COLUMBIAN

STAMP COMPANY INC

BUILDING AND BUYING GREAT STAMP COLLECTIONS

HARRY HAGENDORF

DEALER IN RARE STAMPS

700 WHITE PLAINS ROAD SCARSDALE NY 10583 TELEPHONE 914 725 2290 FAX 914 725 2576
E-MAIL: harryhagendorf@aol.com

SCOTT

2007
Specialized Catalogue of United States Stamps & Covers

EIGHTY-FIFTH EDITION

CONFEDERATE STATES • CANAL ZONE • DANISH WEST INDIES
GUAM • HAWAII • UNITED NATIONS

UNITED STATES ADMINISTRATION:
Cuba • Puerto Rico • Philippines • Ryukyu Islands

EDITOR	James E. Kloetzel
ASSOCIATE EDITOR	William A. Jones
ASSISTANT EDITOR /NEW ISSUES & VALUING	Martin J. Frankevicz
VALUING ANALYST	Steven R. Myers
ADMINISTRATIVE ASSISTANT/IMAGE COORDINATOR	Beth L. Brown
DESIGN MANAGER	Teresa M. Wenrick
ADVERTISING	Renee Davis
CIRCULATION / PRODUCT PROMOTION MANAGER	Tim Wagner
VICE PRESIDENT/EDITORIAL AND PRODUCTION	Steve Collins
VICE PRESIDENT/OPERATIONS	William Fay

Released October 2006
Includes New Stamp Listings through the November 2006 *Scott Stamp Monthly* Catalogue Update

Copyright© 2006 by

Scott Publishing Co.

911 Vandemark Road, Sidney, OH 45365-0828
A division of AMOS PRESS, INC., publishers of *Linn's Stamp News, Coin World* and *Scott Stamp Monthly* magazine.

Copyright Notice

Trademark Notice

Please Note

Scott Publishing Co.

SCOTT 911 VANDEMARK ROAD, SIDNEY, OHIO 45365   937-498-0802

Dear Scott Catalogue User:

Marketplace activity in the highest grades of United States stamps, which we discussed in last year's Letter From the Editor, has remained frenetic during the past year. Once again, this has not universally translated into huge value increases in stamps that are in the grade of very fine or less, but it has given the market a certain soundness that has been felt in stamps of very fine grade. As a result, there have been a relatively large number of value increases in the *2007 Specialized Catalogue of United States Stamps and Covers*. The increases are small compared to the increases in value seen for stamps in the grades of Extremely Fine and Superb. For those values, we recommend our Scott 2007 Fall Edition of the *United States Specialized Valuing Supplement*, which values the more valuable U.S. stamps in seven different grades, from Very Good to Superb.

Where are values changing?

There are almost 14,000 value changes in the 2007 U.S. Specialized Catalogue, and more than 2,500 of these are in the Postage section up to Scott 771. In the entire Postage section, there are more than 4,000 value changes, almost all increases. The other value changes are well spread throughout the entire volume, with large numbers of changes seen in Special Deliveries, Postage Dues, Officials, Newspapers and Periodicals, Revenues and United Nations.

There are value increases in selected classic issues beginning with Scott 1, the 1847 5¢ red brown Franklin, which moves to $600 from $575 in the 2006 U.S. Specialized. Scott 2, its 10¢ counterpart, climbs to $1,400 from $1,350 last year. Among the 1861 issues, Scott 63, the 1¢ blue stamp, moves to $375 unused and $50 used, from $350 unused and $40 used in 2006.

At the top end of the market, the 1867 1¢ Z Grill, Scott 85A, skyrockets to $3,000,000 used from last year's $935,000, based on the now-famous late-2005 trade of the Inverted Jenny plate block of 4, Scott C3a, for the 1¢ Z Grill. The Scott C3a plate block had just been purchased at auction for $2,970,000. The trade elevates the catalogue value of both items to $3,000,000, and the 1¢ Z Grill becomes by far the most valuable single stamp in the 2007 U.S. Specialized Catalogue.

The 1875 Reissues of the 1861-66 issues, Scott 166-177, all increase in value unused by about 10 percent, with even larger increases in the used column. Many Banknote issues from 1870 on rise in value unused and/or used. The 1870 2¢ red brown, Scott 146, moves to $400 unused and $17.50 used, from $350 unused and $15 used last year. The 1880 Special Printings of the 1879 issue, Scott 192-204, generally show increased values.

There are frequent, scattered value increases in the 1908-1921 Washington/Franklin issues, Scott 331-547. Changes from 1922 to the 1930s are more scattered, but those seen are overwhelmingly increases.

In modern postage, there are numerous value increases for items that have become somewhat or very elusive in the marketplace. Some value increases in the modern material are very large. The 2000 pane with Road Runner and Wile E. Coyote with an imperforate stamp at the right, Scott 3392, zips to $40 mint never hinged from just $9 last year and $14 in the 2007 Volume 1. The 2001 Porky Pig pane with imperforate stamp, Scott 3535, zooms to $60 mint never hinged from $12.50 last year and $30 in the 2007 Volume 1.

Other items of note include the 2000 Berries coil, Scott 3404-3407; the 2000 (37¢) nondenominated Flowers coil, Scott 3462-3465; and plate blocks of four with water-activated gum, Scott 3467, 3616, 3620 and 3629F. Some of the value increases here are huge.

Almost all Special Deliveries have increased in value, as have Postage Dues through the 1930 issue. Officials likewise see increases almost across the board, often significantly so. Newspapers and Periodicals follow the same trend. There also are many value increases in the Vending and Affixing Machine Perforations, both unused and used, as well as increases for unused Imperforate Flat Plate Coils.

Editorial enhancements also have been made.

Many new Earliest Documented Use dates have been recorded. There are 27 in the Postage section, four in the Vending and Affixing Machine Perforations area, and two new dates in the Imperforate Flat Plate Coils.

Watermark orientation errors have been listed for the first time for the 1¢ deep green and 2¢ orange red regular issues of 1898-1900, Scott 279 and 279Bd. These errors are vertical watermarks on sheet stamps that were supposed to be printed only on horizontally watermarked paper. The new numbers for the vertically watermarked errors are Scott 279a and 2798Be. The 2¢ booklet pane of six, formerly Scott 279Be, has been moved to the end of the 2¢ sheet stamps and becomes Scott 279Bj. In addition, stamps with normal watermark orientations (not errors) have been listed for the 2¢ booklet pane, now Scott 279Bk, and for the 10¢ orange brown type II sheet stamp, now Scott 283a. These two items exist normally with two watermark orientations due to their having been printed from both 360-subject plates and 180-subject plates (Scott 279Bj and 279Bk) or from 400-subject plates and 200-subject plates (Scott 283 and 283a). In addition, illustrations are now included in the catalogue that show all possible horizontal and vertical watermark orientations: normal, reversed, inverted and inverted reversed. A Special Feature article touching on all these changes, by long-time First Bureau issue collector and researcher Kenneth E. Diehl, is included in the catalogue.

In the 1942-43 Overrun Countries issue, a new "reverse printing" variety has been listed for the Netherlands stamps, Scott 913a, and a partial "reverse printing" has been added for France, Scott 915b. A double impression of the black has been added for Yugoslavia, Scott 917b. The "normal printing" of the flag with dark blue shading over pale blue flag stripes has been added for Greece, Scott 916a, and the main listing makes clear that the 35¢ catalogue value for the major Scott 916 listing is for the so-called "reverse printing" variety, which is a different situation than exists for all the rest of the stamps in this issue. Hopefully, the new Greece listings will stop the offerings in the retail and auction markets of the Greece "reverse printings" at grossly inflated prices.

Values for never-hinged stamps have been added for all early Postage Dues, Scott J1-J7 and J15-J28, that were previously valued only hinged. The listings for Newspaper and Periodical Stamps have grown more sophisticated with the additions of listings for unused stamps without gum and the inclusion of used values for Scott PR9-PR32 for both manuscript cancels and handstamp or blue brush cancels. Collectors and dealers should find the new listings much more informative than the previous listings.

Many new major listings for 20th century essays have been added, based on the 2006 sale of the W. Curtis Livingston essay and proof collection.

Following the comprehensive new listings of Test Stamps and Booklets in last year's U.S. Specialized, the anticipated influx of information and additional items came to pass, resulting in myriad new major-number listings, plus enhanced information on items already listed.

Many new color images have been added this year, as well as new and expanded footnotes and explanatory notes. See the Additions, Deletions & Number Changes listings for additional, important information.

Happy Collecting,

James E Kloetzel

James E. Kloetzel/Catalogue Editor

Table of contents

Acknowledgments

Our appreciation and gratitude go to the following individuals and organizations who have assisted us in preparing information included in this year's edition of the Scott Specialized Catalogue of U.S. Stamps and Covers. Some helpers prefer anonymity. Those individuals have generously shared their stamp knowledge with others through the medium of the Scott Catalogue.

Those who follow provided information that is in addition to the hundreds of dealer price lists and advertisements and scores of auction catalogues and realizations which were used in producing the Catalogue Values provided herein. It is from those noted here that we have been able to obtain information on items not normally seen in published lists and advertisements. Support from these people of course goes beyond data leading to Catalogue Values, for they also are key to editorial changes.

Michael E. Aldrich (Michael E. Aldrich, Inc.)
Arthur L.-F. Askins
Roland Austin
Steven R. Belasco
Alan Berkun
John Birkinbine II
Victor Bove (AVB Stamps)
John D. Bowman (Carriers and Locals Society)
Roger S. Brody
Lawrence A. Bustillo (Suburban Stamp Inc.)
James R. Callis, Jr. (Precancel Stamp Society)
Alan C. Campbell
Gil Celli (Gold Mine Cover Co.)
Richard A. Champagne (Richard A. Champagne, Ltd.)
Leroy P. Collins III (United Postal Stationery Society)
Harry Corrigan
Francis J. Crown, Jr.
Tony L. Crumbley (Carolina Coin & Stamp, Inc.)
Stephen R. Datz
John DeStefanis
Kenneth E. Diehl
Bob Dumaine
Mark Eastzer (Markest Stamp Co.)
Stephen G. Esrati
Jeremiah Farrington
Henry Fisher
Jeffrey M. Forster
Robert S. Freeman
Richard Friedberg
Melvin Getlan

Henry L. Gitner (Henry Gitner Philatelists, Inc.)
Stan Goldfarb
Fred F. Gregory
Harry Hagendorf
John B. Head
Bruce Hecht (Bruce L. Hecht Co.)
Robert R. Hegland
Steven Hines
Wilson Hulme
Doug Iams
Tom Jacks (Mountainside Stamps)
Eric Jackson
Allan Katz (Ventura Stamp Co.)
Patricia A. Kaufmann
Jim Kotanchik
Eliot Landau
Maurice J. Landry (Maurice J. Landry Covers)
Lester C. Lanphear III
John L. Larson
Richard L. Lazorow (The Plate Block Stamp Co.)
James E. Lee
Ronald E. Lesher, Sr.
Steve Levine
John R. Lewis (The William Henry Stamp Co.)
William A. Litle
Larry Lyons
Robert L. Markovits (Quality Investors, Ltd.)
Frank Marrelli (F & M Stamps)
Peter Martin (State Revenue Society)
William K. McDaniel

Timothy M. McRee
Allen Mintz
Jack E. Molesworth
William E. Mooz
Gary M. Morris (Pacific Midwest Co.)
Bruce M. Moyer (Moyer Stamps & Collectibles)
Joseph M. Napp
Gerald Nylander
Michael O. Perry
Stanley M. Piller (Stanley M. Piller & Associates)
Peter W. W. Powell
Louis E. Repeta
Peter A. Robertson
Peter Robin
Richard H. Salz
Byron Sandfield (Park Cities Stamps)
Jacques C. Schiff, Jr. (Jacques C. Schiff, Jr., Inc.)
Terry Scott
Craig Selig
J. Randall Shoemaker (Professional Stamp Experts, Inc.)
Merle Spencer (The Stamp Gallery)
Frank J. Stanley, III
Gordon Stimmell
Jerry Summers
Alan Thomson (Plate Number Coil Collectors' Club)
David R. Torre
Scott R. Trepel (Robert A. Siegel Auction Galleries, Inc.)

Dan Undersander
Steven R. Unkrich
Philip T. Wall
Daniel C. Warren
Dr. Gary B. Weiss
William R. Weiss, Jr. (Weiss Auctions)
Alan B. Whitman
Kirk Wolford (Kirk's Stamp Company)
Robert Wurdeman
Robert F. Yacano (K-Line Philippines)

Expertizing Services

The following organizations will, for a fee, provide expert opinions about stamps submitted to them. Collectors should contact these organizations to find out about their fees and requirements before submitting philatelic material to them. The listing of these groups here is not intended as an endorsement by Scott Publishing Co.

General Expertizing Services

American Philatelic Expertizing Service (a service of the American Philatelic Society)
100 Match Factory Place
Bellefonte PA 16823-1367
Ph: (814) 933-3803
Fax: (814) 933-6128
www.stamps.org
E-mail: apsinfo@stamps.org

Philatelic Foundation
70 West 40th St., 15th Floor
New York NY 10018
Ph: (212) 221-6555
Fax: (212) 221-6208
www.philatelicfoundation.org
E-mail: philatelicfoundation@verizon.net

Professional Stamp Experts
PO Box 6170
Newport Beach CA 92658
Ph: (877) STAMP-88
Fax: (949) 833-7955
www.collectors.com/pse
E-mail: pseinfo@collectors.com

Expertizing Services Covering Specific Fields Or Countries

American First Day Cover Society Expertizing Committee
P.O. Box 141379
Columbus, OH 43214

Confederate Stamp Alliance Authentication Service
c/o Patricia A. Kaufmann
10194 N. Old State Road
Lincoln, DE 19960-9797
Ph: (302) 422-2656
Fax: (302) 424-1990
www.webuystamps.com/csaauth.htm
E-mail: trishkauf@comcast.net

Errors, Freaks and Oddities Collectors Club Expertizing Service
138 East Lakemont Dr.
Kingsland GA 31548
Ph: (912) 729-1573

Hawaiian Philatelic Society Expertizing Service
PO Box 10115
Honolulu HI 96816-0115

Addresses, Telephone Numbers & E-Mail Addresses of General & Specialized Philatelic Societies

Collectors can contact the following groups for information about the philately of the areas within the scope of these societies, or inquire about membership in these groups. Many more specialized philatelic societies exist than those listed below. Aside from the general societies, we limit this list to groups which specialize in areas covered by the Scott U.S. Specialized Catalogue. These addresses were compiled two months prior to publication, and are, to the best of our knowledge, correct and current. Groups should inform the editors of address changes whenever they occur. The editors also want to hear from other such specialized groups not listed.

American Air Mail Society
Stephen Reinhard
P.O. Box 110
Mineola NY 11501
www.americanairmailsociety.org
E-mail: sr1501@aol.com

American First Day Cover Society
Douglas Kelsey
P.O. Box 65960
Tucson AZ 85728-5960
Ph: (520) 321-0880
http://www.afdcs.org
E-mail: afdcs@aol.com

American Philatelic Society
100 Match Factory Place
Bellefonte PA 16823-1367
Ph: (814) 933-3803
http://www.stamps.org
E-mail: apsinfo@stamps.org

American Revenue Association
Eric Jackson
P.O. Box 728
Leesport PA 19533-0728
Ph: (610) 926-6200
http://www.revenuer.org
E-mail: eric@revenuer.com

American Society for Philatelic
Pages and Panels
Gerald N. Blankenship
539 North Gum Gully
Crosby TX 77532
Ph: (281) 324-2709
www.asppp.org
E-mail: asppp134@aol.com

American Stamp Dealers
Association
Joseph Savarese
3 School St.
Glen Cove NY 11542
Ph: (516) 759-7000
http://www.asdaonline.com
E-mail: asda@erols.com

American Topical Association
Ray E. Cartier
P.O. Box 57
Arlington TX 76004-0057
Ph: (817) 274-1181
http://americantopicalassn.org
E-mail: americantopical@msn.com

Canal Zone Study Group
Richard H. Salz
60 27th Ave.
San Francisco CA 94121

Carriers and Locals Society
John D. Bowman
232 Leaf Lane
Alabaster AL 35007
Ph: (205) 621-8449
http://www.pennypost.org
E-mail: johndbowman@charter.net

Christmas Seal & Charity Stamp
Society
John Denune
234 East Broadway
Granville OH 43023
Ph: (740) 587-0276
http://cscss.home.att.net
E-mail: webmaster@christmasseals.net

Confederate Stamp Alliance
Kevin Baker
3015 Fieldview Dr..
Murfreesboro TN 37128
www.csalliance.org
E-mail: kr.baker@comcast.net

Errors, Freaks, and Oddities
Collectors Club
Jim McDevitt
955 S Grover Blvd., #65
Kingsland GA 31548-5263
Ph: (912) 729-1573
www.efoers.org
E-mail: cwouscg@aol.com

Hawaiian Philatelic Society
Kay H. Hoke
P.O. Box 10115
Honolulu HI 96816-0115
Ph: (808) 521-5721
E-mail: bannan@pixi.com

International Philippine Philatelic
Society
Robert F. Yacano
P.O. Box 100
Toast NC 27049
Ph: (336) 783-0768
E-mail: ryacano@triad.rr.com

International Society of Reply
Coupon Collectors
Dr. Allan Hauck
P.O. Box 165
Somers WI 53171-0165

National Duck Stamp Collectors
Society
Anthony J. Monico
P.O. Box 43
Harleysville PA 19438-0043
http://www.hwcn.org/links/ndscs
E-mail: ndscs@hwcn.org

Official Seal Study Group
Fred Scheuer
P.O. Box1518
Waldport OR 97394
Ph: (541) 563-4442

Perfins Club
Kurt Ottenheimer
462 West Walnut St.
Long Beach NY 11561
Ph: (516) 431-3412
E-mail: oak462@juno.com

Plate Number Coil Collectors Club
Ronald E. Maifeld
P.O. Box 54622
Cincinnati OH 45254-0622
http://www.pnc3.org
E-mail: ron.maifeld@pnc3.org

Post Mark Collectors Club
Dave Proulx
7629 Homestead Dr.
Baldwinsville NY 13207
E-mail: stampdance@baldcom.net

Postal History Society
Kalman V. Illyefalvi
8207 Daren Court
Pikesville MD 21208-2211
Ph: (410) 653-0665

Precancel Stamp Society
Arthur Damm
176 Bent Pine Hill
North Wales PA 19454
Ph: (215) 368-6082
E-mail: sandadamm@enter.net

Ryukyu Philatelic Specialist Society
Carmine J. Di Vincenzo
P.O. Box 381
Clayton CA 94517-0381

Souvenir Card Collectors Society
Dana Marr
P.O. Box 4155
Tulsa OK 74159-0155
Ph: (918) 664-6724
E-mail: dmarr5569@aol.com

State Revenue Society
Scott Troutman
P.O. Box 421
Duncansville PA 16635-0421
http://hillcity-mail.com/SRS

United Nations Philatelists
Blanton Clement, Jr.
P. O. Box 146
Morrisville PA 19067-0146
http://www.unpi.com
E-mail: bclemjr@yahoo.com

United Postal Stationery Society
Cora Collins
P.O. Box 1792
Norfolk VA 23501-1792
http://www.upss.org
E-mail: poststat@juno.com

U.S. Cancellation Club
Roger Rhoads
6160 Brownstone Ct.
Mentor OH 44060
http://www/geocities.com/athens/2088/uscchome.html
E-mail: rrrhoads@aol.com

U.S. Philatelic Classics Society
Mark D. Rogers
P.O. Box 80708
Austin TX 78708-0708
http://www.uspcs.org
E-mail: mdr3@swbell.net

U.S. Possessions Philatelic Society
David S. Durbin
1608 S. 22nd St.
Blue Springs MO 64015
Ph: (816) 224-3666

United States Stamp Society
P.O. Box 6634
Katy TX 77491-6634
http://www.usstamps.org
E-mail: webmaster@usstamps.org

Information on Catalogue Values, Grade and Condition

Catalogue Value

The Scott Catalogue value is a retail value; that is, an amount you could expect to pay for a stamp in the grade of Very Fine with no faults. Any exceptions to the grade valued will be noted in the text. The general introduction on the following pages and the individual section introductions further explain the type of material that is valued. The value listed for any given stamp is a reference that reflects recent actual dealer selling prices for that item.

Dealer retail price lists, public auction results, published prices in advertising and individual solicitation of retail prices from dealers, collectors and specialty organizations have been used in establishing the values found in this catalogue. Scott Publishing Co. values stamps, but Scott is not a company engaged in the business of buying and selling stamps as a dealer.

Use this catalogue as a guide for buying and selling. The actual price you pay for a stamp may be higher or lower than the catalogue value because of many different factors, including the amount of personal service a dealer offers, or increased or decreased interest in the country or topic represented by a stamp or set. An item may occasionally be offered at a lower price as a "loss leader," or as part of a special sale. You also may obtain an item inexpensively at public auction because of little interest at that time or as part of a large lot.

Stamps that are of a lesser grade than Very Fine, or those with condition problems, generally trade at lower prices than those given in this catalogue. Stamps of exceptional quality in both grade and condition often command higher prices than those listed.

Values for pre-1900 unused issues are for stamps with approximately half or more of their original gum. Stamps with most or all of their original gum may be expected to sell for more, and stamps with less than half of their original gum may be expected to sell for somewhat less than the values listed. On rarer stamps, it may be expected that the original gum will be somewhat more disturbed than it will be on more common issues. Post-1900 unused issues are assumed to have full original gum. From breakpoints in most countries' listings, stamps are valued as never hinged, due to the wide availability of stamps in that condition. These notations are prominently placed in the listings and in the country information preceding the listings. Some countries also feature listings with dual values for hinged and never-hinged stamps.

Grade

A stamp's grade and condition are crucial to its value. The accompanying illustrations show examples of Very Fine stamps from different time periods, along with examples of stamps in Fine to Very Fine and Extremely Fine grades as points of reference. When a stamp seller offers a stamp in any grade from fine to superb without further qualifying statements, that stamp should not only have the centering grade as defined, but it also should be free of faults or other condition problems.

FINE stamps (illustrations not shown) have designs that are noticeably off center on two sides. Imperforate stamps may have small margins, and earlier issues may show the design touching one edge of the stamp design. For perforated stamps, perfs may barely clear the design on one side, and very early issues normally will have the perforations slightly cutting into the design. Used stamps may have heavier than usual cancellations.

FINE-VERY FINE stamps may be somewhat off center on one side, or slightly off center on two sides. Imperforate stamps will have two margins of at least normal size, and the design will not touch any edge. For perforated stamps, the perfs are well clear of the design, but are still noticeably off center. *However, early issues of a country may be printed in such a way that the design naturally is very close to the edges. In these cases, the perforations may cut into the design very slightly.* Used stamps will not have a cancellation that detracts from the design.

VERY FINE stamps may be slightly off center on one or two sides, but the design will be well clear of the edge. The stamp will present a nice, balanced appearance. Imperforate stamps will have three normal-sized margins. *However, early issues of many countries may be printed in such a way that the perforations may touch the design on one or more sides. Where this is the case, a boxed note will be found defining the centering and margins of the stamps being valued.* Used stamps will have light or otherwise neat cancellations. This is the grade used to establish Scott Catalogue values.

EXTREMELY FINE stamps are close to being perfectly centered. Imperforate stamps will have even margins that are larger than normal. Even the earliest perforated issues will have perforations clear of the design on all sides.

Scott Publishing Co. recognizes that there is no formally enforced grading scheme for postage stamps, and that the final price you pay or obtain for a stamp will be determined by individual agreement at the time of transaction.

Condition

Grade addresses only centering and (for used stamps) cancellation. *Condition* refers to factors other than grade that affect a stamp's desirability.

Factors that can increase the value of a stamp include exceptionally wide margins, particularly fresh color, the presence of selvage, and plate or die varieties. Unusual cancels on used stamps (particularly those of the 19th century) can greatly enhance their value as well.

Factors other than faults that decrease the value of a stamp include loss of original gum, regumming, a hinge remnant or foreign object adhering to the gum, natural inclusions, straight edges, and markings or notations applied by collectors or dealers.

Faults include missing pieces, tears, pin or other holes, surface scuffs, thin spots, creases, toning, short or pulled perforations, clipped perforations, oxidation or other forms of color changelings, soiling, stains, and such man-made changes as reperforations or the chemical removal or lightening of a cancellation.

Grading Illustrations

On the following two pages are illustrations of various stamps from countries appearing in this volume. These stamps are arranged by country, and they represent early or important issues that are often found in widely different grades in the marketplace. The editors believe the illustrations will prove useful in showing the margin size and centering that will be seen on the various issues.

In addition to the matters of margin size and centering, collectors are reminded that the very fine stamps valued in the Scott catalogues also will possess fresh color and intact perforations, and they will be free from defects.

Examples shown are computer-manipulated images made from single digitized master illustrations.

Stamp Illustrations Used in the Catalogue

It is important to note that the stamp images used for identification purposes in this catalogue may not be indicative of the grade of stamp being valued. Refer to the written discussion of grades on this page and to the grading illustrations on the following two pages for grading information.

	1847 ISSUE	1851-57 ISSUES	1857-61 ISSUES	1857-61 ISSUES	1861-67 ISSUES	1869 ISSUE
Fine-Very Fine →						
SCOTT CATALOGUES VALUE STAMPS IN THIS GRADE **Very Fine** →						
Extremely Fine →						

	1870-88 ISSUES	1898 TRANS-MISSISSIPPIS	1902-03 ISSUES	1908-20 WASHINGTON-FRANKLIN ISSUES	1922-25 ISSUES
Fine-Very Fine →					
SCOTT CATALOGUES VALUE STAMPS IN THIS GRADE **Very Fine** →					
Extremely Fine →					

For purposes of helping to determine the gum condition and value of an unused stamp, Scott Publishing Co. presents the following chart which details different gum conditions and indicates how the conditions correlate with the Scott values for unused stamps. Used together, the Illustrated Grading Chart on the previous page and this Illustrated Gum Chart should allow catalogue users to better understand the grade and gum condition of stamps valued in the *Scott U.S. Specialized Catalogue.*

Gum Categories:	MINT N.H.	ORIGINAL GUM (O.G.)				NO GUM
	Mint Never Hinged *Free from any disturbance*	**Lightly Hinged** *Faint impression of a removed hinge over a small area*	**Hinge Mark or Remnant** *Prominent hinged spot with part or all of the hinge remaining*	**Large part o.g.** *Approximately half or more of the gum intact*	**Small part o.g.** *Approximately less than half of the gum intact*	**No gum** *Only if issued with gum*
Commonly Used Symbol:	★★	★	★	★	★	(★)
PRE-1882 ISSUES	*Very fine pre-1890 stamps in these categories trade at a premium over Scott value*			Scott Value for "Unused"		Scott "No Gum" Values thru No. 218
1882-1935 ISSUES	Scott "Never Hinged" Values for Nos. 205-771	Scott Value for "Unused" (Actual value will be affected by the degree of hinging of the full o.g.)				
1935 TO DATE	Scott Value for "Unused"					

Never Hinged (NH; ★★): A never-hinged stamp will have full original gum that will have no hinge mark or disturbance. The presence of an expertizer's mark does not disqualify a stamp from this designation.

Original Gum (OG; ★): Pre-1890 stamps should have approximately half or more of their original gum. On rarer stamps, it may be expected that the original gum will be somewhat more disturbed that it will be on more common issues. Stamps issued in 1890 or later should have full original gum. Original gum will show some disturbance caused by a previous hinge(s) which may be present or entirely removed. The actual value of an 1890 or later stamp will be affected by the degree of hinging of the full original gum.

Disturbed Original Gum: Gum showing noticeable effects of humidity, climate or hinging over more than half of the gum. The significance of gum disturbance in valuing a stamp in any of the Original Gum categories depends on the degree of disturbance, the rarity and normal gum condition of the issue and other variables affecting quality.

Regummed (RG; (★)): A regummed stamp is a stamp without gum that has had some type of gum privately applied at a time after it was issued. This normally is done to deceive collectors and/or dealers into thinking that the stamp has original gum and therefore has a higher value. A regummed stamp is considered the same as a stamp with none of its original gum for purposes of grading.

IMPORTANT INFORMATION REGARDING VALUES FOR NEVER-HINGED STAMPS

Collectors should be aware that the values given for never-hinged stamps from No. 219 on are for stamps in the grade of very fine. The never-hinged premium as a percentage of value will be larger for stamps in extremely fine or superb grades, and the premium will be smaller for fine-very-fine, fine or poor examples. This is particulary true of the issues of the late-19th and early 20th centuries. For example, in the grade of very fine, an unused stamp from this time period may be valued at $100 hinged and $180 never hinged. The never-hinged premium is thus 80%. But in a grade of extremely fine, this same stamp will not only sell for more hinged, but the never-hinged premium will increase, perhaps to 100%-300% or more over the higher extremely fine value. In a grade of superb, a hinged copy will sell for much more than a very fine copy, and additionally the never-hinged premium will be much larger, perhaps as large as 300%-400%. On the other hand, the same stamp in a grade of fine or fine-very fine not only will sell for less than a very fine stamp in hinged condition, but additionally the never-hinged premium will be smaller than the never-hinged premium on a very fine stamp, perhaps as small as 15%-30%.

Please note that the above statements and percentages are NOT a formula for arriving at the values of stamps in hinged or never-hinged condition in the grades of fine, fine to very fine, extremely fine or superb. The percentages given apply only to the size of the premium for never-hinged condition that might be added to the stamp value for hinged condition. The marketplace will determine what this value will be for grades other than very fine. Further, the percentages given are only generalized estimates. Some stamps or grades may have percentages for never-hinged condition that are higher or lower than the ranges given.

Never-Hinged Plate Blocks

Values given for never-hinged plate blocks are for blocks in which all stamps have original gum that has never been hinged and has no disturbances, and all selvage, whether gummed or ungummed, has never been hinged.

Catalogue Listing Policy

It is the intent of Scott Publishing Co. to list all postage stamps of the world in the *Scott Standard Postage Stamp Catalogue*. The only strict criteria for listing is that stamps be decreed legal for postage by the issuing country and that the issuing country actually have an operating postal system. Whether the primary intent of issuing a given stamp or set was for sale to postal patrons or to stamp collectors is not part of our listing criteria. Scott's role is to provide basic comprehensive postage stamp information. It is up to each stamp collector to choose which items to include in a collection.

It is Scott's objective to seek reasons why a stamp should be listed, rather than why it should not. Nevertheless, there are certain types of items that will not be listed. These include the following:

1. Unissued items that are not officially distributed or released by the issuing postal authority. If such items are officially issued at a later date by the country, they will be listed. Unissued items consist of those that have been printed and then held from sale for reasons such as change in government, errors found on stamps or something deemed objectionable about a stamp subject or design.

2. Stamps "issued" by non-existent postal entities or fantasy countries, such as Nagaland, Occusi-Ambeno, Staffa, Sedang, Torres Straits and others. Also, stamps "issued" in the names of legitimate, stamp-issuing countries that are not authorized by those countries.

3. Semi-official or unofficial items not required for postage. Examples include items issued by private agencies for their own express services. When such items are required for delivery, or are valid as prepayment of postage, they are listed.

4. Local stamps issued for local use only. Postage stamps issued by governments specifically for "domestic" use, such as Haiti Scott 219-228, or the United States non-denominated stamps, are not considered to be locals, since they are valid for postage throughout the country of origin.

5. Items not valid for postal use. For example, a few countries have issued souvenir sheets that are not valid for postage. This area also includes a number of worldwide charity labels (some denominated) that do not pay postage.

6. Intentional varieties, such as imperforate stamps that look like their perforated counterparts and are usually issued in very small quantities. Also, other egregiously exploitative issues such as stamps sold for far more than face value, stamps purposefully issued in artificially small quantities or only against advance orders, stamps awarded only to a selected audience such as a philatelic bureau's standing order customers, or stamps sold only in conjunction with other products. All of these kinds of items are usually controlled issues and/or are intended for speculation. These items normally will be included in footnotes.

7. Items distributed by the issuing government only to a limited group, such as a stamp club, philatelic exhibition or a single stamp dealer, or other private company. These items normally will be included in a footnote.

The fact that a stamp has been used successfully as postage, even on international mail, is not in itself sufficient proof that it was legitimately issued. Numerous examples of so-called stamps from non-existent countries are known to have been used to post letters that have successfully passed through the international mail system.

There are certain items that are subject to interpretation. When a stamp falls outside our specifications, it may be listed along with a cautionary footnote.

A number of factors are considered in our approach to analyzing how a stamp is listed. The following list of factors is presented to share with you, the catalogue user, the complexity of the listing process.

Additional printings — "Additional printings" of a previously issued stamp may range from an item that is totally different to cases where it is impossible to differentiate from the original. At least a minor number (a small-letter suffix) is assigned if there is a distinct change in stamp shade, noticeably redrawn design, or a significantly different perforation measurement. A major number (numeral or numeral and capital-letter combination) is assigned if the editors feel the "additional printing" is sufficiently different from the original that it constitutes a different issue.

Commemoratives — Where practical, commemoratives with the same theme are placed in a set. For example, the U.S. Civil War Centennial set of 1961-65 and the Constitution Bicentennial series of 1989-90 appear as sets. Countries such as Japan and Korea issue such material on a regular basis, with an announced, or at least predictable, number of stamps known in advance. Occasionally, however, stamp sets that were released over a period of years have been separated. Appropriately placed footnotes will guide you to each set's continuation.

Definitive sets — Blocks of numbers generally have been reserved for definitive sets, based on previous experience with any given country. If a few more stamps were issued in a set than originally expected, they often have been inserted into the original set with a capital-letter suffix, such as U.S. Scott 1059A. If it appears that many more stamps than the originally allotted block will be released before the set is completed, a new block of numbers will be reserved, with the original one being closed off. In some cases, such as the U.S. Transportation and Great Americans series, several blocks of numbers exist. Appropriately placed footnotes will guide you to each set's continuation.

New country — Membership in the Universal Postal Union is not a consideration for listing status or order of placement within the catalogue. The index will tell you in what volume or page number the listings begin.

"No release date" items — The amount of information available for any given stamp issue varies greatly from country to country and even from time to time. Extremely comprehensive information about new stamps is available from some countries well before the stamps are released. By contrast some countries do not provide information about stamps or release dates. Most countries, however, fall between these extremes. A country may provide denominations or subjects of stamps from upcoming issues that are not issued as planned. Sometimes, philatelic agencies, those private firms hired to represent countries, add these later-issued items to sets well after the formal release date. This time period can range from weeks to years. If these items were officially released by the country, they will be added to the appropriate spot in the set. In many cases, the specific release date of a stamp or set of stamps may never be known.

Overprints — The color of an overprint is always noted if it is other than black. Where more than one color of ink has been used on overprints of a single set, the color used is noted. Early overprint and surcharge illustrations were altered to prevent their use by forgers.

Se-tenants — Connected stamps of differing features (se-tenants) will be listed in the format most commonly collected. This includes pairs, blocks or larger multiples. Se-tenant units are not always symmetrical. An example is Australia Scott 508, which is a block of seven stamps. If the stamps are primarily collected as a unit, the major number may be assigned to the multiple, with minors going to each component stamp. In cases where continuous-design or other unit se-tenants will receive significant postal use, each stamp is given a major Scott number listing. This includes issues from the United States, Canada, Germany and Great Britain, for example.

Understanding the Listings

On the opposite page is an enlarged "typical" listing from this catalogue. Following are detailed explanations of each of the highlighted parts of the listing.

1 Scott number — Stamp collectors use Scott numbers to identify specific stamps when buying, selling, or trading stamps, and for ease in organizing their collections. Each stamp issued by a country has a unique number. Therefore, U.S. Scott 219 can only refer to a single stamp. Although the Scott Catalogue usually lists stamps in chronological order by date of issue, when a country issues a set of stamps over a period of time the stamps within that set are kept together without regard to date of issue. This follows the normal collecting approach of keeping stamps in their natural sets.

When a country is known to be issuing a set of stamps over a period of time, a group of consecutive catalogue numbers is reserved for the stamps in that set, as issued. If that group of numbers proves to be too few, capital-letter suffixes are added to numbers to create enough catalogue numbers to cover all items in the set. Scott uses a suffix letter, e.g., "A," "b," etc., only once. If there is a Scott 296B in a set, there will not be a Scott 296b also.

There are times when the block of numbers is too large for the set, leaving some numbers unused. Such gaps in the sequence also occur when the editors move an item elsewhere in the catalogue or remove it from the listings entirely. Scott does not attempt to account for every possible number, but rather it does attempt to assure that each stamp is assigned its own number.

Scott numbers designating regular postage normally are only numerals. Scott numbers for other types of stamps, e.g., air post, special delivery, and so on, will have a prefix of either a capital letter or a combination of numerals and capital letters.

2 Illustration number — used to identify each illustration. Where more than one stamp in a set uses the same illustration number, that number needs to be used with the description line (noted below) to be certain of the exact variety of the stamp within the set. Illustrations normally are 75, 100, or 150 percent of the original size of the stamp. An effort has been made to note all illustrations not at those percentages. Overprints are shown at 100 percent of the original, unless otherwise noted. Letters *in parentheses* which follow an illustration number refer to illustrations of overprints or surcharges.

3 Listing styles — there are two principal types of catalogue listings: major and minor.
Majors may be distinguished by having as their catalogue number a numeral with or without a capital-letter suffix and with or without a prefix.
Minors have a small-letter suffix (or, only have the small letter itself shown if the listing is immediately beneath its major listing). These listings show a variety of the "normal," or major item. Examples include color variation or a different watermark used for that stamp only.
Examples of major numbers are 9X1, 16, 28A, 6LB1, C13, RW1, and TS1. Examples of minor numbers are 22b, 279Bc and C3a.

4 Denomination — normally value printed on the stamp (generally known as the *face value*), which is — unless otherwise stated — the cost of the stamp at the time of issue.

5 Basic information on stamp or set — introducing each stamp issue, this section normally includes the date of issue, method of printing, perforation, watermark, and sometimes addi-

tional information. New information on method of printing, watermark or perforation measurement may appear when that information changes. Dates of issue are as precise as Scott is able to confirm, either year only, month and year, or month, day and year.

In stamp sets issued over more than one date, the year or span of years will be in bold type above the first catalogue number. Individual stamps in the set will have a date-of-issue appearing in italics. Stamps without a year listed appeared during the first year of the span. Dates are not always given for minor varieties.

6 Color or other description — this line provides information to solidify identification of the stamp. Historically, when stamps normally were printed in a single color, only the color appeared here. With modern printing techniques, which include multicolor presses which mix inks on the paper, earlier methods of color identification are no longer applicable. When space permits, a description of the stamp design will replace the terms "multi" or "multicolored." The color of the paper is noted in italic type when the paper used is not white.

7 Date of issue — As precisely as Scott is able to confirm, either year only; month and year, or month, day and year. In some cases, the earliest known use (eku) is given. All dates, especially where no official date of issue has been given, are subject to change as new information is obtained. Many cases are known of inadvertent sale and use of stamps prior to dates of issue announced by postal officials. These are not listed here.

8 Value unused and **Value used** — the catalogue values are in U. S. dollars and are based on stamps that are in a grade of Very Fine unless stated otherwise. Unused values refer to items that have not seen postal or other duty for which they were intended. For pre-1890 issues, unused stamps must have at least most of their original gum; for later issues, complete gum is expected. Stamps issued without gum are noted. Unused values are for never-hinged stamps beginning at the point immediately following a prominent notice in the actual listing. Scott values for used self-adhesive stamps are for examples either on piece or off piece.

Some sections in this book have more than two columns for values. Check section introductions and watch for value column headers. See the sections "Catalogue Values" and "Understanding Valuing Notations" for an explanation of the meaning of these values.

9 Changes in basic set information — bold or other type is used to show any change in the basic data between stamps within a set of stamps, e.g., perforation from one stamp to the next or a different paper or printing method or watermark.

10 Other varieties — these include additional shades, plate varieties, multiples, used on cover, plate number blocks. coil line pairs, coil plate number strips of three or five, ZIP blocks, etc.

On early issues, there may be a "Cancellation" section. Values in this section refer to single stamps off cover, unless otherwise noted. Values with a "+" are added to the basic used value. See "Basic Stamp Information" for more details on stamp and cancellation varieties.

11 Footnote — Where other important details about the stamps can be found.

HARDING MEMORIAL ISSUE
Tribute to the memory of President Warren G.
Harding, who died in San Francisco, Aug. 2, 1923

Warren Gamaliel
Harding – A177

Plates of 400 subjects in four panes of 100 each.
FLAT PLATE PRINTINGS
Stamp designs: 19¼x22¼ mm

1923   **Perf.11**

610	A177	2¢**black,** *Sept. 1, 1923*	.55	.25
		intense black	.55	.25
		grayish black	.55	.25
		Never hinged	1.10	
		On cover		.30
		P# block of 6	20.00	—
		Never hinged	30.00	
		Double transfer	1.75	.50
a.		Horiz. pair, imperf. vert	1,750.	

Imperf

611	A177	2¢ **black,** *Nov. 15, 1923*	5.00	4.00
		Never hinged	10.50	
		On philatelic cover		8.00
		On commercial cover		15.00
		Pair	11.00	10.00
		Never Hinged	23.00	
		Corner margin block of 4	24.00	22.50
		Margin block of 4, arrow	25.00	22.50
		Center line block	60.00	40.00
		P# block of 6	70.00	—
		Never hinged	95.00	

ROTARY PRESS PRINTINGS
Stamp designs 19¼mm by 22½mm
Perf. 10

612	A177	2¢ **black,** *Sept. 12, 1923*	15.00	1.75
		gray black	15.00	1.75
		Never hinged	32.50	
		On cover		3.25
		P# block of 4	300.00	
		Never hinged	475.00	
		Pair with full vertical gutter between	350.00	

Perf. 11

613	A177	2¢ **black**	45,000.	
		pair	95,000.	

No. 613 was produced from rotary press sheet waste. It is
valued in the grade of fine.

SCOTT NUMBER ❶

ILLUS. NUMBER ❷

LISTING STYLES ❸   MINORS   MAJORS

DENOMINATION ❹

⑤ BASIC INFORMATION ON STAMP OR SET

⑥ COLOR OR OTHER DESCRIPTION

⑦ DATE OF ISSUE

USED   **⑧ CATALOGUE VALUES**   UNUSED

⑨ CHANGES IN BASIC SET INFORMATION

⑩ OTHER VARIETIES

⑪ FOOTNOTE

Scott Numbering Practices and Special Notices

Classification of stamps

The *Scott Specialized Catalogue of United States Stamps* lists the stamps of the United States and its possessions and territories and the stamps of the United Nations. The next level is a listing by section on the basis of the function of the stamps or postal stationery. In each case, the items are listed in specialized detail. The principal sections cover regular postage stamps; air post stamps; postage due stamps, special delivery, and so on. Except for regular postage, catalogue numbers for most sections include a prefix letter (or number-letter combination) denoting the class to which the stamp belongs.

The Table of Contents, on page 4A, notes each section and, where pertinent, the prefix used. Some, such as souvenir cards and encased postage, do not have prefixes. Some sections, such as specimens and private perforations, have suffixes only.

New issue listings

Updates to this catalogue appear each month in the *Scott Stamp Monthly*. Included are corrections and updates to the current edition of this catalogue.

From time to time there will be changes in the listings from the *Scott Stamp Monthly* to the next edition of the catalogue, as additional information becomes available.

The catalogue update section of the *Scott Stamp Monthly* is the most timely presentation of this material available. For current subscription rates, see advertisements in this catalogue or write Scott Publishing Co., P.O. Box 828, Sidney, OH 45365-0828.

Additions, deletions & number changes

A list of catalogue additions, deletions, and number changes from the previous edition of the catalogue appears in each volume. See Catalogue Additions, Deletions & Number Changes in the Table of Contents for the location of this list..

Understanding valuing notations

The *absence of a value* does not necessarily suggest that a stamp is scarce or rare. In the U.S. listings, a dash in the value column means that the stamp is known in a stated form or variety, but information is lacking or insufficient for purposes of establishing a usable catalogue value. These could include rarities, such as Scott 3X4 on cover, or items that have a limited market, such as used plate blocks of Scott 1097.

Stamp values in *italics* generally refer to items which are difficult to value accurately. For expensive items, e.g., value at $1,000 or more, a value in italics represents an item which trades very seldom, such as a unique item. For inexpensive items, a value in italics represents a warning.

The Scott Catalogue values for used stamps reflect canceled-to-order material when such are found to predominate in the marketplace for the issue involved. Frequently notes appear in the stamp listings to specify items which are valued as canceled-to-order (Canal Zone Scott O1-O8) or if there is a premium for postally used examples.

Scott values for used stamps are not for precanceled examples, unless so stated. Precanceled copies must not have additional postal cancellations.

An example of a warning to collectors is a stamp that used has a value considerably higher than the unused version. Here, the collector is cautioned to be certain the used version has a readable, contemporaneous cancellation.

The *minimum catalogue value* of a stamp is 20 cents, to cover a dealer's costs of purchase and preparation for resale. The minimum catalogue value of a first day cover is one dollar. As noted, the sum of these values does not properly represent the "value" of a packet of unsorted or unmounted stamps sold in bulk. Such large collections, mixtures or packets generally consist of the lower-valued stamps.

stamps. There are examples where the catalogue value of a block of stamps is less than the sum of the values of the individual stamps. This situation is caused by the overhead involved in handling single stamps, and should not be considered a suggestion that all blocks be separated into individual stamps to achieve a higher market value.

Values in the "unused" column are for stamps with original gum, if issued with gum. The stamp is valued as hinged if the listing appears *before* the point at which stamps are valued as never hinged. This point is marked by prominent notes in many sections. A similar note will appear at the beginning of the section's listing, noting exactly where the dividing point between hinged and never hinged is for each section of the listings. Where a value for a used stamp is considerably higher than for the unused stamp, the value applies to a stamp showing a distinct contemporaneous cancellation.

Covers

Prices paid for stamps on original covers vary greatly according to condition, appearance, cancellation or postmark and usage. Values given in this volume are for the commonest form with stamps in a grade of very fine "tied on" by the cancellation. A stamp is said to be "tied" to an envelope or card when the cancellation or postmark falls on both the stamp and envelope or card. Letters addressed to foreign countries showing unusual rates and transit markings normally are much in demand and often command large premiums.

Values are for covers bearing a single copy of the stamp referenced and used during the period when the stamp was on sale at post offices unless stated otherwise. If the postage rate was higher than the denomination of the stamp, then the stamp must represent the highest denomination possible to use in making up this rate. In this case, the value is the on-cover value of the stamp plus the used values of the additional stamps. As a general rule, the stamp must be tied to the cover.

Values for patriotic covers of the Civil War period (bearing pictorial designs of a patriotic nature) are for the commonest designs. Approximately 10,000 varieties of designs are known.

Cancellations

A complete treatment of this subject is impossible in a catalogue of this limited size. Only postal markings of meaning — those which were necessary to the proper function of the postal service — are recorded here, while those of value owing to their fanciness only are disregarded. The latter are the results of the whim of some postal official. Many of these odd designs, however, command high prices, based on their popularity, scarcity and clearness of impression.

Although there are many types of most of the cancellations listed, only one of each is illustrated. The values quoted are for the most common type of each.

Values for cancellation varieties are for stamp specimens off cover. Some cancellation varieties (e.g., pen, precancel, cut) are valued individually. Other varieties on pre-1900 stamps (e.g., less common colors, specific dates, foreign usages) are valued using premiums (denoted by "+") which are added to the stated value for the used stamp. When listed on cover, the distinctive cancellation must be on the stamp in order to merit catalogue valuation. Postal markings that denote origin or a service (as distinguished from canceling a stamp) merit catalogue valuation when on a cover apart from the stamp, provided the stamp is otherwise tied to the cover by a cancellation.

One type of "Paid" cancellation used in Boston, and shown in this introduction under "Postal Markings," is common and values given are for types other than this.

Examination

Scott Publishing Co. will not pass upon the genuineness, grade or condition of stamps, because of the time and responsibility involved. Rather, there are several expertizing groups which undertake this work for both collectors and dealers. Neither will Scott Publishing Co. appraise or identify philatelic material. The Company cannot take responsibility for unsolicited stamps or covers.

How to order from your dealer

It is not necessary to write the full description of a stamp as listed in this catalogue. All that you need is the name of the country or *U.S. Specialized* section, the Scott Catalogue number and whether the item is unused or used. For example, "U.S. Scott 833" is sufficient to identify the stamp of the United States listed as the 2-dollar value of a set of stamps issued between 1938-43. This stamp was issued September 29, 1938. It is yellow green and black in color, has a perforation of 11, and is printed on paper without a watermark by a flat plate press. Sections without a prefix or suffix must be mentioned by name.

Abbreviations

Scott Publishing Co. uses a consistent set of abbreviations throughout this catalogue and the *Standard Postage Stamp Catalogue* to conserve space while still providing necessary information. The first block shown here refers to color names only:

COLOR ABBREVIATIONS

amb	amber	ind	indigo
anil	aniline	int	intense
ap	apple	lav	lavender
aqua	aquamarine	lem	lemon
az	azure	lil	lilac
bis	bister	lt	light
bl	blue	mag	magenta
bld	blood	man	manila
blk	black	mar	maroon
bril	brilliant	mv	mauve
brn	brown	multi	multicolored
brnsh	brownish	mlky	milky
brnz	bronze	myr	myrtle
brt	bright	ol	olive
brnt	burnt	olvn	olivine
car	carmine	org	orange
cer	cerise	pck	peacock
chlky	chalky	pnksh	pinkish
cham	chamois	Prus	Prussian
chnt	chestnut	pur	purple
choc	chocolate	redsh	reddish
chr	chrome	res	reseda
cit	citron	ros	rosine
cl	claret	ryl	royal
cob	cobalt	sal	salmon
cop	copper	saph	sapphire
crim	crimson	scar	scarlet
cr	cream	sep	sepia
dk	dark	sien	sienna
dl	dull	sil	silver
dp	deep	sl	slate
db	drab	stl	steel
emer	emerald	turq	turquoise
gldn	golden	ultra	ultramarine
grysh	grayish	ven	venetian
grn	green	ver	vermilion
grnsh	greenish	vio	violet
hel	heliotrope	yel	yellow
hn	henna	yelsh	yellowish

When no color is given for an overprint or surcharge, black is the color used. Abbreviations for colors used for overprints and surcharges are: "(B)" or "(Blk)," black; "(Bl)," blue; "(R)," red; "(G)," green; etc.

Additional abbreviations used in this catalogue are shown below:

Adm.	Administration
AFL	American Federation of Labor
Anniv.	Anniversary
APU	Arab Postal Union
APS	American Philatelic Society
ASEAN	Association of South East Asian Nations
ASPCA	American Society for the Prevention of Cruelty to Animals
Assoc.	Association
b	Born
BEP	Bureau of Engraving and Printing
Bicent.	Bicentennial
Bklt.	Booklet
Brit.	British
btwn.	Between
Bur.	Bureau
c. or ca.	Circa
CAR	Central African Republic
Cat.	Catalogue
Cent.	Centennial, century, centenary
CEPT	Conference Europeenne des Administrations des Postes et des Telecommunications
CIO	Congress of Industrial Organizations
Conf.	Conference
Cong.	Congress
Cpl.	Corporal
CTO	Canceled to order
d	Died
Dbl.	Double
DDR	German Democratic Republic (East Germany)
EC	European Community
ECU	European currency unit
EEC	European Economic Community
EKU	Earliest known use
Engr.	Engraved
Exhib.	Exhibition
Expo.	Exposition
FAO	Food and Agricultural Organization of the United Nations
Fed.	Federation
FIP	Federation International de Philatelie
GB	Great Britain
Gen.	General
GPO	General post office
Horiz.	Horizontal
ICAO	International Civil Aviation Organization
ICY	International Cooperation Year
ILO	International Labor Organization
Imperf.	Imperforate
Impt.	Imprint
Intl.	International
Invtd.	Inverted
IQSY	International Quiet Sun Year
ITU	International Telecommunications Union
ITY	International Tourism Year
IWY	International Women's Year
IYC	International Year of the Child
IYD	International Year of the Disabled
IYSH	International Year of Shelter for the Homeless
IYY	International Youth Year
L	Left
Lieut.	Lieutenant
Litho.	Lithographed

LL................Lower left
LR ....Lower right

mm..............Millimeter
Ms...............Manuscript

NASA ....National Aeronautics and Space Administration
Natl. ....National
NATO........North Atlantic Treaty Organization
No...............Number
NY..............New York
NYC ....New York City

OAU...........Organization of African Unity
OPEC ....Organization of Petroleum Exporting Countries
Ovpt. ....Overprint
Ovptd. ....Overprinted

P#...............Plate number
Perf.............Perforated, perforation
Phil.............Philatelic
Photo..........Photogravure
PO..............Post office
Pr................Pair
P.R. ....Puerto Rico
PRC...........People's Republic of China (Mainland China)
Prec............Precancel, precanceled
Pres. ....President

R ....Right
Rio..............Rio de Janeiro
ROC ....Republic of China (Taiwan)

SEATO........South East Asia Treaty Organization
Sgt...............Sergeant
Soc. ....Society
Souv. ....Souvenir
SSR.............Soviet Socialist Republic
St................Saint, street
Surch..........Surcharge

Typo. ....Typographed

UAE............United Arab Emirate
UAMPT ......Union of African and Malagasy Posts and Telecommunications
UL..............Upper left
UN ....United Nations
UNESCO ....United Nations Educational, Scientific and Cultural Organization
UNICEF......United Nations Children's Fund
Univ ....University
UNPA ....United Nations Postal Administration
Unwmkd ....Unwatermarked
UPU ....Universal Postal Union
UR..............Upper Right
US ....United States
USPO ....United States Post Office Department
USPS ....United States Postal Service (also "U.S. Postage Stamp" when referring to the watermark)
USSR ....Union of Soviet Socialist Republics

Vert ....Vertical
VP ....Vice president

WCY ....World Communications Year
WFUNA......World Federation of United Nations Associations
WHO..........World Health Organization
Wmk ....Watermark
Wmkd ....Watermarked
WMO ....World Meteorological Organization
WRY ....World Refugee Year
WWF.........World Wildlife Fund
WWI ....World War I
WWII ....World War II

YAR ....Yemen Arab Republic
Yemen PDR . Yemen People's Democratic Republic

Postmasters General of the United States

1775 Benjamin Franklin, July 26.
1776 Richard Bache, Nov. 7.
1782 Ebenezer Hazard, Jan. 28.
1789 Samuel Osgood, Sept. 26.
1791 Timothy Pickering, Aug. 12.
1795 Joseph Habersham, Feb. 25.
1801 Gideon Granger, Nov. 28.
1814 Return J. Meigs, Jr., Apr. 11.
1823 John McLean, July 1.
1829 William T. Barry, Apr. 6.
1835 Amos Kendall, May 1.
1840 John M. Niles, May 26.
1841 Francis Granger, Mar. 8.
1841 Charles A. Wickliffe, Oct. 13.
1845 Cave Johnson, Mar. 7.
1849 Jacob Collamer, Mar. 8.
1850 Nathan K. Hall, July 23.
1852 Samuel D. Hubbard, Sept. 14.
1853 James Campbell, Mar. 8.
1857 Aaron V. Brown, Mar. 7.
1859 Joseph Holt, Mar. 14.
1861 Horatio King, Feb. 12.
1861 Montgomery Blair, Mar. 9.
1864 William Dennison, Oct. 1.
1866 Alexander W. Randall, July 25.

1869 John A.J. Creswell, Mar. 6.
1874 Jas. W. Marshall, July 7.
1874 Marshall Jewell, Sept. 1.
1876 James N. Tyner, July 13.
1877 David McK. Key, Mar. 13.
1880 Horace Maynard, Aug. 25.
1881 Thomas L. James, Mar. 8.
1882 Timothy O. Howe, Jan. 5.
1883 Walter Q. Gresham, Apr. 11.
1884 Frank Hatton, Oct. 14.
1885 Wm. F. Vilas, Mar. 7.
1888 Don M. Dickinson, Jan. 17.
1889 John Wanamaker, Mar. 6.
1893 Wilson S. Bissell, Mar. 7.
1895 William L. Wilson, Apr. 4.
1897 James A. Gary, Mar. 6.
1898 Charles Emory Smith, Apr. 22.
1902 Henry C. Payne, Jan. 15.
1904 Robert J. Wynne, Oct. 10.
1905 Geo. B. Cortelyou, Mar. 7.
1907 Geo. von L. Meyer, Mar. 4.
1909 Frank H. Hitchcock, Mar. 6.
1913 Albert S. Burleson, Mar. 5.
1921 Will H. Hays, Mar. 5.
1922 Hubert Work, Mar. 4.

1923 Harry S. New, Mar. 4.
1929 Walter F. Brown, Mar. 6.
1933 James A. Farley, Mar. 4.
1940 Frank C. Walker, Sept. 11.
1945 Robert E. Hannegan, July 1.
1947 Jesse M. Donaldson, Dec. 16.
1953 Arthur E. Summerfield, Jan. 21.
1961 J. Edward Day, Jan. 21.
1963 John A. Gronouski, Sept. 30.
1965 Lawrence F. O'Brien, Nov. 3.
1968 W. Marvin Watson, Apr. 26.
1969 Winton M. Blount, Jan. 22.

U.S. POSTAL SERVICE

1971 Elmer T. Klassen, Dec. 7.
1975 Benjamin Bailar, Feb. 15.
1978 William F. Bolger, Mar. 1.
1985 Paul N. Carlin, Jan. 1.
1986 Albert V. Casey, Jan. 6.
1986 Preston R. Tisch, Aug. 17.
1988 Anthony M. Frank, Mar. 1.
1992 Marvin T. Runyon, Jr., July 6.
1998 William J. Henderson, May 16.
2001 John E. Potter, June 1

Basic Stamp Information

A stamp collector's knowledge of the combined elements that make a given issue of a stamp unique determines his or her ability to identify stamps. These elements include paper, watermark, method of separation, printing, design and gum. On the following pages these important areas are described in detail.

The guide below will direct you to those philatelic terms which are not major headings in the following introductory material. The major headings are:

Plate   Paper   Gum   Postal Markings
Printing   Perforations Luminescence General Glossary

Guide to Subjects

Arrows .... See Plate Markings
Bisect .... See General Glossary
Blocks .... See Plate
Booklet Panes .... See Plate
Booklets .... See Plate
Booklets A.E.F. .... See Plate
Bureau Issues .... See General Glossary
Bureau Prints .... See Postal Markings
Cancellations .... See Postal Markings
Carrier Postmark .... See Postal Markings
Center Line Block .... See Plate
Coarse Perforation .... See Perforations
Coils .... See Plate
Coil Waste .... See Plate
Color Registration Markings .... See Plate Markings
Color Trials .... See Printing
Commemorative Stamps .... See General Glossary
Compound Perforation .... See Perforations
Corner Blocks .... See Plate
Cracked Plate .... See Plate
Crystallization Cracks .... See Plate
Curvature Cracks .... See Plate
Cut Square .... See General Glossary
Diagonal Half .... See General Glossary (Bisect)
Die .... See Plate
Double Impression .... See Printing
Double Paper .... See Paper
Double Perforation .... See Perforations
Double Transfer .... See Plate
Dry Printings .... See note after Scott 1029
Electric Eye .... See Perforations
Embossed Printing .... See Printing
End Roller Grills .... See Paper
Engraving .... See Printing
Error .... See General Glossary
Essay .... See Printing
Fine Perforation .... See Perforations
First Day Covers .... See General Glossary
Flat Plate Printing .... See Printing
Flat Press Printing .... See Printing
Foreign Entry .... See Plate
Giori Press .... See Printing
Gridiron Cancellation .... See Postal Markings
Grills .... See Paper
Gripper Cracks .... See Plate
Guide Dots .... See Plate
Guide Lines .... See Plate Markings
Guide line Blocks .... See Plate
Gum Breaker Ridges .... See General Glossary
Gutter .... See Plate Markings
Hidden Plate Number .... See Plate
Horizontal Half .... See General Glossary (Bisect)
Imperforate .... See Perforations

Imprint .... See Plate Markings
Imprint Blocks .... See Plate
India Paper .... See Paper
Intaglio .... See Printing
Inverted Center .... See Printing
Joint Line Pair .... See Plate
Laid Paper .... See Paper
Line Engraved .... See Printing
Line Pair .... See Plate
Lithography .... See Printing
Luminescent Coating .... See Luminescence
Manila Paper .... See Paper
Margin .... See Plate Markings
Margin Blocks .... See Plate
Multicolored Stamps .... See Printing
New York City Foreign
Mail Cancellations .... See Postal Markings
Offset Printing .... See Printing
Original Gum .... See General Glossary
Overprint .... See Printing
Pair Imperf. Between .... See Perforations
Pane .... See Plate
Part Perforate .... See Perforations
Paste-up .... See Plate
Paste-up Pair .... See Plate
Patent Cancellations .... See Postal Markings
Patriotic Covers .... See General Glossary
Pelure Paper .... See Paper
Phosphor Tagged .... See Luminescence
Plate Arrangement .... See Plate
Plate Flaws .... See Plate
Plate Markings .... See Plate
Postmarks .... See Postal Markings
Precancels .... See Postal Markings
Printed on Both Sides .... See Printing
Proofs .... See Printing
Propaganda Covers .... See General Glossary
Railroad Postmarks .... See Postal Markings
Receiving Mark .... See Postal Markings
Recut .... See Plate
Re-engraved .... See Plate
Re-entry .... See Plate
Re-issue .... See Printing
Relief .... See Plate
Reprints .... See Printing
Retouch .... See Plate
Rosette Crack .... See Printing
Rotary Press Printings .... See Printing
Rotary Press Double Paper .... See Paper
Rough Perforation .... See Perforations
Rouletting .... See Perforations
Se-Tenant .... See General Glossary
Service Indicators .... See Postal Markings
Sheet .... See Plate
Shifted Transfer .... See Plate
Ship Postmarks .... See Postal Markings
Short Transfer .... See Plate
Silk Paper .... See Paper
Specialization .... See General Glossary
Special Printings .... See Printing
Split Grill .... See Paper
Stampless Covers .... See Plate
Stitch Watermark .... See Paper
Strip .... See General Glossary
Surface Printing .... See Printing
Supplementary Mail Cancellations .... See Postal Markings
Surcharges .... See Printing

Plate

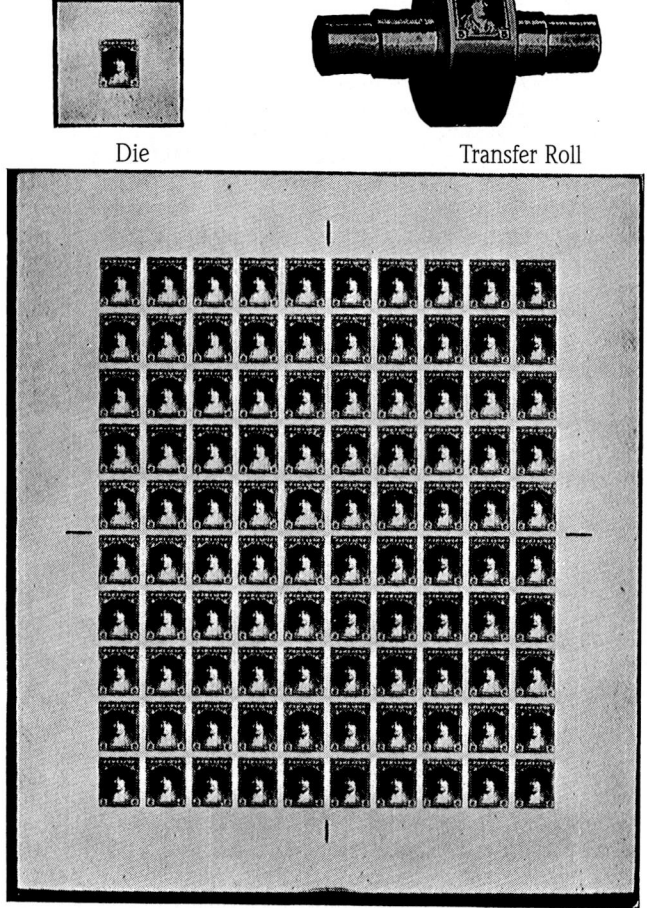

Die   Transfer Roll

Plate

LINE ENGRAVING (INTAGLIO)

Die — Making the die is the initial operation in developing the intaglio plate. The die is a small flat piece of soft steel on which the subject (design) is recess-engraved in reverse. Dies are usually of a single-subject type, but dies exist with multiple subjects of the same design, or even different designs. After the engraving is completed, the die is hardened to withstand the stress of subsequent operations.

Transfer Roll — The next operation is making the transfer roll, which is the medium used to transfer the subject from the die to the plate. A blank roll of soft steel, mounted on a mandrel, is placed under the bearers of a transfer press. The hardened die is placed on the bed of the press and the face of the roll is brought to bear on the die. The bed is then rocked backed and forth under increasing pressure until the soft steel of the roll is forced into every line of the die.

die. The resulting impression on the roll is known as a "relief" or "relief transfer." Several reliefs usually are rocked in on each roll. After the required reliefs are completed, the roll is hardened.

Relief — A relief is the normal reproduction of the design on the die, in reverse. A defective relief, caused by a minute piece of foreign material lodging on the die, may occur during the rocking-in process, or from other causes. Imperfections in the steel of the transfer roll may also result in a breaking away of parts of the design. If the damaged relief is continued in use, it will transfer a repeating defect to the plate. Also reliefs sometime are deliberately altered. "Broken relief" and "altered relief" are terms used to designate these changed conditions.

Plate — A flat piece of soft steel replaces the die on the bed of the transfer press and one of the reliefs on the transfer roll is brought to bear on this soft steel. The position of the plate is determined by position dots, which have been lightly marked on the plate in advance. After the position of the relief is determined, pressure is brought to bear and, by following the same method used in the making of the transfer roll, a transfer is entered. This transfer reproduces, in reverse, every detail of the design of the relief. As many transfers are entered on the plate as there are to be subjects printed at one time.

After the required transfers have been entered, the positions dots, layouts and lines, scratches, etc., are burnished out. Also, any required guide lines, plate numbers, or other marginal markings are added. A proof impression is then taken and if certified (approved), the plate is machined for fitting to the press, hardened and sent to the plate vault until used.

Rotary press plates, after being certified, require additional machining. They are curved to fit the press cylinder and gripper slots are cut into the back of each plate to receive the grippers, which hold the plate securely to the press. The rotary press plate is not hardened until these additional processes are completed.

Transfer — An impression entered on the plate by the transfer roll. A relief transfer is made when entering the design of the die onto the transfer roll.

Double Transfer — The condition of a transfer on a plate that shows evidences of a duplication of all or a portion of the design. A double transfer usually is the result of the changing of the registration between the relief and the plate during the rolling of the original entry.

Occasionally it is necessary to remove the original transfer from a plate and enter the relief a second time. When the finished re-transfer shows indications of the original transfer, because of incomplete erasure, the result is known as a double transfer.

Triple Transfer — Similar to a double transfer, this situation shows evidences of a third entry or two duplications.

Foreign Entry — When original transfers are erased incompletely from a plate, they can appear with new transfers of a different design which are entered subsequently on the plate.

Re-entry — When executing a re-entry, the transfer roll is reapplied to the plate at some time after the latter has been put to press. Thus, worn-out designs may be resharpened by carefully re-entering the transfer roll. If the transfer roll is not carefully entered, the registration will not be true and a double transfer will result. With the protective qualities of chromium plating, it is no longer necessary to resharpen the plate. In fact, after a plate has been curved for the rotary press, it is impossible to make a re-entry.

Shifted Transfer (Shift) — In transferring, the metal displaced on the plate by the entry of the ridges, constituting the design on the transfer roll, is forced ahead of the roll as well as pressed out at the sides. The amount of displaced metal increases with the depth of the entry. When the depth is increased evenly, the design will uniformly entered. Most of the displaced metal is pressed ahead of the roll. If too much pressure is exerted on any pass (rocking), the impression on the previous partial entry may be floated (pushed) ahead of the roll and cause a duplication of the final design. The duplication appears as an increased width of frame lines or a doubling of the lines.

The ridges of the displaced metal are flattened out by the hammering or rolling back of the plate along the space occupied by the subject margins.

Short Transfer — Occasionally the transfer roll is not rocked its entire length in the entering of a transfer onto a plate, with the result that the finished transfer fails to show the complete design. This is known as a short transfer.

Short transfers are known to have been made deliberately, as in the Type III of the 1-cent issue of 1851-60 (Scott 8, 21), or accidentally, as in the 10-cent 1847 (Scott 2).

Re-engraved — Either the die that has been used to make a plate or the plate itself may have its temper drawn (softened) and be re-cut. The resulting impressions for such re-engraved die or plate may differ very slightly from the original issue and are given the label "re-engraved."

Re-cut — A re-cut is the strengthening or altering of a line by use of an engraving tool on unhardened plates.

Retouching — A retouch is the strengthening or altering of a line by means of etching.

PLATE ARRANGEMENT

Arrangement — The first engraved plates used to produce U.S. postage stamps in 1847 contained 200 subjects. The number of subjects to a plate varied between 100 and 300 until the issue of 1890, when the 400-subject plate was first laid down. Since that time, this size of plate has been used for a majority of the regular postal issues (those other than commemoratives). Exceptions to this practice exist, particularly among the more recent issues, and are listed under the headings of the appropriate issues in the catalogue.

Sheet — In single-color printings, the complete impression from a plate is termed a sheet. A sheet of multicolored stamps (two or more colors) may come from a single impression of a plate, i.e., many Giori-type press printings from 1957, or from as many impressions from separate plates as there are inks used for the particular stamp. Combination process printings may use both methods of multicolor production: Giori-type intaglio with offset lithography or with photogravure.

The Huck multicolor press used plates of different format (40, 72 or 80 subjects). The sheet it produced had 200 subjects for normal-sized commemoratives or 400 subjects for regular-issue stamps, similar to the regular products of other presses.

See the note on the Combination Press following the listing for Scott 1703.

In casual usage, a "pane" often is referred to as a "sheet."

Pane — A pane is the part of the original sheet that is issued for sale at post offices. A pane may be the same as an entire sheet, where the plate is small, or it may be a half, quarter, or some other fraction of a sheet where the plate is large.

The illustration shown later under the subtopic "Plate Markings" shows the layout of a 400-subject sheet from a flat plate, which for issuance would have been divided along the intersecting guide lines into four panes of 100.

Panes are classified into normal reading position according to their location on the printed sheet: U.L., upper left; U.R., upper right; L.L., lower left; and L.R., lower right. Where only two panes appear on a sheet, they are designed "R" (right) and "L" (left) or "T" (top) and "B" (bottom), on the basis of the division of the sheet vertically or horizontally.

To fix the location of a particular stamp on any pane, except for those printed on the Combination press, the pane is held with the subjects in the normal position, and a position number is given to each stamp starting with the first stamp in the upper left corner and proceeding horizontally to the right, then staring on the second row at the left and counting across to the right, and so on to the last stamp in the lower right corner.

In describing the location of a stamp on a sheet of stamps issued prior to 1894, the practice is to give the stamp position number first, then the pane position and finally the plate number, i.e., "1R22." Beginning with the 1894 issue and on all later issues the method used is to give the plate number first, then the position of the pane, and finally the position number of the stamp, i.e., "16807LL48" to identify an example of Scott 619 or "2138L2" to refer to an example of Scott 323.

BOOKLET STAMPS

Plates for Stamp Booklets — These are illustrated and described preceding the listing of booklet panes and covers in this catalogue.

Booklet Panes — Panes especially printed and cut to be sold in booklets which are a convenient way to purchase and store stamps. U.S. Booklet panes are straight-edged on three sides, but perforated between the stamps. Die cut, ATM and other panes will vary from this. Except for BK64 and BK65, the A.E.F. booklets, booklets were sold by the Post Office Department for a one-cent premium until 1962. Other sections of this catalogue with listings for booklet panes include Savings, Telegraphs and Canal Zone.

A.E.F. Booklets — These were special booklets prepared principally for use by the U.S. Army Post Office in France during World War I. They were issued in 1-cent and 2-cent denominations with 30 stamps to a pane (10 x 3), bound at right or left. As soon as Gen. John J. Pershing's organization reached France, soldiers' mail was sent free by means of franked envelopes.

Stamps were required during the war for the civilian personnel, as well as for registered mail, parcel post and other types of postal service. See the individual listings for Scott 498f and 499f and booklets BK64 and BK65.

COIL STAMPS

First issued in 1908-09, coils (rolls) originally were produced in two sizes, 500 and 1,000 stamps, with the individual stamps arranged endways or sideways and with and without perforations between.

Rolls of stamps for use in affixing or vending machines were first constructed by private companies and later by the Bureau of Engraving and Printing. Originally, it was customary for the Post Office Department to sell to the private vending companies and others imperforate sheets of stamps printed from the ordinary 400-subject flat plates. These sheets were then pasted together end-to-end or side-to-side by the purchaser and cut into rolls as desired, with the perforations being applied to suit the requirements of the individual machines. Such stamps with private perforations are listed in this catalogue under "Vending and Affixing Machine Perforations."

Later the Bureau produced coils by the same method, also in rolls of 500 and 1,000. These coils were arranged endways or sideways and were issued with or without perforation.

With the introduction of the Stickney rotary press, curved plates made for use on these presses were put into use at the Bureau of Engraving and Printing, and the sale of imperforate sheets was discontinued. This move marked the end of the private perforation. Rotary press coils have been printed on a number of presses over the years and have been made in sizes of 100, 500, 1,000, 3,000 and 10,000 stamps, etc.

Paste-up — the junction of two flat-plate printings joined by pasting the edge of one sheet onto the edge of another sheet to make coils. A two-stamp example of this joining is a "paste-up pair." See Splice.

Guide Line Pair — attached pair of flat-plate-printed coil stamps with printed line between. This line is identical with the guide line (See listing under "Plate Markings") found in sheets.

Joint Line — The edges of two curved plates do not meet exactly on the press and the small space between the plates takes ink and prints a line. A pair of rotary-press-printed stamps with such a line is called a "joint line pair."

Coil stamps printed on the Multicolor Huck Press do not consistently produce such lines. Occasionally accumulated ink will print partial lines in one or more colors, and very occasionally complete lines will be printed. Stamps resulting from such situations are not listed in this Catalogue. The "B" and "C" presses do not print joint lines at all.

Splice — the junction of two rotary-press printings by butting the ends of the web (roll) of paper together and pasting a strip of perforated translucent paper on the back of the junction. The two-stamp specimen to show this situation is a "spliced pair."

Splices occur when a web breaks and is repaired or when one web is finished and another begins.

Plate Number — for U.S. coil stamps prior to Scott 1891, Scott 1947, War Savings Coils and Canal Zone:

On a rotary-press horizontal coil the top or bottom part of a plate number may show. On a vertical coil, the left or right part of a plate number may show. The number was entered on the plate to be cut off when the web was sliced into coils and is found only when the web was sliced off center. Every rotary press coil plate number was adjacent to a joint line, so both features could occur together in one strip.

For U.S. stamps from Scott 1891 onward (excluding Scott 1947) and Official coils:

The plate number is placed in the design area of the stamp, so it will not be trimmed off. Such items are normally collected unused with the stamp containing the plate number in the center of a strip of three or five stamps. They normally are collected used as singles. The line, if any, will be at the right of the plate-number stamp. On the Cottrell press, the number occurs every 24th stamp, on the "B" press every 52nd stamp, on the "C," "D" and "F" presses every 48th stamp.

Unused plate number strips of three and five are valued in this catalogue.

Hidden Plate Number — A plate number may be found entirely on a coil made from flat plates, but usually is hidden by a part of the next sheet which has been lapped over it.

Coil Waste — an occurrence brought about by stamps issued in perforated sheets from a printing intended for coils. These stamps came from short lengths of paper at the end of the coil run. Sometimes the salvaged sections were those which had been laid aside for mutilation because of some defect. Because the paper had been moistened during printing, it sometimes stretched slightly and provided added printing area. Sheets of 70, 100, and 170 are known. See Scott 538-541, 545-546, 578-579, and 594-595.

"T" — Letter which appears in the lower design area of Scott 2115b, which was printed on a experimental pre-phosphored paper. The stamp with the plate number is inscribed "T1."

SHEET STAMPS

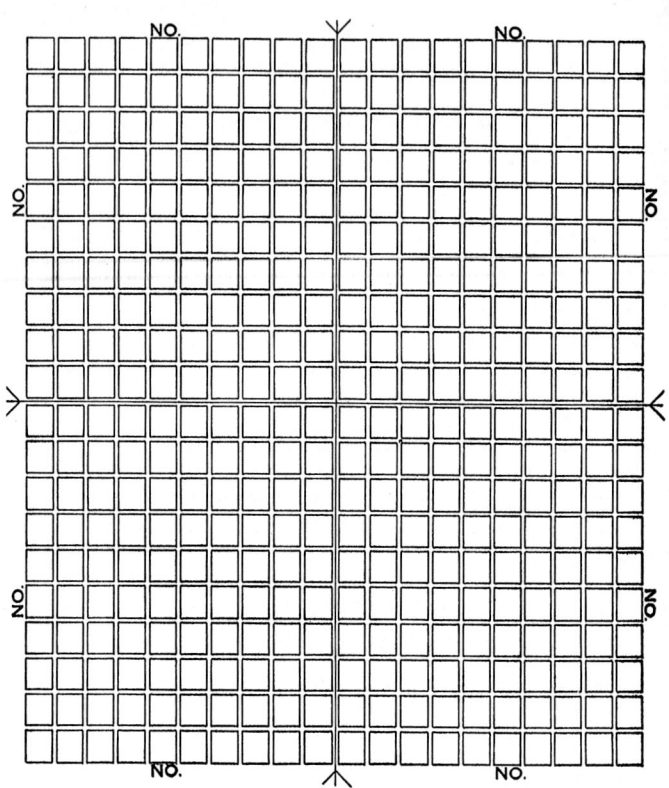

A typical 400-subject plate of 1922

Plate Markings — The illustration above shows a typical 400-subject plate of the 1922 issue with markings as found on this type of plate. Other layouts and markings are found further in the Catalogue text.

Guide Lines — Horizontal or vertical colored lines between the stamps, extending wholly or partially across the sheet. They serve as guides for the operators of perforating machines or to indicate the point of separation of the sheet into panes.

A block of stamps divided by any of the guide lines is known as a "line block" or "guide line block." The block of stamps from the exact center of the sheet, showing the crossed guide lines, is a "center line block."

Gutters — When guide lines are used to mark the division of the sheet into panes, the space between the stamps at the edge of the pane is no different than the space between any other stamps on the sheet. Some plates provide a wide space, or gutter, between the panes. These plates do not produce guide lines.

A pair of stamps with the wide space between is known as a "gutter pair", and blocks with that situation are "gutter blocks." A block of stamps from the exact center of the sheet, showing the two wide spaces crossing, is a "center gutter block" or "cross gutter block."

Gutter pairs or gutter blocks must contain complete stamps on both sides of the gutter, intact including perforation teeth unless imperforate. The stamps on either side of the gutter may or may not be creased; either way they qualify as the listed variety.

Arrows — arrow-shaped markings were used in the margins of stamp sheets, in place of guide lines, on the issues of 1870 through 1894. Since 1894, guide lines with arrows at both ends have been the standard practice on flat-plate printings.

A margin block of at least four stamps, showing the arrow centered at one edge, is known as a "margin block with arrow."

Color Registration Markings — marks of different sizes and shapes used as an aid in properly registering the colors in producing a bicolored or multicolored stamp.

Imprint — design containing the name of the producer of the stamps which appears on the sheet margin usually near the plate number.

A block of stamps with the sheet margin attached, bearing the imprint, is known as the "imprint block." Imprints and plate numbers usually are collected in blocks of six, or of sufficient length to include the entire marking. From 1894 until about 1907, one fashion was to collect the imprints in strips of three, and these have been noted in this Catalogue.

The imprint and plate number combination are found in eight types I-VII, which are illustrated at Scott 245 and Scott E3. Example: "T V" refers to Type V.

Plate Numbers — Serial numbers assigned to plates, appearing on one or more margins of the sheet or pane to identify the plate.

Flat Press Plate Numbers — usually collected in a margin block of six stamps with the plate number centered in the margin.

Rotary Press Plate Numbers — usually collected in a corner margin block large enough to show the plate number(s) and position along the margin and complete selvage on two sides. For issues with a single plate number at the corner of the pane a block of four normally suffices.

During 1933-39, some plates had the number opposite the third stamp (up or down) from the corner of the sheet and for these the number is customarily collected in a corner block of no less than eight stamps. Multicolored stamps may have more than one plate number in the margin and the "plate block" may then be expanded to suit the collector's desire.

The Catalogue listing for plate blocks includes enough stamps to accommodate all numbers on the plate. Plate block listings for se-tenant issues include all the designs as part of the block. When a continuous design is involved, such as Scott 1629-31, the complete design will be included in the plate number block. The entire pane constitutes the plate number block for issues such as the State Birds and Flowers (Scott 1953-2002).

Plate numbers take a further designation from the position on the sheet on which they appear, e.g. U.L. refers to upper left pane, etc.

See note following Scott 1703 for description of combination press markings.

Private Contractor Marks — On rotary plates from Scott 1789 onward: "A" denotes issues produced by private contractor American Bank Note Co., "B" by Banknote Corp of America, "D" by Dittler Brothers, "G" by Guilford Gravure, "K" by KCS Industries, "M" by 3M Corp., "P" by Ashton-Potter (USA) Ltd., "S" by Stamp Venturers, Inc. (now Sennett Security Products), "U" by U.S. Bank Note Co., "V" by Avery Dennison.

Stars — used on the flat plates to indicate a change from the previous spacing of the stamps. They also were used as a check on the assignment of the printed sheets to a perforating machine of the proper setting. Stars appear on certain rotary plates used for printing stamps for coils, appearing adjacent to the plate joint line and above stamp No. 1 on the 170-subject plates, and to the left of stamp No. 141 on the 150-subject plates.

"A" — On flat plates; used on plates having uniform vertical spacing between rows of subjects, but wider than those with the star marking.

"C.S." and "C" — plate has been chromium plated.

"E.I." — abbreviation for Electrolytic Iron. The designation is for plates made by the electrolytic process.

"F" — used to indicate the plate is ready for hardening. This appears only on flat plates and generally precedes the upper right plate number.

plates of some bicolored issues. This marking is used to check printings for "inverts." Beginning with the 6-cent bicolored airpost issue of 1938 (Scott C23), bicolored crosses also were used as an additional check.

"Coil Stamps" — appearing on the side sheet margins, designates plates used in the production of endwise coils.

"S 20," "S 30," "S 40" — marginal markings appearing on certain 150- and 170-subject rotary press plates to designate experimental variations in the depth and character of the frame line to over-come excess inking. "S 30" was adopted as the standard. Blocks showing these markings are listed as "Margin Block with S 20," etc., in this Catalogue.

Initials — used in sheet margins to identify individuals in the Bureau of Engraving and Printing who participated in the production or use of the plates.

Gutter Dashes — on the first 400-subject rotary plates, 3/16-inch horizontal dashes appear in the gutter between the 10th and 11th vertical rows of stamps. This arrangement was superseded by dashes 3/16-inch at the extreme ends of the vertical and horizontal gutters, and a 1/4-inch cross at the central gutter intersection. This latter arrangement continued until replaced by the scanning marks on the Electric Eye plates. See Electric Eye.

Margin — border outside the printed design or perforated area of a stamp, also known as selvage, or the similar border of a sheet of stamps. A block of stamps from the top, side or bottom of a sheet or pane to which is attached the selvage (margin) is known as a "margin block." A block of stamps from the corner of a sheet with full selvage attached to two adjoining sides is known as a "corner block."

NOTE — The descriptions and definitions above indicate that a certain number of stamps make up an arrow or plate number block. Any block of stamps, no matter how large or small, which had an arrow or plate number on its margin would be considered by that name. The usual practice is to collect flat-plate numbers in margin blocks of six and arrow blocks in margin blocks of four. Plate number blocks from rotary press printings generally are collected in blocks of 4 when the plate number appears beside the stamp at any of the four corners of the sheet. Particularly relative to bi-colored stamps, an arrow block is now separated from a plate number block. Thus, in those situations, the two individual types of blocks might form a block of eight or 10, as the situation dictates.

PRINTING

Methods Used — all four basic forms of printing have been used in producing U.S. stamps, engraved, photogravure, lithography, and typography. Holography has been used on some envelopes.

Engraved (Recess or Intaglio) — process where ink is received and held in lines depressed below the surface of the plate. Initially, in printing from such plate damp paper was forced into the depressed lines and therefore picked up ink. Consequently, ink lines on the stamp are slightly raised. This also is noted from the back of the stamp, where depressions mark where ink is placed on the front.

When the ornamental work for a stamp is engraved by a machine, the process is called "engine turned" or lathe-work engraving. An example of such lathe-work background is the 3-cent stamp of 1861 (Scott Illustration No. A25).

Engraved stamps were printed only with flat plates until 1914, when rotary press printing was introduced. "Wet" and "dry" printings are explained in the note in the text of the Catalogue following Scott 1029. The Giori press, used to print some U.S. stamps from 1957 (see Scott 1094, 4-cent Flag issue), applied two or three different colored inks simultaneously.

The Huck Multicolor press, put into service at the Bureau of

Engraving and Printing in 1968, was used first to produce the 1969 Christmas stamp (Scott 1363) and the 6-cent flag coil of 1969 (Scott 1338A). Developed by the Bureau's technical staff and the firm of graphic arts engineers whose name it bears, the Huck press printed, tagged with phosphor ink, gummed and perforated stamps in a continuous operation. Printing was accomplished in as many as nine colors. Fed by paper from a roll, the Huck Multicolor used many recess-engraved plates of smaller size than any used previously for U.S. stamp printing. Its product has certain characteristics which other U.S. stamps do not have. Post office panes of the 1969 Christmas stamp, for example, show seven or eight plate numbers in the margins. Joint lines appear after every two or four stamps. Other presses providing multiple plate numbers are the Andreotti, Champlain, Combination, Miller Offset, A Press, D Press and more.

Photogravure — the design of a stamp to be printed by photogravure usually is photographed through an extremely fine screen, lined in minute quadrille. The screen breaks up the reproduction into tiny dots, which are etched onto the plate and the depressions formed hold the ink. Somewhat similarly to engraved printing, the ink is lifted out of the lines by the paper, which is pressed against the plate. Unlike engraved printing, however, the ink does not appear to be raised relative to the surface of the paper.

Gravure is most often used for multicolored stamps, generally using the three primary colors (red, yellow and blue) and black. By varying the dot matrix pattern and density of these colors, virtually any color can be reproduced. A typical full-color gravure stamp will be created from four printing cylinders (one for each color). The original multicolored image will have been photographically separated into its component colors.

For U.S. stamps, photogravure first appeared in 1967 with the Thomas Eakins issue (Scott 1335). The early photogravure stamps were printed by outside contractors until the Bureau obtained the multicolor Andreotti press in 1971. The earliest stamp printed on that press was the 8-cent Missouri Statehood issue of 1971 (Scott 1426).

Color control bars, dashes or dots are printed in the margin of one pane in each "Andreotti" sheet of 200, 160 or 128 stamps. These markings generally are collected in blocks of 20 or 16 (two full rows of one pane), which include the full complement of plate numbers, Mr. Zip and the Zip and Mail Early slogans.

Details on the Combination Press follow the listing for Scott 1703.

Modern gravure printing may use computer-generated dot-matrix screens, and modern plates may be of various types including metal-coated plastic. The catalogue designation of Photogravure (or "Photo") covers any of these older and more modern gravure methods of printing.

Lithography — this is the most common and least expensive process for printing stamps. In this method, the design is drawn by hand or transferred in greasy ink from an original engraving to the surface of a lithographic stone or metal plate. The stone or plate is wet with an acid fluid, which causes it to repel the printing ink except at the greasy lines of the design. A fine lithographic print closely resembles an engraving, but the lines are not raised on the face or depressed on the back. Thus there usually is a more dull appearance to the lithograph than to the engraving.

Offset Printing or Offset Lithography — a modern development of the lithographic process. Anything that will print — type, woodcuts, photoengravings, plates engraved or etched in intaglio, halftone plates, linoleum blocks, lithographic stones or plates, photogravure plates, rubber stamps, etc. — may be used. Greasy ink is applied to the dampened plate or form and an impression made on a rubber blanket. Paper immediately is pressed against the blanket, which transfers the ink. Because of its greater flexibility, offset printing has largely displaced lithography.

Because the processes and results obtained are similar, stamps printed by either of these two methods normally are considered to be "lithographed."

The first application of lithographic printing for any U.S. items listed in this Catalogue was for Post Office seals, probably using stone printing bases. See also some Confederates States general issues. Offset lithography was used for the 1914 documentary revenues (Scott R195-R216). Postage stamps followed in 1918-20 (Scott 525-536) because of war-time shortages of ink, plates, and manpower relative to the regular intaglio production.

The next use of offset lithography for postage stamps was in 1964 with the Homemakers issue (Scott 1253), in combination with intaglio printing. Many similar issues followed, including the U.S. Bicentennial souvenir sheets of 1976 (Scott 1686-1689), all of which were produced by the combination of the two printing methods. The combination process serves best for soft backgrounds and tonal effects.

Typography — an exact reverse of engraved-plate printing, this process provides for the parts of the design which are to show in color to be left at the original level of the plate and the spaces between cut away. Ink is applied to the raised lines and the pressure of the printing forces these lines, more or less into the paper. The process impresses the lines on the face of the stamp and slightly raises them on the back. Normally, a large number of electrotypes of the original are made and assembled into a plate with the requisite number of designs for printing a sheet of stamps. Stamps printed by this process show greater uniformity, and the stamps are less expensive to print than with intaglio printing.

The first U.S. postal usage of an item printed by typography, or letterpress, under national authority was the 1846 "2" surcharge on the United States City Despatch Post 3-cent carrier stamp (Scott 6LB7). The next usage was the 1865 newspaper and periodical stamp issue, which for security reasons combined the techniques of machine engraving, colorless embossing and typography. This created an unusual first.

Most U.S. stamp typography consists of overprints, such as those for the Canal Zone, the Molly Pitcher and Hawaii Sesquicentennial stamps of 1928 (Scott 646-648), the Kansas-Nebraska control markings (Scott 658-679), Bureau-printed precancels, and "specimen" markings.

Embossed (relief) Printing — method in which the design is sunk in the metal of the die and the printing is done against a platen that is forced into the depression, thus forming the design on the paper in relief. Embossing may be done without ink (blind embossing), totally with ink, or a combination thereof. The U.S. stamped envelopes are an example of this form of printing.

Typeset — made from movable type.

Typeset Stamps — printed from ordinary printer's type. Sometimes electrotype or stereotype plates are made, but because such stamps usually are printed only in small quantities for temporary use, movable type often is used for the purpose. This method of printing is apt to show broken type and lack of uniformity. See Hawaii Scott 1-4 and 12-26.

Holograms — for objects to appear as holograms on stamps, a model exactly the same size as it is too appear on the hologram must be created. Rather than using photographic film to capture the image, holography records an image on a photoresist material. in processing, chemicals eat away at certain exposed areas, leaving a pattern of constructive and destructive interference. When the photoresist is developed, the result is a pattern of uneven ridges that acts as a mold. This mold is then coated with metal, and the resulting form is used to press copies in much the same way phonograph records are produced.

A typical reflective hologram used for stamps consists of a reproduction of the uneven patterns on a plastic film that is applied to a reflective background, ususally a silver or gold foil. Light is reflected off the background through the film, making the pattern present on the film visible. Because of the uneven pattern of the film, the viewer will perceive the objects in their proper three-dimensional relationships with appropriate brightness.

The first hologram on a stamp was produced by Austria in 1988 (Scott 1441).

Foil Application — A modern tecnique of applying color to stamps involves the application of metallic foil to the stamp paper. A pattern of foil is applied to the stamp paper by use of a stamping die. The foil usually is flat, but it may be textured. Canada Scott 1735 has three different foil applications in pearl, bronze, and gold. The gold foil was texured using a chemical-etch copper embossing die. The printing of this stamp also involved two-colored offset lithography plus embossing.

ADDITIONAL TERMS

Multicolored Stamps — until 1957 when the Giori press was introduced, bicolored stamps were printed on a flat-bed press in two runs, one for each color (example: Norse-American Issue of 1925, Scott 620-621). In the flat-press bicolors, if the sheet were fed to the press on the second run in reversed position, the part printed in the second color would be upside down, producing an "invert" such as the famed Scott C3a.

With the Giori press and subsequent presses, stamps could be printed in more than one color at the same time.

Many bicolored and multicolored stamps show varying degrees of poor color registration (alignment). Such varieties are not listed in this Catalogue.

Color Changeling — a stamp which, because of exposure to the environment, has naturally undergone a change of ink colors. Orange U.S. stamps of the early 1900's are notorious for turning brown as the ink reacts with oxygen. Exposure to light can cause some inks to fade. These are not considered color omitted errors. Exposure to other chemicals can cause ink colors to change. These stamps are merely altered stamps, and their value to collectors is greatly diminished.

Color Trials — printings in various colors, made to facilitate selection of color for the issued stamp.

Double Impression — a second impression of a stamp over the original impression.

This is not to be confused with a "double transfer," which is a plate imperfection and does not show a doubling of the entire design. A double impression shows every line clearly doubled. See also "Printed on Both Sides."

Essay — A proposed design, a designer's model or an incomplete engraving. Its design differs in some way — great or small — from the issued item.

Inverted Center — bicolored or multicolored stamp with the center printed upside down relative to the remainder of the design. A stamp may be described as having an inverted center even if the center is printed first. See "Multicolored Stamps."

Flat Plate Printing — stamp printed on a flat-bed press, rather than on a rotary press. See "Plate."

Overprint — any word, inscription or device printed across the face of a stamp to alter its use or locality or otherwise to serve a special purpose. An example is U.S. Scott 646, the "Molly Pitcher" overprint, which is Scott 634 with a black overprinted inscription as a memorial to the Revolutionary War heroine. See "Surcharge."

Printed on Both Sides — Occasionally a sheet of stamps already printed will, through error, be turned over and passed through the press a second time, creating the rare "printed on both sides" variety.

ety. On one side the impression is almost always poor or incomplete. This often is confused with an "offset," which occurs when sheets of stamps are stacked while the ink is still wet.

The "printed on both sides" variety will show the design as a positive (all inscriptions reading correctly) and the offset shows a reverse impression. See "Double Impression."

Progressive Proof — a type of essay that is an incomplete engraving of the finished accepted die.

Proofs — trial printings of a stamp made from the original die or the finished plate.

Reprints and Reissues — are impressions of stamps (usually obsolete) made from the original plates or stones. If they are valid for postage and reproduce obsolete issues (such as U.S. Scott 102-111), the stamps are *reissues*. If they are from current issues, they are designated as *second, third,* etc., *printing*. If designated for a particular purpose, they are called *special printings*.

When special printings are not valid for postage, but are made from original dies and plates by authorized persons, they are *official reprints*. *Private reprints* are made from the original plates and dies by private hands. An example of a private reprint is that of the 1871-1932 reprints made from the original die of the 1845 New Haven, Conn., postmaster's provisional. *Official reproductions* or imitations are made from new dies and plates by government authorization. Scott will list those reissues that are valid for postage if they differ significantly from the original printing.

The U.S. government made special printings of its first postage stamps in 1875. Produced were official imitations of the first two stamps (listed as Scott 3-4), reprints of the demonetized pre-1861 issues (Scott 40-47) and reissues of the 1861 stamps, the 1869 stamps and the then-current 1875 denominations. Even though the official imitations and the reprints were not valid for postage, Scott lists all of these U.S. special printings.

Most reprints or reissues differ slightly from the original stamp in some characteristic, such as gum, paper, perforation, color or watermark. Sometimes the details are followed so meticulously that only a student of that specific stamp is able to distinguish the reprint or reissue from the original.

Rotary Press Printings — stamps which have been printed on a rotary-type press from curved plates. Rotary press-printed stamps are longer or wider than stamps of the same design printed from flat plates. All rotary press printings through 1953, except coil waste (such as Scott 538), exist with horizontal "gum breaker ridges" varying from one to four per stamp. See: "Plate."

Surcharge — overprint which alters or restates the face value or denomination of the stamp to which it was applied. An example is Scott K1, where U.S. stamps were surcharged for use by U.S. Offices in China. Many surcharges are typeset. See: "Overprint" and "Typeset."

COMMON FLAWS

Cracked Plate — A term to describe stamps which show evidences that the plate from which they were printed was cracked.

Plate cracks have various causes, each which may result in a different formation and intensity of the crack. Cracks similar to the above illustration are quite common in older issues and are largely due to the plate being too-quickly immersed in the cooling bath when being tempered. These cracks are known as crystallization cracks. A jagged line running generally in one direction and most often in the gutter between stamps is due to the stress of the steel during the rolling in or transferring process.

In curved (rotary) plates, there are two types of cracks. Once is the bending or curving crack, which is quite marked and always runs in the direction in which the plate is curved.

The accompanying illustration shows the second type, the gripper crack. This type is caused by the cracking of the plate over the slots cut in the underside of the plate, which receive the "grippers" that fasten the plate to the press. These occur only on curved plates and are to be found in the row of stamps adjoining the plate joint. These appear on the printed impression as light irregularly colored lines, usually parallel to the plate joint line.

Rosette Crack — cluster of fine cracks radiating from a central point in irregular lines. These usually are caused by the plate receiving a blow.

Scratched Plate — caused by foreign matter scratching the plate, these usually are too minor to mention. See: "Gouge."

Gouge — exceptionally heavy and usually short scratches, these may be caused by a tool falling onto the plate.

Surface Stains — irregular surface marks resembling the outline of a point on a map. Experts differ on the cause. These are too minor to list.

PAPER

Paper falls broadly into two types: wove and laid. The difference in the appearance is caused by the wire cloth upon which the pulp is first formed.

Paper also is distinguished as thick or thin, hard or soft, and by its color (such as bluish, yellowish, greenish, etc.).

Wove — where the wire cloth is of even and closely woven nature, producing a sheet of uniform texture throughout. This type shows no light or dark figures when held to the light.

Laid — where the wire cloth is formed of closely spaced parallel wires crossed at much wider intervals by cross wires. The resultant paper shows alternate light and dark lines. The distances between the widely spaced lines and the thickness of these lines may vary, but on any one piece of paper they will be the same.

Pelure — type of paper which is very thin and semi-transparent. It may be either wove or laid.

Bluish — The 1909 so-called "bluish" paper was made with 35 percent rag stock instead of all wood pulp. The bluish (actually grayish-blue) color goes through the paper, showing clearly on back and face. See the note with Scott 331.

Manila — a coarse paper formerly made of Manila hemp fiber. Since about 1890, so-called "manila" paper has been manufactured entirely from wood fiber. It is used for cheaper grades of envelopes and newspaper wrappers and normally is a natural light brown. Sometimes color is added, such as in the U.S. "amber manila" envelopes. It may be either wove or laid.

Silk — refers to two kinds of paper found by stamp collectors.

One type has one or more threads of silk embedded in the substance of the paper, extending across the stamp. In the catalogues, this type of paper usually is designated as "with silk threads."

The other type, used to print many U.S. revenue stamps, has shortsilk fibers strewn over it and impressed into it during manufacture. This is simply called "silk paper."

Ribbed — paper which shows fine parallel ridges on one or both sides of a stamp.

India — a soft, silky appearing wove paper, usually used for proof impressions.

Double Paper — as patented by Charles F. Steel, this style of paper consists of two layers, a thin surface paper and a thicker backing paper. Double paper was supposed to be an absolute safeguard against cleaning cancellations off stamps to permit reuse, for any attempt to remove the cancellation would result in the destruction of the upper layer. The Continental Bank Note Co. experimented with this paper in the course of printing Scott 156-165. See "Rotary Press Double Paper."

China Clay Paper — See note preceding Scott 331.

Fluorescent or Bright Paper — See "Luminescence."

Rotary Press Double Paper — Rotary press printings occasionally are found on a double sheet of paper. The web (roll) of paper used on these press must be continuous. Therefore, any break in the web during the process of manufacture must be lapped and pasted. The overlapping portion, when printed upon, is known as a "double paper" variety. More recently, the lapped ends are joined with colored or transparent adhesive tape.

Such results of splicing normally are removed from the final printed material, although some slip through quality control efforts.

In one instance known, two splices have been made, thus leaving three thicknesses of paper. All rotary press stamps may exist on double paper.

Watermarks — Closely allied to the study of paper, watermarks normally are formed in the process of paper manufacture. Watermarks used on U.S. items consist of the letters "USPS" (found on postage stamps). "USPOD" (found on postal cards), the Seal of the United States (found on official seals), "USIR" (found on revenue items), and various monograms of letters, numbers, and so on, found on stamped envelopes.

The letters may be single- or double-lined and are formed from dies made of wire or cut from metal and soldered to the frame on which the pulp is caught or to a roll under which it is passed. The action of these dies is similar to the wires causing the prominent lines of laid paper, with the designs making thin places in the paper which show by more easily transmitting light.

The best method of detecting watermarks is to lay the stamp face down on a dark tray and immerse the stamp in a commercial brand of watermark fluid, which brings up the watermark in dark lines against a lighter background.

Note: This method of detecting watermarks may damage certain stamps printed with inks that run when immersed (such a U.S. Scott 1260 and 1832). It is advisable to first test a damaged stamp of the same type, if possible.

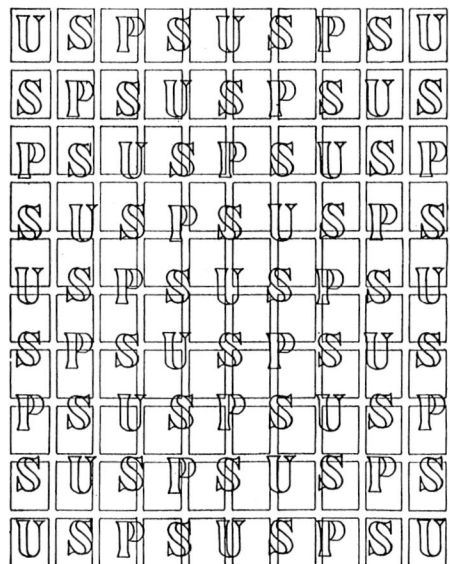

Wmk. 191
PERIOD OF USE
Postage: 1895-1910   Revenue: none
In the 1895-1903 U.S. issues, the paper was fed through the press so that the watermark letter read horizontally on 400 subject sheets and vertically on 200 subject sheets.

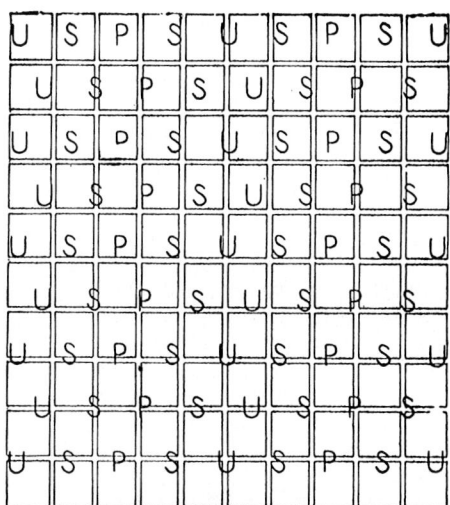

Wmk. 190
PERIOD OF USE
Postage: 1910-1916   Revenue: 1914

USIR
Wmk. 191R
PERIOD OF USE
Postage (unintentionally): 1895   Revenue: 1878-1958
(Scott 271a, 272a), 1951 (832b)

Paper watermarked "USPOD" was used for postal cards from 1873 to 1875. For watermarks used on stamped envelopes, see Envelope Section in the text.

Watermarks may be found normal, reversed, inverted, inverted reversed and sideways, as seen from the back of the stamp.

Stitch Watermark — a type of watermark consisting of a row of short parallel lines. This is caused by the stitches which join the ends of the band on which the paper pulp is first formed. Stitch watermarks have been found on a great many issues, and may exist on all.

GRILLS

The grill consists of small square pyramids in parallel rows, impressed or embossed on the stamp. The object of the process is to break the fibers of the paper so that the ink from the cancellation would soak into the paper and make washing for reuse impossible. Grill impressions, when viewed from the face of the stamp, may be either "points up" or "points down." This process was used on U.S. Scott 79-101, 112-122 and 134-144 as well as some examples of 156-165 and 178-179.

Regular   Continuous   Split Grill
Grill   Marginal Grill

Continuous Marginal Grill — includes continuous rows of grill points impressed by the untrimmed parts of the ends of the grill rollers, noted as "end roller grill" on the 1870 and 1873 issues, and those grills which came from a continuous band lengthwise of the roller.

Split Grill — situation on a stamp showing portions of two or more grills, caused by a sheet being fed under the grill roller off center.

Double (or Triple) Grill — stamp showing two or more separate grill impressions. This is not to be confused with a split grill, which shows two or four partial impressions from a single grill impression.

Rotary Grills — grilled appearance occasionally found on rotary press printings that was produced unintentionally by a knurled roller during the perforating process.

Similarly, grill-like impressions can be left on stamps dispensed from vending machines.

SEPARATION

"Separation" is the general term used to describe methods used to separate stamps. The standard forms currently in use in the United States are perforating and die-cutting. These methods are done during the stamp production process, after printing. Sometimes these methods are done on-press or sometimes as a separate step. The earliest issues, such as the 1847 5¢ Franklin (Scott 1), did not have any means provided for separation. It was expected the stamps would be cut apart with scissors or folded and torn. These are examples of imperforate stamps. Many stamps were first issued in imperforate formats and were later issued with perforations. Therefore, care must be observed in buying single imperforate stamps to be certain they were issued imperforate and are not perforated copies that have been altered by having the perforations trimmed away. Stamps issued imperforate usually are valued as singles. However, imperforate varieties of normally perforated stamps should be collected in pairs or larger pieces as indisputable evidence of their imperforate character.

PERFORATIONS

The chief style of separation of U.S. stamps has been perforating. This is produced by cutting away the paper between the stamps in a line of holes (usually round) and leaving little bridges of paper between the stamps. These little bridges are the "teeth" of the perforation and, of course, project from the stamp when it is torn from the pane.

As the gauge of the perforation often is the distinguishing difference among stamps, it is necessary to measure and describe them by a gauge number. The standard for this measurement is the number of such teeth within two centimeters. Thus, we say that a stamp is perforated 12 or 10½ to note that there are either 12 or 10½ teeth counted within two centimeters.

Some later U.S. stamps are "stroke" perforated rather than "line" perforated. While it is difficult to tell the difference on a single stamp, with a block of four or more stamps the difference is more easily seen where the horizontal and vertical perforations cross. On the "stroke"-perforated items, the crossing point is clean and no holes are out of line. On the "line"-perforated stamps, the crossing point only rarely is perfect and generally there is a roughness.

Perforation Gauge — tool for measuring perforation, as described above.

Fine Perforation — perforation with small holes and teeth close together.

Coarse Perforation — perforation with large holes and teeth far apart, frequently irregularly spaced.

Rough Perforation — holes not clean cut, but jagged.

Compound Perforation — normally where perforations at the top and bottom differ from the perforations at the sides of the stamp. In describing compound perforations, the gauge of the top is given first, then the sides.

Some stamps are found where one side will differ from the other three, and in this case the reading will be the top first, then the right side, then the bottom, then the left side.

Double Perforations — often found on early U.S. revenue stamps and occasionally on postage issues, double perforations are applied in error. They do not generally command a premium over catalogue values of properly perforated stamps and are not to be confused with a variety found on occasional rotary press printings where stamps adjacent to the center gutters will show the entire width of the gutter and a line of perforations on the far end of the gutter. These are caused by the sheet having been cut off center and are called "gutter snipes." They command a small premium.

Many double perforations were privately made to increase the value of the stamp, and are to be considered damaged stamps.

Electric Eye — an electronically controlled mechanical device acting as a guide in the operation of the perforating machine. Positive identification of stamps perforated by the electric eye process may be made by means of the distinctive marks in the gutters and margins of the full sheets on the printed web of paper. The original marks consisted of a series of heavy dashes dividing the vertical sheet gutter between the left and right panes (illustration A), together with a single line (margin line, illustration B), in the right sheet margin at the end of the horizontal sheet gutter between the upper and lower panes.

They first were used in 1933 on 400-subject plates for Scott 634, which was distributed to post offices in 1935 (used were plates 21149-50 and 21367-68). On these plates the plate numbers were placed opposite the ends of the third row of stamps from the top or bottom of the full sheet.

In later experiments, the margin line was broken into closely spaced thin vertical lines. Then it was again returned to its original form, but somewhat narrower.

In 1939, the Bureau of Engraving and Printing installed a new perforating machine which required a different layout to operate the centering mechanism. The vertical dashes remained the same, but the margin line was removed from the right sheet margin and a corresponding line ("gutter bar," illustration C) was placed in the left sheet margin at the end of the horizontal sheet gutter. Additional horizontal lines ("frame bars," illustration D) were added in the left sheet margin opposite the top frame line of the adjacent stamp design of all horizontal rows except the upper horizontal row of each left pane, where the frame bar is omitted. The plate numbers were moved back to their normal positions adjoining the corner stamps. Plates for the two types of machines could not be interchanged.

Later in 1939 a "convertible" plate was employed, consisting of a combination of the two previous layouts, the current one with the addition of a margin line (B) in its former position in the right sheet margin, thus making the perforation possible on either machine.

Originally laid out as 400-subject plates, electric eye plates were later used for 200-subject horizontal or vertical format (commemorative, special delivery and airpost issues), 280-subject (Famous Americans and those with similar formats) and 180- and 360-subject plates (booklet panes of definitives, airpost, postal savings and war savings issues).

In laying out the plates for the 400-subject and 200-subject horizontal format issues, the marks retained the same relative position to the stamp designs. This was changed, however, in entering the design for the stamps of the 200-subject vertical format and 280-subject issues because the stamp designs were turned 90 degrees. That is, the designs were entered on the plates with the longer dimension horizontal. Although the electric eye marks were entered on the plates in the usual positions, on the printed sheet they appear as though shifted 90 degrees when the stamps are held in the customary upright position.

Thus a "horizontal" mark on a 400-subject or 200-subject horizontal format sheet would become a "vertical" mark on a 200-subject vertical format or 280-subject sheet. This situation has caused confusion among collectors and dealers in determining a definite description of the various marks. The designation of the position of the plate numbers also has not been uniform for the "turned" designs.

To solve this confusion, the United States Stamp Society (formerly the Bureau Issues Association) adopted a standard terminology for all the marks appearing on the electric eye sheets. Dashes (A), Margin Line (B), Gutter Bar (C) and Frame Bars (D), whereby each type of mark may be identified readily without referring to its plate number position. The plate number designation of the panes will continue to be established by holding the pane of stamps with the designs in an upright position; the corner of the pane on which the plate number appears will determine the pane is upper left, upper right, lower left, or lower right.

DIE CUTTING

The other major form of U.S. stamp separation is die-cutting. This is a method where a die in the pattern of separation is created that later cuts the stamp paper in a stroke motion. This process is used for self-adhesive postage stamps. Die-cutting can appear in straight lines, such as U.S. Scott 2522; shapes, such as U.S. Scott 1552; or imitating the appearance of perforations, such as U.S. Scott 2920.

On stamps where the die cutting is unintentionally omitted, the terms "die cutting omitted" or "imperforate" may be used interchangeably.

GUM

The Illustrated Gum Chart in the first part of this introduction shows and defines various types of gum condition. Because gum condition has an important impact on the value of unused stamps, we recommend studying this chart and the accompanying text carefully.

The gum on the back of a stamp may be shiny, dull, smooth, rough, dark, white, colored or tinted. Most stamp gumming adhesives use gum arabic or dextrine as a base. Certain polymers such as polyvinyl alcohol (PVA) have been used extensively since World War II.

The *Scott Standard Postage Stamp Catalogue* does not list items by types of gum. The *Scott Specialized Catalogue of United States Stamps* does differentiate among some types of gum for certain issues.

As collectors generally prefer unused stamps with original gum, many unused stamps with no gum have been regummed to make them more desirable (and costly) to collectors who want stamps with full original gum. Some used stamps with faint cancels have had these cancels chemically removed and have been regummed. Skillful regumming can be difficult to detect, particularly on imperforate stamps. Certification of such stamps by competent authorities is suggested.

Reprints of stamps may have gum differing from the original issues. In addition, some countries have used different gum formulas for different seasons. These adhesives have different properties that may become more apparent over time.

Many stamps have been issued without gum, and the catalogue will note this fact. See United States Scott PR33-PR56.

LUMINESCENCE

Kinds of Luminescence — Fluorescence and phosphorescence, two different luminescent qualities, are found in U.S. postage stamps and postal stationery. While all luminescent stamps glow when exposed to short-wave ultraviolet (UV) light, only those with phosphorescent properties display brief afterglow when the UV light source is extinguished.

Fluorescent or "Hi-Bright" Papers — The Bureau of Engraving and Printing, at one point accepting paper for the printing of stamps without regard to fluorescent properties, unknowingly used a mix of paper with infinitely varying amounts of fluorescent optical brighteners added during the papermaking process. In March 1964, to preserve uniformity of product and as a safeguard for an emerging but still incomplete plan for nationwide use of luminescent stamps, BEP purchasing specifications were amended to limit the use of fluorescent paper brighteners. The amended specification permitted paper with some brightener content, but excluded brilliantly glowing papers known in the printing trade as "hi-bright."

Stamps printed on such papers emit a distinctive, intense whitish-violet glow when viewed with either long or short-wave UV. In following years, stamps were produced on papers with lower levels of fluorescence permitted by amended specifications.

Tagged Stamps — The Post Office Department (now the U.S. Postal Service) field-tested automated mail-handling equipment to face, cancel and sort mail at rates up to 30,000 pieces an hour, by sensing UV-light-activated afterglow from phosphorescent substances. For the first tests at Dayton, Ohio, started after August 1, 1963, the 8-cent carmine airpost stamp (Scott C64a) was over-printed (tagged) with a so-called "nearly-invisible" calcium silicate compound which phosphoresces orange-red when exposed to short-wave UV. A facer-canceler, with modifications that included a rapidly cycling on-off UV light, activated the phosphor-tagged airpost stamps and extracted envelopes bearing them from the regular flow of mail.

While the airpost extraction test was still in progress, the entire printing of the City Mail Delivery commemorative (Scott 1238) was ordered tagged with a yellow-green glowing zinc orthosilicate compound intended for use with the automated recognition circuits to be tested with surface transported letter mail.

After the first-day ceremonies October 26, 1963, at Washington, D.C., it was learned the stamps had been tagged to publicize the innovative test by coupling tagging with stamps memorializing "100 years of postal progress" and to provide the first national distribution of tagged stamps for collectors. Between October 28 and November 2, to broaden the scope of the test in the Dayton area, the 4-cent and 5-cent denominations of the regular issue then in use were issued with the same green glowing compound applied in an experimental tagging format (Scott 1036b, 1213b, 1213c, and 1229a).

By June 1964, testing had proven sufficiently effective for the Post Office Department to order all 8-cent airpost adhesive stamps phosphor-tagged for general distribution. By January 1966, all airpost stamps, regardless of denomination, were ordered tagged. Meanwhile, from 1963 through 1965, limited quantities of the Christmas issues were tagged for use in the continuing test in the Dayton area on the use of tagging to automatically position (face) and cancel mail. (Scott 1240a, 1254a-1257a, and 1276a).

On May 19, 1966, the use of phosphor-tagged stamps was expanded to the Cincinnati Postal Region, which then included offices in Ohio, Kentucky and Indiana. During the last half of 1966, primarily to meet postal needs of that region, phosphor-tagged issues were authorized to include additional denominations of regular issues, some postal stationery, and about 12 percent of each commemorative issue starting with the National Park Service 5-cent issue (Scott 1314a) and continuing through the Mary Cassatt 5-cent commemorative (Scott 1322a). After January 1, 1967, most regular values through the 16-cent, all commemoratives, and additional items of postal stationery were ordered tagged.

Adhesive stamps precanceled by the Bureau of Engraving and Printing (Bureau precancels), however, were not tagged, with the exception of Scott 1394, 1596, 1608, and 1610. Because there was no need to cancel mail with these stamps and since precancel permit holders post such mail already faced, postal officials by-passed facer-canceler operations and avoided the cost of tagging.

Overall phosphorescent overprints, when newly issued, are practically invisible in ordinary light. After aging three to five years, the tagging can discolor and become more easily visible. When viewed with UV light, there is little change in the hue of either orange-red or yellow-green emitted light. Even though observable discoloration exists, the presence or absence of tagging is best determined by examination with UV light.

Bar, or block, tagging, instead of the usual overall phosphorescent overprint, was used for some stamps beginning with the Andreotti-printed Mail Order Business commemorative (Scott 1468). These are much easier to identify than the overall overprint, often without need for a UV light.

Band tagging, a bar extending across two or more stamps, was first used with Scott 1489-1498.

Beginning in the 1990s, many stamps are printed on prephosphored paper. Unlike overall tagging, in which the tagging substance is applied to the entire stamp after it is printed, prephosphored paper has the tagging substance added to the surface of the paper during the paper-making process, before printing occurs.

In the late 1990s, some stamps appeared with the tagging formed in the shape of the stamp design elements.

Most of the luminescent issues exist with the luminescent coating unintentionally omitted.

In some postal stationery, such as Scott U551, UC40, UX48a, and UX55, the luminescent element is in the ink with which the stamp design is printed. The luminescent varieties of stamp envelopes Scott U550 and UC37 were made by adding a vertical phosphorescent bar or panel at left of the stamp. On Scott UC42, this "glow-bar" passes through the tri-globe design.

The *Scott Specialized Catalogue of U.S. Stamps and Covers* lists different tagging types when more than one type is known on a stamp. Currently, these types can be large or small block tagging, overall tagging and prephosphored paper. Prephosphored paper is further broken down into two types, each listed separately. It can have a "mottled tagging" appearance, which results from the application of the tagging substance to uncoated paper, or it can have a "solid tagging" appearance, either absolutely uniform or just slightly "grainy." The solid tagging appearance results from the application of the tagging substance to coated paper. Information in the catalogue reflects the most recent findings. Research on tagging is ongoing.

NOTE: Users of UV light should avoid prolonged exposure, which can burn the eyes. Sunglasses (particularly those that feature a "UV block") or prescription eyeglasses, tinted or plain, screen the rays and provide protection.

POSTAL MARKINGS

Postal markings are those marks placed by postal employees of this and other countries on the stamp or cover or both. These marks may indicate the mailing place of a letter, date, rate, route, accounting between post offices, and so on.

In addition to the basis town designations, there are many varieties of supplemental markings. Among these are rate marks, route marks, obliterators, special dating markings usually found on advertised or dead letter covers, transportation markings (rail, steam, ship, airpost, etc.), and service markings (advertised, forwarded, missent, second delivery, mail route, too late, charged, paid box, due, returned for postage, soldier's letter, held for postage, short paid, unpaid, not paid, paid, free, dead letter office, etc.).

These markings originated, for material mailed in what is now the United States, in the Colonial period when manuscript postal markings were first introduced under the Ordinance of December 10, 1672, of New York, which established an inland postal system between the colonies. A "Post Payd" is found on the first letter ever sent under the system, on January 22, 1673. Manuscript postal markings continued in use right through the pre-stamp period and even can be found on some letters today.

The earliest handstamp associated with the American service is a "NEW/YORK" blank handstamp found on letters conveyed via the Bristol Packet line in 1710-12 between New York and England. Following the demise of this operation, the first regular handstamp postal markings were introduced at New York in 1756, when a post office packet service was established between Falmouth, England, and New York. The marking merely was "NEW YORK" on two lines of type. The marking (see illustration), with each word of the city name on a separate line, is represented in presentations such as this as "NEW/YORK." Similar markings were later introduced at other towns, such as ANNA/POLIS, by 1766; CHARLES/TOWN, by 1770; PHILA/DELPHIA, by 1766; HART/FORD, by 1766; while other offices received a single line marking: BOSTON, by 1769; ALBANY, by 1773; PENSACOLA, by 1772; SAVANNA, by 1765, BALTIMORE, by 1772, and WMSBURG, by 1770.

Some of these early letters also bear a circular date stamp containing the month in abbreviated form, i.e., "IV" for June and "IY" for July, and the date in a 14-17mm circle. Known from at least nine towns, these are called "Franklin marks" after Benjamin Franklin, then deputy postmaster general for the English crown. The marks also are known as "American Bishopmarks" to distinguish them from the Bishopmark used in England, which has a center line.

First U.S. Handstamp

Franklin Mark

During 1774-1775, an American provisional postal system was established in opposition to that of the English crown. Both manuscript and handstamp markings have been attributed to it. This system was taken over by Congress on July 26, 1775, and the same markings were continued in use. The earliest reported Congressional marks are a manuscript "Camb Au 8" and a blue-green straightline "NEW*YORK*AU*24." Postal markings are known throughout the

Congressional marks are a manuscript "Camb Au 8" and a blue-green straightline "NEW*YORK*AU*24." Postal markings are known throughout the Revolution, including English occupation markings. Most are manuscript.

In the post-war Confederation period, handstamped circular markings were introduced at Charleston, South Carolina, in 1778-1780, and later at New London, Connecticut. Straightlines and manuscripts continued to dominate until the use of oval markings became widespread about 1800, with circles becoming the predominant markings shortly thereafter.

Handstamp rate markings are known as early as the 1789 pennyweight markings of Albany. Such types of markings became more common in the 1830's and almost the standard by the "5" and "10"-cent rate period which began on July 1, 1845. This period also is when envelopes began to replace folded letter sheets. Before that date, envelopes were charged with an extra rate of postage. These "5," "10," and succeeding "3," "6," "5," and "10" rates of 1851-56 were common on domestic mail until prepayment became compulsory April 1, 1855, on all but drop or local letters domestically. The markings were common on foreign mail through about 1875.

Only 1.3 percent of all letters posted between 1847 and 1852 bore stamps. This proportion increased to 25 percent in 1852, 32 percent in 1853, 34 percent in 1854, 40 percent in 1855, and 64 percent in 1856. Stampless covers are commonplace, although there are some which are highly prized on the basis of their markings. Most are more common than stamped covers of the same period.

While the government began issuing handstamps as early as 1799 and obliterators in 1847, many postmasters were required, or at least permitted, to purchase their own canceling devices or to use pen strokes. Pen cancellations continued to be common in the smaller offices into the 1880's. Because of collector prejudice against pen-canceled stamps, many have ended up being "cleaned" (having the pen cancel removed). These are sold either as unused or with a different, faked cancellation to cover the evidence of cleaning. Ultraviolet light (long-wave) usually will reveal traces of the original pen markings.

From around 1850 until 1900, many postmasters used obliterators cut from wood or cork. Many bear fanciful designs, such as bees, bears, chickens, locks, eagles, Masonic symbols, flags, numerals and so on. Some of the designs symbolized the town of origin. These are not listed in this Catalogue, for they owe their origin to the whim of some individual rather than a requirement of the postal regulations. Many command high prices and are eagerly sought by collectors. This has led to extensive forgery of such markings so that collectors are advised to check them carefully.

Rapid machine cancellations were introduced at Boston in 1880-90 and later spread across the country. Each of the various canceling machine types had identifiable characteristics and collectors form collections based on type. One sub-specialty is that of flag cancellations. While handstamp flag designs are known earlier, the first machine flag cancellation was that of Boston in November-December 1894.

Specialists have noted that different canceling inks are used at different times, depending partly on the type of canceling device used. Rubber handstamps, prohibited in 1893 although used for parcel post and precanceling after that date, require a different type of ink from the boxwood or type-metal cancelers of the classic period, while a still different ink is used for the steel devices of the machine cancels.

Registry of letters was first authorized in this country in the Dutch colony of New Netherlands on overseas mail. Records of valuable letters were kept by postmasters throughout the stampless period while an "R" marking was introduced at Philadelphia in 1845 for registered mail. Cincinnati also had such a registry system. The first appearance of the word "registered" appears on mail in November 1847, in manuscript, and in handstamp in May 1850. The official registration for U.S. mail, however, did not begin until July 1, 1855.

In recent years, the handstamped and machine types of cancellations have been standardized by the Post Office Department and its successor and supplied to the various post offices.

Postmarks — markings to indicate the office of origin or manner of postal conveyance. In general terms, the postmark refers to the post office of origin, but sometimes there also are receiving postmarks of the post office of destination or of transit. Other post office markings include: advertised, forwarded, mail route, missent, paid, not paid, second delivery, too late, etc. Postmarks often serve to cancel postage stamps with or without additional obliterating cancels.

Cancellations — postal markings which make further use of the postage stamps impossible. As used in the listings in this Catalogue, cancellations include both postmarks used as cancellations and obliterations intended primarily to cancel (or "kill") the stamp.

Carrier Postmarks — usually show the words "Carrier" "City Delivery," or "U.S.P.O. Dispatch." They were applied to letters to indicate the delivery of mail by U.S. Government carriers. These markings should not be confused with those of local posts or other private mail services which used postmarks of their own. Free delivery of city mail by carriers was begun on July 1, 1863.

Free — handstamp generally used on free, franked mail. The marking occasionally is seen on early adhesives of the United States used as a canceling device.

Railroad Postmarks — usually handstamps, the markings were used to postmark unpouched mail received by route agents of the Post Office Department traveling on trains on railway mail route. The route name in an agent's postmark often was similar to the name of the railroad or included the terminals of the route. The earliest known use of the word "Railroad" as a postmark is 1838. Route agents gradually became R.P.O. clerks and some continued to use their handstamps after the route agent service ceased June 30, 1882. The railroad postmarks of the 1850 period and later usually carried the name of the railroad.

A sub-group of railroad postmarks is made up of those applied in the early days by railroad station agents, using the railroad's ticket dating handstamp as a postmark. Sometimes the station agent was also the postmaster.

In 1864, the Post Office Department equipped cars for the general distribution of mails between Chicago and Clinton, Iowa.

Modern railroad marks, such as "R.P.O." (Railway Mail Service) is a mark indicating transportation by railroad, and includes Railway Post Office, Terminal Railway Post Office, Transfer Office, Closed Mail Service, Air Mail Field, and Highway Post Office.

Effective November 1, 1949, the Railway Mail Service was merged with others of like nature under the consolidated title Postal Transportation Service (PTS). The service was discontinued June 30, 1977.

The modern "railway marks" are quite common and are not the types referred to under cancellations as listed in the Catalogue.

Way Markings — Way letters are those received by a mail carrier on his way between post offices and delivered at the first post office he reached. The postmaster ascertained where the carrier received them and charged, in his postbills, the postage from those places to destination. He wrote "Way" against those charges in his bills and also wrote or stamped "Way" on each letter. If the letter was exempt from postage, it should have been marked "Free."

The term "mail carrier" above refers to any carrier under contract to carry U.S. mail: a stage line, a horseback rider, or a steamboat or railroad that did not have a route agent on board. Only unpouched mail (not previously placed in a post office) was eligible for a Way fee of one cent. The postmaster paid this fee to the carrier, if demanded, for the carrier's extra work of bringing the letter individually to the post office. For a limited time at certain post offices, the Way fee was added to the regular postage. This explains the use of a numeral with the "Way" marking.

Packet Markings — Packet markings listed in this Catalogue are those applied on a boat traveling on inland or coastal waterways. This group does not include mail to foreign countries that contains the words "British Packet," "American Packet," etc, or their abbreviations. These are U.S. foreign-mail exchange-office markings.

Listed packet markings are in two groups: 1) waterways route-agent markings which denote service exactly the same as that of the railroad route-agent markings, except that the route agent traveled on a boat instead of a train; 2) name-of-boat markings placed on the cover to advertise the boat or, as some believe, to expedite payment of Way and Steam fees at the post office where such letters entered the U.S. mails.

Occasionally waterways route-agent markings included the name of a boat, or "S.B.," "STEAMBOAT," or merely a route number. Such supplemental designations do not alter the character of the markings as those of a route-agent.

19th Century U.S. Express Mail Postmarks — In pre-stamp days these represented either an extra-fast mail service or mail under the care of an express-mail messenger who also carried out-of-mail-express packages. The service was permitted as a practical means of competing with package express companies that also carried mail in competition with the U.S. Mail. Several of these early postmarks were later used by U.S. Mail route agents on the New York-Boston and New York-Albany runs, or by U.S. steamboat letter carriers on the coastal run between Boston and St. John, New Brunswick.

Steamboat or **Steam Markings** — Except for the circular markings "Maysville Ky. Steam" and "Terre Haute Stb." and the rectangular "Troy & New York Steam Boat," these markings contain only the word "STEAMBOAT" or "STEAM," with or without a rating numeral. They represent service the same as that of Way markings, except that the carrier was an inland or coastal steamer that had no contract to carry U.S. mails. Such boats, however, were required by law to carry to the nearest post office any mail given them at landings. The boat owner was paid a two-cent fee for each letter so delivered, except on Lake Erie where the fee was one-cent. At some post offices, the Steamboat fee was added to regular postage. In 1861, the two-cent fee was again added to the postage, and in 1863 double postage was charged.

Ship Postmarks — postal markings indicating arrival on a private ship (one not under contract to carry mail). This marking was applied to letters delivered by such ships to the post office at their port of entry as required by law, for which they received a fee and the letter were taxed with a specified fee for the service in place of the ordinary open postage.

The use of U.S. postage stamps on ship letters is unusual, except for letters from Hawaii, because the U.S. inland postage on ship letters from a foreign point did not need to be prepaid. "U.S. SHIP" is a special marking applied to mail posted on naval vessels, especially during the Civil War period.

Steamship Postmarks — akin to Ship postmarks, but they appear to have been used mostly on mail from Caribbean or Pacific ports to New Orleans or Atlantic ports carried on steamships having a U.S. mail contract. An associated numeral usually designates the through rate from where the letter was received by the ship to its inland destination.

Receiving Mark — impression placed on the back of envelopes by the receiving post office to indicate the name of the office and date of arrival. It also is known as a "backstamp." Generally discontinued about 1913, the marking was employed for a time on air mail service until it was found the practice slowed the service. The markings now are used on registry and special delivery mail.

Miscellaneous Route Markings — wordings associated with the previously described markings include Bay Route, River Mail, Steamer, Mail Route, etc. Classification of the marking ordinarily is evident from the usage, or it can be identified from publications on postal markings.

U.S. Foreign-Mail Exchange-Office Markings — These served to meet the accounting requirements of the various mail treaties before the Universal Postal Union was established. The markings usually designate the exchange office or the carrier (British Packet, Bremen Packet, American Packet, etc.). Sometimes these markings are a restatement of the through rate, or a numeral designating the amount credited or debited to the foreign country as a means of allocating the respective parts of the total postage, according to conditions of route, method of transit, weight, etc.

Gridiron Cancellation — commonest types of cancellations on early U.S. stamps. The markings consist of circles enclosing parallel lines. There are, however, many varieties of grid cancellations.

Paid Markings — generally consist of the word "PAID," sometimes within a frame, indicating regular postage prepaid by the sender of a letter. They are found as separate handstamps, within town or city postmarks, and as a part of obliterating cancels. In each case, the "paid" marking may be used with or without an accompany or combined rate numeral indication.

Precancels — stamps having the cancellation applied before the article is presented for mailing. The purpose is to reduce handling and speed up the mails. A permit is required for use by the public, except for special cases, such as the experiments using Scott 1384a, 1414a-1418a, or 1552 for Christmas mail. Normally the precanceling is done with devices not used for ordinary postal service. Most precancellations consist of the city and state names between two lines or bars.

Precancels are divided into two groups: locals and Bureaus. Locals are printed, usually from 100-subject plates, or handstamped, usually by means of a 10- or 25-subject device having a rubber, metal or vinyl surface, at the town using the stamps. Most locals are made with devices furnished by the Postal Service, but a number have been made with devices created in the city using them. Early locals include the printed "PAID" or "paid" on Scott 7 and 9, "CUMBERLAND, ME." on Scott 24-26 and the Glen Allen, Virginia stars.

Many styles of precancellation are known. More than 600,000 different precancels exist from more than 20,000 post offices in the United States.

The Bureaus, or Bureau Prints, are precancels furnished to the post offices by the Post Office Department in Washington. For 75 years these were printed by the Bureau of Engraving and Printing, hence the name "Bureaus." In late 1991, the American Bank Note Co. and J.W. Fergusson and Sons for Stamp Venturers also began producing precanceled stamps under contract with the Postal Service. Other companies have followed. Since the stamps go to the local post office from the same source, the Postal Service, and the method of production is essentially the same as used by the BEP, the term "Bureau precancel" has been retained in this catologue. The cancellations consist of the name of the city and state where the stamps are to be used, lines or the class of mail. They originated in 1916 when postal officials were seeking ways to reduce costs as well as increase the legibility of the overprint. The BEP was low bidder in three cities, which resulted in the "experimentals." These 16 denominations, including two postage dues, were issued for Augusta, Maine (one value); Springfield, Massachusetts (14 values); and New Orleans (six values) in quanities ranging from 4,000,000 down to 10,000. Electrotype plates mounted on a flat bed press were used to print the precancellations.

Regular production of Bureau Prints began on May 2, 1923, with Scott 581 precanceled "New York, N.Y." All regular Bureaus until 1954 were produced by the Stickney rotary press, whereby the stamps, immediately after printing, pass under the precanceling plates. Then the roll is gummed, perforated and cut into sheets or coils. Since 1954, a variety of printing methods have been used.

Precancels are listed in the Catalogue only if the precanceled stamp is different from the nonprecanceled version (untagged stamps such as Scott 1582a); or, if the stamp only exists precanceled (Scott 2265). Classical locals and experimental bureaus are also included as cancellations. See Service Indicators.

Service Indicators — inscription included in the design of the stamp to indicate the category of postal service to be rendered. The first regular postage stamp to include a service indicator was the 7.9-cent Drum stamp of the Americana series, which was for bulk rate mailings. This stamp was issued with Bureau precancels for proper usage from 107 cities. Copies without the Bureau precancellation were for philatelic purposes.

A second category of service indicators came about when the USPS began to include the postal service between the lines of the Bureau precancellation. Examples of this group are "Bulk Rate" and "Nonprofit Organization."

Finally, with the 16.7-cent Transportation coil (Scott 2261), issued July 7, 1988, the USPS went back to including the service indicator in the design with the indicator serving as the cancellation. With the precancellation now part of the design, the USPS stopped offering tagged versions of the stamps for collectors.

In all cases, the "service indicator" stamp does not normally receive an additional cancellation when used for the indicated service. For examples see Postal Markings - Bureau Precancels.

Tied On — when the cancellation (or postmark) extends from the stamp to the envelope.

Postal Markings, Cancellations Examples

Numerals
Values are for rating marks such as those illustrated. Later types of numerals in grids targets, etc., are common.

PAID ALL
PAID

The common Boston Paid cancellation (Values are for types other than this)

STEAMBOAT
SHIP **STEAM**
FREE

Steamship

Steamboat
(Route agent marking)

Packet Boat
(Name-of-boat marking)

Packet Boat
(Name-of-boat marking)

Packet Boat
(Name-of-boat marking)

Railroad
(Route agent marking)

U.S. Express Mail
(Route agent marking)

(In red on letter to Germany via Prussian Closed Mail, via British Packet. Credits 7 cent to Prussia.)

Carrier

Canadian

Fort

Vera Cruz, Mexico 1914

Exposition Station
Used while exposition is open. Many styles.

Exposition advertising.
Used before exposition opens. Many styles.

Express Company

Army Field Post

Town

Year dated

U.S. Postmark used in China

U.S. Postmark used in Japan

New York City Foreign Mail

New York City Foreign Mail — A group of design cancellations used between 1871 and 1877 in New York City on outgoing foreign mail only. This group of handstamps totals about 200 different fancy stars, geometric designs, wheels conventionalized flowers, etc., the majority within a circle 26-29 mm in diameter.

Patent Defacing Cancellations

Patent Defacing Cancellations — When adhesive stamps came into general use, the Post Office Department made constant efforts to find a type of cancellation which would make the re-use of the stamp impossible. Many patents were granted to inventors and some of the cancellations (killers) came into more or less general use. Some of them appear in combination with the town postmarks.

About 125 different types are known on the stamps issues up to about 1887. Their principal use and greatest variety occur on Scott 65, 147, 158, 183 and 184.

Patent cancellations generally fall into three groups:

1) Small pins or punches which pierce the paper or depress it sufficiently to break the fiber.

2) Sharp blades or other devices for cutting the paper.

3) Rotation of a portion of the canceler so that part of the paper is scraped away.

1. Dot punches through paper   2. Blades cut the paper

2. Small circle cuts the paper   3. Scraped in the shaded circle

Supplementary Mail

Supplementary Mail — markings which designate the special post office service of dispatching mail after the regular mail closed. Two kinds of supplementary mail were available:

1. Foreign mail. For New York, the postmaster general established in 1853 a fee of double the regular rate. This paid to get the mail aboard ship after the regular mail closing and before sailing time. The service continued until 1939. Postmark Types A, D, E, F, and G were used.

2. Domestic mail. For Chicago, at no extra fee, supplementary mail entitled a letter to catch the last eastbound train. Postmark Types B and C were used. No foreign destination was implied.

Similar service with "Supplementary" in the postmark apparently available in Philadelphia and possibly elsewhere.

Type A   Type D   Type E

Type F
Combination Handstamp
(Also comes with numeral "1")
(Stamps with numeral cancel alone do not qualify for Supplementary Mail cancel premiums.)

Type G (also with other numerals)

Type B   Type C

World War I Soldiers' Letters

World War I Soldiers' Letters — At the time the United States declared war against Germany on April 6, 1917, a postal regulation existed which permitted soldiers, sailors and Marines to send letters without prepayment of postage by endorsing them "Soldier letter" and having them countersigned by an officer. The single postage rate would then be collected from the recipient. Few of the enlisted men, however, took advantage of this privilege in sending letters while in the United States and practically all letters sent by soldiers from some 200 World War I military post offices in the United States bear regular postage stamps.

Fig. A

Soon after the arrival of the first units of the American Expeditionary Force in France, this regulation was modified to include letters which although not endorsed, bore the postmark of the United States Army Postal Service. The War Revenue Act of Congress of October 3, 1917, provided free postage for soldiers, sailors and marines assigned to duty overseas.

Therefore, letters from members of the A.E.F. sent before October 1917 without postage stamps were properly charged with postage due, while those sent after that time went through post free.

This provision for free postage did not ordinarily apply to civilians permitted to accompany the army, such as welfare workers, Post Office Department representatives, war correspondents and others. Neither did it apply to the registration fee on soldiers' letters nor to parcel post matter. It was necessary to pay such postage by means of postage stamps.

Fig. B   Fig. C

The first U.S. Army post office, known as an A.P.O., was established at St. Nazaire, France, on July 10, 1917. The A.P.O.'s were at first operated by the Post Office Department, but in May 1918 the Military Express Service was established and the army took over the operation. Later the name was changed to Postal Express Service.

Fig. D   Fig. E

Army post offices were given code numbers and were at first numbered from No. 1 (St. Nazaire) to No. 18 (Saumur). In December 1917, they were renumbered 701, 702, etc., and some 169 A.P.O.'s were established on the Western Front, including offices in Italy, Belgium, Netherlands, Luxembourg, and Germany after the Armistice. Most of the A.P.O.'s were located at fixed places, but "mobile" post offices were assigned to divisions, army corps and armies and were moved from place to place. Many A.P.O.'s had stations or branches, some of which used postmarks with different code numbers from those assigned to the main office.

Until July 1919, all A.E.F. mail was censored, and letters will be found with "company" censor marks (Fig. E) as well as "regimental" censor marks (Fig. F). Distinctive censor marks were used at the base censor's office in Paris (Fig. G).

Fig. F   Fig. G

An interesting variety of subsidiary markings may be found on soldiers' letters: "ADDRESSEE RETURNED TO U.S.A.," "CANNOT BE FOUND," "DECEASED - VERIFIED," "NO RECORD," "SOLDIER'S MAIL," and "UNIT RETURNED TO U.S."

Many styles of stationery were used, mainly those furnished by welfare organizations. Only a few pictorial envelopes were used, but a considerable variety of patriotic and pictorial postcards may be found in addition to officially printed-form postcards.

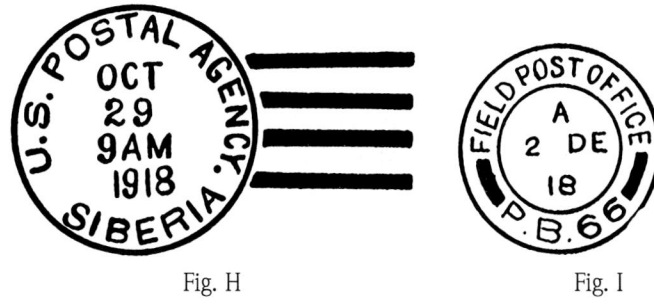

Fig. H   Fig. I

A postal agency was in operation in Siberia from 1918 to 1920 and distinctive postmarks and censor marks were used there (Fig. H). A few American soldiers were sent to North Russia, and postmarks used there were those of the British Expeditionary Force's North Russia postal service (Fig. I).

World War I postmarks have been classified by collectors and the "American Classification System" prepared by the War Cover Club is in general use by collectors of these items.

World War II — Beginning in January 1941, U.S. post offices were established in Newfoundland, Bermuda and other naval bases acquired as a result of the exchange of destroyers with Great Britain. The names of the bases were at first included in the postmark. Later A.P.O. code numbers were adopted, in a similar manner to A.P.O. numbers were cut out of the postmark so that nothing appears to indicate the A.P.O. at which a letter was mailed, although the already established practice was continued of the writer giving the A.P.O. number in the return address. Early in 1943, A.P.O. numbers were replaced in the postmarks at many military post offices.

More than 1,000 different A.P.O. numbers were used. At least 90 types of postmarks exist, of which 45 are handstamped and 40 machine struck.

The armed services, both at home and abroad, were given the franking privilege early in April 1942, the frank consisting of the written word "Free" in the upper right corner of the envelope.

A wide variety of censor marks was used, differing radically in design from those used in World War I.

Bureau Precancels

AUGUSTA
MAINE

NEW
ORLEANS
LA.

SPRINGFIELD
MASS.

Experimentals

PERU
IND.

LANSING
MICH.

SAINT LOUIS
MO.

New Orleans
La.

San Francisco
Calif.

PORTLAND
ME.

LAKEWOOD
N. J.

KANSAS
CITY
MO.

POUGHKEEPSIE
N.Y.

LONG ISLAND
CITY, N.Y.

CORPUS
CHRISTI
TEXAS

ATLANTA
GEORGIA

ATLANTA
GA.

PEORIA
IL

CINCINNATI
OH

Service Indicators

Blk. Rt.
CAR-RT
SORT

Bulk Rate

Nonprofit
Org.

Nonprofit
Org.

PRESORTED
FIRST-CLASS

ZIP+4

Local Precancels

QUINCY
ILLINOIS

FITCHBURG
MASS.

LOS ANGELES
CALIF.

Fergus Falls
Minn.

COVINGTON
KY.

REDWOOD CITY
CALIF.

BELMONT
CALIF.

ELGIN
ILLINOIS

Electroplates

Ashland
Wis.

PALMYRA
N. Y.

Northhampton
MASS.

DES PLAINES
ILL.

RICHMOND
VA.

BROOKFIELD
ILLINOIS

PAONIA
COLO.

GOSHEN
IND

TOWER CITY
N. DAK.

NEW BRUNSWICK
N. J.

ORLANDO,
FLA.

RICHTON PARK
ILL.

MULINO,
OREG.

PINE HILL
N.Y.

FARRELL,
PA

SACRAMENTO
CA

Handstamps

General Glossary

Scott Publishing Co. uses the following terms in its Catalogues, as appropriate. Definitions follow each term.

Imperforate — stamps without perforations, rouletting, or other form of separation. Self-adhesive stamps are die cut, though they look imperforate.

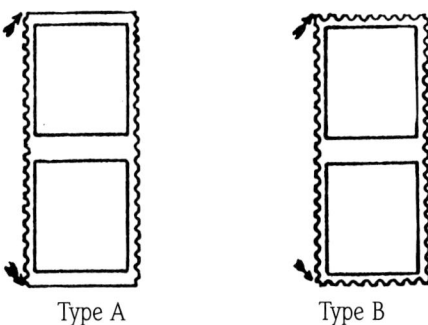

Type A   Type B

Part-Perforate — Stamps with perforations on the two opposite sides, the other two sides remaining imperforate. See coils.

Vertical Pair, Imperforate Horizontally — (Type A illustrated) indicating that a pair of stamps is fully perforated vertically, but has no horizontal perforations.

Horizontal Pair, Imperforate Vertically — (Type A) indicating that a pair of stamps is fully perforated horizontally but has no vertical perforations.

Vertical Pair, Imperforate Between — (Type B illustrated) indicating that the vertical pair is fully perforated at the top, side and bottom, but has no perforations between the stamps.

Horizontal Pair, Imperforate Between — (Type B) indicating that the horizontal pair is fully perforated at the top, sides, and bottom, but has no perforations between the stamps.

Note: Of the above two types (A and B), Type A is the more common.

Blind Perforations — the slight impressions left by the perforating pins if they fail to puncture the paper. While multiples of stamps showing blind perforations may command a slight premium over normally perforated stamps, they are not imperforate errors. Fakers have removed gum from stamps to make blind perforations less evident.

  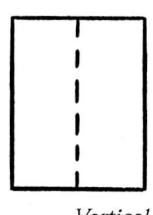

Diagonal   *Horizontal*   *Vertical*

Bisect — Stamps cut in half so that each portion prepaid postage. These items were used in emergencies where no stamps of the lower denomination were available. These may be diagonal, horizontal or vertical. Listings are for bisects on full covers with the bisected stamp tied to the cover on the cut side. Those on piece or part of a cover sell for considerably less. "Half-stamps" that receive a surcharge or overprint are not considered bisects.

This catalogue does not list unofficial bisects after the 1880's.

Block of Four, Imperforate Within — Examples exist of blocks of four stamps that are perforated on all four outside edges, but lack both horizontal and vertical perforations within the block. Scott

accidental example of this phenomenon. Scott RS173j and RS174j are examples of a situation where internal perforations were omitted intentionally to create 4-cent "stamps" from four 1-cent stamps.

Rouletting — short consecutive cuts in the paper to facilitate separation of the stamps, made with a toothed wheel or disc.

Booklets — Many countries have issued stamps in booklets for the convenience of users. This idea is becoming increasingly popular today in many countries. Booklets have been issued in all sizes and forms, often with advertising on the covers, on the panes of stamps or on the interleaving.

The panes may be printed from special plates or made from regular sheets. All panes from booklets issued by the United States and many from those of other countries are imperforate on three sides, but perforated between the stamps. Any stamplike unit in the pane, either printed or blank, which is not a postage stamp, is considered a *label* in the Catalogue listings. The part of the pane through which stitches or staples bind the booklet together, or which affixes the pane to the booklet cover, is considered to be a *binding stub* or *tab*.

Scott lists and values booklets in this volume. Except for panes from Canal Zone, handmade booklet panes are not listed when they are fashioned from existing sheet stamps and, therefore, are not distinguishable from the sheet-stamp foreign counterparts.

Panes usually do not have a "used" value because there is little market activity in used panes, even though many exist used.

Cancellations — the marks or obliterations put on a stamp by the authorities to show that it has done service and is no longer valid for use. If made with a pen, it is a "pen cancellation." When the location of the post office appears in the cancellation, it is a "town cancellation." When calling attention to a cause or celebration, it is a "slogan cancellation." Many other types and styles of cancellations exist, such as duplex, numerals, targets, etc.

Coil Stamps — stamps issued in rolls for use in dispensers, affixing and vending machines. Those of the United States, and its territories are perforated horizontally or vertically only, with the outer edges imperforate. Coil stamps of some countries, such as Great Britain, are perforated on all four sides.

Commemorative Stamps — Special issues which commemorate some anniversary or event or person. Usually such stamps are used for a limited period concurrently with the regular issue of stamps. Examples of commemorative issues are Scott 230-245, 620-621, 946, 1266, C68, and U218-U221.

Covers — envelopes, with or without adhesive postage stamps, which have passed through the mail and bear postal or other markings of philatelic interest. Before the introduction of envelopes in about 1840, people folded letters and wrote the address on the outside. Many people covered their letters with an extra sheet of paper on the outside for the address, producing the term "cover." Used air letter sheets and stamped envelopes also are considered covers. Stamps on paper used to cover parcels are said to be "on wrapper." ("Wrapper" also is the term used for postal stationery items which were open at both sides and wrapped around newspapers or pamphlets.) Often stamps with high face values are rare on cover, but more common on wrapper. Some stamps and postal stationery items are difficult to find used in the manner for which they were intended, but quite common when used to make philatelic items such as flight or first day covers. High face-value stamps also may be more common on package address tags. See postal cards.

Earliest Documented Use (EDU) — For stamps that do not have a designated first day of issue, the earliest documented use is the date when a stamp was first used in the U.S. mails. These dates are listed in the U.S. Specialized catalog, and new dates must be documented with recognized certificates from leading expertizing committees.

Error — stamps having some unintentional major deviation from the normal. Errors include, but are not limited to, mistakes in color, paper, or watermark, inverted centers or frames on multicolor printing, missing color, inverted or double surcharges or overprints, imperforates and part-perforates, unintentionally omitted tagging, and double impressions. A factually wrong or misspelled inscription, if it appears on all examples of a stamp, even if corrected later, is not classified as a philatelic error.

Color-Omitted Errors — This term refers to stamps where a missing color is caused by the complete failure of the printing plate to deliver ink to the stamp paper or any other paper. Generally, this is caused by the printing plate not being engaged on the press or the ink station running dry of ink during printing.

Color-Missing Errors — This term refers to stamps where a color or colors were printed somewhere but do not appear on the finished stamp. There are four different classes of color-missing errors, and the catalog indicates with a two-letter code appended to each such listing what caused the color to be missing:

FO = A *foldover* of the stamp sheet during printing may block ink from appearing on a stamp. Instead, the color will appear on the back of the foldover (where it might fall on the back of the selvage or perhaps on the back of another stamp). FO also will be used in the case of foldunders, where the paper may fold underneath the other stamp paper and the color will print on the platen.

EP = A piece of *extraneous paper* falling across the plate or stamp paper will receive the printed ink. When the extraneous paper is removed, an unprinted portion of stamp paper remains and shows partially or totally missing colors.

CM = A misregistration of the printing plates during printing will result in a *color misregistration*, and such a misregistration may result in a color not appearing on the finished stamp.

PS = A *perforation shift* after printing may remove a color from the finished stamp. Normally, this will occur on a row of stamps at the edge of the stamp pane.

First Day Cover — A philatelic term to designate the use of a certain stamp (on cover) or postal stationery item on the first day of sale at a place officially designated for such sale or so postmarked. Current U.S. stamps may have such a postal marking applied considerably after the actual issue date.

Gum Breaker Ridges — Colorless marks across the backs of some rotary press stamps, impressed during manufacture to prevent curling. Many varieties of "gum breaks" exist.

Original Gum — A stamp is described as "O.G." if it has the original gum as applied when printed. Some are issued without gum, such as Scott 730, 731, 735, 752, etc; government reproductions, such as Scott 3 and 4; and official reprints.

Overprinted and Surcharged Stamps — Overprinting is a wording or design placed on stamps to alter the place of use (e.g., "Canal Zone" on U.S. stamps), to adapt them for a special purpose ("I.R." on 1-cent and 2-cent U.S. stamps of the 1897-1903 regular issue for use as revenue stamps. Scott R153-R155A) or for a special occasion (U.S. Scott 646-648).

Surcharge is an overprint which changes or restates the face value of the item.

Surcharges and overprints may be handstamped, typeset or, occasionally, lithographed or engraved. A few hand-written overprints and surcharges are known. The world's first surcharge was a handstamped "2" on the United States City Despatch Post stamps of 1846.

Postal Cards — cards that have postage printed on them. Ones without printed stamps are referred to as "postcards."

Proofs and Essays — Proofs are impressions taken from an approved die, plate or stone in which the design and color are the same as the stamp issued to the public. Trial color proofs are impressions taken from approved dies, plates or stones in varying colors. An essay is the impression of a design that differs in some way from the stamp as issued.

Provisionals — stamps issued on short notice and intended for temporary use pending the arrival of regular (definitive) issues. They usually are issued to meet such contingencies as changes in government or currency, shortage of necessary values, or military occupation.

In the 1840's, postmasters in certain American cities issued stamps that were valid only at specific post offices. Postmasters of the Confederate States also issued stamps with limited validity. These are known as "postmaster's provisionals." See U.S. Scott 9X1-9X3 and Confederate States Scott 51X1.

Se-Tenant — joined, referring to an unsevered pair, strip or block of stamps differing in design, denomination or overprint. See U.S. Scott 2158a. Unless the se-tenant item has a continuous design (see U.S. Scott 1451a, 1694a) the stamps do not have to be in the same order as shown in the catalogue (see U.S. Scott 2158a).

Tete Beche — A pair of stamps in which one is upside down in relation to the other. Some of these are the result of international sheet arrangements, i.e. Morocco Scott B10-B11. Others occurred when one or more electrotypes accidentally were placed upside down on the plate. See Hawaii Scott 21a and 22a. Separation of the stamps, of course, destroys the tete beche variety.

Specimens — One of the regulations of the Universal Postal Union requires member nations to send samples of all stamps they put into service to the International Bureau in Switzerland. Member nations, of the UPU receive these specimens as samples of what stamps are valid for postage. Many are overprinted, handstamped or initial-perforated "Specimen," "Canceled" or "Muestra." Stamps distributed to government officials or for publicity purposes, and stamps submitted by private security printers for official approval also may receive such defacements.

These markings prevent postal use, and all such items generally are known as "specimens." There is a section in this volume devoted to this type of material. U.S. officials with "specimen" overprints and printings are listed in the Special Printings section.

Territorial and Statehood Dates

	Territorial Date	Statehood Date	
Alabama	Sept. 25, 1817	Dec. 14, 1819	Territory by enabling act of March 3, 1817, effective Sept. 25, 1817. Created out of part of existing Mississippi Territory.
Alaska	Oct. 18, 1867	Jan. 3, 1959	A district from Oct. 18, 1867, until it became an organized territory Aug. 24, 1912.
Arizona	Feb. 24, 1863	Feb. 14, 1912	This region was sometimes called Arizona before 1863 though still in the Territory of New Mexico.
Arkansas	July 5, 1819*	June 15, 1836	The territory was larger than the state. After statehood, the left-over area to the west had post offices that continued for some years to use an Arkansas abbreviation in the postmarks although really they were in the "Indian Country."
California		Sept. 9, 1850	Ceded by Mexico by the Treaty of Guadalupe-Hidalgo, concluded Feb. 2, 1848, and proclaimed July 4, 1848. From then until statehood, California had first a military government until Dec. 20, 1849, and then a local civil government. It never had a territorial form of government.
Colorado	Feb. 28, 1861	Aug. 1, 1876	
Connecticut		Jan. 9, 1788	The fifth of the original 13 colonies.
Delaware		Dec. 7, 1787	The first of the original 13 colonies.
Dakota	March 2, 1861	Nov. 2, 1889	Became two states: North and South Dakota.
Deseret	March 5, 1849		Brigham Young created the unofficial territory of Deseret. In spite of the fact that Utah Territory was created Sept. 9, 1850, Deseret continued to exist unofficially, in what is now Utah, at least as late as 1862.
Frankland or Franklin			This unofficial state was formed in Aug. 1784, in the northeast corner of what is now Tennessee, and the government existed until 1788. In reality it was part of North Carolina.
Florida	March 30, 1822	March 3, 1845	
Georgia		Jan. 2, 1788	The fourth of the original 13 colonies.
Hawaii	Aug. 12, 1898	Aug. 21, 1959	The territorial date given is that of the formal transfer to the United States, with Sanford B. Dole as first Governor.
Idaho	March 3, 1863	July 3, 1890	
Illinois	March 2, 1809*	Dec. 3, 1818	
Indiana	July 5, 1800*	Dec. 11, 1816	There was a residue of Indiana Territory which continued to exist under that name from Dec. 11, 1816 until Dec. 3, 1818, when it was attached to Michigan Territory.
Indian Territory		Nov. 16, 1907	In the region first called the "Indian Country," established June 30, 1834. It never had a territorial form of government. Finally, with Oklahoma Territory, it became the State of Oklahoma on Nov. 16, 1907.
Iowa	July 4, 1838	Dec. 28, 1846	
Jefferson	Oct. 24, 1859		An unofficial territory from Oct. 24, 1859, to Feb. 28, 1861. In reality it included parts of Kansas, Nebraska, Utah and New Mexico Territories, about 30% being in each of the first three and 10% in New Mexico. The settled portion was mostly in Kansas Territory until Jan. 29, 1861, when the State of Kansas was formed from the eastern part of Kansas Territory. From this date the heart of "Jefferson" was in unorganized territory until Feb. 28, 1861, when it became the Territory of Colorado.
Kansas	May 30, 1854	Jan. 29, 1861	
Kentucky		June 1, 1792	Never a territory, it was part of Virginia until statehood.
District of Louisiana	Oct. 1, 1804		An enormous region, it encompassed all of the Louisiana Purchase except the Territory of Orleans. Created by Act of March 26, 1804, effective Oct. 1, 1804, and attached for administrative purposes to the Territory of Indiana.
Territory of Louisiana	July 4, 1805		By Act of March 3, 1805, effective July 4, 1805, the District of Louisiana became the Territory of Louisiana.
Louisiana		April 30, 1812	With certain boundary changes, had been the Territory of Orleans.
District of Maine		March 16, 1820	Before statehood, what is now the State of Maine was called the District of Maine and belonged to Massachusetts.
Maryland		April 28, 1788	The seventh of the original 13 colonies.

	Territorial Date	Statehood Date	
Massachusetts		Feb. 6, 1788	The sixth of the original 13 colonies.
Michigan	July 1, 1805	Jan. 26, 1837	
Minnesota	March 3, 1849	May 11, 1858	
Mississippi	May 7, 1798	Dec. 10, 1817	Territory by Act of April 7, 1798, effective May 7, 1798.
Missouri	Dec. 7, 1812	Aug. 10, 1821	The state was much smaller than the territory. The area to the west and northwest of the state, which had been in the territory, was commonly known as the "Missouri Country" until May 30, 1854, and certain of the post offices in this area show a Missouri abbreviation in the postmark.
Montana	May 26, 1864	Nov. 8, 1889	
Nebraska	May 30, 1854	March 1, 1867	
Nevada	March 2, 1861	Oct. 31, 1864	
New Hampshire		June 21, 1788	The ninth of the original 13 colonies.
New Jersey		Dec. 18, 1787	The third of the original 13 colonies.
New Mexico	Dec. 13, 1850	Jan. 6, 1912	
New York		July 26, 1788	The 11th of the original 13 colonies.
North Carolina		Nov. 21, 1789	The 12th of the original 13 colonies.
North Dakota		Nov. 2, 1889	Had been part of the Territory of Dakota.
Northwest Territory	July 13, 1787		Ceased to exist March 1, 1803, when Ohio became a state. The date given is in dispute, Nov. 29, 1802 often being accepted.
Ohio		March 1, 1803	Had been part of Northwest Territory until statehood.
Oklahoma	May 2, 1890	Nov. 16, 1907	The state was formed from Oklahoma Territory and Indian Territory.
Oregon	Aug. 14, 1848	Feb. 14, 1859	
Orleans	Oct. 1, 1804		A territory by Act of March 26, 1804, effective Oct. 1, 1804. With certain boundary changes, it became the State of Louisiana, April 30, 1812.
Pennsylvania		Dec. 12, 1787	The second of the original 13 colonies.
Rhode Island		May 29, 1790	The 13th of the original 13 colonies.
South Carloina		May 23, 1788	The eighth of the original 13 colonies.
South Dakota		Nov. 2, 1889	Had been part of Dakota Territory.
Southwest Territory			Became the State of Tennessee, with minor boundary changes, June 1, 1796.
Tennessee		June 1, 1796	Had been Southwest Territory before statehood.
Texas		Dec. 29, 1845	Had been an independent Republic before statehood.
Utah	Sept. 9, 1850	Jan. 4, 1896	
Vermont		March 4, 1791	Until statehood, had been a region claimed by both New York and New Hampshire.
Virginia		June 25, 1788	The 10th of the original 13 colonies.
Washington	March 2, 1853	Nov. 11, 1889	
West Virginia		June 20, 1863	Had been part of Virginia until statehood.
Wisconsin	July 4, 1836	May 29, 1848	The state was smaller than the territory, and the left-over area continued to be called the Territory of Wisconsin until March 3, 1849.
Wyoming	July 29, 1868	July 10, 1890	

* The dates followed by an asterisk are one day later than those generally accepted. The reason is that the Act states, with Arkansas for example, "from and after July 4." While it was undoubtedly the intention of Congress to create Arkansas as a Territory on July 4, the U.S. Supreme Court decided that "from and after July 4," for instance, meant "July 5."

Territorial and statehood data compiled by Dr. Carroll Chase and Richard McP. Cabeen.

Domestic Letter Rates

Effective Date	Prepaid	Collect
1845, July 1		
Reduction from 6¢ to 25¢ range on single-sheet letters		
Under 300 miles, per ½ oz	5¢	5¢
Over 300 miles, per ½ oz	10¢	10¢
Drop letters	2¢	
1847-1848		
East, to or from Havana (Cuba) per ½ oz	12½¢	12½¢
East, to or from Chagres (Panama) per ½ oz	20¢	20¢
East, to or from Panama, across Isthmus, per ½ oz.	30¢	30¢
To or from Astoria (Ore.) or Pacific Coast, per ½ oz	40¢	40¢
Along Pacific Coast, per ½ oz	12½¢	12½¢
1847, July 1		
Unsealed circulars		
1 oz. or less	3¢	
1851, July 1		
Elimination of rates of 1847-1848 listed above		
Up to 3,000 miles, per ½ oz.	3¢	5¢
Over 3,000 miles, per ½ oz	6¢	10¢
Drop letters	1¢	
Unsealed circular		
1 oz. or less up to 500 miles	1¢	
Over 500 miles to 1,500 miles	2¢	
Over 1,500 miles to 2,500 miles	3¢	
Over 2,500 miles to 3,500 miles	4¢	
Over 3,500 miles	5¢	
1852, September 30		
Unsealed circulars		
3 oz. or less anywhere in U.S.	1¢	
Each additional ounce	1¢	
(Double charge if collect)		
1855, April 1		
Prepayment made compulsory		
Not over 3,000 miles, per ½ oz.	3¢	
Over 3,000 miles, per ½ oz.	10¢	
Drop letters	1¢	
1863, July 1		
Distance differential eliminated		
All parts of United States, per ½ oz.	3¢	
1883, October 1		
Letter rate reduced one-third		
All parts of United States, per ½ oz.	2¢	
1885, July 1		
Weight increased to 1 oz.		
All parts of United States, per 1 oz.	2¢	
1896, October 1		
Rural Free Delivery started		
1917, November 2		
War emergency		
All parts of United States, per 1 oz.		3¢
1919, July 1		
Restoration of pre-war rate		
All parts of United States, per 1 oz.		2¢

Effective Date	Prepaid
1932, July 6	
Rise due to depression	
All parts of United States, per 1 oz.	3¢
1958, August 1	
All parts of United States, per 1 oz.	4¢
1963, January 7	
All parts of United States, per 1 oz.	5¢
1968, January 7	
All parts of United States, per 1 oz.	6¢
1971, May 16	
All parts of United States, per 1 oz.	8¢
1974, March 2	
All parts of United States, per 1 oz.	10¢
1975, December 31	
All parts of United States, 1st oz.	13¢
1978, May 29	
All parts of United States, 1st oz.	15¢
1981, March 22	
All parts of United States, 1st oz.	18¢
1981, November 1	
All parts of United States, 1st oz.	20¢
1985, February 17	
All parts of United States, 1st oz.	22¢
1988, April 3	
All parts of United States, 1st oz.	25¢
1991, February 3	
All parts of United States, 1st oz.	29¢
1995, January 1	
All parts of United States, 1st oz.	32¢
1999, January 10	
All parts of United States, 1st oz.	33¢
2001, January 7	
All parts of United States, 1st oz.	34¢
2002, June 30	
All parts of United States, 1st oz.	37¢
2006, January 8	
All parts of United States, 1st oz.	39¢

Domestic Air Mail Rates

Effective Date	Prepaid
1911-1916 – The Pioneer Period	
Special official Post Office Flights at Fairs, aviation meets, etc., per 1 oz.	2¢
Postal cards and postcards	1¢
(Regulations prohibited an additional charge for air service on Post Office authorized flights.)	
1918, May 15 - July 13, 1918	
Service between Washington, DC, New York and Philadelphia (including 10¢ special delivery fee), per 1 oz.	24¢
1918, July 15-Dec. 14, 1918	
Service between Washington, DC, New York and Philadelphia (including 10¢ special delivery fee), per 1 oz.	16¢
Additional ounces	6¢
1918, Dec. 15-July 17, 1919	
Service between selected cities (other cities added later, special delivery no longer included), per 1 oz.	6¢
1919, July 18-June 29, 1924	
No specific airmail rate: mail carried by airplane on space available basis but airmail service not guaranteed, per 1 oz.	2¢
Postal cards and postcards, per 1 oz.	1¢
1924, June 30-Jan. 31, 1927	
Airmail service per zone (New York-Chicago; Chicago-Cheyenne, Wyo.; Cheyenne-San Francisco), per 1 oz. (each zone or portion thereof)	8¢
1925, July 1-Jan. 31, 1927	
Special overnight service New York-Chicago (with three intermediate stops), per 1 oz.	10¢
1926, Feb. 15-Jan. 31, 1927	
Contract routes not exceeding 1,000 miles (first flight Feb. 15) per 1 oz. (each route or portion thereof)	10¢
Contract routes between 1,000 and 1,500 miles (Seattle-Los Angeles, first flight Sept. 15) per 1 oz.	15¢
Mail traveling less than entire Seattle-Los Angeles route per 1 oz.	10¢
Contract routes exceeding 1,500 miles (none established during this rate period) per 1 oz.	20¢
Additional service on govt. route, per 1 oz. (each route or portion thereof)	5¢
1927, Feb. 1-July 31, 1928	
All contract routes or govt. zones, or combinations thereof, per ½ oz.	10¢
1928, Aug. 1-July 5, 1932	
All routes, 1st oz.	5¢
Each additional ounce or fraction thereof	10¢

Effective Date	Prepaid
1932, July 6-June 30, 1934	
All routes, 1st oz.	8¢
Each additional ounce or fraction thereof	13¢
1934, July 1-Mar. 25, 1944	
All routes, per oz.	6¢
1944, Mar. 26-Sept. 30, 1946	
All routes, per oz.	8¢
1946, Oct. 1-Dec. 31, 1948	
All routes, per oz.	5¢
1949, Jan. 1-July 31, 1958	
All routes, per oz.	6¢
Postal cards and postcards, per oz.	4¢
1958, Aug. 1-Jan. 6, 1963	
All routes, per oz.	7¢
Postal cards and postcards, per oz.	5¢
1963, Jan. 7-Jan. 6, 1968	
All routes, per oz.	8¢
Postal cards and postcards, per oz.	6¢
1968, Jan. 7-May 15, 1971	
All routes, per oz.	10¢
Postal cards and postcards, per oz.	8¢
1971, May 16-Mar. 1, 1974	
All routes, per oz.	11¢
Postal cards and postcards, per oz.	9¢
1974, Mar. 2-Oct. 10, 1975	
All routes, per oz.	13¢
Postal cards and postcards, per oz.	11¢

As of Oct. 11, 1975, separate domestic airmail service was abolished, although at least one more airmail rate was published; effective Dec. 28, 1975, 17¢ per 1st oz., 15¢ each additional oz., 14¢ for postal cards and postcards. It lasted until May 1, 1977.

Many thanks to the American Air Mail Society for sharing information on airmail rates. For further study, we highly recommend the society's book, *Via Airmail, An Aerophilatelic Survey of Events, Routes, and Rates;* Simine Short, editor; James R. Adams, author (available from the American Airmail Society, P.O. Box 110, Mineola, NY 11501. Price: $20, plus $2.50 postage to U.S. addresses; $3.50 to addresses outside the U.S.).

IDENTIFIER OF DEFINITIVE ISSUES — ARRANGED BY TYPE NUMBERS

This section covers only listed postage stamps. See the Proofs section for imperforate items in the stamp colors mentioned which are not listed here and the Trial Color Proofs section for items in other colors.

ISSUES OF 1847-75

Benjamin Franklin — A1

Reproduction — A3

5¢ On the originals the left side of the white shirt frill touches the oval on a level with the top of the "F" of "Five." On the reproductions it touches the oval about on a level with the top of the figure "5."

George Washington — A2

Reproduction — A4

Top image original, bottom image reproduction

10¢ On the originals line of coat (A) points to "T" of TEN and (B) it points between "T" and "S" of CENTS.

On the reproductions line of coat (A) points to right tip of "X" and line of coat (B) points to center of "S."

On the reproductions the eyes have a sleepy look, the line of the mouth is straighter, and in the curl of the hair near the left cheek is a strong black dot, while the originals have only a faint one.

Imperforate and Unwatermarked

Design Number		Scott Number
A1	5¢ red brown	1
A1	5¢ blue (reproduction)	948a
A3	5¢ red brown (reproduction, Special Printing)	3
A2	10¢ black	2
A2	10¢ brown orange (reproduction)	948b
A4	10¢ black (reproduction, Special Printing)	4

ISSUE OF 1851-75

Franklin — A5

A5

Type I Has a curved line outside the labels with "U.S. Postage" and "One Cent." The scrolls below the lower label are turned under, forming little balls. The scrolls and outer line at top are complete.

A6

Type Ia Same as I at bottom but top ornaments and outer line at top are partly cut away.

Type Ib Same as I but balls below the bottom label are not so clear. The plume-like scrolls at the bottom are not complete.

Type Ic Same as type Ia, but bottom right plume and ball ornament is incomplete. The bottom left plume is complete or almost complete.

A7

Type II The little balls of the bottom scrolls and the bottoms of the lower plume ornaments are missing. The side ornaments are complete.

A8

Type III The top and bottom curved lines outside the labels are broken in the middle. The side ornaments are complete.

Type IIIa Similar to III with the outer line broken at top or bottom but not both. Type IIIa from Plate IV generally shows signs of plate erasure between the horizontal rows. Those from Plate IE show only a slight break in the line at top or bottom.

A9 Type IV

A20 Type V

Type IV Similar to II, but with the curved lines outside the labels recut at top or bottom or both.

The seven types listed account for most of the varieties of recutting.

Type V Similar to type III of 1851-56 but with side ornaments partly cut away.

A5	1¢ blue, type I, imperf.	5
A5	1¢ blue, type Ib, imperf.	5A
A5	1¢ blue, type I, perf. 15½	18
A5	1¢ bright blue, perf. 12 (Special Printing)	40
A6	1¢ blue, type Ia, imperf.	6
A6	1¢ blue, type Ic, imperf.	6b
A6	1¢ blue, type Ia, perf. 15½	19
A6	1¢ blue, type Ic, perf. 15½	19b
A7	1¢ blue, type II, imperf.	7
A7	1¢ blue, type II, perf. 15½	20
A8	1¢ blue, type III, imperf.	8
A8	1¢ blue, type IIIa, imperf.	8A
A8	1¢ blue, type III, perf. 15½	21
A8	1¢ blue, type IIIa, perf. 15½	22
A9	1¢ blue, type IV, imperf.	9
A9	1¢ blue, type IV, perf. 15½	23
A20	1¢ blue, type V, perf. 15½	24
A20	1¢ blue, type V, perf. 15½, laid paper	24b

Washington, Type I — A10

A10 Type I There is an outer frame line on all four sides.

A21 Type II The outer line has been removed at top and bottom.

Type IIa The side frame lines extend only to the top and bottom of the stamp design. All type IIa stamps are from plates 10 and 11 (each exists in 3 states), and these plates produced only type IIa. The side frame lines were recut individually for each stamp, thus being broken between the stamps vertically.
Beware of type II stamps with frame lines that stop at the top of the design (from top row of plate) or bottom of the design (from bottom row of plate). These are sometimes offered as No. 26a.

Jefferson, Type I There are projections on all four sides. — A11

Type II, The projections at top and bottom are partly cut away. Several minor types could be made according to the extent of cutting of the projections. — A22

Nos. 40-47 are reprints produced by the Continental Bank Note Co. The stamps are on white paper without gum, perf. 12. They were not good for postal use. They also exist imperforate.

A10	3¢ orange brown, type I, imperf.	10
A10	3¢ dull red, type I, imperf.	11
A10	3¢ rose, type I, perf. 15½	25
A10	3¢ scarlet, perf. 12 (Special Printing)	41
A21	3¢ dull red, type II, perf. 15½	26
A21	3¢ dull red, type IIa, perf. 15½	26a
A11	5¢ red brown, type I, imperf.	12
A11	5¢ brick red, type I, perf. 15½	27
A11	5¢ red brown, type I, perf. 15½	28
A11	5¢ Indian red, type I, perf. 15½	28A
A11	5¢ brown, type I, perf. 15½	29
A22	5¢ orange brown, type II, perf. 15½	30
A22	5¢ brown, type II, perf. 15½	30A
A22	5¢ orange brown, type II, perf. 12 (Special Printing)	42

Washington, Type I — A12

Washington — A16

A12 Type I The shells at the lower corners are practically complete. The outer line below the label is very nearly complete. The outer lines are broken above the middle of the top label and the "X" in each upper corner.

A13 Type II The design is complete at the top. The outer line at the bottom is broken in the middle. The shells are partly cut away.

A14 Type III The outer lines are broken above the top label and the "X" numerals. The outer line at the bottom and the shells are partly cut away as in Type II.

A15 Type IV The outer lines have been recut at top or bottom or both.

A23 Type V The side ornaments are slightly cut away. Usually only one peral remains at each end of the lower label but some copies show two or three pearls at the right side. At the bottom, the outer line is complete and the shells nearly so. The outer lines at top are complete except over the right "X."

A12	10¢ green, type I, imperf.	13
A12	10¢ green, type I, perf. 15½	31
A12	10¢ blue green, perf. 12 (Special Printing)	43
A13	10¢ green, type II, imperf.	14
A13	10¢ green, type II, perf. 15½	32
A14	10¢ green, type III, imperf.	15
A14	10¢ green, type III, perf. 15½	33
A15	10¢ green, type IV, imperf.	16
A15	10¢ green, type IV, perf. 15½	34
A23	10¢ green, type V, perf. 15½	35
A16	12¢ black, imperf.	17
A16	12¢ black, plate I, perf. 15½	36
A16	12¢ black, plate III	36b
A16	12¢ greenish black, perf. 12	44

Washington — A17

Franklin — A18

Washington — A19

A17	24¢ gray lilac, perf. 15½	37

A17	24¢ blackish violet, perf. 12 (Special Printing)	4
A18	30¢ orange, perf. 15½	3
A18	30¢ yellow orange, perf. 12 (Special Printing)	4
A19	90¢ blue, perf. 15½	39
A19	90¢ deep blue, perf. 12 (Special Printing)	47

ISSUES OF 1861-75

Franklin — A24

A24 See the essay section for type A24 in indigo on perf. 12 thin, semi-transparent paper without the dash under the tip of the ornament at the right of the numeral in the upper left corner.

A24	1¢ blue, perf. 12	63
A24	1¢ blue, same, laid paper	63c
A24	1¢ blue, grill 11x14mm	85A
A24	1¢ blue, grill 11x13mm	86
A24	1¢ blue, grill 9x13mm	92
A24	1¢ blue, no grill, hard white paper (Special Printing)	102

Washington — A25

A25 See the essay section for type A25 in brown rose on perf. 12 thin, semi-transparent paper with smaller ornaments in the corners which do not end in a small ball.

A25	3¢ pink, no grill, perf. 12	64
A25	3¢ lake, same (Special Printing)	66
A25	3¢ scarlet, same (Special Printing)	74
A25	3¢ rose, same	65
A25	3¢ rose, same, laid paper	65b
A25	3¢ rose, grilled all over	79
A25	3¢ rose, grill 18x15mm	82
A25	3¢ rose, grill 13x16mm	83
A25	3¢ rose, grill 12x14mm	85
A25	3¢ rose, grill 11x14mm	85C
A25	3¢ rose, grill 11x13mm	88
A25	3¢ red, grill 9x13mm	94
A25	3¢ brown red, no grill, hard white paper (Special Printing)	104

Jefferson — A26

A26 See the essay section for type A26 in brown on perf. 12 thin, semi-transparent paper without the leaflet in the foliated ornament at each corner.

A26   5¢ buff, no grill **67**
A26   5¢ red brown, no grill **75**
A26   5¢ brown, no grill **76**
A26   5¢ brown, laid paper **76b**
A26   5¢ brown, grilled all over **80**
A26   5¢ brown, grill 9x13mm **95**
A26   5¢ brown, no grill, hard white paper **105**

A27a

Washington — A27

A27 A heavy curved line has been cut below the stars and an outer line added to the ornaments above them.

A27a   10¢ dark green, thin paper **62B**
A27   10¢ yellow green, see illustration A27 .... **68**
A27   10¢ green, grill 11x14mm **85D**
A27   10¢ green, grill 11x13mm **89**
A27   10¢ yellow green, grill 9x13mm **96**
A27   10¢ green, no grill, hard white paper (Special Printing) **106**

Washington — A28

A28 See the essay section for type A28 in black on perf. 12 thin, semi-transparent paper without corner ornaments.

A28   12¢ black, no grill **69**
A28   12¢ black, grill 11x14mm **85E**
A28   12¢ black, grill 11x13mm **90**
A28   12¢ black, grill 9x13mm **97**
A28   12¢ black, no grill, hard white paper, (Special Printing) **107**

Washington — A29   Franklin — A30

See the Trial Color proof section for type A29 in dark violet on perf. 12 thin paper without grill and type A30 in red orange on perf. 12 thin paper without grill.

A29   24¢ red lilac, no grill **70**
A29   24¢ violet, no grill, thin, transparent paper **70c**

A29   24¢ lilac, no grill **78**
A29   24¢ gray lilac, grill 9x13mm **99**
A29   24¢ deep violet, no grill, hard white paper, (Special Printing) **109**
A30   30¢ orange, no grill **71**
A30   30¢ orange, grilled all over **81**
A30   30¢ orange, grill 9x13mm **100**
A30   30¢ brownish orange, no grill, hard white paper, (Special Printing) **110**

Washington — A31

A31 See the essay section for type A31 in dull blue on perf. 12 thin semi-transparent paper without dashes between the parallel lines which form the angle above the ribbon with "U.S. Postage," and without the point of color at the apex of the lower line.

A31   90¢ blue, no grill **72**
A31   90¢ blue, grill 9x13mm **101**
A31   90¢ blue, no grill, hard white paper, (Special Printing) **111**

ISSUES OF 1861-75

Jackson — A32   Lincoln — A33

Perf. 12, Unwmkd.

A32   2¢ black, no grill **73**
A32   2¢ black, laid paper **73d**
A32   2¢ black, grill 12x14mm **84**
A32   2¢ black, grill 11x14mm **85B**
A32   2¢ black, grill 11x13mm **87**
A32   2¢ black, grill 9x13mm **93**
A32   2¢ black, no grill, hard white paper, (Special Printing) **103**
A33   15¢ black, no grill **77**
A33   15¢ black, grill 11x14mm **85F**
A33   15¢ black, grill 11x13mm **91**
A33   15¢ black, grill 9x13mm **98**
A33   15¢ black, no grill, hard white paper, (Special Printing) **108**

ISSUES OF 1869-80

Franklin — A34

A34   1¢ buff, grill 9½x9mm **112**
A34   1¢ buff, no grill **112b**
A34   1¢ buff, no grill, hard white paper (Special Printing) **123**
A34   1¢ buff, no grill, soft porous paper (Special Printing) **133**
A34   1¢ brown orange, same without gum (Special Printing) **133a**

Pony Express — A35   Baldwin 4-4-0 Locomotive, c. 1857 — A36

A35   2¢ brown, grill 9½x9mm **113**
A35   2¢ brown, no grill **113b**
A35   2¢ brown, no grill, hard white paper (Special Printing) **124**
A36   3¢ ultramarine, grill 9½x9mm **114**
A36   3¢ ultramarine, no grill **114a**
A36   3¢ blue, no grill, hard white paper (Special Printing) **125**

Washington — A37   Shield and Eagle — A38

S.S. Adriatic — A39

A37   6¢ ultramarine, grill 9½x9mm **115**
A37   6¢ blue, no grill, hard white paper (Special Printing) **126**
A38   10¢ yellow, grill 9½x9mm **116**
A38   10¢ yellow, no grill, hard white paper (Special Printing) **127**
A39   12¢ green, grill 9½x9mm **117**
A39   12¢ green, no grill, hard white paper (Special Printing) **128**

Landing of Columbus — A40

A40 Type I Picture unframed

A40a Type II Picture framed

Type III same as Type I but without the fringe of brown shading lines around central vignette.

A40   15¢ brown & blue, type I, grill 9½x9mm **118**
A40   15¢ brown & blue, type I, no grill **118a**
A40   15¢ brown & blue, type III, no grill, hard white paper (Special Printing) **129**
A40a   15¢ brown & blue, type II, grill 9½x9mm **119**

The Declaration of
Independence — A41

Shield, Eagle and
Flags — A42

Lincoln — A43

A41	24¢ green & violet, grill 9½x9mm	120
A41	24¢ green & violet, no grill	120a
A41	24¢ green & violet, no grill, hard white paper (Special Printing)	130
A42	30¢ ultramarine & carmine, grill 9½x9mm.......	121
A42	30¢ ultramarine & carmine, no grill..........	121a
A42	30¢ ultramarine & carmine, no grill, hard white paper (Special Printing)............................	131
A43	90¢ carmine & black, grill 9½x9mm...........	122
A43	90¢ carmine & black, no grill	122a
A43	90¢ carmine & black, no grill, hard white paper (Special Printing)............................	132
A43	90¢ carmine & black, 28x28mm, imperf., litho. & engraved..	2433a
A43	90¢ blue & brown, 28x28mm, imperf., litho. & engraved	2433b
A43	90¢ green & blue, 28x28mm, imperf., litho. & engraved	2433c
A43	90¢ scarlet & blue, 28x28mm, imperf., litho. & engraved	2433d

ISSUES OF 1870-88

The secret mark shown in the detail of A45a is seldom found on the actual stamps. Stamps Nos. 146 and 157 are best identified by color which is red brown for No. 146 and brown for No. 157.

Note I: Special printings of 1880-83 — All denominations of this series were printed on special order from the Post Office Department during the period the stamps were current. The paper being the same as used on current issue, the special printings are extremely difficult to identify. The 2¢ brown, 7¢ scarlet vermilion, 12¢ blackish purple and 24¢ dark violet are easily distinguished by the soft porous paper as these denominations were never previously printed on soft paper. The other denominations can be distinguished by shades only, those of the special printings being slightly deeper and richer than the regular issue. The special printings except No. 211B were issued without gum. The only certain way to identify them is by comparison with stamps previously established as special printings.

Franklin — A44

A44

A44a With secret mark In the pearl at the left of the numeral "1" there is a small dash.

A44b Re-engraved The vertical lines in the upper part of the stamp have been so deepened that the background often appears to be solid. Lines of shading have been added to the upper arabesques.

A44	1¢ ultramarine, with grill	134
A44	1¢ ultramarine, no grill	145
A44a	1¢ ultramarine, white wove paper no grill...	156
A44a	1¢ ultramarine, with grill	156e
A44a	1¢ ultramarine, hard white paper, without gum (Special Printing)	167
A44a	1¢ dark ultra, soft porous paper	182
A44a	1¢ dark ultra, soft porous paper, without gum (Special Printing, see note I)....................	192
A44b	1¢ gray blue...	206

Jackson — A45

A45

A45a Under the scroll at the left of "U.S." there is a small diagonal line.

A45	2¢ red brown, with grill...............................	135
A45	2¢ red brown, no grill	146
A45a	2¢ brown, white wove paper no grill	157
A45a	2¢ brown, with grill.....................................	157c
A45a	2¢ dark brown, hard white paper, without gum (Special Printing)	168
A45a	2¢ black brown, soft porous paper, without gum (Special Printing)	193
A45a	2¢ vermilion, yellowish paper.....................	178
A45a	2¢ vermilion, same, with grill.....................	178c
A45a	2¢ vermilion, soft porous paper	183
A45a	2¢ carmine vermilion, hard white paper, without gum (Special Printing)	180
A45a	2¢ scarlet vermilion, soft porous paper, without gum (Special Printing, see note I)......	203

Washington — A46

A46

A46a With secret mark The under part of the tail of the left ribbon is heavily shaded.

A46b Re-engraved The shading at the sides of the central oval appears only about one half the previous width. A short horizontal dash has been cut about 1mm. below the "TS" of "CENTS."

A46	3¢ green, with grill......................................	136
A46	3¢ green, no grill	147
A46a	3¢ green, white wove paper, no grill...........	158
A46a	3¢ green, same, with grill...........................	158e
A46a	3¢ blue green, hard white paper, without gum (Special Printing)	169
A46a	3¢ green, soft porous paper........................	184
A46a	3¢ blue green, soft porous paper, without gum (Special Printing see note I)	194
A46b	3¢ blue green, re-engraved	207
A46b	3¢ vermilion re-engraved............................	214

Lincoln — A47

A47

A47a With secret mark The first four vertical lines of the shading in the lower part of the left ribbon have been strengthened.

A47b Re-engraved. 6¢ on the original stamps four vertical lines can be counted from the edge of the panel to the outside of the stamp. On the re-engraved stamps there are but three lines in the same place.

A47	6¢ carmine, with grill	137
A47	6¢ carmine, no grill	148
A47a	6¢ dull pink, no grill, white wove paper	159
A47a	6¢ dull pink, with grill.................................	159b
A47a	6¢ dull rose, hard white paper, without gum (Special Printing)	170
A47a	6¢ pink, soft porous paper	186
A47a	6¢ dull rose, soft porous paper, without gum (Special Printing see note I).....................	195
A47b	6¢ rose, re-engraved	208

Edwin McMasters
Stanton — A48

Thomas
Jefferson — A49

A48

A48a With secret mark Two small semi-circles are drawn around the ends of the lines which outline the ball in the lower right hand corner.

A49

A49a With secret mark A small semi-circle in the scroll at the right end of the upper label.

A49b Re-engraved On the original stamps there are five vertical lines between the left side of the oval and the edge of the shield. There are only four lines on the re-engraved stamps. In the lower part of the re-engraved stamps the horizontal lines of the background have been strengthened.

Henry Clay — A50

A50

A50a With secret mark The balls of the figure "2" are crescent shaped.

A48	7¢ vermilion, with grill		138
A48	7¢ vermilion, no grill		149
A48a	7¢ orange verm., white wove paper no grill		160
A48a	7¢ orange verm., same, with grill		160a
A48a	7¢ reddish verm., hard white paper, without gum (Special Printing)		171
A48a	7¢ scarlet verm., soft porous paper, without gum (Special Printing)		196
A49	10¢ brown, with grill		139
A49	10¢ brown, no grill		150
A49	10¢ brown, soft porous paper		187
A49a	10¢ brown, white wove paper no grill		161
A49a	10¢ brown, with grill		161c
A49a	10¢ pale brown, hard white paper, without gum (Special Printing)		172
A49a	10¢ brown, soft porous paper		188
A49a	10¢ deep brown, soft porous paper, without gum (Special Printing, see note I)		197
A49b	10¢ brown, re-engraved		209
A50	12¢ dull violet, with grill		140
A50	12¢ dull violet, no grill		151
A50a	12¢ blackish violet, white wove paper, no grill		162
A50a	12¢ blackish violet, with grill		162a
A50a	12¢ dark violet, hard white paper, without gum (Special Printing)		173
A50a	12¢ blackish purple, soft porous paper, without gum (Special Printing)		198

Webster — A51   A51

A51a With secret mark In the lower part of the triangle in the upper left corner two lines have been made heavier forming a "V." This mark can be found on some of the Continental and American (1879) printings, but not all stamps show it.

A51	15¢ orange, with grill		141
A51	15¢ bright orange, no grill		152
A51a	15¢ yellow orange, white wove paper, no grill		163
A51a	15¢ yellow orange, with grill		163a
A51a	15¢ bright orange, hard white paper, without gum (Special Printing)		174
A51a	15¢ red orange, soft porous paper		189
A51a	15¢ orange, soft porous paper, without gum (Special Printing, see note I)		199

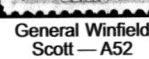

General Winfield Scott — A52   Hamilton — A53

Perry — A54

Secret marks were added to the dies of the 24¢, 30¢ and 90¢ but new plates were not made from them. The various printings of these stamps can be distinguished only by the shades and paper.

A52	24¢ purple, with grill		142
A52	24¢ purple, no grill		153
A52	24¢ purple, vertically ribbed white wove paper, no grill		164
A52	24¢ dull purple, hard white paper, without gum (Special Printing)		175
A52	24¢ dark violet, soft porous paper, without gum (Special Printing)		200
A53	30¢ black, with grill		143
A53	30¢ black, no grill		154
A53	30¢ full black, soft porous paper		190
A53	30¢ gray black, white wove paper, no grill		165
A53	30¢ greenish black, with grill		165c
A53	30¢ greenish black, hard white paper, without gum (Special Printing)		176
A53	30¢ greenish black, soft porous paper, without gum (Special Printing, see note I)		201
A53	30¢ orange brown		217
A54	90¢ carmine, with grill		144
A54	90¢ carmine, no grill		155
A54	90¢ carmine, soft porous paper		191
A54	90¢ rose carmine, white wove paper		166
A54	90¢ violet carmine, hard white paper, without gum (Special Printing)		177
A54	90¢ dull carmine, soft porous paper, without gum (Special Printing, see note I)		202
A54	90¢ purple		218

ISSUES OF 1875-88

Taylor — A55   Garfield — A56

Perf. 12, Unwmkd.

A55	5¢ blue, yellowish wove paper, no grill		179
A55	5¢ blue, with grill		179c
A55	5¢ bright blue, hard, white wove paper, without gum (Special Printing)		181
A55	5¢ blue, soft porous paper		185
A55	5¢ deep blue, soft porous paper, without gum (Special Printing, see note I)		204
A56	5¢ yellow brown		205
A56	5¢ gray brown, soft porous paper, without gum (Special Printing, see note I)		205C
A56	5¢ indigo		216

Washington — A57   Jackson — A58

A57	2¢ red brown		210
A57	2¢ pale red brown, soft porous paper (Special Printing, see note I)		211B
A57	2¢ green		213
A58	4¢ blue green		211
A58	4¢ deep blue green, soft porous paper, without gum (Special Printing, see note I)		211D
A58	4¢ carmine		215

Franklin — A59

A59	1¢ ultramarine		212

ISSUES OF 1890-93

Franklin — A60   Washington — A61

Jackson — A62   Lincoln — A63

Grant — A64

Garfield — A65

William T. Sherman — A66

Daniel Webster — A67

Henry Clay — A68

Jefferson — A69

Perry — A70

A60	1¢ dull blue	219
A61	2¢ lake	219D
A61	2¢ carmine	220
A62	3¢ purple	221
A63	4¢ dark brown	222
A64	5¢ chocolate	223
A65	6¢ brown red	224
A66	8¢ lilac	225
A67	10¢ green	226
A68	15¢ indigo	227
A69	30¢ black	228
A70	90¢ orange	229

ISSUES OF 1894-1903

This series, the first to be printed by the Bureau of Engraving and Printing, closely resembles the 1890 series but is identified by the triangles which have been added to the upper corners of the designs.

The Catalogue divides this group into three separate series, the first of which was issued in 1894 and is unwatermarked. In 1895 the paper used was watermarked with the double line letters USPS (United States Postage Stamp). The stamps show one complete letter of the watermark or parts of two or more letters.

This watermark appears on all United States stamps issued from 1895 until 1910.

In 1898 the colors of some of the denominations were changed, which created the third series noted in the Catalogue.

Other than the watermark, or lack of it, there are three styles of the corner triangles used on the 2 cent stamps and two variations of designs are noted on the 10 cent and $1 denomination. In the following list all of these variations are illustrated and described immediately preceding the denominations on which they appear.

USPS
Wmkd. (191) Horizontally

USPS
or Vertically

(Actual size of letter)

Franklin — A87

Washington — A88

Jackson — A89

Lincoln — A90

Grant — A91

Garfield — A92

Sherman — A93

Clay — A95

Webster — A94

Jefferson — A96

Perry — A97

James Madison — A98

John Marshall — A99

A87	1¢ ultramarine, unwmkd.	246
A87	1¢ blue, unwmkd.	247
A87	1¢ blue, wmkd.	264

A87	1¢ deep green, wmkd.	27
A87	1¢ on 1¢ yellow green, "CUBA"	Cuba 22
A87	1¢ deep green, "GUAM"	Guam
A87	1¢ yellow green, "PHILIPPINES"	Phil. 21
A87	1¢ yellow green, "PORTO RICO"	P.R. 21
A87	1¢ yellow green, "PUERTO RICO"	P.R. 215

Triangle A (Type I) *The horizontal lines of the ground work run across the triangle and are of the same thickness within it as without.*

Triangle B (Type II) *The horiztonal lines cross the triangle but are thinner within it than without. Other minor differences exist, but the change to Triangle B is a sufficient determinant.*

Triangle C (Types III & IV) Type III: *The horizontal lines do not cross the double lines of the triangle. The lines within the triangle are thin, as in Triangle B.*

The rest of the design is the same as Type II, except that most of the designs had the dot in the "S" of "CENTS" removed. Stamps with this dot are listed; some specialists refer to them as "Type IIIa" varieties.

Type IV: Same triangle C as type III, but other design differences including (1) recutting and lengthening of hairline, (2) shaded toga button, (3) strengthening of lines on sleeve, (4) additional dots on ear, (5) "T" of "TWO" straight at right, (6) background lines extend into white oval opposite "U" of "UNITED." Many other differences exist.

A88	2¢ pink, type I, unwmkd.	248
A88	2¢ carmine lake, type I, unwmkd.	249
A88	2¢ carmine, type I, unwmkd.	250
A88	2¢ carmine, type I, wmkd.	265
A88	2¢ carmine, type II, unwmkd.	251
A88	2¢ carmine, type II, wmkd.	266
A88	2¢ carmine, type III, unwmkd.	252

A88 2¢ carmine, type III, wmkd.............................267
A88 2¢ red, type IV, wmkd.................................279B
A88 2¢ booklet pane of 6, wmkd., single stamps
      with 1 or 2 straight edges......................279Bj
A88 2c on 2¢ reddish carmine, type III "CUBA" ......
      ....Cuba 222
A88 2c on 2¢ reddish carmine, type IV, "CUBA" ...
      ....Cuba 222A
A88 2½c on 2¢ reddish carmine, type III, "CUBA"
      ....Cuba 223
A88 2½c on 2¢ reddish carmine, type IV, "CUBA"
      ....Cuba 223A
A88 2¢ red, type IV, "GUAM"...................Guam 2
A88 2¢ red, type IV, "PHILIPPINES".......Phil. 214
A88 Same, booklet pane of 6.................Phil. 214b
A88 2¢ reddish carmine, type IV, "PORTO RICO"
      ....P.R. 211
A88 Same, "PUERTO RICO"....................P.R. 216
A89 3¢ purple, unwmkd.................................253
A89 3¢ purple, wmkd....................................268
A89 3¢ on 3¢ purple, "CUBA"..............Cuba 224
A89 3¢ purple, "GUAM".........................Guam 3
A89 3¢ purple "PHILIPPINES"...............Phil. 215
A90 4¢ dark brown, unwmkd..........................254
A90 4¢ dark brown, wmkd..............................269
A90 4¢ rose brown, wmkd...............................280
A90 4¢ lilac brown, "GUAM"...................Guam 4
A90 4¢ orange brown, "PHILIPPINES"......Phil. 220
A91 5¢ chocolate, unwmkd............................255
A91 5¢ chocolate, wmkd................................270
A91 5¢ dark blue, wmkd................................281
A91 5¢ on 5¢ blue, "CUBA"..................Cuba 225
A91 5¢ blue, "GUAM"...........................Guam 5
A91 5¢ blue, "PHILIPPINES"..................Phil. 216
A91 5¢ blue, "PORTO RICO" ..................P.R. 212
A92 6¢ dull brown, unwmkd............................256
A92 6¢ dull brown, wmkd. USPS....................271
A92 6¢ dull brown, wmkd. USIR....................271a
A92 6¢ lake, wmkd.......................................282
A92 6¢ lake, "GUAM".............................Guam 6
A92 6¢ lake, "PHILIPPINES" ....Phil. 221
A93 8¢ violet brown, unwmkd.........................257
A93 8¢ violet brown, wmkd. USPS..................272
A93 8¢ violet brown, wmkd. USIR..................272a
A93 8¢ violet brown, "GUAM"..................Guam 7
A93 8¢ violet brown, "PHILIPPINES".......Phil. 222
A93 8¢ violet brown, "PORTO RICO"........P.R. 213

Type I *The tips of the foliate ornaments do not impinge on the white curved line below "ten cents."*

Type II *The tips of the ornaments break the curved line below the "e" of "ten" and the "t" of "cents."*

A94 10¢ dark green, unwmkd. 258
A94 10¢ dark green, wmkd. 273
A94 10¢ brown, type I, wmkd. 282C
A94 10¢ orange brown, type II, wmkd. 283
A94 10¢ on 10¢ brown, type I, "CUBA" ...Cuba 226
A94 Same, type II, "CUBA" ....Cuba 226A
A94 10¢ brown, type I, "GUAM" ....Guam 8
A94 10¢ brown, type II, "GUAM" ....Guam 9
A94 10¢ brown, type I, "PHILIPPINES".....Phil. 217
A94 10¢ orange brown, type II, "PHILIPPINES" ......
      ....Phil. 217A
A94 10¢ brown, type I, "PORTO RICO" .....P.R. 214
A95 15¢ dark blue, unwmkd...........................259
A95 15¢ dark blue, wmkd...............................274
A95 15¢ olive green, wmkd............................284
A95 15¢ olive green, "GUAM"................Guam 10
A95 15¢ olive green, "PHILIPPINES" ....Phil. 218
A96 50¢ orange, unwmkd...............................260
A96 50¢ orange, wmkd..................................275
A96 50¢ orange, "GUAM"......................Guam 11
A96 50¢ orange, unwmkd., "PHILIPPINES".............
      ....Phil. 212
A96 50¢ orange, wmkd., "PHILIPPINES" Phil. 219

A97 Type I *The circles enclosing "$1" are broken where they meet the curved line below "One Dollar."*

A97 Type II *The circles are complete.*

A97 $1 black, type I, unwmkd. 261
A97 $1 black, type I, wmkd. 276
A97 $1 black, type II, unwmkd. 261A
A97 $1 black, type II, wmkd. 276A
A97 $1 black, type I, "GUAM"................Guam 12
A97 $1 black, type II, "GUAM"..............Guam 13
A97 $1 black, type I, "PHILIPPINES".......Phil. 223
A97 $1 black, type II, "PHILIPPINES" .....Phil. 223A
A98 $2 bright blue, unwmkd. 262
A98 $2 blue, perf. 11, tagged....................2875a
A98 $2 bright blue, wmkd. 277
A98 $2 dark blue, "PHILIPPINES" ....Phil. 224
A99 $5 dark green, unwmkd. 263
A99 $5 dark green, wmkd. 278
A99 $5 dark green, "PHILIPPINES" ....Phil. 225

ISSUES OF 1902-17

Franklin — A115

Washington — A116

Jackson — A117

Grant — A118

Lincoln — A119

Garfield — A120

Martha Washington — A121

Daniel Webster — A122

Benjamin Harrison — A123

Henry Clay — A124

Jefferson — A125

David G. Farragut — A126

Madison — A127

Marshall — A128

**Unless otherwise noted all stamps are
Perf. 12 and Wmkd. (191)**

Single stamps from booklet panes show 1 or 2 straight edges.

A115 1¢ blue green 300
A115 1¢ booklet pane of 6 ....300b
A115 1¢ blue green, imperf. 314
A115 1¢ blue green, perf. 12 horiz., pair 316
A115 1¢ blue green, perf. 12 vert., pair 318
A115 1¢ blue green, "CANAL ZONE PANAMA"
      ....C.Z. 4
A115 1¢ blue green, "PHILIPPINES"..........Phil. 226
A116 2¢ carmine..301
A116 2¢ booklet pane of 6 ....301c
A116 2¢ carmine, "PHILIPPINES" ....Phil. 227
A117 3¢ bright violet....................................302
A117 3¢ bright violet, "PHILIPPINES" ....Phil. 228
A118 4¢ brown...303
A118 4¢ brown, imperf. 314A
A118 4¢ brown, "PHILIPPINES" ....Phil. 229
A119 5¢ blue...304
A119 5¢ blue, imperf. 315
A119 5¢ blue, perf. 12 horiz. pair 317
A119 5¢ blue, "CANAL ZONE PANAMA" .........C.Z. 6
A119 5¢ blue, "PHILIPPINES" ....Phil. 230
A120 6¢ claret...305
A120 6¢ brownish lake, "PHILIPPINES".....Phil. 231
A121 8¢ violet black.....................................306
A121 8¢ violet black, "CANAL ZONE PANAMA".......
      ....C.Z. 7
A121 8¢ violet black, "PHILIPPINES" ....Phil. 232
A122 10¢ pale red brown 307
A122 10¢ pale red brown, "CANAL ZONE PANAMA"
      ....C.Z. 8
A122 10¢ pale red brown, "PHILIPPINES" ....
      ....Phil. 233
A123 13¢ purple black.................................308
A123 13¢ purple black, "PHILIPPINES" ......Phil. 234
A124 15¢ olive green....................................309
A124 15¢ olive green, "PHILIPPINES" ....Phil. 235
A125 50¢ orange..310
A125 50¢ orange, "PHILIPPINES"...............Phil. 236
A126 $1 black...311
A126 $1 black, "PHILIPPINES" ....Phil. 237
A127 $2 dark blue..312
A127 $2 dark blue, unwmkd., perf. 10 479
A127 $2 dark blue, "PHILIPPINES" ....Phil. 238
A128 $5 dark green......................................313
A128 $5 light green, unwmkd., perf. 10 480
A128 $5 dark green, "PHILIPPINES" ....Phil. 239

ISSUES OF 1903

Washington — A129

Type I

Type II

Specialists recognize over a hundred shades of this stamp in various hues of vermilion, red, carmine and lake. The Scott Catalogue lists only the most striking differences.
    The Government coil stamp, No. 322 should not be confused with the scarlet vermilion coil of the International Vending Machine Co., which is perforated 12½ to 13.

A129 2¢ carmine, type I, wmkd............................319
A129 2¢ lake, type II..319f
A129 2¢ carmine, type I, booklet pane of 6....319g
A129 Same, type II...319h
A129 2¢ carmine, type I, imperf. 320
A129 2¢ lake, type II, imperf. 320a

A129 2¢ carmine, perf. 12 horiz. pair.................. **321**
A129 2¢ carmine, perf. 12 vert. pair **322**
A129 2¢ carmine, "CANAL ZONE PANAMA".... **C.Z. 5**
A129 2¢ carmine, "PHILIPPINES"................ **Phil. 240**
A129 2¢ carmine, same, booklet pane of 6..............
.... **Phil. 240a**

ISSUES OF 1908-09

This series introduces for the first time the single line water-mark USPS. Only a small portion of several letters is often all that can be seen on a single stamp.

Franklin — A138

Washington — A139

Wmk. 190

A138 1¢ green, perf. 12, double line wmk. **331**
A138 1¢ green, same, China clay paper.............**331b**
A138 1¢ green, perf. 12, single line wmk. **374**
A138 1¢ green, perf. 12, bluish paper.................. **357**
A138 1¢ green, imperf., double line wmk. **343**
A138 1¢ green, imperf., single line wmk. **383**
A138 1¢ green, perf. 12 horiz., double line wmk.
.... **348**
A138 1¢ green, perf. 12 horiz., single line wmk. ......
.... **385**
A138 1¢ green, perf. 12 vert., double line wmk. .....
.... **352**
A138 1¢ green, perf. 12 vert., single line wmk. ......
.... **387**
A138 1¢ green, perf. 8½ horiz., single line wmk. ...
.... **390**
A138 1¢ green, perf. 8½ vert., single line wmk. **392**
A139 2¢ carmine, perf. 12, double line wmk. **332**
A139 2¢ carmine, same, China clay paper.......**332b**
A139 2¢ carmine, perf. 12, single line wmk......... **375**
A139 2¢ carmine, perf. 12, bluish paper.............. **358**
A139 2¢ carmine, perf. 11, double line wmk. **519**
A139 2¢ carmine, imperf., double line wmk......... **344**
A139 2¢ carmine, imperf., single line wmk. **384**
A139 2¢ carmine, perf. 12 horiz., double line wmk.
.... **349**
A139 2¢ carmine, perf. 12 horiz., single line wmk. ....
.... **386**
A139 2¢ carmine, perf. 12 vert., double line wmk. ....
.... **353**
A139 2¢ carmine, perf. 12 vert., single line wmk. ....
.... **388**
A139 2¢ carmine, perf. 8½ horiz. single line wmk. ....
.... **391**
A139 2¢ carmine, perf. 8½ vert., single line wmk. ....
.... **393**

Single stamps from booklet panes show 1 or 2 straight edges.

A138 1¢ green, perf. 12, double line wmk., booklet
pane of 6... **331a**
A138 1¢ green, perf.12, single line wmk., booklet
pane of 6... **374a**
A139 2¢ carmine, perf. 12, double line wmk.,
booklet pane of 6............................ **332a**
A139 2¢ carmine, perf. 12, single line wmk., booklet
pane of 6... **375a**

ISSUES OF 1908-21
FLAT BED AND ROTARY PRESS STAMPS

The Rotary Press Stamps are printed from plates that are curved to fit around a cylinder. This curvature produces stamps that are slightly larger, either horizontally or vertically, than those printed from flat plates. Designs of stamps from flat plates measure about 18½-19mm. wide by 22mm. high. When the impressions are placed sidewise on the curved plates the designs are 19½-20mm. wide; when they are placed vertically the designs are 22½ to 23mm. high. A line of color (not a guide line) shows where the curved plates meet or join on the press.

Rotary Press Coil Stamps were printed from plates of 170 subjects for stamps coiled sidewise, and from plates of 150 subjects for stamps coiled endwise.

Washington — A140

1¢ A138 Portrait of Franklin, value in words.
2¢ A139 Portrait of Washington, value in words.
A140 Portrait of Washington, value in numerals.

A140 1¢ green, perf. 12, single line wmk. **405**
A140 1¢ green, same, booklet pane of 6............**405b**
A140 1¢ green, perf. 11, flat plate, unwmkd........ **498**
A140 1¢ green, same, booklet pane of 6............**498e**
A140 1¢ green, same, booklet pane of 30..........**498f**
A140 1¢ green, perf. 11, rotary press measuring
19mmx22½mm, unwmkd........................... **544**
A140 1¢ green, same, measuring 19½ to
20mmx22mm **545**
A140 1¢ gray green, perf. 11, offset, unwmkd....**525**
A140 1¢ gray green, perf. 12½ **536**
A140 1¢ green, perf. 11x10................................. **538**
A140 1¢ green, perf. 10x11................................. **542**
A140 1¢ green, perf. 10, single line wmk. **424**
A140 1¢ green, same, perf. 12x10....................**423A**
A140 1¢ green, same, perf. 10x12....................**423D**
A140 1¢ green, perf.10, single line wmk., booklet
pane of 6 ....**424d**
A140 1¢ green, perf. 10, flat plate, unwmkd........ **462**
A140 1¢ green, same, booklet pane of 6..........**462a**
A140 1¢ green, perf. 10, rotary press, unwmkd. ....
.... **543**
A140 1¢ green, imperf., single line wmk. **408**
A140 1¢ green, imperf., unwmkd. **481**
A140 1¢ green, imperf., offset **531**
A140 1¢ green, perf. 10 horiz., flat plate, single line
wmk.. **441**
A140 1¢ green, same, rotary press..................... **448**
A140 1¢ green, perf. 10 horiz., rotary press,
unwmkd. **486**
A140 1¢ green, perf. 10 vert., flat plate, single line
wmk.. **443**
A140 1¢ green, same, rotary press..................... **452**
A140 1¢ green, perf. 10 vert., rotary press, unwmkd. ....
.... **490**
A140 1¢ green, perf. 8½ horiz. single line wmk. ......
.... **410**
A140 1¢ green, perf. 8½ vert., same **412**

TYPES OF TWO CENTS

TYPE I

TYPE IA

Type Ia *The design characteristics are similar to type I except that all of the lines of the design are stronger.*
The toga button, toga rope and rope shading lines are heavy. The latter characteristics are those of type II, which, however, occur only on impressions from rotary plates.
Used only on flat plates 10208 and 10209.

TYPE II

Type II *Shading lines in ribbons as on type I.*
The toga button, rope and rope shading lines are heavy. The shading lines of the face at the lock of hair end in a strong, vertical curved line.
Used on rotary press printings only.

TYPE III

Type III

Type III *Two lines of shading in the curves of the ribbons. Other characteristics similar to type II.*
Used on rotary press printings only.

TYPE IV

Type IV *Top line of the toga rope is broken.*
The shading lines in the toga button are so arranged that the curving of the first and last form "ID."
The line of color in the left "2" is very thin and usually broken. Used on offset printings only.

TYPE V

Type V *Top line of the toga is complete.*
There are five vertical shading lines in the toga button.
The line of color in the left "2" is very thin and usually broken.
The shading dots on the nose are as shown on the diagram.
Used on offset printings only.

TYPE VA

Type Va *Characteristics are the same as type V except in the shading lines of the nose. The third row of dots from the bottom has four dots instead of six. The overall height is ⅓mm shorter than type V.*
Used on offset printings only.

TYPE VI

Type VI *General characteristics the same as type V except that the line of color in the left "2" is very heavy. Used on offset printings only.*

TYPE VII

Type VII *The line of color in the left "2" is invariably continuous, clearly defined and heavier than in type V or Va but not as heavy as type VI.*
An additional vertical row of dots has been added to the upper lip.
Numerous additional dots have been added to the hair on top of the head.

Used on offset printings only.

A140 2¢ carmine, perf. 12, type I, single line wmk. **406**
A140 2¢ carmine, same, booklet pane of 6.......**406a**
A140 2¢ pale car. red, perf. 11, single line wmk., type I..**461**
A140 2¢ rose, perf. 11, flat plate, unwmkd., type I.... ....**499**
A140 2¢ rose, same, booklet pane of 6.............**499e**
A140 2¢ rose, same, booklet pane of 30..........**499f**
A140 2¢ deep rose, perf. 11, unwmkd., type Ia..**500**
A140 2¢ carmine rose, perf. 11, rotary press, unwmkd., type III **546**
A140 2¢ carmine, perf. 11, offset, unwmkd., type IV **526**
A140 2¢ carmine, same, type V..........................**527**
A140 2¢ carmine, same, type Va........................**528**
A140 2¢ carmine, same, type VI.......................**528A**
A140 2¢ carmine, same, type VII......................**528B**
A140 2¢ carmine rose, perf. 11x10, type II........**539**
A140 2¢ carmine rose, same, type III.................**540**
A140 2¢ rose red, perf. 10x12, single line wmk., type I..**423B**
A140 2¢ rose red, perf. 12x10, single line wmk., type I..**423E**
A140 2¢ rose red, perf. 10, single line wmk., type I **425**
A140 2¢ rose red, same, perf. 10, booklet pane of 6 ....**425e**
A140 2¢ carmine, perf. 10, unwmkd., type I........**463**
A140 2¢ carmine, same, booklet pane of 6.......**463a**
A140 2¢ carmine, imperf., flat plate, single line wmk., type I **409**
A140 2¢ carmine, imperf., rotary press, single line wmk., type I **459**
A140 2¢ carmine, imperf., flat plate, unwmkd., type I **482**
A140 2¢ deep rose, same, type Ia....................**482A**
A140 2¢ carmine rose, imperf., offset, unwmkd., type IV **532**
A140 2¢ carmine rose, same, type V..................**533**
A140 2¢ carmine rose, same, type Va................**534**
A140 2¢ carmine, same, type VI......................**534A**
A140 2¢ carmine, same, type VII.....................**534B**
A140 2¢ carmine, perf. 10 horiz., flat plate, single line wmk., type I **442**
A140 2¢ red, same, rotary press........................**449**
A140 2¢ carmine, same, type III........................**450**
A140 2¢ carmine, perf. 10 horiz., rotary press unwmkd., type II **487**
A140 2¢ carmine, same, type III........................**488**
A140 2¢ carmine, perf. 10 vert., flat plate, single line wmk., type I **444**
A140 2¢ carmine rose, same, rotary press..........**453**
A140 2¢ red, same, type II.................................**454**
A140 2¢ carmine, same, type III........................**455**
A140 2¢ carmine, perf. 10 vert., rotary press, unwmkd., type II **491**
A140 2¢ carmine, same, type VII......................**492**
A140 2¢ carmine, perf. 8½ horiz., type I **411**
A140 2¢ carmine, perf. 8½ vert., type I **413**

TYPES OF THREE CENTS

TYPE I

Type I *The top line of the toga rope is weak and the rope shading lines are thin. The 5th line from the left is missing. The line between the lips is thin.*

TYPE II

Type II *The top line of the toga rope is strong and the rope shading lines are heavy and complete.*
The line between the lips is heavy.
Used on both flat plate and rotary press printings.

TYPE III

Type III *The top line of the toga rope is strong but the 5th shading line is missing as in type I.*
Center shading line of the toga button consists of two dashes with a central dot.
The "P" and "O" of "POSTAGE" are separated by a line of color.
The frame line at the bottom of the vignette is complete.
Used on offset printings only.

TYPE IV

Type IV *The shading lines of the toga rope are complete.*
The second and fourth shading lines in the toga button are broken in the middle and the third line is continuous with a dot in the center.
The "P" and "O" of "POSTAGE" are joined.
The frame line at the bottom of the vignette is broken.
Used on offset printings only.

A140 3¢ deep violet, perf. 12, double line wmk., type I...**333**
A140 3¢ deep violet, same, China clay paper ...**333a**
A140 3¢ deep violet, perf. 12, single line wmk., type I...**376**
A140 3¢ deep violet, perf. 12, bluish paper, type I.... ....**359**
A140 3¢ light violet, perf. 11, unwmkd., type I.....**501**
A140 3¢ light violet, same, booklet pane of 6....**501b**
A140 3¢ dark violet, perf. 11, unwmkd., type II...**502**
A140 3¢ dark violet, same, booklet pane of 6 ...**502b**
A140 3¢ violet, perf. 11, offset, type III................**529**
A140 3¢ purple, same, type IV **530**
A140 3¢ violet, perf. 11x10, type II....................**541**
A140 3¢ deep violet, perf. 10, single line wmk., type I...**426**
A140 3¢ violet, perf. 10, unwmkd., type I **464**
A140 3¢ deep violet, imperf., double line wmk., type I...**345**

A140 3¢ violet, imperf., unwmkd., type I.............**483**
A140 3¢ violet, same, type II.................................**484**
A140 3¢ violet, imperf., offset, type IV...............**535**
A140 3¢ deep violet, perf. 12 vert., single line wmk., type I...**389**
A140 3¢ violet, perf. 10 vert., flat plate, single line wmk., type I...**445**
A140 3¢ violet, perf. 10 vert., rotary press, single line wmk., type I...**456**
A140 3¢ violet, perf. 10 vert., rotary press, unwmkd., type I..**493**
A140 3¢ violet, same, type II.................................**494**
A140 3¢ violet, perf. 10 horiz., type I..................**489**
A140 3¢ deep violet, perf. 8½ vert., type I..........**394**
A140 4¢ orange brown, perf. 12, double line wmk. **334**
A140 4¢ orange brown, same, China clay paper...**334a**
A140 4¢ orange brown, perf. 12, bluish paper.......**360**
A140 4¢ brown, perf. 12, single line wmk. **377**
A140 4¢ brown, perf. 11, unwmkd. **503**
A140 4¢ brown, perf. 10, single line wmk............**427**
A140 4¢ orange brown, perf. 10, unwmkd. **465**
A140 4¢ orange brown, imperf.............................**346**
A140 4¢ orange brown, perf. 12 horiz..................**350**
A140 4¢ orange brown, perf. 12 vert. **354**
A140 4¢ brown, perf. 10 vert., flat plate, single line wmk...**446**
A140 4¢ brown, same, rotary press **457**
A140 4¢ orange brown, perf. 10 vert., rotary press, unwmkd...**495**
A140 4¢ brown, perf. 8½ vert., single line wmk..**395**
A140 5¢ blue, perf. 12, double line wmk..............**335**
A140 5¢ blue, same China clay paper **335a**
A140 5¢ blue, perf. 12 bluish paper.....................**361**
A140 5¢ blue, perf. 12, single line wmk...............**378**
A140 5¢ blue, perf. 11, unwmkd. **504**
A140 5¢ rose (error), same **505**
A140 5¢ carmine (error), perf. 10, unwmkd. **467**
A140 5¢ blue, perf. 10, single line wmk...............**428**
A140 5¢ blue, perf. 12x10 ....**423C**
A140 5¢ blue, perf. 10, unwmkd...........................**466**
A140 5¢ blue, imperf...**347**
A140 5¢ carmine (error), imperf. **485**
A140 5¢ blue, perf. 12 horiz.................................**351**
A140 5¢ blue, perf. 12 vert...................................**355**
A140 5¢ blue, perf. 10 vert., flat plate, single line wmk...**447**
A140 5¢ blue, same, rotary press **458**
A140 5¢ blue, perf. 10 vert., rotary press, unwmkd. **496**
A140 5¢ blue, perf. 8½ vert..................................**396**
A140 6¢ red orange, perf. 12, double line wmk...**336**
A140 6¢ red orange, same, China clay paper ...**336a**
A140 6¢ red orange, perf. 12, bluish paper **362**
A140 6¢ red orange, perf. 12, single line wmk.....**379**
A140 6¢ red orange, perf. 11, unwmkd.................**506**
A140 6¢ red orange, perf. 10, single line wmk.....**429**
A140 6¢ red orange, perf. 10, unwmkd.................**468**
A140 7¢ black, perf. 12, single line wmk. **407**
A140 7¢ black, perf. 11, unwmkd..........................**507**
A140 7¢ black, perf. 10, single line wmk..............**430**
A140 7¢ black, perf. 10, unwmkd. **469**
A140 8¢ olive green, perf. 12, double line wmk...**337**
A140 8¢ olive green, same, China clay paper ...**337a**
A140 8¢ olive green, perf. 12, bluish paper..........**363**
A140 8¢ olive green, perf. 12, single line wmk.....**380**
A140 10¢ yellow, perf. 12, double line wmk. **338**
A140 10¢ yellow, same, China clay paper **338a**
A140 10¢ yellow, perf. 12, bluish paper...............**364**
A140 10¢ yellow, perf. 12, single line wmk..........**381**
A140 10¢ yellow, perf. 12 vert..............................**356**
A140 13¢ blue green, perf. 12, double line wmk. **339**
A140 13¢ blue green, same, China clay paper..**339a**
A140 13¢ blue green, perf. 12, bluish paper........**365**
A140 15¢ pale ultra, perf. 12, double line wmk.   **340**
A140 15¢ pale ultramarine, same, China clay paper..**340a**
A140 15¢ pale ultra, perf. 12, bluish paper..........**366**
A140 15¢ pale ultra, perf. 12, single line wmk....**382**
A140 50¢ violet..**341**
A140 $1 violet brown **342**

ISSUES OF 1912-19

A148

Franklin — A149

Designs of 8¢ to $1 denominations differ only in figures of value.

A148 8¢ pale olive green, perf. 12, single line wmk. **414**
A148 8¢ olive bister, perf. 11, unwmkd. **508**
A148 8¢ pale olive grn., perf. 10, single line wmk...**431**
A148 8¢ olive green, perf. 10, unwmkd. **470**
A148 9¢ salmon red, perf. 12, single line wmk....**415**
A148 9¢ salmon red, perf. 11, unwmkd................**509**
A148 9¢ salmon red, perf. 10, single line wmk....**432**
A148 9¢ salmon red, perf. 10, unwmkd................**471**
A148 10¢ orange yellow, perf. 12, single line wmk. **416**
A148 10¢ orange yellow, perf. 11, unwmkd.........**510**
A148 10¢ orange yellow, perf. 10, single line wmk. **433**
A148 10¢ orange yellow, perf. 10, unwmkd.........**472**
A148 10¢ orange yellow, perf. 10 vert., same **497**
A148 11¢ light green, perf. 11, unwmkd. **511**
A148 11¢ dark green, perf. 10, single line wmk. **434**
A148 11¢ dark green, perf. 10, unwmkd..............**473**
A148 12¢ claret brown, perf. 12, single line wmk...**417**
A148 12¢ claret brown, perf. 11, unwmkd...........**512**
A148 12¢ claret brown, perf. 10, single line wmk. **435**
A148 12¢ claret brown, perf. 10, unwmkd...........**474**
A148 13¢ apple green, perf. 11, unwmkd.............**513**
A148 15¢ gray, perf. 12, single line wmk.............**418**
A148 15¢ gray, perf. 11, unwmkd.........................**514**
A148 15¢ gray, perf. 10, single line wmk.............**437**
A148 15¢ gray, perf. 10, unwmkd.........................**475**
A148 20¢ ultramarine, perf. 12, single line wmk...**419**
A148 20¢ light ultra., perf. 11, unwmkd................**515**
A148 20¢ ultramarine, perf. 10, single line wmk...**438**
A148 20¢ light ultra, perf. 10, unwmkd.................**476**
A148 30¢ orange red, perf. 12, single line wmk...**420**
A148 30¢ orange red, perf. 11, unwmkd..............**516**
A148 30¢ orange red, perf. 10, single line wmk...**439**
A148 30¢ orange red, perf. 10, unwmkd..............**476A**
A148 50¢ violet, perf. 12, single line wmk...........**421**
A148 50¢ violet, perf. 12, double line wmk..........**422**
A148 50¢ red violet, perf. 11, unwmkd.................**517**
A148 50¢ violet, perf. 10, single line wmk...........**440**
A148 50¢ light violet, perf. 10, unwmkd..............**477**
A148 $1 violet brown, perf. 12, double line wmk...**423**
A148 $1 violet brown, perf. 11, unwmkd..............**518**
A148 $1 violet black, perf. 10, double line wmk. **460**
A148 $1 violet black, perf. 10, unwmkd...............**478**

ISSUES OF 1918-20
Perf. 11 Unwmkd.

A149 $2 orange red & black.................................**523**
A149 $2 carmine & black **547**
A149 $5 deep green & black **524**

ISSUES OF 1922-32

Nathan Hale — A154

Franklin — A155

Warren G. Harding — A156

Washington — A157

Lincoln — A158

Martha Washington — A159

Theodore Roosevelt — A160

Garfield — A161

McKinley — A162

Grant — A163

Jefferson — A164

Monroe — A165

Hayes — A166

Cleveland — A167

American Indian — A168

Statue of Liberty — A169

Golden Gate — A170

Niagara Falls — A171

Buffalo — A172

Arlington Amphitheater and Tomb of the Unknown Soldier — A173

Lincoln Memorial — A174

United States Capitol — A175

"America" — A176

Canal Zone Overprints:
Type A has flat-topped "A's" in "CANAL."
Type B has sharp-pointed "A's" in "CANAL."

Unwmkd.

A154	½¢ olive brown, perf. 11	551
A154	½¢ olive brown, perf. 11x10½	653
A154	½¢ olive brown, "CANAL ZONE"	C.Z. 70
A155	1¢ deep green, perf. 11, flat plate	552
A155	1¢ deep green, booklet pane of 6	552a
A155	1¢ green, perf. 11, rotary press 19¾x22¼mm	594
A155	1¢ green, same, 19¼x22½mm (used)	596
A155	1¢ green, perf. 11x10, rotary press	578
A155	1¢ green, perf. 10	581
A155	1¢ green, perf. 11x10½	632
A155	1¢ green, booklet pane of 6	632a
A155	1¢ green, ovpt. Kans.	658
A155	1¢ green, ovpt. Nebr.	669
A155	1¢ green, imperf.	575
A155	1¢ green, perf. 10 vert.	597
A155	1¢ yellow green, perf. 10 horiz.	604
A155	1¢ deep green, "CANAL ZONE" type A, perf. 11	C.Z. 71
A155	1¢ deep green, same, booklet pane of 6	C.Z. 71e
A155	1¢ green, "CANAL ZONE" type B, perf. 11x10½	C.Z. 100
A156	1½¢ yellow brown, perf. 11	553
A156	1½¢ yellow brown, perf. 11x10½	633
A156	1½¢ brown, ovpt. Kans	659
A156	1½¢ brown, ovpt. Nebr.	670
A156	1½¢ brown, perf. 10	582
A156	1½¢ brown, perf. 10 vert.	598
A156	1½¢ yellow brown, perf. 10 horiz.	605
A156	1½¢ yellow brown, imperf., flat plate	576
A156	1½¢ yellow brown, imperf., rotary press, 19¼x22½mm	631
A156	1½¢ yellow brown "CANAL ZONE"	C.Z. 72

Type I

No heavy hair lines at top center of head. Outline of left acanthus scroll generally faint at top and toward base at left side.

Type II

Three heavy hair lines at top center of head; two being outstanding in the white area. Outline of left acanthus scroll very strong and clearly defined at top (under left edge of lettered panel) and at lower curve (above and to left of numeral oval).

A157	2¢ carmine, perf. 11, flat plate	554
A157	2¢ carmine, same, booklet pane of 6	554c
A157	2¢ carmine, perf. 11, rotary press, 19¾x22¼mm	595
A157	2¢ carmine, perf. 11x10	579
A157	2¢ carmine, perf. 11x10½, type I	634
A157	2¢ carmine, perf. 11x10½, type II	634A
A157	2¢ carmine lake, same, type I	634b
A157	2¢ carmine lake, same, booklet pane of 6	634d
A157	2¢ carmine, overprt. Molly Pitcher	646
A157	2¢ carmine, overprt. Hawaii 1778-1928	647
A157	2¢ carmine, overprt. Kans.	660
A157	2¢ carmine, overprt. Nebr.	671
A157	2¢ carmine, perf. 10	583
A157	2¢ carmine, same, booklet pane of 6	583a
A157	2¢ carmine, imperf.	577
A157	2¢ carmine, perf. 10 vert., type I	599
A157	2¢ carmine, same type II	599A
A157	2¢ carmine, perf. 10 horiz.	606
A157	2¢ carmine, "CANAL ZONE" type A, perf. 11	C.Z. 73
A157	2¢ carmine, same, booklet pane of 6	C.Z. 73a
A157	2¢ carmine, "CANAL ZONE" type B, perf. 11	C.Z. 84
A157	2¢ carmine, same, booklet pane of 6	C.Z. 84d
A157	2¢ carmine, "CANAL ZONE" type B, perf. 10	C.Z. 97
A157	2¢ carmine, same, booklet pane of 6	C.Z. 97b
A157	2¢ carmine, "CANAL ZONE" type B, perf. 11x10½	C.Z. 101
A157	2¢ carmine, same, booklet pane of 6	C.Z. 101a
A158	3¢ violet, perf. 11	555
A158	3¢ violet, perf. 11x10½	635
A158	3¢ violet, overprt. Kans.	661
A158	3¢ violet, overprt. Nebr.	672
A158	3¢ violet, perf. 10	584
A158	3¢ violet, perf. 10 vert.	600
A158	3¢ violet, "CANAL ZONE" perf. 11	C.Z. 85
A158	3¢ violet, "CANAL ZONE" perf. 10	C.Z. 98
A158	3¢ violet, "CANAL ZONE" perf. 11x10½	C.Z. 102
A159	4¢ yellow brown, perf. 11	556
A159	4¢ yellow brown, perf. 11x10½	636
A159	4¢ yellow brown, ovrpt. Kans.	662
A159	4¢ yellow brown, ovrpt. Nebr.	673
A159	4¢ yellow brown, perf. 10	585
A159	4¢ yellow brown, perf. 10 vert.	601

A160	5¢ dark blue, perf. 11	557
A160	5¢ dark blue, perf. 11x10½	637
A160	5¢ dark blue, ovpt. Hawaii 1778-1928	648
A160	5¢ deep blue, ovpt. Kans.	663
A160	5¢ deep blue, ovpt. Nebr.	674
A160	5¢ blue, perf. 10	586
A160	5¢ dark blue, perf. 10 vert.	602
A160	5¢ dark blue, "CANAL ZONE" type A, perf. 11	C.Z. 74
A160	5¢ dark blue, same, type B	C.Z. 86
A160	5¢ dark blue, same, perf. 11x10½	C.Z. 103
A161	6¢ red orange, perf. 11	558
A161	6¢ red orange, perf. 11x10½	638
A161	6¢ red orange, ovrpt. Kans.	664
A161	6¢ red orange, ovrpt. Nebr.	675
A161	6¢ red orange, perf. 10	587
A161	6¢ deep orange, perf. 10 vert.	723
A162	7¢ black, perf. 11	559
A162	7¢ black, perf. 11x10½	639
A162	7¢ black, ovrpt. Kans.	665
A162	7¢ black, ovrpt. Nebr.	676
A162	7¢ black, perf. 10	588
A163	8¢ olive green, perf. 11	560
A163	8¢ olive green, perf. 11x10½	640
A163	8¢ olive green, ovrpt. Kans.	666
A163	8¢ olive green, ovrpt. Nebr.	677
A163	8¢ olive green, perf. 10	589
A164	9¢ rose, perf. 11	561
A164	9¢ orange red, perf. 11x10½	641
A164	9¢ light rose, ovrpt. Kans.	667
A164	9¢ light rose, ovrpt. Nebr.	678
A164	9¢ rose, perf. 10	590
A165	10¢ orange, perf. 11	562
A165	10¢ orange, perf. 11x10½	642
A165	10¢ orange yellow, ovrpt. Kans.	668
A165	10¢ orange yellow, ovrpt. Nebr.	679
A165	10¢ orange, perf. 10	591
A165	10¢ orange, perf. 10 vert.	603
A165	10¢ orange, "CANAL ZONE" type A, perf. 11	C.Z. 75
A165	10¢ orange, same, type B	C.Z. 87
A165	10¢ orange, same, perf. 10	C.Z. 99
A165	10¢ orange, same, perf. 11x10½	C.Z. 104
A166	11¢ light blue, perf. 11	563
A166	11¢ light blue, perf. 11x10½	692
A167	12¢ brown violet, perf. 11	564
A167	12¢ brown violet, perf. 11x10½	693
A167	12¢ brown violet, "CANAL ZONE" type A	C.Z. 76
A167	12¢ brown violet, same, type B	C.Z. 88
A168	14¢ blue, perf. 11	565
A168	14¢ dark blue, perf. 11x10½	695
A168	14¢ dark blue, "CANAL ZONE" type A, perf. 11	C.Z. 77
A168	14¢ dark blue, same, type B	C.Z. 89
A168	14¢ dark blue, same, perf. 11x10½	C.Z. 116
A169	15¢ gray, perf. 11	566
A169	15¢ gray, perf. 11x10½	696
A169	15¢ gray, "CANAL ZONE" type A	C.Z. 78
A169	15¢ gray, "CANAL ZONE" type B	C.Z. 90
A170	20¢ carmine rose, perf. 11	567
A170	20¢ carmine rose, perf. 10½x11	698
A170	20¢ carmine rose, "CANAL ZONE"	C.Z. 92
A171	25¢ yellow green, perf. 11	568
A171	25¢ blue green, perf. 10½x11	699
A172	30¢ olive brown, perf. 11	569
A172	30¢ brown, perf. 10½x11	700
A172	30¢ olive brown, "CANAL ZONE" type A	C.Z. 79
A172	30¢ olive brown, "CANAL ZONE" type B	C.Z. 93
A173	50¢ lilac, perf. 11	570
A173	50¢ lilac, perf. 10½x11	701
A173	50¢ lilac, "CANAL ZONE" type A	C.Z. 80
A173	50¢ lilac, "CANAL ZONE" type B	C.Z. 94
A174	$1 violet black, perf. 11	571
A174	$1 violet black, perf. 10¾x10½	4075a
A174	$1 violet brown, "CANAL ZONE" type A	C.Z. 81
A174	$1 violet brown, "CANAL ZONE" type B	C.Z. 95
A175	$2 deep blue, perf. 11	572
A175	$2 deep blue, perf. 10¾x10½	4075b
A176	$5 carmine & blue, perf. 11	573
A176	$5 carmine & blue, perf. 10¾x10½	4075c

REGULAR ISSUES OF 1925-26, 1930 and 1932

Harrison — A186

Wilson — A187

A186	13¢ green, perf. 11	622

A186 13¢ yellow green, perf. 11x10½...............**694**
A187 17¢ black, perf. 11.......................................**623**
A187 17¢ black, perf. 10½x11.........................**697**
A187 17¢ black, "CANAL ZONE" ...............**C.Z. 91**

Harding — A203

Taft — A204

A203 1½¢ brown, perf. 11x10½ **684**
A203 1½¢ brown, perf. 10 vert.............................**686**
A204 4¢ brown, perf. 11x10½.............................**685**
A204 4¢ brown, perf. 10 vert..............................**687**

Washington — A226

A226 3¢ deep violet, perf. 11x10½ **720**
A226 3¢ deep violet, same, booklet pane of 6 **720b**
A226 3¢ deep violet, perf. 10 vert........................**721**
A226 3¢ deep violet, perf. 10 horiz. **722**
A226 3¢ deep violet, "CANAL ZONE" ..........**C.Z. 115**

PRESIDENTIAL ISSUE OF 1938

Benjamin
Franklin — A275

George
Washington — A276

Martha Washington
A277

John Adams
A278

Thomas
Jefferson — A279

James
Madison — A280

The White
House — A281

James
Monroe — A282

John Quincy
Adams — A283

Martin Van
Buren — A285

John Tyler — A287

Zachary
Taylor — A289

Franklin
Pierce — A291

Abraham
Lincoln — A293

Ulysses S.
Grant — A295

Andrew
Jackson — A284

William H.
Harrison — A286

James K.
Polk — A288

Millard
Fillmore — A290

James
Buchanan — A292

Andrew
Johnson — A294

Rutherford B.
Hayes — A296

James A.
Garfield — A297

Grover
Cleveland — A299

William
McKinley — A301

William Howard
Taft — A303

Warren G.
Harding — A305

Chester A.
Arthur — A298

Benjamin
Harrison — A300

Theodore
Roosevelt — A302

Woodrow
Wilson — A304

Calvin
Coolidge — A306

Rotary Press Printing
Unwmkd.

A275 ½¢ deep orange, perf. 11x10½.................**803**
A275 ½¢ red orange, "CANAL ZONE" ........**C.Z. 118**
A276 1¢ green, perf. 11x10½ **804**
A276 1¢ green, booklet pane of 6...................**804b**
A276 1¢ green, perf. 10 vert.............................**839**
A276 1¢ green, perf. 10 horiz............................**848**
A277 1½¢ bister brown, perf. 11x10½.............**805**
A277 1½¢ bister brown, perf. 10 vert................**840**
A277 1½¢ bister brown, perf. 10 horiz..............**849**
A277 1½¢ bister brown, "CANAL ZONE" ....**C.Z. 119**
A278 2¢ rose carmine, perf. 11x10½ **806**
A278 2¢ booklet pane of 6...............................**806b**
A278 2¢ rose carmine, perf. 10 vert. **841**
A278 2¢ rose carmine, perf. 10 horiz................**850**
A279 3¢ deep violet, perf. 11x10½ **807**
A279 3¢ deep violet, booklet pane of 6 ....**807a**
A279 3¢ deep violet, perf. 10 vert.....................**842**
A279 3¢ deep violet, perf. 10 horiz....................**851**
A280 4¢ red violet, perf. 11x10½ **808**
A280 4¢ red violet, perf. 10 vert.......................**843**
A281 4½¢ dark gray, perf. 11x10½....................**809**
A281 4½¢ dark gray, perf. 10 vert.....................**844**
A282 5¢ bright blue, perf. 11x10½....................**810**
A282 5¢ bright blue, perf. 10 vert.....................**845**
A283 6¢ red orange, perf. 11x10½....................**811**
A283 6¢ red orange, perf. 10 vert.....................**846**
A284 7¢ sepia, perf. 11x10½.............................**812**
A285 8¢ olive green, perf. 11x10½....................**813**
A286 9¢ rose pink, perf. 11x10½.......................**814**
A287 10¢ brown red, perf. 11x10½....................**815**
A287 10¢ brown red, perf. 10 vert. **847**

A288 11¢ ultramarine, perf. 11x10½ 816
A289 12¢ bright violet, perf. 11x10½ 817
A290 13¢ blue green, perf. 11x10½ 818
A291 14¢ blue, perf. 11x10½ 819
A292 15¢ blue gray, perf. 11x10½ 820
A293 16¢ black, perf. 11x10½ 821
A294 17¢ rose red, perf. 11x10½ 822
A295 18¢ brn. carmine, perf. 11x10½ 823
A296 19¢ bright violet, perf. 11x10½ 824
A297 20¢ bright blue green, perf. 11x10½......... 825
A298 21¢ dull blue, perf. 11x10½ 826
A299 22¢ vermilion, perf. 11x10½ 827
A300 24¢ gray black, perf. 11x10½ 828
A301 25¢ dp. red lilac, perf. 11x10½ 829
A302 30¢ deep ultra, perf. 11x10½ 830
A303 50¢ lt. red violet, perf. 11x10½ 831

Flat Plate Printing
Perf. 11

A304 $1 pur. & blk., unwmkd. 832
A304 $1 pur. & blk., wmkd. USIR 832b
A304 $1 red vio. & blk., thick white paper, smooth
        colorless gum 832c
A305 $2 yellow green & black 833
A306 $5 carmine & black 834

LIBERTY ISSUE 1954-73

Benjamin Franklin
A477

George Washington
A478

Palace of the
Governors, Santa Fe
— A478a

Mount Vernon — A479

Thomas
Jefferson — A480

Bunker Hill
Monument and
Massachusetts Flag
1776 — A481

Statue of
Liberty — A482

Abraham
Lincoln — A483

The Hermitage — A484

James
Monroe — A485

Theodore
Roosevelt — A486

Statue of Liberty
(Rotary and flat
plate
printing) — A488

A489a John J.
Pershing — 1042A

Independence
Hall — A491

Benjamin
Harrison — A492

Monticello — A494

Robert E.
Lee — A496

Woodrow
Wilson — A487

Design slightly
altered; see
position of torch
(Giorgi press
printing) — A489

The Alamo — A490

A491a Statue of
Liberty

John Jay — A493

Paul
Revere — A495

John
Marshall — A497

Susan B.
Anthony — A498

Patrick
Henry — A499

Alexander Hamilton — A500

Unwmkd.

A477 ½¢ red orange, perf. 11x10½ 1030
A478 1¢ dark green, perf. 11x10½ 1031
A478 1¢ dark green, perf. 10 vert. 1054
A478a 1¼¢ turquoise, perf. 10½x11 .... 1031A
A478a 1¼¢ turquoise, perf. 10 horiz. 1054A
A479 1½¢ brown carmine, perf. 10½x11 1032
A480 2¢ carmine rose, perf. 11x10 1033
A480 2¢ carmine rose, perf. 10 vert. 1055
A481 2½¢ gray blue, perf. 11x10½ 1034
A481 2½¢ gray blue, perf. 10 vert. 1056
A482 3¢ deep violet, perf. 11x10½ 1035
A482 3¢ deep violet, perf. 10 vert. 1057
A482 3¢ deep violet, imperf., size: 24x28mm..........
        .... 1075a
A483 4¢ red violet, perf. 11x10½ 1036
A483 4¢ red violet, perf. 10 vert. 1058
A484 4½¢ blue green, perf. 10½x11 1037
A484 4½¢ blue green, perf. 10 horiz. 1059
A485 5¢ deep blue, perf. 11x10½ 1038
A486 6¢ carmine, perf. 11x10½ 1039
A487 7¢ rose carmine, same 1040
A488 8¢ dark violet blue & carmine, flat plate
        printing, perf. 11, mapprox. 22.7mm high......
        1041
A488 8¢ dark violet blue & carmine, rotary press
        printing, perf. 11, appprox. 22.9mm high.......
        .... 1041B
A488 8¢ dark violet blue & carmine, imperf., size:
        24x28mm............... 1075b
A489 8¢ dark violet blue & carmine, perf. 11 ... 1042
A489a 8¢ brown, perf. 11x10½ 1042A
A490 9¢ rose lilac, perf. 10½x11 1043
A491 10¢ rose lake, same 1044
A491a 11¢ carmine & dark violet blue, perf. 11
        .... 1044A
A492 12¢ red, perf. 11x10½ 1045
A493 15¢ rose lake, perf. 11x10½ 1046
A494 20¢ ultramarine, perf. 10½x11 1047
A495 25¢ green, perf. 11x10½ 1048
A495 25¢ green, perf. 10 vert. 1059A
A496 30¢ black, perf. 11x10½ 1049
A497 40¢ brown red, perf. 11x10½ 1050
A498 50¢ bright purple, perf. 11x10½ 1051
A499 $1 purple, perf. 11x10½ 1052
A500 $5 black, perf. 11 1053

ISSUE OF 1962-66

Andrew
Jackson — A646

George
Washington — A650

A646 1¢ green, perf. 11x10½ 1209
A646 1¢ green, perf. 10 vert. 1225
A650 5¢ dk. bl. gray, perf. 11x10½ 1213
A650 5¢ dk. bl. gray, perf. 10 vert. 1229

PROMINENT AMERICANS ISSUE 1965-81

Thomas Jefferson — A710

Albert Gallatin — A711

Fiorello H. LaGuardia and New York skyline — A817a

Oliver Wendell Holmes — A720

Frank Lloyd Wright and Guggenheim Museum, New York — A712

Francis Parkman — A713

Ernest (Ernie) Taylor Pyle — A818

Dr. Elizabeth Blackwell — A818a

Abraham Lincoln A714

George Washington A715

George C. Marshall — A721

Amadeo P. Giannini — A818b

Re-engraved — A715a

Franklin D. Roosevelt — A716

Frederick Douglass — A722

John Dewey — A723

Franklin D. Roosevelt (vertical coil)

Benjamin Franklin and his signature — A727a – A816

Thomas Paine — A724

Lucy Stone — A725

Albert Einstein — A717

Andrew Jackson — A718

Eugene O'Neill — A726

John Bassett Moore — A727

Henry Ford and 1909 Model I — A718a

John F. Kennedy — A719

Types of 15¢:

I — Necktie barely touches coat at bottom; cross-hatching of tie strong and complete. Flag of "5" is true horizontal. Crosshatching of "15" is colorless when visible.

II — Necktie does not touch coat at bottom; LL to UR crosshatching lines strong, UL to LR lines very faint. Flag of "5" slants down slightly at right. Crosshatching of "15" is colored and visible when magnified.

A third type, used only for No. 1288B, is smaller in overall size, and "15¢" is ¾mm closer to head.

Unwmkd.
Rotary Press Printing

A710   1¢ green, perf. 11x10½ **1278**

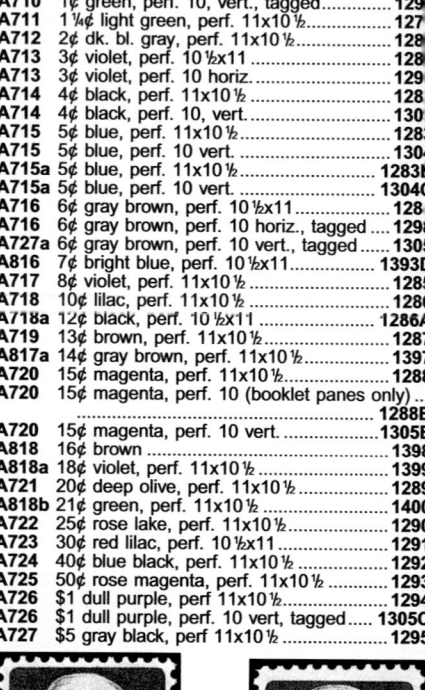

A710	1¢ green, perf. 10, vert., tagged	129
A711	1¼¢ light green, perf. 11x10½	127
A712	2¢ dk. bl. gray, perf. 11x10½	128
A713	3¢ violet, perf. 10½x11	128
A713	3¢ violet, perf. 10 horiz.	129
A714	4¢ black, perf. 11x10½	128
A714	4¢ black, perf. 10, vert.	130
A715	5¢ blue, perf. 11x10½	128
A715	5¢ blue, perf. 10 vert.	130
A715a	5¢ blue, perf. 11x10½	1283t
A715a	5¢ blue, perf. 10 vert.	1304C
A716	6¢ gray brown, perf. 10½x11	128
A716	6¢ gray brown, perf. 10 horiz., tagged	129
A727a	6¢ gray brown, perf. 10 vert., tagged	130
A816	7¢ bright blue, perf. 10½x11	1393D
A717	8¢ violet, perf. 11x10½	128
A718	10¢ lilac, perf. 11x10½	128
A718a	12¢ black, perf. 10½x11	1286A
A719	13¢ brown, perf. 11x10½	1287
A817a	14¢ gray brown, perf. 11x10½	1397
A720	15¢ magenta, perf. 11x10½	1288
A720	15¢ magenta, perf. 10 (booklet panes only)	1288B
A720	15¢ magenta, perf. 10 vert.	1305E
A818	16¢ brown	1398
A818a	18¢ violet, perf. 11x10½	1399
A721	20¢ deep olive, perf. 11x10½	1289
A818b	21¢ green, perf. 11x10½	1400
A722	25¢ rose lake, perf. 11x10½	1290
A723	30¢ red lilac, perf. 10½x11	1291
A724	40¢ blue black, perf. 11x10½	1292
A725	50¢ rose magenta, perf. 11x10½	1293
A726	$1 dull purple, perf 11x10½	1294
A726	$1 dull purple, perf. 10 vert, tagged	1305C
A727	$5 gray black, perf 11x10½	1295

Dwight D. Eisenhower — A815

A815a

A815	6¢ dark blue gray, perf. 11x10½	1393
A815	6¢ dk. bl. gray, perf. 10, vert.	1401
A815	8¢ deep claret, perf. 11x10½ (Booklet panes only)	1395
A815	8¢ deep claret, perf. 10 vert	1402
A815a	8¢ blk., red & bl. gray, perf. 11	1394

FLAG ISSUE 1978-71

Flag and White House — A760

A760	6¢ dark blue, red & green, perf. 11, size: 19x22mm	1338
A760	6¢ dark blue, red & green, perf. 11x10½, size: 18¼x21mm	1338D
A760	6¢ dark blue, red & green, perf. 10 vert., size: 18¼x21mm	1338A
A760	8¢ multicolored, perf. 11x10½	1338F
A760	8¢ multicolored, perf. 10 vert.	1338G

REGULAR ISSUE 1971-74

U.S. Postal Service Emblem — A817

50-Star and 13-Star Flags — A923

Jefferson Memorial and quotation from Declaration of Independence A924

Mail Transport and "Zip Code" A925

Liberty Bell — A926

A817	8¢ multicolored, perf. 11x10½	1396
A923	10¢ red & blue, perf 11x10½	1509
A923	10¢ red & blue, perf. 10 vert.	1519
A924	10¢ blue, perf. 11x10½	1510
A924	10¢ blue, perf. 10 vert.	1520
A925	10¢ multicolored, perf. 11x10½	1511
A926	6.3¢ brick red, perf. 10 vert.	1518

AMERICANA ISSUE 1975-81

Inkwell and Quill — A984

Speaker's Stand — A985

Early Ballot Box — A987

Books, Bookmark, Eyeglasses — A988

Dome of Capitol — A994

Contemplation of Justice — A995

Early American Printing Press — A996

Torch Statue of Liberty — A997

Liberty Bell — A998

Ft. McHenry Flag — A1001

Old North Church — A1003

Sandy Hook Lighthouse A1005

Iron "Betty" Lamp Plymouth Colony, 17th-18th Centuries — A1007

Kerosene Table Lamp — A1009

COIL STAMPS

Six-string guitar — A1011

Eagle and Shield — A999

Head Statue of Liberty — A1002

Ft. Nisqually — A1004

Morris Township School No. 2, Devil's Lake A1006

Rush Lamp and Candle Holder — A1008

Railroad Conductors Lantern, c. 1850 — A1010

Weaver violins — A1199

Saxhorns — A1012

Drum — A1013

Steinway Grand Piano, 1857 — A1014

A984	1¢ dark blue, greenish, perf. 11x10½	1581
A984	1¢ dark blue, greenish, perf. 10 vert.	1811
A985	2¢ red brown, greenish, perf. 11x10½	1582
A987	3¢ olive, greenish, perf 11x10½	1584
A988	4¢ rose magenta, cream, perf. 11x10½	1585
A994	9¢ slate green, gray, perf. 11x10½ (booklet panes only)	1590
A994	9¢ slate green, gray, perf. 10x9¾ (booklet panes only)	1590A
A994	9¢ slate green, gray, perf. 11x10½	1591
A994	9¢ slate green, gray, perf. 10 vert.	1616
A995	10¢ violet, gray, perf. 10 vert.	1617
A995	10¢ violet, gray, perf. 11x10½	1592
A996	11¢ orange, gray, perf. 11x10½	1593
A997	12¢ red brown, beige, perf. 11x10½	1594
A997	12¢ red brown, beige, perf. 10 vert.	1816
A998	13¢ brown, perf. 11x10½	1595
A998	13¢ brown, perf. 10 vert.	1618
A999	13¢ multicolored	1596
A1001	15¢ gray, dark blue & red, perf. 11	1597
A1001	15¢ gray, dark blue & red, perf. 11x10½ (booklet panes only)	1598
A1001	15¢ gray, dark blue & red, perf. 10 vert.	1618C
A1002	16¢ blue, perf. 11x10½	1599
A1002	16¢ blue, perf. 10 vert.	1619
A1003	24¢ red, blue, perf. 11x10½	1603
A1004	28¢ brown, blue, perf. 11x10½	1604
A1005	29¢ blue, blue, perf. 11x10½	1605
A1006	30¢ green, perf. 11x10½	1606
A1007	50¢ black & orange, perf. 11	1608
A1008	$1 brown, orange & yellow, tan, perf. 11	1610
A1009	$2 dark green & red, tan, perf. 11	1611
A1010	$5 red brown, yellow & orange, tan, perf. 11	1612
A1011	3.1¢ brown, yellow, perf. 10 vert.	1613
A1199	3.5¢ purple, yellow, perf. 10 vert.	1813
A1012	7.7¢ brown, bright yellow, perf. 10 vert.	1614
A1013	7.9¢ carmine, yellow, perf. 10 vert.	1615
A1014	8.4¢ dark blue, yellow, perf. 10 vert.	1615C

FLAG ISSUE 1975-77

13-star Flag over Independence Hall — A1015

Flag over Capitol — A1016

A1015	13¢ dark blue & red, perf. 11x10¾	1622
A1015	13¢ dark blue & red, perf. 11¼	1622C
A1015	13¢ dark blue & red, perf. 10 vert.	1625
A1016	13¢ blue & red, perf. 11x10½ (booklet panes only)	1623
A1016	13¢ blue & red, perf. 10x9¾ (booklet panes only)	1623B

REGULAR ISSUE 1978

Indian Head,
Penny, 1877
A1123

Dolley Madison
A1209

Red Masterpiece and
Medallion Roses — A1126

A1123 13¢ brown & blue, green, bister, perf. 11........
....**1734**
A1126 15¢ multicolored, perf 10 (booklet panes
only)..**1737**
A1209 15¢ red brown & sepia, perf. 11..............**1822**

REGULAR ISSUE 1978-85

"A" Eagle — A1124

"B" Eagle — A1207

"C" Eagle — A1332

"C" Eagle
(Booklet) — A1333

"D" Eagle
A1496

"D" Eagle
(Booklet)
A1497

A1124 (15¢) orange, perf. 11................................**1735**
A1124 (15¢) orange, perf. 11x10½ (booklet panes
only)..**1736**
A1124 (15¢) orange, perf. 10 vert.......................**1743**
A1207 (18¢) violet, perf. 11x10½.........................**1818**
A1207 (18¢) violet, perf. 10 (booklet panes only) ......
....**1819**
A1207 (18¢) violet, perf. 10 vert. **1820**
A1332 (20¢) brown, perf. 11x10½.......................**1946**
A1332 (20¢) brown, perf. 10 vert.......................**1947**
A1333 (20¢) brown, perf. 11x10½ (booklet panes
only)..**1948**
A1496 (22¢) green, perf. 11................................**2111**
A1496 (22¢) green, perf. 10 vert.......................**2112**
A1497 (22¢) green, perf. 11 (booklet panes only)......
....**2113**

GREAT AMERICANS ISSUE 1980-99

 Dorothea Dix A1231
 Igor Stravinsky A1232
 Henry Clay A1233
 Carl Schurz A1234
 Pearl Buck A1235
 Luis Muñoz Marin A1556
 Abraham Baldwin A1237
 Sylvanus Thayer A1239

 Margaret Mitchell A1551
 Mary Lyon A1552
 Paul Dudley White MD A1553
 Father Flanagan A1554
 Hugo L. Black A1555
 Walter Lippmann A1236
 Henry Knox A1238
 Richard Russell A1240

 Red Cloud A1557
 Crazy Horse A1242
 Julia Ward Howe A1558
 Rachel Carson A1244
 George Mason A1245
 Ralph Bunche A1247
 Harry S Truman A1249
 Chester Carlson A1562

 Alden Partridge A1241
 Sinclair Lewis A1243
 Buffalo Bill Cody A1559
 Belva Ann Lockwood A1560
 Sequoyah A1246
 Thomas H. Gallaudet A1248
 Virginia Apgar A1561
 John J. Audubon A1250

A1563 Mary Cassatt 23 USA
A1564 Jack London USA 25
A1570 Harvey Cushing MD 45 USA
A2253 Ruth Benedict USA 46 ANTHROPOLOGIST
A1565 Sitting Bull USA 28
A1566 Earl Warren 1891-1974 Chief Justice of the U.S. USA 29
A1256 Chester W. Nimitz USA 50
A1571 Hubert H. Humphrey USA 52 VICE PRESIDENT
A1567 Thomas Jefferson USA 29
A1251 Frank C. Laubach USA 30c
A2255 Alice Hamilton, MD USA 55 SOCIAL REFORMER
A2256 Justin S. Morrill USA 55 LAND-GRANT COLLEGES
A2248 Milton S. Hershey USA 32 INDUSTRIALIST
A2249 Cal Farley USA 32 HUMANITARIAN
A1572 John Harvard USA 56
A1573 H.H.'Hap'Arnold USA 65
A2250 Henry R. Luce USA 32 EDITOR
A2251 Lila and DeWitt Wallace USA 32 PHILANTHROPISTS
A1574 Wendell Willkie 1892-1944 75 USA Statesman
A2257 Mary Breckinridge USA 77 Frontier Nursing Service
A1252 Charles R Drew MD USA 35c
A1568 Dennis Chavez USA 35 United States Senator
A2258 Alice Paul USA 78 SUFFRAGIST
A1575 Bernard Revel USA $1
A1253 Robert Millikan 37c USA
A1254 Grenville Clark USA 39
A1576 Johns Hopkins USA $1
A1577 Bryan $2 USA William Jennings
A1255 Lillian M. Gilbreth USA 40c
A1569 Claire Chennault USA 40 Flying Tigers 1940s
A1578 Bret Harte USA $5

Type	Description	No.
A1231	1¢ black, perf. 11	1844
A1551	1¢ brownish vermilion, perf. 11	2168
A1232	2¢ brown black, perf. 11x10½	1845
A1552	2¢ bright blue, perf. 11	2169
A1233	3¢ olive green, perf. 11x10½	1846
A1553	3¢ bright blue, perf. 11	2170
A1234	4¢ violet, perf. 11x10½	1847
A1554	4¢ blue violet, perf. 11	2171
A1235	5¢ henna brown, perf. 11x10½	1848
A1555	5¢ dark olive green, perf. 11	2172
A1556	5¢ carmine, perf. 11	2173
A1236	6¢ orange vermilion, perf. 11	1849
A1237	7¢ bright carmine, perf. 11	1850
A1238	8¢ olive black, perf. 11	1851
A1239	9¢ dark green, perf. 11	1852
A1240	10¢ Prussian blue, perf. 11	1853
A1557	10¢ lake, perf. 11	2175
A1241	11¢ dark blue, perf. 11	1854
A1242	13¢ light maroon, perf. 11x10½	1855
A1243	14¢ slate green, perf. 11	1856
A1558	14¢ crimson, perf. 11	2176
A1559	15¢ claret, perf. 11	2177
A1244	17¢ green, perf. 11x10½	1857
A1560	17¢ dull blue green, perf. 11	2178
A1245	18¢ dark blue, perf. 11x10½	1858
A1246	19¢ brown, perf. 11x10½	1859
A1247	20¢ claret, perf. 11x10½	1860
A1248	20¢ green, perf. 11x10½	1861
A1249	20¢ black, perf. 11	1862
A1561	20¢ red brown, perf. 11	2179
A1562	21¢ blue violet, perf. 11	2180
A1250	22¢ dark chalky blue, perf. 11	1863
A1563	23¢ purple, perf. 11	2181
A1564	25¢ blue, perf. 11	2182
A1564	25¢ blue, perf. 10	2197
A1565	28¢ myrtle green, perf. 11	2183
A1566	29¢ blue, perf. 11	2184
A1567	29¢ indigo, perf. 11½x11	2185
A1251	30¢ olive gray, perf. 11	1864
A2248	32¢ brown, perf.11.1	2933
A2249	32¢ green, perf. 11.2	2934
A2250	32¢ lake, perf. 11.2	2935
A2251	32¢ blue, perf. 11.2x11.1	2936
A1252	35¢ gray, perf. 11x10½	1865
A1568	35¢ black, perf. 11	2186
A1253	37¢ blue, perf. 11x10½	1866
A1254	39¢ rose lilac, perf. 11	1867
A1255	40¢ dark green, perf. 11	1868
A1569	40¢ dark blue, perf. 11	2187
A1570	45¢ bright blue, perf. 11	2188
A2253	46¢ carmine, perf. 11.1	2938
A1256	50¢ brown, perf. 11	1869
A1571	52¢ purple, perf. 11	2189
A2255	55¢ green, perf. 11	2940
A2256	55¢ black, serpentine die cut 11½, self-adhesive	2941
A1572	56¢ scarlet, perf. 11	2190
A1573	65¢ dark blue, perf. 11	2191
A1574	75¢ deep magenta, perf. 11	2192
A2257	77¢ blue, perf.11.8x11.6	2942
A2258	78¢ purple, perf. 11.2	2943
A1575	$1 dark Prussian green, perf. 11	2193
A1576	$1 dark blue, perf. 11	2194
A1577	$2 bright violet, perf. 11	2195
A1578	$5 copper red, perf. 11	2196

WILDLIFE ISSUES 1981-82

Bighorn — A1267
Puma — A1268
Harbor Seal — A1269
Bison — A1270
Brown bear — A1271
Polar bear — A1272

Elk (wapiti) — A1273

Moose — A1274

White-tailed deer A1275

Pronghorn A1276

Rocky Mountain Bighorn — A1334

A1277 18¢ multicolored, perf. 11 ....**1890**
A1278 18¢ multicolored, perf. 10 vert. **1891**
A1279 6¢ perf. 11 (booklet panes only).............**1892**
A1280 18¢ perf. 11 (booklet panes only)...........**1893**
A1281 20¢ black, dark blue & red, perf. 11........**1894**
A1281 20¢ black, dark blue & red, perf. 10 vert. ....
....**1895**
A1281 20¢ black, dark blue & red, perf. 11x10½ (booklet panes only)............................**1896**
A1498 22¢ blue, red & black, perf. 11 ....**2114**
A1498 22¢ blue, red & black, perf. 10 vert. **2115**
A1499 22¢ blue, red & black, perf. 10 horiz. (booklet panes only)..**2116**

TRANSPORTATION ISSUE 1981-95

FROM BOOKLET PANES

A1267 18¢ dark brown, perf. 11 ....**1880**
A1268 18¢ dark brown, perf. 11 ....**1881**
A1269 18¢ dark brown, perf. 11 ....**1882**
A1270 18¢ dark brown, perf. 11 ....**1883**
A1271 18¢ dark brown, perf. 11 ....**1884**
A1272 18¢ dark brown, perf. 11 ....**1885**
A1273 18¢ dark brown, perf. 11 ....**1886**
A1274 18¢ dark brown, perf. 11 ....**1887**
A1275 18¢ dark brown, perf. 11 ....**1888**
A1276 18¢ dark brown, perf. 11 ....**1889**
A1334 20¢ dark blue, perf. 11 ....**1949**

FLAG ISSUES 1981-85

Field of 1777 flag — A1279

A1277

A1278

A1280

A1281   A1498

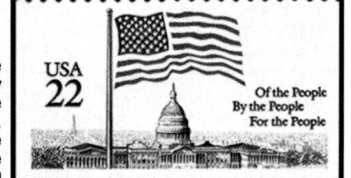
Of the People, By the People, For the People A1499

A1283

A1604a

A1284

A1604b

A1284a

A1622

A1506

A1285

A1810

A1507

A1286

A1623

A1811

A1811a

A1812

Sleigh 1880s A1287

A1624

A1508

A1288

A1509

A1510

A1289

A1625

A1511

A1626

A1512

A1290

A1627

A1816

A1513

Hansom Cab 1890s
USA 10.9c
Bulk Rate

A1291

RR Caboose 1890s
USA 11c
Bulk Rate

A1292

Cog Railway 1870s
20 USA

A1822

Fire Engine 1900s
20.5 USA
ZIP+4
Presort

A1634

Stutz Bearcat 1933
11 USA

A1514

Stanley Steamer 1909
USA
12

A1515

Railroad Mail Car 1920s
Presorted
First-Class
21 USA

A1635

Lunch Wagon 1890s
23 USA

A1823

Pushcart 1880s
12.5
USA

A1516

Patrol Wagon 1880s
USA
13
Presorted
First-Class

A1628

Tandem Bicycle 1890s
24.1 USA
ZIP+4

A1636

Bread Wagon 1880s
25 USA

A1519

Coal Car 1870s
13.2 Bulk Rate
USA

A1629

Iceboat 1880s
USA
14

A1517

Ferryboat 1900s
32 USA

A1825

$1 USA
Seaplane 1914

A1827

Tugboat 1900s
USA
15

A1630

Popcorn Wagon
16.7 USA 1902
Bulk Rate

A1631

Electric Auto 1917
USA 17c

A1293

Dog Sled 1920s
17 USA

A1518

Racing Car 1911
USA
17.5

A1632

Surrey 1890s
USA 18c

A1294

Fire Pumper 1860s
USA 20c

A1295

USA 20
Cable Car 1880s

A1633

A1517	14¢ sky blue	2134
A1630	15¢ violet	2260
A1631	16.7¢ rose, (Bureau precanceled)	2261
A1293	17¢ ultramarine	1906
A1518	17¢ sky blue	2135
A1632	17.5¢ dark violet	2262
A1294	18¢ dark brown	1907
A1295	20¢ vermilion	1908
A1633	20¢ blue violet	2263
A1822	20¢ green	2463
A1634	20.5¢ rose, (Bureau precanceled)	2264
A1635	21¢ olive green, (Bureau precanceled)	2265
A1823	23¢ dark blue	2464
A1636	24.1¢ deep ultramarine, (Bureau precanceled)	2266
A1519	25¢ orange brown	2136
A1825	32¢ blue	2466
A1827	$1 dark blue & scarlet	2468

REGULAR ISSUE 1983-99

A1894

A1897

A1898

A2532

A1283	1¢ violet	1897
A1604a	1¢ violet	2225
A1284	2¢ black	1897A
A1604b	2¢ black	2226
A1284a	3¢ dark green	1898
A1622	3¢ claret	2252
A1506	3.4¢ dark bluish green	2123
A1285	4¢ reddish brown, inscription 19 ½mm long	1898A
A1285	4¢ reddish brown, inscription 17mm long	2228
A1810	4¢ claret	2451
A1507	4.9¢ brown black	2124
A1286	5¢ gray green	1899
A1623	5¢ black	2253
A1811	5¢ carmine, engraved	2452
A1811	5¢ carmine, photogravure	2452B
A1811a	5¢ carmine	2452D
A1812	5¢ brown, engraved (Bureau precanceled)	2453
A1812	5¢ red, photogravure (Bureau precanceled)	2454
A1287	5.2¢ carmine	1900
A1624	5.3¢ black (Bureau precanceled)	2254
A1508	5.5¢ deep magenta	2125
A1288	5.9¢ blue	1901
A1509	6¢ red brown	2126
A1510	7.1¢ lake	2127
A1289	7.4¢ brown	1902
A1625	7.6¢ brown (Bureau precanceled)	2255
A1511	8.3¢ green, inscription 18 ½mm long	2128
A1511	8.3¢ green, same, untagged (Bureau precanceled)	2128a
A1511	8.3¢ green, inscription 18mm long, untagged (Bureau precanceled)	2231
A1626	8.4¢ deep claret, (Bureau precanceled)	2256
A1512	8.5¢ dark Prussian green	2129
A1290	9.3¢ carmine rose	1903
A1627	10¢ sky blue	2257
A1816	10¢ green, engraved (Bureau precanceled)	2457
A1816	10¢ green, photogravure (Bureau precanceled)	2458
A1513	10.1¢ slate blue	2130
A1291	10.9¢ purple	1904
A1292	11¢ red	1905
A1514	11¢ dark green	2131
A1515	12¢ dark blue	2132
A1516	12.5¢ olive green	2133
A1628	13¢ black, (Bureau precanceled)	2258
A1629	13.2¢ slate green, (Bureau precanceled)	2259

USA $8.75

A1758

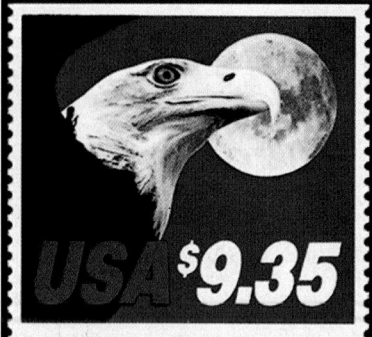

Eagle and Moon — A1296

A1895

Eagle and Half Moon — A1505

A1898a

A2533

A1896

A1894	$2.90 multicolored, perf. 11	**2540**
A1897	$2.90 multicolored, perf. 11x10 ½	**2543**
A1898	$3 multicolored, perf. 11	**2544**
A2532	$3.20 multicolored, serpentine die cut 11.5	**3261**
A1758	$8.75 multicolored, perf. 11	**2394**
A1296	$9.35 multicolored, perf. 10 vert. (booklet panes only)	**1909**
A1296	$9.35 multicolored, booklet pane of 3	**1909a**
A1895	$9.95 multicolored, perf. 11	**2541**
A1505	$10.75 multicolored, perf. 10 vert. (booklet panes only)	**2122**
A1898a	$10.75 multicolored, perf. 11	**2544A**
A2533	$11.75 multicolored, serpentine die cut 11.5	**3262**
A1896	$14 multicolored, perf. 11	**2542**

REGULAR ISSUE 1982-85

George Washington
Washington
Monument — A1532

Consumer
Education — A1390

Sealed Envelopes — A1533

A1532	18¢ multicolored, perf. 10 vert.	**2149**
A1532	18¢ multicolored, same, untagged (Bureau precanceled)	**2149a**
A1390	20¢ sky blue, perf. 10 vert.	**2005**
A1533	21.1¢ multicolored, perf. 10 vert.	**2150**
A1533	21.1¢ multicolored, same, untagged (Bureau precanceled)	**2150a**

REGULAR ISSUE 1987-88

A1646

A1647

A1648

A1649

A1646	22¢ multicolored, perf. 11	**2276**
A1647	(25¢) multicolored, perf. 11	**2277**
A1647	(25¢) multicolored, perf. 10	**2282**
A1647	(25¢) multicolored, perf. 10 vert.	**2279**
A1648	25¢ multicolored, perf. 11	**2278**
A1648	25¢ multicolored, perf. 10	**2285A**
A1649	25¢ multicolored, perf. 10 vert.	**2280**

FLORA & FAUNA ISSUE 1988-2001

A1840

A1841

A2335

A1842

A2336

A1843

A1847

A2350

A1649a

A1649b

A1649c

A1649d

A1848

A1849

A1852

A1853

A1854

A1875

A1879

A1844

A1850

A1851

A2351

A2550

A2551

A2552

A2553

A2634

A2635

A2636

A2637

A2694

A2695

A1845

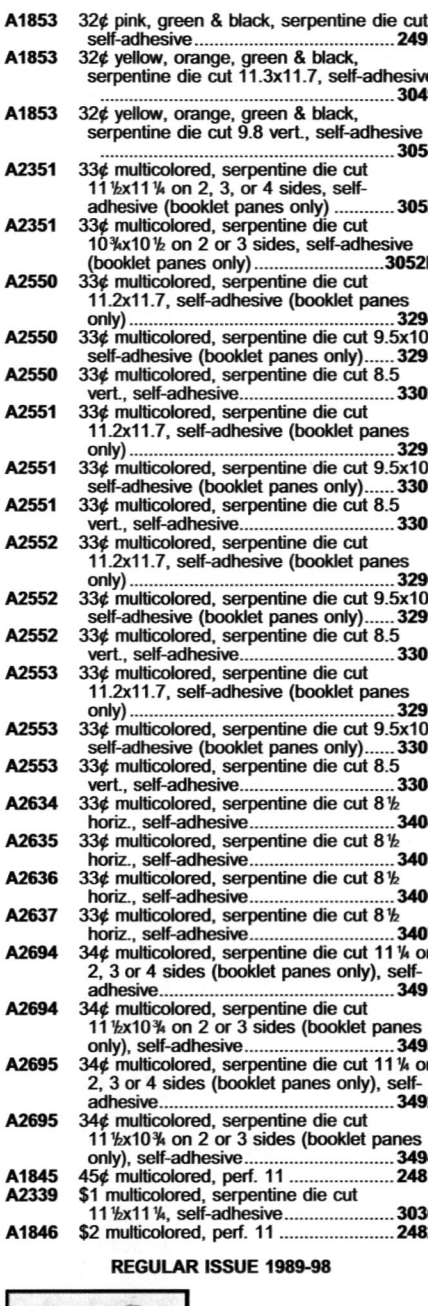

A2339

A1846

A1840	1¢ multicolored, perf. 11	2476
A1841	1¢ multicolored, perf. 11	2477
A1841	1¢ multicolored, serpentine die cut 10½, self-adhesive	3031
A1841	1¢ multicolored, blue inscriptions, serpentine die cut 11¼, self-adhesive	3031A
A1841	1¢ multicolored, perf. 9.8 vert.	3044
A2335	2¢ multicolored, perf. 11.1	3032
A2335	2¢ multicolored, perf. 9¾ vert.	3045
A1842	3¢ multicolored, perf. 11	2478
A2336	3¢ multicolored, perf. 11.1	3033
A1843	19¢ multicolored, perf. 11½x11	2479
A1847	20¢ multicolored, perf. 11x10 (booklet panes only)	2483
A1847	20¢ multicolored, serpentine die cut 10½x11, self-adhesive	3048
A1847	20¢ multicolored, serpentine die cut 11½ vert, self-adhesive	3053
A2350	20¢ multicolored, serpentine die cut 11¼, self-adhesive	3050
A2350	20¢ multicolored, serpentine die cut 10.6 on top and 10.6 on bottom or 10.6 on top and 10.4 on bottom, self-adhesive (booklet panes only)	3051
A2350	20¢ multicolored, serpentine die cut 10.6x10.4 on 3 sides, self-adhesive (booklet panes only)	3051A
A2350	20¢ multicolored, serpentine die cut 9¾ vert., self-adhesive	3055
A1649a	25¢ multicolored, perf. 11 (booklet panes only)	2283
A1649b	25¢ multicolored, perf. 10 (booklet panes only)	2284
A1649c	25¢ multicolored, perf. 10	2285
A1649d	25¢ multicolored, perf. 10 vert.	2281
A1848	29¢ black & multicolored, perf. 10 (booklet panes only)	2484
A1848	29¢ red & multicolored, perf. 11 (booklet panes only)	2485
A1849	29¢ multicolored, perf. 10x11 (booklet panes only)	2486
A1852	29¢ multicolored, die cut, self-adhesive	2489
A1853	29¢ red, green & black, die cut, self-adhesive	2490
A1854	29¢ multicolored, die cut, self-adhesive	2491
A1875	(29¢) yellow, black, red & yellow green, perf. 13	2517
A1875	(29¢) yellow, black, dull red & dark yellow green, perf. 10 vert.	2518
A1875	(29¢) yellow, black, dull red & dark green, bullseye perf. 11.2 (booklet panes only)	2519
A1875	(29¢) pale yellow, black, red & brightgreen, perf. 11 (booklet panes only)	2520
A1879	29¢ dull yellow, black, red & yellow green, perf. 11	2524
A1879	29¢ dull yellow, black, red & yellow green, perf. 13x12¾	2524A
A1879	29¢ pale yellow, black, red & yellow green, roulette 10 vert.	2525
A1879	29¢ pale yellow, black, red & yellow green, perf. 10 vert.	2526
A1879	29¢ pale yellow, black, red & bright green, perf. 11 (booklet panes only)	2527
A1844	30¢ multicolored, perf. 11½x11	2480
A1850	32¢ multicolored, perf. 11x10 (booklet panes only)	2487
A1850	32¢ multicolored, serpentine die cut, self-adhesive	2493
A1850	32¢ multicolored, serpentine die cut vert., self-adhesive	2495
A1851	32¢ multicolored, perf. 11x10 (booklet panes only)	2488
A1851	32¢ multicolored, serpentine die cut, self-adhesive	2494
A1851	32¢ multicolored, serpentine die cut vert., self-adhesive	2495A

A1853	32¢ pink, green & black, serpentine die cut, self-adhesive	2492
A1853	32¢ yellow, orange, green & black, serpentine die cut 11.3x11.7, self-adhesive	3049
A1853	32¢ yellow, orange, green & black, serpentine die cut 9.8 vert., self-adhesive	3054
A2351	33¢ multicolored, serpentine die cut 11½x11¼ on 2, 3, or 4 sides, self-adhesive (booklet panes only)	3052
A2351	33¢ multicolored, serpentine die cut 10¾x10½ on 2 or 3 sides, self-adhesive (booklet panes only)	3052E
A2550	33¢ multicolored, serpentine die cut 11.2x11.7, self-adhesive (booklet panes only)	3294
A2550	33¢ multicolored, serpentine die cut 9.5x10, self-adhesive (booklet panes only)	3298
A2550	33¢ multicolored, serpentine die cut 8.5 vert., self-adhesive	3302
A2551	33¢ multicolored, serpentine die cut 11.2x11.7, self-adhesive (booklet panes only)	3295
A2551	33¢ multicolored, serpentine die cut 9.5x10, self-adhesive (booklet panes only)	3300
A2551	33¢ multicolored, serpentine die cut 8.5 vert., self-adhesive	3303
A2552	33¢ multicolored, serpentine die cut 11.2x11.7, self-adhesive (booklet panes only)	3296
A2552	33¢ multicolored, serpentine die cut 9.5x10, self-adhesive (booklet panes only)	3299
A2552	33¢ multicolored, serpentine die cut 8.5 vert., self-adhesive	3305
A2553	33¢ multicolored, serpentine die cut 11.2x11.7, self-adhesive (booklet panes only)	3297
A2553	33¢ multicolored, serpentine die cut 9.5x10, self-adhesive (booklet panes only)	3301
A2553	33¢ multicolored, serpentine die cut 8.5 vert., self-adhesive	3304
A2634	33¢ multicolored, serpentine die cut 8½ horiz., self-adhesive	3404
A2635	33¢ multicolored, serpentine die cut 8½ horiz., self-adhesive	3405
A2636	33¢ multicolored, serpentine die cut 8½ horiz., self-adhesive	3406
A2637	33¢ multicolored, serpentine die cut 8½ horiz., self-adhesive	3407
A2694	34¢ multicolored, serpentine die cut 11¼ on 2, 3 or 4 sides (booklet panes only), self-adhesive	3491
A2694	34¢ multicolored, serpentine die cut 11½x10¾ on 2 or 3 sides (booklet panes only), self-adhesive	3493
A2695	34¢ multicolored, serpentine die cut 11¼ on 2, 3 or 4 sides (booklet panes only), self-adhesive	3492
A2695	34¢ multicolored, serpentine die cut 11½x10¾ on 2 or 3 sides (booklet panes only), self-adhesive	3494
A1845	45¢ multicolored, perf. 11	2481
A2339	$1 multicolored, serpentine die cut 11½x11¼, self-adhesive	3036
A1846	$2 multicolored, perf. 11	2482

REGULAR ISSUE 1989-98

A1793

A1834

A1877

A1884

A1947

A1950

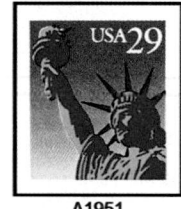

A1951

A1793 25¢ multicolored, die cut, self-adhesive..........
.... **2431**
A1834 25¢ dark red & dark blue, die cut, self-
adhesive.. **2475**
A1877 (29¢) black, blue & dark red, die cut, self-
adhesive.. **2522**
A1884 29¢ black, gold & green, die cut, self-
adhesive.. **2531A**
A1947 29¢ brown & multicolored, die cut, self-
adhesive.. **2595**
A1947 29¢ green & multicolored, die cut, self-
adhesive.. **2596**
A1947 29¢ red & multicolored, die cut, self-
adhesive.. **2597**
A1950 29¢ red, cream & blue, die cut, self-adhesive
.... **2598**
A1951 29¢ multicolored, die cut, self-adhesive
.... **2599**
A1951 32¢ red, light blue, dark blue & yellow,
serpentine die cut 11, self-adhesive..... **3122**
A1951 32¢ red, light blue, dark blue & yellow,
serpentine die cut 11.5x11.8, self-adhesive
.... **3122E**

REGULAR ISSUE 1991-94

A1876

A1881

A1882

A1878

A1880

A1883

A1876 (4¢) bister & carmine, perf. 11 .... **2521**
A1881 19¢ multicolored, perf. 10 vert. **2529**
A1881 19¢ multicolored, perf. 10 vert., two rope
loops on piling.................................... **2529**
A1881 19¢ multicolored, perf. 10 vert., one rope
loop on piling................................. **2529C**
A1882 19¢ multicolored, perf. 10 (booklet panes
only) **2530**
A1878 29¢ multicolored, engraved, perf. 10 vert. .....
.... **2523**
A1878 29¢ multicolored, photogravure, perf. 10 vert.
.... **2523A**
A1880 29¢ multicolored, perf. 11 (booklet panes
only) **2528**

A1883 29¢ multicolored, perf. 11 .... **2531**

REGULAR ISSUE 1991-98

A1956   A1957

A2534   A1959

A1960   A1946

A1961   A1939

A1942

A1944

A1956 (10¢) multicolored, perf. 10 vert. (Bureau
precanceled) **2602**
A1957 (10¢) orange yellow & multicolored, perf. 10
vert. (Bureau precanceled) **2603**
A1957 (10¢) gold & multicolored, perf. 10 vert.
(Bureau precanceled) **2604**
A1957 (10¢) gold & multicolored, serpentine die cut
11.5 vert., self-adhesive **2907**
A2534 (10¢) multicolored, perf. 9.9 vert. (Bureau
precanceled) **3270**
A2534 (10¢) multicolored, serpentine die cut 9.9
vert., self-adhesive (Bureau precanceled)....
.... **3271**
A1959 (23¢) multicolored, perf. 10 vert. (Bureau
precanceled) **2605**
A1960 23¢ multicolored, perf. 10 vert. (Bureau
precanceled) **2606**
A1960 23¢ multicolored, perf. 10 vert., "23" 7mm
long (Bureau precanceled) **2607**

A1960 23¢ violet blue, red & black, perf. 10 vert.,
"First Class" 8½mm long (Bureau
precanceled) **260**
A1946 29¢ black & multicolored, perf. 10 (booklet
panes only) **259**
A1946 29¢ black & multicolored, perf. 11x10
(booklet panes only) **2593**
A1946 29¢ red & multicolored, perf. 11x10 (booklet
panes only) **259**
A1961 29¢ blue & red, perf. 10 vert. **260**
A1939 32¢ red brown, perf. 11.2 .... **258**
A1942 $1 blue, perf. 11½ **2590**
A1944 $5 slate green, perf. 11½ **2592**

G RATE ISSUE 1994-95

A2206

A2210

A2207   A2209

A2208

A2206 (3¢) tan, bright blue & red, perf. 11x10.8 ......
.... **2877**
A2206 (3¢) tan, dark blue & red, perf. 10.8x10.9 ......
.... **2878**
A2210 (5¢) green & multicolored, perf. 9.8 vert.
(Bureau precanceled) **2893**
A2207 (20¢) black "G," yellow & multicolored, perf.
11.2x11.1 .... **2879**
A2207 (20¢) red "G," yellow & multicolored, perf.
11x10.9 .... **2880**
A2209 (25¢) black "G," blue & multicolored, perf.
9.8 vert.(Bureau precanceled) **2888**
A2208 (32¢) black "G" & multicolored, perf.
11.2x11.1 .... **2881**
A2208 (32¢) black "G" & multicolored, perf. 10x9.9
(booklet panes only) **2883**
A2208 (32¢) black "G" & multicolored, die cut, self-
adhesive, small number of blue shading
dots in white stripes below blue field ... **2886**
A2208 (32¢) black "G" & multicolored, die cut, self-
adhesive, thin translucent paper, more blue
shading dots in white stripes below blue
field... **2887**
A2208 (32¢) black "G" & multicolored, perf. 9.8 vert.
.... **2889**
A2208 (32¢) red "G" & multicolored, perf. 11x10.9,
distance from bottom of "G" to top of flag is
13¾mm **2882**
A2208 (32¢) red "G" & multicolored, perf. 11x10.9
on 2 or 3 sides (booklet panes only),
distance from bottom of "G" to top of flag is
13½mm **2885**
A2208 (32¢) red "G" & multicolored, perf. 9.8 vert.
.... **2891**
A2208 (32¢) red "G" & multicolored, rouletted. 9.8
vert. **2892**
A2208 (32¢) blue "G" & multicolored, perf. 10.9
(booklet panes only) **2884**
A2208 (32¢) blue "G" & multicolored, perf. 9.8 vert.
.... **2890**

REGULAR ISSUE 1995-2004

A2217

A2218

A2489

A2853

A2220

A2509

A2223

A2724

A2225

A2490

A2212

A2230

A2217 (5¢) yellow, red & blue, perf. 9.8 vert. (Bureau precanceled) **2902**
A2217 (5¢) yellow, red & blue, serpentine die cut 11.5 vert, self-adhesive (Bureau precanceled) **2902B**
A2218 (5¢) purple & multicolored, perf. 9.9 vert. (Bureau precanceled) **2903**
A2218 (5¢) purple & multicolored, serpentine die cut 11.2 vert., self-adhesive (Bureau precanceled) **2904A**
A2218 (5¢) purple & multicolored, serpentine die cut 9.8 vert., self-adhesive (Bureau precanceled) **2904B**
A2218 (5¢) blue & multicolored, perf. 9.9 vert. (Bureau precanceled) **2904**
A2489 (5¢) multicolored, perf. 10 vert. (Bureau precanceled) **3207**
A2489 (5¢) multicolored, serpentine die cut 9.7 vert., self-adhesive (Bureau precanceled)....**3207A**
A2853 (5¢) multicolored, serpentine die cut 8½ vert., self-adhesive (Bureau precanceled)....**3693**
A2853 (5¢) multicolored, perf. 9¾ vert., "2003" date in blue, unclear dots in surf (Bureau precanceled) **3775**

A2853 (5¢) multicolored, serpentine die cut 9½x10 (coil stamp), self-adhesive (Bureau precanceled) **3785**
A2853 (5¢) multicolored, perf. 9¾ vert., "2004" date in black, rows of dots in surf (Bureau precanceled) **3864**
A2853 (5¢) multicolored, serpentine die cut 10 vert., self-adhesive (Bureau precanceled) **3874**
A2853 (5¢) multicolored, serpentine die cut 11½ vert., "2004" date, self-adhesive (Bureau precanceled) **3875**
A2220 (10¢) black, red brown & brown, perf. 9.8 vert. (Bureau precanceled) **2905**
A2220 (10¢) black, red brown & brown, serpentine die cut 11.5 vert., self-adhesive (Bureau precanceled) **2906**
A2509 (10¢) multicolored, serpentine die cut 9.8 vert., self-adhesive (Bureau precanceled)....**3228**
A2509 (10¢) multicolored, perf 9.9 vert. (Bureau precanceled) **3229**
A2223 (15¢) dark orange, yellow & multicolored (dark, bold colors, heavy shading lines, heavily shaded chrome), perf. 9.8 vert........**2908**
A2223 (15¢) buff & multicolored (more subdued colors, finer details, shinier chrome), perf. 9.8 vert. **2909**
A2223 (15¢) buff & multicolored, serpentine die cut 11.5 vert., self-adhesive.......................**2910**
A2724 (15¢) multicolored, serpentine die cut 11½ vert., self-adhesive (Bureau precanceled **3522**
A2225 (25¢) dark red, dark yellow green & multicolored (dark, saturated colors, dark blue lines in music selection board), perf.9.8 vert. **2911**
A2225 (25¢) dark red, yellow green & multicolored, serpentine die cut 9.8 vert, self-adhesive **2912B**
A2225 (25¢) bright orange red, bright yellow green & multicolored (bright colors, less shading and light blue lines in music selection board), perf. 9.8 vert. **2912**
A2225 (25¢) bright orange red, bright yellow green & multicolored, serpentine die cut 11.5 vert., self-adhesive.............................**2912A**
A2225 (25¢) bright orange red, bright yellow green & multicolored, imperf, with simulated perforations, self-adhesive...................**3132**
A2490 (25¢) multicolored, perf. 10 vert. **3208**
A2490 (25¢) multicolored, serpentine die cut 9.7 vert., self-adhesive (Bureau precanceled)..**3208A**
A2212 32¢ multicolored, perf. 10.4 ....**2897**
A2212 32¢ blue, tan, brown, red & light blue, perf. 10.8x9.8 (booklet panes only) **2916**
A2212 32¢ blue, tan, brown, red & light blue (pronounced blue shading in flag and red "1995"), perf. 9.8 vert..........................**2913**
A2212 32¢ blue, yellow brown, red & gray (gray shading in flag and blue "1995"), perf. 9.8 vert. **2914**
A2212 32¢ multicolored, serpentine die cut 8.7 vert., self-adhesive.............................**2915**
A2212 32¢ dark blue, tan, brown, red & light blue, red "1996," serpentine die cut 9.8 vert., self-adhesive.............................**2915A**
A2212 32¢ dark blue, tan, brown, red & light blue, red "1997," serpentine die cut 9.8 vert., straight cut at bottom and top with 9 teeth between, self-adhesive **2915D**
A2212 32¢ dark blue, tan, brown, red & light blue (sky shows color graduation at lower right, blue "1996"), serpentine die cut 9.9 vert., self-adhesive.............................**3133**
A2212 32¢ dark blue, tan, brown, red & light blue, serpentine die cut 10.9 vert., self-adhesive **2915C**
A2212 32¢ dark blue, tan, brown, red & light blue, serpentine die cut 11.5 vert., self-adhesive **2915B**
A2212 32¢ multicolored, serpentine die cut 8.8 on 2, 3 or 4 adjacent sides, dated "1995" in blue, self-adhesive (booklet panes only) **2920**
A2212 32¢ multicolored, serpentine die cut 11.3 on 2, 3 or 4 adjacent sides, dated "1996" in blue, self-adhesive (booklet panes only) **2920D**
A2212 32¢ dark blue, tan, brown, red & light blue, serpentine die cut 9.8 on 2 or 3 adjacent sides, dated "1996" in red, self-adhesive (booklet panes only) **2921**
A2212 32¢ dark blue, tan, brown, red & light blue, serpentine die cut 9.8 on 2 or 3 adjacent sides, dated "1997" in red, self-adhesive (booklet panes only) **2921b**
A2230 32¢ multicolored, die cut, self-adhesive........ ....**2919**

H RATE ISSUE 1999

A2529

A2530

A2531

A2529 (1¢) multicolored, white USA, black "1998," perf. 11.2 ....**3257**
A2529 (1¢) multicolored, pale blue USA, blue "1998," perf. 11.2 ....**3258**
A2530 22¢ multicolored, serpentine die cut 10.8, self-adhesive.............................**3259**
A2530 22¢ multicolored, serpentine die cut 9.9 vert, self-adhesive.............................**3263**
A2530 22¢ multicolored, perf. 9¾ vert. **3353**
A2531 (33¢) multicolored, perf. 11.2 ....**3260**
A2531 (33¢) multicolored, perf. 9.8 vert. **3264**
A2531 (33¢) multicolored, serpentine die cut 9.9 vert., stamp corners at right angles, backing paper same size as stamp, self-adhesive.............................**3265**
A2531 (33¢) multicolored, serpentine die cut 9.9 vert., stamp corners rounded, backing paper larger than stamp, self-adhesive........ ....**3266**
A2531 (33¢) multicolored, serpentine die cut 9.9, (booklet panes only), self-adhesive **3267**
A2531 (33¢) multicolored, serpentine die cut 11.2x11.1 (booklet panes only), self-adhesive.............................**3268**
A2531 (33¢) multicolored, die cut 8 (booklet panes only), self-adhesive **3269**

REGULAR ISSUE 1999

A2540

A2541

A2540 33¢ multicolored, perf. 11.2.....................**3277**
A2540 33¢ multicolored, serpentine die cut 11.1, self-adhesive.............................**3278**
A2540 33¢ multicolored, serpentine die cut 11½x11¾, self-adhesive **3278F**
A2540 33¢ multicolored, serpentine die cut 9.8 (booklet panes only), self-adhesive **3279**
A2540 33¢ multicolored, perf. 9.9 vert. **3280**
A2540 33¢ multicolored, serpentine die cut 9.8 vert., stamp corners at right angles, backing paper same size as stamp, self-adhesive.............................**3281**
A2540 33¢ multicolored, serpentine die cut 9.8 vert., stamp corners rounded, backing paper same larger than stamp, self-adhesive.............................**3282**
A2541 33¢ multicolored, serpentine die cut 7.9 (booklet panes only), self-adhesive **3283**

DISTINGUISHED AMERICANS ISSUE 2000-06

A2650

A2652

A2656

A2658

A2686

A2687

A2696

A2661

A2662

A2678

A2679

A2663

A2664

A2680

A2681

A2650 10¢ red & black, perf 11 .... **3420**
A2652 23¢ red & black, litho. & engr., serpentine
die cut 11¼x10¾, self-adhesive **3422**
A2652 23¢ red & black, litho., serpentine die cut
11¼x10¾ on 3 sides, self-adhesive
(booklet panes only) **3436**
A2656 33¢ red & black, perf 11 .... **3426**
A2658 63¢ red & black, serpentine die cut 11¼x11,
self-adhesive **3428**
A2661 76¢ red & black, serpentine die cut 11, self-
adhesive **3431**
A2661 76¢ red & black, serpentine die cut 11½x11,
self-adhesive **3432**
A2662 83¢ red & black, serpentine die cut 11x11¾,
self-adhesive **3433**
A2663 83¢ red & black, serpentine die cut 11¼,
self-adhesive **3434**
A2664 87¢ red & black, serpentine die cut 11¼x11,
self-adhesive **3435**

AMERICAN CULTURE ISSUE 2000-03

A2682

A2683

A2684

A2685

A2677

A2722

A2688

A2689

A2875

A2677 (10¢) multicolored, serpentine die cut 11½
vert., self adhesive (Bureau precanceled)....
.... **3447**
A2677 (10¢) multicolored, perf. 10 vert. (Bureau
precanceled) **3769**
A2722 (10¢) multicolored, serpentine die cut 8½
vert., self-adhesive (Bureau precanceled)....
.... **3520**
A2722 (10¢) multicolored, serpentine die cut 11
vert., self-adhesive (Bureau precanceled)....
.... **3770**
A2875 $1 multicolored, serpentine die cut 11¼x11
vert., self-adhesive **3766**

REGULAR ISSUE 2000-03

A2690

A2691

A2692

A2693

A2686 20¢ dark carmine, serpentine die cut
11¼x11 on 3 sides (booklet panes only),
self-adhesive **34**
A2686 20¢ dark carmine, serpentine die cut
10½x11 on 3 sides (booklet panes only),
self-adhesive **3483**
A2687 21¢ multicolored, perf. 11¼ **3467**
A2687 21¢ multicolored, serpentine die cut 11¼ on
3 sides, self-adhesive (booklet panes only)
.... **3484**
A2687 21¢ multicolored, serpentine die cut
10½x11¼ on 3 sides, self-adhesive
(booklet panes only) **3484A**
A2687 21¢ multicolored, serpentine die cut 11, self-
adhesive **3468**
A2687 21¢ multicolored, serpentine die cut 8½
vert., self-adhesive **3475**
A2686 23¢ green, perf. 11¼ **3616**
A2686 23¢ green, serpentine die cut 11¼x11¾,
self-adhesive **3468A**
A2686 23¢ green, serpentine die cut 8½ vert., self-
adhesive (Banknote Corp. Printing) **3475A**
A2686 23¢ gray green, serpentine die cut 8½ vert.,
self-adhesive (Avery Printing) **3617**
A2686 23¢ green, serpentine die cut 11¼ on 3
sides, self-adhesive (booklet panes only......
.... **3618**
A2686 23¢ green, serpentine die cut 10½x11¼ on
3 sides, self-adhesive (booklet panes only)
.... **3619**
A2686 23¢ gray green, serpentine die cut 11, self-
adhesive (Avery Printing) **3819**
A2678 (34¢) multicolored, perf. 111/4 .... **3448**
A2678 (34¢) multicolored, serpentine die cut 11¼,
self-adhesive **3449**
A2678 (34¢) multicolored, serpentine die cut 8 on
2, 3 or 4 sides (booklet panes only), self-
adhesive **3450**
A2679 (34¢) multicolored, serpentine die cut 11 on
2, 3 or 4 sides (booklet panes only), self-
adhesive **3451**
A2680 (34¢) multicolored, perf. 9¾ vert. **3452**
A2680 (34¢) multicolored, serpentine die cut 10
vert., self-adhesive **3453**
A2681 (34¢) purple & multicolored, serpentine die
cut 10½x10¾ on 2 or 3 sides (booklet
panes only), self-adhesive **3454**
A2681 (34¢) purple & multicolored, serpentine die
cut 11½x11¾ on 2 or 3 sides (booklet
panes only), self-adhesive **3458**
A2681 (34¢) purple & multicolored, serpentine die
cut 8½ vert., self-adhesive **3465**
A2682 (34¢) tan & multicolored, serpentine die cut
10½x10¾ on 2 or 3 sides (booklet panes
only), self-adhesive **3455**
A2682 (34¢) tan & multicolored, serpentine die cut
11½x11¾ on 2 or 3 sides (booklet panes
only), self-adhesive **3459**
A2682 (34¢) tan & multicolored, serpentine die cut
8½ vert., self-adhesive **3464**
A2683 (34¢) green & multicolored, serpentine die
cut 10½x10¾ on 2 or 3 sides (booklet
panes only), self-adhesive **3456**
A2683 (34¢) green & multicolored, serpentine die
cut 11½x11¾ on 2 or 3 sides (booklet
panes only), self-adhesive **3460**
A2683 (34¢) green & multicolored, serpentine die
cut 8½ vert., self-adhesive **3462**
A2684 (34¢) red & multicolored, serpentine die cut
10½x10¾ on 2 or 3 sides (booklet panes
only), self-adhesive **3457**
A2684 (34¢) red & multicolored, serpentine die cut
11½x11¾ on 2 or 3 sides (booklet panes
only), self-adhesive **3461**
A2684 (34¢) red & multicolored, serpentine die cut
8½ vert., self-adhesive **3463**
A2685 34¢ multicolored, serpentine die cut 9¾
vert., stamp corners rounded, backing
paper larger than stamp, self-adhesive........
.... **3466**
A2685 34¢ multicolored, perf. 9¾ vert. **3476**
A2685 34¢ multicolored, serpentine die cut 9¾
vert., stamp corners at right angles,
backing paper same size as stamp, self-
adhesive **3477**
A2688 34¢ multicolored, perf. 11¼ **3469**
A2688 34¢ multicolored, serpentine die cut 11¼,
self-adhesive **3470**

A2688 34¢ multicolored, serpentine die cut 8 on 2, 3 or 4 sides, self-adhesive (booklet panes only).. **3495**

A2689 34¢ multicolored, serpentine die cut 11 on 2, 3 or 4 sides (booklet panes only), self-adhesive... **3485**

A2690 34¢ green & multicolored, serpentine die cut 8½ vert., self-adhesive........................... **3478**

A2690 34¢ green & multicolored, serpentine die cut 10½x10¾ on 2 or 3 sides (booklet panes only), self-adhesive **3489**

A2691 34¢ red & multicolored, serpentine die cut 8½ vert., self-adhesive........................... **3479**

A2691 34¢ red & multicolored, serpentine die cut 10½x10¾ on 2 or 3 sides (booklet panes only), self-adhesive **3490**

A2692 34¢ tan & multicolored, serpentine die cut 8½ vert., self-adhesive........................... **3480**

A2692 34¢ tan & multicolored, serpentine die cut 10½x10¾ on 2 or 3 sides (booklet panes only), self-adhesive **3488**

A2693 34¢ purple & multicolored, serpentine die cut 8½ vert., self-adhesive........................... **3481**

A2693 34¢ purple & multicolored, serpentine die cut 10½x10¾ on 2 or 3 sides (booklet panes only), self-adhesive **3487**

A2696 55¢ multicolored, serpentine die cut 10¾, self-adhesive **3471**

A2696 57¢ multicolored, serpentine die cut 10¾, self-adhesive **3471A**

WASHINGTON VIEWS ISSUE 2001-03

A2697

A2818

A2698

A2819

A2697 $3.50 multicolored, serpentine die cut 11¼x11½, self-adhesive **3472**

A2818 $3.85 multicolored, serpentine die cut 11¼, self-adhesive **3647**

A2818 $3.85 multicolored, serpentine die cut 11x10¾, self-adhesive **3647A**

A2698 $12.25 multicolored, serpentine die cut 11¼x11½, self-adhesive **3473**

A2819 $13.65 multicolored, serpentine die cut 11¼, self-adhesive **3648**

UNITED WE STAND ISSUE 2001-02

A2744

A2744 34¢ multicolored, serpentine die cut 11¼ on 2, 3 or 4 sides, self-adhesive (booklet panes only) **3549**

A2744 34¢ multicolored, serpentine die cut 10½x10¾ on 2 or 3 sides, self-adhesive (booklet panes only) **3549B**

A2744 34¢ multicolored, serpentine die cut 9¾ vert., stamp corners at right angles, backing paper same size as stamp, self-adhesive **3550**

A2744 34¢ multicolored, serpentine die cut 9¾ vert., stamp corners rounded, backing paper larger than stamp, self-adhesive........ .... **3550A**

AMERICAN DESIGN ISSUE 2002-05

A2866

A2858

A2868

A2859

A2805

A2860

A2866 1¢ multicolored, perf. 10 vert. **3757**

A2858 2¢ multicolored, serpentine die cut 11, self-adhesive, dated "2004" **3749**

A2858 2¢ multicolored, without microprinting, serpentine die cut 11¼x11½, self-adhesive, dated "2006" **3749A**

A2858 2¢ multicolored, with microprinting, serpentine die cut 11¼x11, self-adhesive, dated "2006" **3749B**

A2868 3¢ multicolored, perf. 9¾ **3759**

A2859 4¢ multicolored, serpentine die cut 10¾x10¼, self-adhesive........................ **3750**

A2805 5¢ multicolored, perf. 10 vert. **3612**

A2805 5¢ multicolored, serpentine die cut 11¼x11¾, self-adhesive **3750A**

A2860 10¢ multicolored, serpentine die cut 11¼x11½, self-adhesive **3751**

REGULAR ISSUE 2002-05

A2806

A2807

A2808

A2809

A2810

A2811

A2813

A2814

A2815

A2816

A2812

A2817

A2806 3¢ red, blue & black, serpentine die cut 11, self-adhesive, lithographed, year at lower left **3613**

A2806 3¢ red, blue & black, serpentine die cut 10, self-adhesive, photogravure, year at lower right **3614**

A2806 3¢ red, blue & black, perf. 10 vert., photogravure, year at lower left............ **3615**

A2807 (37¢) multicolored, perf. 11¼x11............ **3620**

A2807 (37¢) multicolored, serpentine die cut 11¼x11, self-adhesive **3621**

A2807 (37¢) multicolored, serpentine die cut 10 vert., self-adhesive **3622**

A2807 (37¢) multicolored, serpentine die cut 11¼ on 2, 3 or 4 sides, self-adhesive (booklet panes only) **3623**

A2807 (37¢) multicolored, serpentine die cut 10½x10¾ on 2 or 3 sides, self-adhesive (booklet panes only) **3624**

A2807 (37¢) multicolored, serpentine die cut 8 on 2, 3 or 4 sides, self-adhesive (booklet panes only) **3625**

A2808 (37¢) multicolored, serpentine die cut 11 on 2, 3 or 4 sides, self-adhesive (booklet panes only) **3626**

A2809 (37¢) multicolored, serpentine die cut 11 on 2, 3 or 4 sides, self-adhesive (booklet panes only) **3627**

A2810 (37¢) multicolored, serpentine die cut 11 on 2, 3 or 4 sides, self-adhesive (booklet panes only) **3628**

A2811 (37¢) multicolored, serpentine die cut 11 on 2, 3 or 4 sides, self-adhesive (booklet panes only).................................**3629**

A2812 37¢ multicolored, perf. 11¼...........**3629F**
A2812 37¢ multicolored, serpentine die cut 11¼x11, self-adhesive....................**3630**
A2812 37¢ multicolored, perf. 10 vert. **3631**
A2812 37¢ multicolored, serpentine die cut 9¾ vert., self-adhesive........................**3632**
A2812 37¢ multicolored, serpentine die cut 10¼ vert., self-adhesive, lacking points of stars at upper left.............**3632A**
A2812 37¢ multicolored, serpentine die cut 11¾ vert., self-adhesive.....................**3632C**
A2812 37¢ multicolored, serpentine die cut 8½ vert., rounded corners, self-adhesive ...**3633**
A2812 37¢ multicolored, serpentine die cut 8½ vert., right angle corners, self-adhesive.....**3633A**
A2812 37¢ multicolored, serpentine die cut 9½ vert., with microprinted "USA" in top red stripe, self-adhesive **3633B**
A2812 37¢ multicolored, serpentine die cut 11 on 3 sides, self-adhesive (booklet panes only) **3634**
A2812 37¢ multicolored, serpentine die cut 11¼ on 2 or 3 sides, self-adhesive (booklet panes only) **3635**
A2812 37¢ multicolored, serpentine die cut 10½x10¾ on 2 or 3 sides, self-adhesive (booklet panes only) **3636**
A2812 37¢ multicolored, serpentine die cut 11¼x11 on 2 or 3 sides, self-adhesive (booklet panes only) **3636D**
A2812 37¢ multicolored, serpentine die cut 8 on 2, 3 or 4 sides, self-adhesive (booklet panes only) **3637**
A2813 37¢ multicolored, serpentine die cut 8½ horiz., self-adhesive **3638**
A2813 37¢ multicolored, serpentine die cut 11 on 2, 3 or 4 sides, self-adhesive (booklet panes only) **3643**
A2814 37¢ multicolored, serpentine die cut 8½ horiz., self-adhesive **3639**
A2814 37¢ multicolored, serpentine die cut 11 on 2, 3 or 4 sides, self-adhesive (booklet panes only) **3642**
A2815 37¢ multicolored, serpentine die cut 8½ horiz., self-adhesive **3640**
A2815 37¢ multicolored, serpentine die cut 11 on 2, 3 or 4 sides, self-adhesive (booklet panes only) **3645**
A2816 37¢ multicolored, serpentine die cut 8½ horiz., self-adhesive **3641**
A2816 37¢ multicolored, serpentine die cut 11 on 2, 3 or 4 sides, self-adhesive (booklet panes only) **3644**
A2817 60¢ multicolored, serpentine die cut 11x11¼ self-adhesive **3646**

PURPLE HEART ISSUE 2003-06

A2891

A2891 37¢ multicolored, serpentine die cut 11¼x10¾, self-adhesive....................**3784**
A2891 37¢ multicolored, serpentine die cut 10¾x10¼, self-adhesive..................**3784A**
A2891 39¢ multicolored, serpentine die cut 11¼x11, self-adhesive **4032**

EAGLE ISSUE 2003-04

A2898

A2899

A2898 (25¢) gray & gold, serpentine die 11¾ vert. **3792**
A2898 (25¢) gray & gold, perf. 9¾ vert. **3844**
A2898 (25¢) dull blue & gold, serpentine die 11¾ vert. **3794**

A2898 (25¢) dull blue & gold, perf. 9¾ vert. **3852**
A2898 (25¢) green & gold, serpentine die 11¾ vert. **3796**
A2898 (25¢) green & gold, perf. 9¾ vert...........**3850**
A2898 (25¢) Prussian blue & gold, serpentine die 11¾ vert. **3798**
A2898 (25¢) Prussian blue & gold, perf. 9¾ vert. **3848**
A2898 (25¢) red & gold, serpentine die 11¾ vert.....**3800**
A2898 (25¢) red & gold, perf. 9¾ vert. **3846**
A2899 (25¢) gold & red, serpentine die 11¾ vert.....**3793**
A2899 (25¢) gold & red, perf. 9¾ vert. **3853**
A2899 (25¢) gold & Prussian blue, serpentine die 11⅓ vert. **3795**
A2899 (25¢) gold & Prussian blue, perf. 9¾ vert. **3851**
A2899 (25¢) gold & gray, serpentine die 11¾ vert.....**3797**
A2899 (25¢) gold & gray, perf. 9¾ vert............**3849**
A2899 (25¢) gold & dull blue, serpentine die 11¾ vert.....**3799**
A2899 (25¢) gold & dull blue, perf. 9¾ vert. **3847**
A2899 (25¢) gold & green, serpentine die 11¾ vert.....**3801**
A2899 (25¢) gold & green, perf. 9¾ vert...........**3845**

SNOWY EGRET ISSUE 2003-05

A2925

A2925 37¢ multicolored, serpentine die cut 8½ vert., self-adhesive..................**3829**
A2925 37¢ multicolored, serpentine die cut 9½ vert., self-adhesive..................**3829A**
A2925 37¢ multicolored, without microprinting, serpentine die cut 11½x11 on 2, 3 or 4 sides, self-adhesive (booklet panes only) **3830**
A2925 37¢ multicolored, with microprinting, serpentine die cut 11½x11 on 2, 3 or 4 sides, self-adhesive (booklet panes only) **3830D**

FLAG AND STATUE OF LIBERTY ISSUE 2005-06

A3038

A3040

A3038 (39¢) multicolored, with microprinting, perf. 11¼.............**3965**
A3038 (39¢) multicolored, with microprinting, serpentine die cut 11¼x11, self-adhesive....**3966**
A3038 (39¢) multicolored, without microprinting, perf. 9¾ vert.....................**3967**
A3038 (39¢) multicolored, without microprinting, serpentine die cut 8½ vert., self-adhesive ...**3968**
A3038 (39¢) multicolored, with microprinting, serpentine die cut 10¼ vert., self-adhesive ...**3969**
A3038 (39¢) multicolored, with microprinting, serpentine die cut 9½ vert., self-adhesive ...**3970**
A3038 (39¢) multicolored, lithographed, without microprinting, serpentine die cut 11¼x10¾ on 2 or 3 sides, self-adhesive (booklet panes only) ...**3972**
A3038 (39¢) multicolored, without microprinting, serpentine die cut 10¼x10¾ on 2 or 3 sides, self-adhesive (booklet panes only) **3973**
A3038 (39¢) multicolored, photogravure, without microprinting, serpentine die cut 11¼x11 on 2 or 3 sides, self-adhesive (booklet panes only) **3974**
A3038 (39¢) multicolored, without microprinting, serpentine die cut 8 on 2, 3 or 4 sides, self-adhesive (booklet panes only).......**3975**

A3040 39¢ multicolored, with microprinting, serpentine die cut 11¼x10¾, self-adhesive **3978**
A3040 39¢ multicolored, without microprinting, perf. 10 vert....................**3979**
A3040 39¢ multicolored, without microprinting, serpentine die cut 11 vert., self-adhesive **3980**
A3040 39¢ multicolored, with microprinting, serpentine die cut 9½ vert., self-adhesive **3981**
A3040 39¢ multicolored, without microprinting, serpentine die cut 10¼ vert., self-adhesive...**3982**

REGULAR ISSUE 2006

A3053

A3054

A3055

A3056

A3057

A3058

A3053 24¢ multicolored, perf. 11¼...................**4000**
A3053 24¢ multicolored, serpentine die cut 11, self-adhesive..........................**4001**
A3053 24¢ multicolored, serpentine die cut 8½horiz., self-adhesive **4002**
A3054 39¢ multicolored, serpentine die cut 10¼horiz., self-adhesive **4003**
A3054 39¢ multicolored, serpentine die cut 10¾x10½ on 2 or 3 sides, self-adhesive (booklet panes only) **4012**
A3054 39¢ multicolored, serpentine die cut 10¾x11¼ on 2 or 3 sides, self-adhesive (booklet panes only) **4013**
A3055 39¢ multicolored, serpentine die cut 10¼horiz., self-adhesive **4004**
A3055 39¢ multicolored, serpentine die cut 10¾x10½ on 2 or 3 sides, self-adhesive (booklet panes only) **4011**
A3055 39¢ multicolored, serpentine die cut 10¾x11¼ on 2 or 3 sides, self-adhesive (booklet panes only) **4017**
A3056 39¢ multicolored, serpentine die cut 10¼horiz., self-adhesive **4005**
A3056 39¢ multicolored, serpentine die cut 10¾x10½ on 2 or 3 sides, self-adhesive (booklet panes only) **4010**
A3056 39¢ multicolored, serpentine die cut 10¾x11¼ on 2 or 3 sides, self-adhesive (booklet panes only) **4016**
A3057 39¢ multicolored, serpentine die cut 10¼horiz., self-adhesive **4006**
A3057 39¢ multicolored, serpentine die cut 10¾x10½ on 2 or 3 sides, self-adhesive (booklet panes only) **4009**
A3057 39¢ multicolored, serpentine die cut 10¾x11¼ on 2 or 3 sides, self-adhesive (booklet panes only) **4015**
A3058 39¢ multicolored, serpentine die cut 10¼horiz., self-adhesive **4007**
A3058 39¢ multicolored, serpentine die cut 10¾x10½ on 2 or 3 sides, self-adhesive (booklet panes only) **4008**
A3058 39¢ multicolored, serpentine die cut 10¾x11¼ on 2 or 3 sides, self-adhesive (booklet panes only) **4014**

X-PLANES ISSUE 2006

A3059

A3060

A3059 $4.05 multicolored, serpentine die cut
10¾x10½, self-adhesive **4018**
A3060 $14.40 multicolored, serpentine die cut
10¾x10½, self-adhesive **4019**

SUBJECT INDEX OF REGULAR, COMMEMORATIVE & AIR POST ISSUES

Additions, Deletions & Number Changes

Number in 2006 Catalogue	Number in 2007 Catalogue
new	279a
new	279Be
279Be	279Bj
new	279Bk
new	283a
new	530c
new	599b
new	606a
new	913a
new	915b
new	916a
new	917b
new	920a
new	1382b
new	1385a
new	1418g
new	1687t
new	1689x
new	1731b
new	1782b
new	1800c
new	1841c
new	1895h
new	2171c
new	2193a
new	2217k
new	2218 l
new	2223d
new	2520c
new	2605a
new	2703d
new	2790c
new	2915Aj
new	2934a
new	2936a
new	2982a
new	2992c
new	3103b
3052i	3052j
new	3111c
new	3178b
new	3187p
new	3252g
new	3281d
new	3281e
new	3307d
new	3436d
new	3447b
new	3453b
new	3634e
new	3634f
new	3908a
new	3909c
new	3909d

Air Post

new	C23c
new	C63c
new	C83b

Computer Vended Postage

CVP39	CVP42
CVP40	CVP41
CVP41	CVP39
CVP42	CVP40
CVP63	CVP64
CVP64	CVP65
CVP65	CVP66
CVP66	CVP67
CVP67 (Aug. '06 update)	CVP63

Local Stamps

new	34LU4a
new	34LU16
new	75L1a
new	75L2a

Envelopes

new	U505b
new	U611c
new	U655a
new	UC22b

Postal Cards

new	UX9e
new	UX245a

Duck Hunting Permit Stamps (Federal)

new	RW52a
new	RW72c

Junior Duck Stamps

JDS1-JDS14	new

Duck Hunting Permit Stamps (State)

Arizona

new	15b
new	16b

Connecticut

new	9a

Delaware

new	25a

New Hampshire

new	18b
new	19b
new	20b

Rhode Island

new	14b
new	15b

Utah

new	10b

Revenue Stamps

new	R5e
R5e	R5f
new	R6f
new	R13f
new	R16e
R16e	R16f
new	R24e
new	R24f
new	R27e
new	R28e
new	R33e
new	R34f
new	R36e
new	R37e
new	R39e
new	R40e
new	R42e
new	R46e
new	R56e
new	R56f
new	R58e
new	R59e
new	R60e
new	R68e
new	R70e
new	R71e
new	R81e
new	R82e
new	R83e
new	R84e
new	R97f
new	R106a
new	R106b
new	R109b
new	R109c
new	RE147a
new	RE151a
RE151a	deleted
RE151b	deleted
RJM1a	deleted
RJMib	RJM1a

Essays

1-E1	deleted
1-E2	deleted
new	328-E2
new	397-E2
new	398-E2A
new	399-E2A
new	400-E1A
new	499-E1a
new	499-E1b
new	523-E4

Essays

new	537-E1a
new	537-E1b
new	537-E2a

Essays

new	537-E2b
new	548-E2
new	549-E3a
new	549-E3b
new	615-E1
new	617-E1
new	618-E3
new	690-E1
new	742-E1
new	786-E1
new	791-E1
new	791-E2
new	793-E1
new	899-E1
new	909-921-E1
new	923-E2
new	930-933-E1
new	1140-E1
new	C25-C31-E1
new	PR28-E2

Trial Color Proofs

new	157TC deep rose
new	PR1TC deep reddish brown
new	PR1TC dark orange
new	PR1TC green

Specimen Stamps

new	129S

Post Office Seals

new	OX33A
LOX2a	LOX2c
new	LOX2a
new	LOX2b

Test Stamps

new	TD9a
new	TD9B
TD15a	deleted
new	TD24c
new	TD24d
new	TD24E
new	TD33A
new	TD36A
new	TD51A
new	TD57A
new	TD60
new	TD60A
new	TD61
TD61	TD61A
new	TD63A
new	TD63B
new	TD70A
new	TD78A
new	TD78B
new	TD87A
new	TD87B
TD94a	deleted
new	TD94A
new	TD99a
TD109a	deleted
new	TD127A
new	TD127B
new	TD130A
new	TD130B
new	TD138
new	TD139

Test Booklets

new	TDB19a
new	TDB89A

Sanitary Fair

new	WV13TC

Encased Postage

EP14	deleted
EP94	deleted

Confederate Postmasters' Provisionals

new	62X3c

Hawaii

new	71h

United Nations

new	UXC2a

POSTMASTERS' PROVISIONALS

The Act of Congress of March 3, 1845, effective July 1, 1845, established rates of postage as follows:

"For every single letter in manuscript or paper of any kind by or upon which information shall be asked or communicated in writing or by marks designs, conveyed in the mail, for any distance under 300 miles, five cents; and for any distance over 300 miles, ten cents; and for a double letter there shall be charged double these rates; and for a treble letter, treble these rates; and for a quadruple letter, quadruple these rates; and every letter or parcel not exceeding half an ounce in weight shall be deemed a single letter, and every additional weight of half an ounce, shall be charged with an additional single postage. All drop letters, or letters placed in any post office, not for transmission through the mail but for delivery only, shall be charged with postage at the rate of two cents each."

Circulars were charged 2 cents, magazines and pamphlets 2½ cents; newspapers according to size.

Between the time of the Act of 1845, effecting uniform postage rates, and the Act of Congress of March 3, 1847, authorizing the postmaster-general to issue stamps, postmasters in various cities issued provisional stamps.

Before adhesive stamps were introduced, prepaid mail was marked "Paid" either with pen and ink or handstamps of various designs. Unpaid mail occasionally was marked "Due." Most often, however, unpaid mail did not have a "Due" marking, only the amount of postage to be collected from the recipient, e.g. "5," "10," "18¾," etc. Thus, if a letter was not marked "Paid," it was assumed to be unpaid. These "stampless covers" are found in numerous types and usually carry the town postmark.

New York Postmaster Robert H. Morris issued the first postmaster provisional in July 1845. Other postmasters soon followed. The provisionals served until superseded by the federal government's 5c and 10c stamps issued July 1, 1847.

Postmasters recognized the provisionals as indicating postage prepaid. On several provisionals, the signature of initials of the postmaster vouched for their legitimate use.

On July 12, 1845, Postmaster Morris sent examples of his new stamp to the postmasters of Boston, Philadelphia, Albany and Washington, asking that they be treated as unpaid until they reached the New York office. Starting in that year, the New York stamps were distributed to other offices. Postmaster General Cave Johnson reportedly authorized this practice with the understanding that these stamps were to be sold for letters directed to or passing through New York. This was an experiment to test the practicality of the use of adhesive postage stamps.

ALEXANDRIA, VA.

Daniel Bryan, Postmaster

A1

All known copies cut to shape.
Type I — 40 asterisks in circle.
Type II — 39 asterisks in circle.

1846		Typeset	*Imperf.*
1X1	A1	5c **black,** *buff,* type I	—
a.		5c black, *buff,* type II	100,000.
		On cover (I or II)	200,000.
1X2	A1	5c **black,** *blue,* type I, on cover	—

Cancellations

Red circular town
Black "PAID"
Black ms. accounting number ("No. 45," "No. 70")

The approximately 6 copies of Nos. 1X1 and 1X1a known on cover or cover front are generally not tied by postmark and some are uncanceled. The value for "on cover" is for a stamp obviously belonging on a cover which bears the proper circular dated town, boxed "5" and straight line "PAID" markings.

No. 1X2 is unique. It is canceled with a black straight line "PAID" marking which is repeated on the cover. The cover also bears a black circular "Alexandria Nov. 25" postmark.

E1

1846	Printed in upper right corner of envelope	
2XU1	E1 5c **carmine red,** *white*	300,000.

No. 2XU1 exists in two sizes of envelope.
Envelopes and letter sheets are known showing the circular design and figure "2" handstamped in blue or red. They were used locally. Value, blue $3,000, red $5,000.

Letter sheets are known showing the circular design and figure "5" handstamped in blue or red. Value, blue $3,500, red $5,000.

Similar circular design in blue without numeral or "PAID" is known to have been used as a postmark.

BALTIMORE, MD.

James Madison Buchanan, Postmaster

Signature of Postmaster — A1

Printed from a plate of 12 (2x6) containing nine 5c stamps (Pos. 1-6, 8, 10, 12) and three 10c (Pos. 7, 9, 11).

1845		Engr.		*Imperf.*
3X1	A1	5c **black**		5,500.
		On cover		12,500.
		Vertical pair on cover		30,000.
3X2	A1	10c **black,** on cover		60,000.
3X3	A1	5c **black,** *bluish*	65,000.	5,500.
		On cover		12,500.
3X4	A1	10c **black,** *bluish*		60,000.
		On cover		—

Nos. 3X3-3X4 preceded Nos. 3X1-3X2 in use.
No. 3X3 unused is unique. Value is based on 1997 auction sale.

Cancellations

Blue circular town
Blue straight line
"PAID"
Blue "5" in oval
Blue "10" in oval
Black pen

Off cover values are for stamps canceled by either pen or handstamp. Stamps on cover tied by handstamps command

---

E1

Three Separate Handstamps

The "PAID" and "5" in oval were handstamped in blue or red, always both in the same color on the same entire. "James M. Buchanan" was handstamped in black, blue or red. Blue town and rate with black signature was issued first and sells for more.

The paper is manila, buff, white, salmon or grayish. Manila is by far the most frequently found 5c envelope. All 10c envelopes are rare, with manila or buff the more frequent. Of the 10c on salmon, only one example is known.

The general attractiveness of the envelope and the clarity of the handstamps primarily determine the value.
The color listed is that of the "PAID" and "5" in oval.

1845			Various Papers	Handstamped
3XU1	E1	5c	**blue**	6,500.
3XU2	E1	5c	**red**	9,000.
3XU3	E1	10c	**blue**	16,000.
3XU4	E1	10c	**red**	19,000.

Earliest documented uses: Apr. 27, 1846 (No. 3XU2); June 12, 1846 (No. 3XU4).

Cancellations

Blue circular town
Blue "5" in oval

The second "5" in oval on the unlisted "5 + 5" envelopes is believed not to be part of the basic prepaid marking, but envelopes bearing this marking merit a premium over the values for Nos. 3XU1-3XU2.

BOSCAWEN, N.H.

Worcester Webster, Postmaster

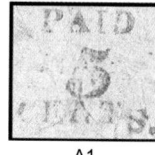

A1

1846 (?)   **Typeset**   *Imperf.*
4X1 A1 5c **dull blue**, *yellowish*, on cover   300,000.
    One copy known, uncanceled on cover with ms. postal markings.

BRATTLEBORO, VT.

Frederick N. Palmer, Postmaster

Initials of Postmaster (FNP) — A1

    Printed from plate of 10 (5x2) separately engraved subjects with imprint "Eng'd by Thos. Chubbuck, Bratto." below the middle stamp of the lower row (Pos. 8).

1846   *Imperf.*
Thick Softwove Paper Colored Through
5X1 A1 5c **black**, *buff*   10,000.
     On cover   35,000.
     Two singles on cover   110,000.
    Earliest documented use: Aug. 28, 1846.

Cancellations
    Red straight line "PAID"
    Red pen
    Blue "5"

    The red pen-marks are small and lightly applied. They were used to invalidate a single sample sheet. One copy of each plate position is known so canceled.

LOCKPORT, N.Y.

Hezekiah W. Scovell, Postmaster

A1

    "Lockport, N.Y." oval and "PAID" separately handstamped in red, "5" in black ms.

1846   *Imperf.*
6X1 A1 5c **red**, *buff*, on cover   300,000.
Cancellation
    Black ms. "X"
    One copy of No. 6X1 is known. Small fragments of two other copies adhering to one cover have been found.

MILLBURY, MASS.

Asa H. Waters, Postmaster

George Washington — A1

Printed from a woodcut, singly, on a hand press.

1846   *Imperf.*
7X1 A1 5c **black**, *bluish*   130,000.   50,000.
     On cover   125,000.
    Earliest documented use: Aug. 21, 1846.

Cancellations
    Red straight line "PAID"
    Red circular "MILBURY, MS.,"
      date in center

NEW HAVEN, CONN.

Edward A. Mitchell, Postmaster
ENVELOPES

E1

    Impressed from a brass handstamp at upper right of envelope.
    Signed in blue, black or magenta ms., as indicated in parenthesis.

1845
8XU1 E1 5c **red** (Bl or M)   100,000.
     Cut square   25,000.
     Cut to shape   10,000.
8XU2 E1 5c **red**, *light bluish* (Bk)   125,000.
8XU3 E1 5c **dull blue**, *buff* (Bl)   125,000.
     Cut to shape (Bk)   12,500.
8XU4 E1 5c **dull blue** (Bl)   125,000.
    Values of Nos. 8XU1-8XU4 are a guide to value. They are based on auction realizations and take condition into consideration. All New Haven envelopes are of almost equal rarity. An entire of No. 8XU2 is the finest example known. The other envelopes and cut squares are valued according to condition as much as rarity.

REPRINTS

    Twenty reprints in dull blue on white paper, signed by E. A. Mitchell in lilac rose ink, were made in 1871 for W. P. Brown and others, value $1,000. Thirty reprints in carmine on hard white paper, signed in dark blue or red, were made in 1874 for Cyrus B. Peets, Chief Clerk for Mitchell, value $750. Unsigned reprints were made for N. F. Seebeck and others about 1872, value $300.
    Edward A. Mitchell, grandson of the Postmaster, in 1923 delivered reprints in lilac on soft white wove paper, dated "1923" in place of the signature, value $300.
    In 1932, the New Haven Philatelic Society bought the original handstamp and gave it to the New Haven Colony Historical Society. To make the purchase possible (at the $1000 price) it was decided to print 260 stamps from the original handstamp. Of these, 130 were in red and 130 in dull blue, all on hard, white wove paper, value approximately $200 each.
    According to Carroll Alton Means' booklet on the New Haven Provisional Envelope, after this last reprinting the brass handstamp was so treated that further reprints cannot be made. The reprints were sold originally at $5 each. A facsimile signature of the postmaster, "E. A. Mitchell," (blue on the red reprints, black on the blue) was applied with a rubber handstamp. These 260 reprints are all numbered to correspond with the number of the booklet issued then.

NEW YORK, N.Y.

Robert H. Morris, Postmaster

George Washington — A1

    Printed by Rawdon, Wright & Hatch from a plate of 40 (5x8). The die for Washington's head on the contemporary bank notes was used for the vignette. It had a small flaw—a line extending from the corner of the mouth down the chin—which is quite visible on the paper money. This was corrected for the stamp.
    The stamps were usually initialed "ACM" (Alonzo Castle Monson) in magenta ink as a control before being sold or passed through the mails. There are four or five styles of these initials. The most common is "ACM" without periods. The scarcest is "A.C.M.", believed written by Marcena Monson. The rare initials

---

"RHM" (Robert H. Morris, the postmaster) and "MMJr (Marcena Monson) are listed separately.
    The stamps were printed on a variety of wove papers varying in thickness from pelure to thick, and in color from gray to bluish and blue. A thick brown gum was used first, succeeded by a thin whitish transparent gum. Some stamps appear to have a slight ribbing or mesh effect. A few also show letters of a double-line papermaker's watermark, a scarce variety. All used true blue copies carry "ACM" without periods; of the three unused copies, two lack initials.

    Nos. 9X1-9X3 and varieties unused are valued without gum. Examples with original gum are extremely scarce and will command higher prices.

    Earliest documented use: July 15, 1845 (Nos. 9X1, 9X1e).

1845-46   **Engr.**   **Bluish Wove Paper**   *Imperf.*
9X1 A1 5c **black,** signed ACM, connected,

1846	1,500.	525.
On cover		650.
On cover to France or England		2,250.
On cover to other European countries		5,500.
Pair	5,750.	1,350.
Pair on cover		2,100.
Pair on cover to England		4,500.
Pair on cover to Canada		5,500.
Strip of 3		4,500.
Strip of 3 on cover		9,000.
Strip of 4	12,500.	
Strip of 4 on cover		20,000.
Block of 4		45,000.
Double transfer at bottom (Pos. 2)	1,700.	600.
Double transfer at top (Pos. 7)	1,700.	600.
Bottom frame line double (Pos. 31)	1,700.	600.
Top frame line double (Pos. 36)	1,700.	600.

    The only blocks currently known are a used block of 4 off cover (faulty) and a block of 9 on cover.

Cancellations

Blue pen	525.
Black pen	+25.
Magenta pen	+100.
Red square grid (New York)	+50.
Black circular date stamp	
Red round grid (Boston)	+350.
Blue numeral (Philadelphia)	+750.
Red "U.S" in octagon frame (carrier)	+1,200.
Red "PAID"	+50.
Red N.Y. circular date stamp	+100.
Large red N.Y. circular date stamp containing "5"	+125.
Small red "5"	

a.	Signed ACM, AC connected,	1,750.	575.
	On cover		725.
	On cover to France or England		2,250.
	On cover to other European countries		6,000.
	Pair	5,750.	1,600.
	Pair, Nos. 9X1, 9X1a		4,500.
	Pair on cover		2,100.
	Double transfer at bottom (Pos. 2)	1,800.	700.
	Double transfer at top (Pos. 7)	1,800.	700.
	Bottom frame line double (Pos. 31)	1,800.	700.
	Top frame line double (Pos. 36)	1,800.	700.

Cancellations

Blue pen	575.
Black pen	+25.
Magenta pen	+100.
Red N.Y. circular date stamp	+125.
Large red N.Y. circular date stamp with "5"	+150.
Red square grid	+100.
Red "PAID"	+50.

b.	Signed A.C.M.	3,750.	700.
	On cover		850.
	On cover to France or England		2,750.
	On cover to other European countries		6,000.
	Pair		2,400.
	Pair on cover		3,250.
	Double transfer at bottom (Pos. 2)	—	950.
	Double transfer at top (Pos. 7)	—	950.
	Bottom frame line double (Pos. 31)		950.
	Top frame line double (Pos. 36)		950.

Cancellations

Blue pen	700.
Black pen	+25.
Red square grid	+100.
Red N.Y. circular date stamp	+100.
Large red N.Y. circular date stamp containing "5"	+150.
Red "PAID"	+50.

c.	Signed MMJr		10,000.
	On cover		
	Pair on cover front		26,500.
d.	Signed RHM	13,000.	3,500.
	Pair		12,000.
	On cover		5,500.
	On cover from New Hamburgh, N.Y.		12,500.

Cancellations

Blue pen		3,250.
Black pen		+150.
Red square grid		+250.
Red N.Y. circular date stamp		+400.
Red "PAID"		+300.

Earliest documented use: July 17, 1845.

e.	Without signature	3,500.	750.
	On cover		1,250.
	On cover to France or England		2,250.
	On cover to other European countries		6,000.
	On cover, July 15, 1845		30,000.
	Pair		2,400.
	Pair on cover		2,600.
	Double transfer at bottom (Pos. 2)	3,750.	850.
	Double transfer at top (Pos. 7)	3,750.	850.
	Bottom frame line double (Pos. 31)	3,750.	850.
	Top frame line double (Pos. 36)	3,750.	850.
	Ribbed paper	—	

Cancellations

Blue pen	750.
Black pen	+25.
Red square grid	+100.
Red N.Y. circular date stamp	+100.
Large red N.Y. circular date stamp containing "5"	+150.
Red "PAID"	+100.

Known used from Albany, Boston, Jersey City, N.J., New Hamburgh, N.Y., Philadelphia, Sing Sing, N.Y., Washington, D.C., and Hamilton, Canada, as well as by route agents on the Baltimore R.R. Covers originating in New Hamburgh are known only with No. 9X1d (one also bearing the U.S. City Despatch Post carrier); one also known used to Holland.

1847		Engr.	Blue Wove Paper	**Imperf.**
9X2	A1 5c	**black,** signed ACM connected	6,500.	3,500.
		On cover		5,750.
		Pair		13,000.
		Pair on cover		
		Double transfer at bottom (Pos. 2)		4,000.
		Double transfer at top (Pos. 7)		4,000.
		Bottom frame line double (Pos. 31)		4,000.
		Top frame line double (Pos. 36)		4,000.
a.		Signed RHM		—
b.		Signed ACM, AC connected		5,000.
d.		Without signature	11,000.	7,250.

Earliest documented use: Mar. 4, 1847.

Cancellations

Red square grid	3,500.
Red "PAID"	+100.
Red N.Y. circular date stamp	+650.

On the only example known of No. 9X2a the "R" is illegible and does not match those of the other "RHM" signatures.

1847		Engr.	Gray Wove Paper	**Imperf.**
9X3	A1 5c	**black,** signed ACM connected	5,250.	2,250.
		On cover		5,250.
		On cover to Europe		8,500.
		Pair		7,750.
		Pair on cover		8,750.
		Double transfer at bottom (Pos. 2)		2,600.
		Double transfer at top (Pos. 7)		2,600.
		Bottom frame line double (Pos. 31)		2,600.
		Top frame line double (Pos. 36)		2,600.
a.		Signed RHM		7,000.
b.		Without signature		12,000.

Earliest documented use: Feb. 8, 1847.

Cancellations

Red square grid	2,250.
Red N.Y. circular date stamp	2,250.
Red "PAID"	+100.

All known used copies of No. 9X3a have red square grid or red "PAID" in arc cancel.

The first plate was of nine subjects (3x3). Each subject differs slightly from the others, with Position 8 showing the white stock shaded by crossed diagonal lines. At some point prints were struck from this plate in black on deep blue and white bond paper, as well as in blue, green, scarlet and brown on white bond paper. These are listed in the Proof and Trial Color Proof sections. Stamps from this plate were not issued, and it is possible that it is an essay, as the design differs slightly from the issued stamps from the sheet of 40.

ENVELOPES

Postmaster Morris, according to newspaper reports of July 2 and 7, 1845, issued envelopes. The design was not stated and no example has been seen.

PROVIDENCE, R.I.

Welcome B. Sayles, Postmaster

A1 & A2

Engraved on copper plate containing 12 stamps (3x4). Upper right corner stamp (Pos. 3) "TEN"; all others "FIVE." The stamps were engraved directly on the plate, each differing from the other. The "TEN" and Pos. 4, 5, 6, 9, 11 and 12 have no period after "CENTS."

Yellowish White Handmade Paper

Earliest documented use: Aug. 25, 1846 (No. 10X1).

1846, Aug. 24				**Imperf.**
10X1	A1	5c	**gray black**	350.	1,750.
			On cover, tied by postmark		20,000.
			On cover, pen canceled		4,500.
			Two on cover		—
			Pair	725.	
			Block of four	1,450.	
10X2	A2	10c	**gray black**	1,150.	15,000.
			On cover, pen canceled		35,000.
a.			Se-tenant with 5c	2,000.	
			Complete sheet	5,500.	

Cancellations

Black pen check mark
Red circular town
Red straight line "PAID" (2 types)
Red "5"

All canceled copies of Nos. 10X1-10X2, whether or not bearing an additional handstamped cancellation, are obliterated with a black pen check mark. There is only one known certified used example off cover of No. 10X2, and it has a minor fault. Value represents a 1997 sale. All genuine covers must bear the red straight line "PAID," the red circular town postmark, and the red numeral "5" or "10" rating mark.

Reprints were made in 1898. In general, each stamp bears one of the following letters on the back: B. O. G. E. R. T. D. U. R. B. I. N. However, some reprint sheets received no such printing on the reverse. All reprints are without gum. Value for 5c, $50; for 10c, $125; for sheet, $725. Reprints without the printing on the reverse sell for more.

ST. LOUIS, MO.

John M. Wimer, Postmaster

A1

A2

A3

Missouri Coat of Arms

Printed from a copper plate of 6 (2x3) subjects separately engraved by J. M. Kershaw.

The plate in its first state, referred to as Plate 1, comprised: three 5c stamps in the left vertical row and three 10c in the right vertical row. The stamps vary slightly in size, measuring from 17¾ to 18¼ by 22 to 22½mm.

Later a 20c denomination was believed necessary. So two of the 5c stamps, types I (pos. 1) and II (pos. 3) were changed to 20c by placing the plate face down on a hard surface and hammering on the back of the parts to be altered until the face was driven flush at those points. The new numerals were then engraved. Both 20c stamps show broken frame lines and the paw of the right bear on type II is missing. The 20c type II (pos. 3) also shows retouching in the dashes under "SAINT" and "LOUIS." The characteristics of types I and II of the 5c also serve to distinguish the two types of the 20c. This altered, second state of the plate is referred to as Plate 2. It is the only state to contain the 20c.

The demand for the 20c apparently proved inadequate, and the plate was altered again. The "20" was erased and "5" engraved in its place, resulting in noticeable differences from the 5c stamps from Plate 1. In type I (pos. 1) reengraved, the "5" is twice as far from the top frame line as in the original state, and the four dashes under "SAINT" and "LOUIS" have disappeared except for about half of the upper dash under each

word. In type II (pos. 3) reengraved, the ornament in the flag of the "5" is a diamond instead of a triangle; the diamond in the bow is much longer than in the first state, and the ball of the "5," originally blank, contains a large dot. At right of the shading of the "5" there is a short curved line which is evidently a remnant of the "0" of "20." Type III (pos. 5) of the 5c was slightly retouched. This second alteration of the plate is referred to as Plate 3.

Type characteristics common to Plates 1, 2 and 3:
5 Cent. Type I (pos. 1). Haunches of both bears almost touch frame lines.
Type II (pos. 3). Bear at right almost touches frame line, but left bear is about ¼mm from it.
Type III (pos. 5). Haunches of both bears about ½mm from frame lines. Small spur on "S" of "POST."
10 Cent. Type I (pos. 2). Three dashes below "POST OFFICE."
Type II (pos. 4). Three pairs of dashes.
Type III (pos. 6). Pairs of dashes (with rows of dots between) at left and right. Dash in center with row of dots above it.
20 Cent. Type I. See 5c Type I.
Type II. See 5c Type II.

Nos. 11X1-11X8 unused are valued without gum.

Wove Paper Colored Through

1845, Nov.-1846					**Imperf.**
11X1	A1	5c	**black,** *greenish*	10,000.	6,500.
			On cover		14,500.
			Pair	25,000.	15,000.
			Two on cover		21,000.
			Strip of 3		27,500.
			Strip of 3 plus single on cover		40,000.
11X2	A2	10c	**black,** *greenish*	10,000.	6,500.
			On cover		11,000.
			Pair		15,000.
			Pair on cover		17,500.
			Strip of 3		27,500.
			Strip of 3 on cover		32,500.
			Five on cover		200,000.
			On cover, #11X2, 11X6		50,000.
11X3	A3	20c	**black,** *greenish*	85,000.	
			On cover, #11X5, two #11X3		200,000.

Printed from Plate 1 (3 varieties each of the 5c and 10c) and Plate 2 (1 variety of the 5c, 3 of the 10c, 2 of the 20c).

1846					
11X4	A1	5c	**black,** *gray lilac*	—	25,000.
			On cover		25,000.
11X5	A2	10c	**black,** *gray lilac*	10,000.	6,000.
			On cover		9,000.
			Pair		15,000.
			Pair, 10c (III), 5c		75,000.
			Strip of 3		27,500.
			Strip of 3 on cover		37,500.
			Pair 10c (II), 10c (III) se-tenant with 5c		47,500.
			Strip of 3 10c (I, II, III) se-tenant with 5c		165,000.
11X6	A3	20c	**black,** *gray lilac*	82,500.	25,000.
			On cover		35,000.
			Pair		30,000.
			Pair on cover		70,000.
			On cover, #11X6 and #11X5		42,500.
			Pair, #11X6 and #11X5		100,000.
			Pair, #11X6 and #11X5, on cover		175,000.
			Strip of 3, 2#11X6 and #11X4		80,000.

Printed from Plate 2 (1 variety of the 5c, 3 of the 10c, 2 of the 20c).

No. 11X6 unused is unique. It is in the grade of fine and is valued thus.

The used pair of No. 11X6 is unique. The left margin cuts into the frameline, and it is valued thus.

1846				**Pelure Paper**
11X7	A1	5c	**black,** *bluish*	—	8,000.
			On cover		11,000.
			Two on cover		25,000.
11X8	A2	10c	**black,** *bluish*	8,000.	8,000.
			On cover		11,000.
a.			Impression of 5c on back		

Printed from Plate 3 (3 varieties each of the 5c, 10c).
Earliest documented use: Nov. 25, 1846 (#11X8).

Cancellations, Nos. 11X1-11X8

Black pen
Ms. initials of postmaster (#11X2, type I)
Red circular town
Red straight line "PAID"
Red grid (#11X7)

Values of Nos. 11X7-11X8, on and off cover, reflect the usual poor condition of these stamps, which were printed on fragile pelure paper. Attractive copies with minor defects sell for considerably more.

Values for used off-cover stamps are for pen-canceled copies. Handstamp canceled copies sell for much more. Values for stamps on cover are pen cancels. Covers with the stamps tied by handstamp sell at considerable premiums depending upon the condition of the stamps and the general attractiveness of the cover. In general, covers with multiple frankings (unless separately valued) are valued at the "on cover" value of the highest item, plus the "off cover" value of the other stamps.

For Tuscumbia, Alabama, formerly listed as United States postmasters' provisional No. 12XU1, see the "3c 1861 Postmasters' Provisionals" section before the Confederate States of America Postmasters' Provisionals.

POSTAGE

Issues from 1847 through 1894 are unwatermarked.

Benjamin Franklin — A1

Double transfer of top frame line — (A) position 80R1

Double transfer of top and bottom frame lines — (B) position 90R1

Double transfer of bottom frame line and lower part of left frame line — (C)

Double transfer of top, bottom and left frame lines, also numerals — (D)

Double transfer of "U," "POST OFFICE" and left numeral — (E)

Double transfer of top frame line, upper part of side frame lines, "U," and "POST OFFICE" — (F)

This issue was authorized by an Act of Congress, approved March 3, 1847, to take effect July 1, 1847, from which date the use of Postmasters' Stamps or any which were not authorized by the Postmaster General became illegal.
This issue was declared invalid as of July 1, 1851.

Produced by Rawdon, Wright, Hatch & Edson.
Plates of 200 subjects in two panes of 100 each.

1847, July 1			Engr.		Imperf.
		Thin Bluish Wove Paper			
1	A1	5c **red brown**		6,500.	600.
		pale brown		6,500.	600.
		brown		6,500.	600.
		No gum		2,500.	
		On cover			675.
		On cover to England or France			2,750.
		On cover to other European countries			3,250.
		Pair		15,500.	1,250.
		Pair on cover			1,400.
		Strip of 3		25,000.	2,400.
		Block of 4		42,500.	27,500.
		Block of 4 on cover			240,000.
		Dot in "S" in upper right corner		6,750.	625.
		Cracked plate (69R1)			625.
a.		5c **dark brown**		8,500.	675.
		No gum		3,250.	
		Pair		20,000.	1,750.

	Block of 4	55,000.	
	grayish brown	8,750.	800.
	No gum	3,400.	
	Pair		2,000.
	blackish brown	9,000.	900.
	No gum	3,500.	
	Pair	22,500.	2,000.
b.	5c orange brown	9,000.	850.
	No gum	3,650.	
	Pair		2,250.
	Block of 4 on cover		—
	No gum	5,000.	
c.	5c red orange	17,500.	5,500.
	No gum	7,500.	
	Pair		20,000.
d.	5c brown orange	—	1,750.
	No gum	4,500.	
	Pair on cover		—
e.	Double impression		
(A)	Double transfer of top frame line (80R1)		725.
(B)	Double transfer of top and bottom frame lines (90R1)	—	725.
(C)	Double transfer of bottom frame line and lower part of left frame line		3,250.
(D)	Double transfer of top, bottom and left frame lines, also numerals		3,250.
(E)	Double transfer of "U," "POST OF-FICE" and left numeral		1,500.
(F)	Double transfer of top frame line, upper part of side frame lines, "U," and "POST OFFICE"		—

The only known double impression shows part of the design doubled.

Some students believe that the "E double transfer" actually shows plate scratches instead.

Earliest documented use: July 7, 1847.

Cancellations

Red	600.
Red town	+200.
Orange red	+15.
Orange red town	+220.
Blue	+35.
Blue town	+125.
Black	+100.
Black town	+400.
Magenta	+250.
Orange	+750.
Ultramarine	+1,000.
Violet	+900.
Violet town	
Green	+1,250.
"Paid"	+50.
"Paid" in grid (demonetized usage)	+300.
"Free"	+400.
Railroad	+200.

U. S. Express Mail (on the cover)		+100.
U. S. Express Mail (on stamp)		—
U. S. Express Mail in black (on stamp) (demonetized usage)		+12,500.
"Way"		+250.
"Way" with numeral		+500.
"Steamboat"		+350.
"Steam"		+200.
"Steamship"		+300.
Philadelphia RR		
Hotel (on the cover)		+2,000.
Numeral		+100.
Canada		+3,000.
Wheeling, Va., grid		+6,000.
Pen		300.

George Washington — A2

Double transfer in "X" at lower right — 1R1A

Double transfer in "Post Office" 31R1B

Double transfer in "X" at lower right — 2R1C

Double transfer of left and bottom frame line — 41R1D

2	A2	10c **black**	32,500.	1,400.
		gray black	32,500.	1,400.
		No gum	15,000.	
		greenish black		1,750.
		On cover		1,700.
		On cover to Canada		2,100.
		On cover to Great Britain		3,250.
		On cover to France		5,250.
		On cover with 5c No. 1		45,000.
		Pair	75,000.	3,350.
		Pair on cover		3,850.
		Strip of 3	110,000.	11,000.
		Block of 4	150,000.	75,000.

	Short transfer at top	35,000.	1,50
	Vertical line through second "F" of "OFFICE" (68R1)	—	2,00
	With "Stick Pin" in tie (52L1)	—	2,00
	With "harelip" (57L1)	—	2,00
a.	Diagonal half used as 5c on cover		13,00
b.	Vertical half used as 5c on cover		35,00
c.	Horizontal half used as 5c on cover		—
(A)	Double transfer in "X" at lower right (1R1)	—	2,100
(B)	Double transfer in "Post Office" (31R1)	—	2,800
(C)	Double transfer in "X" at lower right (2R1)	—	2,100
(D)	Double transfer of left and bottom frame line (41R1)	—	2,100

Earliest documented use: July 2, 1847.

Two examples of the unused block are recorded. Value represents 1998 auction sale price of the only example available to collectors.

The value for the used block of 4 represents a block with manuscript cancel. One block is recorded with a handstamp cancellation and it is worth significantly more.

Cancellations

Red	1,400.
Orange red	+25.
Blue	+50.
Orange	+500.
Black	+350.
Magenta	+650.
Violet	+850.
Green	+2,000.
Ultramarine	+900.
"Paid"	+100.
"Free"	+800.
Railroad	+1,000.
Philadelphia RR straightline	+500.
U.S. Express Mail (on the cover)	+500.
"Way"	+550.
Numeral	+250.
"Steam"	+350.
"Steamship"	+400.
"Steamboat"	+650.
"Steamer 10"	+1,000.
Canada	+3,000.
Panama	
Wheeling, Va., grid	+5,500.
Pen	750.

A3   A4

REPRODUCTIONS of 1847 ISSUE

Actually, official imitations made from new plates of 50 subjects made by the Bureau of Engraving and Printing by order of the Post Office Department. These were not valid for postal use.

Reproductions. The letters R. W. H. & E. at the bottom of each stamp are less distinct on the reproductions than on the originals.

5c. On the originals the left side of the white shirt frill touches the oval on a level with the top of the "F" of "Five." On the reproductions it touches the oval about on a level with the top of the figure "5." On the originals, the bottom of the right leg of the "N" in "CENTS" is blunt. On the reproductions, the "N" comes to a point at the bottom.

10c. On the originals line of coat (A) points to "T" of TEN and (B) it points between "T" and "S" of "CENTS."

On the reproductions line of coat (A) points to right tip of "X" and line of coat (B) points to center of "S."

The bottom of the right leg of the "N" of "CENTS" shows the same difference as on the 5c originals and reproductions.

On the reproductions the eyes have a sleepy look, the line of the mouth is straighter, and in the curl of the hair near the left cheek is a strong black dot, while the originals have only a faint one.

(See Nos. 948a and 948b for 1947 reproductions — 5c blue and 10c brown orange in larger size.)

1875		**Bluish paper, without gum**	*Imperf.*
3	A3	5c red brown *(4779)*	800.
		brown	800.
		dark brown	800.
		Pair	1,750.
		Block of 4	5,250.
4	A4	10c **black** *(3883)*	975.
		gray black	975.
		Pair	2,100.
		Block of 4	6,500.

Numbers in parentheses are quantities sold.

Produced by Toppan, Carpenter, Casilear & Co.

Stamps of the 1851-57 series were printed from plates consisting of 200 subjects and the sheets were divided into two panes of 100 each. Stamps printed from different positions on the plate often have characteristics which make them more valuable than the basic listing. It is, therefore, necessary to be able to clearly identify each position on the plates used to print these stamps. In order that each stamp in the sheet and within each pane could be identified easily in regard to its relative position it was devised that the stamps in each pane be numbered from one to one hundred, starting with the top horizontal row and numbering consecutively from left to right. Thus the first stamp at the upper left corner would be 1 and the last stamp at the bottom right corner, would be 100. The left and right panes are indicated by the letters "L" or "R." The number of the plate is given last. As an example, the best-known of the scarce type III, one cent 1851 being the 99th stamp in the right pane of Plate No. 2 is listed as (99R2),*i.e.* 99th stamp, right pane, Plate No. 2.

One plate of the one cent and several plates of the three cents were reentered after they had been in use. The original state of the plate is called "Early" and the reentered state is termed "Late." If the plate was reentered twice, the inbetween state is called "Intermediate." Identification of "Early," "Intermediate" or "Late" state is explained by the addition of the letters "E," "I" or "L" after the plate numbers. The sixth stamp of the right pane of Plate No. 1 from the "Early" state would be 6R1E. The same plate position from the "Late" state would be 6R1L.

One plate of the three cent stamp never had a plate number and is referred to by specialists as "Plate O."

The position of the stamp in the sheet is placed within parentheses, for example: (99R2).

The different values of this issue were intended primarily for the payment of specific rates, though any value might be used in making up a rate. The one cent stamp was to pay the postage on newspapers, drop letters and circulars, and the one cent carrier fee in some cities from 1856. The three cent stamp represented the rate on ordinary letters and two of them made up the rate for distances over 3000 miles prior to Apr. 1, 1855. The five cent stamp was originally for the registration fee but the fee was usually paid in cash. Occasionally two of them were used to pay the rate over 3000 miles, after it was changed in April, 1855. Singles paid the "Shore to ship" rate to certain foreign countries and, from 1857, triples paid the fifteen-cent rate to France. Ten cents was the rate to California and points distant more than 3000 miles. The twelve cent stamp was for quadruple the ordinary rate. Twenty-four cents represented the single letter rate to Great Britain. Thirty cents was the rate to Germany. The ninety cent stamp was apparently intended to facilitate the payment of large amounts of postage.

Act of Congress, March 3, 1851. "From and after June 30, 1851, there shall be charged the following rates: Every single letter not exceeding 3000 miles, prepaid postage, 3 cents; not prepaid, 5 cents; for any greater distance, double these rates. Every single letter or paper conveyed wholly or in part by sea, and to or from a foreign country over 2500 miles, 20 cents; under 2500 miles, 10 cents. Drop or local letters, 1 cent each. Letters uncalled for and advertised, to be charged 1 cent in addition to the regular postage."

Act of Congress, March 3, 1855. "For every single letter, in manuscript or paper of any kind, in writing, marks or signs, conveyed in the mail between places in the United States not exceeding 3000 miles, 3 cents; and for any greater distance, 10 cents. Drop or local letters, 1 cent."

The Act of March 3, 1855, made the prepayment of postage on domestic letters compulsory April 1, 1855, and prepayment of postage on domestic letters compulsory by stamps effective Jan. 1, 1856.

The Act authorized the Postmaster to establish a system for the registration of valuable letters, and to require prepayment of postage on such letters as well as registration fee of five cents. Stamps to prepay the registry fee were not required until June 1, 1867.

In Nos. 5-17 the 1c, 3c and 12c have very small margins between the stamps. The 5c and 10c have moderate size margins. The values of these stamps take the margin size into consideration.

Franklin — A5

ONE CENT. Issued July 1, 1851.

Type I. Has complete curved lines outside the labels with "U. S. Postage" and "One Cent." The scrolls below the lower label are turned under, forming little balls. The ornaments at top are substantially complete.

Type Ib. As type I, but balls below bottom label are not so clear. Plume-like scrolls at bottom are incomplete.

1851-57				*Imperf.*
5	A5	1c **blue,** type I (7R1E)	225,000.	55,000.
		On cover		65,000.
		Pair, types I, Ib		80,000.
		On cover, pair, one stamp type I		—
		On cover, strip of 3, one stamp type I		100,000.

Earliest documented use: July 5, 1851.

Cancellations

Blue	+750.
Blue town	—
Red grid	+2,500.
Red town	—
Red "Paid"	—

Values for No. 5 are for copies with margins touching or cutting slightly into the design, or for copies with four margins and minor faults. Very few sound copies with the design untouched exist, and these sell for much more than the values shown.

Value for No. 5 unused is for copy with no gum. Only one example unused with original gum is recorded. It is in a larger multiple and is creased.

5A	A5	1c **blue,** type Ib, *July 1, 1851* (Less distinct examples 3-5, 9R1E)	17,500.	8,000.
		No gum	7,500.	
		Pair	37,500.	16,500.
		On cover		8,500.
		blue, type Ib (Best examples 6, 8R1E)	25,000.	15,000.
		No gum	12,000.	
		On cover		17,000.
		Pair, type Ib, II		12,500.
		Block of 4, pair type Ib, pair type IIIa (8-9, 18-19R1E)		—

Earliest documented use: July 1, 1851 (FDC).

Cancellations

Blue town	+200.
Red town	—
Red Carrier	—
Red "Paid"	+450.
Pen (3, 4, 5 or 9R1E)	3,750.
Pen (6 or 8R1E)	6,750.

A6

Type Ia. Same as type I at bottom, but top ornaments and outer line at top are partly cut away. Type Ia comes only from the bottom row of both panes of Plate 4. All type Ia stamps have the flaw below "U" of "U.S.," but this flaw also appears on some stamps of types Ic, III and IIIa of Plate 4.

Type Ic. Same as type Ia, but bottom right plume and ball ornament incomplete. Bottom left plume complete or nearly complete. Best examples are from bottom row, "F" relief, positions 91 and 96R4. Less distinct examples are "E" reliefs from 5th and 9th rows, positions 47L, 49L, 83L, 49R, 81R, 82R, and 89R, Plate 4, and early impressions of 41R4.

6	A6	1c **blue,** type Ia, *1857*	40,000.	12,500.
		No gum	20,000.	
		On cover		17,000.
		Pair	—	30,000.
		Strip of 3 on cover		75,000.
		Pair, types Ia, Ic		26,000.
		Horizontal strip of 3, (95-97R4) types Ia, Ic, Ia		35,000.
		Vertical pair, types Ia, III	57,500.	17,500.
		Vertical pair, types Ia, IIIa	47,500.	16,500.

Visualize selling.

Lilly 1967

Kapiloff 1992

Honolulu Advertiser 1995

Zoellner 1998

Golden 1999

Hall 2001

LeBow 2004

Scarsdale 2006

The next great
Siegel sale could have
your name on it.

AUCTION GALLERIES, INC.

60 EAST 56th STREET, 4th FLOOR
NEW YORK, N.Y. 10022
Ph. (212) 753-6421 Fax (212) 753-6429
E-mail: stamps@siegelauctions.com

www.siegelauctions.com

Block of 4, types Ia, IIIa	95,000.	
"Curl on shoulder" (97L4)	42,500.	13,500.
"Curl in C" (97R4)	42,500.	13,500.

The horizontal strip of 3 represents positions 95-97R4, position 96R4 being type 1c.

Earliest documented use: Apr. 19, 1857.

Cancellations

Blue		+100.
Black Carrier		+350.
Red Carrier		+350.
Pen		6,000.

6b A6 1c **blue,** type Ic ("E" relief, less

distinct examples)	7,000.	2,750.
No gum	3,250.	
On cover		4,250.
Horizontal pair (81-82R4)		—
Pair, types Ic, III		—
Pair, types Ic, IIIa		
blue, type Ic ("F" relief, best examples, 91, 96R4)	27,500.	9,000.
No gum	15,000.	
On cover		10,000.
Vertical pair (81-91R4)		—

Earliest documented use: May 20, 1857 (dated cancel on off-cover stamp); June 6, 1857 (on cover).

Cancellations

Blue ("E" relief)		—
Red ("E" relief)		—
Blue town ("F" relief)		—
Red ("F" relief)		—
Pen ("E" relief)		1,500.
Pen ("F" relief)		3,500.

A7

Type II — Same as Type I at top, but the little balls of the bottom scrolls and the bottoms of the lower plume ornaments are missing. The side ornaments are substantially complete.

7 A7 1c **blue,** type II, (Plates 1E, 2);

July 1, 1851 (Plate 1E)	1,200.	170.
No gum	500.	
On cover		200.
Pair	2,750.	375.
Strip of 3	4,100.	575.
Block of 4 (Plate 1E)	—	
Block of 4 (Plate 2)	5,500.	1,150.
P# block of 8, Impt. (Plate 2)	37,500.	
Design complete at top (10R1E only)	—	2,000.
Pair, types II, IIIa (Plate 1E)	6,150.	1,350.
Double transfer (Plate 1E or 2)	1,250.	180.
Double transfer (89R2)	1,300.	220.
Double transfer, one inverted (71L1E)	1,600.	390.
Triple transfer, one inverted (91L1E)	1,600.	410.
Cracked Plate (2L, 12L, 13L, 23L and 33L, Plate 2)	1,450.	390.
Plate 1L (4R1L only, double transfer), *June 1852*	2,000.	360.
Pair, types II (4R1L), IV	3,900.	650.
Plate 3, *May, 1856*	9,000.	1,500.
On cover		1,750.
Pair	—	3,250.
Block of 4	—	
Double transfer		1,650.
Major plate crack (22L, 24L, 31L, 33L, 34L, 8R, Plate 3)		1,800.
Plate 4, *April, 1857*	3,500.	1,100.
On cover		1,350.
Pair	—	2,300.
Pair (vert.), types II, IIIa	—	—
Block of 4, type II and types III, IIIa	—	—
"Curl in hair" (3R, 4R4)	—	1,200.
Double transfer (10R4)	—	—
Perf. 12½, unofficial	22,500.	8,500.
On cover		35,000.

In addition to the cracked plates listed above (Plate 2) there exist a number of surface cracks coming from the rare Plate 3. These are valued at approximately $600 used.

See note concerning unofficial perfs following listings for No. 11.

Earliest documented uses: July 1, 1851 (Plate 1E) (FDC); Dec. 5, 1855 (Plate 2); May 6, 1856 (Plate 3).

Cancellations

Blue	+7.50
Red	+20.00
Magenta	+40.00
Ultramarine	+50.00
Green	+350.00
Orange	
1855 year date	+10.00
1856 year date	+5.00
1857 year date	+2.50
1858 year date	
"Paid"	+5.00
"Way"	+35.00
Red "Too Late"	+200.00
Numeral	+15.00
Railroad	+50.00
"Steam"	+50.00
"Steamboat"	+70.00
Red Carrier	+35.00

Black Carrier	+25.00
U. S. Express Mail	+25.00
Printed precancel "PAID"	+2,500.
Printed precancel "paid"	+2,500.
Pen	80.00

A8

Type III — The top and bottom curved lines outside the labels are broken in the middle. The side ornaments are substantially complete.

The most desirable examples of type III are those showing the widest breaks in the top and bottom framelines.

A special example is 99R2. All other stamps come from plate 4 and almost all show the breaks in the lines less clearly defined. Some of these breaks, especially of the bottom line, are very small.

Type IIIa — Similar to III with the outer line broken at top or, rarely, at bottom but not both. The side ornaments are substantially complete.

8 A8 1c **blue,** type III (Plate 4) see

below for 99R2	20,000.	3,250.
No gum	7,500.	
On cover		3,500.
Pair	42,500.	6,750.
Pair, types III, IIIa	27,500.	5,000.
Strip of 3		10,500.
Block of 4, types III, IIIa	—	—

Earliest documented use: July 7, 1857 (on off-cover stamp); July 21, 1857 (on cover).

Cancellations

Blue	+60.
Red	+150.
Red Carrier	+200.
Black Carrier	+250.
Pen	1,625.

Values for type III are for at least a 2mm break in each outer line. Examples of type III with wider breaks in outer lines command higher prices; those with smaller breaks sell for much less.

(8) A8 1c **blue,** type III (99R2)

	27,500.	12,000.
No gum	13,000.	
Pair, types III (99R2), II		13,000.
Pair, types III (99R2), IIIa	35,000.	
Block of 4, type III (99R2), 3 type II	40,000.	
On cover (99R2)		17,500.

Cancellations

Blue	+150.00
Green	—
"Paid"	—
Red Carrier	+500.00

8A A8 1c **blue,** type IIIa (Plate 1E) *July 1, 1851*

	5,000.	1,100.
No gum	2,200.	
On cover		1,200.
Pair	10,500.	2,700.
Double transfer, one inverted (81L1E)	5,500.	1,350.
Plate 1E (100R), break in lower line	—	—
Plate 2 (100R), break in lower line	—	—
Plate 4, *April, 1857*	5,250.	1,150.
No gum	2,250.	
On cover		1,300.
Pair	11,500.	2,400.
Block of 4		9,000.

Earliest documented uses: July 3, 1851 (Plate 1E); Apr. 4, 1857 (Plate 4).

Cancellations

Blue	+50.00
Red	+100.00
"Paid"	+90.00
Black Carrier	+160.00
Red Carrier	+150.00
Pen	500.00

Values are for stamps with at least a 2mm break in the top outer line. Examples with a wider break or a break in the lower line command higher prices, those with a smaller break sell for less.

"Paid" Cancellations
Values for "Paid" cancellations are for those OTHER than the common Boston type. See Postal Markings in the Introduction for illustrations.

A9

Type IV. Similar to type II, but with the curved lines outside the labels recut at top or bottom or both.

9 A9 1c **blue,** type IV. *1852*

	850.00	130.00
No gum	325.00	
On cover		150.00
Pair	1,850.	275.00
Strip of 3	2,800.	450.00
Block of 4	4,000.	2,000.
P# block of 8, Impt. (Plate 1)	—	
Double transfer	950.00	140.00
Triple transfer, one inverted (71L1L, 81L1L and 91L1L)	1,000.	180.00
Cracked plate	1,000.	180.00
Bottom frameline broken (89R1L)	—	275.00
Perf. 12½, unofficial		12,500.
Strip of 3		—

a. Printed on both sides, reverse inverted | | — |

See note concerning unofficial perfs following listings for No. 11.

VARIETIES OF RECUTTING

Stamps of this type were printed from Plate 1 after it had been reentered and recut in 1852. All but one stamp (4R, see No. 7 for listings) were recut and all varieties of recutting are listed below:

Recut once at top and once at bottom, (113 on plate)	800.00	130.00
Recut once at top, (40 on plate)	825.00	135.00
Recut once at top and twice at bottom, (21 on plate)	850.00	140.00
Recut twice at bottom, (11 on plate)	875.00	150.00
Recut once at bottom, (8 on plate)	850.00	160.00
Recut once at bottom and twice at top, (4 on plate)	925.00	170.00
Recut twice at bottom and twice at top, (2 on plate)	950.00	225.00

Earliest documented use: June 5, 1852.

Cancellations

Blue	+5.00
Red	+30.00
Ultramarine	+90.00
Brown	+150.00
Green	+350.00
Violet	+300.00
1853 year date	+250.00
1855 year date	+10.00
1856 year date	+7.50
1857 year date	+10.00
"Paid"	+10.00
"U. S. PAID"	+50.00
"Way"	+50.00
"Free"	+75.00
Railroad	+75.00
"Steam"	+60.00
Numeral	+10.00
"Steamboat"	+90.00
"Steamship"	+60.00
Red Carrier	+15.00
Black Carrier	+25.00
U. S. Express Mail	+60.00
Express Company	
Packet boat	
Printed precancel "PAID"	+2,500.
Printed precancel "paid"	+2,500.
Pen	65.00

These 1c stamps were often cut apart carelessly, destroying part or all of the top and bottom lines. When this is so, it makes it difficult to determine whether a stamp is type II, III, IIIa or IV without identifying the position. Such mutilated examples sell for much less.

VALUES FOR NEVER-HINGED STAMPS PRIOR TO SCOTT No. 205

This catalogue does not value pre-1882 stamps in never-hinged condition. Premiums for never-hinged condition in the classic era invariably are even larger than those premiums listed for the post-1890 issues. Generally speaking, the earlier the stamp is listed in the catalogue, the larger will be the never-hinged premium. On some early classics, the premium will be several multiples of the unused, hinged values given in the catalogue.

Washington — A10

THREE CENTS. Issued July 1, 1851 (Plate 1E).
Type I — There is an outer frame line on all four sides.

10	A10	3c	**orange brown,** type I	4,000.	140.00
			No gum	1,750.	
			deep orange brown	4,250.	180.00
			No gum	1,850.	
			copper brown	5,000.	1,000.
			No gum	2,250.	
			On cover, orange brown		210.00
			Pair	9,000.	525.00
			Pair on cover		575.00
			Strip of 3	14,000.	1,250.
			Block of 4	20,000.	—
			Double transfer		170.00
			Triple transfer		425.00
			Gash on shoulder		150.00

Dot in lower right diamond block (69L5E)	275.00	
a. On part-India paper	1,100.	
Printed on both sides	12,000.	

Only one example of No. 10a is recorded.

VARIETIES OF RECUTTING

All of these stamps were recut at least to the extent of four outer frame lines and usually much more. Some of the most prominent varieties are listed below (others are described in "The 3c Stamp of U.S. 1851-57 Issue," by Carroll Chase). Basic values for No. 10 are for copies with recut inner frame lines:

No inner frame lines	4,250.	150.00
Left inner line only recut		170.00
Right inner line only recut		150.00
1 line recut in upper left triangle	4,250.	145.00
2 lines recut in upper left triangle		145.00
3 lines recut in upper left triangle		175.00
5 lines recut in upper left triangle (47L0)		750.00
1 line recut in lower left triangle		150.00
1 line recut in lower right triangle		145.00
2 lines recut in lower right triangle (57L0)		750.00
2 lines recut in upper left triangle and 1 line recut in lower right triangle		210.00
1 line recut in upper right triangle		160.00
Upper part of top label and diamond block recut	4,250.	145.00
Top label and right diamond block joined		150.00
Top label and left diamond block joined		210.00
Lower label and right diamond block joined		200.00
2 lines recut at top of upper right diamond block		190.00
1 line recut at bottom of lower left diamond block (34R2E)		800.00

Earliest documented uses: July 1, 1851 (Plate 1E) (FDC); July 12, 1851 (Plate 1i); July 23, 1851 (Plate 2E); July 19, 1851 (Plate 5E); Sept. 6, 1851 (Plate 0).

Cancellations

Blue	+3.00
Red	+5.00
Orange red	+10.00
Orange	—
Brown	+40.00
Ultramarine	+25.00
Green	+225.00
Violet	+150.00
1851 year date	+350.00
1852 year date	+350.00
"Paid"	+5.00
"Way"	+40.00
"Way" with numeral	+150.00
"Free"	+50.00
Numeral	+15.00
Railroad	+50.00
U. S. Express Mail	+20.00
"Steam"	+35.00
"Steamship"	+60.00
"Steamboat"	+70.00
Packet Boat	+300.00
Black Carrier (circular)	+400.00
Blue Carrier (circular)	+600.00
Blue Carrier (New Orleans "snowshovel")	+400.00
Green Carrier (New Orleans "snowshovel")	+500.00
Canadian	—
Territorial	+200.00
Pen	60.00

11	A10 3c	**dull red** (1853-54-55), type I	300.00	14.00
		orange red (1855)	300.00	14.00
		rose red (1854-55)	300.00	14.00
		No gum	100.00	
		brownish carmine (1851-52 and 1856)	325.00	17.00
		No gum	115.00	
		claret (1852 and 1857)	350.00	20.00
		No gum	130.00	
		deep claret (1857)	375.00	22.50
		No gum	150.00	
		experimental orange brown	—	350.00
		plum (1857)	—	2,000.
		No gum	—	
		pinkish		3,500.
		On cover, dull red		16.50
		On cover, orange red		18.00
		On cover, brownish carmine		22.50
		On cover, claret		25.00
		On cover, experimental orange brown	—	500.00
		On cover, plum	—	
		On propaganda cover, dull red		400.00
		Pair	675.00	60.00
		Pair on cover		65.00
		Strip of 3	1,100.	135.00
		Block of 4	2,000.	1,000.
		P# block of 8, Impt.	4,000.	
		Double transfer in "Three Cents"	325.00	17.00
		Double transfer line through "Three Cents" and rosettes double (92L1L)	450.00	67.50
		Double transfer, "Gents" instead of "Cents" (66R2L)	440.00	52.50
		Triple transfer (92L2L)	440.00	52.50
		Gash on shoulder	325.00	16.00

Dot in lower right diamond block (69L5L)	390.00	30.00
Major cracked plate (84L, 94L, 9R, Plate 5L)	825.00	160.00
Intermediate cracked plate (80L, 96L, 71R, Plate 5L)	550.00	80.00
Minor cracked plate (8L, 27L, 31L, 44L, 45L, 51L, 55L, 65L, 74L, 78L, 79L, 7R, 71R, and 72R, Plate 5L)	425.00	60.00
Worn plate	300.00	12.50
Perf. about 11, unofficial	6,500.	
Block of 4		27,500
Perf. 12½, unofficial	6,000	
On cover		9,000.
Pair on cover		—
c. Vertical half used as 1c on cover		5,000.
Strip of 4 No. 11c used as 6c on cover		15,000.
d. Diagonal half used as 1c on cover		5,000.
e. Double impression		5,000.

The unofficial perf varieties listed represent the first perforated stamps in the U. S. made using a true perforating machine. Known as the "Chicago perfs," both were made by Dr. Elijah W. Hadley, using a machine of his construction. None of the perf 11 stamps are believed to have been used.

The strip of 4 No. 11c on cover is the only recorded multiple of a bisected stamp in United States philately.

VARIETIES OF RECUTTING

All of these stamps were recut at least to the extent of three frame lines and usually much more. Some of the most prominent varieties are listed below (others are described in "The 3c Stamp of U.S. 1851-57 Issue," by Carroll Chase):

Recut inner frame lines	300.00	14.00
No inner frame lines	300.00	14.00
Right inner line only recut	325.00	17.50
1 line recut in upper left triangle	325.00	12.50
2 lines recut in upper left triangle	325.00	13.00
3 lines recut in upper left triangle	340.00	13.50
5 lines recut in upper left triangle (95L1L)	650.00	140.00
1 line recut in lower left triangle	340.00	13.50
1 line recut in lower right triangle	320.00	13.00
1 line recut in upper right triangle	440.00	17.50
1 line recut in UL, LL and LR triangles (49L1L)	500.00	30.00
Recut button on shoulder (10R2L)	500.00	90.00
Lines on bust and bottom of medallion circle recut (47R6)	1,200.	400.00
Upper part of top label and diamond block recut	300.00	14.00
Top label and right diamond block joined	320.00	15.00
Top label and left diamond block joined	340.00	16.50
Lower label and right diamond block joined	340.00	16.50
1 extra vertical line outside of left frame line (29L, 39L, 49L, 59L, 69L, 79L, Plate 3)	325.00	16.50
2 extra vertical lines outside of left frame line (89L, 99L, Plate 3)	390.00	30.00
1 extra vertical line outside of right frame line (58L, 68L, 78L, 88L, 98L, Plate 3)	450.00	17.50
No inner line and frame line close to design at right (9L, 19L, Plate 3)	390.00	30.00
No inner line and frame line close to design at left (70, 80, 90, 100L, Plate 3)	340.00	17.50

Earliest documented uses: Oct. 6, 1851 (Plate 1L); Jan. 7, 1852 (Plate 2L); Jan. 15, 1852 (Plate 3); Mar. 28, 1855 (Plate 4); July 13, 1855 (Plate 5L); Feb. 18, 1856 (Plate 6); Feb. 9, 1856 (Plate 7); Apr. 14, 1856 (Plate 8).

Cancellations

Blue	+.75
Red	+1.00
Orange red	+5.00
Orange	+250.00
Brown	+30.00
Magenta	+40.00
Ultramarine	+40.00
Green	+175.00
Violet	+125.00
Purple	+125.00
Olive	+100.00
Yellow	+5,000.
Yellow, on cover	10,000.
1852 year date	+300.00
1853 year date	+100.00
1854 year date	—
1855 year date	+12.50
1858 year date	+.75
1859 year date	—
"Paid"	+1.25
"Way"	+10.00
"Way" with numeral	+60.00
"Free"	+25.00
Numeral	+7.50
Railroad	+20.00
U. S. Express Mail	+5.00
Supplemental Mail Type A	+2,500.
"Steam"	+15.00
"Ship"	+20.00
"New York Ship"	+35.00
"Steamboat"	+45.00
"Steamship"	+45.00
Packet boat	+120.00
Express Company	+120.00
Black Carrier	+60.00

Red Carrier (New York)   +50.00
Green Carrier (New Orle-
ans)   +350.00
Blue Carrier (New Orleans)   +200.00
Canada   —
Territorial   +100.00
Pen   6.50

Thomas Jefferson — A11

FIVE CENTS.
Type I — Projections on all four sides.

12	A11 5c	**red brown,** type I, *1856*	*21,000.*	950.
		dark red brown	*21,000.*	950.
		No gum	*9,500.*	
		On domestic cover		1,450.
		Single on cover to France		1,800.
		Strip of 3 on cover to France		5,750.
		Pair	*47,500.*	2,200.
		Strip of 3	*70,000.*	4,750.
		Block of 4	*165,000.*	45,000.
		Double transfer (40R1)		1,200.
		Defective transfer (23R1)		1,400.

Earliest documented use: Mar. 24, 1856.

Cancellations

Red   +150.
Magenta   +200.
Blue   +125.
Green   +900.
1856 year date   +25.
1857 year date   +25.
1858 year date   —
"Paid"   +200.
"Steamship"   +200.
U.S. Express Mail   +200.
Express Company   +400.
"Steamboat"   +350.
Railroad   +400.
Numeral   +1,000.
Pen   500.

Washington — A12

TEN CENTS
Type I — The "shells" at the lower corners are practically complete. The outer line below the label is very nearly complete. The outer lines are broken above the middle of the top label and the "X" in each upper corner. Beware of type V perforated (No. 35) trimmed to resemble type I imperforate (No. 13).
Types I, II, III and IV have complete ornaments at the sides of the stamps, and three pearls at each outer edge of the bottom panel.
Type I comes only from the bottom row of both panes of Plate 1.

13	A12 10c	**green,** type I, *1855*	*18,000.*	900.
		dark green	*18,000.*	900.
		yellowish green	*18,000.*	900.
		No gum	*7,750.*	
		On domestic cover		1,000.
		Pair	*40,000.*	2,100.

Strip of 3   3,100.
Vert. pair, types III, I   *25,000.*   1,500.
Vert. pair, types IV, I (86,
96L1)   5,250.
Vertical strip of 3, types II,
III, I   4,250.
Block of 4, types III, I   *55,000.* 10,500.
Block of 4, types III, IV, I   16,000.
Double transfer (100R1)   *19,000.*   1,000.
"Curl" in left "X" (99R1) *19,000.*   1,000.

Earliest documented use: July 11, 1855.

Cancellations

Blue   +40.
Red   +75.
Magenta   +200.
Orange   —
1855 year date   +25.
1856 year date   +25.
1857 year date   +25.
"Paid"   +50.
"Steamship"   +150.
Railroad   +175.
Territorial   +400.
Numeral   +50.
U.S. Express Mail   —
Pen   450.

A13

Type II — The design is complete at the top. The outer line at the bottom is broken in the middle. The shells are partly cut away.

14	A13 10c	**green,** type II, *1855*	5,500.	200.
		dark green	5,500.	200.
		yellowish green	5,500.	200.
		No gum	2,200.	
		On domestic cover		260.
		Pair	12,000.	450.
		Strip of 3	18,500.	775.
		Block of 4	*25,000.*	4,000.
		Pair, types II, III	11,500.	450.
		Pair, types II, IV	*42,500.*	2,100.
		Vertical strip of 3, types II, III, IV		2,500.
		Block of 4, types II, III	—	3,500.
		Block of 4, types II, IV		
		Block of 4, types II, III, IV		10,000.
		Double transfer (31L, 51L, and 20R, Plate 1)	6,000.	280.
		"Curl" opposite "X" (10R1)	6,000.	300.

Earliest documented use: May 12, 1855.

Cancellations

Blue   +10.
Red   +25.
Brown   +75.
Ultramarine   +100.
Magenta   +100.
Green   +200.
Violet   +150.
1855 year date   —
1856 year date   +50.
1857 year date   +10.
1858 year date   +10.
"Paid"   +25.
"Way"   +50.
"Free"   +75.
Railroad   +75.
Steamship   +75.
Steamboat   +100.
Numeral   +50.
Territorial   +150.
Express Company   +200.
U. S. Express Mail   +75.
Pen   90.

A14

Type III — The outer lines are broken above the top label and the "X" numerals. The outer line at the bottom and the shells are partly cut away similar to type II.

15	A14 10c	**green,** type III, *1855*	5,500.	200.
		dark green	5,500.	200.
		yellowish green	5,500.	200.
		No gum	2,200.	
		On domestic cover		260.
		Pair	12,000.	450.
		Strip of 3	18,500.	775.
		Pair, types III, IV	40,000.	2,100.
		Double transfer at top and at bottom		—
		"Curl" on forehead (85L1)	6,000.	300.
		"Curl" to right of left "X" (87R1)	6,000.	300.

Earliest documented use: May 19, 1855.

Cancellations

Blue   +10.
Red   +25.
Orange red   +35.

Magenta   +100
Violet   +150
Brown   +75
Orange   —
Green   +200
1855 year date   —
1856 year date   +50
1857 year date   +10
1858 year date   +10
"Paid"   +25
Steamship   +75
U. S. Express Mail   +75
Express Company   +200
Packet boat   —
Canada (on cover)   +1000
Territorial   +150
Railroad   +75
Numeral   +50
Pen   90.

A15

Type IV — The outer lines have been recut at top or bottom or both.

16	A15 10c	**green,** type IV, *1855*	*35,000.*	1,600.
		dark green	*35,000.*	1,600.
		yellowish green	*35,000.*	1,600.
		No gum	*16,000.*	
		On domestic cover		1,900.
		Pair	—	4,250.
		Block of 4 (54-55, 64-65L)		

VARIETIES OF RECUTTING

Eight stamps on Plate 1 were recut. All are listed below.

Outer line recut at top (65L,
74L, 86L, and 3R, Plate 1) *35,000.* 1,600.
Outer line recut at bottom
(54L, 55L, 76L, Plate 1)   *36,500.* 1,700.
Outer line recut at top and
bottom (64L1)   *40,000.* 2,000.

Positions 65L1 and 86L1 have both "X" ovals recut at top, as well as the outer line.

Earliest documented use: June 4, 1855.

Cancellations

Blue   +75.
Red   +150.
Brown   —
1857 year date   —
1859 year date   —
"Paid"   +150.
Steamship   +300.
Territorial   +500.
Express Company   +750.
Numeral   +150.
Pen   900.

Types I, II, III and IV occur on the same sheet, so it is possible to obtain pairs and blocks showing combinations of types. For listings of type combinations in pairs and blocks, see Nos. 13-15.

Washington — A16

17	A16 12c	**black,** *July 1, 1851*	6,500.	350.
		gray black	6,500.	350.
		intense black	6,500.	350.
		No gum	2,400.	
		Single, on cover		1,500.
		Single on cover with No. 11 to France		1,150.
		Pair	15,000.	750.
		Pair, on cover to England		850.
		Block of 4	35,000.	5,500.
		Double transfer	6,750.	375.
		Triple transfer (5R1 & 49R1)	7,000.	500.
		Not recut in lower right corner	6,750.	375.
		Recut in lower left corner (43L, 53L, 63L, 73L and 100L, Plate 1)	6,750.	425.
		Cracked plate (32R1)		
		On part-India paper	—	1,100.
a.		Diagonal half used as 6c on cover		2,750.

Diagonal half used as 6c on		
"Via Nicaragua" cover		5,750.
b. Vertical half used as 6c on cover		8,500.
c. Printed on both sides		25,000.

Earliest documented use: Aug. 4, 1851.

Cancellations
Red	+20.
Orange red	+45.
Blue	+10.
Brown	+60.
Magenta	+75.
Orange	—
Green	+600.
"Paid"	+25.
"Way"	+75.
Steamship	+100.
Steamboat	+125.
Supplementary Mail Type A	+125.
Railroad	+100.
"Honolulu" in red (on cover)	+400.
U. S. Express Mail	+125.
Pen	175.

Please Note:
Stamps are valued in the grade of very fine unless otherwise indicated.

Values for early and valuable stamps are for examples with certificates of authenticity from acknowledged expert committees, or examples sold with the buyer having the right of certification. This applies to examples with original gum as well as examples without gum. Beware of stamps offered "as is," as the gum on some unused stamps offered with "original gum" may be fraudulent, and stamps offered as unused without gum may in some cases be altered or faintly canceled used stamps.

SAME DESIGNS AS 1851-57 ISSUES
Printed by Toppan, Carpenter & Co.

Nos. 18-39 have small or very small margins. The values take into account the margin size.

1857-61 · *Perf. 15½*

18	A5 1c **blue,** type I (Plate 12), *1861*	2,400.	650.
	No gum	950.	
	On cover		800.
	On patriotic cover		1,350.
	Pair	5,250.	1,400.
	Strip of 3	8,000.	2,400.
	Block of 4	13,500.	
	Pair, types I, II	4,000.	1,000.
	Pair, types I, IIIa	5,500.	1,300.
	Block of 4, types I, II	9,500.	5,250.
	Block of 4, types I, II, IIIa	10,500.	6,500.
	Double transfer	2,650.	700.
	Cracked plate (91R12)		900.

Plate 12 consists of types I & II. A few positions are type IIIa. Late printings of position 46L12 are type III.

Earliest documented use: Jan. 25, 1861.

Cancellations
Blue	+10.
Red	+35.
Violet	+100.
Steamboat	+100.
"Paid"	+25.
"Free"	+750.
Black Carrier	+85.
Red Carrier	+85.
Pen	325.

19	A6 1c **blue,** type Ia (Plate 4)	35,000.	10,000.
	No gum	17,500.	
	On cover		11,500.
	Pair	77,500.	22,500.
	Strip of 3	120,000.	36,000.
	Vertical pair, types Ia, III	57,500.	14,000.
	Vertical pair, types Ia, IIIa	42,500.	11,500.
	Pair, types Ia, Ic	—	—
	Strip of 3, types Ia, Ia, Ic	—	—
	Block of 4, types Ia, Ic, and IIIa	90,000.	
	Block of 4, pair type Ia and types III or IIIa	—	—
	"Curl on shoulder" (97L4)	37,500.	10,500.

Copies of this stamp exist with perforations not touching the design at any point. Such copies command very high prices.

Type Ia comes only from the bottom row of both panes of Plate 4.

Earliest documented use: Sept. 9, 1857. No. 19 is known on a folded circular with Aug. 1 postmark, but the year of use has not been certified.

Cancellations
Red Carrier	+200.
Green	+1,750.
Pen	4,250.

19b	A6 1c **blue,** type Ic ("E" relief, less distinct examples)	4,500.	2,250.
	No gum	2,100.	
	On cover		3,000.
	Horizontal pair (81-82R4)		
	Pair, types Ic, III	—	—
	Pair, types Ic, IIIa	—	—

---

blue, type Ic ("F" relief, best
  examples, 91, 96R4)   *20,000.*   7,000.
  No gum   *9,000.*
  On cover   8,000.

Type Ic — Same as Ia, but bottom right plume and ball ornament incomplete. Bottom left plume complete or nearly complete. Best examples are from bottom row, "F" relief, positions
91 and 96R4. Less distinct examples are "E" reliefs from 5th
and 9th rows, positions 47L, 49L, 83L, 49R, 81R, 82R, and
89R, Plate 4, and early impressions of 41R4. Several combination type multiples can be found in the unused complete left
pane of 100 from Plate 4.

Copies of the "F" relief type Ic stamps exist with perforations
not touching the design at any point. Such copies command a
substantial premium.

Cancellations

Pen ("E" relief)		*650.*
Pen ("F" relief)		*1,600.*

20	A7 1c **blue,** type II (Plate 2)	1,250.	275.
	No gum	525.	
	On cover		325.
	Pair	2,650.	625.
	Strip of 3	4,000.	950.
	Block of 4	*6,000.*	2,400.
	Double transfer (Plate 2)	1,300.	310.
	Double transfer (89R2)	*1,750.*	500.
	Cracked plate (2L, 12L, 13L,		
	23L & 33L, Plate 2)	3,000.	775.
	Plate 1L (4R1L only, double		
	transfer), *July 1857*		775.
	Pair, types II (4R1L), IV		2,000.
	Plate 4	3,250.	900.
	On cover		1,050.
	Pair	7,000.	1,900.
	Strip of 3		
	Double transfer (10R4)	3,500.	*1,450.*
	"Curl in hair" (3R, 4R4)		*1,000.*
	Plate 11	1,750.	500.
	On cover		400.
	On patriotic cover		775.
	Pair	3,000.	750.
	Strip of 3		
	Double transfer		
	Plate 12	1,200.	275.
	On cover		325.
	On patriotic cover		675.
	Pair	2,500.	600.
	Strip of 3	4,000.	950.
	Block of 4	*6,000.*	2,400.
	Double transfer		

Earliest documented uses: July 26, 1857 (Plate 2), July 26,
1857 (Plate 4), Jan. 12, 1861 (Plate 11), Jan. 21, 1861 (Plate
12).

No. 20, plate 2, is also known on two folded circulars dated
July 24 and July 25, respectively, but no postal year date or
docketing verifies the actual day of mailing.

Cancellations

Blue	+5.
Red	+20.
Green	+200.
1857 year date	+10.
1858 year date	+5.
1861 year date	+5.
"FREE"	—
1863 year date	+200.
"Paid"	+15.
Railroad	+60.
"Way"	+75.
Steamboat	+75.
Red Carrier	+35.
Black Carrier	+50.
Pen	135.

21	A8 1c **blue,** type III (Plate 4), see		
	below for 99R2	*17,500.*	2,750.
	No gum	*7,750.*	
	On cover		3,250.
	Pair	*40,000.*	6,250.
	Strip of 3		9,500.
	Block of 4		
	Pair, types III, IIIa	*22,500.*	3,500.
	Vertical pair, types III, II		
	Block of 4, types III, IIIa		
	Plate 12 (46L12)		
a.	Horiz. pair, imperf between		23,000.

Earliest documented use: Sept. 18, 1857.

Cancellations

Blue	+35.
Red	+60.
Green	+500.
1858 year date	+35.
"Paid"	+60.
Black Carrier	+175.
Red Carrier	+150.
Pen	1,350.

Values for type III are for at least a 2mm break in each outer
line. Examples of type III with wider breaks in outer lines command higher prices; those with smaller breaks sell for less.

No. 21a is unique and is contained in a strip of three. Value
reflects auction sale in 1999.

(21)	A8 1c **blue,** type III (99R2)		20,000.
	On cover		—
	Pair, types III (99R2), II		—
	Pair, types III (99R2), IIIa		—
	Strip of 3, types III (99R2),		
	II, IIIa		—
	Block of 9, one type III		
	(99R2), others type II	*110,000.*	

The only recorded unused copy is the one in the block of 9.
Only two covers are recorded bearing No. 21 (99R2).

Earliest documented use: Oct. 27, 1857.

22	A8 1c **blue,** type IIIa (Plate 4)	2,750.	550.

No gum	1,100.	
On cover		600.
On patriotic cover		900.
Pair	6,000.	1,200.
Vertical pair, types IIIa, II		*1,900.*
Strip of 3	9,000.	1,900.
Block of 4	13,000.	5,500.
Block of 4, types IIIa, II		
Double transfer	2,850.	600.
Plate 2 (100R)		
Plate 11 and Plate 12	2,850.	575.
On cover		625.
On patriotic cover		1,050.
Pair	6,250.	1,250.
Vert. pair, types IIIa, II		
(Plate 11)	5,500.	1,250.
Strip of 3	9,000.	1,800.
Strip of 3, types IIIa, II, I		
(46-48L12)		—
Block of 4	13,000.	
Block of 4, types IIIa, II		
(Plate 11)	12,500.	4,250.
Double transfer	3,000.	600.
Triple transfer (Plate 11)		—
Bottom line broken		
(46L12)		2,000.
b.	Horizontal pair, imperf. between		5,000.

One pair of No. 22b is reported. Beware of numerous pairs
that have blind perforations. These are not to be confused with
No. 22b.

Earliest documented uses: July 26, 1857 (Plate 4), Dec. 1860
(day unknown) (dated cancel on off-cover stamp) (Plate 11),
Dec. 31, 1860, (on cover) (Plate 11), Jan. 25, 1861 (Plate 12).

Cancellations

Blue	+5.
Red	+30.
Green	+250.
1857 year date	—
1858 year date	—
1861 year date	—
1863 year date	—
"Paid"	+25.
"Steamboat"	—
Red Carrier	+35.
Black Carrier	+50.
Blue Carrier	+100.
Pen	325.

23	A9 1c **blue,** type IV	9,000.	800.
	No gum	4,000.	
	On cover		1,000.
	Pair	20,000.	1,800.
	Strip of 3	30,000.	2,750.
	Block of 4		25,000.
	Double transfer	9,750.	850.
	Triple transfer, one inverted		
	(71L1L, 81L1L and 91L1L)	15,000.	4,000.
	Cracked plate	9,250.	925.
	Bottom line broken (89R1L)		1,550.

Three or four used blocks of No. 23 are presently known.
Value of used block of four is based on 1998 auction sale of the
well-centered block of 5 sold at auction in 1998. Other blocks
are poorly centered and will sell for much less.

VARIETIES OF RECUTTING

Recut once at top and once		
at bottom, (113 on plate)	9,000.	800.
Recut once at top, (40 on		
plate)	9,250.	825.
Recut once at top and twice		
at bottom, (21 on plate)	9,500.	825.
Recut twice at bottom, (11		
on plate)	9,250.	850.
Recut once at bottom, (8 on		
plate)	9,500.	875.
Recut twice at top and once		
at bottom, (4 on plate)	9,750.	900.
Recut twice at top and twice		
at bottom, (2 on plate)	10,000.	950.

One example of the "recut twice at top and once at bottom"
variety is pos. 71L1L, valued separately under the main listing.

Earliest documented use: July 25, 1857.

Cancellations

Blue	+5.
Red	+45.
1857 year date	+50.
"Paid"	+25.
Red Carrier	+80.
Black Carrier	+80.
Railroad	+100.
"Way"	+120.
"Steamboat"	+135.
"Steam"	+100.
Pen	425.

Franklin — A20

Type V — Similar to type III of 1851-57 but with side ornaments partly cut away. About one-half of all positions have side
scratches. Wide breaks in top and bottom framelines.

Type Va — Stamps from Plate 5 with almost complete ornaments at right side and no side scratches. Many, but not all,
stamps from Plate 5 are Type Va, the remainder being Type V.

24	A20 1c **blue,** type V (Plates 5, 7, 8, 9,		
	10) *1857*	180.00	45.00
	No gum	75.00	
	On cover		52.50
	On patriotic cover		300.00
	Pair	400.00	97.50
	Strip of 3	600.00	160.00
	Block of 4	800.00	425.00
	P# strip of 4, Impt.	1,400.	
	P# block of 8, Impt.	3,500.	—
	Double transfer at top (8R and		
	10R, Plate 8)	240.00	90.00
	Double transfer at bottom		
	(52R9)	300.00	100.00
	Curl on shoulder, (57R, 58R,		
	59R, 98R, 99R, Plate 7)	240.00	72.50
	With "Earring" below ear (10L9)	600.00	100.00
	"Curl" over "C" of "Cent"	250.00	72.50
	"Curl" over "E" of "Cent" (41R		
	and 81R8)	275.00	87.50
	"Curl in hair," 23L7; 39, 69L8;		
	34, 74R9	240.00	62.50
	"Curl" in "O" of "ONE" (62L5)		—
	Horizontal dash in hair (24L7)	350.00	90.00
	Horizontal dash in hair (36L8)	350.00	90.00
	Long double "curl" in hair (52,		
	92R8)	300.00	85.00
	Type Va	500.00	200.00
	On cover (Type Va)		300.00
	Pair (Type Va)		—
	Strip of 3 (Type Va)		—
	Block of 4 (Type Va)		—
	"Curl" on shoulder (48L5)		—
b.	Laid paper		1,750.

Earliest documented uses: Dec. 2, 1857 (Plate 5); Dec. 31,
1857 (Plate 7); Nov. 17, 1857 (Plate 8); Aug. 2, 1859 (Plate 9);
June 14, 1860 (Plate 10).

Cancellations

Blue	+2.50
Red	+15.00
Green	+250.00
Brown	+150.00
Magenta	+150.00
Ultramarine	+100.00
1857 year date	+70.00
1858 year date	+2.50
1859 year date	+2.50
1860 year date	+2.50
1861 year date	+2.50
1862 year date	—
1863 year date	+250.00
Printed Precancel "CUMBER-	
LAND, ME." (on cover)	—
"Paid"	+5.00
"Free"	+25.00
Railroad	+50.00
Numeral	+12.50
Express Company	+90.00
Steamboat	+55.00
"Steam"	+30.00
Steamship	+40.00
Packet boat	—
Supp. Mail Type A, B, or C	+55.00
"Way"	+30.00
Red Carrier	+20.00
Black Carrier	+12.50
Blue Carrier	+50.00
"Old Stamps-Not Recognized"	+1,500.
Territorial	+80.00
Pen	18.00

25	A10 3c **rose,** type I (no inner frame-		
	lines), (Plates 4, 6, 7, 8)	3,000.	125.00
	rose red	3,000.	125.00
	dull red	3,000.	125.00
	No gum	1,250.	
	On cover		140.00
	claret	3,250.	140.00
	No gum	1,300.	
	On patriotic cover		500.00
	Pair	6,500.	300.00
	Strip of 3	10,000.	475.00
	Block of 4	16,000.	7,000.
	Gash on shoulder	3,250.	130.00
	Double transfer	3,300.	160.00

Worn plate	3,000.	125.00
Major cracked plate (47R, 48R, Plate 1)	4,500.	600.00

b. Vert. pair, imperf. horizontally — 10,000.

All type I stamps were printed from 7 of the plates used for the imperfs., so many varieties exist both imperf. and perf.

VARIETIES OF RECUT STAMPS

Lines on bust and bottom of medallion circle recut (47R6)	—	1,400.
Recut inner lines (Plates 2L, 3, 5L)	4,500.	300.00
Recut inner line only at right (Plate 5L)		400.00
1 extra vertical line outside of left frame line (29L, 39L, 49L, 59L, 69L, 79L, Plate 3)	—	425.00
2 extra vertical lines outside of left frame line (89L, 99L, Plate 3)	—	450.00
1 extra vertical line outside of right frame line (58L, 68L, 78L, 88L, 98L, Plate 3)	—	425.00
No inner line and frame line close to design at right (9L, 19L, Plate 3)	—	450.00
No inner line and frame line close to design at left (70L, 80L, 90L, 100L, Plate 3)	—	425.00
Recut button (10R2L)		1,500.
Double transfer "Gents" instead of "Cents" (66R2L)	—	700.00
Triple transfer (92L2L)	—	700.00
Dot in lower right diamond block (69L5L)	—	350.00
Major cracked plate (84L, 94L, 9R, Plate 5L)	5,500.	600.00
Intermediate cracked plate (80L, 96L, 71R, Plate 5L)	5,000.	400.00
Minor cracked plate (8L, 27L, 31L, 44L, 45L, 51L, 55L, 65L, 74L, 78L, 79L, 7R, 71R, and 72R, Plate 5L)	4,750.	325.00

Except for "5 lines recut in upper left triangle" listed under No. 11 are found on No. 25.

Earliest documented use: Feb. 28, 1857 (Plate 7).

Cancellations

Blue	+1.50
Red	+5.00
Orange red	+15.00
Orange	+150.00
Brown	+100.00
Ultramarine	+100.00
Green	+200.00
1857 year date	+1.00
1858 year date	+1.00
1859 year date	+1.00
"Paid"	+2.50
"Way"	+20.00
Railroad	+25.00
Numeral	+7.50
"Steam"	+20.00
Steamship	+35.00
Steamboat	+45.00
Packet Boat	+50.00
Supplementary Mail Type A	+40.00
U. S. Express Mail	+5.00
Express Company	+65.00
Black Carrier	+30.00
"Old Stamps-Not Recognized"	+1,000.
Territorial	+50.00
Printed precancel "Cumberland, Me." (on cover)	—
Pen	55.00

Washington — A21

Type II — There are no outer frame lines at top and bottom. The side frame lines were recut so as to be continuous from the top to the bottom of the plate. Stamps from the top or bottom rows show the ends of the side frame lines and may be mistaken for Type IIa.

Type IIa — The side frame lines extend only to the top and bottom of the stamp design. All Type IIa stamps are from plates 10 and 11 (each of which exists in three states), and these plates produced only Type IIa. The side frame lines were recut individually for each stamp, thus being broken between the stamps vertically.

Beware of type II stamps with frame lines that stop at the top of the design (from top row of plate) or bottom of the design (from bottom row of plate). These are often offered as No. 26a.

26	A21	3c **dull red,** type II	75.00	8.00
		red	75.00	8.00
		rose	75.00	8.00
		No gum	27.50	
		brownish carmine	150.00	19.00
		No gum	57.50	
		claret	170.00	25.00
		No gum	70.00	
		orange brown	—	—
		plum	—	—
		On cover, dull red		9.50
		On cover, orange brown		950.00
		On patriotic cover		125.00
		On Confederate patriotic cover		2,000.
		On Pony express cover		
		Pair	160.00	19.00

Strip of 3	240.00	40.00
Block of 4	400.00	175.00
P# block of 8, Impt.	3,250.	
Double transfer	110.00	19.00
Double transfer, rosettes double and line through "Postage" and "Three Cents" (87R15)	—	1,000.
Left frame line double	110.00	19.00
Right frame line double	110.00	19.00
Cracked plate (62L, 71L, 72L, Plate 18)	750.00	250.00
Damaged transfer above lower left rosette	85.00	10.00
Same, retouched	105.00	11.00
Same, retouched with 2 vertical lines	140.00	12.00
Same, both damaged areas retouched	300.00	100.00
"Quadruple" plate flaw (18L28)	—	1,250.
1 line recut in upper left triangle	—	30.00
5 lines recut in upper left triangle (52L25)		500.00
Inner line recut at left		500.00
Inner line recut at right	—	350.00
Worn plate	85.00	8.50

b. Horiz. pair, imperf. vertically 4,000.
c. Vert. pair, imperf. horizontally 12,000.
d. Horizontal pair, imperf. between —
e. Double impression 2,500.

Frame line double varieties are separate and distinct for virtually the entire length of the stamp. Copies with partly split lines are worth considerably less.

Earliest documented use: Sept. 14, 1857.

Cancellations

Blue	+.25
Red	+1.50
Orange red	+2.50
Orange	+150.00
Brown	+100.00
Ultramarine	+100.00
Violet	+100.00
Green	+150.00
1857 year date	+3.00
1858-1861 year date	+.25
Printed Circular Precancel "Cumberland, Me." (on cover)	—
"Paid"	+.50
"Paid All"	+15.00
"Free"	+20.00
"Collect"	+40.00
Numeral	+2.50
"Steam"	+12.50
Steamer	
Steamboat	+22.50
Steamship	+22.50
"Way"	+12.50
Railroad	+15.00
U. S. Express Mail	+20.00
Express Company	+65.00
Packet boat	+65.00
Supp. Mail Type A, B or C	+100.00
Black Carrier	+30.00
Red Carrier	+25.00
"Southn. Letter Unpaid"	—
Territorial	+20.00
"Old Stamps-Not Recognized"	+500.00
Pen	3.25

26a	A21	3c **dull red,** type IIa	300.00	75.00
		brownish carmine	300.00	75.00
		rose	300.00	75.00
		No gum	100.00	
		claret	325.00	85.00
		No gum	110.00	
		On cover		110.00
		On patriotic cover		350.00
		Pair	650.00	200.00
		Strip of 3	1,250.	350.00
		Block of 4	4,000.	1,500.
		P# block of 8, Impt.	10,000.	
		Double transfer	400.00	150.00
		Double transfer, line through rosettes (61R10i, 61R10L, 98R10i, 98R10L)	—	750.00
		Double transfer of rosettes and lower part of stamp (91R11L)	—	220.00
		Triple transfer	—	425.00
		Damaged transfer above lower left rosette	350.00	95.00
		Same, retouched	325.00	90.00
		Same, both damaged areas retouched		275.00
		Inner line recut at right		275.00
		Inner line recut at left (79L10)		475.00
		Left frame line double (70, 80, 90, 100R11)	—	170.00
		Worn plate	300.00	75.00

f. Horiz. strip of 3, imperf. vert., on cover 14,500.

No. 26f is unique.

Earliest documented use: July 11, 1857.

Cancellations

Blue	+2.50
Red	+10.00
Orange red	+15.00
Orange	+150.00
Brown	+100.00
Ultramarine	+100.00

Violet	+150.0
Green	+175.0
1857 year date	+2.5
1858 or 1859 year date	+1.5
"Paid"	+2.5
"Paid All"	+15.0
"Free"	+20.0
"Collect"	+40.0
Numeral	+2.5
"Steam"	+15.0
Steamer	
Steamboat	+25.0
Steamship	+25.0
"Way"	+15.0
Railroad	+17.5
U. S. Express Mail	+17.5
Express Company	+65.0
Packet boat	+65.0
Black Carrier	+30.0
Red Carrier	+20.0
Territorial	+30.0
Pen	27.50

27	A11	5c **brick red,** type I, *1858*	30,000.	1,700.
		No gum	12,500.	
		On cover		2,100.
		On patriotic cover		5,000.
		Pair	65,000.	4,000.
		Strip of 3		6,250.
		Block of 4	175,000.	40,000.
		Defective transfer (23R1)	—	

The unused block of 4 is unique.

Earliest documented use: Oct. 6, 1858.

Cancellations

Blue	+150.
Red	+175.
Ultramarine	+450.
1859 year date	+50.
1860 year date	+50.
"Paid"	+50.
Supplementary Mail Type A	+150.
"Steamship"	+150.
Pen	950.

28	A11	5c **red brown,** type I	6,500.	1,150.
		pale red brown	6,500.	1,150.
		No gum	2,600.	
		On cover		1,350.
		Pair	14,000.	2,600.
		Strip of 3		4,000.
		Block of 4	50,000.	7,750.
		Defective transfer (23R1)	—	
b.		**Bright red brown**	7,000.	1,500.
		No gum	3,100.	

Earliest documented use: Aug. 23, 1857 (No. 28).

Cancellations

Blue	+25.
Ultramarine	
Red	+45.
1857 year date	+20.
1858 year date	+15.
"Paid"	+35.
Railroad	+75.
"Short Paid"	
Pen	500.

28A	A11	5c **Indian red,** type I, *1858*	80,000.	3,500.
		No gum	25,000.	
		On cover		5,000.
		Pair		7,500.
		Strip of 3		12,500.
		Block of 4		

There are only three recorded examples of No. 28A with any amount of original gum. Value is for a fine stamp, the highest recorded grade (two thus).

Earliest documented use: Mar. 31, 1858.

Cancellations

Red	+75.
Blue	+100.
1858 year date	+50.
1859 year date	+25.
Pen	1,750.

29	A11	5c **brown,** type I, *1859*	3,000.	425.
		pale brown	3,000.	425.
		deep brown	3,000.	425.
		yellowish brown	3,000.	425.
		No gum	1,250.	
		On cover		550.
		Pair	6,500.	900.
		Strip of 3	10,500.	1,450.
		Block of 4	38,500.	5,000.
		Defective transfer (23R1)	—	

Earliest documented use: Mar. 21, 1859.

Cancellations

Blue	+10.
Ultramarine	
Red	+25.
Brown	+75.
Magenta	+125.
Green	+350.
1859 year date	+10.
1860 year date	+10.
"Paid"	+15.
"Steam"	+75.
Steamship	+100.
Numeral	+80.
Pen	185.

WE DON'T ALWAYS GET OUTSTANDING RESULTS.
SOMETIMES THEY'RE SIMPLY AMAZING.

#11X2 Cat. $6,000

Realized $20,900

#2 Cat. $1,350

Realized $7,425

#292 Cat. $3,250

Realized $35,750

#16 Cat. $1,600

Realized $8,800

#21 Cat. $2,750

Realized $9,350

#78 Cat. $200

Realized $6,325

#10 Cat. $200   **Realized $29,700**

#85B Cat. $1,300

Realized $10,450

#89 Cat. $325

Realized $4,950

#460 Cat. $1,850

Realized $28,600

#1 Cat. $550

Realized $20,900

#101 Cat. $1,750

Realized $38,500

#10 Cat. $130

Realized $5,775

There's a price to pay for not choosing the right auction house. And there's a reward if you make the right choice.

Rumsey Auctions has the keen knowledge, experience and integrity to make sure you get the highest prices for your stamps. Let us show you how much we can do for you.

Jefferson — A22

FIVE CENTS.
Type II — The projections at top and bottom are partly cut away. Several minor types could be made according to the extent of cutting of the projections.

30	A22	5c **orange brown**, Type II,		
		1861	1,250.	1,300.
		deep orange brown	1,250.	1,300.
		No gum	550.	
		On cover		*2,400.*
		On patriotic cover		
		Pair	2,600.	*3,250.*
		Strip of 3	4,100.	
		Block of 4	6,500.	—

Earliest documented use: May 8, 1861.

Cancellations

Blue	+30.
Red	+75.
Green	—
"Paid"	+75.
Steamship	+110.
Supplementary Mail Type A	+150.
Railroad	—
Pen	700.

30A	A22	5c **brown**, type II, *1860*	2,250.	325.
		dark brown	2,250.	325.
		yellowish brown	2,250.	325.
		No gum	975.	
		On cover		375.
		On patriotic cover		
		Pair	4,850.	675.
		Strip of 3	7,500.	1,050.

	Block of 4	11,500.	3,250.
	Cracked plate	—	
b.	Printed on both sides		40,000.

Earliest documented use: May 4, 1860.

Cancellations

Blue	+5.
Red	+20.
Magenta	+75.
Green	+350.
"Paid"	+20.
Supplementary Mail Type A	+50.
"Steamship"	+50.
"Steam"	+40.
Express Company	+250.
Railroad	—
Packet boat	—
Pen	160.

31	A12	10c **green**, type I	25,000.	1,200.
		dark green	26,000.	1,200.
		bluish green	25,000.	1,200.
		yellowish green	25,000.	1,200.
		No gum	10,000.	
		On domestic cover		1,400.
		On patriotic cover		3,250.
		Pair	55,000.	2,600.
		Vertical pair, types III, I	35,000.	1,600.
		Vertical pair, types IV, I (86, 96 L I)		—
		Strip of 3		—
		Vertical strip of 3, types II, III, I		—
		Block of 4, types III, I	60,000.	
		Block of 4, types III, IV, I		9,500.
		Vertical block of 6, 2 each types II, III, I	80,000.	
		Double transfer (100R1)	27,500.	1,300.
		"Curl" in left "X" (99R1)	27,500.	1,300.

Type I comes only from the bottom row of both panes of Plate 1.

Earliest documented use: Aug. 25, 1857.

Cancellations

Blue	+15.
Red	+50.
Green	+500.
Supplementary Mail Type A	—
"Steamship"	+100.
Canadian	—
Pen	650.

Act of February 27, 1861. Ten cent rate of postage to be prepaid on letters conveyed in the mail from any point in the United States east of the Rocky Mountains to any State or Territory on the Pacific Coast and vice versa, for each half-ounce.

32	A13	10c **green**, type II	6,500.	300.
		dark green	6,500.	300.
		bluish green	6,500.	300.
		yellowish green	6,500.	300.
		No gum	2,750.	
		On domestic cover		350.
		On pony express cover		8,500.
		Pair	13,500.	625.
		Strip of 3	—	950.
		Block of 4	30,000.	4,500.
		Pair, types II, III	13,500.	700.
		Pair, types II, IV	47,500.	2,700.
		Vertical strip of 3, types II, III, IV		—
		Block of 4, types II, III	30,000.	3,500.
		Block of 4, types II, IV		—
		Block of 4, types II, III, IV	95,000.	18,000.
		Double transfer (31L, 51L and 20R, Plate 1)	6,750.	325.
		"Curl opposite left X" (10R1)		375.

Earliest documented use: July 27, 1857 (dated cancel on off-cover stamp).

Cancellations

Blue	+10.
Red	+30.
Brown	+125.
Green	+300.
"Paid"	+20.
1857 year date	+10.
Supplementary Mail Type A	—
Steamship	+50.
Packet boat	—
Railroad	—
Express Company	—
Pen	160.

33	A14	10c **green**, type III	6,500.	300.
		dark green	6,500.	300.
		bluish green	6,500.	300.
		yellowish green	6,500.	300.
		No gum	2,750.	
		On domestic cover		350.
		Pair	13,500.	625.
		Strip of 3	—	950.
		Pair, types III, IV		2,700.
		"Curl" on forehead (85L1)		375.
		"Curl in left X" (87R1)		375.

Earliest documented use: Oct. 6, 1857.

Cancellations

Blue	+10.
Red	+30.
Brown	+125.
Ultramarine	+100.
1857 year date	+10.
"Paid"	+20.
"Steam"	+45.
Steamboat	—
Steamship	+50.
Numeral	+15.

		Packet boat		—
		Pen		160.
34	A15	10c **green**, type IV	45,000.	2,250.
		dark green	45,000.	2,250.
		bluish green	45,000.	2,250.
		yellowish green	45,000.	2,250.
		No gum	22,500.	
		On domestic cover		2,650.
		Pair		*5,750.*
		Block of 4 (54-55, 64-65L)		

VARIETIES OF RECUTTING

Eight stamps on Plate I were recut. All are listed below.

Outer line recut at top (65L, 74L, 86L and 3R, Plate I)	37,500.	2,250.
Outer line recut at bottom (54L, 55L, 76L, Plate 1)	39,000.	2,300.
Outer line recut at top and bottom (64L1)	41,000.	2,350.

Earliest documented use: Oct. 5, 1857.

Cancellations

Blue	+40.
Red	+75.
Steamship	+200.
Packet boat	—
Pen	1,250.

Types I, II, III and IV occur on the same sheet, so it is possible to obtain pairs and blocks showing combinations of types. For listings of type combinations in pairs and blocks, see Nos. 31-33.

Washington (Two typical examples) — A23

Type V — The side ornaments are slightly cut away. Usually only one pearl remains at each end of the lower label, but some copies show two or three pearls at the right side. At the bottom the outer line is complete and the shells nearly so. The outer lines at top are complete except over the right "X."

35	A23	10c **green**, type V, (Plate 2),		
		1859	275.00	65.00
		dark green	275.00	65.00
		yellowish green	275.00	65.00
		No gum	110.00	
		On domestic cover		77.50
		On patriotic cover		625.00
		On pony express cover		—
		On cover to Canada		125.00
		Pair	575.00	140.00
		Block of 4	1,200.	650.00
		P# block of 8, Impt.	*17,500.*	
		Double transfer at bottom (47R2)	350.00	90.00
		Small "Curl" on forehead (37, 78L2)	325.00	77.50
		Curl in "e" of "cents" (93L2)	350.00	90.00
		Curl in "t" of "cents" (73R2)	350.00	90.00
		Cracked plate	—	

Earliest documented use: Apr. 29, 1859.

Cancellations

Red	+7.50
Orange red	+12.50
Brown	+100.00
Blue	+5.00
Orange	+150.00
Magenta	+100.00
Green	+250.00
1859 year date	+5.00
"Paid"	+5.00
"Paid All"	—
Red carrier	—
Railroad	+40.00
Steamship	+35.00
"Steam"	+30.00
Numerals	+15.00
Supp. Mail Type A or C	+60.00
Express Company	+135.00
"Southn Letter Unpaid"	—
Territorial	—
Pen	30.00

TWELVE CENTS. Printed from two plates.
Plate I — Outer frame lines complete. Very narrow spacing of stamps on the plate.
Plate III — Outer frame lines noticeably uneven or broken, sometimes partly missing. Somewhat wider spacing of stamps on the plate.

36	A16	12c **black** (Plate 1)	2,000.	350.
		gray black	2,000.	350.
		No gum	875.	

Single on cover			625.
Single on cover with No. 26			
to France			400.
Pair on cover to England			800.
Pair on patriotic cover			
Pair		4,500.	750.
Block of 4		11,000.	2,500.
Not recut in lower right corner			
ner		2,150.	375.
Recut in lower left corner			
(43, 53, 63, 73, 100L)		2,200.	360.
Double transfer		2,200.	375.
Triple transfer		2,400.	—
a. Diagonal half used as 6c on cover			17,500.
c. Horizontal pair, imperf. between			12,500.

Earliest documented use: July 30, 1857.

Cancellations

Blue	+5.
Red	+10.
Brown	+75.
Magenta	+55.
Green	+250.
1857 year date	+20.
"Paid"	+10.
Supplementary Mail Type A	+60.
Express Company	—
Railroad	+60.
Numeral	+20.
"Southn Letter Unpaid"	—
Pen	150.

36b	A16	12c **black** (Plate 3)	825.	225.
		intense black	825.	225.
		No gum	360.	
		Single on cover		650.
		Single on cover with No. 26		
		to France		325.
		Pair on cover to England		550.
		Pair	1,700.	500.
		Block of 4	5,000.	2,400.
		Double frame line at right	875.	250.
		Double frame line at left	875.	250.
		Vertical line through rosette		
		(95R3)	1,000.	300.

Earliest documented use: June 1, 1860. (The previously listed Dec. 3, 1859, cover requires expertization in order to be considered.)

Washington — A17

Franklin — A18

37	A17	24c **gray lilac**, *1860*	1,700.	400.
a.		24c **gray**	1,700.	400.
		No gum	650.	
		On cover to England		1,050.
		On patriotic cover		*4,000.*
		Pair	3,750.	875.
		Block of 4, gray lilac	9,750.	6,500.
		P# block of 12, Impt.	32,500.	

The technical configuration of a No. 37 plate block is eight stamps. The unique plate block currently is contained in the listed block of twelve stamps.

Earliest documented use: July 7, 1860.

Cancellations

Blue	+10.
Red	+40.
Magenta	+80.
Violet	+110.
Green	+450.
1860 year date	+15.
"Paid"	+25.
"Paid All"	+50.
"Free"	+100.
Supplementary Mail Type A	+150.
Railroad	+150.
Packet Boat	+200.
Red Carrier	—
Numeral	+40.
"Southn Letter Unpaid"	—
Pen	190.

See Trial Color Proofs for the 24c red lilac.

38	A18	30c **orange**, *1860*	2,250.	500.
		yellow orange	2,250.	500.
		reddish orange	2,250.	500.
		No gum	950.	
		On cover to Germany or		
		France		*1,350.*
		On patriotic cover		*9,000.*
		Pair	5,000.	1,100.
		Block of 4	13,000.	6,750.
		Double transfer (89L1 and		
		99L1)	2,500.	575.
		Recut at bottom (52L1)	2,700.	625.
		Cracked plate	—	—

Earliest documented use: Aug. 8, 1860.

Cancellations

Blue	+20.
Red	+40.
Magenta	+90.
Violet	+200.
Green	+1000.
1860 year date	+30.
"Paid"	+35.
"Free"	—
Black town	+30.
Supplementary Mail Type A	+125.
Steamship	—
Express Company	—
Pen	250.

Washington — A19

39	A19	90c **blue**, *1860*	3,500.	9,000.
		deep blue	3,500.	9,000.
		No gum	1,500.	
		On cover		225,000.
		Pair	7,000.	
		Block of 4	30,000.	45,000.
		Double transfer at bottom	3,750.	—
		Double transfer at top	3,750.	—
		Short transfer at bottom		
		right and left (13L1 and		
		68R1)	3,750.	

The used block of 4 is believed to be unique and has perfs trimmed off at left and bottom clear of design. Value is based on 1993 auction sale.

Earliest documented use: Sept. 11, 1860.

Cancellations

Red	8,000.
Black	+200.
Blue	+300.
Red town	+1,000.
Black town	+1,000.
1861 year date	+1,000.
Boston "Paid"	+750.

Red Carrier	—
N.Y. Ocean Mail	+1,000.
Pen	2,750.

Genuine cancellations on the 90c are very scarce. All used examples of No. 39 must be accompanied by certificates of authenticity issued by recognized expertizing committees.

See Die and Plate Proofs for imperfs. on stamp paper.

REPRINTS OF 1857-60 ISSUE

These were not valid for postal use, though one example each of Nos. 43 and 45 are known with contemporaneous cancels.
Produced by the Continental Bank Note Co.
White paper, without gum.
The 1, 3, 10 and 12c were printed from new plates of 100 subjects each differing from those used for the regular issue.

1875					Perf. 12	
40	A5	1c	**bright blue** (3846)		625.	
			Pair		1,350.	
			Block of 4		3,500.	
			Cracked plate, pos. 91		775.	
			Double transfer, pos. 94		775.	
41	A10	3c	**scarlet** (479)		3,250.	
42	A22	5c	**orange brown** (878)		1,400.	
			Pair		3,250.	
			Vertical margin strip of 4, Impt. & P#		11,500.	
43	A12	10c	**blue green** (516)		3,000.	—
			Pair		7,000.	
44	A16	12c	**greenish black** (489)		3,250.	
			Pair		7,500.	
45	A17	24c	**blackish violet** (479)		3,250.	—
46	A18	30c	**yellow orange** (480)		3,250.	
47	A19	90c	**deep blue** (454)		4,750.	

Nos. 41-46 are valued in the grade of fine.
Nos. 40-47 exist imperforate. Value, set of singles, $25,000. One set of imperforate pairs is recorded. A horizontal strip of 3 of No. 44 also is recorded.
Numbers in parentheses are quantities sold.

Produced by the National Bank Note Co.

Franklin — A24

Washington — A25

Jefferson — A26

Washington — A27

A27a

A27

Washington — A28

A29   A30
Washington   Franklin

Washington — A31

1c — There is a dash under the tip of the ornament at right of the numeral in upper left corner.
3c — Ornaments at corners end in a small ball.
5c — There is a leaflet in the foliated ornaments at each corner.
10c (A27) — A heavy curved line has been cut below the stars and an outer line added to the ornaments above them.
12c — There are corner ornaments consisting of ovals and scrolls.
90c — Parallel lines form an angle above the ribbon with "U. S. Postage"; between these lines there is a row of dashes and a point of color at the apex of the lower line.

Patriotic Covers covering a wide range of historical interest were used during the Civil War period, in the North as well as the South, and are collected in State groups as well as generally, both used and unused. There are believed to be as many as 12,000 varieties.
During the war, these stamps were used as small change until Postage Currency was issued.
The Act of Congress of March 3, 1863, effective July 1, 1863, created a rate of three cents for each half ounce, first class domestic mail. This Act was the first law which established uniform rate of postage regardless of the distance. This rate remained in effect until Oct. 1, 1883.

Plates of 200 subjects in two panes of 100 each.

The following items, formerly listed here as Nos. 55-62, are considered to be essays or trial color proofs. They will be found in their respective sections as follows. Previous No. 58 has been combined with No. 62B.

Formerly	Currently	Formerly	Currently
55	63-E11e	59	69-E6e
56	65-E15h	60	70eTC
57	67-E9e	61	71bTC
58	62B	62	72-E7h

The paper of Nos. 62B-72 is thicker and more opaque than the essays and trial color proofs, except Nos. 62B, 70c, and 70d.

1861					Perf. 12	
62B	A27a	10c	**dark green**		8,000.	1,350.
			dark yellow green		8,000.	1,350.
			No gum		3,750.	
			On cover			1,700.
			On patriotic cover			2,900.
			Pair		17,500.	3,000.
			Block of 4		37,500.	12,500.
			Foreign entry 94R4		9,250.	
			Block of 4, one stamp 94R4			

The foreign entry is of the 90c 1861.

Earliest documented use: Sept. 17, 1861.

Cancellations

Red	+80
Blue	+50
"Paid"	+60
Steamship	+100
Express Company	+200
Supplementary Mail Type A	+125

1861-62						Perf. 12
63	A24	1c	**blue,** *Aug. 17, 1861*		375.00	50.00
			pale blue		375.00	50.00
			bright blue		375.00	50.00
			No gum		140.00	
			On cover (single)			57.50
			On prisoner's letter			225.00
			On patriotic cover			225.00
			Pair		800.00	105.00
			Block of 4		1,750.	500.00
			P# block of 8, Impt.		6,500.	
			Double transfer		—	62.50
			Dot in "U"		400.00	55.00
a.			1c **ultramarine**		2,200.	600.00
			No gum		1,000.	
b.			1c **dark blue**		750.00	300.00
			No gum		275.00	
c.			Laid paper, horiz. or vert.		6,000.	4,000.
d.			Vertical pair, imperf. horiz.			
e.			Printed on both sides		—	4,000.

Earliest documented use: Aug. 17, 1861 (dated cancel on off-cover stamp); Aug. 21, 1861 (on cover).

Cancellations

Blue	+2.00
Red	+7.50
Magenta	+50.00
Green	+250.00
Violet	+50.00
1861 year date	+7.50
1865 year date	+2.00
1866 year date	+2.00
"Free"	+40.00
"Paid"	+2.50
"Paid All"	+15.00
Supp. Mail Type A or B	+30.00
Steamship	+35.00
Steam	+30.00
Express Company	+175.00
Red Carrier	+10.00
Black Carrier	+10.00
Railroad	+30.00
Numeral	+10.00
"Steamboat"	+50.00
Printed Precancel "CUM-BERLAND, ME."	

64	A25	3c	**pink,** *Aug. 17, 1861*		14,000.	950.00
			No gum		5,500.	
			On cover			1,050.
			On patriotic cover			1,250.
			Pair		30,000.	2,250.
			Block of 4		65,000.	

Earliest documented use: Aug. 17, 1861 (FDC).

Cancellations

Blue	+25.00
Red	+90.00
Green	+500.00
1861 date	
"Paid"	+25.00
"Free"	+175.00
"Ship"	+85.00
Supplementary Mail Type B	+150.00
Railroad	+125.00
Steamboat	+175.00

a.			3c **pigeon blood pink**		30,000.	3,750.
			No gum		13,000.	
			On cover			4,500.
			On patriotic cover			6,750.

Earliest documented use: Aug. 21, 1861.

b.			3c **rose pink,** *Aug. 17, 1861*		600.00	160.00
			No gum		260.00	
			On cover			190.00
			On patriotic cover			250.00
			Pair		1,350.	350.00
			Block of 4		3,250.	875.00

Earliest documented use: Aug. 17, 1861 (FDC).

Cancellations

Blue	+10.00
Red	+20.00
Orange red	+25.00
Green	+150.00
Orange	
"Paid"	+10.00
"Free"	+75.00
Supplementary Mail Type C	
"Ship"	+30.00
Railroad	+60.00
Steamboat	+90.00

65	A25	3c	**rose**		150.00	3.00
			bright rose		150.00	3.00
			dull red		150.00	3.00
			rose red		150.00	3.00
			No gum		50.00	
			On cover			3.50
			On patriotic cover			40.00
			On prisoner's letter			150.00
			On pony express cover			
			Pair		325.00	6.75
			Block of 4		700.00	42.50
			P# block of 8, Impt.		4,250.	
			Double transfer		175.00	6.00
			Cracked plate		—	
			brown red		290.00	5.50
			No gum		115.00	
			pale brown red		225.00	5.50

	No gum	85.00	
	dull brown red	260.00	5.50
	No gum	105.00	
	Block of 4	1,300.	
	deep pinkish rose	290.00	25.00
	On cover		
b.	Laid paper, horiz. or vert.	—	500.00
d.	Vertical pair, imperf. horiz.	6,000.	750.00
e.	Printed on both sides	22,500.	5,000.
	Pair	47,500.	
f.	Double impression		7,500.

See Die and Plate Proofs for imperfs. on stamp paper.

Earliest documented use: Aug. 19, 1861.

Cancellations

Blue	+.25
Ultramarine	+2.75
Brown	+50.00
Red	+3.00
Orange red	+3.50
Violet	+35.00
Magenta	+8.00
Green	+100.00
Olive	+100.00
Orange	+150.00
Yellow	+3,500.
1861 year date	+.50
1867 or 1868 year date	+.50
"Paid"	+.35
"Paid All"	+7.50
"Mails Suspended"	—
Railroad	+12.50
"Way"	+20.00
"Free"	+20.00
"Collect"	+35.00
"Ship"	+15.00
"U. S. Ship"	+35.00
"Steam"	+12.00
Steamship	+15.00
Steamboat	+20.00
"Ship Letter"	+35.00
Red Carrier	+15.00
Blue Carrier	+25.00
Black Carrier	+20.00
Supplementary Mail Type A, B or C	+15.00
Numeral	+3.00
Express Company	+90.00
Army Field Post	+60.00
Packet Boat	+40.00
"Registered"	+30.00
"Postage Due"	+25.00
"Advertised"	+15.00
Territorial	+25.00
St. Thomas	—
China	—

The 3c lake can be found under No. 66 in the Trial Color Proofs section.

67	A26	5c **buff**	21,000.	1,050.
		No gum	9,500.	
		On cover		1,300.
		On patriotic cover		4,000.
		Pair	45,000.	2,250.
		Block of 4	11,500.	12,500.
a.		5c **brown yellow**	25,000.	1,100.
		No gum	11,000.	
b.		5c **olive yellow**		2,000.

The unused block of 4 is unique but very faulty. Value is based on actual 1993 sale.

Earliest documented uses: Aug. 19, 1861 (No. 67); Aug. 21, 1861 (No. 67a).

Cancellations

Red	+40.00
Blue	+20.00
Magenta	+125.00
Green	—
1861 year date	+10.00
"Paid"	+25.00
Supplementary Mail Type A	+100.00
Express Company	+250.00
Numeral	+50.00
"Steamship"	+100.00

Values of Nos. 67, 67a, 67b reflect the normal small margins.

68	A27	10c **green**	1,200.	55.00
		yellow green	1,200.	55.00
		No gum	475.	
		On cover		70.00
		On patriotic cover		375.00
		On cover to Canada		95.00
		Pair	2,500.	120.00
		Block of 4	5,500.	625.00
		P# block of 8, Impt.	12,500.	
		Double transfer	1,300.	60.00
		deep yellow green on thin paper	1,350.	65.00
a.		10c **dark green**	1,300.	65.00
		blue green	1,300.	67.50
		No gum	525.	
b.		Vertical pair, imperf. horiz.		3,500.

Earliest documented use: Aug. 20, 1861.

Cancellations

Blue	+2.00
Red	+5.00
Purple	+50.00
Magenta	+50.00
Brown	+50.00
Green	+250.00
1865 year date	+3.50

"Paid"	+2.50
"Collect"	+32.50
"Short Paid"	+50.00
"P.D." in circle	+30.00
"Free"	+25.00
Numeral	+7.50
Red Carrier	+45.00
Railroad	+20.00
Steamship	+15.00
"Steamboat"	+35.00
Supplementary Mail Type A	+30.00
Red Supp. Mail Type D	
Express Company	+70.00
China	
Japan	+200.00
St. Thomas	

> **Stamps are valued in the grade of very fine unless otherwise indicated.**

Please Note:

Values for early and valuable stamps are for examples with certificates of authenticity from acknowledged expert committees, or examples sold with the buyer having the right of certification.

This applies to examples with original gum as well as examples without gum.

Beware of stamps offered "as is," as the gum on some unused stamps offered with "original gum" may be fraudulent, and stamps offered as unused without gum may in some cases be altered or faintly canceled used stamps.

69	A28	12c **black**	2,100.	110.00
		gray black	2,100.	120.00
		No gum	875.	
		intense black	2,200.	125.00
		No gum	900.	
		On domestic cover		150.00
		On patriotic cover		900.00
		On cover to France or Germany with #65		170.00
		Pair	4,750.	260.00
		Block of 4	10,500.	1,100.
		Double transfer of top frame line	2,200.	140.00
		Double transfer of bottom frame line	2,200.	140.00
		Double transfer of top and bottom frame lines	2,300.	145.00

Earliest documented use: Aug. 30, 1861.

Cancellations

Blue	+2.50
Red	+20.00
Purple	+50.00
Magenta	+100.00
Green	+550.00
1861 year date	+5.00
"Paid"	+5.00
"Registered"	+35.00
Supp. Mail Type A, B or C	+45.00
Express Company	+175.00
Railroad	+50.00
Numeral	+15.00

70	A29	24c **red lilac**	2,750.	300.00
		No gum	1,100.	
		On cover		350.00
		On patriotic cover		3,000.
		Pair	6,000.	625.00
		Block of 4	14,500.	3,000.
		Scratch under "A" of "Postage"		—
a.		24c **brown lilac**	2,750.	225.00
		No gum	1,100.	
		Block of 4	14,500.	3,500.
b.		24c **steel blue** ('61)	11,000.	900.00
		No gum	4,500.	
		On cover		1,350.
		Block of 4	55,000.	
c.		24c **violet**, thin paper, Aug. 20, 1861	35,000.	1,700.
		No gum	14,000.	
d.		24c **pale gray violet**, thin paper	17,500.	2,500.
		No gum	6,000.	

There are numerous shades of the 24c stamp in this and the following issue.

Color changelings, especially of No. 78, are frequently offered as No. 70b. Obtaining a certificate from an acknowledged expert committee is strongly advised.

Nos. 70c and 70d are on a thinner, harder and more transparent paper than Nos. 70, 70a, 70b or the latter Nos. 78, 78a, 78b and 78c. No. 70eTC (formerly No. 60, see Trial Color Proofs section) is distinguished by its distinctive dark color.

Earliest documented uses: Jan. 7, 1862 (No. 70); Feb. 5, 1862 (No. 70a); Sept. 21, 1861 (No. 70b); Aug. 20, 1861 (No. 70c); Sept. 10, 1861 (No. 70d).

Cancellations, No. 70

Blue	+5.00
Red	+15.00
Magenta	+200.00
Brown	+125.00
Green	+300.00
1865 year date	+5.00
"Paid"	+15.00
Supp. Mail Types A or B	+75.00
Express Company	+350.00

71	A30	30c **orange**	2,250.	200.
		deep orange	2,250.	200.
		No gum	900.	

	On cover to France or Germany		400
	On patriotic cover		3,500
	Pair	4,750.	450
	Block of 4	15,000.	2,500
	P# strip of 4, Impt.		—
a.	Printed on both sides		—

Values for No. 71 are for copies with small margins, especially at sides. Large-margined examples sell for much more.

Earliest documented use: Aug. 20, 1861.

Cancellations

Blue	+10.00
Magenta	+100.00
Brown	+100.00
Red	+25.00
"Paid"	+15.00
"Paid All"	+35.00
Railroad	—
Packet Boat	—
"Steamship"	+75.00
Supplementary Mail Type A	+75.00
Red Supp. Mail Type D	—
Express Company	+350.00
Japan	—

72	A31	90c **blue**	3,500.	500
		dull blue	3,500.	500.
		No gum	1,500.	
		On cover		25,000.
		Pair	7,500.	1,100.
		Block of 4	28,000.	5,000.
		P# strip of 4, Impt.	25,000.	
a.		90c **pale blue**	3,500.	500.
		No gum	1,500.	
b.		90c **dark blue**	4,250.	650.
		No gum	1,800.	

The unique plate number and imprint strip of 4 of No. 72 has no gum and is valued thus.

Earliest documented use: Nov. 27, 1861.

Cancellations

Blue	+15.
Red	+40.
Green	+750.
1865 year date	+35.
"Paid"	+25.
"Registered"	+75.
Express Company	+500.
Supplementary Mail Type A	+100.

Nos. 68a, 69, 71 and 72 exist as imperforate sheet-margin singles with pen cancel. They were not regularly issued.

The 90c was distributed to several post offices in the last two weeks of August, 1861.

Owing to the Civil War, stamps and stamped envelopes in current use or available for postage in 1860, were demonetized by various post office orders, beginning in August, 1861, and extending to early January, 1862.

P. O. Department Bulletin.

"A reasonable time after hostilities began in 1861 was given for the return to the Department of all these (1851-56) stamps in the hands of postmasters, and as early as 1863 the Department issued an order declining to longer recognize them."

The Act of Congress, approved March 3, 1863, abolished carriers' fees and established a prepaid rate of two cents for drop letters, making necessary the 2-cent Jackson (No. 73).

Free City Delivery was authorized by the Act of Congress of March 3, 1863, effective in 49 cities with 449 carriers, beginning July 1, 1863.

Produced by the National Bank Note Co.
DESIGNS AS 1861 ISSUE

Andrew Jackson — A32   Abraham Lincoln — A33

1861-66   *Perf. 12*

73	A32	2c **black**, *1863*	400.00	65.00
		gray black	400.00	65.00
		intense black	400.00	70.00
		No gum	150.00	
		On cover		85.00
		On prisoner's letter		
		On patriotic cover		2,000.
		Pair	850.00	140.00
		Block of 4	4,000.	1,300.
		P# strip of 4, Impt.	4,500.	
		P# block of 8, Impt.	15,000.	
		Double transfer	450.00	70.00
		Major double transfer of top left corner and "Postage" ("Atherton shift")		13,500.
		Major double transfer of right side, pos. 81, right pane ("Preston shift")	5,000.	4,500.
		Major double transfer of frame in all corners plus hair and chin ("Metzger shift")		—
		Triple transfer		—
		Short transfer	400.00	70.00

	Cracked plate	— —
a.	Diagonal half used as 1c as part of 3c rate on cover	1,750.
b.	Diagonal half used alone as 1c on cover	3,000.
c.	Horiz. half used as 1c as part of 3c rate on cover	3,500.
d.	Vert. half used as 1c as part of 3c rate on cover	2,000.
e.	Vert. half used alone as 1c on cover	4,000.
f.	Printed on both sides	— 15,000.
g.	Laid paper	— 5,000.

Earliest documented use: July 1, 1863 (dated cancel on off-cover stamp); July 6, 1863 (on cover).

Cancellations

Blue	+5.00
Brown	+75.00
Red	+50.00
Orange red	+60.00
Magenta	+200.00
Ultramarine	+150.00
Orange	+200.00
Green	+850.00
1863 year date	+5.00
Printed Precancel "Jefferson, Ohio"	—
"PAID ALL"	+40.00
"Paid"	+10.00
Numeral	+15.00
"Way"	+150.00
Railroad	+300.00
"Steam"	+40.00
Steamship	+100.00
"Steamboat"	+65.00
"Ship Letter"	+150.00
Black Carrier	+20.00
Blue Carrier	+35.00
Supp. Mail Type A or B	+100.00
Express Company	+300.00
"Short Paid"	+250.00
Territorial	+100.00
China	—

The 3c scarlet, design A25, can be found under No. 74 in the Trial Color Proofs section.

75	A26	5c **red brown**	5,500.	525.
		dark red brown	5,500.	525.
		No gum	2,100.	
		On cover		750.
		On patriotic cover		2,500.
		Pair	11,500.	1,100.
		Block of 4	60,000.	7,500.
		Double transfer	5,750.	575.

Values for No. 75 reflect the normal small margins.

Earliest documented use: Jan. 2, 1862.

Cancellations

Blue	+10.
Red	+35.
Magenta	+65.
"Paid"	+25.
Supplementary Mail Type A	+50.
Express Company	+300.

76	A26	5c **brown**, *1863*	1,600.	150.
		pale brown	1,600.	150.
		dark brown	1,600.	150.
		No gum	625.	
		On cover		200.
		On patriotic cover		850.
		Pair	3,500.	325.
		Block of 4	8,000.	1,200.
		P# strip of 4, Impt.	15,000.	
		Double transfer of top frame line	1,700.	160.
		Double transfer of bottom frame line	1,700.	160.
		Double transfer of top and bottom frame lines	1,750.	175.
a.		5c black brown	1,900.	275.
		No gum	750.	
		Block of 4	8,250.	1,800.
b.		Laid paper		

Values of Nos. 76, 76a reflect the normal small margins. The plate no. strip of 4 with imprint of No. 76 is unique.

Earliest documented use: Feb. 3, 1863.

Cancellations

Blue	+5.00
Magenta	+75.00
Red	+15.00
Brown	+75.00
Green	+650.00
1865 year date	+10.00
"Paid"	+15.00
"Short Paid"	+75.00
Supp. Mail Type A or F	+55.00
Express Company	+175.00
"Steamship"	+65.00
Packet boat	—

77	A33	15c **black**, *April, 1866*	4,000.	200.
		full black	4,000.	200.
		No gum	1,500.	
		On cover to France or Germany		275.
		Pair	8,500.	425.
		Block of 4	30,000.	1,000.
		P# block of 8, Impt.	—	
		Double transfer	4,250.	225.
		Cracked plate	—	

Earliest documented use: April 21, 1866.

Cancellations

Blue	+5.
Indigo	+10.
Purple	+60.
Lavender	+150.
Violet	+75.
Magenta	+100.
Red	+35.
Brown	+125.
Green	+375.
Ultramarine	+75.
"Paid"	+15.
"Short Paid"	+85.
"Insufficiently Paid" or "Insufficiently Prepaid"	+150.
"Ship"	+50.
Steamship	+50.
Supplementary Mail Type A	+70.

78	A29	24c **lilac**, *1862*	2,500.	250.
		dark lilac	2,500.	250.
a.		24c **grayish lilac**	2,500.	300.
b.		24c **gray**	2,500.	300.
		No gum	800.	
		On cover		325.
		Pair	5,250.	525.
		Block of 4	15,000.	1,850.
		Scratch under "A" of "Postage"	—	—
c.		24c **blackish violet**	60,000.	7,500.
		No gum	25,000.	
		On cover		9,500.

Only two examples are recorded of No. 78c unused with original gum. No. 78c unused with and without gum are valued in the grade of fine-very fine.

d.	Printed on both sides	25,000.	
	On cover	32,500.	

Earliest documented uses: Oct. 23, 1862 (No. 78a); May 1, 1863 (No. 78c).

Cancellations

Blue	+7.50
Red	+15.00
Magenta	+90.00
Green	+400.00
"Paid"	+15.00
Numeral	+20.00
Supplementary Mail Type A	+50.00
"Free"	+100.00

Nos. 73, 76-78 exist as imperforate sheet-margin singles, all with pen cancel except No. 76 which is uncanceled. They were not regularly issued.

SAME DESIGNS AS 1861-66 ISSUES
Printed by the National Bank Note Co.

Grill

Embossed with grills of various sizes. Some authorities believe that more than one size of grill probably existed on one of the grill rolls.

A peculiarity of the United States issues from 1867 to 1870 is the grill or embossing. The object was to break the fiber of the paper so that the ink of the canceling stamp would soak in and make washing for a second using impossible. The exact date at which grilled stamps came into use is unsettled. Luff's "Postage Stamps of the United States" places the date as probably August 8, 1867.

Horizontal measurements are given first.

GRILL WITH POINTS UP

Grills A and C were made by a roller covered with ridges shaped like an inverted V. Pressing the ridges into the stamp paper forced the paper into the pyramidal pits between the ridges, causing irregular breaks in the paper. Grill B was made by a roller with raised bosses.

A. GRILL COVERING THE ENTIRE STAMP.

1867   *Perf. 12*

79	A25	3c **rose**	8,500.	1,500.
		No gum	2,750.	
		On cover		2,000.
		Pair	18,000.	3,500.
		Block of 4	55,000.	
b.		Printed on both sides	—	

Earliest documented use: Aug. 13, 1867.

Cancellations

Blue	+75.
Ultramarine	+250.
Railroad	—

Values for No. 79 are for fine-very fine copies with minor perf. faults.

An essay (#79-E15) which is often mistaken for No. 79 shows the points of the grill as small squares faintly impressed in the paper but not cutting through it. On the issued stamp the grill generally breaks through the paper. Copies without defects are rare.

See Die and Plate Proofs for imperf. on stamp paper.

80	A26	5c **brown**	—	130,000.
a.		5c **dark brown**		130,000.
81	A30	30c **orange**		80,000.

Eight copies of Nos. 80 and 80a (four unused and four used), and eight copies of No. 81 (one in a museum and not available to collectors) are known. All are more or less faulty and/or off center. Values are for off-center examples with small perforation faults.

B. GRILL ABOUT 18x15mm
(22x18 POINTS)

82	A25	3c **rose**		190,000.

The four known copies of No. 82 are valued in the grade of fine.

Earliest documented use: Feb. 1?, 1869 (dated cancel on off-cover stamp).

C. GRILL ABOUT 13x16mm
(16 TO 17 BY 18 TO 21 POINTS)

The grilled area on each of four C grills in the sheet may total about 18x15mm when a normal C grill adjoins a fainter grill extending to the right or left edge of the stamp. This is caused by a partial erasure on the grill roller when it was changed to produce C grills instead of the all-over A grill. Do not mistake these for the B grill. Unused exists and is very rare, value unused $7,500; value used $2,750; on cover $4,500.

83	A25	3c **rose**	6,500.	1,100.
		No gum	2,500.	
		On cover		1,300.
		Pair	14,000.	3,250.
		Block of 4	30,000.	
		Double grill	7,750.	2,400.
		Grill with points down	7,250.	1,350.

Earliest documented use: Nov. 16, 1867.

Cancellation

Blue	+25.

See Die and Plate Proofs for imperf. on stamp paper.
The 1c, 3c, 5c, 10c, 12c, 30c of 1861 are known with experimental C grills. They are listed in the Essays section. The 3c differs slightly from No. 83.

GRILL WITH POINTS DOWN

The grills were formed by rollers with the surface covered, or partly covered, by pyramidal bosses. On the D, E and F grills the tips of the pyramids are vertical ridges. On the Z grill the ridges are horizontal.

D. GRILL ABOUT 12x14mm
(15 BY 17 TO 18 POINTS)

84	A32	2c	black	16,000.	4,500.
			No gum	8,000.	
			On cover		5,000.
			Pair	35,000.	9,250.
			Block of 4	80,000.	—
			Double transfer	—	
			Split grill		4,750.

No. 84 is valued in the grade of fine.

Earliest documented use: Feb. 15, 1868.

Cancellations

Red	+100.
Blue	+500.
"Paid All"	+100.

85	A25	3c	rose	6,750.	1,100.
			No gum	3,000.	
			On cover		1,250.
			Pair	14,000.	2,500.
			Block of 4	35,000.	—
			Double grill	—	
			Split grill		1,200.

Earliest documented use: Feb. 2, 1868.

Cancellations

Blue	+20.
Green	+400.
"Paid"	+50.

Z. GRILL ABOUT 11x14mm
(13 TO 14 BY 18 POINTS)

85A	A24	1c	blue		3,000,000.

Two copies of No. 85A are known. One is contained in the New York Public Library collection.

85B	A32	2c	black	10,000.	1,400.
			No gum	4,250.	
			On cover		1,550.
			Pair	21,500.	3,150.
			Block of 4	50,000.	—
			Double transfer	10,500.	1,450.
			Double grill	—	
			Split grill		—

Earliest documented use: Jan. 17, 1868 (on piece); Feb. 11, 1868 (on cover).

Cancellations

Blue	+50.
Red	+100.
Black Carrier	+75.
"Paid All"	+75.

85C	A25	3c	rose	25,000.	3,750.
			No gum	9,500.	
			On cover		4,250.

Pair			—
Block of 4	120,000.		—
Double grill	27,000.		—

Earliest documented use: Feb. 12, 1868.

Cancellations

Green	+250.
Blue	+25.
Red	+75.
"Paid"	+50.

85D	A27	10c	green		125,000.

Six copies of No. 85D are known. One is contained in the New York Public Library collection. Value is for a well-centered example with small faults.

85E	A28	12c	intense black	14,000.	2,400.
			black	14,000.	2,400.
			No gum	5,750.	
			On cover		3,000.
			Strip of 3	—	
			Block of 4	—	
			Double transfer of top frame line		2,500.

Earliest documented use: Feb. 12, 1868.

85F	A33	15c	black		500,000.

Two copies of No. 85F are documented, one in the grade of very good, the other extremely fine. Value is for the extremely fine example.

E. GRILL ABOUT 11x13mm
(14 BY 15 TO 17 POINTS)

86	A24	1c	blue	3,500.	525.
			No gum	1,500.	
a.		1c	dull blue	3,500.	500.
			No gum	1,500.	
			On cover		625.
			Pair (blue)	7,250.	1,100.
			Block of 4 (blue)	17,500.	3,250.
			Double grill		650.
			Split grill	3,700.	575.
			Very thin paper		—

Earliest documented use: Mar. 9, 1868.

Cancellations

Blue	+10.
Red	+60.
Green	+400.
"Paid"	+25.
Steamboat	+90.
Red Carrier	+80.

87	A32	2c	black	1,750.	200.
			gray black	1,750.	200.
			No gum	725.	
			intense black	1,700.	225.
			No gum	725.	
			On cover		300.
			Pair	3,500.	425.
			Block of 4	8,000.	6,250.
			P# strip of 4, Impt.	9,000.	
			Double grill	—	
			Double grill, one split	—	
			Triple grill	—	
			Split grill	1,750.	210.
			Grill with points up	—	
			Double transfer	1,750.	210.
a.			Diagonal half used as 1c on cover		2,000.
b.			Vertical half used as 1c on cover		2,000.

Earliest documented use: Mar. 7, 1868.

Cancellations

Blue	+7.50
Purple	+40.00
Brown	+40.00
Red	+50.00
Green	+1,000.
"Paid"	+10.00
Steamship	+60.00
Black Carrier	+35.00
"Paid All"	+20.00
"Short Paid"	+65.00
Japan	

88	A25	3c	rose	1,200.	25.
			pale rose	1,200.	25.
			rose red	1,200.	25.
			No gum	450.	
			On cover		30.
			Pair	2,500.	50.
			Block of 4	6,000.	350.
			P# block of 8, Impt.	13,000.	
			Double grill	—	
			Triple grill	—	
			Split grill	1,300.	30.
			Very thin paper	1,250.	30.
a.		3c	lake red	1,200.	50.
			No gum	450.	

Earliest documented use: Feb. 12, 1868.

Cancellations

Blue	+2.50
Red	+5.00
Ultramarine	+3.00
Green	+80.00
"Paid"	+3.00
"Way"	+20.00
Numeral	+2.00
Steamboat	+35.00
Railroad	+25.00
Express Company	+80.00

89	A27	10c	green	5,500.	325.
			dark green	5,500.	325.
			blue green	5,500.	325.
			No gum	2,400.	
			On cover		425.
			Pair	11,500.	700.

			Block of 4	26,000.	3,500.
			Double grill	7,000.	525.
			Split grill	5,750.	350.
			Double transfer		350.
			Very thin paper	5,750.	350.

Earliest documented use: Feb. 21, 1868.

Cancellations

Blue	+20.
Red	+60.
"Paid"	+15.
Steamship	+50.
Japan	+225.

90	A28	12c	black	5,000.	400.
			gray black	5,000.	400.
			intense black	5,000.	400.
			No gum	2,200.	
			On cover		550.
			Pair	10,500.	850.
			Block of 4	31,500.	2,750.
			Double transfer of top frame line	5,250.	425.
			Double transfer of bottom frame line	5,250.	425.
			Double transfer of top and bottom frame lines	5,500.	475.
			Double grill	5,750.	750.
			Split grill	5,250.	425.

Earliest documented use: Mar. 3, 1868.

Cancellations

Blue	+20.
Red	+65.
Purple	+225.
Green	+60.
Railroad	+20.
"Paid"	

91	A33	15c	black	11,000.	675.
			gray black	11,000.	675.
			No gum	4,500.	
			On cover		900.
			Pair	24,000.	1,400.
			Block of 4	60,000.	12,500.
			Double grill	—	975.
			Split grill	—	700.

Earliest documented use: May 2, 1868.

Cancellations

Blue	+15.
Magenta	+100.
Red	+100.
"Paid"	+30.
Supplementary Mail Type A	+100.

F. GRILL ABOUT 9x13mm
(11 TO 12 BY 15 TO 17 POINTS)

92	A24	1c	blue	3,250.	525.
			dark blue	3,250.	525.
			No gum	975.	
a.		1c	pale blue	2,750.	450.
			No gum	775.	
			On cover		575.
			Pair	6,500.	1,100.
			Block of 4	15,500.	3,000.
			Double transfer	3,500.	575.
			Double grill		900.
			Split grill	3,500.	575.
			Double grill, one split		—
			Very thin paper	3,500.	550.

Earliest documented use: Aug. 11 1868.

Cancellations

Blue	+5.00
Red	+20.00
Green	+250.00
"Paid"	+10.00
Red Carrier	+25.00
"Paid All"	+15.00

93	A32	2c	black	500.	55.00
			gray black	500.	55.00
			No gum	200.	
			On cover		70.00
			Pair	1,050.	120.00
			Block of 4	2,500.	500.00
			P# strip of 4, Impt.	6,250.	
			P# block of 8, Impt.	—	
			Double transfer	550.	62.50
			Double grill	—	180.00
			Split grill	550.	62.50
			Double grill, one split		—
			Double grill, one quadruple split	1,050.	—
			Very thin paper	550.	62.50
a.			Vertical half used as 1c as part of 3c rate on cover		1,250.
b.			Diagonal half used as 1c as part of 3c rate on cover		1,250.
c.			Horizontal half used alone as 1c on cover		2,500.
d.			Diagonal half used alone as 1c on cover		2,500.

Earliest documented use: Mar. 27, 1868.

Cancellations

Blue	+5.00
Red	+15.00
Green	+200.00
"Paid"	+5.00
"Paid All"	+15.00
Black Carrier	+20.00
Red Carrier	+30.00
Japan	+350.00

94	A25	3c	red	425.	10.00
			rose red	425.	10.00
a.		3c	rose	425.	10.00

No gum	150.	
On cover		11.00
Pair	900.	21.00
Block of 4	3,000.	135.00
P# block of 8, Impt.	8,750.	
Double transfer	475.	12.50
Double grill		
Double grill, one normal, one partial with points up	—	—
Triple grill	—	160.00
End roller grill		350.00
Split grill	450.	10.50
Quadruple split grill	750.	130.00
Double grill, one quadruple split	—	—
Grill with points up		
Very thin paper	425.	10.50

c. Vertical pair, imperf. horiz. — 1,500.
Block of 4 — 10,000.
d. Printed on both sides — 7,500.

Seven examples of No. 94d are recorded. Six are in the top row of an unused top margin imprint block of 18 (6x3).

Earliest documented use: Mar. 21, 1868.

Cancellations

Blue	+.25
Ultramarine	+3.00
Red	+3.50
Violet	+5.50
Green	+70.00
Numeral	+3.00
"Paid"	+2.25
"Paid All"	+12.50
"Free"	+20.00
Railroad	+30.00
Steamboat	+40.00
Packet boat	+80.00
Express Company	+50.00

See Die and Plate Proofs for imperf. on stamp paper.

95	A26 5c **brown**	3,750.	875.
	No gum	1,400.	
	dark brown	3,900.	975.
	No gum	1,450.	
	On cover		925.
	Pair	7,750.	1,850.
	Block of 4	17,500.	8,500.
	Double transfer of top frame line	—	—
	Double transfer of bottom frame line	—	—
	Double grill	—	—
	Split grill	4,250.	925.
	Very thin paper	4,000.	900.
a.	5c **black brown**	4,250.	1,200.
	No gum	1,600.	

Earliest documented use: Aug. 19, 1868.

Cancellations

Blue	+10.
Magenta	+55.
Violet	+60.
Red	+50.
Green	+200.
"Paid"	+25.
"Free"	+50.
"Steamship"	+100.

Values of Nos. 95, 95a reflect the normal small margins.

96	A27 10c **yellow green**	3,500.	250.
	green	3,500.	250.
	blue green	3,500.	250.
a.	10c **dark green**	3,500.	350.
	No gum	1,150.	
	On cover		300.
	Pair	7,250.	525.
	Block of 4	26,500.	3,500.
	P# strip of 4, Impt.	29,000.	
	Double transfer	—	—
	Double grill		425.
	Split grill	3,700.	280.
	Quadruple split grill		700.
	Very thin paper	3,700.	280.

Earliest documented use: May 28, 1868.

Cancellations

Blue	+5.00
Red	+25.00
Magenta	+30.00
Green	+200.00
"Paid"	+10.00
"Free"	+50.00
Supplementary Mail Type A	
Steamship	+75.00
Japan	+200.00
China	—

97	A28 12c **black**	3,500.	275.
	gray black	3,500.	275.
	No gum	1,400.	
	On cover		325.
	Pair	7,250.	575.
	Block of 4	30,000.	2,400.
	P# strip of 4, Impt.	32,500.	
	Double transfer of top frame line	3,900.	300.
	Double transfer of bottom frame line	3,900.	300.
	Double transfer of top and bottom frame lines	—	325.
	Double grill	—	500.
	Triple grill	—	
	Split grill	3,900.	300.
	End roller grill		
	Very thin paper	3,900.	300.

Earliest documented use: May 27, 1868.

Cancellations

Blue	+5.00
Red	+50.00
Magenta	+50.00
Brown	+50.00
Green	+250.00
Purple	+150.00
"Paid"	+15.00
"Insufficiently Prepaid"	+100.00
"Paid All"	+25.00
Supplementary Mail Type A	+50.00

98	A33 15c **black**	4,500.	300.
	gray black	4,500.	300.
	No gum	1,750.	
	On cover		350.
	Pair	9,500.	625.
	Block of 4	35,000.	2,750.
	P# block of 8, Impt.	47,500.	
	Double transfer of upper right corner	—	—
	Double grill		450.
	Split grill	4,750.	325.
	Quadruple split grill	5,250.	625.
	Very thin paper	4,750.	300.

Value for the plate block is for an example in fine condition.
Earliest documented use: May 4, 1868.

Cancellations

Blue	+2.50
Magenta	+75.00
Red	+150.00
Orange red	+40.00
Green	+275.00
Orange	+175.00
Purple	
Lavender	+150.00
"Paid"	+20.00
"Insufficiently Prepaid"	+135.00
"Insufficiently Paid"	+135.00
Japan	+300.00
Supplementary Mail Type A	+80.00

99	A29 24c **gray lilac**	8,000.	1,300.
	gray	8,000.	1,300.
	No gum	3,500.	
	On cover		2,250.
	Pair	17,000.	2,750.
	Block of 4	40,000.	8,500.
	P# block of 8, Impt.	85,000.	
	Double grill	9,000.	2,200.
	Split grill	8,250.	1,400.
	Scratch under "A" of "Postage"	—	—

Earliest documented use: Jan. 5, 1869.

Cancellations

Blue	+15.
Red	+100.
"Paid"	+50.

100	A30 30c **orange**	8,000.	900.
	deep orange	8,000.	900.
	No gum	3,250.	
	On cover		2,000.
	Pair	17,000.	1,900.
	Block of 4	40,000.	9,000.
	Double grill	10,500.	1,800.
	Split grill	8,250.	950.
	Double grill, one split	—	—
	Triple grill, two split	—	—

Values for No. 100 are for copies with small margins, especially at sides. Large-margined examples sell for much more.

Earliest documented use: Nov. 10, 1868.

Cancellations

Blue	+10.
Red	+65.
Magenta	+75.
"Paid"	+50.
Supplementary Mail Type A	+100.
Japan	+400.

101	A31 90c **blue**	14,500.	1,900.
	dark blue	14,500.	1,900.
	No gum	5,850.	
	On cover		100,000.
	Pair	31,500.	4,100.
	Block of 4	75,000.	22,500.
	Double grill	19,000.	
	Split grill	15,000.	2,000.

Two usages on cover are recorded (one being a cover front). Value is for use on full cover to Peru.

Earliest documented use: May 8, 1869.

Cancellations

Blue	+40.
Red	+100.
Japan	+600.
"Paid"	+50.

RE-ISSUE OF 1861-66 ISSUES
Produced by the National Bank Note Co.
Without grill, hard white paper, with white crackly gum.
The 1, 2, 5, 10 and 12c were printed from new plates of 100 subjects each.

1875　　　　　　　　　　　　　　　　**Perf. 12**

102	A24 1c **blue** (3195)	950.	1,250.
	No gum	450.	
	On cover		—
	Block of 4	7,250.	
103	A32 2c **black** (979)	4,500.	6,500.
	No gum	2,500.	
	Block of 4	27,500.	
104	A25 3c **brown red** (465)	4,500.	8,500.

	No gum	2,500.		
	Block of 4	32,500.		5,500
105	A26 5c **brown** (672)	3,500.	5,500
	No gum	1,850.		
	Block of 4	24,000.		
106	A27 10c **green** (451)	4,250.	15,000.
	No gum	2,200.		
	Block of 4	27,500.		
107	A28 12c **black** (389)	5,000.	8,000.
	No gum	2,700.		
	Block of 4	30,000.		
108	A33 15c **black** (397)	5,500.	15,000.
	No gum	3,000.		
	Block of 4	37,500.		
109	A29 24c **deep violet** (346)	6,500.	15,000.
	No gum	3,500.		
	Block of 4	45,000.		
110	A30 30c **brownish orange** (346)	7,000.	15,000.
	No gum	4,000.		
	Pair	17,500.		
	Block of 4	50,000.		
111	A31 90c **blue** (317)	7,250.	75,000.
	No gum	4,150.		

Earliest documented uses: No. 102, July 25, 1881; No. 104, July ?, 1883 (dated cancel on off-cover stamp); No. 111, Nov. 30, 1888 (dated cancel on off-cover stamp).

These stamps can be distinguished from the 1861-66 issue by the brighter colors, the sharper proof-like impressions and the paper which is very white instead of yellowish. The gum is almost always somewhat yellowed with age, and unused stamps with original gum are valued with such gum.

Numbers in parentheses are quantities sold.

Five examples are recorded of No. 111 used, one of which has a non-contemporaneous cancel. Value is for centered and sound example (two are known thus).

PLEASE NOTE:
Stamps are valued in the grade of very fine unless otherwise indicated.

Values for early and valuable stamps are for examples with certificates of authenticity from acknowledged expert committees, or examples sold with the buyer having the right of certification. This applies to examples with original gum as well as examples without gum. Beware of stamps offered "as is," as the gum on some unused stamps offered with "original gum" may be fraudulent, and unused stamps offered without may in some cases be altered or faintly canceled used stamps.

VALUES FOR NEVER-HINGED STAMPS PRIOR TO SCOTT No. 205
This catalogue does not value pre-1882 stamps in never-hinged condition. Premiums for never-hinged condition in the classic era invariably are even larger than those premiums listed for the post-1890 issues. Generally speaking, the earlier the stamp is listed in the catalogue, the larger will be the never-hinged premium. On some early classics, the premium will be several multiples of the unused, hinged values given in the catalogue.

Produced by the National Bank Note Co.

Plates for the 1c, 2c, 3c, 6c, 10c and 12c consisted of 300 subjects in two panes of 150 each. For the 15c, 24c, 30c and 90c plates of 100 subjects each.

NOTE: Stamps of the 1869 issue without grill cannot be guaranteed except when unused and with the original gum or traces of the original gum. This does not apply to No. 114 on gray paper.

Franklin — A34　　　　　　　Post Horse and Rider — A35

G. Grill measuring 9½x9mm
(12 by 11 to 11½ points)

1869　　　　**Hard Wove Paper**　　　**Perf. 12**

112	A34 1c **buff**	850.	175.
	brown orange	850.	175.
	dark brown orange	900.	200.
	No gum	360.	
	On cover, single		300.
	Pair	1,750.	375.
	Block of 4	6,000.	2,250.
	Margin block of 4, arrow	6,250.	
	P# block of 10, Impt.	—	—
	Double transfer		
	Double grill	1,250.	350.
	Split grill	950.	225.
	Double grill, one split		
	Double grill, one quadruple split		
b.	Without grill, original gum	9,000.	

Earliest documented use: Apr. 1, 1869.

HOW WOULD GEMS LIKE THESE LOOK IN YOUR COLLECTION?

Cancellations

Blue		+15.
Ultramarine		+60.
Magenta		+55.
Purple		+75.
Red		+50.
Green		+1,000.
"Paid"		+50.
Numeral		+100.
Steamship		+95.
Black town		+30.
Blue town		+30.
Red town		+80.
Black Carrier		+80.
Blue Carrier		+100.
Japan		+600.

113 A35 2c **brown**		800.	100.
pale brown		800.	100.
dark brown		800.	100.
yellow brown		800.	100.
No gum		325.	
On cover, single			140.
Pair		1,700.	230.
Block of 4		3,750.	1,350.
Margin block of 4, arrow		3,850.	
P# block of 10, Impt.		—	
Double grill		—	325.
Split grill		950.	125.
Quadruple split grill			450.
End roller grill		1,250.	
Double transfer			120.
b. Without grill, original gum		2,800.	
c. Half used as 1c on cover, diagonal, vertical or horizontal		6,000.	
d. Printed on both sides		9,000.	

Earliest documented use: Mar. 20, 1869.

Cancellations

Blue	+15.
Red	+30.
Orange red	+35.
Orange	+85.
Magenta	+35.
Purple	+40.
Ultramarine	+50.
Green	+450.
Brown	
"Paid"	+15.
"Paid All"	+25.
Steamship	+60.
Black town	+10.
Blue town	+30.
Japan	+250.
Blue Carrier	+90.
Black Carrier	+80.
China	—
Printed Precancellation "Jefferson, Ohio"	—

Locomotive — A36

114 A36 3c **ultramarine**		350.	20.00
pale ultramarine		350.	20.00
dark ultramarine		350.	20.00
No gum		140.	
blue		625.	100.00
No gum		275.	
violet blue		200.00	
On cover			26.00
Pair		750.	42.50
Block of 4		1,700.	450.00
Margin block of 4, arrow		1,850.	
P# block of 10, Impt.		7,500.	
Double transfer		425.	37.50
Double grill		650.	110.00
Triple grill		—	
Sextuple grill		—	6,500.
Split grill		400.	40.00
Quadruple split grill		700.	150.00
Double grill, one split		—	
Double grill, one quadruple split		—	
End roller grill		—	—
Grill with points up		—	
Gray paper		—	97.50
On cover			850.00
Without grill		—	
Cracked plate		—	160.00
a. Without grill, original gum		1,750.	
b. Vert. one-third used as 1c on cover		—	
c. Vert. two-thirds used as 2c on cover		5,000.	
e. Printed on both sides		—	

The grill-with-points-up variety is found on a unique margin "pair" of stamps where the paper was folded over prior to perforating and grilling. The stamps have drastic freak perfs.

Earliest documented use: Mar. 27, 1869.

Cancellations

Blue	+5.
Ultramarine	+25.
Magenta	+35.
Purple	+75.
Violet	+65.

Red	+15.
Orange red	+20.
Brown	+200.
Green	+450.
Orange	—
Yellow	—
Black town	+3.
Blue town	+7.
Red town	+30.
Numeral	+15.
"Paid"	+20.
"Paid All"	+15.
"Steamboat"	—
"Steamship"	+50.
Ship	+35.
"U. S. Ship"	+450.
Railroad	+30.
Packet Boat	+100.
Black Carrier	+30.
Blue Carrier	+40.
Express Company	+250.
"Way"	—
"Free"	+150.
Alaska	—
Japan	+600.

The authenticity of the yellow cancel has been questioned by some specialists. The editors would like to see an expertizing certificate for this stamp and cancel.

115 A37 6c **ultramarine**		3,250.	250.
pale ultramarine		3,250.	250.
No gum		1,350.	
On cover			450.
Pair		6,750.	600.
Block of 4		16,500.	9,000.
Margin block of 4, arrow		17,500.	
Double grill			675.
Split grill		3,500.	325.
Quadruple split grill		—	850.
Double transfer			290.
b. Vertical half used as 3c on cover		50,000.	

Earliest documented use: Apr. 26, 1869.
No. 115b is unique.

Cancellations

Blue	+5.
Brown	+80.
Magenta	+40.
Purple	+75.
Red	+50.
Green	+1,000.
"Paid"	+15.
"Paid All"	+25.
Black town	+30.
"Short Paid"	+75.
"Insufficiently Paid"	+75.
Steamship	+45.
Railroad	+50.
Japan	+1,500.

Shield and Eagle — A38

S.S. "Adriatic" — A39

116 A38 10c **yellow**		2,500.	150.
yellowish orange		2,500.	150.
No gum		1,000.	
On cover			425.
Pair		5,250.	325.
Block of 4		13,000.	8,000.
Margin block of 4, arrow		13,500.	
Double grill			425.
Split grill		2,700.	175.
End roller grill		—	

Earliest documented use: Apr. 1, 1869.

Cancellations

Blue	+35.
Magenta	+30.
Purple	+100.
Red	+40.
Ultramarine	+60.
Green	+5,000.
Black town	+20.
Steamship	+35.
Railroad	+45.
"Paid"	+15.
"Paid All"	+30.
"Insufficiently Paid"	+50.
Supplementary Mail Type A	+150.
Express Company	
Alaska	+5,000.
St. Thomas	—
Hawaii	—
Japan	+150.
China	—

117 A39 12c **green**		2,600.	160.
yellowish green		2,600.	160.
bluish green		2,750.	200.
No gum		1,100.	
On cover			500.
Pair		5,500.	340.
Block of 4		13,000.	1,800.
Margin block of 4, arrow		13,500.	
Double grill		—	425.
Split grill		3,100.	190.

Double grill, one quadruple split		—
End roller grill		600

Earliest documented use: Apr. 1, 1869.

Cancellations

Blue	+150.
Magenta	+125.
Purple	+250.
Brown	+200.
Red	+150.
Green	+4,000.
Numeral	+125.
"Paid"	+25.
"Paid All"	+40.
"Too Late"	+100.
"Insufficiently Paid"	+125.
Black town	+35.
Red town	+200.
Japan	+500.

Landing of Columbus — A40

No. 118 has horizontal shading lines at the left and right sides of the vignette.

118 A40 15c **brown & blue**, type I, Picture unframed		9,500.	750.
dark brown & blue		9,500.	750.
No gum		4,250.	
On cover			1,900.
Pair		21,000.	1,750.
Block of 4		57,500.	30,000.
Double grill		18,000.	950.
Split grill		9,750.	800.
a. Without grill, original gum		13,000.	

Earliest documented use: Mar. 31, 1869 (dated cancel on off-cover stamp); Apr. 2, 1869 (on cover).

Cancellations

Blue	+65.
Red	+90.
Brown	+150.
"Paid"	+50.
"Paid All"	+100.
"Insufficiently Paid"	+150.
Black town	+50.
Blue town	+120.
Steamship	+100.

A40a

No. 119 has diagonal shading lines at the left and right sides of the vignette.

119 A40a 15c **brown & blue**, type II, Picture framed		4,000.	275.
dark brown & blue		4,000.	275.
No gum		1,750.	
On cover			900.
Pair		8,500.	600.
Block of 4		18,500.	9,000.
P# block of 8, Impt.		45,000.	
Double transfer			
Double grill		6,250.	525.
Split grill		4,000.	350.
b. Center inverted		415,000.	17,500.
No gum		—	
c. Center double, one inverted			80,000.

Earliest documented use: Apr. 5, 1869.

Cancellations

Blue	+60.
Purple	+110.
Magenta	+110.
Red	+150.
Brown	+200.
Green	+1,500.
Numeral	+75.
"Paid"	+20.
"Paid All"	+35.
Black town	+30.
Blue town	+75.
Red town	+110.

"Steamship"		+75.	
Supp. Mail Type A or F		+40.	
Japan		+500.	

Most copies of No. 119b are faulty. Values are for fine centered copies with only minimal faults. Three examples of No. 119b unused are recorded; only one has original gum.

Three examples of No. 119c are recorded. Value is for the finer of the two sound examples.

The Declaration of
Independence — A41

120	A41	24c **green & violet**	9,500.	775.
		bluish green & violet	9,500.	775.
		No gum	4,250.	
		On cover		20,000.
		Pair	21,000.	1,650.
		Block of 4	52,500.	25,000.
		Double grill	—	2,250.
		Split grill	9,750.	900.
a.		Without grill, original gum	13,500.	
b.		Center inverted	285,000.	20,000.
		On cover		105,000.
		Pair		57,500.
		Block of 4		600,000.

Earliest documented use: Apr. 7, 1869 (No. 120); Mar. 1874 (No. 120b).

Cancellations

Blue	+250.
Red	+300.
Black town	+100.
Red town	+400.
"Paid All"	+150.
"Steamship"	+250.
Supp. Mail Type A	+200.
China	+750.

Most copies of No. 120b are faulty. Values are for fine centered copies with only minimal faults. No. 120b unused is valued without gum, as all of the three examples available to collectors are without gum.

Shield, Eagle and
Flags — A42

Lincoln — A43

121	A42	30c **ultramarine & carmine**	8,000.	550.
		ultramarine & dark carmine	8,000.	550.
		No gum	3,750.	
		On cover		32,500.
		Pair	17,500.	1,150.
		Block of 4	40,000.	3,250.
		Double grill	—	1,100.
		Split grill	8,500.	600.
		Double paper (without grill), original gum	8,750.	
a.		Without grill, original gum	12,000.	
		Block of 4	50,000.	
		P# block of 8, Impt.	—	
b.		Flags inverted	275,000.	80,000.
		No gum	210,000.	

Seven examples of No. 121b unused are recorded. Only one has part of its original gum.

Earliest documented use: May 22, 1869.

Cancellations

Blue	+200.
Red	+250.
Brown	+600.
Purple	+1,000.
Green	+7,500.
"Paid"	+50.
"Paid All"	+250.
Black town	+100.
Steamship	+85.
"Steam"	+70.
Supp. Mail Type A	+75.
Japan	+600.
China	—

122	A43	90c **carmine & black**	12,000.	2,250.
		carmine rose & black	12,000.	2,250.
		No gum	5,250.	
		On cover		—
		Pair	30,000.	5,500.
		Block of 4	110,000.	50,000.
		Split grill	—	
a.		Without grill, original gum	18,500.	

Cancellations

Blue	+1,500.
Red	+500.
Orange red	+600.
Brown	+2,000.

Purple	+3,000.
Ultramarine	+1,200.
Black town	+1,500.
Red town	+1,750.
Magenta town	+2,500.
"Paid"	—
"Paid All"	—
N.Y. steamship	+1,000.

Nos. 112, 114, 117, 118, 120b, 121, 122 exist as imperf. singles. They were not regularly issued.

CANCELLATIONS

The common type of cancellation on the 1869 issue is the block or cork similar to illustrations above. Japanese cancellations seen on this issue (not illustrated) resulted from the sale of U.S. stamps in Japanese cities where post offices were maintained for mail going from Japan to the United States.

RE-ISSUE OF 1869 ISSUE
Produced by the National Bank Note Co.
Without grill, hard white paper, with white crackly gum.

The gum is almost always somewhat yellowed with age, and unused stamps with original gum are valued with such gum.

A new plate of 150 subjects was made for the 1c and for the frame of the 15c. The frame on the 15c is the same as type I but without the fringe of brown shading lines around central vignette.

1875				**Perf. 12**
123	A34	1c **buff** (10,000)	675.	400.
		No gum	325.	
		Block of 4	3,500.	
		On cover		3,000.
124	A35	2c **brown** (4755)	800.	600.
		No gum	375.	
		Block of 4	4,500.	
		On cover		10,000.
125	A36	3c **blue** (1406)	5,500.	27,500.
		No gum	3,250.	
		On cover		—

Cancellation

Supplementary Mail Type F   —

Very few authenticated sound used copies of No. 125 are recorded. The used value is for an attractive fine to very fine example with minimal faults. Copies of No. 114 with faint or pressed-out grill are frequently offered as No. 125. Expertization by competent authorities is required.

126	A37	6c **blue** (2226)	2,250.	2,500.
		No gum	1,050.	
		Block of 4	24,000.	
		On cover		—
127	A38	10c **yellow** (1947)	2,250.	1,750.
		No gum	1,150.	
		Block of 4	19,000.	
		On cover		22,500.
128	A39	12c **green** (1584)	3,000.	3,250.
		No gum	1,600.	
		Block of 4	30,000.	
		On cover		—
129	A40	15c **brown & blue,** Type III, (1981)	1,900.	1,300.
		No gum	1,050.	
		Pair		6,000.
		Block of 4	29,000.	
		On cover		22,500.
a.		Imperf. horizontally, single	6,000.	7,000.
		No gum	4,250.	
130	A41	24c **green & violet** (2091)	2,750.	1,600.
		No gum	1,200.	
		Pair		10,000.
		On cover		27,500.
131	A42	30c **ultra & carmine** (1535)	3,250.	3,000.
		No gum	1,700.	
		Pair		28,000.
132	A43	90c **carmine & black** (1356)	4,750.	6,500.
		No gum	2,500.	
		Pair		30,000.
		Block of 4	35,000.	
		P# block of 10, Impt.	325,000.	

Numbers in parentheses are quantities sold.
Two used examples of No. 129a are recorded. Both are faulty and are valued thus.

Earliest documented uses:
No. 123, Dec. 9, 1877;
No. 124, Mar. 20, 1880;
No. 127, Nov. 11, 1880;
No. 128, Mar. 20, 1880;
No. 129, Mar. 20, 1880;
No. 130, Mar. 27, 1880.

RE-ISSUE OF 1869 ISSUE
Produced by the American Bank Note Co.
Without grill, soft porous paper.

1880-81				
133	A34	1c **buff,** issued with gum (+23,252)	375.	275
		No gum	170.	
		Block of 4, with gum	1,850.	
		Margin block of 10, Impt. & P#	22,500.	
		On cover		1,900
a.		1c **brown orange,** issued without gum, 1881	250.	250
		Block of 4, without gum	1,150.	
		Margin block of 10, Impt. & P#, without gum	22,500.	

+ This quantity includes No. 133a.

Earliest documented use: Oct. 5, 1880 (No. 133).

PRODUCED BY THE NATIONAL BANK NOTE COMPANY
Plates of 200 subjects in two panes of 100 each.

Franklin — A44

Jackson — A45

Washington — A46

Lincoln — A47

Edwin M. Stanton — A48

Jefferson — A49

Henry Clay — A50

Daniel Webster — A51

Two varieties of grill are known on this issue.

H. Grill about 10x12mm (11 to 13 by 14 to 16 points.) On all values 1c to 90c.

I. Grill about 8½x10mm (10 to 11 by 10 to 13 points.) On 1, 2, 3, 6, 7, 10 and 15c.

On the 1870-71 stamps the grill impressions are usually faint or incomplete. This is especially true of the H grill, which often shows only a few points.

Values for 1c-7c are for stamps showing well-defined grills.

Killer cancellation of the oval grid type with letters or numeral centers was first used in 1876 Bank Note issues. By order of the Postmaster-General (July 23, 1860) it was prohibited to use the town mark as a canceling instrument, and a joined town and killer cancellation was developed.

Numeral cancellations-see "Postal Markings-Examples."

White Wove Paper, Thin to Medium Thick.

1870-71   *Perf. 12*

134 A44	1c	**ultramarine,** *Apr. 1870*	2,750.	190.00
		pale ultramarine	2,750.	190.00
		dark ultramarine	2,750.	190.00
		No gum	1,100.	
		On cover		220.00
		Pair	5,750.	400.00
		Block of 4	12,500.	1,050.
		Double transfer	3,000.	210.00
		Double grill	—	325.00
		Split grill	3,150.	210.00
		Quadruple split grill	—	525.00
		End roller grill		700.00

Earliest documented use: Apr. 9, 1870.

Cancellations

Blue	+5.00
Red	+15.00
Green	+100.00
"Paid"	+10.00
"Paid All"	+20.00
"Steamship"	+45.00

135 A45	2c	**red brown,** *Apr. 1870*	1,300.	80.00
		pale red brown	1,300.	80.00
		dark red brown	1,300.	80.00
		No gum	550.	
		On cover		105.00
		Pair	2,750.	170.00
		Block of 4	6,000.	475.00
		Double grill	1,700.	150.00
		Split grill	1,350.	95.00
		Quadruple split grill	2,500.	240.00
		End roller grill	2,000.	400.00
		Grill with points up		500.00
a.		Diagonal half used as 1c on cover		—
b.		Vertical half used as 1c on cover		—

Earliest documented use: July 14, 1870.

Cancellations

Blue	+3.00
Red	+10.00
Brown	+8.00
Green	+100.00
"Paid"	+5.00
"Paid All"	+10.00
Numeral	+5.00
China	—

136 A46	3c	**green,** *Mar. 1870*	800.	27.50
		pale green	800.	27.50
		yellow green	800.	27.50

---

		deep green	800.	27.50
		No gum	325.	
		On cover		32.50
		Pair	1,650.	57.50
		Block of 4	3,500.	220.00
		P# block of 10, Impt.	9,000.	
		P# block of 12, Impt.	11,000.	
		Printed on both sides	—	
		Double transfer	—	32.50
		Double grill	1,200.	85.00
		Split grill	850.	32.50
		Quadruple split grill		150.00
		End roller grill	—	275.00
		Cracked plate	—	100.00
a.		Pair, one without grill, on cover		—

Earliest documented use: Mar. 24, 1870.

Cancellations

Blue	+1.00
Purple	+2.50
Magenta	+5.00
Red	+5.00
Orange red	+6.00
Orange	+10.00
Brown	+2.50
Green	+45.00
"Paid"	+2.50
Railroad	+10.00
"Steamship"	+20.00
"Paid All"	+15.00
Numeral	+4.00
"Free"	+25.00

See Die and Plate Proofs for imperf. on stamp paper.

137 A47	6c	**carmine,** *Apr. 1870*	5,500.	525.00
		pale carmine	5,500.	525.00
		carmine rose	5,500.	525.00
		No gum	2,200.	
		On cover		750.00
		Pair	11,500.	1,100.
		Block of 4	26,000.	
		Double grill		900.00
		Split grill	5,750.	550.00
		Quadruple split grill	—	950.00
		End roller grill	7,000.	1,100.

Earliest documented use: Apr. 11, 1870.

Cancellations

Blue	+10.
Red	+35.
"Paid"	+35.

138 A48	7c	**vermilion,** *1871*	4,500.	525.
		deep vermilion	4,500.	525.
		No gum	1,800.	
		On cover		700.
		Pair	9,250.	1,100.
		Block of 4	20,000.	
		Double grill		825.
		Split grill	4,750.	550.
		Quadruple split grill		875.
		End roller grill		1,000.

Earliest documented use: Feb. 12, 1871.

Cancellations

Blue	+10.00
Purple	+20.00
Red	+35.00
Green	+200.00
"Paid"	+25.00

The 7c stamps, Nos. 138 and 149, were issued for a 7c rate of July 1, 1870, to Prussia, German States and Austria, including Hungary, via Hamburg (on the Hamburg-American Line steamers), or Bremen (on North German Lloyd ships), but issue was delayed by the Franco-Prussian War.

The rate for this service was reduced to 6c in 1871.

For several months there was no 7c rate, but late in 1871 the Prussian closed mail rate via England was reduced to 7c which revived an important use for the 7c stamps.

The rate to Denmark direct via Baltic Lloyd ships, or via Bremen and Hamburg as above, was 7c from Jan. 1, 1872.

139 A49	10c	**brown,** *Apr. 1870*	7,000.	775.
		yellow brown	7,000.	775.
		dark brown	7,000.	775.
		No gum	2,750.	
		On cover		1,000.
		Pair	14,500.	1,600.
		Block of 4	32,500.	—
		Double grill		1,350.
		Split grill	7,250.	825.
		End roller grill		1,700.

Earliest documented use: May 6, 1870.

Cancellations

Blue	+15.
Red	+50.
"Steamship"	+50.
"Honolulu Paid All"	—

140 A50	12c	**dull violet,** *Apr. 1870*	27,500.	3,250.
		No gum	14,000.	
		On cover		6,500.
		Pair	60,000.	7,500.
		Strip of 3		15,000.
		Strip of 4		18,500.
		Block of 4	130,000.	
		Split grill		3,500.
		End roller grill		6,750.

Earliest documented use: June 17, 1870.

Cancellations

Blue	+50.
Red	+100.

		"Paid all"		
141 A51	15c	**orange,** *Apr. 1870*	8,500.	1,200
		bright orange	8,500.	1,200
		deep orange	8,500.	1,200
		No gum	3,250.	
		On cover		1,900
		Pair	18,000.	2,600
		Block of 4	42,500.	
		Double grill		3,750
		Split grill	8,750.	1,250
		Quadruple split grill		

Earliest documented use: June 2, 1870.

Cancellations

Blue	+20
Purple	+50
Red	+90
Green	+300

General Winfield Scott — A52   Alexander Hamilton — A53

142 A52	24c	**purple**	—	6,500.
		On cover		—
		Pair, double grill		—
		Split grill		—
		End roller grill		—
		Grill with points up	7,000.	

Earliest documented use: July 11, 1872.

Cancellations

Red	+500.
Blue	+500.
Purple	—

The pair of No. 142 is the unique multiple of this stamp.

143 A53	30c	**black,** *Apr. 1870*	19,000.	3,500.
		full black	19,000.	3,500.
		No gum	8,250.	
		On cover		4,500.
		Pair	41,000.	7,250.
		Block of 4	95,000.	
		Double grill		—
		End roller grill		4,750.

Earliest documented use: Aug. 18, 1870.

Cancellations

Blue	+65.
Red	+125.

Commodore Oliver Hazard Perry — A54

144 A54	90c	**carmine,** *Apr. 12, 1870*	20,000.	2,400.
		dark carmine	20,000.	2,400.
		No gum	9,000.	
		On cover		—
		Pair	42,500.	5,250.
		Block of 4	95,000.	12,000.
		Double grill		—
		Split grill		2,500.

Cancellations

Blue	+80.
Red	+140.

PRODUCED BY THE NATIONAL BANK NOTE COMPANY.

White Wove Paper, Thin to Medium Thick.
Issued (except 3c, 6c and 7c) in April, 1870.
Without Grill.

1870-71   *Perf. 12*

145 A44	1c	**ultramarine**	700.	20.00
		pale ultramarine	700.	20.00
		dark ultramarine	700.	20.00
		gray blue	700.	20.00
		No gum	260.	
		On cover		22.50
		Pair	1,450.	42.50
		Block of 4	3,250.	125.00

P# block of 12, Impt.		*4,500.*	
Double transfer		—	25.00
Worn plate		700.	20.00

Only one plate block of No. 145 is known in private hands. It of average condition and is without gum. Value is based on 998 auction sale.

Earliest documented use: May 7, 1870.

Cancellations

Blue	+.1.00
Ultramarine	+2.50
Magenta	+2.00
Purple	+2.00
Brown	+2.00
Red	+5.00
Green	+55.00
"Paid"	+3.00
"Paid All"	+15.00
"Steamship"	+25.00
Railroad	+20.00
Numeral	+2.00

146 A45	2c **red brown**	400.	17.50
	pale red brown	400.	17.50
	dark red brown	400.	17.50
	No gum	160.	
	orange brown	425.	19.00
	No gum	170.	
	On cover		20.00
	Pair	825.	37.50
	Block of 4	1,750.	120.00
	P# block of 10, Impt.	*7,000.*	
	Double transfer	—	20.00
a.	Diagonal half used as 1c on cover		*700.00*
b.	Vertical half used as 1c on cover		*800.00*
c.	Horiz. half used as 1c on cover		*800.00*
d.	Double impression	6,500.	

The No. 146 plate block is unique. Value is 1998 auction realization. No. 146d is also unique. It has VG-Fine centering and faults and is valued thus.

Earliest documented use: May 7, 1870.

Cancellations

Blue	+.50
Purple	+.75
Red	+3.00
Green	+55.00
Brown	+1.00
"Paid"	+2.00
"Paid All"	+10.00
Numeral	+2.00
"Steamship"	+22.50
Black Carrier	+12.50
Japan	—
China	—
Curacao	—

147 A46	3c **green**	325.	1.75
	pale green	325.	1.75
	dark green	325.	1.75
	No gum	120.	
	yellow green	350.	1.85
	No gum	130.	
	On cover		2.25
	Pair	675.	3.60
	Block of 4	1,450.	24.00
	P# block of 10, Impt.	*3,750.*	
	Double transfer		12.00
	Short transfer at bottom	350.	20.00
	Cracked plate	—	55.00
	Worn plate	325.	1.75
a.	Printed on both sides		*12,500.*
b.	Double impression		*40,000.*
	On cover		—

See Die and Plate Proofs for imperf. on stamp paper.

Earliest documented use: Mar. 1, 1870.

Cancellations

Blue	+.10
Purple	+.35
Magenta	+.35
Brown	+1.50
Red	+2.50
Ultramarine	+2.00
Green	+55.00
"Paid"	+2.00
"Paid All"	+10.00
"Free"	+15.00
Numeral	+2.00
Railroad	+10.00
Express Company	
"Steamboat"	+20.00
"Steamship"	+17.50
Ship	+15.00
Japan	+75.00

148 A47	6c **carmine**	1,100.	35.00
	dark carmine	1,100.	35.00
	rose	1,100.	35.00
	No gum	450.	
	On cover		50.00
	Pair	2,300.	75.00
	Block of 4	5,000.	350.00
	Double transfer	—	45.00
	Double paper		100.00
	brown carmine	1,150.	65.00
	No gum	475.	
	violet carmine	1,300.	90.00
	No gum	525.	
a.	Vertical half used as 3c on cover		*3,500.*
b.	Double impression		*1,500.*
	On cover		*3,000.*

Earliest documented use: Mar. 28, 1870.

Cancellations

Blue	+.1.00
Purple	+1.50
Violet	+1.50
Ultramarine	+3.00
Brown	+1.50
Red	+5.00
Claret	+10.00
Orange red	+7.00
Orange	+10.00
Green	+115.00
"Paid"	+3.00
"Steamship"	+25.00
"Paid All"	+15.00
Numeral	—
Supp. Mail Type A or D	+25.00
China	+75.00
Japan	+150.00

149 A48	7c **vermilion**, *Mar. 1871*	1,300.	95.00
	deep vermilion	1,300.	95.00
	No gum	500.	
	On cover		160.00
	Pair	2,700.	210.00
	Block of 4	6,250.	*750.00*
	Cracked plate	—	—

Earliest documented use: May 11, 1871.

Cancellations

Blue	+2.50
Purple	+7.50
Ultramarine	+12.50
Red	+10.00
Green	+450.00
Japan	+150.00

150 A49	10c **brown**	1,750.	30.00
	dark brown	1,750.	30.00
	yellow brown	1,750.	30.00
	No gum	675.	
	On cover		45.00
	Pair	3,750.	62.50
	Block of 4	8,000.	275.00
	P# block of 10, Impt.	—	
	Double transfer	—	85.00

Earliest documented use: May 14, 1870 (stamp on piece); May 25, 1870 (on cover).

Cancellations

Blue	+.50
Purple	+2.00
Magenta	+2.00
Ultramarine	+4.00
Red	+4.00
Orange red	+5.00
Orange	+10.00
Green	+120.00
Brown	+3.00
"Paid All"	+20.00
"Steamship"	+20.00
Supp. Mail Type A or D	+25.00
Japan	+120.00
China	—
St. Thomas	—

151 A50	12c **dull violet**	3,000.	200.00
	violet	3,000.	200.00
	dark violet	3,000.	200.00
	No gum	1,200.	
	On cover		450.00
	Pair	6,250.	425.00
	Block of 4	14,000.	2,150.

Earliest documented use: July 9, 1870.

Cancellations

Blue	+5.00
Magenta	+10.00
Red	+15.00
Orange	—
Green	+150.00
"Paid All"	+25.00
"Steamship"	+50.00
Supp. Mail Type A or D	+40.00
Japan	—

152 A51	15c **bright orange**	3,000.	200.00
	deep orange	3,000.	200.00
	No gum	1,200.	
	On cover		350.00
	Pair	6,250.	425.00
	Block of 4	14,000.	1,750.
a.	Double impression		6,000.

Earliest documented use: June 24, 1870.

Cancellations

Blue	+2.50
Magenta	+7.50
Ultramarine	+10.00
Red	+15.00
"Paid"	+12.50
"Steamship"	+40.00
Supp. Mail Type A or F	+30.00
China	—

153 A52	24c **purple**	2,200.	160.00
	bright purple	2,200.	160.00
	No gum	875.	
	On cover		1,500.
	Pair	4,750.	350.00
	Block of 4	13,500.	3,500.
	Double paper	—	—

Earliest documented use: Nov. 18, 1870.

Cancellations

Red	+15.00
Blue	+5.00
Purple	+7.50
China	—
"Paid"	+25.00
Town	+15.00
"Steamship"	—

	Supp. Mail Type A, D or F		+30.00
154 A53	30c **black**	7,250.	275.00
	full black	7,250.	275.00
	No gum	3,000.	
	On cover		825.00
	Pair	15,500.	575.00
	Block of 4	37,500.	

Earliest documented use: July 13, 1870.

Cancellations

Blue	+5.00
Brown	+50.00
Magenta	+15.00
Red	+50.00
"Steamship"	+55.00
Supplementary Mail Type A	+40.00

155 A54	90c **carmine**	5,000.	350.00
	dark carmine	5,000.	350.00
	No gum	2,000.	
	On cover		—
	Pair	10,500.	725.00
	Block of 4	24,000.	2,250.
	P# strip of 5, Impt.	*32,500.*	

Earliest documented use: Sept. 1, 1872.

Cancellations

Blue	+10.00
Purple	+15.00
Magenta	+15.00
Green	+275.00
Red	+50.00
Town	+20.00
Supp. Mail Type A or F	+40.00
Japan	—

PLEASE NOTE:

Stamps are valued in the grade of very fine unless otherwise indicated.

Values for early and valuable stamps are for examples with certificates of authenticity from acknowledged expert committees, or examples sold with the buyer having the right of certification. This applies to examples with original gum as well as examples without gum. Beware of stamps offered "as is," as the gum on some unused stamps offered with "original gum" may be fraudulent, and stamps offered as unused without gum may in some cases be altered or faintly canceled used stamps.

VALUES FOR NEVER-HINGED STAMPS PRIOR TO SCOTT No. 205

This catalogue does not value pre-1882 stamps in never-hinged condition. Premiums for never-hinged condition in the classic era invariably are even larger than those premiums listed for the post-1890 issues. Generally speaking, the earlier the stamp is listed in the catalogue, the larger will be the never-hinged premium. On some early classics, the premium will be several multiples of the unused, hinged values given in the catalogue.

PRINTED BY THE CONTINENTAL BANK NOTE COMPANY

Plates of 200 subjects in two panes of 100 each.

Designs of the 1870-71 Issue with secret marks on the values from 1c to 15c, as described and illustrated:

The object of secret marks was to provide a simple and positive proof that these stamps were produced by the Continental Bank Note Company and not by their predecessors.

Franklin — A44a

1c. In the pearl at the left of the numeral "1" there is a small crescent.

Jackson — A45a

2c. Under the scroll at the left of "U. S." there is a small diagonal line. This mark seldom shows clearly. The stamp, No. 157, can be distinguished by its color.

Washington — A46a

3c. The under part of the upper tail of the left ribbon is heavily shaded.

Lincoln — A47a

6c. The first four vertical lines of the shading in the lower part of the left ribbon have been strengthened.

Stanton — A48a

7c. Two small semi-circles are drawn around the ends of the lines that outline the ball in the lower right hand corner.

Jefferson — A49a

10c. There is a small semi-circle in the scroll at the right end of the upper label.

Clay — A50a

12c. The balls of the figure "2" are crescent shaped.

Webster — A51a

15c. In the lower part of the triangle in the upper left corner two lines have been made heavier forming a "V." This mark can be found on some of the Continental and American (1879) printings, but not all stamps show it.

Secret marks were added to the dies of the 24c, 30c and 90c but new plates were not made from them. The various printings of the 30c and 90c can be distinguished only by the shades and paper.

J. Grill about 7x9½mm exists on all values except 24c and 90c. Grill was composed of truncated pyramids and was so strongly impressed that some points often broke through the paper.

White Wove Paper, Thin to Thick

1873, July (?)   Perf. 12

156	A44a	1c ultramarine	300.	5.00
		pale ultramarine	300.	5.00
		gray blue	300.	5.00
		blue	300.	5.00
		No gum	100.	
		dark ultramarine	325.	5.00
		No gum	120.	
		On cover		6.50
		Pair	625.	10.50
		Block of 4	1,300.	47.50
		P# block of 12, Impt.	6,250.	
		Double transfer	375.	9.00
		Double paper	1,000.	200.00
		Ribbed paper	425.	16.00
		Paper with silk fibers	—	27.50
		Cracked plate		—
		Paper cut with "cogwheel" punch	450.	
e.		With grill	2,000.	
f.		Imperf., pair		1,500.

The No. 156 plate block is unique. Value is 1998 auction sale. No. 156f may not have been regularly issued.

Earliest documented use: Aug. 22, 1873.

Cancellations

Blue	+.25
Purple	+.35
Magenta	+.35
Ultramarine	+1.00
Red	+3.50
Orange red	+4.00
Orange	+5.00
Brown	+20.00
Green	+60.00
"Paid All"	+7.00
"Paid"	+1.00
Railroad	+12.00
"Free"	+12.00
Black carrier	+15.00
Numeral	+2.50
Alaska	—
Japan	—
Printed "G." Precancel (Glastonbury, Conn.)	+200.00
Printed Star Precancel (Glen Allen, Va.)	+100.00

157	A45a	2c brown	450.	22.50
		dark brown	450.	22.50
		dark reddish brown	450.	22.50
		yellowish brown	450.	22.50
		No gum	175.	
		With secret mark	475.	25.00
		No gum	185.	
		On cover		27.50
		Pair	925.	47.50
		Block of 4	2,000.	175.00
		P# block of 12, Impt.	6,250.	
		P# block of 14, Impt.	10,000.	
		Double paper	1,050.	105.00
		Ribbed paper	550.	45.00
		Double transfer	—	27.50
		Cracked plate		—
c.		With grill	1,850.	750.00
d.		Double impression	—	5,000.
e.		Vertical half used as 1c on cover		—

Earliest documented use: July 12, 1873.

Cancellations

Blue	+.75
Magenta	+1.00
Purple	+1.00
Red	+5.00
Orange red	+5.50
Orange	+7.50
Green	+100.00
"Paid"	+2.50
"Insufficiently Paid"	—
"Paid All"	+13.50
"P. D." in circle	+15.00
Town	+2.00
Numeral	+1.50
Black Carrier	+8.50
"Steamship"	+15.00

		Supplementary Mail Type F		+5.
		China		
		Japan		+100.
		Printed Star Precancellation (Glen Allen, Va.)		
158	A46a	3c green	140.	1.0
		bluish green	140.	1.0
		yellow green	140.	1.0
		dark yellow green	140.	1.0
		dark green	140.	1.0
		No gum	45.	
		olive green, ribbed paper	375.	15.0
		No gum	150.	
		On cover		1.2
		Pair	290.	2.1
		Block of 4	625.	14.5
		P# strip of 5, Impt.	825.	
		P# strip of 6, Impt.	975.	
		P# block of 10, Impt.	2,800.	
		P# block of 12, Impt.	3,750.	
		P# block of 14, Impt.	4,750.	
		Double paper	425.	50.0
		Paper cut with "cogwheel" punch	280.	225
		Ribbed paper	310.	5.25
		Paper with silk fibers	—	5.25
		Cracked plate	—	32.50
		Major plate crack at bottom		350.00
		Double transfer	—	6.00
		Short transfer at bottom		15.00
e.		With grill	500.	
		End roller grill	950.	425
h.		Horizontal pair, imperf. vert.		—
i.		Horizontal pair, imperf. between		1,300.
j.		Double impression		3,750.
k.		Printed on both sides		7,500.

See Die and Plate Proofs for imperfs. on stamp paper, with and without grill.

Earliest documented use: July 17, 1873.

Cancellations

Blue	+.10
Magenta	+.20
Purple	+.20
Ultramarine	+1.25
Red	+2.50
Orange red	+2.75
Orange	+3.50
Green	+25.00
Town	+.05
"Paid"	+2.50
"Paid All"	+20.00
"Free"	+15.00
Numeral	+1.00
China	
Railroad	+7.00
"R. P. O."	+1.50
"P. D." in circle	
"Steamboat"	
"Steamship"	
Supplementary Mail Type D	+11.00
Supplementary Mail Type F	+8.50
Express Company	
Black Carrier	+8.00
Red Carrier	+25.00
Japan	+65.00
Alaska	

159	A47a	6c dull pink	475.	20.00
		brown rose	475.	20.00
		No gum	180.	
		On cover		47.50
		Pair	1,000.	42.50
		Block of 4	2,250.	150.00
		P# block of 12, Impt.	16,000.	
		Double paper	—	—
		Ribbed paper	—	42.50
		Paper with silk fibers	—	42.50
a.		Diagonal half used as 3c on cover		4,000.
b.		With grill	1,800.	
		End roller grill	2,400.	

Earliest documented use: June 8, 1873.
No. 159a is unique.
No. 159b is valued in the grade of fine.

Cancellations

Blue	+1.00
Indigo	+2.50
Magenta	+1.50
Purple	+1.50
Violet	+3.00
Ultramarine	+2.50
Red	+7.50
Orange red	+9.00
Green	+100.00
Numeral	+1.50
"Paid"	+10.00
"Paid All"	+15.00
Supp. Mail Type D, E or F	+15.00
Japan	+100.00
China	+125.00
Railroad	+6.00
"R. P. O."	+3.00

160	A48a	7c orange vermilion	1,500.	90.00
		vermilion	1,500.	90.00
		No gum	600.	
		On cover		175.00
		Pair	3,150.	190.00
		Block of 4	6,500.	
		P# block of 12, Impt.	14,500.	
		Double transfer of "7 cents" (1R22)	—	210.00
		Double transfer in lower left corner	—	160.00
		Double paper		

	Ribbed paper	—	105.00
	Paper with silk fibers	2,000.	140.00
a.	With grill	3,500.	

The plate block of 12 is in fine condition. It is unique.

Earliest documented use: Sept. 10, 1873.

Cancellations

Blue		+4.00
Red		+10.00
Purple		+10.00
Brown		+5.00
"Paid"		+15.00

161 A49a 10c	brown	1,300.	25.00
	dark brown	1,300.	25.00
	yellow brown	1,300.	25.00
	No gum	500.	
	On cover		40.00
	Pair	2,750.	52.50
	Block of 4	6,250.	200.00
	P# block of 10, Impt.	16,500.	
	P# block of 12, Impt.	21,500.	
	Double paper	—	55.00
	Ribbed paper	—	55.00
	Paper with silk fibers	1,800.	55.00
	Double transfer	—	55.00
c.	With grill	3,750.	
d.	Horizontal pair, imperf. between		2,750.

Earliest documented use: Aug. 2, 1873.

Cancellations

Blue		+1.50
Purple		+2.00
Red		+6.00
Orange red		+7.00
Orange		+10.00
Magenta		+2.00
Brown		+20.00
Green		+100.00
"Paid"		+4.00
"P. D." in circle		+20.00
"Steamship"		+15.00
Supplementary Mail Type E		+7.00
Supplementary Mail Type F		+2.50
Japan		+100.00
China		—
Alaska		—

162 A50a 12c	blackish violet	2,750.	125.00
	No gum	1,150.	
	On cover		325.00
	Pair	5,750.	260.00
	Block of 4	12,500.	950.00
	Ribbed paper	—	210.00
a.	With grill	5,500.	

Earliest documented use: Jan. 3, 1874.

Cancellations

Blue		+2.50
Ultramarine		+15.00
Brown		+5.00
Red		+15.00
Supplementary Mail Type D		+15.00
Japan		+200.00

163 A51a 15c	yellow orange	3,000.	140.00
	pale orange	3,000.	140.00
	reddish orange	3,000.	140.00
	No gum	1,250.	
	On cover		325.00
	Pair	6,250.	300.00
	Block of 4	14,000.	1,150.
	Double paper	—	—
	Paper with silk fibers	3,250.	190.00
	Vertical ribbed paper	3,150.	190.00
a.	With grill	5,750.	

Earliest documented use: July 22, 1873.

Cancellations

Blue		+5.00
Purple		+10.00
Red		+20.00
Green		+350.00
Brown		—
Supplementary Mail Type E		—
Supplementary Mail Type F		+10.00
"Steamship"		—
Numeral		+7.50
Puerto Rico		—
China		—

164 A52 24c	purple		357,500.

The Philatelic Foundation has certified as genuine a 24c on vertically ribbed paper, and that is the unique stamp listed as No. 164. Specialists believe that only Continental used ribbed paper. It is not known for sure whether or not Continental also printed the 24c value on regular paper; if it did, specialists currently are not able to distinguish these from No. 153. The catalogue value represents a 2004 auction sale price realized.

165 A53 30c	gray black	3,500.	130.
	greenish black	3,500.	130.
	No gum	1,400.	
	On cover		725.
	Pair	7,500.	275.
	Block of 4	17,500.	1,200.
	Double transfer		160.
	Double paper	—	—
	Ribbed paper	3,750.	150.
	Paper with silk fibers	—	—
c.	With grill	22,500.	

Earliest documented use: Oct. 14, 1874.

Cancellations

Purple		+10.00
Blue		+5.00
Red		+25.00

Brown		+30.00
Magenta		+10.00
"Steamship"		—
Supplementary Mail Type E		+10.00
Supplementary Mail Type F		+5.00
Japan		+200.00

166 A54 90c	rose carmine	2,750.	275.00
	pale rose carmine	2,750.	275.00
	No gum	1,250.	
	On cover		7,500.
	Pair	5,750.	575.00
	Block of 4	12,000.	2,500.
	P# strip of 5, Impt.	15,000.	

Earliest documented use: June 25, 1875.

Cancellations

Blue		+10.
Purple		+40.
Red		+40.
Supplementary Mail Type F		+30.

SPECIAL PRINTING OF 1873 ISSUE
Produced by the Continental Bank Note Co.

1875　　　　　　　　　　　　　　*Perf. 12*

Hard, white wove paper, without gum

167 A44a	1c	ultramarine	16,000.
168 A45a	2c	dark brown	7,500.
169 A46a	3c	blue green	20,000.
		On cover	—
170 A47a	6c	dull rose	20,000.
171 A48a	7c	reddish vermilion	5,000.
172 A49a	10c	pale brown	19,000.
173 A50a	12c	dark violet	6,500.
		Horizontal pair	—
174 A51a	15c	bright orange	19,000.
175 A52	24c	dull purple	4,500.　5,000.
		Horizontal pair	—
176 A53	30c	greenish black	15,000.
177 A54	90c	violet carmine	19,000.

Although perforated, these stamps were usually cut apart with scissors. As a result, the perforations are often much mutilated and the design is frequently damaged.

These can be distinguished from the 1873 issue by the shades; also by the paper, which is very white instead of yellowish.

These and the subsequent issues listed under the heading of "Special Printings" are special printings of stamps then in current use which, together with the reprints and re-issues, were made for sale to collectors. They were available for postage except for the Officials, Newspaper and Periodical, and demonetized issues.

Only No. 169 is documented on cover (unique; postmarked Mar. 5, 1876).

Only one example of No. 175 used has been certified. It is off-center and creased, and it is valued thus.

PRINTED BY THE CONTINENTAL BANK NOTE COMPANY
REGULAR ISSUE
Yellowish Wove Paper

1875					Perf. 12
178	A45a	2c	**vermilion**, June 1875	475.	12.50
			No gum	190.	
			On cover		15.00
			Pair	1,000.	26.00
			Block of 4	2,100.	130.00
			P# strip of 6, Impt.	3,250.	
			P# block of 12, Impt.	—	
			P# block of 14, Impt.	7,500.	
			Double transfer	—	—
			Double paper	—	—
			Ribbed paper	—	—
			Paper with silk fibers	500.	17.50
b.			Half used as 1c on cover		750.00
c.			With grill	900.	2,750.

See Die and Plate Proofs for imperf. on stamp paper.

Earliest documented use: July 15, 1875.

Cancellations

Blue	+.25
Purple	+.50
Magenta	+.50
Red	+6.00
"Paid"	+8.00
"Steamship"	
Supplementary Mail Type F	+5.50
Black Carrier	+15.00
Railroad	+12.50

Zachary Taylor — A55

179	A55	5c	blue, June 1875	850.	25.00
			dark blue	850.	25.00
			bright blue	850.	25.00
			light blue	850.	25.00
			No gum	325.	
			greenish blue	875.	30.00
			No gum	350.	
			On cover		37.50
			Pair	1,800.	52.50
			Block of 4	4,000.	375.00
			Cracked plate	—	170.00
			Double transfer	—	37.50
			Double paper	1,000.	
			Ribbed paper	—	
			Paper with silk fibers	—	37.50
c.			With grill	4,500.	
			End roller grill	—	

Earliest documented use: July 10, 1875.

Cancellations

Blue	+1.00
Ultramarine	+3.00
Purple	+2.00
Magenta	+2.00
Red	+10.00
Green	+70.00

Numeral	+5.00
Railroad	+17.50
"Steamship"	+12.50
Ship	+12.50
Supplementary Mail Type E	+5.00
Supplementary Mail Type F	+2.00
China	
Japan	+100.00
Peru	

The five cent rate to foreign countries in the Universal Postal Union began on July 1, 1875. No. 179 was issued for that purpose.

SPECIAL PRINTING OF 1875 ISSUE
Produced by the Continental Bank Note Co.
Hard, White Wove Paper, without gum

1875				
180	A45a	2c	carmine vermilion	60,000.
181	A55	5c	bright blue	115,000.

Unlike Nos. 167-177, Nos. 180-181 were seldom cut apart with scissors.

PRINTED BY THE AMERICAN BANK NOTE COMPANY

The Continental Bank Note Co. was consolidated with the American Bank Note Co. on February 4, 1879. The American Bank Note Company used many plates of the Continental Bank Note Company to print the ordinary postage, Departmental and Newspaper stamps. Therefore, stamps bearing the Continental Company's imprint were not always its product.

The A. B. N. Co. also used the 30c and 90c plates of the N. B. N. Co. Some of No. 190 and all of No. 217 were from A. B. N. Co. plate 405.

Early printings of No. 188 were from Continental plates 302 and 303 which contained the normal secret mark of 1873. After those plates were re-entered by the A. B. N. Co. in 1880, pairs or multiple pieces contained combinations of normal, hairline or missing marks. The pairs or other multiples usually found contain at least one hairline mark which tended to disappear as the plate wore.

A. B. N. Co. plates 377 and 378 were made in 1881 from the National transfer roll of 1870. No. 187 from these plates has no secret mark.

Identification by Paper Type:

Collectors traditionally have identified American Bank Note Co. issues by the soft, porous paper on which they were printed. However, the Continental Bank Note Co. used a soft paper from August 1878 through early 1879, before the consolidation of the companies. When the consolidation occurred in the late afternoon of Feb. 4, 1879, American Bank Note Co. took over the presses, plates, paper, ink, and the employees of Continental. Undoubtedly they also acquired panes of finished stamps and sheets of printed stamps that had not yet been gummed and/or perforated. Since the soft paper that was in use at the time of the consolidation and after is approximately the same texture and thickness as the soft paper that American Bank Note Co. began using regularly in June or July of 1879, all undated soft paper stamps have traditionally been classified as American Bank Note Co. printings.

However, if a stamp bears a dated cancellation or is on a dated cover from Feb. 4, 1879 or earlier, collectors (especially specialist collectors) must consider the stamp to be a Continental Bank Note printing. Undated stamps off cover, and stamps and covers dated Feb. 5 or later, have traditionally been considered to be American Bank Note Co. printings since that company held the contract to print U.S. postage stamps beginning on that date. The most dedicated and serious specialist students sometimes attempt to determine the stamp printer of the issues on soft, porous paper in an absolute manner (by scientifically testing the paper and/or comparing printing records).

Earliest documented uses for American Bank Note Co. issues are given for stamps on the soft, porous paper that has been traditionally associated with that company. But, for reasons given above, sometimes that date will precede the Feb. 4, 1879 consolidation date.

SAME AS 1870-75 ISSUES
Soft Porous Paper

1879					Perf. 12
182	A44a	1c	**dark ultramarine**	350.	4.50
			blue	350.	4.50
			gray blue	350.	4.50
			No gum	125.	
			On cover		4.75
			Pair	725.	9.00
			Block of 4	1,600.	62.50
			P# block of 10, Impt.	4,750.	
			Double transfer	—	11.50

Earliest documented use: Jan. 3, 1879.

Cancellations

Blue	+.05
Magenta	+.10
Purple	+.10
Red	+7.00
Printed Star Precancellation (Glen Allen, Va.)	+75.00
Green	+35.00
"Paid"	+4.00

Supplementary Mail Type F	+10.0
Railroad	+12.5
Printed "G." Precancellation (Glastonbury, Conn.)	+100.0

183	A45a	2c	**vermilion**	150.	3.2
			orange vermilion	150.	3.2
			No gum	55.	
			On cover		3.7
			Pair	310.	6.7
			Block of 4	675.	50.0
			P# block of 10, Impt.	2,000.	
			P# block of 12, Impt.	2,500.	
			Double transfer	—	
a.			Double impression	—	5,500

Earliest documented use: Aug. 19, 1878.

Cancellations

Blue	+.2
Purple	+.4
Magenta	+.4
Red	+6.0
Green	+175.00
"Paid"	+5.00
"Paid All"	
"Ship"	
Numeral	+4.00
Railroad	+15.00
Supplementary Mail Type F	+8.00
China	
Printed Star Precancellation in black (Glen Allen, Va.)	+350.00
Printed Star Precancellation in red (Glen Allen, Va.)	+1,750.

184	A46a	3c	**green**	120.	.80
			light green	120.	.80
			dark green	120.	.80
			No gum	40.	
			On cover		.90
			Pair	250.	1.70
			Block of 4	525.	11.50
			P# block of 10, Impt.	1,450.	
			P# block of 12, Impt.	1,750.	
			P# block of 14, Impt.	2,150.	
			Double transfer	—	
			Short transfer	—	6.25
b.			Double impression	—	5,500.

See Die and Plate Proofs for imperf. on stamp paper.

Earliest documented use: July 2, 1878.

Cancellations

Blue	+.10
Magenta	+.15
Purple	+.15
Violet	+.15
Brown	+1.00
Red	+7.50
Green	+25.00
"Paid"	+3.00
"Free"	+15.00
Numeral	+2.00
Railroad	+12.50
"Steamboat"	
Supplementary Mail Type F	+8.00
Printed Star Precancel (Glen Allen, Va.)	—
China	+60.00
Alaska	

185	A55	5c	blue	550.	15.00
			light blue	550.	15.00
			bright blue	550.	15.00
			dark blue	550.	15.00
			No gum	220.	
			On cover		25.00
			Pair	1,150.	32.50
			Block of 4	2,400.	180.00
			P# block of 12, Impt.	12,500.	
			Double transfer		

Earliest documented use: Jan. 16, 1879.

Cancellations

Blue	+.25
Purple	+1.00
Magenta	+1.00
Ultramarine	+3.50
Red	+7.50
Railroad	+20.00
Numeral	+2.00
Supplementary Mail Type F	+1.50
"Steamship"	+35.00
China	+60.00
Peru	
Panama	

186	A47a	6c	**pink**	1,100.	27.50
			dull pink	1,100.	27.50
			brown rose	1,100.	27.50
			No gum	450.	
			On cover		47.50
			Pair	2,300.	57.50
			Block of 4	5,000.	625.00

Earliest documented use: July 1, 1879.

Cancellations

Blue	+.50
Ultramarine	+3.00
Purple	+1.00
Magenta	+1.00
Red	+12.00
Supplementary Mail Type F	+4.00
Railroad	+22.50
Numeral	+4.00
China	+70.00

187	A49	10c	**brown**, without secret mark	3,500.	27.50
			yellow brown	3,500.	27.50
			No gum	1,400.	

On cover			50.00
Pair		7,250.	57.50
Block of 4		16,000.	
Double transfer		—	47.50
Double paper		6,000.	

Earliest documented use: Sept. 5, 1879.

Cancellations

Blue		+.50
Magenta		+1.50
Red		+10.00
"Paid"		+3.50
Supplementary Mail Type F		+3.00
China		+70.00

188	A49a	10c **brown**, with secret mark	2,500.	27.50
		yellow brown	2,500.	27.50
		No gum	1,000.	
		black brown	2,750.	40.00
		No gum	1,100.	
		On cover		42.50
		Pair	5,250.	57.50
		Block of 4	11,500.	300.00
		Pair, one stamp No. 187	8,500.	725.00
		Double transfer		47.50
		Cracked plate	—	—

Earliest documented use: Oct. 5, 1878.

Cancellations

Blue		+.50
Ultramarine		+3.00
Purple		+2.00
Magenta		+2.00
Red		+10.00
Green		+70.00
"Paid"		+7.50
Supplementary Mail Type F		+5.00
Numeral		+3.00
Printed Star Precancel (Glen Allen, Va.)		—

189	A51a	15c **red orange**	350.	25.00
		orange	350.	25.00
		yellow orange	350.	25.00
		No gum	140.	
		On cover		87.50
		Pair	725.	52.50
		Block of 4	1,750.	230.00
		P# block of 12, Impt.	7,250.	
		Double transfer	—	

Earliest documented use: Jan. 20, 1879.

Cancellations

Blue		+1.50
Purple		+3.00
Magenta		+3.00
Ultramarine		+5.00
Red		+12.00
"Steamship"		+22.50
Supplementary Mail Type E		
Supplementary Mail Type F		+5.00
Japan		+120.00
China		

190	A53	30c **full black**	1,100.	80.00
		greenish black	1,100.	80.00
		No gum	450.	
		On cover		425.00
		Pair	2,300.	175.00
		Block of 4	5,000.	500.00
		P# block of 10, Impt.	15,000.	

Earliest documented use: April 5, 1881.

Cancellations

Blue		+1.50
Purple		+3.00
Magenta		+3.00
Red		+20.00
Supplementary Mail Type F		+6.00
"Steamship"		+35.00
Tahiti		
Samoa		

191	A54	90c **carmine**	2,500.	325.00
		rose	2,500.	325.00
		carmine rose	2,500.	325.00
		No gum	1,000.	
		On cover		5,000.
		Pair	5,500.	675.00
		Block of 4	13,000.	1,750.
		Double paper	—	

See Die and Plate Proofs for imperf. on stamp paper.

Earliest documented use: May 27, 1882 (dated cancel on off-cover stamp), June 24, 1882 (on cover).

Cancellations

Blue		+15.00
Purple		+20.00
Red		+45.00
Supplementary Mail Type F		+20.00

SPECIAL PRINTING OF 1879 ISSUE
Produced by the American Bank Note Co.

1880   *Perf. 12*

Soft porous paper, without gum

192	A44a	1c **dark ultramarine**	50,000.
193	A45a	2c **black brown**	19,000.
194	A46a	3c **blue green**	65,000.
195	A47a	6c **dull rose**	45,000.
196	A48a	7c **scarlet vermilion**	7,000.
197	A49a	10c **deep brown**	40,000.
198	A50a	12c **blackish purple**	10,000.
199	A51a	15c **orange**	35,000.
200	A52	24c **dark violet**	9,500.
201	A53	30c **greenish black**	24,000.

202	A54	90c **dull carmine**	35,000.
203	A45a	2c **scarlet vermilion**	70,000.
204	A55	5c **deep blue**	100,000.

Nos. 192 and 194 are valued in the grade of fine.

No. 197 was printed from Continental plate 302 (or 303) after plate was re-entered. Therefore, the stamp may show normal, hairline or missing secret mark.

The Post Office Department did not keep separate records of the 1875 and 1880 Special Printings of the 1873 and 1879 issues, but the total quantity sold of both is recorded.

Unlike the 1875 hard-paper Special Printings (Nos. 167-177), the 1880 soft-paper Special Printings were never cut apart with scissors.

Numbers Sold of 1875 and 1880 Special Printings.

1c ultramarine & dark ultramarine *(388)*
2c dark brown & black brown *(416)*
2c carmine vermilion & scarlet vermilion *(917)*
3c blue green *(267)*
5c bright blue & deep blue *(317)*
6c dull rose *(185)*
7c reddish vermilion & scarlet vermilion *(473)*
10c pale brown & deep brown *(180)*
12c dark violet & blackish purple *(282)*
15c bright orange & orange *(169)*
24c dull purple & dark violet *(286)*
30c greenish black *(179)*
90c violet carmine & dull carmine *(170)*

IMPORTANT INFORMATION REGARDING VALUES FOR NEVER-HINGED STAMPS

Collectors should be aware that the values given for never-hinged stamps from No. 205 on are for stamps in the grade of very fine, just as the values for all stamps in the catalogue are for very fine stamps unless indicated otherwise. The never-hinged premium as a percentage of value will be larger for stamps in extremely fine or superb grades, and the premium will be smaller for fine-very fine, fine or poor examples. This is particularly true of the issues of the late-19th and early-20th centuries. For example, in the grade of very fine, an unused stamp from this time period may be valued at $100 hinged and $180 never hinged. The never-hinged premium is thus 80%. But in a grade of extremely fine, this same stamp will not only sell for more hinged, but the never-hinged premium will increase, perhaps to 100%-300% or more over the higher extremely fine value. In a grade of superb, a hinged copy will sell for much more than a very fine copy, and additionally the never-hinged premium will be much larger, perhaps as large as 300%-400%. On the other hand, the same stamp in a grade of fine or fine-very fine not only will sell for less than a very fine stamp in hinged condition, but additionally the never-hinged premium will be smaller than the never-hinged premium on a very fine stamp, perhaps as small as 15%-30%.

Please note that the above statements and percentages are NOT a formula for arriving at the values of stamps in hinged or never-hinged condition in the grades of very good, fine, fine to very fine, extremely fine or superb. The percentages given apply only to the size of the premium for never-hinged condition that might be added to the stamp value for hinged condition. Further, the percentages given are only generalized estimates. Some stamps or grades may have percentages for never-hinged condition that are higher or lower than the ranges given. For values of the most popular U.S. stamps in the grades of very good, fine, fine to very fine, extremely fine and superb, see the *Scott Valuing Supplement*, updated and issued twice each year in April and October.

VALUES FOR NEVER-HINGED STAMPS PRIOR TO SCOTT 205

This catalogue does not value pre-1882 stamps in never-hinged condition. Premiums for never-hinged condition in the classic era invariably are even larger than those premiums listed for the post-1882 issues. Generally speaking, the earlier the stamp is listed in the catalogue, the larger will be the never-hinged premium. On some early classics, the premium will be several multiples of the unused, hinged values given in the catalogue.

NEVER-HINGED PLATE BLOCKS

Values given for never-hinged plate blocks are for blocks in which all stamps have original gum that has never been hinged and has no disturbances, and all selvage, whether gummed or ungummed, has never been hinged.

REGULAR ISSUE
Printed by the American Bank Note Co.

James A. Garfield — A56

1882, Apr. 10   *Perf. 12*

205	A56	5c **yellow brown**	325.	10.00
		brown	325.	10.00
		gray brown	325.	10.00
		Never hinged	1,000.	
		No gum	120.	
		On cover		18.50
		Pair	675.	22.50
		Block of 4	1,400.	120.00
		P# strip of 5, Impt.	1,950.	
		P# strip of 6, Impt.	2,300.	
		P# block of 10, Impt.	5,750.	
		P# block of 12, Impt.	6,500.	

Earliest documented use: Feb. 18, 1882.

Cancellations

Blue		+.50
Purple		+.75
Magenta		+.75
Red		+7.00
"Ship"		
Numeral		+2.00
Supplementary Mail Type F		+2.50
Red Express Co.		
China		+125.00
Japan		+125.00
Samoa		+150.00
Puerto Rico		

SPECIAL PRINTING
Printed by the American Bank Note Co.

1882   *Perf. 12*

Soft porous paper, without gum

205C	A56	5c **gray brown**	65,000.

Although Post Office records indicate that 2,463 copies of the 5c Garfield Special Printing were sold, almost all of these stamps appear to have been from supplies of the regular issue No. 205. The actual Special Printings, No. 205C, came from a small supply sent to the Third Assistant Post Master General before the regular issue was available. Only 22 examples have been certified as genuine Special Printings.

DESIGNS OF 1873 RE-ENGRAVED

Franklin — A44b

1c — The vertical lines in the upper part of the stamp have been so deepened that the background often appears to be solid. Lines of shading have been added to the upper arabesques.

1881-82

206	A44b	1c **gray blue**, *Aug. 1881*	95.00	1.00
		ultramarine	95.00	1.00
		dull blue	95.00	1.00
		slate blue	95.00	1.00
		Never hinged	300.00	
		No gum	27.50	
		On cover		1.50
		Pair	200.00	2.10
		Block of 4	450.00	16.00
		P# strip of 5, Impt.	575.00	
		P# strip of 6, Impt.	675.00	
		P# block of 10, Impt.	1,900.	
		P# block of 12, Impt.	2,100.	
		Double transfer	120.00	6.00
		Punched with 8 small holes in a circle	200.00	
		P# block of 10, Impt. (8-hole punch)	2,750.	

Earliest documented use: Nov. 2, 1881.

Cancellations

Purple		+.10
Magenta		+.10
Blue		+.20
Red		+3.00
Orange red		+3.50
Orange		+5.00
Green		+50.00
"Paid"		+4.75
"Paid All"		+12.00
Numeral		+3.50
Supplementary Mail Type F		+5.00
Railroad		+10.00
Printed Star Precancel (Glen Allen, Va.)		+55.00
China		

Graded or ungraded, a certificate is only as good as the experience behind it.

The Philatelic Foundation Certificate—the standard of excellence in the hobby since the organization opened its doors in 1945. Since then, we have issued more than 435,000 certs and have created an unequaled, multimillion dollar reference collection comprised of more than half a million stamps. Only the PF boasts five full-time, on-staff expertisers, with several dozen additional consultants on call. Last year, in response to collector demand, the option for **numerical grading** was added.

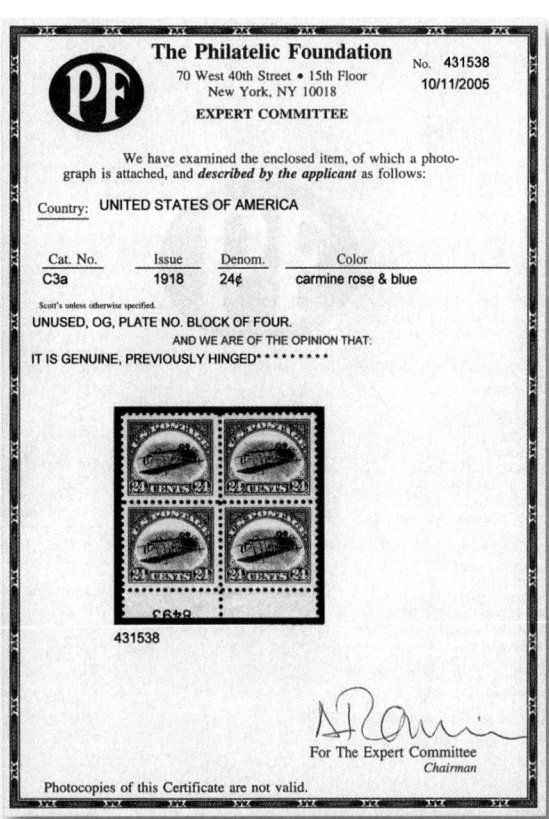

When it comes to your certified stamps, savor the experience.

Washington — A46b

3c. The shading at the sides of the central oval appears only about one-half the previous width. A short horizontal dash has been cut about 1mm below the "TS" of "CENTS."

207	A46b	3c	**blue green**, *July 16, 1881*	100.00	.55
			green	100.00	.55
			yellow green	100.00	.55
			Never hinged	325.00	
			No gum	30.00	
			On cover		.70
			Pair	210.00	1.15
			Block of 4	450.00	30.00
			P# strip of 5, Impt.	600.00	
			P# block of 10, Impt.	*1,900.*	
			Double transfer	—	12.00
			Cracked plate		
			Punched with 8 small holes in a circle	*220.00*	
			P# block of 10, Impt. (8-hole punch)	*3,000.*	
c.			Double impression	—	

Earliest documented use: Aug. 7, 1881.

Cancellations

Purple	+.10
Magenta	+.10
Blue	+.25
Brown	+1.50
Red	+2.50
"Paid"	+3.00
"Paid All"	
Numeral	+2.50
"Ship"	
Railroad	+5.00
Supplementary Mail Type F	+8.00
Printed Star Precancellation (Glen Allen, Va.)	—

Lincoln — A47b

6c. On the original stamps four vertical lines can be counted from the edge of the panel to the outside of the stamp. On the re-engraved stamps there are but three lines in the same place.

208	A47b	6c	**rose**	700.	100.00
			dull rose	700.	100.00
			Never hinged	2,500.	
			No gum	225.	
			On cover (rose)		180.00
			Pair (rose)	1,450.	210.00
			Block of 4 (rose)	3,500.	850.00
			P# block of 10, Impt.	*9,000.*	
			Double transfer	825.	120.00
a.			6c **deep brown red**	650.	160.00
			Never hinged	2,000.	
			No gum	200.	
			pale brown red	575.	110.00
			Never hinged	1,750.	
			No gum	180.	
			On cover (deep brown red)		*425.00*
			Pair (deep brown red)	1,300.	330.00
			Block of 4 (deep brown red)	3,000.	1,200.
			P# strip of 5, Impt.	3,750.	
			P# strip of 6, Impt.	4,500.	
			P# block of 10, Impt.	*9,000.*	
			P# block of 12, Impt.	—	

Earliest documented use: June 1, 1882.

Cancellations

Magenta	+3.00
Purple	+3.00
Blue	+5.00
Red	+15.00
Supplementary Mail Type F	+10.00

Jefferson — A49b

10c. On the original stamps there are five vertical lines between the left side of the oval and the edge of the shield. There are only four lines on the re-engraved stamps. In the lower part of the latter, also, the horizontal lines of the background have been strengthened.

209	A49b	10c	**brown**, *Apr. 1882*	200.	6.00
			yellow brown	200.	6.00
			orange brown	200.	6.00
			Never hinged	550.	
			No gum	60.	
			dark brown	210.	6.50
			purple brown	210.	6.50
			olive brown	210.	6.50
			Never hinged	575.	
			No gum	65.	
			On cover		11.00
			Pair	425.	12.50

	Block of 4	975.	40.00
	P# strip of 5, Impt.	1,350.	
	P# strip of 6, Impt.	1,575.	
	P# block of 10, Impt.	*3,900.*	
	P# block of 12, Impt.	*4,600.*	
	Never hinged	8,750.	
b.	10c **black brown**	2,500.	325.00
	Never hinged	5,000.	
	No gum	825.	
	On cover		*525.00*
	Pair	—	675.00
	Block of 4	—	—
c.	Double impression	—	—

Specimen stamps (usually overprinted "Sample") without overprint exist in a brown shade that differs from No. 209. The unoverprinted brown specimen is cheaper than No. 209. Expertization is recommended.

Earliest documented use: May 4, 1882.

Cancellations

Purple	+.50
Magenta	+.50
Blue	+1.00
Red	+4.00
Green	+35.00
Numeral	+2.00
"Paid"	+2.50
Supplementary Mail Type F	+3.00
Express Company	
Japan	+75.00
China	—
Samoa	—

Printed by the American Bank Note Company.

Washington — A57

Jackson — A58

Nos. 210-211 were issued to meet the reduced first class rate of 2 cents for each half ounce, and the double rate, which Congress approved Mar. 3, 1883, effective Oct. 1, 1883.

1883, Oct. 1   *Perf. 12*

210	A57	2c	**red brown**	50.00	.60
			dark red brown	50.00	.60
			orange brown	50.00	.60
			Never hinged	160.00	
			No gum	17.50	
			On cover		.70
			Pair	105.00	1.25
			Block of 4	225.00	12.00
			P# strip of 5, Impt.	290.00	
			P# strip of 6, Impt.	360.00	
			P# block of 10, Impt.	*1,100.*	
			P# block of 12, Impt.	*1,300.*	
			Double transfer	55.00	2.25

See Die and Plate Proofs for imperf. on stamp paper.

Earliest documented use: Oct. 1, 1883 (FDC).

Cancellations

Purple	+.10
Margenta	+.10
Blue	+.20
Violet	+.30
Brown	+.30
Red	+3.50
Green	+25.00
Numeral	+2.50
"Paid"	+3.00
Railroad	+5.00
Express Company	
Supplementary Mail Type F	+5.00
"Ship"	—
"Steamboat"	—
China	—

211	A58	4c	**blue green**	350.	22.50
			deep blue green	350.	22.50
			Never hinged	1,100.	
			No gum	120.	
			On cover		50.00
			Pair	725.	47.50
			Block of 4	1,500.	120.00
			P# strip of 5, Impt.	2,100.	
			P# strip of 6, Impt.	2,500.	
			P# block of 10, Impt.	5,500.	
			P# block of 12, Impt.	6,400.	
			Never hinged	9,000.	
			Double transfer	—	—
			Cracked plate	—	—

See Die and Plate Proofs for imperf. on stamp paper.

Earliest documented use: Oct. 1, 1883 (FDC).

Cancellations

Purple	+1.00
Magenta	+1.00
Green	+50.00

Blue	+1.00
Numeral	+2.00
Supplementary Mail Type F	+5.00

SPECIAL PRINTING
Printed by the American Bank Note Company.

1883-85   **Soft porous paper**   *Perf. 12*

211B	A57	2c	**pale red brown**, with gum ('85)	450.	
			Never hinged	950.	
			No gum	175.	
			Block of 4	1,950.	
c.			Horizontal pair, imperf. between	2,000.	
			Never hinged	3,000.	
			Top margin strip of 6, "Steamer - American Bank Note Co." imprint	5,000.	
			Never hinged	7,000.	

Earliest documented use: May 23, 1885 (dated cancel on off-cover stamp).

211D	A58	4c	**deep blue green**, without gum	*45,000.*

Postal records indicate that 26 copies of No. 211D were sold. Records also indicate an 1883 delivery and sales of 55 copies of the 2c red brown stamp, but there is no clear evidence that these can be differentiated from no gum examples of No. 210.

No. 211B is from a special trial printing by a new steam-powered American Bank Note Company press. Approximately 1,000 of these stamps (in sheets of 200 with an imperf gutter between the panes of 100) were delivered as samples to the Third Assistant Postmaster General and subsequently made their way to the public market.

REGULAR ISSUE
Printed by the American Bank Note Company.

Franklin — A59

1887   *Perf. 12*

212	A59	1c	**ultramarine**, *June*	120.00	2.25
			bright ultramarine	120.00	2.25
			Never hinged	400.00	
			No gum	45.00	
			On cover		3.00
			Pair	250.00	4.75
			Block of 4	550.00	35.00
			P# strip of 5, Impt.	675.00	
			P# strip of 6, Impt.	825.00	
			P# block of 10, Impt.	*1,675.*	
			P# block of 12, Impt.	*2,000.*	
			Double transfer	—	

See Die and Plate Proofs for imperf. on stamp paper.

Earliest documented use: July 15, 1887. The previously listed July 7, 1887, cover has not been adequately documented. The editors would like to see authenticated evidence of its existence.

Cancellations

Purple	+.10
Magenta	+.10
Blue	+.10
Red	+5.50
Numeral	+2.00
Railroad	+10.00
Supplementary Mail Type F	+5.00
China	—

213	A57	2c	**green**, *Sept. 10*	50.00	.50
			bright green	50.00	.50
			dark green	50.00	.50
			Never hinged	150.00	
			No gum	17.50	
			On cover		.65
			Pair	105.00	1.10
			Block of 4	230.00	10.00
			P# strip of 5, Impt.	300.00	
			P# strip of 6, Impt.	375.00	
			P# block of 10, Impt.	*1,250.*	
			Never hinged	*2,250.*	
			P# block of 12, Impt.	*1,500.*	
			Double transfer	—	3.25
b.			Printed on both sides	—	—

See Die and Plate Proofs for imperf. on stamp paper.

Earliest documented use: Sept. 20, 1887 (dated cancel on off-cover stamp); Sept. 21, 1887 (on cover).

Cancellations

Purple	+.10
Magenta	+.10
Blue	+.90
Red	+5.00
Green	+25.00
"Paid"	+5.00
Railroad	+12.00
Numeral	+2.00
"Steam"	—
"Steamboat"	—
Supplementary Mail Type F	+7.50
China	—

		Japan		—
214	A46b	3c **vermilion,** *Sept.*	80.00	62.50
		Never hinged	240.00	
		No gum	27.50	
		On cover (single)		105.00
		Pair	170.00	130.00
		Block of 4	375.00	350.00
		P# strip of 5, Impt.	475.00	
		P# strip of 6, Impt.	550.00	
		P# block of 10, Impt.	1,400.	
		Never hinged	3,250.	
		P# block of 12, Impt.	1,600.	

Earliest documented use: Sept. 23, 1887.

Cancellations

Purple	+5.00
Magenta	+5.00
Green	+150.00
Blue	+10.00
Supplementary Mail Type F	+15.00
Railroad	+30.00

Printed by the American Bank Note Company.
SAME AS 1870-83 ISSUES

1888   *Perf. 12*

215	A58	4c **carmine,** *Nov.*	250.	22.50
		rose carmine	250.	22.50
		pale rose	250.	22.50
		Never hinged	800.	
		No gum	90.	
		On cover		45.00
		Pair	525.	47.50
		Block of 4	1,100.	150.00
		P# strip of 5, Impt.	1,550.	
		Never hinged	3,250.	
		P# strip of 6, Impt.	1,850.	
		P# block of 10, Impt.	4,750.	
		P# block of 12, Impt.	5,500.	

Earliest documented use: Jan. 18, 1889.

Cancellations

Blue	+1.00
Red	+5.00
Purple	+2.00
Magenta	+2.00
Supplementary Mail Type F	+5.00

216	A56	5c **indigo,** *Feb.*	275.	15.00
		deep blue	275.	15.00
		Never hinged	900.	
		No gum	100.	
		On cover		27.50
		Pair	575.	32.50
		Block of 4	1,200.	130.00
		P# strip of 5, Impt.	1,600.	
		P# strip of 6, Impt.	2,000.	
		P# block of 10, Impt.	7,500.	
		P# block of 12, Impt.	9,000.	

Earliest documented use: Mar. 15, 1888.

Cancellations

Purple	+1.00
Magenta	+1.00
Blue	+1.00
Supplementary Mail Type F	+3.00
China	+85.00
Japan	+85.00
Puerto Rico	+75.00
Samoa	—

217	A53	30c **orange brown,** *Jan.*	475.	120.00
		deep orange brown	475.	120.00
		Never hinged	1,500.	
		No gum	170.	
		On cover		1,400.
		Pair	1,000.	260.00
		Block of 4	2,100.	675.00
		P# strip of 5, Impt.	2,850.	
		P# block of 10, Impt.	7,250.	
		P# block of 12, Impt.	—	

Earliest documented use: Aug. 18, 1888 (dated cancel on off-cover stamp); Sept. 7, 1888 (on cover).

Cancellations

Blue	+5.00
Magenta	+10.00
Supplementary Mail Type F	+10.00
"Paid All"	+25.00
"Paid"	+15.00

218	A54	90c **purple,** *Feb.*	1,200.	260.00
		bright purple	1,200.	260.00
		Never hinged	4,000.	
		No gum	475.	
		On cover		10,000.
		Pair	2,500.	575.00
		Block of 4	5,750.	1,450.
		P# strip of 5, Impt.	7,000.	
		P# block of 10, Impt.	23,500.	
		P# block of 12, Impt.	—	

Earliest documented use: Sept. (day ?), 1888 (dated cancel on off-cover stamp); Oct. 29, 1888 (on cover).

Cancellations

Blue	+10.00
Purple	+15.00
Supplementary Mail Type F	+25.00

See Die and Plate Proofs for imperfs. on stamp paper.

Printed by the American Bank Note Company.
Plates for the 1c and 2c were of 400 subjects in 4 panes of 100 each. All other values were from plates of 200 subjects in two panes of 100 each.

Franklin — A60

Washington — A61

Jackson — A62

Lincoln — A63

Ulysses S. Grant — A64

Garfield — A65

William T. Sherman — A66

Daniel Webster — A67

Henry Clay — A68

Jefferson — A69

Perry — A70

1890-93   *Perf. 12*

219	A60	1c **dull blue,** *Feb. 22, 1890*	30.	.60
		deep blue	30.	.60
		ultramarine	30.	.60
		Never hinged	90.	
		On cover		.65
		Block of 4	130.	4.75
		P# strip of 5, Impt. & letter	175.	
		P# strip of 6, Impt. & letter	240.	
		P# strip of 7, Impt. & letter	275.	
		P# block of 10, Impt. & letter	800.	
		P# block of 12, Impt. & letter	1,100.	
		P# block of 14, Impt. & letter	1,500.	
		Never hinged	3,500.	
		Double transfer	—	—

Earliest documented use: Feb 27, 1890.

Cancellations

Samoa	—
China	—

219D	A61	2c **lake,** *Feb. 22, 1890*	250.	1.75
		Never hinged	800.	
		On cover		2.40
		Block of 4	1,050.	17.50

		P# strip of 5, Impt.	1,350.	
		P# block of 10, Impt.	4,000.	
		Double transfer		

Earliest documented use: Feb. 22, 1890 (FDC).

Cancellation

Supplementary Mail Type F	+3.0

220	A61	2c **carmine,** *1890*	27.50	.5
		dark carmine	27.50	.5
		carmine rose	27.50	.5
		rose	27.50	.7
		Never hinged	70.00	
		On cover		.6
		Block of 4	120.00	2.2
		P# strip of 5, Impt. & letter	170.00	
		P# strip of 6, Impt. & letter	225.00	
		Never hinged	400.00	
		P# strip of 7, Impt. & letter	265.00	
		P# block of 10, Impt. & letter	600.00	
		P# block of 12, Impt. & letter	850.00	
		P# block of 14, Impt. & letter	1,100.	
		Never hinged	—	
		Double transfer		3.25
a.		Cap on left "2" (Plates 235-236, 246-247-248)	150.00	10.00
		Never hinged	410.00	
		Block of 4	700.00	150.00
		Pair, Nos. 220, 220a	—	
		Never hinged	—	
c.		Cap on both "2"s (Plates 245, 246)	700.00	30.00
		Never hinged	1,900.	
		Pair, Nos. 220a, 220c	—	
		Never hinged	—	

Earliest documented uses: Mar. 11, 1890 (No. 220); Sept. 9, 1892 (No. 220a); July 7, 1892 (No. 220c).

Cancellations

Blue	+.05
Purple	+.05
Supp. Mail Types F or G	+3.00
China	+20.00

221	A62	3c **purple,** *Feb. 22, 1890*	90.00	7.50
		bright purple	90.00	7.50
		dark purple	90.00	7.50
		Never hinged	275.00	
		On cover		16.00
		Block of 4	400.00	50.00
		P# strip of 5, Impt.	550.00	
		P# block of 10, Impt.	2,900.	
		Never hinged	—	

Earliest documented use: Feb. 28, 1890.

Cancellation

Samoa	—

222	A63	4c **dark brown,** *June 2, 1890*	120.00	4.00
		blackish brown	120.00	4.00
		Never hinged	360.00	
		On cover		15.00
		Block of 4	500.00	30.00
		P# strip of 5, Impt.	725.00	
		P# block of 10, Impt.	3,500.	
		Never hinged	5,500.	
		Double transfer	135.00	—

Earliest documented use: July 16, 1890.

Cancellation

China	+40.00

223	A64	5c **chocolate,** *June 2, 1890*	100.00	4.00
		yellow brown	100.00	4.00
		Never hinged	300.00	
		On cover		14.00
		Block of 4	425.00	26.50
		P# strip of 5, Impt.	550.00	
		P# block of 10, Impt.	3,000.	
		Never hinged	—	
		Double transfer	115.00	3.75

Earliest documented use: June 14, 1890.

Cancellations

China	+35.00
Samoa	—
Supp. Mail Types F or G	+3.00

224	A65	6c **brown red,** *Feb. 22, 1890*	90.00	20.00
		dark brown red	90.00	20.00
		Never hinged	275.00	
		On cover		35.00
		Block of 4	375.00	110.00
		P# strip of 5, Impt.	525.00	
		P# block of 10, Impt.	2,900.	
		Never hinged	4,500.	

Earliest documented use: May 8, 1890.

Cancellation

Supplementary Mail Type F	+3.00

225	A66	8c **lilac,** *Mar. 21, 1893*	70.00	14.00
		grayish lilac	70.00	14.00
		magenta	70.00	14.00
		Never hinged	200.00	
		On cover		30.00
		Block of 4	290.00	90.00
		P# strip of 5, Impt.	400.00	
		P# block of 10, Impt.	1,950.	
		Never hinged	3,750.	

The 8c was issued because the registry fee was reduced from 10 to 8 cents effective Jan. 1, 1893.

Earliest documented use: May 4, 1893.

226	A67	10c **green,** *Feb. 22, 1890*	225.00	3.75
		bluish green	225.00	3.75
		dark green	225.00	3.75
		Never hinged	675.00	
		On cover		10.00
		Block of 4	950.00	37.50
		P# strip of 5, Impt.	1,150.	

We'll buy your U.S. stamp collection <u>now</u> and pay a price that just might amaze you.

Dr. Bob Friedman has been buying all kinds of U.S. stamp collections for over 30 years.

We are a long-established family-owned business and take great pride in our reputation for honesty and integrity. Count on us to examine all of the philatelic material you have for sale and make you an attractive, viable and Full Market Value offer for every bit of it —whether a small collection of U.S. material or huge accumulation.

We have $1.5 million available for this purpose right now. *Our relationships are personal and confidential between you and Bob Friedman, himself, and over 95% of our offers for collections have been accepted.*

HERE ARE SOME SERIOUS FACTORS TO CONSIDER:

• **We will always buy it all.** We won't just pick a few nice things from your collections then tell you to keep the rest. Dr. Bob Friedman will buy everything you have.

• **Do you need a quick response? Ship your collection to us right now —our insurance covers it up to $10,000 per package if you let us know in advance of sending.** Dr. Bob will send you his check for his best offer within 24 hours. Cash it or return it. The amount will be larger than Dr. Bob's offer if he traveled to your location because he'll save the time and travel costs. *Or...*

• **Let Dr. Bob travel to you.** No heavy lifting, no headaches, no need to pack and ship. Dr. Bob can often come to you, give you a check, then pack and move your collections right away for shipment.

• **Quick Payment.** No waiting. When you accept Dr. Bob's offer during his visit, he'll give you cash or a cashier's check on the spot.

Call Toll Free & Ask For Dr. Bob:
1-800-588-8100

Dr. Robert Friedman

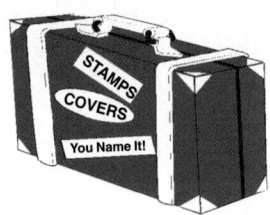

	P# block of 10, Impt.	4,250.	
	Never hinged	*7,000.*	
	Double transfer	—	—

Earliest documented use: Mar. 5, 1890.

Cancellations

		Samoa		—	
		Supp. Mail Type F or G			+2.50
227	A68	15c	**indigo,** *Feb. 22, 1890*	300.00	25.00
		deep indigo		300.00	25.00
		Never hinged		925.00	
		On cover			65.00
		Block of 4		1,300.	135.00
		P# strip of 5, Impt.		1,800.	
		P# block of 10, Impt.		*9,500.*	
		Never hinged		—	
		Double transfer		—	
		Triple transfer		—	

Earliest documented use: May 16, 1890.

Cancellation

		Supplementary Mail Type F			+3.00
228	A69	30c	**black,** *Feb. 22, 1890*	450.00	35.00
		gray black		450.00	35.00
		full black		450.00	35.00
		Never hinged		1,400.	
		On cover			600.00
		Block of 4		1,900.	200.00
		P# strip of 5, Impt.		2,650.	
		P# block of 10, Impt.		*13,500.*	
		Never hinged		—	
		Double transfer		—	

Earliest documented use: April 14, 1890.

Cancellation

		Supplementary Mail Type F			+5.00
229	A70	90c	**orange,** *Feb. 22, 1890*	700.00	140.00
		yellow orange		700.00	140.00
		red orange		700.00	140.00
		Never hinged		2,150.	
		On cover			
		Block of 4		3,000.	725.00
		P# strip of 5, Impt.		4,000.	
		P# block of 10, Impt.		27,500.	
		Never hinged		*42,500.*	
		Short transfer at bottom		—	

Earliest documented use: (?) 16, 1890 (dated cancel on off-cover stamp); Feb. 7, 1892 (on cover).

Cancellation

Supp. Mail Type F or G			+10.00
Nos. 219-229 (12)		2,452.	256.15

VALUES FOR VERY FINE STAMPS
Please note: Stamps are valued in the grade of Very Fine unless otherwise indicated.

COLUMBIAN EXPOSITION ISSUE

World's Columbian Exposition, Chicago, Ill., May 1 - Oct. 30, 1893, celebrating the 400th anniv. of the discovery of America by Christopher Columbus.

See Nos. 2624-2629 for souvenir sheets containing stamps of designs A71-A86 but with "1992" at upper right.

Columbus in Sight of Land — A71

Landing of Columbus — A72

"Santa Maria," Flagship of Columbus — A73

Fleet of Columbus — A74

Columbus Soliciting Aid from Queen Isabella — A75

Columbus Welcomed at Barcelona — A76

Columbus Restored to Favor — A77

Columbus Presenting Natives — A78

Columbus Announcing His Discovery — A79

Columbus at La Rábida — A80

Recall of Columbus — A81

Queen Isabella Pledging Her Jewels — A82

Columbus in Chains — A83

Columbus Describing His Third Voyage — A84

Queen Isabella and Columbus — A85

Columbus — A86

No. 57

Type of imprint and plate number

Exposition Station Handstamp Postmark

Printed by the American Bank Note Company.
Plates of 200 subjects in two panes of 100 each (1c, 2c).
Plates of 100 subjects in two panes of 50 each (2c-$5).
Issued (except 8c) Jan. 1 (a Sunday) and Jan. 2 (Monday), 1893. Jan. 1 and Jan. 2 first day covers are documented for the 1c, 2c, 3c, 4c, 5c and 10c. Jan. 2-only first day covers exist for the 6c and $2. See the First Day Cover section for values.

1893   *Perf. 12*

230	A71	1c **deep blue**	22.50	.40
		blue	22.50	.40
		pale blue	22.50	.40
		Never hinged	57.50	
		On cover		.90
		Pair on cover, Expo. station machine canc.		100.00
		Pair on cover, Expo. station duplex handstamp canc.		175.00
		Block of 4	95.00	7.00
		P# strip of 3, Impt.	82.50	
		P# strip of 4, Impt. & letter	110.00	
		P# block of 6, Impt.	450.00	
		Never hinged	650.00	
		P# block of 8, Impt. & letter	700.00	
		Never hinged	1,025.	
		Double transfer	27.50	.75
		Cracked plate	90.00	

Earliest documented use: Jan. 1, 1893 (FDC).

Cancellation

China		—
Philippines		—

"Broken hat" variety

231	A72	2c **brown violet**	21.00	.30
		deep brown violet	21.00	.30
		gray violet	21.00	.30
		Never hinged	55.00	
		On cover		.35
		On cover or card, Expo. station machine cancel		55.00
		On cover or card, Expo. station duplex handstamp cancel		110.00
		Block of 4	87.50	3.50
		P# strip of 3, Impt.	75.00	
		P# strip of 4, Impt. & letter	100.00	
		Never Hinged	190.00	
		P# block of 6, Impt.	425.00	
		Never hinged	550.00	
		P# block of 8, Impt. & letter	600.00	
		Never hinged	900.00	
		Double transfer	26.00	.35
		Triple transfer	62.50	—
		Quadruple transfer	95.00	
		Broken hat on third figure to left of Columbus	65.00	.45
		Never hinged	160.00	
		Broken frame line	22.50	.35
		Recut frame lines	22.50	—
		Cracked plate	87.50	

There are a number of different versions of the broken hat variety, some of which may be progressive.
Earliest documented use: Jan. 1, 1893 (FDC).

Cancellations

China		—
Supplementary Mail Type G		+3.50

See Die and Plate Proofs for the 2c, imperf. on stamp paper.

232	A73	3c **green**	60.00	15.00
		dull green	60.00	15.00
		dark green	60.00	15.00
		Never hinged	150.00	
		On cover		32.50
		On cover, Expo. station machine canc.		225.00
		On cover, Expo. station duplex handstamp cancel		325.00
		Block of 4	260.00	100.00
		P# strip of 3, Impt.	240.00	
		Never hinged	450.00	
		P# strip of 4, Impt. & letter	310.00	
		Never hinged	600.00	
		P# block of 6, Impt.	725.00	
		Never hinged	1,300.	
		P# block of 8, Impt. & letter	1,200.	
		Never hinged	2,200.	
		Double transfer	80.00	—

Earliest documented use: Jan. 1, 1893 (FDC).

Cancellations

China		—
Supp. Mail Type F or G		+7.50

233	A74	4c **ultramarine**	90.00	7.50
		dull ultramarine	90.00	7.50
		deep ultramarine	90.00	7.50
		Never hinged	225.00	
		On cover		22.50
		On cover, Expo. station machine canc.		275.00
		On cover, Expo. station duplex handstamp cancel		400.00
		Block of 4	390.00	55.00
		P# strip of 3, Impt.	350.00	
		P# strip of 4, Impt. & letter	450.00	—
		P# block of 6, Impt.	1,050.	
		Never hinged	1,750.	
		P# block of 8, Impt. & letter	2,200.	
		Never hinged	3,750.	

		Double transfer	125.00	—
a.		4c blue (error)	19,000.	16,500.
		Never hinged	34,000.	
		Block of 4	92,500.	—
		Never hinged	150,000.	
		P# strip of 4, Impt., letter	150,000.	

No. 233a exists in two shades.

Earliest documented use: Jan. 1, 1893 (FDC).

Cancellation

		Supplementary Mail Type G		+3.00
234	A75	5c **chocolate**	95.00	8.00
		pale brown	95.00	8.00
		yellow brown	95.00	8.00
		dark chocolate	95.00	8.00
		Never hinged	250.00	
		On cover		22.50
		On cover, Expo. station machine canc.		275.00
		On cover, Expo. station duplex handstamp cancel		400.00
		Block of 4	400.00	60.00
		P# strip of 3, Impt.	375.00	
		P# strip of 4, Impt. & letter	525.00	
		P# block of 6, Impt.	1,400.	
		Never hinged	2,400.	
		P# block of 8, Impt. & letter	2,750.	
		Never hinged	4,700.	
		Double transfer	145.00	—

Earliest documented use: Jan. 1, 1893 (FDC).

Cancellations

China		—
Philippines		—
Supplementary Mail Type F		+3.00

235	A76	6c **purple**	90.00	22.50
		dull purple	90.00	22.50
		Never hinged	225.00	
a.		6c red violet	90.00	22.50
		Never hinged	225.00	
		On cover		50.00
		On cover, Expo. station machine canc.		300.00
		On cover, Expo. station duplex handstamp cancel		450.00
		Block of 4	390.00	115.00
		P# strip of 3, Impt.	350.00	
		P# strip of 4, Impt. & letter	450.00	
		P# block of 6, Impt.	1,175.	
		Never hinged	2,000.	
		P# block of 8, Impt. & letter	2,150.	
		Never hinged	3,650.	
		Double transfer	115.00	30.00

Earliest documented use: Jan. 2, 1893 (FDC).

Cancellations

China		—
Supplementary Mail Type F		+5.00

236	A77	8c **magenta,** *Mar. 1893*	80.00	11.00
		light magenta	80.00	11.00
		dark magenta	80.00	11.00
		Never hinged	200.00	
		On cover		22.50
		On cover, Expo. station machine canc.		300.00
		On cover, Expo. station duplex handstamp cancel		475.00
		Block of 4	350.00	65.00
		P# strip of 3, Impt.	300.00	
		P# strip of 4, Impt. & letter	400.00	
		P# block of 6, Impt.	825.00	
		Never hinged	1,450.	
		P# block of 8, Impt. & letter	1,450.	
		Never hinged	2,500.	
		Double transfer	90.00	—

Earliest documented use: Mar. 18, 1893.

Cancellations

China		—
Supplementary Mail Type F		+4.50

237	A78	10c **black brown**	150.00	8.00
		dark brown	150.00	8.00
		gray black	150.00	8.00
		Never hinged	350.00	
		On cover		32.50
		On cover, Expo. station machine canc.		400.00
		On cover, Expo. station duplex handstamp cancel		550.00
		Block of 4	625.00	60.00
		P# strip of 3, Impt.	600.00	
		P# strip of 4, Impt. & letter	750.00	
		Never hinged	1,450.	
		P# block of 6, Impt.	3,750.	
		Never hinged	6,500.	
		P# block of 8, Impt. & letter	6,000.	
		Never hinged	9,500.	
		Double transfer	180.00	12.50
		Triple transfer		

Earliest documented use: Jan. 1, 1893 (FDC).

Cancellations

Philippines		—
Supp. Mail Types F or G		+4.00

238	A79	15c **dark green**	250.00	70.00
		green	250.00	70.00
		dull green	250.00	70.00
		Never hinged	750.00	
		On cover		225.00
		On cover, Expo. station machine canc.		700.00
		On cover, Expo. station duplex handstamp cancel		1,000.
		Block of 4	1,050.	450.00
		P# strip of 3, Impt.	1,000.	

		P# strip of 4, Impt. & letter	1,250.	
		P# block of 6, Impt.	4,000.	
		Never hinged	6,750.	
		P# block of 8, Impt. & letter	7,000.	
		Never hinged	12,000.	
		Double transfer		—

Earliest documented use: Jan. 26, 1893.

Cancellations

China		+75.00
Supp. Mail Type F or G		+10.00

239	A80	30c **orange brown**	300.00	90.00
		bright orange brown	300.00	90.00
		Never hinged	900.00	
		On cover		400.00
		On cover, Expo. station machine canc.		1,250.
		On cover, Expo. station duplex handstamp cancel		1,750.
		Block of 4	1,250.	600.00
		P# strip of 3, Impt.	1,200.	
		P# strip of 4, Impt. & letter	1,600.	
		P# block of 6, Impt.	8,500.	
		Never hinged	14,500.	
		P# block of 8, Impt. & letter	12,000.	
		Never hinged	20,000.	

Earliest documented use: Jan. 10, 1893 (dated cancel on off-cover stamp); Feb. 8, 1893 (cover).

Cancellations

		Supp. Mail Types F or G		+25.00
240	A81	50c **slate blue**	600.00	180.00
		dull state blue	600.00	180.00
		Never hinged	1,750.	
		On cover		625.00
		On cover, Expo. station machine canc.		1,750.
		On cover, Expo. station duplex handstamp cancel		2,250.
		Block of 4	2,600.	1,100.
		P# strip of 3, Impt.	2,500.	
		P# strip of 4, Impt. & letter	3,750.	
		Never hinged	8,000.	
		P# block of 6, Impt.	14,000.	
		Never hinged	23,500.	
		P# block of 8, Impt. & letter	22,500.	
		Never hinged	37,500.	
		Double transfer	—	
		Triple transfer	—	

Earliest documented use: Feb. 8, 1893.

Cancellation

		Supp. Mail Types F or G		+30.00
241	A82	$1 **salmon**	1,200.	650.
		dark salmon	1,200.	650.
		Never hinged	4,000.	
		No gum	625.	
		On cover		2,000.
		On cover, Expo. station machine canc.		3,500.
		On cover, Expo. station duplex handstamp cancel		4,500.
		Block of 4	5,000.	4,500.
		P# strip of 3, Impt.	5,000.	
		P# strip of 4, Impt. & letter	6,500.	
		P# block of 6, Impt.	47,500.	
		P# block of 8, Impt. & letter	80,000.	
		Never hinged	125,000.	
		Double transfer	—	

Earliest documented use: Jan. 11, 1893 (dated cancel on off-cover stamp); Jan. 21, 1893 (on cover).

Cancellations

		Supp. Mail Types F or G		+50.
242	A83	$2 **brown red**	1,250.	600.
		deep brown red	1,250.	600.
		Never hinged	4,100.	
		No gum	625.	
		On cover		2,100.
		On cover, Expo. station machine canc.		3,500.
		On cover, Expo. station duplex handstamp cancel		4,500.
		Block of 4	5,250.	3,250.
		P# strip of 3, Impt.	5,500.	
		P# strip of 4, Impt. & letter	9,000.	
		P# block of 6, Impt.	67,500.	
		P# block of 8, Impt. & letter	85,000.	

Earliest documented use: Jan. 2, 1893 (FDC).

Cancellations

Supplementary Mail Type G		+50.

The No. 242 plate block of 8 is believed to be unique.

243	A84	$3 **yellow green**	1,900.	1,000.
		pale yellow green	1,900.	1,000.
		Never hinged	6,250.	
		No gum	1,000.	
a.		$3 olive green	1,900.	1,000.
		Never hinged	6,250.	
		No gum	1,000.	
		On cover		2,600.
		On cover, Expo. station machine canc.		5,000.
		On cover, Expo. station duplex handstamp cancel		7,000.
		Block of 4	9,000.	9,000.
		P# strip of 3, Impt.	9,000.	
		P# strip of 4, Impt. & letter	11,000.	
		P# block of 6, Impt.	85,000.	

Earliest documented use: Mar. 24, 1893.

244	A85	$4 **crimson lake**	2,600.	1,300.
		Never hinged	8,500.	
		No gum	1,300.	
a.		$4 rose carmine	2,600.	1,300.

pale aniline rose	2,600.	1,300.
Never hinged	8,500.	
No gum	1,300.	
On cover		4,000.
On cover, Expo. station ma-		
chine canc.		6,500.
On cover, Expo. station du-		
plex handstamp cancel		9,000.
Block of 4	11,500.	12,500.
P# strip of 3, Impt.	10,750.	
P# strip of 4, Impt. & letter	15,500.	
P# block of 6, Impt.	250,000.	
P# block of 8, Impt. & letter	310,000.	

The No. 244 plate block of 8 is unique; it has full original gum with light hinge marks.

Earliest documented use: Mar. 24, 1893.

245	A86	$5 black	3,000.	1,500.
		grayish black	3,000.	1,500.
		Never hinged	10,000.	
		No gum	1,500.	
		On cover		4,750.
		On cover, Expo. station ma-		
		chine canc.		15,000.
		On cover, Expo. station du-		
		plex handstamp cancel		17,500.
		Block of 4	13,500.	12,500.
		P# strip of 3, Impt.	13,500.	
		P# strip of 4, Impt. & letter	22,500.	
		Never hinged	45,000.	
		P# block of 6, Impt.	190,000.	
		Never hinged	260,000.	
		P# block of 8, Impt. & letter	250,000.	

Earliest documented use: Jan. 6, 1893.

The No. 245 plate block of 8 is unique; it has traces of original gum.

See Nos. 2624-2629 for souvenir sheets containing stamps of designs A71-A86 but with "1992" at upper right.

Nos. 230-245 exist imperforate; not issued. See Die and Plate proofs for the 2c.

Never-Hinged Stamps

See note before No. 205 regarding premiums for never-hinged stamps.

BUREAU ISSUES

In the following listings of postal issues mostly printed by the Bureau of Engraving and Printing at Washington, D.C., the editors acknowledge with thanks the use of material prepared by the Catalogue Listing Committee of the Bureau Issues Association.

The Bureau-printed stamps until 1965 were engraved except the Offset Issues of 1918-19 (Nos. 525-536). Engraving and lithography were combined for the first time for the Homemakers 5c (No. 1253). The Bureau used photogravure first in 1971 on the Missouri 8c (No. 1426).

Stamps in this section which were not printed by the Bureau begin with Nos. 909-921 and are so noted.

"On cover" listings carry through No. 701. Beyond this point a few covers of special significance are listed. Many Bureau Issue stamps are undoubtedly scarce properly used on cover. Most higher denominations exist almost exclusively on pieces of package wrapping and usually in combination with other values. Collector interest in covers is generally limited to fancy cancellations, attractive corner cards, uses abroad and other special usages.

Plate number blocks are valued unused. Although many exist used, and are scarcer in that condition, they tend to sell for less than the value of the unused examples because they are less sought after.

IMPRINTS AND PLATE NUMBERS

In listing the Bureau of Engraving & Printing Imprints, the editors have followed the classification of types adopted by the Bureau Issues Association. Types I, II, IV, V and VIII occur on postage issues and are illustrated below. Types III, VI and VII occur only on Special Delivery plates, so are illustrated with the listings of those stamps; other types are illustrated with the listings of the issues on which they occur.

Type I   II   IV   V   VIII

In listing Imprint blocks and strips, the editors have designated for each stamp the various types known to exist. If, however, the Catalogue listing sufficiently describes the Imprint, no type number is given. Thus a listing reading: "P# block of 6, Impt. (Imprint) & A" in the 1912-14 series would not be followed by a type number as the description is self-explanatory. Values are for the commonest types.

PLATE POSITIONS

At the suggestion of the Catalogue Listing Committee of the Bureau Issues Association (now the United States Stamp Society), all plate positions of these issues are indicated by giving the plate number first, next the pane position, and finally the stamp position. For example: 20234 L.L. 58.

Franklin — A87

Washington — A88

Jackson — A89

Lincoln — A90

Grant — A91

Garfield — A92

Sherman — A93

Webster — A94

Clay — A95

Jefferson — A96

Perry — A97

James
Madison — A98

John Marshall — A99

REGULAR ISSUE

Plates for the issue of 1894 were of two sizes: 400 subjects for all 1c, 2c and 10c denominations; 200 subjects for all 6c, 8c, 15c, 50c, $1.00, $2.00 and $5.00, and both 400 and 200 subjects for the 3c, 4c and 5c denominations; all issued in panes of 100 each.

1894		Unwmk.	Perf. 12	
246	A87	1c **ultramarine,** *Oct. 1894*	32.50	5.00
		bright ultramarine	32.50	5.00
		dark ultramarine	32.50	5.00
		Never hinged	95.00	
		On cover		20.00
		Block of 4	140.00	35.00
		P# strip of 3, Impt., T I	145.00	

		Never hinged	325.00	
		P# block of 6, Impt., T I	450.00	
		Never hinged	900.00	
		Double transfer	40.00	6.00

Earliest documented use: Oct. 17, 1894.

Cancellation

		China	—	
247	A87	1c **blue**	75.00	3.00
		bright blue	75.00	3.00
		dark blue	75.00	3.00
		Never hinged	225.00	
		On cover		17.50
		Block of 4	325.00	22.50
		P# strip of 3, Impt., T I or II	325.00	
		Never hinged	675.00	
		P# block of 6, Impt., T I or II	900.00	
		Never hinged	1,700.	
		Double transfer	—	4.50

Earliest documented use: Nov. 5, 1894.

TWO CENTS:

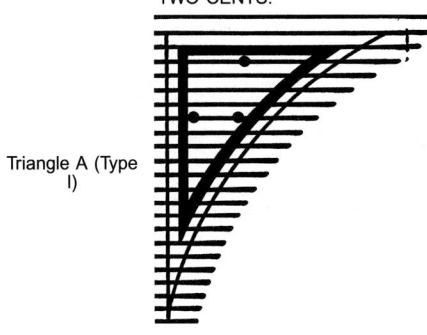

Triangle A (Type I)

Type I (Triangle A). The horizontal lines of the ground work run across the triangle and are of the same thickness within it as without.

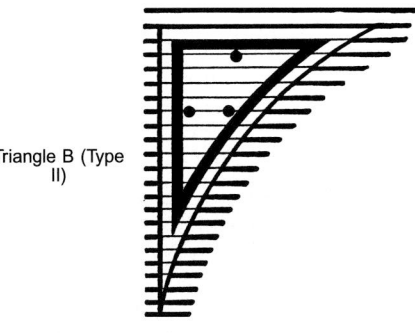

Triangle B (Type II)

Type II (Triangle B). The horizontal lines cross the triangle but are thinner within it than without. Other minor design differences exist, but the change to Triangle B is a sufficient determinant.

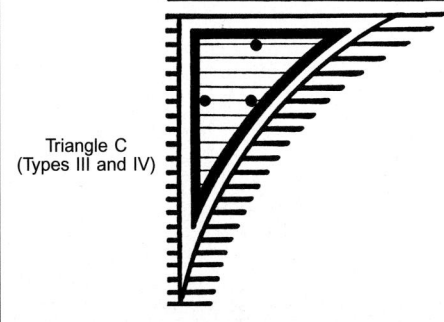

Triangle C (Types III and IV)

Type III (Triangle C). The horizontal lines do not cross the double lines of the triangle. The lines within the triangle are thin, as in Type II. The rest of the design is the same as Type II, except that most of the designs had the dot in the "S" of "CENTS" removed. Stamps with this dot present are listed; some specialists refer to them as "Type IIIa" varieties.

Type IV (Triangle C). See No. 279B and its varieties. Type IV is from a new die with many major and minor design variations including, (1) re-cutting and lengthening of hairline, (2) shaded toga button, (3) strengthening of lines on sleeve, (4) additional dots on ear, (5) "T" of "TWO" straight at right, (6) background lines extend into white oval opposite "U" of "UNITED." Many other differences exist.

For further information concerning type IV, see also George Brett's article in the Sept. 1993 issue of the "The United States Specialist" and the 23-part article by Kenneth Diehl in the Dec. 1994 through Aug. 1997 issues of the "The United States Specialist."

248	A88	2c **pink,** type I, *Oct. 1894*	30.00	7.50
		pale pink	30.00	7.50
		Never hinged	87.50	
		On cover		15.00
		Block of 4	130.00	42.50
		P# strip of 3, Impt., T I or II	120.00	
		Never hinged	275.00	
		P# block of 6, Impt., T I or II	300.00	
		Never hinged	675.00	
		Double transfer	—	—
a.		Vert. pair, imperf horiz.	5,500.	

Earliest documented use: Oct. 16, 1894.

249	A88	2c **carmine lake,** type I, *Oct. 1894*	175.00	5.50
		dark carmine lake	175.00	5.50
		Never hinged	525.00	
		On cover		11.50
		Block of 4	750.00	40.00
		P# strip of 3, Impt., T I or II	700.00	
		Never hinged	1,650.	
		P# block of 6, Impt., T I or II	2,500.	
		Never hinged	5,000.	
		Double transfer	—	6.50

Earliest documented use: Oct. 11, 1894.

250	A88	2c **carmine,** type I, *Oct. 1894*	30.00	2.50
		dark carmine	30.00	4.50
		Never hinged	85.00	
		On cover		3.50
		Block of 4	130.00	18.00
a.		2c **rose,** type I, *Oct. 1894*	30.00	4.50
		Never hinged	85.00	
		On cover		5.50
		Block of 4	130.00	20.00
b.		2c **scarlet,** type I, *Jan. 1895*	30.00	1.00
		Never hinged	85.00	
		On cover		1.50
		Block of 4	130.00	7.50
		P# strip of 3, Impt., T I or II	120.00	
		Never hinged	300.00	
		P# block of 6, Impt., T I or II	375.00	
		Never hinged	750.00	
		Double transfer	—	5.00
d.		Horizontal pair, imperf. between	2,000.	

Earliest documented uses: Oct. 15, 1894 (No. 250), Oct. 13, 1894 (No. 250a), Jan. 17, 1895 (No. 250b).

251	A88	2c **carmine,** type II, *Feb. 1895*	350.00	11.00
		dark carmine	350.00	11.00
		Never hinged	1,000.	
		On cover		20.00
		Block of 4	1,250.	100.00
a.		2c **scarlet,** type II, *Feb. 1895*	300.00	7.50
		Never hinged	1,000.	
		On cover		13.50
		Block of 4	1,250.	65.00
		P# strip of 3, Impt., T II	1,200.	
		Never hinged	3,000.	
		P# block of 6, Impt., T II	3,250.	
		Never hinged	6,500.	

Earliest documented uses: Feb. 12, 1895 (No. 251, dated cancel on off-cover stamp); Feb. 16, 1895 (No. 251, on cover); Feb. 19, 1895 (No. 251a).

252	A88	2c **carmine,** type III, *Mar. 1895*	130.00	11.00
		pale carmine	130.00	11.00
		Never hinged	400.00	
a.		2c **scarlet,** type III, *Mar. 1895*	130.00	11.00

POSTAGE — 51

Never hinged 400.00
On cover — 15.00
Block of 4 550.00 100.00
P# strip of 3, Impt., T II or IV 525.00
 Never hinged 1,400.
P# block of 6, Impt., T II or IV 1,900.
 Never hinged 4,000.
Dot in "S" of "CENTS" (carmine) 150.00 5.75
 Never hinged 390.00
b. Horiz. pair, imperf. vert. 5,000.
c. Horiz. pair, imperf. between 5,500.
Former Nos. 252a, 252b are now Nos. 252b, 252c.

Earliest documented uses: Apr. 2, 1895 (dated cancel tying No. 252 dot in "S" variety on piece); Apr. 5, 1895 (No. 252); Apr. 17, 1895 (No. 252a).

253 A89 3c purple, Sept. 1894 125.00 10.00
 dark purple 125.00 10.00
 Never hinged 375.00
 On cover — 25.00
 Block of 4 550.00 75.00
 Margin block of 4, arrow, R or L 575.00
 P# strip of 3, Impt., T I or II 500.00
  Never hinged 1,200.
 P# block of 6, Impt., T I or II 1,500.
  Never hinged 3,250.

Earliest documented use: Oct. 20, 1894 (dated cancel on off-cover stamp); Nov. 15, 1894 (on cover).

See Die and Plate Proofs for imperf. on stamp paper.

254 A90 4c dark brown, Sept. 1894 175.00 7.50
 brown 175.00 7.50
 Never hinged 525.00
 On cover — 21.00
 Block of 4 750.00 42.50
 Margin block of 4, arrow, R or L 775.00
 P# strip of 3, Impt., T I or II 700.00
  Never hinged 1,750.
 P# block of 6, Impt., T I or II 2,000.
  Never hinged 4,000.

Earliest documented use: Oct. 16, 1894 (dated cancel on off-cover stamp); Nov. 21, 1894 (on cover).

See Die and Plate Proofs for imperf. on stamp paper.

Cancellations
Supplementary Mail Type F +2.00

255 A91 5c chocolate, Sept. 1894 125.00 7.00
 deep chocolate 125.00 7.00
 yellow brown 125.00 7.00
 Never hinged 375.00
 On cover — 20.00
 Block of 4 550.00 50.00
 Margin block of 4, arrow, R or L 575.00
 P# strip of 3, Impt., T I, II or IV 550.00
  Never hinged 1,250.
 P# block of 6, Impt., T I, II or IV 1,350.
  Never hinged 2,750.
 Double transfer 150.00 6.50
 Worn plate, diagonal lines missing in oval background 125.00 5.00
c. Vert. pair, imperf. horiz. 4,000.
 P# block of 6, Impt., T IV —

See Die and Plate Proofs for imperf. on stamp paper.

Earliest documented use: Oct. 23, 1894.

Cancellations
Supplementary Mail Type G +2.00
China —

256 A92 6c dull brown, July 1894 175.00 25.00
 Never hinged 500.00
 On cover — 47.50
 Block of 4 750.00 175.00
 Margin block of 4, arrow, R or L 775.00
 P# strip of 3, Impt., T I 750.00
  Never hinged 1,750.
 P# block of 6, Impt., T I 2,750.
  Never hinged 5,750. —
a. Vert. pair, imperf. horiz. 2,000.
 P# block of 6, Impt., T I 14,000.

Earliest documented use: Aug. 11, 1894.

257 A93 8c violet brown, Mar. 1895 175.00 18.50
 bright violet brown 175.00 18.50
 Never hinged 500.00
 On cover — 45.00
 Block of 4 750.00 130.00
 Margin block of 4, arrow, R or L 775.00
 P# strip of 3, Impt., T I 750.00
  Never hinged 1,750.
 P# block of 6, Impt., T I 2,500.
  Never hinged 5,000.

Earliest documented use: May 8, 1895.

258 A94 10c dark green, Sept. 1894 325.00 15.00
 green 325.00 15.00
 dull green 325.00 15.00
 Never hinged 975.00
 On cover — 35.00
 Block of 4 1,350. 85.00
 P# strip of 3, Impt., T I 1,300.
  Never hinged 3,250.
 P# block of 6, Impt., T I 3,500.
  Never hinged 7,250.
 Double transfer 375.00 15.00

See Die and Plate Proofs for imperf. on stamp paper.

Earliest documented use: Nov. 19, 1894.

Cancellations
China —
Supp. Mail Types F, G +2.00
259 A95 15c dark blue, Oct. 1894 325.00 60.00
 indigo 325.00 60.00
 Never hinged 975.00
 On cover — 115.00
 Block of 4 1,350. 400.00
 Margin block of 4, arrow, R or L 1,400.
 P# strip of 3, Impt., T I 1,500.
  Never hinged 3,250.
 P# block of 6, Impt., T I 5,000.
  Never hinged 9,500.

Earliest documented use: Dec. 6, 1894.

Cancellation
China —
260 A96 50c orange, Nov. 1894 600. 135.
 deep orange 600. 135.
 Never hinged 1,800.
 On cover — 1,000.
 Block of 4 2,750. 1,100.
 Margin block of 4, arrow, R or L 2,850.
 P# strip of 3, Impt., T I 2,600.
  Never hinged 5,750.
 P# block of 6, Impt., T I 10,500.
  Never hinged 17,500.

Earliest documented use: Dec. 12, 1894 (dated cancel on off-cover stamp); Jan. 15, 1895 (on cover).

Cancellations
Supp. Mail Type F or G —
China —

Type I

Type II

ONE DOLLAR
Type I. The circles enclosing "$1" are broken where they meet the curved line below "One Dollar."
Type II. The circles are complete.
The fifteen left vertical rows of impressions from plate 76 are Type I, the balance being Type II.

261 A97 $1 black, type I, Nov. 1894 1,200. 350.
 grayish black 1,200. 350.
 Never hinged 3,250.
 No gum 375.
 On cover — 2,750.
 Block of 4 5,500. 2,100.
 Margin block of 4, arrow, L 5,750.
 P# strip of 3, Impt., T V 4,750.
 P# block of 6, Impt., T V 18,500.

Earliest documented use: Jan. 18, 1895.

261A A97 $1 black, type II, Nov. 1894 2,400. 750.
 Never hinged 6,750.
 No gum 750.
 On cover — 4,500.
 Block of 4 10,000. 4,750.
 Margin block of 4, arrow, R 10,500.
 Horizontal pair, types I and II 4,250. 1,400.
 Block of 4, two each of types I and II 9,500. —
 P# strip of 3, Impt., T V, one stamp No. 261 7,000.
 P# block of 6, Impt., T V, two stamps No. 261 27,500.

Earliest documented use: Mar. 22, 1895. A Mar. 11, 1895, cover has been reported. The editors would like to see evidence of certification of this date.

262 A98 $2 bright blue, Dec. 1894 3,250. 1,250.
 Never hinged 9,750.
 No gum 1,250.
 dark blue 3,400. 1,300.
  Never hinged 8,750.
 On cover — 5,000.
 Block of 4 14,500. 7,250.
 Margin block of 4, arrow, R or L 15,000.
 P# strip of 3, Impt., T V 14,000.
 P# block of 6, Impt., T V 42,500.

Earliest documented use: July 6, 1895 (dated cancel on off-cover stamp); July 15, 1895 (on cover).

263 A99 $5 dark green, Dec. 1894 5,000. 2,600.

Never hinged 15,000.
No gum 2,600.
On cover —
Block of 4 22,500. 14,500.
Margin block of 4, arrow, R or L 23,500.
P# strip of 3, Impt., T V 23,500.

Earliest documented use: July 6, 1896 (dated cancel on off-cover stamp).

REGULAR ISSUE

(Actual size of letter)

repeated in rows, thus

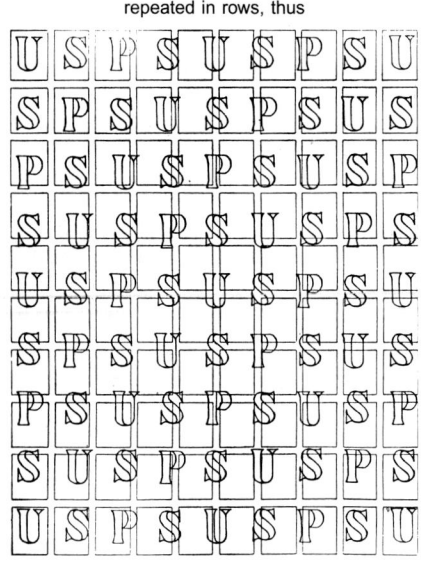

Watermark 191

The letters stand for "United States Postage Stamp."

Plates for the 1895 issue were of two sizes:
400 subjects for all 1c, 2c and 10c denominations; 200 subjects for all 3c, 4c, 5c, 6c, 8c, 15c, 50c, $1, $2 and $5; all issued in panes of 100 each.

Printings from the 400 subject plates show the watermark reading horizontally; on the 200 subject printings the watermark reads vertically (with the tops and bottoms of the letters toward the vertical sides of the stamps).

HORIZONTAL WATERMARK ORIENTATIONS

Normal	Reversed

Inverted	Inverted Reversed

VERTICAL WATERMARK ORIENTATIONS

Normal	Reversed	Inverted	Inverted Reversed

Wmk. 191 Horizontally or Vertically

1895   *Perf. 12*

264	A87	1c	**blue,** *Apr. 1895*	6.50	.50
			dark blue	6.50	.50
			pale blue	6.50	.50
			Never hinged	19.00	
			On cover		1.25
			Block of 4	27.50	5.00
			P# strip of 3, Impt., T I, II, IV or V	27.50	
			Never hinged	70.00	
			P# block of 6, Impt., T I, II, IV or V	250.00	
			Never hinged	450.00	
			Double transfer	—	1.00

Earliest documented use: May 16, 1895.

Cancellations

China	—
Philippines	—
Samoa	—

265	A88	2c	**carmine,** type I, *May 1895*	30.00	3.00
			deep carmine	30.00	3.00
			Never hinged	90.00	
			On cover		5.00
			Block of 4	130.00	16.00

P# strip of 3, Impt., T II	120.00
Never hinged	325.00
P# block of 6, Impt., T II	400.00
Never hinged	800.00
Double transfer	45.00 6.75

Earliest documented use: May 2, 1895.

266	A88	2c	**carmine,** type II, *May 1895*	35.00	5.00
			Never hinged	110.00	
			On cover		8.50
			Block of 4	200.00	40.00
			Horizontal pair, types II and III	125.00	17.50
			Never hinged	350.00	
			P# strip of 3, Impt., T II or IV	140.00	
			Never hinged	375.00	
			P# block of 6, Impt., T II or IV	500.00	
			Never hinged	1,000.	

Earliest documented use: May 27, 1895.

267	A88	2c	**carmine,** type III *May 1895*	5.50	.40
			deep carmine	5.50	.40
			reddish carmine	5.50	.40
			Never hinged	16.00	
			On cover		.55
			Block of 4	24.00	3.25
			P# strip of 3, Impt., T II, IV or V	22.50	
			Never hinged	57.50	
			P# block of 6, Impt., T II, IV or V	190.00	
			Never hinged	325.00	
			Dot in "S" of "CENTS"	7.50	.50
			Never hinged	22.50	
			Double transfer	16.50	1.25
a.			2c **pink,** type III, *Nov. 1897*	8.50	1.00
			Never hinged	25.00	
			bright pink	13.50	4.50
			Never hinged	40.00	
			On cover		1.25
			Block of 4	37.50	7.50
			P# strip of 3, Impt., T II, IV or V	32.50	
			Never hinged	85.00	
			P# block of 6, Impt., T II, IV or V	250.00	
			Never hinged	475.00	
			Dot in "S" of "CENTS"	16.00	.75
			Never hinged	47.50	
b.			2c **vermilion,** type III, *early 1899*	37.50	6.00
c.			2c **rose carmine,** type III, *Mar. 1899*	—	—

Earliest documented uses:
No. 267, May 28, 1895;
No. 267 with dot in "S", July 15, 1895;
No. 267a, Dec. 8, 1897;
No. 267a with dot in "S", Mar. 18, 1898.

Cancellations

Green	—
China	—
Hawaii	—
Philippines	—
Samoa	—

The three left vertical rows of impressions from plate 170 are Type II, the balance being Type III.

268	A89	3c	**purple,** *Oct. 1895*	37.50	2.00
			dark purple	37.50	2.00
			Never hinged	110.00	
			On cover		8.00
			Block of 4	160.00	20.00
			Margin block of 4, arrow, R or L	175.00	
			P# strip of 3, Impt., T II or V	150.00	
			Never hinged	375.00	
			P# block of 6, Impt., T II or IV	725.00	
			Never hinged	1,300.	
			Double transfer	45.00	4.50

Earliest documented use: Dec. 1, 1895.

Cancellations

Guam	—
China	—
Philippines	—

269	A90	4c	**dark brown,** *June, 1895*	50.00	3.00
			dark yellow brown	50.00	3.00
			Never hinged	145.00	
			On cover		11.00
			Block of 4	210.00	27.50
			Margin block of 4, arrow, R or L	225.00	
			P# strip of 3, Impt., T I, II, IV or V	200.00	
			Never hinged	500.00	
			P# block of 6, Impt., T I, II, IV or V	825.00	
			Never hinged	1,650.	
			Double transfer	55.00	5.00

Earliest documented use: July 22, 1895.

Cancellations

Philippines	—
China	—
Samoa	—

270	A91	5c	**chocolate,** *June, 1895*	37.50	3.00
			deep brown	37.50	3.00
			chestnut	37.50	3.00
			Never hinged	110.00	
			On cover		7.50
			Block of 4	160.00	27.50
			Margin block of 4, arrow, R or L	170.00	

P# strip of 3, Impt., T I, II, IV or V	150.00
Never hinged	375.00
P# block of 6, Impt., T I, II, IV or V	700.00
Never hinged	1,300.
Double transfer	45.00 4.50
Worn plate, diagonal lines missing in oval background	40.00 3.25

Earliest documented use: Sept. 12, 1895.

Cancellations

China	—
Supplementary Mail G	+2.50

271	A92	6c	**dull brown,** *Aug. 1895*	130.00	7.50
			claret brown	130.00	7.50
			Never hinged	375.00	
			On cover		27.50
			Block of 4	600.00	65.00
			Margin block of 4, arrow, R or L	625.00	
			P# strip of 3, Impt., T I, IV or V	525.00	
			Never hinged	1,200.	
			P# block of 6, Impt., T I, IV or V	3,000.	
			Never hinged	5,250.	
			Very thin paper	150.00	7.50
a.			Wmkd. USIR	*12,500.*	*8,000.*
			Pair	—	
			P# strip of 3, Impt.	—	

Earliest documented use: Sept. 14, 1895.

Cancellation

Philippines	—

Nos. 271a, 272a must have an identifiable portion of the letters "I" or "R." Single stamps from the same sheets, but showing the "U" or "S" are considered to be Nos. 271 and 272.

272	A93	8c	**violet brown,** *July 1895*	75.00	2.50
			dark violet brown	75.00	2.50
			Never hinged	210.00	
			On cover		14.00
			Block of 4	325.00	17.50
			Margin block of 4, arrow, R or L	340.00	
			P# strip of 3, Impt., T I, IV or V	310.00	
			Never hinged	725.00	
			P# block of 6, Impt., T I, IV or V	1,000.	
			Never hinged	2,100.	
			Double transfer	90.00	4.00
a.			Wmkd. USIR	*6,000.*	*900.00*
			Block of 4		*5,000.*
			P# strip of 3 Impt., T I	*20,000.*	

Earliest documented use: Sept. 11, 1895.

Cancellations

China	—
Guam	—
Philippines	—
Puerto Rico, 1898	—
Samoa	—
Supplementary Mail Type G	+2.50

273	A94	10c	**dark green,** *June 1895*	100.00	2.00
			green	100.00	2.00
			Never hinged	300.00	
			On cover		15.00
			Block of 4	425.00	20.00
			P# strip of 3, Impt., T I or IV	425.00	
			Never hinged	975.00	
			P# block of 6, Impt., T I or IV	1,750.	
			Never hinged	3,500.	
			Double transfer	125.00	4.50

Earliest documented use: July 25, 1895.

Cancellations

Green	—
China	—
Cuba	—
Philippines	—
Supp. Mail Types F, G	+2.00

274	A95	15c	**dark blue,** *Sept. 1895*	250.00	15.00
			indigo	250.00	15.00
			Never hinged	725.00	
			On cover		55.00
			Block of 4	1,050.	95.00
			Margin block of 4, arrow, R or L	1,075.	
			P# strip of 3, Impt., T I or IV	1,000.	
			Never hinged	2,250.	
			P# block of 6, Impt., T I or IV	3,750.	
			Never hinged	*10,000.*	

Earliest documented use: May 5, 1896.

Cancellations

China	—
Philippines	—
Supplementary Mail Type G	+3.00

275	A96	50c	**orange,** *Nov. 1895*	325.	35.00
			Never hinged	925.	
			On cover		400.00
			Block of 4	1,400.	200.00
			Margin block of 4, arrow, R or L	1,450.	
			P# strip of 3, Impt., T I	1,250.	
			P# block of 6, Impt., T I	6,000.	
			Never hinged	*12,500.*	
a.			50c **red orange**	375.	42.50

Never hinged	1,050.	
On cover		400.00
Block of 4	1,600.	250.00
Margin block of 4, arrow, R or L	1,650.	
P# strip of 3, Impt., T I	1,450.	
P# block of 6, Impt., T I	6,500.	

Earliest documented use: May 5, 1896.

Cancellations

China		—
Philippines		—
Supp. Mail Types F, G		+5.

276 A97 $1 **black**, type I, *Aug. 1895* 700. 95.00

greenish black	700.	95.00
Never hinged	2,000.	
No gum	200.	
On cover		2,250.
Block of 4	3,000.	675.
Margin block of 4, arrow, L	3,100.	
P# strip of 3, Impt., T V	2,900.	
Never hinged	6,500.	
P# block of 6, Impt., T V	14,000.	

Earliest documented use: Mar. 1, 1898.

Cancellation

Philippines		—

276A A97 $1 **black**, type II, *Aug. 1895* 1,500. 225.

greenish black	1,500.	225.
Never hinged	4,250.	
No gum	475.	
On cover		3,750.
Block of 4	6,500.	1,550.
Margin block of 4, arrow, R	6,750.	
Horizontal pair, types I and II	2,600.	2,600.
Block of 4, two each of types I and II	6,500.	6,500.
P# strip of 3, Impt., T V, one stamp No. 276	5,250.	
P# block of 6, Impt., T V, two stamps No. 276	25,000.	

Earliest documented use: Apr. 6, 1896.

Cancellation

China		—
Philippines		—

The fifteen left vertical rows of impressions from plate 76 are Type I, the balance being Type II.

277 A98 $2 **bright blue** 1,200. 450.

Never hinged	3,250.	
No gum	400.	

a. $2 **dark blue** 1,200. 450.

Never hinged	3,250.	
No gum	400.	
On cover		3,500.
Block of 4	5,250.	2,750.
Margin block of 4, arrow, R or L	5,500.	
P# strip of 3, Impt., T V	4,500.	—
P# block of 6, Impt., T V	21,000.	

Earliest documented use: July 18, 1895.

Cancellation

Supplementary Mail Type G		—

278 A99 $5 **dark green**, *Aug. 1895* 2,400. 650.

Never hinged	6,750.	
No gum	900.	
On cover		12,500.
Block of 4	10,500.	3,750.
Margin block of 4, arrow, R or L	11,000.	
P# strip of 3, Impt., T V	9,750.	
P# block of 6, Impt., T V	75,000.	

Earliest documented use: Nov. 3, 1896.

See Die and Plate Proofs for imperf. or horiz. pair, imperf. vert. (1c) on stamp paper.

REGULAR ISSUE
Wmk. 191 Horizontally or Vertically
1897-1903   *Perf. 12*

Plates for the 1897-1903 issue were of two sizes:

400 subjects for the 1c and 2c denominations; 200 subjects for all 4c, 5c, 6c and 15c denominations; and both 400 and 200 for the 10c denomination; all issued in panes of 100 each.

Printings from the 400 subject plates show the watermark reading horizontally, on the 200 subject plate printings the watermark reads vertically.

In January, 1898, the color of the 1-cent stamp was changed to green and in March, 1898, that of the 5-cents to dark blue in order to conform to the colors assigned these values by the Universal Postal Union. These changes necessitated changing the colors of the 10c and 15c denominations in order to avoid confusion.

279 A87 1c **deep green**, horizontal watermark, *Jan. 1898* 9.00 .50

green	9.00	.50
yellow green	9.00	.50
dark yellow green	9.00	.50
Never hinged	25.00	
On cover		.60
Block of 4	37.50	5.00
P# strip of 3, Impt., T V	37.50	—
Never hinged	85.00	
P# block of 6, Impt., T V	185.00	
Never hinged	350.00	
Double transfer	12.00	1.10

a. 1c **deep green**, vertical watermark (error), *May 1902* 40.00 7.50

Never hinged	115.00	
On cover		22.50
Block of 4	200.00	
P# strip of 3, Impt., T V	250.00	
Never hinged	650.00	

Earliest documented use: Jan. 31, 1898.

Cancellations

China		—
Guam		—
Puerto Rico, 1898		—
Philippines		-

279B A88 2c **red**, type IV *May 1899* 9.00 .40

light red, *May 1899*	9.00	.40
Never hinged	25.00	
deep red, *Sept. 1901*	13.50	1.25
Never hinged	32.50	
On cover		.50
Block of 4	37.50	3.00
P# strip of 3, Impt., T V	37.50	
Never hinged	85.00	
P# block of 6, Impt., T V	200.00	
Never hinged	360.00	
P# strip of 4, Impt., T V (plate 802, UR position)	250.00	
P# block of 8, Impt., T V (plate 802, UR position)	750.00	
Double transfer	18.00	.75
Triple transfer	—	
Triangle at upper right without shading	22.50	6.00

c. 2c **rose carmine**, type IV, *Mar. 1899* 300.00 100.00

bright carmine rose, *Mar. 1899*	300.00	100.00
Never hinged	750.00	
Block of 4	1,250.	—
P# strip of 3, Impt., T V	1,200.	
Never hinged	2,500.	
P# block of 6, Impt., T V	3,250.	

d. 2c **orange red**, type IV, horizontal watermark, *June 1900* 11.50 .55

pale orange red	11.50	.55
dark orange red, *Sept. 1902*	11.50	.55
deep orange red, *Jan. 1903*	11.50	.55
Never hinged	32.50	
On cover		.70
Block of 4	50.00	4.00
P# strip of 3, Impt., T V	42.50	
Never hinged	115.00	
P# block of 6, Impt., T V	220.00	
Never hinged	400.00	

e. 2c **orange red**, type IV, vertical watermark (error), *May 1902* 35.00 5.00

Never hinged	100.00	
On cover		17.50
Block of 4	175.00	

P# strip of 3, Impt., T V	300.00	
Never hinged	750.00	

f. 2c **carmine**, type IV, *Nov. 1897* 10.00 .50

reddish carmine, *Dec. 1898*	10.00	.50
Never hinged	27.50	
On cover		.65
Block of 4	42.50	3.00
P# strip of 3, Impt., T V	40.00	
Never hinged	95.00	
P# block of 6, Impt., T V	220.00	
Never hinged	385.00	

g. 2c **pink**, type IV, *Nov. 1897* 15.00 1.75

Never hinged	40.00	
bright pink	20.00	2.00
Never hinged	55.00	
On cover		2.00
Block of 4	65.00	12.50
P# strip of 3, Impt., T V	55.00	
Never hinged	140.00	
P# block of 6, Impt., T V	250.00	
Never hinged	475.00	

h. 2c **vermilion**, type IV, *Jan. 1899* 11.00 .55

pale vermilion	11.00	.55
Never hinged	30.00	
On cover		.75
Block of 4	47.50	4.00
P# strip of 3, Impt., T V	45.00	
Never hinged	115.00	
P# block of 6, Impt., T V	235.00	
Never hinged	425.00	

i. 2c **brown orange**, type IV, *Jan. 1899* 100.00 10.00

Never hinged	275.00	
P# strip of 3, Impt., T V	450.00	

j. Booklet pane of 6, **red**, type IV, horizontal watermark, *Apr. 18, 1900* 450.00 1,250.

light red	450.00	1,250.
orange red, *1901*	450.00	1,250.
Never hinged	900.00	

k. Booklet pane of 6, **red**, type IV, vertical watermark 450.00 1,250.

Never hinged	900.00	

Earliest documented uses:
No. 279B, July 6, 1899;
No. 279Bc, Mar 30, 1899;
No. 279Bc in bright rose carmine, July 16, 1899;
No. 279Bd, June 8, 1900;
No. 279Bf, Nov. 18, 1897;
No. 279Bg, Dec. 1, 1897;
No. 279Bh, Feb. 27, 1899.
No. 279Bj booklet single (red), May 4, 1900;
No. 279Bj booklet single (orange red), May 7, 1902;

Cancellations

Puerto Rico, 1898		—
Philippines, 1898		—
Guam, 1899 or 1900		—

Selected watermark orientation varieties added to the U.S. Specialized Catalogue

Kenneth E. Diehl

The 2007 edition of the *Scott Specialized Catalogue of United States Stamps and Covers* introduces lettered minor listings for two interesting watermark orientation errors plus two other minor listings for stamps with non-error differences in watermark orientation. The new error listings are Scott 279a and 279Be, while the non-error listings are Scott 279Bk and 283a.

The stamps of the First Bureau Issue produced by the Bureau of Engraving and Printing were printed on watermarked paper initially in April 1895 and may be located with horizontal as well as vertical double-line "USPS" watermarks. Denominations having the most use, namely the 1¢, 2¢ and 10¢ stamps, were printed on sheets containing 400 subjects. The 400-subject plates used to print stamps on paper with a horizontal watermark consisted of four 100-subject panes separated by guidelines. They were separated along these guidelines by cutting and eventually sent to Post Offices for sale. The remaining denominations between the 3¢ and the $5 stamps, including the final press run for the type II 10¢ denomination Scott 283, were printed from 200-subject plates on paper with vertical watermarks, consisting of two 100-subject panes printed side by side. These were separated along the vertical guideline into two 100-subject panes for eventual sale. The 2¢ booklet panes from this issue were printed from 360-subject plates (on paper with horizontal watermarks) and 180-subject plates (on paper with vertical watermarks).

The normal watermark orientation used for the 400-subject size sheet was required to have the double line "USPS" letters reading horizontally across the stamps from left to right. The 200-subject size sheets were required to have the "USPS" letters reading vertically. The Scott U.S. Specialized Catalogue indicates watermarks should be viewed from the back of the stamp; therefore all watermark orientation descriptions described here conform to this method of designation.

Inspecting plate strips of these stamps indicates that the horizontal watermark may be located in four different orientations. The paper manufacturer, the printing press operator or both could cause these different variations. The paper manufacturer was instructed to make a 45 degree cut in the lower right corner of the sheets to indicate to the printer which side of the paper had the better surface for printing. After the sheets were cut to the proper size for the printer, stacks of these sheets were moved to another cutter to make the 45 degree corner cut. Turning these stacks of sheets over sidewise, endwise, or rotating them 180 degrees during this transfer would still maintain the horizontal integrity of the watermark but result in three additional horizontal variations. Some pressmen with years of printing experience felt that in some instances the reverse side of the paper supplied would produce a better impression and turned or flipped over the sheets for printing. Any of these operations would cause a change in the horizontal watermark orientation, and all four varieties are known. The corner cut having being located on the other corners of sheets and strips has confirmed this.

The first of the four watermark designations is the "normal" arrangement where the letters are normal and upright and read "USPS" from left to right. The second variety is called "reversed" and results from the sheet being turned over, like the page in a book, causing the letters to remain upright but reversed and reading backwards from right to left. The third variety is called "inverted"

and resulted front the sheet being turned end over end, or upside down from its normal position, causing the letters to be inverted but reading from left to right. The fourth and final configuration is called "inverted reversed" and is the result of the sheet being rotated 180 degrees from its normal position, causing the watermark to be upside down in relation to the stamp design and reading backwards from right to left. The four different orientations are illustrated in Figure 1.

HORIZONTAL WATERMARK ORIENTATIONS

Figure 1. The four horizontal "USPS" watermark orientations are shown and named.

The normal orientation for the vertical watermark on the 200-subject printing sheet has the letters reading from the bottom to the top of the stamp with the tops of the letters pointing to the left when viewed from the back side of the stamp. This would be equivalent to rotating a horizontal watermark copy 90 degrees counter clockwise. The same four types of variations found for the horizontal watermark have also been located in the vertical format as illustrated in Figure 2.

VERTICAL WATERMARK ORIENTATIONS

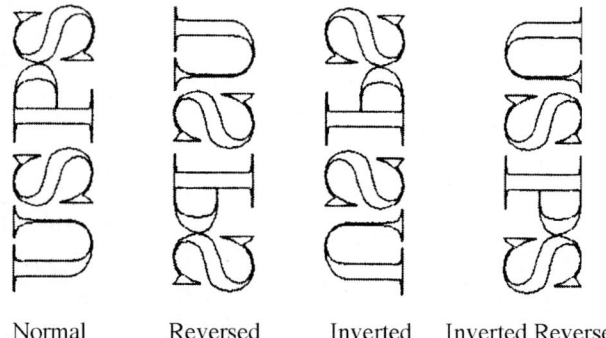

Figure 2. Shown and named are the four possible vertical "USPS" watermark orientations.

Figure 3. These plate number strips were photographed face down on a light table to better show the watermarks. The "large perf hole" appearance is due to the use of the light table. All four orientations of the horizontal watermark are shown and identified.

Normal

Reversed

Inverted

Inverted Reversed

I checked 1460 2¢ plate strips and found the four orientations for the horizontal watermark varied between a low of 19 percent and a high of 30 percent, indicating the four different orientations were produced in almost equal quantities and none should be considered scarce. Figure 3 shows plate number and imprint strips of three with each of the four horizontal watermark orientations.

In 1976, Fred Pitcher first reported an unlisted variety of the 1¢ green stamp, Scott 279, with double-line watermark that had a vertical orientation reading from bottom to top. He reported this in the June 1976 issue of *The Bureau Specialist*, the monthly publication of the Bureau Issues Association, currently known as the United States Stamp Society, and called it the "wrong way" watermark.

The 400-subject printing plate was 20 stamps wide and 20 stamps high, with the stamp height greater than its width. This required the watermarked printing sheet to also be rectangular in shape, and it was 18-1/2 inches wide by 20-3/4 inches tall. This sheet size and configuration prevented the possibility of the printing sheets being accidentally turned 90 degrees when placed

on the printing plate, creating a vertical watermark orientation. The sheet of paper would not cover the entire vertical columns of 20 stamps if rotated 90 degrees either way, and this would be obvious to the printing team and the paper would be removed for destruction. The only other possible source of vertically watermarked paper was that used for the 200-subject sheet stamps. These sheets, however, were only 11-1/4 inches tall by 18-1/2 inches wide and would not be large enough to cover the 400-subject printing plate.

It became obvious that the origin of the vertically watermarked paper for Scott 279 had to be the paper manufacturer. Apparently, they had accidentally cut the 400-subject sheets in the same direction as used for the 200-subject vertically watermarked sheets. This error was not noticed by the paper manufacturer before shipment nor by the Bureau of Engraving and Printing personnel before or after printing, resulting in the issuing of this variety.

It took 74 years before Pitcher's article brought this variety to the attention of collectors. Publication of his article produced several other examples of the 1¢ stamp from BIA members and

Normal   **Reversed**   **Inverted**   **Inverted Reverse**

Figure 4. All four orientations of the vertical watermark are known. These illustrations show and identify them all.

also reports of the discovery of a similar variety on the 2¢ sheet stamp, Scott 279B, resulting in a total of six 1¢ and five 2¢ examples being reported. Additional reports of this variety did not materialize and news about the variety became dormant. In the early 1990s, while working on a 23-part article on the 2¢ triangle stamp varieties, subsequently published in *The United States Specialist*, I made an attempt to determine the printing period for the vertically watermarked variety.

Using the reported plate numbers found with the vertical watermark and checking the Bureau of Engraving and Printing records published by the United States Stamp Society, the approximate printing period was determined to be during April and May 1902. The printing records indicated that five presses were used daily for 1¢ stamp production during this printing period and ten presses for the 2¢ plates. Each press used four plates for printing which required a total of twenty 1¢ plates and forty 2¢ plates on the presses each day during this time interval.

Several years later, in an attempt to acquire more data, I contacted several collectors having substantial holdings of the 1¢ and 2¢ plate numbers. In addition I wrote an article in Linn's about the vertical watermark variety and contacted several other stamp publications requesting the help of their readers by participating in a survey reporting any copies of these varieties in their possession.

Consolidating the data from these different sources, plus the originally reported examples, resulted in a total of 23 1¢ and 21 2¢ plate number copies being reported on vertically watermarked paper.

A total of 131 plate number examples of the twenty plates believed used for the 1¢ vertical watermark printings were inspected to locate the twenty three vertical 1¢ examples. Currently the twenty three examples of the 1¢ stamp have been reported on 14 different plate numbers: 1206, 1207, 1315, 1318,

1328, 1329, 1330, 1340, 1341, 1342, 1343, 1377, 1378 and 1379. The 23 plate positions reported consist of 9 plate number singles and 9 plate strips of three plus 5 without any designation reported. Currently no plate blocks have been reported.

For the 2¢ stamp, 495 plate number examples of the forty plates believed used were inspected with 21 vertical 2¢ examples reported. The 21 examples were located on 14 different plate numbers: 1267, 1270, 1298, 1300, 1311, 1312, 1313, 1344, 1347, 1348, 1350, 1359, 1360 and 1367. The 2¢ plate positions consist of 10 plate singles, 1 plate pair, 7 plate strips of three and 3 without a designation. No plate blocks have been reported for the 2¢ vertically watermarked stamp. Each possible orientation of the vertical watermark orientation is shown in Figure 4.

Plates on press prior to and after the April-May proposed printing period were inspected for the vertical watermark printings. For the 1¢ stamp, twenty-eight possible plates were checked and 219 copies were reported without a single vertical watermark copy being located. For the 2¢ stamp, twenty-four possible plates were checked totaling 354 copies, and again no copies of the vertical watermark were uncovered for any of these plates.

Reviewing the printing history of the 1¢ and 2¢ plates suspected of being involved with the vertical-watermark printing led to the conclusion that any plate cancelled on or before April 15, 1902, was not involved with the vertical printing since none was reported with a vertical watermark. All fourteen 2¢ plates located on vertically watermarked paper were on press between April 16 and May 26. In addition, all reported 1¢ plates printed on vertically watermarked paper were on press between April 16 and at least May 5. This pinned down April 16 as the earliest possible start of the vertical watermark printing. Sixteen of the 20 1¢ plates were on press through at least May 26, while plates 1204-1207 were on press through May 5, 1902. They were replaced on May 5 by plates 1392-1395, which remained on press through June 24, 1902. A total of 29 copies of plates 1392-1395 have not had a single vertical watermark report, while plates 1204-1207 had three vertical reports out of 41 reports. This would indicate that the vertical watermark printing period was between April 16 and May 5, 1902, at the latest, a maximum of 17 working days.

Calculations for the 1¢ stamp indicated a printing period of 11.3 days necessary to print the vertically watermarked examples reported in relation to all the horizontal watermarked copies reported for these plates. For the 2¢ stamp, the results indicated a printing period of 6.5 days would be required. Both figures are less that the projected printing period. The calculated days are subject to change and will fluctuate as more examples are reported for either the vertical or horizontal examples of these plates.

The 2007 edition of the Scott U.S. Specialized Catalogue contains listings for these new 1¢ and 2¢ vertically watermarked error varieties. This has required several numbering revisions and additions to the 2007 catalogue. The 1¢ stamp with horizontal watermark retains its current number as Scott 279. The new 1¢ vertically watermarked error variety becomes Scott 279a. The 2¢ vertical watermark error variety has only been located in the orange red color so the horizontal variety remains as Scott 279Bd with the new vertically watermarked orange red stamp becoming Scott 279Be. The other 2¢ color varieties are not known on vertically watermarked paper so their previous numbers have been retained as the horizontal variety only. The booklet pane listings have been moved to a new position following the various sheet color varieties, Scott 279B through 279Bi. The horizontally watermarked booklet pane variety from the 360-subject printings changes from its old Scott 279Be designation to Scott 279Bj, with a new vertically watermarked booklet pane listing from the 180-subject printings becoming Scott 279Bk. As indicated earlier in this discussion, the vertical watermark orientation on the booklet pane was not an error in the paper, as were the 1¢ and 2¢ sheet stamp varieties, but rather was the result of printing on the 180-subject sheets, which normally had a vertical watermark format.

When checking mint or used singles of the 2¢ stamps for the vertical watermark variety be aware that not all straight edge copies can be guaranteed as coming from the sheet stamp printings. Keep in mind that all booklet pane singles have either one or two straight edges, and the vertically watermarked 180-subject booklet pane stamps were printed in substantial quantities. Therefore, straight- edge vertically watermarked examples may be found from these booklet panes as well as examples originating from the sheet stamps. The only way to guarantee that a single having a vertical watermark is from the sheet variety is if it is perforated on all four sides or is a straight-edge copy not available as a booklet pane single. While straight-edge copies might possibly come from a pane of 100 stamps, there is a good chance they may have come from the booklet pane variety. The only positively identifiable straight-edge copies from panes of 100 are the eighteen bottom straight-edge stamps or the eighteen top straight-edge stamps which are perforated on the other three sides, plus single corner examples having a straight edge at top and right or single corner copies with a straight edge at top and left. These are the only types of straight-edge stamps from the sheet printings that are not available from the booklet pane stamps.

The other 38 straight-edge copies from a pane of 100, 18 copies with a vertical straight edge at left and the 18 copies with a vertical straight edge at right plus the corner copies with straight edge at left and bottom and the one with straight edge at right and bottom, are also found on the booklet panes. There is no way these specific vertically watermarked examples can be guaranteed as coming from the sheet stamps.

Only 362 copies can be authenticated as coming from a sheet of 400 stamps, the 324 fully perforated copies plus the 38 selective straight-edge copies described above, while the other 38 straight-edge copies cannot be guaranteed since they could conceivably have originated from a booklet pane. Therefore, based on the scarcity of verifiable 2¢ sheet stamps with the vertical watermark orientation, there is a good chance that a straight-edge copy from the 38 non-verifiable sheet positions is actually from a booklet pane printing. However, a horizontal pair or larger with a straight edge at either left or right would be indicative of stamps from a sheet printing.

As mentioned above, the 10¢ type II stamp, Scott 283, was printed on both horizontally and vertically watermarked paper. Like the 2¢ booklet panes of this series with horizontal and vertical watermark orientations, this was by design and not by accident, as happened for the 1¢ and 2¢ stamps. With the listing of the 1¢ and 2¢ vertically watermarked stamps and the 2¢ vertically watermarked booklet panes, it is time also to list the 10¢ type II vertically watermarked variety. The final printing of the 10¢ stamps on 400-subject horizontally watermarked paper ended on September 16, 1901, using plates 996-999. The final four plates, 1336-1339, were made in the 200-subject size, initially going to press on January 15, 1902. They were on the press on four separate occasions, with the final printing ending January 15, 1903. The original horizontally watermarked variety has retained its original Scott 283 catalog number, with the new vertical watermark variety now listed as Scott 283a.

There is one other watermark error variety that will be mentioned briefly. It is part of the Second Bureau Series of 1902-1903. The 2¢ booklet panes of this issue, Scott 319g, were printed in sheets containing 180-subjects only. No 360-subject size plates were ever produced. The normal watermark was therefore vertical in orientation as it was for the First Bureau issue 180-subject booklet pane printings. However, a horizontal variety was located and initially listed in the 1973 edition of the Scott U.S. Specialized Catalogue. These sheets were printed in error on paper that was improperly cut by the paper manufacturer, resulting in a horizontal orientation of the watermark, in a similar manner to what occurred for the First Bureau 1¢ and 2¢ sheets stamps. The four plates involved in this printing, 3299, 3300, 3302 and 3307, have all been reported.

Kenneth E. Diehl is a long-time collector and avid researcher in the First Bureau issues of 1894-1903. His last Special Feature article was for the 1999 Scott U.S. Specialized Catalogue on the topic of the Scott Catalogue debut of the 2¢ Type IV stamp.

With the listing of the new vertical watermark for the 1¢ stamp, Scott 279a, and the 2¢, Scott 279Be, a new group of collectors are now aware of these varieties. As indicated in the article, the plate numbers involved and the printing period were determined by results obtained from collectors participating in a survey Mr. Diehl conducted a number of years ago.

In an attempt to increase the data base for the vertically watermarked printing, Mr. Diehl would like to reactivate the survey and respectfully requests the aid of current readers of the 2007 edition of the Scott Specialized Catalogue of United States Stamps and Covers to participate in supplying additional information on their holdings. Requested forms will be supplied containing the plate numbers currently found or probably used for printing on vertically watermarked paper as well as plates not yet reported but possibly used for printing on vertically watermarked paper. Information is requested for the vertically watermarked variety as well as for examples located on horizontally watermarked paper. Reports on the horizontal variety are important and necessary to determine the relative scarcity of each variety as well as provide information to determine the vertical printing period.

Those who would like to participate in this survey should write to Kenneth E. Diehl, P. O. Box 4275, Scottsdale AZ 85261-4275 requesting the forms. There will be no cost to you for participating in the survey since prepaid return envelopes will be supplied as well as return of your initial postage. Your only expense will be your time filling out the forms.

	Supplementary Mail Type				
	G			+4.00	
	Cuba, 1898			—	
	China			—	
	Samoa			—	
280	A90	4c **rose brown,** *Oct. 1898*		30.00	3.00
		Never hinged		85.00	
a.		4c **lilac brown**		30.00	3.00
		brownish claret		30.00	3.00
		Never hinged		85.00	
b.		4c **orange brown**		30.00	3.00
		Never hinged		85.00	
		On cover			11.00
		Block of 4		130.00	25.00
		Margin block of 4, arrow, R or L		140.00	
		P# strip of 3, Impt., T V		120.00	
		Never hinged		275.00	
		P# block of 6, Impt., T V		700.00	
		Never hinged		1,100.	
		Double transfer		35.00	4.50
		Extra frame line at top (Plate 793 R 62)		50.00	9.00

Earliest documented use: Nov. 13, 1898.

Cancellations

Supplementary Mail Type		
G	+3.00	
China	—	
Philippines	—	

281	A91	5c **dark blue,** *Mar. 1898*		35.00	2.00
		blue		35.00	2.00
		bright blue		35.00	2.00
		Never hinged		100.00	
		On cover			10.00
		Block of 4		150.00	13.00
		Margin block of 4, arrow, R or L		160.00	
		P# strip of 3, Impt., T V		140.00	
		Never hinged		350.00	
		P# block of 6, Impt., T V		650.00	
		Never hinged		1,250.	
		Double transfer		45.00	4.00
		Worn plate (diagonal lines missing in oval background)		40.00	2.25

Earliest documented use: Mar. 19, 1898.

Cancellations

Puerto Rico, 1898	—	
Supplementary Mail Type		
G	+4.00	
China	—	
Cuba	—	
Guam	—	
Philippines	—	

282	A92	6c **lake,** *Dec. 1898*		50.00	6.00
		claret		50.00	6.00
		Never hinged		140.00	
		On cover			17.50
		Block of 4		200.00	47.50
		Margin block of 4, arrow, R or L		200.00	
		P# strip of 3, Impt., T V		190.00	
		Never hinged		475.00	
		P# block of 6, Impt., T V		900.00	
		Never hinged		1,650.	
		Double transfer		60.00	8.50
a.		6c **purple lake**		75.00	12.50
		Never hinged		210.00	
		Block of 4		325.00	85.00
		Margin block of 4, arrow		340.00	
		P# strip of 3, Impt., T V		300.00	
		Never hinged		675.00	
		P# block of 6, Impt., T V		1,250.	
		Never hinged		2,200.	

Earliest documented use: Mar. 13, 1899.

Cancellations

Supplementary Mail Type		
G	+4.00	
China	—	
Philippines	—	

Type I. The tips of the foliate ornaments do not impinge on the white curved line below "ten cents."

282C	A94	10c **brown,** type I, *Nov. 1898*		210.00	6.00
		dark brown		210.00	6.00
		Never hinged		625.00	
		On cover			17.50
		Block of 4		900.00	55.00
		P# strip of 3, Impt., T IV or V		825.00	
		Never hinged		1,800.	
		P# block of 6, Impt., T IV or V		2,600.	
		Never hinged		4,250.	
		Double transfer		240.00	10.00

Earliest documented use: Dec. 10, 1898.

Cancellation

Supplementary Mail Type G	+2.50

Type II. The tips of the ornaments break the curved line below the "e" of "ten" and the "t" of "cents."

283	A94	10c **orange brown,** type II, horizontal watermark		160.00	5.00
		brown		160.00	5.00
		yellow brown		160.00	5.00
		Never hinged		450.00	
		On cover			17.50
		Block of 4		700.00	47.50
		Margin block of 4, arrow, R or L		725.00	—
		P# strip of 3, Impt., T V		575.00	
		Never hinged		1,500.	
		P# block of 6, Impt., T V		1,900.	
		Never hinged		3,250.	
		Pair, type I and type II		15,000.	—
a.		10c **orange brown,** type II, vertical watermark, *early 1900*		225.00	10.00
		Never hinged		625.00	
		On cover			35.00
		Block of 4		950.00	
		P# strip of 3, Impt., T V		1,000.	
		Never hinged		2,250.	
		P# block of 6, Impt., T V		2,850.	
		Never hinged		4,500.	

Earliest documented use: Mar. 13, 1899.

Cancellations

Supplementary Mail Type G	+2.50	
China	—	
Puerto Rico	—	

On the 400 subject plate 932, all are Type I except the following: UL 20; UR 11, 12, 13; LL 61, 71, 86, these 7 being Type II.

284	A95	15c **olive green,** *Nov. 1898*		175.00	10.00
		dark olive green		175.00	10.00
		Never hinged		475.00	
		On cover			32.50
		Block of 4		750.00	85.00
		Margin block of 4, arrow, R or L		800.00	
		P# strip of 3, Impt., T IV		700.00	
		Never hinged		1,750.	
		P# block of 6, Impt., T IV		2,250.	
		Never hinged		4,000.	

Earliest documented use: Mar. 18, 1899.

Cancellations

Supp. Mail Type F or G	+2.50	
China	—	
Samoa	—	

Nos. 279-284 (8)		678.00	32.90

VALUES FOR VERY FINE STAMPS
Please note: Stamps are valued in the grade of Very Fine unless otherwise indicated.

TRANS-MISSISSIPPI EXPOSITION ISSUE
Omaha, Nebr., June 1 - Nov. 1, 1898.

Jacques Marquette on the Mississippi A100

Farming in the West — A101

Indian Hunting Buffalo — A102

John Charles Frémont on the Rocky Mountains A103

Troops Guarding Wagon Train — A104

Hardships of Emigration A105

Western Mining Prospector A106

Western Cattle in Storm — A107

Mississippi River Bridge, St. Louis — A108

Exposition Station Handstamp Postmark

Plates of 100 (10x10) subjects, divided vertically into 2 panes of 50.

See Nos. 3209-3210 for bi-colored reproductions of Nos. 285-293.

1898, June 17   Wmk. 191   *Perf. 12*

285	A100	1c **dark yellow green**		30.00	6.50
		yellow green		30.00	6.50
		green		30.00	6.50
		Never hinged		80.00	
		On cover			9.75
		On card, Expo. station canc.			200.00
		Pair, on cover, Expo. station canc.			300.00
		Block of 4		130.00	45.00
		Margin block of 4, arrow, R or L		140.00	—
		P# pair, Impt., T VIII		67.50	
		Never hinged		170.00	
		P# strip of 3, Impt., T VIII		110.00	
		Never hinged		275.00	
		P# block of 4, Impt., T VIII		250.00	
		Never hinged		400.00	
		P# block of 6, Impt., T VIII		400.00	
		Never hinged		675.00	
		Double transfer		40.00	7.50

Earliest documented use: June 17, 1898 (FDC).

When it comes to stamp grading, we wrote the book.

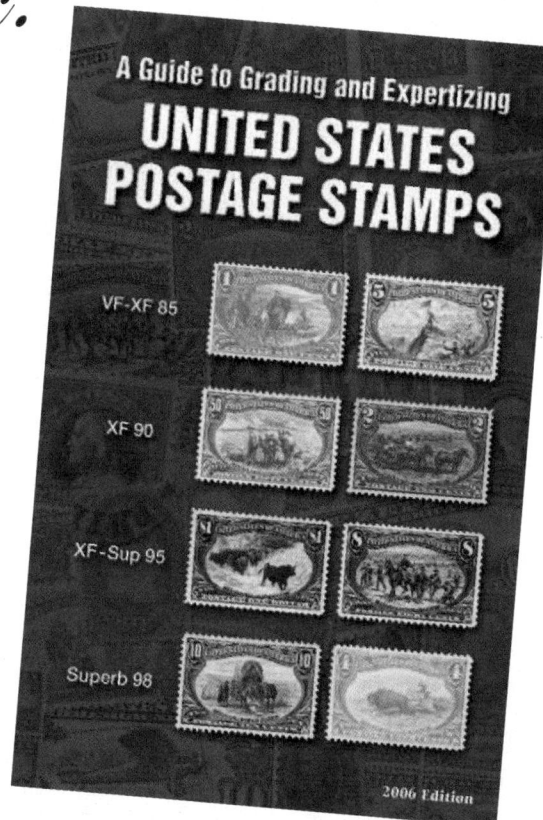

The grading of U.S. stamps has become a popular topic. And for good reason.

Stamps impartially graded by an independent third party provide buyers with consistency, value and liquidity. Rather important considerations when you're parting with your hard-earned cash.

And who better to trust your grading opinions to than the folks who created and defined the modern stamp grading system?

Over the past six years, Professional Stamp Experts has expertized and graded over 50,000 U.S. stamps. Accurately, consistently and in a timely manner. So much so in fact, that today, we are the *#1 expertizing service in the world,* with a volume of over 3,000 stamps per month. A review of prices realized at major auctions over the past year or so will underscore the unparalleled market respect afforded our opinions.

If you'd like to see for yourself what stamp grading is all about, and why PSE is the undisputed grading authority in today's philatelic market, send today for your free copy of *A Guide to Grading and Expertizing United States Postage Stamps.*

We also publish the *Stamp Market Quarterly* four times a year. In it you'll find the most accurate market values for PSE graded stamps available. This publication is also available from us free of charge.

Did you get that? **FREE.** We're even paying the freight. Write or call us today at the address below.

Cancellations

Supp. Mail Type F or G		+1.50
China		—
Philippines		—
Puerto Rico, 1898		—

286	A101	2c **copper red**	30.00	2.50
		brown red	30.00	2.50
		light brown red	30.00	2.50
		Never hinged	80.00	
		On cover		3.50
		On cover, Expo. station canc.		175.00
		Block of 4	130.00	15.00
		Margin block of 4, arrow, R or L	140.00	—
		P# pair, Impt., T VIII	67.50	
		Never hinged	170.00	
		P# strip of 3, Impt., T VIII	110.00	
		Never hinged	275.00	
		P# block of 4, Impt., T VIII	225.00	
		Never hinged	375.00	
		P# block of 6, Impt., T VIII	400.00	
		Never hinged	625.00	
		Double transfer	45.00	3.75
		Worn plate	32.50	3.00

Earliest documented use: June 17, 1898 (FDC).

Cancellations

China		—
Hawaii		—
Puerto Rico, 1898		—
Philippines		—

287	A102	4c **orange**	140.	24.00
		deep orange	140.	24.00
		Never hinged	350.	
		On cover		57.50
		On cover, Expo. station canc.		750.
		Block of 4	600.	185.
		Margin block of 4, arrow, R or L	625.	—
		P# pair, Impt., T VIII	350.	
		Never hinged	750.00	
		P# strip of 3, Impt., T VIII	600.	
		Never hinged	1,200.	
		P# block of 4, Impt., T VIII	1,000.	
		Never hinged	1,600.	
		P# block of 6, Impt., T VIII	1,750.	
		Never hinged	2,750.	

Earliest documented use: June 17, 1898 (FDC).

Cancellations

Supp. Mail Type F or G		+5.
China		—
Philippines		—

288	A103	5c **dull blue**	140.	22.50
		bright blue	140.	22.50
		Never hinged	350.	
		On cover		50.
		On cover, Expo. station canc.		500.
		Block of 4	600.	150.
		Margin block of 4, arrow, R or L	625.	—
		P# pair, Impt., T VIII	350.	
		Never hinged	750.	
		P# strip of 3, Impt., T VIII	600.	
		Never hinged	1,200.	
		P# block of 4, Impt., T VIII	900.	
		Never hinged	1,600.	
		P# block of 6, Impt., T VIII	1,500.	
		Never hinged	2,750.	

Earliest documented use: June 17, 1898 (FDC).

Cancellations

Supp. Mail Type F or G		+5.
China		—
Philippines		—
Puerto Rico, 1898		—

289	A104	8c **violet brown**	200.	45.00
		dark violet brown	200.	45.00
		Never hinged	550.	
		On cover		115.
		On cover, Expo. station canc.		1,000.
		Block of 4	850.	275.
		Margin block of 4, arrow, R or L	875.	—
		P# pair, Impt., T VIII	450.	
		P# strip of 3, Impt., T VIII	800.	
		P# block of 4, Impt., T VIII	2,000.	
		Never hinged	3,350.	
		P# block of 6, Impt., T VIII	3,250.	
		Never hinged	5,250.	
a.		Vert. pair, imperf. horiz.	25,000.	
		P# block of 4, Impt., T VIII	100,000.	

Earliest documented use: June 17, 1898 (FDC).

Cancellations

Philippines		—
Samoa		—

290	A105	10c **gray violet**	180.	32.50
		blackish violet	180.	32.50
		Never hinged	500.	
		On cover		90.00
		On cover, Expo. station canc.		750.
		Block of 4	775.	200.
		Margin block of 4, arrow, R or L	800.	—
		P# pair, Impt., T VIII	425.	
		Never hinged	1,000.	
		P# strip of 3, Impt., T VIII	650.	
		Never hinged	1,450.	
		P# block of 4, Impt., T VIII	2,100.	

		Never hinged	3,500.	
		P# block of 6, Impt., T VIII	3,500.	
		Never hinged	6,000.	

Earliest documented use: June 17, 1898 (FDC).

Cancellations

Supplementary Mail Type G		+5.
China		—
Philippines		—

291	A106	50c **sage green**	700.	190.
		dark sage green	700.	190.
		Never hinged	2,000.	
		On cover		1,750.
		Block of 4	3,250.	1,250.
		Margin block of 4, arrow, R or L	3,400.	
		P# pair, Impt., T VIII	1,950.	
		Never hinged	4,750.	
		P# strip of 3, Impt., T VIII	2,800.	
		Never hinged	6,000.	
		P# block of 4, Impt., T VIII	14,000.	
		Never hinged	23,000.	
		P# block of 6, Impt., T VIII	26,000.	

Earliest documented use: June 17, 1898 (FDC).

Cancellations

Supp. Mail Type F or G		+25.
Cuba		—
Philippines		—

292	A107	$1 **black**	1,250.	600.
		Never hinged	3,500.	
		No gum	650.	
		On cover		4,000.
		Block of 4	5,750.	4,000.
		Margin block of 4, arrow, R or L	6,000.	
		P# pair, Impt., T VIII	3,000.	
		Never hinged	7,500.	
		P# strip of 3, Impt., T VIII	5,500.	
		Never hinged	11,000.	
		P# block of 4, Impt., T VIII	35,000.	
		Never hinged	50,000.	
		P# block of 6, Impt., T VIII	50,000.	
		Never hinged	67,500.	

Earliest documented use: June 17, 1898 (FDC).

Cancellation

Philippines		—

293	A108	$2 **orange brown**	2,250.	1,000.
		dark orange brown	2,250.	1,000.
		Never hinged	6,250.	
		No gum	1,050.	
		On cover		12,500.
		Block of 4	9,500.	6,000.
		Margin block of 4, arrow, R or L	10,000.	
		P# pair, Impt., T VIII	5,250.	
		P# strip of 3, Impt., T VIII	9,000.	
		P# block of 4, Impt., T VIII	80,000.	
		Never hinged		
		P# block of 6, Impt., T VIII	150,000.	

Earliest documented use: June 24, 1898.

Nos. 285-293 (9) 4,920. 1,923.

Never-Hinged Stamps
See note before No. 205 regarding premiums for never-hinged stamps.

PAN-AMERICAN EXPOSITION ISSUE
Buffalo, N.Y., May 1 - Nov. 1, 1901.
On sale May 1-Oct. 31, 1901.

Fast Lake Navigation (Steamship "City of Alpena") — A109

Empire State Express — A110

Electric Automobile in Washington — A111

Bridge at Niagara Falls — A112

Canal Locks at Sault Ste. Marie — A113

Fast Ocean Navigation (Steamship "St. Paul") — A114

BUFFALO, N.Y. SEP 7 3:30 PM 1901

PAN-AMERICAN STATION — D

Exposition Station Machine Cancellation

Plates of 200 subjects in two panes of 100 each.

1901, May 1   **Wmk. 191**   *Perf. 12*

294	A109	1c **green & black**	20.00	3.00
		dark blue green & black	20.00	3.00
		Never hinged	45.00	
		On cover		4.50
		On Expo. cover or card, Expo. station machine canc.		50.00
		On Expo. cover or card, Expo. station duplex handstamp canc.		150.00
		Block of 4	85.00	25.00
		Margin block of 4, top arrow & markers	87.50	
		Margin block of 4, bottom arrow & markers & black P#	90.00	
		P# strip of 3, Impt., T V	87.50	
		Never hinged	170.00	
		P# block of 6, Impt., T V	300.00	
		Never hinged	475.00	
		Margin strip of 5, bottom Impt. T V, two P#, arrow & markers	125.00	
		Never hinged	260.00	
		Margin block of 10, bottom Impt., T V, two P#, arrow & markers	700.00	
		Never hinged	1,050.	
		Double transfer	27.50	5.25
a.		Center inverted	11,000.	13,000.
		Never hinged	19,000.	
		On cover		—
		Block of 4	47,500.	
		P# strip of 4, Impt.	150,000.	

Earliest documented uses: May 1, 1901 (No. 294 FDC); Aug. 2, 1901 (No. 294a). The No. 294a cover sold at auction in 1999 for $121,000. Two other uses on cover are recorded.

295	A110	2c **carmine & black**	17.50	1.00
		carmine & gray black	17.50	1.00
		dark carmine & black	17.50	1.00
		rose carmine & black	17.50	1.00
		scarlet & black	17.50	1.00
		Never hinged	42.50	
		On cover		1.50
		On Expo. cover or card, Expo. sta. machine cancel		60.00
		On Expo. cover or card, Expo. sta. duplex handstamp canc.		200.00
		Block of 4	72.50	8.00
		Margin block of 4, top arrow & markers	75.00	
		P# block of 4, bottom arrow & markers and black P#	77.50	
		P# strip of 3, Impt., T V	72.50	
		Never hinged	140.00	
		P# block of 6, Impt., T V	300.00	
		Never hinged	475.00	
		P# strip of 5, bottom Impt., T V, two P#, arrow & markers	130.00	
		Never hinged	240.00	
		P# block of 10, bottom Impt., T V, two P#, arrow & markers	700.00	
		Never hinged	1,050.	

	Double transfer	25.00	2.25
a.	Center inverted	*45,000.*	*55,000.*
	Block of 4	*425,000.*	

Almost all unused copies of No. 295a have partial or disturbed gum. Values are for examples with full original gum that is slightly disturbed. Value for No. 295a used is for a well-centered example with faults, as there are no known fault-free examples.

Earliest documented use: May 1, 1901 (No. 295 FDC); Feb. 26, (1902?) (No. 295a, dated cancel on off-cover stamp). The dated No. 295a stamp is the only used example showing a date of any kind. Sold at auction in 2001 for $66,000.

296	A111	**4c deep red brown & black**	85.00	15.00
		chocolate & black	85.00	15.00
		Never hinged	190.00	
		On cover		37.50
		On cover, Expo. station machine cancel		350.00
		On cover, Expo. station duplex handstamp canc.		*750.00*
		Block of 4	340.00	125.00
		Margin block of 4, top arrow & markers	360.00	
		P# block of 4, bottom arrow & markers & black P#	375.00	
		P# strip of 3, Impt., T V	325.00	
		Never hinged	700.00	
		P# block of 6, Impt., T V	2,100.00	
		Never hinged	*3,500.*	
		P# strip of 5, bottom Impt., T V, two P#, arrow & markers	600.00	
		Never hinged	1,200.	
		P# block of 10, bottom Impt., T V, two P#, arrow & markers	*4,250.*	
		Never hinged	*6,000.*	
a.		Center inverted	35,000.	—
		Block of 4	150,000.	
		P# strip of 4, Impt.	175,000.	

No. 296a was a Special Printing.
Almost all unused copies of No. 296a have partial or disturbed gum. Values are for examples with full orginal gum that is slightly disturbed.
See No. 296a-S, "Specimen" Stamps.
Earliest documented use: May 1, 1901 (FDC).

297	A112	**5c ultramarine & black**	95.00	14.00
		dark ultramarine & black	95.00	14.00
		Never hinged	210.00	
		On cover		40.00
		On cover, Expo. station machine cancel		350.00
		On cover, Expo. station duplex handstamp canc.		*750.00*
		Block of 4	400.00	110.00
		Margin block of 4, top arrow & markers	425.00	
		P# block of 4, bottom arrow & markers & black P#	450.00	
		P# strip of 3, Impt., T V	375.00	
		Never hinged	725.00	
		P# block of 6, Impt., T V	2,250.00	
		Never hinged	*3,750.*	
		P# strip of 5, bottom Impt., T V, two P#, arrow & markers	700.00	
		Never hinged	1,350.	
		P# block of 10, bottom Impt., T V, two P#, arrow & markers	*4,250.*	
		Never hinged	*6,000.*	

Earliest documented use: May 1, 1901 (FDC).

298	A113	**8c brown violet & black**	120.00	50.00
		purplish brown & black	120.00	50.00
		Never hinged	275.00	
		On cover		110.00
		On cover, Expo. station machine cancel		*750.00*
		On cover, Expo. station duplex handstamp canc.		*1,250.*
		Block of 4	500.00	400.00
		Margin block of 4, top arrow & markers	525.00	
		P# block of 4, bottom arrow & markers & black P#	550.00	
		P# strip of 3, Impt., T V	475.00	
		Never hinged	975.00	
		P# block of 6, Impt., T V	*4,000.*	
		Never hinged	*6,000.*	
		P# strip of 5, bottom Impt., T V, two P#, arrow & markers	875.00	
		Never hinged	1,750.	
		P# block of 10, bottom Impt., T V, two P#, arrow & markers	*7,000.*	
		Never hinged	*9,500.*	

Earliest documented use: May 1, 1901 (FDC).

299	A114	**10c yellow brown & black**	160.00	25.00
		dark yellow brown & black	160.00	30.00
		Never hinged	375.00	
		On cover		125.00
		On cover, Expo. station machine cancel		*1,000.*
		On cover, Expo. station duplex handstamp canc.		*1,500.*
		Block of 4	675.00	250.00
		Margin block of 4, top arrow & markers	700.00	

	P# block of 4, bottom arrow & markers & black P#	750.00	
	P# strip of 3, Impt., T V	650.00	
	Never hinged	1,350.	
	P# block of 6, Impt., T V	6,750.	
	Never hinged	*9,000.*	
	P# strip of 5, bottom Impt., T V, two P#, arrow & markers	1,175.	
	Never hinged	2,250.	
	P# block of 10, bottom Impt., T V, two P#, arrow & markers	10,000.	
	Never hinged	*13,000.*	
	Nos. 294-299 (6)	497.50	108.00
	Nos. 294-299, never hinged	1,138.	

Earliest documented use: May 1, 1901 (FDC).

VALUES FOR VERY FINE STAMPS
Please note: Stamps are valued in the grade of Very Fine unless otherwise indicated.

Franklin — A115

Washington — A116

Jackson — A117

Grant — A118

Lincoln — A119

Garfield — A120

Martha Washington — A121

Daniel Webster — A122

Benjamin Harrison — A123

Henry Clay — A124

Jefferson — A125

David G. Farragut — A126

Madison — A127

Marshall — A128

REGULAR ISSUE

Plates of 400 subjects in four panes of 100 each for all values from 1c to 15c inclusive. Certain plates of 1c, 2c type A129, 3c and 5c show a round marker in margin opposite the horizontal guide line at right or left.
Plates of 200 subjects in two panes of 100 each for 15c, 50c, $1, $2 and $5.

1902-03			**Wmk. 191**	*Perf. 12*

Many stamps of this issue are known with blurred printing due to having been printed on dry paper.

300	A115	**1c blue green,** *Feb. 1903*	12.00	.25
		green	12.00	.25
		deep green	12.00	.25
		gray green	12.00	.25
		yellow green	12.00	.25
		Never hinged	27.50	
		On cover		.30
		Block of 4	50.00	3.50
		P# strip of 3, Impt., T V	47.50	
		Never hinged	95.00	
		P# block of 6, Impt., T V	225.00	
		Never hinged	350.00	
		Double transfer	17.50	1.00
		Worn plate	13.00	.35
		Cracked plate	14.00	.30
b.		Booklet pane of 6, *Mar. 6, 1907*	600.00	*12,500.*
		Never hinged	1,150.	

Earliest documented uses: Feb. 3, 1903 (No. 300); Mar. 22, 1907 (No. 300b single).

301	A116	**2c carmine,** *Jan. 22, 1903*	16.00	.40
		bright carmine	16.00	.40
		deep carmine	16.00	.40
		carmine rose	16.00	.40
		Never hinged	37.50	
		On cover		.45
		Block of 4	67.50	5.00
		P# strip of 3, Impt., T V	65.00	
		Never hinged	130.00	
		P# block of 6, Impt., T V	275.00	
		Never hinged	425.00	
		Double transfer	27.50	1.25

	Cracked plate	—	1.25
c.	Booklet pane of 6, *Jan. 24, 1903*	500.00	2,250.
	Never hinged	950.00	

Earliest documented use: Feb. 2, 1903 (No. 301); Mar. 28, 1903 (No. 301c single); Apr. 4, 1903 (No. 301c pane).
Four unused single imperforate sheet margin examples of No. 301 are recorded. These are considered printer's waste.

302	A117	**3c bright violet,** *Feb. 1903*	55.00	3.50
		violet	55.00	3.50
		deep violet	55.00	3.50
		Never hinged	130.00	
		On cover		11.00
		Block of 4	230.00	30.00
		P# strip of 3, Impt., T V	220.00	
		Never hinged	450.00	
		P# block of 6, Impt., T V	800.00	
		Never hinged	1,350.	
		Double transfer	77.50	4.75
		Cracked plate	—	

Earliest documented use: Mar. 19, 1903.

303	A118	**4c brown,** *Feb. 1903*	60.00	2.30
		dark brown	60.00	2.30
		yellow brown	60.00	2.30
		orange brown	60.00	2.30
		red brown	60.00	2.30
		Never hinged	140.00	
		On cover		12.50
		Block of 4	250.00	25.00
		P# strip of 3, Impt., T V	240.00	
		Never hinged	475.00	
		P# block of 6, Impt., T V	825.00	
		Never hinged	1,375.	
		Double transfer	77.50	2.75

Earliest documented use: Mar. 10, 1903 (on cover front).

304	A119	**5c blue,** *Jan. 1903*	60.00	2.00
		pale blue	60.00	2.00
		bright blue	60.00	2.00
		dark blue	60.00	2.00
		Never hinged	140.00	
		On cover		7.50
		Block of 4	250.00	15.00
		P# strip of 3, Impt., T V	240.00	
		Never hinged	475.00	
		P# block of 6, Impt., T V	825.00	—
		Never hinged	1,375.	
		Double transfer	82.50	3.75
		Cracked plate	70.00	4.75

Earliest documented use: Feb. 9, 1903.

305	A120	**6c claret,** *Feb. 1903*	72.50	5.00
		deep claret	72.50	5.00
		brownish lake	72.50	5.00
		dull brownish lake	72.50	5.00
		Never hinged	170.00	
		On cover		15.00
		Block of 4	310.00	45.00
		P# strip of 3, Impt., T V	290.00	
		Never hinged	600.00	
		P# block of 6, Impt., T V	925.00	
		Never hinged	1,600.	
		Double transfer	77.50	4.50

Earliest documented use: May 8, 1903.

306	A121	**8c violet black,** *Dec. 1902*	45.00	3.00
		black	45.00	3.00
		slate black	45.00	3.00
		gray lilac	45.00	3.00
		Never hinged	105.00	
		lavender	55.00	3.75
		Never hinged	130.00	
		On cover		8.00
		Block of 4	190.00	27.50
		P# strip of 3, Impt., T V	180.00	
		Never hinged	350.00	
		P# block of 6, Impt., T V	750.00	
		Never hinged	1,250.	
		Double transfer	90.00	3.75

Earliest documented use: Dec. 27, 1902.

307	A122	**10c pale red brown,** *Feb. 1903*	70.00	2.80
		red brown	70.00	2.80
		dark red brown	70.00	2.80
		Never hinged	165.00	
		On cover		9.00
		Block of 4	280.00	17.50
		P# strip of 3, Impt., T V	275.00	
		Never hinged	550.00	
		P# block of 6, Impt., T V	1,100.	
		Never hinged	1,850.	
		Double transfer		10.00

Earliest documented use: Mar. 12, 1903.

308	A123	**13c purple black,** *Nov. 1902*	50.00	9.00
		brown violet	50.00	9.00
		Never hinged	115.00	
		On cover		37.50
		Block of 4	210.00	95.00
		P# strip of 3, Impt., T V	200.00	
		Never hinged	400.00	
		P# block of 6, Impt., T V	700.00	
		Never hinged	1,150.	

Earliest documented use: Nov. 18, 1902.

309	A124	**15c olive green,** *May 27, 1903*	200.00	12.00
		dark olive green	200.00	12.00
		Never hinged	475.00	
		On cover		80.00
		Block of 4	800.00	100.00
		Margin block of 4, arrow	825.00	
		P# strip of 3, Impt., T V	750.00	
		Never hinged	1,600.	

	P# block of 6, Impt., T V	3,400.	
	Never hinged	5,750.	
	Double transfer	230.00	14.00

Earliest documented use: July 1903 (on registry tag); Sept. 11, 1903 (on cover).

310	A125	**50c orange,** *Mar. 23, 1903*	475.	27.50
		deep orange	475.	27.50
		Never hinged	1,300.	
		On cover		700.00
		Block of 4	2,000.	225.00
		Margin block of 4, arrow	2,100.	
		P# strip of 3, Impt., T V	1,900.	
		Never hinged	4,250.	
		P# block of 6, Impt., T V	7,500.	

Earliest documented use: Oct. 6, 1903 (on cover front).

311	A126	**$1 black,** *June 5, 1903*	750.00	75.00
		graylsh black	750.00	75.00
		Never hinged	2,100.	
		No gum	180.00	
		On cover		1,500.
		Block of 4	3,150.	500.00
		Margin block of 4, arrow	3,300.	
		P# strip of 3, Impt., T V	3,000.	
		P# block of 6, Impt., T V	20,000.	

Earliest documented use: Sept. 30, 1903.

312	A127	**$2 dark blue,** *June 5, 1903*	1,200.	200.00
		blue	1,200.	200.00
		Never hinged	3,000.	
		No gum	300.00	
		On cover		2,500.
		Block of 4	5,250.	1,750.
		Margin block of 4, arrow	5,500.	
		P# strip of 3, Impt., T V	5,000.	
		P# block of 6, Impt., T V	32,500.	

Earliest documented use: Feb. 17, 1904.

313	A128	**$5 dark green,** *June 5, 1903*	3,000.	750.00
		Never hinged	7,250.	
		No gum	850.00	
		On cover		5,000.
		Block of 4	14,000.	6,000.
		Margin block of 4, arrow	14,500.	
		P# strip of 3, Impt., T V	12,500.	
		P# block of 6, Impt., T V	125,000.	

Earliest documented use: Feb. 17, 1904.

	Nos. 300-313 (14)	6,065.	1,092.

For listings of designs A127 and A128 with Perf. 10 see Nos. 479 and 480.

Earliest documented use dates for imperforates are for the imperforate sheet stamps, not for imperforate stamps with vending and affixing machine perforations or for flat plate imperforate coil stamps. EDU dates for VAMP and flat plate imperf coil stamps are shown in their respective sections later in the catalogue.

1906-08				***Imperf.***
314	A115	**1c blue green,** *Oct. 2, 1906*	16.00	15.00
		green	16.00	15.00
		deep green	16.00	15.00
		Never hinged	35.00	
		On cover		22.50
		Pair	35.00	31.00
		Never hinged	70.00	
		Block of 4	70.00	75.00
		Never hinged	140.00	
		Corner margin block of 4	77.50	72.50
		Margin block of 4, arrow	80.00	75.00
		Margin block of 4, arrow & round marker	175.00	125.00
		Center line block	135.00	100.00
		P# block of 6, Impt.	200.00	—
		Never hinged	300.00	
		Double transfer	30.00	17.50

Earliest documented use: Dec. 20, 1906.

314A	A118	**4c brown,** *Apr. 1908*	75,000.	45,000.
		Never hinged	120,000.	
		On cover		130,000.
		Pair	175,000.	
		Guide line pair	240,000.	

This stamp was issued imperforate but all copies were privately perforated with large oblong perforations at the sides (Schermack type III).
Beware of examples of No. 303 with trimmed perforations and fake private perfs. added.
Used and on-cover values are for contemporary usage.

Earliest documented use: May 27, 1908.

315	A119	**5c blue,** *May 12, 1908*	240.	1,000.
		Never hinged	425.	
		On cover, pair		45,000.
		Pair	500.	4,000.
		Never hinged	875.	
		Block of 4	1,000.	9,000.
		Never hinged	1,750.	
		Corner margin block of 4	1,100.	
		Margin block of 4, arrow	1,600.	
		Margin block of 4, arrow & round marker	2,500.	
		Center line block	10,000.	
		P# block of 6, Impt.	2,750.	
		Never hinged	4,000.	

Earliest documented use: Sept. 15, 1908.

Beware of examples of No. 304 with perforations removed. Used examples of No. 315 must have contemporaneous cancels. Single copies of No. 315 on cover are not known to exist.

COIL STAMPS

Warning! Imperforate stamps are known fraudulently perforated to resemble coil stamps and part-perforate varieties. Fully perforated stamps and booklet stamps also are known with perforations fraudulently trimmed off to resemble coil stamps.

1908			***Perf. 12 Horizontally***
316	A115	**1c blue green,** *Feb. 18*	55,000.	
		Pair	150,000.	
		Guide line pair	240,000.	
317	A119	**5c blue,** *Feb. 24*	6,000.	—
		Never hinged	17,500.	
		Pair	17,500.	
		Never hinged	45,000.	
		Guido lino pair	55,000.	
		Never hinged	150,000.	

Earliest documented use: Sept. 18, 1908.

			Perf. 12 Vertically
318	A115	**1c blue green,** *July 31*	6,000.	
		Never hinged	11,500.	
		Pair	16,500.	
		Guide line pair	35,000.	
		Double transfer		

The No. 318 mint never hinged single is valued in the grade of fine.

Coil stamps for use in vending and affixing machines are perforated on two sides only, either horizontally or vertically. They were first issued in 1908, using perf. 12. This was changed to 8½ in 1910, and to 10 in 1914.
Imperforate sheets of certain denominations were sold to the vending machine companies which applied a variety of private perforations and separations (see Vending and Affixing Machine Perforations section of this catalogue).
Several values of the 1902 and later issues are found on an apparently coarse-ribbed paper. This is caused by worn blankets on the printing presses and is not a true paper variety.
All examples of Nos. 316-318 must be accompanied by certificates of authenticity issued by recognized expertizing committees.

Washington — A129

Plate of 400 subjects in four panes of 100 each.

Type I

Type II

1903			**Wmk. 191**		***Perf. 12***
319	A129	**2c carmine,** type I, *Nov. 12, 1903*	6.00	.25
		bright carmine	6.00	.25
		red	6.00	.25
		Never hinged	12.50	
		On cover		.30
		Block of 4	25.00	2.50
		P# strip of 3, Impt., T V	24.00	
		Never hinged	45.00	
		P# block of 6, Impt., T V	180.00	
		Never hinged	310.00	
		Double transfer	12.50	2.00
a.		**2c lake,** type I	—	—
		carmine lake	—	
b.		**2c carmine rose,** type I	10.00	.40
		Never hinged	22.50	
		On cover		.60
		Block of 4	42.50	9.00
		P# strip of 3, Impt., T V	40.00	
		Never hinged	75.00	
		P# block of 6, Impt., T V	250.00	
		Never hinged	375.00	
c.		**2c scarlet,** type I	7.00	.30
		Never hinged	15.00	
		On cover		.35
		Block of 4	30.00	4.50
		P# strip of 3, Impt., T V	27.50	
		Never hinged	57.50	
		P# block of 6, Impt., T V	190.00	
		Never hinged	325.00	
d.		Vert. pair, imperf. horiz., No. 319	7,500.	
		Never hinged		
e.		Vertical pair, imperf. between, No. 319	2,500.	
		As "e," rouletted between	3,250.	

No. 319e comes from a single pane of stamps on which a line of horizontal perfs is omitted between rows 9 and 10. Additionally, during the use of this stamp, the Postmaster at San Francisco discovered in his stock sheets of No. 319, each of which had the horizontal perforations missing between the two p rows of stamps. To facilitate their separation, the imperf. ws were rouletted, and the stamps sold over the counter. So ertical pairs are found from this source with regular perfora- ons all around and rouletted between.

"Gash on Face"
Variety

The gash may appear as double lines due to different plate wiping techniques.

f.	2c **lake**, type II	10.00	.30
	carmine lake	10.00	.30
	Never hinged	22.50	
	On cover		.35
	Block of 4	42.50	5.50
	P# strip of 3, Impt., T V	45.00	
	Never hinged	90.00	
	P# block of 6, Impt., T V	325.00	
	Never hinged	475.00	
	"Gash on face" plate flaw (car- mine lake, 4671 LL 16)	—	
g.	Booklet pane of 6, **car.**, type I	125.00	550.00
	Never hinged	240.00	
	Wmk. horizontal	1,500.	
	Never hinged	2,500.	
h.	Booklet pane of 6, **car.**, type II	500.00	
	Never hinged	850.00	
i.	2c **carmine**, type II	75.00	50.00
	red	75.00	50.00
	Never hinged	160.00	
	On cover		150.00
j.	2c **carmine rose**, type II	70.00	1.75
	Never hinged	150.00	
	Block of 4	300.00	20.00
	P# block of 6, Impt., T V	1,100.	
k.	2c **scarlet**, type II	50.00	.65
	Never hinged	105.00	
	Block of 4	225.00	5.00
	P# block of 6, Impt., T V	1,000.	
n.	Booklet pane of 6, **car. rose** (I)	250.00	650.00
	Never hinged	450.00	
p.	Booklet pane of 6, **scarlet** (I)	185.00	575.00
	Never hinged	350.00	
q.	Booklet pane of 6, **lake** (II)	300.00	750.00
	Never hinged	575.00	

Earliest documented uses:
No. 319, Nov. 19, 1903;
No. 319a, Sept. 23, 1904;
No. 319b, Nov. 3, 1903;
No. 319c, Dec. 16, 1903;
No. 319f, Sept. 25, 1908;
No. 319g single, Jan. 22, 1904;
No. 319h single, June 8, 1908;
No. 319i, June 5, 1908;
No. 319j, June 30, 1908;
No. 319k, June 11, 1908
No. 319p single, Apr. 12, 1904.

1906   **Imperf.**

320	A129 2c **carmine**, type I *Oct. 2*	16.00	17.50
	Never hinged	35.00	
	On cover		22.50
	Pair	35.00	37.50
	Never hinged	72.50	
	Block of 4	70.00	75.00
	Corner margin block of 4	72.50	100.00
	Margin block of 4, arrow	75.00	110.00
	Margin block of 4, arrow & round marker	—	
	Center line block	150.00	200.00
	P# block of 6, Impt., T V, car- mine	200.00	—
	Never hinged	325.00	
	Double transfer	24.00	21.50

Earliest documented use: Oct. 26, 1906.

a.	2c **lake**, type II	45.00	45.00
	carmine lake	45.00	45.00
	Never hinged	100.00	
	On cover		—
	Pair	100.00	110.00
	Never hinged	225.00	
	Block of 4	200.00	260.00
	Corner margin block of 4	205.00	
	Margin block of 4, arrow	210.00	
	Center line block	425.00	
	P# block of 6, Impt., T V	725.00	—
	Never hinged	1,150.	
	"Gash on face" plate flaw (see No. 319f)	—	
b.	2c **scarlet**, type I	18.50	12.50
	Never hinged	40.00	
	On cover		20.00
	Pair	39.00	
	Never hinged	85.00	
	Block of 4	77.50	
	Corner margin block of 4	80.00	
	Margin block of 4, arrow	82.50	—
	Center line block	205.00	
	P# block of 6, Impt., T V	225.00	—
	Never hinged	350.00	
c.	2c **carmine rose**, type I	60.00	40.00
	Never hinged	130.00	
d.	2c **carmine**, type II	120.00	250.00
	Never hinged	175.00	
	On cover		600.00

	Pair	225.00	
	Never hinged	425.00	
	Guide line pair	450.00	

No. 320d was issued imperforate, but all copies were pri- vately perforated with large oblong perforations at the sides (Schermack type III).

COIL STAMPS

1908   *Perf. 12 Horizontally*

321	A129 2c **carmine**, type I, pair, *Feb.*		
	18	375,000.	
	On cover, single		225,000.
	Guide line pair	—	

Four authenticated unused pairs of No. 321 are known and available to collectors. A fifth, unauthenticated pair is in the New York Public Library Miller collection. The value for an unused pair is for a fine-very fine example. Two fine pairs are recorded and one very fine pair. There are no authenticated unused single stamps recorded. There are 2 authenticated examples of the single used on cover, both used from Indianapolis in 1908. Numerous counterfeits exist.

Earliest documented use: Oct. 2, 1908.

Perf. 12 Vertically

322	A129 2c **carmine**, type II, *July 31*	6,000.	—
	Never hinged	11,000.	
	Pair	16,000.	
	Guide line pair	27,500.	
	Double transfer		—

This Government Coil Stamp should not be confused with those of the International Vending Machine Co., which are per- forated 12½.

All examples of Nos. 321-322 must be accompanied by certif- icates of authenticity issued by recognized expertizing committees.

VALUES FOR VERY FINE STAMPS
Please note: Stamps are valued in the grade of Very Fine unless otherwise indicated.

LOUISIANA PURCHASE EXPOSITION ISSUE
St. Louis, Mo., Apr. 30 - Dec. 1, 1904

Robert R. Livingston — A130

Thomas Jefferson — A131

James Monroe — A132

William McKinley — A133

Map of Louisiana Purchase — A134

Plates of 100 (10x10) subjects, divided vertically into 2 panes of 50.

Exposition Station Machine Cancellation

1904, Apr. 30		**Wmk. 191**		***Perf. 12***
323	A130 1c **green**		30.00	5.00
	dark green		30.00	5.00
	Never hinged		70.00	
	On cover			7.00
	On Expo. card, Expo. station machine canc.			40.00
	On Expo. card, Expo. station duplex handstamp canc.			100.00
	Block of 4		125.00	35.00

Margin block of 4, arrow, R or L	130.00	—
P# pair, Impt., T V	82.50	
Never hinged	180.00	
P# strip of 3, Impt., T V	120.00	
Never hinged	250.00	
P# block of 4, Impt., T V	175.00	
Never hinged	325.00	
P# block of 6, Impt., T V	300.00	
Never hinged	500.00	
Diagonal line through left "1" (2138 L 2)	50.00	12.50
Double transfer	—	

Earliest documented use: Apr. 30, 1904 (FDC).

324	A131 2c **carmine**	27.50	2.00
	bright carmine	27.50	2.00
	Never hinged	65.00	
	On cover		3.00
	On Expo. cover, Expo. station machine canc.		60.00
	On Expo. cover, Expo. station duplex handstamp canc.		150.00
	Block of 4	120.00	17.50
	Margin block of 4, arrow, R or L	130.00	—
	P# pair, Impt., T V	75.00	
	Never hinged	160.00	
	P# strip of 3, Impt., T V	110.00	
	Never hinged	230.00	
	P# block of 4, Impt., T V	175.00	
	Never hinged	325.00	
	P# block of 6, Impt., T V	300.00	
	Never hinged	500.00	
a.	Vertical pair, imperf. horiz.	17,500.	
	Block of 4	40,000.	
	P# block of 4, Impt., T V	55,000.	

Earliest documented use: Apr. 30, 1904 (FDC).

325	A132 3c **violet**	90.00	30.00
	Never hinged	210.00	
	On cover		65.00
	On cover, Expo. station machine canc.		200.00
	On cover, Expo. station duplex handstamp canc.		400.00
	Block of 4	375.00	225.00
	Margin block of 4, arrow, R or L	390.00	—
	P# pair, Impt., T V	225.00	
	Never hinged	500.00	
	P# strip of 3, Impt., T V	350.00	
	Never hinged	725.00	
	P# block of 4, Impt., T V	625.00	
	Never hinged	1,075.	
	P# block of 6, Impt., T V	950.00	
	Never hinged	1,750.	
	Double transfer	—	

Earliest documented use: Apr. 30, 1904 (FDC).

326	A133 5c **dark blue**	95.00	25.00
	Never hinged	225.00	
	On cover		50.00
	On cover, Expo. station machine canc.		400.00
	On cover, Expo. station duplex handstamp canc.		500.00
	Block of 4	400.00	200.00
	Margin block of 4, arrow, R or L	425.00	—
	P# pair, Impt., T V	230.00	
	Never hinged	525.00	
	P# strip of 3, Impt., T V	375.00	
	Never hinged	800.00	
	P# block of 4, Impt., T V	675.00	
	Never hinged	1,150.	
	P# block of 6, Impt., T V	1,000.	
	Never hinged	1,850.	

Earliest documented use: Apr. 30, 1904 (FDC).

327	A134 10c **red brown**	175.00	30.00
	dark red brown	175.00	30.00
	Never hinged	400.00	
	On cover		125.00
	On cover, Expo. station machine canc.		450.00
	On cover, Expo. station duplex handstamp canc.		750.00
	Block of 4	725.00	225.00
	Margin block of 4, arrow, R or L	775.00	—
	P# pair, Impt., T V	425.00	
	Never hinged	900.00	
	P# strip of 3, Impt., T V	725.00	
	Never hinged	1,400.	
	P# block of 4, Impt., T V	1,325.	
	Never hinged	2,250.	
	P# block of 6, Impt., T V	2,250.	
	Never hinged	3,850.	

Earliest documented use: Apr. 30, 1904 (FDC).

	Nos. 323-327 (5)	417.50	92.00
	Nos. 323-327, never hinged	970.00	

JAMESTOWN EXPOSITION ISSUE
Hampton Roads, Va., Apr. 26 - Dec. 1, 1907

Captain John Smith — A135

Founding of Jamestown — A136

Pocahontas — A137

Plates of 200 subjects in two panes of 100 each.

Exposition Station Machine Cancellation

1907	Wmk. 191		Perf. 12
328	A135 1c **green**, *Apr. 26*	30.00	5.00
	dark green	30.00	5.00
	Never hinged	70.00	
	On cover		8.00
	On Expo. card, Expo. station machine canc.		25.00
	On Expo. card, Expo. station duplex handstamp canc.		125.00
	Block of 4	125.00	50.00
	Margin block of 4, arrow	130.00	—
	P# strip of 3, Impt., T V	110.00	
	Never hinged	240.00	
	P# block of 6, Impt., T V	400.00	
	Never hinged	600.00	
	Double transfer	35.00	6.00

Earliest documented use: Apr. 26, 1907 (FDC).

329	A136 2c **carmine**, *Apr. 26*	35.00	4.50
	bright carmine	35.00	4.50
	Never hinged	80.00	
	On cover		6.00
	On Expo. cover, Expo. station machine canc.		100.00
	On Expo. cover, Expo. station duplex handstamp canc.		150.00
	Block of 4	150.00	35.00
	Margin block of 4, arrow	160.00	
	P# strip of 3, Impt., T V	125.00	
	Never hinged	275.00	
	P# block of 6, Impt., T V	500.00	
	Never hinged	725.00	
	Double transfer	42.50	6.00

Earliest documented use: Apr. 26, 1907 (FDC).

330	A137 5c **blue**	150.00	30.00
	deep blue	150.00	30.00
	Never hinged	350.00	
	On cover		82.50
	On cover, Expo. station machine canc.		350.00
	On cover, Expo. station duplex handstamp canc.		500.00
	Block of 4	650.00	210.00
	Margin block of 4, arrow	675.00	—
	P# strip of 3, Impt., T V	525.00	
	Never hinged	1,200.	
	P# block of 6, Impt., T V	2,750.	
	Never hinged	5,250.	
	Double transfer	150.00	35.00

Earliest documented use: May 8, 1907.

	Nos. 328-330 (3)	215.00	39.50
	Nos. 328-330, never hinged	500.00	

REGULAR ISSUE

Plates of 400 subjects in four panes of 100 each for all values 1c to 15c inclusive.

Plates of 200 subjects in two panes of 100 each for 50c and $1 denominations.

In 1909 the Bureau prepared certain plates with horizontal spacings of 3mm between the outer seven vertical stamp rows and 2mm between the others. This was done to try to counteract the effect of unequal shrinkage of the paper. *However, some unequal*

shrinkage still did occur and intermediate spacings are frequently found. The listings of 2mm and 3mm spacings are for exact measurements. Intermediate spacings sell for approximately the same as the cheaper of the two listed spacings.

All such plates were marked with an open star added to the imprint and exist on the 1c, 2c, 3c, 4c and 5c denominations only. A small solid star was added to the imprint and plate number for 1c plate No. 4980, 2c plate No. 4988 and for the 2c Lincoln. All other plates for this issue are spaced 2mm throughout.

There are several types of some of the 2c and 3c stamps of this and succeeding issues. These types are described under the dates at which they first appeared. Illustrations of Types I-VII of the 2c (A140) and Types I-IV of the 3c (A140) are reproduced by permission of H. L. Lindquist.

Imprint, plate number and open star	✿	4968
Imprint, plate number and small solid star	●	4976
Imprint, plate number and "A"	A	5557

(Illustrations reduced in size)

"A" and number only	A	5805
Number only		988

The above illustrations are several of the styles used on plates of issues from 1908 to date.

China Clay Paper.

A small quantity of Nos. 331-340 was printed on paper containing a high mineral content (5-20%), instead of the specified 2%. The minerals, principally aluminum silicate, produced China clay paper. It is thick, hard and grayish, often darker than "bluish" paper.

Franklin — A138   Washington — A139

1908-09	Wmk. 191		Perf. 12
331	A138 1c **green**, *Dec. 1908*	7.25	.40
	bright green	7.25	.40
	dark green	7.25	.40
	yellow green	7.25	.40
	Never hinged	17.50	
	On cover		.55
	Block of 4 (2mm spacing)	32.50	2.50
	Block of 4 (3mm spacing)	35.00	3.00
	P# block of 6, Impt., T V	82.50	
	Never hinged	150.00	
	P# block of 6, Impt. & star	77.50	
	Never hinged	135.00	
	P# block of 6, Impt. & small solid star (plate 4980)	1,500.	
	Never hinged	2,250.	
	Double transfer	9.50	.75
	Cracked plate	—	
a.	Booklet pane of 6, *Dec. 1908*	160.00	450.00
	Never hinged	285.00	
b.	"China Clay" paper	1,000.	

No. 331 exists in horizontal pair, imperforate between, a variety resulting from booklet experiments. Not regularly issued. Value, $2,500.

No. 331a used is valued with a contemporaneous cancel. A certificate of authenticity is advised.

Earliest documented uses: Dec. 1, 1908 (No. 331); Dec. 2, 1908 (No. 331a single) (FDC).

332	A139 2c **carmine**, *Nov. 1908*	6.75	.35
	light carmine	6.75	.35
	dark carmine	6.75	.35
	Never hinged	16.00	
	On cover		.40
	Block of 4 (2mm spacing)	30.00	2.00
	Block of 4 (3mm spacing)	32.50	2.50
	P# block of 6, Impt., T V	77.50	
	Never hinged	135.00	
	P# block of 6, Impt. & star	72.50	
	Never hinged	125.00	
	P# block of 6, Impt. & small solid star (plate 4988)	1,750.	
	Never hinged	2,750.	
	Double transfer	12.50	
	Foreign entry, design of 1c (plate 5299)	1,750.	2,750.
	On cover		
	Rosette crack	—	

	Cracked plate	—	—
a.	Booklet pane of 6	135.00	*400.00*
	Never hinged	230.00	
b.	"China Clay" paper	*1,300.*	

No. 332a used is valued with a contemporaneous cancel. A certificate of authenticity is advised.
No. 332 used with foreign entry, used, is valued in the grade of Fine.

Earliest documented uses: Dec. 3, 1908 (No. 332), Nov. 16, 1908 (No. 332a single).

Washington — A140

TYPE I

THREE CENTS.
Type I. The top line of the toga rope is weak and the rope shading lines are thin. The 5th line from the left is missing. The line between the lips is thin. (For descriptions of 3c types II, III and IV, see notes and illustrations preceding Nos. 484, 529-530.)
Used on both flat plate and rotary press printings.

333	A140	**3c deep violet,** type I, *Dec.*		
		1908	35.00	3.00
		violet	35.00	3.00
		light violet	35.00	3.00
		Never hinged	80.00	
		On cover		8.50
		Block of 4 (2mm spacing)	145.00	26.50
		Block of 4 (3mm spacing)	150.00	29.00
		P# block of 6, Impt., T V	350.00	
		Never hinged	575.00	
		P# block of 6, Impt. & star	375.00	
		Never hinged	625.00	
		Double transfer	37.50	5.75
a.		"China Clay" paper	*1,000.*	
		P# block of 6, Impt., T V	*7,500.*	

Earliest documented use: Jan. 12, 1909.

334	A140	**4c orange brown,** *Dec. 1908*		
		brown	42.50	1.50
		light brown	42.50	1.50
		dark brown	42.50	1.50
			42.50	1.50
		Never hinged	95.00	
		On cover		7.00
		Block of 4 (2mm spacing)	180.00	12.50
		Block of 4 (3mm spacing)	190.00	14.00
		P# block of 6, Impt., T V	425.00	
		Never hinged	700.00	
		P# block of 6, Impt. & star	425.00	
		Never hinged	700.00	
		Double transfer	55.00	—
a.		"China Clay" paper	*1,300.*	

Earliest documented use: Jan. 12, 1909.

335	A140	**5c blue,** *Dec. 1908*		
		bright blue	55.00	2.50
		dark blue	55.00	2.50
			55.00	2.50
		Never hinged	125.00	
		On cover		8.50
		Block of 4 (2mm spacing)	230.00	20.00
		Block of 4 (3mm spacing)	240.00	17.50
		P# block of 6, Impt., T V	525.00	
		Never hinged	1,000.	
		P# block of 6, Impt. & star	550.00	
		Never hinged	1,050.	
		Double transfer	60.00	—
a.		"China Clay" paper	*1,000.*	
		P# block of 6, Impt. & star	—	

Earliest documented use: Jan. 12, 1909.

336	A140	**6c red orange,** *Jan. 1909*		
		pale red orange	70.00	6.50
		orange	70.00	6.50
			70.00	6.50
		Never hinged	160.00	
		On cover		22.50
		Block of 4	275.00	50.00
		P# block of 6, Impt., T V	750.00	
		Never hinged	1,300.	
a.		"China Clay" paper	*1,000.*	
		Never hinged		

Earliest documented use: Jan. 6, 1909.

337	A140	**8c olive green,** *Dec. 1908*		
		deep olive green	50.00	3.00
			50.00	3.00

	Never hinged	110.00	
	On cover		18.00
	Block of 4	210.00	25.00
	P# block of 6, Impt., T V	525.00	
	Never hinged	875.00	
	Double transfer	57.50	—
a.	"China Clay" paper	*1,000.*	

Earliest documented use: Jan. 8, 1909.

338	A140	**10c yellow,** *Jan. 1909*		
		Never hinged	75.00	2.00
		On cover	170.00	
				10.00
		Block of 4	300.00	15.00
		P# block of 6, Impt., T V	800.00	
		Never hinged	1,450.	
		Double transfer	—	
		Very thin paper	—	
a.		"China Clay" paper	*1,000.*	

Earliest documented use: Jan. 18, 1909.

339	A140	**13c blue green,** *Jan. 1909*		
		deep blue green	42.50	19.00
			42.50	19.00
		Never hinged	95.00	
		On cover		110.00
		Block of 4	190.00	175.00
		P# block of 6, Impt., T V	500.00	
		Never hinged	850.00	
		Line through "TAG" of "POSTAGE" (4948 LR 96)	70.00	—
a.		"China Clay" paper	*1,000.*	
		P# block of 6, Impt., T V	*7,500.*	

Earliest documented use: Mar. 5, 1909.

340	A140	**15c pale ultramarine,** *Jan. 1909*		
		ultramarine	70.00	6.50
			70.00	6.50
		Never hinged	160.00	
		On cover		125.00
		Block of 4	290.00	65.00
		P# block of 6, Impt., T V	650.00	
		Never hinged	1,100.	
a.		"China Clay" paper	*1,000.*	
		P# block of 6, Impt., T V	*9,000.*	

Earliest documented use: Mar. 12, 1909.

341	A140	**50c violet,** *Jan. 13, 1909*		
		dull violet	350.00	20.00
			350.00	20.00
		Never hinged	800.00	
		On cover		5,000.
		Block of 4	1,500.	150.00
		Margin block of 4, arrow, right or left	1,550.	
		P# block of 6, Impt., T V	7,000.	
		Never hinged	12,500.	

Earliest documented use: Oct. 23, 1909 (on registry tag); June 2, 1916 (on cover).

342	A140	**$1 violet brown,** *Jan. 29, 1909*		
		light violet brown	550.00	100.00
			550.00	100.00

	Never hinged	1,250.	
	On cover		*6,000.*
	Block of 4	2,400.	700.00
	Margin block of 4, arrow, right or left	2,500.	725.00
	P# block of 6, Impt., T V	*17,500.*	
	Double transfer	—	—

Earliest documented use: July 26, 1909.

	Nos. 331-342 (12)	*1,354.*	*164.75*

For listings of other perforated sheet stamps of A138, A139 and A140 see:
Nos. 357-366 Bluish paper
Nos. 374-382, 405-407 Single line wmk. Perf. 12
Nos. 423A-423C Single line wmk. Perf 12x10
Nos. 423D-423E Single line wmk. Perf 10x12
Nos. 424-430 Single line wmk. Perf. 10
Nos. 461 Single line wmk. Perf. 11
Nos. 462-469 unwmk. Perf. 10
Nos. 498-507 unwmk. Perf. 11
Nos. 519 Double line wmk. Perf. 11
Nos. 525-530 and 536 Offset printing
Nos. 538-546 Rotary press printing

Plate Blocks
Scott values for plate blocks printed from flat plates are for very fine side and bottom positions. Top position plate blocks with full wide selvage sell for more.

Earliest documented use dates for imperforates are for the imperforate sheet stamps, not for imperforate stamps with vending and affixing machine perforations or for flat plate imperforate coil stamps. EDU dates for VAMP and flat plate imperf coil stamps are shown in their respective sections later in the catalogue.

Imperf				
343	A138	**1c green,** *Dec. 1908*	4.50	4.50
		dark green	4.50	4.50
		yellowish green	4.50	4.50
		Never hinged	9.50	
		On cover		10.00
		Pair	9.50	10.00
		Never hinged	20.00	
		Block of 4 (2mm or 3mm spacing)	20.00	20.00
		Corner margin block of 4, 2mm or 3mm	21.00	21.00
		Margin block of 4, arrow, 2mm or 3mm	22.50	21.00
		Center line block	30.00	30.00
		P# block of 6, Impt., T V	47.50	—
		Never hinged	75.00	
		P# block of 6, Impt. & star	57.50	—

Never hinged	90.00	
P# block of 6, Impt. & small solid star (plate 4980)	675.00	
Never hinged	1,050.	
Double transfer	11.00	7.00

Earliest documented use: Jan. 4, 1909.

344 A139 2c **carmine**, *Dec. 1908* — 5.50 3.00
- light carmine — 5.50 3.00
- dark carmine — 5.50 3.00
- Never hinged — 11.50
- On cover — 7.50
- Pair — 11.50 7.50
  - Never hinged — 24.00
- Block of 4 (2mm or 3mm spacing) — 24.00 15.00
- Corner margin block of 4, 2mm or 3mm — 26.50 21.00
- Margin block of 4, arrow, 2mm or 3mm — 30.00 21.00
- Center line block — 37.50 37.50
- P# block of 6, Impt., T V — 77.50 —
  - Never hinged — 120.00
- P# block of 6, Impt. & star — 70.00 —
  - Never hinged — 110.00
- Double transfer — 12.50 4.00
- Foreign entry, design of 1c (plate 5299) — 1,250. —

Earliest documented use: Dec. 7, 1908.

The existence of the foreign entry on the imperforate sheet stamp No. 344 has been questioned by specialists. The editors would like to see evidence of the existence of the item, either unused or used.

345 A140 3c **deep violet**, type I, *1909* — 10.50 20.00
- violet — 10.50 20.00
- Never hinged — 22.00
- On cover — 60.00
- Pair — 22.00 50.00
  - Never hinged — 46.00
- Block of 4 — 45.00 100.00
- Corner margin block of 4 — 47.50 105.00
- Margin block of 4, arrow — 52.50 105.00
- Center line block — 75.00 125.00
- P# block of 6, Impt., T V — 155.00 —
  - Never hinged — 240.00
- Double transfer — 22.50 —

Earliest documented use: Feb. 13, 1909.

346 A140 4c **orange brown**, *Feb. 25, 1909* — 17.50 22.50
- brown — 17.50 22.50
- Never hinged — 37.50
- On cover — 90.00
- Pair — 37.50 57.50
  - Never hinged — 77.50
- Block of 4 (2 or 3mm spacing) — 77.50 115.00
- Corner margin block of 4 (2 or 3mm spacing) — 82.50 120.00
- Margin block of 4, arrow, (2 or 3mm spacing) — 87.50 120.00
- Center line block — 120.00 200.00
- P# block of 6, Impt., T V — 175.00 —
  - Never hinged — 275.00
- P# block of 6, Impt. & star — 210.00 —
  - Never hinged — 325.00
- Double transfer — 37.50 —

Earliest documented use: Mar. 13, 1909.

347 A140 5c **blue**, *Feb. 25, 1909* — 32.50 35.00
- dark blue — 32.50 35.00
- Never hinged — 70.00
- On cover — 125.00
- Pair — 67.50 100.00
  - Never hinged — 145.00
- Block of 4 — 145.00 200.00
- Corner margin block of 4 — 155.00 225.00
- Margin block of 4, arrow — 165.00 235.00
- Center line block — 220.00 300.00
- P# block of 6, Impt., T V — 275.00 —
  - Never hinged — 500.00
- Cracked plate — —

Earliest documented use: Mar. 4, 1909.

Nos. 343-347 (5) — 70.50 85.00
Nos. 343-347, never hinged — 150.50

For listings of other imperforate stamps of designs A138, A139 and A140 see Nos. 383, 384, 408, 409 and 459 Single line wmk.
Nos. 481-485 unwmk.
Nos. 531-535 Offset printing

COIL STAMPS

1908-10   *Perf. 12 Horizontally*

348 A138 1c **green**, *Dec. 29, 1908* — 37.50 25.00
- dark green — 37.50 25.00
- Never hinged — 80.00
- On cover — 50.00
- Pair — 100.00 105.00
  - Never hinged — 210.00
- Guide line pair — 290.00 575.00
  - Never hinged — 600.00

Earliest documented use: Jan. 25, 1909.

349 A139 2c **carmine**, *Jan. 1909* — 80.00 20.00
- dark carmine — 80.00 20.00
- Never hinged — 175.00
- On cover — 37.50
- Pair — 225.00 140.00
  - Never hinged — 450.00
- Guide line pair — 550.00 650.00

Never hinged	1,200.	
Foreign entry, design of 1c (plate 5299)	—	3,000.

Earliest documented use: May 14, 1909.

350 A140 4c **orange brown**, *Aug. 15, 1910* — 160.00 140.00
- Never hinged — 350.00
- On cover — 250.00
- Pair — 370.00 550.00
  - Never hinged — 800.00
- Guide line pair — 1,250. 2,500.
  - Never hinged — 2,750.

Earliest documented use: Mar. 22, 1912.

351 A140 5c **blue**, *Jan. 1909* — 175.00 175.00
- dark blue — 175.00 175.00
- Never hinged — 375.00
- On cover — 625.00
- Pair — 475.00 700.00
  - Never hinged — 1,000.
- Guide line pair — 1,250. 2,750.
  - Never hinged — 2,750.

Earliest documented use: Sept. 21, 1909.

1909   *Perf. 12 Vertically*

352 A138 1c **green**, *Jan. 1909* — 95.00 90.00
- dark green — 95.00 90.00
- Never hinged — 200.00
- On cover — 100.00
- Pair (2mm spacing) — 250.00 425.00
  - Never hinged — 550.00
- Pair (3mm spacing) — 235.00 400.00
  - Never hinged — 525.00
- Guide line pair — 825.00 1,250.
  - Never hinged — 1,800.
- Double transfer — —

353 A139 2c **carmine**, *Jan. 12, 1909* — 95.00 30.00
- dark carmine — 95.00 30.00
- Never hinged — 200.00
- On cover — 35.00
- Pair (2mm spacing) — 250.00 135.00
  - Never hinged — 550.00
- Pair (3mm spacing) — 235.00 125.00
  - Never hinged — 525.00
- Guide line pair — 750.00 850.00
  - Never hinged — 1,600.

Earliest documented use: June 14, 1909.

354 A140 4c **orange brown**, *Feb. 23, 1909* — 220.00 150.00
- Never hinged — 475.00
- On cover — 190.00
- Pair (2mm spacing) — 550.00 550.00
  - Never hinged — 1,200.
- Pair (3mm spacing) — 525.00 550.00
  - Never hinged — 1,150.
- Guide line pair — 1,500. 1,300.
  - Never hinged — 3,250.

Earliest documented use: June 9, 1909.

355 A140 5c **blue**, *Feb. 23, 1909* — 235.00 160.00
- Never hinged — 500.00
- On cover — 275.00
- Pair — 575.00 700.00
  - Never hinged — 1,250.
- Guide line pair — 1,500. 1,600.
  - Never hinged — 3,250.

Earliest documented use: Oct. 25, 1909.

These Government Coil Stamps, Nos. 352-355, should not be confused with those of the International Vending Machine Co., which are perf. 12½-13.

356 A140 10c **yellow**, *Jan. 7, 1909* — 3,000. 3,250.
- Never hinged — 6,500.
- On cover — 10,000.
- Pair — 7,000. 9,000.
  - Never hinged — 14,000.
- Guide line pair — 15,000. 29,000.
  - Never hinged — 55,000.

Earliest documented use: Mar. 9, 1909 (dated cancel on off-cover stamp).

The used guide line pair of No. 356 is unique. Value reflects price realized at auction in 2002.

For listings of other coil stamps of designs A138 A139 and A140 see:
Nos. 385-396, 410-413, 441-459, single line watermark.
Nos. 486-496, unwatermarked.

Beware of stamps offered as No. 356 which may be examples of No. 338 with perfs. trimmed at top and/or bottom. Beware also of plentiful fakes in the marketplace of Nos. 348-355, made by fraudulently perforating imperforate stamps or by fraudulently trimming perforations off fully perforated stamps. Authentication of all these coils is advised.

BLUISH PAPER

This was made with 35 per cent rag stock instead of all wood pulp. The "bluish" color (actually grayish blue) goes through the paper showing clearly on the back as well as on the face.

1909   *Perf. 12*

357 A138 1c **green**, *Feb. 16, 1909* — 100.00 100.00
- Never hinged — 210.00
- On postcard — 120.00
- On cover — 220.00
- Block of 4 (2mm spacing) — 425.00 600.00
- Block of 4 (3mm spacing) — 800.00
- P# block of 6, Impt., T V — 1,100.

Never hinged	1,850.	
P# block of 6, Impt. & star	3,100.	
Never hinged	5,200.	

Earliest documented use: Feb. 21, 1909.

358 A139 2c **carmine**, *Feb. 16, 1909* — 90.00 100.00
- Never hinged — 190.00
- On cover — 190.00
- Block of 4 (2mm spacing) — 375.00 650.00
- Block of 4 (3mm spacing) — 475.00
- P# block of 6, Impt., T V — 1,000.
  - Never hinged — 1,800.
- P# block of 6, Impt. & star — 1,550.
  - Never hinged — 2,650.
- Double transfer — —

Earliest documented use: Feb. 23, 1909.

359 A140 3c **deep violet**, type I — 2,000. 5,000.
- Never hinged — 4,250.
- On cover — —
- Block of 4 — 8,500.
- P# block of 6, Impt., T V — 22,500.
  - Never hinged — 31,000.

Earliest documented use: Dec. 27, 1910.

360 A140 4c **orange brown** — 24,000.
- Never hinged — 37,500.
- Block of 4 — 110,000.
- P# strip of 3, Impt., T V — 125,000.

The No. 360 plate number strip of three is unique.

361 A140 5c **blue** — 6,000. 15,000.
- Never hinged — 15,000.
- On cover — 27,500.
- Block of 4 — 26,000.
- P# block of 6, Impt., T V — 90,000.

The No. 361 plate block is unique.

Earliest documented use: May 18, 1910.

362 A140 6c **red orange** — 1,500. 5,000.
- Never hinged — 3,750.
- On cover — 15,000.
- Block of 4 — 6,250.
- P# block of 6, Impt., T V — 16,000.
  - Never hinged — 30,000.

Earliest documented use: Sept. 14, 1911.

363 A140 8c **olive green** — 27,500.
- Never hinged — 40,000.
- Block of 4 — 125,000.
- P# strip of 3, Impt., T V — 125,000.

The No. 363 plate number strip of three is unique.

364 A140 10c **yellow** — 1,900. 6,250.
- Never hinged — 4,500.
- On cover — —
- Block of 4 — 8,000.
- P# block of 6, Impt., T V — 33,500.

Earliest documented use: Feb. 3, 1910.

365 A140 13c **blue green** — 3,000. 2,250.
- Never hinged — 6,500.
- On cover — —
- Block of 4 — 13,000. 10,000.
- P# block of 6, Impt., T V — 30,000.

366 A140 15c **pale ultramarine** — 1,500. 11,000.
- Never hinged — 3,250.
- On cover — —
- Block of 4 — 6,250.
- P# block of 6, Impt., T V — 11,500.
  - Never hinged — 20,000.

Earliest documented use: Jan. 15, 1911.

Nos. 360 and 363 were not regularly issued.
Used examples of Nos. 357-366 must bear contemporaneous cancels, and Nos. 359-366 used must be accompanied by certificates of authenticity issued by recognized expertizing committees.

IMPORTANT INFORMATION REGARDING VALUES FOR NEVER-HINGED STAMPS

Collectors should be aware that the values given for never-hinged stamps from No. 205 on are for stamps in the grade of very fine, just as the values for all stamps in the catalogue are for very fine stamps unless indicated otherwise. The never-hinged premium as a percentage of value will be larger for stamps in extremely fine or superb grades, and the premium will be smaller for fine-very fine, fine or poor examples. This is particularly true of the issues of the late-19th and early-20th centuries. For example, in the grade of very fine, an unused stamp from this time period may be valued at $100 hinged and $180 never-hinged. The never-hinged premium is thus 80%. But in grade of extremely fine, this same stamp will not only sell for more hinged, but the never-hinged premium will increase, perhaps to 100%-300% or more over the higher extremely fine value. In a grade of superb, a hinged copy will sell for much more than a very fine copy, and additionally the never-hinged premium will be much larger, perhaps as large as 300%-400%. On the other hand, the same stamp in a grade of fine or fine-very fine not only will sell for less than a very fine stamp in hinged condition, but additionally the never-hinged premium will be smaller than the never-hinged premium on a very fine stamp, perhaps as small as 15%-30%.

Please note that the above statements and percentages are NOT a formula for arriving at the values of stamps in hinged or never-hinged condition in the grades of very good, fine, fine to very fine, extremely fine or superb. The percentages given apply only to the size of the premium for never-hinged condition that might be added to the stamp value for hinged condition. Further, the percentages given are only generalized estimates. Some stamps or grades may have percentages for never-hinged condition that are higher or lower than the ranges given. For values of the most popular U.S. stamps in the grades of very good, fine, fine to very fine, extremely fine and superb, see the *Scott Valuing Supplement*, updated and issued twice each year in April and October.

VALUES FOR NEVER-HINGED STAMPS PRIOR TO SCOTT 205

This catalogue does not value pre-1882 stamps in never-hinged condition. Premiums for never-hinged condition in the classic era invariably are even larger than those premiums listed for the post-1882 issues. Generally speaking, the earlier the stamp is listed in the catalogue, the larger will be the never-hinged premium. On some early classics, the premium will be several multiples of the unused, hinged values given in the catalogue.

NEVER-HINGED PLATE BLOCKS

Values given for never-hinged plate blocks are for blocks in which all stamps have original gum that has never been hinged and has no disturbances, and all selvage, whether gummed or ungummed, has never been hinged.

Lincoln — A141   William H. Seward — A142

LINCOLN CENTENARY OF BIRTH ISSUE

Plates of 400 subjects in four panes of 100 each

1909	Wmk. 191	Perf. 12	
367 A141 2c **carmine,** *Feb. 12*		5.50	2.00
bright carmine		5.50	2.00
Never hinged		11.00	
On cover			4.00
Block of 4 (2mm spacing)		22.50	16.00
Block of 4 (3mm spacing)		22.50	15.00
P# block of 6, Impt. & small solid star		200.00	
Never hinged		275.00	
Double transfer		7.50	2.75

Earliest documented use: Feb. 12, 1909 (FDC).

Imperf

368 A141 2c **carmine,** *Feb. 12*		19.00	22.50
Never hinged		37.50	
On cover			35.00
Pair		40.00	50.00
Never hinged		80.00	
Block of 4 (2mm or 3mm spacing)		82.50	95.00
Corner margin block of 4		87.50	95.00
Margin block of 4, arrow		90.00	100.00
Center line block		145.00	125.00

P# block of 6, Impt. & small solid star		190.00	—
Never hinged		390.00	
Double transfer		42.50	30.00

Earliest documented use: Feb. 12, 1909 (FDC).

BLUISH PAPER
Perf. 12

369 A141 2c **carmine,** *Feb.*		225.00	275.00
Never hinged		425.00	
On cover			425.00
Block of 4 (2mm or 3mm spacing)		1,000.	1,250.
P# block of 6, Impt. & small solid star		3,000.	
Never hinged		4,500.	

Earliest documented use: Feb. 27, 1909 (dated cancel on off-cover stamp); Mar. 27, 1909 (on cover).

ALASKA-YUKON-PACIFIC EXPOSITION ISSUE

Seattle, Wash., June 1 - Oct. 16, 1909
Plates of 280 subjects in four panes of 70 each

1909	Wmk. 191	Perf. 12	
370 A142 2c **carmine,** *June 1*		8.75	2.25
bright carmine		8.75	2.25
Never hinged		17.50	
On cover			5.00
On Expo. card or cover, Expo. station machine canc.			65.00
On Expo. card or cover, Expo. station duplex handstamp canc.			250.00
Block of 4		36.00	19.00
P# block of 6, Impt., T V		200.00	
Never hinged		320.00	
Double transfer (5249 UL 8)		10.50	5.00

Earliest documented use: June 1, 1909 (FDC).

Imperf

371 A142 2c **carmine,** *June*		21.00	24.00
Never hinged		42.50	
On cover			42.50
On cover, Expo. station machine canc.			450.00
Pair		45.00	52.50
Never hinged		85.00	
Block of 4		92.50	130.00
Corner margin block of 4		97.50	
Margin block of 4, arrow		100.00	140.00
Center line block		175.00	175.00
P# block of 6, Impt., T V		225.00	—
Never hinged		350.00	
Double transfer		35.00	30.00

Earliest documented use: June 7, 1909.

HUDSON-FULTON CELEBRATION ISSUE

Tercentenary of the discovery of the Hudson River and the centenary of Robert Fulton's steamship, the "Clermont."

Henry Hudson's "Half Moon" and Fulton's Steamship "Clermont" A143

Plates of 240 subjects in four panes of 60 each

1909, Sept. 25	Wmk. 191	Perf. 12	
372 A143 2c **carmine**		12.00	4.75
Never hinged		24.00	
On cover			8.50
Block of 4		50.00	30.00
P# block of 6, Impt., T V		280.00	
Never hinged		425.00	
Double transfer (5393 and 5394)		16.00	5.00

Earliest documented use: Sept. 25, 1909 (FDC).

Imperf

373 A143 2c **carmine**		25.00	27.50
Never hinged		50.00	
On cover			40.00
Pair		52.50	60.00
Never hinged		105.00	
Block of 4		105.00	130.00
Corner margin block of 4		110.00	—
Margin block of 4, arrow		115.00	135.00
Center line block		210.00	160.00
P# block of 6, Impt., T V		240.00	—
Never hinged		375.00	
Double transfer (5393 and 5394)		45.00	32.50

Earliest documented use: Sept. 25, 1909 (FDC).

Earliest documented use dates for imperforates are for the imperforate sheet stamps, not for imperforate stamps with vending and affixing machine perforations or for flat plate imperforate coil stamps. EDU dates for VAMP and flat plate imperf coil stamps are shown in their respective sections later in the catalogue.

REGULAR ISSUE
DESIGNS OF 1908-09 ISSUES

In this issue the Bureau used three groups of plates:
 (1) The old standard plates with uniform 2mm spacing throughout (6c, 8c, 10c and 15c values);
 (2) Those having an open star in the margin and showing spacings of 2mm and 3mm between stamps (for all values 1c to 10c); and
 (3) A third set of plates with uniform spacing of approximately 2¾mm between all stamps. These plates have imprints showing
 a. "Bureau of Engraving & Printing," "A" and number.
 b. "A" and number only.
 c. Number only.
 (See above No. 331)
 These were used for the 1c, 2c, 3c, 4c and 5c values.
 On or about Oct. 1, 1910 the Bureau began using paper watermarked with single-lined letters:

(Actual size of letter)

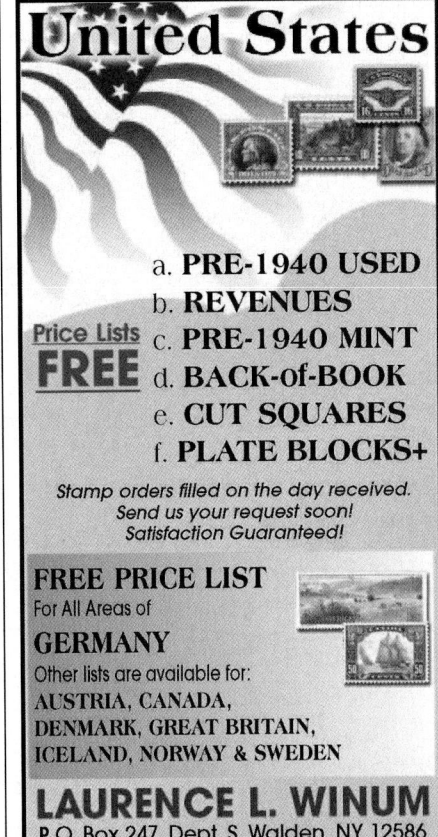

repeated in rows, this way:

U	S	P	S	U	S	P	S	U
U	S	P	S	U	S	P	S	
U	S	P	S	U	S	P	S	U
U	S	P	S	U	S	P	S	
U	S	P	S	U	S	P	S	U
U	S	P	S	U	S	P	S	
U	S	P	S	U	S	P	S	U
U	S	P	S	U	S	P	S	

Watermark 190
Plates of 400 subjects in four panes of 100 each

1910-11	Wmk. 190	Perf. 12	
374 A138	1c **green**, *Nov. 23, 1910*	7.00	.25
	light green	7.00	.25
	dark green	7.00	.25
	Never hinged	16.00	
	On cover		.30
	Block of 4 (2mm spacing)	30.00	3.25
	Block of 4 (3mm spacing)	32.50	3.00
	P# block of 6, Impt., & star	85.00	
	Never hinged	140.00	
	P# block of 6, Impt. & "A"	100.00	—
	Never hinged	160.00	
	Double transfer	14.00	—
	Cracked plate	—	—
	Pane of 60	1,750.	—
a.	Booklet pane of 6, *Oct. 7, 1910*	225.00	300.00
	Never hinged	375.00	

Earliest documented uses: Feb. 7, 1911 (No. 374); Feb. 28, 1911 (No. 374a single).

Panes of 60 of No. 374 were regularly issued in Washington, D.C. during Sept. and Oct., 1912. They were made from the six outer vertical rows of imperforate "Star Plate" sheets that had been rejected for use in vending machines on account of the 3mm spacing.

These panes have sheet margins on two adjoining sides and are imperforate along the other two sides. Upper and lower right panes show plate number, star and imprint on both margins; upper and lower left panes show plate number, star and imprint on side margins, but only the imprint on top or bottom margins.

375 A139	2c **carmine**, *Nov. 23, 1910*	7.00	.25
	bright carmine	7.00	.25
	dark carmine	7.00	.25
	Never hinged	16.00	
	On cover		.30
	Block of 4 (2mm spacing)	30.00	2.00
	Block of 4 (3mm spacing)	29.00	1.75
	P# block of 6, Impt. & star	100.00	
	Never hinged	160.00	
	P# block of 6, Impt. & "A"	110.00	
	Never hinged	175.00	
	Cracked plate	—	—
	Double transfer	12.00	—
	Foreign entry, design of 1c (plate 5299)	—	1,450.
a.	Booklet pane of 6, *Nov. 30, 1910*	125.00	200.00
	Never hinged	200.00	
b.	2c **lake**	900.00	
	Never hinged	1,900.	
c.	Double impression	600.00	
	Never hinged	1,200.	

Earliest documented use: Dec. 29, 1910 (No. 375); May 10, 1911 (No. 375a single).

376 A140	3c **deep violet**, type I, *Jan. 16, 1911*	21.50	2.00
	violet	21.50	2.00
	Never hinged	47.50	
	lilac	26.00	2.25
	Never hinged	55.00	
	On cover		8.00
	Block of 4 (2mm spacing)	90.00	15.00
	Block of 4 (3mm spacing)	92.50	14.00
	P# block of 6, Impt. & star	220.00	
	Never hinged	375.00	
	P# block of 6	250.00	
	Never hinged	400.00	

Earliest documented use: June 9, 1911.

377 A140	4c **brown**, *Jan. 20, 1911*	34.00	1.00
	dark brown	34.00	1.00
	orange brown	34.00	1.00
	Never hinged	75.00	
	On cover		7.50
	Block of 4 (2mm spacing)	150.00	6.50
	Block of 4 (3mm spacing)	145.00	6.00
	P# block of 6, Impt. & star	260.00	
	Never hinged	425.00	

	P# block of 6	310.00	
	Never hinged	500.00	
	Double transfer	—	—

Earliest documented use: Mar. 7, 1911.

378 A140	5c **blue**, *Jan. 25, 1911*	34.00	.75
	light blue	34.00	.75
	dark blue	34.00	.75
	bright blue	34.00	.75
	Never hinged	75.00	
	On cover		5.25
	Block of 4 (2mm spacing)	150.00	6.00
	Block of 4 (3mm spacing)	145.00	5.00
	P# block of 6, Impt., T V	310.00	
	Never hinged	500.00	
	P# block of 6, Impt. & star	310.00	
	Never hinged	500.00	
	P# block of 6, "A"	350.00	
	Never hinged	550.00	
	P# block of 6	350.00	
	Never hinged	550.00	
	Double transfer		—

Earliest documented use: Feb. 14, 1911.

379 A140	6c **red orange**, *Jan. 1911*	37.50	1.00
	light red orange	37.50	1.00
	Never hinged	85.00	
	On cover		13.00
	Block of 4 (2mm spacing)	160.00	12.50
	Block of 4 (3mm spacing)	155.00	11.00
	P# block of 6, Impt., T V	500.00	
	Never hinged	800.00	
	P# block of 6, Impt. & star	440.00	
	Never hinged	700.00	

Earliest documented use: Jan. 12, 1911.

380 A140	8c **olive green**, *Feb. 8, 1911*	115.00	15.00
	dark olive green	115.00	15.00
	Never hinged	260.00	
	On cover		45.00
	Block of 4 (2mm spacing)	475.00	100.00
	Block of 4 (3mm spacing)	475.00	95.00
	P# block of 6, Impt., T V	1,100.	
	Never hinged	1,900.	
	P# block of 6, Impt. & star	1,300.	
	Never hinged	2,200.	

Earliest documented use: May 27, 1911.

381 A140	10c **yellow**, *Jan. 24, 1911*	110.00	6.00
	Never hinged	250.00	
	On cover		22.50
	Block of 4 (2mm spacing)	460.00	50.00
	Block of 4 (3mm spacing)	460.00	47.50
	P# block of 6, Impt., T V	1,150.	
	Never hinged	2,000.	
	P# block of 6, Impt. & star	1,250.	
	Never hinged	2,250.	

Earliest documented use: Feb. 17, 1911.

382 A140	15c **pale ultramarine**, *Mar. 1, 1911*	275.00	17.50
	Never hinged	625.00	
	On cover		100.00
	Block of 4	1,150.	125.00
	P# block of 6, Impt., T V	2,500.	
	Never hinged	4,500.	

Earliest documented use: April 25, 1911.

Nos. 374-382 (9)		641.00	43.75

Earliest documented use dates for imperforates are for the imperforate sheet stamps, not for imperforate stamps with vending and affixing machine perforations or for flat plate imperforate coil stamps. EDU dates for VAMP and flat plate imperf coil stamps are shown in their respective sections later in the catalogue.

1910, Dec.			*Imperf.*
383 A138	1c **green**	2.25	2.00
	dark green	2.25	2.00
	yellowish green	2.25	2.00
	bright green	2.25	2.00
	Never hinged	4.50	
	On cover		5.00
	Pair	5.00	4.50
	Never hinged	10.00	
	Block of 4 (2mm or 3mm spacing)	10.50	14.00
	Corner margin block of 4	11.50	
	Margin block of 4, arrow	12.00	13.50
	Center line block	24.00	16.00
	P# block of 6, Impt., & star	45.00	—
	Never hinged	67.50	
	P# block of 6, Impt. & "A"	82.50	—
	Never hinged	125.00	
	Double transfer	6.50	—

Earliest documented use: Jan. 28, 1911.

Rosette plate crack on head

384 A139	2c **carmine**	3.75	2.
	light carmine	3.75	2.
	Never hinged	7.50	
	dark carmine	55.00	12.
	On cover		3.
	Horizontal pair	11.50	7.
	Never hinged	23.00	
	Vertical pair	8.50	6.
	Never hinged	17.00	
	Block of 4 (2mm or 3mm spacing)	25.00	16.
	Corner margin block of 4	27.50	20.
	Margin block of 4, arrow	27.50	21.
	Center line block	50.00	50.0
	P# block of 6, Impt. & star	130.00	
	Never hinged	200.00	
	P# block of 6, Impt. & "A"	170.00	
	Never hinged	260.00	
	Double transfer	7.50	
	Rosette plate crack on head	150.00	

Earliest documented use: Dec. 8, 1910.

COIL STAMPS

1910, Nov. 1		Perf. 12 Horizontal	
385 A138	1c **green**	45.00	25.0
	dark green	45.00	25.0
	Never hinged	90.00	
	On cover		45.0
	Pair	110.00	100.0
	Never hinged	230.00	
	Guide line pair	450.00	600.0
	Never hinged	1,000.	
386 A139	2c **carmine**	90.00	30.0
	light carmine	90.00	30.0
	Never hinged	190.00	
	On cover		60.0
	Pair	300.00	180.0
	Never hinged	625.00	
	Guide line pair	1,400.	850.0
	Never hinged	3,250.	

Earliest documented use: Dec. 9, 1910.

1910-11		Perf. 12 Vertically	
387 A138	1c **green**, *Nov. 1, 1910*	200.00	90.0
	Never hinged	425.00	
	On cover		110.0
	Pair (2mm spacing)	475.00	290.0
	Never hinged	1,000.	
	Pair (3mm spacing)	500.00	275.0
	Never hinged	1,050.	
	Guide line pair	1,000.	875.0
	Never hinged	2,250.	

Earliest documented use: Nov. 5, 1910.

388 A139	2c **carmine**, *Nov. 1, 1910*	1,250.	550.00
	Never hinged	2,750.	
	On cover		1,300.
	Pair (2mm spacing)	3,250.	7,000.
	Never hinged	6,750.	
	Pair (3mm spacing)	3,500.	7,500.
	Never hinged	7,250.	
	Guide line pair	8,500.	23,000.
	Never hinged	16,000.	

The used guide line pair of No. 388 is unique. It is fine-very fine and valued thus.

Stamps offered as No. 388 frequently are privately perforated examples of No. 384, or copies of No. 375 with top and/or bottom perfs trimmed.

Earliest documented use: Jan. 4, 1911.

389 A140	3c **deep vio.**, type I, *Jan. 24, 1911*	65,000.	10,000.
	Never hinged	150,000.	
	On cover		27,500.
	Pair	140,000.	37,500.

No. 389 is valued in the grade of fine.

Only a small supply of this coil was used at Orangeburg, N.Y. The used pair listed is part of a strip of 3 (three such strips exist). Each strip is in average grade or condition, and the pairs are valued thus. No other used multiples are recorded. There is only one mint, never-hinged example recorded.

Stamps offered as No. 389 sometimes are examples of No. 376 with top and/or bottom perfs trimmed. Expertization by competent authorities is recommended.

Earliest documented use: Mar. 8, 1911.

Beware of plentiful fakes in the marketplace of Nos. 385-389, made by fraudulently perforating the 1c and 2c imperforate stamps or by fraudulently trimming perforations off fully perforated stamps.

910   *Perf. 8½ Horizontally*

90	A138	1c **green**, *Dec. 12, 1910*	5.00	7.00
		dark green	5.00	7.00
		Never hinged	11.00	
		On cover		11.00
		Pair	11.50	*37.50*
		Never hinged	24.00	
		Guide line pair	37.50	*95.00*
		Never hinged	80.00	—
		Double transfer		—

Earliest documented use: Oct. 5, 1911.

91	A139	2c **carmine**, *Dec. 23, 1910*	42.50	17.50
		light carmine	42.50	17.50
		Never hinged	90.00	
		On cover		32.50
		Pair	110.00	115.00
		Never hinged	230.00	
		Guide line pair	260.00	*1,350.*
		Never hinged	550.00	

Earliest documented use: May 3, 1911.

910-13   *Perf. 8½ Vertically*

392	A138	1c **green**, *Dec. 12, 1910*	30.00	27.50
		dark green	30.00	27.50
		Never hinged	60.00	
		On cover		57.50
		Pair	75.00	125.00
		Never hinged	160.00	
		Guide line pair	200.00	*425.00*
		Never hinged	425.00	
		Double transfer		—

Earliest documented use: Dec. 16, 1910.

393	A139	2c **carmine**, *Dec. 16, 1910*	47.50	12.50
		dark carmine	47.50	12.50
		Never hinged	100.00	
		On cover		25.00
		Pair	125.00	85.00
		Never hinged	275.00	
		Guide line pair	300.00	250.00
		Never hinged	650.00	

Earliest documented use: Dec. 27, 1910.

394	A140	3c **deep violet**, type I, *Sept. 1911*	60.00	55.00
		violet	60.00	55.00
		red violet	60.00	55.00
		Never hinged	130.00	
		On cover		110.00
		Pair (2mm spacing)	150.00	*170.00*
		Never hinged	325.00	
		Pair (3mm spacing)	145.00	*160.00*
		Never hinged	310.00	
		Guide line pair	425.00	*575.00*
		Never hinged	900.00	

Earliest documented use: Sept. 18, 1911.

395	A140	4c **brown**, *Apr. 15, 1912*	62.50	55.00
		dark brown	62.50	55.00
		Never hinged	135.00	
		On cover		105.00
		Pair (2mm spacing)	160.00	150.00
		Never hinged	350.00	
		Pair (3mm spacing)	150.00	150.00
		Never hinged	325.00	
		Guide line pair	475.00	*575.00*
		Never hinged	1,100.	

Earliest documented use: June 21, 1912.

396	A140	5c **blue**, *Mar. 1913*	60.00	52.50
		dark blue	60.00	52.50
		Never hinged	130.00	
		On cover		105.00
		Pair	160.00	150.00
		Never hinged	350.00	
		Guide line pair	425.00	*750.00*
		Never hinged	900.00	

Earliest documented use: April 5, 1913.

Beware of plentiful fakes in the marketplace of Nos. 390-393, made by fraudulently perforating imperforate stamps.

PANAMA-PACIFIC EXPOSITION ISSUE
San Francisco, Cal., Feb. 20 - Dec. 4, 1915

Vasco Nunez de
Balboa — A144

Pedro Miguel Locks,
Panama Canal — A145

Golden Gate — A146

Discovery of San
Francisco Bay — A147

Exposition Station Cancellation.

Plates of 280 subjects in four panes of 70 each.

1913   **Wmk. 190**   *Perf. 12*

397	A144	1c **green**, *Jan. 1, 1913*	20.00	2.00
		deep green	20.00	2.00
		yellowish green	20.00	2.00
		Never hinged	45.00	
		On cover		3.50
		On Expo. card, Expo. station 1915 machine cancel		*30.00*
		Pair on cover, Expo. station 1915 duplex handstamp cancel		*150.00*
		Block of 4	82.50	14.00
		P# block of 6	275.00	
		Never hinged	400.00	
		Double transfer	24.00	3.25

Earliest documented use: Jan. 1, 1913 (FDC).

398	A145	2c **carmine**, *Jan. 1913*	20.00	1.00
		deep carmine	20.00	1.00
		Never hinged	45.00	
		On cover		1.75
		On cover, Expo. station 1915 machine cancel		75.00
		On cover, Expo. station 1915 duplex handstamp cancel		*250.00*
		Block of 4	82.50	10.00
		P# block of 6	350.00	
		Never hinged	550.00	
		Double transfer	40.00	3.50
a.		2c carmine lake	1,500.	
		Never hinged	2,500.	
b.		2c lake	5,000.	

Earliest documented use: Jan. 17, 1913.

399	A146	5c **blue**, *Jan. 1, 1913*	80.00	10.00
		dark blue	80.00	10.00
		Never hinged	180.00	
		On cover		27.50
		On cover, Expo. station 1915 machine cancel		300.00
		Block of 4	325.00	70.00
		P# block of 6	1,900.	
		Never hinged	3,200.	

Earliest documented use: Jan. 1, 1913 (FDC).

400	A147	10c **orange yellow**, *Jan. 1, 1913*	135.00	22.50
		Never hinged	300.00	
		On cover		57.50
		On cover, Expo. station 1915 machine cancel		500.00
		Block of 4	575.00	150.00
		P# block of 6	2,350.	
		Never hinged	3,850.	

Earliest documented use: Jan. 1, 1913 (FDC).

400A	A147	10c **orange**, *Aug. 1913*	225.00	19.00
		Never hinged	500.00	
		On cover		75.00
		On cover, Expo. station 1915 machine cancel		550.00
		Block of 4	950.00	105.00
		P# block of 6	12,000.	
		Never hinged	20,000.	

Earliest documented use: Nov. 12, 1913.

Nos. 397-400A (5)	480.00	54.50
Nos. 397-400A, never hinged	1,070.	

1914-15   *Perf. 10*

401	A144	1c **green**, *Dec. 1914*	27.50	7.00
		dark green	27.50	7.00
		Never hinged	62.50	
		On cover		16.00
		On Expo. card, Expo. station 1915 machine cancel		75.00
		Block of 4	120.00	47.50
		P# block of 6	400.00	
		Never hinged	650.00	

Earliest documented use: Dec. 21, 1914.

402	A145	2c **carmine**, *Jan. 1915*	75.00	2.75
		deep carmine	75.00	2.75
		red	75.00	2.75
		Never hinged	175.00	
		On cover		6.50
		On cover, Expo. station 1915 machine cancel		150.00
		On cover, Expo. station 1915 duplex handstamp cancel		450.00
		Block of 4	325.00	19.00
		P# block of 6	1,950.	
		Never hinged	3,250.	

Earliest documented use: Jan. 13, 1915.

403	A146	5c **blue**, *Feb. 1915*	175.00	19.00
		dark blue	175.00	19.00
		Never hinged	400.00	
		On cover		55.00
		On cover, Expo. station 1915 machine cancel		450.00
		Block of 4	750.00	130.00
		P# block of 6	4,000.	
		Never hinged	6,750.	

Earliest documented use: Feb. 6, 1915.

404	A147	10c **orange**, *July 1915*	900.00	70.00
		Never hinged	2,000.	
		On cover		175.00
		On cover, Expo. station 1915 machine cancel		600.00
		Block of 4	3,800.	450.00
		P# block of 6	12,500.	
		Never hinged	20,000.	

Earliest documented use: Aug. 27, 1915.

Nos. 401-404 (4)	1,177.	98.75
Nos. 401-404, never hinged	2,637.	

VALUES FOR VERY FINE STAMPS
Please note: Stamps are valued in the grade of Very Fine unless otherwise indicated.

REGULAR ISSUE

Washington — A140

The plates for this and later issues were the so-called "A" plates with uniform spacing of 2¾mm between stamps.

Plates of 400 subjects in four panes of 100 each for all values 1c to 50c inclusive.

Plates of 200 subjects in two panes of 100 each for $1 and some of the 50c (No. 422) denomination.

1912-14	Wmk. 190	Perf. 12	
405 A140 1c **green**, *Feb. 1912*	7.00	.25
light green	7.00	.25
dark green	7.00	.25
yellowish green	7.00	.25
Never hinged	16.00	
On cover		.30
Block of 4	30.00	2.50
P# block of 6, Impt. & "A"	110.00	
Never hinged	185.00	
P# block of 6, "A"	100.00	
Never hinged	170.00	
P# block of 6	95.00	
Never hinged	155.00	
Cracked plate	14.50	—
Double transfer	8.50	—
a. Vert. pair, imperf. horiz.	1,750.	—
b. Booklet pane of 6, *1912*	65.00	75.00
Never hinged	110.00	
c. Double impression		1,250.

Earliest documented uses: Feb. 2, 1912 (No. 405); Jan. 16, 1912 (No. 405b single).

TYPE I

TWO CENTS

Type I. There is one shading line in the first curve of the ribbon above the left "2" and one in the second curve of the ribbon above the right "2."

The button of the toga has only a faint outline.

The top line of the toga rope, from the button to the front of the throat, is also very faint.

The shading lines of the face terminate in front of the ear with little or no joining, to form a lock of hair.

Used on both flat plate and rotary press printings.

406 A140 2c **carmine**, type I, *Feb. 1912*	7.00	.25
bright carmine	7.00	.25
Never hinged	16.00	
dark carmine	7.50	.25
Never hinged	17.00	
On cover		.30
Block of 4	30.00	2.50
P# block of 6, Impt. & "A"	130.00	
Never hinged	220.00	
P# block of 6, "A"	125.00	
Never hinged	210.00	
P# block of 6	105.00	
Never hinged	170.00	
Margin block of 6, Electrolytic, (Pl. 6023)	1,500.	
Never hinged	2,500.	
Double transfer	9.00	—
a. Booklet pane of 6, *Feb. 8, 1912*	65.00	90.00
Never hinged	110.00	
b. Double impression	—	
c. 2c **lake**, type I	2,000.	2,750.
Never hinged	4,500.	

Earliest documented uses: Feb. 15, 1912 (No. 406); May 2, 1912 (No. 406a single).

407 A140 7c **black**, *Apr. 1914*	80.00	14.00
grayish black	80.00	14.00
intense black	80.00	14.00
Never hinged	180.00	
On cover		75.00
Block of 4	350.00	100.00
P# block of 6	1,200.	
Never hinged	2,000.	

Earliest documented use: May 1, 1914.

Earliest documented use dates for imperforates are for the imperforate sheet stamps, not for imperforate stamps with vending and affixing machine perforations or for flat plate imperforate coil stamps. EDU dates for VAMP and flat plate imperf coil stamps are shown in their respective sections later in the catalogue.

Plate Blocks

Scott values for plate blocks printed from flat plates are for very fine side and bottom positions. Top position plate blocks with full wide selvage sell for more.

1912 Imperf.

408 A140 1c **green**, *Mar. 1912*	1.00	.65
yellowish green	1.00	.65
dark green	1.00	.65
Never hinged	2.00	
On cover		1.20
Pair	2.10	1.50
Never hinged	4.20	
Block of 4	4.20	3.00
Corner margin block of 4	4.30	3.10
Margin block of 4, arrow	4.40	3.25
Center line block	10.00	10.00
P# block of 6, Impt. & "A," T, B or L	45.00	—
Never hinged	75.00	
P# block of 6, Impt. & "A," at right	550.00	—
Never hinged	850.00	
P# block of 6, "A"	26.00	—
Never hinged	45.00	
P# block of 6	18.00	—
Never hinged	29.00	
Double transfer	2.40	1.00
Cracked plate	—	—

Earliest documented use: April 26, 1912.

409 A140 2c **carmine**, type I, *Feb. 1912*	1.20	.65
deep carmine	1.20	.65
scarlet	1.20	.65
Never hinged	2.40	
On cover		1.20
Pair	2.50	1.50
Never hinged	5.00	
Block of 4	5.00	3.00
Corner margin block of 4	5.25	
Margin block of 4, arrow	5.50	3.25
Center line block	11.00	10.00
P# block of 6, Impt. & "A"	47.50	—
Never hinged	80.00	
P# block of 6, "A"	45.00	—
Never hinged	75.00	
P# block of 6	35.00	—
Never hinged	57.50	
Cracked plate (Plates 7580, 7582)	14.00	

Earliest documented use: Apr. 15, 1912.

In late 1914, the Post Office at Kansas City, Missouri, had on hand a stock of imperforate sheets of 400 of stamps Nos. 408 and 409, formerly sold for use in vending machines, but not then in demand. In order to make them salable, they were rouletted with ordinary tracing wheels and were sold over the counter with official approval of the Post Office Department given January 5, 1915.

These stamps were sold until the supply was exhausted. Except for one full sheet of 400 of each kind, all were cut into panes of 100 before being rouletted and sold. They are known as "Kansas City Roulettes". Value, authenticated blocks of 4, 1c $100, 2c $200.

Earliest documented uses of "Kansas City Roulettes": Oct. 22, 1914 (No. 408); Nov. 25, 1914 (No. 409).

COIL STAMPS

1912 Perf. 8½ Horizontally

410 A140 1c **green**, *Mar. 1912*	6.00	5.50
dark green	6.00	5.50
Never hinged	13.00	
On cover		8.50
Pair	15.00	25.00
Never hinged	32.50	
Guide line pair	30.00	55.00
Never hinged	65.00	
Double transfer	—	—

Earliest documented use: Apr. 17, 1912.

411 A140 2c **carmine**, type I, *Mar. 1912*	10.00	5.00
deep carmine	10.00	5.00
Never hinged	22.50	
On cover		12.50
Pair	25.00	25.00
Never hinged	55.00	
Guide line pair	55.00	75.00
Never hinged	125.00	
Double transfer	12.50	—

Earliest documented use: June 12, 1912.

Perf. 8½ Vertically

412 A140 1c **green**, *Mar. 18, 1912*	25.00	6.50
deep green	25.00	6.50
Never hinged	55.00	
On cover		15.00
Pair	60.00	30.00
Never hinged	130.00	
Guide line pair	120.00	105.00
Never hinged	260.00	

Earliest documented use: May 21, 1912.

413 A140 2c **carmine**, type I, *Mar. 1912*	55.00	2.25
dark carmine	55.00	2.25
Never hinged	120.00	
On cover		8.50
Pair	115.00	30.00
Never hinged	250.00	
Guide line pair	300.00	120.00
Never hinged	625.00	
Double transfer	52.50	—

Earliest documented use: April 16, 1912.

Beware of plentiful fakes in the marketplace of Nos. 410-413, made by fraudulently perforating imperforate stamps.

Franklin — A148

1912-14	Wmk. 190	Perf. 1	
414 A148 8c **pale olive green**, *Feb. 1912*	45.00	2.0
olive green	45.00	2.0
Never hinged	100.00	
On cover		15.0
Block of 4	200.00	15.0
P# block of 6, Impt. & "A"	475.00	
Never hinged	775.00	
415 A148 9c **salmon red**, *Apr. 1914*	55.00	13.5
rose red	55.00	13.5
Never hinged	120.00	
On cover		50.0
Block of 4	240.00	125.00
P# block of 6	650.00	
Never hinged	1,100.	

Earliest documented use: May 1, 1914.

416 A148 10c **orange yellow**, *Jan. 1912*	45.00	.7
yellow	45.00	.7
Never hinged	100.00	
On cover		2.7
Block of 4	200.00	5.0
P# block of 6, Impt. & "A"	500.00	
Never hinged	825.00	
P# block of 6, "A"	550.00	
Never hinged	900.00	
Double transfer	—	—
a. 10c **brown yellow**	1,200.	
Never hinged	2,500.	

Earliest documented use: Feb. 12, 1912.

417 A148 12c **claret brown**, *Apr. 1914*	50.00	5.00
deep claret brown	50.00	5.00
Never hinged	110.00	
On cover		25.00
Block of 4	225.00	37.50
P# block of 6	625.00	
Never hinged	1,050.	
Double transfer	55.00	
Triple transfer	72.50	—

Earliest documented use: May 5, 1914.

418 A148 15c **gray**, *Feb. 1912*	85.00	4.50
dark gray	85.00	4.50
Never hinged	190.00	
On cover		17.50
Block of 4	350.00	35.00
P# block of 6, Impt. & "A"	675.00	
Never hinged	1,300.	
P# block of 6, "A"	850.00	
Never hinged	1,450.	
P# block of 6	1,000.	
Never hinged	1,600.	
Double transfer	—	—

Earliest documented use: Apr. 26, 1912.

419 A148 20c **ultramarine**, *Apr. 1914*	200.00	18.50
dark ultramarine	200.00	18.50
Never hinged	430.00	
On cover		150.00
Block of 4	825.00	135.00
P# block of 6	2,000.	
Never hinged	3,400.	

Earliest documented use: May 1, 1914.

420 A148 30c **orange red**, *Apr. 1914*	125.00	17.50
dark orange red	125.00	17.50
Never hinged	270.00	
On cover		250.00
Block of 4	525.00	130.00
P# block of 6	1,450.	
Never hinged	2,350.	

Earliest documented use: May 1, 1914.

421 A148 50c **violet**, *1914*	450.00	30.00
bright violet	450.00	30.00
Never hinged	975.00	
On cover		2,000.
Block of 4	1,900.	200.00
P# block of 6	10,000.	
Never hinged	16,000.	

Earliest documented use: May 1, 1914.

No. 421 almost always has an offset of the frame lines on the back under the gum. Nos. 422 does not have this offset.

1912, Feb. 12	Wmk. 191	
422 A148 50c **violet**	250.00	22.00
Never hinged	575.00	
On cover		2,000.
Block of 4	1,050.	150.00
Margin block of 4, arrow, R or L	1,100.	
P# block of 6, Impt. & "A"	4,750.	
Never hinged	7,500.	

Earliest documented use: Oct. 31, 1914.

423 A148 $1 **violet brown**	525.00	75.00
Never hinged	1,150.	
On cover		7,000.
Block of 4	2,200.	800.00

Margin block of 4, arrow, R or L	2,250.	
P# block of 6, Impt. & "A"	12,000.	
Never hinged	19,000.	
Double transfer (5782 L 66)	550.00	—

Earliest documented use: July 15, 1915.

During the United States occupation of Vera Cruz, Mexico, from April to November, 1914, letters sent from there show provisional Postmarks.
For other listings of perforated sheet stamps of design A148, see:

Nos. 431-440 — Single line wmk. Perf. 10
Nos. 460 — Double line wmk. Perf. 10
Nos. 470-478 — Unwmkd. Perf. 10
Nos. 508-518 — Unwmkd. Perf. 11

1914 Compound Perforations

As the Bureau of Engraving and Printing made the changeover to perf 10 from perf 12, in the normal course of their stamp production they perforated limited quantities of 1c, 2c and 5c stamps with the old 12-gauge perforations in one direction and the new 10-gauge perforations in the other direction. These were not production errors. These compound-perforation stamps previously were listed as Nos. 424a, 424b, 425c, 425d and 428a.

All examples of Nos. 423A-423E must be accompanied by certificates of authenticity issued by a recognized expertizing committee. Fakes made from perf 12, perf 10 and imperfs exist.

1914		Wmk. 190	Perf. 12x10	
423A	A140	1c green	7,500.	5,750.
		Never hinged	—	
		Pair	—	12,500.
		Block of 4	21,000.	
		On postcard	10,000.	
		On cover, pair		11,000.

Formerly No. 424a. Seventeen unused and 53 used examples are recorded. Value for unused is for a sound stamp with perfs touching or just cutting the design. Value for used is for a sound stamp in the grade of fine-very fine. Of the used examples, 23 are precanceled Quincy IL (very scarce) or Chicago (usually inverted). The block of four, single on postcard and pair on cover are each unique (top stamp of pair on cover with small piece missing). The block of 4 has perfs slightly cutting at top and is valued thus.

423B	A140	2c rose red, type I	175,000.	18,500.

Formerly No. 425d. One unused (a plate #7082 single) and 28 used examples are recorded. Value for used is for a sound stamp in the grade of fine-very fine. There are no precancels known on this issue.

423C	A140	5c blue	20,000.	
		Pair	—	

Formerly No. 428a. 24 used examples are recorded. No unused examples are recorded. Three examples are precanceled: Tampa FL (2) and Rahway NJ (1). Value is for a sound stamp in the grade of fine-very fine. The pair is unique (one stamp creased, the other with a small tear).
Earliest documented use: April 14, 1915 (dated cancel on off-cover stamp).

1914		Wmk. 190	Perf. 10x12	
423D	A140	1c green	13,500.	

Formerly No. 424b. 36 used examples are recorded. No unused examples are recorded. 32 examples are precanceled: Dayton OH (29), Buffalo NY (2) and Elkhart IN (1). Value is for a sound stamp in the grade of fine-very fine.

423E	A140	2c rose red, type I	—	

Formerly No. 425c. Only one used example has been certified (by the Philatelic Foundation). It is well centered, has a machine cancel, and has small thinning and a crease.

Plates of 400 subjects in four panes of 100 each.

Type of plate number and imprint used for the 12 special 1c and 2c plates designed for the production of coil stamps.

1913-15		Wmk. 190	Perf. 10	
424	A140	1c green, Sept. 5, 1914	2.50	.20
		bright green	2.50	.20
		deep green	2.50	.20
		yellowish green	2.50	.20
		Never hinged	5.25	
		On cover		.25
		Block of 4	10.50	1.50
		P# block of 6	42.50	
		Never hinged	67.50	
		Block of ten with imprint "COIL STAMPS" and number (6581-82, 85, 89)	135.00	
		Never hinged	220.00	
		Cracked plate	—	—
		Double transfer	4.75	—
c.		Vert. pair, imperf. horiz.	2,800.	2,500.
		Never hinged	4,250.	
d.		Booklet pane of 6	5.25	7.50

		Never hinged	8.75	
e.		As "d," imperf.	1,600.	
f.		Vert. pair, imperf. between and with straight edge at top	9,000.	

For former Nos. 424a and 424b, see Nos. 423A and 423D.
All known examples of No. 424e are without gum.
The unique example of No. 424f is never hinged, and it is valued thus.

Earliest documented uses: Oct. 21, 1914 (No. 424); Dec. 20, 1913 (No. 424d single).

425	A140	2c rose red, type I, Sept. 5, 1914	2.30	.20
		dark rose red	2.30	.20
		carmine rose	2.30	.20
		carmine	2.30	.20
		dark carmine	2.30	.20
		scarlet	2.30	.20
		red	2.30	.20
		Never hinged	4.75	
		On cover		.25
		Block of 4	9.50	1.50
		P# block of 6	27.50	
		Never hinged	45.00	
		Block of 10 with imprint "COIL STAMPS" and number (6568, 70-72)	145.00	
		Never hinged	230.00	
		Cracked plate	9.50	—
		Double transfer	—	—
e.		Booklet pane of 6, Jan. 1914	17.50	25.00
		Never hinged	30.00	

For former Nos. 425c and 425d, see Nos. 423E and 423B.
The aniline inks used on some printings of Nos. 425, 426 and 435a caused a pink tinge to permeate the paper and appear on the back. These are called "pink backs."

Earliest documented uses: Nov. 6, 1914 (No. 425); Jan. 6, 1914 (No. 425e single).

426	A140	3c deep violet, type I, Sept. 18, 1914	15.00	1.50
		violet	16.00	1.50
		bright violet	16.00	1.50
		reddish violet	16.00	1.50
		Never hinged	35.00	
		On cover		3.50
		Block of 4	62.50	12.50
		P# block of 6	210.00	
		Never hinged	350.00	

See "pink backs" note after No. 425.

Earliest documented use: Oct. 11, 1914.

427	A140	4c brown, Sept. 7, 1914	35.00	1.00
		dark brown	35.00	1.00
		orange brown	35.00	1.00
		yellowish brown	35.00	1.00
		Never hinged	80.00	
		On cover		5.25
		Block of 4	145.00	9.00
		P# block of 6	475.00	
		Never hinged	775.00	
		Double transfer	45.00	—

Earliest documented use: Jan. 2, 1915.

428	A140	5c blue, Sept. 14, 1914	35.00	1.00
		bright blue	35.00	1.00
		dark blue	35.00	1.00
		indigo blue	35.00	1.00
		Never hinged	80.00	
		On cover		3.00
		Block of 4	145.00	8.00
		P# block of 6	390.00	
		Never hinged	625.00	

For former No. 428a, see No. 423C.

Earliest documented use: Dec. 2, 1914.

429	A140	6c red orange, Sept. 28, 1914	50.00	2.00
		deep red orange	50.00	2.00
		pale red orange	50.00	2.00
		Never hinged	115.00	
		On cover		9.00
		Block of 4 (2mm spacing)	215.00	16.00
		Block of 4 (3mm spacing)	210.00	15.00
		P# block of 6, Impt. & star	425.00	
		Never hinged	725.00	
		P# block of 6	525.00	
		Never hinged	875.00	

430	A140	7c black, Sept. 10, 1914	100.00	5.00
		gray black	100.00	5.00
		intense black	100.00	5.00
		Never hinged	225.00	
		On cover		37.50
		Block of 4	425.00	40.00
		P# block of 6	1,000.	
		Never hinged	1,650.	

Earliest documented use: April 14, 1915.

431	A148	8c pale olive green, Sept. 26, 1914	37.50	3.00
		olive green	37.50	3.00
		Never hinged	82.50	
		On cover		8.00
		Block of 4	160.00	25.00
		P# block of 6, Impt. & "A"	450.00	
		Never hinged	725.00	
		P# block of 6, "A"	550.00	
		Never hinged	900.00	
		Double impression	—	
		Double impression	—	

Earliest documented use: Jan. 20, 1915.

432	A148	9c salmon red, Oct. 6, 1914	50.00	9.00
		dark salmon red	50.00	9.00
		Never hinged	115.00	
		On cover		27.50

		Block of 4	210.00	70.00
		P# block of 6	725.00	
		Never hinged	1,150.	

Earliest documented use: Oct. 7, 1915 (dated cancel on off-cover block of 4); Feb. 25, 1916 (on cover).

433	A148	10c orange yellow, Sept. 9, 1914	50.00	1.00
		golden yellow	50.00	1.00
		Never hinged	115.00	
		On cover		7.75
		Block of 4	210.00	6.50
		P# block of 6, Impt. & "A"	650.00	
		Never hinged	1,100.	
		P# block of 6, "A"	950.00	
		Never hinged	1,600.	
		P# block of 6	825.00	
		Never hinged	1,400.	

Earliest documented use: Nov. 13, 1914.

434	A148	11c dark green, Aug. 11, 1915	25.00	8.50
		bluish green	25.00	8.50
		Never hinged	60.00	
		On cover		25.00
		Block of 4	105.00	65.00
		P# block of 6	275.00	
		Never hinged	450.00	

435	A148	12c claret brown, Sept. 10, 1914	27.50	6.00
		deep claret brown	27.50	6.00
		Never hinged	65.00	
		On cover		17.50
		Block of 4	115.00	45.00
		P# block of 6	325.00	
		Never hinged	500.00	
		Double transfer	35.00	—
		Triple transfer	40.00	—
a.		12c copper red	32.50	7.00
		Never hinged	75.00	
		On cover		20.00
		Block of 4	125.00	50.00
		P# block of 6	325.00	
		Never hinged	550.00	

All so-called vertical pairs, imperf. between, have at least one perf. hole or "blind perfs" between the stamps.
See "pink backs" note after No. 425.

Earliest documented use: Feb. 22, 1915.

437	A148	15c gray, Sept. 16, 1914	135.00	7.25
		dark gray	135.00	7.25
		Never hinged	300.00	
		On cover		52.50
		Block of 4	575.00	70.00
		P# block of 6, Impt. & "A"	1,050.	
		Never hinged	2,100.	
		P# block of 6, "A"	1,225.	
		Never hinged	2,250.	
		P# block of 6	1,125.	
		Never hinged	2,150.	

Earliest documented use: Sept. 21, 1915.

438	A148	20c ultramarine, Sept. 19, 1914	220.00	6.00
		dark ultramarine	220.00	6.00
		Never hinged	500.00	
		On cover		150.00
		Block of 4	900.00	45.00
		P# block of 6	3,250.	
		Never hinged	5,500.	

Earliest documented use: Nov. 28, 1914.

439	A148	30c orange red, Sept. 19, 1914	260.00	16.00
		dark orange red	260.00	16.00
		Never hinged	600.00	
		On cover		250.00
		Block of 4	1,050.	135.00
		P# block of 6	4,100.	
		Never hinged	6,750.	

Earliest documented use: Feb. 13, 1915.

440	A148	50c violet, Dec. 10, 1915	575.00	16.00
		Never hinged	1,300.	
		On cover		1,750.
		Block of 4	2,250.	120.00
		P# block of 6	15,000.	
		Nos. 424-440 (16)	1,619.	83.65

COIL STAMPS

1914			Perf. 10 Horizontally	
441	A140	1c green, Nov. 14, 1914	1.00	1.00
		deep green	1.00	1.00
		Never hinged	2.00	
		On cover		2.25
		Pair	2.75	4.25
		Never hinged	5.75	
		Guide line pair	8.00	12.50
		Never hinged	17.50	
442	A140	2c carmine, type I, July 22, 1914	10.00	6.00
		deep carmine	10.00	6.00
		Never hinged	21.00	
		On cover		15.00
		Pair	25.00	35.00
		Never hinged	55.00	
		Guide line pair	60.00	130.00
		Never hinged	130.00	

1914			Perf. 10 Vertically	
443	A140	1c green, May 29, 1914	30.00	7.50
		deep green	30.00	7.50
		Never hinged	65.00	
		On cover		15.00
		Pair	75.00	25.00

Never hinged	160.00	
Guide line pair	155.00	110.00
Never hinged	325.00	

Earliest documented use: June. 19, 1914.

444 A140 2c **carmine**, type I, *Apr. 25, 1914*	50.00	3.50
deep carmine	50.00	3.50
red	50.00	3.50
Never hinged	110.00	
On cover		12.50
Pair	130.00	22.50
Never hinged	275.00	
Guide line pair	325.00	80.00
Never hinged	675.00	
a. 2c **lake**		*1,250.*

Earliest documented use: May 19, 1914.

445 A140 3c **violet**, type I, *Dec. 18, 1914*	250.00	150.00
deep violet	250.00	150.00
Never hinged	550.00	
On cover		*250.00*
Pair	575.00	675.00
Never hinged	1,250.	
Guide line pair	1,300.	*2,750.*
Never hinged	2,800.	

Earliest documented use: August 13, 1915.

446 A140 4c **brown**, *Oct. 2, 1914*	140.00	65.00
Never hinged	300.00	
On cover		*125.00*
Pair	325.00	325.00
Never hinged	700.00	
Guide line pair	750.00	*950.00*
Never hinged	1,600.	

Earliest documented use: Aug. 4, 1915.

447 A140 5c **blue**, *July 30, 1914*	50.00	32.50
Never hinged	110.00	
On cover		*57.50*
Pair	115.00	*300.00*
Never hinged	240.00	
Guide line pair	260.00	*850.00*
Never hinged	550.00	

Earliest documented use: May 9, 1916.

Beware of plentiful fakes in the marketplace of Nos. 441-447, made by fraudulently perforating imperforate stamps or by fraudulently trimming perforations off fully perforated stamps.

ROTARY PRESS STAMPS

The Rotary Press Stamps are printed from plates that are curved to fit around a cylinder. This curvature produces stamps that are slightly larger, either horizontally or vertically, than those printed from flat plates. Designs of stamps from flat plates measure about 18½-19mm wide by 22mm high.

When the impressions are placed sidewise on the curved plates the designs are 19½-20mm wide; when they are placed vertically the designs are 22½ to 23mm high. A line of color (not a guide line) shows where the curved plates meet or join on the press.

Rotary Press Coil Stamps were printed from plates of 170 subjects for stamps coiled sidewise, and from plates of 150 subjects for stamps coiled endwise.

Double paper varieties of Rotary Press stamps are not listed in this catalogue. Collectors are referred to the note on "Rotary Press Double Paper" in the "Information for Collectors" in the front of the catalogue.

ROTARY PRESS COIL STAMPS
Stamp designs: 18½-19x22½mm

1915		**Perf. 10 Horizontally**
448 A140 1c **green**, *Dec., 1915*	7.50	4.00
light green	7.50	4.00
Never hinged	16.00	
On cover		8.50
Pair	17.50	15.00
Never hinged	40.00	
Joint line pair	50.00	42.50
Never hinged	110.00	

Earliest documented use: Dec. 11, 1915.

TYPE II

TWO CENTS.
Type II. Shading lines in ribbons as on type I.

The toga button, rope and rope shading lines are heavy. The shading lines of the face at the lock of hair end in a strong vertical curved line.
Used on rotary press printings only.

TYPE III

Type III. Two lines of shading in the curves of the ribbons. Other characteristics similar to type II.
Used on rotary press printings only.

449 A140 2c **red**, type I, *1915*	3,000.	600.00
Never hinged	6,500.	
carmine rose, type I	—	
On cover, type I		*1,350.*
Pair, type I	7,000.	*5,000.*
Never hinged	14,500.	
Joint line pair, type I	16,000.	*13,000.*
Never hinged	32,500.	

Earliest documented uses: Oct. 29, 1915 (on cover front or dated cancel on off-cover stamp); Nov. 4, 1915 (on cover).

450 A140 2c **carmine**, type III, *1915*	12.50	6.50
carmine rose, type III	12.50	6.50
red, type III	12.50	6.50
Never hinged	27.50	
On cover, type III		11.50
Pair, type III	30.00	27.50
Never hinged	65.00	
Joint line pair, type III	150.00	*175.00*
Never hinged	350.00	

Earliest documented use: Dec. 21, 1915.

1914-16		**Perf. 10 Vertically**
Stamp designs: 19½-20x22mm		
452 A140 1c **green**, *Nov. 11, 1914*	10.00	4.00
Never hinged	21.00	
On cover		5.00
Pair	25.00	15.00
Never hinged	55.00	
Joint line pair	75.00	30.00
Never hinged	160.00	

Earliest documented use: Nov. 25, 1914.

453 A140 2c **carmine rose**, type I, *July 3, 1914*	150.00	7.50
Never hinged	325.00	
On cover, type I		11.00
Pair, type I	325.00	25.00
Never hinged	675.00	
Joint line pair, type I	725.00	350.00
Never hinged	1,550.	
Cracked plate, type I	—	—

Earliest documented use: Sept. 26, 1914.

454 A140 2c **red**, type II, *June, 1915*	82.50	10.00
carmine, type II	82.50	10.00
Never hinged	175.00	
On cover, type II		37.50
Pair, type II	175.00	45.00
Never hinged	375.00	
Joint line pair, type II	425.00	275.00
Never hinged	900.00	

Earliest documented use: July 7, 1915.

455 A140 2c **carmine**, type III, *Dec. 1915*	8.50	1.40
carmine rose, type III	8.50	1.40
Never hinged	19.00	
On cover, type III		2.60
Pair, type III	21.00	7.50
Never hinged	45.00	
Joint line pair, type III	50.00	27.50
Never hinged	110.00	

Earliest documented use: Dec. 15, 1915.

Fraudulently altered examples of Type III (Nos. 455, 488, 492 and 540) have had one line of shading scraped off to make them resemble Type II (Nos. 454, 487, 491 and 539).

456 A140 3c **violet**, type I, *Feb. 2, 1916*	250.00	110.00
deep violet	250.00	110.00
red violet	250.00	110.00
Never hinged	525.00	
On cover		210.00
Pair	600.00	475.00
Never hinged	1,250.	
Joint line pair	1,250.	*1,500.*
Never hinged	2,600.	

Earliest documented use: Apr. 13, 1916.

457 A140 4c **brown**, *1915*	25.00	22.50
light brown	25.00	22.50
Never hinged	55.00	
On cover		47.50
Pair	60.00	80.00
Never hinged	130.00	

Joint line pair	150.00	*190.0*
Never hinged	325.00	
Cracked plate	35.00	–

Earliest documented use: Nov. 5, 1915.

458 A140 5c **blue**, *Mar. 9, 1916*	30.00	22.5
Never hinged	65.00	
On cover		47.5
Pair	72.50	62.5
Never hinged	160.00	
Joint line pair	180.00	190.0
Never hinged	375.00	
Double transfer	—	–

Earliest documented use: Apr. 6, 1916.

Horizontal Coil

1914, June 30		***Imperf***
459 A140 2c **carmine**, type I	220.	*1,200*
Never hinged	350.	
Pair	450.	*3,500*
Never hinged	725.	
Joint line pair, with crease	750.	
Never hinged	1,250.	
Joint line pair, without crease	1,150.	*21,000*
Never hinged	2,200.	

Most line pairs of No. 459 are creased. The value for joint line pair with crease is for a pair creased vertically between the stamps, but not touching the design.

When the value for a used stamp is higher than the unused value, the stamp must have a contemporaneous cancel. Valuable stamps of this type should be accompanied by certificates of authenticity issued by recognized expertizing committees. The used value for No. 459 is for an example with such a certificate.

Beware of examples of No. 453 with perforations fraudulently trimmed to resemble single examples of No. 459.

Earliest documented use: Dec. 1914 (dated cancel on a used joint line pair, off cover).

FLAT PLATE PRINTINGS

1915	**Wmk. 191**	**Perf. 10**
460 A148 $1 **violet black**, *Feb. 8*	850.	140.
Never hinged	1,850.	
On cover		*12,000.*
Block of 4	3,750.	750.00
Margin block of 4, arrow, R or L	3,850.	
P# block of 6, Impt. & "A"	12,500.	
Never hinged	19,500.	
Double transfer (5782 L. 66)	900.	175.

Earliest documented uses: May 25, 1916 (dated cancel on stamp on mailing tag); June 2, 1916 (unique usage on cover is from Shanghai, China).

Wmk. 190		**Perf. 11**
461 A140 2c **pale car. red**, type I, *June 17*	150.	*325.*
Never hinged	325.	
On cover		*1,200.*
Block of 4	625.	*2,500.*
P# block of 6	1,500.	
Never hinged	2,600.	

Beware of fraudulently perforated examples of #409 being offered as #461.
See note on used stamps following No. 459.

Earliest documented use: June 24, 1915.

VALUES FOR VERY FINE STAMPS
Please note: Stamps are valued in the grade of Very Fine unless otherwise indicated.

FLAT PLATE PRINTINGS

Plates of 400 subjects in four panes of 100 each for all values 1c to 50c inclusive.

Plates of 200 subjects in two panes of 100 each for $1, $2 and $5 denominations.

The Act of Oct. 3, 1917, effective Nov. 2, 1917, created a 3 cent rate. Local rate, 2 cents.

1916-17	**Unwmk.**	**Perf. 10**
462 A140 1c **green**, *Sept. 27, 1916*	7.00	.35
light green	7.00	.35
dark green	7.00	.35
bluish green	7.00	.35
Never hinged	16.00	
On cover		.50
Block of 4	30.00	3.25
P# block of 6	160.00	
Never hinged	275.00	
Experimental bureau precancel, New Orleans		10.00
Experimental bureau precancel, Springfield, Mass.		10.00
Experimental bureau precancel, Augusta, Me.		25.00
a. Booklet pane of 6, *Oct. 15, 1916*	9.50	12.50
Never hinged	16.00	

Earliest documented use: Apr. 5, 1917 (No. 462a single).

463 A140 2c **carmine**, type I, *Sept. 1916*	4.50	.40
dark carmine	4.50	.40
rose red	4.50	.40
Never hinged	10.00	
On cover		.45
Block of 4	20.00	3.50
P# block of 6	130.00	
Never hinged	220.00	
Double transfer	6.50	–

Experimental bureau precan-
cel, New Orleans   *500.00*
Experimental bureau precan-
cel, Springfield, Mass.   22.50
a.   Booklet pane of 6, *Oct. 8, 1916*   110.00   110.00
Never hinged   180.00

See No. 467 for P# block of 6 from plate 7942.

Earliest documented uses: Sept. 12, 1916 (No. 463).

464 A140 3c **violet,** type I, *Nov. 11, 1916*   75.00   17.50
deep violet   75.00   17.50
Never hinged   170.00
On cover   42.50
Block of 4   325.00 150.00
P# block of 6   1,350.
Never hinged   2,250.
Double transfer in "CENTS" *90.00*   —
Experimental bureau precan-
cel, New Orleans   *1,000.*
Experimental bureau precan-
cel, Springfield, Mass.   200.00

Earliest documented use: Mar. 9, 1917.

465 A140 4c **orange brown,** *Oct. 7, 1916*   45.00   2.50
deep brown   45.00   2.50
brown   45.00   2.50
Never hinged   100.00
On cover   11.00
Block of 4   190.00   25.00
P# block of 6   650.00
Never hinged   1,100.   —
Double transfer   —   —
Experimental bureau precan-
cel, Springfield, Mass.   175.00

466 A140 5c **blue,** *Oct. 17, 1916*   75.00   2.50
dark blue   75.00   2.50
Never hinged   170.00
On cover   13.00
Block of 4   310.00   22.50
P# block of 6   950.00
Never hinged   1,600.
Experimental bureau precan-
cel, Springfield, Mass.   175.00

Earliest documented use: Dec. 7, 1916.

467 A140 5c **carmine** (error in plate of
2c)   550.00 850.00
Never hinged   1,100.
On cover   *5,000.*
Block of 9, #467 in middle   1,050. *1,600.*
Never hinged   1,750.
Block of 12, two middle
stamps #467   2,150. *3,000.*
Never hinged   3,400.
P# block of 6 2c stamps
(#463), P#7942   140.00
Never hinged   250.00

No. 467 is an error caused by using a 5c transfer roll in re-
entering three subjects: 7942 UL 74, 7942 UL 84, 7942 LR 18;
the balance of the subjects on the plate being normal 2c
entries. No. 467 imperf. is listed as No. 485. The error perf 11
on unwatermarked paper is No. 505.
The first value given for the error in blocks of 9 and 12 is for
blocks with the error stamp(s) never hinged. The second value
given is for blocks in which all stamps are never hinged. See
note on used stamps following No. 459.

Earliest documented use: May 22, 1917.

468 A140 6c **red orange,** *Oct. 10, 1916*   95.00   9.00
Never hinged   210.00
On cover   37.50
Block of 4   400.00   70.00
P# block of 6   1,350.
Never hinged   2,500.
Double transfer   —   —
Experimental bureau precan-
cel, New Orleans   *2,500.*
Experimental bureau precan-
cel, Springfield, Mass.   175.00

Earliest documented use: April 19, 1917.

469 A140 7c **black,** *Oct. 10, 1916*   130.00   15.00
gray black   130.00   15.00
Never hinged   290.00
On cover   45.00
Block of 4   550.00 125.00
P# block of 6   1,350.
Never hinged   2,500.
Experimental bureau precan-
cel, Springfield, Mass.   175.00

Earliest documented use: Feb. 19, 1917.

470 A148 8c **olive green,** *Nov. 13, 1916*   60.00   8.00
dark olive green   60.00   8.00
Never hinged   135.00
On cover   27.50
Block of 4   250.00   65.00
P# block of 6, Impt. & "A"   550.00
Never hinged   900.00
P# block of 6, "A"   600.00
Never hinged   1,050.
Experimental bureau precan-
cel, Springfield, Mass.   165.00

Earliest documented use: Jan. 26, 1917 (dated cancel on off-
cover stamp); Feb. 13, 1917 (on cover).

471 A148 9c **salmon red,** *Nov. 16, 1916*   60.00   18.50
Never hinged   135.00
On cover   42.50
Block of 4   250.00 135.00
P# block of 6   750.00
Never hinged   1,250.
Experimental bureau precan-
cel, Springfield, Mass.   150.00

Earliest documented use: Dec. 27, 1917.

---

472 A148 10c **orange yellow,** *Oct. 17,
1916*   110.00   2.50
Never hinged   250.00
On cover   8.50
Block of 4   460.00   16.50
P# block of 6   1,350.
Never hinged   2,250.
Experimental bureau precan-
cel, Springfield, Mass.   160.00

Earliest documented use: Oct. 24, 1916.

473 A148 11c **dark green,** *Nov. 16, 1916*   45.00   18.50
Never hinged   95.00
On cover   47.50
Block of 4   175.00 140.00
P# block of 6   360.00
Never hinged   625.00
Experimental bureau precan-
cel, Springfield, Mass.   *575.00*

Earliest documented use: Apr. 13, 1917.

474 A148 12c **claret brown,** *Oct. 1916*   60.00   7.50
Never hinged   135.00
On cover   22.50
Block of 4   230.00   55.00
P# block of 6   625.00
Never hinged   1,050.
Double transfer   65.00   8.50
Triple transfer   77.50   11.00
Experimental bureau precan-
cel, Springfield, Mass.   200.00

Earliest documented uses: Oct. 6, 1916 (dated cancel on off-
cover pair); Oct. 13, 1916 (on cover).

475 A148 15c **gray,** *Nov. 16, 1916*   200.00   16.00
dark gray   200.00   16.00
Never hinged   440.00
On cover   87.50
Block of 4   850.00 125.00
P# block of 6   3,000.
Never hinged   5,250.
P# block of 6, Impt. & "A"   —
Experimental bureau precan-
cel, Springfield, Mass.   150.00

Earliest documented use: Mar. 2, 1917.

476 A148 20c **light ultramarine,** *Dec. 5,
1916*   250.00   17.50
ultramarine   250.00   17.50
Never hinged   575.00
On cover   *725.00*
Block of 4   1,050. 135.00
P# block of 6   3,600.
Never hinged   6,000.
Experimental bureau precan-
cel, Springfield, Mass.   125.00

476A A148 30c **orange red**   4,500.
Never hinged   9,000.
Block of 4   20,000.
Never hinged   45,000.
P# block of 6, never
hinged   75,000.

No. 476A is valued in the grade of fine.

477 A148 50c **light violet,** *Mar. 2, 1917*   1,100.   80.00
Never hinged   2,400.
On cover   *2,250.*
Block of 4   4,750. 575.00
P# block of 6   *57,500.*
Never hinged   —

Earliest documented use: Aug. 31, 1917.

478 A148 $1 **violet black,** *Dec. 22, 1916*   800.00   25.00
Never hinged   1,800.
On cover   *3,000.*
Block of 4   3,500. 175.00
Margin block of 4, arrow, R
or L   3,650.
P# block of 6, Impt. & "A"   *13,000.*
Never hinged   *21,000.*
Double transfer (5782 L 66)   825.00   32.50

Earliest documented use: May 24, 1917 (on large part of
parcel label).

TYPES OF 1902-03 ISSUE
1917, Mar. 22   Unwmk.   Perf. 10
479 A127 $2 **dark blue**   260.00   42.50
Never hinged   550.00
On cover (other than first flight
or Zeppelin)   *1,250.*
On first flight cover   *350.00*
On Zeppelin flight cover   *750.00*
Block of 4   1,150. 325.00
Margin block of 4, arrow, R or L 1,300.
P# block of 6   4,000.
Never hinged   6,500.
Double transfer   —

Earliest documented use (on large piece of reg'd parcel wrapper): Apr. 6, 1917.

480 A128 $5 **light green**   220.00   40.00
Never hinged   450.00
On cover   *1,250.*
Block of 4   925.00 300.00
Margin block of 4, arrow, R or L 1,025.
P# block of 6   3,100.
Never hinged   5,000.

Earliest documented use: Apr. 6, 1917 (on large piece of
reg'd parcel wrapper).

Earliest documented use dates for imperforates a[...]
for the imperforate sheet stamps, not for imperforat[...]
stamps with vending and affixing machine perforation[...]
or for flat plate imperforate coil stamps. EDU dates fo[...]
VAMP and flat plate imperf coil stamps are shown i[...]
their respective sections later in the catalogue.

1916-17   Imper[...]
481 A140 1c **green,** *Nov. 1916*   .95   .6[...]
bluish green   .95   .6[...]
deep green   .95   .6[...]
Never hinged   1.90
On cover   1.5[...]
Pair   2.00   1.6[...]
Never hinged   4.00
Block of 4   4.00   3.5[...]
Corner margin block of 4   4.25   5.5[...]
Margin block of 4, arrow   4.40   3.7[...]
Center line block   8.50   6.7[...]
P# block of 6   30.00   —
Never hinged   30.00
Margin block of 6, Electrolytic (Pl.
13376)   450.00
Never hinged   800.00
Margin block of 6, Electrolytic (Pl.
13377)   750.00
Never hinged   1,250.
Double transfer   2.50   1.5[...]

Earliest documented use: Nov. 17, 1916.

During September, 1921, the Bureau of Engraving and Printing issued a 1c stamp printed from experimental electrolytic
plates made in accordance with patent granted to George U[...]
Rose. Tests at that time did not prove satisfactory and the
method was discontinued. Four plates were made, viz., 13376,
13377, 13389 and 13390 from which stamps were issued. They
are difficult to distinguish from the normal varieties. (See No.
498).

TYPE Ia

TWO CENTS
Type Ia. The design characteristics are similar to type I except
that all of the lines of the design are stronger.
The toga button, toga rope and rope and rope shading lines
are heavy.
The latter characteristics are those of type II, which, however,
occur only on impressions from rotary plates.
Used only on flat plates 10208 and 10209.

482 A140 2c **carmine,** type I, *Dec. 8,
1916*   1.30   1.25
deep carmine   1.30   1.25
carmine rose   1.30   1.25
deep rose   1.30   1.25
Never hinged   2.60
On cover   2.50
Pair   2.75   2.75
Never hinged   5.50
Block of 4   5.50   6.50
Corner margin block of 4   5.75   5.75
Margin block of 4, arrow   6.00   6.00
Center line block   8.50   8.00
P# block of 6   30.00
Never hinged   45.00
Cracked plate   —   —

Earliest documented use: Dec. 16, 1916.

See No. 485 for P# block of 6 from plate 7942.

482A A140 2c **deep rose,** type Ia   *50,000.*
On cover   *55,000.*
Pair   *110,000.*

Earliest documented use: Feb. 17, 1920.

The imperforate, type Ia, was issued but all known copies
were privately perforated with large oblong perforations at the
sides (Schermack type III).
The No. 482A pair is unique.

TYPE II

THREE CENTS
Type II. The top line of the toga rope is strong and the rope shading lines are heavy and complete.
The line between the lips is heavy.
Used on both flat plate and rotary press printings.

483	A140	3c **violet,** type I, *Oct. 13, 1917*	11.00	7.50
		light violet	11.00	7.50
		Never hinged	24.00	
		On cover		20.00
		Pair	24.00	17.50
		Never hinged	50.00	
		Block of 4	47.50	40.00
		Corner margin block of 4	50.00	42.50
		Margin block of 4, arrow	52.50	42.50
		Center line block	75.00	70.00
		P# block of 6	115.00	—
		Never hinged	190.00	
		Double transfer	17.50	—
		Triple transfer	220.00	—

Earliest documented use: Nov. 8, 1917.

484	A140	3c **violet,** type II	8.50	5.00
		deep violet	8.50	5.00
		Never hinged	19.00	
		On cover		11.50
		Pair	18.00	13.50
		Never hinged	37.50	
		Block of 4	36.00	32.50
		Corner margin block of 4	38.00	35.00
		Margin block of 4, arrow	40.00	35.00
		Center line block	67.50	60.00
		P# block of 6	87.50	—
		Never hinged	145.00	
		Double transfer	12.50	—

Earliest documented use: Apr. 30, 1918.

485	A140	5c **carmine** (error), *Mar. 1917*	12,000.	
		Never hinged	20,000.	
		Block of 9, #485 in middle	22,500.	
		Never hinged	32,500.	
		Block of 12, two middle stamps		
		#485	42,500.	
		Never	52,500.	
		P# block of six 2c stamps		
		(#482), P#7942	130.00	

No. 485 is usually seen either as the center stamp in a block of 9 with 8 No. 482 (the first value given being with No. 485 never hinged) or as two center stamps in a block of 12 (the first value given being with both examples of No. 485 never hinged). A second value is given for each block with all stamps in the block never hinged.
See note under No. 467.

ROTARY PRESS COIL STAMPS
(See note over No. 448)

1916-19   **Perf. 10 Horizontally**
Stamp designs: 18½-19x22½mm

486	A140	1c **green,** *Jan. 1918*	.85	.80
		yellowish green	.85	.80
		Never hinged	1.75	
		On cover		1.10
		Pair	2.00	2.10
		Never hinged	4.25	
		Joint line pair	4.50	5.00
		Never hinged	9.50	
		Cracked plate	—	—
		Double transfer	2.25	

Earliest documented use: June 30, 1918.

487	A140	2c **carmine,** type II, *Nov. 15, 1916*	12.50	5.00
		Never hinged	26.00	
		On cover		10.00
		Pair	30.00	14.00
		Never hinged	65.00	
		Joint line pair	110.00	50.00
		Never hinged	250.00	
		Cracked plate	—	

Earliest documented use: Sept. 21, 1917.

(See note after No. 455)

488	A140	2c **carmine,** type III, *1916*	2.40	2.25
		carmine rose	2.40	2.25
		Never hinged	5.00	
		On cover		4.25
		Pair	5.75	8.00
		Never hinged	12.00	
		Joint line pair	25.00	40.00
		Never hinged	55.00	
		Cracked plate	12.00	8.00

Earliest documented use: Apr. 25, 1917.

489	A140	3c **violet,** type I, *Oct. 10, 1917*	4.50	2.00
		dull violet	4.50	2.00

---

	bluish violet	4.50	2.00
	Never hinged	10.00	
	On cover		3.25
	Pair	10.50	6.00
	Never hinged	22.50	
	Joint line pair	32.50	22.50
	Never hinged	70.00	

Rosette plate crack on head

1916-22   *Perf. 10 Vertically*
Stamp designs: 19½-20x22mm

490	A140	1c **green,** *Nov. 17, 1916*	.50	.50
		yellowish green	.50	.50
		Never hinged	1.05	
		On cover		.75
		Pair	1.25	2.00
		Never hinged	2.60	
		Joint line pair	3.25	3.75
		Never hinged	7.00	
		Double transfer	—	—
		Cracked plate (horizontal)	7.50	—
		Cracked plate (vertical) re-touched	9.00	—
		Rosette plate crack on head	60.00	—

Earliest documented use: Jan. 3, 1917 (dated cancel on off-cover pair); March 6, 1917 (on cover).

491	A140	2c **carmine,** type II, *Nov. 17, 1916*	2,500.	750.00
		Never hinged	5,000.	
		On cover, type II		1,100.
		Pair, type II	6,000.	3,750.
		Never hinged	12,500.	
		Joint line pair, type II	14,000.	12,000.
		Never hinged	27,500.	

Earliest documented use: Jan. 2, 1917.
See note after No. 455.

492	A140	2c **carmine,** type III	9.00	.90
		carmine rose, type III	9.00	.90
		Never hinged	19.00	
		On cover, type III		1.25
		Pair, type III	21.50	3.50
		Never hinged	45.00	
		Joint line pair, type III	55.00	25.00
		Never hinged	115.00	
		Double transfer, type III	—	—
		Cracked plate		

Earliest documented use: April 1, 1917.

493	A140	3c **violet,** type I, *July 23, 1917*	14.00	3.50
		reddish violet, type I	14.00	3.50
		Never hinged	30.00	
		On cover, type I		7.50
		Pair, type I	35.00	10.00
		Never hinged	75.00	
		Joint line pair, type I	110.00	60.00
		Never hinged	230.00	

Earliest documented use: Nov. 2, 1917.

494	A140	3c **violet,** type II, *Feb. 4, 1918*	10.00	1.75
		dull violet, type II	10.00	1.75
		gray violet, type II	10.00	1.75
		Never hinged	21.50	
		On cover, type II		2.00
		Pair, type II	24.00	5.50
		Never hinged	50.00	
		Joint line pair, type II	75.00	11.00
		Never hinged	160.00	

Earliest documented use: Apr. 16, 1918.

495	A140	4c **orange brown,** *Apr. 15, 1917*	10.00	5.00
		Never hinged	21.50	
		On cover		9.50
		Pair	24.00	15.00
		Never hinged	50.00	
		Joint line pair	75.00	30.00
		Never hinged	160.00	
		Cracked plate	25.00	—

Earliest documented use: June 20, 1917.

496	A140	5c **blue,** *Jan. 15, 1919*	3.25	1.40
		Never hinged	7.00	
		On cover		1.90
		Pair	8.00	4.25
		Never hinged	17.50	
		Joint line pair	30.00	14.00
		Never hinged	65.00	

Earliest documented use: April 15, 1919.

497	A148	10c **orange yellow,** *Jan. 31, 1922*	19.00	11.00
		Never hinged	40.00	
		On cover		17.00
		Pair	45.00	50.00

	Never hinged	95.00	
	Joint line pair	130.00	145.00
	Never hinged	280.00	

Earliest documented use: Jan. 31, 1922 (FDC).

Blind Perfs
Listings of imperforate-between varieties are for examples which show no trace of "blind perfs," traces of impressions from the perforating pins which do not cut into the paper.
Some unused stamps have had the gum removed to eliminate the impressions from the perforating pins. These copies do not qualify as the listed varieties.

FLAT PLATE PRINTINGS
Plates of 400 subjects in four panes of 100.
TYPES OF 1913-15 ISSUE

1917-19   Unwmk.   Perf. 11

498	A140	1c **green,** *Mar. 1917*	.35	.25
		light green	.35	.25
		dark green	.35	.25
		yellowish green	.35	.25
		Never hinged	.75	
		On cover		.30
		Block of 4	1.40	1.50
		P# block of 6	16.50	
		Never hinged	27.50	
		Margin block of 6, Electrolytic (Pl. 13376-7, 13389-90)		
		See note after No. 481	1,000.	
		Never hinged	1,750.	
		Cracked plate (10656 UL and 10645 LR)	7.50	—
		Double transfer	5.50	2.00
a.		Vertical pair, imperf. horiz.	900.00	
		Never hinged	1,750.	
b.		Horizontal pair, imperf. between	500.00	
		Never hinged	950.00	
c.		Vertical pair, imperf. between	700.00	—
d.		Double impression	250.00	4,000.
e.		Booklet pane of 6, *March 1917*	2.50	2.00
		Never hinged	4.25	
f.		Booklet pane of 30, *Aug. 1917*	1,150.	
		Never hinged	1,800.	
g.		Perf. 10 at top or bottom	7,500.	20,000.
		Never hinged	11,500.	

Earliest documented use: March 30, 1917 (No. 498e booklet pair); Aug. 8, 1917 (No. 498f single).

No. 498g also known as a transitional stamp gauging 10 at left bottom and 11 at right bottom (bottom center stamp in a plate block of 6).
See No. 505 for P# block of 6 from plate 7942.

499	A140	2c **rose,** type I, *Mar. 1917*	.35	.25
		dark rose, type I	.35	.25
		carmine rose, type I	.35	.25
		deep rose, type I	.35	.25
		Never hinged	.75	
		On cover, type I		.30
		Block of 4, type I	1.40	1.50
		P# block of 6, type I	16.50	
		Never hinged	27.50	
		Double impression, type I, 15mm wide	—	—
		Cracked plate, type I	1,500.	2,300.
		Recut in hair, type I	1,500.	2,300.
		Never hinged	3,000.	
		Double transfer, type I	6.00	—
a.		Vertical pair, imperf. horiz., type I	600.00	
		Never hinged	1,200.	
b.		Horiz. pair, imperf. vert., type I	375.00	225.00
		Never hinged	750.00	
c.		Vert. pair, imperf. btwn., type I	1,000.	300.00
e.		Booklet pane of 6, type I, *Mar. 31, 1917*	4.00	2.50
		Never hinged	6.75	
f.		Booklet pane of 30, type I, *Aug. 1917*	28,000.	
		Never hinged	38,000.	
g.		Double impression, type I	200.00	
		Never hinged	400.00	
		On cover		750.00
h.		2c **lake,** type I	500.00	350.00
		Never hinged	1,000.	
		On cover		—

No. 499b is valued in the grade of fine.
No. 499h occurs in two different lake shades. The true lake is similar to the lake on other lake shades noted elsewhere in this catalogue. A somewhat more common lake shade is known as "Boston lake," and it is a very distinctive and duller shade. Certificates of authenticity recommended for these and all listed lake shades.
Earliest documented uses: Mar. 27, 1917 (No. 499); July 19, 1917 (No. 499e single); Aug. 7, 1917 (No. 499f single).

500	A140	2c **deep rose,** type Ia	280.00	240.00
		Never hinged	600.00	
		On cover, type Ia		650.00
		Block of 4, type Ia	1,200.	1,500.
		P# block of 6, type Ia	2,150.	
		Never hinged	3,750.	—
		P# block of 6, two stamps type I (P# 10208 LL)	12,500.	
		Never hinged	18,500.	
		Pair, types I and Ia (10208 LL 95 or 96)	1,275.	

Earliest documented use: Dec. 15, 1919.
No. 500 exists with imperforate top sheet margin. Copies have been altered by trimming perforations. Some also have faked Schermack perfs.

501	A140	3c **light violet,** type I, *Mar. 1917*	11.00	.40
		violet, type I	11.00	.40

	dark violet, type I		11.00	.40
	reddish violet, type I		11.00	.40
	Never hinged		25.00	
	On cover, type I			.50
	Block of 4, type I		45.00	4.00
	P# block of 6, type I		125.00	
	Never hinged		220.00	
	Double transfer, type I		12.00	
b.	Bklt. pane of 6, type I, *Oct. 17, 1917*		75.00	60.00
	Never hinged		125.00	
c.	Vert. pair, imper. horiz., type I		2,500.	
	Never hinged		3,500.	
d.	Double impression		2,750.	2,750.
	Never hinged		5,000.	

Earliest documented uses: June 5, 1917 (No. 501); Feb. 8, 1918 (No. 501b single).

502	A140	3c **dark violet,** type II	14.00	.75
		violet, type II	14.00	.75
		Never hinged	32.50	
		On cover, type II		1.00
		Block of 4, type II	57.50	5.50
		P# block of 6, type II	140.00	
		Never hinged	250.00	
b.		Bklt. pane of 6, type II, *Feb. 25, 1918*	60.00	55.00
		Never hinged	100.00	
c.		Vert. pair, imperf. horiz., type II	1,400.	750.00
		Never hinged	2,750.	
		On cover		1,500.
d.		Double impression	750.00	300.00
		Never hinged	1,500.	
e.		Perf. 10 at top or bottom	15,000.	12,500.
		Never hinged	21,500.	

Earliest documented uses: Jan. 30, 1918 (No. 502); June 12, 1918 (No. 502b single).

503	A140	4c **brown,** *Mar. 1917*	10.00	.40
		dark brown	10.00	.40
		orange brown	10.00	.40
		yellow brown	10.00	.40
		Never hinged	22.50	
		On cover		2.10
		Block of 4	40.00	3.50
		P# block of 6	130.00	
		Never hinged	225.00	
		Double transfer	15.00	—
b.		Double impression	—	
504	A140	5c **blue,** *Mar. 1917*	9.00	.35
		light blue	9.00	.35
		dark blue	9.00	.35
		Never hinged	20.00	
		On cover		.45
		Block of 4	37.50	3.00
		P# block of 6	125.00	
		Never hinged	210.00	
		Double transfer	11.00	—
a.		Horizontal pair, imperf. between	3,250.	—
b.		Double impression	2,000.	900.00

Earliest documented use: June 5, 1917.

505	A140	5c **rose** (error)	350.00	550.00
		Never hinged	700.00	
		On cover		2,250.
		Block of 9, middle stamp #505	725.00	1,100.
		Never hinged	1,150.	
		Block of 12, two middle stamps #505	1,450.	2,100.
		Never hinged	2,250.	
		Margin block of six 2c stamps (#499), P# 7942	25.00	
		Never hinged	40.00	

Earliest documented use: Mar. 27, 1917.

Value notes under No. 467 also apply to No. 505.

506	A140	6c **red orange,** *Mar. 1917*	12.00	.40
		orange	12.00	.40
		Never hinged	27.50	
		On cover		2.50
		Block of 4	52.50	4.00
		P# block of 6	170.00	
		Never hinged	285.00	
		Double transfer	—	—
a.		Perf. 10 at top or bottom	4,750.	6,500.
507	A140	7c **black,** *Mar. 1917*	27.50	1.25
		gray black	27.50	1.25
		intense black	27.50	1.25
		Never hinged	65.00	
		On cover		7.75
		Block of 4	115.00	12.50
		P# block of 6	250.00	
		Never hinged	450.00	
		Double transfer	—	—
a.		Perf. 10 at top	20,000.	

Only two examples of No. 507a are recorded, being the top two stamps in a block of four with two normal No. 507.

508	A148	8c **olive bister,** *Mar. 1917*	12.00	.65
		dark olive green	12.00	.65
		olive green	12.00	.65
		Never hinged	27.50	
		On cover		2.75
		Block of 4	50.00	6.50
		P# block of 6, Impt. & "A"	170.00	
		Never hinged	285.00	
		P# block of 6, "A"	220.00	
		Never hinged	370.00	
		P# block of 6	140.00	
		Never hinged	240.00	
b.		Vertical pair, imperf. between	—	—
c.		Perf. 10 at top or bottom		15,000.
509	A148	9c **salmon red,** *Mar. 1917*	13.00	1.75
		salmon	13.00	1.75
		Never hinged	30.00	
		On cover		13.00
		Block of 4	57.50	19.00
		P# block of 6	140.00	

		Never hinged	240.00	
		Double transfer	20.00	4.50
a.		Perf. 10 at top or bottom	4,000.	6,500.
		Never hinged	6,500.	

No. 509a also exists as a transitional stamp gauging partly perf 10 and partly perf 11 at top or bottom. Value thus the same as normal 509a.

510	A148	10c **orange yellow,** *Mar. 1917*	17.50	.25
		golden yellow	17.50	.25
		Never hinged	40.00	
		On cover		2.00
		Block of 4	70.00	2.00
		P# block of 6, "A"	290.00	
		Never hinged	475.00	
		P# block of 6	180.00	
		Never hinged	310.00	
a.		10c **brown yellow**	1,250.	
		Never hinged	2,250.	

Earliest documented use: Mar. 27, 1917.

511	A148	11c **light green,** *May 1917*	9.00	2.50
		green	9.00	2.50
		Never hinged	20.00	
		dark green	10.00	2.50
		Never hinged	20.00	
		On cover		8.50
		Block of 4	37.50	22.50
		P# block of 6	125.00	
		Never hinged	220.00	
		Double transfer	12.50	3.25
a.		Perf. 10 at top or bottom	5,000.	4,000.
		Never hinged	7,500.	

No. 511a also exists as a transitional stamp gauging partly perf 10 and partly perf 11 at top or bottom. Value thus the same as normal 511a.

512	A148	12c **claret brown,** *May 1917*	9.00	.40
		Never hinged	20.00	
		On cover		4.00
		Block of 4	37.50	3.75
		P# block of 6	125.00	
		Never hinged	220.00	
		Double transfer	12.50	—
		Triple transfer	20.00	—
a.		12c **brown carmine**	10.00	.50
		Never hinged	22.50	
		On cover		4.50
		Block of 4	40.00	4.50
		P# block of 6	130.00	
		Never hinged	230.00	
b.		Perf. 10 at top or bottom	17,500.	6,000.

Earliest documented use: Aug. 15, 1917 (No. 512a).

513	A148	13c **apple green,** *Jan. 10, 1919*	11.00	6.00
		pale apple green	11.00	6.00
		Never hinged	25.00	
		deep apple green	12.50	6.50
		Never hinged	30.00	
		On cover		19.00
		Block of 4	45.00	45.00
		P# block of 6	125.00	
		Never hinged	220.00	

Earliest documented use: Jan. 25, 1919.

514	A148	15c **gray,** *May 1917*	37.50	1.50
		dark gray	37.50	1.50
		Never hinged	85.00	
		On cover		25.00
		Block of 4	160.00	12.50
		P# block of 6	550.00	—
		Never hinged	900.00	
		Double transfer	—	—
a.		Perf. 10 at bottom		10,000.

Earliest documented use: Nov. 15, 1917.

515	A148	20c **light ultramarine,** *May 1917*	45.00	.45
		gray blue	45.00	.45
		Never hinged	95.00	
		deep ultramarine	50.00	.55
		Never hinged	105.00	
		On cover		75.00
		Block of 4	200.00	3.50
		P# block of 6	600.00	
		Never hinged	1,000.	
		Double transfer	—	—
b.		Vertical pair, imperf. between	2,000.	1,750.
c.		Double impression	1,250.	
d.		Perf. 10 at top or bottom	—	15,000.

No. 515b is valued in the grade of fine.
Beware of pairs with blind perforations inside the design of the top stamp that are offered as No. 515b.

Earliest documented use: May 4, 1918.

516	A148	30c **orange red,** *May 1917*	37.50	1.50
		dark orange red	37.50	1.50
		Never hinged	85.00	
		On cover		150.00
		Block of 4	160.00	12.50
		P# block of 6	600.00	
		Never hinged	925.00	
		Double transfer	—	—
a.		Perf. 10 at top or bottom	20,000.	7,500.
		Never hinged	40,000.	
b.		Double impression	—	

Earliest documented use: Jan. 12, 1918.

517	A148	50c **red violet,** *May 1917*	65.00	.75
		Never hinged	150.00	
		violet	75.00	.75
		Never hinged	150.00	
		light violet	80.00	.75
		Never hinged	180.00	
		On cover		400.00
		Block of 4	290.00	5.00
		P# block of 6	1,600.	
		Never hinged	2,550.	

		Double transfer	100.00	1.
b.		Vertical pair, imperf. between & at bottom	—	10,00
c.		Perf. 10 at top or bottom		

No. 517b is valued in average condition and may be a uniq used pair (precanceled). The editors would like to see authen cated evidence of an unused pair.

Earliest documented use: Dec. 28, 1917 (on registry tag).

518	A148	$1 **violet brown,** *May 1917*	50.00	1.5
		violet black	50.00	1.5
		Never hinged	120.00	
		On cover		550.0
		Block of 4	210.00	12.5
		Margin block of 4, arrow right or left	230.00	
		P# block of 6, Impt. & "A"	1,300.	—
		Never hinged	2,100.	
		Double transfer (5782 L. 66)	70.00	2.0
b.		$1 **deep brown**	1,800.	1,05
		Never hinged	3,750.	
		Block of 4		4,75
		P# block of 6, Impt. & "A," never hinged	32,500.	

Earliest documented use: May 19, 1917.

No. 518b is valued in the grade of fine to very fine.

Nos. 498-504, 506-518 (20)	670.70	261.3

TYPE OF 1908-09 ISSUE

1917, Oct. 10	Wmk. 191		*Perf. 1*

This is the result of an old stock of No. 344 which was returned to the Bureau in 1917 and perforated with the the current gauge 11.

519	A139	2c **carmine**	450.00	*1,250*
		Never hinged	900.00	
		On cover		*2,750*
		Block of 4	2,000.	—
		P# block of 6, T V, Impt.	3,500.	—
		Never hinged	6,500.	—

Beware of copies of No. 344 fraudulently perforated and offered as No. 519. Obtaining a certificate from a recognized expertizing committee is strongly recommended.
Warning: See note following No. 459 regarding used stamps.

Earliest documented use: Oct. 10, 1917.

Franklin — A149

Plates of 100 subjects.

1918, Aug.		Unwmk.		*Perf. 11*
523	A149	$2 **orange red & black**	625.	240.
		red orange & black	625.	240.
		Never hinged	1,300.	
		On cover		*2,000.*
		Block of 4	2,600.	1,300.
		Margin block of 4, arrow	2,700.	
		Center line block	2,900.	1,400.
		P# block of 8, 2# & arrow	12,000.	
		Never hinged	18,000.	

Earliest documented use: Dec. 17, 1918.

524	A149	$5 **deep green & black**	200.	35.
		Never hinged	425.	
		On cover		*2,500.*
		Block of 4	850.00	200.
		Margin block of 4, arrow	900.00	210.
		Center line block	1,100.	225.
		P# block of 8, 2# & arrow	4,500.	
		Never hinged	7,000.	

Earliest documented use: Mar. 20, 1920.

For other listing of design A149 see No. 547.

OFFSET PRINTING

Plates of 400, 800 or 1600 subjects in panes of 100 each, as follows:
No. 525 — 400 and 1600 subjects
No. 526 — 400, 800 and 1600 subjects
No. 529 — 400 subjects
No. 531 — 400 subjects
No. 532 — 400, 800 and 1600 subjects
No. 535 — 400 subjects
No. 536 — 400 and 1600 subjects

TYPES OF 1917-19 ISSUE

1918-20		Unwmk.		*Perf. 11*
525	A140	1c **gray green,** *Dec. 1918*	2.50	.90
		Never hinged	5.50	
		emerald	3.50	1.25
		Never hinged	7.75	
		On cover		1.75
		Block of 4	10.50	6.00
		P# block of 6	22.50	
		Never hinged	42.50	
		"Flat nose"		
a.		1c **dark green**	6.00	1.75

Never hinged		13.00	
Horizontal pair, imperf. between		100.00	*700.00*
Double impression		40.00	—
Never hinged		85.00	

Earliest documented use: Dec. 24, 1918.

TYPE IV

TWO CENTS

Type IV — Top line of the toga rope is broken.
The shading lines in the toga button are so arranged that the curving of the first and last form "D (reversed) ID."
The line of color in the left "2" is very thin and usually broken.
Used on offset printings only.

TYPE V

Type V — Top line of the toga is complete.
There are five vertical shading lines in the toga button.
The line of color in the left "2" is very thin and usually broken.
The shading dots on the nose are as shown on the diagram.
Used on offset printings only.

TYPE Va

Type Va — Characteristics are the same as type V except in the shading dots of the nose. The third row of dots from the bottom has four dots instead of six. The overall height is ⅓mm shorter than type V.
Used on offset printings only.

TYPE VI

Type VI — General characteristics the same as type V except that the line of color in the left "2" is very heavy.
Used on offset printings only.

TYPE VII

Type VII — The line of color in the left "2" is invariably continuous, clearly defined and heavier than in type V or Va but not as heavy as type VI.
An additional vertical row of dots has been added to the upper lip.
Numerous additional dots have been added to the hair on top of the head.
Used on offset printings only.
Dates of issue of types after type IV are not known but official records show the first plate of each type to have been certified as follows:
Type IV, Mar. 6, 1920
Type V, Mar. 20, 1920
Type Va, May 4, 1920
Type VI, June 24, 1920
Type VII, Nov. 3, 1920

526	A140	2c **carmine**, type IV, *1920*	27.50	4.00
		rose carmine, type IV	27.50	4.00
		Never hinged	62.50	
		On cover, type IV		11.00
		Block of 4, type IV	120.00	30.00
		P# block of 6, type IV	240.00	
		Never hinged	450.00	
		Gash on forehead, type IV	60.00	—
		Never hinged	125.00	
		Malformed "2" at left, type IV		
		(10823 LR 93)	40.00	6.00

Earliest documented use: Mar. 15, 1920 (FDC).

527	A140	2c **carmine**, type V, *1920*	20.00	1.25
		bright carmine, type V	20.00	1.25
		rose carmine, type V	20.00	1.25
		Never hinged	45.00	
		On cover		2.75
		Block of 4, type V	85.00	10.00
		Block of 6, P# only, type V	165.00	
		Never hinged	325.00	
		Line through "2" & "EN," type V	35.00	—
		Never hinged	75.00	
a.		Double impression, type V	75.00	
		Never hinged	160.00	
b.		Vert. pair, imperf. horiz., type V	850.00	
c.		Horiz. pair, imperf. vert., type V	*1,000.*	—

Earliest documented use: Apr. 20, 1920.

528	A140	2c **carmine**, type Va, *1920*	9.50	.40
		Never hinged	22.50	
		On cover, type Va		.75
		Block of 4, type Va	40.00	3.50
		Block of 6, P# only, type Va	85.00	
		Never hinged	150.00	
		Block of 6, monogram over P#	175.00	
		Never hinged	165.00	
		Retouches in "P" of Postage		
		type Va	*52.50*	—
		Retouched on toga, type Va		—
		Variety C"R"NTS, type Va	*37.50*	
		Never hinged	85.00	
		Top margin P# block of 6 containing the C"R"NTS variety,		
		type Va	450.00	
c.		Double impression, type Va	55.00	
		Never hinged	125.00	
g.		Vert. pair, imperf. between	*2,500.*	

Earliest documented use: June 18, 1920.

528A	A140	2c **carmine**, type VI, *1920*	52.50	2.00
		bright carmine, type VI	52.50	2.00
		Never hinged	115.00	
		On cover, type VI		3.75
		Block of 4, type VI	225.00	15.00
		P# block of 6, type VI	425.00	
		Never hinged	750.00	
		Block of 6, monogram over P#	525.00	
		Never hinged	750.00	
d.		Double impression, type VI	160.00	—
		Never hinged	325.00	
f.		Vert. pair, imperf. horiz., type VI		—
h.		Vert. pair, imperf. between	*1,000.*	

Earliest documented use: July 30, 1920.

528B	A140	2c **carmine**, type VII, *1920*	22.50	.75
		Never hinged	50.00	
		On cover, type VII		1.00
		Block of 4, type VII	95.00	6.00
		P# block of 6, type VII	175.00	
		Never hinged	340.00	
		Gash on cheek, type VII	*300.00*	—
		Retouched on cheek, type VII	*750.00*	—
		Vertical plate scratch through		
		face, type VII	*200.00*	
e.		Double impression, type VII	80.00	*400.00*

Earliest documented use: Nov. 10, 1920.

TYPE III

THREE CENTS

Type III — The top line of the toga rope is strong but the 5th shading line is missing as in type I.
Center shading line of the toga button consists of two dashes with a central dot.
The "P" and "O" of "POSTAGE" are separated by a line of color.
The frame line at the bottom of the vignette is complete.
Used on offset printings only.

TYPE IV

Type IV — The shading lines of the toga rope are complete.

79

1921, May — Perf. 10
Plates of 400 subjects in four panes of 100 each
Stamp design: 19x22½mm

543	A140 1c	**green**	.70	.40
		deep green	.70	.40
		Never hinged	1.40	
		On cover		.45
		Block of 4	2.80	2.00
		Vertical margin block of 6, P# opposite center horizontal row	32.50	
		Never hinged	57.50	
		Corner margin block of 4, P# only	14.00	
		Never hinged	25.00	
		Double transfer	—	
		Triple transfer	—	
a.		Horizontal pair, imperf. between	2,750.	

Earliest documented use: May 21, 1921.

1922 — Perf. 11
Rotary press sheet waste
Stamp design: 19x22½mm

544	A140 1c	**green**	22,500.	3,750.
		Never hinged	36,500.	
		On cover		5,000.

No. 544 is valued in the grade of fine.
Earliest documented use: Dec. 21, 1922.

1921, May
Issued in panes of 170 stamps (coil waste), later in panes of 70 and 100
Stamp designs: 19½-20x22mm

545	A140 1c	**green**	200.00	210.00
		yellowish green	200.00	210.00
		Never hinged	425.00	
		On cover		1,800.
		Block of 4	825.00	1,050.
		P# block of 4, "S 30"	1,100.	
		Never hinged	1,850.	
		P# block of 4	1,150.	
		Never hinged	1,900.	
		P# block of 4, star	1,200.	
		Never hinged	2,250.	

Earliest documented use: June 25, 1921.

546	A140 2c	**carmine rose,** type III	125.00	175.00
		deep carmine rose	125.00	175.00
		Never hinged	260.00	
		On cover		775.00
		Block of 4	525.00	850.00
		P# block of 4, "S 30"	750.00	
		Never hinged	1,400.	
		P# block of 4	775.00	
		Never hinged	1,450.	
		P# block of 4, star	800.00	
		Never hinged	1,500.	
		Recut in hair	140.00	185.00
a.		Perf. 10 on left side	7,500.	10,000.

Earliest documented use: May 5, 1921.

FLAT PLATE PRINTING
Plates of 100 subjects

1920, Nov. 1 — Perf. 11

547	A149 $2	**carmine & black**	160.	40.
		Never hinged	330.	
		On cover (commercial)		1,000.
		On flown cover (philatelic)		250.
		Block of 4	675.	200.
		Margin block of 4, arrow	700.	
		Center line block	850.	—
		Margin block of 8, two P#, & arrow	4,500.	
		Never hinged	7,000.	
a.		$2 **lake & black**	225.	40.
		Never hinged	475.	

Earliest documented use: Dec. 6, 1920 (on piece).

From No. 548 forward, almost all U.S. stamps have had officially designated first days of sale and use. Therefore, from this point, earliest documented uses are given only for those stamps for which there were not designated first days of sale. For first day covers, see the First Day Cover section later in the catalogue.

PILGRIM TERCENTENARY ISSUE
Landing of the Pilgrims at Plymouth, Mass.

The "Mayflower" — A151

Landing of the Pilgrims — A152

Signing of the Compact — A153

Designed by Clair A. Huston

Plates of 280 subjects in four panes of 70 each

1920, Dec. 21 — Unwmk. — Perf. 11

548	A151 1c	**green**	4.75	2.25
		dark green	4.75	2.25
		Never hinged	11.00	
		On cover		3.50
		Block of 4	20.00	14.00
		P# block of 6	60.00	
		Never hinged	85.00	—
549	A152 2c	**carmine rose**	6.50	1.60
		carmine	6.50	1.60
		rose	6.50	1.60
		Never hinged	14.00	
		On cover		2.50
		Block of 4	27.50	9.00
		P# block of 6	75.00	
		Never hinged	110.00	

Cancellation

		China		—
550	A153 5c	**deep blue**	45.00	14.00
		dark blue	45.00	14.00
		Never hinged	100.00	
		On cover		22.50
		Block of 4	200.00	75.00
		P# block of 6	475.00	
		Never hinged	700.00	
		Nos. 548-550 (3)	56.25	17.85
		Nos. 548-550, never hinged	125.00	

REGARDING VALUES FOR
NEVER-HINGED STAMPS

Collectors should be aware that the values given for never-hinged stamps from No. 205 on are for stamps in the grade of very fine, just as the values for all stamps in the catalogue are for very fine stamps unless indicated otherwise. The never-hinged premium as a percentage of value will be larger for stamps in extremely fine or superb grades, and the premium will be smaller for fine-very fine, fine or poor examples. This is particularly true of the issues of the late-19th and early-20th centuries. For example, in the grade of very fine, an unused stamp from this time period may be valued at $100 hinged and $180 never hinged. The never-hinged premium is thus 80%. But in a grade of extremely fine, this same stamp will not only sell for more hinged, but the never-hinged premium will increase, perhaps to 100%-300% or more over the higher extremely fine value. In a grade of superb, a hinged copy will sell for much more than a very fine copy, and additionally the never-hinged premium will be much larger, perhaps as large as 300%-400%. On the other hand, the same stamp in a grade of fine or fine-very fine not only will sell for less than a very fine stamp in hinged condition, but additionally the never-hinged premium will be smaller than the never-hinged premium on a very fine stamp, perhaps as small as 15%-30%.

Please note that the above statements and percentages are NOT a formula for arriving at the values of stamps in hinged or never-hinged condition in the grades of very good, fine, fine to very fine, extremely fine or superb. The percentages given apply only to the size of the premium for never-hinged condition that might be added to the stamp value for hinged condition. Further, the percentages given are only generalized estimates. Some stamps or grades may have percentages for never-hinged condition that are higher or lower than the ranges given. For values of the most popular U.S. stamps in the grades of very good, fine, fine to very fine, extremely fine and superb, see the *Scott Valuing Supplement*, updated and issued twice each year in April and October.

VALUES FOR NEVER-HINGED STAMPS
PRIOR TO SCOTT 205

This catalogue does not value pre-1882 stamps in never-hinged condition. Premiums for never-hinged condition in the classic era invariably are even larger than those listed for the post-1882 issues. Generally speaking, the earlier the stamp is listed in the catalogue, the larger will be the never-hinged premium. On some early classics, the premium will be several multiples of the unused, hinged values given in the catalogue.

NEVER-HINGED PLATE BLOCKS

Values given for never-hinged plate blocks are for blocks in which all stamps have original gum that has never been hinged and has no disturbances, and all selvage, whether gummed or ungummed, has never been hinged.

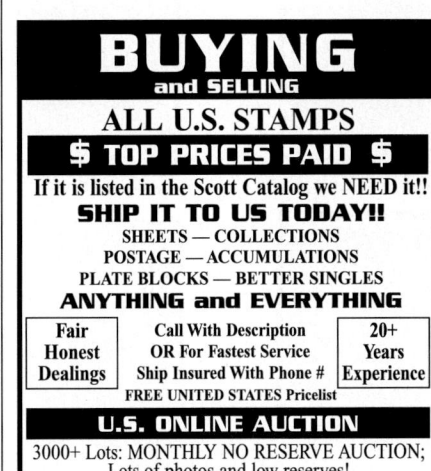

BUYING
and SELLING
ALL U.S. STAMPS
$ TOP PRICES PAID $
If it is listed in the Scott Catalog we NEED it!!
SHIP IT TO US TODAY!!
SHEETS — COLLECTIONS
POSTAGE — ACCUMULATIONS
PLATE BLOCKS — BETTER SINGLES
ANYTHING and EVERYTHING

Fair Honest Dealings	Call With Description OR For Fastest Service Ship Insured With Phone #	20+ Years Experience

FREE UNITED STATES Pricelist

U.S. ONLINE AUCTION
3000+ Lots: MONTHLY NO RESERVE AUCTION;
Lots of photos and low reserves!

WWW.MALACK.COM
Steve Malack Stamps
P.O. Box 5628 Endicott, NY 13763
607-862-9441 (Phone/Fax) EMAIL: MALACKWEB@aol.com
SEE OUR OTHER AD ON PAGE 21

REGULAR ISSUE

Nathan Hale — A154

Franklin — A155

Warren G. Harding — A156

Washington — A157

Lincoln — A158

Martha Washington — A159

Theodore Roosevelt — A160

Garfield — A161

McKinley — A162

Grant — A163

Jefferson — A164

Monroe — A165

Rutherford B. Hayes — A166

Grover Cleveland — A167

American Indian — A168

Statue of Liberty — A169

Golden Gate — A170

Niagara Falls — A171

American Buffalo — A172

Arlington Amphitheater — A173

Lincoln Memorial — A174

United States Capitol — A175

Head of Freedom Statue, Capitol Dome — A176

Plates of 400 subjects in four panes of 100 each for all values ½c to 50c inclusive.

Plates of 200 subjects for $1 and $2. The sheets were cut along the horizontal guide line into two panes, upper and lower, of 100 subjects each.

Plates of 100 subjects for the $5 denomination, and sheets of 100 subjects were issued intact.

The Bureau of Engraving and Printing in 1925 in experimenting to overcome the loss due to uneven perforations, produced what is known as the "Star Plate." The vertical rows of designs on these plates are spaced 3mm apart in place of 2¾mm as on the regular plates. Most of these plates were identified with a star added to the plate number.

Designed by Clair Aubrey Huston.

FLAT PLATE PRINTINGS

1922-25 Unwmk. Perf. 11

551	A154	½c **olive brown**, Apr. 4, 1925	.25	.20
		pale olive brown	.25	.20
		deep olive brown	.25	.20
		Never hinged	.50	
		On 1c stamped envelope (3rd class)		2.50
		Block of 4	1.00	.50
		P# block of 6	10.00	
		Never hinged	20.00	
		"Cap" on fraction bar (Pl. 17041)	.75	.20
552	A155	1c **deep green**, Jan. 17, 1923	1.30	.20
		green	1.30	.20
		pale green	1.30	.20
		Never hinged	2.75	
		On postcard		.25
		Block of 4	5.25	.40
		P# block of 6	30.00	
		Never hinged	45.00	
		Double transfer	3.50	—
a.		Booklet pane of 6, Aug. 11, 1923	7.50	4.00
		Never hinged	12.50	

Earliest documented use: Dec. 26, 1923 (No. 552a single).

553	A156	1½c **yellow brown**, Mar. 19, 1925	2.30	.20
		pale yellow brown	2.30	.20
		brown	2.30	.20
		Never hinged	4.75	
		On 3rd class cover		2.25
		Block of 4	9.50	1.10

		P# block of 6	55.00	—
		Never hinged	75.00	
		Double transfer	—	
554	A157	2c **carmine**, Jan. 15, 1923	1.20	.2
		light carmine	1.20	.2
		Never hinged	2.50	
		On cover		.2
		Block of 4	5.00	.3
		P# block of 6	32.50	
		Never hinged	45.00	
		P# block of 6 & small 5 point star, top only	550.00	
		Never hinged	775.00	
		P# block of 6 & large 5 point star, side only	65.00	
		Never hinged	97.50	
		Same, large 5-pt. star, top	600.00	
		Never hinged	900.00	
		Same, large 6-pt. star, top	750.00	
		Never hinged	1,100.	
		Same, large 6-pt. star, side only (Pl. 17196)	900.00	
		Never hinged	1,500.	
		Double transfer	2.50	.80
a.		Horiz. pair, imperf. vert.	250.00	
b.		Vert. pair, imperf. horiz.	4,000.	
		Never hinged	—	
c.		Booklet pane of 6, Feb. 10, 1923	7.00	3.00
		Never hinged	12.00	
d.		Perf. 10 at top or bottom	7,000.	5,000
		On cover		8,000

No. 554d unused is unique. It is never hinged and has a natural straight edge at left. Value represents the sale price at 2001 auction.

Earliest documented use: Feb. 10, 1923 (No. 554c single).

555	A158	3c **violet**, Feb. 12, 1923	17.50	1.25
		deep violet	17.50	1.25
		dark violet	17.50	1.25
		red violet	17.50	1.25
		bright violet	17.50	1.25
		Never hinged	37.50	
		On 2c stamped envelope (single UPU rate)		8.00
		Block of 4	72.50	9.00
		P# block of 6	225.00	
		Never hinged	350.00	
556	A159	4c **yellow brown**, Jan. 15, 1923	20.00	.50
		brown	20.00	.50
		Never hinged	42.50	
		On cover		9.00
		Block of 4	82.50	3.00
		P# block of 6	250.00	
		Never hinged	400.00	
		Double transfer	—	—
a.		Vert. pair, imperf. horiz.	10,500.	
b.		Perf. 10 at top or bottom	3,000.	15,000.

No. 556a is unique. It resulted from a sheet that was damaged and patched during production.

No. 556b also exists as a transitional stamp gauging 10 at left top and 11 at right top. Value the same.

557	A160	5c **dark blue**, Oct. 27, 1922	20.00	.30
		deep blue	20.00	.30
		Never hinged	42.50	
		On UPU-rate cover		6.00
		Block of 4	82.50	2.00
		P# block of 6	250.00	
		Never hinged	400.00	
		Double transfer (15571 UL 86)	—	350.00
a.		Imperf., pair	2,000.	
		Never hinged	3,500.	
		P# block of 6	8,250.	
b.		Horiz. pair, imperf. vert.	—	
c.		Perf. 10 at top or bottom	—	9,500.
		On cover		15,000.

Earliest documented use: Nov. 12, 1923 (No. 557c).

558	A161	6c **red orange**, Nov. 20, 1922	37.50	1.00
		pale red orange	37.50	1.00
		Never hinged	80.00	
		Pair on special delivery cover		17.50
		Block of 4	155.00	7.50
		P# block of 6	400.00	
		Never hinged	650.00	
		Double transfer (Plate 14169 LR 60 and 70)	57.50	2.00
		Same, recut	57.50	2.00
559	A162	7c **black**, May 1, 1923	8.50	.75
		gray black	8.50	.75
		Never hinged	18.00	
		On registered cover with other values		27.50
		Block of 4	37.50	6.00
		P# block of 6	110.00	
		Never hinged	170.00	
		Double transfer	—	—
560	A163	8c **olive green**, May 1, 1923	50.00	1.00
		pale olive green	50.00	1.00
		Never hinged	105.00	
		Pair on airmail cover		12.50
		Block of 4	210.00	7.50
		P# block of 6	575.00	
		Never hinged	900.00	
		Double transfer	—	—
561	A164	9c **rose**, Jan. 15, 1923	14.00	1.25
		pale rose	14.00	1.25
		Never hinged	29.00	
		On registered cover with other values		22.50
		Block of 4	57.50	9.00
		P# block of 6	250.00	
		Never hinged	400.00	
562	A165	10c **orange**, Jan. 15, 1923	17.50	.35
		pale orange	17.50	.35

Never hinged	37.50		
On special delivery cover with 2c			6.00
Block of 4	72.50		2.00
P# block of 6	275.00		
Never hinged	425.00		
a. Vert. pair, imperf. horiz.	2,250.		
Never hinged	3,250.		
b. Imperf., pair	2,500.		
P# block of 6	11,000.		
c. Perf. 10 at top or bottom	—		8,500.
Pair			18,000.

No. 562b is valued without gum and without blue pencil defacing lines.

563 A166	11c **light blue,** Oct. 4, 1922	1.40	.60	
	greenish blue	1.40	.60	
	Never hinged	2.90		
	On registered cover with other values		12.50	
	Block of 4	5.75	3.50	
	P# block of 6	47.50		
	Never hinged	70.00		
a.	11c **light bluish green**	1.40	.60	
	Never hinged	2.90		
	On registered cover with other values		14.00	
	Block of 4	5.75	4.00	
	P# block of 6	30.00		
	Never hinged	50.00		
	light yellow green	1.40	.60	
	Never hinged	2.50		
d.	Imperf., pair		20,000.	

Many other intermediate shades exist for Nos. 563 and 563a, all falling within the blue or green color families.

564 A167	12c **brown violet,** Mar. 20, 1923	6.00	.35	
	deep brown violet	6.00	.35	
	Never hinged	13.00		
	On special delivery cover		12.50	
	Block of 4	25.00	3.00	
	P# block of 6	100.00		
	Never hinged	150.00		
	P# block of 6 & large 5 point star, side only	140.00		
	Never hinged	220.00		
	P# block of 6 & large 6 point star, side only	250.00		
	Never hinged	400.00		
	Double transfer, (14404 UL 73 & 74)	12.50	1.10	
a.	Horiz. pair, imperf. vert.	1,750.		
565 A168	14c **blue,** May 1, 1923	4.00	.90	
	deep blue	4.00	.90	
	Never hinged	8.50		
	On registered cover with other values		15.00	
	Block of 4	16.50	7.50	
	P# block of 6	70.00		
	Never hinged	120.00		
	Double transfer	—	—	

Horizontal pairs of No. 565 are known with spacings up to 3mm instead of 2mm between. These are from the 5th and 6th vertical rows of the right panes of Plate 14515 and also between stamps Nos. 3 and 4 of the same pane. A plate block of Pl. 14512 is known with 3mm spacing.

566 A169	15c **gray,** Nov. 11, 1922	20.00	.30	
	light gray	20.00	.30	
	Never hinged	42.50		
	On registered cover with 2c		3.50	
	Block of 4	85.00	2.00	
	P# block of 6	275.00		
	Never hinged	425.00		
	P# block of 6 & large 5 point star, side only	550.00		
	Never hinged	825.00		
567 A170	20c **carmine rose,** May 1, 1923	20.00	.30	
	deep carmine rose	20.00	.30	
	Never hinged	42.50		
	On registered UPU-rate cover		12.50	
	Block of 4	85.00	2.00	
	P# block of 6	300.00		
	Never hinged	450.00		
	P# block of 6 & large 5 point star, side only	575.00		
	Never hinged	850.00		
a.	Horiz. pair, imperf. vert.	2,000.		
	Never hinged	3,500.		

"Bridge over Falls" plate scratches

568 A171	25c **yellow green,** Nov. 11, 1922	18.00	.75	
	green	18.00	.75	
	deep green	18.00	.75	
	Never hinged	37.50		
	On contract airmail cover		27.50	
	Block of 4	75.00	6.00	
	P# block of 6	300.00		
	Never hinged	425.00		
	Double transfer	—	—	

	Plate scratches ("Bridge over Falls")	5,000.	—	
b.	Vert. pair, imperf. horiz.	2,000.		
c.	Perf. 10 at one side	5,000.	11,000.	
	Never hinged	7,500.		

No. 568b is valued in the grade of fine.

Double Transfer

569 A172	30c **olive brown,** Mar. 20, 1923	30.00	.60	
	Never hinged	65.00		
	On registered cover with other values		20.00	
	Block of 4	140.00	5.00	
	P# block of 6	300.00		
	Never hinged	450.00		
	Double transfer (16065 UR 52)	55.00	—	
570 A173	50c **lilac,** Nov. 11, 1922	47.50	.40	
	dull lilac	47.50	.40	
	Never hinged	100.00		
	On Federal airmail cover		27.50	
	Block of 4	200.00	2.00	
	P# block of 6	575.00		
	Never hinged	900.00		
571 A174	$1 **violet black,** Feb. 12, 1923	45.00	.65	
	violet brown	45.00	.65	
	Never hinged	95.00		
	On post-1932 registered cover with other values		22.50	
	Block of 4	190.00	4.50	
	Margin block of 4, arrow, top or bottom	200.00		
	P# block of 6	325.00		
	Never hinged	575.00		
	Double transfers, Pl. 18642 L 30 and Pl. 18682	95.00	1.60	
572 A175	$2 **deep blue,** Mar. 20, 1923	80.00	9.00	
	Never hinged	175.00		
	On post-1932 registered cover with other values		55.00	
	Block of 4	335.00	65.00	
	Margin block of 4, arrow, top or bottom	350.00		
	P# block of 6	750.00		
	Never hinged	1,200.		
573 A176	$5 **carmine & blue,** Mar. 20, 1923	110.00	15.00	
	Never hinged	240.00		
	On post-1932 registered cover with other values		175.00	
	Block of 4	475.00	95.00	
	Margin block of 4, arrow	500.00		
	Center line block	600.00	105.00	
	Never hinged	1,050.		
	P# block of 8, two P# & arrow	2,250.	—	
	Never hinged	3,500.		
a.	$5 **carmine lake & dark blue**	200.00	20.00	
	Never hinged	375.00		
	On post-1932 registered cover with other values		190.00	
	Block of 4	850.00	140.00	
	Margin block of 4, arrow	875.00		
	Center line block	950.00	175.00	
	Never hinged	1,600.		
	P# block of 8, two P# & arrow	3,000.		
	Never hinged	4,500.		
	Nos. 551-573 (23)	571.95	36.05	
	Nos. 551-573, never hinged	1,222.		

For other listings of perforated stamps of designs A154 to A176 see:
Nos. 578 & 579, Perf. 11x10
Nos. 581-591, Perf. 10
Nos. 594-596, Perf. 11
Nos. 632-642, 653, 692-696, Perf. 11x10½
Nos. 697-701, Perf. 10½x11
This series also includes #622-623 (perf. 11), 684-687 & 720-723.

Plate Blocks
Scott values for plate blocks printed from flat plates are for very fine side and bottom positions. Top position plate blocks with full wide selvage sell for more.

Earliest documented use dates for imperforates are for the imperforate sheet stamps, not for imperforate stamps with vending and affixing machine perforations or for flat plate imperforate coil stamps. EDU dates for VAMP and flat plate imperf coil stamps are shown in their respective sections later in the catalogue.

1923-25			**Imperf.**	
	Stamp design 19¼x22¼mm			
575 A155	1c **green,** Mar. 1923	5.25	5.00	
	deep green	5.25	5.00	
	Never hinged	11.00		
	On commercial cover		100.00	
	On philatelic cover		8.50	

	Pair	11.50	12.50	
	Never hinged	24.00		
	Block of 4	23.00	27.50	
	Corner margin block of 4	26.00	27.50	
	Margin block of 4, arrow	28.00	30.00	
	Center line block	40.00	40.00	
	P# block of 6	70.00		
	Never hinged	100.00		

Earliest documented use: Mar. 16, 1923.

576 A156	1½c **yellow brown,** Apr. 4, 1925	1.30	1.50	
	pale yellow brown	1.30	1.50	
	brown	1.30	1.50	
	Never hinged	2.70		
	On commercial cover		25.00	
	On philatelic cover		6.00	
	Pair	2.90	3.75	
	Never hinged	6.00		
	Block of 4	5.80	8.50	
	Corner margin block of 4	6.00	8.00	
	Margin block of 4, arrow	6.25	10.00	
	Center line block	11.00	20.00	
	P# block of 6	25.00		
	Never hinged	40.00		
	Double transfer	—	—	

The 1½c A156 Rotary press imperforate is listed as No. 631.

577 A157	2c **carmine**	1.40	1.25	
	light carmine	1.40	1.25	
	Never hinged	2.90		
	On commercial cover		20.00	
	On philatelic cover		6.00	
	Pair	3.00	3.00	
	Never hinged	6.25		
	Block of 4	6.00	7.00	
	Corner margin block of 4	6.25	8.00	
	Margin block of 4, arrow	6.50	10.00	
	Center line block	13.00	15.00	
	P# block of 6	25.00		
	Never hinged	40.00		
	P# block of 6, large 5 point star	67.50	—	
	Never hinged	95.00		
	Nos. 575-577 (3)	7.95	7.75	
	Nos. 575-577, never hinged	16.60		

ROTARY PRESS PRINTINGS
(See note over No. 448)
Issued in sheets of 70, 100 or 170 stamps, coil waste of Nos. 597, 599
Stamp designs: 19¾x22¼mm

1923			**Perf. 11x10**	
578 A155	1c **green**	85.00	160.00	
	Never hinged	180.00		
	On cover		700.00	
	Block of 4	360.00	1,000.	
	P# block of 4, star	875.00		
	Never hinged	1,350.		

Earliest documented use: Nov. 7, 1923.

579 A157	2c **carmine**	80.00	140.00	
	deep carmine	80.00	140.00	
	Never hinged	170.00		
	Block of 4	340.00	1,750.	
	On cover		400.00	
	P# block of 4, star	600.00		
	Never hinged	1,000.		
	Recut in eye, plate 14731	110.00	150.00	

Earliest documented use: Feb. 20, 1923.

Warning: See note following No. 459 regarding used stamps.

Plates of 400 subjects in four panes of 100 each
Stamp designs: 19¼x22½mm

1923-26 *Perf. 10*

581 A155	1c **green**, *Apr. 21, 1923*	11.00	.75
	yellow green	11.00	.75
	pale green	11.00	.75
	Never hinged	22.50	
	On postcard		.85
	On 3rd class cover		1.35
	Block of 4	47.50	4.50
	P# block of 4	160.00	
	Never hinged	225.00	

Earliest documented use: May 18, 1923.

582 A156	1½c **brown**, *Mar. 19, 1925*	5.50	.65
	dark brown	5.50	.65
	Never hinged	11.50	
	On 3rd class cover		6.00
	Block of 4	24.00	4.00
	P# block of 4	75.00	
	Never hinged	110.00	
	Pair with full horiz. gutter btwn.	160.00	
	Pair with full vert. gutter btwn.	210.00	

No. 582 was available in full sheets of 400 subjects but was not regularly issued in that form.

583 A157	2c **carmine**, *Apr. 14, 1924*	2.75	.30
	deep carmine	2.75	.30
	Never hinged	5.75	
	On cover		2.50
	Block of 4	13.00	2.00
	P# block of 4	60.00	
	Never hinged	95.00	
a.	Booklet pane of 6, *Aug. 27, 1926*	95.00	150.00
	Never hinged	175.00	

Earliest documented use (unprecanceled): May 15, 1924.

584 A158	3c **violet**, *Aug. 1, 1925*	30.00	3.00
	Never hinged	62.50	
	On postcard (UPU rate)		12.50
	Block of 4	140.00	17.50
	P# block of 4	275.00	
	Never hinged	425.00	
585 A159	4c **yellow brown**, *Mar. 1925*	18.00	.65
	deep yellow brown	18.00	.65
	Never hinged	37.50	
	On cover		15.00
	Block of 4	80.00	4.00
	P# block of 4	275.00	
	Never hinged	425.00	
586 A160	5c **blue**, *Dec. 1924*	18.00	.40
	deep blue	18.00	.40
	Never hinged	37.50	
	On UPU-rate cover		6.00
	Block of 4	80.00	3.00
	P# block of 4	275.00	
	Never hinged	425.00	
	Double transfer	—	—
a.	Horizontal pair, imperf. vertically		8,000.

No. 586a is unique, precanceled, with average centering and small faults, and it is valued as such.

587 A161	6c **red orange**, *Mar. 1925*	9.25	.60
	pale red orange	9.25	.60
	Never hinged	20.00	
	On registered cover with other values		15.00
	Block of 4	40.00	4.00
	P# block of 4	200.00	
	Never hinged	300.00	
588 A162	7c **black**, *May 29, 1926*	12.50	6.25
	Never hinged	26.00	
	On registered cover with other values		30.00
	Block of 4	57.50	45.00
	P# block of 4	175.00	
	Never hinged	275.00	
589 A163	8c **olive green**, *May 29, 1926*	27.50	4.50
	pale olive green	27.50	4.50
	Never hinged	57.50	
	On airmail cover		22.50
	Block of 4	125.00	25.00
	P# block of 4	300.00	
	Never hinged	450.00	
590 A164	9c **rose**, *May 29, 1926*	6.00	2.50
	Never hinged	13.00	
	On registered cover with other values		22.50
	Block of 4	26.00	17.50
	P# block of 4	125.00	
	Never hinged	200.00	
591 A165	10c **orange**, *June 8, 1925*	60.00	.50
	Never hinged	125.00	
	On airmail cover		17.50
	Block of 4	275.00	3.00
	P# block of 4	475.00	
	Never hinged	750.00	
	Nos. 581-591 (11)	200.50	20.10
	Nos. 581-591, never hinged	433.75	

Bureau Precancels: 1c, 64 diff., 1½c, 76 diff., 2c, 58 diff., 3c, 41 diff., 4c, 36 diff., 5c, 38 diff., 6c, 36 diff., 7c, 18 diff., 8c, 18 diff., 9c, 13 diff., 10c, 39 diff.

Issued in sheets of 70 or 100 stamps, coil waste of Nos. 597, 599
Stamp designs approximately 19¾x22¼mm

1923 *Perf. 11*

594 A155	1c **green**	16,000.	6,750.
	On cover		17,500.
	Pair		14,500.

No. 594 unused is valued without gum; both unused and used are valued with perforations just touching frameline on one side.

Earliest documented use: Mar. 25, 1924.

595 A157	2c **carmine**	275.00	350.00
	deep carmine	275.00	350.00
	Never hinged	550.00	
	On cover		550.00
	Block of 4	1,200.	1,750.
	P# block of 4, star	2,150.	—
	Never hinged	3,100.	
	Recut in eye, plate 14731	—	

Earliest documented uses: Mar. 31, 1923 (dated cancel on off-cover pair of stamps); June 29, 1923 (on cover).

Rotary press sheet waste
Stamp design approximately 19¼x22½mm

596 A155	1c **green**, machine cancel	130,000.	
	With Bureau precancel	110,000.	

A majority of copies of No. 596 carry the Bureau precancel "Kansas City, Mo."
No. 596 is valued in the grade of fine.

COIL STAMPS
ROTARY PRESS

1923-29 *Perf. 10 Vertically*
Stamp designs aproximately 19¾x22¼mm

597 A155	1c **green**, *July 18, 1923*	.25	.20
	yellow green	.25	.20
	Never hinged	.50	
	Three on cover		2.25
	Pair	.55	.25
	Never hinged	1.20	
	Joint line pair	2.00	.75
	Never hinged	4.00	
	Gripper cracks	2.60	1.00
	Double transfer	2.60	1.00
598 A156	1½c **brown**, *Mar. 19, 1925*	.90	.20
	deep brown	.90	.20
	Never hinged	1.80	
	On 3rd class cover		6.00
	Pair	1.90	.25
	Never hinged	3.80	
	Joint line pair	4.50	.75
	Never hinged	9.00	

TYPE I

TYPE II

TYPE I

TYPE II

TYPE I. No heavy hair lines at top center of head. Outline of left acanthus scroll generally faint at top and toward base at left side.
TYPE II. Three heavy hair lines at top center of head; two being outstanding in the white area. Outline of left acanthus scroll very strong and clearly defined at top (under left edge of lettered panel) and at lower curve (above and to left of numeral oval). This type appears only on Nos. 599A and 634A.

599 A157	2c **carmine**, type I, *Jan. 1923*	.35	.20
	deep carmine, type I	.35	.20
	Never hinged	.70	
	On cover		1.10
	Pair, type I	.75	.20
	Never hinged	1.50	

	Joint line pair, type I	2.25	.5
	Never hinged	4.50	
	Double transfer, type I	1.90	1.0
	Gripper cracks, type I	2.30	2.0
b.	2c carmine lake, type I, never hinged	650.00	
	Pair, never hinged	1,400.	
	Joint line pair, never hinged		

Earliest documented use: Jan. 10, 1923 (precanceled version).

599A A157	2c **carmine**, type II, *Mar. 1929*	120.00	11.0
	Never hinged	225.00	
	On cover		30.0
	Pair, type II	240.00	30.0
	Never hinged	475.00	
	Joint line pair, type II	650.00	225.00
	Never hinged	1,300.	
	Joint line pair, types I & II	750.00	1,000
	Never hinged	1,400.	

Earliest documented use: Mar. 29, 1929.

600 A158	3c **violet**, *May 10, 1924*	6.25	.20
	deep violet	6.25	.20
	Never hinged	12.50	
	On cover		6.00
	Pair	13.00	.35
	Never hinged	25.00	
	Joint line pair	22.50	2.50
	Never hinged	45.00	
	Cracked plate	—	
601 A159	4c **yellow brown**, *Aug. 5, 1923*	3.75	.35
	brown	3.75	.35
	Never hinged	7.50	
	On cover		14.00
	Pair	8.25	.95
	Never hinged	16.50	
	Joint line pair	27.50	6.00
	Never hinged	55.00	

Earliest documented use: Sept. 14, 1923.

602 A160	5c **dark blue**, *Mar. 5, 1924*	1.50	.20
	Never hinged	3.00	
	On UPU-rate cover		6.00
	Pair	3.25	.35
	Never hinged	6.50	
	Joint line pair	9.50	1.50
	Never hinged	19.00	
603 A165	10c **orange**, *Dec. 1, 1924*	3.50	.20
	Never hinged	7.00	
	On special delivery cover with 2c		22.50
	Pair	8.00	.25
	Never hinged	16.00	
	Joint line pair	25.00	2.00
	Never hinged	50.00	

The 6c design A161 coil stamp is listed as No. 723.
Bureau Precancels: 1c, 296 diff., 1½c, 188 diff., 2c, type I, 113 diff., 2c, type II, Boston, Detroit, 3c, 62 diff., 4c, 34 diff., 5c, 36 diff., 10c, 32 diff.

1923-25 *Perf. 10 Horizontally*
Stamp designs: 19¼x22½mm

604 A155	1c **green**, *July 19, 1924*	.30	.20
	yellow green	.30	.20
	Never hinged	.60	
	Three on cover		6.00
	Pair	.70	.20
	Never hinged	1.40	
	Joint line pair	3.50	.55
	Never hinged	7.00	
605 A156	1½c **yellow brown**, *May 9, 1925*	.30	.20
	brown	.30	.20
	Never hinged	.60	
	On 3rd class cover		17.50
	Pair	.70	.35
	Never hinged	1.40	
	Joint line pair	3.00	.75
	Never hinged	6.00	
606 A157	2c **carmine**, *Dec. 31, 1923*	.30	.20
	Never hinged	.60	
	On cover		3.50
	Pair	.65	.45
	Never hinged	1.40	
	Joint line pair	2.25	1.00
	Never hinged	4.50	
	Cracked plate	5.25	2.00
a.	2c carmine lake, never hinged	350.00	
	Pair, never hinged	750.00	
	Joint line pair, never hinged	2,750.	
	Nos. 597-599,600-606 (10)	17.40	2.15
	Nos. 597-599, 600-606, never hinged	34.80	

HARDING MEMORIAL ISSUE
Tribute to the memory of President Warren G. Harding, who died in San Francisco, Aug. 2, 1923.

Warren Gamaliel
Harding — A177

Plates of 400 subjects in four panes of 100 each
FLAT PLATE PRINTINGS
Stamp designs: 19¼x22¼mm

1923				**Perf. 11**	
610	A177	2c	**black,** *Sept. 1, 1923*	.55	.25
			intense black	.55	.25
			grayish black	.55	.25
			Never hinged	1.10	
			On cover		.30
			P# block of 6	20.00	—
			Never hinged	30.00	
			Double transfer	1.75	.50
a.			Horiz. pair, imperf. vert.	1,750.	

Imperf

611	A177	2c	**black,** *Nov. 15, 1923*	5.00	4.00
			Never hinged	10.50	
			On philatelic cover		8.00
			On commercial cover		15.00
			Pair	11.00	10.00
			Never hinged	23.00	
			Corner margin block of 4	24.00	22.50
			Margin block of 4, arrow	25.00	22.50
			Center line block	60.00	40.00
			P# block of 6	70.00	—
			Never hinged	95.00	

ROTARY PRESS PRINTINGS
Stamp designs: 19¼x22½mm
Perf. 10

612	A177	2c	**black,** *Sept. 12, 1923*	15.00	1.75
			gray black	15.00	1.75
			Never hinged	32.50	
			On cover		3.25
			P# block of 4	300.00	
			Never hinged	475.00	
			Pair with full vertical gutter between	350.00	

Perf. 11

613	A177	2c	**black**	45,000.	
			Pair	95,000.	

No. 613 was produced from rotary press sheet waste. It is valued in the grade of fine.

Ship "Nieu Nederland"
A178

Walloons Landing at Fort Orange (Albany) — A179

Jan Ribault Monument at Duval County, Fla. — A180

"Broken Circle" flaw

Designed by Clair Aubrey Huston

FLAT PLATE PRINTINGS
Plates of 200 subjects in four panes of 50 each

1924, May 1				**Perf. 11**	
614	A178	1c	**dark green**	2.25	3.25
			green	2.25	3.25
			Never hinged	4.25	
			On cover		4.50
			P# block of 6	42.50	—
			Never hinged	75.00	
			Double transfer	6.50	6.50
615	A179	2c	**carmine rose**	4.50	2.25
			dark carmine rose	4.50	2.25
			Never hinged	8.75	
			On cover		3.50
			P# block of 6	60.00	—
			Never hinged	90.00	
			Double transfer	12.00	3.50
616	A180	5c	**dark blue**	19.00	13.00
			deep blue	19.00	13.00
			Never hinged	37.50	
			On UPU-rate cover		20.00
			P# block of 6	225.00	—
			Never hinged	375.00	
			Added line at bottom of white circle around right numeral, "broken circle" plate flaw (15754 UR 2, 3, 4, 5)	45.00	15.00
			Nos. 614-616 (3)	25.75	18.50
			Nos. 614-616, never hinged	50.50	

LEXINGTON-CONCORD ISSUE

150th anniv. of the Battle of Lexington-Concord.

Washington at Cambridge

A182

The Minute Man, by Daniel Chester French — A183

Plates of 200 subjects in four panes of 50 each

1925, Apr. 4				**Perf. 11**	
617	A181	1c	**deep green**	2.00	2.50
			green	2.00	2.50
			Never hinged	4.00	
			On cover		3.75
			P# block of 6	40.00	—
			Never hinged	65.00	
618	A182	2c	**carmine rose**	4.25	4.00
			pale carmine rose	4.25	4.00
			Never hinged	8.00	
			On cover		5.50
			P# block of 6	60.00	—
			Never hinged	90.00	
619	A183	5c	**dark blue**	17.50	13.00
			blue	17.50	13.00
			Never hinged	35.00	
			On UPU-rate cover		20.00
			P# block of 6	225.00	—
			Never hinged	330.00	
			Line over head (16807 LL 48)	42.50	19.00
			Nos. 617-619 (3)	23.75	19.50
			Nos. 617-619, never hinged	47.00	

NORSE-AMERICAN ISSUE

Arrival in New York, on Oct. 9, 1825, of the sloop "Restaurationen" with the first group of immigrants from Norway.

Sloop "Restaurationen"
A184

Viking Ship
A185

Designed by Clair Aubrey Huston.

Plates of 100 subjects.

1925, May 18 — *Perf. 11*

620	A184	2c	**carmine & black**	3.75 3.00
			deep carmine & black	3.75 3.00
			Never hinged	7.00
			On cover	4.50
			Margin block of 4, arrow	17.50
			Center line block	24.00
			P# block of 8, two P# & arrow	200.00 —
			Never hinged	300.00 —
			P# block of 8, carmine & arrow; black P# omitted	3,250. —
621	A185	5c	**dark blue & black**	12.00 11.00
			Never hinged	24.00
			On UPU-rate cover	17.50
			Margin block of 4, arrow	62.50
			Center line block	75.00
			P# block of 8, two P# & arrow	500.00 —
			Never hinged	700.00

REGULAR ISSUE

Benjamin Harrison — A186

Woodrow Wilson — A187

Plates of 400 subjects in four panes of 100.

1925-26 — *Perf. 11*

622	A186	13c	**green**, *Jan. 11, 1926*	12.00 .75
			light green	12.00 .75
			Never hinged	22.50
			On registered cover with other values	17.50
			P# block of 6	200.00 —
			Never hinged	300.00 —
			P# block of 6, large 5 point star, right side only	2,100. —
			Never hinged	2,750.
623	A187	17c	**black**, *Dec. 28, 1925*	13.00 .30
			gray black	13.00 .30
			Never hinged	25.00
			On registered cover	6.00
			P# block of 6	220.00 —
			Never hinged	325.00

Plate Blocks

Scott values for plate blocks printed from flat plates are for very fine side and bottom positions. Top position plate blocks with full wide selvage sell for more.

SESQUICENTENNIAL EXPOSITION ISSUE

Sesquicentennial Exposition, Philadelphia, Pa., June 1 - Dec. 1, 1926, and 150th anniv. of the Declaration of Independence.

Liberty Bell — A188

Designed by Clair Aubrey Huston.

Plates of 200 subjects in four panes of 50.

1926, May 10 — *Perf. 11*

627	A188	2c	**carmine rose**	2.75 .50
			Never hinged	4.50
			On cover	1.00
			On cover, Expo. station machine canc.	7.50
			On cover, Expo. station duplex handstamp canc.	35.00
			P# block of 6	37.50 —
			Never hinged	50.00
			Double transfer	— —

ERICSSON MEMORIAL ISSUE

Unveiling of the statue of John Ericsson, builder of the "Monitor," by the Crown Prince of Sweden, Washington, D.C., May 29, 1926.

Statue of John Ericsson — A189

Designed by Clair Aubrey Huston.

Plates of 200 subjects in four panes of 50.

1926, May 29 — *Perf. 11*

628	A189	5c	**gray lilac**	6.00 3.25
			Never hinged	9.50
			On UPU-rate cover	8.00
			P# block of 6	60.00 —
			Never hinged	95.00

BATTLE OF WHITE PLAINS ISSUE

150th anniv. of the Battle of White Plains, N. Y.

Alexander Hamilton's Battery — A190

Designed by Clair Aubrey Huston.

Plates of 400 subjects in four panes of 100.

1926, Oct. 18 — *Perf. 11*

629	A190	2c	**carmine rose**	2.00 1.70
			Never hinged	3.25
			On cover	2.25
			P# block of 6	40.00 —
			Never hinged	62.50

INTERNATIONAL PHILATELIC EXHIBITION ISSUE
Souvenir Sheet

A190a

Illustration reduced.
Plates of 100 subjects in four panes of 25 each, separated by one inch wide gutters with central guide lines.
Condition valued:
Centering: Overall centering will average very fine, but individual stamps may be better or worse.
Perforations: No folds along rows of perforations.
Gum: There may be some light gum bends but no gum creases.
Hinging: There may be hinge marks in the selvage and on up to two or three stamps, but no heavy hinging or hinge remnants (except in the ungummed portion of the wide selvage.
Margins: Top panes should have about ½ inch bottom margin and 1 inch top margin.
Bottom panes should have about ½ inch top margin and just under ¾ inch bottom margin. Both will have one wide side (usually 1 inch plus) and one narrow (½ inch) side margin. The wide margin corner will have a small diagonal notch on top panes.

1926, Oct. 18 — *Perf. 11*

630	A190a	2c	**carmine rose**, sheet of 25	375.00 450.00
			Never hinged	600.00
			On cover	—

Dot over first "S" of "States" 18774 LL 9 or 18773 LL 11, sheet 400.00 475.00

Issued in sheets measuring 158-160¼x136-146½mm con taining 25 stamps with inscription "International Philatelic Exh. bition, Oct. 16th to 23rd, 1926" in top margin.

VALUES FOR VERY FINE STAMPS
Please note: Stamps are valued in the grade o Very Fine unless otherwise indicated.

REGULAR ISSUE
ROTARY PRESS PRINTINGS
(See note over No. 448.)
Plates of 400 subjects in four panes of 100 each
Stamp designs 19¼x22½mm

1926, Aug. 27 — *Imperf.*

631	A156	1½c	**yellow brown**	1.90 1.70
			light brown	1.90 1.70
			Never hinged	2.75
			On philatelic cover	12.50
			Pair	4.00 4.00
			Never hinged	5.75
			Pair, vert. gutter between	4.50 5.00
			Pair, horiz. gutter between	4.50 5.00
			Margin block with dash (left, right, top or bottom)	10.00 14.00
			Center block with crossed gutters and dashes	25.00 27.50
			P# block of 4	57.50
			Never hinged	85.00
			Without gum breaker ridges	80.00
			Pair, vert. gutter between	200.00
			Pair, horiz. gutter btwn.	200.00
			Margin block with dash (left, right, top or bottom)	550.00
			Center block with crossed gutters and dashes	1,250.
			Never hinged	1,750.
			P# block of 4	700.00
			Never hinged	1,100.

1926-34 — *Perf. 11x10½*

632	A155	1c	**green**, *June 10, 1927*	.20 .20
			yellow green	.20 .20
			Never hinged	.20
			Three on cover	1.25
			P# block of 4	2.00
			Never hinged	3.00
			Pair with full vertical gutter btwn.	150.00 —
			Cracked plate	— —
a.			Booklet pane of 6, *Nov. 2, 1927*	5.00 4.00
			Never hinged	8.00
b.			Vertical pair, imperf. between	3,500. 125.00
			Never hinged	5,500.
c.			Horiz. pair, imperf. between	5,000.

No. 632c is valued in the grade of fine and never hinged. It is possibly unique.

633	A156	1½c	**yellow brown**, *May 17, 1927*	1.70 .20
			deep brown	1.70 .20
			Never hinged	2.60
			On 3rd class cover	2.50
			P# block of 4	70.00
			Never hinged	120.00

Normal

Recut ("long ear")

634	A157	2c	**carmine**, type I, *Dec. 10, 1926*	.20 .20
			Never hinged	.20
			On cover	.20
			P# block of 4, type I, # opposite corner stamp	3.25

	Never hinged		5.25	

Vertical P# block of 10, # opposite 3rd horizontal row from top or bottom (Experimental Electric Eye plates) 5.00 —
Never hinged 7.50
Margin block of 4, Electric Eye marking .45 .25
Pair with full vertical gutter between 200.00
Recut ("long ear"), type I, 20342 UR 34 400.00 —
Recut face, type I, 20234 LL 58 —
b. 2c **carmine lake,** type I 700.00 —
Never hinged 1,200.
P# block of 4 —
c. Horizontal pair, type I, imperf. between 7,000.
d. Booklet pane of 6, type I, *Feb. 25, 1927* 1.50 1.50
Never hinged 2.50
e. As "d," carmine lake 2,000.
Never hinged 4,000.

Shades of the carmine exist.
No. 634, Type I, exists on a thin, tough experimental paper.
No. 634c is valued in the grade of fine.

Earliest documented use: FDC (No. 634); Dec. 20, 1929 (No. 634b).

634A A157 2c **carmine,** type II, *Dec. 1928* 350.00 13.50
Never hinged 650.00
On cover 21.00
P# block of 4, type II 2,200.
Never hinged 3,000.
Pair with full horiz. gutter btwn. 850.00 —
Never hinged 1,400.
Pair with full vert. gutter btwn. 850.00 —
Never hinged 1,400.
Center block with crossed gutters 2,750.
Never hinged 4,250.

Earliest documented use: Dec. 15, 1928.

No. 634A, Type II, was available in full sheet of 400 subjects but was not regularly issued in that form.

635 A158 3c **violet,** *Feb. 3, 1927* .45 .20
Never hinged .60
On cover 2.00
P# block of 4 17.50 —
Never hinged 32.50
a. 3c **bright violet,** *Feb. 7, 1934* re-issue, Plates 21185 & 21186 .20 .20
Never hinged .30
On cover .25
P# block of 4 11.00 —
Never hinged 20.00
Gripper cracks 3.25 2.00
636 A159 4c **yellow brown,** *May 17, 1927* 2.00 .20
Never hinged 3.00
On cover 8.00
P# block of 4 75.00 —
Never hinged 120.00
Pair with full vert. gutter btwn. 200.00
637 A160 5c **dark blue,** *Mar. 24, 1927* 2.00 .20
Never hinged 3.00
On UPU-rate cover 4.50
P# block of 4 17.50 —
Never hinged 25.00
Pair with full vert. gutter btwn. 275.00
Double transfer —
638 A161 6c **red orange,** *July 27, 1927* 2.00 .20
Never hinged 3.00
On airmail cover 6.00
P# block of 4 15.00 —
Never hinged 22.50
Pair with full horiz. gutter btwn. —
Pair with full vert. gutter btwn. 200.00
639 A162 7c **black,** *Mar. 24, 1927* 2.00 .20
Never hinged 3.00
On registered cover with other values 15.00
P# block of 4 15.00 —
Never hinged 22.50
a. Vertical pair, imperf. between 325.00 250.00
Never hinged 500.00
640 A163 8c **olive green,** *June 10, 1927* 2.00 .20
olive bister 2.00 .20
Never hinged 3.00
On airmail cover 8.00
P# block of 4 14.00 —
Never hinged 21.00
641 A164 9c **rose,** *May 17, 1927* 2.00 .20
salmon rose 2.00 .20
orange red, *1931* 2.00 .20
Never hinged 3.00
On registered cover with other values 8.00
P# block of 4 13.00 —
Never hinged 22.50
Pair with full vert. gutter btwn. —
642 A165 10c **orange,** *Feb. 3, 1927* 3.25 .20
Never hinged 5.00
On special delivery cover with 2c 6.00
P# block of 4 22.50 —

Never hinged 30.00
Double transfer 2.20
Nos. 632-634,635-642 (11) 17.80
Nos. 632-634, 635-642 never hinged 26.60

The 1½c, 2c, 4c, 5c, 6c, 8c imperf. (dry print) are printer's waste.
See No. 653.
Bureau Precancels: 1c, 292 diff., 1½c, 147 diff., 2c, type I, 99 diff., 2c, type II, 4 diff., 3c, 101 diff., 4c, 60 diff., 5c, 91 diff., 6c, 78 diff., 7c, 66 diff., 8c, 78 diff., 9c, 60 diff., 10c, 97 diff.

VERMONT SESQUICENTENNIAL ISSUE

Battle of Bennington, 150th anniv. and State independence.

Green Mountain Boy — A191

FLAT PLATE PRINTING
Plates of 400 subjects in four panes of 100.

1927, Aug. 3 *Perf. 11*
643 A191 2c **carmine rose** 1.20 .80
Never hinged 2.00
On cover 1.50
P# block of 6 35.00 —
Never hinged 55.00

BURGOYNE CAMPAIGN ISSUE

Battles of Bennington, Oriskany, Fort Stanwix and Saratoga.

"The Surrender of General Burgoyne at Saratoga," by John Trumbull A192

Plates of 200 subjects in four panes of 50.

1927, Aug. 3 *Perf. 11*
644 A192 2c **carmine rose** 3.25 2.10
Never hinged 5.50
On cover 3.00
P# block of 6 32.50 —
Never hinged 45.00

VALLEY FORGE ISSUE

150th anniversary of Washington's encampment at Valley Forge, Pa.

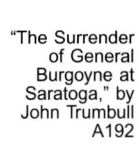

Washington at Prayer — A193

Plates of 400 subjects in four panes of 100.

1928, May 26 *Perf. 11*
645 A193 2c **carmine rose** 1.00 .50
Never hinged 1.50
On cover .75
P# block of 6 25.00 —
Never hinged 40.00
a. 2c **lake** —
Never hinged —

BATTLE OF MONMOUTH ISSUE

150th anniv. of the Battle of Monmouth, N.J., and "Molly Pitcher" (Mary Ludwig Hayes), the heroine of the battle.

No. 634 Overprinted

ROTARY PRESS PRINTING

1928, Oct. 20 *Perf. 11x10½*
646 A157 2c **carmine** 1.10 1.10
Never hinged 1.60
On cover 1.60
P# block of 4 37.50 —
Never hinged 55.00
Wide spacing, vert. pair 50.00
a. "Pitcher" only 500.00

No. 646a is valued in the grade of fine.
The normal space between a vertical pair of the overprints is 18mm, but pairs are known with the space measuring 28mm.

HAWAII SESQUICENTENNIAL ISSUE

Sesquicentennial Celebration of the discovery of the Hawaiian Islands.

Nos. 634 and 637 Overprinted

ROTARY PRESS PRINTING

1928, Aug. 13 *Perf. 11x10½*
647 A157 2c **carmine** 4.50 4.50
Never hinged 7.25
On cover 5.75
P# block of 4 150.00 —
Never hinged 250.00
Wide spacing, vert. pair 125.00
648 A160 5c **dark blue** 12.50 13.50
Never hinged 21.50
On cover 20.00
P# block of 4 275.00 —
Never hinged 425.00

Nos. 647-648 were sold at post offices in Hawaii and at the Postal Agency in Washington, D.C. They were valid throughout the nation.
Normally the overprints were placed 18mm apart vertically, but pairs exist with a space of 28mm between the overprints.

AERONAUTICS CONFERENCE ISSUE

Intl. Civil Aeronautics Conf., Washington, D.C., Dec. 12 - 14, 1928, and 25th anniv. of the 1st airplane flight by the Wright Brothers, Dec. 17, 1903.

Wright Airplane A194

Globe and
Airplane
A195

"Prairie
Dog"
plate
flaw

FLAT PLATE PRINTING
Plates of 200 subjects in four panes of 50.

1928, Dec. 12			Perf. 11	
649 A194	2c carmine rose		1.10	.80
	Never hinged		1.75	
	On cover			1.50
	P# block of 6		10.00	—
	Never hinged		17.50	
650 A195	5c blue		4.50	3.25
	Never hinged		7.25	
	On UPU-rate cover			5.00
	P# block of 6		45.00	—
	Never hinged		70.00	
	Plate flaw "prairie dog" (19658 LL 50)		27.50	12.50

GEORGE ROGERS CLARK ISSUE
150th anniv. of the surrender of Fort Sackville, the present site of Vincennes, Ind., to Clark.

Surrender of
Fort Sackville
A196

Plates of 100 subjects in two panes of 50.

1929, Feb. 25			Perf. 11	
651 A196	2c carmine & black		.75	.50
	Never hinged		1.10	
	On cover			1.00
	Margin block of 4, arrow (line only) right or left		3.25	
	P# block of 6, two P# & "Top"		10.50	—
	Never hinged		16.00	
	P# block of 10, red P# only			—
	Double transfer (19721 R 14, 29 & 44)		4.25	2.25

REGULAR ISSUE
Type of 1922-26 Issue
ROTARY PRESS PRINTING
Plates of 400 subjects in four panes of 100.

1929, May 25			Perf. 11x10½	
653 A154	½c olive brown		.20	.20
	Never hinged		.25	
	On 1c stamped envelope (3rd class)			1.00
	P# block of 4		1.60	—
	Never hinged		2.75	
	Damaged plate, (19652 LL 72)		1.50	.75
	Retouched plate, (19652 LL 72)		1.50	.75
	Pair with full horiz. gutter btwn.		150.00	

Bureau Precancels: 99 diff.

Edison's First
Lamp — A197

Major General John
Sullivan — A198

ELECTRIC LIGHT'S GOLDEN JUBILEE ISSUE
Invention of the 1st incandescent electric lamp by Thomas Alva Edison, Oct. 21, 1879, 50th anniv.

Designed by Alvin R. Meissner.

FLAT PLATE PRINTING
Plates of 400 subjects in four panes of 100.

1929			Perf. 11	
654 A197	2c carmine rose, June 5		.65	.70
	Never hinged		1.00	
	On cover			1.10
	P# block of 6		25.00	—
	Never hinged		45.00	

ROTARY PRESS PRINTING
Perf. 11x10½

655 A197	2c carmine rose, June 11		.60	.20
	Never hinged		.90	
	On cover			.25
	P# block of 4		35.00	—
	Never hinged		55.00	

ROTARY PRESS COIL STAMP
Perf. 10 Vertically

656 A197	2c carmine rose, June 11		13.00	1.75
	Never hinged		21.00	
	On cover			2.75
	Pair		27.50	4.00
	Never hinged		45.00	
	Joint line pair		65.00	27.50
	Never hinged		110.00	

SULLIVAN EXPEDITION ISSUE
150th anniversary of the Sullivan Expedition in New York State during the Revolutionary War.

PLAT PLATE PRINTING
Plates of 400 subjects in four panes of 100.

1929, June 17			Perf. 11	
657 A198	2c carmine rose		.65	.60
	Never hinged		1.00	
	On cover			1.00
	P# block of 6		22.50	—
	Never hinged		37.50	
a.	2c lake		360.00	300.00
	Never hinged		575.00	
	P# block of 6		2,750.	
	Never hinged		3,750.	

REGULAR ISSUE

Nos. 632 to 642 Overprinted

Officially issued May 1, 1929.
Some values known canceled as early as Apr. 15.

This special issue was authorized as a measure of preventing losses from post office burglaries. Approximately a year's supply was printed and issued to postmasters. The P.O. Dept. found it desirable to discontinue the State overprinted stamps after the initial supply was used.

ROTARY PRESS PRINTING

1929, May 1			Perf. 11x10½	
658 A155	1c green		2.25	2.00
	Never hinged		4.00	
	P# block of 4		40.00	—
	Never hinged		60.00	
	Wide spacing, pair		32.50	
a.	Vertical pair, one without ovpt.		375.00	
659 A156	1½c brown		3.75	2.90
	Never hinged		6.25	
	P# block of 4		50.00	—
	Never hinged		75.00	
	Wide spacing, pair		70.00	
a.	Vertical pair, one without ovpt.		425.00	
660 A157	2c carmine		4.25	1.00
	Never hinged		7.00	
	P# block of 4		50.00	—
	Never hinged		75.00	
	Wide spacing, pair		55.00	
661 A158	3c violet		20.00	15.00
	Never hinged		37.50	
	P# block of 4		200.00	—
	Never hinged		300.00	
a.	Vertical pair, one without ovpt.		525.00	

662 A159	4c yellow brown		20.00	9.00
	Never hinged		675.00	
	Never hinged		37.50	
	P# block of 4		200.00	—
	Never hinged		300.00	
a.	Vertical pair, one without ovpt.		500.00	
663 A160	5c deep blue		12.50	9.75
	Never hinged		24.00	
	P# block of 4		150.00	—
	Never hinged		250.00	
664 A161	6c red orange		30.00	18.00
	Never hinged		55.00	
	P# block of 4		450.00	—
	Never hinged		650.00	
665 A162	7c black		30.00	27.50
	Never hinged		55.00	
	P# block of 4		500.00	—
	Never hinged		725.00	
666 A163	8c olive green		95.00	70.00
	Never hinged		180.00	
	P# block of 4		800.00	—
	Never hinged		1,200.	
667 A164	9c light rose		14.00	11.25
	Never hinged		26.00	
	P# block of 4		250.00	—
	Never hinged		375.00	
668 A165	10c orange yellow		25.00	12.00
	Never hinged		45.00	
	P# block of 4		350.00	—
	Never hinged		550.00	
	Pair with full horizontal gutter between		4,750.	
	Nos. 658-668 (11)		256.75	178.40
	Nos. 658-668, never hinged		477.25	

See notes following No. 679.

Overprinted

1929, May 1				
669 A155	1c green		3.75	2.25
	Never hinged		6.25	
	P# block of 4		50.00	—
	Never hinged		75.00	
	Wide spacing, pair		40.00	—
b.	No period after "Nebr." (19338, 19339 UR 26, 36)		50.00	
670 A156	1½c brown		3.50	2.50
	Never hinged		5.75	
	P# block of 4		55.00	—
	Never hinged		80.00	
	Wide spacing, pair		37.50	
671 A157	2c carmine		3.50	1.30
	Never hinged		5.75	
	P# block of 4		42.50	—
	Never hinged		65.00	
	Wide spacing, pair		57.50	
672 A158	3c violet		13.50	12.00
	Never hinged		24.00	
	P# block of 4		175.00	—
	Never hinged		275.00	
	Wide spacing, pair		80.00	
a.	Vertical pair, one without ovpt.		500.00	
673 A159	4c yellow brown		20.00	15.00
	Never hinged		35.00	
	P# block of 4		250.00	—
	Never hinged		360.00	
	Wide spacing, pair		120.00	
674 A160	5c deep blue		18.00	15.00
	Never hinged		32.50	
	P# block of 4		275.00	—
	Never hinged		400.00	
675 A161	6c red orange		42.50	24.00
	Never hinged		75.00	
	P# block of 4		525.00	—
	Never hinged		750.00	
676 A162	7c black		22.50	18.00
	Never hinged		42.50	
	P# block of 4		300.00	—
	Never hinged		500.00	
677 A163	8c olive green		35.00	25.00
	Never hinged		65.00	
	P# block of 4		400.00	—
	Never hinged		600.00	
	Wide spacing, pair		175.00	
678 A164	9c light rose		40.00	27.50
	Never hinged		70.00	
	P# block of 4		525.00	—
	Never hinged		750.00	
	Wide spacing, pair		160.00	
a.	Vertical pair, one without ovpt.		750.00	
679 A165	10c orange yellow		120.00	22.50
	Never hinged		230.00	
	P# block of 4		925.	
	Never hinged		1,300.	
	Nos. 669-679 (11)		322.25	165.05
	Nos. 669-679, never hinged		591.75	

Nos. 658-661, 669-673, 677-678 are known with the overprints on vertical pairs spaced 32mm apart instead of the normal 22mm.

Important: Nos. 658-679 with original gum have either one horizontal gum breaker ridge per stamp or portions of two at the extreme top and bottom of the stamps, 21mm apart. Multiple complete gum breaker ridges indicate a fake overprint. Absence of the gum breaker ridge indicates either regumming or regumming and a fake overprint.

General Wayne
Memorial — A199

Lock No. 5,
Monongahela
River — A200

BATTLE OF FALLEN TIMBERS ISSUE

Memorial to Gen. Anthony Wayne and for 135th
anniv. of the Battle of Fallen Timbers, Ohio.

FLAT PLATE PRINTING

Plates of 400 subjects in four panes of 100.

1929, Sept. 14			*Perf. 11*	
680	A199	2c **carmine rose**	.75	.75
		deep carmine rose	.75	.75
		Never hinged	1.10	
		On cover		1.10
		P# block of 6	20.00	—
		Never hinged	32.50	

OHIO RIVER CANALIZATION ISSUE

Completion of the Ohio River Canalization Project,
between Cairo, Ill. and Pittsburgh, Pa.

Plates of 400 subjects in four panes of 100.

1929, Oct. 19			*Perf. 11*	
681	A200	2c **carmine rose**	.65	.65
		Never hinged	.95	
		On cover		1.10
		P# block of 6	14.00	—
		Never hinged	25.00	

Massachusetts Bay
Colony Seal — A201

Gov. Joseph West
and Chief Shadoo, a
Kiowa — A202

MASSACHUSETTS BAY COLONY ISSUE

300th anniversary of the founding of the Massachusetts Bay Colony.

Plates of 400 subjects in four panes of 100.

1930, Apr. 8			*Perf. 11*	
682	A201	2c **carmine rose**	.55	.50
		Never hinged	.85	
		On cover		1.00
		P# block of 6	22.50	—
		Never hinged	35.00	

CAROLINA-CHARLESTON ISSUE

260th anniv. of the founding of the Province of Carolina and the 250th anniv. of the city of Charleston, S.C.

Plates of 400 subjects in four panes of 100.

1930, Apr. 10			*Perf. 11*	
683	A202	2c **carmine rose**	1.10	1.10
		Never hinged	1.65	
		On cover		1.40
		P# block of 6	40.00	—
		Never hinged	57.50	

REGULAR ISSUE

Harding — A203

Taft — A204

Type of 1922-26 Issue
ROTARY PRESS PRINTING

1930			*Perf. 11x10½*	
684	A203	1½c **brown,** *Dec.1*	.35	.20
		yellow brown	.35	.20
		Never hinged	.50	
		On 3rd class cover		2.00
		P# block of 4	1.75	—
		Never hinged	3.00	

		Pair with full horiz. gutter btwn.	*175.00*	
		Pair with full vert. gutter btwn.	—	
685	A204	4c **brown,** *June 4*	.80	.25
		deep brown	.80	.25
		Never hinged	1.25	
		On cover		5.00
		P# block of 4	15.00	—
		Never hinged	25.00	
		Gouge on right "4" (20141 UL 24)	2.10	.60
		Recut right "4" (20141 UL 24)	2.10	.65
		Pair with full horiz. gutter btwn.	—	

Bureau Precancels: 1½c, 96 diff., 4c, 46 diff.

ROTARY PRESS COIL STAMPS
Perf. 10 Vertically

686	A203	1½c **brown,** *Dec. 1*	1.75	.20
		Never hinged	2.50	
		On 3rd class cover		5.00
		Pair	3.60	.20
		Never hinged	5.25	
		Joint line pair	6.50	.75
		Never hinged	10.50	
687	A204	4c **brown,** *Sept. 18*	3.25	.45
		Never hinged	4.50	
		On cover		10.00
		Pair	6.75	1.00
		Never hinged	9.50	
		Joint line pair	13.00	2.50
		Never hinged	20.00	

Bureau Precancels: 1½c, 107 diff., 4c, 23 diff.

Statue of George
Washington — A205

General von
Steuben — A206

BRADDOCK'S FIELD ISSUE

175th anniversary of the Battle of Braddock's Field,
otherwise the Battle of Monongahela.

Designed by Alvin R. Meissner.

FLAT PLATE PRINTING

Plates of 400 subjects in four panes of 100.

1930, July 9			*Perf. 11*	
688	A205	2c **carmine rose**	.90	.85
		Never hinged	1.40	
		On cover		1.00
		P# block of 6	32.50	—
		Never hinged	45.00	

VON STEUBEN ISSUE

Baron Friedrich Wilhelm von Steuben (1730-1794),
participant in the American Revolution.

FLAT PLATE PRINTING

Plates of 400 subjects in four panes of 100.

1930, Sept. 17			*Perf. 11*	
689	A206	2c **carmine rose**	.50	.50
		Never hinged	.75	
		On cover		1.05
		P# block of 6	17.50	—
		Never hinged	30.00	
a.		Imperf., pair	*2,750.*	
		Never hinged	*3,500.*	
		P# block of 6	*12,500.*	

The No. 689a plate block is unique but damaged. The value
is for the item in its damaged condition.

General Casimir
Pulaski — A207

"The Greatest
Mother" — A208

PULASKI ISSUE

150th anniversary (in 1929) of the death of Gen.
Casimir Pulaski, Polish patriot and hero of the American Revolutionary War.

Plates of 400 subjects in four panes of 100.

1931, Jan. 16			*Perf. 11*	
690	A207	2c **carmine rose**	.30	.25
		deep carmine rose	.30	.25
		Never hinged	.40	

		On cover		.50
		P# block of 6	10.00	—
		Never hinged	17.50	

REGULAR ISSUE
TYPE OF 1922-26 ISSUES
ROTARY PRESS PRINTING

1931			*Perf. 11x10½*	
692	A166	11c **light blue,** *Sept. 4*	2.50	.25
		Never hinged	3.75	
		On registered cover with other values		10.00
		P# block of 4	14.00	—
		Never hinged	25.00	
		Retouched forehead (20617 LL 2, 3)	20.00	1.00
693	A167	12c **brown violet,** *Aug. 25*	5.00	.20
		violet brown	5.00	.20
		Never hinged	8.00	
		Pair on registered cover		8.00
		P# block of 4	22.50	—
		Never hinged	40.00	
694	A186	13c **yellow green,** *Sept. 4*	1.90	.25
		light yellow green	1.90	.25
		blue green	1.90	.25
		Never hinged	3.00	
		On special delivery cover		25.00
		P# block of 4	15.00	—
		Never hinged	25.00	
		Pair with full vert. gutter btwn.	150.00	
695	A168	14c **dark blue,** *Sept. 8*	3.50	.45
		Never hinged	5.50	
		On registered cover with other values		20.00
		P# block of 4	26.00	—
		Never hinged	40.00	
696	A169	15c **gray,** *Aug. 27*	7.75	.25
		dark gray	8.00	.25
		Never hinged	12.00	
		On registered cover with 3c		5.00
		P# block of 4	37.50	—
		Never hinged	52.50	

			Perf. 10½x11	
697	A187	17c **black,** *July 25*	4.25	.25
		Never hinged	6.50	
		On registered cover		5.00
		P# block of 4	37.50	—
		Never hinged	52.50	
698	A170	20c **carmine rose,** *Sept. 8*	7.75	.25
		Never hinged	12.00	
		On registered UPU-rate cover		12.50
		P# block of 4	37.50	—
		Never hinged	60.00	
		Double transfer (20538 LR 26)	20.00	—
699	A171	25c **blue green,** *July 25*	8.00	.25
		Never hinged	12.50	
		On Federal airmail cover		20.00
		P# block of 4	47.50	—
		Never hinged	75.00	
700	A172	30c **brown,** *Sept. 8*	14.00	.25
		Never hinged	22.50	
		On Federal airmail cover		17.50
		P# block of 4	75.00	—
		Never hinged	105.00	
		Retouched in head (20552 UL 83)	27.50	.85
		Cracked plate (20552 UR 30)	26.00	.85
701	A173	50c **lilac,** *Sept. 4*	32.50	.25
		red lilac	32.50	.25
		Never hinged	52.50	
		On Federal airmail cover		25.00
		P# block of 4	180.00	—
		Never hinged	250.00	
		Nos. 692-701 (10)	87.15	2.65
		Nos. 692-701, never hinged	137.50	

Bureau Precancels: 11c, 33 diff., 12c, 33 diff., 13c, 28 diff.,
14c, 27 diff., 15c, 33 diff., 17c, 29 diff., 20c, 37 diff., 25c, 29 diff.,
30c, 31 diff., 50c, 28 diff.

RED CROSS ISSUE

50th anniversary of the founding of the American
Red Cross Society.

FLAT PLATE PRINTING

Plates of 200 subjects in two panes of 100.

1931, May 21			*Perf. 11*	
702	A208	2c **black & red**	.20	.20
		Never hinged	.30	
		Margin block of 4, arrow right or left	1.05	
		P# block of 4, two P#	1.90	—
		Never hinged	2.40	
		Double transfer	1.50	.50
a.		Red cross missing (FO)	*40,000.*	

The cross tends to shift, appearing in many slightly varied
positions.
One example of No. 702a is documented; believed to be
unique. Value reflects most recent sale price at auction in 1994.

YORKTOWN ISSUE

Surrender of Cornwallis at Yorktown, 1781.

Rochambeau, Washington, de Grasse A209

First Plate Layout — Border and vignette plates of 100 subjects in two panes of 50 subjects each. Plate numbers between 20461 and 20602.

Second Plate Layout — Border plates of 100 subjects in two panes of 50 each, separated by a 1 inch wide vertical gutter with central guide line and vignette plates of 50 subjects. Plate numbers between 20646 and 20671.

Issued in panes of 50 subjects.

1931, Oct. 19			Perf. 11	
703	A209 2c	**carmine rose & black**	.35	.25
		Never hinged	.50	
		Margin block of 4, arrow marker, right or left	1.70	
		Center line block	1.80	
		P# block of 4, 2#	2.40	—
		Never hinged	3.00	
		P# block of 4, 2# & arrow & marker block	2.50	—
		Never hinged	3.25	
		P# block of 6, 2# & "TOP," arrow & marker	3.00	—
		Never hinged	4.00	
		P# block of 8, 2# & "TOP"	3.75	—
		Never hinged	5.00	
		Double transfer	1.75	.75
a.		2c **lake & black**	4.50	.75
		Never hinged	6.25	
b.		2c **dark lake & black**	450.00	
		Never hinged	800.00	
		P# block of 4, 2#	2,250.	
		Never hinged	3,000.	
c.		Horiz. pair, imperf. vertically	5,000.	
		Never hinged	6,250.	
		Center line block of 10	17,000.	
		P# block of 10, top, 2#, arrow, marker and "TOP," block	28,500.	
		P# block of 10, bottom, 2#, arrow and marker	23,000.	

WASHINGTON BICENTENNIAL ISSUE

200th anniversary of the birth of George Washington. Various Portraits of George Washington.

By Charles Willson Peale, 1777 — A210

From Houdon Bust, 1785 — A211

By Charles Willson Peale, 1772 — A212

By Gilbert Stuart, 1796 — A213

By Charles Willson Peale, 1777 — A214

By Charles Peale Polk — A215

By Charles Willson Peale, 1795 — A216

By John Trumbull, 1780 — A218

By W. Williams, 1794 — A220

By John Trumbull, 1792 — A217

By Charles B. J. F. Saint Memin, 1798 — A219

By Gilbert Stuart, 1795 — A221

Broken Circle

ROTARY PRESS PRINTINGS
Plates of 400 subjects in four panes of 100 each

1932, Jan. 1			Perf. 11x10½	
704	A210	½c **olive brown**	.20	.20
		Never hinged	.20	
		P# block of 4	6.00	—
		Never hinged	8.50	
		Broken circle (20560 U.R. 8)	.75	.20
705	A211	1c **green**	.20	.20
		Never hinged	.20	
		P# block of 4	4.00	—
		Never hinged	6.00	
		Gripper cracks (20742 UL and UR)	2.75	1.75
706	A212	1½c **brown**	.40	.20
		Never hinged	.55	
		P# block of 4	15.00	—
		Never hinged	30.00	
707	A213	2c **carmine rose**	.20	.20
		Never hinged	.20	
		P# block of 4	1.25	—
		Never hinged	2.25	
		Pair with full vert. gutter between	—	
		Gripper cracks (20752 LR, 20755 LL & LR, 20756 LL, 20774 LR, 20792 LL & LR, 20796 LL & LR)	1.75	.65

Double Transfer

Nº 708
3 Cent Bicentennial
BROKEN TOP FRAME
L.L. 20847 - Stamp Nº 8
King

708	A214 3c	**deep violet**	.55	.20
		Never hinged	.80	
		P# block of 4	17.50	—
		Never hinged	25.00	
		Double transfer	1.75	.65
		Broken top frame line (20847 LL 8)	4.00	.90

Retouch in Eyes — 4c			Cracked Plate — 5c	

709	A215 4c	**light brown**	.25	.2□
		Never hinged	.35	
		P# block of 4	5.00	—
		Never hinged	8.00	
		Double transfer (20568 LR 60)	1.50	.2□
		Retouch in eyes (20568 LR 89)	2.00	.3□
		P# block of 4 with variety		
		Broken bottom frame line (20568 LR 100)	1.50	.5□
		P# block of 4 with variety		
710	A216 5c	**blue**	1.50	.2□
		Never hinged	2.25	
		P# block of 4	15.00	—
		Never hinged	25.00	
		Cracked plate (20637 UR 80)	5.25	1.1□
711	A217 6c	**red orange**	3.00	.2□
		Never hinged	4.50	
		P# block of 4	52.50	—
		Never hinged	72.50	

Double Transfer

712	A218 7c	**black**	.25	.20
		Never hinged	.35	
		P# block of 4	9.00	—
		Never hinged	14.00	
		Double transfer (20563 UL 1 or 20564 LL 91)	1.25	.25
		P# block of 4 with variety	—	
713	A219 8c	**olive bister**	2.75	.50
		Never hinged	4.00	
		P# block of 4	50.00	—
		Never hinged	70.00	
		Pair with full vert. gutter between		
714	A220 9c	**pale red**	2.25	.20
		orange red	2.25	.20
		Never hinged	3.25	
		P# block of 4	35.00	—
		Never hinged	50.00	
715	A221 10c	**orange yellow**	10.00	.20
		Never hinged	15.00	
		P# block of 4	90.00	—
		Never hinged	130.00	
		Nos. 704-715 (12)	21.55	2.70
		Nos. 704-715, never hinged	31.65	

Skier — A222

Boy and Girl Planting Tree — A223

OLYMPIC WINTER GAMES ISSUE

3rd Olympic Winter Games, held at Lake Placid, N.Y., Feb. 4-13, 1932.

FLAT PLATE PRINTING
Plates of 400 subjects in four panes of 100.

1932, Jan. 25			Perf. 11	
716	A222 2c	**carmine rose**	.40	.20
		carmine	.40	.20
		Never hinged	.50	
		P# block of 6	10.00	—
		Never hinged	14.00	
		Cracked plate (20823 UR 41, 42; UL 48, 49, 50)	5.00	1.65
		Recut (20823 UR 61)	3.50	1.50
		Colored "snowball" (20815 UR 64)	25.00	5.00
a.		2c **lake**	—	
		Never hinged	—	
		carmine lake	—	
		Never hinged	—	

ARBOR DAY ISSUE

1st observance of Arbor Day in the state of Nebraska, Apr. 1872, 60th anniv., and cent. of the birth of Julius Sterling Morton, who conceived the plan and the name "Arbor Day," while he was a member of the Nebraska State Board of Agriculture.

ROTARY PRESS PRINTING
Plates of 400 subjects in four panes of 100.

1932, Apr. 22   *Perf. 11x10½*
17 A223 2c carmine rose   .20   .20
   Never hinged   .20
   P# block of 4   5.50 —
   Never hinged   7.50

OLYMPIC GAMES ISSUE
Issued in honor of the 10th Olympic Games, held at Los Angeles, Calif., July 30 to Aug. 14, 1932.

Runner at Starting Mark — A224

Myron's Discobolus — A225

Designed by Victor S. McCloskey, Jr.

ROTARY PRESS PRINTING
Plates of 400 subjects in four panes of 100.

1932, June 15   *Perf. 11x10½*
718 A224 3c violet   1.40 .20
   deep violet   1.40 .20
   Never hinged   1.75
   P# block of 4   12.00 —
   Never hinged   18.50
   Gripper cracks (20906 UL 1)   4.25 .75
   P# block of 4 with variety
719 A225 5c blue   2.20 .20
   deep blue   2.20 .20
   Never hinged   2.75
   P# block of 4   20.00 —
   Never hinged   27.50
   Gripper cracks (20868 UL & UR)   4.25 1.00

Washington, by Gilbert Stuart — A226

REGULAR ISSUE
ROTARY PRESS PRINTING
Plates of 400 subjects in four panes of 100.

1932   *Perf. 11x10½*
720 A226 3c deep violet, *June 16*   .20 .20
   light violet   .20 .20
   Never hinged   .20
   P# block of 4   1.30 —
   Never hinged   1.60
   Double transfer   1.00 .30
   Recut face (20986 UR 15)   2.00 .75
   Gripper cracks   1.25 .30
   Pair with full vert. gutter btwn.   200.00
   Pair with full horiz. gutter btwn.   200.00
b.   Booklet pane of 6, *July 25*   35.00 12.50
   Never hinged   60.00
c.   Vertical pair, imperf. between   700.00 1,350.
   Never hinged   1,400.

Bureau Precancels: 64 diff.

ROTARY PRESS COIL STAMPS
1932   *Perf. 10 Vertically*
721 A226 3c deep violet, *June 24*   2.75 .20
   light violet   2.75 .20
   Never hinged   3.50
   Pair   5.75 .25
   Never hinged   7.00
   Joint line pair   10.00 1.50
   Never hinged   12.50
   Gripper cracks
   Recut face (20995, pos. 29)   —
   Recut lines around eyes   —

Perf. 10 Horizontally
722 A226 3c deep violet, *Oct. 12*   1.50 .35
   light violet   1.50 .35
   Never hinged   2.00
   Pair   3.25 .80
   Never hinged   4.25
   Joint line pair   6.25 2.75
   Never hinged   8.00

Bureau Precancels: No. 721, 46 diff.

TYPE OF 1922-26 ISSUES
1932, Aug. 18   *Perf. 10 Vertically*
723 A161 6c deep orange   11.00 .30
   Never hinged   15.00
   Pair   24.00 .70

   Never hinged   32.50
   Joint line pair   60.00 5.00
   Never hinged   82.50

Bureau Precancels: 5 diff.

William Penn — A227

Daniel Webster (1782-1852), Statesman — A228

WILLIAM PENN ISSUE
250th anniv. of the arrival in America of Penn (1644-1718), English Quaker and founder of Pennsylvania.

FLAT PLATE PRINTING
Plates of 400 subjects in four panes of 100 each.

1932, Oct. 24   *Perf. 11*
724 A227 3c violet   .35 .20
   Never hinged   .50
   P# block of 6   8.00 —
   Never hinged   14.00
a.   Vert. pair, imperf. horiz.   —

DANIEL WEBSTER ISSUE
FLAT PLATE PRINTING
Plates of 400 subjects in four panes of 100.

1932, Oct. 24   *Perf. 11*
725 A228 3c violet   .35 .25
   light violet   .35 .25
   Never hinged   .50
   P# block of 6   16.50 —
   Never hinged   22.50

Gen. James Edward Oglethorpe — A229

Washington's Headquarters at Newburgh, N.Y. — A230

GEORGIA BICENTENNIAL ISSUE
200th anniv. of the founding of the Colony of Georgia, and honoring Oglethorpe, who landed from England, Feb. 12, 1733, and personally supervised the establishing of the colony.

FLAT PLATE PRINTING
Plates of 400 subjects in four panes of 100.

1933, Feb. 12   *Perf. 11*
726 A229 3c violet   .35 .20
   Never hinged   .50
   P# block of 6   10.00 —
   Never hinged   12.50
   P# block of 10, "CS"   14.00 —
   Never hinged   17.50
   Bottom margin block of 20, no P#   —

PEACE OF 1783 ISSUE
150th anniv. of the issuance by George Washington of the official order containing the Proclamation of Peace marking officially the ending of hostilities in the War for Independence.

ROTARY PRESS PRINTING
Plates of 400 subjects in four panes of 100 each.

1933, Apr. 19   *Perf. 10½x11*
727 A230 3c violet   .20 .20
   Never hinged   .20
   P# block of 4   3.00 —
   Never hinged   5.50
   Pair with horiz. gutter between   100.00
   Pair with vert. gutter between   100.00
   Center block with crossed gutters and dashes   —

No. 727 was available in full sheets of 400 subjects with gum, but was not regularly issued in that form. All examples of No. 727 must have original gum, including the gutter pairs and blocks, which are from the full sheets of 400. These should not be confused with similar blocks without gum, which are from the No. 752 Special Printing.

See No. 752 in the Special Printings following No. 751.

CENTURY OF PROGRESS ISSUES
"Century of Progress" Intl. Exhibition, Chicago, which opened June 1, 1933, and centenary of the incorporation of Chicago as a city.

Restoration of Fort Dearborn — A231

Federal Building — A232

ROTARY PRESS PRINTING
Plates of 400 subjects in four panes of 100.

1933, May 25   *Perf. 10½x11*
728 A231 1c yellow green   .20 .20
   Never hinged   .25
   On card, Expo. station machine canc.   1.00
   On card, Expo. station duplex handstamp canc.   3.00
   P# block of 4   1.75 —
   Never hinged   2.75
   Pair with horizontal gutter between 200.00
   Pair with vertical gutter between 200.00
   Center block with crossed gutters and dashes   3,500.
   Gripper cracks (21133 UR & LR)   2.00 —
729 A232 3c violet   .25 .20
   Never hinged   .35
   On cover, Expo. station machine canc.   2.00
   On cover, Expo. station duplex handstamp canc.   6.00
   P# block of 4   2.40 —
   Never hinged   3.50
   Pair with horiz. gutter between 200.00
   Pair with vert. gutter between 200.00
   Center block with crossed gutters and dashes   3,500.

Nos. 728 and 729 were not regularly issued in full sheets of 400 with gum. The gutter pairs and blocks come from a very few non-issued sheets that were retained by Postmaster James A. Farley.

AMERICAN PHILATELIC SOCIETY ISSUE
SOUVENIR SHEETS

A231a

A232a

Illustrations reduced.

FLAT PLATE PRINTING
Plates of 225 subjects in nine panes of 25 each.

1933, Aug. 25   *Imperf.*
Without Gum
730 A231a 1c deep yellow green, sheet of 25   27.50 27.50
a.   Single stamp   .75 .50
   Single on card, Expo. station machine canc.   1.50
   Single on card, Expo. station duplex handstamp canc.   5.00
731 A232a 3c deep violet, sheet of 25   25.00 25.00
a.   Single stamp   .65 .50

| Single on cover, Expo. station machine canc. | 3.00 |
| Single on cover, Expo. station duplex handstamp canc. | 7.50 |

Issued in sheets measuring 134x120mm containing twenty-five stamps, inscribed in the margins: PRINTED BY THE TREASURY DEPARTMENT, BUREAU OF ENGRAVING AND PRINTING, — UNDER AUTHORITY OF JAMES A. FARLEY, POSTMASTER-GENERAL, AT CENTURY OF PROGRESS, — IN COMPLIMENT TO THE AMERICAN PHILATELIC SOCIETY FOR ITS CONVENTION AND EXHIBITION — CHICAGO, ILLINOIS, AUGUST, 1933. PLATE NO. 21145.

Also used were plates 21159 (1c), 21146 and 21160 (3c).

See Nos. 766-767 in the Special Printings following No. 751.

NATIONAL RECOVERY ACT ISSUE

Issued to direct attention to and arouse the support of the nation for the National Recovery Act.

Group of Workers — A233

ROTARY PRESS PRINTING
Plates of 400 subjects in four panes of 100.

1933, Aug. 15		Perf. 10½x11
732 A233 3c **violet**	.20	.20
Never hinged	.20	
P# block of 4	1.50	—
Never hinged	2.00	
Gripper cracks (21151 UL & UR, 21153 UR & LR)	1.50	—
Recut at right (21151 UR 47)	4.00	

BYRD ANTARCTIC ISSUE

Issued in connection with the Byrd Antarctic Expedition of 1933 and for use on letters mailed through the Little America Post Office established at the Base Camp of the Expedition in the territory of the South Pole.

A Map of the World (on van der Grinten's Projection) — A234

Designed by Victor S. McCloskey, Jr.

FLAT PLATE PRINTING
Plates of 200 subjects in four panes of 50 each

1933, Oct. 9		Perf. 11
733 A234 3c **dark blue**	.50	.50
Never hinged	.60	
P# block of 6	12.00	—
Never hinged	15.00	
Double transfer (21167 LR 2)	2.75	1.00

In addition to the postage charge of 3 cents, letters sent by the ships of the expedition to be canceled in Little America were subject to a service charge of 50 cents each.

See No. 753 in the Special Printings following No. 751.

KOSCIUSZKO ISSUE

Kosciuszko (1746-1807), Polish soldier and statesman served in the American Revolution, on the 150th anniv. of the granting to him of American citizenship.

Statue of General Tadeusz Kosciuszko — A235

Designed by Victor S. McCloskey, Jr.

FLAT PLATE PRINTING
Plates of 400 subjects in four panes of 100 each

1933, Oct. 13		Perf. 11
734 A235 5c **blue**	.55	.25
Never hinged	.65	
P# block of 6	27.50	—
Never hinged	35.00	
Cracked plate	—	
a. Horizontal pair, imperf. vertically	2,250.	
Never hinged	2,800.	
P# block of 8	40,000.	

The No. 734a plate block is unique but damaged.

NATIONAL STAMP EXHIBITION ISSUE
SOUVENIR SHEET

A235a

Illustration reduced.

TYPE OF BYRD ISSUE
Plates of 150 subjects in 25 panes of six each.

1934, Feb. 10		Imperf.
Without Gum		
735 A235a 3c **dark blue,** sheet of 6	12.00	10.00
a. Single stamp	1.90	1.65

Issued in sheets measuring 87x93mm containing six stamps, inscribed in the margins: "Printed by the Treasury Department, Bureau of Engraving and Printing, under authority of James A. Farley, Postmaster General, in the National Stamp Exhibition of 1934. New York, N. Y., February 10-18, 1934. Plate No. 21184." Plate No. 21187 was used for sheets printed at the Exhibition, but all these were destroyed.

See No. 768 in the Special Printings following No. 751.

MARYLAND TERCENTENARY ISSUE

300th anniversary of the founding of Maryland.

"The Ark" and "The Dove" — A236

Designed by Alvin R. Meissner.

FLAT PLATE PRINTING
Plates of 400 subjects in four panes of 100.

1934, Mar. 23		Perf. 11
736 A236 3c **carmine rose**	.20	.20
Never hinged	.20	
P# block of 6	6.25	—
Never hinged	9.50	
Double transfer (21190 UL 1)	—	
a. Horizontal pair, imperf between	7,000.	

MOTHERS OF AMERICA ISSUE

Issued to commemorate Mother's Day.

Adaptation of Whistler's Portrait of his Mother — A237

Designed by Victor S. McCloskey, Jr.

Plates of 200 subjects in four panes of 50.
ROTARY PRESS PRINTING

1934, May 2		Perf. 11x10½
737 A237 3c **deep violet**	.20	.20
Never hinged	.20	
P# block of 4	1.00	—
Never hinged	1.50	

FLAT PLATE PRINTING
Perf. 11

1934		
738 A237 3c **deep violet**	.20	.20
Never hinged	.20	
P# block of 6	4.25	—
Never hinged	5.50	

See No. 754 in the Special Printings following No. 751.

WISCONSIN TERCENTENARY ISSUE

Arrival of Jean Nicolet, French explorer, on the shores of Green Bay, 300th anniv. According to historical records, Nicolet was the 1st white man to reach the territory now comprising the State of Wisconsin.

Nicolet's Landing A238

Designed by Victor S. McCloskey, Jr.

FLAT PLATE PRINTING
Plates of 200 subjects in four panes of 50.

1934, July 7		Perf. 11
739 A238 3c **deep violet**	.25	.20
violet	.25	.20
Never hinged	.40	
P# block of 6	2.90	—
Never hinged	4.25	
a. Vert. pair, imperf. horiz.	350.00	
Never hinged	600.00	
b. Horiz. pair, imperf. vert.	500.00	
Never hinged	850.00	
P# block of 6	2,000.	

See No. 755 in the Special Printings following No. 751.

NATIONAL PARKS YEAR ISSUE

El Capitan, Yosemite (California) — A239

Old Faithful, Yellowstone (Wyoming) — A243

View of Grand Canyon (Arizona) A240

Mt. Rainier and Mirror Lake (Washington) A241

Cliff Palace,
Mesa Verde
Park (Colorado)
A242

Crater Lake
(Oregon)
A244

Great Head,
Acadia Park
(Maine)
A245

Great White Throne,
Zion Park
(Utah) — A246

Great Smoky
Mountains (North
Carolina) — A248

Mt. Rockwell
(Mt. Sinopah)
and Two
Medicine Lake,
Glacier
National Park
(Montana)
A247

FLAT PLATE PRINTING
Plates of 200 subjects in four panes of 50.

1934		Unwmk.	Perf. 11	
740	A239	1c **green,** *July 16*	.20	.20
		light green	.20	.20
		Never hinged	.25	
		P# block of 6	1.00	—
		Never hinged	1.75	
		Recut	1.50	.50
a.		Vert. pair, imperf. horiz., with gum	1,500.	
		Never hinged	2,100.	
741	A240	2c **red,** *July 24*	.20	.20
		orange red	.20	.20
		Never hinged	.25	
		P# block of 6	1.50	—
		Never hinged	2.00	
		Double transfer	1.25	—
a.		Vert. pair, imperf. horiz., with gum	475.00	
		Never hinged	800.00	
		P# block of 6	—	
b.		Horiz. pair, imperf. vert., with gum	575.00	
		Never hinged	975.00	
		P# block of 6	2,000.	
		Never hinged	3,250.	
742	A241	3c **deep violet,** *Aug. 3*	.20	.20
		Never hinged	.25	
		P# block of 6	1.80	—
		Never hinged	2.25	
		Recut	1.50	
a.		Vert. pair, imperf. horiz., with gum	700.00	
		Never hinged	1,200.	
743	A242	4c **brown,** *Sept. 25*	.40	.40
		light brown	.40	.40
		Never hinged	.60	
		P# block of 6	7.00	—
		Never hinged	9.00	
a.		Vert. pair, imperf. horiz., with gum	1,000.	
		Never hinged	1,700.	
744	A243	5c **blue,** *July 30*	.70	.65

		light blue	.70	.65
		Never hinged	1.00	
		P# block of 6	9.00	
		Never hinged	12.00	
a.		Horiz. pair, imperf. vert., with gum	600.00	
		Never hinged	1,000.	
		P# block of 6		
745	A244	6c **dark blue,** *Sept. 5*	1.10	.85
		Never hinged	1.60	
		P# block of 6	17.50	
		Never hinged	25.00	
746	A245	7c **black,** *Oct. 2*	.60	.75
		Never hinged	.90	
		P# block of 6	9.00	
		Never hinged	12.00	
		Double transfer	3.00	1.25
a.		Horiz. pair, imperf. vert., with gum	600.00	
		Never hinged	1,000.	
		P# block of 6, never hinged	6,000.	
747	A246	8c **sage green,** *Sept. 18*	1.60	1.50
		Never hinged	2.40	
		P# block of 6	17.50	
		Never hinged	25.00	
748	A247	9c **red orange,** *Aug. 27*	1.50	.65
		orange	1.50	.65
		Never hinged	2.25	
		P# block of 6	15.00	—
		Never hinged	22.50	
749	A248	10c **gray black,** *Oct. 8*	3.00	1.25
		gray	3.00	1.25
		Never hinged	4.50	
		P# block of 6	22.50	
		Never hinged	32.50	
		Nos. 740-749 (10)	9.50	6.65
		Nos. 740-749, never hinged	14.00	

Imperforate varieties of the 2c and 5c exist as errors of the perforated Parks set, but are virtually impossible to distinguish from gummed copies from the imperforate sheets of 200.

Also, beware of fakes of the part-perforate errors of Nos. 740-749, including those with gum (see "without gum" note before No. 752.)

AMERICAN PHILATELIC SOCIETY ISSUE
SOUVENIR SHEET

A248a

Illustration reduced.

Plates of 120 subjects in 20 panes of 6 stamps each.

1934, Aug. 28			Imperf.	
750	A248a	3c **deep violet,** sheet of 6	30.00	27.50
		Never hinged	37.50	
a.		Single stamp	3.50	3.25
		Never hinged	4.50	

Issued in sheets measuring approximately 98x93mm containing six stamps, inscribed in the margins: PRINTED BY THE TREASURY DEPARTMENT, BUREAU OF ENGRAVING AND PRINTING, — UNDER AUTHORITY OF JAMES A. FARLEY, POSTMASTER GENERAL, — IN COMPLIMENT TO THE AMERICAN PHILATELIC SOCIETY FOR ITS CONVENTION AND EXHIBITION, — ATLANTIC CITY, NEW JERSEY, AUGUST, 1934. PLATE NO. 21303.

See No. 770 in the Special Printings following No. 751.

TRANS-MISSISSIPPI PHILATELIC EXPOSITION ISSUE
SOUVENIR SHEET

A248b

Illustration reduced.

Plates of 120 subjects in 20 panes of 6 stamps each.

1934, Oct. 10			Imperf.	
751	A248b	1c **green,** sheet of 6	12.50	12.50
		Never hinged	16.00	
a.		Single stamp	1.40	1.60
		Never hinged	1.85	

Issued in sheets measuring approximately 92x99mm containing six stamps, inscribed in the margins: PRINTED BY THE TREASURY DEPARTMENT, BUREAU OF ENGRAVING AND PRINTING, — UNDER AUTHORITY OF JAMES A. FARLEY, POSTMASTER GENERAL, — IN COMPLIMENT TO THE TRANS-MISSISSIPPI PHILATELIC EXPOSITION AND CONVENTION, OMAHA, NEBRASKA, — OCTOBER, 1934. PLATE NO. 21341.

See No. 769 in the Special Printings that follow.

SPECIAL PRINTING
(Nos. 752-771 inclusive)

"Issued for a limited time in full sheets as printed, and in blocks thereof, to meet the requirements of collectors and others who may be interested." — From Postal Bulletin No. 16614.

Issuance of the following 20 stamps in complete sheets resulted from the protest of collectors and others at the practice of presenting, to certain government officials, complete sheets of unsevered panes, imperforate (except Nos. 752 and 753) and generally ungummed.

Designs of Commemorative Issues
Without Gum

NOTE: In 1940 the P.O. Department offered to and did gum full sheets of Nos. 756-765 and 769-770 sent in by owners. No other Special Printings were accepted for gumming.

TYPE OF PEACE ISSUE

Issued in sheets of 400, consisting of four panes of 100 each, with vertical and horizontal gutters between and plate numbers at outside corners at sides.

ROTARY PRESS PRINTING

1935, Mar. 15		Unwmk.	Perf. 10½x11	
752	A230	3c **violet**	.20	.20
		Pair with horiz. gutter between	5.75	
		Pair with vert. gutter between	9.50	
		Gutter block of 4 with dash (left or right)	12.50	—
		Gutter block of 4 with dash (top or bottom)	20.00	—
		Center block with crossed gutters and dashes	50.00	—
		P# block of 4	27.50	

TYPE OF BYRD ISSUE

Issued in sheets of 200, consisting of four panes of 50 each, with vertical and horizontal guide lines in gutters between panes, and plate numbers centered at top and bottom of each pane. This applies to Nos. 753-765 and 771.

FLAT PLATE PRINTING
Perf. 11

753	A234	3c **dark blue**	.50	.45
		Pair with horiz. line between	2.25	—
		Pair with vert. line between	27.50	—
		Margin block of 4, arrow & guide line (left or right)	4.75	
		Margin block of 4, arrow & guideline (top or bottom)	57.50	—

	Center line block	72.50	15.00
	P# block of 6, number at top or bottom	20.00	—

No. 753 is similar to No. 733. Positive identification is by blocks or pairs showing guide line between stamps. These lines between stamps are found only on No. 753.

TYPE OF MOTHERS OF AMERICA ISSUE
Issued in sheets of 200
FLAT PLATE PRINTING
Imperf

754	A237	3c deep violet	.60	.60
		Pair with horiz. line between	1.75	—
		Pair with vert. line between	1.40	—
		Margin block of 4, arrow & guideline (left or right)	3.75	—
		Margin block of 4, arrow & guideline (top or bottom)	3.00	—
		Center line block	7.25	—
		P# block of 6, number at top or bottom	14.00	—

TYPE OF WISCONSIN ISSUE
Issued in sheets of 200
FLAT PLATE PRINTING
Imperf

755	A238	3c deep violet	.60	.60
		Pair with horiz. line between	1.75	—
		Pair with vert. line between	1.40	—
		Margin block of 4, arrow & guideline (left or right)	3.75	—
		Margin block of 4, arrow & guideline (top or bottom)	3.00	—
		Center line block	7.25	—
		P# block of 6, number at top or bottom	14.00	—

TYPES OF NATIONAL PARKS ISSUE
Issued in sheets of 200
FLAT PLATE PRINTING
Imperf

756	A239	1c green	.20	.20
		Pair with horiz. line between	.45	—
		Pair with vert. line between	.55	—
		Margin block of 4, arrow & guideline (left or right)	1.00	—
		Margin block of 4, arrow & guideline (top or bottom)	1.25	—
		Center line block	3.00	—
		P# block of 6, number at top or bottom	4.50	—

See note above No. 766.

757	A240	2c red	.25	.25
		Pair with horiz. line between	.70	—
		Pair with vert. line between	.55	—
		Margin block of 4, arrow & guideline (left or right)	1.60	—
		Margin block of 4, arrow & guideline (top or bottom)	1.25	—
		Center line block	3.50	—
		P# block of 6, number at top or bottom	5.75	—
		Double transfer	—	—
758	A241	3c deep violet	.50	.45
		Pair with horiz. line between	1.40	—
		Pair with vert. line between	1.25	—
		Margin block of 4, arrow & guideline (left or right)	3.10	—
		Margin block of 4, arrow & guideline (top or bottom)	2.75	—
		Center line block	5.25	—
		P# block of 6, number at top or bottom	14.00	—
759	A242	4c brown	.95	.95
		Pair with horiz. line between	2.75	—
		Pair with vert. line between	2.25	—
		Margin block of 4, arrow & guideline (left or right)	5.75	—
		Margin block of 4, arrow & guideline (top or bottom)	4.75	—
		Center line block	8.50	—
		P# block of 6, number at top or bottom	21.00	—
760	A243	5c blue	1.50	1.40
		Pair with horiz. line between	3.50	—
		Pair with vert. line between	4.25	—
		Margin block of 4, arrow & guideline (left or right)	7.50	—
		Margin block of 4, arrow & guideline (top or bottom)	9.00	—
		Center line block	15.00	—
		P# block of 6, number at top or bottom	25.00	—
		Double transfer	—	—
761	A244	6c dark blue	2.40	2.25
		Pair with horiz. line between	6.50	—
		Pair with vert. line between	5.50	—
		Margin block of 4, arrow & guideline (left or right)	14.00	—
		Margin block of 4, arrow & guideline (top or bottom)	12.50	—
		Center line block	20.00	—
		P# block of 6, number at top or bottom	37.50	—
762	A245	7c black	1.50	1.40
		Pair with horiz. line between	4.25	—
		Pair with vert. line between	3.75	—
		Margin block of 4, arrow & guideline (left or right)	9.25	—
		Margin block of 4, arrow & guideline (top or bottom)	8.25	—
		Center line block	14.00	—

		P# block of 6, number at top or bottom	30.00	—
		Double transfer	—	—
763	A246	8c sage green	1.60	1.50
		Pair with horiz. line between	3.75	—
		Pair with vert. line between	4.75	—
		Margin block of 4, arrow & guideline (left or right)	8.75	—
		Margin block of 4, arrow & guideline (top or bottom)	11.00	—
		Center line block	17.50	—
		P# block of 6, number at top or bottom	37.50	—
764	A247	9c red orange	1.90	1.75
		Pair with horiz. line between	5.00	—
		Pair with vert. line between	4.50	—
		Margin block of 4, arrow & guideline (left or right)	11.50	—
		Margin block of 4, arrow & guideline (top or bottom)	10.50	—
		Center line block	22.50	—
		P# block of 6, number at top or bottom	42.50	—
765	A248	10c gray black	3.75	3.50
		Pair with horiz. line between	9.00	—
		Pair with vert. line between	10.50	—
		Margin block of 4, arrow & guideline (left or right)	20.00	—
		Margin block of 4, arrow & guideline (top or bottom)	24.00	—
		Center line block	30.00	—
		P# block of 6, number at top or bottom	50.00	—
		Nos. 756-765 (10)	14.55	13.65

SOUVENIR SHEETS

Note: Single items from these sheets are identical with other varieties, 766 and 730, 766a and 730a, 767 and 731, 767a and 731a, 768 and 735, 768a and 735a, 769 and 756, 770 and 758.

Positive identification is by blocks or pairs showing wide gutters between stamps. These wide gutters occur only on Nos. 766-770 and measure, horizontally, 13mm on Nos. 766-767; 16mm on No. 768, and 23mm on Nos. 769-770.

TYPE OF CENTURY OF PROGRESS ISSUE

Issued in sheets of 9 panes of 25 stamps each, with vertical and horizontal gutters between panes.

FLAT PLATE PRINTING
Imperf

766	A231a	1c yellow green, pane of 25	25.00	25.00
a.		Single stamp	.70	.50
		Block of 4	2.80	1.70
		Pair with horiz. gutter between	5.50	—
		Pair with vert. gutter between	7.00	—
		Block with crossed gutters	15.00	—
		Block of 50 stamps (two panes)	70.00	—
767	A232a	3c violet, pane of 25	23.50	23.50
a.		Single stamp	.60	.50
		Pair with horiz. gutter between	5.25	—
		Pair with vert. gutter between	6.75	—
		Block with crossed gutters	15.00	—
		Block of 50 stamps (two panes)	65.00	—

NATIONAL EXHIBITION ISSUE
TYPE OF BYRD ISSUE

Issued in sheets of 25 panes of 6 stamps each, with vertical and horizontal gutters between panes.

FLAT PLATE PRINTING
Imperf

768	A235a	3c dark blue, pane of six	20.00	15.00
a.		Single stamp	2.80	2.40
		Pair with horiz. gutter between	7.50	—
		Pair with vert. gutter between	9.00	—
		Block of 4 with crossed gutters	20.00	—
		Block of 12 stamps (two panes)	47.50	—

TYPES OF NATIONAL PARKS ISSUE

Issued in sheets of 20 panes of 6 stamps each, with vertical and horizontal gutters between panes.

FLAT PLATE PRINTING
Imperf

769	A248b	1c green, pane of six	12.50	11.00
a.		Single stamp	1.85	1.80
		Pair with horiz. gutter between	6.00	—
		Pair with vert. gutter between	9.00	—
		Block of 4 with crossed gutters	15.00	—
		Block of 12 stamps (two panes)	30.00	—
770	A248a	3c deep violet, pane of six	30.00	24.00
a.		Single stamp	3.25	3.10
		Pair with horiz. gutter between	12.50	—
		Pair with vert. gutter between	11.00	—
		Block of 4 with crossed gutters	30.00	—
		Block of 12 stamps (two panes)	70.00	—

TYPE OF AIR POST SPECIAL DELIVERY

Issued in sheets of 200, with vertical and horizontal guide lines between panes.

FLAT PLATE PRINTING
Imperf

771	APSD1	16c dark blue	2.60	2.60
		Pair with horiz. line between	7.25	—
		Pair with vert. line between	6.00	—
		Margin block of 4, arrow & guideline (left or right)	17.50	—
		Margin block of 4, arrow & guideline (top or bottom)	15.00	—

	Center line block	65.00	
	P# block of 6, number at top or bottom	52.50	

> **Catalogue values for unused stamps in this section, from this point to the end, are for Never Hinged items.**

VALUES FOR HINGED STAMPS AFTER NO. 771
This catalogue does not value unused stamps after No. 771 in hinged condition. Hinged unused stamps from No. 772 to the present are worth considerably less than the values given for unused stamps, which are for never-hinged examples.

CONNECTICUT TERCENTENARY ISSUE
300th anniv. of the settlement of Connecticut.

The Charter Oak — A249

ROTARY PRESS PRINTING
Plates of 200 subjects in four panes of 50.

1935, Apr. 26　　Unwmk.　　Perf. 11x10½

772	A249	3c violet	.25	.20
		rose violet	.25	.20
		P# block of 4	1.75	
		Defect in cent sign (21395 UR 4)	5.00	4.00

CALIFORNIA PACIFIC EXPOSITION ISSUE
California Pacific Exposition at San Diego.

View of San Diego Exposition A250

ROTARY PRESS PRINTING
Plates of 200 subjects in four panes of 50.

1935, May 29　　Unwmk.　　Perf. 11x10½

773	A250	3c purple	.25	.20
		On cover, Expo. station machine canc. (non-first day)		2.50
		On cover, Expo. station duplex handstamp canc. (non-first day)		20.00
		P# block of 4	1.10	
		Pair with full vertical gutter between	—	

BOULDER DAM ISSUE
Dedication of Boulder Dam.

Boulder Dam (Hoover Dam) — A251

FLAT PLATE PRINTING
Plates of 200 subjects in four panes of 50.

1935, Sept. 30　　Unwmk.　　Perf. 11

774	A251	3c purple	.20	.20
		deep purple	.20	.20
		P# block of 6	1.65	

MICHIGAN CENTENARY ISSUE
Advance celebration of Michigan Statehood centenary.

Michigan State Seal — A252

Designed by Alvin R. Meissner.

ROTARY PRESS PRINTING
Plates of 200 subjects in 4 panes of 50.

1935, Nov. 1	Unwmk.	Perf. 11x10½
775 A252 3c purple		.25 .20
P# block of 4		1.50 —

TEXAS CENTENNIAL ISSUE
Centennial of Texas independence.

Sam Houston, Stephen F. Austin and the Alamo — A253

Designed by Alvin R. Meissner.

ROTARY PRESS PRINTING
Plates of 200 subjects in four panes of 50.

1936, Mar. 2	Unwmk.	Perf. 11x10½
776 A253 3c purple		.25 .20
On cover, Expo. station machine canc.		2.00
On cover, Expo. station duplex handstamp canc.		40.00
P# block of 4		1.25

RHODE ISLAND TERCENTENARY ISSUE
300th anniv. of the settlement of Rhode Island.

Statue of Roger Williams — A254

ROTARY PRESS PRINTING
Plates of 200 subjects in four panes of 50.

1936, May 4	Unwmk.	Perf. 10½x11
777 A254 3c purple		.35 .20
rose violet		.35 .20
P# block of 4		1.25
Pair with full gutter between		200.00

THIRD INTERNATIONAL PHILATELIC EXHIBITION ISSUE
SOUVENIR SHEET

A254a

Illustration reduced.

Plates of 120 subjects in thirty panes of 4 each.
FLAT PLATE PRINTING

1936, May 9	Unwmk.	Imperf.
778 A254a violet, sheet of 4		1.75 1.25
a. 3c Type A249		.40 .30
b. 3c Type A250		.40 .30
c. 3c Type A252		.40 .30
d. 3c Type A253		.40 .30

Issued in sheets measuring 98x66mm containing four stamps, inscribed in the margins: "Printed by the Treasury Department, Bureau of Engraving and Printing, under authority of James A. Farley, Postmaster General, in compliment to the third International Philatelic Exhibition of 1936. New York, N. Y., May 9-17, 1936. Plate No. 21557 (or 21558)."

ARKANSAS CENTENNIAL ISSUE
100th anniv. of the State of Arkansas.

Arkansas Post, Old and New State Houses A255

ROTARY PRESS PRINTING
Plates of 200 subjects in four panes of 50.

1936, June 15	Unwmk.	Perf. 11x10½
782 A255 3c purple		.30 .20
P# block of 4		1.40 —

OREGON TERRITORY ISSUE
Opening of the Oregon Territory, 1836, 100th anniv.

Map of Oregon Territory A256

ROTARY PRESS PRINTING
Plates of 200 subjects in four panes of 50.

1936, July 14	Unwmk.	Perf. 11x10½
783 A256 3c purple		.20 .20
P# block of 4		1.10 —
Double transfer (21579 UL 3)		4.00 2.50

SUSAN B. ANTHONY ISSUE
Susan Brownell Anthony (1820-1906), woman-suffrage advocate, and 16th anniv. of the ratification of the 19th Amendment which grants American women the right to vote.

Susan B. Anthony — A257

ROTARY PRESS PRINTING
Plates of 400 subjects in four panes of 100.

1936, Aug. 26	Unwmk.	Perf. 11x10½
784 A257 3c dark violet		.20 .20
P# block of 4		.75 —
Period missing after "B" (21590 LR 100)		4.00 2.00

ARMY ISSUE
Issued in honor of the United States Army.

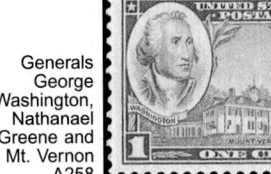

Generals George Washington, Nathanael Greene and Mt. Vernon A258

Maj. Gen. Andrew Jackson, Gen. Winfield Scott and the Hermitage A259

Generals William T. Sherman, Ulysses S. Grant and Philip H. Sheridan A260

Generals Robert E. Lee, "Stonewall" Jackson and Stratford Hall — A261

U. S. Military Academy, West Point — A262

ROTARY PRESS PRINTING
Plates of 200 subjects in four panes of 50.

1936-37	Unwmk.	Perf. 11x10½
785 A258 1c green, Dec. 15, 1936		.20 .20
yellow green		.20 .20
P# block of 4		.85 —
Pair with full vertical gutter between		
786 A259 2c carmine, Jan. 15, 1937		.20 .20
P# block of 4		.85 —
787 A260 3c purple, Feb. 18, 1937		.30 .20
P# block of 4		1.75 —
788 A261 4c gray, Mar. 23, 1937		.50 .20
P# block of 4		8.50 —
789 A262 5c ultramarine, May 26, 1937		.55 .25
P# block of 4		8.00 —
Nos. 785-789 (5)		1.75 1.05

NAVY ISSUE
Issued in honor of the United States Navy.

John Paul Jones and John Barry — A263

Stephen Decatur and Thomas MacDonough A264

Admirals David G. Farragut and David D. Porter — A265

Admirals William T. Sampson, George Dewey and Winfield S. Schley A266

Seal of US Naval Academy and Naval Midshipmen A267

ROTARY PRESS PRINTING
Plates of 200 subjects in four panes of 50.

1936-37			Unwmk.	Perf. 11x10½	
790	A263	1c	green, Dec. 15, 1936	.20	.20
			yellow green	.20	.20
			P# block of 4	.85	
791	A264	2c	carmine, Jan. 15, 1937	.20	.20
			P# block of 4	.75	—
792	A265	3c	purple, Feb. 18, 1937	.20	.20
			P# block of 4	1.00	—
793	A266	4c	gray, Mar. 23, 1937	.40	.20
			P# block of 4	9.00	—
794	A267	5c	ultramarine, May 26, 1937	.55	.25
			P# block of 4	8.75	—
			Pair with full vert. gutter btwn.	—	
			Nos. 790-794 (5)	1.55	1.05

ORDINANCE OF 1787 SESQUICENTENNIAL ISSUE

150th anniv. of the adoption of the Ordinance of 1787 and the creation of the Northwest Territory.

Manasseh Cutler, Rufus Putnam and Map of Northwest Territory A268

ROTARY PRESS PRINTING
Plates of 200 subjects in four panes of 50.

1937, July 13			Unwmk.	Perf. 11x10½	
795	A268	3c	red violet	.25	.20
			P# block of 4	1.25	—

VIRGINIA DARE ISSUE

350th anniv. of the birth of Virginia Dare, 1st child born in America of English parents (Aug. 18, 1587), and the settlement at Roanoke Island.

Virginia Dare and Parents — A269

FLAT PLATE PRINTING

Plates of 192 subjects in four panes of 48 each, separated by 1¼ inch wide gutters with central guide lines.

1937, Aug. 18			Unwmk.	Perf. 11	
796	A269	5c	gray blue	.30	.20
			P# block of 6	6.50	—

SOCIETY OF PHILATELIC AMERICANS ISSUE
SOUVENIR SHEET

A269a

Illustration reduced.

TYPE OF NATIONAL PARKS ISSUE
Plates of 36 subjects
FLAT PLATE PRINTING

1937, Aug. 26			Unwmk.	Imperf.	
797	A269a	10c	blue green	.60	.40

Issued in sheets measuring 67x78mm, inscribed in margins: "Printed by the Treasury Department, Bureau of Engraving and Printing — Under the Authority of James A. Farley, Postmaster General — In Compliment to the 43rd Annual Convention of the Society of Philatelic Americans - Asheville, N.C., August 26-28, 1937. Plate Number 21695 (6)."

CONSTITUTION SESQUICENTENNIAL ISSUE

150th anniversary of the signing of the Constitution on September 17, 1787.

"Adoption of the Constitution" A270

ROTARY PRESS PRINTING
Plates of 200 subjects in four panes of 50.

1937, Sept. 17			Unwmk.	Perf. 11x10½	
798	A270	3c	bright red violet	.35	.20
			P# block of 4	1.50	—

TERRITORIAL ISSUES
Hawaii

Statue of Kamehameha I, Honolulu — A271

Alaska

Mt. McKinley A272

Puerto Rico

La Fortaleza, San Juan — A273

Virgin Islands

Charlotte Amalie Harbor, St. Thomas A274

ROTARY PRESS PRINTING
Plates of 200 subjects in panes of 50.

1937			Unwmk.	Perf. 10½x11	
799	A271	3c	violet, Oct. 18	.25	.20
			P# block of 4	1.25	—
			Perf. 11x10½		
800	A272	3c	violet, Nov. 12	.25	.20
			P# block of 4	1.10	—
			Pair with full gutter between	—	
801	A273	3c	bright violet, Nov. 25	.25	.20
			P# block of 4	1.25	—
802	A274	3c	light violet, Dec. 15	.25	.20
			P# block of 4	1.25	—
			Pair with full vertical gutter between	275.00	
			Nos. 799-802 (4)	1.00	.80

PRESIDENTIAL ISSUE

Benjamin Franklin — A275

George Washington — A276

Martha Washington — A277

John Adams — A278

Thomas Jefferson — A279

James Madison — A280

The White House — A281

James Monroe — A282

John Quincy
Adams — A283

Andrew
Jackson — A284

James A.
Garfield — A297

Chester A.
Arthur — A298

Martin Van
Buren — A285

William H.
Harrison — A286

Grover
Cleveland — A299

Benjamin
Harrison — A300

John Tyler — A287

James K.
Polk — A288

William
McKinley — A301

Theodore
Roosevelt — A302

Zachary
Taylor — A289

Millard
Fillmore — A290

William Howard
Taft — A303

Woodrow
Wilson — A304

Franklin
Pierce — A291

James
Buchanan — A292

Warren G.
Harding — A305

Calvin
Coolidge — A306

Abraham
Lincoln — A293

Andrew
Johnson — A294

ROTARY PRESS PRINTING

Ordinary and Electric Eye (EE) Plates of 400 subjects in four panes of 100. (For details of EE Markings, see Information for Collectors in first part of this Catalogue.)

1938		Unwmk.	Perf. 11x10½	
803	A275	½c **deep orange,** *May 19*	.20	.20
		P# block of 4	.50	—
804	A276	1c **green,** *Apr. 25*	.20	.20
		light green	.20	—
		P# block of 4	.30	—
		Pair with full vert. gutter btwn.	160.00	—
b.		Booklet pane of 6	2.00	.50
c.		Horiz. pair, imperf between (from booklet pane)		—
805	A277	1½c **bister brown,** *May 5*	.20	.20
		buff ('43)	.20	.20
		P# block of 4	.30	—
		Pair with full horiz. gutter btwn.	175.00	—
		Pair with full vert. gutter btwn.		—
b.		Horiz. pair, imperf. between	160.00	20.00

No. 805b used is always Bureau precanceled St. Louis, Mo., and is generally with gum. Value is for gummed pair.

806	A278	2c **rose carmine,** *June 3*	.20	.20
		rose pink ('43)	.20	.20
		P# block of 4, # opposite corner stamp	.30	—
		Vertical margin block of 10, P# opposite 3rd horizontal row (Experimental EE plates)	4.00	
		Recut at top of head, Pl. 22156 U.L. 3	3.00	1.50
		Pair with full horiz. gutter btwn.	125.00	
		Pair with full vert. gutter btwn.		
b.		Booklet pane of 6	4.75	.85

Ulysses S.
Grant — A295

Rutherford B.
Hayes — A296

807	A279	3c **deep violet,** *June 16*	.20	.20
		P# block of 4, # opposite corner stamp	.30	.25
		Vertical margin block of 10, P# opposite 3rd horizontal row (Experimental EE plates)	60.00	
		Pair with full vert. gutter btwn.	150.00	
		Pair with full horiz. gutter btwn.	200.00	
a.		Booklet pane of 6	8.50	2.00
		Horiz. booklet pair with full vert. gutter between		
b.		Horiz. pair, imperf. between	1,500.	—
c.		Imperf., pair	2,750.	—
d.		As "a," imperf between vert.		—
808	A280	4c **red violet,** *July 1*	.75	.20
		rose violet ('43)	.75	.20
		P# block of 4	2.25	
809	A281	4½c **dark gray,** *July 11*	.20	.20
		gray ('43)	.20	.20
		P# block of 4	1.50	
810	A282	5c **bright blue,** *July 21*	.20	.20
		light blue	.20	.20
		P# block of 4	1.00	
		Pair with full vert. gutter btwn.	—	
811	A283	6c **red orange,** *July 28*	.20	.20
		P# block of 4	1.00	
812	A284	7c **sepia,** *Aug. 4*	.35	.20
		violet brown	.35	.20
		P# block of 4	1.50	
813	A285	8c **olive green,** *Aug. 11*	.30	.20
		light olive green ('43)	.30	.20
		olive ('42)	.30	.20
		P# block of 4	1.50	
814	A286	9c **rose pink,** *Aug. 18*	.30	.20
		pink ('43)	.30	.20
		P# block of 4	1.40	
		Pair with full vert. gutter btwn.	—	
815	A287	10c **brown red,** *Sept. 2*	.25	.20
		pale brown red ('43)	.25	.20
		P# block of 4	1.40	
816	A288	11c **ultramarine,** *Sept. 8*	.65	.20
		bright ultramarine	.65	.20
		P# block of 4	3.25	
817	A289	12c **bright violet,** *Sept. 14*	.90	.20
		P# block of 4	4.00	
818	A290	13c **blue green,** *Sept. 22*	1.25	.20
		deep blue green	1.25	.20
		P# block of 4	7.00	
819	A291	14c **blue,** *Oct. 6*	.90	.20
		P# block of 4	4.50	
820	A292	15c **blue gray,** *Oct. 13*	.40	.20
		P# block of 4	1.90	
821	A293	16c **black,** *Oct. 20*	1.10	.25
		P# block of 4	6.00	
822	A294	17c **rose red,** *Oct. 27*	.90	.20
		deep rose red	.90	.20
		P# block of 4	4.50	
823	A295	18c **brown carmine,** *Nov. 3*	2.00	.20
		rose brown ('43)	2.00	.20
		P# block of 4	9.00	
824	A296	19c **bright violet,** *Nov. 10*	1.25	.35
		P# block of 4	6.50	
825	A297	20c **bright blue green,** *Nov. 10*	.85	.20
		deep blue green ('43)	.85	.20
		P# block of 4	3.75	
826	A298	21c **dull blue,** *Nov. 22*	1.25	.20
		P# block of 4	7.50	
827	A299	22c **vermilion,** *Nov. 22*	1.00	.40
		P# block of 4	9.00	
828	A300	24c **gray black,** *Dec. 2*	3.50	.20
		P# block of 4	15.00	
829	A301	25c **deep red lilac,** *Dec. 2*	.80	.20
		rose lilac ('43)	.80	.20
		P# block of 4	3.50	
		Pair with full vert. gutter btwn.	900.00	
830	A302	30c **deep ultramarine,** *Dec. 8*	3.50	.20
		P# block of 4	15.00	
a.		30c blue	15.00	—
b.		30c deep blue	250.00	—
831	A303	50c **light red violet,** *Dec. 8*	5.00	.20
		P# block of 4	22.50	

Bureau Precancels: ½c, 199 diff., 1c, 701 diff., 1½c, 404 diff., 2c, 161 diff., 3c, 87 diff., 4c, 30 diff., 4½c, 27 diff., 5c, 44 diff., 6c, 45 diff., 7c, 44 diff., 8c, 44 diff., 9c, 38 diff., 10c, 43 diff. Also, 11c, 41 diff., 12c, 33 diff., 13c, 28 diff., 14c, 23 diff., 15c, 38 diff., 16c, 6 diff., 17c, 27 diff., 18c, 5 diff., 19c, 8 diff., 20c, 39 diff., 21c, 5 diff., 22c, 4 diff., 24c, 8 diff., 25c, 23 diff., 30c, 27 diff., 50c, 24 diff.

FLAT PLATE PRINTING
Plates of 100 subjects

1938			Perf. 11	
832	A304	$1 **purple & black,** *Aug. 29*	6.50	.20
		Margin block of 4, bottom or side arrow	27.50	—
		Center line block	31.50	4.00
		Top P# block of 4, 2#	32.50	
		Top P# block of 20, 2#, arrow, 2 TOP, 2 registration markers and denomination	145.00	—
a.		Vert. pair, imperf. horiz.	1,500.	
		Top P# blk of 8, imperf horiz.	8,500.	
b.		Watermarked USIR ('51)	175.00	65.00
		Hinged	110.00	
		Center line block		
		P# block of 4, 2#	1,650.	
c.		$1 red violet & black, *Aug. 31, 1954*	6.00	.20
		Top or bottom P# block of 4, 2#	30.00	
d.		As "c," vert. pair, imperf. horiz.	1,500.	
e.		Vertical pair, imperf. between	2,750.	
f.		As "c," vert. pair, imperf. btwn.	8,500.	

No. 832c is dry printed from 400-subject flat plates on thick white paper with smooth, colorless gum.

833	A305	$2	**yellow green & black**, *Sept. 29*		18.00	3.75
			green & black ('43)		18.00	3.75
			Margin block of 4, bottom or side arrow		77.50	—
			Center line block		82.50	35.00
			Top P# block of 4, 2#		95.00	—
			Top P# block of 20, 2#, arrow, 2 TOP, 2 registration markers and denominations		450.00	—
			Top P# block of 20, 2#, black # and marginal markings only (yellow green # and markings omitted)		3,000.	—
834	A306	$5	**carmine & black**, *Nov. 17*		90.00	3.00
			dark red & black		—	—
			Margin block of 4, bottom or side arrow		375.00	—
			Center line block		400.00	25.00
			Top P# block of 4, 2#		400.00	—
			Top P# block of 20, 2#, arrow, 2 TOP, 2 registration markers and denominations		2,200.	—
a.		$5	**red brown & black**		3,000.	7,000.
			Hinged		2,000.	
			Top P# block of 4, 2#		15,000.	
			Hinged		9,500.	
			Nos. 803-834 (32)		143.30	13.15
			Nos. 803-834, P# blocks of 4		718.10	

Top plate number blocks of Nos. 832, 833 and 834 are found both with and without top arrow or registration markers.
No. 834 can be chemically altered to resemble Scott 834a. No. 834a should be purchased only with competent expert certification.

Watermarks
All stamps from No. 835 on are unwatermarked.

CONSTITUTION RATIFICATION ISSUE
150th anniversary of the ratification of the United States Constitution.

Old Courthouse, Williamsburg, Va. — A307

ROTARY PRESS PRINTING
Plates of 200 subjects in four panes of 50.

1938, June 21				*Perf. 11x10½*		
835	A307	3c	**deep violet**		.45	.20
			P# block of 4		3.50	—

SWEDISH-FINNISH TERCENTENARY ISSUE
Tercentenary of the founding of the Swedish and Finnish Settlement at Wilmington, Delaware.

"Landing of the First Swedish and Finnish Settlers in America," by Stanley M. Arthurs — A308

FLAT PLATE PRINTING
Plates of 192 subjects in four panes of 48 each, separated by 1¼ inch wide gutters with central guide lines.

1938, June 27				*Perf. 11*		
836	A308	3c	**red violet**		.30	.20
			P# block of 6		2.25	—

NORTHWEST TERRITORY SESQUICENTENNIAL

"Colonization of the West," by Gutzon Borglum — A309

ROTARY PRESS PRINTING
Plates of 400 subjects in four panes of 100.

1938, July 15				*Perf. 11x10½*		
837	A309	3c	**bright violet**		.30	.20
			rose violet		.30	.20
			P# block of 4		6.00	—

IOWA TERRITORY CENTENNIAL ISSUE

Old Capitol, Iowa City — A310

ROTARY PRESS PRINTING
Plates of 200 subjects in four panes of 50.

1938, Aug. 24				*Perf. 11x10½*		
838	A310	3c	**violet**		.35	.20
			P# block of 4		6.00	—
			Pair with full vertical gutter between			

REGULAR ISSUE
ROTARY PRESS COIL STAMPS
Types of 1938

1939, Jan. 20				*Perf. 10 Vertically*		
839	A276	1c	**green**		.30	.20
			light green		.30	.20
			Pair		.60	.20
			Joint line pair		1.40	.35
840	A277	1½c	**bister brown**		.30	.20
			buff		.30	.20
			Pair		.60	.20
			Joint line pair		1.50	.75
841	A278	2c	**rose carmine**		.40	.20
			Pair		.80	.20
			Joint line pair		1.75	.35
842	A279	3c	**deep violet**		.50	.20
			violet		.50	.20
			Pair		1.00	.20
			Joint line pair		2.00	.35
			Gripper cracks		—	
			Thin translucent paper		2.50	—
843	A280	4c	**red violet**		7.50	.40
			Pair		16.50	.40
			Joint line pair		27.50	5.00
844	A281	4½c	**dark gray**		.70	.40
			Pair		1.50	.80
			Joint line pair		5.00	2.25
845	A282	5c	**bright blue**		5.00	.35
			Pair		10.50	.70
			Joint line pair		27.50	5.00
846	A283	6c	**red orange**		1.10	.20
			Pair		2.25	.40
			Joint line pair		7.50	1.50
847	A287	10c	**brown red**		11.00	1.00
			Pair		24.00	2.25
			Joint line pair		42.50	4.50

Bureau Precancels: 1c, 269 diff., 1½c, 179 diff., 2c, 101 diff., 3c, 46 diff., 4c, 13 diff., 4½c, 3 diff., 5c, 6 diff., 6c, 8 diff., 10c, 4 diff.

1939, Jan. 27				*Perf. 10 Horizontally*		
848	A276	1c	**green**		.85	.20
			Pair		1.75	.25
			Joint line pair		2.75	.75
849	A277	1½c	**bister brown**		1.25	.30
			Pair		2.50	.60
			Joint line pair		4.50	2.00
850	A278	2c	**rose carmine**		2.50	.40
			Pair		5.00	.80
			Joint line pair		6.50	3.50
851	A279	3c	**deep violet**		2.50	.40
			Pair		5.00	.70
			Joint line pair		7.25	3.75
			Nos. 839-851 (13)		33.90	4.45

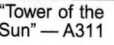

"Tower of the Sun" — A311

Trylon and Perisphere — A312

GOLDEN GATE INTL. EXPOSITION, SAN FRANCISCO
ROTARY PRESS PRINTING
Plates of 200 subjects in four panes of 50.

1939, Feb. 18				*Perf. 10½x11*		
852	A311	3c	**bright purple**		.25	.20
			On cover, Expo. station machine canc. (non-first day)		3.00	
			On cover, Expo. station duplex handstamp canc. (non-first day)		15.00	
			P# block of 4		1.25	

NEW YORK WORLD'S FAIR ISSUE
ROTARY PRESS PRINTING
Plates of 200 subjects in four panes of 50.

1939, Apr. 1				*Perf. 10½x11*		
853	A312	3c	**deep purple**		.30	.20
			On cover, Expo. station machine canc. (non-first day)		3.00	
			On cover, Expo. station duplex handstamp canc.		10.00	
			P# block of 4		1.75	—

WASHINGTON INAUGURATION ISSUE
Sesquicentennial of the inauguration of George Washington as First President.

Washington Taking Oath of Office, Federal Building, New York City — A313

FLAT PLATE PRINTING
Plates of 200 subjects in four panes of 50.

1939, Apr. 30				*Perf. 11*		
854	A313	3c	**bright red violet**		.55	.20
			P# block of 6		3.50	—

BASEBALL CENTENNIAL ISSUE

Sandlot Baseball Game — A314

Designed by William A. Roach.

ROTARY PRESS PRINTING
Plates of 200 subjects in four panes of 50.

1939, June 12				*Perf. 11x10½*		
855	A314	3c	**violet**		1.75	.20
			P# block of 4		7.50	—

PANAMA CANAL ISSUE
25th anniv. of the opening of the Panama Canal.

Theodore Roosevelt, Gen. George W. Goethals and Ship in Gaillard Cut — A315

Designed by William A. Roach.

FLAT PLATE PRINTING
Plates of 200 subjects in four panes of 50.

1939, Aug. 15				*Perf. 11*		
856	A315	3c	**deep red violet**		.30	.20
			P# block of 6		3.50	—

PRINTING TERCENTENARY ISSUE
Issued in commemoration of the 300th anniversary of printing in Colonial America. The Stephen Daye press is in the Harvard University Museum.

Stephen Daye
Press — A316

Designed by William K. Schrage.

ROTARY PRESS PRINTING
E.E. Plates of 200 subjects in four panes of 50.

1939, Sept. 25			**Perf. 10½x11**	
857	A316	3c violet	.20	.20
		P# block of 4	.90	—

50th ANNIVERSARY OF STATEHOOD ISSUE

Map of North
and South
Dakota,
Montana and
Washington
A317

ROTARY PRESS PRINTING
E.E. Plates of 200 subjects in four panes of 50.

1939, Nov. 2			**Perf. 11x10½**	
858	A317	3c rose violet	.25	.20
		P# block of 4	1.25	—

FAMOUS AMERICANS ISSUES
ROTARY PRESS PRINTING
E.E. Plates of 280 subjects in four panes of 70.
AMERICAN AUTHORS

Washington
Irving — A318

James Fenimore
Cooper — A319

Ralph Waldo
Emerson — A320

Louisa May
Alcott — A321

Samuel L. Clemens (Mark
Twain) — A322

1940			**Perf. 10½x11**	
859	A318	1c bright blue green, Jan. 29	.20	.20
		P# block of 4	.95	—
860	A319	2c rose carmine, Jan. 29	.20	.20
		P# block of 4	.95	—
861	A320	3c bright red violet, Feb. 5	.20	.20
		P# block of 4	1.25	—
862	A321	5c ultramarine, Feb. 5	.30	.20
		P# block of 4	8.25	—

863	A322	10c dark brown, Feb. 13	1.65	1.20
		P# block of 4	32.50	—
		Nos. 859-863 (5)	2.55	2.00

AMERICAN POETS

Henry Wadsworth
Longfellow — A323

John Greenleaf
Whittier — A324

James Russell
Lowell — A325

Walt Whitman — A326

James Whitcomb
Riley — A327

864	A323	1c bright blue green, Feb. 16	.20	.20
		P# block of 4	1.75	—
865	A324	2c rose carmine, Feb. 16	.20	.20
		P# block of 4	1.75	—
866	A325	3c bright red violet, Feb. 20	.20	.20
		P# block of 4	2.25	—
867	A326	5c ultramarine, Feb. 20	.35	.20
		P# block of 4	9.50	—
868	A327	10c dark brown, Feb. 24	1.75	1.25
		P# block of 4	32.50	—
		Nos. 864-868 (5)	2.70	2.05

AMERICAN EDUCATORS

Horace Mann — A328

Mark Hopkins — A329

Charles W.
Eliot — A330

Frances E.
Willard — A331

Booker T.
Washington — A332

869	A328	1c bright blue green, Mar. 14	.20	.20
		P# block of 4	1.90	—
870	A329	2c rose carmine, Mar. 14	.20	.20
		P# block of 4	1.50	—
871	A330	3c bright red violet, Mar. 28	.20	.20
		P# block of 4	2.00	—
872	A331	5c ultramarine, Mar. 28	.40	.20
		P# block of 4	9.00	—
873	A332	10c dark brown, Apr. 7	2.00	1.10
		P# block of 4	27.50	—
		Nos. 869-873 (5)	3.00	1.90

AMERICAN SCIENTISTS

John James
Audubon — A333

Dr. Crawford W.
Long — A334

Luther Burbank — A335

Dr. Walter
Reed — A336

Jane Addams — A337

874	A333	1c bright blue green, Apr. 8	.20	.20
		P# block of 4	.90	—
875	A334	2c rose carmine, Apr. 8	.20	.20
		P# block of 4	.95	—
876	A335	3c bright red violet, Apr. 17	.20	.20
		P# block of 4	1.10	—
877	A336	5c ultramarine, Apr. 17	.25	.20
		P# block of 4	5.00	—
878	A337	10c dark brown, Apr. 26	1.10	.85
		P# block of 4	16.00	—
		Nos. 874-878 (5)	1.95	1.65

AMERICAN COMPOSERS

Stephen Collins
Foster — A338

John Philip
Sousa — A339

Victor Herbert — A340

Edward A.
MacDowell — A341

Ethelbert Nevin — A342

879	A338	1c	bright blue green, *May 3*	.20	.20
			P# block of 4	.95	—
880	A339	2c	rose carmine, *May 3*	.20	.20
			P# block of 4	1.00	—
881	A340	3c	bright red violet, *May 13*	.20	.20
			P# block of 4	1.10	—
882	A341	5c	ultramarine, *May 13*	.40	.20
			P# block of 4	9.25	—
883	A342	10c	dark brown, *June 10*	3.75	1.35
			P# block of 4	32.50	—
			Nos. 879-883 (5)	4.75	2.15

AMERICAN ARTISTS

Gilbert Charles
Stuart — A343

James A. McNeill
Whistler — A344

Augustus Saint-
Gaudens — A345

Daniel Chester
French — A346

Frederic Remington — A347

884	A343	1c	bright blue green, *Sept. 5*	.20	.20
			P# block of 4	1.00	—
885	A344	2c	rose carmine, *Sept. 5*	.20	.20
			P# block of 4	.95	—
886	A345	3c	bright red violet, *Sept. 16*	.30	.20
			P# block of 4	1.40	—
887	A346	5c	ultramarine, *Sept. 16*	.50	.20
			P# block of 4	8.00	—
888	A347	10c	dark brown, *Sept. 30*	1.75	1.25
			P# block of 4	20.00	—
			Nos. 884-888 (5)	2.95	2.05

AMERICAN INVENTORS

Eli Whitney — A348

Samuel F. B.
Morse — A349

Cyrus Hall
McCormick — A350

Elias Howe — A351

Alexander Graham
Bell — A352

889	A348	1c	bright blue green, *Oct. 7*	.25	.20
			P# block of 4	2.25	—
890	A349	2c	rose carmine, *Oct. 7*	.30	.20
			P# block of 4	1.50	—
891	A350	3c	bright red violet, *Oct. 14*	.25	.20
			P# block of 4	1.50	—
892	A351	5c	ultramarine, *Oct. 14*	1.10	.30
			P# block of 4	12.50	—
893	A352	10c	dark brown, *Oct. 28*	11.00	2.00
			P# block of 4	57.50	—
			Nos. 889-893 (5)	12.90	2.90
			Nos. 859-893 (35)	30.80	14.70
			Nos. 859-894, P# blocks of 4	303.35	

PONY EXPRESS, 80th ANNIV. ISSUE

Pony Express
Rider — A353

ROTARY PRESS PRINTING
E.E. Plates of 200 subjects in four panes of 50.

1940, Apr. 3   *Perf. 11x10½*
| 894 | A353 | 3c | henna brown | .40 | .20 |
| | | | P# block of 4 | 2.75 | — |

PAN AMERICAN UNION ISSUE
Founding of the Pan American Union, 50th anniv.

The Three Graces
(Botticelli) — A354

ROTARY PRESS PRINTING
E.E. Plates of 200 subjects in four panes of 50.

1940, Apr. 14   *Perf. 10½x11*
| 895 | A354 | 3c | light violet | .30 | .20 |
| | | | P# block of 4 | 2.75 | — |

IDAHO STATEHOOD, 50th ANNIV.

Idaho State
Capitol
A355

ROTARY PRESS PRINTING
E.E. Plates of 200 subjects in four panes of 50.

1940, July 3   *Perf. 11x10*
| 896 | A355 | 3c | bright violet | .25 | .2 |
| | | | P# block of 4 | 1.75 | |

WYOMING STATEHOOD, 50th ANNIV.

Wyoming State
Seal — A356

ROTARY PRESS PRINTING
E.E. Plates of 200 subjects in four panes of 50.

1940, July 10   *Perf. 10½x11*
| 897 | A356 | 3c | brown violet | .25 | .20 |
| | | | P# block of 4 | 1.50 | |

CORONADO EXPEDITION, 400th ANNIV.

"Coronado
and His
Captains"
Painted by
Gerald
Cassidy
A357

ROTARY PRESS PRINTING
E.E. Plates of 200 subjects in four panes of 50.

1940, Sept. 7   *Perf. 11x10½*
| 898 | A357 | 3c | violet | .25 | .20 |
| | | | P# block of 4 | 1.60 | |

NATIONAL DEFENSE ISSUE

Statue of
Liberty — A358

90-millimeter Anti-
aircraft Gun — A359

Torch of Enlightenment — A360

ROTARY PRESS PRINTING
E.E. Plates of 400 subjects in four panes of 100

1940, Oct. 16   *Perf. 11x10½*
899	A358	1c	bright blue green	.20	.20
			P# block of 4	.45	
			Cracked plate (22684 UR 10)	3.00	
			Gripper cracks	3.00	
			Pair with full vert. gutter between	200.00	
a.			Vertical pair, imperf. between	650.00	—
b.			Horizontal pair, imperf. between	35.00	—

0 A359 2c **rose carmine** .20 .20
P# block of 4 .45
Pair with full vert. gutter between 275.00
a. Horizontal pair, imperf. between 40.00
1 A360 3c **bright violet** .20 .20
P# block of 4 .60
Pair with full vert. gutter between
a. Horizontal pair, imperf. between 25.00
Nos. 899-901 (3) .60 .60

Bureau Precancels: 1c, 316 diff., 2c, 25 diff., 3c, 22 diff.

THIRTEENTH AMENDMENT ISSUE
75th anniv. of the 13th Amendment to the Constitution abolishing slavery.

Emancipation Monument; Lincoln and Kneeling Slave, by Thomas Ball — A361

Designed by William A. Roach.

ROTARY PRESS PRINTING
E.E. Plates of 200 subjects in four panes of 50.

1940, Oct. 20 **Perf. 10½x11**
902 A361 3c **deep violet** .25 .20
dark violet .25 .20
P# block of 4 3.00

VERMONT STATEHOOD, 150th ANNIV.

State Capitol, Montpelier A362

Designed by Alvin R. Meissner.

ROTARY PRESS PRINTING
E.E. Plates of 200 subjects in four panes of 50.

1941, Mar. 4 **Perf. 11x10½**
903 A362 3c **light violet** .45 .20
P# block of 4 2.00

KENTUCKY STATEHOOD, 150th ANNIV.

Daniel Boone and Three Frontiersmen, from Mural by Gilbert White — A363

Designed by William A. Roach.

ROTARY PRESS PRINTING
E.E. Plates of 200 subjects in four panes of 50.

1942, June 1 **Perf. 11x10½**
904 A363 3c **violet** .25 .20
P# block of 4 1.25

WIN THE WAR ISSUE

American Eagle — A364

ROTARY PRESS PRINTING
E.E. Plates of 400 subjects in four panes of 100.

1942, July 4 **Perf. 11x10½**
905 A364 3c **violet** .20 .20
light violet .20 .20
P# block of 4 .40
Pair with full vert. or horiz. gutter between 175.00
b. 3c **purple** 500.00

Bureau Precancels: 26 diff.

All examples of No. 905b are precanceled either Los Angeles, Calif., or Fremont, Ohio. Value is for Los Angeles, which is the more common. Stamps with original gum sell for more.

CHINESE RESISTANCE ISSUE
Issued to commemorate the Chinese people's five years of resistance to Japanese aggression.

Map of China, Abraham Lincoln and Sun Yat-sen, Founder of the Chinese Republic A365

ROTARY PRESS PRINTING
E.E. Plates of 200 subjects in four panes of 50.

1942, July 7 **Perf. 11x10½**
906 A365 5c **bright blue** .85 .20
P# block of 4 9.00

ALLIED NATIONS ISSUE

Allegory of Victory — A366

Designed by Leon Helguera.

ROTARY PRESS PRINTING
E.E. Plates of 400 subjects in four panes of 100.

1943, Jan. 14 **Perf. 11x10½**
907 A366 2c **rose carmine** .20 .20
P# block of 4 .30
Pair with full vert. or horiz. gutter between 225.00

Bureau Precancels: Denver, Baltimore.

FOUR FREEDOMS ISSUE

Liberty Holding the Torch of Freedom and Enlightenment — A367

Designed by Paul Manship.

ROTARY PRESS PRINTING
E.E. Plates of 400 subjects in four panes of 100.

1943, Feb. 12 **Perf. 11x10½**
908 A367 1c **bright blue green** .20 .20
P# block of 4 .60

Bureau Precancels: 20 diff.

OVERRUN COUNTRIES ISSUE
Printed by the American Bank Note Co.
FRAMES ENGRAVED, CENTERS OFFSET LETTERPRESS
ROTARY PRESS PRINTING
Plates of 200 subjects in four panes of 50.

Due to the failure of the printers to divulge detailed information as to printing processes used, the editors omit listings of irregularities, flaws and blemishes which are numerous in this issue. Exceptions are made for certified double impressions, the widely recognized "KORPA" variety, and "reverse" vs. "normal" printings of the flag colors.

Flag of Poland A368

1943-44 **Perf. 12**
909 A368 5c **blue violet, bright red & black,** June 22, 1943 .20 .20
Margin block of 4, Inscribed "Poland" 3.50
Top margin block of 6, with red & blue violet guide markings and "Poland" 4.75
Bottom margin block of 6, with red & black guide markings 1.20
a. Double impression of "Poland"
b. Double impression of black flag color and red "Poland"
c. Reverse printing of flag colors (bright red over black)

Flag of Czechoslovakia — A368a

910 A368a 5c **blue violet, blue, bright red & black,** July 12, 1943 .20 .20
Margin block of 4, inscribed "Czechoslovakia" 2.75
Top margin block of 6, with red & blue violet guide markings and "Czechoslovakia" 3.25
a. Double impression of "Czechoslovakia"
b. Reverse printing of flag colors (blue and bright red over black)

Flag of Norway A368b

911 A368b 5c **blue violet, dark rose, deep blue & black,** July 27, 1943 .20 .20
Margin block of 4, inscribed "Norway" 1.30
Bottom margin block of 6 with dark rose & blue violet guide markings .90
a. Double impression of "Norway"

Flag of Luxembourg A368c

912 A368c 5c **blue violet, dark rose, light blue & black,** Aug. 10, 1943 .20 .20
Margin block of 4, inscribed "Luxembourg" 1.20
Top margin block of 6 with light blue & blue violet guide markings & "Luxembourg" 1.60
a. Double impression of "Luxembourg"
b. Reverse printing of flag colors (dark rose and light blue over black)

Flag of
Netherlands
A368d

913 A368d 5c **blue violet, dark rose, blue & black,** *Aug. 24, 1943* .20 .20
　　Margin block of 4, inscribed
　　　"Netherlands" 1.20 —
　　Bottom margin block of 6 with blue
　　　& blue violet guide markings .90 —
　a. 　Reverse printing of flag colors (dark rose
　　　and blue over black) —

Flag of
Belgium
A368e

914 A368e 5c **blue violet, dark rose, yellow & black,** *Sept. 14, 1943* .20 .20
　　Margin block of 4, inscribed "Belgi-
　　　um" 1.10 —
　　Top margin block of 6, with yellow
　　　& blue violet guide markings and
　　　"Belgium" 1.50 —
　a. 　Double impression of "Belgium" —

Flag of France
A368f

915 A368f 5c **blue violet, deep blue, dark rose & black,** *Sept. 28, 1943* .20 .20
　　Margin block of 4, inscribed
　　　"France" 1.25 —
　　Bottom margin block of 6 with dark
　　　rose & blue violet guide markings .90 —
　a. 　Reverse printing of flag colors (deep blue
　　　and dark rose over black) —
　b. 　Partial reverse printing of flag colors (dark
　　　rose over black and black over deep
　　　blue) —

Flag of Greece
A368g

916 A368g 5c **blue violet, pale blue, greenish blue & black,** reverse printing of
　　flag colors (pale blue flag stripes
　　over pale blue shading), *Oct. 12,
　　1943* .35 .25
　　Margin block of 4, inscribed
　　　"Greece" 11.00 —
　　Top margin block of 6 with pale
　　　blue & blue violet guide markings
　　　& "Greece" 11.50 —
　a. 　"Normal" printing of flag colors (dark blue
　　　shading over pale blue flag stripes) —

Flag of
Yugoslavia
A368h

Normal

YUGOSLAVIA

Reverse Printing of
Flag Colors

YUGOSLAVIA

917 A368h 5c **blue violet, blue, dark rose & black,** *Oct. 26, 1943* .25 .20
　　Margin block of 4, inscribed "Yu-
　　　goslavia" 4.25 —
　　Bottom margin block of 6 with
　　　dark rose & blue violet guide
　　　markings 1.50 —
　a. 　Reverse printing of flag colors (blue and
　　　dark rose over black) —
　b. 　Double impression of black —

Flag of
Albania
A368i

918 A368i 5c **blue violet, dark red & black,** *Nov.
　　9, 1943* .20 .20
　　Margin block of 4, inscribed "Alba-
　　　nia" 4.25 —
　　Top margin block of 6, with dark red
　　　& blue violet guide markings & "Al-
　　　bania" 6.50 —
　a. 　Double impression of "Albania" —

Flag of Austria
A368j

919 A368j 5c **blue violet, red & black,** *Nov. 23,
　　1943* .20 .20
　　Margin block of 4, inscribed "Austria" 3.50 —
　　Bottom margin block of 6, with red &
　　　blue violet guide markings 1.30 —
　a. 　Double impression of "Austria" —

Flag of
Denmark
A368k

920 A368k 5c **blue violet, red & black,** *Dec. 7,
　　1943* .20 .20
　　Margin block of 4, inscribed "Den-
　　　mark" 5.25 —
　　Top margin block of 6, with red &
　　　blue violet guide markings & "Den-
　　　mark" 6.00 —
　a. 　Reverse printing of flag colors (red over
　　　black) —

Flag of Korea
A368m

"KORPA" plate
flaw — 921var

921 A368m 5c **blue violet, red, light blue & gray,** *Nov. 2, 1944* .20 .2
　　Margin block of 4, inscribed
　　　"Korea" 4.50 —
　　Top margin block of 6 with blue
　　　& black guide markings and
　　　"Korea" 5.25 —
　　"KORPA" plate flaw 19.00 12.5
　a. 　Double impression of "Korea" —
　The "P" of "KORPA" is actually a mangled "E." Occurs only o
　some panes, position 26.
　　　Nos. 909-921 (13) 2.80 2.6
　　　Nos. 909-921, Name blocks of
　　　4 46.80

TRANSCONTINENTAL RAILROAD ISSUE
Completion of the 1st transcontinental railroad, 75th
anniv.

"Golden Spike
Ceremony"
Painted by
John
McQuarrie
A369

ENGRAVED
ROTARY PRESS PRINTING
E.E. Plates of 200 subjects in four panes of 50.
1944, May 10　　　　　　***Perf. 11x10½***
922 A369 3c **violet** .25 .20
　　P# block of 4 1.40 —

STEAMSHIP ISSUE
1st steamship to cross the Atlantic, 125th anniv.

"Savannah"
A370

ROTARY PRESS PRINTING
E.E. Plates of 200 subjects in four panes of 50.
1944, May 22　　　　　　***Perf. 11x10½***
923 A370 3c **violet** .20 .20
　　P# block of 4 1.25 —

TELEGRAPH ISSUE
1st message transmitted by telegraph, cent.

Telegraph
Wires and
Morse's First
Transmitted
Words "What
Hath God
Wrought"
A371

ROTARY PRESS PRINTING
E.E. Plates of 200 subjects in four panes of 50.
1944, May 24　　　　　　***Perf. 11x10½***
924 A371 3c **bright red violet** .20 .20
　　P# block of 4 .90 —

PHILIPPINE ISSUE

Final resistance of the US and Philippine defenders in Corregidor to the Japanese invaders in 1942.

Aerial View of Corregidor, Manila Bay — A372

ROTARY PRESS PRINTING
E.E. Plates of 200 subjects in four panes of 50.

1944, Sept. 27   *Perf. 11x10½*
925 A372 3c deep violet   .20 .20
        P# block of 4   1.10   —

MOTION PICTURE, 50th ANNIV.

Motion Picture Showing for Armed Forces in South Pacific — A373

ROTARY PRESS PRINTING
E.E. Plates of 200 subjects in four panes of 50.

1944, Oct. 31   *Perf. 11x10½*
926 A373 3c deep violet   .20 .20
        P# block of 4   .90   —

FLORIDA STATEHOOD, CENTENARY

State Seal, Gates of St. Augustine and Capitol at Tallahassee A374

ROTARY PRESS PRINTING
E.E. Plates of 200 subjects in four panes of 50.

1945, Mar. 3   *Perf. 11x10½*
927 A374 3c bright red violet   .20 .20
        P# block of 4   .90   —

UNITED NATIONS CONFERENCE ISSUE
United Nations Conference, San Francisco, Calif.

"Toward United Nations, April 25, 1945" — A375

ROTARY PRESS PRINTING
E.E. Plates of 200 subjects in four panes of 50.

1945, Apr. 25   *Perf. 11x10½*
928 A375 5c ultramarine   .20 .20
        P# block of 4   .45   —

IWO JIMA (MARINES) ISSUE

Battle of Iwo Jima and honoring the achievements of the US Marines.

Marines Raising American Flag on Mount Suribachi, Iwo Jima, from a photograph by Joe Rosenthal — A376

ROTARY PRESS PRINTING
E.E. Plates of 200 subjects in four panes of 50.

1945, July 11   *Perf. 10½x11*
929 A376 3c yellow green   .30 .20
        P# block of 4   2.00   —

FRANKLIN D. ROOSEVELT ISSUE
Franklin Delano Roosevelt (1882-1945).

Roosevelt and Hyde Park Residence A377

Roosevelt and the "Little White House" at Warm Springs, Ga. — A378

Roosevelt and White House — A379

Roosevelt, Map of Western Hemisphere and Four Freedoms A380

ROTARY PRESS PRINTING
E.E. Plates of 200 subjects in four panes of 50.

1945-46   *Perf. 11x10½*
930 A377 1c blue green, *July 26, 1945*   .20 .20
        P# block of 4   .35
931 A378 2c carmine rose, *Aug. 24, 1945* .20 .20
        P# block of 4   .45
932 A379 3c purple, *June 27, 1945*   .20 .20
        P# block of 4   .60
933 A380 5c bright blue, *Jan. 30, 1946* .20 .20
        P# block of 4   .45
        Nos. 930-933 (4)   .80 .80

ARMY ISSUE
Achievements of the US Army in World War II.

United States Troops Passing Arch of Triumph, Paris — A381

ROTARY PRESS PRINTING
E.E. Plates of 200 subjects in four panes of 50.

1945, Sept. 28   *Perf. 11x10½*
934 A381 3c olive   .20 .20
        P# block of 4   .45   —

NAVY ISSUE
Achievements of the U.S. Navy in World War II.

United States Sailors — A382

ROTARY PRESS PRINTING
E.E. Plates of 200 subjects in four panes of 50.

1945, Oct. 27   *Perf. 11x10½*
935 A382 3c blue   .20 .20
        P# block of 4   .60   —

COAST GUARD ISSUE
Achievements of the US Coast Guard in World War II.

Coast Guard Landing Craft and Supply Ship — A383

ROTARY PRESS PRINTING
E.E. Plates of 200 subjects in four panes of 50.

1945, Nov. 10   *Perf. 11x10½*
936 A383 3c bright blue green   .20 .20
        P# block of 4   .55   —

ALFRED E. SMITH ISSUE

Alfred E. Smith, Governor of New York — A384

ROTARY PRESS PRINTING
E.E. Plates of 400 subjects in four panes of 100.

1945, Nov. 26   *Perf. 11x10½*
937 A384 3c purple   .20 .20
        P# block of 4   .45
        Pair with full vert. gutter btwn.
        Pair with full horiz. gutter btwn.   300.00

TEXAS STATEHOOD, 100th ANNIV.

Flags of the United States and the State of Texas — A385

ROTARY PRESS PRINTING
E.E. Plates of 200 subjects in four panes of 50.

1945, Dec. 29   *Perf. 11x10½*
938 A385 3c dark blue   .20 .20
        P# block of 4   .50   —

MERCHANT MARINE ISSUE
Achievements of the US Merchant Marine in World War II.

Liberty Ship Unloading Cargo — A386

ROTARY PRESS PRINTING
E.E. Plates of 200 subjects in four panes of 50.

1946, Feb. 26		Perf. 11x10½	
939 A386	3c blue green	.20	.20
	P# block of 4	.45	—

VETERANS OF WORLD WAR II ISSUE
Issued to honor all veterans of World War II.

Honorable Discharge Emblem — A387

ROTARY PRESS PRINTING
E.E. Plates of 400 subjects in four panes of 100.

1946, May 9		Perf. 11x10½	
940 A387	3c dark violet	.20	.20
	P# block of 4	.45	—
	Pair with full vert. gutter btwn.	225.00	

TENNESSEE STATEHOOD, 150th ANNIV.

Andrew Jackson, John Sevier and State Capitol, Nashville A388

ROTARY PRESS PRINTING
E.E. Plates of 200 subjects in four panes of 50.

1946, June 1		Perf. 11x10½	
941 A388	3c dark violet	.20	.20
	P# block of 4	.50	—

IOWA STATEHOOD, 100th ANNIV.

Iowa State Flag and Map — A389

ROTARY PRESS PRINTING
E.E. Plates of 200 subjects in four panes of 50.

1946, Aug. 3		Perf. 11x10½	
942 A389	3c deep blue	.20	.20
	P# block of 4	.45	—

SMITHSONIAN INSTITUTION ISSUE
100th anniversary of the establishment of the Smithsonian Institution, Washington, D.C.

Smithsonian Institution A390

ROTARY PRESS PRINTING
E.E. Plates of 200 subjects in four panes of 50.

1946, Aug. 10		Perf. 11x10½	
943 A390	3c violet brown	.20	.20
	P# block of 4	.40	—

KEARNY EXPEDITION ISSUE
100th anniversary of the entry of General Stephen Watts Kearny into Santa Fe.

"Capture of Santa Fe" by Kenneth M. Chapman A391

ROTARY PRESS PRINTING
E.E. Plates of 200 subjects in four panes of 50.

1946, Oct. 16		Perf. 11x10½	
944 A391	3c brown violet	.20	.20
	P# block of 4	.40	—

THOMAS A. EDISON ISSUE

Thomas A. Edison (1847-1931), Inventor — A392

ROTARY PRESS PRINTING
E.E. Plates of 280 subjects in four panes of 70.

1947, Feb. 11		Perf. 10½x11	
945 A392	3c bright red violet	.20	.20
	P# block of 4	.40	—

JOSEPH PULITZER ISSUE

Joseph Pulitzer (1847-1911), Journalist, and Statue of Liberty A393

Designed by Victor S. McCloskey, Jr.

ROTARY PRESS PRINTING
E.E. Plates of 200 subjects in four panes of 50.

1947, Apr. 10		Perf. 11x10½	
946 A393	3c purple	.20	.20
	P# block of 4	.40	—

POSTAGE STAMP CENTENARY ISSUE
Centenary of the first postage stamps issued by the United States Government

Washington and Franklin, Early and Modern Mail-carrying Vehicles A394

Designed by Leon Helguera.

ROTARY PRESS PRINTING
E.E. Plates of 200 subjects in four panes of 50.

1947, May 17		Perf. 11x10½	
947 A394	3c deep blue	.20	.20
	P# block of 4	.40	—

CENTENARY INTERNATIONAL PHILATELIC EXHIBITION ISSUE
SOUVENIR SHEET

A395

Illustration reduced.

FLAT PLATE PRINTING
Plates of 30 subjects

1947, May 19			Imperf	
948 A395	Sheet of 2		.55	.4
a.	5c blue, type A1		.20	.2
b.	10c brown orange, type A2		.25	.2

Sheet inscribed below stamps: "100th Anniversary United States Postage Stamps" and in the margins: "PRINTED BY THE TREASURY DEPARTMENT, BUREAU OF ENGRAVING AND PRINTING. — UNDER AUTHORITY OF ROBERT E. HANNEGAN, POSTMASTER GENERAL. — IN COMPLIMENT TO THE CENTENARY INTERNATIONAL PHILATELIC EXHIBITION. — NEW YORK, N.Y., MAY 17-25, 1947." Sheet size varies: 96-98x66-68mm.

DOCTORS ISSUE
Issued to honor the physicians of America.

"The Doctor" by Sir Luke Fildes — A396

Designed by Charles R. Chickering.

ROTARY PRESS PRINTING
E.E. Plates of 200 subjects in four panes of 50.

1947, June 9		Perf. 11x10½	
949 A396	3c brown violet	.20	.20
	P# block of 4	.40	—

UTAH ISSUE
Centenary of the settlement of Utah.

Pioneers Entering the Valley of Great Salt Lake — A397

Designed by Charles R. Chickering.

ROTARY PRESS PRINTING
E.E. Plates of 200 subjects in four panes of 50.

1947, July 24		Perf. 11x10½	
950 A397	3c dark violet	.20	.20
	P# block of 4	.40	—

U.S. FRIGATE CONSTITUTION ISSUE
150th anniversary of the launching of the U.S. frigate Constitution ("Old Ironsides").

Naval Architect's Drawing of Frigate Constitution A398

Designed by Andrew H. Hepburn.

ROTARY PRESS PRINTING
E.E. Plates of 200 subjects in four panes of 50.

1947, Oct. 21		Perf. 11x10½
51 A398 3c blue green	.20	.20
P# block of 4	.40	—

Great White Heron and Map of Florida — A399

Dr. George Washington Carver — A400

EVERGLADES NATIONAL PARK ISSUE

Dedication of the Everglades National Park, Florida, Dec. 6, 1947.

Designed by Robert I. Miller, Jr.

ROTARY PRESS PRINTING
E.E. Plates of 200 subjects in four panes of 50.

1947, Dec. 5		Perf. 10½x11
952 A399 3c bright green	.20	.20
P# block of 4	.40	—

GEORGE WASHINGTON CARVER ISSUE

5th anniversary of the death of Dr. George Washington Carver, (1864-1943), botanist.

ROTARY PRESS PRINTING
E.E. Plates of 280 subjects in four panes of 70.

1948, Jan. 5		Perf. 10½x11
953 A400 3c bright red violet	.20	.20
P# block of 4	.45	—

CALIFORNIA GOLD CENTENNIAL ISSUE

Sutter's Mill, Coloma, California A401

Designed by Charles R. Chickering.

ROTARY PRESS PRINTING
E.E. Plates of 200 subjects in four panes of 50.

1948, Jan. 24		Perf. 11x10½
954 A401 3c dark violet	.20	.20
P# block of 4	.40	—

MISSISSIPPI TERRITORY ISSUE

Mississippi Territory establishment, 150th anniv.

Map, Seal of Mississippi Territory and Gov. Winthrop Sargent A402

Designed by William K. Schrage.

ROTARY PRESS PRINTING
E.E. Plates of 200 subjects in four panes of 50.

1948, Apr. 7		Perf. 11x10½
955 A402 3c brown violet	.20	.20
P# block of 4	.50	—

FOUR CHAPLAINS ISSUE

George L. Fox, Clark V. Poling, John P. Washington and Alexander D. Goode, the 4 chaplains who sacrificed their lives in the sinking of the S.S. Dorchester, Feb. 3, 1943.

Four Chaplains and Sinking S.S. Dorchester A403

Designed by Charles R. Chickering.

ROTARY PRESS PRINTING
E.E. Plates of 200 subjects in four panes of 50.

1948, May 28		Perf. 11x10½
956 A403 3c gray black	.20	.20
P# block of 4	.50	—

WISCONSIN STATEHOOD, 100th ANNIV.

Map on Scroll and State Capitol A404

Designed by Victor S. McCloskey, Jr.

ROTARY PRESS PRINTING
E.E. Plates of 200 subjects in four panes of 50.

1948, May 29		Perf. 11x10½
957 A404 3c dark violet	.20	.20
P# block of 4	.50	—

SWEDISH PIONEER ISSUE

Centenary of the coming of the Swedish pioneers to the Middle West.

Swedish Pioneer with Covered Wagon Moving Westward A405

Designed by Charles R. Chickering.

ROTARY PRESS PRINTING
E.E. Plates of 200 subjects in four panes of 50.

1948, June 4		Perf. 11x10½
958 A405 5c deep blue	.20	.20
P# block of 4	.45	—

PROGRESS OF WOMEN ISSUE

Century of progress of American Women.

Elizabeth Stanton, Carrie Chapman Catt and Lucretia Mott — A406

Designed by Victor S. McCloskey, Jr.

ROTARY PRESS PRINTING
E.E. Plates of 200 subjects in four panes of 50.

1948, July 19		Perf. 11x10½
959 A406 3c dark violet	.20	.20
P# block of 4	.55	—

WILLIAM ALLEN WHITE ISSUE

William Allen White (1868-1944), Writer and Journalist — A407

ROTARY PRESS PRINTING
E.E. Plates of 280 subjects in four panes of 70.

1948, July 31		Perf. 10½x11
960 A407 3c bright red violet	.20	.20
P# block of 4	.40	—

UNITED STATES-CANADA FRIENDSHIP ISSUE

Century of friendship between the US and Canada.

Niagara Railway Suspension Bridge — A408

Designed by Leon Helguera, modeled by V. S. McCloskey, Jr.

ROTARY PRESS PRINTING
E.E. Plates of 200 subjects in four panes of 50.

1948, Aug. 2		Perf. 11x10½
961 A408 3c blue	.20	.20
P# block of 4	.40	—

FRANCIS SCOTT KEY ISSUE

Francis Scott Key (1779-1843), Maryland lawyer and author of "The Star-Spangled Banner" (1813).

Francis Scott Key and American Flags of 1814 and 1948 — A409

Designed by Victor S. McCloskey, Jr.

ROTARY PRESS PRINTING
E.E. Plates of 200 subjects in four panes of 50.

1948, Aug. 9		Perf. 11x10½
962 A409 3c rose pink	.20	.20
P# block of 4	.40	—

SALUTE TO YOUTH ISSUE

Issued to honor the Youth of America and to publicize "Youth Month," September, 1948.

Girl and Boy Carrying Books — A410

ROTARY PRESS PRINTING
E.E. Plates of 200 subjects in four panes of 50.

1948, Aug. 11		Perf. 11x10½
963 A410 3c deep blue	.20	.20
P# block of 4	.40	—

OREGON TERRITORY ISSUE

Centenary of the establishment of Oregon Territory.

John McLoughlin, Jason Lee and Wagon on Oregon Trail — A411

ROTARY PRESS PRINTING
E.E. Plates of 200 subjects in four panes of 50.

1948, Aug. 14		Perf. 11x10½
964 A411 3c brown red	.20	.20
P# block of 4	.40	—

HARLAN F. STONE ISSUE

Harlan Fiske Stone (1872-1946) of New York, associate justice of the Supreme Court, 1925-1941, and chief justice, 1941-1946.

Chief Justice Harlan F. Stone — A412

ROTARY PRESS PRINTING
E.E. Plates of 280 subjects in four panes of 70.

1948, Aug. 25			Perf. 10½x11
965 A412	3c bright violet	.20	.20
	P# block of 4	.60	—

PALOMAR MOUNTAIN OBSERVATORY ISSUE

Dedication, August 30, 1948.

Observatory, Palomar Mountain, California — A413

Designed by Victor S. McCloskey, Jr.

ROTARY PRESS PRINTING
E.E. Plates of 280 subjects in four panes of 70.

1948, Aug. 30			Perf. 10½x11
966 A413	3c blue	.20	.20
	P# block of 4	.95	
a.	Vert. pair, imperf. between	400.	

CLARA BARTON ISSUE

Clara Barton (1821-1912), Founder of the American Red Cross in 1882 — A414

Designed by Charles R. Chickering.

ROTARY PRESS PRINTING
E.E. Plates of 200 subjects in four panes of 50.

1948, Sept. 7			Perf. 11x10½
967 A414	3c rose pink	.20	.20
	P# block of 4	.50	—

POULTRY INDUSTRY CENTENNIAL ISSUE

Light Brahma Rooster A415

Designed by Charles R. Chickering.

ROTARY PRESS PRINTING
E.E. Plates of 200 subjects in four panes of 50.

1948, Sept. 9			Perf. 11x10½
968 A415	3c sepia	.20	.20
	P# block of 4	.50	—

GOLD STAR MOTHERS ISSUE

Issued to honor the mothers of deceased members of the United States armed forces.

Star and Palm Frond — A416

Designed by Charles R. Chickering.

ROTARY PRESS PRINTING
E.E. Plates of 200 subjects in four panes of 50.

1948, Sept. 21			Perf. 10½x11
969 A416	3c orange yellow	.20	.20
	P# block of 4	.40	—

FORT KEARNY ISSUE

Establishment of Fort Kearny, Neb., centenary.

Fort Kearny and Pioneer Group — A417

ROTARY PRESS PRINTING
E.E. Plates of 200 subjects in four panes of 50.

1948, Sept. 22			Perf. 11x10½
970 A417	3c violet	.20	.20
	P# block of 4	.50	—

VOLUNTEER FIREMEN ISSUE

300th anniv. of the organization of the 1st volunteer firemen in America by Peter Stuyvesant.

Peter Stuyvesant, Early and Modern Fire Engines A418

ROTARY PRESS PRINTING
E.E. Plates of 200 subjects in four panes of 50.

1948, Oct. 4			Perf. 11x10½
971 A418	3c bright rose carmine	.20	.20
	P# block of 4	.50	—

INDIAN CENTENNIAL ISSUE

Centenary of the arrival in Indian Territory, later Oklahoma, of the Five Civilized Indian Tribes: Cherokee, Chickasaw, Choctaw, Muscogee and Seminole.

Map of Indian Territory and Seals of Five Tribes — A419

ROTARY PRESS PRINTING
E.E. Plates of 200 subjects in four panes of 50.

1948, Oct. 15			Perf. 11x10½
972 A419	3c dark brown	.20	.20
	P# block of 4	.45	—

ROUGH RIDERS ISSUE

50th anniversary of the organization of the Rough Riders of the Spanish-American War.

Statue of Capt. William O. (Bucky) O'Neill by Solon H. Borglum A420

Designed by Victor S. McCloskey, Jr.

ROTARY PRESS PRINTING
E.E. Plates of 200 subjects in four panes of 50.

1948, Oct. 27			Perf. 11x10½
973 A420	3c violet brown	.20	.2
	P# block of 4	.45	

JULIETTE LOW ISSUE

Low (1860-1927), founder of the Girl Scouts of America. Mrs. Low organized the 1st Girl Guides troop in 1912 at Savannah. The name was changed to Girl Scouts in 1913 and headquarters moved to New York.

Juliette Gordon Low and Girl Scout Emblem A421

Designed by William K. Schrage.

ROTARY PRESS PRINTING
E.E. Plates of 200 subjects in four panes of 50.

1948, Oct. 29			Perf. 11x10½
974 A421	3c blue green	.20	.20
	P# block of 4	.40	—

Will Rogers — A422

Fort Bliss, El Paso, Texas, and Rocket Firing — A423

WILL ROGERS ISSUE

Will Rogers, (1879-1935), humorist and political commentator.

ROTARY PRESS PRINTING
E.E. Plates of 280 subjects in four panes of 70.

1948, Nov. 4			Perf. 10½x11
975 A422	3c bright red violet	.20	.20
	P# block of 4	.45	—

FORT BLISS CENTENNIAL ISSUE

Designed by Charles R. Chickering.

ROTARY PRESS PRINTING
E.E. Plates of 280 subjects in four panes of 70.

1948, Nov. 5			Perf. 10½x11
976 A423	3c henna brown	.20	.20
	P# block of 4	1.00	—

MOINA MICHAEL ISSUE

Moina Michael (1870-1944), educator who originated (1918) the Flanders Field Poppy Day idea as a memorial to the war dead.

Moina Michael and Poppy Plant — A424

ROTARY PRESS PRINTING
E.E. Plates of 200 subjects in four panes of 50.

1948, Nov. 9 — *Perf. 11x10½*
977 A424 3c rose pink — .20 .20
P# block of 4 — .45 —

GETTYSBURG ADDRESS ISSUE

85th anniversary of Abraham Lincoln's address at Gettysburg, Pennsylvania.

Abraham Lincoln and Quotation from Gettysburg Address A425

Designed by Charles R. Chickering.

ROTARY PRESS PRINTING
E.E. Plates of 200 subjects in four panes of 50.

1948, Nov. 19 — *Perf. 11x10½*
978 A425 3c bright blue — .20 .20
P# block of 4 — .50 —

Torch and Emblem of American Turners — A426

Joel Chandler Harris — A427

AMERICAN TURNERS ISSUE

Formation of the American Turners Soc., cent.

Designed by Alvin R. Meissner.

ROTARY PRESS PRINTING
E.E. Plates of 200 subjects in four panes of 50.

1948, Nov. 20 — *Perf. 10½x11*
979 A426 3c carmine — .20 .20
P# block of 4 — .40 —

JOEL CHANDLER HARRIS ISSUE

Joel Chandler Harris (1848-1908), Georgia writer, creator of "Uncle Remus" and newspaperman.

ROTARY PRESS PRINTING
E.E. Plates of 280 subjects in four panes of 70.

1948, Dec. 9 — *Perf. 10½x11*
980 A427 3c bright red violet — .20 .20
P# block of 4 — .55 —

MINNESOTA TERRITORY ISSUE

Establishment of Minnesota Territory, cent.

Pioneer and Red River Oxcart — A428

ROTARY PRESS PRINTING
E.E. Plates of 200 subjects in four panes of 50.

1949, Mar. 3 — *Perf. 11x10½*
981 A428 3c blue green — .20 .20
P# block of 4 — .45 —

WASHINGTON AND LEE UNIVERSITY ISSUE

Bicentenary of Washington and Lee University.

George Washington, Robert E. Lee and University Building, Lexington, Va. — A429

ROTARY PRESS PRINTING
E.E. Plates of 200 subjects in four panes of 50.

1949, Apr. 12 — *Perf. 11x10½*
982 A429 3c ultramarine — .20 .20
P# block of 4 — .40 —

PUERTO RICO ELECTION ISSUE

First gubernatorial election in the Territory of Puerto Rico, Nov. 2, 1948.

Puerto Rican Farmer Holding Cogwheel and Ballot Box — A430

ROTARY PRESS PRINTING
E.E. Plates of 200 subjects in four panes of 50.

1949, Apr. 27 — *Perf. 11x10½*
983 A430 3c green — .20 .20
P# block of 4 — .40 —

ANNAPOLIS TERCENTENARY ISSUE

Founding of Annapolis, Maryland, 300th anniv.

James Stoddert's 1718 Map of Regions about Annapolis, Redrawn A431

ROTARY PRESS PRINTING
E.E. Plates of 200 subjects in four panes of 50.

1949, May 23 — *Perf. 11x10½*
984 A431 3c aquamarine — .20 .20
P# block of 4 — .40 —

G.A.R. ISSUE

Final encampment of the Grand Army of the Republic, Indianapolis, Aug. 28 - Sept. 1, 1949.

Union Soldier and G.A.R. Veteran of 1949 — A432

Designed by Charles R. Chickering.

ROTARY PRESS PRINTING
E.E. Plates of 200 subjects in four panes of 50.

1949, Aug. 29 — *Perf. 11x10½*
985 A432 3c bright rose carmine — .20 .20
P# block of 4 — .40 —

EDGAR ALLAN POE ISSUE

Edgar Allan Poe (1809-1849), Boston-born poet, story writer and editor.

Edgar Allan Poe — A433

ROTARY PRESS PRINTING
E.E. Plates of 280 subjects in four panes of 70.

1949, Oct. 7 — *Perf. 10½x11*
986 A433 3c bright red violet — .20 .20
P# block of 4 — .45 —
Thin outer frame line at top, inner
line missing (24143 LL 42) — 6.00

AMERICAN BANKERS ASSOCIATION ISSUE

75th anniv. of the formation of the Association.

Coin, Symbolizing Fields of Banking Service A434

Designed by Charles R. Chickering.

ROTARY PRESS PRINTING
E.E. Plates of 200 subjects in four panes of 50.

1950, Jan. 3 — *Perf. 11x10½*
987 A434 3c yellow green — .20 .20
P# block of 4 — .40 —

SAMUEL GOMPERS ISSUE

Samuel Gompers (1850-1924), British-born American labor leader.

Samuel Gompers — A435

ROTARY PRESS PRINTING
E.E. Plates of 280 subjects in four panes of 70.

1950, Jan. 27 — *Perf. 10½x11*
988 A435 3c bright red violet — .20 .20
P# block of 4 — .40 —

NATIONAL CAPITAL SESQUICENTENNIAL ISSUE

150th anniversary of the establishment of the National Capital, Washington, D.C.

Statue of Freedom on Capitol Dome — A436

Executive Mansion A437

Supreme Court Building A438

United States Capitol — A439

ROTARY PRESS PRINTING
E.E. Plates of 200 subjects in four panes of 50.

1950			Perf. 10½x11, 11x10½	
989	A436	3c bright blue, *Apr. 20*	.20	.20
		P# block of 4	.40	—
990	A437	3c deep green, *June 12*	.20	.20
		P# block of 4	.40	—
991	A438	3c light violet, *Aug. 2*	.20	.20
		P# block of 4	.30	—
992	A439	3c bright red violet, *Nov. 22*	.20	.20
		P# block of 4	.40	—
		Gripper cracks (24285 UL 11)	4.50	3.00
		Nos. 989-992 (4)	.80	.80

RAILROAD ENGINEERS ISSUE

Issued to honor the Railroad Engineers of America. Stamp portrays John Luther (Casey) Jones (1864-1900), locomotive engineer killed in train wreck near Vaughn, Miss.

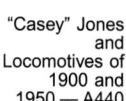

"Casey" Jones and Locomotives of 1900 and 1950 — A440

ROTARY PRESS PRINTING
E.E. Plates of 200 subjects in four panes of 50.

1950, Apr. 29			Perf. 11x10½	
993	A440	3c violet brown	.20	.20
		P# block of 4	.40	—

KANSAS CITY, MISSOURI, CENTENARY ISSUE

Kansas City, Missouri, incorporation.

Kansas City Skyline, 1950 and Westport Landing, 1850 — A441

ROTARY PRESS PRINTING
E.E. Plates of 200 subjects in four panes of 50.

1950, June 3			Perf. 11x10½	
994	A441	3c violet	.20	.20
		P# block of 4	.40	—

BOY SCOUTS ISSUE

Honoring the Boy Scouts of America on the occasion of the 2nd National Jamboree, Valley Forge, Pa.

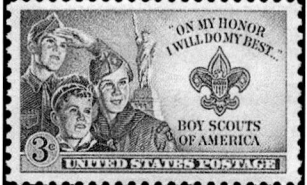

Three Boys, Statue of Liberty and Scout Badge A442

ROTARY PRESS PRINTING
E.E. Plates of 200 subjects in four panes of 50.

1950, June 30			Perf. 11x10½	
995	A442	3c sepia	.20	.20
		P# block of 4	.50	—

INDIANA TERRITORY ISSUE

Establishment of Indiana Territory, 150th anniv.

Gov. William Henry Harrison and First Indiana Capitol, Vincennes A443

ROTARY PRESS PRINTING
E.E. Plates of 200 subjects in four panes of 50.

1950, July 4			Perf. 11x10½	
996	A443	3c bright blue	20	20
		P# block of 4	.50	—

CALIFORNIA STATEHOOD ISSUE

Gold Miner, Pioneers and S.S. Oregon A444

ROTARY PRESS PRINTING
E.E. Plates of 200 subjects in four panes of 50.

1950, Sept. 9			Perf. 11x10½	
997	A444	3c yellow orange	.20	.20
		P# block of 4	.50	—

UNITED CONFEDERATE VETERANS FINAL REUNION ISSUE

Final reunion of the United Confederate Veterans, Norfolk, Virginia, May 30, 1951.

Confederate Soldier and United Confederate Veteran A445

ROTARY PRESS PRINTING
E.E. Plates of 200 subjects in four panes of 50.

1951, May 30			Perf. 11x10½	
998	A445	3c gray	.20	.20
		P# block of 4	.45	—

NEVADA CENTENNIAL ISSUE

Centenary of the settlement of Nevada.

Carson Valley, c. 1851 — A446

Designed by Charles R. Chickering.

ROTARY PRESS PRINTING
E.E. Plates of 200 subjects in four panes of 50.

1951, July 14			Perf. 11x10½	
999	A446	3c light olive green	.20	.20
		P# block of 4	.50	—

LANDING OF CADILLAC ISSUE

250th anniversary of the landing of Antoine de la Mothe Cadillac at Detroit.

Detroit Skyline and Cadillac Landing A447

ROTARY PRESS PRINTING
E.E. Plates of 200 subjects in four panes of 50.

1951, July 24			Perf. 11x10	
1000	A447	3c blue	.20	
		P# block of 4	.30	

COLORADO STATEHOOD, 75th ANNIV.

Colorado Capitol, Mount of the Holy Cross, Columbine and Bronco Buster by Proctor A448

ROTARY PRESS PRINTING
E.E. Plates of 200 subjects in four panes of 50.

1951, Aug. 1			Perf. 11x10½	
1001	A448	3c blue violet	.20	.20
		P# block of 4	.40	—

AMERICAN CHEMICAL SOCIETY ISSUE

75th anniv. of the formation of the Society.

A.C.S. Emblem and Symbols of Chemistry A449

ROTARY PRESS PRINTING
E.E. Plates of 200 subjects in four panes of 50.

1951, Sept. 4			Perf. 11x10½	
1002	A449	3c violet brown	.20	.20
		P# block of 4	.40	—

BATTLE OF BROOKLYN, 175th ANNIV.

Gen. George Washington Evacuating Army; Fulton Ferry House at Right — A450

ROTARY PRESS PRINTING
E.E. Plates of 200 subjects in four panes of 50.

1951, Dec. 10			Perf. 11x10½	
1003	A450	3c violet	.20	.20
		P# block of 4	.40	—

BETSY ROSS ISSUE

200th anniv. of the birth of Betsy Ross, maker of the first American flag.

"Birth of Our Nation's Flag," by Charles H. Weisgerber — Betsy Ross Showing Flag to Gen. George Washington, Robert Morris and George Ross — A451

ROTARY PRESS PRINTING
E.E. Plates of 200 subjects in four panes of 50.

1952, Jan. 2			Perf. 11x10½	
1004	A451	3c carmine rose	.20	.20
		P# block of 4	.40	—

4-H CLUB ISSUE

Farm, Club Emblem, Boy and Girl — A452

ROTARY PRESS PRINTING
E.E. Plates of 200 subjects in four panes of 50.

952, Jan. 15   *Perf. 11x10½*
005 A452 3c blue green   .20 .20
    P# block of 4   .50 —

B. & O. RAILROAD ISSUE

125th anniv. of the granting of a charter to the Baltimore and Ohio Railroad Company by the Maryland Legislature.

Charter and Three Stages of Rail Transportation A453

ROTARY PRESS PRINTING
E.E. Plates of 200 subjects in four panes of 50.

1952, Feb. 28   *Perf. 11x10½*
1006 A453 3c bright blue   .20 .20
    P# block of 4   .45 —

A. A. A. ISSUE

50th anniversary of the formation of the American Automobile Association.

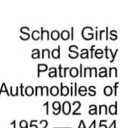

School Girls and Safety Patrolman Automobiles of 1902 and 1952 — A454

ROTARY PRESS PRINTING
E.E. Plates of 200 subjects in four panes of 50.

1952, Mar. 4   *Perf. 11x10½*
1007 A454 3c deep blue   .20 .20
    P# block of 4   .40 —

NATO ISSUE

Signing of the North Atlantic Treaty, 3rd anniv.

Torch of Liberty and Globe — A455

ROTARY PRESS PRINTING
E.E. Plates of 400 subjects in four panes of 100.

1952, Apr. 4   *Perf. 11x10½*
1008 A455 3c deep violet   .20 .20
    P# block of 4   .40 —

GRAND COULEE DAM ISSUE

50 years of Federal cooperation in developing the resources of rivers and streams in the West.

Spillway, Grand Coulee Dam — A456

ROTARY PRESS PRINTING
E.E. Plates of 200 subjects in four panes of 50.

1952, May 15   *Perf. 11x10½*
1009 A456 3c blue green   .20 .20
    P# block of 4   .40 —

LAFAYETTE ISSUE

175th anniversary of the arrival of Marquis de Lafayette in America.

Marquis de Lafayette, Flags, Cannon and Landing Party — A457

Designed by Victor S. McCloskey, Jr.

ROTARY PRESS PRINTING
E.E. Plates of 200 subjects in four panes of 50.

1952, June 13   *Perf. 11x10½*
1010 A457 3c bright blue   .20 .20
    P# block of 4   .45 —

MT. RUSHMORE MEMORIAL ISSUE

Dedication of the Mt. Rushmore National Memorial in the Black Hills of South Dakota, 25th anniv.

Sculptured Heads on Mt. Rushmore — A458

Designed by William K. Schrage.

ROTARY PRESS PRINTING
E.E. Plates of 200 subjects in four panes of 50.

1952, Aug. 11   *Perf. 10½x11*
1011 A458 3c blue green   .20 .20
    P# block of 4   .60 —

ENGINEERING CENTENNIAL ISSUE

American Society of Civil Engineers founding.

George Washington Bridge and Covered Bridge of 1850's A459

ROTARY PRESS PRINTING
E.E. Plates of 200 subjects in four panes of 50.

1952, Sept. 6   *Perf. 11x10½*
1012 A459 3c violet blue   .20 .20
    P# block of 4   .45 —

SERVICE WOMEN ISSUE

Women in the United States Armed Services.

Women of the Marine Corps, Army, Navy and Air Force — A460

ROTARY PRESS PRINTING
E.E. Plates of 200 subjects in four panes of 50.

1952, Sept. 11   *Perf. 11x10½*
1013 A460 3c deep blue   .20 .20
    P# block of 4   .40 —

GUTENBERG BIBLE ISSUE

Printing of the 1st book, the Holy Bible, from movable type, by Johann Gutenberg, 500th anniv.

Gutenberg Showing Proof to the Elector of Mainz — A461

ROTARY PRESS PRINTING
E.E. Plates of 200 subjects in four panes of 50.

1952, Sept. 30   *Perf. 11x10½*
1014 A461 3c violet   .20 .20
    P# block of 4   .40 —

NEWSPAPER BOYS ISSUE

Newspaper Boy, Torch and Group of Homes A462

ROTARY PRESS PRINTING
E.E. Plates of 200 subjects in four panes of 50.

1952, Oct. 4   *Perf. 11x10½*
1015 A462 3c violet   .20 .20
    P# block of 4   .40 —

RED CROSS ISSUE

Globe, Sun and Cross — A463

ROTARY PRESS PRINTING
Cross Typographed
E.E. Plates of 200 subjects in four panes of 50.

1952, Nov. 21   *Perf. 11x10½*
1016 A463 3c deep blue & carmine   .20 .20
    P# block of 4   .40 —

NATIONAL GUARD ISSUE

National Guardsman, Amphibious Landing and Disaster Service A464

ROTARY PRESS PRINTING
E.E. Plates of 200 subjects in four panes of 50.

1953, Feb. 23		Perf. 11x10½
1017 A464 3c **bright blue**	.20	.20
P# block of 4	.40	—

OHIO STATEHOOD, 150th ANNIV.

Ohio Map, State Seal, Buckeye Leaf — A465

ROTARY PRESS PRINTING
E.E. Plates of 280 subjects in four panes of 70.

1953, Mar. 2		Perf. 11x10½
1018 A465 3c **chocolate**	.20	.20
P# block of 4	.45	—

WASHINGTON TERRITORY ISSUE

Organization of Washington Territory, cent.

Medallion, Pioneers and Washington Scene — A466

ROTARY PRESS PRINTING
E.E. Plates of 200 subjects in four panes of 50.

1953, Mar. 2		Perf. 11x10½
1019 A466 3c **green**	.20	.20
P# block of 4	.40	—

LOUISIANA PURCHASE, 150th ANNIV.

James Monroe, Robert R. Livingston and Marquis Francois de Barbé-Marbois A467

ROTARY PRESS PRINTING
E.E. Plates of 200 subjects in four panes of 50.

1953, Apr. 30		Perf. 11x10½
1020 A467 3c **violet brown**	.20	.20
P# block of 4	.50	—

OPENING OF JAPAN CENTENNIAL ISSUE

Centenary of Commodore Matthew Calbraith Perry's negotiations with Japan, which opened her doors to foreign trade.

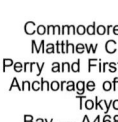

Commodore Matthew C. Perry and First Anchorage off Tokyo Bay — A468

ROTARY PRESS PRINTING
E.E. Plates of 200 subjects in four panes of 50.

1953, July 14		Perf. 11x10½
1021 A468 5c **green**	.20	.20
P# block of 4	.65	—

AMERICAN BAR ASSOCIATION, 75th ANNIV.

Section of Frieze, Supreme Court Room — A469

ROTARY PRESS PRINTING
E.E. Plates of 200 subjects in four panes of 50.

1953, Aug. 24		Perf. 11x10½
1022 A469 3c **rose violet**	.20	.20
P# block of 4	.40	—

SAGAMORE HILL ISSUE

Opening of Sagamore Hill, Theodore Roosevelt's home, as a national shrine.

Home of Theodore Roosevelt A470

ROTARY PRESS PRINTING
E.E. Plates of 200 subjects in four panes of 50.

1953, Sept. 14		Perf. 11x10½
1023 A470 3c **yellow green**	.20	.20
P# block of 4	.40	—

FUTURE FARMERS ISSUE

25th anniversary of the organization of Future Farmers of America.

Agricultural Scene and Future Farmer A471

ROTARY PRESS PRINTING
E.E. Plates of 200 subjects in four panes of 50.

1953, Oct. 13		Perf. 11x10½
1024 A471 3c **deep blue**	.20	.20
P# block of 4	.40	—

TRUCKING INDUSTRY ISSUE

50th anniv. of the Trucking Industry in the US.

Truck, Farm and Distant City — A472

ROTARY PRESS PRINTING
E.E. Plates of 200 subjects in four panes of 50.

1953, Oct. 27		Perf. 11x10½
1025 A472 3c **violet**	.20	.20
P# block of 4	.40	—

GENERAL PATTON ISSUE

Honoring Gen. George S. Patton, Jr. (1885-1945), and the armored forces of the US Army.

Gen. George S. Patton, Jr. and Tanks in Action — A473

ROTARY PRESS PRINTING
E.E. Plates of 200 subjects in four panes of 50.

1953, Nov. 11		Perf. 11x10½
1026 A473 3c **blue violet**	.20	
P# block of 4	.45	

NEW YORK CITY, 300th ANNIV.

Dutch Ship in New Amsterdam Harbor A474

ROTARY PRESS PRINTING
E.E. Plates of 200 subjects in four panes of 50.

1953, Nov. 20		Perf. 11x10½
1027 A474 3c **bright red violet**	.20	.2
P# block of 4	.40	—

GADSDEN PURCHASE ISSUE

Centenary of James Gadsden's purchase of territory from Mexico to adjust the US-Mexico boundary.

Map and Pioneer Group — A475

ROTARY PRESS PRINTING
E.E. Plates of 200 subjects in four panes of 50.

1953, Dec. 30		Perf. 11x10½
1028 A475 3c **copper brown**	.20	.20
P# block of 4	.40	—

COLUMBIA UNIVERSITY, 200th ANNIV.

Low Memorial Library A476

ROTARY PRESS PRINTING
E.E. Plates of 200 subjects in four panes of 50.

1954, Jan. 4		Perf. 11x10½
1029 A476 3c **blue**	.20	.20
P# block of 4	.40	—

Wet and Dry Printings

In 1953 the Bureau of Engraving and Printing began experiments in printing on "dry" paper (moisture content 5-10 per cent). In previous "wet" printings the paper had a moisture content of 15-35 per cent.

The new process required a thicker, stiffer paper, special types of inks and greater pressure to force the paper into the recessed plates. The "dry" printings show whiter paper, a higher sheen on the surface, feel thicker and stiffer, and the designs stand out more clearly than on the "wet" printings.

Nos. 832c and 1041 (flat plate) were the first "dry" printings to be issued of flat-plate, regular-issue stamps. No. 1063 was the first rotary press stamp to be produced entirely by "dry" printing.

Stamps printed by both the "wet" and "dry" process are Nos. 1030, 1031, 1035, 1035a, 1036, 1039, 1049, 1050-1052, 1054, 1055, 1057, 1058, C34-C36, C39, C39a, J78, J80-J84, QE1-QE3, RF26-RF28, S1, S1a, S2, S2a, S3. The "wet" printed 4c coil, No. 1058, exists only Bureau precanceled.

In the Liberty Issue listings that follow, wet printings are listed first, followed by dry printings. Where only one type of printing of a stamp is indicated, it is "dry."

All postage stamps have been printed by the "dry" process since the late 1950s.

LIBERTY ISSUE

Benjamin Franklin — A477

George Washington — A478

Palace of the Governors, Santa Fe — A478a

Mount Vernon — A479

Thomas Jefferson — A480

Bunker Hill Monument and Massachusetts Flag, 1776 — A481

Statue of Liberty — A482

Abraham Lincoln — A483

The Hermitage, Home of Andrew Jackson, near Nashville — A484

James Monroe — A485

Theodore Roosevelt — A486

Woodrow Wilson — A487

Statue of Liberty — A488

Statue of Liberty — A489

John J. Pershing — A489a

The Alamo, San Antonio — A490

Independence Hall — A491

Statue of Liberty — A491a

Benjamin Harrison — A492

John Jay — A493

Monticello, Home of Thomas Jefferson, near Charlottesville, Va. — A494

Paul Revere — A495

Robert E. Lee — A496

John Marshall — A497

Susan B. Anthony — A498

Patrick Henry — A499

Alexander Hamilton — A500

ROTARY PRESS PRINTING
E.E. Plates of 400 subjects in four panes of 100

1954-68   **Perf. 11x10½**

1030a	A477	½c **red orange,** wet printing, *Oct. 20, 1955*	.20	.20
		P# block of 4	.35	—

1030	A477	½c **red orange,** dry printing, *May 1958*	.20	.20
		P# block of 4 (#25980 and up)	.25	—
1031b	A478	1c **dark green,** wet printing, *Aug. 26, 1954*	.20	.20
		P# block of 4	.25	—
1031	A478	1c **dark green,** dry printing, *Mar. 1956*	.20	.20
		P# block of 4 (#25326 and up)	.25	—
		Pair with full vert. gutter between	150.00	
		Pair with full horiz. gutter between	150.00	

Perf. 10½x11

1031A	A478a	1¼c **turquoise,** *June 17, 1960*	.20	.20
		P# block of 4	.45	
1032	A479	1½c **brown carmine,** *Feb. 22, 1956*	.20	.20
		P# block of 4	1.75	

Perf. 11x10½

1033	A480	2c **carmine rose,** *Sept. 15, 1954*	.20	.20
		P# block of 4	.25	
		Pair with full vert. gutter between	—	
		Pair with full horiz. gutter between	—	
a.		Silkote paper	500.	
		P# block of 4	2,750.	

Silkote paper was used in 1954 for an experimental printing of 50,000 stamps. The stamps were put on sale at the Westbrook, Maine post office in Dec. 1954. Only plates 25061 and 25062 were used to print No. 1033a (these plates also used to print No. 1033 on normal paper). Competent expertization is required for No. 1033a.

1034	A481	2½c **gray blue,** *June 17, 1959*	.20	.20
		P# block of 4	.50	—
1035e	A482	3c **deep violet,** wet printing, *June 24, 1954*	.20	.20
		P# block of 4	.35	—
a.		Booklet pane of 6, *June 30, 1954*	4.00	1.25
g.		As "a," vert. imperf. between	5,000.	
1035	A482	3c **deep violet,** dry printing	.20	.20
		P# block of 4 (#25235 and up)	.25	—
		Pair with full vert. gutter between	150.00	
		Pair with full horiz. gutter between	150.00	
b.		Tagged, *July 6, 1966*	.30	.25
		P# block of 4	5.50	
c.		Imperf., pair	2,000.	
d.		Horiz. pair, imperf. between	—	
f.		Booklet pane of 6, dry printing	5.00	1.50

No. 1057a measures about 19½x22mm; No. 1035c, about 18¾x22½mm.

1036c	A483	4c **red violet,** wet printing, *Nov. 19, 1954*	.20	.20
		P# block of 4	.50	—
1036	A483	4c **red violet,** dry printing	.20	.20
		P# block of 4 (#25445 and up)	.35	—
		Pair with full vert. gutter between	675.00	
		Pair with full horiz. gutter between	900.00	
a.		Booklet pane of 6, *July 31, 1958*	2.75	1.25
b.		Tagged, *Nov. 2, 1963*	.60	.40

			8.50	—
d.	As "a," imperf. horiz.		—	
e.	Horiz. pair, imperf between		3,500.	

No. 1036e resulted from a booklet pane foldover after perforating and before cutting into panes.

Perf. 10½x11

1037	A484	4½c **blue green,** *Mar. 16, 1959*	.20	.20
		P# block of 4	.65	

Perf. 11x10½

1038	A485	5c **deep blue,** *Dec. 2, 1954*	.20	.20
		P# block of 4	.45	
		Pair with full vert. gutter btwn.	200.00	
1039a	A486	6c **carmine,** wet printing, *Nov. 18, 1955*	.40	.20
		P# block of 4	2.00	
1039	A486	6c **carmine,** dry printing	.25	.20
		P# block of 4 (#25427 and up)	1.25	
b.	Imperf., block of 4 (unique)	23,000.		
1040	A487	7c **rose carmine,** *Jan. 10, 1956*	.20	.20
		P# block of 4	1.00	—
a.	7c **dark rose carmine**	.20	.20	
	P# block of 4	1.00		

FLAT PLATE PRINTING
Plates of 400 subjects in four panes of 100 each
Size: 22.7mm high
Perf. 11

1041	A488	8c **dark violet blue & carmine,** *Apr. 9, 1954*	.25	.20
		P# block of 4, 2#	2.00	—
		Corner P# block of 4, blue # only	—	
		Corner P# block of 4, red # only	—	
a.	Double impression of carmine	575.00		

FLAT PRINTING PLATES
Frame: 24912-13-14-15, 24926, 24929-30, 24932-33.
Vignette: 24916-17-18-19-20, 24935-36-37, 24939.
See note following No. 1041B.

ROTARY PRESS PRINTING
Plates of 400 subjects in four panes of 100 each
Size: 22.9mm high
Perf. 11

1041B	A488	8c **dark violet blue & carmine,** *Apr. 9, 1954*	.40	.20
		P# block of 4, 2#	3.50	—

ROTARY PRINTING PLATES
Frame: 24923-24, 24928, 24940, 24942.
Vignette: 24927, 24938.
No. 1041B is slightly taller than No. 1041, about the thickness of one line of engraving.

GIORI PRESS PRINTING
Plates of 400 subjects in four panes of 100 each
Redrawn design
Perf. 11

1042	A489	8c **dark violet blue & carmine rose,** *Mar. 22, 1958*	.20	.20
		P# block of 4	.90	

ROTARY PRESS PRINTING
E.E. Plates of 400 subjects in four panes of 100 each
Perf. 11x10½

1042A	A489a	8c **brown,** *Nov. 17, 1961*	.20	.20
		P# block of 4	.90	

Perf. 10½x11

1043	A490	9c **rose lilac,** *June 14, 1956*	.30	.20
		P# block of 4	1.30	—
a.	9c **dark rose lilac**	.30	.20	
	P# block of 4	1.30		
1044	A491	10c **rose lake,** *July 4, 1956*	.30	.20
		P# block of 4	1.40	—
b.	10c **dark rose lake**	.25	.20	
	P# block of 4	1.10		
d.	Tagged, *July 6, 1966*	2.00	1.00	
	P# block of 4	35.00		

No. 1044b is from later printings and is on a harder, whiter paper than No. 1044.

GIORI PRESS PRINTING
Plates of 400 subjects in four panes of 100.
Perf. 11

1044A	A491a	11c **carmine & dark violet blue,** *June 15, 1961*	.30	.20
		P# block of 4	1.50	
c.	Tagged, *Jan. 11, 1967*	2.00	1.60	
	P# block of 4	35.00		

ROTARY PRESS PRINTING
E.E. Plates of 400 subjects in four panes of 100 each
Perf. 11x10½

1045	A492	12c **red,** *June 6, 1959*	.35	.20
		P# block of 4	1.50	—
a.	Tagged, *1968*	.35	.20	

			P# block of 4	4.00	—
1046	A493	15c **rose lake,** *Dec. 12, 1958*	.60	.20	
		P# block of 4	3.00	—	
a.	Tagged, *July 6, 1966*	1.10	.80		
	P# block of 4	13.00			

Perf. 10½x11

1047	A494	20c **ultramarine,** *Apr. 13, 1956*	.40	.20
		P# block of 4	1.75	—
a.	20c **deep bright ultramarine**	.40	.20	
	P# block of 4	1.75	—	

No. 1047a is from later printings and is on a harder, whiter paper than No. 1047.

Perf. 11x10½

1048	A495	25c **green,** *Apr. 18, 1958*	1.10	.75
		P# block of 4	4.75	—
1049a	A496	30c **black,** wet printing, *Sept. 21, 1955*	1.10	.75
		P# block of 4	5.00	—
1049	A496	30c **black,** dry printing, *June 1957*	.70	.20
		P# block of 4 (#25487 and up)	4.00	—
b.	30c **intense black**	.70	.20	
	P# block of 4	3.50	—	

No. 1049b is from later printings and is on a harder, whiter paper than No. 1049.

1050a	A497	40c **brown red,** wet printing, *Sept. 24, 1955*	1.75	.25
		P# block of 4	9.00	
1050	A497	40c **brown red,** dry printing, *Apr. 1958*	1.50	.20
		P# block of 4 (#25571 and up)	7.50	
1051a	A498	50c **bright purple,** wet printing, *Aug. 25, 1955*	1.75	.20
		P# block of 4	11.00	
		Cracked plate (25231 UL 1)	—	
1051	A498	50c **bright purple,** dry printing, *Apr. 1958*	1.50	.20
		P# block of 4 (#25897 and up)	7.00	
1052a	A499	$1 **purple,** wet printing, *Oct. 7, 1955*	5.25	1.00
		P# block of 4	22.50	
1052	A499	$1 **purple,** dry printing, *Oct. 1958*	4.50	.20
		P# block of 4 (#25541 and up)	19.00	

FLAT PLATE PRINTING
Plates of 400 subjects in four panes of 100.
Perf. 11

1053	A500	$5 **black,** *Mar. 19, 1956*	60.00	6.75
		P# block of 4	275.00	

Bureau Precancels: ½c, 37 diff., 1c, 113 diff., 1¼c, 142 diff., 1½c, 45 diff.
2c, 86 diff., 2½c, 123 diff., 3c, 106 diff., 4c, 95 diff., 4½c, 23 diff., 5c, 20 diff., 6c, 23 diff., 7c, 16 diff.
Also, No. 1041, 12 diff., No. 1042, 12 diff., No. 1042A, 16 diff., 9c, 15 diff., 10c, 16 diff., 11c, New York, 12c, 6 diff.
15c, 12 diff., 20c, 20 diff., 25c, 11 diff., 30c, 17 diff., 40c, 10 diff., 50c, 19 diff., $1, 5 diff.

Large Holes

Small Holes

With the change from 384-subject plates to 432-subject plates the size of the perforation holes was reduced. While both are perf. 10 the later holes are smaller than the paper between them. The difference is most noticible on pairs.

ROTARY PRESS COIL STAMPS
1954-80   Perf. 10 Vertically

1054c	A478	1c **dark green,** large holes, wet printing, *Oct. 8, 1954*	.35	
		Pair	.70	
		Joint line pair	1.75	
1054	A478	1c **dark green,** small holes, *Feb. 1960*	.20	.20
		Pair	.40	
		Joint line pair	1.00	
		Large holes, dry printing, *Aug. 1957*	1.00	
		Pair	2.00	
		Joint line pair	4.00	
b.	Imperf., pair	2,500.		

Perf. 10 Horizontally

1054A	A478a	1¼c **turquoise,** *June 17, 1960,* small holes	.20	
		Pair	.25	
		Joint line pair	2.25	
		Large holes	6.00	
		Pair	15.00	
		Joint line pair	150.00	

Perf. 10 Vertically

1055d	A480	2c **carmine rose,** large holes, wet printing, *Oct. 22, 1954*	.40	
		Pair	.80	
		Joint line pair	3.50	
1055	A480	2c **carmine rose,** large holes, dry printing, *May 1957*	.35	
		Pair	.80	
		Joint line pair	1.50	
		Small holes, *Aug. 1961*	2.00	
		Pair	5.00	
		Joint line pair	25.00	
a.	Tagged, small holes, shiny gum, *May 6, 1968*	.20		
	Pair	.20		
	Joint line pair	.75		
	Dull gum, tagged, small holes	.50		
	Pair	1.00		
	Joint line pair	2.50		
b.	Imperf., pair, untagged, shiny gum (Bureau precanceled, Riverdale, MD)	475.00		
	Joint line pair	1,200.		
c.	Imperf. pair, tagged, shiny gum	550.00		
	Joint line pair	1,200.		
1056	A481	2½c **gray blue,** large holes, *Sept. 9, 1959*	.30	.25
		Pair	.60	.50
		Joint line pair	3.50	1.75
		Small holes, *Jan. 1961*	400.00	100.00
		Pair	850.00	200.00
		Joint line pair	3,000.	400.00

No. 1056 with small holes only known with Bureau precancels. It was against postal regulations to make mint precanceled stamps available other than to permit holders for their use. Resale was prohibited. Since some mint examples do exist in the marketplace, values are furnished here.

1057c	A482	3c **deep violet,** large holes, wet printing, *July 20, 1954*	.35	.20
		Pair	.80	.25
		Joint line pair	2.75	.60
		Small holes, *Jan. 1961*	—	
		Pair	—	
		Joint line pair	—	
1057	A482	3c **deep violet,** large holes, dry printing, *Oct. 1956*	.35	.20
		Pair	.80	.20
		Joint line pair	2.75	.25
		Gripper cracks	—	
		Small holes, *Mar. 1958*	.20	.20
		Pair	.20	.20
		Joint line pair	.55	.20
a.	Imperf., pair	1,500.	850.00	
	Joint line pair	2,750.		
b.	Tagged, small holes, philatelic printing, *June 26, 1967*	1.00	.50	
	Pair	3.00	1.00	
	Joint line pair	25.00		
d.	Tagged, small holes, Look magazine printing, *Oct. 1966*	4.00	4.00	
	Pair	11.00	8.00	
	Joint line pair	250.00		

Earliest known use No. 1057d: Dec. 29, 1966.

No. 1057a measures about 19½x22mm; No. 1035c, about 18¾x22½mm.

The second tagged printing (No. 1057b) was a "philatelic reprint" made when the original stock of tagged stamps was exhausted. The original tagged printing (No. 1057d, specially printed for "Look" magazine) has a less intense color, the impression is less sharp and the tagging is brighter.

The reprint was printed on a slightly fluorescent paper, while the original paper is dead under longwave UV light.

1058b	A483	4c **red violet,** large holes, wet printing (Bureau precanceled)	27.50	.50
		Pair	60.00	
		Joint line pair	375.00	

It was against postal regulations to make mint precanceled copies of No. 1058b available other than to permit holders for their use. Resale was prohibited. Since some mint examples do exist in the marketplace, values are furnished here.

1058	A483	4c **red violet,** large holes, dry printing, *July 31, 1958*	.50	.20

		Pair	1.50	.30
		Joint line pair	2.50	.40
	Small holes		.20	.20
		Pair	.35	.20
		Joint line pair	.70	.25
a.	Imperf., pair		90.00	75.00
		Joint line pair	200.00	

Perf. 10 Horizontally

1059	A484	4½c **blue green**, large holes, *May 1, 1959*		1.50	1.00
		Pair	3.00	2.25
		Joint line pair	14.00	3.00
	Small holes		12.00	
		Pair	35.00	
		Joint line pair	450.00	—

Perf. 10 Vertically

1059A	A495	25c **green**, *Feb. 25, 1965*		.50	.30
		Pair	1.00	.60
		Joint line pair	2.00	1.20
b.	Tagged, shiny gum, *Apr. 3, 1973*		.80	.20
		Pair	1.60	.40
		Joint line pair	3.25	1.25
	Tagged, dull gum, *1980*		1.75	
		Pair	3.50	
		Joint line pair	7.00	
c.	Imperf., pair		40.00	
		Joint line pair	80.00	

Value for No. 1059Ac is for fine centering.

Bureau Precancels: 1c, 118 diff., 1¼c, 105 diff., 2c, 191 diff., 2½c, 94 diff., 3c, 142 diff., 4c, 83 diff., 4½c, 23 diff.

NEBRASKA TERRITORY ISSUE

Establishment of the Nebraska Territory, centenary.

"The Sower," Mitchell Pass and Scotts Bluff — A507

ROTARY PRESS PRINTING
E.E. Plates of 200 subjects in four panes of 50.

1954, May 7			**Perf. 11x10½**	
1060	A507 3c **violet**		.20	.20
	P# block of 4		.45	—

KANSAS TERRITORY ISSUE

Establishment of the Kansas Territory, centenary

Wheat Field and Pioneer Wagon Train — A508

ROTARY PRESS PRINTING
E.E. Plates of 200 subjects in four panes of 50.

1954, May 31			**Perf. 11x10½**	
1061	A508 3c **brown orange**		.20	.20
	P# block of 4		.55	—

GEORGE EASTMAN ISSUE

Eastman (1854-1932), inventor of photographic dry plates, flexible film and the Kodak camera; Rochester, N.Y., industrialist.

George Eastman — A509

ROTARY PRESS PRINTING
E.E. Plates of 280 subjects in four panes of 70.

1954, July 12			**Perf. 10½x11**	
1062	A509 3c **violet brown**		.20	.20
	P# block of 4		.40	—

LEWIS AND CLARK EXPEDITION

150th anniv. of the Lewis and Clark expedition.

Meriwether Lewis, William Clark and Sacagawea Landing on Missouri Riverbank A510

ROTARY PRESS PRINTING
E.E. Plates of 200 subjects in four panes of 50.

1954, July 28			**Perf. 11x10½**	
1063	A510 3c **violet brown**		.20	.20
	P# block of 4		.60	—

PENNSYLVANIA ACADEMY OF THE FINE ARTS ISSUE

150th anniversary of the founding of the Pennsylvania Academy of the Fine Arts, Philadelphia.

Charles Willson Peale in his Museum, Self-portrait — A511

ROTARY PRESS PRINTING
E.E. Plates of 200 subjects in four panes of 50.

1955, Jan. 15			**Perf. 10½x11**	
1064	A511 3c **rose brown**		.20	.20
	P# block of 4		.45	—

LAND GRANT COLLEGES ISSUE

Centenary of the founding of Michigan State College and Pennsylvania State University, first of the land grant institutions.

Open Book and Symbols of Subjects Taught A512

ROTARY PRESS PRINTING
E.E. Plates of 200 subjects in four panes of 50.

1955, Feb. 12			**Perf. 11x10½**	
1065	A512 3c **green**		.20	.20
	P# block of 4		.45	—

ROTARY INTERNATIONAL, 50th ANNIV.

Torch, Globe and Rotary Emblem A513

ROTARY PRESS PRINTING
E.E. Plates of 200 subjects in four panes of 50.

1955, Feb. 23			**Perf. 11x10½**	
1066	A513 8c **deep blue**		.25	.20
	P# block of 4		1.25	—

ARMED FORCES RESERVE ISSUE

Marine, Coast Guard, Army, Navy and Air Force Personnel A514

ROTARY PRESS PRINTING
E.E. Plates of 200 subjects in four panes of 50.

1955, May 21			**Perf. 11x10½**	
1067	A514 3c **purple**		.20	.20
	P# block of 4		.40	—

NEW HAMPSHIRE ISSUE

Sesquicentennial of the discovery of the "Old Man of the Mountains."

Great Stone Face — A515

ROTARY PRESS PRINTING
E.E. Plates of 200 subjects in four panes of 50.

1955, June 21			**Perf. 10½x11**	
1068	A515 3c **green**		.20	.20
	P# block of 4		.70	—

SOO LOCKS ISSUE
Centenary of the opening of the Soo Locks.

Map of Great
Lakes and Two
Steamers
A516

ROTARY PRESS PRINTING
E.E. Plates of 200 subjects in four panes of 50.

1955, June 28   *Perf. 11x10½*
1069 A516 3c **blue**   .20   .20
    P# block of 4   .40   —

ATOMS FOR PEACE ISSUE
Issued to promote an Atoms for Peace policy.

Atomic Energy
Encircling the
Hemispheres
A517

Designed by George R. Cox.

ROTARY PRESS PRINTING
E.E. Plates of 200 subjects in four panes of 50.

1955, July 28   *Perf. 11x10½*
1070 A517 3c **deep blue**   .20   .20
    P# block of 4   .40   —

FORT TICONDEROGA ISSUE
Bicentenary of Fort Ticonderoga, New York.

Map of the
Fort, Ethan
Allen and
Artillery
A518

Designed by Enrico Arno.

ROTARY PRESS PRINTING
E.E. Plates of 200 subjects in four panes of 50.

1955, Sept. 18   *Perf. 11x10½*
1071 A518 3c **light brown**   .20   .20
    P# block of 4   .40   —

Andrew W.
Mellon — A519

"Franklin Taking
Electricity from the
Sky," by Benjamin
West — A520

ANDREW W. MELLON ISSUE
Andrew W. Mellon (1855-1937), US Secretary of the
Treasury (1921-32), financier and art collector.

Designed by Victor S. McCloskey, Jr.

ROTARY PRESS PRINTING
E.E. Plates of 280 subjects in four panes of 70.

1955, Dec. 20   *Perf. 10½x11*
1072 A519 3c **rose carmine**   .20   .20
    P# block of 4   .40   —

BENJAMIN FRANKLIN ISSUE
250th anniv. of the birth of Benjamin Franklin.

Designed by Charles R. Chickering.

ROTARY PRESS PRINTING
E.E. Plates of 200 subjects in four panes of 50.

1956, Jan. 17   *Perf. 10½x11*
1073 A520 3c **bright carmine**   .20   .20
    P# block of 4   .40   —

BOOKER T. WASHINGTON ISSUE
Washington (1856-1915), black educator, founder
and head of Tuskegee Institute in Alabama.

Log
Cabin — A521

Designed by Charles R. Chickering.

ROTARY PRESS PRINTING
E.E. Plates of 200 subjects in four panes of 50.

1956, Apr. 5   *Perf. 11x10½*
1074 A521 3c **deep blue**   .20   .20
    P# block of 4   .40   —

FIFTH INTERNATIONAL PHILATELIC EXHIBITION ISSUES
FIPEX, New York City, Apr. 28 - May 6, 1956.

SOUVENIR SHEET

A522

Illustration reduced.

FLAT PLATE PRINTING
Plates of 24 subjects

1956, Apr. 28   *Imperf.*
1075 A522   Sheet of 2   2.00   1.50
  a.   A482 3c deep violet   .80   .60
  b.   A488 8c dark violet blue & carmine 1.00   .75

No. 1075 measures 108x73mm. Nos. 1075a and 1075b measure 24x28mm.
Inscriptions printed in dark violet blue; scrolls and stars in
carmine.

New York
Coliseum and
Columbus
Monument
A523

Designed by William K. Schrage.

ROTARY PRESS PRINTING
E.E. Plates of 200 subjects in four panes of 50.

1956, Apr. 30   *Perf. 11x10½*
1076 A523 3c **deep violet**   .20   .20
    P# block of 4   .30   —

WILDLIFE CONSERVATION ISSUE
Issued to emphasize the importance of Wildlife Conservation in America.

Wild Turkey
A524

Pronghorn
Antelope
A525

King Salmon
A526

Designed by Robert W. (Bob) Hines.

ROTARY PRESS PRINTING
E.E. Plates of 200 subjects in four panes of 50.

1956   *Perf. 11x10½*
1077 A524 3c **rose lake,** *May 5*   .20   .20
    P# block of 4   .35   —
1078 A525 3c **brown,** *June 22*   .20   .20
    P# block of 4   .35   —
1079 A526 3c **blue green,** *Nov. 9*   .20   .20
    P# block of 4   .35   —
    Nos. 1077-1079 (3)   .60   .60

PURE FOOD AND DRUG LAWS, 50th ANNIV.

Harvey Washington
Wiley — A527

Designed by Robert L. Miller.

ROTARY PRESS PRINTING
E.E. Plates of 200 subjects in four panes of 50.

1956, June 27   *Perf. 10½x11*
1080 A527 3c **dark blue green**   .20   .20
    P# block of 4   .50   —

WHEATLAND ISSUE

Pres.
Buchanan's
Home,
Lancaster,
Pa. — A528

ROTARY PRESS PRINTING
E.E. Plates of 200 subjects in four panes of 50.

1956, Aug. 5   *Perf. 11x10½*
1081 A528 3c **black brown**   .20   .20
    P# block of 4   .40   —

LABOR DAY ISSUE

Mosaic, AFL-CIO
Headquarters — A529

Designed by Victor S. McCloskey, Jr.

ROTARY PRESS PRINTING
E.E. Plates of 200 subjects in four panes of 50.

1956, Sept. 3		*Perf. 10½x11*	
1082 A529 3c **deep blue**		.20	.20
P# block of 4		.40	—

NASSAU HALL ISSUE

200th anniv. of Nassau Hall, Princeton University.

Nassau Hall,
Princeton,
N.J. — A530

ROTARY PRESS PRINTING
E.E. Plates of 200 subjects in four panes of 50.

1956, Sept. 22		*Perf. 11x10½*	
1083 A530 3c **black,** *orange*		.20	.20
P# block of 4		.50	—

DEVILS TOWER ISSUE

Issued to commemorate the 50th anniversary of the Federal law providing for protection of American natural antiquities. Devils Tower National Monument, Wyoming, is an outstanding example.

Devils Tower — A531

Designed by Charles R. Chickering.

ROTARY PRESS PRINTING
E.E. Plates of 200 subjects in four panes of 50.

1956, Sept. 24		*Perf. 10½x11*	
1084 A531 3c **violet**		.20	.20
P# block of 4		.45	—
Pair with full horiz. gutter btwn.		—	

CHILDREN'S ISSUE

Issued to promote friendship among the children of the world.

Children of the
World — A532

Designed by Ronald Dias.

ROTARY PRESS PRINTING
E.E. Plates of 200 subjects in four panes of 50.

1956, Dec. 15		*Perf. 11x10½*	
1085 A532 3c **dark blue**		.20	.20
P# block of 4		.40	—

ALEXANDER HAMILTON (1755-1804)

Alexander
Hamilton and
Federal
Hall — A533

Designed by William K. Schrage.

ROTARY PRESS PRINTING
E.E. Plates of 200 subjects in four panes of 50.

1957, Jan. 11		*Perf. 11x10½*	
1086 A533 3c **rose red**		.20	.20
P# block of 4		.40	—

POLIO ISSUE

Honoring "those who helped fight polio," and on for 20th anniv. of the Natl. Foundation for Infantile Paralysis and the March of Dimes.

Allegory — A534   Major Plate Crack

Designed by Charles R. Chickering.

ROTARY PRESS PRINTING
E.E. Plates of 200 subjects in four panes of 50.

1957, Jan. 15		*Perf. 10½x11*	
1087 A534 3c **red lilac**		.20	.20
P# block of 4		.40	—
Major plate crack (25605 UL 1)		—	

COAST AND GEODETIC SURVEY ISSUE

150th anniversary of the establishment of the Coast and Geodetic Survey.

Flag of Coast
and Geodetic
Survey and
Ships at
Sea — A535

Designed by Harold E. MacEwen.

ROTARY PRESS PRINTING
E.E. Plates of 200 subjects in four panes of 50.

1957, Feb. 11		*Perf. 11x10½*	
1088 A535 3c **dark blue**		.20	.20
P# block of 4		.40	—

ARCHITECTS ISSUE

American Institute of Architects, centenary.

Corinthian
Capital and
Mushroom
Type Head
and
Shaft — A536

Designed by Robert J. Schultz.

ROTARY PRESS PRINTING
E.E. Plates of 200 subjects in four panes of 50.

1957, Feb. 23		*Perf. 11x10½*	
1089 A536 3c **red lilac**		.20	.20
P# block of 4		.40	—

STEEL INDUSTRY ISSUE

Centenary of the steel industry in America.

American Eagle and
Pouring Ladle — A537

Designed by Anthonio Petruccelli.

ROTARY PRESS PRINTING
E.E. Plates of 200 subjects in four panes of 50.

1957, May 22		*Perf. 10½x11*	
1090 A537 3c **bright ultramarine**		.20	.20
P# block of 4		.40	—

INTERNATIONAL NAVAL REVIEW ISSUE

Issued to commemorate the International Naval Review and the Jamestown Festival.

Aircraft Carrier
and
Jamestown
Festival
Emblem
A538

Designed by Richard A. Genders.

ROTARY PRESS PRINTING
E.E. Plates of 200 subjects in four panes of 50.

1957, June 10		*Perf. 11x10½*	
1091 A538 3c **blue green**		.20	.20
P# block of 4		.40	—

OKLAHOMA STATEHOOD, 50th ANNIV.

Map of
Oklahoma,
Arrow and
Atom Diagram
A539

Designed by William K. Schrage.

ROTARY PRESS PRINTING
E.E. Plates of 200 subjects in four panes of 50.

1957, June 14		*Perf. 11x10½*	
1092 A539 3c **dark blue**		.20	.20
P# block of 4		.40	—

SCHOOL TEACHERS ISSUE

Teacher and
Pupils — A540

ROTARY PRESS PRINTING
E.E. Plates of 200 subjects in four panes of 50.

1957, July 1		*Perf. 11x10½*	
1093 A540 3c **rose lake**		.20	.20
P# block of 4		.40	—

FLAG ISSUE

"Old Glory" (48 Stars) — A541

Designed by Victor S. McCloskey, Jr.

GIORI PRESS PRINTING
Plates of 200 subjects in four panes of 50.

1957, July 4   *Perf. 11*
1094 A541 4c **dark blue & deep carmine**   .20   .20
P# block of 4   .40   —

"Virginia of Sagadahock" and Seal of Maine — A542

Ramon Magsaysay — A543

SHIPBUILDING ISSUE

350th anniversary of shipbuilding in America.

Designed by Ervine Metzel, Mrs. William Zorach, A. M. Main, Jr., and George F. Cary II.

ROTARY PRESS PRINTING
E.E. Plates of 280 subjects in four panes of 70.

1957, Aug. 15   *Perf. 10½x11*
1095 A542 3c **deep violet**   .20   .20
P# block of 4   .45   —

CHAMPION OF LIBERTY ISSUE

Magsaysay (1907-57), Pres. of the Philippines.

Designed by Arnold Copeland, Ervine Metzl and William H. Buckley.

GIORI PRESS PRINTING
Plates of 192 subjects in four panes of 48 each.

1957, Aug. 31   *Perf. 11*
1096 A543 8c **carmine, ultramarine & ocher** .20   .20
P# block of 4, 2#   .85   —
P# block of 4, ultra. # omitted   —

Marquis de Lafayette (1757-1834) — A544

Whooping Cranes — A545

LAFAYETTE BICENTENARY ISSUE

Designed by Ervine Metzl.

ROTARY PRESS PRINTING
E.E. Plates of 200 subjects in four panes of 50.

1957, Sept. 6   *Perf. 10½x11*
1097 A544 3c **rose lake**   .20   .20
P# block of 4   .40   —

WILDLIFE CONSERVATION ISSUE

Issued to emphasize the importance of Wildlife Conservation in America.

Designed by Bob Hines and C.R. Chickering.

GIORI PRESS PRINTING
Plates of 200 subjects in four panes of 50.

1957, Nov. 22   *Perf. 11*
1098 A545 3c **blue, ocher & green**   .20   .20
P# block of 4   .40   —

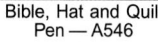

Bible, Hat and Quill Pen — A546

"Bountiful Earth" — A547

RELIGIOUS FREEDOM ISSUE

300th anniv. of the Flushing Remonstrance.

Designed by Robert Geissmann.

ROTARY PRESS PRINTING
E.E. Plates of 200 subjects in four panes of 50.

1957, Dec. 27   *Perf. 10½x11*
1099 A546 3c **black**   .20   .20
P# block of 4   .40   —

GARDENING HORTICULTURE ISSUE

Issued to honor the garden clubs of America and in connection with the centenary of the birth of Liberty Hyde Bailey, horticulturist.

Designed by Denver Gillen.

ROTARY PRESS PRINTING
E.E. Plates of 200 subjects in four panes of 50.

1958, Mar. 15   *Perf. 10½x11*
1100 A547 3c **green**   .20   .20
P# block of 4   .40   —

BRUSSELS EXHIBITION ISSUE

Issued in honor of the opening of the Universal and International Exhibition at Brussels, April 17.

US Pavilion at Brussels A551

Designed by Bradbury Thompson.

ROTARY PRESS PRINTING
E.E. Plates of 200 subjects in four panes of 50.

1958, Apr. 17   *Perf. 11x10½*
1104 A551 3c **deep claret**   .20   .20
On cover, Expo. station ("U.S. Pavilion") canc.   3.00
P# block of 4   .40   —

JAMES MONROE ISSUE

Monroe (1758-1831), 5th President of the US.

James Monroe — A552

Designed by Frank P. Conley.

ROTARY PRESS PRINTING
E.E. Plates of 280 subjects in four panes of 70.

1958, Apr. 28   *Perf. 11x10½*
1105 A552 3c **purple**   .20   .20
P# block of 4   .40   —

MINNESOTA STATEHOOD, 100th ANNIV.

Minnesota Lakes and Pines — A553

Designed by Homer Hill.

ROTARY PRESS PRINTING
E.E. Plates of 200 subjects in four panes of 50.

1958, May 11   *Perf. 11x10½*
1106 A553 3c **green**   .20   .20
P# block of 4   .45   —

GEOPHYSICAL YEAR ISSUE

International Geophysical Year, 1957-58.

Solar Disc and Hands from Michelangelo's "Creation of Adam" — A554

Designed by Ervine Metzl.

GIORI PRESS PRINTING
Plates of 200 subjects in four panes of 50.

1958, May 31   *Perf. 11*
1107 A554 3c **black & red orange**   .20   .20
P# block of 4   .40   —

GUNSTON HALL ISSUE

Issued for the bicentenary of Gunston Hall and to honor George Mason, author of the Constitution of Virginia and the Virginia Bill of Rights.

Gunston Hall, Virginia A555

Designed by Rene Clarke.

ROTARY PRESS PRINTING
E.E. Plates of 200 subjects in four panes of 50.

1958, June 12   *Perf. 11x10½*
1108 A555 3c **light green**   .20   .20
P# block of 4   .40   —

Mackinac Bridge — A556

Simon Bolívar — A557

MACKINAC BRIDGE ISSUE

Dedication of Mackinac Bridge, Michigan.

Designed by Arnold J. Copeland.

ROTARY PRESS PRINTING
E.E. Plates of 200 subjects in four panes of 50.

1958, June 25   *Perf. 10½x11*
1109 A556 3c **bright greenish blue**   .20   .20
P# block of 4   .40   —

CHAMPION OF LIBERTY ISSUE

Simon Bolívar, South American freedom fighter.

ROTARY PRESS PRINTING

E.E. Plates of 280 subjects in four panes of 70.

1958, July 24		*Perf. 10½x11*
1110 A557 4c **olive bister**	.20	.20
P# block of 4	.40	—

GIORI PRESS PRINTING

Plates of 288 subjects in four panes of 72 each.
Perf. 11

1111 A557 8c **carmine, ultramarine & ocher**	.20	.20
P# block of 4, 2#	1.25	—
P# block of 4, ocher # only	—	

ATLANTIC CABLE CENTENNIAL ISSUE

Centenary of the Atlantic Cable, linking the Eastern and Western hemispheres.

Neptune, Globe and Mermaid A558

Designed by George Giusti.

ROTARY PRESS PRINTING

E.E. Plates of 200 subjects in four panes of 50.

1958, Aug. 15		*Perf. 11x10½*
1112 A558 4c **reddish purple**	.20	.20
P# block of 4	.40	—

LINCOLN SESQUICENTENNIAL ISSUE

Sesquicentennial of the birth of Abraham Lincoln. No. 1114 also for the centenary of the founding of Cooper Union, New York City. No. 1115 marks the centenary of the Lincoln-Douglas Debates.

Lincoln by George Healy — A559

Lincoln by Gutzon Borglum — A560

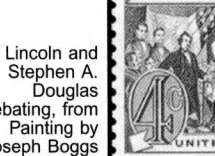

Lincoln and Stephen A. Douglas Debating, from Painting by Joseph Boggs Beale — A561

Daniel Chester French Statue of Lincoln as Drawn by Fritz Busse — A562

Designed by Ervine Metzl.

ROTARY PRESS PRINTING

E.E. Plates of 200 subjects in four panes of 50.

1958-59		*Perf. 10½x11*
1113 A559 1c **green,** *Feb. 12, 1959*	.20	.20
P# block of 4	.25	—
1114 A560 3c **purple,** *Feb. 27, 1959*	.20	.20
P# block of 4	.40	—

	Perf. 11x10½	
1115 A561 4c **sepia,** *Aug. 27, 1958*	.20	.20
P# block of 4	.60	—
1116 A562 4c **dark blue,** *May 30, 1959*	.20	.20
P# block of 4	.40	—
Nos. 1113-1116 (4)	.80	.80

Lajos Kossuth — A563

Early Press and Hand Holding Quill — A564

CHAMPION OF LIBERTY ISSUE

Lajos Kossuth, Hungarian freedom fighter.

ROTARY PRESS PRINTING

E.E. Plates of 280 subjects in four panes of 70.

1958, Sept. 19		*Perf. 10½x11*
1117 A563 4c **green**	.20	.20
P# block of 4	.40	—

GIORI PRESS PRINTING

Plates of 288 subjects in four panes of 72 each.
Perf. 11

1118 A563 8c **carmine, ultramarine & ocher**	.20	.20
P# block of 4, 2#	1.10	—

FREEDOM OF PRESS ISSUE

Honoring Journalism and freedom of the press in connection with the 50th anniv. of the 1st School of Journalism at the University of Missouri.

Designed by Lester Beall and Charles Goslin.

ROTARY PRESS PRINTING

E.E. Plates of 200 subjects in four panes of 50.

1958, Sept. 22		*Perf. 10½x11*
1119 A564 4c **black**	.20	.20
P# block of 4	.40	—

OVERLAND MAIL ISSUE

Centenary of Overland Mail Service.

Mail Coach and Map of Southwest US — A565

Designed by William H. Buckley.

ROTARY PRESS PRINTING

E.E. Plates of 200 subjects in four panes of 50.

1958, Oct. 10		*Perf. 11x10½*
1120 A565 4c **crimson rose**	.20	.20
P# block of 4	.40	—

Noah Webster — A566

Forest Scene — A567

NOAH WEBSTER ISSUE

Webster (1758-1843), lexicographer and author.

Designed by Charles R. Chickering.

ROTARY PRESS PRINTING

E.E. Plates of 280 subjects in four panes of 70.

1958, Oct. 16		*Perf. 10½x11*
1121 A566 4c **dark carmine rose**	.20	.20
P# block of 4	.40	—

FOREST CONSERVATION ISSUE

Issued to publicize forest conservation and the protection of natural resources and to honor Theodore Roosevelt, a leading forest conservationist, on the centenary of his birth.

Designed by Rudolph Wendelin.

GIORI PRESS PRINTING

Plates of 200 subjects in four panes of 50.

1958, Oct. 27		*Perf. 11*
1122 A567 4c **green, yellow & brown**	.20	.20
P# block of 4	.40	—

FORT DUQUESNE ISSUE

Bicentennial of Fort Duquesne (Fort Pitt) at future site of Pittsburgh.

British Capture of Fort Duquesne, 1758; Brig. Gen. John Forbes on Litter, Colonel Washington Mounted A568

Designed by William H. Buckley and Douglas Gorsline.

ROTARY PRESS PRINTING

E.E. Plates of 200 subjects in four panes of 50.

1958, Nov. 25		*Perf. 11x10½*
1123 A568 4c **blue**	.20	.20
P# block of 4	.40	—

OREGON STATEHOOD, 100th ANNIV.

Covered Wagon and Mt. Hood — A569

Designed by Robert Hallock.

ROTARY PRESS PRINTING

E.E. Plates of 200 subjects in four panes of 50.

1959, Feb. 14		*Perf. 11x10½*
1124 A569 4c **blue green**	.25	.20
P# block of 4	1.10	—

José de San Martin — A570

NATO Emblem — A571

CHAMPION OF LIBERTY ISSUE

San Martin, So. American soldier and statesman.

ROTARY PRESS PRINTING

E.E. Plates of 280 subjects in four panes of 70.

1959, Feb. 25		*Perf. 10½x11*
1125 A570 4c **blue**	.20	.20
P# block of 4	.40	—
a. Horiz. pair, imperf. between	1,250.	

GIORI PRESS PRINTING

Plates of 288 subjects in four panes of 72 each.
Perf. 11

1126 A570 8c **carmine, ultramarine & ocher**	.20	.20
P# block of 4	.90	—

NATO ISSUE

North Atlantic Treaty Organization, 10th anniv.

Designed by Stevan Dohanos.

ROTARY PRESS PRINTING
E.E. Plates of 280 subjects in four panes of 70.

1959, Apr. 1		Perf. 10½x11	
1127 A571 4c **blue**		.20	.20
P# block of 4		.40	—

ARCTIC EXPLORATIONS ISSUE

Conquest of the Arctic by land by Rear Admiral Robert Edwin Peary in 1909 and by sea by the submarine "Nautilus" in 1958.

North Pole, Dog Sled and "Nautilus" A572

Designed by George Samerjan.

ROTARY PRESS PRINTING
E.E. Plates of 200 subjects in four panes of 50.

1959, Apr. 6		Perf. 11x10½	
1128 A572 4c **bright greenish blue**		.20	.20
P# block of 4		.40	—

WORLD PEACE THROUGH WORLD TRADE ISSUE

Issued in conjunction with the 17th Congress of the International Chamber of Commerce, Washington, D.C., April 19-25.

Globe and Laurel — A573

Designed by Robert Baker.

ROTARY PRESS PRINTING
E.E. Plates of 200 subjects in four panes of 50.

1959, Apr. 20		Perf. 11x10½	
1129 A573 8c **rose lake**		.20	.20
P# block of 4		.85	

SILVER CENTENNIAL ISSUE

Discovery of silver at the Comstock Lode, Nevada.

Henry Comstock at Mount Davidson Site — A574

Designed by Robert L. Miller and W.K. Schrage.

ROTARY PRESS PRINTING
E.E. Plates of 200 subjects in four panes of 50.

1959, June 8		Perf. 11x10½	
1130 A574 4c **black**		.20	.20
P# block of 4		.40	—

ST. LAWRENCE SEAWAY ISSUE

Opening of the St. Lawrence Seaway.

Great Lakes, Maple Leaf and Eagle Emblems A575

Designed by Arnold Copeland, Ervine Metzl, William H. Buckley and Gerald Trottier.

GIORI PRESS PRINTING
Plates of 200 subjects in four panes of 50.

1959, June 26		Perf. 11	
1131 A575 4c **red & dark blue**		.20	.20
P# block of 4		.40	—
Pair with full horiz. gutter btwn.		—	

See Canada No. 387.

49-STAR FLAG ISSUE

U.S. Flag, 1959 — A576

Designed by Stevan Dohanos.

GIORI PRESS PRINTING
Plates of 200 subjects in four panes of 50.

1959, July 4		Perf. 11	
1132 A576 4c **ocher, dark blue & deep carmine**		.20	.20
P# block of 4		.40	

SOIL CONSERVATION ISSUE

Issued as a tribute to farmers and ranchers who use soil and water conservation measures.

Modern Farm — A577

Designed by Walter Hortens.

GIORI PRESS PRINTING
Plates of 200 subjects in four panes of 50.

1959, Aug. 26		Perf. 11	
1133 A577 4c **blue, green & ocher**		.20	.20
P# block of 4		.40	—

PETROLEUM INDUSTRY ISSUE

Centenary of the completion of the nation's first oil well at Titusville, Pa.

Oil Derrick — A578

Designed by Robert Foster.

ROTARY PRESS PRINTING
E.E. Plates of 200 subjects in four panes of 50.

1959, Aug. 27		Perf. 10½x11	
1134 A578 4c **brown**		.20	.20
P# block of 4		.40	—

DENTAL HEALTH ISSUE

Issued to publicize Dental Health and for the centenary of the American Dental Association.

Children A579

Designed by Charles Henry Carter.

ROTARY PRESS PRINTING
E.E. Plates of 200 subjects in four panes of 50.

1959, Sept. 14		Perf. 11x10	
1135 A579 4c **green**		.20	.20
P# block of 4		.40	—

Ernst Reuter — A580

Dr. Ephraim McDowell — A581

CHAMPION OF LIBERTY ISSUE

Ernst Reuter, Mayor of Berlin, 1948-53.

ROTARY PRESS PRINTING
E.E. Plates of 280 subjects in four panes of 70.

1959, Sept. 29		Perf. 10½x1	
1136 A580 4c **gray**		.20	.2
P# block of 4		.40	—

GIORI PRESS PRINTING
Plates of 288 subjects in four panes of 72 each.
Perf. 11

1137 A580 8c **carmine, ultramarine & ocher**		.20	.2
P# block of 4		.90	
a.	Ocher missing (EP)	4,250.	
b.	Ultramarine missing (EP)	4,250.	
c.	Ocher & ultramarine missing (EP)	4,500.	
d.	All colors missing (EP)	2,500.	

DR. EPHRAIM McDOWELL ISSUE

Honoring McDowell (1771-1830) on the 150th anniv. of the 1st successful ovarian operation in the US, performed at Danville, Ky., 1809.

Designed by Charles R. Chickering.

ROTARY PRESS PRINTING
E.E. Plates of 280 subjects in four panes of 70.

1959, Dec. 3		Perf. 10½x11	
1138 A581 4c **rose lake**		.20	.20
P# block of 4		.40	—
a.	Vert. pair, imperf. btwn.	450.00	
b.	Vert. pair, imperf. horiz.	300.00	

VALUES FOR HINGED STAMPS AFTER NO. 771
This catalogue does not value unused stamps after No. 771 in hinged condition. Hinged unused stamps from No. 772 to the present are worth considerably less than the values given for unused stamps, which are for never-hinged examples.

AMERICAN CREDO ISSUE

Issued to re-emphasize the ideals upon which America was founded and to honor those great Americans who wrote or uttered the credos.

Quotation from Washington's Farewell Address, 1796 — A582

Benjamin Franklin Quotation A583

Thomas Jefferson Quotation A584

Francis Scott
Key Quotation
A585

Abraham
Lincoln
Quotation
A586

Patrick Henry
Quotation
A587

Designed by Frank Conley.

GIORI PRESS PRINTING
Plates of 200 subjects in four panes of 50.

1960-61				**Perf. 11**	
1139	A582	4c	**dark violet blue, & carmine,**		
			Jan. 20, 1960,	.20	.20
			P# block of 4	.40	—
1140	A583	4c	**olive bister & green,** *Mar. 31,*		
			1960	.20	.20
			P# block of 4	.40	—
1141	A584	4c	**gray & vermilion,** *May 18, 1960*	.20	.20
			P# block of 4	.45	—
1142	A585	4c	**carmine & dark blue,** *Sept. 14,*		
			1960	.20	.20
			P# block of 4	.50	—
1143	A586	4c	**magenta & green,** *Nov. 19,*		
			1960	.20	.20
			P# block of 4	.50	—
			Pair with full horiz. gutter between	525.	
1144	A587	4c	**green & brown,** *Jan. 11, 1961*	.20	.20
			P# block of 4	.50	—
			Nos. 1139-1144 (6)	1.20	1.20

BOY SCOUT JUBILEE ISSUE

50th anniv. of the Boy Scouts of America.

Boy Scout
Giving Scout
Sign — A588

Designed by Norman Rockwell.

GIORI PRESS PRINTING
Plates of 200 subjects in four panes of 50.

1960, Feb. 8				**Perf. 11**	
1145	A588	4c	**red, dark blue & dark bister**	.20	.20
			P# block of 4	.55	—

Olympic Rings and
Snowflake — A589

Thomas G.
Masaryk — A590

OLYMPIC WINTER GAMES ISSUE

Opening of the 8th Olympic Winter Games, Squaw Valley, Feb. 18-29, 1960.

Designed by Ervine Metzl.

ROTARY PRESS PRINTING
E.E. Plates of 200 subjects in four panes of 50.

1960, Feb. 18				**Perf. 10½x11**	
1146	A589	4c	**dull blue**	.20	.20
			P# block of 4	.40	—

CHAMPION OF LIBERTY ISSUE

Issued to honor Thomas G. Masaryk, founder and president of Czechoslovakia (1918-35), on the 110th anniversary of his birth.

ROTARY PRESS PRINTING
E.E. Plates of 280 subjects in four panes of 70.

1960, Mar. 7				**Perf. 10½x11**	
1147	A590	4c	**blue**	.20	.20
			P# block of 4	.40	—
a.			Vert. pair, imperf. between	2,750.	

GIORI PRESS PRINTING
Plates of 288 subjects in four panes of 72 each.
Perf. 11

1148	A590	8c	**carmine, ultramarine & ocher**	.20	.20
			P# block of 4	.95	—
a.			Horiz. pair, imperf. between		

WORLD REFUGEE YEAR ISSUE

World Refugee Year, July 1, 1959-June 30, 1960.

Family Walking
Toward New
Life — A591

Designed by Ervine Metzl.

ROTARY PRESS PRINTING
E.E. Plates of 200 subjects in four panes of 50.

1960, Apr. 7				**Perf. 11x10½**	
1149	A591	4c	**gray black**	.20	.20
			P# block of 4	.40	—

WATER CONSERVATION ISSUE

Issued to stress the importance of water conservation and to commemorate the 7th Watershed Congress, Washington, D.C.

Water: From
Watershed to
Consumer
A592

Designed by Elmo White.

GIORI PRESS PRINTING
Plates of 200 subjects in four panes of 50.

1960, Apr. 18				**Perf. 11**	
1150	A592	4c	**dark blue, brown orange &**		
			green	.20	.20
			P# block of 4	.40	—
a.			Brown orange missing (EP)	2,400.	

SEATO ISSUE

South-East Asia Treaty Organization and for the SEATO Conf., Washington, D.C., May 31-June 3.

SEATO Emblem — A593

Designed by John Maass.

ROTARY PRESS PRINTING

E.E. plates of 280 subjects in four panes of 70.

1960, May 31				**Perf. 10½x11**	
1151	A593	4c	**blue**	.20	.20
			P# block of 4	.40	—
a.			Vertical pair, imperf. between	140.00	

AMERICAN WOMAN ISSUE

Issued to pay tribute to American women and their accomplishments in civic affairs, education, arts and industry.

Mother and
Daughter
A594

Designed by Robert Sivard.

ROTARY PRESS PRINTING
E.E. Plates of 200 subjects in four panes of 50.

1960, June 2				**Perf. 11x10½**	
1152	A594	4c	**deep violet**	.20	.20
			P# block of 4	.40	—

50-STAR FLAG ISSUE

US Flag, 1960 — A595

Designed by Stevan Dohanos.

GIORI PRESS PRINTING
Plates of 200 subjects in four panes of 50.

1960, July 4				**Perf. 11**	
1153	A595	4c	**dark blue & red**	.20	.20
			P# block of 4	.40	—

PONY EXPRESS CENTENNIAL ISSUE

Pony Express
Rider — A596

Designed by Harold von Schmidt.

ROTARY PRESS PRINTING
E.E. Plates of 200 subjects in four panes of 50.

1960, July 19				**Perf. 11x10½**	
1154	A596	4c	**sepia**	.20	.20
			P# block of 4	.65	—

Man in Wheelchair
Operating Drill
Press — A597

World Forestry
Congress Seal — A598

EMPLOY THE HANDICAPPED ISSUE

Promoting the employment of the physically handi-capped and publicizing the 8th World Congress of the Intl. Soc. for the Welfare of Cripples, New York City.

Designed by Carl Bobertz.

ROTARY PRESS PRINTING
E.E. Plates of 200 subjects in four panes of 50.

1960, Aug. 28			**Perf. 10½x11**
1155	A597	4c **dark blue**	.20 .20
		P# block of 4	.40 —

WORLD FORESTRY CONGRESS ISSUE

5th World Forestry Cong., Seattle, Wash., Aug. 29-Sept. 10.

ROTARY PRESS PRINTING
E.E. Plates of 200 subjects in four panes of 50.

1960, Aug. 29			**Perf. 10½x11**
1156	A598	4c **green**	.20 .20
		P# block of 4	.40 —

Independence
Bell — A599

Washington Monument
and Cherry
Blossoms — A600

MEXICAN INDEPENDENCE, 150th ANNIV.

Designed by Leon Helguera and Charles R. Chickering.

GIORI PRESS PRINTING
Plates of 200 subjects in four panes of 50.

1960, Sept. 16			**Perf. 11**
1157	A599	4c **green & rose red**	.20 .20
		P# block of 4	.40 —

See Mexico No. 910.

US-JAPAN TREATY ISSUE

Centenary of the United States-Japan Treaty of Amity and Commerce.

Designed by Gyo Fujikawa.

GIORI PRESS PRINTING
Plates of 200 subjects in four panes of 50.

1960, Sept. 28			**Perf. 11**
1158	A600	4c **blue & pink**	.20 .20
		P# block of 4	.40 —

Ignacy Jan
Paderewski — A601

Robert A. Taft — A602

CHAMPION OF LIBERTY ISSUE

Jan Paderewski, Polish statesman and musician.

ROTARY PRESS PRINTING
E.E. Plates of 280 subjects in four panes of 70.

1960, Oct. 8			**Perf. 10½x11**
1159	A601	4c **blue**	.20 .20
		P# block of 4	.40 —

GIORI PRESS PRINTING
Plates of 288 subjects in four panes of 72 each.
Perf. 11

1160	A601	8c **carmine, ultramarine & ocher**	.20 .20
		P# block of 4	.90 —

SENATOR TAFT MEMORIAL ISSUE

Senator Robert A. Taft (1889-1953) of Ohio.

Designed by William K. Schrage.

ROTARY PRESS PRINTING
E.E. Plates of 280 subjects in four panes of 70.

1960, Oct. 10			**Perf. 10½x11**
1161	A602	4c **dull violet**	.20 .20
		P# block of 4	.45 —

WHEELS OF FREEDOM ISSUE

Issued to honor the automotive industry and in con-nection with the National Automobile Show, Detroit, Oct. 15-23.

Globe and
Steering
Wheel with
Tractor, Car
and
Truck — A603

Designed by Arnold J. Copeland.

ROTARY PRESS PRINTING
E.E. Plates of 200 subjects in four panes of 50.

1960, Oct. 15			**Perf. 11x10½**
1162	A603	4c **dark blue**	.20 .20
		P# block of 4	.40 —

BOYS' CLUBS OF AMERICA ISSUE

Boys' Clubs of America movement, centenary.

Profile of Boy — A604

Designed by Charles T. Coiner.

GIORI PRESS PRINTING
Plates of 200 subjects in four panes of 50.

1960, Oct. 18			**Perf. 11**
1163	A604	4c **indigo, slate & rose red**	.20 .20
		P# block of 4	.40 —

FIRST AUTOMATED POST OFFICE IN THE US ISSUE

Publicizing the opening of the 1st automated post office in the US at Providence, R.I.

Architect's
Sketch of New
Post Office,
Providence,
R.I. — A605

Designed by Arnold J. Copeland and Victor S. McCloskey, Jr.

GIORI PRESS PRINTING
Plates of 200 subjects in four panes of 50.

1960, Oct. 20			**Perf. 11**
1164	A605	4c **dark blue & carmine**	.20 .20
		P# block of 4	.40 —

Baron Gustaf
Mannerheim — A606

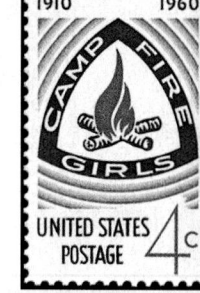

Camp Fire Girls
Emblem — A607

CHAMPION OF LIBERTY ISSUE

Baron Karl Gustaf Emil Mannerheim (1867-1951) Marshal and President of Finland.

ROTARY PRESS PRINTING
E.E. Plates of 280 subjects in four panes of 70.

1960, Oct. 26			**Perf. 10½x11**
1165	A606	4c **blue**	.20 .20
		P# block of 4	.40 —

GIORI PRESS PRINTING
Plates of 288 subjects in four panes of 72 each.
Perf. 11

1166	A606	8c **carmine, ultramarine & ocher**	.20 .20
		P# block of 4	.80 —

CAMP FIRE GIRLS ISSUE

50th anniv. of the Camp Fire Girls' movement and in connection with the Golden Jubilee Convention cele-bration of the Camp Fire Girls.

Designed by H. Edward Oliver.

GIORI PRESS PRINTING
Plates of 200 subjects in four panes of 50.

1960, Nov. 1			**Perf. 11**
1167	A607	4c **dark blue & bright red**	.20 .20
		P# block of 4	.65 —

Giuseppe
Garibaldi — A608

Walter F.
George — A609

CHAMPION OF LIBERTY ISSUE

Giuseppe Garibaldi (1807-1882), Italian patriot and freedom fighter.

ROTARY PRESS PRINTING
E.E. Plates of 280 subjects in four panes of 70.

1960, Nov. 2			**Perf. 10½x11**
1168	A608	4c **green**	.20 .20
		P# block of 4	.40 —

GIORI PRESS PRINTING
Plates of 288 subjects in four panes of 72 each.
Perf. 11

1169	A608	8c **carmine, ultramarine & ocher**	.20 .20
		P# block of 4	.85 —

SENATOR GEORGE MEMORIAL ISSUE

Walter F. George (1878-1957) of Georgia.

Designed by William K. Schrage.

ROTARY PRESS PRINTING
E.E. Plates of 280 subjects in four panes of 70.

1960, Nov. 5			**Perf. 10½x11**
1170	A609	4c **dull violet**	.20 .20
		P# block of 4	.45 —

Andrew Carnegie — A610

John Foster Dulles — A611

ANDREW CARNEGIE ISSUE

Carnegie (1835-1919), industrialist & philanthropist.

Designed by Charles R. Chickering.

ROTARY PRESS PRINTING
E.E. Plates of 280 subjects in four panes of 70.

1960, Nov. 25   *Perf. 10½x11*
1171 A610 4c **deep claret**   .20   .20
         P# block of 4   .40   —

JOHN FOSTER DULLES MEMORIAL ISSUE

Dulles (1888-1959), Secretary of State (1953-59).

Designed by William K. Schrage.

ROTARY PRESS PRINTING
E.E. Plates of 280 subjects in four panes of 70.

1960, Dec. 6   *Perf. 10½x11*
1172 A611 4c **dull violet**   .20   .20
         P# block of 4   .40   —

ECHO I — COMMUNICATIONS FOR PEACE ISSUE

World's 1st communications satellite, Echo I, placed in orbit by the Natl. Aeronautics and Space Admin., Aug. 12, 1960.

Radio Waves Connecting Echo I and Earth — A612

Designed by Ervine Metzl.

ROTARY PRESS PRINTING
E.E. Plates of 200 subjects in four panes of 50.

1960, Dec. 15   *Perf. 11x10½*
1173 A612 4c **deep violet**   .20   .20
         P# block of 4   .65   —

CHAMPION OF LIBERTY ISSUE

Mohandas K. Gandhi, leader in India's struggle for independence.

Mahatma Gandhi — A613

ROTARY PRESS PRINTING
E.E. Plates of 280 subjects in four panes of 70.

1961, Jan. 26   *Perf. 10½x11*
1174 A613 4c **red orange**   .20   .20
         P# block of 4   .40   —

GIORI PRESS PRINTING
Plates of 288 subjects in four panes of 72 each.
                            Perf. 11
1175 A613 8c **carmine, ultramarine & ocher**   .20   .20
         P# block of 4   1.00 —

RANGE CONSERVATION ISSUE

Issued to stress the importance of range conservation and to commemorate the meeting of the American Society of Range Management, Washington, D.C. "The Trail Boss" from a drawing by Charles M. Russell is the Society's emblem.

The Trail Boss and Modern Range — A614

Designed by Rudolph Wendelin.

GIORI PRESS PRINTING
Plates of 200 subjects in four panes of 50.

1961, Feb. 2   *Perf. 11*
1176 A614 4c **blue, slate & brown orange**   .20   .20
         P# block of 4   .40   —

HORACE GREELEY ISSUE

Greeley (1811-1872), publisher and editor.

Horace Greeley — A615

Designed by Charles R. Chickering.

ROTARY PRESS PRINTING
E.E. Plates of 280 subjects in four panes of 70.

1961, Feb. 3   *Perf. 10½x11*
1177 A615 4c **dull violet**   .20   .20
         P# block of 4   .45   —

CIVIL WAR CENTENNIAL ISSUE

Centenaries of the firing on Fort Sumter (No. 1178), the Battle of Shiloh (No. 1179), the Battle of Gettysburg (No. 1180), the Battle of the Wilderness (No. 1181) and the surrender at Appomattox (No. 1182).

Sea Coast Gun of 1861 — A616

Rifleman at Battle of Shiloh, 1862 — A617

Blue and Gray at Gettysburg, 1863 — A618

Battle of the Wilderness, 1864 — A619

Appomattox, 1865 — A620

Designed by Charles R. Chickering (Sumter), Noel Sickles (Shiloh), Roy Gjertson (Gettysburg), B. Harold Christenson (Wilderness), Leonard Fellman (Appomattox).

ROTARY PRESS PRINTING
E.E. Plates of 200 subjects in four panes of 50.

1961-65   *Perf. 11x10½*
1178 A616 4c **light green,** *Apr. 12, 1961*   .30   .20
         P# block of 4   1.25 —
1179 A617 4c **black,** *peach blossom, Apr. 7, 1962* .20   .20
         P# block of 4   .75   —

GIORI PRESS PRINTING
Plates of 200 subjects in four panes of 50.
                            Perf. 11
1180 A618 5c **gray & blue,** *July 1, 1963*   .20   .20
         P# block of 4   .85   —
1181 A619 5c **dark red & black,** *May 5, 1964*   .20   .20
         P# block of 4   .60   —
         Margin block of 4, Mr. Zip and
         "Use Zip Code"   .55   —
1182 A620 5c **Prus. blue & black,** *Apr. 9,*
         1965   .35   .20
         P# block of 4   1.50 —
         Margin block of 4, Mr. Zip and
         "Use Zip Code"   1.30 —
   a.   Horiz. pair, imperf. vert.   4,500.
         Nos. 1178-1182 (5)   1.25 1.00

KANSAS STATEHOOD, 100th ANNIV.

Sunflower, Pioneer Couple and Stockade A621

GIORI PRESS PRINTING
Plates of 200 subjects in four panes of 50.

1961, May 10   *Perf. 11*
1183 A621 4c **brown, dark red & green,** *yellow*   .20   .20
         P# block of 4   .50   —

SENATOR NORRIS ISSUE

Senator George W. Norris of Nebraska, and Norris Dam — A622

Designed by Charles R. Chickering.

ROTARY PRESS PRINTING
E.E. Plates of 200 subjects in four panes of 50.

1961, July 11   *Perf. 11x10½*
1184 A622 4c **blue green**   .20   .20
         P# block of 4   .40   —

NAVAL AVIATION, 50th ANNIV.

Navy's First Plane (Curtiss A-1 of 1911) and Naval Air Wings — A623

Designed by John Maass.

ROTARY PRESS PRINTING
E.E. Plates of 200 subjects in four panes of 50.

1961, Aug. 20   *Perf. 11x10½*
1185 A623 4c **blue**   .20   .20
   P# block of 4   .40
   Pair with full vert. gutter btwn.   150.00

WORKMEN'S COMPENSATION ISSUE
50th anniv. of the 1st successful Workmen's Compensation Law, enacted by the Wisconsin legislature.

Scales of Justice, Factory, Worker and Family — A624

Designed by Norman Todhunter.

ROTARY PRESS PRINTING
E.E. Plates of 200 subjects in four panes of 50.

1961, Sept. 4   *Perf. 10½x11*
1186 A624 4c **ultramarine**, *grayish*   .20   .20
   P# block of 4   .40
   P# block of 4 inverted   .60

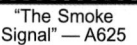

"The Smoke Signal" — A625

Sun Yat-sen — A626

FREDERIC REMINGTON ISSUE
Remington (1861-1909), artist of the West. The design is from an oil painting, Amon Carter Museum of Western Art, Fort Worth, Texas.

Designed by Charles R. Chickering.

GIORI PRESS PRINTING
Panes of 200 subjects in four panes of 50.

1961, Oct. 4   *Perf. 11*
1187 A625 4c **multicolored**   .20   .20
   P# block of 4   .40

REPUBLIC OF CHINA ISSUE
50th anniversary of the Republic of China.

ROTARY PRESS PRINTING
E.E. Plates of 200 subjects in four panes of 50.

1961, Oct. 10   *Perf. 10½x11*
1188 A626 4c **blue**   .20   .20
   P# block of 4   .45

Basketball — A627

Student Nurse Lighting Candle — A628

NAISMITH — BASKETBALL ISSUE
Honoring basketball and James Naismith (1861-1939), Canada-born director of physical education, who invented the game in 1891 at Y.M.C.A. College, Springfield, Mass.

Designed by Charles R. Chickering.

ROTARY PRESS PRINTING
E.E. Plates of 200 subjects in four panes of 50.

1961, Nov. 6   *Perf. 10½x11*
1189 A627 4c **brown**   .20   .20
   P# block of 4   .50

NURSING ISSUE
Issued to honor the nursing profession.

Designed by Alfred Charles Parker.

GIORI PRESS PRINTING
Plates of 200 subjects in four panes of 50.

1961, Dec. 28   *Perf. 11*
1190 A628 4c **blue, green, orange & black**   .20   .20
   P# block of 4, 2#   .50

NEW MEXICO STATEHOOD, 50th ANNIV.

Shiprock A629

Designed by Robert J. Jones.

GIORI PRESS PRINTING
Plates of 200 subjects in four panes of 50.

1962, Jan. 6   *Perf. 11*
1191 A629 4c **lt. blue, maroon & bister**   .20   .20
   P# block of 4   .40

ARIZONA STATEHOOD, 50th ANNIV.

Giant Saguaro Cactus — A630

Designed by Jimmie E. Ihms and James M. Chemi.

GIORI PRESS PRINTING
Plates of 200 subjects in four panes of 50.

1962, Feb. 14   *Perf. 11*
1192 A630 4c **carmine, violet blue & green**   .20   .20
   P# block of 4   .40

PROJECT MERCURY ISSUE
1st orbital flight of a US astronaut, Lt. Col. John H. Glenn, Jr., Feb. 20, 1962.

"Friendship 7" Capsule and Globe — A631

GIORI PRESS PRINTING
Plates of 200 subjects in four panes of 50.

1962, Feb. 20   *Perf. 11*
1193 A631 4c **dark blue & yellow**   .20   .20
   P# block of 4   .40

Imperfs. are printers waste.

MALARIA ERADICATION ISSUE
World Health Organization's drive to eradicate malaria.

Great Seal of US and WHO Symbol A632

Designed by Charles R. Chickering.

GIORI PRESS PRINTING
Plates of 200 subjects in four panes of 50.

1962, Mar. 30   *Perf.*
1194 A632 4c **blue & bister**   .20
   P# block of 4   .40

Charles Evans Hughes — A633

"Space Needle" and Monorail — A634

CHARLES EVANS HUGHES ISSUE
Hughes (1862-1948), Governor of New York, Chief Justice of the US.

Designed by Charles R. Chickering.

ROTARY PRESS PRINTING
E.E. Plates of 200 subjects in four panes of 50.

1962, Apr. 11   *Perf. 10½x11*
1195 A633 4c **black**, *buff*   .20   .20
   P# block of 4   .40

SEATTLE WORLD'S FAIR ISSUE
"Century 21" International Exposition, Seattle, Wash., Apr. 21-Oct. 21.

Designed by John Maass.

GIORI PRESS PRINTING
Plates of 200 subjects in four panes of 50.

1962, Apr. 25   *Perf. 11*
1196 A634 4c **red & dark blue**   .20   .20
   On cover, "Century 21" Expo. cancel   5.00
   On cover, "Space Needle" Expo. cancel 2.00
   P# block of 4   .40

LOUISIANA STATEHOOD, 150th ANNIV.

Riverboat on the Mississippi A635

Designed by Norman Todhunter.

GIORI PRESS PRINTING
Plates of 200 subjects in four panes of 50.

1962, Apr. 30   *Perf. 11*
1197 A635 4c **blue, dark slate green & red**   .20   .20
   P# block of 4   .50

HOMESTEAD ACT, CENTENARY

Sod Hut and Settlers A636

Designed by Charles R. Chickering.

ROTARY PRESS PRINTING
E.E. Plates of 200 subjects in four panes of 50.

1962, May 20		**Perf. 11x10½**	
1198 A636 4c slate		.20	.20
P# block of 4		.40	—

GIRL SCOUTS ISSUE

50th anniversary of the Girl Scouts of America.

Senior Girl Scout and Flag — A637

Designed by Ward Brackett.

ROTARY PRESS PRINTING
E.E. Plates of 200 subjects in four panes of 50.

1962, July 24		**Perf. 11x10½**	
1199 A637 4c rose red		.20	.20
P# block of 4		.40	—
Pair with full vertical gutter between		250.00	

SENATOR BRIEN McMAHON ISSUE

McMahon (1903-52) of Connecticut had a role in opening the way to peaceful uses of atomic energy through the Atomic Energy Act establishing the Atomic Energy Commission.

Brien McMahon and Atomic Symbol A638

Designed by V. S. McCloskey, Jr.

ROTARY PRESS PRINTING
E.E. Plates of 200 subjects in four panes of 50.

1962, July 28		**Perf. 11x10½**	
1200 A638 4c purple		.20	.20
P# block of 4		.40	—

APPRENTICESHIP ISSUE

National Apprenticeship Program and 25th anniv. of the National Apprenticeship Act.

Machinist Handing Micrometer to Apprentice A639

Designed by Robert Geissmann.

ROTARY PRESS PRINTING
E.E. Plates of 200 subjects in four panes of 50.

1962, Aug. 31		**Perf. 11x10½**	
1201 A639 4c black, *yellow bister*		.20	.20
P# block of 4		.40	—

SAM RAYBURN ISSUE

Rayburn (1882-1961), Speaker of the House of Representatives.

Sam Rayburn and Capitol — A640

Designed by Robert L. Miller.

GIORI PRESS PRINTING
Plates of 200 subjects in four panes of 50.

1962, Sept. 16		**Perf. 11**	
1202 A640 4c dark blue & red brown		.20	.20
P# block of 4		.45	—

DAG HAMMARSKJOLD ISSUE

Hammarskjold, UN Sec. General, 1953-61.

UN Headquarters and Dag Hammarskjold, UN Sec. Gen., 1953-61 A641

Designed by Herbert M. Sanborn.

GIORI PRESS PRINTING
Plates of 200 subjects in four panes of 50.

1962, Oct. 23		**Perf. 11**	
1203 A641 4c black, brown & yellow		.20	.20
P# block of 4, 2#		.40	—
a. Yellow inverted, on cover, see note			—

No. 1203a can only be collected on a cover postmarked before Nov. 16, 1962 (the date the Hammarskjold Special Printing, No. 1204, was issued). Covers are known machine postmarked Cuyahoga Falls, Ohio, Nov. 14, 1962, and notarized in the lower left corner by George W. Schwartz, Notary Public. Other covers are reported postmarked Oct. 26, 1962, Brooklyn, NY, Vanderveer Station. Unaddressed, uncacheted first day covers also exist. Other covers may exist. All covers must be accompanied by certificates from recognized expertizing committees.

An unused pane of 50 was signed in the salvage by ten well-known philatelists attesting to its genuineness. This pane was donated to the American Philatelic Society in 1987.

An unknown number of "first day covers" exist bearing Artmaster cachets. These were contrived using examples of No. 1204.

Hammarskjold Special Printing

No. 1204 was issued following discovery of No. 1203 with yellow background inverted.

GIORI PRESS PRINTING
Plates of 200 subjects in four panes of 50.

1962, Nov. 16		**Perf. 11**	
1204 A641 4c black, brown & yel (yellow inverted)		.20	.20
P# block of 4, 2#, yellow # inverted		1.25	—

The inverted yellow impression is shifted to the right in relation to the black and brown impression. Stamps of first vertical row of UL and LL panes show no yellow at left side for a space of 11-11½mm in from the perforations.

Stamps of first vertical row of UR and LR panes show vertical no-yellow strip 9¾mm wide, covering UN Building. On all others, the vertical no-yellow strip is 3½mm wide, and touches UN Building.

CHRISTMAS ISSUE

Wreath and Candles — A642

Designed by Jim Crawford.

GIORI PRESS PRINTING
Plates of 400 subjects in four panes of 100.
Panes of 90 and 100 exist
without plate numbers due to provisional use of smaller paper.
Value per pane thus $50.

1962, Nov. 1		**Perf. 11**	
1205 A642 4c green & red		.20	.20
P# block of 4		.40	—

HIGHER EDUCATION ISSUE

Higher education's role in American cultural and industrial development and the centenary celebrations of the signing of the law creating land-grant colleges and universities.

Map of U.S. and Lamp — A643

Designed by Henry K. Bencsath.

GIORI PRESS PRINTING
Plates of 200 subjects in panes of 50.

1962, Nov. 14		**Perf. 11**	
1206 A643 4c blue green & black		.20	.20
P# block of 4, 2#		.40	—

WINSLOW HOMER ISSUE

Homer (1836-1910), painter, showing his oil, "Breezing Up," which hangs in the National Gallery, Washington, D.C.

"Breezing Up" — A644

Designed by Victor S. McCloskey, Jr.

GIORI PRESS PRINTING
Plates of 200 subjects in four panes of 50.

1962, Dec. 15		**Perf. 11**	
1207 A644 4c multicolored		.20	.20
P# block of 4		.45	—
a. Horiz. pair, imperf. btwn. and at right		6,750.	

FLAG ISSUE

Flag over White House — A645

Designed by Robert J. Jones.

GIORI PRESS PRINTING
Plates of 400 subjects in four panes of 100.

1963-66		**Perf. 11**	
1208 A645 5c blue & red, *Jan. 9, 1963*		.20	.20
P# block of 4		.40	—
Pair with full horiz. gutter between		—	
a. Tagged, *Aug. 25, 1966*		.20	.20
P# block of 4		2.00	—
b. Horiz. pair, imperf. between, tagged		1,500.	

Beware of pairs with faint blind perfs between offered as No. 1208b.

REGULAR ISSUE

Andrew
Jackson — A646

George
Washington — A650

Designed by William K. Schrage.

ROTARY PRESS PRINTING
E.E. Plates of 400 subjects in four panes of 100.

1962-66				Perf. 11x10½	
1209	A646 1c	green, *Mar. 22, 1963*		.20	.20
		P# block of 4		.20	—
		Pair with full vert. gutter btwn.		—	
a.		Tagged, *July 6, 1966*		.20	.20
		P# block of 4		.40	—
1213	A650 5c	dark blue gray, *Nov. 23, 1962*		.20	.20
		P# block of 4		.40	—
		Pair with full vert. gutter btwn.		—	
		Pair with full horiz. gutter btwn.		450.00	
a.		Booklet pane of 5 + label		3.00	2.00
b.		Tagged, *Oct. 28, 1963*		.50	.20
		P# block of 4		4.50	—
c.		As "a," tagged, *Oct. 28, 1963*		2.00	1.50
d.		Horiz. pair, imperf between		2,750.	

Bureau Precancels: 1c, 10 diff., 5c, 18 diff.

No. 1213d resulted from a paper foldover after perforating and before cutting into panes. At least six individually unique panes exist, including at least one that contains two error pairs. Recent auction prices for panes have ranged between $1,400 and $4,000.

COIL STAMPS
(Rotary Press)

1962-66				Perf. 10 Vertically	
1225	A646 1c	green, *May 31, 1963*		.20	.20
		Pair		.30	.20
		Joint line pair		2.00	.20
a.		Tagged, *July 6, 1966*		.20	.20
		Joint line pair		.75	.20
1229	A650 5c	dark blue gray, *Nov. 23, 1962*		1.10	.20
		Pair		2.25	.20
		Joint line pair		3.50	.35
a.		Tagged, *Oct. 28, 1963*		1.40	.20
		Joint line pair		6.50	.20
b.		Imperf., pair		375.00	
		Joint line pair		1,000.	

Bureau Precancels: 1c, 5 diff., 5c, 14 diff.

See Luminescence note in "Basic Stamp Information" in the introduction.

CAROLINA CHARTER ISSUE

Tercentenary of the Carolina Charter granting to 8 Englishmen lands extending coast-to-coast roughly along the present border of Virginia to the north and Florida to the south. Original charter on display at Raleigh.

First Page of
Carolina
Charter
A662

Designed by Robert L. Miller.

GIORI PRESS PRINTING
Plates of 200 subjects in four panes of 50.

1963, Apr. 6				Perf. 11	
1230	A662 5c	dark carmine & brown		.20	.20
		P# block of 4		.40	—

FOOD FOR PEACE-FREEDOM FROM HUNGER ISSUE

American "Food for Peace" program and the "Freedom from Hunger" campaign of the FAO.

Wheat — A663

Designed by Stevan Dohanos.

GIORI PRESS PRINTING
Plates of 200 subjects in four panes of 50.

1963, June 4				Perf. 11	
1231	A663 5c	green, buff & red		.20	.20
		P# block of 4		.40	—

WEST VIRGINIA STATEHOOD, 100th ANNIV.

Map of West
Virginia and
State Capitol
A664

Designed by Dr. Dwight Mutchler.

GIORI PRESS PRINTING
Plates of 200 subjects in four panes of 50.

1963, June 20				Perf. 11	
1232	A664 5c	green, red & black		.20	.20
		P# block of 4		.40	—

EMANCIPATION PROCLAMATION ISSUE

Centenary of Lincoln's Emancipation Proclamation freeing about 3,000,000 slaves in 10 southern states.

Severed
Chain — A665

Designed by Georg Olden.

GIORI PRESS PRINTING
Plates of 200 subjects in four panes of 50.

1963, Aug. 16				Perf. 11	
1233	A665 5c	dark blue, black & red		.20	.20
		P# block of 4		.50	—

ALLIANCE FOR PROGRESS ISSUE

2nd anniv. of the Alliance for Progress, which aims to stimulate economic growth and raise living standards in Latin America.

Alliance
Emblem
A666

Designed by William K. Schrage.

GIORI PRESS PRINTING
Plates of 200 subjects in four panes of 50.

1963, Aug. 17				Perf. 11	
1234	A666 5c	ultramarine & green		.20	.20
		P# block of 4		.40	—

CORDELL HULL ISSUE

Hull (1871-1955), Secretary of State (1933-44).

Cordell Hull — A667

Designed by Robert J. Jones.

ROTARY PRESS PRINTING
E.E. Plates of 200 subjects in four panes of 50.

1963, Oct. 5				Perf. 10½x11	
1235	A667 5c	blue green		.20	.20
		P# block of 4		.50	—

ELEANOR ROOSEVELT ISSUE

Mrs. Franklin D. Roosevelt (1884-1962).

Eleanor
Roosevelt
A668

Designed by Robert L. Miller.

ROTARY PRESS PRINTING
E.E. Plates of 200 subjects in four panes of 50.

1963, Oct. 11				Perf. 11x10½	
1236	A668 5c	bright purple		.20	.20
		P# block of 4		.45	—

SCIENCE ISSUE

Honoring the sciences and in connection with the centenary of the Natl. Academy of Science.

"The Universe"
A669

Designed by Antonio Frasconi.

GIORI PRESS PRINTING
Plates of 200 subjects in four panes of 50.

1963, Oct. 14				Perf. 11	
1237	A669 5c	Prussian blue & black		.20	.20
		P# block of 4		.40	—

CITY MAIL DELIVERY ISSUE

Centenary of free city mail delivery.

Letter Carrier, 1863 — A670

Designed by Norman Rockwell.

GIORI PRESS PRINTING
Plates of 200 subjects in four panes of 50.

1963, Oct. 26		Tagged		Perf. 11	
1238	A670 5c	gray, dark blue & red		.20	.20
		P# block of 4		.50	—
a.		Tagging omitted		7.50	

RED CROSS CENTENARY ISSUE

Cuban Refugees on S.S. Morning Light and Red Cross Flag — A671

Designed by Victor S. McCloskey, Jr.

GIORI PRESS PRINTING
Plates of 200 subjects in four panes of 50.

1963, Oct. 29			Perf. 11
1239 A671 5c	bluish black & red	.20	.20
	P# block of 4	.50	—

CHRISTMAS ISSUE

National Christmas Tree and White House — A672

Designed by Lily Spandorf; modified by Norman Todhunter.

GIORI PRESS PRINTING
Plates of 400 subjects in four panes of 100.

1963, Nov. 1			Perf. 11
1240 A672 5c	dark blue, bluish black & red	.20	.20
	P# block of 4	.50	—
a.	Tagged, Nov. 2, 1963	.65	.50
	P# block of 4	5.00	—
	Pair with full horiz. gutter between	—	

"Columbia Jays" by Audubon — A673

Sam Houston — A674

JOHN JAMES AUDUBON ISSUE

Audubon (1785-1851), ornithologist and artist. The birds pictured are actually Collie's magpie jays. See No. C71.

Designed by Robert L. Miller.

GIORI PRESS PRINTING
Plates of 200 subjects in four panes of 50.

1963, Dec. 7			Perf. 11
1241 A673 5c	dark blue & multicolored	.20	.20
	P# block of 4	.45	—

SAM HOUSTON ISSUE

Houston (1793-1863), soldier, president of Texas, US senator.

Designed by Tom Lea.

ROTARY PRESS PRINTING
E.E. Plates of 200 subjects in four panes of 50.

1964, Jan. 10			Perf. 10½x11
1242 A674 5c	black	.25	.20
	P# block of 4	1.05	—
	Margin block of 4, Mr. Zip and "Use Zip Code"	1.00	—

CHARLES M. RUSSELL ISSUE

Russell (1864-1926), painter. The design is from a painting, Thomas Gilcrease Institute of American History and Art, Tulsa, Okla.

"Jerked Down" — A675

Designed by William K. Schrage.

GIORI PRESS PRINTING
Plates of 200 subjects in four panes of 50.

1964, Mar. 19			Perf. 11
1243 A675 5c	multicolored	.20	.20
	P# block of 4	.40	—
	Margin block of 4, Mr. Zip and "Use Zip Code"	.35	—

NEW YORK WORLD'S FAIR ISSUE

New York World's Fair, 1964-65.

Mall with Unisphere and "Rocket Thrower" by Donald De Lue — A676

Designed by Robert J. Jones.

ROTARY PRESS PRINTING
E.E. Plates of 200 subjects in four panes of 50.

1964, Apr. 22			Perf. 11x10½
1244 A676 5c	blue green	.20	.20
	On cover, Expo. station machine cancel (non-first day)	2.00	
	On cover, Expo. station handstamp cancel (non-first day)	10.00	
	P# block of 4	.45	—
	Margin block of 4, Mr. Zip and "Use Zip Code"	.40	—

JOHN MUIR ISSUE

Muir (1838-1914), naturalist and conservationist.

John Muir and Redwood Forest — A677

Designed by Rudolph Wendelin.

GIORI PRESS PRINTING
Plates of 200 subjects in four panes of 50.

1964, Apr. 29			Perf. 11
1245 A677 5c	brown, green, yellow green & olive	.20	.20
	P# block of 4	.45	—

KENNEDY MEMORIAL ISSUE

President John Fitzgerald Kennedy, (1917-1963).

John F. Kennedy and Eternal Flame — A678

Designed by Raymond Loewy/William Snaith, Inc.

Photograph by William S. Murphy.

ROTARY PRESS PRINTING
E.E. Plates of 200 subjects in four panes of 50.

1964, May 29			Perf. 11x10½
1246 A678 5c	blue gray	.20	.20
	P# block of 4	.60	—

NEW JERSEY TERCENTENARY ISSUE

300th anniv. of English colonization of New Jersey. The design is from a mural by Howard Pyle in the Essex County Courthouse, Newark, N.J.

Philip Carteret Landing at Elizabethtown, and Map of New Jersey — A679

Designed by Douglas Allen.

ROTARY PRESS PRINTING
E.E. Plates of 200 subjects in four panes of 50.

1964, June 15			Perf. 10½x11
1247 A679 5c	brt. ultramarine	.20	.20
	P# block of 4	.50	—
	Margin block of 4, Mr. Zip and "Use Zip Code"	.40	—

NEVADA STATEHOOD, 100th ANNIV.

Virginia City and Map of Nevada A680

Designed by William K. Schrage.

GIORI PRESS PRINTING
Plates of 200 subjects in four panes of 50.

1964, July 22			Perf. 11
1248 A680 5c	red, yellow & blue	.25	.20
	P# block of 4	1.05	—
	Margin block of 4, Mr. Zip and "Use Zip Code"	1.00	—

Flag — A681

William Shakespeare — A682

REGISTER AND VOTE ISSUE

Campaign to draw more voters to the polls.

Designed by Victor S. McCloskey, Jr.

GIORI PRESS PRINTING
Plates of 200 subjects in four panes of 50.

1964, Aug. 1			Perf. 11
1249 A681 5c	dark blue & red	.20	.20
	P# block of 4	.45	—
	Margin block of 4, Mr. Zip and "Use Zip Code"	.40	—

SHAKESPEARE ISSUE

William Shakespeare (1564-1616).

Designed by Douglas Gorsline.

ROTARY PRESS PRINTING
E.E. Plates of 200 subjects in four panes of 50.

1964, Aug. 14			**Perf. 10½x11**	
1250	A682	5c	**black brown,** *tan*	.20 .20
			P# block of 4	.40 —
			Margin block of 4, Mr. Zip and "Use Zip Code"	.35 —

DOCTORS MAYO ISSUE

Dr. William James Mayo (1861-1939) and his brother, Dr. Charles Horace Mayo (1865-1939), surgeons who founded the Mayo Foundation for Medical Education and Research in affiliation with the Univ. of Minnesota at Rochester. Heads on stamp are from a sculpture by James Earle Fraser.

Drs. William and Charles
Mayo — A683

ROTARY PRESS PRINTING
E.E. Plates of 200 subjects in four panes of 50.

1964, Sept. 11			**Perf. 10½x11**	
1251	A683	5c	**green**	.20 .20
			P# block of 4	.60 —
			Margin block of 4, Mr. Zip and "Use Zip Code"	.40 —

AMERICAN MUSIC ISSUE

50th anniv. of the founding of the American Society of Composers, Authors and Publishers (ASCAP).

Lute, Horn,
Laurel, Oak
and Music
Score — A684

Designed by Bradbury Thompson.

GIORI PRESS PRINTING
Plates of 200 subjects in four panes of 50.

1964, Oct. 15			**Perf. 11**	
Gray Paper with Blue Threads				
1252	A684	5c	**red, black & blue**	.20 .20
			P# block of 4	.40 —
			Margin block of 4, Mr. Zip and "Use Zip Code"	.35 —
a.			Blue omitted	900.00
b.			Blue missing (PS)	

Beware of copies offered as No. 1252a which have traces of blue.

HOMEMAKERS ISSUE

Honoring American women as homemakers and for the 50th anniv. of the passage of the Smith-Lever Act. By providing economic experts under an extension service of the U.S. Dept. of Agriculture, this legislation helped to improve homelife.

Farm Scene
Sampler
A685

Designed by Norman Todhunter.

Plates of 200 subjects in four panes of 50.
Engraved (Giori Press); Background Lithographed

1964, Oct. 26			**Perf. 11**	
1253	A685	5c	**multicolored**	.20 .20
			P# block of 4	.40 —
			Margin block of 4, Mr. Zip and "Use Zip Code"	.35 —

CHRISTMAS ISSUE

Holly — A686

Mistletoe — A687

Poinsettia — A688

Sprig of
Conifer — A689

Designed by Thomas F. Naegele.

GIORI PRESS PRINTING
Plates of 400 subjects in four panes of 100.
Panes contain 25 subjects each of Nos. 1254-1257

1964, Nov. 9			**Perf. 11**	
1254	A686	5c	**green, carmine & black**	.25 .20
a.			Tagged, *Nov. 10*	.65 .50
b.			Printed on gummed side	
1255	A687	5c	**carmine, green & black**	.25 .20
a.			Tagged, *Nov. 10*	.65 .50
1256	A688	5c	**carmine, green & black**	.25 .20
a.			Tagged, *Nov. 10*	.65 .50
1257	A689	5c	**black, green & carmine**	.25 .20
a.			Tagged, *Nov. 10*	.65 .50
b.			Block of 4, #1254-1257	1.00 1.00
			P# block of 4	1.10
			Margin block of 4, Zip and "Use Zip Code"	1.00 —
c.			Block of 4, tagged	2.60 2.25
			P# block of 4	5.50 —
			Zip block of 4	3.00 —

No. 1254b resulted from a paper foldover before printing and perforating.

VERRAZANO-NARROWS BRIDGE ISSUE

Opening of the Verrazano-Narrows Bridge connecting Staten Island and Brooklyn.

Verrazano-Narrows Bridge
and Map of New York
Bay — A690

ROTARY PRESS PRINTING
E.E. Plates of 200 subjects in four panes of 50.

1964, Nov. 21			**Perf. 10½x11**	
1258	A690	5c	**blue green**	.20 .20
			P# block of 4	.45 —
			Margin block of 4, Mr. Zip and "Use Zip Code"	.40 —

FINE ARTS ISSUE

Abstract
Design by
Stuart
Davis — A691

GIORI PRESS PRINTING
Plates of 200 subjects in four panes of 50.

1964, Dec. 2			**Perf. 11**	
1259	A691	5c	**ultra., black & dull red**	.20 .20
			P# block of 4, 2#	.45 —
			Margin block of 4, Mr. Zip and "Use Zip Code"	.40 —

AMATEUR RADIO ISSUE

Issued to honor the radio amateurs on the 50th anniversary of the American Radio Relay League.

Radio Waves and
Dial — A692

Designed by Emil J. Willett.

ROTARY PRESS PRINTING
E.E. Plates of 200 subjects in four panes of 50.

1964, Dec. 15			**Perf. 10½x11**	
1260	A692	5c	**red lilac**	.20 .20
			P# block of 4	.60 —
			Margin block of 4, Mr. Zip and "Use Zip Code"	.40 —

BATTLE OF NEW ORLEANS ISSUE

Battle of New Orleans, Chalmette Plantation, Jan. 8-18, 1815, established 150 years of peace and friendship between the US and Great Britain.

General Andrew Jackson and Sesquicentennial
Medal — A693

Designed by Robert J. Jones.

GIORI PRESS PRINTING
Plates of 200 subjects in four panes of 50.

1965, Jan. 8			**Perf. 11**	
1261	A693	5c	**deep carmine, violet blue & gray**	.20 .20
			P# block of 4	.60 —
			Margin block of 4, Mr. Zip and "Use Zip Code"	.50 —

Discus
Thrower — A694

Microscope and
Stethoscope — A695

PHYSICAL FITNESS-SOKOL ISSUE

Publicizing the importance of physical fitness and for the centenary of the founding of the Sokol (athletic) organization in America.

Designed by Norman Todhunter.

GIORI PRESS PRINTING
Plates of 200 subjects in four panes of 50.

1965, Feb. 15			**Perf. 11**	
1262	A694	5c	**maroon & black**	.20 .20
			P# block of 4	.50 —
			Margin block of 4, Mr. Zip and "Use Zip Code"	.40 —

CRUSADE AGAINST CANCER ISSUE

Issued to publicize the "Crusade Against Cancer" and to stress the importance of early diagnosis.

Designed by Stevan Dohanos.

GIORI PRESS PRINTING
Plates of 200 subjects in four panes of 50.

1965, Apr. 1		Perf. 11	
1263 A695 5c black, purple & red orange		.20	.20
P# block of 4, 2#		.40	
Margin block of 4, Mr. Zip and "Use Zip Code"		.35	

CHURCHILL MEMORIAL ISSUE
Sir Winston Spencer Churchill (1874-1965), British statesman and World War II leader.

Winston Churchill — A696

Designed by Richard Hurd.

ROTARY PRESS PRINTING
E.E. Plates of 200 subjects in four panes of 50.

1965, May 13		Perf. 10½x11	
1264 A696 5c black		.20	.20
P# block of 4		.40	
Margin block of 4, Mr. Zip and "Use Zip Code"		.35	

MAGNA CARTA ISSUE
750th anniversary of the Magna Carta, the basis of English and American common law.

Procession of Barons and King John's Crown — A697

Designed by Brook Temple.

GIORI PRESS PRINTING
Plates of 200 subjects in four panes of 50.

1965, June 15		Perf. 11	
1265 A697 5c black, yellow ocher & red lilac		.20	.20
P# block of 4, 2#		.40	
Margin block of 4, Mr. Zip and "Use Zip Code"		.35	
Corner block of 4, black # omitted		—	

INTERNATIONAL COOPERATION YEAR
ICY, 1965, and 20th anniv. of the UN.

International Cooperation Year Emblem A698

Designed by Herbert M. Sanborn and Olav S. Mathiesen.

GIORI PRESS PRINTING
Plates of 200 subjects in four panes of 50.

1965, June 26		Perf. 11	
1266 A698 5c dull blue & black		.20	.20
P# block of 4		.40	
Margin block of 4, Mr. Zip and "Use Zip Code"		.35	

SALVATION ARMY ISSUE
Centenary of the founding of the Salvation Army by William Booth in London.

A699

Designed by Sam Marsh.

GIORI PRESS PRINTING
Plates of 200 subjects in four panes of 50.

1965, July 2		Perf. 11	
1267 A699 5c red, black & dark blue		.20	.20
P# block of 4		.40	
Margin block of 4, Mr. Zip and "Use Zip Code"		.35	

Dante after a 16th Century Painting — A700

Herbert Hoover — A701

DANTE ISSUE
Dante Alighieri (1265-1321), Italian poet.

Designed by Douglas Gorsline.

ROTARY PRESS PRINTING
E.E. Plates of 200 subjects in four panes of 50.

1965, July 17		Perf. 10½x11	
1268 A700 5c maroon, tan		.20	.20
P# block of 4		.40	
Margin block of 4, Mr. Zip and "Use Zip Code"		.35	

HERBERT HOOVER ISSUE
President Herbert Clark Hoover, (1874-1964).

Designed by Norman Todhunter; photograph by Fabian Bachrach, Sr.

ROTARY PRESS PRINTING
E.E. Plates of 200 subjects in four panes of 50.

1965, Aug. 10		Perf. 10½x11	
1269 A701 5c rose red		.20	.20
P# block of 4		.55	
Margin block of 4, Mr. Zip and "Use Zip Code"		.40	

ROBERT FULTON ISSUE
Fulton (1765-1815), inventor of the 1st commercial steamship.

Robert Fulton and the Clermont A702

Designed by John Maass; bust by Jean Antoine Houdon.

GIORI PRESS PRINTING
Plates of 200 subjects in four panes of 50.

1965, Aug. 19		Perf. 11	
1270 A702 5c black & blue		.20	.20
P# block of 4		.40	
Margin block of 4, Mr. Zip and "Use Zip Code"		.35	

FLORIDA SETTLEMENT ISSUE
400th anniv. of the settlement of Florida, and the 1st permanent European settlement in the continental US, St. Augustine, Fla.

Spanish Explorer, Royal Flag of Spain and Ships — A703

Designed by Brook Temple.

GIORI PRESS PRINTING
Plates of 200 subjects with four panes of 50.

1965, Aug. 28		Perf. 11	
1271 A703 5c red, yellow & black		.20	.20
P# block of 4, 3#		.50	
Margin block of 4, Mr. Zip and "Use Zip Code"		.40	
a. Yellow omitted		275.00	

See Spain No. 1312.

TRAFFIC SAFETY ISSUE
Issued to publicize traffic safety and the prevention of traffic accidents.

Traffic Signal — A704

Designed by Richard F. Hurd.

GIORI PRESS PRINTING
Plates of 200 subjects in four panes of 50.

1965, Sept. 3		Perf. 11	
1272 A704 5c emerald, black & red		.20	.20
P# block of 4, 2#		.45	
Margin block of 4, Mr. Zip and "Use Zip Code"		.40	

JOHN SINGLETON COPLEY ISSUE
Copley (1738-1815), painter. The portrait of the artist's daughter is from the oil painting "The Copley Family," which hangs in the National Gallery of Art, Washington, D.C.

Elizabeth Clarke Copley — A705

Designed by John Carter Brown.

GIORI PRESS PRINTING
Plates of 200 subjects in four panes of 50.

1965, Sept. 17		Perf. 11	
1273 A705 5c black, brown & olive		.20	.20
P# block of 4		.50	
Margin block of 4, Mr. Zip and "Use Zip Code"		.40	

INTERNATIONAL TELECOMMUNICATION UNION, 100th ANNIV.

Galt Projection World Map and Radio Sine Wave — A706

Designed by Thomas F. Naegele.

GIORI PRESS PRINTING

Plates of 200 subjects with four panes of 50.

1965, Oct. 6   *Perf. 11*
1274 A706 11c **black, carmine & bister**   .35   .20
P# block of 4, 2#   2.00
Margin block of 4, Mr. Zip and
"Use Zip Code"   1.50   —

ADLAI STEVENSON ISSUE

Adlai Ewing Stevenson (1900-65), governor of Illinois, US ambassador to the UN.

Adlai E. Stevenson — A707

Designed by George Samerjan; photograph by Philippe Halsman.

LITHOGRAPHED, ENGRAVED (Giori)

Plates of 200 subjects in four panes of 50.

1965, Oct. 23   *Perf. 11*
1275 A707 5c **pale blue, black, carmine & violet blue**   .20   .20
P# block of 4   .40

CHRISTMAS ISSUE

Angel with Trumpet, 1840 Weather Vane — A708

Designed by Robert Jones.

After a watercolor by Lucille Gloria Chabot of the 1840 weather vane from the People's Methodist Church, Newburyport, Mass.

GIORI PRESS PRINTING

Plates of 400 subjects in four panes of 100.

1965, Nov. 2   *Perf. 11*
1276 A708 5c **carmine, dark olive green & bister**   .20   .20
P# block of 4   .40
Margin block of 4, Mr. Zip and "Use Zip Code"   .35   —
Pair with full vert. gutter btwn.   —
a.   Tagged, *Nov. 15*   .75   .25
P# block of 4   5.50
Zip block of 4   3.50   —

PROMINENT AMERICANS ISSUE

Thomas Jefferson — A710

Albert Gallatin — A711

Frank Lloyd Wright and Guggenheim Museum, New York — A712

Abraham Lincoln A714

George Washington (redrawn) — A715a

Albert Einstein — A717

Henry Ford and 1909 Model T — A718a

Oliver Wendell Holmes — A720

Frederick Douglass — A722

Francis Parkman — A713

George Washington A715

Franklin D. Roosevelt — A716

Andrew Jackson — A718

John F. Kennedy — A719

George Catlett Marshall — A721

John Dewey — A723

Thomas Paine — A724

Lucy Stone — A72[?]

Eugene O'Neill — A726

John Bassett Moore — A727

Designers: 1c, Robert Geissmann, after portrait by Rembrandt Peale. 1¼c, Robert Gallatin. 2c, Patricia Amarantides; photograph by Blackstone-Shelburne. 3c, Bill Hyde. 4c, Bill Hyde; photograph by Mathew Brady. 5c, Bill Hyde, after portrait by Rembrandt Peale. 5c, No. 1283B, Redrawn by Stevan Dohanos. 6c, Richard L. Clark. 8c, Frank Sebastiano; photograph by Philippe Halsman. 10c, Lester Beall. 12c, Norman Todhunter. 13c, Stevan Dohanos; photograph by Jacques Lowe. 15c, Richard F. Hurd. 20c, Robert Geissmann. 25c, Walter DuBois Richards. 40c, Robert Geissmann, after portrait by John Wesley Jarvis. 50c, Mark English. $1, Norman Todhunter. $5, Tom Laufer.

ROTARY PRESS PRINTING

E.E. Plates of 400 subjects in four panes of 100

1965-78   *Perf. 11x10½, 10½x11*

Types of 15c:
I. Necktie barely touches coat at bottom; crosshatching of tie strong and complete. Flag of "5" is true horizontal. Crosshatching of "15" is colorless when visible.
II. Necktie does not touch coat at bottom; LL to UR crosshatching lines strong, UL to LR lines very faint. Flag of "5" slants down slightly at right. Crosshatching of "15" is colored and visible when magnified.
A third type, used only for No. 1288B, is smaller in overall size and "15¢" is ¾mm closer to head.

1278 A710   1c **green,** tagged, shiny gum, *Jan. 12, 1968*   .20   .20
P# block of 4   .20   —
Margin block of 4, "Use Zip Codes"   .20   —
Dull gum (from bklt. pane)   .20
a.   Booklet pane of 8, shiny gum, *Jan. 12, 1968*   1.00   .75
Dull gum   2.00
b.   Bklt. pane of 4+2 labels, *May 10, 1971*   .80   .60
c.   Untagged (Bureau precanceled)   6.25   1.25
P# block of 4   175.00
Margin block of 4, "Use Zip Codes"   30.00
d.   Tagging omitted (not Bureau precanceled)   3.50   —
e.   As "a," dull gum, tagging omitted   75.00
1279 A711   1¼c **light green,** *Jan. 30, 1967*   .20   .20
P# block of 4   5.50
1280 A712   2c **dark blue gray,** tagged, shiny gum, *June 8, 1966*   .20   .20
P# block of 4   .25
Margin block of 4, "Use Zip Codes"   .20   —
Pair with full vert. gutter between   —
Dull gum (from bklt. pane)   .20
a.   Bklt. pane of 5 + label, *Jan. 8, 1968*   1.25   .80
b.   Untagged (Bureau precanceled)   1.35   .40
P# block of 4   27.50
Margin block of 4, "Use Zip Codes"   7.50
c.   Bklt. pane of 6, shiny gum, *May 7, 1971*   1.00   .75
Dull gum   1.10
d.   Tagging omitted (not Bureau precanceled)   3.50   —
1281 A713   3c **violet,** tagged, *Sept. 16, 1967*   .20   .20
P# block of 4   .25   —
Margin block of 4, "Use Zip Codes"   .20   —
a.   Untagged (Bureau precanceled)   3.00   .75
P# block of 4   —
Margin block of 4, "Use Zip Codes"   30.00
b.   Tagging omitted (not Bureau precanceled)   4.50   —
1282 A714   4c **black,** *Nov. 19, 1965*   .20   .20
P# block of 4   .40
a.   Tagged, *Dec. 1, 1965*   .20   .20
P# block of 4   .55
Pair with full horiz. gutter between   700.00
1283 A715   5c **blue,** *Feb. 22, 1966*   .20   .20
P# block of 4   .50
a.   Tagged, *Feb. 23, 1966*   .20   .20

	P# block of 4		.60	—
	Pair with full vert. gutter between		—	
1283B A715a	5c **blue**, tagged, shiny gum, *Nov. 17, 1967*		.20	.20
	P# block of 4		.50	—
	Pair with full horiz. gutter between		175.00	
	Dull gum		.20	
	P# block of 4		1.40	
d.	Untagged (Bureau precanceled)		12.50	1.00
	P# block of 4		1.00	
e.	Tagging omitted (not Bureau precanceled), shiny gum		4.50	
	Dull gum		4.50	

No. 1283B is redrawn; highlights, shadows softened.

1284 A716	6c **gray brown**, *Jan. 29, 1966*		.20	.20
	P# block of 4		.60	—
	Margin block of 4, "Use Zip Codes" (Bureau precanceled)		3.00	
	Pair with full horiz. gutter between		150.00	
	Pair with full vert. gutter between		150.00	
a.	Tagged, *Dec. 29, 1966*		.20	.20
	P# block of 4		.80	—
	Margin block of 4, "Use Zip Codes"		.65	—
b.	Booklet pane of 8, *Dec. 28, 1967*		1.50	1.00
c.	Bklt. pane of 5+ label, *Jan. 9, 1968*		1.50	1.00
d.	Horiz. pair, imperf. between		1,500.	
e.	As "b," tagging omitted		50.00	

For untagged sheet stamps, "Use Zip Codes" and "Mail Early in the Day" marginal markings are found only on panes with Bureau precancels.

1285 A717	8c **violet**, *Mar. 14, 1966*		.20	.20
	P# block of 4		.85	—
a.	Tagged, *July 6, 1966*		.20	.20
	P# block of 4		.85	—
	Margin block of 4, "Use Zip Codes"		.85	—
1286 A718	10c **lilac**, tagged, *Mar. 15, 1967*		.20	.20
	P# block of 4		1.00	—
	Margin block of 4, "Use Zip Codes"		.85	—
b.	Untagged (Bureau precanceled)		57.50	1.75
	P# block of 4		275.00	
	Margin block of 4, "Use Zip Codes"		275.00	
e.	Tagging omitted (not Bureau precanceled)		10.00	
1286A 718a	12c **black**, tagged, *July 30, 1968*		.25	.20
	P# block of 4		1.00	—
	Margin block of 4, "Use Zip Codes"		1.00	—
c.	Untagged (Bureau precanceled)		4.75	1.00
	P# block of 4		145.00	
	Margin block of 4, "Use Zip Codes"		27.50	
d.	Tagging omitted (not Bureau precanceled)		25.00	
1287 A719	13c **brown**, tagged, *May 29, 1967*		.30	.20
	P# block of 4		1.50	—
	Pair with full horiz. gutter between		—	
a.	Untagged (Bureau precanceled)		6.00	1.00
	P# block of 4		100.00	
b.	Tagging omitted (not Bureau precanceled)		15.00	—
1288 A720	15c **magenta**, type I, tagged, *Mar. 8, 1968*		.30	.20
	P# block of 4		1.25	—
	Margin block of 4, "Use Zip Codes"		1.25	—
	Pair with full horiz. gutter between		200.00	
a.	Untagged (Bureau precanceled)		.75	.75
	P# block of 4		29.50	
	Margin block of 4, "Use Zip Codes"		7.50	
d.	Type II		.55	.20
	P# block of 4		8.00	—
	Zip block of 4		3.50	—
	Pair with full vert. gutter between		300.00	
f.	As "d," tagging omitted (not Bureau precanceled)		7.50	—
h.	As No. 1288, tagging omitted (not Bureau precanceled)		20.00	—

Imperforates exist from printer's waste.

Values for No. 1288a are for the bars-only precancel. Also exists with city precancels, and worth more thus.

1288B A720	15c **magenta**, tagged, perf. 10 (from blkt. pane)		.35	.20
c.	Booklet pane of 8, *June 14, 1978*		2.80	1.75
e.	As "c," vert. imperf between		1,750.	
g.	Tagging omitted		10.00	—
i.	As "c," tagging omitted		85.00	

No. 1288B issued in booklets only. All stamps have one or two straight edges. Plates made from redrawn die.

1289 A721	20c **deep olive**, shiny gum, *Oct. 24, 1967*		.40	.20
	P# block of 4		1.75	—
	Margin block of 4, "Use Zip Codes"		1.65	—
	Dull gum		.45	
	P# block of 4		2.10	—
	Zip block of 4		1.90	—
a.	Tagged, shiny gum, *Apr. 3, 1973*		.40	.20

	P# block of 4		1.75	—
	Zip block of 4		1.65	—
b.	20c **black olive**, tagged, dull gum		.50	.20
	P# block of 4		3.50	
	Zip block of 4		2.25	
1290 A722	25c **rose lake**, *Feb. 14, 1967*		.55	.20
	P# block of 4		2.25	—
	Margin block of 4, "Use Zip Codes"		2.20	—
a.	Tagged, shiny gum, *Apr. 3, 1973*		.45	.20
	P# block of 4		2.00	—
	Zip block of 4		1.90	—
	Dull gum		.45	
	P# block of 4		2.00	—
	Zip block of 4		1.90	—
b.	25c **magenta**		25.00	—
	On cover		—	
	P# block of 4		150.00	
1291 A723	30c **red lilac**, *Oct. 21, 1968*		.65	.20
	P# block of 4		2.90	—
	Margin block of 4, "Use Zip Codes"		2.70	—
a.	Tagged, *Apr. 3, 1973*		.50	.20
	P# block of 4		2.25	—
	Zip block of 4		2.10	—
1292 A724	40c **blue black**, *Jan. 29, 1968*		.80	.20
	P# block of 4		3.25	—
	Margin block of 4, "Use Zip Codes"		3.25	—
a.	Tagged, shiny gum, *Apr. 3, 1973*		.65	.20
	P# block of 4		2.75	—
	Zip block of 4		2.65	—
	Dull gum		.70	
	P# block of 4		3.00	
	Zip block of 4		2.90	
1293 A725	50c **rose magenta**, *Aug. 13, 1968*		1.00	.20
	P# block of 4		4.25	—
	Margin block of 4, "Use Zip Codes"		4.00	—
	Pair with full vert. gutter btwn.		—	
a.	Tagged, *Apr. 3, 1973*		.80	.20
	P# block of 4		3.50	—
	Zip block of 4		3.25	—
1294 A726	$1 **dull purple**, *Oct. 16, 1967*		2.25	.20
	P# block of 4		10.00	—
	Margin block of 4, "Use Zip Codes"		9.25	—
a.	Tagged, *Apr. 3, 1973*		1.65	.20
	P# block of 4		6.75	—
	Zip block of 4		6.65	—
1295 A727	$5 **gray black**, *Dec. 3, 1966*		10.00	2.25
	P# block of 4		42.50	—
a.	Tagged, *Apr. 3, 1973*		8.50	2.00
	P# block of 4		35.00	—
	Nos. 1278-1295 (21)		18.85	6.25
	Nos. 1278-1288, 1289-1295, P# blocks of 4 (20)		78.65	

Bureau Precancels: 1c, 19 diff., 1¼c, 14 diff., 2c, 41 diff., 3c, 11 diff., 4c, 49 diff., No. 1283, 7 diff., No. 1283B, 29 diff., 6c, 35 diff., 8c, 18 diff., 10c, 12 diff., 12c, 3 diff., 13c, 3 diff., No. 1288a, 9 diff., 20c, 14 diff., 25c, 9 diff., 30c, 14 diff., 40c, 7 diff., 50c, 14 diff., $1, 8 diff.

See Luminescence note in "Information for Collectors" at front of book.

COIL STAMPS

1967-75	**Tagged**		**Perf. 10 Horizontally**	
1297 A713	3c **violet**, shiny gum, *Nov. 4, 1975*		.20	.20
	Pair		.20	.20
	Joint line pair		.45	.20
	Dull gum		.75	
	Joint line pair		2.00	
a.	Imperf., pair, shiny gum		22.50	
	Imperf., joint line pair		45.00	
	Imperf, pair, dull gum		25.00	
	Imperf. joint line pair		50.00	
b.	Untagged (Bureau precanceled), shiny gum		.40	.25
	Pair		.80	.50
	Joint line pair		62.50	3.75
	Dull gum		.25	
	Pair		.50	
	Joint line pair		3.75	
c.	As "b," imperf. pair		6.00	—
	Joint line pair		22.50	

No. 1297c is precanceled "Nonprofit Org. / CAR RT SORT."

1298 A716	6c **gray brown**, *Dec. 28, 1967*		.20	.20
	Pair		.30	.20
	Joint line pair		1.10	.25
a.	Imperf., pair		2,000.	
	Imperf., joint line pair		5,000.	
b.	Tagging omitted		6.00	

Bureau Precancels: 3c, 9 diff.

Franklin D. Roosevelt —
A727a

Revised design by Robert J. Jones and Howard C. Mildner.

COIL STAMPS

1966-81	**Tagged**		**Perf. 10 Vertically**	
1299 A710	1c **green**, *Jan. 12, 1968*		.20	.20
	Pair		.20	.20
	Joint line pair		.25	.20
a.	Untagged (Bureau precanceled)		8.00	1.75
	Pair		17.50	4.00
	Joint line pair		295.00	
b.	Imperf., pair		25.00	
	Imperf., joint line pair		55.00	
1303 A714	4c **black**, *May 28, 1966*		.20	.20
	Pair		.30	.20
	Joint line pair		.75	.20
a.	Untagged (Bureau precanceled)		8.75	.75
	Pair		19.00	1.75
	Joint line pair		250.00	
b.	Imperf., pair		750.00	
	Imperf., joint line pair		1,750.	
c.	Tagging omitted (not Bureau precanceled)		12.50	—
	Pair		35.00	
	Joint line pair		135.00	
1304 A715	5c **blue**, shiny gum, *Sept. 8, 1966*		.20	.20
	Pair		.25	.20
	Joint line pair		.40	.20
	Dull gum		.75	
	Joint line pair		5.00	
a.	Untagged (Bureau precanceled)		6.50	.65
	Pair		14.00	1.40
	Joint line pair		195.00	
b.	Imperf., pair		150.00	
	Joint line pair		275.00	
e.	As "a," imperf., pair		300.00	
	Joint line pair		900.00	
f.	Tagging omitted (not Bureau precanceled)		—	

No. 1304b is valued in the grade of fine.

No. 1304e is precanceled Mount Pleasant, Iowa. Also exists from Chicago, Illinois; value $1,500 for pair.

1304C A715a	5c **blue**, *1981*		.20	.20
	Pair		.30	.20
	Joint line pair		1.25	
d.	Imperf., pair		600.00	
1305 A727a	6c **gray brown**, *Feb. 28, 1968*		.20	.20
	Pair		.30	.20
	Joint line pair		.55	.20
a.	Imperf., pair		65.00	
	Joint line pair		125.00	
b.	Untagged (Bureau precanceled)		20.00	1.00
	Pair		42.50	2.25
	Joint line pair		675.00	—
k.	Tagging omitted (not Bureau precanceled)		3.50	
1305E A720	15c **magenta**, type I, shiny gum, *June 14, 1978*		.25	.20
	Pair		.50	.20
	Joint line pair		1.10	.30
	Dull gum		.60	
	Joint line pair		3.50	
f.	Untagged (Bureau precanceled, Chicago, IL)		35.00	—
	Pair		80.00	—
	Joint line pair		1,250.	
g.	Imperf., pair, shiny gum		25.00	
	Joint line pair		60.00	
	Imperf., pair, dull gum		35.00	
	Joint line pair		75.00	
h.	Pair, imperf. between		160.00	
	Joint line pair		500.00	
i	Type II, dull gum		.60	.20
	Joint line pair		2.75	
j.	Type II, dull gum, Imperf., pair		75.00	
	Joint line pair		150.00	
l	Tagging omitted		—	
1305C A726	$1 **dull purple**, shiny gum, *Jan. 12, 1973*		2.00	.40
	Pair		4.00	.80
	Joint line pair		5.50	1.50
	Dull gum		2.75	
	Joint line pair		9.00	
d.	Imperf., pair		2,000.	
	Joint line pair		4,250.	
	Nos. 1297-1305C (9)		3.65	2.00

Bureau Precancels: 1c, 5 diff., 4c, 35 diff., No. 1304a, 45 diff., 6c, 30 diff.

MIGRATORY BIRD TREATY ISSUE

Migratory Birds over Canada-US Border
A728

Designed by Burt E. Pringle.

GIORI PRESS PRINTING
Plates of 200 subjects in four panes of 50.

1966, Mar. 16			**Perf. 11**	
1306 A728	5c **black, crimson & dark blue**		.20	.20
	P# block of 4, 2#		.40	—
	Margin block of 4, Mr. Zip and "Use Zip Code"		.35	—

HUMANE TREATMENT OF ANIMALS ISSUE

Issued to promote humane treatment of all animals and for the centenary of the American Society for the Prevention of Cruelty to Animals.

Mongrel
A729

Designed by Norman Todhunter.

LITHOGRAPHED, ENGRAVED (Giori)
Plates of 200 subjects in four panes of 50.

1966, Apr. 9   *Perf. 11*
1307 A729 5c orange brown & black   .20   .20
             P# block of 4   .40   —
             Margin block of 4, Mr. Zip and "Use
             Zip Code"   .35   —

Clown — A731

Sesquicentennial Seal;
Map of Indiana with
19 Stars and old
Capitol at
Corydon — A730

INDIANA STATEHOOD, 150th ANNIV.

Designed by Paul A. Wehr.

GIORI PRESS PRINTING
Plates of 200 subjects in four panes of 50.

1966, Apr. 16   *Perf. 11*
1308 A730 5c ocher, brown & violet blue   .20   .20
             P# block of 4, 2#   .50   —
             Margin block of 4, Mr. Zip and "Use
             Zip Code"   .40   —

AMERICAN CIRCUS ISSUE

Issued to honor the American Circus on the centenary of the birth of John Ringling.

Designed by Edward Klauck.

GIORI PRESS PRINTING
Plates of 200 subjects in four panes of 50.

1966, May 2   *Perf. 11*
1309 A731 5c multicolored   .20   .20
             P# block of 4, 2#   .50   —
             Margin block of 4, Mr. Zip and "Use
             Zip Code"   .40   —

SIXTH INTERNATIONAL PHILATELIC EXHIBITION ISSUES

Sixth International Philatelic Exhibition (SIPEX), Washington, D.C., May 21-30.

Stamped
Cover — A732

Designed by Thomas F. Naegele.

LITHOGRAPHED, ENGRAVED (Giori)
Plates of 200 subjects in four panes of 50.

1966   *Perf. 11*
1310 A732 5c multicolored, *May 21*   .20   .20
             P# block of 4   .40   —
             Margin block of 4, Mr. Zip and "Use
             Zip Code"   .35   —

A733

SOUVENIR SHEET
Designed by Brook Temple.

Plates of 24 subjects
Illustration reduced.

Imperf
1311 A733 5c multicolored, *May 23*   .20   .20

No. 1311 measures 108x74mm. Below the stamp appears a line drawing of the Capitol and Washington Monument. Marginal inscriptions and drawing are green.

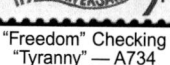

"Freedom" Checking
"Tyranny" — A734

Polish Eagle and
Cross — A735

BILL OF RIGHTS, 175th ANNIV.

Designed by Herbert L. Block (Herblock).

GIORI PRESS PRINTING
Plates of 200 subjects in four panes of 50.

1966, July 1   *Perf. 11*
1312 A734 5c carmine, dark & light blue   .20   .20
             P# block of 4, 2#   .45   —
             Margin block of 4, Mr. Zip and "Use
             Zip Code"   .40   —

POLISH MILLENNIUM ISSUE

Adoption of Christianity in Poland, 1000th anniv.

Designed by Edmund D. Lewandowski.

ROTARY PRESS PRINTING
E.E. Plates of 200 subjects in four panes of 50.

1966, July 30   *Perf. 10½x11*
1313 A735 5c red   .20   .20
             P# block of 4   .45   —
             Margin block of 4, Mr. Zip and "Use
             Zip Code"   .40   —

NATIONAL PARK SERVICE ISSUE

50th anniv. of the Natl. Park Service of the Interior Dept. The design "Parkscape U.S.A." identifies Natl. Park Service facilities.

National Park
Service
Emblem
A736

Designed by Thomas H. Geismar.

LITHOGRAPHED, ENGRAVED (Giori)
Plates of 200 subjects in four panes of 50.

1966, Aug. 25   *Perf. 11*
1314 A736 5c yellow, black & green   .20   .20
             P# block of 4   .45   —
             Margin block of 4, Mr. Zip and "Use
             Zip Code"   .40   —
      a.   Tagged, *Aug. 26*   .35   .35
             P# block of 4   2.25   —
             Zip block of 4   1.50   —

MARINE CORPS RESERVE ISSUE

US Marine Corps Reserve founding, 50th anniv.

Combat Marine, 1966;
Frogman; World War II Flier;
World War I "Devil Dog" and
Marine, 1775 — A737

Designed by Stella Grafakos.

LITHOGRAPHED, ENGRAVED (Giori)
Plates of 200 subjects in four panes of 50.

1966, Aug. 29   *Perf. 11*
1315 A737 5c black, bister, red & ultra.   .20   .20
             P# block of 4   .45   —
             Margin block of 4, Mr. Zip and
             "Use Zip Code"   .40   —
      a.   Tagged   .40   .20
             P# block of 4   2.25   —
             Zip block of 4   1.70   —
      b.   Black & bister (engraved) missing (EP) 16,000.

GENERAL FEDERATION OF WOMEN'S CLUBS ISSUE

75 years of service by the General Federation of Women's Clubs.

Women of
1890 and
1966 — A738

Designed by Charles Henry Carter.

GIORI PRESS PRINTING
Plates of 200 subjects in four panes of 50.

1966, Sept. 12   *Perf. 11*
1316 A738 5c black, pink & blue   .20   .20
             P# block of 4, 2#   .45   —
             Margin block of 4, Mr. Zip and "Use
             Zip Code"   .40   —
      a.   Tagged, *Sept. 13*   .40   .20
             P# block of 4, 2#   2.25   —
             Zip block of 4   1.70   —

AMERICAN FOLKLORE ISSUE
Johnny Appleseed

Issued to honor Johnny Appleseed (John Chapman 1774-1845), who wandered over 100,000 square miles planting apple trees, and who gave away and sold seedlings to Midwest pioneers.

Johnny Appleseed — A739

Designed by Robert Bode.

GIORI PRESS PRINTING
Plates of 200 subjects in four panes of 50.

1966, Sept. 24   *Perf. 11*
1317 A739 5c green, red & black   .20   .20
             P# block of 4, 2#   .45   —
             Margin block of 4, Mr. Zip and "Use
             Zip Code"   .40   —
      a.   Tagged, *Sept. 26*   .40   .20
             P# block of 4, 2#   2.25   —
             Zip block of 4   1.70   —

BEAUTIFICATION OF AMERICA ISSUE

Issued to publicize President Johnson's "Plant for a more beautiful America" campaign.

Jefferson
Memorial,
Tidal Basin
and Cherry
Blossoms
A740

Designed by Miss Gyo Fujikawa.

GIORI PRESS PRINTING
Plates of 200 subjects in four panes of 50.

1966, Oct. 5		Perf. 11	
1318 A740 5c emerald, pink & black		.20	.20
P# block of 4, 2#		.45	—
Margin block of 4, Mr. Zip and "Use Zip Code"		.40	—
a. Tagged		.40	.20
P# block of 4, 2#		2.25	—
Zip block of 4		1.70	—

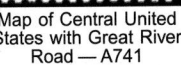

Map of Central United
States with Great River
Road — A741

Statue of Liberty and
"Old Glory" — A742

GREAT RIVER ROAD ISSUE

Issued to publicize the 5,600-mile Great River Road connecting New Orleans with Kenora, Ontario, and following the Mississippi most of the way.

Designed by Herbert Bayer.

LITHOGRAPHED, ENGRAVED (Giori)
Plates of 200 subjects in four panes of 50.

1966, Oct. 21			
1319 A741 5c vermilion, yellow, blue & green		.20	.20
P# block of 4		.60	—
Margin block of 4, Mr. Zip and "Use Zip Code"		.40	—
a. Tagged, Oct. 22		.40	.20
P# block of 4		2.50	—
Zip block of 4		1.70	—

SAVINGS BOND-SERVICEMEN ISSUE

25th anniv. of US Savings Bonds, and honoring American servicemen.

Designed by Stevan Dohanos, photo by Bob Noble.

LITHOGRAPHED, ENGRAVED (Giori)
Plates of 200 subjects in four panes of 50.

1966, Oct. 26		Perf. 11	
1320 A742 5c red, dark blue, light blue & black		.20	.20
P# block of 4		.45	—
Margin block of 4, Mr. Zip and "Use Zip Code"		.40	—
a. Tagged, Oct. 27		.40	.20
P# block of 4		2.00	—
Zip block of 4		1.70	—
b. Red, dark blue & black missing (EP)		4,250.	
c. Dark blue (engr.) missing (EP)		5,500.	

CHRISTMAS ISSUE

Madonna and Child, by Hans
Memling — A743

Designed by Howard C. Mildner.

Modeled after "Madonna and Child with Angels," by the Flemish artist Hans Memling (c.1430-1494), Mellon Collection, National Gallery of Art, Washington, D.C.

LITHOGRAPHED, ENGRAVED (Giori)
Plates of 400 subjects in four panes of 100.

1966, Nov. 1		Perf. 11	
1321 A743 5c multicolored		.20	.20
P# block of 4		.40	—
Margin block of 4, Mr. Zip and "Use Zip Code"		.35	—
a. Tagged, Nov. 2		.40	.20
P# block of 4		2.00	—
Zip block of 4		1.70	—

MARY CASSATT ISSUE

Cassatt (1844-1926), painter. The painting "The Boating Party" is in the Natl. Gallery of Art, Washington, D.C.

"The Boating
Party" — A744

Designed by Robert J. Jones.

GIORI PRESS PRINTING
Plates of 200 subjects in four panes of 50.

1966, Nov. 17		Perf. 11	
1322 A744 5c multicolored		.20	.20
P# block of 4, 2#		.60	—
Margin block of 4, Mr. Zip and "Use Zip Code"		.50	—
a. Tagged		.40	.25
P# block of 4, 2#		2.00	—
Zip block of 4		1.70	—

NATIONAL GRANGE ISSUE

Centenary of the founding of the National Grange, American farmers' organization.

Grange Poster,
1870 — A745

Designed by Lee Pavao.

GIORI PRESS PRINTING
Plates of 200 subjects in four panes of 50.

1967, Apr. 17	Tagged	Perf. 11	
1323 A745 5c orange, yellow, brown, green & black		.20	.20
P# block of 4, 2#		.40	—
Margin block of 4, Mr. Zip and "Use Zip Code"		.35	—
a. Tagging omitted		6.00	

CANADA CENTENARY ISSUE

Centenary of Canada's emergence as a nation.

Canadian
Landscape
A746

Designed by Ivan Chermayeff.

GIORI PRESS PRINTING
Plates of 200 subjects in four panes of 50.

1967, May 25	Tagged	Perf. 11	
1324 A746 5c lt. blue, dp. green, ultra. & olive & black		.20	.20
On cover, Expo. station ("U.S. Pavilion") machine canc.		1.00	
On cover, Expo. station handstamp canc.		2.50	

		.40	—
P# block of 4, 2#			
Margin block of 4, Mr. Zip and "Use Zip Code"		.35	—
a. Tagging omitted		6.00	

ERIE CANAL ISSUE

150th anniversary of the Erie Canal ground-breaking ceremony at Rome, N.Y. The canal links Lake Erie and New York City.

Stern of Early
Canal
Boat — A747

Designed by George Samerjan.

LITHOGRAPHED, ENGRAVED (Giori)
Plates of 200 subjects in four panes of 50.

1967, July 4	Tagged	Perf. 11	
1325 A747 5c ultra., greenish blue, black & crimson		.20	.20
P# block of 4		.40	—
Margin block of 4, Mr. Zip and "Use Zip Code"		.35	—
a. Tagging omitted		11.00	

"SEARCH FOR PEACE" — LIONS ISSUE

Issued to publicize the search for peace. "Search for Peace" was the theme of an essay contest for young men and women sponsored by Lions International on its 50th anniversary.

Peace
Dove — A748

Designed by Bradbury Thompson.

GIORI PRESS PRINTING
Plates of 200 subjects in four panes of 50.

1967, July 5	Tagged	Perf. 11	
Gray Paper with Blue Threads			
1326 A748 5c blue, red & black		.20	.20
P# block of 4		.40	—
Margin block of 4, Mr. Zip and "Use Zip Code"		.35	—
a. Tagging omitted		7.50	

HENRY DAVID THOREAU ISSUE

Henry David Thoreau (1817-1862), writer.

Henry David
Thoreau — A749

Designed by Leonard Baskin.

GIORI PRESS PRINTING
Plates of 200 subjects in four panes of 50.

1967, July 12	Tagged	Perf. 11	
1327 A749 5c carmine, black & blue green		.20	.20
P# block of 4		.50	—
Margin block of 4, Mr. Zip and "Use Zip Code"		.40	—
a. Tagging omitted		—	

NEBRASKA STATEHOOD, 100th ANNIV.

Hereford Steer and Ear of Corn — A750

Designed by Julian K. Billings.

LITHOGRAPHED, ENGRAVED (Giori)
Plates of 200 subjects in four panes of 50.

1967, July 29	Tagged	Perf. 11
1328 A750 5c dark red brown, lemon & yellow	.20	.20
P# block of 4	.45	—
Margin block of 4, Mr. Zip and "Use Zip Code"	.40	—
a. Tagging omitted	7.50	—

VOICE OF AMERICA ISSUE

25th anniv. of the radio branch of the United States Information Agency (USIA).

Radio Transmission Tower and Waves — A751

Designed by Georg Olden.

LITHOGRAPHED, ENGRAVED (Giori)
Plates of 200 subjects in four panes of 50.

1967, Aug. 1	Tagged	Perf. 11
1329 A751 5c red, blue, black & carmine	.20	.20
P# block of 4	.40	—
Margin block of 4, Mr. Zip and "Use Zip Code"	.35	—
a. Tagging omitted	15.00	—

AMERICAN FOLKLORE ISSUE

Davy Crockett (1786-1836), frontiersman, hunter, and congressman from Tennessee who died at the Alamo.

Davy Crockett and Scrub Pine — A752

Designed by Robert Bode.

LITHOGRAPHED, ENGRAVED (Giori)
Plates of 200 subjects in four panes of 50.

1967, Aug. 17	Tagged	Perf. 11
1330 A752 5c green, black, & yellow	.20	.20
P# block of 4	.60	—
Margin block of 4, Mr. Zip and "Use Zip Code"	.40	—
a. Vertical pair, imperf. between	7,000.	—
b. Green (engr.) missing (FO)	—	
c. Black & green (engr.) missing (FO)	—	
e. Tagging omitted	8.00	—

A foldover on a pane of No. 1330 resulted in one example each of Nos. 1330b-1330c. Part of the colors appear on the back of the selvage and one freak stamp. An engraved black-and-green-only impression appears on the gummed side of one almost-complete "stamp."

ACCOMPLISHMENTS IN SPACE ISSUE

US accomplishments in space. Printed with continuous design in horizontal rows of 5. In the left panes the astronaut stamp is 1st, 3rd and 5th, the spaceship 2nd and 4th. This arrangement is reversed in the right panes.

Space-Walking Astronaut A753

Gemini 4 Capsule A754

Designed by Paul Calle.

LITHOGRAPHED, ENGRAVED (Giori)
Plates of 200 subjects in four panes of 50.

1967, Sept. 29	Tagged	Perf. 11
1331 A753 5c multicolored	.50	.20
b. Tagging omitted	25.00	—
1332 A754 5c multicolored	.50	.20
P# block of 4	2.25	
Margin block of 4, Mr. Zip and "Use Zip Code"	2.10	—
Plate flaw (red stripes of flag on capsule omitted; 29322, 29325 UL 19)	210.00	
a. Tagging omitted	25.00	—
b. Pair, #1331-1332	1.10	1.25
c. As "b," tagging omitted	60.00	—

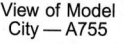

View of Model City — A755

Finnish Coat of Arms — A756

URBAN PLANNING ISSUE

Publicizing the importance of Urban Planning in connection with the Intl. Conf. of the American Institute of Planners, Washington, D.C., Oct. 1-6.

Designed by Francis Ferguson.

LITHOGRAPHED, ENGRAVED (Giori)
Plates of 200 subjects in four panes of 50.

1967, Oct. 2	Tagged	Perf. 11
1333 A755 5c dark blue, light blue & black	.20	.20
P# block of 4	.50	—
Margin block of 4, Mr. Zip and "Use Zip Code"	.40	—
a. Tagging omitted	37.50	—

FINNISH INDEPENDENCE, 50th ANNIV.

Designed by Bradbury Thompson.

ENGRAVED (Giori)
Plates of 200 subjects in four panes of 50.

1967, Oct. 6	Tagged	Perf. 11
1334 A756 5c blue	.20	.20
P# block of 4	.50	—
Margin block of 4, Mr. Zip and "Use Zip Code"	.40	—
a. Tagging omitted		

THOMAS EAKINS ISSUE

Eakins (1844-1916), painter and sculptor. The painting is in the Natl. Gallery of Art, Washington, D.C.

"The Biglin Brothers Racing" (Sculling on Schuylkill River, Philadelphia) A757

Printed by Photogravure & Color Co., Moonachie, N.J.

PHOTOGRAVURE
Plates of 200 subjects in four panes of 50.

1967, Nov. 2	Tagged	Perf.
1335 A757 5c gold & multicolored	.20	
P# block of 4, 6#	.50	
a. Tagging omitted	35.00	

Plate number blocks from upper left or lower left panes sho[w] clipped corner of margin.

CHRISTMAS ISSUE

Madonna and Child, by Hans Memling — A758

LITHOGRAPHED, ENGRAVED (Giori)
Plates of 200 subjects in four panes of 50.

1967, Nov. 6	Tagged	Perf. 1[1]
1336 A758 5c multicolored	.20	.2[0]
P# block of 4	.40	—
Margin block of 4, Mr. Zip and "Use Zip Code"	.35	—
a. Tagging omitted	5.00	—

See note on painting above No. 1321.

MISSISSIPPI STATEHOOD, 150th ANNIV.

Magnolia A759

Designed by Andrew Bucci.

GIORI PRESS PRINTING
Plates of 200 subjects in four panes of 50.

1967, Dec. 11	Tagged	Perf. 11
1337 A759 5c brt. greenish blue, green & red brown	.20	.20
P# block of 4, 2#	.60	—
Margin block of 4, Mr. Zip and "Use Zip Code"	.40	—
a. Tagging omitted	10.00	—

FLAG ISSUE

Flag and White House — A760

Designed by Stevan Dohanos.

GIORI PRESS PRINTING
Plates of 400 subjects in four panes of 100.

1968, Jan. 24	Tagged	Perf. 11
	Size: 19x22mm	
1338 A760 6c dark blue, red & green	.20	.20
P# block of 4	.45	
Margin block of 4, "Use Zip Code"	.40	

	Pair with full vert. gutter btwn.	—
k.	Vert. pair, imperf. btwn.	450.00 200.00
m.	Tagging omitted	4.00
s.	Red missing (FO)	—
u.	Vert. pair, imperf horiz.	—

Beware of regumming on No. 1338u. Most examples have had the gum washed off to make it difficult or impossible to detect blind perfs. Check carefully for blind perfs. Value is for air with original gum.

No. 1338s is unique.

COIL STAMP
MULTICOLOR HUCK PRESS

1969, May 30	Tagged	Perf. 10 Vertically
	Size: 18¼x21mm	
1338A A760 6c dark blue, red & green		.20 .20
	Pair	.30 .20
b.	Imperf., pair	500.00
q.	Tagging omitted	8.50

MULTICOLOR HUCK PRESS
Panes of 100 (10x10) each

1970-71	Tagged	Perf. 11x10½
	Size: 18¼x21mm	
1338D A760 6c dark blue, red & green, *Aug.*		
7, 1970		.20 .20
	Margin block of 20+	2.60
e.	Horiz. pair, imperf. between	150.00
n.	Tagging omitted	5.00
1338F A760 8c dark blue, red & slate green,		
May 10, 1971		.20 .20
	Margin block of 20+	3.00
i.	Imperf., vert. pair	40.00
j.	Horiz. pair, imperf. between	50.00
o.	Tagging omitted	5.00
p.	Slate green omitted	350.00
t.	Horiz. pair, imperf. vertically	—

+ Margin blocks of 20 come in four versions: (1) 2 P#, 3 ME, 3 zip; (2) 3 P#, 2 ME, 2 zip; (3) 2 P#, 3 ME, 2 zip; (4) 3 P#, 2 ME, 3 zip.

COIL STAMP
MULTICOLOR HUCK PRESS

1971, May 10	Tagged	Perf. 10 Vertically
	Size: 18¼x21mm	
1338G A760 8c dk blue, red & slate green		.20 .20
	Pair	.40 .20
h.	Imperf., pair	50.00
r.	Tagging omitted	6.00

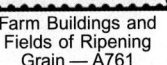

Farm Buildings and Fields of Ripening Grain — A761

Map of North and South America and Lines Converging on San Antonio — A762

ILLINOIS STATEHOOD, 150th ANNIV.
Designed by George Barford.

LITHOGRAPHED, ENGRAVED (Giori)
Plates of 200 subjects in four panes of 50.

1968, Feb. 12	Tagged	Perf. 11
1339 A761 6c dk blue, blue, red & ocher		.20 .20
	P# block of 4	.60
	Margin block of 4, Mr. Zip and "Use Zip Code"	.45
a.	Tagging omitted	—

HEMISFAIR '68 ISSUE

HemisFair '68 exhibition, San Antonio, Texas, Apr. 6-Oct. 6, for the 250th anniv. of San Antonio.

Designed by Louis Macouillard.

LITHOGRAPHED, ENGRAVED (Giori)
Plates of 200 subjects in four panes of 50.

1968, Mar. 30	Tagged	Perf. 11
1340 A762 6c blue, rose red & white		.20 .20
	On cover, Expo. station machine canc.	10.00
	On cover, Expo. roller canc.	25.00
	P# block of 4	.50
	Margin block of 4, Mr. Zip and "Use Zip Code"	.45 —
a.	White omitted	1,200.

AIRLIFT ISSUE

Issued to pay for airlift of parcels from and to US ports to servicemen overseas and in Alaska, Hawaii and Puerto Rico. Valid for all regular postage. On Apr. 26, 1969, the Post Office Department ruled that henceforth No. 1341 "may be used toward paying the postage or fees for special services on *airmail* articles."

Eagle Holding Pennant A763

Designed by Stevan Dohanos.

After a late 19th century wood carving, part of the Index of American Design, National Gallery of Art.

LITHOGRAPHED, ENGRAVED (Giori)
Plates of 200 subjects in four panes of 50.

1968, Apr. 4	Untagged	Perf. 11
1341 A763 $1 sepia, dk. blue, ocher & brown red		2.00 1.25
	P# block of 4	8.50
	Margin block of 4, Mr. Zip and "Use Zip Code"	8.25
	Pair with full horiz. gutter btwn.	—

"SUPPORT OUR YOUTH" — ELKS ISSUE

Support Our Youth program, and honoring the Benevolent and Protective Order of Elks, which extended its youth service program in observance of its centennial year.

Girls and Boys — A764

Designed by Edward Vebell.

LITHOGRAPHED, ENGRAVED (Giori)
Plates of 200 subjects in four panes of 50.

1968, May 1	Tagged	Perf. 11
1342 A764 6c ultramarine & orange red		.20 .20
	P# block of 4	.55
	Margin block of 4, Mr. Zip and "Use Zip Code"	.45 —
a.	Tagging omitted	7.50

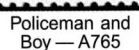

Policeman and Boy — A765

Eagle Weather Vane — A766

LAW AND ORDER ISSUE

Publicizing the policeman as protector and friend and to encourage respect for law and order.

Designed by Ward Brackett.

GIORI PRESS PRINTING
Plates of 200 subjects in four panes of 50 each

1968, May 17	Tagged	Perf. 11
1343 A765 6c chalky blue, black & red		.20 .20
	P# block of 4	.55
	Margin block of 4, Mr. Zip and "Use Zip Code"	.45 —
a.	Tagging omitted	—

REGISTER AND VOTE ISSUE

Campaign to draw more voters to the polls. The weather vane is from an old house in the Russian Hill section of San Francisco, Cal.

Designed by Norman Todhunter and Bill Hyde; photograph by M. Halberstadt.

LITHOGRAPHED, ENGRAVED (Giori)
Plates of 200 subjects in four panes of 50.

1968, June 27	Tagged	Perf. 11
1344 A766 6c black, yellow & orange		.20 .20
	P# block of 4	.50
	Margin block of 4, Mr. Zip and "Use Zip Code"	.45 —
a.	Tagging omitted	—

HISTORIC FLAG SERIES

Flags carried by American colonists and by citizens of the new United States. Printed se-tenant in vertical rows of 10. The flag sequence on the 2 upper panes is as listed. On the 2 lower panes the sequence is reversed with the Navy Jack in the 1st row and the Fort Moultrie flag in the 10th.

Ft. Moultrie, 1776 — A767

Ft. McHenry, 1795-1818 A768

Washington's Cruisers, 1775 — A769

Bennington, 1777 — A770

Rhode Island, 1775 — A771

First Stars and Stripes, 1777 — A772

Bunker Hill,
1775 — A773

Grand Union,
1776 — A774

Philadelphia
Light Horse,
1775 — A775

First Navy
Jack,
1775 — A776

ENGR. (Giori) (#1345-1348, 1350);
ENGR. & LITHO. (#1349, 1351-1354)
Plates of 200 subjects in four panes of 50.

1968, July 4		Tagged		Perf. 11	
1345	A767	6c dark blue		.40	.25
1346	A768	6c dark blue & red		.40	.25
1347	A769	6c dark blue & olive green		.30	.25
1348	A770	6c dark blue & red		.30	.25
1349	A771	6c dark blue, yellow & red		.30	.25
1350	A772	6c dark blue & red		.30	.25
1351	A773	6c dark blue, olive green & red		.30	.25
1352	A774	6c dark blue & red		.30	.25
1353	A775	6c dark blue, yellow & red		.30	.25
1354	A776	6c dark blue, red & yellow		.30	.25
a.		Strip of ten, #1345-1354		3.25	3.25
		P# block of 20, inscriptions, #1345-1354		6.75	—
b.		#1345b-1354b, any single, tagging omitted		—	
c.		As "a," imperf		—	

WALT DISNEY ISSUE

Walt Disney (1901-1966), cartoonist, film producer and creator of Mickey Mouse.

Walt Disney and Children of
the World — A777

Designed by C. Robert Moore.

Designed after portrait by Paul E. Wenzel.
Printed by Achrovure Division of Union-Camp Corp., Englewood, N.J.

PHOTOGRAVURE
Plates of 400 subjects in eight panes of 50.

1968, Sept. 11		Tagged		Perf. 12	
1355	A777	6c multicolored		.40	.20
		P# block of 4, 5#		1.75	—
		P# block of 4, 5#, 5 dashes		1.75	—
		Margin block of 4, Mr. Zip and "Use Zip Code"		1.60	—
a.		Ocher omitted ("Walt Disney," "6c," etc.)		500.00	

b.	Vert. pair, imperf. horiz.	650.00	
c.	Imperf., pair	550.00	
d.	Black omitted	2,000.	
e.	Horiz. pair, imperf. between	4,750.	
f.	Blue omitted	2,000.	
g.	Tagging omitted	15.00	—

FATHER MARQUETTE ISSUE

Father Jacques Marquette (1637-1675), French Jesuit missionary, who together with Louis Jolliet explored the Mississippi River and its tributaries.

Father
Marquette and
Louis Jolliet
Exploring the
Mississippi
A778

Designed by Stanley W. Galli.

GIORI PRESS PRINTING
Plates of 200 subjects in four panes of 50.

1968, Sept. 20		Tagged		Perf. 11	
1356	A778	6c black, apple green & orange brown		.20	.20
		P# block of 4		.60	
		Margin block of 4, Mr. Zip and "Use Zip Code"		.65	—
a.		Tagging omitted		6.00	—

AMERICAN FOLKLORE ISSUE

Daniel Boone (1734-1820), frontiersman and trapper.

Pennsylvania
Rifle, Powder
Horn,
Tomahawk Pipe
and
Knife — A779

Designed by Louis Macouillard.

LITHOGRAPHED, ENGRAVED (Giori)
Plates of 200 subjects in four panes of 50.

1968, Sept. 26		Tagged		Perf. 11	
1357	A779	6c yellow, deep yellow, maroon & black		.20	.20
		P# block of 4		.50	
		Margin block of 4, Mr. Zip and "Use Zip Code"		.45	—
a.		Tagging omitted		—	

ARKANSAS RIVER NAVIGATION ISSUE

Opening of the Arkansas River to commercial navigation.

Ship's Wheel,
Power
Transmission
Tower and
Barge — A780

Designed by Dean Ellis.

LITHOGRAPHED, ENGRAVED (Giori)
Plates of 200 subjects in four panes of 50.

1968, Oct. 1		Tagged		Perf. 11	
1358	A780	6c bright blue, dark blue & black		.20	.20
		P# block of 4		.50	
		Margin block of 4, Mr. Zip and "Use Zip Code"		.45	—
a.		Tagging omitted		—	

LEIF ERIKSON ISSUE

Leif Erikson, 11th century Norse explorer, called the 1st European to set foot on the American continent, at a place he called Vinland. The statue by the American sculptor A. Stirling Calder is in Reykjavik, Iceland.

Leif Erikson by A. Stirling
Calder — A781

Designed by Kurt Weiner.

LITHOGRAPHED & ENGRAVED
Plates of 200 subjects in four panes of 50.

1968, Oct. 9		Tagged		Perf. 11	
1359	A781	6c light gray brown & black brown		.20	.20
		P# block of 4		.50	—
		Margin block of 4, Mr. Zip and "Use Zip Code"		.45	—

The luminescent element is in the light gray brown ink of the background. The engraved parts were printed on a rotary currency press.

CHEROKEE STRIP ISSUE

75th anniversary of the opening of the Cherokee Strip to settlers, Sept. 16, 1893.

Racing for
Homesteads in
Cherokee Strip,
1893 — A782

Designed by Norman Todhunter.

ROTARY PRESS PRINTING
E.E. Plates of 200 subjects in four panes of 50.

1968, Oct. 15		Tagged		Perf. 11x10½	
1360	A782	6c brown		.20	.20
		P# block of 4		.60	—
		Margin block of 4, Mr. Zip and "Use Zip Code"		.50	—
a.		Tagging omitted		7.50	—

JOHN TRUMBULL ISSUE

Trumbull (1756-1843), painter. The stamp shows Lt. Thomas Grosvenor and his attendant Peter Salem. The painting hangs at Yale University.

Detail from "The Battle of
Bunker's Hill" — A783

Modeled by Robert J. Jones.

LITHOGRAPHED, ENGRAVED (Giori)
Plates of 200 subjects in four panes of 50.

1968, Oct. 18		Tagged		Perf. 11	
1361	A783	6c multicolored		.20	.20
		P# block of 4		.60	—
		Margin block of 4, Mr. Zip and "Use Zip Code"		.50	—
a.		Tagging omitted		—	
b.		Black (engr.) missing (FO)		11,000.	

WATERFOWL CONSERVATION ISSUE

Wood Ducks — A784

Designed by Stanley W. Galli.

LITHOGRAPHED, ENGRAVED (Giori)
Plates of 200 subjects in four panes of 50.

1968, Oct. 24		Tagged	Perf. 11	
362 A784 6c	**black & multicolored**		.20	.20
	P# block of 4		.65	—
	Margin block of 4, Mr. Zip and "Use Zip Code"		.60	—
a.	Vertical pair, imperf. between		300.00	—
b.	Red & dark blue omitted		800.00	—
c.	Red omitted		1,750.	

Dangerous fakes exist of Nos. 1362b and 1362c. Authentication by experts is required.

Angel Gabriel, from "The Annunciation" by Jan van Eyck — A785

Chief Joseph, by Cyrenius Hall — A786

CHRISTMAS ISSUE

"The Annunciation" by the 15th century Flemish painter Jan van Eyck is in the National Gallery of Art, Washington, D.C.

Designed by Robert J. Jones.

ENGRAVED (Multicolor Huck press)
Panes of 50 (10x5)

1968, Nov. 1		Tagged	Perf. 11	
1363 A785 6c	**multicolored**		.20	.20
	P# block of 10 +		2.00	—
a.	Untagged, *Nov. 2*		.20	.20
	P# block of 10 +		2.00	—
b.	Imperf., pair, tagged		200.00	
c.	Light yellow omitted		55.00	
d.	Imperf., pair, untagged		275.00	

+ P# blocks come in two versions: (1) 7 P#, 3 ME; (2) 8 P#, 2 ME.

AMERICAN INDIAN ISSUE

Honoring the American Indian and to celebrate the opening of the Natl. Portrait Gallery, Washington, D.C. Chief Joseph (Indian name, Thunder Traveling over the Mountains), a leader of the Nez Percé, was born in eastern Oregon about 1840 and died at the Colesville Reservation in Washington State in 1904.

Designed by Robert J. Jones; lettering by Crimilda Pontes.

LITHOGRAPHED, ENGRAVED (Giori)
Plates of 200 subjects in four panes of 50.

1968, Nov. 4		Tagged	Perf. 11	
1364 A786 6c	**black & multicolored**		.20	.20
	P# block of 4		.75	—
	Margin block of 4, Mr. Zip and "Use Zip Code"		.60	—
a.	Tagging omitted			—

BEAUTIFICATION OF AMERICA ISSUE

Publicizing the Natural Beauty Campaign for more beautiful cities, parks, highways and streets. In the left panes Nos. 1365 and 1367 appear in 1st, 3rd and 5th place, Nos. 1366 and 1368 in 2nd and 4th place. This arrangement is reversed in the right panes.

Capitol, Azaleas and Tulips — A787

Washington Monument, Potomac River and Daffodils A788

Poppies and Lupines along Highway A789

Blooming Crabapples Lining Avenue A790

Designed by Walter DuBois Richards.

LITHOGRAPHED, ENGRAVED (Giori)
Plates of 200 subjects in four panes of 50.

1969, Jan. 16		Tagged	Perf. 11	
1365 A787 6c	**multicolored**		.25	.20
1366 A788 6c	**multicolored**		.25	.20
1367 A789 6c	**multicolored**		.25	.20
1368 A790 6c	**multicolored**		.25	.20
a.	Block of 4, #1365-1368		1.00	1.25
	P# block of 4		1.25	
	Margin block of 4, Mr. Zip and "Use Zip Code"		1.10	
b.	#1365b-1368b, tagging omitted		—	

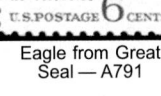

Eagle from Great Seal — A791

July Fourth, by Grandma Moses — A792

AMERICAN LEGION, 50th ANNIV.

Designed by Robert Hallock.

LITHOGRAPHED, ENGRAVED (Giori)
Plates of 200 subjects in four panes of 50.

1969, Mar. 15		Tagged	Perf. 11	
1369 A791 6c	**red, blue & black**		.20	.20
	P# block of 4		.45	—
	Margin block of 4, Mr. Zip and "Use Zip Code"		.40	—
a.	Tagging omitted			—

AMERICAN FOLKLORE ISSUE

Grandma Moses (Anna Mary Robertson Moses, 1860-1961), primitive painter of American life.

Designed by Robert J. Jones.

LITHOGRAPHED, ENGRAVED (Giori)
Plates of 200 subjects in four panes of 50.

1969, May 1		Tagged	Perf. 11	
1370 A792 6c	**multicolored**		.20	.20
	P# block of 4		.50	—
	Margin block of 4, Mr. Zip and "Use Zip Code"		.45	—
a.	Horizontal pair, imperf. between		200.00	
b.	Engraved black ("6c U.S. Postage") & Prus. blue ("Grandma Moses") omitted		750.00	
c.	Tagging omitted		7.50	—

Beware of pairs with blind perfs. being offered as No. 1370a. No. 1370b often comes with mottled or disturbed gum. Such stamps sell for about two-thirds as much as copies with perfect gum.

APOLLO 8 ISSUE

Apollo 8 mission, which 1st put men into orbit around the moon, Dec. 21-27, 1968. The astronauts were: Col. Frank Borman, Capt. James Lovell and Maj. William Anders.

Moon Surface and Earth — A793

Designed by Leonard E. Buckley after a photograph by the Apollo 8 astronauts.

GIORI PRESS PRINTING
Plates of 200 subjects in four panes of 50.

1969, May 5		Tagged	Perf. 11	
1371 A793 6c	**black, blue & ocher**		.20	.20
	P# block of 4		.65	—
	Margin block of 4, Mr. Zip and "Use Zip Code"		.60	—

Imperfs. exist from printer's waste.

W.C. HANDY ISSUE

Handy (1873-1958), jazz musician and composer.

William Christopher Handy — A794

Designed by Bernice Kochan.

LITHOGRAPHED, ENGRAVED (Giori)
Plates of 200 subjects in four panes of 50.

1969, May 17		Tagged	Perf. 11	
1372 A794 6c	**violet, deep lilac & blue**		.20	.20
	P# block of 4		.65	—
	Margin block of 4, Mr. Zip and "Use Zip Code"		.45	—
a.	Tagging omitted		7.50	—

CALIFORNIA SETTLEMENT, 200th ANNIV.

Carmel Mission Belfry — A795

Designed by Leonard Buckley and Howard C. Mildner.

LITHOGRAPHED, ENGRAVED (Giori)
Plates of 200 subjects in four panes of 50.

1969, July 16	Tagged	*Perf. 11*	
1373 A795 6c **orange, red, black & light blue**	.20	.20
P# block of 4	.60	—
Margin block of 4, Mr. Zip and "Use Zip Code"	.45	—
a. Tagging omitted	9.00	—
b. Red (engr.) missing (CM)	—	

JOHN WESLEY POWELL ISSUE

Powell (1834-1902), geologist who explored the Green and Colorado Rivers 1869-75, and ethnologist.

Major Powell Exploring Colorado River, 1869 — A796

Designed by Rudolph Wendelin.

LITHOGRAPHED, ENGRAVED (Giori)
Plates of 200 subjects in four panes of 50.

1969, Aug. 1	Tagged	*Perf. 11*	
1374 A796 6c **black, ocher & light blue**	.20	.20
P# block of 4	.60	—
Margin block of 4, Mr. Zip and "Use Zip Code"	.45	—
a. Tagging omitted	9.00	—

ALABAMA STATEHOOD, 150th ANNIV.

Camellia and Yellow-shafted Flicker — A797

Designed by Bernice Kochan.

LITHOGRAPHED, ENGRAVED (Giori)
Plates of 200 subjects in four panes of 50.

1969, Aug. 2	Tagged	*Perf. 11*	
1375 A797 6c **magenta, rose red, yellow, dark green & brown**	.20	.20
P# block of 4	.75	—
Margin block of 4, Mr. Zip and "Use Zip Code"	.45	—
a. Tagging omitted	—	

BOTANICAL CONGRESS ISSUE

11th Intl. Botanical Cong., Seattle, Wash., Aug. 24-Sept. 2. In left panes Nos. 1376 and 1378 appear in 1st, 3rd and 5th place; Nos. 1377 and 1379 in 2nd and 4th place. This arrangement is reversed in right panes.

Douglas Fir (Northwest) A798

Lady's-slipper (Northeast) A799

Ocotillo (Southwest) A800

Franklinia (Southeast) A801

Designed by Stanley Galli.

LITHOGRAPHED, ENGRAVED (Giori)
Plates of 200 subjects in four panes of 50.

1969, Aug. 23	Tagged	*Perf. 11*	
1376 A798 6c **multicolored**	.35	.20
1377 A799 6c **multicolored**	.35	.20
1378 A800 6c **multicolored**	.35	.20
1379 A801 6c **multicolored**	.35	.20
a. Block of 4, #1376-1379	1.50	1.75
P# block of 4	1.75	—
Margin block of 4, Mr. Zip and "Use Zip Code"	1.60	—

DARTMOUTH COLLEGE CASE ISSUE

150th anniv. of the Dartmouth College Case, which Daniel Webster argued before the Supreme Court, reasserting the sanctity of contracts.

Daniel Webster and Dartmouth Hall — A802

Designed by John R. Scotford, Jr.

ROTARY PRESS PRINTING
E.E. Plates of 200 subjects in four panes of 50.

1969, Sept. 22	Tagged	*Perf. 10½x11*	
1380 A802 6c **green**	.20	.20
P# block of 4	.50	—
Margin block of 4, Mr. Zip and "Use Zip Code"	.45	—

PROFESSIONAL BASEBALL, 100th ANNIV.

Batter — A803

Designed by Alex Ross.

LITHOGRAPHED, ENGRAVED (Giori)
Plates of 200 subjects in four panes of 50.

1969, Sept. 24	Tagged	*Perf. 11*	
1381 A803 6c **yellow, red, black & green**	.55	.20
P# block of 4	2.50	—
Margin block of 4, Mr. Zip and "Use Zip Code"	2.25	—
a. Black omitted ("1869-1969, United States, 6c, Professional Baseball")	850.00	
b. Tagging omitted	—	

INTERCOLLEGIATE FOOTBALL, 100th ANNIV.

Football Player and Coach — A804

Designed by Robert Peak.

LITHOGRAPHED, ENGRAVED (Giori)
Plates of 200 subjects in four panes of 50.

1969, Sept. 26	Tagged	*Perf.*	
1382 A804 6c **red & green**	.20	.20
P# block of 4	1.00	—
Margin block of 4, Mr. Zip and "Use Zip Code"	.60	—
a. Tagging omitted	—	
b. Vert. pair, imperf between	—	

The engraved parts were printed on a rotary currency press

DWIGHT D. EISENHOWER ISSUE

Dwight D. Eisenhower, 34th President (1890-1969) — A805

Designed by Robert J. Jones; photograph by Bernie Noble.

GIORI PRESS PRINTING
Plates of 128 subjects in 4 panes of 32 each.

1969, Oct. 14	Tagged	*Perf. 11*	
1383 A805 6c **blue, black & red**	.20	.20
P# block of 4	.55	—
Margin block of 4, Mr. Zip and "Use Zip Code"	.45	—
a. Tagging omitted	—	
b. Blue ("U.S. 6c Postage") missing (PS)	—	

CHRISTMAS ISSUE

The painting, painted about 1870 by an unknown primitive artist, is the property of the N.Y. State Historical Association, Cooperstown, N.Y.

Winter Sunday in Norway, Maine A806

Designed by Stevan Dohanos.

ENGRAVED (Multicolor Huck)
Panes of 50 (5x10)

1969, Nov. 3	Tagged	*Perf. 11x10½*	
1384 A806 6c **dark green & multicolored**	.20	.20
P# block of 10, 5#, 2-3 zip, 2-3	1.40	—
Mail Early		—
Precancel	.50	.20
b. Imperf., pair	900.00	—
c. Light green omitted	25.00	
d. Light green, red & yellow omitted	750.00	—
e. Yellow omitted	2,250.	
f. Tagging omitted	5.00	—
g. Red & yellow omitted	3,000.	
h. Light green and yellow omitted	—	
i. Light green and red omitted	—	

The precancel value applies to the least expensive of experimental precancels printed locally in four cities, on tagged stamps, with the names between lines 4½mm apart: in black or green, "ATLANTA, GA" and in green only "BALTIMORE, MD," "MEMPHIS, TN" and "NEW HAVEN, CT." They were sold freely to the public and could be used on any class of mail at all post offices during the experimental program and thereafter. The Baltimore precancel is known with tagging omitted; value, unused $50.

Most copies of No. 1384c show orange where the offset green was. Value is for this variety. Copies without orange sell for more.

On No. 1384i, almost all of the yellow is also omitted. Do not confuse with No. 1384d.

Cured Child — A807

HOPE FOR CRIPPLED ISSUE

Issued to encourage the rehabilitation of crippled children and adults and to honor the National Society for Crippled Children and Adults (Easter Seal Society) on its 50th anniversary.

Designed by Mark English.

LITHOGRAPHED, ENGRAVED (Giori)
Plates of 200 subjects in four panes of 50.

1969, Nov. 20	Tagged	Perf. 11
1385 A807 6c **multicolored**	.20	.20
P# block of 4	.50	—
Margin block of 4, Mr. Zip and "Use Zip Code"	.45	—
a. Tagging omitted		

WILLIAM M. HARNETT ISSUE

"Old Models" — A808

Harnett (1848-1892), painter. The painting hangs in the Museum of Fine Arts, Boston.

Designed by Robert J. Jones.

LITHOGRAPHED, ENGRAVED (Giori)
Plates of 128 subjects in 4 panes of 32 each.

1969, Dec. 3	Tagged	Perf. 11
1386 A808 6c **multicolored**	.20	.20
P# block of 4	.55	
Margin block of 4, Mr. Zip and "Use Zip Code"	.45	—

NATURAL HISTORY ISSUE

Centenary of the American Museum of Natural History, New York City. Nos. 1387-1388 alternate in 1st row, Nos. 1389-1390 in 2nd row. This arrangement is repeated throughout the pane.

American Bald Eagle — A809

African Elephant Herd — A810

Tlingit Chief in Haida Ceremonial Canoe — A811

Brontosaurus, Stegosaurus and Allosaurus from Jurassic Period — A812

Designers: No. 1387, Walter Richards; No. 1388, Dean Ellis; No. 1389, Paul Rabut; No. 1390, detail from mural by Rudolph Zallinger in Yal Peabody Museum, adapted by Robert J. Jones.

LITHOGRAPHED, ENGRAVED (Giori)
Plates of 128 subjects in 4 panes of 32 each (4x8).

1970, May 6	Tagged	Perf. 11
1387 A809 6c **multicolored**	.20	.20
1388 A810 6c **multicolored**	.20	.20
1389 A811 6c **multicolored**	.20	.20
1390 A812 6c **multicolored**	.20	.20
a. Block of 4, #1387-1390	.55	.60
P# block of 4	.70	—
Margin block of 4, Mr. Zip and "Use Zip Code"	.60	—
b. As "a," tagging omitted		

MAINE STATEHOOD, 150th ANNIV.

The painting hangs in the Metropolitan Museum of Art, New York City.

The Lighthouse at Two Lights, Maine, by Edward Hopper A813

Designed by Stevan Dohanos.

LITHOGRAPHED, ENGRAVED (Giori)
Plates of 200 subjects in four panes of 50.

1970, July 9	Tagged	Perf. 11
1391 A813 6c **black & multicolored**	.20	.20
P# block of 4	.60	—
Margin block of 4, Mr. Zip and "Use Zip Code"	.45	—
a. Tagging omitted		

WILDLIFE CONSERVATION ISSUE

American Buffalo — A814

Designed by Robert Lougheed.

ROTARY PRESS PRINTING
E.E. Plates of 200 subjects in four panes of 50.

1970, July 20	Tagged	Perf. 11x10½
1392 A814 6c **black,** *light brown*	.20	.20
P# block of 4	.55	—
Margin block of 4, Mr. Zip and "Use Zip Code"	.45	—

REGULAR ISSUE
Dwight David Eisenhower

Dot between "R" and "U" — A815

No Dot between "R" and "U" — A815a

Benjamin Franklin — A816

U.S. Postal Service Emblem — A817

Fiorello H. LaGuardia — A817a

Ernest Taylor Pyle — A818

Dr. Elizabeth Blackwell — A818a

Amadeo P. Giannini — A818b

Designers: Nos. 1393-1395, 1401-1402, Robert Geissman; photograph by George Tames. 7c, Bill Hyde. No. 1396, Raymond Loewy/William Smith, Inc. 14c, Robert Geissman; photograph by George Fayer. 16c, Robert Geissman; photograph by Alfred Eisenstadt. 18c, Robert Geissman; painting by Joseph Kozlowski. 21c, Robert Geissman.

ROTARY PRESS PRINTING
E.E. Plates of 400 subjects in four panes of 100.

1970-74	Tagged	Perf. 11x10½
1393 A815 6c **dark blue gray,** shiny gum, *Aug. 6, 1970*	.20	.20
P# block of 4	.50	—
Margin block of 4, "Use Zip Codes"	.45	—
Dull gum	.20	
P# block of 4	1.00	
Zip block of 4	.55	
a. Booklet pane of 8, shiny gum	1.50	.75
Dull gum	1.90	
b. Booklet pane of 5 + label	1.50	.75
c. Untagged (Bureau precanceled)	12.75	3.00

	P# block of 4	175.00	
	Margin block of 4, "Use Zip Codes"	75.00	
g.	Tagging omitted (not Bureau pre-canceled)	—	—
h.	As "a," tagging omitted, shiny gum	175.00	—
	Dull gum	—	

Perf. 10½x11

1393D	A816 7c **bright blue**, shiny gum, Oct. 20, 1972	.20	.20
	P# block of 4	.60	—
	Margin block of 4, "Use Zip Codes"	.55	
	Dull gum	.20	
	P# block of 4	1.25	
	Zip block of 4	.90	
e.	Untagged (Bureau precanceled)	4.25	1.00
	P# block of 4	52.50	
	Margin block of 4, "Use Zip Codes"	22.50	
f.	Tagging omitted (not Bureau pre-canceled)	4.00	—

GIORI PRESS PRINTING
Plates of 400 subjects in four panes of 100.
Perf. 11

1394	A815a 8c **black, red & blue gray**, May 10, 1971	.20	.20
	P# block of 4	.60	—
	Margin block of 4, "Use Zip Codes"	.55	
	Pair with full vert. gutter btwn.	—	
a.	Tagging omitted	4.50	—
b.	Red missing (PS)	—	
c.	Red and blue missing (PS)	—	

ROTARY PRESS PRINTING
Perf. 11x10½ on 2 or 3 sides

1395	A815 8c **deep claret**, shiny gum (from blkt. pane)	.20	.20
	Dull gum	.20	
a.	Booklet pane of 8, shiny gum, May 10, 1971	1.80	1.25
b.	Booklet pane of 6, shiny gum, May 10, 1971	1.25	1.10
c.	Booklet pane of 4 + 2 labels, dull gum, Jan. 28, 1972	1.65	1.00
d.	Booklet pane of 7 + label, dull gum, Jan. 28, 1972	1.90	1.10
e.	Vert. pair, imperf between	850.00	
f.	As "a," tagging omitted	175.00	—
g.	As "b," tagging omitted	50.00	—
h.	As "c," tagging omitted	35.00	—
i.	As "d," tagging omitted	—	

No. 1395 was issued only in booklets.
1395e resulted from a paper foldover after perforating and before cutting into panes. At least 4 pairs are recorded from 3 panes (one No. 1395a and two 1395d) with different foldover patterns. A pane of No. 1395d also is known with a foldover resulting in a vertical pair of stamp and label, imperf between.

PHOTOGRAVURE (Andreotti)
Plates of 400 subjects in four panes of 100.
Perf. 11x10½

1396	A817 8c **multicolored**, July 1, 1971	.20	.20
	P# block of 12, 6#	2.00	
	P# block of 20, 6#, "Mail Early in the Day," "Use Zip Codes" and rectangular color contents (UL pane)	3.25	
	Margin block of 4, "Use Zip Codes"	.65	

ROTARY PRESS PRINTING
E.E. Plates of 400 subjects in four panes of 100.

1397	A817a 14c **gray brown**, Apr. 24, 1972	.25	.20
	P# block of 4	1.15	
	Margin block of 4, "Use Zip Codes"	—	
a.	Untagged (Bureau precanceled)	140.00	17.50
	Margin block of 4, "Use Zip Codes"	—	
1398	A818 16c **brown**, May 7, 1971	.35	.20
	P# block of 4	2.50	
	Margin block of 4, "Use Zip Codes"	1.50	
a.	Untagged (Bureau precanceled)	22.50	5.00
	P# block of 4		
	Margin block of 4, "Use Zip Codes"	95.00	
b.	Tagging omitted (not Bureau precanceled)	—	—
1399	A818a 18c **violet**, Jan. 23, 1974	.35	.20
	P# block of 4	1.50	
	Margin block of 4, "Use Zip Codes"	1.40	
1400	A818b 21c **green**, June 27, 1973	.40	.20
	P# block of 4	1.65	
	Margin block of 4, "Use Zip Codes"	1.60	
	Nos. 1393-1400 (9)	2.35	1.80

Bureau Precancels: 6c, 6 diff., 7c, 13 diff., No. 1394, 24 diff., 14c, 3 diff., 16c, NYC, 3 diff. Greensboro, NC.

COIL STAMPS
ROTARY PRESS PRINTING

1970-71	**Tagged**	**Perf. 10 Vert.**	
1401	A815 6c **dark blue gray**, shiny gum, Aug. 6, 1970	.20	.20
	Pair	.30	.20

	Joint line pair	.50	.20
	Dull gum	.75	
	Joint line pair	3.00	
a.	Untagged (Bureau precanceled)	19.50	3.00
	Pair	42.50	6.50
	Joint line pair	525.00	
b.	Imperf., pair	2,000.	
	Joint line pair	—	
1402	A815 8c **deep claret**, May 10, 1971	.20	.20
	Pair	.30	.20
	Joint line pair	.60	.20
a.	Imperf., pair	40.00	
	Joint line pair	70.00	
b.	Untagged (Bureau precanceled)	6.75	.75
	Pair	15.00	1.60
	Joint line pair	185.00	
c.	Pair, imperf between	6,250.	

Bureau Precancels: 6c, 4 diff., 8c, 34 diff.

EDGAR LEE MASTERS ISSUE

Edgar Lee Masters (1869-1950), Poet —A819

Designed by Fred Otnes.

LITHOGRAPHED, ENGRAVED (Giori)
E.E. Plates of 200 subjects in four panes of 50.

1970, Aug. 22	**Tagged**	**Perf. 11**	
1405	A819 6c **black & olive bister**	.20	.20
	P# block of 4	.50	—
	Margin block of 4, Mr. Zip and "Use Zip Code"	.45	
a.	Tagging omitted	—	—

WOMAN SUFFRAGE ISSUE
50th anniversary of the 19th Amendment, which gave the vote to women.

Suffragettes, 1920, and Woman Voter, 1970 —A820

Designed by Ward Brackett.

GIORI PRESS PRINTING
Plates of 200 subjects in four panes of 50.

1970, Aug. 26	**Tagged**	**Perf. 11**	
1406	A820 6c **blue**	.20	.20
	P# block of 4	.50	—
	Margin block of 4, Mr. Zip and "Use Zip Code"	.45	—

SOUTH CAROLINA ISSUE
300th anniv. of the founding of Charles Town (Charleston), the 1st permanent settlement of South Carolina. Against a background of pine wood the line drawings of the design represent the economic and historic development of South Carolina: the spire of St. Phillip's Church, Capitol, state flag, a ship, 17th century man and woman, a Fort Sumter cannon, barrels, cotton, tobacco and yellow jasmine.

Symbols of South Carolina A821

Designed by George Samerjan.

LITHOGRAPHED, ENGRAVED (Giori)
Plates of 200 subjects in four panes of 50.

1970, Sept. 12	**Tagged**	**Perf. 1**	
1407	A821 6c **bister, black & red**	.20	.2
	P# block of 4	.55	—
	Margin block of 4, Mr. Zip and "Use Zip Code"	.45	—

STONE MOUNTAIN MEMORIAL ISSUE
Dedication of the Stone Mountain Confederate Memorial, Georgia, May 9, 1970.

Robert E. Lee, Jefferson Davis and "Stonewall" Jackson A822

Designed by Robert Hallock.

GIORI PRESS PRINTING
Plates of 200 subjects in four panes of 50.

1970, Sept. 19	**Tagged**	**Perf. 11**	
1408	A822 6c **gray**	.20	.20
	P# block of 4	.50	—
	Margin block of 4, Mr. Zip and "Use Zip Code"	.45	—

FORT SNELLING ISSUE
150th anniv. of Fort Snelling, Minnesota, an important outpost for the opening of the Northwest.

Fort Snelling, Keelboat and Tepees A823

Designed by David K. Stone.

LITHOGRAPHED, ENGRAVED (Giori)
Plates of 200 in four panes of 50.

1970, Oct. 17	**Tagged**	**Perf. 11**	
1409	A823 6c **yellow & multicolored**	.20	.20
	P# block of 4	.55	—
	Margin block of 4, Mr. Zip and "Use Zip Code"	.45	—
a.	Tagging omitted	—	—

ANTI-POLLUTION ISSUE
Issued to focus attention on the problems of pollution.
In left panes Nos. 1410 and 1412 appear in 1st, 3rd and 5th place; Nos. 1411 and 1413 in 2nd and 4th place. This arrangement is reversed in right panes.

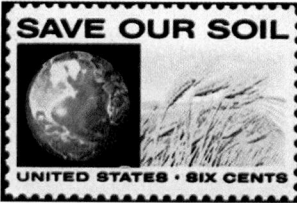

Globe and Wheat — A824

Globe and City — A825

Globe and Bluegill A826

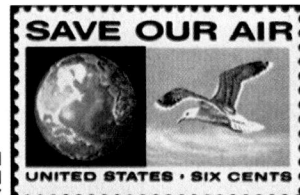

Globe and
Seagull
A827

Designed by Arnold Copeland and Walter DuBois Richards. Printed by Bureau of Engraving and Printing at Guilford Gravure, Inc., Guilford, Conn.

PHOTOGRAVURE
Plates of 200 subjects in four panes of 50.

1970, Oct. 28	Tagged	Perf. 11x10½	
1410 A824 6c **multicolored**		.25	.20
1411 A825 6c **multicolored**		.25	.20
1412 A826 6c **multicolored**		.25	.20
1413 A827 6c **multicolored**		.25	.20
a.	Block of 4, #1410-1413	1.10	1.25
	P# block of 10, 5#	2.25	—
	Margin block of 4, Mr. Zip and "Use Zip Code"	1.25	—

CHRISTMAS ISSUE

In left panes Nos. 1415 and 1417 appear in 1st, 3rd and 5th place; Nos. 1416 and 1418 in 2nd and 4th place. This arrangement is reversed in right panes.

Nativity, by Lorenzo
Lotto — A828

Tin and Cast-
iron
Locomotive
A829

Toy Horse on
Wheels
A830

Mechanical
Tricycle
A831

Doll Carriage
A832

Designers: No. 1414, Howard C. Mildner, from a painting by Lorenzo Lotto (1480-1556) in the National Gallery of Art, Washington, D.C. Nos. 1415-1418, Stevan Dohanos, from a drawing

(locomotive) by Charles Hemming and from "Golden Age of Toys" by Fondin and Remise.
Printed by Guilford Gravure, Inc., Guilford, Conn.

PHOTOGRAVURE
Plates of 200 subjects in four panes of 50.

1970, Nov. 5	Tagged	Perf. 10½x11	
1414 A828 6c **multicolored**		.20	.20
	P# block of 8, 4#	1.10	—
	Margin block of 4, Mr. Zip and "Use Zip Code"	.50	—
a.	Precanceled	.20	.20
	P# block of 8, 4#	1.90	—
	Margin block of 4, Mr. Zip and "Use Zip Code"	.70	—
b.	Black omitted	475.00	—
c.	As "a," blue omitted	1,500.	—
d.	Type II	.20	.20
	P# block of 8, 4#	2.75	—
	Zip block of 4	.85	—
e.	Type II, precanceled	.25	.20
	P# block of 8, 4#	4.00	—
	Zip block of 4	1.25	—

No. 1414 has pregummed paper, a slightly blurry impression, snowflaking in the sky and no gum breaker ridges. No. 1414d has shiny surfaced paper, sharper impression, no snowflaking and vertical and horizontal gum breaker ridges.

No. 1414a has a slightly blurry impression, snowflaking in the sky, no gum breaker ridges and the precancel is grayish black. No. 1414e has sharper impression, no snowflaking, gum breaker ridges and the precancel is intense black.

	Perf. 11x10½		
1415 A829 6c **multicolored**		.30	.20
a.	Precanceled	.75	.20
b.	Black omitted	2,500.	—
c.	Tagging omitted		—
1416 A830 6c **multicolored**		.30	.20
a.	Precanceled	.75	.20
b.	Black omitted	2,500.	—
c.	Imperf., pair (#1416, 1418)		2,500.
1417 A831 6c **multicolored**		.30	.20
a.	Precanceled	.75	.20
b.	Black omitted	2,500.	—
c.	Tagging omitted		—
1418 A832 6c **multicolored**		.30	.20
a.	Precanceled	.75	.20
b.	Block of 4, #1415-1418	1.25	1.40
	P# block of 8, 4#	3.00	—
	Margin block of 4, Mr. Zip and "Use Zip Code"	1.25	—
c.	As "b," precanceled	3.25	3.50
	P# block of 8, 4P#	6.25	—
	Margin block of 4, Mr. Zip and "Use Zip Code"	3.50	—
d.	Black omitted	2,500.	—
e.	As "b," black omitted	10,000.	—
f.	As "b," black omitted on #1417 & 1418	5,000.	—
g.	P# block of 8, black omitted on #1415 & 1416	5,000.	—

The precanceled stamps, Nos. 1414a-1418a, were furnished to 68 cities. The plates include two straight (No. 1414a) or two wavy (Nos. 1415a-1418a) black lines that make up the precancellation. Unused values are for copies with gum and used values are for copies with an additional cancellation or without gum.

UNITED NATIONS, 25th ANNIV.

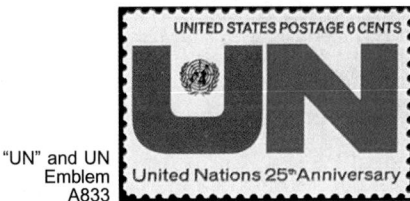

"UN" and UN
Emblem
A833

Designed by Arnold Copeland.

LITHOGRAPHED, ENGRAVED (Giori)
Plates of 200 subjects in four panes of 50.

1970, Nov. 20	Tagged	Perf. 11	
1419 A833 6c **black, verm. & ultra.**		.20	.20
	P# block of 4	.50	—
	Margin block of 4, Mr. Zip and "Use Zip Code"	.45	—
	Pair with full horiz. gutter btwn.		—
a.	Tagging omitted	25.00	—

LANDING OF THE PILGRIMS ISSUE

350th anniv. of the landing of the Mayflower.

Mayflower and
Pilgrims — A834

Designed by Mark English.

LITHOGRAPHED, ENGRAVED (Giori)
Plates of 200 subjects in four panes of 50.

1970, Nov. 21	Tagged	Perf. 11	
1420 A834 6c **blk., org., yel., magenta, bl. & brn.**		.20	.20
	P# block of 4	.50	—
	Margin block of 4, Mr. Zip and "Use Zip Code"	.45	—
a.	Orange & yellow omitted	750.00	—
b.	Tagging omitted		—

DISABLED AMERICAN VETERANS AND SERVICEMEN ISSUE

No. 1421 for the 50th anniv. of the Disabled Veterans of America Organization; No. 1422 honors the contribution of servicemen, particularly those who were prisoners of war, missing or killed in action. Nos. 1421-1422 are printed se-tenant in horizontal rows of 10.

Disabled American
Veterans
Emblem — A835

A836

Designed by Stevan Dohanos.

LITHOGRAPHED, ENGRAVED (Giori)
Plates of 200 subjects in four panes of 50.

1970, Nov. 24	Tagged	Perf. 11	
1421 A835 6c **dark blue, red & multicolored**		.20	.20

ENGRAVED

1422 A836 6c **dark blue, black & red**		.20	.20
a.	Pair, #1421-1422	.30	.30
	P# block of 4	1.00	—
	Margin block of 4, Mr. Zip and "Use Zip Code"	.65	—
b.	As "a," tagging omitted		—

Ewe and Lamb — A837

Gen. Douglas
MacArthur — A838

AMERICAN WOOL INDUSTRY ISSUE

450th anniv. of the introduction of sheep to the North American continent and the beginning of the American wool industry.

Designed by Dean Ellis.

LITHOGRAPHED, ENGRAVED (Giori)
Plates of 200 subjects in four panes of 50.

1971, Jan. 19   **Tagged**   **Perf. 11**
1423 A837 6c **multicolored** .20 .20
    P# block of 4 .55 —
    Margin block of 4, Mr. Zip and
    "Use Zip Code" .45 —
a.   Tagging omitted 11.00 —
b.   Teal blue ("United States") missing
    (CM) 600.00

GEN. DOUGLAS MacARTHUR ISSUE

MacArthur (1880-1964), Chief of Staff, Supreme Commander for the Allied Powers in the Pacific Area during World War II and Supreme Commander in Japan after the war.

Designed by Paul Calle; Wide World photograph.

GIORI PRESS PRINTING
Plates of 200 subjects in four panes of 50.

1971, Jan. 26   **Tagged**   **Perf. 11**
1424 A838 6c **black, red & dark blue** .20 .20
    P# block of 4 .60 —
    Margin block of 4, Mr. Zip and "Use
    Zip Code" .45 —
a.   Red missing (PS) —
b.   Tagging omitted —
c.   Blue missing (PS) —

BLOOD DONOR ISSUE

Salute to blood donors and spur to increased participation in the blood donor program.

"Giving Blood Saves Lives" — A839

Designed by Howard Munce.

LITHOGRAPHED, ENGRAVED (Giori)
Plates of 200 subjects in four panes of 50.

1971, Mar. 12   **Tagged**   **Perf. 11**
1425 A839 6c **blue, scarlet & indigo** .20 .20
    P# block of 4 .50 —
    Margin block of 4, Mr. Zip and
    "Use Zip Code" .45 —
a.   Tagging omitted 11.00 —

MISSOURI STATEHOOD, 150th ANNIV.

The stamp design shows a Pawnee facing a hunter-trapper and a group of settlers. It is from a mural by Thomas Hart Benton in the Harry S Truman Library, Independence, Mo.

"Independence and the Opening of the West," Detail, by Thomas Hart Benton A840

Designed by Bradbury Thompson.

PHOTOGRAVURE (Andreotti)
Plates of 200 subjects in four panes of 50.

1971, May 8   **Tagged**   **Perf. 11x10½**
1426 A840 8c **multicolored** .20 .20
    P# block of 12, 6# 3.00 —
    Margin block of 4, Mr. Zip and "Use
    Zip Code" .65 —
a.   Tagging omitted —

See note on Andreotti printings and their color control markings in Information for Collectors under Printing, Photogravure.

WILDLIFE CONSERVATION ISSUE

Nos. 1427-1428 alternate in first row, Nos. 1429-1430 in second row. This arrangement repeated throughout pane.

Trout A841

Alligator — A842

Polar Bear and Cubs A843

California Condor — A844

Designed by Stanley W. Galli.

LITHOGRAPHED, ENGRAVED (Giori)
Plates of 128 subjects in 4 panes of 32 each (4x8).

1971, June 12   **Tagged**   **Perf. 11**
1427 A841 8c **multicolored** .20 .20
a.   Red omitted 1,250.
b.   Green (engr.) omitted
1428 A842 8c **multicolored** .20 .20
1429 A843 8c **multicolored** .20 .20
1430 A844 8c **multicolored** .20 .20
a.   Block of 4, #1427-1430 .80 .90
    P# block of 4 .90
    Margin block of 4, Mr. Zip and
    "Use Zip Code" .85 —
b.   As "a," light green & dark green omitted from #1427-1428 4,500.
c.   As "a," red omitted from #1427, 1429-1430 7,000.

ANTARCTIC TREATY ISSUE

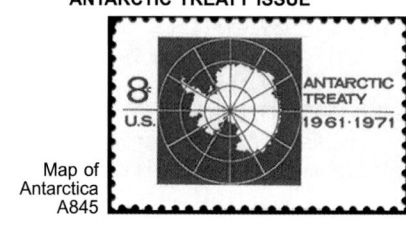

Map of Antarctica A845

Designed by Howard Koslow.

Adapted from emblem on official documents of Consultative Meetings.

GIORI PRESS PRINTING
Plates of 200 subjects in four panes of 50.

1971, June 23   **Tagged**   **Perf. 11**
1431 A845 8c **red & dark blue** .20 .20
    P# block of 4 .65 —
    Margin block of 4, Mr. Zip and
    "Use Zip Code" .60 —
a.   Tagging omitted 10.00
b.   Both colors missing (EP) 500.00

No. 1431b should be collected se-tenant with a normal stamp and/or a partially printed stamp.

AMERICAN REVOLUTION BICENTENNIAL

Bicentennial Commission Emblem — A846

Designed by Chermayeff & Geismar.

LITHOGRAPHED, ENGRAVED (Giori)
Plates of 200 subjects in four panes of 50.

1971, July 4   **Tagged**   **Perf. 11**
1432 A846 8c **gray, red, blue & black** .20 .20
    P# block of 4 .85 —
    Margin block of 4, Mr. Zip and
    "Use Zip Code" .80 —
a.   Gray & black missing (EP) 600.00
b.   Gray ("U.S. Postage 8c") missing (EP) 1,000.

JOHN SLOAN ISSUE

John Sloan (1871-1951), painter. The painting hangs in the Phillips Gallery, Washington, D.C.

The Wake of the Ferry — A847

Designed by Bradbury Thompson.

LITHOGRAPHED, ENGRAVED (Giori)
Plates of 200 subjects in four panes of 50.

1971, Aug. 2   **Tagged**   **Perf. 11**
1433 A847 8c **multicolored** .20 .20
    P# block of 4 .70 —
    Margin block of 4, Mr. Zip and
    "Use Zip Code" .65 —
a.   Tagging omitted —
b.   Red engr. ("John Sloan" and "8") missing (CM) 1,000.

SPACE ACHIEVEMENT DECADE ISSUE

Decade of space achievements and the Apollo 15 moon exploration mission, July 26-Aug. 7. In the left panes the earth and sun stamp is 1st, 3rd and 5th, the rover 2nd and 4th. This arrangement is reversed in the right panes.

Earth, Sun and Landing Craft on Moon — A848

Lunar Rover and Astronauts A849

Designed by Robert McCall.

LITHOGRAPHED, ENGRAVED (Giori)
Plates of 200 subjects in four panes of 50.

971, Aug. 2	**Tagged**	**Perf. 11**	
434 A848 8c **black, blue, gray, yellow & red**		.20	.20
a. Tagging omitted		30.00	
435 A849 8c **black, blue, gray, yellow & red**		.20	.20
a. Tagging omitted		30.00	
b. Pair, #1434-1435		.40	.45
P# block of 4		.65	
Margin block of 4, Mr. Zip and			
"Use Zip Code"		.60	—
c. As "b," tagging omitted		80.00	
d. As "b," blue & red (litho.) omitted		1,350.	

Emily Elizabeth Dickinson (1830-1886), Poet — A850

Sentry Box, Morro Castle, San Juan — A851

EMILY DICKINSON ISSUE

Designed by Bernard Fuchs after a photograph.

LITHOGRAPHED, ENGRAVED (Giori)
Plates of 200 subjects in four panes of 50.

1971, Aug. 28	**Tagged**	**Perf. 11**	
1436 A850 8c **multicolored,** *greenish*		.20	.20
P# block of 4		.65	—
Margin block of 4, Mr. Zip and			
"Use Zip Code"		.60	—
a. Black & olive (engr.) omitted		650.00	
b. Pale rose missing (EP)		6,500.	
c. Red omitted		—	
d. Tagging omitted		—	—

SAN JUAN ISSUE

450th anniversary of San Juan, Puerto Rico.

Designed as a woodcut by Walter Brooks.

LITHOGRAPHED, ENGRAVED (Giori)
Plates of 200 subjects in four panes of 50.

1971, Sept. 12	**Tagged**	**Perf. 11**	
1437 A851 8c **pale brown, black, yellow & dark brown**		.20	.20
P# block of 4		.65	—
Margin block of 4, Mr. Zip and "Use Zip Code"		.60	—
a. Tagging omitted		9.00	

VALUES FOR HINGED STAMPS AFTER NO. 771
This catalogue does not value unused stamps after No. 771 in hinged condition. Hinged unused stamps from No. 772 to the present are worth considerably less than the values given for unused stamps, which are for never-hinged examples.

Young Woman Drug Addict — A852

Hands Reaching for CARE — A853

PREVENT DRUG ABUSE ISSUE

Drug Abuse Prevention Week, Oct. 3-9.

Designed by Miggs Burroughs.

PHOTOGRAVURE (Andreotti)
Plates of 200 subjects in four panes of 50.

1971, Oct. 4	**Tagged**	**Perf. 10½x11**	
1438 A852 8c **blue, deep blue & black**		.20	.20
P# block of 6, 3#		1.00	—
Margin block of 4, "Use Zip Code"		.65	—

CARE ISSUE

25th anniversary of CARE, a US-Canadian Cooperative for American Relief Everywhere.

Designed by Soren Noring

PHOTOGRAVURE (Andreotti)
Plates of 200 subjects in four panes of 50.

1971, Oct. 27	**Tagged**	**Perf. 10½x11**	
1439 A853 8c **blue, blk., vio. & red lilac**		.20	.20
P# block of 8, 4#		1.25	—
Margin block of 4, Mr. Zip and "Use Zip Code"		.65	—
a. Black omitted		2,750.	
b. Tagging omitted		5.00	

HISTORIC PRESERVATION ISSUE

Nos. 1440-1441 alternate in 1st row, Nos. 1442-1443 in 2nd row. This arrangement is repeated throughout the pane.

Decatur House, Washington, D.C. — A854

Whaling Ship Charles W. Morgan, Mystic, Conn. — A855

Cable Car, San Francisco — A856

San Xavier del Bac Mission, Tucson, Ariz. — A857

Designed by Melbourne Brindle.

LITHOGRAPHED, ENGRAVED (Giori)

1971, Oct. 29	**Tagged**	**Perf. 11**	
1440 A854 8c **black brown & ocher,** *buff*		.20	.20
1441 A855 8c **black brown & ocher,** *buff*		.20	.20
1442 A856 8c **black brown & ocher,** *buff*		.20	.20
1443 A857 8c **black brown & ocher,** *buff*		.20	.20
a. Block of 4, #1440-1443		.75	.85

P# block of 4		.90	—
Margin block of 4, Mr. Zip and "Use Zip Code"		.80	—
b. As "a," black brown omitted		1,800.	
c. As "a," ocher omitted		—	
d. As "a," tagging omitted		75.00	

CHRISTMAS ISSUE

Adoration of the Shepherds, by Giorgione — A858

"Partridge in a Pear Tree" — A859

Designers: No. 1444, Bradbury Thompson, using a painting by Giorgione in the National Gallery of Art, Washington, D.C. No. 1445, Jamie Wyeth.

PHOTOGRAVURE (Andreotti)
Plates of 200 subjects in four panes of 50.

1971, Nov. 10	**Tagged**	**Perf. 10½x11**	
1444 A858 8c **gold & multicolored**		.20	.20
P# block of 12, 6#		1.80	—
Margin block of 4, Mr. Zip and "Use Zip Code"		.60	—
a. Gold omitted		425.00	
b. Tagging omitted		—	
1445 A859 8c **dark green, red & multicolored**		.20	.20
P# block of 12, 6#		1.80	—
Margin block of 4, Mr. Zip and "Use Zip Code"		.60	—

Sidney Lanier — A860

Peace Corps Poster, by David Battle — A861

SIDNEY LANIER ISSUE

Lanier (1842-81), poet, musician, lawyer, educator.

Designed by William A. Smith.

GIORI PRESS PRINTING
Plates of 200 subjects in four panes of 50.

1972, Feb. 3	**Tagged**	**Perf. 11**	
1446 A860 8c **black, brown & light blue**		.20	.20
P# block of 4		.65	—
Margin block of 4, Mr. Zip and "Use Zip Code"		.60	—
a. Tagging omitted			

PEACE CORPS ISSUE

Designed by Bradbury Thompson.

PHOTOGRAVURE (Andreotti)
Plates of 200 subjects in four panes of 50.

1972, Feb. 11	**Tagged**	**Perf. 10½x11**	
1447 A861 8c **dark blue, light blue & red**		.20	.20
P# block of 6, 3#		1.00	—
Margin block of 4, Mr. Zip and "Use Zip Code"		.65	—
a. Tagging omitted		5.00	

NATIONAL PARKS CENTENNIAL ISSUE

Centenary of Yellowstone National Park, the 1st National Park, and of the entire National Park System. See No. C84.

A862   A863

A864   A865
Cape Hatteras National Seashore

Wolf Trap Farm, Va. — A866

Old Faithful, Yellowstone — A867

Mt. McKinley, Alaska — A868

Designers: 2c, Walter D. Richards; 6c, Howard Koslow; 8c, Robert Handville; 15c, James Barkley.

LITHOGRAPHED, ENGRAVED (Giori)

1972   **Tagged**   *Perf. 11*

Plates of 400 subjects in 4 panes of 100 each

1448	A862	2c **black & multi.**, Apr. 5	.20	.20
1449	A863	2c **black & multi.**, Apr. 5	.20	.20
1450	A864	2c **black & multi.**, Apr. 5	.20	.20
1451	A865	2c **black & multi.**, Apr. 5	.20	.20
a.		Block of 4, #1448-1451	.25	.30
		P# block of 4	.50	
		Margin block of 4, "Use Zip Codes"	.30	—
b.		As "a," black (litho.) omitted	1,500.	
c.		As "a," tagging omitted	150.00	

Plates of 200 subjects in four panes of 50 each

1452	A866	6c **black & multicolored**, June 26	.20	.20
		P# block of 4	.55	
		Margin block of 4, Mr. Zip and "Use Zip Code"	.50	—
a.		Tagging omitted	11.00	

Plates of 128 subjects in four panes of 32 (8x4)

1453	A867	8c **blk., blue, brn. & multi.**, Mar. 1	.20	.20
		P# block of 4	.70	—
		Margin block of 4, Mr. Zip and "Use Zip Code"	.65	—
a.		Tagging omitted		

Plates of 200 subjects in four panes of 50 each

1454	A868	15c **black & multi.**, July 28	.30	.20
		P# block of 4	1.30	
		Margin block of 4, Mr. Zip	1.25	
a.		Tagging omitted	—	
b.		Yellow omitted	5,750.	

FAMILY PLANNING ISSUE

Family — A869

LITHOGRAPHED, ENGRAVED (Giori)
Plates of 200 subjects in four panes of 50.

1972, Mar. 18   **Tagged**   *Perf. 11*

1455	A869	8c **black & multicolored**	.20	.20
		P# block of 4	.65	—
		Margin block of 4, Mr. Zip and "Use Zip Code"	.60	—
a.		Yellow omitted	425.00	
c.		Dark brown missing (FO)	9,000.	
d.		Tagging omitted	—	

AMERICAN BICENTENNIAL ISSUE
Colonial American Craftsmen

In left panes Nos. 1456 and 1458 appear in 1st, 3rd and 5th place; Nos. 1457 and 1459 in 2nd and 4th place. This arrangement is reversed in right panes.

Glass Blower A870

Silversmith A871

Wigmaker A872

Hatter — A873

Designed by Leonard Everett Fisher.

ENGRAVED
E.E. Plates of 200 subjects in four panes of 50.

1972, July 4   **Tagged**   *Perf. 11x10½*

1456	A870	8c **deep brown**, *dull yellow*	.20	.20
1457	A871	8c **deep brown**, *dull yellow*	.20	.20
1458	A872	8c **deep brown**, *dull yellow*	.20	.20
1459	A873	8c **deep brown**, *dull yellow*	.20	.20
a.		Block of 4, #1456-1459	.65	.75
		P# block of 4	.80	
		Margin block of 4, Mr. Zip and "Use Zip Code"	.70	—
b.		As "a," tagging omitted	150.00	

Margin includes Bicentennial Commission emblem and inscription: USA BICENTENNIAL / HONORS COLONIAL / AMERICAN CRAFTSMEN.

OLYMPIC GAMES ISSUE

11th Winter Olympic Games, Sapporo, Japan, Feb 3-13 and 20th Summer Olympic Games, Munich, Germany, Aug. 26-Sept. 11. See No. C85.

Bicycling and Olympic Rings — A874

Bobsledding and Olympic Rings — A875

Running and Olympic Rings — A876

"Broken red ring" Cylinder Flaw

Designed by Lance Wyman.

PHOTOGRAVURE (Andreotti)
Plates of 200 subjects in four panes of 50.

1972, Aug. 17   **Tagged**   *Perf. 11x10½*

1460	A874	6c **black, blue, red, emerald & yellow**	.20	.20
		P# block of 10, 5#	1.25	
		Margin block of 4, Mr. Zip and "Use Zip Code"	.50	—
		Cylinder flaw (broken red ring) (33313 UL 43)	10.00	
1461	A875	8c **black, blue, red, emerald & yellow**	.20	.20
		P# block of 10, 5#	1.60	
		Margin block of 4, Mr. Zip and "Use Zip Code"	.65	—
a.		Tagging omitted	7.50	
1462	A876	15c **black, blue, red, emerald & yel**	.30	.20
		P# block of 10, 5#	3.00	
		Margin block of 4, Mr. Zip and "Use Zip Code"	1.15	—
	Nos. 1460-1462 (3)		.70	.60

PARENT TEACHER ASSN., 75th ANNIV.

Blackboard A877

Designed by Arthur S. Congdon III.

PHOTOGRAVURE (Andreotti)
Plates of 200 subjects in four panes of 50.

1972, Sept. 15   **Tagged**   *Perf. 11x10½*

1463	A877	8c **yellow & black**	.20	.20
		P# block of 4, 2#	.65	—
		P# block of 4, yellow # reversed	.75	
		Margin block of 4, Mr. Zip and "Use Zip Code"	.60	—

WILDLIFE CONSERVATION ISSUE

Nos. 1464-1465 alternate in 1st row, Nos. 1468-1469 in 2nd row. This arrangement repeated throughout pane.

Fur Seals A878

Cardinal — A879

Brown Pelican — A880

Bighorn Sheep — A881

Designed by Stanley W. Galli.

LITHOGRAPHED, ENGRAVED (Giori)
Plates of 128 subjects in 4 panes of 32 (4x8).

1972, Sept. 20	Tagged	Perf. 11	
1464 A878 8c **multicolored**		.20	.20
1465 A879 8c **multicolored**		.20	.20
1466 A880 8c **multicolored**		.20	.20
1467 A881 8c **multicolored**		.20	.20
a. Block of 4, #1464-1467		.65	.75
P# block of 4		.75	
Margin block of 4, Mr. Zip and "Use Zip Code"		.70	—
b. As "a," brown omitted		4,000.	
c. As "a," green & blue omitted		4,000.	
d. As "a," red & brown omitted		4,000.	
e. As "a," tagging omitted		—	

MAIL ORDER BUSINESS ISSUE

Centenary of mail order business, originated by Aaron Montgomery Ward, Chicago. Design based on Headsville, W.Va., post office in Smithsonian Institution, Washington, D.C.

Rural Post Office Store — A882

Designed by Robert Lambdin.

PHOTOGRAVURE (Andreotti)
Plates of 200 subjects in four panes of 50.

1972, Sept. 27	Tagged	Perf. 11x10½	
1468 A882 8c **multicolored**		.20	.20
P# block of 12, 6#		1.75	
Margin block of 4, Mr. Zip and "Use Zip Code"		.60	

The tagging on No. 1468 consists of a vertical bar of phosphor 10mm wide.

Man's Quest for Health — A883

Tom Sawyer, by Norman Rockwell — A884

OSTEOPATHIC MEDICINE ISSUE

75th anniv. of the American Osteopathic Assoc., founded by Dr. Andrew T. Still (1828-1917), who developed the principles of osteopathy in 1874.

Designed by V. Jack Ruther.

PHOTOGRAVURE (Andreotti)
Plates of 200 subjects in four panes of 50.

1972, Oct. 9	Tagged	Perf. 10½x11	
1469 A883 8c **multicolored**		.20	.20
P# block of 6, 3#		1.10	
Margin block of 4, Mr. Zip and "Use Zip Code"		.65	

AMERICAN FOLKLORE ISSUE
Tom Sawyer

Designed by Bradbury Thompson.

LITHOGRAPHED, ENGRAVED (Giori)
Plates of 200 subjects in four panes of 50.

1972, Oct. 13	Tagged	Perf. 11	
1470 A884 8c **black, red, yellow, tan, blue & rose red**		.20	.20
P# block of 4		.65	
Margin block of 4, Mr. Zip and "Use Zip Code"		.60	—
a. Horiz. pair, imperf. between		4,500.	
b. Red & black (engr.) omitted		1,500.	
c. Yellow & tan (litho.) omitted		2,250.	
d. Tagging omitted		—	

CHRISTMAS ISSUE

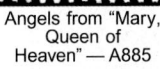

Angels from "Mary, Queen of Heaven" — A885

Santa Claus — A886

Designers: No. 1471, Bradbury Thompson, using detail from a painting by the Master of the St. Lucy legend, in the National Gallery of Art, Washington, D.C. No. 1472, Stevan Dohanos.

PHOTOGRAVURE (Andreotti)
Plates of 200 subjects in four panes of 50.

1972, Nov. 9	Tagged	Perf. 10½x11	
1471 A885 8c **multicolored**		.20	.20
P# block of 12, 6#		1.75	
Margin block of 4, Mr. Zip and "Use Zip Code"		.60	
a. Pink omitted		125.00	
b. Black omitted		3,500.	
1472 A886 8c **multicolored**		.20	.20
P# block of 12, 6#		1.75	
Margin block of 4, Mr. Zip and "Use Zip Code"		.60	

PHARMACY ISSUE

Honoring American druggists in connection with the 120th anniversary of the American Pharmaceutical Association.

Mortar and Pestle, Bowl of Hygeia, 19th Century Medicine Bottles — A887

Designed by Ken Davies.

LITHOGRAPHED, ENGRAVED (Giori)
Plates of 200 subjects in four panes of 50.

1972, Nov. 10	Tagged	Perf. 11	
1473 A887 8c **black & multicolored**		.20	.20
P# block of 4		.65	
Margin block of 4, Mr. Zip and "Use Zip Code"		.60	—
a. Blue & orange omitted		750.00	
b. Blue omitted		1,900.	
c. Orange omitted		1,900.	
d. Tagging omitted		—	
e. Vertical pair, imperf horiz.		—	

STAMP COLLECTING ISSUE

Issued to publicize stamp collecting.

U.S. No. 1 under Magnifying Glass — A888

Designed by Frank E. Livia.

LITHOGRAPHED, ENGRAVED (Giori)
Plates of 160 subjects in four panes of 40.

1972, Nov. 17	Tagged	Perf. 11	
1474 A888 8c **multicolored**		.20	.20
P# block of 4		.65	
Margin block of 4, Mr. Zip and "Use Zip Code"		.60	—
a. Black (litho.) omitted		550.00	

LOVE ISSUE

"Love," by Robert Indiana A889

Designed by Robert Indiana.

PHOTOGRAVURE (Andreotti)
Plates of 200 subjects in four panes of 50.

1973, Jan. 26	Tagged	Perf. 11x10½	
1475 A889 8c **red, emerald & violet blue**		.20	.20
P# block of 6, 3#		1.00	
Margin block of 4, Mr. Zip and "Use Zip Code"		.65	—

AMERICAN BICENTENNIAL ISSUE
Communications in Colonial Times

Printer and Patriots Examining Pamphlet A890

Posting a
Broadside
A891

Postrider
A892

Drummer
A893

Designed by William A. Smith.

GIORI PRESS PRINTING
Plates of 200 subjects in four panes of 50.

1973		Tagged	Perf. 11	
1476	A890	8c **ultra., greenish blk. & red,** Feb. 16	.20	.20
		P# block of 4	.65	
		Margin block of 4, Mr. Zip and "Use Zip Code"	.60	—
a.		Tagging omitted		—
1477	A891	8c **black, vermilion & ultra.,** Apr. 13	.20	.20
		P# block of 4	.65	
		Margin block of 4, Mr. Zip and "Use Zip Code"	.60	—
		Pair with full horiz. gutter btwn.		—

LITHOGRAPHED, ENGRAVED (Giori)
1478	A892	8c **blue, black, red & green,** June 22	.20	.20
		P# block of 4	.65	—
		Margin block of 4, Mr. Zip and "Use Zip Code"	.60	—
a.		Red missing (CM)		—
1479	A893	8c **blue, black, yellow & red,** Sept. 28	.20	.20
		P# block of 4	.65	—
		Margin block of 4, Mr. Zip and "Use Zip Code"	.60	—
		Nos. 1476-1479 (4)	.80	.80

Margin of Nos. 1477-1479 includes Bicentennial Commission emblem and inscription.

AMERICAN BICENTENNIAL ISSUE
Boston Tea Party

In left panes Nos. 1480 and 1482 appear in 1st, 3rd and 5th place, Nos. 1481 and 1483 appear in 2nd and 4th place. This arrangement is reversed in right panes.

British Merchantman A894

British Three-master A895

Boats and Ship's Hull — A896

Boat and Dock — A897

Designed by William A. Smith.

LITHOGRAPHED, ENGRAVED (Giori)
Plates of 200 subjects in four panes of 50.

1973, July 4		Tagged	Perf. 11	
1480	A894	8c **black & multicolored**	.20	.20
1481	A895	8c **black & multicolored**	.20	.20
1482	A896	8c **black & multicolored**	.20	.20
1483	A897	8c **black & multicolored**	.20	.20
a.		Block of 4, #1480-1483	.65	.75
		P# block of 4	.75	—
		Margin block of 4, Mr. Zip and "Use Zip Code"	.70	—
b.		As "a," black (engraved) omitted	1,250.	
c.		As "a," black (litho.) omitted	1,250.	
d.		As "a," tagging omitted		—

Margin includes Bicentennial Commission emblem and inscription.

AMERICAN ARTS ISSUE

George Gershwin (1898-1937), composer (No. 1484); Robinson Jeffers (1887-1962), poet (No. 1485); Henry Ossawa Tanner (1859-1937), black painter (No. 1486); Willa Cather (1873-1947), novelist (No. 1487).

Gershwin, Sportin' Life, Porgy and Bess — A898

Robinson Jeffers, Man and Children of Carmel with Burro — A899

Henry Ossawa Tanner, Palette and Rainbow A900

Willa Cather, Pioneer Family and Covered Wagon A901

Designed by Mark English.

PHOTOGRAVURE (Andreotti)
Plates of 160 subjects in four panes of 40.

1973		Tagged	Perf. 1	
1484	A898	8c **dp. green & multi.,** Feb. 28	.20	.2
		P# block of 12, 6#	1.75	
		Margin block of 4, Mr. Zip, "Use Zip Code" and "Mail Early in the Day"	.60	
		P# block of 16, 6#, Mr. Zip and slogans	2.50	—
a.		Vertical pair, imperf. horiz.	200.00	
1485	A899	8c **Prussian blue & multi.,** Aug. 13	.20	.2
		P# block of 12, 6#	1.75	
		Margin block of 4, Mr. Zip, "Use Zip Code" "Mail Early in the Day"	.60	
		P# block of 16, 6#, Mr. Zip and slogans	2.50	—
a.		Vertical pair, imperf. horiz.	250.00	
1486	A900	8c **yellow brown & multi.,** Sept. 10	.20	.20
		P# block of 12, 6#	1.75	
		Margin block of 4, Mr. Zip, "Use Zip Code" "Mail Early in the Day"	.60	
		P# block of 16, 6#, Mr. Zip and slogans	2.50	—
1487	A901	8c **deep brown & multi.,** Sept. 20	.20	.20
		P# block of 12, 6#	1.75	
		Margin block of 4, Mr. Zip, "Use Zip Code" "Mail Early in the Day"	.60	
		P# block of 16, 6#, Mr. Zip and slogans	2.50	—
a.		Vertical pair, imperf. horiz.	250.00	
		Nos. 1484-1487 (4)	.80	.80

COPERNICUS ISSUE

Nicolaus Copernicus (1473-1543), Polish Astronomer — A902

Designed by Alvin Eisenman after 18th century engraving.

LITHOGRAPHED, ENGRAVED (Giori)
Plates of 200 subjects in four panes of 50.

1973, Apr. 23		Tagged	Perf. 11	
1488	A902	8c **black & orange**	.20	.20
		P# block of 4	.65	—
		Margin block of 4, Mr. Zip and "Use Zip Code"	.60	—
a.		Orange omitted	875.00	
b.		Black (engraved) omitted	900.00	
c.		Tagging omitted		—

The orange can be chemically removed. Expertization of No. 1488a is required.

POSTAL SERVICE EMPLOYEES ISSUE

A tribute to US Postal Service employees. Nos. 1489-1498 are printed se-tenant in horizontal rows of 10. Emerald inscription on back, printed beneath gum in water-soluble ink, includes Postal Service emblem, "People Serving You" and a statement, differing for each of the 10 stamps, about some aspect of postal service.

Each stamp in top or bottom row has a tab with blue inscription enumerating various jobs in postal service.

Stamp Counter — A903

Mail Collection — A904

Letter Facing on Conveyor Belt — A905

Parcel Post Sorting — A906

Mail Canceling — A907

Manual Letter Routing — A908

Electronic Letter Routing — A909

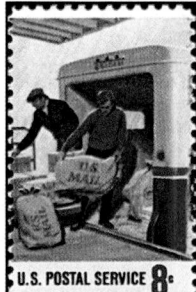
Loading Mail on Truck — A910

Mailman — A911

Rural Mail Delivery — A912

Designed by Edward Vebell.

PHOTOGRAVURE (Andreotti)
Plates of 200 subjects in four panes of 50.

1973, Apr. 30	Tagged	Perf. 10½x11	
1489 A903 8c multicolored		.20	.20
1490 A904 8c multicolored		.20	.20
1491 A905 8c multicolored		.20	.20
1492 A906 8c multicolored		.20	.20
1493 A907 8c multicolored		.20	.20
1494 A908 8c multicolored		.20	.20
1495 A909 8c multicolored		.20	.20
1496 A910 8c multicolored		.20	.20
1497 A911 8c multicolored		.20	.20
1498 A912 8c multicolored		.20	.20
a.	Strip of 10, #1489-1498	1.75	1.90
	P# block of 20, 5# and 10 tabs	3.75	—
b.	As "a," tagging omitted	175.00	—

The tagging on Nos. 1489-1498 consists of a ½-inch horizontal band of phosphor.

HARRY S. TRUMAN ISSUE

Harry S Truman, 33rd President, (1884-1972) — A913

Designed by Bradbury Thompson; photograph by Leo Stern.

GIORI PRESS PRINTING
Plates of 128 subjects in four panes of 32 each.

1973, May 8	Tagged	Perf. 11	
1499 A913 8c carmine rose, black & blue		.20	.20
	P# block of 4	.75	—
a.	Tagging omitted	11.00	

ELECTRONICS PROGRESS ISSUE
See No. C86.

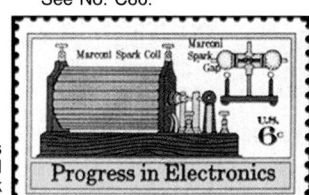
Marconi's Spark Coil and Spark Gap — A914

Transistors and Printed Circuit Board — A915

Microphone, Speaker, Vacuum Tube and TV Camera Tube — A916

Designed by Walter and Naiad Einsel.

LITHOGRAPHED, ENGRAVED (Giori)
Plates of 200 subjects in four panes of 50.

1973, July 10	Tagged	Perf. 11	
1500 A914 6c lilac & multicolored		.20	.20
	P# block of 4	.55	—
	Margin block of 4, Mr. Zip and "Use Zip Code"	.50	—
a.	Tagging omitted	—	
1501 A915 8c tan & multicolored		.20	.20
	P# block of 4	.70	—
	Margin block of 4, Mr. Zip and "Use Zip Code"	.65	—
a.	Black (inscriptions & "U.S. 8c") omitted	400.00	
b.	Tan (background) & lilac omitted	1,100.	

Many examples of No. 1501b are hinged. Value about one-half never hinged value.

1502 A916 15c gray green & multicolored		.30	.20
	P# block of 4	1.30	—
	Margin block of 4, Mr. Zip and "Use Zip Code"	1.20	—
a.	Black (inscriptions & "U.S. 15c") omitted	1,350.	
	Nos. 1500-1502 (3)	.70	.60

LYNDON B. JOHNSON ISSUE

Lyndon B. Johnson, 36th President (1908-1973) — A917

Designed by Bradbury Thompson, portrait by Elizabeth Shoumatoff.

PHOTOGRAVURE (Andreotti)
Plates of 128 subjects in four panes of 32 each.

1973, Aug. 27	Tagged	Perf. 11	
1503 A917 8c black & multicolored, Aug. 27		.20	.20
	P# block of 12, 6#	2.20	—
a.	Horiz. pair, imperf. vert.	300.00	

RURAL AMERICA ISSUE

Centenary of the introduction of Aberdeen Angus cattle into the US (#1504); of the Chautauqua Institution (#1505); and of the introduction of hard winter wheat into Kansas by Mennonite immigrants (#1506).

Angus and Longhorn Cattle — A918

Chautauqua Tent and Buggies A919

Wheat Fields and Train — A920

No. 1504 modeled by Frank Waslick after painting by F. C. "Frank" Murphy. Nos. 1505-1506 designed by John Falter.

LITHOGRAPHED, ENGRAVED (Giori)
Plates of 200 subjects in four panes of 50.

1973-74	Tagged	Perf. 11	
1504 A918 8c multicolored, Oct. 5, 1973		.20	.20
	P# block of 4	.65	—
	Margin block of 4, Mr. Zip and "Use Zip Code"	.60	—
a.	Green & red brown omitted	850.00	
b.	Vert. pair, imperf. between		5,000.
c.	Tagging omitted	—	
1505 A919 10c multicolored, Aug. 6, 1974		.20	.20
	P# block of 4	.85	—
	Margin block of 4, Mr. Zip and "Use Zip Code"	.80	—
a.	Black (litho.) omitted		2,000.
b.	Tagging omitted	—	
1506 A920 10c multicolored, Aug. 16, 1974		.20	.20
	P# block of 4	.85	—
	Margin block of 4, Mr. Zip and "Use Zip Code"	.80	—
a.	Black and blue (engr.) omitted	700.00	
b.	Tagging omitted	—	
	Nos. 1504-1506 (3)	.60	.60

CHRISTMAS ISSUE

Small Cowper Madonna, by Raphael — A921

Christmas Tree in Needlepoint — A922

Designers: No. 1507, Bradbury Thompson, using a painting in the National Gallery of Art, Washington, D.C. No. 1508, Dolli Tingle.

PHOTOGRAVURE (Andreotti)
Plates of 200 subjects in four panes of 50.

1973, Nov. 7   Tagged   Perf. 10½x11

1507	A921 8c multicolored	.20	.20
	P# block of 12, 6#	1.75	—
	Margin block of 4, Mr. Zip and "Use Zip Code"	.60	—
	Pair with full vert. gutter btwn.	—	
1508	A922 8c multicolored	.20	.20
	P# block of 12, 6#	1.75	—
	Margin block of 4, Mr. Zip and "Use Zip Code"	.60	—
	Pair with full horiz. gutter btwn.	—	
a.	Vertical pair, imperf. between	275.00	

The tagging on Nos. 1507-1508 consists of a 20x12mm horizontal bar of phosphor.

50-Star and 13-Star Flags — A923

Jefferson Memorial and Signature — A924

Mail Transport — A925

Liberty Bell — A926

Designers: No. 1509, Ren Wicks. No. 1510, Dean Ellis. No. 1511, Randall McDougall. 6.3c, Frank Lionetti.

MULTICOLOR HUCK PRESS
Panes of 100 (10x10)

1973-74   Tagged   Perf. 11x10½

1509	A923 10c red & blue, Dec. 8, 1973	.20	.20
	P# block of 20, 4-6#, 2-3 "Mail Early" and 2-3 "Use Zip Code"	4.25	—
a.	Horizontal pair, imperf. between	50.00	—
b.	Blue omitted	175.00	—
c.	Imperf., vert. pair	900.00	—
d.	Horiz. pair, imperf. vert.	1,000.	—
e.	Tagging omitted	9.00	—
f.	Vert. pair, imperf between	—	

ROTARY PRESS PRINTING
E.E. Plates of 400 subjects in four panes of 100.

1510	A924 10c blue, Dec. 14, 1973	.20	.20
	P# block of 4	.85	—
	Margin block of 4, "Use Zip Codes"	.80	—
a.	Untagged (Bureau precanceled)	4.00	1.00
	P# block of 4	50.00	
	Margin block of 4, "Use Zip Codes"	25.00	
b.	Booklet pane of 5 + label	1.65	.90
c.	Booklet pane of 8	1.65	1.00
	Pair with full vert. gutter btwn.	225.00	
d.	Booklet pane of 6, Aug. 5, 1974	5.25	1.75
e.	Vert. pair, imperf. horiz.	450.00	
f.	Vert. pair, imperf. between	500.00	

g.	As No. 1510, tagging omitted (not Bureau precanceled)	5.00	
h.	As "c," tagging omitted	—	

Bureau Precancels: 10 different.
No. 1510f resulted from a paper foldover after perforating and before cutting into booklet panes.

PHOTOGRAVURE (Andreotti)
Plates of 400 subjects in four panes of 100.

1511	A925 10c multicolored, Jan. 4, 1974	.20	.20
	P# block of 8, 4#	1.75	—
	Margin block of 4, "Use Zip Codes"	.80	—
	Pair with full horiz. gutter btwn.	—	
a.	Yellow omitted	50.00	

Beware of copies with yellow chemically removed offered as No. 1511a.

COIL STAMPS
ROTARY PRESS PRINTING

1973-74   Tagged   Perf. 10 Vert.

1518	A926 6.3c brick red, Oct. 1, 1974	.20	.20
	Pair	.25	.20
	Joint line pair	.80	
a.	Untagged (Bureau precanceled)	.35	.20
	Pair	.70	.30
	Joint line pair	1.65	1.65
b.	Imperf., pair	175.00	
	Joint line pair	475.00	
c.	As "a," imperf., pair	90.00	
	Joint line pair	200.00	

A total of 129 different Bureau precancels were used by 117 cities.
No. 1518c is precanceled Washington, DC, Columbus, Ohio and Garden City, N.Y. Values for Columbus pair $550, for Garden City pair $850.

MULTICOLOR HUCK PRESS

1519	A923 10c red & blue, Dec. 8, 1973	.20	.20
	Pair	.40	.20
a.	Imperf., pair	35.00	
b.	Tagging omitted	12.50	

ROTARY PRESS PRINTING

1520	A924 10c blue, Dec. 14, 1973	.25	.20
	Pair	.50	.20
	Joint line pair	.75	
a.	Untagged (Bureau precanceled)	5.50	1.25
	Pair	12.00	2.75
	Joint line pair	185.00	—
b.	Imperf., pair	35.00	
	Joint line pair	65.00	

Bureau Precancels: No. 1520a, 14 diff.

VETERANS OF FOREIGN WARS ISSUE

75th anniversary of Veterans of Spanish-American and Other Foreign Wars.

Emblem and Initials of Veterans of Foreign Wars — A928

Designed by Robert Hallock.

GIORI PRESS PRINTING
Plates of 200 subjects in 4 plates of 50.

1974, Mar. 11   Tagged   Perf. 11

1525	A928 10c red & dark blue	.20	.20
	P# block of 4	.85	—
	Margin block of 4, Mr. Zip and "Use Zip Code"	.80	—
a.	Tagging omitted	15.00	
b.	Blue missing (PS)	—	

ROBERT FROST ISSUE

Robert Frost (1873-1963), Poet — A929

Designed by Paul Calle; photograph by David Rhinelander.

ROTARY PRESS PRINTING
E.E. Plates of 200 subjects in four panes of 50.

1974, Mar. 26   Tagged   Perf. 10½x11

1526	A929 10c black	.20	
	P# block of 4	.85	
	Margin block of 4, Mr. Zip and "Use Zip Code"	.80	

EXPO '74 WORLD'S FAIR ISSUE

EXPO '74 World's Fair "Preserve the Environmen[t]" Spokane, Wash., May 4-Nov. 4.

"Cosmic Jumper" and "Smiling Sage" — A93[0]

Designed by Peter Max.

PHOTOGRAVURE (Andreotti)
Plates of 160 subjects in four panes of 40.

1974, Apr. 18   Tagged   Perf. 1[1]

1527	A930 10c multicolored	.20	.[20]
	On cover, Expo. station hand-stamp canc.		12.[5]
	P# block of 12, 6#	2.50	
	Margin block of 4, Mr. Zip, "Use Zip Code" and "Mail Early in the Day"	.80	
	P# block of 16, 6#, Mr. Zip and slogans	3.40	

HORSE RACING ISSUE

Kentucky Derby, Churchill Downs, centenary.

Horses Rounding Turn — A931

Designed by Henry Koehler.

PHOTOGRAVURE (Andreotti)
Plates of 200 subjects in four panes of 50.

1974, May 4   Tagged   Perf. 11x10½

1528	A931 10c yellow & multicolored	.25	.20
	P# block of 12, 6#	3.50	
	Margin block of 4, Mr. Zip and "Use Zip Code"	1.10	
a.	Blue ("Horse Racing") omitted	825.00	
b.	Red ("U.S. postage 10 cents") omitted	2,500.	
c.	Tagging omitted	—	

Beware of stamps offered as No. 1528b that have traces o[f] red.

SKYLAB ISSUE

First anniversary of the launching of Skylab I, honoring all who participated in the Skylab project.

Skylab — A932

Designed by Robert T. McCall.

LITHOGRAPHED, ENGRAVED (Giori)
Plates of 200 subjects in four panes of 50.

1974, May 14   Tagged   Perf. 11

1529	A932 10c multicolored	.20	.20
	P# block of 4	.85	—
	Margin block of 4, Mr. Zip and "Use Zip Code"	.80	—
a.	Vert. pair, imperf. between	—	
b.	Tagging omitted	10.00	

UNIVERSAL POSTAL UNION ISSUE

UPU cent. In the 1st row Nos. 1530-1537 are in sequence as listed. In the 2nd row Nos. 1534-1537 are in llowed by Nos. 1530-1533. Every row of 8 and every horizontal block of 8 contains all 8 designs. The letter writing designs are from famous works of art; some e details. The quotation on every second stamp, etters mingle souls," is from a letter by poet John onne.

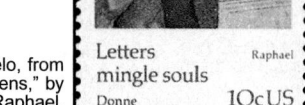

Michelangelo, from "School of Athens," by Raphael, 1509 — A933

"Five Feminine Virtues," by Hokusai, c. 1811 — A934

"Old Scraps," by John Fredrick Peto, 1894 — A935

"The Lovely Reader," by Jean Etienne Liotard, 1746 — A936

"Lady Writing Letter," by Gerard Terborch, 1654 — A937

Inkwell and Quill, from "Boy with a Top," by Jean-Baptiste Simeon Chardin, 1738 — A938

Mrs. John Douglas, by Thomas Gainsborough, 1784 — A939

Don Antonio Noriega, by Francisco de Goya, 1801 — A940

Designed by Bradbury Thompson.

PHOTOGRAVURE (Andreotti)
Plates of 128 subjects in four panes of 32 each.

1974, June 6		Tagged	Perf. 11	
1530	A933	10c multicolored	.20	.20
1531	A934	10c multicolored	.20	.20
1532	A935	10c multicolored	.20	.20
1533	A936	10c multicolored	.20	.20
1534	A937	10c multicolored	.20	.20
1535	A938	10c multicolored	.20	.20
1536	A939	10c multicolored	.20	.20
1537	A940	10c multicolored	.20	.20
a.		Block or strip of 8 (#1530-1537)	1.75	1.75

	P# block of 16, 5#, "Mail Early in the Day," Mr. Zip and "Use Zip Code"	3.50	—
	P# block of 10, 5#; no slogans	2.25	—
b.	As "a," (block), imperf. vert.	7,500.	

MINERAL HERITAGE ISSUE

The sequence of stamps in 1st horizontal row is Nos. 1538-1541, 1538-1539. In 2nd row Nos. 1540-1541 are followed by Nos. 1538-1541.

Petrified Wood A941

Tourmaline A942

Amethyst A943

Rhodochrosite — A944

Designed by Leonard F. Buckley.

LITHOGRAPHED, ENGRAVED (Giori)
Plates of 192 subjects in four panes of 48 (6x8).

1974, June 13		Tagged	Perf. 11	
1538	A941	10c blue & multicolored	.20	.20
a.		Light blue & yellow (litho.) omitted	—	
1539	A942	10c blue & multicolored	.20	.20
a.		Light blue (litho.) omitted	—	
b.		Black & purple (engr.) omitted	—	
1540	A943	10c blue & multicolored	.20	.20
a.		Light blue & yellow (litho.) omitted	—	
1541	A944	10c blue & multicolored	.20	.20
a.		Block or strip of 4, #1538-1541	.80	.90

	P# block of 4	.90	—
	Margin block of 4, Mr. Zip and "Use Zip Code"	.85	—
b.	As "a," light blue & yellow (litho.) omitted	1,750.	—
c.	Light blue (litho.) omitted	—	
d.	Black & red (engr.) omitted	—	
e.	Block of 4, two right stamps being Nos. 1539b and 1541d	4,500.	
f.	As "a," tagging omitted	—	

No. 1541e is usually collected as a transition block of six or larger.

KENTUCKY SETTLEMENT, 150th ANNIV.
Fort Harrod, first settlement in Kentucky.

Covered Wagons at Fort Harrod — A945

Designed by David K. Stone.

LITHOGRAPHED, ENGRAVED (Giori)
Plates of 200 subjects in four panes of 50.

1974, June 15	Tagged	Perf. 11	
1542 A945 10c green & multicolored		.20	.20
P# block of 4		.85	—
Margin block of 4, Mr. Zip and "Use Zip Code"		.80	
a. Dull black (litho.) omitted		700.00	
b. Green (engr. & litho.), black (engr. & litho.) & blue missing (EP)		3,000.	
c. Green (engr.) missing (EP)		3,750.	
d. Green (engr.) & black (litho.) missing (EP)		—	
e. Tagging omitted		—	
f. Blue (litho.) omitted		—	

No. 1542f was caused by an occurrence that seems to be unique for U.S. total color omitted/missing errors. According to the BEP, oil on the printing blanket made a small area unreceptive to the blue ink. No blue at all was printed on one unique error stamp.

AMERICAN REVOLUTION BICENTENNIAL ISSUE
First Continental Congress

Nos. 1543-1544 alternate in 1st row, Nos. 1545-1546 in 2nd row. This arrangement is repeated throughout the pane.

Carpenters' Hall, Philadelphia A946

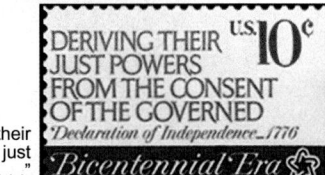

"We ask but for peace . . ." A947

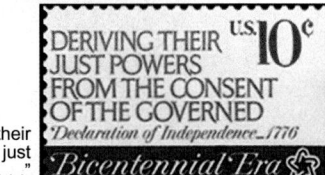

"Deriving their just powers . . ." A948

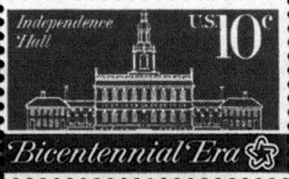

Independence Hall — A949

Designed by Frank P. Conley.

GIORI PRESS PRINTING
Plates of 200 subjects in four panes of 50.

1974, July 4	Tagged	Perf. 11	
1543 A946 10c dark blue & red		.20	.20
1544 A947 10c gray, dark blue & red		.20	.20
1545 A948 10c gray, dark blue & red		.20	.20
1546 A949 10c red & dark blue		.20	.20
a. Block of 4, #1543-1546		.80	.90
P# block of 4		.90	
Margin block of 4, Mr. Zip and "Use Zip Code"		.85	
b. As "a," tagging omitted		60.00	

Margin includes Bicentennial Commission emblem and inscription.

ENERGY CONSERVATION ISSUE
Publicizing the importance of conserving all forms of energy.

Molecules and Drops of Gasoline and Oil — A950

Designed by Robert W. Bode.

LITHOGRAPHED, ENGRAVED (Giori)
Plates of 200 subjects in four panes of 50.

1974, Sept. 23	Tagged	Perf. 11	
1547 A950 10c multicolored		.20	.20
P# block of 4		.85	—
Margin block of 4, Mr. Zip and "Use Zip Code"		.80	—
a. Blue & orange omitted		825.00	
b. Orange & green omitted		550.00	
c. Green omitted		825.00	
d. Tagging omitted		7.50	

AMERICAN FOLKLORE ISSUE
Legend of Sleepy Hollow

The Headless Horseman in pursuit of Ichabod Crane from "Legend of Sleepy Hollow," by Washington Irving.

Headless Horseman and Ichabod A951

Designed by Leonard Everett Fisher.

LITHOGRAPHED, ENGRAVED (Giori)
Plates of 200 subjects in four panes of 50.

1974, Oct. 12	Tagged	Perf. 11	
1548 A951 10c dk. bl., blk., org. & yel.		.20	.20
P# block of 4		.85	—
Margin block of 4, Mr. Zip and "Use Zip Code"		.80	—
a. Tagging omitted		—	

RETARDED CHILDREN ISSUE
Retarded Children Can Be Helped, theme of annual convention of the National Association of Retarded Citizens.

Retarded Child — A952

Designed by Paul Calle.

GIORI PRESS PRINTING
Plates of 200 subjects in four panes of 50.

1974, Oct. 12	Tagged	Perf. 11	
1549 A952 10c brown red & dark brown		.20	.20
P# block of 4		.85	—
Margin block of 4, Mr. Zip and "Use Zip Code"		.80	—
a. Tagging omitted		7.50	

CHRISTMAS ISSUE

Angel — A953

"The Road-Winter," by Currier and Ives — A954

Dove Weather Vane atop Mount Vernon — A955

Designers: No. 1550, Bradbury Thompson, using detail from the Pérussis altarpiece painted by anonymous French artist, 1480, in Metropolitan Museum of Art, New York City. No. 1551, Stevan Dohanos, using Currier and Ives print from drawing by Otto Knirsch. No. 1552, Don Hedin and Robert Geissman.

PHOTOGRAVURE (Andreotti)
Plates of 200 subjects in four panes of 50.

1974, Oct. 23	Tagged	Perf. 10½x11	
1550 A953 10c multicolored		.20	.20
P# block of 10, 5#		2.10	
Margin block of 4, Mr. Zip and "Use Zip Code"		.80	
	Perf. 11x10½		
1551 A954 10c multicolored		.20	.20
P# block of 12, 6#		2.50	
Margin block of 4, Mr. Zip and "Use Zip Code"		.80	
a. Buff omitted		10.00	
b. Tagging omitted		—	

No. 1551a is difficult to identify. Competent expertization is necessary.

Die Cut, Paper Backing Rouletted
1974, Nov. 15 **Untagged**
Self-adhesive; Inscribed "Precanceled"

1552	A955 10c multicolored	.20	.20
	P# block of 20, 6#, 5 slogans	4.25	
	P# block of 12, 6#, 5 different slogans	2.60	
	Nos. 1550-1552 (3)	.60	.60

Unused value of No. 1552 is for copy on rouletted paper backing as issued. Used value is for copy on piece, with or without postmark. **Most copies are becoming discolored, probably from the adhesive. The Catalogue value is for discolored copies.**

Die cutting includes crossed slashes through dove, applied to prevent removal and re-use of the stamp. The stamp will separate into layers if soaked.

Two different machines were used to roulette the sheet.

AMERICAN ARTS ISSUE
Benjamin West (1738-1820), painter (No. 1553); Paul Laurence Dunbar (1872-1906), poet (No. 1554); David (Lewelyn) Wark Griffith (1875-1948), motion picture producer (No. 1555).

Self-portrait — A956   A957

A958

Designers: No. 1553, Bradbury Thompson; No. 1554, Walter D. Richards; No. 1555, Fred Otnes.

PHOTOGRAVURE (Andreotti)
Plates of 200 subjects in four panes of 50.

1975	**Tagged**	**Perf. 10½x11**	
1553	A956 10c multicolored, *Feb. 10*	.20	.20
	P# block of 10, 5#	2.10	
	Margin block of 4, Mr. Zip and "Use Zip Code"	.80	

Perf. 11

1554	A957 10c multicolored, *May 1*	.20	.20
	P# block of 10, 5#	2.10	
	Margin block of 4, Mr. Zip and "Use Zip Code"	.80	
a.	Imperf., pair	1,250.	

LITHOGRAPHED, ENGRAVED (Giori)
Perf. 11

1555	A958 10c brown & multicolored, *May 27*	.20	.20
	P# block of 4	.85	
	Margin block of 4, Mr. Zip and "Use Zip Code"	.80	
a.	Brown (engr.) omitted	625.00	
	Nos. 1553-1555 (3)	.60	.60

SPACE ISSUES
US space accomplishments with unmanned craft. Pioneer 10 passed within 81,000 miles of Jupiter, Dec. 10, 1973. Mariner 10 explored Venus and Mercury in 1974 and Mercury again in 1975.

Pioneer 10 Passing Jupiter A959

Mariner 10, Venus and Mercury A960

Designed by Robert McCall (No. 1556); Roy Gjertson (No. 1557).

LITHOGRAPHED, ENGRAVED (Giori)
Plates of 200 subjects in four panes of 50.

1975	**Tagged**	**Perf. 11**	
1556	A959 10c light yellow, dark yellow, red, blue & 2 dark blues		
	Feb. 28	.20	.20
	P# block of 4	.85	—
	Margin block of 4, Mr. Zip and "Use Zip Code"	.80	—
a.	Red & dark yellow omitted	1,200.	
b.	Dark blues (engr.) omitted	800.00	
c.	Tagging omitted	11.00	
d.	Dark yellow omitted		

Imperfs. exist from printer's waste.

1557	A960 10c black, red, ultra. & bister, *Apr. 4*	.20	.20
	P# block of 4	.85	—
	Margin block of 4, Mr. Zip and "Use Zip Code"	.80	—
a.	Red omitted	400.00	
b.	Ultramarine & bister omitted	1,750.	
c.	Tagging omitted	11.00	
d.	Red missing (PS)	—	

COLLECTIVE BARGAINING ISSUE
Collective Bargaining law, enacted 1935, in Wagner Act.

"Labor and Management" A961

Designed by Robert Hallock.

PHOTOGRAVURE (Andreotti)
Plates of 200 subjects in four panes of 50.

1975, Mar. 13	**Tagged**	**Perf. 11**	
1558	A961 10c multicolored	.20	.20
	P# block of 8, 4#	1.75	—
	Margin block of 4, Mr. Zip and "Use Zip Code"	.80	—

Imperforates exist from printer's waste.

AMERICAN BICENTENNIAL ISSUE
Contributors to the Cause

Sybil Ludington, age 16, rallied militia, Apr. 26, 1777; Salem Poor, black freeman, fought in Battle of Bunker Hill; Haym Salomon, Jewish immigrant, raised money to finance Revolutionary War; Peter Francisco, Portuguese-French immigrant, joined Continental Army at 15. Emerald inscription on back, printed beneath gum in water-soluble ink, gives thumbnail sketch of portrayed contributor.

Sybil Ludington A962

Salem Poor — A963

Haym Salomon A964

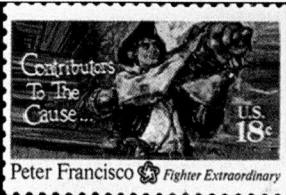

Peter Francisco A965

Designed by Neil Boyle.

PHOTOGRAVURE (Andreotti)
Plates of 200 subjects in four panes of 50.

1975, Mar. 25	**Tagged**	**Perf. 11x10½**	
1559	A962 8c multicolored	.20	.20
	P# block of 10, 5#	1.50	
	Margin block of 4, Mr. Zip and "Use Zip Code"	.65	—
a.	Back inscriptions omitted	200.00	
1560	A963 10c multicolored	.20	.20
	P# block of 10, 5#	2.10	
	Margin block of 4, Mr. Zip and "Use Zip Code"	.80	—
a.	Back inscription omitted	200.00	
1561	A964 10c multicolored	.20	.20
	P# block of 10, 5#	2.10	
	Margin block of 4, Mr. Zip and "Use Zip Code"	.80	—
a.	Back inscription omitted	200.00	
b.	Red omitted	250.00	
1562	A965 18c multicolored	.35	.20
	P# block of 10, 5#	3.60	
	Margin block of 4, Mr. Zip and "Use Zip Code"	1.45	—
	Nos. 1559-1562 (4)	.95	.80

Lexington-Concord Battle, 200th Anniv.

"Birth of Liberty," by Henry Sandham A966

Designed by Bradbury Thompson.

PHOTOGRAVURE (Andreotti)
Plates of 160 subjects in four panes of 40.

1975, Apr. 19	**Tagged**	**Perf. 11**	
1563	A966 10c multicolored	.20	.20
	P# block of 12, 6#	2.50	
	Margin block of 4, Mr. Zip, "Use Zip Code" and "Mail Early in the Day"	.80	—
	P# block of 16, 6 P#, Mr. Zip and slogans	3.40	—
a.	Vert. pair, imperf. horiz.	425.00	

Bunker Hill Battle, 200th Anniv.

Battle of Bunker Hill, by John Trumbull — A967

Designed by Bradbury Thompson.

PHOTOGRAVURE (Andreotti)
Plates of 160 subjects in four panes of 40.

1975, June 17	**Tagged**	*Perf. 11*	
1564 A967 10c **multicolored**		.20	.20
P# block of 12, 6#		2.50	—
Margin block of 4, Mr. Zip, "Use Zip Code" and "Mail Early in the Day"		.80	—
P# block of 16, 6#, Mr. Zip and slogans		3.40	—

Military Uniforms

Bicentenary of US Military Services. Nos. 1565-1566 alternate in one row, Nos. 1567-1568 in next row.

Soldier with Flintlock Musket, Uniform Button — A968

Sailor with Grappling Hook, First Navy Jack, 1775 — A969

Marine with Musket, Fullrigged Ship — A970

Militiaman with Musket and Powder Horn — A971

Designed by Edward Vebell.

PHOTOGRAVURE (Andreotti)
Plates of 200 subjects in four panes of 50.

1975, July 4	**Tagged**	*Perf. 11*	
1565 A968 10c **multicolored**		.20	.20
1566 A969 10c **multicolored**		.20	.20
1567 A970 10c **multicolored**		.20	.20
1568 A971 10c **multicolored**		.20	.20
a. Block of 4, #1565-1568		.85	.90
P# block of 12, 6#		2.50	
P# block of 20, 6#, Mr. Zip and slogans		4.50	—
Margin block of 4, Mr. Zip and "Use Zip Code"		1.00	—

APOLLO SOYUZ SPACE ISSUE

Apollo Soyuz space test project, Russo-American cooperation, launched July 15; link-up, July 17. Nos. in the 1st row, No. 1569 is in 1st and 3rd space, No. 1570 is 2nd space; in the 2nd row No. 1570 is in 1st and 3rd space, No. 1569 in 2nd space, etc.

Participating US and USSR crews: Thomas P. Stafford, Donald K. Slayton, Vance D. Brand, Aleksei A. Leonov, Valery N. Kubasov.

Apollo and Soyuz after Link-up, and Earth — A972

Spacecraft before Link-up, Earth and Project Emblem — A973

Illustrations reduced.

Designed by Robert McCall (No. 1569) and Anatoly M. Aksamit of USSR (No. 1570).

PHOTOGRAVURE (Andreotti)
Plates of 96 subjects in four panes of 24 each.

1975, July 15	**Tagged**	*Perf. 11*	
1569 A972 10c **multicolored**		.20	.20
Pair with full horiz. gutter btwn.		—	
1570 A973 10c **multicolored**		.20	.20
a. Pair, #1569-1570		.45	.40
P# block of 12, 6#		2.50	—
Margin block of 4, Mr. Zip, "Use Zip Code"		.85	—
P# block of 16, 6#, Mr. Zip, "Use Zip Code"		3.40	—
Pair with full horiz. gutter btwn.		—	
b. As "a," tagging omitted		30.00	—
c. As "a," vert. pair imperf. horiz.		2,250.	
d. As "a," yellow omitted			

Nos. 1569-1570 totally imperforate are printer's waste. See Russia Nos. 4339-4340.

INTERNATIONAL WOMEN'S YEAR ISSUE
International Women's Year 1975.

Worldwide Equality for Women A974

Designed by Miriam Schottland.

PHOTOGRAVURE (Andreotti)
Plates of 200 subjects in four panes of 50.

1975, Aug. 26	**Tagged**	*Perf. 11x10½*	
1571 A974 10c **blue, orange & dark blue**		.20	.20
P# block of 6, 3#		1.30	—
Margin block of 4, Mr. Zip and "Use Zip Code"		.80	—
a. Tagging omitted		—	

US POSTAL SERVICE BICENTENNIAL ISSUE

Nos. 1572-1573 alternate in 1st row, Nos. 1574-1575 in 2nd row. This arrangement is repeated throughout the pane.

Stagecoach and Trailer Truck — A975

Old and New Locomotives A976

Early Mail Plane and Jet — A977

Satellite for Transmission of Mailgrams A978

Designed by James L. Womer.

PHOTOGRAVURE (Andreotti)
Plates of 200 subjects in four panes of 50.

1975, Sept. 3	**Tagged**	*Perf. 11x10*	
1572 A975 10c **multicolored**		.20	
1573 A976 10c **multicolored**		.20	
1574 A977 10c **multicolored**		.20	
1575 A978 10c **multicolored**		.20	
a. Block of 4, #1572-1575		.85	
P# block of 12, 6#		2.50	
P# block of 20, 6#, Mr. Zip and slogans		4.50	
Margin block of 4, Mr. Zip and "Use Zip Code"		1.00	
b. As "a," red "10c" omitted		7,500.	

WORLD PEACE THROUGH LAW ISSUE

A prelude to 7th World Law Conference of the World Peace Through Law Center at Washington, D.C., Oct. 12-17.

Law Book, Gavel, Olive Branch and Globe — A979

Designed by Melbourne Brindle.

GIORI PRESS PRINTING
Plates of 200 subjects in four panes of 50.

1975, Sept. 29	**Tagged**	*Perf.*	
1576 A979 10c **green, Prussian blue & rose brown**		.20	
P# block of 4		.85	
Margin block of 4, Mr. Zip and "Use Zip Code"		.80	
a. Tagging omitted		10.00	
b. Horiz. pair, imperf vert.		7,500.	

BANKING AND COMMERCE ISSUE

Banking and commerce in the U.S., and for the Centennial Convention of the American Bankers Association.

Designed by V. Jack Ruther.

Engine Turning, Indian Head Penny, Morgan-type Silver Dollar — A980

Seated Liberty Quarter, $20 Gold Double Eagle and Engine Turning A981

LITHOGRAPHED, ENGRAVED (Giori)
Plates of 160 subjects in four panes of 40.

1975, Oct. 6	**Tagged**	*Perf.*	
1577 A980 10c **multicolored**		.25	
1578 A981 10c **multicolored**		.25	
a. Pair, #1577-1578		.50	

P# block of 4	1.20	—
Margin block of 4, Mr. Zip and "Use Zip Code"	1.00	—
b. As "a," brown & blue (litho) omitted	2,250.	
c. As "a," brown, blue & yellow (litho) omitted	2,750.	
d. As No. 1578, tagging omitted		

CHRISTMAS ISSUE

Madonna and Child, by Domenico Ghirlandaio — A982

Christmas Card, by Louis Prang, 1878 — A983

Designed by Stevan Dohanos.

PHOTOGRAVURE (Andreotti)
Plates of 200 subjects in four panes of 50.

1975, Oct. 14	Tagged	Perf. 11	
1579 A982 (10c) multicolored		.20	.20
P# block of 12, 6#		2.50	—
Margin block of 4, Mr. Zip and "Use Zip Code"		.80	—
a. Imperf., pair		100.00	
Plate flaw ("d" damaged) (36741-36746 LL 47)		5.00	—

	Perf. 11.2		
1580 A983 (10c) multicolored		.20	.20
P# block of 12, 6#		2.50	—
Margin block of 4, Mr. Zip and "Use Zip Code"		.80	—
a. Imperf., pair		100.00	
c. Perf. 10.9		.25	.20
P# block of 12, 6#		3.50	—
Margin block of 4, Mr. Zip and "Use Zip Code"		1.00	—

	Perf. 10.5x11.3		
1580B A983 (10c) multicolored,		.65	.20
P# block of 12, 6#		15.00	—
Margin block of 4, Mr. Zip and "Use Zip Code"		2.75	—

AMERICANA ISSUE

Inkwell and Quill — A984

Speaker's Stand — A985

Early Ballot Box — A987

Books, Bookmark, Eyeglasses — A988

Dome of Capitol — A994

Contemplation of Justice, by J. E. Fraser — A995

Early American Printing Press — A996

Liberty Bell — A998

Fort McHenry Flag (15 Stars) — A1001

Old North Church, Boston — A1003

Sandy Hook Lighthouse, NJ — A1005

Iron "Betty" Lamp, Plymouth Colony, 17th-18th Centuries — A1007

Kerosene Table Lamp — A1009

Torch, Statue of Liberty — A997

Eagle and Shield — A999

Head, Statue of Liberty — A1002

Fort Nisqually, Wash. — A1004

Morris Township School No. 2, Devils Lake, ND — A1006

Rush Lamp and Candle Holder — A1008

Railroad Conductor's Lantern, c. 1850 — A1010

Designed by: 2c, 4c, 15c, V. Jack Ruther Robert Hallock. 3c, Clarence Holbert. 9c, 10c, 11c, Walter Brooks. 12c, George Mercer. No. 1595, Bernard Glassman. No. 1596, James L. Womer.

ROTARY PRESS PRINTING
E.E. Plates of 400 subjects in four panes of 100.

1975-81	Tagged	Perf. 11x10½	
	Size: 18½x22½mm		
1581 A984 1c dark blue, greenish, shiny gum, Dec. 8, 1977		.20	.20
P# block of 4		.25	—
Margin block of 4, "Use Zip Code"		.20	—
Dull gum		.20	
P# block of 4		.50	
Zip block of 4		.20	
Pair with full vert. gutter btwn.			
a. Untagged (Bureau precanceled)		4.50	1.50
P# block of 4		22.50	
Margin block of 4, "Use Zip Codes"		18.50	
c. White paper, dull gum			—
d. Tagging omitted (not Bureau precanceled), shiny gum		4.50	
Dull gum		—	
1582 A985 2c red brown, greenish, shiny gum, Dec. 8, 1977		.20	.20
P# block of 4		.25	—
Margin block of 4, "Use Zip Code"		.20	—
Dull gum		.20	
P# block of 4		2.50	
Zip block of 4		.50	
a. Untagged (Bureau precanceled)		4.50	1.50
P# block of 4		22.50	
Zip block of 4		18.50	
b. Cream paper, dull gum, 1981		.20	.20
P# block of 4		.25	
Zip block of 4		.20	
c. Tagging omitted (not Bureau precanceled)		4.50	
1584 A987 3c olive, greenish, shiny gum, Dec. 8, 1977		.20	.20
P# block of 4		.30	
Margin block of 4, "Use Zip Code"		.25	—
Dull gum		.20	
P# block of 4		.50	
Zip block of 4		.30	
Pair with full horiz. gutter btwn.		—	
a. Untagged (Bureau precanceled)		.75	.50
P# block of 4		9.50	
Zip block of 4		5.00	
b. Tagging omitted (not Bureau precanceled)		7.50	

Values for No. 1584a are for the bars-only precancel. Also known with city precancels, and worth more thus.

1585 A988 4c rose magenta, cream, shiny gum, Dec. 8, 1977		.20	.20
P# block of 4		.40	—
Margin block of 4, "Use Zip Code"		.35	—
Dull gum		.20	
P# block of 4		1.10	
Zip block of 4		.65	
a. Untagged (Bureau precanceled)		1.00	.75
P# block of 4		13.50	
Zip block of 4		6.00	
b. Tagging omitted (not Bureau precanceled), dull gum		25.00	
Shiny gum		35.00	

Values for No. 1585a are for the bars-only precancel. Also known with city precancels, and worth more thus.

	Size: 17½x20½mm		
1590 A994 9c slate green (from bklt. pane #1623a), Mar. 11, 1977		.45	.20
Pair with full horiz. gutter between			

	Perf. 10x9¾		
1590A A994 9c slate green (from bklt. pane #1623Bc), Mar. 11, 1977		20.00	15.00
	Size: 18x22½mm		
	Perf. 11x10½		
1591 A994 9c slate green, gray, shiny gum, Nov. 24, 1975		.20	.20
P# block of 4		.85	—
Margin block of 4, "Use Zip Code"		.80	—
Dull gum		1.00	
P# block of 4		5.00	
Zip block of 4		4.25	
a. Untagged (Bureau precanceled)		1.75	1.00
P# block of 4		50.00	
Zip block of 4		11.50	
b. Tagging omitted (not Bureau precanceled)		5.00	

Values for No. 1591a are for the bars-only precancel. Also known with city precancels, and worth more thus.

1592 A995 10c violet, gray, shiny gum, Nov. 17, 1977		.20	.20
P# block of 4		.90	—
Margin block of 4, "Use Zip Code"		.80	—
Dull gum		.20	
P# block of 4		.90	
Zip block of 4		.80	
a. Untagged (Bureau precanceled, Chicago)		9.50	5.00

	P# block of 4		95.00	
	Zip block of 4		42.50	
b.	Tagging omitted (not Bureau precanceled)		7.50	
1593	A996 11c **orange,** *gray, Nov. 13, 1975*		.20	.20
	P# block of 4		.90	—
	Margin block of 4, "Use Zip Code"		.85	
	Pair with full horiz. gutter between		—	
a.	Tagging omitted		4.00	
1594	A997 12c **red brown,** *beige, Apr. 8, 1981*		.25	.20
	P# block of 4		1.60	—
	Zip block of 4		1.10	—
a.	Tagging omitted		7.50	
1595	A998 13c **brown** (from bklt. pane), *Oct. 31, 1975*		.30	.20
a.	Booklet pane of 6		2.25	1.00
b.	Booklet pane of 7 + label		2.25	1.00
c.	Booklet pane of 8		2.25	1.00
d.	Booklet pane of 5 + label, *Apr. 2, 1976*		1.75	1.00
e.	Vert. pair, imperf. btwn.		1,250.	
f.	Tagging omitted		—	
g.	Horiz. pair, imperf. btwn.		—	

Nos. 1595e and 1595g resulted from paper foldovers after perforating and before cutting into panes. Beware of printer's waste consisting of complete panes with perfs around all outside edges.

PHOTOGRAVURE (Andreotti)
Plates of 400 subjects in four panes of 100.
Perf. 11.2

1596	A999 13c **multicolored,** *Dec. 1, 1975*		.25	.20
	P# block of 12, 6#		3.25	—
	P# block of 20, 6# and slogans		5.50	—
	Margin block of 4, "Use Zip Code"		1.00	—
	Pair with full horiz. gutter btwn.		150.00	
a.	Imperf., pair		45.00	
b.	Yellow omitted		125.00	
d.	Line perforated		27.50	
	P# block of 12, 6#		375.00	

On No. 1596 the entire sheet is perforated at one time so the perforations meet perfectly at the corners of the stamp. On No. 1596d the perforations do not line up perfectly and are perf. 11.

ENGRAVED (Combination Press)
Plates of 460 subjects (20x23) in panes of 100 (10x10)

1597	A1001 15c **gray, dark blue & red,** large block tagging, *June 30, 1978*		.30	.20
	P# block of 6		1.90	—
	P# block of 20, 1-2#		6.50	—
a.	Small block tagging		.30	.20
	P# block of 6		1.90	—
	P# block of 20, 1-2#		6.50	—
b.	Gray omitted		475.00	
c.	Vert. strip of 3, imperf. btwn. and at top or bottom		500.00	
d.	Tagging omitted		3.00	
e.	Imperf., vert. pair		17.50	

Plate number appears 3 times on each plate of 23 rows. With no separating gutters, each pane has only left or right sheet margin. Plate numbers appear on both margins; there are no slogans.

ENGRAVED
Perf. 11x10½

1598	A1001 15c **gray, dark blue & red** (from bklt. pane), *June 30, 1978*		.40	.20
a.	Booklet pane of 8		4.25	.80

1599	A1002 16c **blue,** *Mar. 31, 1978*		.35	.20
	P# block of 4		1.90	—
	Margin block of 4, "Use Correct Zip Code"		1.40	—
1603	A1003 24c **red,** *blue, Nov. 14, 1975*		.50	.20
	P# block of 4		2.25	—
	Margin block of 4, "Use Zip Code"		2.00	—
a.	Tagging omitted		11.00	
1604	A1004 28c **brown,** *blue, shiny gum, Aug. 11, 1978*		.55	.20
	P# block of 4		2.40	—
	Margin block of 4, "Use Correct Zip Code"		2.25	—
	Dull gum		1.10	
	P# block of 4		10.00	
	Zip block of 4		5.00	
1605	A1005 29c **blue,** *light blue, shiny gum, Apr. 14, 1978*		.60	.20
	P# block of 4		3.00	—
	Margin block of 4, "Use Correct Zip Code"		2.40	—
	Dull gum		2.00	
	P# block of 4		15.00	
	Zip block of 4		9.00	
1606	A1006 30c **green,** *blue, Aug. 27, 1979*		.55	.20
	P# block of 4		2.40	—
	Margin block of 4, "Use Correct Zip Code"		2.25	—
a.	Tagging omitted		15.00	

LITHOGRAPHED AND ENGRAVED
Perf. 11

1608	A1007 50c **tan, black & orange,** *Sept. 11, 1979*		.85	.20
	P# block of 4		3.75	—
	Margin block of 4, "Use Correct Zip Code"		3.50	—
a.	Black omitted		275.00	
b.	Vert. pair, imperf. horiz.		1,750.	
c.	Tagging omitted		16.00	

Beware of examples offered as No. 1608b that have blind perfs.

1610	A1008 $1 **tan, brown, orange & yellow,** *July 2, 1979*		2.00	.20
	P# block of 4		8.50	—
	Margin block of 4, "Use Correct Zip Code"		8.00	—
	Pair with full vert. gutter btwn.		—	
a.	Brown (engraved) omitted		250.00	
b.	Tan, orange & yellow omitted		275.00	
c.	Brown inverted		22,500.	
d.	Tagging omitted		15.00	
1611	A1009 $2 **tan, dark green, orange & yellow,** *Nov. 16, 1978*		3.75	.75
	P# block of 4		16.00	—
	Margin block of 4, "Use Correct Zip Code"		15.00	—
a.	Tagging omitted		—	
1612	A1010 $5 **tan, red brown, yellow & orange,** *Aug. 23, 1979*		8.50	1.75
	P# block of 4		36.00	—
	Margin block of 4, "Use Correct Zip Code"		34.00	—
	Nos. 1581-1612 (23)		41.00	21.50

Nos. 1590, 1590A, 1595, 1598, 1623 and 1623b were issued only in booklets. All stamps have one or two straight edges.
Bureau Precancels: 1c, 3 diff., 2c, Chicago, Greensboro, NC, 3c, 6 diff., 4c, Chicago, lines only, No. 1591a, 4 diff., No. 1596, 5 diff., 30c, lines only, 50c, 2 spacings, lines only, $1, 2 spacings, lines only. The 30c, 50c, $1 and No. 1596 are precanceled on tagged stamps.

Six-string
Guitar — A1011

Drum — A1013

Saxhorns — A1012

Steinway Grand
Piano,
1857 — A1014

Designers: 3.1c, George Mercer. 7.7c, Susan Robb. 7.9c, Bernard Glassman. 10c, Walter Brooks. 15c, V. Jack Ruther.

COIL STAMPS
ENGRAVED

1975-79			**Perf. 10 Vertically**	
1613	A1011 3.1c **brown,** *yellow, Oct. 25, 1979*		.20	.20
	Pair		.25	.20

	Joint line pair		1.25	—
a.	Untagged (Bureau precanceled, lines only)		.35	.3
	Pair		.70	.7
	Joint line pair		5.25	—
b.	Imperf., pair		1,300.	
	Joint line pair		3,000.	
1614	A1012 7.7c **brown,** *bright yellow, Nov. 20, 1976*		.20	.2
	Pair		.40	.2
	Joint line pair		.90	—
a.	Untagged (Bureau precanceled)		.40	.3
	Pair		.80	.6
	Joint line pair		3.25	—
b.	As "a," imperf., pair		1,600.	
	Joint line pair		3,000.	

A total of 160 different Bureau precancels were used by 153 cities.
No. 1614b is precanceled Washington, DC. Also exists with Marion, OH precancel; value $1,950 for pair.

1615	A1013 7.9c **carmine,** *yellow, shiny gum, Apr. 23, 1976*		.20	.20
	Pair		.40	.20
	Joint line pair		.75	—
	Dull gum		.60	
	Pair		1.20	
	Joint line pair		2.25	
a.	Untagged (Bureau precanceled), shiny gum		.40	.40
	Pair		.80	.80
	Joint line pair		2.75	
	Dull gum		.45	
	Pair		.90	
	Joint line pair		4.50	
b.	Imperf., pair		575.00	

A total of 109 different Bureau precancels were used by 107 cities plus two types of CAR. RT./SORT.

1615C	A1014 8.4c **dark blue,** *yellow, shiny gum, July 13, 1978*		.20	.20
	Pair		.40	.20
	Joint line pair		3.25	.30
d.	Untagged (Bureau precanceled), shiny gum		.50	.40
	Pair		1.00	.80
	Joint line pair		4.25	
	Dull gum		.40	
	Pair		.80	
	Joint line pair		3.25	
e.	As "d," pair, imperf. between		50.00	
	Joint line pair		125.00	
f.	As "d," imperf., pair		17.50	
	Joint line pair		27.50	

A total of 145 different Bureau precancels were used by 144 cities.
No. 1615Ce is precanceled with lines only. No. 1615Cf is precanceled with lines only (value shown) and also exists in pairs precanceled Newark, N.J. ($27.50), Brownstown, Ind. ($1,000.), Oklahoma City, Okla. ($1,500.) and Washington, DC ($1,500).

1616	A994 9c **slate green,** *gray, Mar. 5, 1976*		.20	.20
	Pair		.40	.20
	Joint line pair		.90	—
a.	Imperf., pair		150.00	
	Joint line pair		350.00	
b.	Untagged (Bureau precanceled), shiny gum		1.15	.75
	Pair		2.30	1.50
	Joint line pair		42.50	
	Dull gum		.75	
	Pair		1.50	
	Joint line pair		19.50	
c.	As "b," imperf., pair		700.00	
	Joint line pair		—	

Values for No. 1616b with shiny gum are for the bars-only precancel. Also known with city precancels, and worth more thus.
No. 1616c is precanceled Pleasantville, NY.

1617	A995 10c **violet,** *gray, shiny gum, Nov. 4, 1977*		.20	.20
	Pair		.40	.20
	Joint line pair		1.00	
	Dull gum		.30	
	Pair		.60	
	Joint line pair		2.50	
a.	Untagged (Bureau precanceled, shiny gum)		42.50	1.35
	Pair		90.00	2.75
	Joint line pair		1,150.	
	Dull gum		1.35	
	Pair		2.75	
	Joint line pair		47.50	
b.	Imperf., pair, shiny gum		60.00	
	Joint line pair, shiny gum		125.00	
	Imperf., pair, dull gum		60.00	
	Joint line pair, dull gum		125.00	
1618	A998 13c **brown,** *shiny gum, Nov. 25, 1975*		.25	.20
	Pair		.50	.20
	Joint line pair		.75	
	Dull gum		.90	
	Pair		1.80	
	Joint line pair		4.50	
a.	Untagged (Bureau precanceled), shiny gum		5.75	.75
	Pair		12.00	1.50
	Joint line pair		90.00	
	Dull gum		.75	
	Pair		1.50	
	Joint line pair		35.00	
b.	Imperf., pair		25.00	

g.	Joint line pair	50.00		
g.	Vertical pair, imperf. between	—		
h.	As "a," imperf., pair	—		

Values for No. 1618a with shiny gum are for the bars-only precancel. Also known with city precancels, and worth more s.

18C	A1001	15c **gray, dark blue & red**, *June 30, 1978*	.50	.20
		Pair	1.00	.20
d.		Imperf., pair	20.00	
e.		Pair, imperf. between	150.00	
f.		Gray omitted	35.00	
i.		Tagging omitted	20.00	
19	A1002	16c **ultramarine**, overall tagging, *Mar. 31, 1978*	.35	.20
		Pair	.70	.20
		Joint line pair	1.50	
a.		Block tagging	.50	.20
		Pair	1.00	.25
		Nos. 1613-1619 (9)	2.30	1.80

No. 1619a (the Huck press printing) has a white background without bluish tinge, is a fraction of a millimeter smaller than No. 619 (the Cottrell press printing) and has no joint lines. Nos. 1615a, 1615d, 1616b, 1617a, 1618a, issued also with ll gum.

Bureau Precancels: 9c, 7 diff., 10c, 3 diff., 13c, 12 diff.
See Nos. 1811, 1813, 1816.

13-Star Flag over Independence Hall — A1015

Flag over Capitol — A1016

Designers: No. 1622, Melbourne Brindle. No. 1623, Esther Porter.

Panes of 100 (10x10) each.

975-81   *Perf. 11x10¾*

622	A1015	13c **dk blue, red & brown red**, *Nov. 15, 1975*	.25	.20
		P# block of 20, 2-3#, 2-3 Zip, 2-3 Mail Early	5.75	—
a.		Horiz. pair, imperf. between	50.00	
b.		Vertical pair, imperf.	450.00	
e.		Horiz. pair, imperf. vert.	—	
f.		Tagging omitted	4.00	

No. 1622 was printed on the Multicolored Huck Press. Plate markings are at top or bottom of pane. It has large block tagging and nearly vertical multiple gum ridges.
See note after No. 1338F for marginal markings.

Perf. 11¼

1622C	A1015	13c **dk blue, red & brown red**, *1981*	1.00	.25
		P# block of 20, 1-2#, 1-2 Zip	37.50	
		P# block of 6	20.00	
d.		Vertical pair, imperf	135.00	

No. 1622C was printed on the Combination Press. Plate markings are at sides of pane. It has small block tagging and shiny flat gum.
See note after No. 1703.

BOOKLET STAMPS

1977, Mar. 11   **Engr.**   *Perf. 11x10½*

1623	A1016	13c **blue & red**	.25	.20
a.		Booklet pane, 1 #1590 + 7 #1623	2.25	1.25
d.		Pair, #1590 & 1623	.70	1.00
f.		Tagging omitted	—	

Perf. 10x9¾

1623B	A1016	13c **blue & red**	.80	.80
c.		Booklet pane, 1 #1590A + 7 #1623B	25.00	—
e.		Pair, #1590A & #1623B	21.00	21.00

COIL STAMP

1975, Nov. 15   *Perf. 10 Vertically*

1625	A1015	13c **dk blue, red & brown red**	.25	.20
		Pair	.50	.20
a.		Imperf., pair	22.50	
b.		Tagging omitted	—	

No. 1625 was printed on both the Huck and "B" presses. Huck press printings have pebbled gum (gummed on press), while "B" press printings have smooth gum (pregummed paper). Huck press printings often show portions of a joint line, but this feature is not consistent. Values for coils and imperf coils are the same for both varieties.

AMERICAN BICENTENNIAL ISSUE
The Spirit of '76

Designed after painting by Archibald M. Willard in Abbot Hall, Marblehead, Massachusetts. Nos. 1629-1631 printed in continuous design.
Left panes contain 3 No. 1631a and one No. 1629; right panes contain one No. 1631 and 3 No. 1631a.

Drummer Boy — A1019   Old Drummer — A1020

Fifer — A1021

Designed by Vincent E. Hoffman.

PHOTOGRAVURE (Andreotti)
Plates of 200 subjects in four panes of 50.

1976, Jan. 1   **Tagged**   *Perf. 11*

1629	A1019	13c **blue violet & multi**	.25	.20
a.		Imperf., vert. pair	—	
1630	A1020	13c **blue violet & multi**	.25	.20
1631	A1021	13c **blue violet & multi**	.25	.20
a.		Strip of 3, #1629-1631	.75	.75
		P# block of 12, 5#	3.50	—
		P# block of 20, 5#, slogans	5.75	—
b.		As "a," imperf.	950.00	
c.		Imperf., vert. pair, #1631	800.00	

INTERPHIL ISSUE

Interphil 76 International Philatelic Exhibition, Philadelphia, Pa., May 29-June 6.

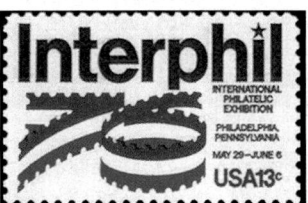

"Interphil 76" A1022

Designed by Terrence W. McCaffrey.

LITHOGRAPHED, ENGRAVED (Giori)
Plates of 200 subjects of four panes of 50.

1976, Jan. 17   **Tagged**   *Perf. 11*

1632	A1022	13c **dark blue & red (engr.), ultra. & red (litho.)**	.20	.20
		P# block of 4	1.00	—
		Margin block of 4, Mr. Zip and "Use Zip Code"	1.00	—
a.		Dark blue & red (engr.) missing (CM)	—	
b.		Tagging omitted	—	
c.		Red (engr,) missing (CM)	—	

AMERICAN BICENTENNIAL ISSUE
Illustration reduced.

Designed by Walt Reed.

PHOTOGRAVURE (Andreotti)
Plates of 200 subjects in four panes of 50.

1976, Feb. 23   **Tagged**   *Perf. 11*

1633	A1023	13c Delaware	.30	.25
1634	A1024	13c Pennsylvania	.30	.25
1635	A1025	13c New Jersey	.30	.25
1636	A1026	13c Georgia	.30	.25
1637	A1027	13c Connecticut	.30	.25
1638	A1028	13c Massachusetts	.30	.25
1639	A1029	13c Maryland	.30	.25
1640	A1030	13c South Carolina	.30	.25
1641	A1031	13c New Hampshire	.30	.25
1642	A1032	13c Virginia	.30	.25
1643	A1033	13c New York	.30	.25
1644	A1034	13c North Carolina	.30	.25
1645	A1035	13c Rhode Island	.30	.25
1646	A1036	13c Vermont	.30	.25
1647	A1037	13c Kentucky	.30	.25
1648	A1038	13c Tennessee	.30	.25
1649	A1039	13c Ohio	.30	.25
1650	A1040	13c Louisiana	.30	.25
1651	A1041	13c Indiana	.30	.25
1652	A1042	13c Mississippi	.30	.25
1653	A1043	13c Illinois	.30	.25
1654	A1044	13c Alabama	.30	.25
1655	A1045	13c Maine	.30	.25
1656	A1046	13c Missouri	.30	.25
1657	A1047	13c Arkansas	.30	.25
1658	A1048	13c Michigan	.30	.25
1659	A1049	13c Florida	.30	.25
1660	A1050	13c Texas	.30	.25
1661	A1051	13c Iowa	.30	.25
1662	A1052	13c Wisconsin	.30	.25
1663	A1053	13c California	.30	.25
1664	A1054	13c Minnesota	.30	.25
1665	A1055	13c Oregon	.30	.25
1666	A1056	13c Kansas	.30	.25
1667	A1057	13c West Virginia	.30	.25
a.		Tagging omitted		.25
1668	A1058	13c Nevada	.30	.25
1669	A1059	13c Nebraska	.30	.25
1670	A1060	13c Colorado	.30	.25
1671	A1061	13c North Dakota	.30	.25
1672	A1062	13c South Dakota	.30	.25
1673	A1063	13c Montana	.30	.25
1674	A1064	13c Washington	.30	.25
1675	A1065	13c Idaho	.30	.25
1676	A1066	13c Wyoming	.30	.25
1677	A1067	13c Utah	.30	.25
1678	A1068	13c Oklahoma	.30	.25
1679	A1069	13c New Mexico	.30	.25
1680	A1070	13c Arizona	.30	.25
1681	A1071	13c Alaska	.30	.25
1682	A1072	13c Hawaii	.30	.25
a.		Pane of 50	17.50	15.00

TELEPHONE CENTENNIAL ISSUE

Centenary of first telephone call by Alexander Graham Bell, March 10, 1876.

Bell's Telephone Patent Application, 1876 — A1073

Designed by George Tscherny.

ENGRAVED (Giori)
Plates of 200 subjects in four panes of 50.

1976, Mar. 10   **Tagged**   *Perf. 11*

1683	A1073	13c **black, purple & red**, *tan*	.25	.20
		P# block of 4	1.10	—
		Margin block of 4, Mr. Zip and "Use Zip Code"	1.00	—
a.		Black & purple missing (EP)	500.00	
b.		Red missing (EP)	—	
c.		All colors missing (EP)	—	

On No. 1683a, the errors have only tiny traces of red present, so are best collected as a horiz. strip of 5 with 2 or 3 error stamps. No. 1683c also must be collected as a transitional strip.

COMMERCIAL AVIATION ISSUE

50th anniversary of first contract airmail flights: Dearborn, Mich. to Cleveland, Ohio, Feb. 15, 1926; and Pasco, Wash. to Elko, Nev., Apr. 6, 1926.

Ford-Pullman Monoplane and Laird Swallow Biplane A1074

Designed by Robert E. Cunningham.

PHOTOGRAVURE (Andreotti)
Plates of 200 subjects in four panes of 50 each

1976, Mar. 19   **Tagged**   *Perf. 11*

1684	A1074	13c **blue & multicolored**	.25	.20
		P# block of 10, 5#	2.75	—
		Margin block of 4, Mr. Zip and "Use Zip Code"	1.00	—
a.		Tagging omitted		

Stamp sheet of State Flags — each 13¢ USA, labeled "BICENTENNIAL ERA 1776-1976":

Row 1: Delaware, Pennsylvania, New Jersey, Georgia, Connecticut — USE ZIP CODE
Row 2: Massachusetts, Maryland, South Carolina, New Hampshire, Virginia
Row 3: New York, North Carolina, Rhode Island, Vermont, Kentucky
Row 4: Tennessee, Ohio, Louisiana, Indiana, Mississippi — MAIL EARLY IN THE DAY
Row 5: Illinois, Alabama, Maine, Missouri, Arkansas — 36787
Row 6: Michigan, Florida, Texas, Iowa, Wisconsin — 36786
Row 7: California, Minnesota, Oregon, Kansas, West Virginia — 37244
Row 8: Nevada, Nebraska, Colorado, North Dakota, South Dakota — 36784
Row 9: Montana, Washington, Idaho, Wyoming, Utah — 36783
Row 10: Oklahoma, New Mexico, Arizona, Alaska, Hawaii

State Flags A1023-A1072

CHEMISTRY ISSUE

Honoring American chemists, in conjunction with the centenary of the American Chemical Society.

Various Flasks, Separatory Funnel, Computer Tape — A1075

Designed by Ken Davies.

PHOTOGRAVURE (Andreotti)
Plates of 200 subjects in four panes of 50.

1976, Apr. 6	Tagged	Perf. 11	
1685 A1075 13c multicolored		.25	.20
P# block of 12, 6#		3.25	—
Margin block of 4, Mr. Zip and "Use Zip Code"		1.00	—
Pair with full vert. gutter btwn.		—	

AMERICAN BICENTENNIAL ISSUES
SOUVENIR SHEETS

Designs, from Left to Right, No. 1686: a, Two British officers. b, Gen. Benjamin Lincoln. c, George Washington. d, John Trumbull, Col. Cobb, von Steuben, Lafayette, Thomas Nelson. e, Alexander Hamilton, John Laurens, Walter Stewart (all vert.).
No. 1687: a, John Adams, Roger Sherman, Robert R. Livingston. b, Jefferson, Franklin. c, Thomas Nelson, Jr., Francis Lewis, John Witherspoon, Samuel Huntington. d, John Hancock, Charles Thomson. e, George Read, John Dickinson, Edward Rutledge (a, d, vert., b, c, e, horiz.).
No. 1688: a, Boatsman. b, Washington. c, Flag bearer. d, Men in boat. e, Men on shore (a, d, horiz., b, c, e, vert.).

No. 1689: a, Two officers. b, Washington. c, Officer, black horse. d, Officer, white horse. e, Three soldiers (a, c, e, horiz., b, d, vert.).

Surrender of Cornwallis at Yorktown, by John
Trumbull — A1076

Declaration of Independence, by John
Trumbull — A1077

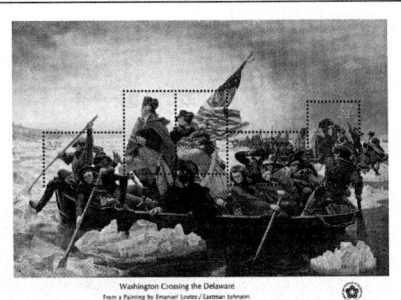

Washington Crossing the Delaware, by Emmanuel
Leutze / Eastman Johnson — A1078

Washington Reviewing Army at Valley Forge, by
William T. Trego — A1079

Illustrations reduced.

Designed by Vincent E. Hoffman.

LITHOGRAPHED
Plates of 30 subjects in six panes of 5 each.

1976, May 29		**Tagged**		**Perf. 11**
1686	A1076	Sheet of 5	3.25	2.25
a.-e.		13c **multicolored**	.45	.40
f.		"USA/13c" omitted on "b," "c" &		
		"d," imperf, tagging omitted	—	2,000.
g.		"USA/13c" omitted on "a" & "e"	450.00	
h.		Imperf., tagging omitted		2,250.
i.		"USA/13c" omitted on "b," "c" &		
		"d"	450.00	
j.		"USA/13c" double on "b"		
k.		"USA/13c" omitted on "c" & "d"	750.00	
l.		"USA/13c" omitted on "e"	550.00	
m.		"USA/13c" omitted, imperf., tag-		
		ging omitted		
n.		As "g," imperf., tagging omitted	—	
o.		"USA/13c" missing on "a" (PS)	—	

p.		As No. 1686, tagging omitted	—	—
q.		"USA/13c" omitted on "a"	—	
1687	A1077	Sheet of 5	4.25	3.25
a.-e.		18c **multicolored**	.55	.55
f.		Design & marginal inscriptions		
		omitted	3,250.	
g.		"USA/18c" omitted on "a" & "c"	600.00	
h.		"USA/18c" omitted on "b," "d" &		
		"e"	450.00	
i.		"USA/18c" omitted on "d"	475.00	475.00
j.		Black omitted in design	2,000.	
k.		"USA/18c" omitted, imperf., tag-		
		ging omitted	2,000.	
m.		"USA/18c" omitted on "b" & "e"	500.00	
n.		"USA/18c" omitted on "b" & "d"	1,000.	
p.		Imperf. (tagged)	1,000.	
q.		"USA/18c" omitted on "c"	—	
r.		Yellow omitted	—	
s.		"USA/18c" missing on "a," "c" and		
		"d" (PS)	—	
t.		"USA/18c" missing on "a" and "d"		
		(PS)	—	
1688	A1078	Sheet of 5	5.25	4.25
a.-e.		24c **multicolored**	.70	.70
f.		"USA/24c" omitted, imperf., tag-		
		ging omitted	1,500.	
g.		"USA/24c" omitted on "d" & "e"	450.00	450.00
h.		Design & marginal inscriptions		
		omitted	2,750.	
i.		"USA/24c" omitted on "a," "b" &		
		"c"	500.00	500.00
j.		Imperf., tagging omitted	1,750.	
k.		"USA/24c" of "d" & "e" inverted	3,250.	—
l.		As "i," imperf, tagging omitted	3,250.	—
m.		Tagging omitted on "e" and "f"	450.00	
n.		As No. 1688, perfs inverted	—	
o.		As No. 1688, tagging omitted	—	
1689	A1079	Sheet of 5	6.25	5.25
a.-e.		31c **multicolored**	.85	.85
f.		"USA/31c" omitted, imperf.	1,500.	
g.		"USA/31c" omitted on "a" & "c"	400.00	
h.		"USA/31c" omitted on "b," "d" &		
		"e"	500.00	—
i.		"USA/31c" omitted on "e"	450.00	
j.		Black omitted in design	1,500.	
k.		Imperf., tagging omitted		2,000.
l.		"USA/31c" omitted on "b" & "d"	600.00	
m.		"USA/31c" omitted on "a," "c" &		
		"e"	—	
n.		As "m," imperf., tagging omitted	—	
p.		As "h," imperf., tagging omitted		2,000.
q.		As "g," imperf., tagging omitted	2,750.	
r.		"USA/31c" omitted on "d" & "e"	600.00	
s.		As "f," tagging omitted	2,250.	
t.		"USA/31c" omitted on "d"	750.00	
u.		As No. 1689, tagging omitted	—	
v.		As No. 1689, perfs inverted	—	
w.		"USA/31c" missing on "a," "b," "c"		
		and "d" (PS)	—	
x.		As No. 1689, tagging omitted	—	
		Nos. 1686-1689 (4)	19.00	

Issued in connection with Interphil 76 International Philatelic
Exhibition, Philadelphia, Pa., May 29-June 6. Size of sheets:
153x204mm; size of stamps: 25x39½mm, 39½x25mm.

Benjamin Franklin

American Bicentennial: Benjamin Franklin (1706-
1790), deputy postmaster general for the colonies
(1753-1774) and statesman. Design based on marble
bust by anonymous Italian sculptor after terra cotta
bust by Jean Jacques Caffieri, 1777. Map published by
R. Sayer and J. Bennett in London.

Franklin and
Map of North
America,
1776 — A1080

Designed by Bernard Reilander (Canada).

LITHOGRAPHED, ENGRAVED (Giori)
Plates of 200 subjects in four panes of 50.

1976, June 1		**Tagged**		**Perf. 11**
1690	A1080	13c **ultramarine & multicolored**	.25	.20
		P# block of 4	1.10	—
		Margin block of 4, Mr. Zip and		
		"Use Zip Code"	1.00	—
a.		Light blue omitted	225.00	
b.		Tagging omitted	7.50	

See Canada No. 691.

Declaration of Independence

Designed after painting of Declaration of Independence, by John Trumbull, in the Rotunda of the Capitol, Washington, D.C. Nos. 1691-1694 printed in continuous design. Left panes contain 10 No. 1694a and 5
each of Nos. 1691-1692; right panes contain 5 each of
Nos. 1693-1694 and 10 No. 1694a.

A1081   A1082

A1083   A1084

Designed by Vincent E. Hoffman.

PHOTOGRAVURE (Andreotti)
Plates of 200 subjects in four panes of 50.

1976, July 4		**Tagged**		**Perf. 11**
1691	A1081	13c **blue & multicolored**	.30	.20
1692	A1082	13c **blue & multicolored**	.30	.20
1693	A1083	13c **blue & multicolored**	.30	.20
1694	A1084	13c **blue & multicolored**	.30	.20
a.		Strip of 4, #1691-1694	1.20	1.10
		P# block of 20, 5#, "Mail Early in		
		the Day," Mr. Zip and "Use Zip		
		Code"	7.25	—
		P# block of 16, 5#, "Mail Early in		
		the Day"	6.00	—
		Margin block of 4, Mr. Zip and		
		"Use Zip Code"	1.25	—

OLYMPIC GAMES ISSUE

12th Winter Olympic Games, Innsbruck, Austria,
Feb. 4-15, and 21st Summer Olympic Games, Montreal, Canada, July 17-Aug. 1. Nos. 1695-1696 alternate in one row, Nos. 1697-1698 in other row.

Diving — A1085   Skiing — A1086

Running — A1087   Skating — A1088

Designed by Donald Moss.

PHOTOGRAVURE (Andreotti)
Plates of 200 subjects in four panes of 50.

1976, July 16	Tagged	Perf. 11
1695 A1085 13c multicolored	.30	.20
1696 A1086 13c multicolored	.30	.20
1697 A1087 13c multicolored	.30	.20
1698 A1088 13c multicolored	.30	.20
a. Block of 4, #1695-1698	1.20	1.20
P# block of 12, 6#	4.00	—
P# block of 20, 6#, Mr. Zip and slogans	8.75	—
Margin block of 4, Mr. Zip and "Use Zip Code"	1.40	—
b. As "a," imperf.	625.00	

CLARA MAASS ISSUE
Clara Louise Maass (1876-1901), volunteer in fight against yellow fever, birth centenary.

Clara Maass and Newark German Hospital Pin — A1089

Designed by Paul Calle.

PHOTOGRAVURE (Andreotti)
Plates of 160 subjects in four panes of 40.

1976, Aug. 18	Tagged	Perf. 11
1699 A1089 13c multicolored	.25	.20
P# block of 12, 6#	4.00	—
Margin block of 4, Mr. Zip, "Use Zip Code" and "Mail Early in the Day"	1.00	—
a. Horiz. pair, imperf. vert.	425.00	

ADOLPH S. OCHS ISSUE
Adolph S. Ochs (1858-1935), publisher of the New York Times, 1896-1935.

Adolph S. Ochs — A1090

Designed by Bradbury Thompson; photograph by S. J. Woolf.

GIORI PRESS PRINTING
Plates of 128 subjects in four panes of 32 (8x4).

1976, Sept. 18	Tagged	Perf. 11
1700 A1090 13c black & gray	.25	.20
P# block of 4	1.10	—
Margin block of 4, Mr. Zip and "Use Zip Code"	.90	—
a. Tagging omitted	50.00	—

CHRISTMAS ISSUE

Nativity, by John Singleton Copley A1091

"Winter Pastime," by Nathaniel Currier A1092

Designers: No. 1701, Bradbury Thompson after 1776 painting in Museum of Fine Arts, Boston. No. 1702, Stevan Dohanos after 1855 lithograph in Museum of the City of New York.

PHOTOGRAVURE (Andreotti)
Plates of 200 subjects in four panes of 50.

1976, Oct. 27	Tagged	Perf. 11
1701 A1091 13c multicolored	.25	.20
P# block of 12, 6#	3.25	—
Margin block of 4, Mr. Zip and "Use Zip Code"	1.00	—
a. Imperf., pair	90.00	
1702 A1092 13c multi, overall tagging	.25	.20
P# block of 10, 5#	2.75	—
Margin block of 4, Mr. Zip and "Use Zip Code"	1.00	—
a. Imperf., pair	100.00	

Plates of 230 (10x23) subjects in panes of 50 (5x10)

	Tagged, Block	
1703 A1092 13c multicolored	.25	.20
P# block of 20, 5-8#	6.00	—
a. Imperf., pair	100.00	
b. Vert. pair, imperf. between	350.00	
c. Tagging omitted	12.50	
d. Red omitted	—	
e. Yellow omitted	—	

No. 1702 has overall tagging. Lettering at base is black and usually ½mm below design. As a rule, no "snowflaking" in sky or pond. Pane of 50 has margins on 4 sides with slogans. Plate Nos. 37465-37478.

No. 1703 has block tagging the size of printed area. Lettering at base is gray black and usually ¾mm below design. "Snowflaking" generally in sky and pond. Plate Nos. 37617-37621 or 37634-37638.

Copies of No. 1703 are known with various amounts of red or yellow missing. Nos. 1703d-1703e are stamps with the colors totally omitted. Expertization is recommended.

COMBINATION PRESS
Cylindrical plates consist of 23 rows of subjects, 10 across for commemoratives (230 subjects), 20 across for definitives (460 subjects), with selvage on the two outer edges only. Guillotining through the perforations creates individual panes of 50 or 100 with selvage on one side only.

Failure of the guillotine to separate through the perforations resulted in straight edges on some stamps. Perforating teeth along the center column and the tenth rows were removed for issues released on or after May 31, 1984 (the 10c Richard Russell, for definitives; the 20c Horace Moses, for commemoratives), creating panes with straight edged stamps on three sides.

Three sets of plate numbers, copyright notices (starting with No. 1787), and zip insignia (starting with No. 1927) are arranged identically on the left and right sides of the plate so that each pane has at least one of each marking. The markings adjacent to any particular row are repeated either seven or eight rows away on the cylinder.

Fifteen combinations of the three marginal markings and blank rows are possible on panes.

AMERICAN BICENTENNIAL ISSUE
Washington at Princeton
Washington's Victory over Lord Cornwallis at Princeton, N.J., bicentenary.

Washington, Nassau Hall, Hessian Prisoners and 13-star Flag, by Charles Willson Peale — A1093

Designed by Bradbury Thompson.

PHOTOGRAVURE (Andreotti)
Plates of 160 subjects in four panes of 40.

1977, Jan. 3	Tagged	Perf.
1704 A1093 13c multicolored	.25	
P# block of 10, 5#	2.75	
Margin block of 4, Mr. Zip and "Use Zip Code", "Mail Early in the Day"	1.00	
a. Horiz. pair, imperf. vert.	525.00	

SOUND RECORDING ISSUE
Centenary of the invention of the phonograph. Thomas Alva Edison and development of sophis-cated recording industry.

Tin Foil Phonograph A1094

Designed by Walter and Naiad Einsel.

LITHOGRAPHED, ENGRAVED (Giori)
Plates of 200 subjects in four panes of 50.

1977, Mar. 23	Tagged	Perf.
1705 A1094 13c black & multicolored	.25	
P# block of 4	1.10	
Margin block of 4, Mr. Zip and "Use Zip Code"	1.00	

AMERICAN FOLK ART SERIES
Pueblo Pottery
Pueblo art, 1880-1920, from Museums in New Mexico, Arizona and Colorado.

Nos. 1706-1709 are printed in blocks and strips of in panes of 40. In the 1st row Nos. 1706-1709 are i sequence as listed. In the 2nd row Nos. 1708-1709 ar followed by Nos. 1706-1709, 1708-1709.

Zia Pot — A1095

San Ildefonso Pot — A1096

Hopi Pot — A1097

Pueblo Art USA 13c
Acoma: School of American Research

Acoma Pot — A1098

Designed by Ford Ruthling.

PHOTOGRAVURE (Andreotti)
Plates of 160 subjects in four panes of 40.

1977, Apr. 13	Tagged	Perf. 11	
1706 A1095 13c **multicolored**		.25	.20
1707 A1096 13c **multicolored**		.25	.20
1708 A1097 13c **multicolored**		.25	.20
1709 A1098 13c **multicolored**		.25	.20
a. Block or strip of 4, #1706-1709		1.00	1.00
P# block of 10, 5#		2.75	—
P# block of 16, 5#; Mr. Zip and			
slogans		4.25	—
Margin block of 6, Mr. Zip and			
"Use Zip Code" "Mail Early in			
the Day"		1.50	—
b. As "a," imperf. vert.		2,250.	

LINDBERGH FLIGHT ISSUE

Charles A. Lindbergh's solo transatlantic flight from New York to Paris, 50th anniversary.

Spirit of St. Louis A1099

Designed by Robert E. Cunningham.

PHOTOGRAVURE (Andreotti)
Plates of 200 subjects in four panes of 50.

1977, May 20	Tagged	Perf. 11	
1710 A1099 13c **multicolored**		.25	.20
P# block of 12, 6#		3.25	—
Margin block of 4, Mr. Zip and			
"Use Zip Code"		1.00	—
a. Imperf., pair		900.00	

Beware of private overprints on No. 1710.

COLORADO STATEHOOD ISSUE

Issued to honor Colorado as the "Centennial State." It achieved statehood in 1876.

Columbine and Rocky Mountains — A1100

Designed by V. Jack Ruther.

PHOTOGRAVURE (Andreotti)
Plates of 200 subjects in four panes of 50.

1977, May 21	Tagged	Perf. 11	
1711 A1100 13c **multicolored**		.25	.20
P# block of 12, 6#		3.25	—
Margin block of 4, Mr. Zip and			
"Use Zip Code"		1.00	—
a. Horiz. pair, imperf. between		—	
b. Horiz. pair, imperf. vertically		800.00	
c. Perf. 11.2		.35	.25
P# block of 12, 6#		20.00	

Perforations do not run through the sheet margin on about 10 percent of the sheets of No. 1711.

BUTTERFLY ISSUE

Nos. 1712-1713 alternate in 1st row, Nos. 1714-1715 in 2nd row. This arrangement is repeated throughout the pane. Butterflies represent different geographic US areas.

Swallowtail A1101

Checkerspot A1102

Dogface A1103

Orange-Tip A1104

Designed by Stanley Galli.

PHOTOGRAVURE (Andreotti)
Plates of 200 subjects in four panes of 50.

1977, June 6	Tagged	Perf. 11	
1712 A1101 13c **tan & multicolored**		.25	.20
1713 A1102 13c **tan & multicolored**		.25	.20
1714 A1103 13c **tan & multicolored**		.25	.20
1715 A1104 13c **tan & multicolored**		.25	.20
a. Block of 4, #1712-1715		1.00	1.00
P# block of 12, 6#		3.25	—
P# block of 20, 6#, Mr. Zip			
and slogans		5.50	—
Margin block of 4, Mr. Zip			
and "Use Zip Code"		1.05	—
b. As "a," imperf. horiz.		15,000.	

AMERICAN BICENTENNIAL ISSUES
Marquis de Lafayette

200th anniversary of Lafayette's Landing on the coast of South Carolina, north of Charleston.

Marquis de Lafayette — A1105

Designed by Bradbury Thompson.

GIORI PRESS PRINTING
Plates of 160 subjects in four panes of 40.

1977, June 13	Tagged	Perf. 11	
1716 A1105 13c **blue, black & red**		.25	.20
P# block of 4		1.10	—
Margin block of 4, Mr. Zip and			
"Use Zip Code"		1.00	—
a. Red missing (PS)		—	

Skilled Hands for Independence

Nos. 1717-1718 alternate in 1st row, Nos. 1719-1720 in 2nd row. This arrangement is repeated throughout the pane.

Seamstress A1106

Blacksmith A1107

Wheelwright A1108

Leatherworker A1109

Designed by Leonard Everett Fisher.

PHOTOGRAVURE (Andreotti)
Plates of 200 subjects in four panes of 50.

1977, July 4	Tagged	Perf. 11	
1717 A1106 13c **multicolored**		.25	.20
1718 A1107 13c **multicolored**		.25	.20
1719 A1108 13c **multicolored**		.25	.20
1720 A1109 13c **multicolored**		.25	.20
a. Block of 4, #1717-1720		1.00	1.00
P# block of 12, 6#		3.25	
P# block of 20, 6#, Mr. Zip and			
slogans		5.50	—
Margin block of 4, Mr. Zip and			
"Use Zip Code"		1.05	—

PEACE BRIDGE ISSUE

50th anniversary of the Peace Bridge, connecting Buffalo (Fort Porter), N.Y. and Fort Erie, Ontario.

Peace Bridge and Dove — A1110

Designed by Bernard Brussel-Smith (wood-cut).

ENGRAVED
Plates of 200 subjects in four panes of 50.

1977, Aug. 4	Tagged	Perf. 11x10½	
1721 A1110 13c **blue**		.25	.20
P# block of 4		1.10	—
Margin block of 4, Mr. Zip and			
"Use Zip Code"		1.00	—

AMERICAN BICENTENNIAL ISSUE
Battle of Oriskany

200th anniv. of the Battle of Oriskany, American Militia led by Brig. Gen. Nicholas Herkimer (1728-77).

Herkimer at
Oriskany, by
Frederick
Yohn
A1111

Designed by Bradbury Thompson after painting in Utica, N.Y.
Public Library.

PHOTOGRAVURE (Andreotti)
Plates of 160 subjects in four panes of 40.

1977, Aug. 6		Tagged	Perf. 11	
1722	A1111	13c **multicolored**	.25	.20
		P# block of 10, 5#	2.75	—
		Margin block of 6, Mr. Zip and		
		"Use Zip Code" and "Mail Early		
		in the Day"	1.50	—

ENERGY ISSUE
Conservation and development of nation}s energy
resources. Nos. 1723-1724 se-tenant vertically.

"Conservation"
A1112

"Development"
A1113

Designed by Terrance W. McCaffrey.

PHOTOGRAVURE (Andreotti)
Plates of 160 subjects in four panes of 40.

1977, Oct. 20		Tagged	Perf. 11	
1723	A1112	13c **multicolored**	.25	.20
1724	A1113	13c **multicolored**	.25	.20
a.		Pair, #1723-1724	.50	.50
		P# block of 12, 6#	3.25	—
		Margin block of 4, Mr. Zip, "Use		
		Zip Code" and "Mail Early in the		
		Day"	1.00	—

ALTA CALIFORNIA ISSUE
Founding of El Pueblo de San José de Guadalupe,
first civil settlement in Alta California, 200th
anniversary.

Farm Houses
A1114

Designed by Earl Thollander.

LITHOGRAPHED, ENGRAVED (Giori)
Plates of 200 subjects in four panes of 50.

1977, Sept. 9		Tagged	Perf. 11	
1725	A1114	13c **black & multicolored**	.25	.20
		P# block of 4	1.10	—
		Margin block of 4, Mr. Zip and		
		"Use Zip Code"	1.00	—
a.		Tagging omitted		—

AMERICAN BICENTENNIAL ISSUE
Articles of Confederation
200th anniversary of drafting the Articles of Confederation, York Town, Pa.

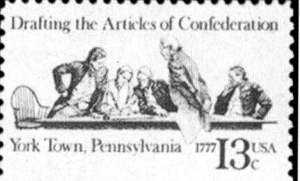

Members of
Continental
Congress in
Conference
A1115

Designed by David Blossom.

ENGRAVED (Giori)
Plates of 200 subjects in four panes of 50.

1977, Sept. 30		Tagged	Perf. 11	
1726	A1115	13c **red & brown**, *cream*	.25	.20
		P# block of 4	1.10	—
		Margin block of 4, Mr. Zip		
		and "Use Zip Code"	1.00	—
a.		Tagging omitted		—
b.		Red omitted	600.00	
c.		Red & brown omitted	400.00	

No. 1726b also has most of the brown omitted. No. 1726c
must be collected as a transition multiple, certainly with No.
1726b and preferably also with No. 1726.

TALKING PICTURES, 50th ANNIV.

Movie
Projector and
Phonograph
A1116

Designed by Walter Einsel.

LITHOGRAPHED, ENGRAVED (Giori)
Plates of 200 subjects in four panes of 50.

1977, Oct. 6		Tagged	Perf. 11	
1727	A1116	13c **multicolored**	.25	.20
		P# block of 4	1.10	—
		Margin block of 4, Mr. Zip and		
		"Use Zip Code"	1.00	—

AMERICAN BICENTENNIAL ISSUE
Surrender at Saratoga
200th anniversary of Gen. John Burgoyne's surrender at Saratoga.

Surrender of
Burgoyne, by
John Trumbull
A1117

Designed by Bradbury Thompson.

PHOTOGRAVURE (Andreotti)
Plates of 160 subjects in four panes of 40.

1977, Oct. 7		Tagged	Perf. 11	
1728	A1117	13c **multicolored**	.25	.20
		P# block of 10, 5#	2.75	—
		Margin block of 6, Mr. Zip, "Use		
		Zip Code" and "Mail Early in the		
		Day"	1.50	—

CHRISTMAS ISSUE

Washington at
Valley
Forge — A1118

Rural
Mailbox — A1119

Designers: No. 1729, Stevan Dohanos, after painting by J. C.
Leyendecker. No. 1730, Dolli Tingle.

PHOTOGRAVURE (Combination Press)
Plates of 460 subjects (20x23) in panes of 100
(10x10).

1977, Oct. 21		Tagged	Perf. 1	
1729	A1118	13c **multicolored**	.25	.2(
		P# block of 20, 5-8#	5.75	
a.		Imperf., pair	70.00	

See Combination Press note after No. 1703.

PHOTOGRAVURE (Andreotti)
Plates of 400 subjects in 4 panes of 100.

1730	A1119	13c **multicolored**	.25	.2(
		P# block of 10, 5#	2.75	
		Margin block of 4, Mr. Zip and		
		"Use Zip Code"	1.00	—
		Pair with full vert. gutter btwn.		—
a.		Imperf., pair	250.00	

CARL SANDBURG ISSUE
Carl Sandburg (1878-1967), poet, biographer and
collector of American folk songs, birth centenary.

Carl Sandburg, by William
A. Smith, 1952 — A1120

Designed by William A. Smith.

GIORI PRESS PRINTING
Plates of 200 subjects in four panes of 50.

1978, Jan. 6		Tagged	Perf. 11	
1731	A1120	13c **black & brown**	.25	.20
		P# block of 4	1.25	—
		Margin block of 4, Mr. Zip	1.05	—
a.		Brown omitted	2,250.	
b.		Tagging omitted		

CAPTAIN COOK ISSUE
Capt. James Cook, 200th anniversary of his arrival
in Hawaii, at Waimea, Kauai, Jan. 20, 1778, and of
his anchorage in Cook Inlet, near Anchorage, Alaska,
June 1, 1778. Nos. 1732-1733 printed in panes of 50,
containing 25 each of Nos. 1732-1733 including 5 No.
1732a.

Capt. Cook, by Nathaniel
Dance — A1121

"Resolution"
and
"Discovery," by
John Webber
A1122

Designed by Robert F. Szabo (No. 1732; Jak Katalan (No.
1733.

GIORI PRESS PRINTING
Plates of 200 subjects in four panes of 50.

1978, Jan. 20		Tagged	Perf. 11	
1732	A1121	13c **dark blue**	.25	.20
1733	A1122	13c **green**	.25	.20
a.		Vert. pair, imperf. horiz.		
b.		Pair, #1732-1733	.50	.50
		P# block of 4, #1732 or 1733	1.10	
		Margin block of 4, Mr. Zip,		
		#1732 or 1733	1.05	—

	P# block of 20, 10 each #1732-1733, P# and slogans	5.25	—
c.	As "b," imperf. between	4,250.	—
d.	As "b," tagging omitted		—

Indian Head Penny, 1877 — A1123

Eagle — A1124

Red Masterpiece and Medallion Roses — A1126

ENGRAVED (Giori)
Plates of 600 subjects in four panes of 150.

1978	Tagged	Perf. 11	
1734	A1123 13c **brown & blue green**, *bister, Jan. 11, 1978*	.25	.20
	P# block of 4	1.25	—
	Margin block of 4, "Use Correct Zip Code"	1.00	—
	Vert. pair with full horiz. gutter between		—
a.	Horiz. pair, imperf. vert.	275.00	
b.	Tagging omitted		—

PHOTOGRAVURE (Andreotti)
Plates of 400 subjects in four panes of 100.

1735	A1124 (15c) **orange**, *May 22, 1978*	.30	.20
	P# block of 4	1.40	—
	Margin block of 4, "Use Zip Code"	1.25	—
	Vert. pair with full horiz. gutter between		—
a.	Imperf., pair	90.00	
b.	Vert. pair, imperf. horiz.	650.00	
c.	Perf. 11.2	.35	.20
	P# block of 4	1.80	—
	Zip block of 4	1.50	—

BOOKLET STAMPS
ENGRAVED
Perf. 11x10½ on 2 or 3 sides

1736	A1124 (15c) **orange**	.30	.20
a.	Booklet pane of 8, *May 22, 1978*	2.50	1.50
b.	As "a," tagging omitted		—
c.	Vert. pair, imperf between	900.00	

Perf. 10

1737	A1126 15c **multicolored**	.30	.20
a.	Booklet pane of 8, *July 11, 1978*	2.50	1.50
b.	Imperf, pair	500.00	
c.	As "a," imperf	2,300.	
d.	As "a," tagging omitted	50.00	

A1127   A1128   A1129

A1130   A1131

Designed by Ronald Sharpe.

BOOKLET STAMPS
ENGRAVED

1980, Feb. 7	Tagged	Perf. 11 on 2 or 3 sides	
1738	A1127 15c **sepia**, *yellow*	.30	.20
1739	A1128 15c **sepia**, *yellow*	.30	.20
1740	A1129 15c **sepia**, *yellow*	.30	.20
1741	A1130 15c **sepia**, *yellow*	.30	.20

1742	A1131 15c **sepia**, *yellow*	.30	.20
a.	Booklet pane of 10, 2 each #1738-1742	3.50	3.00
b.	Strip of 5, #1738-1742	1.50	1.40

COIL STAMP

1978, May 22		Perf. 10 Vert.	
1743	A1124 (15c) **orange**	.30	.20
	Pair	.60	.20
	Joint line pair	.75	
a.	Imperf., pair	85.00	
	Joint line pair		—

No. 1743a is valued in the grade of fine.

BLACK HERITAGE SERIES
Harriet Tubman (1820-1913), born a slave, helped more than 300 slaves escape to freedom.

Harriet Tubman and Cart Carrying Slaves — A1133

Designed by Jerry Pinkney after photograph.

PHOTOGRAVURE (Andreotti)
Plates of 200 subjects in four panes of 50.

1978, Feb. 1	Tagged	Perf. 10½x11	
1744	A1133 13c **multicolored**	.25	.20
	P# block of 12, 6#	3.25	—
	Margin block of 4, Mr. Zip	1.00	—

AMERICAN FOLK ART SERIES
Quilts
Nos. 1745-1746 alternate in 1st row, Nos. 1747-1748 in 2nd.

Basket Design

A1134   A1135

A1136   A1137

Designed by Christopher Pullman after 1875 quilt made in New York City. Illustration reduced.

PHOTOGRAVURE (Andreotti)
Plates of 192 subjects in four panes of 48 (6x8).

1978, Mar. 8		Perf. 11	
1745	A1134 13c **multicolored**	.25	.20
1746	A1135 13c **multicolored**	.25	.20
1747	A1136 13c **multicolored**	.25	.20
1748	A1137 13c **multicolored**	.25	.20
a.	Block of 4, #1745-1748	1.00	1.00
	P# block of 12, 6#	3.25	—
	P# block of 16, 6#, Mr. Zip and copyright	4.50	—
	Margin block of 4, Mr. Zip, copyright	1.05	—

AMERICAN DANCE ISSUE
Nos. 1749-1750 alternate in 1st row, Nos. 1751-1752 in 2nd.

Ballet A1138

Theater A1139

Folk Dance A1140

Modern Dance A1141

Designed by John Hill.

PHOTOGRAVURE (Andreotti)
Plates of 192 subjects in four panes of 48 (6x8).

1978, Apr. 26	Tagged	Perf. 11	
1749	A1138 13c **multicolored**	.25	.20
1750	A1139 13c **multicolored**	.25	.20
1751	A1140 13c **multicolored**	.25	.20
1752	A1141 13c **multicolored**	.25	.20
a.	Block of 4, #1749-1752	1.00	1.00
	P# block of 12, 6#	3.25	—
	P# block of 16, 6#, Mr. Zip and copyright	4.50	—
	Margin block of 4, Mr. Zip, copyright	1.05	—

AMERICAN BICENTENNIAL ISSUE
French Alliance, signed in Paris, Feb. 6, 1778 and ratified by Continental Congress, May 4, 1778.

King Louis XVI and
Benjamin Franklin, by
Charles Gabriel
Sauvage — A1142

Designed by Bradbury Thompson after 1785 porcelain sculpture in Du Pont Winterthur Museum, Delaware.

GIORI PRESS PRINTING
Plates of 160 subjects in four panes of 40.

1978, May 4	Tagged	Perf. 11	
1753 A1142 13c blue, black & red		.25	.20
P# block of 4		1.10	—
Margin block of 4, Mr. Zip		1.00	—
a. Red missing (PS)			

EARLY CANCER DETECTION ISSUE

George Papanicolaou, M.D. (1883-1962), cytologist and developer of Pap Test, early cancer detection in women.

Dr. Papanicolaou and
Microscope — A1143

Designed by Paul Calle.

ENGRAVED
Plates of 200 subjects in four panes of 50.

1978, May 18	Tagged	Perf. 10½x11	
1754 A1143 13c brown		.25	.20
P# block of 4		1.10	—
Margin block of 4, Mr. Zip		1.00	—

PERFORMING ARTS SERIES

Jimmie Rodgers (1897-1933), the "Singing Brakeman, Father of Country Music" (No. 1755); George M. Cohan (1878-1942), actor and playwright (No. 1756).

Jimmie Rodgers with
Guitar and Brakeman's
Cap,
Locomotive — A1144

George M. Cohan,
"Yankee Doodle Dandy"
and Stars — A1145

Designed by Jim Sharpe.

PHOTOGRAVURE (Andreotti)
Plates of 200 subjects in four panes of 50.

1978	Tagged	Perf. 11	
1755 A1144 13c multicolored, May 24		.25	.20
P# block of 12, 6#		4.00	—
Margin block of 4, Mr. Zip		1.25	—
1756 A1145 15c multicolored, July 3		.30	.20
P# block of 12, 6#		4.00	—
Margin block of 4, Mr. Zip		1.25	—

CAPEX ISSUE

CAPEX '78, Canadian International Philatelic Exhibition, Toronto, Ont., June 9-18.

Wildlife from Canadian-United States
Border — A1146

Illustration reduced.

Designed by Stanley Galli.

LITHOGRAPHED, ENGRAVED (Giori)
Plates of 24 subjects in four panes of 6 each.

1978, June 10	Tagged	Perf. 11	
1757 A1146 Block of 8, multicolored		2.00	1.75
a. 13c Cardinal		.25	.20
b. 13c Mallard		.25	.20
c. 13c Canada goose		.25	.20
d. 13c Blue jay		.25	.20
e. 13c Moose		.25	.20
f. 13c Chipmunk		.25	.20
g. 13c Red fox		.25	.20
h. 13c Raccoon		.25	.20
P# block of 8		2.25	—
Margin block of 8, Mr. Zip and copyright		2.10	—
Pane of 6 No. 1757, P#, Mr. Zip and copyright		13.00	—
i. As No. 1757, yellow, green, red, brown, blue, black (litho) omitted		7,000.	
j. Strip of 4 (a-d), imperf. vert.		5,000.	
k. Strip of 4 (e-h), imperf. vert.		3,250.	
l. As No. 1757, "d" and "h" with black (engr.) omitted		—	
m. As No. 1757, "b" with blue missing (PS)		—	

No. 1757k is worth more when contained in the sheet of 8. Value is for strip only.

PHOTOGRAPHY ISSUE

Photography's contribution to communications and understanding.

Camera, Lens, Color
Filters, Adapter Ring,
Studio Light Bulb and
Album — A1147

Designed by Ben Somoroff.

PHOTOGRAVURE (Andreotti)
Plates of 160 subjects in four panes of 40.

1978, June 26	Tagged	Perf. 11	
1758 A1147 15c multicolored		.30	.20
P# block of 12, 6#		4.00	—
Margin block of 4, Mr. Zip and copyright		1.25	—
P# block of 16, 6#, Mr. Zip and copyright		5.00	—

VIKING MISSIONS TO MARS ISSUE

Second anniv. of landing of Viking 1 on Mars.

Viking 1
Lander
Scooping up
Soil on
Mars — A1148

Designed by Robert McCall.

LITHOGRAPHED, ENGRAVED (Giori)
Plates of 200 subjects in four panes of 50.

1978, July 20	Tagged	Perf. 1	
1759 A1148 15c multicolored		.30	
P# block of 4		1.35	
Margin block of 4, Mr. Zip		1.25	
a. Tagging omitted		57.50	

AMERICAN OWLS ISSUE
Nos. 1760-1761 alternate in one horizontal rov
Nos. 1762-1763 in the next.

Great Gray
Owl — A1149

Saw-whet
Owl — A1150

Barred Owl — A1151

Great Horned
Owl — A1152

Designed by Frank J. Waslick.

LITHOGRAPHED, ENGRAVED (Giori)
Plates of 200 subjects in four panes of 50.

1978, Aug. 26	Tagged	Perf. 11	
1760 A1149 15c multicolored		.30	.20
1761 A1150 15c multicolored		.30	.20
1762 A1151 15c multicolored		.30	.20
1763 A1152 15c multicolored		.30	.20
a. Block of 4, #1760-1763		1.25	1.25
P# block of 4		1.40	—
Margin block of 4, Mr. Zip		1.25	—
b. As "a," tagging omitted			

AMERICAN TREES ISSUE
Nos. 1764-1765 alternate in 1st row, Nos. 1766-1767 in 2nd.

Giant Sequoia
A1153

White
Pine — A1154

White Oak — A1155

Gray Birch — A1156

Designed by Walter D. Richards.

PHOTOGRAVURE (Andreotti)
Plates of 160 subjects in four panes of 40.

1978, Oct. 9   **Tagged**   *Perf. 11*

1764	A1153	15c	multicolored	.30 .20
1765	A1154	15c	multicolored	.30 .20
1766	A1155	15c	multicolored	.30 .20
1767	A1156	15c	multicolored	.30 .20
a.			Block of 4, #1764-1767	1.25 1.25
			P# block of 12, 6#	4.00
			P# block of 16, 6#, Mr. Zip and copyright	5.25
			Margin block of 4, Mr. Zip, copyright	1.30 —
b.			As "a," imperf. horiz.	17,500.

No. 1767b is unique.

CHRISTMAS ISSUE

Madonna and Child with Cherubim, by Andrea della Robbia — A1157

Child on Hobby Horse and Christmas Trees — A1158

Designed by Bradbury Thompson (No. 1768) after terra cotta sculpture in National Gallery, Washington, D.C. by Dolli Tingle (No. 1769).

PHOTOGRAVURE (Andreotti)
Plates of 400 subjects in four panes of 100.

1978, Oct. 18   *Perf. 11*

1768	A1157	15c	blue & multicolored	.30 .20
			P# block of 12, 6#	4.00
			Margin block of 4, "Use Correct Zip Code"	1.25 —
a.			Imperf., pair	90.00

Value for No. 1768a is for an uncreased pair.

1769	A1158	15c	red & multicolored	.30 .20
			P# block of 12, 6#	4.00
			Margin block of 4, "Use Correct Zip Code"	1.25 —
			Pair with full horiz. gutter btwn.	—
a.			Imperf., pair	90.00
b.			Vert. pair, imperf. horiz.	1,700.

Robert F. Kennedy — A1159

Martin Luther King, Jr. and Civil Rights Marchers — A1160

ROBERT F. KENNEDY ISSUE

Designed by Bradbury Thompson after photograph by Stanley Tretick.

ENGRAVED
Plates of 192 subjects in four panes of 48 (8x6).

1979, Jan. 12   **Tagged**   *Perf. 11*

1770	A1159	15c	blue	.35 .20
			P# block of 4	1.75 —
			Margin block of 4, Mr. Zip	1.50 —
a.			Tagging omitted	50.00

BLACK HERITAGE SERIES

Dr. Martin Luther King, Jr. (1929-1968), Civil Rights leader.

Designed by Jerry Pinkney.

PHOTOGRAVURE (Andreotti)
Plates of 200 subjects in four panes of 50.

1979, Jan. 13   **Tagged**   *Perf. 11*

1771	A1160	15c	multicolored	.40 .20
			P# block of 12, 6#	5.75
			Margin block of 4, Mr. Zip	1.75 —
a.			Imperf., pair	1,500.

INTERNATIONAL YEAR OF THE CHILD ISSUE

Children of Different Races — A1161

Designed by Paul Calle.

ENGRAVED
Plates of 200 subjects in four panes of 50.

1979, Feb. 15   **Tagged**   *Perf. 11*

1772	A1161	15c	orange red	.30 .20
			P# block of 4	1.40 —
			Margin block of 4, Mr. Zip	1.25 —

John Steinbeck (1902-1968), Novelist — A1162

Albert Einstein (1879-1955), Theoretical Physicist — A1163

LITERARY ARTS SERIES

Designed by Bradbury Thompson after photograph by Philippe Halsman.

ENGRAVED
Plates of 200 subjects in four panes of 50.

1979, Feb. 27   **Tagged**   *Perf. 10½x11*

1773	A1162	15c	dark blue	.30 .20
			P# block of 4	1.40 —
			Margin block of 4, Mr. Zip	1.25 —

ALBERT EINSTEIN ISSUE

Designed by Bradbury Thompson after photograph by Hermann Landshoff.

ENGRAVED
Plates of 200 subjects in four panes of 50.

1979, Mar. 4   **Tagged**   *Perf. 10½x11*

1774	A1163	15c	chocolate	.35 .20
			P# block of 4	1.75 —
			Margin block of 4, Mr. Zip	1.50 —
			Pair, horiz. gutter btwn.	

AMERICAN FOLK ART SERIES
Pennsylvania Toleware, c. 1800

Coffeepot — A1164

Tea Caddy — A1165

Sugar Bowl — A1166

Coffeepot — A1167

Designed by Bradbury Thompson.

PHOTOGRAVURE (Andreotti)
Plates of 160 subjects in four panes of 40.

1979, Apr. 19   **Tagged**   *Perf. 11*

1775	A1164	15c	multicolored	.30 .20
1776	A1165	15c	multicolored	.30 .20
1777	A1166	15c	multicolored	.30 .20
1778	A1167	15c	multicolored	.30 .20
a.			Block of 4, #1775-1778	1.25 1.25
			P# block of 10, 5#	3.25
			P# block of 16, 5#; Mr. Zip and copyright	5.25
			Margin block of 6, Mr. Zip and copyright	2.00 —
b.			As "a," imperf. horiz.	4,000.

AMERICAN ARCHITECTURE SERIES

Nos. 1779-1780 alternate in 1st row, Nos. 1781-1782 in 2nd.

Virginia Rotunda, by Thomas Jefferson — A1168

Baltimore Cathedral, by Benjamin Latrobe — A1169

Boston State House, by Charles Bulfinch — A1170

Philadelphia Exchange, by William Strickland — A1171

Designed by Walter D. Richards.

ENGRAVED (Giori)

Plates of 192 subjects in four panes of 48 (6x8).

1979, June 4			Tagged	Perf. 11	
1779	A1168	15c	black & brick red	.30	.20
1780	A1169	15c	black & brick red	.30	.20
1781	A1170	15c	black & brick red	.30	.20
1782	A1171	15c	black & brick red	.30	.20
a.	Block of 4, #1779-1782			1.25	1.25
	P# block of 4			1.45	—
	Margin block of 4, Mr. Zip			1.30	—
b.	As "a," tagging omitted			—	

ENDANGERED FLORA ISSUE

Nos. 1783-1784 alternate in one horizontal row. Nos. 1785-1786 in the next.

Persistent Trillium — A1172

Hawaiian Wild Broadbean — A1173

Contra Cocta Wallflower — A1174

Antioch Dunes Evening Primrose — A1175

Designed by Frank J. Waslick.

PHOTOGRAVURE (Andreotti)

Plates of 200 subjects in four panes of 50.

1979, June 7			Tagged	Perf. 11	
1783	A1172	15c	multicolored	.30	.20
1784	A1173	15c	multicolored	.30	.20
1785	A1174	15c	multicolored	.30	.20
1786	A1175	15c	multicolored	.30	.20
a.	Block of 4, #1783-1786			1.25	1.25
	P# block of 12, 6#			4.00	
	P# block of 20, 6#, Mr. Zip and copyright			6.50	—
	Margin block of 4, Mr. Zip			1.30	—
	As "a," full vert. gutter btwn.				
b.	As "a," imperf.			300.00	

SEEING EYE DOGS ISSUE

1st guide dog program in the US, 50th anniv.

German Shepherd Leading Man — A1176

Designed by Joseph Csatari.

PHOTOGRAVURE (Combination Press)

Plates of 230 (10x23) subjects in panes of 50 (10x5).

1979, June 15			Tagged	Perf. 11	
1787	A1176	15c	multicolored	.30	.20
	P# block of 20, 5-8#, 1-2 copyright			6.50	—
a.	Imperf., pair			425.00	
b.	Tagging omitted			12.00	

See Combination Press note after No. 1703.

Child Holding Winner's Medal — A1177

John Paul Jones, by Charles Willson Peale — A1178

SPECIAL OLYMPICS ISSUE

Special Olympics for special children, Brockport, N.Y., Aug. 8-13.

Designed by Jeff Cornell.

PHOTOGRAVURE (Andreotti)

Plates of 200 subjects in four panes of 50.

1979, Aug. 9			Tagged	Perf. 11	
1788	A1177	15c	multicolored	.30	.20
	P# block of 10, 5#			3.25	—
	Zip block of 4			1.25	—

JOHN PAUL JONES ISSUE

John Paul Jones (1747-1792), Naval Commander American Revolution.

Designed after painting in Independence National Historic Park, Philadelphia.

Printed by American Bank Note Co. and J. W. Fergusson and Sons.

Designed by Bradbury Thompson.

PHOTOGRAVURE (Champlain)

Plates of 200 subjects in four panes of 50.

1979, Sept. 23			Tagged	Perf. 11x1	
1789	A1178	15c	multicolored	.30	.2
	P# block of 10, 5#			3.25	-
	Zip block of 4			1.25	-
c.	Vert. pair, imperf. horiz.			175.00	

Numerous varieties of printer's waste exist. These include imperforates, perforated or imperforate gutter pairs or blocks and shifted or missing colors.

			Perf. 11		
1789A	A1178	15c	multicolored	.55	.2
	P# block of 10, 5#			4.00	-
	Zip block of 4			3.25	-
d.	Vertical pair, imperf. horiz.			140.00	
			Perf. 12		
1789B	A1178	15c	multicolored	3,500.	3,500
	P# block of 10, 5#			40,000.	
	Zip block of 4			15,000.	-

OLYMPIC GAMES ISSUE

22nd Summer Olympic Games, Moscow, July 19 Aug. 3, 1980. Nos. 1791-1792 alternate in one horizontal row, Nos. 1793-1794 in next.

Javelin — A1179

Running A1180

Swimming A1181

Rowing A1182

Equestrian A1183

Designed by Robert M. Cunningham.

PHOTOGRAVURE
Plates of 200 subjects in four panes of 50.

1979, Sept. 5   **Tagged**   *Perf. 11*
790 A1179 10c **multicolored**   .20   .20
    P# block of 12, 6#   3.00 —
    Zip block of 4   .85

1979, Sept. 28
791 A1180 15c **multicolored**   .30   .20
792 A1181 15c **multicolored**   .30   .20
793 A1182 15c **multicolored**   .30   .20
794 A1183 15c **multicolored**   .30   .20
   a.   Block of 4, #1791-1794   1.25   1.25
    P# block of 12, 6#   4.00
    Zip block of 4   1.30
    P# block of 20, 6#, zip, copyright   6.50
   b.   As "a," imperf.   1,500.

OLYMPIC GAMES ISSUE
13th Winter Olympic Games, Lake Placid, N.Y., Feb. 12-24. Nos. 1795-1796 alternate in one horizontal row, Nos. 1797-1798 in next.

Speed Skating A1184

Downhill Skiing A1185

Ski Jump — A1186

Ice Hockey A1187

Designed by Robert M. Cunningham.

PHOTOGRAVURE
Plates of 200 subject in four panes of 50.

1980, Feb. 1   **Tagged**   *Perf. 11¼x10½*
1795 A1184 15c **multicolored**   .35   .20
1796 A1185 15c **multicolored**   .35   .20
1797 A1186 15c **multicolored**   .35   .20
1798 A1187 15c **multicolored**   .35   .20
   b.   Block of 4, #1795-1798   1.50   1.40
    P# block of 12, 6#   4.50
    Zip block of 4   1.55
    P# block of 20, 6#, zip and copyright   7.50

Perf. 11
1795A A1184 15c **multicolored**   1.10   .60
1796A A1185 15c **multicolored**   1.10   .60
1797A A1186 15c **multicolored**   1.10   .60
1798A A1187 15c **multicolored**   1.10   .60
   c.   Block of 4, #1795A-1798A   4.50   3.50
    P# block of 12, 6#   15.00
    Zip block of 4   4.75
    P# block of 20, 6#, zip and copyright   27.50

CHRISTMAS ISSUE

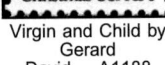
Virgin and Child by Gerard David — A1188

Santa Claus, Christmas Tree Ornament — A1189

Designed by Bradbury Thompson (No. 1799) and by Eskil Ohlsson (No. 1800).

No. 1799 is designed after a painting in National Gallery of Art, Washington, D.C.

PHOTOGRAVURE (Andreotti)
Plates of 400 subjects in four panes of 100.

1979, Oct. 18   **Tagged**   *Perf. 11*
1799 A1188 15c **multicolored**   .30   .20
    P# block of 12, 6#   4.00
    Zip block of 4   1.25
    P# block of 20, 6#, zip, copyright   6.50
   a.   Imperf., pair   90.00
   b.   Vert. pair, imperf. horiz.   650.00
   c.   Vert. pair, imperf. between   1,200.
   d.   Tagging omitted
1800 A1189 15c **multicolored**   .30   .20
    P# block of 12, 6#   4.00
    Zip block of 4   1.25
    P# block of 20, 6#, zip, copyright   6.50
   a.   Green & yellow omitted   550.00
   b.   Green, yellow & tan omitted   550.00
   c.   Vert. se-tenant pair, #1800a & 1800b   1,500.

Nos. 1800a and 1800b always have the remaining colors misaligned.
Nos. 1800a, 1800b and 1800c are valued in the grade of fine.

VALUES FOR HINGED STAMPS AFTER NO. 771
This catalogue does not value unused stamps after No. 771 in hinged condition. Hinged unused stamps from No. 772 to the present are worth considerably less than the values given for unused stamps, which are for never-hinged examples.

PERFORMING ARTS SERIES
Will Rogers (1879-1935), actor and humorist.

Will Rogers — A1190

Designed by Jim Sharpe.

PHOTOGRAVURE (Andreotti)
Plates of 200 subjects in four panes of 50.

1979, Nov. 4   **Tagged**   *Perf. 11*
1801 A1190 15c **multicolored**   .30   .20
    P# block of 12, 6#   4.00
    Zip block of 4   1.25
    P# block of 20, 6#, zip, copyright   6.50
   a.   Imperf., pair   200.00

VIETNAM VETERANS ISSUE
A tribute to veterans of the Vietnam War.

Ribbon for Vietnam Service Medal A1191

Designed by Stevan Dohanos.

PHOTOGRAVURE (Andreotti)
Plates of 200 subjects in four panes of 50.

1979, Nov. 11   **Tagged**   *Perf. 11*
1802 A1191 15c **multicolored**   .30   .20
    P# block of 10, 5#   3.25
    Zip block of 4   1.25

W.C. Fields — A1192

Benjamin Banneker — A1193

PERFORMING ARTS SERIES
W.C. Fields (1880-1946), actor and comedian.

Designed by Jim Sharpe.

PHOTOGRAVURE
Plates of 200 subjects in four panes of 50.

1980, Jan. 29   **Tagged**   *Perf. 11*
1803 A1192 15c **multicolored**   .30   .20
    P# block of 12, 6#   4.00
    Zip block of 4   1.25
    P# block of 20, 6#, zip, copyright   6.50
   a.   Imperf., pair

BLACK HERITAGE SERIES
Benjamin Banneker (1731-1806), astronomer and mathematician.

Designed by Jerry Pinkney.

Printed by American Bank Note Co. and J. W. Fergusson and Sons.

PHOTOGRAVURE
Plates of 200 subjects in four panes of 50.

1980, Feb. 15   **Tagged**   *Perf. 11*
1804 A1193 15c **multicolored**   .35   .20
    P# block of 12, 6#   4.50
    Zip block of 4   1.50
    Plate block of 20, 6#, zip, copyright   6.50
   a.   Horiz. pair, imperf. vert.   500.00

Imperfs, including gutter pairs and blocks, exist from printer's waste. These have been fraudulently perforated to simulate No. 1804a. Genuine examples of No. 1804a do not have colors misregistered.

NATIONAL LETTER WRITING WEEK ISSUE
National Letter Writing Week, Feb. 24-Mar. 1. Nos. 1805-1810 are printed vertically se-tenant.

Letters Preserve Memories — A1194

P.S. Write Soon — A1195

Letters Lift Spirits — A1196

Letters Shape Opinions — A1197

Designed by Randall McDougall.

Plates of 240 subjects in four panes of 60 (10x6) each.

PHOTOGRAVURE

1980, Feb. 25		Tagged	Perf. 11	
1805 A1194	15c	multicolored	.30	.20
1806 A1195	15c	purple & multi	.30	.20
1807 A1196	15c	multicolored	.30	.20
1808 A1195	15c	green & multi	.30	.20
1809 A1197	15c	multicolored	.30	.20
1810 A1195	15c	red & multi	.30	.20
a.		Vertical strip of 6, #1805-1810	1.85	2.00
		P# block of 36, 6#	13.00	—
		Zip block of 12	3.75	—
		Nos. 1805-1810 (6)	1.80	1.20

AMERICANA TYPE

Weaver Violins — A1199

Designer: 3.5c, George Mercer.

COIL STAMPS

1980-81		Engr.	Perf. 10 Vertically	
1811 A984	1c	dark blue, greenish, shiny gum, Mar. 6, 1980	.20	.20
		Pair	.20	.20
		Joint line pair	.40	—
		Dull gum	.20	
		Joint line pair	.50	
a.		Imperf., pair	175.00	
		Joint line pair	275.00	
b.		Tagging omitted	—	
1813 A1199	3.5c	purple, yellow, June 23, 1980	.20	.20
		Pair	.20	.20
		Joint line pair	1.00	—
a.		Untagged (Bureau precanceled, lines only)	.20	.20
		Pair	.35	.35
		Joint line pair	1.95	—
b.		Imperf., pair	175.00	
		Joint line pair	450.00	
1816 A997	12c	red brown, beige, Apr. 8, 1981	.25	.20
		Pair	.50	.20
		Joint line pair	1.50	—
a.		Untagged (Bureau precanceled), red brown, beige	1.15	1.15
		Pair	2.40	2.40
		Joint line pair	47.50	—
b.		Imperf., pair	175.00	
		Joint line pair	325.00	
c.		As "a," brownish red, reddish beige	1.65	1.65
		Pair	3.50	3.50
		Joint line pair	67.50	—
		Nos. 1811-1816 (3)	.65	.60

Bureau Precancels: No. 1816a, lines only, PRESORTED/FIRST CLASS; No. 1816c, PRESORTED/FIRST CLASS.

Eagle — A1207

PHOTOGRAVURE

Plates of 400 subjects in four panes of 100.

1981, Mar. 15		Tagged	Perf. 11x10½	
1818 A1207	(18c)	violet	.35	.20
		P# block of 4	1.60	—
		Zip block of 4	1.50	—
		Pair with full vert. gutter between		

BOOKLET STAMP
ENGRAVED
Perf. 10

1819 A1207	(18c)	violet	.40	.20
a.		Booklet pane of 8	3.75	2.25

COIL STAMP
Perf. 10 Vert.

1820 A1207	(18c)	violet	.40	.20
		Pair	.80	.20
		Joint line pair	1.60	—
a.		Imperf., pair	90.00	
		Joint line pair	160.00	

Frances Perkins A1208

Dolley Madison A1209

FRANCES PERKINS ISSUE

Frances Perkins (1882-1965), Secretary of Labor, 1933-1945 (first woman cabinet member).

Designed by F.R. Petrie.

ENGRAVED

Plates of 200 subjects in four panes of 50.

1980, Apr. 10		Tagged	Perf. 10½x11	
1821 A1208	15c	Prussian blue	.30	.20
		P# block of 4	1.30	—
		Zip block of 4	1.25	—

DOLLEY MADISON ISSUE

Dolley Madison (1768-1849), First Lady, 1809-1817.

Designed by Esther Porter.

ENGRAVED

Plates of 600 subjects in four panes of 150.

1980, May 20		Tagged	Perf. 11	
1822 A1209	15c	red brown & sepia	.30	.20
		P# block of 4	1.40	—
		Zip block of 4	1.25	—
a.		Red brown missing (PS)		

Emily Bissell — A1210

Helen Keller and Anne Sullivan — A1211

EMILY BISSELL ISSUE

Emily Bissell (1861-1948), social worker; introduced Christmas seals in United States.

Designed by Stevan Dohanos.

ENGRAVED

Plates of 200 subjects in four panes of 50.

1980, May 31		Tagged	Perf.	
1823 A1210	15c	black & red	.35	
		P# block of 4	1.75	
		Zip block of 4	1.50	
a.		Vert. pair, imperf. horiz.	375.00	
b.		All colors missing (EP)		
c.		Red missing (FO)		

HELEN KELLER ISSUE

Helen Keller (1880-1968), blind and deaf writer and lecturer taught by Anne Sullivan (1867-1936).

Designed by Paul Calle.

LITHOGRAPHED AND ENGRAVED

Plates of 200 subjects in four panes of 50.

1980, June 27		Tagged	Perf. 1	
1824 A1211	15c	multicolored	.30	.2
		P# block of 4	1.30	—
		Zip block of 4	1.25	—

Veterans Administration Emblem — A1212

Gen. Bernardo de Galvez — A1213

VETERANS ADMINISTRATION, 50th ANNIV.

Designed by Malcolm Grear.

Printed by American Bank Note Co. and J. W. Fergusson and Sons.

PHOTOGRAVURE

Plates of 200 subjects in four panes of 50.

1980, July 21		Tagged	Perf. 11	
1825 A1212	15c	carmine & violet blue	.30	.20
		P# block of 4, 2#	1.30	—
		Zip block of 4	1.25	—
a.		Horiz. pair, imperf. vert.	450.00	

BERNARDO DE GALVEZ ISSUE

Gen. Bernardo de Galvez (1746-1786), helped defeat British in Battle of Mobile, 1780.

Designed by Roy H. Andersen.

LITHOGRAPHED & ENGRAVED

Plates of 200 subjects in four panes of 50.

1980, July 23		Tagged	Perf. 11	
1826 A1213	15c	multicolored	.30	.20
		P# block of 4	1.30	—
		Zip block of 4	1.25	—
a.		Red, brown & blue (engr.) omitted	700.00	
b.		Blue, brown, red (engr.) & yellow (litho.) omitted	1,250.	

CORAL REEFS ISSUE

Nos. 1827-1828 alternate in one horizontal row, Nos. 1829-1830 in the next.

Brain Coral, Beaugregory Fish — A1214

Elkhorn Coral, Porkfish — A1215

Chalice Coral, Moorish Idol — A1216

Finger Coral, Sabertooth Blenny — A1217

Designed by Chuck Ripper.

PHOTOGRAVURE
Plates of 200 subjects in four panes of 50.

1980, Aug. 26	**Tagged**	**Perf. 11**	
1827 A1214 15c **multi**		.30	.20
1828 A1215 15c **multi**		.30	.20
1829 A1216 15c **multi**		.30	.20
1830 A1217 15c **multi**		.30	.20
	Cylinder flaw (period between "Finger coral" and "Hawaii" instead of colon) (39390 LR 48)	—	—
a.	Block of 4, #1827-1830	1.25	1.10
	P# block of 12, 6#	4.00	—
	Zip block of 4	1.30	—
b.	As "a," imperf.	500.00	
c.	As "a," vert. imperf. between	—	
d.	As "a," imperf. vert.	3,500.	

American Bald Eagle — A1218

Edith Wharton — A1219

ORGANIZED LABOR ISSUE
Designed by Peter Cocci.

PHOTOGRAVURE
Plates of 200 subjects in four panes of 50.

1980, Sept. 1	**Tagged**	**Perf. 11**	
1831 A1218 15c **multi**		.30	.20
	P# block of 12, 6#	3.50	—
	Zip block of 4	1.25	—
a.	Imperf., pair	325.00	

LITERARY ARTS SERIES
Edith Wharton (1862-1937), novelist.

Designed by Bradbury Thompson after 1905 photograph.

ENGRAVED
Plates of 200 subjects in four panes of 50.

1980, Sept. 5	**Tagged**	**Perf. 10½x11**	
1832 A1219 15c **purple**		.30	.20
	P# block of 4	1.30	—
	Zip block of 4	1.25	—

EDUCATION ISSUE

"Homage to the Square: Glow" by Josef Albers — A1220

Designed by Bradbury Thompson

Printed by American Bank Note Co. and J. W. Fergusson and Sons.

PHOTOGRAVURE
Plates of 200 subjects in four panes of 50.

1980, Sept. 12	**Tagged**	**Perf. 11**	
1833 A1220 15c **multi**		.30	.20
	P# block of 6, 3#	1.90	—
	Zip block of 4	1.25	—
a.	Horiz. pair, imperf. vert.	225.00	

AMERICAN FOLK ART SERIES
Pacific Northwest Indian Masks

Heiltsuk, Bella Bella Tribe — A1221

Chilkat Tlingit Tribe — A1222

Tlingit Tribe — A1223

Bella Coola Tribe — A1224

Designed by Bradury Thompson after photographs.

PHOTOGRAVURE
Plates of 160 subjects in four panes of 40.

1980, Sept. 25	**Tagged**	**Perf. 11**	
1834 A1221 15c **multi**		.35	.20
1835 A1222 15c **multi**		.35	.20
1836 A1223 15c **multi**		.35	.20
1837 A1224 15c **multi**		.35	.20
a.	Block of 4, #1834-1837	1.50	1.25
	P# block of 10, 5#	5.00	—
	Zip, copyright block of 6	2.25	—

AMERICAN ARCHITECTURE SERIES

Smithsonian A1225

Trinity Church A1226

Penn Academy A1227

Lyndhurst A1228

Designed by Walter D. Richards.

ENGRAVED (Giori)
Plates of 160 subjects in four panes of 40.

1980, Oct. 9	**Tagged**	**Perf. 11**	
1838 A1225 15c **black & red**		.30	.20
1839 A1226 15c **black & red**		.30	.20
1840 A1227 15c **black & red**		.30	.20
1841 A1228 15c **black & red**		.30	.20
a.	Block of 4, #1838-1841	1.25	1.25
	P# block of 4	1.50	—
	Zip block of 4	1.30	—
b.	As "a," red missing on Nos. 1838, 1839 (PS)	400.00	
c.	As "a," tagging omitted	—	

CHRISTMAS ISSUE

Madonna and Child — A1229

Wreath and Toys — A1230

Designed by Esther Porter (No. 1842) after Epiphany Window, Washington Cathedral, and by Bob Timberlake (No. 1843).

PHOTOGRAVURE
Plate of 200 subjects in four panes of 50.

1980, Oct. 31   Tagged   **Perf. 11**

1842	A1229 15c **multi**	.30	.20
	P# block of 12, 6#	4.00	—
	Zip block of 4	1.25	—
a.	Imperf., pair	60.00	
	Pair with full vert. gutter btwn.		

PHOTOGRAVURE (Combination Press)
Plates of 230 subjects (10x23) in panes of 50 (10x5).

1843	A1230 15c **multi**	.30	.20
	P# block of 20, 5-8 #, 1-2 copyright	6.50	—
a.	Imperf., pair	70.00	
b.	Buff omitted	25.00	
c.	Vert. pair, imperf. horiz.		
d.	Horiz. pair, imperf. between	4,000.	
e.	Tagging omitted		

No. 1843b is difficult to identify and should have a competent certificate.

See Combination Press note after No. 1703.

GREAT AMERICANS ISSUE

A1231

A1232

A1233

A1234

A1235

A1236

A1237

A1238

A1239

A1240

A1241

A1242

A1243

A1244

A1245

A1246

A1247

A1248

A1249

A1250

A1251

A1252

A1253

A1254

A1255

A1256

Designers: 1c, Bernie Fuchs. 2c, Burt Silverman, 3c, 17c, 40c, Ward Brackett. 4c, 7c, 10c, 18c, 30c, Richard Sparks. 5c, Paul Calle. 6c, No. 1861, Dennis Lyall. 8c, Arthur Lidov. 9c, 11c, Robert Alexander Anderson. 13c, Brad Holland. 14c, Bradbury Thompson. 19c, 39c, Roy H. Andersen. No. 1860, Jim Sharpe. No. 1862, 22c, 50c, 37c, Christopher Calle. 35c, Nathan Jones.

ENGRAVED

1980-85   Tagged   **Perf. 11x10½**
Perf. 11 (1c, 6c-11c, 14c, No. 1862, 22c, 30c, 39c, 40c, 50c)

1844	A1231 1c **black,** perf. 11.2, small block tagging, *Sept. 23, 1983*	.20	.20
	P# block of 6	.35	—

	P# block of 20, 1-2 #, 1-2 copyright	2.00	
a.	Imperf., pair	375.00	
b.	Vert. pair, imperf. btwn. and at bottom	2,000.	
c.	Perf. 10.9, small block tagging	.20	
	P# block of 6	.35	
	P# block of 20, 1-2 #, 1-2 copyright	2.00	
d.	Perf. 10.9, large block tagging, *1985*	.20	
	P# block of 6	.35	
	P# block of 20, 1-2 #, 1-2 copyright	2.00	
e.	Vert. pair, imperf. horiz.		
1845	A1232 2c **brn blk,** overall tagging, *Nov. 18, 1982*	.20	.2
	P# block of 4	.35	
	Zip block of 4	.25	
	Vert. pair, full gutter between	—	
a.	Tagging omitted		
1846	A1233 3c **olive green,** overall tagging, *July 13, 1983*	.20	.2
	P# block of 4	.55	—
	Zip block of 4	.30	—
a.	Tagging omitted	7.00	
1847	A1234 4c **violet,** overall tagging, *June 3, 1983*	.20	.2
	P# block of 4	.65	—
	Zip block of 4	.35	—
a.	Tagging omitted	5.00	
1848	A1235 5c **henna brown,** overall tagging, *June 25, 1983*	.20	.2
	P# block of 4	.70	—
	Zip block of 4	.45	—
1849	A1236 6c **orange vermilion,** large block tagging, *Sept. 19, 1985*	.20	.2
	P# block of 6	.85	—
	P# block of 20, 1-2 #, 1-2 zip, 1-2 copyright	5.00	—
a.	Vert. pair, imperf. between and at bottom	2,000.	
1850	A1237 7c **bright carmine,** small block tagging, *Jan. 25, 1985*	.20	.2C
	P# block of 6	.95	—
	P# block of 20, 1-2 #, 1-2 zip, 1-2 copyright	4.00	—
1851	A1238 8c **olive black,** overall tagging, *July 25, 1985*	.20	.20
	P# block of 4	.85	—
	Zip block of 4	.60	—
a.	Tagging omitted		
1852	A1239 9c **dark green,** small block tagging, *June 7, 1985*	.20	.20
	P# block of 4	1.30	—
	P# block of 20, 1-2 #. 1-2 zip, 1-2 copyright	5.00	—
1853	A1240 10c **Prus. blue,** small block tagging, *May 31, 1984*	.25	.20
	P# block of 6	2.00	—
	P# block of 20, 1-2 #, 1-2 copyright, 1-2 zip	9.00	—
a.	Large block tagging	.30	.20
	P# block of 6	2.25	—
	P# block of 20, 1-2 #, 1-2 copyright, 1-2 zip	9.00	—
b.	Vert. pair, imperf. between	850.00	
c.	Horiz. pair, imperf. between	2,000.	
d.	Vert. pair, imperf horiz.	—	

Completely imperforate tagged or untagged stamps are from printer's waste.

1854	A1241 11c **dark blue,** overall tagging, *Feb. 12, 1985*	.40	.20
	P# block of 4	2.00	—
	Zip block of 4	1.60	—
a.	Tagging omitted	25.00	
1855	A1242 13c **light maroon,** overall tagging, *Jan. 15, 1982*	.40	.20
	P# block of 4	2.25	—
	Zip block of 4	1.60	—
a.	Tagging omitted	7.50	
1856	A1243 14c **slate green,** small block tagging, *Mar. 21, 1985*	.30	.20
	P# block of 6	2.25	—
	P# block of 20, 1-2 #, 1-2 zip, 1-2 copyright	9.00	—
a.	Large block tagging	.30	.20
	P# block of 6	2.25	—
	P# block of 20, 1-2 #, 1-2 zip, 1-2 copyright	9.00	—
b.	Vert. pair, imperf. horiz.	120.00	
c.	Horiz. pair, imperf. between	9.00	
d.	Vert. pair, imperf. between	1,750.	
e.	All color omitted	—	

No. 1856e comes from a partially printed pane and should be collected as a vertical strip of 10, one stamp normal, one stamp transitional and 8 stamps with color omitted.

1857	A1244 17c **green,** overall tagging, *May 28, 1981*	.35	.20
	P# block of 4	2.00	—
	Zip block of 4	1.40	—
a.	Tagging omitted	15.00	
1858	A1245 18c **dark blue,** overall tagging, *May 7, 1981*	.35	.20
	P# block of 4	3.00	—
	Zip block of 4	1.40	—
	Pair with full horiz. gutter between	—	
a.	Tagging omitted	6.50	
1859	A1246 19c **brown,** overall tagging, *Dec. 27, 1980*	.45	.20
	P# block of 4	2.75	—
	Zip block of 4	1.90	—
1860	A1247 20c **claret,** overall tagging, *Jan. 12, 1982*	.40	.20
	P# block of 4	3.75	—
	Zip block of 4	1.65	—
a.	Tagging omitted	7.50	

61 A1248 20c **green,** overall tagging, *June 10, 1983* .50 .20
P# block of 4 4.00 —
Zip block of 4 2.00 —
a. Tagging omitted —
62 A1249 20c **black,** perf 10.9, small block tagging, dull gum, *Jan. 26, 1984* .40 .20
P# block of 6 4.50 —
P# block of 20, 1-2 #, 1-2 copyright, 1-2 zip 12.00 —
a. Perf. 11.2, large block tagging, dull gum .40 .20
Corner P# block of 4 3.00 —
Zip block of 4 1.60 —
b. Perf. 11.2, overall tagging, dull gum, *1990* .40 .20
Corner P# block of 4 3.75 —
Zip block of 4 1.60 —
c. Tagging omitted, perf. 11.2 11.50 —
d. Prephosphored uncoated paper (mottled tagging), shiny gum, perf. 11.2, *1993* .40 .20
Corner P# block of 4 2.50 —
Zip block of 4 1.60 —
863 A1250 22c **dark chalky blue,** small block tagging, *Apr. 23, 1985* .75 .20
P# block of 6 7.50 —
P# block of 20, 1-2 #, 1-2 zip, 1-2 copyright 17.50 —
a. Large block tagging 1.00 .20
P# block of 6 8.00 —
P# block of 20, 1-2 #, 1-2 zip, 1-2 copyright 22.50 —
b. Perf. 11.2, large block tagging, *1987* .55 .20
Corner P# block of 4 7.00 —
Zip block of 4 2.25 —
c. Tagging omitted 7.50 —
d. Vert. pair, imperf. horiz. 2,000. —
e. Vert. pair, imperf. between —
f. Horiz. pair, imperf. between 2,000. —
864 A1251 30c **olive gray,** small block tagging, *Sept. 2, 1984* .60 .20
P# block of 6 3.50 —
P# block of 20, 1-2 #, 1-2 copyright, 1-2 zip 17.50 —
a. Perf. 11.2, large block tagging .55 .20
Corner P# block of 4 3.25 —
Zip block of 4 2.50 —
b. Perf. 11.2, overall tagging 1.75 .20
Corner P# block of 4 22.50 —
Zip block of 4 7.25 —
c. Tagging omitted —
865 A1252 35c **gray,** overall tagging, *June 3, 1981* .75 .20
P# block of 4 4.25 —
Zip block of 4 3.25 —
a. Tagging omitted —
866 A1253 37c **blue,** overall tagging, *Jan. 26, 1982* .80 .20
P# block of 4 3.75 —
Zip block of 4 3.25 —
a. Tagging omitted 12.50 —
867 A1254 39c **rose lilac,** perf 10.9, small block tagging, *Mar. 20, 1985* .90 .20
P# block of 6 5.75 —
P# block of 20, 1-2 #, 1-2 zip, 1-2 copyright 22.50 —
a. Vert. pair, imperf. horiz. 525.00 —
b. Vert. pair, imperf. between 2,000. —
c. Large block tagging, perf 10.9 .90 .20
P# block of 6 5.75 —
P# block of 20, 1-2 #, 1-2 zip, 1-2 copyright 20.00 —
d. Perf. 11.2, large block tagging .90 .20
Corner P# block of 4 5.75 —
Zip block of 4 3.75 —
868 A1255 40c **dark green,** perf 10.9, small block tagging, *Feb. 24, 1984* .90 .20
P# block of 6 6.50 —
P# block of 20, 1-2 #, 1-2 copyright, 1-2 zip 20.00 —
a. Perf. 11.2, large block tagging .90 .20
Corner P# block of 4 6.50 —
Zip block of 4 3.75 —
869 A1256 50c **brown,** perf 10.9, overall tagging, shiny gum, *Feb. 22, 1985* .95 .20
P# block of 4 7.50 —
Zip block of 4 4.00 —
a. Perf. 11.2, large block tagging, dull gum .95 .20
P# block of 4 6.25 —
Zip block of 4 4.00 —
b. Tagging omitted 11.00 —
c. Tagging omitted, perf. 11.2, dull gum 9.00 —
d. Perf. 11.2, overall tagging 1.50 .20
P# block of 4 8.50 —
Zip block of 4 6.75 —
e. Perf. 11.2, prephosphored uncoated paper (mottled tagging), shiny gum, *1992* .90 .20
P# block of 4 5.00 —
Zip block of 4 4.00 —
Nos. 1844-1869 (26) 11.25 5.20

A1261

A1262

EVERETT DIRKSEN (1896-1969)
Senate minority leader, 1960-1969.

Designed by Ron Adair.

ENGRAVED
Plates of 200 subjects in four panes of 50.

1981, Jan. 4   **Tagged**   *Perf. 11*
1874 A1261 15c **gray** .30 .20
P# block of 4 1.40 —
Zip block of 4 1.25 —
a. All color omitted 500.00

No. 1874a comes from a partially printed pane and may be collected as a vertical strip of 3 or 5 (1 or 3 stamps normal, one stamp transitional and one stamp with color omitted) or as a pair with one partially printed stamp.

BLACK HERITAGE SERIES
Whitney Moore Young, Jr. (1921-1971), civil rights leader.

Designed by Jerry Pinkney.

PHOTOGRAVURE
Plates of 200 subjects in four panes of 50.

1981, Jan. 30   **Tagged**   *Perf. 11*
1875 A1262 15c **multi** .35 .20
P# block of 4, 6# 1.75 —
Zip block of 4 1.50 —

FLOWER ISSUE

A1263   A1264

A1265   A1266

Illustration reduced.

Designed by Lowell Nesbitt.

PHOTOGRAVURE
Plates of 192 subjects in four panes of 48 (8x6).

1981, Apr. 23   **Tagged**   *Perf. 11*
1876 A1263 18c **multicolored** .35 .20
1877 A1264 18c **multicolored** .35 .20
1878 A1265 18c **multicolored** .35 .20
1879 A1266 18c **multicolored** .35 .20
a. Block of 4, #1876-1879 1.40 1.25
P# block of 4, 6# 1.75 —
Zip block of 4 1.45 —

American Wildlife

A1267

A1268

A1269

A1270

A1271

A1272

A1273

A1274

A1275

A1276

Designs from photographs by Jim Brandenburg.

ENGRAVED
1981, May 14   **Tagged**   *Perf. 11*
Dark brown
1880 A1267 18c Bighorn .75 .20
a. Tagging omitted —
1881 A1268 18c Puma .75 .20
1882 A1269 18c Harbor seal .75 .20
1883 A1270 18c American Buffalo .75 .20
1884 A1271 18c Brown bear .75 .20
1885 A1272 18c Polar bear .75 .20
1886 A1273 18c Elk (wapiti) .75 .20
a. Tagging omitted —
1887 A1274 18c Moose .75 .20
a. Tagging omitted —
1888 A1275 18c White-tailed deer .75 .20
1889 A1276 18c Pronghorn .75 .20
a. Booklet pane of 10, #1880-1889 7.50 6.00
b. Tagging omitted —

Nos. 1880-1889 issued in booklet only. All stamps have one or two straight edges.
Imperfs are from printer's waste.

FLAG AND ANTHEM ISSUE

A1277

A1278

A1279

A1280

Designed by Peter Cocci.

ENGRAVED
Plates of 460 subjects (20x23) in panes of 100 (10x10).

1981, Apr. 24   **Tagged**   *Perf. 11*
1890 A1277 18c **multicolored** .35 .20
P# block of 6 2.25 —
P# block of 20, 1-2 # 10.00 —
a. Imperf., pair 100.00
b. Vert. pair, imperf. horiz. 750.00

See Combination Press note after No. 1703.

Coil Stamp
Perf. 10 Vert.

1891 A1278 18c **multicolored**		.35	.20
Pair		.70	.20
P# strip of 3, #1		85.00	
P# strip of 3, #2		16.00	
P# strip of 3, #3		200.00	
P# strip of 3, #4		6.00	
P# strip of 3, #5		4.00	
P# strip of 3, #6		*1,000.*	
P# strip of 3, #7		26.00	
P# strip of 5, #1		360.00	
P# strip of 5, #2		50.00	
P# strip of 5, #3		800.00	
P# strip of 5, #4		7.00	
P# strip of 5, #5		4.75	
P# strip of 5, #6		*3,750.*	
P# strip of 5, #7		30.00	
P# single, #1		—	2.50
P# single, #2		—	1.00
P# single, #3		—	10.00
P# single, #4		—	1.00
P# single, #5		—	1.00
P# single, #6		—	*700.00*
P# single, #7		—	25.00
a.	Imperf., pair	20.00	
	P#2-5		
b.	Pair, imperf. between	*1,250.*	
c.	Tagging omitted	—	
	P#2		

Beware of pairs offered as No. 1891b that have faint blind perfs.

Vertical pairs and blocks exist from printer's waste.

Booklet Stamps
Perf. 11

1892 A1279 6c **multicolored**		.50	.20
1893 A1280 18c **multicolored**		.30	.20
a.	Booklet pane of 8 (2 #1892, 6 #1893)	3.00	2.50
b.	As "a," vert. imperf. between	75.00	
c.	Se-tenant pair, #1892 & #1893	.90	1.00
d.	As "a," tagging omitted	—	

Bureau Precanceled Coils

Starting with No. 1895b, Bureau precanceled coil stamps are valued unused as well as used. The coils issued with dull gum may be difficult to distinguish.

When used normally these stamps do not receive any postal markings so that used stamps with an additional postal cancellation of any kind are worth considerably less than the values shown here.

FLAG OVER SUPREME COURT ISSUE

A1281

Designed by Dean Ellis

ENGRAVED
Plates of 460 subjects (20x23) in panes of 100 (10x10)

1981, Dec. 17		**Tagged**	**Perf. 11**	
1894 A1281 20c black, dark blue & red, dull				
	gum		.40	.20
	P# block of 6		2.75	
	P# block of 20, 1-2 #		9.00	—
a.	Vert. pair, imperf.		35.00	
b.	Vert. pair, imperf. horiz.		475.00	
c.	Dark blue omitted		75.00	
d.	Black omitted		300.00	
e.	Perf. 11.2, shiny gum		.35	.20
	P# block of 6		2.50	
	P# block of 20, 1-2 #		8.50	—
f.	Tagging omitted		—	

Coil Stamp
Perf. 10 Vert.

1895 A1281 20c black, dark blue & red, wide			
	block tagging	.40	.20
	Pair	.80	.20
	P# strip of 3, #1	5.00	
	P# strip of 3, #2	7.75	
	P# strip of 3, #3	3.50	
	P# strip of 3, #5	3.50	
	P# strip of 3, #11	8.00	
	P# strip of 3, #13, 14	3.25	
	P# strip of 5, #1	72.50	
	P# strip of 5, #2	8.00	
	P# strip of 5, #3	5.00	
	P# strip of 5, #5	4.25	
	P# strip of 5, #11	9.00	
	P# strip of 5, #13, 14	4.25	
	P# single, #1	—	.75
	P# single, #2-3	—	.50
	P# single, #5	—	.50
	P# single, #11	—	3.00
	P# single, #13, 14	—	1.00
a.	Narrow block tagging	.40	.20
	Pair	.80	.20
	P# strip of 3, #4	35.00	
	P# strip of 3, #6	85.00	
	P# strip of 3, #8	3.50	
	P# strip of 3, #9-10	3.25	
	P# strip of 3, #12	6.50	
	P# strip of 5, #4	525.00	
	P# strip of 5, #6	200.00	
	P# strip of 5, #8	12.50	
	P# strip of 5, #9	4.25	
	P# strip of 5, #10	4.75	
	P# strip of 5, #12	8.25	
	P# single, #4	—	.90
	P# single, #6	—	2.50
	P# single, #8	—	.50
	P# single, #9	—	.50
	P# single, #10	—	.70
	P# single, #12	—	.90
b.	Untagged (Bureau precanceled, lines only)	.50	.50
	P# strip of 3, #14	57.50	
	P# strip of 5, #14	60.00	
	P# single, #14		50.00
c.	Tagging omitted (not Bureau precanceled		
	P# strip of 3, #4	—	
	P# strip of 3, #3, 5, 8, 10, 11, 14	—	
	P# strip of 5, #5, 10, 11, 14	—	
	P# single, #5, 8-11, 14	—	
d.	Imperf., pair	8.00	
	P#1-6, 8-14		
e.	Pair, imperf. between	*850.00*	
f.	Black omitted	50.00	
g.	Dark blue omitted	*1,500.*	
h.	Black field of stars instead of blue	—	

The wide block tagging on No. 1895 and narrow block tagging on No. 1895a differentiate stamps printed on two different presses. The wide blocks are approximately 20-21mm high by 18mm wide with a 4mm untagged gutter between tagging blocks.

The narrow blocks are approximately 21-22mm high and approximately 16-16½mm wide with a 5½-6½ untagged gutter between tagging blocks.

BOOKLET STAMP
Perf. 11x10½

1896 A1281 20c black, dark blue & red,			
	small block tagging	.40	.20
a.	Booklet pane of 6	3.00	2.25
	Scored perforations	3.00	2.25
b.	Booklet pane of 10, *June 1, 1982*	5.25	3.25
c.	As "b," tagging omitted		

d.	Large block tagging ('83)	.40	
e.	As "d," booklet pane of 10	5.25	3
	Scored perforations	5.25	3
f.	As "a," tagging omitted	—	

Booklets containing two panes of ten of No. 1896e were issued Nov. 17, 1983.

The small block tagging is 16x18mm (Nos. 1896-1896b). large block tagging is 18x21mm (Nos. 1896d-1896e).

TRANSPORTATION ISSUE

A1283   A1284

Designer: 1c, 2c, David Stone.

COIL STAMPS
ENGRAVED

1981-84		**Tagged**	**Perf. 10 Ver**	
1897 A1283	1c **violet,** *Aug. 19, 1983*		.20	.2
	Pair		.20	.2
	P# strip of 3, line, #1, 2		.30	
	P# strip of 3, line, #3, 4		.50	
	P# strip of 3, line, #5, 6		.30	
	P# strip of 5, line, #1, 2		.45	
	P# strip of 5, line, #3, 4		.60	
	P# strip of 5, line, #5, 6		.50	
	P# single, #1, 2		—	.2
	P# single, #3, 4		—	.6
	P# single, #5, 6		—	.3
b.	Imperf., pair		600.00	
	P#5-6			
	Joint line pair		—	
1897A A1284	2c **black,** *May 20, 1982*		.20	.2
	Pair		.20	.2
	P# strip of 3, line, #2-4, 6, 8, 10		.45	
	P# strip of 5, line, #2-4, 6, 8, 10		.50	
	P# single, #2-4, 6, 8, 10		—	.4
c.	Imperf., pair		50.00	
	P#3-4, 8, 10			
	Joint line pair		—	
d.	Tagging omitted		27.50	
	P#8			

A1284a   A1285

Designers: 3c, Walter Brooks. 4c, Jim Schleyer.

1898 A1284a	3c **dark green,** *Mar. 25, 1983*	.20	.20
	Pair	.20	.20
	P# strip of 3, line, #1-4	.65	
	P# strip of 5, line, #1-4	.70	
	P# single, #1-4	—	.55
1898A A1285	4c **reddish brown,** *Aug. 19, 1982*	.20	.20
	Pair	.20	.20
	P# strip of 3, line, #1-4	.95	
	P# strip of 3, line, #5-6	2.10	
	P# strip of 5, line, #1-4	1.00	
	P# strip of 5, line, #5-6	2.25	
	P# single, #1-4	—	.75
	P# single, #5-6	—	2.00
b.	Untagged (Bureau precanceled, Nonprofit Org.)	.20	.20
	P# strip of 3, line, #3-6	4.75	
	P# strip of 5, line, #3-6	5.00	
	P# single, #3, 4	—	4.00
	P# single, #5, 6	—	4.25
c.	As "b," imperf., pair	725.00	
	P#5-6		
d.	As No. 1898A, imperf. pair	800.00	—
	P#1-2		
e.	Tagging omitted (not Bureau precanceled)		
	P# strip of 5, #3	150.00	
	P# strip of 5, #4	250.00	

See also No. 2228.

A1286   A1287

Designers: 5c, 5.2c, Walter Brooks.

1899 A1286	5c **gray green,** Oct. 10, 1983	.20	.20
	Pair	.25	.20
	P# strip of 3, line, #1-4	.85	
	P# strip of 5, line, #1-4	.90	
	P# single, #1-4	—	.75
a.	Imperf., pair	2,750.	
	P#1-2		
b.	Tagging omitted	22.50	—
	P# strip of 5, line, #1, 2	450.00	
	P# single, #1, 2	—	350.00
1900 A1287	5.2c **carmine,** Mar. 21, 1983	.20	.20
	Pair	.25	.20
	P# strip of 3, line, #1-2	6.00	
	P# strip of 3, line, #3	160.00	
	P# strip of 3, line, #5	140.00	
	P# strip of 5, line, #1-2	8.25	
	P# strip of 5, line, #3	290.00	
	P# strip of 5, line, #5	190.00	
	P# single, #1-2	—	5.50
	P# single, #3	—	170.00
	P# single, #5	—	140.00
a.	Untagged (Bureau precanceled, lines only)	.20	.20
	P# strip of 3, line, #1-3	9.25	
	P# strip of 3, line, #4	12.50	
	P# strip of 3, line, #5	9.25	
	P# strip of 3, line, #6	12.50	
	P# strip of 5, line, #1-3	10.00	
	P# strip of 5, line, #4, 6	13.00	
	P# strip of 5, line, #5	10.00	
	P# single, #1, 2	—	3.00
	P# single, #3	—	2.00
	P# single, #4	—	10.00
	P# single, #5	—	2.00
	P# single, #6	—	10.00
b.	Tagging omitted		—

A1288   A1289

Designers: 5.9c, David Stone. 7.4c, Jim Schleyer.

1901 A1288	5.9c **blue,** Feb. 17, 1982	.25	.20
	Pair	.50	.20
	P# strip of 3, line, #3-4	6.75	
	P# strip of 5, line, #3-4	13.00	
	P# single, #3-4	—	5.75
a.	Untagged (Bureau precanceled, lines only)	.20	.20
	P# strip of 3, line, #3-4	22.50	
	P# strip of 3, line, #5-6	80.00	
	P# strip of 5, line, #3-4	30.00	
	P# strip of 5, line, #5-6	100.00	
	P# single, #3-4	—	5.50
	P# single, #5-6	—	75.00
b.	As "a," imperf., pair	160.00	
	P#3-4		
	Joint line pair	—	
1902 A1289	7.4c **brown,** Apr. 7, 1984	.20	.20
	Pair	.40	.20
	P# strip of 3, #2	8.00	
	P# strip of 5, #2	8.25	
	P# single, #2		6.00
a.	Untagged (Bureau precanceled, Blk. Rt. CAR-RT SORT)	.20	.20
	P# strip of 3, #2	5.00	
	P# strip of 5, #2	5.50	
	P# single, #2	—	4.00

A1290   A1291

Designers: 9.3c, Jim Schleyer. 10.9c, David Stone.

1903 A1290	9.3c **carmine rose,** Dec. 15	.30	.20
	Pair	.60	.20
	P# strip of 3, line, #1-2	7.50	
	P# strip of 3, line, #3-4	20.00	

	P# strip of 3, line, #5-6	250.00	
	P# strip of 5, line, #1-2	12.00	
	P# strip of 5, line, #3-4	32.50	
	P# strip of 5, line, #5	325.00	
	P# strip of 5, line, #6	300.00	
	P# single, #1-2	—	7.00
	P# single, #3-4	—	17.50
	P# single, #5-6	—	200.00
a.	Untagged (Bureau precanceled, lines only)	.25	.25
	P# strip of 3, line, #1	11.50	
	P# strip of 3, line, #2	10.50	
	P# strip of 3, line, #3	21.00	
	P# strip of 3, line, #4	16.00	
	P# strip of 3, line, #5-6	2.50	
	P# strip of 3, line, #8	225.00	
	P# strip of 5, line, #1	12.00	
	P# strip of 5, line, #2	11.00	
	P# strip of 5, line, #3	26.00	
	P# strip of 5, line, #4	18.00	
	P# strip of 5, line, #5-6	2.75	
	P# strip of 5, line, #8	260.00	
	P# single, #1-2	—	10.00
	P# single, #3	—	12.50
	P# single, #4	—	10.00
	P# single, #5-6	—	1.75
	P# single, #8	—	240.00
b.	As "a," imperf., pair	110.00	
	P#1-2		
	Joint line pair	200.00	
1904 A1291	10.9c **purple,** Mar. 26, 1982	.30	.20
	Pair	.60	.20
	P# strip of 3, line, #1-2	15.00	
	P# strip of 5, line, #1-2	29.00	
	P# single, #1-2	—	12.00
a.	Untagged (Bureau precanceled, lines only)	.30	.25
	P# strip of 3, line, #1-2	20.00	
	P# strip of 3, line, #3-4	300.00	
	P# strip of 5, line, #1-2	29.00	
	P# strip of 5, line, #3-4	325.00	
	P# single, #1-2	—	8.75
	P# single, #3-4	—	50.00
b.	As "a," imperf., pair	150.00	
	P#1-2		
	Joint line pair	—	

A1292   A1293

Designers: 11c, Jim Schleyer. 17c Chuck Jaquays.

1905 A1292	11c **red,** Feb. 3, 1984	.30	.20
	Pair	.60	.20
	P# strip of 3, #1	3.50	
	P# strip of 5, #1	3.75	
	P# single, #1	—	3.00
a.	Untagged Sept. 1991	.25	.20
	Pair	.50	.20
	P# strip of 3, #1	3.00	
	P# strip of 3, #2, precanceled	2.25	
	P# strip of 5, #1	3.75	
	P# strip of 5, #2, precanceled	2.75	
	P# single, #1	—	2.75
	P# single, #2, precanceled	—	2.00

Untagged stamps from plate 1 come only Bureau precanceled with lines. Untagged stamps from plate 2 come both without and with Bureau precancel lines.

1906 A1293	17c **ultramarine,** June 25	.35	.20
	Pair	.70	.20
	P# strip of 3, line, #1-5	2.00	
	P# strip of 3, line, #6	13.00	
	P# strip of 3, line, #7	5.00	
	P# strip of 5, line, #1-5	2.25	
	P# strip of 5, line, #6	13.50	
	P# strip of 5, line, #7	5.25	
	P# single, #1-5	—	1.50
	P# single, #6	—	12.00
	P# single, #7	—	4.75
a.	Untagged (Bureau precanceled, Presorted First Class)	.35	.35
	P# strip of 3, line, #1, 2	9.00	
	P# strip of 3, line, #3-5	3.50	
	P# strip of 3, line, #6, 7	11.00	
	P# strip of 5, line, #1, 2	9.25	
	P# strip of 5, line, #3-5	3.75	
	P# strip of 5, line, #6-7	11.50	
	P# single, #1, 2	—	7.25
	P# single, #3-5	—	3.00
	P# single, #6, 7	—	9.00

Three different precancel styles exist in four different lengths: "PRESORTED" measuring 11.3mm, 12.8mm, 13.4mm and 14.1mm. These measurements can vary slightly. The most common is the 11.3mm. Combination pairs exist of the 11.3mm and 12.8mm varieties. The 13.4mm and 14.1mm legths have the same "type" style and vary in length, and as a result many coil collectors prefer to refer to, and collect, only the three different "type" styles.

b.	Imperf., pair	160.00	

```
                    P#1-4
                    Joint line pair              —
  c.    As "a," imperf., pair      575.00
                    P#3-4
                    Joint line pair              —
```

A1294

A1295

Designers: 18c, David Stone. 20c, Jim Schleyer.

1907 A1294 18c **dark brown,** *May 18* .35 .20

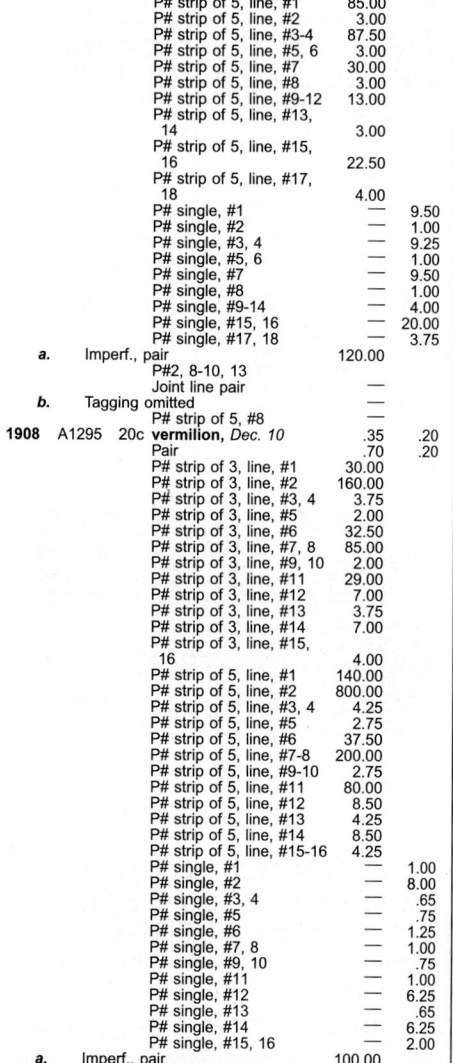

Pair	.70	.20
P# strip of 3, line, #1	55.00	
P# strip of 3, line, #2	2.75	
P# strip of 3, line, #3, 4	62.50	
P# strip of 3, line, #5, 6	2.75	
P# strip of 3, line, #7	30.00	
P# strip of 3, line, #8	2.75	
P# strip of 3, line, #9-12	12.00	
P# strip of 3, line, #13, 14	2.75	
P# strip of 3, line, #15, 16	19.00	
P# strip of 3, line, #17, 18	3.50	
P# strip of 5, line, #1	85.00	
P# strip of 5, line, #2	3.00	
P# strip of 5, line, #3-4	87.50	
P# strip of 5, line, #5, 6	3.00	
P# strip of 5, line, #7	30.00	
P# strip of 5, line, #8	3.00	
P# strip of 5, line, #9-12	13.00	
P# strip of 5, line, #13, 14	3.00	
P# strip of 5, line, #15, 16	22.50	
P# strip of 5, line, #17, 18	4.00	
P# single, #1	—	9.50
P# single, #2	—	1.00
P# single, #3, 4	—	9.25
P# single, #5, 6	—	1.00
P# single, #7	—	9.50
P# single, #8	—	1.00
P# single, #9-14	—	4.00
P# single, #15, 16	—	20.00
P# single, #17, 18	—	3.75

```
  a.    Imperf., pair               120.00
              P#2, 8-10, 13
              Joint line pair          —
  b.    Tagging omitted               —
              P# strip of 5, #8         —
```

1908 A1295 20c **vermilion,** *Dec. 10* .35 .20

Pair	.70	.20
P# strip of 3, line, #1	30.00	
P# strip of 3, line, #2	160.00	
P# strip of 3, line, #3, 4	3.75	
P# strip of 3, line, #5	2.00	
P# strip of 3, line, #6	32.50	
P# strip of 3, line, #7, 8	85.00	
P# strip of 3, line, #9, 10	2.00	
P# strip of 3, line, #11	29.00	
P# strip of 3, line, #12	7.00	
P# strip of 3, line, #13	3.75	
P# strip of 3, line, #14	7.00	
P# strip of 3, line, #15, 16	4.00	
P# strip of 5, line, #1	140.00	
P# strip of 5, line, #2	800.00	
P# strip of 5, line, #3, 4	4.25	
P# strip of 5, line, #5	2.75	
P# strip of 5, line, #6	37.50	
P# strip of 5, line, #7-8	200.00	
P# strip of 5, line, #9-10	2.75	
P# strip of 5, line, #11	80.00	
P# strip of 5, line, #12	8.50	
P# strip of 5, line, #13	4.25	
P# strip of 5, line, #14	8.50	
P# strip of 5, line, #15-16	4.25	
P# single, #1	—	1.00
P# single, #2	—	8.00
P# single, #3, 4	—	.65
P# single, #5	—	.75
P# single, #6	—	1.25
P# single, #7, 8	—	1.00
P# single, #9, 10	—	.75
P# single, #11	—	1.00
P# single, #12	—	6.25
P# single, #13	—	.65
P# single, #14	—	6.25
P# single, #15, 16	—	2.00

```
  a.    Imperf., pair               100.00
              P#1-5, 9-10, 15-16
              Joint line pair          300.00    —
  b.    Tagging omitted               —
          Nos. 1897-1908 (14)        3.60    2.80
              See Nos. 2225-2228.
```

Eagle and Moon — A1296

Booklet Stamp
PHOTOGRAVURE

1983, Aug. 12 **Untagged** *Perf. 10 Vert.*
1909 A1296 $9.35 **multicolored** 22.50 15.00
  a. Booklet pane of 3 67.50 —

A1297

A1298

AMERICAN RED CROSS CENTENNIAL

Designed by Joseph Csatari.

PHOTOGRAVURE
Plates of 200 subjects in four panes of 50.

1981, May 1 **Tagged** *Perf. 10½x11*
1910 A1297 18c **multicolored** .35 .20
  P# block of 4, 6# 1.50 —
  Zip block of 4 1.40 —

SAVINGS & LOAN SESQUICENTENNIAL

Designed by Don Hedin.

PHOTOGRAVURE
Plates of 200 subjects in four panes of 50.

1981, May 8 **Tagged** *Perf. 11*
1911 A1298 18c **multicolored** .35 .20
  P# block of 4, 6# 1.50 —
  Zip block of 4 1.40 —

SPACE ACHIEVEMENT ISSUE

A1299

A1302

A1300

A1301

A1303

A1306

A1304

A1305

Designed by Robert McCall.

Designs: A1299, Moon walk. A1300-A1301, A1304-A1305, Columbia space shuttle. A1302, Skylab. A1303, Pioneer 11. A1306, Telescope. Se-tenant in blocks of 8.

PHOTOGRAVURE
Plates of 192 subjects in four panes of 48 each.

1981, May 21 **Tagged** *Perf. 11*
1912	A1299	18c	**multicolored**	.40	.20
1913	A1300	18c	**multicolored**	.40	.20
1914	A1301	18c	**multicolored**	.40	.20
1915	A1302	18c	**multicolored**	.40	.20
1916	A1303	18c	**multicolored**	.40	.20
1917	A1304	18c	**multicolored**	.40	.20
1918	A1305	18c	**multicolored**	.40	.20
1919	A1306	18c	**multicolored**	.40	.20

```
  a.    Block of 8, #1912-1919      3.25    3.00
              P# block of 8, 6#       3.75    —
              Zip, copyright block of 8  3.25   —
  b.    As "a," imperf.              7,500.
  c.    As "a," tagging omitted       —
```

PROFESSIONAL MANAGEMENT EDUCATION CENTENARY

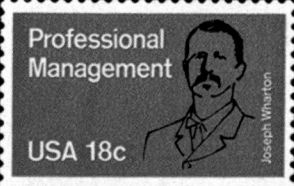

Joseph Wharton (Founder of Wharton School of Business)
A1307

Designed by Rudolph de Harak.

PHOTOGRAVURE
Plates of 200 subject in four panes of 50.

1981, June 18   **Tagged**   **Perf. 11**
1920 A1307 18c **blue & black**   .35   .20
      P# block of 4, 2#   1.50
      Zip block of 4   1.40   —

PRESERVATION OF WILDLIFE HABITATS

Great Blue Heron — A1308

Badger — A1309

Grizzly Bear — A1310

Ruffed Grouse — A1311

Designed by Chuck Ripper

PHOTOGRAVURE
Plates of 200 subjects in four panes of 50.

1981, June 26   **Tagged**   **Perf. 11**
1921 A1308 18c **multicolored**   .35   .20
1922 A1309 18c **multicolored**   .35   .20
1923 A1310 18c **multicolored**   .35   .20
1924 A1311 18c **multicolored**   .35   .20
  a. Block of 4, #1921-1924   1.50 1.25
      P# block of 4, 5#   2.00
      Zip block of 4   1.55   —

INTERNATIONAL YEAR OF THE DISABLED

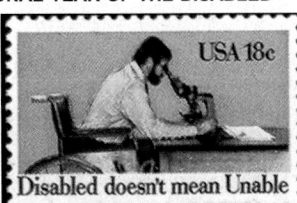

Man Using Microscope A1312

Designed by Martha Perske

PHOTOGRAVURE
Plates of 200 subjects in four panes of 50.

1981, June 29   **Tagged**   **Perf. 11**
1925 A1312 18c **multicolored**   .35   .20
      P# block of 4, 6#   1.50
      Zip block of 4   1.40   —
  a. Vert. pair, imperf. horiz.   2,750.

EDNA ST. VINCENT MILLAY ISSUE

A1313

Designed by Glenora Case Richards

LITHOGRAPHED AND ENGRAVED
Plates of 200 subjects in four panes of 50.

1981, July 10   **Tagged**   **Perf. 11**
1926 A1313 18c **multicolored**   .35   .20
      P# block of 4, 7#   1.50
      Zip block of 4   1.40   —
  a. Black (engr., inscriptions) omitted   300.00

ALCOHOLISM

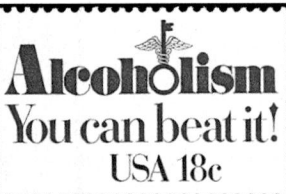

A1314

Designed by John Boyd

ENGRAVED
Plates of 230 (10x23) subjects in panes of 50 (5x10).

1981, Aug. 19   **Tagged**   **Perf. 11**
1927 A1314 18c **blue & black**   .45   .20
      P# block of 6   10.00
      P# block of 20, 1-2 #, 1-2 copyright, 1-2 Zip   20.00
  a. Imperf., pair   400.00
  b. Vert. pair, imperf. horiz.   2,500.

See Combination Press note after No. 1703.

AMERICAN ARCHITECTURE SERIES

New York University Library by Stanford White A1315

Biltmore House By Richard Morris Hunt — A1316

Palace of the Arts by Bernard Maybeck A1317

National Farmer's Bank by Louis Sullivan A1318

Designed by Walter D. Richards

ENGRAVED
Plates of 160 subjects in four panes of 40.

1981, Aug. 28   **Tagged**   **Perf. 11**
1928 A1315 18c **black & red**   .40   .20
  a. Tagging omitted

1929 A1316 18c **black & red**   .40   .20
1930 A1317 18c **black & red**   .40   .20
  a. Tagging omitted
1931 A1318 18c **black & red**   .40   .20
  a. Block of 4, #1928-1931   1.65 1.65
      P# block of 4   2.10
      Zip block of 4   1.80   —
  b. As "a," tagging omitted

SPORTS PERSONALITIES

Mildred Didrikson Zaharias — A1319

Robert Tyre Jones — A1320

Designed by Richard Gangel

ENGRAVED
Plates of 200 subjects in four panes of 50.

1981, Sept. 22   **Tagged**   **Perf. 10½x11**
1932 A1319 18c **purple**   .40   .20
      P# block of 4   3.00
      Zip block of 4   1.75   —
1933 A1320 18c **green**   .60   .20
      P# block of 4   3.25
      Zip block of 4   2.50   —

FREDERIC REMINGTON

Coming Through the Rye — A1321

Designed by Paul Calle

LITHOGRAPHED AND ENGRAVED
Plates of 200 in four panes of 50.

1981, Oct. 9   **Tagged**   **Perf. 11**
1934 A1321 18c **gray, olive green & brown**   .35   .20
      P# block of 4, 3#   1.60
      Zip block of 4   1.50   —
  a. Vert. pair, imperf. between   250.00
  b. Brown omitted   425.00

JAMES HOBAN

Irish-American Architect of the White House A1322

Designed by Ron Mercer and Walter D. Richards.

PHOTOGRAVURE
Plates of 200 in four panes of 50.

1981, Oct. 13   **Tagged**   **Perf. 11**
1935 A1322 18c **multicolored**   .35   .20
      P# block of 4, 6#   1.60
      Zip block of 4   1.50   —
1936 A1322 20c **multicolored**   .35   .20
      P# block of 4, 6#   1.65
      Zip block of 4   1.50   —

See Ireland No. 504.

AMERICAN BICENTENNIAL

Battle of Yorktown A1323

Battle of the Virginia Capes A1324

Designed by Cal Sacks.

LITHOGRAPHED AND ENGRAVED
Plates of 200 in four panes of 50.

1981, Oct. 16	Tagged	Perf. 11
1937 A1323 18c multicolored	.35	.20
1938 A1324 18c multicolored	.35	.20
a. Pair, #1937-1938	.90	.75
P# block of 4, 7#	2.00	—
Zip block of 4	1.65	—
b. As "a," black (engr., inscriptions) omitted	375.00	
c. As "a," tagging omitted	—	

CHRISTMAS

Madonna and Child, Botticelli — A1325

Felt Bear on Sleigh A1326

Designed by Bradbury Thompson (No. 1939) and by Naiad Einsel (No. 1940).

PHOTOGRAVURE
Plates of 400 in four panes of 100 (No. 1939)
Plates of 200 in four panes of 50 (No. 1940)

1981, Oct. 28	Tagged	Perf. 11
1939 A1325 (20c) multicolored	.40	.20
P# block of 4, 6#	1.75	—
Zip block of 4	1.65	—
a. Imperf., pair	110.00	
b. Vert. pair, imperf. horiz.	1,250.	
c. Tagging omitted	15.00	
1940 A1326 (20c) multicolored	.40	.20
P# block of 4, 5#	1.75	—
Zip block of 4	1.65	—
a. Imperf., pair	225.00	
b. Vert. pair, imperf. horiz.	3,000.	

JOHN HANSON

First President of the Continental Congress — A1327

Designed by Ron Adair.

PHOTOGRAVURE
Plates of 200 in panes of 50

1981, Nov. 5	Tagged	Perf. 11
1941 A1327 20c multicolored	.40	.20
P# block of 4, 5#	1.75	—
Zip block of 4	1.65	—

DESERT PLANTS

Barrel Cactus — A1328

Saguaro — A1331

Agave — A1329

Beavertail Cactus — A1330

Designed by Frank J. Waslick.

LITHOGRAPHED AND ENGRAVED
Plates of 160 in four panes of 40

1981 Dec. 11	Tagged	Perf. 11
1942 A1328 20c multicolored	.35	.20
1943 A1329 20c multicolored	.35	.20
1944 A1330 20c multicolored	.35	.20
1945 A1331 20c multicolored	.35	.20
a. Block of 4, #1942-1945	1.50	1.25
P# block of 4, 7#	1.90	—
Zip block of 4	1.55	—
b. As "a," deep brown (litho.) omitted	4,250.	
c. No. 1945 imperf., vert. pair	3,500.	
d. As "a," tagging omitted	—	

A1332   A1333

Designed by Bradbury Thompson.

PHOTOGRAVURE
Plates of 400 in panes of 100.

1981, Oct. 11	Tagged	Perf. 11x10½
1946 A1332 (20c) brown	.40	.20
P# block of 4	2.00	—
Zip block of 4	1.65	—
a. Tagging omitted	9.00	
b. All color omitted	—	

No. 1946b comes from a partially printed pane with most stamps normal. It must be collected as a vertical pair or strip with normal or partially printed stamps attached.

ENGRAVED
COIL STAMP
Perf. 10 Vert.

1947 A1332 (20c) brown	.60	.20
Pair	1.20	.20
Joint line pair	1.50	—
a. Imperf. pair	1,000.	
Joint line pair	—	

BOOKLET STAMPS
Perf. 11

1948 A1333 (20c) brown	.40	.20
a. Booklet pane of 10	4.50	3.25

Rocky Mountain Bighorn — A1334

BOOKLET STAMP
ENGRAVED

1982, Jan. 8	Tagged	Perf. 11
1949 A1334 20c dark blue	.55	.20
a. Booklet pane of 10	5.50	2.50
b. As "a," imperf. between	100.00	
c. Type II	1.40	.20
d. Type II, booklet pane of 10	14.00	—
e. As #1949, tagging omitted	5.00	—
f. As "e," booklet pane of 10	50.00	—

No. 1949 is 18¾mm wide and has overall tagging. No. 1949c is 18½mm wide and has block tagging.

FRANKLIN DELANO ROOSEVELT

A1335

Designed by Clarence Holbert.

ENGRAVED
Plates of 192 in four panes of 48

1982, Jan. 30	Tagged	Perf. 11
1950 A1335 20c blue	.40	.20
P# block of 4	1.75	—
Zip block of 4	1.65	—

LOVE ISSUE

A1336

Designed by Mary Faulconer.

PHOTOGRAVURE
Plates of 200 in four panes of 50.

1982, Feb. 1	Tagged	Perf. 11¼	
1951 A1336 20c **multicolored**		.40	.20
	P# block of 4, 5#	1.75	—
	Zip block of 4	1.65	—
b.	Imperf., pair	250.00	
c.	Blue omitted	225.00	
d.	Yellow omitted	1,000.	
e.	Purple omitted	—	
f.	Tagging omitted		—

No. 1951c is valued in the grade of fine.

Perf. 11¼x10½

1951A A1336 20c **multicolored**		.75	.25
	P# block of 4, 5#	3.50	—
	Zip block of 4	3.00	—

GEORGE WASHINGTON

A1337

Designed by Mark English.

PHOTOGRAVURE
Plates of 200 in four panes of 50.

1982, Feb. 22	Tagged	Perf. 11	
1952 A1337 20c **multicolored**		.40	.20
	P# block of 4, 6#	1.75	—
	Zip block of 4	1.65	—

STATE BIRDS AND FLOWERS ISSUE

Illustration reduced.

Designed by Arthur and Alan Singer.

PHOTOGRAVURE (Andreotti)
Plates of 200 subjects in four panes of 50.

1982, Apr. 14	Tagged	Perf. 10½x11¼	
1953 A1338 20c Alabama		.55	.30
1954 A1339 20c Alaska		.55	.30
1955 A1340 20c Arizona		.55	.30
1956 A1341 20c Arkansas		.55	.30
1957 A1342 20c California		.55	.30
1958 A1343 20c Colorado		.55	.30
1959 A1344 20c Connecticut		.55	.30
1960 A1345 20c Delaware		.55	.30
1961 A1346 20c Florida		.55	.30
1962 A1347 20c Georgia		.55	.30
1963 A1348 20c Hawaii		.55	.30
1964 A1349 20c Idaho		.55	.30
1965 A1350 20c Illinois		.55	.30
1966 A1351 20c Indiana		.55	.30
1967 A1352 20c Iowa		.55	.30
1968 A1353 20c Kansas		.55	.30
1969 A1354 20c Kentucky		.55	.30
1970 A1355 20c Louisiana		.55	.30
1971 A1356 20c Maine		.55	.30
1972 A1357 20c Maryland		.55	.30
1973 A1358 20c Massachusetts		.55	.30
1974 A1359 20c Michigan		.55	.30
1975 A1360 20c Minnesota		.55	.30
1976 A1361 20c Mississippi		.55	.30
1977 A1362 20c Missouri		.55	.30
1978 A1363 20c Montana		.55	.30
1979 A1364 20c Nebraska		.55	.30
1980 A1365 20c Nevada		.55	.30
1981 A1366 20c New Hampshire		.55	.30
b.	Black missing (EP)	6,000.	
1982 A1367 20c New Jersey		.55	.30
1983 A1368 20c New Mexico		.55	.30
1984 A1369 20c New York		.55	.30
1985 A1370 20c North Carolina		.55	.30
1986 A1371 20c North Dakota		.55	.30
1987 A1372 20c Ohio		.55	.30
1988 A1373 20c Oklahoma		.55	.30
1989 A1374 20c Oregon		.55	.30
1990 A1375 20c Pennsylvania		.55	.30
1991 A1376 20c Rhode Island		.55	.30
b.	Black missing (EP)	6,000.	
1992 A1377 20c South Carolina		.55	.30
1993 A1378 20c South Dakota		.55	.30
1994 A1379 20c Tennessee		.55	.30
1995 A1380 20c Texas		.55	.30
1996 A1381 20c Utah		.55	.30
1997 A1382 20c Vermont		.55	.30
1998 A1383 20c Virginia		.55	.30
1999 A1384 20c Washington		.55	.30
2000 A1385 20c West Virginia		.55	.30
2001 A1386 20c Wisconsin		.55	.30
b.	Black missing (EP)	6,000.	
2002 A1387 20c Wyoming		.55	.30
b.	A1338-A1387 Pane of 50, Nos. 1953-2002	27.50	20.00
d.	Pane of 50, imperf.	27,500.	

Perf. 11¼x11

1953A A1338 20c Alabama		.65	.30
1954A A1339 20c Alaska		.65	.30
1955A A1340 20c Arizona		.65	.30
1956A A1341 20c Arkansas		.65	.30
1957A A1342 20c California		.65	.30
1958A A1343 20c Colorado		.65	.30
1959A A1344 20c Connecticut		.65	.30
1960A A1345 20c Delaware		.65	.30
1961A A1346 20c Florida		.65	.30
1962A A1347 20c Georgia		.65	.30
1963A A1348 20c Hawaii		.65	.30
1964A A1349 20c Idaho		.65	.30
1965A A1350 20c Illinois		.65	.30
1966A A1351 20c Indiana		.65	.30
1967A A1352 20c Iowa		.65	.30
1968A A1353 20c Kansas		.65	.30
1969A A1354 20c Kentucky		.65	.30
1970A A1355 20c Louisiana		.65	.30
1971A A1356 20c Maine		.65	.30
1972A A1357 20c Maryland		.65	.30
1973A A1358 20c Massachusetts		.65	.30
1974A A1359 20c Michigan		.65	.30
1975A A1360 20c Minnesota		.65	.30
1976A A1361 20c Mississippi		.65	.30
1977A A1362 20c Missouri		.65	.30
1978A A1363 20c Montana		.65	.30
1979A A1364 20c Nebraska		.65	.30
1980A A1365 20c Nevada		.65	.30
1981A A1366 20c New Hampshire		.65	.30
1982A A1367 20c New Jersey		.65	.30
1983A A1368 20c New Mexico		.65	.30
1984A A1369 20c New York		.65	.30
1985A A1370 20c North Carolina		.65	.30
1986A A1371 20c North Dakota		.65	.30
1987A A1372 20c Ohio		.65	.30
1988A A1373 20c Oklahoma		.65	.30
1989A A1374 20c Oregon		.65	.30
1990A A1375 20c Pennsylvania		.65	.30
1991A A1376 20c Rhode Island		.65	.30
1992A A1377 20c South Carolina		.65	.30
1993A A1378 20c South Dakota		.65	.30
1994A A1379 20c Tennessee		.65	.30
1995A A1380 20c Texas		.65	.30
1996A A1381 20c Utah		.65	.30
1997A A1382 20c Vermont		.65	.30
1998A A1383 20c Virginia		.65	.30
1999A A1384 20c Washington		.65	.30
2000A A1385 20c West Virginia		.65	.30
2001A A1386 20c Wisconsin		.65	.30
2002A A1387 20c Wyoming		.65	.30
c.	A1338-A1387 Pane of 50, Nos. 1953A-2002A	32.50	22.50

US-NETHERLANDS

200th Anniv. of Diplomatic Recognition by The Netherlands
A1388

Designed by Heleen Tigler Wybrandi-Raue.

PHOTOGRAVURE
Plates of 230 (10x23) subjects in panes of 50 (5x10).

1982, Apr. 20	Tagged	Perf. 11	
2003 A1388 20c **verm., brt. blue & gray blk.**		.40	.20
	P# block of 6	3.50	—
	P# block of 20, 1-2 #, 1-2 copyright, 1-2 zip	10.00	—
a.	Imperf., pair	300.00	

See Combination Press note after No. 1703.
See Netherlands Nos. 640-641.

LIBRARY OF CONGRESS

A1389

Designed by Bradbury Thompson.

ENGRAVED
Plates of 200 subjects in four panes of 50.

1982, Apr. 21	Tagged	Perf. 11	
2004 A1389 20c **red & black**		.40	.20
	P# block of 4	1.75	—
	Zip block of 4	1.65	—
a.	All color missing	—	

No. 2004a must be collected as a right margin horiz. strip of 5 or 3 with 3 (or 1) normal, one transitional and one with color omitted.

A1390

Designed by John Boyd.

ENGRAVED
Coil Stamp

1982, Apr. 27	Tagged	Perf. 10 Vert.	
2005 A1390 20c **sky blue**		.55	.20
	Pair	1.10	.20
	P# strip of 3, line, #1-4	22.50	
	P# strip of 5, line, #1-2	160.00	
	P# strip of 5, line, #3-4	100.00	
	P# single, #1-4		1.50
a.	Imperf., pair	100.00	
	P#1-4		
	Joint line pair	400.00	
b.	Tagging omitted	7.50	

KNOXVILLE WORLD'S FAIR

A1391

A1392

A1393

State Birds and Flowers
A1338-A1387

A1394

Illustration reduced.

Designed by Charles Harper.

PHOTOGRAVURE
Plates of 200 in four panes of 50.

1982, Apr. 29	**Tagged**	*Perf. 11*	
2006 A1391 20c	**multicolored**	.45	.20
2007 A1392 20c	**multicolored**	.45	.20
2008 A1393 20c	**multicolored**	.45	.20
2009 A1394 20c	**multicolored**	.45	.20
	Any single on cover, Expo. station handstamp cancel		10.00
a.	Block of 4, #2006-2009	1.80	1.50
	P# block of 4, 6#	2.40	—
	Zip block of 4	1.90	—

HORATIO ALGER

A1395

Designed by Robert Hallock.

ENGRAVED
Plates of 200 in four panes of 50.

1982, Apr. 30	**Tagged**	*Perf. 11*	
2010 A1395 20c	**red & black,** *tan*	.40	.20
	P# block of 4	1.75	—
	Zip block of 4	1.65	—
a.	Red and black omitted		—
b.	Tagging omitted		—

The Philatelic Foundation has issued a certificate for a pane of 50 with red and black colors omitted. Recognition of this error is by the paper and by a tiny residue of red ink from the tagging roller. The engraved plates did not strike the paper.

AGING TOGETHER

A1396

Designed by Paul Calle.

ENGRAVED
Plates of 200 in four panes of 50.

1982, May 21	**Tagged**	*Perf. 11*	
2011 A1396 20c	**brown**	.40	.20
	P# block of 4	1.75	—
	Zip block of 4	1.65	—

john, Ethel and Lionel Barrymore — A1397

A1398

PERFORMING ARTS SERIES
Designed by Jim Sharpe.

PHOTOGRAVURE
Plates of 200 in four panes of 50.

1982, June 8	Tagged	Perf. 11	
1396 A1397 20c multicolored		.40	.20
P# block of 4, 6#		1.75	—
Zip block of 4		1.65	—

DR. MARY WALKER
Designed by Glenora Richards.

PHOTOGRAVURE
Plate of 200 in four panes of 50.

1982, June 10	Tagged	Perf. 11	
1397 A1398 20c multicolored		.40	.20
P# block of 4, 6#		1.75	—
Zip block of 4		1.65	—

INTERNATIONAL PEACE GARDEN

Dunseith, ND-Boissevain, Manitoba — A1399

Designed by Gyo Fujikawa.

LITHOGRAPHED AND ENGRAVED
Plate of 200 in four panes of 50.

1982, June 30	Tagged	Perf. 11	
1398 A1399 20c multicolored		.50	.20
P# block of 4, 5#		2.25	—
Zip block of 4		2.00	—
a. Black (engr.) omitted		250.00	

A1400 A1401

AMERICA'S LIBRARIES
Designed by Bradbury Thompson.

ENGRAVED
Plate of 200 subjects in four panes of 50.

1982, July 13	Tagged	Perf. 11	
1399 A1400 20c red & black		.40	.20
P# block of 4		1.75	—
Zip block of 4		1.65	—
a. Vert. pair, imperf. horiz.		275.00	
b. Tagging omitted		7.50	
c. All colors missing (EP)		—	

BLACK HERITAGE SERIES
Jackie Robinson (1919-72), baseball player.

Designed by Jerry Pinkney.

PHOTOGRAVURE
Plate of 200 subjects in four panes of 50.

1982, Aug. 2	Tagged	Perf. 10½x11	
2016 A1401 20c multicolored		1.10	.20
P# block of 4, 5#		5.50	—
Zip block of 4		4.75	—

TOURO SYNAGOGUE

Oldest Existing Synagogue Building in the U.S. — A1402

Designed by Donald Moss and Bradbury Thompson.

PHOTOGRAVURE AND ENGRAVED
Plates of 230 (10x23) subjects in panes of 50 (5x10).

1982, Aug. 22	Tagged	Perf. 11	
2017 A1402 20c multicolored		.45	.20
P# block of 20, 6-12 #, 1-2 copyright, 1-2 zip		12.50	—
a. Imperf., pair		2,500.	

See Combination Press note after No. 1703.

WOLF TRAP FARM PARK

A1403

Designed by Richard Schlecht.

PHOTOGRAVURE
Plates of 200 in four panes of 50.

1982, Sept. 1	Tagged	Perf. 11	
2018 A1403 20c multicolored		.40	.20
P# block of 4, 5#		1.75	—
Zip block of 4		1.65	—

AMERICAN ARCHITECTURE SERIES

A1404

A1405

A1406

A1407

Designed by Walter D. Richards.

ENGRAVED
Plates of 160 subjects in four panes of 40.

1982, Sept. 30	Tagged	Perf. 11	
2019 A1404 20c black & brown		.45	.20
a. Tagging omitted			
b. Red missing (PS)			
2020 A1405 20c black & brown		.45	.20
a. Red missing (PS)			
2021 A1406 20c black & brown		.45	.20
2022 A1407 20c black & brown		.45	.20
a. Block of 4, #2019-2022		2.00	1.75
P# block of 4		2.50	—
Zip block of 4		2.10	—

FRANCIS OF ASSISI

A1408

Designed by Ned Seidler.

Printed by American Bank Note Co. and J.W. Fergusson and Sons.

PHOTOGRAVURE
Plates of 200 subjects in four panes of 50.

1982, Oct. 7	Tagged	Perf. 11	
2023 A1408 20c multicolored		.40	.20
P# block of 4, 6#		1.75	—
Zip block of 4		1.65	—

PONCE DE LEON

A1409

Designed by Richard Schlecht.

PHOTOGRAVURE (Combination press)
Plates of 230 subjects (10x23) in panes of 50 (5x10).

1982, Oct. 12	Tagged	Perf. 11	
2024 A1409 20c multicolored		.50	.20
P# block of 6, 5#		3.50	—
P# block of 20, 5 or 10 #, 1-2 zip, 1-2 copyright		12.00	—
a. Imperf., pair		450.00	
b. Vert. pair, imperf. between and at top		—	

See Combination Press note after No. 1703.

CHRISTMAS ISSUES

A1410

A1411

A1412

A1413

A1414

A1415

PHOTOGRAVURE
Plates of 200 subjects in four panes of 50

Designed by Chuck Ripper.

1982, Nov. 3		Tagged	
2025	A1410 13c **multicolored**	.25	.20
	P# block of 4	1.40	—
	Zip block of 4	1.10	—
a.	Imperf., pair	500.00	

PHOTOGRAVURE (Combination Press)
Plates of 230 subjects (10x23) in panes of 50 (5x10).

Designed by Bradbury Thompson.

1982, Oct. 28		Tagged	
2026	A1411 20c **multicolored**	.40	.20
	P# block of 20, 5 or 10 #, 1-2 copyright, 1-2 zip	11.00	—
a.	Imperf. pair	150.00	—
b.	Horiz. pair, imperf. vert.	—	
c.	Vert. pair, imperf. horiz.	—	

See Combination Press note after No. 1703.

PHOTOGRAVURE
Plates of 200 in four panes of 50.

Designed by Dolli Tingle.

2027	A1412 20c **multicolored**	.50	.20
2028	A1413 20c **multicolored**	.50	.20
2029	A1414 20c **multicolored**	.50	.20
2030	A1415 20c **multicolored**	.50	.20
a.	Block of 4, #2027-2030	2.10	1.50
	P# block of 4, 4#	2.50	—
	Zip block of 4	2.10	—
b.	As "a," imperf.	2,000.	
c.	As "a," imperf. horiz.	850.00	

SCIENCE & INDUSTRY

A1416

Designed by Saul Bass.

LITHOGRAPHED AND ENGRAVED
Plates of 200 in four panes of 50.

1983, Jan. 19		Tagged		Perf. 11
2031	A1416 20c **multicolored**	.40	.20	
	P# block of 4, 4#	1.75	—	
	Zip block of 4	1.65	—	
a.	Black (engr.) omitted	1,250.		
b.	Tagging omitted	—		

BALLOONS

Intrepid — A1417

Explorer II — A1420

A1418

A1419

Designed by Davis Meltzer.

PHOTOGRAVURE
Plates of 160 in four panes of 40.

1983, Mar. 31		Tagged		Perf. 11
2032	A1417 20c **multicolored**	.50	.20	
2033	A1418 20c **multicolored**	.50	.20	
2034	A1419 20c **multicolored**	.50	.20	
2035	A1420 20c **multicolored**	.50	.20	
a.	Block of 4, #2032-2035	2.00	1.50	
	P# block of 4, 5#	2.25		
	Zip block of 4	2.10		
b.	As "a," imperf.	4,000.		
c.	As "a," right stamp perf., otherwise imperf.	4,500.		

US-SWEDEN

Benjamin Franklin A1421

Designed by Czeslaw Slania, court engraver of Sweden.

ENGRAVED
Plates of 200 in four panes of 50.

1983, Mar. 24		Tagged		Perf. 11
2036	A1421 20c **blue, blk & red brn**	.40	.20	
	P# block of 4	1.75		
	Zip block of 4	1.65	—	

See Sweden No. 1453.

CCC, 50th ANNIV.

A1422

Designed by David K. Stone.

PHOTOGRAVURE
Plates of 200 in four panes of 50.

1983, Apr. 5		Tagged		Perf. 11
2037	A1422 20c **multicolored**	.40	.20	
	P# block of 4, 6#	1.75		
	Zip block of 4	1.65	—	
a.	Imperf., pair	3,000.		
b.	Vert. pair, imperf. horiz.	—		

JOSEPH PRIESTLEY

Discoverer of Oxygen — A1423

Designed by Dennis Lyall.

Printed by American Bank Note Company and J.W. Fergusson and Sons.

PHOTOGRAVURE
Plates of 200 in four panes of 50.

1983, Apr. 13		Tagged		Perf. 11
2038	A1423 20c **multicolored**	.40	.20	
	P# block of 4, 6#	1.75	—	
	Zip block of 4	1.65	—	

VOLUNTARISM

A1424

Designed by Paul Calle.

ENGRAVED (Combination Press)
lates of 230 subjects (10x23) in panes of 50 (5x10).

1983, Apr. 20	Tagged	Perf. 11	
)39 A1424 20c red & black		.40	.20
P# block of 6		3.00	
P# block of 20, 1-2 #, 1-2 copyright, 1-2 zip		10.00	—
a.	Imperf., pair	350.00	

See Combination Press note after No. 1703.

US-GERMANY

A1425

Designed by Richard Schlecht.

ENGRAVED
Plates of 200 in four panes of 50.

1983, Apr. 29	Tagged	Perf. 11	
2040 A1425 20c brown		.40	.20
P# block of 4		1.75	
Zip block of 4		1.65	—
a.	Tagging omitted	—	

See Germany No. 1397.

BROOKLYN BRIDGE

A1426

Normal

"Unfinished Bridge" Short Transfer

Designed by Howard Koslow.

ENGRAVED
Plates of 200 in four panes of 50.

1983, May 17	Tagged	Perf. 11	
2041 A1426 20c blue		.40	.20
P# block of 4		1.75	
Zip block of 4		1.65	—
Short transfer (unfinished bridge) (UL 2)		9.00	.75
P# block of 4		15.00	—
a.	Tagging omitted	—	
b.	All color missing (EP)	75.00	

On No. 2041b, an albino impression of the stamp is evident.

TVA

Norris Hydroelectric Dam — A1427

Designed by Howard Koslow.

PHOTOGRAVURE AND ENGRAVED (Combination Press)
Plates of 230 in panes of 50

1983, May 18	Tagged	Perf. 11	
2042 A1427 20c multicolored		.40	.20
P# block of 20, 5-10 #, 1-2 copyright, 1-2 zip		10.00	—

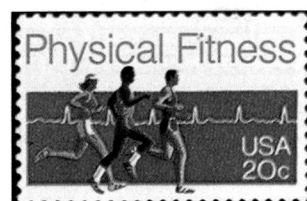

Runners, Electrocardiograph Tracing — A1428

Designed by Donald Moss.

PHOTOGRAVURE (Combination Press)
Plates of 230 in panes of 50.

1983, May 14	Tagged	Perf. 11	
2043 A1428 20c multicolored		.40	.20
P# block of 6, 4#		3.00	
P# block of 20, 4-8 #, 1-2 copyright, 1-2 zip		10.00	—

BLACK HERITAGE SERIES
Scott Joplin (1868-1917), Ragtime composer.

A1429

Designed by Jerry Pinkney.

PHOTOGRAVURE
Plates of 200 in four panes of 50.

1983, June 9	Tagged	Perf. 11	
2044 A1429 20c multicolored		.50	.20
P# block of 4, 6#		2.40	
Zip block of 4		2.10	—
a.	Imperf., pair	450.00	
b.	Tagging omitted	—	

MEDAL OF HONOR

A1430

Designed by Dennis J. Hom.

LITHOGRAPHED AND ENGRAVED
Plates of 160 in four panes of 40.

1983, June 7	Tagged	Perf. 11	
2045 A1430 20c multicolored		.55	.20
P# block of 4, 5#		2.50	
Zip block of 4		2.25	—
a.	Red omitted	250.00	

A1431   A1432

GEORGE HERMAN RUTH (1895-1948)
Designed by Richard Gangel.

ENGRAVED
Plates of 200 in four panes of 50.

1983, July 6	Tagged	Perf. 10½x11	
2046 A1431 20c blue		1.40	.20
P# block of 4		6.50	
Zip block of 4		5.75	—

LITERARY ARTS SERIES
Nathaniel Hawthorne (1804-1864), novelist.

Designed by Bradbury Thompson after 1851 painting by Cephus Giovanni Thompson.

PHOTOGRAVURE
Plates of 200 in four panes of 50.

1983, July 8	Tagged	Perf. 11	
2047 A1432 20c multicolored		.45	.20
P# block of 4, 4#		2.10	
Zip block of 4		1.90	—

1984 SUMMER OLYMPICS
Los Angeles, July 28-August 12

Discus A1433

High Jump — A1434

Archery
A1435

Boxing
A1436

Designed by Bob Peak.

PHOTOGRAVURE
Plates of 200 in four panes of 50.

1983, July 28		Tagged	Perf. 11	
2048	A1433 13c **multicolored**		.35	.20
2049	A1434 13c **multicolored**		.35	.20
2050	A1435 13c **multicolored**		.35	.20
2051	A1436 13c **multicolored**		.35	.20
a.	Block of 4, #2048-2051		1.50	1.25
	P# block of 4, 4#		1.75	—
	Zip block of 4		1.65	—

SIGNING OF TREATY OF PARIS

John Adams,
B. Franklin,
John Jay,
David Hartley
A1437

Designed by David Blossom based on unfinished painting by Benjamin West in Winterthur Museum.

PHOTOGRAVURE
Plates of 160 in four panes of 40.

1983, Sept. 2		Tagged	Perf. 11	
2052	A1437 20c **multicolored**		.40	.20
	P# block of 4, 4#		1.75	—
	Zip block of 4		1.65	—
a.	Tagging omitted			—

CIVIL SERVICE

A1438

Designed by MDB Communications, Inc.

PHOTOGRAVURE AND ENGRAVED
Plates of 230 in four panes of 50.

1983, Sept. 9		Tagged	Perf. 11	
2053	A1438 20c **buff, blue & red**		.40	.20
	P# block of 6		3.00	—
	P# block of 20, 1-2P#, 1-2 Zip,			
	1-2 Copyright		10.00	—
a.	Tagging omitted			—

METROPOLITAN OPERA

Original State Arch and Current 5-arch Entrance
A1439

Designed by Ken Davies.

LITHOGRAPHED AND ENGRAVED
Plates of 200 in four panes of 50.

1983, Sept. 14		Tagged	Perf. 11	
2054	A1439 20c **yellow & maroon**		.40	.20
	P# block of 4, 2#		1.75	—
	Zip block of 4		1.65	—
a.	Tagging omitted		8.50	

AMERICAN INVENTORS

Charles Steinmetz and Curve on Graph
A1440

Edwin Armstrong and Frequency Modulator
A1441

Nikola Tesla and Induction Motor — A1442

Philo T. Farnsworth and First Television Camera
A1443

Designed by Dennis Lyall.

LITHOGRAPHED AND ENGRAVED
Plates of 200 in four panes of 50.

1983, Sept. 21		Tagged	Perf. 11	
2055	A1440 20c **multicolored**		.50	.20
2056	A1441 20c **multicolored**		.50	.20
2057	A1442 20c **multicolored**		.50	.20
2058	A1443 20c **multicolored**		.50	.20
a.	Block of 4, #2055-2058		2.00	1.50
	P# block of 4, 2#		2.75	—
	Zip block of 4		2.10	—
b.	As "a," black omitted		350.00	

STREETCARS

A1444

A1445

A1446

A1447

Designed by Richard Leech.

PHOTOGRAVURE AND ENGRAVED
Plates of 200 in four panes of 50.

1983, Oct. 8		Tagged	Perf. 11	
2059	A1444 20c **multicolored**		.50	.20
2060	A1445 20c **multicolored**		.50	.20
2061	A1446 20c **multicolored**		.50	.20
2062	A1447 20c **multicolored**		.50	.20
a.	Block of 4, #2059-2062		2.00	1.50
	P# block of 4, 5#		2.60	—
	Zip block of 4		2.10	—
b.	As "a," black omitted		400.00	
c.	As "a," black omitted on #2059, 2061		—	

CHRISTMAS

Niccolini-Cowper Madonna, by Raphael — A1448

Santa Claus
A1449

Designed by Bradbury Thompson (No. 2063), and John Berkey (No. 2064).

PHOTOGRAVURE
Plates of 200 in four panes of 50 (No. 2063),
Plates of 230 in panes of 50 (Combination Press, No. 2064)

1983, Oct. 28		Tagged	Perf. 11	
2063	A1448 20c **multicolored**		.40	.20
	P# block of 4, 5#		1.75	—
	Zip block of 4		1.65	—
2064	A1449 20c **multicolored**		.40	.20
	P# block of 6, 5#		3.00	—
	P# block of 20, 5-10 P#, 1-2			
	copyright, 1-2 zip		11.50	—
a.	Imperf., pair		150.00	
b.	Tagging omitted			

See Combination Press note after No. 1703.

German Religious
Leader, Founder of
Lutheran Church
1483-1546) — A1450

Caribou and Alaska
Pipeline — A1451

MARTIN LUTHER

Designed by Bradbury Thompson.

Printed by American Bank Note Company.

PHOTOGRAVURE
Plates of 200 in four panes of 50.

1983, Nov. 11	Tagged	Perf. 11
)65 A1450 20c **multicolored**	.40	.20
P# block of 4, 5#	1.75	
Zip block of 4	1.65	—

ALASKA STATEHOOD, 25th ANNIV.

Designed by Bill Bond.

Printed by American Bank Note Company and J.W. Ferguson and Sons.

PHOTOGRAVURE
Plates of 200 in four panes of 50.

1984, Jan. 3	Tagged	Perf. 11
)66 A1451 20c **multicolored**	.40	.20
P# block of 4, 5#	1.75	
Zip block of 4	1.65	—

14th WINTER OLYMPIC GAMES, Sarajevo, Yugoslavia, Feb. 8-19

Ice Dancing — A1452

Downhill
Skiing — A1453

Cross-country
Skiing — A1454

Hockey — A1455

Designed by Bob Peak.

PHOTOGRAVURE
Plates of 200 in four panes of 50.

1984, Jan. 6	Tagged	Perf. 10½x11
2067 A1452 20c **multicolored**	.55	.20
2068 A1453 20c **multicolored**	.55	.20
2069 A1454 20c **multicolored**	.55	.20
2070 A1455 20c **multicolored**	.55	.20
a. Block of 4, #2067-2070	2.20	1.75
P# block of 4, 4#	3.00	—
Zip block of 4	2.25	

Pillar, Dollar
Sign — A1456

A1457

FEDERAL DEPOSIT INSURANCE CORPORATION, 50TH ANNIV.

Designed by Michael David Brown.

PHOTOGRAVURE
Plates of 200 in four panes of 50
(1 pane each #2071, 2074, 2075 and 2081)

1984, Jan. 12	Tagged	Perf. 11
2071 A1456 20c **multicolored**	.40	.20
P# block of 4, 6#, UL only	1.75	
Zip block of 4	1.65	—

LOVE

Designed by Bradbury Thompson.

PHOTOGRAVURE AND ENGRAVED (Combination Press)
Plates of 230 in four panes of 50.

1984, Jan. 31	Tagged	Perf. 11x10½
2072 A1457 20c **multicolored**	.40	.20
P# block of 20, 6-12#, 1-2 copyright, 1-2 zip	11.50	—
a. Horiz. pair, imperf. vert.	175.00	
b. Tagging omitted	5.00	

See Combination Press note after No. 1703.

A1458

A1459

BLACK HERITAGE SERIES

Carter G. Woodson (1875-1950), Black Historian.

Designed by Jerry Pinkney.

Printed by American Bank Note Company.

PHOTOGRAVURE
Plates of 200 in four panes of 50.

1984, Feb. 1	Tagged	Perf. 11
2073 A1458 20c **multicolored**	.40	.20
P# block of 4, 6#	2.00	—
Zip block of 4	1.65	—
a. Horiz. pair, imperf. vert.	1,250.	

SOIL & WATER CONSERVATION

Designed by Michael David Brown.

See No. 2071 for printing information.

1984, Feb. 6	Tagged	Perf. 11
2074 A1459 20c **multicolored**	.40	.20
P# block of 4, 6#, UR only	1.75	
Zip block of 4	1.65	—

50TH ANNIV. OF CREDIT UNION ACT

Dollar Sign, Coin — A1460

Designed by Michael David Brown.

See No. 2071 for printing information.

1984, Feb. 10	Tagged	Perf. 11
2075 A1460 20c **multicolored**	.40	.20
P# block of 4, 6#, LR only	1.75	—
Zip block of 4	1.65	

ORCHIDS

Wild Pink — A1461

Yellow Lady's-slipper
A1462

Spreading
Pogonia — A1463

Pacific
Calypso — A1464

Designed by Manabu Saito.

PHOTOGRAVURE
Plates of 192 in four panes of 48.

1984, Mar. 5	Tagged	Perf. 11
2076 A1461 20c **multicolored**	.50	.20
2077 A1462 20c **multicolored**	.50	.20
2078 A1463 20c **multicolored**	.50	.20
2079 A1464 20c **multicolored**	.50	.20
a. Block of 4, #2076-2079	2.00	1.50
P# block of 4, 5#	2.50	—
Zip block of 4	2.10	—

HAWAII STATEHOOD, 25th ANNIV.

Eastern Polynesian Canoe, Golden Plover, Mauna Loa Volcano A1465

Designed by Herb Kane.

Printed by American Bank Note Company.

PHOTOGRAVURE
Plates of 200 in four panes of 50.

1984, Mar. 12		Tagged	Perf. 11	
2080	A1465	20c multicolored	.40	.20
		P# block of 4, 5#	1.70	—
		Zip block of 4	1.65	—

50TH ANNIV., NATIONAL ARCHIVES

Abraham Lincoln, George Washington — A1466

Designed by Michael David Brown.

See No. 2071 for printing information.

1984, Apr. 16		Tagged	Perf. 11	
2081	A1466	20c multicolored	.40	.20
		P# block of 4, 6#, LL only	1.70	—
		Zip block of 4	1.65	—

LOS ANGELES SUMMER OLYMPICS
July 28-August 12

Diving — A1467

Long Jump — A1468

Wrestling — A1469

Kayak — A1470

Designed by Bob Peak.

PHOTOGRAVURE
Plates of 200 in four panes of 50.

1984, May 4		Tagged	Perf. 11	
2082	A1467	20c multicolored	.55	.20
2083	A1468	20c multicolored	.55	.20
2084	A1469	20c multicolored	.55	.20
2085	A1470	20c multicolored	.55	.20
a.		Block of 4, #2082-2085	2.40	1.90

			3.50	—
		P# block of 4, 4#	2.50	—
		Zip block of 4		
b.		As "a," imperf between vertically	—	

LOUISIANA WORLD EXPOSITION
New Orleans, May 12-Nov. 11

Bayou Wildlife A1471

Designed by Chuck Ripper.

PHOTOGRAVURE
Plates of 160 in four panes of 40.

1984, May 11		Tagged	Perf. 11	
2086	A1471	20c multicolored	.50	.20
		On cover, Expo. station pictorial handstamp cancel	2.50	
		P# block of 4, 5#	2.60	—
		Zip block of 4	2.10	—

HEALTH RESEARCH

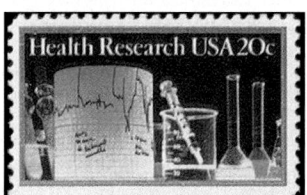

Lab Equipment A1472

Designed by Tyler Smith.

Printed by American Bank Note Company.

PHOTOGRAVURE
Plates of 200 in four panes of 50.

1984, May 17		Tagged	Perf. 11	
2087	A1472	20c multicolored	.40	.20
		P# block of 4, 5#	1.75	—
		Zip block of 4	1.65	—

Actor Douglas Fairbanks (1883-1939) — A1473

A1474

PERFORMING ARTS

Designed by Jim Sharpe.

PHOTOGRAVURE AND ENGRAVED (Combination Press)
Plates of 230 in panes of 50.

1984, May 23		Tagged	Perf. 11	
2088	A1473	20c multicolored	.40	.20
		P# block of 20, 5-10#, 1-2 copyright, 1-2 zip	11.00	—
a.		Tagging omitted	15.00	
b.		Horiz. pair, imperf between		

See Combination Press note after No. 1703.

JIM THORPE, 1888-1953

Designed by Richard Gangel.

ENGRAVED
Plates of 200 in four panes of 50.

1984, May 24		Tagged	Perf. 11	
2089	A1474	20c dark brown	.40	.20
		P# block of 4	2.00	—
		Zip block of 4	1.65	—

PERFORMING ARTS

John McCormack (1884-1945), Operatic Tenor — A1475

Designed by Jim Sharpe (US) and Ron Mercer (Ireland).

PHOTOGRAVURE
Plates of 200 in four panes of 50.

1984, June 6		Tagged	Perf.	
2090	A1475	20c multicolored	.40	
		P# block of 4, 5#	1.75	
		Zip block of 4	1.65	

See Ireland No. 594.

ST. LAWRENCE SEAWAY, 25th ANNIV.

Aerial View of Seaway, Freighters A1476

Designed by Ernst Barenscher (Canada).

Printed by American Bank Note Company.

PHOTOGRAVURE
Plates of 200 in four panes of 50.

1984, June 26		Tagged	Perf. 1	
2091	A1476	20c multicolored	.40	.2
		P# block of 4, 4#	1.75	
		Zip block of 4	1.65	—

WATERFOWL PRESERVATION ACT, 50th ANNIV.

"Mallards Dropping In" by Jay N. Darling A1477

Design adapted from Darling's work (No. RW1) by Donald M McDowell.

ENGRAVED
Plates of 200 in four panes of 50.

1984, July 2		Tagged	Perf. 11	
2092	A1477	20c blue	.50	.20
		P# block of 4	2.50	—
		Zip block of 4	2.25	—
a.		Horiz. pair, imperf. vert.	350.00	

The Elizabeth — A1478

A1479

ROANOKE VOYAGES

Designed by Charles Lundgren.

Printed by American Bank Note Company.

PHOTOGRAVURE
Plates of 200 in four panes of 50.

1984, July 13	Tagged	Perf. 11	
2093 A1478 20c multicolored		.40	.20
P# block of 4, 5#		1.75	—
Zip block of 4		1.65	—
Pair with full horiz. gutter btwn.		—	

LITERARY ARTS SERIES
Herman Melville (1819-1891), Author

Designed by Bradbury Thompson.

ENGRAVED
Plates of 200 in four panes of 50.

1984, Aug. 1	Tagged	Perf. 11	
2094 A1479 20c sage green		.40	.20
P# block of 4		1.75	—
Zip block of 4		1.65	—
a.	Tagging omitted		

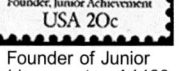

Founder of Junior Achievement — A1480

Smokey Bear — A1481

HORACE MOSES (1862-1947)
Designed by Dennis Lyall.

ENGRAVED (Combination Press)
Plates of 200 in panes of 50.

1984, Aug. 6	Tagged	Perf. 11	
2095 A1480 20c orange & dark brown		.45	.20
P# block of 6		3.50	—
P# block of 20, 1-2#, 1-2 copyright, 1-2 zip		12.50	—

See Combination Press note after No. 1703.

SMOKEY BEAR
Designed by Rudolph Wendelin.

LITHOGRAPHED AND ENGRAVED
Plates of 200 in panes of 50.

1984, Aug. 13	Tagged	Perf. 11	
2096 A1481 20c multicolored		.40	.20
P# block of 4, 5#		2.00	—
Zip block of 4		1.65	—
a.	Horiz. pair, imperf. btwn.	275.00	
b.	Vert. pair, imperf. btwn.	225.00	
c.	Block of 4, imperf. btwn. vert. and horiz.	5,500.	
d.	Horiz. pair, imperf. vert.	1,500.	
e.	Tagging omitted	—	

ROBERTO CLEMENTE (1934-1972)

Clemente Wearing Pittsburgh Pirates Cap, Puerto Rican Flag — A1482

Designed by Juan Lopez-Bonilla.

PHOTOGRAVURE
Plates of 200 in panes of 50.

1984, Aug. 17	Tagged	Perf. 11	
2097 A1482 20c multicolored		1.50	.20
P# block of 4, 6#		6.50	—
Zip block of 4		6.25	—
a.	Horiz. pair, imperf. vert.	2,000.	

DOGS

Beagle and Boston Terrier A1483

Chesapeake Bay Retriever and Cocker Spaniel A1484

Alaskan Malamute and Collie A1485

Black and Tan Coonhound and American Foxhound A1486

Designed by Roy Andersen.

PHOTOGRAVURE
Plates of 160 in panes of 40.

1984, Sept. 7	Tagged	Perf. 11	
2098 A1483 20c multicolored		.50	.20
2099 A1484 20c multicolored		.50	.20
2100 A1485 20c multicolored		.50	.20
2101 A1486 20c multicolored		.50	.20
a.	Block of 4, #2098-2101	2.00	1.90
	P# block of 4, 4#	3.00	—
	Zip block of 4	2.10	—
b.	As "a," imperf horiz.	—	

CRIME PREVENTION

McGruff, the Crime Dog — A1487

Designed by Randall McDougall.

Printed by American Bank Note Company.

PHOTOGRAVURE
Plates of 200 in panes of 50.

1984, Sept. 26	Tagged	Perf. 11	
2102 A1487 20c multicolored		.40	.20
P# block of 4, 4#		1.75	—
Zip block of 4		1.65	—

HISPANIC AMERICANS

A1488

Designed by Robert McCall.

PHOTOGRAVURE
Plates of 160 in four panes of 40.

1984, Oct. 31	Tagged	Perf. 11	
2103 A1488 20c multicolored		.40	.20
P# block of 4, 6#		1.75	—
Zip block of 4		1.65	—
a.	Vert. pair, imperf. horiz.	2,250.	

FAMILY UNITY

Stick Figures — A1489

Designed by Molly LaRue.

PHOTOGRAVURE AND ENGRAVED (Combination Press)
Plates of 230 in panes of 50.

1984, Oct. 1	Tagged	Perf. 11	
2104 A1489 20c multicolored		.40	.20
P# block of 20, 3-6#, 1-2 copyright, 1-2 zip		12.50	—
a.	Horiz. pair, imperf. vert.	500.00	
b.	Tagging omitted	7.50	
c.	Vert. pair, imperf. btwn. and at bottom	—	
d.	Horiz. pair, imperf. between	—	

See Combination Press note after No. 1703.
Used untagged imperfs exist from printer's waste.

A1490

Abraham Lincoln Reading to Son, Tad — A1491

ELEANOR ROOSEVELT (1884-1962)
Designed by Bradbury Thompson.

ENGRAVED
Plates of 192 in panes of 48.

1984, Oct. 11	Tagged	Perf. 11	
2105 A1490 20c deep blue		.40	.20
P# block of 4		2.00	—
Zip block of 4		1.65	—

NATION OF READERS

Design adapted from Anthony Berger daguerrotype by Bradbury Thompson.

ENGRAVED

Plates of 200 in panes of 50.

1984, Oct. 16	Tagged	Perf. 11	
2106 A1491 20c **brown & maroon**		.40	.20
P# block of 4		1.90	
Zip block of 4		1.65	—

CHRISTMAS

Madonna and Child by Fra Filippo Lippi — A1492

Santa Claus — A1493

Designed by Bradbury Thompson (No. 2107) and Danny La Boccetta (No. 2108).

PHOTOGRAVURE

Plates of 200 in panes of 50.

1984, Oct. 30	Tagged	Perf. 11	
2107 A1492 20c **multicolored**		.40	.20
P# block of 4, 5#		1.70	
Zip block of 4		1.65	—
2108 A1493 20c **multicolored**		.40	.20
P# block of 4, 5#		1.70	
Zip block of 4		1.65	—
a. Horiz. pair, imperf. vert.		925.00	

No. 2108a is valued in the grade of fine.

VIETNAM VETERANS MEMORIAL

Memorial and Visitors — A1494

Designed by Paul Calle.

ENGRAVED

Plates of 160 in panes of 40.

1984, Nov. 10	Tagged	Perf. 11	
2109 A1494 20c **multicolored**		.40	.20
P# block of 4		2.25	
Zip block of 4		1.65	—
a. Tagging omitted		—	

PERFORMING ARTS

Jerome Kern (1885-1945), Composer — A1495

Designed by Jim Sharpe.

Printed by the American Bank Note Company.

PHOTOGRAVURE

Plates of 200 in four panes of 50.

1985, Jan. 23	Tagged	Perf. 11	
2110 A1495 22c **multicolored**		.40	.20
P# block of 4, 5#		1.75	
Zip block of 4		1.65	—
a. Tagging omitted		7.50	

A1496

A1497

Designed by Bradbury Thompson.

PHOTOGRAVURE

Plates of 460 (20x23) in panes of 100.

1985, Feb. 1	Tagged	Perf. 11	
2111 A1496 (22c) **green**		.60	.20
P# block of 6		4.50	
P# block of 20, 1-2 #, 1-2			
Zip, 1-2 Copyright		20.00	—
a. Vert. pair, imperf.		40.00	
b. Vert. pair, imperf. horiz.		*1,350.*	
c. Tagging omitted		—	

COIL STAMP
Perf. 10 Vert.

2112 A1496 (22c) **green**		.60	.20
Pair		1.20	.20
P# strip of 3, #1, 2		5.00	
P# strip of 5, #1, 2		6.50	
P# single, #1, 2		—	.50
a. Imperf., pair		45.00	
P#1, 2			
b. As "a," tagging omitted		100.00	
P#1, 2			
c. As No. 2112, tagging omitted		—	
P#1, 2			

ENGRAVED
BOOKLET STAMP
Perf. 11

2113 A1497 (22c) **green**		.80	.20
a. Booklet pane of 10		8.50	3.00
b. As "a," imperf. btwn. horiz.			

A1498

Flag Over Capitol Dome A1499

Designed by Frank Waslick.

ENGRAVED

Plates of 400 subjects in panes of 100.

1985, Mar. 29	Tagged	Perf. 11	
2114 A1498 22c **blue, red & black**		.40	.20
P# block of 4		1.90	
Zip block of 4		1.65	—
Pair with full horizontal gutter		—	
a. All color missing (EP)		—	
b. Tagging omitted		—	

No. 2114a should be collected se-tenant with a normal or a partially printed stamp.

COIL STAMP
Perf. 10 Vert.

2115 A1498 22c **blue, red & black,** wide			
block tagging, 19mmx21.5mm (B press)		.40	.20
Pair		.80	.20
P# strip of 3, #2		3.00	
P# strip of 3, #4		4.75	
P# strip of 3, #6		6.00	
P# strip of 3, #10		3.50	
P# strip of 3, #13		10.50	
P# strip of 3, #14		24.00	
P# strip of 3, #15		3.00	
P# strip of 3, #16		4.25	
P# strip of 3, #21		5.00	
P# strip of 5, #2		3.50	
P# strip of 5, #4		5.50	
P# strip of 5, #6		6.50	
P# strip of 5, #10		3.75	
P# strip of 5, #13		12.50	
P# strip of 5, #14		29.00	
P# strip of 5, #15		3.25	
P# strip of 5, #16		5.50	
P# strip of 5, #21		6.00	
P# single, #2		—	.50

P# single, #4		—	.5
P# single, #6		—	6.5
P# single, #10		—	.6
P# single, #13		—	9.0
P# single, #14		—	27.5
P# single, #15		—	1.5
P# single, #16		—	2.2
P# single, #21		—	2.2
a. Narrow block tagging, 17.5mmx21.5mm (C press)		.40	.2
P# strip of 3, #1, 3		10.00	
P# strip of 3, #5		4.50	
P# strip of 3, #7		10.50	
P# strip of 3, #8		3.00	
P# strip of 3, #11		5.75	
P# strip of 3, #12		3.00	
P# strip of 3, #17, 18		5.00	
P# strip of 3, #19		3.00	
P# strip of 3, #20		5.00	
P# strip of 3, #22		3.00	
P# strip of 5, #1		12.00	
P# strip of 5, #3		47.50	
P# strip of 5, #5		5.75	
P# strip of 5, #7		12.00	
P# strip of 5, #8		3.25	
P# strip of 5, #11		6.00	
P# strip of 5, #12		3.25	
P# strip of 5, #17-18		6.00	
P# strip of 5, #19		3.25	
P# strip of 5, #20		6.00	
P# strip of 5, #22		3.25	
P# single, #1, 3, 5		—	.5
P# single, #7-8		—	.6
P# single, #11		—	1.0
P# single, #12		—	.65
P# single, #17-18		—	2.0
P# single, #19		—	.65
P# single, #20		—	2.25
P# single, #22		—	.65
b. Wide and tall block tagging, 19.5mmx23mm (D press)		.40	.20
P# strip of 3, #8		—	
P# strip of 3, #18		—	
P# strip of 3, #20		—	
P# strip of 3, #22		—	
P# strip of 5, #8		150.00	
P# strip of 5, #18		80.00	
P# strip of 5, #20		100.00	
P# strip of 5, #22		125.00	
P# single, #8		—	50.00
P# single, #18		—	50.00
P# single, #20		—	50.00
P# single, #22		—	50.00
c. Inscribed "T" at bottom, *May 23, 1987*		.50	.40
P# strip of 3, #1		3.00	
P# strip of 5, #1		3.50	
P# single, #1		—	3.00
d. Black field of stars		—	
e. Tagging omitted		12.50	
f. Imperf., pair		12.50	
P#1-8, 10-12, 15, 17-20, 22			

No. 2115 is known with capitol in bluish black color, apparently from contaminated ink. Specialists often refer to this as "Erie blue."

BOOKLET STAMP
Perf. 10 Horiz.

2116 A1499 22c **blue, red & black**		.50	.20
a. Booklet pane of 5		2.50	1.25
Scored perforations		2.50	

BOOKLET STAMPS

Frilled Dogwinkle — A1500

Reticulated Helmet — A1501

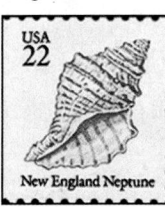

New England Neptune — A1502

Calico Scallop — A1503

Lightning Whelk — A1504

Designed by Pete Cocci.

ENGRAVED

1985, Apr. 4   **Tagged**   *Perf. 10*

117	A1500	22c	**black & brown**	.40	.20
a.		Tagging omitted			
118	A1501	22c	**black & multi**	.40	.20
119	A1502	22c	**black & brown**	.40	.20
a.		Tagging omitted			
120	A1503	22c	**black & violet**	.40	.20
121	A1504	22c	**black & multi**	.40	.20
a.		Booklet pane of 10, 2 ea #2117-2121		4.00	3.00
b.		As "a," violet omitted on both Nos. 2120		600.00	
c.		As "a," vert. imperf. between		550.00	—
d.		As "a," imperf.		—	
e.		Strip of 5, Nos. 2117-2121		2.00	—

Eagle and Half Moon — A1505

Designed by Young & Rubicam.

TYPE I: washed out, dull appearance most evident in the black of the body of the eagle, and the red in the background between the eagle's shoulder and the moon. "$10.75" appears splotchy or grainy (P# 11111).
TYPE II: brighter, more intense colors most evident in the black on the eagle's body, and red in the background. "$10.75" appears smoother, brighter, and less grainy (P# 22222).

PHOTOGRAVURE

1985, Apr. 29   **Untagged**   *Perf. 10 Vert.*

2122	A1505	$10.75	**multicolored,** type I	19.00	7.50
a.		Booklet pane of 3		60.00	—
b.		Type II, *June 19,* 1989		21.00	10.00
c.		As "b," booklet pane of 3		65.00	—

Coil Plate No. Strips of 3
Beginning with No. 2123, coil plate No. strips of 3 usually sell at the level of strips of 5 minus the face value of two stamps.

TRANSPORTATION ISSUE

School Bus 1920s
3.4 USA

A1506

Star Route Truck
5.5 USA 1910s

A1508

Tractor 1920s
7.1 USA

A1510

Buckboard 1880s
USA 4.9

A1507

Tricycle 1880s
6 USA

A1509

Ambulance 1860s
8.3 USA

A1511

Tow Truck 1920s
8.5 USA

A1512

Stutz Bearcat 1933
11 USA

A1514

Pushcart 1880s
12.5 USA

A1516

Dog Sled 1920s
17 USA

A1518

Oil Wagon 1890s
10.1 USA

A1513

Stanley Steamer 1909
USA 12

A1515

Iceboat 1880s
USA 14

A1517

Bread Wagon 1880s
25 USA

A1519

Designers: 3.4c, 17c, Lou Nolan. 4.9c, 8.5c, 14c, 25c, William H. Bond. 5.5c, David K. Stone. 6c, 8.3c, 10.1c, 12.5c. James Schleyer. 7.1c, 11c, 12c, Ken Dallison.

COIL STAMPS
ENGRAVED

1985-87   **Tagged**   *Perf. 10 Vert.*

2123	A1506	3.4c	**dark bluish green,** *June 8*	.20	.20
		Pair		.20	.20
		P# strip of 5, line, #1-2		.90	
		P# single, #1-2		—	.80
a.		Untagged (Bureau precancel, Non-profit Org. CAR-RT SORT)		.20	.20
		P# strip of 5, line, #1-2		4.25	
		P# single, #1-2		—	3.75
2124	A1507	4.9c	**brown black,** *June 21*	.20	.20
		Pair		.20	.20
		P# strip of 5, line, #3-4		.85	
		P# single, #3-4		—	.80
a.		Untagged (Bureau precancel, Non-profit Org.)		.20	.20
		P# strip of 5, line, #1-6		1.40	
		P# single, #1-6		—	1.25
2125	A1508	5.5c	**deep magenta,** *Nov. 1, 1986*	.20	.20
		Pair		.20	.20
		P# strip of 5, #1		1.50	
		P# single, #1		—	1.25
a.		Untagged (Bureau precancel, Non-profit Org. CAR-RT SORT)		.20	.20
		P# strip of 5, #1		1.75	
		P# strip of 5, #2		2.25	
		P# single, #1		—	1.00
		P# single, #2		—	1.75

On No. 2125a, both vignette and the precancel inscription were printed from a single printing sleeve.

2126	A1509	6c	**red brown,** *May 6*	.20	.20
		Pair		.25	.20
		P# strip of 5, #1		1.50	
		P# single, #1		—	1.00
a.		Untagged (Bureau precancel, Non-profit Org.)		.20	.20
		P# strip of 5, #1		1.75	
		P# strip of 5, #2		7.00	
		P# single, #1		—	1.00
		P# single, #2		—	2.75
b.		As "a," imperf., pair		225.00	
		P#2			
2127	A1510	7.1c	**lake,** *Feb. 6, 1987*	.20	.20
		Pair		.30	.20
		P# strip of 5, #1		2.10	
		P# single, #1		—	1.50
a.		Untagged (Bureau precancel "Non-profit Org." in black), *Feb. 6, 1987*		.20	.20

		P# strip of 5, #1		3.00	
		P# single, #1		—	1.75
b.		Untagged (Bureau precancel "Non-profit 5-Digit Zip + 4" in black), *May 26, 1989*		.20	.20
		P# strip of 5, #1		1.75	
		P# single, #1		—	1.25

On Nos. 2127a and 2127b, both the vignette and the precancel inscription were printed from a single printing sleeve.

2128	A1511	8.3c	**green,** *June 21*	.20	.20
		Pair		.40	.20
		P# strip of 5, line, #1-2		1.50	
		P# single, #1-2		—	1.00
a.		Untagged (Bureau precancel, Blk. Rt. CAR-RT SORT)		.20	.20
		P# strip of 5, line, #1-2		1.50	
		P# strip of 5, line, #3-4		4.50	
		P# single, #1-2		—	1.25
		P# single, #3-4		—	3.75

On No. 2231 "Ambulance 1860s" is 18mm long; on No. 2128, 18½mm long.

2129	A1512	8.5c	**dark Prussian green,** *Jan. 24, 1987*	.20	.20
		Pair		.40	.20
		P# strip of 5, #1		3.00	
		P# single, #1		—	2.25
a.		Untagged (Bureau precancel, Non-profit Org.)		.20	.20
		P# strip of 5, #1		2.75	
		P# strip of 5, #2		12.00	
		P# single, #1		—	2.00
		P# single, #2		—	8.00
2130	A1513	10.1c	**slate blue,** *Apr. 18*	.25	.20
		Pair		.50	.20
		P# strip of 5, #1		2.50	
		P# single, #1		—	2.00
a.		Untagged (Bureau precancel "Bulk Rate Carrier Route Sort" in red)		.25	.25
		P# strip of 5, #2-3		2.25	
		P# single, #2-3		—	2.00
		Untagged (Bureau precancel "Bulk Rate" and lines in black)		.25	.25
		P# strip of 5, #1-2		2.50	
		P# single, #1-2		—	1.75
b.		As "a," red precancel, imperf, pair		15.00	
		P# strip of 6, #3		200.00	
		As "a," black precancel, imperf, pair		85.00	
		P# strip of 6, #1		400.00	
2131	A1514	11c	**dark green,** *June 11*	.25	.20
		Pair		.50	.20
		P# strip of 5, line, #1-4		1.40	
		P# single, #1-4		—	1.00
a.		Tagging omitted			
2132	A1515	12c	**dark blue,** type I, *Apr. 2*	.25	.20
		Pair		.50	.20
		P# strip of 5, line, #1-2		2.25	
		P# single, #1-2		—	1.50
a.		Untagged, type I (Bureau precancel, PRESORTED FIRST-CLASS), *Apr. 2*		.25	.25
		P# strip of 5, line, #1-2		2.40	
		P# single, #1-2		—	1.75
b.		Untagged, type II, (Bureau precancel, PRESORTED FIRST-CLASS) *1987*		.40	.30
		P# strip of 5, no line, #1		19.00	
		P# single, #1		—	17.00
c.		Tagging omitted, type I, (not Bureau precanceled), *1987*		12.50	
		P# strip of 5, #1, 2		150.00	
		P# single, #1, 2		—	140.00

Type II has "Stanley Steamer 1909" ½mm shorter (17⅞mm) than No. 2132 (18mm).

2133	A1516	12.5c	**olive green,** *Apr. 18*	.25	.20
		Pair		.50	.20
		P# strip of 5, #1		3.00	
		P# strip of 5, #2		4.75	
		P# single, #1		—	2.25
		P# single, #2		—	3.00
a.		Untagged (Bureau precancel, Bulk Rate)		.25	.25
		P# strip of 5, #1		3.00	
		P# strip of 5, #2		3.50	
		P# single, #1		—	1.75
		P# single, #2		—	3.00
b.		As "a," imperf., pair		45.00	
		P#1			

All No. 2133 from plate 1 and some No. 2133a from plate 1 were printed with luminescent ink that is orange under long wave UV light.

2134	A1517	14c	**sky blue,** type I, *Mar. 23*	.30	.20
		Pair		.60	.20
		P# strip of 5, line, #1-4		2.25	
		P# single, #1-4		—	1.50
a.		Imperf., pair		100.00	
		P#1-2			
b.		Type II, *Sept. 30, 1986*		.30	.20
		P# strip of 5, no line, #2		3.25	
		P# single, #2		—	2.50
c.		Tagging omitted, type I		15.00	—

Type II design is ¼mm narrower (17¼mm) than the original stamp (17½mm) and has block tagging. No. 2134 has overall tagging.

2135	A1518	17c	**sky blue,** *Aug. 20, 1986*	.35	.20
		Pair		.70	.20
		P# strip of 5, #2		3.25	
		P# single, #2		—	1.50
a.		Imperf., pair		400.00	
		P#2			
2136	A1519	25c	**orange brown,** *Nov. 22, 1986*	.45	.20
		Pair		.90	.20
		P# strip of 5, #1-5		3.50	

P# single, #1	—	1.25
P# single, #2-4	—	.65
P# single, #5	—	2.50
P#2-5		
a. Imperf., pair	10.00	
P#2-5		
b. Pair, imperf. between	*650.00*	
c. Tagging omitted	27.50	
P# strip of 5, #1	250.00	
Nos. 2123-2136 (14)	3.50	2.80

Precancellations on Nos. 2125a, 2127a do not have lines.
Precancellation on No. 2129a is in red. See No. 2231.

BLACK HERITAGE SERIES

Mary McLeod Bethune (1875-1955), educator.

A1520

Designed by Jerry Pinkney from a photograph.

Printed by American Bank Note Company.

PHOTOGRAVURE
Plates of 200 in four panes of 50.

1985, Mar. 5	Tagged		*Perf. 11*
2137 A1520 22c **multicolored**		.60	.20
P# block of 4, 6#		3.25	
Zip block of 4		2.50	—
a. Tagging omitted		—	

AMERICAN FOLK ART SERIES
Duck Decoys

Broadbill
A1521

Mallard
A1522

Canvasback
A1523

Redhead
A1524

Designed by Stevan Dohanos.

Printed by American Bank Note Company.

PHOTOGRAVURE
Plates of 200 in four panes of 50.

1985, Mar. 22	Tagged		*Perf. 11*
2138 A1521 22c **multicolored**		1.00	.20
2139 A1522 22c **multicolored**		1.00	.20
2140 A1523 22c **multicolored**		1.00	.20

2141 A1524 22c **multicolored**		1.00	.20
a. Block of 4, #2138-2141		4.00	2.75
P# block of 4, 5#		4.50	
Zip block of 4		4.25	—

WINTER SPECIAL OLYMPICS

Ice Skater, Emblem, Skier — A1525

Designed by Jeff Carnell.

PHOTOGRAVURE
Plates of 160 in four panes of 40.

1985, Mar. 25	Tagged		*Perf. 11*
2142 A1525 22c **multicolored**		.40	.20
P# block of 4, 6#		1.75	
Zip block of 4		1.65	—
a. Vert. pair, imperf. horiz.		*475.00*	

LOVE

A1526

Designed by Corita Kent.

PHOTOGRAVURE
Plates of 200 in four panes of 50.

1985, Apr. 17	Tagged		*Perf. 11*
2143 A1526 22c **multicolored**		.40	.20
P# block of 4, 6#		1.70	
Zip block of 4		1.65	—
a. Imperf., pair		*1,500.*	

RURAL ELECTRIFICATION ADMINISTRATION

REA Power Lines, Farmland A1527

Designed by Howard Koslow.

PHOTOGRAVURE & ENGRAVED (Combination Press)
Plates of 230 in panes of 50.

1985, May 11	Tagged		*Perf. 11*
2144 A1527 22c **multicolored**		.45	.20
P# block of 20, 5-10 #, 1-2 Zip,			
1-2 Copyright		17.50	
a. Vert. pair, imperf between		—	

See Combination Press note after No. 1703.

AMERIPEX '86

US No. 134 — A1528

Designed by Richard Sheaff.

LITHOGRAPHED & ENGRAVED
Plates of 192 in four panes of 48

1985, May 25	Tagged		*Perf. 1*
2145 A1528 22c **multicolored**		.40	
P# block of 4, 3#		1.75	
Zip block of 4		1.65	
a. Red, black & blue (engr.) omitted		190.00	
b. Red & black omitted		*1,250.*	
c. Red omitted		*1,750.*	
d. Black missing (PS)		—	

ABIGAIL ADAMS (1744-1818)

A1529

Designed by Bart Forbes.

PHOTOGRAVURE
Plates of 200 in four panes of 50.

1985, June 14	Tagged		*Perf. 11*
2146 A1529 22c **multicolored**		.40	.20
P# block of 4, 4#		2.00	
Zip block of 4		1.65	—
a. Imperf., pair		*250.00*	

FREDERIC AUGUSTE BARTHOLDI (1834-1904)

Architect and Sculptor, Statue of Liberty A1530

Designed by Howard Paine from paintings by Jose Frappa and James Dean.

LITHOGRAPHED & ENGRAVED
Plates of 200 in four panes of 50.

1985, July 18	Tagged		*Perf. 11*
2147 A1530 22c **multicolored**		.40	.20
P# block of 4, 5#		1.90	
Zip block of 4		1.65	—

Examples of No. 2147 exist with most, but not all, of the engraved black omitted.

George Washington, Washington Monument — A1532

Sealed Envelopes — A1533

Designed by Thomas Szumowski (#2149) based on a portrait by Gilbert Stuart, and Richard Sheaff (#2150).

COIL STAMPS
PHOTOGRAVURE

1985		*Perf. 10 Vertically*	
2149 A1532 18c **multicolored, low gloss gum,** *Nov. 6*		.35	.20
Pair		.70	.20
P# strip of 5, #1112		3.00	
P# strip of 5, #3333		4.25	
P# single, #1112		—	2.10
P# single, #3333		—	3.25
a. Untagged (Bureau precanceled), low gloss gum		.35	.35
P# strip of 5, #11121		6.00	
P# strip of 5, #33333		3.00	
P# single, #11121		—	5.00
P# single, #33333		—	2.00
Dull gum		.35	
P# strip of 5, #33333		4.00	
P# strip of 5, #43444		6.50	
P# single, #43444		—	5.50
b. Imperf., pair		*950.00*	

	P#1112		
c.	As "a," imperf., pair	750.00	
	P#33333		
d.	Tagging omitted (not Bureau precan-celed)	—	—
e.	As "a," tagged (error), dull gum	2.00	1.75
	Pair	4.00	3.75
	P# strip of 5, #33333	50.00	
	P# single, #33333	—	35.00
	Low gloss gum	2.00	
	P# strip of 5, #33333	50.00	
	P# single, #33333	—	35.00
2150	A1533 21.1c **multicolored,** *Oct. 22*	.40	.20
	Pair	.80	.20
	P# strip of 5, #111111	3.25	
	P# strip of 5, #111121	4.75	
	P# single, #111111	—	2.50
	P# single, #111121	—	3.75
a.	Untagged (Bureau Precancel)	.40	.40
	Pair	.80	.80
	P# strip of 5, #111111	3.25	
	P# strip of 5, #111121	4.75	
	P# single, #111111	—	2.50
	P# single, #111121	—	3.75
b.	As "a," tagged (error)	2.50	2.50
	Pair	5.00	5.00
	P# strip of 5, #111111	30.00	
	P# strip of 5, #111121	4.75	
	P# single, #111111	—	—
	P# single, #111121	—	3.75

Precancellations on Nos. 2149a ("PRESORTED FIRST-CLASS"), 2150a and 2150b ("ZIP+4") do not have lines.

KOREAN WAR VETERANS

American Troops in Korea A1535

Designed by Richard Sheaff from a photograph by David D. Duncan.

ENGRAVED
Plates of 200 in four panes of 50.

1985, July 26	**Tagged**	*Perf. 11*	
2152 A1535 22c **gray green & rose red**		.40	.20
P# block of 4		2.50	—
Zip block of 4		1.75	—

SOCIAL SECURITY ACT, 50th ANNIV.

Men, Women, Children, Corinthian Columns A1536

Designed by Robert Brangwynne.

Printed by American Bank Note Company.

PHOTOGRAVURE
Plates of 200 in four panes of 50.

1985, Aug. 14	**Tagged**	*Perf. 11*	
2153 A1536 22c **deep & light blue**		.40	.20
P# block of 4, 2#		1.90	—
Zip block of 4		1.70	—

WORLD WAR I VETERANS

The Battle of Marne, France A1537

Designed by Richard Sheaff from Harvey Dunn's charcoal drawing.

ENGRAVED
Plates of 200 in four panes of 50.

1985, Aug. 26	**Tagged**	*Perf. 11*	
2154 A1537 22c **gray green & rose red**		.40	.20
P# block of 4		2.25	—
Zip block of 4		1.85	—
a.	Red missing (PS)	—	
b.	Tagging omitted	—	

HORSES

Quarter Horse A1538

Morgan A1539

Saddlebred A1540

Appaloosa A1541

Designed by Roy Andersen.

PHOTOGRAVURE
Plates of 160 in four panes of 40.

1985, Sept. 25	**Tagged**	*Perf. 11*	
2155 A1538 22c **multicolored**		1.25	.20
2156 A1539 22c **multicolored**		1.25	.20
2157 A1540 22c **multicolored**		1.25	.20
2158 A1541 22c **multicolored**		1.25	.20
a.	Block of 4, #2155-2158	6.00	5.00
	P# block of 4, 5#	7.50	—
	Zip block of 4	6.25	—

PUBLIC EDUCATION IN AMERICA

Quill Pen, Apple, Spectacles, Penmanship Quiz — A1542

Designed by Uldis Purins.

Printed by American Bank Note Company

PHOTOGRAVURE
Plates of 200 in four panes of 50.

1985, Oct. 1	**Tagged**	*Perf. 11*	
2159 A1542 22c **multicolored**		.45	.20
P# block of 4, 5#		2.75	—
Zip block of 4		1.85	—
a.	Tagging omitted	—	

INTERNATIONAL YOUTH YEAR

YMCA Youth Camping, Cent. — A1543

Boy Scouts, 75th Anniv. A1544

Big Brothers / Big Sisters Federation, 40th Anniv. A1545

Camp Fire Inc., 75th Anniv. A1546

Designed by Dennis Luzak.

Printed by American Bank Note Company.

PHOTOGRAVURE
Plates of 200 in four panes of 50.

1985, Oct. 7	**Tagged**	*Perf. 11*	
2160 A1543 22c **multicolored**		.70	.20
2161 A1544 22c **multicolored**		.70	.20
2162 A1545 22c **multicolored**		.70	.20
2163 A1546 22c **multicolored**		.70	.20
a.	Block of 4, #2160-2163	3.00	2.25
	P# block of 4, 5#	4.00	—
	Zip block of 4	3.25	—

HELP END HUNGER

Youths and Elderly Suffering from Malnutrition A1547

Designed by Jerry Pinkney.

Printed by the American Bank Note Company.

PHOTOGRAVURE
Plates of 200 in four panes of 50.

1985, Oct. 15	**Tagged**	*Perf. 11*	
2164 A1547 22c **multicolored**		.45	.20
P# block of 4, 5#		2.00	—
Zip block of 4		1.90	—
a.	Tagging omitted	—	

CHRISTMAS

Genoa Madonna, Enameled
Terra-Cotta by Luca Della
Robbia (1400-
1482) — A1548

Poinsettia
Plants
A1549

Designed by Bradbury Thompson (No. 2165) and James
Dean (No. 2166).

PHOTOGRAVURE

Plates of 200 in panes of 50.

1985, Oct. 30	Tagged		Perf. 11	
2165 A1548	22c **multicolored**		.40	.20
	P# block of 4, 4#		1.75	—
	Zip block of 4		1.65	—
a.	Imperf., pair		80.00	
b.	Tagging omitted		—	
2166 A1549	22c **multicolored**		.40	.20
	P# block of 4, 5#		1.70	—
	Zip block of 4		1.65	—
a.	Imperf., pair		120.00	

ARKANSAS STATEHOOD, 150th ANNIV.

Old State
House, Little
Rock — A1550

Designed by Roger Carlisle.

Printed by the American Bank Note Company

PHOTOGRAVURE

Plates of 200 in four panes of 50.

1986, Jan. 3	Tagged		Perf. 11	
2167 A1550	22c **multicolored**		.75	.20
	P# block of 4, 6#		3.75	—
	Zip block of 4		3.10	—
a.	Vert. pair, imperf. horiz.		—	
b.	Tagging omitted		—	

Marginal Inscriptions
**Beginning with the Luis Munoz Marin issue a
number of stamps include a descriptive inscription
in the selvage.**

GREAT AMERICANS ISSUE

A1551   A1552

Designed by Ron Adair.

Printed by the Bureau of Engraving & Printing.

ENGRAVED
Panes of 100 (#2168-2193, 2195), Panes of 20
(#2194, 2196)

Perf. 11, 11¹⁄₂x11 (#2185), 11.2x11.1 (20c)

1986-94		Tagged		
2168 A1551	1c **brownish vermilion**, large block tagging, *June 30*		.20	.20
	P# block of 4		.25	—
	Zip block of 4		.20	—
a.	Tagging omitted		5.00	
2169 A1552	2c **bright blue**, large block tagging, *Feb. 28, 1987*		.20	.20
	P# block of 4		.30	—
	Zip block of 4		.20	—
a.	Untagged		.20	.20
	P# block of 4		.35	—
	Zip block of 4		.20	—
b.	Tagging omitted		—	

The tagging omitted error No. 2169b appeared before No.
2169a was issued. Plate blocks from plate 1 are the error if
untagged. No. 2169a is from plate 2. Other blocks and
singles can be distinguished if se-tenant with tagged stamps. No.
2169a and 2169b also can be distinguished using a long wave
ultraviolet light. The paper of No. 2169b will appear brownish,
while the paper of No. 2169a appears almost white.

A1553

A1554

Designed by Christopher Calle.

Printed by the Bureau of Engraving & Printing.

2170 A1553	3c **bright blue**, large block tagging, dull gum, *Sept. 15*		.20	.20
	P# block of 4		.50	—
	Zip block of 4		.25	—
a.	Untagged, dull gum, *1994*		.20	.20
	P# block of 4		.50	—
	Zip block of 4		.25	—
	Shiny gum, *1994*		.20	
	P# block of 4		.50	—
	Zip block of 4		.25	—
b.	Tagging omitted		—	

The tagging omitted error No. 2170b appeared before No.
2170a was issued. Plate blocks from plates 2 and 3 are the
error if untagged. No. 2170a is from plate 4. Other blocks and
singles are indistiguishable, unless se-tenant with tagged
stamps.

2171 A1554	4c **blue violet**, large block tagging, *July 14*		.20	.20
	P# block of 4		.60	—
	Zip block of 4		.40	—
a.	4c **grayish violet**, untagged		.20	.20
	P# block of 4		.40	—
	Zip block of 4		.35	—
b.	4c **deep grayish blue**, untagged, *1993*		.20	.20
	P# block of 4		.50	—
	Zip block of 4		.40	—
c.	As No. 2171, tagging omitted		—	

No. 2171c was found on a USPS souvenir page with first day
cancel. No. 2171a and 2171b were not available on the first day
of issue.

A1555

A1556

Designers: No. 2172, Christopher Calle. No. 2173, Juan
Maldonado.

Printed by the Bureau of Engraving & Printing.

2172 A1555	5c **dark olive green**, large block tagging, *Feb. 27*		.20	.20
	P# block of 4		1.00	—
	Zip block of 4		.45	—
a.	Tagging omitted		80.00	
2173 A1556	5c **carmine**, overall tagging, *Feb. 18, 1990*		.20	.20
	P# block of 4		.75	—
	P# zip block of 4		.90	—
	Zip block of 4		.45	—
a.	Untagged, *1991*		.20	.20

	P# block of 4		.60	
	P# zip block of 4		.75	
	Zip block of 4		.45	
b.	Tagging omitted			

The tagging omitted error No. 2173b appeared before N
2173a was issued. Plate blocks from plate 1 are the error
untagged. No. 2173a is from plate 2. Other blocks and singl
are indistinguishable, unless se-tenant with tagged stamps.

A1557

A1558

Designers: 10c, Robert Anderson. 14c, Ward Brackett.

Printed by the Bureau of Engraving & Printing.

2175 A1557	10c **lake**, large block tagging, dull gum, *Aug. 15, 1987*		.25	.2
	P# block of 4		1.10	—
	Zip block of 4		1.00	—
a.	Overall tagging, dull gum, *1990*		.60	.2
	P# block of 4		10.00	—
	Zip block of 4		2.00	—
b.	Tagging omitted		12.50	
c.	Prephosphored coated paper (solid tagging), dull gum, *1991*		.90	.2
	P# block of 4		4.00	—
	Zip block of 4		3.60	—
d.	Prephosphored uncoated paper (mottled tagging), shiny gum, *1993*		.90	.2
	P# block of 4		4.00	—
	Zip block of 4		3.60	—
e.	10c **carmine**, prephosphored uncoated paper (mottled tagging), shiny gum, *1994*		.30	.2
	P# block of 4		1.50	—
	Zip block of 4		1.20	—
f.	As "c," all color omitted		—	

No. 2157f must be collected se-tenant with a partially printe
stamp or longer vertical strip.

2176 A1558	14c **crimson**, large block tagging, *Feb. 12, 1987*		.30	.2
	P# block of 4		1.50	—
	Zip block of 4		1.20	—
a.	Tagging omitted		—	

A1559

A1560

Designers: 15c, Jack Rosenthal. 17c, Christopher Calle.

Printed by the Bureau of Engraving & Printing.

2177 A1559	15c **claret**, large block tagging, *June 6, 1988*		.35	.20
	P# block of 4		10.00	—
	Zip block of 4		1.50	—
a.	Overall tagging, *1990*		.30	—
	P# block of 4		3.25	—
	Zip block of 4		1.20	—
b.	Prephosphored coated paper (solid tagging)		.40	—
	P# block of 4		3.25	—
	Zip block of 4		1.60	—
c.	Tagging omitted		15.00	—
d.	All color omitted		—	

No. 2177d resulted from partially printed panes. It must be
collected se-tenant with a partially printed stamp or in a longer
horizontal strip showing error stamps plus partially/completely
printed stamps.

2178 A1560	17c **dull blue green**, large block tagging, *June 18*		.35	.20
	P# block of 4		2.00	—
	Zip block of 4		1.40	—
	Pair with full horizontal gutter between		—	
a.	Tagging omitted		10.00	

A1561

A1562

A1566

A1567

Designers: 20c, Robert Anderson. 21c, Susan Sanford.

Printed by: 20c, Banknote Corporation of America. 21c, Bureau of Engraving & Printing.

2179	A1561	20c **red brown**, prephosphored coated paper (grainy solid tagging), *Oct. 24, 1994*	.40 .20
		P# block of 4, 1#+B	2.00 —
a.		20c **orange brown**, prephosphored coated paper (grainy solid tagging)	.45 .20
		P# block of 4, 1#+B	2.25 —
b.		20c **bright red brown**, prephosphored coated paper (grainy solid tagging)	1.00 .25
		P# block of 4, 1#+B	6.00 —
2180	A1562	21c **blue violet**, large block tagging, *Oct. 21, 1988*	.45 .20
		P# block of 4	2.50 —
		Zip block of 4	1.65 —
a.		Tagging omitted	—

No. 2180 is known with worn tagging mats on which horizontal untagged areas have taggant giving the appearance of vertical band tagging.

A1563

A1564

A1565

Designers: 23c, Dennis Lyall. 25c, Richard Sparks. 28c, Robert Anderson.

Printed by the Bureau of Engraving & Printing.

2181	A1563	23c **purple**, large block tagging, dull gum, *Nov. 4, 1988*	.45 .20
		P# block of 4	2.50 —
		Zip block of 4	1.90 —
a.		Overall tagging, dull gum	.65 —
		P# block of 4	5.00 —
		Zip block of 4	2.60 —
b.		Prephosphored coated paper (solid tagging), dull gum	.60 —
		P# block of 4	3.50 —
		Zip block of 4	2.40 —
c.		Prephosphored uncoated paper (mottled tagging), shiny gum	.65 .20
		P# block of 4	5.00 —
		Zip block of 4	2.60 —
d.		Tagging omitted	7.50
2182	A1564	25c **blue**, large block tagging, *Jan. 11*	.50 .20
		P# block of 4	2.75 —
		Zip block of 4	2.00 —
a.		Booklet pane of 10, *May 3, 1988*	5.00 3.75
b.		As #2182, tagging omitted	—
c.		As "a," tagging omitted	—
d.		Horiz. pair, imperf between	—
e.		As "a," all color omitted on right stamps	—
f.		As No. 2182 (sheet stamp), vert. pair, bottom stamp all color omitted	—

No. 2182f may be collected se-tenant with a partially printed stamp or longer vertical strip.
See Nos. 2197, 2197a.

2183	A1565	28c **myrtle green**, large block tagging, *Sept. 14, 1989*	.65 .20
		P# block of 4	3.50 —
		Zip block of 4	2.60 —

Designed by Christopher Calle.

Printed by: No. 2184, Canadian Bank Note Co. for Stamp Venturers. No. 2185, Stamp Venturers.

2184	A1566	29c **blue**, prephosphored uncoated paper (mottled tagging), *Mar. 9, 1992*	.65 .20
		P# block of 4, #+S	3.50 —
		Zip block of 4	2.60 —
2185	A1567	29c **indigo**, prephosphored coated paper (solid tagging), *Apr. 13, 1993*	.65 .20
		P# block of 4, 1#+S	3.50 —
		Zip block of 4	2.60 —

A1568

A1569

A1570

Designers: 35c, 40c, Christopher Calle. 45c, Bradbury Thompson.

Printed by: 35c, Canadian Bank Note Co. for Stamp Venturers. 40c, 45c, Bureau of Engraving & Printing.

2186	A1568	35c **black**, prephosphored uncoated paper (mottled tagging), *Apr. 3, 1991*	.75 .20
		P# block of 4, #+S	4.25 —
		Zip block of 4	3.00 —
2187	A1569	40c **dark blue**, overall tagging, dull gum, *Sept. 6, 1990*	.85 .20
		P# block of 4	4.50 —
		Zip block of 4	3.40 —
a.		Prephosphored coated paper (solid tagging), dull gum	1.00 .35
		P# block of 4	5.50 —
		Zip block of 4	4.00 —
b.		Prephosphored coated paper (grainy solid tagging), low gloss gum, *1998*	.85 .35
		P# block of 4	4.50 —
		Zip block of 4	3.40 —
c.		Prephosphored uncoated paper (mottled tagging), shiny gum, *1994*	1.00 .20
		P# block of 4	10.00 —
		Zip block of 4	4.00 —
d.		Tagging omitted	—
2188	A1570	45c **bright blue**, large block tagging, *June 17, 1988*	1.00 .20
		P# block of 4	5.00 —
		Zip block of 4	4.00 —
a.		45c **blue**, overall tagging, *1990*	2.25 .20
		P# block of 4	17.50 —
		Zip block of 4	8.00 —
b.		Tagging omitted	20.00

The blue on No. 2188a is noticeably lighter than on No. 2188. Color variety specialists, as well as tagging specialists, will want to consider it as a second variety of this stamp.

A1571

A1572

Designers: 52c, John Berkey. 56c, Robert Anderson.

Printed by the Bureau of Engraving & Printing.

2189	A1571	52c **purple**, prephosphored coated paper (solid tagging), dull gum, *June 3, 1991*	1.10 .20
		P# block of 4	7.50 —
		Zip block of 4	4.50 —
a.		Prephosphored uncoated paper (mottled tagging), shiny gum, *1993*	1.25 —
		P# block of 4	8.00 —
		Zip block of 4	5.00 —

Selvage inscriptions from the original printing of No. 2189 from plate 1 show the incorrect dates for Humphrey's vice-presidential term ("1964 to 1968"). Corrected plate 1 and plate 2 printings (No. 2189a) show the dates correctly as 1965 to 1969. Values for the two varieties of inscription blocks of 6 are approximately the same: $8.50.

2190	A1572	56c **scarlet**, large block tagging, *Sept. 3*	1.20 .20
		P# block of 4	7.00 —
		Zip block of 4	4.80 —
a.		Tagging omitted	—

No. 2190 known with a "tagging spill" making stamp appear overall tagged.

A1573

A1574

Designed by Christopher Calle.

Printed by the Bureau of Engraving & Printing.

2191	A1573	65c **dark blue**, large block tagging, *Nov. 5, 1988*	1.30 .20
		P# block of 4	6.50 —
		Zip block of 4	5.20 —
a.		Tagging omitted	20.00
2192	A1574	75c **deep magenta**, prephosphored coated paper (solid tagging), dull gum, *Feb. 16, 1992*	1.60 .20
		P# block of 4	7.50 —
		Zip block of 4	6.40 —
a.		Prephosphored uncoated paper (mottled tagging), shiny gum	1.75 —
		P# block of 4	9.00 —
		Zip block of 4	7.00 —

A1575

"Lipstick on Shirt Front" double gouge plate flaw

A1576

Designers: No. 2193, Tom Broad. No. 2194, Bradbury Thompson.

Printed by the Bureau of Engraving & Printing.

2193	A1575	$1 **dark Prussian green**, large block tagging, *Sept. 23*	3.00 .50
		P# block of 4	15.00 —
		Zip block of 4	12.00 —
a.		All color omitted	—

No. 2193a must be collected se-tenant vertically with partially printed stamps.

2194	A1576	$1 **intense deep blue**, large block tagging, dull gum, *June 7, 1989*	2.25 .50
		P# block of 4	12.00 —
		Pane of 20	48.00 —
		Double gouge plate flaw ("Lipstick on Shirt Front"), (pos. 6 on one plate #1 pane)	—
b.		$1 **deep blue**, overall tagging, dull gum, *1990*	2.50 .50
		P# block of 4	13.00 —
		Pane of 20	52.50 —
c.		Tagging omitted	10.00
d.		$1 **dark blue**, prephosphored coated paper (solid tagging), dull gum, *1992*	2.50 .50

	P# block of 4	13.00	—
	Pane of 20	52.50	—

e. $1 **blue**, prephosphored uncoated paper (mottled tagging), shiny gum, *1993* — 2.75 .60

	P# block of 4	14.00	—
	Pane of 20	58.00	—

f. $1 **blue**, prephosphored coated paper (grainy solid tagging), low gloss gum, *1998* — 2.75 .50

	P# block of 4	14.00	—
	Pane of 20	58.00	—

No. 2194 issued in pane of 20 (see No. 2196.)
The intense deep blue of No. 2194 is much deeper than the deep blue and dark blue of the other $1 varieties.
The "Lipstick on Shirt Front" flaw was discovered during production and the position was repaired. Very few have been found.

A1577

A1578

Designers: $2, Tom Broad. $5, Arthur Lidov.

Printed by the Bureau of Engraving & Printing.

2195 A1577 $2 **bright violet**, large block tagging, *Mar. 19* — 4.50 .50
	P# block of 4	20.00	—
	Zip block of 4	17.00	—
a.	Tagging omitted	*45.00*	

No. 2195 is known with worn tagging mats on which horizontal untagged areas have taggant giving the appearance of vertical band tagging.

2196 A1578 $5 **copper red**, large block tagging, *Aug. 25, 1987* — 9.00 1.00
	P# block of 4	42.50	—
	Pane of 20	185.00	—
a.	Tagging omitted	—	—
b.	Prephosphored coated paper (solid tagging), *1992*	11.00	—
	P# block of 4	45.00	—
	Pane of 20	220.00	—
	Nos. 2168-2196 (28)	32.75	7.30

Booklet Stamp
Perf. 10 on 2 or 3 sides

2197 A1564 25c **blue**, large block tagging, *May 3, 1988* — .55 .20
a.	Booklet pane of 6	3.30	2.50
b.	Tagging omitted	4.50	
c.	As "b," booklet pane of 6	60.00	

UNITED STATES - SWEDEN
STAMP COLLECTING

Handstamped Cover, Philatelic Memorabilia A1581

Boy Examining Stamp Collection A1582

No. 836 Under Magnifying Glass, Sweden Nos. 260, 271 — A1583

1986 Presidents Miniature Sheet — A1584

Designed by Richard Sheaff and Eva Jern (No. 2200).

BOOKLET STAMPS
LITHOGRAPHED & ENGRAVED
Perf. 10 Vert. on 1 or 2 Sides

1986, Jan. 23   **Tagged**
2198 A1581 22c **multicolored** — .45 .20
2199 A1582 22c **multicolored** — .45 .20
2200 A1583 22c **multicolored** — .45 .20
2201 A1584 22c **multicolored** — .45 .20
a.	Bklt. pane of 4, #2198-2201	2.00	1.75
b.	As "a," black omitted on Nos. 2198, 2201	45.00	—
c.	As "a," blue (litho.) omitted on Nos. 2198-2200	2,400.	—
d.	As "a," buff (litho.) omitted	—	

See Sweden Nos. 1585-1588.

LOVE ISSUE

A1585

Designed by Saul Mandel.

Plates of 200 in four panes of 50.
PHOTOGRAVURE

1986, Jan. 30   **Tagged**   *Perf. 11*
2202 A1585 22c **multicolored** — .55 .20
	P# block of 4, 5#	2.75	—
	Zip block of 4	2.25	—
a.	Tagging omitted	—	

Sojourner Truth (c. 1797-1883), Human Rights Activist — A1586

Texas State Flag and Silver Spur — A1587

BLACK HERITAGE SERIES
Designed by Jerry Pinkney.

Printed by American Bank Note Co.

Plates of 200 in four panes of 50
PHOTOGRAVURE

1986, Feb. 4   **Tagged**   *Perf. 1*
2203 A1586 22c **multicolored** — .55 .2
	P# block of 4, 6#	2.75	.2
	Zip block of 4	2.25	—

REPUBLIC OF TEXAS, 150th ANNIV.
Designed by Don Adair.

Printed by the American Bank Note Co.

Plates of 200 in four panes of 50.
PHOTOGRAVURE

1986, Mar. 2   **Tagged**   *Perf. 1*
2204 A1587 22c **dark blue, dark red & grayish black** — .55 .2
	P# block of 4, 3#	2.75	.2
	Zip block of 4	2.25	—
a.	Horiz. pair, imperf. vert.	1,000.	
b.	Dark red omitted	2,500.	
c.	Dark blue omitted	8,000.	

FISH

Muskellunge — A1588

Atlantic Cod A1589

Largemouth Bass — A1590

Bluefin Tuna A1591

Catfish
A1592

Designed by Chuck Ripper.

BOOKLET STAMPS
PHOTOGRAVURE

1986, Mar. 21   Tagged   Perf. 10 Horiz.

2205 A1588 22c multicolored	.75	.20
2206 A1589 22c multicolored	.75	.20
2207 A1590 22c multicolored	.75	.20
2208 A1591 22c multicolored	.75	.20
2209 A1592 22c multicolored	.75	.20
a. Bklt. pane of 5, #2205-2209	5.50	2.75

No. 2209a apparently lacking the red color is reported. It is believed no genuine error examples exist. Panes apparently lacking red must be certified, and examples presently with certificates should be recertified.

PUBLIC HOSPITALS

A1593

Designed by Uldis Purins.

Printed by the American Bank Note Co.

PHOTOGRAVURE
Plates of 200 in four panes of 50.

1986, Apr. 11   Tagged   Perf. 11

2210 A1593 22c multicolored	.40	.20
P# block of 4, 5#	1.75	
Zip block of 4	1.65	—
a. Vert. pair, imperf. horiz.	300.00	
b. Horiz. pair, imperf. vert.	1,250.	

PERFORMING ARTS

Edward Kennedy "Duke" Ellington (1899-1974), Jazz Composer — A1594

Designed by Jim Sharpe.
Printed by the American Bank Note Co.

PHOTOGRAVURE
Plates of 200 in four panes of 50.

1986, Apr. 29   Tagged   Perf. 11

2211 A1594 22c multicolored	.40	.20
P# block of 4, 6#	1.90	
Zip block of 4	1.75	—
a. Vert. pair, imperf. horiz.	825.00	

AMERIPEX '86 ISSUE
Miniature Sheets

35 Presidents — A1599a

A1599b

A1599c

A1599d

Illustrations reduced.

Designs: No. 2216: a, George Washington. b, John Adams. c, Thomas Jefferson. d, James Madison. e, James Monroe. f, John Quincy Adams. g, Andrew Jackson. h, Martin Van Buren. i, William H. Harrison.

No. 2217: a, John Tyler. b, James Knox Polk. c, Zachary Taylor. d, Millard Fillmore. e, Franklin Pierce. f, James Buchanan. g, Abraham Lincoln. h, Andrew Johnson. i, Ulysses S. Grant.

No. 2218: a, Rutherford B. Hayes. b, James A. Garfield. c, Chester A. Arthur. d, Grover Cleveland. e, Benjamin Harrison. f, William McKinley. g, Theodore Roosevelt. h, William H. Taft. i, Woodrow Wilson.

No. 2219: a, Warren G. Harding. b, Calvin Coolidge. c, Herbert Hoover. d, Franklin Delano Roosevelt. e, White House. f, Harry S. Truman. g, Dwight D. Eisenhower. h, John F. Kennedy. i, Lyndon B. Johnson.

Designed by Jerry Dadds.

LITHOGRAPHED & ENGRAVED

1986, May 22   Tagged   Perf. 11

2216 A1599a Sheet of 9	5.00	4.00
a.-i. 22c, any single	.55	.40
j. Blue (engr.) omitted	2,500.	
k. Black inscription omitted	2,000.	
l. Imperf.	10,500.	
m. As "k," double impression of red	—	

2217	A1599b	Sheet of 9	5.00	4.00
a.-i.		22c, any single	.55	.40
j.		Black inscription omitted	*2,500.*	
k.		Tagging omitted	—	
2218	A1599c	Sheet of 9	5.00	4.00
a.-i.		22c, any single	.55	.40
j.		Brown (engr.) omitted	—	
k.		Black inscription omitted	*2,500.*	
l.		Tagging omitted	—	
2219	A1599d	Sheet of 9	5.00	4.00
a.-i.		22c, any single	.55	.40
j.		Blackish blue (engr.) inscription omit-		
		ted on a-b, d-e, g-h	*2,500.*	
k.		Tagging omitted on c, f, i	*4,000.*	
l.		Blackish blue (engr.) omitted on all		
		stamps	—	
		Nos. 2216-2219 (4)	20.00	16.00

Issued in conjunction with AMERIPEX '86 Intl. Philatelic Exhibition, Chicago, IL May 22-June 1. Sheet size: 120x207mm (sheet size varied).

ARCTIC EXPLORERS

Elisha Kent Kane — A1600

Adolphus W. Greely A1601

Vilhjalmur Stefansson A1602

Robert E. Peary, Matthew Henson A1603

Designed by Dennis Lyall.
Printed by the American Bank Note Company

PHOTOGRAVURE
Plates of 200 in four panes of 50.

1986, May 28			**Tagged**		***Perf. 11***
2220	A1600	22c	**multicolored**	.65	.20
2221	A1601	22c	**multicolored**	.65	.20
2222	A1602	22c	**multicolored**	.65	.20
2223	A1603	22c	**multicolored**	.65	.20
a.		Block of 4, #2220-2223		2.75	2.25
		P# block of 4, 5#		4.50	—
		Zip block of 4		3.00	—
b.		As "a," black omitted		*5,500.*	
c.		As "a," Nos. 2220, 2221 black omitted		—	
d.		As "a," Nos. 2222, 2223 black omitted		—	

STATUE OF LIBERTY, 100th ANNIV.

A1604

Designed by Howard Paine.

ENGRAVED
Plates of 200 in four panes of 50.

1986, July 4			**Tagged**		***Perf. 11***
2224	A1604	22c	**scarlet & dark blue**	.40	.20
		P# block of 4		2.25	—
		Zip block of 4		1.65	—
a.		Scarlet omitted		—	

On No. 2224a, virtually all of the dark blue also is omitted, so the error stamp should be collected as part of a transition strip. See France No. 2014.

> **Coil Plate No. Strips of 3**
> Beginning with No. 2123, coil plate no. strips of 3 usually sell at the level of strips of 5 minus the face value of two stamps.

TRANSPORTATION ISSUE

A1604a

A1604b

Designers: 1c, 2c, David Stone.

COIL STAMPS
ENGRAVED

1986-87			**Tagged**		***Perf. 10 Vert.***
2225	A1604a	1c	**violet,** large block tagging, dull gum, *Nov. 26*	.20	.20
		Pair		.20	.20
		P# strip of 5, #1		.60	
		P# strip of 5, #2		.65	
		P# single, #1		—	.40
		P# single, #2		—	.50
a.		Prephosphored uncoated paper (mottled tagging) (error), shiny gum		.20	.20
		Pair		.20	.20
		P# strip of 5, #3		27.50	
		P# single, #3		—	13.00
b.		Untagged, dull gum		.20	.20
		Pair		.20	.20
		P# strip of 5, #2-3		.65	
		P# single, #2-3		—	.45
		Shiny gum		.20	
		P# strip of 5, #3		.80	
		Low gloss gum		.20	
		P# strip of 5, #3		.80	
c.		Imperf., pair		*2,000.*	
2226	A1604b	2c	**black,** dull gum, *Mar. 6, 1987*	.20	.20
		Pair		.20	.20
		P# strip of 5, #1		.70	
		P# single, #1		—	.45
a.		Untagged, dull gum		.20	.20
		Pair		.20	.20
		P# strip of 5, #2		.70	
		P# single, #2		—	.50
		Shiny gum		.20	
		P# strip of 5, #2		1.75	

REDUCED SIZE

2228	A1285	4c	**reddish brown,** large block tagging, *Aug.*	.20	.20
		Pair		.20	.20
		P# strip of 5, #1		1.25	
		P# single, #1		—	.95
a.		Overall tagging, *1990*		.70	.20
		Pair		1.40	.20
		P# strip of 5, #1		11.00	
		P# single, #1		—	9.00
b.		Imperf., pair		250.00	
		P#1		—	

Earliest known usage of No. 2228: Aug. 15, 1986.
On No. 2228 "Stagecoach 1890s" is 17¾mm long; on No. 1898A, 19½mm long.

UNTAGGED

2231	A1511	8.3c	**green** (Bureau precancel, Blk. Rt./CAR-RT/SORT), *Aug. 29*	.40	.20
		Pair		.80	.40
		P# strip of 5, #1		6.00	
		P# strip of 5, #2		8.00	
		P# single, #1		—	3.00
		P# single, #2		—	4.75

On No. 2231 "Ambulance 1860s" is 18mm long; on No. 2128, 18½mm long.
Joint lines do not appear on Nos. 2225-2231.

AMERICAN FOLK ART SERIES
Navajo Art

A1605

A1606

A1607

A1608

Designed by Derry Noyes.

LITHOGRAPHED & ENGRAVED
Plates of 200 in four panes of 50.

1986, Sept. 4			**Tagged**		***Perf. 11***
2235	A1605	22c	**multicolored**	.80	.20
2236	A1606	22c	**multicolored**	.80	.20
2237	A1607	22c	**multicolored**	.80	.20
2238	A1608	22c	**multicolored**	.80	.20
a.		Block of 4, #2235-2238		3.25	2.25
		P# block of 4, 5#		4.25	
		Zip block of 4		3.50	
b.		As "a," black (engr.) omitted		375.00	

LITERARY ARTS SERIES

T.S. Eliot (1888-1965), Poet — A1609

Designed by Bradbury Thompson.

ENGRAVED
Plates of 200 in four panes of 50.

1986, Sept. 26			**Tagged**		***Perf. 11***
2239	A1609	22c	**copper red**	.55	.20
		P# block of 4		2.75	
		Zip block of 4		2.25	—
a.		Tagging omitted		—	

AMERICAN FOLK ART SERIES
Woodcarved Figurines

A1610

A1611

A1612

A1613

Designed by Bradbury Thompson.
Printed by the American Bank Note Company

PHOTOGRAVURE
Plates of 200 in four panes of 50.

1986, Oct. 1		Tagged	Perf. 11	
2240	A1610	22c multicolored	.50	.20
2241	A1611	22c multicolored	.50	.20
2242	A1612	22c multicolored	.50	.20
2243	A1613	22c multicolored	.50	.20
a.		Block of 4, #2240-2243	2.00	1.50
		P# block of 4, 5#	3.75	—
		Zip block of 4	2.25	—
b.		As "a," imperf. vert.	1,350.	

CHRISTMAS

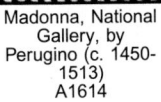

Madonna, National
Gallery, by
Perugino (c. 1450-
1513)
A1614

Village Scene
A1615

Designed by Bradbury Thompson (#2244) & Dolli Tingle (#2245).

PHOTOGRAVURE
Plates of 200 in four panes of 50.

1986, Oct. 24		Tagged	Perf. 11	
2244	A1614	22c multicolored	.40	.20
		P# block of 4, 6#	2.00	
		Zip block of 4	1.65	—
a.		Imperf., pair	650.00	
2245	A1615	22c multicolored	.40	.20
		P# block of 4, 6#	1.90	—
		Zip block of 4	1.65	—

MICHIGAN STATEHOOD, 150th ANNIV.

White Pine — A1616

Designed by Robert Wilbert.

PHOTOGRAVURE
Plates of 200 in four panes of 50.

1987, Jan. 26		Tagged	Perf. 11	
2246	A1616	22c multicolored	.55	.20
		P# block of 4, 5#	2.75	—
		Zip block of 4	2.25	—
		Pair with full vert. gutter between	—	

PAN AMERICAN GAMES
Indianapolis, Aug. 7-25

Runner in Full
Stride
A1617

Designed by Lon Busch.

PHOTOGRAVURE
Plates of 200 in four panes of 50.

1987, Jan.. 29		Tagged	Perf. 11	
2247	A1617	22c multicolored	.40	.20
		P# block of 4, 5#	1.90	—
		Zip block of 4	1.65	—
a.		Silver omitted	1,500.	

No. 2247a is valued in the grade of fine.

LOVE ISSUE

A1618

Designed by John Alcorn.

PHOTOGRAVURE
Panes of 100

1987, Jan. 30		Tagged	Perf. 11½x11	
2248	A1618	22c multicolored	.40	.20
		P# block of 4, 5#	1.90	—
		Zip block of 4	1.65	—
		Pair with full horiz. gutter between		

BLACK HERITAGE SERIES

Jean Baptiste Pointe du
Sable (c. 1750-1818),
Pioneer Trader, Founder of
Chicago — A1619

Designed by Thomas Blackshear.

PHOTOGRAVURE
Plates of 200 in four panes of 50.

1987, Feb. 20		Tagged	Perf. 11	
2249	A1619	22c multicolored	.50	.20
		P# block of 4, 5#	2.60	—
		Zip block of 4	2.10	—
a.		Tagging omitted	10.00	

Enrico Caruso (1873-
1921), Opera Tenor
A1620

Fourteen
Achievement
Badges
A1621

PERFORMING ARTS SERIES

Designed by Jim Sharpe.
Printed by American Bank Note Co.

PHOTOGRAVURE & ENGRAVED
Plates of 200 in four panes of 50.

1987, Feb. 27		Tagged	Perf. 11	
2250	A1620	22c multicolored	.40	.20
		P# block of 4, 4#	1.90	—
		Zip block of 4	1.65	—
a.		Black (engr.) omitted	5,000.	

GIRL SCOUTS, 75TH ANNIVERSARY
Designed by Richard Sheaff.

LITHOGRAPHED & ENGRAVED
Plates of 200 in four panes of 50.

1987, Mar. 12		Tagged	Perf. 11	
2251	A1621	22c multicolored	.40	.20
		P# block of 4, 6#	1.90	—
		Zip block of 4	1.65	—
a.		All litho. colors omitted	2,500.	
b.		Red & black (engr.) omitted	2,000.	

All known examples of No. 2251a have been expertized and certificate must accompany purchase. The unique pane of No. 2251b has been expertized and a certificate exists for the pane of 50.

Coil Plate No. Strips of 3
Beginning with No. 2123, coil plate no. strips of 3 usually sell at the level of strips of 5 minus the face value of two stamps.

TRANSPORTATION ISSUE

A1622

A1623

A1624

A1625

A1626

A1627

A1628

A1629

A1630

A1631

A1632

A1633

A1634

A1635

A1636

Designers: 3c, 7.6c, 13.2c, 15c, Richard Schlecht. 5c. 5.3c, 16.7c, Lou Nolan. 8.4c, 20.5c, 24.1c, Christopher Calle. 10c, William H. Bond. 13c, Joe Brockert. 17.5c, Tom Broad. 20c, Dan Romano. 21c, David Stone.

COIL STAMPS
ENGRAVED

1987-88   *Perf. 10 Vert.*
Tagged, Untagged (5.3c, 7.6c, 8.4c, 13c, 13.2c, 16.7c, 20.5c, 24.1c)

2252	A1622	3c **claret,** dull gum, *Feb. 29, 1988*	.20	.20
		Pair	.20	.20
		P# strip of 5, #1	.90	
		P# single, #1	—	.60
a.		Untagged, dull gum	.20	.20
		P# strip of 5, #2-3	1.25	
		P# single, #2	—	.95
		P# single, #3	—	.80
		Shiny gum, *1995*	.20	
		P# strip of 5, #3	1.25	
		P# strip of 5, #5	5.25	
		P# strip of 5, #6	2.10	
		P# single, #5	—	2.50
		P# single, #6	—	2.00
		Low gloss gum	.20	
		P# strip of 5, #5	8.00	
b.		As "a," imperf pair, shiny gum		

The plate #5 on No. 2252a with low gloss gum is smaller than the #5 on No. 2252a with shiny gum. The smaller plate #5 represents a different printing sleeve (plate).

2253	A1623	5c **black,** *Sept. 25*	.20	.20
		Pair	.20	.20
		P# strip of 5, #1	.90	
		P# single, #1	—	.75
2254	A1624	5.3c **black** (Bureau precancel "Nonprofit Carrier Route Sort" in red), *Sept. 16, 1988*	.20	.20
		Pair	.20	.20
		P# strip of 5, #1	1.10	
		P# single, #1	—	.70
2255	A1625	7.6c **brown** (Bureau precancel "Nonprofit" in red), *Aug. 30, 1988*	.20	.20
		Pair	.30	.30

		P# strip of 5, #1-2	2.25	
		P# strip of 5, #3	6.25	
		P# single, #1-2	—	1.50
		P# single, #3	—	4.00
2256	A1626	8.4c **deep claret** (Bureau precancel "Nonprofit" in red), *Aug. 12, 1988*	.20	.20
		Pair	.30	.30
		P# strip of 5, #1-2	1.90	
		P# strip of 5, #3	13.50	
		P# single, #1-2	—	1.00
		P# single, #3	—	5.50
a.		Imperf., pair	600.00	
		P#1		
2257	A1627	10c **blue,** large block tagging, dull gum, *Apr. 11*	.40	.20
		Pair	.80	.20
		P# strip of 5, #1	3.50	
		P# single, #1	—	1.00
a.		Overall tagging, dull gum, *1993*	.20	.20
		Pair	.40	.20
		P# strip of 5, #1	4.00	
		P# single, #1	—	3.25
		Shiny gum, *1994*	.20	.20
		Pair	.20	.20
		P# strip of 5, #4	3.50	
		P# single, #4	—	2.00
b.		Prephosphored uncoated paper (mottled tagging), shiny gum	.20	.20
		Pair	.40	.20
		P# strip of 5, #1, 2	3.25	
		P# strip of 5, #3, 4	3.75	
		P# single, #1, 2	—	2.50
		P# single, #3, 4	—	2.75
c.		Prephosphored coated paper (solid tagging), low gloss gum	.20	.20
		Pair	.40	.20
		P# strip of 5, #5	5.75	
		P# single, #5	—	4.00
d.		Tagging omitted	27.50	
		P# strip of 5, #4	250.00	
e.		Imperf, pair, large block tagging	1,850.	
2258	A1628	13c **black** (Bureau precancel "Presorted First-Class" in red), *Oct. 29, 1988*	.30	.25
		Pair	.60	.50
		P# strip of 5, #1	3.25	
		P# single, #1	—	2.00
2259	A1629	13.2c **slate green** (Bureau precancel "Bulk Rate" in red), *July 19, 1988*	.25	.25
		Pair	.50	.50
		P# strip of 5, #1-2	2.75	
		P# single, #1-2	—	1.50
a.		Imperf., pair	100.00	
		P#1-2		
2260	A1630	15c **violet,** large block tagging, *July 12, 1988*	.25	.20
		Pair	.50	.20
		P# strip of 5, #1	2.00	
		P# strip of 5, #2	2.50	
		P# single, #1-2	—	1.50
a.		Overall tagging, *1990*	.25	.20
		Pair	.50	.20
		P# strip of 5, #2	3.25	
		P# single, #2	—	2.75
b.		Tagging omitted	3.75	
		P# strip of 5, #2	225.00	
		P# single, #2	—	200.00
c.		Imperf., pair	700.00	
		P#2		
2261	A1631	16.7c **rose** (Bureau precancel "Bulk Rate " in black), *July 7, 1988*	.30	.30
		Pair	.60	.60
		P# strip of 5, #1	2.75	
		P# strip of 5, #2	3.75	
		P# single, #1	—	1.75
		P# single, #2	—	2.75
a.		Imperf., pair	175.00	
		P#1		

All known copies of No. 2261a are miscut top to bottom.

2262	A1632	17.5c **dark violet,** *Sept. 25*	.50	.20
		Pair	1.00	.20
		P# strip of 5, #1	3.50	
		P# single, #1	—	2.50
a.		Untagged (Bureau Precancel "ZIP + 4 Presort" in red)	.50	.30
		P# strip of 5, #1	3.50	
		P# single, #1	—	2.75
b.		Imperf., pair	2,500.	
		P#1		
2263	A1633	20c **blue violet,** large block tagging, *Oct. 28, 1988*	.35	.20
		Pair	.70	.20
		P# strip of 5, #1-2	3.50	
		P# single, #1-2	—	1.50
a.		Imperf., pair	50.00	
		P#2		
b.		Overall tagging, *1990*	.35	.20
		Pair	.70	.20
		P# strip of 5, #2	8.00	
		P# single, #2	—	5.00
2264	A1634	20.5c **rose** (Bureau precancel "ZIP + 4 Presort" in black), *Sept. 28, 1988*	.50	.40
		Pair	1.00	.80
		P# strip of 5, #1	5.25	
		P# single, #1	—	3.25
2265	A1635	21c **olive green** (Bureau precancel "Presorted First-Class" in red), *Aug. 16, 1988*	.40	.40
		Pair	.80	.80
		P# strip of 5, #1-2	3.50	
		P# single, #1-2	—	2.50
a.		Imperf., pair	45.00	

		P#1		
2266	A1636	24.1c **deep ultra** (Bureau precancel ZIP + 4 in red), *Oct. 26, 1988*	.60	
		Pair	1.20	
		P# strip of 5, #1	4.00	
		P# single, #1	—	2.5
		Nos. 2252-2266 (15)	4.85	3.8

5.3c, 7.6c, 8.4c, 13.2c, 16.7c, 20.5c, 21c and 24.1c or available precanceled.

SPECIAL OCCASIONS

A1637

A1638

A1639

A1640

A1641

A1642

A1643

A1644

Designed by Oren Sherman.

BOOKLET STAMPS
PHOTOGRAVURE

1987, Apr. 20   Tagged   *Perf. 10 on 1, 2 or 3 Sides*

2267	A1637	22c **multicolored**	.65	.20
2268	A1638	22c **multicolored**	.80	.20
2269	A1639	22c **multicolored**	.80	.20
2270	A1640	22c **multicolored**	.80	.20
2271	A1641	22c **multicolored**	.80	.20
2272	A1642	22c **multicolored**	.65	.20
2273	A1643	22c **multicolored**	1.40	.20
2274	A1644	22c **multicolored**	.80	.20
a.		Bklt. pane of 10 (#2268-2271, 2273-2274, 2 each #2267, 2272)	10.00	5.00

UNITED WAY, 100th ANNIV.

United Way
1887-1987
Uniting Communities USA 22
Six Profiles
A1645

Designed by Jerry Pinkney.

LITHOGRAPHED & ENGRAVED
Plates of 200 in four panes of 50.

1987, Apr. 28		**Tagged**		*Perf. 11*
2275 A1645	22c	**multicolored**	.40	.20
		P# block of 4, 6#	1.90	
		Zip block of 4	1.65	—

A1646

A1647

A1648

A1649

Pheasant — A1649a

Grosbeak — A1649b

Owl — A1649c

Honeybee — A1649d

Designs: Nos. 2276, 2278, 2280, Peter Cocci. Nos. 2277, 2279, 2282, Robert McCall. Nos. 2281, 2283-2285, Chuck Ripper.

PHOTOGRAVURE (Nos. 2276-2279)
Panes of 100

1987-88		**Tagged**		*Perf. 11*
2276 A1646	22c	**multicolored**, *May 9*	.40	.20
		P# block of 4, 4#	1.90	
		Zip block of 4	1.65	—
a.		Booklet pane of 20, *Nov. 30*	8.50	—
b.		As "a," vert. pair, imperf. btwn.	1,500.	
2277 A1647	(25c)	**multi**, *Mar. 22, 1988*	.45	.20
		P# block of 4, 4#	2.00	—
		Zip block of 4	1.85	—
2278 A1648	25c	**multi**, *May 6, 1988*	.45	.20
		P# block of 4, 4#	1.90	—
		Zip block of 4	1.85	—
		Pair with full vert. gutter between	125.00	

COIL STAMPS
Perf. 10 Vert.

2279 A1647	(25c)	**multi**, *Mar. 22, 1988*	.45	.20
		Pair	.90	.20
		P# strip of 5, #1111	2.75	
		P# strip of 5, #1211	4.25	
		P# strip of 5, #1222	2.75	
		P# strip of 5, #2222	4.50	
		P# single, #1111	—	.65
		P# single, #1211	—	1.25

		P# single, #1222	—	.65
		P# single, #2222	—	3.50
a.		Imperf., pair	65.00	
		P#1111, 1211, 2222		

ENGRAVED

2280 A1649	25c	**multi**, large block tagging, *May 20, 1988*	.45	.20
		Pair	.90	.20
		P# strip of 5, #1	6.25	
		P# strip of 5, #2-5	3.50	
		P# strip of 5, #7	6.25	
		P# strip of 5, #8	3.50	
		P# strip of 5, #9	9.50	
		P# single, #1	—	2.50
		P# single, #2-5	—	.75
		P# single, #7	—	2.50
		P# single, #8	—	.75
		P# single, #9	—	2.00
a.		Prephosphored uncoated paper (mottled tagging) *Feb. 14, 1989*	.45	.20
		P# strip of 5, #1	37.50	
		P# strip of 5, #2, 3	3.50	
		P# strip of 5, #5	6.50	
		P# strip of 5, #6	11.50	
		P# strip of 5, #7-11, 13-14	3.50	
		P# strip of 5, #15	6.25	
		P# single, #1	—	30.00
		P# single, #2	—	.75
		P# single, #3	—	.55
		P# single, #5	—	1.25
		P# single, #6	—	5.75
		P# single, #7-11, 13-14	—	.75
		P# single, #15	—	2.00
b.		Imperf., pair, large block tagging	25.00	
		P#2-9		
c.		Imperf., pair, prephosphored paper (mottled tagging)	10.00	
		P#2-3, 5-11, 13-15		
d.		Tagging omitted	7.50	
		P# strip of 5, #7, 8		
e.		Black trees	100.00	—
		P# strip of 5, #4, 5, 9	550.00	—
f.		Pair, imperf. between	400.00	

LITHOGRAPHED AND ENGRAVED

2281 A1649d	25c	**multi**, small block tagging *Sept. 2, 1988*	.45	.20
		Pair	.90	.20
		P# strip of 5, #1	3.75	
		P# single, #1	—	.65
a.		s No. 2281, imperf., pair	50.00	
		P#1-2		
b.		Black (engr.) omitted	60.00	—
c.		Black (litho.) omitted	475.00	
d.		Pair, imperf. between	750.00	
e.		Yellow (litho.) omitted	1,100.	
f.		Large block tagging	.45	.20
		Pair	.90	
		P# strip of 5, #2	3.75	
		P# single, #2	—	.65
g.		As "f," imperf. pair	50.00	
h.		As "f," tagging omitted		

No. 2281h can be distinguished as having come from the large block tagging stamp by its deeper colors and jet black "25," which is a characteristic of the plate 2 large block tagged printing.

No. 2281 from plate #1 is known with two types of "1" on the plate-numbered stamps. The original tall "1" was later shortened manually by removing the top of the "1," including the serif, so it would not penetrate the design. Value of plate # strip of 5 with tall "1," $24.

Beware of stamps with traces of the litho. black that are offered as No. 2281c.

Vertical pairs or blocks of No. 2281 and imperfs. with the engr. black missing are from printer's waste.

BOOKLET STAMPS

Printed by American Bank Note Co. (#2283)

PHOTOGRAVURE
Perf. 10, 11 (#2283)

2282 A1647	(25c)	**multi**, *Mar. 22, 1988*	.50	.20
a.		Booklet pane of 10	6.50	3.50
2283 A1649a	25c	**multi**, *Apr. 29, 1988*	.50	.20
a.		Booklet pane of 10	6.00	3.50
b.		25c multicolored, red removed from sky		.20
c.		As "b," bklt. pane of 10	70.00	
d.		Vert. pair, imperf. btwn.		

Imperf. panes exist from printers waste, and a large number exist. No. 2283d resulted from a foldover. Non-foldover pairs and multiples are printer's waste.

2284 A1649b	25c	**multi**, *May 28, 1988*	.50	.20
2285 A1649d	25c	**multi**, *May 28, 1988*	.50	.20
b.		Bklt. pane of 10, 5 each #2284-2285	5.00	3.50
d.		Pair, Nos. 2284-2285	1.10	.25
e.		As "d," tagging omitted	12.50	
2285A A1648	25c	**multi**, *July 5, 1988*	.50	.20
c.		Booklet pane of 6	3.00	2.00

NORTH AMERICAN WILDLIFE
Illustration reduced.

Designed by Chuck Ripper.

PHOTOGRAVURE
Plates of 200 in four panes of 50.

1987, June 13		**Tagged**		*Perf. 11*
2286 A1650	22c	Barn swallow	.95	.50
2287 A1651	22c	Monarch butterfly	.95	.50
2288 A1652	22c	Bighorn sheep	.95	.50
2289 A1653	22c	Broad-tailed hummingbird	.95	.50
2290 A1654	22c	Cottontail	.95	.50

2291 A1655	22c	Osprey	.95	.50
2292 A1656	22c	Mountain lion	.95	.50
2293 A1657	22c	Luna moth	.95	.50
2294 A1658	22c	Mule deer	.95	.50
2295 A1659	22c	Gray squirrel	.95	.50
2296 A1660	22c	Armadillo	.95	.50
2297 A1661	22c	Eastern chipmunk	.95	.50
2298 A1662	22c	Moose	.95	.50
2299 A1663	22c	Black bear	.95	.50
2300 A1664	22c	Tiger swallowtail	.95	.50
2301 A1665	22c	Bobwhite	.95	.50
2302 A1666	22c	Ringtail	.95	.50
2303 A1667	22c	Red-winged blackbird	.95	.50
2304 A1668	22c	American lobster	.95	.50
2305 A1669	22c	Black-tailed jack rabbit	.95	.50
2306 A1670	22c	Scarlet tanager	.95	.50
2307 A1671	22c	Woodchuck	.95	.50
2308 A1672	22c	Roseate spoonbill	.95	.50
2309 A1673	22c	Bald eagle	.95	.50
2310 A1674	22c	Alaskan brown bear	.95	.50
2311 A1675	22c	Iiwi	.95	.50
2312 A1676	22c	Badger	.95	.50
2313 A1677	22c	Pronghorn	.95	.50
2314 A1678	22c	River otter	.95	.50
2315 A1679	22c	Ladybug	.95	.50
2316 A1680	22c	Beaver	.95	.50
2317 A1681	22c	White-tailed deer	.95	.50
2318 A1682	22c	Blue jay	.95	.50
2319 A1683	22c	Pika	.95	.50
2320 A1684	22c	American buffalo	.95	.50
2321 A1685	22c	Snowy egret	.95	.50
2322 A1686	22c	Gray wolf	.95	.50
2323 A1687	22c	Mountain goat	.95	.50
2324 A1688	22c	Deer mouse	.95	.50
2325 A1689	22c	Black-tailed prairie dog	.95	.50
2326 A1690	22c	Box turtle	.95	.50
2327 A1691	22c	Wolverine	.95	.50
2328 A1692	22c	American elk	.95	.50
2329 A1693	22c	California sea lion	.95	.50
2330 A1694	22c	Mockingbird	.95	.50
2331 A1695	22c	Raccoon	.95	.50
2332 A1696	22c	Bobcat	.95	.50
2333 A1697	22c	Black-footed ferret	.95	.50
2334 A1698	22c	Canada goose	.95	.50
2335 A1699	22c	Red fox	.95	.50
a.		A1650-A1699 Pane of 50, #2286-2335	50.00	35.00
2286b-2335b		Any single, red omitted	2,500.	

RATIFICATION OF THE CONSTITUTION BICENTENNIAL

Dec 7, 1787 USA
Delaware 22
A1700

Dec 12, 1787 USA
Pennsylvania
A1701

Dec 18, 1787 USA
New Jersey 22
A1702

January 2, 1788 USA
Georgia
A1703

January 9, 1788
Connecticut
A1704

Feb 6, 1788
Massachusetts
A1705

April 28, 1788 USA
Maryland 22
A1706

May 23, 1788
South Carolina 25
A1707

July 26, 1788 USA
New York 25
A1710

November 21, 1789 25 USA
North Carolina
A1711

25 USA
June 21, 1788
New Hampshire
A1708

June 25, 1788 USA
Virginia 25
A1709

25 USA
May 29, 1790
Rhode Island
A1712

Designers: Nos. 2336-2337, 2341 Richard Sheaff. No. 23
Jim Lamb. No. 2339, Greg Harlin. No. 2340, Christopher Ca
No. 2342, Stephen Hustvedt. Nos. 2343, 2347, Bob Timberla
No. 2344, Thomas Szumowski. No. 2345, Pierre Mion.
2346, Bradbury Thompson. No. 2348, Robert Brangwynne.

Printed by the Bureau of Engraving & Printing or t
American Bank Note Co. (Nos. 2343-2344, 2347).
LITHOGRAPHED & ENGRAVED, PHOTOGRAVU
(#2337, 2339, 2343-2344, 2347), ENGRAVED
(#2341).
Plates of 200 in four panes of 50.

1987-90		Tagged	Perf.	
2336	A1700	22c **multi**, *July 4*	.60	
		P# block of 4, 5#	2.75	
		Zip block of 4	2.50	
2337	A1701	22c **multi**, *Aug. 26*	.60	
		P# block of 4, 5#	2.75	
		Zip block of 4	2.50	
2338	A1702	22c **multi**, *Sept. 11*	.60	
		P# block of 4, 5#	2.75	
		Zip block of 4	2.50	
a.		Black (engr.) omitted	5,500.	
2339	A1703	22c **multi**, *Jan. 6, 1988*	.60	
		P# block of 4, 5#	2.75	
		Zip block of 4	2.50	
2340	A1704	22c **multi**, *Jan. 9, 1988*	.60	
		P# block of 4, 5#	2.75	
		Zip block of 4	2.50	
2341	A1705	22c **dark blue & dark red**, *Feb. 6, 1988*	.60	
		P# block of 4, 1#	2.75	
		Zip block of 4	2.50	
2342	A1706	22c **multi**, *Feb. 15, 1988*	.60	
		P# block of 4, 6#	2.75	
		Zip block of 4	2.50	
2343	A1707	25c **multi**, *May 23, 1988*	.60	
		P# block of 4, 5#	2.75	
		Zip block of 4	2.50	
a.		Strip of 3, vert. imperf btwn.	12,500.	
b.		Red missing (PS)		

NORTH AMERICAN WILDLIFE ISSUE
A1650-A1699

344 A1708 25c **multi**, *June 21, 1988*	.60	.20
P# block of 4, 4#	2.75	—
Zip block of 4	2.50	—
345 A1709 25c **multi**, *June 25, 1988*	.60	.20
P# block of 4, 5#	2.75	—
Zip block of 4	2.50	—
2346 A1710 25c **multi**, *July 26, 1988*	.60	.20
P# block of 4, 5#	2.75	—
Zip block of 4	2.50	—
2347 A1711 25c **multi**, *Aug. 22, 1989*	.60	.20
P# block of 4, 5#	2.75	—
Zip block of 4	2.50	—
2348 A1712 25c **multi**, *May 29, 1990*	.60	.20
P# block of 4, 7#	3.00	—
Zip block of 4	2.50	—
Nos. 2336-2348 (13)	7.80	2.60

No. 2343b resulted either from a shifting of all colors or from a shift of both the perforations and the cutting of the pane.

Arabesque, Dar Batha Palace Door, Fez — A1713

William Faulkner (1897-1962), Novelist — A1714

US-MOROCCO DIPLOMATIC RELATIONS, 200th ANNIV.

Designed by Howard Paine.

LITHOGRAPHED & ENGRAVED
Plates of 200 in four panes of 50.

1987, July 17	**Tagged**	**Perf. 11**	
2349 A1713 22c **scarlet & black**		.55	.20
P# block of 4, 2#		1.75	—
Zip block of 4		1.65	—
a. Black (engr.) omitted		275.00	

See Morocco No. 642.

LITERARY ARTS SERIES

Designed by Bradbury Thompson.

ENGRAVED
Plates of 200 in four panes of 50

1987, Aug. 3	**Tagged**	**Perf. 11**	
2350 A1714 22c **bright green**		.55	.20
P# block of 4		2.75	—
Zip block of 4		2.25	—

Used untagged imperfs exist from printer's waste.

AMERICAN FOLK ART SERIES
Lacemaking

Lacemaking USA 22 — A1715

Lacemaking USA 22 — A1716

Lacemaking USA 22 — A1717

Lacemaking USA 22 — A1718

Designed by Libby Thiel.

LITHOGRAPHED & ENGRAVED
Plates of 160 in four panes of 40.

1987, Aug. 14	**Tagged**	**Perf. 11**	
2351 A1715 22c **ultra & white**		.45	.20
2352 A1716 22c **ultra & white**		.45	.20
2353 A1717 22c **ultra & white**		.45	.20
2354 A1718 22c **ultra & white**		.45	.20
a. Block of 4, #2351-2354		1.90	1.90
P# block of 4, 4#		3.25	—
Zip block of 4		2.00	—
b. As "a," white omitted		600.00	

DRAFTING OF THE CONSTITUTION BICENTENNIAL
Excerpts from the Preamble

A1719

A1720

A1721

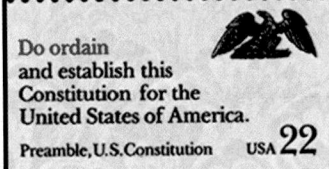

A1722

A1723

Designed by Bradbury Thompson.

BOOKLET STAMPS
PHOTOGRAVURE

1987, Aug. 28	**Tagged**	**Perf. 10 Horiz.**	
2355 A1719 22c **multicolored**		.75	.20
a. Grayish green (background) omitted			
2356 A1720 22c **multicolored**		.75	.20
a. Grayish green (background) omitted			
2357 A1721 22c **multicolored**		.75	.20
a. Grayish green (background) omitted			
2358 A1722 22c **multicolored**		.75	.20
a. Grayish green (background) omitted			
2359 A1723 22c **multicolored**		.75	.20
a. Bklt. pane of 5, #2355-2359		3.75	2.25
b. Grayish green (background) omitted			
c. As No. 2359a, grayish green (background) omitted		—	

A1724

A1725

SIGNING OF THE CONSTITUTION

Designed by Howard Koslow.

LITHOGRAPHED & ENGRAVED
Plates of 200 in four panes of 50.

1987, Sept. 17	**Tagged**	**Perf. 11**	
2360 A1724 22c **multicolored**		.55	.20
P# block of 4, 6#		2.75	—
Zip block of 4		2.25	—

CERTIFIED PUBLIC ACCOUNTING

Designed by Lou Nolan.

LITHOGRAPHED & ENGRAVED
Plates of 200 in four panes of 50.

1987, Sept. 21	**Tagged**	**Perf. 11**	
2361 A1725 22c **multicolored**		1.50	.20
P# block of 4, 5#		7.50	—
Zip block of 4		6.00	—
a. Black (engr.) omitted		725.00	

LOCOMOTIVES

Stourbridge Lion, 1829 A1726

Best Friend of Charleston, 183 A1727

John Bull, 1831 A1728

Brother Jonathan, 1832 A1729

Gowan & Marx, 1839 — A1730

Designed by Richard Leech.

BOOKLET STAMPS
LITHOGRAPHED & ENGRAVED

1987, Oct. 1	Tagged	Perf. 10 Horiz.
2362 A1726 22c multicolored	.55	.20
2363 A1727 22c multicolored	.55	.20
2364 A1728 22c multicolored	.55	.20
2365 A1729 22c multicolored	.55	.20
a. Red omitted	1,100.	225.00
2366 A1730 22c multicolored	.55	.20
a. Bklt. pane of 5, #2362-2366	2.75	2.50
b. As No. 2366, black (engr.) omitted (single)	—	
c. As No. 2366, blue omitted (single)	—	

CHRISTMAS

Moroni Madonna — A1731

Christmas Ornaments — A1732

Designed by Bradbury Thompson (No. 2367) and Jim Dean (No. 2368).

PHOTOGRAVURE
Plates of 800 in eight panes of 100.

1987, Oct. 23	Tagged	Perf. 11
2367 A1731 22c multicolored	.45	.20
P# block of 4, 6#	2.25	
Zip block of 4	1.90	—
2368 A1732 22c multicolored	.45	.20
P# block of 4, 6#	2.10	
Zip block of 4	1.90	—
Pair with full vert. gutter between	—	

1988 WINTER OLYMPICS, CALGARY

Skiing — A1733

Designed by Bart Forbes.

Printed by the American Bank Note Company

PHOTOGRAVURE
Plates of 200 in four panes of 50.

1988, Jan. 10	Tagged	Perf. 11
2369 A1733 22c multicolored	.45	.20
P# block of 4, 4#	2.10	
Zip block of 4	1.90	—

AUSTRALIA BICENTENNIAL

Caricature of an Australian Koala and an American Bald Eagle — A1734

Designed by Roland Harvey.

PHOTOGRAVURE
Plates of 160 in four panes of 40.

1988, Jan. 26	Tagged	Perf. 11
2370 A1734 22c multicolored	.45	.20
P# block of 4, 5#	2.10	
Zip block of 4	1.90	—

See Australia No. 1052.

BLACK HERITAGE SERIES

James Weldon Johnson (1871-1938), Author and Lyricist — A1735

Designed by Thomas Blackshear.

Printed by the American Bank Note Co.

PHOTOGRAVURE
Plates of 200 in four panes of 50.

1988, Feb. 2	Tagged	
2371 A1735 22c multicolored	.50	.20
P# block of 4, 5#	2.60	—
Zip block of 4	2.10	—
a. Tagging omitted	—	

CATS

Siamese and Exotic Shorthair A1736

Abyssinian and Himalayan A1737

Maine Coon and Burmese A1738

American Shorthair and Persian A1739

Designed by John Dawson.

Printed by the American Bank Note Co.

PHOTOGRAVURE
Plates of 160 in four panes of 40.

1988, Feb. 5	Tagged	
2372 A1736 22c multicolored	.70	.2
2373 A1737 22c multicolored	.70	.2
2374 A1738 22c multicolored	.70	.2
2375 A1739 22c multicolored	.70	.2
a. Block of 4, #2372-2375	2.80	1.9
P# block of 4, 5#	4.00	—
Zip block of 4	3.00	—

AMERICAN SPORTS

Knute Rockne (1883-1931), Notre Dame footba coach.
Francis Ouimet (1893-1967), 1st amateur golfer t win the US Open championship.

A1740   A1741

Designed by Peter Cocci and Thomas Hipschen.

LITHOGRAPHED & ENGRAVED
Plates of 200 in four panes of 50.

1988, Mar. 9	Tagged	
2376 A1740 22c multicolored	.50	.20
P# block of 4, 7#	2.60	
Zip block of 4	2.10	

Designed by M. Gregory Rudd.
Printed by the American Bank Note Co.

PHOTOGRAVURE
Plates of 200 in four panes of 50.

1988, June 13	Tagged	
2377 A1741 25c multicolored	.60	.20
P# block of 4, 5#	3.00	—
Zip block of 4	2.50	—

LOVE ISSUE
Roses

A1742   A1743

Designed by Richard Sheaff.

PHOTOGRAVURE
Plates of 400 in four panes of 100 (25c).
Plates of 200 in four panes of 50 (45c).

1988	Tagged	
2378 A1742 25c multicolored, *July 4*	.50	.20
P# block of 4, 5#	2.25	
Zip block of 4	2.10	—
Pair with full horiz. gutter between	—	
a. Imperf., pair	1,900.	
2379 A1743 45c multicolored, *Aug, 8*	.85	.20
P# block of 4, 4#	3.75	
Zip block of 4	3.50	

1988 SUMMER OLYMPICS, SEOUL

Gymnastic Rings A1744

Designed by Bart Forbes.

PHOTOGRAVURE
Plates of 200 in four panes of 50

1988, Aug. 19 — Tagged
2380 A1744 25c multicolored — .50 .20
P# block of 4, 5# — 2.25 —
Zip block of 4 — 2.10 —

CLASSIC AUTOMOBILES

1928 Locomobile A1745

1929 Pierce-Arrow — A1746

1931 Cord A1747

1932 Packard A1748

1935 Duesenberg — A1749

Designed by Ken Dallison.

LITHOGRAPHED & ENGRAVED
BOOKLET STAMPS

1988, Aug. 25 — Tagged — Perf. 10 Horiz.
2381 A1745 25c multicolored — .80 .20
2382 A1746 25c multicolored — .80 .20
2383 A1747 25c multicolored — .80 .20
2384 A1748 25c multicolored — .80 .20
2385 A1749 25c multicolored — .80 .20
a. Bklt. pane of 5, #2381-2385 — 6.00 3.50

ANTARCTIC EXPLORERS

Nathaniel Palmer (1799-1877) A1750

Lt. Charles Wilkes (1798-1877) A1751

Richard E. Byrd (1888-1957) A1752

Lincoln Ellsworth (1880-1951) A1753

Designed by Dennis Lyall.

Printed by the American Bank Note Co.

PHOTOGRAVURE
Plates of 160 in four panes of 40.

1988, Sept. 14 — Tagged — Perf. 11
2386 A1750 25c multicolored — .65 .20
2387 A1751 25c multicolored — .65 .20
2388 A1752 25c multicolored — .65 .20
2389 A1753 25c multicolored — .65 .20
a. Block of 4, #2386-2389 — 2.75 2.00
P# block of 4, 6# — 4.50 —
Zip block of 4 — 3.00 —
b. As "a," black omitted — 1,350.
c. As "a," imperf. horiz. — 2,150.

AMERICAN FOLK ART SERIES
Carousel Animals

Deer — A1754
Horse — A1755
Camel — A1756
Goat — A1757

Designed by Paul Calle.

LITHOGRAPHED & ENGRAVED
Plates of 200 in four panes of 50.

1988, Oct. 1 — Tagged — Perf. 11
2390 A1754 25c multicolored — .65 .20
2391 A1755 25c multicolored — .65 .20
2392 A1756 25c multicolored — .65 .20
2393 A1757 25c multicolored — .65 .20
a. Block of 4, #2390-2393 — 3.00 2.00
P# block of 4, 7# — 4.00 —
Zip block of 4 — 3.25 —

EXPRESS MAIL RATE

Eagle and Moon — A1758

Designed by Ned Seidler.

LITHOGRAPHED & ENGRAVED
Panes of 20

1988, Oct. 4 — Tagged — Perf. 11
2394 A1758 $8.75 multicolored — 13.50 8.00
P# block of 4, 7# — 54.00 —

SPECIAL OCCASIONS

Happy Birthday A1759

Best Wishes A1760

Thinking of You A1761

Love You A1762

Designed by Harry Zelenko.

Printed by the American Bank Note Co.

BOOKLET STAMPS
PHOTOGRAVURE

1988, Oct. 22 — Tagged — Perf. 11
2395 A1759 25c multicolored — .50 .20
2396 A1760 25c multicolored — .50 .20
a. Bklt. pane of 6, 3 #2395 + 3 #2396 with gutter between — 3.50 3.25
2397 A1761 25c multicolored — .50 .20
2398 A1762 25c multicolored — .50 .20
a. Bklt. pane of 6, 3 #2397 + 3 #2398 with gutter between — 3.50 3.25
b. As "a," imperf. horiz. — —
c. As "a," imperf. — —

CHRISTMAS

Madonna and Child, by Botticelli — A1763

One-horse Open Sleigh and Village Scene — A1764

"Missing Curlicue on Sleigh Runner" Cylinder Flaw

Designed by Bradbury Thompson (No. 2399) and Joan Landis (No. 2400).

LITHOGRAPHED & ENGRAVED (No. 2399), PHOTOGRAVURE (No. 2400)

Plates of 300 in 6 Panes of 50

1988, Oct 20	Tagged	Perf. 11½	
2399 A1763 25c multicolored		.50	.20
P# block of 4, 5+1#		2.25	
Zip, copyright block of 4		2.10	—
Pair with full vert. gutter btwn.		—	
a. Gold omitted		25.00	
2400 A1764 25c multicolored		.50	.20
P# block of 4, 5#		2.25	
Zip, copyright block of 4		2.10	—
Pair with full vert. gutter btwn.		—	
Cylinder flaw (missing curlicue on sleigh runner, 11111 UR19)		8.50	

MONTANA STATEHOOD, 100th ANNIV.

C.M. Russell and Friends, by Charles M. Russell (1865-1926) A1765

Designed by Bradbury Thompson.

LITHOGRAPHED & ENGRAVED

Plates of 200 in four panes of 50.

1989, Jan. 15	Tagged	Perf. 11	
2401 A1765 25c multicolored		.55	.20
P# block of 4, 5#		2.75	
Zip block of 4		2.25	—

Imperfs without gum exist from printer's waste.

BLACK HERITAGE SERIES

Asa Philip Randolph (1889-1979), Labor and Civil Rights Leader — A1766

Designed by Thomas Blackshear.

PHOTOGRAVURE

Plates of 200 in four panes of 50.

1989, Feb. 3	Tagged	Perf. 11	
2402 A1766 25c multicolored		.50	.20
P# block of 4, 5#		2.25	
Zip block of 4		2.10	—

NORTH DAKOTA STATEHOOD, 100th ANNIV.

Grain Elevator on the Prairie A1767

Designed by Wendell Minor.

Printed by the American Bank Note Co.

PHOTOGRAVURE

Plates of 200 in four panes of 50.

1989, Feb. 21	Tagged	Perf. 11	
2403 A1767 25c multicolored		.50	.20
P# block of 4, 4#		2.25	
Zip block of 4		2.10	—

WASHINGTON STATEHOOD, 100th ANNIV.

Mt. Rainier — A1768

Designed by Howard Rogers.

Printed by the American Bank Note Co.

PHOTOGRAVURE

Plates of 200 in four panes of 50.

1989, Feb. 22	Tagged	Perf. 11	
2404 A1768 25c multicolored		.50	.20
P# block of 4, 4#		2.25	
Zip block of 4		2.10	—

STEAMBOATS

Experiment, 1788-90 — A1769

Phoenix, 1809 A1770

New Orleans, 1812 A1771

Washington, 1816 — A1772

Walk in the Water, 1818 A1773

Designed by Richard Schlecht.

LITHOGRAPHED & ENGRAVED BOOKLET STAMPS

Perf. 10 Horiz. on 1 or 2 Sides

1989, Mar. 3			Tagged	
2405 A1769 25c multicolored			.50	
2406 A1770 25c multicolored			.50	
2407 A1771 25c multicolored			.50	
2408 A1772 25c multicolored			.50	
2409 A1773 25c multicolored			.50	
a. Booklet pane of 5, #2405-2409			2.50	1.7
b. As "a," tagging omitted				

No. 122 — A1774

Arturo Toscanini (1867-1957), Conductor — A1775

WORLD STAMP EXPO '89

Nov. 17-Dec. 3. Washington, D.C.

Designed by Richard Sheaff.

LITHOGRAPHED & ENGRAVED

Plates of 200 in four panes of 50.

1989, Mar. 16	Tagged	Perf. 11	
2410 A1774 25c grayish brn, blk & car rose		.50	.20
P# block of 4, 4#		2.25	
Zip block of 4		2.10	—

PERFORMING ARTS

Designed by Jim Sharpe

Printed by the American Bank Note Co.

PHOTOGRAVURE

Plates of 200 in four panes of 50.

1989, Mar. 25	Tagged	Perf. 11	
2411 A1775 25c multicolored		.50	.20
P# block of 4, 5#		2.25	
Zip block of 4		2.10	—

CONSTITUTION BICENTENNIAL SERIES

House of Representatives A1776

Senate A1777

Executive Branch — A1778

Supreme Court — A1779

Designed by Howard Koslow.

LITHOGRAPHED & ENGRAVED
Plates of 200 in four panes of 50.

		Tagged		Perf. 11	
1989-90					
2412	A1776	25c **multi**, *Apr. 4, 1989*		.50	.20
		P# block of 4, 4#		2.25	—
		Zip block of 4		2.10	—
2413	A1777	25c **multi**, *Apr. 6, 1989*		.50	.20
		P# block of 4, 4#		2.75	—
		Zip block of 4		2.10	—
2414	A1778	25c **multi**, *Apr. 16, 1989*		.50	.20
		P# block of 4, 4#		2.25	—
		Zip block of 4		2.10	—
2415	A1779	25c **multi**, *Feb. 2, 1990*		.50	.20
		P# block of 4, 4#		2.25	—
		Zip block of 4		2.10	—

SOUTH DAKOTA STATEHOOD, 100th ANNIV.

Pasque Flowers, Pioneer Woman and Sod House on Grasslands A1780

Designed by Marian Henjum.

Printed by the American Bank Note Co.

PHOTOGRAVURE
Plates of 200 in four panes of 50.

		Tagged	Perf. 11	
1989, May 3				
2416	A1780	25c **multicolored**	.60	.20
		P# block of 4, 4#	2.75	—
		Zip block of 4	2.50	—

AMERICAN SPORTS

Henry Louis "Lou" Gehrig (1903-1941), New York Yankee Baseball Player — A1781

Designed by Bart Forbes.

Printed by the American Bank Note Co.

PHOTOGRAVURE
Plates of 200 in four panes of 50.

		Tagged	Perf. 11	
1989, June 10				
2417	A1781	25c **multicolored**	.60	.20
		P# block of 4, 6#	3.00	—
		Zip block of 4	2.50	—

LITERARY ARTS SERIES

Ernest Miller Hemingway (1899-1961), Nobel Prize winner for Literature in 1954 — A1782

Designed by M. Gregory Rudd.

Printed by the American Bank Note Co.

PHOTOGRAVURE
Plates of 200 in four panes of 50.

		Tagged	Perf. 11	
1989, July 17				
2418	A1782	25c **multicolored**	.50	.20
		P# block of 4, 5#	2.25	—
		Zip block of 4	2.10	—
a.		Vert. pair, imperf horiz.	1,850.	

MOON LANDING, 20TH ANNIVERSARY

Raising of the Flag on the Lunar Surface, July 20, 1969 — A1783

Designed by Christopher Calle.

LITHOGRAPHED & ENGRAVED
Panes of 20

		Tagged	Perf. 11x11½	
1989, July 20				
2419	A1783	$2.40 **multicolored**	4.75	2.00
		P# block of 4, 6#	20.00	—
		Pane of 20	100.00	—
a.		Black (engr.) omitted	2,250.	
b.		Imperf., pair	700.00	
c.		Black (litho.) omitted	2,500.	

No. 2419 exists with a gray background instead of the normal dark blue. Some of these may have been caused by a chemical wiping of the blue plate. However, the same or extremely similar stamps can be produced by exposing normal stamps to sunlight or fluorescent light for varying time periods.

LETTER CARRIERS

A1784

Designed by Jack Davis.

Printed by the American Bank Note Co.

PHOTOGRAVURE
Plates of 160 in four panes of 40.

		Tagged	Perf. 11	
1989, Aug. 30				
2420	A1784	25c **multicolored**	.50	.20
		P# block of 4, 5#	2.25	—
		Zip block of 4	2.10	—

CONSTITUTION BICENTENNIAL

Bill of Rights — A1785

Designed by Lou Nolan.

LITHOGRAPHED & ENGRAVED
Plates of 200 in four panes of 50.

		Tagged	Perf. 11	
1989, Sept. 25				
2421	A1785	25c **multicolored**	.50	.20
		P# block of 4	3.25	—
		Zip block of 4	2.10	—
a.		Black (engr.) omitted	275.00	

PREHISTORIC ANIMALS

Tyrannosaurus Rex — A1786

Pteranodon A1787

Stegosaurus A1788

Brontosaurus A1789

Designed by John Gurche.

LITHOGRAPHED & ENGRAVED
Plates of 160 in four panes of 40.

		Tagged	Perf. 11	
1989, Oct. 1				
2422	A1786	25c **multicolored**	.70	.20
2423	A1787	25c **multicolored**	.70	.20
2424	A1788	25c **multicolored**	.70	.20
2425	A1789	25c **multicolored**	.70	.20
a.		Block of 4, #2422-2425	2.80	2.00
		P# block of 4, 6#	4.00	—
		Zip block of 4	3.00	—
b.		As "a," black (engr.) omitted	475.00	

The correct scientific name for Brontosaurus is Apatosaurus. Copyright block margin includes ad and Stamposaurus character trademark.

No. 2425b is valued in the grade of fine. Very fine blocks exist and sell for approximately $600.

PRE-COLUMBIAN AMERICA ISSUE

Southwest Carved Figure, A.D. 1150-1350 — A1790

Designed by Lon Busch.

Printed by the American Bank Note Company.

PHOTOGRAVURE
Plate of 200 in four panes of 50.

1989, Oct. 12	Tagged	Perf. 11	
2426 A1790 25c **multicolored**		.60	.20
P# block of 4, 6#		3.00	—
Zip block of 4		2.50	—

See No. C121.

CHRISTMAS

Madonna and Child, by Caracci — A1791

Sleigh Full of Presents — A1792

Designed by Bradbury Thompson (#2427) and Steven Dohanos (#2428-2429).

Printed by the Bureau of Engraving and Printing (#2427-2428) and American Bank Note Company (#2429).

LITHOGRAPHED & ENGRAVED, PHOTOGRAVURE (#2428-2429)
Sheets of 300 in six panes of 50.

1989, Oct. 19	Tagged	Perf. 11½	
2427 A1791 25c **multicolored**		.50	.20
P# block of 4, 5#		2.25	—
Zip, copyright block of 4		2.10	—
Pair with full horiz. gutter between		—	
a.	Booklet pane of 10	5.00	3.50
b.	Red (litho.) omitted	750.00	
c.	As "a," imperf.	—	

	Perf. 11		
2428 A1792 25c **multicolored**		.50	.20
P# block of 4, 5#		2.25	—
Zip, copyright block of 4		2.10	—
a.	Vert. pair, imperf. horiz.	850.00	

BOOKLET STAMP
Perf. 11½ on 2 or 3 sides

2429 A1792 25c **multicolored**		.50	.20
a.	Booklet pane of 10	5.00	3.50
b.	Vert. pair, imperf between	—	
c.	As "a," imperf between	—	
d.	As "a," red omitted	3,500.	
e.	Imperf., pair	—	

Marked differences exist between Nos. 2428 and 2429: No. 2429 was printed in four colors, No. 2428 in five colors. The runners on the sleigh in No. 2429 are twice as thick as those on No. 2428. On No. 2429 the package at the upper left in the sleigh has a red bow, whereas the same package in No. 2428 has a red and black bow; and the ribbon on the upper right package in No. 2429 is green, whereas the same ribbon in No. 2428 is black.

Eagle and Shield — A1793

Designed by Jay Haiden.

Printed by the American Bank Note Company.

PHOTOGRAVURE
BOOKLET STAMP

1989, Nov. 10	Tagged	Self-Adhesive	*Die Cut*	
2431 A1793 25c **multicolored**			.50	.20
a.	Booklet pane of 18		11.00	
b.	Vert. pair, die cutting omitted between		500.00	
c.	Die cutting omitted, pair		275.00	

Panes sold for $5.
Also available in strips of 18 with stamps spaced for use in affixing machines to service first day covers. Sold for $5.
No. 2431c will include part of the margins around the stamps.
Sold only in 15 test cities (Atlanta, Chicago, Cleveland, Columbus, OH, Dallas, Denver, Houston, Indianapolis, Kansas City, MO, Los Angeles, Miami, Milwaukee, Minneapolis, Phoenix, St. Louis) and through the philatelic agency.

WORLD STAMP EXPO '89
Washington, DC, Nov. 17-Dec. 3

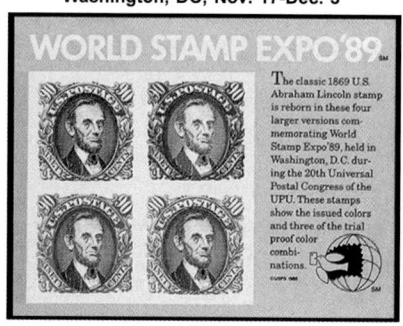

A1794

Illustration reduced.

Designed by Richard Sheaff.

LITHOGRAPHED & ENGRAVED

1989, Nov. 17	Tagged	Imperf.	
2433 A1794	Sheet of 4	13.50	12.00
a.	90c like No. 122	3.00	2.50
b.	90c like 132TC (blue frame, brown center)	3.00	2.50
c.	90c like 132TC (green frame, blue center)	3.00	2.50
d.	90c like 132TC (scarlet frame, blue center)	3.00	2.50
e.	As No. 2433, tagging omitted	—	

20th UPU CONGRESS
Traditional Mail Delivery

Stagecoach, c. 1850 — A1795

Paddlewheel Steamer — A1796

Biplane — A1797

Depot-hack Type Automobile — A1798

Designed by Mark Hess.

LITHOGRAPHED & ENGRAVED
Plates of 160 in four panes of 40.

1989, Nov. 19	Tagged	Perf. 1	
2434 A1795 25c **multicolored**		.50	.2
2435 A1796 25c **multicolored**		.50	.2
2436 A1797 25c **multicolored**		.50	.2
2437 A1798 25c **multicolored**		.50	.2
a.	Block of 4, #2434-2437	2.00	1.7
	P# block of 4, 5#	3.75	—
	Zip block of 4	2.25	—
b.	As "a," dark blue (engr.) omitted	500.00	
c.	As No. 2437a, tagging omitted	—	

No. 2437b is valued in the grade of fine. Very fine blocks exis and sell for approximately $700.

Souvenir Sheet
LITHOGRAPHED & ENGRAVED

1989, Nov. 28	Tagged	Imper	
2438	Sheet of 4	5.00	3.7
a.	A1795 25c multicolored	1.10	.8
b.	A1796 25c multicolored	1.10	.8
c.	A1797 25c multicolored	1.10	.8
d.	A1798 25c multicolored	1.10	.8
e.	Dark blue & gray (engr.) omitted	5,000.	

20th Universal Postal Union Congress.

VALUES FOR HINGED STAMPS AFTER NO. 771
This catalogue does not value unused stamps after No. 771 in hinged condition. Hinged unused stamps from No. 772 to the present are worth considerably less than the values given for unused stamps, which are for never-hinged examples.

IDAHO STATEHOOD, 100th ANNIV.

Mountain Bluebird, Sawtooth Mountains — A1799

Designed by John Dawson.

Printed by the American Bank Note Company.

PHOTOGRAVURE
Plates of 200 in four panes of 50.

1990, Jan. 6	Tagged	Perf. 11	
2439 A1799 25c **multicolored**		.55	.20
P# block of 4, 5#		2.75	—
Zip block of 4		2.25	—

LOVE

A1800

Designed by Jayne Hertko.

Printed by the U.S. Banknote Company (#2440) and the Bureau of Engraving and Printing (#2441).

PHOTOGRAVURE
Plates of 200 in four panes of 50.

1990, Jan. 18	Tagged	Perf. 12½x13
440 A1800 25c black, bright blue, dark pink		
& emerald green	.50	.20
P# block of 4, 4#	2.25	—
Zip, copyright block of 4	2.10	—
a. Imperf., pair	750.00	

BOOKLET STAMP
Perf. 11½ on 2 or 3 sides

441 A1800 25c black, ultramarine, bright		
pink & dark green	.50	.20
a. Booklet pane of 10	5.00	3.50
b. Bright pink omitted	175.00	
c. As "a," bright pink omitted	1,800.	

No. 2441b may be obtained from booklet panes containing both normal and color-omitted stamps.

BLACK HERITAGE SERIES

Ida B. Wells (1862-1931), Journalist — A1801

Designed by Thomas Blackshear.

Printed by American Bank Note Company.

PHOTOGRAVURE
Plates of 200 in four panes of 50.

1990, Feb. 1	Tagged	Perf. 11
2442 A1801 25c multicolored	.75	.20
P# block of 4, 5#	3.75	—
Zip block of 4	3.25	—

Beach Umbrella — A1802

Designed by Pierre Mion.

BOOKLET STAMP
PHOTOGRAVURE

1990, Feb. 3	Tagged	Perf. 11
2443 A1802 15c multicolored	.30	.20
a. Booklet pane of 10	3.00	2.00
b. Blue omitted	150.00	
c. As "a," blue omitted	1,500.	

WYOMING STATEHOOD, 100th ANNIV.

High Mountain Meadows, by Conrad Schwiering A1803

Designed by Jack Rosenthal.

LITHOGRAPHED & ENGRAVED
Plates of 200 in four panes of 50.

1990, Feb. 23	Tagged	Perf. 11
2444 A1803 25c multicolored	.50	.20
P# block of 4, 5#	2.25	—
Zip block of 4	2.10	—
a. Black (engr.) omitted	1,500.	—

CLASSIC FILMS

Judy Garland and Toto (The Wizard of Oz) — A1804

Clark Gable & Vivien Leigh (Gone With the Wind) — A1805

Gary Cooper (Beau Geste) — A1806

John Wayne (Stagecoach) A1807

Designed by Thomas Blackshear.

Printed by the American Bank Note Company.

PHOTOGRAVURE
Plates of 160 in four panes of 40.

1990, Mar. 23	Tagged	Perf. 11
2445 A1804 25c multicolored	1.50	.20
2446 A1805 25c multicolored	1.50	.20
2447 A1806 25c multicolored	1.50	.20
2448 A1807 25c multicolored	1.50	.20
a. Block of 4, #2445-2448	6.00	3.50
P# block of 4, 5#	6.50	—
Zip block of 4	6.25	—

LITERARY ARTS SERIES

Marianne Moore (1887-1972), Poet — A1808

Designed by M. Gregory Rudd.

Printed by the American Bank Note Company.

PHOTOGRAVURE
Plates of 200 in four panes of 50.

1990, Apr. 18	Tagged	Perf. 11
2449 A1808 25c multicolored	.60	.20
P# block of 4, 3#	2.75	—
Zip block of 4	2.50	—
a. All colors missing (EP)	—	

No. 2449a must be collected se-tenant with a partially printed stamp or in longer horizontal strips with a partially printed stamp and normal stamps.

> **Coil Plate No. Strips of 3**
> Beginning with No. 2123, coil plate no. strips of 3 usually sell at the level of strips of 5 minus the face value of two stamps.

TRANSPORTATION ISSUE

A1810

A1811

A1811a

A1812

A1816

A1822

A1823

A1825

A1827

Designers: 4c, 32c, Richard Schlecht. Nos. 2452, 2452B, 2452D, Susan Sanford. No. 2453, Paul Calle. 10c, David K. Stone. 20c, 23c, Robert Brangwynne. $1, Chuck Hodgson.

Printed by: Guilford Gravure for American Bank Note Co. (No. 2452B), J.W. Fergusson & Sons for Stamp Venturers (No. 2454), Stamp Venturers (No, 2452D), others by BEP.

COIL STAMPS
ENGRAVED, PHOTOGRAVURE (#2452B, 2452D, 2454, 2458)
Tagged, Untagged (Nos. 2452B, 2452D, 2453, 2454, 2457-2458)

1990-95				*Perf. 9.8 Vert.*
2451	A1810	4c **claret**, *Jan. 25, 1991*	.20	.20
		Pair	.20	.20
		P# strip of 5, #1	1.10	
		P# single, #1	—	.95
a.		Imperf., pair	575.00	
		P#1		
b.		Untagged	.20	.20
		Pair	.20	.20
		P# strip of 5, #1	1.10	
		P# single, #1	—	.95
2452	A1811	5c **carmine**, dull gum, *Aug. 31*	.20	.20
		Pair	.20	.20
		P# strip of 5, #1	1.25	
		P# single, #1	—	.90
a.		Untagged, dull gum	.20	.20
		Pair	.20	.20
		P# strip of 5, #1	1.25	
		P# single, #1	—	1.00
		Low gloss gum	.20	.20
		Pair	.20	.20
		P# strip of 5, #2	1.40	
		P# single, #2	—	1.20
c.		Imperf., pair	650.00	
2452B	A1811	5c **carmine**, *Dec. 8, 1992*	.20	.20
		Pair	.20	.20
		P# strip of 5, #A1-A2	1.50	
		P# single, #A1-A2	—	1.00
f.		Printed with luminescent ink	.20	.20
		Pair	.20	.20
		P# strip of 5, #A3	2.10	
		P# single, #A3	—	2.00
2452D	A1811a	5c **carmine**, low gloss gum, *Mar. 20, 1995*	.20	.20
		Pair	.20	.20
		P# strip of 5, #S1-S2	1.60	
		P# single, #S1-S2	—	1.10
e.		Imperf., pair	150.00	
g.		Printed with luminescent ink, shiny gum	.20	.20
		Pair	.20	.20
		P# strip of 5, #S2	1.90	
		P# single, #S2	—	1.75
		Low gloss gum	.20	
		P# strip of 5, #S3	1.90	
2453	A1812	5c **brown** (Bureau precancel, Additional Nonprofit Postage Paid, in gray), *May 25, 1991*	.20	.20
		Pair	.20	.20
		P# strip of 5, #1-3	1.50	
		P# single, #1-3	—	1.00
a.		Imperf., pair	250.00	
		P#1		
b.		Gray omitted	—	
2454	A1812	5c **red** (Bureau precancel, Additional Nonprofit Postage Paid, in gray), shiny gum, *1991, Oct. 22*	.30	.20
		Pair	.60	.20
		P# strip of 5, #S11	2.00	
		P# single, #S11	—	1.25
		Low gloss gum	.50	
		Pair	1.00	
		P# strip of 5, #S11	10.00	
2457	A1816	10c **green** (Bureau precancel, Additional Presort Postage Paid, in gray), *May 25, 1991*	.20	.20
		Pair	.40	.40
		P# strip of 5, #1	2.10	
		P# single, #1	—	1.50
a.		Imperf., pair	140.00	
		P#1		
b.		All color omitted	—	

No. 2457b must be collected as part of a transitional strip with normal stamps having freak perfs.

2458	A1816	10c **green** (Bureau precancel, Additional Presort Postage Paid, in black), *May 25, 1994*	.30	.20
		Pair	.60	.40
		P# strip of 5, #11, 22	2.50	
		P# single, #11	—	2.25
		P# single, #22	—	2.00
2463	A1822	20c **green**, *June 9, 1995*	.40	.20
		Pair	.80	.20
		P# strip of 5, #1-2	4.00	
		P# single, #1-2	—	2.25
a.		Imperf., pair	95.00	
2464	A1823	23c **dark blue**, prephosphored coated paper (solid tagging), dull gum, *Apr. 12, 1991*	.45	.20
		Pair	.90	.20
		P# strip of 5, #2-3	3.75	
		P# single, #2-3	—	2.00
a.		Prephosphored uncoated paper (mottled tagging), dull gum, *1993*	.45	.20

		Pair	.90	.20
		P# strip of 5, #3	4.50	
		Shiny gum, *1993*	.45	
		Pair	.90	
		P# strip of 5, #3	4.50	
		P# strip of 5, #4	4.75	
		P# strip of 5, #5	11.50	
		P# single, #3-4	—	2.75
		P# single, #5	—	5.00
b.		Imperf., pair	125.00	
		P#2		
2466	A1825	32c **blue**, prephosphored uncoated paper (mottled tagging), shiny gum, *June 2, 1995*	.65	.20
		Pair	1.30	.30
		P# strip of 5, #2	5.50	
		P# strip of 5, #3	5.75	
		P# strip of 5, #4	5.50	
		P# strip of 5, #5	11.00	
		P# single, #2, 3	—	2.25
		P# single, #4	—	2.50
		P# single, #5	—	2.75
		Low gloss gum	.60	
		Pair	1.20	
		P# strip of 5, #3	9.00	
		P# strip of 5, #4	15.00	
		P# strip of 5, #5	8.00	
		P# single, #3	—	2.25
		P# single, #4	—	2.50
		P# single, #5	—	2.75
a.		Imperf., pair, shiny gum	550.00	
		Low gloss gum	550.00	
b.		32c **bright blue**, prephosphored uncoated paper (mottled tagging), low gloss gum	6.00	4.50
		Pair	12.00	11.00
		P# strip of 5, #5	140.00	
		P# single, #5	—	110.00

Some specialists refer to No. 2466b as "Bronx blue," and it is considered to be an error of color.

2468	A1827	$1 **blue & scarlet**, overall tagging, dull gum, *Apr. 20*	1.75	.50
		Pair	3.50	1.00
		P# strip of 5, #1	10.00	
		P# single, #1	—	3.00
a.		Imperf., pair	2,750.	—
b.		Prephosphored uncoated paper (mottled tagging), shiny gum, *1993*	1.75	.50
		Pair	3.50	1.00
		P# strip of 5, #3	10.00	
		P# single, #3	—	3.00
c.		Prephosphored coated paper (grainy solid tagging), low gloss gum, *1998*	2.25	.50
		Pair	4.50	1.00
		P# strip of 5, #3	15.00	
		P# single, #3	—	3.00
		Nos. 2451-2468 (12)	5.05	2.70

Some mint pairs of No. 2468 appear to be imperf. but have faint blind perforations on the gum.

LIGHTHOUSES

Admiralty Head, WA — A1829

Cape Hatteras, NC — A1830

West Quoddy Head, ME — A1831

American Shoals, FL — A1832

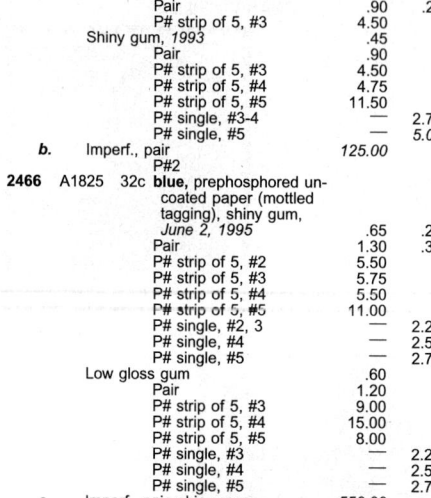

Sandy Hook, NJ — A1833

Designed by Howard Koslow.

BOOKLET STAMPS
LITHOGRAPHED & ENGRAVED
Perf. 10 Vert. on 1 or 2 sides

1990, Apr. 26					Tagged
2470	A1829	25c **multicolored**		1.40	.20
2471	A1830	25c **multicolored**		1.40	.20
2472	A1831	25c **multicolored**		1.40	.20
2473	A1832	25c **multicolored**		1.40	.20
2474	A1833	25c **multicolored**		1.40	.20
a.		Bklt. pane of 5, #2470-2474		7.00	2.00
b.		As "a," white ("USA 25") omitted		75.00	

Perforations on Lighthouse booklet panes separate very easily. Careful handling is required.

FLAG

A1834

Designed by Harry Zelenko.

Printed by Avery International Corp.

PHOTOGRAVURE
1990, May 18   Untagged Self-adhesive *Die Cut* Printed on Plastic

2475	A1834	25c **dark red & dark blue**	.55	.25
a.		Pane of 12	6.60	

Sold only in panes of 12; peelable plastic backing inscribed in light ultramarine. Available for a test period of six months at 22 First National Bank automatic teller machines in Seattle.

FLORA and FAUNA

American Kestrel — A1840

A1841

Eastern Bluebird — A1842

Fawn — A1843

Cardinal — A1844

Pumpkinseed Sunfish — A1845

Bobcat
A1846

Designers: 1c, 3c, 45c, Michael Matherly. 19c, Peter Cocci.
30c, Robert Giusti. $2, Chuck Ripper.

Printed by: No. 2476 and No. 2478, American Bank Note Co.
No. 2477, No. 2479, and No. 2482, Bureau of Engraving &
Printing. No. 2480 and No. 2482, Stamp Venturers. No. 2481,
Stamp Venturers (engraved) and The Press, Inc. (lithographed).

LITHOGRAPHED
Panes of 100

1990-95		**Untagged**	**Perf. 11, 11.2 (#2477)**	
2476	A1840	1c **multicolored,** June 22, 1991	.20	.20
		P# block of 4, 4#+A	.20	
		Zip block of 4	.20	—

Imperfs of No. 2476 are from printer's waste.

2477	A1841	1c **multicolored,** shiny gum, May 10, 1995	.20	.20
		P# block of 4, 4#	.20	
		Low gloss gum	.20	
		P# block of 4, 4#	.20	
a.		Tagged (error), shiny gum	—	
2478	A1842	3c **multicolored,** June 22, 1991	.20	.20
		P# block of 4, 4#+A	.30	
		Zip block of 4	.25	—
a.		Vert. pair, imperf horiz.	—	
b.		Double impression of all colors except yellow	—	

Imperfs of No. 2478 are from printer's waste.

See Nos. 3032/3053. Compare design A1842 with design A2336.

PHOTOGRAVURE
Plates of 400 in four panes of 100.

		Tagged	**Perf. 11½x11**	
2479	A1843	19c **multicolored,** Mar. 11, 1991	.35	.20
		P# block of 4, 5#	1.75	
		Zip block of 4	1.50	—
a.		Tagging omitted	10.00	
b.		Red omitted	750.00	
c.		Imperf, pair	—	

On No. 2479b other colors are shifted.

2480	A1844	30c **multicolored,** June 22, 1991	.60	.20
		P# block of 4, 4#+S	2.75	
		Zip block of 4	2.50	—

LITHOGRAPHED & ENGRAVED
Panes of 100
Perf. 11

2481	A1845	45c **multicolored,** Dec. 2, 1992	.90	.20
		P# block of 4, 5#+S	4.25	
		Zip block of 4	3.75	—
a.		Black (engr.) omitted	450.00	

Panes of 20

2482	A1846	$2 **multicolored,** June 1, 1990	3.50	1.25
		P# block of 4, 5#	14.00	
		Pane of 20	70.00	
a.		Black (engr.) omitted	250.00	
b.		Tagging omitted	15.00	

Blue Jay — A1847

Wood Duck — A1848

African Violets — A1849

Peach — A1850

Pear — A1851

Rose — A1853

Red Squirrel — A1852

Pine Cone — A1854

Designed by Robert Giusti (#2483-2485), Ned Seidler
(#2486-2488, 2493-2495A), Michael R. Matherly (#2489), Gyo
Fujikawa (#2490), Paul Breeden (#2491), Gyo Fujikawa
(#2492).

Printed by Stamp Venturers (#2483, 2492), Bureau of
Engraving and Printing (#2484, 2487-2488), J.W. Fergusson &
Sons for KCS Industries, Inc. (#2485), KCS Industries (#2486),
Dittler Brothers, Inc. (#2489), Stamp Venturers (#2490), Bank-
note Corporation of America (#2491), Avery-Dennison (#2493-
2495, 2495A).

PHOTOGRAVURE
BOOKLET STAMPS

1991-95			**Perf. 10.9x9.8**	
		Tagged		
2483	A1847	20c **multicolored,** June 15, 1995	.50	.20
a.		Booklet pane of 10	5.25	2.25
b.		As "a," imperf	—	

		Perf. 10 on 2 or 3 sides		
2484	A1848	29c **black & multi,** overall tagging, Apr. 12, 1991	.60	.20
a.		Booklet pane of 10	6.00	3.75
b.		Vert. pair, imperf. horiz.	200.00	
c.		As "b," bklt. pane of 10	1,000.	
d.		Prephosphored coated paper (solid tagging)	.60	.20
e.		As "d," booklet pane of 10	6.00	3.75
f.		Vert. pair, imperf between and with natural straight edge at bottom	—	
g.		As "f," bklt. pane of 10	—	

		Perf. 11 on 2 or 3 Sides		
2485	A1848	29c **red & multi,** Apr. 12, 1991	.60	.20
a.		Booklet pane of 10	6.00	4.00
b.		Vert. pair, imperf. between	3,000.	
c.		Imperf, pair	2,500.	

		Perf. 10x11 on 2 or 3 Sides		
2486	A1849	29c **multicolored,** Oct. 8, 1993	.60	.20
a.		Booklet pane of 10	6.00	4.00

		Perf. 11x10 on 2 or 3 Sides		
2487	A1850	32c **multicolored,** July 8, 1995	.65	.20
2488	A1851	32c **multicolored,** July 8, 1995	.65	.20
a.		Booklet pane, 5 each #2487-2488	6.50	4.25
b.		Pair, #2487-2488	1.30	.30

1993-95			**Tagged**	
		Die Cut		
2489	A1852	29c **multicolored,** June 25	.65	.20
a.		Booklet pane of 18	12.00	
b.		As "a," die cutting omitted	—	
2490	A1853	29c **red, green & black,** Aug. 19	.65	.20
a.		Booklet pane of 18	12.00	

Nos. 2489-2490 also available in strips with stamps spaced
for use in affixing machines to service first day covers. No plate
numbers. Stamps removed from strips are indistinquishable
from booklet stamps.

2491	A1854	29c **multicolored,** Nov. 5	.60	.20
a.		Booklet pane of 18	11.00	
b.		Horiz. pair, die cutting omitted between	225.00	
c.		Coil with plate # B1		5.00
		P# strip of 5, #B1	8.00	

Stamps without plate # from coil strips are indistinquishable
from booklet stamps once they are removed from the backing
paper.

		Serpentine Die Cut 11.3x11.7 on 2, 3 or 4 Sides		
2492	A1853	32c **pink, green & black,** June 2, 1995	.65	.20
a.		Booklet pane of 20+label	13.00	
b.		Booklet pane of 15+label	9.75	
c.		Horiz. pair, die cutting omitted between	—	
d.		As "a," 2 stamps and parts of 7 others printed on backing liner	—	
e.		Booklet pane of 14	21.00	
f.		Booklet pane of 16	21.00	
g.		Coil with plate # S111		3.75

		P# strip of 5, #S111	7.00
h.		Vert. pair, die cutting omitted between (from No. 2492b)	—

Stamps on plate # strips are separated on backing larger
than the stamps. Stamps without plate # from coil strips are
indistinquishable from interior position booklet stamps once
they are removed from the backing paper.

For booklet panes containing No. 2492f with one stamp
removed, see Nos. BK178B, BK178D-BK178E in Booklets
section.

		Serpentine Die Cut 8.8 on 2, 3 or 4 Sides		
2493	A1850	32c **multicolored,** July 8, 1995	.65	.20
2494	A1851	32c **multicolored,** July 8, 1995	.65	.20
a.		Booklet pane, 10 each #2493-2494+label	13.00	
b.		Pair, #2493-2494	1.30	
c.		As "b," die cutting omitted	—	

COIL STAMPS
Serpentine Die Cut 8.8 Vert.

2495	A1850	32c **multicolored,** July 8, 1995	1.50	.20
2495A	A1851	32c **multicolored,** July 8, 1995	1.50	.20
b.		Pair, #2495-2495A	3.00	
		P# strip of 5, 3 #2495A, 2 #2495, P#V11111	12.50	
		P# single, #V11111		4.25

See Nos. 3048, 3053-3054.

Scott values for used self-adhesive stamps are
for examples either on piece or off piece.

OLYMPIANS

Jesse Owens, 1936 — A1855

Ray Ewry, 1900-08 A1856

Hazel Wightman, 1924 — A1857

Eddie Eagan, 1920, 1932 — A1858

Helene Madison, 1932 — A1859

Designed by Bart Forbes.

Printed by the American Bank Note Company.

PHOTOGRAVURE
Panes of 35.

1990, July 6		Tagged		*Perf. 11*
2496	A1855 25c **multicolored**		.60	.20
2497	A1856 25c **multicolored**		.60	.20
2498	A1857 25c **multicolored**		.60	.20
2499	A1858 25c **multicolored**		.60	.20
2500	A1859 25c **multicolored**		.60	.20
a.	Strip of 5, #2496-2500		3.25	2.50
	P# block of 10, 4#		8.00	—
	Zip, inscription block of 10		6.50	
b.	As "a," blue omitted		—	

INDIAN HEADDRESSES

Assiniboin
A1860

Cheyenne
A1861

Comanche
A1862

Flathead
A1863

Shoshone
A1864

Designed by Lunda Hoyle Gill.

LITHOGRAPHED & ENGRAVED
BOOKLET STAMPS

1990, Aug. 17	Tagged	*Perf. 11 on 2 or 3 Sides*	
2501	A1860 25c **multicolored**	1.20	.20
2502	A1861 25c **multicolored**	1.20	.20
2503	A1862 25c **multicolored**	1.20	.20
2504	A1863 25c **multicolored**	1.20	.20
2505	A1864 25c **multicolored**	1.20	.20
a.	Bklt. pane of 10, 2 each #2501-2505	12.00	7.50
b.	As "a," black (engr.) omitted	3,500.	
c.	Strip of 5, #2501-2505	6.00	2.50
d.	As "a," horiz. imperf. between	—	

The one example of No. 2505d that has been reported is actually split at the booklet fold and is a block of 4 and a block of 6.

MICRONESIA & MARSHALL ISLANDS

Canoe and Flag of the Federated States of Micronesia
A1865

Stick Chart, Canoe and Flag of the Republic of the Marshall Islands
A1866

LITHOGRAPHED & ENGRAVED
Sheets of 200 in four panes of 50.

1990, Sept. 28		Tagged		*Perf. 11*
2506	A1865 25c **multicolored**		.50	.20
2507	A1866 25c **multicolored**		.50	.20
a.	Pair, #2506-2507		1.00	.60
	P# block of 4, 6#		2.50	
	Zip block of 4		2.10	
b.	As "a," black (engr.) omitted		3,000.	

See Micronesia Nos. 124-126, Marshall Islands No. 381.

SEA CREATURES

Killer Whales
A1867

Northern Sea Lions — A1868

Sea Otter — A1869

Common Dolphin
A1870

Designed by Peter Cocci (Nos. 2508, 2511), Vladimir Beilin, USSR (Nos. 2509-2510).

LITHOGRAPHED & ENGRAVED
Sheets of 160 in four panes of 40.

1990, Oct. 3		Tagged		*Perf. 11*
2508	A1867 25c **multicolored**		.55	.20
2509	A1868 25c **multicolored**		.55	.20
2510	A1869 25c **multicolored**		.55	.20

2511	A1870 25c **multicolored**		.55	.2
a.	Block of 4, #2508-2511		2.25	1.9
	P# block of 4, 5#		2.50	
	Zip block of 4		2.30	—
b.	As "a," black (engr.) omitted		450.00	

See Russia Nos. 5933-5936.

PRE-COLUMBIAN AMERICA ISSUE

Grand Canyon
A1871

Designed by Mark Hess.

Printed by the American Bank Note Company.

PHOTOGRAVURE
Plates of 200 in four panes of 50.
(3 panes of #2512, 1 pane of #C127)

1990, Oct. 12		Tagged		*Perf. 11*
2512	A1871 25c **multicolored**		.55	.20
	P# block of 4, 4#, UR, LL, LR		2.75	
	Zip block of 4		2.25	—

See No. C127.

DWIGHT D. EISENHOWER, BIRTH CENTENARY

A1872

Designed by Ken Hodges.

Printed by the American Bank Note Company.

PHOTOGRAVURE
Plates of 160 in four panes of 40.

1990, Oct. 13		Tagged		*Perf. 11*
2513	A1872 25c **multicolored**		.90	.20
	P# block of 4, 5#		4.00	
	P# block of 8, 5# and inscriptions		8.00	—
	Zip block of 4		3.75	—
a.	Imperf., pair		2,250.	

CHRISTMAS

Madonna & Child, by Antonello — A1873

Christmas Tree — A1874

Designed by Bradbury Thompson (#2514) and Libby Thiel (#2515-2516).

Printed by the Bureau of Engraving and Printing or the American Bank Note Company (#2515).

LITHOGRAPHED & ENGRAVED
Sheets of 300 in six panes of 50 (#2414-2415).

1990, Oct. 18		Tagged		*Perf. 11½*
2514	A1873 25c **multicolored**, large block tagging		.50	.20
	P# block of 4, 5#		2.25	—
	Zip, copyright block of 4		2.10	—
a.	Large block tagging over prephosphored coated paper (solid tagging)		.50	.20
b.	As "a," bklt. pane of 10		5.00	3.25

PHOTOGRAVURE
Perf. 11

15 A1874 25c multicolored		.50	.20
P# block of 4, 4#		2.25	—
Zip block of 4		2.10	—
a.	Vert. pair, imperf. horiz.		1,100.
b.	All colors missing (EP)		

No. 2515b must be collected se-tenant with normal and/or partially printed stamp(s).

BOOKLET STAMP
Perf. 11½x11 on 2 or 3 sides

516 A1874 25c multicolored		.50	.20
a.	Booklet pane of 10	5.00	3.25

Marked differences exist between Nos. 2515 and 2516. The background red on No. 2515 is even while that on No. 2516 is blotchy. The bands across the tree and "Greetings" are blue green on No. 2515 and yellow green on No. 2516.

A1875

A1876

Designed by Wallace Marosek (Nos. 2517-2520), Richard Sheaff (No. 2521).

Printed by U.S. Bank Note Company (No. 2517), Bureau of Engraving and Printing (No. 2518-2519), KCS Industries (No. 2520), American Bank Note Company (No. 2521).

PHOTOGRAVURE
Sheets of 100

1991, Jan. 22	**Tagged**	**Perf. 13**	
2517 A1875 (29c) yel, blk, red & yel grn		.60	.20
P# block of 4, 4#		2.75	—
Zip block of 4		2.50	—
a.	Imperf., pair		700.00
b.	Horiz. pair, imperf. vert.		1,250.

Do not confuse No. 2517a with No. 2518a. See note after No. 2518.

COIL STAMP
Perf. 10 Vert.

2518 A1875 (29c) yel, blk, dull red & dk yel grn		.60	.20
Pair		1.20	.20
P# strip of 5, #1111		3.50	
P# strip of 5, #1211		18.00	
P# strip of 5, #1222		3.50	
P# strip of 5, #2211		4.75	
P# strip of 5, #2222		3.50	
P# single, #1111		—	.75
P# single, #1211		—	14.00
P# single, #1222		—	.75
P# single, #2211		—	3.00
P# single, #2222		—	.75
a.	Imperf., pair		35.00
P#1111, 1222, 2211, 2222			

"For U.S. addresses only" is 17½mm long on No. 2517, 16½mm long on No. 2518. Design of No. 2517 measures 21½x17½mm, No. 2518, 21x18mm.

BOOKLET STAMPS
Perf. 11 on 2 or 3 Sides

2519 A1875 (29c) yel, blk, dull red & dk grn		.60	.20
a.	Booklet pane of 10	6.50	4.50
2520 A1875 (29c) pale yel, blk, red & brt grn		1.75	.20
a.	Booklet pane of 10	18.00	4.50
b.	As "a," imperf. horiz.	—	
c.	Horiz. pair, imperf btwn.		

No. 2519 has bullseye perforations that measure approximately 11.2. No. 2520 has less pronounced black lines in the leaf, which is a much brighter green than on No. 2519.
No. 2520c is from a paper foldover before perforating.

LITHOGRAPHED
Panes of 100

1991, Jan. 22	**Untagged**	**Perf. 11**	
2521 A1876 (4c) bister & carmine		.20	.20
P# block of 4, 2#		.40	—
Zip block of 4		.30	—
a.	Vert. pair, imperf. horiz.		100.00
b.	Imperf., pair		65.00

FLAG

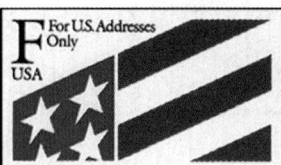

A1877

Designed by Harry Zelenko. Printed by Avery International Corp.

PHOTOGRAVURE

1991, Jan. 22 Untagged Self-Adhesive Die Cut Printed on Plastic

2522 A1877 (29c) blk, blue & dk red		.60	.25
a.	Pane of 12	7.25	

Sold only in panes of 12; peelable plastic backing inscribed in light ultramarine. Available during a test period at First National Bank automatic teller machines in Seattle.

Flag Over Mt. Rushmore — A1878

Designed by Clarence Holbert.

COIL STAMP
ENGRAVED

1991, Mar. 29	**Tagged**	**Perf. 10 Vert.**	
2523 A1878 29c blue, red & claret, prephosphored uncoated paper (mottled tagging)		.65	.20
Pair		1.30	.20
P# strip of 5, #1-7		4.25	
P# strip of 5, #8		6.00	
P# strip of 5, #9		9.00	
P# single, #1		—	.60
P# single, #2-4		—	.50
P# single, #5		—	2.25
P# single, #6, 7		—	.60
P# single, #8		—	2.00
P# single, #9		—	2.00
b.	Imperf., pair	20.00	
P#1, 3-4, 6-7, 9			
c.	29c blue, red & brown, prephosphored uncoated paper (mottled tagging)	5.00	
Pair		10.00	
P# strip of 5, #1		3,500.	
P# strip of 5, #7		190.00	
P# single, #1		—	
P# single, 7		—	160.00
d.	Prephosphored coated paper (solid tagging)	5.00	
Pair		10.00	
P# strip of 5, #2		1,250.	
P# strip of 5, #6		260.00	
P# single, #2		—	200.00
P# single, #6		—	150.00

Specialists often call No. 2523c the "Toledo brown" variety, and No. 2523d "Lenz paper." It was from No. 2523d that it was discovered that "solid tagging" on prephosphored paper resulted from the application of taggant to coated paper.

COIL STAMP
PHOTOGRAVURE

Printed by American Bank Note Co.

1991, July 4		**Perf. 10 Vert.**	
2523A A1878 29c blue, red & brown		.60	.20
Pair		1.20	.20
P# strip of 5, #A11111, A22211		4.00	
P# single, #A11111, A22211		—	2.50

On No. 2523A, USA and 29 are not outlined in white and are farther from the bottom of the design.

A1879

Designed by Wallace Marosek.

Printed by U.S. Bank Note Co. (#2524), J.W. Fergusson & Sons for Stamp Venturers (#2525, 2526), J.W. Fergusson & Sons, Inc. for KCS Industries, Inc. (#2527).

PHOTOGRAVURE
Panes of 100

1991-92	**Tagged**	**Perf. 11**	
2524 A1879 29c dull yel, blk, red & yel grn, Apr. 5, 1991		.60	.20
P# block of 4, 4#+U		2.75	—
Zip block of 4		2.50	—

See note after No. 2527.

Perf. 13x12¾

2524A A1879 29c dull yel, blk, red & yel grn, Apr. 5, 1991		1.00	.20
P# block of 4, 4#+U		50.00	—

Zip block of 4	7.50	

COIL STAMPS
Rouletted 10 Vert.

2525 A1879 29c pale yel, blk, red & yel grn, Aug. 16, 1991		.60	.20
Pair		1.20	.30
P# strip of 5, #S1111, S2222		4.50	
P# single, #S1111, S2222		—	.75

No. 2525 was issued in attached coils so that "blocks" and "vertical pairs" exist.

Perf. 10 Vert.

2526 A1879 29c pale yel, blk, red & yel grn, Mar. 3, 1992		.60	.20
Pair		1.20	.30
P# strip of 5, #S2222		4.50	
P# single, #S2222		—	2.50

BOOKLET STAMP
Perf. 11 on 2 or 3 Sides

2527 A1879 29c pale yel, blk, red & bright grn, Apr. 5		.60	.20
a.	Booklet pane of 10	6.00	3.50
b.	Horiz. pair, imperf. between	—	
c.	Horiz. pair, imperf. vert.	200.00	
d.	As "a," imperf. horiz.	1,000.	

Flower on Nos. 2524-2524A has grainy appearance, inscriptions look rougher.
No. 2527b resulted from a foldover.

Flag, Olympic Rings — A1880

Designed by John Boyd.

Printed by KCS Industries, Inc.

BOOKLET STAMP
PHOTOGRAVURE

1991, Apr. 21	**Tagged**	**Perf. 11 on 2 or 3 Sides**	
2528 A1880 29c multicolored		.60	.20
a.	Booklet pane of 10	6.00	3.50
c.	Vert. pair, imperf between, perfed at top and bottom	275.00	
d.	Vert. strip of 3, top or bottom pair imperf between	—	
e.	Vert. pair, imperf horiz.	750.00	

No. 2528c comes from misperfed booklet panes. No. 2528d resulted from paper foldovers after normal perforating and before cutting into panes. Two No. 2528d are known. No. 2528e is valued in the grade of fine.

Fishing Boat — A1881

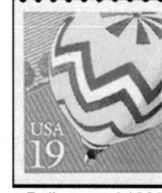

Balloon — A1882

Designed by Pierre Mion.

Printed by: Multi-Color Corp. for American Bank Note Co (type I); Guilford Gravure (type II); J. W. Fergusson & Sons for Stamp Venturers (No. 2529C).

COIL STAMPS
PHOTOGRAVURE

1991, Aug. 8	**Tagged**	**Perf. 9.8 Vert.**	
2529 A1881 19c multicolored		.40	.20
Pair		.80	.30
P# strip of 5, #A1111, A1212, A2424		3.25	
P# strip of 5, #A1112		6.25	
P# single, #A1111, A1212, A2424		—	2.25
P# single, #A1112		—	5.00
a.	Type II, 1993	.40	.20
Pair		.80	.30
P# strip of 5, #A5555, A5556, A6667, A7667, A7679, A7766, A7779		3.75	
P# single, same #		—	2.50
b.	As "a," untagged, 1993	1.00	.40
Pair		2.00	.80
P# strip of 5, #A5555		7.50	
P# single, #A5555		—	

Design on Type II stamps is created by a finer dot pattern. Vertical sides of "1" are smooth on Type II and jagged on Type I stamps.
Imperforates are from printer's waste. Also, No. 2529a, Plate #A7767 is known only from printer's waste.

1994, June 25   Tagged   Perf. 9.8 Vert.
2529C A1881 19c **multicolored**   .50   .20
           Pair   1.00   .30
           P# strip of 5, #S111   5.25
           P# single, #S111   —   2.40

No. 2529C has one loop of rope tying boat to piling.

BOOKLET STAMP

1991, May 17   Tagged   Perf. 10 on 2 or 3 Sides
2530 A1882 19c **multicolored**   .40   .20
a.   Booklet pane of 10   4.00   2.75

Flags on Parade — A1883

Designed by Frank J. Waslick and Peter Cocci.

PHOTOGRAVURE
Panes of 100

1991, May 30   Tagged   Perf. 11
2531 A1883 29c **multicolored**, overall tagging   .60   .20
           P# block of 4, 4#   2.75
           Zip block of 4   2.50   —
b.   Prephosphored coated paper (solid tag-
           ging)   .75   .25
           P# block of 4, 4#   6.50   —
           Zip block of 4   3.25

Liberty Torch — A1884

Designed by Harry Zelenko.

Printed by Avery Dennison Co.

PHOTOGRAVURE

1991, June 25   Tagged   Die Cut
Self-Adhesive
2531A A1884 29c **black, gold & green**,
                prephosphored coat-
                ed paper (solid tag-
                ging)   .60   .25
b.   Booklet pane of 18   11.00
c.   Die cutting omitted, pair   2,000.
d.   Overall tagging, *1992*   .60   .25
e.   As "d," booklet pane of 18   11.00

Sold only in panes of 18; peelable paper backing inscribed in
light blue. Available for consumer testing at First National Bank
automatic teller machines in Seattle, WA.

SWITZERLAND

Switzerland,
700th Anniv.
A1887

Designed by Hans Hartman, Switzerland.

Printed by the American Bank Note Company.

PHOTOGRAVURE
Plates of 160 in four panes of 40

1991, Feb. 22   Tagged   Perf. 11
2532 A1887 50c **multicolored**   1.00   .25
           P# block of 4, 5#   5.00
           Zip block of 4   4.25   —
a.   Vert. pair, imperf. horiz.   2,500.

See Switzerland No. 888.
Imperfs exist from printer's waste.

A1888

A1889

VERMONT STATEHOOD, 200th ANNIV.

Designed by Sabra Field.

Printed by the American Bank Note Company.

PHOTOGRAVURE
Plates of 200 in four panes of 50

1991, Mar. 1   Tagged   Perf. 11
2533 A1888 29c **multicolored**   .90   .20
           P# block of 4, 4#+A   4.50   —
           Zip block of 4   3.75   —

SAVINGS BONDS, 50TH ANNIVERSARY

Designed by Primo Angeli.

1991, Apr. 30   Tagged   Perf. 11
2534 A1889 29c **multicolored**   .60   .20
           P# block of 4, 6#   2.75   —
           Zip block of 4   2.50   —
a.   Tagging omitted

LOVE

A1890

A1891

Designed by Harry Zelenko (#2535-2536) and Nancy L.
Krause (#2537).

Printed by U.S. Banknote Co. (#2535), the Bureau of Engraving and Printing (#2536) and American Bank Note Co. (#2537).

PHOTOGRAVURE
Panes of 50

1991, May 9   Tagged   Perf. 12½x13
2535 A1890 29c **multicolored**   .60   .20
           P# block of 4, 5#+U   2.75   —
           Zip, copyright block of 4   2.50   —
b.   Imperf., pair   2,000.

Perf. 11
2535A A1890 29c **multicolored**   .85   .20
           P# block of 4, 5#+U   4.00   —
           Zip, copyright block of 4   3.50   —

BOOKLET STAMP
Perf. 11.1x11.3 on 2 or 3 Sides
2536 A1890 29c **multicolored**   .60   .20
a.   Booklet pane of 10   6.00   3.50

"29" is closer to edge of design on No. 2536 than on No.
2535.

Sheets of 200 in panes of 50
Perf. 11
2537 A1891 52c **multicolored**   .90   .20
           P# block of 4, 3#+A   4.50   —
           Zip block of 4   4.00

LITERARY ARTS SERIES

William Saroyan
A1892

Designed by Ren Wicks.

Printed by J.W. Fergusson for American Bank Note Co.

PHOTOGRAVURE
Sheets of 200 in four panes of 50

1991, May 22   Tagged   Perf.
2538 A1892 29c **multicolored**   .60
           P# block of 4, 5#+A   2.75
           Zip block of 4   2.50

See Russia No. 6002.

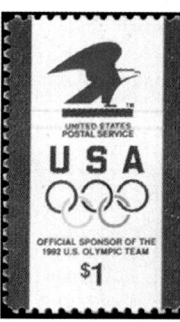

Eagle, Olympic
Rings — A1893

A1894

A1895

A1896

Futuristic
Space Shuttle
A1897

Space Shuttle
Challenger
A1898

Space Shuttle
Endeavour —
A1898a

Designed by: Terrence McCaffrey (Nos. 2539-2541), Timothy
Knapp (No. 2542), Ken Hodges (No. 2543), Phil Jordan (Nos.
2544-2544A).

Printed by: J.W. Fergusson & Sons for Stamp Venturers (No.
2539); American Bank Note Co (Nos. 2540-2541); Jeffries
Banknote Co. for the American Bank Note Co (No. 2542).

Nos. 2540, 2543-2544 for priority mail rate. Nos. 2541, 2544A
for domestic express mail rate. No. 2542 for international
express mail rate. Nos. 2544-2544A printed by Ashton-Potter (USA) Ltd.

Sheet of 180 in nine panes of 20 (No. 2539)
Sheet of 120 in six panes of 20 (Nos. 2540-2542,
2544-2544A)
Pane of 40 (No. 2543)
PHOTOGRAVURE
Copyright information appears in the center
of the top and bottom selvage.

1991, Sept. 29	Tagged	Perf. 11	
2539 A1893 $1 **gold & multi**		1.90	.50
P# block of 4, 6#+S		8.00	—
Pane of 20		40.00	
a. Black omitted		—	

LITHOGRAPHED & ENGRAVED
1991, July 7	Tagged	Perf. 11	
2540 A1894 $2.90 **multicolored**		6.00	1.50
P# block of 4, 5#+A		24.00	—
Pane of 20		120.00	
a. Vert. pair, imperf horiz.		—	
b. Black (engr.) omitted		—	

No. 2540 exists imperf and with color missing from printer's waste.

1991, June 16	Untagged	Perf. 11	
2541 A1895 $9.95 **multicolored**		20.00	6.00
P# block of 4, 5#+A		80.00	—
Pane of 20		400.00	
a. Imperf., pair		—	

No. 2541 exists imperf plus black (engr.) omitted from printer's waste.

1991, Aug. 31	Untagged	Perf. 11	
2542 A1896 $14 **multicolored**		25.00	10.00
P# block of 4, 5#+A		100.00	—
Pane of 20		500.00	
a. Red (engr. inscriptions) omitted		—	

No. 2542 exists imperf plus red omitted from printer's waste.

1993, June 3	Tagged	Perf. 11x10½	
2543 A1897 $2.90 **multicolored**		6.00	1.75
P# block of 4, 6#		27.50	—
Zip block of 4		25.00	—
a. Tagging omitted		—	

1995, June 22	Tagged	Perf. 11.2	
2544 A1898 $3 **multicolored**, dated "1995"		5.75	1.75
b. Dated "1996"		5.75	1.75
P# block of 4, 5#+P		23.50	—
Pane of 20		120.00	
c. As "b," horiz. pair, imperf between		—	
d. As "b," imperf pair		1,500.	

1995, Aug. 4	Tagged	Perf. 11	
2544A A1898a $10.75 **multicolored**		20.00	9.00
P# block of 4, 5#+P		82.50	—
Pane of 20		425.00	

FISHING FLIES

Royal
Wulff — A1899

Jock
Scott — A1900

Apte Tarpon
Fly — A1901

Lefty's
Deceiver
A1902

Muddler
Minnow
A1903

Designed by Chuck Ripper.

Printed by American Bank Note Co.

PHOTOGRAVURE
BOOKLET STAMPS
1991, May 31	Tagged	Perf. 11 Horiz.	
2545 A1899 29c **multicolored**		2.00	.20
a. Black omitted			
2546 A1900 29c **multicolored**		2.00	.20
a. Black omitted			
2547 A1901 29c **multicolored**		2.00	.20
a. Black omitted			
2548 A1902 29c **multicolored**		2.00	.20
2549 A1903 29c **multicolored**		2.00	.20
a. Bklt. pane of 5, #2545-2549		10.00	3.50

Horiz. pairs, imperf vert,. exist from printer's waste.

Cole Porter (1891-
1964),
Composer — A1904

S. W. Asia Service
Medal — A1905

PERFORMING ARTS
Designed by Jim Sharpe.

Printed by American Bank Note Co.

PHOTOGRAVURE
Panes of 50
1991, June 8	Tagged	Perf. 11	
2550 A1904 29c **multicolored**		.60	.20
P# block of 4, 5#+A		2.75	—
Zip block of 4		2.50	—
a. Vert. pair, imperf. horiz.		575.00	

OPERATIONS DESERT SHIELD & DESERT STORM
Designed by Jack Williams.

Printed by J.W. Fergusson Co. for Stamp Venturers (No.
2551), Multi-Color Corp. for the American Bank Note Co. (No.
2552).

PHOTOGRAVURE
Panes of 50
1991, July 2	Tagged	Perf. 11	
2551 A1905 29c **multicolored**		.60	.20
P# block of 4, 7#+S		2.75	—
Zip block of 4		2.50	—
a. Vert. pair, imperf. horiz.		1,500.	

No. 2551 is 21mm wide.

BOOKLET STAMP
Perf. 11 Vert. on 1 or 2 Sides
2552 A1905 29c **multicolored**		.60	.20
a. Booklet pane of 5		3.00	2.25

No. 2552 is 20½mm wide. Inscriptions are shorter than on
No. 2551.
No. 2552 Vert. pairs, imperf horiz., are from printer's waste.

1992 SUMMER OLYMPICS, BARCELONA

Pole
Vault — A1907

Discus
A1908

Women's
Sprints
A1909

Javelin
A1910

Women's
Hurdles
A1911

Designed by Joni Carter.

Printed by the American Bank Note Co.

PHOTOGRAVURE
Panes of 40

1991, July 12		Tagged	Perf. 11	
2553	A1907	29c multicolored	.60	.20
2554	A1908	29c multicolored	.60	.20
2555	A1909	29c multicolored	.60	.20
2556	A1910	29c multicolored	.60	.20
2557	A1911	29c multicolored	.60	.20
a.		Strip of 5, #2553-2557	3.00	2.25
		P# block of 10, 5#+A	8.00	—
		Zip block of 10	6.00	—

NUMISMATICS

1858 Flying Eagle Cent,
1907 Standing Liberty
Double Eagle, Series 1875
$1 Note, Series 1902 $10
National Currency
Note — A1912

Designed by V. Jack Ruther.

LITHOGRAPHED & ENGRAVED
Sheets of 200 in four panes of 50

1991, Aug. 13		Tagged	Perf. 11	
2558	A1912	29c multicolored	.60	.20
		P# block of 4, 7#	2.75	
		Zip block of 4	2.50	

WORLD WAR II

A1913

Illustration reduced.

Designed by William H. Bond.

Designs and events of 1941: a, Military vehicles (Burma Road, 717-mile lifeline to China). b, Recruits (America's first peacetime draft). c, Shipments for allies (U.S. supports allies with Lend-Lease Act). d, Franklin D. Roosevelt, Winston Churchill (Atlantic Charter sets war aims of allies). e, Tank (America becomes the "arsenal of democracy.") f, Sinking of Destoyer Reuben James, Oct. 31. g, Gas mask, helmet (Civil defense mobilizes Americans at home). h, Liberty Ship, sea gull (First Liberty ship delivered December 30). i, Sinking ships (Japanese bomb Pearl Harbor, December 7). j, Congress in session (U.S. declares war on Japan, December 8). Central label is the size of 15 stamps and shows world map, extent of axis control.

LITHOGRAPHED & ENGRAVED
Plates of eight subjects in four panes of 2 each

1991, Sept. 3		Tagged	Perf. 11	
2559	A1913	Block of 10	7.50	5.00
		Pane of 20	15.00	—
a.-j.		29c any single	.75	.45
k.		Black (engr.) omitted	12,500.	

No. 2559 has selvage at left and right and either top or bottom.

BASKETBALL, 100TH ANNIVERSARY

Basketball, Hoop, Players'
Arms — A1914

Designed by Lon Busch.

PHOTOGRAVURE
Sheets of 200 in four panes of 50

1991, Aug. 28		Tagged	Perf. 11	
2560	A1914	29c multicolored	.60	.20
		P# block of 4, 4#	2.75	—
		Zip block of 4	2.50	—

DISTRICT OF COLUMBIA BICENTENNIAL

Capitol
Building from
Pennsylvania
Avenue, Circa
1903 — A1915

Designed by Pierre Mion.

LITHOGRAPHED & ENGRAVED
Plates of 200 in four panes of 50

1991, Sept. 7		Tagged	Perf. 11	
2561	A1915	29c multicolored	.60	.20
		P# block of 4, 5#	2.75	—
		Zip block of 4	2.50	—
a.		Black (engr.) omitted	110.00	

COMEDIANS

Stan Laurel
(1890-1965)
and Oliver
Hardy (1892-
1957)
A1916

Edgar Bergen
(1903-1978)
and Charlie
McCarthy
A1917

Jack Benny
(1894-1974)
A1918

Fanny Brice
(1891-1951)
A1919

Bud Abbott
(1895-1974)
and Lou
Costello (1908-
1959)
A1920

Designed by Al Hirschfeld.

LITHOGRAPHED & ENGRAVED
BOOKLET STAMPS

1991, Aug. 29		Tagged	Perf. 11 on 2 or 3 Side	
2562	A1916	29c multicolored	.85	.2
2563	A1917	29c multicolored	.85	.2
2564	A1918	29c multicolored	.85	.2
2565	A1919	29c multicolored	.85	.2
2566	A1920	29c multicolored	.85	.2
a.		Bklt. pane of 10, 2 each #2562-2566	9.00	5.0
b.		As "a," scar & brt violet (engr.) omitted	700.00	
c.		Strip of 5, #2562-2566	4.25	2.5

BLACK HERITAGE SERIES

Jan E. Matzeliger (1852-
1889), Inventor — A1921

Designed by Higgins Bond.
Printed by J.W. Fergusson & Sons for the American Bank Note Co.

PHOTOGRAVURE
Plates of 200 in four panes of 50

1991, Sept. 15		Tagged	Perf. 11	
2567	A1921	29c multicolored	.60	.20
		P# block of 4, 6#+A	2.75	—
		Zip block of 4	2.40	—
a.		Horiz. pair, imperf. vert.	1,500.	
b.		Vert. pair, imperf. horiz.	1,450.	
c.		Imperf., pair	500.00	

SPACE EXPLORATION

Mercury,
Mariner 10
A1922

Venus,
Mariner 2
A1923

Earth, Landsat
A1924

Moon, Lunar Orbiter A1925

Mars, Viking Orbiter A1926

Jupiter, Pioneer 11 A1927

Saturn, Voyager 2 A1928

Uranus, Voyager 2 A1929

Neptune, Voyager 2 A1930

Pluto — A1931

Designed by Ron Miller.

PHOTOGRAVURE
BOOKLET STAMPS

1991, Oct. 1	Tagged	Perf. 11 on 2 or 3 Sides		
2568	A1922	29c multicolored	.85	.20
2569	A1923	29c multicolored	.85	.20
2570	A1924	29c multicolored	.85	.20
2571	A1925	29c multicolored	.85	.20
2572	A1926	29c multicolored	.85	.20
2573	A1927	29c multicolored	.85	.20
2574	A1928	29c multicolored	.85	.20
2575	A1929	29c multicolored	.85	.20
2576	A1930	29c multicolored	.85	.20
2577	A1931	29c multicolored	.85	.20
a.		Bklt. pane of 10, #2568-2577	9.00	4.50

CHRISTMAS

Madonna and Child by Antoniazzo Romano — A1933

Santa Claus in Chimney — A1934

Santa Checking List — A1935

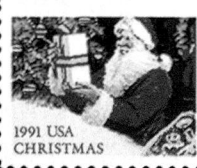

Santa with Present — A1936

Santa at Fireplace — A1937

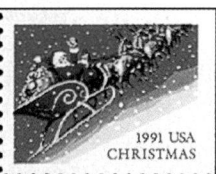

Santa and Sleigh — A1938

Designed by Bradbury Thompson (#2578) and John Berkey (#2579-2585).
Printed by the Bureau of Engraving and Printing (#2578); J.W. Fergusson & Sons (#2579) and Multi-Color Corp. (#2580-2585) for the American Bank Note Co.

LITHOGRAPHED & ENGRAVED
Sheets of 300 in six panes of 50

1991, Oct. 17	Tagged	Perf. 11	
2578	A1933 (29c) multicolored	.60	.20
	P# block of 4, 5#	2.75	—
	Zip, copyright block of 4	2.50	—
a.	Booklet pane of 10	6.00	3.25
b.	Red & black (engr.) omitted	3,500.	

PHOTOGRAVURE

2579	A1934 (29c) multicolored	.60	.20
	P# block of 4, 3#+A	2.50	—
	Zip block of 4	2.25	—
a.	Horiz. pair, imperf. vert.	275.00	
b.	Vert. pair, imperf. horiz.	500.00	

Booklet Stamps
Size: 25x18½mm
Perf. 11 on 2 or 3 Sides

2580	A1934 (29c) Type I	2.00	.20
2581	A1934 (29c) Type II	2.00	.20
a.	Pair, #2580-2581	4.00	.50
b.	Bklt. pane, 2 each, #2580, 2581	9.00	1.25
2582	A1935 (29c) multicolored	.60	.20
a.	Bklt. pane of 4	2.40	1.25
2583	A1936 (29c) multicolored	.60	.20
a.	Bklt. pane of 4	2.40	1.25
2584	A1937 (29c) multicolored	.60	.20
a.	Bklt. pane of 4	2.40	1.25
2585	A1938 (29c) multicolored	.60	.20
a.	Bklt. pane of 4	2.40	1.25
	Nos. 2578-2585 (8)	7.60	1.60

The far left brick from the top row of the chimney is missing from Type II, No. 2581.
Imperfs of Nos. 2581, 2583-2585 are printer's waste.

James K. Polk (1795-1849) A1939

"The Surrender of General Burgoyne at Saratoga," by John Trumbull A1942

Washington and Jackson — A1944

Designed by John Thompson (No. 2587), based on painting by John Trumbull (No. 2590), Richard D. Sheaff (No. 2592).
Printed by Banknote Corporation of America (No. 2587), Stamp Venturers (Nos. 2590, 2592).

ENGRAVED
Sheets of 400 in four panes of 100 (No. 2587)
Sheets of 120 in six panes of 20 (Nos. 2590, 2592)

1994-95	Tagged	Perf. 11.2	
2587	A1939 32c red brown, Nov. 2, 1995	.65	.20
	P# block of 4, 1#+B	3.25	—
	Perf. 11.5		
2590	A1942 $1 blue, May 5, 1994	1.90	.50
	P# block of 4, 1#+S	7.60	—
	Pane of 20	38.00	—
2592	A1944 $5 slate green, Aug. 19, 1994	8.00	2.50
	P# block of 4, 1#+S	40.00	—
	Pane of 20	160.00	—

Some plate blocks contain either inscription or plate position diagram.

A1946

Eagle and Shield — A1947

A1950

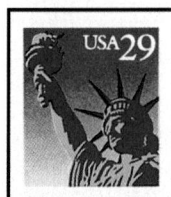

Statue of Liberty — A1951

Designed by Lou Nolan (#2593-2594), Jay Haiden (#2595-2597), Richard Sheaff (#2598), Tom Engeman (#2599).
Printed by Bureau of Engraving & Printing (#2593), Stamp Venturers for KCS Industries (#2594), Banknote Corporation of America (#2595), Dittler Brothers, Inc. (#2596, 2599), Stamp Venturers (#2597), National Label Co. for 3M (#2598).

BOOKLET STAMPS
PHOTOGRAVURE

1992, Sept. 8	Tagged	Perf. 9.8 on 2 or 3 sides	
2593	A1946 29c black & multi	.60	.20
a.	Booklet pane of 10	6.00	4.25

d.	Imperf, pair	—	

Perf. 11x10 on 2 or 3 sides

2593B	A1946	29c **black & multi**, shiny gum	1.40	.50
		Low gloss gum	3.00	
c.		Bklt. pane of 10, shiny gum	14.00	7.50
		Low gloss gum	30.00	

1993, Apr. 8(?)　　Perf. 11x10 on 2 or 3 Sides

2594	A1946	29c **red & multi**	.65	.20
a.		Booklet pane of 10	6.50	4.25

Denomination is red on #2594 and black on #2593 and 2593B.

LITHOGRAPHED & ENGRAVED

1992, Sept. 25　　Tagged　　Die Cut

Self-Adhesive

2595	A1947	29c **brown & multicolored**	.60	.25
a.		Bklt. pane of 17 + label	13.00	
b.		Die cutting omitted, pair	150.00	
c.		Brown omitted	375.00	
d.		As "a," die cutting omitted	1,250.	
2596	A1947	29c **green & multicolored**	.60	.25
a.		Bklt. pane of 17 + label	12.00	

PHOTOGRAVURE

2597	A1947	29c **red & multicolored**	.60	.25
a.		Bklt. pane of 17 + label	10.50	

Plate No. and inscription reads down on No. 2595a and up on Nos. 2596a-2597a. Design is sharper and more finely detailed on Nos. 2595, 2597.

Nos. 2595a-2597a sold for $5 each.

Nos. 2595-2597 also available in strips with stamps spaced for use in affixing machines to service first day covers.

PHOTOGRAVURE

1994　　Tagged　　Die Cut

Self-Adhesive

2598	A1950	29c **red, cream & blue**, *Feb. 4*	.60	.20
a.		Booklet pane of 18	11.00	
b.		Coil with P#111	—	3.75
		P# strip of 5, #111	6.75	
2599	A1951	29c **multicolored**, *June 24*	.60	.20
a.		Booklet pane of 18	11.00	
b.		Coil with P#D1111	—	4.00
		P# strip of 5, #D1111	6.75	

Except for Nos. 2598b and 2599b with plate numbers, coil stamps of these issues are indistinguishable from booklet stamps once they are removed from the backing paper.

See Nos. 3122-3122E.

> **Scott values for used self-adhesive stamps are for examples either on piece or off piece.**

Eagle and
Shield — A1956

Eagle and
Shield — A1957

A1959

A1960

Flag Over White
House — A1961

Designed by Chris Calle (#2602-2604), Terrence McCaffrey (#2605), Lon Busch (#2606-2608), V. Jack Ruther (29c).

Printed by Guildford Gravure, Inc. for the American Bank Note Co. (#2602, 2606), Bureau of Engraving and Printing (#2603, 2607), Stamp Venturers (#2604, 2608), American Bank Note Co. (#2605)

PHOTOGRAVURE
COIL STAMPS

1991-93　　Untagged　　Perf. 10 Vert.

2602	A1956	(10c) **multi** (Bureau precancel, Bulk Rate, in blue), *Dec. 13*	.20	.20
		Pair	.40	.40
		P# strip of 5, #A11111, A11112, A21112, A21113, A22112, A22113, A33333, A43325, A43326, A43334, A43335, A53335, A54444, A54445, A77777, A88888	2.50	
		P# strip of 5, #A12213	19.00	
		P# strip of 5, #A34424, A34426, A43324, A88889	3.75	
		P# strip of 5, #A32333	280.00	
		P# strip of 5, #A33334	70.00	
		P# strip of 5, #A33335, A43426, A89999, A99998, A99999, A1010101010, A1011101011, A1011101012, A1110101010, A1110111010, A1111101010, A1111111010, A1411101010, A1411101011, A1412111110, A1412111111	3.00	
		P# strip of 5, #A99999	2.75	
		P# strip of 5, #A1011101010	5.00	
		P# strip of 5, #A1211101010	4.75	
		P# strip of 5, #A1110101011	11.50	
		P# single, #A11111, A11112, A21112, A21113, A22112, A22113, A43324, A43325, A43326, A43334, A43335, A43426, A54444, A54445, A77777, A88888, A89999, A99998, A99999	—	2.25
		P# single, #A12213	—	17.00
		P# single, #A32333	—	275.00
		P# single, #A33335, A33335, A34424, A34426	—	3.25
		P# single, #A33334	—	80.00
		P# single, #A53335, A88889, A1010101010, A1011101011, A1011101012, A1110101010, A1110111010, A1111101010, A1111111010, A1411101010, A1411101011, A1412111110, A1412111111	—	2.50
		P# single, #A1011101010	—	3.50
		P# single, #A1211101010	—	4.00
		P# single, #A1110101011	—	9.00
a.		Imperf., pair	—	
2603	A1957	(10c) **org yel & multi**, shiny gum (Bureau precancel, Bulk Rate, in red), *May 29, 1993*	.20	.20
		Pair	.40	.40
		P# strip of 5, #11111, 22221, 22222	3.00	
		P# single, same	—	1.75
		Low gloss gum	.20	
		Pair	.40	
		P# strip of 5, #22222, 33333, 44444	3.00	
		P# strip of 5, #11111	67.50	
		P# single, #33333, 44444	—	2.50
a.		Imperf., pair	25.00	
b.		Tagged (error), shiny gum	2.00	1.50
		Pair	4.00	3.50
		P# strip of 5, #11111, 22221	13.00	
		P# strip of 5, #22222	450.00	
		P# single, #11111, 22221	—	12.00
		P# single, #22222	—	300.00

All examples of Nos. 2603, 2603a and 2603b were printed with luminescent ink.

See No. 2907.

2604	A1957	(10c) **gold & multi**, shiny gum (Bureau precancel, Bulk Rate, in red), *May 29, 1993*	.20	.20
		Pair	.40	.40
		P# strip of 5, #S22222	3.25	
		P# single, same	—	1.75
		Low gloss gum	.20	
		Pair	.40	
		P# strip of 5, #S11111	3.00	
		P# strip of 5, #S22222	2.75	
		P# single, #S11111	—	2.00
2605	A1959	23c **multi** (Bureau precancel in blue), *Sept. 27*	.45	.40
		Pair	.90	.80
		P# strip of 5, #A111, A212, A222	3.50	
		P# strip of 5, #A112, A122, A333	4.50	
		P# single, #A111, A112, A122, A212, A222, A333	—	2.25
a.		Imperf, pair	—	
2606	A1960	23c **multi** (Bureau precanceled), *July 21, 1992*	.45	.40
		Pair	.90	.80
		P# strip of 5, #A1111, A2222, A2232, A2233, A3333, A4364, A4443, A4444, A4453	4.00	
		P# single, same #	—	2.50

"First-Class" is 9½mm long and "23" is 6mm long on No. 2606.

2607	A1960	23c **multi**, shiny gum (Bureau precanceled), *Oct. 9, 1992*	.45	.40

	Pair	.90	.8
	P# strip of 5, #1111	4.00	
	P# single, #1111	—	2.5
	Low gloss gum	.45	
	Pair	.90	
	P# strip of 5, #1111	4.00	
a.	Tagged (error), shiny gum	5.00	4.5
	Pair	10.00	9.0
	P# strip of 5, #1111	140.00	
	P# single, #1111	—	70.0
c.	Imperf., pair	75.00	

"First-Class" is 9mm long and "23" is 6½mm long on No. 2607.

2608	A1960	23c **vio bl, red & blk** (Bureau precanceled), *May 14, 1993*	.45	.4
		Pair	.90	.8
		P# strip of 5, #S111	4.25	
		P# single, #S111	—	2.5

"First-Class" is 8½mm long and "23" is 6½mm long on No. 2608.

ENGRAVED
Tagged

2609	A1961	29c **blue & red**, *Apr. 23, 1992*	.60	.20
		Pair	1.20	.20
		P# strip of 5, #1-8	4.50	
		P# strip of 5, #9-16	5.50	
		P# strip of 5, #18	6.00	
		P# single, #1-4	—	.75
		P# single, #5	—	2.25
		P# single, #6-8	—	.75
		P# single, #9	—	2.50
		P# single, #10-16	—	1.00
		P# single, #18	—	4.00
a.		Imperf., pair	15.00	
		P#3-7		
b.		Pair, imperf. between	95.00	

Beware of pairs with blind perfs sometimes offered as No. 2609b.

WINTER OLYMPICS

Hockey
A1963

Figure Skating
A1964

Speed Skating
A1965

Skiing
A1966

Bobsledding
A1967

Designed by Lon Busch. Printed by J.W. Fergusson & Sons Stamp Venturers.

PHOTOGRAVURE
Panes of 35

1992, Jan. 11	Tagged	Perf. 11
2611 A1963 29c multicolored	.60	.20
2612 A1964 29c multicolored	.60	.20
2613 A1965 29c multicolored	.60	.20
2614 A1966 29c multicolored	.60	.20
2615 A1967 29c multicolored	.60	.20
a. Strip of 5, #2611-2615	3.00	2.50
P# block of 10, 4#+S	7.00	—
Zip, copyright block of 15	9.00	—

Inscriptions on six marginal tabs.

Features detail from
No. 129 — A1968

W.E.B. Du Bois (1868-
1963) — A1969

WORLD COLUMBIAN STAMP EXPO
Designed by Richard Sheaff.

LITHOGRAPHED & ENGRAVED
Plates of 200 in four panes of 50

1992, Jan. 24	Tagged	Perf. 11
2616 A1968 29c multicolored	.60	.20
P# block of 4, 4#	2.75	—
Zip block of 4	2.50	—
a. Tagging omitted	8.50	

BLACK HERITAGE SERIES
W.E.B. Du Bois (1868-1963), Writer and Civil Rights
Leader
Designed by Higgins Bond.

LITHOGRAPHED & ENGRAVED
Plates of 200 in four panes of 50

1992, Jan. 31	Tagged	Perf. 11
2617 A1969 29c multicolored	.60	.20
P# block of 4, 7#	2.75	—
Zip block of 4	2.50	—

A1970

A1971

LOVE
Designed by Uldis Purins. Printed by the U.S. Bank Note Co.

PHOTOGRAVURE
Panes of 50

1992, Feb. 6	Tagged	Perf. 11
2618 A1970 29c multicolored	.60	.20
P# block of 4, U+5#	2.75	—
Zip, copyright block of 4	2.50	—
a. Horiz. pair, imperf. vert.	700.00	
b. As "a," green omitted on right stamp	3,250.	

OLYMPIC BASEBALL
Designed by Anthony DeLuz.

PHOTOGRAVURE
Plates of 200 in four panes of 50

1992, Apr. 3	Tagged	Perf. 11
2619 A1971 29c multicolored	.60	.20
P# block of 4, 5#	2.75	—
Zip block of 4	2.50	—

VOYAGES OF COLUMBUS

Seeking
Queen
Isabella's
Support
A1972

Crossing the
Atlantic
A1973

Approaching
Land
A1974

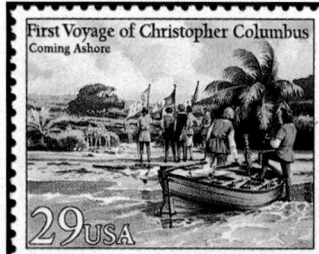

Coming
Ashore
A1975

Designed by Richard Schlecht.

LITHOGRAPHED & ENGRAVED
Plates of 160 in four panes of 40

1992, Apr. 24	Tagged	Perf. 11
2620 A1972 29c multicolored	.60	.20
2621 A1973 29c multicolored	.60	.20
2622 A1974 29c multicolored	.60	.20
2623 A1975 29c multicolored	.60	.20
a. Block of 4, #2620-2623	2.40	2.00
P# block of 4, 5#	2.75	—
Zip block of 4	2.50	—

See Italy Nos. 1877-1880.

Souvenir Sheets

A1976

A1977

A1978

A1979

A1980

A1981

Illustrations reduced.

Designed by Richard Sheaff.

Printed by the American Bank Note Co. Margins on Nos. 2624-2628 are lithographed. Nos. 2624a-2628c, 2629 are similar in design to Nos. 230-245 but are dated 1492-1992.

LITHOGRAPHED & ENGRAVED

1992, May 22   ***Perf. 10½***
Tagged (15c-$5), Untagged

2624	A1976	Sheet of 3	2.00	1.25
a.	A71	1c **deep blue**	.20	.20
b.	A74	4c **ultramarine**	.20	.20
c.	A82	$1 **salmon**	1.75	1.00
d.		As No. 2624, tagging omitted on "c"	—	
2625	A1977	Sheet of 3	7.25	5.00
a.	A72	2c **brown violet**	.20	.20
b.	A73	3c **green**	.20	.20
c.	A85	$4 **crimson lake**	7.00	4.00
2626	A1978	Sheet of 3	1.60	1.25
a.	A75	5c **chocolate**	.20	.20
b.	A80	30c **orange brown**	.60	.30
c.	A81	50c **slate blue**	.90	.50
d.		As No. 2626, tagging omitted on "c"	—	
2627	A1979	Sheet of 3	5.75	3.50
a.	A76	6c **purple**	.20	.20
b.	A77	8c **magenta**	.20	.20
c.	A84	$3 **yellow green**	5.50	3.00
2628	A1980	Sheet of 3	4.00	3.00
a.	A78	10c **black brown**	.20	.20
b.	A79	15c **dark green**	.30	.20
c.	A83	$2 **brown red**	3.50	2.00
d.		As No. 2628, tagging omitted on "b"	—	
2629	A1981	$5 Sheet of 1	8.75	6.00
a.	A86	$5 **black**, single stamp	8.50	6.00
		Nos. 2624-2629 (6)	29.35	20.00

See Italy Nos. 1883-1888, Portugal Nos. 1918-1923 and Spain Nos. 2677-2682.

Imperforate examples are known of all the Columbus souvenir sheets, but these are not listed in this catalogue. Their appearance several years after the issue date, in substantial quantities of all six sheets at the same time and, evidently, from a single source, with many small faults such as wrinkles and light creases that are not normally seen on these sheets, raises serious concerns about the legitimacy of these imperforate sheets as issued errors.

These circumstances have led the Scott editors to adopt the position that these imperforate sheets are indeed almost certainly printer's waste rather than issued errors. While it is possible that actual imperforate errors of one or more of the sheets may exist that were legitimately sold by the USPS, it is not possible to separate these (should they exist) from the many more numerous examples that apparently are printer's waste.

NEW YORK STOCK EXCHANGE BICENTENNIAL

A1982

Designed by Richard Sheaff.

Printed by the Jeffries Bank Note Co. for the American Bank Note Co.

LITHOGRAPHED & ENGRAVED

1992, May 17   **Tagged**   ***Perf. 11***

2630	A1982	29c **green, red & black**	.60	.20
		P# block of 4, 3#+A	2.75	—
		Zip, Olympic block of 4	2.50	—
a.		Black missing (EP)	—	
b.		Black missing (CM)	8,000.	
c.		Center (black engr.) inverted	26,000.	

No. 2630a must be collected se-tenant with a normal stamp or with a stamp with half of black engraving missing, or se-tenant with a normal stamp and an additional 2630a.

No. 2630b may be collected alone or se-tenant with No. 2630c.

Two panes, each containing 28 No. 2630c and 12 No. 2630b, have been documented. One pane sold for $488,750 in a 2002 auction. The other pane (with small thins on two No. 2620c) sold for $373,750 in a 2005 auction. A single No. 2630c from the first pane sold for $28,600 in a 2005 auction, and two others sold for $26,450 and $25,875 in separate 2006 auctions. A corner margin block from the first pane, containing two No. 2630c and two No. 2630b sold for $66,125 in a 2006 auction.

The unique pane containing 4 No. 2630a, one stamp with half of black center missing and 35 normal stamps sold at a 2002 auction for $18,400.

SPACE ACCOMPLISHMENTS

Cosmonaut, US Space Shuttle — A1983

Astronaut, Russian Space Station, Russian Space Shuttle — A1984

Sputnik, Vostok, Apollo Command & Lunar Modules — A1985

Soyuz, Mercury & Gemini Spacecraft — A1986

Designed by Vladimir Beilin (Russia) and Robert T. McCall.

PHOTOGRAVURE
Plates of 200 in four panes of 50

1992, May 29   **Tagged**   ***Perf. 11***

2631	A1983	29c **multicolored**	.60	.20
2632	A1984	29c **multicolored**	.60	.20
2633	A1985	29c **multicolored**	.60	.20
2634	A1986	29c **multicolored**	.60	.20
a.		Block of 4, #2631-2634	2.40	1.90
		P# block of 4, 4#	3.25	—
		Zip block of 4	2.50	—
b.		As "a," yellow omitted	—	

See Russia Nos. 6080-6083.

ALASKA HIGHWAY, 50th ANNIVERSARY

A1987

Designed by Byron Birdsall.

LITHOGRAPHED & ENGRAVED
Plates of 200 in four panes of 50

1992, May 30   **Tagged**   ***Perf.***

2635	A1987	29c **multicolored**	.60	
		P# block of 4, 6#	2.75	
		Zip block of 4	2.50	
a.		Black (engr.) omitted	825.00	

Almost half the recorded No. 2635a errors are poorly centered. These sell for approximately $475.

KENTUCKY STATEHOOD BICENTENNIAL

A1988

Designed by Joseph Petro.

Printed by J.W. Fergusson & Sons for Stamp Venturers.

PHOTOGRAVURE
Plates of 200 in four panes of 50

1992, June 1   **Tagged**   ***Perf. 1***

2636	A1988	29c **multicolored**	.60	.2
		P# block of 4, 5#+S	2.75	—
		Zip block of 4	2.50	—
a.		Dark blue missing (EP)	—	
b.		Dark blue and red missing (EP)	—	
c.		All colors missing (EP)	—	

Nos. 2636a-2636c must be collected se-tenant with norma stamps.

SUMMER OLYMPICS

Soccer
A1989

Gymnastics
A1990

Volleyball
A1991

Boxing
A1992

Swimming
A1993

Designed by Richard Waldrep.

Printed by J.W. Fergusson & Sons for Stamp Venturers.

PHOTOGRAVURE
Panes of 35

1992, June 11		Tagged		Perf. 11	
2637	A1989	29c	multicolored	.60	.20
2638	A1990	29c	multicolored	.60	.20
2639	A1991	29c	multicolored	.60	.20
2640	A1992	29c	multicolored	.60	.20
2641	A1993	29c	multicolored	.60	.20
a.			Strip of 5, #2637-2641	3.00	2.50
			P# block of 10, 5#+S	6.50	—
			Zip, copyright block of 15	9.00	—

Inscriptions on six marginal tabs.

HUMMINGBIRDS

Ruby-throated
A1994

Broad-billed
A1995

Costa's — A1996

Rufous — A1997

Calliope — A1998

Designed by Chuck Ripper.

Printed by Multi-Color Corp. for the American Bank Note Co.

PHOTOGRAVURE
BOOKLET STAMPS
Perf. 11 Vert. on 1 or 2 sides

1992, June 15				Tagged	
2642	A1994	29c	multicolored	.60	.20
2643	A1995	29c	multicolored	.60	.20
2644	A1996	29c	multicolored	.60	.20
2645	A1997	29c	multicolored	.60	.20
2646	A1998	29c	multicolored	.60	.20
a.			Bklt. pane of 5, #2642-2646	3.00	2.50

Imperfs of No. 2646a are printer's waste.

WILDFLOWERS

Illustration reduced.

Designed by Karen Mallary.

Printed by Ashton-Potter America, Inc.

LITHOGRAPHED
Plates of 300 in six panes of 50 and
Plates of 200 in four panes of 50

1992, July 24			Tagged	Perf. 11	
2647	A1999	29c	Indian paintbrush	.75	.60
2648	A2000	29c	Fragrant water lily	.75	.60
2649	A2001	29c	Meadow beauty	.75	.60
2650	A2002	29c	Jack-in-the-pulpit	.75	.60
2651	A2003	29c	California poppy	.75	.60
2652	A2004	29c	Large-flowered trillium	.75	.60
2653	A2005	29c	Tickseed	.75	.60
2654	A2006	29c	Shooting star	.75	.60
2655	A2007	29c	Stream violet	.75	.60
2656	A2008	29c	Bluets	.75	.60
2657	A2009	29c	Herb Robert	.75	.60
2658	A2010	29c	Marsh marigold	.75	.60
2659	A2011	29c	Sweet white violet	.75	.60
2660	A2012	29c	Claret cup cactus	.75	.60
2661	A2013	29c	White mountain avens	.75	.60
2662	A2014	29c	Sessile bellwort	.75	.60
2663	A2015	29c	Blue flag	.75	.60
2664	A2016	29c	Harlequin lupine	.75	.60
2665	A2017	29c	Twinflower	.75	.60
2666	A2018	29c	Common sunflower	.75	.60
2667	A2019	29c	Sego lily	.75	.60
2668	A2020	29c	Virginia bluebells	.75	.60
2669	A2021	29c	Ohi'a lehua	.75	.60
2670	A2022	29c	Rosebud orchid	.75	.60
2671	A2023	29c	Showy evening primrose	.75	.60
2672	A2024	29c	Fringed gentian	.75	.60
2673	A2025	29c	Yellow lady's slipper	.75	.60
2674	A2026	29c	Passionflower	.75	.60
2675	A2027	29c	Bunchberry	.75	.60
2676	A2028	29c	Pasqueflower	.75	.60
2677	A2029	29c	Round-lobed hepatica	.75	.60
2678	A2030	29c	Wild columbine	.75	.60
2679	A2031	29c	Fireweed	.75	.60
2680	A2032	29c	Indian pond lily	.75	.60
2681	A2033	29c	Turk's cap lily	.75	.60
2682	A2034	29c	Dutchman's breeches	.75	.60
2683	A2035	29c	Trumpet honeysuckle	.75	.60
2684	A2036	29c	Jacob's ladder	.75	.60
2685	A2037	29c	Plains prickly pear	.75	.60
2686	A2038	29c	Moss campion	.75	.60
2687	A2039	29c	Bearberry	.75	.60
2688	A2040	29c	Mexican hat	.75	.60
2689	A2041	29c	Harebell	.75	.60
2690	A2042	29c	Desert five spot	.75	.60
2691	A2043	29c	Smooth Solomon's seal	.75	.60
2692	A2044	29c	Red maids	.75	.60
2693	A2045	29c	Yellow skunk cabbage	.75	.60
2694	A2046	29c	Rue anemone	.75	.60
2695	A2047	29c	Standing cypress	.75	.60
2696	A2048	29c	Wild flax	.75	.60
a.			A1999-A2048 Pane of 50, #2647-2696	40.00	—

Sheet margin selvage contains a diagram of the plate layout with each pane's position shaded in gray.

WORLD WAR II

A2049

Illustration reduced.

Designed by William H. Bond.

Designs and events of 1942: a, B-25's take off to raid Tokyo, Apr. 18. b, Ration coupons (Food and other commodities rationed). c, Divebomber and deck crewman (US wins Battle of the Coral Sea, May). d, Prisoners of war (Corregidor falls to Japanese, May 6). e, Dutch Harbor buildings on fire (Japan invades Aleutian Islands, June). f, Headphones, coded message (Allies decipher secret enemy codes). g, Yorktown lost, U.S. wins at Midway. h, Woman with drill (Millions of women join war effort). i, Marines land on Guadalcanal, Aug. 7. j, Tank in desert (Allies land in North Africa, Nov.).

Central label is the size of 15 stamps and shows world map, extent of axis control.

LITHOGRAPHED & ENGRAVED
Plates of 80 in four panes of 20 each

1992, Aug. 17			Tagged	Perf. 11	
2697	A2049		Block of 10	7.50	5.00
			Pane of 20	15.00	
a.-j.		29c	any single	.75	.30
k.			Red (litho.) omitted	5,000.	

No. 2697 has salvage at left and right and either top or bottom.

Dorothy
Parker — A2050

Von Karman (1881-1963), Rocket Scientist — A2051

LITERARY ARTS SERIES

Designed by Greg Rudd.

Printed by J.W. Fergusson & Sons for Stamp Venturers.

PHOTOGRAVURE
Plates of 200 in four panes of 50

1992, Aug. 22			Tagged	Perf. 11	
2698	A2050	29c	multicolored	.60	.20
			P# block of 4, 5# + S	2.75	
			Zip block of 4	2.50	—

THEODORE VON KARMAN

Designed by Chris Calle.

Printed by J.W. Fergusson & Sons for Stamp Venturers.

PHOTOGRAVURE
Plates of 200 in four panes of 50

1992, Aug. 31			Tagged	Perf. 11	
2699	A2051	29c	multicolored	.60	.20
			P# block of 4, 4# + S	2.75	
			Zip block of 4	2.50	—

MINERALS

Azurite — A2052

Copper — A2053

Variscite — A2054

Wulfenite — A2055

Designed by Len Buckley.

LITHOGRAPHED & ENGRAVED
Sheets of 160 in four panes of 40.

1992, Sept. 17	Tagged		Perf. 11
2700 A2052 29c multicolored		.60	.20
2701 A2053 29c multicolored		.60	.20
2702 A2054 29c multicolored		.60	.20

2703 A2055 29c multicolored	.60	.2
a. Block or strip of 4, #2700-2703	2.40	2.0
P# block of 4, 6#	2.75	
Zip block of 4	2.50	
b. As "a," silver (litho.) omitted	8,500.	
c. As "a," red (litho.) omitted	—	
d. As "a," silver omitted on two stamps	—	

JUAN RODRIGUEZ CABRILLO

Cabrillo (d. 1543), Ship,
Map of San Diego Bay
Area — A2056

Designed by Ren Wicks.

Printed by The Press and J.W. Fergusson & Sons for Stamp Venturers.

LITHOGRAPHED & ENGRAVED
Plates of 200 in four panes of 50

1992, Sept. 28	Tagged		Perf. 11
2704 A2056 29c multicolored		.60	.20
P# block of 4, 7# + 2 "S"s		2.75	—
Zip, Olympic block of 4		2.50	—
a. Black (engr.) omitted		3,500.	

WILDFLOWERS
A1999-A2048

WILD ANIMALS

Giraffe
A2057

Giant Panda
A2058

Flamingo
A2059

King Penguins
A2060

White Bengal
Tiger — A2061

Designed by Robert Giusti.

Printed by J.W. Fergusson & Sons for Stamp Venturers.

PHOTOGRAVURE
BOOKLET STAMPS

1992, Oct. 1			**Tagged**		**Perf. 11 Horiz.**
2705	A2057	29c	**multicolored**	.65	.20
2706	A2058	29c	**multicolored**	.65	.20
2707	A2059	29c	**multicolored**	.65	.20
2708	A2060	29c	**multicolored**	.65	.20
2709	A2061	29c	**multicolored**	.65	.20
a.		Booklet pane of 5, #2705-2709		3.25	2.25
b.		As "a," imperf.		2,500.	

CHRISTMAS

Madonna and Child, by
Giovanni Bellini — A2062

A2063

A2064
A2065

A2066

Designed by Bradbury Thompson (#2710) and Lou Nolan (#2711-2719). Illustration reduced.

Printed by the Bureau of Engraving and Printing, Ashton-Potter America, Inc. (#2711-2714), the Multi-Color Corporation for American Bank Note Company (#2715-2718), and Avery Dennison (#2719).

LITHOGRAPHED & ENGRAVED
Sheets of 300 in six panes of 50 (#2710, 2714a)

1992			**Tagged**		**Perf. 11½x11**
2710	A2062	29c	**multicolored**, Oct. 22	.60	.20
		P# block of 4, 5#		2.75	—
		Zip, copyright block of 4		2.50	—
a.		Booklet pane of 10		6.00	3.50

LITHOGRAPHED

2711	A2063	29c	**multicolored**, Oct. 22	.75	.20
2712	A2064	29c	**multicolored**, Oct. 22	.75	.20
2713	A2065	29c	**multicolored**, Oct. 22	.75	.20
2714	A2066	29c	**multicolored**, Oct. 22	.75	.20
a.		Block of 4, #2711-2714		3.00	1.10
		P# block of 4, 5# + P		3.75	—
		Zip, copyright block of 6		4.50	—

Booklet Stamps
PHOTOGRAVURE
Perf. 11 on 2 or 3 Sides

2715	A2063	29c	**multicolored**, Oct. 22	.85	.20
2716	A2064	29c	**multicolored**, Oct. 22	.85	.20
2717	A2065	29c	**multicolored**, Oct. 22	.85	.20
2718	A2066	29c	**multicolored**, Oct. 22	.85	.20
a.		Booklet pane of 4, #2715-2718		3.50	1.25
b.		As "a," imperf. horiz.			

No. 2718a completely imperf is printer's waste.

Self-Adhesive
Die Cut

2719	A2064	29c	**multicolored**, Oct. 28	.60	.20
a.		Booklet pane of 18		11.00	

"Greetings" is 27mm long on Nos. 2711-2714, 25mm long on Nos. 2715-2718 and 21½mm long on No. 2719. Nos. 2715-2719 differ in color from Nos. 2711-2714.

CHINESE NEW YEAR

Year of the
Rooster
A2067

Designed by Clarence Lee.

Printed by the American Bank Note Co.
LITHOGRAPHED & ENGRAVED
Panes of 20

1992, Dec. 30			**Tagged**		**Perf. 11**
2720	A2067	29c	**multicolored**, prephosphored paper (mottled tagging) plus block tagging under the engraved portion of the design	.60	.20
		P# block of 4, 5#+A		2.50	—
		Pane of 20		11.50	—
a.		Prephosphored paper (mottled tagging) plus block tagging on top of printed design		3.00	—
		P# block of 4, 5#+A			
b.		Prephosphored paper (mottled tagging)		75.00	—

See No. 3895i.

AMERICAN MUSIC SERIES

Elvis Presley
A2068

Oklahoma!
A2069

Hank Williams
A2070

Elvis Presley
A2071

Bill Haley
A2072

Clyde
McPhatter
A2073

Ritchie Valens
A2074

Otis Redding
A2075

Buddy
Holly — A2076

Dinah
Washington
A2077

Designed by Mark Stutzman (#2721, 2724-2725, 2727, 2729, 2731-2732, 2734, 2736), Wilson McLean (#2722), Richard Waldrep (#2723), John Berkey (#2726, 2728, 2730, 2733, 2735, 2737).

Printed by the Bureau of Engraving and Printing (#2721), Stamp Venturers (#2722-2730), Multi-color Corp. (#2731-2737).

PHOTOGRAVURE
Panes of 40, Panes of 35 (#2724-2730)

1993			**Tagged**	**Perf. 11**	
2721	A2068	29c **multicolored**, *Jan. 8*		.60	.20
		P# block of 4, 5#		2.75	
		Zip, copyright block of 4		2.50	—
a.	Imperf, pair			—	

Perf. 10

2722	A2069	29c **multicolored**, *Mar. 30*	.60	.20
		P# block of 4, 4#+S	4.00	—
		Zip block of 4	2.50	
2723	A2070	29c **multicolored**, *June 9*	.75	.20
		P# block of 4, 6#+S	4.25	—
		Zip block of 4	3.25	

Perf. 11.2x11.5

2723A	A2070	29c **multicolored**, *June 9*	22.50	10.00
		P# block of 4, 6#+S	140.00	
		Zip block of 4	100.00	—

1993, June 16				**Perf. 10**	
2724	A2071	29c **multicolored**		.70	.20
2725	A2072	29c **multicolored**		.70	.20
2726	A2073	29c **multicolored**		.70	.20
2727	A2074	29c **multicolored**		.70	.20
2728	A2075	29c **multicolored**		.70	.20
2729	A2076	29c **multicolored**		.70	.20
2730	A2077	29c **multicolored**		.70	.20
a.	Vert. strip of 7, #2724-2730			5.50	
	Horiz. P# block of 10, 2				
	sets of 6P#+S, + top label			10.00	—
	Vert. P# block of 8, 6#+S			7.75	—
	Pane of 35			29.00	—

No. 2730a with Nos. 2724-2730 in numerical sequence cannot be obtained from the pane of 35.

Booklet Stamps
Perf. 11 Horiz.

2731	A2071	29c **multicolored**	.60	.20
2732	A2072	29c **multicolored**	.60	.20
2733	A2073	29c **multicolored**	.60	.20
2734	A2074	29c **multicolored**	.60	.20
2735	A2075	29c **multicolored**	.60	.20
2736	A2076	29c **multicolored**	.60	.20
2737	A2077	29c **multicolored**	.60	.20
a.	Booklet pane, 2 #2731, 1 each #2732-2737		5.00	2.25
b.	Booklet pane, #2731, 2735-2737 + tab		2.40	1.50

Nos. 2731-2737 have smaller design sizes, brighter colors and shorter inscriptions than Nos. 2724-2730, as well as framelines around the designs and other subtle design differences.
No. 2737b without tab is indistinguishable from broken No. 2737a.
See Nos. 2769, 2771, 2775 and designs A2112-A2117.

SPACE FANTASY

A2086

A2087

A2088

A2089

A2090

Designed by Stephen Hickman.

PHOTOGRAVURE
BOOKLET STAMPS

1993, Jan. 25		**Tagged**	**Perf. 11 Vert.**	
2741	A2086	29c **multicolored**	.60	.20
2742	A2087	29c **multicolored**	.60	.20
2743	A2088	29c **multicolored**	.60	.20
2744	A2089	29c **multicolored**	.60	.20
2745	A2090	29c **multicolored**	.60	.20
a.	Booklet pane of 5, #2741-2745		3.00	2.25

BLACK HERITAGE SERIES

Porcy Lavon Julian (1899-1975), Chemist — A2091

Designed by Higgins Bond.

LITHOGRAPHED & ENGRAVED
Panes of 50

1993, Jan. 29		**Tagged**	**Perf. 11**	
2746	A2091	29c **multicolored**	.60	.20
		P# block of 4, 7#	2.75	—
		Zip block of 4	2.50	—

OREGON TRAIL

A2092

Designed by Jack Rosenthal.

LITHOGRAPHED & ENGRAVED
Panes of 50

1993, Feb. 12		**Tagged**	**Perf. 11**	
2747	A2092	29c **multicolored**	.60	.20
		P# block of 4, 6#	2.75	
		Zip block of 4	2.50	—
a.	Tagging omitted		22.50	
b.	Blue omitted			

WORLD UNIVERSITY GAMES

A2093

Designed by David Buck.

PHOTOGRAVURE
Panes of 50

1993, Feb. 25		**Tagged**	**Perf. 11**	
2748	A2093	29c **multicolored**	.60	.20
		P# block of 4, 5#	2.75	—
		Zip block of 4	2.50	—

GRACE KELLY (1929-1982)

Actress, Princess of
Monaco — A2094

Designed by Czeslaw Slania.

Printed by Stamp Venturers.

ENGRAVED
Panes of 50

1993, Mar. 24	Tagged	Perf. 11	
49 A2094 29c blue		.60	.20
P# block of 4, 1# +S		2.75	—
Zip block of 4		2.50	—

See Monaco No. 1851.

CIRCUS

Clown — A2095

Ringmaster — A2096

Trapeze
Artist — A2097

Elephant — A2098

Designed by Steve McCracken.

Printed by Ashton Potter America.

LITHOGRAPHED
Panes of 40

1993, Apr. 6	Tagged	Perf. 11	
2750 A2095 29c multicolored		.60	.20
2751 A2096 29c multicolored		.60	.20
2752 A2097 29c multicolored		.60	.20
2753 A2098 29c multicolored		.60	.20
a. Block of 4, #2750-2753		2.40	1.75
P# block of 6, 5#+P		5.75	—
Zip block of 6		3.75	—

Plate and zip blocks of 6 and copyright blocks of 9 contain one #2753a with continuous design (complete spotlight).

CHEROKEE STRIP LAND RUN, CENTENNIAL

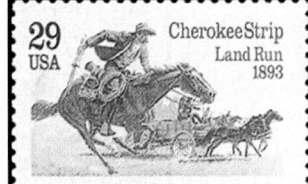

A2099

Designed by Harold T. Holden.

Printed by American Bank Note. Co.

LITHOGRAPHED & ENGRAVED
Panes of 20

1993, Apr. 17	Tagged	Perf. 11	
2754 A2099 29c multicolored		.60	.20
P# block of 4, 5#+A		2.50	—
Pane of 20		12.50	—

DEAN ACHESON (1893-1971)

Secretary of State — A2100

Designed by Christopher Calle.

Printed by Stamp Venturers.

ENGRAVED
Sheets of 300 in six panes of 50

1993, Apr. 21		Perf. 11	
2755 A2100 29c greenish gray		.60	.20
P# block of 4, 1#+S		2.75	—
Zip block of 4		2.50	—

SPORTING HORSES

Steeplechase
A2101

Thoroughbred
Racing
A2102

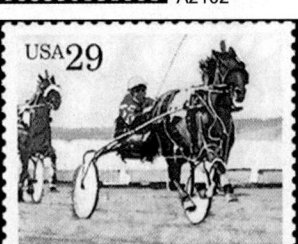

Harness
Racing
A2103

Polo — A2104

Designed by Michael Dudash.

Printed by Stamp Venturers.

LITHOGRAPHED & ENGRAVED
Panes of 40

1993, May 1	Tagged	Perf. 11x11½	
2756 A2101 29c multicolored		.60	.20
2757 A2102 29c multicolored		.60	.20
2758 A2103 29c multicolored		.60	.20
2759 A2104 29c multicolored		.60	.20
a. Block of 4, #2756-2759		2.40	2.00
P# block of 4, 5#+S		2.75	—
Zip block of 4		2.50	—
b. As "a," black (engr.) omitted		1,000.	

GARDEN FLOWERS

Hyacinth — A2105

Daffodil — A2106

Tulip — A2107

Iris — A2108

Lilac — A2109

Designed by Ned Seidler.

LITHOGRAPHED & ENGRAVED
BOOKLET STAMPS

1993, May 15	Tagged	Perf. 11 Vert.	
2760 A2105 29c multicolored		.60	.20
2761 A2106 29c multicolored		.60	.20
2762 A2107 29c multicolored		.60	.20
2763 A2108 29c multicolored		.60	.20
2764 A2109 29c multicolored		.60	.20
a. Booklet pane of 5, #2760-2764		3.00	2.25
b. As "a," black (engr.) omitted		200.00	
c. As "a," imperf.		1,250.	

WORLD WAR II

A2110

Illustration reduced.

Designed by William H. Bond.

Designs and events of 1943: a, Destroyers (Allied forces battle German U-boats). b, Military medics treat the wounded. c, Amphibious landing craft on beach (Sicily attacked by Allied forces, July). d, B-24s hit Ploesti refineries, August. e, V-mail delivers letters from home. f, PT boat (Italy invaded by Allies, Sept.).

g, Nos. WS7, WS8, savings bonds, (Bonds and stamps help war effort). h, "Willie and Joe" keep spirits high. i, Banner in window (Gold Stars mark World War II losses). j, Marines assault Tarawa, Nov.

Central label is the size of 15 stamps and shows world map with extent of Axis control and Allied operations.

LITHOGRAPHED & ENGRAVED
Plates of 80 in four panes of 20 each

1993, May 31		Tagged	Perf. 11	
2765	A2110	Block of 10	7.50	5.00
		Pane of 20	15.00	—
a.-j.		29c any single	.75	.40

No. 2765 has selvage at left and right and either top or bottom.

JOE LOUIS (1914-1981)

A2111

Designed by Thomas Blackshear.

LITHOGRAPHED & ENGRAVED
Plates of 200 in four panes of 50

1993, June 22		Tagged	Perf. 11	
2766	A2111	29c multicolored	.60	.20
		P# block of 4, 5#	2.75	
		Zip block of 4	2.50	—

AMERICAN MUSIC SERIES
Oklahoma! Type and

Show Boat — A2112

Porgy & Bess — A2113

My Fair Lady — A2114

Designed by Wilson McLean.

Printed by Multi-Color Corp.

BOOKLET STAMPS
PHOTOGRAVURE
Perf. 11 Horiz. on 1 or 2 Sides

1993, July 14			Tagged	
2767	A2112	29c multicolored	.60	.20
2768	A2113	29c multicolored	.60	.20
2769	A2069	29c multicolored	.60	.20
2770	A2114	29c multicolored	.60	.20
a.		Booklet pane of 4, #2767-2770	2.75	2.25

No. 2769 has smaller design size, brighter colors and shorter inscription than No. 2722, as well as a frameline around the design and other subtle design differences.

Imperfs of No. 2770a are printer's waste.

AMERICAN MUSIC SERIES
Hank Williams Type and

Patsy Cline — A2115

The Carter Family A2116

Bob Wills — A2117

Designed by Richard Waldrep.

Printed by Stamp Venturers (#2771-2774) and American Bank Note Co. (#2775-2778).

PHOTOGRAVURE
Panes of 20

1993, Sept. 25		Tagged	Perf. 10	
2771	A2070	29c multicolored		.75	.20
2772	A2115	29c multicolored		.75	.20
2773	A2116	29c multicolored		.75	.20
2774	A2117	29c multicolored		.75	.20
a.		Block or horiz. strip of 4, #2771-2774	3.00	1.75
		Horiz. P# block of 8, 2 sets of 6#+S + top label	6.50	—
		P# block of 4, 6#+S	3.25	—
		Pane of 20	16.00	—

Booklet Stamps
Perf. 11 Horiz. on one or two sides
With Black Frameline

2775	A2070	29c multicolored	.60	.20
2776	A2116	29c multicolored	.60	.20
2777	A2115	29c multicolored	.60	.20

2778	A2117	29c multicolored		.60	
a.		Booklet pane of 4, #2775-2778		2.50	2
b.		As "a," imperf			

Inscription at left measures 27½mm on No. 2723, 27mm No. 2771 and 22mm on No. 2775. No. 2723 shows only t tuning keys on guitar, while No. 2771 shows those two a parts of two others.

NATIONAL POSTAL MUSEUM

Independence Hall, Benjamin Franklin, Printing Press, Colonial Post Rider — A2118

Pony Express Rider, Civil War Soldier, Concord Stagecoach A2119

JN-4H Biplane, Charles Lindbergh, Railway Mail Car, 1931 Model A Ford Mail Truck A2120

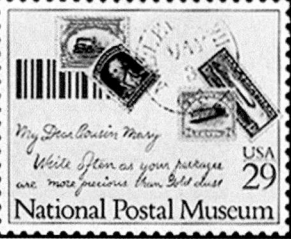

California Gold Rush Miner's Letter, Nos. 39, 295, C3a, C13, Barcode and Circular Date Stamp A2121

Designed by Richard Schlecht.

Printed by American Bank Note Co.

LITHOGRAPHED AND ENGRAVED

1993, July 30		Tagged	Perf. 11	
2779	A2118	29c multicolored	.60	.20
2780	A2119	29c multicolored	.60	.20
2781	A2120	29c multicolored	.60	.20
2782	A2121	29c multicolored	.60	.20
a.		Block or strip of 4, #2779-2782	2.40	2.00
		P# block of 4, 7#+A	2.50	
		Pane of 20	12.50	—
b.		As "a," engr. maroon (USA/29) and black ("My dear...") omitted	—	
c.		As "a," imperf	3,500.	

AMERICAN SIGN LANGUAGE

A2122

A2123

Designed by Chris Calle.

Printed by Stamp Venturers.

PHOTOGRAVURE

1993, Sept. 20	Tagged	Perf. 11½
ᵈ83 A2122 29c **multicolored**		.60 .20
ᵈ84 A2123 29c **multicolored**		.60 .20
a.	Pair, #2783-2784	1.20 .75
	P# block of 4, 4#+S	2.50 —
	Pane of 20	12.50 —

CLASSIC BOOKS

A2124

A2125

A2126

A2127

Designed by Jim Lamb.

Printed by American Bank Note Co.
Designs: No. 2785, Rebecca of Sunnybrook Farm, by Kate Douglas Wiggin. No. 2786, Little House on the Prairie, by Laura

Ingalls Wilder. No. 2787, The Adventures of Huckleberry Finn, by Mark Twain. No. 2788, Little Women, by Louisa May Alcott.

LITHOGRAPHED & ENGRAVED
Panes of 40

1993, Oct. 23	Tagged	Perf. 11
2785 A2124 29c **multicolored**		.60 .20
2786 A2125 29c **multicolored**		.60 .20
2787 A2126 29c **multicolored**		.60 .20
2788 A2127 29c **multicolored**		.60 .20
a.	Block or horiz. strip of 4, #2785-2788	2.40 2.00
	P# block of 4, 5#+A	5.00 —
	Zip block of 4	2.50 —
b.	As "a," imperf	2,750.

CHRISTMAS

Madonna and Child in a Landscape, by Giovanni Battista Cima — A2128

Jack-in-the-Box A2129

Red-Nosed Reindeer A2130

Snowman — A2131

Toy Soldier Blowing Horn — A2132

Designed by Bradbury Thompson (#2789-2790), Peter Good (#2791-2803).

Printed by Bureau of Engraving and Printing (#2789, 2791-2798), KCS Industries (#2790), Avery Dennison (#2799-2803).

LITHOGRAPHED & ENGRAVED
Panes of 50 (#2789, 2791-2794)

1993, Oct. 21	Tagged	Perf. 11
2789 A2128 29c **multicolored**		.60 .20
	P# block of 4, 4#	2.75 —
	Zip, copyright block of 4	2.50 —

Booklet Stamp
Size: 18x25mm
Perf. 11½x11 on 2 or 3 Sides

2790 A2128 29c **multicolored**		.60 .20
a.	Booklet pane of 4	2.40 1.75
b.	Imperf., pair	—
c.	As "a," imperf	—

Nos. 2789-2790 have numerous design differences.

1993

PHOTOGRAVURE
Perf. 11½

2791 A2129 29c **multicolored**, Oct. 21	.60 .20
2792 A2130 29c **multicolored**, Oct. 21	.60 .20
2793 A2131 29c **multicolored**, Oct. 21	.60 .20
2794 A2132 29c **multicolored**, Oct. 21	.60 .20
a.	Block or strip of 4, #2791-2794	2.40 2.00
	P# block of 4, 6#	4.00 —
	Zip, copyright block of 4	2.50 —

Snowman on Nos. 2793, 2799 has three buttons and seven snowflakes beneath nose (placement differs on both stamps). No. 2796 has two buttons and five snowflakes beneath nose. No. 2803 has two orange buttons and four snowflakes beneath nose.

Booklet Stamps
Size: 18x21mm
Perf. 11x10 on 2 or 3 Sides

2795 A2132 29c **multicolored**, Oct. 21	.85 .20
2796 A2131 29c **multicolored**, Oct. 21	.85 .20
2797 A2130 29c **multicolored**, Oct. 21	.85 .20
2798 A2129 29c **multicolored**, Oct. 21	.85 .20
a.	Booklet pane, 3 each #2795-2796, 2 each #2797-2798	8.50 4.00
b.	Booklet pane, 3 each #2795-2796, 2 each #2797-2798, 2 each #2797-2798	8.50 4.00
c.	Block of 4, #2795-2798	3.40 1.75

Self-Adhesive
Size: 19½x26½mm
Die Cut

2799 A2131 29c **multicolored**, Oct. 28	.65 .20
a.	Coil with plate # V1111111	— 3.50
	P# strip of 5, 1 each #2799-2801, 2 #2802, P#V1111111	6.00
	P# strip of 8, 2 each #2799-2802, P#V1111111	9.75
2800 A2132 29c **multicolored**, Oct. 28	.65 .20
2801 A2129 29c **multicolored**, Oct. 28	.65 .20
2802 A2130 29c **multicolored**, Oct. 28	.65 .20
a.	Booklet pane, 3 each #2799-2802	8.00
b.	Block of 4, #2799-2802	2.60

Except for No. 2799a with plate number, coil stamps are indistinguishable from booklet stamps once they are removed from the backing paper.

Size: 17x20mm

2803 A2131 29c **multicolored**, Oct. 28	.60 .20
a.	Booklet pane of 18	11.00

Snowman on Nos. 2793, 2799 has three buttons and seven snowflakes beneath nose (placement differs on both stamps). No. 2796 has two buttons and five snowflakes beneath nose. No. 2803 has two orange buttons and four snowflakes beneath nose.

MARIANA ISLANDS

A2133

Designed by Herb Kane.

LITHOGRAPHED AND ENGRAVED

1993, Nov. 4	Tagged	Perf. 11
2804 A2133 29c **multicolored**		.60 .20
	P# block of 4, 6#	2.50 —
	Pane of 20	12.50 —

COLUMBUS' LANDING IN PUERTO RICO, 500th ANNIVERSARY

A2134

Designed by Richard Schlecht.

Printed by Stamp Venturers.

PHOTOGRAVURE
Panes of 50

1993, Nov. 19	Tagged	Perf. 11.2
2805 A2134 29c **multicolored**		.60 .20
	P# block of 4, 5#+S	2.75 —
	Zip block of 4	2.50 —

AIDS AWARENESS

A2135

Designed by Tom Mann.
Printed by Stamp Venturers.

PHOTOGRAVURE
Panes of 50

1993, Dec. 1	Tagged	Perf. 11.2	
2806 A2135 29c **black & red**		.60	.20
	P# block of 4, 3#+S	2.75	—
	Zip, copyright block of 6	2.50	—
a.	Perf. 11 vert. on 1 or 2 sides, from bklt. pane	.60	.20
b.	As "a," booklet pane of 5	3.00	2.00

WINTER OLYMPICS

Slalom — A2136

Luge — A2137

Ice Dancing — A2138

Cross-Country
Skiing — A2139

Ice Hockey — A2140

Designed by Lon Busch.
Printed by Ashton-Potter.

LITHOGRAPHED
Sheets of 120 in six panes of 20

1994, Jan. 6	Tagged	Perf. 11.2	
2807 A2136 29c **multicolored**		.60	.20
2808 A2137 29c **multicolored**		.60	.20
2809 A2138 29c **multicolored**		.60	.20
2810 A2139 29c **multicolored**		.60	.20
2811 A2140 29c **multicolored**		.60	.20
a.	Strip of 5, #2807-2811	3.00	2.50
	Horiz. P# block of 10, 2 sets of 4#+P and inscriptions	6.50	—
	Horiz. P# block of 10, 2 sets of 4#+P	6.00	—
	Pane of 20	12.50	—

EDWARD R. MURROW, JOURNALIST (1908-65)

A2141

Designed by Chris Calle.

ENGRAVED
Panes of 50

1994, Jan. 21	Tagged	Perf. 11.2	
2812 A2141 29c **brown**		.60	.20
	P# block of 4, 1#	2.75	—

LOVE

A2142

A2143

A2144

Designed by Peter Goode (#2813), Lon Busch (#2814-2815).

Printed by Banknote Corp. of America (#2813), American Banknote Co. (#2814) and Bureau of Engraving and Printing (#2814C, 2815).

Booklet Stamps
LITHOGRAPHED & ENGRAVED

1994	Tagged	Die Cut	
	Self-adhesive		
2813	A2142 29c **multicolored**, *Jan. 27*	.60	.20
a.	Booklet pane of 18	11.00	
b.	Coil with plate # B1	—	3.75
	P# strip of 5, #B1	6.75	

Except for No. 2813b with plate number, coil stamps are indistinguishable from booklet stamps once they are removed from the backing paper.

PHOTOGRAVURE
Perf. 10.9x11.1 on 2 or 3 sides

2814	A2143 29c **multicolored**, *Feb. 14*	.60	.20
a.	Booklet pane of 10	6.00	3.50
b.	Imperf, pair		

Horiz. pairs, imperf between, are printer's waste.

LITHOGRAPHED & ENGRAVED
Sheets of 300 in six panes of 50
Tagged
Perf. 11.1

2814C	A2143 29c **multicolored**, *June 11*	.70	.20
	P# block of 4, 5#	3.00	—

Size of No. 2814C is 20x28mm. No. 2814 is 18x24½mm.

PHOTOGRAVURE & ENGRAVED
Sheet of 300 in six panes of 50
Perf. 11.2

2815	A2144 52c **multicolored**, *Feb. 14*	1.00	.20
	P# block of 4, 5#	5.00	—
	P# block of 10, 2 sets of 5#, plate diagram, copyright and pane price inscriptions	11.00	—

BLACK HERITAGE SERIES

Dr. Allison Davis (1902-83)
Social Anthropologist,
Educator — A2145

Designed by Chris Calle.

Printed by Stamp Venturers.

ENGRAVED

1994, Feb. 1	Tagged	Perf. 11.	
2816 A2145 29c **red brown & brown**		.60	.2
	P# block of 4, 1#+S	2.50	
	Pane of 20	12.50	

CHINESE NEW YEAR

Year of the
Dog — A2146

Designed by Clarence Lee.

Printed by J.W. Fergusson & Sons for Stamp Venturers.

PHOTOGRAVURE
Sheets of 180 in nine panes of 20

1994, Feb. 5	Tagged	Perf. 11.2	
2817 A2146 29c **multicolored**		.80	.20
	P# block of 4, 4#+S	3.50	—
	Pane of 20	17.50	—

See No. 3895j.

BUFFALO SOLDIERS

A2147

Designed by Mort Kuntsler.

Printed by Stamp Venturers.

LITHOGRAPHED & ENGRAVED
Plates of 180 in nine panes of 20

1994, Apr. 22	Tagged	Perf. 11.5x11.2	
2818 A2147 29c **multicolored**		.60	.20
	P# block of 4, 5#+S	2.50	—
	Pane of 20	12.50	—
a.	Double impression (second impression light) of red brown (engr. inscriptions)		

SILENT SCREEN STARS

Rudolph Valentino
(1895-1926) — A2148

Clara Bow (1905-
65) — A2149

Charlie Chaplin (1889-
1977) — A2150

Lon Chaney (1883-
1930) — A2151

John Gilbert (1895-
1936) — A2152

Zasu Pitts (1898-
1963) — A2153

Harold Lloyd (1894-
1971) — A2154

Keystone
Cops — A2155

Theda Bara (1885-
1955) — A2156

Buster Keaton (1895-
1966) — A2157

Designed by Al Hirschfeld.

LITHOGRAPHED & ENGRAVED
Plates of 160 in four panes of 40

1994, Apr. 27		**Tagged**	**Perf. 11.2**
2819	A2148 29c **red, black & bright violet**	1.10	.30
2820	A2149 29c **red, black & bright violet**	1.10	.30
2821	A2150 29c **red, black & bright violet**	1.10	.30
2822	A2151 29c **red, black & bright violet**	1.10	.30
2823	A2152 29c **red, black & bright violet**	1.10	.30
2824	A2153 29c **red, black & bright violet**	1.10	.30
2825	A2154 29c **red, black & bright violet**	1.10	.30
2826	A2155 29c **red, black & bright violet**	1.10	.30
2827	A2156 29c **red, black & bright violet**	1.10	.30
2828	A2157 29c **red, black & bright violet**	1.10	.30
a.	Block of 10, #2819-2828	11.00	4.00
	P# block of 10, 4#, plate diagram and copyright inscription	12.00	—
	Half pane of 20	23.00	—
b.	As "a," black (litho.) omitted		
c.	As "a," blk, red & brt vio (litho.) omitted	—	

GARDEN FLOWERS

Lily — A2158

Zinnia — A2159

Gladiola — A2160

Marigold — A2161

Rose — A2162

Designed by Ned Seidler.

LITHOGRAPHED & ENGRAVED

1994, Apr. 28		**Tagged**	**Perf. 10.9 Vert.**
		Booklet Stamps	
2829	A2158 29c **multicolored**	.60	.20
2830	A2159 29c **multicolored**	.60	.20
2831	A2160 29c **multicolored**	.60	.20
2832	A2161 29c **multicolored**	.60	.20
2833	A2162 29c **multicolored**	.60	.20
a.	Booklet pane of 5, #2829-2833	3.00	2.25
b.	As "a," imperf	1,750.	
c.	As "a," black (engr.) omitted	250.00	
d.	As "a," tagging omitted	—	

1994 WORLD CUP SOCCER CHAMPIONSHIPS

A2163   A2164

A2165

Illustration reduced.

Designed by Michael Dudash.

Printed by J.W. Fergusson & Sons for Stamp Venturers.
Design: 40c, Soccer player, diff.

PHOTOGRAVURE
Plates of 180 in nine panes of 20

1994, May 26		**Tagged**	**Perf. 11.1**
2834	A2163 29c **multicolored**	.60	.20
	P# block of 4, 4#+S	2.50	—
	Pane of 20	12.50	—
2835	A2163 40c **multicolored**	.80	.20
	P# block of 4, 4#+S	3.20	—
	Pane of 20	16.00	—
2836	A2164 50c **multicolored**	1.00	.20
	P# block of 4, 4#+S	4.00	—
	Pane of 20	20.00	—
	Souvenir Sheet		
2837	A2165 Sheet of 3, #a.-c.	4.00	3.00

Nos. 2834-2836 are printed on phosphor-coated paper while
Nos. 2837a (29c), 2837b (40c), 2837c (50c) are block tagged.
No. 2837c has a portion of the yellow map in the LR corner.

WORLD WAR II

A2166

Illustration reduced.

Designed by William H. Bond.

Designs and events of 1944: a, Allied forces retake New
Guinea. b, P-51s escort B-17s on bombing raids. c, Troops
running from landing craft (Allies in Normandy, D-Day, June 6).
d, Airborne units spearhead attacks. e, Officer at periscope
(Submarines shorten war in Pacific). f, Parade (Allies free
Rome, June 4; Paris, Aug. 25).
g, Soldier firing flamethrower (US troops clear Saipan
bunkers). h, Red Ball Express speeds vital supplies. i, Battleship firing main battery (Battle for Leyte Gulf, Oct. 23-26). j,
Soldiers in snow (Bastogne and Battle of the Bulge, Dec.).
Central label is size of 15 stamps and shows world map with
extent of Axis control and Allied operations.

LITHOGRAPHED & ENGRAVED
Plates of eight subjects in four panes of 2 each

1994, June 6		**Tagged**	**Perf. 10.9**
2838	A2166 Block of 10	15.00	10.00
	Pane of 20	30.00	—
a.-j.	29c any single	1.50	.50

No. 2838 has selvage at left and right and either top or
bottom.

NORMAN ROCKWELL

A2167

A2168

Illustration reduced.

Designed by Richard Sheaff based on Rockwell's works.

LITHOGRAPHED & ENGRAVED
Sheets of 200 in four panes of 50

1994, July 1		**Tagged**		*Perf. 10.9x11.1*	
2839	A2167	29c	multicolored	.60	.20
		P# block of 4, 5#		2.75	—

Souvenir Sheet
LITHOGRAPHED

2840	A2168	Sheet of 4		4.00	2.75
a.		50c Freedom From Want		1.00	.65
b.		50c Freedom From Fear		1.00	.65
c.		50c Freedom of Speech		1.00	.65
d.		50c Freedom of Worship		1.00	.65

Panes of No. 2839 contain two plate blocks, one containing a plate position diagram.

Moon Landing, 25th Anniv.

A2169

A2170

Designed by Paul and Chris Calle.

Printed by Stamp Venturers (#2841) and Banknote Corp. of America (#2842).

Miniature Sheet
LITHOGRAPHED

1994, July 20		**Tagged**		*Perf. 11.2x11.1*	
2841	A2169	29c Sheet of 12		9.00	
a.		Single stamp		.75	.60

LITHOGRAPHED & ENGRAVED
Sheets of 120 in six panes of 20
Perf. 10.7x11.1

2842	A2170	$9.95	multicolored	20.00	16.00
		P# block of 4, 5#+B		82.50	

LOCOMOTIVES

Hudson's
General
A2171

McQueen's
Jupiter
A2172

Eddy's No.
242 — A2173

Ely's No.
10 — A2174

Buchanan's
No.
999 — A2175

Designed by Richard Leech.

Printed by J.W. Ferguson & Sons for Stamp Venturers.

PHOTOGRAVURE

1994, July 28		**Tagged**		*Perf. 11 Horiz.*	
		Booklet Stamps			
2843	A2171	29c	multicolored	.70	.20
2844	A2172	29c	multicolored	.70	.20
2845	A2173	29c	multicolored	.70	.20
2846	A2174	29c	multicolored	.70	.20
2847	A2175	29c	multicolored	.70	.20
a.		Booklet pane of 5, #2843-2847		3.50	2.00
b.		As "a," imperf.		—	

GEORGE MEANY, LABOR LEADER (1894-1980)

A2176

Designed by Chris Calle.

ENGRAVED
Sheets of 200 in four panes of 50

1994, Aug. 16		**Tagged**		*Perf. 11.1x1*	
2848	A2176	29c	blue	.60	.20
		P# block of 4, 1#		2.50	—

Panes of No. 2848 contain two plate blocks, one containing a plate position diagram.

AMERICAN MUSIC SERIES
Popular Singers

Al Jolson
(1886-1950)
A2177

Bing Crosby
(1904-77)
A2178

Ethel Waters
(1896-1977)
A2179

Nat "King"
Cole (1919-65)
A2180

Ethel Merman
(1908-84)
A2181

Jazz Singers

Bessie Smith
(1894-1937)
A2182

Muddy Waters
(1915-83)
A2183

Billie Holiday
(1915-59)
A2184

Robert
Johnson
(1911-38)
A2185

Jimmy
Rushing
(1902-72)
A2186

"Ma" Rainey
(1886-1939)
A2187

Mildred Bailey
(1907-51)
A2188

Howlin' Wolf
(1910-76)
A2189

Designed by Chris Payne (#2849-2853), Howard Koslow (#2854, 2856, 2858, 2860), Julian Allen (#2855, 2857, 2859, 2861).

Printed by J.W. Fergusson & Sons for Stamp Venturers (#2849-2853), Manhardt-Alexander for Ashton-Potter (USA) Ltd. (#2854-2861).

PHOTOGRAVURE
Plates of 180 in nine panes of 20, Plates
of 210 in six panes of 35 (#2854-2861)

1994, Sept. 1		Tagged	Perf. 10.1x10.2	
2849	A2177	29c multicolored	.75	.20
2850	A2178	29c multicolored	.75	.20
2851	A2179	29c multicolored	.75	.20
2852	A2180	29c multicolored	.75	.20
2853	A2181	29c multicolored	.75	.20
a.		Vert. strip of 5, #2849-2853	3.75	2.00
		Vert. P# block of 6, 6#+S	7.00	—
		Horiz. P# block of 12, 2 sets of 6#+S, + top label	14.00	—
		Pane of 20	20.00	—
b.		Pane of 20, imperf	4,600.	

Some plate blocks of 6 will contain plate position diagram and copyright inscription, others will contain pane price inscription.

1994, Sept. 17			Perf. 11x10.8	
		LITHOGRAPHED		
2854	A2182	29c multicolored	.75	.20
2855	A2183	29c multicolored	.75	.20
2856	A2184	29c multicolored	.75	.20
2857	A2185	29c multicolored	.75	.20
2858	A2186	29c multicolored	.75	.20
2859	A2187	29c multicolored	.75	.20
2860	A2188	29c multicolored	.75	.20
2861	A2189	29c multicolored	.75	.20
a.		Block of 8, #2854-2861 +2 additional stamps	7.50	4.50
		Vert. P# block of 10, 5#+P	9.00	—
		P# block of 10, 2 sets of 5#+P, + top label	9.00	—
		Pane of 35	27.50	—

Vertical plate blocks contain either pane price inscription or copyright inscription.

Nos. 2854-2861 were available on the first day in 9 other cities.

LITERARY ARTS SERIES

James Thurber (1894-1961) — A2190

Designed by Richard Sheaff based on drawing by James Thurber.

LITHOGRAPHED & ENGRAVED
Plates of 200 in four panes of 50

1994, Sept. 10		Tagged	Perf. 11	
2862	A2190	29c multicolored	.60	.20
		P# block of 4, 2#	2.75	

Panes of No. 2862 contain two plate blocks, one containing a plate position diagram.

WONDERS OF THE SEA

Diver,
Motorboat
A2191

Diver,
Ship — A2192

Diver, Ship's
Wheel
A2193

Diver,
Coral — A2194

Designed by Charles Lynn Bragg.

Printed by Barton Press for Banknote Corporation of America.

LITHOGRAPHED
Plates of 216 in nine panes of 24

1994, Oct. 3		Tagged	Perf. 11x10.9	
2863	A2191	29c multicolored	.60	.20
2864	A2192	29c multicolored	.60	.20
2865	A2193	29c multicolored	.60	.20
2866	A2194	29c multicolored	.60	.20
a.		Block of 4, #2863-2866	2.40	1.50
		P# block of 4, 4#+B	2.50	—
		Pane of 24	16.00	—
b.		As "a," imperf	1,500.	

CRANES

Black-Necked
A2195

Whooping — A2196

Designed by Clarence Lee based on illustrations by Zhan Gengxi.

Printed by Barton Press for Banknote Corporation of America.

LITHOGRAPHED & ENGRAVED
Sheets of 120 in six panes of 20

1994, Oct. 9	Tagged	Perf. 10.8x11

2867 A2195 29c multicolored .70 .20
2868 A2196 29c multicolored .70 .20
a. Pair, #2867-2868 1.40 .75
  P# block of 4, 5#+B 3.00 —
  Pane of 20 14.50
b. As "a," black & magenta (engr.) omitted 1,750.
c. As "a," double impression of engr. black (Birds' names and "USA") & magenta ("29") 5,000.
d. As "a," double impression of engr. black ("USA") & magenta ("29") —

LEGENDS OF THE WEST

A2197

Illustration reduced.

g. Bill Pickett (1870-1932) (Revised)

Vertical Pair with Horizontal Gutter

Horizontal Pair with Vertical Gutter

Illustration reduced.

Designed by Mark Hess.

Printed by J.W. Fergusson & Sons for Stamp Venturers.

Designs: a, Home on the Range. b, Buffalo Bill Cody (1846-1917). c, Jim Bridger (1804-81). d, Annie Oakley (1860-1926). e, Native American Culture. f, Chief Joseph (c. 1840-1904). h, Bat Masterson (1853-1921). i, John C. Fremont (1813-90). j, Wyatt Earp (1848-1929). k, Nellie Cashman (c. 1849-1925). l, Charles Goodnight (1826-1929). m, Geronimo (1823-1909). n, Kit Carson (1809-68). o, Wild Bill Hickok (1837-76). p, Western Wildlife. q, Jim Beckwourth (c. 1798-1866). r, Bill Tilghman (1854-1924). s, Sacagawea (c. 1787-1812). t, Overland Mail.

PHOTOGRAVURE
Sheets of 120 in six panes of 20

1994, Oct. 18	Tagged	Perf. 10.1x10

2869 A2197 Pane of 20 15.00 10.00
a.-t. 29c any single .75 .50
  Sheet of 120 (6 panes) 90.00
  Cross gutter block of 20 25.00 —
  Vert. pairs with horiz. gutter (each) 2.50 —
  Horiz. pairs with vert. gutter (each) 2.50 —
u. As No. 2869, a.-e. imperf. f.-j. part perf. —

Cross gutter block of 20 consists of six stamps from each of two panes and four stamps from each of two other panes with the cross gutter between.

LEGENDS OF THE WEST (Recalled)

g. Bill Pickett (Recalled)

Nos. 2870b-2870d, 2870f-2870o, 2870q-2870s have a frameline around the vignette that is half the width of the frameline on similar stamps in No. 2869. Other design differences may exist.

PHOTOGRAVURE
Sheets of 120 in six panes of 20

1994	Tagged	Perf. 10.1x10

2870 A2197 29c Pane of 20 240.00 —

150,000 panes of No. 2870 were made available through a drawing. Panes were delivered in an envelope. Value is for pane without envelope.

CHRISTMAS

Madonna and Child, by Elisabetta Sira — A2200

Stocking — A2201

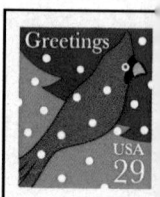

Santa Claus — A2202

Cardinal in Snow — A2203

Designed by Bradbury Thompson (#2871), Lou Nola (#2872), Harry Zelenko (#2873), Peter Good (#2874).

Printed by Bureau of Engraving and Printing (#2871), Ashton Potter USA, Ltd. (#2872), Avery Dennison (#2873-2874).

LITHOGRAPHED & ENGRAVED
Sheets of 300 in six panes of 50

1994, Oct. 20	Tagged	Perf. 11¼

2871 A2200 29c multicolored, shiny gum .70 .20
  P# block of 4, 5# 3.00
  Low gloss gum .70
  P# block of 4, 5# 3.00

BOOKLET STAMP
Perf. 9¾x11

2871A A2200 29c multicolored .60 .20
b. Booklet pane of 10 6.25 3.50
c. Imperf, pair 550.00

LITHOGRAPHED
Sheets of 400 in eight panes of 50
Perf. 11¼

2872 A2201 29c multicolored .60 .20
  P# block of 4, 5#+P 2.50
a. Booklet pane of 20 12.50 4.00
b. Imperf., pair
c. Vert. pair, imperf. horiz.
d. Quadruple impression of black, triple impression of blue, double impressions of red and yellow, green normal —
e. Vert. pair, imperf between —

Panes of Nos. 2871-2872 contain four plate blocks, one containing pane position diagram.

PHOTOGRAVURE
BOOKLET STAMPS
Self-Adhesive
Die Cut

2873 A2202 29c multicolored .60 .20
a. Booklet pane of 12 7.25
b. Coil with plate # V1111 — 4.75
  P# strip of 5, P#V1111 6.75

Except for No. 2873b with plate number, coil stamps are indistinguishable from booklet stamps once they are removed from the backing paper.

2874 A2203 29c multicolored .60 .20
a. Booklet pane of 18 11.00

BUREAU OF ENGRAVING & PRINTING
Souvenir Sheet

A2204

Illustration reduced.

Major Double Transfer

©USPS 1994

Minor Double Transfer

Designed by Peter Cocci, using original die for Type A98.

LITHOGRAPHED & ENGRAVED

1994, Nov. 3	Tagged		Perf. 11	
2875 A2204	$2 Sheet of 4		16.00	13.50
a.	Single stamp		4.00	2.00
	Sheet of 4 with major double transfer on right stamp		90.00	—
	Major double transfer, single stamp		—	—
	Sheet of 4 with minor double transfer on right stamp		35.00	—
	Minor double transfer, single stamp		—	—

CHINESE NEW YEAR

Year of the
Boar — A2205

Designed by Clarence Lee.

Printed by Stamp Venturers.

PHOTOGRAVURE
Panes of 20

1994, Dec. 30	Tagged		Perf. 11.2x11.1	
2876 A2205	29c multicolored		.70	.20
	P# block of 4, 5#+S		3.00	—
	Pane of 20		15.00	—

See No. 3895k.

The first class rate was increased to 32c on Jan. 1, 1995.

A2206

A2207

A2208

A2208a

A2209

Designed by Richard D. Sheaff (#2877-2878), Lou Nolan (#2879-2892).

Printed by American Bank Note Co. (#2877, 2884, 2890), Bureau of Engraving and Printing (#2879, 2881, 2883, 2889),

Stamp Venturers (#2878, 2880, 2882, 2888, 2891-2892), KCS Industries (#2885), Avery-Dennison (#2886-2887).

Coil Plate No. Strips of 3
Beginning with No. 2123, coil plate no. strips of 3 usually sell at the level of strips of 5 minus the face value of two stamps.

LITHOGRAPHED
Sheets of 100

1994, Dec. 13	Untagged		Perf. 11x10.8	
2877 A2206	(3c) tan, bright blue & red		.20	.20
	P# block of 4, 3#+A		.30	—
	Zip block of 4		.25	—
a.	Imperf., pair		150.00	—
b.	Double impression of red		175.00	—

No. 2877 imperf and with blue omitted is known from printer's waste.

		Perf. 10.8x10.9		
2878 A2206	(3c) tan, dark blue & red		.20	.20
	P# block of 4, 3#+S		.40	—
	Zip block of 4		.25	—

Inscriptions on #2877 are in a thin typeface. Those on #2878 are in heavy, bold type.

PHOTOGRAVURE
Tagged

		Perf. 11.2x11.1		
2879 A2207	(20c) black "G," yellow & multi		.40	.20
	P# block of 4, 5#		7.00	—
	Zip block of 4		1.75	—
a.	Imperf., pair		—	

		Perf. 11x10.9		
2880 A2207	(20c) red "G," yellow & multi		.75	.20
	P# block of 4, 5#+S		10.00	—
	Zip block of 4		3.25	—

		Perf. 11.2x11.1		
2881 A2208	(32c) black "G" & multi		1.00	.20
	P# block of 4, 4#		70.00	—
	Zip block of 4		5.50	—
a.	Booklet pane of 10		6.00	3.75

		Perf. 11x10.9		
2882 A2208a	(32c) red "G" & multi		.60	.20
	P# block of 4, 4#+S		4.00	—
	Zip block of 4		2.75	—

Distance on #2882 from bottom of red G to top of flag immediately above is 13¾mm. Illustration A2208a shows #2885 superimposed over #2882.

BOOKLET STAMPS
Perf. 10x9.9 on 2 or 3 Sides

2883 A2208	(32c) black "G" & multi		.65	.20
a.	Booklet pane of 10		6.50	3.75

Perf. 10.9 on 2 or 3 Sides

2884 A2208	(32c) blue "G" & multi		.65	.20
a.	Booklet pane of 10		6.50	3.75
b.	As "a," imperf		1,750.	

Perf. 11x10.9 on 2 or 3 Sides

2885 A2208a	(32c) red "G" & multi		.85	.20
a.	Booklet pane of 10		8.50	4.50
b.	Horiz. pair, imperf vert.		—	
c.	Horiz. pair, imperf between		—	

Distance on #2885 from bottom of red G to top of flag immediately above is 13½mm. See note below #2882.
No. 2885c resulted from a paper foldover after perforating and before cutting into panes.

A2208b

A2208c

Self-Adhesive			Die Cut	
2886 A2208b	(32c) gray, blue, light blue, red & black		.75	.20
a.	Booklet pane of 18		14.00	—
b.	Coil with plate # V11111		—	3.25
	P# strip of 5, same #		5.50	—

No. 2886 is printed on surface-tagged paper which is opaque, thicker and brighter than that of No. 2887 and has only a small number of blue shading dots in the white stripes immediately below the flag's blue field.
Except for No. 2886b with plate number, coil stamps are indistinguishable from booklet stamps once they are removed from the backing paper.

2887 A2208c	(32c) black, blue & red		.75	.20
a.	Booklet pane of 18		14.00	—

No. 2887 has noticeable blue shading in the white stripes immediately below the blue field and has overall tagging. The paper is translucent, thinner and duller than No. 2886.

COIL STAMPS
Perf. 9.8 Vert.

2888 A2209	(25c) black "G," blue & multi		.80	.50
	Pair		1.60	1.00
	P# strip of 5, #S11111		5.00	—
	P# single, #S11111		—	2.50
2889 A2208	(32c) black "G" & multi		1.50	.20
	Pair		3.00	.30

	P# strip of 5, #1111, 2222	11.50	
	P# single, #1111, 2222		6.00
a.	Imperf., pair	300.00	
2890 A2208	(32c) blue "G" & multi	.65	.20
	Pair	1.25	.30
	P# strip of 5, #A1111, A1112, A1113, A1211, A1212, A1311, A1313, A1324, A2211, A2212, A2213, A2214, A3113, A3314, A3323, A3324, A3433, A3435, A3436, A4427, A5327, A5417, A5427	5.00	
	P# strip of 5, #A1222, A1314, A4426, A5437	6.25	
	P# strip of 5, #A1417, A2223	9.00	
	P# strip of 5, #A1433	9.75	
	P# strip of 5, #A2313	10.00	
	P# strip of 5, #A3114, A3315, A3423	7.25	
	P# strip of 5, #A3426	7.25	
	P# strip of 5, #A4435	240.00	
	P# single, #A1111, A1313, A2214, A3113, A3314, A3324, A4427, A5427	—	1.00
	P# single, #A1212, A3323	—	3.00
	P# single, #A2212, A3435	—	3.50
	P# single, #A1112, A1311, A1324, A2213, A5327	—	2.50
	P# single, #A1113, A5437	—	3.75
	P# single, #A3315, A3423, A3426	—	4.75
	P# single, #A1222, A2211, A3114	—	4.25
	P# single, #A1211, A1314, A4426	—	4.00
	P# single, #A1417, A1433	—	6.75
	P# single, #A2223, A2313	—	6.00
	P# single, #A3433, A3436	—	2.00
	P# single, #A4435	—	225.00
	P# single, #A5417	—	3.00
2891 A2208	(32c) red "G" & multi	.85	.20
	Pair	1.70	.30
	P# strip of 5, #S1111	5.75	
	P# single, #S1111	—	1.00

Rouletted 9.8 Vert.

2892 A2208	(32c) red "G" & multi	.75	.20
	Pair	1.50	.30
	P# strip of 5, #S1111, S2222	6.00	
	P# single, #S1111, S2222	—	1.00

See note under No. 2525.

A2210

Flag Over
Porch — A2212

Designed by Lou Nolan (#2893), Dave LaFleur (#2897).

Printed by American Bank Note Co. (#2893), Stamp Venturers (#2897).

PHOTOGRAVURE
COIL STAMP

1995	Untagged		Perf. 9.8 Vert.	
2893 A2210	(5c) green & multi		.30	.20
	Pair		.60	.20
	P# strip of 5, #A11111, A21111		2.50	—
	P# single, #A11111, A21111		—	1.50

No. 2893 was only available through the Philatelic Fullfillment Center (and, for a short time, at the L'Enfant Plaza Philatelic Center in Washington, DC) after its announcement 1/12/95. Covers submitted for first day cancels received a 12/13/94 cancel, even though the stamps were not available on that date.

Sheets of 400 in four panes of 100

1995	Tagged		Perf. 10.4	
2897 A2212	32c multicolored, low gloss gum		.65	.20
	P# block of 4, 5#+S		4.25	—
	Very low gloss gum		.65	
	P# block of 4, 5#+S		4.25	
a.	Imperf., vert. pair		70.00	

See Nos. 2913-2916D, 2920-2921, 3133. For booklet see No. BK243.

Butte — A2217

Mountain — A2218

Auto — A2220

Auto Tail
Fin — A2223

Juke Box — A2225

Flag Over
Field — A2230

Designed by Tom Engeman (#2902-2904B), Robert Brangwynne (#2905-2906), Chris Calle (#2907), Bill Nelson (#2908-2912B), Dave LaFleur (#2913-2916, 2921), Sabra Field (#2919).

Printed by J.W. Fergusson & Sons for Stamp Venturers (#2902, 2905, 2909, 2912, 2914), Bureau of Engraving and Printing (#2903, 2904B, 2908, 2911, 2912B, 2913, 2915A, 2915C-2915D, 2919, 2921), Stamp Venturers (#2902B, 2904, 2906-2907, 2910, 2912A, 2915B), Avery Dennison (#2904A, 2915, 2919, 2920).

Coil Plate No. Strips of 3
Beginning with No. 2123, coil plate No. strips of 3 usually sell at the level of strips of 5 minus the face value of two stamps.

COIL STAMPS
PHOTOGRAVURE

1995-97	**Untagged**	*Perf. 9.8 Vert.*

Self-Adhesive (#2902B, 2904A-2904B, 2906-2907, 2910, 2912A, 2912B, 2915-2915D, 2919-2921)

2902	A2217	(5c) yellow, red & blue, Mar. 10	.20	.20
		Pair	.20	.20
		P# strip of 5, #S111, S222, S333	1.50	
		P# single, #S111, S222, S333	—	1.00
a.		Imperf., pair	650.00	

Serpentine Die Cut 11.5 Vert.

2902B	A2217	(5c) yellow, red & blue, June 15, 1996	.20	.20
		Pair	.20	
		P# strip of 5, #S111	1.50	
		P# single, #S111	—	1.10

Perf. 9.8 Vert.

2903	A2218	(5c) purple & multi, Mar. 16, 1996	.25	.20
		Pair	.50	.20
		P# strip of 5, #11111	1.50	
		P# single, #11111	—	1.00
a.		Tagged (error)	4.00	3.50
		P# strip of 5, #11111	85.00	
		P# single, #11111	—	72.50

Letters of inscription "USA NONPROFIT ORG." outlined in purple on #2903.

2904	A2218	(5c) blue & multi, Mar. 16, 1996	.20	.20
		Pair	.40	.20
		P# strip of 5, #S111	1.50	
		P# single, #S111	—	1.00
c.		Imperf., pair	450.00	

Letters of inscription have no outline on #2904.

Serpentine Die Cut 11.2 Vert.

2904A	A2218	(5c) purple & multi, June 15, 1996	.20	.20
		Pair	.40	
		P# strip of 5, #V222222, V333323, V333342	1.75	
		P# strip of 5, #V333333	1.60	
		P# strip of 5, #V333343	2.50	
		P# single, #V222222, V333323, V333333, V333342	—	1.25
		P# single, #V333343	—	2.10

Serpentine Die Cut 9.8 Vert.

2904B	A2218	(5c) purple & multi, Jan. 24, 1997	.20	.20
		pair	.40	
		P# strip of 5, #1111	1.50	
		P# single, #1111	—	1.25

Letters of inscription outlined in purple on #2904B, not outlined on No. 2904A.

Perf. 9.8 Vert.

2905	A2220	(10c) black, red brown & brown, small "1995" date, Mar. 10	.20	.20
		Pair	.40	.40
		P# strip of 5, #S111, S222	2.40	
		P# single, #S111, S222	—	1.75
a.		Large "1995" date, 1996	.20	.20
		Pair	.40	.40
		P# strip of 5, #S333	2.40	
		P# single, #S333	—	1.50

Date on 2905 is approximately 1.5mm long, on No. 2905a 2mm long.

Serpentine Die Cut 11.5 Vert.

2906	A2220	(10c) black, brown & red brown, June 15, 1996	.20	.20
		Pair	.40	
		P# strip of 5, #S111	2.50	
		P# single, #S111	—	1.75
2907	A1957	(10c) gold & multi, May 21, 1996	.35	.20
		Pair	.70	
		P# strip of 5, #S11111	3.00	
		P# single, #S11111	—	2.00

Perf. 9.8 Vert.

2908	A2223	(15c) dark orange yellow & multi, tagged, Mar. 17	.30	.30
		Pair	.60	.60
		P# strip of 5, #11111	3.00	
		P# single, #11111	—	2.00

No. 2908 has dark, bold colors, heavy shading lines and heavily shaded chrome.

2909	A2223	(15c) buff & multi, Mar. 17	.30	.30
		Pair	.60	.60
		P# strip of 5, #S11111	2.75	
		P# single, #S11111	—	1.75

No. 2909 has shinier chrome, more subdued colors and finer details than No. 2908.

Serpentine Die Cut 11.5 Vert.

2910	A2223	(15c) buff & multi, June 15, 1996	.30	.30
		Pair	.60	
		P# strip of 5, #S11111	2.90	
		P# single, #S11111	—	1.75

Perf. 9.8 Vert.

2911	A2225	(25c) dark red, dark yellow green & multi, tagged, Mar. 17	.50	.50
		Pair	1.00	1.00
		P# strip of 5, #111111, 212222, 222222	4.25	
		P# strip of 5, #332222	4.75	
		P# single, #111111, 212222, 222222	—	2.50
		P# single, #332222	—	3.00
a.		Imperf, pair	—	

No. 2911 has dark, saturated colors and dark blue lines in the music selection board.

2912	A2225	(25c) bright orange red, bright yellow green & multi, Mar. 17	.50	.50
		Pair	1.00	1.00
		P# strip of 5, #S11111, S22222	3.75	
		P# single, same #	—	2.25

No. 2912 has bright colors, less shading and light blue lines in the music selection board.

Serpentine Die Cut 11.5 Vert.

2912A	A2225	(25c) bright orange red, bright yellow green & multi, June 15, 1996	.50	.50
		Pair	1.00	
		P# strip of 5, #S11111, S22222	4.50	
		P# single, same #	—	2.10

Serpentine Die Cut 9.8 Vert.

2912B	A2225	(25c) dark red, dark yellow green & multi, Jan. 24, 1997	.65	.50
		pair	1.30	
		P# strip of 5, #111111	4.00	
		P# strip of 5, #222222	4.50	
		P# single, #111111, 222222	—	2.00

See No. 3132.

Tagged
Perf. 9.8 Vert.

2913	A2212	32c blue, tan, brown, red & light blue, shiny gum, May 19	.65	.20
		Pair	1.30	.30
		P# strip of 5, #11111, 22221	5.25	
		P# strip of 5, #22222	5.50	
		P# single, #11111, 22222	—	1.00
		P# single, #22221	—	3.50
		Low gloss gum	.65	
		Pair	1.30	
		P# strip of 5, #11111, 22222, 33333, 34333, 44444, 45444, 66646, 77767, 78767, 91161, 99969	5.00	

		P# strip of 5, #22322	12.00	
		P# strip of 5, #66666	11.00	
		P# single, #22322	—	6
		P# single, #33333, 34333, 44444, 45444, 66646, 77767	—	1
		P# single, #66666	—	8
		P# single, #78767, 91161, 99969	—	2
a.		Imperf., pair	35.00	

No. 2913 has pronounced light blue shading in the flag and red "1995" at left bottom. See No. 3133.

2914	A2212	32c blue, yellow brown, red & gray, May 19	.65	
		Pair	1.30	
		P# strip of 5, #S11111	4.50	
		P# single, #S11111	—	2

No. 2914 has pale gray shading in the flag and blue "1995" left bottom.

Serpentine Die Cut 8.7 Vert.

2915	A2212	32c multicolored, Apr. 18	1.25	
		Pair	2.50	
		P# strip of 5, #V11111	8.50	
		P# single, #V11111	—	4.

Serpentine Die Cut 9.8 Vert.

2915A	A2212	32c dk blue, tan, brown, red & light blue, May 21, 1996	.65	2
		Pair	1.30	
		P# strip of 5, #11111, 22222, 23222, 33333, 44444, 45444, 55555, 66666, 78777, 88888, 11111A, 13231A, 13311A, 22222A, 33333A, 44444A, 55555A, 66666A, 77777A, 78777A, 88888A, 99999	5.00	
		P# strip of 5, #87888	60.00	
		P# strip of 5, #87898	15.00	
		P# strip of 5, #88898	275.00	
		P# strip of 5, #89878, 97898	7.75	
		P# strip of 5, #89888	20.00	
		P# strip of 5, #89898	8.00	
		P# strip of 5, #89899	525.00	
		P# strip of 5, #99899	35.00	
		P# strip of 5, #13211A	80.00	
		P# single, #11111, 22222, 23222, 33333, 44444, 45444, 55555, 66666, 78777, 88888, 99999, 11111A, 13231A, 13311A, 22222A, 33333A, 44444A, 55555A, 66666A, 77777A, 78777A, 88888A	—	1.2
		P# single, #87888	—	25.00
		P# single, #87898, 89878, 97898	—	4.50
		P# single, #88898	—	75.00
		P# single, #89888	—	8.00
		P# single, #89898	—	2.75
		P# single, #89899	—	225.00
		P# single, #99899	—	32.50
		P# single, #13211A	—	75.00
h.		Die cutting omitted, pair	35.00	
i.		Tan omitted		2,000.
j.		Double die cutting	30.00	

No. 2915A has red "1996" at left bottom.

Die cutting on No. 2915A shows either 10 serpentine "peaks" on each side, 11 "peaks" on the left side and 10 "peaks" on the right side, or 10 "peaks" on the left side and 11 "peaks" on the right side. The last configuration is considered by specialists to be an error, and it is rare.

Sky on No. 2915A shows color gradation at LR not on No. 3133.

On No. 2915Ai all other colors except brown are severely shifted.

On No. 2915Aj, the second die cutting is a different gauge than normal 9.8.

Plate number 99999 strips of No. 2915A are known with the brown date number shifted one stamp to the right of the stamp with the other plate numbers. Such strips are scarce. Value of mint never hinged P# strip of 5 or 6, $750. Used examples are rare.

Serpentine Die Cut 11.5 Vert.

2915B	A2212	32c dk blue, tan, brown, red & light blue, June 15, 1996	1.00	.90
		Pair	2.00	
		P# strip of 5, #S11111	8.00	
		P# single, #S11111	—	2.75

Serpentine Die Cut 10.9 Vert.

2915C	A2212	32c dk blue, tan, brown, red & light blue, May 21, 1996	1.50	.40
		Pair	3.00	
		P# strip of 5, #55555, 66666	22.50	
		P# single, #55555, 66666	—	3.75
		P# single, #88888		

Plate number 55555 strips of No. 2915C are known with the tan plate number shifted one stamp to the left of the stamp with the other plate numbers. Extremely scarce. Last reported auction sale price (2006) was approximately $5,250.

Serpentine Die Cut 9.8 Vert.

2915D	A2212	32c dark blue, tan, brown, red & light blue, Jan. 24, 1997	1.75	.90
		pair	3.50	
		P# strip of 5, #11111	9.00	
		P# single, #11111	—	3.25

No. 2915D shows 9 "peaks" at left and 10 at right or 10 "peaks" at left and 10 at right.

Beach Clean-Up
A2269

Designed by Christy Millard (#2951), Jennifer Michalove (#2952), Brian Hailes (#2953) and Melody Kiper (#2954).
Printed by Ashton-Potter (USA) Ltd.

LITHOGRAPHED
Sheets of 96 in six panes of 16

1995, Apr. 20		Tagged	Perf. 11.1x11	
2951	A2266	32c multicolored	.65	.20
2952	A2267	32c multicolored	.65	.20
2953	A2268	32c multicolored	.65	.20
2954	A2269	32c multicolored	.65	.20
a.		Block of 4, #2951-2954	2.60	1.75
		P# block of 4, 5#+P	2.60	
		Horiz. P# block of 8, 2 sets of 5#+P, + top or bottom label	5.25	—
		Pane of 16	10.50	—

A2270 A2271

RICHARD M. NIXON
37th President (1913-94)

Designed by Daniel Schwartz.
Printed by Barton Press and Bank Note Corp. of America.

LITHOGRAPHED & ENGRAVED
Sheets of 200 in four panes of 50

1995, Apr. 26		Tagged	Perf. 11.2	
2955	A2270	32c multicolored	.65	.20
		P# block of 4, 5#+B	3.00	
a.		Red (engr.) missing (CM)	1,250.	

No. 2955 is known with red (engr. "Richard Nixon") inverted, and with red engr. omitted but only half the Nixon portrait present, both from printer's waste. No. 2955a shows a complete Nixon portrait.

BLACK HERITAGE SERIES
Bessie Coleman (d. 1926), Aviator

Designed by Chris Calle.

ENGRAVED
Sheets of 200 in four panes of 50

1995, Apr. 27		Tagged	Perf. 11.2	
2956	A2271	32c red & black	.75	.20
		P# block of 4, 1#	3.25	—

LOVE

A2272 A2273

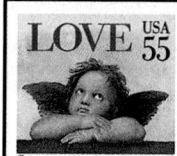

Cherubs from Sistine Madonna, by Raphael — A2274

Designed by Terry McCaffrey.
Printed by Bureau of Engraving and Printing (#2957-2959), Bank Note Corp. of America (#2960).

LITHOGRAPHED & ENGRAVED
Sheets of 300 in six panes of 50

1995, May 12		Tagged	Perf. 11.2	
2957	A2272	32c multicolored	.65	.20
		P# block of 4, 5#	3.00	
		Copyright block of 6	4.25	—

Compare with No. 3030. For booklet see No. BK244.

2958	A2273	55c multicolored	1.10	.20
		P# block of 4, 5#	5.50	—

BOOKLET STAMPS
Perf. 9.8x10.8

2959	A2272	32c multicolored	.65	.20
a.		Booklet pane of 10	6.50	3.25
b.		Imperf, pair	—	

Self-Adhesive
Die Cut

2960	A2274	55c multicolored	1.10	.20
a.		Booklet pane of 20 + label	22.50	

RECREATIONAL SPORTS

Volleyball
A2275

Softball
A2276

Bowling
A2277

Tennis
A2278

Golf — A2279

Designed by Don Weller.
Printed by Bank Note Corp. of America.

LITHOGRAPHED
Sheets of 120 in six panes of 20

1995, May 20		Tagged	Perf. 11.	
2961	A2275	32c multicolored	.65	.2
2962	A2276	32c multicolored	.65	.2
2963	A2277	32c multicolored	.65	.2
2964	A2278	32c multicolored	.65	.2
2965	A2279	32c multicolored	.65	.2
a.		Vert. strip of 5, #2961-2965	3.25	2.0
		P# block of 10, 2 sets of 4#+B	6.50	
		Pane of 20	13.00	—
b.		As "a," imperf	2,500.	
c.		As "a," yellow omitted	2,250.	
d.		As "a," yellow, blue & magenta omitted	2,250.	

PRISONERS OF WAR & MISSING IN ACTION

A2280

Designed by Carl Herrman.
Printed by Ashton-Potter (USA) Ltd.

LITHOGRAPHED
Sheets of 160 in eight panes of 20

1995, May 29		Tagged	Perf. 11.2	
2966	A2280	32c multicolored	.65	.20
		P# block of 4, 5#+P	2.50	—
		Pane of 20	12.50	—

The five plate numbers do not include a sixth plate number for the plate that applied a transparent laquer "color."

LEGENDS OF HOLLYWOOD

Marilyn Monroe (1926-62) — A2281

Cross Gutter Block of 8

Illustration reduced.

Designed by Michael Deas.
Printed by Stamp Venturers.

PHOTOGRAVURE
Sheets of 120 in six panes of 20

1995, June 1		Tagged	Perf. 11.1	
2967	A2281	32c multicolored	.85	.20
		P# block of 4, 6#+S	5.50	—
		Pane of 20	25.00	
		Sheet of 120 (six panes)	150.00	—
		Cross gutter block of 8	55.00	
		Block of 8 with vertical gutter	45.00	—

	Horiz. pair with vert. gutter	7.50	—
	Vert. pair with horiz. gutter	4.00	—
a.	Imperf., pair	550.00	
	Pane of 20, imperf.	5,750.	

Perforations in corner of each stamp are star-shaped.

TEXAS STATEHOOD

A2282

Designed by Laura Smith.
Printed by Sterling Sommer for Ashton-Potter (USA) Ltd.

LITHOGRAPHED
Sheets of 120 in six panes of 20

		1995, June 16	**Tagged**	**Perf. 11.2**	
2968	A2282	32c **multicolored**		.75	.20
		P# block of 4, 6#+P		3.00	—
		Pane of 20		15.00	—

GREAT LAKES LIGHTHOUSES

Split Rock, Lake
Superior — A2283

St. Joseph, Lake
Michigan — A2284

Spectacle Reef, Lake
Huron — A2285

Marblehead, Lake
Erie — A2286

Thirty Mile Point, Lake
Ontario — A2287

Designed by Howard Koslow.
Printed by Stamp Venturers.

PHOTOGRAVURE
BOOKLET STAMPS

		1995, June 17	**Tagged**	**Perf. 11.2 Vert.**	
2969	A2283	32c **multicolored**		1.00	.30
2970	A2284	32c **multicolored**		1.00	.30
2971	A2285	32c **multicolored**		1.00	.30
2972	A2286	32c **multicolored**		1.00	.30
2973	A2287	32c **multicolored**		1.00	.30
a.		Booklet pane of 5, #2969-2973		5.00	3.00

U.N., 50th ANNIV.

A2288

Designed by Howard Paine.
Printed by Banknote Corp. of America.

ENGRAVED
Sheets of 180 in nine panes of 20

		1995, June 26	**Tagged**	**Perf. 11.2**	
2974	A2288	32c **blue**		.65	.20
		P# block of 4, 1#+B		2.60	—
		Pane of 20		13.00	—

CIVIL WAR

A2289

Illustration reduced.

Designed by Mark Hess.

Printed by Stamp Venturers.

Designs: a, Monitor and Virginia. b, Robert E. Lee. c, Clara Barton. d, Ulysses S. Grant. e, Battle of Shiloh. f, Jefferson Davis. g, David Farragut. h, Frederick Douglass. i, Raphael Semmes. j, Abraham Lincoln. k, Harriet Tubman. l, Stand Watie. m, Joseph E. Johnston. n, Winfield Hancock. o, Mary Chesnut. p, Battle of Chancellorsville. q, William T. Sherman. r, Phoebe Pember. s, "Stonewall" Jackson. t, Battle of Gettysburg.

PHOTOGRAVURE
Sheets of 120 in six panes of 20

		1995, June 29	**Tagged**	**Perf. 10.1**	
2975	A2289	Pane of 20		35.00	17.50
a.-t.		32c any single		1.50	.60
		Sheet of 120 (6 panes)		200.00	
		Cross gutter block of 20		42.50	—
		Vert. pairs with horiz. gutter (each)		5.00	—
		Horiz. pairs with vert. gutter (each)		5.00	—
u.		As No. 2975, a.-e. imperf, f.-j. part perf		—	
v.		As No. 2975, k.-t. imperf, f.-j. part perf		—	
w.		As No. 2975, imperf		1,500.	
x.		Block of 9 (f.-h., k.-m., p.-r.) k.-l. & p.-q. imperf. vert.		—	

Cross gutter block of 20 consists of six stamps from each of two panes and four stamps from each of two other panes with the cross gutter between.

AMERICAN FOLK ART SERIES
Carousel Horses

A2290

A2291

A2292

A2293

Designed by Paul Calle.
Printed at Sterling Sommer for Ashton-Potter (USA) Ltd.

LITHOGRAPHED
Sheets of 160 in eight panes of 20

		1995, July 21	**Tagged**	**Perf. 11**	
2976	A2290	32c **multicolored**		.65	.20
2977	A2291	32c **multicolored**		.65	.20
2978	A2292	32c **multicolored**		.65	.20
2979	A2293	32c **multicolored**		.65	.20
a.		Block of 4, #2976-2979		2.60	2.00
		P# block of 4, 5#+P		2.60	—
		Pane of 20		13.00	—

WOMAN SUFFRAGE

A2294

Designed by April Greiman.
Printed by Ashton-Potter (USA) Ltd.

LITHOGRAPHED & ENGRAVED
Sheets of 160 in four panes of 40

		1995, Aug. 26	**Tagged**	**Perf. 11.1x11**	
2980	A2294	32c **multicolored**		.65	.20
		P# block of 4, 5#+P		3.00	—
a.		Black (engr.) omitted		400.00	
b.		Imperf., pair		1,500.	

No. 2980a is valued in the grade of fine. Very fine examples exist and sell for much more.

WORLD WAR II

A2295

Illustration reduced.

Designed by Bill Bond.

Designs and events of 1945: a, Marines raise flag on Iwo Jima. b, Fierce fighting frees Manila by March 3, 1945. c, Soldiers advancing (Okinawa, the last big battle). d, Destroyed bridge (US and Soviets link up at Elbe River). e, Allies liberate Holocaust survivors. f, Germany surrenders at Reims. g, Refugees (By 1945, World War II has uprooted millions). h, Truman announces Japan's surrender. i, Sailor kissing nurse (News of victory hits home). j, Hometowns honor their returning veterans.

Central label is size of 15 stamps and shows world map with extent of Axis control and Allied operations.

LITHOGRAPHED & ENGRAVED
Plates of eight subjects in four panes of 2 each

1995, Sept. 2	Tagged		Perf. 11.1	
2981 A2295	Block of 10		12.50	7.50
	Pane of 20		25.00	—
a.-j.	32c any single		1.25	.50

No. 2981 has selvage at left and right and either top or bottom.

AMERICAN MUSIC SERIES

Louis Armstrong (1901-71) A2296

Coleman Hawkins (1904-69) A2297

James P. Johnson (1894-1955) A2298

Jelly Roll Morton (1890-1941) A2299

Charlie Parker (1920-55) A2300

Eubie Blake (1883-1983) A2301

Charles Mingus (1922-79) A2302

Thelonious Monk (1917-82) A2303

John Coltrane (1926-67) A2304

Erroll Garner (1921-77) A2305

Designed by Dean Mitchell (#2982-2984, 2987, 2989, 2991-2992) and Thomas Blackshear (others).

Printed by Ashton-Potter (USA) Ltd. (#2982), Sterling Sommer for Ashton-Potter (USA) Ltd. (#2983-2992).

LITHOGRAPHED
Plates of 120 in six panes of 20

1995		Tagged		Perf. 11.1x11	
2982 A2296	32c	white denomination, Sept. 1		.80	.20
		P# block of 4, 4#+P		3.20	—
		Pane of 20		16.00	—
a.		Imperf, pair			
2983 A2297	32c	multicolored, Sept. 16		1.20	.20
2984 A2296	32c	black denomination, Sept. 16		1.20	.20
2985 A2298	32c	multicolored, Sept. 16		1.20	.20
2986 A2299	32c	multicolored, Sept. 16		1.20	.20
2987 A2300	32c	multicolored, Sept. 16		1.20	.20
2988 A2301	32c	multicolored, Sept. 16		1.20	.20
2989 A2302	32c	multicolored, Sept. 16		1.20	.20
2990 A2303	32c	multicolored, Sept. 16		1.20	.20
2991 A2304	32c	multicolored, Sept. 16		1.20	.20
2992 A2305	32c	multicolored, Sept. 16		1.20	.20
a.		Vert. block of 10, #2983-2992		12.00	—
		P# block of 10		15.00	—
		Pane of 20		30.00	—
b.		Pane of 20, dark blue (inscriptions) omitted		—	
c.		Imperf pair of Nos. 2991-2992		—	

GARDEN FLOWERS

Aster A2306

Chrysanthemum A2307

Dahlia — A2308

Hydrangea — A2309

Rudbeckia — A2310

Designed by Ned Seidler.

LITHOGRAPHED & ENGRAVED
BOOKLET STAMPS

1995, Sept. 19		Tagged	Perf. 10.9 Vert.	
2993 A2306	32c	multicolored	.65	.20
2994 A2307	32c	multicolored	.65	.20
2995 A2308	32c	multicolored	.65	.20
2996 A2309	32c	multicolored	.65	.20
2997 A2310	32c	multicolored	.65	.20
a.		Booklet pane of 5, #2993-2997	3.25	2.25
b.		As "a," imperf		

EDDIE RICKENBACKER (1890-1973), AVIATOR

A2311

Designed by Davis Meltzer.

PHOTOGRAVURE
Panes of 50

1995, Sept. 25		Tagged	Perf. 11¼	
2998 A2311	60c	multicolored, small "1995" year date	1.40	.50
		P# block of 4, 5#	9.00	—
a.		Large "1995" date, Oct., 1999	2.00	.50
		P# block of 4, 5#	12.00	—

Date on No. 2998 is 1mm long, on No. 2998a 1½mm long.

REPUBLIC OF PALAU

A2312

Designed by Herb Kane.
Printed by Sterling Sommer for Ashton-Potter (USA) Ltd.

LITHOGRAPHED
Sheets of 200 in four panes of 50

1995, Sept. 29	Tagged	Perf. 11.1
2999 A2312 32c multicolored		.65 .20
P# block of 4, 5#+P		3.00 —

See Palau Nos. 377-378.

COMIC STRIPS

A2313

Illustration reduced.

Designed by Carl Herrman.

Printed by Stamp Venturers.

Designs: a, The Yellow Kid. b, Katzenjammer Kids. c, Little Nemo in Slumberland. d, Bringing Up Father. e, Krazy Kat. f, Rube Goldberg's Inventions. g, Toonerville Folks. h, Gasoline Alley. i, Barney Google. j, Little Orphan Annie. k, Popeye. l, Blondie. m, Dick Tracy. n, Alley Oop. o, Nancy. p, Flash Gordon. q, Li'l Abner. r, Terry and the Pirates. s, Prince Valiant. t, Brenda Starr, Reporter.

PHOTOGRAVURE
Sheets of 120 in six panes of 20

1995, Oct. 1	Tagged	Perf. 10.1
3000 A2313 Pane of 20		13.00 10.00
a.-t. 32c any single		.65 .50
Sheet of 120 (6 panes)		105.00
Cross gutter block of 20		35.00 —
Vert. pairs with horiz. gutter (each)		3.75 —
Horiz. pairs with vert. gutter (each)		3.75 —
u. As No. 3000, a.-h. imperf., i.-l. part perf		—
v. As No. 3000, m.-t. imperf., i.-l. part perf		—
w. As No. 3000, a.-l. imperf.,m.-t. imperf vert.		—
x. As No. 3000, imperf		—

Inscriptions on back of each stamp describe the comic strip.
Cross gutter block of 20 consists of six stamps from each of two panes and four stamps from each of two other panes with the cross gutter between.

U.S. NAVAL ACADEMY, 150th ANNIVERSARY

A2314

Designed by Dean Ellis. Printed by Sterling-Sommer for Aston-Potter (USA) Ltd.

LITHOGRAPHED
Sheets of 160 in eight panes of 20

1995, Oct. 10	Tagged	Perf. 10.9
3001 A2314 32c multicolored		.65 .20
P# block of 4, 5#+P		2.60 —
Pane of 20		13.00 —

LITERARY ARTS SERIES

Tennessee Williams (1911-83)
A2315

Designed by Michael Deas. Printed by Sterling-Sommer for Ashton-Potter (USA) Ltd.

LITHOGRAPHED
Sheets of 160 in eight panes of 20

1995, Oct. 13	Tagged	Perf. 11.1
3002 A2315 32c multicolored		.65 .20
P# block of 4, 5#+P		2.60 —
Pane of 20		13.00 —

CHRISTMAS

Madonna and Child, by Giotto di Bondone — A2316

Santa Claus Entering Chimney — A2317

Child Holding Jumping Jack — A2318

Child Holding Tree — A2319

Santa Claus Working on Sled — A2320

Midnight Angel — A2321

Children Sledding — A2322

Designed by Richard Sheaff (#3003), John Grossman & Laura Alders (#3004-3018).

Printed by Bureau of Engraving and Printing (#3003), Sterling-Sommer for Ashton-Potter (USA) Ltd. (#3004-3007), Avery Dennison (#3008-3011, 3013-3017), Banknote Corporation of America (#3012, 3018).

LITHOGRAPHED & ENGRAVED
Sheets of 300 in six panes of 50

1995	Tagged	Perf. 11.2
3003 A2316 32c multicolored, Oct. 19		.65 .20
c. Black (engr., denomination) omitted		225.00

BOOKLET STAMP
Perf. 9.8x10.9

3003A A2316 32c multicolored, Oct. 19		.65 .20
b. Booklet pane of 10		6.50 4.00

LITHOGRAPHED
Sheets of 200 in four panes of 50
Perf. 11.25

3004 A2317 32c multicolored, Sept. 30		.65 .20
3005 A2318 32c multicolored, Sept. 30		.65 .20
3006 A2319 32c multicolored, Sept. 30		.65 .20
3007 A2320 32c multicolored, Sept. 30		.65 .20
a. Block or strip of 4, #3004-3007		2.60 1.25
P# block of 4, 4#+P		3.00 —
b. Booklet pane of 10, 3 each #3004-3005, 2 each #3006-3007		6.50 4.00
c. Booklet pane of 10, 2 each #3004-3005, 3 each #3006-3007		6.50 4.00
d. As "a," imperf		600.00

PHOTOGRAVURE
Self-Adhesive Stamps
Serpentine Die Cut 11.25 on 2, 3 or 4 sides

3008 A2320 32c multicolored, Sept. 30		.85 .20
3009 A2318 32c multicolored, Sept. 30		.85 .20
3010 A2317 32c multicolored, Sept. 30		.85 .20
3011 A2319 32c multicolored, Sept. 30		.85 .20
a. Booklet pane of 20, 5 each #3008-3011 + label		17.50

LITHOGRAPHED
Serpentine Die Cut 11.3x11.6 on 2, 3 or 4 sides

3012 A2321 32c multicolored, Oct. 19		.65 .20
a. Booklet pane of 20 + label		13.00
b. Vert. pair, die cutting omitted between		—
c. Booklet pane of 15 + label, 1996		10.00
d. Booklet pane of 15		45.00

No. 3012a comes either with no die cutting in the label (1995 printing) or with the die cutting (and deeper colors) from the 1996 printing.
No. 3012d is a pane of 16 with one stamp removed. The missing stamp can be from either row 1, 2, 3, 7 or 8 of the pane. No. 3012d cannot be made from No. 3012c, a pane of 15 + label. The label is die cut. If the label is removed, an impression of the die cutting appears on the backing paper.

PHOTOGRAVURE
Die Cut

3013 A2322 32c multicolored, Oct. 19		.65 .20
a. Booklet pane of 18		12.00
b. As "a," tagging omitted		—

Self-Adhesive Coil Stamps
Serpentine Die Cut 11.2 Vert.

3014 A2320 32c multicolored, Sept. 30		1.00 .30
3015 A2318 32c multicolored, Sept. 30		1.00 .30
3016 A2317 32c multicolored, Sept. 30		1.00 .30
3017 A2319 32c multicolored, Sept. 30		1.00 .30
a. Strip of 4, #3014-3017		4.00
P# strip of 5, 1 each #3014-3017 + 1 stamp, P#V1111		10.00
P# strip of 8, 2 each #3014-3017, P#V1111		22.50
P# single (#3017), #V1111		— 3.00

LITHOGRAPHED
Serpentine Die Cut 11.6 Vert.

3018 A2321 32c multicolored, Oct. 19		.80 .30
P# strip of 5, #B1111		7.50
P# single, #B1111		— 3.00

Nos. 3014-3018 were only available through the Philatelic Fullfillment Center in Kansas City.
Nos. 3005-3006 have "USA" printed in green. It is red on the self-adhesive stamps.

ANTIQUE AUTOMOBILES

1893 Duryea A2323

1894 Haynes A2324

1898 Columbia A2325

1899 Winton A2326

1901 White A2327

Designed by Ken Dallison.
Printed by Stamp Venturers.

PHOTOGRAVURE
Sheets of 200 in eight panes of 25

1995, Nov. 3	Tagged	Perf. 10.1x11.1		
3019	A2323 32c multicolored		.90	.20
3020	A2324 32c multicolored		.90	.20
3021	A2325 32c multicolored		.90	.20
3022	A2326 32c multicolored		.90	.20
3023	A2327 32c multicolored		.90	.20
a.	Vert. or horiz. strip of 5, #3019-3023		4.50	2.00
	Vert. or Horiz. P# block of 10, 2 sets of 4#+S		10.00	—
	Pane of 25		24.00	—

Vert. and horiz. strips are all in different order.

UTAH STATEHOOD CENTENARY

Delicate Arch, Arches Natl. Park — A2328

Designed by McRay Magleby.
Printed by Sterling Sommer for Ashton-Potter (USA) Ltd.

LITHOGRAPHED
Sheets of 200 in four panes of 50

1996, Jan. 4	Tagged	Perf. 11.1		
3024	A2328 32c multicolored		.75	.20
	P# block of 4, 5#+P		3.50	—

For booklet see No. BK245.

GARDEN FLOWERS

Crocus — A2329

Winter Aconite — A2330

Pansy — A2331

Snowdrop — A2332

Anemone — A2333

Designed by Ned Seidler.

LITHOGRAPHED & ENGRAVED
BOOKLET STAMPS

1996, Jan. 19	Tagged	Perf. 10.9 Vert.		
3025	A2329 32c multicolored		.75	.20
3026	A2330 32c multicolored		.75	.20
3027	A2331 32c multicolored		.75	.20
3028	A2332 32c multicolored		.75	.20
3029	A2333 32c multicolored		.75	.20
a.	Booklet pane of 5, #3025-3029		3.75	2.50
b.	As "a," imperf.			

LOVE

Cherub from Sistine Madonna, by Raphael — A2334

Designed by Terry McCaffrey.
Printed by Banknote Corporation of America.

LITHOGRAPHED & ENGRAVED
BOOKLET STAMP
Serpentine Die Cut 11.3x11.7

1996, Jan. 20		Tagged		
Self-Adhesive				
3030	A2334 32c multicolored		.65	.20
a.	Booklet pane of 20 + label		13.00	
b.	Booklet pane of 15 + label		10.00	
c.	Red (engr.) omitted		225.00	

d.	Red (engr.) missing (CM)		—	
e.	Double impression of red (engr.)		—	
f.	Die cutting omitted, pair		300.00	

No. 3030d must be collected se-tenant with a stamp bear the red engraving.

FLORA AND FAUNA SERIES
Kestrel, Blue Jay and Rose Types of 1993-95 an

Red-headed Woodpecker A2335

Eastern Bluebird A2336

Red Fox — A2339

Ring-necked Pheasant — A2350

Coral Pink Rose — A2351

Designed by Michael Matherly (#3031-3033, 3044-3045 Terry McCaffrey (#3050-3051, 3055); Derry Noyes (#3036 3052, 3052E).
Printed by Banknote Corporation of America (#3031A, 3036 Bureau of Engraving & Printing (#3031-3033, 3044-3045 Stamp Venturers (#3048-3049, 3053); Avery Dennison (#3050 3051A). American Packaging Corp. for Sennett Security Prod ucts (#3052); Sennett Security Products (#3052E).

LITHOGRAPHED
Sheets of 300 in six panes of 50 (#3031).
Sheets of 400 in eight panes of 50 (#3031A).
Sheets of 400 in four panes of 100 (#3032-3033).
Sheets of 120 in six panes of 20 (#3036).
Sheets of 200 in ten panes of 20 (#3036a)

1996-2002	Untagged	Serpentine Die Cut 10½		
	Self-Adhesive (#3031, 3031A)			
3031	A1841 1c multicolored, Nov. 19, 1999		.20	.20
	P# block of 4, 4# or 4# + A		.25	
	Serpentine Die Cut 11¼			
3031A	A1841 1c multicolored, Oct. 2000		.20	.20
	P# block of 4, 6# + B		.20	
b.	Die cutting omitted, pair			

No. 3031A has blue inscription and year.

	Perf. 11			
3032	A2335 2c multicolored, Feb. 2		.20	.20
	P# block of 4, 5#		.25	—
3033	A2336 3c multicolored, Apr. 3		.20	.20
	P# block of 4, 5#		.25	—

Some plate blocks contain plate position diagram.

	Tagged			
	Serpentine Die Cut 11½x11¼			
	Self-Adhesive			
3036	A2339 $1 multicolored, Aug. 14, 1998		2.00	.50
	P# block of 4, 4#+B		8.00	
	Pane of 20		40.00	
a.	Serpentine die cut 11¾x11, 2002		2.75	.50
	P# block of 4, 4#+B		11.00	
	Pane of 20		55.00	

The tagging of No. 3036 has a bright yellow-green appear ance under shortwave ultraviolet light while that of No. 3036a appears light blue green.

COIL STAMPS
Untagged
Perf. 9¾ Vert.

3044	A1841 1c multicolored, small date, Jan. 20		.20	.20
	Pair		.20	.20
	P# strip of 5, #1111 in black, yellow, blue, magenta order		.60	
	P# single, same			.40
	P# strip of 5, #1111 in black, blue, yellow, magenta order		.95	

	P# single, same	— .65
a.	Large date	.20 .20
	Pair	.20 .20
	P# strip of 5, #1111, 2222, 3333, 4444 in yellow, magenta, blue, black order	.85
	P# strip of 5, same	.55

Date on No. 3044 is 1mm long, on No. 3044a 1.5mm long.

Untagged

045	A2335	2c	multicolored, *June 22, 1999*	.20 .20
		Pair		.20 .20
		P# strip of 5, #11111		.80 —
		P# strip of 5, #22222		1.90 —
		P# single, #11111		— .65
		P# single, #22222		— .75

BOOKLET STAMPS
PHOTOGRAVURE
Serpentine Die Cut 10.4x10.8 on 3 Sides

1996-2000   **Tagged**

Self-Adhesive

048	A1847	20c	multicolored, *Aug. 2, 1996*	.40 .20
a.		Booklet pane of 10		4.00
b.		Booklet pane of 4		22.50
c.		Booklet pane of 6		37.50

Nos. 3048b-3048c are from the vending machine booklet No. BK237 that has a glue strip at the top edge of the top pane, the peelable strip removed and the rouletting line 2mm lower than on No. 3048a on some booklets, when the panes are compared with bottoms aligned. Vending booklets with plate #52222 always have gauge 8½ rouletting on booklet covers. Convertible booklets (No. 3048a) with plate #52222 always have gauge 12½ rouletting on booklet covers. Vending booklets with plate #51111 can have eith 8½ or 12½ gauge rouletting on booklet cover, and it may be impossible to tell a vending booklet with 12½ gauge rouletting and plate #51111 from a convertible booklet with peelable strip removed.

Serpentine Die Cut 11.3x11.7 on 2, 3 or 4 Sides

3049	A1853	32c	yellow, orange, green & black, *Oct. 24, 1996*	.65 .20
a.		Booklet pane of 20 + label		13.00
b.		Booklet pane of 4, *Dec. 1996*		2.60
c.		Booklet pane of 5 + label, *Dec. 1996*		3.50
		P# single, #S1111		.85 1.00
d.		Booklet pane of 6, *Dec. 1996*		4.00
		Booklet pane of 6 containing		
		P# single		6.00
		P# single, #S1111		2.50 1.00

The plate # single in No. 3049c is on the lower left stamp. In No. 3049d it is the lower right stamp on the bottom pane of the booklet.

Serpentine Die Cut 11.2 on 3 Sides

3050	A2350	20c	multicolored, *July 31, 1998*	.50 .20
a.		Booklet pane of 10, all stamps upright		5.00
b.		Serpentine die cut 11		1.25 .20
c.		As "b," booklet pane of 10, all stamps upright		12.50

Serpentine Die Cut 10½x11 on 3 Sides

3051	A2350	20c	multicolored, *July 1999*	.60 .20

No. 3051 represents the eight upright stamps on the booklet panes Nos. 3051Ab and 3051Ac. The two stamps turned sideways on those panes are No. 3051A.

Specialists should note that 3051 can be either die cut 10.4 at top and 10.6 at bottom or 10.6 at top and 10.4 at bottom. These two varieties exist in equal numbers.

Serpentine Die Cut 10.6x10.4 on 3 Sides

3051A	A2350	20c	multicolored,	4.50 .50
b.		Booklet pane of 5, 4 #3051, 1 #3051A turned sideways at top		7.50
c.		Booklet pane of 5, 4 #3051, 1 #3051A turned sideways at bottom		7.50

Serpentine Die Cut 11½x11¼ on 2, 3 or 4 Sides

3052	A2351	33c	multicolored, *Aug. 13, 1999*	.90 .20
a.		Booklet pane of 4		3.60
b.		Booklet pane of 5 + label		4.50
c.		Booklet pane of 6		5.50
d.		Booklet pane of 20 + label		17.50
j.		Die cutting omitted, pair		—

Serpentine Die Cut 10¾x10½ on 2 or 3 sides

3052E	A2351	33c	multicolored, *Apr. 7, 2000*	.65 .20
f.		Booklet pane of 20		13.00
g.		Black ("33 USA," etc.) omitted		400.00
h.		As "f," all 12 stamps on one side with black omitted		—
i.		Horiz. pair, die cutting omitted between		—

No. 3052Ef is a double-sided booklet pane with 12 stamps on one side and 8 stamps plus label on the other side.

COIL STAMPS
Serpentine Die Cut 11½ Vert.

3053	A1847	20c	multicolored, *Aug. 2, 1996*	.50 .20
		Pair		1.00
		P# strip of 5, #S1111		3.25
		P# single, #S1111		— 2.00

Yellow Rose, Ring-necked Pheasant Types of 1996-98

Printed by Bureau of Engraving and Printing (#3054-3055).

COIL STAMPS
LITHOGRAPHED

1997-98   **Tagged**   *Serpentine Die Cut 9¾ Vert.*
Self-Adhesive

3054	A1853	32c	yellow, magenta, black & green, *Aug. 1, 1997*	.65 .20
		Pair		1.30
		P# strip of 5, #1111, 1112, 1122, 2222, 2223, 2333, 3344, 4455, 5455, 5555, 5556, 5566, 5666, 6666		5.25
		P# strip of 5, #2233, 3444, 6677, 6777		6.75
		P# strip of 5, #7777, 8888		5.75
		P# single, #1111, 1112, 1122, 4455, 5555, 5556, 5566, 5666, 6666, 7777		— 2.00
		P# single, #2222, 2333		— 2.50
		P# single, #2223, 8888		— 2.75
		P# single, #2233, 3444		— 3.50
		P# single, #3344, 5455, 6677		— 3.50
		P# single, #6777		— 5.50
a.		Die cutting omitted, pair		90.00
b.		Black, yellow & green omitted		—
c.		Black, yellow & green omitted, die cutting omitted, pair		—
d.		Black omitted		—
e.		Black omitted, die cutting omitted, pair		—
f.		All colors omitted, die cutting omitted		—
g.		Pair, die cutting omitted, containing one stamp each of "c" and "e"		—

Nos. 3054b and 3054d also are miscut and with shifted die cuttings.

No. 3054f must be collected se-tenant with a partially printed stamp(s).

3055	A2350	20c	multicolored, *July, 31, 1998*	.40 .20
		Pair		.80
		P# strip of 5, P#1111, 2222		3.50
		P# single, same		— 2.25
a.		Die cutting omitted, pair		200.00

BLACK HERITAGE SERIES

Ernest E. Just (1883-1941), Marine Biologist — A2358

Designed by Richard Sheaff.
Printed by Banknote Corporation of America.

LITHOGRAPHED
Sheets of 160 in eight panes of 20

1996, Feb. 1			**Tagged**	**Perf. 11.1**
3058	A2358	32c	gray & black	.65 .20
		P# block of 4, 4#+B		2.60 —
		Pane of 20		13.00 —

SMITHSONIAN INSTITUTION, 150TH ANNIVERSARY

A2359

Designed by Tom Engeman.
Printed by Ashton-Potter (USA) Ltd.

LITHOGRAPHED
Sheets of 160 in eight panes of 20

1996, Feb. 7			**Tagged**	**Perf. 11.1**
3059	A2359	32c	multicolored	.65 .20
		P# block of 4, 4#+P		2.60 —
		Pane of 20		13.00 —

CHINESE NEW YEAR

Year of the Rat — A2360

Designed by Clarence Lee.
Printed by Stamp Venturers.

PHOTOGRAVURE
Sheets of 180 in nine panes of 20

1996, Feb. 8			**Tagged**	**Perf. 11.1**
3060	A2360	32c	multicolored	.90 .20
		P# block of 4, 4#+S		4.25 —
		Pane of 20		19.00 —
a.		Imperf., pair		800.00

See No. 3895a.

PIONEERS OF COMMUNICATION

Eadweard Muybridge (1830-1904), Photographer A2361

Ottmar Mergenthaler (1854-99), Inventor of Linotype A2362

Frederic E. Ives (1856-1937), Developer of Halftone Process A2363

William Dickson (1860-1935), Co-developer of Kinetoscope A2364

Designed by Fred Otnes.
Printed by Ashton-Potter USA.

LITHOGRAPHED
Sheets of 120 in six panes of 20

1996, Feb. 22			**Tagged**	**Perf. 11.1x11**
3061	A2361	32c	multicolored	.65 .20
3062	A2362	32c	multicolored	.65 .20
3063	A2363	32c	multicolored	.65 .20
3064	A2364	32c	multicolored	.65 .20
a.		Block or strip of 4, #3061-3064		2.60 2.00
		P# block of 4, 5#+P		2.60 —
		Pane of 20		13.00 —

FULBRIGHT SCHOLARSHIPS, 50th ANNIVERSARY

A2365

Designed by Richard D. Sheaff.

LITHOGRAPHED & ENGRAVED
Sheets of 200 in four panes of 50

1996, Feb. 28	Tagged	Perf. 11.1	
3065	A2365 32c **multicolored**	.75	.20
	P# block of 4, 5#	4.25	—

For booklet see No. BK246.

JACQUELINE COCHRAN (1910-80), PILOT

A2366

Designed by Davis Meltzer.

LITHOGRAPHED & ENGRAVED
Sheets of 300 in six panes of 50

1996, Mar. 9	Tagged	Perf. 11.1	
3066	A2366 50c **multicolored**	1.00	.40
	P# block of 4, 5#	5.00	—
a.	Black (engr.) omitted	60.00	

MARATHON

A2367

Designed by Michael Bartalos.

Printed by Banknote Corporation of America.

LITHOGRAPHED
Sheets of 160 in eight panes of 20

1996, Apr. 11	Tagged	Perf. 11.1	
3067	A2367 32c **multicolored**	.65	.20
	P# block of 4, 4#+B	2.60	—
	Pane of 20	13.00	—

1996 SUMMER OLYMPIC GAMES

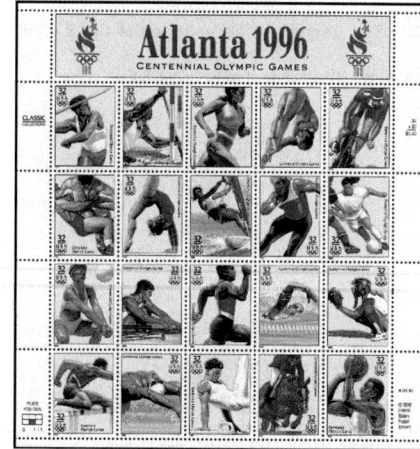

A2368

Illustration reduced.

Designed by Richard Waldrep. Printed by Stamp Venturers.

Designs: a, Decathlon (javelin). b, Men's canoeing. c, Women's running. d, Women's diving. e, Men's cycling. f, Freestyle wrestling. g, Women's gymnastics. h, Women's sailboarding. i, Men's shot put. j, Women's soccer. k, Beach volleyball. l, Men's rowing. m, Men's sprints. n, Women's swimming. o, Women's softball. p, Men's hurdles. q, Men's swimming. r, Men's gymnastics (pommel horse). s, Equestrian. t, Men's basketball.

PHOTOGRAVURE
Sheets of 120 in six panes of 20

1996, May 2	Tagged	Perf. 10.1	
3068	A2368 Pane of 20	13.00	10.00
a.-t.	32c any single	.65	.50
	Sheet of 120 (6 panes)	120.00	
	Cross gutter block of 20	45.00	—
	Vert. pairs with horiz. gutter (each)	4.00	—
	Horiz. pairs with vert. gutter (each)	4.00	—
u.	As No. 3068, imperf	1,250.	
v.	As No. 3068, back inscriptions omitted on a., f., k. & p., incorrect back inscriptions on others	—	

Inscription on back of each stamp describes the sport shown. Cross gutter block of 20 consists of six stamps from each of two panes and four stamps from each of two other panes with the cross gutter between.

GEORGIA O'KEEFFE (1887-1986)

A2369

Designed by Margaret Bauer. Printed by Stamp Venturers.

PHOTOGRAVURE
Sheets of 90 in six panes of 15

1996, May 23	Tagged	Perf. 11.6x11.4	
3069	A2369 32c **multicolored**	.85	.20
	P# block of 4, 5#+S	5.00	—
	Pane of 15	14.50	9.00
a.	Imperf., pair	150.00	
	Pane of 15, imperf.	1,250.	—

For booklet see No. BK247.

TENNESSEE STATEHOOD BICENTENNIAL

A2370

Designed by Phil Jordan. Printed by Stamp Venturers.

PHOTOGRAVURE
Sheets of 200 in four panes of 50.

1996, May 31	Tagged	Perf. 11.1	
3070	A2370 32c **multicolored**	.65	.20
	P# block of 4, 5#+S	3.00	—

For booklet see No. BK248.

Booklet Stamp
Self-Adhesive
Serpentine Die Cut 9.9x10.8

3071	A2370 32c **multicolored**	.70	.30
a.	Booklet pane of 20, #S11111	14.00	
b.	Horiz. pair, die cutting omitted btwn.	—	
c.	Die cutting omitted, pair	—	
d.	Horiz. pair, die cutting omitted vert.	—	—

AMERICAN INDIAN DANCES

Fancy — A2371   Butterfly — A2372

Traditional — A2373   Raven — A2374

Hoop — A2375

Designed by Keith Birdsong. Printed by Ashton-Potter (USA) Ltd.

LITHOGRAPHED
Sheets of 120 in six panes of 20.

996, June 7	Tagged	Perf. 11.1
072 A2371 32c multicolored	.80	.20
073 A2372 32c multicolored	.80	.20
074 A2373 32c multicolored	.80	.20
075 A2374 32c multicolored	.80	.20
076 A2375 32c multicolored	.80	.20
a. Strip of 5, #3072-3076	4.00	2.50
P# block of 10, 4#+P	10.00	—
Pane of 20	20.00	—

For booklet see No. BK249.

PREHISTORIC ANIMALS

Eohippus
A2376

Woolly
Mammoth
A2377

Mastodon
A2378

Saber-tooth
Cat — A2379

Designed by Davis Meltzer. Printed by Ashton-Potter (USA) Ltd.

LITHOGRAPHED
Sheets of 120 in six panes of 20

1996, June 8	Tagged	Perf. 11.1x11
3077 A2376 32c multicolored	.65	.20
3078 A2377 32c multicolored	.65	.20
3079 A2378 32c multicolored	.65	.20
3080 A2379 32c multicolored	.65	.20
a. Block or strip of 4, #3077-3080	2.60	2.00
P# block of 4, 4#+P	2.60	—
Pane of 20	13.00	—

A2380

A2381

BREAST CANCER AWARENESS
Designed by Tom Mann. Printed by Ashton-Potter (USA) Ltd.

LITHOGRAPHED
Sheets of 120 in six panes of 20

1996, June 15	Tagged	Perf. 11.1
3081 A2380 32c multicolored	.65	.20
P# block of 4, 5#+P	2.60	—
Pane of 20	13.00	—

LEGENDS OF HOLLYWOOD
James Dean (1931-55)

Designed by Michael Deas.

Printed by Stamp Venturers.

PHOTOGRAVURE
Sheets of 120 in six panes of 20.

1996, June 24	Tagged	Perf. 11.1
3082 A2381 32c multicolored	.65	.20
P# block of 4, 7#+S	4.00	—
Pane of 20	18.50	10.00
Sheet of 120 (six panes)	110.00	
Cross gutter block of 8	30.00	—
Block of 8 with vertical gutter	20.00	—
Horiz. pair with vert. gutter	4.75	—
Vert. pair with horiz. gutter	3.00	—
a. Imperf., pair	200.00	
Pane of 20, imperf.	2,250.	
b. As "a," red (USA 32c) missing (CM) and tan (JAMES DEAN) omitted	—	
c. As "a," tan (JAMES DEAN) omitted	—	
d. As "a," top stamp red missing (CM) and tan (JAMES DEAN) omitted, bottom stamp tan omitted	—	

Perforations in corner of each stamp are star-shaped. No. 3082 was also available on the first day of issue in at least 127 Warner Bros. Studio stores.

Cross-gutter block consists of 3 stamps vertically from 2 upper panes and 1 stamp each from 2 lower panes.

For booklet see No. BK250.

Nos. 3082b-3082d come from the same error pane. The top row is No. 3082b; rows 2-4 are No. 3082c. No. 3082d is a vertical pair with one stamp from No. 3082b at top and one stamp from No. 3082c at bottom.

FOLK HEROES

A2382

A2383

A2384

A2385

Designed by David LaFleur.

Printed by Ashton-Potter (USA) Ltd.

LITHOGRAPHED
Sheets of 120 in six panes of 20

1996, July 11	Tagged	Perf. 11.1x11
3083 A2382 32c multicolored	.65	.20
3084 A2383 32c multicolored	.65	.20
3085 A2384 32c multicolored	.65	.20
3086 A2385 32c multicolored	.65	.20
a. Block or strip of 4, #3083-3086	2.60	2.00
P# block of 4, 4#+P	2.60	—
Pane of 20	13.00	—

For booklet see No. BK251.

Myron's
Discobolus — A2386

Young Corn, by Grant
Wood — A2387

CENTENNIAL OLYMPIC GAMES
Designed by Carl Herrman.

Printed by Ashton-Potter (USA) Ltd.

ENGRAVED
Sheets of 80 in four panes of 20

1996, July 19	Tagged	Perf. 11.1
3087 A2386 32c brown	.80	.20
P# block of 4, 1#+P	4.50	—
Pane of 20	21.50	10.00

Sheet margin of the pane of 20 is lithographed.
For booklet see No. BK252.

IOWA STATEHOOD, 150TH ANNIVERSARY
Designed by Carl Herrman.

Printed by Ashton-Potter (USA) Ltd. (#3088), Banknote Corporation of America (#3089).

LITHOGRAPHED
Sheets of 200 in four panes of 50

1996, Aug. 1	Tagged	Perf. 11.1
3088 A2387 32c multicolored	.80	.20
P# block of 4, 4#+P	3.75	—

For booklet see No. BK253.

BOOKLET STAMP
Self-Adhesive
Serpentine Die Cut 11.6x11.4

3089 A2387 32c multicolored	.70	.30
a. Booklet pane of 20	14.00	

RURAL FREE DELIVERY, CENT.

A2388

Designed by Richard Sheaff.

LITHOGRAPHED & ENGRAVED
Sheets of 120 in six panes of 20

1996, Aug. 7	Tagged	Perf. 11.2x11
3090 A2388 32c multicolored	.65	.20
P# block of 4, 5#	2.60	—
Pane of 20	13.00	—

For booklet see No. BK254.

RIVERBOATS

Robt. E.
Lee — A2389

Sylvan
Dell — A2390

Far West
A2391

Rebecca
Everingham
A2392

Bailey Gatzert
A2393

Designed by Dean Ellis.

Printed by Avery Dennison.

PHOTOGRAVURE
Sheets of 200 in 10 panes of 20
Serpentine Die Cut 11x11.1

1996, Aug. 22　　　　　　　　　**Tagged**

Self-Adhesive

3091	A2389	32c	**multicolored**	.65	.20
3092	A2390	32c	**multicolored**	.65	.20
3093	A2391	32c	**multicolored**	.65	.20
3094	A2392	32c	**multicolored**	.65	.20
3095	A2393	32c	**multicolored**	.65	.20
a.	Vert. strip of 5, #3091-3095			3.25	
	P# block of 10, 5#+V			6.50	
	Pane of 20			13.00	
b.	Strip of 5, #3091-3095, with special				
	die cutting			*80.00*	*50.00*
	P# block of 10, 5#+V			*160.00*	
	Pane of 20			*320.00*	

The serpentine die cutting runs through the peelable backing to which Nos. 3091-3095 are affixed. No. 3095a exists with stamps in different sequences.

On the long side of each stamp in No. 3095b, the die cutting is missing 3 "perforations" between the stamps, one near each end and one in the middle. This allows a complete strip to be removed from the backing paper for use on a first day cover. No. 3095b was also used to make Souvenir Page No. 1215.

For booklet see No. BK255.

AMERICAN MUSIC SERIES
Big Band Leaders

Count Basie
A2394

Tommy &
Jimmy Dorsey
A2395

Glenn Miller
A2396

Benny
Goodman
A2397

Songwriters

Harold Arlen
A2398

Johnny Mercer
A2399

Dorothy Fields
A2400

Hoagy
Carmichael
A2401

Designed by Bill Nelson (#3096-3099), Gregg Rudd (#3100-3103).

Printed by Ashton-Potter (USA) Ltd.

LITHOGRAPHED
Sheets of 120 in six panes of 20

1996, Sept. 11　　　**Tagged**　　　*Perf. 11.1x11*

3096	A2394	32c	**multicolored**	.65	.20
3097	A2395	32c	**multicolored**	.65	.20
3098	A2396	32c	**multicolored**	.65	.20
3099	A2397	32c	**multicolored**	.65	.20
a.	Block or strip of 4, #3096-3099			2.60	2.00
	P# block of 4, 6#+P			3.50	—
	P# block of 8, 2 sets of P# +				
	top label			6.75	—
	Pane of 20			17.00	—

3100	A2398	32c	**multicolored**	.70	
3101	A2399	32c	**multicolored**	.70	
3102	A2400	32c	**multicolored**	.70	
3103	A2401	32c	**multicolored**	.70	
a.	Block or strip of 4, #3100-3103			2.80	2.
	P# block of 4, 6#+P			3.00	
	P# block of 8, 2 sets of P# +				
	top label			5.75	
	Pane of 20			15.00	

LITERARY ARTS SERIES

F. Scott
Fitzgerald
(1896-1940)
A2402

Designed by Michael Deas.

PHOTOGRAVURE
Sheets of 200 in four panes of 50

1996, Sept. 27　　　**Tagged**　　　*Perf. 11.*

3104	A2402	23c	**multicolored**	.55	.2
	P# block of 4, 4#			4.00	—

ENDANGERED SPECIES

A2403

Illustration reduced.

Designed by James Balog. Printed by Ashton-Potter (USA) Ltd.

Designs: a, Black-footed ferret. b, Thick-billed parrot. c, Hawaiian monk seal. d, American crocodile. e, Ocelot. f, Schaus swallowtail butterfly. g, Wyoming toad. h, Brown pelican. i, California condor. j, Gila trout. k, San Francisco garter snake. l, Woodland caribou. m, Florida panther. n, Piping plover. o, Florida manatee.

LITHOGRAPHED
Sheets of 90 in six panes of 15

1996, Oct. 2　　　**Tagged**　　　*Perf. 11.1x11*

3105	A2403	Pane of 15		10.50	8.00
a.-o.	32c any single			.70	.50

See Mexico No. 1995. For booklet see No. BK256.

COMPUTER TECHNOLOGY

A2404

Designed by Nancy Skolos & Tom Wedell.

Printed by Ashton-Potter (USA) Ltd.

LITHOGRAPHED & ENGRAVED
Sheets of 160 in four panes of 40

96, Oct. 8	Tagged	Perf. 10.9x11.1
06 A2404 32c multicolored		.65 .20
P# block of 4, 6#+P		3.00 —

CHRISTMAS

Madonna and Child from
Adoration of the Shepherds,
y Paolo de Matteis — A2405

Family at
Fireplace — A2406

Decorating
Tree — A2407

Dreaming of Santa
Claus — A2408

Holiday
Shopping — A2409

Skaters — A2410

Designed by Richard D. Sheaff (#3107, 3112), Julia Talcott (#3108-3111, 3113-3117).

Printed by Bureau of Engraving and Printing (#3107, 3112), Ashton-Potter (USA) Ltd. (#3108-3111), Banknote Corporation of America (#3113-3116), Avery-Dennison (#3117).

LITHOGRAPHED & ENGRAVED
Sheets of 300 in six panes of 50

1996	Tagged	Perf. 11.1x11.2
3107 A2405 32c multicolored, Nov. 1		.65 .20
P# block of 4, 5#		3.00 —

For booklet see No. BK257.

LITHOGRAPHED
Perf. 11.3

3108 A2406 32c multicolored, Oct. 8		.65 .20
3109 A2407 32c multicolored, Oct. 8		.65 .20
3110 A2408 32c multicolored, Oct. 8		.65 .20
3111 A2409 32c multicolored, Oct. 8		.65 .20
a.	Block or strip of 4, #3108-3111	2.60 1.75
	P# block of 4, 4#+P	3.00 —
b.	Strip of 4, #3110-3111, 3108-3109, with #3109 imperf., #3108 imperf. at right	—
c.	Strip of 4, #3108-3111, with #3111 imperf, #3110 imperf at right	—

BOOKLET STAMPS
Self-Adhesive

LITHOGRAPHED & ENGRAVED
Serpentine Die Cut 10 on 2, 3 or 4 Sides

3112 A2405 32c multicolored, Nov. 1		.65 .20
a.	Booklet pane of 20 + label	13.00
b.	Die cutting omitted, pair	75.00
c.	As "a," die cutting omitted	

LITHOGRAPHED
Serpentine Die Cut 11.8x11.5 on 2, 3 or 4 Sides

3113 A2406 32c multicolored, Oct. 8		.65 .20
3114 A2407 32c multicolored, Oct. 8		.65 .20
3115 A2408 32c multicolored, Oct. 8		.65 .20
3116 A2409 32c multicolored, Oct. 8		.65 .20
a.	Booklet pane of 20, 5 ea #3113-3116	13.00
b.	Strip of 4, #3113-3116, die cutting omitted	600.00
c.	Block of 6, die cutting omitted	800.00
d.	As "a," die cutting omitted	2,250.

PHOTOGRAVURE
Die Cut

3117 A2410 32c multicolored, Oct. 8		.65 .20
a.	Booklet pane of 18	12.00

HANUKKAH

A2411

Designed by Hannah Smotrich.

Printed by Avery Dennison.

PHOTOGRAVURE
Sheets of 200 in 10 panes of 20

1996, Oct. 22	Tagged	Serpentine Die Cut 11.1
Self-Adhesive		
3118 A2411 32c multicolored		.65 .20
P# block of 4, 5#+V		2.60
Pane of 20		13.00

Backing on No. 3118 is die cut with a continuous horizontal wavy line. The 1997 reprint is die cut with two short horizontal lines on each side of a semi-circle on the backing of each stamp.

See No. 3352, Israel No. 1289. For booklet see No. BK258.

CYCLING
Souvenir Sheet

A2412

Illustration reduced.

Designed by McRay Magleby.

Printed by Stamp Venturers.

PHOTOGRAVURE

1996, Nov. 1	Tagged	Perf. 11x11.1
3119 A2412	Sheet of 2	2.25 2.00
a.	50c orange & multi	1.10 1.00
b.	50c blue green & multi	1.10 1.00

CHINESE NEW YEAR

Year of the
Ox — A2413

Designed by Clarence Lee.

Printed by Stamp Venturers.

PHOTOGRAVURE
Sheets of 180 in 9 panes of 20

1997, Jan. 5	Tagged	Perf. 11.2
3120 A2413 32c multicolored		.80 .20
P# block of 4, 4#+S		3.20 —
Pane of 20		16.00

See No. 3895b.

BLACK HERITAGE SERIES

Brig. Gen. Benjamin O.
Davis, Sr. (1880-
1970) — A2414

Designed by Richard Sheaff.

Printed by Banknote Corp. of America.

LITHOGRAPHED
Sheets of 120 in six panes of 20

1997, Jan. 28	Tagged	Serpentine Die Cut 11.4
Self-Adhesive		
3121 A2414 32c multicolored		.65 .20
P# block of 4, 4#+B		2.60
Pane of 20		13.00

Statue of Liberty Type of 1994
Printed by Avery-Dennison.

PHOTOGRAVURE
Serpentine Die Cut 11 on 2, 3 or 4 Sides

1997, Feb. 1		Tagged
Self-Adhesive		
3122 A1951 32c red, light blue, dark blue & yellow		.65 .20
a.	Booklet pane of 20 + label	13.00
b.	Booklet pane of 4	2.60
c.	Booklet pane of 5 + label	3.50
	P# single, #V1111	.85 1.00
d.	Booklet pane of 6	4.00
	Booklet pane of 6 containing P# single	6.00
	P# single, #V1111	2.50 1.00
h.	As "a," die cutting omitted	

The plate # single in No. 3122c is the lower left stamp and should be collected unused with the reorder label to its right to differentiate it from the plate # single in No. 3122d which is the lower left stamp in the bottom pane of the booklet and should be collected with a normal stamp adjoining it at right. In used condition, these plate # singles are indistinguishable.

Serpentine Die Cut 11.5x11.8 on 2, 3 or 4 Sides

1997		Tagged
Self-Adhesive		
3122E A1951 32c red, light blue, dark blue & yellow		1.10 .20
f.	Booklet pane of 20 + label	35.00
g.	Booklet pane of 6	7.00
	Booklet pane of 6 containing P# single	12.50
	P# single, #V1111	5.00 2.00

The plate # single in No. 3122Eg is the lower left stamp in the bottom pane of the booklet.

LOVE

Swans

A2415   A2416

Designed by Marvin Mattelson.

Printed by Banknote Corp. of America.

LITHOGRAPHED
Serpentine Die Cut 11.8x11.6 on 2, 3 or 4 Sides

1997, Feb. 4		Tagged
Self-Adhesive		
3123 A2415 32c multicolored		.65 .20
a.	Booklet pane of 20 + label	13.00
b.	Die cutting omitted, pair	150.00
c.	As "a," die cutting omitted	1,500.
d.	As "a," black omitted	600.00

Serpentine Die Cut 11.6x11.8 on 2, 3 or 4 Sides

3124 A2416 55c multicolored		1.10 .20
a.	Booklet pane of 20 + label	22.00

HELPING CHILDREN LEARN

A2417

Designed by Chris Van Allsburg.

Printed by Avery-Dennison.

PHOTOGRAVURE
Sheets of 160 in eight panes of 20
Serpentine Die Cut 11.6x11.7

1997, Feb. 18   **Tagged**
Self-Adhesive

3125 A2417 32c **multicolored** .65 .20
    P# block of 4, 4#+V 2.60
    Pane of 20 13.00

The die cut perforations of #3125 are fragile and separate easily.

MERIAN BOTANICAL PRINTS

Citron, Moth, Larvae, Pupa, Beetle A2418

Flowering Pineapple, Cockroaches A2419

No. 3128 (r), No. 3129 (l), No. 3128a below

Designed by Phil Jordan based on works by Maria Sibylla Merian (1647-1717).

Printed by Stamp Venturers.

PHOTOGRAVURE
Serpentine Die Cut 10.9x10.2 on 2, 3 or 4 Sides
1997, Mar. 3   **Tagged**
Self-Adhesive

3126 A2418 32c **multicolored** .65 .20
3127 A2419 32c **multicolored** .65 .20
a.   Booklet pane, 10 ea #3126-3127 + label 13.00
b.   Pair, #3126-3127 1.30
c.   Vert. pair, die cutting omitted between 500.00

Size: 18.5x24mm
Serpentine Die Cut 11.2x10.8 on 2 or 3 Sides

3128 A2418 32c **multicolored** 1.00 .20
a.   See footnote 3.00 .25
b.   Booklet pane, 2 ea #3128-3129, 1 #3128a 7.00

3129 A2419 32c **multicolored** 1.00 .20
a.   See footnote 4.50 .35
b.   Booklet pane, 2 ea #3128-3129, 1 #3129a 9.00
c.   Pair, #3128-3129 2.00

Nos. 3128a-3129a are placed sideways on the pane and are serpentine die cut 11.2 on top and bottom, 10.8 on left side. The right side is 11.2 broken by a lsloping die cut where the stamp meets the vertical die cutting of the two stamps above it. See illustration above.

PACIFIC 97

Sailing Ship — A2420

Stagecoach — A2421

Designed by Richard Sheaff.

Printed by Banknote Corporation of America.

ENGRAVED
Sheets of 96 in six panes of 16
1997, Mar. 13   **Tagged**   *Perf. 11.2*
3130 A2420 32c blue .65 .20
3131 A2421 32c red .65 .20
a.   Pair, #3130-3131 1.30 .60
   P# block of 4, 1#+B 2.60
   Pane of 16 10.50 7.50
   Sheet of 96 (6 panes) 80.00
   Cross gutter block of 16 (8 #3131a) 30.00 —
   Vert. pairs with horiz. gutter (each) 10.00 —
   Horiz. pairs with vert. gutter (each) 5.00 —

Juke Box and Flag Over Porch Types of 1995
Designed by Bill Nelson (#3132), Dave LaFleur (#3133).

Printed by Stamp Venturers.

PHOTOGRAVURE
COIL STAMPS
1997, Mar. 14   **Untagged**   *Imperf.*
Self-Adhesive
3132 A2225 (25c) **bright orange red, bright yellow green & multi** 1.00 .50
   Pair 2.00
   P# strip of 5, #M11111 5.50
   P#, single, #M11111 2.50

Tagged
Serpentine Die Cut 9.9 Vert.
3133 A2212 32c **dark blue, tan, brown, red & light blue** .85 .20
   Pair 1.70
   P# strip of 5, #M11111 6.50
   P#, single, #M11111 3.75

Nos. 3132-3133 were issued without backing paper. No. 3132 has simulated perforations ending in black bars at the top and bottom edges of the stamp. Sky on No. 3133 shows color gradation at LR not on Nos. 2915A or 2915D, and it has blue "1996" at left bottom.

LITERARY ARTS SERIES

Thornton Wilder (1897-1975) A2422

Designed by Phil Jordan.

Printed by Ashton-Potter (USA) Ltd.

LITHOGRAPHED
Sheets of 180 in nine panes of 20
1997, Apr. 17   **Tagged**   *Perf. 11*
3134 A2422 32c **multicolored** .65
   P# block of 4, 4#+P 2.60
   Pane of 20 13.00

RAOUL WALLENBERG (1912-47)

Wallenberg and Jowich Refugees A2423

Designed by Howard Paine.

Printed by Sterling Sommer for Ashton-Potter (USA) Ltd.

LITHOGRAPHED
Sheets of 180 in nine panes of 20
1997, Apr. 24   **Tagged**   *Perf. 11*
3135 A2423 32c **multicolored** .65
   P# block of 4, 4#+P 2.60
   Pane of 20 13.00

DINOSAURS

A2424

Illustration reduced.

Designed by James Gurney.
Printed by Sterling Sommer for Ashton-Potter (USA) Ltd.

Designs: a, Ceratosaurus. b, Camptosaurus. c, Camarasaurus. d, Brachiosaurus. e, Goniopholis. f, Stegosaurus. g, Allosaurus. h, Opisthias. i, Edmontonia. j, Einiosaurus. k, Daspletosaurus. l, Palaeosaniwa. m, Corythosaurus. n, Ornithomimus. o, Parasaurolophus.

LITHOGRAPHED
1997, May 1   **Tagged**   *Perf. 11x11.1*
3136 A2424 Sheet of 15 10.00 8.00
a.-o.   32c any single .65 .50
p.   As No. 3136, bottom 7 stamps imperf. 4,000.
q.   As No. 3136, top 8 stamps imperf 4,000.
r.   As No. 3136, all colors and tagging missing (EP) —

No. 3136r resulted from double sheeting in the sheet-fed press. It is properly gummed and perforated.

BUGS BUNNY

A2425

Cross Gutter Block of 12

Illustration reduced.

Designed by Warner Bros.

Printed by Avery Dennison.

PHOTOGRAVURE

| 1997, May 22 | Tagged | Serpentine Die Cut 11 |
| | **Self-Adhesive** | |

137	Pane of 10		6.75	
a.	A2425 32c single		.65	.20
b.	Booklet pane of 9 #3137a		6.00	
c.	Booklet pane of 1 #3137a		.65	
	Sheet of 60 (six panes) top		375.00	
	Sheet of 60 (six panes) bottom, with			
	plate #		625.00	
	Pane of 10 from uncut press sheet		70.00	
	Pane of 10 with plate #		350.00	
	Cross gutter block of 9 or 10		200.00	
	Cross gutter block of 12		250.00	
	Vert. pair with horiz. gutter		25.00	
	Horiz. pair with vert. gutter		50.00	

Die cutting on #3137 does not extend through the backing paper.

Booklet pane of 10 with P# comes from bottom uncut sheet of 60.

Nos. 3137b-3137c and 3138b-3138c are separated by a vertical line of microperforations that are absent on the uncut sheet of 60.

The horiz. pair with vert. gutter consists of a stamp at the left, from No. 3137b, part of the illustration of Bugs Bunny, the small gutter between the panes, and a stamp at the right from the left row of 3137b. Some pairs may include the single stamp from No. 3137c in addition to the two stamps at the right and left.

3138	Pane of 10	140.00
a.	A2425 32c single	3.50
b.	Booklet pane of 9 #3138a	25.00
c.	Booklet pane of 1, no die cutting	100.00

Die cutting on #3138b extends through the backing paper.

An untagged promotional piece similar to No. 3137c exists on the same backing paper as the booklet pane, with the same design image, but without Bugs' signature and the single stamp. Replacing the stamp is an enlarged "32 / USA" in the same style as used on the stamp. This promotional piece was not valid for postage.

PACIFIC 97

Franklin — A2426   Washington — A2427

Designed by Richard Sheaff. Selvage on Nos. 3139-3140 is lithographed.

LITHOGRAPHED & ENGRAVED

1997		Tagged	Perf. 10.5x10.4	
3139	Pane of 12, May 29		12.00	9.00
a.	A2426 50c single		1.00	.50
3140	Pane of 12, May 30		14.50	11.00
a.	A2427 60c single		1.20	.60

Nos. 3139-3140 were sold through June 8.

MARSHALL PLAN, 50TH ANNIV.

Gen. George C. Marshall, Map of Europe
A2428

Designed by Richard Sheaff.

Printed by Stevens Security Press for Ashton-Potter (USA) Ltd.

LITHOGRAPHED & ENGRAVED
Sheets of 120 in six panes of 20

1997, June 4		Tagged	Perf. 11.1	
3141	A2428 32c multicolored		.65	.20
	P# block of 4, 5#+P		2.60	—
	Pane of 20		13.00	—

CLASSIC AMERICAN AIRCRAFT

A2429

Illustration reduced.

Designed by Phil Jordan.

Printed by Stamp Venturers.

Designs: a, Mustang. b, Model B. c, Cub. d, Vega. e, Alpha. f, B-10. g, Corsair. h, Stratojet. i, GeeBee. j, Staggerwing. k, Flying Fortress. l, Stearman. m, Constellation. n, Lightning. o, Peashooter. p, Tri-Motor. q, DC-3. r, 314 Clipper. s, Jenny. t, Wildcat.

PHOTOGRAVURE
Sheets of 120 in six panes of 20

1997, July 19		Tagged	Perf. 10.1	
3142	A2429 Pane of 20		13.00	10.00
a.-t.	32c any single		.65	.50
	Sheet of 120 (6 panes)		85.00	
	Cross gutter block of 20		22.50	
	Vert. pairs with horiz. gutter			
	(each)		2.40	—
	Horiz. pairs with vert. gutter			
	(each)		2.40	—

Inscriptions on back of each stamp describe the airplane.
Cross gutter block of 20 consists of six stamps from each of two panes and four stamps from each of two other panes with the cross gutter between.

FOOTBALL COACHES

Bear Bryant
A2430

Pop Warner
A2431

Vince Lombardi
A2432

George Halas
A2433

Designed by Carl Herrman.

Printed by Sterling Sommer for Ashton-Potter (USA) Ltd.

LITHOGRAPHED
Sheets of 120 in six panes of 20

1997		Tagged	Perf. 11.2	
3143	A2430 32c multicolored, July 25		.65	.20
3144	A2431 32c multicolored, July 25		.65	.20
3145	A2432 32c multicolored, July 25		.65	.20
3146	A2433 32c multicolored, July 25		.65	.20
a.	Block or strip of 4, #3143-3146		2.60	—
	P# block of 4, 5#+P		2.60	1.75
	P# block of 8, 2 sets of P# +			
	top label		5.25	—
	Pane of 20		13.00	

With Red Bar Above Coach's Name
Perf. 11

3147	A2432 32c multicolored, Aug. 5		.65	.30
	P# block of 4, 4#+P		3.00	—
	Pane of 20		14.50	—
3148	A2430 32c multicolored, Aug. 7		.65	.30
	P# block of 4, 4#+P		3.00	—
	Pane of 20		14.50	—
3149	A2431 32c multicolored, Aug. 8		.65	.30
	P# block of 4, 4#+P		3.00	—
	Pane of 20		14.50	—
3150	A2433 32c multicolored, Aug. 16		.65	.30
	P# block of 4, 4#+P		3.00	—
	Pane of 20		14.50	—

AMERICAN DOLLS

A2434

Illustration reduced.

Designed by Derry Noyes.

Printed by Sterling Sommer for Ashton-Potter (USA) Ltd.

Designs: a, "Alabama Baby," and doll by Martha Chase. b, "Columbian Doll." c, Johnny Gruelle's "Raggedy Ann." d, Doll by Martha Chase. e, "American Child." f, "Baby Coos." g, Plains Indian. h, Doll by Izannah Walker. i, "Babyland Rag." j, "Scootles." k, Doll by Ludwig Greiner. l, "Betsy McCall." m, Percy Crosby's "Skippy." n, "Maggie Mix-up." o, Dolls by Albert Schoenhut.

LITHOGRAPHED
Sheets of 90 in six panes of 15

1997, July 28		Tagged		Perf. 10.9x11.1
3151	A2434	Pane of 15	13.50	—
a.-o.		32c any single	.90	.60

For booklet see No. BK266.

A2435

A2436

LEGENDS OF HOLLYWOOD
Humphrey Bogart (1899-1957).

Designed by Carl Herrman.

Printed by Stamp Venturers.

PHOTOGRAVURE
Sheets of 120 in six panes of 20

1997, July 31		Tagged		Perf. 11.1
3152	A2435	32c **multicolored**	.85	.20
		P# block of 4, 5#+S	3.50	—
		Pane of 20	18.50	—
		Sheet of 120 (6 panes)	95.00	—
		Cross gutter block of 8	17.50	—
		Block of 8 with vertical gutter	13.50	—
		Horiz. pair with vert. gutter	3.50	—
		Vert. pair with horiz. gutter	2.50	—

Perforations in corner of each stamp are star-shaped. Cross-gutter block consists of 6 stamps from upper panes and 2 stamps from panes below.
For booklet see No. BK267.

"THE STARS AND STRIPES FOREVER!"
Designed by Richard Sheaff.

Sheets of 300 in six panes of 50
PHOTOGRAVURE

1997, Aug. 21		Tagged		Perf. 11.1
3153	A2436	32c **multicolored**	.65	.20
		P# block of 4, 4#	3.00	—

For booklet see No. BK268.

AMERICAN MUSIC SERIES
Opera Singers

Lily Pons — A2437

Richard Tucker
A2438

Lawrence Tibbett
A2439

Rosa Ponselle
A2440

Classical Composers & Conductors

Leopold Stokowski
A2441

Arthur Fiedler
A2442

George Szell — A2443

Eugene Ormandy
A2444

Samuel Barber
A2445

Ferde Grofé
A2446

Charles Ives — A2447

Louis Moreau Gottschalk
A2448

Designed by Howard Paine.

Printed by Ashton-Potter (USA) Ltd.

LITHOGRAPHED
Sheets of 120 in six panes of 20

1997		Tagged		Perf. 1
3154	A2437	32c **multicolored,** *Sept. 10*	.65	.2
3155	A2438	32c **multicolored,** *Sept. 10*	.65	.2
3156	A2439	32c **multicolored,** *Sept. 10*	.65	.2
3157	A2440	32c **multicolored,** *Sept. 10*	.65	.2
a.		Block or strip of 4, #3154-3157	2.60	2.0
		P# block of 4, 5#+P	2.60	
		P# block of 8, 2 sets of P# +		
		top label	5.00	—
		Pane of 20	12.50	—
3158	A2441	32c **multicolored,** *Sept. 12*	.75	.2
3159	A2442	32c **multicolored,** *Sept. 12*	.75	.2
3160	A2443	32c **multicolored,** *Sept. 12*	.75	.20
3161	A2444	32c **multicolored,** *Sept. 12*	.75	.20
3162	A2445	32c **multicolored,** *Sept. 12*	.75	.20
3163	A2446	32c **multicolored,** *Sept. 12*	.75	.20
3164	A2447	32c **multicolored,** *Sept. 12*	.75	.20
3165	A2448	32c **multicolored,** *Sept. 12*	.75	.20
a.		Block of 8, #3158-3165	6.00	4.00
		P# block of 8, 2 sets of 5P#+P		
		+ top label	9.00	—
		Pane of 20	20.00	

PADRE FÉLIX VARELA (1788-1853)

A2449

Designed by Carl Herrman.

Printed by Sterling Sommer for Ashton-Potter (USA) Ltd.

LITHOGRAPHED
Sheets of 120 in six panes of 20

1997, Sept. 15		Tagged		Perf. 11.2
3166	A2449	32c **purple**	.65	.20
		P# block of 4, 1#+P	2.60	—
		Pane of 20	13.00	—

DEPARTMENT OF THE AIR FORCE, 50TH ANNIV.

Thunderbirds Aerial Demonstration Squadron A2450

Designed by Phil Jordan.

Printed by Sterling Sommer for Ashton-Potter (USA) Ltd.

LITHOGRAPHED
Sheets of 180 in nine panes of 20

1997, Sept. 18	**Tagged**	***Perf. 11.2x11.1***	
3167 A2450	32c multicolored	.65	.20
	P# block of 4, 4#+P	2.60	—
	Pane of 20	13.00	—

A hidden 3-D design can be seen on the stamp when it is viewed with a special viewer sold by the post office.

CLASSIC MOVIE MONSTERS

Lon Chaney as The Phantom of the Opera — A2451

Bela Lugosi as Dracula — A2452

Boris Karloff as Frankenstein's Monster — A2453

Boris Karloff as The Mummy — A2454

Lon Chaney, Jr. as The Wolf Man — A2455

Cross Gutter Block of 8

Designed by Derry Noyes.

Printed by Stamp Venturers.

PHOTOGRAVURE
Sheets of 180 in nine panes of 20

1997, Sept. 30	**Tagged**	***Perf. 10.2***	
3168 A2451	32c multicolored	.75	.20
3169 A2452	32c multicolored	.75	.20
3170 A2453	32c multicolored	.75	.20
3171 A2454	32c multicolored	.75	.20
3172 A2455	32c multicolored	.75	.20
a.	Strip of 5, #3168-3172	3.75	2.25
	P# block of 10, 5#+S	7.50	—
	Pane of 20	15.00	—
	Sheet of 180 (9 panes)	130.00	
	Cross-gutter block of 8	17.50	
	Block of 10 with horiz. gutter	12.50	
	Vert. pairs with horiz. gutter (each)	2.50	—
	Horiz. pairs with vert. gutter (each)	2.50	—

Plate blocks may contain top label. See note after No. 3167. For booklet see No. BK269.

FIRST SUPERSONIC FLIGHT, 50TH ANNIV.

A2456

Designed by Phil Jordan.

Printed by Banknote Corporation of America.

LITHOGRAPHED
Sheets of 180 in nine panes of 20

1997, Oct. 14	**Tagged**	***Serpentine Die Cut 11.4***	
	Self-Adhesive		
3173 A2456	32c multicolored	.65	.20
	P# block of 4, 4#+B	2.60	
	Pane of 20	13.00	

WOMEN IN MILITARY SERVICE

A2457

Designed by Derry Noyes.

Printed by Banknote Corporation of America.

LITHOGRAPHED
Sheets of 120 in six panes of 20

1997, Oct. 18	**Tagged**	***Perf. 11.1***	
3174 A2457	32c multicolored	.65	.20
	P# block of 4, 6#+B	2.60	—
	Pane of 20	13.00	

KWANZAA

A2458

Designed by Synthia Saint James. Printed by Avery Dennison.

PHOTOGRAVURE
Sheets of 250 in five panes of 50

1997, Oct. 22	**Tagged**	***Serpentine Die Cut 11***	
	Self-Adhesive		
3175 A2458	32c multicolored	.65	.20
	P# block of 4, 4#+V	3.00	
	Sheet of 250 (5 panes)	550.00	
	P# block of 4, 4#+V and 4 sets of #+VO	225.00	
	Horiz. pair with vert. gutter	11.00	

See Nos. 3348, 3368, 3673.

CHRISTMAS

Madonna and Child, by Sano di Pietro — A2459

Holly — A2460

Designed by Richard D. Sheaff (#3176), Howard Paine (#3177).

Printed by Bureau of Engraving and Printing (#3176), Banknote Corporation of America (#3177).

LITHOGRAPHED
Serpentine Die Cut 9.9 on 2, 3 or 4 Sides

1997			**Tagged**
	Booklet Stamps		
	Self-Adhesive		
3176 A2459	32c multicolored, *Oct. 27*	.65	.20
a.	Booklet pane of 20 + label	13.00	

Serpentine Die Cut 11.2x11.8 on 2, 3 or 4 Sides

3177 A2460	32c multicolored, *Oct. 30*	.65	.20
a.	Booklet pane of 20 + label	13.00	
b.	Booklet pane of 4	2.60	
c.	Booklet pane of 5 + label	3.25	
d.	Booklet pane of 6	3.90	

MARS PATHFINDER
Souvenir Sheet

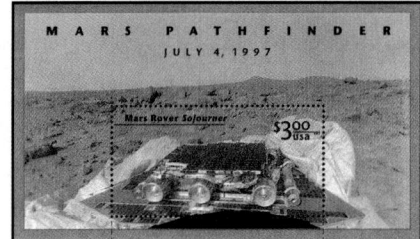

Mars Rover Sojourner — A2461

Illustration reduced.

Designed by Terry McCaffrey. Printed by Stamp Venturers.

PHOTOGRAVURE

1997, Dec. 10   **Tagged**   *Perf. 11x11.1*
3178 A2461 $3 **multicolored**   6.00 4.00
   a. $3, single stamp   5.50 3.00
   b.   Single souvenir sheet from sheet of 18   7.00 —
     Sheet of 18   125.00
     Vert. pair with horiz. gutter   15.00 —

The perforations at the bottom of the stamp contain the letters "USA." Vertical rouletting extends from the vertical perforations of the stamp to the bottom of the souvenir sheet.

Sheet of 18 has vertical perforations separating the three rows of souvenir sheets. These were cut away when No. 3178 was produced. Thus, the souvenir sheet from sheet of 18 is wider and has vertical perforations on one or two sides.

See note after No. 3167.

CHINESE NEW YEAR

Year of the Tiger
A2462

Designed by Clarence Lee. Printed by Stamp Venturers.

PHOTOGRAVURE
Sheets of 180 in nine panes of 20

1998, Jan. 5   **Tagged**   *Perf. 11.2*
3179 A2462 32c **multicolored**   .80 .20
    P# block of 4, 4#+S   3.75 —
    Pane of 20   18.00

See No. 3895c.

A2463   A2464

ALPINE SKIING
Designed by Michael Schwab.

Printed by Banknote Corporation of America.

LITHOGRAPHED
Sheets of 180 in nine panes of 20

1998, Jan. 22   **Tagged**   *Perf. 11.2*
3180 A2463 32c **multicolored**   .65 .20
    P# block of 4, 6#+B   2.60
    Pane of 20   13.00

BLACK HERITAGE SERIES
Madam C.J. Walker (1867-1919), Entrepreneur

Designed by Richard Sheaff. Printed by Banknote Corp. of America.

LITHOGRAPHED
Sheets of 180 in nine panes of 20
Serpentine Die Cut 11.6x11.3

1998, Jan. 28   **Tagged**
     Self-Adhesive
3181 A2464 32c **sepia & black**   .65 .20
    P# block of 4, 3#+B   2.60
    Pane of 20   13.00

CELEBRATE THE CENTURY

1900s — A2465

No. 3182: a, Model T Ford. b, Theodore Roosevelt. c, Motion picture "The Great Train Robbery," 1903. d, Crayola Crayons introduced, 1903. e, St. Louis World's Fair, 1904. f, Design used on Hunt's Remedy stamp (#RS56), Pure Food & Drug Act, 1906. g, Wright Brothers first flight, Kitty Hawk, 1903. h, Boxing match shown in painting "Stag at Sharkey's," by George Bellows of the Ash Can School. i, Immigrants arrive. j, John Muir, preservationist. k, "Teddy" Bear created. l, W.E.B. Du Bois, social activist. m, Gibson Girl. n, First baseball World Series, 1903. o, Robie House, Chicago, designed by Frank Lloyd Wright.

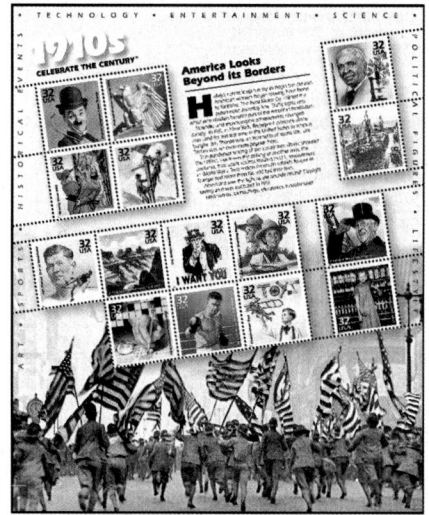

1910s — A2466

No. 3183: a, Charlie Chaplin as the Little Tramp. b, Federal Reserve System created, 1913. c, George Washington Carver. d, Avant-garde art introduced at Armory Show, 1913. e, First transcontinental telephone line, 1914. f, Panama Canal opens, 1914. g, Jim Thorpe wins decathlon at Stockholm Olympics, 1912. h, Grand Canyon National Park, 1919. i, U.S. enters World War I. j, Boy Scouts started in 1910, Girl Scouts formed in 1912. k, Woodrow Wilson. l, First crossword puzzle published, 1913. m, Jack Dempsey wins heavyweight title, 1919. n, Construction toys. o, Child labor reform.

1920s — A2467

No. 3184: a, Babe Ruth. b, The Gatsby style. c, Prohibition enforced. d, Electric toy trains. e, 19th Amendment (woman voting). f, Emily Post's Etiquette. g, Margaret Mead, anthropologist. h, Flappers do the Charleston. i, Radio entertains America. j, Art Deco style (Chrysler Building). k, Jazz flourishes. l, Four Horsemen of Notre Dame. m, Lindbergh flies the Atlantic. n, American realism (The Automat, by Edward Hopper). o, Stock Market crash, 1929.

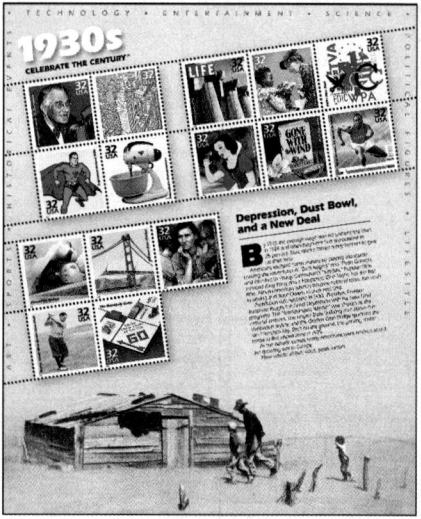

1930s — A2468

No. 3185: a, Franklin D. Roosevelt. b, The Empire State Building. c, 1st Issue of Life Magazine, 1936. d, Eleanor Roosevelt. e, FDR's New Deal. f, Superman arrives, 1938. g, Household conveniences. h, "Snow White and the Seven Dwarfs," 1937. i, "Gone with the Wind," 1936. j, Jesse Owens. k, Streamline design. l, Golden Gate Bridge. m, America survives the Depression. n, Bobby Jones wins golf Grand Slam, 1938. o, The Monopoly Game.

1940s — A2469

No. 3186: a, World War II. b, Antibiotics save lives. c, Jackie Robinson. d, Harry S Truman. e, Women support war effort. f, TV entertains America. g, Jitterbug sweeps nation. h, Jackson Pollock, Abstract Expressionism. i, GI Bill, 1944. j, Big Band Sound. k, Intl. style of architecture (UN Headquarters). l, Postwar baby boom. m, Slinky, 1945. n, "A Streecar Named Desire," 1947. o, Orson Welles' "Citizen Kane."

1950s — A2470

No. 3187: a, Polio vaccine developed. b, Teen fashions. c, The "Shot Heard 'Round the World." d, US launches satellites. e, Korean War. f, Desegregating public schools. g, Tail fins, chrome. h, Dr. Seuss' "The Cat in the Hat." i, Drive-in movies. j, World Series rivals. k, Rocky Marciano, undefeated boxer. l, "I Love Lucy." m, Rock 'n Roll. n, Stock car racing. o, Movies go 3-D.

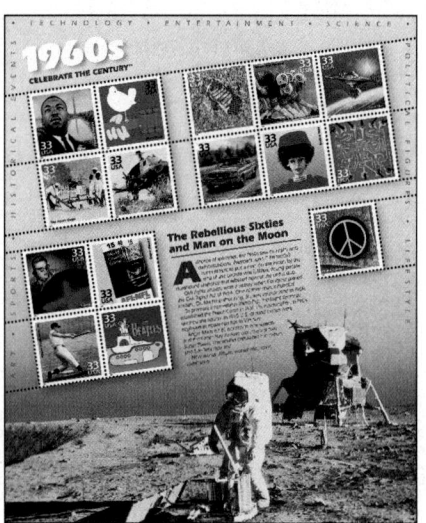

1960s — A2471

No. 3188: a, Martin Luther King, Jr., "I Have a Dream." b, Woodstock. c, Man walks on the moon. d, Green Bay Packers. e, Star Trek. f, The Peace Corps. g, Viet Nam War. h, Ford Mustang. i, Barbie Doll. j, Integrated circuit. k, Lasers. l, Super Bowl I. m, Peace symbol. n, Roger Maris, 61 in '61. o, The Beatles "Yellow Submarine."

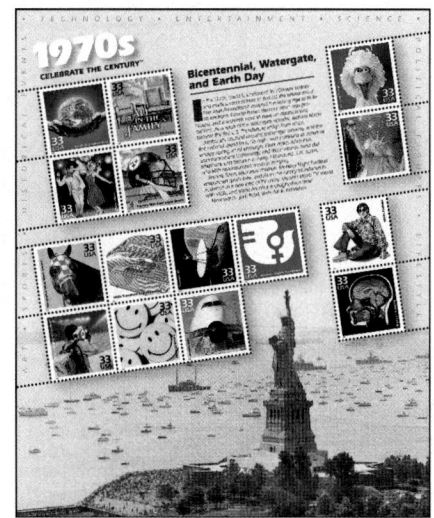

1970s — A2472

No. 3189: a, Earth Day celebrated. b, "All in the Family" television series. c, "Sesame Street" television series character, Big Bird. d, Disco music. e, Pittsburgh Steelers win four Super Bowls. f, US Celebrates 200th birthday. g, Secretariat wins Triple Crown. h, VCRs transform entertainment. i, Pioneer 10. j, Women's rights movement. k, 1970s fashions. l, "Monday Night Football." m, Smiley face buttons. n, Jumbo jets. o, Medical imaging.

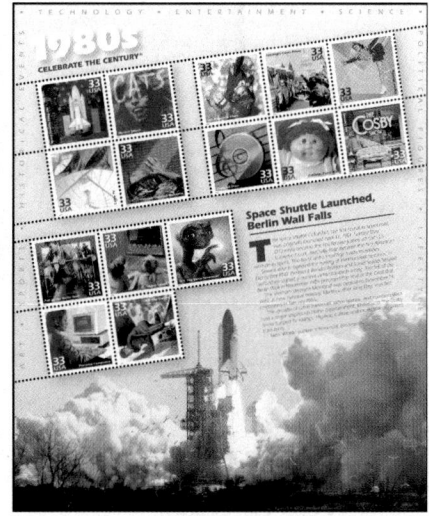

1980s — A2473

No. 3190: a, Space shuttle program. b, "Cats" Broadway show. c, San Francisco 49ers. d, Hostages in Iran come home. e, Figure skating. f, Cable TV. g, Vietnam Veterans Memorial. h, Compact discs. i, Cabbage Patch Kids. j, "The Cosby Show" television series. k, Fall of the Berlin Wall. l, Video games. m, "E. T. The Extra-Terrestrial" movie. n, Personal computers. o, Hip-hop culture.

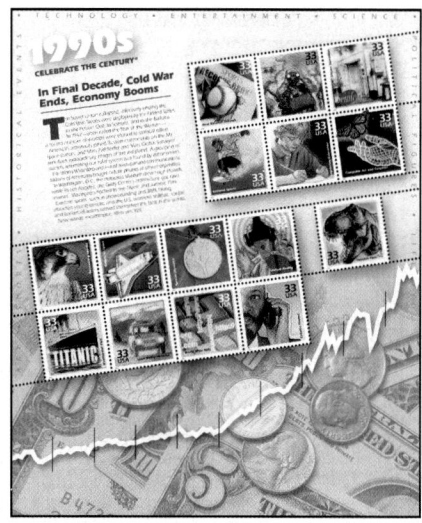

1990s — A2474

No. 3191: a, New baseball records. b, Gulf War. c, "Seinfeld" television series. d, Extreme sports. e, Improving education. f, Computer art and graphics. g, Recovering species. h, Return to space. i, Special Olympics. j, Virtual reality. k, Movie "Jurassic Park." l, Movie "Titanic." m, Sport utility vehicles. n, World Wide Web. o, Cellular phones.

Designed by Richard Waldrep (#3182), Dennis Lyall (#3183), Carl Herrman (#3184, 3188, 3190), Howard Paine (#3185-3187, 3189, 3191).

All illustrations reduced.

Printed by Ashton-Potter (USA) Ltd.

LITHOGRAPHED, ENGRAVED (#3182m, 3183f, 3184m, 3185b, 3186k, 3187a, 3188c, 3189h)

1998-2000		Tagged	Perf. 11½	
3182	A2465	Pane of 15, *Feb. 3, 1998*	11.50	8.50
a.-o.		32c any single	.75	.65
		Sheet of 4 panes	46.00	
p.		Engr. red (No. 3182m, Gibson girl) omitted, in pane of 15	—	
3183	A2466	Pane of 15, *Feb. 3, 1998*	11.50	8.50
a.-o.		32c any single	.75	.65
		Sheet of 4 panes	46.00	
p.		Nos. 3183g, 3183 l-3183o imperf, in pane of 15	1,250.	
3184	A2467	Pane of 15, *May 28, 1998*	11.50	8.50
a.-o.		32c any single	.75	.65
		Sheet of 4 panes	46.00	
3185	A2468	Pane of 15, *Sept. 10, 1998*	11.50	8.50
a.-o.		32c any single	.75	.65
		Sheet of 4 panes	46.00	
3186	A2469	Pane of 15, *Feb. 18, 1999*	12.00	8.50
a.-o.		33c any single	.80	.65
		Sheet of 4 panes	48.00	
p.		Tagging omitted on b-j and m-o	—	
3187	A2470	Pane of 15, *May 26, 1999*	12.00	8.50
a.-o.		33c any single	.80	.65
		Sheet of 4 panes	48.00	
p.		Tagging omitted	—	
3188	A2471	Pane of 15, *Sept. 17, 1999*	12.00	8.50
a.-o.		33c any single	.80	.65
		Sheet of 4 panes	48.00	
3189	A2472	Pane of 15, *Nov. 18, 1999*	12.00	8.50
a.-o.		33c any single	.80	.65
		Sheet of 4 panes	48.00	
3190	A2473	Pane of 15, *Jan. 12, 2000*	12.00	8.50
a.-o.		33c any single	.80	.65
		Sheet of 4 panes	48.00	
3191	A2474	Pane of 15, *May 2, 2000*	12.00	8.50
a.-o.		33c any single	.80	.65
		Sheet of 4 panes	48.00	

"REMEMBER THE MAINE"

A2475

Designed by Richard Sheaff.

LITHOGRAPHED & ENGRAVED
Sheets of 120 in six panes of 20

1998, Feb. 15		Tagged	Perf. 11.2x11	
3192	A2475	32c **red & black**	.65	.20
		P# block of 4, 2#	2.60	
		Pane of 20	13.00	

FLOWERING TREES

Southern
Magnolia — A2476

Blue
Paloverde — A2477

Yellow
Poplar — A2478

Prairie Crab
Apple — A2479

Pacific
Dogwood — A2480

Designed by Howard Paine.

Printed by Banknote Corporation of America.

LITHOGRAPHED
Sheets of 120 in six panes of 20

1998, Mar. 19	Tagged			Die Cut Perf 11.3

Self-Adhesive

3193	A2476	32c	multicolored	.65	.20
3194	A2477	32c	multicolored	.65	.20
3195	A2478	32c	multicolored	.65	.20
3196	A2479	32c	multicolored	.65	.20

3197	A2480	32c	multicolored	.65	.20

a.	Strip of 5, #3193-3197		3.25
	P# block of 10, 2 sets of B+6#		6.50
	Pane of 20		13.00
b.	As "a," die cutting omitted		—

ALEXANDER CALDER (1898-1976), SCULPTOR

Black Cascade, 13
Verticals,
1959 — A2481

Untitled,
1965 — A2482

Rearing Stallion,
1928 — A2483

Portrait of a Young
Man,
c. 1945 — A2484

Un Effet du Japonais,
1945 — A2485

Designed by Derry Noyes. Printed by Stamp Venturers.

PHOTOGRAVURE
Sheets of 120 in six panes of 20

1998, Mar. 25	Tagged			Perf. 1

3198	A2481	32c	multicolored		.65
3199	A2482	32c	multicolored		.65
3200	A2483	32c	multicolored		.65
3201	A2484	32c	multicolored		.65
3202	A2485	32c	multicolored		.65

a.	Strip of 5, #3198-3202	3.25	2
	P# block of 10, 2 sets of S+6#	6.50	
	Pane of 20	13.00	
	Sheet of 120 (6 panes)	110.00	
	Cross gutter block of 20	37.50	
	Block of 10 with horiz. gutter	22.50	
	Vert. pairs with horiz. gutter (each)	4.00	
	Horiz. pairs with vert. gutter (each)	5.50	

Cross gutter block of 20 consists of six stamps from each
two panes and four stamps from each of two other panes w
the cross gutter between. The sheet of 120 was quickly s
out.

A2486

CINCO DE MAYO

Designed by Carl Herrman.

Printed by Stamp Venturers.

PHOTOGRAVURE
Sheets of 180 in nine panes of 20
Serpentine Die Cut 11.7x10.9

1998, Apr. 16		Tagge

Self-Adhesive

3203	A2486	32c	multicolored	.65	.2
		P# block of 4, 5#+S		2.60	
		Pane of 20		13.00	
		Sheet of 180 (9 panes)		115.00	
		Cross gutter block of 4		13.00	
		Vert. pair with horiz. gutter		2.25	
		Horiz. pair with vert. gutter		2.25	

See Mexico #2066. For 33c version, see #3309.

A2487   A2488

SYLVESTER & TWEETY

Designed by Brenda Guttman.

Printed by Avery Dennison.

PHOTOGRAVURE

1998, Apr. 27	Tagged	*Serpentine Die Cut 11.1*

Self-Adhesive

3204		Pane of 10	6.75	
a.		A2487 32c single	.65	.20
b.		Booklet pane of 9 #3204a	6.00	
c.		Booklet pane of 1 #3204a	.65	
		Sheet of 60 (six panes) top	70.00	
		Sheet of 60 (six panes) bottom, with plate #	110.00	
		Pane of 10 from sheet of 60	12.50	
		Pane of 10 with plate #	50.00	
		Cross gutter block of 9 or 10	45.00	
		Cross gutter block of 12	50.00	
		Vert. pair with horiz. gutter	7.00	
		Horiz. pair with vert. gutter	14.00	

Die cutting on #3204b does not extend through the backing
paper. Pane with plate number comes from bottom uncut sheet
of 60.

The horiz. pair with vert. gutter consists of a stamp at the left
from either No. 3204b, part of the illustration of Sylvester &
Tweety, the small gutter between the panes, and a stamp at the
right from the left row of No. 3204b. Some pairs may include the

Sister Rosetta
Tharpe (1921-
73)
A2500

Designed by Howard Paine.
Printed by American Packaging Corp. for Sennett Security
Products.

PHOTOGRAVURE
Sheets of 120 in six panes of 20

1998, July 15		Tagged	Perf. 10.1x10.3	
3216	A2497	32c	multicolored	.65	.20
3217	A2498	32c	multicolored	.65	.20
3218	A2499	32c	multicolored	.65	.20
3219	A2500	32c	multicolored	.65	.20
a.	Block or strip of 4, #3216-3219			2.60	2.00
	P# block of 4, 6#+S			3.50	—
	P# block of 8, 2 sets of P# + top label			7.00	—
	Pane of 20			17.00	—

SPANISH SETTLEMENT OF THE SOUTHWEST

La Mision de
San Miguel de
San Gabriel,
Espanola,
NM — A2501

Designed by Richard Sheaff.
Printed by Banknote Corporation of America.

LITHOGRAPHED
Sheets of 180 in nine panes of 20

1998, July 11		Tagged	Perf. 11.2	
3220	A2501	32c	multicolored	.65	.20
	P# block of 4, 4#+B			2.60	—
	Pane of 20			13.00	—

LITERARY ARTS SERIES

Stephen
Vincent Benét
(1898-43)
A2502

Designed by Carl Herrman.
Printed by Ashton-Potter (USA) Ltd.

LITHOGRAPHED
Sheets of 180 in nine panes of 20

1998, July 22		Tagged	Perf. 11.2	
3221	A2502	32c	multicolored	.65	.20
	P# block of 4, 4#+P			2.60	—
	Pane of 20			13.00	—

TROPICAL BIRDS

Antillean
Euphonia
A2503

Green-throated Carib — A2504

Crested
Honeycreeper
A2505

Cardinal
Honeyeater
A2506

Designed by Phil Jordan.
Printed by Banknote Corporation of America.

LITHOGRAPHED
Sheets of 180 in nine panes of 20

1998, July 29		Tagged	Perf. 11.2	
3222	A2503	32c	multicolored	.65	.20
3223	A2504	32c	multicolored	.65	.20
3224	A2505	32c	multicolored	.65	.20
3225	A2506	32c	multicolored	.65	.20
a.	Block or strip of 4, #3222-3225			2.60	2.00
	P# block of 4, 4#+P			2.60	—
	Pane of 20			13.00	—

For booklet see No. BK272.

LEGENDS OF HOLLYWOOD

Alfred Hitchcock (1899-
1980) — A2507

Designed by Richard Sheaff.
Printed at American Packaging Corp. for Sennett Security
Products.

PHOTOGRAVURE
Sheets of 120 in six panes of 20

1998, Aug. 3		Tagged	Perf. 11.1	
3226	A2507	32c	multicolored	.75	.20
	P# block of 4, 4#+S			4.25	—
	Pane of 20			20.00	12.50
	Sheet of 120 (6 panes)			85.00	
	Cross gutter block of 8			19.00	—
	Block of 8 with vert. gutter			13.50	—
	Horiz. pair with vert. gutter			3.50	—
	Vert. pair with horiz. gutter			2.25	—

Perforations in corner of each stamp are star-shaped. Cross-
gutter block consists of 6 stamps from upper panes and 2
stamps from panes below. Hitchcock's profile in the UL corner
of each stamp is laser cut.

ORGAN & TISSUE DONATION

A2508

Designed by Richard Sheaff. Printed by Avery Dennison.

PHOTOGRAVURE
Sheets of 160 in eight panes of 20

1998, Aug. 5		Tagged	Serpentine Die Cut 11.	
			Self-Adhesive		
3227	A2508	32c	multicolored	.65	.20
	P# block of 4 5#+V			2.60	
	Pane of 20			13.00	

MODERN BICYCLE

A2509

Designed by Richard Sheaff. Printed by Bureau of Engraving
and Printing (#3228), Sennett Security Printers (#3229).

PHOTOGRAVURE
COIL STAMP
Serpentine Die Cut 9.8 Vert.

1998, Aug. 14				Untagged	
			Self-Adhesive (#3228)		
3228	A2509	(10c)	multicolored, small "1998" year date	.20	.20
	Pair			.40	
	P# strip of 5, P#111, 221, 222, 333, 344, 444, 555			2.75	
	P# single, same #			—	1.75
a.	Large date			.25	.20
	Pair			.50	
	P# strip of 5, #666, 777, 888			2.75	
	P# strip of 5, #999			3.00	
	P# single, #666, 888			—	2.50
	P# single, #777, 999			—	1.75

Date on No. 3228a is approximately 1½mm; on No. 3228
approximately 1mm.

Untagged
Perf. 9.9 Vert.

3229	A2509	(10c)	multicolored	.20	.20
	Pair			.40	.25
	P# strip of 5, P#S111			2.50	
	P# single, same #			—	1.75

BRIGHT EYES

Dog — A2510

Fish — A2511

Cat — A2512

Parakeet
A2513

Hamster
A2514

Designed by Carl Herrman. Printed at Guilford Gravure for
Banknote Corp. of America.

PHOTOGRAVURE
Sheets of 180 in nine panes of 20

1998, Aug. 20		Tagged	*Serpentine Die Cut 9.9*		
			Self-Adhesive		
3230	A2510	32c	multicolored	.75	.20
3231	A2511	32c	multicolored	.75	.20
3232	A2512	32c	multicolored	.75	.20
3233	A2513	32c	multicolored	.75	.20
3234	A2514	32c	multicolored	.75	.20
a.		Strip of 5, #3230-3234		3.75	
		P# block of 8, 2 sets of 6#+B		7.50	
		Pane of 20		15.00	

Hidden 3-D designs can be seen on each stamp when
viewed with a special viewer sold by the post office.
Plate blocks may contain top label.

KLONDIKE GOLD RUSH, CENTENNIAL

A2515

Designed by Howard Paine. Printed at Sterling Sommer for
Ashton Potter (USA) Ltd.

LITHOGRAPHED
Sheets of 180 in nine panes of 20

1998, Aug. 21		Tagged		*Perf. 11.1*	
3235	A2515	32c	multicolored	.65	.20
		P# block of 4, 5#+P		2.60	—
		Pane of 20		13.00	—

AMERICAN ART

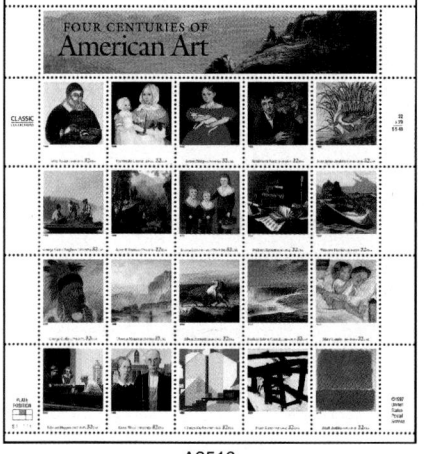

A2516

Illustration reduced.

Designed by Howard Paine. Printed by Sennett Security
Products.

Paintings: a, "Portrait of Richard Mather," by John Foster. b, "Mrs. Elizabeth Freake and Baby Mary," by The Freake Limner. c, "Girl in Red Dress with Cat and Dog," by Ammi Phillips. d, "Rubens Peale with a Geranium," by Rembrandt Peale. e, "Long-billed Curlew, Numenius Longrostris," by John James Audubon. f, "Boatmen on the Missouri," by George Caleb Bingham. g, "Kindred Sprits," by Asher B. Durand. h, "The Westwood Children," by Joshua Johnson. i, "Music and Literature," by William Harnett. j, "The Fog Warning," by Winslow Homer. k, "The White Cloud, Head Chief of the Iowas," by George Catlin. l, "Cliffs of Green River," by Thomas Moran. m, "The Last of the Buffalo," by Alfred Bierstadt. n, "Niagara," by Frederic Edwin Church. o, "Breakfast in Bed," by Mary Cassatt. p, "Nighthawks," by Edward Hopper. q, "American Gothic," by Grant Wood. r, "Two Against the White," by Charles Sheeler. s, "Mahoning," by Franz Kline. t, "No. 12," by Mark Rothko.

PHOTOGRAVURE
Sheets of 120 stamps in six panes of 20

1998, Aug. 27		Tagged		*Perf. 10.2*	
3236	A2516	Pane of 20		15.00	10.00
a.-t.		32c any single		.75	.60
		Sheet of 120 (six panes)		85.00	
		Cross gutter block of 20		27.50	—
		Vert. pairs with horiz. gutter (each)		3.00	—
		Horiz. pairs with vert. gutter (each)		3.00	—

Inscriptions on the back of each stamp describe the painting
and the artist.
Cross gutter block of 20 consists of six stamps from each of
two panes and four stamps from each of two other panes with
the cross gutter between.

AMERICAN BALLET

A2517

Designed by Derry Noyes. Printed by Sterling Sommer for
Ashton-Potter (USA) Ltd.

LITHOGRAPHED
Sheets of 120 in six panes of 20

1998, Sept. 16		Tagged		*Perf. 10.9x11.1*	
3237	A2517	32c	multicolored	.65	.20
		P# block of 4, 4#+P		3.00	—
		Pane of 20		14.50	—
		Sheet of 120 (six panes)		85.00	
		Cross gutter block of 4		14.00	—
		Vert. pair with horiz. gutter		2.25	—
		Horiz. pair with vert. gutter		2.25	—

For booklet see No. BK273.

SPACE DISCOVERY

A2518

A2519

A2520

A2521

A2522

Designed by Phil Jordan. Printed at American Packaging
Corp. for Sennett Security Products.

PHOTOGRAVURE
Sheets of 180 in nine panes of 20

1998, Oct. 1		Tagged		*Perf. 11.1*	
3238	A2518	32c	multicolored	.65	.20
3239	A2519	32c	multicolored	.65	.20
3240	A2520	32c	multicolored	.65	.20
3241	A2521	32c	multicolored	.65	.20
3242	A2522	32c	multicolored	.65	.20
a.		Strip of 5, #3238-3242		3.25	2.25
		P# block of 10, 2 sets of 5#+S		6.50	—
		Pane of 20		13.00	
		Sheet of 180 (9 panes)		110.00	
		Cross gutter block of 10		17.50	—
		Vert. block of 10 with horiz. gutter		10.00	—
		Horiz. pair (#3238, 3242) with vert. gutter		2.00	—
		Vert. pairs with horiz. gutter (each)		2.00	—
		Pane of 20 from sheet of 180		12.00	—

Hidden 3-D designs can be seen on each stamp when
viewed with a special viewer sold by the post office.
Plate blocks may contain top label.
Cross gutter block of 10 consists of two stamps from each of
two panes and three stamps from each of two other panes with
the cross gutter between. Pane of 20 from sheet of 180 has
vertical perforations on one or both sides and is wider than
pane sold in local post offices.
For booklet see No. BK274.

GIVING AND SHARING

A2523

Designed by Bob Dinetz.

Printed by Avery Dennison.

PHOTOGRAVURE
Sheets of 200 in ten panes of 20

1998, Oct. 7		Tagged		*Serpentine Die Cut 11.1*	
				Self-Adhesive	
3243	A2523	32c	multicolored	.65	.20
		P# block of 4, 4#+V		2.60	—
		Pane of 20		13.00	—

CHRISTMAS

Madonna and Child, Florence,
15th Cent. — A2524

Evergreen
Wreath — A2525

Victorian
Wreath — A2526

Chili Pepper
Wreath — A2527

Tropical
Wreath — A2528

Designed by Richard D. Sheaff (#3244), Lilian Dinihanian (A2525), George de Bruin (A2526), Chris Crinklaw (A2527), Micheale Thunin (A2528).

Printed by Bureau of Engraving and Printing (#3244), Banknote Corporation of America (#3245-3252).

LITHOGRAPHED
Sheets of 160 in 8 panes of 20 (#3249-3252)

Serpentine Die Cut 10.1x9.9 on 2, 3 or 4 Sides
1998, Oct. 15   Tagged

Self-Adhesive
Booklet Stamps

3244	A2524	32c	**multicolored**	.65	.20
a.	Booklet pane of 20 + label			13.00	
b.	Die cutting omitted, pair			—	

Serpentine Die Cut 11.3x11.7 on 2 or 3 Sides

3245	A2525	32c	**multicolored**	5.00	.20
3246	A2526	32c	**multicolored**	5.00	.20
3247	A2527	32c	**multicolored**	5.00	.20
3248	A2528	32c	**multicolored**	5.00	.20
a.	Booklet pane of 4, #3245-3248			22.50	
b.	Booklet pane of 5, #3245-3246, 3248, 2 #3247 + label			27.50	
c.	Booklet pane of 6, #3247-3248, 2 each #3245-3246			32.50	
d.	As "a," die cutting omitted			—	
e.	As "b," die cutting omitted			—	
f.	As "c," die cutting omitted			—	

Size: 23x30mm

Serpentine Die Cut 11.4x11.5 on 2, 3, or 4 Sides

3249	A2525	32c	**multicolored**	1.00	.20
a.	Serp. die cut 11.7x11.6 on 2, 3, or 4 sides			1.50	.20
3250	A2526	32c	**multicolored**	1.00	.20
a.	Serp. die cut 11.7x11.6 on 3 or 4 sides			1.50	.20
3251	A2527	32c	**multicolored**	1.00	.20
a.	Serp. die cut 11.7x11.6 on 3 or 4 sides			1.50	.20
3252	A2528	32c	**multicolored + label**	1.00	.20
a.	Serp. die cut 11.7x11.6 on 2, 3, or 4 sides			1.50	.20
b.	Block or strip of 4, #3249-3252			4.00	
	P#block of 4, 6#+B			4.50	
	Pane of 20			22.00	
c.	Booklet pane of 20, 5 each #3249-3252 + label			22.50	
d.	Block or strip of 4, #3249a-3252a			6.00	
e.	Booklet pane of 20, 5 each #3249a-3252a + label			30.00	
f.	Block or strip of 4, #3249-3252, red ("Greetings 32 USA" and "1998") omitted on #3249, 3252			750.00	
g.	Block or strip of 4, #3249-3252, red ("Greetings 32 USA" and "1998") omitted on #3249, 3252; green (same) omitted on #3250, 3251			—	

Dedicated printing plates were used to print the red and green denominations, salutations and dates. Red and green appearing in the wreaths come from other plates and, therefore, are not part of the color omissions.

Specialists will want to note that the "1998" date on the flat pane of 20 is about .1mm wider than the date on the corresponding booklet pane (No. 3252c). The measurements are approximately 1.3mm versus 1.2mm, respectively. Therefore, unused and used singles can be distinguished.

Weather
Vane — A2529

Uncle Sam — A2530

Uncle Sam's Hat — A2531

Space Shuttle
Landing
A2532

Piggyback
Space Shuttle
A2533

Designed by Terry McCaffrey (#3257-3258, 3260, 3264-3269), Richard Sheaff (#3259, 3263), Phil Jordan (#3261-3262).

Printed by Ashton Potter (USA) Ltd. (#3257), American Packaging Corp. for Sennett Security Products (#3259), Stamp Venturers (#3260), Banknote Corporation of America (#3258, 3261-3262), Bureau of Engraving and Printing (#3263-3267), Avery Dennison (#3268-3269).

LITHOGRAPHED
Sheets of 400 in eight panes of 50 (#3257, 3260), Sheets of 300 in six panes of 50 (#3258), Sheets of 160 in eight panes of 20 (#3259), Sheets of 120 in six panes of 20 (#3261-3262)

1998		**Untagged**	**Perf. 11.2**	
3257	A2529	(1c) **multicolored** *Nov. 9*	.20	.20
		P# block of 4, 5# + P	.25	
a.	Black omitted		150.00	
3258	A2529	(1c) **multicolored,** *Nov. 9*	.20	.20
		P# block of 4, 5# + B	.25	

No. 3257 is 18mm high, has thin letters, white USA, and black 1998. No. 3258 is 17mm high, has thick letters, pale blue USA and blue 1998.

PHOTOGRAVURE
Tagged
Serpentine Die Cut 10.8
Self-Adhesive (#3259, 3261-3263, 3265-3269)

3259	A2530	22c **multicolored,** *Nov. 9*	.45	.20
a.	Die cut 10.8x10.5		2.50	.25
b.	Vert. pair, No. 3259 + 3259a		3.50	
	P# block of 4, 4# + S, all No. 3259		2.50	
	P# block of 4, top stamps No. 3259, bottom stamps No. 3259a		—	
	P# block of 4, top stamps No. 3259a, bottom stamps No. 3259		7.50	
	Pane of 20, all No. 3259		9.00	
	Pane of 20, row 1 No. 3259a, rows 2-4 No. 3259		—	
	Pane of 20, row 2 No. 3259a, rows 1, 3-4 No. 3259		35.00	
	Pane of 20, row 3 No. 3259a, rows 1-2, 4 No. 3259		15.00	
	Pane of 20, row 4 No. 3259a, rows 1-3 No. 3259		30.00	

See No. 3353.

Perf. 11.2

3260	A2531	(33c) **multicolored,** shiny gum, *Nov. 9*	.65	.20
		P# block of 4 4#+S	2.60	—
		Low-gloss gum	.65	.20
		P# block of 4 4#+S	2.60	

LITHOGRAPHED
Serpentine Die Cut 11.5

3261	A2532	$3.20 **multicolored,** *Nov. 9*	6.00	1.50
		P# block of 4, 4#+B	24.00	
		Pane of 20	120.00	
3262	A2533	$11.75 **multicolored,** *Nov. 9*	22.50	10.00
		P# block of 4, 4#+B	90.00	
		Pane of 20	450.00	

COIL STAMPS
PHOTOGRAVURE
Serpentine Die Cut 9.9 Vert.

3263	A2530	22c **multicolored,** *Nov. 9*	.45	.20
		Pair	.90	
		P# strip of 5, #1111	3.50	
		P# single, same #	—	2.50
a.	Die cutting omitted, pair		—	

See No. 3353.

Perf. 9.8 Vert.

3264	A2531	(33c) **multicolored,** *Nov. 9*	.65	.2
		Pair	1.30	.3
		P# strip of 5, #1111, 3333, 3343, 3344, 3444	5.00	
		P# single, same #		2.5

On No. 3264, the black plate #1 of plate #1111 used printing rolls of 100 places the plate digit "1" farther from th black printing in the vignette than does the black plate #1 plate #1111 used in printing rolls of 3,000. These are referred t as "Low black 1" and "Hi black 1" and are used by plate numbe specialists to distinguish the different printings from plate #1111.

Serpentine Die Cut 9.9 Vert.

3265	A2531	(33c) **multicolored,** *Nov. 9*	.80	.20
		Pair	1.60	
		P# strip of 5, #1111, 1131, 2222, 3333	6.25	
		P# single, same #		2.25
a.	Die cutting omitted, pair		95.00	—
b.	Red omitted		650.00	
c.	Black omitted		—	
d.	Black omitted, die cutting omitted, pair		—	

Unused examples of No. 3265 are on backing paper the same size as the stamps. Corners of the stamp are 90 degree angles.

On No. 3265b, the blue and gray colors are shifted down and to the right.

Serpentine Die Cut 9.9 Vert.

3266	A2531	(33c) **multicolored,** *Nov. 9*	1.00	.20
		Pair	2.00	
		P# strip of 5, #1111	8.00	
		P# single, same #		3.50

Unused examples of No. 3266 are on backing paper larger than the stamps, and the stamps are spaced approximately 2mm. apart. Corners of stamps are rounded.

BOOKLET STAMPS
Serpentine Die Cut 9.9 on 2 or 3 Sides

3267	A2531	(33c) **multicolored,** *Nov. 9*	.65	.20
a.	Booklet pane of 10		6.50	

Serpentine Die Cut 11¼ on 3 Sides (#3268, 3268a)
or 11 on 2, 3 or 4 sides (#3268b, 3268c)

3268	A2531	(33c) **multicolored,** *Nov. 9*	.65	.20
a.	Booklet pane of 10		6.50	
b.	Serpentine die cut 11		.65	.20
c.	As "b," booklet pane of 20 + label		13.00	

Die Cut 8 on 2, 3 or 4 Sides

3269	A2531	(33c) **multicolored,** *Nov. 9*	.65	.20
a.	Booklet pane of 18		12.00	

Used examples of an "H" nondenominated stamp inscribed "Postcard Rate" exist in the marketplace. There is no evidence that these stamps were ever officially issued.

A2534

Designed by Chris Calle.

PHOTOGRAVURE
COIL STAMPS

1998, Dec. 14		**Untagged**	**Perf. 9.8 Vert.**	
3270	A2534	(10c) **multicolored,** small date	.20	.20
		Pair	.40	.40
		P# strip of 5, #11111	2.75	
		P# single, #11111		1.75
a.	Large date		.35	.20
		Pair	.70	.40
		P# strip of 5, #22222	7.00	
		P# single, same #	—	2.25

Self-Adhesive
Serpentine Die Cut 9.9 Vert.

3271	A2534	(10c) **multicolored,** small date	.20	.20
		Pair	.40	
		P# strip of 5, #11111, 22222	2.75	
		P# single, #11111, 22222		1.75
a.	Large date		.60	.20
		Pair	1.20	
		P# strip of 5, #33333	3.25	
		P# single, #33333	—	1.75
b.	Tagged (error)		1.25	.75
		Pair	2.50	
		P# strip of 5, #11111	10.50	
		P# single, #11111	—	9.50

No. 3271 is known with eagle in red brown rather than the normal golden brown, apparently from contaminated ink. Values slightly higher than normal No. 3271.

Dates on Nos. 3270a and 3271a are approximately 1¾mm; on Nos. 3270-3271 approximately 1¼mm.

Compare to Nos. 2602-2604, 2907.

Scott values for used self-adhesvive stamps are for examples either on piece or off piece.

CHINESE NEW YEAR

Year of the
Rabbit
A2535

Designed by Clarence Lee.

Printed at American Packaging Corp. for Sennett Security Printers.

PHOTOGRAVURE
Sheets of 180 in nine panes of 20

1999, Jan. 5	**Tagged**		**Perf. 11.2**
3272 A2535 33c multicolored		.80	.20
P# block of 4, 4#+S		3.25	
Pane of 20		17.00	—

See No. 3895d.

BLACK HERITAGE SERIES

Malcolm X (1925-65), Civil
Rights Activist — A2536

Designed by Richard Sheaff. Printed by Banknote Corp. of America.

LITHOGRAPHED
Sheets of 180 in nine panes of 20

1999, Jan. 20	**Tagged**	**Serpentine Die Cut 11.4**	
		Self-Adhesive	
3273 A2536 33c multicolored		.85	.20
P# block of 4, 3#+B		3.40	
Pane of 20		17.00	—

LOVE

A2537   A2538

Designed by John Grossman, Holly Sudduth.

Printed by Avery Dennison.

PHOTOGRAVURE

1999, Jan. 28	**Tagged**		**Die Cut**
	Booklet Stamp		
	Self-Adhesive		
3274 A2537 33c multicolored		.65	.20
a. Booklet pane of 20		13.00	
b. Die cutting omitted, pair		200.00	
c. As "a," die cutting omitted		2,000.	
Sheets of 160 in eight panes of 20			
3275 A2538 55c multicolored		1.10	.20
P# block of 4, 7#+B		4.40	
Pane of 20		22.00	

HOSPICE CARE

A2539

Designed by Phil Jordan.

Printed by Banknote Corp. of America.

LITHOGRAPHED
Sheets of 120 in six panes of 20

1999, Feb. 9	**Tagged**	**Serpentine Die Cut 11.4**	
3276 A2539 33c multicolored		.65	.20
P# block of 4, 4#+B		2.80	
Pane of 20		13.50	

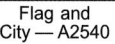

Flag and   Flag and
City — A2540   Chalkboard — A2541

Designed by Richard Sheaff. Printed by Bureau of Engraving and Printing (#3277, 3279-3282), Avery Dennison (#3278, 3278F, 3283).

PHOTOGRAVURE
Sheets of 400 in four panes of 100 (#3277),
Sheets of 200 in ten panes of 20 (#3278)

1999, Feb. 25	**Tagged**		**Perf. 11.2**
Self-Adhesive (#3278, 3278F, 3279, 3281-3282)			
3277 A2540 33c multicolored		.70	.20
P# block of 4, 4#		47.50	—

No. 3277 has red date.

Serpentine Die Cut 11 on 2, 3 or 4 Sides

3278 A2540 33c multicolored		.65	.20
P# block of 4, 4#+V		4.25	
Pane of 20		20.00	
a. Booklet pane of 4		2.60	
b. Booklet pane of 5 + label		3.25	
P# single, #V1111, V1112, V1121, V1122, V1212, V2212		.80	1.00
c. Booklet pane of 6		3.90	
d. Booklet pane of 10		12.50	
e. Booklet pane of 20 + label		13.00	
h. As "e," die cutting omitted		—	
i. Serpentine die cut 11¼		1.40	.20
j. As "i," booklet pane of 10		14.00	

No. 3278 has black date.
The plate # single in No. 3278b is the lower left single.

BOOKLET STAMPS
Serpentine Die Cut 11½x11¾ on 2, 3 or 4 Sides

3278F A2540 33c multicolored		.85	.20
g. Booklet pane of 20 + label		17.50	

No. 3278F has black date.

Serpentine Die Cut 9.8 on 2 or 3 Sides

3279 A2540 33c multicolored		.75	.20
a. Booklet pane of 10		7.50	

No. 3279 has red date.

COIL STAMPS
Perf. 9.9 Vert.

3280 A2540 33c multicolored, small "1999" year date		.65	.20
Pair		1.30	.30
P# strip of 5, #1111, 2222		5.00	
P# single, same #			2.50
a. Large date		.75	.20
Pair		1.50	.30
P# strip of 5, #3333		8.00	
P# single, same #			5.00
b. As No. 3280, imperf pair		—	

Serpentine Die Cut 9.8 Vert.

Two types of No. 3281: Type I, Long vertical feature at left and right of tallest building consists of 3 separate lines; Type II, Same features consist of solid color.

3281 A2540 33c multicolored, type I, large "1999" year date		.65	.20
Pair		1.30	
P# strip of 5, #6666, 7777, 8888, 9999, 1111A, 2222A, 3333A, 4444A, 5555A, 6666A, 7777A, 8888A, 1111B, 2222B		5.00	
P# single, same #			1.25
P# single, #7777A, 8888A, 1111B, 2222B		—	2.25
a. Die cutting omitted, pair		30.00	
b. Light blue and yellow omitted		*600.00*	
c. Small date, type II		.65	.20
Pair		1.30	
P# strip of 5, #1111, 2222, 3333, 3433, 4443, 4444, 5555		5.00	
P# single, same #			1.25
d. Small date, type I		.75	.20
Pair		1.50	
P# strip of 5, #9999A		7.50	
P# single, same #			2.25
e. As "c," die cutting omitted, pair		—	

Corners are square on #3281. Unused examples are on backing paper the same size as the stamps, and the stamps are adjoining.
Date on Nos. 3280a and 3281 is approximately 1¾mm; on Nos. 3280, 3281c and 3281d approximately 1¼mm.

3282 A2540 33c multicolored		.65	.20
Pair		1.30	
P# strip of 5, #1111, 2222		5.00	
P# single, same #			3.25

Corners are rounded on #3282. Unused examples are on backing paper larger than the stamps, and the stamps are spaced approximately 2mm. apart.

PHOTOGRAVURE
Serpentine Die Cut 7.9 on 2, 3 or 4 Sides

1999, Mar. 13		**Tagged**

Self-Adhesive
BOOKLET STAMP

3283 A2541 33c multicolored		.65	.20
a. Booklet pane of 18		12.00	

IRISH IMMIGRATION

A2542

Designed by Howard Paine. Printed by Ashton-Potter (USA) Ltd.

LITHOGRAPHED
Sheets of 180 in nine panes of 20

1999, Feb. 26	**Tagged**		**Perf. 11.2**
3286 A2542 33c multicolored		.65	.20
P# block of 4, 4#+P		2.60	—
Pane of 20		13.00	—

See Ireland No. 1168.

PERFORMING ARTS SERIES
Alfred Lunt (1892-1977), Lynn Fontanne (1887-1983), Actors

A2543

Designed by Carl Herrman. Printed by Sterling Sommer for Ashton-Potter (USA) Ltd.

LITHOGRAPHED
Sheets of 180 in nine panes of 20

1999, Mar. 2	**Tagged**		**Perf. 11.2**
3287 A2543 33c multicolored		.65	.20
P# block of 4, 4#+P		2.60	—
Pane of 20		13.00	—

ARCTIC ANIMALS

Arctic Hare — A2544

Arctic Fox — A2545

Snowy Owl — A2546

Polar Bear — A2547

Gray Wolf — A2548

Designed by Derry Noyes. Printed by Banknote Corp. of America.

LITHOGRAPHED
Sheets of 90 in six panes of 15

1999, Mar. 12	Tagged		Perf. 11	
3288	A2544	33c multicolored	.85	.20
3289	A2545	33c multicolored	.85	.20
3290	A2546	33c multicolored	.85	.20
3291	A2547	33c multicolored	.85	.20

3292	A2548	33c multicolored	.85	.20
a.		Strip of 5, #3288-3292	4.25	—
		Pane of 15, 6#+B	12.00	—

While the normal definition of a plate block dictates a block of 10, this would require collectors to discard the decorative label and top row of stamps from the pane of 15. To avoid destroying the more collectible entire, Scott is listing the entire pane as the plate block, and will provide space for this item in the Commemorative Plate Block supplement.

SONORAN DESERT

A2549

Illustration reduced.

Designed by Ethel Kessler. Printed by Banknote Corporation of America.

Designs: a, Cactus wren, brittlebush, teddy bear cholla. b, Desert tortoise. c, White-winged dove, prickly pear. d, Gambel quail. e, Saguaro cactus. f, Desert mule deer. g, Desert cottontail, hedgehog cactus. h, Gila monster. i, Western diamondback rattlesnake, cactus mouse. j, Gila woodpecker.

LITHOGRAPHED
Sheets of 60 in six panes of 10
Serpentine Die Cut Perf 11.2

1999, Apr. 6			Tagged	
		Self-Adhesive		
3293	A2549	Pane of 10	6.50	
a.-j.		33c any single	.65	.50
		Sheet of 6 panes	40.00	

BERRIES

Blueberries
A2550

Raspberries
A2551

Strawberries
A2552

Blackberries
A2553

Designed by Howard Paine. Printed by Guilford Gravure for Banknote Corporation of America.

PHOTOGRAVURE
Serpentine Die Cut 11¼x11½ on 2, 3 or 4 Sides (Nos. 3294-3297), or 2 or 3 sides (Nos. 3294a-3297a)

1999, Apr. 10			Tagged	
		Self-Adhesive		
3294	A2550	33c multicolored	.65	.20
a.		Dated "2000," Mar. 15, 2000	.75	.20
3295	A2551	33c multicolored	.65	.20
a.		Dated "2000," Mar. 15, 2000	.75	.20
3296	A2552	33c multicolored	.65	.20
a.		Dated "2000," Mar. 15, 2000	.75	.20
3297	A2553	33c multicolored	.65	.20
a.		Dated "2000," Mar. 15, 2000	.75	.20
b.		Booklet pane of 20, 5 each #3294-3297 + label	13.00	
c.		Block of 4, #3294-3297	2.60	
d.		Booklet pane of 20, 5 #3297e + label	15.00	
e.		Block of 4, #3294a-3297a	3.00	

No. 3297d is a double-sided booklet pane, with 12 stamps on one side and eight stamps plus label on the other side.

Serpentine Die Cut 9½x10 on 2 or 3 Sides

3298	A2550	33c multicolored	.85	.
3299	A2552	33c multicolored	.85	.
3300	A2551	33c multicolored	.85	.
3301	A2553	33c multicolored	.85	.
a.		Booklet pane of 4, #3298-3301	3.40	
b.		Booklet pane of 5, #3298, 3299, 3301, 2 #3300 + label	4.25	
c.		Booklet pane of 6, #3300, 3301, 2 #3298, 3299	5.35	
d.		Block of 4, #3298-3301	3.40	

COIL STAMPS
Serpentine Die Cut 8.5 Vert.

3302	A2550	33c multicolored	.75	.
3303	A2551	33c multicolored	.75	.
3304	A2553	33c multicolored	.75	.
3305	A2552	33c multicolored	.75	.
a.		Strip ot 4, #3302-3305	3.00	
		P# strip of 5, 2 #3302, 1 ea #3303-3305, P#B1111, B1112, B2211, B2221, B2222	5.50	
		P# strip of 9, 2 ea #3302-3303, 3305, 3 #3304, same P#	8.25	
		P# single (#3304), same P#	—	1.5

A2554   A2555

DAFFY DUCK

Designed by Ed Wieczyk.
Printed by Avery Dennison.

PHOTOGRAVURE
1999, Apr. 16   Tagged   Serpentine Die Cut 11.1
Self-Adhesive

3306		Pane of 10	6.75	
a.		A2554 33c single	.65	.20
b.		Booklet pane of 9 #3306a	6.00	
c.		Booklet pane of 1 #3306a	.65	
		Sheet of 60 (six panes) top	40.00	
		Sheet of 60 (six panes) bottom, with plate # in selvage	47.50	
		Pane of 10 from sheet of 60	8.00	
		Pane of 10 with plate # in selvage	15.00	
		Cross gutter block of 9 or 10	15.00	
		Cross gutter block of 12	18.00	
		Vert. pair with horiz. gutter	2.00	
		Horiz. pair with vert. gutter	4.00	

Nos. 3306b-3306c and 3307b-3307c are separated by a vertical line of microperforations, which is absent on the uncut sheet of 60.
Die cutting on #3306b does not extend through the backing paper.

3307		Pane of 10	14.00	
a.		A2554 33c single	1.25	
b.		Booklet pane of 9 #3307a	12.00	
c.		Booklet pane of 1, no die cutting	1.75	
d.		As "a," vert. pair, imperf between		

Die cutting on #3307a extends through the backing paper.
Nos. 3306b-3306c and 3307b-3307c are separated by a vertical line of microperforations.

LITERARY ARTS SERIES
Ayn Rand (1905-82).

Designed by Phil Jordan.

Printed by Sterling Sommer for Ashton-Potter (USA) Ltd.

LITHOGRAPHED
Sheets of 180 in nine panes of 20

1999, Apr. 22		Tagged	Perf. 11.2	
3308	A2555	33c multicolored	.65	.20
		P# block of 4, 4#+P	2.60	
		Pane of 20	13.00	—

Cinco De Mayo Type of 1998
Designed by Carl Herrman.

Printed by Banknote Corporation of America.

LITHOGRAPHED
Sheets of 160 in eight panes of 20
Serpentine Die Cut 11.6x11.3

1999, Apr. 27				Tagged
		Self-Adhesive		
3309	A2486	33c multicolored	.65	.20
		P# block of 4, 6#+B	2.60	
		Pane of 20	13.00	

TROPICAL FLOWERS

Bird of
Paradise
A2556

Royal
Poinciana
A2557

Gloriosa
Lily — A2558

Chinese
Hibiscus
A2559

Designed by Carl Herrman.

Printed by Sennett Security Products.

PHOTOGRAVURE
BOOKLET STAMPS
Serpentine Die Cut 10.9 on 2 or 3 Sides

1999, May 1			Tagged	
Self-Adhesive				
3310	A2556	33c **multicolored**	.65	.20
3311	A2557	33c **multicolored**	.65	.20
3312	A2558	33c **multicolored**	.65	.20
3313	A2559	33c **multicolored**	.65	.20
a.		Block of 4, #3310-3313	2.60	
b.		Booklet pane, 5 each #3313a	13.00	

No. 3313b is a double-sided booklet pane with 12 stamps on one side and 8 stamps plus label on the other side.

A2560

A2561

JOHN (1699-1777) & WILLIAM (1739-1823) BARTRAM, BOTANISTS

Designed by Phil Jordan. Printed by Banknote Corporation of America.

LITHOGRAPHED
Sheets of 180 in nine panes of 20

1999, May 18	Tagged	*Serpentine Die Cut 11½*
Self-Adhesive		
3314	A2560	33c Franklinia alatamaha, by William Bartram	.65	.20
	P# block of 4, 4#+B	2.60	
	Pane of 20	13.00	

PROSTATE CANCER AWARENESS

Designed by Michael Cronan. Printed by Avery Dennison.

PHOTOGRAVURE
Sheets of 200 in ten panes of 20

1999, May 28	Tagged	*Serpentine Die Cut 11*
Self-Adhesive		
3315	A2561	33c **multicolored**	.65	.20
	P# block of 4, 5#+V	2.60	
	Pane of 20	13.00	

CALIFORNIA GOLD RUSH, 150TH ANNIV.

A2562

Designed by Howard Paine. Printed by Ashton-Potter (USA) Ltd.

LITHOGRAPHED
Sheets of 180 in nine panes of 20

1999, June 18	Tagged	*Perf. 11¼*
3316	A2562	33c **multicolored**	.65	.20
	P# block of 4, 5#+P	2.60	—
	Pane of 20	13.00	—

AQUARIUM FISH
Reef Fish

A2563

A2564

A2565

A2566

Designed by Richard Sheaff. Printed by Banknote Corporation of America.

Designs: No. 3317, Yellow fish, red fish, cleaner shrimp. No. 3318, Fish, thermometer. No. 3319, Red fish, blue & yellow fish. No. 3320, Fish, heater/aerator.

LITHOGRAPHED
Sheets of 120 in six panes of 20

1999, June 24	Tagged	*Serpentine Die Cut 11½*
Self-Adhesive			
3317	A2563	33c **multicolored**, block tagging	.65	.20
a.	Overall tagging	12.50	10.00
3318	A2564	33c **multicolored**, block tagging	.65	.20
a.	Overall tagging	12.50	10.00
3319	A2565	33c **multicolored**, block tagging	.65	.20
a.	Overall tagging	12.50	10.00
3320	A2566	33c **multicolored**, block tagging	.65	.20
a.	Overall tagging	12.50	10.00
b.	Strip of 4, #3317-3320	2.60	
	P# block of 8, 2 sets of 4#+B	5.20	
	Pane of 20	13.00	
	Sheet of 6 panes	80.00	
	Cross gutter block of 8	20.00	
	Block of 8 with horiz. gutter	9.00	
	Horiz. pair with vert. gutter	2.00	
	Vert. pairs with horiz. gutter (each)	2.25	
c.	Strip of 4, #3317a-3320a	55.00	
	P# block of 8, 2 sets of 4#+B	125.00	
	Pane of 20	300.00	

Plate blocks will have either top label or list of fish shown on bottom selvage. Cross gutter block of 8 consists of 4 horiz. pairs separated by vert. gutter with horiz. gutter between.
Press sheets were printed with large block tagging.

EXTREME SPORTS

Skateboarding — A2567

Snowboarding — A2569

Inline Skating — A2570

Designed by Carl Herrman. Printed by Avery Dennison.

PHOTOGRAVURE
Sheets of 160 in eight panes of 20

1999, June 25	Tagged	*Serpentine Die Cut 11*
Self-Adhesive			
3321	A2567	33c **multicolored**	.75	.20
3322	A2568	33c **multicolored**	.75	.20
3323	A2569	33c **multicolored**	.75	.20
3324	A2570	33c **multicolored**	.75	.20
a.	Block or strip of 4, #3321-3324	3.00	
	P# block of 4, 4#+V	3.00	
	Pane of 20	15.00	
	Sheet of 80 (four panes) top	62.50	
	Sheet of 80 (four panes) bottom, with plate # in sheet margin	67.50	
	Pane of 20 with extra selvage from sheet of 80	15.00	
	Pane of 20 with plate # in sheet margin	22.50	
	Cross gutter block of 8	7.50	
	Vert. pairs with horiz. gutter (each)	2.00	
	Horiz. pairs with vert. gutter (each)	2.00	
	Block of 4 with horiz. gutter	5.00	
	Block of 8 with vert. gutter	10.00	

Cross gutter block of 8 consists of 4 horiz. pairs separated by vert. gutter with horiz. gutter between

AMERICAN GLASS

Free-Blown
Glass — A2571

Mold-Blown
Glass — A2572

Pressed Glass — A2573   Art Glass — A2574

Designed by Richard Sheaff. Printed by Sterling Sommer for
Ashton-Potter (USA) Ltd.

LITHOGRAPHED
Sheets of 90 in six panes of 15

1999, June 29			**Tagged**		**Perf. 11**
3325	A2571	33c	multicolored	1.00	.20
3326	A2572	33c	multicolored	1.00	.20
3327	A2573	33c	multicolored	1.00	.20
3328	A2574	33c	multicolored	1.00	.20
a.			Strip or block of 4, #3325-3328	4.00	2.00
			Pane of 15, 4 each #3325, 3327-3328, 3 #3326	15.00	8.00

A2575   A2576

LEGENDS OF HOLLYWOOD
James Cagney (1899-1986)

Designed by Howard Paine.

Printed by Sennett Security Products.

PHOTOGRAVURE
Sheets of 120 in six panes of 20

1999, July 22			**Tagged**		**Perf. 11**
3329	A2575	33c	multicolored	.80	.20
			P# block of 4, 5#+S	4.25	—
			Pane of 20	20.00	—
			Sheet of 120 (6 panes)	85.00	—
			Cross gutter block of 8	17.50	—
			Block of 8 with vertical gutter	11.00	—
			Horiz. pair with vert. gutter	3.00	—
			Vert. pair with horiz. gutter	2.00	—

Perforations in corner of each stamp are star-shaped. Cross-gutter block consists of 2 stamps from upper panes and 6 stamps from panes below.

GEN. WILLIAM "BILLY" L. MITCHELL (1879-1936), AVIATION PIONEER

Designed by Phil Jordan.
Printed by Guilford Gravure for Banknote Corporation of America.

PHOTOGRAVURE
Sheets of 180 in nine panes of 20

1999, July 30	**Tagged**		***Serpentine Die Cut 9³⁄₄x10***		
			Self-Adhesive		
3330	A2576	55c	multicolored	1.10	.30
			P# block of 4, 5#+B	4.40	
			Pane of 20	22.00	

HONORING THOSE WHO SERVED

A2577

Designed by Richard Sheaff and Uldis Purins.
Printed by Avery Dennison.

PHOTOGRAVURE
Sheets of 200 in 10 panes of 20

1999, Aug. 16	**Tagged**		***Serpentine Die Cut 11***		
			Self-Adhesive		
3331	A2577	33c	black, blue & red	.65	.20
			P# block of 4, 3#+V	2.60	
			Pane of 20	13.00	

UNIVERSAL POSTAL UNION

A2578

Designed by Gerald Gallo.
Printed by Sterling Sommer for Ashton-Potter (USA) Ltd.

LITHOGRAPHED
Sheets of 180 in nine panes of 20

1999, Aug. 25			**Tagged**		**Perf. 11**
3332	A2578	45c	multicolored	.90	.45
			P# block of 4, 3#+P	3.60	—
			Pane of 20	18.00	—

FAMOUS TRAINS

Daylight
A2579

Congressional
A2580

20th Century
Limited
A2581

Hiawatha
A2582

Super Chief
A2583

Designed by Howard Paine.
Printed by Ashton-Potter (USA) Ltd.

LITHOGRAPHED
Sheets of 120 in six panes of 20

1999, Aug. 26			**Tagged**		**Perf. 11**
3333	A2579	33c	multicolored	.75	.20
3334	A2580	33c	multicolored	.75	.20
3335	A2581	33c	multicolored	.75	.20
3336	A2582	33c	multicolored	.75	.20
3337	A2583	33c	multicolored	.75	.20
a.			Strip of 5, #3333-3337	3.75	—
			Pane of 20, 4 #3337a	15.00	—
			P# block of 8, 2 sets of 4#+P	6.00	—
			Sheet of 120 (6 panes)	90.00	—
			Block of 10 with vert. gutter	15.00	—
			Cross gutter block of 8	17.50	—
			Horiz. pairs with vert. gutter (each)	2.25	—
			Vert. pairs with horiz. gutter (each)	2.25	—

Stamps in No. 3337a are arranged in four different orders. Plate block may contain top label.

FREDERICK LAW OLMSTED (1822-1903), LANDSCAPE ARCHITECT

A2584

Designed by Ethel Kessler.
Printed by Ashton-Potter (USA) Ltd.

LITHOGRAPHED
Sheets of 120 in six panes of 20

1999, Sept. 12			**Tagged**		**Perf. 11**
3338	A2584	33c	multicolored	.65	.20
			P# block of 4, 4#+P	2.60	—
			Pane of 20	13.00	—

AMERICAN MUSIC SERIES
Hollywood Composers

Max Steiner
(1888-1971)
A2585

Dimitri Tiomkin (1894-1975) A2586

Bernard Herrmann (1911-75) A2587

Franz Waxman (1906-67) A2588

Alfred Newman (1907-70) A2589

Erich Wolfgang Korngold (1897-1957) A2590

Designed by Howard Paine.
Printed by Sterling Sommer for Ashton-Potter (USA) Ltd.

LITHOGRAPHED
Sheets of 120 in six panes of 20

1999, Sept. 16		Tagged	Perf. 11	
3339	A2585	33c multicolored	.70	.20
3340	A2586	33c multicolored	.70	.20
3341	A2587	33c multicolored	.70	.20
3342	A2588	33c multicolored	.70	.20
3343	A2589	33c multicolored	.70	.20
3344	A2590	33c multicolored	.70	.20
a.		Block of 6, #3339-3344	4.25	—
		P# block of 6, 5#+P	4.25	—
		P# block of 8, 2 sets of 5#+P +		
		top label	5.75	—
		Pane of 20	14.50	—

AMERICAN MUSIC SERIES
Broadway Songwriters

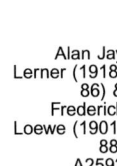

Ira (1896-1983) & George (1898-1937) Gershwin A2591

Alan Jay Lerner (1918-86) & Frederick Loewe (1901-88) A2592

Lorenz Hart (1895-1943) A2593

Richard Rodgers (1902-79) & Oscar Hammerstein II (1895-1960) A2594

Meredith Willson (1902-84) A2595

Frank Loesser (1910-69) A2596

Designed by Howard Paine.
Printed by Sterling Sommer for Ashton-Potter (USA) Ltd.

LITHOGRAPHED
Sheets of 120 in six panes of 20

1999, Sept. 21		Tagged	Perf. 11	
3345	A2591	33c multicolored	.70	.20
3346	A2592	33c multicolored	.70	.20
3347	A2593	33c multicolored	.70	.20
3348	A2594	33c multicolored	.70	.20
3349	A2595	33c multicolored	.70	.20
3350	A2596	33c multicolored	.70	.20
a.		Block of 6, #3345-3350	4.25	—

P# block of 6, 5#+P	4.25	—
P# block of 8, 2 sets of 5#+P +		
top label	5.75	—
Pane of 20	14.50	—

INSECTS & SPIDERS

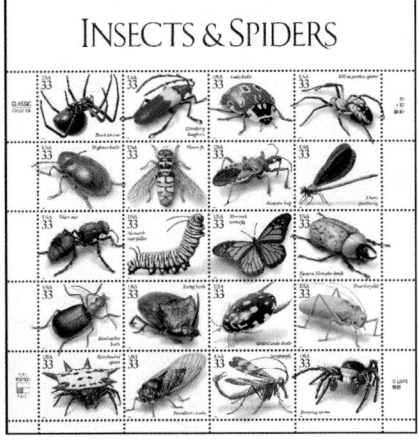

A2597

Illustration reduced.

Designed by Carl Herrman.
Printed by Ashton-Potter (USA) Ltd.

Designs: a, Black widow. b, Elderberry longhorn. c, Lady beetle. d, Yellow garden spider. e, Dogbane beetle. f, Flower fly. g, Assassin bug. h, Ebony jewelwing. i, Velvet ant. j, Monarch caterpillar. k, Monarch butterfly. l, Eastern Hercules beetle. m, Bombardier beetle. n, Dung beetle. o, Spotted water beetle. p, True katydid. q, Spinybacked spider. r, Periodical cicada. s, Scorpionfly. t, Jumping spider.

LITHOGRAPHED
Sheets of 80 in four panes of 20

1999, Oct. 1		Tagged	Perf. 11	
3351	A2597	Pane of 20	13.00	10.00
a.-t.		33c any single	.65	.50
		Sheet of 4 panes	52.50	
		Cross gutter block of 20	20.00	
		Vert. pair with horiz. gutter		
		(each)	1.60	
		Horiz. pair with vert. gutter		
		(each)	1.60	

Cross gutter block of 20 consists of six stamps from each of two panes and four stamps from each of the two other panes with the cross gutter between.

Hanukkah Type of 1996

Designed by Hannah Smotrich.
Printed by Avery Dennison.

PHOTOGRAVURE
Sheets of 200 in 10 panes of 20

1999, Oct. 8		Tagged	Serpentine Die Cut 11	
			Self-Adhesive	
3352	A2411	33c multicolored	.65	.20
		P# block of 4, 5#+V	2.60	
		Pane of 20	13.00	

Uncle Sam Type of 1998

Designed by Richard Sheaff.
Printed by Bureau of Engraving and Printing.

COIL STAMP
PHOTOGRAVURE

1999, Oct. 8		Tagged	Perf. 9¾ Vert.	
3353	A2530	22c multicolored	.45	.20
		Pair	.90	.30
		P# strip of 5, #1111	3.50	
		P# single, same #	—	2.50

NATO, 50TH ANNIV.

A2598

Designed by Michael Cronan.
Printed by Ashton-Potter (USA) Ltd.

LITHOGRAPHED
Sheets of 180 in nine panes of 20

1999, Oct. 13   Tagged   *Perf. 11¼*
3354 A2598 33c multicolored   .65   .20
    P# block of 4, 4#+P   2.60   —
    Pane of 20   13.00

CHRISTMAS

Madonna and Child, by
Bartolomeo Vivarini — A2599

Deer — A2600

Designed by Richard Sheaff (#3355), Tom Nikosey (#3356-3367).
Printed by Banknote Corp. of America.

LITHOGRAPHED
Serpentine Die Cut 11¼ on 2 or 3 sides
1999, Oct. 20   Tagged
Booklet Stamp
Self-Adhesive
3355 A2599 33c multicolored   .75   .15
  a. Booklet pane of 20   15.00

Sheets of 120 in six panes of 20
Serpentine Die Cut 11¼
3356 A2600 33c gold & red   .75   .20
3357 A2600 33c gold & blue   .75   .20
3358 A2600 33c gold & purple   .75   .20
3359 A2600 33c gold & green   .75   .20
  a. Block or strip of 4, #3356-3359   3.00
    P# block of 4, 6#+B   3.00
    Pane of 20   15.00

Booklet Stamps
Serpentine Die Cut 11¼ on 2, 3 or 4 sides
3360 A2600 33c gold & red   1.50   .20
3361 A2600 33c gold & blue   1.50   .20
3362 A2600 33c gold & purple   1.50   .20
3363 A2600 33c gold & green   1.50   .20
  a. Booklet pane of 20, 5 each #3360-3363 30.00
  b. Block of 4, #3360-3363   6.00
  c. As "b," die cutting omitted   —
  d. As "a," die cutting omitted   —

Size: 21x19mm
Serpentine Die Cut 11½x11¼ on 2 or 3 sides
3364 A2600 33c gold & red   1.75   .20
3365 A2600 33c gold & blue   1.75   .20
3366 A2600 33c gold & purple   1.75   .20
3367 A2600 33c gold & green   1.75   .20
  a. Booklet pane of 4, #3364-3367   7.00
  b. Booklet pane of 5, #3364, 3366, 3367, 2
    #3365 + label   8.75
  c. Booklet pane of 6, #3365, 3367, 2 each
    #3364 & 3366   10.50
  d. Block of 4, #3364-3367   7.00

The frame on Nos. 3356-3359 is narrow and the space
between it and the hoof is a hairline. The frame on Nos. 3360-
3363 is much thicker, and the space between it and the hoof is
wider.

Kwanzaa Type of 1997
Designed by Synthia Saint James
Printed by Avery Dennison.

PHOTOGRAVURE
Sheets of 240 in twelve pane of 20
1999, Oct. 29   Tagged   *Serpentine Die Cut 11*
Self-Adhesive
3368 A2458 33c multicolored   .65   .20
    P# block of 4, 4#+V   2.60
    Pane of 20   13.00

YEAR 2000

Baby New Year — A2601

Designed by Carl Herrman.
Printed by Banknote Corporation of America.

LITHOGRAPHED
Sheets of 120 in six panes of 20
1999, Dec. 27   Tagged   *Serpentine Die Cut 11¼*
Self-Adhesive
3369 A2601 33c multicolored   .65   .20
    P# block of 4, 5#+B   3.00
    Pane of 20   14.50

CHINESE NEW YEAR

Year of the
Dragon
A2602

Designed by Clarence Lee.
Printed by Sterling Sommer.

LITHOGRAPHED
Sheets of 180 in nine panes of 20
2000, Jan. 6   Tagged   *Perf. 11¼*
3370 A2602 33c multicolored   .80   .20
    P# block of 4, 4#+P   3.25   —
    Pane of 20   15.50   —
    See No. 3895e.

BLACK HERITAGE SERIES

Patricia Roberts Harris
(1924-85), First Black
Woman Cabinet
Secretary — A2603

Designed by Richard Sheaff.
Printed by Ashton-Potter (USA) Ltd.

LITHOGRAPHED
Sheets of 180 in nine panes of 20
Serpentine Die Cut 11½x11¼
2000, Jan. 27   Tagged
Self-Adhesive
3371 A2603 33c indigo   .65   .20
    P# block of 4, 4#+P   2.60
    Pane of 20   13.00

SUBMARINES

S Class
A2604

Los Angeles
Class
A2605

Ohio Class
A2606

USS Holland
A2607

Gato Class — A2608

Illustration of No. 3377 reduced.

Designed by Carl Herrman.
Printed by Banknote Corporation of America.

LITHOGRAPHED
Sheets of 180 in nine panes of 20
2000, Mar. 27   Tagged   *Perf. 11*
3372 A2605 33c multicolored, with
    microprinted "USPS" at base
    of sail   .75   .20
    P# block of 4, 4#+B   3.00   —
    Pane of 20   15.00   —

BOOKLET STAMPS
3373 A2604 22c multicolored   1.15   .75
3374 A2605 33c multicolored, no microprint-
    ing   1.60 1.00
3375 A2606 55c multicolored   2.40 1.25
3376 A2607 60c multicolored   2.60 1.50
3377 A2608 $3.20 multicolored   14.75 5.00
  a. Booklet pane of 5, #3373-3377   22.50   —

No. 3377a was issued with two types of text in the selvage.

PACIFIC COAST RAIN FOREST

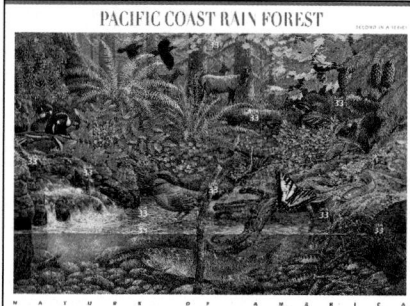

A2609

Illustration reduced.

Designed by Ethel Kessler.
Printed by Banknote Corporation of America.

Designs: a, Harlequin duck. b, Dwarf oregongrape, snail-eat-
ing ground beetle. c, American dipper, horiz. d, Cutthroat trout,
horiz. e, Roosevelt elk. f, Winter wren. g, Pacific giant salamander, Rough-skinned newt. h, Western tiger swallowtail, horiz. i,
Douglas squirrel, foliose lichen. j, Foliose lichen, banana slug.

LITHOGRAPHED
Sheets of 60 in six panes of 10
Serpentine Die Cut 11¼x11½, 11½ (horiz. stamps)
2000, Mar. 29   Tagged

Self-Adhesive

3378 A2609	Pane of 10	8.00	
a.-j.	33c any single	.80	.50
	Sheet of 6 panes	50.00	

LOUISE NEVELSON (1899-1988), SCULPTOR

Silent Music I — A2610

Royal Tide I — A2611

Black Chord — A2612

Nightsphere-Light A2613

Dawn's Wedding Chapel I — A2614

Designed by Ethel Kessler.

Printed by Ashton-Potter (USA) Ltd.

LITHOGRAPHED
Sheets of 80 in four panes of 20.

				Perf. 11x11¼
2000, Apr. 6		**Tagged**		
3379	A2610	33c	multicolored	.65 .20
3380	A2611	33c	multicolored	.65 .20
3381	A2612	33c	multicolored	.65 .20
3382	A2613	33c	multicolored	.65 .20
3383	A2614	33c	multicolored	.65 .20
a.		Strip of 5, #3379-3383		3.25 —
		P# block of 10, 4#+P		6.50 —
		Pane of 20		13.00 —

HUBBLE SPACE TELESCOPE IMAGES

Eagle Nebula — A2615   Ring Nebula — A2616

Lagoon Nebula — A2617   Egg Nebula — A2618

Galaxy NGC 1316 — A2619

Designed by Phil Jordan. Printed at American Packaging Corp. for Sennett Security Products.

PHOTOGRAVURE
Sheets of 120 in six panes of 20.

				Perf. 11
2000, Apr. 10		**Tagged**		
3384	A2615	33c	multicolored	.65 .20
3385	A2616	33c	multicolored	.65 .20
3386	A2617	33c	multicolored	.65 .20
3387	A2618	33c	multicolored	.65 .20
3388	A2619	33c	multicolored	.65 .20
a.		Strip of 5, #3384-3388		3.25 —
		P# block of 10, 6#+S		6.50 —
		Pane of 20		13.00 —
b.		As "a," imperf		1,250.
		As "b," pane of 20		5,000.

AMERICAN SAMOA

Samoan Double Canoe A2620

Designed by Howard Paine.
Printed by Ashton-Potter (USA) Ltd.

LITHOGRAPHED
Sheets of 120 in six panes of 20

				Perf. 11
2000, Apr. 17		**Tagged**		
3389	A2620	33c	multicolored	.65 .20
		P# block of 4, 4#+P		2.60 —
		Pane of 20		13.00 —

LIBRARY OF CONGRESS

Interior Dome and Arched Windows in Main Reading Room, Thomas Jefferson Building — A2621

Designed by Ethel Kessler.
Printed by Ashton-Potter (USA) Ltd.

LITHOGRAPHED
Sheets of 120 in six panes of 20

				Perf. 11
2000, Apr. 24		**Tagged**		
3390	A2621	33c	multicolored	.65 .20
		P# block of 4, 5#+P		2.60 —
		Pane of 20		13.00 —

ROAD RUNNER & WILE E. COYOTE

A2622

Cross Gutter Block of 9

Illustration reduced.

Designed by Ed Wleczyk, Warner Bros.
Printed by Banknote Corp. of America, Inc.

LITHOGRAPHED

2000, Apr. 26   **Tagged**   *Serpentine Die Cut 11*
Self-Adhesive

3391	Pane of 10	9.00	
a.	A2622 33c single	.85	.20
b.	Booklet pane of 9 #3391a	7.75	
c.	Booklet pane of 1 #3391a	1.25	
	Sheet of 60 (six panes) top, with plate # in selvage on reverse	55.00	
	Sheet of 60 (six panes) bottom, with plate # in selvage	57.50	
	Pane of 10 from sheet of 60	9.50	
	Two panes of 10 with plate numbers on front	22.50	
	Cross gutter block of 9 or 10	16.00	
	Vert. pair with horiz. gutter	2.00	
	Horiz. pair with vert. gutter	4.00	
d.	All die cutting omitted, pane of 10	*2,500.*	

Die cutting on #3391b does not extend through the backing paper.

3392	Pane of 10	*40.00*	
a.	A2622 33c single	*2.75*	
b.	Booklet pane of 9 #3392a	*30.00*	
c.	Booklet pane of 1, imperf.	*5.00*	

Die cutting on #3392a extends through the backing paper. Used examples of No. 3392a are identical to those of No. 3391a.
Nos. 3391b-3391c and 3392b-3392c are separated by a vertical line of microperforations.

DISTINGUISHED SOLDIERS

Maj. Gen. John
L. Hines
(1868-1968)
A2623

Gen. Omar N.
Bradley (1893-
1981)
A2624

Sgt. Alvin C.
York (1887-
1964)
A2625

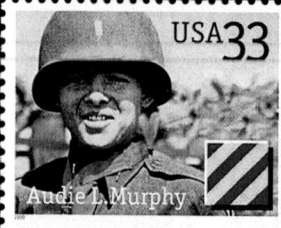

Second Lt.
Audie L.
Murphy (1924-
71)
A2626

Designed by Phil Jordan.
Printed by Sterling Sommer for Ashton-Potter (USA) Ltd.

LITHOGRAPHED
Sheets of 120 in six panes of 20

2000, May 3			**Tagged**	*Perf. 11*	
3393	A2623	33c	multicolored	.65	.20
3394	A2624	33c	multicolored	.65	.20
3395	A2625	33c	multicolored	.65	.20
3396	A2626	33c	multicolored	.65	.20
a.			Block or strip of 4, #3393-3396	2.60	—
			P# block of 4, 4#+P	2.60	—
			Pane of 20	13.00	—

SUMMER SPORTS

Runners
A2627

Designed by Richard Sheaff.
Printed by Ashton-Potter (USA) Ltd.

LITHOGRAPHED
Sheets of 120 in six panes of 20

2000, May 5			**Tagged**	*Perf. 11*	
3397	A2627	33c	multicolored	.65	.20
			P# block of 4, 4#+P	2.60	—
			Pane of 20	13.00	—

ADOPTION

Stick Figures — A2628

Designed by Greg Berger.
Printed by Banknote Corporation of America.

LITHOGRAPHED
Sheets of 120 in six panes of 20

2000, May 10			**Tagged**	*Serpentine Die Cut 11½*	
			Self-Adhesive		
3398	A2628	33c	multicolored	.75	.20
			P# block of 4, 5#+B	3.00	
			Pane of 20	15.00	
a.			Die cutting omitted, pair	—	

YOUTH TEAM SPORTS

Basketball — A2629

Football — A2630

Soccer — A2631

Baseball — A2632

Designed by Derry Noyes.
Printed by Sterling Sommer for Ashton-Potter (USA) Ltd.

LITHOGRAPHED
Sheets of 120 in six panes of 20

2000, May 27			**Tagged**	*Perf. 11*	
3399	A2629	33c	multicolored	.65	.20
3400	A2630	33c	multicolored	.65	.20
3401	A2631	33c	multicolored	.65	.20
3402	A2632	33c	multicolored	.65	.20
a.			Block or strip of 4, #3399-3402	2.60	—
			P# block of 4, 4#+P	2.60	—
			Pane of 20	13.00	—

THE STARS AND STRIPES

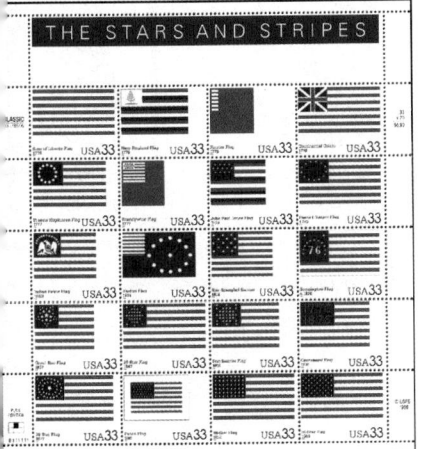

A2633

Illustration reduced.

Designed by Richard Sheaff.
Printed by Banknote Corp. of America.

Designs: a, Sons of Liberty Flag, 1775. b, New England Flag, 1775. c, Forster Flag, 1775. d, Continental Colors, 1776. e, Francis Hopkinson Flag, 1777. f, Brandywine Flag, 1777. g, John Paul Jones Flag, 1779. h, Pierre L'Enfant Flag, 1783. i, Indian Peace Flag, 1803. j, Easton Flag, 1814. k, Star-Spangled Banner, 1814. l, Bennington Flag, c. 1820. m, Great Star Flag, 1837. n, 29-Star Flag, 1847. o, Fort Sumter Flag, 1861. p, Centennial Flag, 1876. q, 38-Star Flag, 1877. r, Peace Flag, 1891. s, 48-Star Flag, 1912. t, 50-Star Flag, 1960.

LITHOGRAPHED

2000, June 14   Tagged   Perf. 10½x11

3403	A2633	Pane of 20	15.00	11.00
a.-t.		33c any single	.75	.50
		Sheet of 120 (6 panes)	85.00	
		Cross gutter block of 20	25.00	—
		Vert. pairs with horiz. gutter (each)	2.50	—
		Horiz. pairs with vert. gutter (each)	2.50	—

Inscriptions on the back of each stamp describe the flag.
Cross gutter block of 20 consists of six stamps from each of two panes and four stamps from each of two other panes with the cross gutter between.

BERRIES

Blueberries — A2634

Strawberries — A2635

Blackberries — A2636

Raspberries — A2637

Designed by Howard Paine. Printed by Guilford Gravure.
See designs A2550-A2553.

PHOTOGRAVURE
COIL STAMPS

Serpentine Die Cut 8½ Horiz.

2000, June 16   Tagged

Self-Adhesive

3404	A2634	33c multicolored	2.00	.20
3405	A2635	33c multicolored	2.00	.20
3406	A2636	33c multicolored	2.00	.20
3407	A2637	33c multicolored	2.00	.20
a.		Strip of 4, #3404-3407	8.00	
		P# strip of 5, 2 #3404, 1 each #3405-3407, #G1111	12.00	
		P# strip of 9, 2 each #3404-3405, 3407, 3 #3406, #G1111	20.00	
		P# single (#3406), #G1111	—	1.50

Nos. 3404-3407 are linerless coils issued without backing paper. The adhesive is strong and can remove the ink from stamps in the roll.

LEGENDS OF BASEBALL

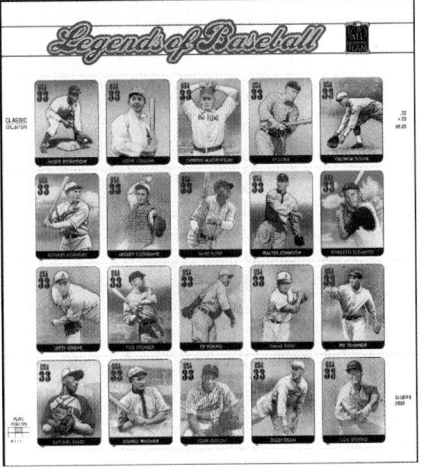

A2638

Illustration reduced.

Designed by Phil Jordan. Printed by Ashton-Potter (USA) Ltd.

Designs: a, Jackie Robinson. b, Eddie Collins. c, Christy Mathewson. d, Ty Cobb. e, George Sisler. f, Rogers Hornsby. g, Mickey Cochrane. h, Babe Ruth. i, Walter Johnson. j, Roberto Clemente. k, Lefty Grove. l, Tris Speaker. m, Cy Young. n, Jimmie Foxx. o, Pie Traynor. p, Satchel Paige. q, Honus Wagner. r, Josh Gibson. s, Dizzy Dean. t, Lou Gehrig.

LITHOGRAPHED
Sheets of 120 in six panes of 20

2000, July 6   Tagged   Serpentine Die Cut 11¼
Self-Adhesive

3408	A2638	Pane of 20	13.00	
a.-t.		33c any single	.65	.50
		Sheet of 120 (6 panes)	80.00	
		Cross gutter block of 20	22.50	—
		Vert. pairs with horiz. gutter (each)	2.25	—
		Horiz. pairs with vert. gutter (each)	2.25	—

Cross gutter block of 20 consists of six stamps from each of two panes and four stamps from each of two other panes with the cross gutter between.

SPACE
Souvenir Sheets

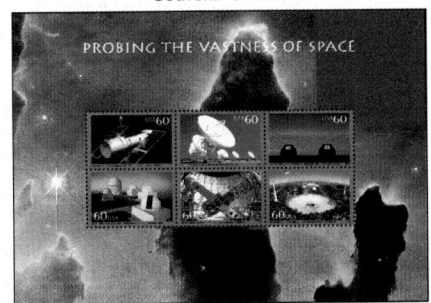

Probing the Vastness of Space — A2639

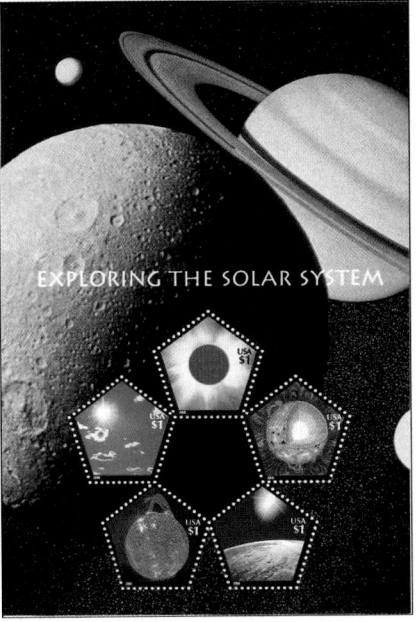
Exploring the Solar System — A2640

Escaping the Gravity of Earth — A2641

Space Achievement and Exploration — A2642

Landing on the Moon — A2643

Designed by Richard Sheaff. Printed by American Packaging Corporation for Sennett Security Products.

Designs: No. 3409: a, Hubble Space Telescope. b, Radio interferometer very large array, New Mexico. c, Optical and infrared telescopes, Keck Observatory, Hawaii. d, Optical telescopes, Cerro Tololo Observatory, Chile. e, Optical telescope, Mount Wilson Observatory, California. f, Radio telescope, Arecibo Observatory, Puerto Rico.
No. 3410: a, Sun and corona. b, Cross-section of sun. c, Sun and earth. d, Sun and solar flare. e, Sun and clouds.
No. 3411: a, Space Shuttle and Space Station. b, Astronauts working in space.
Illustrations reduced.

PHOTOGRAVURE

2000		**Tagged**	**Perf. 10½x11**	
3409	A2639	Sheet of 6, *July 10*	10.00	7.00
a.-f.		60c any single	1.60	1.00

Perf. 10¾

3410	A2640	Sheet of 5 + label, *July 11*	15.00	10.00
a.-e.		$1 any single	2.75	1.75
f.		As No. 3410, imperf	3,250.	
g		As No. 3410, with hologram from No. 3411b applied	—	

Untagged
Photogravure with Hologram Affixed
Perf. 10½, 10¾ (#3412)

3411	A2641	Sheet of 2, *July 9*	20.00	10.00
a.-b.		$3.20 any single	9.00	4.00
c.		Hologram omitted on right stamp	—	
3412	A2642	**multicolored**, *July 7*	32.50	17.50
a.		$11.75 single	30.00	15.00
b.		Hologram omitted	—	
c.		Hologram omitted on No. 3412 in uncut sheet of 5 panes	—	
3413	A2643	**multicolored**, *July 8*	32.50	17.50
		Uncut sheet of 5 panes, #3409-3413	100.00	
a.		$11.75 single	30.00	15.00
b.		Double hologram	—	
c.		Double hologram on No. 3413 in uncut sheet of 5 panes	—	
d.		Hologram omitted on No. 3413 in uncut sheet of 5 panes	—	
		Nos. 3409-3413 (5)	110.00	62.00

Warning: Soaking in water may affect holographic images.

STAMPIN' THE FUTURE CHILDREN'S STAMP DESIGN CONTEST WINNERS

By Zachary Canter A2644

By Sarah Lipsey A2645

By Morgan Hill — A2646

By Ashley Young A2647

Designed by Richard Sheaff. Printed by Ashton-Potter (USA) Ltd.

LITHOGRAPHED
Sheets of 120 in six panes of 20

2000, July 13	**Tagged**		**Serpentine Die Cut 11¼**	
		Self-Adhesive		
3414	A2644	33c **multicolored**	.65	.20
3415	A2645	33c **multicolored**	.65	.20
3416	A2646	33c **multicolored**	.65	.20
3417	A2647	33c **multicolored**	.65	.20
a.		Horiz. strip of 4, #3414-3417	2.60	
		P# block of 8, 2 sets of 5#+P	5.25	
		Pane of 20	13.00	

Plate block may contain top label.

DISTINGUISHED AMERICANS

Gen. Joseph W. Stilwell (1883-1946) A2650

Wilma Rudolph (1940-94), Athlete A2652

Sen. Claude Pepper (1900-89) — A2656

Dr. Jonas Salk (1914-95), Polio Vaccine Pioneer — A2658

Sen. Hattie Caraway (1878-1950) A2661

Edna Ferber (1887-1968), Writer A2662

Edna Ferber (With Curving Shoulder) — A2663

Dr. Albert Sabin (1906-93), Polio Vaccine Pioneer — A2664

Designed by: 10c, 23c, 33c, 63c, 76c, 83c, 87c Richard Sheaff.
Printed by Banknote Corporation of America (#3420-3433), Ashton-Potter (USA) Ltd. (#3422, 3428, 3434).

LITHOGRAPHED & ENGRAVED, LITHOGRAPHED (#3436)
Sheets of 120 in six panes of 20
Perf. 11 (#3420, 3426), Serpentine Die Cut 11¼x10¾ (#3422), 11¼x11 (#3428), 11 (#3431), 11½x11 (#3432), 11x11¾ (#3433), 11¼ (#3434)

2000-06				**Tagged**
		Self-Adhesive (#3422, 3431-3434, 3436)		
3420	A2650	10c **red & black**, *Aug. 24*	.20	.20
		P# block of 4, 3#+B	.80	—
		Pane of 20	4.00	—
a.		Imperf, pair	500.00	
3422	A2652	23c **red & black**, *July 14, 2004*	.45	.20
		P# block of 4, 2#+P	1.80	
		Pane of 20	9.00	
3426	A2656	33c **red & black**, *Sept. 7*	.65	.20
		P# block of 4, 3#+B	2.60	—
		Pane of 20	13.00	—
3428	A2658	63c **red & black** *Marc. 8, 2006*	1.25	.20
		P# block of 4, 3#+P	5.00	
		Pane of 20	25.00	
a.		Black (litho.) omitted	—	
3431	A2661	76c **red & black**, *Feb. 21, 2001*	1.50	.20
		P# block of 4, 3#+B	6.00	
		Pane of 20	30.00	
3432	A2661	76c **red & black**,	3.50	2.00
		P# block of 4, 3#+B	14.00	
		Pane of 20	70.00	
3433	A2662	83c **red & black**, *July 29, 2002*	1.60	.30
		P# block of 4, 3#+B1	6.50	
		Pane of 20	32.50	

The previously listed "Big Mouth" flaw on No. 3433 has been discovered to be not a constant plate flaw but rather the result of extraneous matter on the plate affecting a reported 15 panes before the matter fell off, or was removed from, the plate.

3434	A2663	83c **red & black**, *Aug. 2003*	1.60	.30
		P# block of 4, 3#+P	6.50	
		Pane of 20	32.50	
3435	A2664	87c **red & black**, *Marc. 8, 2006*	1.75	.30
		P# block of 4, 2#+S	7.00	
		Pane of 20	35.00	

BOOKLET STAMP
Serpentine Die Cut 11¼x10¾ on 3 Sides
Self-Adhesive

3436	A2652	23c **red & black**, *July 14, 2004*	.45	.20
a.		Booklet pane of 4	1.80	
b.		Booklet pane of 6	2.70	
c.		Booklet pane of 10	4.50	
d.		As "c," die cutting omitted	—	

This is an ongoing set. Numbers may change.

CALIFORNIA STATEHOOD, 150TH ANNIV.

Big Sur and Iceplant — A2668

Designed by Carl Herrman.
Printed by Avery Dennison.

PHOTOGRAVURE
Sheets of 200 in ten panes of 20

2000, Sept. 8	**Tagged**		**Serpentine Die Cut 11**	
		Self-Adhesive		
3438	A2668	33c **multicolored**	.75	.20
		P# block of 4, 5#+V	3.00	
		Pane of 20	15.00	

DEEP SEA CREATURES

Fanfin Anglerfish
A2669

Sea Cucumber
A2670

Fangtooth
A2671

Amphipod
A2672

Medusa
A2673

Designed by Ethel Kessler.
Printed by American Packaging Corp. for Sennett Security Products.

PHOTOGRAVURE
Sheets of 135 in nine panes of 15

2000, Oct. 2		Tagged	Perf. 10x10¼	
3439	A2669	33c multicolored	.65	.20
3440	A2670	33c multicolored	.65	.20
3441	A2671	33c multicolored	.65	.20
3442	A2672	33c multicolored	.65	.20
3443	A2673	33c multicolored	.65	.20
a.		Vert. strip of 5, #3439-3443	3.25	2.00
		Pane of 15, 4#+S	9.75	—
		Sheet of 135 (nine panes)	90.00	—
		Cross gutter block of 10	15.00	—
		Horiz. block of 10 with vert. gutter	10.00	—
		Horiz. pairs with vert. gutter (each)	2.00	—
		Vert. pair with horiz. gutter	1.75	—

See note under No. 3292 regarding lack of plate block listing.
Cross gutter block of 10 consists of three stamps from each of two panes and two stamps from each of the other two panes with the cross gutter between.

LITERARY ARTS SERIES

Thomas Wolfe
(1900-38),
Novelist
A2674

Designed by Phil Jordan.
Printed by Ashton-Potter (USA) Ltd.

LITHOGRAPHED
Sheets of 120 in six panes of 20

2000, Oct. 3		Tagged	Perf. 11	
3444	A2674	33c multicolored	.65	.20
		P# block of 4, 5#+P	2.60	—
		Pane of 20	13.00	—

WHITE HOUSE, 200TH ANNIV.

A2675

Designed by Derry Noyes.
Printed by Ashton-Potter (USA) Ltd.

LITHOGRAPHED
Sheets of 180 in nine panes of 20

2000, Oct. 18	Tagged	Serpentine Die Cut 11¼	
Self-Adhesive			
3445	A2675 33c multicolored	1.00	.20
	P# block of 4, 4#+P	4.00	
	Pane of 20	20.00	

LEGENDS OF HOLLYWOOD

Edward G. Robinson (1893-1973) — A2676

Designed by Howard Paine.
Printed by American Packaging Corporation for Sennett Security Products.

PHOTOGRAVURE
Sheets of 120 in six panes of 20

2000, Oct. 24		Tagged	Perf. 11	
3446	A2676	33c multicolored	.80	.20
		P# block of 4, 7#+S	5.00	—
		Pane of 20	24.00	12.50
		Sheet of 120 (6 panes)	95.00	
		Cross gutter block of 8	22.50	
		Block of 8 with vertical gutter	14.00	
		Horiz. pair with vert. gutter	3.50	
		Vert. pair with horiz. gutter	2.50	

Perforations in corner of each stamp are star-shaped. Cross gutter block consists of 6 stamps from upper panes and 2 stamps from panes below.

New York Public Library
Lion — A2677

Designed by Carl Herrman.
Printed by American Packaging Corporation for Sennett Security Products.

PHOTOGRAVURE
COIL STAMP
Serpentine Die Cut 11½ Vert.

2000, Nov. 9			Untagged	
Self-Adhesive				
3447	A2677	(10c) multicolored, "2000" year date	.20	.20
		Pair	.40	
		P# strip of 5, #S11111, S22222, S33333, S44444, S66666	3.00	
		P# single, #S11111, S22222, S33333, S44444, S66666	—	1.75
a.		"2003" year date	.20	.20
		Pair	.40	
		P# strip of 5, #S55555	3.00	
		P# single, #S55555	—	1.75
b.		As No. 3447, prephosphored coated paper (solid tagging)	—	—

No. 3447 also is known with extremely faint phosphor splotches. No. 3447b has full-strength tagging.
See No. 3769.

Flag Over Farm — A2678

Designed by Richard Sheaff.
Printed by Sterling Sommer for Ashton-Potter (USA) Ltd. (#3448), Ashton-Potter (USA) Ltd. (#3449), Avery Dennison (#3450).

LITHOGRAPHED (#3448-3449), PHOTOGRAVURE (#3450)
Sheets of 120 in six panes of 20

2000, Dec. 15		Tagged	Perf. 11¼	
3448	A2678	(34c) multicolored	.65	.20
		P# block of 4, 4# + P	3.00	—
		Pane of 20	14.50	—
Self-Adhesive				
Serpentine Die Cut 11¼				
3449	A2678	(34c) multicolored	.65	.20
		P# block of 4, 4# + P	3.00	
		Pane of 20	14.50	
Booklet Stamp				
Self-Adhesive				
Serpentine Die Cut 8 on 2, 3 or 4 sides				
3450	A2678	(34c) multicolored	.75	.20
a.		Booklet pane of 18	14.00	

A2679

Statue of
Liberty — A2680

Designed by Derry Noyes.
Printed by Avery Dennison (#3451), Bureau of Engraving and Printing (#3452-3453).

PHOTOGRAVURE
Serpentine Die Cut 11 on 2, 3 or 4 sides

2000, Dec. 15			Tagged	
Self-Adhesive (#3451, 3453)				
Booklet Stamp				
3451	A2679	(34c) multicolored	.65	.20
a.		Booklet pane of 20	13.00	
b.		Booklet pane of 4	3.50	
		Booklet pane of 4 containing P# single	3.50	
		P# single, #V1111	.90	.70
c.		Booklet pane of 6	5.25	
d.		As "a," die cutting omitted	—	
Coil Stamps				
Perf. 9¾ Vert.				
3452	A2680	(34c) multicolored	.65	.20
		Pair	1.30	.30
		P# strip of 5, #1111	5.00	
		P# single, same #	—	2.50
Serpentine Die Cut 10 Vert.				
3453	A2680	(34c) multicolored, small date	.65	.20
		Pair	1.30	
		P# strip of 5, #1111	7.50	
		P# single, same #	—	2.00
a.		Die cutting omitted, pair		
b.		Large date	.70	.20

Pair		1.40
P# strip of 5, #1111		10.00
P# single, same #		— 2.50

The date on No. 3453 is 1⅛mm long, on No. 3453b 1½mm long and darker in color.

A2681

A2682

A2683

Flowers — A2684

Designed by Derry Noyes.
Printed by American Packaging Corporation for Sennett Security Products (#3454-3461), Guilford Gravure for Banknote Corporation of America, Inc. (#3462-3465).

PHOTOGRAVURE
Serpentine Die Cut 10½x10¾ on 2 or 3 sides
2000, Dec. 15   **Tagged**

Booklet Stamps
Self-Adhesive

3454	A2681	(34c)	purple & multi	1.00 .20
3455	A2682	(34c)	tan & multi	1.00 .20
3456	A2683	(34c)	green & multi	1.00 .20
3457	A2684	(34c)	red & multi	1.00 .20
a.			Block of 4, #3454-3457	4.00
b.			Booklet pane of 4, #3454-3457	4.00
c.			Booklet pane of 6, #3456, 3457, 2 each #3454-3455	6.00
d.			Booklet pane of 6, #3454, 3455, 2 each #3456-3457	6.00
e.			Booklet pane of 20, 5 each #3454-3457 + label	20.00

No. 3457e is a double-sided booklet pane, with 12 stamps on one side and eight stamps plus label on the other side.

Serpentine Die Cut 11½x11¾ on 2 or 3 sides

3458	A2681	(34c)	purple & multi	2.50 .25
3459	A2682	(34c)	tan & multi	2.50 .25
3460	A2683	(34c)	green & multi	2.50 .25
3461	A2684	(34c)	red & multi	2.50 .25
a.			Block of 4, #3458-3461	10.00
b.			Booklet pane of 20, 2 each #3461a, 3 each #3457a	32.00
c.			Booklet pane of 20, 2 each #3457a, 3 each #3461a	38.00

Nos. 3461b and 3461c are double-sided booklet panes, with 12 stamps on one side and eight stamps plus label on the other side.

Coil Stamps
Serpentine Die Cut 8½ Vert.

3462	A2683	(34c)	green & multi	3.50 .20
3463	A2684	(34c)	red & multi	3.50 .20
3464	A2682	(34c)	tan & multi	3.50 .20
3465	A2681	(34c)	purple & multi	3.50 .20
a.			Strip of 4, #3462-3465	14.00
			P# strip of 5, 2 #3462, 1 each #3463-3465, P#B1111	20.00
			P# strip of 9, 2 each #3462-3463, 3465, 3 each #3464, same P#	30.00
			P# single (#3464)	— 1.25

Lettering on No. 3462 has black outline not found on No. 3456. Zeroes of "2000" are rounder on Nos. 3454-3457 than on Nos. 3462-3465.

Statue of Liberty
A2685

George Washington
A2686

American Buffalo — A2687

Flag Over Farm — A2688

Statue of Liberty — A2689

A2690

A2691

A2692

Flowers — A2693

Apple — A2694

Orange — A2695

Eagle — A2696

Capitol Dome — A2697

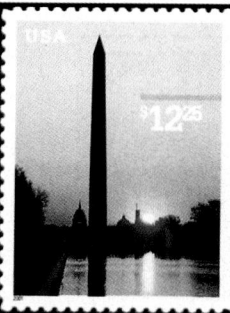
Washington Monument — A2698

Designed by Sterling Sommer for Ashton-Potter (USA) Ltd. (#3467), Carl Herrman (#3467, 3468, 3471, 3471A, 3475, 3484, 3484A), Richard Sheaff (#3468A, 3469, 3470, 3475A,

3482-3483, 3495), Derry Noyes (#3466, 3472-3473, 347... 3477-3481, 3485, 3487-3490), Ned Seidler (#3491-3494).
Printed by Avery Dennison (#3468, 3475, 3485, 3495) As...ton-Potter (USA) Ltd. (#3469-3470, 3482-3484A), America... Packaging Corporation for Sennett Security Printers (#347... 3471A, 3487-3490), Bureau of Engraving and Printing (#346... 3476-3477), Guilford Gravure, Inc. for Banknote Corporation... America (#3475A, 3478-3481), Banknote Corporation... America (#3468A, 3472-3473, 3491-3494).

PHOTOGRAVURE
Serpentine Die Cut 9¾ Vert.
2001, Jan. 7   **Tagge...**

Coil Stamp
Self-Adhesive

3466	A2685	34c	multicolored	.65 .2...
			Pair	1.30
			P# strip of 5, #1111, 2222	5.00
			P# single, same #	— 2.5...

Sheets of 400 in four panes of 100 (#3467), Sheets of 200 in ten panes of 20 (#3468), Sheets of 200 in two panes of 100 (#3469), Sheets of 120 in six panes of 20 (#3468A, 3470-3473), Sheets of 160 in eight panes of 20 (#3471A)
Self-Adhesive (#3468-3468A, 3470-3473)

2001		**Photo.**	**Tagged**	**Perf. 11¼x1...**
3467	A2687	21c	multicolored, Sept. 20	.50 .2...
			P# block of 4, 6#+P	18.00 —

Serpentine Die Cut 11

3468	A2687	21c	multicolored, Feb. 22	.40 .2...
			P# block of 4, 4#+V	1.60
			Pane of 20	8.00

Litho.
Serpentine Die Cut 11¼x11¾

3468A	A2686	23c	green, Sept. 20	.45 .2...
			P# block of 4, 3#+B	1.80
			Pane of 20	9.00

Photo.
Perf. 11¼

3469	A2688	34c	multicolored, Feb. 7	.75 .2...
			P# block of 4, 4#+P	25.00 —

Serpentine Die Cut 11¼

3470	A2688	34c	multicolored, Mar. 6	.65 .20
			P# block of 4, 4#+P	2.60
			Pane of 20	13.00

Photo.
Serpentine Die Cut 10¾

3471	A2696	55c	multicolored, Feb. 22	1.10 .20
			P# block of 4, 5#+S	4.40
			Pane of 20	22.00

Serpentine Die Cut 10¾

3471A	A2696	57c	multicolored, Sept. 20	1.10 .20
			P# block of 4, 5#+S	4.40
			Pane of 20	22.00

LITHOGRAPHED
Serpentine Die Cut 11¼x11½

3472	A2697	$3.50	multicolored, Jan. 29	7.00	2.00
			P# block of 4, 4#+B	28.00	
			Pane of 20	140.00	
a.			Die cutting omitted, pair	—	
3473	A2698	$12.25	multicolored, Jan. 29	22.50	10.00
			P# block of 4, 4#+B	90.00	
			Pane of 20	450.00	

COIL STAMPS
Self-Adhesive (#3475-3475A, 3477-3481)
Photo.
Serpentine Die Cut 8½ Vert.

3475	A2687	21c	multicolored, Feb. 22	.50 .20
			Pair	1.00 .30
			P# strip of 5, #V1111, V2222	3.50
			P# single, same #	— 1.25
3475A	A2686	23c	green, Sept. 20	.50 .20
			Pair	1.00
			P# strip of 5, #B11	3.50
			P# single, same #	— 2.00

Compare No. 3475A ("2001" date at lower left) with No. 3617 ("2002" date at lower left).

Perf. 9¾ Vert.

3476	A2685	34c	multicolored, prephosphored coated paper (grainy solid tagging), Feb. 7	.65 .20
			Pair	1.30 .30
			P# strip of 5, #1111	5.00
			P# single, same #	— 2.50
a.			Prephosphored coated paper (solid tagging)	.65 .20
			Pair	1.30 .30
			P# strip of 5, #1111	5.00
			P# single, same #	— 2.00

Serpentine Die Cut 9¾ Vert.

3477	A2685	34c	multicolored, Feb. 7	.65 .20
			Pair	1.30 .30
			P# strip of 5, #1111, 2222, 3333, 4444, 5555, 6666	5.00
			P# strip of 5, #7777	7.50

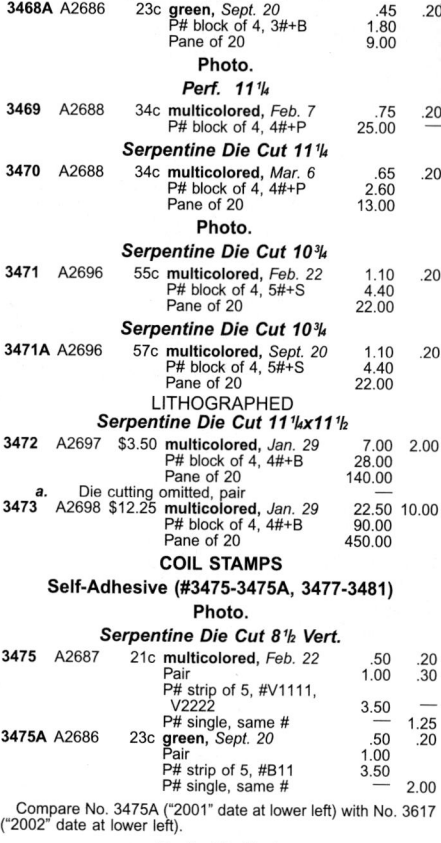

	P# single, same #	—	1.00	
	P# single, #7777	—	3.25	
a.	Die cutting omitted, pair			

No. 3477 has right angle corners and backing paper as high ...he stamp. No. 3466 has rounded corners and is on backing ...er larger than the stamp.

Serpentine Die Cut 8½ Vert.

8	A2690	34c green & multi, *Feb. 7*	.65	.20
9	A2691	34c red & multi, *Feb. 7*	.65	.20
40	A2692	34c tan & multi, *Feb. 7*	.65	.20
1	A2693	34c purple & multi, *Feb. 7*	.65	.20
a.		Strip of 4, #3478-3481	2.60	
		P# strip of 5, 2 #3478, 1 each #3479-3481, P#B1111, B2111, B2122, B2211, B2222	4.50	
		P# strip of 9, 3 #3480, 2 each #3478-3479, 3481, P# B1111, B2111, B2122, B2211, B2222	6.50	—
		P# single, (#3480), same #	—	2.00

BOOKLET STAMPS
Litho.
Self-Adhesive, Tagged
Serpentine Die Cut 11¼x11 on 3 Sides

82	A2686	20c dark carmine, *Feb. 22*	.40	.20
a.		Booklet pane of 10	4.00	
b.		Booklet pane of 4	1.60	
c.		Booklet pane of 6	2.40	

Serpentine Die Cut 10½x11 on 3 Sides

483	A2686	20c dark carmine, *Feb. 22*	1.75	1.50
a.		Booklet pane of 4, 2 #3482 at L, 2 #3483 at R	9.00	
b.		Booklet pane of 6, 3 #3482 at L, 3 #3483 at R	15.00	
c.		Booklet pane of 10, 5 #3482 at L, 5 #3483 at R	16.00	
d.		Booklet pane of 4, 2 #3483 at L, 2 #3482 at R	9.00	
e.		Booklet pane of 6, 3 #3483 at L, 3 #3482 at R	15.00	
f.		Booklet pane of 10, 5 #3483 at L, 5 #3482 at R	16.00	
g.		Pair, #3482 at L, #3483 at R	4.00	
h.		Pair, #3483 at L, #3482 at R	4.00	

Serpentine Die Cut 11¼ on 3 Sides

484	A2687	21c multicolored, *Sept. 20*	.50	.20
b.		Booklet pane of 4	2.00	
c.		Booklet pane of 6	3.00	
d.		Booklet pane of 10	5.00	

Serpentine Die Cut 10½x11¼

484A	A2687	21c multicolored, *Sept. 20*	3.50	1.50
e.		Booklet pane of 4, 2 #3484 at L, 2 #3484A at R	9.00	
f.		Booklet pane of 6, 3 #3484 at L, 3 #3484A at R	15.00	
g.		Booklet pane of 10, 5 #3484 at L, 5 #3484A at R	20.00	
h.		Booklet pane of 4, 2 #3484A at L, 2 #3484 at R	9.00	
i.		Booklet pane of 6, 3 #3484A at L, 3 #3484 at R	15.00	
j.		Booklet pane of 10, 5 #3484A at L, 5 #3484 at R	20.00	
k.		Pair, #3484 at L, #3484A at R	4.00	
l.		Pair, #3484A at L, #3484 at R	4.00	

Photo.
Serpentine Die Cut 11 on 2, 3 or 4 Sides

3485	A2689	34c multicolored, *Feb. 7*	.65	.20
a.		Booklet pane of 10	6.50	
b.		Booklet pane of 20	13.00	
c.		Booklet pane of 4	3.00	
		Booklet pane of 4 containing P# single	4.00	
		P# single, #V1111, V1122, V2212, V2222	1.50	1.50
		P# single, #V1112, V1121	—	—
d.		Booklet pane of 6	4.50	
e.		Die cutting omitted, pair (from No. 3485b)	—	
		As "e," booklet pane of 20	—	

Serpentine Die Cut 10½x10¾ on 2 or 3 Sides

3487	A2693	34c purple & multi, *Feb. 7*	.75	.20
3488	A2692	34c tan & multi, *Feb. 7*	.75	.20
3489	A2690	34c green & multi, *Feb. 7*	.75	.20
3490	A2691	34c red & multi, *Feb. 7*	.75	.20
a.		Block of 4, #3487-3490	3.00	
b.		Booklet pane of 4, #3487-3490	3.00	
c.		Booklet pane of 6, #3489-3490, 2 each #3487-3488	4.50	
d.		Booklet pane of 6, #3487-3488, 2 each #3489-3490	4.50	
e.		Booklet pane of 20, 5 each #3490a + label	15.00	

No. 3490e is a double-sided booklet pane, with 12 stamps on one side and eight stamps plus label on the other side.

Litho.
Serpentine Die Cut 11¼ on 2, 3 or 4 Sides

3491	A2694	34c multicolored, *Mar. 6*	.65	.20
3492	A2695	34c multicolored, *Mar. 6*	.65	.20
a.		Pair, #3491-3492	1.30	
b.		Booklet pane, 10 each #3491-3492	13.00	
c.		As "a," black ("34 USA") omitted	—	
d.		As "a," die cutting omitted		

e.	As "b," die cutting omitted	—		

Serpentine Die Cut 11½x10¾ on 2 or 3 Sides

3493	A2694	34c multicolored, *May*	1.00	.20
3494	A2695	34c multicolored, *May*	1.00	.20
a.		Pair, #3493-3494	2.00	
b.		Booklet pane, 2 each #3493-3494	4.00	
		Booklet pane, 2 each #3493-3494, containing P# single	6.00	
		P# single, #B1111	2.00	2.00
c.		Booklet pane, 3 each #3493-3494, #3493 at UL	6.00	
d.		Booklet pane, 3 each #3493-3494, #3494 at UL	6.00	

Serpentine Die Cut 8 on 2, 3 or 4 sides

3495	A2688	34c multicolored, *Dec. 17*	.80	.20
a.		Booklet pane of 18	15.00	

LOVE

Rose, Apr. 20, 1763 Love Letter by John Adams — A2699

Rose, Apr. 20, 1763 Love Letter by John Adams — A2700

Rose, Aug. 11, 1763 Love Letter by Abigail Smith (Abigail Adams in 1764) — A2701

Designed by Lisa Catalone. Printed by Banknote Corporation of America, Inc.

LITHOGRAPHED
Sheets of 180 in nine panes of 20 (#3499)

Serpentine Die Cut 11¼ on 2, 3 or 4 Sides
2001   **Tagged**

Self-Adhesive
Booklet Stamps (Nos. 3496-3498)

3496	A2699	(34c) multicolored, *Jan. 19*	.75	.20
a.		Booklet pane of 20	15.00	
b.		Vert. pair, die cutting omitted between	—	

Serpentine Die Cut 11¼ on 2, 3 or 4 Sides

3497	A2700	34c multicolored, *Feb. 14*	.75	.20
a.		Booklet pane of 20	15.00	
b.		Vertical pair, die cutting omitted between	—	

Size: 18x21mm

Serpentine Die Cut 11½x10¾ on 2 or 3 Sides

3498	A2700	34c multicolored, *Feb. 14*	1.00	.20
a.		Booklet pane of 4	4.00	
		Booklet pane of 4 containing P# single	6.00	
		P# single, #B1111	2.00	2.00
b.		Booklet pane of 6	6.00	

Plate number single on No. 3498 is on the lower left stamp of the bottom pane of 4 of the booklet.

Serpentine Die Cut 11¼

3499	A2701	55c multicolored, *Feb. 14*	1.10	.20
		P# block of 4, 4#+B	4.50	
		Pane of 20	22.50	

See No. 3551.

CHINESE NEW YEAR

Year of the Snake — A2702

Designed by Clarence Lee. Printed by Sterling Sommer for Ashton-Potter (USA) Ltd.

LITHOGRAPHED
Sheets of 180 in nine panes of 20

2001, Jan. 20		**Tagged**		**Perf. 11¼**	
3500	A2702	34c multicolored		.70	.20
		P# block of 4, 5#+P		2.80	—
		Pane of 20		14.00	

See No. 3895f.

BLACK HERITAGE SERIES

Roy Wilkins (1901-81), Civil Rights Leader — A2703

Designed by Richard Sheaff. Printed by Ashton-Potter (USA) Ltd.

LITHOGRAPHED
Sheets of 180 in nine panes of 20

Serpentine Die Cut 11½x11¼
2001, Jan. 24   **Tagged**

Self-Adhesive

3501	A2703	34c blue	.65	.20
		P# block of 4, 2#+P	2.60	
		Pane of 20	13.00	

AMERICAN ILLUSTRATORS

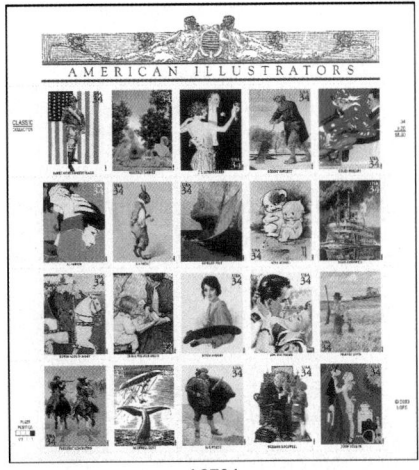

A2704

Illustration reduced.

Designed by Carl Herrman.
Printed by Avery Dennison.

Designs: a, Marine Corps poster "First in the Fight, Always Faithful," by James Montgomery Flagg. b, "Interlude (The Lute Players)," by Maxfield Parrish. c, Advertisement for Arrow Collars and Shirts, by J. C. Leyendecker. d, Advertisement for Carrier Corp. Refrigeration, by Robert Fawcett. e, Advertisement for Luxite Hosiery, by Coles Phillips. f, Illustration for correspondence school lesson, by Al Parker. g, "Br'er Rabbit," by A. B. Frost. h, "An Attack on a Galleon," by Howard Pyle. i, Kewpie and Kewpie Doodle Dog, by Rose O'Neill. j, Illustration for cover of True Magazine, by Dean Cornwell. k, "Galahad's Departure," by Edwin Austin Abbey. l, "The First Lesson," by Jessie Willcox Smith. m, Illustration for cover of McCall's Magazine, by Neysa McMein. n, "Back Home For Keeps," by Jon Whitcomb. o, "Something for Supper," by Harvey Dunn. p, "A Dash for the Timber," by Frederic Remington. q, Illustration for "Moby Dick," by Rockwell Kent. r, "Captain Bill Bones," by N. C. Wyeth. s, Illustration for cover of The Saturday Evening Post, by Norman Rockwell. t, "The Girl He Left Behind," by John Held, Jr.

PHOTOGRAVURE
Sheets of 80 in four panes of 20

2001, Feb. 1   **Tagged**   *Serpentine Die Cut 11¼*
Self-Adhesive

3502	A2704	Pane of 20	17.50	
a.-t.		34c any single	.85	.60
		Sheet of 80 (4 panes)	52.50	
		Block of 20 different stamps with vert. gutter between any 2 columns	27.50	
		Pairs with vert. gutter between (each)	2.00	

DIABETES AWARENESS

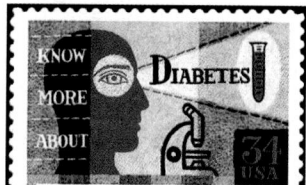

A2705

Designed by Richard Sheaff. Printed by Ashton-Potter (USA) Ltd.

LITHOGRAPHED
Sheets of 180 in nine panes of 20
Serpentine Die Cut 11 1/4x11 1/2

2001, Mar. 16   **Tagged**
Self-Adhesive
3503 A2705 34c **multicolored**   .65   .20
            P# block of 4, 4#+P   2.60
            Pane of 20   13.00

NOBEL PRIZE CENTENARY

Alfred Nobel and Obverse of Medals
A2706

Designed by Olof Baldursdottir of Sweden. Printed by De La Rue Security Printing.

LITHOGRAPHED & ENGRAVED
Sheets of 120 in six panes of 20

2001, Mar. 22   **Tagged**   **Perf. 11**
3504 A2706 34c **multicolored**   .65   .20
            P# block of 4, 3#+S   2.60   —
            Pane of 20   13.00   —
a.   Imperf, pair   —
          See Sweden No. 2415.

PAN-AMERICAN EXPOSITION INVERT STAMPS, CENT.

A2707

Illustration reduced.
Reproductions (dated 2001) of: a, #294a. b, #295a. c, #296a. d, Commemorative "cinderella" stamp depicting a buffalo.
Designed by Richard Sheaff. Printed by Banknote Corporation of America.

LITHOGRAPHED (#3505d), ENGRAVED (others)
Sheets of 28 in four panes of 7

2001, Mar. 29   **Perf. 12 (#3505d), 12 1/2x12 (others)**
Tagged (#3505d), Untagged (others)
3505 A2707 Pane of 7, #3505a-3505c, 4
            #3505d   9.00   7.00
a.   A109 1c **green & black**   .60   .20
b.   A110 2c **carmine & black**   .60   .20
c.   A111 4c **deep red brown & black**   .60   .20
d.   80c **red & blue**   1.75   .35
            Sheet of 4 panes   45.00
            Pane with vertical gutter, 80c
            stamps at left; "a," "b" & "c" at
            right (from sheet of 4 panes)   20.00

GREAT PLAINS PRAIRIE

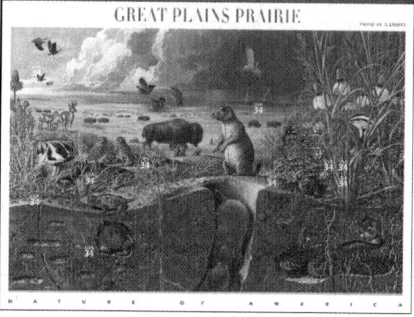

A2708

Illustration reduced.

Designed by Ethel Kessler. Printed by Ashton-Potter (USA) Ltd.

Wildlife and flowers: a, Pronghorns, Canada geese. b, Burrowing owls, American buffalos. c, American buffalo, Black-tailed prairie dogs, wild alfalfa, horiz. d, Black-tailed prairie dog, American buffalos,. e, Painted lady butterfly, American buffalo, prairie coneflowers, prairie wild roses, horiz. f, Western meadowlark, camel cricket, prairie coneflowers, prairie wild roses. g, Badger, harvester ants. h, Eastern short-horned lizard, plains pocket gopher. i, Plains spadefoot, dung beetle, prairie wild roses, horiz. j, Two-striped grasshopper, Ord's kangaroo rat.

LITHOGRAPHED
Sheets of 60 in six panes of 10

2001, Apr. 19   Tagged   *Serpentine Die Cut 10*
Self-Adhesive
3506 A2708   Pane of 10   10.00
a.-j.   34c Any single   .90   .50
              Sheet of 6 panes   55.00

PEANUTS COMIC STRIP

Snoopy
A2709

Designed by Paige Braddock. Printed by Ashton-Potter (USA) Ltd.

LITHOGRAPHED
Sheets of 180 in nine panes of 20
Serpentine Die Cut 11 1/4x11 1/2

2001, May 17   **Tagged**
Self-Adhesive
3507 A2709 34c **multicolored**   .75   .20
            P# block of 4, 5#+P   3.00
            Pane of 20   15.00

HONORING VETERANS

A2710

Designed by Carl Herrman. Printed by Ashton-Potter (USA) Ltd.

LITHOGRAPHED
Sheets of 180 in nine panes of 20
Serpentine Die Cut 11 1/4x11 1/2

2001, May 23   **Tagged**
Self-Adhesive
3508 A2710 34c **multicolored**   .65   .20
            P# block of 4, 4#+P   2.60
            Pane of 20   13.00 11.00

FRIDA KAHLO (1907-54), PAINTER

Self-portrait — A2711

Designed by Richard Sheaff. Printed by Sterling Sommer Ashton-Potter (USA) Ltd..

LITHOGRAPHED
Sheets of 80 in four panes of 20

2001, June 21   **Tagged**   **Perf. 11**
3509 A2711 34c **multicolored**   .65
            P# block of 4, 4#+P   2.60
            Pane of 20   13.00

LEGENDARY PLAYING FIELDS

Ebbets Field — A2712

Tiger Stadium A2713

Crosley Field — A2714

Yankee Stadium A2715

Polo Grounds A2716

Forbes Field — A2717

Fenway Park — A2718

Comiskey Park — A2719

Shibe Park — A2720

Wrigley Field — A2721

Designed by Phil Jordan. Printed by Avery Dennison.

PHOTOGRAVURE
Sheets of 160 in eight panes of 20
Serpentine Die Cut 11¼x11½

2001, June 27   **Tagged**

Self-Adhesive

3510 A2712 34c multicolored .80 .60
3511 A2713 34c multicolored .80 .60
3512 A2714 34c multicolored .80 .60
3513 A2715 34c multicolored .80 .60
3514 A2716 34c multicolored .80 .60
3515 A2717 34c multicolored .80 .60
3516 A2718 34c multicolored .80 .60
3517 A2719 34c multicolored .80 .60
3518 A2720 34c multicolored .80 .60
3519 A2721 34c multicolored .80 .60
  a. Block of 10, #3510-3519 8.00
    P# block of 10, 4#+V 8.00
    Pane of 20 16.00
    Sheet of 160 (8 panes) 115.00
    Cross-gutter block of 12 20.00
    Horiz. block of 10 with vert. gutter 10.00
    Block of 4 with horiz. gutter 4.50
    Vert. pairs with horiz. gutter (each) 2.00
    Horiz. pairs with vert. gutter (each) 2.00

Cross gutter block contains one each Nos. 3510-3517, two each of Nos. 3518-3519, and vertical and horizontal gutters.

ATLAS STATUE, NEW YORK CITY

A2722

Designed by Kevin Newman. Printed by Banknote Corporation of America.

PHOTOGRAVURE
COIL STAMP
Serpentine Die Cut 8½ Vert.

2001, June 29   **Untagged**

Self-Adhesive

3520 A2722 (10c) multicolored .20 .20
    Pair .40
    P# strip of 5, #B1111 2.75
    P# single, same # — 1.75
    See No. 3770.

LEONARD BERNSTEIN (1918-90), CONDUCTOR

A2723

Designed by Howard Paine. Printed by Sterling Sommer for Ashton-Potter (USA) Ltd.

LITHOGRAPHED
Sheets of 180 in nine panes of 20

2001, July 10   **Tagged**   *Perf. 11¼*
3521 A2723 34c multicolored .65 .20
    P# block of 4, 4#+P 2.60 —
    Pane of 20 13.00 —

WOODY WAGON

A2724

Designed by Kevin Newman. Printed by American Packaging Corporation for Sennett Security Products.

PHOTOGRAVURE
COIL STAMP
Serpentine Die Cut 11½ Vert.

2001, Aug. 3   **Untagged**

Self-Adhesive

3522 A2724 (15c) multicolored .30 .20
    Pair .60
    P# strip of 5, #S11111 3.00
    P# single, same # — 1.75

LEGENDS OF HOLLYWOOD

Lucille Ball (1911-89) — A2725

Designed by Derry Noyes. Printed by Banknote Corporation of America.

LITHOGRAPHED
Sheets of 180 in nine panes of 20

2001, Aug. 6   **Tagged**   *Serpentine Die Cut 11*
Self-Adhesive
3523 A2725 34c multicolored .85 .20
    P# block of 4, 4#+B 3.75
    Pane of 20 18.50 13.00
    Sheet of 180 (9 panes) 130.00
    Cross-gutter block of 8 20.00
    Block of 8 with vert. gutter 11.50
    Horiz. pair with vert. gutter 3.25

    Vert. pairs with horiz. gutter 2.25
  a. Die cutting omitted, pair —
    As "a," pane of 20 —

Cross gutter block consists of 6 stamps from upper panes and 2 stamps from lower panes.

AMERICAN TREASURES SERIES
Amish Quilts

Diamond in the Square, c. 1920 — A2726

Lone Star, c. 1920 — A2727

Sunshine and Shadow, c. 1910 — A2728

Double Ninepatch Variation — A2729

Designed by Derry Noyes. Printed by Ashton-Potter (USA) Ltd.

LITHOGRAPHED
Sheets of 120 in six panes of 20
Serpentine Die Cut 11¼x11½

2001, Aug. 9   **Tagged**

Self-Adhesive

3524 A2726 34c multicolored .65 .20
3525 A2727 34c multicolored .65 .20
3526 A2728 34c multicolored .65 .20
3527 A2729 34c multicolored .65 .20
  a. Block or strip of 4, #3524-3527 2.60
    P# block of 4, 5#+P 2.60
    Pane of 20 13.00

CARNIVOROUS PLANTS

Venus Flytrap — A2730

Yellow Trumpet — A2731

Cobra Lily — A2732

English Sundew — A2733

Designed by Steve Buchanan.
Printed by Avery Dennison.

PHOTOGRAVURE
Sheets of 160 in eight panes of 20
2001, Aug. 23   Tagged   *Serpentine Die Cut 11½*
Self-Adhesive

3528	A2730	34c multicolored	.65	.20
3529	A2731	34c multicolored	.65	.20
3530	A2732	34c multicolored	.65	.20
3531	A2733	34c multicolored	.65	.20
a.		Block or strip of 4, #3528-3531	2.60	
		P# block of 4, 4#+V	2.60	
		Pane of 20	13.00	

EID

"Eid Mubarak" — A2734

Designed by Mohamed Zakariya.
Printed by Avery Dennison.

PHOTOGRAVURE
Sheets of 240 in twelve panes of 20
2001, Sept. 1   Tagged   *Serpentine Die Cut 11¼*
Self-Adhesive

3532	A2734	34c multicolored	.65	.20
		P# block of 4, 3#+V	2.60	
		Pane of 20	13.00	

See No. 3674.

ENRICO FERMI (1901-54), PHYSICIST

A2735

Designed by Richard Sheaff. Printed by Sterling Sommer for Ashton-Potter (USA) Ltd.

LITHOGRAPHED
Sheets of 180 in nine panes of 20
2001, Sept. 29   Tagged   *Perf. 11*

3533	A2735	34c multicolored	.65	.20
		P# block of 4, 4#+P	2.60	
		Pane of 20	13.00	—

THAT'S ALL FOLKS!

Porky Pig at Mailbox — A2736

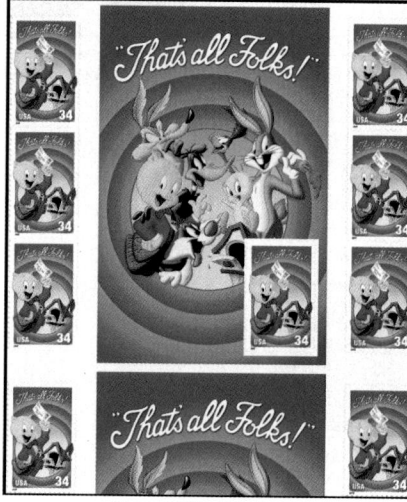

Cross Gutter Block of 9

Illustration reduced.
Designed by Ed Wleczyk, Warner Bros.
Printed by Avery Dennison.

PHOTOGRAVURE
2001, Oct. 1   Tagged   *Serpentine Die Cut 11*
Self-Adhesive

3534		Pane of 10	6.50	
a.		A2736 34c single	.65	.20
b.		Booklet pane of 9 or 10 #3534a	5.85	
c.		Booklet pane of 1 #3534a	.65	
		Sheet of 60 (six panes) no plate numbers	47.50	
		Sheet of 60 (six panes) with plate # in selvage on front and reverse	50.00	
		Pane of 10 from sheet of 60	8.00	
		Pane of 10 with plate numbers on front	12.50	
		Cross gutter block of 9 or 10	16.00	
		Cross gutter block of 12	18.00	
		Vert. pair with horiz. gutter	2.00	
		Horiz. pair with vert. gutter	4.00	

Die cutting on No. 3534b does not extend through the backing paper.

3535		Pane of 10	60.00	
a.		A2736 34c single	5.00	
b.		Booklet pane of 9 #3535a	50.00	
c.		Booklet pane of 1, no die cutting	7.50	

Die cutting on No. 3535a extends through backing paper.
Nos. 3534b-3534c and 3535b-3535c are separated by a vertical line of microperforations.

CHRISTMAS

Virgin and Child, by Lorenzo Costa — A2737

A2738   A2739

A2740   A2741

19th Century Chromolithographs of Santa Claus

Designed by Richard Sheaff.
Printed by Guilford Gravure, Inc., for Banknote Corporation America (#3536), American Packaging Corporation for Senn Security Products (#3537-3540), Avery Dennison (#354 3544).

PHOTOGRAVURE
Sheets of 160 in eight panes of 20 (#3537-3540)
Serpentine Die Cut 11½ on 2, 3 or 4 Sides
2001, Oct. 10   Tagge
Self-Adhesive
Booklet Stamps (#3536, 3537a-3540a, 3537b, 3538b, 3539b, 3540e, 3541-3544)

3536	A2737	34c multicolored	.65	.2
a.		Booklet pane of 20	13.00	

Serpentine Die Cut 10¾x11
Black Inscriptions

3537	A2738	34c multicolored, large date	.65	.2
a.		Small date (from booklet pane)	.65	.2
b.		Large date (from booklet pane)	1.75	.2
3538	A2739	34c multicolored, large date	.65	.2
a.		Small date (from booklet pane)	.65	.2
b.		Large date (from booklet pane)	1.75	.2
3539	A2740	34c multicolored, large date	.65	.2
a.		Small date (from booklet pane)	.65	.2
b.		Large date (from booklet pane)	1.75	.2
3540	A2741	34c multicolored, large date	.65	.2
a.		Small date (from booklet pane)	.65	.2
b.		Block of 4, #3537-3540	2.60	
		P# block of 4, 4#+S	2.60	
		Pane of 20	13.00	
c.		Block of 4, small date, #3537a-3540a	2.60	
d.		Booklet pane of 20, 5 #3540c + label	13.00	
e.		Large date (from booklet pane)	1.75	.20
f.		Block of 4, large date, #3537b-3539b, 3540e	7.00	
g.		Booklet pane of 20, 5 #3540f + label	35.00	

Nos. 3540d and 3540g are double-sided booklet panes, with 12 stamps on one side and eight stamps plus label on the other side.

Numerals "3" and "4" are distinctly separate on Nos. 3537-3540, and touching or separated by a slight hairline on the booklet pane stamps.
Designs of Nos. 3537a-3540a are slightly taller than Nos. 3537-3540.

Serpentine Die Cut 11 on 2 or 3 Sides
Size: 21x18½mm
Green and Red Inscriptions

3541	A2738	34c multicolored	.65	.20
3542	A2739	34c multicolored	.65	.20
3543	A2740	34c multicolored	.65	.20
3544	A2741	34c multicolored	.65	.20
a.		Block of 4, #3541-3544	2.60	
b.		Booklet pane of 4, #3541-3544	2.60	
c.		Booklet pane of 6, #3543-3544, 2 #3541-3542	3.90	
d.		Booklet pane of 6, #3541-3542, 2 #3543-3544	3.90	
		Nos. 3536-3544 (9)	5.85	1.80

JAMES MADISON (1751-1836)

Madison and His Home, Montpelier A2742

Designed by John Thompson.

Printed by Banknote Corporation of America.

LITHOGRAPHED & ENGRAVED
Sheets of 120 in six panes of 20

01, Oct. 18 **Tagged** *Perf. 11x11¼*

45	A2742 34c	green & black	.65	.20
		P# block of 4, 2#+B	2.60	—
		Pane of 20	13.00	—
		Sheet of 120	80.00	
		Cross gutter block of 4	8.25	—
		Horiz. pair with vert. gutter	3.00	—
		Vert. pair with horiz. gutter	2.00	—

THANKSGIVING

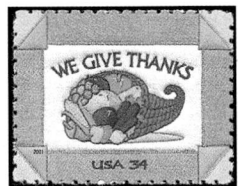

Cornucopia — A2743

Designed by Richard Sheaff.

Printed by Ashton-Potter (USA) Ltd.

LITHOGRAPHED
Sheets of 180 in nine panes of 20

2001, Oct. 19 **Tagged** *Serpentine Die Cut 11¼*
Self-Adhesive

546	A2743 34c	multicolored	.65	.20
		P# block of 4, 4#+P	2.60	
		Pane of 20	13.00	

Hanukkah Type of 1996
Designed by Hannah Smotrich.

Printed by Avery Dennison.

PHOTOGRAVURE
Sheets of 200 in ten panes of 20

2001, Oct. 21 **Tagged** *Serpentine Die Cut 11*
Self-Adhesive

547	A2411 34c	multicolored	.65	.20
		P# block of 4, 5#+V	2.60	
		Pane of 20	13.00	

Kwanzaa Type of 1997
Designed by Synthia Saint James.

Printed by Avery Dennison.

PHOTOGRAVURE
Sheets of 240 in twelve panes of 20

2001, Oct. 21 **Tagged** *Serpentine Die Cut 11*
Self-Adhesive

3548	A2458 34c	multicolored	.65	.20
		P# block of 4, 4#+V	2.60	
		Pane of 20	13.00	

UNITED WE STAND

A2744

Designed by Terry McCaffrey.

Printed by Banknote Corporation of America (#3549), Bureau of Engraving and Printing (#3550).

LITHOGRAPHED
BOOKLET STAMPS
Serpentine Die Cut 11¼ on 2, 3, or 4 Sides
2001, Oct. 24 **Tagged**
Self-Adhesive

3549	A2744 34c	multicolored	.65	.20
a.		Booklet pane of 20	13.00	

PHOTOGRAVURE
Serpentine Die Cut 10½x10¾ on 2 or 3 Sides
2002, Jan. **Tagged**
Self-Adhesive

3549B	A2744 34c	multicolored, *Jan. 2002*	.80	.20
c.		Booklet pane of 4	3.20	
d.		Booklet pane of 6	4.80	
e.		Booklet pane of 20	16.00	

No. 3549Be is a double-sided booklet pane, with 12 stamps on one side and eight stamps plus label on the other side. "First day covers" of No. 3549B are dated Oct. 24, 2001.

COIL STAMP

Serpentine Die Cut 9¾ Vert.
2001, Oct. 24 **Tagged**
Self-Adhesive

3550	A2744 34c	multicolored, perpendicular corners	.80	.20
		Pair	1.60	
		P# strip of 5, #1111, 2222	7.00	
		P# strip of 5, #3333	9.00	
		P# single, same #	—	1.00
		P# single, #3333	—	2.75
3550A	A2744 34c	multicolored	.80	.20
		Pair	1.60	
		P# strip of 5, #1111	7.00	
		P# single, same #	—	2.00

No. 3550 has right angle corners and backing paper as high as the stamp. No. 3550A has rounded corners, the backing paper larger than the stamp, and the stamps are spaced approximately 2mm apart.

Love Letters Type of 2001
Designed by Lisa Catalone.
Printed by Banknote Corporation of America.

LITHOGRAPHED
Sheets of 160 in eight panes of 20

2001, Nov. 19 **Tagged** *Serpentine Die Cut 11¼*
Self-Adhesive

3551	A2701 57c	multicolored	1.10	.20
		P# block of 4, 4# + B	5.00	
		Pane of 20	24.00	

WINTER OLYMPICS

Ski Jumping
A2745

Snowboarding
A2746

Ice Hockey
A2747

Figure Skating
A2748

Designed by Jager Di Paola Kemp. Printed by American Packaging Corporation for Sennett Security Products.

PHOTOGRAVURE
Sheets of 180 in nine panes of 20
Serpentine Die Cut 11½x10¾
2002, Jan. 8 **Tagged**
Self-Adhesive

3552	A2745 34c	multicolored	.65	.20
3553	A2746 34c	multicolored	.65	.20
3554	A2747 34c	multicolored	.65	.20
3555	A2748 34c	multicolored	.65	.20
a.		Block or strip of 4, #3552-3555	2.60	
		P# block of 4, 6#+S (UL and UR only)	3.00	
		Pane of 20	15.00	
		Sheet of 180 (9 panes)	125.00	
		Cross gutter block of 8	15.00	
		Block of 4 with vert. gutter	4.00	
		Block of 8 with horiz. gutter	8.00	
		Vert. pair with horiz. gutter, each	1.75	

		Horiz. pair with vert. gutter, each	1.75
b.		Die cutting inverted, pane of 20	—
c.		Die cutting omitted, block of 4	850.00
		As "c," pane of 20	—

Cross gutter blocks of 8 may be either 2x4 or 4x2 in configuration. The former will not show equal numbers of each stamp; the latter will.

Blocks of 4 with vertical gutter must show one of each of the stamps.

MENTORING A CHILD

Child and Adult — A2749

Designed by Lance Hidy. Printed by American Packaging Corporation for Sennett Security Products.

PHOTOGRAVURE
Sheets of 120 in six panes of 20
Serpentine Die Cut 11x10¾
2002, Jan. 10 **Tagged**
Self-Adhesive

3556	A2749 34c	multicolored	.65	.20
		P# block of 4, 5#+S	2.60	
		Pane of 20	13.00	

BLACK HERITAGE SERIES

Langston Hughes (1902-67), Writer — A2750

Designed by Richard Sheaff. Printed by Banknote Corporation of America.

LITHOGRAPHED
Sheets of 120 in six panes of 20
Serpentine Die Cut 10¼x10½
2002, Feb. 1 **Tagged**
Self-Adhesive

3557	A2750 34c	multicolored	.65	.20
		P# block of 4, 5#+B	3.00	
		Pane of 20	15.00	
a.		Die cutting omitted, pair	—	
		As "a," pane of 20	—	

Beware of pairs/panes with extremely faint die cutting offered as imperf errors.

HAPPY BIRTHDAY

A2751

Designed by Harry Zelenko. Printed by Avery Dennison.

PHOTOGRAVURE
Sheets of 200 in ten panes of 20

2002, Feb. 8 **Tagged** *Serpentine Die Cut 11*
Self-Adhesive

3558	A2751 34c	multicolored	.65	.20
		P# block of 4, 4#+V	2.60	
		Pane of 20	13.00	

See No. 3695.

CHINESE NEW YEAR

Year of the Horse
A2752

Designed by Clarence Lee. Printed by Banknote Corporation of America.

LITHOGRAPHED
Sheets of 120 in six panes of 20
Serpentine Die Cut 10¹⁄₂x10¹⁄₄

2002, Feb. 11		Tagged		
Self-Adhesive				
3559	A2752	34c **multicolored**	.75	.20
		P# block of 4, 5#+B	3.00	
		Pane of 20	15.00	
		See No. 3895g.		

U.S. MILITARY ACADEMY, BICENT.

Military Academy Coat of Arms — A2753

Designed by Derry Noyes. Printed by American Packaging Corp. for Sennett Security Products.

PHOTOGRAVURE
Sheets of 180 in nine panes of 20
Serpentine Die Cut 10¹⁄₂x11

2002, Mar. 16		Tagged		
Self-Adhesive				
3560	A2753	34c **multicolored**	.65	.20
		P# block of 4, 6#+S	2.60	
		Pane of 20	13.00	

GREETINGS FROM AMERICA

A2754-A2803

Illustration reduced.
Designed by Richard Sheaff. Printed by American Packaging Corp. for Sennett Security Products.

PHOTOGRAVURE
Sheets of 100 in two panes of 50

2002, Apr. 4		Tagged	*Serpentine Die Cut 10³⁄₄*
Self-Adhesive			
3561	A2754	34c Alabama	.65 .45
3562	A2755	34c Alaska	.65 .45
3563	A2756	34c Arizona	.65 .45
3564	A2757	34c Arkansas	.65 .45

3565	A2758	34c California	.65	.45
3566	A2759	34c Colorado	.65	.45
3567	A2760	34c Connecticut	.65	.45
3568	A2761	34c Delaware	.65	.45
3569	A2762	34c Florida	.65	.45
3570	A2763	34c Georgia	.65	.45
3571	A2764	34c Hawaii	.65	.45
3572	A2765	34c Idaho	.65	.45
3573	A2766	34c Illinois	.65	.45
3574	A2767	34c Indiana	.65	.45
3575	A2768	34c Iowa	.65	.45
3576	A2769	34c Kansas	.65	.45
3577	A2770	34c Kentucky	.65	.45
3578	A2771	34c Louisiana	.65	.45
3579	A2772	34c Maine	.65	.45
3580	A2773	34c Maryland	.65	.45
3581	A2774	34c Massachusetts	.65	.45
3582	A2775	34c Michigan	.65	.45
3583	A2776	34c Minnesota	.65	.45
3584	A2777	34c Mississippi	.65	.45
3585	A2778	34c Missouri	.65	.45
3586	A2779	34c Montana	.65	.45
3587	A2780	34c Nebraska	.65	.45
3588	A2781	34c Nevada	.65	.45
3589	A2782	34c New Hampshire	.65	.45
3590	A2783	34c New Jersey	.65	.45
3591	A2784	34c New Mexico	.65	.45
3592	A2785	34c New York	.65	.45
3593	A2786	34c North Carolina	.65	.45
3594	A2787	34c North Dakota	.65	.45
3595	A2788	34c Ohio	.65	.45
3596	A2789	34c Oklahoma	.65	.45
3597	A2790	34c Oregon	.65	.45
3598	A2791	34c Pennsylvania	.65	.45
3599	A2792	34c Rhode Island	.65	.45
3600	A2793	34c South Carolina	.65	.45
3601	A2794	34c South Dakota	.65	.45
3602	A2795	34c Tennessee	.65	.45
3603	A2796	34c Texas	.65	.45
3604	A2797	34c Utah	.65	.45
3605	A2798	34c Vermont	.65	.45
3606	A2799	34c Virginia	.65	.45
3607	A2800	34c Washington	.65	.45
3608	A2801	34c West Virginia	.65	.45
3609	A2802	34c Wisconsin	.65	.45
3610	A2803	34c Wyoming	.65	.45
a.		Pane of 50, #3561-3610	32.50	
		Sheet of 100 (two panes)	65.00	
		Block of 50 different stamps with vert. gutter between any 2 columns	32.50	
		Pair with vert. gutter between (each)	2.00	

LONGLEAF PINE FOREST

A2804

Illustration reduced.
Designed by Ethel Kessler. Printed by American Packaging Corp. for Sennett Security Products.

Wildlife and flowers: a, Bachman's sparrow. b, Northern bobwhite, yellow pitcher plants. c, Fox squirrel, red-bellied woodpecker. d, Brown-headed nuthatch. e, Broadhead skink, yellow pitcher plants, pipeworts. f, Eastern towhee, yellow pitcher plants, Savannah meadow beauties, toothache grass. g, Gray fox, gopher tortoise, horiz. h, Blind click beetle, sweetbay, pine woods treefrog. i, Rosebud orchid, pipeworts, southern toad, yellow pitcher plants. j, Grass-pink orchid, yellow-sided skimmer, pipeworts, yellow pitcher plants, horiz.

PHOTOGRAVURE
Sheets of 90 in nine panes of 10
Serpentine Die Cut 10¹⁄₂x10³⁄₄, 10³⁄₄x10¹⁄₂

2002, Apr. 26			Tagged
Self-Adhesive			
3611	A2804	Pane of 10	12.00
a.-j.		34c Any single	1.10 .50
		Sheet of 9 panes	100.00
k.		As No. 3611, die cutting omitted	—

AMERICAN DESIGN SERIES

Toleware Coffeepot — A2805

Designed by Derry Noyes.
Printed by American Packaging Corp. for Sennett Security Products.

PHOTOGRAVURE
COIL STAMP

2002, May 31		Untagged	*Perf. 10 Ve*
3612	A2805	5c **multicolored**	.20
		Pair	.20
		P# strip of 5, #S1111111	1.60
		P# single, #S1111111	— 1.

Star — A2806

Designed by Phil Jordan. Printed by Banknote Corporation America.

LITHOGRAPHED, PHOTOGRAVURE (No. 3614, 3615)
Sheets of 400 in eight panes of 50

2002, June 7		Untagged	*Serpentine Die Cut 1*
Self-Adhesive (#3613-3614)			
Year at Lower Left			
3613	A2806	3c **red, blue & black**	.20 .2
		P# block of 4, 3#+B	.25
a.		Die cutting omitted, pair	—
Serpentine Die Cut 10			
Year at Lower Right			
3614	A2806	3c **red, blue & black**	.20 .2
		P# block of 4, 3#+B	.25
Coil Stamp			
Perf. 10 Vert.			
Year at Lower Left			
3615	A2806	3c **red, blue & black**	.20 .2
		Pair	.20 .2
		P# strip of 5, #S111	1.00 —
		P# single, same #	— .65
a.		Prephosphored paper (solid tagging) (error)	.20 .20
		Pair	.20 .20
		P# strip of 5, #S111	1.00 —
		P# single, same #	— .65

Washington Type of 2001

Designed by Richard Sheaff. Printed by Ashton-Potter (USA) Ltd. (#3616, 3618, 3619), Avery Dennison (#3617).

LITHOGRAPHED, PHOTOGRAVURE (#3617)
Sheets of 400 in four panes of 100 (#3616)

2002, June 7		Tagged	*Perf. 11¹⁄*
3616	A2686	23c **green**	.50 .20
		P# block of 4, 1#+P	15.00
Self-Adhesive			
Coil Stamp			
Serpentine Die Cut 8¹⁄₂ Vert.			
3617	A2686	23c **gray green**	.45 .20
		Pair	.90
		P# strip of 5, #V11, V13, V21, V22, V24, V35, V36, V45, V46	3.00
		P# single, same #	— .60
a.		Die cutting omitted, pair	—

Compare No. 3617 ("2002" date at lower left) with No. 3475A ("2001" date at lower left).

Booklet Stamps
Serpentine Die Cut 11¹⁄₄x11 on 3 Sides

3618	A2686	23c **green**	.45 .20
a.		Booklet pane of 4	1.80
b.		Booklet pane of 6	2.70
c.		Booklet pane of 10	4.50
Serpentine Die Cut 10¹⁄₂x11 on 3 Sides			
3619	A2686	23c **green**	2.25 1.75
a.		Booklet pane of 4, 2 #3619 at L, 2 #3618 at R	6.00
b.		Booklet pane of 6, 3 #3619 at L, 3 #3618 at R	9.50
c.		Booklet pane of 4, 2 #3618 at L, 2 #3619 at R	6.00
d.		Booklet pane of 6, 3 #3618 at L, 3 #3619 at R	9.50
e.		Booklet pane of 10, 5 #3619 at L, 5#3618 at R	13.50
f.		Booklet pane of 10, 5 #3618 at L, 5 #3619 at R	13.50
g.		Pair, #3619 at L, #3618 at R	2.75
h.		Pair, #3618 at L, #3619 at R	2.75

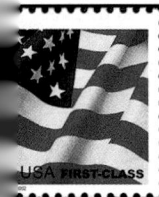

Flag — A2807

Designed by Terrence W. McCaffrey. Printed by Sterling Sommer for Ashton-Potter (USA) Ltd. (#3620), Ashton-Potter (USA) Ltd. (#3621), Bureau of Engraving and Printing (#3622), Banknote Corporation of America (#3623), American Packaging Corporation for Sennett Security Products (#3624), Avery Dennison (#3625).

LITHOGRAPHED, PHOTOGRAVURE (#3622, 3624, 3625)

Sheets of 400 in four panes of 100 (#3620), Sheets of 120 in six panes of 20 (#3621)

2002, June 7		**Tagged**		Perf. 11¼x11
3620	A2807	(37c) multicolored	.85	.20
		P# block of 4, 4#+P	25.00	

Self-Adhesive
Serpentine Die Cut 11¼x11

3621	A2807	(37c) multicolored	.75	.20
		P# block of 4, 4#+P	3.00	
		Pane of 20	15.00	

Coil Stamp
Serpentine Die Cut 10 Vert.

3622	A2807	(37c) multicolored	.75	.20
		Pair	1.50	
		P# strip of 5, #1111, 2222	6.00	
		P# single, same #	— 2.00	
a.		Die cutting omitted, pair	—	

Booklet Stamps
Serpentine Die Cut 11¼ on 2, 3 or 4 Sides

3623	A2807	(37c) multicolored	.75	.20
a.		Booklet pane of 20	15.00	

Serpentine Die Cut 10½x10¾ on 2 or 3 Sides

3624	A2807	(37c) multicolored	.75	.20
a.		Booklet pane of 4	3.00	
b.		Booklet pane of 6	4.50	
c.		Booklet pane of 20	15.00	

Serpentine Die Cut 8 on 2, 3 or 4 sides

3625	A2807	(37c) multicolored	.75	.20
a.		Booklet pane of 18	13.50	

Toy Mail Wagon — A2808 · Toy Locomotive — A2809 · Toy Taxicab — A2810 · Toy Fire Pumper — A2811

Designed by Derry Noyes. Printed by Avery Dennison

PHOTOGRAVURE
Serpentine Die Cut 11 on 2, 3 or 4 Sides
2002, June 7 **Tagged**
Booklet Stamps
Self-Adhesive

3626	A2808	(37c) multicolored	.75	.20
3627	A2809	(37c) multicolored	.75	.20
3628	A2810	(37c) multicolored	.75	.20
3629	A2811	(37c) multicolored	.75	.20
a.		Block of 4, #3626-3629	3.00	
b.		Booklet pane of 4, #3626-3629	3.00	
c.		Booklet pane of 6, #3627, 3629, 2 each #3626, 3628	4.50	
d.		Booklet pane of 6, #3626, 3628, 2 each #3627, 3629	4.50	
e.		Booklet pane of 20, 5 each #3626-3629	15.00	

Flag — A2812

Designed by Terrence W. McCaffrey. Printed by Ashton-Potter (USA) Ltd. (#3629F, 3630, 3633B), American Packaging Corporation for Sennett Security Products (#3631, 3632A, 3632C, 3636), Bureau of Engraving and Printing (#3632), Banknote Corporation of America (#3633, 3635), Guilford Gravure for Banknote Corporation of America (#3633A), Avery Dennison (#3634, 3634b, 3636D, 3637).

LITHOGRAPHED, PHOTOGRAVURE (#3631-3633, 3634, 3636, 3636D)
Sheets of 400 in four panes of 100

2002-05		**Tagged**		Perf. 11¼
3629F	A2812	37c multicolored, Nov. 24, 2003	.85	.20
		P# block of 4, 4#+P	25.00	

No. 3629F has microprinted "USA" in top red stripe of flag.

Sheets of 120 in six panes of 20
Serpentine Die Cut 11¼x11
Self-Adhesive

3630	A2812	37c multicolored	.75	.20
		P# block of 4, 4#+P	5.00	
		Pane of 20	22.50	

No. 3630 has microprinted "USA" in top red stripe of flag.

COIL STAMPS
Water-Activated Gum
Perf. 10 Vert.

3631	A2812	37c multicolored, June 7	.75	.20
		Pair	1.50	
		P# strip of 5, #S1111	5.25	
		P# single, same #	— 2.00	

No. 3631 is known printed with non-reactive red ink and also with luminescent red ink that glows orange under long wave ultraviolet light.

Self-Adhesive
Serpentine Die Cut 9¾ Vert.

3632	A2812	37c multicolored, June 7	.75	.20
		Pair	1.50	
		P# strip of 5, #1111, 2222, 3333, 4444, 5555, 6666, 7777, 8888, 9999, 1111A, 2222A, 3333A, 4444A, 5555A, 6666A	5.25	
		P# single, same #	— 2.00	
b.		Die cutting omitted, pair	100.00	

On plate #s 1111 through 9999 and 5555A-6666A, the color laydown order of plate numbers is yellow, magenta, cyan, black. Plate #s 1111A through 4444A have a laydown order of cyan, magenta, yellow, black.

Serpentine Die Cut 10¼ Vert.

3632A	A2812	37c multicolored, prephosphored paper (solid tagging), Aug. 7, 2003	.75	.20
		Pair	1.50	
		P# strip of 5, #S1111, S2222, S3333	5.25	
		P# strip of 5, #S4444	150.00	
		P# single, same #	— 2.00	
e.		Prephosphored paper (mottled tagging)	.75	.20
		Pair	1.50	
		P# strip of 5, #S3333, S4444	5.25	
		P# single, P#S1111, S2222, S3333	— 2.00	
		P# single, P#S4444	— 50.00	
f.		Die cutting omitted, pair		

No. 3632A lacks points of stars at margin at left top, and was printed in "logs" of adjacent coil rolls that are connected at the top or bottom, wherein each roll could be separated from an adjacent roll as needed.
No. 3632 has "2002" date at left bottom. No. 3632A has "2003" date at left bottom.
On No. 3632A, P# S3333 was printed with red ink that glows orange under long wave ultraviolet light as well as with non-reactive red ink. P# S4444 was printed with and without luminescent red ink. Values below.

Serpentine Die Cut 11¾ Vert.

3632C	A2812	37c multicolored, prephosphored paper (solid tagging), 2004	.75	.20
		Pair	1.50	
		P# strip of 5, #S1111	5.25	
		P# single, same #	— 2.00	
d.		Prephosphored paper (mottled tagging)	.75	.20
		Pair	1.50	
		P# strip of 5, #S1111	5.25	
		P# single, same #	— 2.00	

Backing paper of 3632C is larger than the stamp, and stamps are spaced 3½mm apart. Dated "2004" at left bottom.

Serpentine Die Cut 8½ Vert.

3633	A2812	37c multicolored, June 7	.75	.20
		Pair	1.50	
		P# strip of 5, #B1111	7.50	
		P# single, same #	— 2.00	

Backing paper of No. 3633 is larger than the stamp.

3633A	A2812	37c multicolored April, 2003	1.75	.20
		Pair	3.50	
		P# strip of 5 #B1111	12.00	
		P# single, same #	— 2.00	

No. 3633A has right angle corners and backing paper as high as the stamp, and is dated "2003." No. 3633 is dated "2002," has rounded corners, the backing paper larger than the stamp, and the stamps are spaced approximately 2mm apart.

Serpentine Die Cut 9½ Vert.
Coil Stamp

3633B	A2812	37c multicolored June 7, 2005	.90	.20
		Pair	1.80	
		P# strip of 5, #P1111	6.50	
		P# single, #P1111	— 2.00	

No. 3633B has microprinted "USA" in top red stripe of flag, and has "2005" date at bottom left.

Booklet Stamps
Serpentine Die Cut 11.1 on 3 Sides (#3634) or 2 or 3 sides (#3634b-3634d)

3634	A2812	37c multicolored, large "2002" year date, June 7	.75	.20
a.		Booklet pane of 10	7.50	
b.		Small "2003," Oct. 23, 2003	.75	.20
c.		Booklet pane, 4 #3634b	3.00	
d.		Booklet pane, 6 #3634b	4.50	
e.		As #3634, die cut 11.3	.75	.20
f.		As "e," booklet pane of 10	7.50	

Serpentine Die Cut 11.3 on 2, 3 or 4 Sides

3635	A2812	37c multicolored, June 7	.75	.20
a.		Booklet pane of 20	15.00	

No. 3635 has "USPS" microprinted in the top red flag stripe and has a small "2002" year date.

Serpentine Die Cut 10½x10¾ on 2 or 3 Sides

3636	A2812	37c multicolored, June 7	.75	.20
a.		Booklet pane of 4	3.00	
b.		Booklet pane of 6	4.50	
c.		Booklet pane of 20	15.00	

No. 3636c is a double-sided booklet pane, with 12 stamps on one side and eight stamps plus label on the other side.
Nos. 3636a and 3636b were issued on three types of prephosphored paper, with solid, grainy solid and mottled tagging characteristics. No. 3636c was issued on two types of prephosphored paper, with solid and mottled tagging.

Serpentine Die Cut 11¼x11 on 2 or 3 Sides

3636D	A2812	37c multicolored, July, 2004	.90	.20
e.		Booklet pane of 6	18.00	

No. 3636D lacks points of stars at margin at UL. No. 3636De is a double-sided booklet pane with 12 stamps on one side and eight stamps plus label on the other side.

Serpentine Die Cut 8 on 2, 3 or 4 Sides
Tagged

3637	A2812	37c multicolored, Feb. 4, 2003	.75	.20
a.		Booklet pane of 18	13.50	

Toy Locomotive — A2813 · Toy Mail Wagon — A2814 · Toy Fire Pumper — A2815 · Toy Taxicab — A2816

Designed by Derry Noyes. Printed by Banknote Corporation of America, Avery Dennison (#3642-3645)

PHOTOGRAVURE
Serpentine Die Cut 8½ Horiz.
2002, July 26 **Tagged**
Self-Adhesive
Coil Stamps

3638	A2813	37c multicolored	.75	.20
3639	A2814	37c multicolored	.75	.20
3640	A2815	37c multicolored	.75	.20
3641	A2816	37c multicolored	.75	.20
a.		Strip of 4, #3638-3641	3.00	
		P# strip of 5, 2 #3638, 1 each #3639-3641, #B11111, B12222	5.50	

P# strip of 9, 2 each #3638-
3639, 3641, 3 #3640,
#B11111, B12222   8.75
P# single (#3640), #B11111,
B12222   — 2.00

Serpentine Die Cut 11 on 2, 3 or 4 Sides
Booklet Stamps

3642	A2814 37c **multicolored,** "2002" year date	.75 .20
a.	Serpentine die cut 11x11¼ on 2 or 3 sides, dated "2003," Sept. 3, 2003	.75 .20
3643	A2813 37c **multicolored,** "2002" year date	.75 .20
a.	Serpentine die cut 11x11¼ on 2 or 3 sides, dated "2003," Sept. 3, 2003	.75 .20
3644	A2816 37c **multicolored,** "2002" year date	.75 .20
a.	Serpentine die cut 11x11¼ on 2 or 3 sides, dated "2003," Sept. 3, 2003	.75 .20
3645	A2815 37c **multicolored,** "2002" year date	.75 .20
a.	Block of 4, #3642-3645	3.00
b.	Booklet pane of 4, #3642-3645	3.00
c.	Booklet pane of 6, #3643, 3645, 2 each #3642, 3644	4.50
d.	Booklet pane of 6, #3642, 3644, 2 each #3643, 3645	4.50
e.	Booklet pane of 20, 5 each #3642-3645	15.00
f.	Serpentine die cut 11x11¼ on 2 or 3 sides, dated "2003," Sept. 3, 2003	.75 .20
g.	Block of 4, #3642a, 3643a, 3644a, 3645f	3.00
h.	Booklet pane of 20, 5 #3645g	15.00

No. 3645h is a double-sided booklet with 12 stamps on one side and 8 stamps plus label (booklet cover on the other side. Nos. 3642a, 3643a, 3644a and 3645f have slightly narrower designs than Nos. 3642-3645.

Coverlet Eagle — A2817

Designed by Richard Sheaff. Printed by Ashton-Potter (USA) Ltd.

LITHOGRAPHED
Sheets of 120 in six panes of 20
Serpentine Die Cut 11x11¼

2002, July 12   **Tagged**

Self-Adhesive

3646	A2817 60c **multicolored**	1.25	.25
	P# block of 4, 4#+P	5.00	
	Pane of 20	25.00	

Jefferson Memorial A2818

Capitol Dome — A2819

Designed by Derry Noyes. Printed by Banknote Corporation of America (#3647-3648), American Packaging Corporation for Sennett Security Printers (#3647A).

LITHOGRAPHED
Sheets of 180 in nine panes of 20
Serpentine Die Cut 11¼ (#3647, 3648), 11x10¾ (#3647A)

2002-03   **Tagged**

Self-Adhesive

3647	A2818 $3.85 **multicolored,** *July 30*	7.50	2.00
	P# block of 4, 4#+B	30.00	
	Pane of 20	150.00	
3647A	A2818 $3.85 **multicolored,** *Nov. 2003*	7.50	2.00
	P# block of 4, 5#+S	30.00	
	Pane of 20	150.00	

3648	A2819 $13.65 **multicolored,** *July 30*	27.50	10.00
	P# block of 4, 4#+B	110.00	
	Pane of 20	550.00	

No. 3647A is dated 2003.

MASTERS OF AMERICAN PHOTOGRAPHY

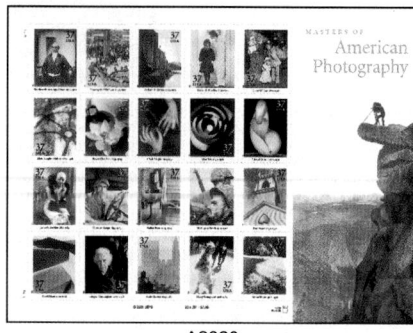

A2820

Illustration reduced.
Designed by Derry Noyes. Printed by American Packaging Corporation for Sennett Security Products.

Designs: a, Portrait of Daniel Webster, by Albert Sands Southworth and Josiah Johnson Hawes. b, Gen. Ulysses S. Grant and Officers, by Timothy H. O'Sullivan. c, "Cape Horn, Columbia River," by Carleton E. Watkins. d, "Blessed Art Thou Among Women," by Gertrude Käsebier. e, "Looking for Lost Luggage, Ellis Island," by Lewis W. Hine. f, "The Octopus," by Alvin Langdon Coburn. g, "Lotus, Mount Kisco, New York," by Edward Steichen. h, "Hands and Thimble," by Alfred Stieglitz. i, "Rayograph," by Man Ray. j, "Two Shells," by Edward Weston. k, "My Corsage," by James VanDerZee. l, "Ditched, Stalled, and Stranded, San Joaquin Valley, California," by Dorothea Lange. m, "Washroom and Dining Area of Floyd Burroughs' Home, Hale County, Alabama," by Walker Evans. n, "Frontline Soldier with Canteen, Saipan," by W. Eugene Smith. o, "Steeple," by Paul Strand. p, "Sand Dunes, Sunrise," by Ansel Adams. q, "Age and Its Symbols," by Imogen Cunningham. r, New York cityscape, by André Kertész. s, Photograph of pedestrians, by Garry Winogrand. t, "Bristol, Vermont," by Minor White.

PHOTOGRAVURE
Sheets of 120 in six panes of 20
Serpentine Die Cut 10½x10¾

2002, June 13   **Tagged**

Self-Adhesive

3649	A2820 Pane of 20	15.00	
a.-t.	37c Any single	.75	.50
	Sheet of 120 (6 panes)	90.00	
	Cross-gutter block of 20	30.00	
	Horiz. block of 8 with vert. gutter	11.00	
	Vert. block of 10 with horiz. gutter	14.00	
	Vert. pairs with horiz. gutter (each)	2.50	
	Horiz. pairs with vert. gutter (each)	2.50	

Cross gutter block of 20 consists of six stamps from each of two panes and four stamps from each of two other panes with the cross gutter between.

AMERICAN TREASURES SERIES

Scarlet and Louisiana Tanagers, by John James Audubon — A2821

Designed by Derry Noyes. Printed by American Pacakaging Corporation for Sennett Security Products.

PHOTOGRAVURE
Sheets of 120 in six panes of 20

2002, June 27   **Tagged**   *Serpentine Die Cut 10¾*

Self-Adhesive

3650	A2821 37c **multicolored**	1.00	.20
	P# block of 4, 7#+S	6.00	
	Pane of 20	27.50	

HARRY HOUDINI (1874-1926), MAGICIAN

A2822

Designed by Richard Sheaff. Printed by Ashton-Potter (USA) Ltd.

LITHOGRAPHED
Sheets of 180 in nine panes of 20

2002, July 3   **Tagged**   *Serpentine Die Cut 11*

Self-Adhesive

3651	A2822 37c **multicolored**	.75	
	P# block of 4, 4#+P	3.00	
	Pane of 20	15.00	

ANDY WARHOL (1928-87), ARTIST

Self-Portrait — A2823

Designed by Richard Sheaff.
Printed by American Packaging Corporation for Sennett Security Products.

PHOTOGRAVURE
Sheets of 80 in four panes of 20
Serpentine Die Cut 10½x10¾

2002, Aug. 9   **Tagged**

Self-Adhesive

3652	A2823 37c **multicolored**	.75	.20
	P# block of 4, 6#+S	3.00	
	Pane of 20	15.00	

TEDDY BEARS, CENTENNIAL

Bruin Bear, c. 1907 — A2824

"Stick" Bear, 1920s — A2825

Gund Bear, c.
1948 — A2826

Ideal Bear, c.
1905 — A2827

Designed by Margaret Bauer.
Printed by American Packaging Corporation for Sennett
Security Products.

PHOTOGRAVURE
Sheets of 120 in six panes of 20

**2002, Aug. 15   Tagged   *Serpentine Die Cut 10½*
Self-Adhesive**

3653	A2824	37c **multicolored**	1.00	.20
3654	A2825	37c **multicolored**	1.00	.20
3655	A2826	37c **multicolored**	1.00	.20
3656	A2827	37c **multicolored**	1.00	.20
a.		Block or vert. strip of 4, #3653-3656	4.00	
		P# block of 4, 7#+S	5.00	
		P# block of 10, 2 sets of P# +		
		top label	15.00	
		Pane of 20	27.50	
		Sheet of 120 (six panes)	125.00	
		Cross gutter block of 8	22.50	
		Block of 8 with vert. gutter	11.00	
		Block of 4 with horiz. gutter	6.00	
		Vert. pair with horiz. gutter		
		(each)	2.50	
		Horiz. pair with vert. gutter		
		(each)	2.50	

Cross gutter block can be either a vertical or horizontal block
showing all designs.

LOVE

A2828

A2829

Designed by Michael Osborne.
Printed by Banknote Corporation of America (#3657), Avery
Dennison.

LITHOGRAPHED (#3657), PHOTOGRAVURE
Sheets of 200 in ten panes of 20 (#3658)
Serpentine Die Cut 11 on 2, 3 or 4 Sides

**2002, Aug. 16   Tagged
Booklet Stamp (#3657)
Self-Adhesive**

3657	A2828	37c **multicolored**	.75	.20
a.		Booklet pane of 20	15.00	

Serpentine Die Cut 11

3658	A2829	60c **multicolored**	1.25	.25
		P# block of 4, 5#+V	5.00	
		Pane of 20	25.00	

OGDEN NASH (1902-7187), POET

Nash and
Poems
A2830

Designed by Carl T. Herrman.
Printed by Avery Dennison.

PHOTOGRAVURE
Sheets of 200 in ten panes of 20

**2002, Aug. 19   Tagged   *Serpentine Die Cut 11*
Self-Adhesive**

3659	A2830	37c **multicolored**	.75	.20
		P# block of 4, 8#+V	3.00	
		Pane of 20	15.00	

DUKE KAHANAMOKU (1890-1968), "FATHER OF SURFING" AND OLYMPIC SWIMMER

Kahanamoku and
Surfers at Waikiki
Beach — A2831

Designed by Carl T. Herrman.
Printed by Avery Dennison.

PHOTOGRAVURE
Sheets of 200 in ten panes of 20
Serpentine Die Cut 11½x11¾

**2002, Aug. 24   Tagged
Self-Adhesive**

3660	A2831	37c **multicolored**	.75	.20
		P# block of 4, 4#+V	3.00	
		Pane of 20	15.00	

AMERICAN BATS

Red
Bat — A2832

Leaf-nosed
Bat — A2833

Pallid
Bat — A2834

Spotted
Bat — A2835

Designed by Phil Jordan.
Printed by American Packaging Corporation for Sennett
Security Products.

PHOTOGRAVURE
Sheets of 200 in six panes of 20

**2002, Sept. 13   Tagged   *Serpentine Die Cut 10¾*
Self-Adhesive**

3661	A2832	37c **multicolored**	.75	.20
3662	A2833	37c **multicolored**	.75	.20
3663	A2834	37c **multicolored**	.75	.20

3664	A2835	37c **multicolored**	.75	.20
a.		Block or horiz. strip of 4, #3661-3664	3.00	
		P# block of 4, 7#+S	3.25	
		P# block of 8, 2 sets of P# +		
		top label	6.50	
		Pane of 20	16.00	

WOMEN IN JOURNALISM

Nellie Bly
(1864-1922)
A2836

Ida M. Tarbell
(1857-1944)
A2837

Ethel L. Payne
(1911-91)
A2838

Marguerite
Higgins (1920-
66)
A2839

Designed by Fred Otnes.
Printed by American Packaging Corporation for Sennett
Security Products.

PHOTOGRAVURE
Sheets of 120 in six panes of 20
Serpentine Die Cut 11x10½

**2002, Sept. 14   Tagged
Self-Adhesive**

3665	A2836	37c **multicolored**	.75	.20
3666	A2837	37c **multicolored**	.75	.20
3667	A2838	37c **multicolored**	.75	.20
3668	A2839	37c **multicolored**	.75	.20
a.		Block or horiz. strip of 4, #3665-3668	3.00	
		P# block of 4, 5#+S	3.25	
		P# block of 8, 2 sets of P# +		
		top label	6.50	
		Pane of 20	16.00	

IRVING BERLIN (1888-1989), COMPOSER

Berlin and Score of "God
Bless America" — A2840

Designed by Greg Berger.
Printed by Avery Dennison.

PHOTOGRAVURE
Sheets of 200 in ten panes of 20

2002, Sept. 15   Tagged   *Serpentine Die Cut 11*
Self-Adhesive

3669 A2840 37c **multicolored**   .75   .20
      P# block of 4, 4#+V   3.00
      Pane of 20   15.00

NEUTER AND SPAY

Kitten — A2841

Puppy
A2842

Designed by Derry Noyes. Printed by American Packaging
Corporation for Sennett Security Products.

PHOTOGRAVURE
Sheets of 120 in six panes of 20

Serpentine Die Cut 10³⁄₄x10¹⁄₂

2002, Sept. 20   Tagged
Self-Adhesive

3670 A2841 37c **multicolored**   1.00   .20
3671 A2842 37c **multicolored**   1.00   .20
   a. Horiz. or vert. pair, #3670-3671   2.00
       P# block of 4, 5#+S   4.00
       P# block of 8, 2 sets of P# +
          top label   8.00
       Pane of 20   20.00

Hanukkah Type of 1996

Designed by Hannah Smotrich.
Printed by Avery Dennison.

PHOTOGRAVURE
Sheets of 200 in ten panes of 20

2002, Oct. 10   Tagged   *Serpentine Die Cut 11*
Self-Adhesive

3672 A2411 37c **multicolored**   .75   .20
      P# block of 4, 5#+V   3.00
      Pane of 20   15.00

Kwanzaa Type of 1997

Designed by Synthia Saint James.
Printed by Avery Dennison.

PHOTOGRAVURE
Sheets of 200 in ten panes of 20

2002, Oct. 10   Tagged   *Serpentine Die Cut 11*
Self-Adhesive

3673 A2458 37c **multicolored**   .75   .20
      P# block of 4, 4#+V   3.00
      Pane of 20   15.00

Eid Type of 2001

Designed by Mohamed Zakariya.
Printed by Avery Dennison.

PHOTOGRAVURE
Sheets of 240 in twelve panes of 20

2002, Oct. 10   Tagged   *Serpentine Die Cut 11*
Self-Adhesive

3674 A2734 37c **multicolored**   .75   .20
      P# block of 4, 3#+V   3.00
      Pane of 20   15.00

CHRISTMAS

Madonna and Child, by Jan
Gossaert — A2843

Designed by Richard Sheaff.
Printed by Banknote Corporation of America.

LITHOGRAPHED
Serpentine Die Cut 11x11¹⁄₄ on 2, 3 or 4 Sides
2002, Oct. 10   Tagged

Self-Adhesive
Booklet Stamp
Design size: 19x27mm

3675 A2843 37c **multicolored**   .75   .20
   a. Booklet pane of 20   15.00

   Compare to No. 3820, which measures 19¹⁄₂x28mm

CHRISTMAS

Snowman with Red
and Green Plaid
Scarf — A2844

Snowman with Blue
Plaid Scarf — A2845

Snowman with
Pipe — A2846

Snowman with Top
Hat — A2847

Snowman with Blue
Plaid Scarf — A2848

Snowman with
Pipe — A2849

Snowman with Top
Hat — A2850

Snowman with Red
and Green Plaid
Scarf — A2851

Designed by Derry Noyes.

Printed by Avery Dennison (#3676-3679, 3688-3691),
Guilford Gravure (#3680-3683), and American Packaging Corp.
for Sennett Security Products (#3684-3687).

PHOTOGRAVURE
Sheets of 200 in ten panes of 20

2002, Oct. 28   Tagged   *Serpentine Die Cut*
Self-Adhesive

3676 A2844 37c **multicolored**   .75
3677 A2845 37c **multicolored**   .75
3678 A2846 37c **multicolored**   .75
3679 A2847 37c **multicolored**   .75
   a. Block or vert. strip of 4, #3676-3679   3.00
       P# block of 4, 4#+V   3.00
       Pane of 20   15.00

COIL STAMPS
Serpentine Die Cut 8¹⁄₂ Vert.

3680 A2848 37c **multicolored**   .90
3681 A2849 37c **multicolored**   .90
3682 A2850 37c **multicolored**   .90
3683 A2851 37c **multicolored**   .90
   a. Strip of 4, #3680-3683   3.60
       P# strip of 5, 2 #3680, 1 each
          #3681-3683, #G1111, G1112   6.00
       P# strip of 9, 2 each #3680,
          3681, 3683, 3 #3682, same #   9.00
       P# single (#3682), same #   — 2.

BOOKLET STAMPS
Serpentine Die Cut 10³⁄₄x11 on 2 or 3 Sides

3684 A2844 37c **multicolored**   .90
3685 A2845 37c **multicolored**   .90
3686 A2846 37c **multicolored**   .90
3687 A2847 37c **multicolored**   .90
   a. Block of 4, #3684-3687   3.60
   b. Booklet pane of 20, 5 #3687a + label   18.00

No. 3687b is a double-sided booklet pane with 12 stamps
one side and eight stamps plus label on the other side.

Serpentine Die Cut 11 on 2 or 3 Sides

3688 A2851 37c **multicolored**   1.00
3689 A2848 37c **multicolored**   1.00
3690 A2849 37c **multicolored**   1.00
3691 A2850 37c **multicolored**   1.00
   a. Block of 4, #3688-3691   4.00
   b. Booklet pane of 4, #3688-3691   4.00
   c. Booklet pane of 6, #3690-3691, 2 each
          #3688-3689   6.00
   d. Booklet pane of 6, #3688-3689, 2 each
          #3690-3691   6.00
   Nos. 3676-3691 (16)   11.20 3.2

Colors of Nos. 3684-3687 are deeper and designs are slight
smaller than those found on Nos. 3676-3679.

LEGENDS OF HOLLYWOOD

Cary Grant (1904-86),
Actor — A2852

Designed by Carl Herrman.

Printed by American Packaging Corporation for Sennett
Security Products.

PHOTOGRAVURE
Sheets of 120 in six panes of 20

2002, Oct. 15   Tagged   *Serpentine Die Cut 10³⁄₄*
Self-Adhesive

3692 A2852 37c **multicolored**   .90   .20
      P# block of 4, 6#+S   3.60
      Pane of 20   18.00
      Sheet of 120 (6 panes)   90.00
      Cross gutter block of 8   17.50
      Block of 8 with vertical gutter 12.50
      Horiz. pair with vert. gutter   3.00
      Vert. pair with horiz. gutter   2.00

   Cross gutter block consists of 6 stamps from upper panes
and 2 stamps from panes below.

Sea Coast — A2853

Designed by Tom Engelman.

Printed by Banknote Corporation Of America.

PHOTOGRAVURE
COIL STAMP
Serpentine Die Cut 8½ Vert.

⟩2, Oct. 21   **Tagged**

Self-Adhesive

⟩3	A2853	(5c) **multicolored**	.20	.20
		Pair	.20	
		P# strip of 5, #B111	1.50	
		P# single, #B111	—	1.00

See Nos. 3775, 3785, 3864, 3874, 3875.

HAWAIIAN MISSIONARY STAMPS

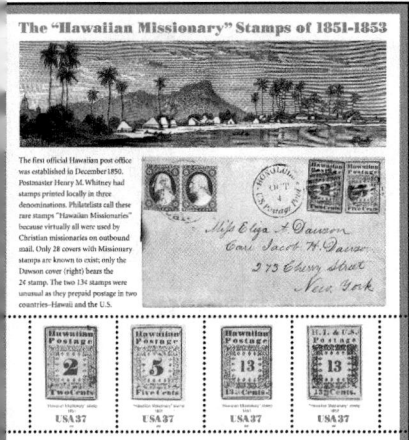

A2854

Illustration reduced.

Designed by Richard Sheaff.

Printed by Banknote Corporation of America.

Designs: a, 2c stamp of 1851 (Hawaii Scott 1). b, 5c stamp of ⟩851 (Hawaii Scott 2) c, 13c stamp of 1851 (Hawaii Scott 3). d, ⟩3c stamp of 1852 (Hawaii Scott 4).

LITHOGRAPHED
Sheets of 24 in six panes of 4

⟩002, Oct. 24   **Tagged**   ***Perf. 11***

⟩694	A2854	Pane of 4	3.50	2.50
⟩.-d.		37c Any single	.85	.50
		Sheet of 6 panes	25.00	

Happy Birthday Type of 2002
Designed by Harry Zelenko.

Printed by Avery Dennison.

PHOTOGRAVURE
Sheets of 200 in ten panes of 20

⟩002, Oct. 25   **Tagged**   ***Serpentine Die Cut 11***
Self-Adhesive

⟩695	A2751	37c **multicolored**	.75	.20
		P# block of 4, 4#+V	3.00	
		Pane of 20	15.00	

Greetings From America Type of 2002
Designed by Richard Sheaff. Printed by American Packaging ⟩orp. for Sennett Security Products.

PHOTOGRAVURE
Sheets of 100 in two panes of 50

⟩002, Oct. 25   **Tagged**   ***Serpentine Die Cut 10¾***
Self-Adhesive

3696	A2754	37c Alabama	.75	.60
3697	A2755	37c Alaska	.75	.60
3698	A2756	37c Arizona	.75	.60
3699	A2757	37c Arkansas	.75	.60
3700	A2758	37c California	.75	.60
3701	A2759	37c Colorado	.75	.60
3702	A2760	37c Connecticut	.75	.60
3703	A2761	37c Delaware	.75	.60
3704	A2762	37c Florida	.75	.60
3705	A2763	37c Georgia	.75	.60
3706	A2764	37c Hawaii	.75	.60
3707	A2765	37c Idaho	.75	.60
3708	A2766	37c Illinois	.75	.60
3709	A2767	37c Indiana	.75	.60
3710	A2768	37c Iowa	.75	.60
3711	A2769	37c Kansas	.75	.60
3712	A2770	37c Kentucky	.75	.60
3713	A2771	37c Louisiana	.75	.60
3714	A2772	37c Maine	.75	.60
3715	A2773	37c Maryland	.75	.60
3716	A2774	37c Massachusetts	.75	.60
3717	A2775	37c Michigan	.75	.60
3718	A2776	37c Minnesota	.75	.60
3719	A2777	37c Mississippi	.75	.60
3720	A2778	37c Missouri	.75	.60
3721	A2779	37c Montana	.75	.60
3722	A2780	37c Nebraska	.75	.60
3723	A2781	37c Nevada	.75	.60
3724	A2782	37c New Hampshire	.75	.60
3725	A2783	37c New Jersey	.75	.60
3726	A2784	37c New Mexico	.75	.60
3727	A2785	37c New York	.75	.60
3728	A2786	37c North Carolina	.75	.60
3729	A2787	37c North Dakota	.75	.60
3730	A2788	37c Ohio	.75	.60
3731	A2789	37c Oklahoma	.75	.60
3732	A2790	37c Oregon	.75	.60
3733	A2791	37c Pennsylvania	.75	.60
3734	A2792	37c Rhode Island	.75	.60
3735	A2793	37c South Carolina	.75	.60
3736	A2794	37c South Dakota	.75	.60
3737	A2795	37c Tennessee	.75	.60
3738	A2796	37c Texas	.75	.60
3739	A2797	37c Utah	.75	.60
3740	A2798	37c Vermont	.75	.60
3741	A2799	37c Virginia	.75	.60
3742	A2800	37c Washington	.75	.60
3743	A2801	37c West Virginia	.75	.60
3744	A2802	37c Wisconsin	.75	.60
3745	A2803	37c Wyoming	.75	.60
a.		Pane of 50, #3696-3745	37.50	

BLACK HERITAGE SERIES

Thurgood Marshall (1908-93), Supreme Court Justice — A2855

Designed by Richard Sheaff. Printed by Ashton-Potter (USA) Ltd.

LITHOGRAPHED
Sheets of 180 in nine panes of 20

2003, Jan. 7   **Tagged**   ***Serpentine Die Cut 11½***
Self-Adhesive

3746	A2855	37c **black & gray**	.75	.20
		P# block of 4, 3#+P	3.00	
		Pane of 20	15.00	

CHINESE NEW YEAR

Year of the Ram — A2856

Designed by Clarence Lee. Printed by Banknote Corporation of America.

LITHOGRAPHED
Sheets of 120 in six panes of 20

2003, Jan. 15   **Tagged**   ***Serpentine Die Cut 11½***
Self-Adhesive

3747	A2856	37c **multicolored**	.75	.20
		P# block of 4, 4#+B	3.00	
		Pane of 20	15.00	

See No. 3895h.

LITERARY ARTS

Zora Neale Hurston (1891-1960), Writer A2857

Designed by Howard E. Paine. Printed by American Packaging Corporation for Sennett Security Products.

PHOTOGRAVURE
Sheets of 120 in six panes of 20

2003, Jan. 24   **Tagged**   ***Serpentine Die Cut 10¾***
Self-Adhesive

3748	A2857	37c **multicolored**	.75	.20
		P# block of 4, 5#+S	3.00	
		Pane of 20	15.00	

AMERICAN DESIGN SERIES

Navajo Necklace — A2858

Chippendale Chair — A2859

American Clock — A2860

Tiffany Lamp — A2866

Silver Coffeepot — A2868

Designed by Derry Noyes. Printed by Ashton-Potter (USA) Ltd. (#3749B, 3750, 3751), American Packaging Corp. for Sennett Security Products (#3749A, 3750A, 3757, 3759).

LITHOGRAPHED, PHOTOGRAVURE (#3749A, 3750A)
Sheets of 280 in fourteen panes of 20

2003-05   **Untagged**   ***Serpentine Die Cut 11***
Self-Adhesive

3749	A2858	2c **multicolored**, *Aug. 20, 2004*	.20	.20
		P# block of 4, 5#+V	.20	
		Pane of 20	.80	

A reprinting of No. 3749 shows the borders in a much brighter deep turquoise blue shade.

Serpentine Die Cut 11¼x11½

3749A	A2858	2c **multicolored**, *Dec. 8, 2005*	.20	.20
		P# block of 4, 6#+S	.20	
		Pane of 20	.80	

Serpentine Die Cut 11¼x11
With "USPS" Microprinting

3749B	A2858	2c **multicolored**, *Dec. 8, 2005*	.20	.20
		P# block of 4, 5#+P	.20	
		Pane of 20	.80	

Microprinted "USPS" on No. 3749B is found on top silver appendage next to and below the middle turquoise stone on the right side of the necklace. Nos. 3749A and 3749B are dated "2006."

Sheets of 120 in six panes of 20, Sheets of 160 in eight panes of 20 (#3750A)

Untagged   ***Serpentine Die Cut 10¾x10¼***
Self-Adhesive

3750	A2859	4c **multicolored**, *Mar. 5, 2004*	.20	.20
		P# block of 4, 4#+P	.35	
		Pane of 20	1.60	

Serpentine Die Cut 11¼x11¾

3750A	A2805	5c **multicolored**, *June 25, 2004*	.20	.20
		P# block of 4, 7#+S	.40	
		Pane of 20	2.00	

Serpentine Die Cut 11¼x11
Tagged

3751	A2860	10c **multicolored**, *Jan. 24*	.20	.20
		P# block of 4, 4#+P	.80	
		Pane of 20	4.00	

PHOTOGRAVURE
COIL STAMP

Untagged   ***Perf. 10 Vert.***

3757	A2866	1c **multicolored**, *Mar. 1*	.20	.20
		Pair	.20	.20
		P# strip of 5, #S11111	.60	—
		P# single, #S11111	—	.30
3759	A2868	3c **multicolored**, *Sept. 16, 2005*	.20	.20
		Pair	.20	.20
		P# strip of 5, #S1111	1.00	—
		P# single, #S1111	—	.65

This is an ongoing set. Numbers may change.

AMERICAN CULTURE SERIES

Wisdom, Rockefeller Center, New York City — A2875

Designed by Carl Herrman. Printed by Ashton-Potter (USA) Ltd.

LITHOGRAPHED
Sheets of 120 in six panes of 20
Serpentine Die Cut 11¼x11

2003, Feb. 28   **Tagged**
Self-Adhesive
3766 A2875 $1 **multicolored**		2.00	.40
P# block of 4, 5# + P		8.00	
Pane of 20		40.00	

New York Public Library Lion Type of 2000
Designed by Carl Herrman. Printed by American Packaging Corporation for Sennett Security Products.

PHOTOGRAVURE
COIL STAMP

2003, Feb. 4   **Untagged**   *Perf. 10 Vert.*
3769 A2677 (10c) **multicolored**		.20	.20
Pair		.40	.20
P# strip of 5, #S11111		3.00	
P# single, #S11111		—	1.75

Atlas Statue Type of 2001
Designed by Kevin Newman. Printed by Avery Dennison.

PHOTOGRAVURE
Serpentine Die Cut 11 Vert.

2003, Nov.   **Untagged**
Coil Stamp
Self-Adhesive
3770 A2722 (10c) **multicolored**		.20	.20
Pair		.40	
P# strip of 5, #V11111,			
V11222, V12222, V21111,			
V21211, V22111, V22112,			
V22212, V23113, V32332,			
V33333		2.75	
P# strip of 5, #V12111		—	
P# strip of 5, #V22222		4.50	
P# single, same #		—	1.75
P# single, # V12111			*100.00*
P# single, V13222, V33332			
P# single, # V22222			3.00

No. 3770 is dated 2003.

SPECIAL OLYMPICS

Athlete with Medal — A2879

Designed by Derry Noyes. Printed by Avery Dennison.

PHOTOGRAVURE
Sheets of 200 in ten panes of 20
2003, Feb. 13   Tagged   Serpentine Die Cut 11
Self-Adhesive
3771 A2879 80c **multicolored**		1.60	.35
P# block of 4, 6# + V		6.40	
Pane of 20		32.00	

AMERICAN FILMMAKING: BEHIND THE SCENES

A2880

Block of 10 With Vertical Gutter Between

Illustrations reduced.

Designed by Imaginary Forces. Printed by American Packaging Corporation for Sennett Security Products.

Designs: a, Screenwriting (segment of script from *Gone With the Wind*). b, Directing (John Cassavetes). c, Costume design (Edith Head). d, Music (Max Steiner working on score). e, Makeup (Jack Pierce working on Boris Karloff's makeup for *Frankenstein*). f, Art direction (Perry Ferguson working on sketch for *Citizen Kane*). g, Cinematography (Paul Hill, assistant cameraman for *Nagana*). h, Film editing (J. Watson Webb editing *The Razor's Edge*). i, Special effects (Mark Siegel working on model for *E.T. The Extra-Terrestrial*). j, Sound (Gary Summers works on control panel).

PHOTOGRAVURE
Sheets of 60 in six panes of 10
Serpentine Die Cut 11 Horiz.

2003, Feb. 25   **Tagged**
Self-Adhesive
3772 A2880 Pane of 10		10.00	
a.-j. 37c Any single		1.00	.50
Sheet of 6 panes		60.00	
Block of 10 with vertical gutter between		12.50	

OHIO STATEHOOD BICENTENNIAL

Aerial View of Farm Near Marietta — A2881

Designed by Phil Jordan. Printed by Banknote Corporatio[n] America.

LITHOGRAPHED
Sheets of 120 in six panes of 20
Serpentine Die Cut 11¾x11½

2003, Mar. 1   Tagg[ed]
Self-Adhesive
3773 A2881 37c **multicolored**		.75	
P# block of 4, 4# + B		3.00	
Pane of 20		15.00	

PELICAN ISLAND NATIONAL WILDLIFE REFUG[E] CENT.

Brown Pelican — A2882

Designed by Carl T. Herrman. Printed by Banknote Corpora[ra]tion of America.

LITHOGRAPHED
Sheets of 120 in six panes of 20
Serpentine Die Cut 12x11½

2003, Mar. 14   Tagge[d]
Self-Adhesive
3774 A2882 37c **multicolored**		.75	.[..]
P# block of 4, 4#+B		3.00	
Pane of 20		15.00	

Sea Coast Type of 2002
Designed by Tom Engeman. Printed by Banknote Corpora[r]tion of America.

PHOTOGRAVURE
COIL STAMP

2003, Mar. 19   **Untagged**   *Perf. 9¾ Ver[t.]*
3775 A2853 (5c) **multicolored**		.20	.[..]
Pair		.20	[..]
P# strip of 5, #B111		1.50	
P# single, #B111			1.[..]

See No. 3864. No. 3775 has "2003" year date in blue, do[ts] that run together in surf area, and a distinct small orange clou[d.] No. 3864 has "2004" year date in black, rows of distinctly sepa[a]rated dots in surf area, and the small orange cloud is indistin[ct.]

OLD GLORY

Uncle Sam on Bicycle with Liberty Flag, 20th Cent. — A2883

1888 Presidential Campaign Badge — A2884

1893 Silk Bookmark — A2885

Modern Hand Fan — A2886

Carving of Woman with Flag and Sword, 19th Cent. — A2887

Designed by Richard Sheaff. Printed by Ashton-Potter (USA) Ltd.

LITHOGRAPHED
BOOKLET STAMPS

2003, Apr. 3   Tagged   *Serpentine Die Cut 10x9¾*
Self-Adhesive

3776	A2883	37c	multicolored	.75	.50
3777	A2884	37c	multicolored	.75	.50
3778	A2885	37c	multicolored	.75	.50
3779	A2886	37c	multicolored	.75	.50
3780	A2887	37c	multicolored	.75	.50
a.		Horiz. strip of 5, #3776-3780		3.75	
b.		Booklet pane, 2 #3780a		7.50	

No. 3780b was issued with two types of backing.

CESAR E. CHAVEZ (1927-93), LABOR ORGANIZER

A2888

Designed by Carl Herrman. Printed by Banknote Corporation of America.

LITHOGRAPHED
Sheets of 120 in six panes of 20
Serpentine Die Cut 11¾x11½

2003, Apr. 23   Tagged
Self-Adhesive

3781	A2888	37c	multicolored	.75	.20
		P# block of 4, 4# + B		3.00	
		Pane of 20		15.00	

LOUISIANA PURCHASE, BICENT.

English Translation of Treaty, Map of U.S., Treaty Signers — A2889

Designed by Richard Sheaff. Printed by American Packaging Corporation for Sennett Security Products

PHOTOGRAVURE
Sheets of 120 in six panes of 20

2003, Apr. 30   Tagged   *Serpentine Die Cut 10¾*
Self-Adhesive

3782	A2889	37c	multicolored	.75	.40
		P# block of 4, 6# + S		3.00	
		Pane of 20		15.00	

FIRST FLIGHT OF WRIGHT BROTHERS, CENT.

Orville Wright Piloting 1903 Wright Flyer — A2890

Designed by McRay Magleby. Printed by Avery Dennison.

PHOTOGRAVURE
BOOKLET STAMP

2003, May 22   Tagged   *Serpentine Die Cut 11*
Self-Adhesive

3783	A2890	37c	multicolored	.75	.40
a.		Booklet pane of 9		6.75	
b.		Booklet pane of 1		.75	

PURPLE HEART

A2891

Designed by Carl Herrman. Printed by Banknote Corporation of America (#3784), Ashton-Potter (USA) Ltd. (#3784A).

LITHOGRAPHED
Sheets of 200 in ten panes of 20 (#3784), Sheets of 120 in six panes of 20 (#3784A)

2003   Tagged   *Serpentine Die Cut 11¼x10¾*
Self-Adhesive

3784	A2891	37c	multicolored, *May 30*	.75	.20
		P# block of 4, 4#+B		3.00	
		Pane of 20		15.00	
b.		Printed on back of backing paper		—	

Serpentine Die Cut 10¾x10¼

3784A	A2891	37c	multicolored, *Aug. 1*	.75	.20
		P# block of 4, 4#+P		3.00	
		Pane of 20		15.00	
c.		Die cutting omitted, pane of 20		1,750.	

Sea Coast Type of 2002

Designed by Tom Engeman. Printed by J.W. Ferguson & Sons for Ashton-Potter (USA) Ltd.

PHOTOGRAVURE
COIL STAMP

2003, June   Untagged   *Serpentine Die Cut 9½x10*
Self-Adhesive

3785	A2853	(5c)	multicolored	.20	.20
		Pair		.20	
		P# strip of 5, #P1111		1.50	
		P# single, same #		—	1.00
a.		Serp. die cut 9¼x10		.20	.20
		Pair		.20	
		P# strip of 5, #P2222		1.50	
		P# single, same #		—	1.00
b.		As "a," tagged (error)		5.00	2.00
		P# strip of 5, #P2222		65.00	
		P# single, same #		—	7.00

No. 3785 has more of a scarlet shade in sky than does No. 3785a. Both have black "2003" year date.

LEGENDS OF HOLLYWOOD

Audrey Hepburn (1929-93), Actress — A2892

Designed by Michael J. Deas. Printed by American Packaging Corporation for Sennett Security Products.

PHOTOGRAVURE
Sheets of 120 in six panes of 20

2003, June 11   Tagged   *Serpentine Die Cut 10¾*
Self-Adhesive

3786	A2892	37c	multicolored	.90	.20
		P# block of 4, 6#+S		3.60	
		Pane of 20		18.00	
		Sheet of 120 (6 panes)		85.00	
		Cross gutter block of 8		17.50	
		Block of 8 with vertical gutter		10.00	
		Horiz. pair with vert. gutter		3.00	
		Vert. pair with horiz. gutter		2.00	

Cross gutter block consists of 6 stamps from upper panes and 2 stamps from panes below.

SOUTHEASTERN LIGHTHOUSES

Old Cape Henry, Virginia — A2893

Cape Lookout, North Carolina — A2894

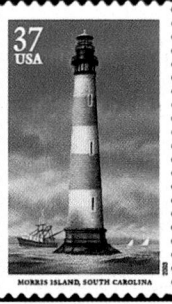

Morris Island, South Carolina — A2895

Tybee Island, Georgia — A2896

Hillsboro Inlet, Florida — A2897

Designed by Howard E. Paine. Printed by American Packaging Corporation for Sennett Security Products.

PHOTOGRAVURE
Sheets of 120 in six panes of 20

2003, June 13   Tagged   *Serpentine Die Cut 10¾*
Self-Adhesive

3787	A2893	37c	multicolored	.95	.20
3788	A2894	37c	multicolored	.95	.20
a.		Bottom of "USA" even with top of upper half-diamond of lighthouse (pos. 2)		4.00	2.50
3789	A2895	37c	multicolored	.95	.20
3790	A2896	37c	multicolored	.95	.20
3791	A2897	37c	multicolored	.95	.20
a.		Strip of 5, #3587-3791		5.00	
b.		Strip of 5, #3787, 3788a, 3789-3791		8.50	
		P# block of 10, 2 sets of 6#+S		10.00	
		Pane of 20		23.50	

Eagle in Gold on
Colored
Background
A2898

Colored Eagle on
Gold Background
A2899

Designed by Tom Engeman. Printed by American Packaging
Corporation for Sennett Security Products.

PHOTOGRAVURE
COIL STAMPS
Dated "2003"

Serpentine Die Cut 11¾ Vert.

2003, June 26			Untagged	
		Self-Adhesive		
3792	A2898	(25c) gray & gold	.50	.20
3793	A2899	(25c) gold & red	.50	.20
3794	A2899	(25c) dull blue & gold	.50	.20
3795	A2899	(25c) gold & Prussian blue	.50	.20
3796	A2898	(25c) green & gold	.50	.20
3797	A2899	(25c) gold & gray	.50	.20
3798	A2899	(25c) Prussian blue & gold	.50	.20
3799	A2899	(25c) gold & dull blue	.50	.20
3800	A2899	(25c) red & gold	.50	.20
3801	A2899	(25c) gold & green	.50	.20
a.		Strip of 10, #3792-3801	5.00	
		P# strip of 11, 2 # 3801, 1 each #3792-3800, #S1111111, S2222222, S3333333	7.50	
		P# strip of 21, 3 # 3796, 2 each #3792-3795, 3797-3801, same #	15.00	
		P# single (#3796), same #	—	2.00

Dated "2005"

2005, Aug. 5		*Serpentine Die Cut 11½ Vert.*		
3792a	A2898	(25c) gray & gold	.50	.20
3793a	A2899	(25c) gold & red	.50	.20
3794a	A2899	(25c) dull blue & gold	.50	.20
3795a	A2899	(25c) gold & Prussian blue	.50	.20
3796a	A2898	(25c) green & gold	.50	.20
3797a	A2899	(25c) gold & gray	.50	.20
3798a	A2898	(25c) Prussian blue & gold	.50	.20
3799a	A2899	(25c) gold & dull blue	.50	.20
3800a	A2898	(25c) red & gold	.50	.20
3801b	A2899	(25c) gold & green	.50	.20
c.		Strip of 10, #3792a-3801b	5.00	
		P# strip of 11, 2 #3801b, 1 each #3792a-3800a, P#S1111111	7.50	
		P# strip of 21, 3 #3796a, 2 each #3792a-3795a, 3797a-3800a, 3801b, P#S1111111	15.00	
		P# single (#3796a), #S1111111		1.75

ARCTIC TUNDRA

A2900

Illustration reduced.

Designed by Ethel Kessler. Printed by Banknote Corporation
of America.

Wildlife and vegetation: a, Gyrfalcon. b, Gray wolf, vert. c,
Common raven, vert. d, Musk oxen and caribou, vert. e, Grizzly
bears, caribou. f, Caribou, willow ptarmigans. g, Arctic ground
squirrel, vert. h, Willow ptarmigan, bearberry. i, Arctic grayling. j,
Singing vole, thin-legged wolf spider, lingonberry, Labrador tea.

LITHOGRAPHED
Sheets of 80 in eight panes of 10
Serpentine Die Cut 10¾x10½, 10½x10¾

2003, July 2			Tagged	
		Self-Adhesive		
3802	A2900	Pane of 10	7.50	
a.-j.		37c Any single	.75	.50
		Sheet of 8 panes	65.00	
		Pair of tete-beche panes	15.00	

KOREAN WAR VETERANS MEMORIAL

Memorial in
Snow — A2901

Designed by Richard Sheaff. Printed by Banknote Corporation of America.

LITHOGRAPHED
Sheets of 120 in six panes of 20
Serpentine Die Cut 11½x11¾

2003, July 27			Tagged	
		Self-Adhesive		
3803	A2901	37c multicolored	.75	.20
		P# block of 4, 4#+B	3.00	
		Pane of 20	15.00	

MARY CASSATT PAINTINGS

Young Mother,
1888 — A2902

Children Playing on the
Beach, 1884 — A2903

On a Balcony, 1878-
79 — A2904

Child in a Straw Hat, c.
1886 — A2905

Designed by Derry Noyes. Printed by American Packaging
Corporation for Sennett Security Products.

PHOTOGRAVURE
Serpentine Die Cut 10¾ on 2 or 3 Sides

2003, Aug. 7			Tagged	
		Self-Adhesive		
		Booklet Stamps		
3804	A2902	37c multicolored	.75	.20
3805	A2903	37c multicolored	.75	.20
3806	A2904	37c multicolored	.75	.20
3807	A2905	37c multicolored	.75	.20
a.		Block of 4, #3804-3807	3.00	
b.		Booklet pane of 20, 5 #3807a	15.00	

No. 3807b is a double-sided booklet with 12 stamps on one
side and 8 stamps plus label (booklet cover) on the other side.

EARLY FOOTBALL HEROES

Bronko Nagurski
(1908-90) — A2906

Ernie Nevers (1903-
76) — A2907

Walter Camp (1859-
1925) — A2908

Red Grange (1903-
91) — A2909

Designed by Richard Sheaff. Printed by Avery Dennison.

PHOTOGRAVURE
Sheets of 200 in ten panes of 20
Serpentine Die Cut 11½x11¾

2003, Aug. 8			Tagged	
		Self-Adhesive		
3808	A2906	37c multicolored	.75	.20
3809	A2907	37c multicolored	.75	.20
3810	A2908	37c multicolored	.75	.20
3811	A2909	37c multicolored	.75	.20
a.		Block of 4, #3808-3811	3.00	
		P# block of 4, 7#+V	3.00	
		Pane of 20	15.00	

ROY ACUFF

Acuff (1903-92), Country
Music Artist, and
Fiddle — A2910

Designed by Richard Sheaff.
Printed by Avery Dennison.

PHOTOGRAVURE
Sheets of 200 in ten panes of 20

2003, Sept. 13   Tagged   *Serpentine Die Cut 11*
Self-Adhesive

3812 A2910 37c **multicolored**   .75   .20
      P# block of 4, 4#+V   3.00
      Pane of 20   15.00

DISTRICT OF COLUMBIA

Map, National Mall, Row Houses and Cherry
Blossoms — A2911

Designed by Greg Berger.
Printed by American Packaging Corporation for Sennett
Security Products.

PHOTOGRAVURE
Sheets of 128 in eight panes of 16

2003, Sept. 23   Tagged   *Serpentine Die Cut 11*
Self-Adhesive

3813 A2911 37c **multicolored**   .75   .20
      P# block of 4, 8#+S   3.50
      Pane of 16   17.00

REPTILES AND AMPHIBIANS

Scarlet
Kingsnake
A2912

Reticulate
Collared
Lizard
A2914

Ornate
Chorus
Frog — A2915

Ornate Box
Turtle
A2916

Designed by Steve Buchanan. Printed by Avery Dennison.

PHOTOGRAVURE
Sheets of 200 in ten panes of 20

2003, Oct. 7   Tagged   *Serpentine Die Cut 11*
Self-Adhesive

3814 A2912 37c **multicolored**   .75   .20
3815 A2913 37c **multicolored**   .75   .20
3816 A2914 37c **multicolored**   .75   .20
3817 A2915 37c **multicolored**   .75   .20
3818 A2916 37c **multicolored**   .75   .20
  a.   Vert. strip of 5, #3814-3818   3.75
           P# block of 10, 4#+V   7.50
           Pane of 20   15.00

Washington Type of 2002
Designed by Richard Sheaff.

Printed by Avery Dennison.

PHOTOGRAVURE
Sheets of 200 in ten panes of 20

2003, Oct.   Tagged   *Serpentine Die Cut 11*
Self-Adhesive

3819 A2686 23c **gray green**   .45   .20
      P# block of 4, 2#+V   1.80
      Pane of 20   9.00

Christmas Type of 2002
Designed by Richard Sheaff.

Printed by Ashton-Potter (USA) Ltd.

LITHOGRAPHED
Serpentine Die Cut 11x11¼ on 2 or 3 Sides
2003, Oct. 23   Tagged
Self-Adhesive
Booklet Stamp
Size: 19½x28mm

3820 A2843 37c **multicolored**   .75   .20
  a.   Booklet pane of 20   15.00
  b.   Die cutting omitted, pair

No. 3820a is a double-sided booklet with 12 stamps on one
side and 8 stamps plus label (booklet cover) on the other side.
Compare to No. 3675, which measures 19x27mm.

CHRISTMAS

Reindeer with Pan
Pipes — A2917

Santa Claus with
Drum — A2918

Santa Claus with
Trumpet — A2919

Reindeer with
Horn — A2920

Reindeer with Pan
Pipes — A2921

Santa Claus with
Drum — A2922

Santa Claus with
Trumpet — A2923

Reindeer with
Horn — A2924

Designed by Ethel Kessler.

Printed by American Packaging Corp. for Sennett Security
Products.

PHOTOGRAVURE
Sheets of 160 in eight panes of 20
Serpentine Die Cut 11¾x11
2003, Oct. 23   Tagged
Self-Adhesive

3821 A2917 37c **multicolored**   .75   .20
3822 A2918 37c **multicolored**   .75   .20
3823 A2919 37c **multicolored**   .75   .20
3824 A2920 37c **multicolored**   .75   .20
  a.   Block of 4, #3821-3824   3.00
           P# block of 4, 4#+S   15.00
           Pane of 20   15.00
  b.   Booklet pane of 20, 5 each #3821-3824 15.00

BOOKLET STAMPS
Serpentine Die Cut 10½x10¾ on 2 or 3 Sides

3825 A2921 37c **multicolored**   .75   .20
3826 A2922 37c **multicolored**   .75   .20
3827 A2923 37c **multicolored**   .75   .20
3828 A2924 37c **multicolored**   .75   .20
  a.   Block of 4, #3825-3828   3.00
  b.   Booklet pane of 4, #3825-3828   3.00
  c.   Booklet pane of 6, #3827-3828, 2 each
           #3825-3826   4.50
  d.   Booklet pane of 6, #3825-3826, 2 each
           #3827-3828   4.50

No. 3824b is a double-sided booklet with 12 stamps on one
side and 8 stamps plus label (booklet cover) on the other side.

Blue-Spotted
Salamander
A2913

Snowy Egret — A2925

Designed by Carl T. Herrman.

Printed by Avery Dennison (#3829), Ashton-Potter (USA) Ltd. (#3829A, 3830, 3830D).

COIL STAMPS

2003-05   Tagged   *Serpentine Die Cut 8½ Vert.*
Self-Adhesive
PHOTOGRAVURE

3829	A2925 37c **multicolored,** *Oct. 24,*		
	2003	.75	.20
	Pair	1.50	
	P# strip of 5, #V1111,		
	V2111, V3212, V3222	5.25	
	P# strip of 5, #V3211	—	
	P# strip of 5, #V3221	175.00	
	P# single, same #	—	2.00
	P# single, #V2121	—	—
	P# single, #V3211	—	—
	P# single, #V3221		8.00

LITHOGRAPHED
Serpentine Die Cut 9½ Vert.

3829A	A2925 37c **multicolored,** *Mar., 2004*	.75	.20
	Pair	1.50	
	P# strip of 5, #P11111,		
	P22222, P33333, P44444,		
	P55555	5.25	
	P# single, same #		2.00

Serpentine Die Cut 11½x11 on 2, 3 or 4 Sides
Booklet Stamps
PHOTOGRAVURE

3830	A2925 37c **multicolored,** *Jan. 30,*		
	2004	.75	.20
a.	Booklet pane of 20	15.00	
b.	Die cutting omitted, pair	—	
c.	As "a," die cutting omitted	—	

With "USPS" Microprinted on Bird's Breast

3830D	A2925 37c **multicolored,** *2005(?)*	.75	.20
e.	Booklet pane of 20	15.00	

PACIFIC CORAL REEF

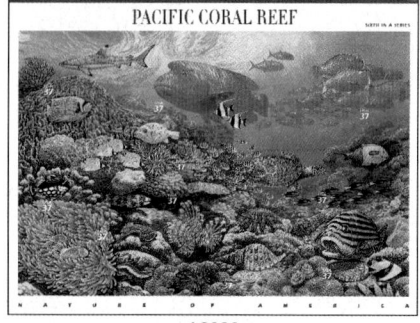

A2926

Illustration reduced.

Designed by Ethel Kessler. Printed by Avery Dennison.

Marine life: a, Emperor angelfish, blue coral, mound coral, vert. b, Humphead wrasse, Moorish idol. c, Bumphead parrotfish, vert. d, Black-spotted puffer, threadfin butterflyfish, staghorn coral. e, Hawksbill turtle, palette surgeonfish. f, Pink anemonefish, magnificent sea anemone, vert. g, Snowflake moray eel, Spanish dancer. h, Lionfish, vert. i, Triton's trumpet. j, Oriental sweetlips, bluestreak cleaner wrasse, mushroom coral, vert.

PHOTOGRAVURE
Sheets of 80 in eight panes of 10

2004, Jan. 2   Tagged   *Serpentine Die Cut 10¾*
Self-Adhesive

3831	A2926 Pane of 10	7.50	
a.-j.	37c Any single	.75	.20
	Sheet of 8 panes	57.50	

CHINESE NEW YEAR

Year of the Monkey A2927

Designed by Clarence Lee. Printed by American Packaging Corporation for Sennett Security Products.

PHOTOGRAVURE
Sheets of 120 in six panes of 20

2004, Jan. 13   Tagged   *Serpentine Die Cut 10¾*
Self-Adhesive

3832	A2927 37c **multicolored**	.75	.20
	P# block of 4, 4# + S	3.00	
	Pane of 20	15.00	

LOVE

Candy Hearts — A2928

Designed by Michael Osborne. Printed by Avery Dennison.

PHOTOGRAVURE
BOOKLET STAMP
Serpentine Die Cut 10¾ on 2, 3 or 4 Sides

2004, Jan. 14   Tagged
Self-Adhesive

3833	A2928 37c **multicolored**	.75	.20
a.	Booklet pane of 20	15.00	

BLACK HERITAGE SERIES

Paul Robeson (1898-1976), Actor, Singer, Athlete and Activist — A2929

Designed by Richard Sheaff. Printed by American Packaging Corporation for Sennett Security Products.

PHOTOGRAVURE
Sheets of 120 in six panes of 20

2004, Jan. 20   Tagged   *Serpentine Die Cut 10¾*
Self-Adhesive

3834	A2929 37c **multicolored**	.75	.20
	P# block of 4, 4# + S	3.00	
	Pane of 20	15.00	

THEODOR SEUSS GEISEL (DR. SEUSS)

Dr. Seuss (1904-91), Children's Book Writer, and Book Characters A2930

Designed by Carl T. Herrman. Printed by American Packaging Corporation for Sennett Security Products.

PHOTOGRAVURE
Sheets of 180 in nine panes of 20
Serpentine Die Cut 10¾x10½

2004, Mar. 2   Tagge
Self-Adhesive

3835	A2930 37c **multicolored**	.75	
	P# block of 4, 6#+S	3.25	
	Pane of 20	16.00	
a.	Die cutting omitted, pair	—	

FLOWERS

White Lilacs and Pink Roses — A2931

Five Varieties of Pir... Roses — A2932

Designed by Richard Sheaff. Printed by Ashton-Potter (US. Ltd. (#3836), American Packaging Corporation for Senne Security Products.

LITHOGRAPHED (#3836), PHOTOGRAVURE
BOOKLET STAMP (#3836)
Sheets of 160 in eight panes of 20 (#3837)
Serpentine Die Cut 10¾ on 2, 3 or 4 Sides

2004, Mar. 4   Tagge
Self-Adhesive

3836	A2931 37c **multicolored**	.75	.2
a.	Booklet pane of 20	15.00	

Serpentine Die Cut 11½x11

3837	A2932 60c **multicolored**	1.25	.2
	P# block of 4, 5#+S	5.00	
	Pane of 20	25.00	

UNITED STATES AIR FORCE ACADEMY, 50TH ANNIV.

Cadet Chapel A2933

Designed by Phil Jordan. Printed by American Packaging Corporation for Sennett Security Products.

PHOTOGRAVURE
Sheets of 120 in six panes of 20

2004, Apr. 1   Tagged   *Serpentine Die Cut 10¾*
Self-Adhesive

3838	A2933 37c **multicolored**	.75	.20
	P# block of 4, 6# + S	3.00	
	Pane of 20	15.00	

HENRY MANCINI

Henry Mancini (1924-94), Composer, and Pink Panther A2934

Designed by Carl Herrman. Printed by American Packaging Corporation for Sennett Security Products.

PHOTOGRAVURE
Sheets of 120 in six panes of 20

2004, Apr. 13   Tagged   *Serpentine Die Cut 10¾*
Self-Adhesive

3839	A2934 37c **multicolored**	.75	.20
	P# block of 4, 6#+S	3.00	
	Pane of 20	15.00	

AMERICAN CHOREOGRAPHERS

Martha Graham (1893-1991) A2935

Alvin Ailey (1931-89), and Dancers A2936

Agnes de Mille (1909-93), and Dancers A2937

George Balanchine (1904-83), and Dancers A2938

Designed by Ethel Kessler. Printed by Ashton-Potter (USA) Ltd.

LITHOGRAPHED
Sheets of 120 in six panes of 20

2004, May 4   Tagged   *Serpentine Die Cut 10¾*
Self-Adhesive

3840	A2935	37c	multicolored	.75	.20
3841	A2936	37c	multicolored	.75	.20
3842	A2937	37c	multicolored	.75	.20
3843	A2938	37c	multicolored	.75	.20
a.	Horiz. strip of 4, #3840-3843		3.00	
	P# block of 8, 2 sets of P#, 6#+P		6.00	
	Pane of 20		15.00	
b.	Strip of 4, die cutting omitted		—	
	As "b," pane of 20		—	

Eagle Types of 2003

Designed by Tom Engeman. Printed by American Packaging Corporation for Sennett Security Products.

PHOTOGRAVURE
COIL STAMPS

2004, May 12		Untagged		Perf. 9¾ Vert.	
3844	A2898	(25c)	gray & gold	.50	.20
3845	A2899	(25c)	gold & green	.50	.20
3846	A2898	(25c)	red & gold	.50	.20
3847	A2899	(25c)	gold & dull blue	.50	.20
3848	A2899	(25c)	Prussian blue & gold	.50	.20
3849	A2899	(25c)	gold & gray	.50	.20
3850	A2898	(25c)	green & gold	.50	.20
3851	A2899	(25c)	gold & Prussian blue	.50	.20
3852	A2898	(25c)	dull blue & gold	.50	.20
3853	A2899	(25c)	gold & red	.50	.20
a.	Strip of 10, #3844-3853			5.00	—
	P# strip of 11, 2 # 3844, 1 each # 3845-3853, #S1111111			7.50	—
	P# single (#3849), same #			—	2.00

LEWIS & CLARK EXPEDITION, BICENT.

Meriwether Lewis (1774-1809) and William Clark (1770-1838) On Hill — A2939

Lewis — A2940

Clark — A2941

Designed by Michael J. Deas. Printed by Banknote Corporation of America for Sennett Security Products (#3854), Ashton-Potter (USA) Ltd.

LITHOGRAPHED & ENGRAVED
Sheets of 180 in nine panes of 20

2004, May 14   Tagged   *Serpentine Die Cut 10¾*
Self-Adhesive

3854	A2939	37c	green & multicolored	.85	.20
	P# block of 4, 6#+S		3.50	
	Pane of 20		17.50	
	Sheet of 180 (9 panes)		160.00	
	Cross gutter block of 4		12.50	
	Horiz. pair with vert. gutter		2.00	
	Vert. pair with horiz. gutter		2.00	

Booklet Stamps
Serpentine Die Cut 10½x10¾

3855	A2940	37c	blue & multicolored	.90	.45
3856	A2941	37c	red & multicolored	.90	.45
a.	Horiz. or vert. pair, #3855-3856		1.80	
b.	Booklet pane, 5 each #3855-3856		9.00	

Nos. 3855-3856 were issued in booklets containing two No. 3856b, each with a different backing. The booklets sold for $8.95.

ISAMU NOGUCHI (1904-88), SCULPTOR

Akari 25N — A2942

Margaret La Farge Osborn — A2943

Black Sun — A2944

Mother and Child — A2945

Figure (Detail) — A2946

Designed by Derry Noyes. Printed by Ashton-Potter (USA) Ltd.

LITHOGRAPHED
Sheets of 120 in six panes of 20
Serpentine Die Cut 10½x10¾

2004, May 18				Tagged	
			Self-Adhesive		
3857	A2942	37c	black	.75	.20
3858	A2943	37c	black	.75	.20
3859	A2944	37c	black	.75	.20
3860	A2945	37c	black	.75	.20
3861	A2946	37c	black	.75	.20
a.	Horiz. strip of 5, #3857-3861			3.75	
	P# block of 6 (3 across x 2 down), 2#+P			4.50	
	P# block of 8, 2 sets of 2#+P + left label			6.00	
	Pane of 20			15.00	
	Sheet of 120 (6 panes)			85.00	
	Cross gutter block of 8			17.50	
	Block of 8 with vert. gutter			10.00	
	Block of 10 with horiz. gutter			11.00	
	Horiz. pair with vert. gutter			2.25	
	Vert. pair with horiz. gutter			2.25	

The cross gutter block consists of 1 stamp from each of the two upper panes and three stamps vertically from each of the two lower panes.

NATIONAL WORLD WAR II MEMORIAL

A2947

Designed by Howard E. Paine. Printed by Ashton-Potter (USA) Ltd.

LITHOGRAPHED
Sheets of 180 in nine panes of 20

2004, May 29   Tagged   *Serpentine Die Cut 10¾*
Self-Adhesive

3862 A2947 37c **multicolored**   .75   .20
           P# block of 4, 4#+P   3.00
           Pane of 20   15.00

SUMMER OLYMPIC GAMES, ATHENS, GREECE

Stylized
Runner
A2948

Designed by Richard Sheaff. Printed by Ashton-Potter (USA) Ltd.

LITHOGRAPHED
Sheets of 120 in six panes of 20

2004, June 9   Tagged   *Serpentine Die Cut 10¾*
Self-Adhesive

3863 A2948 37c **multicolored**   .75   .20
           P# block of 4, 4#+P   3.00
           Pane of 20   15.00

Sea Coast Type of 2002
Designed by Tom Engeman. Printed by American Packaging Corp. for Sennett Security Products.

PHOTOGRAVURE
COIL STAMP

2004, June 11   Untagged   *Perf. 9¾ Vert.*
3864 A2853 (5c) **multicolored**   .20   .20
           Pair   .20   —
           P# strip of 5, #S1111   1.50   —
           P# single, same #   —   1.00

No. 3864 has "2004" year date in black, rows of distinctly separated dots in surf area, and the small orange cloud is indistinct. No. 3775 has "2003" year date in blue, dots that run together in surf area, and a distinct small orange cloud.

No. 3864 known with red ink that glows orange under long wave ultraviolet light. Values the same.

DISNEY CHARACTERS

Goofy, Mickey Mouse,
Donald Duck — A2949

Bambi,
Thumper — A2950

Mufasa,
Simba — A2951

Jiminy Cricket,
Pinocchio — A2952

Designed by David Pacheco. Printed by American Packaging Corporation for Bamknote Corporation of America/Sennett Security Products.

LITHOGRAPHED
Sheets of 180 in nine panes of 20
Serpentine Die Cut 10½x10¾

2004, June 23   Tagged
Self-Adhesive

3865 A2949 37c **multicolored**   .75   .20
3866 A2950 37c **multicolored**   .75   .20
3867 A2951 37c **multicolored**   .75   .20
3868 A2952 37c **multicolored**   .75   .20
  a.   Block or vert. strip of 4, #3865-3868 3.00
           P# block of 4, 4#+S   3.00
           Pane of 20   15.00

U.S.S. CONSTELLATION

A2953

Designed by Howard E. Paine. Printed by Ashton-Potter (USA) Ltd.

ENGRAVED
Sheets of 180 in nine panes of 20

2004, June 30   Tagged   *Serpentine Die Cut 10½*
Self-Adhesive

3869 A2953 37c **brown**   .75   .20
           P# block of 4, 1#+P   3.00
           Pane of 20   15.00

R. BUCKMINSTER FULLER (1895-1983),
ENGINEER

Time Magazine Cover
Depicting Fuller, by
Boris
Artzybasheff — A2954

Designed by Carl T. Herrman. Printed by Ashton-Potter (USA) Ltd.

LITHOGRAPHED
Sheets of 120 in six panes of 20
Serpentine Die Cut 10½x10¾

2004, July 12   Tagg
Self-Adhesive

3870 A2954 37c **multicolored**   .75
           P# block of 4, 5#+P   3.00
           Pane of 20   15.00

LITERARY ARTS

James Baldwin
(1924-87),
Writer
A2955

Designed by Phil Jordan. Printed by Ashton-Potter (USA) L

LITHOGRAPHED
Sheets of 180 in nine panes of 20

2004, July 23   Tagged   *Serpentine Die Cut 10*
Self-Adhesive

3871 A2955 37c **multicolored**   .75   .2
           P# block of 4, 5#+P   3.00
           Pane of 20   15.00

AMERICAN TREASURES SERIES

Giant
Magnolias on
a Blue Velvet
Cloth, by
Martin
Johnson
Heade
A2956

Designed by Derry Noyes. Printed by American Packaging Corporation for Sennett Security Products.

PHOTOGRAVURE
BOOKLET STAMP
Serpentine Die Cut 10¾ on 2 or 3 Sides

2004, Aug. 12   Tagge
Self-Adhesive

3872 A2956 37c **multicolored**   .70   .2
  a.   Booklet pane of 20   15.00
  b.   Die cutting omitted, pair   —

No. 3872a is a double-sided booklet pane with 12 stamps or one side and eight stamps plus label on the other side.

ART OF THE AMERICAN INDIAN

A2957

Designed by Richard Sheaff. Printed by Avery Dennison. Designs: a, Mimbres bowl. b, Kutenai parfleche. c, Tlingit sculptures. d, Ho-Chunk bag. e, Seminole doll. f, Mississippian effigy. g, Acoma pot. h, Navajo weaving. i, Seneca carving. j, Luiseño basket.

PHOTOGRAVURE
Serpentine Die Cut 10¾x11

2004, Aug. 21   Tagged
Self-Adhesive

3873 A2957   Pane of 10   7.50
  a.-j. 37c Any single   .75   .20
Sea Coast Type of 2002
Designed by Tom Engeman.

Printed by Ashton-Potter (USA), Ltd. (#3874); American Packaging Corporation for Sennett Security Products (#3875).

PHOTOGRAVURE
COIL STAMPS
004-05 Untagged *Serpentine Die Cut 10 Vert.*
Self-Adhesive

3874 A2853 (5c) **multicolored**, large "2003" year
date .20 .20
Pair .20
P# strip of 5, #P2222 1.50
P# single, #P2222 — 1.00
a. Small "2003" year date ('05) .20 .20
Pair .20
P# strip of 5, #P3333, P4444,
P5555, P6666, P7777 1.50
P# single, same numbers — 1.00

On No. 3874 the color laydown oder of plate numbers is cyan, magenta, yellow, black. On No. 3874a, the order is BCMY.

Serpentine Die Cut 11½ Vert.

4875 A2853 (5c) **multicolored**, "2004" year date .20 .20
Pair .20
P# strip of 5, #S1111 1.50
P# single, #S1111 — 1.00

On No. 3875, the stamps are spaced on backing paper that is aller than the stamps.

LEGENDS OF HOLLYWOOD

John Wayne (1907-79),
Actor — A2958

Designed by Derry Noyes.

Printed by American Packaging Corporation for Sennett Security Products.

PHOTOGRAVURE
Sheets of 120 in six panes of 20
2004, Sept. 9 Tagged *Serpentine Die Cut 10¾*
Self-Adhesive

3876 A2958 37c **multicolored** .75 .20
P# block of 4, 6#+S 3.00
Pane of 20 15.00
Sheet of 120 (6 panes) 85.00
Cross gutter block of 8 17.50
Block of 8 with vertical gutter 10.00
Horiz. pair with vert. gutter 3.00
Vert. pair with horiz. gutter 2.00

SICKLE CELL DISEASE AWARENESS

Mother and Child — A2959

Designed by Howard Paine.

Printed by Avery Dennison.

PHOTOGRAVURE
Sheets of 200 in ten panes of 20
2004, Sept. 29 Tagged *Serpentine Die Cut 11*
Self-Adhesive

3877 A2959 37c **multicolored** .75 .20
P# block of 4, 6#+V 3.00
Pane of 20 15.00

CLOUDSCAPES

A2960

Designed by Howard E. Paine.

Printed by Avery Dennison.

Clouds: a, Cirrus radiatus. b, Cirrostratus fibratus. c, Cirrocumulus undulatus. d, Cumulonimbus mammatus. e, Cumulonimbus incus. f, Altocumulus stratiformis. g, Altostratus translucidus. h, Altocumulus undulatus. i, Altocumulus castellanus. j, Altocumulus lenticularis. k, Stratocumulus undulatus. l, Stratus opacus. m, Cumulus humilis. n, Cumulus congestus. o, Cumulonimbus with tornado.

PHOTOGRAVURE
2004, Oct. 4 Tagged *Serpentine Die Cut 11*
Self-Adhesive

3878 A2960 Pane of 15 12.50
a.-o. 37c Any single .80 .20

CHRISTMAS

Madonna and Child, by
Lorenzo Monaco — A2961

Designed by Richard Sheaff.
Printed by Ashton-Potter (USA), Ltd.

LITHOGRAPHED
BOOKLET STAMP
Serpentine Die Cut 10¾x11 on 2 or 3 Sides
2004, Oct. 14 Tagged
Self-Adhesive

3879 A2961 37c **multicolored** .75 .20
a. Booklet pane of 20 15.00

No. 3879a is a double-sided booklet pane with 12 stamps on one side and eight stamps plus label that serves as a booklet cover on the other side.

HANUKKAH

Dreidel — A2962

Designed by Ethel Kessler.
Printed by Banknote Corporation of America for Sennett Security Products.

LITHOGRAPHED
Sheets of 300 in fifteen panes of 20
2004, Oct. 15 Tagged *Serpentine Die Cut 10¾*
Self-Adhesive

3880 A2962 37c **multicolored** .75 .20
P# block of 4, 4#+S 3.00
Pane of 20 15.00

KWANZAA

People in
Robes — A2963

Designed by Derry Noyes.
Printed by Ashton-Potter (USA), Ltd.

LITHOGRAPHED
Sheets of 160 in eight panes of 20
2004, Oct. 16 Tagged *Serpentine Die Cut 10¾*
Self-Adhesive

3881 A2963 37c **multicolored** .75 .20
P# block of 4, 6#+P 3.00
Pane of 20 15.00

MOSS HART (1904-61), PLAYWRIGHT

A2964

Designed by Ethel Kessler.
Printed by Avery Dennison.

PHOTOGRAVURE
Sheets of 200 in ten panes of 20
2004, Oct. 25 Tagged *Serpentine Die Cut 11*
Self-Adhesive

3882 A2964 37c **multicolored** .75 .20
P# block of 4, 5#+V 3.00
Pane of 20 15.00

CHRISTMAS

Purple Santa
Ornament — A2965

Green Santa
Ornament — A2966

Blue Santa
Ornament — A2967

Red Santa
Ornament — A2968

Purple Santa
Ornament — A2969

Green Santa
Ornament — A2970

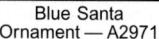

Blue Santa
Ornament — A2971

Red Santa
Ornament — A2972

Designed by Derry Noyes. Printed by American Packaging Corporation for Sennett Security Printers. (#3883-3890), Avery Dennison (#3891-3894).

PHOTOGRAVURE
Sheets of 160 in eight panes of 20
Serpentine Die Cut 11¹/₂x11

2004, Nov. 16				Tagged
Self-Adhesive				
3883	A2965	37c	purple & multicolored	.75	.20
3884	A2966	37c	green & multicolored	.75	.20
3885	A2967	37c	blue & multicolored	.75	.20
3886	A2968	37c	red & multicolored	.75	.20
a.		Block or strip of 4, #3883-3886		3.00	
		P# block of 4, 4#+S		3.00	
		Pane of 20		15.00	
b.		Booklet pane of 20, 5 #3886a blocks		15.00	

Booklet Stamps
Serpentine Die Cut 10¹/₄x10³/₄ on 2 or 3 Sides

3887	A2969	37c	purple & multicolored	.75	.20
3888	A2970	37c	green & multicolored	.75	.20
3889	A2971	37c	blue & multicolored	.75	.20
3890	A2972	37c	red & multicolored	.75	.20
a.		Block of 4, #3887-3890		3.00	
b.		Booklet pane of 4, #3887-3890		3.00	
c.		Booklet pane of 6, #3889-3890, 2 each #3887-3888		4.50	
d.		Booklet pane of 6, #3887-3888, 2 each #3889-3890		4.50	

Serpentine Die Cut 8 on 2, 3 or 4 Sides

3891	A2970	37c	green & multicolored	.75	.20
3892	A2969	37c	purple & multicolored	.75	.20
3893	A2972	37c	red & multicolored	.75	.20
3894	A2971	37c	blue & multicolored	.75	.20
a.		Block of 4, #3891-3894		3.00	
b.		Booklet pane of 18, 6 each #3891, 3893, 3 each #3892, 3894		13.50	
		Nos. 3883-3894 (12)		9.00	2.40

No. 3886b is a double-sided booklet with 12 stamps on one side and 8 stamps plus label that serves as a booklet cover on the other side.

The design of No. 3894b shows ornaments in a wooden box. The pattern of the wooden box dividers creates three types of each design. Rows 1 and 4 are Type 1, with a top horizontal strip of frame extending from edge to edge while the bottom strip of frame stops at the design's width. Rows 2 and 5 are Type 2, with both top and bottom strips of frame stopping at the design's width. Rows 3 and 6 are Type 3, with the top strip of frame stopping at design's width while the bottom strip of frame extends from edge to edge. Each variety is equally common.

Chinese New Year Types of 1992-2004
Designed by Clarence Lee. Printed by American Packaging Corporation for Sennett Security Products.

PHOTOGRAVURE

2005, Jan. 6	Tagged	*Serpentine Die Cut 10³/₄*
Self-Adhesive		
3895		Double sided pane of 24, 2 each #a-l	18.00	
a.	A2360	37c Rat	.75	.20
b.	A2413	37c Ox	.75	.20
c.	A2462	37c Tiger	.75	.20
d.	A2535	37c Rabbit	.75	.20
e.	A2602	37c Dragon	.75	.20
f.	A2702	37c Snake	.75	.20
g.	A2752	37c Horse	.75	.20
h.	A2856	37c Ram	.75	.20
i.	A2927	37c Monkey	.75	.20
j.	A2067	37c Rooster	.75	.20
k.	A2146	37c Dog	.75	.20
l.	A2205	37c Boar	.75	.20
m.		As No. 3895, die cutting omitted on "a," "b," and "c" on reverse side	—	

No. 3895h has "2005" year date and is photogravure while No. 3747 has "2003" year date and is lithographed.

Stamps are on the right side of the front and on the left side of the reverse.

BLACK HERITAGE SERIES

Marian Anderson (1897-1993), Singer — A2973

Designed by Richard Sheaff. Printed by American Packaging Corporation for Sennett Security Products.

PHOTOGRAVURE
Sheets of 120 in six panes of 20

2005, Jan. 27	Tagged	*Serpentine Die Cut 10³/₄*
Self-Adhesive		
3896	A2973	37c multicolored	.75	.20
		P# block of 4, 4# + S	3.00	
		Pane of 20	15.00	

RONALD REAGAN

Ronald Reagan (1911-2004), 40th President — A2974

Designed by Howard E. Paine. Printed by American Packaging Corporation for Sennett Security Products.

PHOTOGRAVURE
Sheets of 120 in six panes of 20

2005, Feb. 9	Tagged	*Serpentine Die Cut 10³/₄*
Self-Adhesive		
3897	A2974	37c multicolored	.75	.20
		P# block of 4, 4#+S	3.00	
		Pane of 20	15.00	
		Sheet of 120 (6 panes)	90.00	
		Cross gutter block of 4	8.25	
		Horiz. pair with vert. gutter	3.00	
		Vert. pair with horiz. gutter	2.00	

The bottom center stamp (pos. 18) shows a small portion of the pane position diagram in the bottom margin, due to the too-high placement of the diagram in the selvage. There are three varieties of the portion appearing on the stamp, depending on the pane position on the press sheet.

LOVE

Hand and Flower
Bouquet — A2975

Designed by Derry Noyes. Printed by Avery Dennison.

PHOTOGRAVURE
BOOKLET STAMP
Serpentine Die Cut 10³/₄x11 on 2, 3 or 4 Sides

2005, Feb. 18			Tagged
Self-Adhesive			
3898	A2975	37c multicolored	.75	.20
a.		Booklet pane of 20	15.00	

NORTHEAST DECIDUOUS FOREST

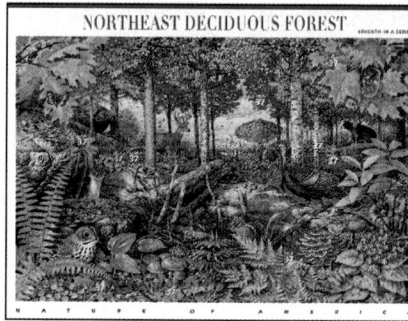

A2976

Illustration reduced.

Designed by Ethel Kessler. Printed by Avery Dennison.

Wildlife: a, Eastern buckmoth, vert. b, Red-shouldered hawk. c, Eastern red bat. d, White-tailed deer. e, Black bear. f, Long-tailed weasel, vert. g, Wild turkey, vert. h, Ovenbird, vert. i, Red eft. j, Eastern chipmunk.

PHOTOGRAVURE
Sheets of 80 in eight panes of 10

2005, Mar. 3	Tagged	*Serpentine Die Cut 10³/₄*
Self-Adhesive		
3899	A2976	Pane of 10	7.50	
a.-j.		37c Any single	.75	.20
		Sheet of 8 panes	60.00	

SPRING FLOWERS

Hyacinth — A2977

Daffodil — A2978

Tulip — A2979

Iris — A2980

Designed by Derry Noyes. Printed by Ashton-Potter (USA) Ltd.

LITHOGRAPHED
BOOKLET STAMPS
Serpentine Die Cut 10³/₄ on 2 or 3 Sides

2005, Mar. 15			Tagged
Self-Adhesive			
3900	A2977	37c multicolored	.75	.20
3901	A2978	37c multicolored	.75	.20
3902	A2979	37c multicolored	.75	.20
3903	A2980	37c multicolored	.75	.20
a.		Block of 4, #3900-3903	3.00	
b.		Booklet pane, 5 each #3900-3903	15.00	

No. 3903b is a double-sided booklet with 12 stamps on one side and 8 stamps plus label (booklet cover) on the other side.

LITERARY ARTS

Robert Penn Warren (1905-89), Writer A2981

Designed by Carl Herrman. Printed by American Packaging Corporation for Sennett Security Products.

PHOTOGRAVURE
Sheets of 120 in six panes of 20

005, Apr. 22   Tagged   *Serpentine Die Cut 10¾*
Self-Adhesive

04	A2981	37c **multicolored**	.75	.20
		P# block of 4, 5#+S	3.00	
		Pane of 20	15.00	

EDGAR Y. "YIP" HARBURG

arburg (1896-
1981), Lyricist
A2982

Designed by Ethel Kessler. Printed by Banknote Corporation
f America for Sennett Security Products.

LITHOGRAPHED
Sheets of 120 in six panes of 20

005, Apr. 28   Tagged   *Serpentine Die Cut 10¾*
Self-Adhesive

905	A2982	37c **multicolored**	.75	.20
		P# block of 4, 4#+S	3.00	
		Pane of 20	15.00	

AMERICAN SCIENTISTS

Barbara
McClintock
(1902-92),
Geneticist
A2983

Josiah Willard Gibbs (1839-1903),
Thermodynamicist — A2984

John von
Neumann
(1903-57),
Mathematician
A2985

Richard
Feynman
(1918-88),
Physicist
A2986

Designed by Carl Herrman. Printed by Banknote Corporation
of America for Sennett Security Products.

LITHOGRAPHED
Sheets of 180 in nine panes of 20

2005, May 4   Tagged   *Serpentine Die Cut 10¾*
Self-Adhesive

3906	A2983	37c **multicolored**	.75	.20
3907	A2984	37c **multicolored**	.75	.20
3908	A2985	37c **multicolored**	.75	.20
a.		Vert. pair, die cutting omitted, #3906 & 3908	—	
3909	A2986	37c **multicolored**	.75	.20
a.		Block or horiz. strip of 4, #3906-3909	3.00	
		P# block of 8, 2 sets of P# + top label, 5#+S	6.00	
		P# block of 4, 5#+S	3.00	
		Pane of 20	15.00	
b.		All colors omitted, tagging omitted, pane of 20	—	

c.		As "a," printing on back of stamps omitted	—	
d.		Vert. pair, die cutting omitted, #3907 & 3909	—	

On No. 3909b, the printing on the back of the pane and all die
cutting is normal.

MODERN AMERICAN ARCHITECTURE

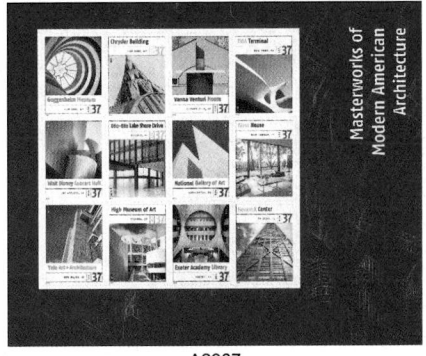

A2987

Illustration reduced.

Designed by Margaret Bauer. Printed by Ashton-Potter (USA)
Ltd.

Buildings: a, Guggenheim Museum, New York. b, Chrysler
Building, New York. c, Vanna Venturi House, Philadelphia. d,
TWA Terminal, New York. e, Walt Disney Concert Hall, Los
Angeles. f, 860-880 Lake Shore Drive, Chicago. g, National
Gallery of Art, Washington, DC. h, Glass House, New Canaan,
CT. i, Yale Art and Architecture Building, New Haven, CT. j,
High Museum of Art, Atlanta. k, Exeter Academy Library, Exe-
ter, NH. l, Hancock Center, Chicago.

LITHOGRAPHED
Serpentine Die Cut 10¾x11

2005, May 19   Tagged
Self-Adhesive

3910	A2987	Pane of 12	9.00	
a.-l.		37c Any single	.75	.20
m.		As No. 3910, orange yellow omitted	—	—

No. 3910m exists on a first day cover.

LEGENDS OF HOLLYWOOD

Henry Fonda (1905-82),
Actor — A2988

Designed by Derry Noyes. Printed by Ashton-Potter (USA)
Ltd.

LITHOGRAPHED
Sheets of 180 in nine panes of 20
Serpentine Die Cut 11x10¾

2005, May 20   Tagged
Self-Adhesive

3911	A2988	37c **multicolored**	.75	.20
		P# block of 4, 5#+P	3.00	
		Pane of 20	15.00	
		Sheet of 180 (9 panes)	135.00	
		Cross gutter block of 8	17.50	
		Block of 8 with vert. gutter	10.00	
		Horiz. pair with vert. gutter	3.00	
		Vert. pair with horiz. gutter	2.00	

The cross gutter block consists of 4 stamps from the two
upper panes and 4 stamps from the two lower panes.

DISNEY CHARACTERS

Pluto, Mickey
Mouse — A2989

Mad Hatter,
Alice — A2990

Flounder,
Ariel — A2991

Snow White,
Dopey — A2992

Designed by David Pacheco. Printed by Banknote Corporation of America for Sennett Security Products.

LITHOGRAPHED
Sheets of 180 in nine panes of 20
Serpentine Die Cut 10½x10¾

2005, June 30   Tagged
Self-Adhesive

3912	A2989	37c **multicolored**	.75	.20
3913	A2990	37c **multicolored**	.75	.20
3914	A2991	37c **multicolored**	.75	.20
3915	A2992	37c **multicolored**	.75	.20
a.		Block or vert. strip of 4, #3912-3915	3.00	
		P# block of 4, 6#+S	3.00	
		P# block of 10, 2 sets of P# + top label	7.50	
		Pane of 20	15.00	
b.		Die cutting omitted, pane of 20	—	
c.		Printed on backing paper, pane of 20	—	

ADVANCES IN AVIATION

Boeing 247 — A2993

Consolidated PBY Catalina A2994

Grumman F6F Hellcat A2995

Republic P-47 Thunderbolt A2996

Engineering and Research Corporation Ercoupe 415 — A2997

Lockheed P-80 Shooting Star — A2998

Consolidated B-24 Liberator A2999

Boeing B-29 Superfortress A3000

Beechcraft 35 Bonanza A3001

Northrop YB-49 Flying Wing — A3002

Designed by Phil Jordan. Printed by Ashton-Potter (USA) Ltd.

LITHOGRAPHED
Sheets of 180 in nine panes of 20
Serpentine Die Cut 10¾x10½

2005, July 29   **Tagged**

Self-Adhesive

3916	A2993	37c	multicolored	.75	.20
3917	A2994	37c	multicolored	.75	.20
3918	A2995	37c	multicolored	.75	.20
3919	A2996	37c	multicolored	.75	.20
3920	A2997	37c	multicolored	.75	.20
3921	A2998	37c	multicolored	.75	.20
3922	A2999	37c	multicolored	.75	.20
3923	A3000	37c	multicolored	.75	.20
3924	A3001	37c	multicolored	.75	.20
3925	A3002	37c	multicolored	.75	.20
a.		Block of 10, #3916-3925		7.50
		P# block of 10, 7#+P		7.50
		Pane of 20		15.00

RIO GRANDE BLANKETS

A3003

A3004

A3005

A3006

Designed by Derry Noyes. Printed by Ashton-Potter (USA) Ltd.

LITHOGRAPHED
BOOKLET STAMPS
Serpentine Die Cut 10¾ on 2 or 3 Sides

2005, July 30   Tagge

Self-Adhesive

3926	A3003	37c	multicolored	.75	
3927	A3004	37c	multicolored	.75	
3928	A3005	37c	multicolored	.75	
3929	A3006	37c	multicolored	.75	
a.		Block of 4, #3926-3929		3.00
b.		Booklet pane, 5 each #3926-3929		15.00

No. 3929b is a double-sided booklet with 12 stamps on o
side and 8 stamps plus label (booklet cover) on the other sid

PRESIDENTIAL LIBRARIES ACT, 50th ANNIV.

Presidential Seal — A3007

Designed by Howard E. Paine. Printed by Banknote Corpora
tion of America for Sennett Security Products.

LITHOGRAPHED
Sheets of 180 in nine panes of 20

2005, Aug. 4   Tagged   *Serpentine Die Cut 10³*
Self-Adhesive

3930	A3007	37c	multicolored	.75	.20
		P# block of 4, 3#+S		3.00
		Pane of 20		15.00
		Sheet of 180 (9 panes)		135.00
		Cross gutter block of 4		8.25
		Horiz. pair with vert. gutter		3.00
		Vert. pair with horiz. gutter		2.00

SPORTY CARS OF THE 1950S

1953 Studebaker Starliner A3008

1954 Kaiser Darren A3009

1953 Chevrolet Corvette A3010

1952 Nash Healey A3011

1955 Ford
Thunderbird
A3012

Designed by Art M. Fitzpatrick. Printed by Ashton-Potter
(USA) Ltd.

LITHOGRAPHED
BOOKLET STAMPS
Serpentine Die Cut 10¾ on 2 or 3 Sides

2005, Aug. 20			**Tagged**	

Self-Adhesive

3931	A3008	37c multicolored	.75	.20
3932	A3009	37c multicolored	.75	.20
3933	A3010	37c multicolored	.75	.20
3934	A3011	37c multicolored	.75	.20
3935	A3012	37c multicolored	.75	.20
a.		Vert. strip of 5, #3931-3935	3.75	
b.		Booklet pane, 4 each #3931-3935	15.00	

Stamps in No. 3935a are not adjacent, as rows of salvage are
between stamps one and two, and between stamps three and
four.

No. 3935b is a double-sided booklet pane with 12 stamps on
one side (2 each #3931, 3933, 3935, and 3 each #3932, 3934)
and eight stamps (1 each #3932, 3934, and 2 each #3931,
3933, 3935) plus label on the other side.

ARTHUR ASHE

Arthur Ashe (1943-93),
Tennis Player — A3013

Designed by Carl T. Herrman. Printed by Ashton-Potter
(USA) Ltd.

LITHOGRAPHED
Sheets of 240 in twelve panes of 20

2005, Aug. 27	**Tagged**	**Serpentine Die Cut 10¾**		

Self-Adhesive

3936	A3013	37c multicolored	.75	.20
		P# block of 4, 5#+P	3.00	
		Pane of 20	15.00	

TO FORM A MORE PERFECT UNION

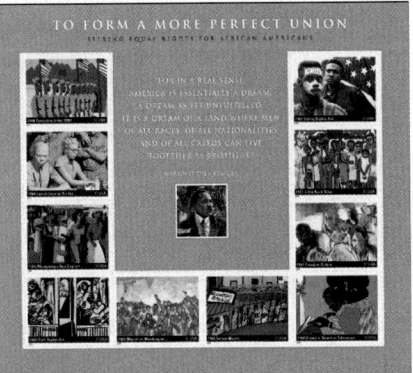

A3014

Designed by Ethel Kessler. Printed by Ashton-Potter (USA)
Ltd.

Inscriptions and artwork: a, 1948 Executive Order 9981
(Training for War, by William H. Johnson). b, 1965 Voting Rights
Act (Youths on the Selma March, 1965, photograph by Bruce
Davidson). c, 1960 Lunch Counter Sit-ins (National Civil Rights
Museum exhibits, by StudioEIS). d, 1957 Little Rock Nine
(America Cares, by George Hunt). e, 1955 Montgomery Bus
Boycott (Walking, by Charles Alston). f, 1961 Freedom Riders
(Freedom Riders, by May Stevens). g, 1964 Civil Rights Act
(Dixie Café, by Jacob Lawrence). h, 1963 March on Washington
(March on Washington, by Alma Thomas). i, 1965 Selma March
(Selma March, by Bernice Sims). j, 1954 Brown v. Board of
Education (The Lamp, by Romare Bearden).

LITHOGRAPHED
Serpentine Die Cut 10¾x10½

2005, Aug. 30			**Tagged**	

Self-Adhesive

3937	A3014	Pane of 10	7.50	
a.-j.		37c Any single	.75	.20

CHILD HEALTH

Child and
Doctor — A3015

Designed by Craig Frazier.

Printed by Avery Dennison.

PHOTOGRAVURE
Sheets of 200 in ten panes of 20
Serpentine Die Cut 10½x11

2005, Sept. 7			**Tagged**	

Self-Adhesive

3938	A3015	37c multicolored	.75	.20
		P# block of 4, 4#+V	3.00	
		Pane of 20	15.00	

LET'S DANCE

Merengue — A3016

Salsa — A3017

Cha Cha
Cha — A3018

Mambo — A3019

Designed by Ethel Kessler.

Printed by American Packaging Corporation for Sennett
Security Products.

PHOTOGRAVURE
Sheets of 120 in six panes of 20

2005, Sept. 17	**Tagged**	**Serpentine Die Cut 10¾**		

Self-Adhesive

3939	A3016	37c multicolored	.75	.20
3940	A3017	37c multicolored	.75	.20
3941	A3018	37c multicolored	.75	.20
3942	A3019	37c multicolored	.75	.20
a.		Vert. strip of 4, #3939-3942	3.00	
		P# block of 8, 8#+S	6.00	
		Pane of 20	15.00	

Stamps in the vertical strip are not adjacent as rows of
selvage are between the stamps. The backing paper of stamps
from the 2nd and 4th columns have Spanish inscriptions, while
the other columns have English inscriptions.

GRETA GARBO

Garbo (1905-90),
Actress — A3020

Designed by Carl T. Herrman.

Printed by Banknote Corporation of America for Sennett
Security Products.

ENGRAVED
Sheets of 120 in six panes of 20

2005, Sept. 23	**Tagged**	**Serpentine Die Cut 10¾**		

Self-Adhesive

3943	A3020	37c black	.75	.20
		P# block of 4, 1#+S	3.00	
		Pane of 20	15.00	

See Sweden No. 2517.

JIM HENSON AND THE MUPPETS

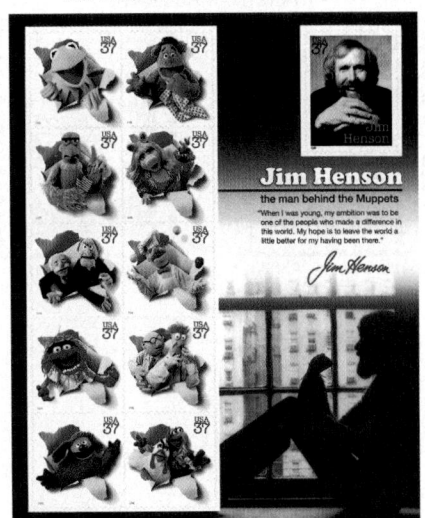

A3021

Designed by Edward Eyth.

Printed by Avery Dennison.
No. 3944: a, Kermit the Frog. b, Fozzie Bear. c, Sam the Eagle and flag. d, Miss Piggy. e, Statler and Waldorf. f, The Swedish Chef and fruit. g, Animal. h, Dr. Bunsen Honeydew and Beaker. i, Rowlf the Dog. j, The Great Gonzo and Camilla the Chicken. k, Jim Henson.
Nos. 3944a-3944j are 30x30mm; No. 3944k, 28x37mm.

PHOTOGRAVURE
Serpentine Die Cut 10½, 10½x10¾ (#3944k)
2005, Sept. 28   **Tagged**
Self-Adhesive

3944	A3021	Pane of 11	8.25	
a.-k.		37c Any single	.75	.20

CONSTELLATIONS

Leo — A3022   Orion — A3023

Lyra — A3024   Pegasus — A3025

Designed by McRay Magleby.

Printed by Ashton-Potter (USA) Ltd.

LITHOGRAPHED
Sheets of 240 in twelve panes of 20
2005, Oct. 3   **Tagged**   *Serpentine Die Cut 10¾*
Self-Adhesive

3945	A3022	37c **multicolored**	.75	.20
3946	A3023	37c **multicolored**	.75	.20
3947	A3024	37c **multicolored**	.75	.20
3948	A3025	37c **multicolored**	.75	.20
a.		Block or vert. strip of 4, #3945-3948	3.00	
		P# block of 4, 6#+P	3.00	
		P# block of 10, 2 sets of P# + top label	7.50	
		Pane of 20	15.00	
b.		As "a," die cutting omitted	—	

CHRISTMAS COOKIES

Santa Claus — A3026   Snowmen — A3027

Angel — A3028   Elves — A3029

Santa Claus — A3030   Snowmen — A3031

Angel — A3032   Elves — A3033

Designed by Derry Noyes.

Printed by Banknote Corporation of America for Sennett Security Products (#3949-3952), American Packaging Corporation for Sennett Security Products (#3953-3960).

LITHOGRAPHED, PHOTOGRAVURE (#3953-3960)
Serpentine Die Cut 10¾x11
2005, Oct. 20   **Tagged**
Self-Adhesive
Design Size: 19x26mm

3949	A3026	37c **multicolored**	.75	.20
3950	A3027	37c **multicolored**	.75	.20
3951	A3028	37c **multicolored**	.75	.20
3952	A3029	37c **multicolored**	.75	.20
a.		Block or vert. strip of 4, #3949-3952	3.00	
		P# block of 4, 4#+S	3.00	
		Pane of 20	15.00	

Booklet Stamps
Serpentine Die Cut 10¾x11 on 2 or 3 Sides
Design Size: 19½x27mm

3953	A3026	37c **multicolored**	.75	.20
3954	A3027	37c **multicolored**	.75	.20
3955	A3028	37c **multicolored**	.75	.20
3956	A3029	37c **multicolored**	.75	.20
a.		Block of 4, #3953-3956	3.00	
b.		Booklet pane of 20, 5 #3956a	15.00	

Serpentine Die Cut 10½x10¾

3957	A3030	37c **multicolored**	1.50	.20
3958	A3031	37c **multicolored**	1.50	.20
3959	A3032	37c **multicolored**	1.50	.20
3960	A3033	37c **multicolored**	1.50	.20
a.		Block of 4, #3957-3960	6.00	
b.		Booklet pane of 4, #3957-3960	6.00	
c.		Booklet pane of 6, #3959-3960, 2 each #3957-3958	9.00	
d.		Booklet pane of 6, #3957-3958, 2 each #3959-3960	9.00	

No. 3956b is a double-sided booklet pane with 12 stamps on one side and eight stamps plus label that serves as a booklet cover on the other side. Nos. 3949-3952 have a small "2005" year date, while Nos. 3953-3956 have a large year date. Other design differences caused by different cropping of the images can be found, with Nos. 3953-3956 showing slightly more design features on one or more sides.

DISTINGUISHED MARINES

Lt. Gen. John A. Lejeune (1867-1942), 2nd Infantry Division Insignia A3034

Lt. Gen. Lewis B. Puller (1898-1971), 1st Marine Division Insignia A3035

Sgt. John Basilone (1916-45), 5th Marine Division Insignia A3036

Sgt. Major Daniel J. Daly (1873-1937), 73rd Machine Gun Company 6th Marine Regiment Insignia A3037

Designed by Phil Jordan. Printed by Ashton-Potter (USA) Ltd.

LITHOGRAPHED
Sheets of 180 in nine panes of 20
Serpentine Die Cut 11x10½
2005, Nov. 10   **Tagged**
Self-Adhesive

3961	A3034	37c **multicolored**	.75	.20
3962	A3035	37c **multicolored**	.75	.20
3963	A3036	37c **multicolored**	.75	.20
3964	A3037	37c **multicolored**	.75	.20
a.		Block or horiz. strip of 4, #3961-3964	3.00	
		P# block of 4, 6#+P	3.00	
		P# block of 8, 2 sets of P# + top panel	6.00	
		Pane of 20	15.00	

Flag and Statue of Liberty — A3038

Designed by Carl and Ann Purcell. Printed by Sterling Sommer, Inc. for Ashton-Potter (USA) Ltd. (#3965), Ashton-Potter (USA) Ltd. (#3966, 3970), American Packaging Corporation for Sennett Security Printers (#3967, 3969, 3973), Avery Dennison (#3968, 3972, 3975), Banknote Corporation of America for Sennett Security Products (#3974).

LITHOGRAPHED (#3965, 3966, 3970, 3974), PHOTOGRAVURE
Sheets of 400 in four panes of 100 (#3965), Sheets of 120 in six panes of 20 (#3966)

2005, Dec. 8		**Tagged**	*Perf. 11¼*	
3965	A3038	(39c) **multicolored**	.80	.20
		P# block of 4, 4#+P	3.20	—

Self-Adhesive (#3966, 3968, 3969-3970, 3972, 3974-3975)
Serpentine Die Cut 11¼x11

3966	A3038	(39c) **multicolored**	.80	.20
		P# block of 4, 4#+P	3.20	
		Pane of 20	16.00	
a.		Booklet pane of 20	16.00	
b.		As "a," die cutting omitted	—	

COIL STAMPS
Perf. 9¾ Vert.

3967	A3038	(39c) **multicolored**	.80	.20
		Pair	1.60	—
		P# strip of 5, #S1111	5.75	
		P# single, #S1111		2.00

Serpentine Die Cut 8½ Vert.

3968	A3038	(39c) **multicolored**	.80	.20
		Pair	1.60	
		P# strip of 5, #V1111	5.75	
		P# single, #V1111		2.00
3969	A3038	(39c) **multicolored**	.80	.20
		Pair	1.60	
		P# strip of 5, #S1111	5.75	
		P# single, #S1111		2.00

No. 3969 is dated "2006."

Serpentine Die Cut 9½ Vert.

3970	A3038	(39c) **multicolored**	.80	.20
		Pair	1.60	
		P# strip of 5, #P1111	7.00	
		P# strip of 5, #P2222	5.75	
		P# single, #P1111, P2222		2.00

BOOKLET STAMPS

Serpentine Die Cut 11¼x10¾ on 2 or 3 Sides

3972	A3038	(39c) **multicolored**	.80	.20
a.		Booklet pane of 20	16.00	

Serpentine Die Cut 10¼x10¾ on 2 or 3 Sides

3973	A3038	(39c) **multicolored**	.80	.20
a.		Booklet pane of 20	16.00	

On No. 3973, the sky immediately above the date is bright blue and extends from the left side to beyond the "6" in the date, the left arm of the star at upper left barely touches the frame line and is without the "USPS" microprinting, but is most easily distinguishable by the die cutting. No. 3973a is a double-sided booklet pane with 12 stamps on one side and eight stamps plus label that serves as a booklet cover on the other side.

No. 3973 was not available until January 2006.

Serpentine Die Cut 11¼x11 on 2 or 3 Sides

3974	A3038	(39c) **multicolored**	.80	.20
a.		Booklet pane of 4	3.20	
b.		Booklet pane of 6	4.80	

Serpentine Die Cut 8 on 2, 3 or 4 Sides

3975	A3038	(39c) **multicolored**	.80	.20
a.		Booklet pane of 18	14.50	
		Nos. 3965-3975 (10)	8.00	2.00

Nos. 3965-3975 are dated "2006."

On No. 3966, the sky immediately above the date is bright blue and extends from the left side to beyond the "6" in the date, the left arm of the star at upper left is clear of the top frame, and "USPS" is microprinted on the top red flag stripe.

On No. 3974, the sky immediately above the date is dark blue and extends from the left side to the second "0" in the date, the left arm of the star at upper left touches the top frame, and lacks the microprinting found on No. 3966.

Nos. 3965 and 3970 also have "USPS" microprinted on the top red flag stripe.

Nos. 3966a and 3972a are double-sided booklet panes with 12 stamps on one side and eight stamps plus label that serves as a booklet cover on the other side. On No. 3966a, the stamps on one side are upside-down with relation to the stamps on the other side. On No. 3972a the stamps are all aligned the same on both sides.

Birds — A3039

Designed by Craig Frazier. Printed by Avery Dennison.

PHOTOGRAVURE
Serpentine Die Cut 11 on 2, 3, or 4 Sides

2006, Jan. 3   **Tagged**

BOOKLET STAMP
Self-Adhesive

3976	A3039	(39c) **multicolored**	.80	.20
a.		Booklet pane of 20	16.00	

Flag and Statue of Liberty — A3040

Designed by Carl and Ann Purcell. Printed by American Packaging Corporation for Sennett Security Products (#3979, 3982), Ashton-Potter (USA) Ltd. (#3978, 3981). Avery Dennison (#3980).

LITHOGRAPHED (#3978, 3981), PHOTOGRAVURE (#3979-80)
Sheets of 120 in six panes of 20

2006   **Tagged**   *Serpentine Die Cut 11¼x10¾*
Self-Adhesive

3978	A3040	39c **multicolored**, *Apr. 8*	.80	.20
		P# block of 4, 4#+P	3.20	
		Pane of 20	16.00	
a.		Booklet pane of 10	8.00	
b.		Booklet pane of 20	16.00	

No. 3978 has "USPS" microprinted on top red flag stripe.
No. 3978b is a double-sided booklet with 12 stamps on one side and 8 stamps plus label (booklet cover) on the other side.

Serpentine Die Cut 11 Vert.
COIL STAMPS

3979	A3040	39c **multicolored**, *Mar. 8*	.80	.20
		Pair	1.60	—
		P# strip of 5, #S1111	5.75	—
		P# single, #S1111	—	2.00
3980	A3040	39c **multicolored**, *Jan. 9*	.80	.20
		Pair	1.60	
		P# strip of 5, #V1111	5.75	
		P# single, #V1111		2.00

No. 3980 has rounded corners and lacks microprinting. Unused examples are on backing paper taller than the stamp, and the stamps are spaced approximately 3mm apart.

Serpentine Die Cut 9½ Vert.

3981	A3040	39c **multicolored**, *Apr. 8*	.80	.20
		Pair	1.60	
		P# strip of 5, #P1111	5.75	
		P# single, #P1111		2.00

No. 3981 has "USPS" microprinted on top red flag stripe.

Serpentine Die Cut 10¼ Vert.

3982	A3040	39c **multicolored**, *Apr. 8*	.80	.20
		Pair	1.60	
		P# strip of 5, #S1111	5.75	
		P# single, #S1111		2.00

No. 3982 was not made available until June, despite the official first day of issue.

CHILDREN'S BOOK ANIMALS

The Very Hungry Caterpillar, from *The Very Hungry Caterpillar*, by Eric Carle — A3041

Wilbur, from *Charlotte's Web*, by E. B. White — A3042

Fox in Socks, from *Fox in Socks*, by Dr. Seuss — A3043

Maisy, from *Maisy's ABC*, by Lucy Cousins — A3044

Wild Thing, from *Where the Wild Things Are,* by Maurice Sendak — A3045

Curious George, from *Curious George,* by Margaret and H. A. Rey — A3046

Olivia, from *Olivia,* by Ian Falconer — A3047

Frederick, from *Frederick,* by Leo Lionni — A3048

Designed by Derry Noyes. Printed by American Packaging Corporation for Sennett Security Products.

PHOTOGRAVURE
Sheets of 96 in six panes of 16

2006, Jan. 10   Tagged   *Serpentine Die Cut 10¾*
Self-Adhesive

3987	A3041	39c	multicolored	.80	.20
3988	A3042	39c	multicolored	.80	.20
3989	A3043	39c	multicolored	.80	.20
3990	A3044	39c	multicolored	.80	.20
3991	A3045	39c	multicolored	.80	.20
3992	A3046	39c	multicolored	.80	.20
3993	A3047	39c	multicolored	.80	.20
3994	A3048	39c	multicolored	.80	.20

a.   Block of 8, #3987-3994   6.50
P# block of 8, 9# + S   6.50
Pane of 20   13.00
Sheet of 96   80.00
Cross gutter block of 8   15.00
Block of 8 with horiz. gutter   9.00
Block of 8 different stamps with vert. gutter   8.00
Horiz. pair with vert. gutter   2.00
Vert. pair with horiz. gutter   2.00

See Great Britain Nos. 2340-2341.

2006 WINTER OLYMPICS, TURIN, ITALY

Skier — A3049

Designed by Derry Noyes. Printed by Banknote Corporation of America for Sennett Security Products.

LITHOGRAPHED
Sheets of 240 in twelve panes of 20

2006, Jan. 11   Tagged   *Serpentine Die Cut 10¾*
Self-Adhesive

3995 A3049 39c multicolored   .80   .20
P# block of 4, 4# + S   3.20
Pane of 20   16.00

BLACK HERITAGE SERIES

Hattie McDaniel (1895-1952), Actress — A3050

Designed by Ethel Kessler. Printed by Banknote Corporation of America for Sennett Security Products.

LITHOGRAPHED
Sheets of 240 in twelve panes of 20

2006, Jan. 25   Tagged   *Serpentine Die Cut 10¾*
Self-Adhesive

3996 A3050 39c multicolored   .80   .20
P# block of 4, 4# + S   3.20
Pane of 20   16.00

Chinese New Year Types of 1992-2004

Designed by Clarence Lee. Printed by Banknote Corporation of America for Sennett Security Products.

LITHOGRAPHED

2006, Jan. 29   Tagged   *Serpentine Die Cut 10¾*
Self-Adhesive

3997   Pane of 12   9.75
a.   A2360 39c Rat   .80   .20
b.   A2413 39c Ox   .80   .20
c.   A2462 39c Tiger   .80   .20
d.   A2535 39c Rabbit   .80   .20
e.   A2602 39c Dragon   .80   .20
f.   A2702 39c Snake   .80   .20
g.   A2752 39c Horse   .80   .20
h.   A2856 39c Ram   .80   .20
i.   A2927 39c Monkey   .80   .20
j.   A2067 39c Rooster   .80   .20
k.   A2146 39c Dog   .80   .20
l.   A2205 39c Boar   .80   .20

WEDDING DOVES

Dove Facing Left — A3051

Dove Facing Right — A3052

Designed by Michael Osborne. Printed by Ashton-Potter (USA) Ltd.

LITHOGRAPHED
BOOKLET STAMPS
Serpentine Die Cut 10¾x11 on 2, 3 or 4 Sides
2006, Mar. 1   Tagged
Self-Adhesive

3998 A3051 39c pale lilac & bluish lilac   .80   .20
a.   Booklet pane of 20   16.00

Serpentine Die Cut 10¾x11

3999 A3052 63c pale green & dull green   1.25   .25
a.   Booklet pane, 20 each #3998-3999   37.50
b.   Horiz. pair, #3998-3999 with vertical gutter between   2.10   1.00

Common Buckeye Butterfly — A3053

Designed by Carl T. Herrman. Printed by Sterling Somme Inc. for Ashton-Potter (USA) Ltd. (#4000), Avery Dennison (#4001-4002).

LITHOGRAPHED (#4000), PHOTOGRAVURE (#4001-4002)
Sheets of 400 in four panes of 100 (#4000), Sheets of 280 in fourteen panes of 20 (#4001)

2006, Mar. 8   Tagged   *Perf. 11*
4000 A3053 24c multicolored   .50   .20
P# block of 4, 4#+P   2.00

Self-Adhesive
Serpentine Die Cut 11
4001 A3053 24c multicolored   .50   .20
P# block of 4, 4#+V   2.00
Pane of 20   10.00
a.   Serpentine die cut 10¾x11¼ on 3 sides (from booklet panes)   .50   .20
b.   Booklet pane of 10 #4001a   5.00
c.   Booklet pane of 4 #4001a   2.00
d.   Booklet pane of 6 #4001a   3.00

COIL STAMP
Serpentine Die Cut 8½ Horiz.
4002 A3053 24c multicolored   .50   .20
Pair   1.00
P# strip of 5, #V1111   3.75
P# single, #V1111   — 2.00

No. 4001b is a convertible booklet that was sold flat. It has a self-adhesive panel that covers the rouletting on the inside of the booklet cover. Nos. 4001c and 4001d are component panes of a vending machine booklet, which was sold pre-folded and sealed, and which does not have the self-adhesive panel covering the rouletting on the inside of the booklet cover.

CROPS OF THE AMERICAS

Chili Peppers — A3054

Beans — A3055

Sunflower and Seeds — A3056

Squashes — A3057

Corn — A3058

Designed by Phil Jordan. Printed by American Packaging Corporation for Sennett Security Products (#4003-4012), Banknote Corporation of America for Sennett Security Products (#4013-4017).

PHOTOGRAVURE (#4003-4012), LITHOGRAPHED (#4013-4017)
Serpentine Die Cut 10¼ Horiz.
2006, Mar. 16   Tagged
Self-Adhesive
Coil Stamps

4003	A3054	39c multicolored	.80	.20
4004	A3055	39c multicolored	.80	.20
4005	A3056	39c multicolored	.80	.20
4006	A3057	39c multicolored	.80	.20
4007	A3058	39c multicolored	.80	.20

a.   Strip of 5, #4003-4007   4.00
P# strip of 5, #4003-4007, #S1111   5.75
P# strip of 11, 3 #4005, 2 each #4003-4004, 4006-4007   11.00
P# single (#4005), #S1111   — 2.00

Booklet Stamps
Serpentine Die Cut 10¾x10½ on 2 or 3 Sides

08	A3058	39c multicolored	.80	.20
09	A3057	39c multicolored	.80	.20
10	A3056	39c multicolored	.80	.20
11	A3055	39c multicolored	.80	.20
12	A3054	39c multicolored	.80	.20
a.		Horiz. strip of 5, #4008-4012	4.00	
b.		Booklet pane, 4 each #4008-4012	16.00	

No. 4012b is a double-sided booklet with 12 stamps on one
e and 8 stamps plus label (booklet cover) on the other side.
"USA" is at right of "39" on No. 4004, at left of "39" on No.
11, 4017. Top of "USA" is aligned with top of "39" on No.
13, with bottom of "39" on Nos. 4003, 4012.
The peelable salvage strips were removed by the manufac-
er from 1 million of the 11 million vending booklets produced
ontaining Nos. 4017b, 4017c and 4017d).

Serpentine Die Cut 10¾x11¼ on 2 or 3 Sides

13	A3054	39c multicolored	.80	.20
14	A3058	39c multicolored	.80	.20
15	A3057	39c multicolored	.80	.20
16	A3056	39c multicolored	.80	.20
a.		Booklet pane of 4, #4013-4016	3.20	
17	A3055	39c multicolored	.80	.20
a.		Horiz. strip of 5, #4013-4017	4.00	
b.		Booklet pane of 4, #4013-4015, 4017	3.20	
c.		Booklet pane of 6, #4013-4016, 2 #4017	4.80	
d.		Booklet pane of 6, #4013-4015, 4017, 2 #4016	4.80	

X-PLANES

A3059

A3060

Designed by Phil Jordan. Printed by Banknote Corporation of
America for Sennett Security Products.

LITHOGRAPHED WITH HOLOGRAM AFFIXED
Sheets of 120 in six panes of 20
Serpentine Die Cut 10¾x10½

2006, Mar. 17   **Tagged**
Self-Adhesive

4018	A3059	$4.05 multicolored	8.00	5.00
		P# block of 4, 4#+S	40.00	
		Pane of 20	160.00	
a.		Silver foil ("X") omitted	—	
4019	A3060	$14.40 multicolored	27.50	15.00
		P# block of 4, 4#+S	110.00	
		Pane of 20	550.00	

SUGAR RAY ROBINSON (1921-89), BOXER

A3061

Designed by Carl T. Herrman. Printed by Avery Dennison.

PHOTOGRAVURE
Sheets of 200 in ten panes of 20

2006, Apr. 7   Tagged   Serpentine Die Cut 11
Self-Adhesive

4020	A3061	39c red & blue	.80	.20
		P# block of 4, 2#+V	3.20	
		Pane of 20	16.00	

BENJAMIN FRANKLIN (1706-90)

Statesman
A3062

Scientist
A3063

Printer
A3064

Postmaster
A3065

Designed by Richard Sheaff. Printed by Avery Dennison.

PHOTOGRAVURE
Sheets of 200 in ten panes of 20

2006, Apr. 7   Tagged   Serpentine Die Cut 11
Self-Adhesive

4021	A3062	39c multicolored	.80	.20
4022	A3063	39c multicolored	.80	.20
4023	A3064	39c multicolored	.80	.20
4024	A3065	39c multicolored	.80	.20
a.		Block or horiz. strip of 4	3.20	
		P# block of 4, 4#+V	3.20	
		Pane of 20	16.00	

DISNEY CHARACTERS

Mickey and Minnie
Mouse — A3066

Cinderella and Prince
Charming — A3067

Beauty and the
Beast — A3068

Lady and Tramp
A3069

Designed by David Pacheco. Printed by Ashton-Potter (USA) Ltd.

LITHOGRAPHED
Sheets of 180 in nine panes of 20
Serpentine Die Cut 10½x10¾

2006, Apr. 21			Tagged		
		Self-Adhesive			
4025	A3066	39c multicolored		.80	.20
4026	A3067	39c multicolored		.80	.20
4027	A3068	39c multicolored		.80	.20
4028	A3069	39c multicolored		.80	.20
a.		Block or vert. strip of 4, #4025-4028		3.20	
		P# block of 4, 6#+P		3.20	
		Pane of 20		16.00	

Birds — A3070

Designed by Craig Frazier. Printed by Avery Dennison.

PHOTOGRAVURE
Serpentine Die Cut 11 on 2, 3 or 4 Sides

2006, May 1			Tagged		
		Self-Adhesive			
		Booklet Stamp			
4029	A3070	39c multicolored		.80	.20
a.		Booklet pane of 20		16.00	

LITERARY ARTS

Katherine Anne Porter (1890-1980), Author
A3071

Designed by Derry Noyes. Printed by Banknote Corporation of America for Sennett Security Products.

LITHOGRAPHED
Sheets of 240 in twelve panes of 20

2006, May 15		Tagged	*Serpentine Die Cut 10¾*		
		Self-Adhesive			
4030	A3071	39c multicolored		.80	.20
		P# block of 4, 4#+S		3.20	
		Pane of 20		16.00	

AMBER ALERT

Mother and Child — A3072

Designed by Derry Noyes. Printed by Avery Dennison.

PHOTOGRAVURE
Sheets of 160 in eight panes of 20

2006, May 25		Tagged	*Serpentine Die Cut 10¾*		
		Self-Adhesive			
4031	A3072	39c multicolored		.80	.20
		P# block of 4, 6#+V		3.20	
		Pane of 20		16.00	

Purple Heart Type of 2003

Designed by Carl T. Herrman. Printed by Ashton-Potter (USA) Ltd.

LITHOGRAPHED
Sheets of 120 in six panes of 20
Serpentine Die Cut 11¼x11

2006, May 26			Tagged		
		Self-Adhesive			
4032	A2891	39c multicolored		.80	.20
		P# block of 4, 4#+P		3.20	
		Pane of 20		16.00	

WONDERS OF AMERICA

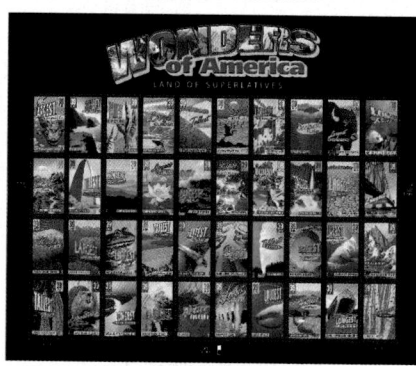

A3073-A3112

Illustration reduced.

Designed by Richard Sheaff. Printed by Avery Dennison.

Designs: No. 4033, American alligator, largest reptile. No. 4034, Moloka'i, highest sea cliffs. No. 4035, Saguaro, tallest cactus. No. 4036, Bering Glacier, largest glacier. No. 4037, Great Sand Dunes, tallest dunes. No. 4038, Chesapeake Bay, largest estuary. No. 4039, Cliff Palace, largest cliff dwelling. No. 4040, Crater Lake, deepest lake. No. 4041, American bison, largest land mammal. No. 4042, Off the Florida Keys, longest reef. No. 4043, Pacific Crest Trail, longest hiking trail. No. 4044, Gateway Arch, tallest man-made monument. No. 4045, Appalachians, oldest mountains. No. 4046, American lotus, largest flower. No. 4047, Lake Superior, largest lake. No. 4048, Pronghorn, fastest land animal. No. 4049, Bristlecone pines, oldest trees. No. 4050, Yosemite Falls, tallest waterfall. No. 4051, Great Basin, largest desert. No. 4052, Verrazano-Narrows Bridge, longest span. No. 4053, Mount Washington, windiest place. No. 4054, Grand Canyon, largest canyon. No. 4055, American bullfrog, largest frog. No. 4056, Oroville Dam, tallest dam. No. 4057, Peregrine falcon, fastest bird. No. 4058, Mississippi River Delta, largest delta. No. 4059, Steamboat, tallest geyser. No. 4060, Rainbow Bridge, largest natural bridge. No. 4061, White sturgeon, largest freshwater fish. No. 4062, Rocky Mountains, longest mountain chain. No. 4063, Coast redwoods, tallest trees. No. 4064, American beaver, largest rodent. No. 4065, Mississippi-Missouri, longest river system. No. 4066, Mount Wai'ale'ale, rainiest spot. No. 4067, Kilauea, most active volcano. No. 4068, Mammoth Cave, longest cave. No. 4069, Blue whale, loudest animal. No. 4070, Death Valley, hottest spot. No. 4071, Cornish-Windsor Bridge, longest covered bridge. No. 4072, Quaking aspen, largest plant.

PHOTOGRAVURE
Sheets of 80 in two panes of 40

2006, May 27		Tagged	*Serpentine Die Cut 10¾*		
		Self-Adhesive			
4033	A3073	39c multicolored		.80	.20
4034	A3074	39c multicolored		.80	.20
4035	A3075	39c multicolored		.80	.20
4036	A3076	39c multicolored		.80	.20
4037	A3077	39c multicolored		.80	.20
4038	A3078	39c multicolored		.80	.20
4039	A3079	39c multicolored		.80	.20
4040	A3080	39c multicolored		.80	.20
4041	A3081	39c multicolored		.80	.20
4042	A3082	39c multicolored		.80	.20
4043	A3083	39c multicolored		.80	.20
4044	A3084	39c multicolored		.80	.20
4045	A3085	39c multicolored		.80	.20
4046	A3086	39c multicolored		.80	.20
4047	A3087	39c multicolored		.80	.20
4048	A3088	39c multicolored		.80	.20
4049	A3089	39c multicolored		.80	.20
4050	A3090	39c multicolored		.80	.20
4051	A3091	39c multicolored		.80	.20
4052	A3092	39c multicolored		.80	.20
4053	A3093	39c multicolored		.80	.20
4054	A3094	39c multicolored		.80	.20
4055	A3095	39c multicolored		.80	.20
4056	A3096	39c multicolored		.80	.20
4057	A3097	39c multicolored		.80	.20
4058	A3098	39c multicolored		.80	.20
4059	A3099	39c multicolored		.80	.20
4060	A3100	39c multicolored		.80	.20

4061	A3101	39c multicolored		.80	
4062	A3102	39c multicolored		.80	
4063	A3103	39c multicolored		.80	
4064	A3104	39c multicolored		.80	
4065	A3105	39c multicolored		.80	
4066	A3106	39c multicolored		.80	
4067	A3107	39c multicolored		.80	
4068	A3108	39c multicolored		.80	
4069	A3109	39c multicolored		.80	
4070	A3110	39c multicolored		.80	
4071	A3111	39c multicolored		.80	
4072	A3122	39c multicolored		.80	
a.		Pane of 40, #4033-4072		32.00	
		Sheet of 80 (two panes)		65.00	
		Block of 40 different stamps with horiz. gutter between any two rows		32.00	
		Pair with horiz. gutter between (each)		2.00	

EXPLORATION OF EAST COAST BY SAMUEL D CHAMPLAIN, 400TH ANNIV.

Ship and Map — A3113

A3114

Designed by Rejean Myette and Francois Martin, Canada (#4073), Terrence W. McCaffrey and Francois Martin (#4074). Printed by Ashton-Potter (USA) Ltd. Illustration A3114 is reduced.

LITHOGRAPHED & ENGRAVED
Sheets of 120 in six panes of 20 (#4073), Sheets of 24 in six panes of 4 (#4074)

2006, May 28		Tagged	*Serpentine Die Cut 10¾*		
		Self-Adhesive (#4073)			
4073	A3113	39c multicolored		.80	.20
		P# block of 4, 6#+P		3.20	
		Pane of 20		16.00	
		Souvenir Sheet			
		Perf. 11			
4074	A3114	Sheet, 2 each #4074a, Canada #2156a		3.50	2.00
a.	A3113	39c multicolored		.80	.20
		Sheet of 24		21.00	—
		Cross gutter block of 4 Canadian and 4 American stamps		8.00	—
		Block of 2 Canadian and 2 American stamps with horiz. gutter between		4.00	—
		Horiz. pair of Canadian and American stamps with vert. gutter between		2.00	—

Washington 2006 World Philatelic Exhibition (#4074). Canada No. 2156, which was sold only by Canada Post, has a bar code in the lower left margin of the sheet. No. 4074, which was sold only by the United States Postal Service for $1.75, lacks this bar code.

WASHINGTON 2006 WORLD PHILATELIC EXHIBITION
Souvenir Sheet

A3115

Designed by Richard Sheaff. Printed by Banknote Corporation of America for Sennett Security Products.

LITHOGRAPHED (MARGIN) & ENGRAVED
Sheets of 18 in six panes of 3

006, May 29	Tagged		Perf. 10¾x10½	
075 A3115	Pane of 3		16.00	6.00
a.	A174 $1 violet black		2.00	.50
b.	A175 $2 deep blue		4.00	1.00
c.	A176 $5 carmine & blue		10.00	2.50
	Sheet of 6 panes		96.00	—
	Cross gutter block of 4 panes		64.00	—
	Vert. pair of panes with horiz. gutter between		32.00	—
	Horiz. pair of panes with vert. gutter between		32.00	—

DISTINGUISHED AMERICAN DIPLOMATS
Souvenir Sheet

A3116

Designed by Howard E. Paine. Printed by Avery Dennison.

No. 4076: a, Robert D. Murphy (1894-1978). b, Frances E. Willis (1899-1983). c, Hiram Bingham IV (1903-88). d, Philip C. Habib (1920-92). e, Charles E. Bohlen (1904-74). f, Clifton R. Wharton, Sr. (1899-1990).

PHOTOGRVURE
Sheets of 90 in fifteen panes of 6

2006, May 29	Tagged	Serpentine Die Cut 10¾		
	Self-Adhesive			
4076 A3116	Pane of 6		4.80	
a.-f.	39c any single		.80	.20
	Sheet of 15 panes		72.00	
	Cross gutter block of 6		7.00	
	Block of 6 with vert. gutter between		7.00	
	Block of 6 with horiz. gutter between		7.00	
	Horiz. pair with vert. gutter (each)		2.00	
	Vert. pair with horiz. gutter (each)		2.00	

The cross gutter block consists of 1 stamp from each of two panes and 2 stamps from each of two adjacent panes. Plate number, 1#+V, is on margin of backing paper.

LEGENDS OF HOLLYWOOD

Judy Garland (1922-69), Actress — A3117

Designed by Ethel Kessler. Printed by Banknote Corporation of America for Sennett Security Products.

LITHOGRAPHED
Sheets of 120 in six panes of 20

2006, June 10	Tagged	Serpentine Die Cut 10¾		
	Self-Adhesive			
4077 A3117	39c multicolored		.80	.20
	P# block of 4, 4#+S		3.20	
	Pane of 20		16.00	
	Sheet of 120 (6 panes)		97.50	
	Cross gutter block of 8		17.50	
	Block of 8 with vertical gutter		10.00	
	Horiz. pair with vert. gutter		3.00	
	Vert. pair with horiz. gutter		2.00	

Cross gutter block consists of 6 stamps from upper panes and 2 stamps from panes below.

Ronald Reagan Type of 2005

Designed by Howard E. Paine. Printed by American Packaging Corporation for Sennett Security Products.

PHOTOGRAVURE
Sheets of 120 in six panes of 20

2006, June 14	Tagged	Serpentine Die Cut 10¾		
	Self-Adhesive			
4078 A2974	39c multicolored		.80	.20
	P# block of 4, 4#+S		3.20	
	Pane of 20		16.00	

Happy Birthday Type of 2002

Designed by Harry Zelenko. Printed by Avery Dennison.

PHOTOGRAVURE
Sheets of 200 in ten panes of 20

2006, June 23	Tagged	Serpentine Die Cut 11		
	Self-Adhesive			
4079 A2751	39c multicolored		.80	.20
	P# block of 4, 4#+V		3.20	
	Pane of 20		16.00	

BASEBALL SLUGGERS

Roy Campanella (1921-93) — A3118

Hank Greenberg (1911-86) — A3119

Mel Ott (1909-58) — A3120

Mickey Mantle (1931-95) — A3121

Designed by Phil Jordan. Printed by Avery Dennison.

PHOTOGRAVURE
Sheets of 120 in six panes of 20

2006, July 15   Tagged   Serpentine Die Cut 10¾
Self-Adhesive

4080	A3118	39c	multicolored	.80	.20
4081	A3119	39c	multicolored	.80	.20
4082	A3120	39c	multicolored	.80	.20
4083	A3121	39c	multicolored	.80	.20

a.	Block or vert. strip of 4, #4080-4083	3.20
	P# block of 4, 6#+V	3.20
	P# block of 10, 2 sets of P# + top label	8.00
	Pane of 20	16.00
	Sheet of 120 (six panes)	97.50
	Cross gutter block of 8	17.50
	Block of 4 with horiz. gutter	6.00
	Horiz. pair with vert. gutter	3.00
	Vert. pair with horiz. gutter	3.00

Cross gutter block of 8 consists of four stamps from top two panes and four stamps from bottom two panes with the cross gutter between.

DC COMICS SUPERHEROES

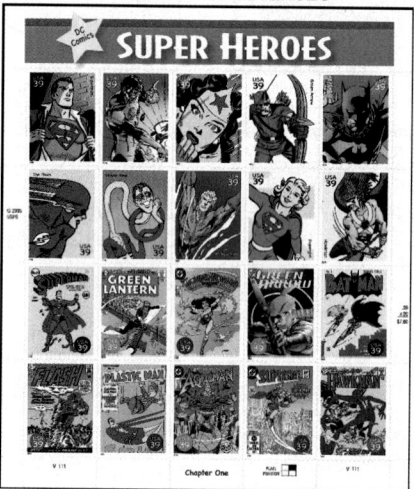

A3122

Designed by Carl T. Herrman. Printed by Avery Dennison. No. 4084: a, Superman. b, Green Lantern. c, Wonder Woman. d, Green Arrow. e, Batman. f, The Flash. g, Plastic Man. h, Aquaman. i, Supergirl. j, Hawkman. k, Cover of *Superman #11*. l, Cover of *Green Lantern #4*. m, Cover of *Wonder Woman #22 (Second Series)*. n, Cover of *Green Arrow #15*. o, Cover of *Batman #1*. p, Cover of *The Flash #111*. q, Cover of *Plastic Man #4*. r, Cover of *Aquaman #5 (of 5)*. s, Cover of *The Daring New Adventures of Supergirl #1*. t, Cover of *The Brave and the Bold Presents Hawkman #36*.

PHOTOGRAVURE
Sheets of 80 in four panes of 20
Serpentine Die Cut 10½x10¾

2006, July 20   Tagged
Self-Adhesive

4084	A3122	Pane of 20	16.00	
a.-t.		39c Any single	.80	.20
		Sheet of 80 (4 panes)	65.00	
		Cross gutter block of 20	24.00	
		Horiz. pair with vert. gutter (each)	3.00	
		Vert. pair with horiz. gutter (each)	3.00	

Cross gutter block consists of 12 stamps from the panes on one side of the sheet and 8 stamps from the panes on the other side of the sheet.

2006 END-OF-YEAR ISSUES
The USPS has announced that the following items will be released in late 2006. Dates, denominations and cities are tentative.

American Clock, American Design Series, 10c coil stamp, *Aug. 4,* Independence, OH

American Motorcycles, 4x39c block or horizontal strip depicting 1940 Indian 4, 1918 Cleveland A-2, generic chopper motorcycle, and 1965 Harley-Davidson Electra-Glide, *Aug. 7,* Sturgis, SD.

Quilts of Gee's Bend, Alabama, American Treasure Series, 10x39c pane of self-adhesive stamps depicting Housetop quilt by Mary Lee Bendolph, Chinese Coins quilt by Arlonzia Pettway, Roman Stripes quilt by Loretta Pettway, Medallion with Checkerboard Center quilt by Patty Ann Williams, Housetop and Half-Log Cabin quilt by Lottie Mooney, Bars and String-pieced Columns quilt by Jessie T. Pettway, Nine Patch quilt by Ruth P. Mosely, Medallion quilt by Loretta Pettway, Pig in a Pen Medallion quilt by Minnie Sue Coleman, and Blocks and Strips quilt by Annie Mae Young, *Aug. 24,* Des Plaines, IL.

Southern Florida Wetlands, Nature of America Series, 10x39c pane of self-adhesive stamps depicting Smail kite, American crocodile, Cape Sable seaside sparrow, Wood stork, Roseate spoonbills, American alligator, Florida panther, White ibis, Bald eagle and cowhorn orchid, and Everglades mink, *Oct. 4,* Naples, FL.

Christmas, 4x39c block of self-adhesive stamps, *Oct. 5,* New York NY

Christmas, 4x39c block of self-adhesive booklet stamps in convertible booklet of 20, *Oct. 5,* New York NY

Christmas, 4x39c block of self-adhesive booklet stamps in vending machine booklet of 20, *Oct. 5,* New York NY

Hanukkah, 39c self-adhesive stamp, *Oct. 6,* New York NY

Kwanzaa, 39c self-adhesive stamp, *Oct. 6,* New York NY

Eid, 39c self-adhesive stamp, *Oct. 6,* New York NY

Christmas, 39c self-adhesive booklet stamp depicting Madonna and Child with Bird, *Oct. 17,* Denver, CO.
Listings as of Noon, Aug. 10, 2006.

SEMI-POSTAL STAMPS

The genesis of the U.S. semi-postal stamp program was a July 1997 bill passed by both houses of Congress that directed the USPS to issue a stamp benefit breast-cancer research. On August 13, the President signed it into law. The surcharge was to be up to 25% of the current first-class rate.

BREAST CANCER RESEARCH

SP1

Designed by Ethel Kessler. Printed by Avery Dennison.

PHOTOGRAVURE
Sheets of 160 in eight panes of 20

1998, July 29   Tagged   Serpentine Die Cut 11
Self-Adhesive

B1 SP1 (32c+8c) **multicolored**   .75   .20
          P# block of 4, 6#+V   3.00
          Pane of 20   15.00

The 8c surtax was for cancer research. After the Jan. 10, 1999, first class postage rate changes, No. B1 became a 33c stamp with a 7c surtax; after Jan. 7, 2001, it became a 34c stamp with a 6c surtax. Effective Mar. 23, 2002, the stamp was sold for 45c, but the face value remained at 34c until June 30, 2002, at which time the face value rose to 37c.
Sales of No. B1 were suspended Jan. 1, 2004, but resumed Feb. 2, 2004, after Congress extended the sales period through Dec. 31, 2005.

HEROES OF 2001

Firemen Atop World Trade Center Rubble — SP2

Designed by Derry Noyes. Printed by Ashton-Potter (USA) Ltd..

LITHOGRAPHED
Sheets of 120 in six panes of 20

2002, June 7   Tagged   Serpentine Die Cut 11¼
Self-Adhesive

B2 SP2 (34c+11c) **multicolored**   .80   .45
          P# block of 4, 4#+P   3.25
          Pane of 20   15.50

The 11c surtax was for assistance to families of emergency relief personnel killed or permanently disabled in the line of duty in connection with the terrorist attacks of Sept. 11, 2001. No. B2 became a 37c stamp with an 8c surtax June 30, 2002.

STOP FAMILY VIOLENCE

SP3

Designed by Carl T. Herrman.
Printed by Avery Dennison.

PHOTOGRAVURE
Sheets of 200 in ten panes of 20

2003, Oct. 8   Tagged   Serpentine Die Cut 11
Self-Adhesive

B3 SP3 (37c+8c) **multicolored**   .85   .50
          P# block of 4, 4#+V   3.50
          Pane of 20   17.00

AIR POST STAMPS

Air mail in the U. S. postal system developed in three stages: pioneer period (with many unofficial or semi-official flights before 1918), government flights and contract air mail (C.A.M.). Contract air mail began on February 15, 1926.
All C.A.M. contracts were canceled on February 19, 1934, and air mail was carried by Army planes for six months. After that the contract plan was resumed. Separate domestic airmail service was abolished Oct. 11, 1975.
See Domestic Air Mail Rates chart in introduction.

Curtiss Jenny — AP1

No. C3 first used on airplane mail service between Washington, Philadelphia and New York, on May 15, 1918, but was valid for ordinary postage. The rate of postage was 24 cents per ounce, which included immediate individual delivery.
Rate of postage was reduced to 16 cents for the first ounce and 6 cents for each additional ounce, which included 10 cents for immediate individual delivery, on July 15, 1918, by Postmaster General's order of June 26, 1918. No. C2 was first used for air mail in the tri-city service on July 15.
Rate of postage was reduced on December 15, 1918, by Postmaster General's order of November 30, 1918, to 6 cents per ounce. No. C1 was first used for air mail (same three-way service) on Dec. 16.

FLAT PLATE PRINTINGS
Plates of 100 subjects.

1918	Unwmk.	Engr.	Perf. 11	
C1 AP1	6c **orange**, Dec. 10		60.	30.
	pale orange		60.	30.
	Never hinged		125.	
	On cover			50.
	First flight cover, Dec. 16			2,000.
	Margin block of 4, arrow top or left		275.	140.
	Center line block		290.	150.
	P# block of 6, arrow		725.	
	Never hinged		1,050.	
	Double transfer (#9155-14)		90.	45.
C2 AP1	16c **green**, July 11		70.	35.
	dark green		70.	35.
	Never hinged		150.	
	On cover			55.
	First flight cover, July 15			800.

	Margin block of 4, arrow top or left		310.	175.
	Center line block		340.	190.
	P# block of 6, arrow		1,000.	—
	Never hinged		1,500.	
C3 AP1	24c **carmine rose & blue**, May 13		70.	35.
	dark carmine rose & blue		75.	35.
	Never hinged		150.	
	On cover			75.
	First flight cover, May 15			750.
	Margin block of 4, arrow top or left		310.	150.
	Margin block of 4, arrow bottom		360.	160.
	Margin block of 4, arrow right		400.	200.
	Center line block		350.	175.
	P# block of 4, red P# only		400.	—
	P# block of 12, two P#, arrow & two "TOP"		1,225.	
	Never hinged		2,000.	
	P# block of 12, two P#, arrow & blue "TOP" only		12,500.	
a.	Center inverted		275,000.	
	Never hinged		375,000.	
	Block of 4		1,250,000.	
	Block of 4 with horiz. guide line		1,350,000.	
	Corner margin block of 4 with siderographer's initials		1,750,000.	
	Center line block		1,350,000.	
	P# block of 4, blue P#		3,000,000.	
	Nos. C1-C3 (3)		200.00	100.00
	Nos. C1-C3, never hinged		425.00	

Plate Blocks
Scott values for plate blocks printed from flat plates are for very fine side and bottom positions. Top position plate blocks with full wide selvage sell for more.

Airplane Radiator and
Wooden
Propeller — AP2

Air Service
Emblem — AP3

DeHavilland Biplane — AP4

Nos. C4-C6 were issued primarily for use in the new night-flying air mail service between New York and San Francisco, but valid for all purposes. Three zones were established; New York-Chicago, Chicago-Cheyenne, Cheyenne-San Francisco, and the rate of postage was 8 cents an ounce for each zone. Service was inaugurated on July 1, 1924.

These stamps were placed on sale at the Philatelic Agency at Washington on the dates indicated in the listings but were not issued to postmasters at that time.

Plates of 400 subjects in four panes of 100 each.

1923		Unwmk.		Perf. 11	
C4	AP2	8c **dark green,** *Aug. 15*	22.50	14.00
		deep green	22.50	14.00
		Never hinged	40.00	
		On cover		22.50
		P# block of 6	250.00	—
		Never hinged	350.00	
		Double transfer	40.00	22.50
C5	AP3	16c **dark blue,** *Aug. 17*	70.00	30.00
		Never hinged	150.00	
		On cover		47.50
		P# block of 6	1,550.	—
		Never hinged	2,350.	
		Double transfer	120.00	50.00
C6	AP4	24c **carmine,** *Aug. 21*	80.00	30.00
		Never hinged	160.00	
		On cover		42.50
		P# block of 6	2,050.	—
		Never hinged	3,100.	
		Double transfer (Pl. 14841)	160.00	42.50
		Nos. C4-C6 (3)	172.50	74.00
		Nos. C4-C6, never hinged	350.00	

Map of United States and Two Mail Planes — AP5

Double Transfer

The Act of Congress of February 2, 1925, created a rate of 10 cents per ounce for distances to 1000 miles, 15 cents per ounce for 1500 miles and 20 cents for more than 1500 miles on contract air mail routes.

Plates of 200 subjects in four panes of 50 each.

1926-27		Unwmk.		Perf. 11	
C7	AP5	10c **dark blue,** *Feb. 13, 1926*	2.50	.35
		light blue	2.50	.35
		Never hinged	4.50	
		P# block of 6	35.00	—
		Never hinged	47.50	
		Double transfer (18246 UL 11)	5.75	1.10
C8	AP5	15c **olive brown,** *Sept. 18, 1926*	2.75	2.50
		light brown	2.75	2.50
		Never hinged	5.25	
		P# block of 6	35.00	—
		Never hinged	50.00	
C9	AP5	20c **yellow green,** *Jan. 25, 1927*	7.00	2.00
		green	7.00	2.00
		Never hinged	13.50	
		P# block of 6	75.00	—
		Never hinged	105.00	
		Nos. C7-C9 (3)	12.25	4.85
		Nos. C7-C9, never hinged	23.25	

Lindbergh's Plane "Spirit of St. Louis" and Flight Route — AP6

A tribute to Col. Charles A. Lindbergh, who made the first non-stop (and solo) flight from New York to Paris, May 20-21, 1927.

Plates of 200 subjects in four panes of 50 each.

1927, June 18		Unwmk.		Perf. 11	
C10	AP6	10c **dark blue**	7.00	2.50
		Never hinged	13.00	
		P# block of 6	90.00	—
		Never hinged	130.00	
		Double transfer	11.50	3.25
a.		Booklet pane of 3, *May 26, 1928*	80.00	65.00
		Never hinged	130.00	

Beacon on Rocky Mountains AP7

Issued to meet the new rate, effective August 1, of 5 cents per ounce.

Plates of 100 subjects in two panes of 50

1928, July 25		Unwmk.		Perf. 11	
C11	AP7	5c **carmine and blue**	4.75	.75
		Never hinged	9.00	
		On cover, first day of 5c airmail rate, Aug. 1		3.00
		Margin block of 4, arrow, (line) right or left	22.50	4.50
		P# block of 6, two P# & red "TOP"	40.00	—
		Never hinged	55.00	
		P# block of 6, two P# & blue "TOP"	40.00	—
		Never hinged	55.00	
		P# block of 6, two P# & double "TOP"	110.00	—
		Never hinged	160.00	
		P# block of 8, two P# only (no "TOP")	190.00	—
		Never hinged	275.00	

	Recut frame line at left	6.50	1.
	Double transfer		
a.	Vert. pair, imperf. between	7,000.	

Winged Globe — AP8

Plates of 200 subjects in four panes of 50 each.

1930, Feb. 10		Unwmk.		Perf. 1	
		Stamp design: 46½x19mm			
C12	AP8	5c **violet**	9.00	.5
		Never hinged	17.50	
		P# block of 6	135.00	—
		Never hinged	200.00	
		Double transfer (Pl. 20189)	19.00	1.2
a.		Horiz. pair, imperf. between	4,500.	

See Nos. C16-C17, C19.

GRAF ZEPPELIN ISSUE

Zeppelin Over Atlantic Ocean — AP9

Zeppelin Between Continents — AP10

Zeppelin Passing Globe — AP11

Issued for use on mail carried on the first Europe-Pan-America round trip flight of the Graf Zeppelin in May, 1930. They were withdrawn from sale June 30, 1930.

Plates of 200 subjects in four panes of 50 each.

1930, Apr. 19		Unwmk.		Perf. 11	
C13	AP9	65c **green**	250.	160.
		Never hinged	425.	
		On cover or card		175.
		Block of 4	1,050.	700.
		P# block of 6	2,300.	—
		Never hinged	3,250.	
C14	AP10	$1.30 **brown**	500.	375.
		Never hinged	900.	
		On cover		400.
		Block of 4	2,250.	1,500.
		P# block of 6	5,750.	—
		Never hinged	8,000.	
C15	AP11	$2.60 **blue**	775.	575.
		Never hinged	1,200.	
		On cover		600.
		Block of 4	3,400.	2,500.
		P# block of 6	8,500.	—
		Never hinged	12,000.	
		Nos. C13-C15 (3)	1,525.	1,110.
		Nos. C13-C15, never hinged	2,525.	

ROTARY PRESS PRINTING
Plates of 200 subjects in four panes of 50 each.

1931-32		Unwmk.		Perf. 10½x11	
		Stamp design: 47½x19mm			
C16	AP8	5c **violet,** *Aug. 19, 1931*	5.00	.60
		Never hinged	8.75	
		Block of 4	22.00	2.00
		P# block of 4	75.00	—
		Never hinged	100.00	

Issued to conform with new air mail rate of 8 cents per ounce which became effective July 6, 1932.

17	AP8 8c **olive bister,** *Sept. 26, 1932*	2.25	.40
	Never hinged	4.00	
	Block of 4	10.00	2.00
	P# block of 4	27.50	
	Never hinged	37.50	

CENTURY OF PROGRESS ISSUE

"Graf Zeppelin," Federal Building at Chicago Exposition and Hangar at Friedrichshafen — AP12

Issued in connection with the flight of the airship "Graf Zeppelin" in October, 1933, to Miami, Akron and Chicago and from the last city to Europe.

FLAT PLATE PRINTING
Plates of 200 subjects in four panes of 50 each.

1933, Oct. 2	Unwmk.	Perf. 11	
C18	AP12 50c **green**	55.00	55.00
	Never hinged	100.00	
	On cover		80.00
	Block of 4	230.00	290.00
	P# block of 6	500.00	
	Never hinged	750.00	

Catalogue values for unused stamps in this section, from this point to the end, are for Never Hinged items.

Type of 1930 Issue
ROTARY PRESS PRINTING
Issued to conform with new air mail rate of 6 cents per ounce which became effective July 1, 1934.

Plates of 200 subjects in four panes of 50 each.

1934, June 30	Unwmk.	Perf. 10½x11	
C19	AP8 6c **dull orange**	3.50	.25
	On cover, first day of 6c airmail rate, July 1		10.00
	Block of 4	14.00	1.10
	P# block of 4	20.00	—
	Horiz. pair with full vert. gutter btwn.	425.00	
	Vert. pair with full horiz. gutter btwn.	—	

TRANSPACIFIC ISSUES

"China Clipper" over Pacific AP13

Issued to pay postage on mail transported by the Transpacific air mail service, inaugurated Nov. 22, 1935.

FLAT PLATE PRINTING
Plates of 200 subjects in four panes of 50 each.

1935, Nov. 22	Unwmk.	Perf. 11	
C20	AP13 25c **blue**	1.40	1.00
	P# block of 6	22.50	—

"China Clipper" over Pacific — AP14

Issued primarily for use on the Transpacific service to China, but valid for all air mail purposes.

FLAT PLATE PRINTING
Plates of 200 subjects in four panes of 50 each.

1937, Feb. 15	Unwmk.	Perf. 11	
C21	AP14 20c **green**	11.00	1.75
	dark green	11.00	1.75
	Block of 4	45.00	8.50
	P# block of 6	100.00	—

C22	AP14 50c **carmine**	11.00	5.00
	Block of 4	45.00	21.00
	P# block of 6	100.00	

Wide full selvage top margin plate blocks of No. C22 are extremely scarce and sell for six to seven times the value listed.

Eagle Holding Shield, Olive Branch and Arrows — AP15

FLAT PLATE PRINTING
Frame plates of 100 subjects in two panes of 50 each separated by a 1½-inch wide vertical gutter with central guide line, and vignette plates of 50 subjects. Some plates were made of iron, then chromed; several of these carry an additional imprint, "E.I." (Electrolytic Iron).

1938, May 14	Unwmk.	Perf. 11	
C23	AP15 6c **dark blue & carmine**	.50	.20
	Margin block of 4, bottom or side arrow	2.25	.55
	P# block of 4, 2 P#	6.50	
	Center line block	2.75	.95
	Top P# block of 10, with two P#, arrow, two "TOP" and two registration markers	13.50	
a.	Vert. pair, imperf. horiz.	325.00	—
	P# block of 4, 2 P#	1,250.	
b.	Horiz. pair, imperf. vert.	12,500.	
	P# block of 4, 2 P#	37,500.	
c.	Ultramarine & carmine	150.00	1,500.
	P# block of 4, 2 P#	1,500.	

Top plate number blocks of No. C23 are found both with and without top arrow.

The plate block of No. C23b is unique and never hinged; value is based on 1994 auction sale.

TRANSATLANTIC ISSUE

Winged Globe — AP16

Inauguration of Transatlantic air mail service.

FLAT PLATE PRINTING
Plates of 200 subjects in four panes of 50 each.

1939, May 16	Unwmk.	Perf. 11	
C24	AP16 30c **dull blue**	12.00	1.50
	P# block of 6	130.00	—

Twin-Motored Transport Plane — AP17

ROTARY PRESS PRINTING
E. E. Plates of 200 subjects in four panes of 50 each.

1941-44	Unwmk.	Perf. 11x10½	
C25	AP17 6c **carmine,** *June 25, 1941*	.20	.20
	P# block of 4	.60	—
	Pair with full vert. gutter btwn.	225.00	
	Pair with full horiz. gutter btwn.		
a.	Booklet pane of 3, *Mar. 18, 1943*	5.00	1.50
b.	Horiz. pair, imperf. between	2,250.	

Singles from No. C25a are imperf. at sides or at sides and bottom.

Value of No. C25b is for pair without blue crayon P. O. rejection mark on front. Very fine pairs with crayon mark sell for about $1,750.

C26	AP17 8c **olive green,** *Mar. 21, 1944*	.20	.20
	P# block of 4	1.10	—
	Pair with full horiz. gutter btwn.	325.00	
C27	AP17 10c **violet,** *Aug. 15, 1941*	1.25	.20
	P# block of 4	5.50	—
C28	AP17 15c **brown carmine,** *Aug. 19, 1941*	2.25	.35
	P# block of 4	10.00	—
C29	AP17 20c **bright green,** *Aug. 27, 1941*	2.25	.30
	P# block of 4	10.00	—
C30	AP17 30c **blue,** *Sept. 25, 1941*	2.25	.35
	P# block of 4	10.00	—

C31	AP17 50c **orange,** *Oct. 29, 1941*	11.00	3.25
	P# block of 4	50.00	—
	Nos. C25-C31 (7)	19.40	4.85

DC-4 Skymaster AP18

ROTARY PRESS PRINTING
E. E. Plates of 200 subjects in four panes of 50 each.

1946, Sept. 25	Unwmk.	Perf. 11x10½	
C32	AP18 5c **carmine**	.20	.20
	P# block of 4	.45	—

DC-4 Skymaster — AP19

ROTARY PRESS PRINTING
E. E. Plates of 400 subjects in four panes of 100 each.

1947, Mar. 26	Unwmk.	Perf. 10½x11	
C33	AP19 5c **carmine**	.20	.20
	P# block of 4	.60	—

Pan American Union Building, Washington, D.C., and Martin 2-0-2 — AP20

Statue of Liberty, New York Skyline and Lockheed Constellation AP21

San Francisco-Oakland Bay Bridge and Boeing B377 Stratocruiser — AP22

Designed by Victor S. McCloskey, Jr., Leon Helguera and William K. Schrage.

ROTARY PRESS PRINTING
E. E. Plates of 200 subjects in four panes of 50 each.

1947	Unwmk.	Perf. 11x10½	
C34	AP20 10c **black,** *Aug. 30*	.25	.20
	P# block of 4	1.10	—
a.	Dry printing	.40	.20
	P# block of 4 (#25613, 25614)	1.75	—
C35	AP21 15c **bright blue green,** *Aug. 20*	.35	.20
	blue green	.35	.20
	P# block of 4	1.50	—
	Pair with full horiz. gutter btwn.	650.00	
a.	Horiz. pair, imperf. between	2,500.	
b.	Dry printing	.55	.20
	P# block of 4 (#25492 and up)	2.50	—
C36	AP22 25c **blue,** *July 30*	.90	.20
	P# block of 4	3.75	—
a.	Dry printing	1.10	.20
	P# block of 4 (#25615 and up)	4.75	—
	Nos. C34-C36 (3)	1.50	.60

See note on wet and dry printings following No. 1029.
No. C35a is valued in the grade of fine.

ROTARY PRESS COIL STAMP
Type of 1947

1948, Jan. 15   Unwmk.   *Perf. 10 Horizontally*
C37 AP19 5c **carmine**   1.00 .80
      Pair   2.10 1.75
      Joint line pair   10.00 3.00

NEW YORK CITY ISSUE

Map of Five Boroughs,
Circular Band and
Planes — AP23

50th anniv. of the consolidation of the five boroughs of New
York City.

ROTARY PRESS PRINTING
E. E. Plates of 400 subjects in four panes of 100
each.

1948, July 31   Unwmk.   *Perf. 11x10½*
C38 AP23 5c **bright carmine**   .20 .20
      P# block of 4   3.50 —

Type of 1947
ROTARY PRESS PRINTING
E. E. Plates of 400 subjects in four panes of 100
each.

1949   Unwmk.   *Perf. 10½x11*
C39 AP19 6c **carmine**, *Jan. 18*   .20 .20
      P# block of 4   .50 —
      Pair with full horiz. gutter btwn.   600.00
a.   Booklet pane of 6, *Nov. 18*   10.00 5.00
b.   Dry printing   .50 .20
      P# block of 4 (#25340 and up)   2.25 —
c.   As "a," dry printing   20.00 —

See note on wet and dry printings following No. 1029.

ALEXANDRIA BICENTENNIAL ISSUE

Home of John
Carlyle,
Alexandria
Seal and
Gadsby's
Tavern
AP24

200th anniv. of the founding of Alexandria, Va.

ROTARY PRESS PRINTING
E. E. Plates of 200 subjects in four panes of 50
each.

1949, May 11   Unwmk.   *Perf. 11x10½*
C40 AP24 6c **carmine**   .20 .20
      P# block of 4   .50 —

ROTARY PRESS COIL STAMP
Type of 1947

1949, Aug. 25   Unwmk.   *Perf. 10 Horizontally*
C41 AP19 6c **carmine**   3.00 .20
      Pair   6.25 .20
      Joint line pair   14.00 1.35

UNIVERSAL POSTAL UNION ISSUE

Post Office
Department
Building
AP25

Globe and
Doves
Carrying
Messages
AP26

Boeing
Stratocruiser
and
Globe — AP27

Universal Postal Union, 75th Anniv.

ROTARY PRESS PRINTING
E. E. Plates of 200 subjects in four panes of 50
each.

1949   Unwmk.   *Perf. 11x10½*
C42 AP25 10c **violet**, *Nov. 18*   .20 .20
      P# block of 4   1.40 —
C43 AP26 15c **ultramarine**, *Oct. 7*   .30 .25
      P# block of 4   1.25 —
C44 AP27 25c **rose carmine**, *Nov. 30*   .60 .40
      P# block of 4   4.00 —
      Nos. C42-C44 (3)   1.10 .85

WRIGHT BROTHERS ISSUE

Wilbur and
Orville Wright
and their
Plane,
1903 — AP28

46th anniv. of the 1st successful flight in a motor-powered
airplane, Dec. 17, 1903, at Kill Devil Hill near Kitty Hawk, NC, by
Wilbur (1867-1912) and Orville Wright (1871-1948) of Dayton,
OH. The plane flew 852 feet in 59 seconds.

ROTARY PRESS PRINTING
E. E. Plates of 200 subjects in four panes of 50
each.

1949, Dec. 17   Unwmk.   *Perf. 11x10½*
C45 AP28 6c **magenta**   .20 .20
      P# block of 4   .70 —

Diamond
Head,
Honolulu,
Hawaii
AP29

ROTARY PRESS PRINTING
E. E. Plates of 200 subjects in four panes of 50
each.

1952, Mar. 26   Unwmk.   *Perf. 11x10½*
C46 AP29 80c **bright red violet**   5.00 1.25
      P# block of 4   22.50 —

POWERED FLIGHT, 50th ANNIV.

First Plane and
Modern
Plane — AP30

ROTARY PRESS PRINTING
E. E. Plates of 200 subjects in four panes of 50
each.

1953, May 29   Unwmk.   *Perf. 11x10½*
C47 AP30 6c **carmine**   .20 .20
      P# block of 4   .55 —

Eagle in Flight — AP31

Issued primarily for use on domestic post cards.

ROTARY PRESS PRINTING
E. E. Plates of 400 subjects in four panes of 100
each.

1954, Sept. 3   Unwmk.   *Perf. 11x10*
C48 AP31 4c **bright blue**   .20
      P# block of 4   1.25

AIR FORCE, 50th ANNIV.

B-52
Stratofortress
and F-104
Starfighters
AP32

Designed by Alexander Nagy, Jr.

ROTARY PRESS PRINTING
E. E. Plates of 200 subjects in four panes of 50
each.

1957, Aug. 1   Unwmk.   *Perf. 11x10*
C49 AP32 6c **blue**   .20 .2
      P# block of 4   .65 —

Type of 1954
Issued primarily for use on domestic post cards.

1958, July 31   Unwmk.   *Perf. 11x10*
C50 AP31 5c **red**   .20 .2
      P# block of 4   1.10 —

Silhouette of Jet
Airliner — AP33

Designed by William H. Buckley and Sam Marsh.

ROTARY PRESS PRINTING
E. E. Plates of 400 subjects in four panes of 100
each.

1958, July 31   Unwmk.   *Perf. 10½x11*
C51 AP33 7c **blue**   .20 .20
      P# block of 4   .60 —
a.   Booklet pane of 6   10.00 7.00
b.   Vert. pair, imperf. between (from booklet
      pane)

No. C51b resulted from a paper foldover after perforating and
before cutting into panes. Two pairs are known.

ROTARY PRESS COIL STAMP
Perf. 10 Horizontally

C52 AP33 7c **blue**   2.00 .20
      Pair   4.25 .40
      Joint line pair   14.00 1.25
      Small holes   10.00
      Pair   20.00
      Joint line pair   200.00

ALASKA STATEHOOD ISSUE

Big Dipper,
North Star and
Map of
Alaska — AP34

Designed by Richard C. Lockwood.

ROTARY PRESS PRINTING
E. E. Plates of 200 subjects in four panes of 50
each.

1959, Jan. 3   Unwmk.   *Perf. 11x10½*
C53 AP34 7c **dark blue**   .20 .20
      P# block of 4   .60 —

BALLOON JUPITER ISSUE

Balloon and Crowd — AP35

Designed by Austin Briggs.

Centenary of the carrying of mail by the balloon Jupiter from Lafayette to Crawfordsville, Ind.

GIORI PRESS PRINTING
Plates of 200 subjects in four panes of 50 each.

1959, Aug. 17	Unwmk.	Perf. 11		
C54 AP35 7c **dark blue & red**			.30	.20
P# block of 4			1.25	—

HAWAII STATEHOOD ISSUE

Alii Warrior, Map of Hawaii and Star of Statehood AP36

Designed by Joseph Feher.

ROTARY PRESS PRINTING
E. E. Plates of 200 subjects in four panes of 50 each.

1959, Aug. 21	Unwmk.	Perf. 11x10½		
C55 AP36 7c **rose red**			.20	.20
P# block of 4			.60	—

PAN AMERICAN GAMES ISSUE

Runner Holding Torch — AP37

Designed by Suren Ermoyan.

3rd Pan American Games, Chicago, Aug. 27-Sept. 7, 1959.

GIORI PRESS PRINTING
Plates of 200 subjects in four panes of 50 each.

1959, Aug. 27	Unwmk.	Perf. 11		
C56 AP37 10c **violet blue & bright red**			.25	.25
P# block of 4			1.25	—

Liberty Bell — AP38

Statue of Liberty AP39

Abraham Lincoln AP40

GIORI PRESS PRINTING
Plates of 200 subjects in four panes of 50 each.

1959-66	Unwmk.	Perf. 11		
C57 AP38 10c **black & green,** *June 10, 1960*			1.00	.70
P# block of 4			4.50	—
C58 AP39 15c **black & orange,** *Nov. 20, 1959*			.35	.20
P# block of 4			1.50	—
C59 AP40 25c **black & maroon,** *Apr. 22, 1960*			.50	.20
P# block of 4			2.00	—
a.	Tagged, *Dec. 29, 1966*		.60	.30
P# block of 4			2.50	—
Nos. C57-C59 (3)			1.85	1.10

See Luminescence data in Information for Collectors section.

Type of 1958
ROTARY PRESS PRINTING
E. E. Plates of 400 subjects in four panes of 100 each.

1960, Aug. 12	Unwmk.	Perf. 10½x11		
C60 AP33 7c **carmine**			.20	.20
P# block of 4			.60	—
Pair with full horiz. gutter btwn.			125.00	—
a.	Booklet pane of 6, *Aug. 19*		11.00	8.00
b.	Vert. pair, imperf between (from booklet pane)		5,500.	

No. C60b resulted from a paper foldover after perforating and before cutting into panes. Two pairs are known.

Type of 1958
ROTARY PRESS COIL STAMP

1960, Oct. 22	Unwmk.	Perf. 10 Horizontally		
C61 AP33 7c **carmine**			4.00	.25
Pair			8.25	.55
Joint line pair			35.00	3.75

Type of 1959-60 and

Statue of Liberty AP41

GIORI PRESS PRINTING
Plates of 200 subjects in four panes of 50 each.

1961-67	Unwmk.	Perf. 11		
C62 AP38 13c **black & red,** *June 28, 1961*			.40	.20
P# block of 4			1.65	—
a.	Tagged, *Feb. 15, 1967*		.75	.50
P# block of 4			5.00	—
C63 AP41 15c **black & orange,** *Jan. 13, 1961*			.30	.20
P# block of 4			1.25	—
a.	Tagged, *Jan. 11, 1967*		.35	.20
P# block of 4			1.50	—
b.	As "a," horiz. pair, imperf. vert.		15,000.	
c.	Horiz. pair, imperf between and at left		—	

Jet Airliner over Capitol — AP42

Designed by Henry K. Bencsath.

ROTARY PRESS PRINTING
E.E. Plates of 400 subjects in four panes of 100 each.

1962, Dec. 5	Unwmk.	Perf. 10½x11		
C64 AP42 8c **carmine**			.20	.20
P# block of 4			.65	—
a.	Tagged, *Aug. 1, 1963*		.20	.20
P# block of 4			.65	—
	As "a," pair with full horiz. gutter between			
b.	Booklet pane of 5 + label		7.00	3.00
c.	As "b," tagged, *1964*		2.00	.75

Nos. C64a and C64c were made by overprinting Nos. C64 and C64b with phosphorescent ink. No. C64a was first issued at Dayton, O., for experiments in high speed mail sorting. The tagging is visible in ultraviolet light.

COIL STAMP; ROTARY PRESS
Perf. 10 Horizontally

C65 AP42 8c **carmine**		.40	.20
Pair		.80	.20
Joint line pair		3.75	.35
a.	Tagged, *Sept. 1964*	.35	.20
Pair		.70	.20
Joint line pair		1.50	.30

Earliest documented use of C65a: Jan. 14, 1965.

MONTGOMERY BLAIR ISSUE

Montgomery Blair — AP43

Designed by Robert J. Jones

Montgomery Blair (1813-83), Postmaster General (1861-64), who called the 1st Intl. Postal Conf., Paris, 1863, forerunner of the UPU.

GIORI PRESS PRINTING
Plates of 200 subjects in four panes of 50 each.

1963, May 3	Unwmk.	Perf. 11		
C66 AP43 15c **dull red, dark brown & blue**			.60	.55
P# block of 4			2.50	—

Bald Eagle — AP44

Designed by V. S. McCloskey, Jr.

Issued primarily for use on domestic post cards.

ROTARY PRESS PRINTING
E.E. Plates of 400 subjects in four panes of 100 each.

1963, July 12	Unwmk.	Perf. 11x10½		
C67 AP44 6c **red**			.20	.20
P# block of 4			1.40	—
a.	Tagged, *Feb. 15, 1967*		4.00	3.00
P# block of 4			55.00	—

AMELIA EARHART ISSUE

Amelia Earhart and Lockheed Electra — AP45

Designed by Robert J. Jones.

Amelia Earhart (1898-1937), 1st woman to fly across the Atlantic.

GIORI PRESS PRINTING
Plates of 200 subjects in four panes of 50 each.

1963, July 24	Unwmk.	Perf. 11	
C68 AP45 8c carmine & maroon		.20	.20
P# block of 4		1.00	—

ROBERT H. GODDARD ISSUE

Robert H. Goddard, Atlas Rocket and Launching Tower, Cape Kennedy AP46

Designed by Robert J. Jones.

Dr. Robert H. Goddard (1882-1945), physicist and pioneer rocket researcher.

GIORI PRESS PRINTING
Plates of 200 subjects in four panes of 50 each.

1964, Oct. 5	Tagged	Perf. 11	
C69 AP46 8c blue, red & bister		.40	.20
P# block of 4		1.75	—
Margin block of 4, Mr. Zip and "Use Zip Code"		1.65	—
a. Tagging omitted			—

Luminescence
Air Post stamps issued after mid-1964 are tagged.

ALASKA PURCHASE ISSUE

Tlingit Totem, Southern Alaska — AP47

Designed by Willard R. Cox

Centenary of the Alaska Purchase. The totem pole shown is in the Alaska State Museum, Juneau.

GIORI PRESS PRINTING
Plates of 200 subjects in four panes of 50 each.

1967, Mar. 30	Unwmk.	Perf. 11	
C70 AP47 8c brown		.25	.20
P# block of 4		1.10	—
Margin block of 4, Mr. Zip and "Use Zip Code"		1.05	—

"Columbia Jays" by John James Audubon — AP48

Fifty-Star Runway — AP49

GIORI PRESS PRINTING
Designed by Robert J. Jones.

Plates of 200 subjects in four panes of 50 each.

1967, Apr. 26		Perf. 11	
C71 AP48 20c multicolored		.80	.20
P# block of 4		3.50	—
Margin block of 4, Mr. Zip and "Use Zip Code"		3.25	—
a. Tagging omitted		10.00	—

See note over No. 1241.

ROTARY PRESS PRINTING
Designed by Jaan Born.

E. E. Plates of 400 subjects in four panes of 100 each.

1968, Jan. 5	Unwmk.	Perf. 11x10½	
C72 AP49 10c carmine		.20	.20
P# block of 4		.90	—
Margin block of 4, "Use Zip Codes"		.85	—
Vert. pair with full horiz. gutter between			—
b. Booklet pane of 8		2.00	.75
c. Booklet pane of 5 + label, Jan. 6		3.75	.75
d. Vert. pair, imperf. between (from bklt. pane)		4,000.	—
e. Tagging omitted		10.00	—
f. As "b," tagging omittod			—

Red is the normal color of the tagging. Copies of No. C72b exist that have a mixture of the two tagging compounds. No. C72d resulted from a paper foldover after perforating and before cutting into panes. Two pairs are recorded from different panes.

ROTARY PRESS COIL STAMP
Perf. 10 Vertically

C73 AP49 10c carmine		.30	.20
Pair		.65	.20
Joint line pair		1.75	.20
a. Imperf., pair		600.00	
Joint line pair		900.00	

$1 Air Lift
This stamp, listed as No. 1341, was issued Apr. 4, 1968, to pay for airlift of parcels to and from U.S. ports to servicemen overseas and in Alaska, Hawaii and Puerto Rico.

It was "also valid for paying regular rates for other types of mail," the Post Office Department announced to the public in a philatelic release dated Mar. 10, 1968. The stamp is inscribed "U.S. Postage" and is untagged.

On Apr. 26, 1969, the P.O.D. stated in its Postal Manual (for postal employees) that this stamp "may be used toward paying the postage or fees for special services on airmail articles." On Jan. 1, 1970, the Department told postal employees through its Postal Bulletin that this $1 stamp "can only be used to pay the airlift fee or toward payment of postage or fees on airmail articles."

Some collectors prefer to consider No. 1341 an airmail stamp.

50th ANNIVERSARY OF AIR MAIL ISSUE

Curtiss Jenny — AP50

Designed by Hordur Karlsson.

50th anniv. of regularly scheduled air mail service.

LITHOGRAPHED, ENGRAVED (GIORI)
Plates of 200 subjects in four panes of 50 each.

1968, May 15		Perf. 11	
C74 AP50 10c blue, black & red		.25	.20
P# block of 4		1.60	—
Margin block of 4, Mr. Zip and "Use Zip Code"		1.05	—
b. Tagging omitted		10.00	—

"USA" and Jet — AP51

Designed by John Larrecq.

LITHOGRAPHED, ENGRAVED (GIORI)
Plates of 200 subjects in four panes of 50 each.

1968, Nov. 22		Perf. 11	
C75 AP51 20c red, blue & black		.35	.20
P# block of 4		1.75	—
Margin block of 4, Mr. Zip and "Use Zip Code"		1.50	—
a. Tagging omitted		12.50	—

MOON LANDING ISSUE

Designed by Paul Calle.

Man's first landing on the moon July 20, 1969, by U.S. astronauts Neil A. Armstrong and Col. Edwin E. Aldrin, Jr., with Lieut. Col. Michael Collins piloting Apollo 11.

LITHOGRAPHED, ENGRAVED (GIORI)
Plates of 128 subjects in four panes of 32 each.

1969, Sept. 9		Perf.	
C76 AP52 10c yellow, black, lt. blue, ultra., rose red & carmine		.25	
P# block of 4		1.10	
Margin block of 4, Mr. Zip and "Use Zip Code"		1.05	—
a. Rose red (litho.) omitted		525.00	
b. Tagging omitted			—

On No. C76a, the lithographed rose red is missing from the entire vignette-the dots on top of the yellow areas as well as the flag shoulder patch.

Silhouette of Delta Wing Plane — AP53

Silhouette of Jet Airliner — AP54

Winged Airmail Envelope — AP55

Statue of Liberty AP56

Designed by George Vander Sluis (9c, 11c), Nelson Gruppo (13c) and Robert J. Jones (17c).

ROTARY PRESS PRINTING
E. E. Plates of 400 subjects in four panes of 100 each.

1971-73		Perf. 10½x11	
C77 AP53 9c red, May 15, 1971		.20	.20
P# block of 4		.90	—
Margin block of 4, "Use Zip Codes"		.85	—

No. C77 issued primarily for use on domestic post cards.

	Perf. 11x10½		
C78 AP54 11c carmine, May 7, 1971		.20	.20
P# block of 4		.90	—
Margin block of 4, "Use Zip Codes"		.85	—
Pair with full vert. gutter btwn.			—
a. Booklet pane of 4 + 2 labels		1.25	.75
b. Untagged (Bureau precanceled)		.85	.85
P# block of 4		27.50	
Margin block of 4, "Use Zip Codes"		13.75	
c. Tagging omitted (not Bureau precanceled)		7.50	
C79 AP55 13c carmine, Nov. 16, 1973		.25	.20
P# block of 4		1.10	—
Margin block of 4, "Use Zip Codes"		1.05	—
a. Booklet pane of 5 + label, Dec. 27, 1973		1.50	.75
b. Untagged (Bureau precanceled)		.85	.85

	P# block of 4	11.50	—
	Margin block of 4, "Use Zip Codes"	9.50	—
c.	Green instead of red tagging (single from booklet pane)		—
d.	Tagging omitted (not precanceled)	7.50	—

No. C78b Bureau precanceled "WASHINGTON D.C." (or C" - more valuable thus), No. C79b "WASHINGTON DC" ly; both for use of Congressmen, but available to any permit lder.

Red is the normal color of the tagging. Copies also exist that ave a mixture of the two tagging compounds.

GIORI PRESS PRINTING
Panes of 200 subjects in four panes of 50 each.
Perf. 11

80 AP56	17c **bluish black, red, & dark green,** *July 13, 1971*	.35	.20
	P# block of 4	1.60	—
	Margin block of 4, Mr. Zip and "Use Zip Code"	1.50	—
a.	Tagging omitted	10.00	

"USA" & Jet Type of 1968
LITHOGRAPHED, ENGRAVED (GIORI)
Plates of 200 subjects in four panes of 50 each.
Perf. 11

81 AP51	21c **red, blue & black,** *May 21, 1971*	.40	.20
	P# block of 4	2.00	—
	Margin block of 4, Mr. Zip and "Use Zip Code"	1.75	—
a.	Tagging omitted	10.00	
b.	Black (engr.) missing (FO)	2,750.	

The two recorded examples of No. C81b are in a single full- ane. Catalogue value is for both errors.

COIL STAMPS
ROTARY PRESS PRINTING

1971-73		*Perf. 10 Vertically*	
82 AP54	11c **carmine,** *May 7, 1971*	.25	.20
	Pair	.50	.25
	Joint line pair	.80	.35
a.	Imperf., pair	250.00	
	Joint line pair	425.00	
b.	Tagging omitted	8.00	
83 AP55	13c **carmine,** *Dec. 27, 1973*	.30	.20
	Pair	.60	.25
	Joint line pair	1.10	
a.	Imperf., pair	75.00	
	Joint line pair	150.00	
b.	Tagging omitted		—

NATIONAL PARKS CENTENNIAL ISSUE
City of Refuge, Hawaii

Kii Statue and
Temple — AP57

Designed by Paul Rabut.

Centenary of national parks. This 11c honors the City of Refuge National Historical Park, established in 1961 at Honaunau, island of Hawaii.

LITHOGRAPHED, ENGRAVED (GIORI)
Plates of 200 subjects in four panes of 50 each.

1972, May 3		*Perf. 11*	
C84 AP57	11c **orange & multicolored**	.20	.20
	P# block of 4	.90	—
	Margin block of 4, Mr. Zip and "Use Zip Code"	.85	—
a.	Blue & green (litho.) omitted	750.00	
b.	Tagging omitted		—

OLYMPIC GAMES ISSUE

Skiing and
Olympic
Rings — AP58

Designed by Lance Wyman.

11th Winter Olympic Games, Sapporo, Japan, Feb. 3-13, and 20th Summer Olympic Games, Munich, Germany, Aug. 26- Sept. 11.

PHOTOGRAVURE (Andreotti)
Plates of 200 subjects in four panes of 50 each.

1972, Aug. 17		*Perf. 11x10½*	
C85 AP58	11c **black, blue, red, emerald & yel-low**	.20	.20
	P# block of 10, 5 P#	2.40	—
	Margin block of 4, "Use Zip Code"	.85	—

ELECTRONICS PROGRESS ISSUE

De Forest
Audions
AP59

Designed by Walter and Naiad Einsel.

LITHOGRAPHED, ENGRAVED (GIORI)
Plates of 200 subjects in four panes of 50 each.

1973, July 10		*Perf. 11*	
C86 AP59	11c **vermilion, lilac, pale lilac, ol-ive, brown, deep carmine & black**	.30	.20
	P# block of 4	1.25	—
	Margin block of 4, Mr. Zip and "Use Zip Code"	1.20	—
a.	Vermilion & olive (litho.) omitted	900.00	
b.	Tagging omitted	25.00	
c.	Olive omitted		

Statue of
Liberty
AP60

Mt. Rushmore
National
Memorial
AP61

Designed by Robert (Gene) Shehorn.

GIORI PRESS PRINTING
Panes of 200 subjects in four panes of 50 each.

1974		*Perf. 11*	
C87 AP60	18c **carmine, black & ultramarine,** *Jan. 11*	.35	.30
	P# block of 4, 2#	1.50	—
	Margin block of 4, Mr. Zip and "Use Zip Code"	1.45	—
a.	Tagging omitted	17.50	
C88 AP61	26c **ultramarine, black & carmine,** *Jan. 2*	.60	.20
	P# block of 4	2.30	—
	Margin block of 4, Mr. Zip and "Use Zip Code"	2.20	—
	Pair with full vert. gutter btwn.		—
a.	Tagging omitted	25.00	
b.	Yellow-green instead of orange-red tag-ging		—

Plane and
Globes
AP62

Plane, Globes
and
Flags — AP63

Designed by David G. Foote.

GIORI PRESS PRINTING
Panes of 200 subjects in four panes of 50 each.

1976, Jan. 2		*Perf. 11*	
C89 AP62	25c **red, blue & black**	.50	.20
	P# block of 4	2.25	—
	Margin block of 4, Mr. Zip and "Use Zip Code"	2.10	—
a.	Tagging omitted		—
C90 AP63	31c **red, blue & black**	.60	.20
	P# block of 4	2.60	—
	Margin block of 4, Mr. Zip and "Use Zip Code"	2.50	—
a.	Tagging omitted	15.00	

WRIGHT BROTHERS ISSUE

Orville and Wilbur   Wright Brothers,
Wright, and   Flyer A and
Flyer A — AP64   Shed — AP65

Designed by Ken Dallison.

75th anniv. of 1st powered flight, Kill Devil Hill, NC, Dec. 17, 1903.

LITHOGRAPHED, ENGRAVED (GIORI)
Plates of 400 subjects in four panes of 100 each.

1978, Sept. 23		*Perf. 11*	
C91 AP64	31c **ultramarine & multicolored**	.65	.30
C92 AP65	31c **ultramarine & multicolored**	.65	.30
a.	Vert. pair, #C91-C92	1.30	1.20
	P# block of 4	3.00	—
	Margin block of 4, "Use Correct Zip Code"	2.75	—
b.	As "a," ultra. & black (engr.) omitted	700.00	
c.	As "a," black (engr.) omitted	2,500.	
d.	As "a," black, yellow, magenta, blue & brown (litho.) omitted	2,250.	

OCTAVE CHANUTE ISSUE

Chanute and   Biplane Hang-glider
Biplane Hang-   and
glider — AP66   Chanute — AP67

Designed by Ken Dallison.

Octave Chanute (1832-1910), civil engineer and aviation pioneer.

LITHOGRAPHED, ENGRAVED (GIORI)
Plates of 400 subjects in four panes of 100 each.

1979, Mar. 29		**Tagged**	*Perf. 11*
C93 AP66	21c **blue & multicolored**	.70	.35
C94 AP67	21c **blue & multicolored**	.70	.35
a.	Vert. pair, #C93-C94	1.40	1.20
	P# block of 4	3.00	—
	Margin block of 4, Mr. Zip	2.85	—
b.	As "a," ultra & black (engr.) omitted	4,500.	

WILEY POST ISSUE

Wiley Post and "Winnie Mae" — AP68

NR-105-W, Post in Pressurized Suit, Portrait — AP69

Designed by Ken Dallison.

Wiley Post (1899-1935), first man to fly around the world alone and high-altitude flying pioneer.

LITHOGRAPHED, ENGRAVED (GIORI)
Plates of 400 subjects in four panes of 100 each.

1979, Nov. 20	Tagged	Perf. 11	
C95	AP68 25c blue & multicolored	1.10	.45
C96	AP69 25c blue & multicolored	1.10	.45
a.	Vert. pair, #C95-C96	2.25	1.50
	P# block of 4	4.60	—
	Margin block of 4, Mr. Zip	4.50	—

OLYMPIC GAMES ISSUE

High Jump — AP70

Designed by Robert M. Cunningham.

22nd Olympic Games, Moscow, July 19-Aug. 3, 1980.

PHOTOGRAVURE
Plates of 200 subjects in four panes of 50 each.

1979, Nov. 1	Tagged	Perf. 11	
C97	AP70 31c multicolored	.70	.30
	P# block of 12, 6#	9.50	—
	Zip block of 4	3.00	—

PHILIP MAZZEI (1730-1816)

Italian-born Political Writer — AP71

Designed by Sante Graziani

PHOTOGRAVURE
Plates of 200 subjects in four panes of 50 each.

1980, Oct. 13	Tagged	Perf. 11	
C98	AP71 40c multicolored	.80	.20
	P# block of 12, 6#	10.00	—
	Zip block of 4	3.50	—
b.	Imperf., pair	3,500.	
d.	Tagging omitted	10.00	

1982	Tagged	Perf. 10½x11¼	
C98A	AP71 40c multicolored	7.50	1.50
	P# block of 12, 6#	125.00	—
c.	Horiz. pair, imperf. vert.	4,250.	

BLANCHE STUART SCOTT (1886-1970)

First Woman Pilot — AP72

Designed by Paul Calle.

PHOTOGRAVURE
Plates of 200 subjects in four panes of 50.

1980, Dec. 30	Tagged	Perf. 11	
C99	AP72 28c multicolored	.60	.20
	P# block of 12, 6#	8.50	—
	Zip block of 4	2.50	—
a.	Imperf., pair	2,750.	

GLENN CURTISS (1878-1930)

Aviation Pioneer and Aircraft Designer AP73

Designed by Ken Dallison.

PHOTOGRAVURE
Plates of 200 subjects in four panes of 50.

1980, Dec. 30	Tagged	Perf. 11	
C100	AP73 35c multicolored	.65	.20
	P# block of 12, 6#	9.00	—
	Zip block of 4	2.75	—

SUMMER OLYMPICS 1984

Women's Gymnastics — AP74

Hurdles — AP75

Women's Basketball — AP76

Soccer — AP77

Shot Put — AP78

Men's Gymnastics AP79

Women's Swimming AP80

Weight Lifting AP81

Women's Fencing AP82

Cycling AP83

Women's Volleyball AP84

Pole Vaulting AP85

Designed by Robert Peak.

23rd Olympic Games, Los Angeles, July 28-Aug. 12, 1984.

PHOTOGRAVURE
Plates of 200 subjects in four panes of 50.

1983, June 17	Tagged	Perf. 11	
C101	AP74 28c multicolored	1.00	.30
C102	AP75 28c multicolored	1.00	.30
C103	AP76 28c multicolored	1.00	.30
C104	AP77 28c multicolored	1.00	.30
a.	Block of 4, #C101-C104	4.25	2.50
	P# block of 4, 4#	5.50	—
	Zip block of 4	4.25	—
b.	As "a," imperf. vert.	7,500.	

1983, Apr. 8	Tagged	Perf. 11.2 Bullseye	
C105	AP78 40c multicolored	.90	.40
a.	Perf. 11 line	1.00	.45
C106	AP79 40c multicolored	.90	.40
a.	Perf. 11 line	1.00	.45
C107	AP80 40c multicolored	.90	.40
a.	Perf. 11 line	1.00	.45
C108	AP81 40c multicolored	.90	.40
a.	Perf. 11 line	1.00	.45
b.	Block of 4, #C105-C108	4.25	3.00
	P# block of 4, 4#	5.00	
	Zip block of 4	4.50	
c.	Block of 4, #C105a-C108a	5.00	4.00
	P# block of 4, 4#	7.50	
d.	Block of 4, imperf.	1,100.	

983, Nov. 4   **Tagged**   *Perf. 11*

109	AP82 35c **multicolored**	.90	.55
110	AP83 35c **multicolored**	.90	.55
111	AP84 35c **multicolored**	.90	.55
112	AP85 35c **multicolored**	.90	.55
a.	Block of 4, #C109-C112	4.00	3.25
	P# block of 4, 4#	6.50	—
	Zip block of 4	4.25	—

AVIATION PIONEERS

Alfred V. Verville (1890-1970), Inventor, Verville-Sperry R-3 Army Racer — AP86

Lawrence Sperry (1892-1931), Aircraft Designer, and Father Elmer (1860-1930), Designer and Pilot, 1st Seaplane AP87

Designed by Ken Dallison (No. C113) and Howard Koslow (No. C114)

PHOTOGRAVURE
Plates of 200 in four panes of 50
(2 panes each, No. C113 and No. C114)
Plates of 200 in four panes of 50 (No. C114)

1985, Feb. 13   **Tagged**   *Perf. 11*

C113	AP86 33c **multicolored**	.65	.20
	P# block of 4, 5#, UL, LR	3.25	—
	Zip block of 4	2.90	—
a.	Imperf., pair	850.00	
C114	AP87 39c **multicolored**	.80	.25
	P# block of 4, 5#, UR, LL	3.75	—
	Zip block of 4	3.50	—
a.	Imperf., pair	1,750.	

Philatelic Foundation certificates issued prior to August 1994 for No. C114 with magenta missing have been rescinded. At this time no true magenta missing copies are known.

TRANSPACIFIC AIRMAIL
50th Anniversary

Martin M-130 China Clipper AP88

Designed by Chuck Hodgson.

PHOTOGRAVURE
Plates of 200 in four panes of 50

1985, Feb. 15   **Tagged**   *Perf. 11*

C115	AP88 44c **multicolored**	.85	.25
	P# block of 4, 4#	4.00	—
	Zip block of 4	3.50	—
a.	Imperf., pair	800.00	

FR. JUNIPERO SERRA (1713-1784)
California Missionary

Outline Map of Southern California, Portrait, San Gabriel Mission AP89

Designed by Richard Schlecht from a Spanish stamp.

PHOTOGRAVURE
Plates of 200 in four panes of 50

1985, Aug. 22   **Tagged**   *Perf. 11*

C116	AP89 44c **multicolored**	1.00	.35
	P# block of 4	8.00	—
	Zip block of 4	4.25	—
a.	Imperf., pair	1,500.	

SETTLING OF NEW SWEDEN, 350th ANNIV.

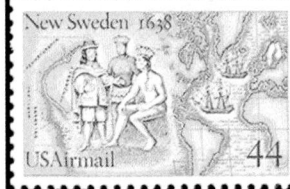

Settler, Two Indians, Map of New Sweden, Swedish Ships "Kalmar Nyckel" and "Fogel Grip" — AP90

Designed by Goran Osterland based on an 18th century illustration from a Swedish book about the Colonies.

LITHOGRAPHED AND ENGRAVED
Plates of 200 in four panes of 50

1988, Mar. 29   **Tagged**   *Perf. 11*

C117	AP90 44c **multicolored**	1.00	.25
	P# block of 4, 5#	6.50	—
	Zip block of 4	5.00	—

See Sweden No. 1672 and Finland No. 768.

SAMUEL P. LANGLEY (1834-1906)

Langley and Unmanned Aerodrome No. 5 — AP91

Designed by Ken Dallison.

LITHOGRAPHED AND ENGRAVED
Plates of 200 in four panes of 50

1988, May 14   **Tagged**   *Perf. 11*

C118	AP91 45c **multicolored,** large block tagging	.90	.20
	P# block of 4, 7#	4.00	—
	Zip block of 4	4.00	—
a.	Overall tagging	3.00	.50
	P# block of 4, 7#	30.00	—
	Zip block of 4	14.00	—

IGOR SIKORSKY (1889-1972)

Sikorsky and 1939 VS300 Helicopter AP92

Designed by Ren Wicks.

PHOTOGRAVURE AND ENGRAVED
Plates of 200 in four panes of 50

1988, June 23   **Tagged**   *Perf. 11*

C119	AP92 36c **multicolored**	.70	.25
	P# block of 4, 6#	3.25	—
	Zip block of 4	3.10	—
a.	Red, dk blue & black (engraved) omitted		

Beware of copies with traces of engraved red offered as "red omitted" varieties.

FRENCH REVOLUTION BICENTENNIAL

Liberty, Equality and Fraternity — AP93

Designed by Richard Sheaff.

LITHOGRAPHED AND ENGRAVED
Plates of 120 in four panes of 30.

1989, July 14   **Tagged**   *Perf. 11½x11*

C120	AP93 45c **multicolored**	.95	.20
	P# block of 4, 4#	4.75	—
	Zip block of 4	4.00	—

See France Nos. 2143-2145a.

PRE-COLUMBIAN AMERICA ISSUE

Southeast Carved Figure, 700-1430 A.D. — AP94

Designed by Lon Busch.
Printed by American Bank Note Co.

PHOTOGRAVURE
Plates of 200 in four panes of 50

1989, Oct. 12   **Perf. 11**

C121	AP94 45c **multicolored**	.90	.20
	P# block of 4, 4#	5.25	—
	Zip block of 4	3.75	—

20th UPU CONGRESS
Futuristic Mail Delivery

Spacecraft — AP95

Air-suspended Hover Car — AP96

Moon Rover — AP97

Space Shuttle — AP98

Designed by Ken Hodges.

LITHOGRAPHED & ENGRAVED
Plates of 160 in four panes of 40.

1989, Nov. 27		**Tagged**	**Perf. 11**	
C122 AP95	45c **multicolored**		1.00	.50
C123 AP96	45c **multicolored**		1.00	.50
C124 AP97	45c **multicolored**		1.00	.50
C125 AP98	45c **multicolored**		1.00	.50
a.	Block of 4, #C122-C125		4.00	3.00
	P# block of 4, 5#		5.50	—
	Zip block of 4		4.50	—
b.	As "a," light blue (engr.) omitted		750.00	

Souvenir Sheet
LITHOGRAPHED & ENGRAVED

1989, Nov. 24		**Tagged**	**Imperf.**	
C126	Sheet of 4		4.75	3.75
a.	AP95 45c multicolored		1.00	.50
b.	AP96 45c multicolored		1.00	.50
c.	AP97 45c multicolored		1.00	.50
d.	AP98 45c multicolored		1.00	.50
e.	As No. C126, tagging omitted		—	

PRE-COLUMBIAN AMERICA ISSUE

Tropical
Coast — AP99

Designed by Mark Hess.
Printed by the American Bank Note Company.

PHOTOGRAVURE
Plates of 200 in four panes of 50
(3 panes of #2512, 1 pane of #C127)

1990, Oct. 12		**Tagged**	**Perf. 11**	
C127 AP99	45c **multicolored**		.90	.20
	P# block of 4, 4#, UL only		7.00	—
	Zip block of 4		3.75	—

HARRIET QUIMBY, 1ST AMERICAN WOMAN PILOT

Quimby (1884-
1912), Bleriot
Airplane
AP100

Designed by Howard Koslow. Printed by Stamp Venturers.

PHOTOGRAVURE
Panes of 200 in four panes of 50

1991, Apr. 27		**Tagged**	**Perf. 11**	
C128 AP100	50c **multicolored**, overall tagging		1.00	.25
	P# block of 4, S1111		5.25	—
	Zip block of 4		4.25	—
a.	Vert. pair, imperf. horiz.		1,750.	
b.	Perf. 11.2, prephosphored uncoated			
	paper (mottled tagging), *1993*		1.10	.25
	P# block of 4, S2222		5.75	—
	Zip block of 6		4.50	—

WILLIAM T. PIPER, AIRCRAFT MANUFACTURER

Piper and
Piper
Cub — AP101

Designed by Ren Wicks.
Printed by J. W. Fergusson and Sons for American Bank
Note Co.

PHOTOGRAVURE
Panes of 200 in four panes of 50

1991, May 17		**Tagged**	**Perf. 11**	
C129 AP101	40c **multicolored**		.80	.20
	P# block of 4, 4#+A		3.75	—
	Zip block of 4		3.50	—

Blue sky is plainly visible all the way across stamp above
Piper's head.
See No. C132.

ANTARCTIC TREATY, 30TH ANNIVERSARY

AP102

Designed by Howard Koslow. Printed by Stamp Venturers.

PHOTOGRAVURE
Panes of 50

1991, June 21		**Tagged**	**Perf. 11**	
C130 AP102	50c **multicolored**		1.00	.35
	P# block of 4, 4#+S		5.00	—
	Zip block of 4		4.25	—

PRE-COLUMBIAN AMERICA ISSUE

Bering Land
Bridge
AP103

Designed by Richard Schlect.

PHOTOGRAVURE
Plates of 200 in 4 panes of 50

1991, Oct. 12		**Tagged**	**Perf. 11**	
C131 AP103	50c **multicolored**		1.00	.35
	P# block of 4, 6#		5.25	—
	Zip block of 4		4.75	—

Piper Type of 1991
Printed by Stamp Venturers.

PHOTOGRAVURE
Panes of 200 in four panes of 50

1993		**Tagged**	**Perf. 11.2**	
C132 AP101	40c **multicolored**		2.00	.60
	P# block of 4, 4#+S		45.00	—
	Zip block of 4		9.00	—

Piper's hair touches top edge of design. No inscriptions.
Bullseye perf.

"All LC (Letters and Cards) mail receives First-Class
Mail service in the United States, is dispatched by the
fastest transportation available, and travels by airmail
or priority service in the destination country. All LC
mail should be marked 'AIRMAIL' or 'PAR AVION.'"
(U.S. Postal Service, Pub. 51).

No. C133 listed below was issued to meet the LC
rate to Canada and Mexico and is inscribed with the
silhouette of a jet plane next to the denomination indicating the need for airmail service. This is unlike No.
2998, which met the LC rate to other countries, but
contained no indication that it was intended for that
use.

Future issues that meet a specific international airmail rate and contain the airplane silhouette will be
treated by Scott as Air Post stamps. Stamps similar to
No. 2998 will be listed in the Postage section.

NIAGARA FALLS

AP104

Designed by Ethel Kessler. Printed by Avery Dennison.

PHOTOGRAVURE
Sheets of 200 in ten panes of 20

1999, May 12		**Tagged**	**Perf. 11**	
		Self-Adhesive		
C133 AP104	48c **multicolored**		.95	.20
	P# block of 4, 5#+V		4.00	
	Pane of 20		20.00	

RIO GRANDE

AP105

Designed by Ethel Kessler. Printed by Avery Dennison.

PHOTOGRAVURE
Sheets of 200 in ten panes of 20

1999, July 30		**Tagged**	*Serpentine Die Cut 1*	
		Self-Adhesive		
C134 AP105	40c **multicolored**		.80	.6
	P# block of 4, 5#+V		3.20	
	Pane of 20		16.00	

GRAND CANYON

AP106

Designed by Ethel Kessler.
Printed by Banknote Corp. of America.

LITHOGRAPHED
Sheets of 180 in nine panes of 20
Serpentine Die Cut 11¼x11½

2000, Jan. 20			Tagge
		Self-Adhesive	
C135 AP106 60c **multicolored**		1.25	.2
	P# block of 4, 4#+B	5.00	
	Pane of 20	25.00	
a.	Die cutting omitted, pair	2,250.	
b.	Vert. pair, die cutting omitted horiz.	—	
c.	Horiz. pair, die cutting omitted between	—	
d.	Horiz. pair, vert. die cutting omitted	—	

NINE-MILE PRAIRIE, NEBRASKA

AP107

Designed by Ethel Kessler. Printed by Ashton-Potter (USA)
Ltd.

LITHOGRAPHED
Sheets of 180 in nine panes of 20
Serpentine Die Cut 11¼x11½

2001, Mar. 6			**Tagged**
		Self-Adhesive	
C136 AP107 70c **multicolored**		1.40	.30
	P# block of 4, 5#+P	5.60	
	Pane of 20	28.00	

MT. MCKINLEY

AP108

Designed by Ethel Kessler. Printed by Avery Dennison.

PHOTOGRAVURE
Sheets of 200 in ten panes of 20.

2001, Apr. 17		**Tagged**	*Serpentine Die Cut 11*
		Self-Adhesive	
C137 AP108 80c **multicolored**		1.60	.35
	P# block of 4, 5 #+V	6.40	
	Pane of 20	32.00	

ACADIA NATIONAL PARK

AP109

Designed by Ethel Kessler. Printed by Banknote Corporation of America.

LITHOGRAPHED
Sheets of 180 in nine panes of 20 (#C138), Sheets of 120 in six panes of 20 (#C138a)
Serpentine Die Cut 11.25x11.5 (No. C138), 11.5x11.9 (No. C138a)

01-05			**Tagged**

Self-Adhesive

38	AP109 60c **multicolored**, prephosphored coated paper (solid tagging), *May 30, 2001*	1.25	.25
	P# block of 4, #B1111	5.00	
	Pane of 20	25.00	
a.	Overall tagging, *March 2003*	1.25	.25
	P# block of 4, 4# + B	5.00	
	Pane of 20	25.00	
b.	As "a," with "2005" year date, *Jan. 2005*	1.25	.25
	P# block of 4, 4#+S	5.00	
	Pane of 20	25.00	
c.	As "b," printed on back of backing paper	—	

SCENIC AMERICAN LANDSCAPES

Bryce Canyon National Park — AP110

Great Smoky Mountains National Park — AP111

Yosemite National Park — AP112

Designed by Ethel Kessler. Printed by Banknote Corporation of America for Sennett Security Products (#C139), Ashton-Potter (USA) Ltd. (#C140), Avery Dennison (#C141).

LITHOGRAPHED, PHOTOGRAVURE (#C141)
Sheets of 180 in nine panes of 20 (#C139), Sheets of 120 in six panes of 20 (#C140), Sheets of 200 in ten panes of 20 (#C141)

2006, Feb. 24   **Tagged**   *Serpentine Die Cut 10¾*
Self-Adhesive

C139	AP110 63c **multicolored**	1.25	.25
	P# block of 4, 5#+S	5.00	
	Pane of 20	25.00	
C140	AP111 75c **multicolored**	1.50	.35
	P# block of 4, 5#+P	6.00	
	Pane of 20	30.00	

Serpentine Die Cut 11

C141	AP112 84c **multicolored**	1.75	.35
	P# block of 4, 5#+S	7.00	
	Pane of 20	35.00	
	Nos. C139-C141 (3)	4.50	.95

AIR POST SPECIAL DELIVERY STAMPS

Great Seal of United States
APSD1

No. CE1 was issued for the prepayment of the air postage and the special delivery fee in one stamp. First day sale was at he American Air Mail Society Convention.

FLAT PLATE PRINTING
Plates of 200 subjects in four panes of 50 each.

1934, Aug. 30	**Unwmk.**		**Perf. 11**
CE1	APSD1 16c **dark blue**	.60	.70
	blue	.60	.70
	Never hinged	.80	
	P# block of 6	17.50	—

Never hinged	22.50	
First day cover, Chicago *(40,171)*	25.00	
First day cover, Washington, D.C., *Aug. 31*	15.00	

For imperforate variety see No. 771.

Type of 1934
Frame plates of 100 subjects in two panes of 50 each separated by a 1½ inch wide vertical gutter with central guide line, and vignette plates of 50 subjects.

The "seal" design for No. CE2 was from a new engraving, slightly smaller than that used for No. CE1.

Top plate number blocks of No. CE2 are found both with and without top arrow.

Issued in panes of 50 each.

1936, Feb. 10			
CE2	APSD1 16c **red & blue**	.40	.25
	Never hinged	.50	
	Margin block of 4, bottom or side arrow	2.00	1.50

Center line block		2.50	2.25
P# block of 4, 2#		7.50	
Never hinged		10.00	
P# block of 4, 2#, blue dotted registration marker		85.00	
Never hinged		110.00	
Same, arrow, thick red registration marker		80.00	
Never hinged		100.00	
P# block of 10, 2#, two "TOP" and two registration markers		20.00	6.00
Never hinged		25.00	
First day cover Washington, D.C. *(72,981)*			17.50
a. Horiz. pair, imperf. vert.		*3,750.*	
P# block of 6, 2#, two "TOP" and registration markers		*40,000.*	

The No. CE2a plate block is unique. Value represents sale in 1997.

Quantities issued: #CE1, 9,215,750; #CE2, 72,517,850.

AIR POST SEMI-OFFICIAL STAMPS

Buffalo Balloon

This stamp was privately issued by John F. B. Lillard, a Nashville reporter. It was used on covers carried on a balloon ascension of June 18, 1877, which began at Nashville and landed at Gallatin, Tenn., and possibly on other flights. The balloon was owned and piloted by Samuel Archer King. The stamp was reported to have been engraved by (Mrs.?) J. H. Snively and printed in tete beche pairs from a single die. Lillard wrote that 300 were printed and 23 used.

Buffalo Balloon — APSO1

1877, June 18	**Typo.**		**Imperf.**
CL1	APSO1 5c **deep blue**	*7,500.*	
	Never hinged	*10,000.*	
	On cover with 3c #158	—	

	On cover with 1c #156 & 2c #178		—
a.	Tête bêche pair, vertical	*21,500.*	
	Never hinged	—	

A black proof exists of No. CL1, value *$7,500.*

Rodgers Aerial Post

This stamp was privately issued by Calbraith Perry Rodgers' wife who acted as unofficial postmaster during her husband's cross-country airplane flight in 1911. Rodgers was competing for the $50,000 prize offered by William Randolph Hearst to whomever completed the trip within a 30-day period. Rodgers' flight was sponsored by the Armour meat-packing company, makers of the soft drink, Vin Fiz.

The stamp probably was first available in Texas about October 19. Recorded dated examples exist from Oct. 19 to Nov. 8.

Each of the thirteen known copies is trimmed close to the design on one or more sides.

APSO2

1911, Oct.   *Imperf.*
CL2 APSO2 25c **black**   *35,000.*
          Tied on postcard with 1c
          #374   *50,000.*
No. CL2 is the first stamp in the world to picture an airplane.

R.F. OVERPRINTS

Authorized as a control mark by the United States Fleet Post Office during 1944-45 for the accommodation of and exclusive use by French naval personnel on airmail correspondence to the United States and Canada. All "R.F." (Republique Francaise) mail had to be posted on board French ship or at one of their western Mediterranean or northwest African naval bases and had to bear the return address, rank and/or serial number of a Frenc officer or seaman. It also had to be reviewed by a censor.

All "R.F." overprints were handstamped by the French naval authorities after the stamps were affixed for mailing. The stamps had to be canceled a special French naval cancellation. The status of unused copies seems questionable; they are alleged to have been handstamped at a later dat

Several types of "R.F." overprints other than those illustrated are known, but their validity is doubtful.

United States No. C25 Handstamped in Black

R. F. a		R.. F. b	R.F. g	RF h
R.F c	R..F d		RF i	
RF e	RF f		R. F. j	

1944-45   **Unwmk.**   *Perf. 11x10½*
CM1 AP17 (a) 6c **carmine**, on cover   300.00
CM2 AP17 (b) 6c **carmine**, on cover   475.00
CM3 AP17 (c) 6c **carmine**, on cover   300.00
CM4 AP17 (d) 6c **carmine**, on cover   350.00
CM5 AP17 (e) 6c **carmine**, on cover   425.00
CM6 AP17 (f) 6c **carmine**, on cover   350.00
CM7 AP17 (g) 6c **carmine**, on cover   600.00

CM8 AP17 (h) 6c **carmine**, on cover   600.
CM9 AP17 (i) 6c **carmine**, on cover   750.
CM10 AP17 (j) 6c **carmine**, on cover
          Counterfeits of several types exist.
No. 907 is known with type "c" overprint; No. C19 with typ
"e" or "h"; No. C25a (single) with type "c", and No. C26 with ty
"a," "d" or "f." Type "i" exists in several very minor variations

STAMPED ENVELOPES
Nos. UC3, UC4 or UC6 Handstamped in Black
1944-45
UCM1 UC2 (a) 6c **orange**, entire   300.0
UCM2 UC2 (b) 6c **orange**, entire   550.0
UCM3 UC2 (d) 6c **orange**, entire   450.0
UCM4 UC2 (f) 6c **orange**, entire   550.0
UCM5 UC2 (h) 6c **orange**, entire
UCM6 UC2 (i) 6c **orange**, entire
UCM7 UC2 (j) 6c **orange**, entire
          Values for Nos. UCM1-UCM7 reflect the scarcity of the actu
overprint types. Use of No. UC6 envelopes was by far the mos
common. Overprints on Nos. UC3 or UC4 merit a premium.

SPECIAL DELIVERY STAMPS

Special Delivery service was instituted by the Act of Congress of March 3, 1885, and put into operation on October 1, 1885. The Act limited the service to free delivery offices and such others as served places with a population of 4,000 or more, and its privileges were thus operative in but 555 post offices. The Act of August 4, 1886, made the stamps and service available at all post offices and upon any article of mailable matter, beginning Oct. 1, 1886. To consume the supply of stamps of the first issue, Scott No. E2 was withheld until September 6, 1888.

A Special Delivery stamp, when affixed to any stamped letter or article of mailable matter, secured later delivery during daytime and evening at mos post offices, so that the item did not have to wait until the next day for delivery.

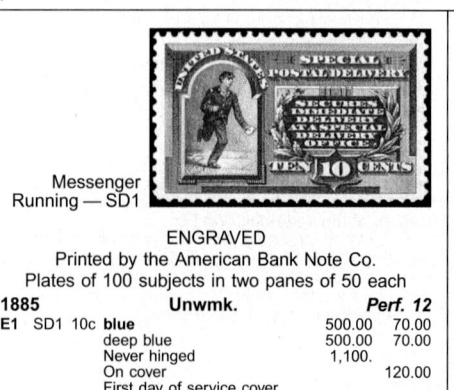

Messenger
Running — SD1

ENGRAVED
Printed by the American Bank Note Co.
Plates of 100 subjects in two panes of 50 each
1885   **Unwmk.**   *Perf. 12*
E1 SD1 10c **blue**   500.00   70.00
          deep blue   500.00   70.00
          Never hinged   1,100.
          On cover   120.00
          First day of service cover
          (Oct. 1)   20,000.

Block of four   2,250.
P# block of 8, Impt. 495 or
     496   15,000.
Margin strip of 4, same   4,500.
Double transfer at top   800.00   200.00
     Earliest documented use: Sept. 29, 1885, on a cover deliv-
ered Oct. 1. There is also a Sept. 30 cover recorded, received
for delivery at 7:00 a.m. Oct. 1.

Messenger
Running
SD2

1888, Sept. 6
E2 SD2 10c **blue**   475.00   30.00
          deep blue   475.00   30.00
          Never hinged   1,050.
          On cover   80.00
          Block of four   2,150.
          P# block of 8, Impt. 73 or
               552   15,000.
          Never hinged   21,500.
          Margin strip of 4, same   4,750.
     Earliest documented use: Dec. 18, 1888.
See note above No. E3.

COLUMBIAN EXPOSITION ISSUE
     Though not issued expressly for the Exposition, No.
E3 is considered to be part of that issue. It was
released in orange because No. E2 was easily confused with the 1c Columbian, No. 230.
     From Jan. 24, 1893, until Jan. 5, 1894, the special
delivery stamp was printed in orange; the issue in that
color continued until May 19, 1894, when the stock on

and was exhausted. The stamp in blue was not [is]sued from Jan. 24, 1893 to May 19, 1894. However, [i]n Jan. 5, 1894, printing of the stamp in blue was [re]sumed. Presumably it was reissued from May 19, [1]894 until the appearance of No. E4 on Oct. 10, 1894. [T]he emissions of the blue stamp of this design before [J]an. 24, 1893 and after Jan. 5, 1894 are [in]distinguishable.

[1]893, Jan. 24

[E]3	SD2 10c	**orange**	260.00	40.00
		deep orange	260.00	40.00
		Never hinged	600.00	
		On cover		120.00
		On cover, Columbian Expo. station machine canc.		1,000.
		On cover, Columbian Expo. station duplex handstamp cancel		1,250.
		Block of four	1,150.	
		P# block of 8, Impt. 73 or 552	10,000.	
		Never hinged	12,500.	
		Margin strip of 4, same	3,750.	

Earliest documented use: Feb. 11, 1893.

Messenger Running — SD3

Type III	Type VI	Type VII

Printed by the Bureau of Engraving and Printing.

1894, Oct. 10

Line under "TEN CENTS"

E4	SD3 10c	**blue**	850.00	55.00
		dark blue	850.00	55.00
		bright blue	1,000.	75.00
		Never hinged	2,100.	
		On cover		200.00
		Block of four	3,600.	
		Margin block of 4, arrow	3,750.	
		P#77 block of 6, T III Impt.	17,500.	
		Never hinged	25,000.	
		Margin strip of 3, same	5,000.	
		Never hinged	7,500.	
		Double transfer	—	—

Earliest documented use: Oct. 25, 1894.

Imperfs of No. E4 on stamp paper, currently listed as No. E4aP, may not be proofs, but it is also unlikely that they were regularly issued. They most likely are from printer's waste.

1895, Aug. 16   **Wmk. 191**

E5	SD3 10c	**blue**	210.00	10.00
		dark blue	210.00	10.00
		deep blue	210.00	10.00
		Never hinged	470.00	
		On cover		20.00
		Block of four	900.00	
		Margin block of 4, arrow	925.00	

P# block of 6, T III, VI or VII Impt.	4,750.	
Never hinged	6,750.	
Margin strip of 3, same	900.00	
Never hinged	1,600.	
Double transfer	—	32.50
Line of color through "POSTAL DELIVERY," from bottom row of Plates 1257-1260	300.00	35.00
Never hinged	625.00	
a. Dots in curved frame above messenger (Pl. 882)	275.00	15.00
Never hinged	600.00	
b. Printed on both sides	—	

Earliest documented use: Oct. 3, 1895.

The existence of No. E5b has been questioned by specialists. The editors would like to see authenticated evidence of its existence.

See Die and Plate Proofs for imperf. on stamp paper.

Messenger on Bicycle — SD4

1902, Dec. 9

E6	SD4 10c	**ultramarine**	200.00	10.00
		dark ultramarine	210.00	10.00
		pale ultramarine	200.00	10.00
		Never hinged	450.00	
a.		**10c blue**	200.00	10.00
		Never hinged	450.00	
		On cover		17.50
		Block of four	850.00	
		Margin block of 4, arrow	875.00	
		P# block of 6, T VII Impt.	3,000.	
		Never hinged	4,250.	
		Margin strip of 3, same	725.00	
		Never hinged	1,250.	
		P# block of 6, "09"	2,750.	
		Never hinged	4,000.	
		Margin strip of 3, same	750.	
		Never hinged	1,200.	
		Double transfer	—	—
		Damaged transfer under "N" of "CENTS"	220.00	15.00

Earliest documented use: Jan. 22, 1903.

No. E6 was re-issued in 1909 from new plates 5240, 5243-5245. After a few months use the Bureau added "09" to these plate numbers. The stamp can be identified only by plate number. The plate numbers without the "09" are scarcer and worth more.

Helmet of Mercury — SD5

Designed by Whitney Warren.

Plates of 280 subjects in four panes of 70 each

1908, Dec. 12

E7	SD5 10c	**green**	70.00	45.00
		dark green	70.00	45.00
		yellowish green	70.00	45.00
		Never hinged	150.00	
		On cover		175.00
		Block of four	300.00	
		P# block of 6, T V Impt.	1,000.	—
		Never hinged	1,400.	
		Margin strip of 3, same	300.00	
		Never hinged	500.00	
		Double transfer	160.00	100.00

Earliest documented use: Dec. 14, 1908.

Plates of 200 subjects in four panes of 50 each

1911, Jan.   **Wmk. 190**   **Perf. 12**

E8	SD4 10c	**ultramarine**	105.00	8.00
		pale ultramarine	105.00	8.00
		dark ultramarine	105.00	8.00
		Never hinged	230.00	
b.		**10c violet blue**	120.00	12.00
		Never hinged	270.00	
		On cover		15.00
		Block of four	440.00	
		P# block of 6, T VII Impt.	1,850.	
		Never hinged	2,750.	
		P# block of 6	1,700.	
		Never hinged	2,500.	

Top frame line missing (Pl. 5514)	145.00	20.00
Never hinged	325.00	

Earliest documented use: Jan. 14, 1911.

1914, Sept.   **Perf. 10**

E9	SD4 10c	**ultramarine**	190.00	12.00
		pale ultramarine	190.00	12.00
		Never hinged	425.00	
		On cover		40.00
		Block of four	800.00	
		P# block of 6, T VII Impt.	4,000.	
		Never hinged	6,000.	
		P# block of 6	3,000.	
		Never hinged	4,500.	
		Margin block of 8, T VII Impt. & P# (side)	—	
a.		**10c blue**	240.00	15.00
		Never hinged	525.00	
		On cover		37.50
		Block of four	1,050.	
		P# block of 6, T VII Impt.	5,000.	
		Never hinged	6,500.	
		P# block of 6	4,000.	
		Never hinged	5,250.	
		Margin block of 8, T VII Impt. & P# (side)	—	

Earliest documented use: Oct. 26, 1914.

1916, Oct. 19   **Unwmk.**   **Perf. 10**

E10	SD4 10c	**pale ultramarine**	320.00	45.00
		ultramarine	340.00	50.00
		Never hinged	700.00	
		On cover		90.00
		Block of four	1,400.	
		P# block of 6, T VII Impt. 5520	5,500.	
		Never hinged	7,250.	
		P# block of 6	5,000.	
		Never hinged	6,500.	
a.		**10c blue**	350.00	50.00
		Never hinged	750.00	
		On cover		100.00
		Block of four	1,550.	
		P# block of 6, T VII Impt. 5520	5,750.	
		P# block of 6	5,000.	

Earliest documented use: Nov. 4, 1916.

1917, May 2   **Unwmk.**   **Perf. 11**

E11	SD4 10c	**ultramarine**	20.00	.75
		pale ultramarine	20.00	.75
		dark ultramarine	25.00	2.00
		Never hinged	45.00	
		On cover		4.00
		Block of four	85.00	
		P# block of 6, T VII Impt.	725.00	
		Never hinged	1,100.	
		P# block of 6	225.00	
		Never hinged	325.00	
		Margin block of 8, T VII Impt. & P# (side)	—	
b.		**10c gray violet**	30.00	3.00
		Never hinged	65.00	
c.		**10c blue**	60.00	4.00
		Never hinged	125.00	
		On cover		15.00
		Block of four	250.00	
		P# block of 6, T VII Impt.	2,000.	
		P# block of 6	600.00	
		Margin block of 8, T VII Impt. & P# (side)	—	
d.		Perf. 10 at left	—	

Earliest documented use: June 12, 1917.

The aniline ink used on some printings of No. E11 permeated the paper causing a pink tinge to appear on the back. Such stamps are called "pink backs." They are scarce and valued higher than the normal stamp.

Motorcycle Delivery SD6

Post Office Truck — SD7

1922, July 12   **Unwmk.**   **Perf. 11**

E12	SD6 10c	**gray violet**	40.00	1.00
		Never hinged	90.00	
		On cover		2.00
		First day cover		500.00
		P# block of 6	450.00	
		Never hinged	700.00	

		Double transfer	—	—
a.	10c	**deep ultramarine**	50.00	2.00
		Never hinged	110.00	
		On cover		3.50
		P# block of 6	525.00	—
		Never hinged	775.00	
		Double transfer	—	—

FLAT PLATE PRINTING

1925		**Unwmk.**		***Perf. 11***

Issued to facilitate special delivery service for parcel post.

E13	SD6	15c	**deep orange,** *Apr. 11, 1925*	27.50	1.75
			Never hinged	55.00	
			On cover		12.50
			First day cover		350.00
			P# block of 6	350.00	—
			Never hinged	500.00	
			Double transfer	37.50	3.00
E14	SD7	20c	**black,** *Apr. 25, 1925*	2.00	1.00
			Never hinged	4.25	
			On cover		1.50
			First day cover		125.00
			P# block of 6	35.00	
			Never hinged	50.00	

Motorcycle Type of 1922
ROTARY PRESS PRINTING

1927-31			**Unwmk.**	***Perf. 11x10½***	
E15	SD6	10c	**gray violet,** *Nov. 29, 1927*	.65	.25
			violet	.65	.25
			Never hinged	1.20	
a.		10c	**red lilac**	.65	.25
			Never hinged	1.20	
b.		10c	**gray lilac**	.65	.25
			Never hinged	1.20	
			On cover		.30
			First day cover		110.00
			First day cover, electric eye plate, *Sept. 8, 1941*		30.00
			P# block of 4	3.75	—
			Never hinged	6.25	
			Gouged plate	—	—
			Cracked plate 19280 LR	35.00	
c.			Horizontal pair, imperf. between	325.00	
			Never hinged	550.00	
E16	SD6	15c	**orange,** *Aug. 1931*	.70	.25
			Never hinged	1.05	
			On cover		.30

First day cover, Washington, D.C., *Aug. 13, 1931*		125.00	
P# block of 4		2.75	
Never hinged		4.50	

The Washington, D.C. Aug. 13, 1931 first day cover reflects the first day of sale at the philatelic agency. The actual earliest documented use of No. E16 is Aug. 6, 1931, at Easton, PA; value, $2,500.

> **Catalogue values for unused stamps in this section, from this point to the end, are for Never Hinged items.**

Motorcycle Type of 1922
ROTARY PRESS PRINTING
E. E. Plates of 200 subjects in four panes of 50 each.

1944-51			**Unwmk.**	***Perf. 11x10½***	
E17	SD6	13c	**blue,** *Oct. 30, 1944*	.60	.20
			First day cover		15.00
			P# block of 4	2.75	—
E18	SD6	17c	**orange yellow,** *Oct. 30, 1944*	3.00	2.25
			First day cover		12.00
			First day cover, Nos. E17 & E18		30.00
			P# block of 4	22.50	—
E19	SD7	20c	**black,** *Nov. 30, 1951*	1.25	.20
			First day cover		5.00
			P# block of 4	5.50	—

Special Delivery Letter, Hand to Hand — SD8

ROTARY PRESS PRINTING
E.E. Plates of 200 subjects in four panes of 50 each

1954, Oct. 13			**Unwmk.**	***Perf. 11x10***	
E20	SD8	20c	**deep blue**	.40	
			light blue		
			First day cover, Boston *(194,043)*		3.
			P# block of 4	2.00	

1957, Sept. 3					
E21	SD8	30c	**lake**	.50	.
			First day cover, Indianapolis, Ind. *(111,451)*		2.
			P# block of 4	2.25	

Arrows SD9

Designed by Norman Ives.

GIORI PRESS PRINTING
Plates of 200 subjects in four panes of 50 each

1969, Nov. 21			**Unwmk.**	***Perf. 1***	
E22	SD9	45c	**carmine & violet blue**	1.25	.2
			First day cover, New York, N.Y.		4.0
			P# block of 4	5.50	—
			Margin block of 4, Mr. Zip and "Use Zip Code"	5.10	—

1971, May 10				***Perf. 1***	
E23	SD9	60c	**violet blue & carmine**	1.25	.2
			First day cover, Phoenix, Ariz. *(129,562)*		3.5
			P# block of 4	5.50	—
			Margin block of 4, Mr. Zip and "Use Zip Code"	5.25	—

REGISTRATION STAMP

The Registry System for U.S. mail went into effect July 1, 1855, the fee being 5 cents. On June 30, 1863, the fee was increased to 20 cents. On January 1, 1869, the fee was reduced to 15 cents and on January 1, 1874, to 8 cents. On July 1, 1875, the fee was increased to 10 cents. On January 1, 1893, the fee was again reduced to 8 cents and again it was increased to 10 cents on November 1, 1909.

Early registered covers with various stamps, rates and postal markings are of particular interest to collectors.

Registry stamps (10c ultramarine) were issued on December 1, 1911, to prepay registry fees (not postage), but ordinary stamps were valid for registry fees then as now. These special stamps were abolished May 28, 1913, by order of the Postmaster General, who permitted their use until supplies on hand were exhausted.

Eagle — RS1

ENGRAVED

1911, Dec. 1		**Wmk. 190**		***Perf. 12***	
F1	RS1	10c	**ultramarine**	70.00	9.00
			pale ultramarine	70.00	9.00
			Never hinged	150.00	
			On cover		45.00
			Block of 4	325.00	75.00
			P# block of 6, Impt. & "A"	*1,600.*	—
			Never hinged	*2,500.*	
			First day cover		17,500.

CERTIFIED MAIL STAMP

Certified Mail service was started on June 6, 1955, for use on first class mail for which no indemnity value is claimed, but for which proof of mailing and proof of delivery are available at less cost than registered mail. The mailer receives one receipt and the addressee signs another when the postman delivers the letter. The second receipt is kept on file at the post office for six months. The Certified Mail charge, originally 15 cents, is in addition to regular postage, whether surface mail, air mail, or special delivery.

Catalogue value for the unused stamp in this section is for a Never Hinged item.

Letter Carrier — CM1

ROTARY PRESS PRINTING
E. E. Plates of 200 subjects in four panes of 50

1955, June 6		**Unwmk.**		*Perf. 10½x11*	
FA1	CM1	15c **red**		.45	.30
		P# block of 4		4.25	—
		First day cover			5.00

POSTAGE DUE STAMPS

Postage due stamps were authorized by an act of Congress, approved March 3, 1879, and effective July 1, 1879. By law, postage due stamps were to be affixed by clerks to any piece of mailable matter to denote the amount collected from the addressee because of insufficient prepayment of postage.

Although the Post Office Department required postage to be prepaid beginning in 1855, there were many instances when full postage was not required, and postage due payment had to be collected in cash from the addressees. These instances included insufficiently prepaid letters, advertised letters, and unpaid ship letters and steamboat letters.

The reason for the appearance of postage due stamps may be summed up in one word: accountability. The 1880 *Report of the Postmaster General* noted that the former system of collecting postage due had one great weakness: "In securing the full returns of the department was entirely dependent on the fidelity of the postmasters." Postage due stamps, affixed to underpaid mail as receipts for the underpayment collected, solved that problem by requiring postmasters to account for cash receipts that would balance any postage due stamps no longer in stock, in the same way that they had to account for regular postage stamp sales.

The last postage due stamps were printed in early November, 1985. With the advent of postage meters, the scrapping of the last Cottrell press in November 1985 (the last press capable of printing the current postage due stamps as designed), and finally new regulations requiring full prepayment of postage in all cases, postage due stamps became anachronistic, and their use ceased.

Printed by the American Bank Note Co.
Plates of 200 subjects in two panes of 100 each.

D1   D2

1879		**Unwmk.**	**Engr.**	*Perf. 12*
J1	D1	1c **brown**		90.00 14.00
		Never hinged		250.00
		pale brown		90.00 14.00
		deep brown		90.00 14.00
		Block of 4		400.00 75.00
		P# block of 10, Impt.		1,600.
		Earliest documented use: July 5, 1879.		
J2	D1	2c **brown**		425.00 15.00
		Never hinged		1,100.
		pale brown		425.00 15.00
		Block of 4		1,800. —
		Earliest documented use: July 27, 1879.		
J3	D1	3c **brown**		105.00 6.00
		Never hinged		300.00
		pale brown		105.00 6.00
		deep brown		105.00 6.00
		yellowish brown		115.00 7.00
		Block of 4		460.00 32.50
		P# block of 10, Impt.		1,800.
		Earliest documented use: June 18, 1879.		
J4	D1	5c **brown**		825.00 65.00
		Never hinged		2,100.
		pale brown		825.00 65.00
		deep brown		825.00 65.00
		Block of 4		3,500. —
		Earliest documented use: July 7, 1879.		
J5	D1	10c **brown**, *Sept. 19*		950.00 65.00

	Never hinged	2,500.	
	pale brown	950.00	65.00
	deep brown	950.00	65.00
	Block of 4	4,250.	—
a.	Imperf., pair	3,000.	
	Earliest documented use: Oct. 7, 1879.		
J6	D1 30c **brown**, *Sept. 19*	400.00	60.00
	Never hinged	900.00	
	pale brown	400.00	60.00
	Block of 4	1,700.	—
	P# block of 10, Impt.	5,000.	
J7	D1 50c **brown**, *Sept. 19*	650.00	85.00
	Never hinged	1,750.	
	pale brown	650.00	85.00
	Block of 4	2,900.	—
	P# block of 10, Impt.	12,500.	

SPECIAL PRINTING

1879		**Unwmk.**	*Perf. 12*
		Soft porous paper	
	Printed by the American Bank Note Co.		
J8	D1	1c deep brown *(9,420)*	20,000.
J9	D1	2c deep brown *(1,361)*	15,000.
J10	D1	3c deep brown *(436)*	20,000.
J11	D1	5c deep brown *(249)*	13,500.
J12	D1	10c deep brown *(174)*	8,000.
J13	D1	30c deep brown *(179)*	8,500.
J14	D1	50c deep brown *(179)*	8,000.

Identifying characteristics for the final 8,920 copies of No. J8 delivered to the Post Office are unknown, and it is likely that these were regular issue stamps (No. J1) that were then sold as special printings.

1884		**Unwmk.**	*Perf. 12*
J15	D1	1c **red brown**	75.00 7.00
		Never hinged	200.00
		pale red brown	75.00 7.00
		deep red brown	75.00 7.00
		Block of 4	350.00 45.00
		P# block of 10, Impt.	1,450.
J16	D1	2c **red brown**	90.00 6.00
		Never hinged	250.00
		pale red brown	90.00 6.00
		deep red brown	90.00 6.00
		Block of 4	400.00 37.50
		P# block of 10, Impt.	1,650.
J17	D1	3c **red brown**	1,150. 275.00

	Never hinged	2,500.	
	deep red brown	1,150.	275.00
	Block of 4	5,000.	—
J18	D1 5c **red brown**	625.00	40.00
	Never hinged	1,450.	
	pale red brown	625.00	40.00
	deep red brown	625.00	40.00
	Block of 4	2,850.	
J19	D1 10c **red brown**	625.00	35.00
	Never hinged	1,450.	
	deep red brown	625.00	35.00
	P# block of 10, Impt.	14,000.	
J20	D1 30c **red brown**	225.00	60.00
	Never hinged	550.00	
	deep red brown	225.00	60.00
	Block of 4	1,050.	350.00
	P# block of 10, Impt.	3,500.	
J21	D1 50c **red brown**	1,900.	225.00
	Never hinged	4,250.	
	Block of 4	8,250.	—

1891		**Unwmk.**	*Perf. 12*
J22	D1 1c **bright claret**	35.00	2.00
	Never hinged	95.00	
	light claret	35.00	2.00
	dark claret	35.00	2.00
	Block of 4	160.00	11.00
	P# block of 10, Impt.	625.00	
J23	D1 2c **bright claret**	37.50	2.00
	Never hinged	100.00	
	light claret	37.50	2.00
	dark claret	37.50	2.00
	Block of 4	170.00	11.00
	P# block of 10, Impt.	700.00	
J24	D1 3c **bright claret**	75.00	16.00
	Never hinged	200.00	
	dark claret	75.00	16.00
	Block of 4	350.00	80.00
	P# block of 10, Impt.	1,100.	
J25	D1 5c **bright claret**	110.00	16.00
	Never hinged	325.00	
	light claret	110.00	16.00
	dark claret	110.00	16.00
	Block of 4	500.00	80.00
	P# block of 10, Impt.	1,500.	
J26	D1 10c **bright claret**	180.00	30.00
	Never hinged	550.00	
	light claret	180.00	30.00
	Block of 4	180.00	190.00
	P# block of 10, Impt.	2,500.	

J27 D1 30c **bright claret**	650.00	225.00
Never hinged	1,800.	
Block of 4	2,750.	—
P# block of 10, Impt.	8,750.	
J28 D1 50c **bright claret**	650.00	210.00
Never hinged	1,800.	
dark claret	650.00	210.00
Block of 4	3,000.	—
P# block of 10, Impt.	10,500.	
Nos. J22-J28 (7)	1,737.	501.00

See Die and Plate Proofs for imperfs. on stamp paper.

Printed by the Bureau of Engraving and Printing.

1894		**Unwmk.**		**Perf. 12**
J29 D2 1c **vermilion**	2,400.	725.
pale vermilion	2,400.	725.
Never hinged	5,500.	
Block of 4	10,500.	3,250.
P# block of 6, Impt.	—	
J30 D2 2c **vermilion**	850.	350.
deep vermilion	850.	350.
Never hinged	2,100.	
Block of 4	3,750.	
P# block of 6, Impt.	7,000.	

1894-95

J31 D2 1c **deep claret**, *Aug. 14, 1894*	80.00	12.00
claret	80.00	12.00
lake	80.00	12.00
Never hinged	300.00	
Block of 4	360.00	65.00
P# block of 6, Impt.	675.00	
Never hinged	1,900.	
b. Vertical pair, imperf. horiz.	—	

See Die and Plate Proofs for imperf. on stamp paper.

J32 D2 2c **deep claret**, *July 20, 1894*	70.00	10.00
claret	70.00	10.00
lake	70.00	10.00
Never hinged	275.00	
Block of 4	300.00	65.00
P# block of 6, Impt.	625.00	
Never hinged	1,750.	
J33 D2 3c **deep claret**, *Apr. 27, 1895*	220.00	50.00
lake	220.00	50.00
Never hinged	600.00	
Block of 4	950.00	—
P# block of 6, Impt.	2,400.	
Never hinged	4,250.	
J34 D2 5c **deep claret**, *Apr. 27, 1895*	350.00	55.00
claret	350.00	55.00
Never hinged	1,000.	

Block of 4	1,500.	—
P# block of 6, Impt.	2,750.	
Never hinged	6,500.	
J35 D2 10c **deep claret**, *Sept. 24, 1894*	400.00	40.00
Never hinged	1,100.	
Block of 4	1,750.	—
P# block of 6, Impt.	3,000.	
J36 D2 30c **deep claret**, *Apr. 27, 1895*	600.00	225.00
claret	600.00	225.00
Never hinged	1,400.	
Block of 4	2,750.	—
P# block of 6, Impt.	4,750.	
Never hinged	9,000.	
a. 30c **carmine**	600.00	225.00
Never hinged	1,400.	
Block of 4	2,750.	—
P# block of 6, Impt.	4,750.	
Never hinged	9,000.	
b. 30c **pale rose**	475.00	200.00
Never hinged	1,200.	
Block of 4	2,150.	—
P# block of 6, Impt.	4,000.	
Never hinged	8,000.	
J37 D2 50c **deep claret**, *Apr. 27, 1895*	1,800.	725.00
Never hinged	4,250.	
Block of 4	7,750.	—
a. 50c **pale rose**	1,800.	725.00
Never hinged	4,250.	
Block of 4	7,750.	—
P# block of 6, Impt.	13,000.	

Shades are numerous in the 1894 and later issues.

Wmk. 191 Horizontally or Vertically

1895-97				**Perf. 12**
J38 D2 1c **deep claret**, *Aug. 29, 1895*	15.00	1.00
claret	15.00	1.00
carmine	15.00	1.00
lake	15.00	1.00
Never hinged	40.00	
Block of 4	65.00	8.50
P# block of 6, Impt.	260.00	
Never hinged	420.00	
J39 D2 2c **deep claret**, *Sept. 14, 1895*	15.00	1.00
claret	15.00	1.00
carmine	15.00	1.00
lake	15.00	1.00
Never hinged	40.00	
Block of 4	65.00	8.50
P# block of 6, Impt.	260.00	
Never hingod	420.00	
Double transfer	—	

In October, 1895, the Postmaster at Jefferson, Iowa, surcharged a few 2 cent stamps with the words "Due I cent" in black on each side, subsequently dividing the stamps vertically and using each half as a 1 cent stamp. Twenty of these were used.

J40 D2 3c **deep claret**, *Oct. 30, 1895*	110.00	4.00
claret	110.00	4.00
rose red	110.00	4.00
carmine	110.00	4.00
Never hinged	275.00	
Block of 4	475.00	22.50
P# block of 6, Impt.	1,000.	
Never hinged	1,800.	
J41 D2 5c **deep claret**, *Oct. 15, 1895*	115.00	4.00
claret	115.00	4.00
carmine rose	115.00	4.00
Never hinged	290.00	
Block of 4	500.00	22.50
P# block of 6, Impt.	1,000.	
Never hinged	1,900.	
J42 D2 10c **deep claret**, *Sept. 14, 1895*	115.00	6.00
claret	115.00	6.00
carmine	115.00	6.00
lake	115.00	6.00
Never hinged	290.00	
Block of 4	500.00	37.50
P# block of 6, Impt.	1,000.	
Never hinged	1,900.	
J43 D2 30c **deep claret**, *Aug. 21, 1897*	700.00	70.00
claret	700.00	70.00
Never hinged	1,800.	
Block of 4	3,000.	425.00
P# block of 6, Impt.	6,250.	
J44 D2 50c **deep claret**, *Mar. 17, 1896*	450.00	50.00
claret	450.00	50.00
Never hinged	1,200.	
Block of 4	2,000.	250.00
P# block of 6, Impt.	4,600.	—
Nos. J38-J44 (7)	1,520.	136.00

Plates of 400 subjects in four panes of 100.

1910-12		**Wmk. 190**		**Perf. 12**
J45 D2 1c **deep claret**, *Aug. 30, 1910*	45.00	5.00
Never hinged	130.00	
a. 1c **rose carmine**	40.00	5.00
Never hinged	120.00	
Block of 4 (2 or 3mm spacing)	200.00	20.00
P# block of 6, Impt. & star	525.00	
Never hinged	800.00	
J46 D2 2c **deep claret**, *Nov. 25, 1910*	45.00	2.00
lake	45.00	2.00
Never hinged	130.00	
a. 2c **rose carmine**	40.00	2.00
Never hinged	120.00	
Block of 4 (2 or 3mm spacing)	200.00	7.50
P# block of 6, Impt. & star	500.00	
Never hinged	775.00	
P# block of 6	525.00	
Never hinged	800.00	
Double transfer	—	
J47 D2 3c **deep claret**, *Aug. 31, 1910*	675.00	50.00
lake	675.00	50.00

Never hinged	1,750.	
Block of 4 (2 or 3mm spacing)	2,900.	275
P# block of 6, Impt. & star	6,000.	
Never hinged	11,500.	
J48 D2 5c **deep claret**, *Aug. 31, 1910*	130.00	11.
Never hinged	300.00	
a. 5c **rose carmine**	130.00	11.
Never hinged	300.00	
Block of 4 (2 or 3mm spacing)	550.00	60.
P# block of 6, Impt. & star	1,150.	
Never hinged	1,900.	
J49 D2 10c **deep claret**, *Aug. 31, 1910*	140.00	20.
Never hinged	360.00	
Block of 4 (2 or 3mm spacing)	600.00	120.
P# block of 6, Impt. & star	1,500.	
a. 10c **rose carmine**	140.00	20.
Never hinged	360.00	
J50 D2 50c **deep claret**, *Sept. 23, 1912*	1,150.	175.
Never hinged	3,000.	
Block of 4 (2 or 3mm spacing)	5,000.	
P# block of 6, Impt. & star	10,000.	

1914				**Perf. 1**
J52 D2 1c **carmine lake**	85.00	15.
deep carmine lake	85.00	15.
Never hinged	250.00	
Block of 4 (2 or 3mm spacing)	375.00	80.
P# block of 6, Impt. & star	700.00	—
Never hinged	1,500.	
a. 1c **dull rose**	90.00	15.
Never hinged	260.00	
Block of 4 (2 or 3mm spacing)	400.00	85.
P# block of 6, Impt. & star	725.00	
Never hinged	1,600.	
J53 D2 2c **carmine lake**	60.00	1.
Never hinged	170.00	
Block of 4	250.00	8.
P# block of 6	550.00	
Never hinged	1,100.	
a. 2c **dull rose**	65.00	2.
Block of 4	190.00	15.
b. 2c **vermilion**	65.00	2.
Never hinged	190.00	
Block of 4	275.00	14.
P# block of 6	600.00	
Never hinged	1,250.	
J54 D2 3c **carmine lake**	1,150.	70.
Never hinged	3,300.	
Block of 4 (2 or 3mm spacing)	5,250.	
P# block of 6, Impt. & star	9,500.	—
a. 3c **dull rose**	1,100.	70.
Never hinged	3,250.	
Block of 4 (2 or 3mm spacing)	5,000.	
P# block of 6, Impt. & star	9,000.	—
J55 D2 5c **carmine lake**	55.00	5.
Never hinged	160.00	
Block of 4 (2 or 3mm spacing)	240.00	30.
P# block of 6, Impt. & star	475.00	
Never hinged	1,050.	
a. 5c **dull rose**	85.00	4.00
carmine rose	45.00	4.00
Never hinged	150.00	
deep claret	—	
Block of 4 (2 or 3mm spacing)	200.00	20.00
P# block of 6, Impt. & star	400.00	
Never hinged	1,000.	
J56 D2 10c **carmine lake**	80.00	4.00
Never hinged	220.00	
Block of 4 (2 or 3mm spacing)	350.00	22.50
P# block of 6, Impt. & star	775.00	
a. 10c **dull rose**	85.00	5.00
carmine rose	85.00	5.00
Never hinged	240.00	
Block of 4 (2 or 3mm spacing)	375.00	25.00
P# block of 6, Impt. & star	900.00	
Never hinged	1,600.	
J57 D2 30c **carmine lake**	250.00	25.00
Never hinged	575.00	
Block of 4 (2 or 3mm spacing)	1,100.	150.00
P# block of 6, Impt. & star	2,900.	
J58 D2 50c **carmine lake**	17,500.	1,350.
Never hinged	32,500.	
Precanceled		725.00
Block of 4 (2 or 3mm spacing)	75,000.	6,500.
P# block of 6, Impt. & star	125,000.	

No. J58, precanceled, was used at Buffalo (normal, inverted) and Chicago (normal, inverted, double, double inverted).

1916		**Unwmk.**		**Perf. 10**
J59 D2 1c **rose**	4,500.	625.00
Never hinged	10,000.	
Block of 4 (2 or 3mm spacing)	21,000.	3,250.
P# block of 6, Impt. & star	31,500.	
Experimental bureau precancel, New Orleans	350.00	
J60 D2 2c **rose**	250.00	75.00
Never hinged	650.00	
Block of 4	1,100.	350.00
P# block of 6	2,150.	—
Experimental bureau precancel, New Orleans	35.00	

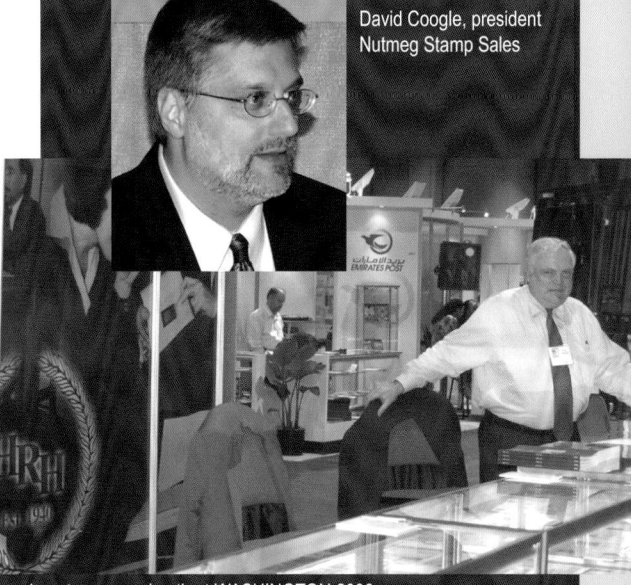

17   Unwmk.   *Perf. 11*

1	D2	1c **carmine rose**	3.00	.25
		dull rose	3.00	.25
		Never hinged	10.00	
a.		1c **rose red**	3.00	.25
		Never hinged	10.00	
b.		1c **deep claret**	3.00	.25
		claret brown	3.00	.25
		Never hinged	10.00	
		Block of 4 (2 or 3mm spacing)	13.00	2.00
		P# block of 6, Impt. & star	125.00	—
		Never hinged	250.00	
		P# block of 6	45.00	—
		Never hinged	90.00	
2	D2	2c **carmine rose**	3.00	.25
		Never hinged	10.00	
a.		2c **rose red**	3.00	.25
		Never hinged	10.00	
b.		2c **deep claret**	3.00	.25
		claret brown	3.00	1.10
		Never hinged	10.00	
		Block of 4	13.00	2.00
		Never hinged	42.50	
		P# block of 6	45.00	—
		Never hinged	90.00	
		Double transfer	—	—
63	D2	3c **carmine rose**	15.00	.80
		Never hinged	40.00	
a.		3c **rose red**	15.00	.80
		Never hinged	40.00	
b.		3c **deep claret**	15.00	.80
		claret brown	15.00	.80
		Never hinged	40.00	
		Block of 4 (2 or 3mm spacing)	65.00	5.00
		P# block of 6, Impt. & star	150.00	—
		Never hinged	275.00	
		P# block of 6	125.00	—
		Never hinged	260.00	
64	D2	5c **carmine rose**	12.50	.80
		carmine rose	12.50	.80
		Never hinged	37.50	
a.		5c **rose red**	12.50	.80
		Never hinged	37.50	
b.		5c **deep claret**	12.50	.80
		claret brown	12.50	.80
		Never hinged	37.50	
		Block of 4 (2 or 3mm spacing)	52.50	6.00
		P# block of 6, Impt. & star	125.00	—
		Never hinged	250.00	
		P# block of 6	105.00	—
		Never hinged	240.00	
65	D2	10c **carmine rose**	25.00	1.00
		Never hinged	70.00	
a.		10c **rose red**	25.00	1.00
		Never hinged	70.00	
b.		10c **deep claret**	25.00	1.00
		claret brown	25.00	1.00
		Never hinged	70.00	
		Block of 4 (2 or 3mm spacing)	110.00	7.50
		P# block of 6, Impt. & star	220.00	—
		Never hinged	450.00	
		P# block of 6	240.00	—
		Never hinged	500.00	
		Double transfer	—	—
66	D2	30c **carmine rose**	90.00	2.00
		Never hinged	260.00	
a.		30c **deep claret**	90.00	2.00
		claret brown	90.00	2.00
		Never hinged	260.00	
		Block of 4 (2 or 3mm spacing)	390.00	14.00
		P# block of 6, Impt. & star	725.00	—
		P# block of 6	750.00	—
67	D2	50c **carmine rose**	150.00	1.00
		Never hinged	370.00	
a.		50c **rose red**	150.00	1.00
		Never hinged	370.00	
b.		50c **deep claret**	150.00	1.00
		claret brown	150.00	1.00
		Never hinged	370.00	
		Block of 4 (2 or 3mm spacing)	625.00	7.50
		P# block of 6, Impt. & star	1,100.	—
		Never hinged	2,500.	
		P# block of 6	1,150.	

1925, Apr. 13

J68	D2	½c **dull red**	1.00	.25
		Never hinged	1.75	
		Block of 4	4.00	1.50
		P# block of 6	12.50	—
		Never hinged	17.50	

D3   D4

1930   Unwmk.   *Perf. 11*

Design measures 19x22mm

J69	D3	½c **carmine**	4.50	1.90
		Never hinged	10.00	
		P# block of 6	42.50	—
		Never hinged	70.00	
J70	D3	1c **carmine**	3.00	.35
		Never hinged	7.00	
		P# block of 6	30.00	—
		Never hinged	50.00	

J71	D3	2c **carmine**	4.00	.35
		Never hinged	9.00	
		P# block of 6	45.00	—
		Never hinged	70.00	
J72	D3	3c **carmine**	21.00	2.75
		Never hinged	50.00	
		P# block of 6	275.00	—
		Never hinged	425.00	
J73	D3	5c **carmine**	19.00	5.00
		Never hinged	45.00	
		P# block of 6	250.00	—
		Never hinged	400.00	
J74	D3	10c **carmine**	45.00	2.00
		Never hinged	95.00	
		P# block of 6	475.00	—
		Never hinged	700.00	
J75	D3	30c **carmine**	150.00	4.00
		Never hinged	325.00	
		P# block of 6	1,150.	—
		Never hinged	2,150.	
J76	D3	50c **carmine**	200.00	2.00
		Never hinged	450.00	
		P# block of 6	1,750.	—
		Never hinged	3,000.	

Design measures 22x19mm

J77	D4	$1 **carmine**	35.00	.35
		Never hinged	70.00	
		P# block of 6	250.00	—
		Never hinged	475.00	
a.		$1 **scarlet**	30.00	.35
		Never hinged	60.00	
		P# block of 6	275.00	—
		Never hinged	500.00	
J78	D4	$5 **carmine**	40.00	.35
		Never hinged	90.00	
		P# block of 6	300.00	—
		Never hinged	600.00	
a.		$5 **scarlet**	35.00	.35
		Never hinged	75.00	
		P# block of 6	260.00	—
		Never hinged	525.00	
b.		As "a," wet printing	40.00	.35
		Never hinged	90.00	
		P# block of 6	300.00	—
		Never hinged	600.00	

See note on Wet and Dry Printings following No. 1029.

Type of 1930-31 Issue
Rotary Press Printing
Ordinary and Electric Eye Plates
Design measures 19x22½mm

1931   Unwmk.   *Perf. 11x10½*

J79	D3	½c **dull carmine**	.90	.20
		Never hinged	1.30	
a.		½c **scarlet**	.90	.20
		Never hinged	1.30	
		P# block of 4	20.00	—
		Never hinged	30.00	
J80	D3	1c **dull carmine**	.20	.20
		Never hinged	.30	
a.		1c **scarlet**	.20	.20
		Never hinged	.30	
		P# block of 4 (#25635, 25636)	1.50	—
		Never hinged	2.25	
b.		As "a," wet printing	.20	.20
		Never hinged	.20	
		P# block of 4	1.75	—
		Never hinged	2.50	
		Pair with full vertical gutter between	—	
J81	D3	2c **dull carmine**	.20	.20
		Never hinged	.30	
a.		2c **scarlet**	.20	.20
		Never hinged	.30	
		P# block of 4 (#25637, 25638)	1.50	—
		Never hinged	2.25	
b.		As "a," wet printing	.20	.20
		Never hinged	.30	
		P# block of 4	2.00	—
		Never hinged	2.75	
J82	D3	3c **dull carmine**	.25	.20
		Never hinged	.40	
a.		3c **scarlet**	.25	.20
		Never hinged	.40	
		P# block of 4 (#25641, 25642)	2.25	—
		Never hinged	3.25	
b.		As "a," wet printing	.30	.20
		Never hinged	.45	
		P# block of 4	2.50	—
		Never hinged	3.50	
J83	D3	5c **dull carmine**	.40	.20
		Never hinged	.60	
a.		5c **scarlet**	.40	.20
		Never hinged	.60	
		P# block of 4 (#25643, 25644)	3.00	—
		Never hinged	4.25	
b.		As "a," wet printing	.50	.20
		Never hinged	.75	
		P# block of 4	3.50	—
		Never hinged	4.75	
J84	D3	10c **dull carmine**	1.10	.20
		Never hinged	1.80	
a.		10c **scarlet**	1.10	.20
		Never hinged	1.80	
		P# block of 4 (#25645, 25646)	6.50	—
		Never hinged	8.75	
b.		As "a," wet printing	1.25	.20
		Never hinged	1.90	
		P# block of 4	7.00	—
		Never hinged	9.25	
J85	D3	30c **dull carmine**	7.50	.25
		Never hinged	11.50	
a.		30c **scarlet**	7.50	.25
		Never hinged	11.50	
		P# block of 4	35.00	—
		Never hinged	50.00	

J86	D3	50c **dull carmine**	9.00	.25
		Never hinged	15.00	
a.		50c **scarlet**	9.00	.25
		Never hinged	15.00	
		P# block of 4	52.50	—
		Never hinged	75.00	

Design measures 22½x19mm

1956   *Perf. 10½x11*

J87	D4	$1 **scarlet**	30.00	.25
		Never hinged	47.50	
		P# block of 4	190.00	—
		Never hinged	275.00	
		Nos. J79-J87 (9)	49.55	1.95

> **Catalogue values for unused stamps in this section, from this point to the end, are for Never Hinged items.**

D5

Rotary Press Printing

Denominations added in black by rubber plates in an operation similar to precanceling.

1959, June 19   Unwmk.   *Perf. 11x10½*
Denomination in Black

J88	D5	½c **carmine rose**	1.50	1.10
		P# block of 4	150.00	
J89	D5	1c **carmine rose**, shiny gum	.20	.20
		P# block of 4	.35	—
		Dull gum	.25	
		P# block of 4	4.50	
a.		Denomination omitted	250.00	
b.		Pair, one without "1 CENT"	500.00	
J90	D5	2c **carmine rose**, shiny gum	.20	.20
		P# block of 4	.45	
		Wide spacing, pair	120.00	
		Dull gum	.40	
		P# block of 4	12.50	
J91	D5	3c **carmine rose**, shiny gum	.20	.20
		P# block of 4	.50	
		Dull gum	.50	
		P# block of 4	15.00	
a.		Pair, one without "3 CENTS"	675.00	
J92	D5	4c **carmine rose**	.20	.20
		P# block of 4	.60	—
		Wide spacing, pair	120.00	
J93	D5	5c **carmine rose**, shiny gum	.20	.20
		P# block of 4	.65	
		Dull gum	.45	
		P# block of 4	8.00	
a.		Pair, one without "5 CENTS"	1,500.	
J94	D5	6c **carmine rose**, shiny gum	.20	.20
		P# block of 4	.70	—
		Pair with full vertical gutter between		
		Dull gum	100.00	
		P# block of 4	1,250.	
a.		Pair, one without "6 CENTS"	850.00	

J95	D5	7c **carmine rose**, shiny gum	.20	.20

J95 D5 7c **carmine rose**, shiny gum .20 .20
      P# block of 4 .80
      Wide spacing, pair 120.00
      Dull gum 750.00
      P# block of 4 7,500.
J96 D5 8c **carmine rose** .20 .20
      P# block of 4 .90
      Wide spacing, pair 120.00
  a. **Pair, one without "8 CENTS"** 850.00
J97 D5 10c **carmine rose**, shiny gum .20 .20
      P# block of 4 1.00
      Dull gum .35
      P# block of 4 5.00
J98 D5 30c **carmine rose**, shiny gum .75 .20
      P# block of 4 3.50
      Dull gum 1.00
      P# block of 4 16.00
J99 D5 50c **carmine rose**, shiny gum 1.10 .20

      P# block of 4 5.00 —
      Dull gum 1.75
      P# block of 4 20.00
Straight Numeral Outlined in Black
J100 D5 $1 **carmine rose**, shiny gum 2.00 .20
      P# block of 4 8.50
      Dull gum 2.50
      P# block of 4 22.50
J101 D5 $5 **carmine rose**, shiny gum 9.00 .20
      P# block of 4 40.00
      Dull gum 11.00
      P# block of 4 65.00
      Nos. J88–J101 (14) 16.15 3.70
All single copies with denomination omitted are catalogued as No. J89a.

	Rotary Press Printing	
1978-85		*Perf. 11x1●*
	Denomination in Black	

J102 D5 11c **carmine rose**, *Jan. 2, 1978* .25
      P# block of 4 2.00
J103 D5 13c **carmine rose**, *Jan. 2, 1978* .25
      P# block of 4 2.00
J104 D5 17c **carmine rose**, *June 10, 1985* .40
      P# block of 4 22.50

U.S. POSTAL AGENCY IN CHINA

Postage stamps of the 1917-19 U.S. series (then current) were issued to the U.S. Postal Agency, Shanghai, China, surcharged at double the origina●
value of the stamps.

These stamps were intended for sale at Shanghai at their surcharged value in local currency, valid for prepayment on mail despatched from the U.S●
Postal Agency at Shanghai to addresses in the U.S.

Stamps were first issued May 24, 1919, and were placed on sale at Shanghai on July 1, 1919. These stamps were not issued to postmasters in th●
U.S. The Shanghai post office, according to the U.S.P.O. Bulletin, was closed in December 1922. The stamps were on sale at the Philatelic Agency ●
Washington, D.C. for a short time after that.

Italicized numbers in parentheses indicate quantities shipped to the postal agency in Shanghai and to the Washington Philatelic Agency. In the cas●
of Nos. K17-K18, the numbers are the quantity locally overprinted. All Nos. K16a, K17 and K18 are believed to have been sold. The final disposition ●
remainders of the others is not known. Neither the records of the Shanghai Postal Agency nor the records of the Washington Philatelic Agency hav●
been located at this time. Authority for quantities shipped is the research of Joseph M. Napp, who in turn benefitted by the research of Meyer Tuchinsk●

The cancellations of the China office included "U.S. Postal Agency Shanghai China", "U.S. Pos. Service Shanghai China" duplexes, and th●
Shanghai parcel post roller cancel.

United States Stamps #498-
499, 502-504, 506-510, 512,
514-518 Surcharged in Black
or Red (Nos. K7, K16)

1919   Unwmk.   Perf. 11
K1 A140 2c on 1c **green** (*355,000*) 25.00 35.00
      Never hinged 70.00
      Block of 4 110.00 210.00
      P# block of 6 300.00 —
      Never hinged 600.00
      Double transfer 42.50
      Never hinged 110.00

      Earliest documented use: July 2, 1919.

K2 A140 4c on 2c **rose**, type I (*355,000*) 25.00 35.00
      Never hinged 70.00
      Block of 4 110.00 220.00
      P# block of 6 300.00 —
      Never hinged 600.00

      Earliest documented use: July 2, 1919.

K3 A140 6c on 3c **violet**, type II,
      (*113,000*) 57.50 85.00
      Never hinged 140.00
      Block of 4 250.00 450.00
      P# block of 6 650.00 —
      Never hinged 1,100.
K4 A140 8c on 4c **brown** (*113,000*) 57.50 85.00
      Never hinged 140.00
      Block of 4 250.00 475.00
      P# block of 6 650.00 —
      Never hinged 1,100.
K5 A140 10c on 5c **blue** (*113,000*) 65.00 85.00
      Never hinged 170.00
      Block of 4 280.00 450.00
      P# block of 6 600.00 —
      Never hinged 1,100.
K6 A140 12c on 6c **red orange** (*113,000*) 85.00 120.00
      Never hinged 220.00
      Block of 4 375.00 700.00
      P# block of 6 800.00 —
      Never hinged 1,500.
K7 A140 14c on 7c **black** (*113,000*) 87.50 140.00
      Never hinged 210.00
      Block of 4 400.00 850.00
      P# block of 6 1,050.
      Never hinged 1,650.
K8 A148 16c on 8c **olive bister** (*13,000*) 65.00 90.00
      Never hinged 170.00
      Block of 4 280.00 575.00
      P# block of 6 600.00
      Never hinged 1,100.
  a. **16c on 8c olive green** (*100,000*) 60.00 75.00
      Never hinged 160.00
      Block of 4 260.00 525.00
      P# block of 6 575.00
      Never hinged 1,000.
K9 A148 18c on 9c **salmon red** (*113,000*) 65.00 100.00
      Never hinged 170.00
      Block of 4 280.00 550.00
      P# block of 6 700.00

            Never hinged 1,200.
K10 A148 20c on 10c **orange yellow**
      (*113,000*) 60.00 80.00
      Never hinged 160.00
      Block of 4 260.00 425.00
      P# block of 6 725.00
      Never hinged 1,300.
K11 A148 24c on 12c **brown carmine**
      (*50,000*) 80.00 90.00
      Never hinged 200.00
      Block of 4 350.00 425.00
      P# block of 6 1,000.
      Never hinged 2,000.
  a. **24c on 12c claret brown** (*8,000*) 105.00 140.00
      Never hinged 270.00
      Block of 4 450.00 725.00
      P# block of 6 1,150.
      Never hinged 2,000.
K12 A148 30c on 15c **gray** (*58,000*) 87.50 160.00
      Never hinged 210.00
      Block of 4 375.00 —
      P# block of 6 1,150.
      Never hinged 2,000.
K13 A148 40c on 20c **deep ultramarine**
      (*58,000*) 130.00 250.00
      Never hinged 300.00
      Block of 4 550.00 1,450.
      P# block of 6 1,300.
      Never hinged 2,250.
K14 A148 60c on 30c **orange red** (*58,000*) 120.00 200.00
      Never hinged 280.00
      Block of 4 525.00 1,250.
      P# block of 6 1,050.
      Never hinged 1,800.
K15 A148 $1 on 50c **light violet** (*14,000*) 575.00 700.00
      Never hinged 1,300.
      Block of 4 2,500. 5,000.
      P# block of 6 17,500.
K16 A148 $2 on $1 **violet brown** (*13,800*) 450.00 575.00
      Never hinged 1,000.
      Block of 4 2,000. 4,750.
      Margin block of 4, arrow, right
      or left 2,100.
      P# block of 6 7,000.
      Never hinged 11,000.
  a. **Double surcharge** (*200*) 7,750. 8,000.
      Never hinged 12,500.
      Block of 4
      Nos. K1–K16 (16) 2,035. 2,830.

A fake of No. K1 has recently been discovered. Other values
exist, but those examined are rather crudely made.

United States Stamps Nos.
498 and 528B Locally
Surcharged

1922, July 3
K17 A140 2c on 1c **green** (*10,000*) 110.00 140.00
      Never hinged 250.00
      Block of 4 475.00 650.00

      P# block of 6 850.00
      Never hinged 1,750.
K18 A140 4c on 2c **carmine**, type VII
      (*10,000*) 100.00 120.0●
      Never hinged 230.00
      Block of 4 425.00 550.0●
      P# block of 6 800.00
      Never hinged 1,400.
  a. **"SHANGHAI" omitted** 5,000.
  b. **"CHINA" only** 15,000.

OFFICIAL STAMPS

The original official stamps were authorized by Act of Congress, approved March 3, 1873, abolishing the franking privilege. Stamps for each executive government department were issued July 1, 1873.

Penalty franks were first authorized in 1877, and their expanded use after 1879 reduced the need for official stamps, the use of which was finally abolished on July 5, 1884.

DESIGNS. Stamps for departments other than the Post Office picture the same busts used in the regular postage issue: 1c Franklin, 2c Jackson, 3c Washington, 6c Lincoln, 7c Stanton, 10c Jefferson, 12c Clay, 15c Webster, 24c Scott, 30c Hamilton, and 90c Perry. William H. Seward appears on the $2, $5, $10 and $20.

Designs of the various denominations are not identical, but resemble those illustrated.

PLATES. Plates of 200 subjects in two panes of 100 were used for Post Office Department 1c, 3c, 6c; Treasury Department 1c, 2c, 3c, and War Department 2c, 3c. Plates of 10 subjects were used for State Department $2, $5, $10 and $20. Plates of 100 subjects were used for all other Official stamps up to No. O120.

CANCELLATIONS. Odd or Town cancellations on Departmental stamps are relatively much scarcer than those appearing on the general issues of the same period. Town cancellations, especially on the 1873 issue, are scarce. The "Kicking Mule" cancellation is found used on stamps of the War Department and has also been seen on some stamps of the other Departments. Black is usual.

Grade, condition and presence of original gum are very important in valuing Nos. O1-O120.
As is done elsewhere in this catalogue, all Officials are valued in the grade of very fine. If unused, they will have original gum.

Printed by the Continental Bank Note Co.
Thin Hard Paper

O1   Franklin — O2

AGRICULTURE

1873   Engr.   Unwmk.   Perf. 12

				Un	Used
O1	O1	1c	**yellow**	270.00	*180.00*
			golden yellow	300.00	*200.00*
			olive yellow	300.00	*200.00*
			No gum	160.00	
			On wrapper		*1,250.*
			Block of 4	1,200.	
			Ribbed paper	325.00	200.00
			Cancellations		
			Magenta		+7.50
			Violet		+7.50
			Blue		+5.00
			Red		+50.00
			Town		+7.50
			Fort		+150.00
O2	O1	2c	**yellow**	230.00	85.00
			golden yellow	250.00	90.00
			olive yellow	250.00	90.00
			No gum	100.00	
			On cover		*3,500.*
			Block of 4	1,000.	
			P# block of 12	—	
			Ribbed paper	230.00	95.00
			Cancellations		
			Blue		+3.00
			Violet		+3.00
			Red		+15.00
			Magenta		+5.00
			Town		+5.00
O3	O1	3c	**yellow**	210.00	16.00
			golden yellow	225.00	20.00
			olive yellow	225.00	20.00
			No gum	80.00	
			On cover		*900.00*
			Block of 4	1,000.	—
			P# block of 12, Impt., never hinged	3,750.	
			Ribbed paper	225.00	16.00
			Double transfer	—	—
			Short transfer at upper left (pos. 10, 18, 28)	—	—

The never hinged, bottom left plate block of No. O3 is the only plate block of this number recorded.

Cancellations		
Blue		+.50
Purple		+1.00
Magenta		+1.00
Violet		+1.00
Red		+17.50
Indigo		+10.00
Green		+200.00
Brown		+20.00
Town		+4.00
"Paid"		+27.50
Numeral		+35.00
Railroad		+75.00
Express Company		+900.00

O4	O1	6c	**yellow**	240.00	60.00
			golden yellow	300.00	80.00
			olive yellow	300.00	80.00
			No gum	95.00	

On cover			*7,500.*
Block of 4	1,150.		
Cancellations			
Blue			+3.00
Magenta			+4.00
Violet			+5.00
Red			+50.00
Town			+7.00
"Paid"			+27.50
Numeral			+35.00
Express Company			—
Revenue			—

O5	O1	10c	**yellow**	500.00	200.00
			golden yellow	550.00	250.00
			olive yellow	550.00	250.00
			No gum	220.00	
			On cover (parcel label)		—
			Block of 4	2,250.	
			Cancellations		
			Violet		+5.00
			Blue		+5.00
			Red		+50.00
			Town		+25.00
O6	O1	12c	**yellow**	425.00	250.00
			golden yellow	525.00	300.00
			olive yellow	525.00	300.00
			No gum	250.00	
			On cover		*11,000.*
			Block of 4	1,850.	
			Cancellations		
			Violet		+10.00
			Blue		+10.00
			Red		+50.00
			Town		+30.00
O7	O1	15c	**yellow**	425.00	220.00
			golden yellow	500.00	250.00
			olive yellow	500.00	250.00
			No gum	225.00	
			Block of 4	1,850.	
			Cancellations		
			Purple		+10.00
			Blue		+10.00
			Recut top left frame line (pos. 100)	—	725.00
O8	O1	24c	**yellow**	425.00	210.00
			golden yellow	500.00	250.00
			No gum	225.00	
			On parcel label		—
			Block of 4	1,850.	
			Cancellation		
			Violet		+10.00
O9	O1	30c	**yellow**	500.00	270.00
			golden yellow	600.00	300.00
			olive yellow	600.00	300.00
			No gum	275.00	
			Block of 4	2,250.	
			Cancellations		
			Blue		+10.00
			Red		+65.00

EXECUTIVE

1873

O10	O2	1c	**carmine**	850.00	475.00
			deep carmine	850.00	475.00
			No gum	450.00	
			On cover with No. O11		*3,000.*
			On cover, single franking		*2,900.*
			Block of 4	4,250.	

The only known block is with original gum and is off-center with perfs just cutting into design. It is valued thus.

Cancellations			
Violet			+10.00
Blue favor			+10.00
Red			+50.00
Town			+30.00

O11	O2	2c	**carmine**	550.00	240.00
			deep carmine	550.00	240.00
			No gum	240.00	
			On cover, single franking		*3,750.*
			Block of 4	3,250.	
			Foreign entry of 6c Agriculture (pos. 40)	2,300.	
			Cancellations		
			Violet		+10.00
			Blue favor		+10.00
			Red		+50.00

O12	O2	3c	**carmine**	700.00	210.00
a.			3c **violet rose**	700.00	210.00

No gum	270.00		
On cover			*1,000.*
On cover from Long Branch, N.J.			*4,500.*
Block of 4	3,250.		
Cancellations			
Blue favor			+10.00
Violet			+10.00
Indigo			+20.00
Red			+50.00
Town			+35.00

O13	O2	6c	**carmine**	825.00	550.00
			pale carmine	825.00	550.00
			deep carmine	825.00	550.00
			No gum	325.00	
			On cover		*3,500.*
			Double transfer (pos. 6)	2,250.	
			Cancellations		
			Violet		+15.00
			Blue favor		+15.00
			Town		+50.00
			New York Foreign Mail		—
O14	O2	10c	**carmine**	1,100.	650.00
			pale carmine	1,100.	650.00
			deep carmine	1,100.	650.00
			No gum	600.00	
			On cover		—
			Block of 4	5,000.	
			Cancellations		
			Violet		+15.00
			Blue favor		+15.00

O3   O4

INTERIOR

1873

O15	O3	1c	**vermilion**	75.00	10.00
			dull vermilion	75.00	10.00
			bright vermilion	75.00	10.00
			No gum	30.00	
			On cover		160.00
			Block of 4	325.00	325.00
			P# block of 10, Impt.	1,000.	
			Never hinged	1,500.	
			Ribbed paper	85.00	20.00
			Short transfer at bottom right (pos. 91)	—	—

Cancellations

Violet		+1.00
Blue		+1.00
Red		+12.50
Ultramarine		+8.00
Town		+3.00

O16	O3	2c	**vermilion**	70.00	12.00
			dull vermilion	70.00	12.00
			bright vermilion	70.00	12.00
			No gum	30.00	
			On cover		65.00
			Block of 4	300.00	300.00
			P# block of 10, Impt.	950.00	
			P# block of 12, Impt.	1,050.	

Cancellations

Purple		+.75
Violet		+.75
Blue		+.75
Red		+6.00
Town		+7.50
Numeral		+20.00
"Paid"		+20.00

O17	O3	3c	**vermilion**	80.00	6.00
			dull vermilion	80.00	6.00
			bright vermilion	80.00	6.00
			No gum	35.00	
			On cover		40.00
			First day cover, Nos. O17, O18, *July 1, 1873*		9,000.
			Block of 4	350.00	350.00
			P# block of 10, Impt.	975.00	
			Ribbed paper	100.00	10.00

Cancellations

Violet		+1.00
Blue		+1.00
Indigo		+3.00
Magenta		+5.00
Red		+15.00
Green		+65.00
Town		+7.50
Numeral		+20.00
Express Company		+75.00
"Paid"		+20.00
Fort		—

O18	O3	6c	**vermilion**	70.00	10.00
			dull vermilion	70.00	10.00
			bright vermilion	70.00	10.00
			scarlet vermilion	70.00	10.00
			No gum	27.50	
			On cover		95.00
			Block of 4	350.00	—
			P# block of 10, Impt.	950.00	

Cancellations

Violet		+1.00
Blue		+1.00
Red		+15.00
Town		+7.50
Express Company		—
Railroad		—
Fort		—

See No. O17 for first day cover listing.

O19	O3	10c	**vermilion**	70.00	20.00
			dull vermilion	70.00	20.00
			bright vermilion	70.00	20.00
			No gum	27.50	
			On cover		450.00
			Block of 4	350.00	—
			P# block of 12, Impt.	950.00	

Cancellations

Violet		+1.00
Blue		+1.00
Indigo		+10.00
Red		+25.00
Town		+10.00
Fort		—
New York Foreign Mail		+300.00

O20	O3	12c	**vermilion**	90.00	12.00
			bright vermilion	90.00	12.00
			No gum	35.00	
			On cover		450.00
			Block of 4	400.00	500.00
			P# block of 10, Impt.	1,150.	
			Short transfer at right (pos. 6)	—	—

Cancellations

Violet		+1.00
Magenta		+1.00
Blue		+1.00
Red		+15.00
Brown		+20.00
Town		+7.50
Fort		—

O21	O3	15c	**vermilion**	200.00	25.00
			bright vermilion	200.00	25.00
			No gum	80.00	
			On cover		650.00
			Block of 4	900.00	—
			P# block of 12, Impt.	—	
			Double transfer of left side	275.00	37.50

Cancellations

Blue		+1.50
Violet		+1.50
Town		+5.00

O22	O3	24c	**vermilion**	180.00	20.00
			dull vermilion	180.00	20.00
			bright vermilion	180.00	20.00
			No gum	60.00	
			On cover		2,500.
			Block of 4	775.00	2,000.
			P# block of 12, Impt.	2,500.	
a.			Double impression		—

Cancellations

Violet		+1.50
Blue		+1.50
Red		+15.00
Town		+5.00

O23	O3	30c	**vermilion**	275.00	20.00
			bright vermilion	275.00	20.00
			No gum	100.00	
			On parcel label		2,850.
			Block of 4	1,200.	—
			P# block of 12, Impt.	4,000.	

Cancellations

Violet		+2.00
Blue		+2.00
Red		+50.00
Town		+7.50

O24	O3	90c	**vermilion**	300.00	50.00
			bright vermilion	300.00	50.00
			No gum	120.00	
			On cover		4,500.
			Block of 4	1,500.	—
			P# block of 12, Impt.	4,500.	
			Double transfer	360.00	
			Major double transfer (Pos. 17)	575.00	250.00
			Short transfer at right (Pos. 56)	—	
			Silk paper	—	

Cancellations

Violet		+4.00
Blue		+4.00
Magenta		+10.00
Red		+50.00
Brown		+60.00
Town		+17.50

JUSTICE

1873

O25	O4	1c	**purple**	250.00	100.00
			dark purple	250.00	100.00
			No gum	100.00	
			On cover		1,750.
			On cover with No. O26		4,000.
			Block of 4	1,100.	
			Double transfer	—	—

Cancellations

Violet		+3.00
Blue		+3.00
Indigo		+5.00
Magenta		+5.00
Red		+20.00
Town		+7.50

O26	O4	2c	**purple**	310.00	110.00
			light purple	310.00	110.00
			No gum	120.00	
			On cover		1,500.
			Block of 4	1,400.	
			Short transfer at right side (pos. 3)	—	

Cancellations

Violet		+4.00
Blue		+4.00
Ultramarine		+10.00
Indigo		+5.00
Magenta		+5.00
Red		+20.00

O27	O4	3c	**purple**	320.00	35.00
			dark purple	320.00	35.00
			bluish purple	320.00	35.00
			No gum	110.00	
			On cover		575.00
			Block of 4	1,450.	
			Double transfer	—	

Cancellations

Violet		+2.00
Magenta		+2.00
Blue		+2.00
Ultramarine		+10.00
Indigo		+5.00
Red		+12.00
Green		+100.00
Town		+15.00

O28	O4	6c	**purple**	310.00	45.00
			light purple	310.00	45.00
			bluish purple	310.00	45.00
			No gum	120.00	
			On cover		1,200.
			Block of 4	1,400.	

Cancellations

Violet		+2.00
Blue		+2.00
Indigo		+5.00
Magenta		+5.00
Red		+15.00
Town		+17.50

O29	O4	10c	**purple**	310.00	100.00
			bluish purple	310.00	100.00
			No gum	120.00	
			On cover		3,750.
			Block of 4	1,400.	—
			P# block of 10, Impt.	6,000.	
			Double transfer	—	—

Cancellations

Violet		+4.00
Blue		+4.00
Magenta		+5.00

			Town		+17.
O30	O4	12c	**purple**	260.00	75.
			dark purple	260.00	75.
			No gum	95.00	
			On cover		1,75
			Block of 4	925.00	

Cancellations

Purple		+2.
Violet		+2.
Blue		+2.
Magenta		+5.
Red		+35.
Town		+17.

O31	O4	15c	**purple**	450.00	200.
			No gum	210.00	
			On cover		1,25
			Block of 4	2,250.	
			Double transfer	—	

Cancellations

Violet		+5.
Blue		+5.
Indigo		+5.
Magenta		+10.0
Red		+35.0
Town		+10.0

The block of 4 of No. O31 is unique. It is in the grade of fin and is valued thus.

O32	O4	24c	**purple**	1,250.	425.0
			No gum	550.00	
			On cover		8,00
			Short transfer (pos. 98)	—	

Cancellations

Violet		+10.0
Blue		+10.0
Magenta		+10.0
Red		+35.0
Town		+40.0

O33	O4	30c	**purple**	1,250.	325.0
			No gum	550.00	
			On cover with Nos. O27 & O28		22,00
			Block of 4	5,000.	
			Double transfer at top	1,350.	350.0

Cancellations

Purple		+10.0
Violet		+10.0
Blue		+10.0
Magenta		+10.0
Red		+50.0
Town		+40.0

The block of 4 of No. O33 is unique. It is in the grade of fin and is valued thus.

O34	O4	90c	**purple**	1,750.	700.0
			dark purple	1,750.	650.0
			No gum	700.00	
			On cover with No. O33		26,000
			Pair	—	
			Double plate scratch	—	
			Triple transfer at top	—	

Cancellations

Purple		+25.0
Violet		+25.0
Blue		+25.0
Magenta		+25.0

No. O34 on cover is unique. The cover bears three No. O34 and four No. O33.

O5　　　　　　　O6

NAVY

1873

O35	O5	1c	**ultramarine**	160.00	50.00
			dark ultramarine	160.00	50.00
			No gum	65.00	
			On cover		750.00
			On cover with No. O36		2,000.
			Block of 4	750.00	
			P# block of 12, Impt.	2,000.	
a.			**1c dull blue**	160.00	50.00
			No gum	65.00	

Cancellations

Violet		+2.00
Blue		+2.00
Indigo		+5.00
Red		+20.00
Town		+7.50
Steamship		+100.00
New York Foreign Mail		

O36	O5	2c	**ultramarine**	160.00	25.00
			dark ultramarine	160.00	25.00
			No gum	65.00	
			On cover		350.00
			Block of 4	750.00	
			P# block of 12, Impt.	1,750.	
			Double transfer	—	
a.			**2c dull blue**	160.00	25.00

gray blue	160.00	25.00
No gum	65.00	
Block of 4	750.00	

The 2c deep green and the 2c black, both perforated and imperforate, are trial color proofs.

Cancellations

Violet	+1.50
Blue	+1.50
Indigo	+5.00
Red	+15.00
Green	+75.00
Town	+10.00
Steamship	+100.00

O37	O5	3c **ultramarine**	170.00	15.00
		pale ultramarine	170.00	15.00
		dark ultramarine	170.00	15.00
		No gum	60.00	
		On cover		*160.00*
		Block of 4	775.00	*1,000.*
		P# block of 12, Impt.	*2,500.*	
		Double transfer	—	
a.		3c **dull blue**	170.00	15.00
		No gum	60.00	

Cancellations

Violet	+1.50
Blue	+1.50
Indigo	+5.00
Ultramarine	+10.00
Magenta	+5.00
Red	+15.00
Town	+5.00
Blue town	+15.00
Steamship	+75.00

O38	O5	6c **ultramarine**	150.00	25.00
		bright ultramarine	150.00	25.00
		No gum	55.00	
		On cover		*750.00*
		Block of 4	700.00	—
		P# block of 12, Impt.	*2,400.*	
		Vertical line through "N" of "Navy"	175.00	35.00
		Double transfer	—	
a.		6c **dull blue**	150.00	25.00
		No gum	55.00	

Cancellations

Violet	+1.50
Purple	+1.50
Blue	+1.50
Magenta	+10.00
Red	+17.50
Green	+100.00
Town	+5.00
Steamship	+100.00
New York Foreign Mail	

O39	O5	7c **ultramarine**	650.00	230.00
		dark ultramarine	650.00	230.00
		No gum	250.00	
		On cover		*3,000.*
		Block of 4	*2,800.*	
		Double transfer	—	
a.		7c **dull blue**	650.00	230.00
		No gum	250.00	

Cancellations

Blue	+10.00
Violet	+10.00
Magenta	+10.00
Red	+45.00
Town	+25.00

O40	O5	10c **ultramarine**	210.00	45.00
		dark ultramarine	210.00	45.00
		No gum	75.00	
		On cover		*4,000.*
		Block of 4	1,150.	
		P# block of 12, Impt.	*2,800.*	
		Plate scratch (pos. 3)	325.00	—
		Ribbed paper	225.00	60.00
a.		10c **dull blue**	210.00	45.00
		No gum	75.00	

Cancellations

Violet	+2.00
Blue	+2.00
Brown	+20.00
Red	+25.00
Town	+10.00
Steamship	+100.00
New York Foreign Mail	

O41	O5	12c **ultramarine**	220.00	45.00
		pale ultramarine	220.00	45.00
		dark ultramarine	220.00	45.00
		No gum	80.00	
		On cover		*3,000.*
		Block of 4	1,100.	
		P# strip of 6, Impt.	—	
		Short transfer at lower right (pos. 10)	—	—
		Double transfer of left side (pos. 50)	400.00	250.00

Cancellations

Violet	+2.50
Magenta	+2.50
Blue	+2.50
Red	+25.00
Town	+10.00
Supplementary Mail	+80.00
Steamship	+200.00
New York Foreign Mail	+325.00

O42	O5	15c **ultramarine**	375.00	75.00
		dark ultramarine	375.00	75.00
		No gum	135.00	
		Block of 4	1,700.	
		P# strip of 6, Impt.	—	
		Short transfer at upper left (pos. 26)	—	

Cancellations

Violet	+2.50
Blue	+2.50
Red	+35.00
Yellow	—
Town	+20.00

O43	O5	24c **ultramarine**	400.00	85.00
		dark ultramarine	400.00	85.00
		No gum	160.00	
		On cover		*20,000.*
		Block of 4	*2,000.*	
		Recut at upper right (pos. 33, 92)	—	
a.		24c **dull blue**	375.00	80.00
		No gum	150.00	

Cancellations

Violet	+5.00
Magenta	+5.00
Red	+50.00
Blue	+5.00
Green	+150.00
Town	+40.00
Steamship	+125.00
New York Foreign Mail	

O44	O5	30c **ultramarine**	325.00	50.00
		dark ultramarine	325.00	50.00
		No gum	125.00	
		Block of 4	1,600.	*3,000.*
		Double transfer	350.00	55.00

Cancellations

Blue	+4.00
Red	+30.00
Violet	+4.00
Town	+20.00
Supplementary Mail	+125.00
New York Foreign Mail	+400.00

O45	O5	90c **ultramarine**	1,050.	375.00
		No gum	450.00	
		Block of 4	*6,250.*	
		Short transfer at upper left (pos. 1, 5)	—	—
a.		Double impression		*20,000.*

Cancellations

Purple	+15.00
Violet	+15.00
Red	+75.00
Town	+40.00

POST OFFICE

Stamps of the Post Office Department are often on paper with a gray surface. This is due to insufficient wiping of the excess ink off plates during printing.

1873

O47	O6	1c **black**	25.00	12.00
		gray black	25.00	12.00
		No gum	12.00	
		On cover		*60.00*
		Block of 4	110.00	
		P# block of 12, Impt.	400.00	
		Never hinged	550.00	

Cancellations

Purple	+1.00
Violet	+1.00
Magenta	+1.00
Blue	+1.00
Red	+12.50
Town	+3.50

O48	O6	2c **black**	30.00	10.00
		gray black	30.00	10.00
		No gum	12.00	
		On cover		*160.00*
		Block of 4	140.00	—
		P# block of 12, Impt.	*475.00*	
a.		Double impression	600.00	400.00

Cancellations

Purple	+1.00
Violet	+1.00
Blue	+1.00
Indigo	+5.00
Magenta	+1.00
Red	+12.50
Town	+3.50
Blue town	+7.50
New York Foreign Mail	

O49	O6	3c **black**	10.00	2.00
		gray black	10.00	2.00
		No gum	3.00	
		On cover		*20.00*
		Block of 4	45.00	
		P# block of 14, Impt.	*200.00*	
		Never hinged	*300.00*	
		Cracked plate	—	—
		Double transfer at bottom	—	—
		Double paper	—	—
		Vertical ribbed paper	—	—
a.		Printed on both sides		*7,500.*

Cancellations

Purple	+.75
Violet	+.75
Blue	+.75
Indigo	+5.00
Ultramarine	+1.50
Magenta	+.75
Red	+10.00
Brown	+20.00
Green	+60.00
Numeral	+20.00
Town	+1.50
Railroad	+25.00
"Paid"	+12.00

O50	O6	6c **black**	30.00	8.00
		gray black	30.00	8.00
		No gum	12.00	
		On cover		*75.00*
		Block of 4	150.00	
		P# block of 14, Impt.	550.00	
		Vertical ribbed paper	—	12.50
		Double transfer of top frame (pos. 96L, 99L)	—	—
a.		Diagonal half used as 3c on cover		*5,000.*
b.		Double impression		*3,000.*

Cancellations

Purple	+.75
Violet	+.75
Magenta	+.75
Blue	+.75
Indigo	+5.00
Red	+12.00
Brown	+20.00
Numeral	+20.00
Town	+2.50
"Paid"	+15.00

O51	O6	10c **black**	140.00	55.00
		gray black	140.00	55.00
		No gum	60.00	
		On cover		*400.00*
		Block of 4	700.00	
		P# block of 12, Impt.	*1,950.*	

Cancellations

Violet	+3.50
Red	+15.00
Magenta	+3.50
Blue	+3.50
Town	+10.00

O52	O6	12c **black**	120.00	12.00
		gray black	120.00	12.00
		No gum	40.00	
		On cover		*1,000.*
		Block of 4	575.00	*1,250.*
		P# block of 12, Impt.	*1,850.*	
		Plate scratch above small "12"	—	

Cancellations

Purple	+1.00
Magenta	+1.00
Blue	+1.00
Indigo	+5.00
Red	+12.50
Town	+4.00

O53	O6	15c **black**	140.00	20.00
		gray black	140.00	20.00
		No gum	50.00	
		On cover		*5,000.*
		Block of 4	675.00	
		P# block of 14, Impt.	*2,250.*	
		Double transfer	—	—

Cancellations

Violet	+1.50
Magenta	+1.50
Red	+20.00
Blue	+1.50
Town	+7.50
New York Foreign Mail	

O54	O6	24c **black**	200.00	25.00
		gray black	200.00	25.00
		No gum	70.00	
		Block of 4	900.00	
		P# block of 12, Impt.	—	
		Double paper	—	—

Cancellations

Violet	+1.50
Blue	+1.50
Red	+20.00
Town	+7.50

O55	O6	30c **black**	200.00	25.00
		gray black	200.00	25.00
		No gum	70.00	
		On cover		—
		Block of 4	900.00	750.00
		P# block of 12, Impt.	*2,750.*	

Cancellations

Purple	+1.50
Blue	+1.50
Red	+20.00
Magenta	+1.50
Town	+12.50

O56	O6	90c **black**	220.00	25.00
		gray black	220.00	25.00
		No gum	80.00	
		Block of 4	950.00	*1,250.*
		P# block of 12, Impt.	*3,000.*	
		Double transfer	—	—
		Double paper	—	—
		Silk paper	—	—

Cancellations

Purple	+1.50
Magenta	+1.50
Blue	+1.50
Town	+6.50

STATE

Franklin — O7   William H. Seward — O8

1873

O57	O7	1c **dark green**	260.00	75.00
		dark yellow green	260.00	75.00
		light green	260.00	75.00
		No gum	110.00	
		On cover		—
		Block of 4	1,250.	
		Plate scratch at left (pos. 51)	—	—

Cancellations
Violet		+2.00
Blue favor		+2.00
Red		+17.50
Town		+7.50

O58	O7	2c **dark green**	310.00	100.00
		dark yellow green	310.00	100.00
		yellow green		
		No gum	120.00	
		On cover		1,000.
		Double transfer at bottom (pos. 98)	600.00	—

Cancellations
Violet		+5.00
Blue favor		+5.00
Indigo		+5.00
Red		+50.00
Town		+25.00

O59	O7	3c **bright green**	220.00	25.00
		yellow green	220.00	25.00
		dark green	220.00	25.00
		No gum	85.00	
		On cover		450.00
		First day cover, *July 1, 1873*		—
		Block of 4	1,100.	
		Double paper	—	—
		Short transfer at right (pos. 85)		—

Cancellations
Violet		+1.50
Blue favor		+1.50
Indigo		+1.50
Red		+10.00
Town		+6.50

O60	O7	6c **bright green**	220.00	30.00
		dark green	220.00	30.00
		yellow green	220.00	30.00
		No gum	85.00	
		On cover		650.00
		Block of 4	1,100.	
		P# block of 12, Impt.	—	
		Double transfer	—	—
		Foreign entry of 6c Executive (pos. 41, 91)	—	500.00
		Double transfer plus foreign entry of 6c Executive (pos. 61)	—	
		Plate scratch in margin (pos. 26, right; 27, left)	325.00	275.00

Cancellations
Violet		+2.00
Blue favor		+10.00
Indigo		+2.00
Red		+20.00
Town		+17.50

O61	O7	7c **dark green**	290.00	65.00
		dark yellow green	290.00	65.00
		No gum	95.00	
		On cover		1,000.
		Block of 4	1,500.	
		Ribbed paper	310.00	70.00

Cancellations
Violet		+2.00
Blue favor		+2.00
Indigo		+2.00
Red		+25.00
Town		+10.00

O62	O7	10c **dark green**	230.00	55.00
		bright green	230.00	55.00
		yellow green	3,000.	—
		No gum	100.00	
		On cover		2,000.
		Block of 4	1,150.	
		P# block of 12, Impt.	—	
		Short transfer (pos. 34)	275.00	67.50

Cancellations
Violet		+2.50
Blue favor		+2.50
Indigo		+2.50
Red		+35.00
Town		+25.00
New York Foreign Mail		+325.00

O63	O7	12c **dark green**	310.00	125.00
		dark yellow green		
		No gum	140.00	
		On cover		1,500.

Block of 4		1,650.	

Cancellations
Violet		+5.00
Blue favor		+5.00
Red		+30.00
Town		+15.00

O64	O7	15c **dark green**	320.00	90.00
		dark yellow green	320.00	90.00
		No gum	130.00	
		On cover		5,750.
		Block of 4	1,750.	
		Short transfer at upper right		450.00
		Plate scratch at lower left (pos. 91)	450.00	
		Plate scratch in margin (pos. 95, right; 96, left)	—	
		Damaged plate at left (pos. 63)	—	—

Cancellations
Violet		+2.50
Blue favor		+2.50
Red		+30.00
Town		+30.00

O65	O7	24c **dark green**	525.00	230.00
		dark yellow green	525.00	230.00
		No gum	275.00	
		On cover		17,500.
		Block of 4	3,100.	
		Short transfer at bottom left (pos. 10)	600.00	
		Plate gashes in forehead (pos. 76)	750.00	
		Plate scratch (pos. 66)	800.00	

Cancellations
Violet		+15.00
Blue favor		+15.00
Indigo		+15.00
Red		+85.00
Town		+55.00

O66	O7	30c **dark green**	500.00	180.00
		dark yellow green	500.00	180.00
		No gum	240.00	
		On cover		—
		Block of 4	4,500.	

Cancellations
Violet		+5.00
Blue favor		+5.00
Indigo		+5.00
Red		+50.00
Town		+50.00

O67	O7	90c **dark green**	1,050.	325.00
		dark yellow green		
		No gum	525.00	
		On parcel wrapper front with Nos. O60 & O66		62,500.

Cancellations
Violet		+15.00
Blue favor		+15.00
Red		+85.00
Red New York Foreign Mail		—
Town		+90.00

O68	O8	$2 **green & black**	1,350.	1,500.
		yellow green & black	1,350.	1,500.
		No gum	650.00	
		On parcel label		175,000.
		Block of 4	18,000.	
		Ribbed paper	—	

Cancellations
Violet		+25.00
Blue favor		+25.00
Red		+175.00
Town		+125.00
Red New York Foreign Mail		+3,000.
Pen		300.00

O69	O8	$5 **green & black**	6,500.	12,000.
		yellow green & black	6,500.	12,000.
		No gum	3,250.	
		Irregular block of 6	50,000.	

Cancellations
Blue favor		+250.00
Red favor		+250.00
Pen		1,600.

O70	O8	$10 **green & black**	4,750.	6,500.
		yellow green & black	4,750.	6,500.
		No gum	2,750.	
		Block of 4	25,000.	
		P# sheet of 10, Impt.	60,000.	
		Ribbed paper	—	

Cancellations
Blue favor		+200.00
Pen		1,150.

O71	O8	$20 **green & black**	4,500.	3,250.
		yellow green & black	4,500.	3,250.
		No gum	2,250.	
		Block of 4	22,500.	
		Block of 4, presentation pen cancel		7,500.
		P# sheet of 10, Impt.	60,000.	

No. O71 used is valued with a blue or red favor cancel.

Cancellations
Blue favor		2,500.
Red favor		2,500.
Pen presentation		1,100.

The design of Nos. O68 to O71 measures 25½x39½mm.

O9   O10

TREASURY

1873

O72	O9	1c **brown**	115.00	10.0
		dark brown	115.00	10.0
		yellow brown	115.00	10.0
		No gum	45.00	
		On cover		100.0
		Block of 4	500.00	325.0
		P# block of 14, Impt.	2,000.	
		Never hinged	2,800.	
		Double transfer	125.00	12.5

Cancellations
Purple		+1.0
Violet		+1.0
Magenta		+1.0
Blue		+1.0
Red		+10.0
Brown		+20.0
Green		+200.0
Town		+2.0
Blue town		+4.0
New York Foreign Mail		

O73	O9	2c **brown**	120.00	8.0
		dark brown	120.00	8.0
		yellow brown	120.00	8.0
		No gum	40.00	
		On cover		75.00
		Block of 4	525.00	325.0
		P# block of 14, Impt.	1,850.	
		Double transfer	—	12.5
		Plate scratch (pos. 3R)		

Cancellations
Purple		+1.00
Violet		+1.00
Magenta		+1.00
Blue		+1.00
Indigo		+3.00
Red		+10.00
Town		+2.00
Blue town		+4.00
New York Foreign Mail		+275.00

O74	O9	3c **brown**	105.00	2.00
		dark brown	105.00	2.00
		yellow brown	105.00	2.00
		No gum	40.00	
		On cover		30.00
		First day cover, *July 1, 1873*		11,000.
		Block of 4	450.00	250.00
		P# block of 14, Impt.	1,750.	
		Double paper	—	
		Shaded circle outside of right frame line	—	—
		Short transfer at bottom (pos. 36 R 29)	—	—
a.		Double impression		5,000.

Cancellations
Purple		+.50
Violet		+.50
Blue		+.50
Indigo		+3.00
Ultramarine		+2.00
Magenta		+.50
Red		+3.50
Brown		+20.00
Green		+200.00
Town		+1.00
Railroad		+20.00
"Paid"		+10.00

O75	O9	6c **brown**	115.00	4.00
		dark brown	115.00	4.00
		yellow brown	115.00	4.00
		No gum	40.00	
		On cover		75.00
		Block of 4	500.00	500.00
		P# block of 12, Impt.	1,800.	
		Never hinged	2,500.	
		Dirty plate	115.00	6.00
		Double transfer	—	

Cancellations
Purple		+.50
Violet		+.50
Magenta		+.50
Blue		+.50
Indigo		+3.00
Ultramarine		+1.50
Red		+5.00
Green		+200.00
"Paid"		+20.00
Town		+1.50
New York Foreign Mail		

O76	O9	7c **brown**	240.00	35.00
		dark brown	240.00	35.00
		yellow brown	240.00	35.00
		No gum	95.00	
		On cover		750.00
		Block of 4	1,050.	1,000.
		P# block of 12, Impt.	—	

Cancellations
Purple		+2.00
Violet		+2.00

			Unused	Used
		Blue		+2.00
		Indigo		+3.00
		Red		+30.00
		Green		+200.00
		Town		+7.50
		Blue town		+12.50
		New York Foreign Mail		—
77	O9	10c **brown**	230.00	12.00
		dark brown	230.00	12.00
		yellow brown	230.00	12.00
		No gum	90.00	
		On cover		450.00
		Block of 4	1,050.	325.00
		P# block of 12, Impt.	—	
		Double paper	—	—
		Double transfer	—	—

Cancellations
- Purple +1.00
- Violet +1.00
- Blue +1.00
- Indigo +3.00
- Ultramarine +4.00
- Magenta +1.00
- Red +12.00
- Brown +20.00
- Green +200.00
- Town +4.00
- Blue town +8.50

78	O9	12c **brown**	290.00	10.00
		dark brown	290.00	10.00
		yellow brown	290.00	10.00
		No gum	100.00	
		On cover		600.00
		Block of 4	1,350.	325.00

Cancellations
- Purple +.50
- Blue +.50
- Ultramarine +10.00
- Red +10.00
- Green +200.00
- Town +2.50
- Railroad +20.00

79	O9	15c **brown**	290.00	12.00
		yellow brown	290.00	12.00
		No gum	100.00	
		On cover		850.00
		Block of 4	1,350.	325.00
		P# block of 12, Impt.	4,000.	
		Never hinged	5,500.	

Cancellations
- Blue +1.00
- Purple +1.00
- Red +10.00
- Green +200.00
- Town +2.50
- Blue town +7.50
- Numeral +15.00
- Steamship +100.00

O80	O9	24c **brown**	650.00	90.00
		dark brown	650.00	90.00
		yellow brown	650.00	90.00
		No gum	270.00	
		Block of 4	3,000.	
		Block of 14	—	
		Double transfer at top	700.00	—
		Short transfer at top (pos. 61)		—

Cancellations
- Violet +10.00
- Blue +5.00
- Ultramarine +10.00
- Magenta +5.00
- Red +30.00
- Brown +20.00
- Town +15.00
- Blue town +25.00
- New York Foreign Mail —

O81	O9	30c **brown**	400.00	12.00
		dark brown	400.00	12.00
		yellow brown	400.00	12.00
		No gum	140.00	
		On cover		5,000.
		Block of 4	1,750.	500.00
		Short transfer at left top (pos. 95)	450.00	25.00
		Short transfer at right top (pos. 45)	450.00	25.00
		Block of 4, one pos. 45	—	
		Short transfer across entire top (pos. 41)	450.00	25.00

Cancellations
- Purple +1.00
- Blue +1.00
- Magenta +1.00
- Red +12.00
- Green +200.00
- Town +3.50
- Blue town +7.50

O82	O9	90c **brown**	400.00	15.00
		dark brown	400.00	15.00
		yellow brown	400.00	15.00
		No gum	140.00	
		Block of 4	1,750.	375.00
		Double paper	—	—

Cancellations
- Purple +1.00
- Magenta +1.00
- Blue +1.00
- Red +30.00
- Brown +7.50
- Green +200.00
- Town +3.50
- Blue town +7.50

WAR

1873

O83	O10	1c **rose**	230.00	15.00
		rose red	230.00	15.00
		No gum	90.00	
		On cover		140.00
		Block of 4	975.00	
		Block of 10	—	
		P# block of 12, Impt.	3,000.	

Cancellations
- Purple +1.00
- Blue +1.00
- Magenta +5.00
- Red +15.00
- Town +3.50
- Fort +100.00
- Numeral +12.50
- "Paid" —

O84	O10	2c **rose**	230.00	15.00
		rose red	230.00	15.00
		No gum	90.00	
		On cover		70.00
		Block of 4	975.00	
		P# block of 14, Impt.	3,500.	
		Ribbed paper	240.00	17.50

Cancellations
- Purple +1.50
- Magenta +1.50
- Blue +1.50
- Red +15.00
- Town +4.00
- Fort +100.00

O85	O10	3c **rose**	230.00	5.00
		rose red	230.00	5.00
		No gum	90.00	
		On cover		40.00
		Block of 4	975.00	550.00
		P# block of 14, Impt.	3,500.	

Cancellations
- Purple +1.00
- Blue +1.00
- Ultramarine +10.00
- Magenta +1.00
- Red +20.00
- Green +35.00
- Town +1.50
- Fort +100.00
- "Paid" +12.00

O86	O10	6c **rose**	600.00	10.00
		pale rose	600.00	10.00
		No gum	250.00	
		On cover		60.00
		Block of 4	2,850.	
		P# block of 12, Impt.	—	

Cancellations
- Purple +1.50
- Blue +1.50
- Indigo +3.00
- Magenta +3.00
- Red +15.00
- Town +3.50
- Blue town +6.50
- Fort +100.00

O87	O10	7c **rose**	160.00	90.00
		pale rose	160.00	90.00
		rose red	160.00	90.00
		No gum	80.00	
		On cover		—
		Block of 4	675.00	
		P# block of 10, Impt.	2,250.	

Cancellations
- Purple +2.50
- Blue +3.50
- Magenta +10.00
- Red +25.00
- Town +7.50

O88	O10	10c **rose**	130.00	25.00
		rose red	130.00	25.00
		No gum	45.00	
		On cover		2,000.
		Block of 4	550.00	900.00
		P# block of 12, Impt.	1,800.	

All copies of No. O88 show a crack at lower left. It was on the original die.

Cancellations
- Purple +1.00
- Blue +1.00
- Town +3.50
- Fort +100.00

O89	O10	12c **rose**	250.00	12.00
		No gum	110.00	
		On cover		450.00
		Block of 4	1,100.	550.00
		P# block of 12, Impt.	3,250.	
		Never hinged	4,500.	
		Ribbed paper	275.00	20.00

Cancellations
- Purple +1.00
- Magenta +1.00
- Blue +1.00
- Indigo +5.00
- Red +10.00
- Town +3.00
- Fort +100.00

O90	O10	15c **rose**	80.00	15.00
		pale rose	80.00	15.00
		rose red	80.00	15.00
		No gum	30.00	
		On cover		3,000.
		Block of 4	350.00	
		P# block of 10, Impt.	1,000.	
		Ribbed paper	87.50	20.00
		Short transfer at upper right (pos. 74)		—

Cancellations
- Purple +1.00
- Blue +1.00
- Ultramarine +10.00
- Magenta +3.00
- Red +10.00
- Town +2.50
- Fort +200.00
- Express Company —

O91	O10	24c **rose**	80.00	12.00
		pale rose	80.00	12.00
		rose red	80.00	12.00
		No gum	30.00	
		On cover		—
		Block of 4	350.00	2,250.
		P# block of 10, Impt.	1,300.	

Cancellations
- Purple +1.00
- Blue +1.00
- Magenta +5.00
- Town +2.50
- Fort +100.00

O92	O10	30c **rose**	125.00	12.00
		rose red	125.00	12.00
		No gum	45.00	
		On cover		—
		Block of 4	550.00	350.00
		P# block of 12, Impt.	1,750.	
		Ribbed paper	135.00	15.00

Cancellations
- Purple +1.00
- Magenta +1.00
- Blue +1.00
- Red +20.00
- Town +2.50
- Fort +100.00

O93	O10	90c **rose**	210.00	50.00
		rose red	210.00	50.00
		No gum	80.00	
		On cover		—
		Block of 4	925.00	975.00
		P# block of 12, Impt.	3,500.	

Cancellations
- Purple +2.00
- Magenta +2.00
- Blue +2.00
- Red +20.00
- Numeral +40.00
- Town +7.50
- Fort +125.00

Printed by the American Bank Note Co.

The Continental Bank Note Co. was consolidated with the American Bank Note Co. on February 4, 1879. The American Bank Note Company used many plates of the Continental Bank Note Company to print the ordinary postage, Departmental and Newspaper stamps. Therefore, stamps bearing the Continental Company's imprint were not always its product.

1879 — **Soft Porous Paper**

AGRICULTURE

O94	O1	1c **yellow** (issued without gum)	6,000.	
		Block of 4	30,000.	
O95	O1	3c **yellow**	550.00	100.00
		No gum	240.00	
		On cover		—
		Block of 4	2,750.	1,300.
		P# block of 12, Impt.	7,250.	

Cancellations
- Purple +5.00
- Blue +5.00
- Town +30.00

INTERIOR

O96	O3	1c **vermilion**	300.00	275.00
		pale vermilion	300.00	275.00
		No gum	160.00	
		Block of 4	1,450.	
		P# block of 12, Impt.	4,500.	
		Short transfer at lower right (pos. 91)	600.00	

Cancellations
- Purple +5.00
- Blue +5.00
- Town +15.00

O97	O3	2c **vermilion**	10.00	3.00
		pale vermilion	10.00	3.00
		scarlet vermilion	10.00	3.00
		No gum	3.00	
		On cover		150.00
		Block of 4	47.50	250.00
		P# block of 12, Impt.	225.00	

Cancellations
- Purple +.50
- Violet +.50
- Blue +.50
- Red +5.00
- Town +1.50
- Blue town +3.00
- Railroad +40.00
- Fort +100.00

O98	O3	3c **vermilion**	10.00	3.00
		pale vermilion	10.00	3.00
		No gum	3.00	
		On cover		30.00
		Block of 4	47.50	—
		P# block of 10, Impt.	225.00	

Cancellations
- Purple +.50
- Violet +.50
- Blue +.50
- Red +5.00
- Town +1.50
- Blue town +3.00
- Railroad +40.00

O99	O3	6c	**vermilion**	15.00	8.00
			pale vermilion	15.00	8.00
			scarlet vermilion	15.00	8.00
			No gum	5.00	
			On cover		200.00
			Block of 4	67.50	
			P# block of 10, Impt.	*275.00*	

Cancellations
Purple		+.50
Blue		+.50
Red		+5.00
Town		+1.50
Fort		+100.00

O100	O3	10c	**vermilion**	110.00	75.00
			pale vermilion	110.00	75.00
			No gum	60.00	
			On cover		*1,200.*
			Block of 4	500.00	
			P# block of 12, Impt.	*1,650.*	

Cancellations
Purple		+5.00
Blue		+5.00
Town		+10.00

O101	O3	12c	**vermilion**	230.00	115.00
			pale vermilion	230.00	115.00
			No gum	130.00	—
			On cover		—
			Block of 4	1,075.	*575.00*
			Block of 6		*1,500.*
			P# block of 12, Impt.	*2,900.*	
			Short transfer at lower right (pos. 6)	—	—

Cancellation
Violet		+5.00

O102	O3	15c	**vermilion**	400.00	260.00
			No gum	200.00	
			Block of 4	1,750.	
			P# block of 12, Impt.	—	
			On cover		—
			Double transfer	450.00	—

Cancellations
Purple		+5.00
Blue		+5.00

O103	O3	24c	**vermilion**	4,400.	
			No gum	2,100.	
			Block of 4	*24,000.*	
			P# strip of 6, Impt.	—	

Cancellation
Blue		—

JUSTICE

O106	O4	3c	**bluish purple**	160.00	100.00
			deep bluish purple	160.00	100.00
			No gum	80.00	
			On cover		700.00
			Block of 4	600.00	

Cancellations
Violet		+5.00
Blue		+5.00
Indigo		+5.00
Ultramarine		+10.00

O107	O4	6c	**bluish purple**	450.00	250.00
			No gum	210.00	
			On cover		—
			Block of 4	2,100.	

Cancellations
Blue		+10.00
Indigo		+5.00
Town		+20.00

POST OFFICE

O108	O6	3c	**black**	30.00	8.00
			gray black	30.00	8.00
			No gum	10.00	
			On cover		—
			Block of 4	130.00	
			P# block of 14, Impt.	*475.00*	

Cancellations
Purple		+1.00
Violet		+1.00
Blue		+1.00
Indigo		+10.00
Magenta		+1.00
Red		+20.00
Green		+40.00
Town		+2.00
"Paid"		+12.00

TREASURY

O109	O9	3c	**brown**	80.00	10.00
			yellow brown	80.00	10.00
			No gum	35.00	
			On cover		110.00
			Block of 4	400.00	*900.00*
			P# block of 14, Impt.	*1,450.*	

Cancellations
Purple		+1.50
Blue		+1.50
Indigo		+3.00
Town		+2.00
Numeral		+7.50

O110	O9	6c	**brown**	200.00	50.00
			yellow brown	200.00	50.00
			dark brown	200.00	50.00
			No gum	65.00	
			On cover		300.00
			Block of 4	950.00	—
			P# block of 12, Impt.	*2,900.*	

Cancellations
Purple		+6.00
Magenta		+6.00
Blue		+6.00

O111	O9	10c	**brown**	260.00	80.00
			yellow brown	260.00	80.00
			dark brown	260.00	80.00

No gum		90.00	
On cover			*750.00*
Block of 4		1,250.	—
P# block of 12, Impt.		*4,500.*	

Cancellations
Purple		+2.50
Blue		+2.50
Magenta		+5.00
Town		+7.50

O112	O9	30c	**brown**	2,400.	425.00
			No gum	875.00	
			Block of 4	*12,000.*	

Cancellations
Blue		+25.00
Indigo		+25.00
Town		+50.00

O113	O9	90c	**brown**	4,500.	525.00
			dark brown	4,500	525.00
			No gum	1,650.	
			Block of 4	*20,000.*	

Cancellations
Purple		+25.00
Blue		+25.00
Town		+75.00

WAR

O114	O10	1c	**rose red**	6.00	4.00
			rose	6.00	4.00
			dull rose red	6.00	4.00
			brown rose	6.00	4.00
			No gum	2.50	
			On cover		55.00
			Block of 4	27.50	
			P# block of 12, Impt.	150.00	
			Never hinged	220.00	

Cancellations
Purple		+.50
Blue		+.50
Town		+1.00
Fort		+100.00

O115	O10	2c	**rose red**	12.00	4.00
			dark rose red	12.00	4.00
			dull vermilion	12.00	4.00
			No gum	4.00	
			On cover		40.00
			Block of 4	52.50	—
			P# block of 12, Impt.	200.00	
			Never hinged	290.00	

Cancellations
Purple		+.50
Blue		+.50
Magenta		+.50
Green		+35.00
Town		+2.00
Fort		+100.00

O116	O10	3c	**rose red**	12.00	2.00
			dull rose red	12.00	2.00
			No gum	4.00	
			On cover		35.00
			Block of 4	52.50	—
			P# block of 12, Impt.	200.00	
			Never hinged	290.00	
			Double transfer	17.50	6.00
			Plate flaw at upper left (32 R 20)	—	—
a.			Imperf., pair	5,000.	
b.			Double impression	6,500.	

Cancellations
Purple		+.50
Violet		+.50
Blue		+.50
Ultramarine		+5.00
Magenta		+1.00
Red		+5.00
Town		+1.00
Fort		+100.00

O117	O10	6c	**rose red**	11.00	3.00
			dull rose red	11.00	3.00
			dull vermilion		—
			No gum	4.00	
			On cover		50.00
			Block of 4	47.50	—
			P# block of 12, Impt.	190.00	

Cancellations
Purple		+.50
Blue		+.50
Magenta		+1.00
Brown		+20.00
Town		+1.00
Fort		+100.00
Numeral		+7.50

O118	O10	10c	**rose red**	65.00	50.00
			dull rose red	65.00	50.00
			No gum	26.00	
			On cover		*1,800.*
			Block of 4	300.00	
			P# block of 10, Impt.	950.00	

Cancellations
Violet		+3.00
Town		+5.00
Fort		+100.00

O119	O10	12c	**rose red**	60.00	14.00
			dull rose red	60.00	14.00
			brown rose	60.00	14.00
			No gum	20.00	
			On cover		—
			Block of 4	260.00	—
			P# block of 10, Impt.	775.00	

Cancellations
Purple		+1.00
Violet		+1.00
Red		+10.00
Town		+2.50
Fort		+150.00

O120	O10	30c	**rose red**	220.00	100.00

dull rose red		220.00	100
No gum		90.00	
Block of 4		950.00	
P# block of 10, Impt.		*3,500.*	

Cancellations
Violet		+5
Town		+10.
Fort		+125

SPECIAL PRINTINGS

Special printings of Official stamps were made 1875 at the time the other Reprints, Re-issues a Special Printings were printed. They are ungumme Though overprinted "SPECIMEN," these stamps a Special Printings, and they are not considered to be the same category as the stamps listed in the Spe men section of this catalogue.

Although perforated, these stamps were sometime (but not always) cut apart with scissors. As a result th perforations may be mutilated and the desig damaged.

Number sold indicated in brackets.

All values exist imperforate.

Blocks of 4 are now listed. All are scarce, a few ar rare. They will be valued when sufficient informatio has been received. Imprint and plate number strips o blocks are very scarce.

The "SEPCIMEN" error appears once on som panes of 100. The error was discovered and correcte part way through the printing. Blocks of 4 or larger wit the "SEPCIMEN" error are rare and worth much mor than the value of the individual stamps.

Printing flaws which resemble broken type (but ar not) are commonly found on the SPECIMEN overprir on these and other overprinted stamps. The variet listed as a "small dotted i" is actually an "i"; it is not on of the printing flaws noted in the preceding sentence All "small dotted 'i'" varieties are on ribbed paper fror the second special printings. They occur in positions and 26.

Printed by the Continental Bank Note Co.

Overprinted in Block Letters

1875		Thin, hard white paper		*Perf. 12*
		Type D		

AGRICULTURE

Carmine Overprint

O1S	D	1c	**yellow** (10,234)		25.00
			Block of 4		*300.00*
a.			"Sepcimen" error		2,250.
b.			Horiz. ribbed paper (10,000)		30.00
			Block of 4		*350.00*
c.			As "b," small dotted "i" in "Specimen"		450.00
O2S	D	2c	**yellow** (4,192)		50.00
			Block of 4		*550.00*
a.			"Sepcimen" error		2,750.
O3S	D	3c	**yellow** (389)		275.00
a.			"Sepcimen" error		10,000.
O4S	D	6c	**yellow** (373)		300.00
a.			"Sepcimen" error		17,500.
O5S	D	10c	**yellow** (390)		300.00
a.			"Sepcimen" error		15,000.
O6S	D	12c	**yellow** (379)		300.00
a.			"Sepcimen" error		10,000.
O7S	D	15c	**yellow** (370)		300.00
a.			"Sepcimen" error		10,000.
O8S	D	24c	**yellow** (352)		300.00
a.			"Sepcimen" error		10,000.
O9S	D	30c	**yellow** (354)		300.00
a.			"Sepcimen" error		12,500.

EXECUTIVE

Blue Overprint

O10S	D	1c	**carmine** (10,000)		25.00
			Block of 4		*300.00*
			P# block of 14, Impt.		*5,000.*
a.			Horiz. ribbed paper (10,000)		30.00
			Block of 4		*350.00*
b.			As "a," small dotted "i" in "Specimen"		450.00
O11S	D	2c	**carmine** (7,430)		45.00
			Block of 4		550.00
			Foreign entry of 6c Agri- culture (pos. 40)		*2,000.*
O12S	D	3c	**carmine** (3,735)		55.00
			Block of 4		—
O13S	D	6c	**carmine** (3,485)		55.00
			Block of 4		—
O14S	D	10c	**carmine** (3,461)		55.00
			Block of 4		—

INTERIOR
Blue Overprint

5S	D	1c **vermilion** (7,194)	45.00	
		Block of 4	550.00	
		P# block of 12, impt.	5,500.	
6S	D	2c **vermilion** (1,263)	70.00	
		Block of 4	900.00	
		P# Block of 12, Impt.	7,500.	
a.		"Sepcimen" error	10,000.	
17S	D	3c **vermilion** (88)	1,250.	
18S	D	6c **vermilion** (83)	1,250.	
19S	D	10c **vermilion** (82)	1,250.	
20S	D	12c **vermilion** (75)	1,250.	
21S	D	15c **vermilion** (78)	1,250.	
		Double transfer at left	2,000.	
22S	D	24c **vermilion** (77)	1,250.	
23S	D	30c **vermilion** (75)	1,250.	
24S	D	90c **vermilion** (77)	1,250.	

JUSTICE
Blue Overprint

25S	D	1c **purple** (10,000)	25.00	
		Block of 4	250.00	
		P# block of 12, Impt.	3,250.	
a.		"Sepcimen" error	1,750.	
b.		Horiz. ribbed paper (9,729)	30.00	
		Block of 4	300.00	
		P# block of 12, Impt.	4,000.	
c.		As "b," small dotted "i" in "Specimen"	450.00	
26S	D	2c **purple** (3,395)	45.00	
		Block of 4	550.00	
		P# block of 12, Impt.	5,500.	
a.		"Sepcimen" error	2,250.	
27S	D	3c **purple** (178)	800.00	
a.		Plate scratches	8,000.	
		"Sepcimen" error		
28S	D	6c **purple** (163)	800.00	
29S	D	10c **purple** (163)	800.00	
30S	D	12c **purple** (154)	800.00	
a.		"Sepcimen" error	12,500.	
31S	D	15c **purple** (157)	800.00	
a.		"Sepcimen" error	12,500.	
32S	D	24c **purple** (150)	800.00	
a.		"Sepcimen" error	12,500.	
33S	D	30c **purple** (150)	800.00	
a.		"Sepcimen" error	12,500.	
34S	D	90c **purple** (152)	800.00	

NAVY
Carmine Overprint

35S	D	1c **ultramarine** (10,000)	30.00	
		Block of 4	350.00	
a.		"Sepcimen" error	2,250.	
b.		Double "Specimen" overprint	1,750.	
36S	D	2c **ultramarine** (1,748)	55.00	
		Block of 4	650.00	
a.		"Sepcimen" error	3,000.	
37S	D	3c **ultramarine** (126)	900.00	
38S	D	6c **ultramarine** (116)	1,000.	
		Vertical line through "N" of "Navy"	1,500.	
39S	D	7c **ultramarine** (501)	400.00	
		Block of 4	4,000.	
a.		"Sepcimen" error	7,500.	
40S	D	10c **ultramarine** (112)	1,000.	
a.		"Sepcimen" error	12,500.	
41S	D	12c **ultramarine** (107)	900.00	
		Double transfer at left side, pos. 50		
a.		"Sepcimen" error	12,500.	
42S	D	15c **ultramarine** (107)	900.00	
a.		"Sepcimen" error	12,500.	
43S	D	24c **ultramarine** (106)	900.00	
a.		"Sepcimen" error	12,500.	
44S	D	30c **ultramarine** (104)	900.00	
		Double transfer		
a.		"Sepcimen" error	12,500.	
45S	D	90c **ultramarine** (102)	900.00	

POST OFFICE
Carmine Overprint

O47S	D	1c **black** (6,015)	37.50	
		Block of 4	450.00	
a.		"Sepcimen" error	1,750.	
b.		Inverted overprint	2,500.	
O48S	D	2c **black** (590)	100.00	
		Block of 4	1,200.	
a.		"Sepcimen" error	3,000.	
O49S	D	3c **black** (91)	1,100.	
a.		"Sepcimen" error		
O50S	D	6c **black** (87)	1,000.	
O51S	D	10c **black** (177)	800.00	
a.		"Sepcimen" error	10,000.	
O52S	D	12c **black** (93)	900.00	
O53S	D	15c **black** (82)	1,000.	
a.		"Sepcimen" error	12,500.	
O54S	D	24c **black** (84)	1,000.	
a.		"Sepcimen" error	10,000.	
O55S	D	30c **black** (81)	1,100.	
O56S	D	90c **black** (82)	1,000.	
a.		"Sepcimen" error		

STATE
Carmine Overprint

O57S	D	1c **bluish green** (10,000)	25.00	
		Block of 4	300.00	
a.		"Sepcimen" error	1,750.	
b.		Horiz. ribbed paper (10,000)	30.00	
		Block of 4	350.00	
c.		As "b," small dotted "i" in "Specimen"	500.00	
d.		Double "Specimen" overprint	3,500.	
		Block of 4		
O58S	D	2c **bluish green** (5,145)	75.00	
		Block of 4	550.00	
a.		"Sepcimen" error	2,250.	

O59S	D	3c **bluish green** (793)	110.00	
		Block of 4	5,500.	
a.		"Sepcimen" error		
O60S	D	6c **bluish green** (467)	250.00	
a.		"Sepcimen" error	7,500.	
O61S	D	7c **bluish green** (791)	110.00	
		Block of 4	1,000.	
a.		"Sepcimen" error	7,500.	
O62S	D	10c **bluish green** (346)	450.00	
		Short transfer, pos. 34	2,000.	
a.		"Sepcimen" error	12,500.	
O63S	D	12c **bluish green** (280)	500.00	
a.		"Sepcimen" error	10,000.	
O64S	D	15c **bluish green** (257)	500.00	
O65S	D	24c **bluish green** (253)	500.00	
a.		"Sepcimen" error	10,000.	
O66S	D	30c **bluish green** (249)	500.00	
a.		"Sepcimen" error	10,000.	
O67S	D	90c **bluish green** (245)	500.00	
a.		"Sepcimen" error	10,000.	
O68S	D	$2 **green & black** (32)	17,500.	
O69S	D	$5 **green & black** (12)	25,000.	
O70S	D	$10 **green & black** (8)	50,000.	
O71S	D	$20 **green & black** (7)	80,000.	

TREASURY
Blue Overprint

O72S	D	1c **dark brown** (2,185)	40.00	
		Block of 4	475.00	
		Double transfer		
O73S	D	2c **dark brown** (309)	200.00	
		Block of 4	2,400.	
O74S	D	3c **dark brown** (84)	1,250.	
O75S	D	6c **dark brown** (85)	1,250.	
O76S	D	7c **dark brown** (198)	750.00	
		Block of 4	4,500.	
		P# block of 12, impt.	17,500.	

The only recorded plate block of No. O76S is contained in a half sheet of 50 stamps.

O77S	D	10c **dark brown** (82)	1,200.	
O78S	D	12c **dark brown** (75)	1,200.	
O79S	D	15c **dark brown** (75)	1,200.	
O80S	D	24c **dark brown** (99)	1,200.	
O81S	D	30c **dark brown** (74)	1,200.	
		Short transfer at left top (pos. 95) (1)	—	
		Short transfer at right top (pos. 45) (1)	—	
O82S	D	90c **dark brown** (72)	1,200.	

WAR
Blue Overprint

O83S	D	1c **deep rose** (9,610)	25.00	
		Block of 4	300.00	
a.		"Sepcimen" error	1,250.	
O84S	D	2c **deep rose** (1,618)	70.00	
		Block of 4	850.00	
		P# block of 12	3,750.	
a.		"Sepcimen" error	1,800.	
O85S	D	3c **deep rose** (118)	900.00	
a.		"Sepcimen" error	10,000.	
O86S	D	6c **deep rose** (111)	900.00	
a.		"Sepcimen" error	15,000.	
O87S	D	7c **deep rose** (539)	300.00	
		Block of 4	2,250.	
a.		"Sepcimen" error	9,000.	
O88S	D	10c **deep rose** (119)	900.00	
a.		"Sepcimen" error	12,500.	
O89S	D	12c **deep rose** (105)	900.00	
a.		"Sepcimen" error	12,500.	
O90S	D	15c **deep rose** (105)	900.00	
a.		"Sepcimen" error	12,500.	
O91S	D	24c **deep rose** (106)	900.00	
a.		"Sepcimen" error	12,500.	
O92S	D	30c **deep rose** (104)	900.00	
a.		"Sepcimen" error	12,500.	
O93S	D	90c **deep rose** (106)	900.00	
a.		"Sepcimen" error	12,500.	

Printed by the American Bank Note Co.
SOFT POROUS PAPER
EXECUTIVE

1881

Blue Overprint

O10xS	D	1c **violet rose** (4,652)	85.00	
		Block of 4	900.00	

NAVY
Carmine Overprint

O35xS	D	1c **gray blue** (4,182)	90.00	
		deep blue	90.00	
		Block of 4	950.00	
a.		Double overprint	1,100.	

STATE

O57xS	D	1c **yellow green** (1,672)	325.00	
		Block of 4	2,100.	

POSTAL SAVINGS MAIL

The Act of Congress, approved June 25, 1910, establishing postal savings depositories, provided:
"Sec. 2. That the Postmaster General is hereby directed to prepare and issue special stamps of the necessary denominations for use, in lieu of penalty or franked envelopes, in the transmittal of free mail resulting from the administration of this act."

The use of postal savings official stamps was discontinued by the Act of Congress, approved September 23, 1914. Postmasters were notified of the discontinuance in mid-October 1914. The unused stamps in the hands of postmasters were returned and destroyed.

O11

Printed by the Bureau of Engraving & Printing

				Engr.	Wmk. 191	
1910-11						
O121	O11	2c **black**, *Dec. 22, 1910*		17.50	2.00	
		Never hinged		40.00		
		On cover			12.50	
		Block of 4 (2mm spacing)		80.00	11.00	
		Block of 4 (3mm spacing)		77.50	10.00	
		P# block of 6, Impt. & Star		350.00		
		Double transfer		22.50	4.00	
O122	O11	50c **dark green**, *Feb. 1, 1911*		160.00	60.00	
		Never hinged		375.00		
		On cover			225.00	
		Block of 4 (2mm spacing)		675.00	300.00	
		Block of 4 (3mm spacing)		650.00	300.00	
		Margin block of 4, arrow		675.00		
		P# block of 6, Impt. & Star		2,400.		
		Never hinged		3,500.		
O123	O11	$1 **ultramarine**, *Feb. 1, 1911*		200.00	15.00	
		Never hinged		450.00		
		On cover			110.00	
		Block of 4 (2mm spacing)		850.00	75.00	
		Block of 4 (3mm spacing)		825.00	75.00	
		Margin block of 4, arrow		850.00		
		P# block of 6, Impt. & Star		2,400.	—	
		Wmk. 190				
O124	O11	1c **dark violet**, *Mar. 27, 1911*		10.00	2.00	
		Never hinged		22.50		
		On cover			15.00	
		Block of 4 (2mm spacing)		45.00	9.00	
		Block of 4 (3mm spacing)		42.50	8.50	
		P# block of 6, Impt. & Star		190.00		
O125	O11	2c **black**		55.00	7.00	
		Never hinged		125.00		
		On cover			25.00	
		Block of 4 (2mm spacing)		240.00	32.50	
		Block of 4 (3mm spacing)		225.00	32.50	
		P# block of 6, Impt. & Star		700.00		
		Double transfer		60.00	8.00	
O126	O11	10c **carmine**, *Feb. 1, 1911*		20.00	2.00	
		Never hinged		47.50		
		On cover			20.00	
		Block of 4 (2mm spacing)		87.50	30.00	
		Block of 4 (3mm spacing)		82.50	10.00	
		P# block of 6, Impt. & Star		370.00		
		Double transfer		25.00	3.50	

> **Catalogue values for unused stamps in this section, from this point to the end, are for Never Hinged items.**

From No. O127 onward, all official stamps are tagged unless noted.

OFFICIAL MAIL

O12

Designed by Bradbury Thompson

Engraved

			Unwmk.	Tagged	*Perf. 11*	
1983, Jan. 12-1985						
O127	O12	1c **red, blue & black**		.20	.20	
		FDC, Washington, DC			1.00	
		P# block of 4, UL or UR		.25		
O128	O12	4c **red, blue & black**		.20	.25	
		FDC, Washington, DC			1.00	
		P# block of 4, LR only		.40		
O129	O12	13c **red, blue & black**		.45	.75	
		FDC, Washington, DC			1.00	
		P# block of 4, UR only		2.00		
O129A	O12	14c **red, blue & black**, *May 15, 1985*		.45	.50	
		FDC, Washington, DC			1.00	
		Zip-copyright block of 6		2.90		
O130	O12	17c **red, blue & black**		.60	.40	
		FDC, Washington, DC			1.00	
		P# block of 4, LL only		3.00		
O132	O12	$1 **red, blue & black**		2.25	1.00	
		FDC, Washington, DC			2.25	
		P# block of 4, UL only		10.00		
O133	O12	$5 **red, blue & black**		9.00	*12.00*	
		FDC, Washington, DC			12.50	
		P# block of 4, LL only		42.50		
		Nos. O127-O133 (7)		13.15	15.10	

No. O129A does not have a "c" after the "14."

COIL STAMPS
Perf. 10 Vert.

O135	O12	20c **red, blue & black**	1.75	2.00
		FDC, Washington, DC		1.00
		Pair	3.50	4.00
		P# strip of 3, P# 1	12.50	
		P# strip of 5, P# 1	57.50	
		P# single, #1	—	20.00
a.		Imperf., pair	2,000.	
O136	O12	22c **red, blue & blk, low gloss gum,** *May 15, 1985*	1.00	2.00
		FDC, Washington, DC		1.00
		Pair	2.00	4.00
		Dull finish gum	75.00	
a.		Tagging omitted	—	

Used Values
of Nos. O135-O138, O140, etc., do not apply to copies removed from first day covers.

Inscribed: Postal Card Rate D

1985, Feb. 4 — **Perf. 11**

O138	O12	(14c) **red, blue & black**	5.25	10.00
		FDC, Washington, DC		1.00
		P# block of 4, LR only	42.50	—

Frame line completely around the design — O13

Inscribed: No. O139, Domestic Letter Rate D; No. O140, Domestic Mail E.

COIL STAMPS

1985-88   Litho., Engr. (#O139)   **Perf. 10 Vert.**

O138A	O13	15c **red, blue & blk,** *June 11, 1988*	.45	.50
		FDC, Corpus Christi, TX		1.25
		Pair	.90	1.00
O138B	O13	20c **red, blue & blk,** *May 19, 1988*	.45	.30
		FDC, Washington		1.25
		Pair	.90	.60
O139	O12	(22c) **red, blue & blk,** *Feb. 4*	5.25	5.25
		FDC, Washington, DC		1.00
		Pair	10.50	
		P# strip of 3, P# 1	27.50	
		P# strip of 5, P# 1	55.00	
		P# single, #1	—	32.50
O140	O13	(25c) **red, blue & black,** *Mar. 22, 1988*	.75	2.00
		FDC, Washington		1.25
		Pair	1.50	—
O141	O13	25c **red, blue & blk,** *June 11, 1988*	.65	.50
		FDC, Corpus Christi, TX		1.25
		Pair	1.30	1.00
a.		Imperf., pair	1,500.	
		Nos. O138A-O141 (5)	7.55	8.55

First day cancellation was applied to 137,721 covers bearing Nos. O138A and O141.

Plates of 400 in four panes of 100.

1989, July 5   Litho.   **Perf. 11**

O143	O13	1c **red, blue & black**	.20	.20
		FDC, Washington, DC		1.25

Type of 1985 and

O14

COIL STAMPS

1991   Litho.   **Perf. 10 Vert.**

O144	O14	(29c) **red, blue & blk,** *Jan. 22*	.80	.50
		FDC, Washington, DC		1.25
		Pair	1.60	—
O145	O13	29c **red, blue & blk,** *May 24*	.65	.30
		FDC, Seattle, WA		1.25
		Pair	1.30	.60

Plates of 400 in four panes of 100.

1991-93   Litho.   **Perf. 11**

O146	O13	4c **red, blue & blk,** *Apr. 6*	.20	.30
		FDC, Oklahoma City, OK		1.25
O146A	O13	10c **red, blue & black,** *Oct. 19, 1993*	.25	.30
		FDC, Washington, DC		1.25
O147	O13	19c **red, blue & blk,** *May 24*	.40	.50
		FDC, Seattle, WA		1.25

O148	O13	23c **red, blue & blk,** *May 24*	.45	.30
		FDC, Seattle, WA		1.25
		Horiz. pair with full vert. gutter between	—	
		Vert. pair with full horiz. gutter between	—	

Imperfs of No. O148 are printer's waste.

O151	O13	$1 **red, blue & black,** *Sept. 1993*	4.75	.75
		Nos. O146-O151 (5)	6.05	2.15

COIL STAMPS

Inscribed: No. O152, For U.S. addresses only G.

Perf. 9.8 Vert.

O152	O14	(32c) **red, blue & black,** *Dec. 13, 1994*	.65	.50
		FDC, Washington, DC		1.25
		Pair	1.30	
O153	O13	32c **red, blue & black,** *May 9, 1995*	1.25	.50
		FDC, Washington, DC		1.25
		Pair	2.50	

Nos. O146A, O151, O153 have a line of microscopic text below the eagle.

1995, May 9   Litho.   **Perf. 11.2**

O154	O13	1c **red, blue & black,** untagged	.20	.50
		FDC, Washington, DC		1.25
		Pair	.20	—
O155	O13	20c **red, blue & black**	.45	.50
		FDC, Washington, DC		1.25
		Pair	.90	—
O156	O13	23c **red, blue & black**	.55	.50
		FDC, Washington, DC		1.25
		Pair	1.10	—

Nos. O154-O156 have a line of microscopic text below the eagle.

COIL STAMP

1999, Oct. 8   Litho.   **Perf. 9¾ Vert.**

O157	O13	33c **red, blue & black**	.65	—
		FDC, Washington, DC		1.25
		Pair	1.30	—

No. O157 has a line of microscopic text below the eagle.

Type of 1985
COIL STAMP

2001, Feb. 27   Litho.   Tagged   **Perf. 9¾ Vert.**

O158	O13	34c **red, blue & black**	.65	.50
		FDC, Washington, DC		1.25
		Pair	1.30	—

Type of 1985
COIL STAMP

2002, Aug. 2   Photo.   Tagged   **Perf. 10 Vert.**

O159	O13	37c **red, blue & black**	.70	.50
		First day cover, Washington, DC		1.25
		First day cover, any other city		1.25
		Pair	1.40	—
		P# strip of 5, P#S111	5.25	—
		P# single, same #		.70

Type of 1985
COIL STAMP

2006, Mar. 8   Photo.   Tagged   **Perf. 10 Vert.**

O160	O13	39c **red, blue & black**	.80	.40
		First day cover, Washington, DC		1.25
		First day cover, any other city		1.25
		Pair	1.60	—
		P# strip of 5, #S111	5.75	—
		P# single, #S111	—	2.00

NEWSPAPER AND PERIODICAL STAMPS

First issued in September 1865 for prepayment of postage on bulk shipments of newspapers and periodicals. From 1875 on, the stamps were affixed pages of receipt books, sometimes canceled, and retained by the post office.

Virtually all used stamps of Nos. PR1-PR4 are canceled by blue brush strokes and have faults such as tears, stains, creases, etc. All are rare. Most used stamps of Nos. PR9-PR32, PR57-PR79 and PR81-PR89 are pen canceled (or uncanceled), with some of Nos. PR9-PR32 also known canceled by a thick blue brush stroke or a handstamp cancellation. Used values for Nos. PR90-PR125 are for stamps with handstamp cancellations.

Discontinued on July 1, 1898.

Washington — N1

Franklin — N2

Lincoln — N3

Values for Nos. PR1-PR8 are for examples with perforations on all four sides. Examples with natural straight edges sell for somewhat less. Some panes were fully perforated, while others have natural straight edges either at top or bottom affecting five stamps in the pane of ten.

Printed by the National Bank Note Co.
Plates of 20 subjects in two panes of 10 each.
Typographed and Embossed
1865   Unwmk.   *Perf. 12*
Thin hard paper, without gum
Size of design: 51x95mm
Colored Border

PR1	N1	5c	**dark blue**	625.00	*2,000.*
			blue	625.00	*2,000.*
			Block of 4	3,000.	—
a.			5c **light blue**	850.00	—
PR2	N2	10c	**blue green**	300.00	*1,800.*
a.			10c **green**	300.00	*1,800.*
			Block of 4	1,400.	—
b.			Pelure paper	300.00	*1,800.*
PR3	N3	25c	**orange red**	325.00	*2,400.*
			Block of 4	1,500.	—
a.			25c **carmine red**	350.00	*2,400.*
			Block of 4	1,600.	—
b.			Pelure paper	325.00	—

Nos. PR1-PR3 used are valued with faults.

White Border
Yellowish paper

PR4	N1	5c	**light blue**	225.00	*2,400.*
			blue	225.00	—
a.			5c **dark blue**	250.00	—
			Block of 4	1,250.	—
b.			Pelure paper	250.00	—

REPRINTS of 1865 ISSUE

Printed by the Continental Bank Note Co. using the original National Bank Note Co. plates
1875   *Perf. 12*
Hard white paper, without gum
5c White Border, 10c and 25c Colored Border

PR5	N1	5c	**dull blue** *(10,000)*	200.00
			dark blue	200.00
			Block of 4	900.00
a.			Printed on both sides	5,750.
PR6	N2	10c	**dark bluish green** *(7765)*	210.00
			deep green	210.00
			Block of 4	925.00
a.			Printed on both sides	4,250.
PR7	N3	25c	**dark carmine** *(6684)*	230.00
			dark carmine red	230.00
			Block of 4	1,050.

750 examples of each value, which were remainders from the regular issue, were sold as reprints because of delays in obtaining Nos. PR5-PR7. These remainders cannot be distinguished from Nos. PR2-PR4, and are not included in the reprint quantities.

The Continental Bank Note Co. made another special printing from new plates, which did not have the colored border. These exist imperforate and perforated, but they were not regularly issued.

On No. PR5, there is no thin line of color in the second white area on each side of the stamp. On No. PR8, there is often a thin line of color in this area, but not all examples of No. PR8 show this line (see illustration below). Expertization is based on color and paper.

#PR5   #PR8

Printed by the American Bank Note Co.
Soft porous paper, without gum
White Border
1881

PR8	N1	5c	**dark blue** *(5645)*	725.00
			Block of 4	3,500.

Statue of Freedom on Capitol Dome, by Thomas Crawford — N4

"Justice" — N5

Ceres — N6

"Victory" — N7

Clio — N8

Minerva — N9

Vesta — N10

"Peace" — N11

"Commerce" — N12

Hebe — N13

Indian Maiden — N14

Values for used examples of Nos. PR9-PR125 are for fine-very fine examples for denominations to $3, and fine for denominations of $3 or higher. Some used Scott numbers may not exist without faults.

Printed by the Continental Bank Note Co.
Plates of 100 subjects in two panes of 50 each
Size of design: 24x35mm

1875, Jan. 1   **Engr.**   *Perf. 12*
Thin hard paper

PR9	N4	2c black	260.00	25.00
		gray black	260.00	25.00
		greenish black	260.00	25.00
		No gum	110.00	
		Handstamp or blue brush cancel		45.00
		Block of 4	1,150.	160.00
PR10	N4	3c black	260.00	27.50
		gray black	260.00	27.50
		No gum	110.00	
		Handstamp or blue brush cancel		45.00
		Block of 4	1,150.	140.00
PR11	N4	4c black	260.00	25.00
		gray black	260.00	25.00
		greenish black	260.00	25.00
		No gum	110.00	
		Handstamp or blue brush cancel		45.00
		Block of 4	1,150.	
PR12	N4	6c black	260.00	27.50
		gray black	260.00	27.50
		greenish black	260.00	27.50
		No gum	110.00	
		Handstamp or blue brush cancel		45.00
		Block of 4	1,150.	
PR13	N4	8c black	300.00	40.00
		gray black	300.00	40.00

		greenish black	300.00	40.00
		No gum	130.00	
		Handstamp or blue brush cancel		80.00
PR14	N4	9c black	450.00	87.50
		gray black	450.00	87.50
		No gum	180.00	
		Handstamp or blue brush cancel		200.00
		Double transfer at top	500.00	100.00
PR15	N4	10c black	325.00	32.50
		gray black	325.00	32.50
		greenish black	325.00	32.50
		No gum	130.00	
		Handstamp or blue brush cancel		60.00
		Block of 4	1,600.	
PR16	N5	12c rose	750.00	82.50
		pale rose	750.00	82.50
		No gum	300.00	
		Handstamp or blue brush cancel		160.00
PR17	N5	24c rose	825.00	100.00
		pale rose	825.00	100.00
		No gum	325.00	
		Handstamp or blue brush cancel		200.00
		Paper with silk fibers	2,000.	
PR18	N5	36c rose	850.00	110.00
		pale rose	850.00	110.00
		No gum	350.00	
		Handstamp or blue brush cancel		250.00
PR19	N5	48c rose	1,250.	175.00
		pale rose	1,250.	175.00
		No gum	500.00	
		Handstamp or blue brush cancel		350.00
PR20	N5	60c rose	1,200.	100.00
		pale rose	1,200.	100.00
		No gum	475.00	
		Handstamp or blue brush cancel		225.00
PR21	N5	72c rose	1,250.	230.00
		pale rose	1,250.	230.00
		No gum	500.00	
		Handstamp or blue brush cancel		475.00
PR22	N5	84c rose	1,850.	330.00
		pale rose	1,850.	330.00
		No gum	700.00	
		Handstamp or blue brush cancel		600.00
PR23	N5	96c rose	1,350.	225.00
		pale rose	1,350.	225.00
		No gum	550.00	
		Handstamp or blue brush cancel		525.00
PR24	N6	$1.92 dark brown	1,600.	225.00
		No gum	675.00	
		Handstamp or blue brush cancel		400.00
PR25	N7	$3 vermilion	1,800.	250.00
		No gum	725.00	
		Handstamp or blue brush cancel		500.00
PR26	N8	$6 ultramarine	3,500.	475.00
		dull ultramarine	3,500.	475.00
		No gum	1,400.	
		Handstamp or blue brush cancel		750.00
PR27	N9	$9 yellow orange	4,000.	525.00
		No gum	1,700.	
		Handstamp or blue brush cancel		900.00
PR28	N10	$12 blue green	4,500.	675.00
		No gum	1,750.	
		Handstamp or blue brush cancel		1,200.
PR29	N11	$24 dark gray violet	4,500.	700.00
		No gum	1,750.	
		Handstamp or blue brush cancel		1,250.
PR30	N12	$36 brown rose	5,000.	850.00
		No gum	2,000.	
		Handstamp or blue brush cancel		1,500.
PR31	N13	$48 red brown	6,250.	1,000.
		No gum	2,300.	
		Handstamp or blue brush cancel		1,750.
PR32	N14	$60 violet	6,500.	1,100.
		No gum	2,400.	
		Handstamp or blue brush cancel		2,000.

SPECIAL PRINTING of 1875 ISSUE
Printed by the Continental Bank Note Co.
Hard white paper, without gum

1875   *Perf. 12*

PR33	N4	2c gray black (5,000)	600.00	
a.		Horizontally ribbed paper (10,000)	400.00	
		Block of 4	3,000.	
PR34	N4	3c gray black (5,000)	600.00	
		Block of 4	3,000.	
a.		Horizontally ribbed paper (1,952)	400.00	
PR35	N4	4c gray black (4451)	650.00	
		Block of 4	3,250.	
a.		Horizontally ribbed paper	800.00	
PR36	N4	6c gray black (2348)	850.00	
PR37	N4	8c gray black (1930)	925.00	
PR38	N4	9c gray black (1795)	1,050.	
PR39	N4	10c gray black (1499)	1,300.	
PR40	N5	12c pale rose (1313)	1,500.	
PR41	N5	24c pale rose (411)	2,100.	
PR42	N5	36c pale rose (330)	2,800.	
PR43	N5	48c pale rose (268)	3,750.	

PR44	N5	60c pale rose (222)	3,750.	
PR45	N5	72c pale rose (174)	4,400.	
PR46	N5	84c pale rose (164)	4,800.	
PR47	N5	96c pale rose (141)	8,500.	
PR48	N6	$1.92 dark brown (41)	22,500.	
PR49	N7	$3 vermilion (20)	45,000.	
PR50	N8	$6 ultramarine (14)	80,000.	
PR51	N9	$9 yellow orange (4)	160,000.	
PR52	N10	$12 blue green (5)	125,000.	
PR53	N11	$24 dark gray violet (2)	—	
PR54	N12	$36 brown rose (2)	250,000.	
PR55	N13	$48 red brown (1)	—	
PR56	N14	$60 violet (1)	—	

Although four examples of No. PR51 were sold, only one currently documented.

No. PR54 is valued in the grade of fine. Although two stamps were sold, only one is currently documented.

All values of this issue, Nos. PR33 to PR56, exist imperforate but were not regularly issued thus. Value, set $60,000.

Numbers in parenthesis are quantities sold.

Printed by the American Bank Note Co.
Soft porous paper

1879   **Unwmk.**   *Perf. 1*

PR57	N4	2c black	50.00	8.5
		gray black	50.00	8.5
		greenish black	50.00	8.5
		No gum	20.00	
		Handstamp cancel		20.0
		Block of 4	225.00	
		Double transfer at top	55.00	14.0
		Cracked plate	—	
PR58	N4	3c black	60.00	10.5
		gray black	60.00	10.5
		intense black	60.00	10.5
		No gum	25.00	
		Handstamp cancel		20.00
		Block of 4	250.00	
		Double transfer at top	65.00	15.00
PR59	N4	4c black	60.00	10.50
		gray black	60.00	10.50
		intense black	60.00	10.50
		greenish black	60.00	10.50
		No gum	25.00	
		Handstamp cancel		30.00
		Block of 4	250.00	
		Double transfer at top	65.00	15.00
PR60	N4	6c black	105.00	21.00
		gray black	105.00	21.00
		intense black	105.00	21.00
		greenish black	105.00	21.00
		No gum	45.00	
		Handstamp cancel		50.00
		Block of 4	500.00	
		Double transfer at top	115.00	26.00
PR61	N4	8c black	115.00	21.00
		gray black	115.00	21.00
		greenish black	115.00	21.00
		No gum	47.50	
		Handstamp cancel		50.00
		Block of 4	525.00	
		Double transfer at top	125.00	26.00
PR62	N4	10c black	115.00	21.00
		gray black	115.00	21.00
		greenish black	115.00	21.00
		No gum	47.50	
		Handstamp cancel		50.00
		Block of 4	525.00	
		Double transfer at top	125.00	
PR63	N5	12c red	475.00	85.00
		No gum	200.00	
		Handstamp cancel		175.00
		Block of 4	2,150.	
PR64	N5	24c red	475.00	85.00
		No gum	200.00	
		Handstamp cancel		175.00
		Block of 4	2,150.	
PR65	N5	36c red	1,000.	240.00
		No gum	475.00	
		Handstamp cancel		500.00
		Block of 4	4,500.	
PR66	N5	48c red	1,000.	180.00
		No gum	450.00	
		Handstamp cancel		450.00
PR67	N5	60c red	1,000.	160.00
		No gum	450.00	
		Handstamp cancel		400.00
		Block of 4	4,500.	
a.		Imperf., pair	4,000.	
PR68	N5	72c red	1,250.	300.00
		No gum	575.00	
		Handstamp cancel		700.00
PR69	N5	84c red	1,250.	225.00
		No gum	575.00	
		Handstamp cancel		575.00
		Block of 4	—	
PR70	N5	96c red	1,200.	160.00
		No gum	525.00	
		Handstamp cancel		375.00
		Block of 4	5,500.	
PR71	N6	$1.92 pale brown	550.00	135.00
		brown	550.00	135.00
		No gum	225.00	
		Handstamp cancel		300.00
		Block of 4	2,500.	
		Cracked plate	600.00	
PR72	N7	$3 red vermilion	625.00	150.00
		No gum	250.00	
		Handstamp cancel		350.00
		Block of 4	2,850.	
PR73	N8	$6 blue	1,050.	230.00
		ultramarine	1,100.	230.00
		No gum	400.00	
		Handstamp cancel		500.00
PR74	N9	$9 orange	800.00	160.00
		No gum	325.00	

R75 N10	$12	**yellow green**	850.00	210.00
		No gum	325.00	
		Handstamp cancel		475.00
R76 N11	$24	**dark violet**	800.00	260.00
		No gum	300.00	
		Handstamp cancel		600.00
R77 N12	$36	**Indian red**	850.00	280.00
		No gum	350.00	
		Handstamp cancel		650.00
R78 N13	$48	**yellow brown**	900.00	390.00
		No gum	350.00	
		Handstamp cancel		775.00
R79 N14	$60	**purple**	850.00	360.00
		bright purple	850.00	360.00
		No gum	350.00	
		Handstamp cancel		750.00

See Die and Plate Proofs for other imperfs. on stamp paper.

SPECIAL PRINTING of 1879 ISSUE
Printed by the American Bank Note Co.
Without gum

1883

R80 N4	2c	**intense black** (4,514)	1,350.
		Block of 4	6,250.

REGULAR ISSUE
Printed by the American Bank Note Co.
With gum

1885, July 1   Unwmk.   *Perf. 12*

PR81 N4	1c	**black**	70.00	7.50
		gray black	70.00	7.50
		intense black	70.00	7.50
		No gum	35.00	
		Handstamp cancel		25.00
		Block of 4	300.00	
		Double transfer at top	75.00	11.00
PR82 N5	12c	**carmine**	180.00	18.00
		deep carmine	180.00	18.00
		rose carmine	180.00	18.00
		No gum	75.00	
		Handstamp cancel		75.00
		Block of 4	875.00	
		Plate crack (pos. 41)	240.00	
PR83 N5	24c	**carmine**	180.00	20.00
		deep carmine	180.00	20.00
		rose carmine	180.00	20.00
		No gum	75.00	
		Handstamp cancel		100.00
		Block of 4	875.00	
PR84 N5	36c	**carmine**	280.00	32.50
		deep carmine	280.00	32.50
		rose carmine	280.00	32.50
		No gum	115.00	
		Handstamp cancel		120.00
		Block of 4	1,300.	
PR85 N5	48c	**carmine**	400.00	47.50
		deep carmine	400.00	47.50
		No gum	175.00	
		Handstamp cancel		190.00
		Block of 4	1,750.	
PR86 N5	60c	**carmine**	525.00	70.00
		deep carmine	525.00	70.00
		No gum	230.00	
		Handstamp cancel		270.00
		Block of 4	2,400.	
PR87 N5	72c	**carmine**	525.00	75.00
		deep carmine	525.00	75.00
		rose carmine	525.00	75.00
		No gum	230.00	
		Handstamp cancel		300.00
		Block of 4	2,400.	
PR88 N5	84c	**carmine**	800.00	175.00
		rose carmine	800.00	175.00
		No gum	300.00	
		Handstamp cancel		450.00
		Block of 4	3,650.	
PR89 N5	96c	**carmine**	700.00	135.00
		rose carmine	700.00	135.00
		No gum	275.00	
		Handstamp cancel		400.00
		Block of 4	3,150.	

See Die and Plate Proofs for imperfs. on stamp paper.

Printed by the Bureau of Engraving and Printing

1894   Unwmk.   *Perf. 12*
Soft wove paper, with pale, whitish gum

PR90 N4	1c	**intense black**	425.00	*750.00*
		No gum	175.00	
		Block of 4	1,850.	
		Double transfer at top	450.00	
PR91 N4	2c	**intense black**	475.00	
		No gum	200.00	
		Block of 4	2,150.	
		Double transfer at top	500.00	
PR92 N4	4c	**intense black**	500.00	—
		No gum	225.00	
		Block of 4	2,400.	
PR93 N4	6c	**intense black**	4,750.	
		No gum	2,200.	
		Block of 4	—	
PR94 N4	10c	**intense black**	1,150.	
		No gum	500.00	
		Block of 4	5,000.	
PR95 N5	12c	**pink**	2,600.	*1,500.*
		No gum	1,100.	
		Block of 4	12,000.	
PR96 N5	24c	**pink**	3,750.	*1,750.*

		No gum	1,850.	
		Block of 4	17,500.	
PR97 N5	36c	**pink**	*50,000.*	
		Block of 4	50,000.	
PR98 N5	60c	**pink**	60,000.	7,500.
		Block of 4	60,000.	
PR99 N5	96c	**pink**	52,500.	
PR100 N7	$3	**scarlet**	60,000.	
		Block of 4	60,000.	
PR101 N8	$6	**pale blue**	60,000.	—
		No gum	30,000.	

Nos. PR95-PR98 used are valued with fine centering and small faults.
No. PR97 unused is valued in the grade of very good to fine.
No. PR98 unused is valued in the grade of fine. Nos. PR99-PR100 unused are valued in the grade of fine-very fine.

Statue of Freedom — N15   N16

N17   N18

N19   N20

N21   N22

1895, Feb. 1   Unwmk.   *Perf. 12*
Size of designs: 1c-50c, 21x34mm
$2-$100, 24x35mm

PR102 N15	1c	**black**	230.00	100.00
		Never hinged	500.00	
		No gum	90.00	
		Block of 4	1,050.	500.00
PR103 N15	2c	**black**	230.00	100.00
		gray black	230.00	100.00
		Never hinged	500.00	
		No gum	90.00	
		Block of 4	1,050.	—
		Double transfer at top	250.00	
PR104 N15	5c	**black**	300.00	150.00
		gray black	300.00	150.00
		Never hinged	650.00	
		No gum	125.00	
		Block of 4	1,350.	
PR105 N15	10c	**black**	550.00	350.00
		Never hinged	1,150.	
		No gum	225.00	
		Block of 4	2,750.	

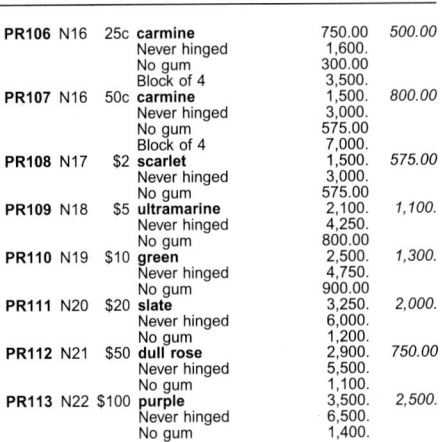

PR106 N16	25c	**carmine**	750.00	500.00
		Never hinged	1,600.	
		No gum	300.00	
		Block of 4	3,500.	
PR107 N16	50c	**carmine**	1,500.	800.00
		Never hinged	3,000.	
		No gum	575.00	
		Block of 4	7,000.	
PR108 N17	$2	**scarlet**	1,500.	575.00
		Never hinged	3,000.	
		No gum	575.00	
PR109 N18	$5	**ultramarine**	2,100.	*1,100.*
		Never hinged	4,250.	
		No gum	800.00	
PR110 N19	$10	**green**	2,500.	*1,300.*
		Never hinged	4,750.	
		No gum	900.00	
PR111 N20	$20	**slate**	3,250.	*2,000.*
		Never hinged	6,000.	
		No gum	1,200.	
PR112 N21	$50	**dull rose**	2,900.	750.00
		Never hinged	5,500.	
		No gum	1,100.	
PR113 N22	$100	**purple**	3,500.	*2,500.*
		Never hinged	6,500.	
		No gum	1,400.	

Nos. PR102-PR113 were printed from plates with arrows in the top, bottom and side margins, but no guidelines between the stamps.

1895-97   **Wmk. 191**   *Perf. 12*

PR114 N15	1c	**black,** *Jan. 11, 1896*	8.00	25.00
		gray black	8.00	25.00
		Never hinged	20.00	
		No gum	2.75	
		Block of 4	35.00	—
PR115 N15	2c	**black,** *Nov. 21, 1895*	8.00	25.00
		gray black	15.00	25.00
		Never hinged	20.00	
		No gum	2.75	
		Block of 4	35.00	—
PR116 N15	5c	**black,** *Feb. 12, 1896*	13.00	40.00
		gray black	13.00	40.00
		Never hinged	27.50	
		No gum	4.25	
		Block of 4	57.50	—
PR117 N15	10c	**black,** *Sept. 13, 1895*	13.00	25.00
		gray black	13.00	25.00
		Never hinged	27.50	
		No gum	4.25	
		Block of 4	57.50	—
PR118 N16	25c	**carmine,** *Oct. 11, 1895*	20.00	65.00
		lilac rose	20.00	65.00
		Never hinged	45.00	
		No gum	7.00	
		Block of 4	87.50	—
PR119 N16	50c	**carmine,** *Sept. 19, 1895*	25.00	75.00
		rose carmine	25.00	75.00
		lilac rose	25.00	75.00
		Never hinged	55.00	
		No gum	8.50	
		Block of 4	110.00	—
PR120 N17	$2	**scarlet,** *Jan. 23, 1897*	30.00	110.00
		scarlet vermilion	30.00	110.00
		Never hinged	75.00	
		No gum	10.00	
		Block of 4	130.00	—
PR121 N18	$5	**dark blue,** *Jan. 16, 1896*	40.00	160.00
		Never hinged	100.00	
		No gum	13.50	
		Block of 4	200.00	
a.		$5 light blue	200.00	450.00
		Never hinged	450.00	
		Block of 4	875.00	700.00
PR122 N19	$10	**green,** *Mar. 5, 1896*	42.50	160.00
		Never hinged	105.00	
		No gum	70.00	
		Block of 4	200.00	—
PR123 N20	$20	**slate,** *Jan. 27, 1896*	45.00	180.00
		Never hinged	110.00	
		No gum	15.00	
		Block of 4	210.00	—
PR124 N21	$50	**dull rose,** *July 31, 1897*	75.00	210.00
		Never hinged	170.00	
		No gum	27.50	
		Block of 4	350.00	
PR125 N22	$100	**purple,** *Jan. 23, 1896*	65.00	240.00
		Never hinged	150.00	
		No gum	22.50	
		Block of 4	300.00	
		Nos. PR114-PR125 (12)	384.50	1,315.
		Nos. PR114-PR125, never hinged	902.50	

Nos. PR114-PR125 were printed from the original plates with guide lines added in November 1895. Top and bottom plate strips and blocks of Nos. PR114-PR119 exist both with and without vertical guidelines.

In 1899 the Government sold 26,989 sets of these stamps, but, as the stock of high values was not sufficient to make up the required number, an additional printing was made of the $5, $10, $20, $50 and $100. These are virtually indistinguishable from earlier printings.

POSTAL NOTE STAMPS

Postal note stamps were issued to supplement the regular money order service. They were a means of sending amounts under $1. One or two Postal note stamps, totaling 1c to 99c, were affixed to United States Postal Notes and canceled by the clerk. The stamps were on the second of three parts, the one retained by the post office redeeming the Postal Note. They were discontinued March 31, 1951.

MO1

ROTARY PRESS PRINTING

1945, Feb. 1		Unwmk.	Perf. 11x10½	
PN1	MO1	1c **black** (155950-155951)	.30	.20
PN2	MO1	2c **black** (156003-156004)	.30	.20
PN3	MO1	3c **black** (156062-156063)	.30	.20
PN4	MO1	4c **black** (156942-156943)	.30	.20
PN5	MO1	5c **black** (156261-156262)	.35	.20
PN6	MO1	6c **black** (156064-156065)	.40	.20
PN7	MO1	7c **black** (156075-156076)	.55	.20
PN8	MO1	8c **black** (156077-156078)	.65	.20
PN9	MO1	9c **black** (156251-156252)	.75	.20
PN10	MO1	10c **black** (156274-156275)	.85	.20
PN11	MO1	20c **black** (156276-156277)	1.75	.20
PN12	MO1	30c **black** (156303-156304)	2.25	.20
PN13	MO1	40c **black** (156283-156284)	2.75	.20

PN14	MO1	50c **black** (156322-156323)	3.25	
PN15	MO1	60c **black** (156324-156325)	4.25	
PN16	MO1	70c **black** (156344-156345)	5.25	
PN17	MO1	80c **black** (156326-156327)	6.00	
PN18	MO1	90c **black** (156352-156353)	6.75	
		Nos. PN1-PN18 (18)	37.00	3.

Blocks of four and plate number blocks of four are valued at and 15 times the unused single value.

Postal note stamps exist on postal note cards with first da cancellation.

Numbers in parentheses are plate Nos.

PARCEL POST STAMPS

The Act of Congress approved Aug. 24, 1912, created postage rates on 4th class mail weighing 4 ounces or less at 1 cent per ounce or fraction. On mail over 4 ounces, the rate was by the pound. These rates were to be prepaid by distinctive postage stamps. Under this provision, the Post Office Department prepared 12 parcel post and 5 parcel post due stamps, usable only on parcel post packages starting Jan. 1, 1913. Other stamps were no usable on parcel post starting on that date.

Beginning on Nov. 27, 1912, the stamps were shipped to post offices offering parcel post service. Approximate shipping dates were: 1c, 2c, 5c, 25c 1c due, 5c due, Nov. 27; 10c, 2c due, Dec. 9; 4c, 10c due, Dec. 12; 15c, 20c, 25c due, Dec. 16; 75c, Dec. 18. There was no prohibition on sale of the stamps prior to Jan. 1, 1913. Undoubtedly many were used on 4th class mail in Dec. 1912. Fourth class mail was expanded by adding former 2nd and 3rd class categories and was renamed "parcel post" effective Jan. 1, 1913. Normally 4th class (parcel post) mail did not receive a dated cancel unless a special service was involved. Small pieces, such as samples, are known with 1st class cancels.

With the approval of the Interstate Commerce Commission, the Postmaster General directed, in Order No. 7241 dated June 26, 1913, and effective July 1, 1913, that regular postage stamps should be valid on parcels. Parcel post stamps then became usable as regular stamps.

Parcel post and parcel post due stamps remained on sale, but no further printings were made. Remainders, consisting of 3,510,345 of the 75c, were destroyed in Sept. 1921.

The 20c was the first government-issued postage stamp of any country to show an airplane.

Post Office Clerk — PP1

City Carrier — PP2

Railway Postal Clerk — PP3

Rural Carrier — PP4

Mail Train and Mail Bag on Rack — PP5

Steamship "Kronprinz Wilhelm" and Mail Tender, New York — PP6

Automobile Service — PP7

Airplane Carrying Mail — PP8

Manufacturing (Steel Plant, South Chicago) — PP9

Dairying — PP10

Harvesting PP11

Fruit Growing (Florida Orange Grove) — PP12

6161   **TEN**

Plate number and imprint consisting of value in words.

Marginal imprints, consisting of value in words, were added to plates on January 27, 1913.

Designed by Clair Aubrey Huston.

Plates of 180 subjects in four panes of 45 each.

1913   Wmk. 190   Engr.   Perf. 12

PP1	1c carmine rose (209,691,094)	5.75	1.75
	carmine	5.75	1.75
	Never hinged	14.00	
	First day cover, *July 1, 1913*		*1,500.*
	On cover, 1913-25		6.00
	Block of 4	25.00	9.00
	P# block of 4, Impt.	45.00	
	P# block of 6, Impt.	105.00	
	P# block of 6	110.00	
	Never hinged	180.00	
	Double transfer	9.50	4.00
PP2	2c carmine rose (206,417,253)	6.75	1.40
	carmine	6.75	1.40
	Never hinged	19.00	
	First day cover, *July 1, 1913*		*1,750.*
	On cover, 1913-25		5.75
	Block of 4	30.00	6.50
	P# block of 4, Impt.	47.50	
	P# block of 6, Impt.	125.00	
	P# block of 6	145.00	
	Never hinged	240.00	
	Double transfer	—	—
a.	2c lake	1,750.	
b.	2c carmine lake	350.00	

No. Q2a is valued in the grade of fine to very fine.

PP3	3c carmine, *Apr. 5, 1913* (29,027,433)	13.50	6.50
	deep carmine	13.50	6.50
	Never hinged	37.50	
	First day cover, *July 1, 1913*		*3,500.*
	On cover, 1913-25		19.00
	Block of 4	57.50	37.50
	P# block of 4, Impt.	100.00	
	P# block of 6, Impt.	260.00	
	P# block of 6	235.00	
	P# block of 8, Impt. (side)	310.00	
	Never hinged	550.00	
	Retouched at lower right corner (No. 6257 LL 7)	26.00	14.50
	Double transfer (No. 6257 LL 6)	26.00	14.50

Q4	PP4	4c carmine rose (76,743,813)	37.50	3.50
		carmine	37.50	3.50
		Never hinged	110.00	
		First day cover, *July 1, 1913*		*3,500.*
		On cover, 1913-25		65.00
		Block of 4	160.00	17.50
		P# block of 4, Impt.	360.00	
		P# block of 6, Impt.	1,050.	
		P# block of 6	1,000.	
		Never hinged	1,700.	
		Double transfer	—	—
Q5	PP5	5c carmine rose (108,153,993)	32.50	2.50
		carmine	32.50	2.50
		Never hinged	90.00	
		First day cover, *July 1, 1913*		*3,500.*
		On cover, 1913-25		42.50
		Block of 4	135.00	15.00
		P# block of 4, Impt.	350.00	
		P# block of 6, Impt.	1,000.	
		P# block of 6	975.00	
		Never hinged	1,600.	
		Double transfer	45.00	6.25
Q6	PP6	10c carmine rose (56,896,653)	52.50	3.50
		carmine	52.50	3.50
		Never hinged	120.00	
		First day cover, *July 1, 1913*		*12,500.*
		On cover, 1913-25		55.00
		Block of 4	240.00	30.00
		P# block of 4, Impt.	440.00	
		P# block of 6, Impt.	1,150.	
		P# block of 6	1,000.	
		Never hinged	1,650.	
		Double transfer	—	—
Q7	PP7	15c carmine rose (21,147,033)	67.50	15.00
		carmine	67.50	15.00
		Never hinged	180.00	
		First day cover, *July 1, 1913*		350.00
		On cover, 1913-25		100.00
		Block of 4	310.00	
		P# block of 4, Impt.	700.00	
		P# block of 6, Impt.	2,600.	
		P# block of 8, Impt.	3,100.	
		P# block of 6	2,300.	
		Never hinged	3,700.	
Q8	PP8	20c carmine rose (17,142,393)	150.00	30.00
		carmine	150.00	30.00
		Never hinged	325.00	
		On cover, 1913-25		750.00
		Block of 4	650.00	150.00

	P# block of 4, Impt.	1,500.	
	P# block of 6, Impt.	6,500.	
	P# block of 8, Impt. (side)	7,000.	
	P# block of 6	6,500.	
	Never hinged	10,000.	
Q9 PP9	25c carmine rose (21,940,653)	67.50	8.50
	carmine	67.50	8.50
	Never hinged	180.00	
	On cover, 1913-25		300.00
	Block of 4	310.00	60.00
	P# block of 6, Impt.	2,700.	
	P# block of 8, Impt. (side)	3,500.	
	P# block of 6	2,400.	
	Never hinged	3,850.	
Q10 PP10	50c carmine rose, *Mar. 15, 1913* (2,117,793)	300.00	50.00
	carmine	300.00	50.00
	Never hinged	700.00	
	On cover, 1913-25		—
	Block of 4	1,350.	325.00
	Never hinged	3,000.	
	P# block of 6, Impt.	22,500.	
	Never hinged	30,000.	
Q11 PP11	75c carmine rose (2,772,615)	110.00	40.00
	carmine	110.00	40.00
	Never hinged	240.00	
	On cover, 1913-25		—
	Block of 4	500.00	225.00
	P# block of 6, Impt.	4,000.	
	P# block of 8, Impt. (side)	3,600.	
	P# block of 6	3,000.	
	Never hinged	4,500.	
Q12 PP12	$1 carmine rose, *Jan. 3, 1913* (1,053,273)	375.00	45.00
	carmine	375.00	45.00
	Never hinged	850.00	
	On cover, 1913-25		1,250.
	Block of 4	1,650.	225.00
	P# block of 6, Impt.	20,000.	
	Never hinged	29,000.	
	P# block of 8, Impt. (side)	21,000.	
	P# block of 6	18,000.	
	Nos. Q1-Q12 (12)	*1,218.*	*207.65*
	Nos. Q1-Q12, never hinged	*2,865.*	

The 1c, 2c, 4c and 5c are known in parcel post usage postmarked Jan. 1, 1913.

PARCEL POST POSTAGE DUE STAMPS

See notes preceding Scott No. Q1. Parcel Post Due stamps were allowed to be used as regular postage due stamps from July 1, 1913.

PPD1

Designed by Clair Aubrey Huston

Plates of 180 subjects in four panes of 45

1913   Wmk. 190   Engr.   Perf. 12

JQ1 PPD1	1c dark green (7,322,400)	10.50	4.50
	yellowish green	10.50	4.50
	Never hinged	26.00	
	On cover, 1913-25		150.00
	Block of 4	47.50	35.00
	P# block of 6	550.00	
	Never hinged	900.00	

Earliest documented use: Feb. 26, 1913.

JQ2 PPD1	2c dark green (3,132,000)	85.00	17.50
	yellowish green	85.00	17.50
	Never hinged	210.00	
	On cover, 1913-25		200.00
	Block of 4	375.00	125.00
	P# block of 6	3,750.	
	Never hinged	6,000.	

Earliest documented use: July 7, 1913.

JQ3 PPD1	5c dark green (5,840,100)	14.00	5.50
	yellowish green	14.00	5.50
	Never hinged	35.00	
	On cover, 1913-25		185.00
	Block of 4	60.00	37.50
	P# block of 6	600.00	
	Never hinged	975.00	

Earliest documented use: Jan. 15, 1913 (dated cancel on off-cover stamp).

JQ4 PPD1	10c dark green (2,124,540)	175.00	45.00
	yellowish green	175.00	45.00
	Never hinged	425.00	
	On cover, 1913-25		650.00

	Block of 4	775.00	375.00
	P# block of 6	9,750.	
	Never hinged	14,000.	

Earliest documented use: July 19, 1913.

JQ5 PPD1	25c dark green (2,117,700)	100.00	5.00
	yellowish green	100.00	5.00
	Never hinged	260.00	
	On cover, 1913-25		—
	Block of 4	450.00	35.00
	P# block of 6	5,000.	
	Never hinged	8,000.	

Earliest documented use: Aug. 30, 1913.

	Nos. JQ1-JQ5 (5)	*384.50*	*77.50*
	Nos. JQ1-JQ5, never hinged	*956.00*	

SPECIAL HANDLING STAMPS

The Postal Service Act, approved February 28, 1925, provided for a special handling stamp of the 25-cent denomination for use on fourth-class m
matter, which would secure for such mail matter the expeditious handling accorded to mail matter of the first class.

PP13

FLAT PLATE PRINTING
Plates of 200 subjects in four panes of 50

1925-55   **Unwmk.**   *Perf. 11*

QE1 PP13 10c **yellow green**, *1955*	2.00	1.00
Never hinged	3.50	
Block of 4	8.50	5.75
P# block of 6	32.50	
Never hinged	47.50	
a. Wet printing, *June 25, 1928*	2.50	1.00
Never hinged	4.25	
P# block of 6	22.50	

Never hinged	32.50	
First day cover		45.00
QE2 PP13 15c **yellow green**, *1955*	2.10	.90
Never hinged	3.60	
Block of 4	8.75	5.75
P# block of 6	42.50	
Never hinged	62.50	
a. Wet printing, *June 25, 1928*	2.75	.90
Never hinged	4.50	
P# block of 6	32.50	
Never hinged	47.50	
First day cover		45.00
QE3 PP13 20c **yellow green**, *1955*	3.25	1.50
Never hinged	5.25	
Block of 4	14.50	11.00
P# block of 6	47.50	
Never hinged	70.00	
a. Wet printing, *June 25, 1928*	4.50	1.50
Never hinged	7.75	
P# block of 6	37.50	
Never hinged	55.00	
First day cover		45.00
First day cover, Nos. QE1a-QE3a		350.00

QE4 PP13 25c **yellow green**, *1929*	18.00	7
Never hinged	32.50	
Block of 4	85.00	32
P# block of 6	260.00	
Never hinged	375.00	
a. 25c **deep green**, *Apr. 11, 1925*	30.00	5
Never hinged	50.00	
First day cover		225.
Block of 4	130.00	30.
P# block of 6	330.00	
Never hinged	475.00	
"A" and second "T" of "States" joined at top (Pl. 17103)	50.00	22.
"A" and second "T" of "States" and "T" and "A" of "Postage" joined at top (Pl. 17103)	75.00	45.
Nos. QE1-QE4 (4)	25.35	10.
Nos. QE1-QE4, never hinged	44.85	

See note on Wet and Dry Printings following No. 1029.

POSTAL INSURANCE STAMPS

Postal insurance stamps were issued to pay insurance on parcels for loss or damage. The stamps come in a booklet of one which also carrie
instructions for use and a receipt form for use if there is a claim. The booklets were sold by vending machine. Values in unused column are for complete
booklets. Values in used column are for used stamps.

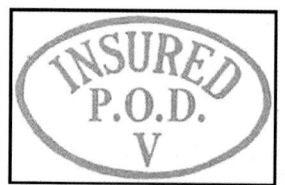

PPI1

1965, Aug.   **Typo.**   *Rouletted 9 at Top*

QI1 PPI1 (10c) **dark red**	135.00	—

No. QI1 paid insurance up to $10. It was sold at the Canoga Park, Calif., automatic post office which opened Aug. 19, 1965. The "V" stands for "Vended."

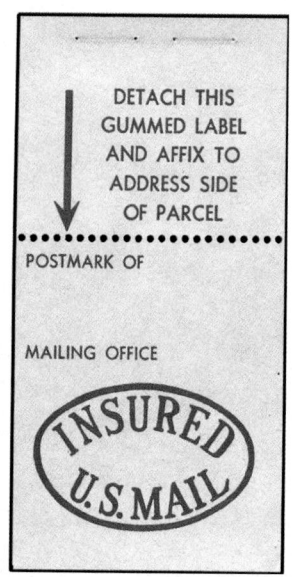

PPI2

1966, Mar. 26   **Litho.**   *Perf. 11 at Top*

QI2 PPI2 (20c) **red**	4.00	—

No. QI2 paid insurance up to $15. The rate increased from 20c to 25c on Apr. 18, 1976, and to 40c on July 18, 1976.

The QI2 booklet comes with two types of front covers, the first beginning "Vended..." and the second "Domestic Vended...." There also are two types of back covers, the first with some white on black lettering, the second with all black on white lettering.

No 25c postal insurance stamps were printed. Existing copies of No. QI2 had 5c postage stamps added and the value on the cover was changed to 25c, usually by hand, but sometimes by handstamp or label. Twenty-cent stamps were added to make the 40c rate since new postal insurance stamps were not issued until 1977. Some 25c provisional booklets were further revalued to 40c by the addition of a 15c stamp. Each provisional booklet comes with both cover types.

Type PPI2 with "FEE PAID THROUGH VENDING MACHINE" Added Below

1977-81   **Litho.**   *Perf. 11 at Top*

QI3 PPI2 (40c) **black**	8.50	—

Available for use by Nov. 28, 1977 or earlier.

QI4 PPI2 (50c) **green**	7.50	—

The rate increased to 50c on May 29, 1978. Examples of QI2 and QI3 exist revalued to 50c by the addition of stamps.

QI5 PPI2 (45c) **red**, *1981*	8.50	—

No. QI3 booklets exist revalued to 45c by the addition of a 5c stamp, and the QI4 booklet is known revalued to 45c on its cover.

FIRST DAY COVERS

All envelopes or cards are postmarked Washington, D.C., unless otherwise stated. Minors and sublistings without dates have the same date and city (if none is otherwise mentioned) as the previous listing. Minors and sublistings with dates differing from the previous listing are postmarked in Washington, D.C. unless otherwise stated.

Values are for first day covers in very fine condition, without tears, stains or smeared postmarks, and with sound stamps that have fresh color and are not badly off center.

Printed cachets on covers before Scott Nos. 772 and C20 sell at a substantial premium. Values for covers of Nos. 772-986 and C20-C45 are for those with the most common cachets and addressed. Unaddressed covers sell at a substantial premium and covers without cachet sell at a substantial discount. Values for covers from Scott 987 and C46 onward are for those with the most common cachets and unaddressed.

Values for 1st class rate stamps are for covers bearing single stamps. Blocks of 4 on first day covers usually sell for about 1½ times as much as singles; Plate number blocks of 4 at about 3 times; Plate number blocks of 6 at about 4 times; coil line pairs at about 3 times. Stamps with denominations less than the first class rate will have the proper multiple to make the rate if practical or additional postage. (See Nos. 899, 907-908, 930-31, etc.)

Dates given are those on which the stamps were first *officially* placed on sale. Many instances are known of stamps being sold in advance, contrary to regulations.

Numbers in parentheses are quantities stated to have received the first day cancel.

Listings from Scott Nos. 551 and C4 are for covers canceled at cities officially designated by the Post Office Department or Postal Service. Some tagged varieties and cities of special interest are exceptions.

Air post first day covers are listed following the Postage first day covers. Envelope, postal card and other first day covers are with the regular listings.

Quantities given for se-tenant issues include the multiple and any single or combination of singles (see No. 2375a).

1851-57

5A	1c **blue**, type Ib, *July 1, 1851,* Boston, Mass.	120,000.
	1c **blue**, type II, *July 1, 1851,* any city	25,000.
	Same on printed circular	4,000.
10	3c **orange brown**, *July 1, 1851,* any city	12,500.

The No. 5A cover is unique. Value is based on 1996 auction sale. The No. 7 cover also is unique.

1861

64	3c **pink**, *Aug. 17, 1861,* Baltimore, Md.	17,500.
64b	3c **rose pink**, *Aug. 17, 1861,* Baltimore, Md.	23,000.

The Nos. 64 and 64b covers are each unique. Values based on 1999 and 1996 auction sales, respectively.

1883

210	2c **red brown**, *Oct. 1,* any city	2,000.
210, 211	2c, 4c **blue green**, *Oct. 1,* New York, N.Y.	36,000.

The Nos. 210, 211 cover is unique. Value is based on 1996 auction sale.

1890

219D	2c **lake**, *Feb. 22,* any city	35,000.

1893

COLUMBIAN EXPOSITION ISSUE

230	1c **deep blue**, *Jan. 1,* any city	9,000.
	Jan. 2, any city	5,000.
231	2c **brown violet**, *Jan. 1,* any city	12,500.
	Jan. 2, any city	5,000.
232	3c **green**, *Jan. 1,* any city	11,000.
	Jan. 2, any city	7,000.
	230, 232 on one cover, *Jan. 2,* Boston, Mass.	8,250.
233	4c **ultramarine**, *Jan. 1,* any city	16,500.
	Jan. 2, any city	10,500.
234	5c **chocolate**, *Jan. 1,* any city	27,500.
	Jan. 2, any city	17,500.
235	6c **purple**, *Jan. 2,* any city	22,500.
237	10c **black brown**, *Jan. 1,* any city	32,500.
	Jan. 2, any city	27,500.
242	$2 **brown red**, *Jan. 2,* any city	65,000.

As Jan. 1, 1893, was a Sunday, specialists recognize both Jan. 1 and 2 as "first day."

1898

TRANS-MISSISSIPPI EXPOSITION ISSUE

285	1c **green**, *June 17,* any city	15,000.
286	2c **copper red**, *June 17,* any city	17,500.
	Pittsburgh, Pa,	15,000.
287	4c **orange**, *June 17*	27,500.
288	5c **dull blue**, *June 17,* any city	20,000.
	285, 287-288 on one cover	75,000.
289	8c **violet brown**, *June 17,* any city	22,500.
290	10c **gray violet**, *June 17*	27,500.
	285-290, all 6 on one cover, *June 17*	100,000.
291	50c **sage green**, *June 17,* any city	50,000.
292	$1 **black**, *June 17,* any city	55,000.

1901

PAN AMERICAN EXPOSITION ISSUE

294	1c **green & black**, *May 1,* any city	5,500.
295	2c **carmine & black**, *May 1,* any city	3,000.
297	5c **ultra. & blk.**, *May 1,* any city	35,000.
	294, 295, 297 on one cover, *May 1,* Boston, Mass.	17,500.
	294, 296, 297 on one cover, *May 1,* Boston, Mass.	27,500.
	295, 298 on one cover, *May 1,* Washington, D.C.	28,500.
	296, 298 on one cover, *May 1,* Boston, Mass.	27,500.
	297, 298 on one cover, *May 1,* Philadelphia, Pa.	27,500.
	294-299, complete set of 6 on one cover *May 1,* any city	35,000.

1904

LOUISIANA PURCHASE EXPOSITION ISSUE

323	1c **green**, *Apr. 30,* any city	7,500.
324	2c **carmine**, *Apr. 30,* any city	5,000.
325	3c **violet**, *Apr. 30,* any city	20,000.
326	5c **dark blue**, *Apr. 30,* any city	22,500.
327	10c **red brown**, *Apr. 30,* any city	24,000.
	323-327, all 5 on one cover, *Apr. 30,* New York	80,000.

The Nos. 323-327 combination cover is unique. Value is based on 1996 auction sale.

1907

328	1c **Jamestown**, *Apr. 26,* any city	10,000.
329	2c **Jamestown**, *Apr. 26,* any city	15,000.

1908

331a	1c **green**, booklet single, *Dec. 2,* Washington, D.C.	17,500.

1909

367	2c **Lincoln**, *Feb. 12,* any city	500.
	On pictorial postcard, *Feb. 12,* Boston	425.

Imperf

368	2c **Lincoln**, *Feb. 12,* any city	13,000.

1909

ALASKA-YUKON ISSUE

370	2c **carmine**, *June 1,* any city	3,000.
	On Expo-related picture postcard, *June 1*	5,000.

1909

HUDSON-FULTON ISSUE

372	2c **carmine**, *Sept. 25,* any city	900.
	On Expo-related picture postcard, *Sept. 25*	1,400.

Imperf

373	2c **carmine**, *Sept. 25,* any city	8,000.

1913

PANAMA-PACIFIC ISSUE

397	1c **green**, *Jan. 1,* any city	5,000.
399	5c **blue**, *Jan. 1*	21,000.
400	10c **orange yellow**, *Jan. 1*	10,000.
	397, 399 & 400, all 3 on one cover, San Francisco, Cal.	10,000.

1916-22

COIL STAMP

497	10c **orange yellow**, *Jan. 31, 1922,* any city	6,000.

1918-20

OFFSET PRINTING

526	2c **carmine**, type IV, *Mar. 15, 1920*	850.

1919

537	3c **Victory**, *Mar. 3,* any city	800.

1919

Perf. 11x10

541	3c **violet**, type II, *June 14, 1919,* any city	9,000.

1920

Perf. 10x11

REGULAR ISSUE

542	1c **green**, *May 26*	1,750.

1920

548	1c **Pilgrim**, *Dec. 21,* any city, pair	1,000.
	Plymouth, Mass.	5,000.
549	2c **Pilgrim**, *Dec. 21,* any city	750.
	Plymouth, Mass.	5,000.
550	5c **Pilgrim**, *Dec. 21*	—
	548-550, complete set of 3 on one cover, *Dec. 21,* any city	2,500.
	Washington, D.C.	3,000.

1922-26   Perf. 11

551	½c **Hale**, *Apr. 4, 1925,* block of 4	19.00
	New Haven, Conn.	25.00
	551 & 576 on one cover, *Apr. 4, 1925,* New Haven, Conn.	165.00
552	1c **Franklin**, *Jan. 17, 1923,* pair	27.50
	Philadelphia, Pa.	47.50
553	1½c **Harding**, *Mar. 19, 1925,* pair	52.50
	553, 582, 598 on one cover, *Mar. 19, 1925*	190.00
554	2c **Washington**, *Jan. 15, 1923*	42.50
555	3c **Lincoln**, *Feb. 12, 1923*	40.00
	Hodgenville, Ky.	325.00
556	4c **Martha Washington**, *Jan. 15, 1923*	65.00
557	5c **Roosevelt**, *Oct. 27, 1922*	135.00
	New York, N.Y.	190.00
	Oyster Bay, N.Y.	1,250.
558	6c **Garfield**, *Nov. 20, 1922*	235.00
559	7c **McKinley**, *May 1, 1923*	185.00
	Niles, O.	275.00
560	8c **Grant**, *May 1, 1923*	190.00
561	9c **Jefferson**, *Jan. 15, 1923*	190.00
562	10c **Monroe**, *Jan. 15, 1923*	190.00
	554, 556, 561 & 562, all 4 stamps issued *Jan. 15* on one cover	3,500.
563	11c **Hayes**, *Oct. 4, 1922*	650.00
	Fremont, O.	3,750.
564	12c **Cleveland**, *Mar. 20, 1923*	185.00
	Boston, Mass. (Philatelic Exhibition)	185.00
	Caldwell, N.J.	210.00
565	14c **American Indian**, *May 1, 1923*	400.00
	Muskogee, Okla.	1,250.
566	15c **Statue of Liberty**, *Nov. 11, 1922*	575.00
567	20c **Golden Gate**, *May 1, 1923*	600.00
	San Francisco, Cal.	2,000.
	559, 560, 565 & 567, all 4 stamps issued *May 1* on one cover	10,000.
568	25c **Niagara Falls**, *Nov. 11, 1922*	650.00
569	30c **American Buffalo**, *Mar. 20, 1923*	800.00
570	50c **Arlington**, *Nov. 11, 1922*	1,250.
571	$1 **Lincoln Memorial**, *Feb. 12, 1923*	7,000.
	Springfield, Ill.	6,500.
572	$2 **U.S. Capitol**, *Mar. 20, 1923*	17,500.
573	$5 **America**, *Mar. 20, 1923*	32,500.

Imperf

576	1½c **Harding**, *Apr. 4, 1925*	42.50

Perf. 10

581	1c **Franklin**, *Oct. 17, 1923,* not pre-canceled	6,000.
582	1½c **Harding**, *Mar. 19, 1925*	40.00
583a	2c **Washington booklet pane of 6**, *Aug. 27, 1926*	1,500.
584	3c **Lincoln**, *Aug. 1, 1925*	55.00
585	4c **Martha Washington**, *Apr. 4, 1925*	50.00
586	5c **Roosevelt**, *Apr. 4, 1925*	60.00
587	6c **Garfield**, *Apr. 4, 1925*	60.00
	585-587, all 3 stamps issued *April 4* on one cover	1,000.
588	7c **McKinley**, *May 29, 1926*	60.00
589	8c **Grant**, *May 29, 1926*	65.00
590	9c **Jefferson**, *May 29, 1926*	77.50
591	10c **Monroe**, *June 8, 1925*	95.00

Perf. 10 Vertically

597	1c **Franklin**, *July 18, 1923*	600.00
598	1½c **Harding**, *Mar. 19, 1925*	65.00
599	2c **Washington**, *Jan. 15, 1923*	1,750.

600	3c	**Lincoln,** *May 10, 1924*	90.00
602	5c	**Roosevelt,** *Mar. 5, 1924*	95.00
603	10c	**Monroe,** *Dec. 1, 1924*	110.00

No. 599 is known used on Jan. 10, 11 and 13, 1923 (one each day). Jan. 15 was the first day of sale in Washington, D. C.

Perf. 10 Horizontally

604	1c	**Franklin,** *July 19, 1924*	90.00
605	1½c	**Harding,** *May 9, 1925*	70.00
606	2c	**Washington,** *Dec. 31, 1923*	125.00

1923

610	2c	**Harding,** perf. 11, *Sept. 1*	37.50
		Marion, O.	22.50
611	2c	**Harding,** imperf., *Nov. 15*	90.00
612	2c	**Harding,** perf. 10, *Sept. 12*	100.00

1924

614	1c	**Huguenot-Walloon,** *May 1,* pair	35.00
		Albany, N.Y	35.00
		Allentown, Pa.	35.00
		Charleston, S.C.	35.00
		Jacksonville, Fla.	35.00
		Lancaster, Pa.	35.00
		Mayport, Fla.	35.00
		New Rochelle, N.Y.	35.00
		New York, N.Y.	35.00
		Philadelphia, Pa.	35.00
		Reading, Pa.	35.00
615	2c	**Huguenot-Walloon,** *May 1*	50.00
		Albany, N.Y.	50.00
		Allentown, Pa.	50.00
		Charleston, S.C.	50.00
		Jacksonville, Fla.	50.00
		Lancaster, Pa.	50.00
		Mayport, Fla.	50.00
		New Rochelle, N.Y.	50.00
		New York, N.Y.	50.00
		Philadelphia, Pa.	50.00
		Reading, Pa.	50.00
616	5c	**Huguenot-Walloon,** *May 1*	75.00
		Albany, N.Y.	75.00
		Allentown, Pa.	75.00
		Charleston, S.C.	75.00
		Jacksonville, Fla.	75.00
		Lancaster, Pa.	75.00
		Mayport, Fla.	75.00
		New Rochelle, N.Y.	75.00
		New York, N.Y.	75.00
		Philadelphia, Pa.	75.00
		Reading, Pa.	75.00
		614-616 on one cover, any city	160.00

1925

617	1c	**Lexington-Concord,** *Apr. 4,* pair	30.00
		Boston, Mass.	30.00
		Cambridge, Mass.	30.00
		Concord, Mass.	32.50
		Concord Junction, Mass.	30.00
		Lexington, Mass.	30.00
618	2c	**Lexington-Concord,** *Apr. 4*	35.00
		Boston, Mass.	35.00
		Cambridge, Mass.	35.00
		Concord, Mass	35.00
		Concord Junction, Mass.	35.00
		Lexington, Mass.	42.50
619	5c	**Lexington-Concord,** *Apr. 4*	75.00
		Boston, Mass.	75.00
		Cambridge, Mass.	75.00
		Concord, Mass.	75.00
		Concord Junction, Mass.	75.00
		Lexington, Mass.	75.00
		617-619 on one cover, Concord Junction or Lexington	175.00
		Set of 3 on one cover, any other city	150.00

1925

620	2c	**Norse-American,** *May 18*	20.00
		Algona, Iowa	20.00
		Benson, Minn.	20.00
		Decorah, Iowa	20.00
		Minneapolis, Minn.	20.00
		Northfield, Minn.	20.00
		St. Paul, Minn.	20.00
621	5c	**Norse-American,** *May 18*	32.50
		Algona, Iowa	32.50
		Benson, Minn.	32.50
		Decorah, Iowa	32.50
		Minneapolis, Minn.	32.50
		Northfield, Minn.	32.50
		St. Paul, Minn.	32.50
		620-621 on one cover, any city	50.00

1925-26

622	13c	**Harrison,** *Jan. 11, 1926*	25.00
		Indianapolis, Ind.	37.50
		North Bend, Ohio (500)	175.00
623	17c	**Wilson,** *Dec. 28, 1925*	30.00
		New York, N.Y.	30.00
		Princeton, N.J.	30.00
		Staunton, Va.	30.00

1926

627	2c	**Sesquicentennial,** *May 10*	15.00
		Boston, Mass.	15.00
		Philadelphia, Pa.	15.00
628	5c	**Ericsson,** *May 29*	40.00
		Chicago, Ill.	40.00
		Minneapolis, Minn.	40.00
		New York, N.Y.	40.00
629	2c	**White Plains,** New York, N.Y., *Oct. 18*	6.25
		New York, N.Y., Inter-Philatelic Exhibition Agency cancellation	6.25
		White Plains, N.Y.	6.25

		Washington, D.C., *Oct. 28*	3.50
630		Sheet of 25, *Oct. 18*	1,500.
		Sheet of 25, *Oct. 28*	1,000.

1926-34　　　　　　　　　　Imperf.

631	1½c	**Harding,** *Aug. 27, 1926,* pair	35.00

Perf. 11x10½

632	1c	**Franklin,** *June 10, 1927,* pair	45.00
632a		Booklet pane of 6, *Nov. 2, 1927*	3,250.
633	1½c	**Harding,** *May 17, 1927,* pair	45.00
634	2c	**Washington,** *Dec. 10, 1926*	47.50
635	3c	**Lincoln,** *Feb. 3, 1927*	47.50
635a		3c **bright violet,** *Feb. 7, 1934*	25.00
636	4c	**Martha Washington,** *May 17, 1927*	50.00
637	5c	**Roosevelt,** *Mar. 24, 1927*	50.00
638	6c	**Garfield,** *July 27, 1927*	57.50
639	7c	**McKinley,** *Mar. 24, 1927*	57.50
		637, 639, both stamps issued *Mar. 24*	500.00
640	8c	**Grant,** *June 10, 1927*	67.50
		632, 640, both stamps issued *June 10*	350.00
641	9c	**Jefferson,** *May 17, 1927*	72.50
		633, 636, 641 all three stamps issued *May 17*	550.00
642	10c	**Monroe,** *Feb. 3, 1927*	90.00

1927

643	2c	**Vermont,** *Aug. 3*	6.00
		Bennington, Vt.	6.00
644	2c	**Burgoyne,** *Aug. 3*	12.50
		Albany, N.Y.	12.50
		Rome, N.Y.	12.50
		Syracuse, N.Y.	12.50
		Utica, N.Y.	12.50

1928

645	2c	**Valley Forge,** *May 26*	4.00
		Cleveland, O.	67.50
		Lancaster, Pa.	4.00
		Norristown, Pa.	4.00
		Philadelphia, Pa.	4.00
		Valley Forge, Pa.	4.00
		West Chester, Pa.	4.00
		Cleveland, Midwestern Philatelic Sta. cancellation	4.00
646	2c	**Molly Pitcher,** *Oct. 20*	15.00
		Freehold, N.J.	15.00
		Red Bank, N.J.	15.00

1928

647	2c	**Hawaii,** *Aug. 13*	15.00
		Honolulu, Hawaii	17.50
648	5c	**Hawaii,** *Aug. 13*	22.50
		Honolulu, Hawaii	25.00
		647-648 on one cover	40.00
649	2c	**Aero Conf.,** *Dec. 12*	7.00
650	5c	**Aero Conf.,** *Dec. 12*	10.00
		649-650 on one cover	15.00

1929

651	2c	**Clark,** Vincennes, Indiana, *Feb. 25*	6.00
		Washington, *Feb. 26,* first day of sale by Philatelic Agency	3.00

Perf. 11x10½

653	½c	**olive brown,** *May 25,* block of four	27.50
654	2c	**Electric Light,** perf. 11, Menlo Park, N.J., *June 5*	10.00
		Washington, D.C., *June 6,* first day of sale by Philatelic Agency	4.00
655	2c	**Electric Light,** perf. 11x10½, *June 11*	80.00
656	2c	**Electric Light,** perf. 10 vert., *June 11*	90.00
657	2c	**Sullivan,** Auburn, N.Y., *June 17*	4.00
		Binghamton, N.Y.	4.00
		Canajoharie, N.Y.	4.00
		Canandaigua, N.Y.	4.00
		Elmira, N.Y.	4.00
		Geneseo, N.Y.	4.00
		Geneva, N.Y.	4.00
		Horseheads, N.Y.	4.00
		Owego, N.Y.	4.00
		Penn Yan, N.Y	4.00
		Perry, N.Y.	4.00
		Seneca Falls, N.Y.	4.00
		Waterloo, N.Y.	4.00
		Watkins Glen, N.Y.	4.00
		Waverly, N.Y.	4.00
		Washington, D.C., *June 18*	2.00

1929

658	1c	**Kansas,** *May 1,* pair	50.00
		Newton, Kan., *Apr. 15*	325.00
659	1½c	**Kansas,** *May 1,* pair	57.50
		Colby, Kan., *Apr. 16*	—
660	2c	**Kansas,** *May 1*	57.50
		Colby, Kan., *Apr. 16*	—
661	3c	**Kansas,** *May 1*	65.00
		Colby, Kan., *Apr. 16*	—
662	4c	**Kansas,** *May 1*	65.00
		Colby, Kan., *Apr. 16*	—
663	5c	**Kansas,** *May 1*	90.00
		Colby, Kan., *Apr. 16*	—
664	6c	**Kansas,** *May 1*	100.00
		Newton, Kan., *Apr. 15*	600.00
665	7c	**Kansas,** *May 1*	100.00
		Colby, Kan., *Apr. 16*	—
666	8c	**Kansas,** *May 1*	125.00
		Newton, Kan., *Apr. 15*	575.00
667	9c	**Kansas,** *May 1*	150.00
		Colby, Kan., *Apr. 16*	—
668	10c	**Kansas,** *May 1*	200.00
		Colby, Kan., *Apr. 16*	—

		658-668 on 1 cover, Washington, D.C., *May 1*	1,5
669	1c	**Nebraska,** *May 1,* pair	50
		Beatrice, Neb., *Apr. 15*	125
670	1½c	**Nebraska,** *May 1,* pair	52
		Hartington, Neb., *Apr. 15*	275
671	2c	**Nebraska,** *May 1*	57
		Auburn, Neb., *Apr. 15*	1,2
		Beatrice, Neb., *Apr. 15*	225
		Hartington, Neb., *Apr. 15*	225
672	3c	**Nebraska,** *May 1*	70
		Beatrice, Neb., *Apr. 15*	275.
		Hartington, Neb., *Apr. 15*	275.
673	4c	**Nebraska,** *May 1*	75
		Beatrice, Neb., *Apr. 15*	240.
		Hartington, Neb., *Apr. 15*	275.
674	5c	**Nebraska,** *May 1*	75.
		Beatrice, Neb., *Apr. 15*	275.
		Hartington, Neb., *Apr. 15*	275.
675	6c	**Nebraska,** *May 1*	100.
		Ravenna, Neb., *Apr. 1?*	
		Wahoo, Neb., *Apr. 17*	
676	7c	**Nebraska,** *May 1*	100.
		Auburn, Neb., *Apr. 17*	275.
677	8c	**Nebraska,** *May 1*	125.
		Humbolt, Neb., *Apr. 17*	250.
		Pawnee City, Neb., *Apr. 17*	275.
678	9c	**Nebraska,** *May 1*	150.
		Cambridge, Neb., *Apr. 17*	250.
679	10c	**Nebraska,** *May 1*	200.
		Tecumseh, Neb., *Apr. 18*	
		669-679 on 1 cover, Washington, D.C., *May 1*	1,50
		658-679 on 1 cover, Washington, D.C., *May 1*	4,25
680	2c	**Fallen Timbers,** Erie, Pa., *Sept. 14*	3.5
		Maumee, O.	3.5
		Perrysburg, O.	3.5
		Toledo, O.	3.5
		Waterville, O.	3.5
		Washington, D.C., *Sept. 16*	2.0
681	2c	**Ohio River,** Cairo, Ill., *Oct. 19*	3.5
		Cincinnati, O.	3.5
		Evansville, Ind.	3.5
		Homestead, Pa.	3.5
		Louisville, Ky.	3.5
		Pittsburgh, Pa.	3.5
		Wheeling, W. Va.	3.5
		Washington, D.C., *Oct. 21*	2.0

1930

682	2c	**Massachusetts Bay Colony,** Boston, Mass. *Apr. 8 (60,000)*	3.5
		Salem, Mass.	3.5
		Washington, D.C., *Apr. 11*	2.0
683	2c	**Carolina-Charleston,** Charleston, S.C. *Apr. 10*	3.5
		Washington, D.C., *Apr. 11*	2.0

Perf. 11x10½

684	1½c	**Harding,** Marion, O., *Dec. 1,* pair	4.5
		Washington, D.C., *Dec. 2*	2.5
685	4c	**Taft,** Cincinnati, O., *June 4*	6.0
		Washington, D.C., *June 5*	3.0

Perf. 10 Vertically

686	1½c	**Harding,** Marion, Ohio, *Dec. 1*	5.00
		Washington, D.C., *Dec. 2*	3.00
687	4c	**Taft,** *Sept. 18*	20.00

Perf. 11

688	2c	**Braddock,** Braddock, Pa., *July 9*	4.00
		Washington, D.C., *July 10*	2.00
689	2c	**Von Steuben,** New York, N.Y., *Sept. 17*	4.00
		Washington, D.C., *Sept. 18*	2.00

1931

690	2c	**Pulaski,** Brooklyn, N.Y., *Jan. 16*	4.00
		Buffalo, N.Y.	4.00
		Chicago, Ill.	4.00
		Cleveland, O.	4.00
		Detroit, Mich.	4.00
		Gary, Ind.	4.00
		Milwaukee, Wis.	4.00
		New York, N.Y.	4.00
		Pittsburgh, Pa.	4.00
		Savannah, Ga.	4.00
		South Bend, Ind.	4.00
		Toledo, O.	4.00
		Washington, D.C., *Jan. 17*	2.00

1931　　　　　　Perf. 11x10½, 10½x11

692	11c	**Hayes,** *Sept. 4*	100.
693	12c	**Cleveland,** *Aug. 25*	100.
694	13c	**Harrison,** *Sept. 4*	100.
695	14c	**American Indian,** *Sept. 8*	100.
696	15c	**Liberty,** *Aug. 27*	120.
697	17c	**Wilson,** *July 25,* Brooklyn, N.Y.	2,750.
		Washington, D.C., *July 27*	400.
698	20c	**Golden Gate,** *Sept. 8*	300.
699	25c	**Niagara Falls,** *July 25,* Brooklyn, N.Y.	2,000.
		Washington, D.C., *July 27*	350.
		697, 699 on one cover, Brooklyn, *July 25*	5,750.
		697, 699 on one cover, Washington, *July 27*	2,500.
700	30c	**American Buffalo,** *Sept. 8*	300.
701	50c	**Arlington,** *Sept. 4*	400.
		Woolrich, Pa., *Sept. 4*	625.

1931

702	2c	**Red Cross,** *May 21*	3.00
		Dansville, N.Y.	3.00
703	2c	**Yorktown,** *Oct. 19,* Wethersfield, Conn.	3.50
		Yorktown, Va.	3.50
		Washington, D.C., *Oct. 20*	3.00

32

WASHINGTON BICENTENNIAL ISSUE

4	½c	Jan. 1, block of 4	5.00
5	1c	Jan. 1, pair	4.00
6	1½c	Jan. 1, pair	4.00
7	2c	Jan. 1	4.00
8	3c	Jan. 1	4.00
9	4c	Jan. 1	4.00
0	5c	Jan. 1	4.00
1	6c	Jan. 1	4.00
2	7c	Jan. 1	4.00
3	8c	Jan. 1	4.50
4	9c	Jan. 1	4.50
5	10c	Jan. 1	4.50
		704-715, set of 12 on one cover, Jan. 1	70.00

32

6	2c	Olympic Winter Games, Jan. 25, Lake Placid, N.Y.	6.00
		Washington, D.C., Jan. 26	1.50
7	2c	Arbor Day, Apr. 22, Nebraska City, Neb.	4.00
		Washington, D.C., Apr. 23	1.50
		Adams, N.Y., Apr. 23	6.50
8	3c	Olympic Summer Games, June 15, Los Angeles, Cal.	6.00
		Washington, D.C., June 16	2.75
9	5c	Olympic Summer Games, June 15, Los Angeles, Cal.	8.00
		Washington, D.C., June 16	2.75
		718, 719 on one cover, Los Angeles, Cal.	10.00
		718, 719 on one cover, Washington, D.C.	4.50
20	3c	Washington, June 16	7.50
20b		Booklet pane of 6, July 25	100.00
21	3c	Washington Coil, Sideways, June 24	15.00
22	3c	Washington Coil, Endways, Oct. 12	15.00
23	6c	Garfield Coil, Sideways, Aug. 18, Los Angeles, Cal.	15.00
		Washington, D.C., Aug. 19	4.00
24	3c	William Penn, Oct. 24, New Castle, Del.	3.25
		Chester, Pa.	3.25
		Philadelphia, Pa.	3.25
		Washington, D.C., Oct. 25	1.25
25	3c	Daniel Webster, Oct. 24, Franklin, N.H.	3.25
		Exeter, N.H.	3.25
		Hanover, N.H.	3.25
		Washington, D.C., Oct. 25	1.25

933

26	3c	Gen. Oglethorpe, Feb. 12, Savannah, Ga., (200,000)	3.25
		Washington, D.C., Feb. 13	1.50
27	3c	Peace Proclamation, Apr. 19, Newburgh, N.Y. (349,571)	3.50
		Washington, D.C., Apr. 20	1.25
28	1c	Century of Progress, May 25, Chicago, Ill., strip of 3	3.00
		Washington, D.C., May 26	1.00
29	3c	Century of Progress, May 25, Chicago, Ill.	3.00
		Washington, D.C., May 26	1.00
		728, 729 on one cover	5.00

Covers mailed May 25, bearing Nos. 728 and 729 total 232,251.

30	1c	American Philatelic Society, sheet of 25, Aug. 25, Chicago, Ill.	100.00
30a	1c	A.P.S., imperf., Aug. 25, Chicago, Ill., strip of 3	3.25
		Washington, D.C., Aug. 28	1.25
31	3c	American Philatelic Society, sheet of 25, Aug. 25, Chicago, Ill.	100.00
31a	3c	A.P.S., single, imperf., Aug. 25, Chicago, Ill.	3.25
		Washington, D.C., Aug. 28	1.25
		730a, 731a on one cover	5.50

Covers mailed Aug. 25 bearing Nos. 730, 730a, 731, 731a total 65,218.

732	3c	National Recovery Administration, Aug. 15,(65,000)	3.25
		Nira, Iowa, Aug. 17	2.50
733	3c	Byrd Antarctic, Oct. 9	10.00
734	5c	Kosciuszko, Oct. 13, Boston, Mass. (23,025)	4.50
		Buffalo, N.Y. (14,981)	5.50
		Chicago, Ill, (26,306)	4.50
		Detroit, Mich. (17,792)	5.25
		Pittsburgh, Pa. (6,282)	32.50
		Kosciuszko, Miss. (27,093)	5.25
		St. Louis, Mo. (17,872)	5.25
		Washington, D.C., Oct. 14	1.60

1934

735	3c	National Exhibition, sheet of 6, Byrd imperf., Feb. 10, New York, N.Y.	40.00
		Washington, D.C., Feb. 19	27.50
735a	3c	National Exhibition, single, imperf., New York, N.Y., Feb. 10 (450,715)	5.00
		Washington, D.C., Feb. 19	2.75
736	3c	Maryland Tercentenary, Mar. 23 St. Mary's City, Md. (148,785)	1.60
		Washington, D.C., Mar. 24	1.00
737	3c	Mothers of America, perf. 11x10½, May 2, any city	1.60
738	3c	Mothers of America, perf. 11, May 2, any city	1.60
		737, 738 on one cover	4.00

Covers mailed at Washington, May 2 bearing Nos. 737 and 738 total 183,359.

739	3c	Wisconsin, July 7, Green Bay, Wisc. (130,000)	1.10
		Washington, D.C., July 9	1.00
740	1c	Parks, Yosemite, July 16 Yosemite, Cal., (60,000), strip of 3	2.25 / 2.75
741	2c	Parks, Grand Canyon, July 24 Grand Canyon, Ariz., (75,000), pair	2.25 / 2.75
742	3c	Parks, Mt. Rainier, Aug. 3 Longmire, Wash., (64,500)	2.50 / 3.00
743	4c	Parks, Mesa Verde, Sept. 25 Mesa Verde, Colo., (51,882)	2.25 / 2.75
744	5c	Parks, Yellowstone, July 30 Yellowstone, Wyo., (87,000)	2.25 / 2.50
745	6c	Parks, Crater Lake, Sept. 5 Crater Lake, Ore., (45,282)	3.00 / 3.25
746	7c	Parks, Arcadia, Oct. 2 Bar Harbor, Maine (51,312)	3.00 / 3.25
747	8c	Parks, Zion, Sept. 18 Zion, Utah, (43,650)	3.25 / 3.75
748	9c	Parks, Glacier Park, Aug. 27 Glacier Park, Mont., (52,626)	3.50 / 3.75
749	10c	Parks, Smoky Mountains, Oct. 8 Sevierville, Tenn., (39,000)	6.00 / 7.50

Imperf

750	3c	American Philatelic Society, sheet of 6, Aug. 28, Atlantic City, N.J.	40.00
750a	3c	A.P.S., single, Aug. 28, Atlantic City, N.J. (40,000)	3.25
		Washington, D.C., Sept. 4	2.00
751	1c	Trans-Mississippi Philatelic Expo., sheet of 6, Oct. 10, Omaha, Neb.	35.00
751a	1c	Trans-Miss. Phil. Expo., Omaha. Neb., Oct. 10 (125,000), strip of 3	3.25
		Washington, D.C., Oct. 15	2.00

1935

SPECIAL PRINTING
Nos. 752-771 issued Mar. 15

752	3c	Peace Commemoration	5.00
753	3c	Byrd	6.00
754	3c	Mothers of America	6.00
755	3c	Wisconsin Tercentenary	6.00
756	1c	Parks, Yosemite, strip of 3	6.00
757	2c	Parks, Grand Canyon, pair	6.00
758	3c	Parks, Mount Rainier	6.00
759	4c	Parks, Mesa Verde	6.50
760	5c	Parks, Yellowstone	6.50
761	6c	Parks, Crater Lake	6.50
762	7c	Parks, Acadia	6.50
763	8c	Parks, Zion	7.50
764	9c	Parks, Glacier Park	7.50
765	10c	Parks, Smoky Mountains	7.50
766a	1c	Century of Progress, strip of 3	5.50
		Pane of 25	250.00
767a	3c	Century of Progress	5.50
		Pane of 25	250.00
768a	3c	Byrd	6.50
		Pane of 25	250.00
769a	1c	Parks, Yosemite, strip of 3	4.00
		Pane of 6	250.00
770a	3c	Parks, Mount Rainier	5.00
		Pane of 6	250.00
771	16c	Airmail Special Delivery	12.50

> Catalogue values from this point to No. 986 are for addressed covers with the most common cachets.

772	3c	Connecticut Tercentenary, Apr. 26, Hartford, Conn. (217,800)	14.00
		Washington, D.C., Apr. 27	2.25
773	3c	California Exposition, May 29, San Diego, Cal. (214,042)	14.00
		Washington, D.C., May 31	1.50
774	3c	Boulder Dam, Sept. 30, Boulder City, Nev. (166,180)	15.00
		Washington, D.C., Oct. 1	2.00
775	3c	Michigan Centenary, Nov. 1, Lansing, Mich. (176,962)	15.00
		Washington, D.C., Nov. 2	1.50

1936

776	3c	Texas Centennial, Mar. 2, Gonzales, Texas (319,150)	20.00
		Washington, D.C., Mar. 3	2.00
777	3c	Rhode Island Tercentenary, May 4, Providence, R.I. (245,400)	12.50
		Washington, D.C., May 5	2.25
778	3c	TIPEX souvenir sheet, May 9 (297,194) New York, N.Y. (TIPEX cancellation)	14.00
		Washington, D.C., May 11	3.50
782	3c	Arkansas Centennial, June 15, Little Rock, Ark. (376,693)	13.00
		Washington, D.C, June 16	1.25
783	3c	Oregon Territory Centennial, July 14, Astoria, Ore. (91,110)	10.00
		Daniel, Wyo., (67,013)	10.00
		Lewiston, Ida., (86,100)	10.00
		Missoula, Mont., (59,883)	11.00
		Walla Walla, Wash., (106,150)	9.00
		Washington, D.C., July 15	1.25
784	3c	Susan B. Anthony, Aug. 26 (178,500)	15.00

1936-37

785	1c	Army, Dec. 15, 1936, strip of 3	8.00
786	2c	Army, Jan. 15, 1937, pair	8.00
787	3c	Army, Feb. 18, 1937	8.00
788	4c	Army, Mar. 23, 1937	8.00
789	5c	Army, May 26, 1937, West Point, N.Y. (160,000)	8.00
		Washington, D.C., May 27	3.00
790	1c	Navy, Dec. 15, 1936, strip of 3	8.00
791	2c	Navy, Jan. 15, 1937, pair	8.00
792	3c	Navy, Feb. 18, 1937	8.00

793	4c	Navy, Mar. 23, 1937	8.00
794	5c	Navy, May 26, 1937, Annapolis, Md., (202,806)	8.00
		Washington, D.C., May 27	3.00

Covers for #785 & 790 total 390, 749; #786 & 791 total 292,570; #787 & 792 total 320,888; #788 & 793 total 331,000.

1937

795	3c	Ordinance of 1787, July 13 Marietta, Ohio (130,531)	9.00
		New York, N.Y. (125,134)	9.00
		Washington, D.C., July 14	1.25
796	5c	Virginia Dare, Aug. 18, Manteo, N.C. (226,730)	11.00
797	10c	Souvenir Sheet, Aug. 26, Asheville, N.C. (164,215)	11.00
798	3c	Constitution, Sept. 17, Philadelphia, Pa. (281,478)	9.00
799	3c	Hawaii, Oct. 18, Honolulu, Hawaii (320,334)	11.00
800	3c	Alaska, Nov. 12, Juneau, Alaska (230,370)	10.00
801	3c	Puerto Rico, Nov. 25, San Juan, P.R. (244,054)	10.00
802	3c	Virgin Islands, Dec. 15, Charlotte Amalie, V.I. (225,469)	10.00

1938

PRESIDENTIAL ISSUE

803	½c	Franklin, May 19, Philadelphia, Pa. (224,901), block of 6	3.00
804	1c	G. Washington, Apr. 25 (124,037), strip of 3	3.00
804b		Booklet pane of 6, Jan. 27, 1939	12.50
805	1½c	M. Washington, May 5 (128,339), pair	3.00
806	2c	J. Adams, June 3 (127,806), pair	3.00
806b		Booklet pane of 6, Jan. 27, 1939	15.00
807	3c	Jefferson, June 16 (118,097)	3.00
807a		Booklet pane of 6, Jan. 27, 1939	17.50
808	4c	Madison, July 1 (118,765)	3.00
809	4½c	White House, July 11 (115,820)	3.00
810	5c	Monroe, July 21 (98,282)	3.00
811	6c	J.Q. Adams, July 28 (97,428)	3.00
812	7c	Jackson, Aug. 4 (98,414)	3.00
813	8c	Van Buren, Aug. 11 (94,857)	3.00
814	9c	W.H. Harrison, Aug. 18 (91,229)	3.00
815	10c	Tyler, Sept. 2 (83,707)	3.00
816	11c	Polk, Sept. 8 (63,966)	5.00
817	12c	Taylor, Sept. 14 (62,935)	5.00
818	13c	Fillmore, Sept. 22 (58,965)	5.00
819	14c	Pierce, Oct. 6 (49,819)	5.00
820	15c	Buchanan, Oct. 13 (52,209)	5.00
821	16c	Lincoln, Oct. 20 (59,566)	7.00
822	17c	A. Johnson, Oct. 27 (55,024)	6.00
823	18c	Grant, Nov. 3 (53,124)	6.00
824	19c	Hayes, Nov. 10 (54,124)	6.00
825	20c	Garfield, Nov. 10 (51,971)	7.00
826	21c	Arthur, Nov. 22 (44,367)	7.00
827	22c	Cleveland, Nov. 22 (44,358)	8.00
828	24c	B. Harrison, Dec. 2 (46,592)	8.00
829	25c	McKinley, Dec. 2 (45,691)	8.00
830	30c	T. Roosevelt, Dec. 8 (43,528)	9.00
831	50c	Taft, Dec. 8 (41,984)	12.50
832	$1	Wilson, purple & black, Aug. 29 (24,618)	50.00
832c		red violet & black, Aug. 31, 1954 (20,202)	25.00
833	$2	Harding, Sept. 29 (19,895)	100.00
834	$5	Coolidge, Nov. 17 (15,615)	175.00

1938

835	3c	Constitution, June 21, Philadelphia, Pa. (232,873)	15.00
836	3c	Swedes and Finns, June 27, Wilmington, Del. (225,617)	15.00
837	3c	Northwest Sesqui., July 15, Marietta, Ohio (180,170)	15.00
838	3c	Iowa, Aug. 24, Des Moines, Iowa (209,860)	15.00

1939

COIL STAMPS
Perf. 10 Vertically

839	1c	G. Washington, Jan. 20, strip of 3	5.00
840	1½c	M. Washington, Jan. 20, pair	5.00
841	2c	J. Adams, Jan. 20, pair	5.00
842	3c	Jefferson, Jan. 20	5.00
843	4c	Madison, Jan. 20	5.00
844	4½c	White House, Jan. 20	5.00
845	5c	Monroe, Jan. 20	5.00
846	6c	J.Q. Adams, Jan. 20	6.50
847	10c	Tyler, Jan. 20	9.00
		839-847 on one cover, Jan. 20	45.00

Perf. 10 Horizontally

848	1c	Strip of 3, Jan. 27	5.00
849	1½c	Pair, Jan. 27	5.00
850	2c	Pair, Jan. 27	5.00
851	3c	Jan. 27	5.50
		848-851 on one cover, Jan. 27	25.00

1939

852	3c	Golden Gate Expo, Feb. 18, San Francisco, Cal. (352,165)	16.00
853	3c	N.Y. World's Fair, Apr. 1, New York, N.Y. (585,565)	20.00
854	3c	Washington Inauguration, Apr. 30, New York, N.Y. (395,644)	17.50
855	3c	Baseball Centennial, June 12, Cooperstown, N.Y. (398,199)	40.00
856	3c	Panama Canal, Aug. 15, U.S.S. Charleston, Canal Zone (230,974)	18.00

857	3c **Printing Tercentenary**, Sept. 25, New York, N.Y. (295,270)	15.00
858	3c **50th Statehood Anniversary**, Bismarck, N.D. Nov. 2 (142,106)	12.50
	Pierre, S.D., Nov. 2 (150,429)	12.50
	Helena, Mont., Nov. 8 (130,273)	12.50
	Olympia, Wash., Nov. 11 (150,429)	12.50

1940

FAMOUS AMERICANS

859	1c **Washington Irving**, Jan. 29, Tarrytown, N.Y. (170,969), strip of 3	3.00
860	2c **James Fenimore Cooper**, Jan. 29, Cooperstown, N.Y. (154,836), pair	3.00
861	3c **Ralph Waldo Emerson**, Feb. 5, Boston, Mass. (185,148)	3.00
862	5c **Louisa May Alcott**, Feb. 5, Concord, Mass. (134,325)	4.00
863	10c **Samuel L. Clemens**, Feb. 13, Hannibal, Mo. (150,492)	8.00
864	1c **Henry W. Longfellow**, Feb. 16, Portland, Me. (160,508), strip of 3	3.00
865	2c **John Greenleaf Whittier**, Feb. 16, Haverhill, Mass. (148,423), pair	3.00
866	3c **James Russell Lowell**, Feb. 20, Cambridge, Mass. (148,735)	3.00
867	5c **Walt Whitman**, Feb. 20, Camden, N.J. (134,185)	4.00
868	10c **James Whitcomb Riley**, Feb. 24, Greenfield, Ind. (131,760)	6.00
869	1c **Horace Mann**, Mar. 14, Boston, Mass. (186,854), strip of 3	3.00
870	2c **Mark Hopkins**, Mar. 14, Williamstown, Mass. (140,286), pair	3.00
871	3c **Charles W. Eliot**, Mar. 28, Cambridge, Mass. (155,708)	3.00
872	5c **Frances E. Willard**, Mar. 28, Evanston, Ill. (140,483)	4.00
873	10c **Booker T. Washington**, Apr. 7, Tuskegee Institute, Ala. (163,507)	10.00
874	1c **John James Audubon**, Apr. 8, St. Francisville, La. (144,123), strip of 3	3.00
875	2c **Dr. Crawford W. Long**, Apr. 8, Jefferson, Ga. (158,128), pair	3.00
876	3c **Luther Burbank**, Apr. 17, Santa Rosa, Cal. (147,033)	3.00
877	5c **Dr. Walter Reed**, Apr. 17 (154,464)	4.00
878	10c **Jane Addams**, Apr. 26, Chicago, Ill. (132,375)	6.00
879	1c **Stephen Collins Foster**, May 3, Bardstown, Ky. (183,461), strip of 3	3.00
880	2c **John Philip Sousa**, May 3 (131,422), pair	4.00
881	3c **Victor Herbert**, May 13, New York, N.Y. (168,200)	3.00
882	5c **Edward A. MacDowell**, May 13, Peterborough, N.H. (135,155)	4.00
883	10c **Ethelbert Nevin**, June 10, Pittsburgh, Pa. (121,951)	6.00
884	1c **Gilbert Stuart**, Sept. 5, Narragansett, R.I. (131,965), strip of 3	3.00
885	2c **James A. McNeill Whistler**, Sept. 5, Lowell, Mass. (130,962), pair	3.00
886	3c **Augustus Saint-Gaudens**, Sept. 16, New York, N.Y. (138,200)	3.00
887	5c **Daniel Chester French**, Sept. 16, Stockbridge, Mass. (124,608)	4.00
888	10c **Frederic Remington**, Sept. 30, Canton, N.Y. (116,219)	7.00
889	1c **Eli Whitney**, Oct. 7, Savannah, Ga. (140,868), strip of 3	3.00
890	2c **Samuel F.B. Morse**, Oct. 7, New York, N.Y. (135,388), pair	3.00
891	3c **Cyrus Hall McCormick**, Oct. 14, Lexington, Va. (137,415)	3.00
892	5c **Elias Howe**, Oct. 14, Spencer, Mass. (126,334)	3.00
893	10c **Alexander Graham Bell**, Oct. 28, Boston, Mass. (125,372)	10.00

1940

894	3c **Pony Express**, Apr. 3, St. Joseph, Mo. (194,589)	12.00
	Sacramento, Cal. (160,849)	12.00
895	3c **Pan American Union**, Apr. 14 (182,401)	9.50
896	3c **Idaho Statehood**, July 3, Boise, Idaho (156,429)	9.50
897	3c **Wyoming Statehood**, July 10 Cheyenne, Wyo. (156,709)	9.50
898	3c **Coronado Expedition**, Sept. 7, Albuquerque, N.M. (161,012)	9.50
899	1c **Defense**, Oct. 16, strip of 3	7.00
900	3c **Defense**, Oct. 16, pair	7.00
901	3c **Defense**, Oct. 16	7.00
	899-901 on one cover	12.00

First day cancel was applied to 450,083 covers bearing one or more of Nos. 899-901.

902	3c **Thirteenth Amendment**, Oct. 20, World's Fair, N.Y. (156,146)	10.00

1941

903	3c **Vermont Statehood**, Mar. 4, Montpelier, Vt. (182,423)	10.00

MacArthur, W. Va.
Apr 15, 1942
First Day Cover

Covers exist with this cancellation. "First Day" refers to the first day of the new name of the town, previously known as Hollywood, W. Va.

1942

904	3c **Kentucky Statehood**, June 1, Frankfort, Ky. (155,730)	10.00
905	3c **"Win the War"**, July 4 (191,168)	10.00
906	5c **Chinese Resistance**, July 7, Denver, Colo. (168,746)	12.00

1943-44

907	2c **Allied Nations**, Jan. 14, 1943 (178,865), pair	5.50
908	1c **Four Freedoms**, Feb. 12, 1943 (193,800), strip of 3	5.50
909	5c **Poland**, June 22, 1943, Chicago, Ill. (88,170)	5.00
	Washington, D.C. (136,002)	4.00
910	5c **Czechoslovakia**, July 12, 1943 (145,112)	4.00
911	5c **Norway**, July 27, 1943 (155,054)	4.00
912	5c **Luxemborg**, Aug. 10, 1943 (166,367)	4.00
913	5c **Netherlands**, Aug. 24, 1943 (148,763)	4.00
914	5c **Belgium**, Sept. 14, 1943 (154,220)	4.00
915	5c **France**, Sept. 28, 1943 (163,478)	4.00
916	5c **Greece**, Oct. 12, 1943 (166,553)	4.00
917	5c **Yugoslavia**, Oct. 26, 1943 (161,835)	4.00
918	5c **Albania**, Nov. 9, 1943 (162,275)	4.00
919	5c **Austria**, Nov. 23, 1943 (172,285)	4.00
920	5c **Denmark**, Dec. 7, 1943 (173,784)	4.00
921	5c **Korea**, Nov. 2, 1944 (192,860)	5.00

1944

922	3c **Railroad**, May 10, Ogden, Utah (151,324)	10.00
	Omaha, Neb. (171,000)	10.00
	San Francisco, Cal. (125,000)	10.00
923	3c **Steamship**, May 22, Kings Point, N.Y. (152,324)	9.00
	Savannah, Ga. (181,472)	9.00
924	3c **Telegraph**, May 24 (141,907)	9.00
	Baltimore, Md. (136,480)	9.00
925	3c **Philippines**, Sept. 27 (214,865)	9.00
926	3c **Motion Picture**, Oct. 31, Hollywood, Cal. (190,660)	10.00
	New York, N.Y. (176,473)	9.00

1945

927	3c **Florida**, Mar. 3, Tallahassee, Fla. (228,435)	9.00
928	5c **United Nations Conference**, Apr. 25, San Francisco, Cal. (417,450)	9.00
929	3c **Iwo Jima**, July 11 (391,650)	15.00

1945-46

930	1c **Roosevelt**, July 26, 1945, Hyde Park, N.Y. (390,219), strip of 3	4.00
931	2c **Roosevelt**, Aug. 24, 1945, Warm Springs, Ga. (426,142), pair	4.00
932	3c **Roosevelt**, June 27, 1945 (391,650)	4.00
933	5c **Roosevelt**, Jan. 30, 1946 (466,766)	4.00

1945

934	3c **Army**, Sept. 28 (392,300)	11.00
935	3c **Navy**, Oct. 27, Annapolis, Md. (460,352)	11.00
936	3c **Coast Guard**, Nov. 10 New York, N.Y. (405,280)	11.00
937	3c **Alfred E. Smith**, Nov. 26 New York, N.Y. (424,950)	3.00
938	3c **Texas**, Dec. 29, Austin, Tex. (397,860)	9.00

1946

939	3c **Merchant Marine**, Feb. 26 (432,141)	9.00
940	3c **Veterans of WWII**, May 9 (492,786)	11.00
941	3c **Tennessee**, June 1, 1946, Nashville, Tenn. (463,512)	4.00
942	3c **Iowa**, Aug. 3, Iowa City, Iowa (517,505)	4.00
943	3c **Smithsonian**, Aug. 10 (402,448)	4.00
944	3c **Kearny Expedition**, Oct. 16, Santa Fe, N.M. (384,300)	4.00

1947

945	3c **Thomas A. Edison**, Feb. 11, Milan, Ohio (632,473)	4.00
946	3c **Joseph Pulitzer**, Apr. 10, New York, N.Y. (580,870)	4.00
947	3c **Stamp Centenary**, May 17, New York, N.Y. (712,873)	4.00
948	5c and 10c **Centenary Exhibition Sheet**, May 19, New York, N.Y. (502,175)	4.50
949	3c **Doctors**, June 9, Atlantic City, N.J. (508,016)	9.00
950	3c **Utah**, July 24, Salt Lake City, Utah (456,416)	3.00
951	3c **"Constitution,"** Oct. 21, Boston, Mass. (683,416)	8.00
952	3c **Everglades Park**, Dec. 5, Florida City, Fla. (466,647)	3.00

1948

953	3c **Carver**, Jan. 5, Tuskegee Institute, Ala. (402,179)	3.00
954	3c **California Gold**, Jan. 24, Coloma, Calif. (526,154)	3.50
955	3c **Mississippi Territory**, Apr. 7, Natchez, Miss. (434,804)	2.00
956	3c **Four Chaplains**, May 28 (459,070)	8.00
957	3c **Wisconsin Centennial**, May 29, Madison, Wis. (470,280)	3.00
958	3c **Swedish Pioneers**, June 4 Chicago, Ill. (364,318)	3.00
959	3c **Women's Progress**, July 19, Seneca Falls, N.Y. (401,923)	3.00
960	3c **William Allen White**, July 31, Emporia, Kans. (385,648)	2.50
961	3c **U.S.-Canada Friendship**, Aug. 2, Niagara Falls, N.Y. (406,467)	3.00

962	3c **Francis Scott Key**, Aug. 9, Frederick, Md. (505,930)	2.
963	3c **Salute to Youth**, Aug. 11 (347,070)	2.
964	3c **Oregon Territory Establishment**, Aug. 14, Oregon City, Ore. (365,898)	3
965	3c **Harlan Fiske Stone**, Aug. 25, Chesterfield, N.H. (362,170)	3.
966	3c **Palomar Observatory**, Aug. 30, Palomar Mountain, Calif. (401,365)	5.
967	3c **Clara Barton**, Sept. 7, Oxford, Mass. (362,000)	3.
968	3c **Poultry Industry**, Sept. 9, New Haven, Conn. (475,000)	3
969	3c **Gold Star Mothers**, Sept. 21 (386,064)	2
970	3c **Fort Kearny**, Sept. 22, Minden, Neb. (429,633)	2.
971	3c **Volunteer Firemen**, Oct. 4, Dover, Del. (399,630)	10
972	3c **Indian Centennial**, Oct. 15, Muskogee, Okla. (459,520)	3
973	3c **Rough Riders**, Oct. 27, Prescott, Ariz. (399,198)	2
974	3c **Juliette Low**, Oct. 29, Savannah, Ga. (476,573)	8.
975	3c **Will Rogers**, Nov. 4, Claremore, Okla. (450,350)	2
976	3c **Fort Bliss**, Nov. 5, El Paso, Tex. (421,000)	5.
977	3c **Moina Michael**, Nov. 9, Athens, Ga. (374,090)	2.
978	3c **Gettysburg Address**, Nov. 19, Gettysburg, Pa. (511,990)	2.
979	3c **American Turners Society**, Nov. 20, Cincinnati, Ohio (434,090)	2.
980	3c **Joel Chandler Harris**, Dec. 9, Eatonton, Ga. (426,199)	2.

1949

981	3c **Minnesota Territory**, Mar. 3, St. Paul, Minn. (458,750)	2.
982	3c **Washington and Lee University**, Apr. 12, Lexington, Va. (447,910)	2.
983	3c **Puerto Rico Election**, Apr. 27, San Juan, P.R. (390,416)	2.
984	3c **Annapolis, Md.**, May 23, Annapolis, Md. (441,802)	3.0
985	3c **G.A.R.**, Aug. 29, Indianapolis, Ind. (471,696)	3.2
986	3c **Edgar Allan Poe**, Oct. 7, Richmond, Va. (371,020)	4.0

Catalogue values from this point to the end of the section are for unaddressed covers with the most common cachets.

1950

987	3c **American Bankers Assoc.**, Jan. 3, Saratoga Springs, N.Y. (388,622)	2.7
988	3c **Samuel Gompers**, Jan. 27 (332,023)	1.7

National Capital Sesquicentennial

989	3c **Freedom**, Apr. 20 (371,743)	1.5
990	3c **Executive**, June 12 (376,789)	1.5
991	3c **Judicial**, Aug. 2 (324,007)	1.5
992	3c **Legislative**, Nov. 22 (352,215)	1.5
993	3c **Railroad Engineers**, Apr. 29, Jackson, Tenn. (420,830)	4.0
994	3c **Kansas City Centenary**, June 3, Kansas City, Mo. (405,390)	1.5
995	3c **Boy Scouts**, June 30, Valley Forge, Pa. (622,972)	12.0
996	3c **Indiana Territory Sesquicentennial**, July 4, Vincennes, Ind. (359,643)	1.75
997	3c **California Statehood**, Sept. 9, Sacramento, Cal. (391,919)	2.50

1951

998	3c **United Confederate Veterans**, May 30, Norfolk, Va. (374,235)	3.00
999	3c **Nevada Centennial**, July 14, Genoa, Nev. (336,890)	1.50
1000	3c **Landing of Cadillac**, July 24, Detroit, Mich. (323,094)	1.50
1001	3c **Colorado Statehood**, Aug. 1, Minturn, Colo. (311,568)	1.50
1002	3c **American Chemical Society**, Sept. 4, New York, N.Y. (436,419)	1.75
1003	3c **Battle of Brooklyn**, Dec. 10, Brooklyn, N.Y. (420,000)	1.50

1952

1004	3c **Betsy Ross**, Jan. 2, Philadelphia, Pa. (314,312)	1.50
1005	3c **4-H Club**, Jan. 15, Springfield, Ohio (383,290)	3.25
1006	3c **B. & O. Railroad**, Feb. 28, Baltimore, Md. (441,600)	4.50
1007	3c **American Automobile Association**, Mar. 4, Chicago, Ill. (520,123)	1.75
1008	3c **NATO**, Apr. 4 (313,518)	1.50
1009	3c **Grand Coulee Dam**, May 15, Grand Coulee, Wash. (341,680)	1.50
1010	3c **Lafayette**, June 13, Georgetown, S.C. (349,102)	1.50
1011	3c **Mt. Rushmore Memorial**, Aug. 11, Keystone, S.D. (337,027)	1.50
1012	3c **Civil Engineers**, Sept. 6, Chicago, Ill. (318,483)	1.50
1013	3c **Service Women**, Sept. 11 (308,062)	1.75
1014	3c **Gutenberg Bible**, Sept. 30 (387,078)	1.50
1015	3c **Newspaper Boys**, Oct. 4, Philadelphia, Pa. (626,000)	1.50
1016	3c **Red Cross**, Nov. 21, New York, N.Y. (439,252)	2.00

53			
7	3c	**National Guard,** *Feb. 23 (387,618)*	2.00
8	3c	**Ohio Sesquicentennial,** *Mar. 2,* Chillicothe, Ohio *(407,983)*	1.50
9	3c	**Washington Territory,** *Mar. 2,* Olympia, Wash. *(344,047)*	1.50
20	3c	**Louisiana Purchase,** *Apr. 30,* St. Louis, Mo. *(425,600)*	1.50
21	3c	**Opening of Japan,** *July 14 (320,541)*	1.75
22	3c	**American Bar Association,** *Aug. 24,* Boston, Mass. *(410,036)*	6.50
23	3c	**Sagamore Hill,** *Sept. 14,* Oyster Bay, N.Y. *(379,750)*	1.50
24	3c	**Future Farmers,** *Oct. 13,* Kansas City, Mo. *(424,193)*	1.50
25	3c	**Trucking Industry,** *Oct. 27,* Los Angeles, Calif. *(875,021)*	1.50
26	3c	**Gen. G.S. Patton, Jr.,** *Nov. 11,* Fort Knox, Ky. *(342,600)*	4.00
27	3c	**New York City,** *Nov. 20,* New York, N.Y. *(387,914)*	1.50
28	3c	**Gadsden Purchase,** *Dec. 30,* Tucson, Ariz. *(363,250)*	1.50
54			
29	3c	**Columbia University,** *Jan. 4,* New York, N.Y. *(550,745)*	1.50

54-67

LIBERTY ISSUE

30a	½c	**Franklin,** *Oct. 20, 1955 (223,122),* block of 6	1.00
31b	1c	**Washington,** *Aug. 26, 1954,* Chicago, Ill. *(272,581),* strip of 3	1.00
31A	1¼c	**Palace of Governors,** *June 17, 1960,* Santa Fe, N.M., strip of 3	1.00
		1031A and 1054A on one cover	1.50

First day cancel was applied to 501,848 covers bearing one more of Nos. 1031A, 1054A.

32	1½c	**Mt. Vernon,** *Feb. 22, 1956,* Mount Vernon, Va. *(270,109),* pair	1.00
33	2c	**Jefferson,** *Sept. 15, 1954,* San Francisco, Cal. *(307,300),* pair	1.00
34	2½c	**Bunker Hill,** *June 17, 1959,* Boston, Mass. *(315,060),* pair	1.00
35e	3c	**Statue of Liberty,** *June 24, 1954,* Albany, N.Y. *(340,001)*	1.00
35a		Booklet pane of 6, *June 30, 1954*	3.50
35b	3c	Tagged, *July 6, 1966*	40.00
36c	4c	**Lincoln,** *Nov. 19, 1954,* New York, N.Y. *(374,064)*	1.25
36a		Booklet pane of 6, *July 31, 1958,* Wheeling, W. Va. *(135,825)*	4.00
36b	4c	Tagged, *Nov. 2, 1963*	50.00

No. 1036b was supposed to have been issued at Dayton Nov. but a mix-up delayed its issuance there until Nov. 4. About 0 Covers received the Nov. 2 cancellation.

37	4½c	**Hermitage,** *Mar. 16, 1959,* Hermitage, Tenn. *(320,000)*	1.00
38	5c	**Monroe,** *Dec. 2, 1954,* Fredericksburg, Va. *(255,650)*	1.00
39a	6c	**T. Roosevelt,** *Nov. 18, 1955,* New York, N.Y. *(257,551)*	1.00
40	7c	**Wilson,** *Jan. 10, 1956,* Staunton, Va. *(200,111)*	1.00
41	8c	**Statue of Liberty** (flat plate), *Apr. 9, 1954*	1.00
41B	8c	**Statue of Liberty** (rotary press), *Apr. 9, 1954*	1.00

First day cancellation was applied to 340,077 covers bearing ne or more of Nos. 1041-1041B.

42	8c	**Statue of Liberty** (Giori press), *Mar. 22, 1958,* Cleveland, O. *(223,899)*	1.00
042A	8c	**Pershing,** *Nov. 17, 1961,* New York, N.Y. *(321,031)*	1.25
43	9c	**Alamo,** *June 14, 1956,* San Antonio, Texas *(207,086)*	1.50
44	10c	**Independence Hall,** *July 4, 1956,* Philadelphia, Pa., *(220,930)*	1.00
44d	10c	Tagged, *July 6, 1966*	40.00
44A	11c	**Statue of Liberty,** *June 15, 1961 (238,905)*	1.25
44Ac	11c	Tagged, *Jan. 11, 1967*	40.00
45	12c	**B. Harrison,** *June 6, 1959,* Oxford, O. *(225,869)*	1.25
45a	12c	Tagged, *May 6, 1968*	40.00
46	15c	**Jay,** *Dec. 12, 1958 (205,680)*	1.25
46a	15c	Tagged, *July 6, 1966*	40.00
47	20c	**Monticello,** *Apr. 13, 1956,* Charlottesville, Va. *(147,860)*	1.25
48	25c	**Revere,** *Apr. 18, 1958,* Boston, Mass. *(196,530)*	1.25
49a	30c	**Lee,** *Sept. 21, 1955,* Norfolk, Va. *(120,166)*	2.00
50a	40c	**Marshall,** *Sept. 24, 1955,* Richmond, Va. *(113,972)*	2.00
51a	50c	**Anthony,** *Aug. 25, 1955,* Louisville, Ky. *(110,220)*	6.00
52a	$1	**Henry,** *Oct. 7, 1955,* Joplin, Mo. *(80,191)*	15.00
53	$5	**Hamilton,** *Mar. 19, 1956,* Paterson, N.J. *(34,272)*	50.00

1954-73

COIL STAMPS

1054c	1c	**Washington,** *Oct. 8, 1954,* Baltimore, Md. *(196,318),* strip of 3	1.00
1054A	1¼c	**Palace of Governors,** *June 17, 1960,* Santa Fe, N.M., strip of 3	1.00
1055d	2c	**Jefferson,** *Oct. 22, 1954,* St. Louis, Mo. *(162,050),* pair	1.00
1055a	2c	Tagged, *May 6, 1968,* pair	32.50

1056	2½c	**Bunker Hill,** *Sept. 9, 1959,* Los Angeles, Calif. *(198,680),* pair	2.00
1057c	3c	**Statue of Liberty,** *July 20, 1954 (137,139)*	1.00
1058	4c	**Lincoln,** *July 31, 1958,* Mandan, N.D. *(184,079)*	1.25
1059	4½c	**Hermitage,** *May 1, 1959,* Denver, Colo. *(202,454)*	1.75
1059A	25c	**Revere,** *Feb. 25, 1965,* Wheaton, Md. *(184,954)*	1.25
1059Ab	25c	Tagged, *Apr. 3, 1973,* New York, N.Y.	40.00

1954

1060	3c	**Nebraska Territory,** *May 7,* Nebraska City, Neb. *(401,015)*	1.00
1061	3c	**Kansas Territory,** *May 31,* Fort Leavenworth, Kans. *(349,145)*	1.00
1062	3c	**George Eastman,** *July 12,* Rochester, N.Y. *(630,448)*	1.00
1063	3c	**Lewis & Clark Expedition,** *July 28,* Sioux City, Iowa *(371,557)*	1.50

1955

1064	3c	**Pennsylvania Academy of the Fine Arts,** *Jan. 15,* Philadelphia, Pa. *(307,040)*	1.00
1065	3c	**Land Grant Colleges,** *Feb. 12,* East Lansing, Mich. *(419,241)*	1.25
1066	8c	**Rotary International,** *Feb. 23,* Chicago, Ill. *(350,625)*	2.75
1067	3c	**Armed Forces Reserve,** *May 21 (300,436)*	1.25
1068	3c	**New Hampshire,** *June 21,* Franconia, N.H. *(330,630)*	2.00
1069	3c	**Soo Locks,** *June 28,* Sault Sainte Marie, Mich. *(316,616)*	1.00
1070	3c	**Atoms for Peace,** *July 28 (351,940)*	1.00
1071	3c	**Fort Ticonderoga,** *Sept. 18,* Fort Ticonderoga, N.Y. *(342,946)*	1.00
1072	3c	**Andrew W. Mellon,** *Dec. 20 (278,897)*	1.00

1956

1073	3c	**Benjamin Franklin,** *Jan. 17,* Philadelphia, Pa. *(351,260)*	1.25
1074	3c	**Booker T. Washington,** *Apr. 5,* Booker T. Washington Birthplace, Va. *(272,659)*	2.00
1075	11c	**FIPEX Souvenir Sheet,** *Apr. 28,* New York, N.Y. *(429,327)*	5.00
1076	3c	**FIPEX,** *Apr. 30,* New York, N.Y. *(526,090)*	1.00
1077	3c	**Wildlife (Turkey),** *May 5,* Fond du Lac, Wis. *(292,121)*	1.75
1078	3c	**Wildlife (Antelope),** *June 22,* Gunnison, Colo. *(294,731)*	1.75
1079	3c	**Wildlife (Salmon),** *Nov. 9,* Seattle, Wash. *(346,800)*	1.75
1080	3c	**Pure Food and Drug Laws,** *June 27,* Washington, D.C. *(411,761)*	1.00
1081	3c	**Wheatland,** *Aug. 5,* Lancaster, Pa. *(340,142)*	1.00
1082	3c	**Labor Day,** *Sept. 3,* Camden, N.J. *(338,450)*	1.00
1083	3c	**Nassau Hall,** *Sept. 22,* Princeton, N.J. *(350,756)*	1.00
1084	3c	**Devils Tower,** *Sept. 24,* Devils Tower, Wyo. *(285,090)*	1.25
1085	3c	**Children,** *Dec. 15 (305,125)*	1.00

1957

1086	3c	**Alexander Hamilton,** *Jan. 11,* New York, N.Y. *(305,117)*	1.00
1087	3c	**Polio,** *Jan. 15 (307,630)*	1.50
1088	3c	**Coast & Geodetic Survey,** *Feb. 11,* Seattle, Wash. *(309,931)*	1.00
1089	3c	**Architects,** *Feb. 23,* New York, N.Y. *(368,840)*	1.25
1090	3c	**Steel Industry,** *May 22,* New York, N.Y. *(473,284)*	1.00
1091	3c	**Naval Review,** *June 10,* U.S.S. Saratoga, Norfolk, Va. *(365,933)*	1.25
1092	3c	**Oklahoma Statehood,** *June 14,* Oklahoma City, Okla. *(327,172)*	1.00
1093	3c	**School Teachers,** *July 1,* Philadelphia, Pa. *(357,986)*	2.00
		(Spelling error) Philadelpia	8.00
1094	4c	**Flag,** *July 4 (523,879)*	1.00
1095	3c	**Shipbuilding,** *Aug. 15,* Bath, Maine *(347,432)*	1.50
1096	8c	**Ramon Magsaysay,** *Aug. 31 (334,558)*	1.00
1097	3c	**Lafayette Bicentenary,** *Sept. 6,* Easton, Pa. *(260,421)*	1.00
		Fayetteville, N.C. *(230,000)*	1.00
		Louisville, Ky. *(207,856)*	1.00
1098	3c	**Wildlife (Whooping Cranes),** *Nov. 22,* New York, N.Y. *(342,970)*	1.25
		New Orleans, La. *(154,327)*	1.25
		Corpus Christi, Tex. *(280,990)*	1.25
1099	3c	**Religious Freedom,** *Dec. 27,* Flushing, N.Y. *(357,770)*	1.00

1958

1100	3c	**Gardening-Horticulture,** *Mar. 15,* Ithaca, N.Y. *(451,292)*	1.00
1104	3c	**Brussels Exhibition,** *Apr. 17,* Detroit, Mich. *(428,073)*	1.00
1105	3c	**James Monroe,** *Apr. 28,* Montross, Va. *(326,988)*	1.00
1106	3c	**Minnesota Statehood,** *May 11,* Saint Paul, Minn. *(475,552)*	1.00
1107	3c	**International Geophysical Year,** *May 31,* Chicago, Ill. *(397,000)*	1.00
1108	3c	**Gunston Hall,** *June 12,* Lorton, Va. *(349,801)*	1.00

1109	3c	**Mackinac Bridge,** *June 25,* Mackinac Bridge, Mich. *(445,605)*	1.00
1110	4c	**Simon Bolivar,** *July 24*	1.50
1111	8c	**Simon Bolivar,** *July 24*	2.25
		1110-1111 on one cover	2.00

First day cancellation was applied to 708, 777 covers bearing one or more of Nos. 1110-1111.

1112	4c	**Atlantic Cable,** *Aug. 15,* New York, N.Y. *(365,072)*	1.00

1958-59

1113	1c	**Lincoln Sesquicentennial,** *Feb. 12, 1959,* Hodgenville, Ky. *(379,862)* block of four	1.75
1114	3c	**Lincoln Sesquicentennial,** *Feb. 12, 1959,* New York, N.Y. *(437,737)*	1.75
1115	4c	**Lincoln-Douglas Debates,** *Aug. 27, 1958,* Freeport, Ill. *(373,063)*	1.75
1116	4c	**Lincoln Sesquicentennial,** *May, 30, 1959 (894,887)*	1.75

1958

1117	4c	**Lajos Kossuth,** *Sept. 19*	1.25
1118	8c	**Lajos Kossuth,** *Sept. 19*	1.50
		1117-1118 on one cover	2.25

First day cancellation was applied to 722,188 covers bearing one or more of Nos. 1117-1118.

1119	4c	**Freedom of Press,** *Sept. 22,* Columbia, Mo. *(411,752)*	1.00
1120	4c	**Overland Mail,** *Oct. 10,* San Francisco, Cal. *(352,760)*	1.00
1121	4c	**Noah Webster,** *Oct. 16,* West Hartford, Conn. *(364,608)*	1.00
1122	4c	**Forest Conservation,** *Oct. 27,* Tucson, Ariz. *(405,959)*	1.00
1123	4c	**Fort Duquesne,** *Nov. 25,* Pittsburgh, Pa. *(421,764)*	1.00

1959

1124	4c	**Oregon Statehood,** *Feb. 14,* Astoria, Ore. *(452,764)*	1.00
1125	4c	**San Martin,** *Feb. 25*	1.50
1126	8c	**San Martin,** *Feb. 25*	2.25
		1125-1126 on one cover	2.00

First day cancellation was applied to 910,208 covers bearing one or more of No. 1125-1126.

1127	4c	**NATO,** *Apr. 1 (361,040)*	1.00
1128	4c	**Arctic Exploration,** *Apr. 6,* Cresson, Pa. *(397,770)*	1.00
1129	8c	**World Trade,** *Apr. 20 (503,618)*	1.00
1130	4c	**Silver Centennial,** *June 8,* Virginia City, Nev. *(337,233)*	1.00
1131	4c	**St. Lawrence Seaway,** *June 26,* Massena, N.Y. *(543,211)*	1.25
1132	4c	**Flag** (49 stars), *July 4,* Auburn, N.Y. *(523,773)*	1.00
1133	4c	**Soil Conservation,** *Aug. 26,* Rapid City, S.D. *(400,613)*	1.00
1134	4c	**Petroleum Industry,** *Aug. 27,* Titusville, Pa. *(801,859)*	1.50
1135	4c	**Dental Health,** *Sept. 14,* New York, N.Y. *(649,813)*	3.50
1136	4c	**Reuter,** *Sept. 29*	1.25
1137	8c	**Reuter,** *Sept. 29*	1.50
		1136-1137 on one cover	2.25

First day cancellation was applied to 1,207,933 covers bearing one or more of Nos. 1136-1137.

1138	4c	**Dr. Ephraim McDowell,** *Dec. 3,* Danville, Ky. *(344,603)*	1.25

1960-61

1139	4c	**Washington "Credo,"** *Jan. 20, 1960,* Mount Vernon, Va. *(438,335)*	1.25
1140	4c	**Franklin "Credo,"** *Mar. 31, 1960,* Philadelphia, Pa. *(497,913)*	1.25
1141	4c	**Jefferson "Credo,"** *May 18, 1960,* Charlottesville, Va. *(454,903)*	1.25
1142	4c	**Francis Scott Key "Credo,"** *Sept. 14, 1960,* Baltimore, Md. *(501,129)*	1.25
1143	4c	**Lincoln "Credo,"** *Nov. 19, 1960,* New York, N.Y. *(467,780)*	1.25
1144	4c	**Patrick Henry "Credo,"** *Jan. 11, 1961,* Richmond, Va. *(415,252)*	1.25

1960

1145	4c	**Boy Scouts,** *Feb. 8 (1,419,955)*	4.00
1146	4c	**Olympic Winter Games,** *Feb. 18,* Olympic Valley, Calif. *(516,456)*	1.00
1147	4c	**Masaryk,** *Mar. 7*	1.25
1148	8c	**Masaryk,** *Mar. 7*	1.50
		1147-1148 on one cover	2.25

First day cancellation was applied to 1,710,726 covers bearing one or more of Nos. 1147-1148.

1149	4c	**World Refugee Year,** *Apr. 7 (413,298)*	1.00
1150	4c	**Water Conservation,** *Apr. 18 (648,988)*	1.00
1151	4c	**SEATO,** *May 31 (514,926)*	1.00
1152	4c	**American Woman,** *June 2 (830,385)*	1.25
1153	4c	**50-Star Flag,** *July 4,* Honolulu, Hawaii *(820,900)*	1.00
1154	4c	**Pony Express Centennial,** *July 19,* Sacramento, Calif. *(520,223)*	1.75
1155	4c	**Employ the Handicapped,** *Aug. 28,* New York, N.Y. *(439,638)*	1.50
1156	4c	**World Forestry Congress,** *Aug. 29,* Seattle, Wash. *(350,848)*	1.00
1157	4c	**Mexican Independence,** *Sept. 16,* Los Angeles, Calif, *(360,297)*	1.00
1158	4c	**U.S.-Japan Treaty,** *Sept. 28 (545,150)*	1.00

1159	4c **Paderewski**, *Oct. 8*	1.25
1160	8c **Paderewski**, *Oct. 8*	1.50
	1159–1160 on one cover	2.25

First day cancellation was applied to 1,057,438 covers bearing one or more of Nos. 1159–1160.

1161	4c **Robert A. Taft**, *Oct. 10*, Cincinnati, Ohio *(312,116)*	1.00
1162	4c **Wheels of Freedom**, *Oct. 15*, Detroit, Mich. *(380,551)*	1.00
1163	4c **Boys' Clubs**, *Oct. 18*, New York, N.Y. *(435,009)*	1.00
1164	4c **Automated P.O.**, *Oct. 20*, Providence, R.I. *(458,237)*	1.00
1165	4c **Mannerheim**, *Oct. 26*	1.25
1166	8c **Mannerheim**, *Oct. 26*	1.50
	1165–1166 on one cover	2.25

First day cancellation was applied to 1,168,770 covers bearing one or more of Nos. 1165–1166.

1167	4c **Camp Fire Girls**, *Nov. 1*, New York, N.Y. *(324,944)*	3.00
1168	4c **Garibaldi**, *Nov. 2*	1.25
1169	8c **Garibaldi**, *Nov. 2*	1.50
	1168–1169 on one cover	2.25

First day cancellation was applied to 1,001,490 covers bearing one or more of Nos. 1168–1169.

1170	4c **Senator George**, *Nov. 5*, Vienna, Ga. *(278,890)*	1.00
1171	4c **Andrew Carnegie**, *Nov. 25*, New York, N.Y. *(318,180)*	1.00
1172	4c **John Foster Dulles**, *Dec. 6 (400,055)*	1.00
1173	4c **Echo I**, *Dec. 15 (583,747)*	2.50

1961-65

1174	4c **Gandhi**, *Jan. 26, 1961*	1.25
1175	8c **Gandhi**, *Jan. 26, 1961*	1.75
	1174–1175 on one cover	2.50

First day cancellation was applied to 1,013,515 covers bearing one or more of Nos. 1174–1175.

1176	4c **Range Conservation**, *Feb. 2, 1961*, Salt Lake City, Utah *(357,101)*	1.00
1177	4c **Horace Greeley**, *Feb. 3, 1961*, Chappaqua, N.Y. *(359,205)*	1.00
1178	4c **Fort Sumter**, *Apr. 12, 1961*, Charleston, S.C. *(602,599)*	4.00
1179	4c **Battle of Shiloh**, *Apr. 7, 1962*, Shiloh, Tenn. *(526,062)*	4.00
1180	5c **Battle of Gettysburg**, *July 1, 1963*, Gettysburg, Pa. *(600,205)*	4.00
1181	5c **Battle of Wilderness**, *May 5, 1964*, Fredericksburg, Va. *(450,904)*	4.00
1182	5c **Appomattox**, *Apr. 9, 1965*, Appomattox, Va. *(653,121)*	4.00

1961

1183	4c **Kansas Statehood**, *May 10*, Council Grove, Kansas *(480,561)*	1.00
1184	4c **Senator Norris**, *July 11 (482,875)*	1.00
1185	4c **Naval Aviation**, *Aug. 20*, San Diego, Calif. *(416,391)*	1.50
1186	4c **Workmen's Compensation**, *Sept. 4*, Milwaukee, Wis, *(410,236)*	1.00
1187	4c **Frederic Remington**, *Oct. 4 (723,443)*	1.25
1188	4c **China Republic**, *Oct. 10 (463,900)*	5.50
1189	4c **Naismith-Basketball**, *Nov. 6*, Springfield, Mass. *(479,917)*	7.50
1190	4c **Nursing**, *Dec. 28 (964,005)*	10.00

1962

1191	4c **New Mexico Statehood**, *Jan. 6*, Sante Fe, N.M. *(365,330)*	2.00
1192	4c **Arizona Statehood**, *Feb. 14*, Phoenix, Ariz. *(508,216)*	1.75
1193	4c **Project Mercury**, *Feb. 20*, Cape Canaveral, Fla. *(3,000,000)*	3.00
	Any other city	5.00
1194	4c **Malaria Eradication**, *Mar. 30 (554,175)*	1.00
1195	4c **Charles Evans Hughes**, *Apr. 11 (544,424)*	1.00
1196	4c **Seattle World's Fair**, *Apr. 25*, Seattle, Wash. *(771,856)*	1.25
1197	4c **Louisiana Statehood**, *Apr. 30*, New Orleans, La. *(436,681)*	1.00
1198	4c **Homestead Act**, *May 20*, Beatrice, Nebr. *(487,450)*	1.00
1199	4c **Girl Scouts**, *July 24*, Burlington, Vt. *(634,347)*	5.00
1200	4c **Brien McMahon**, *July 28*, Norwalk, Conn. *(384,419)*	1.00
1201	4c **Apprenticeship**, *Aug. 31 (1,003,548)*	1.00
1202	4c **Sam Rayburn**, *Sept. 16*, Bonham, Texas *(401,042)*	1.50
1203	4c **Dag Hammarskjold**, *Oct. 23*, New York, N.Y. *(500,683)*	1.00
1203a	4c **Dag Hammarskjold**, original yellow inverted, *Oct. 23*, New York, N.Y.	2,000.
1204	4c **Hammarskjold**, yellow inverted, *Nov. 16*, (about *75,000)*	5.00
1205	4c **Christmas**, *Nov. 1*, Pittsburgh, Pa. *(491,312)*	1.10
1206	4c **Higher Education**, *Nov. 14 (627,347)*	1.25
1207	4c **Winslow Homer**, *Dec. 15*, Gloucester, Mass. *(498,866)*	1.25

1963-66

1208	5c **Flag**, *Jan. 9, 1963 (696,185)*	1.00
1208a	5c Tagged, *Aug. 25, 1966*	30.00

1962-66

REGULAR ISSUE

1209	1c **Jackson**, *Mar. 22, 1963*, New York, N.Y. *(392,363)*, block of 5 or 6	1.00
1209a	1c Tagged, *July 6, 1966*, block of 5 or 6	30.00
1213	5c **Washington**, *Nov. 23, 1962*, New York, N.Y. *(360,531)*	1.00
1213a	Booklet pane of 5 + label, *Nov. 23, 1962*, New York, N.Y. *(111,452)*	4.00
1213b	5c Tagged, *Oct. 28, 1963*, Dayton, Ohio (about *15,000)*	30.00
1213c	Booklet pane of 5 + label, tagged, *Oct. 28, 1963*, Dayton, Ohio Washington, D.C. *(750)*	100.00 110.00
1225	1c **Jackson**, Coil, *May 31, 1963*, Chicago, Ill. *(238,952)*, pair and strip of 3	1.00
1225a	1c Coil, tagged, *July 6, 1966*, pair and strip of 3	30.00
1229	5c **Washington**, Coil, *Nov. 23, 1962*, New York, N.Y. *(184,627)*	1.00
1229a	5c Coil, tagged, *Oct. 28, 1963*, Dayton, Ohio (about *2,000)*	30.00

1963

1230	5c **Carolina Charter**, *Apr. 6*, Edenton, N.C. *(426,200)*	1.00
1231	5c **Food for Peace**, *June 4 (624,342)*	1.00
1232	5c **West Virginia Statehood**, *June 20*, Wheeling, W. Va. *(413,389)*	1.00
1233	5c **Emancipation Proclamation**, *Aug. 16*, Chicago, Ill, *(494,886)*	1.75
1234	5c **Alliance for Progress**, *Aug. 17 (528,095)*	1.00
1235	5c **Cordell Hull**, *Oct. 5* Carthage, Tenn. *(391,631)*	1.00
1236	5c **Eleanor Roosevelt**, *Oct. 11 (860,155)*	1.25
1237	5c **Science**, *Oct. 14 (504,503)*	1.00
1238	5c **City Mail Delivery**, *Oct. 26 (544,806)*	1.25
1239	5c **Red Cross**, *Oct. 29 (557,678)*	1.50
1240	5c **Christmas**, *Nov. 1*, Santa Claus, Ind. *(458,619)*	1.25
1240a	5c **Christmas**, tagged, *Nov. 2*, (about *500)*	60.00

Note below No. 1036b also applies to No. 1240a.

1241	5c **Audubon**, *Dec. 7*, Henderson, Ky. *(518,855)*	1.25

1964

1242	5c **Sam Houston**, *Jan. 10*, Houston, Tex. *(487,986)*	1.75
1243	5c **Charles Russell**, *Mar. 19*, Great Falls, Mont. *(658,745)*	1.25
1244	5c **N.Y. World's Fair**, *Apr. 22*, World's Fair, N.Y. *(1,656,346)*	1.75
1245	5c **John Muir**, *Apr. 29*, Martinez, Calif. *(446,925)*	1.50
1246	5c **John F. Kennedy**, *May 29*, Boston, Mass. *(2,003,096)*	2.50
	Any other city	4.50
1247	5c **New Jersey Tercentenary**, *June 15*, Elizabeth, N.J. *(526,879)*	1.00
1248	5c **Nevada Statehood**, *July 22*, Carson City, Nev. *(584,973)*	1.00
1249	5c **Register & Vote**, *Aug. 1 (533,439)*	1.25
1250	5c **Shakespeare**, *Aug. 14*, Stratford, Conn. *(524,053)*	1.50
1251	5c **Drs. Mayo**, *Sept. 11*, Rochester, Minn. *(674,846)*	3.00
1252	5c **American Music**, *Oct. 15*, New York, N.Y. *(466,107)*	1.50
1253	5c **Homemakers**, *Oct. 26*, Honolulu, Hawaii *(435,392)*	1.00
1257b	5c **Christmas**, *Nov. 9*, Bethlehem, Pa.	3.00
	1254–1257, any single	1.00
1257c	5c Tagged, *Nov. 10*, Dayton, O.	57.50
	1254a–1257a, any single	30.00

First day cancellation was applied to 794,900 covers bearing Nos. 1254–1257 in singles or multiples and at Dayton to about 2,700 covers bearing Nos. 1254a–1257a in singles or multiples.

1258	5c **Verrazano-Narrows Bridge**, *Nov. 21*, Staten Island, N.Y. *(619,780)*	1.00
1259	5c **Fine Arts**, *Dec. 2 (558,046)*	1.00
1260	5c **Amateur Radio**, *Dec. 15*, Anchorage, Alaska *(452,255)*	5.00

1965

1261	5c **Battle of New Orleans**, *Jan. 8*, New Orleans, La. *(466,029)*	1.00
1262	5c **Physical Fitness-Sokol**, *Feb. 15 (864,848)*	1.25
1263	5c **Cancer Crusade**, *Apr. 1 (744,485)*	2.50
1264	5c **Churchill**, *May 13*, Fulton, Mo. *(773,580)*	1.50
1265	5c **Magna Carta**, *June 15*, Jamestown, Va. *(490,065)*	1.00
1266	5c **Intl. Cooperation Year**, *June 26*, San Francisco, Cal. *(402,925)*	1.00
1267	5c **Salvation Army**, *July 2*, New York, N.Y. *(634,228)*	3.00
1268	5c **Dante**, *July 17*, San Francisco, Cal. *(424,893)*	1.00
1269	5c **Herbert Hoover**, *Aug. 10*, West Branch, Iowa *(698,182)*	1.00
1270	5c **Robert Fulton**, *Aug. 19*, Clermont, N.Y. *(550,330)*	1.00
1271	5c **Florida Settlement**, *Aug. 28*, St. Augustine, Fla. *(465,000)*	1.00
1272	5c **Traffic Safety**, *Sept. 3*, Baltimore, Md. *(527,075)*	1.00
1273	5c **Copley**, *Sept. 17 (613,484)*	1.00
1274	11c **Intl. Telecommunication Union**, *Oct. 6 (332,818)*	1.10

1275	5c **Adlai Stevenson**, *Oct. 23*, Bloomington, Ill. *(755,656)*	1
1276	5c **Christmas**, *Nov. 2*, Silver Bell, Ariz. *(705,039)*	
1276a	5c Tagged, *Nov. 15*, (about *300)*	50

1965-78

PROMINENT AMERICANS ISSUE

1278	1c **Jefferson**, *Jan. 12, 1968*, Jeffersonville, Ind., block of 5 or 6	1
1278a	Booklet pane of 8, *Jan. 12, 1968*, Jeffersonville, Ind.	2
1278b	Booklet pane of 4 + 2 labels, *May 10, 1971*	11

First day cancellation was applied to 655,680 covers bearing one or more of Nos. 1278, 1278a and 1299.

1279	1¼c **Gallatin**, *Jan. 30, 1967*, Gallatin, Mo. *(439,010)*	1
1280	2c **Wright**, *June 8, 1966*, Spring Green, Wis. *(460,427)*	1
1280a	Booklet pane of 5 + label, *Jan. 8, 1968*, Buffalo, N.Y. *(147,244)*	3
1280c	Booklet pane of 6, *May 7, 1971*, Spokane, Wash.	15
1281	3c **Parkman**, *Sept. 16, 1967*, Boston, Mass. *(518,355)*	1
1282	4c **Lincoln**, *Nov. 19, 1965*, New York, N.Y. *(445,629)*	1
1282a	4c Tagged, *Dec. 1, 1965*, Dayton, O. (about *2,000)* Washington, D.C. *(1,200)*	30. 32
1283	5c **Washington**, *Feb. 22, 1966* *(525,372)*	1.
1283a	5c Tagged, *Feb. 23, 1966*, (about *900)* Dayton, Ohio (about *200)*	30. 75.
1283B	5c **Washington**, Redrawn, *Nov. 17, 1967*, New York, N.Y. *(328,983)*	1.
1284	6c **Roosevelt**, *Jan. 29, 1966*, Hyde Park, N.Y. *(448,631)*	1.
1284a	6c Tagged, *Dec. 29, 1966*	40.
1284b	Booklet pane of 8, *Dec. 28, 1967*	2.
1284c	Booklet pane of 5 + label, *Jan. 9, 1968*	100.
1285	8c **Einstein**, *Mar. 14, 1966*, Princeton, N.J. *(366,803)*	3.
1285a	8c Tagged, *July 6, 1966*	40.
1286	10c **Jackson**, *Mar. 15, 1967*, Hermitage, Tenn. *(255,945)*	1.
1286A	12c **Ford**, *July 30, 1968*, Greenfield Village, Mich. *(342,850)*	1.
1287	13c **Kennedy**, *May 29, 1967*, Brookline, Mass. *(391,195)*	1.7
1288	15c **Holmes**, type I, *Mar. 8, 1968* *(322,970)*	1.0
1288B	15c **Holmes**, from bklt., *June 14, 1978*, Boston, Mass.	1.0
1288Bc	Booklet pane of 8	

First day cancellation was applied to 387,119 covers bearing one or more of Nos. 1288B and 1305E.

1289	20c **Marshall**, *Oct. 24, 1967*, Lexington, Va. *(221,206)*	1.1
1289a	20c Tagged, *Apr. 3, 1973*, New York, N.Y.	40.0
1290	25c **Douglass**, *Feb. 14, 1967* *(213,730)*	2.5
1290a	25c Tagged, *Apr. 3, 1973*, New York, N.Y.	45.0
1291	30c **Dewey**, *Oct. 21, 1968*, Burlington, Vt. *(162,790)*	1.7
1291a	30c Tagged, *Apr. 3, 1973*, New York, N.Y.	45.0
1292	40c **Paine**, *Jan. 29, 1968*, Philadelphia, Pa. *(157,947)*	1.7
1292a	40c Tagged, *Apr. 3, 1973*, New York, N.Y.	45.0
1293	50c **Stone**, *Aug. 13, 1968*, Dorchester, Mass. *(140,410)*	2.5
1293a	50c Tagged, *Apr. 3, 1973*, New York, N.Y.	45.0
1294	$1 **O'Neill**, *Oct. 16, 1967*, New London, Conn. *(103,102)*	6.0
1294a	$1 Tagged, *Apr. 3, 1973*, New York, N.Y.	60.0
1295	$5 **Moore**, *Dec. 3, 1966*, Smyrna, Del. *(41,130)*	40.0
1295a	$5 Tagged, *Apr. 3, 1973*, New York, N.Y.	120.0

First day cancellation was applied to 17,533 covers bearing one or more of Nos. 1059b, 1289a, 1290a, 1291a, 1292a, 1293a, 1294a and 1295a.

COIL STAMPS

1297	3c **Parkman**, *Nov. 4, 1975*, Pendleton, Ore. *(166,798)*	1.00
1298	6c **Roosevelt**, Perf. 10 Horiz., *Dec. 28, 1967*	1.00

First day cancellation was applied to 312,330 covers bearing one or more of Nos. 1298 and 1284b.

1299	1c **Jefferson**, *Jan. 12, 1968*, Jeffersonville, Ind., pair and strip of 3	1.00
1303	4c **Lincoln**, *May 28, 1966*, Springfield, Ill. *(322,563)*	1.50
1304	5c **Washington**, *Sept. 8, 1966*, Cincinnati, O. *(245,400)*	1.00
1305	6c **Roosevelt**, Perf. 10 vert., *Feb. 28, 1968 (317,199)*	1.00
1305E	15c **Holmes**, type I, *June 14, 1978*, Boston, Mass.	1.00
1305C	$1 **O'Neill**, *Jan. 12, 1973*, Hempstead, N.Y. *(121,217)*	4.00

?66

?06	5c **Migratory Bird Treaty,** *Mar. 16,* Pittsburgh, Pa. *(555,485)*	1.75
?07	5c **Humane Treatment of Animals,** *Apr. 9,* New York, N.Y. *(524,420)*	1.25
?08	5c **Indiana Statehood,** *Apr. 16,* Corydon, Ind. *(575,557)*	1.00
?09	5c **Circus,** *May 2,* Delavan, Wis. *(754,076)*	2.00
?10	5c **SIPEX,** *May 21 (637,802)*	1.00
?11	5c **SIPEX, souvenir sheet,** *May 23 (700,882)*	1.10
?12	5c **Bill of Rights,** *July 1,* Miami Beach, Fla. *(562,920)*	1.75
?13	5c **Polish Millennium,** *July 30 (715,603)*	1.50
?14	5c **Natl. Park Service,** *Aug. 25,* Yellowstone National Park, Wyo. *(528,170)*	1.00
?14a	5c **Tagged,** *Aug. 26*	35.00
?15	5c **Marine Corps Reserve,** *Aug. 29 (585,923)*	1.50
?15a	5c **Tagged,** *Aug. 29*	35.00
?16	5c **Gen. Fed. of Women's Clubs,** *Sept. 12,* New York, N.Y. *(383,334)*	1.25
?16a	5c **Tagged,** *Sept. 13*	35.00
?17	5c **Johnny Appleseed,** *Sept. 24,* Leominster, Mass. *(794,610)*	1.25
?17a	5c **Tagged,** *Sept. 26*	35.00
?18	5c **Beautification of America,** *Oct. 5 (564,440)*	1.00
?18a	5c **Tagged,** *Oct. 5*	35.00
?19	5c **Great River Road,** *Oct. 21,* Baton Rouge, La. *(330,933)*	1.00
?19a	5c **Tagged,** *Oct. 22*	35.00
?20	5c **Savings Bond-Servicemen,** *Oct. 26,* Sioux City, Iowa *(444,421)*	1.00
?20a	5c **Tagged,** *Oct. 27*	35.00
?21	5c **Christmas,** *Nov. 1,* Christmas, Mich. *(537,650)*	1.00
?21a	5c **Tagged,** *Nov. 2*	35.00
?22	5c **Mary Cassatt,** *Nov. 17 (593,389)*	1.00
?22a	5c **Tagged,** *Nov. 17*	35.00

?967

?23	5c **National Grange,** *Apr. 17 (603,460)*	1.00
?24	5c **Canada Centenary,** *May 25,* Montreal, Canada *(711,795)*	1.00
?25	5c **Erie Canal,** *July 4,* Rome, N.Y. *(784,611)*	1.00
?26	5c **Search for Peace-Lions,** *July 5,* Chicago, Ill. *(393,197)*	1.00
?27	5c **Thoreau,** *July 12,* Concord, Mass. *(696,789)*	1.00
?28	5c **Nebraska Statehood,** *July 29,* Lincoln, Nebr. *(1,146,957)*	1.00
?29	5c **Voice of America,** *Aug. 1 (455,190)*	2.00
?30	5c **Davy Crockett,** *Aug. 17,* San Antonio, Tex. *(462,291)*	1.25
?331a	5c **Space Accomplishments,** *Sept. 29,* Kennedy Space Center, Fla. *(667,267)*	8.00
	1331-1332, any single	3.00
?333	5c **Urban Planning,** *Oct. 2 (389,009)*	1.00
?334	5c **Finland Independence,** *Oct. 6,* Finland, Minn. *(408,532)*	1.00
?335	5c **Thomas Eakins,** *Nov. 2 (648,054)*	1.40
?336	5c **Christmas,** *Nov. 6,* Bethlehem, Ga. *(462,118)*	1.25
?337	5c **Mississippi Statehood,** *Dec. 11,* Natchez, Miss. *(379,612)*	1.00

1968-71

?338	6c **Flag** (Giori), *Jan. 24, 1968 (412,120)*	1.00
?338A	6c **Flag coil,** *May 30, 1969,* Chicago, Ill. *(248,434)*	1.00
?338D	6c **Flag** (Huck), *Aug. 7, 1970 (365,280)*	1.00
?338F	6c **Flag,** *May 10, 1971*	1.00
?338G	8c **Flag coil,** *May 10, 1971*	1.00

First day cancellation (May 10) was applied to 235,543 covers bearing one or more of Nos. 1338F-1338G.

1968

?339	6c **Illinois Statehood,** *Feb. 12,* Shawneetown, Ill. *(761,640)*	1.00
?340	6c **HemisFair'68,** *Mar. 30,* San Antonio, Tex. *(469,909)*	1.00
?341	$1 **Airlift,** *Apr. 4,* Seattle, Wash. *(105,088)*	7.00
?342	6c **Youth-Elks,** *May 1,* Chicago, Ill. *(354,711)*	1.00
?343	6c **Law and Order,** *May 17 (407,081)*	2.50
?344	6c **Register and Vote,** *June 27 (355,685)*	1.00
?354a	6c **Historic Flag series of 10,** *July 4,* Pittsburgh, Pa. *(2,924,962)*	15.00
	1345-1354, any single	3.00
?355	6c **Disney,** *Sept. 11,* Marceline, Mo. *(499,505)*	25.00
?356	6c **Marquette,** *Sept. 20,* Sault Ste. Marie, Mich. *(379,710)*	1.00
?357	6c **Daniel Boone,** *Sept. 26,* Frankfort, Ky. *(333,440)*	1.25
?358	6c **Arkansas River,** *Oct. 1,* Little Rock, Ark. *(358,025)*	1.00
?359	6c **Leif Erikson,** *Oct. 9,* Seattle, Wash. *(376,565)*	1.00
?360	6c **Cherokee Strip,** *Oct. 15,* Ponca, Okla. *(339,330)*	1.00
?361	6c **John Trumbull,** *Oct. 18,* New Haven, Conn. *(378,285)*	2.00
?362	6c **Waterfowl Conservation,** *Oct. 24,* Cleveland, Ohio, *(349,719)*	1.25
?363	6c **Christmas,** tagged, *Nov. 1 (739,055)*	1.25
?363a	6c **Untagged,** *Nov. 2*	10.00
?364	6c **American Indian,** *Nov. 4 (415,964)*	1.25

1969

1368a	6c **Beautification of America,** *Jan. 16 (1,094,184)*	4.00
	1365-1368, any single	1.00
1369	6c **American Legion,** *Mar. 15 (632,035)*	1.00
1370	6c **Grandma Moses,** *May 1 (367,880)*	1.50
1371	6c **Apollo 8,** *May 5,* Houston, Texas *(908,634)*	2.25
1372	6c **W.C. Handy,** *May 17,* Memphis, Tenn. *(398,216)*	2.25
1373	6c **California Bicentenary,** *July 16,* San Diego, Calif, *(530,210)*	1.00
1374	6c **J.W. Powell,** *Aug. 1,* Page, Ariz. *(434,433)*	1.00
1375	6c **Alabama Statehood,** *Aug. 2,* Huntsville, Ala. *(485,801)*	1.00
1379a	6c **Botanical Congress,** *Aug. 23,* Seattle, Wash. *(737,935)*	5.00
	1376-1379, any single	1.50
1380	6c **Dartmouth Case,** *Sept. 22,* Hanover, N.H. *(416,327)*	1.00
1381	6c **Professional Baseball,** *Sept. 24,* Cincinnati, Ohio *(414,942)*	12.00
1382	6c **Intercollegiate Football,** *Sept. 26,* New Brunswick, N.J. *(414,860)*	6.50
1383	6c **Dwight D. Eisenhower,** *Oct. 14,* Abilene, Kans. *(1,009,560)*	1.00
1384	6c **Christmas,** *Nov. 3,* Christmas, Fla. *(555,500)*	1.25
1385	6c **Hope for Crippled,** *Nov. 20,* Columbus, Ohio *(342,676)*	1.25
1386	6c **William M. Harnett,** *Dec. 3,* Boston, Mass. *(408,860)*	1.00

1970-74

1390a	6c **National History,** *May 6, 1970,* New York, N.Y. *(834,260)*	4.00
	1387-1390, any single	1.50
1391	6c **Maine Statehood,** *July 9, 1970,* Portland, Maine, *(472,165)*	2.75
1392	6c **Wildlife Conservation,** *July 20, 1970,* Custer, S.D. *(309,418)*	1.00
1393	6c **Eisenhower,** *Aug. 6, 1970*	1.00
1393a	Booklet pane of 8	3.00
1393b	Booklet pane of 5 + label	1.50

First day cancellations were applied to 823,540 covers bearing one or more of Nos. 1393 and 1401.

1393D	7c **Franklin,** *Oct. 20, 1972,* Philadelphia, Pa. *(309,276)*	1.00
1394	8c **Eisenhower** (multi), *May 10, 1971*	1.00
1395	8c **Eisenhower** (claret), *May 10, 1971*	1.00
1395a	Booklet pane of 8	2.50
1395b	Booklet pane of 6	2.50
1395c	Booklet pane of 4 + 2 labels, *Jan. 28, 1972,* Casa Grande, Ariz.	2.25
1395d	Booklet pane of 7 + label, *Jan. 28, 1972,* Casa Grande, Ariz.	2.25

First day cancellations were applied to 813,947 covers bearing one or more of Nos. 1394, 1395 and 1402. First day cancellations were applied to 181,601 covers bearing one or more of Nos. 1395c or 1395d.

1396	8c **Postal Service Emblem,** *July 1, 1971,* any city (est. 16,300,000)	1.00

First day cancels from over 16,000 different cities are known. Some are rare.

1397	14c **Fiorello H. LaGuardia,** *Apr. 24, 1972,* New York, N.Y. *(180,114)*	1.00
1398	16c **Ernie Pyle,** *May 7, 1971 (444,410)*	1.50
1399	18c **Elizabeth Blackwell,** *Jan. 23, 1974,* Geneva, N.Y. *(217,938)*	1.25
1400	21c **Amadeo Giannini,** *June 27, 1973,* San Mateo, Calif. *(282,520)*	1.50
1401	6c **Eisenhower coil,** *Aug. 6, 1970*	1.00
1402	8c **Eisenhower coil,** *May 10, 1971*	1.00

1970

1405	6c **Edgar Lee Masters,** *Aug. 22,* Petersburg Ill. *(372,804)*	1.00
1406	6c **Woman Suffrage,** *Aug. 26,* Adams, Mass. *(508,142)*	1.00
1407	6c **South Carolina Anniv.** *Sept. 12,* Charleston, S.C. *(533,000)*	1.00
1408	6c **Stone Mt. Memorial,** *Sept. 19,* Stone Mountain, Ga. *(558,546)*	1.00
1409	6c **Fort Snelling,** *Oct. 17,* Fort Snelling, Minn. *(497,611)*	1.00
1413a	6c **Anti-Pollution,** *Oct. 28,* San Clemente, Calif. *(1,033,147)*	4.00
	1410-1413, any single	1.25
1414	6c **Christmas (Nativity),** *Nov. 5*	1.25
1414a	6c **Precanceled,** *Nov. 5*	7.50
1418b	6c **Christmas,** *Nov. 5*	5.50
	1415-1418, any single	1.50
	1414-1418 on one cover	8.50
1418c	6c **Precanceled,** *Nov. 5*	15.00
	1415a-1418a, any single	5.00
	1414a-1418a on one cover	30.00

First day cancellation was applied to 2,014,450 covers bearing one or more of Nos. 1414-1418 or 1414a-1418a.

1419	6c **United Nations,** *Nov. 20,* New York, N.Y. *(474,070)*	1.25
1420	6c **Pilgrims' Landing,** *Nov. 21,* Plymouth, Mass. *(629,850)*	1.00
1421	6c **Disabled Veterans,** *Nov. 24,* Cincinnati, Ohio, or Montgomery, Ala.	2.00
1422	6c **U.S. Servicemen,** *Nov. 24,* Cincinnati, Ohio, or Montgomery, Ala.	2.00
1421a		3.00

First day cancellation was applied to 476,610 covers at Cincinnati and 336,417 at Montgomery, each cover bearing one or more of Nos. 1421-1422.

1971

1423	6c **Wool Industry,** *Jan. 19,* Las Vegas, Nev. *(379,911)*	1.00
1424	6c **MacArthur,** *Jan. 26,* Norfolk, Va. *(720,035)*	1.50
1425	6c **Blood Donor,** *Mar. 12,* New York, N.Y. *(644,497)*	1.00
1426	8c **Missouri Sesquicentennial,** *May 8,* Independence, Mo. *(551,000)*	1.00
1430a	8c **Wildlife Conservation,** *June 12,* Avery Island, La. *(679,483)*	3.00
	1427-1430, any single	1.25
1431	8c **Antarctic Treaty,** *June 23 (419,200)*	1.00
1432	8c **American Revolution Bicentennial,** *July 4 (434,930)*	1.00
1433	8c **John Sloan,** *Aug. 2,* Lock Haven, Pa. *(482,265)*	1.00
1434a	8c **Space Achievement Decade,** *Aug. 2,* Kennedy Space Center, Fla. *(1,403,644)*	2.00
	Houston, Texas *(811,560)*	2.00
	Huntsville, Ala. *(524,000)*	2.00
1436	8c **Emily Dickinson,** *Aug. 28,* Amherst, Mass. *(498,180)*	1.00
1437	8c **San Juan,** *Sept. 12,* San Juan, P.R. *(501,668)*	1.00
1438	8c **Drug Abuse,** *Oct. 4,* Dallas, Texas *(425,330)*	1.00
1439	8c **CARE,** *Oct. 27,* New York, N.Y. *(402,121)*	1.00
1443a	8c **Historic Preservation,** *Oct. 29,* San Diego, Calif. *(783,242)*	3.00
	1440-1443, any single	1.25
1444	8c **Christmas (religious),** *Nov. 10*	1.25
1445	8c **Christmas (secular),** *Nov. 10*	1.25
	1444-1445 on one cover	1.50

First day cancellation was applied to 348,038 covers with No. 1444 and 580,062 with No. 1445.

1972

1446	8c **Sidney Lanier,** *Feb. 3,* Macon Ga. *(394,800)*	1.00
1447	8c **Peace Corps,** *Feb. 11 (453,660)*	1.00
1451a	2c **National Parks Centennial,** *Apr. 5,* Hatteras, N.C., block of 4 *(505,697)*	3.00
1452	6c **National Parks,** *June 26,* Vienna, Va. *(403,396)*	1.00
1453	8c **National Parks,** *Mar. 1,* Yellowstone National Park, Wyo. Washington, D.C. *(847,500)*	1.00
1454	15c **National Parks,** *July 28,* Mt. McKinley National Park, Alaska *(491,456)*	1.00
1455	8c **Family Planning,** *Mar. 18,* New York, N.Y. *(691,385)*	1.00
1459a	8c **Colonial Craftsmen** (Rev. Bicentennial), *July 4,* Williamsburg, Va. *(1,914,976)*	2.50
	1456-1459, any single	1.00
1460	6c **Olympics,** *Aug. 17*	1.00
1461	8c **Winter Olympics,** *Aug. 17*	1.00
1462	15c **Olympics,** *Aug. 17*	1.00
	1460-1462 and C85 on one cover	2.00

First day cancellation was applied to 971,536 covers bearing one or more of Nos. 1460-1462 and C85.

1463	8c **P.T.A.,** *Sept. 15,* San Francisco, Cal. *(523,454)*	1.00
1467a	8c **Wildlife,** *Sept. 20,* Warm Springs, Ore. *(733,778)*	3.00
	1464-1467, any single	1.50
1468	8c **Mail Order,** *Sept. 27,* Chicago, Ill. *(759,820)*	1.00
1469	8c **Osteopathy,** *Oct. 9,* Miami, Fla. *(607,160)*	1.50
1470	8c **Tom Sawyer,** *Oct. 13,* Hannibal, Mo. *(459,013)*	1.50
1471	8c **Christmas (religious),** *Nov. 9*	1.00
1472	8c **Christmas (secular),** *Nov. 9*	1.00
	1471-1472 on one cover	2.00

First day cancellation was applied to 713,821 covers bearing one or more of Nos. 1471-1472.

1473	8c **Pharmacy,** *Nov. 10,* Cincinnati, Ohio *(804,320)*	8.00
1474	8c **Stamp Collecting,** *Nov. 17,* New York, N.Y. *(434,680)*	1.25

1973

1475	8c **Love,** *Jan. 26,* Philadelphia, Pa. *(422,492)*	2.00
1476	8c **Pamphleteer** (Rev. Bicentennial), *Feb. 16,* Portland, Ore. *(431,784)*	1.00
1477	8c **Broadside** (Rev. Bicentennial), *Apr. 13,* Atlantic City, N.J. *(423,437)*	1.00
1478	8c **Post Rider** (Rev. Bicentennial), *June 22,* Rochester, N.Y. *(586,850)*	1.00
1479	8c **Drummer** (Rev. Bicentennial), *Sept. 28,* New Orleans, La. *(522,427)*	1.00
1483a	8c **Boston Tea Party** (Rev. Bicentennial), *July 4,* Boston, Mass. *(897,870)*	3.00
	1480-1483, any single	1.00
1484	8c **George Gershwin,** *Feb. 28,* Beverly Hills, Calif. *(448,814)*	1.00
1485	8c **Robinson Jeffers,** *Aug. 13,* Carmel, Calif. *(394,261)*	1.00
1486	8c **Henry O. Tanner,** *Sept. 10,* Pittsburgh, Pa. *(424,065)*	2.50
1487	8c **Willa Cather,** *Sept. 20,* Red Cloud, Nebr. *(435,784)*	1.00
1488	8c **Nicolaus Copernicus,** *Apr. 23 (734,190)*	1.25
1498a	8c **Postal People,** *Apr. 30,* any city *(1,489-1498, any single)*	5.00
	1489-1498, any single	1.00

First day cancellation was applied at Boston to 1,205,212 covers bearing one or more of Nos. 1489-1498. Cancellations at other cities unrecorded.

1499	8c **Harry S Truman**, *May 8*, Independence, Mo. *(938,636)*	1.50
1500	6c **Electronics**, *July 10*, New York, N.Y.	1.00
1501	8c **Electronics**, *July 10*, New York, N.Y.	1.00
1502	15c **Electronics**, *July 10*, New York, N.Y.	1.00
	1500-1502 and C86 on one cover	4.00

First day cancellation was applied to 1,197,700 covers bearing one or more of Nos. 1500-1502 and C86.

1503	8c **Lyndon B. Johnson**, *Aug. 27*, Austin, Texas *(701,490)*	1.00

1973-74

1504	8c **Angus Cattle**, *Oct. 5, 1973*, St. Joseph, Mo. *(521,427)*	1.00
1505	10c **Chautauqua**, *Aug. 6, 1974*, Chautauqua, N.Y. *(411,105)*	1.00
1506	10c **Wheat**, *Aug. 16, 1974*, Hillsboro, Kans. *(468,280)*	1.00
1507	8c **Christmas (religious)**, *Nov. 7, 1973*	1.00
1508	8c **Christmas (secular)**, *Nov. 7, 1973*	1.00
	1507-1508 on one cover	1.10

First day cancellation was applied to 807,468 covers bearing one or both of Nos. 1507-1508.

1509	10c **Crossed Flags**, *Dec. 8, 1973*, San Francisco, Calif.	1.00

First day cancellation was applied to 341,528 covers bearing one or more of Nos. 1509 and 1519.

1510	10c **Jefferson Memorial**, *Dec. 14, 1973*	1.00
1510b	Booklet pane of 5 + label	2.25
1510c	Booklet pane of 8	2.50
1510d	Booklet pane of 6, *Aug. 5, 1974*, Oakland, Calif.	3.00

First day cancellation was applied to 686,300 covers bearing one or more of Nos. 1510, 1510b, 1510c, 1520.

1511	10c **Zip Code**, *Jan. 4, 1974 (335,220)*	1.00
1518	6.3c **Bell Coil**, *Oct. 1, 1974 (221,141)*	1.00
1519	10c **Crossed Flags coil**, *Dec. 8, 1973*, San Francisco, Calif.	1.00
1520	10c **Jefferson Memorial coil**, *Dec. 14, 1973*	1.00

1974

1525	10c **Veterans of Foreign Wars**, *Mar. 11 (543,598)*	1.50
1526	10c **Robert Frost**, *Mar. 26*, Derry, N.H. *(500,425)*	1.00
1527	10c **EXPO '74**, *Apr. 18*, Spokane, Wash. *(565,548)*	1.00
1528	10c **Horse Racing**, *May 4*, Louisville, Ky. *(623,983)*	3.00
1529	10c **Skylab**, *May 14*, Houston, Tex. *(972,326)*	1.50
1537a	10c **UPU Centenary**, *June 6 (1,374,765)*	4.00
	1530-1537, any single	1.00
1541a	10c **Mineral Heritage**, *June 13*, Lincoln, Neb. *(865,368)*	2.75
	1538-1541, any single	1.00
1542	10c **Kentucky Settlement**, *June 15*, Harrodsburg, Ky. *(478,239)*	1.00
1546a	10c **Continental Congress** (Rev. Bicentennial), *July 4*, Philadelphia, Pa. *(2,124,957)*	2.75
	1543-1546, any single	1.00
1547	10c **Energy Conservation**, *Sept. 23*, Detroit, Mich. *(587,210)*	1.00
1548	10c **Sleepy Hollow**, *Oct. 10*, North Tarrytown, N.Y. *(514,836)*	3.00
1549	10c **Retarded Children**, *Oct. 12*, Arlington Tex. *(412,882)*	1.00
1550	10c **Christmas (Religious)**, *Oct. 23*, New York, N.Y. *(634,990)*	1.00
1551	10c **Christmas (Currier & Ives)**, *Oct. 23*, New York, N.Y. *(634,990)*	1.00
	1550-1551 on one cover	1.10
1552	10c **Christmas (Dove)**, *Nov. 15*, New York, N.Y. *(477,410)*	1.50

1975

1553	10c **Benjamin West**, *Feb. 10*, Swarthmore, Pa. *(465,017)*	1.00
1554	10c **Paul L. Dunbar**, *May 1*, Dayton, Ohio *(397,347)*	1.50
1555	10c **D.W. Griffith**, *May 27*, Beverly Hills, Calif. *(424,167)*	1.00
1556	10c **Pioneer-Jupiter**, *Feb. 28*, Mountain View, Calif. *(594,896)*	1.25
1557	10c **Mariner 10**, *Apr. 4*, Pasadena, Calif. *(563,636)*	1.25
1558	10c **Collective Bargaining**, *Mar. 13 (412,329)*	1.00
1559	8c **Sybil Ludington** (Rev. Bicentennial), *Mar. 25*, Carmel, N.Y. *(394,550)*	1.00
1560	10c **Salem Poor** (Rev. Bicentennial), *Mar. 25*, Cambridge, Mass. *(415,565)*	1.50
1561	10c **Haym Salomon** (Rev. Bicentennial), *Mar. 25*, Chicago, Ill. *(442,630)*	1.00
1562	18c **Peter Francisco** (Rev. Bicentennial), *Mar. 25*, Greensboro, N.C. *(415,000)*	1.00
1563	10c **Lexington-Concord** (Rev. Bicentennial), *Apr. 19*, Lexington, Mass., or Concord, Mass. *(975,020)*	1.00
1564	10c **Bunker Hill** (Rev. Bicentennial), *June 17*, Charlestown, Mass. *(557,130)*	1.00
1568a	10c **Military Services** (Rev. Bicentennial), *July 4 (1,134,831)*	2.50
	1565-1568, any single	1.00
1569a	10c **Apollo-Soyuz**, *July 15*, Kennedy Space Center, Fla. *(1,427,046)*	5.00
	1569-1570, any single	3.00
1571	10c **International Women's Year**, *Aug. 26*, Seneca Falls, N.Y. *(476,769)*	1.00

1575a	10c **Postal Service Bicentenary**, *Sept. 3*, Philadelphia, Pa. *(969,999)*	2.50
	1572-1575, any single	1.00
1576	10c **World Peace through Law**, *Sept. 29 (386,736)*	1.25
1577a	10c **Banking-Commerce**, *Oct. 6*, New York, N.Y. *(555,580)*	1.75
	1577-1578, any single	1.00
1579	(10c) **Christmas (religious)**, *Oct. 14*	1.00
1580	(10c) **Christmas (secular)**, *Oct. 14*	1.00
	1579-1580 on one cover	2.00

First day cancellation was applied to 730,079 covers bearing one or more of Nos. 1579-1580.

1975-79

AMERICANA ISSUE

1581	1c **Inkwell**, *Dec. 8, 1977*, St. Louis, Mo., multiple for 1st class rate	1.00
1582	2c **Speaker's Stand**, *Dec. 8, 1977*, St. Louis, Mo., multiple for 1st class rate	1.00
1584	3c **Ballot Box**, *Dec. 8, 1977*, St. Louis, Mo., multiple for 1st class rate	1.00
1585	4c **Books and Eyeglasses**, *Dec. 8, 1977*, St. Louis, Mo., multiple for 1st class rate	1.00

First day cancellation was applied to 530,033 covers bearing one or more of Nos. 1581-1582, 1584-1585.

1590	9c **Capitol Dome**, from bklt., *Mar. 11, 1977*, New York, N.Y., plus postage for 1st class rate	1.00
1591	9c **Capitol Dome**, *Nov. 24, 1975 (190,117)*, multiple for 1st class rate	1.00
1592	10c **Justice**, *Nov. 17, 1977*, New York, N.Y. *(359,050)*, multiple for 1st class rate	1.00
1593	11c **Printing Press**, *Nov. 13, 1975*, Philadelphia, Pa. *(217,755)*, multiple for 1st class rate	1.00
1594	12c **Torch**, *Apr. 8, 1981*, Dallas, TX, multiple for 1st class rate	1.00

First day cancellation was applied to 280,930 covers bearing one or more of Nos. 1594 and 1816.

1595	13c **Liberty Bell**, *Oct. 31, 1975*, Cleveland, Ohio *(256,734)*	1.00
1595a	Booklet pane of 6	2.00
1595b	Booklet pane of 7 + label	2.75
1595c	Booklet pane of 8	2.50
1595d	Booklet pane of 5 + label, *Apr. 2, 1976*, Liberty, Mo.	2.25
1596	13c **Eagle and Shield**, *Dec. 1, 1975*, Juneau, Alaska *(418,272)*	1.00
1597	15c **Flag**, *June 30, 1978*, Baltimore, Md.	1.00
1598	15c **Flag**, from bklt., *June 30, 1978*, Baltimore, Md.	1.00
1598a	Booklet pane of 8	2.50

First day cancellation was applied to 315,359 covers bearing one or more of Nos. 1597, 1598, and 1618C.

1599	16c **Statue of Liberty**, *Mar. 31, 1978*, New York, N.Y.	1.00
1603	24c **Old North Church**, *Nov. 14, 1975*, Boston, Mass. *(208,973)*	1.00
1604	28c **Fort Nisqually**, *Aug. 11, 1978*, Tacoma, Wash. *(159,639)*	1.00
1605	29c **Sandy Hook Lighthouse**, *Apr. 14, 1978*, Atlantic City, N.J. *(193,476)*	1.50
1606	30c **Schoolhouse**, *Aug. 27, 1979*, Devils Lake, N.D. *(186,882)*	1.25
1608	50c **Betty Lamp**, *Sept. 11, 1979*, San Juan, P.R. *(159,540)*	1.50
1610	$1 **Rush Lamp**, *July 2, 1979*, San Francisco, Calif. *(255,575)*	3.00
1611	$2 **Kerosene Lamp**, *Nov. 16, 1978*, New York, N.Y. *(173,596)*	5.00
1612	$5 **Railroad Lantern**, *Aug. 23, 1979*, Boston, Mass. *(129,192)*	12.50

COIL STAMPS

1613	3.1c **Guitar**, *Oct. 25, 1979*, Shreveport, La. *(230,403)*	1.00
1614	7.7c **Saxhorns**, *Nov. 20, 1976*, New York, N.Y. *(285,290)*	1.00
1615	7.9c **Drum**, *Apr. 23, 1976*, Miami, Fla. *(193,270)*	1.00
1615C	8.4c **Piano**, *July 13, 1978*, Interlochen, Mich. *(200,392)*	1.00
1616	9c **Capitol Dome**, *Mar. 5, 1976*, Milwaukee, Wis. *(128,171)*	1.00
1617	10c **Justice**, *Nov. 4, 1977*, Tampa, Fla. *(184,954)*	1.00
1618	13c **Liberty Bell**, *Nov. 25, 1975*, Allentown, Pa. *(320,387)*	1.00
1618C	15c **Flag**, *June 30, 1978*, Baltimore, Md.	1.00
1619	16c **Statue of Liberty**, *Mar. 31, 1978*, New York, N.Y.	1.00

First day cancellation was applied to 376,338 covers bearing one or more of Nos. 1599 and 1619.

1975

1622	13c **13-Star Flag**, *Nov. 15*, Philadelphia, Pa.	1.00
1623	13c **Flag over Capitol**, *Mar. 11*, New York, N.Y.	1.50

1623a	Booklet pane of 8, perf 11 (1 #1590 +7 #1623)	25.
1623Bc	Booklet pane of 8, perf. 10x9¾ (1 #1590A + 7 #1623B)	15.

First day cancellation was applied to 242,208 covers bearing Nos. 1623, 1623a, 1623B or 1623Bc.

1625	13c **13-Star Flag coil**, *Nov. 15*, Philadelphia, PA	1

First day cancellation was applied to 362,959 covers bearing one or more of Nos. 1622 and 1625.

1976

1631a	13c **Spirit of '76**, *Jan. 1*, Pasadena, CA *(1,013,067)*	2
	1629-1631, any single	1.
1632	13c **Interphil '76**, *Jan. 17*, Philadelphia, Pa. *(519,902)*	1.
1002a	13c **State Flags**, *Feb. 23*	27.
	1633-1682, any single	1.
1683	13c **Telephone**, *Mar. 10*, Boston, Mass. *(662,515)*	1.
1684	13c **Commercial Aviation**, *Mar. 19*, Chicago Ill. *(631,555)*	1.
1685	13c **Chemistry**, *Apr. 6*, New York, N.Y. *(557,600)*	1.

Bicentennial Souvenir Sheets of 5

1686	13c **Surrender of Cornwallis**, *May 29*, Philadelphia, Pa.	7.
1687	18c **Declaration of Independence**, *May 29*, Philadelphia, Pa.	7.
1688	24c **Declaration of Independence**, *May 29*, Philadelphia, Pa.	7.5
1689	31c **Washington at Valley Forge**, *May 29*, Philadelphia, Pa.	7.

First day cancellation was applied to 879,890 covers bearing singles, multiples or complete sheets of Nos. 1686-1689.

1690	13c **Franklin**, *June 1*, Philadelphia, Pa. *(588,740)*	1.0
1694a	13c **Declaration of Independence**, *July 4*, Philadelphia, Pa. *(2,093,880)*	2.0
	1691-1694, any single	1.0
1698a	13c **Olympic Games**, *July 16*, Lake Placid, N.Y. *(1,140,189)*	2.0
	1695-1698, any single	1.0
1699	13c **Clara Maass**, *Aug. 18*, Belleville, N.J. *(646,506)*	2.0
1700	13c **Adolph S. Ochs**, *Sept. 18*, New York, N.Y. *(582,580)*	1.0
1701	13c **Christmas (religious)**, *Oct. 27*, Boston, Mass. *(540,050)*	1.0
1702	13c **Christmas (secular)**, *Oct. 27*, Boston, Mass. *(181,410)*	1.0
1703	13c **Christmas (secular)**, block tagged, *Oct. 27*, Boston, Mass. *(330,450)*	1.0
	1701 and 1702 or 1703 on one cover	1.2

1977

1704	13c **Washington at Princeton**, *Jan. 3*, Princeton, N.J. *(695,335)*	1.0
1705	13c **Sound Recording**, *Mar. 23 (632,216)*	1.2
1709a	13c **Pueblo Art**, *Apr. 13*, Santa Fe, N.M. *(1,194,554)*	2.00
	1706-1709, any single	1.00
1710	13c **Lindbergh Flight**, *May 20*, Roosevelt Sta., N.Y. *(3,985,989)*	3.0
1711	13c **Colorado Statehood**, *May 21*, Denver, Colo. *(510,880)*	1.00
1715a	13c **Butterflies**, *June 6*, Indianapolis, Ind. *(1,218,278)*	2.00
	1712-1715, any single	2.00
1716	13c **Lafayette's Landing**, *June 13*, Charleston, S.C. *(514,506)*	1.00
1720a	13c **Skilled Hands**, *July 4*, Cincinnati, Ohio *(1,263,568)*	2.00
	1717-1720, any single	1.00
1721	13c **Peace Bridge**, *Aug. 4*, Buffalo, N.Y. *(512,995)*	1.00
1722	13c **Battle of Oriskany**, *Aug. 6*, Utica, N.Y. *(605,906)*	1.00
1723a	13c **Energy Conservation**, *Oct. 20 (410,299)*	1.50
	1723-1724, any single	1.25
1725	13c **Alta California**, *Sept. 9*, San Jose, Calif. *(709,457)*	1.00
1726	13c **Articles of Confederation**, *Sept. 30*, York, Pa. *(605,455)*	1.00
1727	13c **Talking Pictures**, *Oct. 6*, Hollywood, Calif. *(570,195)*	1.50
1728	13c **Surrender at Saratoga** *Oct. 7*, Schuylerville, N.Y. *(557,529)*	1.00
1729	13c **Christmas (Valley Forge)**, *Oct. 21*, Valley Forge, Pa. *(583,139)*	1.00
1730	13c **Christmas (mailbox)**, *Oct. 21*, Omaha, Nebr. *(675,786)*	1.00

1978

1731	13c **Carl Sandburg**, *Jan. 6*, Galesburg, Ill. *(493,826)*	1.00
1732a	13c **Captain Cook**, *Jan. 20*, Honolulu, Hawaii, or Anchorage, Alaska	1.75
	1732-1733, any single	1.25

First day cancellation was applied to 823,855 covers at Honolulu, and 672,804 at Anchorage, each cover bearing one or both of Nos. 1732-1733.

1734	13c **Indian Head Penny**, *Jan. 11*, Kansas City, Mo. *(512,426)*	1.00

1978-80

REGULAR ISSUE

1735	(15c) "A" Eagle, *May 22*, Memphis, Tenn.	1.00
1736	(15c) "A" Eagle, bklt. single *May 22*, Memphis, Tenn.	1.00
1736a	Booklet pane of 8	2.50
1737	15c Roses, *July 11*, Shreveport, La. *(445,003)*	1.00
1737a	Booklet pane of 8	2.50
1742a	15c Windmills Booklet pane of 10, *Feb. 7, 1980*, Lubbock, TX	3.50
	1738-1742, any single	1.00
1743	15c "A" Eagle coil, *May 22*, Memphis, Tenn.	1.00

First day cancellation was applied to 689,049 covers bearing one or more of Nos. 1735, 1736 and 1743. First day cancellation was applied to 708,411 covers bearing one or more of Nos. 1738-1742a.

1978

1744	13c Harriet Tubman, *Feb. 1 (493,495)*	1.75
1748a	13c American Quilts, *Mar. 8*, Charleston, W.Va.	2.00
	1745-1748, any single	1.00

First day cancellation was applied to 1,081,827 covers bearing one or more of Nos. 1745-1748.

1752a	13c American Dance, *Apr. 26*, New York, N.Y. *(1,626,493)*	2.00
	1749-1752, any single	1.00
1753	13c French Alliance, *May 4*, York, Pa. *(705,240)*	1.00
1754	13c Papanicolaou, *May 18 (535,584)*	1.00
1755	13c Jimmie Rodgers, *May 24*, Meridian, Miss. *(599,287)*	1.00
1756	15c George M. Cohan, *July 3*, Providence, R.I. *(740,750)*	1.25
1757	CAPEX souv. sheet, *June 10*, Toronto, Canada *(1,994,067)*	2.75
1758	15c Photography, *June 26*, Las Vegas, Nev. *(684,987)*	1.00
1759	15c Viking Missions, *July 20*, Hampton, Va. *(805,051)*	1.00
1763a	15c American Owls, *Aug. 26*, Fairbanks, Alas. *(1,690,474)*	2.00
	1760-1763, any single	1.25
1767a	15c American Trees, *Oct. 9*, Hot Springs National Park, Ark. *(1,139,100)*	2.00
	1764-1767, any single	1.25
1768	15c Christmas (Madonna), *Oct. 18 (553,064)*	1.00
1769	15c Christmas (Hobby Horse), *Oct. 18*, Holly, Mich. *(603,008)*	1.00

1979-80

1770	15c Robert Kennedy, *Jan. 12 (624,582)*	1.50
1771	15c Martin L. King, *Jan. 13*, Atlanta, Ga. *(726,149)*	2.00
1772	15c Year of Child, *Feb. 15*, Philadelphia, Pa. *(716,782)*	1.00
1773	15c John Steinbeck, *Feb. 27*, Salinas, Calif. *(709,073)*	1.00
1774	15c Albert Einstein, *Mar. 4*, Princeton, N.J. *(641,423)*	3.00
1778a	15c Toleware, *Apr. 19*, Lancaster, Pa. *(1,581,962)*	2.00
	1775-1778, any single	1.00
1782a	15c American Architecture, *June 4*, Kansas City, Mo. *(1,219,258)*	2.00
	1779-1782, any single	1.00
1786a	15c Endangered Flora, *June 7*, Milwaukee, Wis. *(1,436,268)*	2.00
	1783-1786, any single	1.00
1787	15c Guide Dogs, *June 15*, Morristown, N.J. *(588,826)*	1.25
1788	15c Special Olympics, *Aug. 9*, Brockport, N.Y. *(651,344)*	1.25
1789	15c John Paul Jones, *Sept. 23*, Annapolis, Md.	1.50
1789A	15c John Paul Jones, *Sept. 23*, Annapolis, Md.	1.50

Total for 1789 and 1789A is 587,018.

1790	10c Olympic Javelin, *Sept. 5*, Olympia, Wash. *(305,122)*	1.00
1794a	15c Olympics 1980, *Sept. 28*, Los Angeles, Calif. *(1,561,366)*	2.00
	1791-1794, any single	1.25
1798b	15c Winter Olympics, *Feb. 1, 1980*, Lake Placid, N.Y. *(1,166,302)*	2.00
	1795-1798, any single	1.25

1979

1799	15c Christmas (Madonna), *Oct. 18 (686,990)*	1.25
1800	15c Christmas (Santa Claus), *Oct. 18*, North Pole, Alaska *(511,829)*	1.25
	1799-1800, both stamps issued *Oct. 18*	2.00
1801	15c Will Rogers, *Nov. 4*, Claremore, Okla. *(1,643,151)*	1.50
1802	15c Viet Nam Veterans, *Nov. 11*, Arlington, VA *(445,934)*	3.25

1980

1803	15c W.C. Fields, *Jan. 29*, Beverly Hills, CA *(633,303)*	1.75
1804	15c Benjamin Banneker, *Feb. 15*, Annapolis, MD *(647,126)*	2.00
1810a	15c Letter Writing, *Feb. 25 (1,083,360)*	2.50
	1805-1810, any single	1.00

1980-81

DEFINITIVES

1811	1c Quill Pen, coil, *Mar. 6, 1980*, New York, NY *(262,921)*	1.00
1813	3.5c Violins, coil, *June 23, 1980*, Williamsburg, PA	1.00

FD cancel was applied to 716,988 covers bearing Nos. 1813 or U590.

1816	12c Torch, coil, *Apr. 8, 1981*, Dallas, TX	1.00
1818	(18c) "B" Eagle, *Mar. 15, 1981*, San Francisco, CA	1.25

FD cancel was applied to 511,688 covers bearing one or more of Nos. 1818-1820, U592 or UX88.

1819	(18c) "B" Eagle, bklt. single, *Mar. 15, 1981*, San Francisco, CA	1.00
1819a	Booklet pane of 8	3.00
1820	(18c) "B" Eagle, coil, *Mar. 15, 1981*, San Francisco, CA	1.00

1980

1821	15c Frances Perkins, *Apr. 10 (678,966)*	1.00
1822	15c Dolley Madison, *May 20 (331,048)*	1.00
1823	15c Emily Bissell, *May 31*, Wilmington, DE *(649,509)*	1.00
1824	15c Helen Keller, Anne Sullivan, *June 27*, Tuscumbia, AL *(713,061)*	1.25
1825	15c Veterans Administration, *July 21 (634,101)*	1.50
1826	15c Bernardo de Galvez, *July 23*, New Orleans, LA *(658,061)*	1.00
1830a	15c Coral Reefs, *Aug. 26*, Charlotte Amalie, VI *(1,195,126)*	2.00
	1827-1830, any single	1.00
1831	15c Organized Labor, *Sept. 1 (759,973)*	1.00
1832	15c Edith Wharton, *Sept. 5*, New Haven, CT *(633,917)*	1.00
1833	15c Education, *Sept. 12*,Franklin, MA *(672,592)*	1.50
1837a	15c Indian Masks, *Sept. 25*, Spokane, WA *(2,195,136)*	2.00
	1834-1837, any single	1.00
1841a	15c Architecture, *Oct. 9*, New York, NY *(2,164,721)*	1.75
	1838-1841, any single	1.00
1842	15c Christmas (Madonna), *Oct. 31 (718,614)*	1.00
1843	15c Christmas (Toys), *Oct. 31*, Christmas, MI *(755,108)*	1.25

1980-85

GREAT AMERICANS ISSUE

1844	1c Dorothea Dix, *Sept. 23, 1983*, Hampden, ME *(164,140)*	1.00
1845	2c Igor Stravinsky, *Nov. 18, 1982*, New York, NY *(501,719)*	1.00
1846	3c Henry Clay, *July 13, 1983 (204,320)*	1.00
1847	4c Carl Schurz, *June 3, 1983*, Watertown, WI *(165,010)*	1.00
1848	5c Pearl Buck, *June 25, 1983*, Hillsboro, WV *(231,852)*	1.00
1849	6c Walter Lippman, *Sept. 19, 1985*, Minneapolis, MN *(371,990)*	1.00
1850	7c Abraham Baldwin, *Jan. 25, 1985*, Athens, GA *(402,285)*	1.00
1851	8c Henry Knox, *July 25, 1985*, Thomaston, ME *(315,937)*	1.00
1852	9c Sylvanus Thayer, *June 7, 1985*, Braintree, MA *(345,649)*	1.25
1853	10c Richard Russell, *May 31, 1984*, Winder, GA *(183,581)*	1.00
1854	11c Alden Partridge, *Feb. 12, 1985*, Northfield, VT *(442,311)*	1.25
1855	13c Crazy Horse, *Jan. 15, 1982*, Crazy Horse, SD	1.50
1856	14c Sinclair Lewis, *Mar. 21, 1985*, Sauk Centre, MN *(308,612)*	1.25
1857	17c Rachel Carson, *May 28, 1981*, Springdale, PA *(273,686)*	1.00
1858	18c George Mason, *May 7, 1981*, Gunston Hall, VA *(461,937)*	1.00
1859	19c Sequoyah, *Dec. 27, 1980*, Tahlequah, OK *(241,325)*	1.25
1860	20c Ralph Bunche, *Jan. 12, 1982*, New York, NY	1.75
1861	20c Thomas H. Gallaudet, *June 10, 1983*, West Hartford, CT *(261,336)*	1.25
1862	20c Harry S Truman, *Jan. 26, 1984 (267,631)*	1.25
1863	22c John J. Audubon, *Apr. 23, 1985*, New York, NY *(516,249)*	1.25
1864	30c Frank Laubach, *Sept. 2, 1984*, Benton, PA *(118,974)*	1.25
1865	35c Charles Drew, *June 3, 1981 (383,882)*	1.75
1866	37c Robert Millikan, *Jan. 26, 1982*, Pasadena, CA	1.25
1867	39c Grenville Clark, *Mar. 20, 1985*, Hanover, NH *(297,797)*	1.25
1868	40c Lillian Gilbreth, *Feb. 24, 1984*, Montclair, NJ *(110,588)*	1.50
1869	50c Chester W. Nimitz, *Feb. 22, 1985*, Fredericksburg, TX *(376,166)*	2.00

1981

1874	15c Everett Dirksen, *Jan. 4*, Pekin, IL *(665,755)*	1.00
1875	15c Whitney M. Young, *Jan. 30*, New York, NY *(963,870)*	1.75
1879a	18c Flowers, *Apr. 23*, Fort Valley, GA *(1,966,599)*	2.50
	1876-1879, any single	1.00

DEFINITIVES

1889a	18c Animals Booklet pane of 10, *May 14*, Boise, ID	5.00
	1880-1889, any single	1.00
1890	18c Flag-Anthem (grain), *Apr. 24*, Portland, ME	1.00
1891	18c Flag-Anthem (sea), *Apr. 24*, Portland, ME	1.50
1892	6c Star Circle, *Apr. 24*, Portland, ME	1.00
1893	18c Flag-Anthem (mountain), *Apr. 24*, Portland, ME	1.00
1893a	Booklet pane of 8 (2 #1892, 6 #1893)	2.50

FDC cancel was applied to 691,526 covers bearing one or more of Nos. 1890-1893 & 1893a.

1894	20c Flag-Court, *Dec. 17*	1.00
1895	20c Flag-Court, coil, *Dec. 17*	1.00
1896	20c Flag-Court, perf. 11x10½, *Dec. 17 (185,543)*	1.00
1896a	Booklet pane of 6	6.00
1896b	Booklet pane of 10, *June 1, 1982*	10.00

First day cancellations were applied to 598,169 covers bearing one or more of Nos. 1894-1896.

1981-84

TRANSPORTATION ISSUE

1897	1c Omnibus, *Aug. 19, 1983*, Arlington, VA *(109,463)*	1.00
1897A	2c Locomotive, *May 20, 1982*, Chicago, IL *(290,020)*	1.50
1898	3c Handcar, *Mar. 25, 1983*, Rochester, NY *(77,900)*	1.00
1898A	4c Stagecoach, *Aug. 19, 1982*, Milwaukee, WI *(152,940)*	1.00
1899	5c Motorcycle, *Oct. 10, 1983*, San Francisco, CA *(188,240)*	2.00
1900	5.2c Sleigh, *Mar. 21, 1983*, Memphis, TN *(141,979)*	1.00
1901	5.9c Bicycle, *Feb. 17, 1982*, Wheeling, WV *(814,419)*	1.50
1902	7.4c Baby Buggy, *Apr. 7, 1984*, San Diego, CA	1.00
1903	9.3c Mail Wagon, *Dec. 15, 1981*, Shreveport, LA *(199,645)*	1.00
1904	10.9c Hansom, *Mar. 26, 1982*, Chattanooga, TN	1.00
1905	11c Railroad Caboose, *Feb. 3, 1984*, Chicago, IL *(172,753)*	1.50
1906	17c Electric Auto, *June 25, 1982*, Greenfield Village, MI *(239,458)*	1.00
1907	18c Surrey, *May 18, 1981*, Notch, MO *(207,801)*	1.00
1908	20c Fire Pumper, *Dec. 10, 1981*, Alexandria, VA *(304,668)*	2.00
1909	$9.35 Eagle, *Aug. 12, 1983*, Kennedy Space Center, FL *(77,858)*	50.00
1909a	Booklet pane of 3	125.00

1981

1910	18c Red Cross, *May 1 (874,972)*	1.50
1911	18c Savings & Loan, *May 8*, Chicago, IL *(740,910)*	1.00
1919a	18c Space Achievement, *May 21*, Kennedy Space Center, FL *(7,027,549)*	3.00
	1912-1919, any single	1.00
1920	18c Professional Management, *June 18*, Philadelphia, PA *(713,096)*	1.00
1924a	18c Wildlife Habitats, *June 26*, Reno, NV *(2,327,609)*	2.50
	1921-1924, any single	1.00
1925	18c Year of Disabled, *June 29*, Milford, MI *(714,244)*	1.00
1926	18c Edna St. V. Millay, *July 10*, Austerlitz, NY *(725,978)*	1.00
1927	18c Alcoholism, *Aug. 19 (874,972)*	3.00
1931a	18c Architecture, *Aug. 28*, New York, NY *(1,998,208)*	2.50
	1928-1931, any single	1.00
1932	18c Babe Zaharias, *Sept. 22*, Pinehurst, NC	6.50
1933	18c Bobby Jones, *Sept. 22*, Pinehurst, NC	10.00
	1932-1933, both stamps issued *Sept. 22*, Pinehurst, NC	12.50

First day cancel was applied to 1,231,543 covers bearing one or more of Nos. 1932-1933.

1934	18c Frederic Remington, *Oct. 9*, Oklahoma City, OK *(1,367,099)*	1.25
1935	18c James Hoban, *Oct. 13*	1.00
1936	20c James Hoban, *Oct. 13*	1.00
	1935-1936, both stamps issued *Oct. 13*	2.50

FD cancel was applied to 635,012 covers bearing Nos. 1935-1936.

1938a	18c Yorktown-Va. Capes Battle, *Oct. 16*, Yorktown, VA *(1,098,278)*	1.50
	1937-1938, any single	1.00
1939	(20c) Christmas (Madonna), *Oct. 28*, Chicago, IL *(481,395)*	1.00
1940	(20c) Christmas (Teddy Bear), *Oct. 28*, Christmas Valley, OR *(517,898)*	1.00
1941	20c John Hanson, *Nov. 5*, Frederick, MD *(605,616)*	1.00
1945a	20c Desert Plants, *Dec. 11*, Tucson, AZ *(1,770,187)*	2.50
	1942-1945, any single	1.00

REGULAR ISSUE

1946	(20c) "C" Eagle, *Oct. 11*, Memphis, TN	1.00
1947	(20c) "C" Eagle, coil, *Oct. 11*, Memphis, TN	1.00

1948 (20c) **"C" Eagle,** bklt. single, *Oct. 11,* Memphis, TN 1.00
1948a Booklet pane of 10 .... *3.50*

First day cancellations were applied to 304,404 covers bearing one or more of Nos. 1946-1948.

1982

1949 20c **Bighorn,** *Jan. 8,* Bighorn, MT 1.25
1949a Booklet pane of 10 .... 6.00
1950 20c **F.D. Roosevelt,** *Jan. 30,* Hyde Park, NY 1.00
1951 20c **Love,** *Feb. 1,* Boston, MA *(325,727)* 1.00
1952 20c **Washington,** *Feb. 22,* Mt. Vernon, VA 1.25
2002b 20c **Birds-Flowers,** *Apr. 14,* Washington, DC, or State Capital 30.00
1953-2002, any single 1.25
2003 20c **U.S.-Netherlands,** *Apr. 20* 1.00
2004 20c **Library of Congress,** *Apr. 21* 1.00
2005 20c **Consumer Education,** *Apr. 27* 1.00
2009a 20c **Knoxville Fair,** *Apr. 29,* Knoxville, TN 2.50
2006-2009, any single 1.00
2010 20c **Horatio Alger,** *Apr. 30,* Willow Grove, PA 1.00
2011 20c **Aging,** *May 21,* Sun City, AZ *(510,677)* 1.00
2012 20c **Barrymores,** *June 8,* New York, NY 1.00
2013 20c **Dr. Mary Walker,** *June 10,* Oswego, NY 1.00
2014 20c **Peace Garden,** *June 30,* Dunseith, ND 1.00
2015 20c **America's Libraries,** *July 13,* Philadelphia, PA 1.00
2016 20c **Jackie Robinson,** *Aug. 2,* Cooperstown, NY 6.00
2017 20c **Touro Synagogue,** *Aug. 22,* Newport, RI *(517,264)* 1.50
2018 20c **Wolf Trap Farm Park,** *Sept. 1,* Vienna, VA *(704,361)* 1.00
2022a 20c **Architecture,** *Sept. 30 (1,552,567)* 2.50
2019-2022, any single 1.00
2023 20c **St. Francis,** *Oct. 7,* San Francisco, CA *(530,275)* 1.25
2024 20c **Ponce de Leon,** *Oct. 12,* San Juan, PR *(530,275)* 1.00
2025 13c **Puppy, Kitten,** *Nov. 3,* Danvers, MA *(239,219)* 1.25
2026 20c **Christmas (Madonna),** *Oct. 28 (462,982)* 1.00
2030a 20c **Christmas (Children),** *Oct. 28,* Snow, OK *(676,950)* 2.50
2027-2030, any single 1.00

1983

2031 20c **Science & Industry,** *Jan. 19,* Chicago, IL *(526,693)* 1.00
2035a 20c **Balloons,** *Mar. 31,* Albuquerque, NM or Washington, DC *(989,305)* 2.50
2032-2035, any single 1.00
2036 20c **U.S.-Sweden,** *Mar. 24,* Philadelphia, PA *(526,373)* 1.00
2037 20c **Civilian Conservation Corps.,** *Apr. 5,* Luray, VA *(483,824)* 1.00
2038 20c **Joseph Priestley,** *Apr. 13,* Northumberland, PA *(673,266)* 1.00
2039 20c **Voluntarism,** *Apr. 20 (574,708)* 1.00
2040 20c **U.S.-Germany,** *Apr. 29,* Germantown, PA *(611,109)* 1.00
2041 20c **Brooklyn Bridge,** *May 17,* Brooklyn, NY *(815,085)* 1.75
2042 20c **TVA,** *May 18,* Knoxville, TN *(837,588)* 1.00
2043 20c **Physical Fitness,** *May 14,* Houston, TX *(501,336)* 1.25
2044 20c **Scott Joplin,** *June 9,* Sedalia, MO *(472,667)* 1.75
2045 20c **Medal of Honor,** *June 7 (1,623,995)* 5.50
2046 20c **Babe Ruth,** *July 6,* Chicago, IL *(1,277,907)* 5.00
2047 20c **Nathaniel Hawthorne,** *July 8,* Salem, MA *(442,793)* 1.00
2051a 13c **Summer Olympics,** *July 28,* South Bend, IN *(909,332)* 2.50
2048-2051, any single 1.25
2052 20c **Treaty of Paris,** *Sept. 2 (651,208)* 1.00
2053 20c **Civil Service,** *Sept. 9 (422,206)* 1.00
2054 20c **Metropolitan Opera,** *Sept. 14,* New York, NY *(807,609)* 1.50
2058a 20c **American Inventors,** *Sept. 21 (1,006,516)* 2.50
2055-2058, any single 1.00
2062a 20c **Streetcars,** *Oct. 8,* Kennebunkport, ME *(1,116,909)* 2.50
2059-2062, any single 1.00
2063 20c **Christmas (Madonna),** *Oct. 28 (361,874)* 1.00
2064 20c **Christmas (Santa),** *Oct. 28,* Santa Claus, IN *(388,749)* 1.00
2065 20c **Martin Luther,** *Nov. 11 (463,777)* 1.50

1984

2066 20c **Alaska Statehood,** *Jan. 3,* Fairbanks, AK *(816,591)* 1.00
2070a 20c **Winter Olympics,** *Jan. 6,* Lake Placid, NY *(1,245,807)* 2.50
2067-2070, any single 1.00
2071 20c **Federal Deposit Ins. Corp.,** *Jan. 12 (536,329)* 1.00
2072 20c **Love,** *Jan. 31 (327,727)* 1.00
2073 20c **Carter Woodson,** *Feb. 1 (387,583)* 1.75
2074 20c **Soil & Water Conservation,** *Feb. 6,* Denver, CO *(426,101)* 1.00
2075 20c **Credit Union Act,** *Feb. 10,* Salem, MA *(523,583)* 1.00
2079a 20c **Orchids,** *Mar. 5,* Miami, FL *(1,063,237)* 2.50

2076-2079, any single 1.00
2080 20c **Hawaii Statehood,** *Mar. 12,* Honolulu, HI *(546,930)* 1.00
2081 20c **National Archives,** *Apr. 16 (414,415)* 1.00
2085a 20c **Olympics 1984,** *May 4,* Los Angeles, CA *(1,172,313)* 2.50
2082-2085, any single 1.25
2086 20c **Louisiana Exposition,** *May 11,* New Orleans, LA *(467,408)* 1.00
2087 20c **Health Research,** *May 17,* New York, NY *(845,007)* 1.00
2088 20c **Douglas Fairbanks,** *May 23,* Denver CO *(547,134)* 1.00
2089 20c **Jim Thorpe,** *May 24,* Shawnee, OK *(568,544)* 3.00
2090 20c **John McCormack,** *June 6,* Boston, MA *(464,117)* 1.00
2091 20c **St. Lawrence Seaway,** *June 26,* Massena, NY *(550,173)* 1.00
2092 20c **Waterfowl Preservation Act,** *July 2,* Des Moines, IA *(549,388)* 1.00
2093 20c **Roanoke Voyages,** *July 13,* Manteo, NC *(443,725)* 1.00
2094 20c **Herman Melville,** *Aug. 1,* New Bedford, MA *(378,293)* 1.75
2095 20c **Horace A. Moses,** *Aug. 6,* Bloomington, IN *(459,386)* 1.00
2096 20c **Smokey Bear,** *Aug. 13,* Capitan, NM *(506,833)* 3.00
2097 20c **Roberto Clemente,** *Aug. 17,* Carolina, PR *(547,387)* 9.00
2101a 20c **Dogs,** *Sept. 7,* New York, NY *(1,157,373)* 3.00
2098-2101, any single 1.50
2102 20c **Crime Prevention,** *Sept. 26 (427,564)* 1.25
2103 20c **Hispanic Americans,** *Oct. 31 (416,796)* 1.75
2104 20c **Family Unity,** *Oct. 1,* Shaker Heights, OH *(400,659)* 1.00
2105 20c **Eleanor Roosevelt,** *Oct. 11,* Hyde Park, NY *(479,919)* 1.00
2106 20c **Nation of Readers,** *Oct. 16 (437,559)* 1.00
2107 20c **Christmas (Madonna),** *Oct. 30 (386,385)* 1.00
2108 20c **Christmas (Santa),** *Oct. 30,* Jamaica, NY *(430,843)* 1.00
2109 20c **Vietnam Veterans' Memorial,** *Nov. 10 (434,489)* 5.00

1985

2110 22c **Jerome Kern,** *Jan. 23,* New York, NY *(503,855)* 1.00

REGULAR ISSUE

2111 (22c) **"D" Eagle,** *Feb. 1,* Los Angeles, CA 1.00
2112 (22c) **"D" Eagle, coil,** *Feb. 1,* Los Angeles, CA 1.00
2113 (22c) **"D" Eagle, bklt. single,** *Feb. 1,* Los Angeles, CA 1.00
2113a Booklet pane of 10 .... 7.50

First Day cancel was applied to 513,027 covers bearing one or more of Nos. 2111-2113.

2114 22c **Flag over Capitol Dome,** *Mar. 29* 1.00
2115 22c **Flag over Capitol Dome,** coil, *Mar. 29* 1.00
2115b Inscribed "T" at bottom, *May 23, 1987,* Secaucus, NJ 1.00

First Day Cancel was applied to 268,161 covers bearing one or more of Nos. 2114-2115.

2116 22c **Flag Over Capitol Dome,** bklt. single, *Mar. 29,* Waubeka, WI *(234,318)* 1.00
2116a Booklet pane of 5 .... 3.50
2121a 22c **Seashells Booklet pane of 10,** *Apr. 4,* Boston, MA *(426,290)* 7.50
2117-2121, any single 1.00
2122 $10.75 **Eagle and Half Moon,** type I, *Apr. 29,* San Francisco, CA *(93,154)* 50.00
2122a Booklet pane of 3 .... 125.00
2122b Type II, *June 19, 1989* 350.00
2122c Booklet pane of 3, type II 700.00

1985-87

TRANSPORTATION ISSUE

2123 3.4c **School Bus,** *June 8, 1985,* Arlington, VA *(131,480)* 1.00
2124 4.9c **Buckboard,** *June 21, 1985,* Reno, NV 1.00
2125 5.5c **Star Route Truck,** *Nov. 1, 1986,* Fort Worth, TX *(136,021)* 1.00
2126 6c **Tricycle,** *May 6, 1985,* Childs, MD *(151,494)* 1.25
2127 7.1c **Tractor,** *Feb. 6, 1987,* Sarasota, FL *(167,555)* 1.00
2127a 7.1c **Tractor,** Zip+4 precancel, untagged, *May 26, 1989,* Rosemont, IL *(202,804)* 5.00
2128 8.3c **Ambulance,** *June 21, 1986,* Reno, NV 1.00

First day cancel was applied to 338,765 covers bearing one or more of Nos. 2124 and 2128.

2129 8.5c **Tow Truck,** *Jan. 24, 1987,* Tucson, AZ *(224,285)* 1.25
2130 10.1c **Oil Wagon,** *Apr. 18, 1985,* Oil Center, NM 1.25
2130a 10.1c "Bulk Rate Carrier Route Sort" precancel, *June 27, 1988 (136,428)* 1.25
2131 11c **Stutz Bearcat,** *June 11, 1985,* Baton Rouge, LA *(135,037)* 1.25

2132 12c **Stanley Steamer,** *Apr. 2, 1985,* Kingfield, ME *(173,998)* 1
2133 12.5c **Pushcart,** *Apr. 18, 1985,* Oil Center, NM 1

First day cancel was applied to 319,953 covers bearing one or more of Nos. 2130 and 2133.

2134 14c **Ice Boat,** *Mar. 23, 1985,* Rochester, NY *(324,710)* .... 1.
2135 17c **Dog Sled,** *Aug. 20, 1986,* Anchorage, AK .... 1.
2136 25c **Bread Wagon,** *Nov. 22, 1986,* Virginia Beach, VA *(151,950)* .... 1.

1985

2137 22c **Mary McLeod Bethune,** *Mar. 5 (413,244)* .... 1.
2141a 22c **Duck Decoys,** *Mar. 22,* Shelburne, VT *(932,249)* .... 2.
2138-2141, any single .... 1.
2142 22c **Winter Special Olympics,** *Mar. 25,* Park City, UT *(253,074)* .... 1.
2143 22c **Love,** *Apr. 17,* Hollywood, CA *(283,072)* .... 1.
2144 22c **Rural Electrification Administration,** *May 11,* Madison, SD *(472,895)* .... 1.
2145 22c **AMERIPEX '86,** *May 25,* Rosemont, IL *(457,038)* .... 1.
2146 22c **Abigail Adams,** *June 14,* Quincy, MA *(491,026)* .... 1.
2147 22c **Frederic Auguste Bartholdi,** *July 18,* New York, NY *(594,896)* 1.0
2149 18c **George Washington, Washington Monument,** *Nov. 6 (376,238)* 1.0
2150 21.1c **Envelopes,** *Oct. 22 (119,941)* 1.0
2152 22c **Korean War Veterans,** *July 26 (391,754)* 2.5
2153 22c **Social Security Act,** *Aug. 14,* Baltimore, MD *(265,143)* 1.0
2154 22c **World War I Veterans,** *Aug. 26,* Milwaukee, WI 1.5
2158a 22c **Horses,** *Sept. 25,* Lexington, KY *(1,135,368)* 2.5
2155-2158, any single 1.5
2159 22c **Public Education in America,** *Oct. 1,* Boston, MA *(356,030)* 1.0
2163a 22c **International Youth Year,** *Oct. 7,* Chicago, IL *(1,202,541)* 2.5
2160, 2162-2163, any single 1.0
2161 .... 2.0
2164 22c **Help End Hunger,** *Oct. 15 (299,485)* 1.0
2165 22c **Christmas (Madonna & Child),** *Oct. 30,* Detroit, MI 1.0
2166 22c **Christmas (Poinsettia),** *Oct. 30,* Nazareth, MI *(524,929)* 1.0

1986

2167 22c **Arkansas Statehood,** *Jan. 3,* Little Rock, AR *(364,729)* 1.0

1986-94

GREAT AMERICANS ISSUE

2168 1c **Margaret Mitchell,** *June 30, 1986,* Atlanta, GA *(316,764)* 2.0
2169 2c **Mary Lyon,** *Feb. 28, 1987,* South Hadley, MA *(349,831)* 1.00
2170 3c **Dr. Paul Dudley White,** *Sept. 15, 1986* 1.00
2171 4c **Father Flanagan,** *July 14, 1986,* Boys Town, NE *(367,883)* 1.25
2172 5c **Hugo Black,** *Feb. 27, 1986 (303,012)* 1.00
2173 5c **Luis Munoz Marin,** *Feb. 18, 1990,* San Juan, PR *(269,618)* 1.00
2175 10c **Red Cloud,** *Aug. 15, 1987,* Red Cloud, NE *(300,472)* 1.50
2176 14c **Julia Ward Howe,** *Feb. 12, 1987,* Boston, MA *(454,829)* 1.00
2177 15c **Buffalo Bill Cody,** *June 6, 1988,* Cody, WY *(356,395)* 1.75
2178 17c **Belva Ann Lockwood,** *June 18, 1986,* Middleport, NY *(249,215)* 1.00
2179 20c **Virginia Apgar,** *Oct. 24, 1994,* Dallas, TX *(28,461)* 1.00
2180 21c **Chester Carlson,** *Oct. 21, 1988,* Rochester, NY *(288,073)* 1.00
2181 23c **Mary Cassatt,** *Nov. 4, 1988,* Philadelphia, PA *(322,537)* 1.00
2182 25c **Jack London,** *Jan. 11, 1986,* Glen Ellen, CA *(358,686)* 1.25
2182a Booklet pane of 10, *May 3, 1988,* San Francisco, CA 6.00
2183 28c **Sitting Bull,** *Sept. 14, 1989,* Rapid City, SD *(126,777)* 1.50
2184 29c **Earl Warren,** *Mar. 9, 1992 (175,517)* 1.25
2185 29c **Thomas Jefferson,** *Apr. 13, 1993,* Charlottesville, VA *(202,962)* 1.25
2186 35c **Dennis Chavez,** *Apr. 3, 1991,* Albuquerque, NM *(285,570)* 1.25
2187 40c **Claire Chennault,** *Sept. 6, 1990,* Monroe, LA *(186,761)* 2.00
2188 45c **Harvey Cushing,** *June 17, 1988,* Cleveland, OH *(135,140)* 1.25
2189 52c **Hubert Humphrey,** *June 3, 1991,* Minneapolis, MN *(93,391)* 1.40
2190 56c **John Harvard,** *Sept. 3, 1986,* Cambridge, MA 2.50
2191 65c **Hap Arnold,** *Nov. 5, 1988,* Gladwyne, PA *(129,829)* 2.50
2192 75c **Wendell Willkie,** *Feb. 18, 1992,* Bloomington, IN *(47,086)* 2.50
2193 $1 **Dr. Bernard Revel,** *Sept. 23, 1986,* New York, NY 5.00

▪4	$1 **Johns Hopkins,** *June 7, 1989,* Baltimore, MD *(159,049)*		3.00
▪5	$2 **William Jennings Bryan,** *Mar. 19, 1986,* Salem, IL *(123,430)*		6.00
▪6	$5 **Bret Harte,** *Aug. 25, 1987,* Twain Harte, CA *(111,431)*		15.00
▪7	25c **Jack London,** bklt. single, *May 3, 1988,* San Francisco, CA		1.00
▪7a	Booklet pane of 6		4.00

First day cancel was applied to 94,655 covers bearing one or more of Nos. 2183a, 2197, and 2197a.

▪86
▪01a	22c **Stamp Collecting Booklet pane of 4,** *Jan. 23,* State College, PA		4.00
	2198-2201, any single		1.00

First day cancellation was applied to 675,924 covers bearing ▪e or more of Nos. 2198-2201a.

▪02	22c **Love,** *Jan. 30,* New York, NY		1.00
▪03	22c **Sojourner Truth,** *Feb. 4,* New Paltz, NY *(342,985)*		1.75
▪04	22c **Republic of Texas,** *Mar. 2,* San Antonio, TX *(380,450)*		1.75
▪09a	22c **Fish Booklet pane of 5,** *Mar. 21,* Seattle, WA		5.00
	2205-2209, any single		1.25

First day cancellation was applied to 988,184 covers bearing ▪e or more of Nos. 2205-2209a.

▪10	22c **Public Hospitals,** *Apr. 11,* New York, NY *(403,665)*		1.00
▪11	22c **Duke Ellington,** *Apr. 29,* New York, NY *(397,894)*		2.25
▪16	22c **Presidents Souvenir Sheet of 9 (Washington-Harrison),** *May 22,* Chicago, IL		4.00
▪17	22c **Presidents Souvenir Sheet of 9 (Tyler-Grant),** *May 22,* Chicago, IL		4.00
▪18	22c **Presidents Souvenir Sheet of 9 (Hayes-Wilson),** *May 22,* Chicago, IL		4.00
▪19	22c **Presidents Souvenir Sheet of 9 (Harding-Johnson),** *May 22,* Chicago, IL		4.00
	2216a-2219g, 2219i, any single		1.50
	2219h		2.50

First day cancellation was applied to 9,009,599 covers bearing one or more of Nos. 2216-2219, 2216a-2219i.

▪23a	22c **Polar Explorers,** *May 28,* North Pole, AK *(760,999)*		3.75
	2220-2223, any single		1.25
▪24	22c **Statue of Liberty,** *July 4,* New York, NY *(1,540,308)*		1.25

▪986-87

TRANSPORTATION ISSUE
▪225	1c **Omnibus,** *Nov. 26, 1986 (57,845)*		1.00
▪226	2c **Locomotive,** *Mar. 6, 1987,* Milwaukee, WI *(169,484)*		1.50

▪986
▪238a	22c **Navajo Art,** *Sept. 4,* Window Rock, AZ *(1,102,520)*		2.00
	2235-2238, any single		1.00
▪239	22c **T.S. Eliot,** *Sept. 26,* St. Louis, MO *(304,764)*		1.00
▪243a	22c **Woodcarved Figurines,** *Oct. 1 (629,399)*		2.00
	2240-2243, any single		1.00
▪244	22c **Christmas (Madonna),** *Oct. 24 (467,999)*		1.00
▪245	22c **Christmas (Winter Village),** *Oct. 24,* Snow Hill, MD *(504,851)*		1.00

▪987
▪246	22c **Michigan Statehood Sesquicent.,** *Jan. 26,* Lansing, MI *(379,117)*		1.00
▪247	22c **Pan American Games,** *Jan. 29,* Indianapolis, IN *(344,731)*		1.00
▪248	22c **Love,** *Jan. 30,* San Francisco, CA *(333,329)*		1.00
▪249	22c **Pointe du Sable,** *Feb. 20,* Chicago, IL *(313,054)*		1.50
▪250	22c **Enrico Caruso,** *Feb. 27,* New York, NY *(389,834)*		1.00
▪251	22c **Girl Scouts of America,** *Mar. 12 (556,391)*		2.50

1987-88

TRANSPORTATION ISSUE
▪252	3c **Conestoga Wagon,** *Feb. 29, 1988,* Conestoga, PA *(155,203)*		1.00
▪253	5c **Milk Wagon,** *Sept. 25, 1987,* Indianapolis, IN		1.00

First day cancel was applied to 162,571 covers bearing one ▪or more of Nos. 2253 and 2262.

▪254	5.3c **Elevator,** *Sept. 16, 1988,* New York, NY *(142,705)*		1.00
▪255	7.6c **Carretta,** *Aug. 30, 1988,* San Jose, CA *(140,024)*		1.00
▪256	8.4c **Wheelchair,** *Aug. 12, 1988,* Tucson, AZ *(136,337)*		1.00
▪257	10c **Canal Boat,** *Apr. 11, 1987,* Buffalo, NY *(171,952)*		1.00
▪258	13c **Police Patrol Wagon,** *Oct. 29, 1988,* Anaheim, CA *(132,928)*		1.50
▪259	13.2c **Railway Coal Car,** *July 19, 1988,* Pittsburgh, PA *(123,965)*		1.00
▪260	15c **Tugboat,** *July 12, 1988,* Long Beach, CA *(134,926)*		1.00

2261	16.7c **Popcorn Wagon,** *July 7, 1988,* Chicago, IL *(117,908)*		1.00
2262	17.5c **Racing Car,** *Sept. 25, 1987,* Indianapolis, IN		1.25
2263	20c **Cable Car,** *Oct. 28, 1988,* San Francisco, CA *(150,068)*		1.00
2264	20.5c **Fire Engine,** *Sept. 28, 1988,* San Angelo, TX *(111,431)*		1.50
2265	21c **Railway Mail Car,** *Aug. 16, 1988,* Santa Fe, NM *(124,430)*		1.00
2266	24.1c **Tandem Bicycle,** *Oct. 26, 1988,* Redmond, WA *(138,593)*		1.50

1987
2274a	22c **Special Occasions Booklet pane of 10,** *Apr. 20,* Atlanta, GA		5.00
	2267-2274, any single		1.00

First day cancellation was applied to 1,588,129 covers bearing one or more of Nos. 2267-2274a.

2275	22c **United Way,** *Apr. 28 (556,391)*		1.00

1987-89
2276	22c **Flag and Fireworks,** *May 9, 1987,* Denver, CO *(398,855)*		1.00
2276a	Booklet pane of 20, *Nov. 30, 1987*		8.00
2277	(25c) **"E" Earth,** *Mar. 22, 1988*		1.25
2278	25c **Flag and Clouds,** *May 6, 1988,* Boxborough, MA *(131,265)*		1.25
2279	(25c) **"E" Earth,** coil, *Mar. 22, 1988*		1.25
2280	25c **Flag over Yosemite,** *May 20, 1988,* Yosemite, CA *(144,339)*		1.25
	Prephosphored paper, *Feb. 14, 1989,* Yosemite, CA *(118,874)*		1.25
2281	25c **Honey Bee,** *Sept. 2, 1988,* Omaha, NE *(122,853)*		1.25
2282	(25c) **"E" Earth,** bklt. single, *Mar. 22, 1988*		1.25
2282a	Booklet pane of 10		6.00

First day cancel was applied to 363,639 covers bearing one or more of Nos. 2277, 2279 and 2282.

2283	25c **Pheasant,** *Apr. 29, 1988,* Rapid City, SD *(167,053)*		1.25
2283a	Booklet pane of 10		6.00
2285b	25c **Grosbeak & Owl, booklet pane of 10** *May 28, 1988,* Arlington, VA		6.00
	2284-2285, any single		1.25

First day cancel was applied to 272,359 covers bearing one or more of Nos. 2284 and 2285.

2285A	25c **Flag and Clouds,** bklt. single, *July 5, 1988 (117,303)*		1.00
2285Ac	Booklet pane of 6		4.00
2335a	22c **American Wildlife,** *June 13, 1987,* Toronto, Canada		50.00
	2286-2335, any single		1.50

1987-90   RATIFICATION OF THE CONSTITUTION
2336	22c **Delaware,** *July 4, 1987,* Dover, DE *(505,770)*		1.50
2337	22c **Pennsylvania,** *Aug. 26, 1987,* Harrisburg, PA *(367,184)*		1.50
2338	22c **New Jersey,** *Sept. 11, 1987,* Trenton, NJ *(432,899)*		1.50
2339	22c **Georgia,** *Jan. 6, 1988,* Atlanta, GA *(467,804)*		1.50
2340	22c **Connecticut,** *Jan. 9, 1988,* Hartford, CT *(379,706)*		1.50
2341	22c **Massachusetts,** *Feb. 6, 1988,* Boston, MA *(412,616)*		1.50
2342	22c **Maryland,** *Feb. 15, 1988,* Annapolis, MD *(376,403)*		1.50
2343	22c **South Carolina,** *May 23, 1988,* Columbia, SC *(322,938)*		1.50
2344	22c **New Hampshire,** *June 21, 1988,* Concord, NH *(374,402)*		1.50
2345	22c **Virginia,** *June 25, 1988,* Williamsburg, VA *(474,079)*		1.50
2346	22c **New York,** *July 26, 1988,* Albany, NY *(385,793)*		1.50
2347	25c **North Carolina,** *Aug. 22, 1989,* Fayetteville, NC *(392,953)*		1.50
2348	25c **Rhode Island,** *May 29, 1990,* Pawtucket, RI *(305,566)*		1.50

1987
2349	22c **U.S.-Morocco Diplomatic Relations Bicent.,** *July 17 (372,814)*		1.00
2350	22c **William Faulkner,** *Aug. 3,* Oxford, MS *(480,024)*		1.00
2354a	22c **Lacemaking,** *Aug. 14,* Ypsilanti, MI		2.50
	2351-2354, any single		1.00
2359a	22c **Drafting of Constitution Bicent. Booklet pane of 5,** *Aug. 28*		4.00
	2355-2359, any single		1.25

First day cancellation was applied to 1,008,799 covers bearing one or more of Nos. 2355-2359a.

2360	22c **Signing of Constitution Bicent.,** *Sept. 17,* Philadelphia, PA *(719,975)*		1.25
2361	22c **Certified Public Accounting,** *Sept. 21,* New York, NY *(362,099)*		7.50
2366a	22c **Locomotives booklet pane of 5,** *Oct. 1,* Baltimore, MD		3.00
	2362-2366, any single		1.25

First day cancellation was applied to 976,694 covers bearing one or more of Nos. 2362-2366a.

2367	22c **Christmas (Madonna),** *Oct. 23 (320,406)*		1.25
2368	22c **Christmas (Ornaments),** *Oct. 23,* Holiday-Anaheim, CA *(375,858)*		1.25

1988
2369	22c **Winter Olympics, Calgary,** *Jan. 10,* Anchorage, AK *(395,198)*		1.00
2370	22c **Australia Bicentennial,** *Jan. 26 (523,465)*		1.75
2371	22c **James Weldon Johnson,** *Feb. 2,* Nashville, TN *(465,282)*		1.75
2375a	22c **Cats,** *Feb. 5,* New York, NY *(872,734)*		4.50
	2372-2375, any single		2.00
2376	22c **Knute Rockne,** *Mar. 9,* Notre Dame, IN *(404,311)*		4.00
2377	25c **Francis Ouimet,** *June 13,* Brookline, MA *(383,168)*		4.50
2378	25c **Love,** *July 4,* Pasadena, CA *(399,038)*		1.00
2379	45c **Love,** *Aug. 8,* Shreveport, LA *(121,808)*		1.25
2380	25c **Summer Olympics, Seoul,** *Aug. 19,* Colorado Springs, CO *(402,616)*		1.25
2385a	25c **Automobiles booklet pane of 5,** *Aug. 25,* Detroit, MI		4.00
	2381-2385, any single		1.25

First day cancel was applied to 875,801 covers bearing one or more of Nos. 2381-2385a.

2389a	25c **Antarctic Explorers,** *Sept. 14 (720,537)*		3.00
	2386-2389, any single		1.25
2393a	25c **Carousel Animals,** *Oct. 1,* Sandusky, OH *(856,380)*		3.00
	2390-2393, any single		1.25
2394	$8.75 **Express Mail,** *Oct. 4,* Terre Haute, IN *(66,558)*		27.50
2396a	25c **Special Occasions (Happy Birthday, Best Wishes),** *Oct. 22,* King of Prussia, PA		4.00
	2395-2396, any single		1.25
2398a	25c **Special Occasions (Thinking of You, Love You),** *Oct. 22,* King of Prussia, PA		4.00
	2397-2398, any single		1.25

First day cancel was applied to 126,767 covers bearing one or more of Nos. 2395-2398, 2396a, 2398a.

2399	25c **Christmas (Madonna),** *Oct. 20 (247,291)*		1.25
2400	25c **Christmas (Contemporary),** *Oct. 20,* Berlin, NH *(412,213)*		1.25

1989
2401	25c **Montana,** *Jan. 15,* Helena, MT *(353,319)*		1.25
2402	25c **A. Philip Randolph,** *Feb. 3,* New York, NY *(363,174)*		1.75
2403	25c **North Dakota,** *Feb. 21,* Bismarck, ND *(306,003)*		1.00
2404	25c **Washington Statehood,** *Feb. 22,* Olympia, WA *(445,174)*		1.00
2409a	25c **Steamboats Booklet pane of 5,** *Mar. 3,* New Orleans, LA		3.00
	2405-2409, any single		1.25

First day cancel was applied to 981,674 covers bearing one or more of Nos. 2405-2409a.

2410	25c **World Stamp Expo,** *Mar. 16,* New York, NY *(296,310)*		1.00
2411	25c **Arturo Toscanini,** *Mar. 25,* New York, NY *(309,441)*		1.00

1989-90

BRANCHES OF GOVERNMENT
2412	25c **House of Representatives,** *Apr. 4, 1989 (327,755)*		1.25
2413	25c **Senate,** *Apr. 6, 1989 (341,288)*		1.25
2414	25c **Executive Branch,** *Apr. 16, 1989* Mount Vernon, VA *(387,644)*		1.25
2415	25c **Supreme Court,** *Feb. 2, 1990 (233,056)*		1.25

1989
2416	25c **South Dakota,** *May 3,* Pierre, SD *(348,370)*		1.00
2417	25c **Lou Gehrig,** *June 10,* Cooperstown, NY *(694,227)*		4.00
2418	25c **Ernest Hemingway,** *July 17,* Key West, FL *(345,436)*		1.25
2419	$2.40 **Moon Landing,** *July 20 (208,982)*		7.50
2420	25c **Letter Carriers,** *Aug. 30,* Milwaukee, WI *(372,241)*		1.25
2421	25c **Bill of Rights,** *Sept. 25,* Philadelphia, PA *(900,384)*		1.00
2425a	25c **Dinosaurs,** *Oct. 1,* Orlando, FL *(871,634)*		3.00
	2422-2425, any single		1.50
2426	25c **Southwest Carved Figure,** *Oct. 12,* San Juan, PR *(215,285)*		1.00
2427	25c **Christmas (Madonna),** *Oct. 19 (395,321)*		1.00
2427a	Booklet pane of 10		6.00
2428	25c **Christmas (Sleigh with Presents),** *Oct. 19,* Westport, CT		1.00
2429	25c **Christmas (Sleigh with Presents) from bklt.,** *Oct. 19,* Westport, CT		1.00
2429a	Booklet pane of 10		6.00

First day cancel was applied to 345,931 covers bearing one or more of Nos. 2428-2429a.

2431	25c **Eagle and Shield,** *Nov. 10,* Virginia Beach, VA		1.25
2433	90c **World Stamp Expo '89 Souvenir Sheet,** *Nov. 17 (281,725)*		7.00
2437a	25c **Classic Mail Transportation,** *Nov. 19 (916,389)*		2.50

		2434-2437, any single	1.25
2438	25c	**Classic Mail Transportation Souvenir Sheet,** *Nov. 28 (241,634)*	3.00

1990

2439	25c	**Idaho Statehood,** *Jan. 6,* Boise, ID *(252,493)*	1.25
2440	25c	**Love,** *Jan. 18,* Romance, AR	1.25
2441	25c	**Love, from bklt.,** *Jan. 18,* Romance, AR	1.00
2441a		Booklet pane of 10	6.00

First day cancel was applied to 257,788 covers bearing one or more of Nos. 2440-2441a.

2442	25c	**Ida B. Wells,** *Feb. 1,* Chicago, IL *(229,226)*	2.00
2443	15c	**Beach Umbrella,** *Feb. 3,* Sarasota, FL	1.25
2443a		Booklet pane of 10	4.25

First day cancel was applied to 72,286 covers bearing one or more of Nos. 2443-2443a.

2444	25c	**Wyoming Statehood,** *Feb. 23,* Cheyenne, WY *(317,654)*	1.00
2448a	25c	**Classic Films,** *Mar. 23,* Hollywood, CA *(863,079)*	5.00
		2445-2448, any single	2.50
2449	25c	**Marianne Moore,** *Apr. 18,* Brooklyn, NY *(390,535)*	1.25

1990-95

TRANSPORTATION COILS

2451	4c	**Steam Carriage,** *Jan. 25, 1991,* Tucson, AZ *(100,393)*	1.25
2452	5c	**Circus Wagon,** engraved, *Aug. 31, 1990,* Syracuse, NY *(71,806)*	1.50
2452B	5c	**Circus Wagon,** photogravure, *Dec. 8, 1992,* Cincinnati, OH	1.50
2452D	5c	**Circus Wagon,** with cent sign, photogravure, *Mar. 20, 1995,* Kansas City MO *(20,835)*	2.00
2453	5c	**Canoe,** engraved, *May 25, 1991,* Secaucus, NJ *(108,634)*	1.25
2454	5c	**Canoe,** photogravure, *Oct. 22, 1991,* Secaucus, NJ	1.25
2457	10c	**Tractor Trailer,** engr., *May 25, 1991,* Secaucus, NJ *(84,717)*	1.25
2458	10c	**Tractor Trailer,** photo., *May 25, 1994,* Secaucus, NJ *(15,431)*	1.25
2463	20c	**Cog Railway,** *June 9, 1995,* Dallas, TX *(28,883)*	1.25
2464	23c	**Lunch Wagon,** *Apr. 12, 1991,* Columbus, OH *(115,830)*	1.25
2466	32c	**Ferry Boat,** *June 2, 1995,* McLean VA	1.25

First day cancellation was applied to 59,100 covers bearing one or more of Nos. 2466, 2492.

2468	$1	**Seaplane,** *Apr. 20, 1990* Phoenix, AZ *(244,775)*	2.50

1990

2474a	25c	**Lighthouses booklet pane of 5,** *Apr. 26*	4.00
		2470-2474, any single	1.50

First day cancel was applied to 805,133 covers bearing one or more of Nos. 2470-2474a.

2475	25c	**Flag,** *May 18,* Seattle, WA *(97,567)*	1.00

1990-95

FLORA AND FAUNA ISSUE

2476	1c	**Kestrel,** *June 22,* Aurora, CO *(77,781)*	1.00
2477	1c	**Kestrel, with cent sign,** *May 10, 1995* Aurora, CO *(21,767)*	1.00
2478	3c	**Eastern Bluebird,** *June 22,* Aurora, CO *(76,149)*	1.00
2479	19c	**Fawn,** *Mar. 11 (100,212)*	1.00
2480	30c	**Cardinal,** *June 22,* Aurora, CO *(101,290)*	1.25
2481	45c	**Pumpkinseed Sunfish,** *Dec. 2, 1992 (38,696)*	1.75
2482	$2	**Bobcat,** *June 1,* Arlington, VA *(49,660)*	5.00
2483	20c	**Blue Jay,** booklet single, *June 15, 1995,* Kansas City MO	1.25

First day cancellation was applied to 16,847 covers bearing one or more of Nos. 2483, 2483a.

2484	29c	**Wood Duck,** black denomination bklt. single, *Apr. 12,* Columbus, OH	1.00
2484a		Booklet pane of 10	4.00
2485	29c	**Wood Duck,** red denomination bklt. single, *Apr. 12,* Columbus, OH	1.00
2485a		Booklet pane of 10	4.00

First day cancel was applied to 205,305 covers bearing one or more of Nos. 2484-2485, 2484a-2485a.

2486	29c	**African Violet,** *Oct. 8, 1993,* Beaumont, TX	1.00
2486a		Booklet pane of 10	4.00

First day cancellation was applied to 40,167 covers bearing one or more of Nos. 2486-2486a.

2487	32c	**Peach,** booklet single, *July 8, 1995,* Reno NV	1.25
2488	32c	**Pear,** booklet single, *July 8, 1995,* Reno NV	1.50

First day cancellation was applied to 71,086 covers bearing one or more of Nos. 2487-2488, 2488a, 2493-2495A.

2488a		Booklet pane, 5 each #2488-2489	7.50
2489	29c	**Red Squirrel,** self-adhesive, *June 25, 1993* Milwaukee, WI *(48,564)*	1.25

2490	29c	**Red Rose,** self-adhesive, *Aug. 19, 1993* Houston, TX *(37,916)*	1.25
2491	29c	**Pine Cone,** self-adhesive, *Nov. 5, 1993* Kansas City, MO *(110,924)*	1.25
2492	32c	**Pink Rose,** self-adhesive, *June 2, 1995,* McLean VA	1.25

First day cancellation was applied to 59,100 covers bearing one or more of Nos. 2466, 2492.

2493	32c	**Peach,** self-adhesive, *July 8, 1995,* Reno NV	1.25
2494	32c	**Pear,** self-adhesive, *July 8, 1995,* Reno NV	1.25
2495	32c	**Peach,** self-adhesive, serpentine die cut vert., *July 8, 1995,* Reno NV	1.25
2495A	32c	**Pear,** self-adhesive, serpentine die cut vert., *July 8, 1995,* Reno NV	1.25

First day cancellation was applied to 71,086 covers bearing one or more of Nos. 2487-2488, 2488a, 2493-2495A.

1990

2500a	25c	**Olympians,** *July 6,* Minneapolis, MN *(1,143,404)*	4.00
		2496-2500, any single	1.25
2505a	25c	**Indian Headdresses, booklet pane of 10** *Aug. 17,* Cody, WY	6.00
		2501-2505, any single	1.25

First day cancel was applied to 979,580 covers bearing one or more of Nos. 2501-2505a.

2507a	25c	**Micronesia, Marshall Islands,** *Sept. 28 (343,816)*	2.00
		2506-2507, any single	1.25
2511a	25c	**Sea Creatures,** *Oct. 3,* Baltimore, MD *(706,047)*	3.00
		2508-2511, any single	1.25
2512	25c	**Grand Canyon,** *Oct. 12,* Grand Canyon, AZ *(164,190)*	1.25
2513	25c	**Dwight D. Eisenhower,** *Oct. 13,* Abilene, KS *(487,988)*	1.25
2514	25c	**Christmas (traditional),** *Oct. 18*	1.25
2514a		Booklet pane of 10	6.00

First day cancel was applied to 378,383 covers bearing one or more of Nos. 2514-2514a.

2515	25c	**Christmas (secular),** *Oct. 18,* Evergreen, CO	1.25
2516	25c	**Christmas (secular),** *Oct. 18,* Evergreen, CO	1.00
2516a		Booklet pane of 10	6.00

First day cancel was applied to 230,586 covers bearing one or more of Nos. 2515-2516a.

1991-94

2517	(29c)	**"F" Flower,** *Jan. 22, 1991 (106,698)*	1.25
2518	(29c)	**"F" Flower,** coil, *Jan. 22, 1991 (39,311)*	1.25
2519	(29c)	**"F" Flower,** bklt. single (bullseye perf. 11.2), *Jan. 22, 1991*	1.00
2519a		Booklet pane of 10	7.25
2520	(29c)	**"F" Flower,** bklt. single (perf. 11), *Jan. 22, 1991*	1.25
2520a		Booklet pane of 10	8.00

First day cancel was applied to 32,971 covers bearing one or more of Nos. 2519-2520, 2519a-2520a.

2521	(4c)	**Makeup Stamp,** *Jan. 22, 1991 (51,987)*	1.25
2522	(29c)	**"F" Flag,** *Jan. 22, 1991 (48,821)*	1.25
2523	29c	**Flag over Mt. Rushmore,** engraved, *Mar. 29, 1991* Mt. Rushmore, SD *(233,793)*	1.25
2523A	29c	**Flag over Mt. Rushmore,** photogravure, *July 4, 1991* Mt. Rushmore, SD *(80,662)*	1.25
2524	29c	**Flower,** *Apr. 5, 1991,* Rochester, NY *(132,233)*	1.00
2525	29c	**Flower,** roulette 10 coil, *Aug. 16, 1991,* Rochester, NY *(144,750)*	1.00
2526	29c	**Flower,** perf. 10 coil, *Mar. 3, 1992,* Rochester, NY *(35,877)*	1.00
2527	29c	**Flower,** bklt. single, *Apr. 5, 1991,* Rochester, NY	1.00
2527a		Booklet pane of 10	4.00

First day cancel was applied to 16,975 covers bearing one or more of Nos. 2527-2527a.

2528	29c	**Flag and Olympic Rings,** bklt. single, *Apr. 21, 1991,* Atlanta, GA	1.25
2528a		Booklet pane of 10	5.00

First day cancel was applied to 319,488 covers bearing one or more of Nos. 2528-2528a.

2529	19c	**Fishing Boat,** two loops, *Aug. 8, 1991 (82,698)*	1.50
2529C	19c	**Fishing Boat,** one loop, *June 25, 1994,* Arlington, VA *(14,538)*	1.50
2530	19c	**Balloon,** *May 17, 1991,* Denver, CO	1.25
2530a		Booklet pane of 10	5.00

First day cancel was applied to 96,351 covers bearing one or more of Nos. 2530-2530a.

2531	29c	**Flags on Parade,** *May 30, 1991,* Waterloo, NY *(104,046)*	1.00
2531A	29c	**Liberty Torch,** *June 25, 1991,* New York, NY *(68,456)*	1.25

1991-95

2532	50c	**Switzerland,** *Feb. 22,* Washington, DC *(316,047)*	1.40
2533	29c	**Vermont,** *Mar. 1,* Bennington, VT *(308,105)*	1.50
2534	29c	**Savings Bonds,** *Apr. 30,* Washington, DC *(341,955)*	1.25

2535	29c	**Love,** *May 9,* Honolulu, HI *(336,132)*	
2536	29c	**Love,** bklt. single, *May 9,* Honolulu, HI	
2536a		Booklet pane of 10	

First day cancel was applied to 43,336 covers bearing one or more of Nos. 2536-2536a.

2537	52c	**Love,** *May 9,* Honolulu, HI *(90,438)*	
2538	29c	**William Saroyan,** *May 22,* Fresno, CA *(334,373)*	
2539	$1	**Eagle & Olympic Rings,** *Sept. 29,* Orlando, FL *(69,241)*	
2540	$2.90	**Eagle & Olympic Rings,** *July 7,* San Diego, CA *(79,555)*	
2541	$9.95	**Eagle & Olympic Rings,** *June 16,* Sacramento, CA *(68,657)*	15
2542	$14	**Eagle,** *Aug. 31,* Hunt Valley, MD *(54,727)*	27
2543	$2.90	**Futuristic Space Shuttle,** *June 3, 1993,* Kennedy Space Center, FL *(36,359)*	6
2544	$3	**Space Shuttle Challenger,** *June 22, 1995* Anaheim CA *(16,502)*	6
2544A	$10.75	**Space Shuttle Endeavour,** *Aug. 4, 1995* Irvine CA *(10,534)*	15

1991

2549a	29c	**Fishing Flies booklet pane of 5,** *May 31,* Cuddebackville, NY *(1,045,726)*	3
		2545-2549, any single	1
2550	29c	**Cole Porter,** *June 8,* Peru, IN *(304,363)*	1.
2551	29c	**Desert Storm/ Desert Shield,** *July 2*	2.
2552	29c	**Desert Storm/ Desert Shield,** bklt. single, *July 2*	2.
2552a		Booklet pane of 5	2.

First day cancel was applied to 860,455 covers bearing one or more of Nos. 2551-2552, 2552a.

2557a	29c	**Summer Olympics,** *July 12,* Los Angeles, CA *(886,984)*	3.
		2553-2557, any single	1.
2558	29c	**Numismatics,** *Aug. 13,* Chicago, IL *(288,519)*	1.
2559	29c	**World War II block of 10,** *Sept. 3,* Phoenix, AZ *(1,832,967)*	7.
		2559a-2559j, any single	1.
2560	29c	**Basketball,** *Aug. 28,* Springfield, MA *(295,471)*	2.
2561	29c	**District of Columbia,** *Sept. 7 (299,989)*	1.
2566a	29c	**Comedians booklet pane of 10,** *Aug. 29,* Hollywood, CA	3.
		2562-2566, any single	1.

First day cancel was applied to 954,293 covers bearing one or more of Nos. 2562-2566a.

2567	29c	**Jan Matzeliger,** *Sept. 15,* Lynn, MA *(289,034)*	1.
2577a	29c	**Space Exploration booklet pane of 10,** *Oct. 1,* Pasadena, CA	5.0
		2568-2577, any single	1.

First day cancel was applied to 1,465,111 covers bearing one or more of Nos. 2568-2577a.

2578	(29c)	**Christmas (religious),** *Oct. 17,* Houston, TX	1.
2579	(29c)	**Christmas (secular),** *Oct. 17,* Santa, ID *(169,750)*	1.
2581b	(29c)	**Christmas booklet pane of 4,** *Oct. 17,* Santa, ID	2.5
		2580-2581, any single	1.
2582	(29c)	**Christmas,** bklt. single, *Oct. 17,* Santa, ID	1.
2582a		Booklet pane of 4	2.5
2583	(29c)	**Christmas,** bklt. single, *Oct. 17,* Santa, ID	1.
2583a		Booklet pane of 4	2.5
2584	(29c)	**Christmas,** bklt. single, *Oct. 17,* Santa, ID	1.
2584a		Booklet pane of 4	2.5
2585	(29c)	**Christmas,** bklt. single, *Oct. 17,* Santa, ID	1.
2585a		Booklet pane of 4	2.5

First day cancel was applied to 168,794 covers bearing one or more of Nos. 2580-2585, 2581b, 2582a, 2583a, 2584a and 2585a.

1991-95

2587	32c	**James K. Polk,** *Nov. 2, 1995,* Columbia TN *(189,429)*	1.2
2590	$1	**Surrender of Gen. John Burgoyne,** *May 5, 1994,* New York, NY *(379,629)*	2.50
2592	$5	**Washington & Jackson,** *Aug. 19, 1994,* Pittsburgh, PA *(16,303)*	12.50
2593	29c	**Pledge of Allegiance,** black denomination, *Sept. 8, 1992,* Rome, NY	1.25
2593a		Booklet pane of 10	5.00

First day cancel was applied to 61,464 covers bearing one or more of Nos. 2593-2593a.

2595	29c	**Eagle & Shield,** brown denomination, *Sept. 25, 1992,* Dayton, OH	1.50
2596	29c	**Eagle & Shield,** green denomination, *Sept. 25, 1992,* Dayton, OH	1.50
2597	29c	**Eagle & Shield,** red denomination, *Sept. 25, 1992,* Dayton, OH	1.50

First day cancel was applied to 65,822 covers bearing one or more of Nos. 2595-2597.

2598	29c	**Eagle,** *Feb. 4, 1994,* Sarasota, FL *(67,300)*	1.25

99	29c **Statue of Liberty**, *June 24, 1994,* Haines City, FL *(39,810)*	1.25
02	(10c) **Eagle & Shield**, Bulk Rate USA, *Dec. 13, 1991*, Kansas City, MO *(21,176)*	1.25
03	(10c) **Eagle & Shield**, USA Bulk Rate, *May 29, 1993*, Secaucus, NJ	1.25
04	(10c) **Eagle & Shield**, gold eagle, *May 29, 1993*, Secaucus, NJ	1.25

First day cancellation was applied to 36,444 covers bearing ne or more of Nos. 2603-2604.

05	23c **Flag**, *Sept. 27, 1991*	1.25
06	23c **Reflected Flag**, *July 21, 1992*, Kansas City, MO *(35,673)*	1.25
07	23c **Reflected Flag**, 7mm "23," *Oct. 9, 1992*, Kansas City, MO	1.25
08	23c **Reflected Flag**, 8 ½mm "First Class" *May 14, 1993*, Denver, CO *(15,548)*	1.25
09	29c **Flag over White House**, *Apr. 23, 1992 (56,505)*	1.25

92

15a	29c **Winter Olympics**, *Jan. 11*, Orlando, FL *(1,062,048)*	3.50
	2611-2615, any single	1.25
16	29c **World Columbian Stamp Expo**, *Jan. 24*, Rosemont, IL *(309,729)*	1.25
17	29c **W.E.B. Du Bois**, *Jan. 31*, Atlanta, GA *(196,219)*	1.75
18	29c **Love**, *Feb. 6*, Loveland, CO *(218,043)*	1.25
19	29c **Olympic Baseball**, *Apr. 3*, Atlanta, GA *(105,996)*	2.00
23a	29c **Voyages of Columbus**, *Apr. 24*, Christiansted, VI	2.75
	2620-2623, any single	1.25

First day cancellation was applied to 509,270 covers bearing ne or more of Nos. 2620-2623a.

24	**First Sighting of Land Souvenir Sheet of 3**, *May 22*, Chicago, IL	2.10
24a	1c	1.50
24b	4c	1.50
24c	$1	2.00
25	**Claiming a New World Souvenir Sheet of 3**, *May 22*, Chicago, IL	8.00
25a	2c	1.50
25b	3c	1.50
25c	$4	8.00
26	**Seeking Royal Support Souvenir Sheet of 3**, *May 22*, Chicago, IL	1.75
26a	5c	1.50
26b	30c	1.50
26c	50c	1.50
27	**Royal Favor Restored Souvenir Sheet of 3**, *May 22*, Chicago, IL	6.25
27a	6c	1.50
27b	8c	1.50
27c	$3	6.00
28	**Reporting Discoveries Souvenir Sheet of 3**, *May 22*, Chicago, IL	4.50
28a	10c	1.50
28b	15c	1.50
28c	$2	4.00
629	$5 **Christopher Columbus Souvenir Sheet**, *May 22*, Chicago, IL	10.00

First day cancel was applied to 211,142 covers bearing one r more of Nos. 2624-2629.

630	29c **New York Stock Exchange**, *May 17*, New York, NY *(261,897)*	2.50
634a	29c **Space Accomplishments**, *May 29*, Chicago, IL	2.75
	2631-2634, any single	1.50

First day cancel was applied to 277,853 covers bearing one r more of Nos. 2631-2634a.

635	29c **Alaska Highway**, *May 30*, Fairbanks, AK *(186,791)*	1.25
636	29c **Kentucky**, *June 1*, Danville, KY *(251,153)*	1.25
641a	29c **Summer Olympics**, *June 11*, Baltimore, MD *(713,942)*	3.00
	2637-2641, any single	1.25
646a	29c **Hummingbirds booklet pane of 5**, *June 15*	3.00
	2642-2646, any single	1.25

First day cancel was applied to 995,278 covers bearing one r more of Nos. 2642-2646a.

696a	29c **Wildflowers**, *July 24*, Columbus, OH	30.00
	2647-2696, any single	1.25

First day cancellation was applied to 3,693,972 covers bearing one or more of Nos. 2647-2696a.

2697	29c **World War II block of 10**, *Aug. 17*, Indianapolis, IN *(1,734,880)*	7.00
	2697a-2697j, any single	1.75

First day cancel was applied to 1,734,880 covers bearing one or more of Nos. 2697, 2697a-2697j.

2698	29c **Dorothy Parker**, *Aug. 22*, West End, NJ *(266,323)*	1.50
2699	29c **Theodore von Karman**, *Aug. 31 (256,986)*	1.50
2703a	29c **Minerals**, *Sept. 17*	2.75
	2700-2703, any single	1.25

First day cancellation was applied to 681,416 covers bearing one or more of Nos. 2700-2703.

2704	29c **Juan Rodriguez Cabrillo**, *Sept. 28*, San Diego, CA *(290,720)*	1.25

2709a	29c **Wild Animals booklet pane of 5**, *Oct. 1*, New Orleans, LA	3.25
	Any other city	4.00
	2705-2709, any single	1.25

First day cancel was applied to 604,205 New Orleans covers bearing one or more of Nos. 2705-2709a.

2710	29c **Christmas (religious)**, *Oct. 22*	1.25
2710a	Booklet pane of 10	7.25

First day cancel was applied to 201,576 covers bearing one or more of Nos. 2710-2710a.

2714a	29c **Christmas (secular)**, *Oct. 22*, Kansas City (MO)	2.75
	2711-2714, any single	1.25
2718a	29c **Christmas (secular) booklet pane of 4**, *Oct. 22*, Kansas City, MO	2.75
	2715-2718, any single	1.25

First day cancel was applied to 461,937 covers bearing one or more of Nos. 2711-2714, 2715-2718 and 2718a.

2719	29c **Christmas (secular)**, self-adhesive, *Oct. 28*, New York, NY *(48,873)*	1.25
2720	29c **Chinese New Year**, *Dec. 30*, San Francisco, CA *(138,238)*	2.25

1993

2721	29c **Elvis (Presley)**, *Jan. 8*, Memphis, TN, AM cancellation, *(4,452,815)*	2.00
	Any city, PM cancellation	3.00
2722	29c **Oklahoma!**, *Mar. 30*, Oklahoma City, OK *(283,837)*	1.25
2723	29c **Hank Williams**, perf 10, *June 9*, Nashville, TN	1.25
2723A	29c **Hank Williams**, perf 11.2x11.5, *June 9*, Nashville, TN	—

First day cancel was applied to 311,106 covers bearing one or more of Nos. 2723-2723A.

2730a	29c **Rock & Roll/Rhythm & Blues Musicians**, *June 16*, Cleveland OH or Santa Monica CA	5.00
	Any other city	5.00
	2724-2730, any single	1.25
	Any single, any other city	1.25

Value for No. 2730a is also for any se-tenant configuration of seven different stamps.
First day cancel was applied to 540,809 covers bearing one or more of Nos. 2724-2730a, 2731-2737b.

2737a	29c **Rock & Roll/Rhythm & Blues Musicians booklet pane of 8**, *June 16*, Cleveland, OH or Santa Monica CA	5.25
	Any other city	5.25
	2731-2737, any single	1.25
	Any single, any other city	1.25
2737b	29c **Rock & Roll/Rhythm & Blues Musicians booklet pane of 4**, *June 16*, Cleveland, OH or Santa Monica CA	2.75
	Any other city	2.75

For first day cancellation quantities, see No. 2730a.

2745a	29c **Space Fantasy booklet pane of 5**, *Jan. 25*, Huntsville, AL	3.25
	2741-2745, any single	1.25

First day cancel was applied to 631,203 covers bearing one or more of Nos. 2741-2745a.

2746	29c **Percy Lavon Julian**, *Jan. 29*, Chicago, IL *(120,877)*	1.75
2747	29c **Oregon Trail**, *Feb. 12*, Salem, OR *(436,550)*	1.25

No. 2747 was also available on the first day of issue in 36 cities along the route of the Oregon Trail.

2748	29c **World University Games**, *Feb. 25*, Buffalo, NY *(157,563)*	1.50
2749	29c **Grace Kelly**, *Mar. 24*, Beverly Hills, CA *(263,913)*	3.00
2753a	29c **Circus**, *Apr. 6*	3.00
	2750-2753, any single	1.50

First day cancel was applied to 676,927 covers bearing one or more of Nos. 2750-2753a.

2754	29c **Cherokee Strip Land Run**, *Apr. 17*, Enid, OK *(260,118)*	1.25
2755	29c **Dean Acheson**, *Apr. 21*, *(158,783)*	1.25
2759a	29c **Sporting Horses**, *May 1*, Louisville, KY	3.50
	2756-2759, any single	1.75

First day cancel was applied to 448,059 covers bearing one or more of Nos. 2756-2759a.

2764a	29c **Garden Flowers booklet pane of 5**, *May 15*, Spokane, WA	3.00
	2760-2764, any single	1.50

First day cancel was applied to 492,578 covers bearing one or more of Nos. 2760-2764a.

2765	29c **World War II block of 10**, *May 31*,	7.00
	2765a-2765j, any single	1.75

First day cancel was applied to 543,511 covers bearing one or more of Nos. 2765, 2765a-2765j.

2766	29c **Joe Louis**, *June 22*, Detroit, MI *(229,272)*	3.00
2770a	29c **Broadway Musicals booklet pane of 4**, *July 14*, New York, NY	3.50
	2767-2770, any single	1.25

First day cancel was applied to 308,231 covers bearing one or more of Nos. 2767-2770a.

2774a	29c **Country Music**, *Sept. 25*, Nashville, TN	3.00
	2771-2774, any single	1.25

2778a	29c **Country Music booklet pane of 4**, *Sept. 25*, Nashville, TN	3.00
	2775-2778, any single	1.25

First day cancel was applied to 362,904 covers bearing one or more of Nos. 2771-2774a, 2775-2778a.

2782a	29c **National Postal Museum**, *July 30*	2.75
	2779-2782, any single	1.25

First day cancel was applied to 371,115 covers bearing one or more of Nos. 2779-2782a.

2784a	29c **Deafness/Sign Language**, *Sept. 20*, Burbank, CA	2.50
	2783-2784, any single	1.50

First day cancel was applied to 112,350 covers bearing one or more of Nos. 2783-2784a.

2788a	29c **Classic Books**, *Oct. 23*, Louisville, KY	2.75
	2785-2788, any single	1.25

First day cancel was applied to 269,457 covers bearing one or more of Nos. 2785-2788a.

2789	29c **Christmas (religious)**, *Oct. 21*, Raleigh, NC	1.25
2790	29c **Christmas (religious)**, booklet single, *Oct. 21*, Raleigh, NC	1.25
2790a	Booklet pane of 4	2.50

First day cancellation was applied to 155,192 covers bearing one or more of Nos. 2789-2790a.

2794a	29c **Christmas (secular)**, sheet stamps, *Oct. 21*, New York, NY	2.75
	2791-2794, any single	1.25
2798a	29c **Christmas (secular) booklet pane of 10**, *Oct. 21*, New York, NY	6.50
2798b	29c **Christmas (secular) booklet pane of 10**, *Oct. 21*, New York, NY	6.50
	2795-2798, any single	1.25
2799	29c **Christmas (snowman)**, large self-adhesive, *Oct. 28*, New York, NY	1.25
2800	29c **Christmas (soldier)**, self-adhesive, *Oct. 28*, New York, NY	1.25
2801	29c **Christmas (jack-in-the-box)**, self-adhesive, *Oct. 28*, New York, NY	1.25
2802	29c **Christmas (reindeer)**, self-adhesive, *Oct. 28*, New York, NY	1.25
	2799-2802 on one cover	2.50
2803	29c **Christmas (snowman)**, small self-adhesive, *Oct. 28*, New York, NY	1.25

First day cancel was applied to 384,262 covers bearing one or more of Nos. 2791-2794a, 2795-2798b, 2799-2803.

2804	29c **Mariana Islands**, *Nov. 4*, Saipan, MP *(157,410)*	1.25
2805	29c **Columbus' Landing in Puerto Rico**, *Nov. 19*, San Juan, PR *(222,845)*	1.25
2806	29c **AIDS Awareness**, *Dec. 1*, New York, NY	2.00
2806a	Booklet single, perf. 11 vert.	2.00
2806b	Booklet pane of 5	4.00

First day cancellation was applied to 209,200 covers bearing one or more of Nos. 2806-2806b.

1994

2811a	29c **Winter Olympics**, *Jan. 6*, Salt Lake City, UT	3.00
	2807-2811, any single	1.25

First day cancellation was applied to 645,636 covers bearing one or more of Nos. 2807-2811a.

2812	29c **Edward R. Murrow**, *Jan. 21*, Pullman, WA *(154,638)*	1.25
2813	29c **Love**, self-adhesive, *Jan. 27*, Loveland, OH *(125,146)*	1.25
2814	29c **Love**, booklet single, *Feb. 14*, Niagara Falls, NY	1.25
2814a	Booklet pane of 10	6.50
2814C	29c **Love**, *June 11*, Niagara Falls, NY *(42,109)*	1.25
2815	52c **Love**, *Feb. 14*, Niagara Falls, NY	1.50
2816	29c **Dr. Allison Davis**, *Feb. 1*, Williamstown, MA *(162,404)*	2.00
2817	29c **Chinese New Year**, *Feb. 5*, Pomona, CA *(148,492)*	2.00
2818	29c **Buffalo Soldiers**, *Apr. 22*, Dallas, TX *(107,223)*	2.75

No. 2818 was also available on the first day of issue in forts in Kansas, Texas and Arizona.

2828a	29c **Silent Screen Stars**, *Apr. 27*, San Francisco, CA	6.50
	2819-2828, any single	1.50

First day cancellation was applied to 591,251 covers bearing one or more of Nos. 2819-2828a.

2833a	29c **Garden Flowers booklet pane of 5**, *Apr. 28*, Cincinnati, OH	3.25
	2829-2833, any single	1.25

First day cancellation was applied to 153,069 covers bearing one or more of Nos. 2829-2833a.

2834	29c **World Cup Soccer**, *May 26*, New York, NY	1.50
2835	40c **World Cup Soccer**, *May 26*, New York, NY	1.50
2836	50c **World Cup Soccer**, *May 26*, New York, NY	1.75

First day cancellation was applied to 443,768 covers bearing one or more of Nos. 2834-2836.

2837	**World Cup Soccer souvenir sheet of 3**, *May 26*, New York, NY *(59,503)*	3.50

2838 29c **World War II block of 10,** *June 6,*
USS Normandy 7.00
2838a-2838j, any single 1.75

No. 2838 was also available on the first day of issue in 13 other locations.
First day cancellation was applied to 744,267 covers bearing one or more of Nos. 2838, 2838a-2838j.

2839 29c **Norman Rockwell,** *July 1,* Stockbridge, MA *(232,076)* 1.25
2840 50c **Norman Rockwell Souvenir Sheet of 4,** *July 1,* Stockbridge, MA 3.50
2840a-2840d, any single 1.50

First day cancellation was applied to 19,734 covers bearing one or more of Nos. 2840-2840d.

2841 29c **Moon Landing Sheet of 12,** *July 20,* 6.50
2841a, single stamp 1.50

First day cancellation was applied to 303,707 covers bearing one or more of Nos. 2841-2841a.

2842 $9.95 **Moon Landing,** *July 20 (11,463)* 20.00
2847a 29c **Locomotives booklet pane of 5,** *July 28,* Chama, NM 4.00
2843-2847, any single 1.75

First day cancellation was applied to 169,016 covers bearing one or more of Nos. 2843-2847a.

2848 29c **George Meany,** *Aug. 16 (172,418)* 1.25
2853a 29c **American Music Series,** *Sept. 1,* New York, NY 4.50
2849-2853, any single 1.50

First day cancellation was applied to 156,049 covers bearing one or more of Nos. 2849-2853a.

2861a 29c **American Music Series,** *Sept. 17,* Greenville MS 6.00
2854-2861, any single 1.25

First day cancellation was applied to 483,737 covers bearing one or more of Nos. 2854-2861a.

2862 29c **James Thurber,** *Sept. 10,* Columbus OH *(39,064)* 1.25
2866a 29c **Wonders of the Sea,** *Oct. 3,* Honolulu HI 2.75
2863-2866, any single 1.25

First day cancellation was applied to 284,678 covers bearing one or more of Nos. 2863-2866a.

2868a 29c **Cranes,** *Oct. 9* 2.50
2867-2868, any single 1.25

First day cancellation was applied to 202,955 covers bearing one or more of Nos. 2867-2868a, 24,942 with the People's Republic of China stamps.

2869 29c **Legends of the West Pane of 20,**
Oct. 18, Laramie WY *(429,680)* 15.00
Tucson, AZ *(220,417)* 15.00
Lawton, OK *(191,393)* 15.00
2869a-2869t, any single, any city 1.25

First day cancellation was applied to covers bearing one or more of Nos. 2869-2869t.

2871 29c **Christmas (religious),** perf 11¼, *Oct. 20 (155,192)* 1.25
2871A 29c **Christmas (religious),** perf 9¾x11, *Oct. 20 (155,192)* 1.25
2872 29c **Christmas (stocking),** *Oct. 20,* Harmony MN 1.25
2873 29c **Christmas (Santa Claus),** self-adhesive, *Oct. 20,* Harmony MN 1.25
2874 29c **Christmas (cardinal),** small self-adhesive, *Oct. 20,* Harmony MN 1.25

First day cancellation was applied to 132,005 covers bearing one or more of Nos. 2872, 2872a, 2873, 2874.

2875 $2 **Bureau of Printing and Engraving Souvenir sheet,** *Nov. 3,* New York, NY *(13,126)* 25.00
2876 29c **Chinese New Year (Boar),** *Dec. 30,* Sacramento CA 1.75
2877 (3c) **Dove, bright blue,** *Dec. 13* 1.25
2878 (3c) **Dove, dark blue,** *Dec. 13* 1.25
2879 (20c) **G, black,** *Dec. 13* 1.25
2880 (20c) **G, red,** *Dec. 13* 1.25
2881 (32c) **G, black,** *Dec. 13* 1.25
2881a Booklet pane of 10 6.75
2882 (32c) **G, red,** *Dec. 13* 1.25
2883 (32c) **G, black,** *Dec. 13* 1.25
2883a Booklet pane of 10 6.75
2884 (32c) **G, black,** *Dec. 13* 1.25
2884a Booklet pane of 10 6.75
2885 (32c) **G, red,** *Dec. 13* 1.25
2885a Booklet pane of 10 6.75
2886 (32c) **G, gray, blue, light blue, red & black,** self-adhesive, *Dec. 13* 1.25
2887 (32c) **G, black, blue & red,** self-adhesive, *Dec. 13* 1.25
2888 (25c) **G, black,** coil, *Dec. 13* 1.25
2889 (32c) **G, black,** coil, *Dec. 13* 1.25
2890 (32c) **G, blue,** coil, *Dec. 13* 1.25
2891 (32c) **G, red,** coil, *Dec. 13* 1.25
2892 (32c) **G, red,** rouletted coil, *Dec. 13* 1.25

Originally, No. 2893 (the 5c green Non-profit Presort G rate stamp) was only available through the Philatelic Fullfillment Center after their announcement 1/12/95. Requests for first day cancels received a 12/13/94 cancel, even though they were not available on that date. Value, $1.25.
First day cancellation was applied to 338,107 covers bearing one or more of Nos. 2877-2893(?), and U633-U634.

2897 32c **Flag Over Porch,** *May 19,* Denver CO 1.25

First day cancellation was applied to 66,609 covers bearing one or more of Nos. 2897, 2913-2914, 2916 and possibly, 2920.

1995-98

2902 (5c) **Butte,** coil, *Mar. 10,* State College PA 1.25

First day cancellation was applied to 80,003 covers bearing one or more of Nos. 2902, 2905, and U635-U636.

2902B (5c) **Butte,** self-adhesive coil, *June 15, 1996,* San Antonio TX 1.25

First day cancellation was applied to 87,400 covers bearing one or more of Nos. 2902B, 2904A, 2906, 2910, 2912A, 2915B.

2903 (5c) **Mountain,** purple & multi coil, *Mar. 16, 1996* San Jose CA 1.25
2904 (5c) **Mountain,** blue & multi coil, *Mar. 16,1996* San Jose CA 1.25

First day cancellation was applied to 28,064 covers bearing one or more of Nos. 2903-2904.

2904A (5c) **Mountain,** purple & multi self-adhesive coil, *June 15, 1996,* San Antonio TX 1.25

First day cancellation was applied to 87,400 covers bearing one or more of Nos. 2902B, 2904A, 2906, 2910, 2912A, 2915B.

2904B (5c) **Mountain,** purple & multi self-adhesive coil, inscription outlined, *Jan. 24, 1997,* Tucson, AZ 1.25
2905 (10c) **Auto,** coil, *Mar. 10,* State College PA 1.25
2906 (10c) **Auto,** self-adhesive coil, *June 15, 1996* San Antonio TX 1.25

First day cancellation was applied to 87,400 covers bearing one or more of Nos. 2902B, 2904A, 2906, 2910, 2912A, 2915B.

2907 (10c) **Eagle & Shield,** USA Bulk Rate self-adhesive coil, *May 21, 1996* 1.25

First day cancellation was applied to 54,102 covers bearing one or more of Nos. 2907, 2915A, 2915C, 2921.

2908 (15c) **Auto tail fin (dark orange yellow),** coil, *Mar. 17,* New York NY 1.25
2909 (15c) **Auto tail fin (buff),** coil, *Mar. 17,* New York, NY 1.25

First day cancellation was applied to 93,770 covers bearing one or more of Nos. 2908-2909, 2911-2912, 2919.

2910 (15c) **Auto tail fin (buff),** self-adhesive coil, *June 15, 1996,* San Antonio TX 1.25

First day cancellation was applied to 87,400 covers bearing one or more of Nos. 2902B, 2904A, 2906, 2910, 2915B.

2911 (25c) **Juke box,** coil, *Mar. 17,* New York NY 1.25
2912 (25c) **Juke box,** coil, *Mar. 17,* New York NY 1.25

First day cancellation was applied to 93,770 covers bearing one or more of Nos. 2908-2909, 2911-2912, 2919.

2912A (25c) **Juke box,** self-adhesive coil, bright orange red & multi, microperfs, *June 15, 1996,* New York NY 1.25

First day cancellation was applied to 87,400 covers bearing one or more of Nos. 2902B, 2904A, 2906, 2910, 2912A, 2915B.

2912B (25c) **Juke box,** self-adhesive coil, dark red & multi, *Jan. 24, 1997,* Tucson, AZ 1.25
2913 32c **Flag Over Porch,** coil, *May 19,* Denver CO 1.25
2914 32c **Flag Over Porch,** coil, *May 19,* Denver CO 1.25
2915 32c **Flag Over Porch,** self-adhesive, die cut 8.7 vert., *Apr. 18* 1.25
2915A 32c **Flag Over Porch,** self-adhesive, die cut 9.8 vert., 11 teeth, *May 21, 1996* 1.25
2915B 32c **Flag Over Porch,** self-adhesive die cut 11.5 vert., *June 15, 1996,* San Antonio TX 1.25

First day cancellation was applied to 87,400 covers bearing one or more of Nos. 2902B, 2904A, 2906, 2910, 2912A, 2915B.

2915C 32c **Flag Over Porch,** self-adhesive, die cut 10.9, *May 21, 1996* 2.00
2915D 32c **Flag Over Porch,** self-adhesive coil, self-adhesive die cut 9.8 vert., 9 teeth, *Jan. 24, 1997,* Tucson, AZ 1.25

First day cancellation was applied to 56,774 covers bearing one or more of Nos. 2904B, 2912B, 2915D and 2921b.

2916 32c **Flag Over Porch,** booklet single, *May 19,* Denver CO 1.25
2916a Booklet pane of 10 7.50
2919 32c **Flag Over Field,** self-adhesive, *Mar. 17,* New York NY 1.25

First day cancellation was applied to 93,770 covers bearing one or more of Nos. 2908-2909, 2911-2912, 2919.

2920 32c **Flag Over Porch,** self-adhesive, *Apr. 18* 1.25

First day cancellation was applied to 66,609 covers bearing one or more of Nos. 2897, 2913-2914, 2916 and possibly, 2920.
First day cancellation was applied to 57,639 covers bearing one or more of Nos. 2920d, 3030, 3044.

2921 32c **Flag Over Porch,** self-adhesive, booklet stamp, die cut 9.8 on 2 or 3 sides, *May 21, 1996* 1.25

First day cancellation was applied to 54,102 covers bearing one or more of Nos. 2907, 2915A, 2915C, 2921.

GREAT AMERICANS ISSUE

2933 32c **Milton Hershey,** *July 11,* Hershey PA *(121,228)* 1.
2934 32c **Cal Farley,** *Apr. 26, 1996,* Amarillo TX *(109,440)* 1
2935 32c **Henry Luce,** *Apr. 3, 1998,* New York NY *(76,982)* 1
2936 32c **Wallace,** *July 16, 1998,* Pleasantville NY *(72,183)* 1
2938 46c **Ruth Benedict,** *Oct. 20,* Virginia Beach VA *(24,793)* 1
2940 55c **Alice Hamilton,** *July 11,* Boston MA *(24,225)* 1
2941 55c **Justin Morrill,** *July 17, 1999* Strafford VT *(19,699)* 1
2942 77c **Mary Breckinridge,** *Nov. 9, 1998* Troy, NY 1

First day cancellation was applied to 121,662 covers bearing one or more of Nos. 2942, 3257-3261, 3263-3269.

2943 78c **Alice Paul,** *Aug. 18,* Mount Laurel NJ *(25,071)* 1

1995

2948 (32c) **Love,** *Feb. 1,* Valentines VA 1.
2949 (32c) **Love,** self-adhesive, *Feb. 1,* Valentines VA 1.

First day cancellation was applied to 70,778 covers bearing one or more of Nos. 2948, 2949.

2950 32c **Florida Statehood,** *Mar. 3,* Tallahassee FL *(167,499)* 1
2954a 32c **Earth Day,** *Apr. 20* 2.
2951-2954, any single 1.

First day cancellation was applied to 328,893 covers bearing one or more of Nos. 2951-2954, 2954a.

2955 32c **Richard Nixon,** *Apr. 26,* Yorba Linda CA *(377,605)* 1.
2956 32c **Bessie Coleman,** *Apr. 27,* Chicago IL *(299,834)* 1.
2957 32c **Love,** *May 12,* Lakeville PA 1.2
2958 55c **Love,** *May 12,* Lakeville PA 1.
2959 32c **Love,** booklet single, *May 12,* Lakeville PA 1.2
2959a Booklet pane of 10 7.
2960 55c **Love,** self-adhesive, *May 12,* Lakeville PA 1.

First day cancellation was applied to 273,350 covers bearing one or more of Nos. 2957-2959, 2959a, and U637.

2965a 32c **Recreational Sports,** *May 20,* Jupiter FL 3.2
2961-2965, any single 1.5

First day cancellation was applied to 909,807 covers bearing one or more of Nos. 2961-2965, 2965a.

2966 32c **Prisoners of War & Missing in Action,** *May 29 (231,857)* 2.0
2967 32c **Marilyn Monroe,** *June 1,* Universal City CA *(703,219)* 3.0
Any other city 1.7
2968 32c **Texas Statehood,** *June 16,* Austin TX *(177,550)* 1.7
2973a 32c **Great Lakes Lighthouses booklet pane of 5,** *June 17,* Cheboygan MI 5.0
2969-2973, any single 2.0

First day cancellation was applied to 626,055 covers bearing one or more of Nos. 2969-2973, 2973a.

2974 32c **UN, 50th Anniv.,** *June 26,* San Francisco CA *(160,383)* 1.5
2975 32c **Civil War pane of 20,** *June 29,* Gettysburg PA 16.0
Any other city 16.0
2975a-2975t, any single, Gettysburg PA 1.7
Any other city 1.5

First day cancellation was applied to 1,950,134 covers bearing one or more of Nos. 2975, 2975a-2975t, and UX200-UX219.

2979a 32c **Carousel Horses,** *July 21,* Lahaska PA 3.2
2976-2979, any single 1.2

First day cancellation was applied to 479,038 covers bearing one or more of Nos. 2976-2979, 2979a.

2980 32c **Woman Suffrage,** *Aug. 26 (196,581)* 1.25
2981 32c **World War II block of 10,** *Sept. 2,* Honolulu HI 7.00
2981a-2981j, any single 1.75

First day cancellation was applied to 1,562,094 covers bearing one or more of Nos. 2981, 2981a-2981j.

2982 32c **American Music Series,** *Sept. 1,* New Orleans LA *(258,996)* 1.75
2992a 32c **American Music Series,** *Sept. 16,* Monterey CA 6.50
2983-2992, any single 1.50

First day cancellation was applied to 629,956 covers bearing one or more of Nos. 2983-2992, 2992a.

2997a 32c **Garden Flowers booklet pane of 5,** *Sept. 19,* Encinitas CA 4.00
2993-2997, any single 1.25

First day cancellation was applied to 564,905 covers bearing one or more of Nos. 2993-2997, 2997a.

2998 60c **Eddie Rickenbacker,** *Sept. 25,* Columbus OH *(24,283)* 1.75
2999 32c **Republic of Palau,** *Sept. 29,* Agana GU *(157,377)* 1.25

00	32c **Comic Strips Pane of 20,** *Oct. 1,* Boca Raton FL	13.00
	3000a-3000t, any single	2.00

First day cancellation was applied to 1,362,990 covers bearing one or more of Nos. 3000, 3000a-3000t.

01	32c **US Naval Academy,** *Oct. 10,* Annapolis, MD *(222,183)*	2.00
02	32c **Tennessee Williams,** *Oct. 13,* Clarksdale MS *(209,812)*	1.25
03	32c **Christmas Madonna,** perf 11.2, *Oct. 19*	1.25
03A	32c **Christmas, Madonna,** perf 9.8x10.9. *Oct. 19*	1.25
03Ab	Booklet pane of 10	7.25

First day cancellation was applied to 223,301 covers e or more of Nos. 3003, 3003A-3003Ab.

07a	32c **Christmas (secular) sheet,** *Sept. 30,* North Pole NY	3.25
	3004-3007, any single	1.25
07b	32c **Booklet pane of 10, 3 #3004,** etc.	7.25
07c	32c **Booklet pane of 10, 2 #3004,** etc.	7.25

First day cancellation was applied to 487,816 covers bearing e or more of Nos. 3004-3007, 3007a.

08-3011	32c **Christmas (secular) self-adhesive booklet stamps,** *Sept. 30,* North Pole NY	3.25
	3008-3011, any single	1.25
12	32c **Angel,** *Oct. 19,* Christmas FL	1.25
13	32c **Children sledding,** *Oct. 19,* Christmas FL	1.25

First day cancellation was applied to 77,675 covers bearing ne or more of Nos. 3012, 3013, 3018.

014-3017	32c **Self-adhesive coils,** *Sept. 30,* North Pole NY	2.50
	3014-3017, any single	1.25
018	32c **Self-adhesive coil,** *Oct. 19,* Christmas FL	1.25

First day cancellation was applied to 77,675 covers bearing ne or more of Nos. 3012, 3013, 3018.

023a	32c **Antique Automobiles,** *Nov. 3,* New York NY	3.00
	3019-3023, any single	1.25

First day cancellation was applied to 757,003 covers bearing ne or more of Nos. 3019-3023, 3023a.

1996

024	32c **Utah Statehood Cent.,** *Jan. 4,* Salt Lake City UT *(207,089)*	1.25
029a	32c **Garden Flowers booklet pane,** *Jan. 19,* Kennett Square PA	3.50
	3025-3029, any single	1.25

First day cancellation was applied to 876,176 covers bearing ne or more of Nos. 3025-3029, 3029a.

030	32c **Love, self-adhesive,** *Jan. 20,* New York NY	1.25

First day cancellation was applied to 57,639 covers bearing ne or more of Nos. 2920d, 3030, 3044.

1996-2000

FLORA AND FAUNA

3031	1c **Kestrel,** *Nov. 19, 1999,* New York, NY *(14,431)*	1.50
4032	2c **Red-headed woodpecker,** *Feb. 2,* Sarasota FL *(37,319)*	1.25
3033	3c **Eastern Bluebird,** *Apr. 3 (23,405)*	1.25
3036	$1 **Red Fox,** *Aug. 14, 1998*	3.50

First day cancellation was applied to 46,557 covers bearing ne or more of Nos. 3228-3229, 3036.

3044	1c **American Kestrel, coil,** *Jan. 20,* New York NY	1.25

First day cancellation was applied to 57,639 covers bearing ne or more of Nos. 2920d, 3030, 3044.

3045	2c **Red-Headed Woodpecker,** *June 22, 1999 (14,377)*	1.25
3048	20c **Blue Jay, booklet stamp, self-adhesive,** *Aug. 2,* St. Louis MO	1.25

First day cancellation was applied to 32,633 covers bearing ne or more of Nos. 3048, 3053.

3049	32c **Yellow Rose, booklet stamp, self-adhesive,** *Oct. 24,* Pasadena, CA *(7,849)*	1.25
3050	20c **Ring-necked Pheasant, booklet stamp, self-adhesive,** *July 31, 1998* Somerset NJ	1.25

First day cancellation was applied to 32,220 covers bearing ne or more of Nos. 3050, 3055.

3052	33c **Coral Pink Rose, serpentine die cut 11½x11¼,** *Aug. 13, 1999,* Indianapolis, IN	1.25
3052E	33c **Coral Pink Rose, serpentine die cut 10¾x10½,** *Apr. 7, 2000,* New York, NY *(18,709)*	1.25
3053	20c **Blue Jay, coil, self-adhesive,** *Aug. 2,* St. Louis MO	1.25

3054	32c **Yellow Rose, self-adhesive,** *Aug. 1, 1997,* Falls Church VA *(20,029)*	1.25
3055	20c **Ring-necked Pheasant,coil, self-adhesive,** *July 31, 1998* Somerset NJ	1.25

First day cancellation was applied to 32,220 covers bearing one or more of Nos. 3050, 3055.

1996

3058	32c **Ernest E. Just,** *Feb. 1 (191,360)*	1.75
3059	32c **Smithsonian, 150th anniv.,** *Feb. 7, (221,399)*	1.25
3060	32c **Chinese New Year,** *Feb. 8,* San Francisco CA *(237,451)*	1.75
3064a	32c **Pioneers of Communication,** *Feb. 22,* New York NY	2.50
	3061-3064, any single	1.25

First day cancellation was applied to 567,205 covers bearing one or more of Nos. 3061-3064, 3064a.

3065	32c **Fulbright Scholarships,** *Feb. 28,* Fayetteville AR *(227,330)*	1.25
3066	50c **Jacqueline Cochran,** *Mar. 9,* Indio CA *(30,628)*	1.75
3067	32c **Marathon,** *Apr. 11,* Boston MA *(177,050)*	2.00
3068	32c **Olympics, pane of 20,** *May 2*	13.00
	3068a-3068t, any single	1.25
	Atlanta, GA	—

Washington DC first day cancellation was applied to 1,807,316 covers bearing one or more of Nos. 3068, 3068a-3068t. Atlanta was also an official first day city, and covers postmarked there are scarce.

3069	32c **Georgia O'Keeffe,** *May 23,* Santa Fe NM *(200,522)*	1.50
3070	32c **Tennessee Statehood, Bicen.,** *May 31,* Knoxville, Memphis or Nashville TN	1.25
3071	32c **Tennessee, self-adhesive,** *May 31,* Knoxville, Memphis or Nashville TN	1.25

First day cancellation was applied to 217,281 covers bearing one or more of Nos. 3070-3071.

3076a	32c **American Indian Dances, strip of 5,** *June 7,* Oklahoma City OK	2.75
	3072-3076, any single	1.25

First day cancellation was applied to 653,057 covers bearing one or more of Nos. 3072-3076, 3076a.

3080a	32c **Prehistoric Animals,** *June 8,* Toronto, Canada	2.75
	3077-3080, any single	1.50

First day cancellation was applied to 485,929 covers bearing one or more of Nos. 3077-3080, 3080a.

3081	32c **Breast Cancer Awareness,** *June 15* (183,896)	1.25
	Any other city	1.25
3082	32c **James Dean,** *June 24,* Burbank CA *(263,593)*	2.00
3086a	32c **Folk Heroes,** *July 11,* Anaheim CA	2.75
	3083-3086, any single	1.25

First day cancellation was applied to 739,706 covers bearing one or more of Nos. 3083-3086, 3086a.

3087	32c **Centennial Olympic Games,** *July 19,* Atlanta GA *(269,056)*	1.25
3088	32c **Iowa Statehood, 150th Anniv.,** *Aug. 1,* Dubuque IA	1.25
3089	32c **Iowa Statehood, self-adhesive** *Aug. 1,* Dubuque IA	1.25
	3088, 3089, both stamps issued *Aug. 1,* Dubuque, IA	1.75

First day cancellation was applied to 215,181 covers bearing one or more of Nos. 3088-3089.

3090	32c **Rural Free Delivery,** *Aug. 7,* Charleston WV *(192,070)*	1.25
3091-3095	32c **Riverboats,** *Aug. 22,* Orlando FL	3.50
	3091-3095, any single	1.25
3095b	32c **Riverboats, special die cutting,** *Aug. 22,* Orlando FL	3.50

First day cancellation was applied to 770,384 covers bearing one or more of Nos. 3091-3095, 3095b.

3099a	32c **Big Band Leaders,** *Sept. 11,* New York NY	3.25
	3096-3099, any single	1.25

First day cancellation was applied to 1,235,166 covers bearing one or more of Nos. 3096-3103, 3099a, 3103a.

3103a	32c **Songwriters,** *Sept. 11,* New York NY	3.25
	3100-3103, any single	1.25

First day cancellation was applied to 1,235,166 covers bearing one or more of Nos. 3096-3103, 3099a, 3103a.

3104	23c **F. Scott Fitzgerald,** *Sept. 27,* St. Paul MN *(150,783)*	1.25
3105	32c **Endangered Species,** *Oct. 2,* San Diego CA	7.50
	3105a-3105o, any single	1.25

First day cancellation was applied to 941,442 covers bearing one or more of Nos. 3105, 3105a-3105o.

3106	32c **Computer Technology,** *Oct. 8,* Aberdeen Proving Ground MD *(153,688)*	1.75
3107	32c **Christmas Madonna,** *Nov. 1,* Richmond VA	1.25

First day cancellation was applied to 164,447 covers bearing one or more of Nos. 3107, 3112.

3111a	32c **Christmas (secular),** *Oct. 8,* North Pole AK	2.75
	3108-3111, any single	1.25

First day cancellation was applied to 884,339 covers bearing one or more of Nos. 3108-3111, 3111a, 3113-3117.

3112	32c **As No. 3107, self-adhesive,** *Nov. 1,* Richmond VA	1.25
3113-3116	32c **Christmas (secular), self-adhesive,** *Oct. 8,* North Pole AK	3.25
	3113-3116, any single	1.25
3117	32c **Skaters, self-adhesive,** *Oct. 8,* North Pole AK	1.25

First day cancellation was applied to 884,339 covers bearing one or more of Nos. 3108-3111, 3111a, 3113-3117.

3118	32c **Hanukkah,** *Oct. 22 (179,355)*	1.75
3119	50c **Cycling,** *Nov. 1,* New York NY	4.00
	3119a-3119b, any single	2.00

First day cancellation was applied to 290,091 covers bearing one or more of Nos. 3119, 3119a-3119b.

1997

3120	32c **Chinese New Year,** *Jan. 5,* Honolulu *(233,638)*	1.75
3121	32c **Benjamin O. Davis, Sr.,** *Jan. 28 (166,527)*	1.75
3122	32c **Statue of Liberty, self-adhesive,** *Feb. 1,* San Diego CA *(40,003)*	1.25
3123	32c **Love, Swans, self-adhesive,** *Feb. 4,* Los Angeles CA	1.25
3124	55c **Love, Swans, self-adhesive,** *Feb. 4,* Los Angeles CA	1.50

First day cancellation was applied to 257,380 covers bearing one or more of Nos. 3123-3124.

3125	32c **Helping Children Learn, self-adhesive** *Feb. 18 (175,410)*	1.25
3126	32c **Merian Botanical Prints, Citron, etc., self-adhesive, die cut 10.9x10.2,** *Mar. 3*	1.25
3127	32c **Merian Botanical Prints, Pineapple, etc., self-adhesive, die cut 10.9x10.2,** *Mar. 3*	1.25
3128	32c **Merian Botanical Prints, Citron, etc., self-adhesive, die cut 11.2x10.8,** *Mar. 3*	1.25
3128a	32c **Merian Botanical Prints, Citron, etc., self-adhesive, die cut mixed perf,** *Mar. 3*	1.25
3129	32c **Merian Botanical Prints, Pineapple, etc., self-adhesive, die cut 11.2x10.8,** *Mar. 3*	1.25
3129a	32c **Merian Botanical Prints, Pineapple, etc., self-adhesive, die cut mixed perf,** *Mar. 3*	1.25

First day cancellation was applied to 336,897 covers bearing one or more of Nos. 3126-3129, 3128a-3129a.

3131a	32c **Pacific 97,** *Mar. 13,* New York NY	1.75
	3130-3131, any single	1.25

First day cancellation was applied to 371,908 covers bearing one or more of Nos. 3130-3131, 3131a.

3132	(25c) **Juke Box, self-adhesive** *Mar. 14,* New York NY	1.25
3133	32c **Flag over Porch, Self-adhesive** *Mar. 14,* New York NY	1.25

First day cancellation was applied to 26,0820 covers bearing one or more of Nos. 3132-3133.

3134	32c **Thornton Wilder,** *Apr. 17,* Hamden CT *(157,299)*	1.25
3135	32c **Raoul Wallenberg,** *Apr. 24 (168,668)*	2.00
3136	32c **Dinosaurs, pane of 15** *May 1,* Grand Junction CO	7.50
	3136a-3136o, any single	1.25

First day cancellation was applied to 1,782,1221 covers bearing one or more of Nos. 3136, 3136a-3136o.

3137a	32c **Bugs Bunny,** *May 22,* Burbank CA *(378,142)*	2.00
3139	50c **Pacific 97, Franklin, pane of 12** *May 29,* San Francisco CA	12.00
	3139a, single	2.00
3140	60c **Pacific 97,, pane of 12,** *May 30,* San Francisco CA	12.00
	3140a, single	2.00

First day cancellation was applied to 328,401 covers bearing one or more of Nos. 3139-3140, 3139a-3140b.

3141	32c **Marshall Plan,** *June 4,* Cambridge MA *(157,622)*	1.25
3142	32c **Classic American Aircraft,** *July 19,* Dayton OH	10.00
	3142a-3142t, any single	1.25

First day cancellation was applied to 1,413,833 covers bearing one or more of Nos. 3142, 3142a-3142t.

3146a 32c **Football Coaches** *July 25,*
Canton OH 2.50
3143-3146, any single 1.50

First day cancellation was applied to 586,946 covers bearing
one or more of Nos. 3143-3146.

3147 32c **Bear Bryant,** *Aug. 5,* Green
Bay WI *(119,428)* 1.50
3148 32c **Pop Warner,** *Aug. 7,* Tusca-
loosa AL *(23,858)* 1.50
3149 32c **Vince Lombardi,** *Aug. 8,*
Philadelphia PA *(37,839)* 1.50
3150 32c **George Halas,** *Aug. 16,* Chicago IL *(26,760)* 1.50
3151 32c **American Dolls,** *July 28,*
Anaheim CA 8.00
3151a-3151o, any single 1.25

First day cancellation was applied to 831,359 covers bearing
one or more of Nos. 3151, 3151a-3151o.

3152 32c **Humphrey Bogart,** *July 31,*
Los Angeles CA *(220,254)* 1.75
3153 32c **"The Star and Stripes For-
ever,"** *Aug. 21,* Milwaukee
WI *(36,666)* 1.25
3157a 32c **Opera Singers,** *Sept. 10,*
New York NY 2.75
3154-3157, any single 1.25

First day cancellation was applied to 386,689 covers bearing
one or more of Nos. 3154-3157.

3165a 32c **Classical Composers and
Conductors,** *Sept. 12,* Cincinnati OH 5.25
3158-3165, any single 1.25

First day cancellation was applied to 424,344 covers bearing
one or more of Nos. 3158-3165.

3166 32c **Padre Felix Varela,** *Sept. 15,*
Miami FL *(120,079)* 1.25
3167 32c **Department of the Air
Force,** *Sept. 18 (178,519)* 1.50
3172a 32c **Classic Movie Monsters,**
Sept. 30, Universal City CA 3.75
3168-3172, any single 1.50

First day cancellation was applied to 476,993 covers bearing
one or more of Nos. 3168-3172.

3173 32c **First Supersonic Flight,**
Oct. 14, Edwards AFB CA
(173,778) 1.50
3174 32c **Women in Military Service,**
Oct. 18 (106,121) 1.50
3175 32c **Kwanzaa,** *Oct. 22,* Los Angeles CA *(92,489)* 1.75
3176 32c **Christmas Madonna,** *Oct.
27 (35,809)* 1.25
3177 32c **Holly,** *Oct. 30,* New York NY
(87,332) 1.25
3178 $3 **Mars Pathfinder,** *Dec. 10*
Pasadena CA *(11,699)* 9.00

1998
3179 32c **Chinese New Year,** *Jan. 5,*
Seattle WA *(234,269)* 1.75
3180 32c **Alpine Skiing,** *Jan. 22,* Salt
Lake City UT *(196,504)* 1.25
3181 32c **Madam C. J. Walker,** *Jan.
28,* Indianapolis IN
(146,348) 1.75

1998-2000
CELEBRATE THE CENTURY
3182 32c **1900s,** *Feb. 3 (11,699)* 8.50
3182a-3182o, any single 1.50
3183 32c **1910s,** *Feb. 3* 8.50
3183a-3183o, any single 1.50

First day cancellation was applied to 3,896,387 covers bearing one or more of Nos. 3182-3182o, 3183-3183o.

3184 32c **1920s,** *May 28* 8.50
3184a-3184o, any single 1.75

First day cancellation was applied to 1,057,909 covers bearing one or more of Nos. 3184-3184o.

3185 32c **1930s,** *Sept. 10,* Cleveland
OH 8.50
3185a-3185o, any single 1.75

First day cancellation was applied to 999,017 covers bearing
one or more of Nos. 3185-3185o.

3186 33c **1940s,** *Feb. 18, 1999,* Dob-
bins AFB GA 8.50
3186a-3186o, any single 1.75

First day cancellation was applied to 1,459,138 covers bearing one or more of Nos. 3186-3186o.

3187 33c **1950s,** *May 26, 1999,*
Springfield MA 8.50
3187a-3187o, any single 1.75

First day cancellation was applied to 1,454,906 covers bearing one or more of Nos. 3187-3187o.

3188 33c **1960s,** *Sept. 17, 1999,*
Green Bay, WI 8.50
3188a-3188o, any single 1.75

First day cancellation was applied to 1,252,243 covers bearing one or more of Nos. 3188-3188o.

3189 33c **1970s,** *Nov. 18, 1999,* New
York, NY 8.50
3189a-3189o, any single 1.75

First day cancellation was applied to 894,084 covers bearing
one or more of Nos. 3189-3189o.

3190 33c **1980s,** *Jan. 12, 2000,* Kennedy Space Center, FL 8.50

3190a-3190o, any single 1.75
3191 33c **1990s,** *May 2, 2000,* Escon-
dido, CA 8.50
3191a-3191o, any single 1.75

First day cancellation was applied to 1,172,962 covers bearing one or more of Nos. 3191-3190o.

1998
3192 32c **"Remember the Maine,"**
Feb. 15, Key West FL
(161,657) 1.75
3193-3197 32c **Flowering Trees,** *Mar. 19,*
New York NY 3.75
3193-3197, any single 1.50

First day cancellation was applied to 666,199 covers bearing
one or more of Nos. 3193-3197.

3202a 32c **Alexander Calder,** *Mar. 25* 3.75
3198-3202, any single 1.50

First day cancellation was applied to 588,887 covers bearing
one or more of Nos. 3198-3202, 3202a.

3203 32c **Cinco de Mayo,** *Apr. 16,*
San Antonio TX *(144,443)* 1.25
3204a 32c **Sylvester & Tweety,** *Apr. 27,*
New York NY *(213,839)* 1.25
3206 32c **Wisconsin Statehood,** *May
29,* Madison WI *(130,810)* 1.25

1998-99
3207 (5c) **Wetlands,** *June 5,* McLean
VA 1.25
3207A (5c) **Wetlands, Serpentine die
cut,** *Dec. 14* 1.25
3208 (25c) **Diner,** *June 5,* McLean VA 1.25

First day cancellation was applied to 35,333 covers bearing
one or more of Nos. 3207, 3208; 13,378 covers bearing one of
more of Nos. 3207A, 3270-3271.

3208A (25c) **Diner, Serpentine die cut,**
June 5 (13,984) 1.25

1998
1898 TRANS-MISSISSIPPI STAMPS, CENT.
3209 **Sheet of 9,** *June 18,*
Anaheim CA 6.50
3209a 1c 1.50
3209b 2c 1.50
3209d 4c 1.50
3209e 5c 1.50
3209f 8c 1.50
3209g 10c 1.50
3209h 50c 2.00
3209i $1 2.50
$2 4.50
3210 $1 **Sheet of 9,** *June 18,*
Anaheim CA 15.00

First day cancellation was applied to 203,649 covers bearing
one or more of Nos. 3209-3210, 3209a-3209i.

1998
3211 32c **Berlin Airlift,** *June 26,* Berlin, Germany *(137,894)* 1.25
3215a 32c **Folk Musicians,** *June 26* 3.25
3212-3215, any single 1.25

First day cancellation was applied to 341,015 covers bearing
one or more of Nos. 3212-3215, 3215a.

3219a 32c **Gospel Music,** *July 15,* New
Orleans LA 3.25
3216-3219, any single 1.25

First day cancellation was applied to 330,533 covers bearing
one or more of Nos. 3216-3219, 3219a.

3220 32c **Spanish Settlement of the
Southwest,** *July 11,* Espa-
ñola NM *(122,182)* 1.25
3221 32c **Stephen Vincent Benét,** *July
22,* Harpers Ferry WV
(107,412) 1.25
3225a 32c **Tropical Birds,** *July 29,* Ponce PR 3.00
3222-3225, any single 1.25

First day cancellation was applied to 371,354 covers bearing
one or more of Nos. 3222-3225, 3225a.

3226 32c **Alfred Hitchcock,** *Aug. 3,*
Los Angeles CA *(140,628)* 1.50
3227 32c **Organ & Tissue Donation,**
Aug. 5, Columbus OH
(110,601) 1.25
3228 (10c) **Modern Bicycle, Serpentine
die cut,** *Aug. 14* 1.25
3229 (10c) **Modern Bicycle,** *Aug. 14* 1.25

First day cancellation was applied to 46,557 covers bearing
one or more of Nos. 3228-3229, 3036.

3230-3234 32c **Bright Eyes,** *Aug. 20,* Boston MA 3.25
3230-3234, any single 1.75

First day cancellation was applied to 394,280 covers bearing
one or more of Nos. 3230-3234.

3235 32c **Klondike Gold Rush Cent.,**
Aug. 21, Nome or Skagway
AK *(123,559)* 1.50
3236 32c **American Art, pane of 20,**
Aug. 27, Santa Clara CA 9.00
3236a-3236t, any single 1.25

First day cancellation was applied to 924,031 covers bearing
one or more of Nos. 3236, 3236a-3236t.

3237 32c **American Ballet,** *Sept. 16,*
New York NY *(133,034)* 1.25

3242a 32c **Space Discovery,** *Oct. 1,*
Kennedy Space Center FL 3
3238-3242, any single 1

First day cancellation was applied to 399,807 covers bear
one or more of Nos. 3238-3242, 3242a.

3243 32c **Giving & Sharing,** *Oct. 7,*
Atlanta GA *(124,051)* 1
3244 32c **Christmas, Madonna,** *Oct.
15 (105,835)* 1
3245-3248 32c **Christmas, Secular,** *Oct. 15,*
Christmas MI 3
3245-3248, any single 1
3249-3252 32c **Christmas, Secular, size:
23x30mm,** *Oct. 15,* Christ-
mas MI 3
3249-3252, any single 1.

First day cancellation was applied to 328,199 covers bear
one or more of Nos. 3245-3252.

3257 (1c) **Weather Vane, white USA,**
Nov. 9, Troy NY 1.
3258 (1c) **Weather Vane, pale blue
USA,** *Nov. 9,* Troy NY 1
3259 22c **Uncle Sam,** *Nov. 9,* Troy NY 1.
3260 (33c) **Uncle Sam's Hat,** *Nov. 9,*
Troy NY 1.
3261 $3.20 **Space Shuttle Landing,**
Nov. 9, 5.
3262 $11.75 **Piggyback Space Shuttle,**
Nov. 9, New York NY
(3,703) 25.
3263 22c **Uncle Sam, coil,** *Nov. 9,*
Troy NY 1.
3264 (33c) **Uncle Sam's Hat, coil,** *Nov.
9,* Troy NY 1.
3265 (33c) **Uncle Sam's Hat, self-adhesive coil, die cut 9.9,**
round corners, Nov. 9, Troy
NY 1.
3266 (33c) **Uncle Sam's Hat, self-adhesive coil, die cut 9.9,**
square corners, Nov. 9,
Troy NY 1.
3267 (33c) **Uncle Sam's Hat, self-adhesive booklet single, die
cut 9.9** *Nov. 9,* Troy NY 1.
3268 (33c) **Uncle Sam's Hat, self-adhesive booklet single, die
cut 11.2x11.1** *Nov. 9,* Troy
NY 1.
3269 (33c) **Uncle Sam's Hat, self-adhesive booklet single, die
cut 8** *Nov. 9,* Troy NY 1.

First day cancellation was applied to 121,662 covers bearin
one or more of Nos. 2942, 3257-3261, 3263-3269.

3270 (10c) **Eagle & Shield, Presorted
Std.,** *Dec. 14* 1.
3271 (10c) **Eagle & Shield, Presorted
Std., self-adhesive,
Serpentine die cut,** *Dec.
14* 1.

First day cancellation was applied to 13,378 covers bearin
one of more of Nos. 3207A, 3270-3271.

1999
3272 33c **Chinese New Year,** *Jan. 5,*
Los Angeles CA *(151,436)* 1.7
3273 33c **Malcolm X,** *Jan. 20,* New
York NY *(107,226)* 2.0
3274 33c **Love,** *Jan. 28,* Loveland CO 1.2
3275 55c **Love,** *Jan. 28,* Loveland CO 1.5

First day cancellation was applied to 189,331 covers bearin
one or more of Nos. 3274, 3275, UX300.

3276 33c **Hospice Care,** *Feb. 9,* Largo
FL *(136,976)* 1.2
3277 33c **Flag & City,** *Feb. 25,* Orlando FL 1.2
3278 33c **Flag & City, self-adhesive,
die cut 11.1** *Feb. 25,* Orlan-
do FL 1.2
3279 33c **Flag & City, self-adhesive,
die cut 9.8** *Feb. 25,* Orlan-
do FL 1.25
3280 33c **Flag & City, coil, perf. 9.9
vert.** *Feb. 25,* Orlando FL 1.25
3281 33c **Flag & City, self-adhesive
coil, die cut 9.8 vert,
square corners,** *Feb. 25,*
Orlando FL 1.25
3282 33c **Flag & City, self-adhesive
coil, die cut 9.8 vert.,
round corners,** *Feb. 25,*
Orlando FL 1.25

First day cancellation was applied to 88,569 covers bearing
one or more of Nos. 3277-3282.

3283 33c **Flag & Blackboard, self-adhesive, die cut 7.9,** *Mar. 13*
(26,067) 1.25
3286 33c **Irish Immigration,** *Feb. 26,*
Boston MA *(127,213)* 1.50
3287 33c **Lunt & Fontanne,** *Mar. 2,*
New York NY *(120,423)* 1.25
3292a 33c **Arctic Animals,** *Mar. 12,*
Barrow AK 3.25
3288-3292, any single 1.25

First day cancellation was applied to 476,863 covers bearing
one or more of Nos. 3288-3292, 3292a.

3293 33c **Sonoran Desert, Pane of
10,** *Apr. 6,* Tucson AZ 6.75
3293a-3293j, any single 1.25

First day cancellation was applied to 410,985 covers bearing
one or more of Nos. 3293-3293j.

4-3297	33c	**Christmas Berries, die cut 11.2x11.7** *Apr. 10,* Ponchatoula LA	3.25
		3294-3297, any single	1.25
		3297e, dated 2000, *Mar. 15, 2000,* Ponchatoula LA	3.25
		3294a-3296a, 3297c, any single	1.25

First day cancellation was applied to 101,344 covers bearing one of more of Nos. 3294-3305.

8-3301	33c	**Christmas Berries, die cut 9.5x10** *Apr. 10,* Ponchatoula LA	3.25
		3298-3301, any single	1.25
2-3305	33c	**Christmas Berries, die cut 8.5 vert.** *Apr. 10,* Ponchatoula LA	3.25
		3302-3305, any single	1.25

First day cancellation was applied to 101,344 covers bearing one of more of Nos. 3294-3305.

06a	33c	**Daffy Duck,** *Apr. 16,* Los Angeles CA	1.50

First day cancellation was applied to 177,988 covers bearing ne of more of Nos. 3306-3307c, UX304.

08	33c	**Ayn Rand,** *Apr. 22,* New York NY *(123,660)*	2.00
09	33c	**Cinco de Mayo,** *Apr. 27,* San Antonio TX *(20,904)*	1.25
10-3313	33c	**Tropical Flowers,** *May 1,* Honolulu HI	3.25
		3310-3313, any single	1.25

First day cancellation was applied to 311,495 covers bearing ne of more of Nos. 3310-3313, 3313a, 3313b.

14	33c	**Bartram,** *May 18,* Philadelphia PA *(110,381)*	1.25
15	33c	**Prostate Cancer Awareness,** *July 22,* Austin TX *(113,299)*	1.25
16	33c	**California Gold Rush,** *June 18,* Sacramento CA *(123,648)*	1.25
17-3320	33c	**Aquarium Fish,** *June 24,* Anaheim CA	3.25
		3317-3320, any single	1.25

First day cancellation was applied to 301,719 covers bearing ne of more of Nos. 3317-3320, 3320a-3320c.

321-3324	33c	**Extreme Sports,** *June 25,* San Francisco CA	3.00
		3321-3324, any single	1.25

First day cancellation was applied to 278,068 covers bearing ne of more of Nos. 3321-3324, 3324a.

328a	33c	**American Glass,** *June 29,* Corning NY	3.00
		3325-3328, any single	1.25

First day cancellation was applied to 272,792 covers bearing ne of more of Nos. 3325-3328, 3328a.

329	33c	**James Cagney,** *July 22,* Burbank CA *(135,867)*	1.75
330	55c	**"Billy" Mitchell,** *July 30,* Milwaukee WI	1.50

First day cancellation was applied to 42,144 covers bearing ne of more of Nos. 3330, C134.

331	33c	**Honoring Those Who Served,** *Aug. 16,* Kansas City MO *(130,306)*	1.75
332	45c	**Universal Postal Union,** *Aug. 25,* Beijing, China *(20,371)*	1.25
337a	33c	**Famous Trains,** *Aug. 26,* Cleveland, OH	3.75
		any other city	3.75
		#3333-3337, any single, Cleveland, OH	1.50
		#3333-3337, any single, any other city	1.50

First day cancellation was applied to 518,446 covers bearing ne of more of Nos. 3333-3337, 3337a, UX307-UX311a.

3338	33c	**Frederick Law Olmsted,** *Sept. 12,* Boston, MA *(109,735)*	1.25
3344a	33c	**Hollywood Composers,** *Sept. 16,* Los Angeles, CA	3.75
		#3339-3344, any single, Los Angeles, CA	1.25

First day cancellation was applied to 287,407 covers bearing one of more of Nos. 3339-3344, 3344a.

3350a	33c	**Broadway Songwriters,** *Sept. 21,* New York, NY	3.75
		#3345-3350, any single, New York, NY	1.25

First day cancellation was applied to 284,840 covers bearing one of more of Nos. 3345-3350, 3350a.

3351	33c	**Insects & Spiders,** *Oct. 1,* Indianapolis, IN	10.00
		#3351a-3351t, any single	1.25

First day cancellation was applied to 773,590 covers bearing one of more of Nos. 3351-3351t.

3352	33c	**Hanukkah,** *Oct. 8,* Washington, DC	1.50
3353	22c	**Uncle Sam perforated coil,** *Oct. 8,* Washington, DC	1.25

First day cancellation was applied to 44,534 covers bearing one of more of Nos. 3352-3353, O157.

3354	33c	**NATO,** *Oct. 13,* Brussels, Belgium *(110,415)*	1.25
3355	33c	**Christmas Madonna,** *Oct. 20,* Washington, DC *(110,460)*	1.25

3356-3359	33c	**Christmas Deer, narrow frame (sheet),** *Oct. 20,* Rudolph, WI	3.00
		3356-3359, any single	1.25
3360-3363	33c	**Christmas Deer, thick frame (booklet),** *Oct. 20,* Rudolph, WI	3.00
		3360-3363, any single	1.25
3364-3367	33c	**Christmas Deer, smaller size (booklet),** *Oct. 20,* Rudolph, WI	3.00
		3364-3367, any single	1.25

First day cancellation was applied to 239,350 covers bearing one of more of Nos. 3356-3367, 3359a, 3363a, 3367a-3367c.

3368	33c	**Kwanzaa,** *Oct. 29,* Los Angeles, CA *(20,493)*	1.75
3369	33c	**Year 2000,** *Dec. 27,* Washington, DC *(145,928)*	1.25

2000

3370	33c	**Chinese New Year,** *Jan. 6,* San Francisco, CA *(155,586)*	1.75
3371	33c	**Patricia Roberts Harris,** *Jan. 27,* Washington, DC *(82,211)*	1.75
3372	33c	**Los Angeles Class Submarine, with microprinting,** *Mar. 27,* Groton, CT	1.50
3373	22c	**S Class Submarine,** *Mar. 27,* Groton, CT	1.50
3374	33c	**Los Angeles Class Submarine, no microprinting,** *Mar. 27,* Groton, CT	1.50
3375	55c	**Ohio Class Submarine,** *Mar. 27,* Groton, CT	1.75
3376	60c	**USS Holland,** *Mar. 27,* Groton, CT	1.75
3377	$3.20	**Gato Class Submarine,** *Mar. 27,* Groton, CT	6.00
		3377a, Booklet pane of 5, #3373-3377, either selvage	8.00

First day cancellation was applied to 265,226 covers bearing one of more of Nos. 3372-3377, 3377a.

3378	33c	**Pacific Coast Rain Forest Pane of 10,** *Mar. 29,* Seattle, WA	6.75
		3378a-3378j, any single	1.25

First day cancellation was applied to 435,549 covers bearing one of more of Nos. 3378-3378j.

3383a	33c	**Louise Nevelson,** *Apr. 6,* New York, NY	3.25
		3379-3383, any single	1.25

First day cancellation was applied to 389,200 covers bearing one of more of Nos. 3379-3383, 3383a.

3388a	33c	**Hubble Space Telescope,** *Apr. 10,* Greenbelt, MD	3.25
		3384-3388, any single	1.25

First day cancellation was applied to 411,449 covers bearing one of more of Nos. 3384-3388, 3388a.

3389	33c	**American Samoa,** *Apr. 17,* Pago Pago, AS *(107,346_*	1.25
3390	33c	**Library of Congress,** *Apr. 24,* Washington, DC *(115,679)*	1.25
3391a	33c	**Road Runner & Wile E. Coyote,** *Apr. 26,* Phoenix, AZ	1.25

First day cancellation was applied to 154,903 covers bearing one of more of Nos. 3391-3392, 3391a-3391c, 3392a-3392c.

3396a	33c	**Distinguished Soldiers,** *May 3,* Washington, DC	3.25
		Any other city	3.25
		3393-3396, any single, Washington, DC	1.50
		Any other city	1.25

First day cancellation was applied to 322,278 covers bearing one of more of Nos. 3393-3396, 3396a.

3397	33c	**Summer Sports,** *May 5,* Spokane, WA *(110,768)*	1.25
3398	33c	**Adoption,** *May 10,* Beverly Hills, CA	1.25

First day cancellation was applied to 137,903 covers bearing one of more of Nos. 3398, UX315.

3402a	33c	**Youth Team Sports,** *May 27,* Lake Buena Vista, FL	3.25
		3399-3402, any single	1.25

First day cancellation was applied to 309,349 covers bearing one of more of Nos. 3399-3402, 3402a.

3403	33c	**The Stars and Stripes, pane of 20,** *June 14,* Baltimore, MD	10.00
		3403a-3403t, any single	1.25

First day cancellation was applied to 1,121,071 covers bearing one of more of Nos. 3403-3403t.

3404-3407	33c	**Berries, die cut 8½ horiz.,** *June 16,* Buffalo, NY	3.25
		3404-3707, any single	1.25

First day cancellation was applied to 35,671 covers bearing one of more of Nos. 3404-3407, 3407a.

3408	33c	**Legends of Baseball, pane of 20,** *July 6,* Atlanta, GA	10.00
		3408a-3708t, any single	1.50

First day cancellation was applied to 1,214,413 covers bearing one of more of Nos. 3408-3408t.

3409	60c	**Probing the Vastness of Space,** *July 10,* Anaheim, CA	6.00
		3409a-3409f, any single	1.50

First day cancellation was applied to 296,252 covers bearing one of more of Nos. 3409-3409f.

3410	$1	**Exploring the Solar System,** *July 11,* Anaheim, CA	9.00
		3410a-3410e, any single	2.00

First day cancellation was applied to 49,500 covers bearing one of more of Nos. 3410-3410e.

3411	$3.20	**Escaping the Gravity of Earth,** *July 9,* Anaheim, CA	9.50
		3411a-3411b, any single	3.75

First day cancellation was applied to 22,321 covers bearing one of more of Nos. 3411-3411b.

3412	$11.75	**Space Achievement and Exploration,** *July 7,* Anaheim, CA *(12,070)*	17.50
3413	$11.75	**Landing on the Moon,** *July 8,* Anaheim, CA *(11,639)*	17.50
3414-3417	33c	**Stampin' The Future,** *July 13,* Anaheim, CA	3.25
		3414-3417, any single	1.25

First day cancellation was applied to 294,434 covers bearing one of more of Nos. 3414-3417, 3417a.

Distinguished Americans Issue 2000-2004

3420	10c	**Joseph W. Stilwell,** *Aug. 24,* Providence, RI *(21,669)*	1.50
3422	23c	**Wilma Rudolph, litho. & engr.** *July 14, 2004,* Sacramento, CA	1.25
3426	33c	**Claude Pepper,** *Sept. 7,* Washington, DC *(60,689)*	1.25
3428	63c	**Dr. Jonas Salk,** *Mar. 8,* Washington, DC	2.50
		Any other city	2.50
3431	76c	**Hattie Caraway,** *Feb. 21, 2001,* Little Rock, AR	1.75
3433	83c	**Edna Ferber,** *July 29, 2002,* Appleton, WI	1.75
3435	87c	**Dr. Albert Sabin,** *Mar. 8,* Washington, DC	3.00
		Any other city	3.00
3436	23c	**Wilma Rudolph, litho. booklet stamp** *July 14, 2004,* Sacramento, CA	1.25
3438	33c	**California Statehood,** *Sept. 8,* Sacramento, CA *(119,729)*	1.25
3443a	33c	**Deep Sea Creatures,** *Oct. 2,* Monterey, CA	3.75
		#3439-3443, any single	1.25

First day cancellation was applied to 385,406 covers bearing one of more of Nos. 3439-3443, 3443a.

3444	33c	**Thomas Wolfe,** *Oct. 3,* Asheville, NC *(112,293)*	1.25
3445	33c	**White House,** *Oct. 18,* Washington, DC *(135,844)*	1.25
3446	33c	**Edward G. Robinson,** *Oct. 24,* Los Angeles, CA *(120,125)*	1.50
3447	(10c)	**New York Public Library Lion,** *Nov. 9,* New York, NY *(18,477)*	1.25
3448	(34c)	**Flag Over Farm, perf,** *Dec. 15,* Washington, DC	1.25
3449	(34c)	**Flag Over Farm, litho. self-adhesive,** *Dec. 15,* Washington, DC	1.25
3450	(34c)	**Flag Over Farm, photo. self-adhesive,** *Dec. 15,* Washington, DC	1.25
3451	(34c)	**Statue of Liberty, booklet stamp,** *Dec. 15,* Washington, DC	1.25
3452	(34c)	**Statue of Liberty perforated coil,** *Dec. 15,* Washington, DC	1.25
3453	(34c)	**Statue of Liberty self-adhesive coil,** *Dec. 15,* Washington, DC	1.25
3454-3457	(34c)	**Flowers, booklet stamps die cut 10¾x10¾,** *Dec. 15,* Washington, DC	3.25
		3454-3457, any single	1.25
3458-3461	(34c)	**Flowers, booklet stamps die cut 11½x11¾,** *Dec. 15,* Washington, DC	3.25
		3458-3461, any single	1.25
3462-3465	(34c)	**Flowers, coil stamps,** *Dec. 15,* Washington, DC	3.25
		3462-3465, any single	1.25

First day cancellation was applied to 178,635 covers bearing one of more of Nos. 3448-3465, 3450a, 3451a-3451d, 3457a-3457e, 3461a-3461c, 3465a.

2001

3466	34c	**Statue of Liberty coil (rounded corners),** *Jan. 7,* Washington, DC	1.25
3467	21c	**American Buffalo, perforated sheet stamp,** *Sept. 20,* Washington, DC	1.25
3468	21c	**American Buffalo, perforated sheet stamp,** *Feb. 22,* Wall, SD	1.25
3468A	23c	**George Washington, sheet stamp,** *Sept. 20,* Washington, DC	1.25
3469	34c	**Flag Over Farm, perforated sheet stamp,** *Feb. 7,* New York, NY	1.25
3470	34c	**Flag Over Farm, self-adhesive sheet stamp,** *Mar. 6,* Lincoln, NE	1.25
3471	55c	**Eagle,** *Feb. 22,* Wall, SD	1.50
3471A	57c	**Eagle,** *Sept. 20,* Washington, DC	1.50
3472	$3.50	**Capitol Dome,** *Jan. 29,* Washington, DC	6.25
3473	$12.25	**Washington Monument,** *Jan. 29,* Washington, DC	15.00

3475	21c **American Buffalo coil stamp,** *Feb. 22,* Wall, SD	1.25
3475A	23c **George Washington, coil stamp,** *Sept. 20,* Washington, DC	1.25
3476	34c **Statue of Liberty, perforated coil stamp,** *Feb. 7,* New York, NY	1.25
3477	34c **Statue of Liberty coil stamp (right angle corners),** *Feb. 7,* New York, NY	1.25
3478-3481	34c **Flower coil stamps,** *Feb. 7,* New York, NY	3.25
	3478-3481, any single	1.25

Serpentine Die Cut 11¼

3482	20c **George Washington booklet stamp,** *Feb. 22,* Wall, SD	1.25

Serpentine Die Cut 10½x11¼

3483	21c **George Washington booklet stamp,** *Feb. 22,* Wall, SD	1.25
3484	21c **American Buffalo, booklet stamp, serp. die cut 11¼,** *Sept. 20,* Washington, DC	1.25
3484A	21c **American Buffalo, booklet stamp, serp. die cut 10½x11¼,** *Sept. 20,* Washington, DC	1.25
3485	34c **Statue of Liberty booklet stamp,** *Feb. 7,* New York, NY	1.25
3487-3490	34c **Flower booklet stamps,** *Feb. 7,* New York, NY	3.25
	3487-3490, any single	1.25
3491-3492	34c **Apple & Orange booklet stamps,** *Feb. 7,* Lincoln, NE	2.25
	3491-3492, any single	1.25
3495	34c **Flag Over Farm, booklet stamp,** *Dec. 17,* Washington, DC	1.25
3496	(34c) **Love Letter,** *Jan. 19,* Tucson, AZ	1.25
3497	34c **Love Letters,** *Feb. 14,* Lovejoy, GA	1.25

Serpentine Die Cut 11½x10¾

3498	34c **Love Letters, die cut 11½x10¾,** *Feb. 14,* Lovejoy, GA	1.25
3499	55c **Love Letter,** *Feb. 14,* Lovejoy, GA	1.50
3500	34c **Chinese New Year,** *Jan. 20,* Oakland, CA	1.75
3501	34c **Roy Wilkins,** *Jan. 24,* Minneapolis, MN	1.25
3502	34c **American Illustrators pane of 20,** *Feb. 1,* New York, NY	9.50
	3502a-3502t, any single	1.25
3503	34c **Diabetes Awareness,** *Mar. 16,* Boston, MA	1.25
3504	34c **Nobel Prize Centenary,** *Mar. 22,* Washington, DC	1.50
3505	**Pan-American Inverts Pane,** *Mar. 29,* New York, NY	6.00
3505a	1c	1.25
3505b	2c	1.25
3505c	4c	1.25
3505d	80c	1.75
3506	34c **Great Plains Prairie Pane of 10,** *Apr. 19,* Lincoln, NE	7.00
3507	34c **Peanuts,** *May 17,* Santa Rosa, CA	1.50
3508	34c **Honoring Veterans,** *May 23,* Washington, DC	2.00
	Any other city	1.25
3509	34c **Frida Kahlo,** *June 21,* Phoenix, AZ	1.25
3519a	34c **Legendary Playing Fields,** *June 27,* New York, NY, Boston, MA, Chicago, IL or Detroit, MI	
	3510-3519, any single, New York, NY, Boston, MA, Chicago, IL or Detroit, MI	6.50
3520	(10c) **Atlas Statue,** *June 29,* New York, NY	1.50
3521	34c **Leonard Bernstein,** *July 10,* New York, NY	1.25
3522	(15c) **Woody Wagon,** *Aug. 3,* Denver, CO	1.25
3523	34c **Lucille Ball,** *Aug. 6,* Los Angeles, CA	1.75
3527a	34c **Amish Quilts,** *Aug. 9,* Nappanee, IN	3.25
	3524-3527, any single	1.25
3531a	34c **Carniverous Plants,** *Aug. 23,* Des Plaines, IL	3.25
	3528-3531, any single	1.25
3532	34c **Eid** *Sept. 1,* Des Plaines, IL	1.25
3533	34c **Enrico Fermi,** *Sept. 29,* Chicago, IL	1.25
3534a	34c **That's All Folks!,** *Oct. 1,* Beverly Hills, CA	1.25
3536	34c **Christmas, Madonna,** *Oct. 10,* Philadelphia, PA	1.25
3537-3540	34c **Christmas, Santas, black inscriptions, large date** *Oct. 10,* Santa Claus, IN	3.25
	3537-3540, any single	1.25
	3537a-3540a, small date (from booklet)	3.25
	3537a-3540a, any single	1.25
3541-3544	34c **Christmas, Santas, green and red inscriptions,** *Oct. 10,* Santa Claus, IN	3.25
	3541-3544, any single	1.25
3545	34c **James Madison,** *Oct. 18,* New York, NY	1.25
3546	34c **Thanksgiving,** *Oct. 19,* Dallas, TX	1.25
3547	34c **Hanukkah,** *Oct. 21,* New York, NY	1.25
3548	34c **Kwanzaa,** *Oct. 21,* New York, NY	1.25
3549	34c **United We Stand,** *Oct. 24,* Washington, DC	1.50
3549B	34c **United We Stand,** serpentine die cut 10½x10¾ booklet stamp *Oct. 24,* Washington, DC	

2002

3552-3555	34c **Winter Sports,** *Jan. 8,* Park City, UT	3.25
	3552-3555, any single	1.25
3556	34c **Mentoring a Child,** *Jan. 10,* Annapolis, MD	1.25
3557	34c **Langston Hughes,** *Feb. 1,* New York, NY	1.25
3558	34c **Happy Birthday,** *Feb. 8,* Riverside, CA	1.25
3559	34c **Chinese New Year,** *Feb. 11,* New York, NY	1.50
3560	34c **U.S. Military Academy Bicent.,** *Mar. 16,* West Point, NY	1.50
3610a	34c **Greetings from America Pane,** *Apr. 4,* New York, NY	32.50
	3561-3610, Any single, New York, NY	1.25
	3610a, Any other city	32.50
	3561-3610, Any single, any other city	1.50
	3561-3610, any state capital	1.75
3611	34c **Longleaf Pine Forest Pane of 10,** *Apr. 26,* Tallahassee, FL	7.00
	3611a-3611j, any single	1.25
3612	5c **Toleware Coffeepot,** *May 31,* McLean, VA	1.25
3613	3c **Litho. Star sheet stamp,** *June 7,* Washington, DC	1.25
	Any other city	1.25
3614	3c **Photo. Star sheet stamp,** *June 7,* Washington, DC	1.25
	Any other city	1.25
3615	3c **Star coil stamp,** *June 7,* Washington, DC	1.25
3616	23c **George Washington,** water-activated gum sheet stamp, *June 7,* Washington, DC	1.00
3617	23c **George Washington,** gray green coil stamp, *June 7,* Washington, DC	1.00
3618	23c **George Washington,** booklet stamp, serp. die cut 11¼ on 3 sides, *June 7,* Washington, DC	1.00
3620	(37c) **Flag,** water-activated gum sheet stamp, *June 7,* Washington, DC	1.25
	Any other city	1.25
3621	(37c) **Flag,** self-adhesive sheet stamp, serp. die cut 11¼x11, *June 7,* Washington, DC	1.25
	Any other city	1.25
3622	(37c) **Flag,** coil stamp, *June 7,* Washington, DC	1.25
	Any other city	1.25
3623	(37c) **Flag,** booklet stamp, serp. die cut 11¼ on 2, 3 or 4 sides, *June 7,* Washington, DC	1.25
	Any other city	1.25
3624	(37c) **Flag,** booklet stamp, serp. die cut 10½x10¾ on 2 or 3 sides, *June 7,* Washington, DC	1.25
	Any other city	1.25
3625	(37c) **Flag,** booklet stamp, serp. die cut 8 on 2, 3 or 4 sides, *June 7,* Washington, DC	1.25
	Any other city	1.25
3626-3629	(37c) **Antique Toys,** booklet stamps, *June 7,* Washington, DC	3.25
	Any other city	3.25
	3626-3629, any single	1.25
	3626-3629, any single, any other city	1.25
3629F	37c **Flag,** perf. 11¼, *Nov. 24,* Washington, DC	1.25
3630	37c **Flag,** self-adhesive sheet stamp, serp. die cut 11¼x11, *June 7,* Washington, DC	1.25
	Any other city	1.25
3631	37c **Flag,** water-activated gum coil stamp, *June 7,* Washington, DC	1.25
3632	37c **Flag,** self-adhesive coil stamp, serp. die cut 10 vert., *June 7,* Washington, DC	1.25
3632A	37c **Flag coil, lacking star points at top** *Aug. 7, 2003* Columbus, OH	—
3633	37c **Flag,** self-adhesive coil stamp, serp. die cut 8½ vert., *June 7,* Washington, DC	1.25
3634	37c **Flag,** self-adhesive booklet stamps, serp. die cut 11 on 3 sides, *June 7,* Washington, DC	1.25
3635	37c **Flag,** booklet stamp, serp. die cut 11¼ on 2, 3 or 4 sides, *June 7,* Washington, DC	1.25
3636	37c **Flag,** booklet stamp, serp. die cut 10½x10¾ on 2 or 3 sides, *June 7,* Washington, DC	1.25
3637	37c **Flag,** booklet stamp, serp. die cut 8 on 2, 3 or 4 sides, *Feb. 4, 2003* Washington, DC	1.25
3638-3641	37c **Antique Toys coil stamps,** *July 26,* Rochester, NY	3.25
	3638-3641, any single	1.25
3642-3645	37c **Antique Toys booklet stamps,** *July 26,* Rochester, NY	3.25
	3642-3645, any single	1.25
3642a-3645f	37c **Antique Toys,** booklet stamps, serp. die cut 11x11¼ on 2 or 3 sides, *Sept. 3,* Washington, DC	3.25
	3642a-3645f, any single	1.25
3646	60c **Coverlet Eagle,** *July 12,* Oak Brook, IL	1.50
3647	$3.85 **Jefferson Memorial,** *July 30,* Washington, DC	7.00
	Any other city	7.00

3648	$13.65 **Capitol Dome,** *July 30,* Washington, DC	25
	Any other city	25
3649	37c **Masters of American Photography,** *June 13,* San Diego, CA	10
	3649a-3649t, any single	
3650	37c **John James Audubon,** *June 27,* Santa Clara, CA	1
3651	37c **Harry Houdini,** *July 3,* New York, NY	1
3652	37c **Andy Warhol,** *Aug. 9,* Pittsburgh, PA	1
3653-3656	37c **Teddy Bears,** *Aug. 15,* Atlantic City, NJ	3
	3653-3656, any single	1
3657	37c **Love,** *Aug. 16,* Atlantic City, NJ	1
3658	60c **Love,** *Aug. 16,* Atlantic City, NJ	1
3659	37c **Ogden Nash,** *Aug. 19,* Baltimore, MD	1
3660	37c **Duke Kahanamoku,** *Aug. 24,* Honolulu, HI	1
3661-3664	37c **American Bats,** *Sept. 13,* Austin, TX	3
	3661-3664, any single	1
3665-3668	37c **Women in Journalism,** *Sept. 14,* Fort Worth, TX	3
	3665-3668, any single	1
3669	37c **Irving Berlin,** *Sept. 15,* New York, NY	1
3670-3671	37c **Neuter and Spay,** *Sept. 20,* Washington, DC	2
	Any other city	2
	3670-3671, either single, Washington, DC	1.
	3670-3671, either single, any other city	1.
3672	37c **Hanukkah,** *Oct. 10,* Washington, DC	1
3673	37c **Kwanzaa,** *Oct. 10,* Washington, DC	1
3674	37c **Eid,** *Oct. 10,* Washington, DC	1
3675	37c **Christmas Madonna,** design size 19x27mm, *Oct. 10,* Chicago, IL	1
3676-3679	37c **Christmas Snowmen,** serp. die cut 11 (sheet stamps), *Oct. 28,* Houghton, MI	3.
	3676-3679, any single	1.
3680-3683	37c **Christmas Snowmen,** serp. die cut 8½ vert. (coil stamps), *Oct. 28,* Houghton, MI	3.
	3680-3683, any single	1.
3684-3687	37c **Christmas Snowmen,** serp. die cut 10¾x11 on 2 or 3 sides (large booklet stamps), *Oct. 28,* Houghton, MI	3.
	3684-3687, any single	1.
3688-3691	37c **Christmas Snowmen,** serp. die cut 11 on 2 or 3 sides (small booklet stamps), *Oct. 28,* Houghton, MI	3.
	3688-3691, any single	1.
3692	37c **Cary Grant,** *Oct. 15,* Los Angeles, CA	1.
3693	(5c) **Sea Coast,** *Oct. 21,* Washington, DC	1.
3694	37c **Hawaiian Missionary Stamps sheet,** *Oct. 24,* New York, NY	3.
	3694a-3694d, any single	1.
3695	37c **Happy Birthday,** *Oct. 25,* New York, NY	1.

2003

3745a	37c **Greetings From America,** *Oct. 25,* New York, NY	35.0
	3696-3745, any single	1.
	3696-3745, any state capital	1.5
3746	37c **Thurgood Marshall,** *Jan. 7,* Washington, DC	1.
3747	37c **Chinese New Year,** *Jan. 15,* Chicago, IL	1.5
3748	37c **Zora Neale Hurston,** *Jan. 24,* Eatonville, FL	1.
3749	2c **Navajo Necklace,** *Aug. 20, 2004,* Indianapolis, IN	1.
3749A	2c **Navajo Necklace,** photo., serpentine die cut 11¼x11½, *Dec. 8, 2005* Washington, DC	2.0
	Any other city	2.0
3749B	2c **Navajo Necklace,** litho., serpentine die cut 11¼x11, *Dec. 8, 2005* Washington, DC	2.0
	Any other city	2.0
3750	4c **Chippendale Chair,** *Mar. 5, 2004,* New York, NY	1.2
3750A	5c **Toleware, serpentine die cut 11¼x11¾,** *June 25, 2004* Santa Clara, CA	1.2
3751	10c **American Clock,** *Jan. 24,* Tucson, AZ	1.2

American Design Series

3757	1c **Tiffany Lamp Coil,** *Mar. 1,* Biloxi, MS	1.25
3759	3c **Silver Coffeepot,** *Sept. 16, 2005,* Milwaukee, WI	2.00

American Culture Series

3766	$1 **Wisdom,** *Feb. 28,* Biloxi, MS	2.50
3769	(10c) **New York Public Library Lion,** perf. 10 vert., *Feb. 4,* Washington, DC	1.25
3771	80c **Special Olympics,** *Feb. 13,* Chicago, IL	1.75
3772	37c **American Filmmaking: Behind the Scenes Pane of 10,** *Feb. 25,* Beverly Hills, CA	7.25
	3772a-3772j, any single	1.25
3773	37c **Ohio Statehood Bicentennial,** *Mar. 1,* Chillicothe, OH	1.25
3774	37c **Pelican Island National Wildlife Refuge, Cent.,** *Mar. 14,* Sebastian, FL	1.25

'75	(5c)	**Sea Coast,** perf. 9¾ vert. *Mar. 19,* Washington, DC	1.25
'76-3780	37c	**Old Glory,** *Apr. 3,* New York, NY	4.00
		3776-3780, any single	1.25
'81	37c	**Cesar E. Chavez,** *Apr. 23,* Los Angeles, CA	1.25
'82	37c	**Louisiana Purchase, Bicent.,** *Apr. 30,* New Orleans, LA	1.25
'83	37c	**First Flight,** *May 22,* Dayton, OH or Kill Devil Hills, NC	1.25
'84	37c	**Purple Heart,** *May 30,* Mount Vernon, VA	1.50
'84A	37c	**Purple Heart, serpentine die cut 10¾x10¼,** *Aug. 1,* Somerset, NJ	—
'86	37c	**Audrey Hepburn,** *June 11,* Los Angeles, CA	1.50
'87-3791	37c	**Southeastern Lighthouses,** *June 13,* Tybee Island, GA	4.00
		3787, 3788a, 3789-3791, Tybee Island, GA	4.00
		3787-3791, 3788a, any single	1.25
'792-3801	(25c)	**Eagle coils,** *June 26,* Santa Clara, CA	6.00
		3792-3801, any single	1.25
'792a-3801b	(25c)	**Eagle coil dated "2005",** *Aug. 5,* Grand Rapids, MI	6.00
		3792a-3801b, any single	1.25
'802	37c	**Arctic Tundra,** *July 2,* Fairbanks, AK	7.50
		3802a-3802j, any single	1.25
'803	37c	**Korean War Veterans Memorial,** *July 27,* Washington, DC	1.50
'804-3807	37c	**Mary Cassatt booklet stamps,** *Aug. 7,* Columbus, OH	3.25
		3804-3807, any single	1.25
'808-3811	37c	**Early Football Heroes,** *Aug. 8,* South Bend, IN	3.25
		3808-3811, any single	1.25
'812	37c	**Roy Acuff,** *Sept. 13,* Nashville, TN	1.25
'813	37c	**District of Columbia,** *Sept. 23,* Washington, DC	1.25
'814-3818	37c	**Reptiles and Amphibians,** *Oct. 7,* San Diego, CA	4.00
		3814-3818, any single, San Diego, CA	1.25
'820	37c	**Christmas Madonna,** design size 19½x28mm, *Oct. 23,* New York, NY	1.25
'821-3824	37c	**Christmas Music Makers (sheet stamps),** serp. die cut 11x11¼, *Oct. 23,* New York, NY	3.25
		3821-3824, any single	1.25
'825-3828	37c	**Christmas Music Makers (vending machine booklet stamps),** serp. die cut 11¾x11 on 3 sides, *Oct. 23,* New York, NY	3.25
		3825-3828, any single	1.25
'829	37c	**Snowy Egret coil,** *Oct. 24,* New York, NY	1.25

2004

3830	37c	**Snowy Egret booklet stamp,** *Jan. 30,* Norfolk, VA	1.25
3831	37c	**Pacific Coral Reef,** *Jan. 2,* Honolulu, HI	7.50
		3831a-3831j, any single	1.25
3832	37c	**Chinese New Year,** *Jan. 13,* San Francisco, CA	1.50
3833	37c	**Love Candy Hearts,** *Jan. 14,* Revere, MA	1.25
3834	37c	**Paul Robeson,** *Jan. 20,* Princeton, NJ	1.25
3835	37c	**Theodor Seuss Geisel (Dr. Seuss),** *Mar. 2,* La Jolla, CA	1.25
3836	37c	**Flowers,** *Mar. 4,* New York, NY	1.25
3837	60c	**Flowers,** *Mar. 4,* New York, NY	1.50
3838	37c	**U.S. Air Force Academy,** *Apr. 1,* Colorado Springs, CO	1.50
3839	37c	**Henry Mancini,** *Apr. 13,* Los Angeles, CA	1.25
3840-3843	37c	**American Choreographers,** *May 4,* Newark, NJ	3.25
		3840-3843, any single	1.25
3844-3853	(25c)	**Eagle coils,** perf. 9¾ vert. *May 12,* Washington, DC	6.00
		3844-3853, any single	1.25
3854	37c	**Lewis & Clark,** *May 14,* Astoria, OR	1.50
		Atchison, KS	1.50
		Great Falls, MT	1.50
		Hartford, IL	1.50
		Ilwaco, WA	1.50
		Orofino, ID	1.50
		Omaha, NE	1.50
		Pierre, SD	1.50
		Sioux City, IA	1.50
		St. Charles, MO	1.50
		Washburn, ND	1.50
3855-3856	37c	**Lewis & Clark booklet stamps,** *May 14,* Astoria, OR	2.40
		Atchison, KS	2.40
		Great Falls, MT	2.40
		Hartford, IL	2.40
		Ilwaco, WA	2.40
		Orofino, ID	2.40
		Omaha, NE	2.40
		Pierre, SD	2.40
		Sioux City, IA	2.40
		St. Charles, MO	2.40
		Washburn, ND	2.40
		3855-3856, any single, any of the aforementioned 11 cities	1.40
3857-3861	37c	**Isamu Noguchi,** *May 18,* Long Island City, NY	4.00
		3857-3861, any single	1.25
3862	37c	**National World War II Memorial,** *May 29,* Washington, DC	1.50
		Any other city	1.50

3863	37c	**Summer Olympics,** *June 9,* Philadelphia, PA	1.25
3864	(5c)	**Sea Coast coil with black 2004 date,** *June 11,* Washington, DC	1.25
3865-3868	37c	**Disney Characters,** *June 23,* Anaheim, CA	3.25
		3865-3868, any single	1.25
3869	37c	**U.S.S. Constellation,** *June 30,* Baltimore, MD	1.25
3870	37c	**R. Buckminster Fuller,** *July 12,* Stanford, CA	1.25
3871	37c	**James Baldwin,** *July 23,* New York, NY	1.25
3872	37c	**Martin Johnson Heade,** *Aug. 12,* Sacramento, CA	1.25
3873	37c	**Art of the American Indian pane of 10,** *Aug. 21,* Santa Fe, NM	7.00
		3873a-3873j, any single, Santa Fe, NM	1.25
3876	37c	**John Wayne,** *Sept. 9,* Los Angeles, CA	1.50
3877	37c	**Sickle Cell Disease,** *Sept. 29,* Atlanta, GA	1.25
3878	37c	**Cloudscapes,** *Oct. 4,* Milton, MA	9.00
		3878a-3878o any single	1.25
3879	37c	**Christmas Madonna,** *Oct. 14,* New York, NY	1.25
3880	37c	**Hanukkah,** *Oct. 15,* New York, NY	1.25
3881	37c	**Kwanzaa,** *Oct. 16,* Chicago, IL	1.25
3882	37c	**Moss Hart,** *Oct. 25,* New York, NY	1.25
3883-3886	37c	**Christmas Santa Ornaments,** serpentine die cut 11½x11, *Nov. 16,* New York, NY	3.25
		3883-3886, any single	1.25
3887-3890	37c	**Christmas Santa Ornaments,** serpentine die cut 10¾x10¾ on 2 or 3 sides, *Nov. 16,* New York, NY	3.25
		3887-3890, any single	1.25
3891-3894	37c	**Christmas Santa Ornaments,** serpentine die cut 8 on 2, 3 or 4 sides, *Nov. 16,* New York, NY	3.25
		3891-3894, any single	1.25

2005

3895	37c	**Chinese New Year double-sided pane,** *Jan. 6,* Honolulu, HI	20.00
		3895a-3895l, any single	1.25
3896	37c	**Marian Anderson,** *Jan. 27,* Washington, DC	1.25
3897	37c	**Ronald Reagan,** *Feb. 9,* Simi Valley, CA	1.25
		Any other city	1.25
3898	37c	**Love,** *Feb. 18,* Atlanta, GA	1.25
3899	37c	**Northeast Deciduous Forest,** *Mar. 3,* New York, NY	7.50
		3899a-3899j, any single	1.25
3900-3903	37c	**Spring Flowers,** *Mar. 15,* Chicago, IL	3.25
		3900-3903, any single	1.25
3904	37c	**Robert Penn Warren,** *Apr. 22,* Guthrie, KY	1.25
3905	37c	**Yip Harburg,** *Apr. 28,* New York, NY	1.25
3906-3909	37c	**American Scientists,** *May 4,* New Haven, CT	3.25
		3906-3909, any single	1.25
3910	37c	**Modern American Architecture,** *May 19,* Las Vegas NV	9.00
		Any other city	9.00
		3910a-3910l, any single, Las Vegas, NV	1.25
		3910a-3910l, any single, any other city	1.25
3911	37c	**Henry Fonda,** *May 20,* Los Angeles, CA	1.25
3912-3915	37c	**Disney Characters,** *June 30,* Anaheim, CA	3.25
		3912-3915, any single	1.25
3916-3925	37c	**Advances in Aviation,** *July 29,* Oshkosh, WI	7.50
		3916-3925, Vienna, VA	7.50
		3916-3925, any single, Oshkosh, WI	1.25
		3916-3925, any single, Vienna, VA	1.25
3926-3929	37c	**Rio Grande Blankets,** *July 30,* Santa Fe, NM	3.25
		3926-3929, any single	1.25
3930	37c	**Presidential Libraries Act, 50th Anniv.,** *Aug. 4,* Grand Rapids, MI	1.25
		Abilene, KS	1.25
		Ann Arbor, MI	1.25
		Atlanta, GA	1.25
		Austin, TX	1.25
		Boston, MA	1.25
		College Station, TX	1.25
		Hyde Park, NY	1.25
		Independence, MO	1.25
		Little Rock, AR	1.25
		Simi Valley, CA	1.25
		West Branch, IA	1.25
		Yorba Linda, CA	1.25
3931-3935	37c	**Sporty Cars of the 1950s,** *Aug. 20,* Detroit, MI	5.00
		3931-3935, any single	2.00
3936	37c	**Arthur Ashe,** *Aug. 27,* Flushing, NY	2.00
3937	37c	**To Form a More Perfect Union pane of 10,** *Aug. 30,* Washington, DC	8.75
		Greensboro, NC	8.75
		Jackson, MS	8.75
		Little Rock, AR	8.75
		Memphis, TN	8.75
		Montgomery, AL	8.75
		Selma, AL	8.75
		Topeka, KS	8.75
		Any other city	8.75
		3937a-3937j, any single, Washington, DC	2.00
		3937a-3937j, any single, Greensboro, NC	2.00
		3937a-3937j, any single, Jackson, MS	2.00

		3937a-3937j, any single, Little Rock, AR	2.00
		3937a-3937j, any single, Memphis, TN	2.00
		3937a-3937j, any single, Montgomery, AL	2.00
		3937a-3937j, any single, Selma, AL	2.00
		3937a-3937j, any single, Topeka, KS	2.00
3938	37c	**Child Health,** *Sept. 7,* Philadelphia, PA	2.00
		Any other city	2.00
3939-3942	37c	**Let's Dance,** *Sept. 17,* New York, NY	4.25
		Miami, FL	4.25
		3939-3942, any single, New York, NY	2.00
		3939-3942, any single, Miami, FL	2.00
3943	37c	**Greta Garbo,** *Sept. 23,* New York, NY	2.00
3944	37c	**Jim Henson and the Muppets,** *Sept. 28,* North Hollywood, CA	9.25
		3944a-3944k, any single	2.00
3945-3948	37c	**Constellations,** *Oct. 3,* Bloomfield Hills, MI	4.25
		3945-3948, any single	2.00
3949-3952	37c	**Christmas Cookies,** serpentine die cut 10¾x11, *Oct. 20,* New York, NY	4.25
		Minneapolis, MN	4.25
		3949-3952, any single, New York, NY	2.00
		3949-3952, any single, Minneapolis, MN	2.00
3953-3956	37c	**Christmas Cookies,** convertible booklet stamps, serpentine die cut 10¾x11 on 2 or 3 sides, *Oct. 20,* New York, NY	4.25
		Minneapolis, MN	4.25
		3949-3952, any single, New York, NY	2.00
		3949-3952, any single, Minneapolis, MN	2.00
3957-3960	37c	**Christmas Cookies,** vending machine booklet stamps, serpentine die cut 10½x10¾, *Oct. 20,* New York, NY	4.25
		Minneapolis, MN	4.25
		3949-3952, any single, New York, NY	2.00
		3949-3952, any single, Minneapolis, MN	2.00
3961-3964	37c	**Distinguished Marines,** *Nov. 10,* Washington, DC	4.25
		Oceanside, CA	4.25
		Any other city	4.25
		3961-3964, any single, Washington, DC	2.00
		3961-3964, any single, Oceanside, CA	2.00
		3961-3964, any single, any other city	2.00
3965	(39c)	**Flag and Statue of Liberty,** perf. 11¼, *Dec. 8,* Washington, DC	2.00
		Any other city	2.00
3966	(39c)	**Flag and Statue of Liberty,** self-adhesive, serpentine die cut 11¼x11, *Dec. 8,* Washington, DC	2.00
		Any other city	2.00
3967	(39c)	**Flag and Statue of Liberty,** coil stamp, perf. 9¾ vert., *Dec. 8,* Washington, DC	2.00
		Any other city	2.00
3968	(39c)	**Flag and Statue of Liberty,** self-adhesive coil stamp, photo., serpentine die cut 8½ vert., *Dec. 8,* Washington, DC	2.00
		Any other city	2.00
3969	(39c)	**Flag and Statue of Liberty,** self-adhesive coil stamp, photo., serpentine die cut 10¼ vert., *Dec. 8,* Washington, DC	2.00
		Any other city	2.00
3970	(39c)	**Flag and Statue of Liberty,** self-adhesive coil stamp, litho., serpentine die cut 9½ vert., *Dec. 8,* Washington, DC	2.00
		Any other city	2.00
3972	(39c)	**Flag and Statue of Liberty,** self-adhesive booklet stamp with bright blue spot over date, photo., serpentine die cut 11¼x10¾ on 2 or 3 sides, *Dec. 8,* Washington, DC	2.00
		Any other city	2.00
3973	(39c)	**Flag and Statue of Liberty,** self-adhesive booklet stamp, serpentine die cut 10¼x10¾, *Dec. 8,* Washington, DC	2.00
		Any other city	2.00

Although No. 3973 has an issue date of Dec. 8, it was not known to have been available until January 2006.

3974	(39c)	**Flag and Statue of Liberty,** self-adhesive booklet stamp with dark blue spot over date, litho., serpentine die cut 11¼x11 on 2 or 3 sides, *Dec. 8,* Washington, DC	2.00
		Any other city	2.00
3975	(39c)	**Flag and Statue of Liberty,** self-adhesive booklet stamp, photo., serpentine die cut 8 on 2, 3 or 4 sides, *Dec. 8,* Washington, DC	2.00
		Any other city	2.00

2006

3976	(39c)	**Birds,** self-adhesive booklet stamp, *Jan. 3,* Washington, DC	2.00
		Any other city	2.00
3978	39c	**Flag and Statue of Liberty,** self-adhesive, *Apr. 8,* Washignton, DC	2.00
		Any other city	2.00
3979	39c	**Flag and Statue of Liberty,** coil stamp, perf. 10 vert. *Mar. 8,* Washington, DC	2.00
		Any other city	2.00
3980	39c	**Flag and Statue of Liberty,** self-adhesive coil stamp, serpentine die cut 11 vert. with rounded corners, *Jan. 9,* Washington, DC	2.00
		Any other city	2.00

3981	39c **Flag and Statue of Liberty**, self-adhesive coil stamp, serpentine die cut 9½ vert., *Apr. 8*, Washington, DC		2.00
	Any other city		2.00
3987-3994	39c **Children's Book Animals**, *Jan. 10*, Findlay, OH		7.50
	3987-3994, any single		2.00
3999	39c **2006 Winter Olympics**, *Jan. 11*, Colorado Springs, CO		2.00
3996	39c **Hattie McDaniel**, *Jan. 25*, Beverly Hills, CA		2.00
3997	39c **Chinese New Year pane**, *Jan. 29*, Washington, DC		10.50
	3997a-3997l, any single		2.00
3998	39c **Wedding Dove**, *Mar. 1*, New York, NY		2.00
3999	63c **Wedding Dove**, *Mar. 1*, New York, NY		2.50
4000	24c **Common Buckeye Butterfly**, perf. 11¼, *Mar. 8*, Washington, DC		2.00
	Any other city		2.00
4001	24c **Common Buckeye Butterfly**, self-adhesive, serpentine die cut 11, *Mar. 8*, Washington, DC		2.00
	Any other city		2.00
4001a	24c **Common Buckeye Butterfly**, self-adhesive booklet pane stamp, serpentine die cut 10¾x11¼, *Mar. 8*, Washington, DC		2.00
	Any other city		2.00
4002	24c **Common Buckeye Butterfly**, self-adhesive coil stamp, serpentine die cut 8½ horiz., *Mar. 8*, Washington, DC		2.00
	Any other city		2.00
4003-4007	39c **Crops of the Americas**, self-adhesive coil stamps, *Mar. 16*, New York, NY		5.25
	4003-4007, any single		2.00
4008-4012	39c **Crops of the Americas**, self-adhesive booklet stamps, serpentine die cut 10¾x10½ on 2 or 3 sides, *Mar. 16*, New York, NY		5.25
	4008-4012, any single		2.00

4013-4017	39c **Crops of the Americas**, self-adhesive booklet stamps, serpentine die cut 10¾x11¼ on 2 or 3 sides, *Mar. 16*, New York, NY		5.25
	4013-4017, any single		2.00
4018	$4.05 **X-Plane**, *Mar. 17*, New York, NY		8.00
	Any other city		8.00
4019	$14.40 **X-Plane**, *Mar. 17*, New York, NY		27.50
	Any other city		27.50
4020	39c **Sugar Ray Robinson**, *Apr. 7*, New York, NY		2.00
4021-4024	39c **Benjamin Franklin**, *Apr. 7*, Philadelphia, PA		4.50
	4021-4024, any single		2.00
4025-4028	39c **Disney Characters**, *Apr. 21*, Orlando, FL		4.50
	4025-4028, any single		2.00
4029	39c **Birds**, self-adhesive booklet stamp, *May 1*, Washington, DC		2.00
4030	39c **Katherine Anne Porter**, *May 15*, Kyle, TX		2.00
4031	39c **Amber Alert**, *May 25*, Arlington, TX		2.00
	Washington, DC		2.00
4032	39c **Purple Heart**, *May 26*, Washington, DC		2.00
4072a	39c **Wonders of America**, *May 27*, Washington, DC		32.50
	4033-4072, any single, Washington, DC		2.00
	4072a, any other city		32.50
	4033-4072, any single, any other city		2.00
4073	39c **Samuel de Champlain**, self-adhesive stamp, *May 28*, Washington, DC		2.00
	Ticonderoga, NY		2.00
	Annapolis Royal, Nova Scotia, Canada		2.00
4074	**Samuel de Champlain**, souvenir sheet, *May 28*, Washington, DC		4.75
	Ticonderoga, NY		4.75
	Annapolis Royal, Nova Scotia, Canada		4.75
4075	**Washington 2006 World Philatelic Exhibition**, souvenir sheet, *May 29*, Washington, DC		16.00

4075a	$1		3.
4075b	$2		5.
4075c	$5		10.
4076	39c **Distinguished American Diplomats**, souvenir sheet, *May 30*, Washington, DC		6.
	4076a-4076f, any single		2.
4077	39c **Judy Garland**, *June 10*, New York, NY		2.
4078	39c **Ronald Reagan**, *June 14*, Simi Valley, CA		2.
4079	39c **Happy Birthday**, *June 23*, Santa Clara, CA		2.
4080-4083	39c **Baseball Sluggers**, *July 15*, Bronx, NY		4.
	4080-4083, any single		2.
4084	39c **DC Comics Superheroes**, *July 20*, San Diego, CA		16.
	4084a-4084t, any single		2.

SEMI-POSTAL FIRST DAY COVERS

1998

B1	32c +8c **Breast Cancer**, *July 29*, Washington, DC (51,775)		2.0

2002

B2	(34c+11c) **Heroes of 2001**, *June 7*, New York, NY		3.0
	Any other city		2.0

2003

B3	(37c+8c) **Stop Family Violence**, *Oct. 8*, Washington, DC		1.6
	Any other city		1.6

AIR POST FIRST DAY COVERS

1918

C1	6c **orange**, *Dec. 10*		32,500.
C2	16c **green**, *July 11*		32,500.
C3	24c **carmine rose & blue**, *May 13*		27,500.

1923

C4	8c **dark green**, *Aug. 15*		450.00
C5	16c **dark blue**, *Aug. 17*		650.00
C6	24c **carmine**, *Aug. 21*		850.00

1926-27

C7	10c **dark blue**, *Feb. 13, 1926*		70.00
	Chicago, Ill.		85.00
	Detroit, Mich.		85.00
	Cleveland, Ohio		130.00
	Dearborn, Mich.		130.00
C8	15c **olive brown**, *Sept. 18, 1926*		85.00
C9	20c **yellow green**, *Jan. 25, 1927*		100.00
	New York, N.Y.		125.00
C10	10c **dark blue**, *June 18, 1927*		25.00
	St. Louis, Mo.		25.00
	Little Falls, Minn.		35.00
	Detroit, Mich.		35.00
C10a	Booklet pane of 3, *May 26, 1928*		875.00
	Cleveland Midwestern Philatelic Sta. cancel		800.00
	C10a & 645 on one cover, Washington, D.C.		1,000.

1928-30

C11	5c **carmine & blue**, *July 25, 1928*, pair		50.00
C12	5c **violet**, *Feb. 10, 1930*		12.00
C13	65c **green**, *Apr. 19, 1930*		1,200.
C14	$1.30 **brown**, *Apr. 19, 1930*		1,100.
C15	$2.60 **blue**, *Apr. 19, 1930*		1,200.
	C13-C15 on one cover		15,000.

Values are for first day covers flown on Zeppelin flights with appropriate markings. Non-flown covers sell for less.

1931-33

C16	5c **violet**, *Aug. 19, 1931*		175.00
C17	8c **olive bister**, *Sept. 26, 1932*		15.00
C18	50c **green**, *Oct. 2, 1933*, New York, N.Y. (3,500)		200.00
	Akron, Ohio, *Oct. 4*		300.00
	Washington, D.C., *Oct. 5*		275.00
	Miami, Fla., *Oct. 6*		150.00
	Chicago, Ill., *Oct. 7*		250.00

1934-37

C19	6c **dull orange**, *June 30, 1934*, Baltimore, Md.		190.00
	New York, N.Y.		800.00
	Brooklyn, N.Y.		1,200.
	San Francisco, Calif.		1,500.

	Washington, D.C., *July 1*		10.00

Catalogue values for Nos. C20-C45 are for addressed covers with the most common cachets.

C20	25c **blue**, *Nov. 22, 1935 (10,910)*		40.00
	San Francisco, Cal. (15,000)		35.00
C21	20c **green**, *Feb. 15, 1937*		45.00
C22	50c **carmine**, *Feb. 15, 1937*		50.00
	C21-C22 on one cover		100.00

First day covers of Nos. C21 and C22 total 40,000.

1938-39

C23	6c **dark blue & carmine**, *May 14, 1938*, Dayton, Ohio (116,443)		15.00
	St. Petersburg, Fla. (95,121)		15.00
	Washington, D.C., *May 15*		3.50
C24	30c **dull blue**, *May 16, 1939*, New York, N.Y. (68,634)		47.50

1941-44

C25	6c **carmine**, *June 25, 1941 (99,986)*		3.75
C25a	Booklet pane of 3, *Mar. 18, 1943*		25.00
C26	8c **olive green**, *Mar. 21, 1944 (147,484)*		3.75
C27	10c **violet**, *Aug. 15, 1941*, Atlantic City, N.J. (87,712)		8.00
C28	15c **brown carmine**, *Aug. 19, 1941*, Baltimore, Md. (74,000)		10.00
C29	20c **bright green**, *Aug. 27, 1941*, Philadelphia, Pa. (66,225)		12.50
C30	30c **blue**, *Sept. 25, 1941*, Kansas City, Mo. (57,175)		20.00
C31	50c **orange**, *Oct. 29, 1941*, St. Louis, Mo. (54,580)		40.00

1946-48

C32	5c **carmine**, *Sept. 25, 1946*		2.00

First day covers of Nos. C32 & UC14 total 396,669.

C33	5c **carmine**, *Mar. 26, 1947 (342,634)*		2.00
C34	10c **black**, *Aug. 30, 1947 (265,773)*		2.00
C35	15c **bright blue green**, *Aug. 20, 1947*, New York, N.Y. (230,338)		1.75
C36	25c **blue**, *July 30, 1947*, San Francisco, Cal. (201,762)		2.25
C37	5c **carmine, coil**, *Jan. 15, 1948 (192,084)*		1.75
C38	5c **New York City**, *July 31, 1948*, New York, N.Y. (371,265)		1.75

1949

C39	6c **carmine**, *Jan. 18 (266,790)*		1.50
C39a	Booklet pane of 6, *Nov. 18, 1949*, New York, N.Y.		10.00
C40	6c **Alexandria Bicentennial**, *May 11*, Alexandria, Va. (386,717)		1.50
C41	6c **carmine coil**, *Aug. 25 (240,386)*		1.25
C42	10c **U.P.U.**, *Nov. 18*, New Orleans, La. (270,000)		1.75
C43	15c **U.P.U.**, *Oct. 7*, Chicago, Ill. (246,833)		2.75

C44	25c **U.P.U.**, *Nov. 30*, Seattle, Wash. (220,215)		3.75
C45	6c **Wright Brothers**, *Dec. 17*, Kitty Hawk, N.C. (378,585)		2.75

Catalogue values from this point to the end of the section are for unaddressed covers with the most common cachets.

1952-59

C46	80c **Hawaii**, *Mar. 26, 1952*, Honolulu, Hawaii, (89,864)		20.00
C47	6c **Powered Flight**, *May 29, 1953*, Dayton, Ohio (359,050)		1.50
C48	4c **bright blue**, *Sept. 3, 1954*, Philadelphia, Pa. (295,720)		1.00
C49	6c **Air Force**, *Aug. 1, 1957 (356,683)*		2.75
C50	5c **red**, *July 31, 1958*, Colorado Springs, Colo. (207,954)		1.00
C51	7c **blue**, *July 31, 1958*, Philadelphia, Pa. (204,401)		1.00
C51a	Booklet pane of 6, San Antonio, Tex. (119,769)		9.00
C52	7c **blue coil**, *July 31, 1958*, Miami, Fla. (181,603)		1.00
C53	7c **Alaska Statehood**, *Jan. 3, 1959*, Juneau, Alaska (489,752)		1.50
C54	7c **Balloon Jupiter**, *Aug. 17, 1959*, Lafayette, Ind.(383,556)		1.75
C55	7c **Hawaii Statehood**, *Aug. 21, 1959*, Honolulu, Hawaii (533,464)		1.00
C56	10c **Pan American Games**, *Aug. 27, 1959*, Chicago, Ill. (302,306)		1.00

1959-66

C57	10c **Liberty Bell**, *June 10, 1960*, Miami, Fla. (246,509)		1.25
C58	15c **Statue of Liberty**, *Nov. 20, 1959*, New York, N.Y. (259,412)		1.25
C59	25c **Abraham Lincoln**, *Apr. 22, 1960*, San Francisco, Cal. (211,235)		1.50
C59a	25c Tagged, *Dec. 29, 1966* (about 3,000)		50.00
C60	7c **carmine**, *Aug. 12, 1960*, Arlington, Va. (247,190)		1.00
C60a	Booklet pane of 6, *Aug. 19, 1960*, St. Louis, Mo. (143,363)		8.00
C61	7c **carmine coil**, *Oct. 22, 1960*, Atlantic City, N.J. (197,995)		1.00

1961-67

C62	13c **Liberty Bell**, *June 28, 1961*, New York, N.Y. (316,166)		1.00
C62a	13c Tagged, *Feb. 15, 1967*		50.00
C63	15c **Redrawn Statue of Liberty**, *Jan. 13, 1961*, Buffalo, N.Y. (192,976)		1.00
C63a	15c Tagged, *Jan. 11, 1967*		50.00
C64	8c **carmine**, *Dec. 5, 1962 (288,355)*		1.00
C64b	Booklet pane of 5 + label (146,835)		3.50

C64a	8c Tagged, *Aug. 1, 1963,* Dayton, Ohio *(262,720)*	2.00
C65	8c **carmine coil,** *Dec. 5, 1962 (220,173)*	1.00

1963-69

C66	15c **Montgomery Blair,** *May 3, 1963,* Silver Spring, Md. *(260,031)*	1.50
C67	6c **Bald Eagle,** *July 12, 1963,* Boston, Mass. *(268,265)*	1.00
C67a	6c Tagged, *Feb. 15, 1967*	50.00
C68	8c **Amelia Earhart,** *July 24, 1963,* Atchison, Kan. *(437,996)*	3.50
C69	8c **Robert H. Goddard,** *Oct. 5, 1964,* Roswell, N.M. *(421,020)*	3.00
C70	8c **Alaska Purchase,** *Mar. 30, 1967,* Sitka, Alaska *(554,784)*	1.50
C71	20c **Audubon,** *Apr. 26, 1967,* Audubon (Station of N.Y.C.), N.Y. *(227,930)*	2.00
C72	10c **carmine,** *Jan. 5, 1968,* San Francisco, Cal.	1.00
C72b	Booklet pane of 8	3.75
C72c	Booklet pane of 5 + label, slogan 4 *Jan. 6, 1968*	125.00
	With slogan 5	110.00
C73	10c **carmine coil,** *Jan. 5, 1968,* San Francisco, Cal.	1.00
C74	10c **Air Mail Service,** *May 15, 1968* *(521,084)*	1.50
C75	20c **USA and Jet,** *Nov. 22, 1968,* New York, N.Y. *(276,244)*	1.25
C76	10c **Moon Landing,** *Sept. 9, 1969* *(8,743,070)*	5.00

1971-73

C77	9c **red,** *May 15, 1971,* Kitty Hawk, N.C.	1.00

First day cancellation was applied to 379,442 covers of Nos. C77 and UXC10.

C78	11c **carmine,** *May 7, 1971,* Spokane, Wash.	1.00
C78a	Booklet pane of 4 + 2 labels	2.25
C79	13c **carmine,** *Nov. 16, 1973,* New York, N.Y. *(282,550)*	1.00
C79a	Booklet pane of 5 + label, *Dec. 27, 1973,* Chicago, Ill.	2.25

First day cancellation was applied to 464,750 covers of Nos. C78, C78a and C82, and to 204,756 covers of Nos. C79a and C83.

C80	17c **Statue of Liberty,** *July 13, 1971,* Lakehurst, N.J. *(172,269)*	1.25
C81	21c **USA and Jet,** *May 21, 1971 (293,140)*	1.00
C82	11c **carmine coil,** *May 7, 1971,* Spokane, Wash.	1.00
C83	13c **carmine coil,** *Dec. 27, 1973,* Chicago, Ill.	1.00
C84	11c **National Parks Centennial,** *May 3, 1972,* Honaunau, Hawaii *(364,816)*	1.00
C85	11c **Olympics,** *Aug. 17, 1972*	1.00

First day cancellation was applied to 971,536 covers of Nos. 1460-1462 and C85.

C86	11c **Electronics,** *July 10, 1973,* New York, N.Y.	1.00

First day cancellation was applied to 1,197,700 covers of Nos. 1500-1502 and C86.

1974-79

C87	18c **Statue of Liberty,** *Jan. 11, 1974,* Hempstead, N.Y. *(216,902)*	1.00
C88	26c **Mt. Rushmore,** *Jan. 2, 1974,* Rapid City, S.D. *(210,470)*	1.50
C89	25c **Plane and Globes,** *Jan. 2, 1976,* Honolulu, Hawaii	1.00
C90	31c **Plane, Globes and Flag,** *Jan. 2, 1976,* Honolulu, Hawaii	1.25
C92a	31c **Wright Brothers,** *Sept. 23, 1978,* Dayton, Ohio	4.00
	C91-C92, any single	3.00
C94a	21c **Octave Chanute,** *Mar. 29, 1979,* Chanute, Kan. *(459,235)*	4.00
	C93-C94, any single	3.00
C96a	25c **Wiley Post,** *Nov. 20, 1979,* Oklahoma City, Okla.	4.00
	C95-C96, any single	3.00
C97	31c **Olympics,** *Nov. 1, 1979,* Colorado Springs, CO	1.50

1980

C98	40c **Philip Mazzei,** *Oct. 13*	1.50
C99	28c **Blanche Stuart Scott,** *Dec. 30,* Hammondsport, NY *(238,502)*	1.50
C100	35c **Glenn Curtiss,** *Dec. 30,* Hammondsport, NY *(208,502)*	1.50

1983

C104a	28c **Olympics,** *June 17,* San Antonio, TX *(901,028)*	3.75
	C101-C104, any single	1.75
C108a	40c **Olympics,** *Apr. 8,* Los Angeles, CA *(1,001,657)*	5.00
	C105-C108, any single	1.75
C112a	35c **Olympics,** *Nov. 4,* Colorado Springs, CO *(897,729)*	4.50
	C109-C112, any single	1.75

1985

C113	33c **Alfred V. Verville,** *Feb. 13,* Garden City, NY	1.50
C114	39c **Lawrence & Elmer Sperry,** *Feb. 13,* Garden City, NY	1.50

First day cancel was applied to 429,290 covers bearing one more of Nos. C113-C114.

C115	44c **Transpacific Air Mail,** *Feb. 15,* San Francisco, CA *(269,229)*	1.75

A total of 269,229 first day cancels were applied for Nos. C115 and UXC22.

C116	44c **Junipero Serra,** *Aug. 22,* San Diego, CA *(254,977)*	2.00

1988

C117	44c **Settling of New Sweden,** *Mar. 29,* Wilmington, DE *(213,445)*	1.50
C118	45c **Samuel P. Langley,** *May 14,* San Diego, CA	1.50
C119	36c **Igor Sikorsky,** *June 23,* Stratford, CT *(162,986)*	2.25

1989

C120	45c **French Revolution,** *July 14 (309,975)*	1.50
C121	45c **Southeast Carved Figure,** *Oct. 12,* San Juan, PR *(93,569)*	1.50
C125a	45c **Future Mail Transportation,** *Nov. 27 (765,479)*	6.50
	C122-C125, any single	1.75
C126	45c **Future Mail Transportation Souvenir Sheet,** *Nov. 24 (257,826)*	6.50

1990

C127	45c **Tropical Coast,** *Oct. 12,* Grand Canyon, AZ *(137,068)*	1.50

1991

C128	50c **Harriet Quimby,** *Apr. 27,* Plymouth, MI	1.50
C129	40c **William T. Piper,** *May 17,* Denver, CO	1.50
C130	50c **Antarctic Treaty,** *June 21*	1.50
C131	50c **Bering Land Bridge,** *Oct. 12,* Anchorage, AK	1.50

1999

C133	48c **Niagara Falls,** *May 12,* Niagara Falls, NY *(20,878)*	1.75
C134	40c **Rio Grande,** *July 30,* Milwaukee, WI	1.75
	any other city	1.75

First day cancel was applied to 42,144 covers bearing one more of Nos. 3330, C134.

C135	60c **Grand Canyon,** *Jan. 20,* Grand Canyon, AZ *(64,282)*	1.75

2001

C136	70c **Nine-mile Prairie,** *Mar. 6,* Lincoln, NE	2.00
C137	80c **Mt. McKinley,** *Apr. 17,* Fairbanks, AK	2.00
C138	60c **Acadia National Park,** *May 30,* Bar Harbor, ME	1.75

2006

C139	63c **Bryce Canyon National Park,** *Feb. 24,* St. Louis, MO	1.50
	Any other city	1.50
C140	75c **Great Smoky Mountains National Park,** *Feb. 24,* St. Louis, MO	1.50
	Any other city	1.50
C141	84c **Yosemite National Park,** *Feb. 24,* St. Louis, MO	1.75
	Any other city	1.75

BOOKLETS: PANES & COVERS

Most booklet panes issued before 1962 consist of a vertical block of 6 stamps perforated vertically through the center. The panes are perforate horizontally on all but the bottom edge and the top of the selvage tab. The selvage top, the two sides and the bottom are straight edged. Exceptions fo panes issued before 1962 are the 1917 American Expeditionary Forces panes (30 stamps); Lindbergh and 6¢ 1943 air mails (3), and the Saving Stamps (10). Since 1962, panes have been issued with 3 to 20 stamps and various configurations. They have included one or more labels and two o more stamps se-tenant.

Flat plate booklet panes, with the exceptions noted above, were made from specially designed plates of 180 or 360 subjects. They are collected i plate positions. There are nine collectible positions on the 180-subject plate and 12 on the 360-subject plate.

Rotary booklet panes issued from 1926 to May 1978 (except for Nos. 1623a and 1623c) were made from specially designed plates of 180, 320, 36C and 400 subjects. They also are collected in plate positions. There are five collectible positions on the 360-subject plates which were printed befor electric eye plates came into use, and 20 collectible positions on the Type II "new design" 360-subject rotary plates. There are 21 collectible positions i the rotary air mail 180-subject plate as well as the Type IV "modified design" 360-subject plate. There are 16 collectible positions on the 320-subjec plates and 20 on the 400 subject plates. There are five collectible positions on Defense and War Savings 300-subject plates.

The generally accepted methods of designating pane positions as illustrated and explained hereafter are those suggested by George H. Beans in th May 1913 issue of "Everybody's Philatelist" and by B. H. Mosher in his monograph "Discovering U.S. Rotary Pane Varieties 1926-78." Some collector seek all varieties possible, but the majority collect unused (A) panes and plate number (D) panes from flat plate issues, and plain panes and panes wit electric eye bars and electric eye dashes, where available, from rotary plates.

Starting in 1977, BEP made two major changes in booklet production. Printing of panes was gradually moved from rotary plates to sleeves fo modern high speed presses. Also, booklet production was transferred to Goebel booklet-forming machines. These changes virtually eliminate collectible pane positions for several years. However, beginning with No. BK156 (No. 2276a), BEP and other printers began placing printing proces control marks in pane tabs. As a result, specialist booklet pane collectors actively resumed collecting pane positions. Collectible positions on thes issues are not shown in this catalogue but can be found in the United States Stamp Society's Research Paper No. 2 "Folded Style Checklist," Michae O. Perry, editor. Also, because of the requirements of the Goebel machine, the subject size of printing plates or sleeves varied widely. For thes reasons, plate layouts are not shown for each issue. The plate layout for No. 1288c and the sleeve layout for No. 1623a are shown as typical.

The following panes, issued after Mar. 11, 1977, were printed from pairs of rotary plates and assembled into booklets on the Goebel machine: Nos 1288c, 1742a, 1819a, 1889a, and 1949a. One pane in 12 of those issues may have a join line along either long side of the pane, creating thre collectible positions: no join line, join line top (or right) and join line bottom (or left). Except for Nos. 1736a and 2276a, all other booklet panes issue from Mar. 11, 1977 on were printed from intaglio sleeves, gravure cylinders, and/or offset plates.

At least one pane in every booklet produced on the BEP's Goebel machines contain two register marks in the tab: a cross register line (CRL) 1.5mn wide which runs across the width of the tab and a length register mark (LRM), typically 1.5x5mm, usually placed above the right hand (or top) stamp o the pane. Nos. 1623a and 1623Bc were regularly issued with the LRM over either stamp. Some copies of Nos. 1893a, 2121a and 3003Ab were issue with the LRM over the left stamp.

Starting with No. 1889a (except for No. 1948a), plate numbers (1 to 5 digits) were placed in the tab, normally over the left stamp. On booklets containing Nos. 1889a, 1949a and 2113a, the plate number is supposed to be on the top pane, the second pane not having a number. All subsequen multi-pane booklets have the plate number on each pane. Some multi-pane booklets contain panes with different plate numbers. The booklet value is determined by the top pane.

Some recent booklets have been printed by contractors other than the BEP so markings may differ or be absent.

Panes in all booklets assembled on the Goebel machine will be folded at least once. **Repeated handling of booklets with folded panes may caus the panes to fall apart.**

Booklet panes with tabs attached to the cover by adhesive instead of staples are valued on the basis of the tab intact. Minor damage on the back of the tab due to removal from the booklet does not affect the value. Some of these panes were furnished to first day cover processors unfolded and not pasted into covers. Around 1989, these panes were available to collectors through the Philatelic Agency.

All panes from 1967 to date are tagged, unless otherwise stated.

Dr. William R. Bush, Morton Dean Joyce, Robert E. Kitson, Richard F. Larkin, Dr. Robert Marks, Bruce H. Mosher, the United States Stamp Society (formerly the Bureau Issues Association), and the Booklet Collectors Club helped the editors extensively in compiling the listings and preparing the illustrations of booklets, covers and plate layouts.

180-SUBJECT PLATE — 9 Collectible Positions

Beginning at upper left and reading from left to right, the panes are designated from 1 to 30. All positions not otherwise identifiable are designated by the letter A: Pane 1A, 2A, 3A, 4A, etc.
The identifiable positions are as follows:
A — The ordinary booklet pane without distinguishing features. Occurs in Position 1, 2, 3, 4, 8, 9, 10, 21, 22, 23, 24, 27, 28, 29, 30.
B — Split arrow and guide line at right. Occurs in Position 5 only.
C — Split arrow and guide line at left. Occurs in Position 6 only.
D — Plate number pane. Occurs in Position 7 only.
E — Guide line pane showing horizontal guide line between stamps 1-2 and 3-4 of the pane. Occurs in Positions 11, 12, 13, 14, 17, 18, 19, and 20.
F — Guide line through pane and at right. Occurs in Position 15 only.
G — Guide line through pane and at left. Occurs in Position 16 only.
H — Guide line at right. Occurs in Position 25 only.
I — Guide line at left. Occurs in Position 26 only.
Only positions B, F and H or C, G and I may be obtained from the same sheet, depending on whether the knife which separated the panes fell to right or left of the line.
Side arrows, bottom arrows, or bottom plate numbers are seldom found because the margin of the sheets is usually cut off, as are the sides and bottom of each pane.
In the illustrations, the dotted lines represent the rows of perforations, the unbroken lines represents the knife cut.

360-SUBJECT PLATE — 12 Collectible Positions

As with the 180-Subject Sheets, the position of the various panes is indicated by numbers beginning in the upper left corner with the No. 1 and reading from left to right to No. 60.

The identifiable positions are as follows:

A — The ordinary booklet pane without distinguishing features. Occurs in Positions 1, 2, 3, 4, 8, 9, 10, 11, 12, 13, 14, 17, 18, 19, 20, 41, 42, 43, 44, 47, 48, 49, 50, 51, 52, 53, 54, 57, 58, 59, and 60.

B — Split arrow and guide line at right. Occurs in Position 5 only.

C — Split arrow and guide line at left. Occurs in Position 6 only.

D — Plate number pane. Occurs in Position 7 only.

E, F, G — Do not occur in the 360-Subject Plate.

H — Guide line at right. Occurs in Positions 15, 45, and 55.

I — Guide line at left. Occurs in Positions 16, 46, and 56.

J — Guide line at bottom. Occurs in Positions 21, 22, 23, 24, 27, 28, 29 and 30.

K — Guide line at right and bottom. Occurs in Position 25 only.

L — Guide line at left and bottom. Occurs in Position 26 only.

M — Guide line at top. Occurs in Positions 31, 32, 33, 34, 37, 38, 39 and 40.

N — Guide line at top and right. Occurs in Position 35 only.

O — Guide line at top and left. Occurs in Position 36 only.

Only one each of Positions B or C, K, L, N or O; four positions of H or I, and eight or nine positions of J or M may be obtained from each 360 subject sheet, depending on whether the knife fell to the right or left, top or bottom of the guide lines.

Because the horizontal guide line appears so close to the bottom row of stamps on panes Nos. 21 to 30, Positions M, N, and O occur with great deal less frequency than Positions J, K and L.

The 360-Subject Rotary Press Plate (before Electric Eye) Position A only

The 360-Subject Rotary Press Plate — Electric Eye

A modified design was put into use in 1956. The new plates have 20 frame bars instead of 17.

The A.E.F. Plate — 360-Subject Flat Plate — 8 Collectible Positions (See listings)

The 320-Subject Plate

400-Subject Plate — The 300-Subject plate with double labels has the same layout.

1 A	2 A	3 A	4 A	5 B	6 C	7 A	8 A	9 A	10 A
11 A	12 A	13 A	14 A	15 H	16 I	17 A	18 A	19 A	20 A
21 J	22 J	23 J	24 J	25 K	26 L	27 J	28 J	29 J	30 J
31 M	32 M	33 M	34 M	35 N	36 O	37 M	38 M	39 M	40 M
41 A	42 A	43 A	44 A	45 H	46 I	47 A	48 A	49 A	50 A
51 A	52 A	53 A	54 A	55 H	56 I	57 A	58 A	59 A	60 A

194·25

Lindbergh Booklet Plate-180 Subjects — 11 Collectible Positions

Airmail 180-Subject Rotary Press Plate — Electric Eye

Plate Sizes: No. 1288Bc to date.

Since 1978 numerous plate sizes from 78 to 1080 subjects have been used. Since plate size is not relevant to collecting these panes, we are not including this information in the catalogue.

BOOKLET COVERS

Front covers of booklets of postage and airmail issues are illustrated and numbered.

Included are the Booklet Cover number (BC2A); and the catalogue numbers of the Booklet Panes (300b, 331a). The text of the inside and or back covers changes. Some modern issues have minor changes on the front covers also. When more than one combination of covers exists, the number of possible booklets is noted in parenthesis after the booklet listing.

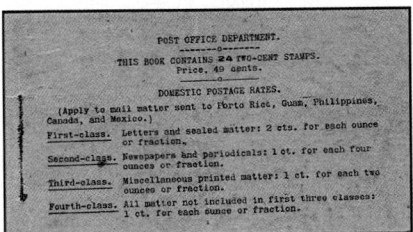

279Be — BC1

1900-03

Text only cover

25c booklet contains 2 panes of six 2c stamps.
49c booklet contains 4 panes of six 2c stamps.
97c booklet contains 8 panes of six 2c stamps.

Booklets sold for 1c more than the face value of the stamps.

300b, 331a — BC2A

279Be, 301c, 319, 332a — BC2B

1900-08

Text cover with price added in upper corners

25c booklet contains 4 panes of six 1c stamps or 2 panes of six 2c stamps.
49c booklet contains 4 panes of six 2c stamps.
97c booklet contains 8 panes of six 2c stamps.

331a, 332a, 374a, 375a, 405b, 406a — BC3

1908-12   **Postrider**

25c booklet contains 4 panes of six 1c stamps.
25c booklet contains 2 panes of six 2c stamps.
49c booklet contains 4 panes of six 2c stamps.
97c booklet contains 8 panes of six 2c stamps.

405b, 424d, 462a, 498e, 632a, 804b — BC4A

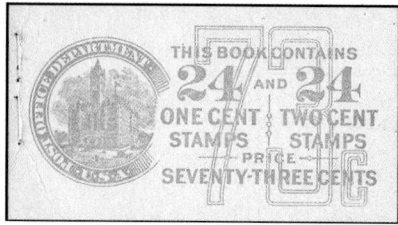

405b, 424d, 462a, 498e, 552a, 632a — BC4B

1912-39   **Washington P.O.**
**Price of booklet in large numerals
behind contents information**
25c booklet contains 4 panes of six 1c stamps.
73c booklet contains 4 panes of six 1c stamps and 4
   panes of six 2c stamps.
97c booklet contains 16 panes of six 1c stamps.

406a, 425e, 463a, 499e, 554c, 583a, 632a, 634d,
804b, 806b — BC5A

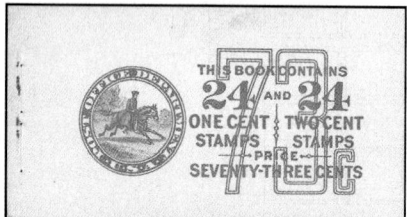

632a, 804b — BC5D

1912-39   **Small Postrider**
Large background numerals
25c booklets contain 4 panes of six 1c stamps or 2
   panes of six 2c stamps.
49c booklet contains 4 panes of six 2c stamps.
73c booklet contains 4 panes of six 1c stamps and 4
   panes of six 2c stamps.
97c booklets contain 16 panes of six 1c stamps or 8
   panes of six 2c stamps.

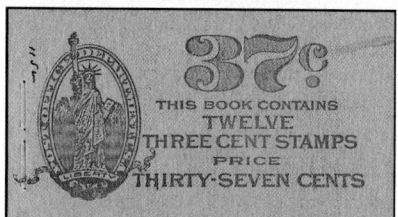

498e, 552a — BC6A

501b, 502b — BC6B

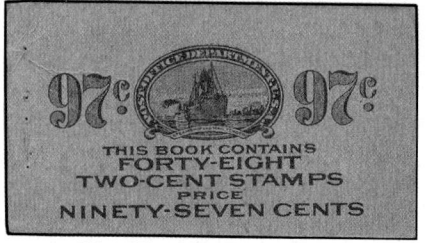

499e, 554c, 583a, 634d — BC6C

1917-27   **Oval designs**
25c booklet contains 4 panes of six 1c stamps.
37c booklet contains 2 panes of six 3c stamps.
97c booklet contains 8 panes of six 2c stamps.

498f, 499f — BC7

Illustration reduced.

1917   **A.E.F.**
$3 booklet contains 10 panes of thirty 1c stamps.
$6 booklet contains 10 panes of thirty 2c stamps.
Booklets sold for face value.

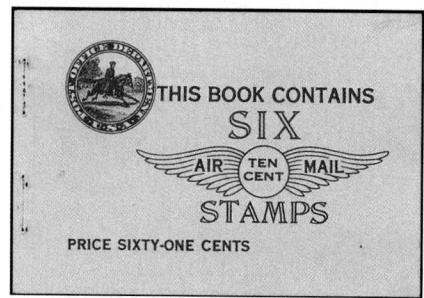

C10a — BC8

1928   **Postrider and Wings**
61c booklet contains 2 panes of three 10c stamps.

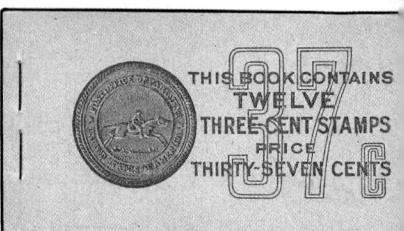

720b, 806b, 807a, 1035a — BC9A

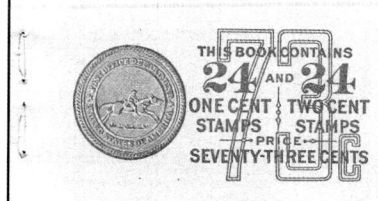

804b — BC9E

1932-54   **Post Office Se**
Large background numerals
25c booklet contains 2 panes of six 2c stamps.
37c booklet contains 2 panes of six 3c stamps.
49c booklet contains 4 panes of six 2c stamps.
73c booklets contain 4 panes of six 3c stamps or 4
   panes of six 1c stamps and 4 panes of six 2c
   stamps.

1036a — BC9F

1036a — BC9G

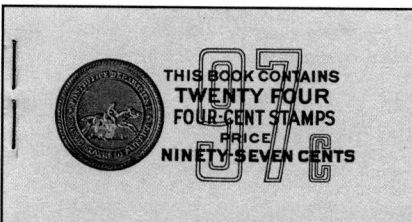

1036a — BC9H

1958
97c booklet contains 4 panes of six 4c stamps.

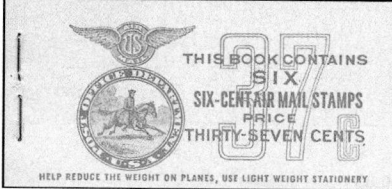

C25a — BC10

Large background numerals
1943   **Postrider and Wings**
37c booklet contains 2 panes of three 6c stamps.
73c booklet contains 4 panes of three 6c stamps.

C39a — BC11A

C51a — BC11B

C51a, C60a — BC11C

C64b, C64c — BC11D

1949-63 **U.S. Airmail Wings**

The 73c and 85c booklets were the last sold for 1c over face value.

73c booklet contains 2 panes of six 6c stamps.
85c booklet contains 2 panes of six 7c stamps.
80c booklet contains 2 panes of five 8c stamps.
$2 booklet contains 5 panes of five 8c stamps.

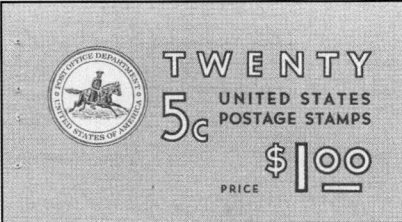

1213a — BC12A

1962-63 **Small Postrider**

$1 booklet contains 4 panes of five 5c stamps.

1213a, 1213c — BC13A

C64b, C64c — BC13B

1963-64 **Mr. Zip**

$1 booklet contains 4 panes of five 5c stamps.
$2 booklet contains 5 panes of five 8c stamps.

1278a, 1284b, 1393a — BC14A

C72b — BC14B

1967-68

$2 booklet contains 4 panes of eight 6c stamps and 1 pane of eight 1c stamps.
$4 booklet contains 5 panes of eight 10c stamps.

1284c, 1393b, 1395b, C72c, C78a — BC15

1968-71

$1 booklets contain 2 panes of five 10c stamps or 2 panes of six 8c stamps and 1 pane of four 1c stamps; 3 panes of five 6c stamps and 1 pane of five 2c stamps or 2 panes of four 11c stamps and 1 pane of six 2c stamps.

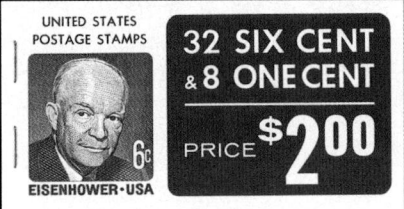

1278a, 1393a, 1395a — BC16

1970-71 **Eisenhower**

$2 booklet contains 4 panes of eight 6c stamps and 1 pane of eight 1c stamps.
$1.92 booklet contains 3 panes of eight 8c stamps.

1395d — BC17A

1510b — BC17B

1510c — BC17C

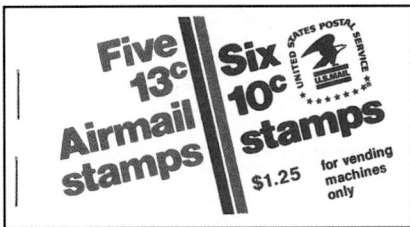

1510d — BC17D

1972-74 **Postal Service Emblem**

$2 booklet contains 3 panes of seven 8c stamps and 1 pane of four 8c stamps.
$1 booklet contains 2 panes of five 10c stamps.
$4 booklet contains 5 panes of eight 10c stamps.
$1.25 booklet contains 1 pane of five 13c stamps and 1 pane of six 10c stamps.

C79a — BC18

1973

$1.30 booklet contains 2 panes of five 13c stamps.

1595a, 1595d — BC19A

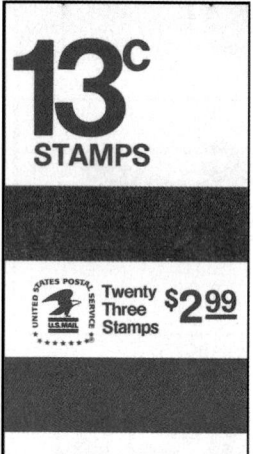

1595c — BC19B

1975-76
    90c booklet contains 1 pane of six 13c stamps and 1
        pane of six 2c stamps.
    $1.30 booklet contains 2 panes of five 13c stamps.
    $2.99 booklet contains 2 panes of eight 13c stamps and
        1 pane of seven 13c stamps.

1623a — BC20

1598a — BC21

1737a — BC22

1288c — BC23

1736c — BC24

BC24 illustration reduced.

1977-78
    $1 booklet contains 1 pane of one 9c stamp and
        seven 13c stamps.
    $1.20 booklet contains 1 pane of eight 15c stamps.
    $2.40 booklet contains 2 panes of eight 15c stamps.
    $3.60 booklet contains 3 panes of eight 15c stamps.

1742a — BC25

1080
    $3 booklet contains 2 panes of ten 15c stamps.

1819a, 1948a, 2113a — BC26

1981-82
    $4.32 booklet contains 3 panes of eight B stamps.
    $4 booklet contains 2 panes of ten C stamps.
    $4.40 booklet contains 2 panes of ten D stamps.

1893a — BC27

1889a — BC28

1981
    $1.20 booklet contains 1 pane of two 6c and six 18c
        stamps.
    $3.60 booklet contains 2 panes of ten 18c stamps.

1896a — BC29

1896b — BC29A

1896b — BC29B

1949a — BC30

1982
$1.20 booklet contains 2 panes of six 20c stamps.
$2 booklet contains 1 pane of ten 20c stamps.
$4 booklet contains 2 panes of ten 20c stamps.

1909a — BC31

2122a — BC31A

2122c — BC31B

1983-89
$28.05 booklet contains 1 pane of three $9.35 stamps.
$32.25 booklet contains 1 pane of three $10.75 stamps.

2116a — BC32

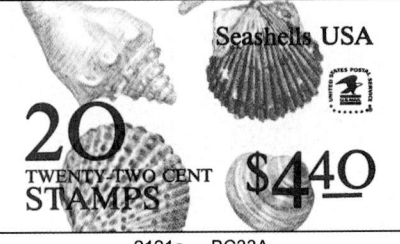

2121a — BC33A

Many different seashell configurations are possible on
BC33A. Seven adjacent covers are necessary to show all 25
shells.

2121a — BC33B

2116a — BC33C

1985
$1.10 booklet contains one pane of five 22c stamps.
$2.20 booklet contains two panes of five 22c stamps.
$4.40 booklet contains two panes of ten 22c stamps.

2201a — BC34

2209a — BC35

1986
$1.76 booklet contains 2 panes of four 22c stamps.
$2.20 booklet contains 2 panes of five 22c stamps.

FOR 22 CENTS, YOU
CAN ADD ONE OF
THESE GREETINGS TO
A LETTER TO
ANYONE IN THE
UNITED STATES,
CANADA OR MEXICO.

Get Well!
Thank You!
Best Wishes!
Keep in Touch!
Love You, Dad!
Happy Birthday!
Congratulations!
Love You, Mother!

10 TWENTY-TWO CENT
U.S. POSTAGE STAMPS $2.20

2274a — BC36

1987
$2.20 booklet contains 1 pane of ten 22c stamps.

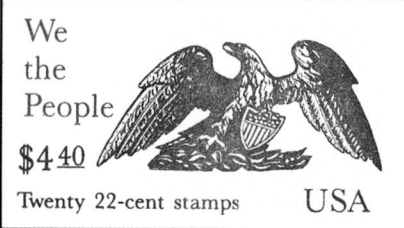

2359a — BC37

1987
$4.40 booklet contains four panes of five 22c stamps.

2366a — BC38

1987
$4.40 booklet contains four panes of five 22c stamps.

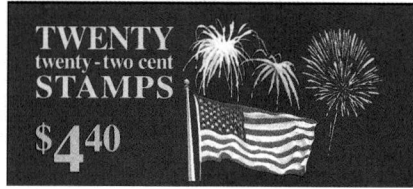

2276a — BC39

Illustration reduced.

1987
$4.40 booklet contains one pane of twenty 22c stamps.

2282a — BC40

1988
$5 booklet contains two panes of ten E stamps.

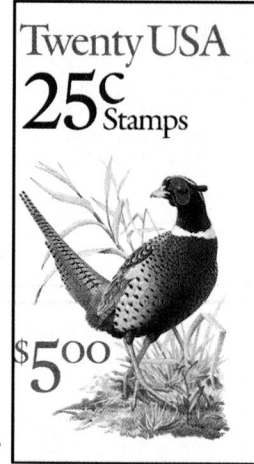

2283a,
2283c — BC41

1988
$5 booklet contains two panes of ten 25c stamps.

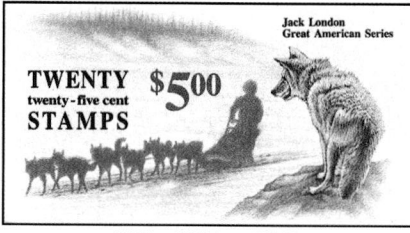

2182a, 2197a — BC43

1988
$1.50 booklet contains one pane of six 25c stamps.
$3 booklet contains two panes of six 25c stamps.
$5 booklet contains two panes of ten 25c stamps.

2285b — BC45

1988
$5 booklet contains two panes of ten 25c stamps.

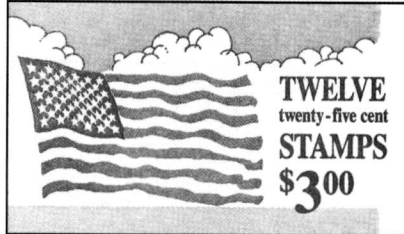

2285c — BC46

1988
$3 booklet contains two panes of six 25c stamps.

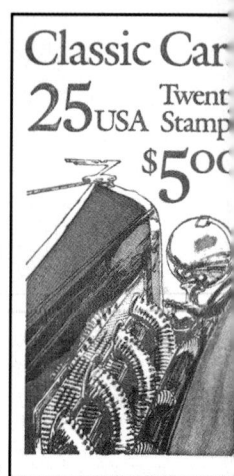

2385a — BC47

1988
$5 booklet contains four panes of five 25c stamps.

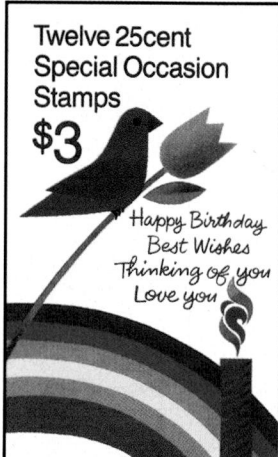

2396a,
2398a — BC48

1988
$3 booklet contains two panes of six 25c stamps.

2409a — BC49

1989
$5 booklet contains four panes of five 25c stamps.

Twenty
Stamps $5.00***

Season's Greetings

2427a — BC50

1989
$5 booklet contains two panes of ten 25c stamps.

2429a — BC51

Illustration reduced.

1989
$5 booklet contains two panes of ten 25c stamps.

2431a — BC52

1989
$5 fold-it-yourself booklet contains eighteen self-adhesive 25c stamps.

2441a — BC53

Illustration reduced.

1990
$5 booklet contains two panes of ten 25c stamps.

For Post Cards

15 USA Twenty Stamps $3.00

2443a — BC54

1990
$3 booklet contains two panes of ten 15c stamps.

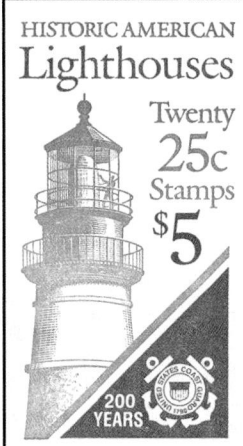

HISTORIC AMERICAN Lighthouses

Twenty 25c Stamps $5

200 YEARS

2474a — BC55

1990
$5 booklet contains four panes of five 25c stamps.

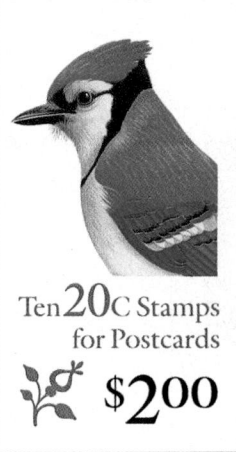

Ten 20c Stamps for Postcards $2.00

2483a — BC56

1995
$2 booklet contains one pane of 10 20c stamps.

Twenty Stamps $5.80

2484a, 2485a — BC57

Illustration reduced.

1991-92
$2.90 booklet contains one pane of 10 29c stamps.
$5.80 booklet contains two panes of 10 29c stamps.

AFRICAN VIOLET
Ten 29c Stamps
$2.90

2486a — BC58

1993
$2.90 booklet contains one pane of 10 29c stamps.
$5.80 booklet contains two panes of 10 29c stamps.

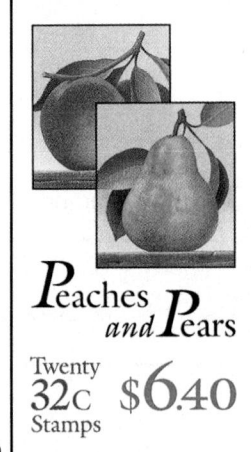

Peaches and Pears
Twenty 32c Stamps $6.40

2488a — BC59

1995
$6.40 booklet contains two panes of 10 32c stamps.

Self-adhesive Stamps

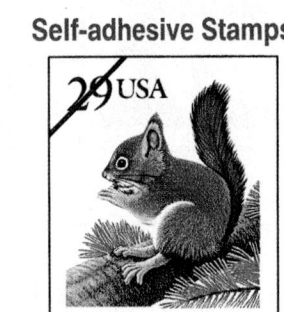

Eighteen Stamps $5.22

2489a
BC60

1993
$5.22 fold-it-yourself booklet contains 18 self-adhesive 29c stamps.

Self-adhesive Stamps

Eighteen
29c Stamps $**5**.22

2490a
BC61

1993
$5.22 fold-it-yourself booklet contains 18 self-adhesive
29c stamps.

Self-adhesive Stamps

Eighteen
Stamps $**5**.22

2491a — BC61A

1993
$5.22 fold-it-yourself booklet contains 18 self-adhesive
stamps.

Twenty
Self-adhesive Stamps

$**6**.40

2492a — BC61B

1995
$6.40 fold-it-yourself booklet contains 20 self-adhesive
32c stamps.

Twenty Self-adhesive Stamps

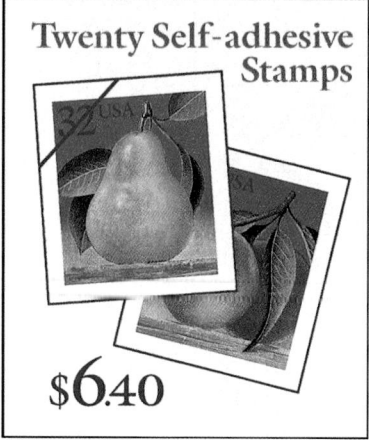

$**6**.40

2494a
BC61C

1995
$6.40 fold-it-yourself booklet contains 20 self-adhesive
32c stamps.

AMERICAN INDIAN
Headdresses

Twenty
25c Stamps $5

2505a — BC62

Twenty
Stamps $**5**.00
***

Season's Greetings

2514a — BC63

Greetings

Twenty
Stamps $**5**.00
***

Season's Greetings

2516a — BC64

1990
$5 booklet contains two panes of 10 25c stamps.

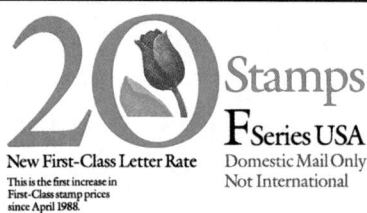

2519a, 2520a — BC65

1991
$2.90 booklet contains one pane of 10 F stamps.
$5.80 booklet contains two panes of 10 F stamps.

Twenty
Stamps

$**5**.80

2527a — BC66

Ten
Stamps

$**2**.90

2528a — BC67

Ten Stamps $2.90

2528a — BC67A

1991
$2.90 booklet contains one pane of 10 29c stamps.

Twenty Stamps $3.80

2530a — BC68

1991
$3.80 booklet contains two panes of 10 19c stamps.

Self-adhesive • DO NOT WET • USPS 1991 • Patent Pending
The U.S. Postal Service offers prestamped First-Class envelopes with printed return addresses at reasonable prices including shipping & handling. Convenient quantities of 50 available, several styles & sizes offered. Ask for an order form at your post office or write to: STAMPED ENVELOPE AGENCY PO BOX 500 WILLIAMSBURG PA 16693-0500

Self-adhesive • DO NOT WET • USPS 1991 • Patent Pending
The U.S. Postal Service offers prestamped First-Class envelopes with printed return addresses at reasonable prices including shipping & handling. Convenient quantities of 50 available, several styles & sizes offered. Ask for an order form at your post office or write to: STAMPED ENVELOPE AGENCY PO BOX 500 WILLIAMSBURG PA 16693-0500

2531Ab — BC68A

Self-adhesive Stamps

29 USA

Convenient: No Licking!

Strong Adhesive: Stays on Envelopes!

Easy to Use: No Tearing!

Eighteen Stamps

2531Ab — BC68B

1991
$5.22 fold-it-yourself booklet contains 18 self-adhesive 29c stamps.

Twenty Stamps $5.80

2536a — BC69

1991
$5.80 booklet contains two panes of 10 29c stamps.

Fishing Flies

Twenty Stamps $5.80 29c

2549a — BC70

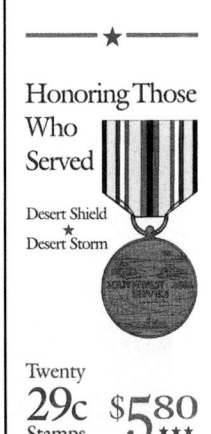

Honoring Those Who Served

Desert Shield
Desert Storm

Twenty 29c Stamps $5.80 ★★★

2552a — BC71

1991
$5.80 booklet contains four panes of 5 29c stamps.

COMEDIANS BY HIRSCHFELD

TWENTY 29 CENT STAMPS $5.80

2566a — BC72

1991
$5.80 booklet contains two panes of ten 29c stamps.

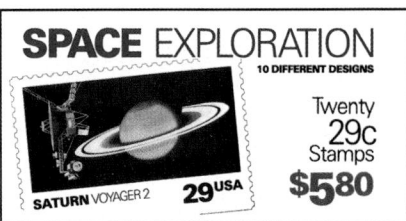

SPACE EXPLORATION
10 DIFFERENT DESIGNS

Twenty 29c Stamps $5.80

2577a — BC73

1991
$5.80 booklet contains two panes of 10 29c stamps.

Christmas 1991 USA
Antoniazzo c.1480 Houston Museum

Twenty Stamps First-Class Letter Rate

Season's Greetings

2578a — BC74

1991
($5.80) booklet contains two panes of 10 (29c) stamps.

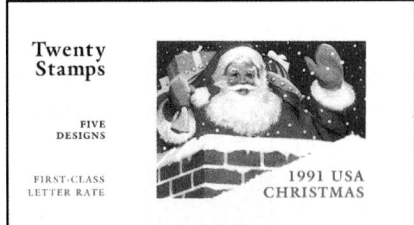

Twenty Stamps

FIVE DESIGNS

FIRST-CLASS LETTER RATE

1991 USA CHRISTMAS

2581b, 2582a-2585a — BC75

1991
($5.80) booklet contains five panes of 4 (29c) stamps.

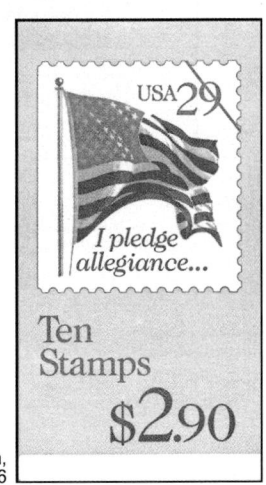

USA 29
I pledge allegiance...

Ten Stamps $2.90

2593a, 2594a — BC76

1992
$2.90 booklet contains one pane of 10 29c stamps.
$5.80 booklet contains two panes of 10 29c stamps.

2595a — BC77

1992

$5 fold-it-yourself booklet contains 17 self-adhesive 29c stamps.

Nos. BC77 differs in size and style of type as well as location of UPC labels.

2598a
BC78

1994

$5.22 fold-it-yourself booklet contains 18 self-adhesive 29c stamps.

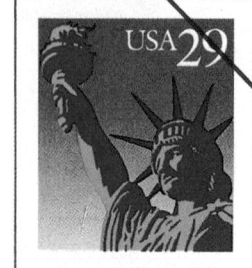

2599a
BC79

1994

$5.22 fold-it-yourself booklet contains 18 self-adhesive 29c stamps.

2646a — BC80

2709a — BC83

1992

$5.80 booklet contains four panes of 5 29c stamps.

CHRISTMAS

2710a — BC83A

1992

$5.80 booklet contains two panes of 10 29c stamps.

2718a — BC84

1992

$5.80 booklet contains five panes of 4 29c stamps

2719a
BC85

1992

$5.22 fold-it-yourself booklet contains 18 self-adhesive 29c stamps.

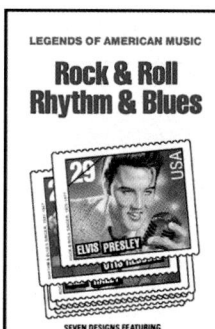

2737a — BC86

1993

$5.80 booklet contains one pane of four 29c stamps and two panes of eight 29c stamps.

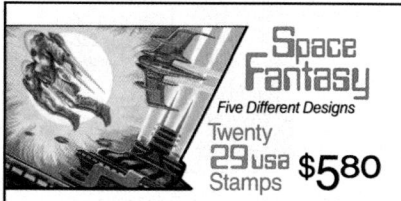

2745a — BC89

1993

$5.80 booklet contains four panes of 5 29c stamps.

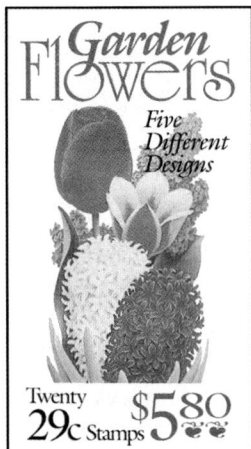

2764a — BC90

1993
$5.80 booklet contains four panes of 5 29c stamps.

2770a — BC91

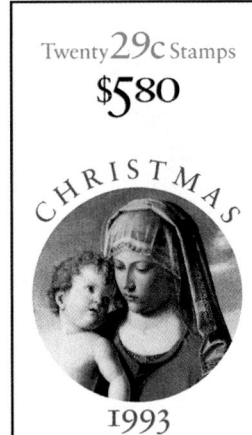

2790a — BC93

1993
$5.80 booklet contains five panes of 4 29c stamps.

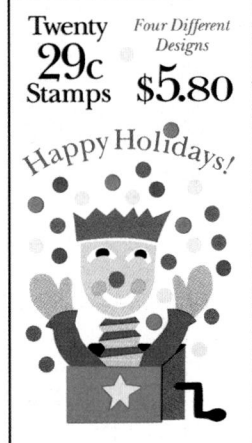

2798a — BC94

1993
$5.80 booklet contains two panes of 10 29c stamps.

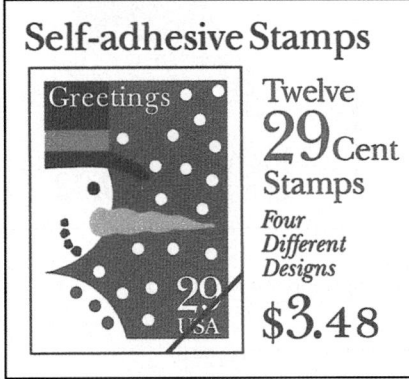

2802a — BC95

1993
$3.48 fold-it-yourself booklet contains 12 self-adhesive 29c stamps.

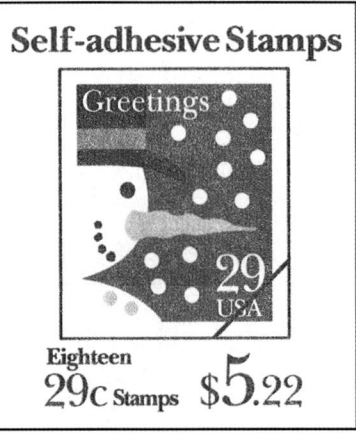

2803a
BC96

1993
$5.22 fold-it-yourself booklet contains 18 self-adhesive 29c stamps.

2806b — BC97

1993
$2.90 booklet contains two panes of 5 29c stamps.

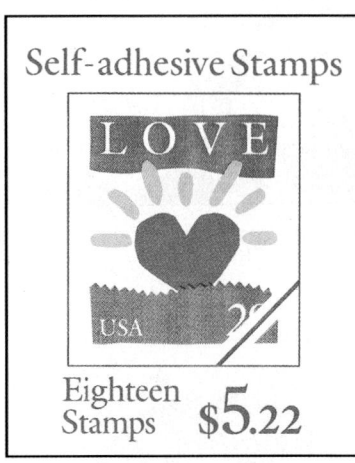

2813a
BC98

1994
$5.22 fold-it-yourself booklet contains 18 self-adhesive 29c stamps.

2778a — BC92

1993
$5.80 booklet contains five panes of 4 29c stamps.

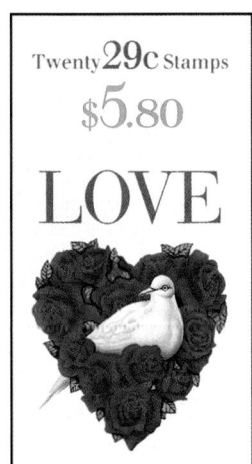

2814a — BC99

1994
$5.80 booklet contains two panes of 10 29c stamps.

2833a — BC100

1994
$5.80 booklet contains four panes of 5 29c stamps.

2847a — BC101

1994
$5.80 booklet contains four panes of 5 29c stamps.

2871Ab — BC102

1994
$5.80 booklet contains two panes of 10 29c stamps.

2872a — BC103

1994
$5.80 booklet contains one pane of 20 29c stamps.

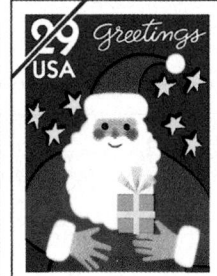

2873a — BC104

1994
$3.48 fold-it-yourself booklet contains 12 self-adhesive 29c stamps.

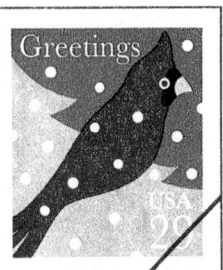

2874a
BC105

1994
$5.22 fold-it-yourself booklet contains 18 self-adhesive 29c stamps.

2881a, 2883a, 2884a, 2885a — BC106

1994
($3.20) booklet contains one pane of 10 G stamps.
($6.40) booklet contains two panes of 10 G stamps.

No. BC106 was printed by three different manufacturers either two- or four-color formats, with G in different colors with other minor design differences.

2886a, 2887a — BC107

1994
($5.76) fold-it-yourself booklet contains 18 self-adhesive G stamps.

2916a — BC108

1995
$3.20 booklet contains one pane of 10 32c stamps.
$6.40 booklet contains two panes of 10 32c stamps.

2919a
BC113

1995
$5.76 fold-it-yourself booklet contains 18 self-adhesive 32c stamps.

Twenty Self-adhesive Stamps

$6.40

920a
C114

95
$6.40 fold-it-yourself booklet contains 20 self-adhesive 32c stamps.

Twenty Self-adhesive Stamps

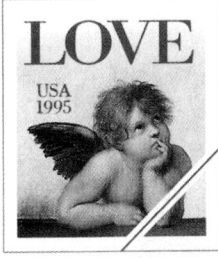

LOVE
USA 1995

First-Class Letter Rate
For Domestic Mail Only / Not for International Use

2949a
BC115

995
($6.40) fold-it-yourself booklet contains 20 self-adhesive non-denominated 32c stamps.

Twenty LOVE Stamps
Twenty
32c Stamps $6.40

2959a — BC116

1995
$6.40 booklet contains two panes of 10 32c stamps.

Twenty Self-adhesive Stamps

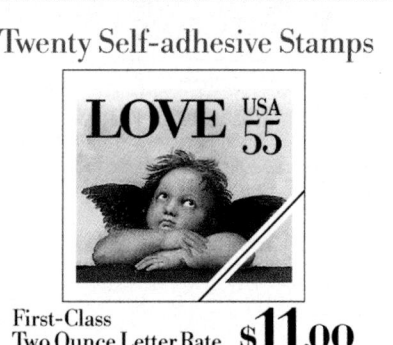

LOVE USA 55

First-Class Two Ounce Letter Rate $11.00

2960a — BC117

1995
$11 fold-it-yourself booklet contains 20 self-adhesive 55c stamps.

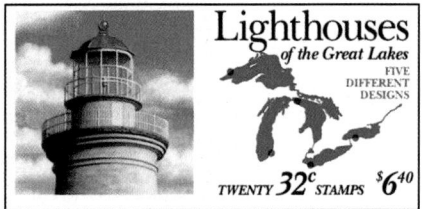

Lighthouses of the Great Lakes
FIVE DIFFERENT DESIGNS
TWENTY 32c STAMPS $6.40

2973a — BC118

1995
$6.40 booklet contains four panes of 5 32c stamps.

Garden Flowers
Five Different Designs
Twenty
32c Stamps $6.40

2997a — BC119

1995
$6.40 booklet contains four panes of 5 32c stamps

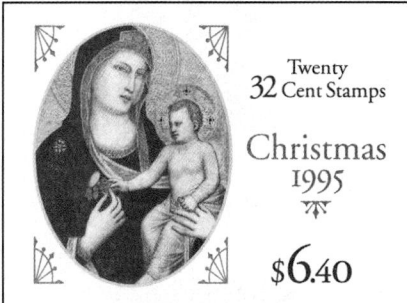

Twenty 32 Cent Stamps
Christmas 1995
$6.40

3003b — BC120

1995
$6.40 booklet contains two panes of 10 32c stamps

Holiday Greetings

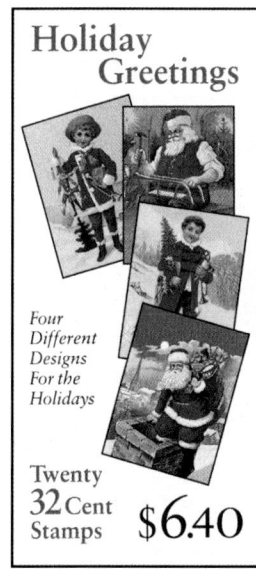

Four Different Designs For the Holidays

Twenty
32 Cent Stamps $6.40

3007b-3007c
BC121

1995
$6.40 booklet contains two panes of 10 32c stamps

Holiday Greetings

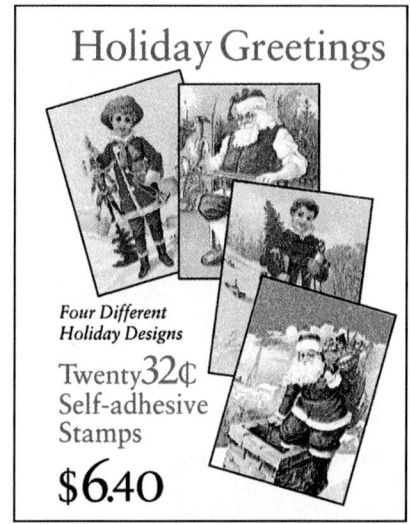

Four Different Holiday Designs

Twenty 32¢ Self-adhesive Stamps

$6.40

3011a — BC122

1995
$6.40 fold-it-yourself booklet contains 20 self-adhesive 32c stamps

Holiday Greetings

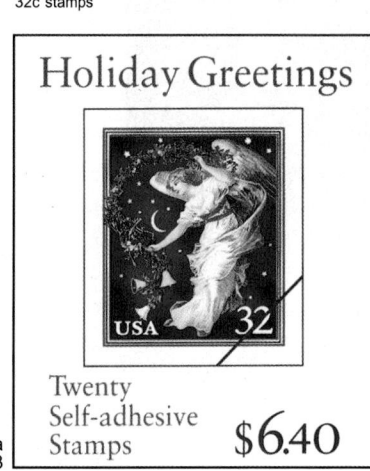

USA 32

Twenty Self-adhesive Stamps $6.40

3012a
BC123

1995
$6.40 fold-it-yourself booklet contains 20 self-adhesive 32c stamps

Eighteen Self-adhesive Stamps

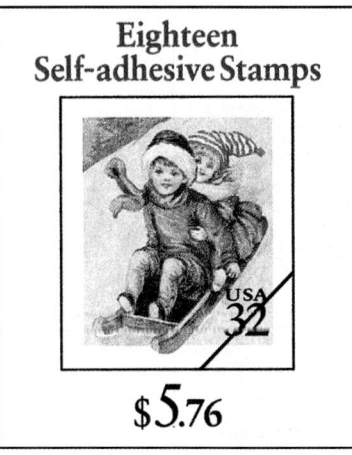

$5.76

3013a
BC124

1995
$5.76 fold-it-yourself booklet contains 18 self-adhesive
32c stamps

3029a — BC125

1996
$6.40 booklet contains four panes of 5 32c stamps

Front

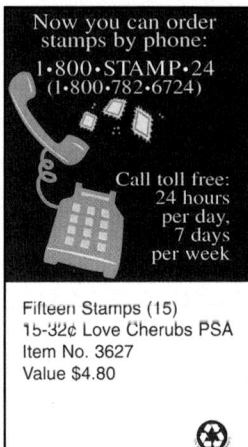

Now you can order
stamps by phone:
1·800·STAMP·24
(1·800·782·6724)

Call toll free:
24 hours
per day,
7 days
per week

Fifteen Stamps (15)
15-32¢ Love Cherubs PSA
Item No. 3627
Value $4.80

Back — BC126

1996
$4.80 booklet contains 15 32c stamps
$9.60 booklet contains 30 32c stamps

  A number of different stamps have been sold in BC126. The
text on the front and back changes to describe the contents of
the booklet. The enclosed stamps are affixed to the cover with a
spot of glue.

Twenty Self-adhesive Stamps

$6.40

UNITED STATES
POSTAL SERVICE.
We Deliver For You.

3071a — BC127

1996
$6.40 fold-it-yourself booklet contains 20 self-adhesive
32c stamps

Ten Self-adhesive Stamps for Postcards

USA
20

$2.00

3048a-3048c
BC128

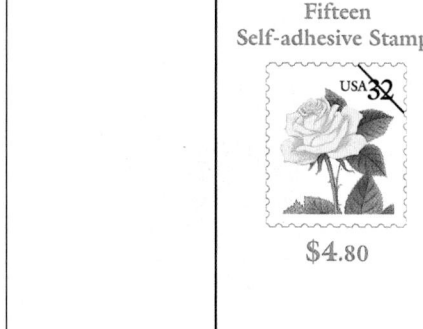

Fifteen
Self-adhesive Stamps

$4.80

UNITED STATES
POSTAL SERVICE.
We Deliver For You.

3049b — BC129

1996
$2.00 fold-it-yourself booklet contains 10 self-adhesive
20c stamps
$2.00 booklet contains 10 self-adhesive 20c stamps

1996
$4.80 booklet contains 15 self-adhesive 32c stamps

Ten Self-adhesive 20¢ Stamps

$2.00

3050a, 3051Ab-
3051Ac
BC130

1998
$2.00 fold-it-yourself booklet contains 10 self-adhesive
20c stamps
$2.00 booklet contains 10 self-adhesive 20c stamps

Coral Pink Rose
Twenty Self-adhesive 33¢ Stamps

$6.60

3052a-3052E — BC131

1999
$4.95 booklet contains 15 self-adhesive 33c stamps + la-
bel
$6.60 fold-it-yourself booklet contains 20 self-adhesive
33c stamps + label

Twenty
Self-adhesive Stamps

$6.40

3089a — BC133

3112a — BC134

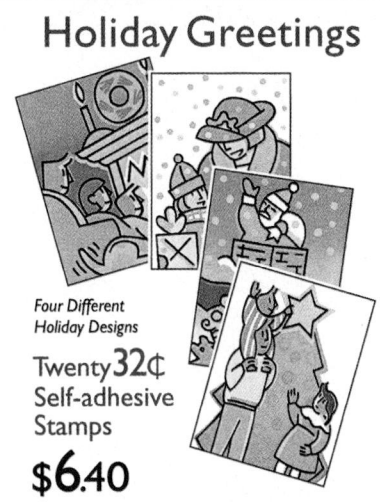

3116a — BC135

1996
$6.40 fold-it-yourself booklet contains 20 self-adhesive
        32c stamps

Eighteen
Self-adhesive Stamps

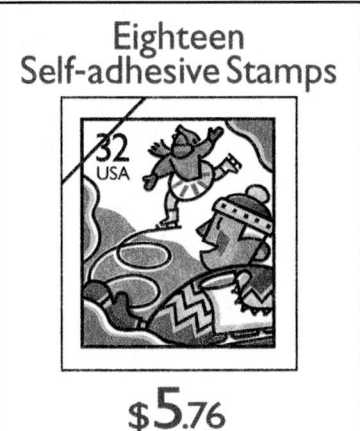

$5.76

3117a
BC136

1996
$5.76 fold-it-yourself booklet contains 18 self-adhesive
        32c stamps

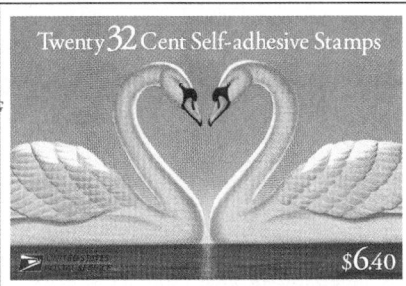

3123a — BC137

1997
$6.40 fold-it-yourself booklet contains 20 self-adhesive
        32c stamps
$11   fold-it-yourself booklet contains 20 self-adhesive
        55c stamps

3127a, 3128b, 3129b — BC138

1997
$4.80 booklet contains 15 32c stamps
$6.40 fold-it-yourself booklet contains 20 32c stamps

3137-3138 — BC139

1997
$3.20 booklet contains 10 32c self-adhesive stamps

3176a — BC140

3177a
BC141

1997
$6.40 fold-it-yourself booklet contains 20 self-adhesive
        32c stamps

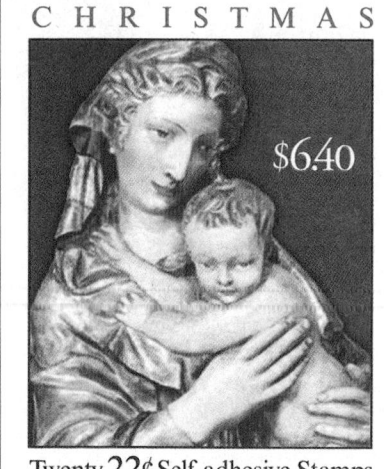

Twenty 32¢ Self-adhesive Stamps

3244a — BC142

3248a-3248c,
3252b — BC143

1998
$4.80 booklet contains 15 self-adhesive 32c stamps
$6.40 fold-it-yourself booklet contains 20 self-adhesive
     32c stamps

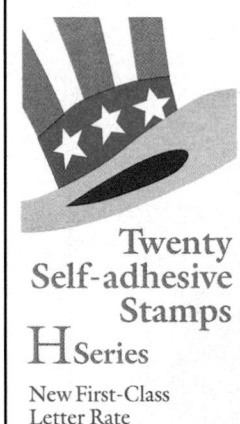

3267a, 3268a-3268b,
3269a — BC144

1998
($6.60) booklet contains 20 self-adhesive (33c) stamps
($3.30) fold-it-yourself booklet contains 10 self-adhesive
     (33c) stamps
($6.60) fold-it-yourself booklet contains 20 self-adhesive
     (33c) stamps
($5.94) fold-it-yourself booklet contains 18 self-adhesive
     (33c) stamps

3274a
BC145

3278a-3278e,
3279a — BC146

1999
$3.30 Fold-it-yourself booklet contains 10 self-adhesive
     33c stamps
$4.95 Booklet contains 15 self-adhesive 33c stamps
$6.60 Fold-it-yourself booklet contains 20 self-adhesive
     33c stamps
$6.60 Booklet contains 20 self-adhesive 33c stamps

3283a — BC147

1999
$5.94 fold-it-yourself booklet contains 18 self-adhesive
     33c stamps

3297
BC14

1999
$6.60 fold-it-yourself booklet contains 20 self-adhesive
     33c stamps + label
$4.95 booklet contains 15 self-adhesive 33c stamps + la-
     bel

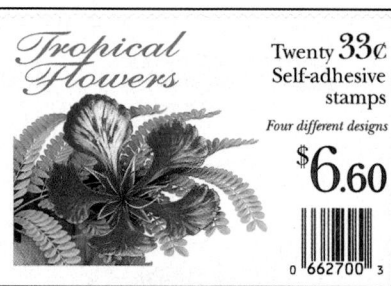

3313b — BC149

1999
$6.60 fold-it-yourself booklet contains 20 self-adhesive
     33c stamps

No. 3355 — BC150

Nos. 3360-3363 — BC151

Nos. 3364-3367 — BC152

1999
$6.60 fold-it-yourself booklets contains 20 self-adhesive 33c stamps
$4.95 fold-it-yourself booklet contains 15 self-adhesive 33c stamps

3377a — BC153

2000
$9.80 booklet contains 2 panes of one 22c, 33c, 55c, 60c and $3.20 stamps and 6 leaves of text.

3436a, 3436b, 3436c — BC153A

2004
$2.30 booklet contains 10 self-adhesive 23c stamps
$2.30 fold-it-yourself booklet contains 10 self-adhesive 23c stamps

3450a — BC154

2000
$6.12 fold-it-yourself booklet contains 18 self-adhesive (34c) stamps

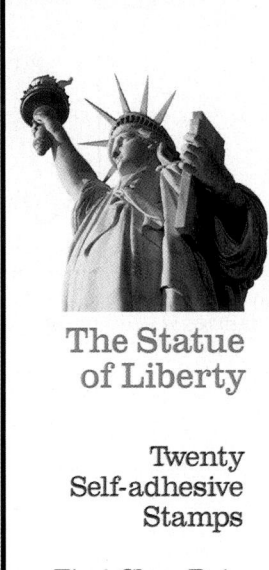

3451a — BC155

2000
$6.80 fold-it-yourself booklet contains 20 self-adhesive (34c) stamps

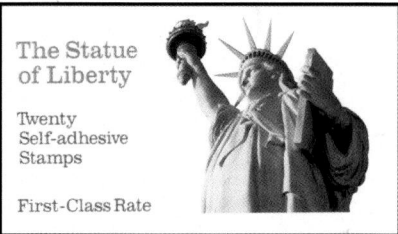

3451b, 3451c — BC156

2000
$6.80 booklet contains 20 self-adhesive (34c) stamps

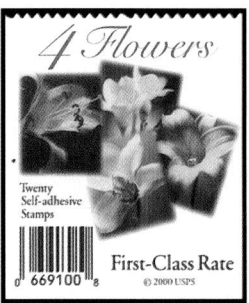

3457a — BC157

2000
$6.80 fold-it-yourself booklet contains 20 self-adhesive (34c) stamps

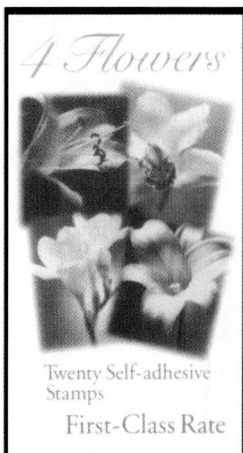

3457b, 3457c, 3457d — BC158

2000
$6.80 booklet contains 20 self-adhesive (34c) stamps

3482a, 3483a, 3483b — BC159

2001
$2 fold-it-yourself booklet contains 10 self-adhesive 20c stamps
$2 booklet contains 10 self-adhesive 20c stamps

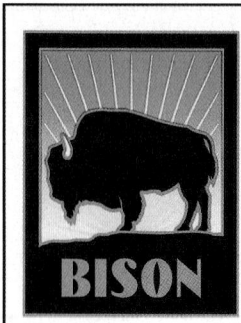

Ten 21 cent
Self-adhesive
Stamps
$2.10

3484b, 3484c, 3484d,
3484Ae, 3484Af,
3484Ag, 3484Ah,
3484Ai,
3484Aj — BC159A

2001
$2.10 fold-it-yourself booklet contains 10 self-adhesive 21c stamps
$2.10 booklet contains 10 self-adhesive 21c stamps

The Statue
of Liberty

Ten 34 cent
Self-adhesive
Stamps   **$3.40**

3485a, 3485b —
BC160

2001
$3.40 fold-it-yourself booklet contains 10 self-adhesive 34c stamps
$6.80 fold-it-yourself booklet contains 20 self-adhesive 34c stamps

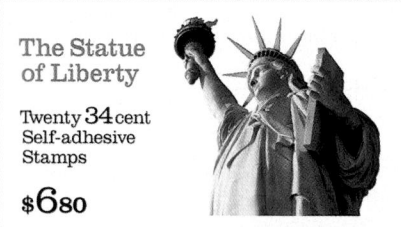

The Statue
of Liberty

Twenty 34 cent
Self-adhesive
Stamps

$6.80

3485c, 3485d — BC160A

2001
$6.80 booklet contains 20 self-adhesive 34c stamps

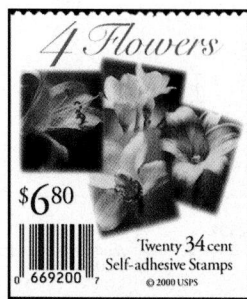

4 Flowers

$6.80

Twenty 34 cent
Self-adhesive Stamps
© 2000 USPS

0 669200 7

3490a — BC161

2001
$6.80 fold-it-yourself booklet contains 20 self-adhesive 34c stamps

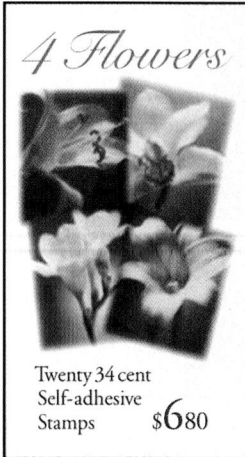

4 Flowers

Twenty 34 cent
Self-adhesive
Stamps   **$6.80**

3490b, 3490c,
3490d — BC162

2001
$6.80 booklet contains 20 self-adhesive 34c stamps

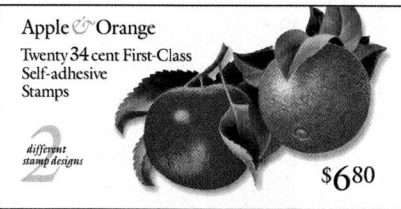

Apple & Orange
Twenty 34 cent First-Class
Self-adhesive
Stamps

2 different stamp designs

$6.80

3492b — BC163

2001
$6.80 fold-it-yourself booklet contains 20 self-adhesive 34c stamps

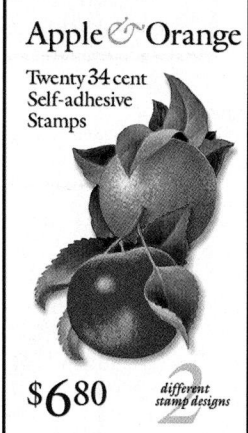

Apple & Orange

Twenty 34 cent
Self-adhesive
Stamps

$6.80   2 different stamp designs

3494b, 3494c,
3494d — BC163A

2001
$6.80 booklet contains 20 self-adhesive 34c stamps

Farm Flag
Eighteen Self-Adhesive Stamps
$6.12

3495a — BC163B

2001
$6.12 booklet contains 18 self-adhesive 34c stamps

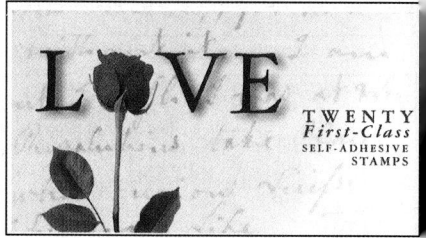

LOVE

TWENTY
First-Class
SELF-ADHESIVE
STAMPS

3496a — BC164

2001
$6.80 fold-it-yourself booklet contains 20 self-adhesive (34c) stamps

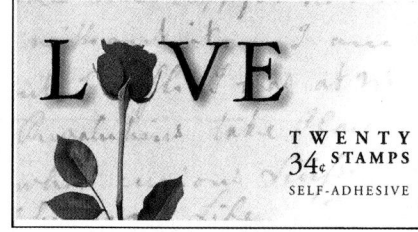

LOVE

TWENTY
34¢ STAMPS
SELF-ADHESIVE

3497a — BC165

2001
$6.80 fold-it-yourself booklet contains 20 self-adhesive 34c stamps

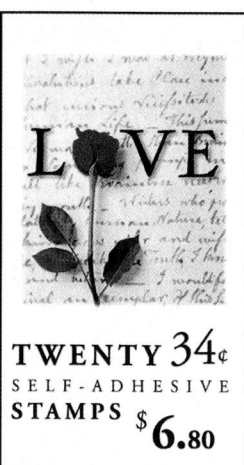

LOVE

TWENTY 34¢
SELF-ADHESIVE
STAMPS   **$6.80**

3498a,
3498b — BC166

2001
$6.80 booklet contains 20 self-adhesive 34c stamps

Seasons Greetings
Twenty **34** cent
First-Class
Self-adhesive
Stamps
$6.80

3536a — BC167

2001
$6.80 fold-it-yourself booklet contains 20 self-adhesive 34c stamps

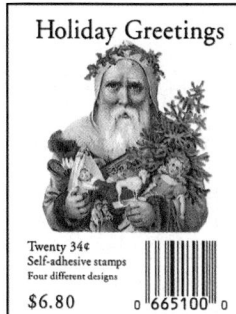

3540d — BC168

2001
$6.80 fold-it-yourself booklet contains 20 self-adhesive 34c stamps

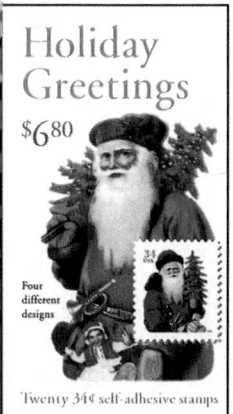

3544b, 3544c, 3544d — BC169

2001
$6.80 booklet contains 20 self-adhesive 34c stamps

3549a — BC170

2001
$6.80 booklet contains 20 self-adhesive 34c stamps

3549Bc,
3549Bd — BC171

2002
$6.80 booklet contains 20 self-adhesive 34c stamps

3549Be — BC172

2002
$6.80 fold-it-yourself booklet contains 20 self-adhesive 34c stamps

3618a, 3618b, 3619a, 3619b — BC173

2002
$2.30 booklet contains 10 self-adhesive 23c stamps

3623a — BC174

2002
$7.40 fold-it-yourself booklet contains 20 self-adhesive (37c) stamps

3624a, 3624b — BC175

2002
$7.40 booklet contains 20 self-adhesive (37c) stamps

3624c — BC176

2002
$7.40 fold-it-yourself booklet contains 20 self-adhesive (37c) stamps

3625a BC177

2002
$6.66 fold-it-yourself booklet contains 18 self-adhesive (37c) stamps

3629b, 3629c, 3629d — BC178

2002
$7.40 booklet contains 20 self-adhesive (37c) stamps

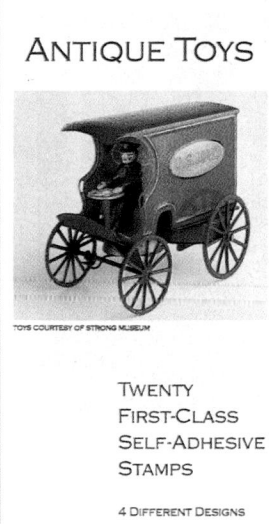

ANTIQUE TOYS

TOYS COURTESY OF STRONG MUSEUM

TWENTY
FIRST-CLASS
SELF-ADHESIVE
STAMPS

4 DIFFERENT DESIGNS

3629e — BC179

2002
    $7.40 fold-it-yourself booklet contains 20 self-adhesive (37c) stamps

U.S. Flag
Ten
37-cent First-Class
self-adhesive stamps
$3⁷⁰

3634a — BC180

2002
    $3.70 fold-it-yourself booklet contains 10 self-adhesive 37c stamps
    $7.40 booklet contains 20 self-adhesive 37c stamps.

U.S. Flag
Twenty
37 cent First-Class
self-adhesive stamps
$7⁴⁰

3635a — BC181

2002
    $7.40 fold-it-yourself booklet contains 20 self-adhesive 37c stamps

3636c — BC183

2002
    $7.40 fold-it-yourself booklet contains 20 self-adhesive 37c stamps

U.S. Flag
Twenty
37-cent First-Class
self-adhesive stamps
$7⁴⁰

3636a,
3636b — BC182

2002
    $7.40 fold-it-yourself booklet contains 20 self-adhesive 37c stamps

U.S. Flag
Eighteen 37-cent First-Class
self-adhesive stamps
$6⁶⁶

3637a—BC184

2003
    $6.66 fold-it-yourself booklet contains 18 self-adhesive 37c stamps

ANTIQUE TOYS
TWENTY 37¢
SELF-ADHESIVE
STAMPS
$7.40
4 DIFFERENT DESIGNS

3645b, 3645c, 3645d — BC185

2002
    $7.40 booklet contains 20 self-adhesive 37c stamps

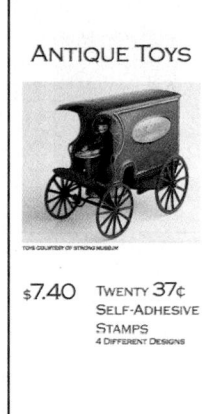

ANTIQUE TOYS
TOYS COURTESY OF STRONG MUSEUM
$7.40   TWENTY 37¢
SELF-ADHESIVE
STAMPS
4 DIFFERENT DESIGNS

3645e — BC186

2002
    $7.40 fold-it-yourself booklet contains 20 self-adhesive 37c stamps

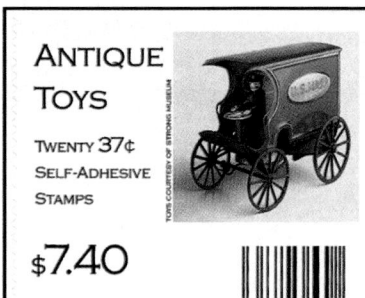

ANTIQUE TOYS
TWENTY 37¢
SELF-ADHESIVE
STAMPS
$7.40
4 DIFFERENT DESIGNS

3645h — BC179A

2003
    $7.40 booklet contains 20 self-adhesive 37c stamps

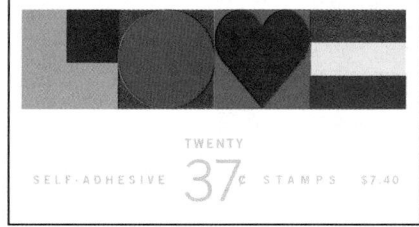

TWENTY
SELF-ADHESIVE 37¢ STAMPS $7.40

3657a — BC187

2002
    $7.40 fold-it-yourself booklet contains 20 self-adhesive 37c stamps

CHRISTMAS
Season's Greetings
$7.40
Twenty 37¢ self-adhesive stamps
UNITED STATES
POSTAL SERVICE

3675a — BC188

2002
    $7.40 fold-it-yourself booklet contains 20 self-adhesive 37c stamps

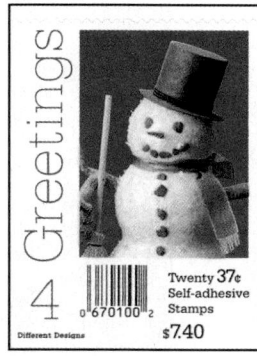

3687b — BC189

2
$7.40 booklet contains 20 self-adhesive 37c stamps

Greetings
4 Different Designs
$7.40 Twenty 37¢ Self-adhesive Stamps

3691b, 3691c, 3691d — BC190

02
$7.40 booklet contains 20 self-adhesive 37c stamps

3780b — BC191

03
$7.40 booklet contains 20 self-adhesive stamps

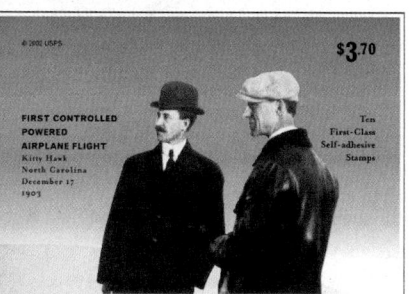

3783a, 3783b — BC192

003
$3.70 fold-it-yourself booklet contains 10 self-adhesive 37c stamps

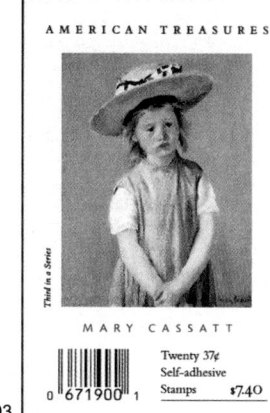

3807b — BC193

2003
$7.40 fold-it-yourself booklet contains 20 self-adhesive 37c stamps

3820a — BC194

2003
$7.40 fold-it-yourself booklet contains 20 self-adhesive 37c stamps

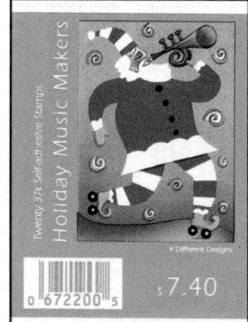

3824b — BC195

2003
$7.40 fold-it-yourself booklet contains 20 self-adhesive 37c stamps

3828b, 3828c, 3828d — BC196

2003
$7.40 booklet contains 20 self-adhesive 37c stamps

BC180 Type of 2002

2003
$7.40 booklet contains 20 self-adhesive 37c stamps

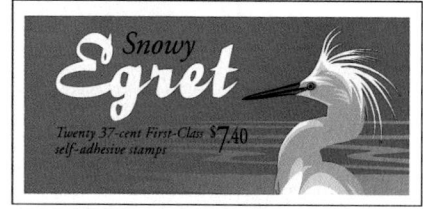

3830a — BC197

2004
$7.40 fold-it-yourself booklet contains 20 self-adhesive 37c stamps

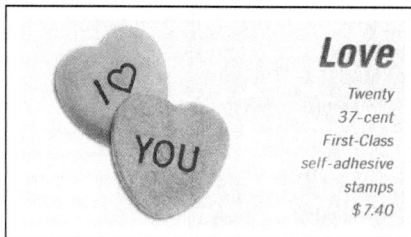

3833a — BC198

2004
$7.40 fold-it-yourself booklet contains 20 self-adhesive 37c stamps

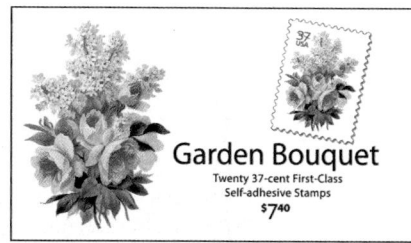

3836a — BC199

2004
$7.40 booklet contains 20 self-adhesive stamps

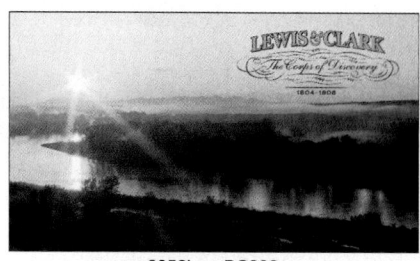

3856b — BC200

2004
$8.95 booklet contains 20 self-adhesive stamps

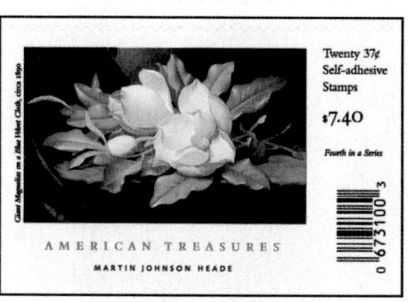

3872a — BC201

2004
$7.40 fold-it-yourself booklet contains 20 self-adhesive 37c stamps

3879a — BC202

2004
$7.40 fold-it-yourself booklet contains 20 self-adhesive 37c stamps

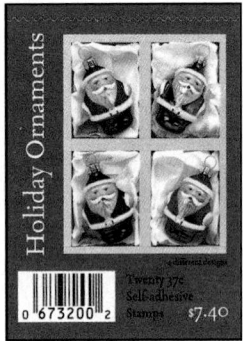

3886b — BC203

2004
$7.40 fold-it-yourself booklet contains 20 self-adhesive 37c stamps

3890b, 3890c,
3890d — BC204

2004
$7.40 booklet contains 20 self-adhesive 37c stamps

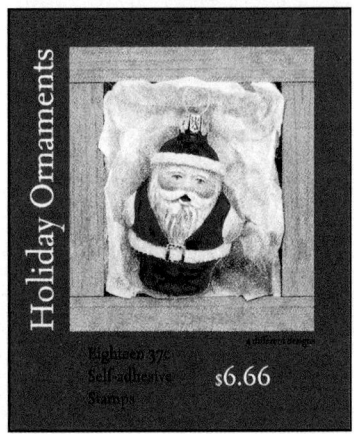

3894b
BC205

2004
$6.66 fold-it-yourself booklet contains 18 self-adhesive 37c stamps

3898a — BC206

2005
$7.40 booklet contains 20 self-adhesive stamps

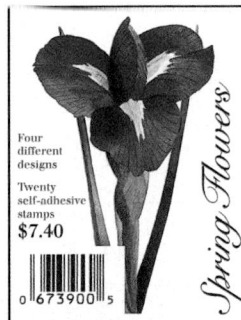

3903b — BC207

2005
$7.40 booklet contains 20 self-adhesive stamps

3908b — BC208

2005
$7.40 booklet contains 20 self-adhesive stamps

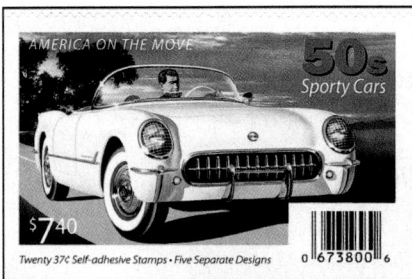

3935b — BC209

2004
$7.40 fold-it-yourself booklet contains 20 self-adhesive 37c stamps

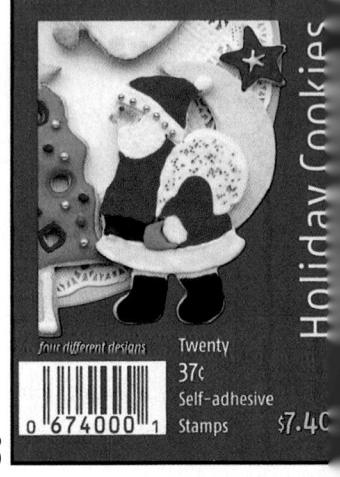

3956b
BC210

2005
$7.40 fold-it-yourself booklet contains 20 self-adhesive 37c stamps

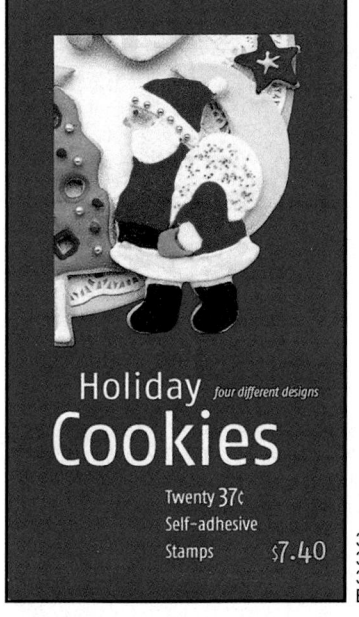

3960b,
3960c,
3960d
BC211

2005
$7.40 booklet contains 20 self-adhesive 37c stamps

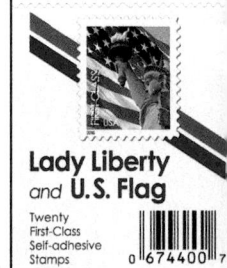

3966a,
3972a — BC212

2005
($7.80) fold-it-yourself booklet contains 20 self-adhesive (39c) stamps (2)

Lady Liberty
and **U.S. Flag**

Twenty
First-Class
Self-adhesive
Stamps

3974a,
3974b — BC213

2005
($7.80) booklet contains 20 self-adhesive (39c) stamps

Lady Liberty
and **U.S. Flag**

Eighteen First-Class
Self-adhesive Stamps

3975a
BC214

2005
($7.02) fold-it-yourself booklet contains 18 self-adhesive (39c) stamps

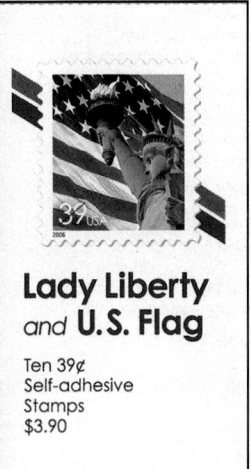

Lady Liberty
and **U.S. Flag**

Ten 39¢
Self-adhesive
Stamps
$3.90

3978a — BC216

2006
$3.90 fold-it-yourself booklet contains 10 self-adhesive 39c stamps

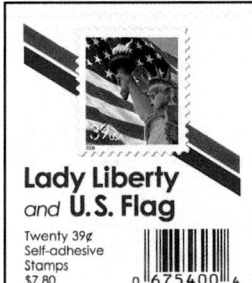

Lady Liberty
and **U.S. Flag**

Twenty 39¢
Self-adhesive
Stamps
$7.80

3978b — BC217

2006
$7.80 fold-it-yourself booklet contains 20 self-adhesive 39c stamps

3976a — BC215

2006
($7.80) fold-it-yourself booklet contains 20 self-adhesive (39c) stamps

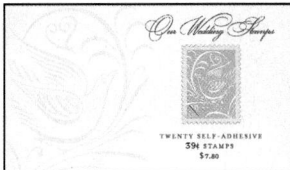

3998a — BC218

2006
$7.80 booklet contains 20 self-adhesive 39c stamps

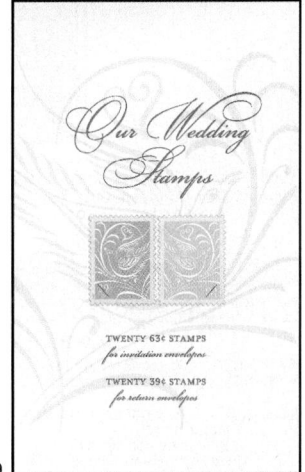

3999a — BC219

2006
$20.40 booklet contains 20 self-adhesive 39c and 20 self-adhesive 63c stamps

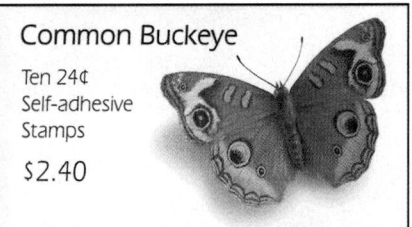

Common Buckeye

Ten 24¢
Self-adhesive
Stamps

$2.40

4001b, 4001c, 4001d — BC220

2006
$4.80 fold-it-yourself booklet contains 10 self-adhesive 24c stamps
$4.80 booklet contains 10 self-adhesive 24c stamps

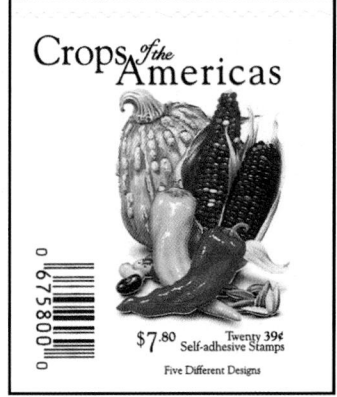

Crops *of the* **Americas**

$7.80 Twenty 39¢
Self-adhesive Stamps

Five Different Designs

4012b
BC221

2006
$7.80 fold-it-yourself booklet contains 20 self-adhesive 39c stamps

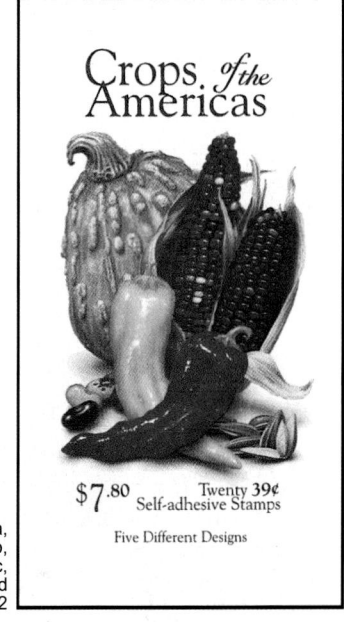

Crops *of the* **Americas**

$7.80 Twenty 39¢
Self-adhesive Stamps

Five Different Designs

4016a,
4017b,
4017c,
4017d
BC222

2006
$7.80 booklet contains 20 self-adhesive 39c stamps

4029a — BC223

2006
$7.80 fold-it-yourself booklet contains 20 self-adhesive 39c stamps

---

BOOKLET PANES

Values for both unused and used booklet panes are for complete panes with selvage, and for panes of six unless otherwise stated. Panes in booklets are Never Hinged. Values for stapled booklets are for those with creasing along the lines of the staples. Values for booklets which were glued shut are for opened booklets without significant damage to the cover.

See other notes in the introduction to this section.

Washington — A88

Wmk. 191 Horizontally or Vertically

1900-03   *Perf. 12*
279Bj A88 2c **red,** horizontal wmk., *Apr. 18*   450. *1,250.*
            light red   450.
            orange red, *1902*   450.
            Never hinged   900.
            With plate number (D)   1,250. *3,000.*
              Never hinged   2,000.
279Bk A88 2c **red,** vertical watermark   450. *1,250.*
            Never hinged   900.
            With plate number (D)   1,250.
              Never hinged   2,000.

360- (horiz. wmk.) and 180- (vert. wmk.) subject plates. All plate positions exist, except J, K, and L, due to the horizontal guide line being placed too far below stamps to appear on the upper panes.

Booklets
BK1 BC1 25c **black,** *cream*   —
BK2 BC1 25c **black,** *buff*   6,000.
BK3 BC1 49c **green,** *cream*   —
BK4 BC1 49c **black,** *buff*   —
BK5 BC1 97c **red,** *cream*   —
BK6 BC1 97c **black,** *gray*   —
BK7 BC2B 25c **black,** *cream* (3)   7,000.
BK8 BC2B 49c **black,** *buff* (3)
BK9 BC2B 97c **black,** *gray* (3)   15,000.

Nos. BK1-BK6 and one type each of Nos. BK7-BK9 exist with specimen overprints handstamped on cover and individual stamps.

All covers of BK7-BK9 exist with "Philippines" overprint in 50mm or 48mm.

Franklin — A115

Washington — A116

1903-07   **Wmk. 191 Vertically**
300b A115 1c **blue green,** *Mar. 6, 1907*   600. *12,500.*
            Never hinged   1,150.
            With plate number (D)   1,300.
              Never hinged   2,250.
            With plate number 3472 over left
              stamp (D)   4,000.

180-Subject Plates only. All plate positions exist.

Booklet
BK10 BC2A 25c **black,** *green* (6)   6,500.

301c A116 2c **carmine,** *Jan. 24, 1903*   500. *2,250.*
            Never hinged   950.
            With plate number (D)   1,500. *3,000.*
              Never hinged   2,500.

180-Subject Plates only. All plate positions exist.

Booklets
BK11 BC2B 25c **black,** *cream*   3,000.
BK12 BC2B 49c **black,** *buff*   4,000.
BK13 BC2B 97c **black,** *gray*   —

Washington — A129

1903   **Wmk. 191 Vertically**
319g A129 2c **carmine,** type I, *Dec. 3,*
            1903   125.00 *550.00*
            Never hinged   240.00
            With plate number (D)   275.00 *850.00*
              Never hinged   500.00
            Wmk. horizontal   1,500.
              Never hinged   2,500.
              With Plate number (D)   5,000.
319n A129 2c **carmine rose** (I)   250.00 *650.00*
            Never hinged   450.00
            With plate number (D)   425.00 *950.00*
              Never hinged   725.00
319p A129 2c **scarlet** (I)   185.00 *575.00*
            Never hinged   350.00
            With plate number (D)   350.00 *900.00*
              Never hinged   625.00
319h A129 2c **carmine,** type II, *1907*   300.00
            Never hinged   850.00
            With plate number (D)   650.00
              Never hinged   1,450.
319q A129 2c **lake** (II)   300.00 *750.00*
            Never hinged   575.00
            With plate number (D)   550.00
              Never hinged   900.00

180-Subject Plates only. All plate positions exist.

Booklet
BK14 BC2B 25c **black,** *cream* (11)   1,100.
BK15 BC2A 49c **black,** *buff* (11)   1,350.
BK16 BC2A 49c **black,** *pink*   2,500.
BK17 BC2B 97c **black,** *gray* (11)   2,750.

Booklet Covers
When more than one combination of covers exists, the number of possible booklets is noted in parenthesis after the booklet listing.

Franklin — A138

Washington — A139

1908   **Wmk. 191 Vertically**
331a A138 1c **green,** *Dec. 1908*   160.00 *450.00*
            Never hinged   285.00
            With plate number (D)   240.00
              Never hinged   400.00

180- and 360-Subject Plates. All plate positions exist.
No. 331 exists in horizontal pair, imperforate between, a variety resulting from booklet experiments. Not regularly issued. Value, unused $2,500.

Booklets
BK18 BC2A 25c **black,** *green* (3)   2,000.
BK19 BC3 25c **black,** *green*   2,250.

332a A139 2c **carmine,** *Nov. 16, 1908*   135.00 *400.00*
            Never hinged   230.00
            With plate number (D)   175.00
              Never hinged   300.00

180- and 360-Subject Plates. All plate positions exist.

Booklets
BK20 BC2B 25c **black,** *cream* (2)   1,250.
BK21 BC2A 49c **black,** *buff* (2)   2,750.
BK22 BC2A 49c **black,** *pink*   2,750.
BK23 BC2B 97c **black,** *gray* (3)   3,000.
BK24 BC3 25c **black,** *cream*   1,250.
BK25 BC3 49c **black,** *pink*   2,500.
BK26 BC3 97c **black,** *gray*   3,000.

1910   **Wmk. 190 Vertically**   *Perf. 12*
374a A138 1c **green,** *Oct. 7, 1910*   225.00 *300.00*
            Never hinged   375.00
            With plate number (D)   300.00
              Never hinged   475.00

360-Subject Plates only. All plate positions exist.

Booklet
BK27 BC3 25c **black,** *green* (2)   2,000.

375a A139 2c **carmine,** *Nov. 30, 1910*   125.00 *200.00*
            Never hinged   200.00
            With plate number (D)   170.00
              Never hinged   290.00

360-Subject Plates only. All plate positions exist.

Booklets
BK28 BC3 25c **black,** *cream* (2)   900.00
BK29 BC3 49c **black,** *pink* (2)   2,500.
BK30 BC3 97c **black,** *gray* (2)   3,000.

Washington — A140

1912   **Wmk. 190 Vertically**
405b A140 1c **green,** *Feb. 8, 1912*   65.00 *75.00*
            Never hinged   110.00
            With plate number (D)   80.00
              Never hinged   140.00

360-Subject Plates only. All plate positions exist.

Ordinary Booklets
BK31 BC3 25c **black,** *green* (2)   1,000.
BK32 BC4A 25c **black,** *green* (3)   1,250.
BK33 BC4A 97c **green,** *lavender*   1,750.

Combination Booklet
BK34 BC4B 73c **red,** 4 #405b + 4 #406a 3,000.

406a A140 2c **carmine,** *Feb. 8, 1912*   65.00 *90.00*
            Never hinged   110.00
            With plate number (D)   80.00
              Never hinged   140.00

360-Subject Plates only. All plate positions exist.

Ordinary Booklets
BK35 BC3 25c **black,** *cream* (2)   825.00
BK36 BC3 49c **black,** *pink* (2)   1,500.
BK37 BC3 97c **black,** *gray* (2)   2,000.
BK38 BC5A 25c **red,** *buff* (3)   1,000.
BK39 BC5A 49c **red,** *pink* (3)   1,750.
BK40 BC5A 97c **red,** *blue,* (3)   2,250.

Combination Booklet

See No. BK34.

1914   **Wmk. 190 Vertically**   *Perf. 10*
424d A140 1c **green**   5.25   7.50
            Never hinged   8.75
            Double transfer, Plate 6363   —   —
            With plate number (D)   14.00
              Never hinged   22.50
            Cracked plate   —
   e.   As "d," imperf.   1,600.
            With plate number (D)

360-Subject Plates only. All plate positions exist.
All known examples of No. 424e are without gum.

Ordinary Booklets
BK41 BC4A 25c **green,** *green* (3)   300.00
BK42 BC4A 97c **green,** *lavender* (2)   135.00

Combination Booklet
BK43 BC4B 73c **red,** 4 #424d + 8 #425e
            (3)   300.00

425e A140 2c **carmine,** *Jan. 6, 1914*   17.50   25.00
            Never hinged   30.00
            With plate number (D)   42.50
              Never hinged   70.00

360-Subject Plates only. All plate positions exist.

Ordinary Booklets
BK44 BC5A 25c **red,** *buff* (3)   500.00
BK45 BC5A 49c **red,** *pink* (3)   1,000.

K46 BC5A 97c **red**, *blue* (3)   1,250.

Combination Booklet
See No. BK43.

16   **Unwmk.**   *Perf. 10*

2a A140 1c **green**, *Oct. 15, 1916*   9.50   *12.50*
   Never hinged   16.00
   Cracked plate at right   225.00   —
    Never hinged   325.00
   Cracked plate at left   310.00
    Never hinged   425.00
   With plate number (D)   25.00
    Never hinged   37.50

360-Subject Plates only. All plate positions exist.

Ordinary Booklets

K47 BC4A 25c **green**, *green*   650.00
K48 BC4A 97c **green**, *lavender*   500.00

Combination Booklets

K49 BC4B 73c **red**, 4 #462a + 4 #463a
    (2)   900.00

63a A140 2c **carmine**, *Oct. 8, 1916*   110.00   *110.00*
   Never hinged   180.00
   With plate number (D)   150.00
    Never hinged   240.00

360-Subject Plates only. All plate positions exist.

Ordinary Booklets

K50 BC5A 25c **red**, *buff*   850.00
K51 BC5A 49c **red**, *pink*   1,500.
K52 BC5A 97c **red**, *blue*   2,500.

Combination Booklets
See No. BK49.

917-18   **Unwmk.**   *Perf. 11*

98e A140 1c **green**, *Apr. 6, 1917*   2.50   *2.00*
   Never hinged   4.25
   Double transfer   —   —
   With plate number (D)   6.00   *2.00*
    Never hinged   9.00

360-Subject Plates only. All plate positions exist.

Ordinary Booklets

K53 BC4A 25c **green**, *green* (2)   300.00
K54 BC4A 97c **green**, *lavender* (4)   85.00
K55 BC6A 25c **green**, *green* (5)   120.00

Combination Booklet

K56 BC4B 73c **red**, 4 #498e + 4 #499e
    (4)   80.00
K57 BC4B 73c **red**, 4 #498e + 4 #554c
    (3)   100.00

499e A140 2c **rose**, type I, *Mar. 31,*
    1917   4.00   *2.50*
   Never hinged   6.75
   With plate number (D)   7.00   *2.25*
    Never hinged   10.00

360-Subject Plates only. All plate positions exist.

Ordinary Booklets

BK58 BC5A 25c **red**, *buff* (5)   250.00
BK59 BC5A 49c **red**, *pink* (4)   400.00
BK60 BC5A 97c **red**, *blue* (3)   750.00
BK61 BC6C 97c **red**, *blue* (2)   1,250.

Combination Booklets
See No. BK56.

501b A140 3c **violet**, type I, *Oct. 17,*
    1917   75.00   *60.00*
   Never hinged   125.00
   With plate number (D)   105.00
    Never hinged   160.00

360-Subject Plates only. All plate positions exist.

Booklet

BK62 BC6B 37c **violet**, *sage*   500.00

502b A140 3c **violet**, type II, *Mar. 1918*   60.00   *55.00*
   Never hinged   100.00
   With plate number (D)   77.50
    Never hinged   120.00

360-Subject Plates only. All plate positions exist.

Booklet

BK63 BC6B 37c **violet**, *sage*   235.00

Washington — A140

A.E.F. Panes of 30

1917, Aug.

498f A140 1c **green** (pane of 30)   *1,150.*
   Never hinged   *1,800.*

Booklet

BK64 BC7 $3 **black**, *green*   25,000.

499f A140 2c **rose**, (pane of 30) type I   *28,000.*
   Never hinged   *38,000.*

Booklet

BK65 BC7 $6 **black**, *pink*

No copies of No. BK65 are known. The number and description is provided only for specialist reference.

Nos. 498f and 499f were for use of the American Expeditionary Force in France.

They were printed from the ordinary 360-Subject Plates, the sheet being cut into 12 leaves of 30 stamps each in place of 60 leaves of 6 stamps each, and, of course, the lines of perforations changed accordingly.

The same system as used for designating plate positions on the ordinary booklet panes is used for designating the war booklet, only each war booklet pane is composed of 5 ordinary panes. Thus, No. W1 booklet pane would be composed of positions 1, 2, 3, 4, and 5 of an ordinary pane, etc.

The A. E. F. booklet panes were bound at side margins which accounts for side arrows sometimes being found on positions W5 and W6. As the top and bottom arrows were always removed when the sheets were cut, positions W1 and W2 cannot be distinguished from W7 and W8. Cutting may remove guidelines on these, but identification is possible by wide bottom margins. Positions W3 and W4 cannot be distinguished from W9 and W10.

There are thus just 8 collectible positions from the sheet as follows:

W1 or W7 Narrow top and wide bottom margins. Guide line at right.

W2 or W8 As W1, but guide line at left.

W3 or W9 Approximately equal top and bottom margins. Guide line at right.

W4 or W10 As W3, but guide line at left.

W5 Narrow bottom margin showing guideline very close to stamps. Wide top margin. Guide line at right. Pane with extra long tab may show part of split arrow at left.

W6 As W5, but guide line at left, split arrow at right. Guide line at left and at bottom. Arrow at lower right may or may not show.

W11 Narrow bottom and wide top margins. Guide line at right. Siderographer initials on left tab.

W12 Narrow bottom and wide top margins. Guide line at left. Finisher initials on right tab.

Franklin — A155

Washington — A157

1923   **Unwmk.**   *Perf. 11*

552a A155 1c **deep green**, *Aug. 1923*   7.50   *4.00*
   Never hinged   12.50
   With plate number (D)   13.00
    Never hinged   21.00

360-Subject Plates only. All plate positions exist.

Ordinary Booklets

BK66 BC6A 25c **green**, *green* (2)   75.00
BK67 BC4A 97c **green**, *lavender* (3)   650.00

Combination Booklet

BK68 BC4B 73c **white**, *red*, 4 #552a + 4
    #554c (3)   85.00

554c A157 2c **carmine**   7.00   *3.00*
   Never hinged   12.00
   With plate number (D)   12.00
    Never hinged   20.00

360-Subject Plates only. All plate positions exist.

Ordinary Booklets

BK69 BC5A 25c **red**, *buff* (3)   *400.00*
BK70 BC5A 49c **red**, *pink* (3)   950.00
BK71 BC6C 97c **red**, *blue* (3)   1,500.

Combination Booklets

See Nos. BK57 and BK68.

ROTARY PRESS PRINTINGS

Two experimental plates were used to print No. 583a. At least one guide line pane (H) is known from these plates. The rest of rotary press booklet panes were printed from specially prepared plates of 360-subjects in arrangement as before, but without the guide lines and the plate numbers are at the sides instead of at the top as on the flat plates.

The only varieties possible are the ordinary pane (A) and partial plate numbers appearing at the right or left of the upper or lower stamps of a booklet pane when the trimming of the sheets is off center. The note applies to Nos. 583a, 632a, 634d, 720b, 804b, 806b and 807a, before Electric Eyes.

1926   *Perf. 10*

583a A157 2c **carmine**, *Aug. 1926*   95.00   *150.00*
   Never hinged   175.00

Ordinary Booklets

BK72 BC5A 25c **red**, *buff* (3)   *725.00*
BK73 BC5A 49c **red**, *pink*   *1,000.*
BK74 BC6C 97c **red**, *blue*   *1,250.*

1927   *Perf. 11x10½*

632a A155 1c **green**, *Nov. 2, 1927*   5.00   *4.00*
   Never hinged   8.00

Ordinary Booklets

BK75 BC5A 25c **green**, *green* (3)   65.00
BK76 BC4A 97c **green**, *lavender*   600.00
BK77 BC5A 97c **green**, *lavender*   —

Combination Booklets

BK78	BC4B	73c **red**, 4 #632a + 4 #634d	—
BK79	BC5D	73c **red**, 4 #632a + 4 #634d (2)	90.00

634d	A157	2c **carmine**, type I, *Feb. 25, 1927*	1.50	*1.50*
		Never hinged	2.50	

Ordinary Booklets

BK80	BC5A	25c **red**, *buff* (2)	10.00
a.		With experimental cellophane interleaving	*1,500.*
BK81	BC5A	49c **red**, *pink* (2)	15.00
BK82	BC5A	97c **red**, *blue* (3)	50.00
BK83	BC6C	97c **red**, *blue*	900.00

Combination Booklets

See Nos. BK78 and BK79.

56,000 booklets of BK80a were produced in 1928 using .00125 inch thick cellophane interleaving. Scarce, as few were saved.

Varieties

634e	A157	2c **carmine lake**, type I	*2,000.*
		Never hinged	*4,000.*

Washington — A226

1932

720b	A226	3c **deep violet**, *July 25, 1932*	35.00	*12.50*
		Never hinged	60.00	

Ordinary Booklets

BK84	BC9A	37c **violet**, *buff* (2)	135.00
a.		With experimental cellophane interleaving	*1,750.*
BK85	BC9A	73c **violet**, *pink* (2)	375.00

30,000 booklets of No. BK84a were made with .001 inch thick cellophane interleaving, similar to but thinner than the experimental interleaving used for No. BK80a. Poor handling qualities during booklet assembly plus higher cost prevented wider use. Placed on sale in Wash. D.C. post office in Sept., 1936. Extremely scarce, as few were saved.

> **Catalogue values for unused panes in this section, from this point to the end, are for Never Hinged items.**

Washington — A276

Adams — A278

Jefferson — A279

In 1942 plates were changed to the Type II "new design" and the E. E. marks may appear at the right or left margins of panes of Nos. 804b, 806b and 807a. Panes printed from E. E. plates have 2½mm vertical gutter; those from pre-E. E. plates have 3mm vertical gutter.

1939-42   *Perf. 11x10½*

804b	A276	1c 3mm vert. gutter, *Jan. 27, 1939*	4.00	*.85*

Ordinary Booklets

BK86	BC5A	25c **green**, *green*	75.00
BK87	BC5A	97c **green**, *lavender*	*500.00*
BK88	BC4A	97c **green**, *lavender*	—

Combination Booklet

BK89	BC5D	73c **red**, 4 #804b + 4 #806b	135.00

804b	A276	1c 2½mm vert. gutter, *Apr. 14, 1942*	2.00	*.50*
		Horiz. pair, perf. only at bottom		

Ordinary Booklets

BK90	BC5A	25c **green**, *green*	8.25
BK91	BC5A	97c **green**, *lavender*	500.00

Combination Booklets

BK92	BC5D	73c **red**, 4 #804b + 4 #806b	30.00
BK93	BC9E	73c **red**, 4 #804b + 4 #806b	37.50

Varieties

804c	A278	2c Horiz. pair, imperf btwn. (from booklet pane)	—
806b	A278	2c 3mm vert. gutter, *Jan. 27, 1939*	20.00 *2.50*

Combination Booklets

BK94	BC5A	97c **red**, *blue*	375.00

Combination Booklets

See No. BK89.

806b	A278	2c 2½mm vert. gutter, *Apr. 25, 1942*	4.75	*.85*

Ordinary Booklets

BK95	BC5A	97c **red**, *blue*	1,250.
BK96	BC5A	25c **red**, *buff*	19.00
BK97	BC9A	25c **red**, *buff*	90.00
BK98	BC5A	49c **red**, *pink*	45.00
BK99	BC9A	49c **red**, *pink*	75.00

Combination Booklets

See Nos. BK92 and BK93.

807a	A279	3c 3mm vert. gutter, *Jan. 27, 1939*	25.00	*3.25*

Booklets

BK100	BC9A	37c **violet**, *buff*	80.00
BK101	BC9A	73c **violet**, *pink*	*750.00*

807a	A279	3c 2½mm vert. gutter, *Mar. 6, 1942*	8.50	*2.00*
		Horiz. pair with full vert. pane gutter btwn.	—	

Booklets

BK102	BC9A	37c **violet**, *buff* (3)	22.50
BK103	BC9A	73c **violet**, *pink* (3)	47.50

Varieties

807d	A279	As "a," imperf between vert.	—

Statue of Liberty — A482

Lincoln — A483

1954-58   *Perf. 11x10½*

1035a	A482	3c pane of 6, *June 30, 1954*	4.00	*1.25*
1035f		Dry printing	5.00	*1.50*

Booklets

BK104	BC9A	37c **violet**, *buff*, with #1035a	20.00
a.		With #1035f	25.00
BK105	BC9A	73c **violet**, *pink*, with #1035a	25.00
a.		With #1035f	30.00

Varieties

1035g		As "a," vert. imperf. betwn.	*5,000.*
1036a	A483	4c pane of 6, *July 31, 1958*	2.75 *1.25*

Booklets

BK106	BC9F	97c on 37c **violet**, *buff*	60.00
BK107	BC9G	97c on 73c **violet**, *pink*	30.00
BK108	BC9H	97c **blue**, *yellow*	150.00

BK109	BC9H	97c **blue**, *pink* (3)	18.00
a.		With experimental silicone interleaving	*150.00*

Varieties

1036d	A483	As "a," imperf. horiz.	—
1036e	A483	Horiz. pair, imperf between	*3,500.*

No. 1036e resulted from a booklet pane foldover after perforating and before cutting into panes.

Washington (Slogan 1) — A650

Slogan 2

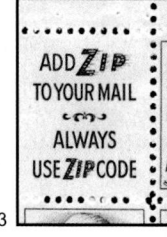

Slogan 3

1962-64   *Perf. 11x10*

Plate of 300 stamps, 60 labels

1213a	A650	5c pane of 5+label, slogan 1, *Nov. 23, 1962*	7.00	*4.0*
		With slogan 2, *1963*	16.00	*7.0*
		With slogan 3, *1964*	3.00	*2.0*

Booklets

BK110	BC12A	$1 **blue**, slogan 1	30.00
BK111	BC12A	$1 **blue**, slogan 2	110.00
BK112	BC13A	$1 **blue**, slogan 2	90.00
BK113	BC13A	$1 **blue**, slogan 3 (4)	15.00

1213c	A650	As No. 1213a, tagged, slogan 2, *Oct. 28, 1963*	50.00	*10.0*
		With slogan 3, *1964*	2.00	*1.5*

Booklets

BK114	BC13A	$1 **blue**, slogan 2	200.00
BK115	BC13A	$1 **blue**, slogan 3 (4)	10.50

Varieties

1213d	A650	Horiz. pair, imperf between	*2,750.*

No. 1213d resulted from a paper foldover after perforating and before cutting into panes. At least six individually unique panes exist, including at least one that contains two error pairs. Recent auction prices have ranged between $1,400 and $4,000.

Jefferson — A710

Wright — A712

Slogan 4

Slogan 5

1967-78 *Perf. 11x10½*

1278a A710   1c pane of 8, shiny gum, *Jan. 12, 1968*   1.00   .75
      Dull gum   2.00

Combination Booklets

See Nos. BK116, BK117B, BK118 and BK119.

1278b A710   1c pane of 4+2 labels, slogans 5 & 4, *May 10, 1971*   .80   .60

Combination Booklet

See No. BK122.

Varieties

1278e A710   As "a," dull gum, tagging omitted   *75.00*

1280a A712   2c pane of 5+label, slogan 4, *Jan. 8, 1968*   1.25   .80
      With slogan 5   1.25   .80

Combination Booklets

See Nos. BK117 and BK120.

1280c A712   2c pane of 6, shiny gum, *May 7, 1971*   1.00   .75
      Dull gum   1.10

Combination Booklets

See Nos. BK127 and BKC22.

The 1c and 6c panes of 8, Nos. 1278a and 1284b, were printed from 320-subject plates and from 400-subject plates, both with electric eye markings. The 2c and 6c panes of 5 stamps plus label, Nos. 1280a and 1284c, were printed from 360-subject plates.

An experimental moisture-resistant gum was used on 1,000,000 panes of No. 1278a and 4,000,000 of No. 1393a released in March, 1971. This dull finish gum shows no breaker ridges. The booklets lack interleaving. This gum was also used for Nos. 1395c, 1395d, 1288c and all engraved panes from No. 1510b on unless noted.

Roosevelt — A716

Oliver Wendell Holmes — A720

Perf. 10½x11

1284b A716   6c pane of 8, *Dec. 28, 1967*   1.50   1.00

Combination Booklet

BK116 BC14A $2 **brown**, 4 #1284b (6c)+1 #1278a(1c)(2)   7.75

1284c A716   6c pane of 5+label, slogan 4, *Jan. 9, 1968*   1.50   1.00
      With slogan 5   1.50   1.00

Combination Booklet

BK117 BC15 $1 **brown**, 3 #1284c (6c) + 1 #1280a (2c) (2)   7.00

No. BK117 contains panes with slogan 4, slogan 5 or combinations of 4 and 5.

Varieties

1284e A716   6c As "b," tagging omitted   *50.00*   —

Perf. 10

1288Bc A720   15c pane of 8, *June 14, 1978*   2.80   1.75

Booklet

BK117A BC23 $3.60 **red & light blue**, no P#   8.75

Varieties

1288Be A720   As "c," vert. imperf. btwn.   *1,750.*
1288Bi A720   As "c," tagging omitted   *50.00*

Eisenhower — A815

Plate of 400 subjects for No. 1393a. Plate of 300 stamps and 60 labels for No. 1393b.

1970 Tagged *Perf. 11x10½*

1393a A815   6c pane of 8, shiny gum, *Aug. 6*   1.50   .75
      Dull gum   1.90

Combination Booklets

BK117B BC14A $2 **blue**, 4 #1393a (6c) + 1 #1278a (1c)   9.00
BK118 BC16 $2 **blue**, 4 #1393a (6c) + 1 #1278a (1c) (2)   7.25
BK119 BC16 $2 **blue**, dull gum, 4 #1393a (6c) + 1 #1278a (1c) (2)   8.75

1393b A815   6c pane of 5+label, slogan 4, *Aug. 6*   1.50   .75
      With slogan 5   1.50   .75

Combination Booklet

BK120 BC15 $1 **blue**, 3 #1393b (6c) + 1 #1280a (2c)   6.00

No. BK120 contains panes with slogan 4, slogan 5 or combinations of 4 and 5.

Varieties

1393h A815   6c As "a," tagging omitted, shiny gum   *175.00*   —
      Dull gum   —

Slogans 6 and 7

Eisenhower — A815a

1971-72		**Shiny Gum**	*Perf. 11x10½*	
1395a	A815a	8c **deep claret**, pane of 8, *May 10, 1971*	1.80	1.25
		Booklet		
BK121	BC16	$1.92 **claret** (2)	6.50	
1395b	A815a	8c pane of 6, *May 10, 1971*	1.25	1.10
		Combination Booklet		
BK122	BC15	$1 **claret**, 2 #1395b (8c) + 1 #1278b (1c) (2)	4.00	
		Dull Gum		
1395c	A815a	8c pane of 4+2 labels, slogans 6 and 7, *Jan. 28, 1972*	1.65	1.00
1395d	A815a	8c pane of 7+label, slogan 4, *Jan. 28, 1972*	1.90	1.10
		With slogan 5	1.90	1.10
		Combination Booklet		
BK123	BC17A	$2 **claret**, *yellow*, 3 #1395d + 1 #1395c	7.75	
		Varieties		
1395e		Vert. pair, imperf between	850.00	
1395f		As "a," tagging omitted	175.00	—
1395g		As "b," tagging omitted	50.00	—
1395h		As "c," tagging omitted	35.00	—
1395i		As "d," tagging omitted	—	

Plate of 400 subjects for No. 1395a. Plate of 360 subjects for No. 1395b. Plate of 300 subjects (200 stamps and 100 double-size labels) for No. 1395c. Plate of 400 subjects (350 stamps and 50 labels) for No. 1395d.

A pane of No. 1395d is known with a foldover resulting in a vertical pair of stamp and label, imperf between.

No. 1395e resulted from a paper foldover after perforating and before cutting into panes. At least 4 pairs are recorded from 3 panes (one 1395a, two 1395d) with different foldover patterns.

No. BK123 exists with covers printed on both thin and thick card stock.

Booklet Covers

When more than one combination of covers exists, the number of possible booklets is noted in parenthesis after the booklet listing.

Slogan 8

Jefferson Memorial — A924

1973-74			*Perf. 11x10½*	
1510b	A924	10c pane of 5+label, slogan 8, *Dec. 14, 1973*	1.65	.90
		Booklet		
BK124	BC17B	$1 **red & blue**	3.75	
1510c	A924	10c pane of 8, *Dec. 14, 1973*	1.65	1.00
		Booklet		
BK125	BC17C	$4 **red & blue**	8.50	
1510d	A924	10c pane of 6, *Aug. 5, 1974*	5.25	1.75
		Combination Booklet		
BK126	BC17D	$1.25 **red & blue**, 1 #1510d (10c) + 1 #C79a (13c)	7.25	

No. BK125 exists with covers printed on both thin and thick card stock.

Varieties

1510f	Vert. pair, imperf between	500.00	
1510h	As "c," tagging omitted	—	

No. 1510f resulted from a paper foldover after perforating and before cutting into panes.

Slogan 9

Liberty Bell — A998

1975-78			*Perf. 11x10*	
1595a	A998	13c pane of 6, *Oct. 31, 1975*	2.25	1.
		Combination Booklet		
BK127	BC19A	90c **red & blue**, 1 #1595a (13c) + 1 #1280c (2c) (2)	3.25	
1595b	A998	13c pane of 7+label, slogan 8, *Oct. 31, 1975*	2.25	1.0
1595c	A998	13c pane of 8, *Oct. 31, 1975*	2.25	1.0
		Combination Booklet		
BK128	BC19B	$2.99 **red & blue**, 2 #1595c (13c) + 1 #1595b (13c) (2)	7.75	

No. BK128 exists with covers printed on both thin and thic card stock.

1595d	A998	13c pane of 5+label, slogan 9, *Apr. 2, 1976*	1.75	1.0
		Booklet		
BK129	BC19A	$1.30 **red & blue**	4.00	
		Varieties		
1595e		Vert. pair, imperf. btwn.	1,250.	
1595f		Tagging omitted	—	—
1595g		Horiz. pair, imperf. btwn.	—	

Nos. 1595e and 1595g resulted from paper foldovers afte perforating and before cutting into panes. Beware of printer' waste consisting of complete panes with perfs around a outside edges.

A994, A1018a

Fort McHenry Flag (15 Stars) — A1001

1977-78			*Perf. 11x10½*	
1598a	A1001	15c pane of 8, *June 30, 1978*	4.25	.80
		Booklet		
BK130	BC21	$1.20 **red & light blue**, no P#	4.50	
1623a	A1018a	Pane of 8 (1 #1590 + 7 #1623), *Mar. 11, 1977*	2.25	1.25
		Booklet		
BK131	BC20	$1 **red & light blue**, no P# (3)	2.50	
		Varieties		
1623d		Pair, Nos. 1590, 1623	.70	1.00

623f		Tagging omitted, single stamp	—	

Perf. 10x9¾

623Bc	A1018a	Pane of 8 (1 #1590A + 7 #1623B), *Mar. 11, 1977*	25.00	—

Booklet

K132	BC20	$1 **red & light blue**, no P# (2)	26.00	

Varieties

623Be		Pair, Nos. 1590A, 1623B	21.00	21.00

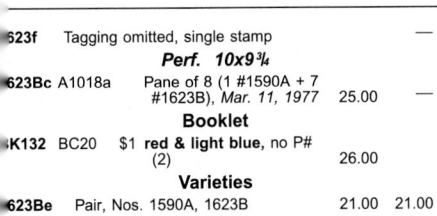

Eagle — A1124

1978   **Tagged**   **Perf. 11x10½**

1736a	A1124	A pane of 8, *May 22*	2.50	1.50

Booklet

BK133	BC24	$3.60 **deep orange**	7.75	

No. BK133 exists with covers printed on both thin and thick card stock.

Varieties

1736b		As "a," tagging omitted	—	
1736c		Vert. pair, imperf between	900.00	

Red Masterpiece and Medallion Roses — A1126

Perf. 10

1737a	A1126	15c pane of 8, *July 11*	2.50	1.50

Booklet

BK134	BC22	$2.40 **rose red & yel grn**, no P# (4)	5.25	

Varieties

1737c		As "a," imperf.	2,300.	
1737d		As "a," tagging omitted	50.00	—

Windmills — A1127-A1131

1980   **Perf. 11**

1742a	A1131	15c pane of 10, *Feb. 7*	3.50	3.00

Booklet

BK135	BC25	$3 **light blue & dark blue**, *blue*, no P#	7.50	

Varieties

1742b		Strip of 5, #1738-1742	1.50	1.40

A1207

A1267-A1276

A1279-A1280

1981

1819a	A1207	B pane of 8, *Mar. 15*	3.75	2.25

Booklet

BK136	BC26	$4.32 **dull violet**, no P#	11.75	
1889a	A1267	18c pane of 10, *May 14*	7.50	6.00

Booklet

BK137	BC28	$3.60 **gray & olive**, P#1-10	17.00	
		P#11-13	40.00	
		P#14-16	35.00	

Varieties

1880a		Tagging omitted	—	
1886a		Tagging omitted	—	
1887a		Tagging omitted	—	
1889b		Tagging omitted	—	

Imperfs of Nos. 1880-1889 are from printer's waste.

1893a	A1279	Pane of 8 (2 #1892, 6 #1893), *Apr. 24*	3.00	2.50

Booklet

BK138	BC27	$1.20 **blue & red**, P#1	3.25	

Varieties

1893b		As "a," vert. imperf. btwn.	75.00	
1893c		Pair, Nos. 1892, 1893	.90	1.00
1893d		As "a," tagging omitted	—	

BK138a	BC27	$1.20 With No. 1893b, P#1	75.00	
BK138b	BC27	$1.20 With No. 1893d, P#1	—	

A1281

1981-83

1896a	A1281	20c pane of 6, small block tagging, *Dec. 17, 1981*	3.00	2.25
		Scored perforations	3.00	—

Booklet

BK139	BC29	$1.20 **blue & red**, P#1 (2)	3.25	
1896b	A1281	20c pane of 10, *June 1, 1982*	5.25	3.25
BK140	BC29A	$2 **blue & red**, P#1 (4)	5.50	
		P#4	47.50	
1896e	A1281	20c pane of 10, large block tagging, *Nov. 17, 1983*	5.25	3.25
		Scored perforations	5.25	

Booklet

BK140A	BC29B	$4 **blue & red**, *Nov. 17, 1983*, P#2	11.00	
		P#3	17.50	
		P#4	—	

Varieties

1896c		As "b," tagging omitted	—	—
1896f		As "a," tagging omitted	—	—

The small block tagging is 16x18mm (Nos. 1896a-1896b). The large block tagging is 18x21mm (No. 1896e).

Booklet Covers

When more than one combination of covers exists, the number of possible booklets is noted in parenthesis after the booklet listing.

A1296

1983

1909a	A1296	$9.35 pane of 3, *Aug. 12*	67.50	

Booklet

BK140B	BC31	28.05 **blue & red**, P#1111	70.00	

A1333

1981

1948a	A1333	C pane of 10, *Oct. 11*	4.50	3.25

Booklet

BK141	BC26	$4 **brown**, *blue*, no P#	10.00	

A1334

1982

1949a	A1334	20c pane of 10, type I, *Jan. 8*	5.50	2.50
1949d		As "a," type II	11.00	—

Booklets

BK142	BC30	$4 **blue & yellow green,** P#1-6, 9-10	16.00	
		P#11, 12, 15	40.00	
		P#14	30.00	
		P#16	75.00	
		P#17-19	55.00	
		P#20, 22-24	100.00	
		P#21, 28, 29	*350.00*	
		P#25-26	*150.00*	
a.		Type II, P#34	22.00	

Varieties

1949b		As "a," vert. imperf. btwn.	*100.00*
1949f		As "a," tagging omitted	50.00	—

Booklets

BK142b		As BK142, with 2 #1949b	—
BK142c		As BK142, with 2 #1949f, P#4, 5, 6	*100.00*

Stamps in No. 1949a are 18¾mm wide and have overall tagging. Stamps in No. 1949d are 18½mm wide and have block tagging.
Plate number does not always appear on top pane in Nos. BK142, BK142a. These booklets sell for more, except P#14 and 15.
Booklet cover BC30 comes in blue & yellow green and in blue & olive green. Both are equally common.

A1497

1985   *Perf. 11*

2113a	A1497	D pane of 10 *Feb. 1*	8.50	3.00

Booklet

BK143	BC26	$4.40 **green,** P#1, 3, 4	17.00
		P#2	*600.00*

Varieties

2113b		As "a," imperf. between, horiz.	—

Plate number does not always appear on top pane in No. BK143. These booklets sell for more except P#4.

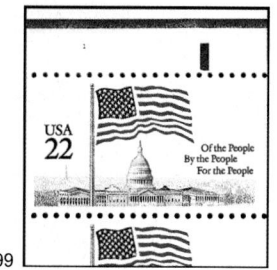

A1499

Perf. 10 Horiz.

2116a	A1499	22c pane of 5, *Mar. 29*	2.50	1.25
		Scored perforations	2.50	—

Booklets

BK144	BC33C	$1.10 **blue & red,** P#1, 3 (2)	2.75
BK145	BC32	$2.20 **blue & red,** P#1, 3 (2)	5.25

A1500-A1504

Perf. 10

2121a	A1500	22c pane of 10, *Apr. 4*	4.00	3.00

Booklets

BK146	BC33A	$4.40 **multicolored,** P#1, 3	8.50
		P#2	10.00
BK147	BC33B	$4.40 **brown & blue,** P#1, 3, 5, 6, 7, 10	8.50
		P#8	10.00

Varieties

2121b		As "a," violet omitted on both Nos. 2120	*600.00*
2121c		As "a," vert. imperf. btwn.	*550.00*
2121d		As "a," imperf.	—
2121e		Strip of 5, Nos. 2117-2121	2.00	—

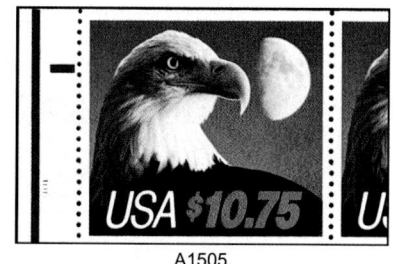

A1505

1985-89   *Perf. 10 Vert.*

2122a	A1505	10.75 type I, pane of 3, *Apr. 29, 1985*	60.00	—

Booklet

BK148	BC31A	32.25 **multicolored,** P#11111	62.50
2122c	A1505	10.75 type II, pane of 3, *June 19, 1989*	65.00	—

Booklet

BK149	BC31B	32.25 **blue & red,** P#22222 (2)	67.50

No. 2182a — A1564

No. 2197a — A1564

1988   *Perf. 1*

2182a	A1564	25c pane of 10, *May 3*	5.00	3.7

Booklet

BK150	BC43	$5 **multicolored,** P#1-2	10.50

Varieties

2182c		As "a," tagging omitted	—
2182d		Horiz. pair, imperf. between	—
2182e		As "a," all color omitted on right stamps	—

Booklet

BK150a	BC43	$5 As BK150, with #2182c	—

Perf. 10 on 2 or 3 Sides

2197a	A1564	25c pane of 6, *May 3*	3.30	2.5

Booklets

BK151	BC43	$1.50 **blue & brown,** P#1	3.30
BK152	BC43	$3 **brown & blue,** P#1	6.60

BK151 and BK152 exist with covers printed on both thin and thick card stock.

Varieties

2197c	A1564	25c As "a," tagging omitted	60.00

Booklet

BK151a	BC43	$1.50 As BK151, with #2197c	65.00

A1581-A1584

1986

2201a	A1581	22c pane of 4, *Jan. 23*	2.00	1.75

Booklet

BK153	BC34	$1.76 **purple & black,** P#1	4.00

Varieties

2201b		As "a," black omitted on Nos. 2198, 2201	45.00
2201c		As "a," blue (litho.) omitted on Nos. 2198-2200	*2,400.*
2201d		As "a," buff (litho.) omitted	—

Booklets

BK153a	BC34	$1.76 As No. BK153, with 2 #2201b	100.00
BK153b	BC34	$1.76 As No. BK153, with 2 #2201c	*5,000.*

A1588-A1592

2209a	A1588	22c pane of 5, *Mar. 21*	5.50	2.75

Booklet

BK154	BC35	$2.20 **blue green and red,** P#11111, 22222	12.00

A1637-A1644

87

'4a A1637 22c pane of 10, *Apr. 20* 10.00 5.00

Booklet

155 BC36 $2.20 **blue & red,** P#111111, 222222 12.50

A1646

Perf. 11

'76a A1646 22c pane of 20, *Nov. 30* 8.50 —

Booklet

K156 BC39 $4.40 **multicolored,** no P# 9.00
P#1111, 2222 12.00
P#2122 19.00

Varieties

'76b As "a," vert. pair, imperf. between *1,500.*

No. 2276a was made from sheets of No. 2276 which had lternating rows of perforations removed and the right sheet argins trimmed off.

A1647

1988 *Perf. 10*

2282a A1647 E pane of 10, *Mar. 22* 6.50 3.50
Scored perforations 6.50 —

Booklet

BK157 BC40 $5 **blue,** P#1111, 2222 13.00
P#2122 15.00

A1649a

Perf. 11

2283a A1649a 25c pane of 10, *Apr. 29* 6.00 3.50

Booklet

BK158 BC41 $5 **multicolored,** P#A1111 12.00

Varieties

2283d Vert. pair, imperf. between —

No. 2283d resulted from a foldover. Non-foldover pairs and multiples are printer's waste, as are imperf panes.

Color Change

2283c A1649a 25c red removed from sky, pane of 10 *70.00* —

Booklet

BK159 BC41 $5 **multicolored,** P#A3111, A3222 *140.00*

A1649b-A1649c

Perf. 10

2285b A1649b 25c pane of 10, *May 28* 5.00 3.50

Booklet

BK160 BC45 $5 **red & black,** P#1111, 1112, 1211, 1433, 1434, 1734, 2121, 2321, 3333, 5955 (2) 12.00
P#1133, 2111, 2122, 2221, 2222, 3133, 3233, 3412, 3413, 3422, 3521, 4642, 4644, 4911, 4941 20.00
P#1414 95.00
P#1634, 3512 50.00
P#3822 40.00
P#5453 165.00

Varieties

2285d Pair, Nos. 2284-2285 1.10 .25
2285e As "d," tagging omitted 12.50

A1648

2285Ac A1648 25c pane of 6, *July 5* 3.00 2.00

Booklet

BK161 BC46 $3 **blue & red,** P#1111 6.00

A1719-A1723

1987

2359a A1719 22c pane of 5, *Aug. 28* 3.75 2.25

Booklet

BK162 BC37 $4.40 **red & blue,** P#1111, 1112 15.00

Varieties

2355a Grayish green (background) omitted, single stamp —
2356a As No. 2355a —
2357a As No. 2355a —
2358a As No. 2355a —
2359b As No. 2355a —
2359c As No. 2359a, grayish green (background) omitted —

A1726-A1730

2366a A1726 22c pane of 5, *Oct. 1* 2.75 2.50

Booklet

BK163 BC38 $4.40 **black & yellow,** P#1, 2 11.00

Varieties

2365a Red omitted, single stamp *1,100.* *225.00*
2366b Black omitted, single stamp —
2366c Blue omitted, single stamp —

A1745-A1749

1988

2385a A1745 25c pane of 5, *Aug. 25* 6.00 3.50

Booklet

BK164 BC47 $5 **black & red,** P#1 25.00

A1759-A1760

A1761-A1762

Perf. 11

2396a	A1759	25c pane of 6, *Oct. 22*	3.50	3.25
2398a	A1761	25c pane of 6, *Oct. 22*	3.50	3.25

Combination Booklet

BK165 BC48 $3 **multicolored,** 1 #2396a,
1 #2398a, P#A1111 (2)   7.00

Varieties

2398b	As "a," imperf. horiz.	—
2398c	As "a," imperf	—

One example of a never-folded pane of No. 2396a exists uncancelled, affixed to a USPS souvenir page.

A1769-A1773

1989   **Perf. 10**
2409a A1769 25c pane of 5, *Mar. 3*   2.50 1.75
Never folded pane, P#1   8.00
P#2   20.00

Booklet
BK166 BC49 $5 **blue & black,** P#1, 2   10.00
Varieties
2409b   As "a," tagging omitted   —

A1791

Perf. 11½

2427a A1701 25c pane of 10, *Oct. 10*   5.00 3.50
Never folded pane, P#1   10.00

Booklet
BK167 BC50 $5 **multicolored,** P#1   10.00
Varieties
2427b   As "a," red (litho.) omitted   750.00
2427c   As "a," imperf   —

A1792

2429a A1792 25c pane of 10, *Oct. 19*   5.00 3.50
Never folded pane, P#1111   17.50

Booklet
BK168 BC51 $5 **multicolored,** P#1111, 2111   10.00
Varieties
2429b   Vert. pair, imperf between   —
2429c   As "a," imperf between   —
2429d   As "a," red omitted   3,500.
2429e   Imperf., pair   —

A1793

Illustration reduced.

Self-adhesive   *Die*
2431a A1793 25c pane of 18, *Nov. 10*, P#A1111   11.00

By its nature, No. 2431a constitutes a complete booklet. & red peelable paper backing is booklet cover (BC52). So $5.

Varieties
2431b   Vert. pair, die cutting omitted between   500.00
2431c   Die cutting omitted, pair   275.00

A1800

1990   **Perf. 1**
2441a A1800 25c pane of 10, *Jan. 18*   5.00 3
Never folded pane, P#1211   25.00

Varieties
2441b   Bright pink omitted, single stamp   175.00
2441c   As "a," bright pink omitted   1,800.

Panes exist containing both normal and bright pink omit stamps. Value is less than that of No. 2441c.

Booklet
BK169 BC53 $5 **multicolored,** P#1211   10.50
P#2111   20.00
P#2211   30.00
P#2222   17.50

A1802

Perf. 11
2443a A1802 15c pane of 10, *Feb. 3*   3.00 2.0
Never folded pane, P#111111   9.00

Booklet
BK170 BC54 $3 **multi,** P#111111   6.00
P#221111   10.00
Varieties
2443b   Blue omitted, single stamp   150.00
2443c   As "a," blue omitted   1,500.

A1829-A1833

Perf. 10
2474a A1829 25c pane of 5, *Apr. 26*   7.00 2.00
Never folded pane, P#1, 3, 5   7.50
P#2   9.50
P#4   —

Booklet
BK171 BC55 $5 **blue & red,** P#1-5 (2)   28.00
Varieties
2474b   As #2474a, white omitted   75.00

Booklet

K171a   As No. BK171, with 4
No. 2474b   300.00

A1847

2483a   A1847   20c **multicolored,** pane of 10, *June 15, 1995*   5.25   2.25
  Never folded pane   6.25

Booklet

BK172   BC56   **$2 multicolored,** P#S1111   5.25

Varieties

2483b   As "a," imperf   —

A1848

Perf. 10

2484a   A1848   29c **black & multi,** overall tagging, pane of 10, *Apr. 12, 1991*   6.00   3.75
  Never folded pane, P#1111   9.50
2484e   A1848   29c **black & multi,** prephosphored paper (solid tagging), pane of 10, *1992*   6.00   3.75

Booklets

BK173   BC57   **$2.90 black & green,** with No. 2484e   6.25
BK174   BC57   **$5.80 black & red,** P#1111, 2222   12.00
  P#1211   125.00
  P#3222, 3333   20.00
BK174a   As No. BK174, with 2 #2484e, P#2122, 2222, 3222, 3333   20.00
  P#3221   125.00
  P#3331   —
  P#4444   15.00

Varieties

2484b   Vert. pair, imperf horiz.   200.00
2484c   As "b," pane of 10   1,000.
2484f   Vert. pair, imperf between and with natural straight edge at bottom   —
2484g   As "f," booklet pane of 10   —

Perf. 11

2485a   A1848   29c **red & multi,** pane of 10, *Apr. 12, 1991*   6.00   4.00
  Never folded pane, P#K11111   12.50

Booklets

BK175   BC57   **$5.80 black & multi,** P#K11111   13.00

Varieties

2485b   Vert. pair, imperf. between   3,000.
2485c   Imperf, pair   2,500.

A1849

2486a   A1849   29c pane of 10, *Oct. 8, 1993*   6.00   4.00
  Never folded pane, P#K1111   6.75

Booklet

BK176   BC58   **$2.90 multicolored,** P#K1111   6.25
BK177   BC58   **$5.80 multicolored,** P#K1111   12.50

A1850-A1851

2488a   A1850   32c **multicolored,** pane of 10, *July 8, 1995*   6.50   4.25
  Never folded pane   7.25

Booklet

BK178   BC59   **$6.40 multicolored,** P#11111   13.00

Varieties

2488b   Pair, Nos. 2487-2488   1.30   .30

A1852

Self-Adhesive   Die Cut

2489a   A1852   29c pane of 18, *June 25, 1993* P#D11111, D22211   12.00
  P#D22221, D22222, D23133   14.50

By its nature, No. 2489a constitutes a complete booklet (BC60). The peelable backing serves as a booklet cover.

Varieties

2489b   As "a," die cutting omitted   —

Red Rose

A1853

Self-Adhesive   Die Cut

2490a   A1853   29c pane of 18, *Aug. 19, 1993,* P#S111   12.00

By its nature, No. 2490a constitutes a complete booklet (BC61). The peelable backing, of which two types are known, serves as a booklet cover.

A1854

Self-Adhesive   Die Cut

2491a   A1854   29c pane of 18, *Nov. 5, 1993,*
  P#B3-11, 13-14, 16   11.00
  P#B1   17.50
  P#B2, 12, 15   15.00

By is nature, No. 2491a constitutes a complete booklet (BC61A). The peelable backing serves as a booklet cover.

Varieties

2491b   Horiz. pair, die cutting omitted between   225.00

Pink Rose (No. 2492a) — A1853

Serpentine Die Cut 11.3x11.7 on 2, 3 or 4 Sides
Self-Adhesive

2492a   A1853   32c pane of 20+label, *June 2, 1995,* P#S111, S112, S333, S444, S555   13.00
2492b   A1853   32c pane of 15+label, *1996*   9.75
2492e   A1853   32c pane of 14, *1996*   21.00
2492f   A1853   32c pane of 16, *1996*   21.00

By its nature, No. 2492a is a complete booklet (BC61B). The peelable backing serves as a booklet cover.

Nos. 2492a and 2492b come either with no die cutting on the label or with die cutting.

No. 2492e contains blocks of 4, 6 and 4 stamps. No. 2492f contains blocks of 6,6, and 4 stamps. The blocks are on rouletted backing paper. The peel-a-way strips that were between the blocks have been removed to fold the pane.

Booklets

BK178A   BC126   **$4.80 blue,** No. 2492b (5)   10.00
BK178B   BC126   **$4.80 blue,** No. 2492f with bottom right stamp removed   40.00
BK178C   BC126   **$9.60 blue,** 2 #2492b, No P# (3)   20.00
BK178D   BC126   **$9.60 blue,** 2 panes of #2492f ea with a stamp removed from either the top or bottom row, No P# (3)   45.00

Combination Booklets

BK178E   BC126   **$9.60 blue,** 1 ea #2492e, 2492f, no P# (3)   47.50
BK178F   BC126   **$9.60 blue,** #2492b, 2492f with bottom right stamp removed, no P#   225.00

No. BK178A was issued wrapped in cellophane and not wrapped in cellophane. The two cellophane-wrapped versions are scarcer.

No. BK178E was sold wrapped in cellophane with the contents of the booklet listed on a label. Three versions exist. No. 2492f is affixed to the booklet cover, and No. 2492e is loose.

The panes of #2492f with one stamp removed that are contained in Nos. BK178B, BK178D and BK178F cannot be made from No. 2492b, a pane of 15 + label. The label is located in the sixth or seventh row of the pane and is sometimes die cut. The panes with one stamp removed all have the stamp removed from the top or bottom row of the pane.

Varieties

2492c   Horiz. pair, die cutting omitted btwn.   —
2492d   As "a," 2 stamps and parts of 7 others printed on backing liner   —
2492h   Vert. pair, die cutting omitted btwn. (from No. 2492b)   —

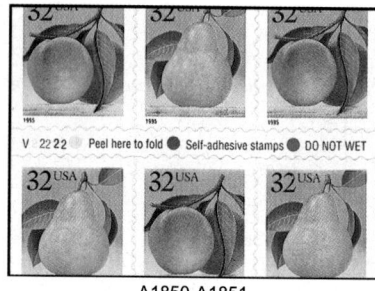

A1850-A1851

Serpentine Die Cut 8.8

2494a	A1850	32c pane of 20+label, *July 8, 1995,*		
		P# list 1	13.00	
		P# list 2	18.00	
		P#V11132, V33353	15.00	
		P#V33323	25.00	—
		P#V11232		—

By its nature, No. 2494a is a complete booklet (BC61C). The peelable backing serves as a booklet cover. It comes either with no die cutting on the label or with die cutting.

List 1 — P#V11111, V11122, V12132, V12211, V12221, V22212, V22222, V33142, V33243, V33333, V33343, V33363, V44424, V44434, V44454, V45434, V45464, V54365, V54565, V55365, V55565.

List 2 — P#V11131, V12131, V12232, V22221, V33143, V33453.

Varieties

2494b		Pair, #2493-2494	1.30
2494c		As "b," die cutting omitted	—

A1860-A1864

1990

Perf. 11

2505a	A1860	25c pane of 10, *Aug. 17*	12.00	7.50
		Never folded pane, P#1-2	17.50	

Booklet

BK179	BC62	$5 multicolored, P#1, 2	20.00

Varieties

2505b		As "a," black (engr.) omitted	3,500.
2505c		Strip of 5, Nos. 2501-2505	6.00 2.50
2505d		As "a," horiz. imperf.	—

A1873

1990

Perf. 11½

2514b	A1873	25c pane of 10, *Oct. 18*	5.00	3.25
		Never folded pane	12.50	

Booklet

BK180	BC63	$5 multicolored, P#1	10.00

A1874

1990

Perf. 11½x11

2516a	A1874	25c pane of 10, *Oct. 18*	5.00	3.25
		Never folded pane, P#1111	—	
		Never folded pane, P#1211	15.00	

Booklet

BK181	BC64	$5 multicolored, P#1211	11.00
		P#1111	—

No. 2519a — A1875

No. 2520a — A1875

1991

Perf. 11.2 Bullseye

2519a	A1875	F pane of 10, *Jan. 22*	6.50	4.50

Booklets

BK182	BC65	($2.90) yellow & multi, P#2222	6.50	
BK183	BC65	($5.80) grn, red & blk, P#1111, 2121, 2222	13.00	
		P#1222, 2111, 2212	25.00	

Perf. 11

2520a	A1875	F pane of 10, *Jan. 22*	18.00	4.50
		Never folded pane, P#K1111	—	

Booklet

BK184	BC65	($2.90) like #BK182, grn, red & blk, P#K1111	18.00

Varieties

2520b		As "a," imperf. horiz.	—

A1879

Perf. 11

2527a	A1879	29c pane of 10, *Apr. 5*	6.00	3.50
		Never folded pane, P#K1111	8.00	

Booklet

BK185	BC66	$5.80 multicolored, P#K1111, K2222, K3333	12.00

Varieties

2527b		Horiz. pair, imperf between	—
2527c		Horiz. pair, imperf vert.	200.00
2527d		As "a," imperf horiz.	1,000.

A1880

Perf. 11

2528a	A1880	29c pane of 10, *Apr. 21*	6.00	3.5
		Never folded pane	7.00	

Booklets

BK186	BC67	$2.90 black & multicolored, P#K11111	5.75	
BK186A	BC67A	$2.90 red & multicolored, P#K11111 (2)	6.75	

Varieties

2528c		Vert. pair, imperf between, perfed at top and bottom	275.00
2528d		Vert. strip of 3, top or bottom pair imperf between	—
2528e		Vert. pair, imperf horiz.	750.00

No. 2528c comes from misperfed booklet panes. No. 2528d resulted from paper foldovers after normal perforating and before cutting into panes. Two No. 2528d are known. No. 2528e is valued in the grade of fine.

Booklet Covers

When more than one combination of covers exists, the number of possible booklets is noted in parenthesis after the booklet listing.

A1882

1991

Perf. 10

2530a	A1882	19c pane of 10, *May 17*	4.00	2.75
		Never folded pane, P#1111	5.00	

Booklet

BK187	BC68	$3.80 black & blue, P#1111, 2222	8.00
		P#1222	32.50

A1884

Self-Adhesive
Die Cut

2531Ab	A1884	29c pane of 18, prephosphored coated paper (solid tagging), *June 25,* no P#	11.00

By its nature, No. 2531Ab constitutes a complete booklet (BC68A). The peelable backing serves as a booklet cover.

Varieties

2531Ac		As "b," die cutting omitted, pair	2,000.
2531Ae		As "b," overall tagging (BC68B), *1992*	11.00

A1890

			Perf. 11	
6a	A1890	29c pane of 10, *May 9*	6.00	3.50
		Never folded pane, P#1111, 1112	8.25	

Booklet

188	BC69	$5.80 **multicolored,** P#1111, 1112	12.00	
		P#1113, 1123, 2223	16.00	
		P#1212	42.50	

A1899-A1903

			Perf. 11	
49a	A1899	29c pane of 5, *May 31*	10.00	3.50
		Never folded pane, P#A23133, A23213	12.50	
		P#A11111, A22122, A22132, A33213	—	
		P#A23124	42.50	
		P#A32225, A33233	27.50	

Booklet

K189	BC70	$5.80 **multicolored,** P#A22122, A23123, A23124, A33235, A44446, A45546, A45547	25.00	
		P#A11111, A22133, A23133, A23213	47.50	
		P#A22132, A32224, A32225, A33233	27.50	
		P#A31224	—	

No. BK189 exists assembled from panes with different plate numbers.
P#33213 has yet to be found as top pane in booklets.

Varieties

2545a	Black omitted, single stamp	—
2546a	Black omitted, single stamp	—
2547a	Black omitted, single stamp	—

A1905

			Perf. 11	
2552a	A1905	29c pane of 5, *July 2*	3.00	2.25
		Never folded pane, P#A11121111	4.75	

Booklet

BK190	BC71	$5.80 **multicolored,** P#A11111111, A11121111	12.00	

A1916-A1920

2566a	A1916	29c pane of 10, *Aug. 29*	9.00	5.00
		Never folded pane, P#1	10.50	

Booklet

BK191	BC72	$5.80 **scar, blk & brt vio,** P#1, 2	19.00	

Varieties

2566b	As "a," scar & brt violet (engr.) omitted	*700.00*	
2566c	Strip of 5, Nos. 2562-2566	4.25	2.50

A1922-A1931

2577a	A1922	29c pane of 10, *Oct. 1*	9.00	4.50
		Never folded pane, P#111111	12.50	

Booklet

BK192	BC73	$5.80 **blue, black & red,** P#111111	19.00	
		P#111112	24.00	

A1933

2578a	A1933	(29c) pane of 10, *Oct. 17*	6.00	3.25
		Never folded pane	8.00	

Booklet

BK193	BC74	($5.80) **multicolored,** P#1	12.00	

Varieties

2578b	Red & black (engr.) omitted	*3,500.*	

A1934

2581b	A1934	(29c) pane, 2 each, #2580, 2581, *Oct. 17*	9.00	1.25
		Never bound pane, P#A11111	11.00	
2582a	A1935	(29c) pane of 4, *Oct. 17*	2.40	1.25
		Never bound pane, P#A11111	3.50	

2583a	A1936	(29c) pane of 4, *Oct. 17*	2.40	1.25
		Never bound pane, P#A11111	3.50	
2584a	A1937	(29c) pane of 4, *Oct. 17*	2.40	1.25
		Never bound pane, P#A11111	3.50	
2585a	A1938	(29c) pane of 4, *Oct. 17*	2.40	1.25
		Never bound pane, P#A11111	3.50	

Combination Booklet

BK194	BC75	($5.80) **multicolored,** 1 each #2581b, 2582a-2585a, P#A11111, A12111	20.00	

Varieties

2581a	Pair, Nos. 2580-2581	4.00	.50

For illustrations A1935-A1938 see regular listings. Panes are similar to A1934.
Nos. 2581b-2585a are unfolded panes.
Imperf examples of Nos. 2582a-2585a are printer's waste.

A1946

1992-94			**Perf. 10**	
2593a	A1946	29c **black & multi,** pane of 10, *Sept. 8*	6.00	4.25
		Never folded pane, P#1111	8.00	

Booklets

BK195	BC76	$2.90 **blue & red,** P#1111, 2222	5.50	
BK196	BC76	$5.80 **blue & red,** P#1111, 2222	11.00	
		P#1211, 2122	—	

Varieties

2593d	A1946	Imperf, pair	—
		Perf. 11x10	
2593Bc	A1946	29c **black & multi,** pane of 10, shiny gum, *1993*	14.00	7.50
		Low gloss gum	20.00	

Booklet

BK197	BC76	$5.80 **blue & red,** P#1111, 1211, 2122, 2222, 2232, 3333	30.00	
		P#2232, 4444, low gloss gum	45.00	
		P#2333	—	
		P#3333, low gloss gum	*125.00*	
2594a	A1946	29c **red & multi,** pane of 10, *1993*	6.50	4.25
		Never folded pane	8.00	

Booklet

BK198	BC76	$2.90 **black, red & blue,** P#K1111	6.00	
BK199	BC76	$5.80 **multicolored,** *1994,* P#K1111	13.50	

A1947

Self-adhesive
Die Cut

2595a	A1947	29c **brown & multi,** pane of 17 + label, *Sept. 25,* P#B1111-1, B1111-2, B2222-1, B2222-2, B3333-1, B3333-3, B3434-1, B3434-3, B4444-1	13.00	
		P#B4344-1, B4444-3	15.00	

P#B4344-3   *200.00*

Varieties

2595b		Die cutting omitted, pair	150.00
2595c		Brown omitted, single	375.00
2595d		As "a," no die cutting	1,250.
2596a	A1947	29c **green & multi,** pane of 17 + label, *Sept. 25, 1992,* P#D11111, D21221, D22322, D32322, D32332, D43352, D43452, D43453, D54563, D54573, D65784	12.00
		P#D54571, D54673, D61384	15.00
		P#D32342, D42342	35.00
		P#D54561	25.00
2597a	A1947	29c **red & multi,** pane of 17 + label, *Sept. 25,* P#S1111	10.50

By their nature, Nos. 2595a-2597a constitute complete booklets (DC77). A peelable paper backing serves as a booklet cover for each. No. 2595a has a black and multicolored backing with serifed type. No. 2596a has a blue and multicolored backing, No. 2597a a black and multicolored backing with unserifed type.

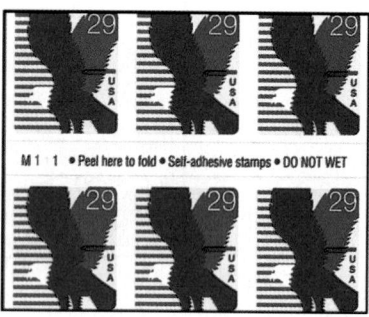

A1950

Self-Adhesive   *Die Cut*

2598a	A1950	29c pane of 18, *Feb. 4, 1994,* P#M111, M112	11.00

By its nature, No. 2598a constitutes a complete booklet (BC78). The peelable backing serves as a booklet cover.

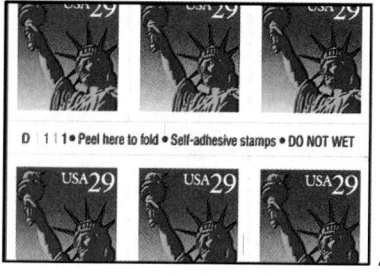

A1951

Self-Adhesive   *Die Cut*

2599a	A1951	29c pane of 18, *June 24, 1994,* P#D1111, D1212	11.00

By its nature, No. 2599a constitutes a complete booklet (BC79). The peelable backing serves as a booklet cover.

A1994-A1998

1992

2646a	A1994	29c pane of 5, *June 15*	3.00 2.50
		Never folded pane, P#A2212112, A2212122, A2222222	4.00
		P#A1111111, A2212222	10.00

Imperfs of No. 2646a are printer's waste.

Booklet

BK201	BC80	$5.80 **multicolored,** P#A1111111, A2212112, A2212122, A2222222	12.00
		P#A2212122	18.00

A2057-A2061

2709a	A2057	29c pane of 5, *Oct. 1*	3.25 2.25
		Never folded pane	4.25

Booklet

BK202	BC83	$5.80 **multicolored,** P#K1111	12.00

Varieties

2709b		As "a," imperf.	2,500.

A2062

2710a	A2062	29c pane of 10, *Oct. 22*	6.00 3.50
		Never folded pane	7.00

Booklet

BK202A	BC83A	$5.80 **multicolored,** P#1	12.00

A2063-A2066

2718a	A2063	29c pane of 4, *Oct. 22*	3.50 1.25
		Never bound pane, P#A111111, A222222	4.50
		P#A112211	

Booklet

BK203	BC84	$5.80 **multi,** P#A111111, A112211, A222222	17.50

Varieties

2718b		As "a," imperf. horiz.	—

No. 2718a completely imperf is printer's waste.

A2064

Self-Adhesive

Die Cut

2719a	A2064	29c **multicolored,** pane of 18, *Oct. 29,* P#V11111	11.00

By its nature, No. 2719a constitutes a complete booklet (BC85). The peelable paper backing serves as a booklet cover.

A2071, A2075-A2077

Tab format on No. 2737a is similar to that shown for No. 2737b.

1993

2737a	A2071	29c pane of 8, 2 #2731, 1 each #2732-2737, *June 16*	5.00 2.2
		Never folded pane, P#A22222	6.25
		P#A13113	—
2737b	A2071	29c pane of 4, #2731, 2735-2737 + tab, *June 16*	2.40 1.5
		Never folded pane, P#A22222	3.50
		P#A13113	—

Combination Booklet

BK204	BC86	$5.80 **multicolored,** 2 #2737a, + 1 #2737b, P#A11111, A22222	12.50
		P#A13113, A44444	15.00

No. 2737b without tab is indistinguishable from broken No. 2737a.

Never folded panes of No. 2737a with P#A11111 exist missing the bottom stamp (found in some USPS mint sets).

No. BK204 exists assembled from panes with different plate numbers.

A2086-A2090

2745a	A2086	29c pane of 5, *Jan. 25*	3.00 2.25
		Never folded pane, P#1111, 1211	4.00
		P#2222	6.50

Booklet

BK207	BC89	$5.80 **multi,** P#1111, 1211, 2222	12.00

A2105-A2109

2764a	A2105	29c pane of 5, *May 15*	3.00	2.25
		Never folded pane, P#1	4.00	

Booklet

BK208	BC90	$5.80 multicolored, P#1, 2	12.00	

Varieties

2764b		As "a," black (engr.) omitted	*200.00*	
2764c		As "a," imperf.	*1,250.*	

Booklet

BK208a		As #BK208, with 4 #2764b	*850.00*	

A2069, A2112-A2114

2770a	A2069	29c pane of 4, *July 14*	2.75	2.25
		Never folded pane, P#A11111, A11121, A22222	3.75	

Booklet

BK209	BC91	$5.80 multicolored, P#A11111, A11121, A22222, A23232, A23233	12.00	

A2070, A2115-A2117

2778a	A2070	29c pane of 4, *Sept. 25, 1993*	2.50	2.00
		Never folded pane, P#A222222	3.50	

Booklet

BK210	BC92	$5.80 multicolored, P#A111111, A222222, A333333, A422222 P#A333323	11.00	

Varieties

2778b		As "a," imperf.	—	

A2128

2790a	A2128	29c pane of 4, *Oct. 21, 1993*	2.40	1.75
		Never bound pane, P#K111111, K133333, K144444,	3.50	
		P#K255555	*85.00*	

Booklet

BK211	BC93	$5.80 multicolored, P#K111111, K133333, K144444, K255555, K266666	12.00	
		P#K222222	35.00	

Varieties

2790b		Imperf., pair	—	
2790c		As "a," imperf.	—	

No. 2798a — A2129-A2132

2798a	A2129	29c pane of 10, 3 each #2795-2796, 2 each #2797-2798, *Oct. 21, 1993*	8.50	4.00
		Never folded pane, P#111111	10.00	
2798b	A2129	29c pane of 10, 3 each #2797-2798, 2 each #2795-2796, *Oct. 21, 1993*	8.50	4.00
		Never folded pane, P#111111	10.00	

Combination Booklet

BK212	BC94	$5.80 multicolored, 1 each #2798a, 2798b, P#111111, 222222	17.50	

Varieties

2798c		Block of 4, Nos. 2795-2798	3.40	1.75

On No. 2798b the plate number appears close to the top row of perfs. Different selvage markings can be found there.

A2129-A2132

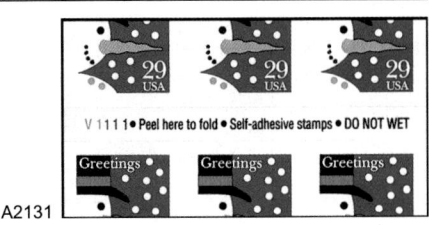

A2131

Self-Adhesive   *Die Cut*

2802a	A2129	29c pane of 3 each #2799-2802, *Oct. 28, 1993*, P#V1111111, V2221222, V2222112, V2222122, V2222221, V2222222	7.25	
		P#V3333333	9.25	
2803a	A2131	29c pane of 18, *Oct. 28, 1993*, P#V1111	11.00	
		P# V2222	14.00	

Varieties

2802b		Block of 4, Nos. 2799-2802	2.60	

By their nature, Nos. 2802a-2803a constitute complete booklets (BC95-BC96). The peelable backing serves as a booklet cover.

A2135

2806b	A2135	29c pane of 5, *Dec. 1, 1993*	3.00	2.00
		Never folded pane	4.00	

Booklet

BK213	BC97	$2.90 black & red, P#K111	6.00	

A2142

1994   **Self-Adhesive**   *Die Cut*

2813a	A2142	29c pane of 18, *Jan. 27*, P#, see list	11.00	
		P#B111-5, B333-14	*75.00*	
		P#B121-5, B444-7, B444-8, B444-9, B444-14	14.00	
		P#B333-5, B333-7, B333-8	22.50	
		P#B334-11	*750.00*	
		P#B344-11	50.00	
		P#B434-10	100.00	

By its nature, No. 2813a constitutes a complete booklet (BC98). The peelable backing serves as a booklet cover.

List — #B111-1, B111-2, B111-3, B111-4, B221-5, B222-4, B222-5, B222-6, B333-9, B333-10, B333-11, B333-12, B333-17, B344-12, B344-13, B444-10, B444-13, B444-15, B444-16, B444-17, B444-18, B444-19, B555-20, B555-21

A2143

2814a	A2143	29c pane of 10, *Feb. 14, 1994*	6.00	3.50
		Never folded pane, P#A11111	7.50	

Booklet

BK214	BC99	$5.80 **multicolored**, P#A11111, A11311, A12112, A21222, A22122, A22322	11.00	
		P#A12111, A12211, A12212, A21311	25.00	
		P#A22222	16.00	

Varieties

2814b	Imperf, pair	—

Horiz. pairs, imperf between, are printer's waste.

A2158-A2162

2833a	A2158	29c pane of 5, *Apr. 28, 1994*	3.00	2.25
		Never folded pane, P#2	3.50	

Booklet

BK215	BC100	$5.80 **multicolored**, P#1, 2	12.00

Varieties

2833b	As "a," imperf	*1,750.*
2833c	As "a," black (engr.) omitted	250.00
2833d	As "a," tagging omitted	—

Booklet

BK215a	As #BK215, with 4 #2833c	*1,050.*

A2171-A2175

2847a	A2171	29c pane of 5, *July 28, 1994*	3.50	2.00
		Never folded pane	4.50	

Booklet

BK216	BC101	$5.80 **multicolored**, P#S11111	14.00

Varieties

2847b	As "a," imperf	—

A2200

2871Ab	A2200	29c pane of 10, *Oct. 20, 1994*	6.25	3.50
		Never folded pane, P#1, 2	7.00	

Booklet

BK217	BC102	$5.80 **multicolored**, P#1, 2	12.50

Varieties

2871Ac	Imperf, pair	*550.00*

A2201

2872a	A2201	29c pane of 20, *Oct. 20, 1994*	12.50	4.00
		Never folded pane, P#P11111, P22222, P44444		
		P#P33333	14.00	—

Booklet

BK218	BC103	$5.80 **multicolored**, P#P11111, P22222, P33333, P44444	12.50

Varieties

2872c	Vert. pair, imperf horiz.	—
2872e	Vert. pair, imperf between	—

A2202

2873a	A2202	29c pane of 12, *Oct. 20, 1994*, P#V1111	7.25	

By is nature, No. 2873a constitutes a complete booklet (BC104). The peelable backing serves as a booklet cover.

A2203

2874a	A2203	29c pane of 18, *Oct. 20, 1994*, P#V1111, V2222	11.00	

By its nature, No. 2874a constitutes a complete booklet (BC105). The peelable backing serves as a booklet cover.

A2208

1994   *Perf. 11.2x11.1*

2881a	A2208	(32c) **black "G" & multi**, pane of 10, *Dec. 13, 1994*	6.00	3.75

Booklet

BK219	BC106	($3.20) **pale blue & red**, P#1111	6.00

Perf. 10x9.9

2883a	A2208	(32c) **black "G" & multi**, pane of 10, *Dec. 13, 1994*	6.50	3.75

Booklets

BK220	BC106	($3.20) **pale blue & red**, P#1111, 2222	6.50
BK221	BC106	($6.40) **blue & red**, P#1111, 2222	13.00

Perf. 10.9

2884a	A2208	(32c) **blue "G" & multi**, pane of 10, *Dec. 13, 1994*	6.50	3.75

Booklet

BK222	BC106	($6.40) **blue "G" & multi**, P#A1111, A1211, A2222, A3333, A4444	13.00

No. BK222 exists with panes that have different plate numbers.

Varieties

2884b	As "a," imperf.	*1,750.*

Perf. 11x10.9

2885a	A2208	(32c) **red "G" & multi**, pane of 10, *Dec. 13, 1994*	8.50	4.50

Booklet

BK223	BC106	($6.40) **red "G" & multi**, P#K1111	17.50

Varieties

2885b	Horiz. pair, imperf vert.	—
2885c	Horiz. pair, imperf between	—

No. 2885c resulted from a paper foldover after perforating and before cutting into panes.

No. 2886a — A2208b

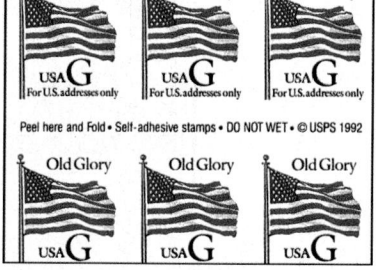

No. 2887a — A2208c

Self-Adhesive   *Die Cut*

2886a	A2208b	(32c) pane of 18, *Dec. 13, 1994*, P#V11111, V22222	14.00
2887a	A2208c	(32c) pane of 18, *Dec. 13, 1994*, no P#	14.00

By their nature, Nos. 2886a and 2887a constitute complete booklets (BC107). The peelable backing serves as a booklet cover. The backing on No. 2886a contains a UPC symbol, while the backing on No. 2887a does not.

A2212

Perf. 10.8x9.8

...6a	A2212	32c blue, tan, brown, red & light blue, pane of 10, *May 19, 1995*	6.50	3.25
		Never folded pane, P#11111	7.25	

Booklets

...225	BC108	$3.20 blue & red, P#11111, 22222, 33332	6.50	
		P#23222, 44444	—	
...226	BC108	$6.40 multicolored, P#11111, 22222, 23222, 33332, 44444	13.00	

Varieties

...6b		As "a," imperf.	—

...2230

		Self-Adhesive	**Die Cut**
...919a	A2230	32c pane of 18, *Mar. 17, 1995*, P#V1111, V1311, V1433, V2222, V2322	12.00
		P#V2111	45.00

Varieties

...919b		Vert. pair, die cutting omitted between	—

By its nature No. 2919a is a complete booklet (BC113). The peelable backing serves as a booklet cover.

Nos. 2920a, 2920c — A2212

Serpentine Die Cut 8.7 on 2 or 3 Sides
Self-Adhesive

2920a	A2212	32c pane of 20+label, large date, *Apr. 18, 1995* (see List 1)	13.00
		P#V23422	25.00
		P#V23522	40.00
		P#V57663	—
2920c	A2212	32c pane of 20+label, small date, *Apr. 18, 1995,*	
		P#V11111	110.00

Varieties

2920g	As "a," partial pane of 10, 3 stamps and parts of 7 stamps printed on backing liner	—
2920i	Die cutting omitted, pair	—
2920j	Dark blue omitted (from 2920a)	—

By their nature Nos. 2920a, 2920c are complete booklets (BC114). The rouletted peelable backing, of which two types are known, serves as a booklet cover.

Date on No. 2920a is nearly twice as large as date on No. 2920c.

No. 2920a comes either with no die cutting on the label or with die cutting.

List 1 — P#V12211, V12212, V12312, V12321, V12322, V12331, V13322, V13831, V13834, V13836, V22211, V23322, V23432, V34743, V34745, V36743, V42556, V45554, V56663, V56665, V56763, V65976, V78989.

Nos. 2920f, 2920h — A2212

Serpentine Die Cut 8.7
Self-Adhesive

2920f	A2212	32c pane of 15+label	10.00
2920h	A2212	32c pane of 15, see note, *1996*	35.00

Booklets

BK226A	BC126	$4.80 blue, 1 #2920f, no P# (4)	10.00
BK226B	BC126	$4.80 blue, 1 #2920h, no P# (3)	65.00
BK227	BC126	$9.60 blue, 2 #2920f (3)	18.00

No. 2920h is a pane of 16 with one stamp removed. The missing stamp is the lower right stamp in the pane or (more rarely) the upper left stamp. No. 2920h cannot be made from No. 2920f, a pane of 15 + label. The label is located in the sixth or seventh row of the pane and is die cut. If the label is removed, an impression of the die cutting appears on the backing paper.

No. 2920De — A2212

Serpentine Die Cut 11.3
Self-Adhesive

2920De	A2212	32c pane of 10, *Jan. 20, 1996*	7.50

By its nature No. 2920De is a complete booklet (BC114). The rouletted peelable backing serves as a booklet cover.

Below is a list of known plate numbers. Some numbers may be scarcer than the value indicated in the listing.

No. 2920De — P#V11111, V12111, V23222, V31121, V32111, V32121, V44322, V44333, V44444, V55555, V66666, V66886, V67886, V68886, V68896, V76989, V77666, V77668, V77766, V77776, V78698, V78886, V78896, V78898, V78986, V78989, V89999.

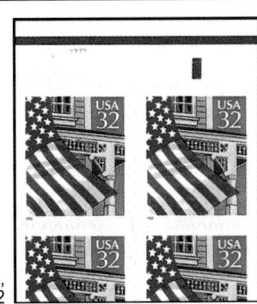

Nos. 2921a, 2921c, 2921d — A2212

Serpentine Die Cut 9.8
Self-Adhesive

2921a	A2212	32c pane of 10, dated red "1996," *May 21, 1996*	7.50
		Never folded pane, P#21221, 22221, 22222	9.00
2921c	A2212	32c pane of 10, dated red "1997," *Jan. 24, 1997*	12.00
		Never folded pane, P#11111	14.00
2921d	A2212	32c pane of 5 + label, dated red "1997," *Jan. 24, 1997*	7.00
		Never folded pane, P#11111	8.50

Combination Booklet

BK227A	BC108	$4.80 multicolored, 1 ea #2921c-2921d P#11111	19.00

Booklets

BK228	BC108	$6.40 blue, red & black, 2 #2921a (5)	15.00

Known numbers for BK228: P#11111, 13111, 21221, 22221, 22222, 44434, 44444, 55555, 55556, 66666, 77777, 88788, 88888, 99999. Some numbers may be scarcer than the value indicated in the listing.

BK228A	BC108	$9.60 multicolored, 3 #2921c, P#11111	22.50

Varieties

2921e		As "a," die cutting omitted	250.00

Booklet

BK228b		As #BK228, with 2 #2921e, P#11111	500.00

A2264

		Self-Adhesive	**Die Cut**
2949a	A2264	(32c) pane of 20 + label, *Feb. 1, 1995*, P#B1111-1, B2222-1, B2222-2, B3333-2	13.00

By its nature, No. 2949a is a complete booklet (BC115). The peelable backing serves as a booklet cover.

Varieties

2949b	As "a," red (engr.) omitted, single stamp	400.00
2949c	As "a," red (engr.) omitted	8,000.
2949d	As "a," red (engr.) missing (CM)	—

No. 2949d must be collected se-tenant with a normal stamp.

A2272

Perf. 9.8x10.8

2959a	A2272	32c pane of 10, *May 12, 1995*	6.50	3.25
		Never folded pane	6.75	

Booklet
BK229　BC116　$6.40 **multicolored**, P#1　　13.00
Varieties
2959b　　　Imperf, pair　　　—

A2274

Self-Adhesive		**Die Cut**

2960a　A2274　55c pane of 20 + label, *May 12, 1995*, P#B1111-1, B2222-1　22.50

By its nature, No. 2960a is a complete booklet (BC117). The peelable backing serves as a booklet cover. It comes either with no die cutting on the label or with die cutting.

A2283-A2287

2973a　A2283　32c pane of 5, *June 17, 1995*　5.00　3.00
　　　　　　　Never folded pane　　　5.50
Booklet
BK230　BC118　$6.40 **multicolored**, P#S11111　20.00

A2306-A2310

2997a　A2306　32c pane of 5, *Sept. 19, 1995*　3.25　2.25
　　　　　　　Never folded pane　　　4.25
Booklet
BK231　BC119　$6.40 **multicolored**, P#2　　13.00
Varieties
2997b　　　As "a," imperf.　　　—

A2316

3003Ab　A2316　32c pane of 10, *Oct. 19, 1995*　6.50　4.00
　　　　　　　Never folded pane　　　7.50
Booklet
BK232　BC120　$6.40 **multicolored**, P#1　　13.00

A2317-A2320

3007b　A2317　32c pane of 10, 3 each
　　　　　　　#3004-3005, 2 each
　　　　　　　#3006-3007, *Sept. 30, 1995*　　6.50　4.00
　　　　　　　Never folded pane,
　　　　　　　P#P1111　　7.50
3007c　A2317　32c pane of 10, 2 each
　　　　　　　#3004-3005, 3 each
　　　　　　　#3006-3007, *Sept. 30, 1995*　　6.50　4.00
　　　　　　　Never folded pane,
　　　　　　　P#P1111　　7.50
Combination Booklet
BK233　BC121　$6.40 **multicolored**, 1 each
　　　　　　　#3007b, 3007c,
　　　　　　　P#P1111, P2222　　13.00
Varieties
3007d　　　As "a," imperf.　　600.00

A2317-A2320

Serpentine Die Cut

3011a　A2317　32c pane of 20 +label, *Sept. 30, 1995*, P#V1111, V1211,
　　　　　　　V3233, V3333, V4444　17.50
　　　　　　　P#V1212　　25.00

By is nature, No. 3011a is a complete booklet (BC122). The peelable backing serves as a booklet cover.

No.
3012a
—
A2321

Serpentine Die Cut

3012a　A2321　32c pane of 20 + label, *Oct. 19, 1995*, P#B1111,
　　　　　　　B2222, B3333　　13.00

By its nature, No. 3012a is a complete booklet (BC123). The peelable backing serves as a booklet cover.
No. 3012a comes either with no die cutting on the label (1995 printing) or with die cutting from the 1996 printing.

3012c　A2321　32c pane of 15 + label,
　　　　　　　1996, no P#　　10.00
3012d　A2321　32c pane of 15, see note,
　　　　　　　1996　　45.00
Booklets
BK233A　BC126　$4.80 **blue**, #3012c (2)　10.00
BK233B　BC126　$4.80 **blue**, #3012d　　—
BK233C　BC126　$9.60 **blue** 2 #3012c (3)　18.00
BK233D　BC126　$9.60 **blue**, 2 #3012d, no P#
　　　　　　　(3)　　25.00
Combination Booklet
BK233E　BC126　$9.60 **blue**, 1 ea #3012c,
　　　　　　　3012d (2)　　55.00

3012b　　　　Vert. pair, die cutting
　　　　　　　omitted between　　—

No. 3012d is a pane of 16 with one stamp removed. missing stamp can be from either row 1, 2, 3, 7 or 8. No. 3 cannot be made from No. 3012c, a pane of 15 + label. The i is die cut. If the label is removed, an impression of the cutting appears on the backing paper.

A2322

Die Cut

3013a　A2322　32c Pane of 18, *Oct. 19, 1995*,
　　　　　　　P#V1111　　12.00

By its nature, No. 3013a is a complete booklet (BC124). peelable backing serves as a booklet cover.

A2329-A2333

3029a　A2329　32c pane of 5, *Jan. 19, 1996*　3.75　2.
　　　　　　　Never folded pane　　4.25
Booklet
BK234　BC125　$6.40 **multicolored**, P#1　　15.00
Varieties
3029b　　　As "a," imperf.　　—

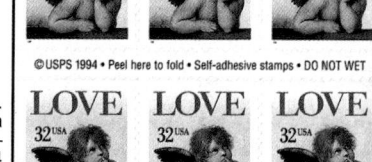

No.
3030a
—
A2334

Serpentine Die Cut 11.3x11.7

3030a　A2334　32c pane of 20+label, *Jan. 20, 1996*　　13.00

By its nature, No. 3030a is a complete booklet (BC115). Th peelable backing serves as a booklet cover.
P#B1111-1, B1111-2, B2222-1, B2222-2.

3030b　A2334　32c pane of 15+label, *1996*　10.00
Booklet
BK235　BC126　$4.80 **blue** (4)　　10.00
BK236　BC126　$9.60 **blue** (3)　　18.00
Varietles
3030c　　　Red (engr.) omitted, sin-
　　　　　　　gle stamp　　225.00
3030d　　　Red (engr.) missing
　　　　　　　(CM), single stamp　　—
3030e　　　Double impression of
　　　　　　　red (engr.)　　—
3030f　　　Die cutting omitted, pair　300.00

No. 3030d must be collected se-tenant with a stamp bearing the red engraving.

A1847

Serpentine Die Cut 10.4x10.8

3048a A1847 20c pane of 10, *Aug. 2, 1996*, P#S1111, S2222 4.00

By is nature, No. 3048a is a complete booklet (BC128). The peelable backing serves as a booklet cover.

3048b A1847 20c Booklet pane of 4 *22.50*
3048c A1847 20c Booklet pane of 6 *37.50*

Nos. 3048b-3048c are from the vending machine booklet No. K237 that has a glue strip at the top edge of the top pane, the peelable strip removed and the rouletting line 2mm lower than No. 3048a when the panes are compared with the bottoms signed

Booklet

K237 BC128 $2.00 **multicolored,** 1 ea #3048b, 3048c, P#S1111, S2222 *60.00*

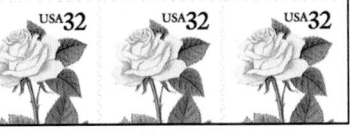

A1853

Serpentine Die Cut 11.3x11.7

3049a A1853 32c pane of 20, *Oct. 24, 1996,* P#S1111, S2222 13.00

By its nature, No. 3049a is a complete booklet (BC61B). The peelable backing, of which three types are known, serves as a booklet cover.

3049b A1853 32c pane of 4, *Dec. 1996,* no P# 2.60
3049c A1853 32c pane of 5 + label, *Dec. 1996,* P#S1111 3.50
3049d A1853 32c pane of 6, *Dec. 1996,* without P# 4.00

Combination Booklet

BK241 BC129 $4.80 **multicolored,** 1 ea #3049b-3049d, P#S1111 10.25

Booklet

BK242 BC129 $9.60 **multicolored,** 5 #3049d, P#S1111 20.00

The backing on Nos. BK241-BK242 is rouletted between each pane.
P# on Nos. 3049c-3049d is on a stamp, not the removable strip.

Varieties

3049c P# single, #S1111 .85 *1.00*
3049d Pane of 6 containing P# single 6.00
P# single, #S1111 2.50 1.00

The plate # single in No. 3049c is on the lower left stamp. In No. 3049d it is the lower right stamp on the bottom pane of the booklet.

A2350

1998 **Serpentine Die Cut 11.2**
3050a A2350 20c pane of 10, *July 31, 1998,* P#V1111, V2222, V2232, V3233 5.00
P#V2342, V2343, V3232 —

Serpentine Die Cut 11
3050c A2350 20c pane of 10, *July 31, 1998,* P#V2333, V2342, V2343, V3232, V3243, V3333 12.50
P#V2232, V2332

By their nature Nos. 3050a and 3050c are complete booklets (BC130). The peelable backing serves as a booklet cover. All stamps in Nos. 3050a and 3050c are upright.

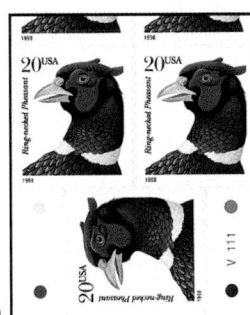

3051Ac — A2350

Serpentine Die Cut 10½x11 on 3 Sides (#3051), 10.6x10.4 on 3 sides (#3051A)

1999

Self-Adhesive

3051Ab A2350 20c pane, 4 #3051, 1 #3051A turned sideways at top, *July 1999* 7.50
3051Ac A2350 20c pane, 4 #3051, 1 #3051A turned sideways at bottom, *July 1999* 7.50

BOOKLET

BK242A BC130 $2.00 **multicolored,** #3051b, 3051c, P#V1111, *July 1999* 15.00

3052a-3052c — A2351

3052d — A2351

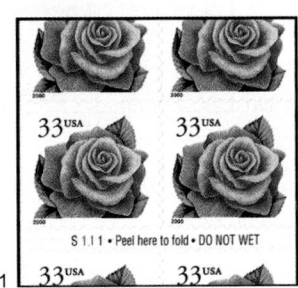

3052Ef — A2351

Serpentine Die Cut 11½x11¼

3052a A2351 33c pane of 4, no P# 3.60
3052b A2351 33c pane of 5 + label, no P# 4.50
3052c A2351 33c pane of 6 5.50
3052d A2351 33c pane of 20 + label, P#S111, S222 17.50

COMBINATION BOOKLET

BK242B BC131 $4.95 **multicolored,** 1 each #3052a-3052c, P#S111, *Aug. 13, 1999* 13.75

Varieties

3052j Die cutting omitted, pair —

No. BK242B has a self-adhesive strip on #3052b that adhers to the plastic-coated peelable backing of #3052a when the booklet is closed. When the booklet is opened, this strip is sticky and my adhere firmly to mounts, album pages, etc. Removal of this strip will damage the backing paper of #3052b. Plate numbers for No. BK242B are on backing paper below bar code.
No. 3052d is a complete booklet (BC131). The peelable backing serves as a booklet cover.

Serpentine Die Cut 10¾x10½ on 2 or 3 Sides

2000
3052Ef A2351 33c pane of 20, *Apr. 7, 2000,* P#S111, S222, S333 13.00

By its nature, No. 3052Ef is a complete booklet. Eight #3052E and the booklet cover (similar to BC131) are printed on one side of the peelable backing and twelve #3052E appear on the other side of the backing.

Varieties

3052Eh As "f," all 12 stamps on one side with black ("33 USA," etc.) omitted —
3052Ei Horiz. pair, die cutting omitted between —

3071a — A2370

Serpentine Die Cut 9.9x10.8

3071a A2370 32c pane of 20, *May 31, 1996,* P#S11111 14.00

Varieties

3071b Horiz. pair, die cutting omitted between —
3071c Die cutting omitted, pair —
3071d Horiz. pair, die cutting omitted vert. — —

By its nature, No. 3071a is a complete booklet (BC127). The peelable backing serves as a booklet cover.

A2387

Serpentine Die Cut 11.6x11.4

3089a A2387 32c pane of 20, *Aug. 1, 1996,* P#B1111 14.00

By its nature, No. 3089a is a complete booklet (BC133). The peelable backing serves as a booklet cover.

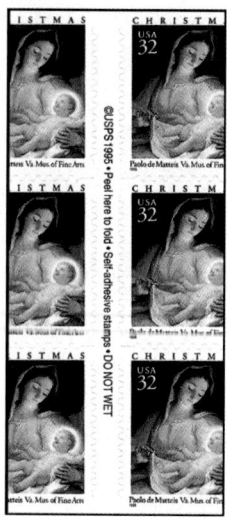

A2405

Serpentine Die Cut 10 on 2, 3 or 4 Sides

3112a	A2405	32c pane of 20 + label, *Nov. 1, 1996*	13.00

Varieties

3112b	Die cutting omitted, pair	75.00
3112c	As "a," die cutting omitted	—

By its nature No. 3112a is a complete booklet (BC134). The peelable backing serves as a booklet cover.

Below is a list of known plate numbers. Some numbers may be scarcer than the value indicated in the listing.

P#1111-1, 1211-1, 2212-1, 2222-1, 2323-1, 3323-1, 3333-1, 3334-1, 4444-1, 5544-1, 5555-1, 5556-1, 5556-2, 5656-2, 6656-2, 6666-1, 6666-2, 6766-1, 7887-1, 7887-2, 7888-2, 7988-2.

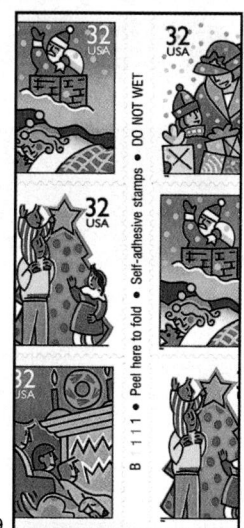

A2406-2409

Serpentine Die Cut 11.8x11.5 on 2, 3 or 4 Sides

3116a	A2406	32c pane of 20 + label, *Oct. 8, 1996*, P#B1111, B2222, B3333,	13.00

Varieties

3116b	Strip of 4, #3113-3116, die cutting omitted	*600.00*
3116c	Block of 6, die cutting omitted	*800.00*
3116d	As "a," die cutting omitted	*2,250.*

By its nature No. 3116a is a complete booklet (BC135). The peelable backing serves as a booklet cover.

A2410

Die Cut

3117a	A2410	32c pane of 18, *Oct. 8, 1996*, P#V1111, V2111	12.00

By its nature No. 3117a is a complete booklet (BC136). The peelable backing serves as a booklet cover.

MAKESHIFT VENDING MACHINE BOOKLETS

The booklets listed below were released in 1996 to meet the need for $4.80 and $9.60 vending machine booklets. The booklets consist of blocks of sheet stamps folded and affixed to a standard cover (BC126) with a spot of glue.

The cover varies from issue to issue in the line of text on the front that indicates the number of stamps contained in the booklet and in the four lines of text on the back that describe the contents of the booklet and list the booklet's item number. Due to the folding required to make stamps fit within the covers, the stamp blocks may easily fall apart when booklets are opened. Stamps may also easily detach from booklet cover.

1996

Booklets

BK243	BC126	$4.80 **blue**, 15 #2897 (32c Flag Over Porch)	11.00
BK244	BC126	$4.80 **blue**, 15 #2957 (32c Cherub/Love)	11.00
BK245	BC126	$4.80 **blue**, 15 #3024 (32c Utah)	12.50
BK246	BC126	$4.80 **blue**, 15 #3065 (32c Fulbright Scholarships)	11.00
BK247	BC126	$4.80 **blue**, 15 #3069 (32c Georgia O'Keeffe)	11.00
BK248	BC126	$4.80 **blue**, 15 #3070 (32c Tennessee)	11.00
BK249	BC126	$4.80 **blue**, 3 #3076a (32c Indian Dances)	11.00
BK250	BC126	$4.80 **blue**, 15 #3082 (32c James Dean)	13.50
BK251	BC126	$4.80 **blue**, 15(#3083-3086) (32c Folk Heroes)	11.00
BK252	BC126	$4.80 **blue**, 15 #3087 (32c Olympic Centennial)	15.00
BK253	BC126	$4.80 **blue**, 15 #3088 (32c Iowa)	11.00
BK254	BC126	$9.60 **blue**, 30 #3090 (32c Rural Free Delivery)	22.50
BK255	BC126	$4.80 **blue**, 3 #3095a (32c Riverboats)	12.50
BK256	BC126	$4.80 **blue**, #3105a-3105o (32c Endangered Species)	11.00
BK257	BC126	$4.80 **blue**, 15 #3107 (32c Madonna Christmas)	11.00
BK258	BC126	$4.80 **blue**, 15 #3118 (32c Hanukkah)	11.00

The contents of #BK251 may vary.
See Nos. BK266-BK269, BK272-BK274, BK277-BK278.

No. 3122a
—
A1951

1997

Serpentine Die Cut 11

3122a	A1951	32c pane of 20 + label, *Feb. 1,* P#V1111, V1211, V1311, V2122, V2222, V2311, V2331, V3233, V3333, V3513, V4532	13.00

Varieties

3122h	As "a," die cutting omitted	—

By its nature, No. 3122a is a complete booklet (BC79). The peelable backing, of which two types are known, serves as booklet cover.

3122b	A1951	32c pane of 4, *Feb. 1,* no P#	2.60
3122c	A1951	32c pane of 5 + label, *Feb. 1,* P#V1111	3.50
3122d	A1951	32c pane of 6, *Feb. 1,* without P#	4.00

Varieties

3122c	P# single, #V1111	.85	1.
3122d	pane of 6 containing P# single	6.00	
	P#Single, #V1111	2.50	1.

The plate # single in No. 3122c is the lower left stamp a should be collected unused with the reorder label to its right differentiate it from the plate # single in No. 3122d which is th lower left stamp in the bottom pane of the booklet and should collected with a normal stamp adjoining it at right. In use condition, these plate # singles are indistinguishable.

Serpentine Die Cut 11.5x11.8 on 2, 3 or 4 Sides

3122Ef	A1951	32c pane of 20 + label, P#V1111, V1211, V2122, V2222	35.00
3122Eg	A1951	32c pane of 6, *1997*, without plate # single	7.00

By its nature, No. 3122Ef is a complete booklet (BC79). Th peelable backing serves as a booklet cover.

Combination Booklet

BK259	BC79	$4.80 **multicolored**, 1 ea #3122b-3122d, P#V1111	10.00

Booklets

BK260	BC79	$9.60 **multicolored**, 5 #3122d, P#V1111	19.00
BK260A	BC79	$9.60 **multicolored**, 5 #3122Eg	37.50

The backing on Nos. BK259-BK260 is rouletted betwee each pane.

Varieties

3122Eg	pane of 6 containing P# single	12.50	
	P# single, #V1111	5.00	2.0

The plate # single in No. 3122Eg is the lower left stamp in th bottom pane of the booklet.

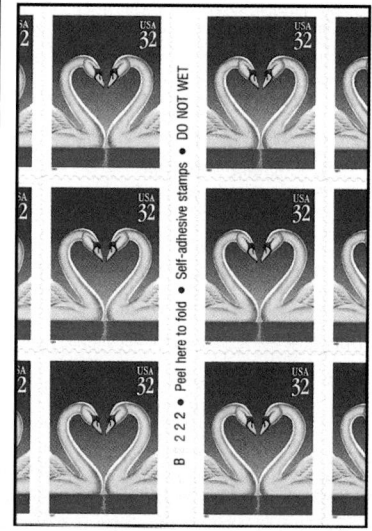

A2415

1997

Serpentine Die Cut 11.8x11.6 on 2, 3 or 4 Sides

3123a	A2415	32c pane of 20 + label, *Feb. 4,* P#B1111, B2222, B3333, B4444, B5555, B6666, B7777	13.00

Serpentine Die Cut 11.6x11.8 on 2, 3 or 4 Sides

3124a	A2416	55c pane of 20 + label, *Feb. 4,* P#B1111, B2222, B3333, B4444	22.00

By their nature, Nos. 3123a-3124a are complete booklets (BC137). The peelable backing serves as a booklet cover.

Varieties

3123b	Die cutting omitted, pair	*150.00*
3123c	As "a," die cutting omitted	*1,500.*
3123d	As "a," black omitted	*600.00*

No. 3127a — A2418-A2419

No. 3128b, 3129b —
A2418-A2419

Serpentine Die Cut 10.9x10.2 on 2, 3 or 4 Sides
1997

3127a	A2418	32c pane of 20, 10 ea #3126-3127 + label, *Mar. 3*, P#S11111, S22222, S33333	13.00

By its nature, No. 3127a is a complete booklet (BC138). The peelable backing serves as a booklet cover.

See Footnote

3128b	A2418	32c pane of 5, 2 ea #3128-3129, 1 #3128a, *Mar. 3*, P#S11111	6.00
3129b	A2419	32c pane of 5, 2 ea #3128-3129, 1 #3129a, *Mar. 3*, no P#	7.50

Combination Booklet

BK261	BC138	$4.80 2 #3128b, 1 #3129b, P#S11111	23.00

Varieties

3127b	Pair, Nos. 3126-3127	1.30
3127c	Vert. pair, die cutting omitted between	500.00
3129c	Pair, Nos. 3128-3129	2.00

Nos. 3128-3129 are serpentine die cut 11.2x10.8 on 2 or 3 sides. Nos. 3128a-3129a are placed sideways on the pane and are serpentine die cut 11.2 on top and bottom, 10.8 on left side. The right side is 11.2 broken by a large perf where the stamp meets the vertical perforations of the two stamps above it.
In No. BK261, No. 3128b at top has no plate #, while the No. 3128b at bottom has a plate # in the selvage.

A2425

1997, May 22

Serpentine Die Cut 11
Self-Adhesive

3137	A2425	32c pane of 10, Nos. 3137b, 3137c, no P#	6.75
3137b	A2425	32c pane of 9, no P#	6.00
3137c	A2425	32c pane of 1, no P#	.65

Varieties

Pane of 10 from uncut press sheet	*70.00*
Pane of 10 with plate #	*350.00*

Die cutting on #3137 does not extend through the backing paper.

3138	A2425	32c pane of 10, Nos. 3138b, 3138c, no P#	140.00
3138b	A2425	32c pane of 9, no P#	*25.00*

No Die Cutting

3138c	A2425	32c pane of 1, no P#	*100.00*

Die cutting on #3138b extends through the backing paper.
By their nature, Nos. 3137-3138 are complete booklets (BC139). The peelable backing serves as a booklet cover.

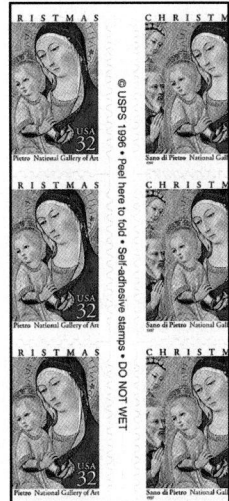

3176a — A2459

Serpentine Die Cut 9.9 on 2, 3 or 4 Sides
1997, Oct. 27   **Tagged**

3176a	A2459	32c pane of 20+label, P#1111, 2222, 3333	13.00

By its nature, No. 3176a is a complete booklet (BC140). The peelable backing serves as a booklet cover.

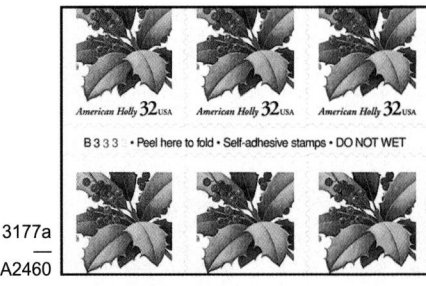

3177a —
A2460

Serpentine Die Cut 11.2x11.8 on 2, 3 or 4 Sides
1997, Oct. 30   **Tagged**
Self-Adhesive

3177a	A2460	32c pane of 20 + label, P#B1111, B2222, B3333	13.00

By its nature No. 3177a is a complete booklet (BC141). The peelable backing serves as a booklet cover.

3177b	A2460	32c Booklet pane of 4, no P#	2.60
3177c	A2460	32c Booklet pane of 5 + label, no P#	3.25
3177d	A2460	32c Booklet pane of 6, no P# or P#B1111	3.90

Combination Booklet

BK264	BC141	$4.80 **black & green**, 1 ea #3177b-3177d, P#B1111	9.75

Booklet

BK265	BC141	$9.60 **black & green**, 5 #3177d, P#B1111	20.00

Panes in Nos. BK264-BK265 are separated by rouletting between each pane.

MAKESHIFT VENDING MACHINE BOOKLETS
See note before No. BK243.
1997

BK266	BC126	$4.80 #3151a-3151o (32c Dolls)	9.00
BK267	BC126	$4.80 15 #3152 (32c Humphrey Bogart)	9.00
BK268	BC126	$4.80 15 #3153 (32c Stars & Stripes)	9.00
BK269	BC126	$4.80 3 ea #3168-3172 (32c Movie Monsters)	9.00

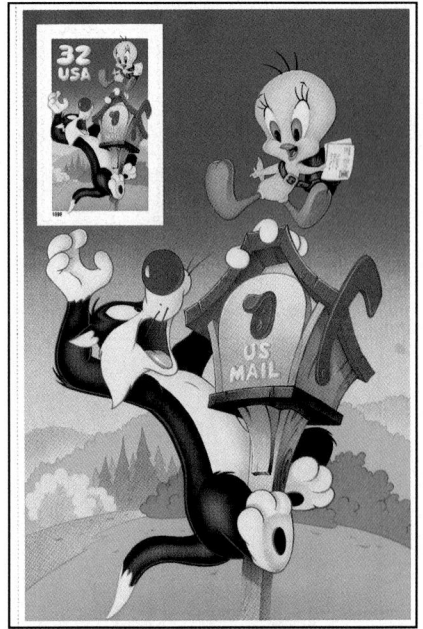

A2487

1998, Apr. 27   **Serpentine Die Cut 11.1**
Self-Adhesive

3204	A2487	32c Pane of 10, 1 each #3204b, 3204c	6.75
3204b	A2487	32c Pane of 9, no P#	6.00
3204c	A2487	32c Pane of 1, no P#	.65
3205	A2487	32c Pane of 10, 1 each #3205b, 3205c	12.50
3205b	A2487	32c Pane of 9, no P#	*9.00*

No Die Cutting

3205c	A2487	32c Pane of 1, no P#	*2.00*

Varieties

Pane of 10 from sheet of 60		*12.50*
Pane of 10 with plate #		*50.00*

Die cutting on No. 3205b extends through the backing paper. By their nature, Nos. 3204 and 3205 are complete booklets. The peelable backing (BC139) serves as a booklet cover.

3244a — A2524

Serpentine Die Cut 10.1x9.9 on 2, 3 or 4 Sides
1998, Oct. 15   **Tagged**

3244a	A2524	32c pane of 20+label, P#11111, 22222, 33333	13.00

No. 3244a is a complete booklet (BC142). The peelable backing serves as a booklet cover.

Varieties

3244b	Die cutting omitted, pair	—

3248a-3248c

3252b — A2525-A2528

Serpentine Die Cut 11.3x11.6 on 2, or 3 Sides
1998, Oct. 15   **Tagged**

3248a	A2525	32c pane of 4, #3245-3248, no P#	22.50
3248b	A2525	32c pane of 5, #3245-3246, 3248, 2 #3247 + label, no P#	27.50
3248c	A2525	32c pane of 6, #3247-3248, 2 each #3245-3246, P#B111111	32.50

Combination Booklet

BK270	BC143	$4.80 **multi,** 1 each #3248a-3248c, P#B111111	85.00

Varieties

3248d	A2525	32c As "a," imperf	—
3248e	A2525	32c As "b," imperf	—
3248f	A2525	32c As "c," imperf	—

Serpentine Die Cut 11.4x11.5 on 2, 3 or 4 Sides

3252c	A2525	32c pane of 5 each #3249-3252 + label, P#B222222, B333333, B444444, B555555	22.50

Serpentine Die Cut 11.7x11.6 on 2, 3 or 4 Sides

3252e	A2525	32c pane of 5 each #3249a-3252a + label, P#B111111, B222222	30.00

Nos. 3252c and 3252e are complete booklets (BC143). The peelable backing serves as a booklet cover.

Varieties

3252b	Block of 4, #3249-3252	4.00
3252d	Block of 4, #3249a-3252a	6.00

3267a, 3268a-3268b, 3269a — A2531

Serpentine Die Cut 9.9 on 2 or 3 Sides
1998, Nov. 9

3267a	A2531	(33c) pane of 10	6.50

Booklet

BK271	BC144	($6.60) **multi** P#1111, 2222, 3333	13.00

Die cut 11¼ on 3 sides (No. 3268a), 11 on 2, 3 or 4 Sides (No. 3268c)

3268a	A2531	(33c) pane of 10, P#V1111, V1211, V2211, V2222	6.50
3268c	A2531	(33c) pane of 20 + label, P#V1111, V1112, V1113, V1213, V1222, V2113, V2122, V2213, V2223	13.00
		P# V1122, V2222	20.00

Die Cut 8

3269a	A2531	(33c) pane of 18, P#V1111	12.00

Nos. 3268a, 3268c, 3269a are complete booklets (BC144). The peelable backing serves as a booklet cover.

MAKESHIFT VENDING MACHINE BOOKLETS
See note before No. BK243.

1998

BK272	BC126	$4.80 15 (#3222-3225) (32c Tropical Birds)	9.00
BK273	BC126	$4.80 15 #3237 (32c Ballet)	9.00
BK274	BC126	$4.80 3 #3242a (32c Space Discovery)	9.00

Configuration of stamps in #BK272 may vary.

3274a — A2537

Tagged   Die C

3274a	A2537	33c pane of 20, *Jan. 28, 1999*	13.00

No. 3274a is a complete booklet (BC145). The peelable backing serves as a booklet cover.

Below is a list of known plate numbers. Some numbers m be scarcer than the value indicated in the listing.
P#V1111, V1112, V1117, V1118, V1211, V1212, V12 V1233, V1313, V1314, V1333, V1334, V1335, V2123, V22 V2222, V2223, V2424, V2425, V2426, V2324, V3123, V31 V3125, V3133, V3134, V3323, V3327, V3333, V3334, V33 V4549, V5650.

Varieties

3274b	Die cutting omitted, pair	200.
3274c	As "a," die cutting omitted	2,000.

Nos. 3278a-3278c

No. 3278d, 3278j

Nos. 3278e, 3278Fg

No. 3279a — A2540

Serpentine Die Cut 11 on 2, 3 or 4 Sides
1999   **Tagged**

Self-Adhesive

3278a	A2540	33c pane of 4, no P#	2.60
3278b	A2540	33c pane of 5 + label, P#V1111, V1112, V1121, V1122, V1212, V2212	3.25
3278c	A2540	33c pane of 6, no P#	3.90
3278d	A2540	33c pane of 10, P#V1112, V1113, V2322, V2324, V3433, V3434, V3545	12.50
		P#V1111	—
3278e	A2540	33c pane of 20 + label, P#V1111, V1211, V2122, V2222, V2223, V3333, V4444	13.00
		P#V8789	—

Nos. 3278d-3278e are complete booklets. The peelable backing serves as a booklet cover and is similar to BC146.

Serpentine Die Cut 11½x11¾ on 2, 3 or 4 Sides

3278Fg	A2540	33c pane of 20 + label	17.50

No. 3278Fg is a complete booklet. The peelable backing serves as a booklet cover and is similar to BC146.

Below is a list of known plate numbers. Some numbers may be scarcer than the value indicated in the listing.
P# V1111, V1131, V2222, V2223, V2227, V2243, V2323, V2423, V2443, V3333, V4444, V5428, V5445, V5446, V5576, V5578, V6423, V6456, V6546, V6556, V6575, V6576, V7567, V7663, V7667, V7676, V8789.

Serpentine Die Cut 11¼

8j	A2540	33c pane of 10, P#V1111, V2222		14.00
		P#V1112, V1113, V2322		

y its nature No. 3278j is a complete booklet. The peelable
king serves as a booklet cover and is similar to BC146.

Serpentine Die Cut 9.8 on 2 or 3 Sides

9a	A2540	33c pane of 10	7.50

COMBINATION BOOKLET

275	BC146	$4.95 **multi,** 1 each #3278a-3278c, P#V1111, V1112, V1121, V1122, V1212, V2212	10.00

BOOKLET

276	BC146	$6.60 **multi,** 2 #3279a, P#1111, 1121	15.00

Varieties

8b	variety, P# single, #V1111, V1112, V1121, V1122, V1212, V2212	.80	1.00
8h	As "e," die cutting omitted	—	

No. 3278 has black date.
he plate # single in No. 3278b is the lower left single.

No. 283a

Serpentine Die Cut 7.9 on 2, 3 or 4 Sides
Tagged

83a	A2541	33c pane of 18, P#V1111	12.00

No. 3283a is a complete booklet (BC147). The peelable back-
serves as a booklet cover.

Nos. 3297b, 3301a

No. 3297d

No. 3301c — A2550-A2553

Serpentine Die Cut 11¼x11½ on 2, 3 or 4 Sides
1999-2000   Tagged
Self-Adhesive

3297b	33c pane of 20, 5 ea #3294-3297 + label	13.00

No. 3297b is a complete booklet (BC148). The peelable back-
ing serves as a booklet cover.
P#B1111, B1112, B2211, B2222, B3331, B3332, B3333,
B4444, B5555.

Serpentine Die Cut 11¼x11½ on 2 or 3 Sides

3297d	33c pane of 20, 5 #3297e + label *Mar. 15, 2000*, P#B1111	15.00

By its nature, No. 3297d is a double-sided complete booklet.
Two #3297e and the booklet cover (similar to BC148) are
printed on one side of the peelable backing and three #3297e
appear on the other side of the backing.

Varieties

3297c	Block of 4, Nos. 3294-3297	2.60
3297e	Block of 4, Nos. 3294a-3297a	3.00

Serpentine Die Cut 9½x10 on 2 or 3 sides

3301a	A2550	33c pane of 4, no P#	3.40
3301b	A2550	33c pane of 5 + label, no P#	4.25
3301c	A2550	33c pane of 6, P#B1111, B1112, B2212, B2222 P#B2221	5.35 —

COMBINATION BOOKLET

BK276A	BC148	$4.95 **multicolored,** 1 each #3301a-3301c, P# see 3301c	13.00

Varieties

3301d	Block of 4, Nos. 3298-3301	3.40

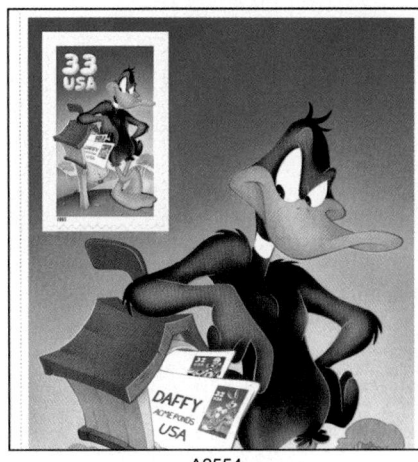

A2554

1999, Apr. 16   Serpentine Die Cut 11.1
Self-Adhesive

3306	33c Pane of 10, 1 each #3306b, 3306c	6.75
3306b	33c Pane of 9, no P#	6.00
3306c	33c Pane of 1, no P#	.65
3307	33c Pane of 10, 1 each #3307b, 3307c	14.00
3307b	33c Pane of 9, no P#	12.00

No Die Cutting

3307c	33c Pane of 1, no P#	1.25

Varieties

	Pane of 10 from sheet of 60	8.00
	Pane of 10 with plate #	15.00

Die cutting on No. 3306b does not extend through the backing paper. Die cutting on No. 3307b extends through the backing paper. Used examples of No. 3306b and 3306c are identical
to those from No. 3307b. By their nature, Nos. 3306 and 3307
are complete booklets. The peelable backing (BC139) serves
as a booklet cover.

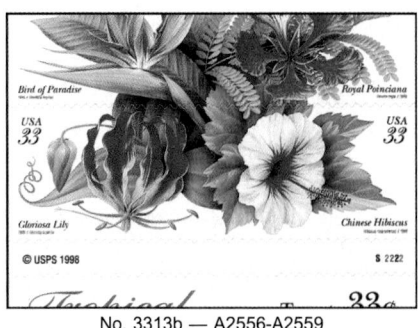

No. 3313b — A2556-A2559

Serpentine Die Cut 10.9 on 2 or 3 Sides
1999   Tagged

3313b	33c pane of 20, all P# (see below) except P#S22444 P#S22444	13.00

By its nature, No. 3313b is a complete booklet. Two #3313a
and the booklet cover (BC149) are printed on one side of the
peelable backing and 3 #3313a appear on the other side of the
backing.
P#S11111, S22222, S22244, S22344, S22444, S22452,
S22462, S23222, S24222, S24224, S24242, S24244, S24422,
S24442, S24444, S26462, S32323, S32333, S32444, S33333,
S44444, S45552, S46654, S55452, S55552, S56462, S62544,
S62562, S64452, S64544, S65544, S65552, S66462, S66544,
S66552, S66562, S66652.

Varieties

3313a	Block of 4, Nos. 3310-3313	2.60

A2599

Nos. 3360-3363 — A2600

Nos. 3364-3367 — A2600

No. 3367c — A2600

1999, Oct. 20   *Serpentine Die Cut 11¼*
Self-Adhesive

3355a	A2599	33c pane of 20, P#B1111, B2222, B3333	15.00
3363a	A2600	33c pane of 20, P#B111111, B222222, B333333, B444444, B555555, B666666, B777777, B888888, B999999, B000000, BAAAAAA, BBBBBBB	17.50

By their nature, Nos. 3355a and 3363a are complete booklets. Twelve #3355 are printed on one side of the peelable backing and 8 #3355 and BC150 appear on the other side of the backing. The peelable backing (BC151) serves as a booklet cover on No. 3363a.

Varieties

3363d	As "a," die cutting omitted	—

Serpentine Die Cut 11½x11¼ on 2 or 3 sides
Stamp Size: 21x19mm

3367a	A2600	33c pane of 4, no P#	7.00
3367b	A2600	33c pane of 5 + label, no P#	8.75
3367c	A2600	33c pane of 6, P#B111111, B222222	10.50

COMBINATION BOOKLET

BK276B	BC152	$4.95 **green & gold**, 1 each #3367a-3367c, P#B see 3367c	26.50

Varieties

3367d	A2600	33c Block of 4, Nos. 3364-3367	7.00

MAKESHIFT VENDING MACHINE BOOKLETS
See note before No. BK243.
1999

BK277	BC126	$4.95 4 each #3325, 3327-3328, 3 #3326 (33c American Glass)	11.00
BK278	BC126	$4.95 3 each #3333-3337 (33c Famous Trains)	11.00

No. 3377a — A2604-A2608

Selvage 1

THE SUBMARINE STAMPS
U.S. Navy Submarines
A Century of Service to America

USS Holland, the U.S. Navy's first submarine, was purchased in 1900.

S-class submarines were designed during WWI.

Gato class submarines played a key role in the destruction of Japanese maritime power in the Pacific during WWII.

Los Angeles class attack submarines, armed with "smart" torpedoes and cruise missiles, are nuclear powered.

Ohio class submarines–also nuclear powered–carry more than half of America's strategic weapons, making them a vital part of America's nuclear deterrence.

Selvage 2

2000, Mar. 27   *Perf. 11*

3377a	pane of 5 with selvage 1	22.50	—
	With selvage 2	22.50	—

Booklet

BK279 BC153 $9.80 **multicolored**, no P#	45.00

No. BK279 contains one pane with selvage 1 and one pane with selvage 2.

A2622

2000, Apr. 26   *Serpentine Die Cut 11*
Self-Adhesive

3391	A2622	33c Pane of 10, 1 each # 3391b, 3391c	9.00
3391b	A2622	33c Pane of 9, no P#	7.75
3391c	A2622	33c Pane of 1, no P#	1.25
3392	A2622	33c Pane of 10, 1 each # 3392b, 3392c	40.00
3392b	A2622	33c Pane of 9, no P#	30.00

No Die Cutting

3392c	A2622	33c Pane of 1, no P#	5.00

Varieties

	Pane of 10 from sheet of 60	9.50
	Two panes of 10 with plate number on front	22.50
3391d	All die cutting omitted, pane of 10	2,500.

Die cutting on No. 3392a extends through backing paper. By their nature, Nos. 3391 and 3392 are complete booklets. The peelable backing (BC139) serves as a booklet cover.

UNITED STATES
POSTAL SERVICE®

Nos. 3436a, 3436b, 3436c — A2652

Serpentine Die Cut 11¼x10¾ on 3 Sides
2004, July 14   **Lit**
Self-Adhesive

3436a	A2652	23c pane of 4, no P#	1.80
3436b	A2652	23c pane of 6, no P#	2.70
3436c	A2652	23c pane of 10, P#P11	4.50

COMBINATION BOOKLET

BK279A	BC153A	$2.30 **multi**, #3436a-3436b, no P#	4.50

By its nature, No. 3436c is a complete booklet (BC153A). T peelable backing serves as a booklet cover. No. BK279A la the self-adhesive panel that covers the rouletting. The back on No. 3436b has a different product code (672900) than t found on the lower portion of No. 3436c (673000).

Varieties

3436d	A2652	23c As "c," die cutting omitted	—

3450a — A2678

2000   *Serpentine Die Cut 8 on 2, 3 or 4 Side*
Self-Adhesive

3450a	A2678	(34c) pane of 18, P#V1111, Dec. 15	14.00

No. 3450a is a complete booklet (BC154). The peelable backing serves as a booklet cover.

3451a — A2679

3451b — A2679

3451c — A2679

Serpentine Die Cut 11 on 2, 3 or 4 Sides
2000, Dec. 15

Self-Adhesive

3451a	A2679	(34c) pane of 20, P#V1111, V2222		13.00

No. 3451a is a complete booklet (BC155). The peelable backing serves as a booklet cover.

3451b	A2679	(34c) pane of 4, without plate #		3.50
3451c	A2679	(34c) pane of 6, no P#		5.25

COMBINATION BOOKLET

BK280	BC156	($6.80) multicolored, 2 each #3451b, 3451c	17.50

P# on No. 3451b is on the lower right stamp of the right pane of 4 of the booklet.

Varieties

3451b	pane of 4, containing P# single	3.50	
	P# single, #V1111, V2222	.90	.70
3451d	As "a," die cutting omitted	—	

3457a — A2681-A2684

3457b, 3457c, 3457d — A2681-A2684

Serpentine Die Cut 10¹⁄₂x10³⁄₄ on 2 or 3 Sides (#3454-3457), 11¹⁄₂x11³⁄₄ on 2 or 3 sides (#3458-3461)

2000

Self-Adhesive

3457e	(34c) pane of 20, 5 each # 3454-3457, P#S1111, Dec. 15	20.00

No. 3457e is a complete booklet. Two #3457a and the booklet cover (BC157) are printed on one side of the peelable backing and three #3457a appear on the other side of the backing.

3457b	(34c) pane of 4, #3454-3457, Dec. 15	4.00
3457c	(34c) pane of 6, #3456, 3457, 2 each #3454-3455, no P#, Dec. 15	6.00
3457d	(34c) pane of 6, #3454, 3455, 2 each #3456-3457, no P#, Dec. 15	6.00

COMBINATION BOOKLET

BK281	BC158 ($6.80) multicolored, #3457c, 3457d, 2 #3457b, P#S1111	20.00

P# on No. BK281 is on the backing paper of the top pane of No. 3457b.

3461b	pane of 20, 2 each #3461a, 3 each #3457a, #S1111, Dec. 15	32.00
3461c	pane of 20, 2 each #3457a, 3 each #3461a, #S1111, Dec. 15	38.00

Nos. 3461b and 3461c are complete booklets. Two blocks of four with the same gauge die cutting and the booklet cover (BC157) are printed on one side of the peelable backing and three blocks of four with the other gauge die cutting appear on the other side of the backing.

Varieties

3457a	Block of 4, #3454-3457	4.00
3461a	Block of 4, #3458-3461	10.00

Nos. 3482a, 3483a, 3483b — A2686

Serpentine Die Cut 11¹⁄₄x11 on 3 Sides
2001, Feb. 22

Self-Adhesive

3482a	A2686	20c pane of 10, P#P1, P2, P3	4.00
3482b	A2686	20c pane of 4, P#P1, P2, P3	1.60
3482c	A2686	20c pane of 6, no P#	2.40

COMBINATION BOOKLET

BK281A	BC159 $2 multicolored, #3482b-3482c, P#P1, P2, P3	4.00

No. BK281A has slightly smaller cover than No. 3482a and lacks self-adhesive panel that covers the rouletting.

Serpentine Die Cut 10¹⁄₂x11 on 3 Sides

3483a	A2686	20c pane of 4, 2 #3482 at L, 2 #3483 at R, P#P1, P2, P3	9.00
3483b	A2686	20c pane of 6, 3 #3482 at L, 3 #3483 at R, no P#	15.00
3483c	A2686	20c pane of 10, 5 #3482 at L, 5 #3483 at R, P#P1, P2, P3	16.00
3483d	A2686	20c pane of 4, 2 #3483 at L, 2 #3282 at R, P#P1, P2, P3	9.00
3483e	A2686	20c pane of 6, 3 #3483 at L, 3 #3282 at R, no P#	15.00
3483f	A2686	20c pane of 10, 5 #3483 at L, 5 #3282 at R, P#P1, P2, P3	16.00

Nos. 3482a, 3483c and 3483f are complete booklets (BC159) and include a self-adhesive panel that covers the rouletting. The peelable backing, which is slightly longer than that on Nos. BK282 and BK282A, serves as a booklet cover.

COMBINATION BOOKLETS

BK282	BC159 $2 multicolored, #3483a-3483b, P#P1, P2, P3	24.00
BK282A	BC159 $2 multicolored, #3483d-3483e, P#P1, P2, P3	24.00

Varieties

3483g	Pair, #3482 at L, #3483 at R	4.00
3483h	Pair, #3483 at L, #3482 at R	4.00

Nos. 3484b, 3484c, 3484d, 3484Ae, 3484Af, 3484Ag, 3484Ah, 3484Ai, 3484Aj — A2687

Serpentine Die Cut 11¹⁄₄ on 3 Sides
2001, Sept. 20

Self-Adhesive

3484b	A2687	21c pane of 4, P#P111111, P333333, P444444	2.00
3484c	A2687	21c pane of 6, no P#	3.00
3484d	A2687	21c pane of 10, P#P111111, P222222, P333333, P444444, P555555	5.00

Serpentine Die Cut 10¹⁄₂x11¹⁄₄ on 3 Sides

3484Ae	A2687	21c pane of 4, 2 #3484 at L, 2# 3484A at R, P#P111111, P333333, P444444	9.00
3484Af	A2687	21c pane of 6, 3 #3484 at L, 3# 3484A at R, no P#	15.00
3484Ag	A2687	21c pane of 10, 5 #3484 at L, 5# 3484A at R, P#P111111, P222222, P333333, P444444, P555555	20.00
3484Ah	A2687	21c pane of 4, 2 #3484A at L, 2# 3484 at R, P#P111111, P333333, P444444	9.00
3484Ai	A2687	21c pane of 6, 3 #3484A at L, 3# 3484 at R, no P#	15.00
3484Aj	A2687	21c pane of 10, 5 #3484A at L, 5# 3484 at R, P#P111111, P222222, P333333, P444444, P555555	20.00

COMBINATION BOOKLETS

BK282B	BC159A $2.10 multi, #3484b-3484c, P#P111111, P333333, P444444	5.00
BK282C	BC159A $2.10 multi, #3484Ae-3484Af, P#P111111, P333333, P444444	24.00
BK282D	BC159A $2.10 multi, #3484Ah-3484Ai, P#P111111, P333333, P444444	24.00

Nos. 3484d, 3484Ag and 3484Aj are complete booklets (BC159A). The peelable backing serves as a booklet cover. Nos. BK282-BK282D lack self-adhesive panel that covers the rouletting. Nos. BK282B-BK282D have a small 662900 UPC code on cover back, while Nos. 3484d, 3484Ag and 3484Aj have a large 662800 UPC code on cover back.

Varieties

| 3484Ak | Pair, #3484 at L, #3484A at R | 4.00 |
| 3484Al | Pair, #3484A at L, #3484 at R | 4.00 |

No. 3485a — A2689

No. 3485b — A2689

No. 3485c — A2689

2001, Feb. 7   *Serpentine Die Cut 11 on 3 Sides*
Self-Adhesive

3485a	A2689	34c pane of 10, P#V1111, V1221	6.50
3485b	A2689	34c pane of 20, P#V1111, V1211, V1221, V2111, V2112, V2121, V2122, V2212, V2222	13.00
3485c	A2689	34c pane of 4, without P#	3.00
3485d	A2689	34c pane of 6, no P#	4.50

COMBINATION BOOKLET

| BK283 | BC160A | $6.80 **multicolored**, 2 each #3485c-3485d, P#V1111, V1122, V2212, V2222 | 15.00 |
| | | P#V1112, V1121 | — |

Varieties

3485c	pane of 4, containing P# single	4.00	
	P# single, #V1111, V1122, V2212, V2222	1.50	1.50
	Pane containing P#V1112, V1121	—	—
	P# single, #V1112, V1121	—	—
3485e	Die cutting omitted, pair (from No. 3485b)	—	
3485f	Die cutting omitted, pane of 20	—	

Nos. 3485a-3485b are complete booklets (BC160). The peelable backing serves as a booklet cover.

Nos. 3490b, 3490c, 3490d — A2690-A2693

No. 3490e — A2690-A2693

Serpentine Die Cut 10½x 10¾ on 2 or 3 Sides
2001, Feb. 7

Self-Adhesive

3490b	34c pane of 4	3.00
3490c	34c pane of 6, #3489-3490, 2 each #3487-3488	4.50
3490d	34c pane of 6, #3487-3488, 2 each #3489-3490	4.50
3490e	34c pane of 20, 5 #3490a, P#S1111, S2222	15.00

COMBINATION BOOKLET

| BK284 | BC162 | $6.80 **multicolored**, #3490c-3490d, 2 #3490b, P#S1111 | 15.00 |

No. 3490e is a complete booklet (BC161) with 12 stamps on one side and eight stamps plus label on the other side. The peelable backing serves as a booklet cover.
P# on No. BK284 is on the backing paper of the bottom pane of No. 3490b.

Varieties

| 3490a | Block of 4, #3487-3490 | 3.00 |

Nos. 3492b — A2694-A2695

Serpentine Die Cut 11¼ on 2, 3 or 4 sides
2001, Mar. 6

Self-Adhesive

| 3492b | 34c pane of 20, 10 each #3491-3492, P# B1111, B2222, B3333, B4444, B5555, B6666, B7777 | 13.00 |

No. 3492b is a complete booklet (BC163). The peelable backing serves as a booklet cover.

Varieties

3492a	Pair, #3491-3492	1.30
3492c	As "a," black ("34 USA") omitted	—
3492d	As "a," die cutting omitted	—
3492e	As "b," die cutting omitted	—

No. 3494b — A2694-A2695

No. 3494c — A2694-A2695

No. 3494d — A2694-A2695

2001, May   *Serpentine Die Cut 11½x10¾*
Self-Adhesive

3494b	34c pane of 4, 2 each #3493-3494, without P#	4.00
3494c	34c pane of 6, 3 each #3493-3494, #3493 at UL, no P#	6.00
3494d	34c pane of 6, 3 each #3493-3494, #3494 at UL, no P#	6.00

COMBINATION BOOKLET

| BK284A | BC163A | $6.80 **multi**, #3494c, 3494d, 2 #3494b, P#B1111 | 22.00 |

Varieties

3494a	Pair, #3493-3494	2.00	
3494b	Pane of 4 with P#	6.00	
	P# single #B1111	2.00	2.00

3495a — A2688

Serpentine Die Cut 8 on 2, 3 or 4 Sides
2001, Dec. 17

Self-Adhesive

| 3495a | 34c pane of 18, #V1111 | 15.00 |

Nos. 3495a is a complete booklet (BC163B). The peelable backing serves as a booklet cover.

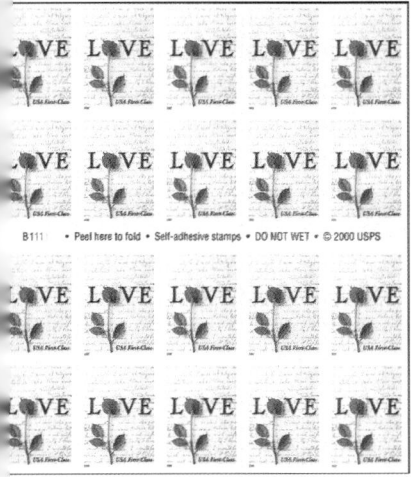

3496a — A2699

01 *Serpentine Die Cut 11¼ on 2, 3, or 4 Sides*
Self-Adhesive

96a A2699 (34c) pane of 20, P#B1111,
B2222, *Jan. 19* 15.00

Varieties

96b A2699 (34c) Vert. pair, die cutting omitted
between —

No. 3496a is a complete booklet (BC164). The peelable back-
serves as a booklet cover.

3497a — A2700

3498a, 3498b —
A2700

01 *Serpentine Die Cut 11¼ on 2, 3 or 4 Sides*
Self-Adhesive

497a A2700 34c pane of 20, P#B1111, B2222,
B3333, B4444, B5555, *Feb.
14* 15.00

Size: 18x21mm

Serpentine Die Cut 11½x10¾

498a A2700 34c pane of 4, without P#, *Feb.
14* 4.00
498b A2700 34c pane of 6, no P#, *Feb. 14* 6.00

COMBINATION BOOKLET

K285 BC166 $6.80 **multicolored,** 2 each
#3498a-3498b, P#B1111 22.00

Varieties

497b Vert. pair, imperf between —
498a pane of 4, containing plate # single 6.00
P# single, #B1111 2.00 2.00

No. 3497a is a complete booklet (BC165). The peelable back-
ng serves as a booklet cover.

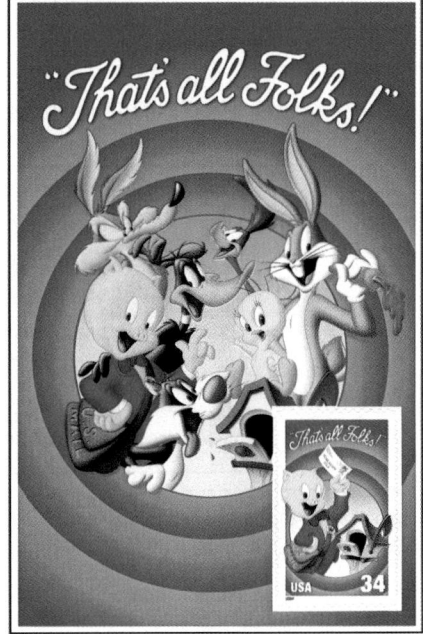

A2736

2001, Oct. 1 *Serpentine Die Cut 11*
Self-Adhesive

3534 A2736 34c pane of 10, 1 each #3534b,
3534c 6.50
3534b A2736 34c pane of 9, no P# 5.85
3534c A2736 34c pane of 1, no P# .65
3535 A2736 34c pane of 10, 1 each #3535b,
3535c 60.00
3535b A2736 34c pane of 9, no P# 50.00

No Die Cutting

3535c A2736 34c pane of 1, no P# 7.50

Die cutting on No. 3535b extends through backing paper. By
their nature, Nos. 3534 and 3535 are complete booklets. The
peelable backing serves as a booklet cover (BC139).

A2737

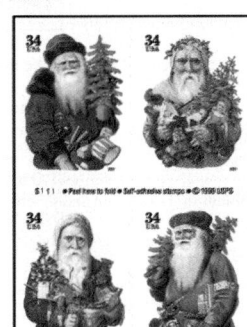

No. 3540d — A2738-
A2741

3544b

Serpentine Die Cut 11½ on 2, 3 or 4 Sides
2001, Oct. 10

Self-Adhesive

3536a A2737 34c pane of 20, P#B1111 13.00

No. 3536a is a complete booklet (BC167). The peelable backing serves as a booklet cover.

Serpentine Die Cut 10¾x11 on 2 or 3 Sides

3540d 34c pane of 20, 5 each #3537a-
3540a + label, P#S1111 13.00
3540g Booklet pane of 20, 5 #3540f
+ label, P#S3333, S4444 35.00

Nos. 3540d and 3540g are complete booklets (BC168) with
12 stamps on one side and eight stamps plus label on the other
side. The peelable backing serves as a booklet cover.

Green Inscriptions
Stamp Size: 21x18½mm

Serpentine Die Cut 11 on 2 or 3 sides

3544b 34c pane of 4, #3541-3544 2.60
3544c 34c pane of 6, #3543-3544, 2
#3541-3542 3.90
3544d 34c pane of 6, #3541-3542, 2
#3543-3544 3.90

COMBINATION BOOKLET

BK286 BC169 $6.80 **multi,** #3544c-3544d, 2
#3544b, P#V1111 13.00

P# on No. BK286 is on the backing paper of the bottom pane
of No. 3544b.

Varieties

3540c Block of 4, #3537a-3540a 2.60
3544a Block of 4, #3541-3544 2.60

Varieties

3540f Block of 4, large date, #3537b-3539b,
3540e 7.00

No. 3549a — A2744

Serpentine Die Cut 11¼ on 2, 3 or 4 Sides
2001, Oct. 24

Self-Adhesive

3549a A2744 34c Pane of 20, P#B1111,
B2222, B3333, B4444 13.00

No. 3549a is a complete booklet (BC170). The peelable backing serves as a booklet cover.

3549Bc, 3549Bd —
A2744

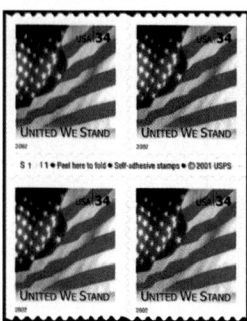

3549Be — A2744

Serpentine Die Cut 10½x10¾ on 2 or 3 Sides
2002, Jan.
Self-Adhesive
3549Bc	A2744	34c pane of 4	3.20
3549Bd	A2744	34c pane of 6	4.80
3549Be	A2744	34c pane of 20, P#S1111	16.00

COMBINATION BOOKLET
BK287 BC171 $6.80 **multi,** 2 each #3549Bc, 3549Bd, P#S1111 ... 16.00

P# on No. BK287 is on the backing paper of the lower example of No. 3549Bd. No. 3549Be is a complete booklet (BC172) with 12 stamps on one side and eight stamps plus label on the other side. The peelable backing serves as a booklet cover.

Washington Type of 2002
2002, June 7   *Serpentine Die Cut 11¼x11*
Self-Adhesive
3618a	A2686	23c pane of 4, P#P1, P2, P4	1.80
3618b	A2686	23c pane of 6, no P#	2.70

Serpentine Die Cut 11¼x11 on 3 Sides
|**3618c**|A2686|23c pane of 10, P#P1, P2, P3|4.50|

COMBINATION BOOKLET
BK288 BC173 $2.30 **multi,** #3618a-3618b, P#P1, P2, P4 ... 4.50

No. BK288 has a 671800 UPC code on cover back, while No. 3618c has a 671000 UPC code on cover back.

Serpentine Die Cut 10½x11 on 3 Sides
3619a	A2686	23c pane of 4, 2 #3619 at L, 2 #3618 at R, P#P1, P2, P4	6.00
3619b	A2686	23c pane of 6, 3 #3619 at L, 3 #3618 at R, no P#	9.50
3619c	A2686	23c pane of 4, 2 #3618 at L, 2 #3619 at R, P#P1, P2, P4	6.00
3619d	A2686	23c pane of 6, 3 #3618 at L, 3 #3619 at R, no P#	9.50

Washington Type of 2002
Serpentine Die Cut 10½x11 on 3 Sides
2002, June 7
Self-Adhesive
3619e A2686 23c pane of 10, 5 #3619 at L, 5 #3618 at R, P#P1, P2, P3 ... 13.50

No. 3619e is a complete booklet (BC173) and includes a self-adhesive panel that covers the rouletting. The peelable backing, which is slightly longer than those on Nos. BK289 and BK289A, serves as a booklet cover.

3619f A2686 23c pane of 10, 5 #3618 at L, 5 #3619 at R, P#P1, P2, P3 ... 13.50

No. 3619f is a complete booklet (BC173) and includes a self-adhesive panel that covers the rouletting. The peelable backing, which is slightly longer than those on Nos. BK289 and BK289A, serves as a booklet cover.

COMBINATION BOOKLET
BK289 BC173 $2.30 **multi,** #3619a-3619b, P#P1, P2, P4 ... 15.50
BK289A BC173 $2.30 **multi,** #3619c-3619d, P#P1, P2, P4 ... 15.50

Variety
3619g	Pair, #3619 at L, #3618 at R	2.75
3619h	Pair, #3618 at L, #3619 at R	2.75

No. 3618c is a complete booklet (BC173) and includes a self-adhesive panel that covers the rouletting. The peelable backing, which is slightly longer than those on Nos. BK289 and BK289A, serves as a booklet cover.

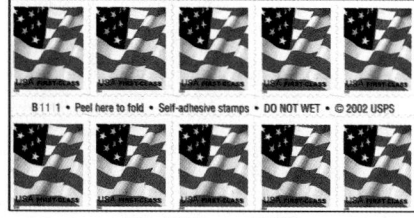

No. 3623a — A2807

Serpentine Die Cut 11¼ on 2, 3 or 4 Sides
2002, June 7   Litho.
Self-Adhesive
3623a A2807 (37c) pane of 20, P#B1111, B2222, B3333 ... 15.00

No. 3623a is a complete booklet (BC174). The peelable backing serves as a booklet cover.

No. 3624a — A2807

No. 3624b — A2807

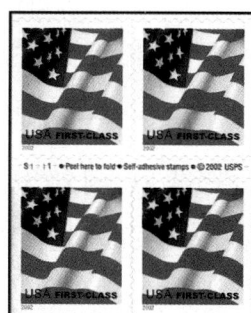

No. 3624c — A2807

Serpentine Die Cut 10½x10¾ on 2 or 3 Sides
2002, June 7   Photo.
Self-Adhesive
3624a	A2807	(37c) pane of 4, no P#	3.00
3624b	A2807	(37c) pane of 6, no P#	4.50
3624c	A2807	(37c) pane of 20, P#S1111	15.00

COMBINATION BOOKLET
BK290 BC175 ($7.40) **multi,** 2 each #3624a, 3624b, P#S11111 ... 15.00

Plate number appears on the backing of the lower example of No. 3624b in No. BK290.

No. 3624c is a complete booklet pane (BC176) with 12 stamps on one side and eight stamps plus label on the other side. The peelable backing serves as a booklet cover.

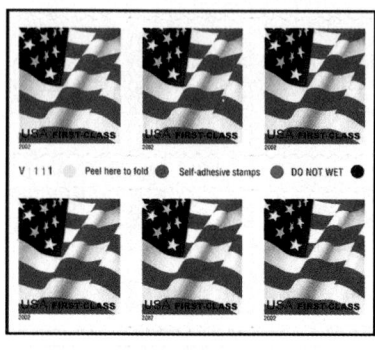

No. 362_ — A28_

Serpentine Die Cut 8 on 2, 3 or 4 Sides
2002, June 7   Pho.
Self-Adhesive
3625a A2807 (37c) pane of 18, P#V1111 ... 13.50

No. 3625a is a complete booklet (BC177). The peelable backing serves as a booklet cover.

No. 3629b — A2808-A2811

No. 3629c — A2808-A2811

No. 3629d — A2808-A2811

No. 3629e —
A2808-A2811

Serpentine Die Cut 11 on 2, 3 or 4 Sides
2002, June 7   **Photo.**
Self-Adhesive

3629b	(37c) pane of 4, #3626-3629, no P#	3.00
3629c	(37c) pane of 6, #3627, 3629, 2 each #3626, 3628, no P#	4.50
3629d	(37c) pane of 6, #3626, 3628, 2 each #3627, 3629, no P#	4.50
3629e	(37c) pane of 20, 5 each #3626-3629, P#V1111, V1112, V2222	15.00

COMBINATION BOOKLET

BK291	BC178 ($7.40) **multi,**#3629c-3629d, 2 #3629b, no P#	15.00

No. 3629e is a complete booklet (BC179). The peelable backing serves as a booklet cover.

Variety

3629a	Block of 4, #3626-3629	3.00

No. 3634a — A2812

Serpentine Die Cut 11.1 on 3 Sides
2002, June 7   **Photo.**
Self-Adhesive

3634a	A2812 37c pane of 10, P#V1111	7.50

No. 3634a is a complete booklet (BC180). The peelable backing serves as a booklet cover.

Serpentine Die Cut 11.3 on 3 Sides
2002?   **Photo.**
Self-Adhesive

3634f	A2812 37c pane of 10, P#V11111	—

No. 3634f is a complete booklet (BC180). The peelable backing serves as a booklet cover.

Serpentine Die Cut 11 on 2 or 3 Sides
2003, Nov.   **Photo.**
Self-Adhesive

3634c	A2812 37c pane of 4 #3634b, no P#	3.00
3634d	A2812 37c pane of 6 #3634b, no P#	4.50

COMBINATION BOOKLET

BK291A	BC180 $7.40 **multi,** 2 each #3634c, 3634d, P#V1111	15.00

Plate number appears on the backing of the lower example of No. 3634d in No. BK291A.

Serpentine Die Cut 11.3 on 3 Sides
Self-Adhesive
Photo.

3634f	A2812 37c pane of 10, P#VIIII	7.50

No. 3634f is a complete booklet (BC180). The peelable backing serves as a booklet cover.

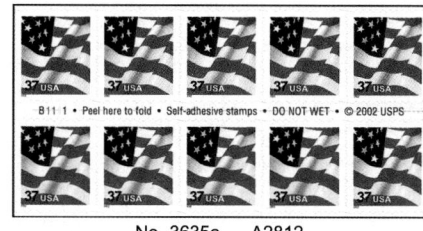

No. 3635a — A2812

Serpentine Die Cut 11¼ on 2, 3 or 4 Sides
2002, June 7   **Litho.**
Self-Adhesive

3635a	A2812 37c pane of 20, P#B1111, B2222, B3333, B4444, B5555, B6666, B7777	15.00

No. 3635a is a complete booklet (BC181). The peelable backing serves as a booklet cover.

No. 3636a — A2812

No. 3636b — A2812

Serpentine Die Cut 10½x10¾ on 2 or 3 Sides
2002, June 7   **Photo.**
Self-Adhesive

3636a	A2812 37c pane of 4, no P#	3.00
3636b	A2812 37c pane of 6, no P#	4.50

COMBINATION BOOKLET

BK291B	BC182 $7.40 **multi,** 2 each #3636a, 3636b, P#S11111	15.00

Plate number appears on the backing of the lower example of No. 3636b in No. BK291B.

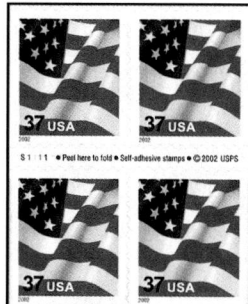

No. 3636c — A2812

Serpentine Die Cut 10½x10¾ on 2 or 3 Sides
2002, June 7   **Photo.**
Self-Adhesive

3636c	A2812 37c pane of 20, P#S1111, S2222, S3333, S4444	15.00

No. 3636c is a complete booklet (BC183) with 12 stamps on one side and eight stamps plus label on the other side. The peelable backing serves as a booklet cover.

Serpentine Die Cut 11¼x11 on 2 or 3 Sides
2004, July   **Photo.**
Self-Adhesive

3636De	A2812 37c pane of 20, P#V1111	18.00

No. 3636De is a complete booklet (BC183) with 12 stamps on one side and eight stamps plus label on the other side. The peelable backing serves as a booklet cover.

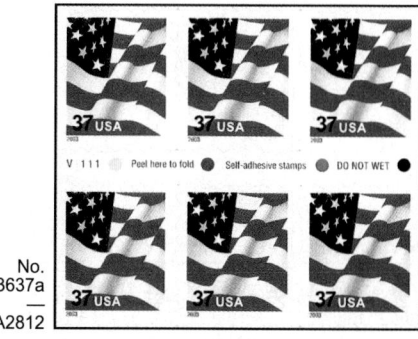

No. 3637a — A2812

Serpentine Die Cut 8 on 2, 3 or 4 Sides
2003, Feb. 4   **Photo.**
Self-Adhesive

3637a	A2812 37c pane of 18, #V1111	13.50

No. 3637a is a complete booklet (BC184). The peelable backing serves as a booklet cover.

No. 3645b —
A2813-A2816

No. 3645c — A2813-A2816

No. 3645d — A2813-A2816

No. 3645e — A2813-A2816

Serpentine Die Cut 11 on 2, 3 or 4 Sides
2002, July 26   Photo.
Self-Adhesive

3645b	37c pane of 4, #3642-3645, no P#		3.00
3645c	37c pane of 6, #3643, 3645, 2 each		
	#3642, 3644, no P#		4.50
3645d	37c pane of 6, #3642, 3644, 2 each		
	#3643, 3645, no P#		4.50
3645e	37c pane of 20, 5 each #3642-3645,		
	P#V1111, V1112, V2221, V2222		15.00

COMBINATION BOOKLET

BK292	BC185	$7.40 **multi**,#3645c-3645d, 2 #3645b, P#V1111	15.00

No. 3645e is a complete booklet (BC186). The peelable backing serves as a booklet cover. Plate number on No. BK292 is on backing paper of No. 3645d.

Variety

3645a		Block of 4, #3642-3645	3.00

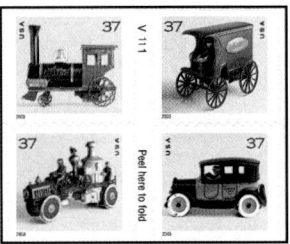

No. 3645h — A2813-A2816

Serpentine Die Cut 11x11¼ on 2 or 3 Sides
2003, Sept. 3   Photo.
Self-Adhesive

3645h	37c pane of 20, P#V1111		15.00

No. 3645h is a complete double-sided booklet. Two # 3645g and the booklet cover (BC179A) are printed on one side of the peelable backing, and three #3645g appear on the other side of the backing.

Variety

3645g		Block of 4, #3642a, 3643a, 3644a, 3645f	3.00

No. 3657a — A2828

Serpentine Die Cut 11 on 2, 3 or 4 Sides
2002, Aug. 16   Litho.
Self-Adhesive

3657a	A2828	37c pane of 20, P#B11111, B22222, B33333, B44444, B55555, B66666, B77777	15.00

No. 3657a is a complete booklet (BC187). The peelable backing serves as a booklet cover.

Nos. 3675a — A2843

Serpentine Die Cut 11x11¼ on 2, 3 or 4 Sides
2002, Oct. 10
Self-Adhesive

3675a	A2843	37c pane of 20, P#B1111, B2222	15.00

No. 3675a is a complete booklet (BC188). The peelable backing serves as a booklet cover.

No. 3687b — A2844-A2847

No. 3691b — A2848-A2851

No. 3691c — A2848-A2851

No. 3691d — A2848-A2851

Serpentine Die Cut 10¾ on 2 or 3 Sides
2002, Oct. 28
Self-Adhesive

3687b	37c Pane of 20, P#S111, S1113, S2222, S4444		18.00

Serpentine Die Cut 11 on 2 or 3 Sides

3691b	37c Pane of 4, #3688-3691, no P#		4.00
3691c	37c Pane of 6, #3690-3691, 2 each		
	#3688-3689, no P#		6.00
3691d	37c Pane of 6, #3688-3689, 2 each		
	#3690-3691, no P#		6.00

COMBINATION BOOKLET

BK293	BC190	$7.40 **multi**, #3691c, 3691d 2 each #3691b, P#V1111	20.00

No. 3687b is a complete booklet (BC189) with 12 stamps on one side and eight stamps plus label on the other side. The peelable backing serves as a booklet cover. Plate number appears on the backing of the upper example of No. 3691b in BK293.

Varieties

3687a		Block of 4, #3684-3687	3.60
3691a		Block of 4, #3688-3691	4.00

No. 3780b — A2883-A2887

Backing 1

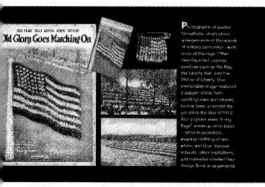

Backing 2

03, Apr. 3   Litho.   *Serpentine Die Cut 10x9¾*
Self-Adhesive
0b   37c Pane of 2 #3780a with backing 1   7.50
      With backing 2   7.50
Booklet
294 BC191 $7.40 **multi,** no P#   15.00
o. BK294 contains one pane with backing 1 and one pane
 backing 2.
Variety
0a   Horiz. strip of 5, #3776-3780   3.75

No. 3783a — A2890

No. 3783b — A2890

3, May 22   Photo.   *Serpentine Die Cut 11*
Self-Adhesive
3a A2890 37c Pane of 9, no P#   6.75
3b A2890 37c Pane of 1, no P#   .75
COMBINATION BOOKLET
295 BC192 $3.70 **multi,** #3783a-3783b, no P# 7.50

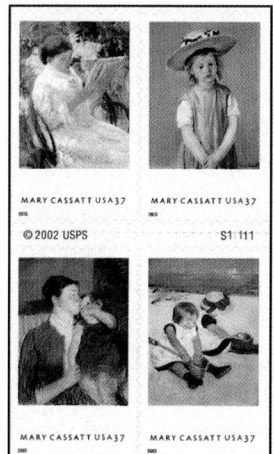

No. 3807b —
A2902-A2905

Serpentine Die Cut 10¾ on 2 or 3 Sides
3, Aug. 7   Photo.
Self-Adhesive
7b   37c pane of 20, 5 #3807a,
      P#S11111   15.00
y its nature, No. 3807b is a complete double-sided booklet.
#3807a and the booklet cover (BC193) are printed on one

side of the peelable backing and three #3807a appear on the
other side of the backing.

Variety
3807a   Block of 4, #3804-3807   3.00

3820a — A2843

Serpentine Die Cut 11x11¼ on 2 or 3 Sides
2003, Oct. 23
Self-Adhesive
Size: 28x19½mm
3820a   37c pane of 20, P#P1111   15.00
No. 3820a is a complete double-sided booklet. Eight stamps
and the booklet cover (BC194) are printed on one side of the
peelable backing, and 12 stamps are printed on the other side
of the backing.

3824b — A2917-
A2920

3828b — A2921-
A2924

3828c — A2921-A2924

3828d — A2921-A2924

Serpentine Die Cut 11¾x11 on 2 or 3 Sides
2003, Oct. 23
Self-Adhesive
3824b   37c Pane of 20, 5 each #3821-3824,
         P#S1111   15.00
Serpentine Die Cut 10½x10¾ on 2 or 3 Sides
3828b   37c Pane of 4, #3825-3828, no P#   3.00
3828c   37c Pane of 6, #3827-3828, 2 each
         #3825-3828, no P#   4.50
3828d   37c Pane of 6, #3825-3826, 2 each
         #3827-3828, no P#   4.50
COMBINATION BOOKLET
BK296 BC196 $7.40 **multi,** #3828c, 3828d, 2
       each #3828b, P#S11111   15.00

No. 3824b is a complete double-sided booklet. Two #3824a
and the booklet cover (BC195) are printed on one side of the
peelable backing, and three #3824a are printed on the other
side of the backing.
Plate number appears on the backing of No. 3828d in BK296.

Varieties
3824a   Block of 4, #3821-3824   3.00
3828a   Block of 4, #3825-3828   3.00

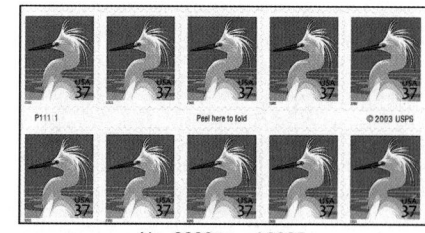

No. 3830a — A2925

Serpentine Die Cut 11½x11 on 2, 3 or 4 Sides
2004, Jan. 30   Litho.
Self-Adhesive
3830a A2925 37c pane of 20, P#P11111   15.00
No. 3830a is a complete booklet (BC197). The peelable backing serves as a booklet cover.

Varieties
3830c   As "a," die cutting omitted   —

Serpentine Die Cut 11½x11 on 2, 3 or 4 Sides
2005?   Photo.
Self-Adhesive
With "USPS" Microprinted on Bird's Breast
3830De A2925 37c pane of 20, P#P33333   15.00
No. 3830De is a complete booklet (BC197). The peelable
backing serves as a booklet cover.

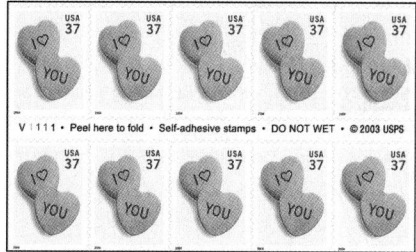

No. 3833a — A2928

Serpentine Die Cut 10¾ on 2, 3 or 4 Sides
2004, Jan. 14   **Photo.**
Self-Adhesive
3833a A2928 37c pane of 20, P#V1111   15.00

No. 3833a is a complete booklet (BC198). The peelable backing serves as a booklet cover.

No. 3836a — A2931

Serpentine Die Cut 10¾ on 2, 3 or 4 Sides
2004, Mar. 4   **Litho.**
Self-Adhesive
3836a A2931 37c pane of 20, #P22222   15.00

No. 3836a is a complete booklet (BC199). The peelable backing serves as a booklet cover.

No. 3856b — A2940-A2941

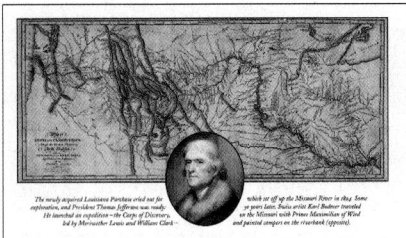

Backing 1

Backing 2

Serpentine Die Cut 10½x10¾
2004, May 14   **Litho. & Engr.**
Self-Adhesive
3856b 37c Pane, 5 each #3855-3856 with
     backing 1   9.00
     With backing 2   9.00
Booklet
BK297 BC200 $8.95 **multi**, no P#   18.00

No. BK297 contains one pane with backing 1 and one pane with backing 2.

Variety
3856a   Horiz. or vert. pair, #3855-3856   1.80

No. 3872a — A2956

Serpentine Die Cut 10¾ on 2 or 3 Sides
2004, Aug. 12   **Photo.**
Self-Adhesive
3872a A2956 37c pane of 20, P#S1111   15.00

No. 3872a is a complete booklet (BC201) with 12 stamps on one side and eight stamps plus label on the other side. The peelable backing serves as a booklet cover.

A2961

Serpentine Die Cut 10¾x11 on 2 or 3 Sides
2004, Oct. 14   **Litho.**
Self-Adhesive
3879a A2961 37c pane of 20, P#P1111   15.00

No. 3879a is a complete booklet with 12 stamps on one side and eight stamps plus a label that serves as a booklet cover (BC202) on the other side.

No. 3886b —A2965-A2968

No. 3890b — A2969-A2972

No. 3890c — A2969-A2972

No. 3890d — A2969-A2972

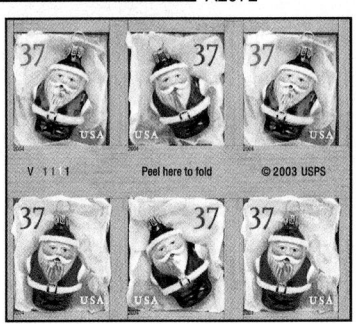

No. 3894b — A2969-A2972

Serpentine Die Cut 11½x11 on 2 or 3 Sides
2004, Nov. 16   **Photo.**
Self-Adhesive
3886b   37c pane of 20, 5 #3886a blocks,
     P#S1111   15.00
Serpentine Die Cut 10¼x10¾ on 2 or 3 Sides
3890b   37c pane of 4 #3887-3890, no P#   3.00
3890c   37c pane of 6 #3889-3890, 2 each
     #3887-3888, no P#   4.50
3890d   37c pane of 6 #3887-3888, 2 each
     #3889-3890, no P#   4.50
Serpentine Die Cut 8 on 2, 3 or 4 Sides
3894b   37c pane of 18, 6 each #3891,
     3893, 3 each #3892, 3894,
     P#V11111   13.50
COMBINATION BOOKLET
BK298 BC204 $7.40 **multi**, #3890c, 3890d, 2
     #3890b, P#S11111   15.00
Varieties
3890a   Block of 4, #3887-3890   3.00
3894a   Block of 4, #3891-3894   3.00

No. 3886b is a complete double-sided booklet. Two #3886 and the booklet cover (BC203) are on one side of the peelable backing and three #3886a are on the other side of the backing.

Plate number appears on the backing of No. 3890d in No. BK291A.

By its nature, No. 3894b is a complete booklet (BC205). The peelable backing serves as a booklet cover.

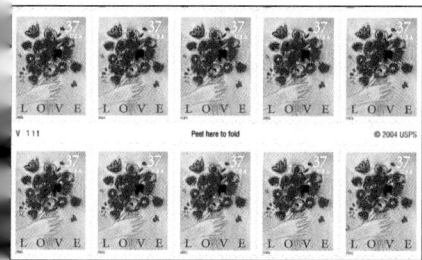

No. 3898a — A2975

Serpentine Die Cut 10³⁄₄x11 on 2, 3 or 4 Sides
2005, Feb. 18 **Photo.**
Self-Adhesive
3898a A2975 37c pane of 20, #V1111 15.00
No. 3898a is a complete booklet (BC206). The peelable backing serves as a booklet cover.

A2977-A2980

Serpentine Die Cut 10³⁄₄ on 2 or 3 Sides
2005, Mar. 15 **Litho.**
Self-Adhesive
3903b 37c pane of 20, P#P1111 15.00
No. 3903b is a complete booklet with 12 stamps on one side and eight stamps plus a label that serves as a booklet cover (BC207) on the other side.

A3003-A3006

Serpentine Die Cut 10³⁄₄ on 2 or 3 Sides
2005, July 30 **Litho.**
Self-Adhesive
3929b 37c pane of 20, P#P1111 15.00
No. 3929b is a complete booklet with 12 stamps on one side and eight stamps plus a label that serves as a booklet cover (BC208) on the other side.

A3008-A3012

Serpentine Die Cut 10³⁄₄ on 2 or 3 Sides
2005, Aug. 20 **Litho.**
Self-Adhesive
3935b 37c pane of 20, P#P1111 15.00
Varieties
3935a Vert. strip of 5, #3931-3935 3.75
No. 3935b is a complete booklet (BC209) with 12 stamps on one side (2 each #3931, 3933, 3935, and 3 each #3932, 3934) and eight stamps (1 each #3932, 3934, and 2 each #3931, 3933, 3935) plus a label that serves as the booklet cover on the other side.

No. 3956b — A3026-A3029

No. 3960b — A3030-A3033

No. 3960c — A3030-A3033

No. 3960d — A3030-A3033

Serpentine Die Cut 10³⁄₄x11 on 2 or 3 Sides
2005, Oct. 20 **Photo.**
Self-Adhesive
3956b 37c pane of 5 #3956a blocks, P#S1111 15.00
Serpentine Die Cut 10¹⁄₂x10³⁄₄ on 2 or 3 Sides
3960b 37c pane of 4 #3957-3960, no P# 6.00
3960c 37c pane of 6 #3959-3960, 2 each #3957-3958, no P# 9.00
3960d 37c pane of 6 #3957-3958, 2 each #3959-3960, no P# 9.00
COMBINATION BOOKLET
BK299 BC211 $7.40 **multi**, #3960c, 3960d, 2 #3960b, P#S1111 30.00
Varieties
3956a Block of 4, #3953-3956 3.00
3960a Block of 4, #3957-3960 6.00
No. 3956b is a complete double-sided booklet. Two #3956a and the booklet cover (BC210) are on one side of the peelable backing and three #3956a are on the other side of the backing.
Plate number appears on the backing of the lower example of No. 3960b in No. BK299.

Nos. 3966a, 3972a, 3973a — A3038

No. 3974a — A3038

No. 3974b — A3038

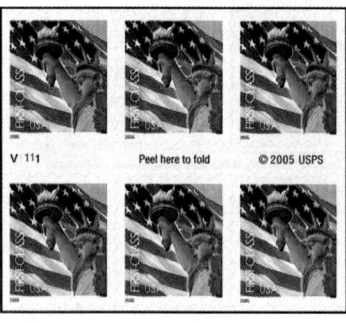

No. 3975a — A3038

Serpentine Die Cut 11¼x11 on 2 or 3 Sides
2005, Dec. 8   Litho.
Self-Adhesive
3966a A3038 (39c) pane of 20, P#P1111   16.00
Photo.
Serpentine Die Cut 11¼x10¾ on 2 or 3 Sides
3972a A3038 (39c) pane of 20, P#V1111   16.00
Serpentine Die Cut 10¼x10¾ on 2 or 3 Sides
3973a A3038 (39c) pane of 20, P#S1111   16.00

No. 3973a is a complete double-sided booklet. Eight stamps and the booklet cover (BC212) are on one side of the peelable backing, and twelve stamps are on the other side of the backing.

Serpentine Die Cut 11¼x11 on 2 or 3 Sides
Litho.
3974a A3038 (39c) pane of 4, no P#   3.20
3975b A3038 (39c) pane of 6, no P#   4.80
Serpentine Die Cut 8 on 2, 3 or 4 Sides
Photo.
3975a A3038 (39c) pane of 18, P#V1111   14.50
COMBINATION BOOKLET
BK300 BC213 ($7.80) **multi,** 2 each #3974a,
    3974b, P#S1111   16.00

Nos. 3966a and 3972a are complete double-sided booklets. Eight stamps and the booklet cover (BC212) are on one side of the peelable backing and twelve stamps are on the other side of the backing. On No. 3966a, the stamps on one side are upside-down with relation to the stamps on the other side. On No. 3972a the stamps are all aligned the same on both sides.

Plate number appears on the backing of the lower example of No. 3974a in No. BK300.

By its nature, No. 3975a is a complete booklet (BC214). The peelable backing serves as a booklet cover.

No. 3976a — A3039

Serpentine Die Cut 11 on 2, 3 or 4 Sides
2006, Jan. 3   Photo.
Self-Adhesive
3976a A3039 (39c) pane of 20, P#V11111   16.00

By its nature, No. 3976a is a complete booklet (BC215). The peelable backing serves as a booklet cover.

No. 3978a—A3040

Serpentine Die Cut 11¼x10¾ on 3 Sides
2006, Apr. 8   Litho.
Self-Adhesive
3978a A3040 39c pane of 10, P#P1111   8.00

No. 3978a is a complete booklet (BC216). The peelable backing serves as a booklet cover.

No. 3978b—A3040

Serpentine Die Cut 11¼x10¾ on 2 or 3 Sides
2006, Apr. 8   Litho.
Self-Adhesive
3978b A3040 39c pane of 20, P#P1111   16.00

No. 3978b is a complete booklet with 12 stamps on one side and eight stamps plus a label that serves as the booklet cover (BC217) on the other side.

No. 3998a — A3051

No. 3999a — A3051-A3052

Serpentine Die Cut 10¾x11 on 2, 3 or 4 Sides
2006, Mar. 1   Litho
Self-Adhesive
3998a A3051 39c pane of 20, #P1   16.00

No. 3998a is a complete booklet (BC218). The peelable backing serves as a booklet cover.

Serpentine Die Cut 10¾x11
3999a   Pane of 40 (20 each #3998-3999),
    #P11   37.50

No. 3999a is a complete booklet (BC219). The peelable backing serves as a booklet cover.

No. 4001b, 4001c—A3053

Serpentine Die Cut 10¾x11¼
2006, Mar. 8   Photo.
Self-Adhesive
4001b A3053 24c pane of 10 #4001a, P#V1111   5.00

No. 4001b is a complete booklet (BC220). The peelable backing serves as a booklet cover. No. 4001b was sold flat. It has a self-adhesive panel that covers the rouletting on the inside of the booklet cover that is not found in BK301. Three large cuts of rouletting separates the two halves of the booklet cover on No. 4001b.

4001c A3053 24c pane of 4 #4001a, P#V1111   2.00
4001d A3053 24c pane of 6 #4001a, no P#   3.00
COMBINATION BOOKLET
BK301 BC220 $2.40 **multi,** #4001c, 4001d,
    P#V1111   5.00

No. BK301 is sold glued shut. When the booklet is opened, the self-adhesive panel found on the right side of No. 4001d sticks to the left side of 4001c, as shown in the illustration above. Fine rouletting separates the two halves of the booklet cover on No. BK301.

No. 4012b—A3054-A3058

A3054, A3056-A3058 — 4016a pane

A3054-A3055, A3057-A3058 — 4017b pane

A3054-A3058 — 4017c pane

A3054-A3058 — 4017d pane

Serpentine Die Cut 10¾x10½ on 2 or 3 Sides
2006, Mar. 16   Photo.
Self-Adhesive
4012b   39c pane of 20, P#S1111   16.00

No. 4012b is a complete booklet with 12 stamps on one side and eight stamps plus a label that serves as a booklet cover (BC221) on the other side.

Serpentine Die Cut 10¾x11¼ on 2 or 3 Sides
Litho.

4016a	39c pane of 4, #4013-4016, no P#	3.20
4017b	39c pane of 4, #4013-4015, 4017, no P#	3.20
4017c	39c pane of 6, #4013-4016, 2 #4017, no P#	4.80
4017d	39c pane of 6, #4013-4015, 4017, 2 #4016, no P#	4.80

COMBINATION BOOKLET
BK302 BC222 $7.80 multi, #4016a, 4017b, 4017c, 4017d, no P#   16.00

Varieties
4012a   Horiz. strip of 5, #4008-4012   4.00
4017a   Horiz. strip of 5, #4013-4017   4.00

No. 4029a — A3070

Serpentine Die Cut 11 on 2, 3 or 4 Sides
2006, May 1   Photo.
Self-Adhesive
4029a   A3070 39c pane of 20, P#V11111   16.00

By its nature, No. 4029a is a complete booklet (BC223). The peelable backing serves as a booklet cover.

AIR POST BOOKLET PANES

Spirit of St. Louis — AP6

FLAT PLATE PRINTING
1928   **Perf. 11**
C10a AP6 10c dark blue, May 26   80.00 65.00
           Never hinged   130.00
           Tab at bottom

No. C10a was printed from specially designed 180-subject plates arranged exactly as a 360-subject plate-each pane of three occupying the relative position of a pane of six in a 360-subject plate. Plate numbers appear at the sides, therefore Position D does not exist except partially on panes which have been trimmed off center. All other plate positions common to a 360-subject plate are known.

Booklet
BKC1 BC8 61c blue   275.00
           Tab at bottom, one pane in complete booklet   13,500.

Catalogue values for unused panes in this section, from this point to the end, are for Never Hinged items.

AP17

ROTARY PRESS PRINTINGS
1943
C25a AP17 6c carmine, Mar. 18   5.00 1.50
180-Subject Plates Electric Eye Convertible.

Booklets
BKC2 BC10 37c red   11.00
BKC3 BC10 73c red   22.50

AP19

1949   **Perf. 10½x11**
C39a AP19 6c carmine, Nov. 18   10.00 5.00
C39c   Dry printing   20.00 —

Booklets
BKC4   BC11A 73c red, with #C39a (4)   25.00
BKC4a BC11A 73c red, with #C39c   50.00

AP33

1958
C51a AP33 7c blue, July 31   10.00 7.00

Booklets
BKC5 BC11B 85c on 73c red   21.00
BKC6 BC11C 85c blue   21.00

Varieties
C51b   Vert. pair, imperf. between (from booklet pane)   —

No. C51b resulted from a paper foldover after perforating and before cutting into panes. Two pairs are known.

1960
C60a AP33 7c carmine, Aug. 19   11.00 8.00

Booklets
BKC7 BC11C 85c blue   23.00
BKC8 BC11C 85c red   23.00

Varieties
C60b   Vert. pair, imperf between   5,500.

No. C60b resulted from a paper foldover after perforating and before cutting into panes. Twp pairs are known.

AP42

1962-64
C64b AP42 8c carmine, pane of 5+label, slogan 1, Dec. 5, 1962   7.00 3.00
           With slogan 2, 1963   50.00 5.00
           With slogan 3, 1964   13.00 2.50

Booklets (No. C64b)
BKC9   BC11D 80c black, pink, slogan 1   22.50
BKC10 BC11D $2 red, pink, slogan 1   35.00
BKC11 BC11D 80c black, pink, slogan 3 (2) 30.00
BKC12 BC11D $2 red, pink, slogan 2   300.00
BKC13 BC13B $2 red, pink, slogan 2   300.00
BKC14 BC13B $2 red, slogan 3   3,500.
BKC15 BC13B $2 red, pink, slogan 3   100.00

C64c AP42 As No. C64b, tagged, slogan 3, 1964 2.00 .75
Plate of 360 subjects (300 stamps, 60 labels).

Booklets (No. C64c)
BKC16 BC11D 80c black (2)   35.00
BKC17 BC11D 80c black, pink   900.00
BKC18 BC13B $2 red, pink   325.00
BKC19 BC13B $2 red (3)   13.00

AP49

AP54

Paying bills? Use Postal Money Orders. Safe. Sure. Convenient.

AP55

1968-73			**Perf. 11x1**
C72b	AP49	10c **carmine**, pane of 8, Jan. 5, 1968	2.00
		Booklet	
BKC20 BC14B		$4 **red** (2)	12.00
C72c	AP49	10c **carmine**, pane of 5+label, slogan 4, Jan. 6, 1968	3.75
		With slogan 5	3.75
		Booklet	
BKC21 BC15		$1 **red** (2)	8.00
		Varieties	
C72d		Vert. pair, imperf. between	4,000.
C72f		As "b," tagging omitted	

No. C72d resulted from a paper foldover after perforating a before cutting into booklet panes. Two pairs are recorded fr different panes.

C78a	AP54	11c **carmine**, pane of 4+2 labels, slogans 5 & 4, May 7, 1971	1.25
		Combination Booklet	
BKC22 BC15		$1 **red**, 2 #C78a + 1 #1280c (2)	3.75
C79a	AP55	13c **carmine**, pane of 5+label, slogan 8, Dec. 27, 1973	1.50
		Booklet	
BKC23 BC18		$1.30 **blue & red** (2)	3.25
		Combination Booklet	
		See No. BK126.	

No. C72b, the 8-stamp pane, was printed from 320-subje plate and from 400-subject plate; No. C72c, C78a and C7 from 360-subject plates.

COMPUTER VENDED POSTAGE STAMPS

Unlike meters, except for the limits of the service requested, computer vended postage stamps are usable from any post office at any date.

Self-service user-interactive mailing system machines which vended computer-printed postage were in service and available to the general public a the Martin Luther King, Jr., Station of the Washington, DC, Post Office, and at the White Flint Mall in Kensington, MD, until May 7, 1990.

Machines were also available for use by delegates to the 20th Universal Postal Congress at the Washington Convention Center between Nov. 13 an Dec. 14, 1989. These machines, Washington Nos. 11 and 12, were not readily accessible by the general public.

A variety of services were available by using the machines, which could weigh items to be sent, determine postage rates through the connecte computer, permit the customer to cancel the transaction or continue with it and generate a postage stamp, a label and a receipt. The stamps produce were valid only for domestic postage.

A tagged orange strip runs along the left side of the stamp. The requested mail service is in a double line box.

The denomination is in the upper box at right under "U.S. Postage." The date of the transaction is below the denomination. Next to the date is a number which indicates the item number within the transaction. The maximum number of items per transaction may be five.

Above the post office location is a box at right which gives the machine number, followed by the transaction or serial number. Stamps from the sam transaction, which are generated and printed at the same time, will have the same transaction number, but different item numbers, even if different ma services are requested. Transaction numbers go back to 00001 every time the machine is reset. Below this is the weight of the item to be mailed.

Along with each stamp generated came an unattached label with one of three slogan types: "We Deliver. . .," used from September to November, "W Deliver. . . / United States Postal Service," used thereafter, and "Developed by / Technology Resource Department," used only on Machine 11 during it limited use.

Listings and values are for the basic denominations of the five postal services, though others are known or possible (45c, 65c, 85c for first class ove 1 oz., $1.10 for certified first class, $3.25 for priority mail, $8.50 for express mail to post office boxes, parcel post weight and zone variations, etc.) Values for used copies are for those with a regular cancellation.

A total of 3,000 unused sets of five different service stamps and unused sets of two 25c (Nos. 02501-12500) first class stamps furnished to th Philatelic Agency have a first day date and serial numbers with the final three digits matching. First day dates Nos. 00101-02500 were sold over th counter at post offices.

Stamps were intended to be dispensed individually. The height of the stamps produced differs from machine to machine. Unsevered strips of stamps are known, as are unsevered strips of a slogan and one or more stamps. Printing varieties such as squeezes (more than one impression condensed o to one stamp) and stretches (impression stretched out so that a complete impression will not fit on the paper) also are known.

Issues starting with No. 31 will be explained with the listings.

CVP1

CVP2

1989, Aug. 23		**Tagged**	**Guillotine**
		Self-Adhesive	
		Washington, DC, Machine 82	
CVP1	CVP1	25c **First Class**, any date other than first day	6.00
a.		First day dated, serial Nos. 12501-15500	4.50
b.		First day dated, serial Nos. 00001-12500	4.50
		On cover with first day cancel	150.0
c.		First day dated, over No. 27500	—
		On cover with first day cancel	150.0
CVP2	CVP1	$1 **Third Class**, any date other than first day	—
a.		First day dated, serial Nos. 24501-27500	—
b.		First day dated, over No. 27500	—
CVP3	CVP2	$1.69 **Parcel Post**, any date other than first day	—
a.		First day dated, serial Nos. 21501-24500	—
b.		First day dated, over No. 27500	—

P4	CVP1	$2.40 **Priority Mail,** any date other than first day	— —
a.		First day dated, serial Nos. 18501-21500	— —
b.		Priority Mail ($2.74), with bar code (CVP2)	100.00
c.		First day, over No. 27500 On cover with first day cancel or verifying receipt	— 500.00
P5	CVP1	$8.75 **Express Mail,** any date other than first day	— —
a.		First day dated, serial Nos. 15501-18500	— —
b.		First day, over No. 27500 On cover with first day cancel or verifying receipt	— —
		Nos. 1a-5a (5)	82.50 —

Washington, DC, Machine 83

P6	CVP1	25c **First Class,** any date other than first day	6.00 —
a.		First day dated, serial Nos. 12501-15500	4.50 —
b.		First day dated, serial Nos. 00001-12500 On cover with first day cancel	4.50 — 150.00
c.		First day, over No. 27500 On cover with first day cancel	— 150.00

Error dates 11/17/90 and 11/18/90 exist.

P7	CVP1	$1 **Third Class,** any date other than first day	— —
a.		First day dated, serial Nos. 24501-27500	— —
b.		First day, over No. 27500	— —
P8	CVP2	$1.69 **Parcel Post,** any date other than first day	— —
a.		First day dated, serial Nos. 21501-24500	— —
b.		First day, over No. 27500	— —
P9	CVP1	$2.40 **Priority Mail,** any date other than first day	— —
a.		First day dated, serial Nos. 18501-21500	— —
b.		First day, over No. 27500 On cover with first day cancel or verifying receipt	— 500.00

Error date 11/17/90 exists.

c.		Priority Mail ($2.74), with bar code (CVP2)	100.00

Error date 11/18/90 exists.

P10	CVP1	$8.75 **Express Mail,** any date other than first day	— —
a.		First day dated, serial Nos. 15501-18500	— —
b.		First day, over No. 27500 On cover with first day cancel or verifying receipt	— —
		Nos. 6a-10a (5)	57.50 —

Error date 11/17/90 exists.

1989, Sept. 1   Kensington, MD, Machine 82

CVP11	CVP1	25c **First Class,** any date other than first day	6.00 —
a.		First day dated, serial Nos. 12501-15500	4.50 —
b.		First day dated, serial Nos. 00001-12500 On cover with first day cancel	4.50 — 100.00
c.		First day, over No. 27500 On cover with first day cancel	— 100.00
CVP12	CVP1	$1 **Third Class,** any date other than first day	— —
a.		First day dated, serial Nos. 24501-27500	— —
b.		First day, over No. 27500	— —
CVP13	CVP2	$1.69 **Parcel Post,** any date other than first day	— —
a.		First day dated, serial Nos. 21501-24500	— —
b.		First day, over No. 27500	— —
CVP14	CVP1	$2.40 **Priority Mail,** any date other than first day	— —
a.		First day dated, serial Nos. 18501-21500	— —
b.		First day, over No. 27500	— —
c.		Priority Mail ($2.74), with bar code (CVP2)	100.00
CVP15	CVP1	$8.75 **Express Mail,** any date other than first day	— —
a.		First day dated, serial Nos. 15501-18500	— —
b.		First day, over No. 27500	— —
		Nos. 11a-15a (5)	57.50 —
		Nos. 1b, 11b (2)	9.00 —

Kensington, MD, Machine 83

CVP16	CVP1	25c **First Class,** any date other than first day	6.00 —
a.		First day dated, serial Nos. 12501-15500	4.50 —
b.		First day dated, serial Nos. 00001-12500 On cover with first day cancel	4.50 — 100.00

CVP17	CVP1	$1 **Third Class,** any date other than first day	— —
a.		First day dated, serial Nos. 24501-27500	— —
b.		First day, over No. 27500	— —
CVP18	CVP2	$1.69 **Parcel Post,** any date other than first day	— —
a.		First day dated, serial Nos. 21501-24500	— —
b.		First day, over No. 27500	— —
CVP19	CVP1	$2.40 **Priority Mail,** any date other than first day	— —
a.		First day dated, serial Nos. 18501-21500	— —
b.		First day, over No. 27500	— —
c.		Priority Mail ($2.74), with bar code (CVP2)	100.00
CVP20	CVP1	$8.75 **Express Mail,** any date other than first day	— —
a.		First day dated, serial Nos. 15501-18500	— —
b.		First day, over No. 27500	— —
		Nos. 16a-20a (5)	57.50 —
		Nos. 6b, 16b (2)	9.00 —

Unsevered pairs and single with advertising label exist for most, if not all, of the machine vended items from Kensington machine #83. Other combinations also exist.

1989, Nov.   Washington, DC, Machine 11

CVP21	CVP1	25c **First Class**	150.00
a.		First Class, with bar code (CVP2)	—

Stamps in CVP1 design with $1.10 denominations exist (certified first class).

CVP22	CVP1	$1 **Third Class**	500.00
CVP23	CVP2	$1.69 **Parcel Post**	500.00
CVP24	CVP1	$2.40 **Priority Mail**	500.00
a.		Priority Mail ($2.74), with bar code (CVP2)	—
CVP25	CVP1	$8.75 **Express Mail**	500.00

No. 21 dated Nov. 30 known on cover, Nos. 24-25 known dated Dec. 2.

Washington, DC, Machine 12

CVP26	CVP1	25c **First Class**	150.00

A $1.10 certified First Class stamp, dated Nov. 20, exists on cover.

CVP27	CVP1	$1 **Third Class**	—

A $1.40 Third Class stamp of type CVP2, dated Dec. 1 is known on a Dec. 2 cover.

CVP28	CVP2	$1.69 **Parcel Post**	—
CVP29	CVP1	$2.40 **Priority Mail**	—
a.		Priority Mail ($2.74), with bar code (CVP2)	—
CVP30	CVP1	$8.75 **Express Mail**	—

Nos. 29-30 known dated Dec. 1. An $8.50 Express Mail stamp, dated Dec. 2, exists on cover.

CVP3 — Type I   CVP3 — Type II

Denomination printed by ECA GARD Postage and Mailing Center machines.

COIL STAMPS

1992, Aug. 20   Engr.   Tagged   Perf. 10 Horiz.

CVP31	CVP3	29c **red & blue,** type I, prephosphored paper (solid tagging), dull gum	.70	.25
		Pair	1.40	
		P# strip of 5, P#1	8.50	
		P# single, #1		5.50
a.		29c Type I, prephosphored paper (mottled tagging), shiny gum	.70	.25
		Pair	1.40	
		P# strip of 5, P#1	8.50	
		P# single, #1		5.50
		First day cover, Oklahoma City, OK		1.25
b.		32c Type II, prephosphored paper (solid tagging), dull gum, *Nov. 1994*	.90	.40
		Pair	1.80	
		P# strip of 5, P#1	10.00	
		P# single, #1		5.50
c.		32c Type II, prephosphored paper (mottled tagging), shiny gum	1.00	.40
		Pair	2.00	
		P# strip of 5, P#1	8.75	
		P# single, #1		6.00

Types I and II differ in style of asterisk, period between dollar and cent figures and font used for figures, as shown in illustrations.

No. 31 was available at five test sites in the Southern Maryland, Miami, Oklahoma City, Detroit and Santa Ana, CA, divisions. They were produced for use in ECA GARD Postage and Mailing Center (PMC) machines which can produce denominations from 1c through $99.99.

For Nos. 31-31a, the 29c value has been listed because it was the current first class rate and was the only value available through the USPS Philatelic Sales Division. The most common denomination available other than 29c will probably be 1c (value 20c) as these were made in quantity, by collectors and dealers, between plate number strips. Later the machines were adjusted to provide only 19c and higher value stamps.

For Nos. 31b-31c, the 32c value has been listed because it was the first class rate in effect for the majority of the period the stamps were in use.

CVP4

Denominations printed by Unisys PMC machines.

1994, Feb. 19   Photo.   Tagged   Perf. 9.9 Vert.

CVP32	CVP4	29c **dark red & dark blue**	.70	.35
		Pair	1.40	—
		P# strip of 5, #A11	8.00	
		P# single, #A11		5.50
		First day cover, Merrifield, VA *(26,390)*		1.25

No. 32 was available at six test sites in northern Virginia. It was produced for use in machines which can produce values from 19c to $99.99. See note following No. 31.

For No. 32, the 29c value has been listed because it was the first class rate in effect at the time the stamp was issued.

1996, Jan. 26   Photo.   Tagged   Perf. 9.9 Vert.

CVP33	CVP4	32c **bright red & blue,** "1996" below design	.70	.25
		Pair	1.40	
		P# strip of 5, same, #11	7.25	
		P# single, #11		6.00

Letters in "USA" on No. 33 are thicker than on No. 32. Numerous other design differences exist in the moire pattern and in the bunting. No. 33 has "1996" in the lower left corner; No. 32 has no date.

For No. 33, the 32c value has been listed because it was the first class rate in effect at the time the stamp was issued.

CVP5

Illustration reduced.

1999   Tagged   Die Cut   Self-Adhesive

CVP34	CVP5	33c **black**	50.00	
		On cover		75.00
a.		"Priority Mail" under encryption at LL	—	—
b.		"Express Mail" under encryption at LL	—	—

No. CVP34 was available from 15 NCR Automated Postal Center machines located in central Florida. Machines could produce values in any denomination required. The backing paper is taller and wider than the stamp.

Sales of No. CVP34 were discontinued in 2000 or 2001.

CVP6

Illustration reduced.

1999, May 7   Tagged   Die Cut   Self-Adhesive
Size: 77 ½x39mm
Microprinting Above Red Orange Line

CVP35	CVP6	33c **black & red orange,** control numbers only at LL, square corners	150.00	—
		Round corners	7.50	—
a.		"Priority Mail" at LL, square corners	150.00	—

b.   "Priority Mail AS" and text string at
     LL, square corners   150.00   —
     Round corners   —   —

No Microprinting Above Red Orange Line

CVP36 CVP6   33c **black & red orange,** control
     numbers only at LL, square
     corners   125.00   —
     Round corners   10.00   —
a.   "Priority Mail" at LL, square corners   125.00   —
     Round corners   —   —
b.   "Priority Mail AS" and text string at
     LL, square corners   125.00   —
     Round corners   —   —

Size: 73½x42mm

CVP37 CVP6   33c **black & pink,** control num-
     bers only at LL   3.75   —
a.   "Priority Mail" at LL   5.00   —
b.   "Priority Mail AS" and text string at LL   5.00   —

Nos. CVP35-CVP37 were available from 18 IBM Neopost machines located in central Florida. The backing paper is taller than the stamp. Any denomination could be printed up to $99.99.

CVP7

Simplypostage.com — CVP8

2000-01   *Serpentine Die Cut 8*
Self-Adhesive

CVP38 CVP7   33c **black, yellow & pink**   —   —
     On cover   —   —
     Pane of 10   —   —

Serpentine Die Cut 8 at Right
Eagle and Stars Background

CVP39 CVP8   34c **black, blue & orange,** *2001*   —   —
     On cover   75.00
     Pane of 4   —   —
CVP40 CVP8   34c **black, blue & orange,** with
     control number at UL, *2001*   —   —
     On cover   75.00
     Pane of 4   —   —

Flag Background

CVP41 CVP8   34c **black, blue & orange,** with
     control number at UL, *2001*   —   —
     On cover   150.00
     Pane of 4   —   —
CVP42 CVP8   34c **black, blue & orange,** con-
     trol number at LL, *2001*   —   —
     On cover   150.00
     Pane of 4   —   —

Customers could print up to five panes of Nos. CVP39-CVP42 in each transaction. Panes were consecutively numbered identifying the total number of stamps and panes in each transaction.

Neopostage.com — CVP9

2002, June -2003   *Serpentine Die Cut 8¾ at Right*
CVP43 CVP9   21c **black, blue & orange,** *June
     2002*   —   —
     On cover   —   —
a.   Booklet pane of 10   —   —
CVP44 CVP9   23c **black, blue & orange,**
     June, 2002   —   —
     On cover   —   —
a.   Booklet pane of 10   —   —
CVP45 CVP9   34c **black, blue & orange,** *June
     2002*   —   —
     On cover   —   —
a.   Booklet pane of 10   —   —
CVP46 CVP9   37c **black, blue & orange,** *July
     1, 2003*

     On cover   —   —
a.   Booklet pane of 10   —   —
CVP47 CVP9   50c **black, blue & orange,** *July
     1, 2003*   —   —
     On cover   —   —
a.   Booklet pane of 10   —   —
CVP48 CVP9   60c **black, blue & orange,** *July
     1, 2003*   —   —
     On cover   —   —
a.   Booklet pane of 10   —   —
CVP49 CVP9   70c **black, blue & orange,** *July
     1, 2003*   —   —
     On cover   —   —
a.   Booklet pane of 10   —   —
CVP50 CVP9   80c **black, blue & orange,** *July
     1, 2003*   —   —
     On cover   —   —
a.   Booklet pane of 10   —   —
CVP51 CVP9 $3.50 **black, blue & orange,** *June
     2002*   —   —
     On cover   —   —
a.   Booklet pane of 1   —   —
b.   Booklet pane of 2   —   —
c.   Booklet pane of 5   —   —
d.   Booklet pane of 10   —   —
CVP52 CVP9 $3.85 **black, blue & orange,** *July
     1, 2003*   —   —
     On cover   —   —
a.   Booklet pane of 1   —   —
b.   Booklet pane of 2   —   —
c.   Booklet pane of 5   —   —
d.   Booklet pane of 10   —   —
CVP53 CVP9 $13.65 **black, blue & orange,** *July
     1, 2003*   —   —
     On cover   —   —
a.   Booklet pane of 1   —   —
b.   Booklet pane of 2   —   —
c.   Booklet pane of 5   —   —
d.   Booklet pane of 10   —   —

Nos. CVP43-CVP53 were printed only with the stated values.
   A 57c denomination (pane of 10) and $12.45 denomination (pane of 1) exist, but may have been produced at a site not accessible by the public.
   While the name on Nos. CVP38-CVP42 reads simplypostage.com and the name on Nos. CVP43-CVP53 reads neopostage.com, both were products of Neopost.

CVP10

IBM Pitney Bowes — CVP11

Illustrations reduced.

2004, Apr. 14   *Die Cut*
CVP54 CVP10   37c **black & pink**   2.00   —
a.   "First Class Mail" under encryption at
     LL   —   —
b.   "Priority Mail" under encryption at LL   —   —
c.   "Parcel Post" under encryption at LL   —   —
d.   "International" under encryption at LL   —   —
CVP55 CVP11   37c **black,** "US Postage" under en-
     cryption at LL   2.00   —
a.   "First Class Mail" under encryption at
     LL   —   —

---

b.   "Priority Mail" under encryption at LL   —
c.   "Parcel Post" under encryption at LL   —
d.   "International" under encryption at LL   —

Nos. CVP54-CVP55 could be printed in any denomination to $99.99.

CVP12

IBM Pitney Bowes — CVP13

Illustrations reduced.

2004, Nov. 19   *Die Cut*
Self-Adhesive

CVP56 CVP12   37c **black & pink**   1.00   .25
a.   "Priority" under denomination   1.25   —
b.   "Parcel Post" under denomination   1.25   —
c.   "Express" under denomination   1.25   —
CVP57 CVP13   37c **black & pink**   1.00   .25
a.   "Priority" under denomination   1.25   —
b.   "Parcel Post" under denomination   1.25   —
c.   "Express" under denomination   1.25   —
d.   "Int Air LP" under denomination   1.25   —

Nos. CVP56-CVP57 could be printed in any denomination. Catalogue values for CVP56a-CVP56c and CVP57a-CVP57d are for stamps with low denominations. Stamps with denominations appropriate to the service described are valued correspondingly higher.

Blank Under Denomination
"IM" and Numbers Under Encryption

CVP58 CVP13   60c **black & pink**   3.00   .50
CVP59 CVP13   80c **black & pink**   3.75   .50

"PM" and Numbers Under Encryption

CVP60 CVP13 $3.85 **black & pink**   15.00   .50

"EM" and Numbers Under Encryption

CVP61 CVP13 $13.65 **black & pink**   42.50   1.00

"IB" and Numbers Under Encryption

CVP62 CVP13 $1 **black & pink**   4.00   .25

Nos. CVP58-CVP61 could only be printed in denominations listed. No. CVP62 could be printed in any denomination above 99c.

IBM Pitney Bowes Type of 2004
2006 ?   *Die Cut*
Self-Adhesive
Blank Under Denomination
"IM" and Numbers Under Encryption

CVP63 CVP13   48c **black & pink**   1.00   .40
CVP64 CVP13   63c **black & pink**   1.25   .50
CVP65 CVP13   84c **black & pink**   1.75   .50

"PM" and Numbers Under Encryption

CVP66 CVP13 $4.05 **black & pink**   8.25   .50

"EM" and Numbers Under Encryption

CVP67 CVP13 $14.40 **black & pink**   26.00   1.00

Nos. CVP63-CVP67 could only be printed in denominations listed.

Machine Set-up Test Labels

Test labels were generated when machines were activated. They were not intended for public distribution.

Other samples, advertizing labels, proofs, etc. exist.

POSTAL CARDS

On July 5, 1990 the first of a number of "Postal Buddy" machines was placed in service at the Merrifield, VA post office. The machine printed out numerous items such as address labels (including monogram if you wished), fax labels, "penalty" cards, denominated postal cards, etc. Certain services were free, such as the penalty card mailed to your post office for change of address. The 15-cent denominated card cost 33-cents each and could be used to notify others of address change, meeting notices, customized messages, etc. Borders, messages, backs are different. The cards also came in sheets of 4.

These machines were tested in at least 30 locations in Virginia, including 16 post offices.

Denominated Postal Cards

10005-90-198-022

Number under design includes machine number, year, date (1 through 366) and transaction number.

1990, July 5

CVUX1	15c	6.00	*10.00*
	First day cancel, Merrifield, VA *(6,500)*		5.00

1991, Feb. 3

CVUX2	19c	3.00	*8.00*
	First day cancel, any location		35.00

Number under design includes ZIP Code of the originating machine (22033 in illustration), machine number (101), last digit of year, numbers of month and day (21203 for Dec. 3, 1992) and transaction number (041).

1992, Nov. 13

CVUX3	19c	6.00	*15.00*
	First day dated, Reston or Chantilly, VA		25.00

A total of 171 machines were used in the greater Washington, DC area including locations in Virginia and Maryland (109), the greater San Diego area (59), and in Denver (3). The machine numbers (011, 012, 021, 101, 111, 121, 131) when combined with the zip code created unique identification numbers for each machine.

No. 3 is known also on fluorescent paper. Two different designs on back known for each paper type.

The contract for Postal Buddy machines was canceled Sept. 16, 1993. After the contract was canceled, the Postal Buddy Corporation sold remaining stocks of card stock to the public with both reverse designs imprinted. By using this stock and a high quality copier, very dangerous counterfeits can be created. The duplication of numbers in the transaction line will be one indicator.

PERSONAL COMPUTER POSTAGE

Personal computer postage, approved by the US Postal Service, was created by subscribing to Stamps.com, an internet website. Customers ordered self-adhesive labels showing vignettes, but lacking any franking value. The franking value portion of the stamps could be printed at the customer's convenience at any computer with an internet connection, using the customer's access codes. Any postage printed would be charged against the customer's account.

Stamps with major listings could be printed in any denomination up to $999.99. Stamps with minor listings could only be printed in denominations calculated by the weight of the piece being mailed. Denominations for minor listings can range from 23c to $133.20. Customers could print the franking value portion of the stamps on whatever they put into their printer, be it envelopes, plain gummed labels or regular paper, but these listings are limited to items on the self-adhesive labels shown, which have tagging that allows the mail the stamp is on to go through the mail stream smoothly.

Stamps.com

Flag and
Star — CVPA1

2002   *Serpentine Die Cut 5¾ at Left*
"Stamps.com" in Lower Case Letters
Identification Code Above Zip Code

1CVP1	CVPA1 37c **black, blue & orange**		4.00	3.00
	On cover			3.50
	Sheet of 25		100.00	
a.	"First Class" below "US Postage"		2.75	2.00
b.	"Priority" below "US Postage"		8.25	2.50
c.	"Express" below "US Postage"		25.00	5.00
d.	"Media Mail" below "US Postage"		7.75	2.50
e.	"Parcel Post" below "US Postage"		7.75	2.50
f.	"Bound Printed Matter" below "US Postage"		7.75	2.50
g.	"BPM" below "US Postage"		7.75	2.50

Identification Code Below Zip Code

1CVP2	CVPA1 37c **black, blue & orange**		7.00	3.00
	On cover			4.00
	Sheet of 25		175.00	
a.	"First Class" below zip code		2.75	2.00
b.	"Priority" below zip code		8.25	2.50

c.	"Express" below zip code		25.00	5.00
d.	"Media Mail" below zip code		7.75	2.50
e.	"Parcel Post" below zip code		7.75	2.50

See Nos. 1CVP9, 1CVP21.

Love — CVPA2

2002   *Serpentine Die Cut 5¾ at Left*

1CVP3	CVPA2 37c **black, blue & orange**		4.00	4.00
	On cover			5.00
	Sheet of 25		100.00	
a.	"First Class" below "US Postage"		2.75	2.00
b.	"Priority" below "US Postage"		8.25	2.50
c.	"Express" below "US Postage"		25.00	5.00
d.	"Media Mail" below "US Postage"		7.75	2.50
e.	"Parcel Post" below "US Postage"		7.75	2.50
f.	"Bound Printed Matter" below "US Postage"		7.75	2.50
g.	"BPM" below "US Postage"		7.75	2.50

Statue of Liberty and
Flag — CVPA3

Liberty Bell and
Flag — CVPA4

Eagle and Flag   CVPA5

George Washington and Flag — CVPA6

Capitol Building and Flag — CVPA7

2003, June   *Serpentine Die Cut 5¾ at Left*

1CVP4	CVPA3 37c **black, blue & orange**	3.50	2.00
	On cover		3.00
a.	"First Class" below "US Postage"	3.25	2.00
b.	"Priority" below "US Postage"	8.00	1.00
c.	"Express" below "US Postage"	25.00	3.00
d.	"Media Mail" below "US Postage"	7.50	1.00
e.	"Parcel Post" below "US Postage"	7.50	1.00
f.	"Bound Printed Matter" below "US Postage"	7.50	1.00
g.	"BPM" below "US Postage"	7.50	1.00
1CVP5	CVPA4 37c **black, blue & orange**	3.50	2.00
	On cover		3.00
a.	"First Class" below "US Postage"	3.25	2.00
b.	"Priority" below "US Postage"	8.00	1.00
c.	"Express" below "US Postage"	25.00	3.00
d.	"Media Mail" below "US Postage"	7.50	1.00
e.	"Parcel Post" below "US Postage"	7.50	1.00
f.	"Bound Printed Matter" below "US Postage"	7.50	1.00
g.	"BPM" below "US Postage"	7.50	1.00
1CVP6	CVPA5 37c **black, blue & orange**	3.50	2.00
	On cover		3.00
a.	"First Class" below "US Postage"	3.25	2.00
b.	"Priority" below "US Postage"	8.00	1.00
c.	"Express" below "US Postage"	25.00	3.00
d.	"Media Mail" below "US Postage"	7.50	1.00
e.	"Parcel Post" below "US Postage"	7.50	1.00
f.	"Bound Printed Matter" below "US Postage"	7.50	1.00
g.	"BPM" below "US Postage"	7.50	1.00
1CVP7	CVPA6 37c **black, blue & orange**	3.50	2.00
	On cover		3.00
a.	"First Class" below "US Postage"	3.25	.20
b.	"Priority" below "US Postage"	8.00	1.00
c.	"Express" below "US Postage"	25.00	3.00
d.	"Media Mail" below "US Postage"	7.50	1.00
e.	"Parcel Post" below "US Postage"	7.50	1.00
f.	"Bound Printed Matter" below "US Postage"	7.50	1.00
g.	"BPM" below "US Postage"	7.50	1.00
1CVP8	CVPA7 37c **black, blue & orange**	3.50	2.00
	On cover		3.00
a.	"First Class" below "US Postage"	3.25	.20
b.	"Priority" below "US Postage"	8.00	1.00
c.	"Express" below "US Postage"	25.00	3.00
d.	"Media Mail" below "US Postage"	7.50	1.00
e.	"Parcel Post" below "US Postage"	7.50	1.00

---

f.	"Bound Printed Matter" below "US Postage"	7.50	1.00
g.	"BPM" below "US Postage"	7.50	1.00
h.	Strip of 5, #1CVP4-1CVP8	17.50	

Flag and Star Type of 2002 Redrawn With "Stamps.com" in Upper Case Letters

2003, June   *Serpentine Die Cut 5¾ at Left*
Identification Code Above Zip Code

1CVP9	CVPA1 37c **black, blue & orange**	2.50	1.50
	On cover		2.50
	Sheet of 25	62.50	
a.	"First Class" below "US Postage"	.75	.20
b.	"Priority" below "US Postage"	8.00	1.00
c.	"Express" below "US Postage"	25.00	3.00
d.	"Media Mail" below "US Postage"	7.50	1.00
e.	"Parcel Post" below "US Postage"	7.50	1.00
f.	"Bound Printed Matter" below "US Postage"	7.50	1.00
g.	"BPM" below "US Postage"	7.50	1.00

Snowman — CVPA8

Snowflakes CVPA9

Holly — CVPA10

Dove — CVPA11

Gingerbread Man and Candy — CVPA12

2003, Dec.   *Serpentine Die Cut 4½ at Left*

1CVP10	CVPA8 37c **black, blue & orange**	2.50	1.5
	On cover		2.5
a.	"First Class" below "US Postage"	2.00	1.0
b.	"Priority" below "US Postage"	8.00	1.0
c.	"Express" below "US Postage"	25.00	3.0
d.	"Media Mail" below "US Postage"	7.50	1.0
e.	"Parcel Post" below "US Postage"	7.50	1.0
f.	"Bound Printed Matter" below "US Postage"	7.50	1.0
g.	"BPM" below "US Postage"	7.50	1.0
1CVP11	CVPA9 37c **black, blue & orange**	2.50	1.5
	On cover		2.5
a.	"First Class" below "US Postage"	2.00	1.0
b.	"Priority" below "US Postage"	8.00	1.0
c.	"Express" below "US Postage"	25.00	3.0
d.	"Media Mail" below "US Postage"	7.50	1.0
e.	"Parcel Post" below "US Postage"	7.50	1.0
f.	"Bound Printed Matter" below "US Postage"	7.50	1.0
g.	"BPM" below "US Postage"	7.50	1.0
1CVP12	CVPA10 37c **black, blue & orange**	2.50	1.5
	On cover		2.50
a.	"First Class" below "US Postage"	2.00	1.00
b.	"Priority" below "US Postage"	8.00	1.00
c.	"Express" below "US Postage"	25.00	3.00
d.	"Media Mail" below "US Postage"	7.50	1.00
e.	"Parcel Post" below "US Postage"	7.50	1.00
f.	"Bound Printed Matter" below "US Postage"	7.50	1.00
g.	"BPM" below "US Postage"	7.50	1.00
1CVP13	CVPA11 37c **black, blue & orange**	2.50	1.50
	On cover		2.50
a.	"First Class" below "US Postage"	2.00	1.00
b.	"Priority" below "US Postage"	8.00	1.00
c.	"Express" below "US Postage"	25.00	3.00
d.	"Media Mail" below "US Postage"	7.50	1.00
e.	"Parcel Post" below "US Postage"	7.50	1.00
f.	"Bound Printed Matter" below "US Postage"	7.50	1.00
g.	"BPM" below "US Postage"	7.50	1.00
1CVP14	CVPA12 37c **black, blue & orange**	2.50	1.50
	On cover		2.50
a.	"First Class" below "US Postage"	2.00	1.00
b.	"Priority" below "US Postage"	8.00	1.00
c.	"Express" below "US Postage"	25.00	3.00
d.	"Media Mail" below "US Postage"	7.50	1.00
e.	"Parcel Post" below "US Postage"	7.50	1.00
f.	"Bound Printed Matter" below "US Postage"	7.50	1.00
g.	"BPM" below "US Postage"	7.50	1.00
h.	Strip of 5, #1CVP10-1CVP14	12.50	

Mailbox — CVPA13

2004, Mar.   *Serpentine Die Cut 6½ at Left*

1CVP15	CVPA13 37c **black, blue & orange**	25.00	15.00
	On cover		35.00
a.	"First Class" below "US Postage"	25.00	15.00
b.	"Priority" below "US Postage"	—	—
c.	"Express" below "US Postage"	—	—
d.	"Media Mail" below "US Postage"	—	—
e.	"Parcel Post" below "US Postage"	—	—
f.	"Bound Printed Matter" below "US Postage"	—	—
g.	"BPM" below "US Postage"	—	—

Blank sheets of No. 1CVP15 were sent free of charge to those who responded to special Stamps.com promotions which offered a fixed amount of free postage as an enticement to new subscribers. The franking portion of the stamps could only be applied after subscribing.

George Washington
CVPA14

Thomas
Jefferson — CVPA15

Abraham
Lincoln — CVPA16

Theodore
Roosevelt — CVPA17

John F.
Kennedy — CVPA18

d.	"Media Mail" below "US Postage"	5.00	2.50
e.	"Parcel Post" below "US Postage"	5.00	2.50
f.	"Bound Printed Matter" below "US Postage"	5.00	2.50
g.	"BPM" below "US Postage"	5.00	2.50
1CVP17	CVPA15 37c **black, blue & orange**	2.00	1.00
	On cover		2.50
a.	"First Class" below "US Postage"	1.10	.75
b.	"Priority" below "US Postage"	5.00	2.50
c.	"Express" below "US Postage"	20.00	5.00
d.	"Media Mail" below "US Postage"	5.00	2.50
e.	"Parcel Post" below "US Postage"	5.00	2.50
f.	"Bound Printed Matter" below "US Postage"	5.00	2.50
g.	"BPM" below "US Postage"	5.00	2.50
1CVP18	CVPA16 37c **black, blue & orange**	2.00	1.00
	On cover		2.50
a.	"First Class" below "US Postage"	1.10	.75
b.	"Priority" below "US Postage"	5.00	2.50
c.	"Express" below "US Postage"	20.00	5.00
d.	"Media Mail" below "US Postage"	5.00	2.50
e.	"Parcel Post" below "US Postage"	5.00	2.50
f.	"Bound Printed Matter" below "US Postage"	5.00	2.50
g.	"BPM" below "US Postage"	5.00	2.50
1CVP19	CVPA17 37c **black, blue & orange**	2.00	1.00
	On cover		2.50
a.	"First Class" below "US Postage"	1.10	.75
b.	"Priority" below "US Postage"	5.00	2.50
c.	"Express" below "US Postage"	20.00	5.00
d.	"Media Mail" below "US Postage"	5.00	2.50
e.	"Parcel Post" below "US Postage"	5.00	2.50
f.	"Bound Printed Matter" below "US Postage"	5.00	2.50
g.	"BPM" below "US Postage"	5.00	2.50
1CVP20	CVPA18 37c **black, blue & orange**	2.00	1.00
	On cover		2.50
a.	"First Class" below "US Postage"	1.10	.75
b.	"Priority" below "US Postage"	5.00	2.50
c.	"Express" below "US Postage"	20.00	5.00
d.	"Media Mail" below "US Postage"	5.00	2.50
e.	"Parcel Post" below "US Postage"	5.00	2.50
f.	"Bound Printed Matter" below "US Postage"	5.00	2.50
g.	"BPM" below "US Postage"	5.00	2.50
h.	Horiz. strip of 5, #1CVP16-1CVP20	10.00	

Flag and Star Type of 2002 Redrawn With Orange Stars and Text at Left

2004, Apr. *Serpentine Die Cut 6½ at Left*
"Stamps.com" in Upper Case Letters
Identification Code Above Zip Code

1CVP21	CVPA1 37c **black, blue & orange**	2.00	1.00
	On cover		2.50
	Sheet of 25	50.00	
a.	"First Class" below "US Postage"	1.35	.75
b.	"Priority" below "US Postage"	6.00	2.50
c.	"Express" below "US Postage"	22.50	5.00
d.	"Media Mail" below "US Postage"	6.00	2.50
e.	"Parcel Post" below "US Postage"	6.00	2.50
f.	"Bound Printed Matter" below "US Postage"	6.00	2.50
g.	"BPM" below "US Postage"	6.00	2.50

Bicycling — CVPA19

Running — CVPA20

Swimming
CVPA21

Boxing — CVPA22

Equestrian
CVPA23

Basketball
CVPA24

Judo — CVPA25

2004, Apr. *Serpentine Die Cut 6½ at Left*

1CVP16	CVPA14 37c **black, blue & orange**	2.00	1.00
	On cover		2.50
a.	"First Class" below "US Postage"	1.10	.75
b.	"Priority" below "US Postage"	5.00	2.50
c.	"Express" below "US Postage"	20.00	5.00

Soccer   CVPA26

Gymnastics
CVPA27

Tennis — CVPA28

2004, Apr.   *Serpentine Die Cut 6½ at Left*

1CVP22	CVPA19 37c **black, blue & orange**		3.00	2.00
	On cover			3.00
a.	"First Class" below "US Postage"		2.50	1.50
b.	"Priority" below "US Postage"		8.00	1.00
c.	"Express" below "US Postage"		25.00	3.00
d.	"Media Mail" below "US Postage"		7.50	1.00
e.	"Parcel Post" below "US Postage"		7.50	1.00
f.	"Bound Printed Matter" below "US Postage"		7.50	1.00
g.	"BPM" below "US Postage"		7.50	1.00
1CVP23	CVPA20 37c **black, blue & orange**		3.00	2.00
	On cover			3.00
a.	"First Class" below "US Postage"		2.50	1.50
b.	"Priority" below "US Postage"		8.00	1.00
c.	"Express" below "US Postage"		25.00	3.00
d.	"Media Mail" below "US Postage"		7.50	1.00
e.	"Parcel Post" below "US Postage"		7.50	1.00
f.	"Bound Printed Matter" below "US Postage"		7.50	1.00
g.	"BPM" below "US Postage"		7.50	1.00
1CVP24	CVPA21 37c **black, blue & orange**		3.00	2.00
	On cover			3.00
a.	"First Class" below "US Postage"		2.50	1.50
b.	"Priority" below "US Postage"		8.00	1.00
c.	"Express" below "US Postage"		25.00	3.00
d.	"Media Mail" below "US Postage"		7.50	1.00
e.	"Parcel Post" below "US Postage"		7.50	1.00
f.	"Bound Printed Matter" below "US Postage"		7.50	1.00
g.	"BPM" below "US Postage"		7.50	1.00
1CVP25	CVPA22 37c **black, blue & orange**		3.00	2.00
	On cover			3.00
a.	"First Class" below "US Postage"		2.50	1.50
b.	"Priority" below "US Postage"		8.00	1.00
c.	"Express" below "US Postage"		25.00	3.00
d.	"Media Mail" below "US Postage"		7.50	1.00
e.	"Parcel Post" below "US Postage"		7.50	1.00
f.	"Bound Printed Matter" below "US Postage"		7.50	1.00
g.	"BPM" below "US Postage"		7.50	1.00
1CVP26	CVPA23 37c **black, blue & orange**		3.00	2.00
	On cover			3.00
a.	"First Class" below "US Postage"		2.50	1.50
b.	"Priority" below "US Postage"		8.00	1.00
c.	"Express" below "US Postage"		25.00	3.00
d.	"Media Mail" below "US Postage"		7.50	1.00
e.	"Parcel Post" below "US Postage"		7.50	1.00
f.	"Bound Printed Matter" below "US Postage"		7.50	1.00

g.	"BPM" below "US Postage"		7.50	1.00
h.	Horiz. strip of 5, #1CVPss-1CVP26		15.00	
1CVP27	CVPA24 37c **black, blue & orange**		3.00	2.00
	On cover			3.00
a.	"First Class" below "US Postage"		2.50	1.50
b.	"Priority" below "US Postage"		8.00	1.00
c.	"Express" below "US Postage"		25.00	3.00
d.	"Media Mail" below "US Postage"		7.50	1.00
e.	"Parcel Post" below "US Postage"		7.50	1.00
f.	"Bound Printed Matter" below "US Postage"		7.50	1.00
g.	"BPM" below "US Postage"		7.50	1.00
1CVP28	CVPA25 37c **black, blue & orange**		3.00	2.00
	On cover			3.00
a.	"First Class" below "US Postage"		2.50	1.50
b.	"Priority" below "US Postage"		8.00	1.00
c.	"Express" below "US Postage"		25.00	3.00
d.	"Media Mail" below "US Postage"		7.50	1.00
e.	"Parcel Post" below "US Postage"		7.50	1.00
f.	"Bound Printed Matter" below "US Postage"		7.50	1.00
g.	"BPM" below "US Postage"		7.50	1.00
1CVP29	CVPA26 37c **black, blue & orange**		3.00	2.00
	On cover			3.00
a.	"First Class" below "US Postage"		2.50	1.50
b.	"Priority" below "US Postage"		8.00	1.00
c.	"Express" below "US Postage"		25.00	3.00
d.	"Media Mail" below "US Postage"		7.50	1.00
e.	"Parcel Post" below "US Postage"		7.50	1.00
f.	"Bound Printed Matter" below "US Postage"		7.50	1.00
g.	"BPM" below "US Postage"		7.50	1.00
1CVP30	CVPA27 37c **black, blue & orange**		3.00	2.00
	On cover			3.00
a.	"First Class" below "US Postage"		2.50	1.50
b.	"Priority" below "US Postage"		8.00	1.00
c.	"Express" below "US Postage"		25.00	3.00
d.	"Media Mail" below "US Postage"		7.50	1.00
e.	"Parcel Post" below "US Postage"		7.50	1.00
f.	"Bound Printed Matter" below "US Postage"		7.50	1.00
g.	"BPM" below "US Postage"		7.50	1.00
1CVP31	CVPA28 37c **black, blue & orange**		3.00	2.00
	On cover			3.00
a.	"First Class" below "US Postage"		2.50	1.50
b.	"Priority" below "US Postage"		8.00	1.00
c.	"Express" below "US Postage"		25.00	3.00
d.	"Media Mail" below "US Postage"		7.50	1.00
e.	"Parcel Post" below "US Postage"		7.50	1.00
f.	"Bound Printed Matter" below "US Postage"		7.50	1.00
g.	"BPM" below "US Postage"		7.50	1.00
h.	Horiz. strip of 5, #1CVP27-1CVP31		15.00	

The item pictured above was produced by Stamps.com for a special promotional mailing of its own and was not made available unused to customers.

Leaning Tower of
Pisa — CVPA29

Sphinx and
Pyramids — CVP...

Sydney Opera
House — CVPA31

Mayan
Pyramid — CVPA32

Asian
Temple — CVPA33

2004, July   *Serpentine Die Cut 6½ at Left*

1CVP32	CVPA29 37c **black, blue & orange**		3.00	2.00
	On cover			3.00
a.	"First Class" below "US Postage"		2.30	1.50
b.	"Priority" below "US Postage"		8.00	1.00
c.	"Express" below "US Postage"		25.00	3.00
d.	"Media Mail" below "US Postage"		7.50	1.00
e.	"Parcel Post" below "US Postage"		7.50	1.00
f.	"Bound Printed Matter" below "US Postage"		7.50	1.00
g.	"BPM" below "US Postage"		7.50	1.00
1CVP33	CVPA30 37c **black, blue & orange**		3.00	2.00
	On cover			3.00
a.	"First Class" below "US Postage"		2.30	1.50
b.	"Priority" below "US Postage"		8.00	1.00
c.	"Express" below "US Postage"		25.00	3.00
d.	"Media Mail" below "US Postage"		7.50	1.00
e.	"Parcel Post" below "US Postage"		7.50	1.00
f.	"Bound Printed Matter" below "US Postage"		7.50	1.00
g.	"BPM" below "US Postage"		7.50	1.00
1CVP34	CVPA31 37c **black, blue & orange**		3.00	2.00
	On cover			3.00
a.	"First Class" below "US Postage"		2.30	1.50
b.	"Priority" below "US Postage"		8.00	1.00
c.	"Express" below "US Postage"		25.00	3.00
d.	"Media Mail" below "US Postage"		7.50	1.00
e.	"Parcel Post" below "US Postage"		7.50	1.00

f.	"Bound Printed Matter" below "US Postage"	7.50	1.00
g.	"BPM" below "US Postage"	7.50	1.00
CVP35	CVPA32 37c **black, blue & orange**	3.00	2.00
	On cover		3.00
a.	"First Class" below "US Postage"	2.30	1.50
b.	"Priority" below "US Postage"	8.00	1.00
c.	"Express" below "US Postage"	25.00	3.00
d.	"Media Mail" below "US Postage"	7.50	1.00
e.	"Parcel Post" below "US Postage"	7.50	1.00
f.	"Bound Printed Matter" below "US Postage"	7.50	1.00
g.	"BPM" below "US Postage"	7.50	1.00
1CVP36	CVPA33 37c **black, blue & orange**	3.00	2.00
	On cover		3.00
a.	"First Class" below "US Postage"	2.30	1.50
b.	"Priority" below "US Postage"	8.00	1.00
c.	"Express" below "US Postage"	25.00	3.00
d.	"Media Mail" below "US Postage"	7.50	1.00
e.	"Parcel Post" below "US Postage"	7.50	1.00
f.	"Bound Printed Matter" below "US Postage"	7.50	1.00
g.	"BPM" below "US Postage"	7.50	1.00
h.	Strip of 5, #1CVP32-1CVP36	15.00	

Computer and Letters — CVPA34

2005, Mar.   *Serpentine Die Cut 6½ at Left*

1CVP37	CVPA34 37c **black, blue & orange**	25.00	15.00
	On cover		75.00
a.	"First Class" below "US Postage"	25.00	15.00
b.	"Priority" below "US Postage"	—	—
c.	"Express" below "US Postage"	—	—
d.	"Media Mail" below "US Postage"	—	—
e.	"Parcel Post" below "US Postage"	—	—
f.	"Bound Printed Matter" below "US Postage"	—	—
g.	"BPM" below "US Postage"	—	—

Blank sheets of No. 1CVP37 were sent free of charge to those who responded to special Stamps.com promotions which offered a fixed amount of free postage as an enticement to new subscribers. The franking portion of the stamps could only be applied after subscribing.

Logo — CVPA35

2005, Aug.   *Die Cut Perf. 6½ at Left*

1CVP38	CVPA35 37c **black, blue & orange**	.75	.20
	On cover		2.50
a.	"Priority" below "US Postage"	8.00	1.00
b.	"Express" below "US Postage"	25.00	3.00
c.	"Media Mail" below "US Postage"	7.50	1.00
d.	"Parcel Post" below "US Postage"	7.50	1.00
e.	"BPM" below "US Postage"	7.50	1.00
f.	"Aerogramme" below "US Postage"	1.40	1.00
g.	"Intl Air Letter" below "US Postage"	1.25	1.00
h.	"Intl Eco Letter" (Economy Letter Mail) below "US Postage"	5.50	1.00
i.	"GXG" (Global Express Guaranteed) below "US Postage"	50.00	6.00
j.	"EMS" (Global Express Mail) below "US Postage"	32.50	4.00
k.	"GPM" (Global Priority Mail) below "US Postage"	8.00	1.00
l.	"Intl Air Parcel" (Air Parcel Post) below "US Postage"	26.00	3.00
m.	"Intl Eco Parcel" (Economy Parcel Post) below "US Postage"	32.50	4.00
n.	"M-Bag (Air)" below "US Postage"	35.00	5.00
o.	"M-Bag (Economy)" below "US Postage"	18.00	3.00
p.	"Mat for Blind" below "US Postage"	.20	—

Values for lettered varieties on Nos. 1CVP38 are based on the prices set as the minimum values for each service classification in the software available at the time the stamps were issued. As of mid-December, the software was changed to allow for a 1c minimum value for any of these lettered varieties.>

In 2006, No. 1CVP38 was made available on a coil roll.

Snowman — CVPA36

Candy Cane — CVPA37

Dove — CVPA38

Stylized Christmas Tree and Window — CVPA39

2005, Nov.   *Die Cut Perf. 6 at Right*

1CVP39	CVPA36 37c **multicolored**	.75	.20
	On cover		2.50
a.	"Priority" below "US Postage"	8.00	1.00
b.	"Express" below "US Postage"	25.00	3.00
c.	"Media Mail" below "US Postage"	7.50	1.00
d.	"Parcel Post" below "US Postage"	7.50	1.00
e.	"BPM" below "US Postage"	7.50	1.00
f.	"Aerogramme" below "US Postage"	1.40	1.00
g.	"Intl Air Letter" below "US Postage"	1.25	1.00
h.	"Intl Eco Letter" (Economy Letter Mail) below "US Postage"	5.50	1.00
i.	"GXG" (Global Express Guaranteed) below "US Postage"	50.00	6.00
j.	"EMS" (Global Express Mail) below "US Postage"	32.50	4.00
k.	"GPM" (Global Priority Mail) below "US Postage"	8.00	1.00
l.	"Intl Air Parcel" (Air Parcel Post) below "US Postage"	26.00	3.00
m.	"Intl Eco Parcel" (Economy Parcel Post) below "US Postage"	32.50	4.00
n.	"M-Bag (Air)" below "US Postage"	35.00	5.00
o.	"M-Bag (Economy)" below "US Postage"	18.00	3.00
p.	"Mat for Blind" below "US Postage"	.20	—
1CVP40	CVPA37 37c **multicolored**	.75	.20
	On cover		2.50
a.	"Priority" below "US Postage"	8.00	1.00
b.	"Express" below "US Postage"	25.00	3.00
c.	"Media Mail" below "US Postage"	7.50	1.00
d.	"Parcel Post" below "US Postage"	7.50	1.00
e.	"BPM" below "US Postage"	7.50	1.00
f.	"Aerogramme" below "US Postage"	1.40	1.00
g.	"Intl Air Letter" below "US Postage"	1.25	1.00
h.	"Intl Eco Letter" (Economy Letter Mail) below "US Postage"	5.50	1.00
i.	"GXG" (Global Express Guaranteed) below "US Postage"	50.00	6.00
j.	"EMS" (Global Express Mail) below "US Postage"	32.50	4.00
k.	"GPM" (Global Priority Mail) below "US Postage"	8.00	1.00
l.	"Intl Air Parcel" (Air Parcel Post) below "US Postage"	26.00	3.00
m.	"Intl Eco Parcel" (Economy Parcel Post) below "US Postage"	32.50	4.00
n.	"M-Bag (Air)" below "US Postage"	35.00	5.00

---

o.	"M-Bag (Economy)" below "US Postage"	18.00	3.00
p.	"Mat for Blind" below "US Postage"	.20	—
1CVP41	CVPA38 37c **multicolored**	.75	.20
	On cover		2.50
a.	"Priority" below "US Postage"	8.00	1.00
b.	"Express" below "US Postage"	25.00	3.00
c.	"Media Mail" below "US Postage"	7.50	1.00
d.	"Parcel Post" below "US Postage"	7.50	1.00
e.	"BPM" below "US Postage"	7.50	1.00
f.	"Aerogramme" below "US Postage"	1.40	1.00
g.	"Intl Air Letter" below "US Postage"	1.25	1.00
h.	"Intl Eco Letter" (Economy Letter Mail) below "US Postage"	5.50	1.00
i.	"GXG" (Global Express Guaranteed) below "US Postage"	50.00	6.00
j.	"EMS" (Global Express Mail) below "US Postage"	32.50	4.00
k.	"GPM" (Global Priority Mail) below "US Postage"	8.00	1.00
l.	"Intl Air Parcel" (Air Parcel Post) below "US Postage"	26.00	3.00
m.	"Intl Eco Parcel" (Economy Parcel Post) below "US Postage"	32.50	4.00
n.	"M-Bag (Air)" below "US Postage"	35.00	5.00
o.	"M-Bag (Economy)" below "US Postage"	18.00	3.00
p.	"Mat for Blind" below "US Postage"	.20	—
1CVP42	CVPA39 37c **multicolored**	.75	.20
	On cover		2.50
a.	"Priority" below "US Postage"	8.00	1.00
b.	"Express" below "US Postage"	25.00	3.00
c.	"Media Mail" below "US Postage"	7.50	1.00
d.	"Parcel Post" below "US Postage"	7.50	1.00
e.	"BPM" below "US Postage"	7.50	1.00
f.	"Aerogramme" below "US Postage"	1.40	1.00
g.	"Intl Air Letter" below "US Postage"	1.25	1.00
h.	"Intl Eco Letter" (Economy Letter Mail) below "US Postage"	5.50	1.00
i.	"GXG" (Global Express Guaranteed) below "US Postage"	50.00	6.00
j.	"EMS" (Global Express Mail) below "US Postage"	32.50	4.00
k.	"GPM" (Global Priority Mail) below "US Postage"	8.00	1.00
l.	"Intl Air Parcel" (Air Parcel Post) below "US Postage"	26.00	3.00
m.	"Intl Eco Parcel" (Economy Parcel Post) below "US Postage"	32.50	4.00
n.	"M-Bag (Air)" below "US Postage"	35.00	5.00
o.	"M-Bag (Economy)" below "US Postage"	18.00	3.00
p.	"Mat for Blind" below "US Postage"	.20	—
q.	Vert. strip, 2 each #1CVP39-1CVP42	6.00	

Values for lettered varieties on Nos. 1CVP39-1CVP42 are based on the prices set as the minimum values for each service classification in the software available at the time the stamps were issued. As of mid-December, the software was changed to allow for a 1c minimum value for any of these lettered varieties.

Endicia.com

CVPA40

CVPA41

Service inscriptions under "US Postage": Nos. 1CVP43, 1CVP47, Postcard. Nos. 1CVP44, 1CVP48, First Class. Nos. 1CVP45, 1CVP49, Intl. Mail. Nos. 1CVP46, 1CVP50, Priority Mail.

2005-06   *Serpentine Die Cut 10¼*

1CVP43	CVPA40 24c **black & bright rose**	.50	.20
	On postcard		2.50
1CVP44	CVPA40 39c **black & bright rose**	.80	.20
	On cover		2.50
1CVP45	CVPA40 63c **black & bright rose**	1.25	1.00
	On cover		2.50
1CVP46	CVPA40 $4.05 **black & bright rose**	8.25	1.00

On cover			6.00	

Coil Stamps
Serpentine Die Cut 10½x10¼ on 2 Sides

1CVP47	CVPA41	24c **black & pink**	.50	.20
		On postcard		2.50
1CVP48	CVPA41	39c **black & pink**	.80	.20
		On cover		2.50
1CVP49	CVPA41	63c **black & pink**	1.25	1.00
		On cover		2.50
1CVP50	CVPA41	$4.05 **black & pink**	8.25	1.00
		On cover		6.00

Issued: Nos. 1CVP43-1CVP46, Nov. 2005; Nos. 1CVP47-1CVP50, Jan. 2006.

Face values of 2c, 52c, 63c, 87c, $1.11, $1.35, $1.59, $1.83, $2.07, $2.31, $2.55, $2.79, $3.03, and $3.27 could also be printed on stamps with the "First class" inscription. Additionally, an 84c face value could be printed on stamps with the "Intl. Mail" inscription, and a $8.10 face value could be printed on stamps with the "Priority Mail" inscription.

Stamps.com

Flag and Mount Rushmore — CVPA42

Flag and Eagle — CVPA43

Flag and Statue of Liberty — CVPA44

Flag and Liberty Bell — CVPA45

2006, Mar.   *Die Cut Perf. 6 at Right*

1CVP51	CVPA42	39c **multicolored**	.80	.20
		On cover		2.50
1CVP52	CVPA43	39c **multicolored**	.80	.20
		On cover		2.50
1CVP53	CVPA44	39c **multicolored**	.80	.20
		On cover		2.50
1CVP54	CVPA45	39c **multicolored**	.80	.20
		On cover		2.50
a.		Vert. strip of 8, 2 each #1CVP51-1CVP54		
			6.50	

Other service inscriptions with any possible face value can be printed on Nos. 1CVP51-1CVP54.

Stamps.com

Leaning Tower of Pisa — CVPA46

Taj Mahal — CVPA47

Eiffel Tower — CVPA48

Parthenon — CVPA49

2006   *Die Cut Perf 6 at Right*

1CVP55	CVPA46	39c **multicolored**	.80	.20
		On cover		2.50
1CVP56	CVPA47	39c **multicolored**	.80	.20
		On cover		2.50
1CVP57	CVPA48	39c **multicolored**	.80	.20
		On cover		2.50
1CVP58	CVPA49	39c **multicolored**	.80	.20
		On cover		2.50
a.		Vert. strip, 2 each #1CVP55-1CVP58	6.50	

With the introduction of the new software in December 2005, any stamp could have any denomination above 1c, and any service classification.

Pitney Bowes Stamp Expressions

CVPA50

Illustration reduced.

2006   *Die Cut Perf. 6 Horiz.*
Inscribed "pitneybowes.com/se" at Right

1CVP59	CVPA50	39c **black + label**	.80	.80
		On cover		4.00

The stamp and label are separated by vertical roulettes. Users could create their own label images on the Pitney Bowes Stamp Expressions website (which required approval of the image from Pitney Bowes before it could be used), or download various pre-approved label images from the website into their personal computers. Stamps could be printed without label images. Stamps were printed on rolls of tagged thermal paper from a device that could be operated without a direct connection to the personal computer. See No. 1CVT1.

COMPUTER VENDED POSTAGE TEST STAMPS
Pitney Bowes Stamp Expressions

CVT1

Illustration reduced.

2006   *Die Cut Perf. 6 Horiz.*
Inscribed "pbstampexpressions.com" at Right

1CVT1	CVT1	39c **black + label**	—	—
		On cover		—

No. 1CVT1 were produced only by beta testers of the Pitney Bowes Stamp Expressions system, and as such were not available to normal subscribers to the system. Examples are known to have passed through the mail. Notes concerning No. 1CVP59 apply to No. 1CVT1.

PERSONALIZED POSTAGE

These stamps, approved by the USPS, were created by individuals accessing an internet website to design stamps using their own digital pictures, ...ch were then produced by the companies and mailed to the customer. Some restrictions were in force to protect copyrighted material and to prevent ...of offensive subjects. Pictures in the frames shown here are for illustrative purposes only as countless other pictures exist for each denomination. ...mps were sold in full sheets at well above the face value, with discounts from the selling price usually available for purchases of multiple sheets. All ...mps are self-adhesive.

...or companies producing stamps with varieties and colors, the correct order for identifying stamps is as follows: major catalogue number, then the ...ety letter, followed by the color letter. Thus the 29mm tall Stamps.com 23c stamp with the tag bar to the right of the denomination with an orange ...ne is No. 2CVP1ag.

Photostamps
Produced by Stamps.com

...amps produced by Stamps.com could be printed in 10 dif- ...nt border colors, all being equally available. The denomina- ...and encryption were always printed in black. Border colors ...c, black. d, dark blue. e, red. f, light blue. g, orange. h, dark ...i, yellow. j, green. k, violet. l, pink. Only the denominations ...d below could be ordered.

CVPB1

Serpentine Die Cut 5 at Right

			Tagged	
...04, Aug.				
...VP1	CVPB1	23c any color, #c-l, tag bar above denomination and encryption	—	—
		On cover		—
a.		29mm tall tag bar at right of denomination and encryption	—	—
		On cover		—
b.		35mm tall tag bar at right of denomination and encryption, die cut perf. 4¾ at right	15.00	—
		On cover		—
...VP2	CVPB1	37c any color, #c-l, tag bar above denomination and encryption	—	—
		On cover		—
a.		29mm tall tag bar at right of denomination and encryption	—	—
		On cover		—
b.		35mm tall tag bar at right of denomination and encryption, die cut perf. 4¾ at right	5.00	—
		On cover		—
...VP3	CVPB1	49c any color, #c-l, tag bar above denomination and encryption	—	—
		On cover		—
a.		29mm tall tag bar at right of denomination and encryption	—	—
		On cover		—
b.		35mm tall tag bar at right of denomination and encryption, die cut perf. 4¾ at right	30.00	—
		On cover		—
...CVP4	CVPB1	60c any color, #c-l, tag bar above denomination and encryption	—	—
		On cover		—
a.		29mm tall tag bar at right of denomination and encryption	—	—
		On cover		—
b.		35mm tall tag bar at right of denomination and encryption, die cut perf. 4¾ at right	15.00	—
		On cover		—
...CVP5	CVPB1	83c any color, #c-l, tag bar above denomination and encryption	—	—
		On cover		—
a.		29mm tall tag bar at right of denomination and encryption	—	—
		On cover		—
b.		35mm tall tag bar at right of denomination and encryption, die cut perf. 4¾ at right	30.00	—
		On cover		—
2CVP6	CVPB1	$1.06 any color, #c-l, tag bar above denomination and encryption	—	—
		On cover		—
a.		29mm tall tag bar at right of denomination and encryption	—	—
		On cover		—
b.		35mm tall tag bar at right of denomination and encryption, die cut perf. 4¾ at right	30.00	—
		On cover		—
2CVP7	CVPB1	$3.85 any color, #c-l, tag bar above denomination and encryption		

---

a.		29mm tall tag bar at right of denomination and encryption	—	—
		On cover		—
b.		35mm tall tag bar at right of denomination and encryption, die cut perf. 4¾ at right	275.00	—
		On cover		—

Earliest known uses: Nos. 2CVP1-2CVP7, 8/7; Nos. 2CVP1a-2CVP7a, 8/23; Nos. 2CVP1b-2CVP7b, 9/1.

CVPB2

2005 — Die Cut Perf. 5 at Right

2CVP8	CVPB2	23c any color, #c-l, tag bar 3½mm wide, roulettes left of denomination	—	—
		On cover		—
a.		3½mm wide tag bar, no roulettes	5.00	—
		On cover		—
b.		15mm wide tag bar, no roulettes	2.00	1.60
		On cover		
2CVP9	CVPB2	37c any color, #c-l, tag bar 3½mm wide, roulettes left of denomination	—	—
		On cover		—
a.		3½mm wide tag bar, no roulettes	5.50	—
		On cover		—
b.		15mm wide tag bar, no roulettes	2.25	1.90
		On cover		
2CVP10	CVPB2	49c any color, #c-l, tag bar 3½mm wide, roulettes left of denomination	—	—
		On cover		—
a.		3½mm wide tag bar, no roulettes	6.50	—
		On cover		—
b.		15mm wide tag bar, no roulettes	2.50	2.25
		On cover		
2CVP11	CVPB2	60c any color, #c-l, tag bar 3½mm wide, roulettes left of denomination	—	—
		On cover		—
a.		3½mm wide tag bar, no roulettes	7.00	—
		On cover		—
b.		15mm wide tag bar, no roulettes	2.75	2.40
		On cover		
2CVP12	CVPB2	83c any color, #c-l, tag bar 3½mm wide, roulettes left of denomination	—	—
		On cover		—
a.		3½mm wide tag bar, no roulettes	8.50	—
		On cover		—
b.		15mm wide tag bar, no roulettes	3.50	3.00
		On cover		
2CVP13	CVPB2	$1.06 any color, #c-l, tag bar 3½mm wide, roulettes left of denomination	—	—
		On cover		—
a.		3½mm wide tag bar, no roulettes	10.00	—
		On cover		—
b.		15mm wide tag bar, no roulettes	4.00	3.50
		On cover		
2CVP14	CVPB2	$3.85 any color, #c-l, tag bar 3½mm wide, roulettes left of denomination	—	—
		On cover		—
a.		3½mm wide tag bar, no roulettes	27.50	—
		On cover		—
b.		15mm wide tag bar, no roulettes	10.50	9.25

Earliest known uses: Nos. 2CVP8-2CVP14, 5/20; Nos. 2CVP8a-2CVP14a, 7/12; Nos. 2CVP8b-2CVP14b, 7/29.

PictureItPostage
Produced by Endicia.com

Stamps produced by Endicia.com could be printed in 18 dif- ferent colors, which were limited by Pictureitpostage.com software based on the amount of contrast with the uploaded picture. Colors are: a, black. b, dark green. c, light green. d, light

---

blue. e, violet. f, gray. g, dark blue. h, orange. i, light purple. j, beige. k, blue. l, brown. m, red. n, blue green. o, gray blue. p, white. q, yellow. r, yellow brown. Only the denominations listed could be ordered.

Horizontal Image — CVPB3

Vertical Image CVPB4

Illustration CVPB3 is reduced.

2005, June 6 — Serpentine Die Cut 10½
Encryption in Black

2CVP15	CVPB3	23c any color, #a-r	2.00	2.00
		On cover, any color		—
2CVP16	CVPB3	37c any color, #a-r	2.40	2.40
		On cover, any color		—
2CVP17	CVPB3	49c any color, #a-r	2.75	2.75
		On cover, any color		—
2CVP18	CVPB3	60c any color, #a-r	3.00	3.00
		On cover, any color		—
2CVP19	CVPB4	23c any color, #a-r	2.00	2.00
		On cover, any color		—
2CVP20	CVPB4	37c any color, #a-r	2.40	2.40
		On cover, any color		—
2CVP21	CVPB4	49c any color, #a-r	2.75	2.75
		On cover, any color		—
2CVP22	CVPB4	60c any color, #a-r	3.00	3.00
		On cover, any color		—

Zazzle.com
Produced by Pitney Bowes

The denomination and encryption of stamps produced by Zazzle.com could only be printed in black, but 216 other colors were available to change the background or border of the pic- ture that was uploaded when creating a stamp image. Only the denominations listed could be ordered.

Horizontal Image — CVPB5

Vertical Image
CVPB6

Illustration CVPB5 is reduced.

2005, July   *Serpentine Die Cut 9¼*
Any Frame Color

2CVP23	CVPB5	23c	black	1.60	1.60
			On cover		—
2CVP24	CVPB5	37c	black	1.90	1.90
			On cover		—
2CVP25	CVPB5	49c	black	2.25	2.25
			On cover		—
2CVP26	CVPB5	60c	black	2.40	2.40
			On cover		—
2CVP27	CVPB5	83c	black	3.00	3.00
			On cover		—
2CVP28	CVPB5	$1.06	black	3.50	3.50
			On cover		—
2CVP29	CVPB5	$3.85	black	9.25	9.25
			On cover		—
2CVP30	CVPB6	23c	black	1.60	1.60
			On cover		—
2CVP31	CVPB6	37c	black	1.90	1.90
			On cover		—
2CVP32	CVPB6	49c	black	2.25	2.25
			On cover		—
2CVP33	CVPB6	60c	black	2.40	2.400
			On cover		—
2CVP34	CVPB6	83c	black	3.00	3.00
			On cover		—
2CVP35	CVPB6	$1.06	black	3.50	3.50
			On cover		—
2CVP36	CVPB6	$3.85	black	9.25	9.25
			On cover		-

Horizontal Stamps

2CVP23a	Dated "2006"	1.60	1.60
2CVP24a	Dated "2006"	1.90	1.90
2CVP25a	Dated "2006"	2.25	2.25
2CVP26a	Dated "2006"	2.40	2.40
2CVP27a	Dated "2006"	3.00	3.00
2CVP28a	Dated "2006"	3.50	3.50
2CVP29a	Dated "2006"	9.25	9.25

Vertical Stamps

2CVP30a	Dated "2006"	1.60	1.60
2CVP31a	Dated "2006"	1.90	1.90
2CVP32a	Dated "2006"	2.25	2.25
2CVP33a	Dated "2006"	2.40	2.40
2CVP34a	Dated "2006"	3.00	3.00
2CVP35a	Dated "2006"	3.50	3.50
2CVP36a	Dated "2006"	9.25	9.25

Zazzle.com Type of 2005

Notes concerning Nos. 2CVP23-2CVP36 apply to Nos. 2CVP37-2CVP50

2005, Nov.   *Serpentine Die Cut 9¼*
Any Frame Color

2CVP37	CVPB5	24c	black	1.50	1.50
			On cover		—
2CVP38	CVPB5	39c	black	1.75	1.75
			On cover		—
2CVP39	CVPB5	52c	black	2.25	2.25
			On cover		—
2CVP40	CVPB5	63c	black	2.50	2.50
			On cover		—
2CVP41	CVPB5	87c	black	3.00	3.00
			On cover		

2CVP42	CVPB5	$1.11	black	3.50	3.50
			On cover		—
2CVP43	CVPB5	$4.05	black	9.00	9.00
			On cover		—
2CVP44	CVPB6	24c	black	1.50	1.50
			On cover		—
2CVP45	CVPB6	39c	black	1.75	1.75
			On cover		—
2CVP46	CVPB6	52c	black	2.25	2.25
			On cover		—
2CVP47	CVPB6	63c	black	2.50	2.50
			On cover		—
2CVP48	CVPB6	87c	black	3.00	3.00
			On cover		—
2CVP49	CVPB6	$1.11	black	3.50	3.50
			On cover		—
2CVP50	CVPB6	$4.05	black	9.00	9.00
			On cover		-

Horizontal Stamps

2CVP37a	Dated "2006"	1.50	1.50
2CVP38a	Dated "2006"	1.75	1.75
2CVP39a	Dated "2006"	2.25	2.25
2CVP40a	Dated "2006"	2.50	2.50
2CVP41a	Dated "2006"	3.00	3.00
2CVP42a	Dated "2006"	3.50	3.50
2CVP43a	Dated "2006"	9.00	9.00

Vertical Stamps

2CVP44a	Dated "2006"	1.50	1.50
2CVP45a	Dated "2006"	1.75	1.75
2CVP46a	Dated "2006"	2.25	2.25
2CVP47a	Dated "2006"	2.50	2.50
2CVP48a	Dated "2006"	3.00	3.00
2CVP49a	Dated "2006"	3.50	3.50
2CVP50a	Dated "2006"	9.00	9.00

Overall Tagging
Horizontal Stamps

2CVP37b	As "a," overall tagging	2.00	2.00
2CVP38b	As "a," overall tagging	2.50	2.50
2CVP39b	As "a," overall tagging	3.00	3.00
2CVP40b	As "a," overall tagging	3.25	3.25
2CVP41b	As "a," overall tagging	4.00	4.00
2CVP42b	As "a," overall tagging	5.00	5.00
2CVP43b	As "a," overall tagging	12.50	12.50

Vertical Stamps

2CVP44b	As "a," overall tagging	2.00	2.00
2CVP45b	As "a," overall tagging	2.50	2.50
2CVP46b	As "a," overall tagging	3.00	3.00
2CVP47b	As "a," overall tagging	3.25	3.25
2CVP48b	As "a," overall tagging	4.00	4.00
2CVP49b	As "a," overall tagging	5.00	5.00
2CVP50b	As "a," overall tagging	12.50	12.50

Nos. 2CVP37a-2CVP50a have frame tagging.

Stamps.com Type of 2005

Nos. 2CVP51-2CVP57 have denomination in same colors (#c-l, as noted above No. 2CVP1) as border, no roulettes, and a 15mm wide tag bar at right. Only the denominations listed below could be ordered.

2005, Dec.   *Die Cut Perf. 5¼ at Right*
Any Frame Color

2CVP51	CVPB2	24c	any color, #c-l	1.75	1.75
			On cover, any color		—
2CVP52	CVPB2	39c	any color, #c-l	2.00	2.00
			On cover, any color		—
2CVP53	CVPB2	52c	any color, #c-l	2.40	2.40
			On cover, any color		—
2CVP54	CVPB2	63c	any color, #c-l	2.75	2.75
			On cover, any color		—
2CVP55	CVPB2	87c	any color, #c-l	3.25	3.25
			On cover, any color		—
2CVP56	CVPB2	$1.11	any color, #c-l	3.75	3.75
			On cover, any color		—
2CVP57	CVPB2	$4.05	any color, #c-l	10.00	10.00
			On cover, any color		—

Endicia.com Type of 2005

Notes pertaining to Nos. 2CVP15-2CVP22 apply to Nos. 2CVP58-2CVP65.

2005, Dec.   *Serpentine Die Cut 10½*
Encryption in Black
Horizontal Stamps

2CVP58	CVPB3	24c	any color, #a-r	2.25	2.25
			On cover, any color		—
2CVP59	CVPB3	39c	any color, #a-r	3.75	3.75
			On cover, any color		—
2CVP60	CVPB3	52c	any color, #a-r	4.50	4.50
			On cover, any color		—
2CVP61	CVPB3	63c	any color, #a-r	5.00	5.00
			On cover, any color		—

Vertical Stamps

2CVP62	CVPB4	24c	any color, #a-r	2.25	2.25
			On cover, any color		—
2CVP63	CVPB4	39c	any color, #a-r	3.75	3.75
			On cover, any color		—
2CVP64	CVPB4	52c	any color, #a-r	4.50	4.50
			On cover, any color		—
2CVP65	CVPB4	63c	any color, #a-r	5.00	5.00
			On cover, any color		—

2006
Horizontal Stamps
6x38mm Vertical Tagging Bar(s)

2CVP58s	6x38mm tagging bar at right	2.25	2.25
2CVP58t	6x38mm tagging bars at left and right	1.75	1.75
2CVP59s	6x38mm tagging bar at right	2.50	2.50

2CVP59t	6x38mm tagging bars at left and right	2.00	
2CVP60s	6x38mm tagging bar at right	3.00	
2CVP60t	6x38mm tagging bars at left and right	2.40	
2CVP61s	6x38mm tagging bar at right	3.50	
2CVP61t	6x38mm tagging bars at left and right	2.75	

Vertical Stamps
Horizontal Tagging Bar(s)

2CVP62s	38x6mm tagging bar at top	2.25	
2CVP62t	38x6mm tagging bars at top and bottom	1.75	
2CVP63s	38x6mm tagging bar at top	2.50	
2CVP63t	38x6mm tagging bars at top and bottom	2.00	
2CVP64s	38x6mm tagging bar at top	3.00	
2CVP64t	38x6mm tagging bars at top and bottom	2.40	
2CVP65s	38x6mm tagging bar at top	3.50	
2CVP65t	38x6mm tagging bars at top and bottom	2.75	

Nos. 2CVP58-2CVP61 have a 4x30mm tagging bar at r
Nos. 2CVP62-2CVP65 have a 30x4mm tagging bar at top
The "s" and "t" varieties of Nos. 2CVP58-2CVP65 are pri
on the same sheet. The "s" varieties are from the left col
only of the 2CVP58-2CVP61 sheets and the bottom row of
2CVP62-2CVP65 sheets. All other stamps on the sheets
the "t" varieties.

Endicia.com Type of 2005

Notes pertaining to Nos. 2CVP15-2CVP22 apply to N
2CVP66-2CVP71.

2006, Jan.   *Serpentine Die Cut 1*
Encryption in Black
Horizontal Stamps
6x38mm Tagging Bar at Right

2CVP66	CVPB3	87c	any color, #a-r	3.25	3
			On cover, any color		
2CVP67	CVPB3	$1.11	any color, #a-r	3.75	3
			On cover, any color		
2CVP68	CVPB3	$4.05	any color, #a-r	10.00	10
			On cover, any color		

Vertical Stamps
38x6 Tagging Bar at Top

2CVP69	CVPB4	87c	any color, #a-r	3.25	3
			On cover, any color		
2CVP70	CVPB4	$1.11	any color, #a-r	3.75	3.
			On cover, any color		
2CVP71	CVPB4	$4.05	any color, #a-r	10.00	10.

Horizontal Stamps
6x38mm Tagging Bars at Left and Right\

2CVP66t	any color, #a-r	3.25	3.
2CVP67t	any color, #a-r	3.75	3.
2CVP68t	any color, #a-r	10.00	10.

Vertical Stamps
38x6mm Tagging Bars at Top and Bottom

2CVP69t	any color, #a-r	3.25	3.2
2CVP70t	any color, #a-r	3.75	3.7
2CVP71t	any color, #a-r	10.00	10.

Nos. 2CVP66-2CVP68 have a 6x38mm tagging bar at righ
and are from the left column only of the sheet. Nos. 2CVP6.
2CVP71 have a 38x6mm tagging bar at top, and are from th
bottom row of sheet. The "t" varieties compose the rest of th
stamps on the sheet.

VENDING & AFFIXING MACHINE PERFORATIONS

Imperforate sheets of 400 were first issued in 1906 on the request of several makers of vending and affixing machines. The machine manufacturers made coils from the imperforate sheets and applied various perforations to suit the particular needs of their machines. These privately applied perforations were used for many years and form a chapter of postal history.

Unused values are for pairs, used values for singles. Used multiples are highly valued, with prices often equalling or exceeding those for unused pairs or strips. "On cover" values are for single stamps used commercially in the proper period when known that way. Several, primarily the Alaska-Yukon and Hudson-Fulton commemoratives, are known almost exclusively on covers from contemporaneous stamp collectors and stamp dealers. Virtually all are rare and highly prized by specialists.

The 2mm and 3mm spacings refer only to the 1908-10 issues. (See note following No. 330 in the Postage section.) Values for intermediate spacings would roughly correspond to the lower-valued of the two listed spacings. Guide line pairs of 1906-10 issues have 2mm spacing except the Alaska-Yukon and Hudson-Fulton issues, which have 3mm spacing. Scott Nos. 408-611 have 3mm spacing, except the "A" plates which have 2¾mm spacing and Scott No. 577, which has both 2¾mm and 3mm spacing. (All spacing measurements are approximate.)

Spacing on paste-up pairs is not a factor in valuing them. Because they were joined together by hand, many different spacings can occur, from less than 2mm to more than 3mm.

Perfins listed here are punched into the stamp at the same time as the perforation. The most common pattern consisted of a 7mm square made up of nine holes. Pins would be removed to create unique perfins for each company using the machines. The catalogue value is for the most common perfin pattern on each stamp.

* — Many varieties are suspected or known to have been perforated for philatelic purposes and not actually used in machines. These are indicated by an asterisk before the number. Several of these privately applied perforation varieties exist in blocks, which were not produced in the regular course of business. They are generally valued at a premium over the multiple of the coil pairs contained, with an additional premium for plate numbers attached.

Counterfeits are prevalent, especially of items having a basic imperf. variety valued far lower than the vending machine coil.

The Vending and Affixing Machine Perforations Committee of the Bureau Issues Association (now the United States Stamp Society) and William R. Weiss, Jr., compiled these listings.

The Attleboro Stamp Co.
See following U.S. Automatic Vending Company.

THE BRINKERHOFF COMPANY
Sedalia, Mo., Clinton, Iowa
Manufacturers of Vending Machines

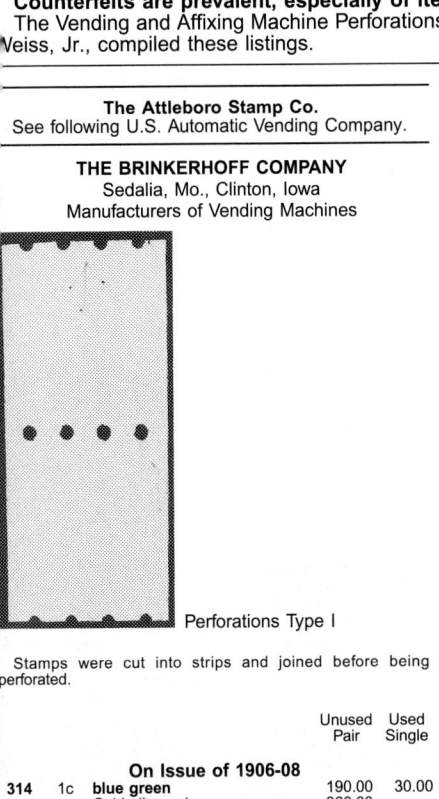

Perforations Type I

Stamps were cut into strips and joined before being perforated.

			Unused Pair	Used Single
On Issue of 1906-08				
314	1c	blue green	190.00	30.00
		Guide line pair	360.00	
320	2c	carmine	210.00	30.00
		Guide line pair	400.00	
		Pasteup pair	300.00	
*320a	2c	lake	160.00	25.00
		Guide line pair	310.00	
		Pasteup pair	225.00	
On Issue of 1908-09				
*343	1c	green	110.00	20.00
		Guide line pair	275.00	
		Pasteup pair	220.00	
*344	2c	carmine	100.00	20.00
		On cover		1,500.
		Guide line pair	200.00	—
		Pasteup pair	175.00	
*345	3c	deep violet	130.00	—
		Guide line pair	260.00	
*346	4c	orange brown	150.00	120.00
		Guide line pair	275.00	
		Pasteup pair	200.00	
*347	5c	blue	290.00	80.00
		On cover		3,000.
		Guide line pair	475.00	
On Lincoln Issue of 1909				
*368	2c	carmine, coiled endwise	160.00	175.00
		Guide line pair	300.00	
On Alaska-Yukon Issue of 1909				
*371	2c	carmine, coiled sideways	550.00	—
		Guide line pair	950.00	
On Issue of 1910				
*383	1c	green	190.00	
		Guide line pair		—
On Issue of 1912				
*408	1c	green	30.00	15.00
		On cover		750.00
		Guide line pair	60.00	

			Unused Pair	Used Single
		Pasteup pair	50.00	
*409	2c	carmine	30.00	15.00
		On cover		1,000.
		Guide line pair	60.00	
		Pasteup pair	50.00	

Type IIa — One knife cut.

Type IIb — Two knife cuts.

Perforations Type II, 2 Holes

The Type II items listed below are without knife cuts and did not pass through the vending machine. Types IIa and IIb (illustrated above) have knife cuts, applied by the vending machine, to help separate the stamps.

	Type			Unused Pair	Used Single
On Issue of 1906-08					
314	*II	1c	blue green	90.00	12.50
			On cover		750.00
	IIa	1c	blue green	75.00	12.50
			Guide line pair	150.00	
	*IIb	1c	blue green	400.00	—
			Pasteup pair	675.00	
320	*II	2c	carmine	190.00	65.00
			Pasteup pair	300.00	
	IIa	2c	carmine	37.50	12.50
			On cover		500.00
			Guide line pair	110.00	
320a	*II	2c	lake	190.00	65.00
			On cover		500.00
	IIa	2c	lake	80.00	12.50
			On cover		500.00
			Guide line pair	160.00	
			Pasteup pair	90.00	
	*IIb	2c	lake	325.00	75.00
On Issue of 1908-09					
343	*II	1c	green	60.00	
			On cover		600.00
			Guide line pair	105.00	
	IIa	1c	green	18.00	3.25
			On cover		600.00
			Pasteup pair	30.00	
	IIb	1c	green	30.00	
			On cover		750.00
			Pasteup pair	52.50	
344	*II	2c	carmine	72.50	
			On cover, pair		600.00
			Guide line pair	155.00	
			Pasteup pair	120.00	

	Type			Unused Pair	Used Single
	IIa	2c	carmine	18.00	3.25
			Guide line pair	35.00	
			On cover		700.00
	IIb	2c	carmine	25.00	6.50
			Guide line pair	70.00	
			Pasteup pair	55.00	
345	*II	3c	deep violet	100.00	12.50
			Guide line pair	250.00	
	*IIa	3c	deep violet	80.00	12.50
			On cover		1,500.
			Guide line pair	160.00	
	*IIb	3c	deep violet	260.00	
346	*II	4c	orange brown	140.00	
			Guide line pair	260.00	
	*IIa	4c	orange brown	120.00	50.00
			On cover		1,200.
			Guide line pair	230.00	
			Pasteup pair	190.00	
	*IIb	4c	orange brown	140.00	50.00
			On cover		1,500.
347	*II	5c	blue	225.00	
			Guide line pair	375.00	
	*IIa	5c	blue	135.00	100.00
			On cover		3,000.
			Pasteup pair	200.00	
	*IIb	5c	blue	170.00	
			Pasteup pair	330.00	
On Lincoln Issue of 1909					
368	*II	2c	carmine	70.00	
			On cover		1,000.
			Guide line pair	140.00	
	IIa	2c	carmine	70.00	14.00
			On cover		1,200.
			Guide line pair	200.00	
	IIb	2c	carmine	200.00	22.50
			On cover		1,500.
			Guide line pair	400.00	
On Alaska-Yukon Issue of 1909					
371	*II	2c	carmine, coiled sideways	150.00	100.00
			On cover		1,000.
			Guide line or pasteup pair	300.00	
	II	2c	carmine, coiled endwise	600.00	
			Guide line pair		1,200.
	IIa	2c	carmine, coiled sideways	160.00	45.00
			On cover		750.00
			Guide line pair	300.00	
On Hudson-Fulton Issue of 1909					
373	*II	2c	carmine, coiled sidewise	250.00	
			Guide line or pasteup pair	450.00	
On Issue of 1910					
383	*II	1c	green	35.00	
			Guide line pair	70.00	
	IIa	1c	green	42.50	9.00
			On cover		800.00
	IIb	1c	green	85.00	50.00
			On cover		1,000.
			Guide line pair	160.00	
384	*II	2c	carmine	35.00	
			On cover		750.00
			Guide line pair	65.00	
	IIa	2c	carmine	110.00	
			On cover		1,000.
			Pasteup pair	175.00	
	IIb	2c	carmine	60.00	9.00
			On cover		1,500.
			Guide line pair	175.00	
			Pasteup pair	120.00	
On Issue of 1912					
408	*II	1c	green	90.00	—
			On cover		800.00
			Guide line pair	140.00	
			Pasteup pair	110.00	
	*IIa	1c	green	110.00	
			Guide line pair	200.00	

Type			Unused Pair	Used Single
IIb	1c	green	22.50	5.50
		On cover		800.00
		Guide line pair	45.00	
409	*II	2c	carmine	65.00	
		On cover		800.00
		Guide line pair	130.00	
		Pasteup pair	120.00	
	*IIa	2c	carmine	250.00	—
		On cover		800.00
		Guide line pair	450.00	
	IIb	2c	carmine	30.00	5.50
		On cover		625.00
		Guide line pair	55.00	

THE FARWELL COMPANY

Chicago, Ill.

A wholesale dry goods firm using Schermack (Mailometer) affixing machines. In 1911 the Farwell Company began to make and perforate their own coils. These were sometimes wrongly called "Chambers" perforations.

Type A

Type B

Stamps were perforated in sheets, then cut into strips and coiled. Blocks exist.

The following listings are grouped according to the number of holes, further divided into two types of spacing, narrow and wide.

The type symbols (3A2) indicate 3 holes over 2 holes with narrow, type A, spacing between groups.

Types A and B occurred in different rows on the same sheet. Left margin or pasteup stamps sometimes show different perforation type on the two sides.

Commercial usages of Farwell perforations are generally, but not always, on printed Farwell Co. corner card covers.

			Unused Pair Spacing 2mm	3mm	Used Single
Group I, no spacing					
On Issue of 1910					
384	2c	carmine, 7 holes	2,500.	2,500.	950.00
		On cover			5,000.
384	2c	carmine, 6 holes	4,000.	4,000.	2,250.
		On cover			5,000.

Type					
Group 2, two and three holes					
On Issue of 1910					
383	2B3	1c	green	375.00	625.00	200.00
	3A2	1c	green	375.00	625.00	
		On cover			—
		Guide line pair	650.00		
384	2A3	2c	carmine	275.00	475.00	200.00
		On cover			950.00
		Guide line pair	950.00	1,000.	
		Pasteup pair		800.00	
	2B3	2c	carmine	600.00	675.00	225.00
		On cover			—
		Pasteup pair		1,000.	
	3A2	2c	carmine	425.00	475.00	210.00
		On cover			1,500.
		Guide line pair	750.00		
	3B2	2c	carmine	375.00	375.00	300.00
		Guide line pair	800.00		

Group 3, three and four holes					
On Issue of 1910					
383	3B4	1c	green	300.00	300.00	200.00
		Pasteup pair	600.00		
	4B3	1c	green	375.00	375.00	200.00
384	3B4	2c	carmine	500.00	500.00	260.00
		On cover			—
		Guide line pair	800.00		

Type					
4B3	2c	carmine	800.00	800.00	400.00
		On cover			700.00
		Guide line pair	—		
4A3	2c	Carmine			

Group 4, four and four holes
On Issue of 1908-09

343	*A	1c	green	225.00		
	*B	1c	green	225.00		
		On cover			500.00
344	*A	2c	carmine	225.00	350.00	
	*B	2c	carmine	175.00	160.00	115.00

On Lincoln Issue of 1909

368	*A	2c	carmine	800.00	800.00	
	*B	2c	carmine	800.00	800.00	

On Issue of 1910

383	A	1c	green	65.00	60.00	60.00
		Guide line pair	130.00		
	B	1c	green	65.00	55.00	
		On cover			250.00
		Guide line pair	130.00		
384	A	2c	carmine	70.00	65.00	25.00
		Guide line pair	140.00		
	B	2c	carmine	70.00	65.00	17.50
		On cover			300.00
		Guide line pair	140.00		
		Pasteup pair	150.00		

On Issue of 1912

408	A	1c	green	35.00		2.75
		On cover			400.00
		Guide line pair	65.00		
	B	1c	green	35.00		2.75
		On cover			200.00
		Guide line pair	65.00		
409	A	2c	carmine	30.00		2.75
		On cover			70.00
	B	2c	carmine	30.00		2.75
		On cover			75.00
		Guide line pair	60.00		

On Issue of 1916-17

482	A	2c	carmine	400.00		60.00
		On cover			1,100.
		Guide line pair	700.00		
		Pasteup pair	600.00		
	B	2c	carmine	425.00		60.00
		On cover			1,100.
		Guide line pair	750.00		

Group 5, four and five holes
On Issue of 1910

383	4A5	1c	green	650.00	600.00	—
		Guide line pair	1,200.		
384	4A5	2c	carmine	800.00	700.00	
		Guide line pair	1,500.		

On Issue of 1912

408	4A5	1c	green	1,100.		
		Guide line pair	2,000.		
	*5A4	1c	green	1,100.		
		Guide line pair	2,000.		
409	*4A5	2c	carmine	1,100.		—
		Guide line or pasteup pair	2,000.		
	*5A4	2c	carmine	1,100.		
		Guide line pair	2,000.		

INTERNATIONAL VENDING MACHINE CO.

Baltimore, Md.

Similar to the Government Coil stamp #322, but approximately perf. 12½ with somewhat inconsistent spacing.

On Issue of 1906-08

320	2c	carmine	3,000.
320b	2c	scarlet	3,000.

On Issue of 1908-09

343	1c	green	2,750.
344	2c	carmine	1,100.
345	3c	deep violet	1,100.
346	4c	orange brown	—
347	5c	blue	5,750.

THE MAILOMETER COMPANY

Detroit, Mich.

Formerly the Schermack Mailing Machine Co., then Mail-om-eter Co., and later the Mail-O-Meter Co. Their round-hole perforations were developed in an attempt to get the Bureau of Engraving and Printing to adopt a larger perforation for coil stamps.

Perforations Type I

Used experimentally in Detroit and Chicago in August, 1909. Later used regularly in the St. Louis branch.

Two varieties exist: six holes 1.95mm in diameter spaced an average 1.2mm apart with an overall length of 17.7mm, and six holes 1.95mm in diameter spaced an average 1.15mm apart with an overall length of 17.45mm.

To date, only the 17.7mm length perfs. have been found on commercial covers.

Values for type I perfs are for the 17.45mm length. Values for the scarcer 17.7mm length are higher.

			Unused Pair Spacing 2mm	3mm	Used Single
On Issue of 1906-08					
*320	2c	carmine	450.00		
*320a	2c	lake	350.00		
		Guide line pair	800.00		
*320b	2c	scarlet	325.00		
On Issue of 1908-09					
343	1c	green	45.00	50.00	25.0
		On cover			500.0
		Guide line pair	70.00		
344	2c	carmine	40.00	45.00	5.0
		On cover, St. Louis			75.0
		On cover, Detroit or Chicago			1,250.
		On cover, Washington, D.C.			1,750.
		Guide line pair	85.00		
		With perforated control mark, single			77.50
		Same, on cover			350.00
345	3c	deep violet	65.00		20.00
		Guide line pair	130.00		
346	4c	orange brown	130.00	90.00	40.00
		Guide line pair	250.00		
347	5c	blue	140.00		40.00
		Guide line pair	250.00		
On Lincoln Issue of 1909					
*368	2c	carmine	180.00	130.00	110.00
		Guide line or pasteup pair	360.00		
On Alaska-Yukon Issue of 1909					
*371	2c	carmine	220.00		110.00
		Guide line pair	400.00		
On Hudson-Fulton Issue of 1909					
*373	2c	carmine	210.00		100.00
		Guide line pair	400.00		
On Issue of 1910					
383	1c	green	42.50	37.50	3.50
		On cover			—
		Guide line pair	80.00		
384	2c	carmine	55.00	45.00	5.00
		On cover			75.00
		Guide line pair	100.00		
On Issue of 1912					
*408	1c	green	25.00		4.50
		Guide line pair	47.50		
*409	2c	carmine	25.00		4.50
		Guide line pair	47.50		

Perforations Type II

Used experimentally: Chicago, 1909; Detroit, 1911. Perforation holes 1.95mm in diameter.

			Unused Pair		Used Single
On Issue of 1906-08					
*320	2c	carmine	700.00		
*320b	2c	scarlet	1,000.		
		Guide line pair	1,400.		
On Issue of 1908-09					
343	1c	green	65.00	65.00	15.00
		Guide line pair	130.00		
344	2c	carmine	75.00	75.00	15.00
		On cover			5,000.
		Guide line pair	150.00		
*345	3c	deep violet	275.00		70.00
		Pasteup pair	400.00		
*346	4c	orange brown	400.00	300.00	

47	5c	blue	600.00		

On Lincoln Issue of 1909

68	2c	carmine	600.00	575.00	

On Alaska-Yukon Issue of 1909

71	2c	carmine	650.00	

On Hudson-Fulton Issue of 1909

73	2c	carmine	375.00	
		Guide line or pasteup pair	650.00	

On Issue of 1910

3	1c	green	150.00	150.00	27.50
		Guide line or pasteup pair	300.00		
4	2c	carmine	160.00	150.00	*55.00*
		On cover			*4,000.*

Perforations Type III

Used experimentally in Detroit in 1910. Perforation holes 1.8mm in diameter.

On Issue of 1906-08

320	2c	carmine	800.00
320b	2c	scarlet	900.00

On Issue of 1908-09

343	1c	green	170.00	170.00
		Guide line pair	340.00	
344	2c	carmine	220.00	220.00
		Guide line pair	450.00	
		Pasteup pair	400.00	
345	3c	deep violet	300.00	
		Guide line pair	550.00	
346	4c	orange brown	425.00	350.00
		Pasteup pair	600.00	
347	5c	blue	*700.00*	
		Pasteup pair		*1,100.*

On Lincoln Issue of 1909

368	2c	carmine	325.00	275.00	100.00
		Pasteup pair	450.00		

On Alaska-Yukon Issue of 1909

371	2c	carmine	750.00	

On Hudson-Fulton Issue of 1909

373	2c	carmine	700.00	
		Guide line pair	*1,400.*	
		Pasteup pair		

Perforations Type IV

Used in St. Louis branch office. Blocks exist but were not regularly produced or issued.

On Issue of 1906-08

*320	2c	carmine	220.00	*80.00*
		Guide line pair	440.00	
		Pasteup pair	400.00	
*320b	2c	scarlet	150.00	*65.00*
		Guide line pair	500.00	

On Issue of 1908-09

343	1c	green	45.00	40.00	9.00
		Guide line pair	95.00		
		Pasteup pair	90.00		
344	2c	carmine	55.00	45.00	9.00
		On cover			
		Guide line or pasteup pair	100.00		
345	3c	deep violet	105.00		
		Guide line pair	210.00		
346	4c	orange brown	165.00	140.00	
		Guide line pair	325.00		
347	5c	blue	200.00		*55.00*
		Guide line pair	375.00		

On Lincoln Issue of 1909

*368	2c	carmine	105.00	105.00	27.50
		Guide line or pasteup pair	200.00		

On Alaska-Yukon Issue of 1909

*371	2c	carmine	*325.00*	
		Guide line pair	*550.00*	
		Pasteup pair	*550.00*	

On Hudson-Fulton Issue of 1909

*373	2c	carmine	*325.00*	
		On cover		
		Guide line pair	*525.00*	

On Issue of 1910

383	1c	green	14.00	10.00	2.25
		On cover			*200.00*
		Guide line pair	22.50		
384	2c	carmine	25.00	22.50	1.25
		On cover			*90.00*
		Guide line pair	40.00		

On Issue of 1912

408	1c	green	7.00	1.25
		On cover		*60.00*
		Guide line or pasteup pair	11.00	
409	2c	carmine	8.00	.75
		On cover		*30.00*
		Guide line pair	14.00	
		Pasteup pair	13.00	

On Issue of 1916-17

482	2c	carmine	110.00	65.00
		On cover		*275.00*
		Guide line pair	*200.00*	
		Pasteup pair	*225.00*	
483	3c	violet, type I	150.00	65.00
		On cover		*275.00*
		Guide line pair	*300.00*	
		Pasteup pair	*225.00*	

THE SCHERMACK COMPANY

Detroit, Mich.

These perforations were developed by the Schermack Mailing Machine Co. before it became the Mailometer Co. The Type III perforation was used in the company's affixing machines from 1908 through 1927 or 1928.

Perforations Type I. Eight Holes

Perforated in sheets, then cut into strips and coiled.

			Unused Pair Spacing 2mm	3mm	Used Single
On Issue of 1906-08					
314	1c	blue green	150.00		*100.00*
		Guide line pair	300.00		
		*Seven holes	1,000.		
		*Pasteup pair	*1,350.*		
		*Six holes	900.00		
		Guide line pair	*2,250.*		
320	2c	carmine	125.00		*55.00*
		On cover			*2,000.*
		Guide line pair	240.00		
		Seven holes	1,100.		*300.00*
		On cover			*8,000.*
		Guide line pair	*1,500.*		
		Pasteup pair	1,100.		
		*Six holes	1,000.		
		Guide line pair	*2,250.*		
*320a	2c	lake	350.00		*110.00*
		*Seven holes	600.00		
		Guide line pair	*1,500.*		
		*Six holes	*1,250.*		
*320b	2c	scarlet, six holes	*1,500.*		
*315	5c	blue	—		
On Issue of 1908-09					
*343	1c	green	250.00	—	80.00
		Guide line pair	—		
*344	2c	carmine	1,000.		
		Guide line pair	*1,400.*		
*345	3c	deep violet	*1,400.*		
		Guide line pair	*1,750.*		
*346	4c	orange brown	600.00	—	
		Guide line pair	—		
*347	5c	blue	600.00		
		Guide line pair	—		
On Lincoln Issue of 1909					
*368	2c	carmine	200.00	225.00	80.00
		Guide line pair	350.00		
		*Seven holes	875.00	—	
		*Six holes	1,000.		

			Unused Pair Spacing 2mm	3mm	Used Single
		Guide line pair		*1,500.*	

Perforations Type II

Cut into strips and joined before being perforated.

			Unused Pair Spacing 2mm	3mm	Used Single
On Issue of 1906-08					
314	1c	blue green	300.00		*80.00*
		On cover			*1,750.*
		Guide line pair	500.00		
320	2c	carmine	150.00		*55.00*
		Guide line pair	275.00		
*320a	2c	lake	260.00		*100.00*
		Guide line pair	450.00		
*315	5c	blue	*12,000.*		*1,750.*
		Guide line pair	—		
On Issue of 1908-09					
*343	1c	green	600.00	625.00	
		Guide line pair	1,050.		
*344	2c	carmine	600.00	575.00	
		Guide line pair	1,100.		
*345	3c	deep violet	600.00		
		Guide line pair	1,100.		
*346	4c	orange brown	800.00	—	
		Guide line pair	1,400.		
*347	5c	blue	750.00		
		Guide line pair	1,500.		
On Lincoln Issue of 1909					
*368	2c	carmine	150.00	135.00	65.00
		Guide line pair	275.00		
On Issue of 1910					
*383	1c	green	—		
		Guide line or pasteup pair	—		
*384	2c	carmine	—		

Existance of genuine copies of Nos. 383-384 has been questioned.

Perforations Type III

Blocks exist but were not regularly produced or issued.

			Unused Pair Spacing 2mm	3mm	Used Single
On Issue of 1906-08					
314	1c	blue green	11.00		2.25
		On cover			*125.00*
		Guide line pair	22.50		
		Pasteup pair	19.00		
320	2c	carmine, type I	16.00		5.50
		On cover			*80.00*
		Guide line pair	30.00		
320a	2c	lake, type II	22.50		2.75
		On cover			*80.00*
		Guide line pair	45.00		
		Pasteup pair	40.00		
		With perforated control mark, single			—
*320b	2c	scarlet, type I	22.50		5.50
		On cover			—
		Guide line pair	40.00		
320c	2c	carmine rose, type I	55.00		
320d	2c	carmine, type II, single	120.00		
		On cover			*600.00*
		Pair	225.00		
		Guide line pair	450.00		
314A	4c	brown, single	75,000.		*45,000.*
		Pair	175,000.		
		On cover			*130,000.*
		Guide line pair	240,000.		
*315	5c	blue	*4,500.*		
On Issue of 1908-09					
343	1c	green	5.50	6.50	1.25
		On cover			*25.00*
		Guide line or pasteup pair	10.00		
		With perforated control mark, single			*52.50*
		Same, on cover			*500.00*
344	2c	carmine	5.50	6.50	1.25
		On cover			*20.00*

No.		Description	2mm	3mm	Used Single
		Guide line or pasteup pair	10.00		
		With perforated control mark, single		50.00	
		Same, on cover			500.00
345	3c	deep violet	22.50	150.00	12.50
		On cover			—
		Guide line pair	50.00		
		Pasteup pair	50.00		
		With perforated control mark, single		775.00	
		Same, on cover			7,500.
346	4c	orange brown	32.50	22.50	17.50
		On cover			3,000.
		Guide line or pasteup pair	55.00		
		With perforated control mark, single		"	1,350.
		On cover			9,000.
347	5c	blue	55.00		17.50
		On cover			2,250.
		Guide line pair	100.00		

On Lincoln Issue of 1909

No.		Description	2mm	3mm	Used Single
368	2c	carmine	65.00	50.00	12.50
		On cover			175.00
		Guide line or pasteup pair	125.00		

On Alaska-Yukon Issue of 1909

No.		Description	2mm	3mm	Used Single
*371	2c	carmine	85.00		
		On cover			4,000.
		Guide line or pasteup pair	160.00		

On Hudson-Fulton Issue of 1909

No.		Description	2mm	3mm	Used Single
*373	2c	carmine	105.00		
		Guide line or pasteup pair	200.00		

On Issue of 1910

No.		Description	2mm	3mm	Used Single
383	1c	green	4.50	3.25	1.25
		On cover			20.00
		Guide line or pasteup pair	8.75		
		With perforated control mark, single		32.50	
		Same, on cover			325.00

Earliest documented use: Feb. 8, 1911.

No.		Description	2mm	3mm	Used Single
384	2c	carmine	10.00	7.75	1.25
		On cover			20.00
		Guide line pair	16.00		
		With perforated control mark, single		32.50	
		Same, on cover			275.00

On Issue of 1912

No.		Description	2mm	3mm	Used Single
408	1c	green	2.25		.60
		On cover			20.00
		Guide line or pasteup pair	4.50		
		With perforated control mark, single		37.50	
		Same, on cover			300.00
409	2c	carmine	2.25		.50
		On cover			20.00
		Guide line or pasteup pair	4.50		
		Aniline ink ("pink back")			—
		With perforated control mark, single		37.50	
		Same, on cover			300.00

Earliest documented use: Mar. 21, 1912.

On Issue of 1916-17

No.		Description	2mm	3mm	Used Single
481	1c	green	3.25		.40
		On cover			20.00
		Guide line or pasteup pair	6.50		
482	2c	carmine, type I	4.50		.60
		On cover			15.00
		Guide line or pasteup pair	8.50		
		Aniline ink ("pink back")			—

Earliest documented use: Dec. 16, 1916.

No.		Description	2mm	3mm	Used Single
482A	2c	deep rose, type Ia, single			50,000.
		Pair			110,000.
		On cover			55,000.
483	3c	violet, type I	11.00		2.75
		On cover			100.00
		Guide line or pasteup pair	19.00		

Earliest documented use: Nov 2, 1917.

No.		Description	2mm	3mm	Used Single
484	3c	violet, type II	16.00		4.50
		On cover			75.00
		Guide line or pasteup pair	30.00		

Earliest documented use: April 5, 1918.

On Issue of 1918-20

No.		Description	2mm	3mm	Used Single
531	1c	green	15.00		4.50
		On cover			100.00
		Guide line or pasteup pair	30.00		
532	2c	carmine, type IV	40.00		3.50
		On cover			75.00
		Guide line or pasteup pair	80.00		

No.		Description	2mm	3mm	Used Single
		Pasteup strip of 4, left pair No. 532, right pair No. 482		1,900.	

Earliest documented use: April 28, 1920.

No.		Description	2mm	3mm	Used Single
533	2c	carmine, type V		350.00	45.00
		On cover			250.00
		Guide line or pasteup pair		1,000.	
534	2c	carmine, type Va		25.00	2.25
		On cover			90.00
		Guide line or pasteup pair		55.00	
534A	2c	carmine, type VI		45.00	4.50
		On cover			75.00
		Guide line or pasteup pair		90.00	

Earliest documented use: Aug. 31, 1920.

No.		Description	2mm	3mm	Used Single
534B	2c	carmine, type VII		1,200.	85.00
		On cover			425.00
		Guide line or pasteup pair		2,000.	
535	3c	violet, type IV		20.00	3.50
		On cover			75.00
		Guide line or pasteup pair		40.00	

On Issue of 1923-26

No.		Description	2mm	3mm	Used Single
575	1c	green		200.00	6.75
		Unused single		22.50	
		On cover			400.00
		Guide line or pasteup pair		375.00	
		Precanceled		4.50	1.25
		On cover, precanceled			100.00
576	1½c	yellow brown		22.50	4.50
		On cover			200.00
		Guide line or pasteup pair		40.00	
		Precanceled		4.50	1.00
		On cover, precanceled			75.00
577	2c	carmine	27.50	22.50	1.25
		On cover			20.00
		Guide line or pasteup pair	50.00	40.00	

On Harding Issue of 1923

No.		Description	2mm	3mm	Used Single
611	2c	black		95.00	17.50
		On cover			7,500.
		Guide line or pasteup pair		160.00	

U.S. AUTOMATIC VENDING COMPANY

New York, N.Y.

Separations Type I

Cut into strips and joined before being perforated.

Two varieties exist: 15½ and 16mm between notches of the perforations.

On Issue of 1906-08
Coiled Endwise

No.		Description	Unused Pair	Used Single
314	1c	blue green	50.00	12.50
		On cover		1,900.
		Guide line or pasteup pair	95.00	
320	2c	carmine	45.00	9.00
		On cover		3,500.
		Guide line pair	90.00	
		Pasteup pair	80.00	
*320a	2c	lake	100.00	9.00
		Guide line or pasteup pair	200.00	
320b	2c	scarlet	55.00	8.00
		On cover		3,500.
		Guide line pair	110.00	
315	5c	blue	750.00	—
		On cover		10,000.

No.		Description	Unused Pair	Used Single
		Guide line pair	2,500.	
		Pasteup pair	2,750.	

On Issue of 1908-09
Coiled Endwise

No.		Description	Unused Pair	Used Single
343	1c	green	11.00	
		On cover		10
		On postcard		6
		Guide line or pasteup	22.00	
344	2c	carmine	9.00	
		On cover		10
		Guide line or pasteup	17.50	
*345	3c	deep violet	32.50	9
		On cover		500
		Guide line or pasteup pair	65.00	
*346	4c	orange brown	50.00	10
		Guide line or pasteup pair	105.00	
347	5c	blue	90.00	
		On cover		2,2
		On cover (pair) with No. 373 USAV type II pair		7,5
		Guide line or pasteup pair	175.00	

On Lincoln Issue of 1909

No.		Description	Unused Pair	Used Single
368	2c	carmine, coiled endwise	40.00	8
		On cover		500
		First day cover, *Feb. 12, 1909*		14,5
		Guide line or pasteup pair	80.00	

On Alaska-Yukon Issue of 1909

No.		Description	Unused Pair	Used Single
*371	2c	carmine, coiled sideways	80.00	12
		On cover		500
		Guide line pair	150.00	
		Type Ia, No T. and B. margins	140.00	17.
		Type Ia, Guide line or pasteup pair	225.00	

Type Ia stamps are a deep shade and have a misplaced position dot in the "S" of "Postage." Beware of trimmed copies No. 371 type I.

On Issue of 1910

No.		Description	Unused Pair	Used Single
383	1c	green	6.50	2.
		On cover		100.
		On postcard		40.
		Guide line or pasteup pair	11.00	
*384	2c	carmine	22.50	5.
		Guide line pair	40.00	

On Issue of 1912

No.		Description	Unused Pair	Used Single
*408	1c	green	11.00	2.
		Guide line pair	19.00	
*409	2c	carmine	14.00	4.
		Guide line pair	22.50	

Separations Type II

Similar to Type I but with notches farther apart and a longer slit. Cut into strips and joined before being perforated.

No.		Description	2mm	3mm	Used Single
		On Issue of 1906-08 — Coiled Sideways			
*314	1c	blue green	50.00		9.00
		On cover			
		Guide line or pasteup	82.50		
*320	2c	carmine	87.50		
		Guide line pair	120.00		
*320b	2c	scarlet	60.00		5.50
		Guide line pair	100.00		
*315	5c	blue	1,400.		
		Guide line pair	2,500.		

On Issue of 1908-09

No.		Description	2mm	3mm	Used Single
343	1c	green	14.00		3.50
		On cover			1,000.
		Guide line or pasteup pair	22.50		
344	2c	carmine	16.00		
		On cover			2,500.
		Guide line pair	25.00		
*345	3c	deep violet	65.00		—
		Guide line pair	110.00		
*346	4c	orange brown	95.00	82.50	
		Guide line pair	160.00		
*347	5c	blue	190.00		
		Guide line pair	300.00		

			Unused Pair Spacing		Used
			2mm	3mm	Single

On Lincoln Issue of 1909

| 68 | 2c | carmine | 100.00 | 87.50 | 22.50 |
| | | Guide line pair | 175.00 | | |

On Alaska-Yukon Issue of 1909

371	2c	carmine	75.00		40.00
		On cover			500.00
		Guide line or pasteup pair	130.00		

On Hudson-Fulton Issue of 1909

373	2c	carmine	80.00		17.50
		On cover			2,000.
		Guide line or pasteup pair	150.00		

See No. 347 USAV type I for combination cover.

On Issue of 1910

83	1c	green	16.00	12.50	
		On cover			1,000.
		Guide line pair	27.50		
84	2c	carmine	22.50	16.00	
		On cover			2,500.
		Guide line pair	40.00		

On Issue of 1912

408	1c	green	11.00		2.25
		On cover			1,500.
		Guide line pair	19.00		
409	2c	carmine	16.00		4.50
		Guide line pair	27.50		

Perforations Type III

Cut into strips and joined before being perforated.

On Issue of 1906-08

*314	1c	blue green	55.00	12.50
		Guide line pair	100.00	
*320	2c	carmine	100.00	
*320b	2c	scarlet	65.00	12.50
		Guide line pair	110.00	
*315	5c	blue	1,200.	
		Guide line or pasteup pair	2,500.	

On Issue of 1908-09

343	1c	green	27.50	25.00	5.50
		Guide line or pasteup pair	45.00		
344	2c	carmine	27.50	35.00	5.50
		Guide line pair	45.00		
*345	3c	deep violet	110.00		
		Guide line pair	190.00		
*346	4c	orange brown	110.00	100.00	14.00
		Guide line pair	190.00		
*347	5c	blue	140.00		
		Guide line pair	250.00		

On Lincoln Issue of 1909

*368	2c	carmine	70.00	60.00	19.00
		Guide line pair	120.00		
		Experimental perf. 12.3	3,250.		
		Guide line pair	5,500.		

On Alaska-Yukon Issue of 1909

*371	2c	carmine	90.00	19.00
		On cover		—
		Guide line or pasteup pair	140.00	

On Hudson-Fulton Issue of 1909

*373	2c	carmine	100.00	19.00
		On cover		—
		Guide line or pasteup pair	140.00	

On Issue of 1910

383	1c	green	15.00	13.00	2.75
		Guide line pair	25.00		
384	2c	carmine	17.50	15.00	2.75
		Guide line pair	27.50		

On Issue of 1912

408	1c	green	10.00	
		Guide line pair	16.00	
409	2c	carmine	17.50	
		Guide line pair	25.00	
		Pasteup pair	25.00	

On 1914 Rotary Press Coil

| 459 | 2c | carmine | 27,500. | 11,500. |

This firm also produced coil strips of manila paper, folded so as to form small "pockets", each "pocket" containing one 1c stamp and two 2c stamps, usually imperforate but occasionally with either government or U.S.A.V. private perforations. The manila "pockets" were perforated type II, coiled sideways. They fit U.S.A.V. ticket vending machines. Multiples exist. Values are for "pockets" with known combinations of stamps, listed by basic Scott Number. Other combinations exist, but

are not listed due to the fact that the stamps may have been added at a later date.

Pocket Type 1 (1908)
("Patents Pending" on front and green advertising on reverse)

| Type 1-1 | 314 + 320 | 2,750. |
| Type 1-2 | 314 + 320b | 2,750. |

Pocket Type 2 (1909)
("Patents Applied For" Handstamped in greenish blue)

Type 2-1	343 + 371	1,500.
Type 2-2	343 + 372	900.
Type 2-3	343 (USAV Type I) + 371	2,000.
Type 2-4	343 + 375	900.

Pocket Type 3 (1909)
("Patents Pending" printed in red)

Type 3-1	347 + 371	1,000.
Type 3-1A	343 + 372	1,000.
Type 3-2	343 + 373	800.
Type 3-3	343 + 375	800.
Type 3-4	383 + 406	800.

Pocket Type 4 (1909)
(No printing on front, serial number on back)

Type 4-1	343 + 344	300.
Type 4-2	343 + 368	300.
Type 4-3	343 + 371	300.
Type 4-4	383 + 344	300.
Type 4-5	383 (USAV Type II) + 344	300.
Type 4-6	383 + 384	300.
Type 4-7	383 + 406	300.

THE ATTLEBORO STAMP COMPANY

Attleboro, Mass.

This Company used an affixing machine to stamp its newsletters during the summer and fall of 1909.

Nos. 343-344

No. 371

			Unused Pair	Used Single
		On Issue of 1908-09		
343	1c	green	1,400.	1,000.
		On Attleboro Philatelist wrapper		5,000.
		On cover		19,000.
		Guide line or pasteup pair	2,500.	
344	2c	carmine	45,000.	
		The No. 344 pair is unique.		
		On Alaska-Yukon Issue of 1909		
371	2c	carmine, coiled sidewise	3,500.	1,100.
		Guide line or pasteup pair	5,500.	—
		On wrapper or cover		8,000.

IMPERFORATE FLAT PLATE COIL STAMPS

These flat plate imperforate coil stamps were made from imperforate sheets of the regular issues, and were issued in coils of 500 or 1,000. Th[e] numbers assigned below are those of the regularly issued imperforate sheet stamps to which "H" or "V" has been added to indicate that the stamps a[re] coiled horizontally (side by side), or vertically (top to bottom). These coil stamps are virtually indistinguishable from the corresponding imperforate she[et] stamps, although they can be authenticated, particularly when in strips of four or longer. Many genuine imperforate coil stamps bear authenticati[ng] signatures of contemporaneous experts.

Values for stamps on cover are for single stamps.

FLAT PLATE PRINTING

1908 — Wmk. 191 — Imperf.

314V A115 1c **blue green,** pair, never hinged	—	—
Strip of 4	—	
Guide line pair	—	
Guide line strip of 4	—	

The Philatelic Foundation has certified one unused No. 314V pair (with coil leader strip attached). The existence of any of the other listed items has been questioned by specialists. The editors would like to see certified evidence of the other listings.

314H A115 1c **blue green,** pair	2,100.	—
Never hinged	3,750.	
On cover		1,300.
Pair on cover	—	2,000.
Strip of 4	—	
Never hinged	8,000.	
Guide line pair	5,000.	
Guide line strip of 4	8,000.	
Pasteup pair	3,500.	
Never hinged	5,500.	
Pasteup strip of 4	5,000.	
Never hinged	8,000.	

Earliest documented use: Mar. 9, 1908.

320V A129 2c **carmine,** pair	1,500.	—
On cover		—
Strip of 4	—	—
Guide line pair	—	
Guide line strip of 4	—	

Earliest documented use: Apr. 9, 1908.

320H A129 2c **carmine,** pair	500.00	—
Strip of 4	—	—
Guide line pair	—	
Guide line strip of 4	—	

Earliest documented use: Sept. 17, 1908.

1908-10 — Imperf.

343V A138 1c **green,** pair	25.00	8.50
Never hinged	40.00	
On cover		10.00
Strip of 4	60.00	—
Guide line pair	60.00	
Guide line strip of 4	85.00	
Pasteup pair	50.00	

Earliest documented use: May 24, 1910.

343H A138 1c **green,** pair	50.00	—
Never hinged	80.00	
Strip of 4	120.00	—
Guide line pair	100.00	
Guide line strip of 4	250.00	
Pasteup pair	80.00	
344V A139 2c **carmine,** pair	30.00	25.00
Never hinged	50.00	
On cover		15.00
Strip of 4	75.00	—
Guide line pair	60.00	—
Guide line strip of 4	105.00	
Pasteup pair	60.00	
Foreign entry, design of 1c	2,500.	3,000.
Never hinged	3,500.	

Earliest documented use: Oct. 13, 1909.

344H A139 2c **carmine,** pair (2mm spacing)	35.00	25.00
Never hinged	55.00	
On cover		—
Strip of 4	90.00	
Guide line pair	80.00	
Guide line strip of 4	140.00	
Pasteup pair	60.00	
Pair (3mm spacing)	40.00	—
Strip of 4	100.00	
Guide line pair	85.00	—
Guide line strip of 4	150.00	

Earliest documented use: March 23, 1909.

345H A140 3c **deep violet,** type I, pair	160.00	
346V A140 4c **orange brown,** pair	125.00	
Never hinged	250.00	
Strip of 4	375.00	—
Never hinged	650.00	
Guide line pair	325.00	75.00
Guide line strip of 4	700.00	
Pasteup pair	250.00	

Earliest documented use: Feb. 18, 1911.

347V A140 5c **blue,** pair	175.00	—
Never hinged	275.00	
On cover		—
Strip of 4	425.00	—
Never hinged	700.00	
Guide line pair	375.00	—
Guide line strip of 4	600.00	

Earliest documented use: April 17, 1909.

1909 — Imperf.

368V A141 2c **carmine,** *Lincoln,* pair	200.00	—
Never hinged	300.00	—
On cover		—
Strip of 4	500.00	—
Never hinged	750.00	
Guide line pair	400.00	
Never hinged	650.00	
Guide line strip of 4	800.00	
Never hinged	1,250.	
Pasteup pair	300.00	
Never hinged	475.00	

Earliest documented use: Feb. 12, 1909.

368H A141 2c **carmine,** *Lincoln,* pair	275.00	
Never hinged	450.00	
On cover		—
Strip of 4	700.00	
Never hinged	1,050.	
Guide line pair	525.00	
Never hinged	900.00	
Guide line strip of 4	900.00	
Pasteup pair	425.00	
Never hinged	650.00	

Earliest documented use: Dec. 9, 1909.

1910 — Wmk. 190 — Imperf.

383V A138 1c **green,** pair	12.00	—
Never hinged	20.00	
On cover		6.00
Strip of 4	27.50	—
Guide line pair	25.00	—
Never hinged	40.00	
Guide line strip of 4	60.00	—
Never hinged	95.00	
Pasteup pair	20.00	
Never hinged	35.00	
Double transfer	—	—

Earliest documented use: Apr. 13, 1911.

383H A138 1c **green,** pair (2mm spacing)	17.50	—
Never hinged	28.00	
Strip of 4	42.50	—
Never hinged	65.00	
Guide line pair	35.00	—
Never hinged	55.00	
Guide line strip of 4	65.00	—
Never hinged	110.00	
Pasteup pair	30.00	
Pair (3mm spacing)	17.50	—
Never hinged	28.00	
Strip of 4	42.50	—
Never hinged	65.00	
Guide line pair	35.00	—
Never hinged	55.00	
Guide line strip of 4	65.00	—
Never hinged	110.00	
384V A139 2c **carmine,** pair	14.00	—
Never hinged	24.00	
On cover		7.00
Strip of 4	30.00	—
Guide line pair	30.00	—
Guide line strip of 4	55.00	—
Pasteup pair	22.50	
Foreign entry, design of 1c	1,500.	—

Earliest documented use: Oct. 21, 1910.

384H A139 2c **carmine,** pair (2mm spacing)	27.50	—
Never hinged	45.00	
Strip of 4	70.00	—
Guide line pair	60.00	—
Guide line strip of 4	105.00	—
Pasteup pair	50.00	
Pair (3mm spacing)	25.00	—
Strip of 4	70.00	—
Guide line pair	55.00	—
Guide line strip of 4	100.00	—

Earliest documented use: Mar. 9, 1912.

1912 — Wmk. 190 — Imperf.

408V A140 1c **green,** pair	4.00	
Never hinged	7.00	
On cover		—
Strip of 4	8.50	
Guide line pair	9.00	
Guide line strip of 4	14.00	
Pasteup pair	7.00	

Earliest documented use: May 17, 1912.

408H A140 1c **green,** pair	5.00	
Never hinged	8.00	
Strip of 4	12.00	
Guide line pair	10.00	
Guide line strip of 4	17.50	
409V A140 2c **carmine,** pair	4.00	
Never hinged	7.00	
Strip of 4	9.00	
Never hinged	15.00	
Guide line pair	8.00	

Never hinged	15.00	
Guide line strip of 4	14.00	
Pasteup pair	7.00	

Earliest documented use: May 29, 1912.

409H A140 2c **carmine,** pair	6.00	
Never hinged	10.00	
Strip of 4	14.00	
Guide line pair	9.00	
Never hinged	16.00	
Guide line strip of 4	15.00	
Pasteup pair	7.00	
Double transfer	7.00	

Earliest documented use: Dec. 17, 1914.

COMMEMORATIVE STAMPS, QUANTITIES ISSUED

Quantities issued fall into four categories. First are stamps where reasonably accurate counts are made of the number of copies sold.
Second are stamps where the counts are approximations of the number sold.
Third are stamps where the count is of quantities shipped to post offices and philatelic sales units, but no adjustments are made for returned or destroyed copies.
Fourth are stamps for which the quantity printed is furnished but no other adjustments are made.
Occasionally more accurate figures are determined. In these cases the quantities here will be adjusted. For example, it is now known that while ,000,000 sets of the Voyages of Columbus souvenir sheets were printed, the number sold was 1,185,170 sets.

Scott No.	Quantity	Scott No.	Quantity	Scott No.	Quantity	Scott No.	Quantity
230	449,195,550	675	980,000			783	74,407,450
231	1,464,588,750	676	850,000			784	269,522,200
232	11,501,250	677	1,480,000			785	105,196,150
233	19,181,550	678	530,000			786	93,848,500
234	35,248,250	679	1,890,000			787	87,741,150
235	4,707,550	680	29,338,274			788	35,794,150
236	10,656,550	681	32,680,900			789	36,839,250
237	16,516,950	682	74,000,774			790	104,773,450
238	1,576,950	683	25,215,574			791	92,054,550
239	617,250	688	25,609,470			792	93,291,650
240	243,750	689	66,487,000			793	34,552,950
241	55,050	690	96,559,400			794	36,819,050
242	45,550	702	99,074,600			795	84,825,250
243	27,650	703	25,006,400			796	25,040,400
244	26,350	704	87,969,700			797	5,277,445
245	27,350	705	1,265,555,100			798	99,882,300
285	70,993,400	706	304,926,800			799	78,454,450
286	159,720,800	707	4,222,198,300			800	77,004,200
287	4,924,500	708	456,198,500			801	81,292,450
288	7,694,180	709	151,201,300			802	76,474,550
289	2,927,200	710	170,565,100			835	73,043,650
290	4,629,760	711	111,739,400			836	58,564,368
291	530,400	712	83,257,400			837	65,939,500
292	56,900	713	96,506,100			838	47,064,300
293	56,200	714	75,709,200			852	114,439,600
294	91,401,500	715	147,216,000			853	101,699,550
295	209,759,700	716	51,102,800			854	72,764,550
296	5,737,100	717	100,869,300			855	81,269,600
297	7,201,300	718	168,885,300			856	67,813,350
298	4,921,700	719	52,376,100			857	71,394,750
299	5,043,700	724	49,949,000			858	66,835,000
323	79,779,200	725	49,538,500			859	56,348,320
324	192,732,400	726	61,719,200			860	53,177,110
325	4,542,600	727	73,382,400			861	53,260,270
326	6,926,700	728	348,266,800			862	22,104,950
327	4,011,200	729	480,239,300			863	13,201,270
328	77,728,794	730	(sheet of 25)	456,704		864	51,603,580
329	149,497,994	730a		11,417,600		865	52,100,510
330	7,980,594	731	(sheet of 25)	441,172		866	51,666,580
367	148,387,191	731a		11,029,300		867	22,207,780
368	1,273,900	732	1,978,707,300			868	11,835,530
369	637,000	733	5,735,944			869	52,471,160
370	152,887,311	734	45,137,700			870	52,366,440
371	525,400	735	(sheet of 6)	811,404		871	51,636,270
372	72,634,631	735a		4,868,424		872	20,729,030
373	216,480	736	46,258,300			873	14,125,580
397 & 401	334,796,926	737	193,239,100			874	59,409,000
398 & 402	503,713,086	738	15,432,200			875	57,888,600
399 & 403	29,088,726	739	64,525,400			876	58,273,180
400 & 404	16,968,365	740	84,896,350			877	23,779,000
537	99,585,200	741	74,400,200			878	15,112,580
548	137,978,207	742	95,089,000			879	57,322,790
549	196,037,327	743	19,178,650			880	58,281,580
550	11,321,607	744	30,980,100			881	56,398,790
610	1,459,487,085	745	16,923,350			882	21,147,000
611	770,000	746	15,988,250			883	13,328,000
612	99,950,300	747	15,288,700			884	54,389,510
614	51,378,023	748	17,472,600			885	53,636,580
615	77,753,423	749	18,874,300			886	55,313,230
616	5,659,023	750	(sheet of 6)	511,391		887	21,720,580
617	15,615,000	750a		3,068,346		888	13,600,580
618	26,596,600	751	(sheet of 6)	793,551		889	47,599,580
619	5,348,800	751a		4,761,306		890	53,766,510
620	9,104,983	752	3,274,556			891	54,193,580
621	1,900,983	753	2,040,760			892	20,264,580
627	307,731,900	754	2,389,288			893	13,726,580
628	20,280,500	755	2,294,948			894	46,497,400
629	40,639,485	756	3,217,636			895	47,700,000
630	(sheet of 25)	107,398	757	2,746,640		896	50,618,150
643	39,974,900	758	2,168,088			897	50,034,400
644	25,628,450	759	1,822,684			898	60,943,700
645	101,330,328	760	1,724,576			902	44,389,550
646	9,779,896	761	1,647,696			903	54,574,550
647	5,519,897	762	1,682,948			904	63,558,400
648	1,459,897	763	1,638,644			906	21,272,800
649	51,342,273	764	1,625,224			907	1,671,564,200
650	10,319,700	765	1,644,900			908	1,227,334,200
651	16,684,674	766	(pane of 25)	98,712		909	19,999,646
654	31,679,200	766a		2,467,800		910	19,999,646
655	210,119,474	767	(pane of 25)	85,914		911	19,999,646
656	133,530,000	767a		2,147,850		912	19,999,646
657	51,451,880	768	(pane of 6)	267,200		913	19,999,646
658	13,390,000	768a		1,603,200		914	19,999,646
659	8,240,000	769	(pane of 6)	279,960		915	19,999,646
660	87,410,000	769a		1,679,760		916	14,999,646
661	2,540,000	770	(pane of 6)	215,920		917	14,999,646
662	2,290,000	770a		1,295,520		918	14,999,646
663	2,700,000	771	1,370,560			919	14,999,646
664	1,450,000	772	70,726,800			920	14,999,646
665	1,320,000	773	100,839,600			921	14,999,646
666	1,530,000	774	73,610,650			922	61,303,000
667	1,130,000	775	75,823,900			923	61,001,450
668	2,860,000	776	124,324,500			924	60,605,000
669	8,220,000	777	67,127,650			925	50,129,350
670	8,990,000	778	(sheet of 4)	2,809,039		926	53,479,400
671	73,220,000	778a		2,809,039		927	61,617,350
672	2,110,000	778b		2,809,039		928	75,500,000
673	1,600,000	778c		2,809,039		929	137,321,000
674	1,860,000	778d		2,809,039		930	128,140,000
		782	72,992,650			931	67,255,000

Scott No.	Quantity	Scott No.	Quantity	Scott No.	Quantity
932	133,870,000	1079	109,275,000	1199	126,515,00
933	76,455,400	1080	112,932,200	1200	130,960,00
934	128,357,750	1081	125,475,000	1201	120,055,00
935	138,863,000	1082	117,855,000	1202	120,715,00
936	111,616,700	1083	122,100,000	1203	121,440,00
937	308,587,700	1084	118,180,000	1204	40,270,00
938	170,640,000	1085	100,975,000	1205	861,970,00
939	135,927,000	1086	115,299,450	1206	120,035,00
940	260,339,100	1087	186,949,627	1207	117,870,00
941	132,274,500	1088	115,235,000	1230	129,945,00
942	132,430,000	1089	106,647,500	1231	135,620,00
943	139,209,500	1090	112,010,000	1232	137,540,00
944	114,684,450	1091	118,470,000	1233	132,435,00
945	156,540,510	1092	102,230,000	1234	135,520,00
946	120,452,600	1093	102,410,000	1235	131,420,00
947	127,104,300	1094	84,054,400	1236	133,170,00
948	10,299,600	1095	126,266,000	1237	130,195,00
949	132,902,000	1096	39,489,600	1238	120,450,00
950	131,968,000	1097	122,990,000	1239	118,665,00
951	131,488,000	1098	174,372,800	1240	1,291,250,00
952	122,362,000	1099	114,365,000	1241	175,175,00
953	121,548,000	1100	122,765,200	1242	125,995,00
954	131,109,500	1104	113,660,200	1243	128,025,00
955	122,650,500	1105	120,196,580	1244	145,700,00
956	121,953,500	1106	120,805,200	1245	120,310,00
957	115,250,000	1107	125,815,000	1246	511,750,00
958	64,198,500	1108	108,415,200	1247	123,845,00
959	117,642,500	1109	107,195,200	1248	122,825,00
960	77,649,600	1110	115,745,280	1249	453,090,00
961	113,474,500	1111	39,743,640	1250	123,245,00
962	120,868,500	1112	114,570,200	1251	123,355,00
963	77,800,500	1113	120,400,200	1252	126,970,00
964	52,214,000	1114	91,160,200	1253	121,250,00
965	53,958,100	1115	114,860,200	1254-1257	1,407,760,00
966	61,120,010	1116	126,500,000	1258	120,005,00
967	57,823,000	1117	120,561,280	1259	125,800,00
968	52,975,000	1118	44,064,576	1260	122,230,00
969	77,149,000	1119	118,390,200	1261	115,695,00
970	58,332,000	1120	125,770,200	1262	115,095,000
971	56,228,000	1121	114,114,280	1263	119,560,000
972	57,832,000	1122	156,600,200	1264	125,180,000
973	53,875,000	1123	124,200,200	1265	120,135,000
974	63,834,000	1124	120,740,200	1266	115,405,000
975	67,162,200	1125	133,623,280	1267	115,855,000
976	64,561,000	1126	45,569,088	1268	115,340,000
977	64,079,500	1127	122,493,280	1269	114,840,000
978	63,388,000	1128	131,260,200	1270	116,140,000
979	62,285,000	1129	47,125,200	1271	116,900,000
980	57,492,610	1130	123,105,000	1272	114,085,000
981	99,190,000	1131	126,105,050	1273	114,880,000
982	104,790,000	1132	209,170,000	1274	26,995,000
983	108,805,000	1133	120,835,000	1275	128,495,000
984	107,340,000	1134	115,715,000	1276	1,139,930,000
985	117,020,000	1135	118,445,000	1306	116,835,000
986	122,633,000	1136	111,685,000	1307	117,470,000
987	130,960,000	1137	43,099,200	1308	123,770,000
988	128,478,000	1138	115,444,000	1309	131,270,000
989	132,090,000	1139	126,470,000	1310	122,285,000
990	130,050,000	1140	124,560,000	1311	14,680,000
991	131,350,000	1141	115,455,000	1312	114,160,000
992	129,980,000	1142	122,060,000	1313	128,475,000
993	122,315,000	1143	120,540,000	1314	119,535,000
994	122,170,000	1144	113,075,000	1315	125,110,000
995	131,635,000	1145	139,325,000	1316	114,853,200
996	121,860,000	1146	124,445,000	1317	124,290,000
997	121,120,000	1147	113,792,000	1318	128,460,000
998	119,120,000	1148	44,215,200	1319	127,585,000
999	112,125,000	1149	113,195,000	1320	115,875,000
1000	114,140,000	1150	121,805,000	1321	1,173,547,420
1001	114,490,000	1151	115,353,000	1322	114,015,000
1002	117,200,000	1152	111,080,000	1323	121,105,000
1003	116,130,000	1153	153,025,000	1324	132,045,000
1004	116,175,000	1154	119,665,000	1325	118,780,000
1005	115,945,000	1155	117,855,000	1326	121,985,000
1006	112,540,000	1156	118,185,000	1327	111,850,000
1007	117,415,000	1157	112,260,000	1328	117,225,000
1008	2,899,580,000	1158	125,010,000	1329	111,515,000
1009	114,540,000	1159	119,798,000	1330	114,270,000
1010	113,135,000	1160	42,696,000	1331-1332	120,865,000
1011	116,255,000	1161	106,610,000	1333	110,675,000
1012	113,860,000	1162	109,695,000	1334	110,670,000
1013	124,260,000	1163	123,690,000	1335	113,825,000
1014	115,735,000	1164	123,970,000	1336	1,208,700,000
1015	115,430,000	1165	124,796,000	1337	113,330,000
1016	136,220,000	1166	42,076,800	1339	141,350,000
1017	114,894,600	1167	116,210,000	1340	144,345,000
1018	118,706,000	1168	126,252,000	1342	147,120,000
1019	114,190,000	1169	42,746,400	1343	130,125,000
1020	113,990,000	1170	124,117,000	1344	158,700,000
1021	89,289,600	1171	119,840,000	1345-1354	228,040,000
1022	114,865,000	1172	117,187,000	1355	153,015,000
1023	115,780,000	1173	124,390,000	1356	132,560,000
1024	115,244,600	1174	112,966,000	1357	130,385,000
1025	123,709,600	1175	41,644,200	1358	132,265,000
1026	114,789,600	1176	110,850,000	1359	128,710,000
1027	115,759,600	1177	98,616,000	1360	124,775,000
1028	116,134,600	1178	101,125,000	1361	128,295,000
1029	118,540,000	1179	124,865,000	1362	142,245,000
1060	115,810,000	1180	79,905,000	1363	1,410,580,000
1061	113,603,700	1181	125,410,000	1364	125,100,000
1062	128,002,000	1182	112,845,000	1365-1368	192,570,000
1063	116,078,150	1183	106,210,000	1369	148,770,000
1064	116,139,800	1184	110,810,000	1370	139,475,000
1065	120,484,800	1185	116,995,000	1371	187,165,000
1066	53,854,750	1186	121,015,000	1372	125,555,000
1067	176,075,000	1187	111,600,000	1373	144,425,000
1068	125,944,400	1188	110,620,000	1374	135,875,000
1069	122,284,600	1189	109,110,000	1375	151,110,000
1070	133,638,850	1190	145,350,000	1376-1379	159,195,000
1071	118,664,600	1191	112,870,000	1380	129,540,000
1072	112,434,000	1192	121,820,000	1381	130,925,000
1073	129,384,550	1193	289,240,000	1382	139,055,000
1074	121,184,600	1194	120,155,000	1383	150,611,200
1075	2,900,731	1195	124,595,000	1384	1,709,795,000
1076	119,784,200	1196	147,310,000	1385	127,545,000
1077	123,159,400	1197	118,690,000	1386	145,788,800
1078	123,138,800	1198	122,730,000	1387-1390	201,794,200

Scott No.	Quantity	Scott No.	Quantity	Scott No.	Quantity
391	171,850,000	1690	164,890,000	2031	118,555,000
392	142,205,000	1691-1694	208,035,000	2032-2035	226,128,000
405	137,660,000	1695-1698	185,715,000	2036	118,225,000
406	135,125,000	1699	130,592,000	2037	114,290,000
407	135,895,000	1700	158,332,800	2038	165,000,000
408	132,675,000	1701	809,955,000	2039	120,430,000
409	134,795,000	1702-1703	963,370,000	2040	117,025,000
410-1413	161,600,000	1704	150,328,000	2041	181,700,000
414-1414a	683,730,000	1705	176,830,000	2042	114,250,000
415-1418,		1706-1709	195,976,000	2043	111,775,000
1415a-1418a	489,255,000	1710	208,820,000	2044	115,200,000
419	127,610,000	1711	192,250,000	2045	108,820,000
420	129,785,000	1712-1715	219,830,000	2046	184,950,000
421-1422	134,380,000	1716	159,852,000	2047	110,925,000
423	136,305,000	1717-1720	188,310,000	2048-2051	395,424,000
424	134,840,000	1721	163,625,000	2052	104,340,000
425	130,975,000	1722	156,296,000	2053	114,725,000
426	161,235,000	1723-1724	158,676,000	2054	112,525,000
427-1430	175,679,600	1725	154,495,000	2055-2058	193,055,000
431	138,700,000	1726	168,050,000	2059-2062	207,725,000
432	138,165,000	1727	156,810,000	2063	715,975,000
433	152,125,000	1728	153,736,000	2064	848,525,000
434-1435	176,295,000	1729	882,260,000	2065	165,000,000
436	142,845,000	1730	921,530,000	2066	120,000,000
437	148,755,000	1731	156,560,000	2067-2070	319,675,000
438	139,080,000	1732-1733	202,155,000	2071	103,975,000
439	130,755,000	1744	156,525,000	2072	554,675,000
440-1443	170,208,000	1745-1748	165,182,400	2073	120,000,000
444	1,074,350,000	1749-1752	157,598,400	2074	106,975,000
445	979,540,000	1753	102,856,000	2075	107,325,000
446	137,355,000	1754	152,270,000	2076-2079	306,912,000
447	150,400,000	1755	94,600,000	2080	120,000,000
448-1451	172,730,000	1756	151,570,000	2081	108,000,000
452	104,090,000	1757	15,170,400	2082-2085	313,350,000
453	164,096,000	1758	161,228,000	2086	130,320,000
454	53,920,000	1759	158,880,000	2087	120,000,000
455	153,025,000	1760-1763	186,550,000	2088	117,050,000
456-1459	201,890,000	1764-1767	168,136,000	2089	115,725,000
460	67,335,000	1768	963,120,000	2090	116,600,000
461	179,675,000	1769	916,800,000	2091	120,000,000
462	46,340,000	1770	159,297,600	2092	123,575,000
463	180,155,000	1771	166,435,000	2093	120,000,000
464-1467	198,364,800	1772	162,535,000	2094	117,125,000
468	185,490,000	1773	155,000,000	2095	117,225,000
469	162,335,000	1774	157,310,000	2096	95,525,000
470	162,789,950	1775-1778	174,096,000	2097	119,125,000
471	1,003,475,000	1779-1782	164,793,600	2098-2101	216,260,000
472	1,017,025,000	1783-1786	163,055,000	2102	120,000,000
473	165,895,000	1787	161,860,000	2103	108,140,000
474	166,508,000	1788	165,775,000	2104	117,625,000
475	320,055,000	1789	160,000,000	2105	112,896,000
476	166,005,000	1790	67,195,000	2106	116,500,000
477	163,050,000	1791-1794	186,905,000	2107	751,300,000
478	159,005,000	1795-1798	208,295,000	2108	786,225,000
479	147,295,000	1799	873,710,000	2109	105,300,000
480-1483	196,275,000	1800	931,880,000	2110	124,500,000
484	139,152,000	1801	161,290,000	2137	120,000,000
485	128,048,000	1802	172,740,000	2138-2141	300,000,000
486	146,008,000	1803	168,995,000	2142	120,580,000
487	139,608,000	1804	160,000,000	2143	729,700,000
488	159,475,000	1805-1810	232,134,000	2144	124,750,000
489-1498	486,020,000	1821	163,510,000	2145	203,496,000
499	157,052,800	1822	256,620,000	2146	126,325,000
500	53,005,000	1823	95,695,000	2147	130,000,000
501	159,775,000	1824	153,975,000	2152	119,975,000
502	39,005,000	1825	160,000,000	2153	120,000,000
503	152,624,000	1826	103,850,000	2154	119,975,000
504	145,840,000	1827-1830	204,715,000	2155-2158	147,940,000
505	151,335,000	1831	166,545,000	2159	120,000,000
506	141,085,000	1832	163,310,000	2160-2163	130,000,000
507	885,160,000	1833	160,000,000	2164	120,000,000
508	939,835,000	1834-1837	152,404,000	2165	759,200,000
525	143,930,000	1838-1841	152,420,000	2166	757,600,000
526	145,235,000	1842	692,500,000	2198-2201	67,996,800
527	135,052,000	1843	718,715,000	2202	947,450,000
528	156,750,000	1874	160,155,000	2203	130,000,000
529	164,670,000	1875	159,505,000	2204	136,500,000
530-1537	190,156,800	1876-1879	210,633,000	2205-2209	219,990,000
538-1541	167,212,800	1910	165,175,000	2210	130,000,000
542	156,265,000	1911	107,240,000	2211	130,000,000
543-1546	195,585,000	1912-1919	337,819,000	2216	5,825,050
547	148,850,000	1920	99,420,000	2217	5,825,050
548	157,270,000	1921-1924	178,930,000	2218	5,825,050
549	150,245,000	1925	100,265,000	2219	5,825,050
550	835,180,000	1926	99,615,000	2220-2223	130,000,000
551	882,520,000	1927	97,535,000	2224	220,725,000
552	213,155,000	1928-1931	167,308,000	2235-2238	240,525,000
553	156,995,000	1932	101,625,000	2239	131,700,000
554	146,365,000	1922	99,170,000	2240-2243	240,000,000
555	148,805,000	1934	101,155,000	2244	690,100,000
556	173,685,000	1935	101,200,000	2245	882,150,000
557	158,600,000	1936	167,360,000	2246	167,430,000
558	153,355,000	1937-1938	162,420,000	2247	166,555,000
559	63,205,000	1939	597,720,000	2248	811,560,000
560	157,865,000	1940	792,600,000	2249	142,905,000
561	166,810,000	1941	167,130,000	2250	130,000,000
562	44,825,000	1942-1945	191,560,000	2251	149,980,000
563	144,028,000	1950	163,939,200	2267-2274	610,425,000
564	139,928,000	1952	180,700,000	2275	156,995,000
565-1568	179,855,000	1953-2002	666,950,000	2286-2335	645,975,000
569-1570	161,863,200	2003	109,245,000	2336	166,725,000
571	145,640,000	2004	112,535,000	2337	186,575,000
572-1575	168,655,000	2006-2009	124,640,000	2338	184,325,000
576	146,615,000	2010	107,605,000	2339	165,845,000
577-1578	146,196,000	2011	173,160,000	2340	155,170,000
579	739,430,000	2012	107,285,000	2341	102,100,000
580	878,690,000	2013	109,040,000	2342	103,325,000
1629-1631	219,455,000	2014	183,270,000	2343	162,045,000
1632	157,825,000	2015	169,495,000	2344	153,295,000
1633-1682	436,005,000	2016	164,235,000	2345	160,245,000
1683	159,915,000	2017	110,130,000	2346	183,290,000
1684	156,960,000	2018	110,995,000	2347	179,800,000
1685	158,470,000	2019-2022	165,340,000	2348	164,130,000
1686	1,990,000	2023	174,180,000	2349	157,475,000
1687	1,983,000	2024	110,261,000	2350	156,225,000
1688	1,953,000	2026	703,295,000	2351-2354	163,980,000
1689	1,903,000	2027-2030	788,880,000	2355-2359	584,340,000

Scott No.	Quantity	Scott No.	Quantity	Scott No.	Quantity
2360	168,995,000	2753a	65,625,000	3095a	32,000,0
2361	163,120,000	2754	110,000,000	3099a	23,025,0
2362-2366	394,776,000	2755	115,870,000	3103a	23,025,0
2367	528,790,000	2759a	40,000,000	3104	300,000,0
2368	978,340,000	2764a	199,784,500	3105	14,910,0
2369	158,870,000	2765	120,000,000	3106	93,612,0
2370	145,560,000	2766	160,000,000	3107	243,575,0
2371	97,300,000	2770a	128,735,000	3111a	56,479,0
2372-2375	158,556,000	2774a	25,000,000	3112	847,750,0
2376	97,300,000	2778a	170,000,000	3116a	451,312,5
2377	153,045,000	2782a	37,500,000	3117	495,504,0
2378	841,240,000	2784a	41,840,000	3118	103,520,0
2379	169,765,000	2788a	37,550,000	3120	106,000,0
2380	157,215,000	2804	88,300,000	3121	112,000,0
2381-2385	635,238,000	2805	105,000,000	3123	1,660,000,0
2386-2389	162,142,500	2806	100,000,000	3124	814,000,0
2390-2393	305,015,000	2806a	250,000,000	3125	122,000,0
2395-2398	480,000,000	2811a	35,800,000	3131a	65,000,0
2399	921,285,000	2812	160,600,000	3131	07,500,0
2400	1,030,850,000	2813	357,949,584	3135	96,000,0
2401	165,495,000	2814	830,000,000	3136	14,600,0
2402	151,675,000	2814C	300,000,000	3137	37,800,0
2403	163,000,000	2815	274,800,000	3138	118,0
2404	264,625,000	2816	155,500,000	3139	593,7
2405-2409	204,984,000	2817	105,000,000	3140	592,8
2410	103,835,000	2818	185,500,000	3141	45,250,0
2411	152,250,000	2828a	18,600,000	3142	8,050,0
2412	138,760,000	2833a	166,000,000	3146a	22,500,0
2413	137,985,000	2834	201,000,000	3147	20,000,0
2414	138,580,000	2835	300,000,000	3148	20,000,0
2415	150,545,000	2836	269,370,000	3149	10,000,00
2416	164,680,000	2837	60,000,000	3150	10,000,00
2417	262,755,000	2838	120,600,000	3151	7,000,0
2418	191,755,000	2839	209,000,000	3152	195,000,0
2420	188,400,000	2840	20,000,000	3153	323,000,0
2421	191,860,000	2841	12,958,000	3157a	21,500,0
2422-2425	406,988,000	2842	100,500,000	3158-3161	12,900,0
2426	137,410,000	2847a	159,200,000	3162-3165	8,600,00
2427	913,335,000	2848	150,500,000	3166	25,250,00
2428	900,000,000	2853a	35,436,000	3167	45,250,00
2429	399,243,000	2854	24,986,000	3172a	36,250,00
2433	2,017,225	2855	24,986,000	3173	173,000,00
2434-2437	163,824,000	2856	24,986,000	3174	37,000,00
2438	2,047,200	2857	19,988,800	3175	133,000,00
2439	173,000,000	2858	19,988,800	3176	882,500,00
2440	886,220,000	2859	19,988,800	3177	1,621,465,00
2441	995,178,000	2860	19,988,800	3178	15,000,00
2442	153,125,000	2861	19,988,800	3179	51,000,00
2444	169,495,000	2862	150,750,000	3180	80,000,00
2445-2448	176,808,000	2866a	56,475,000	3181	45,000,00
2449	150,000,000	2868a	77,748,000	3182	12,533,00
2470-2474	733,608,000	2869	20,000,000	3183	12,533,00
2496-2500	178,587,500	2870	150,186	3184	12,533,00
2501-2505	619,128,000	2871	518,500,000	3185	12,533,00
2506-2507	151,430,000	2872	602,500,000	3186	12,533,00
2508-2511	278,264,000	2873	236,997,600	3187	12,533,00
2512	143,995,000	2874	45,000,000	3188	8,000,00
2513	142,692,000	2875	5,000,000	3189	6,000,00
2514	728,919,000	2876	80,000,000	3190	6,000,00
2515	599,400,000	2948	214,700,000	3191	8,250,00
2516	320,304,000	2949	1,220,970,000	3192	30,000,00
2532	103,648,000	2950	94,500,000	3193-3197	250,000,00
2533	179,990,000	2954a	50,000,000	3198-3202	80,000,00
2534	150,560,000	2955	80,000,000	3203	85,000,00
2538	161,498,000	2956	97,000,000	3204	39,600,00
2545-2549	744,918,000	2957	315,000,000	3205	650,00
2550	149,848,000	2958	300,000,000	3206	32,000,00
2551	200,003,000	2965a	30,000,000	3209	2,200,00
2552	200,000,000	2966	125,000,000	3210	2,200,00
2553-2557	170,025,600	2967	400,000,000	3211	30,000,00
2558	150,310,000	2968	99,424,000	3212-3215	45,000,00
2560	149,810,000	2973a	120,240,000	3216-3219	45,000,00
2561	149,260,000	2974	60,000,000	3220	46,300,00
2562-2566	699,978,000	2975	300,000,000	3221	30,000,00
2567	148,973,000	2979a	62,500,000	3222-3225	70,000,00
2577a	33,394,800	2980	105,000,000	3226	65,000,00
2615a	32,000,000	2981	100,000,000	3227	50,000,00
2616	148,665,000	2982	150,000,000	3230-3234	180,000,00
2617	149,990,000	2983-2992	15,000,000	3235	28,000,00
2618	835,000,000	2992	15,000,000	3236	4,000,00
2619	160,000,000	2997a	200,000,000	3237	130,750,00
2623a	40,005,000	2998	300,000,000	3238-3242	185,000,00
2624	1,185,170	2999	85,000,000	3243	50,000,00
2625	1,185,170	3000	300,000,000	3244	925,200,00
2626	1,185,170	3001	80,000,000	3245-3248	116,760,000
2627	1,185,170	3002	80,000,000	3249-3252	991,750,000
2628	1,185,170	3003	300,000,000	3272	51,000,000
2629	1,185,170	3007a	75,000,000	3273	100,000,000
2630	148,000,000	3008	350,495,000	3274	1,000,000,000
2634a	37,315,000	3009	350,495,000	3275	
2635	146,610,000	3010	350,495,000	3276	100,000,000
2636	160,000,000	3011	350,495,000	3286	40,400,000
2641a	32,000,000	3013	90,000,000	3287	42,500,000
2646a	87,728,000	3023a	30,000,000	3288-3292	73,155,000
2696a	11,000,000	3024	120,000,000	3293a-j	100,000,000
2697	12,000,000	3029a	160,000,000	3306	42,700,000
2698	105,000,000	3030	2,550,000,000	3307	500,000
2699	142,500,000	3058	92,100,000	3308	42,500,000
2703a	36,831,000	3059	115,600,000	3309	105,000,000
2704	85,000,000	3060	93,150,000	3310-3313	1,500,000,000
2709a	80,000,000	3064a	23,292,500	3314	145,375,000
2721	517,000,000	3065	111,000,000	3315	78,100,000
2722	150,000,000	3066	314,175,000	3316	89,270,000
2723	152,000,000	3067	209,450,000	3317-3320	141,175,000
2730a	14,285,715	3068	16,207,500	3321-3324	151,976,000
2731	98,841,000	3069	156,300,000	3325-3328	116,083,500
2732	32,947,000	3070	100,000,000	3329	75,500,000
2733	32,947,000	3071	60,120,000	3330	100,750,000
2734	32,947,000	3076a	27,850,000	3331	101,800,000
2735	65,894,000	3080a	22,218,000	3332	43,150,000
2736	65,894,000	3081	95,600,000	3333-3337	120,000,000
2737	65,894,000	3082	300,000,000	3338	42,500,000
2745a	140,000,000	3086a	23,681,250	3339-3344	42,500,000
2746	105,000,000	3087	133,613,000	3345-3350	42,500,000
2747	110,000,000	3088	103,400,000	3351	4,235,000
2748	110,000,000	3089	60,000,000	3352	65,000,000
2749	172,870,000	3090	134,000,000	3354	44,600,000

Scott No.	Quantity
3355	1,555,560,000
3356-3359	116,500,000
3360-3363	1,785,060,000
3364-3367	118,125,000
3368	95,000,000
3369	120,000,000

Quantities for Nos. 3370-on, and for Nos. 3190, 191 and 3236, are for Quantities ordered.

Scott No.	Quantity
3370	56,000,000
3371	150,000,000
3372	65,150,000
3373-3377	15,000,000
3378a-j	100,000,000
3379-3383	55,000,000
3384-3388	105,350,000
3389	16,000,000
3390	55,000,000
3391	30,000,000
3392	236,000
3393-3396	55,000,000
3397	90,600,000
3398	200,000,000
3399-3402	88,000,000
3403	4,000,000
3408	11,250,000
3409	1,695,000
3410	1,695,000
3411	1,695,000
3412	1,695,000
3413	1,695,000
3414-3417	100,000,000
3438	53,000,000
3439-3443	85,000,000
3444	53,000,000
3445	125,000,000
3446	52,000,000
3496	500,000,000
3497	1,500,000,000
3498	80,000,000
3499	180,000,000
3500	55,000,000
3501	200,000,000
3502	125,000,000
3503	100,000,000
3504	35,000,000
3505	1,598,000
3506a-j	89,600,000
3507	125,000,000
3508	200,000,000
3509	55,000,000
3510-3519	125,000,000
3521	55,000,000
3523	110,000,000
3524-3527	96,000,000
3528-3531	100,000,000
3532	75,000,000
3533	30,000,000
3534a	275,000,000
3535	236,000
3536	800,000,000
3537-3540	125,000,000
3537a-3540a	1,500,000,000
3541-3544	201,000,000
3545	32,000,000
3546	69,000,000
3547	49,000,000
3548	40,000,000
3551	100,000,000
3552-3555	80,000,000
3556	125,000,000
3557	120,000,000
3558	75,000,000
3559	70,000,000
3560	55,000,000
3561-3610	200,000,000
3611a-j	70,000,000
3649a-t	60,000,000
3650	70,000,000
3651	61,000,000
3652	61,000,000
3653-3656	200,000,000
3657	1,500,000,000
3658	150,000,000
3659	75,000,000
3660	62,800,000
3661-3664	111,000,000
3665-3668	61,000,000
3669	61,000,000
3670-3671	200,000,000
3672	35,000,000
3673	40,000,000
3674	35,000,000
3675	739,200,000
3676-3679	125,000,000
3680-3683	300,000,000
3684-3687	1,705,000,000
3688-3691	200,000,000
3692	80,000,000
3694	1,610,000
3695	50,000,000
3696-3745	200,000,000
3746	150,000,000
3747	70,000,000
3748	70,000,000
3771	60,000,000
3772a-j	70,000,000
3773	50,000,000
3774	55,000,000
3776-3780	60,000,000
3781	75,000,000
3782	54,000,000
3783	85,000,000
3786	80,000,000
3787-3791	125,000,000
3802a-j	60,000,000

Scott No.	Quantity
3803	86,800,000
3804-3807	778,800,000
3808-3811	70,000,000
3812	52,000,000
3813	72,000,000
3814-3818	80,000,000
3820	700,000,000
3821-3824	1,875,000,000
3825-3828	200,990,000
3831a-j	76,000,000
3832	80,000,000
3833	750,000,000
3834	130,000,000
3835	172,000,000
3836	750,000,000
3837	150,000,000
3838	60,000,000
3839	80,000,000
3840-3843	57,000,000
3854	62,200,000
3855-3856	20,000,000
3857-3861	57,000,000
3862	96,400,000
3863	71,800,000
3865-3868	284,000,000
3869	45,800,000
3870	60,000,000
3871	50,000,000
3872	794,000,000
3873a-j	87,000,000
3876	100,000,000
3877	96,400,000
3878a-o	125,040,000
3879	776,400,000
3881	60,000,000
3882	45,000,000
3883-3886	125,000,000
3887-3890	200,990,000
3891-3894	270,000,000

AIR POST STAMPS

Cat. No.	Quantity
C1	3,395,854
C2	3,793,887
C3	2,134,888
C4	6,414,576
C5	5,309,275
C6	5,285,775
C7	42,092,800
C8	15,597,307
C9	17,616,350
C10	20,379,179
C11	106,887,675
C12	97,641,200
C13	93,536
C14	72,428
C15	61,296
C16	57,340,050
C17	76,648,803
C18	324,070
C19	302,205,100
C20	10,205,400
C21	12,794,600
C22	9,285,300
C23	349,946,500
C24	19,768,150
C25	4,746,527,700
C26	1,744,878,650
C27	67,117,400
C28	78,434,800
C29	42,359,850
C30	59,880,850
C31	11,160,600
C32	864,753,100
C33	971,903,700
C34	207,976,550
C35	756,186,350
C36	132,956,100
C37	33,244,500
C38	38,449,100
C39	5,070,095,200
C40	75,085,000
C41	260,307,500
C42	21,061,300
C43	36,613,100
C44	16,217,100
C45	80,405,000
C46	18,876,800
C47	78,415,000
C48	50,483,977
C49	63,185,000
C50	72,480,000
C51	1,326,960,000
C52	157,035,000
C53	90,055,200
C54	79,290,000
C55	84,815,000
C56	38,770,000
C57	39,960,000
C58	98,160,000
C59	
C60	1,289,460,000
C61	87,140,000
C62	
C63	
C64	
C65	
C66	42,245,000
C67	
C68	63,890,000
C69	62,255,000

Cat. No.	Quantity
C70	55,710,000
C71	+ 50,000,000
C72	
C73	
C74	+ 60,000,000
C75	
C76	152,364,800
C77	
C78	
C79	
C80	
C81	
C82	
C83	
C84	78,210,000
C85	96,240,000
C86	58,705,000
C87	
C88	
C89	
C90	
C91-C92	
C93-C94	
C95-C96	
C97	
C101-C104	+ 165,000,000
C105-C108	+ 165,000,000
C109-C112	+ 175,000,000
C113	98,600,000
C114	110,475,000
C115	167,625,000
C116	45,700,000
C117	22,975,000
C118	201,150,000
C119	111,550,000
C120	38,532,000
C121	39,325,000
C122-C125	106,360,000
C126	1,944,000
C127	48,000,000
C128	250,000,000
C129	182,400,000
C130	113,000,000
C131	15,260,000
C132	100,000,000
C133	100,750,000
C134	100,750,000
C135	+ 100,800,000
C136	85,000,000
C137	85,000,000
C138	100,000,000

+ Quantity ordered printed.

CARRIERS' STAMPS

The term "Carriers' Stamps" is applied to certain stamps of the United States used to defray delivery to a post office on letters going to another po[st] office, and for collection and delivery in the same city (local letters handled only by the carrier department). A less common usage was for a collectio[n] fee from the addressee at the post office ("drop letters"). During the period when these were in use, the ordinary postage fee defrayed the carriage [of] mail matter from post office to post office only.

In many of the larger cities the private ("Local") posts delivered mail to the post office or to an addressee in the city direct for a fee of 1 or 2 cen[ts] (seldom more), and adhesive stamps were often employed to indicate payment. (See introduction to "Local Stamps" section.)

Carrier service dates back at least to 1689 when the postmaster of Boston was instructed "to receive all letters and deliver them at 1d." In 1794, th[e] law allowed a penny post to collect 2 cents for the delivery of a letter. As these early fees were paid in cash, little evidence survives.

In 1851 the Federal Government, under the acts of 1825 and 1836, began to deliver letters in many cities and so issued Carriers' stamps for loc[al] delivery service. This Act of Congress of March 3, 1851, effective July 1, 1851 (succeeding Act of 1836), provided for the collecting and delivering [of] letters to the post office by carriers, "for which not exceeding 1 or 2 cents shall be charged."

Carriers' stamps were issued under the authority of, or derived from, the postmaster general. The "Official Issues" (Nos. LO1-LO2) were gener[al] issues of which No. LO2 was valid for postage at face value, and No. LO1 at the value set upon sale, in any post office. They were issued under th[e] direct authority of the postmaster general. The "Semi-official Issues" were valid in the city in which they were issued either directly by or sanctioned b[y] the local postmaster under authority derived from the postmaster general.

These "Official" and "Semi-official" Carriers' stamps prepaid the fees of official letter carriers who were appointed by the postmaster general and wer[e] under heavy bond to the United States for the faithful performance of their duties. Some of the letter carriers received fixed salaries from th[e] government. Others were paid from the fees received for the delivery and collection of letters carried by them. After discontinuance of carrier fees o[n] June 30, 1863, all carriers of the United States Post Office were government employees, paid by salary at a yearly rate.

Some Carriers' stamps are often found on cover with the regular government stamps and have the official post office cancellation applied to them a[s] well. Honour's City Express and the other Charleston, S.C., Carrier stamps almost always have the stamp uncanceled or canceled with pen, or les[s] frequently pencil.

Unless indicated otherwise, values for Carriers' stamps on cover are for covers having the stamp tied by a handstamped cancellatio[n] Carriers' stamps, either uncanceled or pen-canceled, **on covers to which they apparently belong,** also are valued where possible. For covers wit[h] stamps canceled by pen or pencil with initials or name of carrier, as sometimes seen on No. LO2 from Washington, and on Baltimore carrier stamp[s] the premium is 75% of the on-cover value.

All Carriers' stamps are imperforate and on wove paper, either white or colored through, unless otherwise stated.

Counterfeits exist of many Carriers' stamps.

GENERAL ISSUE CARRIER STAMPS

Franklin — OC1

Eagle — OC2

Engraved and printed by Toppan, Carpenter, Casilear & Co. Plate of 200 subjects divided into two panes of 100 each, one left, one right

1851, Sept. Unwmk. Imperf.

LO1 OC1 (1c)	**dull blue** (shades),		
	rose	6,000.	6,500.
	On cover from Philadel-phia		17,500.
	On cover from New York		30,000.
	On cover from New Orleans with 3c #10 (a 2nd #LO1 removed)		30,000.
	Pair	14,500.	16,000.
	Strip of 3	22,500.	23,500.
	Major plate crack	—	
	Major plate crack, on cover		60,000.
	Corner plate cracks (91L)	—	—
	Double transfer	—	—
	Double transfer, on cover		30,000.

Earliest known use: Oct. 28, 1851.

Cancellations

Red star (Philadelphia)	6,500.
Blue town (Philadelphia)	+1,000.
Red town (New York)	+1,000.
Black town (New York), unique	+4,000.
Blue grid (New York)	—
Black grid (New York)	—
Black grid (New Orleans)	+4,000.
Green grid (New Orleans)	—

Of the entire issue of 310,000 stamps, 250,000 were sent to New York, 50,000 to New Orleans, 10,000 to Philadelphia. However, the quantity sent to each city is not indicative of proportionate use. More appear to have been used in Philadelphia than in the other two cities. The use in all three cities was notably limited.

No. LO1, major plate crack on cover, is unique. The double transfer on cover also is unique.

U.S.P.O. Despatch

Engraved and printed by Toppan, Carpenter, Casilear & Co. Plate of 200 subjects divided into two panes of 100 each, one upper, one lower

1851, Nov. 17 Unwmk. Imperf.

LO2 OC2	1c **blue** (shades)	25.00	60.00
	On cover, used alone		500.00
	On cover, precanceled		600.00
	On cover, pair or 2 singles		1,500.

On cover with block of 3, 1c #9		4,500.
On cover with 3c #11		400.
On cover with 3c #25		—
On cover with 3c #26		600.
On cover with strip of 3, 3c #26		—
On cover with 5c #30A and 10c #32		33,000.
On cover, tied by town handstamp, with 3c #65 (Washington, D.C.)		4,500.
On 3c envelope #U1, #LO2 pen canceled		—
On 3c envelope #U2, tied by handstamp		—
On 3c envelope #U2, #LO2 pen canceled		—
Pair	70.00	
On 3c envelope #U10, not canceled, with certicate		—
Pair on cover (Cincinnati)		1,000.
Block of 4	275.00	
Margin block of 8, imprint	800.00	
Double transfer	—	—
Double transfer on cover		—

Earliest known use: Jan. 3, 1852.

Cancellations

Red star	60.
Philadelphia	+50.
Cincinnati	+200.
Black grid	—
Blue grid	+300.
Red grid	+300.
Black town	+5.
Blue town	+100.
Red town	+300.
Kensington, Pa. (red)	—
Kensington, Pa. red "3c"	—
Washington, D.C.	+1,000.
Blue squared target	—
Red squared target	—
Railroad	—
Black carrier (Type C32)	—
Red carrier (Type C32)	—
Carrier's initial, manuscript	—

Earliest known use: Jan. 3, 1852. Used principally in Philadelphia, Cincinnati, Washington, D.C., and Kensington, Pa.

GOVERNMENT REPRINTS

Printed by the Continental Bank Note Co.
First reprinting-10,000 copies, on May 19, 1875.
Second reprinting-10,000 copies, on Dec. 22, 1875.

The first reprinting of the Franklin stamp was on the rose paper of the original, obtained from Toppan, Carpenter, Casilear & Co. Two batches of ink were used, both darker than the original. The second reprinting was on much thicker, paler paper in an indigo color. All of these differ under ultraviolet light. The design of the reprints is not as distinct as the original design and may appear a bit "muddy" in the lathework above the vignette.

Most of the reprints of the Eagle stamp are on the same hard white paper used for special printings of the postage issue, but a few have been found on both very

thin and very thick soft porous white paper. A ver[y] small number are known to fluoresce green. Reprin[ts] may be differentiated from the originals under ultravi[o-] let light by the whiteness of the paper. Nos. LO3-LO[6] are ungummed, Nos. LO1-LO2 have brown gum.

1875

Franklin Reprints
Imperf

LO3 OC1 (1c)	**blue,** rose		50.
	indigo, rose		70.
	Block of 4		225.
	Margin block of 4, imprint		—
	Corner plate cracks (91L)		100.
	Short transfer		—

Perf. 12

LO4 OC1 (1c)	**blue**		16,000.
	Pair		35,000.

No. LO4 is valued in the grade of average to fine.

Eagle Reprints
Imperf

LO5 OC2	1c **blue**		25.
	Block of 4		125.
	Margin block of 8, imprint & Pl.#		—

Perf. 12

LO6 OC2	1c **blue**		175.
	Block of 4		1,000.
	Margin block of 8, imprint & Pl.#		12,500.

CITY CARRIER DEPARTMENT STAMPS
All are imperforate.
Baltimore, Md.

C1

1850-55	Typo.	Settings of 10 (2x5) varieties		
1LB1 C1	1c **red** (shades), bluish		180.	160.
	On cover, tied by handstamp			1,000.
	On cover with 1c #9			
	On cover (tied) with 3c #11			500.
1LB2 C1	1c **blue** (shades), bluish		200.	150.
	On cover, tied			1,000.
a.	Bluish laid paper		—	—
1LB3 C1	1c **blue** (shades)		160.	100.
	On cover, tied by handstamp			1,000.
	On cover, tied by ms.			250.
	Block of 4		1,000.	
a.	Laid paper		200.	150.
	On cover, tied by handstamp			1,000.
b.	Block of 14 containing three tete-beche gutter pairs (unique)		6,000.	
1LB4 C1	1c **green**		—	1,000.
	On cover, tied by handstamp			3,500.

On cover, not tied		1,200.
On cover with 1c #7, tied by handstamp		2,250.
On cover with 3c #11, ms. tied		—
On 3c envelope #U10		3,500.
Pair		6,750.

5 C1	1c **red**	2,250.	1,750.
On cover, tied by handstamp			4,500.
On cover, not tied			3,000.
On cover (tied) with 3c #11			5,000.

The No. 1LB4 pair is the unique multiple of this stamp.

Cancellations on Nos. 1LB1-1LB5:

Black grid	—
Blue grid	—
Black cross	—
Black town	—
Blue town	+100.
Black numeral	—
Blue numeral	—
Black pen	—

C2

			Typo.
6 C2	1c **blue** (shades)	130.	90.
On cover			400.
On cover with 3c #11			1,000.
On cover with 3c #25 (both tied)			1,350.
On cover with 3c #26			1,250.
7 C2	1c **red** (shades)	130.	90.
On cover			300.
On cover (tied) with 3c #25			350.
On cover (tied) with 3c #26			350.
On 3c envelope #U9, tied			300.
On 3c envelope #U10, tied			350.
Block of 4		850.	

C3

Plate of 10 (2x5); 10 Varieties

The sheet consisted of at least four panes of 10 placed horizontally, the two center panes tete beche. This makes possible the horizontal tete beche gutter pairs.

57			Typo.
8 C3	1c **black** (shades)	65.	50.
On cover, tied by handstamp			125.
On cover, tied by handstamp, to Germany			3,750.
On cover (tied) with 3c #26			175.
On 3c envelope #U9, tied			225.
On 3c envelope #U10			225.
On 3c envelope #U27, tied			250.
Strip of 3 (not tied), on cover			4,000.
Block of 4		275.	
Pane of 10		1,000.	
Tete beche gutter pair		650.	
a.	"SENT," Pos. 7	100.	75.
On cover, tied by handstamp			175.
On cover with 3c #26			250.
On 3c envelope #U9, tied			250.
On 3c envelope #U10, tied			250.
b.	Short rays, Pos. 2	100.	75.
On cover (tied) with 3c #26			600.

Cancellations

Black pen (or pencil)	20.00
Blue town	+2.50
Black town	+2.50
Black Steamship	—

LB9 C3	1c **red** (shades)	100.	90.
On cover			175.
On cover with 3c #26			300.
On 3c envelope #U9			325.
On 3c envelope #U10			325.
Block of 6		2,750.	
a.	"SENT," Pos. 7	140.	110.
On cover (tied) with 3c #26			500.
b.	Short rays, Pos. 2	140.	110.
c.	As "b," double impression		800.

The block of 6 of No. 1LB9 is the only recorded multiple of this stamp.

Cancellations on Nos. 1LB6-1LB7, 1LB9:

Black town	—
Blue town	—
Blue numeral	—
Black pen	—
Carrier's initial, manuscript	+25.

Boston, Mass.

C6

Several Varieties

1849-50	**Pelure Paper**		**Typeset**
3LB1 C6	1c **blue**	375.	180.
On cover, tied by handstamp			275.
On cover with 5c #1			4,000.
On cover with two 5c #1			8,750.
On cover with 3c #10			450.00
a.	Wrong ornament at left		400.00
On cover, not tied			—

Cancellations

Red town	—
Red grid	—
Black ornate double oval	—
Black "Penny Post Paid" in 3-bar circle	—

C7

1851		**Typeset**

Several Varieties

Wove Paper Colored Through

3LB2 C7	1c **blue** (shades), *slate*	190.	100.
On cover			220.
On cover with 5c #1			12,500.
On cover with 3c #10			500.
On cover with 3c #11			325.
On 3c envelope #U2, #U5 or #U9			350.
Tete beche gutter pair		600.	

Cancellations on Nos. 3LB2:

Black small fancy circle	—
Black diamond grid	+100.00
Red town	—
Black grid	—
Black PAID	—
Black crayon	—
Red small fancy circle	+50.00
Red diamond grid	+100.00
Black railroad	—
Black hollow star	—
Black pencil	—
Red crayon	—
Black "Penny Post Paid" in 3-bar circle	—
Red "Penny Post Paid" in 3-bar circle	—

Charleston, S. C.

John H. Honour was appointed a letter carrier at Charleston, in 1849, and engaged his brother-in-law, E. J. Kingman, to assist him. They separated in 1851, dividing the carrier business of the city between them. At the same time Kingman was appointed a letter carrier. In March, 1858, Kingman retired, being replaced by Joseph G. Martin. In the summer of 1858, John F. Steinmeyer, Jr., was added to the carrier force. When Honour retired in 1860, John C. Beckman was appointed in his place.

Each of these carriers had stamps prepared. These stamps were sold by the carriers. The Federal Government apparently encouraged their use.

Honour's City Express

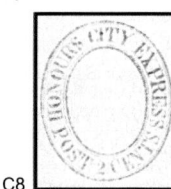

C8

1849	**Typo.**	**Wove Paper Colored Through**		
4LB1 C8	2c **black**, *brown rose*	10,000.		
Cut to shape		4,000.	4,000.	
On cover, not canceled, with certificate			17,000.	
On cover, cut to shape, tied, with 10c #2			40,000.	
4LB2 C8	2c **black**, *yellow*, cut to shape		—	
On cover, not tied, with certificate			12,500.	

On cover, cut to shape, uncanceled	—
On cover, rectangular-cut, tied, with 10c #2	—

Cancellations on Nos. 4LB1-4LB2: Red grid, red town, red crayon.

No. 4LB1 unused is a unique uncanceled stamp on piece. The used cut-to-shape stamp is also unique. Additionally, each of the listed covers bearing No. 4LB1 is unique.

Four examples of No. 4LB2 are recorded, each listing above being unique.

C10

1854	**Wove Paper**		**Typeset**
4LB3 C10	2c **black**		1,500.
On cover, tied by pen cancel			3,000.
On cover with 3c #11, tied			4,500.
On cover with 3c #11, not tied			3,250.

Cancellations

Black town	—
Blue town	—
Black pen	—
Black pencil	—
Brown "PAID"	—
Initial "H"	—

C11

Several Varieties

1849-50			**Typeset**

Wove Paper Colored Through

4LB5 C11	2c **black**, *bluish*, pelure	750.	500.
On cover with pair 5c #1b			—
On cover with two 5c #1b			—
On cover (tied) with 3c #11			4,000.
a.	"Ceuts"	5,750.	
4LB7 C11	2c **black**, *yellow*	750.	1,000.
On cover, tied by handstamp			9,000.
a.	"Ccnts," ms. tied on cover		14,500.

No. 4LB5a is unique. It is without gum and is valued thus. No. 4LB7a also is unique.

The varieties of type C11 on bluish wove (thicker) paper and pink, pelure paper are not believed genuine.

Cancellation Nos. 4LB5, 4LB7:

Red town	—
Black pen	—
Red pen	—
Red crayon	—

C13   C14

C15

Several varieties of each type

1851-58			**Typeset**

Wove Paper Colored Through

4LB8 C13	2c **black**, *bluish*	350.	175.
On cover, tied by handstamp			700.
On cover, not tied			300.
On cover, tied, with 3c #10			1,500.
On cover, tied, with 3c #11			1,500.
On cover, tied, with 3c #26			1,500.
Pair			1,500.
a.	Period after "PAID"	500.	250.
On cover			650.
On cover, ms. tied, with 3c #11			750.
b.	"Cens"	700.	900.
On cover, ms. tied, with 3c #11			3,250.
c.	"Conours" and "Bents"		—
4LB9 C13	2c **black**, *bluish*, pelure	850.	950.
4LB11 C14	(2c) **black**, *bluish*		375.
On cover, tied by handstamp, with 3c #11			12,500.

On cover, ms. tied, with 3c #11		—	3,000.
4LB12 C14 (2c) **black,** *bluish,* pelure		—	
4LB13 C15 (2c) **black,** *bluish* ('58)		750.	400.
On cover with 3c #11, Aiken, S.C. postmark, tied by handstamp (unique)			6,000.
On cover with 3c #26, tied by pen cancel			4,000.
Horiz. pair			3,500.
a. Comma after "PAID"		1,100.	
b. No period after "Post"		1,400.	

The pair of No. 4LB13 is the unique multiple of this stamp.
A 2c of design C13 exists on pink pelure paper. It is believed not to have been issued by the post, but to have been created later and perhaps accidentally.

Cancellations on Nos. 4LB8-4LB13

Black town	—
Blue town	—
Red town	—
Black pen	—
Black pencil	—
Red crayon	—
Brown cork initial "H"	—

Kingman's City Post

 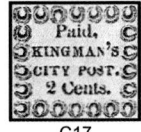

C16   C17

Several varieties of each

1851(?)-58(?)			**Typeset**
Wove Paper Colored Through			
4LB14 C16 2c **black,** *bluish*		1,400.	900.
Vert. pair, ms. tied, on Valentine cover			6,000.
On cover with 3c #11			7,500.
On cover with 3c #26			6,000.
a. "Kingman's" erased			5,000.
4LB15 C17 2c **black,** *bluish*		800.	800.
On cover		—	—
Vertical pair		—	
Horiz. pair, not tied, on Valentine cover			8,750.
Vertical strip of 3		25,000.	
a. "Kingman's" erased, on cover with 3c #11, tied by pen cancel (unique)			4,500.

The No. 4LB14 pair on cover is the only recorded multiple of this stamp.
The 4LB15 pair and strip of 3 actually are uncanceled on covers and are valued thus. The horiz. pair on cover is ms. canceled.

Cancellations on Nos. 4LB14-4LB15: Black town, black pen.

Martin's City Post

C18

Several varieties

1858 Wove Paper Colored Through		**Typeset**
4LB16 C18 2c **black,** *bluish*	8,000.	

Beckman's City Post
Same as C19, but inscribed "Beckmann's City Post."

1860
4LB17 C19 2c **black,** on cover —

No. 4LB17 is unique. It is on cover with 3c No. 26, both tied by black circle townmark: "CHARLESTON, S.C. JUN 18, 1860".

Steinmeyer's City Post

C19   C20

Several varieties of Type C19
Type C20 printed from plate of 10 (2x5) varieties

1859 Wove Paper Colored Through		**Typeset**
4LB18 C19 2c **black,** *bluish*	21,000.	
On cover, uncanceled		—
4LB19 C20 2c **black,** *bluish*	4,500.	—
4LB20 C20 2c **black,** *pink*	200.	—
Block of 4	850.	
Sheet of 10	2,250.	

4LB21 C20 2c **black,** *yellow*	200.	
Block of 4	850.	
Sheet of 10	2,250.	

Sheets of 10 of Nos. 4LB20-4LB21 exist signed by J.F. Steinmeyer Jr. These sell for about 50% more than the unsigned sheets.
Two examples of No. 4LB18 are known on cover, both uncanceled.

Cancellation on Nos. 4LB19-4LB21: Black pen.

Cincinnati, Ohio
Williams' City Post
Organized by C. C. Williams, who was appointed and commissioned by the Postmaster General.

C20a

1854 Wove Paper		**Litho.**
9LB1 C20a 2c **brown**	—	4,000.
On cover, tied by handstamp		—
On cover, tied by pen cancel		4,500.
On cover with 1c #9		10,000.
Pair	7,500.	

Cancellations

Red squared target	—
Black pen	—
Blue company circle	—

Fraser & Co.
Local stamps of designs L146-L147 were carrier stamps when used on cover between Feb. 3, 1848 and June 30, 1849.

Cleveland, Ohio
Bishop's City Post.
Organized by Henry S. Bishop, "Penny Postman" who was appointed and commissioned by the Postmaster General.

C20b   C20c

1854 Wove Paper		**Litho.**
10LB1 C20b **blue**	5,000.	4,000.
On cover, tied by handstamp		15,000.
Pair on cover, canceled by pencil, with 3c #11, with certificate		17,000.
Vertically Laid Paper		
10LB2 C20c 2c **black,** *bluish*	7,000.	7,000.
On cover		—
Pair		—

Cancellations on #10LB1-10LB2

Red town	—
Red boxed numeral	—
Black pencil	—
Black pen	—

Louisville, Ky.
Carrier Service was first established by the Louisville Post Office about 1854, with one carrier. David B. Wharton, appointed a carrier in 1856, issued an adhesive stamp in 1857, but as he was soon thereafter replaced in the service, it is believed that few, if any, of these stamps were used. Brown & McGill, carriers who succeeded Wharton, issued stamps in April, 1858.

Wharton's U.S.P.O. Despatch

C21

Sheet of 50 subjects in two panes of 25 (5x5) ea one upper, one lower

1857 Lithographed by Robyn &		
5LB1 C21 (2c) **bluish green** (shades)	125.	
Block of 4	650.	
Pane of 25	3,250.	
Sheet of 50	7,000.	

Brown & McGill's U. S. P. O. Despatch

C22

1858 Litho. by Hart & Maypo		
5LB2 C22 (2c) **blue** (shades)	250.	
On cover, not tied, with 3c #26		75
On cover with 3c #26, tied by handstamp		6,
Block of 4	1,250.	
5LB3 C22 (2c) **black**	4,500.	15,

The value for No. 5LB3 used refers to the finer of the known used (canceled) examples; it is on a piece with a 3c

Cancellations on Nos. 5LB2-5LB3: Blue town, black pen

New York, N. Y.
UNITED STATES CITY DESPATCH POST
By an order made on August 1, 1842, the Postmaster General established a carrier service in New Y known as the "United States City Despatch Po Local delivery service had been authorized by the of Congress of July 2, 1836.
Greig's City Despatch Post was sold to the U. S O. Department and on August 16, 1842, began ope tion as the "United States City Despatch Post" un the superintendence of Alexander M. Greig who v appointed a U. S. letter carrier for that purpose.
The Greig circular introducing this service sta that letter boxes had been placed throughout the c that letters might be sent prepaid or collect, and registry service was available for an extra 3 cents.
The City Despatch Post stamps were accepted the service of the United States City Despatch P The stamps thus used bear the cancellation of New York Post Office, usually "U.S." in an octag which served to indicate that the carrier service v now a government operation (no longer a private lo post) as well as a cancellation.

 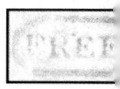

Some examples are canceled by a circular da stamp reading "U.S. CITY DESPATCH POST" infrequently, a New York town postmark. When ca celed "FREE" in frame they were used as lo stamps. See No. 40L1 in Locals section.
No. 6LB3 was the first stamp issued by authority the U.S.P.O. Department. The 3c denominati included 1 cent in lieu of drop letter postage until J 30, 1845, and the maximum legal carrier fee of cents. Service was discontinued late in Novembe 1846.

C23   C24

Engraved and printed by Rawdon, Wright & Hatch.

Plate of 42 (6x7) subjects
Wove Paper Colored Through

1842		
6LB1 C23 3c **black,** *grayish*	2,00	
On cover, tied by handstamp	11,50	
On cover, not tied	10,00	

Cancellations

Red "U.S" in octagon	2,000.
Red circle "U.S. City Despatch Post"	—
Red town	—

Used copies which do not bear the official cancellation of the New York Post Office and unused copies are classed as Local Stamps. See No. 40L1.

1842-45

Wove Paper (unsurfaced) Colored Through

6LB2	C24	3c **black**, *rosy buff*	2,500.	
6LB3	C24	3c **black**, *light blue*	550.	500.
		On cover, tied by hand- stamp		1,750.
		On cover, not tied		750.00
		Pair	2,250.	
6LB4	C24	3c **black**, *green*	11,500.	

Some authorities consider No. 6LB2 to be an essay, and No. 6LB4 a color changeling.

Glazed Paper, Surface Colored

6LB5	C24	3c **black**, *blue green* (shades)	200.	175.
		On cover, tied by hand- stamp		600.
		Five on cover		20,000.
		Pair	—	400.
		Strip of 3		650.
		Strip of 4		800.
		Strip of 5	—	—
		Ribbed paper	—	—
		Double transfer		—
a.		Double impression		1,500.
b.		3c **black**, *blue*	650.	250.
		On cover		750.
		Strip of 3 + single on cover		14,000.
		Strip of 3	2,500.	
		Block of 12	23,000.	—
c.		As "b," double impression		850.
d.		3c **black**, *green*	1,000.	900.
		On cover		
		Strip of 4 + single on cover		36,000.
e.		As "d," double impression		
		On cover		—

Cancellations

Red curved PAID	—
Red "U.S City Despatch Post"	—
Red "U.S" in octagon	—
Red New York	—
Red double line circle "U.S. City Despatch Post"	—

No. 6LB5 has been noted on cover with the 5c New York signed "R.H.M.," No. 9X1d.

6LB6	C24	3c **black**, *pink*, on cover front	14,500.

No. 6LB6 is unique.

C25

1846

No. 6LB5 Surcharged in Red

6LB7	C25	2c on 3c **black**, *bluish green*, on cover, not tied, with certificate	70,000.

The City Dispatch 2c red formerly listed as No. 6LB8 is now listed under Local Stamps as No. 160L1.

U.S. MAIL

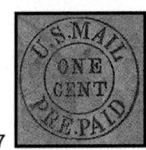

C27

Issued by the Postmaster at New York, N.Y.

1849 — Wove Paper, Colored Through — Typo.

6LB9	C27	1c **black**, *rose*	100.	100.
		On cover, tied by hand- stamp		250.
		On cover with 5c #1		2,000.
		Pair	250.	
		Block of 4	600.	

1849-50

Glazed Surface Paper

6LB10	C27	1c **black**, *yellow*	100.	100.
		On cover, tied by hand- stamp		250.
		On cover with 5c #1		1,500.
		Pair	250.	
		Block of 4	600.	
6LB11	C27	1c **black**, *buff*	100.	100.

	On cover	250.
	On cover, not tied, with 5c #1, with certificate	3,000.
a.	Pair, one stamp sideways	2,850.

Cancellations on #6LB9-6LB11

Red town	—
Red grid	—
Red "PAID"	+50.
Black numeral in circle	—
Red "N.Y. U.S. CITY MAIL" in circle	+150.
Black pen	—
Black pencil	—

Philadelphia, Pa.

C28

Several Varieties
Thick Wove Paper Colored Through

1849-50 — Typeset

7LB1	C28	1c **black**, *rose* (with "L P")	450.	
		On cover, tied by hand- stamp		3,000.
		On cover, not canceled		2,000.
		On cover with 5c #1		
7LB2	C28	1c **black**, *rose* (with "S")	3,000.	
		On cover, not canceled		4,500.
7LB3	C28	1c **black**, *rose* (with "H")	275.	
		On cover, tied by hand- stamp		3,750.
		On cover, not canceled		1,000.
		On cover with 5c #1		
7LB4	C28	1c **black**, *rose* (with "L S")	400.	500.
		On cover, not canceled		3,000.
7LB5	C28	1c **black**, *rose* (with "J J")	7,500.	
		On cover with 5c #1, un- canceled		70,000.

The unique used No. 7LB5 in an uncanceled stamp on a cover front.

C29

Several Varieties

7LB6	C29	1c **black**, *rose*	300.	250.
		On cover, tied by hand- stamp		2,500.
		On cover, uncanceled		500.00
7LB7	C29	1c **black**, *blue*, glazed	1,000.	
		On cover, tied by hand- stamp		6,500.
		On cover, uncanceled		1,500.
		On cover with 5c #1		
7LB8	C29	1c **black**, *vermilion*, glazed	700.	
		On cover, tied by hand- stamp		1,500.
		On cover with 5c dark brown #1a, uncanceled		12,500.
		On cover with 5c orange brown #1b, uncanceled		21,000.
7LB9	C29	1c **black**, *yellow*, glazed	2,750.	2,250.
		On cover, not canceled		4,000.
		On cover with 3c #10, un- canceled		2,000.

Cancellations on Nos. 7LB1-7LB9: Normally these stamps were left uncanceled on the letter, but occasionally were accidentally tied by the Philadelphia town postmark which was normally struck in blue ink.

A 1c black on buff (unglazed) of type C29 is believed to be a color changeling.

C30

Settings of 25 (5x5) varieties (Five basic types)

1850-52 — Litho.

7LB11	C30	1c **gold**, *black*, glazed	175.	110.
		On cover, tied by hand- stamp		600.
		On cover (tied) with 5c #1		3,500.
		On cover (tied) with 3c #10		800.
		On cover (uncanceled) with 3c #10		250.
		Block of 19	8,250.	
7LB12	C30	1c **blue**	400.	275.
		On cover, tied by hand- stamp		1,250.
		On cover (tied) with 3c #10		1,750.
		On cover (tied) with 3c #11		1,250.
		Pair		1,600.
7LB13	C30	1c **black**	750.	550.
		On cover, tied by hand- stamp		2,500.
		On cover (tied) with 3c #10		—
		On cover (not tied) with 3c #11		3,250.

Cancellations on #7LB11-7LB13

Red star	—
Red town	—
Blue town	—

C31

Handstamped

7LB14	C31	1c **blue**, *buff*	3,250.

No. 7LB14 was handstamped on coarse dark buff paper on which rectangles in the approximate size of the type C31 handstamp had been ruled in pencil. The stamps so produced were later cut out and show traces of the adjoining handstamp markings as well as parts of the penciled rectangle. Some uncanceled examples exist on covers.

1855(?)

7LB16	C31	1c **black**	5,000.
		On cover with strip of 3, 1c #9	—
		On cover with 3c 1851 stamp removed, tied by handstamp	7,000.

C32

1856(?) — Handstamped

7LB18	C32	1c **black**	1,250.	2,000.
		On cover (cut diamond- shaped) with pair 1c #7 and single 1c #9		—
		On cover with strip of 3, 1c #7		17,000.
		On cover with 3c #11		9,500.
		On 3c envelope #U5		—

On 3c envelope #U10, not
canceled　　　　　　　9,000.

Cancellations on #7LB16, 7LB18

Black circled grid　　　—
Black town　　　　　　—

Nos. 7LB16 and 7LB18 were handstamped on the sheet
margins of U.S. 1851 1c stamps, cut out and used as adhesives. The paper therefore has some surface bluing, and some
stamps show parts of the plate imprint.

Values are for stamps cut square unless otherwise
mentioned.

ENVELOPES

Handstamps of types C31 and C32 were also used
to make stamped envelopes and letter sheets or circulars. These same types were also used as postmarks
or cancellations in the same period.

A handstamp similar to C32, but with "U.S.P. DES-
PATCH" in serif capitals, is believed to have been used
only as a postmark.

Type C31 exists struck in blue or red, type C32 in
blue, black or red. When found on cover, on various
papers, struck alone, they are probably postmarks and
not prepaid stamped envelopes. As such, these entire
covers, depending upon the clarity of the handstamp
and the general attractiveness of the letter are valued
between $400 and $800.

When found on envelopes with the Carrier stamp
canceled by a handstamp (such as type C31 struck in
blue on a buff envelope canceled by the red solid star
cancellation) they can be regarded as probably having
been sold as prepaid envelopes. Value approximately
$3,000.

Labels of these designs are believed by most specialists not to be carrier stamps. Those seen are
uncanceled, either off cover or affixed to stampless
covers of the early 1850s. Some students believe they
should be given carrier status.

St. Louis, Mo.

C36　　　　　　　C37

Illustrations enlarged to show details of the two types (note
upper corners especially). Sizes of actual designs are 17
1/2x22mm.

1849　　　**White Wove Paper**　　**Lith**
　　　　　　Two Types

8LB1　C36　2c　black　　　　7,000.
8LB2　C37　2c　black　　　　6,000.

Cancellation on Nos. 8LB1-8LB2: Black town.

C38

1857　　　　　　　　　　Lith
8LB3　C38　2c　blue　　　　22,50
　　　On cover, tied by hand-
　　　　stamp　　　　　　55,00
　　　On Valentine cover, ms.
　　　　cancel, not tied　　35,00

The used example off cover is unique. Four covers a
recorded.

Cancellations on No. 8LB3: Black boxed "1ct," "Paid" in
black pen.

LOCAL STAMPS

This listing of Local stamps includes stamps issued by Local Posts (city delivery), Independent Mail Routes and Services, Express Companies an
other private posts which competed with, or supplemented, official services.

The Independent Mail Routes began using stamps early in 1844 and were put out of business by an Act of March, 1845, which became effective Jul
1, 1845. By this Act, the Government reduced the zones to two, reduced the rates to 5c and 10c and applied them to weight instead of the number c
sheets of paper which composed a letter.

Most of the Local Posts still in business were forced to discontinue service by an Act of 1861, except Boyd's and Hussey's which were able t
continue about 20 years longer because of the particular nature of their business. Other posts appeared illegally and sporadically after 1861 and wer
quickly suppressed.

City posts generally charged 1c to deliver a letter to the Post Office (usually the letter bore a government stamp as well) and 2c for intracity deliver
(such letters naturally bore only local stamps). These usages are not catalogued separately because the value of a cover is determined as much by it
attractiveness as its franking, rarity being the basic criterion.

Only a few Local Posts used special handstamps for canceling. The stamps frequently were left uncanceled, were canceled by pen, or less often b
pencil. **Unless indicated otherwise, values for stamps on cover are for covers having the stamp tied by a handstamped cancellation, eithe
private or governmental.** Local stamps, either uncanceled or pen canceled, **on covers to which they apparently belong**, also are valued wher
possible.

The absence of any specific cancellation listed indicates that no company handstamp is known so used, and that the canceling, if any, was done b
pen, pencil or government handstamp. Local stamps used on letters directed out of town (and consequently bearing government stamps) sometimes
because of their position, are tied together with the government stamp by the cancellation used to cancel the latter.

Values for envelopes are for entires unless specifically mentioned.

All Local stamps are imperforate and on wove paper, either white or colored through, unless otherwise stated.

Counterfeits exist of many Local stamps, but most of these are crude reproductions and would deceive only the novice.

Adams & Co.'s Express, California

This post started in September, 1849, operating
only on the Pacific Coast.

D. H. Haskell, Manager
L1　　　　　　　L2
Nos. 1L2-1L5 Printed in Sheets of 40 (8x5).

1854　　　　　　　　　Litho.　—
1L1　L1　25c　black, blue　　2,750.　—
　　　On cover　　　　　　　—
1L2　L2　25c　black (initials in black)　75.00　—
　　　Block of 4　　　　375.00
　　　Sheet of 40　　　　—
a.　Initials in red　　　　—
b.　Without initials　　　—

Cancellation (1L1-1L2): Black Express Co.

Nos. 1L1-1L2 were the earliest adhesive franks issued west
of the Mississippi River.

No. 1L2 usually bear manuscript control markings "LR" for
Louis Reed or less commonly "ICW" for Isaiah C. Wood.

Glazed Surface Cardboard

1L3　L2　25c　black, pink　　　30.00
　　　Block of 4　　　　　160.00
　　　Sheet of 40　　　　2,000.
　　　Retouched flaw above LR "25"　100.00

No. 1L3 was probably never placed in use as a postage
stamp.

L3

**Overprinted in red "Over our California lines
only"**

1L4　L3　25c　black (with initials "LR")　750.00　—

L4　　　　　　　L5

1L5　L4　25c　black (black surcharge)　2,750.　—
1L6　L5　25c　black　　　　　2,000.　—
　　　Pair　　　　　　　6,500.

The pair of No. 1L6 is unique.

NEWSPAPER STAMP

L6

| P1 | L6 | black, *claret* | — | 2,000. |

Cancellation: Blue company oval.

ENVELOPES

L6a   L6b

Typo.

1LU1	L6a	25c blue (cut square)		15,000.
1LU2	L6a	25c black, on U.S. #U9		—
1LU3	L6b	50c black, on U.S. #U9	2,500.	2,500.
1LU4	L6b	50c black, *buff*		15,000.

Nos. 1LU2 and 1LU3 exist cut out and apparently used as adhesives.
Cancellation: Blue company oval.

Adams' City Express Post, New York, N.Y.

L7   L7a

L8

1850-51				Typo.
2L2	L7	2c black, *buff*	5,000.	2,250.
		On cover, canceled, not tied, with certificate		10,000.
2L3	L7a	1c black, *gray*		—
2L4	L8	2c black, *gray*	450.00	450.00
		On cover, tied by handstamp		5,500.

Nos. 2L3-2L4 were reprinted in black and in blue on white wove paper. Some students claim that the 1c and 2c in blue exist as originals. An example of the 2c used on cover recently (2005) received a "genuine usage" certificate from the Philatelic Foundation, strengthening the argument for a catalogue major-number listing. Research is continuing.

Allen's City Dispatch, Chicago, Ill.

Established by Edwin Allen for intracity delivery of letters and circulars. The price of the stamps is believed to have been determined on a quantity basis. Uncanceled and canceled remainders were sold to collectors after suppression of the post in February, 1883.

L9

| 1882 | | Typo. | | Perf. 10 |

Sheet of 100 (10x10)

3L1	L9	pink	7.50	25.00
		On cover		900.00
		Block of 4	40.00	—
	a.	Horizontal pair, imperf. between		—
3L2	L9	black	12.50	100.00
		On cover		55.00
		Block of 4	55.00	
	a.	Horizontal pair, imperf. between		—
3L3	L9	red, *yellow*	.75	20.00
		On cover		800.00
		Block of 4	3.25	
	a.	Imperf., pair	150.00	
	b.	Horizontal pair, imperf. between		—
3L4	L9	blackish purple	120.00	

Cancellations: Violet company oval, violet "eagle."

American Express Co., New York, N.Y.

Believed by some researchers to have been established by Smith & Dobson in 1856, and short-lived.

L10

Typeset
Glazed Surface Paper

| 4L1 | L10 | 2c black, *green* | | 9,000. |

American Letter Mail Co.

Lysander Spooner established this independent mail line operating to and from New York, Philadelphia and Boston.

L12   L13

| 1844 | | | | Engr. |

Sheet of 20 (5x4)

5L1	L12	5c black, thin paper (2nd printing)	7.50	35.00
		Thick paper (1st printing)	35.00	50.00
		On cover		850.00
		Pair on cover		—
		Block of 4, thin paper	40.00	
		Sheet of 20, thin paper	225.00	

No. 5L1 has been extensively reprinted in several colors, distinguishable by the rust marks on the plate, which were mostly removed from the margins and gutters between stamps but remain within the stamp designs. Cancellations: Red dotted star (2 types). Red "PAID," black brush, red brush.

Engr.

5L2	L13	black, *gray*	150.00	250.00
		On cover, tied by handstamp		1,000.
		On cover, ms. tied		500.00
		On cover, not tied		350.00
		Pair on cover		—
		Vertical strip of 4	3,000.	
		Block of 4	4,000.	
5L3	L13	blue, *gray*	2,000.	1,750.
		On cover, uncanceled, with certificate		12,500.

Cancellations: Red "PAID," red company oval.

A. W. Auner's Despatch Post, Philadelphia, Pa.

L13a

| 1851 | | | | Typeset |

Cut to shape

| 154L1 | L13a | black, *grayish* | | 9,000. |
| | | On cover, not tied, with certificate | | 16,500. |

Nos. 154L1 unused and on cover are each unique.

L14

Baker's City Express Post, Cincinnati, Ohio

1849				
6L1	L14	2c black, *pink*		2,250.
		On cover, uncanceled, with certificate		12,500.

Bank & Insurance Delivery Office or City Post
See Hussey's Post.

Barnard's Cariboo Express, British Columbia

The adhesives were used on British Columbia mail and the post did not operate in the United States, so the formerly listed PAID and COLLECT types are omitted. This company had an arrangement with Wells, Fargo & Co. to exchange mail at San Francisco.

Barnard's City Letter Express, Boston, Mass.

Established by Moses Barnard

L19

1845				
7L1	L19	black, *yellow*, glazed paper	1,250.	1,000.
7L2	L19	red	1,000.	
		On cover, ms. cancel, not tied, with certificate		5,000.

No. 7L2 unused and on cover are each unique.

Barr's Penny Dispatch, Lancaster, Pa.
Established by Elias Barr.

L19a   L20

1855   **Typeset**
Five varieties of each
8L1 L19a **red**   1,000. 1,000.
            On cover, ms. cancel, not tied,
            with certificate   2,000.
8L2 L20   **black**, *green*   250.   200.00
            On cover with 3c #11
            Pair   650.

Bayonne City Dispatch, Bayonne City, N.J.
Organized April 1, 1883, to carry mail, with three
daily deliveries. Stamps sold at 80 cents per 100.

L21

1883   **Electrotyped**
Sheet of 10
9L1 L21 1c **black**   200.   275.
            On cover   750.
            On cover with 1c & 2c #183,
            206   2,750.
            On cover with 3c #207   1,600.

Cancellation: Purple concentric circles.

ENVELOPE
1883, May 15   **Handstamped**
9LU1 L21 1c **purple**, *amber*   175.   1,000.

Bentley's Dispatch, New York, N.Y.
Established by H. W. Bentley, who acquired
Cornwell's Madison Square Post Office, operating until
1856, when the business was sold to Lockwood. Bentley's postmark was double circle handstamp.

L22   L22a

1856(?)   **Glazed Surface Paper**
10L1 L22   **gold**   9,000. 9,000.
10L2 L22a **gold**   7,500.
            Pair   10,000.

Two unused examples of No. 10L1 are known, while the used
example is unique.

Cancellation: Black "PAID."

Berford & Co.'s Express, New York, N.Y.
Organized by Richard G. Berford and Loring L. Lom-
bard. Carried letters, newspapers and packages by
steamer to Panama and points on the West Coast,
North and South America. Agencies in West Indies,
West Coast of South America, Panama, Hawaii, etc.

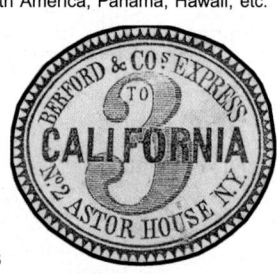

L23

1851
11L1 L23   3c   **black**   5,000. 7,000.
            On cover, not canceled   —   —
11L2 L23   6c   **green**   —   —
            On cover, tied   —   —
11L3 L23   10c **violet**   5,000.
            On cover, not canceled
            Four cut to shape on cover   15,000.
            Pair   —
   a.   Horiz. tete beche pair
            On cover with normal pair   67,500.
            Two tete beche pair on cover   75,000.
11L4 L23   25c **red**   17,000.
            On cover with #11L1 & 2
            #11L2   75,000.

Values of cut to shape copies are about half of those quoted.
No. 11L4 unused and on cover are each unique.
Cancellation: Red "B & Co. Paid" (sometimes impressed with-
out ink). Dangerous counterfeits exist of Nos. 11L1-11L4.

Bicycle Mail Route, California
During the American Railway Union strike, Arthur C.
Banta, Fresno agent for Victor bicycles, established
this post to carry mail from Fresno to San Francisco
and return, employing messengers on bicycles. The
first trip was made from Fresno on July 6, 1894. Service was discontinued on July 18 when the strike
ended. In all, 380 letters were carried. Stamps were
used on covers with U.S. Government adhesive
stamps and on stamped envelopes.

L24

Printed from single die. Sheet of six.
Error of spelling "SAN FRANSISCO"

1894   **Typo.**   **Rouletted 10**
12L1 L24 25c **green**   150.   200.
            On cover   1,500.
            Block of 4   700.
            Pane of 6   1,750.

L25

Retouched die. Spelling error corrected.
12L2   L25 25c **green**   30.   75.
            On cover   1,250.
            Block of 4   125.
            Pane of 6   250.
   a.   "Horiz." pair, imperf. "vert" 75.
            As "a," pane of 6   —

ENVELOPES
12LU1 L25 25c **brown**, on 2c No. U311   200. 1,350.
12LU2 L25 25c **brown**, on 2c No. U312   200. 1,350.

Cancellation: Two black parallel bars 2mm apart.
Stamps and envelopes were reprinted from the defaced die.

Bigelow's Express, Boston, Mass.

Authorities consider items of this design to be express company labels rather than stamps.

Bishop's City Post, Cleveland, Ohio
See Carriers' Stamps, Nos. 10LB1-10LB2.

Blizzard Mail
Organized March, 1888, to carry mail to New Y[ork]
City during the interruption of U.S. mail by the Blizz[ard]
of 1888. Used March 12-16.

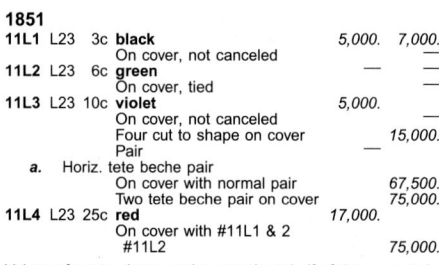

L27

1888, Mar. 12   **Quadrille Paper**   **Typ**
163L1 L27 5c **black**   2,750.

D.O. Blood & Co., Philadelphia, Pa.
I. Philadelphia Despatch Post
Operated by Robertson & Co., predecessor of D.[O.]
Blood & Co.

L28

L29

Initialed "R & Co."

1842   **Handstampe[d]**
Cut to Shape
15L1 L28 3c **red**, *bluish*   1,50[0]
            On cover, not tied   8,50[0]
15L2 L28 3c **black**   1,50[0]
            On cover, not tied, with certi-
            cate   15,00[0]

Cancellations on Nos. 15L1-15L2: Red "3," red pattern [of]
segments.

With or without shading in background.
Initialed "R & Co"

1843   **Litho[.]**
15L3 L29 (3c) **black**, *grayish*   750.
            On cover, tied by handstamp 12,50[0]
            On cover, tied by ms. cancel 5,00[0]
            On cover, not tied, with certif-
            icate   3,50[0]
   a.   Double impression   —

Cancellation on No. 15L3: Red "3"
The design shows a messenger stepping over the Merchants[']
Exchange Building, which then housed the Government Pos[t]
Office, implying that the private post gave faster service.
See illustration L161 for similar design.

II. D.O. Blood & Co.
Formed by Daniel Otis Blood and Walter H. Blood i[n]
1845. Successor to Philadelphia Despatch Post which
issued Nos. 15L1-15L3.

L30

Initialed "Dob & Cos" or "D.O.B. & Co."

845

Shading in background

5L4	L30 (3c)	**black,** *grayish*	600.	
		On cover, tied by handstamp		6,000.
		On cover, not tied		1,500.

L31

L32

1846

15L5	L31 (2c)	**black**	125.	250.
		On cover		
		On cover, not tied, with certificate		800.
		Block of 4	475.	
		Pane of 12	5,500.	

1847

15L6	L32 (2c)	**black**	—	200.
		On cover		
		On cover, not tied, with certificate		1,250.
		On cover, not tied, with 5c #1		—

Cancellations on Nos. 15L4-15L6: Black dot pattern, black cross, red "PAID."
Dangerous counterfeits exist of Nos. 15L3-15L6.

L33

L34

L35

1846-47

15L7	L33 (2c)	**black**	175.00	350.00
		On cover, tied by handstamp		1,750.
		On cover, cut to shape, tied by handstamp		1,100.
		On cover, not tied		750.00
15L8	L34 (2c)	**black**	110.00	75.00
		On cover, tied by handstamp		950.00
		On cover, uncanceled		500.00
15L9	L35 (2c)	**black**	100.00	60.00
		On cover, tied by handstamp		1,500.

	On cover, with 5c #1		—
	On cover, not tied		500.00
	Block of 4		

Values for Nos. 15L7-15L9 cut to shape are half of those quoted.
"On cover" listings of Nos. 15L7-15L9 are for stamps tied by government town postmarks, either Philadelphia, or rarely Baltimore.

L36

L37

1848

15L10	L36 (2c)	**black & blue**	350.00	500.00
		On cover, tied by handstamp		1,250.
		On cover, not canceled		1,000.
		On cover, with 5c #1		
		Pair	1,300.	
15L11	L37 (2c)	**black,** *pale green*	300.00	300.00
		On cover, tied by handstamp		1,250.
		On cover, not tied		800.00

Cancellation: Black grid.

L38

L39

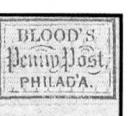

L40

L41

1848-54

15L12	L38 (2c)	**gold,** *black, glazed*	110.00	100.00
		On cover, tied by handstamp		500.00
		On cover, acid tied		200.00
		On cover with 5c #1		
15L13	L39	1c **bronze,** *black, glazed* ('50)	25.00	12.50
		On cover, tied by handstamp		225.00
		On cover, acid tied		75.00
		On cover, acid tied, with 5c #1		1,500.
		On cover with 10c #2		
		On cover, acid tied, with three 1c #7		1,100.
		On cover with, tied by handstamp, 3c #10		250.00
		Block of 4	150.00	
		Pane of 24	1,250.	
15L14	L40 (1c)	**bronze,** *lilac* ('54)	4.25	2.50
		On cover, tied by handstamp		200.00
		On cover, acid tied		30.00
		On cover, acid tied, with 1c #9		300.00
		On cover with 3c #11		375.00
		On cover, tied by handstamp, with 3c #26		200.00
		On cover, acid tied, with 3c #64b		250.00
		Block of 4	50.00	
		Pane of 25	750.00	
a.		Laid paper	—	—
b.		Tete beche pair		
15L15	L40 (1c)	**blue & pink,** *bluish* ('53)	22.50	12.50
		On cover, tied by handstamp		200.00
		On cover, acid tied		50.00
		Block of 4	80.00	
		Pane of 25	1,250.	
a.		Laid paper	—	—
		Block of 4		
15L16	L40 (1c)	**bronze,** *black, glazed* ('54)	30.00	25.00
		On cover, tied by handstamp		225.00
		On cover, acid tied		75.00
		On cover, tied by handstamp, with 3c #11		275.00
15L17	L41 (2c)	**bronze,** *black, glazed*	35.00	20.00
		On cover, tied by handstamp		225.00
		On cover, acid tied		75.00
		On cover, acid tied, with 5c #1		1,250.
		On cover, not tied, with 5c #1		750.
		On cover, handstamp tied, with pair of 5c #1a		11,000.

D.O. Blood & Co. reduced the cost for mailing letters from 2c to 1c as of Jan. 8, 1849, in anticipation of the government carrier rate reduction. As a result, Nos. 15L12 and 15L17 could be purchased for 1c after this date.
Cancellations: Black grid (No. 15L12, 15L17). Nos. 15L13-15L16 were almost always canceled with an acid which discolored both stamp and cover.

III. Blood's Penny Post

Blood's Penny Post was acquired by the general manager, Charles Kochersperger, in 1855, when Daniel O. Blood died.

Henry Clay — L42

1855 **Engr. by Draper, Welsh & Co.**

15L18	L42 (1c)	**black**	35.00	10.00
		On cover		150.00
		On cover, tied by handstamp, with 3c #11		400.00
		On cover, tied by handstamp, with 3c #26		350.00
		On 3c entire #U9		300.00
		Block of 4	175.00	

Cancellations: Black or red circular "Blood's Penny Post," black "1" in frame, red "1" in frame.

ENVELOPES

L42A

L43

L44

1848-60 **Embossed**

15LU1	L42A	**albino embossing,** *white*	—	
15LU1A	L42A	**albino embossing,** *buff*	—	4,500.
15LU1B	L43	**red,** *white*	75.00	100.00
a.		Pink, *white*		100.00
b.		Impressed on US Env. #U9		225.00
15LU2	L43	**red,** *white*	—	150.00
15LU3	L44	**red,** *white*	75.00	160.00
15LU4	L44	**red,** *buff*	75.00	125.00

One example of No. 15LU1 is recorded, uncanceled, with the embossed stamp cut out and reattached. Two examples of No. 15LU1A are recorded, canceled by the "Blood's Despatch/28 So. Sixth" handstamp.

L45

15LU5	L45	**red,** *white*	35.00	75.00
		Used with 3c #11		350.00
		Used with 3c #26		350.00
a.		Impressed on US Env. #U7		250.00
b.		Impressed on US Env. #U9		250.00
c.		Impressed on US Env. #U1		300.00
d.		Impressed on US Env. #U3		500.00
e.		Impressed on US Env. #U2		275.00
15LU6	L45	**red,** *amber*	35.00	100.00
15LU6A	L45	**red,** *buff*		350.00
		On cover with 10c #2		
		On cover with three 1c #9		—
b.		Red, *brown*		500.00

Laid Paper

15LU7	L45	**red,** *white*	35.00	125.00
		Used with acid tied #15L14		200.00
a.		Impressed on US env. #U9		350.00
15LU8	L45	**red,** *buff*	35.00	125.00
		Used with 3c No. 25		200.00
15LU9	L45	**red,** *buff*	35.00	125.00
15LU10	L45	**red,** *blue*		6,500.

Nos. 15LU1-15LU9 exist in several envelope sizes.

Cancellations: Black grid (Nos. 15LU1-15LU4), black company circle (2 sizes and types). When on government envelope, the Blood stamp was often left uncanceled.

Bouton's Post, New York, N.Y.
I. Franklin City Despatch Post
Organized by John R. Bouton

L46

1847		Glazed Surface Paper	Typo.
16L1	L46 (2c) **black,** *green*	7,500.	
a.	"Bouton" in blk. ms. vert. at side	7,000.	
	On cover	14,000.	

II. Bouton's Manhattan Express
Acquired from William V. Barr

L47

1847			Typo.
17L1	L47	2c **black,** *pink*	4,000.
		Cut to shape	900.
		On cover, uncanceled	4,500.

III. Bouton's City Dispatch Post
(Sold to Swarts' in 1849.)

Corner Leaves — L48   Corner Dots — L49

Design: Zachary Taylor

1848			Litho.
18L1	L48	2c **black**	— 600.
		On cover	2,000.
		On cover with 5c #1	27,500.
		On cover with 10c #2	50,000.
18L2	L49	2c **black,** *gray blue*	— 250.
		On cover, tied by handstamp	600.
		On cover tied by Swarts' handstamp	1,000.
		On cover with 5c #1	25,000.
		On cover with 10c #2	7,500.

Cancellations on Nos. 18L1-18L2: Red "PAID BOUTON."

Boyce's City Express Post, New York, N.Y.

L50

Center background has 17 parallel lines

1852		Glazed Surface Paper	Typo.
19L1	L50	2c **black,** *green*	1,500. 1,000.
		Cut to shape	600.00
		On cover, tied by manuscript cancel	4,000.

Boyd's City Express, New York, N.Y.

Boyd's City Express, as a post, was established by John T. Boyd, on June 17, 1844. In 1860 the post was briefly operated by John T. Boyd, Jr., under whose management No. 20L15 was issued.

For about six months in 1860 the post was suspended. It was then sold to William and Mary Blackham who resumed operation on Dec. 24, 1860.

The Blackham issues began with No. 20L16. Boyd's had arrangements to handle local delivery mail for Pomeroy, Letter Express, Brooklyn City Express Post, Staten Island Express Post and possibly others.

L51

Designs L51-L56, L59-L60 have a rectangular frame of fine lines surrounding the design.

1844		Glazed Surface Paper	Litho.
20L1	L51	2c **black,** *green*	1,000.
		On cover	4,000.
		On cover, not tied, with #117L4	7,000.

Cancellation: Red "FREE."

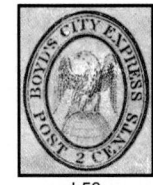

L52   L53

L54

Plain background. Map on globe.

1844			Litho.
20L2	L52	2c **black,** *yellow green*	175.00
		On cover	450.00

Cancellation: Red "FREE."

Plain background. Only globe shaded.

1845			Engr.
20L3	L53	2c **black,** *bluish green*	— 250.00
		On cover	500.00

Cancellation: Red "FREE."

Inner oval frame of two thin lines. Netted background, showing but faintly on late impressions.

1845			Engr.
20L4	L54	2c **black,** *green*	— 15.00
		On cover, tied by handstamp	250.00
		On cover, tied, with 5c U.S. Postmaster Provisional #9X1, on cover front	—
		On cover, tied, with 5c #1	5,000.
		On cover, not tied, with 5c #1	1,500.
		Double transfer	35.00
a.		Diagonal half used as 1c on cover	2,300.

Cancellations: Red "FREE." Black grid.
The 20L4 and 9X1 on cover front is the only recorded usage of a local stamp and a Postmaster Provisional.

1847			
20L5	L54	2c **gold,** *cream*	350.00 600.00
		On cover	1,750.

Designs L54-L59 (except No. 20L23) were also obtainable die cut. An extra charge was made for such stamps. In general, genuine Boyd die-cuts sell for 75% of rectangular cut copies. Stamps hand cut to shape are worth much less.

L55   L56

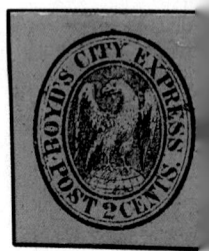

L57

No period after "CENTS." Inner oval frame has heavy inner line.

1848			Engr.
20L7	L55	2c **black,** *green* (glazed)	10.00 15.0
		On cover, tied by handstamp	175.0
		On cover, tied by handstamp, with 5c #1	3,25
		On cover, tied, with 3c #11	275.0
		Block of 4	40.00
a.		2c **black,** *yellow green*	15.0
		On cover	135.0

Cancellation: Black grid.
No. 20L7a is on unglazed surface-colored paper.

1852			Litho.
Period after "CENTS." Inner frame as in L55.			
20L8	L56	2c **black,** *green*	25.00 35.0
		On cover	150.0
		Vert. strip of 3 on cover	300.0
20L9	L56	2c **gold,**	12.50 80.0
		On cover, tied by handstamp	750.0
		On cover with 3c #11	1,25
		Block of 4	80.00

Cancellations on Nos. 20L8-20L9: Black cork. Black "PAID J.T.B."
No. 20L8 was reprinted in 1862 on unglazed paper, and about 1880 on glazed paper without rectangular frame.

1854

Period after "CENTS." Inner oval frame has heavy outer line. Eagle's tail pointed. Upper part of "2" open, with heavy down stroke at left shorter than one at right. "2C" closer than "T2."

20L10	L57	2c **black,** *green*	32.50 25.0
		On cover, tied by handstamp	200.0

Cancellation: Black "PAID J.T.B."

L58   L59

1855	**Unglazed Paper Colored Through**		Typo.
Outer oval frame of three lines, outermost heavy. Solid background.			
20L11	L58	2c **black,** *olive green*	65.00 90.00
		On cover, tied by handstamp	350.00

1856			
20L12	L58	2c **brick red,** *white*	50.00 45.00
		On cover, tied by handstamp	500.00
20L13	L58	2c **dull orange,** *white*	50.00 45.00
		On cover	400.00
a.		Printed on both sides	—

Cancellation on Nos. 20L11-20L13: Black "PAID J.T.B."
Nos. 20L11-20L13 were reprinted in the 1880's for sale to collectors. They were printed from a new small plate of 25 on lighter weight paper and in colors of ink and paper lighter than the originals.

1857	**Glazed Surface Paper**		Litho.
Similar to No. 20L10, but eagle's tail square. Upper part of "2" closed (in well printed specimens) forming a symmetrical "o" with downstrokes equal. "T2" closer than "2C."			
20L14	L59	2c **black,** *green*	12.50 25.00
		On cover	125.00
		On cover, tied by handstamp, with 3c #26	—
		Pair on cover	—
		Block of 4	65.00
a.		Serrate perf.	—

The serrate perf. is probably of private origin.
No. 20L15 was made by altering the stone of No. 20L14, and many traces of the "S" of "CENTS" remain.

60				
L15 L59	1c **black,** *green*		1.00	*50.00*
	On cover, tied by handstamp			*400.00*
	Block of 4		7.50	
a.	"CENTS" instead of "CENT"			—
	On cover			*450.00*

Cancellation on Nos. 20L14-20L15: Black "PAID J.T.B."

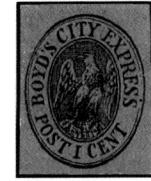

L60   L61

Center dots before "POST" and after "CENTS."

861				
L16 L60	2c **black,** *red*		7.50	*20.00*
	On cover, tied by handstamp			*200.00*
	Block of 4		37.50	
a.	Tete beche pair		45.00	
L17 L60	1c **black,** *lilac*		12.50	*17.50*
	On cover, tied by handstamp			*250.00*
	On cover, tied by handstamp, with 3c #26			*200.00*
	On cover, tied by handstamp, with 3c #65			*500.00*
	Block of 4		50.00	
a.	"CENTS" instead of "CENT"		50.00	*75.00*
	Two on cover (No. 20L17a)			—
b.	"1" inverted			—
L18 L60	1c **black,** *blue gray*		22.50	*35.00*
	On cover, tied by handstamp			*250.00*
	On cover, tied by handstamp, with 3c #26			*225.00*
	On cover, tied by handstamp, with 3c #65			*225.00*
	Block of 4		90.00	
a.	"CENTS" instead of "CENT"		75.00	*90.00*
	On cover			*250.00*
	On cover, tied by handstamp, with 1c #24 and three 3c #26			*2,000.*
b.	"1" inverted			—

Cancellations on Nos. 20L16-20L18: Black or blue company oval, black company circle, black or blue "PAID" in circle.

1861				
L19 L60	2c **gold,**		250.00	
	Block of 4			—
a.	Tete beche pair			—
L20 L60	2c **gold,** *green*		20.00	
	Block of 4			—
a.	Tete beche pair			—
L21 L60	2c **gold,** *dark blue*		12.50	
	On cover, tied by handstamp			*150.00*
	Block of 4			—
a.	Tete beche pair			—
L22 L60	2c **gold,** *crimson*		25.00	
	Block of 4			—
a.	Tete beche pair			—

1866				**Typo.**
L23 L58	2c **black,** *red*		7.50	*25.00*
	On cover, tied by handstamp			*250.00*
	Block of 4		37.50	
a.	Tete beche pair		55.00	

Cancellations: Black company, black "PAID" in circle. *No. 20L23 was reprinted from a new stone on paper of normal color. See note after No. 20L13.*

1866				**Typo.**

No period or center dots.

L24 L61	1c **black,** *lilac*		30.00	*65.00*
	On cover, tied by handstamp			*500.00*
	Block of 4			—
L25 L61	1c **black,** *blue*		6.00	*50.00*
	On cover, tied by handstamp			*500.00*
	Block of 4		30.00	

Cancellation on Nos. 20L24-20L25: Black company. Reprints exist of Nos. 20L24 and 20L25. Originals of No. 20L24 are grayish black on glazed paper, while the reprints are deep black on unglazed paper. Reprints of No. 20L25 are identical to the originals, and it is customary to regard stamps with original gum as originals and those without gum as reprints.

Boyd's City Dispatch
(Change in Name)

L62

1874		**Glazed Surface Paper**		**Litho.**
20L26 L62	2c **light blue**		35.00	*40.00*
	On cover			—
	Block of 4			—

A unique sheet of 100 exists. It demonstrates 10 transfer types (2x5) repeated ten times to produce the printing stone. The same stone was modified to produce Nos. 20L30-20L36.
The 2c black on wove paper, type L62, is a cut-out from the Bank Notices Nos. 20LUX1, 20LUX2, or 20LUX3.

Surface Colored Paper

20L28 L62	2c **black,** *red*			—
20L29 L62	2c **blue,** *red*			*250.00*

The adhesives of type L62 were made from the third state of the envelope die.
Nos. 20L28 and 20L29 are color trials, possibly used postally.

L63   L64

1877				**Litho.**
20L30 L63	2c **lilac,** *roseate*			—
	Laid Paper			
20L31 L63	2c **lilac,** *roseate*			—
	Perf 12½, Wove Paper			
20L32 L63	2c **lilac,** *roseate*		27.50	*25.00*
	On cover			*200.00*
a.	2c **lilac,** *grayish*		27.50	*25.00*
	Laid Paper			
20L33 L63	2c **lilac,** *roseate*			*25.00*
a.	2c **lilac,** *grayish*			—
	Glazed Surface Paper			
20L34 L63	2c **brown,** *yellow*		35.00	*35.00*
	On cover, tied by handstamp			—
a.	Imperf. horizontally			—

1877		**Laid Paper**		**Perf. 11, 12, 12½**
20L35 L64	(1c) **violet,** *lilac*		15.00	*17.50*
	On cover, tied by handstamp			*350.00*
a.	(1c) **red lilac,** *lilac*		27.50	*27.50*
b.	(1c) **gray lilac,** *lilac*		17.50	*17.50*
c.	Vert. pair, imperf. horiz.		400.00	
20L36 L64	(1c) **gray,** *roseate*		15.00	*15.00*
	On cover, tied by handstamp			*250.00*
a.	(1c) **gray,** *grayish*			*15.00*

Cancellations on Nos. 20L30-20L36: Black "PAID" in circle. Purple company oval.

Boyd's Dispatch
(Change in Name)

Mercury Series — Type I — L65

Printed in sheets of 100.
Inner frame line at bottom broken below foot of Mercury.
Printed by C.O. Jones.

1878	**Litho.**	**Wove Paper**		**Imperf.**
20L37 L65	**black,** *pink*		400.00	*300.00*
	Surface Colored Wove Paper			
20L38 L65	**black,** *orange red*		750.00	*500.00*
20L39 L65	**black,** *crimson*		450.00	*300.00*

Laid Paper

20L40 L65	**black,** *salmon*		450.00	
20L41 L65	**black,** *lemon*		450.00	*400.00*
20L42 L65	**black,** *lilac pink*		450.00	

Nos. 20L37-20L42 are color trials, some of which may have been used postally.

Surface Colored Paper
Perf. 12

20L43 L65	**black,** *crimson*		60.00	*50.00*
	On cover, tied by handstamp			*300.00*
a.	**black,** *dull brown red*		40.00	*40.00*
	On cover, tied by handstamp			*300.00*
20L43A L65	**black,** *orange red*		150.00	*150.00*
	On cover, tied by handstamp			*1,000.*

Cancellations on Nos. 20L37-20L43A: Black "PAID" in circle. Purple company oval.

Wove Paper
Perf. 11, 11½, 12, 12½ and Compound

20L44 L65	**black,** *pink*		1.50	*2.50*
	On cover			*200.00*
a.	Horizontal pair, imperf. between			—

1879				**Perf. 11, 11½, 12**
20L45 L65	**black,** *blue*		10.00	*15.00*
	On cover, tied by handstamp			*200.00*
20L46 L65	**blue,** *blue*		27.50	*32.50*
	On cover, tied by handstamp			*400.00*

1880				**Perf. 11, 12, 13½**
20L47 L65	**black,** *lavender*		8.00	*20.00*
	On cover, tied by handstamp			*300.00*
	Block of 4		50.00	
a.	Horizontal pair, imperf. between		400.00	
20L48 L65	**blue,** *lavender*			—

1881		**Laid Paper**		**Perf. 12, 12½, 14**
20L49 L65	**black,** *pink*		350.00	
	On cover, tied by handstamp			*600.00*
20L50 L65	**black,** *lilac pink*		7.00	*25.00*
	On cover, tied by handstamp			*325.00*

Mercury Series — Type II — L65a — 20L51   Mercury Series — Type III — L65b — 20L55

No break in frame, the great toe raised, other toes touching line.
Printed by J. Gibson

1881	**Wove Paper**			**Perf. 12, 16 & Compound.**
20L51 L65a	**black,** *blue*		35.00	*30.00*
20L52 L65a	**black,** *pink*		75.00	*75.00*
	On cover, tied by handstamp			*400.00*
	Laid Paper			
20L53 L65a	**black,** *pink*		7.50	*7.50*
	On cover, tied by handstamp			*125.00*
20L54 L65a	**black,** *lilac pink*		12.50	*10.00*
	On cover			*200.00*

No break in frame, the great toe touching.
Printed by the "Evening Post"

Perf. 10, 11½, 12, 16 & Compound

1882		**Wove Paper**		
20L55 L65b	**black,** *blue*		4.00	*10.00*
	On cover, tied by handstamp			*225.00*
	Pair on cover			*225.00*
20L56 L65b	**black,** *pink*		.40	*1.50*
	On cover, tied by handstamp			*100.00*
	Block of 4		2.00	

Cancellations on Nos. 20L44-20L56: black or purple company ovals of various types, purple company circle, purple "SPECIAL," purple Maltese cross.

ENVELOPES
Boyd's City Post

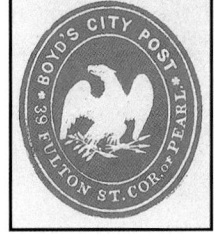

L66

Imprinted in upper right corner.

Used envelopes show Boyd's handstamps.

1864 Diagonally Laid Paper

			Embossed
20LU1	L66	red	175.00
20LU2	L66	red, amber	90.00
20LU3	L66	red, yellow	—
20LU4	L66	blue	175.00
20LU5	L66	blue, amber	175.00
20LU6	L66	blue, yellow	—

Several shades of red and blue.

20LU7	L66	deep blue, orange, cut square	600.00
		Entire	5,500.

Reprinted on pieces of white, fawn and oriental buff papers, vertically, horizontally or diagonally laid.

Wove Paper

20LU8	L66	red, cream	175.00
20LU9	L66	red, orange	— 2,500.
20LU10	L66	blue, cream	—
20LU11	L66	blue, orange	—
		Impression at upper left	4,000.
20LU11A	L66	blue, amber	—

Boyd's City Dispatch

L67a　　　　　　　　　L67b

L67a. Lines and letters sharp and clear. Trefoils at sides pointed and blotchy, middle leaf at right long and thick at end.
L67b. Lines and letters thick and rough. Lobes of trefoils rounded and definitely outlined. Stamp impressed normally in upper right corner of envelope; L67b rarely in upper left.

1867 Diagonally Laid Paper

			Typo.
20LU12	L67	2c red (a) (b)	— 800.00
20LU13	L67	2c red, amber (b)	— 300.00
20LU14	L67	2c red, cream (b)	— 300.00
a.		On horiz. laid paper	—
20LU15	L67	2c red, yellow (a) (b)	— 300.00
20LU16	L67	2c red, orange (b)	— 300.00
a.		Stamp impressed at upper left	—

Wove Paper

20LU17	L67	2c red (a) (b)	— 300.00
20LU18	L67	2c red, cream (a) (b)	— 300.00
20LU19	L67	2c red, yellow (a)	—
20LU20	L67	2c red, orange (a) (b)	—
20LU21	L67	2c red, blue (a) (b)	500.00 400.00

Design as Type L62
First state of die, showing traces of old address.

1874 Diagonally Laid Paper

20LU22	L62	2c red, amber	200.00
20LU23	L62	2c red, cream	— 200.00

Wove Paper

20LU24	L62	2c red, amber	200.00
20LU25	L62	2c red, yellow	200.00

Second state of die, no traces of address.

1875 Diagonally Laid Paper

20LU26	L62	2c red, amber	— 1,250.
20LU27	L62	2c red, cream	— 375.00

Wove Paper

20LU28	L62	2c red, amber	450.00

L68　　　　　　　　　　L69

1877 Laid Paper

20LU29	L68	2c red, amber	800.00

Stamp usually impressed in upper left corner of envelope.

1878 Diagonally Laid Paper

20LU30	L69	(1c) red, amber	— 650.00

Wove Paper

20LU31	L69	(1c) red, cream	—
20LU32	L69	(1c) red, yellow	—

Boyd's Dispatch

L70　　　　　　Mercury Series
　　　　　　　　Type IV — L71

Shading omitted in banner. No period after "Dispatch." Short line extends to left from great toe.

1878 Diagonally Laid Paper

20LU33	L70	black	40.00 100.00
20LU34	L70	black, amber	80.00
20LU35	L70	black, cream	50.00 100.00
20LU36	L70	red	50.00
20LU37	L70	red, amber	35.00 45.00
20LU38	L70	red, cream	35.00 80.00
20LU39	L70	red, yellow green	—
20LU40	L70	red, orange	350.00
20LU41	L70	red, fawn	—

Wove Paper

20LU42	L70	red	— 800.00

Mercury Series-Type V

Colorless crosshatching lines in frame work

1878 Diagonally Laid Paper

20LU43	L71	red	— 450.00
20LU44	L71	red, cream	25.00 50.00

Wove Paper

20LU44A	L71	red	1,000.

Boyd's Bank Notices
IMPORTERS' AND TRADERS' NATIONAL BANK OF NEW YORK

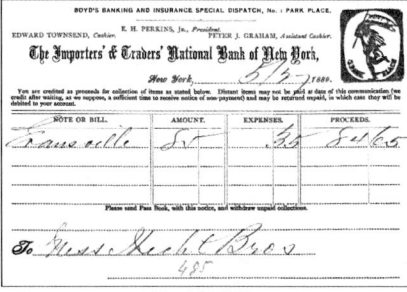

No. 20LUX9a

1874-83 Incomplete Year Date ("187 "), Card Stock

20LUX1	L62	(2c) black, 155x100mm	250.00

Complete Year Date, Medium Wove Paper

20LUX2	L62	2c black, 157x104mm (1875)	—
20LUX3	L62	2c black, 152x104mm (1876)	250.00
20LUX4	L68	2c black, 154x105mm (1876)	—
20LUX5	L68	2c black, 156x108mm (1877)	400.00
20LUX6	L69	(1c) black, 156x108mm (1878)	—
a.		Four officers in masthead instead of three	—
20LUX7	L70	(1c) black, 158x110mm (1879)	250.00
20LUX8	L70	(1c) black, large year date and city, 158x110mm (1879)	250.00
20LUX9	L70	(1c) black, 149x102mm (1880)	75.00
a.		Three officers in masthead instead of four, 156x112mm	400.00
20LUX10	L70	(1c) black, 149x102mm (1881)	—
a.		Four officers in masthead instead of three	—
20LUX11	L71	(1c) black, 152x106mm (1883)	—

Sizes of these cards may vary by up to two millimeters in either dimension from the measurements shown.
Nos. 20LUX5 and 20LUX9 exist on paper with a papermaker's watermark. Nos. 20LUX6, 20LUX9 and 20LUX10 may be found with either three or four bank officers listed in the masthead. The major number is the card that was issued first. No. 20LUX11 is known only unused, and may be a remainder that was printed but not used.

NATIONAL PARK BANK

Medium Wove Paper

1881 (?)

20LUX12	L71	(1c) black, 122x63mm ('83)	175.00

No postmarks or cancellations were used on Bank Notices. Boyd's sometimes added the recipient's address in pencil.

FLEISCHMANN'S MODEL BAKERY
Card Stock

1879

20LUX13	L69	(1c) black, 130x75mm	3,00

This card is imprinted "Fleischmann's Model Bakery."

Bradway's Despatch, Millville, N.J.
Operated by Isaac Bradway

L72

1857

			Type
21L1	L72	gold, lilac, on cover, not tied, with certificate	9,25
		On cover, not tied, with 3c #11, with certificate	12,00

Brady & Co., New York, N.Y.

Operated by Abner S. Brady at 97 Duane St. Successor to Clark & Co.

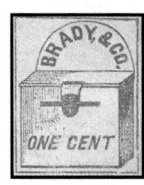

L73

1857

			Typo
22L1	L73	1c red, yellow	1,000. 1,000
		On cover, tied by company handstamp	22,000
		On cover, tied by "PAID" handstamp	10,000

Cancellations: Blue boxed "PAID," blue company oval.
Reprints exist.
No. 22L1 tied on corner by company handstamp is unique. Three covers recorded with stamp tied by "PAID."

Brady & Co.'s Penny Post, Chicago, Ill.

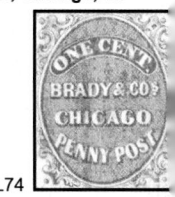

L74

1860(?)

			Litho.
23L1	L74	1c violet	650.00

The authenticity of this stamp has not been fully established.

Brainard & Co.

Established by Charles H. Brainard in 1844, operating between New York, Albany and Troy, Exchanged mail with Hale & Co. by whom Brainard had been employed.

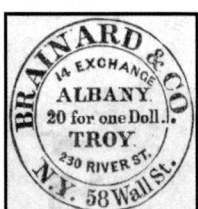

L75

1844

			Typo.
24L1	L75	black	1,000. 1,250.
		On cover, two stamps tied	1,250.
		On cover, not tied	2,000.
		On cover, cut to shape, not tied	1,750.
24L2	L75	blue	1,000. 1,250.
		On cover, not tied	3,250.

Nos. 21L1-24L2 cut to shape are one half of values quoted.

Brigg's Despatch, Philadelphia, Pa.
Established by George W. Briggs

  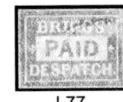

L76   L77

1847
25L1	L76	(2c)	**black**, *yellow buff*	1,000.	
			On cover, not tied, with certificate	11,500.	
25L2	L76	(2c)	**black**, *blue*, cut to shape	7,500.	

No. 25L2 is unique. It is on cover, manuscript "X" cancel, genuine, but Philatelic Foundation has declined to give an opinion as to whether the stamp originated on the cover.

1848
25L4	L77	(2c)	**gold**, *yellow*, glazed	5,500.	
			On cover, not tied		
25L5	L77	(2c)	**gold**, *black*, glazed	4,000.	
			On cover		
25L6	L77	(2c)	**gold**, *pink*	—	

No. 25L4 used and on cover are each unique.

Handstamps formerly illustrated as types L78 and L79 are included in the section "Local Handstamped Covers" at the end of the Local Stamp listings. They were used as postmarks and there is no evidence that any prepaid handstamped envelopes or letter sheets were ever sold.

Broadway Post Office, New York, N.Y.
Started by James C. Harriott in 1848. Sold to Dunham & Lockwood in 1855.

L80

1849(?)   Typo.
26L1	L80	(1c)	**gold**, *black*, glazed	1,000.	1,250.
			Cut to shape		250.
			On cover		—
			Pair on cover		—

1851(?)
26L2	L80	(1c)	**black**	250.	400.
			On cover		1,500.
			On cover with 3c #11		2,750.
			Pair	1,000.	1,000.
			Pair on part of cover		1,500.
			Block of 4	1,750.	

Cancellation: Black oval "Broadway City Express Post-Office 2 Cts."

Bronson & Forbes' City Express Post, Chicago, Ill.
Operated by W.H. Bronson and G.F. Forbes.

L81

1855   Typo.
27L1	L81		**black**, *green*	600.	1,500.
			On cover		
			On cover, tied by handstamp, with 3c #11		10,000.
27L2	L81		**black**, *lilac*		3,500.

Cancellation: Black circle "Bronson & Forbes' City Express Post" (2 types).
No. 27L2 is unique.

Brooklyn City Express Post, Brooklyn, N.Y.
According to the foremost students of local stamps, when this concern was organized its main asset was the business of Kidder's City Express Post, of which Isaac C. Snedeker was the proprietor.

L82   L83

1855-64   **Glazed Surface Paper**   Typo.
28L1	L82	1c	**black**, *blue* (shades)	25.00	80.00
			On cover, tied by handstamp		400.00
			Block of 4	125.00	
a.			Tete beche pair	80.00	
28L2	L82	1c	**black**, *green*	20.00	50.00
			On cover, tied by handstamp		350.00
			On cover, tied by handstamp, with 3c #65		1,250.
			Block of 4	100.00	
a.			Tete beche pair	125.00	
28L3	L83	2c	**black**, *crimson*	60.00	70.00
			On cover, tied by handstamp		400.00
			Block of 4	300.00	
28L4	L83	2c	**black**, *pink*	17.50	100.00
			On cover, tied by handstamp		550.00
			On cover, tied by handstamp, with 3c #65		1,750.
			Block of 4	100.00	
a.			Tete beche pair	60.00	
28L5	L83	2c	**black**, *dark blue*	50.00	90.00
			On cover, tied by handstamp		500.00
			On cover, tied by handstamp, with 3c #11		500.00
			Block of 4	250.00	

No. 28L5 has frame (dividing) lines around design.

28L6	L83	2c	**black**, *orange*	—	—
			On cover		—
a.			Tete beche pair		—

Unsurfaced Paper Colored Through
28L7	L83	2c	**black**, *pink*	300.00	750.00

Cancellations: Black ring, red "PAID."
Reprints exist of Nos. 28L1-28L4, 28L6.

Browne & Co.'s City Post Office, Cincinnati, Ohio
Operated by John W.S. Browne

L84   L85

1852-55   Litho.
29L1	L84	1c	**black** (Brown & Co.)	175.00	150.00
			On cover		1,000.
			On cover with 3c #11		2,750.
			Pair	450.00	
29L2	L85	2c	**black** (Browne & Co.)	175.00	150.00
			On cover, tied by handstamp		4,500.
			On cover with 3c #11		4,000.
			Pair	575.	

Cancellations: Black, blue or red circle "City Post*," red, bright blue or dull blue circle "Browne & Co. City Post Paid."

Browne's Easton Despatch, Easton, Pa.
Established by William J. Browne

L87   L88

1857   **Glazed Surface Paper**   Typeset
30L1	L87	2c	**black**, *red*	—	5,000.
30L2	L88	2c	**black**, *red*	—	

George Washington — L89

                        Wove Paper   Engr.
30L3	L89	2c	**black**	750.	1,000.
			Pair		1,600.
			Block of 6		5,750.

The No. 30L3 block of 6 is the only reported block of this stamp. Three pairs are reported.

Cancellation on No. 30L3: Black oval "Browne's Despatch Easton Pa."

Brown's City Post, New York, N.Y.
Established by stamp dealer William P. Brown for philatelic purposes.

L86

1876   **Glazed Surface Paper**   Typo.
31L1	L86	1c	**black**, *bright red*	200.00	275.00
			On cover		800.00
31L2	L86	1c	**black**, *yellow*	200.00	275.00
			On cover		800.00
31L3	L86	1c	**black**, *green*	200.00	275.00
			On cover		800.00
31L4	L86	1c	**black**, *violet*	200.00	275.00
			On cover		800.00
31L5	L86	1c	**black**, *vermilion*	200.00	275.00
			On cover		800.00

Cancellation: Black circle "Brown's Despatch Paid."

Bury's City Post, New York, N.Y.

L90   L91

1857   **Embossed without color**
32L1	L90	1c	*blue*	8,000.	

                                      Handstamped
32L2	L91		**black**, *blue*	—	

Bush's Brooklyn City Express, Brooklyn, N.Y.

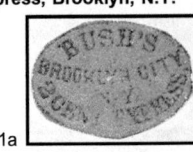

L91a

1848(?)   **Cut to shape**   **Handstamped**
157L1	L91a	2c	**red**, *green*, glazed	27,500.	

No. 157L1 is unique. It is uncanceled on a large piece.
See Bush handstamp in Local Handstamped Covers section.

California City Letter Express Co., San Francisco, Calif.
Organized by J.W. Hoag, proprietor of the Contra-Costa Express, for local delivery. Known also as the California Letter Express Co.

L92

L93

1862-66   Typeset

33L1	L92	10c **red**			—
		On cover, not tied, with 10c #68, with certificate			23,000.
33L2	L92	10c **blue**			—
		On cover, not tied, with certificate			16,500.
33L3	L92	10c **green**		5,500.	
		On cover, uncanceled, with certificate			18,000.
33L4	L93	10c **red**		—	
33L5	L93	10c **blue**			14,000.
33L6	L93	10c **green**		19,000.	
		On cover, not tied, with certificate			31,000.

No side ornaments, "Hoogs & Madison's" in one line

33L7	L93	10c **red**		1,200.	
		On cover, not tied, with certificate			19,000.
33L8	L93	10c **blue**		4,000.	
		On cover, not tied, with 10c #68 with certificate			60,000.

Nos. 33L1 unused, 33L1 on cover with #68, 33L3 used, 33L3 on cover, 33L6 unused, 33L6 on (patriotic) cover, 33L7 used, 33L7 on cover, 33L8 unused and 33L8 on cover with #68 each are unique. The other varieties of Nos. 33L1-33L8 are all rare.

California Penny Post Co.

Established in 1855 by J. P. Goodwin and partners. At first confined its operations to San Francisco, Sacramento, Stockton and Marysville, but branches were soon established at Benicia, Coloma, Nevada, Grass Valley and Mokelumne Hill. Operation was principally that of a city delivery post, as it transported mail to the General Post Office and received mail for local delivery. Most of the business of this post was done by means of prepaid envelopes.

L94

L94a

L95

L95a

1855   Litho.

34L1	L94	2c **blue**		700.	750.
		On cover			20,000.
		Block of 4		3,000.	
34L1A	L94a	3c **blue**			850.
34L2	L95	5c **blue**		250.	425.
		On cover			1,250.
		Block of 4		750.	
34L3	L95a	10c **blue**		475.	—
		On cover			3,000.

Cancellation: Blue circle "Penny Post Co."
Only one example of No. 34L1 on cover is recorded. The stamp is tied by manuscript cancel. Three examples of No. 34L1A are recorded, each uncanceled on cover.

L96

34L4	L96	5c **blue**		600.	1,750.
		On cover			3,000.
		Strip of 3			3,500.

The strip of 3 of No. 34L4 has faults but is unique. Value is for strip in faulty condition.

ENVELOPES

L97

1855-59

34LU1	L97	2c **black**, *white*		200.	900.
		With 1c #9			—
		With 3c #11			9,000.
		With 10c #14			11,000.
a.		Impressed on 3c US env. #U10		250.	1,000.
34LU2	L97	5c **blue**, *blue*		200.	900.
34LU3	L97	5c **black**, *buff*		200.	900.
a.		Impressed on 3c US env. #U10			1,500.
34LU4	L97	7c **black**, *orange buff*		—	
a.		Impressed on 3c US env. #U10			—

L98

34LU6	L98	7c **vermilion** on 3c US env. #U9		200.00	1,000.
34LU7	L98	7c **vermilion** on 3c US env. #U10		225.00	1,750.

PENNY-POSTAGE PAID, 5.

L98A

34LU8	L98A	5c **black**, *white*		150.	1,200.
34LU9	L98A	5c **black**, *buff*		150.	1,200.
		On cover, with 3c #11			—
a.		Impressed on 3c US env. #U10			1,250.
34LU10	L98A	7c **black**, *white*		150.	1,000.
		On cover, with 3c #11			1,750.
a.		Impressed on 3c US env. #U9			—
34LU11	L98A	7c **black**, *buff*		150.00	1,100.
a.		Impressed on 3c US env. #U10			1,500.
34LU11C	L98A	**black**, *buff*, "Collect Penny Postage" (no denomination)		250.	1,500.
		On cover, with 3c #11			—

L98B

34LU11B	L98B	7c **black** on 3c US env. #U10		250.	1,400.
34LU12	L98B	7c **black** on 3c US env. #U9		250.	4,500.

OCEAN PENNY POSTAGE. PAID 5.

L98C

34LU13	L98C	5c **black**, *buff*			—

L98D

34LU13A	L98D	5c **black**, *buff*			—
34LU14	L98D	7c **black**, *buff*		300.	3,00_
		With 3c #11			5,00_
34LU15	L98D	7c **black** on 3c US env. #U9		350.	2,50_
34LU16	L98D	7c **black** on 3c US env. #U10			—

The non-government envelopes of types L97, L98A, L98_ and L98D bear either 1c No. 9 or 3c No. 11 adhesives. These adhesives are normally canceled with the government postma_ of the town of original mailing. Values are for covers of this kin_ The U.S. adhesives are seldom canceled with the Penny Po_ cancellation. When they are, the cover sells for more.

At least eight different varieties of the 34LU14 are known wit_ different printed instructions/addresses, some with room to ad_ U.S. postage.

Carnes' City Letter Express, San Francisco, Calif_

Established by George A. Carnes, former P.O. clerk.

L99

L100

1864   Typo_

35L1	L99	(5c) **rose**		175.	300
		On cover, tied			17,500.
		Block of 4		750.	

Cancellations: Black dots. Blue dots. Blue "Paid." Blue oval "Wm. A. Frey."
See illustration L206

Overprinted "X" in Blue

35L2	L99	10c **rose**			200.00

Litho.

35L3	L100	5c **bronze**			125.00
a.		Tete beche pair			300.00
35L4	L100	5c **gold**			125.00
a.		Tete beche pair			300.00
35L5	L100	5c **silver**			125.00
a.		Tete beche pair			300.00
35L6	L100	5c **black**			125.00
a.		Tete beche pair			300.00
35L7	L100	5c **blue**			100.00
a.		Tete beche pair			250.00
35L8	L100	5c **red**			125.00
a.		Tete beche pair			300.00

Printed in panes of 18 (3x6) from three settings of 6 (3x2), with the bottom setting inverted, creating three tete-beche pairs.

G. Carter's Despatch, Philadelphia, Pa.

Operated by George Carter

L101

1849-51

36L1	L101	2c **black**		—	100.00
		On cover, tied by pen cancel			225.00
		On cover, with 5c #1			—
a.		Ribbed paper		—	140.00
		On cover, tied by pen cancel			300.00

No. 36L1 exists on paper with a blue, red or maroon wash. The origin and status are unclear.
Cancellation: Black circle "Carter's Despatch."

City Dispatch, St. Louis, Mo.

L109

Initials in black ms.

1851 **Litho.**
42L1 L109 2c **black,** *blue* 40,000.

No. 42L1 used is unique. A second example, on cover, is recorded.

City Dispatch Post Office, New Orleans, La.

Stamps sold at 5c each, or 30 for $1.

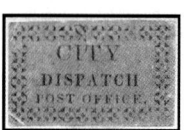

L110

1847 **Glazed Surface Paper** **Typeset**
43L1 L110 (5c) **black,** *green* 6,000.
　　On cover —
43L2 L110 (5c) **black,** *pink* 6,000.
　　On cover, not canceled —

City Express Post, Philadelphia, Pa.

L111　　　　　L112

184-(?) **Typeset**
44L1 L111 2c **black,** on cover, un-
　　canceled, with certificate 11,000.
44L2 L112 (2c) **black,** *pink* 10,000.
　　On cover, uncanceled,
　　with certificate 20,000.
44L3 L112 (2c) **red,** *yellow,* on cover, un-
　　canceled 30,000.

One example recorded of Nos. 44L1 and 44L3. Six No. 44L2 recorded, five of these uncanceled on covers.
See illustration L8.

City Letter Express Mail, Newark, N.J.

Began business under the management of Augustus Peck at a time when there was no free city delivery in Newark.

L113

1856 **Litho.**
45L1 L113 1c **red** 350.00 500.00
　　Cut to shape 100.00
　　On cover —
　　On cover, cut to shape, tied
　　by handstamp, with 3c
　　#11 17,000.
45L2 L113 2c **red,** on cover, cut to shape,
　　uncanceled, with certifi-
　　cate 11,000.

On No. 45L2, the inscription reads "City Letter/Express/City Delivery" in three lines across the top. The example on cover is unique.

City Mail Co., New York, N.Y.

There is evidence that Overton & Co. owned this post.

L114

1845
46L1 L114 (2c) **black,** *grayish* 1,500. 1,500.
　　On cover, not tied, with
　　certificate 8,000.
　　Cancellation: Red "PAID."

City One Cent Dispatch, Baltimore, Md.

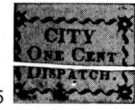

L115

1851
47L1 L115 1c **black,** *pink* (on cover) —

Clark & Co., New York, N.Y.

(See Brady & Co.)

L116

1857 **Typo.**
48L1 L116 1c **red,** *yellow* 600. 900.
　　On cover 2,500.
　　Cancellation: Blue boxed "PAID."

Clark & Hall, St. Louis, Mo.

Established by William J. Clark and Charles F. Hall.

L117

Several varieties

1851 **Typeset**
49L1 L117 1c **black,** *pink,* on cover, un-
　　canceled, with certificate 19,000.

Clarke's Circular Express, New York, N.Y.

Established by Marion M. Clarke

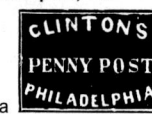

George
Washington — L118

Impression handstamped through inked ribbon.
Cut squares from envelopes or wrappers.

1865-68(?)
50LU1 L118 **blue,** wove paper 5,750.
　a. Diagonally laid paper 4,500.
50LU2 L118 **black,** diag. laid paper 5,750.
　　No. 50LU1 unused is unique.

Cancellation: Blue dated company circle.

Clinton's Penny Post, Philadelphia, Pa.

L118a

Typo.
161L1 L188a (1c) **black** 22,500.

Cook's Dispatch, Baltimore, Md.

Established by Isaac Cook

L119

1853
51L1 L119 (1c) **green,** *white* 4,000. 3,00
　　Cut to shape 1,500.
　　On cover —
　　Cancellation: Red straight-line "I cook."

Cornwell's Madison Square Post Office, New York, N.Y.

Established by Daniel H. Cornwell. Sold to H.W. Bentley.

L120

1856 **Typo.**
52L1 L120 (1c) **red,** *blue* 600. —
52L2 L120 (1c) **red** 250. 600.
　　On cover, tied by hand-
　　stamp 10,000.
　　Pair —

Cancellation: Black oval "Cornwell's Madison Square Post Office." Covers also bear black boxed "Paid Swarts."

Cressman & Co.'s Penny Post, Philadelphia, Pa.

L121

1856
　　Glazed Surface Paper
53L1 L121 (1c) **gold,** *black* 350. 350.
　　Pair 1,200.
53L2 L121 (1c) **gold,** *lilac,* on cover, acid
　　tied 25,000.

The vertical pair of No. 53L1 is unique. No. 53L2 also is unique.

Cancellation: Acid. (See D.O. Blood & Co. Nos. 15L13-15L16.)

Crosby's City Post, New York, N.Y.

Established by Oliver H. Crosby. Stamps printed by J.W. Scott & Co.

L123

1870 **Typo.**
　　Printed in sheets 25 (5x5), imprint at left.
54L1 L123 2c **carmine** (shades) 1.00 50.00
　　On cover 400.00
　　Pair —
　　Sheet of 25 50.00
　　Cancellation: Black oval "Crosby's City Post."

Cummings' City Post, New York, N.Y.

Established by A. H. Cummings.

L124

Glazed Surface Paper   Typo.

.1	L124	2c **black**, *rose*		1,000.
		On cover, tied, with certificate		5,750.
		On cover, not tied, with certificate		—
.2	L124	2c **black**, *green*		650.
		On cover		2,500.
.3	L124	2c **black**, *yellow*		750.
		On cover, tied by handstamp		2,000.
		On cover, not tied, with certificate		1,250.

Cancellations: Red boxed "FREE," red boxed "PAID AHC," black cork (3 types).

L125

.4	L125	2c **black**, *green*	750.00	750.00
.5	L125	2c **black**, *olive*	750.00	750.00

L126

.7	L126	2c **black**, *vermilion*	8,250.
		On cover, uncanceled, with certificate	22,000.

As L124, but "Cummings" erased on cliche

L8	L124	2c **black**, *vermilion*	—

Nos. 55L7 on cover and 55L8 each are unique.

Cutting's Despatch Post, Buffalo, N.Y.

Established by Thomas S. Cutting

L127

Cut to shape

Glazed Surface Paper

L1	L127	2c **black**, *vermilion*	—
		On cover, cut to shape, uncanceled, with certificate	22,000.

Davis's Penny Post, Baltimore, Md.

Established by William D. Davis and brother.

L128

Several varieties   Typeset

L1	L128	(1c) **black**, *lilac*	2,750.
		On cover, tied by handstamp	11,000.
a.		"Pennq," pos. 2	8,250. 8,250.

Cancellation: Red company circle.

Deming's Penny Post, Frankford, Pa.

Established by Sidney Deming

L129

1854   Litho.

5L1	L129	(1c) **black**, *grayish*	5,750.
		On cover, with 3c #11	18,000.

Douglas' City Despatch, New York, N.Y.

Established by George H. Douglas

L130

L131

Printed in sheets of 25

1879   Typo.   Perf. 11

59L1	L130	(1c) **pink**	10.00	15.00
		On cover		300.00
a.		Imperf.	30.00	
59L2	L130	(2c) **blue**	10.00	15.00
		On cover, tied by handstamp		500.00
a.		Imperf.	50.00	
b.		Printed on both sides		—

Printed in sheets of 50 (10x5).

Perf. 11, 12 & Compound

59L3	L131	1c **vermilion**	15.00	35.00
		On cover		325.00
a.		Imperf.	1.00	
59L4	L131	1c **orange**	25.00	50.00
		On cover, tied by handstamp		600.00
59L5	L131	1c **blue**	30.00	50.00
		On cover		300.00
a.		Imperf.	1.00	
59L6	L131	1c **slate blue**	20.00	25.00
a.		Imperf.	7.50	

Cancellations on Nos. 59L1-59L6: Ornate purple design, purple circular design composed of bars and wedges.
Imperforates are believed to be remainders sold by the printer.

Dupuy & Schenck, New York, N.Y.

Established by Henry J. Dupuy and Jacob H. Schenck, formerly carriers for City Despatch Post and U. S. City Despatch Post.

Beehive — L132

1846-47   Engr.

60L1	L132	(1c) **black**, glazed paper	175.	300.
		On cover, tied by handstamp		1,750.
		On cover, tied by ms.		1,250.
60L2	L132	(1c) **black**, *gray*	175.	300.
		On cover, tied by handstamp		1,600.

Cancellation: Red "PAID."

Eagle City Post, Philadelphia, Pa.

Established by W. Stait, an employee of Adams' Express Co.

L133

Black manuscript "WS" on used examples

1847   Pelure Paper   Typeset

61L1	L133	(2c) **black**, *grayish*	14,000.	10,000.
		Cut to shape, on cover		—

No. 61L1 unused is unique. Value reflects a 1997 auction sale.

L134

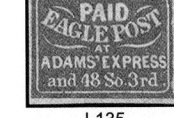
L135

Two types: 39 and 46 points around circle

1846   Litho.

61L2	L134	(2c) **black**	125.00	250.00
		On cover, tied by handstamp		1,500.
		On cover, not tied		1,000.
		Block of 4	600.00	
a.		Tete beche pair	500.00	
		Block of 18, containing 4 tete beche pairs	4,000.	

Paper varies in thickness.
Five types identified of Nos. 61L3-61L4.

1850

61L3	L135	(1c) **red**, *bluish*	225.00	225.00
		On cover, not tied, with certificate		2,250.
61L4	L135	(1c) **blue**, *bluish*	175.00	250.00
		On cover, tied by handstamp		6,500.
		On cover, not tied		400.00
		Block of 4	1,150.	

Cancellations on Nos. 61L2-61L4: Red "PAID" in large box, red circular "Stait's at Adams Express."

East River Post Office, New York, N. Y.

Established by Jacob D. Clark and Henry Wilson in 1850, and sold to Sigmund Adler in 1852.

L136

1852   Typo.

62L1	L136	(1c) **black**, *rose* (on cover)	—

L137

L138

1852-54   Litho.

62L3	L137	(1c) **black**, *green*, glazed	1,000.	—

1855

62L4	L138	(1c) **black**, *green*, glazed	250.00	250.00
		On cover		800.00
		On cover, not tied		400.00
		Vertical pair	2,500.	

The unique No. 62L4 pair is the only recorded multiple of any of the East River Post Office stamps.

Eighth Avenue Post Office, New York, N.Y.

L139

1852   Typo.

63L1	L139	**red**, on cover	19,000.

One example known, uncanceled on cover.

Empire City Dispatch, New York, N.Y.

Established by J. Bevan & Son and almost immediately suppressed by the Government.

L140

1881   Typo.   Laid Paper   Perf. 12

64L1	L140	**black**, *green*	1.50
		Block of 4	7.50
a.		Imperf.	—
b.		Horiz. pair, imperf. btwn.	85.00
c.		Vert. pair, imperf. btwn.	85.00

Essex Letter Express, New York, N.Y.

L141

1856		**Glazed Surface Paper**	**Typo.**
65L1	L141	2c **black**, *red*	1,250.

Though uncanceled examples exist affixed to covers, some authorities doubt that No. 65L1 was placed in use.

Faunce's Penny Post, Atlantic City, N.J.

Established in 1884 by Ancil Faunce to provide local delivery of letters to and from the post office. Discontinued in 1887.

L141a

1885			**Die cut**
152L1	L141a	(1c) **black**, *red*	225. 350.
		On cover	1,500.

Jabez Fearey & Co.'s Mustang Express, Newark, N.J.

Established by Jabez Fearey, Local Agent of the Pacific & Atlantic Telegraph Co.

L142

1887 (?)		**Glazed Surface Paper**	**Typeset**
66L1	L142	**black**, *red*	275.00
		On cover	—

Some authorities consider this item to be an express company label rather than a stamp.

Fiske & Rice

Authorities consider items of this design to be express company labels rather than stamps.

Floyd's Penny Post, Chicago, Ill.

Established by John R. Floyd early in 1860, operated by him until June 20, 1861, then continued by Charles W. Mappa.

John R. Floyd — L144

1860			**Typo.**
68L1	L144	(1c) **blue** (shades)	— 125.
		On cover, tied by handstamp	1,000.
		On cover with 3c #26	—
		On cover with 3c #65	1,500.
		Pair	275.
		Strip of 4	1,250.
68L2	L144	(1c) **brown**	500. 1,000.
		On cover	4,250.

68L3	L144	(1c) **green**	4,500. 3,250.
		On cover	—
		On 3c pink entire	27,500.

Cancellations: Black circle "Floyd's Penny Post Chicago," black circle "Floyd's Penny Post" and sunburst, black or blue oval "Floyd's Penny Post Chicago."

Franklin City Despatch Post, N.Y.

(See Bouton's Manhattan Express.)

Frazer & Co., Cincinnati, Ohio.

Established by Hiram Frazer. Stamps used while he was a Cincinnati letter carrier. Stamps of designs L146 and L147 were carrier stamps when used on cover betweeen Feb, 3, 1848 and June 30, 1849.

L145

Cut to shape

1845

Glazed Surface Paper

69L1	L145	2c **black**, *green*	—
		On cover	—

L146   L147

1845-51		**Wove Paper**	**Litho.**
69L2	L146	2c **black**, *pink*	— 3,500.
		On cover, ms. tied	6,750.
69L3	L146	2c **black**, *green*	2,500. 2,750.
		On 1847 cover, tied by handstamp	11,000.
		On cover, not tied	3,500.
69L4	L146	2c **black**, *yellow*	2,500. 2,500.
69L5	L146	2c **black**, *grayish*	2,500. 2,500.

Two stamps of type L146 show manual ms. erasure of "& Co."

1848-51			
69L6	L147	2c **black**, *rose*	2,750.
		On 1848 cover, not tied, with certificate	6,500.
69L7	L147	2c **black**, *blue* (shades)	3,500. —
69L8	L147	2c **black**, *yellow*	2,750.
		On 1848 part-printed notice	7,500.

Hiram Frazer was a government letter carrier until June 5, 1849. Therefore, any usage before that date is a government-carrier usage, not a local-post usage.

Freeman & Co.'s Express, New York, N.Y.

L147a

1855 (?)			**Litho.**
164L1	L147a	(25c) **blue**	3,500.
		On cover, not tied, with certificate	—

Friend's Boarding School, Barnesville, Ohio.

(Barclay W. Stratton, Supt.)

On Nov. 6, 1877 the school committee decided to charge the students one cent for each letter carried to or from the post office, and one and a half miles away. Adhesive labels were prepared and sold for one cent each. Their sale and use continued until 1884.

L147b — Type I

L147b — Type II

L147b — Type III

Three main types and sizes of frame

1877			**Typ**
151L1	L147b	(1c) **black**	175.00
		On cover, uncanceled, affixed to backflap	400.
		On cover, tied by handstamp, with 3c #158	2,40
		On cover, tied by handstamp, with 2c #210	2,75

No. 151L1 was usually affixed to the back of the envelo and left uncanceled.

Gahagan & Howe City Express, San Francisco, Calif.

Established by Dennis Gahagan and C. E. B. How as successors to John C. Robinson, proprietor of th San Francisco Letter Express. Sold in 1865 to Willia E. Loomis, who later purchased the G. A. Carnes bus ness. Loomis used the adhesive stamps and han stamps of these posts, changing the Carnes stamp b erasing his name.

L148

L149

1849-70			**Typeset**
70L1	L148	5c **light blue**	400. 800.
70L2	L149	(5c) **blue**	150. 400.
a.		Tete beche pair	450.
		Sheet of 20, with 4 tete beche pairs	

Sheets of No. 70L2 contain five vertical rows of 4, the first two rows being reversed against the others, making horizontal tete beche pairs with wide margins between. The pairs were not evenly locked up in the form. There are five different types of No. 70L2.

L150

70L3	L150	(5c) **black**	40.00 45.00
		Pair	100.00
		Strip of 3	175.00

Overprinted "X" in Blue

70L4	L150	10c **black**	750.00

Cancellations: Blue or black oval "Gahagan & Howe," blue or black oval "San Francisco Letter Express" and horseman (Robinson), blue or black oval "PAID" (Loomis).

Glen Haven Daily Mail, Glen Haven, N.Y.

Glen Haven was located at the head of Skaneateles Lake, Cayuga County, N.Y., until 1910 when the City

Syracuse, having purchased the land for reservoir purposes, razed all the buildings.

Glen Haven, by 1848, had become a famous Water Cure resort, with many sanitariums conducted there. The hamlet had a large summer colony interested in dress reform under the leadership of Amelia Jenks Bloomer; also antislavery, and other reform movements.

A local post was established by the hotel and sanitarium managements for their guests' convenience to deliver mail to the U.S. post offices at Homer or Scott, N.Y. The local stamps were occasionally pen canceled. They are known tied to cover with the Homer or Scott town postmark when the local stamp was placed adjacent to the government stamp and received the cancellation accidentally. The local stamps are only known used in conjunction with government stamps.

| L151 | | L152 |

1854-58 | | **Typeset**

Several varieties of each

71L1	L151	1c **black**, *dark green*	1,000.	
	a.	"Glen" instead of "Glen"	3,500.	
		On cover, uncanceled, with 3c #26, with certificate		6,250.

No. 71L1a unused (actually uncanceled on piece) and on cover with #26 each are unique.

Glazed Surface Paper

| 71L2 | L152 | 1c **black**, *green* | 500. | 500. |
| | | On cover | | 2,000. |

| Links at corners — L153 | Varying ornaments at corners — L153a |

Several varieties of each
Glazed Surface Paper

71L3	L153	1c **black**, *green*	200.	225.
		On cover		2,000.
		On cover, tied by handstamp, with 3c #11		1,750.
		On cover, not tied, with 3c #11		500.
		Pair	700.	
71L4	L153a	1c **black**, *green*	300.	350.
		On cover		1,000.
		On 3c entire #U9, tied by handstamp		1,000.
		"Block" of 3	900.00	

The strip of 3 of No. 71L4 is the only known multiple of any Glen Haven stamp. It has faults and is valued thus.

Gordon's City Express, New York, N. Y.

Established by Samuel B. Gordon

L154

1848-52		**Typo.**	**Surface Colored Paper**
72L1	L154	2c **black**, *vermilion*	7,000.	
		On cover, uncanceled, with certificate		15,000.
72L2	L154	2c **black**, *green*	150.	175.
		On cover		650.

Glazed Surface Paper

| 72L3 | L154 | 2c **black**, *green* | 125. | 200. |
| | | On cover | | 650. |

Cancellation: Small black or red "PAID."

Grafflin's Baltimore Despatch, Baltimore, Md.

Established by Joseph Grafflin; operated from Apr. 1, 1855, until June 30, 1863

L155

Printed in sheets of 49

1856				**Litho.**
73L1	L155	1c **black**	200.	350.
		On cover, tied by handstamp		4,000.
		On cover, tied by handstamp, with 3c #11		3,000.
		Block of 4	1,050.	

Originals show traces of a fine horizontal line through tops of most of the letters in "BALTIMORE."

Guy's City Despatch, Philadelphia, Pa.

Established by F. A. Guy, who employed 8 carriers.

L156

Sheets of 25 (5x5)

1879		**Typo.**	**Perf. 11, 12, 12½**
74L1	L156	(1c) **pink**	30.00	35.00
		On cover, tied by handstamp		800.00
		Block of 4	150.00	
	a.	Imperf., pair	—	
74L2	L156	(1c) **blue**	45.00	60.00
		On cover, tied by handstamp		1,500.
		Block of 4	225.00	
	a.	Imperf., pair	—	
	b.	(1c) **Ultramarine**	75.00	100.00

Cancellation: Purple company oval.

Guy's City Despatch was in operation from April to June, 1879. When Guy's was suppressed, the remainders were sold to a New York stamp dealer.

Hackney & Bolte Penny Post, Atlantic City, N.J.

Established in 1886 by Evan Hackney and Charles Bolte to provide delivery of mail to and from the post office. Discontinued in 1887.

L156a

Die cut

153L1	L156a	(1c) **black**, *red*	250.	375.
		On cover		1,500.
		On cover, tied by handstamp, with 2c #210		5,000.

Hale & Co.

Established by James W. Hale at New York, N.Y., to carry mail to points in New England, New York State, Philadelphia and Baltimore. Stamps sold at 6 cents each or "20 for $1.00."

L157

L158

Printed in sheets of 20 (5x4)

Pelure paper was used for initial printings, with medium wove paper used subsequently.

1844				**Typo.**
75L1	L157	(6c) **light blue** (shades)	65.00	40.00
		Cut to shape		17.50
		On cover, tied by handstamp		500.00
		Cut to shape on cover, tied by handstamp		200.00
		Strip of 3 on cover, tied by handstamp		7,000.
		Strip of 3 on cover, not tied		2,750.
	a.	Pelure paper		—
75L2	L157	(6c) **red**, *bluish*	300.00	300.00
		Cut to shape		75.00
		On cover, tied by handstamp		2,500.
		On cover, not tied		500.00
		Cut to shape on cover, tied by handstamp		1,000.
		Pair on cover		—
		Ms. "23 State," cut to shape		1,900.
		On cover		4,000.
	a.	Pelure paper		—

Two covers recorded showing the manuscript change of address.

Same Handstamped in Black or Red,
"City Despatch Office, 23 State St."

75L3	L157	(6c) **red**, *bluish* (Bk), cut to shape		2,000.
		Pair, partly cut to shape		44,000.
75L4	L157	(6c) **blue** (R), cut to shape		2,000.

No. 75L3 single and pair each are unique.

No. 75L3 and 75L4 represent the first handstamped overprints in philately.

Same as Type L157 but street address omitted

75L5	L158	(6c) **blue** (shades)	40.00	20.00
		Cut to shape		5.00
		On cover, tied by handstamp		450.00
		Cut to shape on cover, tied by handstamp		200.00
		Pair on cover		700.00
		Strip of 3 on cover, not tied		—
		Pair	500.00	
		Block of 9	—	
		Block of 15	9,500.	
		Sheet of 20 (5x4)	17,000.	
		Ms. "23 State St.," on cover		2,500.

Cancellations on Nos. 75L1-75L5: Large red "PAID," red, black or blue oval "Hale & Co." (several types and cities), small red ornamental framed box (several types), red negative monogram "WE," magenta ms. "NB" (New Bedford).

The No. 75L5 sheet of 20 is unique.

Hall & Mills' Despatch Post, New York, N.Y.

Established by Gustavus A. Mills and A. C. Hall.

L159

Several Varieties

1847		**Glazed Surface Paper**		**Typeset**
76L1	L159	(2c) **black**, *green*	300.	300.
		On cover		750.
		On cover with 5c #1		2,500.

T.A. Hampton City Despatch, Philadelphia, Pa.

L159a

L159b

Several Varieties of L159a

1847		Cut to shape	Typeset
77L1	L159a	(2c) **black**	1,500.
		On cover, tied by hand-stamp	14,000.
		On cover, uncanceled, with certificate	5,000.
77L2	L159b	**black**, on cover	13,000.

Only one cover known with No. 77L1 tied by handstamp. Five or six covers are known with stamp uncanceled.

Two covers known with No. 77L2, each with stamp canceled, not tied. May 23 cover with certificate is valued above. Second cover is undated Valentine cover.

A handstamp similar to type L159b with denomination "2cts" or "3c" instead of "PAID." in center has been used as a postmark.

Hanford's Pony Express, New York, N.Y.

Established by John W. Hanford.

L160

1845			Glazed Surface Paper	Typo.
78L1	L160	2c	**black**, *orange yellow* (shades)	300. 400.
			Cut to shape	60.
			On cover, tied by handstamp	2,000.

Cancellation: Small red "PAID."

The handstamp in black or red formerly listed as Nos. 78LU1-78LU6 is illustrated in the Local Handstamped Covers section. It was used as a postmark and there is no evidence that any prepaid handstamped envelopes or lettersheets were ever sold.

George S. Harris City Despatch Post, Philadelphia, Pa.

L160a

L160b

1847 (?)			Typeset
79L1	L160a	(2c) **black**, on cover	
79L2	L160b	**black**, on cover	30,000.

One example each known of Nos. 79L1-79L2, each uncanceled on cover, No. 79L2 with certificate.

Hartford, Conn. Mail Route

L161

Plate of 12 (6x2) varieties

1844			Glazed Surface Paper	Engr.
80L1	L161	(5c)	**black**, *yellow*	1,250. 2,000.
			On cover	
			Pair	5,000.
			Pair on cover, not canceled	32,500.
80L3	L161		**black**, *pink*	3,500.

Chemically affected copies of No. 80L1 appear as buff, and of No. 80L3 as salmon.

Cancellations are usually initials or words ("S," "W," "South," etc.) in black ms. This may indicate destination or routing.

Hill's Post, Boston, Mass.

Established by Oliver B. Hill

L162

1849			Typo.
81L1	L162	1c **black**, *rose*, on cover, tied by handstamp	7,500.
		On cover, canceled but not tied, with certificate	6,500.

Only one No. 81L1 tied to cover recorded. Six covers recorded bearing No. 80L1 not tied, all but one of those also uncanceled.

A. M. Hinkley's Express Co., New York, N.Y.

Organized by Abraham M. Hinkley, Hiram Dixon and Hiram M. Dixon, in 1855, and business transferred to the Metropolitan Errand & Carrier Express Co. in same year.

L163

Sheets of 64 (8x8)

1855			Litho.
82L1	L163	1c **red**, *bluish*	400.00
		Block of 4	
a.		Tete-beche pair	

It is doubtful that No. 82L1 was ever placed in use.

Only one example of No. 82L1a is recorded. It is contained in a block of 16 of No. 82L1.

Reprints exist on white paper somewhat thicker than the originals.

Homan's Empire Express, New York, N.Y.

Established by Richard S. Homan

L164

Several varieties

1852			Typeset
83L1	L164	**black**, *yellow*	
a.		"1" for "I" in "PAID"	8,250.

No. 83L1a is unique. It is affixed to a cover front, uncanceled, with certificate.

Hopedale Penny Post, Milford, Mass.

Hopedale was a large farm community southwest Milford, Mass. The community meeting of Feb. 1849, voted to arrange for regular transportation mail to the nearest post office, which was at Milford, mile and a half distant, at a charge of 1c a letter. complete history of this community may be found "The Hopedale Community," published in 1897.

Rayed asterisks in corners — L165

Plain asterisks in corners — L166

Several varieties of Types L165-L166

1849			Glazed Surface Paper	Typese
84L1	L165	(1c)	**black**, *pink*	800.00 800.0
			On cover with 3c #11, handstamp tied	3,75
			On cover with 3c #11, not canceled	1,25
84L2	L166	(1c)	**black**, *pink*	1,000. 1,00

Types L165 and L166 probably were printed together in single small plate.

L167

			Wove Paper	Typo.
84L3	L167	(1c)	**black**, *yellow*	— 2,400
			Cut to shape	900.
			On cover	
84L4	L167	(1c)	**black**, *pink*	600. 600
			Pair	4,500.

The No. 84L4 pair is unique, defective at top. It is the only recorded multiple of any Hopedale Penny Post issue.

J. A. Howell's City Despatch, Philadelphia, Pa.

L167a

184?			Typo.
165L1	L167a	**black**	

Hoyt's Letter Express, Rochester, N.Y.

David Hoyt, agent at Rochester for the express company of Livingston, Wells & Pomeroy, operated a letter and package express by boats on the Genesee Canal between Dansville, N.Y., and Rochester, where connection was also made with Pomeroy's Letter Express.

L168

Several varieties

1844			Glazed Surface Paper	Typeset
85L1	L168	(5c)	**black**, *vermilion*	4,000. —
a.		"Lettcr" instead of "Letter"	
			Pair, #85L1, 85L1a, on cover front	

Humboldt Express, Nevada

A branch of Langton's Pioneer Express, connecting with the main line of Pioneer Express at Carson City, Nevada, and making tri-weekly trips to adjacent points.

L169

3			**Litho.**	
1	L169	25c **brown**	1,750.	1,250.
		Pair		2,750.
		On cover (U.S. Envelopes		
		Nos. U34 or U35)		40,000.
		On cover with 3c #65		—

cancellations: Blue oval "Langton's Pioneer Express Union-
." Red "Langton & Co."

Hussey's Post, New York, N.Y.

Established by George Hussey.
Reprints available for postage are so described.

L170   L171

54			**Litho.**	
L1	L170	(1c) **blue**	500.	
		On cover, tied by hand-stamp		2,750.
		On cover, with U.S. 3c (#11)		—
56				
L2	L171	(1c) **black**	300.	200.
		On cover, tied by hand-stamp		1,200.
L3	L171	(1c) **red**		200.
		On cover, tied by hand-stamp		750.

Cancellation on Nos. 87L1-87L3: Black "FREE."

L172   L173

858				
7L4	L172	1c **brown red**	45.	125.
		On cover, tied by hand-stamp		450.
		Pair on cover		1,000.
7L5	L172	1c **black**	175.	
		On cover		—
		Block of 4		—
		Strip of 7		—

Cancellation on Nos. 87L4-87L5: Black circle "1ct PAID HUS-
SEY 50 Wm. ST," date in center.
The No. 87L5 block of 4 and strip of 7 are unique.

1858				
87L6	L173	(1c) **black**	5.00	
		On cover		—
87L7	L173	(1c) **rose red**	5.00	
		On cover		—
		Sheet of 46	275.00	
87L8	L173	(1c) **red**	60.00	
		On cover		—
		Sheet of 46		—

Type L173 was printed in sheets of 46: 5 horizontal rows of 8,
one row of 6 sideways at bottom. Type L173 saw little, if any,
commercial use and was probably issued mainly for collectors.
Covers exist, many with apparently contemporaneous corner
cards. On-cover stamps bear a black HUSSEY'S POST handstamp, but most if not all of Nos. 87L6-87L8 were canceled after
the post ceased to operate.

 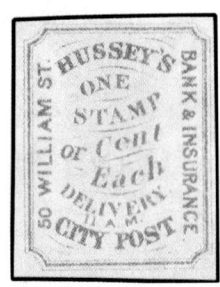

L174   L175

1858			**Typo.**	
87L9	L174	(1c) **blue**	5.00	

1859			**Litho.**	
87L10	L175	1c **rose red**	15.00	40.00
		On cover		400.00

No. 87L10 in orange red is not known to have been placed in
use.
Cancellations: Black "FREE," black company circle "1 CT
PAID HUSSEY 50 WM ST.," no date in center (smaller than
cancel on Nos. 87L4-87L5).

87L11	L175	1c **lake**	—	
87L12	L175	1c **black**	—	

L176   L177

1862				
87L13	L176	1c **black**	25.00	
87L14	L176	1c **blue**	15.00	25.00
		On cover		450.00
87L15	L176	1c **green**	20.00	
		On cover		450.00
87L16	L176	1c **red**	30.00	
87L17	L176	1c **red brown**	30.00	
87L18	L176	1c **brown**	30.00	
87L19	L176	1c **lake**	—	
87L20	L176	1c **purple**	30.00	
87L21	L176	1c **yellow**	30.00	

Similar to L174 but has condensed "50" and shows a
short flourish line over the "I" of "DELIVERY."
Printed in sheets of 49

1862				
87L22	L177	(1c) **blue**	3.00	25.00
		On cover		—

L178   Similar to L171, but no
dots in corners — L179

Printed in sheets of 30

1863				
87L23	L178	(1c) **blue**	7.50	
87L24	L179	(1c) **black**	5.00	
		Sheet of 30	225.00	
87L25	L179	(1c) **red**	6.50	
		Sheet of 30	250.00	
		On cover with 6c #115		17,500.

See No. 87L52.

L180   L182

87L26	L180	1c **brown red**	5.00	25.00
		Block of 4	25.00	
		On cover, tied by hand-stamp		450.00

A so-called "reprint" of No. 87L26, made for J. W. Scott, has a
colored flaw extending diagonally upward from the "I" in "CITY."
*Reprints of types L173, L174, L178, L179 and L180 were
made in 1875-76 on thicker paper in approximately normal colors and were available for postage.*

1863				
		Dated 1863		
87L27	L182	1c **blue**	20.00	
		Cut to shape	12.50	
		On cover, tied by hand-stamp		500.00
87L28	L182	1c **green**	27.50	
		Cut to shape	14.00	
		On cover, tied by hand-stamp		550.00
87L29	L182	1c **yellow**	25.00	
		Cut to shape	12.50	
		On cover, tied by hand-stamp		500.00
87L30	L182	1c **brown**	27.50	
		Cut to shape	14.00	
87L31	L182	1c **red brown**	30.00	
		Cut to shape	15.00	
87L32	L182	1c **red**	27.50	
		Cut to shape	14.00	
87L33	L182	1c **black**	40.00	
		Cut to shape	20.00	
87L34	L182	1c **violet**	40.00	
		Cut to shape	20.00	
87L35	L182	2c **brown**	40.00	75.00
		Cut to shape	20.00	
		On cover, tied by hand-stamp		650.00

The 2c blue dated 1863 exists only as a counterfeit.

1865				
		Dated 1865		
87L38	L182	2c **blue**	35.00	45.00
		On cover, tied by hand-stamp		475.00
1867				
		Dated 1867		
87L39	L182	2c **blue**	45.00	40.00
		On cover, tied by hand-stamp		450.00
1868				
		Dated 1868		
87L40	L182	2c **blue**	40.00	65.00
		On cover, tied by hand-stamp		500.00
1869				
		Dated 1870		
87L41	L182	2c **blue**	45.00	70.00
		On cover, tied by hand-stamp		500.00
1871				
		Dated 1871		
87L42	L182	2c **blue**	40.00	65.00
		On cover, tied by hand-stamp		750.00

L183   L184

1872				
		Wove Paper		
87L43	L183	**black**	5.00	20.00
		On cover, tied by hand-stamp		300.00
		Pair on cover, tied by hand-stamp		1,500.
87L44	L183	**red lilac**	9.00	40.00
		On cover, tied by hand-stamp		300.00
87L45	L183	**blue**	6.00	40.00
		On cover, tied by hand-stamp		300.00
		Pair on cover, tied by hand-stamp		750.00
87L46	L183	**green**	10.00	45.00
		On cover, tied by hand-stamp		300.00

Sheets contain four panes of 28 each. Double periods after
"A.M." on two stamps in two panes, and on four stamps in the
other two panes.
Covers show postmark reading: "HUSSEY'S SPECIAL-MES-
SENGER EXPRESS-PAID-54 PINE ST."

1872				
		Thick Laid paper		
87L47	L184	**black**	10.00	35.00
		On cover		—
		Block of 4	45.00	
87L48	L184	**yellow**	17.50	65.00
87L49	L184	**red brown**	17.50	50.00

87L50	L184	On cover		200.00
		red	17.50	40.00
		On cover		—

L185

L186

1873
Thin Wove Paper

87L51	L185	2c **black**	75.00	150.00
		On cover		500.00

A reprint of No. 87L51, believed to have been made for J. W. Scott, shows a 4mm break in the bottom frameline under "54."

Type of 1863
1875
Thick Wove Paper

87L52	L179	(1c) **blue**	750.00

1875

L186 in imitation of L180, but no corner dots, "S" for "$," etc.

87L53	L186	1c **black**	2.00

Some authorities believe Nos. 87L52-87L53 are imitations made from new stones. Attributed to J. W. Scott.

"Copyright 1877" — L188

L188a

1877
Thick Wove Paper

87L55	L188	**black**	175.00	—
		On cover		600.00

Error of design, used provisionally. Stamp was never copyrighted. Printed singly.

87L56	L188a	**black**	350.00

Thin Wove Paper

87L57	L188a	**blue**	45.00
87L58	L188a	**rose**	30.00
		On cover	—

Perf. 12½

87L59	L188a	**blue**	3.00	10.00
		On cover		250.00
a.		Imperf. horizontally, pair		—
87L60	L188a	**rose**	3.00	10.00
		On cover		250.00

"TRADE MARK"
small — L189

"TRADE MARK" larger, touching "s" of "Easson." — L191

1878   Wove Paper   Perf. 11, 11½, 11x12, 12

87L61	L189	**blue**	15.00	50.00
		On cover, tied by hand-stamp		150.00
87L62	L189	**carmine**	12.50	40.00
		On cover, tied by hand-stamp		200.00
87L63	L189	**black**	100.00	

Nos. 87L61-87L63 exist imperforate.

Perf. 11, 12, 12½, 14, 16 and Compound

87L64	L190	**blue**	5.00	17.50
		On cover, tied by hand-stamp		200.00
87L65	L190	**red**	5.00	10.00
		On cover, tied by hand-stamp		150.00
87L66	L190	**black**		—

The existence of No. 87L66 either perforated or as an imperf reprint has been questioned by specialists. The editors would like to see authenticated evidence of its existence.
Nos. 87L64-87L65 imperf. are reprints.

1879   Perf. 11, 12, and Compound

87L67	L191	**blue**	3.00	10.00
		On cover, tied by handstamp		300.00
87L69	L191	**black**		—

1880   Imperf.

87L70	L191	**blue**	4.00	50.00
		On cover, tied by handstamp		450.00
87L71	L191	**red**	5.00	75.00
87L72	L191	**black**	4.00	

The authenticity of Nos. 87L69-87L72 has not been fully established.

L192

Two types of L192:
I. Imprint "N. F. Seebeck, 97 Wall St. N. Y." is in lower tablet below "R Easson, etc."
II. Imprint in margin below stamp.

1880   Glazed Surface Wove Paper   Perf. 12

87L73	L192	**brown**, type I	10.00	20.00
		On cover, tied by handstamp		250.00
		Block of 4		—
a.		Type II	3.00	5.00
		On cover, tied by handstamp		250.00
b.		Horiz. pair, imperf. between	50.00	
c.		Imperf., pair	50.00	
87L74	L192	**ultramarine**, type I	12.50	25.00
		On cover, tied by handstamp		350.00
a.		Imperf., pair		—
		Imperf (single) on cover		135.00
b.		Deep blue, type II	40.00	
87L75	L192	**red**, type II	1.50	3.50
		On cover, tied by handstamp		175.00
		Block of 4	6.50	
a.		Imperf, single on cover		150.00

1882   Perf. 16, 12

87L76	L192	**brown**, type I	12.50	3
		On cover, tied by handstamp		12
87L77	L192	**ultramarine**, type I	10.00	2
		On cover, tied by handstamp		12

Cancellations: Violet 3-ring target, violet ornamental
Imperf. impressions of Type I in various colors, on horizon
laid paper, ungummed, are color trials.

SPECIAL DELIVERY STAMPS

L181

Typographed; Numerals Inserted Separately
1863   Glazed Surface Pap

87LE1	L181	5c **black**, red	2.00	17
		On cover		350
87LE2	L181	10c **gold**, green	2.50	20
		On cover		350
87LE3	L181	15c **gold**, black	3.50	27
		On cover		400
		On cover with 1c #87L10, tied by handstamps		
87LE4	L181	20c **black**	2.00	17
		On cover		400
87LE5	L181	25c **gold**, blue	4.00	40.
		On cover		400.
87LE6	L181	30c **gold**, red		
87LE7	L181	50c **black**, green		

Nos. 87LE1-87LE7 on cover show Hussey handstamp ca
cellations in various types.
Nos. 87LE4 and 87LE5 are on unglazed paper, the latt
surface colored. Ten minor varieties of each value, except th
30c and 50c, which have the figures in manuscript. Printed
two panes of 10, certain values exist in horizontal cross-gutt
tete beche pairs.
Originals of the 5c to 20c have large figures of value. The 2
has condensed figures with decimal point. Reprints exist wi
both large and condensed figures. Reprints of the 25c also ex
with serifs on large figures.
Most of the Hussey adhesives are known on cover, tied wi
Hussey Express postmarks. Many of these were canceled aft
the post ceased to operate as a mail carrier. "On cover" value
are for original stamps used while the post was operating.

LETTERSHEETS AND WRAPPERS (No. 87LUP2)

L192a

L192b

1856   Handstamped   Inscribed: "82 Broadway"

87LUP1	L192	**black**		— 500.0

1858   Inscribed: "50 William St. Basement"

87LUP2	L192a	**black**, manila		— 600
		With 1c #87L3, tied by handstamp		1,250
87LUP3	L192a	**black**		— 650
		With 1c #87L2, tied by handstamp		2,750
		With 1c #87L3, tied by handstamp		1,750.

Nos. 87LUP1 and 87LUP3 appear on papers of various
colors.

Jefferson Market P. O., New York, N. Y.
Established by Godfrey Schmidt

L193

1850   Glazed Surface Paper   Litho.

88L1	L193	(2c) **black**, pink	7,000.	
88L2	L193	(2c) **black**, blue		
		On cover, tied by handstamp		
		On cover, not tied		3,500.

Four examples recorded of No. 88L1, all unused. Five No.
88L2 recorded, all on covers (two with stamp tied by
handstamp).

Jenkins' Camden Dispatch, Camden, N. J.

Established by Samuel H. Jenkins and continued by Iliam H. Jenkins.

George Washington — L194

There are two types of design L194.

53-54			**Litho.**
L1	L194	**black** (fine impression) (1854)	350.00 450.00
		On cover, tied by ms., with certificate	3,500.

George Washington — L194a

Typo. from Woodcut

9L2	L194a	**black**, *yellow* (coarse impression) (1853)	3,000.
		On cover, tied by ms., with certificate	6,500.

L195

Typeset

89L3	L195	1c **black**, *grayish* (1853)	— —
		On cover, tied by ms.	17,500.

No. 89L3 was probably the first stamp issued by Jenkins. Each of the four known examples is of a different type.

Johnson & Co.'s City Despatch Post, Baltimore, Md.

Operated by Ezekiel C. Johnson, letter carrier

L196

1848			**Typeset**
90L1	L196	2c **black**, *lavender*	—

Two recorded examples of No. 90L1, each uncanceled on cover.

Jones' City Express, Brooklyn, N. Y.

George Washington — L197

1845		**Glazed Surface Paper**	**Engr.**
91L1	L197	2c **black**, *pink*	1,000. 1,500.
		On cover, not tied, with certificate	3,500.

Cancellation: Red oval "Boyd's City Express Post."

Kellogg's Penny Post & City Despatch, Cleveland, Ohio

L198

1853			**Typo.**
92L1	L198	(1c) **vermilion**	1,750.
		On cover, tied by handstamp	
		On cover, tied by handstamp, with 3c #11, with certificate	42,500.
		On cover, not tied, with 3c #11, with certificate	15,000.
		On 3c entire #U2, tied by handstamp	9,000.

Cancellation: Black grid.

Kidder's City Express Post, Brooklyn, N.Y.

In 1847, Henry A. Kidder took over the post of Walton & Co., and with the brothers Isaac C. Snedeker and George H. Snedeker increased its scope. In 1851, the business was sold to the Snedekers. It was operated under the old name until 1853 when the Brooklyn City Express Post was founded.

L199

Stamps bear black manuscript "I S" control in two styles.

1847		**Glazed Surface Paper**	**Typo.**
93L1	L199	2c **black**, *pale blue*	750. 500.
		On cover, tied by handstamp	6,000.
		On cover, not tied	4,500.
		Block of 4	3,500.

Cancellation: Red "PAID."

Reprinted on green paper.

Kurtz Union Despatch Post, New York, N.Y.

L200

Typeset; "T" in Black Ms.

1853

		Glazed Surface Paper	
94L1	L200	2c **black**, *green*	3,500.

Langton & Co.
(See Humboldt Express.)
Ledger Dispatch, Brooklyn, N.Y.

Established by Edwin Pidgeon. Stamps reported to have been sold at 80 cents per 100. Suppressed after a few months.

L201

1882		**Typo.**	**Rouletted 12 in color**
95L1	L201	**rose** (shades)	300. 600.
		Block of 4	1,500.

Letter Express

Established by Henry Wells. Carried mail for points in Western New York, Chicago, Detroit and Duluth.

L202

L203

1844		**Glazed Surface Paper**	**Typo.**
96L1	L202	5c **black**, *pink*	300.00 200.00
		On cover, tied by ms. cancel	1,000.

		On cover, not tied		500.00
		Pair on cover, tied by ms. cancel		2,000.
		Pair on cover, not tied		1,000.
		Pair	700.00	450.00
		Block of 10	28,500.	
96L2	L202	5c **black**, *green*	—	500.00
		On cover, tied by ms. cancel		5,000.
		On cover, not tied		3,500.
		Pair		1,500.
96L3	L203	10c **black**, *pink*	—	500.00
		On cover, tied by ms. cancel		1,500.
		On cover, not tied		750.00
		Pair	1,500.	1,500.
		Strip of 3		9,250.
a.		Bisect on cover, tied by ms. cancel		—

No. 96L3a was sold as a horizontal or vertical bisect. It is known used singly for 5c (rare), or as two bisects for 10c (extremely rare). Stamps are known almost exclusively tied with black ms. "X" covering the cut, and can be authenticated by experts.

The block of 10 of No. 96L1 is the only block recorded of any Letter Express issue. Value represents actual auction sale price in 1999.

L204

96L4	L204	10c **black**, *scarlet*	—	2,500.
		On cover, tied by ms. cancel, with certificate		9,250.
a.		Tete beche pair, one stamp a horiz. bisect, on piece		8,750.

Cancellations: Red large partly boxed "PAID," red boxed "Boyd's City Express Post."

Locomotive Express Post

L205

1847 (?)			**Handstamped**
97L1	L205	**black**	—

Wm. E. Loomis Letter Express, San Francisco, Calif.

William E. Loomis established this post as the successor to the Gahagan & Howe City Express, which he bought in 1865. He continued to use the Gahagan & Howe stamps unchanged. Later Loomis bought Carnes' City Letter Express. He altered the Carnes stamp by erasing "CARNES}" from the plate and adding the address below the oval: "S.E. cor. Sans'e & Wash'n."

L206

1868			**Typo.**
98L1	L206	(5c) **rose**	275.00 650.00

Cancellation: Blue "PAID."

McGreely's Express, Alaska

Established in 1898 by S. C. Marcuse to carry letters and packages by motorboat between Dyea and Skagway, Alaska.

L208

1898　　　　Typo.　　　　*Perf. 14*

155L1 L208　25c **blue**　　　　50.00
　　Block of 4　　　　250.00
　　The status of No. 155L1 is questioned.

McIntire's City Express Post, New York, N.Y.

Established by William H. McIntire

Mercury — L207

1859　　　　　　　　Litho.

99L1 L207　2c **pink**　　　10.00　100.00
　　Block of 4　　　　75.00
　　On cover, tied by handstamp　　3,250.
　a.　Period after CENTS omitted　　—
　Cancellation: Black oval "McIntire's City Express Post Paid."

McMillan's City Dispatch Post, Chicago, Ill.

L208a

1855　　　　　　　Typeset
100L1 L208a　**black,** *rose*　　25,000.
　　No. 100L1 is unique.

Mac & Co's Dispatch, Fallsington-Morrisville, Pa.

L208b

Typo.
166L1 L208b　1c **black,** on 3c entire #U1,
　　uncanceled, with certifi-
　　cate　　14,000.
　　No. 166L1 is unique.

Magic Letter Express, Richmond, Va.

Established by Evans, Porter & Co.

L209　　　　　L209a

1865　　　　　　　Typo.
101L1 L209　1c **black,** on cover, not tied
　　　　by cancel　　40,000.
101L2 L209a　2c **black,** *brown*　14,000.
101L3 L209a　5c **black,** *brown*　—　—
　　Nos. 101L1-101L2 each are unique.

Mason's New Orleans City Express, New Orleans, La.

J. Mason, proprietor

L210

1850-57　　　　　　Typeset
102L1 L210　½c **black,** *blue* (value changed
　　　　to "1" in black ms.)　12,500.
　　On cover, tied

102L2 L210　2c **black,** *yellow*　　—　3,000.
　　On cover, tied by hand-
　　stamp　　10,000.
　Cancellations: Red grid, small red circle "Mason's City Express."

Mearis' City Despatch Post, Baltimore, Md.

Established by Malcom W. Mearis

L211

L212

Black ms. initials "M W M" control on all stamps

1846　　　　　　　Typeset
103L1 L211　1c **black,** *gray*　　—
　　On cover, tied by hand-
　　stamp　　22,000.
103L2 L212　1c **black,** *gray*　　—
103L3 L212　2c **black,** *gray*　　—
　　On cover, uncancelled, with
　　certificate　　16,500.
　a.　Horiz. pair, #103L2-103L3　—
　　Two types of No. 103L3.

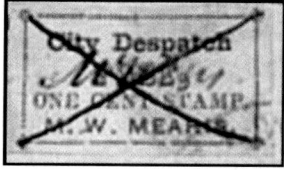

L213

Two types of each.

103L4 L213　1c **black,** *gray*　　—
103L5 L213　2c **black,** *gray*　　—
　a.　Horiz. pair, #103L4-103L5　—

L214

103L6 L214　1c **black,** *gray*　11,000.
　　No. 103L6 is unique; tied on small piece by handstamp.
　　Corner ornaments of Nos. 103L1-103L6 differ on each stamp. All varieties of Nos. 103L1-103L6 contained in one plate.

Menant & Co.'s Express, New Orleans, La.

L215

1853 (?)　　　　　Typo.
104L1 L215　2c **dark red**　15,000.
　　Only four examples are known. Two have Philatelic Foundation Certificates. All four have faults, and the stamp is valued thus.
　Reprints are fairly common and are orange red, not dark red.

Mercantile Library Association, New York, N.Y.

Stamps paid for special delivery service of books ordered from the library, and of forms especially provided to subscribers. The forms bore a government stamp on the outside, a library stamp inside.

L216

1870-75　　　　　　Lith
105L1 L216　5c **black,** *maroon*　250.　3.
105L2 L216　5c **black,** *yellow*　350.　5
105L3 L216　5c **blue**　　350.　5
　　Pair, on postal card　　1,4
105L5 L216　6c **black,** *maroon*　2,250.
105L6 L216　10c **black,** *yellow*　500.　7
　　No. 105L5 is slightly larger than the 5c and 10c stamps. The stamps "on cover" are affixed to cutouts from ord blanks showing order number, title of book desired, and su scriber's name and address. When canceled, the stamps a order blanks show a dull blue double-lined oval inscribed "ME CANTILE LIBRARY ASSOCIATION" and date in center. T stamps are really more a form of receipt for a prepaid par delivery service than postage stamps.

POSTAL CARD
Printed on U.S. Postal Card, First Issue
105LUX1 L216　10c **yellow**　3,500.
　　No. 105LUX1 is unique.

Messenkope's Union Square Post Office, New York, N.Y.

Established by Charles F. Messenkope in 1849 an sold to Joseph E. Dunham in 1850.

L217

1849　　Glazed Surface Paper　Litho
106L1 L217　(1c) **black,** *green*　90.　90
　　On cover, tied by hand-
　　stamp　　500
　　Pair on cover (2c rate), tied
　　by handstamp　　1,750
　　On cover with 5c #1　2,750
　　On cover, tied by hand-
　　stamp, with 3c #10　1,250
　　On cover, tied by hand-
　　stamp, with 3c #11　2,000
　　On cover with 3c #26　950
　　Strip of 3　400.
106L2 L217　(2c) **black,** *pink*　—　—
　　On cover
　　Some examples of No. 106L1 are found with "MES-SENKOPES" crossed through in black ms. in an apparent attempt (by Dunham?) to obliterate it.
　　Cancellations: Red "PAID," red oval "DUNHAMS UNION SQUARE POST OFFICE," red grid of dots.

Metropolitan Errand and Carrier Express Co., New York, N.Y.

Organized Aug. 1, 1855, by Abraham M. Hinkley, Hiram Dixon, and others.

L218

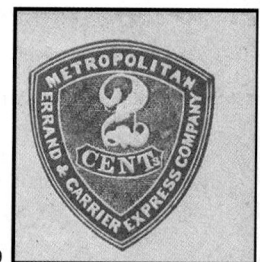

L219

Printed in sheets of 100 (10x10),
each stamp separated by thin ruled lines.

5		Thin to Medium Wove Paper	Engr.	
L1	L218	1c **red orange** (shades)	20.00	25.00
		Cut to shape	5.00	4.00
		On cover, tied by hand-stamp		325.00
		On cover, cut to shape, tied by handstamp		150.00
		On cover, cut to shape, tied by handstamp, with 3c #11		900.00
		Pair	35.00	
		Pair on cover, tied by hand-stamp		—
		Pair on cover, uncanceled		1,000.
		Block of 4	90.00	
L2	L218	5c **red orange**	225.00	
		Cut to shape	60.00	
L3	L218	10c **red orange**	300.00	
		Cut to shape	60.00	
L4	L218	20c **red orange**	325.00	
		Cut to shape	60.00	

Cancellations: Black, blue or green boxed "PAID."
The imprint "Baldwin, Bald & Cousland New York" appears in bottom margin of the two stamps at the bottom right of the sheets.
Nos. 107L1-107L4 have been extensively reprinted in brown and in blue on paper much thicker than the originals.

ENVELOPE
Embossed
Wide Diagonally Laid Paper

LU1	L219	2c **red**, *amber*, entire	125.00

No. 107LU1 has been reprinted on amber wove, diagonally and or horizontally laid paper with narrow lines. The embossing is sharper than on the original.

Metropolitan Post Office, New York, N.Y.

Established by Lemuel Williams who later took William H. Laws as a partner.

L220

L221

L222

L223

Nos. 108L1-108L5 were issued die cut.

1852-53		Glazed Surface Paper	Embossed	
108L1	L220	(2c) **red** (L. Williams)	550.	550.
		On cover, tied by pencil, with certificate		—
		On cover, tied by blue ms., with two 3c #11 and strip of 3 12c #17		—
108L2	L221	(2c) **red** (address and name erased)	1,000.	1,000.
		On cover, uncanceled, with certificate		5,500.
108L3	L222	(2c) **red**	275.	350.
		On cover, tied by hand-stamp		4,000.
108L3A	L222	(2c) **blue**	600.	700.
		On cover, tied by hand-stamp		7,500.
		On cover, tied by hand-stamp, with 3c #11		8,250.

Wove Paper

108L4	L223	1c **red**	75.	90.
		On cover		300.
		On cover, tied by hand-stamp, with 3c #11		1,500.
108L5	L223	1c **blue**	85.	100.
		On cover		350.
		On cover, tied by hand-stamp, with 3c #26		700.

Cancellations: Black circle "METROPOLITAN P. O.," black boxed "PAID W. H. LAWS," black smudge.

G. A. Mills' Despatch Post, New York, N.Y.

Established by Gustavus A. Mills at 6 Wall St., succeeding Hall & Mills.

L224

Several varieties

1847		Glazed Surface Paper	Typeset	
109L1	L224	(2c) **black**, *green*	500.	500.
		On cover		—

Moody's Penny Dispatch, Chicago, Ill.

Robert J. Moody, proprietor

"CHICAGO" 8mm —
L225

Several varieties

1856		Glazed Surface Paper	Typeset	
110L1	L225	(1c) **black**, *red*,	1,750.	1,750.
		On cover, tied by hand-stamp, with 3c #11		16,000.
		On cover with three 1c #9		70,000.
		Vert. strip of 3 showing 3 varieties: period, colon, comma after "Dispatch"	18,000.	6,000.
a.		"CHICAGO" sans serif and 12½mm		2,750.
b.		"Henny" instead of "Penny," on cover, tied by handstamp, with 3c #11		40,000.

Cancellations: Blue circle "Moody's Despatch."
The vertical strip of 3, the cover with the three 1c stamps and No. 110L1b, are each unique.

Morton's Post, Philadelphia, Pa.

L225a

167L1	L225a	2c **black**, *grayish*, on cover, uncanceled, with certificate	13,000.

No. 167L1 is unique.

New York City Express Post, New York, N.Y.

L226

Several varieties

1847		Glazed Surface Paper	Engr.	
111L1	L226	2c **black**, *green*	1,200.	1,500.
		Cut to shape	400.	450.
		On cover, tied by hand-stamp		4,000.
		On cover, cut to shape, tied by handstamp		1,750.

Wove Paper

111L2	L226	2c **orange**	—	—
		On cover		8,000.

One Cent Despatch,
Baltimore, Md.,
Washington, D.C.

Established by J.H. Wiley to deliver mail in Washington, Georgetown and Baltimore. Made as many as five deliveries daily at 1 cent if prepaid, or 2 cents payable on delivery.

L227

L228

Two types:
I. Courier's letter points to "O" of "ONE."

II. Letter points to "N" of "ONE."

1856		Washington, D.C.		Litho.
		Inscribed at bottom "Washington City"		
112L1	L227	1c **violet**	225.	150.
		On cover, tied by hand-stamp		750.
		On cover, tied by hand-stamp, with 3c #11		1,500.
		On 3c entire #U1, tied by handstamp		750.
		Horiz. pair, types I & II		1,250.
		Baltimore, Maryland		
		No name at bottom		
112L2	L228	1c **red**	450.	250.
		On cover, tied by hand-stamp		2,000.
		On cover with 3c #11		2,250.

The No. 112L1 pair is the unique multiple of either One Cent Despatch stamp.

Cancellation on Nos. 112L1-112L2: Black circle "City Despatch."

Overton & Co.

Carried mail principally between New York and Boston; also to Albany. Stamps sold for 6c each, 20 for $1.

L229

1844				
113L1	L229	(6c) **black**, *greenish*	400.	400.
		On cover, tied by ms.		5,000.
		On cover, not tied		2,250.
		Pair		850.
a.		"FREE" printed below design		1,750.
		On cover		4,000.
		Pair on cover, not tied, with certificate		18,500.

Cancellation: Black "PAID." Red "Cd."

Penny Express Co.

Little information is available on this post, but a sheet is known carrying the ms. initials of Henry Reed of the Holladay staff. The post was part of the Holladay Overland Mail and Express Co. system.
In 1866 in the West the "short-bit" or 10 cents was the smallest currency generally used. The word "penny" is believed to refer to the "half-bit" or 5 cents (nickel).

L230

Printed in sheets of 32 (8x4)

1866				Litho.
114L1	L230	5c **black**	400.00	
		Pair	850.00	
a.		Sheet of 32 initialed "HR," black ms., original gum	7,000.	
114L2	L230	5c **blue**	15.00	
		Block of 4	65.00	
		Sheet of 32, no gum	650.00	
114L3	L230	5c **red**	15.00	
		Block of 4	65.00	
		Sheet of 32, no gum	650.00	

Nos. 114L1-114L3 lack gum and probably were never placed in use.

Philadelphia Despatch Post, Philadelphia, Pa.
See D.O. Blood & Co.

Pinkney's Express Post, New York, N.Y.

L231

1851   Glazed Surface Paper   Typo.

115L1	L231	2c **black,** *green*	1,400.
		Cut to shape	800.
		On cover, tied by ms., with certificate	5,750.
		On cover, not canceled, with certificate	9,000.
		On cover, cut to shape, with certificate	3,500.

On the cover with No. 115L1 tied, the stamp is faulty. It is valued thus.

Pips Daily Mail, Brooklyn, N.Y.

L232

1862 (?)   Litho.

116L1	L232	1c **black**	400.	
116L2	L232	1c **black,** *buff*	250.	2,250.
116L3	L232	1c **black,** *yellow*	250.	
116L4	L232	1c **black,** *dark blue*	300.	
116L5	L232	1c **black,** *rose*	300.	
		Block of 4	—	

No. 116L2 used is unique.

Pomeroy's Letter Express.

Established in 1844 by George E. Pomeroy. Carried mail principally to points in New York State. Connected with Letter Express for Western points.

L233

Engraved by John E. Gavit, Albany, N.Y. (Seen as "GAVIT" in bottom part of stamp). Sheets of 40 (8x5).

1844

Surface Colored Wove Paper

117L1	L233	5c **black,** *yellow*	6.50	65.00
		On cover, tied by ms.		900.00
		Pair		250.00
		Pair on cover		3,500.
		Block of 4	40.00	
117L2	L233	**black,** *yellow* (value incomplete)	750.	1,500.
		On cover, tied by ms.		3,000.
		On cover, ms. cancel, not tied		2,250.

Thin Bond Paper

117L3	L233	5c **blue**	5.00	125.00
		On cover, not tied		2,000.
		Pair on cover, not tied		4,000.
117L4	L233	5c **black**	3.50	125.00
		On cover		—
		Strip of 4 on cover		—
		Block of 4	30.00	
		Sheet of 40	—	
117L5	L233	5c **red**	3.50	125.00
		On cover, not tied		3,500.
		Strip of 3 on cover		—
		Block of 4	25.00	
117L6	L233	5c **lake**	200.00	300.00
		On cover, tied by ms.		900.00
		Pair on cover		—
117L7	L233	5c **orange**	7.50	

Cancellations: Large red partly boxed "PAID" (Nos. 117L1, 117L6), red "Cd" (Nos. 117L1-117L2, 117L4); stamps are considered "tied to cover" by this "Cd" when the impression shows through the letter paper.

All stamps except No. 117L2 have "20 for $1" in tablet at the bottom. On No. 117L2 the value is incomplete.

Remainders of Nos. 117L1, 117L3, 117L4 and 117L5 are plentiful in unused condition, including multiples and sheets. A 5c black on yellow paper colored through and a 5c brown were prepared for use but never issued. No. 117L2 was never remaindered.

P. O. Paid, Philadelphia, Pa.

See note in Carriers' Stamps Section.

Price's City Express, New York, N.Y.

L235   L236

1857-58   Glazed Surface Paper   Litho.

119L1	L235	2c **black,** *vermilion*	275.
		On cover, tied by handstamp	5,000.
		On cover, ms. tied	1,000.
		On cover, not tied, with certificate	750.00
		On cover, tied by handstamp, with 3c #26	—
119L2	L235	2c **black,** *green*	250.
		Cut to shape	85.

1858

Sheets of 108 (12x9)

119L3	L236	2c **black,** *green*	5.00	150.00
		On cover		—
		Block of 4	27.50	

Cancellation on #119L3: Black oval "Price's City Express."

Price's Eighth Avenue Post Office, New York, N.Y.

Established by James Price at 350 Eighth Avenue, in 1854, and sold to Russell in the same year.

L237

1854   Litho.

120L1	L237	(2c) **red,** *bluish*	600.00
		On cover, uncanceled, with certificate	7,500.

Priest's Despatch, Philadelphia, Pa.

Established by Solomon Priest

L238   L239

1851   Glazed Surface Paper   Typo.

121L1	L238	(2c) **silver,** *vermilion*	2,250.	—
121L2	L238	(2c) **gold,** *dark blue*	500.	

Wove Paper

121L2A	L238	(2c) **bronze,** *bluish*	500.	1,000.
121L3	L238	(2c) **black,** *yellow*	500.	
		On cover, uncanceled, with 3c #11, with certificate		5,500.
121L4	L238	(2c) **black,** *rose*	500.	
		On cover, uncanceled, with certificate		2,500.
121L5	L238	(2c) **black,** *blue*	1,000.	
121L6	L239	(2c) **black,** *yellow*	500.	
		On cover, uncanceled, with 3c #11, with certificate		4,500.
121L7	L239	(2c) **black,** *blue*	500.	
		On cover, uncanceled, with certificate		3,250.
121L8	L239	(2c) **black,** *rose*	500.00	
121L9	L239	(2c) **black,** *emerald,* uncanceled, on cover		6,500.

No. 121L9 is believed to be unique.

Prince's Letter Dispatch, Portland, Maine

Established by J. H. Prince of Portland. Mail carried nightly by messenger travelling by steamer to Boston. Stamp engraved by Lowell of Lowell & Brett, Boston, his name appearing in the design below the steamship.

L240

Printed in sheets of 40 (5x8)

1861   Li

122L1	L240	**black**	7.50	12
		On cover, tied by handstamp		5,
		On cover, tied by handstamp, with 3c #65		8,
		On cover, tied by handstamp, with 3c #94		4,
		Block of 4	40.00	
		Sheet of 40	550.00	

Cancellations: Black, blue or red Boston datestamps, b company serrated oval, black "Boston & Portland/Express State Street, Boston/34 Exchange Street, Portland" framed bon-marker handstamp.

Private Post Office, San Francisco, Calif. ENVELOPES

L241

(Illustration reduced size.)

Impressed on U.S. Envelopes, 1863-64 Issue

1864   Typ

123LU1	L241	15c **blue,** *orange* (on US #U56)	600.
123LU2	L241	15c **blue,** *buff* (on US #U54)	600.
a.		15c **blue** (on US #U58)	700.00 4,7
b.		15c **blue,** *buff* (on US #U59)	600.00
123LU3	L241	25c **blue,** *buff* (on US #U54)	600.00

Providence Despatch, Providence, R.I.

L242

1849   Types

124L1	L242	**black**	2,000.

Public Letter Office, San Francisco, Calif. ENVELOPES

L243

Illustration reduced.

Impressed on U.S. Envelopes, 1863-64 Issue

1864   Typese

125LU1	L243	**black**	350.00	
125LU2	L243	**blue**	350.00	
125LU3	L243	15c **blue**	400.00	5,00
125LU4	L243	25c **blue**	400.00	

The Private Post Office of San Francisco changed its name to Public Post Office sometime in 1864. The office address was the same for both, 5 Kearny St.

Reed's City Despatch Post, San Francisco, Calif.

Pioneer San Francisco private post. Also serving Adams & Co. for city delivery.

L244

1853-54   Glazed Surface Paper   Litho.

126L1	L244	**black,** *green,* on cover, tied by handstamp	
126L2	L244	**black,** *blue,* on cover, uncanceled	27,500.

No. 126L1 is unique. Two No. 126L2 recorded, each uncanceled on cover.

Cancellation: Blue double-circle "Adams & Co. San Francisco."

Ricketts & Hall, Baltimore, Md.

Successors to Cook's Dispatch

L244a

57 Cut to shape Typo.

'L1 L244a 1c **red,** *bluish* — 9,000.

Robison & Co., Brooklyn, N.Y.

L245

55-56 Typo.

8L1 L245 1c **black,** *blue* 4,750. 4,750.
On cover, tied 7,000.

Cancellation: Blue "PAID."

Roche's City Dispatch, Wilmington, Del.

L246

350 Glazed Surface Paper Typo.

29L1 L246 (2c) **black,** *green* 2,250.
Cut to shape 1,750.
On cover, uncanceled, with certificate 8,250.
On cover, cut to shape, uncanceled, with certificate 3,500.

A black negative handstamp similar to type L246 served olely as a postmark and no evidence exists that any prepaid andstamped envelopes or lettersheets were ever sold.

Rogers' Penny Post, Newark, N.J.

Established by Alfred H. Rogers, bookseller, at 194 road St., Newark, N.J.

L246a

Cut to shape

856 Glazed Surface Paper Handstamped

162L1 L246a (1c) **black,** *green* 30,000.

No. 162L1 is unique. It is on a tiny piece. Value represents 000 auction sale price.

See Rogers' handstamp in Local Handstamp Covers section.

Russell 8th Ave. Post Office, New York, N.Y.

(See Price's Eighth Avenue Post Office.)

L247

1854-58 Wood Engraving

130L1 L247 (2c) **blue,** *rose* 600. 500.
On cover, tied —
130L2 L247 (2c) **black,** *yellow* 750. 650.
On cover, tied 5,000.
On cover, uncanceled, with 3c #11, with certificate 9,250.
130L3 L247 (2c) **red,** *bluish* 900. 750.
On cover, tied by handstamp 8,750.
On cover, not tied, with 3c #11, with certificate 5,750.
130L4 L247 (2c) **blue green,** *green* —

No. 130L4 used is unique.

St. Louis City Delivery Company, St. Louis, Mo.

(See Cincinnati City Delivery.)

L249

1883 Typo. *Perf. 12*

131L1 L249 (1c) **red** 4.00 7.50
Block of 4 17.50
On cover, tied by handstamp 2,750.
a. Imperf., pair —
b. Horiz. pair, imperf between 350.00

Cancellation: Purple target.

Smith & Stephens' City Delivery, St. Louis, Mo.

L284

Typeset

158L1 L284 1c **black,** *pale rose,* on cover, tied by ms. cancel 25,000.

No. 158L1 is unique.

Spaulding's Penny Post, Buffalo, N.Y.

L283

L283a

1848-49

156L1 L283 2c **vermilion** 40,000.
156L2 L283a 2c **carmine** 40,000.
On cover —

Nos. 156L1 unused, 156L2 unused and 156L2 on cover each are unique.

A No. 156L1 on cover, uncanceled, was reported but has not been seen.

Spence & Brown Express Post, Philadelphia, Pa.

L285

L286

(Illustrations reduced size.)

1847 (?) Typeset

159L1 L285 2c **black,** *bluish* 10,000. 11,500.

One each recorded of No. 159L1 unused and used.

1848 Litho.

159L2 L286 (2c) **black** 1,500. —
On cover, tied by ms. 33,000.
Block of 4 6,500.

No. 159L2 on cover is unique.

Squier & Co. City Letter Dispatch, St. Louis, Mo.

(Jordan & Co.)

This post began to operate as a local carrier on July 6, 1859 and was discontinued in the early part of 1860. Squier & Co. used imperforate stamps; their successors (Jordan & Co.) about Jan. 1 1860, used the roulettes.

L248

1859 Litho. *Imperf.*

132L1 L248 1c **green** 150. 175.
On cover 1,500.
On cover, tied by handstamp, with 3c #26 3,500.
On cover, tied by ms., with 3c #26 1,000.
On cover, uncanceled, with 3c #26 600.
Block of 4 750.

1860 *Rouletted 19*

132L2 L248 1c **rose brown** 280. 280.
On cover 1,000.
On cover, with 3c #26, each tied by handstamps (unique) 11,500.
132L3 L248 1c **brownish purple** 280. 280.
On cover 1,000.
132L4 L248 1c **green** 280. 350.
On cover 1,000.
On cover, tied by handstamp, with 3c #26 5,000.

Cancellation: Black circle "Jordan's Penny Post Saint Louis."

Staten Island Express Post, Staten Island, N. Y.

Established by Hagadorn & Co., with office at Stapleton, Staten Island. Connected with Boyd for delivery in New York City.

L250

1849 Typo.

133L1 L250 3c **vermilion** 1,400. 1,100.
On cover, tied by ms. 4,750.
On cover, not tied 3,500.
On cover, uncanceled, with certificate 3,250.
133L2 L250 6c **vermilion** — 3,000.

Stringer & Morton's City Despatch, Baltimore, Md.

According to an advertisement in the Baltimore newspapers, dated October 19, 1850, this post aimed to emulate the successful posts of other cities, and divided the city into six districts, with a carrier in each district. Stamps were made available throughout the city.

L251

1850 Glazed Surface Paper

134L1 L251 (1c) **gold,** *black* 500. —
On cover, uncanceled 700.

Cancellation: Black circle "Baltimore City Despatch & Express Paid."

Sullivan's Dispatch Post, Cincinnati, Ohio

L252

1853		**Glazed Surface Paper**		**Litho.**
135L1	L252	(2c) **black**, *green*, uncanceled, on cover		—

Wove Paper

135L2	L252	(2c) **bluish black**, uncanceled, on magazine, with certificate		40,000.
135L3	L252	(2c) **green**	60,000.	
		On cover		—

Nos. 135L1-135L2 are either die cut octagonally or cut round. They do not exist cut square.

Each listed Sullivan Post item is unique. Additionally, a second No. 135L2 on magazine is in the Smithsonian Institution collection.

Swarts' City Dispatch Post, New York, N.Y.

Established by Aaron Swarts, at Chatham Square, in 1847, becoming one of the largest local posts in the city.

The postmarks of Swarts' Post Office are often found on stampless covers, as this post carried large quantities of mail without using adhesive stamps.

Zachary Taylor   George
L253   Washington
              L254

1849-53		**Glazed Surface Paper**		**Litho.**
136L1	L253	(2c) **black**, *light green*	—	175.00
		On cover, tied by hand-stamp		450.00
		On cover, not tied		300.00
		On cover with 3c #10		450.00
136L2	L253	(2c) **black**, *dark green*	—	135.00
		On cover, tied by hand-stamp		375.00

Wove Paper

136L3	L253	(2c) **pink**	—	35.00
		On cover, tied by hand-stamp		350.00
		On cover with 5c #1		—
136L4	L253	(2c) **red** (shades)	20.00	20.00
		On cover, tied by hand-stamp		275.00
		On cover with 5c #1		5,000.
		On cover, tied by hand-stamp, with 3c #11		325.00
		Block of 4	85.00	
		Sheet of 25	600.00	
136L5	L253	(2c) **pink**, *blue*		60.00
		On cover, tied by hand-stamp		375.00
136L6	L253	(2c) **red**, *blue*		60.00
		On cover, tied by hand-stamp		400.00
136L7	L253	(2c) **black**, *blue gray*	200.00	150.00
		On cover, tied by hand-stamp		400.00
136L8	L253	(2c) **blue**		200.00
		On cover, tied by hand-stamp		650.00
136L9	L254	(1c) **red**	—	40.00
		On cover, tied by hand-stamp		400.00
		On cover with 3c #11		—
136L10	L254	(1c) **pink**	—	30.00
		On cover, tied by hand-stamp		250.00
		On cover, tied by hand-stamp, with 3c #11		800.00
136L11	L254	(1c) **red**, *bluish*	—	100.00
		On cover		500.00
136L12	L254	(1c) **pink**, *bluish*	—	100.00
		On cover		450.00

Bouton's Stamp with Red ms. "Swarts" at Top

136L13	L49	2c **black**, *gray blue*	500.	550.
		On cover, tied by hand-stamp		1,500.
		On cover, not tied		600.

L255

Printed in sheets of 25 (5x5). Five minor varieties, the stamps in each vertical row being identical.

136L14	L255	1c **blue**	15.	60.
		On cover, tied by hand-stamp		175.
		On cover, tied by hand-stamp, with 3c #11		225.
		Block of 4	65.	
a.		Thin paper	8.00	
		Block of 4	35.	
		Sheet of 25	225.00	
136L15	L255	1c **red**		500.
		On cover, tied by hand-stamp		1,000.
		On cover with 3c #10		1,650.
		On cover, tied by hand-stamp, with 3c #11		3,500.
136L16	L255	1c **red**, *bluish*	—	135.
		On cover, tied by hand-stamp		1,000.
136L17	L255	1c **black**, on cover		36,000.

Nos. 136L3-136L4, 136L9-136L10, 136L14-136L15 have been reprinted.

Cancellations: Red boxed "PAID" (mostly on Nos. 136L1-136L8, 136L13), black boxed "PAID SWARTS" (mostly on Nos. 136L9-136L12), black oval "Swarts Post Office Chatham Square" (Nos. 136L9-136L12), black oval "Swarts B Post Chatham Square," black grids (5-bar rectangle, 6-bar circle, solid star, hollow star, star in circle, etc). Other handstamp postmarks of the post have been found as cancellations. Government town postmarks exist on almost all Swarts stamps.

Teese & Co. Penny Post, Philadelphia, Pa.

L256

Printed in sheet of 200 divided into two panes of 100. Each pane includes setting of 20, repeated 5 times. Vertical or horizontal tete beche pairs appear twice in each setting. Twenty varieties.

1852		**Wove Paper**		**Litho.**
137L1	L256	(1c) **blue**, *bluish*	20.00	125.00
		On cover, tied by hand-stamp		3,000.
		On cover, tied by hand-stamp, with 3c #11		—
		Block of 4	90.00	
a.		Tete beche pair	100.00	

Telegraph Despatch P. O., Philadelphia, Pa.

L257

1848			
138L1	L257	1c **black**, *yellowish*	2,750.
		On cover, tied by ms., with certificate	15,000.
		On cover, not tied, with certificate	5,500.
138L2	L257	2c **black**, *yellowish*, on cover with 5c #1	10,500.

The 2c differs in design, including the address, "Office No. 6 Sth 8 St" at bottom.
One example known of No. 138L2.

Third Avenue Post Office, New York, N.Y.

Established by S. Rothenheim, a former carrier for Boyd's City Express. All stamps were cut to shape by hand before being sold and exist only in that form.

L258

1855		**Glazed Surface Paper**		**Handstamped**
139L1	L258	2c **black**, *green*	500.	500.
		On cover, uncanceled		1,250.
		On cover, uncanceled, with 3c #11, with certificate		1,600.
139L1A	L258	2c **blue**, *green*, on cover, uncanceled, with certificate		2,250.
139L2	L258	2c **black**, *maroon*	3,250.	2,250.

Unsurfaced Paper colored through

139L3	L258	2c **black**, *yellow*		2,250.
		On cover, uncanceled, with 3c #11, with certificate		3,
139L4	L258	2c **black**, *blue*		
		On cover, uncanceled, with 3c #11, with certificate		7,
139L5	L258	2c **black**, *brown*		2,250.
139L6	L258	2c **black**, *buff*		2,500.
139L7	L258	2c **black**, *pink*		5,250.
		On cover, uncanceled, with 3c #11		6,5
139L8	L258	2c **black**, *green*	4,150.	2,2

Nos. 139L1A, 139L2, 139L4 on cover, 139L7-139L8 unu and 139L8 used are each unique.

Cancellation on No. 139L1: Black "PAID."

Union Post, New York, N Y

L259

1846				**Handstamp**
		Thick Glazed Surface Paper		
140L3	L259	**blue**, *green* ("UNOIN")		3,000.
140L4	L259	**red**, *blue* ("UNION")		2,000.
		On cover		

Type L259 was used also as a postmark, usually struck blue.

Union Square Post Office, New York, N.Y.

Established by Joseph E. Dunham about 1850. 1851 Dunham acquired Messenkope's Union Squa Post Office, operating the combined posts until 18 or 1855. The business was sold in 1855 to Phineas Godfrey.

L259a   L260

Printed in sheets of 120 (6x20)

1852				**Typ**
141L1	L259a	1c **black**, *dark green*	9.00	45.0
		On cover, tied by hand-stamp		900.0
		On cover, tied by hand-stamp, with 3c #11		1,500
		Block of 4	45.00	
141L2	L259a	1c **black**, *light apple green*	40.00	75.0
		On cover, tied by hand-stamp		700.0
		On cover, tied by hand-stamp, with 3c #11		1,500
		On cover, cut to shape, tied by handstamp, with 3c #11		200.0
141L3	L260	2c **black**, *rose*	3.50	3,000
		On cover		3,500
		Block of 4	17.50	

Used stamps must bear handstamp cancels.

Walton & Co.'s City Express, Brooklyn, N.Y.

Operated by Wellington Walton.

L261

1846		**Glazed Surface Paper**		**Litho.**
142L1	L261	2c **black**, *pink*	700.	900.
		On cover, tied by ms.		
		On cover, ms. cancel, not tied, with certificate		15,000
		On cover, handstamp cancel, not tied		
		On cover, cut to shape, tied by handstamp, with certificate		4,500.
		On cover, cut to shape, handstamp cancel, not tied, with certificate		6,000.

Cancellations: Black "PAID / W. W." Black oblong quad (ties stamp "through" to cover).

Wells, Fargo and Co.

Wells, Fargo & Company entered the Western field about July 1, 1852, to engage in business on the Pacific Coast, and soon began to acquire other express businesses, eventually becoming the most important express company in its territory.

The Central Overland, California and Pikes Peak Express Company, inaugurated in 1860, was the pioneer Pony Express system and was developed to bring about quicker communication between the extreme portions of the United States. Via water the time was 25 to 30 days, with two monthly sailings, and by the overland route the time was 28 days. In 1860 the pioneer Pony Express carried letters only, reducing the time for the 2,100 miles (St. Joseph to San Francisco) to about 12 days. The postage rate was originally $5 per half-ounce.

About April 1, 1861, Wells, Fargo & Company became agents for the Central Overland, California and Pikes Peak Express Company and issued $2 red and $4 green stamps.

During the July 1 to Oct. 24, 1861, period of use of Nos. 143L3-143L6, Wells, Fargo & Co. was under contract with the U.S. government, so stamps used during this period are technically official issues authorized by Congress.

The rates were cut in half about July 1, 1861, and new stamps were issued: the $1 red, $2 green and $4 black, and the $1 garter design.

The revival of the Pony Express in 1862, known as the "Virginia City Pony" resulted in the appearance of the "cents" values, first rate.

Advertisement in the Placerville newspaper, Aug. 7, 1862: "Wells, Fargo & Co.'s Pony Express. On and after Monday, the 11th inst., we will run a Pony Express Daily between Sacramento and Virginia City, carrying letters and exchange papers, through from San Francisco in 24 hours, Sacramento in 15 hours and Placerville in 10 hours. Rates: All letters to be enclosed in our franks, and TEN CENTS PREPAID, in addition, for each letter weighing half an ounce or less, and ten cents for each additional half-ounce."

Wells, Fargo & Company used various handstamps to indicate mail transit. These are illustrated and described in the handbook, "Wells, Fargo & Co.'s Handstamps and Franks" by V. M. Berthold, published by Scott Stamp & Coin Co., Ltd. (out of print). The history of the Pony Express, a study of the stamps and reprints, and a survey of existing covers are covered in "The Pony Express," by M. C. Nathan and Winthrop S. Boggs, published by the Collectors Club, 22 E. 35th., New York, N.Y. 10016.

Wells Fargo stamps of types L262 and L264 were lithographed by Britton & Rey, San Francisco. Type L263 was printed by George F. Nesbitt, New York.

L262

Front hoof missing

The $2 and $4 stamps were printed from plates of 20 (5x4), while the $1 was printed from a plate of 40 (8x5), and divided into two panes of 20 (4x5) each.

1861   (April to July 1)   Litho.
143L1 L262 $2 red   175. 800.
  On US envelope #U10
  On US envelope #U16   12,500.
  On US envelope #U17   12,500.
  On US envelope #U18   12,500.
  On US envelope #U32
  (patriotic cover)   100,000.
  On US envelope #U33   15,000.
  On US envelope #U65
143L2 L262 $4 green   300. 1,250.
  Block of 4   9,000.
  On US envelope #U33

The No. 143L2 block is the only recorded $4 block.

1861   (July 1 to Nov.)
143L3 L262 $1 red   90. 750.
  Block of 4   750.
  Sheet of 40   7,000.
  On US envelope #U11
  On US envelope #U15   8,500.
  On US envelope #U17   8,500.
  On US envelope #U32   9,000.
  On US envelope #U33   9,000.
  On US envelope #U35   8,500.
  On US envelope #U40   9,000.
  On US envelope #U41   8,500.
  Front hoof missing (9R)   1,250. 6,000.
143L4 L262 $2 green   250. 1,750.
  Block of 4   1,200.
  On US envelope #U41   50,000.
143L5 L262 $4 black   175. 6,000.

  Block of 4
On cover to Wash., D.C.,
  tied by handstamp   350,000.

Cancellations: Blue, black or magenta express company.
Nos. 143L1-143L5 and 143L7-143L9 were reprinted in 1897. The reprints are retouched. Shades vary from originals. Originals and reprints are fully described in "The Pony Express," by M. C. Nathan and W. S. Boggs (Collectors Club).

L263

Printed in sheets of 20 (5x4). One example recorded with Nesbitt imprint (pos. 18).

1861   Thin Wove Paper
143L6 L263 $1 blue   750. 1,250.
  Strip of 3
  On 10c US env. #U40   75,000.

No. 143L6 apparently used only from east to west. Most counterfeits have a horizontal line bisecting the shield. Some genuine stamps have a similar line drawn in with blue or red ink. Value for genuine, $300.

L264

Printed in sheets of 40 (8x5), four panes of 10, each pane 2x5.

1862-64
143L7 L264 10c brown (shades)   50. 150.
  Pair   125. 500.
  Block of 4   500.
  On US envelope #U26   5,000.
  On US envelope #U32   3,500.
  On US envelope #U34   4,500.
  On US envelope #U35   3,500.
  On cover with 3c #65
143L8 L264 25c blue   75. 140.
  Pair   175.
  Block of 4   500.
  On plain cover   2,250.
  Strip of 3 on cover
  On US envelope #U10
  On US envelope #U26   2,000.
  On US envelope #U34   4,000.
  On US envelope #U35   4,000.
143L9 L264 25c red   30. 80.
  Pair   80.
  Block of 4   225.
  Sheet of 40   4,500.
  On US envelope #U9
  On US envelope #U10   4,000.
  On US envelope #U34   4,000.
  On US envelope #U35   9,000.
  Pair on US envelope #U35   9,000.
  On US envelope #U59   2,750.

Cancellations on Nos. 143L7-143L9: Blue or black express company, black town.

NEWSPAPER STAMPS

L265

L266

L267

L268

L269

L270

1861-70
143LP1 L265 black   1,250.
  On cover, uncanceled, with
    certificate   11,000.
143LP2 L266 blue   1,250
143LP3 L267 blue   20.00 75.00
  Pair   100.00
  Block of 4
  Sheet of 50
  a. Thin paper   40.00 100.00
143LP4 L268 blue   50.00

    Rouletted 10
143LP5 L267 blue   25.00 125.00
  On wrapper   1,500.
  Pair   55.00
  Block of 4   125.00
  a. Thin paper
143LP6 L268 blue   22.50
  a. Tete beche pair   350.00

Design L267 was printed in sheets of 50 (5x10).

1883-88   *Perf. 11, 12, 12½*
143LP7 L268 blue   12.50 25.00
143LP8 L269 blue   25.00 35.00
143LP9 L270 blue   3.50 5.00
  Double transfer
  On wrapper   1,500.
  Strip of 3 on wrapper
  a. Vertical pair, imperf. between   125.00
  b. Horiz. pair, imperf. vert.   350.00

FOR PUBLISHERS' USE

L271

1876   Typo.
143LP10 L271 blue   8.50 25.00
  Pair   17.50 60.00
  Block of 4   45.00
  Sheet of 50
  On wrapper   1,750.
  On wrapper with #143LP9

Cancellation: Blue company.

ENVELOPES

1862
143LU1 L264 10c red   1,250.
  On US envelope #U34   1,500.
143LU2 L264 10c blue
  On US envelope #U34   9,500.

143LU3 L264 25c **red**   700.
              On "Gould & Curry" over-
                all advertising env.   700.

Westervelt's Post, Chester, N.Y.

Operated by Charles H. Westervelt. Rate was 1 cent for letters and 2 cents for packages carried to the post office. Local and government postage required prepayment.

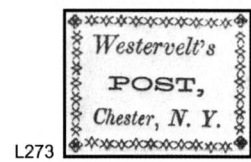

L273

Several varieties

1863 (?)   **Typeset**
144L1 L273 (1c) **black**, *buff*   35.00
              On cover   650.00
              On cover, tied by hand-
                stamp, with 3c #65   1,000.
              Sheet of 6   675.00   —
144L2 L273   **black**, *lavender*   40.00   —
              On cover   —

Indian Chief — L274

General U. S.
Grant — L275

Six varieties

1864 (?)   **Typeset**
144L9 L274 (1c) **red**, *pink*   75.00
              On cover   650.00
              On cover, tied by hand-
                stamp, with 3c #65   2,000.

Six varieties

1865   **Typo.**
144L29 L275 2c **black**, *yellow*   35.00   —
144L30 L275 2c **black**, *gray green*   40.00   —
144L40 L275 2c **red**, *pink*   40.00   —

All of the Westervelt stamps are believed to have a philatelic flavor, although it is possible that Nos. 144L1-144L2 were originally issued primarily for postal purposes. It is possible that Nos. 144L9, 144L29-144L30 and 144L40 were used in the regular course of business, particularly No. 144L9.

However, the large number of varieties on various colors of paper, which exist both as originals as well as contemporaneous and near-contemporaneous reprints, are believed to have been produced solely for sale to collectors. Design L275 was certainly issued primarily for sale to collectors. Many of the unlisted colors in all three types exist only as reprints. Forgeries of all three designs also exist.

L276

ENVELOPES
Impressed at top left

1865   **Typo.**
144LU1 L276   **red**, *white*   —
144LU2 L276   **red brown**, *orange*   — 250.00
144LU3 L276   **black**, *bluish*   —
144LU4 L276   **black**, *buff*   —
144LU5 L276   **black**, *white*   —

It is possible that Nos. 114LU1-144LU5 were corner cards and had no franking value.

Westtown, Westtown, Pa.

The Westtown School at Westtown, Pa., is the oldest of the secondary schools in America, managed by the Society of Friends. It was established in 1799. In 1853 the school authorities decided that all outgoing letters carried by stage should pay a fee of 2 cents. Prepaid stamps were placed on sale at the school. Stamps were usually affixed to the reverse of the letter sheets or envelopes.

At first, letters were usually mailed at West Chester, Pa. After March 4, 1859, letters were sent from Street Road Post Office, located at the railroad station. Later this became the Westtown Post Office. The larger stamp was the first used. The smaller stamp came into use about 1867.

L277 — Type I

L277 — Type II

L277 — Type III

L277 — Type IV

L277a — Type V

L277a — Type VI

L277a — Type VII

1853-67(?)   **Litho.**
145L1 L277 (2c) **gold**   45.   —
              On front of cover, tied
                with 3c #11   4,500.
              On front of cover, un-
                canceled, with 1c #9   1,000.
              On front of cover, un-
                canceled, with 3c #11   150.00
              On front of cover, un-
                canceled, with 3c
                #26a   200.00
145L2 L277a (2c) **gold**   30.   —
              On cover   400.
              On cover, tied by
                handstamp, with 3c
                #158   2,250.
              Block of 4   400.
              Block of 6   1,000.
  a.   Tete beche pair   300.

No. 145L1 in red brown is a fake.

Whittelsey's Express, Chicago, Ill.
Operated by Edmund A. and Samuel M. Whittelsey

George Washington — L278

1857   **Typo.**
146L1 L278 2c **red**   2,000. 6,000.
              Block of 11   20,000.

Cancellation: Blue oval "Whittelsey's Express."

Williams' City Post, Cincinnati, Ohio.
See Carriers' Stamps, No. 9LB1.

Wood & Co. City Despatch, Baltimore, Md.
Operated by W. Wood

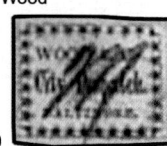

L280

1856   **Typeset**
148L1 L280 (1c) **black**, *yellow,* on cover,
                ms. cancel, not tied, with
                certificate   11,000.
              On printed matter, tied by
                ms.   7,500.
              On 3c red entire #U10,
                tied by ms., with certifi-
                cate   14,500.

W. Wyman, Boston, Mass.
Established to carry mail between Boston and New York

L281

1844   **Lith.**
149L1 L281 5c **black**   — 750.
              On cover, tied by ms., Wy-
                man handstamp   3,8
              On cover, tied by ms.,
                Overton handtsamp   10,
              On cover, not tied   2,0

No. 149L1 may have been sold singly at 6 cents each.

Zieber's One Cent Dispatch, Pittsburgh, Pa.

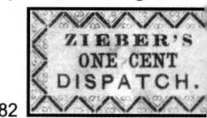

L282

1851   **Types**
150L1 L282 1c **black**, *gray blue*   20,0
              On cover, acid cancel, with
                3c #10

No. 150L1 used and on cover are each unique.

Cancellation: Acid

For Local #151L1 see **Friend's Boarding School.**
For Local #152L1 see **Faunce's Penny Post.**
For Local #153L1 see **Hackney & Bolte Penny Post.**
For Local #154L1 see **A. W. Auner's Despatch Post.**
For Local #155L1 see **McGreely's Express.**
For Local #156L1-156L2 see **Spaulding's Penny Post.**
For Local #157L1 see **Bush's Brooklyn City Express.**
For Local #158L1 see **Smith & Stephens City Delivery.**
For Local #159L1-159L2 see **Spence & Brown Express Post.**
For Local #160L1 see **City Dispatch, New York City.**
For Local #161L1 see **Clinton's Penny Post.**
For Local #162L1 see **Rogers' Penny Post.**
For Local #163L1 see **Blizzard Mail.**
For Local #164L1 see **Freeman & Co.'s Express, New York City.**
For Local #165L1 see **J. A. Howell's City Despatch.**
For Local #166L1 see **Mac & Co's Dispatch.**
For Local #167L1 see **Morton's Post.**

LOCAL HANDSTAMPED COVERS

In 1835-1860 when private companies carried mail, many of them used handstamps on the covers they carried. Examples of these handstamps are shown on this and following pages.

Accessory Transit Co. of Nicaragua

Blue or Black

Red, Black or Blue

A sub-variety shows "Leland" below "MAILS" in lower right corner.

Red or Blue

1853

Barker's City Post, Boston, Mass.

Black

1855-59

Also known with "10" instead of "34" Court Square.

E. N. Barry's Despatch Post, New York, N.Y.

Black

1852

Bates & Co., New Bedford, Mass.
(Agent for Hale & Co. at New Bedford)

Red

1845

Branch Post Office, New York, N. Y.
(Swarts' Chatham Square Post Office)

Red

1847

Brigg's Despatch, Philadelphia, Pa.

Black

1848

Bush's Brooklyn City Express, Brooklyn, N. Y.

Red

1848

Cover shows red PAID.

Central Post Office, New York, N.Y.

Black

1856

Cover shows black PAID.

City Despatch Post, New York, N. Y.
(Used by Mead, successor to United States City Despatch Post.)

Black

1848

City Dispatch Post, Baltimore, Md.

Red

1846-47

City Despatch & Express, Baltimore, Md.

Black

1850

Cole's City Despatch P. O., New York, N. Y.
(Used by Cole with some of the City Despatch Post stamps.)

Black or Red

1848-50

Dunhams Post Office, New York, N. Y.
(See Union Square Post Office).

Red

1850-52

Gay, Kinsley & Co., Boston, Mass.
(A package express)

Red

Hanford's Pony Express Post, New York, N.Y.

Black or Red

1845-51

Hartford Penny Post, Hartford, Conn.

Black

1852-61

Hudson Street Post Office, New York, N. Y.

Red

1850

Cover shows red PAID.

Jones & Russell's Pikes Peak Express Co., Denver, Colo.

Black

1859-60

Kenyon's Letter Office, 91 Wall St., New York City

Red

1846-60

Letter Express, San Francisco, Cal.
(See Gahagan & Howe, San Francisco, Cal.)

Blue

1865-66

Libbey & Co.'s City Post, Boston, Mass.

LIBBEY & CO'S
CITY POST.
Black or Red   10 COURT SQUARE

1852

Cover has 3c 1851 postmarked Boston, Mass.

Manhattan Express, New York, N. Y.
(W. V. Barr. See Bouton's Manhattan Express.)

Red

1847

New York Penny Post,
New York, N. Y.

Black or Red

1840-41

Also known with hour indicated.

Noisy Carriers, San Francisco, Cal.

Blue or Green

Blue

By Mail Steamer FROM NOISY CARRIER'S

Black or Red

Black, Blue or Green

Black

Forwarded Via Independent Line

Black
or
Blue

1853-56

Northern Liberties News Rooms, Philadelphia, Pa.
(Actually a carrier marking mechanically applied)

Black

Black

1835-36

Overton & Co.'s City Mail,
New York, N. Y.

Red

1844-45

Pony Express

Blue or
Red

1860

Blue (Enlarged)

61

Black or Carmine

1860-61

Blue or Red

1853-56

from

St. Joseph, Mo.   Black or Green
Denver City, K. T.   Black
Leavenworth City, K. T. Black
San Francisco, Cal.   Blue

Black or Green

1860-61

Red

Blue

1860

Rogers' Penny Post, Newark, N. J.

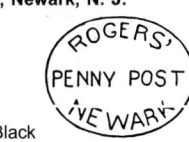

Black

1856

Spark's Post Office, New York, N. Y.

Red, Green, Blue or Black

1848

Spaulding's Penny Post, Buffalo, N. Y.

Black

1848

Spence & Brown Express Post, Philadelphia, Pa.

Black

1848

Stait's Despatch Post, Philadelphia, Pa. (Eagle City Post)

Red or Black

1850-51

Red

1850-55

Stone's City Post, New York, N. Y.

Red

1858-59

J. W. Sullivan's Newspaper Office, San Francisco, Cal.

Black or Red

1854-55

Towle & Co. Letter Delivery, Boston, Mass.

Red

1847

Towle's City Dispatch Post, Boston, Mass.

Red

1849

Towle's City Post, Boston, Mass.

(Also 10 Court Sq.) Red

1849-50

Cover shows PAID.

STAMPED ENVELOPES AND WRAPPERS

Fine-Very Fine →

THE
SCOTT
CATALOGUE
VALUES
CUT SQUARES
IN THIS GRADE

Very Fine →

Extremely Fine →

VALUES

Values for cut squares and most entires are for examples in the grade of very fine. Very fine cut squares will have the design well centered within moderately large margins. The margins on 20th century cut squares should be at least ¼ inch on the cut sides unless indicated otherwise. Cut squares of modern issues should show full tagging bars when they exist. An illustrated grading guide is shown above. These examples are computer-manipulated images made from single digitized master illustrations. Selected issues from both the 19th and 20th centuries are shown in the grades of fine-very fine, very fine and extremely fine. In addition to margin size, collectors are reminded that very fine cut squares (and entires) also will possess a fresh appearance and be free from defects.

Precanceled cut squares must include the entire precancellation. Values for unused entires are for those without printed or manuscript address, and for the most popular sizes. In a number of cases the larger envelopes are less expensive than the values shown here, for example, Nos. U348-U351. Values for letter sheets and wrappers are for folded entires. Unfolded copies sell for more.

"Full corner" cut squares include both back and side flaps. These items generally command a premium of 25% or more above the cut square values shown here, which are not for "full corners."

A plus sign (+) before a Catalogue number indicates that the item was not regularly issued and is not known used.

Envelopes are not available before the First day of issue so most cachets are applied after the envelope has been canceled. First day covers are valued uncacheted. First day covers prior to Nos. U532, UC18 and UO73 are addressed. Minimum values are $1 through 1986, and $1.25 after.

PRECANCELED CUT SQUARES

Precanceled envelopes do not normally receive another cancellation. Since the lack of a cancellation makes it impossible to distinguish between cut squares from used and unused envelopes, they are valued here as used only. Precanceled entires are valued mint and used since entires will show evidence of usage.

HISTORY

STAMPED ENVELOPES were first issued on July 1, 1853. They have always been made by private contractors, after public bidding, usually at four-year intervals. They have always been sold to the public at postage value plus cost of manufacture. They have appeared in many sizes and shapes, made of a variety of papers, with a number of modifications.

George F. Nesbitt & Co. made the government envelopes during the 1853-70 period. The Nesbitt seal or crest on the tip of the top flap was officially ordered discontinued July 7, 1853.

Watermarks in envelope paper, illustrated in this introduction, were mandatory from their first appearance in 1853. One important exception started in 1919 and lasted until the manila newspaper wrappers were discontinued in October 1934. The envelope contractor, due to inability to obtain watermarked Manila paper, was permitted to buy unwatermarked stock in the open market, a procedure that accounts for the wide range of shades and weights in this paper, including glazed and unglazed brown (kraft) paper. No. U615, and other unwatermarked envelopes that follow will be so noted in the listings. Diagonally laid paper has been used for some envelopes beginning with Scott U571.

A few stamped envelopes, in addition to the Manila items noted above, have been found without watermarks or with unauthorized watermarks. Such unusual watermarks or lack of watermarks are errors, bidders' samples or "specimen" envelopes, and most of them are quite rare.

Watermarks usually have been changed with every four-year contract, and thus serve to identify the envelope contractor, and since 1911, the manufacturer of the paper.

Envelope paper watermarks can be seen by spreading the envelope open and holding it against the light.

COLORS IN ENVELOPE PAPER

Stamped envelopes usually have been supplied in several colors and qualities of paper, some of which blend into each other and require study for identification. The following are the principal colors and the approximate years of use for stamped envelopes and wrappers:

Amber: 1870-1920 and 1929-1943; in two qualities; a pale yellow color; its intentional use in the Nesbitt series is doubtful.

Amber-Manila: 1886-98; same as Manila-amber.

Blue: 1874-1943; usually in two qualities; light and dark shades.

Buff: 1853-70; called cream, 1870-78; and oriental buff, 1886-1920; varies widely in shades.

Canary: 1873-78; another designation given to lemon.

Cream: 1870-78; see buff; second quality in 1c and 2c envelopes.

Fawn: 1874-86; very dark buff, almost light chocolate.

Lemon: 1873-78; Post Office official envelopes only; same as canary.

Manila: 1861-1934; second quality envelopes 1886-1928, and most wrappers; light and dark shades 1920-34; also kraft colored paper in later years.

Manila-Amber: 1886-98; amber shade of Manila quality.

Orange: 1861-83; second and third qualities only.

Oriental Buff: 1886-1920; see buff.

White: 1853-date; two qualities 1915-date; three qualities 1915-25; many shades including ivory, light gray, and bluish; far more common than any other color of paper. Envelopes that have no paper color given are white.

Laid paper was used almost exclusively from 1853 to 1915, but there were a few exceptions, mostly in the Manila papers. Wove paper has been the rule since 1915.

EMBOSSING AND PRINTING DIES

Until the modern era, stamped envelopes were always embossed, with the colorless areas slightly ed above the colored (or printed) flat background. ile this process was not made mandatory in the inal act, custom and tradition firmly established policy. In 1977, No. U584 became the first envel- to have no embossing. Since 1977, most enve- es are not embossed. Embossing is an unusual cedure, seldom seen in other printed matter. bossed impressions without color and those where s are raised are not unusual. The method of mak- envelope embossings has few counterparts in the ographic industries, and hence is not well under- od, even by stamp collectors.

hree types of dies are used, closely interrelated in ir derivation, MASTER dies, HUB dies and WORK- (or PRINTING) dies. These types and the ways in ch they are made, have undergone many changes the years, and some of the earlier techniques are ecorded and rather vague. No attempt will be made describe other than the present day-methods. As an to clarity, the design illustrated herewith is the erlocked monogram "US," within a single circular der. Dies with curved faces for rotary printing are d extensively, as well as with straight faces for flat nting; only the latter will be described, since the sic principles are the same for both.

Figure 1

Master Die for Envelope Stamps
Colorless Lines are Recessed Below the Printing urface.
It Reads Backward.

The MASTER die (Figure 1) is engraved on the uared end of a small soft steel cylinder, before hard- ing. The lines that are to remain colorless are cut or graved into the face of this die, leaving the flat area the face to carry the printing ink. The monogram is versed, reading backward, as with any printing type plate. Instead of engraving, a master die may be ade by transfer under heavy pressure, usually with me modification in design, in which case it is called sub-master or supplementary-master die. Sub- aster dies are sometimes made without figures of lue, when the balance of the design is as desired, d only the figures of value engraved by hand. Vari- s other combinations of transfer and engraving are own, always resulting in a reversed design, with cessed lines and figures, from which proofs can be lled, and which accurately represents the printing rface that is desired in the eventual working die. The ft steel of a master die, after engraving and transfer- g is completed, is hardened by heat treatments fore it can be used for making hubs.

Figure 2

Hub Die for Envelope Stamps
Colorless Lines Protrude above the Surface.
The Monogram Reads Forward.

The HUB die (Figure 2), also called HOB die, is ade from soft steel by transfer under pressure from he hardened master or sub-master die, which serves s a matrix or pattern. Since it is a transfer from the aster die, the colorless lines protrude from the sur- ace and it reads forward. This transfer impression of he hub die is made in a depression at the end of a turdy cylinder, as it is subject to extremely hard ser- ice in making many working dies.

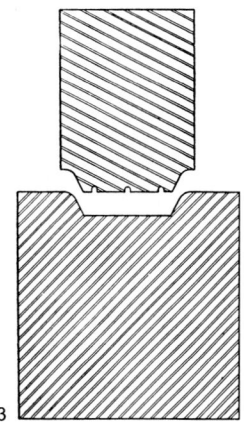

Figure 3

Pressure Transfer From Master Die to Hub Die
Above, Hardened Steel Master Die with Recessed Monogram.
Below, Soft Steel Hub Die Blank.

Figure 3 shows the relative position of the hardened steel master die as it enters the depression in the soft steel hub die blank. Some surplus metal may be squeezed out as the master die is forced into the hub blank, and require removal, leading to possible minor differences between the hub and master dies. At the completion of the pressure transfer the engraver may need to touch up the protruding surfaces to eliminate imperfections, to make letters and figures more sym- metrical, and to improve the facial lines of the bust.

A hub die may be made by normal transfer, as above, the figures of value then ground off, and thus be ready for use in making a sub-master die without figures of value, and in which the figures of value may be engraved or punched. Since a hub die may be used to make a hundred or more working dies, it must be exceedingly sturdy and withstand terrific punishment without damage. Duplicate hub dies are frequently made from master dies, as stand-bys or reserves. After completion, hub dies are hardened. Hub dies cannot be engraved, nor can proof impressions be taken from them.

Figure 4

Working or Printing Die for Envelope Stamps
An exact Replica of the Master Die, except for size and shape of shank, which is designed for Printers} lock-up.
It Reads Backward.

The WORKING, or PRINTING, die (Figure 4) is like the type or plate that printers use, and may be thin to clamp to a base block, or type-high with square sides to lock in a printer's form. Its face reads backward, i.e., in reverse, and it is an exact replica of the master die as well as an exact matrix of the hub die.

Figure 5

Pressure Transfer from Hub to Working Die
Above, Soft Steel Blank for Working Die.
Below, Hardened Steel Hub Die with Protruding Lines.

The process of pressure transfer is shown in Figure 5. where the soft steel blank of the working die is entering the depression on the top end of the hard- ened hub die, In fact the pressure transfer of working dies from hub dies closely resembles that of minting coins, and many of these envelope stamp dies are made at the United States Mint in Philadelphia.

In some cases even working dies may be made without figures of value, and the figures of value indi- vidually engraved thereon. This is known to be the case in Die B of the 6c orange airmail stamped envel- ope die, where the size and position of the "6" has eleven variations.

There are some known instances, as in the case of the 4c and 5c envelopes dies of 1903 and 1907, where the engraved master dies were used as printing dies, since the anticipated demand did not justify the expense of making hub dies.

While working envelope dies are heat treated to the hardest temper known, they do wear down eventually to a point where impressions deteriorate and are unsatisfactory, due to shallow recesses or to broken areas, and such dies are destroyed. In many cases these printing dies can be reworked, or deepened, by annealing the steel, touching up the lines or busts by hand engraving to restore the letters or renew the facial contour lines, and then rehardened for subse- quent use. This recutting is the principal cause for minor die varieties in envelope stamps. When working dies are no longer useful, they are mutilated and even- tually melted down into scrap metal.

The average "life" (in number of good impressions obtained) of a hardened steel working die, as used in envelope printing and embossing machines is around 30,000,000 on flat bed presses, and 43,000,000 on rotary presses. With a production of stamped enve- lopes of approximately 2 billion annually, 60 to 75 working dies are worn out each year, and require replacement with new dies or a reworking of old dies. Some 200 to 250 working dies can be in constant use, since most envelope printing presses are set up for a special size, type or value, and few can be operated continuously at maximum capacity.

Master and hub dies of obsolete envelope issues are kept in the vaults of the Bureau of Engraving and printing in Washington, as are the original dies of adhesive stamps, revenue paper, government securi- ties and paper currency.

PRINTING ENVELOPE STAMPS

Embossed envelope stamps are not printed against a rigid flat platen, as is the normal printed page, but against a somewhat flexible or resilient platen or make-ready (Figure 6). This resilient platen is hard enough to produce a clear full impression from the ink on the face of the working die, and soft enough to push the paper into the uninked recesses that correspond to the engraved lines cut into the master die. The normal result is raised lines or embossments without ink or color, standing out in relief against an inked or colored background. The method differs from the usual embossing technique, where rigid dies are used on both sides of the paper, as in notarial seals. The use of the resilient platen in envelope embossing permits far higher operating speeds than can be obtained with rigid embossing dies, without the need of such accu- rate register between the printing surface and the platen.

Figure 6

Printing Process for Embossed
A. Working Die, Carrying ink on its surface.
B. Resilient Platen, or Make-ready, Pushing Paper into uninked recesses, so that lines of Embossed Mon- ogram receive no color.
C. Paper of Envelope Blank, after Printing and Embossing. Heavy line shows deposit of ink on sur- face of paper, but Embossed Lines are not inked.
D. Front view of Embossed impression.

When these recessed lines in a working die become filled with ink or other foreign material, the paper is not pushed in, the plugged area receives ink, and the cor- responding colorless line does not appear on the stamp. This accounts for missing letters, lines or figures, and is a printing error, not a die variety.

An ALBINO impression is where two or more envel- ope blanks are fed into the printing press. The one adjacent to the printing die receives the color and the embossing, while the others are embossed only. Albi- nos are printing errors and are sometimes worth more than normal, inked impressions. Because of the nature of the printing process, many albinos were produced, and most collectors will not pay much, or any, premium for most of them. Albinos of earlier issues, canceled while current, are scarce.

Before January 1, 1965, stamped envelopes were printed by two processes: (1.) The rotary, with curved dies, on Huckins and Harris presses. (2.) The flat pro- cess, with straight dies, as illustrated, on the O'Connell-type press, which is a redesigned Hartford press. The flat bed presses include a gumming and folding attachment, while the rotary presses, running at higher speeds, require separate folding machines.

Different master dies in every denomination are required for Huckins, Harris and flat bed presses. This difference gives rise to most of the major die varieties in envelope stamps.

Web-fed equipment which converts paper from a roll into finished envelopes in a continuous operation has produced envelopes starting with Nos. U547 and UC37. Albino impressions do not occur on envelopes produced by web-fed equipment.

Some authorities claim that Scott U37, U48, U49, U110, U124, U125, U130, U133A, U137A, U137B, U137C, W138, U140A, U145, U162, U178A, U185, U220, U285, U286, U298, U299, UO3, UO32, UO38, UO45 and UO45A (with plus sign + before number), were not regularly issued and are not known to have been used.

Wrappers are listed with envelopes of corresponding design, and are numbered with the prefix "W" inotoad of "U."

ENVELOPE WATERMARKS

Watermark Illustrations 5, 6, 17 and 18 are condensed. Watermark 4 was used only on Officials. Watermarks 9 and 10 are found on Specimens and Errors. Watermarks 17-18 were the last laid paper watermarks; watermarks 19-21 the first wove paper watermarks. Beginning with No. U615, unwatermarked paper was used for some issues. Beginning with No. U625, unwatermarked paper was used for all issues.

Wmks. 1 (1853-70) & 2 (1870-78)

Wmk. 3 (1876)

Wmk. 4 (1877-82)

Wmk. 5 (1878-82)

Wmk. 6 (1882-86)

Wmks. 7 (1886-90) & 8 (1890-94)

Wmks. 9 (1886-87) & 10 (1886-99)

Wmk. 11 (1893)

Wmks. 12 (1894-98) & 13 (1899-1902)

Wmks. 14 (1903-07) & 15 (1907-11)

Wmks. 15A (1907-11) & 16 (1911-15)

Wmks. 17 & 18 (1911-15)

Wmk. 19, 20 & 21 (1915-19)

Wmks. 22 & 23 (1919-20)

Wmks. 24 & 25 (1921-24)

Wmks. 26 & 27 (1925-28)

Wmks. 28 & 28A (1929-32)

Wmks. 29, 30 & 30A (1929-32)

Wmks. 31, 32, 33 (1933-36)

Wmks. 35 & 36 (1937-40)

Wmks. 38 & 39 (1941-44)

Wmks. 40 & 41 (1945-48)

Wmks. 42 & 43 (1949-52)

Wmks. 44 & 45 (1953-56)

Wmk. 46 (1957-60)

Wmks. 47 & 48 (1961-88)

Wmks. 49 & 50 (1965-92)

Letter Sheet (1886-94)

Official Envelopes (1991)

Washington — U1

"THREE" in short label with curved ends; 13mm wide at top Twelve varieties.

U2

"THREE" in short label with straight ends; 15½mm wide at
o. Three varieties.

U3

"THREE" in short label with octagonal ends. Two varieties.

U4

"THREE" in wide label with straight ends; 20mm wide at top.

U5

"THREE" in medium wide label with curved ends; 14½mm
wide at top. Ten varieties. A sub-variety shows curved lines at
either end of label omitted; both T's have longer cross stroke; R
s smaller (20 varieties).

U6

Four varieties.

U7

"TEN" in short label; 15½mm wide at top.

U8

"TEN" in wide label; 20mm wide at top.

Printed by George F. Nesbitt & Co., New York, N.Y.

1853-55
On Diagonally Laid Paper (Early printings of No. U1 on Horizontally Laid Paper)

U1	U1	3c **red**	400.00	35.00
		Entire	2,250.	45.00
U2	U1	3c **red**, *buff*	100.00	25.00
		Entire	1,000.	30.00
U3	U2	3c **red**	1,300.	45.00
		Entire	6,000.	100.00
U4	U2	3c **red**, *buff*	350.00	40.00
		Entire	2,500.	75.00
U5	U3	3c **red** ('54)	6,250.	550.00
		Entire	37,500.	900.00
U6	U3	3c **red**, *buff* ('54)	4,750.	75.00
		Entire	—	150.00
U7	U4	3c **red**	5,500.	150.00
		Entire	—	300.00
U8	U4	3c **red**, *buff*	8,750.	150.00
		Entire	—	300.00
U9	U5	3c **red** ('54)	40.00	4.00
		Entire	150.00	9.00
U10	U5	3c **red**, *buff* ('54)	22.50	4.00
		Entire	72.50	6.00
U11	U6	6c **red**	325.00	90.00
		Entire	450.00	175.00
U12	U6	6c **red**, *buff*	175.00	90.00
		Entire	275.00	200.00
U13	U6	6c **green**	400.00	125.00
		Entire	750.00	225.00
U14	U6	6c **green**, *buff*	225.00	100.00
		Entire	450.00	225.00
U15	U7	10c **green** ('55)	550.00	100.00
		Entire	950.00	150.00
U16	U7	10c **green**, *buff* ('55)	190.00	75.00
		Entire	500.00	150.00
a.		10c **pale green**, *buff*	150.00	65.00
		Entire	425.00	125.00
U17	U8	10c **green** ('55)	550.00	140.00
		Entire	900.00	225.00
a.		10c **pale green**	400.00	125.00
		Entire	750.00	200.00
U18	U8	10c **green**, *buff* ('55)	400.00	90.00
		Entire	700.00	175.00
a.		10c **pale green**, *buff*	375.00	90.00
		Entire	750.00	175.00

*Nos. U9, U10, U11, U12, U13, U14, U17, and U18 have been
reprinted on white and buff papers, wove or vertically laid, and
are not known entire. The originals are on diagonally laid paper.
Value, set of 8 reprints on laid, $225. Reprints on wove sell for
more.*

Franklin — U9

Period after "POSTAGE." (Eleven varieties.)

Franklin — U10

Bust touches inner frame-line at front and back.

Franklin — U11

No period after "POSTAGE." (Two varieties.)

Washington — U12

Nine varieties of type U12.

Envelopes are on diagonally laid paper.
Wrappers on vertically or horizontally laid paper, or
on unwatermarked wove paper (Nos. W22, W25).

Wrappers of the 1 cent denomination were authorized by an
Act of Congress, February 27, 1861, and were issued in October, 1861. These were suspended in 1863, and their use
resumed in June, 1864.

1860-61

W18B	U9	1c **blue** ('61)	5,750.	
U19	U9	1c **blue**, *buff*	40.00	15.00
		Entire	90.00	32.50
W20	U9	1c **blue**, *buff* ('61)	70.00	50.00
		Entire	125.00	75.00
W21	U9	1c **blue**, *manila* ('61)	60.00	45.00
		Entire	125.00	100.00
U21A	U9	1c **blue**, *orange, entire*	2,750.	
W22	U9	1c **blue**, *orange* ('61)	4,250.	
		Entire	8,000.	
U23	U10	1c **blue**, *orange*	750.00	350.00
		Entire	1,000.	500.00
U24	U11	1c **blue**, *amber*	375.00	125.00
		Entire	725.00	225.00
W25	U11	1c **blue**, *manila* ('61)	7,500.	2,250.
		Entire	20,000.	4,500.
U26	U12	3c **red**	35.00	20.00
		Entire	60.00	32.50
U27	U12	3c **red**, *buff*	26.00	13.00
		Entire	45.00	22.50
U28	U12 + U9	3c + 1c **red & blue**	375.00	275.00
		Entire	825.00	500.00
U29	U12 + U9	3c + 1c **red & blue**, *buff*	375.00	275.00
		Entire	825.00	500.00
U30	U12	6c **red**	3,500.	1,500.
		Entire	6,500.	
U31	U12	6c **red**, *buff*	4,000.	1,500.

			Entire	7,000.	15,000.
U32	U12	10c **green**		1,650.	450.00
			Entire	14,000.	650.00
U33	U12	10c **green**, buff		1,650.	375.00
			Entire	4,500.	550.00

Nos. U26, U27, U30 to U33 have been reprinted on the same vertically laid paper as the reprints of the 1853-55 issue, and are not known entire. Value, Nos. U26-U27, $160; Nos. U30-U33, $100.

Washington — U13

17 varieties for Nos. U34-U35; 2 varieties for No. U36.

Washington — U14   Washington — U15

Washington — U16

Envelopes are on diagonally laid paper.

U36 and U45 come on vertically or horizontally laid paper. U36 appeared in August, 1861, and was withdrawn in 1864. Total issue 211,800.

1861

U34	U13	3c **pink**		32.50	6.00
			Entire	62.50	13.00
U35	U13	3c **pink**, buff		32.50	6.00
			Entire	62.50	13.00
U36	U13	3c **pink**, blue (Letter Sheet)		82.50	60.00
			Entire	290.00	140.00
+U37	U13	3c **pink**, orange		5,500.	
			Entire	8,000.	
U38	U14	6c **pink**		125.00	80.00
			Entire	210.00	190.00
U39	U14	6c **pink**, buff		82.50	62.50
			Entire	225.00	160.00

U40	U15	10c **yellow green**		47.50	30.00
			Entire	82.50	60.00
a.		10c **blue green**		47.50	30.00
			Entire	82.50	60.00
U41	U15	10c **yellow green**, buff		47.50	52.50
			Entire	82.50	52.50
a.		10c **blue green**, buff		47.50	30.00
			Entire	82.50	52.50
U42	U16	12c **red & brown**, buff		275.00	175.00
			Entire	550.00	650.00
a.		12c **lake & brown**, buff		1,400.	
U43	U16	20c **red & blue**, buff		325.00	200.00
			Entire	575.00	1,250.
U44	U16	24c **red & green**, buff		300.00	200.00
			Entire	750.00	1,500.
a.		24c **lake & green**, salmon		325.00	225.00
			Entire	850.00	1,750.
U45	U16	40c **black & red**, buff		375.00	350.00
			Entire	850.00	4,500.

Nos. U38 and U39 have been reprinted on the same papers as the reprints of the 1853-55 issue, and are not known entire. Value, set of 2 reprints, $60.

Jackson — U17

"U.S. POSTAGE" above. Downstroke and tail of "2" unite near the point (seven varieties).

Jackson — U18

"U.S. POSTAGE" above. The downstroke and tail of the "2" touch but do not merge.

Jackson — U19

"U.S. POST" above. Stamp 24-25mm wide (Sixteen varieties).

Jackson — U20

"U.S. POST" above. Stamp 25½-26¼mm wide. (Twenty-five varieties.)

Envelopes are on diagonally laid paper.
Wrappers on vertically or horizontally laid paper.

1863-64

U46	U17	2c **black**, buff		52.50	21.00
			Entire	82.50	37.50
W47	U17	2c **black**, dark manila		80.00	50.00
			Entire	100.00	80.00
+U48	U18	2c **black**, buff		3,250.	
			Entire	6,250.	
+U49	U18	2c **black**, orange		2,750.	
			Entire	5,750.	
U50	U19	2c **black**, buff ('64)		17.50	9.50
			Entire	40.00	21.00
W51	U19	2c **black**, buff ('64)		400.00	200.00
			Entire	600.00	350.00
U52	U19	2c **black**, orange ('64)		18.00	9.50
			Entire	35.00	18.00
W53	U19	2c **black**, dark manila ('64)		50.00	40.00
			Entire	175.00	140.00
U54	U20	2c **black**, buff ('64)		18.00	9.50
			Entire	37.50	16.00
W55	U20	2c **black**, buff ('64)		100.00	65.00
			Entire	150.00	120.00

U56	U20	2c **black**, orange ('64)		21.00	8
			Entire	32.50	16
W57	U20	2c **black**, light manila ('64)		22.50	14
			Entire	35.00	24

Washington — U21

79 varieties for Nos. U58-U61; 2 varieties for Nos. U63-U6

Washington — U22

1864-65

U58	U21	3c **pink**		10.50	1.
			Entire	18.00	3.
U59	U21	3c **pink**, buff		9.50	1.
			Entire	16.00	3.
U60	U21	3c **brown** ('65)		75.00	40.
			Entire	140.00	125.
U61	U21	3c **brown**, buff ('65)		60.00	30.
			Entire	125.00	80.
U62	U21	6c **pink**		110.00	29.
			Entire	190.00	85.
U63	U21	6c **pink**, buff		55.00	27.
			Entire	110.00	50.
U64	U21	6c **purple** ('65)		75.00	26.
			Entire	100.00	55.
U65	U21	6c **purple**, buff ('65)		60.00	20.
			Entire	80.00	55.
U66	U22	9c **lemon**, buff ('65)		450.00	250.
			Entire	625.00	1,00
U67	U22	9c **orange**, buff ('65)		160.00	90.
			Entire	225.00	275.
a.		9c **orange yellow**, buff		160.00	90.
			Entire	225.00	275.
U68	U22	12c **brown**, buff ('65)		325.00	55.
			Entire	625.00	1,20
U69	U22	12c **red brown**, buff ('65)		150.00	55.
			Entire	200.00	360.
U70	U22	18c **red**, buff ('65)		95.00	95.
			Entire	200.00	800.
U71	U22	24c **blue**, buff ('65)		100.00	95.
			entire	200.00	750.
U72	U22	30c **green**, buff ('65)		125.00	80.
			Entire	200.00	1,50
a.		30c **yellow green**, buff		125.00	80.
			Entire	200.00	1,50
U73	U22	40c **rose**, buff ('65)		125.00	250.
			Entire	350.00	2,00

Printed by George H. Reay, Brooklyn, N. Y.
The engravings in this issue are finely executed.

Franklin — U23

Bust points to the end of the "N" of "ONE."

Jackson — U24

Bust narrow at back. Small, thick figures of value.

Washington — U25

*ueue projects below bust.

Lincoln — U26

*leck very long at the back.

Stanton — U27

Bust pointed at the back; figures "7" are normal.

Jefferson — U28

Queue forms straight line with the bust.

Clay — U29

Ear partly concealed by hair, mouth large, chin prominent.

Webster — U30

Has side whiskers.

Scott — U31

Straggling locks of hair at top of head; ornaments around the inner oval end in squares.

Hamilton — U32

Back of bust very narrow, chin almost straight; labels containing figures of value are exactly parallel.

Perry — U33

Front of bust very narrow and pointed; inner lines of shields project very slightly beyond the oval.

1870-71

U74	U23	1c **blue**		45.00	30.00
			Entire	80.00	45.00
a.		1c **ultramarine**		72.50	35.00
			Entire	140.00	60.00
U75	U23	1c **blue,** *amber*		37.50	27.50
			Entire	60.00	40.00
a.		1c **ultramarine,** *amber*		70.00	30.00
			Entire	100.00	55.00
U76	U23	1c **blue,** *orange*		20.00	15.00
			Entire	35.00	22.50
W77	U23	1c **blue,** *manila*		45.00	37.50
			Entire	82.50	70.00
U78	U24	2c **brown**		40.00	16.00
			Entire	60.00	22.50
U79	U24	2c **brown,** *amber*		22.50	10.00
			Entire	40.00	17.50
U80	U24	2c **brown,** *orange*		12.00	6.50
			Entire	17.50	11.00
W81	U24	2c **brown,** *manila*		29.00	22.50
			Entire	62.50	57.50
U82	U25	3c **green**		8.50	1.00
			Entire	17.00	1.00
a.		3c **brown** (error), entire		*13,000.*	
U83	U25	3c **green,** *amber*		7.25	2.00
			Entire	18.00	5.00
U84	U25	3c **green,** *cream*		11.00	4.50
			Entire	17.00	10.00
U85	U26	6c **dark red**		32.50	16.00
			Entire	60.00	21.00
a.		6c **vermilion**		32.50	16.00
			Entire	75.00	20.00
U86	U26	6c **dark red,** *amber*		40.00	20.00
			Entire	75.00	30.00
a.		6c **vermilion,** *amber*		40.00	20.00
			Entire	75.00	30.00
U87	U26	6c **dark red,** *cream*		40.00	20.00
			Entire	80.00	30.00
a.		6c **vermilion,** *cream*		40.00	20.00
			Entire	80.00	30.00
U88	U27	7c **vermilion,** *amber* ('71)		55.00	*190.00*
			Entire	82.50	*900.00*
U89	U28	10c **olive black**		975.00	900.00
			Entire	*1,350.*	*1,250.*
U90	U28	10c **olive black,** *amber*		975.00	900.00
			Entire	*1,350.*	*1,250.*
U91	U28	10c **brown**		92.50	72.50
			Entire	140.00	125.00
U92	U28	10c **brown,** *amber*		110.00	52.50
			Entire	140.00	125.00
a.		10c **dark brown,** *amber*		110.00	75.00
			Entire	140.00	125.00
U93	U29	12c **plum**		125.00	82.50
			Entire	240.00	*450.00*
U94	U29	12c **plum,** *amber*		140.00	110.00
			Entire	240.00	*650.00*
U95	U29	12c **plum,** *cream*		275.00	250.00
			Entire	375.00	
U96	U30	15c **red orange**		85.00	85.00
			Entire	175.00	
a.		15c **orange**		85.00	

			Entire	175.00	
U97	U30	15c **red orange,** *amber*		210.00	*300.00*
			Entire	400.00	
a.		15c **orange,** *amber*		210.00	
			Entire	400.00	
U98	U30	15c **red orange,** *cream*		325.00	350.00
			Entire	425.00	
a.		15c **orange,** *cream*		325.00	
			Entire	425.00	
U99	U31	24c **purple**		150.00	150.00
			Entire	200.00	
U100	U31	24c **purple,** *amber*		200.00	*325.00*
			Entire	375.00	
U101	U31	24c **purple,** *cream*		275.00	500.00
			Entire	475.00	
U102	U32	30c **black**		80.00	110.00
			Entire	300.00	*750.00*
U103	U32	30c **black,** *amber*		250.00	500.00
			Entire	650.00	
U104	U32	30c **black,** *cream*		250.00	500.00
			Entire	400.00	
U105	U33	90c **carmine**		175.00	*350.00*
			Entire	250.00	
U106	U33	90c **carmine,** *amber*		325.00	450.00
			Entire	800.00	*4,500.*
U107	U33	90c **carmine,** *cream*		300.00	*2,500.*
			Entire	800.00	*5,000.*

Printed by Plimpton Manufacturing Co.

U34

Bust forms an angle at the back near the frame. Lettering poorly executed. Distinct circle in "O" of "Postage."

U35

Lower part of bust points to the end of the "E" in "ONE." Head inclined downward.

U36

Bust narrow at back. Thin numerals. Head of "P" narrow. Bust broad at front, ending in sharp corners.

U37

Bust broad. Figures of value in long ovals.

U38

Similar to U37 but the figure "2" at the left touches the oval.

U39

Similar to U37 but the "O" of "TWO" has the center netted instead of plain and the "G" of "POSTAGE" and the "C" of "CENTS" have diagonal crossline.

U40

Bust broad: numerals in ovals short and thick.

U41

Similar to U40 but the ovals containing the numerals are much heavier. A diagonal line runs from the upper part of the "U" to the white frame-line.

U42

Similar to U40 but the middle stroke of "N" in "CENTS" is as thin as the vertical strokes.

U43

Bottom of bust cut almost semi-circularly.

U44

Thin lettering, long thin figures of value.

U45

Thick lettering, well-formed figures of value, queue does not project below bust.

U46

Top of head egg-shaped; knot of queue well marked projects triangularly.

Taylor — U47

Die 1 —
Figures of value with thick, curved tops.

Die 2 —
Figures of value with long, thin tops.

U48

Neck short at back.

U49

Figures of value turned up at the ends.

U50

Very large head.

U51

Knot of queue stands out prominently.

U52

Ear prominent, chin receding.

U53

No side whiskers, forelock projects above head.

U54

Hair does not project; ornaments around the inner oval end in points.

U55

Back of bust rather broad, chin slopes considerably; labels containing figures of value are not exactly parallel.

U56

Front of bust sloping; inner lines of shields project considerably into the inner oval.

1874-86

No.	Die	Description		
U108	U34	1c dark blue	210.00	70.00
		Entire	275.00	110.00
a.		1c light blue	210.00	70.00
		Entire	275.00	125.00
U109	U34	1c dark blue, amber	190.00	75.00
		Entire	210.00	140.00
+U110	U34	1c dark blue, cream	1,750.	
U111	U34	1c dark blue, orange	25.00	17.50
		Entire	35.00	25.00
a.		1c light blue, orange	25.00	17.50
		Entire	35.00	25.00
W112	U34	1c dark blue, manila	72.50	42.50
		Entire	110.00	75.00
U113	U35	1c light blue	1.90	1.00
		Entire	3.00	1.10
a.		1c dark blue	9.00	7.50
		Entire	29.00	20.00
U114	U35	1c light blue, amber	4.50	4.00
		Entire	8.25	6.00
a.		1c dark blue, amber	20.00	10.00
		Entire	30.00	20.00
U115	U35	1c blue, cream	5.25	4.50
		Entire	10.50	6.50
a.		1c dark blue, cream	20.00	8.50
		Entire	32.50	20.00
U116	U35	1c light blue, orange	.80	.40
		Entire	1.25	.75
a.		1c dark blue, orange	4.50	2.50
		Entire	16.00	8.00
U117	U35	1c light blue, blue ('80)	8.50	5.25
		Entire	13.50	9.00
U118	U35	1c light blue, fawn ('79)	8.50	5.25
		Entire	15.00	10.00
U119	U35	1c light blue, manila ('86)	9.00	3.25
		Entire	17.00	5.00
W120	U35	1c light blue, manila	1.60	1.10
		Entire	2.75	1.75
a.		1c dark blue, manila	9.00	8.00
		Entire	16.00	15.00
U121	U35	1c light blue, amber manila ('86)	19.00	10.00
		Entire	29.00	20.00
U122	U36	2c brown	150.00	50.00
		Entire	175.00	85.00
U123	U36	2c brown, amber	72.50	40.00
		Entire	125.00	70.00
+U124	U36	2c brown, cream	1,250.	
+U125	U36	2c brown, orange	25,000.	
		Entire	45,000.	
W126	U36	2c brown, manila	175.00	85.00
		Entire	300.00	160.00
W127	U36	2c vermilion, manila	3,000.	250.00
		Entire	4,750.	5,000.
U128	U37	2c brown	60.00	35.00
		Entire	110.00	75.00
U129	U37	2c brown, amber	85.00	45.00
		Entire	125.00	77.50
+U130	U37	2c brown, cream	50,000.	
W131	U37	2c brown, manila	20.00	17.00
		Entire	29.00	26.00
U132	U38	2c brown	82.50	29.00
		Entire	125.00	80.00
U133	U38	2c brown, amber	350.00	70.00
		Entire	575.00	140.00
+U133A	U38	2c brown, cream	75,000.	
U134	U39	2c brown	1,500.	160.00
		Entire	2,250.	300.00
U135	U39	2c brown, amber	525.00	125.00
		Entire	700.00	160.00
U136	U39	2c brown, orange	57.50	29.00
		Entire	87.50	37.50
W137	U39	2c brown, manila	80.00	40.00
		Entire	125.00	55.00
+U137A	U39	2c vermilion	40,000.	
+U137B	U39	2c vermilion, amber	40,000.	
+U137C	U39	2c vermilion, orange	40,000.	
+W138	U39	2c vermilion, manila	32,500.	
U139	U40	2c brown ('75)	62.50	37.50
		Entire	82.50	47.50
U140	U40	2c brown, amber ('75)	97.50	62.50
		Entire	140.00	77.50
+U140A	U40	2c reddish brown, orange ('75)	25,000.	
		Entire	40,000.	
W141	U40	2c brown, manila ('75)	37.50	27.50
		Entire	45.00	32.50
U142	U40	2c vermilion ('75)	9.00	5.00
		Entire	10.50	7.50
a.		2c pink	9.00	5.00
		Entire	10.50	7.50
U143	U40	2c vermilion, amber ('75)	9.00	4.50
		Entire	10.50	5.75
U144	U40	2c vermilion, cream ('75)	19.00	7.50
		Entire	24.00	12.50
+U145	U40	2c vermilion, orange ('75)	50,000.	
U146	U40	2c vermilion, blue ('80)	140.00	40.00
		Entire	200.00	140.00
U147	U40	2c vermilion, fawn ('75)	9.50	5.00
		Entire	15.00	7.00
W148	U40	2c vermilion, manila ('75)	4.00	3.75
		Entire	8.50	6.50
U149	U41	2c vermilion ('78)	62.50	32.50
		Entire	95.00	42.50
a.		2c pink	62.50	35.00
		Entire	95.00	42.50
U150	U41	2c vermilion, amber ('78)	42.50	17.50
		Entire	62.50	22.50
U151	U41	2c vermilion, blue ('80)	14.00	10.00
		Entire	21.00	15.00
a.		2c pink, blue	13.00	10.00
		Entire	17.50	12.50
U152	U41	2c vermilion, fawn ('78)	13.00	4.75
		Entire	18.00	9.50
U153	U42	2c vermilion ('76)	77.50	27.50
		Entire	110.00	37.50
U154	U42	2c vermilion, amber ('76)	400.00	90.00
		Entire	450.00	175.00
W155	U42	2c vermilion, manila ('76)	24.00	11.00
		Entire	47.50	20.00
U156	U43	2c vermilion ('81)	1,750.	175.00
		Entire	2,250.	500.00
U157	U43	2c vermilion, amber ('81)	57,500.	35,000.
		Entire	70,000.	
W158	U43	2c vermilion, manila ('81)	110.00	62.50
		Entire	190.00	175.00
U159	U44	3c green	37.50	6.75
		Entire	62.50	17.50
U160	U44	3c green, amber	40.00	11.50
		Entire	65.00	20.00
U161	U44	3c green, cream	42.50	15.00
		Entire	70.00	30.00
+U162	U44	3c green, blue	—	
U163	U45	3c green	1.50	.30
		Entire	4.25	2.25
U164	U45	3c green, amber	1.60	.70
		Entire	4.25	2.00
U165	U45	3c green, cream	9.50	6.50
		Entire	19.00	9.00
U166	U45	3c green, blue	8.50	6.25
		Entire	17.00	11.00
U167	U45	3c green, fawn ('75)	5.25	3.50
		Entire	9.25	5.00
U168	U46	3c green ('81)	1,500.	80.00
		Entire	5,000.	275.00
U169	U46	3c green, amber	325.00	110.00
		Entire	625.00	300.00
U170	U46	3c green, blue ('81)	12,500.	3,750.
		Entire	20,000.	4,750.
U171	U46	3c green, fawn ('81)	45,000.	3,250.
		Entire		14,000.
U172	U47	5c blue, die 1 ('75)	15.00	9.00
		Entire	21.00	14.00
U173	U47	5c blue, die 1, amber ('75)	15.00	10.00
		Entire	21.00	14.00
U174	U47	5c blue, die 1, cream ('75)	125.00	42.50
		Entire	190.00	90.00
U175	U47	5c blue, die 1, blue ('75)	40.00	16.00
		Entire	57.50	25.00
U176	U47	5c blue, die 1, fawn ('75)	160.00	60.00
		Entire	300.00	
U177	U47	5c blue, die 2 ('75)	14.00	8.00
		Entire	20.00	16.00
U178	U47	5c blue, die 2, amber ('75)	12.00	8.00
		Entire	21.00	17.00
+U178A	U47	5c blue, die 2, cream ('76)	14,000.	
		Entire	22,500.	
U179	U47	5c blue, die 2, blue ('75)	32.50	11.00
		Entire	47.50	27.50
U180	U47	5c blue, die 2, fawn ('75)	140.00	47.50
		Entire	240.00	140.00
U181	U48	6c red	10.00	6.75
		Entire	15.00	12.50
a.		6c vermilion	10.00	6.75
		Entire	15.00	12.50
U182	U48	6c red, amber	15.00	6.75
		Entire	24.00	15.00
a.		6c vermilion, amber	15.00	6.75
		Entire	24.00	15.00
U183	U48	6c red, cream	55.00	17.50
		Entire	87.50	40.00
a.		6c vermilion, cream	55.00	17.50
		Entire	87.50	40.00
U184	U48	6c red, fawn ('75)	24.00	13.50
		Entire	35.00	29.00
+U185	U49	7c vermilion	1,800.	
U186	U49	7c vermilion, amber	160.00	70.00
		Entire	200.00	
U187	U50	10c brown	45.00	22.50
		Entire	65.00	
U188	U50	10c brown, amber	82.50	35.00
		Entire	160.00	
U189	U51	10c chocolate ('75)	8.00	4.25
		Entire	13.00	9.25
a.		10c bister brown	9.00	5.25
		Entire	13.00	10.50
b.		10c yellow ocher	4,500.	
		Entire	8,500.	
U190	U51	10c chocolate, amber ('75)	9.00	7.25
		Entire	14.50	11.50
a.		10c bister brown, amber	9.00	7.75
		Entire	14.50	11.50
b.		10c yellow ocher amber	3,500.	
		Entire	6,500.	
U191	U51	10c brown, oriental buff ('86)	20.00	8.75
		Entire	22.50	11.50
U192	U51	10c brown, blue ('86)	20.00	8.75
		Entire	22.50	15.00
a.		10c gray black, blue	18.00	8.25
		Entire	21.00	15.00
b.		10c red brown, blue	18.00	8.25
		Entire	21.00	15.00
U193	U51	10c brown, manila ('86)	19.00	10.00
		Entire	24.00	16.00
a.		10c red brown, manila	19.00	10.00
		Entire	24.00	16.00
U194	U51	10c brown, amber manila ('86)	21.00	9.00
		Entire	27.50	17.50
a.		10c red brown, amber manila	21.00	9.00
		Entire	27.50	17.50
U195	U52	12c plum	475.00	100.00
		Entire	700.00	
U196	U52	12c plum, amber	275.00	175.00
		Entire	350.00	
U197	U52	12c plum, cream	225.00	150.00
		Entire	950.00	
U198	U53	15c orange	55.00	40.00
		Entire	92.50	55.00
U199	U53	15c orange, amber	160.00	100.00
		Entire	300.00	
U200	U53	15c orange, cream	600.00	350.00
		Entire	1,100.	
U201	U54	24c purple	175.00	150.00
		Entire	250.00	
U202	U54	24c purple, amber	200.00	125.00
		Entire	260.00	
U203	U54	24c purple, cream	190.00	125.00
		Entire	750.00	
U204	U55	30c black	65.00	27.50
		Entire	90.00	65.00

No.	Die	Denom.	Description		
U205	U55	30c	**black,** *amber*	75.00	60.00
			Entire	140.00	*250.00*
U206	U55	30c	**black,** *cream* ('75)	400.00	375.00
			Entire	800.00	
U207	U55	30c	**black,** *oriental buff* ('81)	100.00	82.50
			Entire	160.00	
U208	U55	30c	**black,** *blue* ('81)	110.00	82.50
			Entire	140.00	
U209	U55	30c	**black,** *manila* ('81)	95.00	80.00
			Entire	160.00	
U210	U55	30c	**black,** *amber manila* ('86)	175.00	85.00
			Entire	210.00	
U211	U56	90c	**carmine** ('75)	110.00	85.00
			Entire	160.00	95.00
U212	U56	90c	**carmine,** *amber* ('75)	225.00	300.00
			Entire	275.00	
U213	U56	90c	**carmine,** *cream* ('75)	1,750.	
			Entire	3,250.	
U214	U56	90c	**carmine,** *oriental buff* ('86)	200.00	275.00
			Entire	300.00	300.00
U215	U56	90c	**carmine,** *blue* ('86)	200.00	250.00
			Entire	275.00	275.00
U216	U56	90c	**carmine,** *manila* ('86)	175.00	250.00
			Entire	275.00	275.00
U217	U56	90c	**carmine,** *amber manila* ('86)	150.00	200.00
			Entire	225.00	275.00

Note: No. U206 has watermark #2; No. U207 watermark #6 or #7. No U213 has watermark #2; No. U214 watermark #7. These envelopes cannot be positively identified except by the watermark.

U57

Single line under "POSTAGE."

U58

Double line under "POSTAGE."

1876
Printed by Plimpton Manufacturing Co.

No.	Die	Denom.	Description		
U218	U57	3c	**red**	52.50	25.00
			Entire	77.50	50.00
U219	U57	3c	**green**	45.00	17.50
			Entire	65.00	40.00
U220	U58	3c	**red**	42,500.	
			Entire	60,000.	
U221	U58	3c	**green**	52.50	25.00
			Entire	85.00	50.00

Garfield — U59

1882-86
Printed by Plimpton Manufacturing Co. and Morgan Envelope Co.

No.	Die	Denom.	Description		
U222	U59	5c	**brown**	5.75	3.00
			Entire	10.50	7.00
U223	U59	5c	**brown,** *amber*	6.00	3.50
			Entire	11.00	8.50
U224	U59	5c	**brown,** *oriental buff* ('86)	140.00	75.00
			Entire	200.00	
U225	U59	5c	**brown,** *blue*	82.50	35.00
U226	U59	5c	**brown,** *fawn*	125.00	75.00
			Entire	375.00	
			Entire	525.00	

Washington — U60

1883, October

No.	Die	Denom.	Description		
U227	U60	2c	**red**	4.50	2.25
			Entire	10.00	3.00
a.		2c	**brown** (error), entire	*10,000.*	
U228	U60	2c	**red,** *amber*	5.75	2.75
			Entire	10.50	6.00
U229	U60	2c	**red,** *blue*	8.50	5.00
			Entire	13.00	8.00
U230	U60	2c	**red,** *fawn*	9.25	5.25
			Entire	15.00	7.00

Washington — U61

Wavy lines fine and clear.

1883, November
Four Wavy Lines in Oval

No.	Die	Denom.	Description		
U231	U61	2c	**red**	4.75	2.50
			Entire	9.00	4.00
U232	U61	2c	**red,** *amber*	5.75	3.75
			Entire	10.50	5.75
U233	U61	2c	**red,** *blue*	10.00	7.50
			Entire	17.00	10.00
U234	U61	2c	**red,** *fawn*	7.00	4.75
			Entire	11.00	6.00
W235	U61	2c	**red,** *manila*	20.00	6.25
			Entire	30.00	12.50

U62

Retouched die. Wavy lines thick and blurred.

1884, June

No.	Die	Denom.	Description		
U236	U62	2c	**red**	13.00	4.00
			Entire	20.00	7.75
U237	U62	2c	**red,** *amber*	16.00	10.00
			Entire	25.00	11.00
U238	U62	2c	**red,** *blue*	29.00	12.00
			Entire	40.00	15.00
U239	U62	2c	**red,** *fawn*	25.00	11.00
			Entire	25.00	12.50

U63

3½ links over left "2."

No.	Die	Denom.	Description		
U240	U63	2c	**red**	100.00	47.50
			Entire	160.00	72.50
U241	U63	2c	**red,** *amber*	1,000.	325.00
U242	U63	2c	**red,** *fawn*	2,750.	750.0
			Entire		*37,50*
			Entire		*55,00*

U64

2 links below right "2."

No.	Die	Denom.	Description		
U243	U64	2c	**red**	140.00	75.0
			Entire	175.00	100.0
U244	U64	2c	**red,** *amber*	350.00	100.0
			Entire	500.00	125.0
U245	U64	2c	**red,** *blue*	500.00	210.0
			Entire	650.00	225.0
U246	U64	2c	**red,** *fawn*	450.00	170.0
			Entire	700.00	275.0

U65

Round "O" in "TWO." White lines above "WO" of "TWO" joined to form thick white dash.

No.	Die	Denom.	Description		
U247	U65	2c	**red**	3,000.	600.0
			Entire	4,000.	*1,000*
U248	U65	2c	**red,** *amber*	5,000.	*1,050*
			Entire	7,500.	*1,500*
U249	U65	2c	**red,** *fawn*	1,250.	425.0
			Entire	2,000.	600.0

Jackson, Die 1 — U66

Die 1	Die 2
Numeral at left is 2¾mm wide.	Numeral at left is 3¼mm wide.

1883-86

No.	Die	Denom.	Description		
U250	U66	4c	**green,** die 1	4.00	3.50
			Entire	6.50	6.00
U251	U66	4c	**green,** die 1, *amber*	5.00	3.50
			Entire	7.50	5.25
U252	U66	4c	**green,** die 1, *oriental buff* ('86)	13.00	9.00
			Entire	18.00	12.50
U253	U66	4c	**green,** die 1, *blue* ('86)	13.00	6.50
			Entire	18.00	8.00
U254	U66	4c	**green,** die 1, *manila* ('86)	16.00	7.50
			Entire	21.00	15.00
U255	U66	4c	**green,** die 1, *amber manila* ('86)	24.00	10.00
			Entire	32.50	15.00
U256	U66	4c	**green,** die 2	11.00	5.00
			Entire	19.00	6.75
U257	U66	4c	**green,** die 2, *amber*	15.00	7.00
			Entire	25.00	10.00
U258	U66	4c	**green,** die 2, *manila* ('86)	15.00	7.50
			Entire	25.00	12.50
U259	U66	4c	**green,** die 2, *amber manila* ('86)	15.00	7.50
			Entire	25.00	12.50

1884, May

260	U61	2c **brown**	17.00	5.75
		Entire	21.00	9.00
261	U61	2c **brown**, *amber*	17.00	6.50
		Entire	21.00	7.50
262	U61	2c **brown**, *blue*	21.00	10.00
		Entire	29.00	14.00
263	U61	2c **brown**, *fawn*	17.00	9.25
		Entire	20.00	12.50
264	U61	2c **brown**, *manila*	19.00	11.50
		Entire	26.00	19.00

1884, June

Retouched Die

265	U62	2c **brown**	20.00	6.50
		Entire	27.50	12.00
266	U62	2c **brown**, *amber*	67.50	40.00
		Entire	75.00	50.00
267	U62	2c **brown**, *blue*	25.00	9.00
		Entire	32.50	15.00
268	U62	2c **brown**, *fawn*	18.00	11.00
		Entire	22.50	15.00
269	U62	2c **brown**, *manila*	30.00	15.00
		Entire	35.00	24.00

2 Links Below Right "2"

270	U64	2c **brown**	140.00	50.00
		Entire	175.00	110.00
271	U64	2c **brown**, *amber*	500.00	110.00
		Entire	600.00	350.00
272	U64	2c **brown**, *fawn*	*10,000.*	*3,000.*
		Entire	*12,000.*	*4,000.*

Round "O" in "Two"

273	U65	2c **brown**	300.00	110.00
		Entire	400.00	200.00
274	U65	2c **brown**, *amber*	300.00	110.00
		Entire	400.00	190.00
275	U65	2c **brown**, *blue*		*20,000.*
		Entire		*47,500.*
276	U65	2c **brown**, *fawn*	1,050.	700.00
		Entire	1,550.	*900.00*

Washington — U67

Extremity of bust below the queue forms a point.

U68

Extremity of bust is rounded. Similar to U61. Two wavy lines in oval.

1884-86

U277	U67	2c **brown**	.50	.20
		Entire	1.00	.40
a.		2c **brown lake**, die 1	22.50	21.00
		Entire	27.50	26.00
U278	U67	2c **brown**, *amber*	.65	.50
		Entire	1.75	.75
a.		2c **brown lake**, *amber*	35.00	25.00
		Entire	42.50	32.50
U279	U67	2c **brown**, *oriental buff* ('86)	5.00	2.10
		Entire	7.50	3.00
U280	U67	2c **brown**, *blue*	3.00	2.10
		Entire	4.50	3.50
U281	U67	2c **brown**, *fawn*	3.75	2.40
		Entire	5.75	4.00
U282	U67	2c **brown**, *manila* ('86)	13.00	4.00
		Entire	17.50	6.50
W283	U67	2c **brown**, *manila*	7.50	5.00
		Entire	11.00	6.50
U284	U67	2c **brown**, *amber manila* ('86)	9.00	5.75
		Entire	15.00	7.00
+U285	U67	2c **red**	775.00	
		Entire	1,650.	
+U286	U67	2c **red**, *blue*	325.00	
		Entire	375.00	
W287	U67	2c **red**, *manila*	150.00	
		Entire	210.00	
U288	U68	2c **brown**	375.00	50.00
		Entire	850.00	150.00
U289	U68	2c **brown**, *amber*	18.00	13.00
		Entire	24.00	17.00
U290	U68	2c **brown**, *blue*	1,900.	300.00
		Entire	2,400.	450.00

U291	U68	2c **brown**, *fawn*	35.00	22.50
		Entire	45.00	27.50
W292	U68	2c **brown**, *manila*	25.00	19.00
		Entire	35.00	22.50

Gen. U.S. Grant — US1

1886

Printed by American Bank Note Co.

Issued August 18, 1886. Withdrawn June 30, 1894.

Letter Sheet, 160x271mm

Stamp in upper right corner

Creamy White Paper

U293	US1	2c **green**, entire	27.50	17.00

Perforation varieties:

83 perforations at top	27.50	17.00
42 perforations at top	50.00	20.00
33 perforations at top	50.00	20.00

All with 41 perforations at top

Inscribed: Series 1	27.50	17.00
Inscribed: Series 2	27.50	17.00
Inscribed: Series 3	27.50	17.00
Inscribed: Series 4	27.50	17.00
Inscribed: Series 5	27.50	17.00
Inscribed: Series 6	27.50	17.00
Inscribed: Series 7	27.50	17.00
No inscription, continuous side perforations	27.50	17.00
No inscription, interrupted side perforations	27.50	17.00

Franklin — U69   Washington — U70

Bust points between third and fourth notches of inner oval "G" of "POSTAGE" has no bar.

U71

Bust points between second and third notches of inner oval; "G" of "POSTAGE" has a bar; ear is indicated by one heavy line; one vertical line at corner of mouth.

U72

Frame same as U71; upper part of head more rounded; ear indicated by two curved lines with two locks of hair in front; two vertical lines at corner of mouth.

Jackson — U73   Grant — U74

There is a space between the beard and the collar of the coat. A button is on the collar.

U75

The collar touches the beard and there is no button.

1887-94

Printed by Plimpton Manufacturing Co. and Morgan Envelope Co., Hartford, Conn.; James Purcell, Holyoke, Mass.

U294	U69	1c **blue**	.55	.20
		Entire	1.00	.50
U295	U69	1c **dark blue** ('94)	7.50	2.50
		Entire	10.50	6.50
U296	U69	1c **blue**, *amber*	3.50	1.25
		Entire	6.00	3.50
U297	U69	1c **dark blue**, *amber* ('94)	47.50	22.50
		Entire	57.50	27.50
+U298	U69	1c **blue**, *oriental buff*	15,000.	
		Entire	20,000.	
+U299	U69	1c **blue**, *blue*	20,000.	
		Entire	30,000.	
U300	U69	1c **blue**, *manila*	.65	.35
		Entire	1.25	.75
W301	U69	1c **blue**, *manila*	.45	.30
		Entire	1.25	.60
U302	U69	1c **dark blue**, *manila* ('94)	30.00	12.50
		Entire	37.50	20.00
W303	U69	1c **dark blue**, *manila* ('94)	17.50	10.00
		Entire	25.00	13.00
U304	U69	1c **blue**, *amber manila*	12.50	5.00
		Entire	17.50	7.50
U305	U70	2c **green**	19.00	10.50
		Entire	35.00	15.00
U306	U70	2c **green**, *amber*	45.00	17.50
		Entire	55.00	22.50
U307	U70	2c **green**, *oriental buff*	97.50	35.00
		Entire	125.00	50.00
U308	U70	2c **green**, *blue*	9,000.	1,250.
		Entire		22,000.
U309	U70	2c **green**, *manila*	17,500.	750.00
		Entire	25,000.	1,050.
U310	U70	2c **green**, *amber manila*	—	1,250.
		Entire	—	3,500.
U311	U71	2c **green**	.35	.20
		Entire	.75	.25
a.		2c **dark green** ('94)	.50	.30
		Entire	1.10	.85
U312	U71	2c **green**, *amber*	.45	.20
		Entire	.80	.30
a.		Double impression	—	
b.		2c **dark green**, *amber* ('94)	.60	.35
		Entire	1.10	.85
U313	U71	2c **green**, *oriental buff*	.60	.25
		Entire	1.20	.40
a.		2c **dark green**, *oriental buff* ('94)	2.00	1.00
		Entire	4.00	4.00
U314	U71	2c **green**, *blue*	.65	.30
		Entire	1.25	.40
a.		2c **dark green** *blue* ('94)	.85	.40
		Entire	1.75	1.50
U315	U71	2c **green**, *manila*	1.75	.50
		Entire	2.75	1.00
a.		2c **dark green** *manila* ('94)	2.75	.75
		Entire	4.00	1.50
W316	U71	2c **green**, *manila*	4.00	2.50
		Entire	11.00	7.00
U317	U71	2c **green**, *amber manila*	2.75	1.90
		Entire	6.00	3.00
a.		2c **dark green**, *amber manila* ('94)	4.00	3.00
		Entire	7.50	4.00
U318	U72	2c **green**	150.00	12.50
		Entire	200.00	45.00
U319	U72	2c **green**, *amber*	190.00	25.00
		Entire	275.00	50.00
U320	U72	2c **green**, *oriental buff*	175.00	40.00
		Entire	240.00	70.00
U321	U72	2c **green**, *blue*	190.00	65.00
		Entire	300.00	82.50
U322	U72	2c **green**, *manila*	275.00	65.00
		Entire	325.00	110.00
U323	U72	2c **green**, *amber manila*	600.00	100.00

		Entire		700.00	175.00
U324	U73	4c **carmine**		3.25	2.00
		Entire		6.00	2.10
a.		4c **lake**		3.50	2.00
		Entire		7.00	3.75
b.		4c **scarlet** ('94)		3.50	2.00
		Entire		7.00	3.75
U325	U73	4c **carmine**, *amber*		3.75	3.50
		Entire		7.50	4.00
a.		4c **lake**, *amber*		3.75	3.50
		Entire		7.75	4.00
b.		4c **scarlet**, *amber* ('94)		4.00	3.75
		Entire		8.00	4.25
U326	U73	4c **carmine**, *oriental buff*		8.00	3.50
		Entire		16.00	6.25
a.		4c **lake**, *oriental buff*		8.00	3.50
		Entire		16.00	6.25
U327	U73	4c **carmine**, *blue*		6.50	4.00
		Entire		13.00	7.00
a.		4c **lake**, *blue*		6.50	4.00
		Entire		13.00	6.00
U328	U73	4c **carmine**, *manila*		9.00	7.00
		Entire		13.00	7.50
a.		4c **lake**, *manila*		9.00	6.00
		Entire		13.00	7.50
b.		4c **pink**, *manila*		15.00	10.00
		Entire		21.00	12.50
U329	U73	4c **carmine**, *amber manila*		7.50	3.25
		Entire		13.50	5.00
a.		4c **lake**, *amber manila*		7.50	3.25
		Entire		13.50	5.00
b.		4c **pink**, *amber manila*		16.00	10.00
		Entire		22.50	12.50
U330	U74	5c **blue**		4.00	4.00
		Entire		8.00	11.00
U331	U74	5c **blue**, *amber*		5.50	2.50
		Entire		10.50	14.00
U332	U74	5c **blue**, *oriental buff*		6.00	4.00
		Entire		17.00	18.00
U333	U74	5c **blue**, *blue*		10.50	6.00
		Entire		17.00	15.00
U334	U75	5c **blue** ('94)		27.50	12.50
		Entire		42.50	22.50
U335	U75	5c **blue**, *amber* ('94)		15.00	7.50
		Entire		20.00	40.00
U336	U55	30c **red brown**		60.00	47.50
		Entire		70.00	475.00
a.		30c **yellow brown**		60.00	47.50
		Entire		70.00	475.00
b.		30c **chocolate**		60.00	47.50
		Entire		70.00	475.00
U337	U55	30c **red brown**, *amber*		60.00	47.50
		Entire		70.00	475.00
a.		30c **yellow brown**, *amber*		60.00	47.50
		Entire		70.00	475.00
b.		30c **chocolate**, *amber*		60.00	47.50
		Entire		70.00	475.00
U338	U55	30c **red brown**, *oriental buff*		60.00	47.50
		Entire		70.00	475.00
a.		30c **yellow brown**, *oriental buff*		60.00	47.50
		Entire		70.00	475.00
U339	U55	30c **red brown**, *blue*		60.00	47.50
		Entire		70.00	475.00
a.		30c **yellow brown**, *blue*		60.00	47.50
		Entire		70.00	475.00
U340	U55	30c **red brown**, *manila*		60.00	47.50
		Entire		70.00	475.00
a.		30c **brown**, *manila*		60.00	47.50
		Entire		70.00	475.00
U341	U55	30c **red brown**, *amber manila*		60.00	47.50
		Entire		70.00	475.00
a.		30c **yellow brown**, *amber manila*		60.00	47.50
		Entire		70.00	475.00
U342	U56	90c **purple**		77.50	90.00
		Entire		110.00	1,050.
U343	U56	90c **purple**, *amber*		92.50	90.00
		Entire		140.00	1,050.
U344	U56	90c **purple**, *oriental buff*		92.50	90.00
		Entire		150.00	1,050.
U345	U56	90c **purple**, *blue*		92.50	90.00
		Entire		150.00	1,050.
U346	U56	90c **purple**, *manila*		100.00	92.50
		Entire		150.00	1,050.
U347	U56	90c **purple**, *amber manila*		100.00	92.50
		Entire		150.00	1,050.

Columbus and Liberty — U76

Four dies were used for the 1c, 2c and 5c:
1 — Meridian behind Columbus' head. Period after "CENTS" and "AMERICA" appears on 1c, 2c and 5c.
2 — No meridian. With periods. Appears on 1c, 2c and 5c.
3 — With meridian. No periods. Appears on 1c, 2c and 10c.
4 — No meridian. No periods. Appears on 2c.

1893

U348	U76	1c **deep blue**		2.25	1.25
		Entire		3.00	1.50
		Entire, Expo. station machine cancel			100.00

		Entire, Expo. station duplex handstamp cancel			250.00	
U349	U76	2c **violet**		1.75	.50	
		Entire		3.50	.60	
		Entire, Expo. station machine cancel			40.00	
		Entire, Expo. station duplex handstamp cancel			85.00	
a.		2c **dark slate** (error)		2,500.		
		Entire		3,500.		
U350	U76	5c **chocolate**		8.50	7.50	
		Entire		13.00	10.00	
		Entire, Expo. station machine cancel			150.00	
		Entire, Expo. station duplex handstamp cancel			250.00	
a.		5c **slate brown** (error)		800.00	950.00	
		Entire		1,100.	1,400.	
U351	U76	10c **slate brown**		35.00	30.00	
		Entire		70.00	60.00	
		Entire, Expo. station machine cancel			250.00	
		Entire, Expo. station duplex handstamp cancel			450.00	

Franklin — U77

Washington — U78

Bust points to first notch of inner oval and is only slightly concave below.

U79

Bust points to middle of second notch of inner oval and is quite hollow below. Queue has ribbon around it.

U80

Same as die 2, but hair flowing. No ribbon on queue.

Lincoln — U81

Bust pointed but not draped.

U82

Bust broad and draped.

U83

Head larger, inner oval has no notches.

Grant — U84

Similar to design of 1887-95 but smaller.

1899

U352	U77	1c **green**		1.10	.2
		Entire		2.75	.5
U353	U77	1c **green**, *amber*		5.50	1.5
		Entire		8.75	2.7
U354	U77	1c **green**, *oriental buff*		14.50	2.7
		Entire		19.00	3.7
U355	U77	1c **green**, *blue*		14.50	7.5
		Entire		19.00	12.5
U356	U77	1c **green**, *manila*		2.40	.9
		Entire		6.50	2.0
W357	U77	1c **green**, *manila*		2.50	1.1
		Entire		9.00	4.0
U358	U78	2c **carmine**		3.00	1.7
		Entire		8.00	3.2
U359	U78	2c **carmine**, *amber*		25.00	15.00
		Entire		32.50	21.00
U360	U78	2c **carmine**, *oriental buff*		24.00	12.5
		Entire		35.00	15.00
U361	U78	2c **carmine**, *blue*		65.00	35.00
		Entire		77.50	50.00
U362	U79	2c **carmine**		.35	.2
		Entire		.65	.3
a.		2c **dark lake**		30.00	30.00
		Entire		37.50	35.00
U363	U79	2c **carmine**, *amber*		1.40	.20
		Entire		3.00	.60
U364	U79	2c **carmine**, *oriental buff*		1.20	.20
		Entire		3.00	.60
U365	U79	2c **carmine**, *blue*		1.50	.55
		Entire		3.50	2.00
W366	U79	2c **carmine**, *manila*		8.00	3.25
		Entire		12.00	7.50
U367	U80	2c **carmine**		6.00	2.75
		Entire		11.00	6.75
U368	U80	2c **carmine**, *amber*		9.00	6.75
		Entire		15.00	12.00
U369	U80	2c **carmine**, *oriental buff*		25.00	12.50
		Entire		32.50	20.00
U370	U80	2c **carmine**, *blue*		12.50	10.00
		Entire		25.00	15.00
U371	U81	4c **brown**		20.00	13.00
		Entire		30.00	18.00
U372	U81	4c **brown**, *amber*		20.00	13.00
		Entire		32.50	24.00
U373	U82	4c **brown**		13,500.	1,250.
		Entire		20,000.	
U374	U83	4c **brown**		15.00	8.00
		Entire		27.50	12.50
U375	U83	4c **brown**, *amber*		65.00	25.00
		Entire		80.00	40.00
W376	U83	4c **brown**, *manila*		20.00	10.00
		Entire		35.00	25.00
U377	U84	5c **blue**		13.00	10.00
		Entire		18.00	17.00
U378	U84	5c **blue**, *amber*		17.00	10.50
		Entire		25.00	18.00

Franklin — U85

Washington — U86

"D" of "UNITED" contains vertical line at right that parallels the left vertical line. One short and two long vertical lines at the right of "CENTS."

Grant — U87

Lincoln — U88

1903
Printed by Hartford Manufacturing Co., Hartford, Conn.

U379	U85	1c	**green**	.70	.20
			Entire	1.20	.35
U380	U85	1c	**green**, *amber*	15.00	2.00
			Entire	21.00	2.50
U381	U85	1c	**green**, *oriental buff*	18.00	2.50
			Entire	25.00	3.00
U382	U85	1c	**green**, *blue*	22.50	2.50
			Entire	32.50	3.00
U383	U85	1c	**green**, *manila*	4.00	.90
			Entire	5.00	1.25
W384	U85	1c	**green**, *manila*	2.50	.40
			Entire	4.00	.80
U385	U86	2c	**carmine**	.40	.20
			Entire	.85	.35
a.			2c **pink**	2.00	1.50
			Entire	3.00	2.00
b.			2c **red**	2.00	1.50
			Entire	3.00	2.00
U386	U86	2c	**carmine**, *amber*	2.00	.20
			Entire	3.50	.80
a.			2c **pink**, *amber*	5.00	3.00
			Entire	7.50	4.00
b.			2c **red**, *amber*	14.00	7.00
			Entire	20.00	10.00
U387	U86	2c	**carmine**, *oriental buff*	2.00	.30
			Entire	2.75	.35
a.			2c **pink**, *oriental buff*	3.25	2.00
			Entire	4.50	3.00
b.			2c **red**, *oriental buff*	3.75	2.25
			Entire	5.00	3.25
U388	U86	2c	**carmine**, *blue*	2.00	.50
			Entire	2.75	.60
a.			2c **pink**, *blue*	22.50	14.00
			Entire	30.00	18.00
b.			2c **red**, *blue*	22.50	14.00
			Entire	30.00	18.00
W389	U86	2c	**carmine**, *manila*	20.00	10.00
			Entire	25.00	15.00
U390	U87	4c	**chocolate**	22.50	12.50
			Entire	30.00	15.00
U391	U87	4c	**chocolate**, *amber*	22.50	12.50
			Entire	30.00	15.00
W392	U87	4c	**chocolate**, *manila*	22.50	12.50
			Entire	40.00	30.00
U393	U88	5c	**blue**	22.50	12.50

			Entire	32.50	17.50
U394	U88	5c	**blue**, *amber*	22.50	12.50
			Entire	32.50	20.00

U89

Re-cut die — "D" of "UNITED" is well rounded at right. The three lines at the right of "CENTS" and at the left of "TWO" are usually all short; the lettering is heavier and the ends of the ribbons slightly changed.

1904
Re-cut Die

U395	U89	2c	**carmine**	.60	.20
			Entire	1.00	.45
a.			2c **pink**	5.00	2.50
U396	U89	2c	**carmine**, *amber*	8.00	1.00
			Entire	12.50	2.00
a.			2c **pink**, *amber*	10.00	3.00
U397	U89	2c	**carmine**, *oriental buff*	5.50	1.10
			Entire	7.50	1.50
a.			2c **pink**, *oriental buff*	7.00	2.75
U398	U89	2c	**carmine**, *blue*	4.00	.90
			Entire	5.50	1.40
a.			2c **pink**, *blue*	5.75	2.50
W399	U89	2c	**carmine**, *manila*	15.00	10.00
			Entire	35.00	25.00
a.			2c **pink**, *manila*	22.50	17.50
			Entire	65.00	85.00

Franklin — U90

U90 Die 1

U90 Die 2

U90 Die 3

U90 Die 4

Die 1 — Wide "D" in "UNITED."
Die 2 — Narrow "D" in "UNITED."
Die 3 — Wide "S-S" in "STATES" (1910).
Die 4 — Sharp angle at back of bust, "N" and "E" of "ONE" are parallel (1912).

1907-16
Printed by Mercantile Corp. and Middle West Supply Co., Dayton, Ohio

U400	U90	1c	**green,** die 1	.30	.20
			Entire	.50	.30
a.		Die 2		.80	.25
			Entire	1.10	.45
b.		Die 3		.80	.35
			Entire	1.20	.65
c.		Die 4		.80	.30
			Entire	1.00	.45
U401	U90	1c	**green,** *amber,* die 1	2.00	.40
			Entire	2.50	.60
a.		Die 2		2.50	.70
			Entire	3.25	.80
b.		Die 3		3.00	.75
			Entire	3.75	.80
c.		Die 4		2.00	.65
			Entire	2.75	.75
U402	U90	1c	**green,** *oriental buff,* die 1	10.00	1.00
			Entire	12.50	1.75
a.		Die 2		12.50	1.50
			Entire	17.50	1.75
b.		Die 3		15.00	1.50

			Entire	20.00	2.50
c.		Die 4		10.00	1.50
			Entire	12.50	2.25
U403	U90	1c	**green,** *blue,* die 1	10.00	1.50
			Entire	12.50	2.25
a.		Die 2		12.00	3.00
			Entire	15.00	4.00
b.		Die 3		12.00	3.00
			Entire	15.00	3.25
c.		Die 4		9.00	1.25
			Entire	12.50	3.00
U404	U90	1c	**green,** *manila,* die 1	3.00	1.90
			Entire	4.50	2.75
a.		Die 3		3.75	3.00
			Entire	5.75	4.50
W405	U90	1c	**green,** *manila,* die 1	.80	.25
			Entire	2.00	1.00
a.		Die 2		60.00	25.00
			Entire	70.00	30.00
b.		Die 3		9.00	4.00
			Entire	35.00	25.00
c.		Die 4		80.00	—

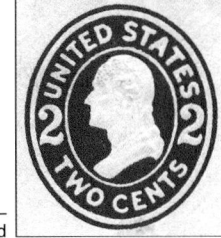

Washington — U91 — brown red

U91 Die 1 — carmine

U91 Die 2

U91 Die 3

U91 Die 4

U91 Die 5

U91 Die 6

U91 Die 7

U91 Die 8

Die 1 — Oval "O" in "TWO" and "C" in "CENTS." Front of bust broad.

Die 2 — Similar to 1 but hair re-cut in two distinct locks at top of head.

Die 3 — Round "O" in "TWO" and "C" in "CENTS," coarse lettering.

Die 4 — Similar to 3 but lettering fine and clear, hair lines clearly embossed. Inner oval thin and clear.

Die 5 — All "S's" wide (1910).

Die 6 — Similar to 1 but front of bust narrow (1913).

Die 7 — Similar to 6 but upper corner of front of bust cut away (1916).

Die 8 — Similar to 7 but lower stroke of "S" in "CENTS" is a straight line. Hair as in Die 2 (1916).

U406	U91	2c **brown red**, die 1	.85	.20
		Entire	2.50	.30
a.	Die 2		42.50	7.00
		Entire	52.50	22.50
b.	Die 3		.65	.20
		Entire	2.50	1.00
U407	U91	2c **brown red**, *amber*, die 1	6.00	2.00
		Entire	8.25	5.00
a.	Die 2		350.00	65.00
		Entire	450.00	100.00
b.	Die 3		4.00	1.25
		Entire	6.50	1.90
U408	U91	2c **brown red**, *oriental buff*, die 1	8.50	1.50
		Entire	11.50	3.75
a.	Die 2		375.00	125.00
		Entire	450.00	150.00
b.	Die 3		7.00	2.50
		Entire	10.00	5.00
U409	U91	2c **brown red**, *blue*, die 1	5.50	2.00
		Entire	7.50	3.75
a.	Die 2		375.00	160.00
		Entire	450.00	450.00
b.	Die 3		5.50	1.75
		Entire	7.50	3.50
W410	U91	2c **brown red**, *manila*, die 1	40.00	32.50
		Entire	50.00	42.50
U411	U91	2c **carmine**, die 1	.25	.20
		Entire	1.00	.35
a.	Die 2		.75	.20
		Entire	2.00	1.50
b.	Die 3		.75	.35
		Entire	1.20	.50
c.	Die 4		.40	.20
		Entire	1.10	.35
d.	Die 5		.55	.30
		Entire	1.50	.50
e.	Die 6		.40	.20
		Entire	1.40	.30
f.	Die 7		40.00	25.00
		Entire	50.00	30.00
g.	Die 8		40.00	25.00
		Entire	50.00	30.00
h.	#U411 with added impression of #U400, entire		375.00	
i.	#U411 with added impression of #U416a, entire		375.00	
U412	U91	2c **carmine**, *amber*, die 1	.25	.20
		Entire	1.00	.20
a.	Die 2		2.00	.25
		Entire	4.00	3.00
b.	Die 3		2.00	.45

c.	Die 4		2.50	.75
		Entire	.40	.25
d.	Die 5		1.00	.40
		Entire	.75	.35
e.	Die 6		1.25	.55
		Entire	.55	.35
f.	Die 7		1.00	.50
		Entire	35.00	25.00
		Entire	40.00	32.50
U413	U91	2c **carmine**, *oriental buff*, die 1	.45	.20
		Entire	.65	.25
a.	Die 2		2.00	.45
		Entire	4.00	3.75
b.	Die 3		8.50	3.00
		Entire	12.50	5.50
c.	Die 4		.40	.20
		Entire	1.00	.40
d.	Die 5		3.25	1.25
		Entire	4.00	3.25
e.	Die 6		.55	.35
		Entire	1.10	.55
f.	Die 7		100.00	45.00
		Entire	125.00	62.50
g.	Die 8		30.00	22.50
		Entire	47.50	27.50
U414	U91	2c **carmine**, *blue*, die 1	.50	.20
		Entire	1.25	.25
a.	Die 2		2.00	.35
		Entire	5.00	5.00
b.	Die 3		2.50	.60
		Entire	3.00	.70
c.	Die 4		.50	.25
		Entire	1.00	.45
d.	Die 5		2.00	.30
		Entire	2.50	.40
e.	Die 6		.55	.30
		Entire	1.00	.40
f.	Die 7		40.00	25.00
		Entire	45.00	35.00
g.	Die 8		40.00	25.00
		Entire	45.00	35.00
W415	U91	2c **carmine**, *manila*, die 1	4.50	2.00
		Entire	7.00	4.75
a.	Die 2		5.00	1.25
		Entire	5.50	4.50
b.	Die 5		5.00	2.50
		Entire	7.50	3.00
c.	Die 7		125.00	97.50
		Entire	160.00	125.00

U90 4c Die 1

U90 4c Die 2

Die 1 — "F" close to (1mm) left "4."
Die 2 — "F" far from (1¾mm) left "4."

U416	U90	4c **black**, die 2	5.00	3.00
		Entire	10.00	5.00
a.	Die 1		5.00	3.00
		Entire	10.00	5.00
U417	U90	4c **black**, *amber*, die 2	7.00	2.50
		Entire	11.50	4.00
a.	Die 1		7.00	2.50
		Entire	11.50	4.00

Die 1 — Tall "F" in "FIVE"

Die 2 — Short "F" in "FIVE"

Die 1 — Tall "F" in "FIVE."
Die 2 — Short "F" in "FIVE."

U418	U91	5c **blue**, die 2	6.50	2.25
		Entire	12.50	6.50
a.	Die 1		6.50	2.25
		Entire	12.50	6.50
b.	5c **blue**, *buff*, die 2 (error)		*3,000.*	
c.	5c **blue**, *blue*, die 2 (error)		*3,000.*	
d.	As "c," die 1 (error), entire		*6,500.*	
U419	U91	5c **blue**, *amber*, die 2	16.00	11.00
		Entire	22.00	13.00
a.	Die 1		15.00	11.00
		Entire	21.00	13.00

On July 1, 1915 the use of laid paper was discontinued and wove paper was substituted. Nos. U400 to W405 and U411 to U419 exist on both papers; U406 to W410 come on laid only. Nos. U429 and U430 exist on laid paper.

Franklin — U92

Die 1

Die 2

Die 3   Die 4   Die 5

(The 1c and 4c dies are the same except for figures of value.)
Die 1 — UNITED nearer inner circle than outer circle.
Die 2 — Large U; large NT closely spaced.
Die 3 — Knob of hair at back of neck. Large NT wide spaced.
Die 4 — UNITED nearer outer circle than inner circle.
Die 5 — Narrow oval C, (also O and G).

Printed by Middle West Supply Co. and International Envelope Corp., Dayton, Ohio.

1915-32

U420	U92	1c **green**, die 1 ('17)	.20	.2
		Entire	.35	.2
a.	Die 2		150.00	55.0
		Entire, size 8	200.00	70.0
b.	Die 3		.30	.2
		Entire	.45	.2
c.	Die 4		.50	.4
		Entire	.70	.5
d.	Die 5		.40	.3
		Entire	.60	.4
U421	U92	1c **green**, *amber*, die 1 ('17)	.50	.3
		Entire	.75	.4
a.	Die 2		475.00	175.0
		Entire, size 8	625.00	200.0
b.	Die 3		1.25	.6
		Entire	1.75	.9
c.	Die 4		1.75	.8
		Entire	2.25	1.2
d.	Die 5		1.00	.5
		Entire	1.40	.8
U422	U92	1c **green**, *oriental buff*, die 1 ('17)	2.25	.9
		Entire	3.00	1.4
a.	Die 4		5.00	1.2
		Entire	7.00	2.7
U423	U92	1c **green**, *blue*, die 1 ('17)	.45	.3
		Entire	.75	.5
a.	Die 3		.75	.4
		Entire	1.00	.7
b.	Die 4		1.25	.6
		Entire	1.95	.9
c.	Die 5		.80	.3
		Entire	1.50	.6
U424	U92	1c **grn**, *manila* (unglazed), die 1 ('16)	6.50	4.0
		Entire	8.50	5.0
W425	U92	1c **grn**, *manila* (unglazed), die 1 ('16)	.20	.2
		Entire	1.00	.2
a.	Die 3		175.00	125.0
		Entire	210.00	140.0
U426	U92	1c **green**, (glazed) *brown*, die 1 ('20)	45.00	15.0
		Entire	55.00	17.5
W427	U92	1c **green**, (glazed) *brown*, die 1 ('20)	65.00	30.0
		Entire	75.00	40.0
U428	U92	1c **green**, (unglazed) *brown*, die 1 ('20)	16.00	7.5
		Entire	22.50	9.0
W428A	U92	1c **green**, (unglazed) *brown*, die 1 ('20), entire	*3,000.*	

All manila envelopes of circular dies are unwatermarked. Manila paper, including that of Nos. U424 and W425, exists in many shades.

Washington — U93

Die 1

Die 2

Die 3

Die 4

Die 5

Die 6

Die 7

Die 8

Die 9

(The 1½c, 2c, 3c, 5c, and 6c dies are the same except for figures of value.)

Die 1 — Letters broad. Numerals vertical. Large head (9¼mm). from tip of nose to back of neck. E closer to inner circle than N of cents.

Die 2 — Similar to 1; but U far from left circle.

Die 3 — Similar to 2; but all inner circles very thin (Rejected die).

Die 4 — Large head as in Die 1. C of CENTS close to circle. Baseline of right numeral "2" slants downward to right. Left numeral "2" is larger.

Die 5 — Small head (8¾mm) from tip of nose to back of neck. T and S of CENTS close at bottom.

Die 6 — Similar to 5; but T and S of CENTS far apart at bottom. Left numeral slopes to right.

Die 7 — Large head. Both numerals slope to right. Clean cut lettering. All letters T have short top strokes.

Die 8 — Similar to 7; but all letters T have long top strokes.

Die 9 — Narrow oval C (also O and G).

U429	U93	2c **carmine,** die 1, *Dec. 20,*		
		1915	.20	.20
		Entire	.35	.20
a.	Die 2		15.00	7.00
		Entire	22.50	10.00
b.	Die 3		45.00	50.00
		Entire	55.00	200.00
c.	Die 4		30.00	15.00
		Entire	37.50	20.00
d.	Die 5		.50	.35
		Entire	.80	.45
e.	Die 6		.60	.30
		Entire	1.10	.60
f.	Die 7		.65	.25
		Entire	.95	.75
g.	Die 8		.45	.20
		Entire	.75	.50
h.	Die 9		.40	.20
		Entire	.75	.45
i.	2c **green** (error), die 1, entire		*14,000.*	
j.	#U429 with added impression of			
	#U420		1,100.	
	Entire		1,500.	
k.	#U429 with added impression of			
	#U416a, entire		1,000.	
l.	#U429 with added impression of			
	#U400, entire		1,000.	
m.	#U429, double impression, entire		1,750.	
U430	U93	2c **carmine,** *amber,* die 1		
		('16)	.25	.20
		Entire	.45	.20
a.	Die 2		20.00	12.50
		Entire	25.00	15.00
b.	Die 4		50.00	25.00
		Entire	62.50	30.00
c.	Die 5		1.50	.35
		Entire	2.00	.60
d.	Die 6		1.10	.40
		Entire	1.90	.75
e.	Die 7		.70	.35
		Entire	1.50	.95
f.	Die 8		.65	.30
		Entire	.95	.45
g.	Die 9		.60	.20
		Entire	.80	.35
U431	U93	2c **carmine,** *oriental buff,*		
		die 1 ('16)	2.25	.65
		Entire	4.50	1.40
a.	Die 2		200.00	75.00
		Entire	250.00	100.00
b.	Die 4		75.00	60.00
		Entire	90.00	75.00
c.	Die 5		3.00	2.00
		Entire	5.00	2.75
d.	Die 6		3.00	2.00
		Entire	5.50	2.75
e.	Die 7		3.00	2.00
		Entire	4.75	3.25
U432	U93	2c **carmine,** *blue,* die 1 ('16)	.25	.20
		Entire	.50	.20
b.	Die 2		40.00	25.00
		Entire	47.50	35.00
c.	Die 3		160.00	90.00
		Entire	200.00	110.00
d.	Die 4		65.00	50.00
		Entire	75.00	55.00
e.	Die 5		1.00	.30
		Entire	1.90	.75
f.	Die 6		1.00	.40

		Entire	1.75	.60
g.	Die 7		.75	.35
		Entire	1.45	.65
h.	Die 8		.60	.25
		Entire	1.25	.50
i.	Die 9		.90	.35
		Entire	2.50	.55
j.	2c purple (error), die 9		—	
U432A	U93	2c **car,** *manila,* die 7, un-		
		watermarked, entire	*35,000.*	
W433	U93	2c **carmine,** *manila,* die 1		
		('16)	.25	.20
		Entire	.45	.30
W434	U93	2c **carmine,** (glazed) *brown*		
		('20), die 1	95.00	50.00
		Entire	120.00	60.00
W435	U93	2c **carmine,** (unglazed)		
		brown, die 1 ('20)	95.00	50.00
		Entire	120.00	60.00
U436	U93	3c **purple,** die 1 ('32)	.30	.20
		Entire	.55	.25
a.	3c **dark violet,** die 1 ('17)		.55	.20
		Entire	.70	.25
b.	3c **dark violet,** die 5 ('17)		1.65	.75
		Entire	3.00	.90
c.	3c **dark violet,** die 6 ('17)		2.00	1.40
		Entire	3.25	1.50
d.	3c **dark violet,** die 7 ('17)		1.40	.95
		Entire	2.50	1.00
e.	3c **purple,** die 7 ('32)		.65	.30
		Entire	1.50	.75
f.	3c **purple,** die 9 ('32)		.40	.20
		Entire	.50	.30
g.	3c **carmine** (error), die 1		40.00	30.00
		Entire	60.00	45.00
h.	3c **carmine** (error), die 5		35.00	30.00
		Entire	55.00	45.00
i.	#U436 with added impression of			
	#U420, entire		900.00	
j.	#U436 with added impression of			
	#U429, entire		900.00	950.00
U437	U93	3c **purple,** *amber,* die 1		
		('32)	.35	.20
		Entire	.60	.35
a.	3c **dark violet,** die 1 ('17)		5.00	1.25
		Entire	9.00	2.25
b.	3c **dark violet,** die 5 ('17)		8.00	2.50
		Entire	12.00	3.00
c.	3c **dark violet,** die 6 ('17)		8.00	2.50
		Entire	12.00	3.00
d.	3c **dark violet,** die 7 ('17)		8.00	2.25
		Entire	12.00	2.50
e.	3c **purple,** die 7 ('32)		.75	.20
		Entire	1.25	.50
f.	3c **purple,** die 9 ('32)		.50	.20
		Entire	1.00	.30
g.	3c **carmine** (error), die 5		500.00	350.00
		Entire	525.00	325.00
h.	3c **black** (error), die 1		200.00	—
		Entire	275.00	
U438	U93	3c **dark violet,** *oriental buff,*		
		die 1 ('17)	25.00	1.65
		Entire	27.50	2.00
a.	Die 5		25.00	1.65
		Entire	27.50	2.00
b.	Die 6		35.00	3.50
		Entire	37.50	4.50
c.	Die 7		35.00	3.50
		Entire	37.50	7.75
U439	U93	3c **purple,** *blue,* die 1 ('32)	.30	.20
		Entire	.75	.25
a.	3c **dark violet,** die 1 ('17)		8.00	2.00
		Entire	14.00	6.00
b.	3c **dark violet,** die 5 ('17)		9.00	6.00
		Entire	14.00	7.50
c.	3c **dark violet,** die 6 ('17)		9.00	6.00
		Entire	14.00	7.50
d.	3c **dark violet,** die 7 ('17)		12.00	6.00
		Entire	17.50	7.50
e.	3c **purple,** die 7 ('32)		.75	.25
		Entire	1.50	.50
f.	3c **purple,** die 9 ('32)		.50	.20
		Entire	1.20	.45
g.	3c **carmine** (error), die 5		375.00	300.00
		Entire	475.00	725.00
U440	U92	4c **black,** die 1 ('18)	1.50	.60
		Entire	3.00	2.00
a.	With added impression of 2c car-			
	mine (#U429), die 1, entire		400.00	
U441	U92	4c **black,** *amber,* die 1 ('18)	3.00	.85
		Entire	4.75	2.00
U442	U92	4c **black,** *blue,* die 1 ('21)	3.25	.85
		Entire	6.00	1.75
U443	U93	5c **blue,** die 1 ('18)	3.25	2.75
		Entire	5.75	3.25
U444	U93	5c **blue,** *amber,* die 1 ('18)	3.75	1.60
		Entire	6.50	3.50
U445	U93	5c **blue,** *blue,* die 1 ('21)	4.00	3.25
		Entire	8.00	4.25

For 1½c and 6c see Nos. U481-W485, U529-U531.

Surcharged Envelopes

The provisional 2c surcharges of 1920-21 were made at central post offices with canceling machines using slugs provided by the Post Office Department.

Double or triple surcharge listings of 1920-25 are for specimens with surcharge directly or partly upon the stamp.

Surcharged on 1874-1920 Envelopes indicated by Numbers in Parentheses

Surcharged

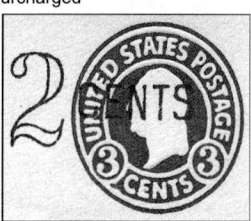

Type 1

1920-21

Surcharged in Black

U446	U93	2c on 3c **dark vio** (U436, die 1)	15.00	10.00
		Entire	22.50	12.50
a.		On No. U436b (die 5)	15.00	10.00
		Entire	22.50	12.50

Surcharged

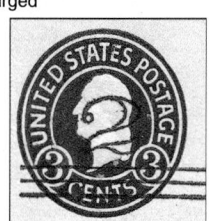

Type 2

Rose Surcharge

U447	U93	2c on 3c **dark vio** (U436, die 1)	9.00	6.50
		Entire	16.00	8.50
b.		On No. U436c (die 6)	12.50	8.50
		Entire	25.00	10.00

Black Surcharge

U447A	U93	2c on 2c **carmine** (U429, die 1)	50,000.	
U447C	U93	2c on 2c **carmine**, *amber* (U430, die 1)	—	
U448	U93	2c on 3c **dark vio** (U436, die 1)	2.50	2.00
		Entire	3.50	2.50
a.		On No. U436b (die 5)	2.50	2.50
		Entire	3.50	2.50
b.		On No. U436c (die 6)	3.25	2.00
		Entire	4.50	2.50
c.		On No. U436d (die 7)	2.50	2.00
		Entire	3.50	2.50
U449	U93	2c on 3c **dark violet**, *amber* (U437, die 1)	7.00	6.00
		Entire	9.00	7.50
a.		On No. U437b (die 5)	12.50	7.50
		Entire	16.00	10.00
b.		On No. U437c (die 6)	9.00	6.00
		Entire	11.50	7.50
c.		On No. U437d (die 7)	8.00	6.50
		Entire	10.50	8.00
U450	U93	2c on 3c **dark violet**, *oriental buff* (U438, die 1)	20.00	15.00
		Entire	22.50	18.00
a.		On No. U438a (die 5)	20.00	15.00
		Entire	22.50	18.00
b.		On No. U438b (die 6)	20.00	15.00
		Entire	22.50	18.00
c.		On No. U438c (die 7)	135.00	90.00
		Entire	175.00	125.00
U451	U93	2c on 3c **dark violet**, *blue* (U439, die 1)	15.00	10.50
		Entire	20.00	11.50
b.		On No. U439b (die 5)	15.00	10.50
		Entire	20.00	11.50
c.		On No. U439c (die 6)	15.00	10.50
		Entire	20.00	11.50
d.		On No. U439d (die 7)	27.50	22.50
		Entire	40.00	27.50

Type 2 exists in three city sub-types.

Surcharged

Type 3

Bars 2mm apart, 25 to 26mm in length

U451A	U90	2c on 1c **green** (U400, die 1)	30,000.	
		Entire	—	
U452	U92	2c on 1c **green** (U420, die 1)	3,750.	

		Entire	4,250.	
a.		On No. U420b (die 3)	3,750.	
		Entire	4,250.	
b.		As No. U452, double surcharge	4,500.	
		Entire	5,000.	
U453	U91	2c on 2c **car** (U411b, die 3)	5,000.	
		Entire	8,000.	
a.		On No. U411 (die 1)	5,000.	
		Entire	8,000.	
U453B	U91	2c on 2c **carmine**, *blue* (U414e, die 6)	3,000.	
		Entire	3,750.	
U453C	U91	2c on 2c **carmine**, *oriental buff* (U413e, die 6)	2,500.	750.00
		Entire	3,250.	
d.		On No. U413 (die 1)	2,500.	
		Entire	3,250.	
U454	U93	2c on 2c **car** (U429e, die 6)	150.00	
		Entire	200.00	
a.		On No. U429 (die 1)	350.00	
		Entire	400.00	
b.		On No. U429d (die 5)	500.00	
		Entire	650.00	
c.		On No. U429f (die 7)	150.00	
		Entire	200.00	
U455	U93	2c on 2c **carmine**, *amber* (U430, die 1)	2,250.	
		Entire	4,250.	
a.		On No. U430d (die 6)	2,250.	
		Entire	4,250.	
b.		On No. U430e (die 7)	2,250.	
		Entire	4,250.	
U456	U93	2c on 2c **carmine**, *oriental buff* (U431a, die 2)	300.00	
		Entire	375.00	
a.		On No. U431c (die 5)	350.00	
		Entire	425.00	
b.		On No. U431e (die 7)	800.00	
		Entire	850.00	
c.		As No. U456, double surcharge	750.00	
U457	U93	2c on 2c **carmine**, *blue* (U432f, die 6)	400.00	
		Entire	450.00	
a.		On No. U432e (die 5)	400.00	
		Entire	500.00	
b.		On No. U432g (die 7)	800.00	
		Entire	850.00	
U458	U93	2c on 3c **dark vio** (U436, die 1)	.50	.35
		Entire	.70	.45
a.		On No. U436b (die 5)	.50	.40
		Entire	.70	.50
b.		On No. U436c (die 6)	.50	.35
		Entire	.70	.45
c.		On No. U436d (die 7)	.50	.35
		Entire	.70	.45
d.		As #U458, double surcharge	25.00	7.50
		Entire	35.00	10.00
e.		As #U458, triple surcharge	110.00	
		Entire	160.00	
f.		As #U458, dbl. surch., 1 in **magenta**	110.00	
		Entire	150.00	
g.		As #U458, dbl. surch., types 2 & 3	140.00	
		Entire	190.00	
h.		As "a," double surcharge	27.50	15.00
		Entire	37.50	20.00
i.		As "a," triple surcharge	110.00	
		Entire	160.00	
j.		As "a," double surch., both **magenta**	110.00	
		Entire	150.00	
k.		As "b," double surcharge	25.00	8.00
		Entire	35.00	11.00
l.		As "c," double surcharge	25.00	8.00
		Entire	35.00	11.00
m.		As "c," triple surcharge	110.00	
		Entire	150.00	
U459	U93	2c on 3c **dark violet**, *amber* (U437c, die 6)	3.00	1.00
		Entire	4.50	1.75
a.		On No. U437 (die 1)	4.00	1.00
		Entire	5.50	1.75
b.		On No. U437b (die 5)	4.00	1.00
		Entire	5.50	1.75
c.		On No. U437d (die 7)	3.00	1.00
		Entire	4.50	1.75
d.		As #U459, double surcharge	35.00	
		Entire	50.00	
e.		As "a," double surcharge	35.00	
		Entire	50.00	
f.		As "b," double surcharge	35.00	
		Entire	50.00	
g.		As "b," double surcharge, types 2 & 3	125.00	
		Entire	175.00	
h.		As "c," double surcharge	35.00	
		Entire	50.00	
U460	U93	2c on 3c **dark violet**, *oriental buff* (U438a, die 5)	4.00	2.00
		Entire	5.00	2.50
a.		On No. U438 (die 1)	4.00	2.00
		Entire	5.00	2.50
b.		On No. U438b (die 6)	4.00	2.00
		Entire	5.00	2.50
c.		As #U460, double surcharge	20.00	
		Entire	30.00	
d.		As "a," double surcharge	20.00	
		Entire	30.00	
e.		As "b," double surcharge	20.00	
		Entire	30.00	
f.		As "b," triple surcharge	150.00	
		Entire	250.00	
U461	U93	2c on 3c **dark violet**, *blue* (U439, die 1)	6.00	1.00
		Entire	8.00	1.50
a.		On No. U439b (die 5)	6.00	1.00

		Entire	8.00	1
b.		On No. U439c (die 6)	6.00	1
		Entire	8.00	1
c.		On No. U439d (die 7)	12.50	2
		Entire	17.50	3
d.		As #U461, double surcharge	20.00	
		Entire	30.00	
e.		As "a," double surcharge	20.00	
		Entire	30.00	
f.		As "b," double surcharge	20.00	
		Entire	30.00	
g.		As "c," double surcharge	20.00	
		Entire	30.00	
U462	U87	2c on 4c **chocolate** (U390)	625.00	260.
		Entire	1,000.	500.
U463	U87	2c on 4c **chocolate**, *amber* (U391)	1,250.	350.
		Entire	1,600.	400.
U463A	U90	2c on 4c **black** (U416, die 2)	1,400.	400.
		Entire	2,000.	
U464	U93	2c on 5c **blue** (U440)	1,400.	
		Entire	2,000.	

Type 3 exists in 11 city sub-types.

Surcharged

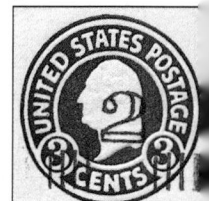

Type 4

Bars 1 mm apart, 21 to 23 mm in length

U465	U92	2c on 1c **green** (U420, die 1)	1,750.	
		Entire	2,900.	
a.		On No. U420b (die 3)	2,000.	
		Entire	3,000.	
U466	U91	2c on 2c **car** (U411e, die 6)	15,000.	
		Entire	27,500.	

The existence of No. U466 as a cut square has been questioned by specialists.

U466A	U93	2c on 2c **carmine** (U429, die 1)	950.00	
		Entire	1,600.	
c.		On No. U429d (die 5)	1,250.	
		Entire	1,750.	
d.		On No. U429e (die 6)	1,250.	
		Entire	1,750.	
e.		On No. U429f (die 7)	1,250.	
		Entire	1,750.	
U466B	U93	2c on 2c **carmine**, *amber* (U430)	15,000.	
U466C	U93	2c on 2c **carmine**, *oriental buff* (U431), entire	—	
U466D	U25	2c on 3c **green**, die 2 (U82)	7,500.	
U467	U45	2c on 3c **green**, die 2 (U163)	425.00	
		Entire	550.00	
U468	U93	2c on 3c **dark vio** (U436, die 1)	.70	.45
		Entire	1.00	.75
a.		On No. U436b (die 5)	.70	.50
		Entire	1.00	.75
b.		On No. U436c (die 6)	.70	.50
		Entire	1.00	.75
c.		On No. U436d (die 7)	.70	.50
		Entire	1.00	.75
d.		As #U468, double surcharge	20.00	
		Entire	30.00	
e.		As #U468, triple surcharge	100.00	
		Entire	150.00	
f.		As #U468, dbl. surch., types 2 & 4	125.00	
		Entire	175.00	
g.		As "a," double surcharge	20.00	
		Entire	30.00	
h.		As "b," double surcharge	20.00	
		Entire	30.00	
i.		As "c," double surcharge	20.00	
		Entire	30.00	
j.		As "c," triple surcharge	100.00	
		Entire	150.00	
k.		As "c," inverted surcharge	75.00	
		Entire	125.00	
l.		2c on 3c **carmine** (error), (U436h)	650.00	
		Entire	800.00	
m.		As #U468, triple surcharge, one inverted, entire		900.00
U469	U93	2c on 3c **dark violet**, *amber* (U437, die 1)	3.50	2.25
		Entire	4.75	2.75
a.		On No. U437b (die 5)	3.50	2.25
		Entire	4.75	2.75
b.		On No. U437c (die 6)	3.50	2.25
		Entire	4.75	2.75
c.		On No. U437d (die 7)	3.50	2.25
		Entire	4.75	2.75
d.		As #U469, double surcharge	30.00	
		Entire	40.00	
e.		As "a," double surcharge	30.00	
		Entire	40.00	
f.		As "a," double surcharge, types 2 & 4	100.00	

	Entire	150.00	
g.	As "b," double surcharge	30.00	
	Entire	40.00	
h.	As "c," double surcharge	30.00	
	Entire	40.00	
0	U93 2c on 3c **dark violet**, *oriental buff* (U438, die 1)	5.50	2.50
	Entire	9.00	4.00
a.	On No. U438a (die 5)	5.50	2.50
	Entire	9.00	4.00
b.	On No. U438b (die 6)	5.50	2.50
	Entire	9.00	4.00
c.	On No. U438c (die 7)	40.00	32.50
	Entire	60.00	45.00
d.	As #U470, double surcharge	25.00	
	Entire	35.00	
e.	As #U470, double surch., types 2 & 4	100.00	
	Entire	150.00	
f.	As "a," double surcharge	25.00	
	Entire	35.00	
g.	As "b," double surcharge	25.00	
	Entire	35.00	
71	U93 2c on 3c **dark violet**, *blue* (U439, die 1)	7.00	1.75
	Entire	12.50	3.50
a.	On No. U439b (die 5)	7.00	1.75
	Entire	12.50	3.50
b.	On No. U439c (die 6)	7.00	1.75
	Entire	12.50	3.50
c.	On No. U439d (die 7)	10.00	6.00
	Entire	20.00	10.00
d.	As #U471, double surcharge	30.00	
	Entire	40.00	
e.	As #U471, double surch., types 2 & 4	175.00	
	Entire	250.00	
f.	As "a," double surcharge	30.00	
	Entire	40.00	
g.	As "b," double surcharge	30.00	
	Entire	40.00	
72	U87 2c on 4c **chocolate** (U390)	14.00	8.00
	Entire	25.00	14.00
a.	Double surcharge	150.00	
73	U87 2c on 4c **chocolate**, *amber* (U391)	16.00	10.00
	Entire	25.00	13.50

Type 4 exists in 30 city sub-types.

Surcharged

Double Surcharge, Type 4 and 1c as above

474	U93 2c on 1c on 3c **dark violet** (U436, die 1)	300.	
	Entire	400.	
a.	On No. U436b (die 5)	400.	
	Entire	575.	
b.	On No. U436d (die 7)	900.	
	Entire	1,150.	
475	U93 2c on 1c on 3c **dark violet**, *amber* (U437, die 1)	300.	
	Entire	475.	

Surcharged

J476	U93 2c on 3c **dark violet**, *amber* (U437, die 1)	300.	
	Entire	475.	
a.	On No. U437c (die 6)	750.	
	Entire	1,000.	
b.	As #U476, double surcharge	—	

Surcharged at Duncan, OK.

Surcharged

U477	U93 2c on 3c **dark vio** (U436, die 1)	140.	
	Entire	190.	
a.	On No. U436b (die 5)	275.	
	Entire	325.	
b.	On No. U436c (die 6)	275.	
	Entire	325.	
c.	On No. U436d (die 7)	275.	
	Entire	325.	
U478	U93 2c on 3c **dark violet**, *amber* (U437, die 1)	350.	
	Entire	450.	

Surcharged at Frederick, OK.

Handstamped Surcharged in Black or Violet

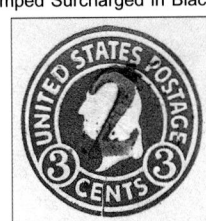

U479	U93 2c on 3c **dark violet** (Bk) (U436, die 1)	450.	
	Entire	550.	
a.	On No. U436b (die 5)	900.	
	Entire	1,100.	
b.	On No. U436d (die 7)	450.	
	Entire	550.	
U480	U93 2c on 3c **dark violet** (V) (U436d, die 7)	6,000.	
	Entire	8,000.	
a.	Double overprint	—	

Expertization by competent authorities is required for Nos. U476-U480.
Surcharged at Daytona, FL (#U479) and Orlando Beach, FL (#U480).

1925

		Type of 1916-32 Issue		
U481	U93	1½c **brown**, die 1, *Mar. 19*	.20	.20
		Entire	.55	.20
		Entire, 1st day cancel	60.00	
a.		Die 8	.60	.25
			.80	.50
b.		1½c purple, die 1 (error) ('34)	90.00	
		Entire	110.00	—
U482	U93	1½c **brown**, die 1, *amber*	.90	.40
			1.50	.60
a.		Die 8	1.75	.75
		Entire	2.25	.80
U483	U93	1½c **brown**, die 1, *blue*	1.50	.95
			2.40	1.25
a.		Die 8	2.25	1.25
		Entire	3.00	1.40
U484	U93	1½c **brown**, die 1, *manila*	6.00	3.00
		Entire	11.00	6.00
W485	U93	1½c **brown**, die 1, *manila*	.80	.20
		Entire	1.25	.45
a.		With added impression of #W433	120.00	—

The manufacture of newspaper wrappers was discontinued in 1934.

New rates on printed matter effective Apr. 15, 1925, resulted in revaluing some of the current envelopes.
Under the caption "Revaluation of Surplus Stocks of the 1 cent envelopes," W. Irving Glover, Third Assistant Postmaster-General, distributed through the Postal Bulletin a notice to postmasters authorizing the surcharging of envelopes under stipulated conditions.
Surcharging was permitted "at certain offices where the excessive quantities of 1 cent stamped envelopes remained in stock on April 15, 1925."
Envelopes were revalued by means of post office canceling machines equipped with special dies designed to imprint "1 ½" in the center of the embossed stamp and four vertical bars over the original numerals "1" in the lower corners.
Postmasters were notified that the revaluing dies would be available for use only in the International and "Universal" Model G machines and that the overprinting of surplus envelopes would be restricted to post offices having such canceling equipment available.

Envelopes of Preceding Issues Surcharged

1925

On Envelopes of 1887

U486	U71	1½c on 2c **green** (U311)	900.	
		Entire	1,300.	
U487	U71	1½c on 2c **green**, *amber* (U312)	1,400.	
		Entire	1,850.	

On Envelopes of 1899

U488	U77	1½c on 1c **green** (U352)	675.	
		Entire	1,000.	
U489	U77	1½c on 1c **green**, *amber* (U353)	125.	60.
		Entire	200.	90.

On Envelopes of 1907-16

U490	U90	1½c on 1c **green** (U400, die 1)	6.50	3.50
		Entire	10.00	5.50
a.		On No. U400a (die 2)	17.50	9.00
		Entire	20.00	12.00
b.		On No. U400b (die 3)	40.00	17.50
		Entire	50.00	22.50
c.		On No. U400c (die 4)	9.50	2.50
		Entire	12.50	4.00
U491	U90	1½c on 1c **green**, *amber* (U401c, die 4)	7.50	2.25
		Entire	11.00	4.50
a.		On No. U401 (die 1)	12.00	2.50
		Entire	16.00	6.00
b.		On No. U401a (die 2)	1200.00	65.00
		Entire	140.00	95.00
c.		On No. U401b (die 3)	50.00	30.00
		Entire	65.00	40.00
U492	U90	1½c on 1c **green**, *oriental buff* (U402a, die 2)	600.00	150.00
		Entire	700.00	175.00
a.		On No. U402c (die 4)	1,200.	250.00
		Entire	1,500.	300.00
U493	U90	1½c on 1c **grn**, *blue* (U403c, die 4)	125.00	70.00
		Entire	160.00	70.00
a.		On No. U403a (die 2)	125.00	70.00
		Entire	160.00	90.00
U494	U90	1½c on 1c **grn**, *manila* (U404, die 1)	400.00	100.00
		Entire	550.00	150.00
a.		On No. U404a (die 3)	1,250.	
		Entire	1,500.	

On Envelopes of 1916-20

U495	U92	1½c on 1c **green** (U420, die 1)	.75	.25
		Entire	1.00	.45
a.		On No. U420a (die 2)	80.00	52.50
		Entire	110.00	90.00
b.		On No. U420b (die 3)	2.00	.70
		Entire	2.50	.85
c.		On No. U420c (die 4)	2.00	.85
		Entire	2.75	1.15
d.		As #U495, double surcharge	10.00	3.00
		Entire	15.00	5.00
e.		As "b," double surcharge	10.00	3.00
		Entire	15.00	5.00
f.		As "c," double surcharge	10.00	3.00
		Entire	15.00	5.00
U496	U92	1½c on 1c **grn**, *amber* (U421, die 1)	20.00	12.50
		Entire	27.50	15.00
a.		On No. U421b (die 3)	600.00	
		Entire	700.00	
b.		On No. U421c (die 4)	20.00	12.50
		Entire	27.50	15.00
U497	U92	1½c on 1c **green**, *oriental buff* (U422, die 1)	4.00	1.90
		Entire	6.50	2.25
a.		On No. U422b (die 4)	65.00	
		Entire	90.00	
U498	U92	1½c on 1c **grn**, *blue* (U423c, die 4)	1.50	.75
		Entire	2.25	1.00
a.		On No. U423 (die 1)	2.50	1.50
		Entire	4.00	2.00
b.		On No. U423b (die 3)	2.00	1.50
		Entire	3.00	2.00
U499	U92	1½c on 1c **green**, *manila* (U424)	12.50	6.00
		Entire	19.00	7.00
U500	U92	1½c on 1c **green**, *brown* (unglazed) (U428)	82.50	30.00
		Entire	95.00	35.00
U501	U92	1½c on 1c **green**, *brown* (glazed) (U426)	82.50	30.00
		Entire	95.00	35.00
U502	U93	1½c on 2c **carmine** (U429, die 1)	300.00	
		Entire	500.00	—
a.		On No. U429d (die 5)	400.00	
		Entire	575.00	
b.		On No. U429f (die 7)	400.00	
		Entire	575.00	
c.		On No. U429e (die 6)	425.00	
		Entire		
d.		On No. U429g (die 8)	550.00	

U503   U93   1½c on 2c **carmine**, oriental buff
(U431c, die 5)   400.00   —
     Entire   525.00   —
   a.   Double surcharge   —
   b.   Double surcharge, one inverted   700.00
U504   U93   1½c on 2c **car**, blue (U432, die 1)   450.00   —
     Entire   525.00   —
   a.   On No. U432g (die 7)   450.00
     Entire   525.00

On Envelopes of 1925

U505   U93   1½c on 1½c **brown** (U481, die 1)   500.00
     Entire   650.00
   a.   On No. U481a (die 8)   500.00
     Entire   650.00
   b.   As No. U505, double surcharge, entire   —
U506   U93   1½c on 1½c **brown**, blue (U483a, die 8)   500.00
     Entire   650.00

The paper of No. U500 is not glazed and appears to be the same as that used for the wrappers of 1920. Type 8 exists in 20 city sub-types.

Surcharged

Black Surcharge
On Envelopes of 1887

U507   U69   1½c on 1c **blue** (U294)   3,250.
     Entire   4,000.
U507A   U69   1½c on 1c **blue**, amber (U296)   —
U507B   U69   1½c on 1c **blue**, manila (U300), entire   4,750.

On Envelope of 1899

U508   U77   1½c on 1c **green**, amber (U353)   70.00
     Entire   100.00

On Envelopes of 1903

U508A   U85   1½c on 1c **green** (U379)   4,750.
     Entire   6,750.
U509   U85   1½c on 1c **green**, amber (U380)   15.00   10.00
     Entire   27.50   15.00
   a.   Double surcharge   75.00
     Entire   100.00
U509B   U85   1½c on 1c **green**, oriental buff (U381)   60.00   40.00
     Entire   70.00   50.00

On Envelopes of 1907-16

U510   U90   1½c on 1c **green** (U400, die 1)   2.75   1.25
     Entire   4.50   1.50
   b.   On No. U400a (die 2)   9.00   4.00
     Entire   12.50   6.00
   c.   On No. U400b (die 3)   35.00   8.00
     Entire   45.00   11.00
   d.   On No. U400c (die 4)   4.00   1.25
     Entire   7.25   2.00
   e.   As No. U510, double surcharge   25.00
     Entire   50.00
U511   U90   1½c on 1c **green**, amber (U401, die 1)   250.00   100.00
     Entire   375.00   150.00
U512   U90   1½c on 1c **green**, oriental buff (U402, die 1)   8.50   4.00
     Entire   15.00   6.50
   a.   On No. U402c (die 4)   20.00   14.00
     Entire   27.50   17.00
U513   U90   1½c on 1c **grn**, blue (U403, die 1)   6.00   4.00
     Entire   9.00   5.00
   a.   On No. U403c (die 4)   6.00   4.00
     Entire   9.00   5.00
U514   U90   1½c on 1c **green**, manila (U404, die 1)   32.50   9.00
     Entire   42.50   22.50
   a.   On No. U404a (die 3)   75.00   37.50
     Entire   85.00   45.00

On Envelopes of 1916-20

U515   U92   1½c on 1c **green** (U420, die 1)   .35   .20
     Entire   .65   .30
   a.   On No. U420a (die 2)   20.00   15.00
     Entire   25.00   20.00
   b.   On No. U420b (die 3)   .35   .20
     Entire   .65   .30
   c.   On No. U420c (die 4)   .35   .20
     Entire   .65   .30
   d.   As #U515, double surcharge   10.00
     Entire   15.00
   e.   As #U515, inverted surcharge   20.00
     Entire   30.00
   f.   As #U515, triple surcharge   20.00
     Entire   30.00
   g.   As #U515, dbl. surch., one invtd., entire   —
   h.   As "b," double surcharge   10.00
     Entire   15.00
   i.   As "b," inverted surcharge   20.00

     Entire   30.00
   j.   As "b," triple surcharge   30.00
     Entire   40.00
   k.   As "c," double surcharge   10.00
     Entire   15.00
   l.   As "c," inverted surcharge   20.00
     Entire   30.00
U516   U92   1½c on 1c **green**, amber (U421c, die 4)   47.50   25.00
     Entire   57.50   35.00
   a.   On No. U421 (die 1)   52.50   30.00
     Entire   62.50   40.00
U517   U92   1½c on 1c **green**, oriental buff (U422, die 1))   6.00   1.25
     Entire   8.00   1.50
   a.   On No. U422a (die 4)   7.00   1.50
     Entire   9.00   2.00
U518   U92   1½c on 1c **green**, blue (U423b, die 4)   5.50   1.25
     Entire   7.50   1.50
   a.   On No. U423 (die 1)   7.50   2.50
     Entire   10.00   3.00
   b.   On No. U423a (die 3)   25.00   7.50
     Entire   32.50   9.00
   c.   As "a," double surcharge   30.00
     Entire   42.50
U519   U92   1½c on 1c **green**, manila (U424, die 1)   30.00   10.00
     Entire   37.50   12.50
   a.   Double surcharge   100.00
U520   U93   1½c on 2c **car** (U429, die 1)   350.00   —
     Entire   500.00   —
   a.   On No. U429d (die 5)   350.00
     Entire   500.00
   b.   On No. U429e (die 6)   350.00
     Entire   500.00
   c.   On No. U429f (die 7)   400.00
     Entire   550.00
U520D   U93   1½c on 2c **car**, amber (U430c, die 5), entire   —

Magenta Surcharge

U521   U92   1½c on 1c **green** (U420b, die 3), Oct. 22, 1925   4.50   3.50
     Entire   6.00   5.50
     Entire, 1st day cancel, Washington, D.C.   100.00
   a.   Double surcharge   75.00
     Entire   125.00

Sesquicentennial Exposition Issue

150th anniversary of the Declaration of Independence.

Liberty Bell — U94

Die 1. The center bar of "E" of "postage" is shorter than top bar.
Die 2. The center bar of "E" of "postage" is of same length as top bar.

1926, July 27

U522   U94   2c **carmine**, die 1   1.10   .50
     Entire   1.60   .95
   a.   Die 2   7.00   3.75
     Entire   11.00   5.50
     Entire, die 2, 1st day cancel, Washington, D.C.   32.50
     Entire, die 2, 1st day cancel, Philadelphia   27.50

Washington Bicentennial Issue

200th anniversary of the birth of George Washington.

Mount Vernon — U95

2c Die 1 — "S" of "Postage" normal.
2c Die 2 — "S" of "Postage" raised.

1932

U523   U95   1c **olive green**, Jan. 1   1.00   .80
     Entire   1.50   1.75
     Entire, 1st day cancel   18.00
U524   U95   1½c **chocolate**, Jan. 1   2.00   1.50
     Entire   2.75   2.50
     Entire, 1st day cancel   18.00
U525   U95   2c **carmine**, die 1, Jan. 1   .40   .20
     Entire   .50   .25
     Entire, 1st day cancel   16.00
   a.   2c carmine, die 2   70.00   20.00
     Entire   85.00   27.50
   b.   2c **carmine**, blue, die 1 (error) entire   27,500.

U526   U95   3c **violet**, June 16   2.00
     Entire   2.50
     Entire, 1st day cancel
U527   U95   4c **black**, Jan. 1   18.00
     Entire   22.50
     Entire, 1st day cancel
U528   U95   5c **dark blue**, Jan. 1   4.00
     Entire   4.75
     Entire, 1st day cancel
     Nos. U523-U528 (6)   27.40

1932, Aug. 18
Type of 1916-32 Issue

U529   U93   6c **orange**, die 7   6.75
     Entire   10.00
     Entire, 1st day cancel, Los Angeles
U530   U93   6c **orange**, amber, die 7   12.50
     Entire   17.50
     Entire, 1st day cancel, Los Angeles
U531   U93   6c **orange**, blue, die 7   12.50
     Entire   17.50
     Entire, 1st day cancel

Franklin — U96

   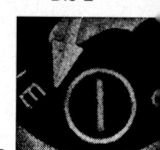

Die 1   Die 2

Die 3

Die 1 — Short (3½mm) and thick "I" in thick circle.
Die 2 — Tall (4½mm) and thin "1" in thin circle; upper and lower bars of E in ONE long and 1mm from circle.
Die 3 — As in Die 2, but E normal and 1½mm from circle.

Printed by International Envelope Corp.
1950

U532   U96   1c **green**, die 1, Nov. 16   5.50   1.7
     Entire   8.75   2.2
     Entire, 1st day cancel, NY, NY   1.0
   a.   Die 2   7.00   3.0
     Entire   10.00   3.7
   b.   Die 3   7.00   3.0
     Entire   9.50   3.7
     Precanceled, die 3   1.2
     Entire, precanceled, die 3   2.50   1.5

Washington — U97

Die 1   Die 2

Die 3   Die 4

Die 1 — Thick "2" in thick circle; toe of "2" is acute angle.
Die 2 — Thin "2" in thin circle; toe of "2" is almost right angle;
..e through left stand of "N" in UNITED and stand of "E" in
.OSTAGE goes considerably below tip of chin; "N" of UNITED
tall; "O" of TWO is high.
Die 3 — Figure "2" as in Die 2. Short UN in UNITED thin
..ossbar in A of STATES.
Die 4 — Tall UN in UNITED; thick crossbar in A of STATES;
..herwise like Die 3.

..533	U97	2c **carmine**, die 3	.75	.25
		Entire	1.25	.35
a.	Die 1, *Nov. 17*		.85	.30
		Entire	1.50	.45
		Entire, 1st day cancel, NY, NY		1.00
b.	Die 2		1.50	.85
		Entire	2.00	.95
c.	Die 4		1.40	.60
		Entire	1.60	.65

Die 1   Die 2

Die 4   Die 5

Die 1 — Thick and tall (4½mm) "3" in thick circle; long top
bars and short stems in T's of STATES.
Die 2 — Thin and tall (4½mm) "3" in medium circle; short top
bars and long stems in T's of STATES.
Die 3 — Thin and short (4mm) "3" in thin circle; lettering wider
than Dies 1 and 2; line from left stand of N to stand of E is
distinctly below tip of chin.
Die 4 — Figure and letters as in Die 3. Line hits tip of chin;
short N in UNITED and thin crossbar in A of STATES.
Die 5 — Figure, letter and chin line as in Die 4; but tall N in
UNITED and thick crossbar in A of STATES.

U534	U97	3c **dark violet**, die 4	.40	.20
		Entire	.50	.25
a.	Die 1, *Nov. 18*		2.00	.70
		Entire	2.50	1.20
		Entire, 1st day cancel, NY, NY		1.00
b.	Die 2, *Nov. 19*		.80	.50
		Entire	1.60	.55
		Entire, 1st day cancel, NY, NY		4.00
c.	Die 3		.60	.25
		Entire	1.10	.45
d.	Die 5		.80	.45
		Entire	1.25	.65

Washington — U98

1952

U535	U98	1½c **brown**	5.50	3.50
		Entire	6.25	4.25
		Precanceled		1.25
		Entire, precanceled	2.50	1.50

Die 1

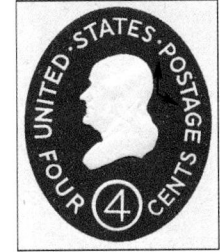

Die 2   Die 3

Die 1 — Head high in oval (2mm below T of STATES). Circle
near (1mm) bottom of colored oval.
Die 2 — Head low in oval (3mm). Circle 1½mm from edge of
oval. Right leg of A in POSTAGE shorter than left. Short leg on
P.
Die 3 — Head centered in oval (2½mm). Circle as in Die 2.
Legs of A of POSTAGE about equal. Long leg on P.

1958

U536	U96	4c **red violet**, die 1, *July 31*	.80	.20
		Entire	.95	.25
		Entire, 1st day cancel, Montpelier, Vt. *(163,746)*		1.00
a.	Die 2		1.05	.20
		Entire	1.30	.25
b.	Die 3		1.05	.20
		Entire	1.30	.25

Nos. U429, U429f, U429h, U533, U533a-U533c
Surcharged in Red at Left of Stamp

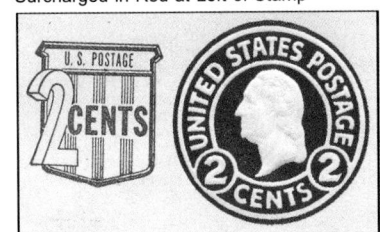

1958

U537	U93	2c + 2c **carmine**, die 1	3.50	1.50
		Entire	5.00	15.00
a.	Die 7		11.00	7.00
		Entire	15.00	15.00
b.	Die 9		5.50	5.00
		Entire	8.00	15.00
U538	U97	2c + 2c **carmine**, die 1	.75	1.25
		Entire	1.50	25.00
a.	Die 2		1.00	1.25
		Entire	2.00	25.00
b.	Die 3		.80	1.25
		Entire	2.00	25.00
c.	Die 4		.80	1.25
		Entire	1.50	25.00

Nos. U436a, U436e-U436f, U534, U534b-U534d
Surcharged in Green at Left of Stamp

a

U539	U93	3c + 1c **purple**, die 1	15.00	11.00
		Entire	17.50	—
a.	Die 7		12.00	9.00
		Entire	15.00	—
b.	Die 9		30.00	15.00
		Entire	35.00	—
U540	U97	3c + 1c **dark violet**, die 3	.50	1.00
		Entire	.60	2.00
a.	Die 2		3,500.	—
		Entire		
b.	Die 4		.75	1.00
		Entire	.90	2.00
c.	Die 5		.75	1.00
		Entire	1.00	2.00

Benjamin   George
Franklin — U99   Washington — U100

Die 1   Die 2

Dies of 1¼c
Die 1 — The "4" is 3mm high. Upper leaf in left cluster is 2mm
from "U."
Die 2 — The "4" is 3½mm high. Leaf clusters are larger.
Upper leaf at left is 1mm from "U."

1960

U541	U99	1¼c **turquoise**, die 1, *June 25, 1960*	.75	.50
		Entire	.90	.55
		Entire, 1st day cancel, Birmingham, Ala. *(211,500)*		1.00
		Precanceled		.20
		Entire, precanceled	.45	.45
a.	Die 2, precanceled		1.50	
		Entire, precanceled	2.00	2.00
U542	U100	2½c **dull blue**, *May 28, 1960*	.85	.50
		Entire	1.00	.60
		Entire, 1st day cancel, Chicago, Ill. *(196,977)*		1.00
		Precanceled		.25
		Entire, precanceled	.55	.55

Pony Express Centennial Issue

Pony Express
Rider — U101

White Outside, Blue Inside.

1960

U543	U101	4c **brown**, *July 19, 1960*	.60	.30
		Entire	.75	.40
		Entire, 1st day cancel, St. Joseph, Mo. *(407,160)*		1.00

Abraham
Lincoln — U102

Die 1

Die 2

Die 3

Die 1 — Center bar of E of POSTAGE is above the middle.
Center bar of E of STATES slants slightly upward. Nose
sharper, more pointed. No offset ink specks inside envelope on
back of die impression.
Die 2 — Center bar of E of POSTAGE in middle. P of POST-
AGE has short stem. Ink specks on back of die impression.
Die 3 — Fl of FIVE closer than Die 1 or 2. Second T of
STATES seems taller than ES. Ink specks on back of die
impression.

1962

U544	U102	5c **dark blue,** die 2, *Nov. 19, 1962*		.85	.20
		Entire		1.10	.30
		Entire, 1st day cancel, Springfield, Ill. *(163,258)*			1.50
a.		Die 1		.85	.25
		Entire		1.10	.30
b.		Die 3		.90	.35
		Entire		1.20	.40
c.		Die 2 with albino impression of 4c (#U536), entire		85.00	—
d.		Die 3 with albino impression of 4c (#U536), entire		85.00	—
e.		Die 3 on complete impression of 4c (#U536), cut square		60.00	

No. U536 Surcharged in Green at left of Stamp

Two types of surcharge:
Type I — "U.S. POSTAGE" 18 ½mm high. Serifs on cross of T
both diagonal. Two lines of shading in C of CENT.
Type II — "U.S. POSTAGE" 17 ½mm high. Right serif on cross
of T is vertical. Three shading lines in C.

1962

U545	U96	4c + 1c **red vio.,** die 1, type I, *Nov. 1962*	1.40	1.25
		Entire	1.60	2.50
a.		Type II	1.40	1.25
		Entire	1.60	2.50

New York World's Fair Issue

Issued to publicize the New York World's Fair, 1964-
65.

Globe with
Satellite
Orbit — U103

1964

U546	U103	5c **maroon,** *Apr. 22, 1964*	.60	.40
		Entire	.75	.50
		Entire, 1st day cancel World's Fair, N.Y. *(466,422)*		1.00

Precanceled cut squares

Precanceled envelopes do not normally receive
another cancellation. Since the lack of a cancellation makes it impossible to distinguish between
cut squares from used and unused envelopes,
they are valued here as used only.

Liberty Bell — U104

Old Ironsides — U105

Eagle — U106

Head of Statue of
Liberty — U107

Printed by the United States Envelope Company, Williamsburg, Pa. Designed (6c) by Howard C. Mildner and (others) by
Robert J. Jones.

1965-69

U547	U104	1 ¼c **brown,** *Jan. 6, 1965*		.20
		Entire	.90	2.00
		Entire, 1st day cancel, Washington, D.C.		1.00
U548	U104	1 ⁴⁄₁₀c **brown,** *Mar. 26, 1968*		.20
		Entire	1.00	2.00
		Entire, 1st day cancel, Springfield, Mass. *(134,832)*		1.00
U548A	U104	1 ⁴⁄₁₀c **orange,** *June 16, 1969*		.20
		Entire	.85	2.00
		Entire, 1st day cancel, Washington, D.C.		1.00
b.		1 ⁴⁄₁₀c **brown (error),** entire		—
U549	U105	4c **bright blue,** *Jan. 6, 1965*	.75	.20
		Entire	.95	.20
		Entire, 1st day cancel, Washington, D.C.		1.00
U550	U106	5c **bright purple,** *Jan. 5, 1965*	.75	.20
		Entire	.85	.25
		Entire, 1st day cancel, Williamsburg, Pa. *(246,496)*		1.00
a.		Bar tagged, *Aug. 15, 1967*	3.00	1.00
		Entire	3.50	5.00
		Entire, tagged, 1st day cancel		3.50
b.		orange-red (air post) instead of yellow-green tagging, entire		—

Tagged

U551	U107	6c **light green,** *Jan. 4, 1968*	.70	.20
		Entire	.80	.25
		Entire, 1st day cancel, New York, N.Y. *(184,784)*		1.25

First day covers of the 1 ¼c and 4c total 451,960.

Nos. U549-U550 Surcharged Types "b" and "a" in
Red or Green at Left of Stamp

1968, Feb. 5

U552	U105	4c + 2c **bright blue** (R)	3.75	2.00
		Entire	4.00	2.50
		Entire, 1st day cancel		6.00
U553	U106	5c + 1c **bright purple** (G)	3.50	2.75
		Entire	4.00	3.25
		Entire, 1st day cancel		6.00
a.		Tagged	3.50	2.75
		Entire	4.00	3.25
		Entire, 1st day cancel		6.00

Tagged

Envelopes from No. U554 onward are tagge[d]
except for bulk-rate and non-profit envelope[s]
which are untagged. The tagging element is in t[he]
ink through No. 608 unless otherwise noted. Fro[m]
No. 611 on, envelopes have bar or block taggi[ng]
unless otherwise noted.

Herman Melville Issue

Issued to honor Herman Melville (1819-189[1]),
writer, and the whaling industry.

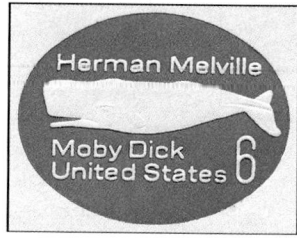

Moby
Dick — U108

1970, Mar. 7

U554	U108	6c **blue**	.50	.2[0]
		Entire	.60	.2[5]
		Entire, 1st day cancel, New Bedford, Mass. *(433,777)*		1.5[0]

Youth Conference Issue

Issued to publicize the White House Conference o[n]
Youth, Estes Park, Colo., Apr. 18-22.

Conference
Emblem
Symbolic of
Man's
Expectant Soul
and of
Universal
Brotherhood
U109

Printed by United States Envelope Company, Williamsburg,
Pa. Designed by Chermayeff and Geismar Associates.

1971, Feb. 24

U555	U109	6c **light blue**	.75	.2[0]
		Entire	.85	.4[0]
		Entire, 1st day cancel, Washington, D.C. *(264,559)*		1.00

Liberty Bell Type of 1965 and U110

Eagle — U110

Printed by the United States Envelope Co., Williamsburg, Pa.
Designed (8c) by Bradbury Thompson.

1971

U556	U104	1 ⁷⁄₁₀c **deep lilac,** untagged, *May 10*		.20
		Entire	.30	.20
		Entire, 1st day cancel, Baltimore, Md. *(150,767)*		1.00
U557	U110	8c **ultramarine,** *May 6*	.40	.20
		Entire	.50	.25
		Entire, 1st day cancel, Williamsburg, Pa. *(193,000)*		1.00

Nos. U551 and U555 Surcharged in Green at Left of
Stamp

71, May 16

61 U107	6c + (2c) **light green**	1.00	1.25
	Entire	1.10	2.50
	Entire, 1st day cancel, Washington, D.C.		2.50
62 U109	6c + (2c) **light blue**	2.00	2.50
	Entire	2.50	3.00
	Entire, 1st day cancel, Washington, D.C.		3.00

Bowling Issue

Issued as a salute to bowling and in connection with 7th World Tournament of the International Bowling deration, Milwaukee, Wis.

Bowling Ball and Pin — U111

Designed by George Giusti.

71, Aug. 21

63 U111	8c **rose red**	.70	.20
	Entire	.80	.20
	Entire, 1st day cancel, Milwaukee, Wis. (281,242)		1.00

Aging Conference Issue

White House Conference on Aging, Washington, .C., Nov. 28-Dec. 2, 1971.

Conference Symbol — U112

Designed by Thomas H. Geismar.

971, Nov. 15

564 U112	8c **light blue**	.50	.20
	Entire	.65	.20
	Entire, 1st day cancel, Washington, D.C. (125,000)		1.00

International Transportation Exhibition Issue

U.S. International Transportation Exhibition, Dulles International Airport, Washington, D.C., May 27-June .

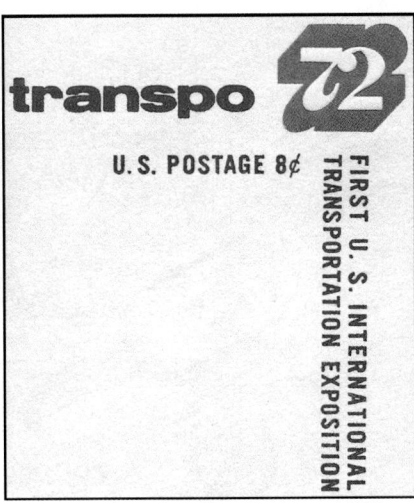

Transportation Exhibition Emblem — U113

Emblem designed by Toshihiki Sakow.

1972, May 2

U565 U113	8c **ultramarine & rose red**	.50	.20
	Entire	.75	.25
	Entire, 1st day cancel, Washington, D.C.		1.00

No. U557 Surcharged Type "b" (like Nos. U537-U538) in Ultramarine at Left of Stamp

1973, Dec. 1

U566 U110	8c + 2c **brt. ultramarine**	.40	1.25
	Entire	.50	2.50
	Entire, 1st day cancel, Washington, D.C.		1.50

Liberty Bell — U114

1973, Dec. 5

U567 U114	10c **emerald**	.40	.20
	Entire	.50	.20
	Entire, 1st day cancel, Philadelphia, Pa. (142,141)		1.00

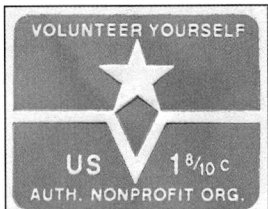

"Volunteer Yourself" — U115

Designed by Norman Ives.

1974, Aug. 23

Untagged

U568 U115	1⁶⁄₁₀c **blue green**		.20
	Entire	.30	2.00
	Entire, 1st day cancel, Cincinnati, Ohio		1.00

Tennis Centenary Issue

Centenary of tennis in the United States.

Tennis Racquet — U116

Designed by Donald Moss.

1974, Aug. 31

Block Tagged

U569 U116	10c **yellow, brt. blue & light green**	.65	.20
	Entire	.75	.25
	Entire, 1st day cancel, Forest Hills, N.Y. (245,000)		1.25

Bicentennial Era Issue

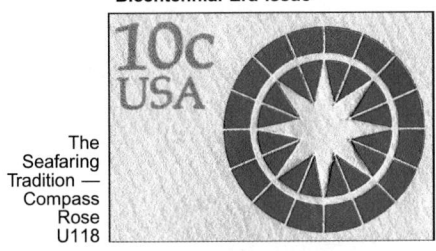

The Seafaring Tradition — Compass Rose U118

The American Homemaker — Quilt Pattern — U119

The American Farmer — Sheaf of Wheat U120

The American Doctor — Mortar U121

The American Craftsman — Tools, c. 1750 U122

Designs (in brown on left side of envelope): 10c, Norwegian sloop Restaurationen. No. U572, Spinning wheel. No. U573, Plow. No. U574, Colonial era medical instruments and bottle. No. U575, Shaker rocking chair.

Designed by Arthur Congdon.

1975-76

Embossed

Diagonally Laid Paper

U571 U118	10c **brown & blue,** light brown, Oct. 13, 1975	.30	.20
	Entire	.45	.20
	Entire, 1st day cancel, Minneapolis, Minn. (255,304)		1.00
a.	Brown ("10c/USA," etc.) omitted, entire	150.00	
U572 U119	13c **brown & blue green,** light brown, Feb. 2, 1976	.35	.20
	Entire	.50	.20
	Entire, 1st day cancel, Biloxi, Miss. (196,647)		1.00
a.	Brown ("13c/USA," etc.) omitted, entire	150.00	
U573 U120	13c **brown & bright green,** light brown, Mar. 15, 1976	.35	.20
	Entire	.50	.20
	Entire, 1st day cancel, New Orleans, La. (214,563)		1.00
a.	Brown ("13c/USA," etc.) omitted, entire	150.00	
U574 U121	13c **brown & orange,** light brown, June 30, 1976	.35	.20
	Entire	.50	.20
	Entire, 1st day cancel, Dallas, Texas		1.50
a.	Brown ("13c/USA," etc.) omitted, entire	150.00	
U575 U122	13c **brown & carmine,** lt. brown, Aug. 6, 1976	.35	.20
	Entire	.50	.20
	Entire, 1st day cancel, Hancock, Mass.		1.00
a.	Brown ("13c/USA," etc.) omitted, entire	150.00	
	Nos. U571-U575 (5)	1.70	1.00

Liberty Tree, Boston, 1646 — U123

Designed by Leonard Everett Fisher.

1975, Nov. 8

Embossed

U576 U123	13c **orange brown**	.30	.20
	Entire	.40	.20
	Entire, 1st day cancel, Memphis, Tenn. (226,824)		1.00

Star and
Pinwheel — U124

U125

U126

Eagle — U127

Uncle
Sam — U128

Designers: 2c, Rudolph de Harak. 2.1c, Norman Ives. 2.7c,
Ann Sforza Clementino. 15c, George Mercer.

1976-78   **Embossed**

U577 U124 2c **red,** untagged, *Sept. 10, 1976*   .20
                Entire   .30 *1.00*
                Entire, 1st day cancel, Hemp-
                stead, N.Y. *(81,388)*   1.00
U578 U125 2.1c **green,** untagged, *June 3, 1977*   .20
                Entire   .30 *1.50*
                Entire, 1st day cancel, Houston,
                Tex. *(120,280)*   1.00
U579 U126 2.7c **green,** untagged, *July 5, 1978*   .20
                Entire   .35 *1.50*
                Entire, 1st day cancel, Raleigh,
                N.C. *(92,687)*   1.00
U580 U127 (15c) **orange,** *May 22, 1978*   .40   .20
                Entire   .55   .20
                Entire, 1st day cancel, Memphis,
                Tenn.   1.00
U581 U128 15c **red,** ink tagged, *June 3, 1978* .40   .20
                Entire   .55   .20
                Entire, 1st day cancel, Williams-
                burg, Pa. *(176,000)*   1.00
  a.   Bar tagged   6.00   —

Bicentennial Issue

Centennial
Envelope,
1876 — U129

1976, Oct. 15   **Embossed**
U582 U129 13c **emerald**   .35   .20
                Entire   .45   .20
                Entire, 1st day cancel, Los Ange-
                les, Cal. *(277,222)*   1.00

Golf Issue

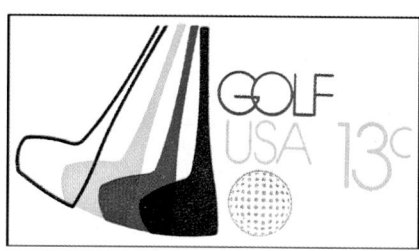

Golf Club in Motion and Golf Ball — U130

Designed by Guy Salvato.

1977, Apr. 7   **Photogravure and Embossed**
U583 U130 13c **black, blue & yellow green** .65   .20
                Entire   .75 *1.00*
                Entire, 1st day cancel, Augusta,
                Ga. *(252,000)*   1.50
  a.   Black omitted, entire   650.00
  b.   Black & blue omitted, entire   550.00
  c.   Black, blue & yellow green omitted, en-
          tire   600.00
          On No. U583c, the embossing is present.

Energy Issue
Conservation and development of national resources.

"Conservation"
U131

"Development"
U132

Designed by Terrance W. McCaffrey.

1977, Oct. 20   **Embossed**
            Bar Tagged
U584 U131 13c **black, red & yellow**   .40   .20
                Entire   .50   .20
                Entire, 1st day cancel, Ridley
                Park, Pa.   1.00
  a.   Red & yellow omitted, entire   250.00
  b.   Yellow omitted, entire   175.00
  c.   Black omitted, entire   175.00
  d.   Black & red omitted, entire   400.00
U585 U132 13c **black, red & yellow**   .40   .20
                Entire   .50   .20
                Entire, 1st day cancel, Ridley
                Park, Pa.   1.00

First day cancellation applied to 353,515 of Nos. U584 and
U585.

Olive Branch and Star — U133

Designed by George Mercer.

1978, July 28   **Emboss**
            Black Surcharge
U586 U133 15c on 16c **blue**   .35
                Entire   .50   *1*
                Entire, 1st day cancel, Wil-
                liamsburg, Pa. *(193,153)*   1
  a.   Surcharge omitted, entire   375.00 *1,0*
  b.   Surcharge on No. U581, entire   100.00
  c.   As "a," with surcharge printed on
          envelope flap   175.00
  d.   Surcharge inverted (in lower left cor-
          ner), entire   450.00

Auto Racing Issue

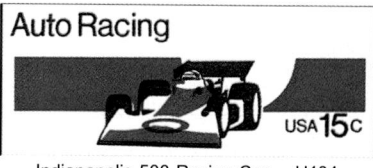

Indianapolis 500 Racing Car — U134

Designed by Robert Peak.

1978, Sept. 2   **Embosse**
U587 U134 15c **red, blue & black**   .35
                Entire   .50 *1.*
                Entire, 1st day cancel, Ontario,
                Cal. *(209,147)*   *1.*
  a.   Black omitted, entire   120.00
  b.   Black & blue omitted, entire   450.00
  c.   Red omitted, entire   120.00
  d.   Red & blue omitted, entire   550.00

No. U576 Surcharged Like No. U586

1978, Nov. 28   **Embosse**
U588 U123 15c on 13c **orange brown**   .35   *.2*
                Entire   .50   *.2*
                Entire, 1st day cancel, Williams-
                burg, Pa. *(137,500)*   *1.0*
  a.   Surcharge inverted (in lower left corner),
          entire   —

U135

Weaver Violins — U136

U137

Eagle — U138

U139

Eagle — U140

1979, May 18   **Untagged**   **Embossed**
U589 U135   3.1c   **ultramarine**   .50
    Entire   .25 *1.50*
    Entire, 1st day cancel, Denver,
      Colo. *(117,575)*   1.00

1980, June 23   **Untagged**   **Embossed**
U590 U136   3.5c   **purple**   .50
    Entire   .30 *1.50*
    Entire, 1st day cancel, Williams-
      burg, Pa.   1.00

1982, Feb. 17   **Untagged**   **Embossed**
U591 U137   5.9c   **brown**   .50
    Entire   .30 *1.50*
    Entire, 1st day cancel, Wheeling,
      WV   1.00

1981, Mar. 15   **Embossed**
U592 U138   (18c)   **violet**   .45 .25
    Entire   .55 .30
    Entire, 1st day cancel, Memphis,
      TN *(179,171)*   1.00

1981, Apr. 2   **Embossed**
U593 U139   18c   **dark blue**   .45 .25
    Entire   .55 .30
    Entire, 1st day cancel, Star City,
      IN *(160,439)*   1.00

1981, Oct. 11   **Embossed**
U594 U140   (20c)   **brown**   .45 .25
    Entire   .55 .30
    Entire, 1st day cancel, Memphis,
      TN *(304,404)*   2.00

Veterinary Medicine Issue

Seal of
Veterinarians
U141

Design at left side of envelope shows 5 animals and bird in brown, "Veterinary Medicine" in gray.
Designed by Guy Salvato.

1979, July 24   **Embossed**
U595 U141   15c   **brown & gray**   .50 .20
    Entire   .60 *1.00*
    Entire, 1st day cancel, Seattle,
      WA *(209,658)*   1.00
  a.   Gray omitted, entire   *1,000.*
  b.   Brown omitted, entire   *1,000.*
  c.   Gray & brown omitted, entire   *450.00*
On No. 595c, the embossing of the seal is present.

Olympic Games Issue
22nd Olympic Games, Moscow, July 19-Aug. 3, 1980.

U142

Design (multicolored on left side of envelope) shows two soccer players with ball.
Designed by Robert M. Cunningham.

1979, Dec. 10   **Embossed**
U596 U142   15c   **red, green & black**   .60 .20
    Entire   .70 *1.00*
    Entire, 1st day cancel, East
      Rutherford, NJ *(179,336)*   1.00
  a.   Red & green omitted, tagging omitted,
      entire   *225.00*
  b.   Black omitted, tagging omitted, entire   *225.00*
  c.   Black & green omitted, entire   *225.00*
  d.   Red omitted, tagging omitted, entire   *400.00*

Highwheeler Bicycle — U143

Design (blue on left side of envelope) shows racing bicycle.
Designed by Robert Hallock.

1980, May 16   **Embossed**
U597 U143   15c   **blue & rose claret**   .40 .20
    Entire   .55 .20
    Entire, 1st day cancel, Balti-
      more, MD *(173,978)*   1.25
  a.   Blue ("15c USA") omitted, entire   *100.00*

Yacht — U144

Designed by Cal Sachs.

1980, Sept. 15   **Embossed**
U598 U144   15c   **blue & red**   .40 .20
    Entire   .55 .20
    Entire, 1st day cancel, Newport,
      RI *(192,220)*   1.00

Italian
Honeybee
and Orange
Blossoms
U145

Bee and petals colorless embossed.
Designed by Jerry Pinkney.

1980, Oct. 10   **Photogravure and Embossed**
U599 U145   15c   **brown, green & yellow**   .35 .20
    Entire   .50 .20
    Entire, 1st day cancel, Paris, IL
      (202,050)   1.00
  a.   Brown ("USA 15c") omitted, entire   *125.00*
  b.   Green omitted, entire
No. U599b also has almost all of the brown color missing.

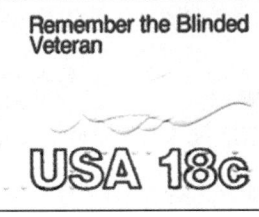

Hand and
Braille — U146

Hand and braille colorless embossed.
Designed by John Boyd.

1981, Aug. 13   **Embossed**
U600 U146   18c   **blue & red**   .45 .20
    Entire   .55 .25
    Entire, 1st day cancel, Arling-
      ton, VA *(175,966)*   1.00
  a.   Blue omitted, entire   *350.00*
  b.   Red omitted, entire   *250.00*

Capitol
Dome — U147

1981, Nov. 13   **Embossed**
U601 U147   20c   **deep magenta, ink** tagged   .45 .20
    Entire   .55 .20
    Entire, 1st day cancel, Los Ange-
      les, CA   1.00
  a.   Bar tagged   3.00 *1.50*

U148

Designed by Bradbury Thompson.

1982, June 15   **Embossed**
U602 U148   20c   **dark blue, black & magenta**   .45 .20
    Entire   .55 .20
    Entire, 1st day cancel, Wash-
      ington, DC *(163,905)*   1.00
  a.   Dark blue omitted, entire   *150.00*
  b.   Dark blue & magenta omitted, entire   —

U149

Designed by John Boyd.

1982, Aug. 6   **Embossed**
U603 U149   20c   **purple & black**   .65 .20
    Entire   .75 .20
    Entire, 1st day cancel, Washing-
      ton, DC *(110,679)*   1.25
  a.   Black omitted, entire   —
  b.   Purple omitted, entire   —

U150

1983, Mar. 21   **Untagged**   **Embossed**
U604 U150 5.2c **orange**   .20
    Entire   .40   *1.00*
    Entire, 1st day cancel, Memphis,
    TN *(141,979)*   1.00

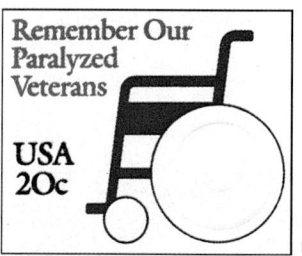

U151

1983, Aug. 3   **Embossed**
U605 U151 20c **red, blue & black**   .45   .20
    Entire   .55   .20
    Entire, 1st day cancel, Port-
    land, OR *(21,500)*   1.00
  a.   Red omitted, entire   *350.00*
  b.   Blue omitted, entire   *350.00*
  c.   Red & black omitted, entire   *150.00*
  d.   Blue & black omitted, entire   *150.00*
  e.   Black omitted, entire   *375.00*

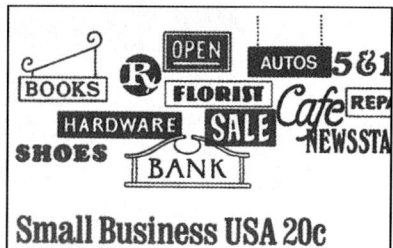

U152

Designed by Peter Spier and Pat Taylor.
Design shows storefronts at lower left. Stamp and design continue on back of envelope.

1984, May 7
U606 U152 20c **multi**   .50   .20
    Entire   .60   .20
    Entire, 1st day cancel, Washing-
    ton, DC *(77,665)*   1.00

U153

Designed by Bradbury Thompson.

1985, Feb. 1   **Embossed**
U607 U153 (22c) **deep green**   .55   .30
    Entire   .65   .40
    Entire, 1st day cancel, Los An-
    geles, CA   1.00

American
Buffalo — U154

Designed by George Mercer.

1985, Feb. 25   **Embossed**
U608 U154 22c **violet brown**, ink tagged   .55   .20
    Entire   .65   .20
    Entire, 1st day cancel, Bison, SD
    (105,271)   1.00
  a.   Untagged, 3 precancel lines, un-
    watermarked, *Nov. 1, 1986*   .20
    Entire   .60   .20
  b.   Bar tagged   2.00   1.00
  c.   As "b," tagging omitted
Original printings of No. U608 were printed with luminescent ink. later printings have a luminescent vertical bar to the left of the stamp.

Frigate U.S.S.
Constitution — U155

Designed by Cal Sacks.

1985, May 3   **Untagged**   **Embossed**
U609 U155 6c **green blue**   .20
    Entire   .25   *1.00*
    Entire, 1st day cancel, Boston,
    MA *(170,425)*   1.25

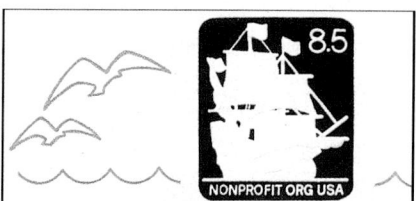

The Mayflower — U156

Designed by Robert Brangwynne.

1986, Dec. 4   **Untagged**   **Embossed**
       Precanceled
U610 U156 8.5c **black & gray**   .20
    Entire   .30   .30
    Entire, 1st day cancel, Plymouth,
    MA *(105,164)*   1.00

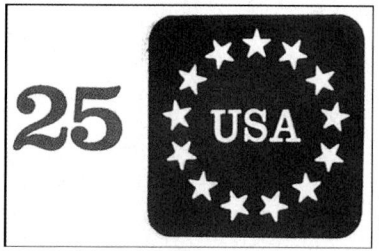

Stars
U157

Designed by Joe Brockert.

1988, Mar. 26   **Typo. & Embossed**
U611 U157 25c **dark red & deep blue**   .60   .20
    Entire   .70   .25
    Entire, 1st day cancel, Star, MS
    (29,393)   1.25
  a.   Dark red (25) omitted, tagging omitted,
    entire   75.00   —
  b.   Tagging omitted, entire   14.00
  c.   Dark red (25) omitted, tagging not omit-
    ted   —

U.S. Frigate Constellation — U158

Designed by Jerry Dadds.

1988, Apr. 12   **Untagged**   **Typo. & Embosse**
       Precanceled
U612 U158 8.4c **black & bright blue**   .30   *1.*
    Entire
    Entire, 1st day cancel, Balti-
    more, MD *(41,420)*   1.
  a.   Black omitted, entire   *600.00*

Snowflake — U159

Designed by Randall McDougall. "Holiday Greetings!" inscribed in lower left.

1988, Sept. 8   **Typo.**
U613 U159 25c **dark red & green**   1.00   *20.0*
    Entire   1.25   *27.5*
    Entire, 1st day cancel, Snow-
    flake, AZ *(32,601)*   1.2

Stars
U160

Designed by Joe Brockert. "Philatelic Mail" and asterisks in dark red below vignette; continuous across envelope face and partly on reverse.

1989, Mar. 10   **Typo.**
U614 U160 25c **dark red & deep blue**   .50   .25
    Entire   .60   .30
    Entire, 1st day cancel, Cleveland,
    OH   1.25
  a.   Tagging omitted, entire   —
    No. U614 was issued only in No. 9 size.

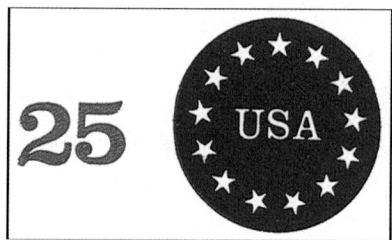

Stars — U161

Designed by Joe Brockert.

1989, July 10   **Typo.**   **Unwmk.**
U615 U161 25c **dark red & deep blue**   .50   .25
    Entire   .60   .30
    Entire, 1st day cancel, Washing-
    ton, DC *(33,461)*   1.25
  a.   Dark red omitted, entire   —
Lined with a blue design to provide security for enclosures. Issued only in No. 9 size.

Love!
U162

Designed by Tim Girvin. Light blue lines printed diagonally over the entire surface of the envelope.

1989, Sept. 22	Litho. & Typo.	Unwmk.	
U616 U162 25c dark red & bright blue		.50	.75
Entire		.60	.85
Entire, 1st day cancel, Mc-Lean, VA (69,498)		1.25	
a. Dark red and bright blue omitted, entire		175.00	
b. Bright blue omitted, entire		—	

No. U616 has light blue lines printed over the entire surface of envelope. Issued only in No. 9 size.

Shuttle Docking at Space Station — U163

Designed by Richard Sheaff.

1989, Dec. 3	Typo.	Unwmk.	
	Die Cut		
U617 U163 25c ultramarine		.90	.60
Entire		1.00	1.00
Entire, 1st day cancel, Washington, DC		1.25	
a. Ultramarine omitted, entire		550.00	

A hologram, visible through the die cut window to the right of "USA 25," is affixed to the inside of the envelope. Available only in No. 9 size.
See Nos. U625, U639.

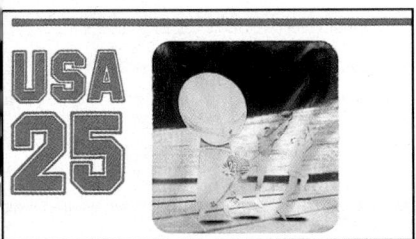

Vince Lombardi Trophy, Football Players — U164

Designed by Bruce Harman.

1990, Sept. 9	Typo.	Unwmk.	Die Cut
U618 U164 25c vermilion		.90	.60
Entire		1.00	.70
Entire, 1st day cancel, Green Bay, WI (54,589)		1.25	

A hologram, visible through the die cut window to the right of "USA 25," is affixed to the inside of the envelope. Issued only in No. 10 size.

Star — U165

Designed by Richard Sheaff.

1991, Jan. 24	Typo. & Embossed	Wmk.	
U619 U165 29c ultramarine & rose		.60	.30
Entire		.70	.35
Entire, unwatermarked, May 1, 1992		.70	.35
Entire, 1st day cancel, Washington, DC (33,025)		1.25	
a. Ultramarine omitted, entire		600.00	
b. Rose omitted, entire		375.00	

Unwatermarked envelopes are on recycled paper, were issued May 1, 1992, and have a "recycled" imprint under the flap.
See No. U623.

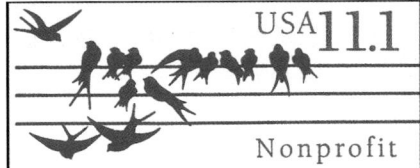

Birds — U166

Designed by Richard Sheaff
Stamp and design continue on back of envelope. Illustration reduced.

1991, May 3	Typo.	Wmk.	
	Untagged, Precanceled		
U620 U166 11.1c blue & red			.50
Entire		.55	1.00
Entire, 1st day cancel, Boxborough, MA (20,720)		1.25	
Entire, unwatermarked, May 1, 1992		.35	.25

Unwatermarked envelopes are on recycled paper, were issued May 1, 1992, and have a "recycled" imprint under the flap.

Love — U167

Designed by Salahattin Kanidinc.

1991, May 9	Litho.	Unwmk.	
U621 U167 29c light blue, maroon & bright rose		.60	.60
Entire		.70	.70
Entire, 1st day cancel, Honolulu, HI (40,110)		1.25	
a. Bright rose omitted, entire		500.00	

Unwatermarked envelopes are on recycled paper, were issued May 1, 1992, and have a "recycled" imprint under the flap.

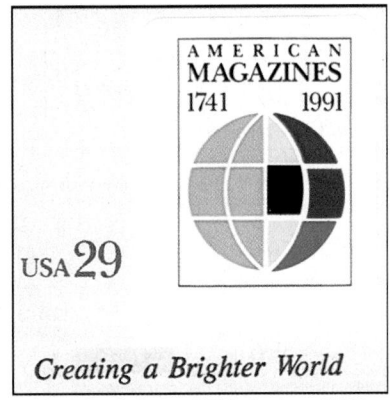

Magazine Industry, 250th Anniv. — U168

Designed by Bradbury Thompson.

1991, Oct. 7	Photo. & Typo.	Unwmk.	
U622 U168 29c multicolored		.60	.50
Entire		.70	1.50
Entire, 1st day cancel, Naples, FL (26,020)		1.25	

The photogravure vignette, visible through the die cut window to the right of "USA 29", is affixed to the inside of the envelope. Issued only in No. 10 size.

Star
U169

Designed by Richard Sheaff.
Stamp and design continue on back of envelope.

1991, July 20	Typo.		
U623 U169 29c ultra & rose		.60	.30
Entire		.70	.35
Entire, 1st day cancel, Washington, DC (16,038)		1.25	
a. Ultra omitted, entire		575.00	
b. Rose omitted, entire		250.00	

Lined with a blue design to provide security for enclosures. Unwatermarked envelopes are on recycled paper, were issued May 1, 1992, and have a "recycled" imprint under the flap. Issued only in No. 9 size.

Country Geese
U170

Designed by Marc Zaref.

1991, Nov. 8	Litho. & Typo.	Wmk.	
U624 U170 29c blue gray & yellow		.60	.60
Entire		.70	.70
Entire, 1st day cancel, Virginia Beach, VA (21,031)		1.25	
Entire, unwatermarked, May 1, 1992		.70	.70

Unwatermarked envelopes are on recycled paper in No. 10 size only, were issued May 1, 1992, and have a "recycled" imprint under the flap.

Space Shuttle Type of 1989

Designed by Richard Sheaff.

1992, Jan. 21	Typo.	Unwmk.	Die Cut
U625 U163 29c yellow green		.90	.50
Entire		1.00	.60
Entire, 1st day cancel, Virginia Beach, VA (37,646)		1.25	

A hologram, visible through the die cut window to the right of "USA 29," is affixed to the inside of the envelope. Examples on recycled paper were issued May 1, 1992 and have a "recycled" imprint under the flap. Issued only in No. 10 size.

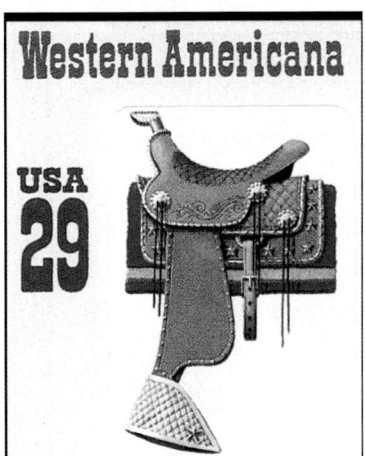

U171

Designed by Harry Zelenko.

1992, Apr. 10   Typo. & Litho.   *Die Cut*
U626 U171 29c **multicolored**   .60   .30
              Entire   .70   *1.25*
              Entire, 1st day cancel, Dodge
                City, KS *(34,258)*   1.25

The lithographed vignette, visible through the die cut window to the right of "USA 29," is affixed to the inside of the envelope. Issued only in the No. 10 size.

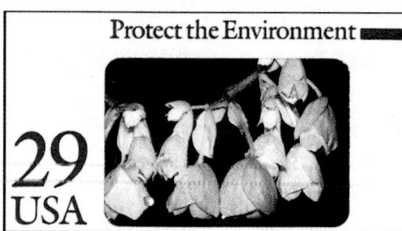

Hillebrandia — U172

Designed by Joseph Brockert. Illustration reduced.

1992, Apr. 22
U627 U172 29c **multicolored**   .60   .30
              Entire   .70   *1.75*
              Entire, 1st day cancel, Chicago,
                IL *(29,432)*   1.25

The lithographed vignette, visible through the die cut window to the right of "29 USA," is affixed to the inside of the envelope. Inscribed "Save the Rain Forests" in the lower left. Issued only in the No. 10 size.

Star — U173

Designed by Joseph Brockert.

1992, May 19   Typo. & Embossed   **Precanceled**
                        Untagged
U628 U173 19.8c **red & blue**   .40
              Entire   .50   *1.00*
              Entire, 1st day cancel, Las
                Vegas, NV *(18,478)*   1.25

              Issued only in No. 10 size.

U174

Designed by Richard Sheaff. Illustration reduced.

1992, July 22   Typo.
U629 U174 29c **red & blue**   .60   .30
              Entire   .70   .35
              Entire, 1st day cancel, Wash-
                ington, DC *(28,218)*   1.25

U175

Designed by Nancy Krause. Illustration reduced.

1993, Oct. 2   Typo. & Litho.   *Die Cut*
U630 U175 29c **multicolored**   .90   .50
              Entire   1.00   *1.50*
              Entire, 1st day cancel, King
                of Prussia, PA *(6,511)*   1.25

The lithographed vignette, visible through the die cut window to the right of "USA 29," is affixed to the inside of the envelope. Issued only in the No. 10 size.

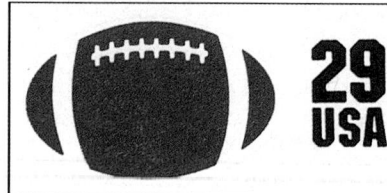

U176

Designed by Richard Sheaff.

1994, Sept. 17   Typo. & Embossed
U631 U176 29c **brown & black**   .60   .50
              Entire   .70   *1.00*
              Entire, 1st day cancel, Can-
                ton, OH *(28,977)*   1.25
     a.   Black ("29/USA") omitted, entire   300.00

              Issued only in No. 10 size.

Liberty Bell — U177

Designed by Richard Sheaff.

1995, Jan. 3   Typo. & Embossed
U632 U177 32c **greenish blue & blue**   .65   .30
              Entire   .75   .40
              Entire, 1st day cancel, Wil-
                liamsburg, PA   1.25
     a.   Greenish blue omitted, entire   450.00
     b.   Blue ("USA 32") omitted, entire   150.00

First day cancellation was applied to 54,102 of Nos. U632, UX198.
              See No. U638.

U178

Design sizes: 49x38mm (#U633), 53x44mm (U634). Stamp and design continue on back of envelope.

1995   **Typo.**
U633 U178 (32c) **blue & red**   .65   .30
              Entire, #6¾   .75   .40
U634 U178 (32c) **blue & red**   .65   .30
              Entire, #10   .75   .40
     a.   Red & tagging omitted, entire   500.00
     b.   Blue omitted, entire   500.00

Originally, Nos. U633-U634 were only available through the Philatelic Fulfillment Center after their announcement 1/12/95. Envelopes submitted for first day cancels received a 12/13/94 cancel, even though they were not available on that date.

U179

Design size: 58x25mm. Stamp and design continue on b[ack] of envelope.
Designed by Douglas Smith.

1995, Mar. 10   Ty[po.]
                   Precanceled, Untagged
U635 U179 (5c) **green & red brown**   .55
              Entire
              Entire, 1st day cancel, State Col-
                lege, PA

Graphic Eagle — U180

Designed by Uldis Purins.

1995, Mar. 10   **Typ[o.]**
                   Precanceled, Untagged
U636 U180 (10c) **dark carmine & blue**
              Entire   .30 1[.]
              Entire, 1st day cancel, State
                College, PA   1[.]

              Issued only in No. 10 size.

Spiral Heart — U181

Designed by Uldis Purins.

1995, May 12   **Typ[o.]**
U637 U181 32c **red,** *light blue*   .65   .[3]
              Entire   .75   .[6]
              Entire, 1st day cancel, Lakeville,
                PA   1.[2]
     a.   Red omitted, entire   — 1.[2]

On No. U637a, the red "RECYCLED" and recycling symb[ol] appear on the bottom backflap.

                   Liberty Bell Type
1995, May 16   **Typ[o.]**
U638 U177 32c **greenish blue & blue**   .65   .[3]
              Entire   .70   .[3]
              Entire, 1st day cancel, Washing-
                ton, DC   1.[2]
     a.   Greenish blue omitted, entire   —

No. U638 was printed on security paper and was issued on[ly] in No. 9 size.

                   Space Shuttle Type of 1989
Designed by Richard Sheaff.

1995, Sept. 22   Typo.   *Die Cu[t]*
U639 U163 32c **carmine rose**   .65   .[3]
              Entire   .70   .[4]
              Entire, 1st day cancel, Milwaukee,
                WI   1.[2]

A hologram, visible through the die cut window to the right [of] "USA 32," is affixed to the inside of the envelope. No. U639 wa[s] issued only in No. 10 size.

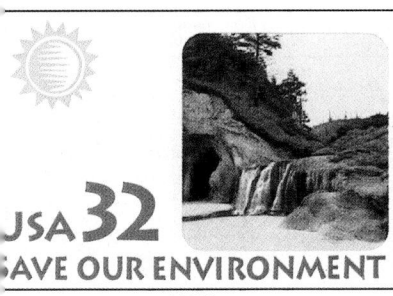

U182

Designed by Richard Sheaff.

6, Apr. 20   **Typo. & Litho.**   *Die Cut*
0 U182 32c **multicolored** .60 .30
    Entire .70 .35
    Entire, 1st day cancel, Chicago,
    IL *(9,921)* 1.25

he lithographed vignette, visible through the die cut window
e right of "USA 32c," is affixed to the inside of the envelope.
ed only in the No. 10 size.

U183

Designed by Brad Copeland. Illustration reduced.

6, May 2
1 U183 32c **multicolored** .60 .30
    Entire .70 .35
    Entire, 1st day cancel, Wash-
    ington, DC 1.25
. Blue & red omitted, entire —
. Blue & gold omitted, entire 500.00
. Red omitted, entire —
. Black & red omitted, entire 450.00
. Blue omitted, entire —

U184

esigner by Richard Sheaff.

9, Jan. 11   **Typo. & Embossed**
2 U184 33c **yellow, blue & red**, tagging
    bar to left of design .65 .30
    Entire .80 .40
    Entire, 1st day cancel, Wash-
    ington, DC 1.25
. Tagging bar to right of design .65 .30
    Entire .80 .40
. As "a," blue omitted, entire —
. As "a," yellow omitted, entire —
. As "a," yellow and blue omitted, entire —
. As "a," blue and red omitted, entire —
. As "a," all colors omitted, entire —

Earliest documented use of No. U642a, 10/12/99.
n No. U642f, the distinctive tagging bar is present. Exper-
ion is required.

9, Jan. 11   **Typo.**
3 U184 33c **blue & red** .65 .30
    Entire .80 .40
    Entire, 1st day cancel, Wash-
    ton, DC 1.25
. Tagging bar to right of design .65 .30
    Entire .80 .40

Issued only in No. 9 size.

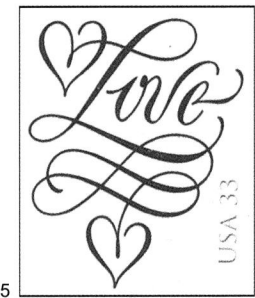

U185

Designed by Julian Waters.

1999, Jan. 28   **Litho.**
U644 U185 33c **violet** .65 .30
    Entire .80 .40
    Entire, 1st day cancel, Love-
    land, CO 1.25
a. Tagging bar to right of design .65 .30
    Entire .80 .40

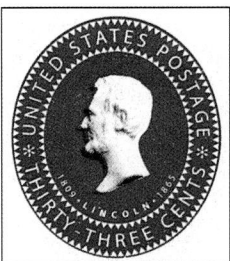

Lincoln — U186

Designed by Richard Sheaff.

1999, June 5   **Typo. & Litho.**
U645 U186 33c **blue & black** .65 .30
    Entire .80 .40
    Entire, 1st day cancel,
    Springfield, IL 1.25

Eagle — U187

Designed by Michael Doret.

2001, Jan. 7   **Typo.**
U646 U187 34c **blue gray & gray** .65 .30
    Entire .85 .40
    Entire, 1st day cancel,
    Washington, DC 1.25
a. Blue gray omitted, entire 350.00

    Many color shades known.
All No. U646 were printed on recycled paper. It was also
produced using a different blue-gray recycled paper starting in
2002.

Lovebirds
U188

Designed by Robert Brangwynne.

2001, Feb. 14   **Litho.**
U647 U188 34c **rose & dull violet** .65 .30
    Entire .85 .40
    Entire, 1st day cancel,
    Lovejoy, GA 1.25

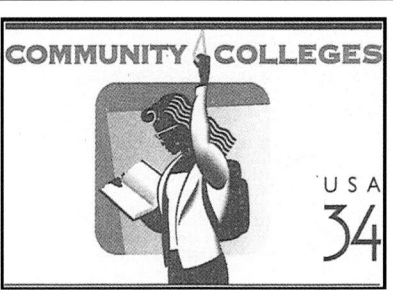

Community Colleges, Cent. — U189

Designed by Howard Paine.

2001, Feb. 20   **Typo.**
U648 U189 34c **dark blue & orange brown** .65 .30
    Entire .85 .40
    Entire, 1st day cancel, Joliet, IL 1.25

Ribbon Star — U190

Designed by Terrence W. McCaffrey.

2002, June 7   **Typo.**
U649 U190 37c **red, blue & gray** .75 .35
    Entire .90 .45
    Entire, 1st day cancel, Washing-
    ton, DC 1.25
    Entire, 1st day cancel, any other
    city 1.25
a. Gray omitted, entire —
b. Blue and gray omitted, entire —

All No. U649 were printed on recycled paper. It was also
produced using a different blue-gray recycled paper starting in
2002.

Type of 1995 Inscribed "USA / Presorted / Standard"
Designed by Uldis Purins.

2002, Aug. 8   **Typo.**
Untagged
Precanceled
U650 U180 (10c) **dark carmine & blue** .20
    Entire .35 1.50
    Entire, 1st day cancel, Washington, DC 1.25

Issued only in No. 10 size.

Nurturing Love — U191

Designed by Craig Frazier.

2003, Jan. 25   **Typo.**
U651 U191 37c **olive green & yellow orange** .75 .35
    Entire .90 .45
    Entire, 1st day cancel, Tucson, AZ 1.25
a. Tagging omitted, entire —

Jefferson Memorial Type
Designed by Derry Noyes.

2003, Dec. 29   **Typo.**
U652 A2818 $3.85 **multicolored** 7.75 6.25
    Entire 7.75 7.00
    Entire, 1st day cancel, Wash-
    ington, DC 5.75

On No. U652, the stamp indicia is printed on the flap of the
envelope.

Disney Type of 2004
Designed by David Pacheco.

2004, June 23   **Litho.**

U653	A2949	37c **multicolored**	2.50	2.10
		Entire	2.50	2.50
		Entire, 1st day cancel, Anaheim, CA		2.50
U654	A2950	37c **multicolored**	2.50	2.10
		Entire	2.50	2.50
		Entire, 1st day cancel, Anaheim, CA		2.50
U655	A2951	37c **multicolored**	2.50	2.10
		Entire	2.50	2.50
		Entire, 1st day cancel, Anaheim, CA		2.50
a.		All color missing on reverse, entire	—	
U656	A2952	37c **multicolored**	2.50	2.10
		Entire	2.50	2.50
		Entire, 1st day cancel, Anaheim, CA		2.50
a.		Booklet of 12 letter sheets, 3 each #U653-U656	30.00	

No. U656a sold for $14.95.

White Lilies and Pink Roses Type of 2004

Designed by Richard Sheaff.

2005, Mar. 3   **Litho.**

U657	A2931	37c **multicolored**	2.50	2.50
		First day cancel, New York, NY		2.50

No. U657 was sold in pads of 12 for $14.95.

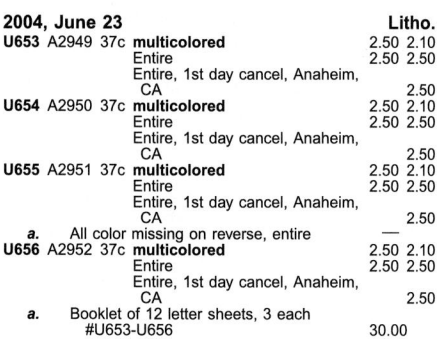

Computer-generated Study of an X-Plane — U192

2006, Jan. 5   **Typo.**   **Unwmk.**

U658	U192	$4.05 **multicolored**	8.25	6.50
		Entire	8.25	7.25
		Entire, 1st day cancel, Kansas City, MO		6.50

Benjamin Franklin — U193

Designed by Richard Sheaff.

2006, Jan. 9   **Typo.**   **Unwmk.**

U659	U193	39c **blue green & black**	.80	.40
		Entire	.95	.50
		Entire, 1st day cancel, Washington, DC		1.25
		Entire, 1st day cancel, any other city		1.25

AIR POST STAMPED ENVELOPES AND AIR LETTER SHEETS

All envelopes have carmine and blue borders, unless noted. There are seven types of borders:

Carmine Diamond in Upper Right Corner.

a — Diamonds measure 9 to 10mm paralled to edge of envelope and 11 to 12mm along oblique side (with top flap open). Sizes 5 and 13 only.

b — Like "a" except diamonds measure 7 to 8mm along oblique side (with top flap open). Sizes 5 and 13 only.

c — Diamonds measure 11 to 12mm parallel to edge of envelope. Size 8 only.

Blue Diamond in Upper Right Corner.

d — Lower points of top row of diamonds point to left. Size 8 only.

e — Lower points of top row of diamonds point to right. Size 8 only.

Diamonds Omitted in Upper Right Corner (1965 Onward)

f — Blue diamond above at left of stamp.

g — Red diamond above at left of stamp.

UC1

5c — Vertical rudder is not semi-circular but slopes down to the left. The tail of the plane projects into the G of POSTAGE. Border types a, b, c, d and e.

UC2

Die 2 (5c and 8c): Vertical rudder is semi-circular. The tail of the plane touches but does not project into the G of POSTAGE. Border types b, d, and e for the 5c; b and d for the 8c.

Die 2 (6c) — Same as UC2 except three types of numeral.

2a — The numeral "6" is 6½mm wide.

2b — The numeral "6" is 6mm wide.

2c — The numeral "6" is 5½mm wide.

Eleven working dies were used in printing the 6c. On each, the numeral "6" was engraved by hand, producing several variations in position, size and thickness.

Nos. UC1 and UC2 occur with varying size blue blobs, caused by a shallow printing die. They are not constant.

Border types b and d for dies 2a and 2b; also without border (June 1944 to Sept. 1945) for dies 2a, 2b and 2c.

Die 3 (6c): Vertical rudder leans forward. S closer to O than to T of POSTAGE. E of POSTAGE has short center bar. Border types b and d, also without border.

No. UC1 with 1933 and 1937 watermarks and No. UC2 with 1933 watermark were issued in Puerto Rico.

No. UC1 in blue black, with 1925 watermark #26 and border type a, is a proof.

1929-44

UC1	UC1	5c **blue,** *Jan. 12, 1929*	3.50	2.00
		Entire, border a or b	4.50	2.25
		Entire, border c, d or e	8.50	5.75
		First day cancel, border a, entire		40.00
		1933 wmk. #33, border d, entire	750.00	750.00
		1933 wmk. #33, border b, entire	—	—
		1937 wmk. #36, border d, entire	—	2,500.
		1937 wmk. #36, border b, entire	—	—
		Bicolored border omitted, entire	1,300.	
a.		Orange and blue border, type b	375.00	
UC2	UC2	5c **blue,** die 2	11.50	5.00
		Entire, border b	13.50	6.50
		Entire, border e	19.50	12.50
		1929 wmk. #28, border d, entire	—	1,500.
		1933 wmk. #33, border b, entire	650.00	—
		1933 wmk. #33, border d, entire	325.00	—
UC3	UC2	6c **orange,** die 2a, *July 1, 1934*	1.50	.40
		Entire, bicolored border	1.75	.60
		Entire, without border	2.50	1.25
		Entire, 1st day cancel		14.00
a.		With added impression of 3c purple (#U436a), entire without border	4,000.	
UC4	UC2	6c **orange,** die 2b ('42)	2.75	2.00
		Entire, bicolored border, 1941 wmk. #39	60.00	20.00
		Entire, without border	4.50	2.00
UC5	UC2	6c **orange,** die 2c ('44)	.75	.30
		Entire, without border	1.00	.45
UC6	UC2	6c **orange,** die 3 ('42)	1.00	.35
		Entire, bicolored border	1.50	.75
		Entire, without border	2.50	.90
		Entire, carmine of border omitted	4,000.	
		Double impression, entire	400.00	
a.		6c orange, *blue,* die 3 (error) Entire, without border	3,500.	2,400.
UC7	UC2	8c **olive green,** die 2, *Sept. 26, 1932*	13.00	3.50
		Entire, bicolored border	16.00	6.50
		Entire, 1st day cancel		11.00

Surcharged in black on envelopes indicated by number in parenthesis

1945

UC8	U93	6c on 2c **carmine** (U429, die 1)	1.25	
		Entire	1.60	
a.		On U429f, die 7	2.25	
		Entire	3.00	2
b.		On U429g, die 8	1.75	
		Entire	2.25	
c.		On U429h, die 9	10.00	7
		Entire	15.00	11
d.		6c on 1c green (error) (U420)	1,750.	
		Entire	2,500.	
e.		6c on 3c purple (error) (U436a)	2,000.	
		Entire	3,250.	
f.		6c on 3c purple (error), *amber* (U437a)	3,000.	
		Entire	3,500.	
g.		6c on 3c violet (error) (U526)	3,000.	
		Entire	3,500.	
UC9	U95	6c on 2c **carmine** (U525)	70.00	35
		Entire	95.00	45

Ten surcharge varieties are found on Nos. UC8-UC9.

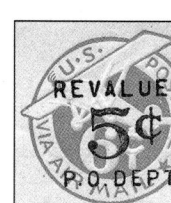

Surcharged in Black on 6c Air Post Envelopes without borders

1946

UC10	UC2	5c on 6c **orange,** die 2a	2.75	1
		Entire	3.50	2
		First day of rate, *Oct. 1, 1946,* entire		100
a.		Double surcharge	75.00	
UC11	UC2	5c on 6c **orange,** die 2b	9.00	5
		Entire	10.00	7
		First day of rate, *Oct. 1, 1946,* entire		150
UC12	UC2	5c on 6c **orange,** die 2c	.75	
		Entire	1.25	
		First day of rate, *Oct. 1, 1946,* entire		75
a.		Double surcharge	75.00	300
UC13	UC2	5c on 6c **orange,** die 3	.80	
		Entire	1.00	
		First day of rate, *Oct. 1, 1946,* entire		75
a.		Double surcharge	75.00	

The 6c borderless envelopes and the revalued envelopes were issued primarily for use to and from members of armed forces. The 5c rate came into effect Oct. 1, 1946. Ten surcharge varieties are found on Nos. UC10-UC13.

DC-4 Skymaster — UC3

Envelopes with borders types b and d.

Die 1 — The end of the wing at the right is a smooth curve. The juncture of the front end of the plane and the engine form an acute angle. The first T of STATES and the E's of UNITED STATES lean to the left.

Die 2 — The end of the wing at the right is a straight line. The juncture of the front end of the plane and the engine is wide open. The first T of STATES and the E's of UNITED STATES lean to the right.

1946

UC14	UC3	5c **carmine,** die 1, *Sept. 25, 1946*	.85	
		Entire, bicolored border	1.10	
		Entire, 1st day cancel		1
		Entire, bicolored border omitted	—	
UC15	UC3	5c **carmine,** die 2	.85	
		Entire, bicolored border	1.10	

No. UC14, printed on flat bed press, measures 21½mm high. No. UC15, printed on rotary press, measures 22mm high. See No. UC18.

DC-4 Skymaster — UC4

1947-55　Typographed, Without Embossing
Letter Sheets for Foreign Postage

C16	UC4	10c	**bright red**, *pale blue*, "Air Letter" on face, 2-line inscription on back, entire	8.50	6.00
			Entire, 1st day cancel, *Apr. 29, 1947*		2.00
			Die cutting reversed, entire	110.00	
C16a	UC4	10c	**bright red**, *pale blue*, Sept. 1951, "Air Letter" on face, 4-line inscription on back, entire	17.50	14.00
			Die cutting reversed, entire	275.00	
b.		10c	chocolate, *pale blue*, entire	450.00	
C16c	UC4	10c	**bright red**, *pale blue*, Nov. 1953, "Air Letter" and "Aerogramme" on face, 4-line inscription on back, entire	45.00	12.50
			Die cutting reversed, entire	150.00	
C16d	UC4	10c	**bright red**, *pale blue*, 1955, "Air Letter" and "Aerogramme" on face, 3-line inscription on back, entire	9.00	8.00
			Die cutting reversed, entire	60.00	
			Dark blue (inscriptions & border diamonds) omitted	—	

Printed on protective tinted paper containing colorless inscription,
UNITED STATES FOREIGN AIR MAIL multiple, repeated in parallel vertical or horizontal lines.

Postage Stamp Centenary Issue

Centenary of the first postage stamps issued by the United States Government.

Washington and Franklin, Early and Modern Mail-carrying Methods — UC5

Two dies: Rotary, design measures 22¼mm high; and flat bed press, design 21¾mm high.

1947, May 21　　Embossed
For Domestic Postage

C17	UC5	5c	carmine (rotary)	.50	.30
			Entire, bicolored border b	.60	.40
			Entire, 1st day cancel, NY, NY		1.25
a.			Flat plate printing	.50	.30
			Entire	.60	.40

Type of 1946

Type I: 6's lean to right.
Type II: 6's upright.

1950

C18	UC3	6c	carmine, type I, Sept. 22, 1950	.40	.25
			Entire, bicolored border	.60	.30
			Entire, 1st day cancel, Philadelphia		1.00
a.			Type II	.75	.25
			Entire	1.00	.30

Several other types differ slightly from the two listed.

Nos. UC14, UC15, UC18 Surcharged in Red at Left of Stamp

1951

UC19	UC3	6c on 5c	**carmine**, die 1	.85	.50
			Entire	1.25	.80
UC20	UC3	6c on 5c	**carmine**, die 2	.85	.50
			Entire	1.25	.80
a.			6c on 6c **carmine** (error) entire	1,500.	
b.			Double surcharge	500.00	—

Nos. UC14 and UC15 Surcharged in Red at Left of Stamp

1952

UC21	UC3	6c on 5c	**carmine**, die 1	27.50	17.50
			Entire	32.50	22.50
UC22	UC3	6c on 5c	**carmine**, die 2, *Aug. 29, 1952*	4.00	2.50
			Entire	5.75	4.25
			Entire, 1st day cancel, Norfolk, Va.		25.00
a.			Double surcharge	200.00	
b.			Triple surcharge, entire	—	

Same Surcharge in Red on No. UC17

UC23	UC5	6c on 5c	**carmine**	1,350.	
			Entire	2,500.	

The 6c on 4c black (No. U440) is believed to be a favor printing.

Fifth International Philatelic Exhibition Issue

FIPEX, the Fifth International Philatelic Exhibition, New York, N.Y., Apr. 28-May 6, 1956.

Eagle in Flight — UC6

1956, May 2

UC25	UC6	6c	red	.75	.50
			Entire	1.00	.80
			Entire, 1st day cancel, New York, N.Y. (363,239)		1.25

Two types exist, differing slightly in the clouds at top.

Skymaster Type of 1946

1958, July 31

UC26	UC3	7c	blue	.65	.50
			Entire	1.00	.55
			Entire, 1st day cancel, Dayton, O. (143,428)		1.00

Nos. UC3-UC5, UC18 and UC25 Surcharged in Green at Left of Stamp

1958

UC27	UC2	6c + 1c	**orange**, die 2a	350.00	250.00
			Entire, without border	375.00	600.00
			Entire, with border	8,000.	
UC28	UC2	6c + 1c	**orange**, die 2b	80.00	80.00
			Entire, without border	120.00	250.00
UC29	UC2	6c + 1c	**orange**, die 2c	50.00	50.00
			Entire	55.00	110.00
UC30	UC3	6c + 1c	**carmine**, type I	1.00	.50
			Entire	1.25	.65
a.			Type II	1.00	.50
			Entire	1.25	.65
UC31	UC6	6c + 1c	**red**	1.00	.50
			Entire	1.40	.85

Jet Airliner — UC7

Letter Sheet for Foreign Postage

Type I: Back inscription in 3 lines.
Type II: Back inscription in 2 lines.

1958-59　Typographed, Without Embossing

UC32	UC7	10c	**blue & red**, *blue*, II, *May, 1959*, entire	6.00	5.00
b.			Red omitted, II, entire	850.00	
c.			Blue omitted, II, entire	850.00	
UC32a	UC7	10c	**blue & red**, *blue*, I, *Sept. 12, 1958*, entire	10.00	5.00
			Entire, 1st day cancel, St. Louis, Mo. (92,400)		1.25
			Die cutting reversed, entire	75.00	
d.			Red omitted, I, entire	1,000.	

Silhouette of Jet Airliner — UC8

1958, Nov. 21　　Embossed

UC33	UC8	7c	blue	.60	.25
			Entire	.70	.30
			Entire, 1st day cancel, New York, N.Y. (208,980)		1.00

1960, Aug. 18

UC34	UC8	7c	carmine	.60	.25
			Entire	.70	.30
			Entire, 1st day cancel, Portland, Ore. (196,851)		1.00

Jet Airliner and Globe — UC9

Letter Sheet for Foreign Postage
Typographed, Without Embossing

1961, June 16

UC35	UC9	11c	**red & blue**, *blue*, entire	2.75	2.25
			Entire, 1st day cancel, Johnstown, Pa. (163,460)		1.00
			Die cutting reversed, entire	35.00	
a.			Red omitted, entire	950.00	
b.			Blue omitted, entire	850.00	

Jet Airliner — UC10

1962, Nov. 17　　Embossed

UC36	UC10	8c	red	.55	.20
			Entire	.75	.30
			Entire, 1st day cancel, Chantilly, Va. (194,810)		1.00

Jet Airliner — UC11

1965-67

UC37	UC11	8c	**red**, *Jan. 7*	.45	.20
			Entire, border "f"	.55	.30
			Entire, border "g"	20.00	
			Entire, 1st day cancel, Chicago, Ill. (226,178)		1.00
a.			Tagged, *Aug. 15, 1967*	3.50	.50
			Entire	5.00	.75
			Tagged, 1st day cancel		3.50

No. UC37a has a 8x24mm panel at left of stamp that glows orange red under ultraviolet light.

Pres. John F. Kennedy and Jet Plane UC12

Letter Sheets for Foreign Postage
Typographed, Without Embossing

1965, May 29
UC38 UC12 11c **red & dark blue**, *blue*, entire 3.25 2.75
    Entire, 1st day cancel, Boston,
    Mass. *(337,122)* 1.50
    Die cutting reversed, entire 40.00

1967, May 29
UC39 UC12 13c **red & dark blue**, *blue*, entire 3.25 2.75
    Entire, 1st day cancel, Chica-
    go, Ill. *(211,387)* 1.50
    Die cutting reversed, entire *100.00*
  a. Red omitted, entire *750.00*
  b. Dark blue omitted, entire *500.00*

Jet Liner — UC13

Designed by Robert J. Jones.

1968, Jan. 8   **Tagged**   **Embossed**
UC40 UC13 10c **red** .50 .20
    Entire .80 .20
    Entire, 1st day cancel, Chicago,
    Ill. *(157,553)* 1.00

No. UC37 Surcharged in Red at Left of Stamp

1968, Feb. 5
UC41 UC11 8c + 2c **red** .65 .20
    Entire .90 .40
    Entire, 1st day cancel, Washing-
    ton, D.C. 8.00

Human Rights Year Issue

Issued for International Human Rights Year, and to commemorate the 20th anniversary of the United Nations' Declaration of Human Rights.

Globes and Flock of Birds — UC14

Printed by Acrovure Division of Union-Camp Corporation, Englewood, N.J. Designed by Antonio Frasconi.

Letter Sheet for Foreign Postage

1968, Dec. 3   **Tagged**   **Photo.**
UC42 UC14 13c **gray, brown, orange & black**,
    blue, entire 8.00 4.00
    Entire, 1st day cancel, Wash-
    ington, D.C. *(145,898)* 1.25
    Die cutting reversed, entire 75.00
  a. Orange omitted, entire *1,000.*
  b. Brown omitted, entire *375.00*
  c. Black omitted, entire —

No. UC42 has a luminescent panel ⅜x1 inch on the right globe. The panel glows orange red under ultraviolet light.

Jet Plane — UC15

Printed by United States Envelope Co., Williamsburg, Pa. Designed by Robert Geissmann.

1971, May 6   **Embossed (Plane)**
Center Circle Luminescent
UC43 UC15 11c **red & blue** .50 .20
    Entire .60 .20
    Entire, 1st day cancel, Williams-
    burg, Pa. *(187,000)* 1.00

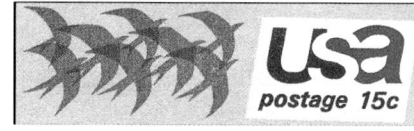

Birds in Flight — UC16

Printed by Bureau of Engraving and Printing. Designed by Soren Noring.

Letter Sheet for Foreign Postage

1971   **Tagged**   **Photo.**
UC44 UC16 15c **gray, red, white & blue**, *blue*,
    entire, *May 28* 1.50 1.10
    Entire, 1st day cancel, Chicago,
    Ill. *(130,669)* 1.25
    Die cutting reversed, entire 30.00
  a. "AEROGRAMME" added to inscription,
    entire, *Dec. 13* 1.50 1.10
    Entire, 1st day cancel, Philadel-
    phia, Pa. 1.25
    Die cutting reversed, entire 30.00

Folding instructions (2 steps) in capitals on No. C44; (4 steps) in upper and lower case on No. UC44a.
On Nos. UC44-UC44a the white rhomboid background of "USA postage 15c" is luminescent. No. UC44 is inscribed: "VIA AIR MAIL-PAR AVION". "postage 15c" is in gray. See No. UC46.

No. UC40 Surcharged in Green at Left of Stamp

1971, June 28   **Embossed**
UC45 UC13 10c + (1c) **red** 1.50 .20
    Entire 1.90 .50
    Entire, 1st day cancel, Washing-
    ton, D.C. 8.00

HOT AIR BALLOONING CHAMPIONSHIPS ISSUE

Hot Air Ballooning World Championships, Albuquerque, N.M., Feb. 10-17, 1973.

"usa" Type of 1971

Design: Three balloons and cloud at left in address section; no birds beside stamp. Inscribed "INTERNATIONAL HOT AIR BALLOONING." "postage 15c" in blue.
Printed by Bureau of Engraving and Printing. Designed by Soren Noring (vignette) and Esther Porter (balloons).

Letter Sheet for Foreign Postage

1973, Feb. 10   **Tagged**   **Photo.**
UC46 UC16 15c **red, white & blue**, *blue*, entire .75 .40
    Entire, 1st day cancel, Albuquer-
    que, N.M. *(210,000)* 1.00

Folding instructions as on No. UC44a. See notes after No. UC44.

Bird in Flight — UC17

1973, Dec. 1   **Luminescent**
UC47 UC17 13c **rose red** .30
    Entire .40
    Entire, 1st day cancel, Memphis,
    Tenn. *(132,658)*

UC18

Printed by the Bureau of Engraving and Printing. Designed by Bill Hyde.

Letter Sheet for Foreign Postage.

1974, Jan. 4   **Tagged**   **Phot**
UC48 UC18 18c **red & blue**, *blue*, entire .90
    Entire, 1st day cancel, Atlanta,
    Ga. *(119,615)* 1
  a. Red omitted, entire —

25TH ANNIVERSARY OF NATO ISSUE

UC19

Design: "NATO" and NATO emblem at left in address section.
Printed by Bureau of Engraving and Printing. Designed by Soren Noring.

Letter Sheet for Foreign Postage

1974, Apr. 4   **Tagged**   **Phot**
UC49 UC19 18c **red & blue**, *blue*, entire .90
    Entire, 1st day cancel, Washing-
    ton, D.C. 1.0

UC20

Printed by Bureau of Engraving and Printing. Designed by Robert Geissmann.

Letter Sheet for Foreign Postage

1976, Jan. 16   **Tagged**   **Photo**
UC50 UC20 22c **red & blue**, *blue*, entire .90
    Entire, 1st day cancel, Tempe,
    Ariz. *(118,303)* 1.0
    Die cutting reversed, entire 15.00

"USA" — UC21

Printed by Bureau of Engraving and Printing. Designed by Soren Noring.

Letter Sheet for Foreign Postage

1978, Nov. 3   **Tagged**   **Photo**
UC51 UC21 22c **blue**, *blue*, entire .70 .2
    Entire, 1st day cancel, St. Pe-
    tersburg, Fla. *(86,099)* 1.00
    Die cutting reversed, entire 25.00

...d OLYMPIC GAMES, MOSCOW, JULY 19-AUG. 3, 1980.

UC22

...Design (multicolored in bottom left corner) shows discus ...wer.
...rinted by Bureau of Engraving and Printing. Designed by ...pert M. Cunningham.

Letter Sheet for Foreign Postage

		Tagged	Photo.
...79, Dec. 5			
...52 UC22	22c **red, black & green**, *bluish*, entire	1.50	.25
	Entire, 1st day cancel, Bay Shore, N.Y.	1.00	

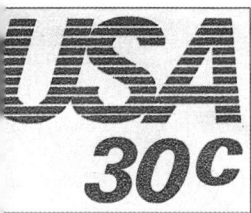

"USA" — UC23

...Design (brown on No. UC53, green and brown on No. UC54): ...ver left, Statue of Liberty. Inscribed "Tour the United States." ...ding area shows tourist attractions.
...Printed by Bureau of Engraving and Printing.
...Designed by Frank J. Waslick.

Letter Sheet for Foreign Postage

		Tagged	Photo.
...80, Dec. 29			
...53 UC23	30c **blue, red & brown**, *blue*, entire	.65	*1.00*
	Entire, 1st day cancel, San Francisco, CA	1.25	
	Die cutting reversed, entire	20.00	
a.	Red (30) omitted, entire	70.00	
	Die cutting reversed, entire		*20.00*

		Tagged	Photo.
...81, Sept. 21			
...54 UC23	30c **yellow, magenta, blue & black**, *blue*, entire	.65	*1.00*
	Entire, 1st day cancel, Honolulu, HI	1.25	
	Die cutting reversed, entire	20.00	

UC24

Design: "Made in USA . . . world's best buys!" on flap, ship, ...actor in lower left. Reverse folding area shows chemicals, jet ...lhouette, wheat, typewriter and computer tape disks. Printed ...y Bureau of Engraving and Printing.
Designed by Frank J. Waslick.

Letter Sheet for Foreign Postage

		Tagged	Photo.
...982, Sept. 16			
...C55 UC24	30c **multi**, *blue*, entire	.65	*1.00*
	Entire, 1st day cancel, Seattle, WA	1.25	
	Die cutting reversed, entire	—	

WORLD COMMUNICATIONS YEAR

World Map Showing Locations of Satellite Tracking Stations — UC25

Design: Reverse folding area shows satellite, tracking station.
Printed by Bureau of Engraving and Printing.
Designed by Esther Porter.

Letter Sheet for Foreign Postage

		Tagged	Photo.
1983, Jan. 7			
UC56 UC25	30c **multi**, *blue*, entire	.65	*1.00*
	Entire, 1st day cancel, Anaheim, CA	1.25	
	Die cutting reversed, entire	25.00	

1984 OLYMPICS

UC26

Indicia in black, multicolor design of woman equestrian at lower left with montage of competitive events on reverse folding area.
Printed by the Bureau of Engraving & Printing.
Designed by Bob Peak.

Letter Sheet for Foreign Postage

		Tagged	Photo.
1983, Oct. 14			
UC57 UC26	30c **black & multi**, *light blue*, entire	.65	*1.50*
	Entire, 1st day cancel, Los Angeles, CA	1.25	
	Die cutting reversed, entire	—	

WEATHER SATELLITES, 25TH ANNIV.

Landsat Infrared and Thermal Mapping Bands UC27

Design: Landsat orbiting the earth at lower left with three Landsat photographs on reverse folding area. Inscribed: "Landsat views the Earth."
Printed by the Bureau of Engraving & Printing.
Designed by Esther Porter.

Letter Sheet for Foreign Postage

		Tagged	Photo.
1985, Feb. 14			
UC58 UC27	36c **multi**, *blue*, entire	.70	*1.00*
	Entire, 1st day cancel, Goddard Flight Center, MD	1.40	
	Die cutting reversed, entire	30.00	

NATIONAL TOURISM WEEK

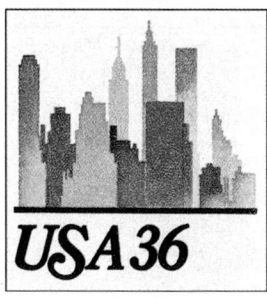

Urban Skyline — UC28

Design: Inscribed "Celebrate America" at lower left and "Travel. . . the perfect freedom" on folding area. Skier, Indian chief, cowboy, jazz trumpeter and pilgrims on reverse folding area.
Printed by the Bureau of Engraving & Printing.
Designed by Dennis Luzak.

Letter Sheet for Foreign Postage

		Tagged	Photo.
1985, May 21			
UC59 UC28	36c **multi**, *blue*, entire	.70	*1.00*
	Entire, 1st day cancel, Washington, DC	1.40	
	Die cutting reversed, entire	25.00	
a.	Black omitted, entire	950.00	—

MARK TWAIN AND HALLEY'S COMET

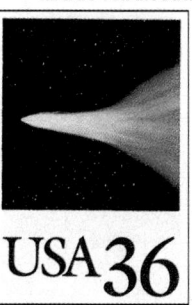

Comet Tail Viewed from Space — UC29

Design: Portrait of Twain at lower left and inscribed "I came in with Halley's Comet in 1835. It is coming again next year, and I expect to go out with it. It will be the greatest disappointment of my life if I don't go out with Halley's Comet." "1835 . Mark Twain . 1910 . Halley's Comet . 1985" and Twain, Huckleberry Finn, steamboat and comet on reverse folding areas.
Printed by the Bureau of Engraving & Printing.
Designed by Dennis Luzak.

Letter Sheet for Foreign Postage

		Tagged	Photo.
1985, Dec. 4			
UC60 UC29	36c **multi**, entire	1.00	*1.50*
	Entire, 1st day cancel, Hannibal, MO	2.00	
	Die cutting reversed, entire	25.00	

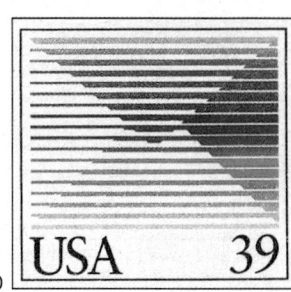

UC30

Printed by the Bureau of Engraving & Printing.

Letter Sheet for Foreign Postage

		Litho.	Tagged
1988, May 9			
UC61 UC30	39c **multi**, entire	.80	*1.00*
	Entire, 1st day cancel, Miami, FL (27,446)	1.60	
a.	Tagging bar to left of design ('89)	.80	*1.00*

On No. UC61, the tagging bar is between "USA" and "39."

MONTGOMERY BLAIR, POSTMASTER GENERAL
1861-64

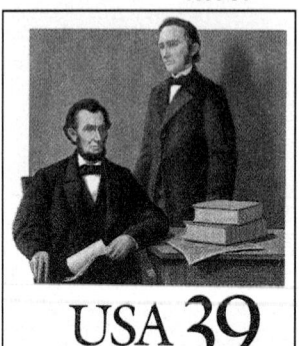

Blair and Pres.
Abraham
Lincoln — UC31

Design: Mail bags and "Free city delivery," "Railway mail service" and "Money order system" at lower left. Globe, locomotive, bust of Blair, UPU emblem and "The Paris conference of 1863, initiated by Postmaster General Blair, led, in 1874, to the founding of the Universal Postal Union" contained on reverse folding area.
Printed by the Bureau of Engraving & Printing.
Designed by Ned Seidler.

Letter Sheet for Foreign Postage

			Tagged	
1989, Nov. 20		**Litho.**		
UC62	UC31	39c **multicolored,** entire	.80	*1.00*
		Entire, 1st day cancel, Washington, DC		1.75
a.		Double impression	—	
b.		Triple impression	—	
c.		Quadruple impression	—	

UC32

Designed by Bradbury Thompson.
Printed by the Bureau of Engraving and Printing.

Letter Sheet for Foreign Postage

			Tagged	
1991, May 17		**Litho.**		
UC63	UC32	45c **gray, red & blue,** *blue,* entire	.90	*1.00*
a.		White paper	.90	*1.00*
		Entire, 1st day cancel, Denver, CO *(19,941)*		1.40

Thaddeus Lowe (1832-1913), Balloonist — UC33

Designed by Davis Meltzer.
Printed by the Bureau of Engraving & Printing.

Letter Sheet for Foreign Postage

			Tagged	
1995, Sept. 23		**Litho.**		
UC64	UC33	50c **multicolored,** *blue,* entire	1.00	1.00
		Entire, 1st day cancel, Tampa, FL		1.25

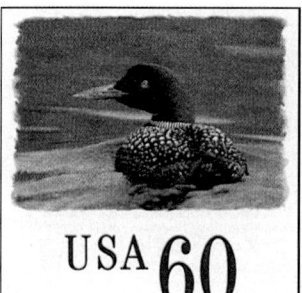

USA 60

Voyageurs
Natl. Park,
Minnesota
UC34

Designed by Phil Jordan.

Printed by Bureau of Engraving & Printing.

Letter Sheet for Foreign Postage

			Tagged	
1999, May 15		**Litho.**		
UC65	UC34	60c **multicolored,** *blue,* entire	1.25	1.00
		Entire, 1st day cancel, Denver, CO		1.50

OFFICIAL ENVELOPES & WRAPPERS

By the Act of Congress, January 31, 1873, the franking privilege of officials was abolished as of July 1, 1873 and the Postmaster General was authorized to prepare official envelopes. At the same time official stamps were prepared for all Departments. Department envelopes became obsolete July 5, 1884. After that, government offices began to use franked envelopes of varied design. These indicate no denomination and lie beyond the scope of this Catalogue.

Post Office Department

UO1

Numeral 9mm high.

UO2

Numeral 9mm high.

UO3

Numeral 9½mm high.

Printed by George H. Reay, Brooklyn, N.Y.

1873

UO1	UO1	2c **black,** *lemon*	24.00	10.00
		Entire	35.00	15.00
UO2	UO2	3c **black,** *lemon*	16.00	6.50
		Entire	29.00	11.00
+UO3	UO2	3c **black**	*22,500.*	

		Entire	*30,000.*	
UO4	UO3	6c **black,** *lemon*	26.00	1
		Entire	35.00	2.

The No. UO3 entire is unique. It has a tear through the st[...] that has been professionally repaired. Value based on au[...] sale in 1999.

UO4

Numeral 9¼mm high.

UO5

Numeral 9¼mm high.

UO6

Numeral 10½mm high.

Printed by Plimpton Manufacturing Co., Hartford, Conn.

1874-79

UO5	UO4	2c **black,** *lemon*	10.50	4.
		Entire	15.00	7.
UO6	UO4	2c **black**	140.00	35.
		Entire	190.00	55.
UO7	UO5	3c **black,** *lemon*	3.25	
		Entire	4.25	1.
UO8	UO5	3c **black**	*3,000.*	2,25
		Entire	*5,750.*	
UO9	UO5	3c **black,** *amber*	150.00	40.[
		Entire	175.00	60.[
UO10	UO5	3c **black,** *blue*	*45,000.*	
		Entire	*50,000.*	
UO11	UO5	3c **blue,** *blue* ('75)	*45,000.*	
		Entire	*50,000.*	
UO12	UO6	6c **black,** *lemon*	16.00	6.[
		Entire	26.00	12.[
UO13	UO6	6c **black**	*3,250.*	1,75
		Entire	*5,750.*	

Fakes exist of Nos. UO3, UO8 and UO13.

Postal Service

UO7

1877

UO14	UO7	**black**	7.00	4.5
		Entire	11.50	6.0
UO15	UO7	**black,** *amber*	225.00	40.0
		Entire	900.00	65.0
UO16	UO7	**blue,** *amber*	210.00	40.0
		Entire	900.00	65.0
UO17	UO7	**blue,** *blue*	9.00	6.7
		Entire	13.50	10.5

War Department

Franklin — UO8

Bust points to the end of "N" of "ONE".

Jackson — UO9

Bust narrow at the back.

Washington — UO10

Queue projects below the bust.

Lincoln — UO11

Neck very long at the back.

Jefferson — UO12

Queue forms straight line with bust.

Clay — UO13

Ear partly concealed by hair, mouth large, chin prominent.

Webster — UO14

Has side whiskers.

Scott — UO15

Hamilton — UO16

Back of bust very narrow; chin almost straight; the labels containing the letters "U S" are exactly parallel.

Printed by George H. Reay.

1873

UO18	UO8	1c	**dark red**	700.00	300.00
			Entire	1,200.	325.00
WO18A	UO8	1c	**dark red,** *manila*		
UO19	UO9	2c	**dark red**	2,250.	400.00
			Entire	3,000.	
UO20	UO10	3c	**dark red**	72.50	42.50
			Entire	100.00	70.00
UO21	UO10	3c	**dark red,** *amber*	40,000.	
			Entire	50,000.	
UO22	UO10	3c	**dark red,** *cream*	1,000.	300.00
			Entire	1,200.	350.00
UO23	UO11	6c	**dark red**	325.00	100.00
			Entire	425.00	250.00
UO24	UO11	6c	**dark red,** *cream*	8,250.	425.00
			Entire	10,000.	2,000.
UO25	UO12	10c	**dark red**	17,500.	2,250.
			Entire	27,500.	4,000.
UO26	UO13	12c	**dark red**	175.00	50.00
			Entire	250.00	—
UO27	UO14	15c	**dark red**	160.00	55.00
			Entire	210.00	375.00
UO28	UO15	24c	**dark red**	175.00	50.00
			Entire	225.00	1,250.
UO29	UO16	30c	**dark red**	550.00	150.00
			Entire	725.00	500.00

1873

UO30	UO8	1c	**vermilion**	200.00	
			Entire	400.00	
WO31	UO8	1c	**vermilion,** *manila*	20.00	14.00
			Entire	35.00	25.00
+UO32	UO9	2c	**vermilion**	500.00	
			Entire		—
WO33	UO9	2c	**vermilion,** *manila*	225.00	
			Entire	375.00	
UO34	UO10	3c	**vermilion**	100.00	40.00
			Entire	175.00	125.00
UO35	UO10	3c	**vermilion,** *amber*	125.00	
			Entire	375.00	
UO36	UO10	3c	**vermilion,** *cream*	17.00	12.50
			Entire	40.00	26.00
UO37	UO11	6c	**vermilion**	100.00	
			Entire	175.00	
+UO38	UO11	6c	**vermilion,** *cream*	575.00	
			Entire	27,500.	
UO39	UO12	10c	**vermilion**	350.00	
			Entire	450.00	
UO40	UO13	12c	**vermilion**	175.00	
			Entire	225.00	
UO41	UO14	15c	**vermilion**	250.00	
			Entire	3,000.	
UO42	UO15	24c	**vermilion**	450.00	
			Entire	650.00	
UO43	UO16	30c	**vermilion**	500.00	
			Entire	625.00	

UO17

Bottom serif on "S" is thick and short; bust at bottom below hair forms a sharp point.

UO18

Bottom serif on "S" is thick and short; front part of bust is rounded.

UO19

Bottom serif on "S" is short; queue does not project below bust.

UO20

Neck very short at the back.

UO21

Knot of queue stands out prominently.

UO22

Ear prominent, chin receding.

UO23

Has no side whiskers; forelock projects above head.

UO24

Back of bust rather broad; chin slopes considerably; the label containing letters "U S" are not exactly parallel.

Printed by Plimpton Manufacturing Co.

1875

UO44	UO17	1c **red**	190.00	85.00
		Entire	250.00	175.00
+**UO45**	UO17	1c **red**, *amber*	1,050.	
+**UO45A**	UO17	1c **red**, *orange*	37,500.	
WO46	UO17	1c **red**, *manila*	4.25	2.75
		Entire	9.50	6.50
UO47	UO18	2c **red**	140.00	—
		Entire	190.00	
UO48	UO18	2c **red**, *amber*	37.50	17.50
		Entire	45.00	27.50
UO49	UO18	2c **red**, *orange*	70.00	17.50
		Entire	80.00	30.00
WO50	UO18	2c **red**, *manila*	100.00	50.00
		Entire	225.00	—
UO51	UO19	3c **red**	17.00	10.00
		Entire	21.00	17.50
UO52	UO19	3c **red**, *amber*	21.00	10.00
		Entire	26.00	16.00
UO53	UO19	3c **red**, *cream*	7.00	3.75
		Entire	9.75	6.50
UO54	UO19	3c **red**, *blue*	3.75	2.75
		Entire	5.50	4.50
UO55	UO19	3c **red**, *fawn*	6.00	2.75
		Entire	10.00	4.00
UO56	UO20	6c **red**	65.00	30.00
		Entire	100.00	—
UO57	UO20	6c **red**, *amber*	95.00	40.00
		Entire	125.00	—
UO58	UO20	6c **red**, *cream*	225.00	85.00
		Entire	275.00	
UO59	UO21	10c **red**	250.00	80.00
		Entire	300.00	
UO60	UO21	10c **red**, *amber*	1,250.	
		Entire	1,650.	
UO61	UO22	12c **red**	65.00	40.00
		Entire	190.00	*250.00*
UO62	UO22	12c **red**, *amber*	800.00	
		Entire	950.00	
UO63	UO22	12c **red**, *cream*	700.00	
		Entire	950.00	
UO64	UO23	15c **red**	250.00	140.00
		Entire	300.00	—
UO65	UO23	15c **red**, *amber*	950.00	
		Entire	1,200.	
UO66	UO23	15c **red**, *cream*	800.00	
		Entire	1,000.	
UO67	UO24	30c **red**	190.00	140.00
		Entire	225.00	—
UO68	UO24	30c **red**, *amber*	950.00	
		Entire	2,400.	
UO69	UO24	30c **red**, *cream*	1,000.	
		Entire	1,350.	

POSTAL SAVINGS ENVELOPES

Issued under the Act of Congress, approved June 25, 1910, in lieu of penalty or franked envelopes. Unused remainders, after mid-October 1914, were overprinted with the Penalty Clause. Regular stamped envelopes, redeemed by the Government, were also overprinted for official use.

UO25

1911

UO70	UO25	1c **green**	75.00	25.00
		Entire	95.00	42.50
UO71	UO25	1c **green**, *oriental buff*	200.00	75.00
		Entire	250.00	90.00
UO72	UO25	2c **carmine**	12.50	4.00
		Entire	21.00	12.00
a.		2c **carmine**, *manila* (error)	1,750.	1,000.
		Entire	2,500.	1,400.

Tagged
Envelopes from No. UO73 onward are tagged unless otherwise noted.

OFFICIAL MAIL

Great Seal — UO26

1983, Jan. 12   **Embossed**
UO73 UO26 20c **blue**, entire   1.25 *30.00*
First day cancel, Washington, DC   1.00

UO27

1985, Feb. 26   **Embossed**
UO74 UO27 22c **blue**, entire   .90 *25.00*
First day cancel, Washington, DC   1.00

UO28

1987, Mar. 2   **Typo.**
UO75 UO28 22c **blue**, entire   1.25 *35.00*
First day cancel, Washington, DC   1.00

Used exclusively to mail U.S. Savings Bonds.

UO29

1988, Mar. 22   **Typo.**
UO76 UO29 (25c) **black & blue**, entire   1.25 *35.00*
First day cancel, Washington, DC   1.25

Used exclusively to mail U.S. Savings Bonds.

UO30

UO31

1988, Apr. 11   **Typo. & Embosse**
UO77 UO30 25c **black & blue**, entire   .80 *20.0*
First day cancel, Washington, DC   1.2
a. Denomination & lettering as on No. UO78, entire   .90 *15.0*

Typo.
UO78 UO31 25c **black & blue**, entire   .90 *35.0*
First day cancel, Washington, DC (*12,017*)   1.2
a. Denomination & lettering as on No. UO77, entire   1.00 *35.0*

No. UO78 used exclusively to mail U.S. Savings Bonds. First day cancellations applied to 12,017 of Nos. UO77, UO78.

1990, Mar. 17   **Typo**
Stars and "E Pluribus Unum" illegible. "Official" is 13mm, "USA" is 16mm long.

UO79 UO31 45c **black & blue**, entire   1.25 —
First day cancel, Springfield, VA (*5,956*)   1.5
UO80 UO31 65c **black & blue**, entire   1.75 —
First day cancel, Springfield, VA (*6,922*)   2.2

Used exclusively to mail U.S. passports.

UO32

Stars and "E Pluribus Unum" clear and sharply printed. "Official" is 14½mm, "USA" is 17mm long.

1990, Aug. 10   **Litho.**
UO81 UO32 45c **black & blue**, entire   1.25 *100.0*
First day cancel, Washington, DC (*7,160*)   1.50
UO82 UO32 65c **black & blue**, entire   1.60 *150.0*
First day cancel, Washington, DC (*6,759*)   2.25

Used exclusively to mail U.S. passports.

UO33

1991, Jan. 22   **Typo.**   **Wmk.**
UO83 UO33 (29c) **black & blue**, entire   1.25 *35.00*
First day cancel, Washington, DC (*30,549*)   1.25

Used exclusively to mail U.S. Savings Bonds.

Official Mail

UO34

91, Apr. 6   Wmk.   Litho. & Embossed
84 UO34 29c **black & blue,** entire   .75   20.00
     First day cancel, Oklahoma
       City, OK (27,841)   1.25
     Entire, unwatermarked, May 1,
       1992   .75   —

Unwatermarked envelopes on recycled paper were issued
y 1, 1992, and have a "recycled" imprint under the flap.

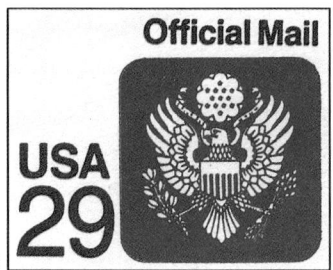

Official Mail

UO35

91, Apr. 17   Typo.   Wmk.
85 UO35 29c **black & blue,** entire   .70   20.00
     First day cancel, Washington,
       DC (25,563)   1.25
     Entire, unwatermarked, May 1,
       1992   .70   —

Used exclusively to mail U.S. Savings Bonds.
watermarked envelopes on recycled paper were issued May
1992, and have a "recycled" imprint under the flap.

Used Values
The appearance in the marketplace of postally
sed examples of the entires used to mail pass-
orts (Nos. UO86-UO87) is so infrequent that it
urrently is not possible to establish accurate
alues.

Consular Service,
Bicent. — UO36

Designed by Zebulon Rogers. Quotation from O. Henry on
ap.

992, July 10   Litho.   Unwmk.
O86 UO36 52c **blue & red,** entire   1.60   125.00
     First day cancel, Washington,
       DC (30,374)   2.25
   a.   52c blue & red, blue-white, entire   1.50   125.00
O87 UO36 75c **blue & red,** entire   3.00   125.00
     First day cancel, Washington,
       DC (25,995)   3.25
   a.   75c blue & red, blue-white, entire   2.50   125.00
     Used exclusively to mail U.S. passports.
Available only in 4⅜ inch x 8⅞ inch size with self-adhesive
ap.
Original issues have "USPS copyright" on left under flap. Re-
ssues (Nos. UO86a and UO87a) have it at right.

Official Mail

UO37

1995-99   Typo. & Embossed   Unwmk.
UO88 UO37 32c **blue & red,** entire, May 9,
       1995   .80   20.00
     First day cancel, Washington,
       DC   1.25
UO89 UO37 33c **blue & red,** entire, Feb. 22,
       1999   .70   20.00
     First day cancel, Washington,
       DC   1.25

Type of 1995
2001   Typo. & Embossed   Tagged   Unwmk.
UO90 UO37 34c **blue & red,** entire, Feb. 27,
       2001   .85   20.00
     First day cancel, Washington,
       DC   1.25

Type of 1995
Typo. & Embossed
2002-2006   Tagged   Unwmk.
UO91 UO37 37c **blue & red,** type I, entire, Aug.
       2, 2002   .90   —
     First day cancel, Washington, DC   1.25
     First day cancel, any other city   1.25
UO91a   Type II, entire, Aug. 2, 2002   .90   —

Type I has 29x28mm blue panel, top of "USA" even with the
bottom of the eagle's neck and is made with "100% recycled
paper" as noted on reverse. Type II has a 27½x27½mm blue
panel, top of "USA" even with the highest arrow, and has no
mention of "100% recycled paper" on reverse.

2006   Typo. & Embossed   Tagged   Unwmk.
UO92 UO37 39c **blue & red,** entire, Jan. 9, 2006   .95   —
     Entire, 1st day cancel, Washing-
       ton, DC   1.25
     Entire, 1st day cancel, any other
       city   1.25

Type I has **29x28mm blue panel, top of "USA"
even with the bottom of the eagle's neck and is
made with "100% recycled paper" as noted on
reverse. Type II has a 27½x27½mm blue panel, top
of "USA" even with the highest arrow, and has no
mention of "100% recycled paper" on reverse.**

Included in listings of Official Envelopes

POSTAL CARDS

Values are for unused cards as sold by the Post Office, without printed or written address or message, and used cards with Post Office cancellati~~on~~ when current. Used cards with postage added to meet higher rates sell for less. Used cards for international rates are for proper usage. Those us~~ed~~ domestically sell for less.

The "Preprinted" values are for unused cards with printed or written address or message.

Starting with No. UX21, all postal cards have been printed by the Government Printing Office.

Nos. UX1-UX48 are typographed; others are lithographed (offset) unless otherwise stated.

Numerous printing varieties exist. Varieties of surcharged cards include (a) inverted surcharge at lower left, (b) double surcharge, one inverted lower left, (c) surcharge in other abnormal positions, including back of card. Such surcharge varieties command a premium.

Colored cancellations sell for more than black in some instances. **All values are for entire cards.**

As of Jan. 1, 1999, postal cards were sold individually for 1c over face value.

See Computer Vended Postage section for "Postal Buddy" cards.

Since 1875 it has been possible to purchase some postal cards in sheets for multiple printing, hence pairs, strips and blocks are available. Some sheets have been cut up so that cards exist with stamp inverted, in center of card, two on one card, in another corner, etc. These are only curiosities and of minimal value.

Liberty — PC1

Wmk. Large "U S P O D" in Monogram, (90x60mm)

1873, May   **Size: 130x76mm**
UX1 PC1 1c **brown,**   375.00   25.00
     Preprinted   70.00
     First day cancel. Boston, New
     York or Washington   12,000.

One card is documented canceled May 10 in Owensboro, Ky.; another May 11 in Providence, R.I.; and another May 12 in Springfield, Mass.

Wmk. Small "U S P O D" in Monogram, (53x36mm)

1873, July 6
UX3 PC1 1c **brown,** *buff*   80.00   2.50
     Preprinted   20.00
  a.   Without watermark   800.00

The watermarks on Nos. UX1, UX3 and UX4 are found in normal position, inverted, reversed, and inverted and reversed. They are often dim, especially on No. UX4. Values listed are for clear watermarks.

No. UX3a is not known unused. Cards offered as such are either unwatermarked proofs, or have partial or vague watermarks. See No. UX65.

Liberty — PC2

Inscribed: "WRITE THE ADDRESS . . ."
1875   **Wmk. Small "U S P O D" in Monogram**
UX4 PC2 1c **black,** *buff,* Sept. 28   4,000.   400.

     Preprinted   750.
     Unwmk.
UX5 PC2 1c **black,** *buff,* Sept. 30   82.50   .45
     Preprinted   7.00

For other postal card of type PC2 see No. UX7.

Liberty — PC3

For International Use

1879, Dec. 1
UX6 PC3 2c **blue,** *buff*   35.00   25.00
     Preprinted   11.50
  a.   2c **dark blue,** *buff*   35.00   25.00
     Preprinted   11.50

See Nos. UX13 and UX16.

Design of PC2, Inscribed "NOTHING BUT THE ADDRESS."

1881, Oct. 17 (?)
UX7 PC2 1c **black,** *buff*   70.00   .40
     Preprinted   6.50
  a.   23 teeth below "ONE CENT"   1,350.   65.00
     Preprinted   225.00
  b.   Printed on both sides   800.00   400.00

Jefferson — PC4

1885, Aug. 24
UX8 PC4 1c **brown,** *buff*   55.00   1.25
     Preprinted   10.00
  c.   1c **dark chocolate,** *buff*   300.00   40.00
     Preprinted   75.00
  d.   Double impression   7,500.
  e.   Double impression, one inverted   9,500.
  f.   Printed on both sides

Card was printed in many shades of brown ink. Earliest documented use: Aug. 29, 1885.

Head of Jefferson facing right, centered on card.

PC5

1886, Dec. 1
UX9 PC5 1c **black,** *buff*   25.00
     Preprinted   1.75
  a.   1c **black,** *dark buff*   75.00   5~~.~~
     Preprinted   20.00
  b.   Double impression   —
  c.   Double impression, one inverted   8,500.
  d.   **1c black,** *salmon pink*   2,000.   3,1~~~~
  e.   Triple impression   3,000.

Grant — PC6

1891, Dec. 16   **Size: 155x95m~~m~~**
UX10 PC6 1c **black,** *buff*   45.00   1~~~~
     Preprinted   6.50
  a.   Double impression, one inverted   3,250.
  b.   Double impression   1,250.
  c.   Triple impression, one inverted   3,250.
  d.   Quintuple impression, three in-
     verted   3,250.

Two types exist of No. UX10.
Earliest documented use: Dec. 23, 1891.

     Size: 117x75mm
UX11 PC6 1c **blue,** *grayish white*   22.50   3~~.~~
     Preprinted   5.00
  b.   Double impression, one inverted   3,000.

Cards printed in black instead of blue are invariably proofs
Earliest documented use: Dec. 21, 1891.

PC7

Head of Jefferson facing left.
Small wreath and name below.
Size: 140x89mm

1894, Jan. 2
UX12 PC7 1c **black,** *buff*   45.00   .6~~~~
     Preprinted   2.25
  a.   Double impression

Two types exist of No. UX12: flat bed printing and rota~~ry~~ press printing.

For International Use

1897, Jan. 25   **Design of PC~~3~~**
     Size: 140x89mm
UX13 PC3 2c **blue,** *cream*   200.00   85.0~~0~~
     Preprinted   85.00

Earliest documented use: Apr. 17, 1897.

PC8

Head same as PC7. Large wreath and name below.

897, Dec. 1
Size: 139x82mm

X14	PC8 1c **black,** *buff*		40.00	.45
	Preprinted		2.75	
a.	Double impression, one inverted		10,000.	8,750.
	Preprinted		—	
b.	Printed both sides		—	—
	Preprinted		3,000.	
c.	Double impression		—	—
	Preprinted		—	—
d.	**Black,** *salmon pink,* preprinted		1,500.	

John Adams — PC9

898
Size: 126x74mm

X15	PC9 1c **black,** *buff, Mar. 31*	47.50	15.00
	Preprinted		12.50	

Design same as PC3, without frame around card.
For International Use
Size: 140x82mm

X16	PC3 2c **black,** *buff*	14.00	17.00
	Preprinted		5.00	

McKinley — PC10

902

JX17	PC10 1c **black,** *buff*	9,000.	
	Preprinted		3,500.	3,500.

Earliest documented use; May 27, 1902.

McKinley — PC11

1902

UX18	PC11 1c **black,** *buff*	16.00	.35
	Preprinted		1.75	

Earliest documented use; July 14, 1902.
Two types exist of Nos. UX18-UX20.

McKinley — PC12

1907

UX19	PC12 1c **black,** *buff*	45.00	.50
	Preprinted		2.25	

Earliest documented use; June 28, 1907.

Same design, correspondence space at left
1908, Jan. 2

UX20	PC12 1c **black,** *buff*	57.50	4.25
	Preprinted		8.50	

PC13

McKinley, background shaded.

1910

UX21	PC13 1c **blue,** *bluish*	105.00	13.00
	Preprinted		17.50	
a.	1c **bronze blue,** *bluish*	400.00	100.00
	Preprinted		150.00	
b.	Double impression	1,200.	
c.	Triple impression	2,500.	
d.	Double impression, one inverted	—	
e.	Four arcs above and below "IS" of inscription to left of stamp impression are pointed	2,250.	400.00
	Preprinted	900.00	

A No. UX21 card exists with Philippines No. UX11 printed on the back.

PC14

Same design, white background.

1910, Apr. 13

UX22	PC14 1c **blue,** *bluish*	19.00	.35
	Preprinted		1.75	
a.	Double impression	600.00	
b.	Triple impression	3,250.	2,250.
c.	Triple impression, one inverted	—	
d.	Quintuple impression	6,000.	

See No. UX24.

PC15

Head of Lincoln, solid background.

1911, Jan. 21
Size: 127x76mm

UX23	PC15 1c **red,** *cream*	10.00	5.50
	Preprinted		3.00	
a.	Triple impression	—	
b.	Double impression	7,250.	

See No. UX26.

Design same as PC14
1911, Aug. 10   **Size: 140x82mm**

UX24	PC14 1c **red,** *cream*	10.00	.35
	Preprinted		1.25	
a.	Double impression	—	
b.	Triple impression	—	

Copies with 1920 2-line surcharge are considered favor items.

Grant — PC16

1911, Oct. 27
For International Use
Size: 140x82mm

UX25	PC16 2c **red,** *cream*	1.50	20.00
	Preprinted		.65	
a.	Double impression	—	

For surcharge see No. UX36.

1913, July 29
Size: 127x76mm

UX26	PC15 1c **green,** *cream*	13.00	7.50
	Preprinted		2.50	

Jefferson — PC17

Die I — End of queue small, sloping sharply downward to right.

Die II (recut) — End of queue large and rounded.

1914-16
Size: 140x82mm

UX27	PC17 1c **green,** *buff,* die I, *June 4*	.25	.25
	Preprinted		.20	
a.	1c **green,** *cream*	4.50	.65
	Preprinted		1.25	
b.	Double impression	2,500.	
e.	Triple impression	5,500.	
f.	Quadruple impression	6,500.	

On gray, rough surfaced card

UX27C	PC17 1c **green,** die I, *1916*	4,000.	190.00
	Preprinted		275.00	
UX27D	PC17 1c **dark green,** die II, *Dec. 22, 1916*	24,000.	160.00
	Preprinted		375.00	

For surcharges see Nos. UX39 and UX41.

Lincoln — PC19

1917, Mar. 14   **Size: 127x76mm**

UX28 PC19 1c **green**, *cream*	.60	.30
Preprinted	.30	
a. 1c **green**, *dark buff*	1.50	.60
Preprinted	.50	
b. Double impression		—
Preprinted	2,250.	

No. UX28 was printed also on light buff and canary.
See No. UX43. For surcharges see Nos. UX40 and UX42.

Jefferson — PC20

Die I — Rough, coarse impression. End of queue slopes sharply downward to right. Left basal ends of "2" form sharp points.

Size: 140x82mm

Die II — Clear fine lines in hair. Left basal ends of "2" form balls.

1917-18

UX29 PC20 2c **red**, *buff*, die I, *Oct. 22*	42.50	2.10
Preprinted	6.50	
a. 2c **lake**, *cream*, die I	50.00	4.00
Preprinted	9.00	
c. 2c **vermilion**, *buff*, die I	925.00	75.00
Preprinted	70.00	
UX30 PC20 2c **red**, *cream*, die II, *Jan. 23, 1918*	30.00	1.60
Preprinted	4.50	

2c Postal Cards of 1917-18 Revalued

Surcharged in one line by canceling machine at Washington, DC

1920, Apr.

UX31 PC20 1c on 2c **red**, *cream*, die II	4,500.	4,500.
Preprinted	2,600.	

Surcharged in two lines by canceling machine (46 Types)

UX32 PC20 1c on 2c **red**, *buff*, die I	52.50	12.50
Preprinted	15.00	
a. 1c on 2c **vermilion**, *buff*	150.00	60.00
Preprinted	60.00	
b. Double surcharge	150.00	100.00
Preprinted	100.00	—
UX33 PC20 1c on 2c **red**, *cream*, die II	12.50	2.00
Preprinted	2.50	
a. Inverted surcharge	100.00	100.00
Preprinted	—	
b. Double surcharge	100.00	75.00
Preprinted	50.00	
c. Double surcharge, one inverted	350.00	
Preprinted	—	
d. Triple surcharge	375.00	

Surcharge varieties with the values listed here for Nos. UX32 and UX33 **must have** the surcharges *on the stamp.* Copies having the surcharge inverted in the lower left corner, either alone or in combination with a normal surcharge, exist in many of the 46 types.

Surcharged in Two Lines by Press Printing

1920

UX34 PC20 1c on 2c **red**, *buff*, die I	550.00	52.50
Preprinted	125.00	
a. Double surcharge	750.00	
UX35 PC20 1c 2c **red**, *cream*, die II	225.00	37.50
Preprinted	55.00	

Surcharges were prepared from (a) special dies fitting International and Universal post office canceling machines (Nos. UX31-UX33), and (b) printing press dies (Nos. UX34-UX35). There are 38 canceling machine types on Die I, and 44 on Die II. There are two printing press types of each die.

UX36 PC16 1c on 2c **red**, *cream* (#UX25)		57,500.

Unused copies of No. UX36 (New York surcharge) were probably made by favor. Used copies of No. UX36 (Los Angeles surcharge, three to four examples used in Long Beach are recorded) are unquestionably authentic. Surcharges on other numbers exist, but their validity is doubtful.

McKinley — PC21

1926, Feb. 1

For International Use

UX37 PC21 3c **red**, *buff*	4.50	15.00
Preprinted	1.75	
First day cancel, Washington, DC		225.00
a. 3c **red**, *yellow*	5.25	15.00
Preprinted	1.75	
b. Double impression	5,000.	

Franklin — PC22

1951, Nov. 16

UX38 PC22 2c **carmine rose**, *buff*	.35	.25
Preprinted	.25	
First day cancel		1.00
a. Double impression	500.00	
b. 2c **carmine rose**, *dark buff*, (error)	700.00	
c. 2c **lake**, *buff*	35.00	25.00

No. UX38b was printed on spacer paper used for counting.
For surcharge see No. UX47.

Nos. UX27 and UX28 Surcharged by Canceling Machine at Left of Stamp in Light Green

1952

UX39 PC17 2c on 1c **green**, *buff, Jan. 1*	.50	.35
Preprinted	.25	
First day cancel, any city		12.00
a. Surcharged vertically, reading down	8.00	10.00
Preprinted	3.00	
b. Double surcharge	20.00	25.00
UX40 PC19 2c on 1c **green**, *cream, Mar. 22*	.65	.45
Preprinted	.40	
First day cancel, Washington, D.C.		22.50
a. Surcharged vertically, reading down	7.00	5.50
Preprinted	4.00	

Nos. UX27 and UX28 with Similar Surcharge Typographed at Left of Stamp in Dark Green.

1952

UX41 PC17 2c on 1c **green**, *buff*	4.50	2.00
Preprinted	1.75	
a. Inverted surcharge at lower left	77.50	125.00
Preprinted	50.00	
UX42 PC19 2c on 1c **green**, *cream*	5.00	2.50
Preprinted	3.00	
a. Surcharged by offset lithography	5.00	2.50
b. Surcharged on back	160.00	

Type of 1917

1952, July 31   **Size: 127x76m**

UX43 PC19 2c **carmine**, *buff*	.30	1
Preprinted	.20	
First day cancel		1

Torch and Arm of Statue of Liberty — PC23

Fifth International Philatelic Exhibition (FIPEX), New Yo City, Apr. 28-May 6, 1956.

1956, May 4

UX44 PC23 2c **deep carmine & dark violet blue**, *buff*	.25	1.
First day cancel, New York, NY (537,474)		1.
a. Dark violet blue omitted	650.00	600.
b. Double impression of dark violet blue	40.00	
c. Double impression of deep carmine	40.00	30.
d. Double impression of deep carmine & dark violet blue	650.00	
e. Double impression of deep carmine, dark violet blue omitted	—	
f. 2c **rose pink & dark violet blue**, *buff*	100.00	75.0
g. As "f," dark violet blue omitted	750.00	
h. 2c **pink & dark violet blue**, *buff*	750.00	750.0
i. As "h," double impression of dark violet blue	—	

Statue of Liberty
PC24   PC25

For International Use

1956, Nov. 16

UX45 PC24 4c **deep red & ultramarine**, *buff*	1.50	90.0
First day cancel, New York, NY (129,841)		1.0

See No. UY16.

1958, Aug. 1

UX46 PC25 3c **purple**, *buff*	.50	.2
First day cancel, Philadelphia, Pa. (180,610)		1.0
a. "N GOD WE TRUST"	14.00	25.0
First day cancel, Philadelphia, Pa.		175.0
b. Double impression	250.00	
c. Double impression one inverted	4,500.	
d. Precanceled with 3 printed purple lines, *1961*	4.25	2.5
e. Indicia omitted (inscription normal)	325.00	
f. 3c **purple**, *dark buff* (error)	900.00	

On No. UX46c, the precanceling lines are incorporated with the design. The earliest documented postmark on this experimental card is Oct. 31, 1961. UX46f was printed on space paper used for counting.
See No. UY17.

No. UX38 Surcharged by Canceling Machine at Left of Stamp in Black

ONE CENT ADDITIONAL PAID

1958

UX47 PC22 2c + 1c **carmine rose**, *buff*	225.00	600.00

The surcharge was applied to 750,000 cards for the use of the General Electric Co., Owensboro, Ky. A variety of the surcharge shows the D of PAID beneath the N of ADDITIONAL All known examples of No. UX47 have a printed advertisement on the back and a small punch hole near lower left corner.

No. UX47 exists with inverted surcharge at lower left. Value, $500.

Used value is for commercially used card.

Lincoln
PC26

62, Nov. 19
Precanceled with 3 printed red violet lines
48 PC26 4c **red violet** .50 .20
   First day cancel, Springfield, IL
   (162,939) 1.25
a. Tagged, *June 25, 1966* .50 .20
   First day cancel, Bellevue, OH 30.00
No. UX48a was printed with luminescent ink.
See note on Luminescence in "Information for Collectors."
See No. UY18.

**Used values are for contemporaneous usage
thout additional postage applied. Used values
r international-rate cards are for proper usage.**

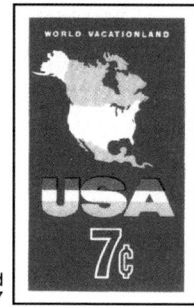
Map of Continental United
States — PC27

Designed by Suren H. Ermoyan

For International Use

963, Aug. 30
X49 PC27 7c **blue & red** 4.00 *65.00*
   First day cancel, New
   York, NY 1.00
a. Blue omitted 7,500.
First day cancellation was applied to 270,464 of Nos. UX49
d UY19. See Nos. UX54, UX59, UY19-UY20.

Flags
and
Map of
U.S.
PC28

175th anniv. of the U.S. Customs Service.

Designed by Gerald N. Kurtz

964, Feb. 22
Precanceled with 3 printed blue lines
X50 PC28 4c **red & blue** .50 *1.00*
   First day cancel, Washington,
   DC *(313,275)* 1.00
a. Blue omitted 650.00
b. Red omitted —
c. Double red impression *650.00*

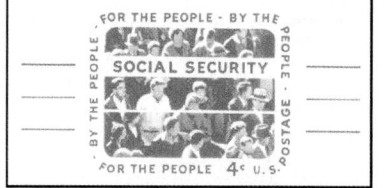
Americans "Moving Forward" (Street Scene) — PC29

Issued to publicize the need to strengthen the US Social
Security system. Released in connection with the 15th conf. of
he Intl. Social Security Association at Washington, DC.

Designed by Gerald N. Kurtz

1964, Sept. 26
Precanceled with a blue and 2 red printed lines
UX51 PC29 4c **dull blue & red** .40 *1.00*
   First day cancel, Washington,
   D.C. *(293,650)* 1.00
a. Red omitted —
b. Dull blue omitted 700.00 650.00

Coast Guard Flag — PC30

175th anniv. of the U.S. Coast Guard.

Designed by Muriel R. Chamberlain

1965, Aug. 4
Precanceled with 3 printed red lines
UX52 PC30 4c **blue & red** .30 *1.00*
   First day cancel, Newburyport,
   Mass. *(338,225)* 1.25
a. Blue omitted 450.00

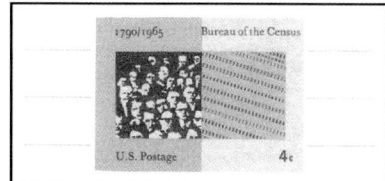
Crowd and Census Bureau Punch Card — PC31

Designed by Emilio Grossi

1965, Oct. 21
Precanceled with 3 bright blue printed lines
UX53 PC31 4c **bright blue & black** .30 *1.00*
   First day cancel, Philadelphia, Pa.
   (275,100) 1.00

Map Type of 1963
For International Use

1967, Dec. 4
UX54 PC27 8c **blue & red** 4.00 *65.00*
   First day cancel, Washington,
   DC 1.00
First day cancellation was applied to 268,077 of Nos. UX54
and UY20.

Lincoln
PC33

Designed by Robert J. Jones

Luminescent Ink

1968, Jan. 4
Precanceled with 3 printed green lines
UX55 PC33 5c **emerald** .30 *.60*
   First day cancel, Hodgenville, Ky. 1.25
a. Double impression —
First day cancellation was applied to 274,000 of Nos. UX55
and UY21.

Woman Marine, 1968, and
Marines of Earlier
Wars — PC34

25th anniv. of the Women Marines.

Designed by Muriel R. Chamberlain

1968, July 26
UX56 PC34 5c **rose red & green** .35 *1.00*
   First day cancel, San Francisco,
   Cal. *(203,714)* 1.25

Tagged
**Postal cards from No. UX57 onward are either
tagged or printed with luminescent ink unless otherwise noted.**

Weather Vane — PC35

Centenary of the Army's Signal Service, the Weather Services (Weather Bureau).

Designed by Robert Geissmann

1970, Sept. 1
UX57 PC35 5c **blue, yellow, red & black** .30 *1.00*
   First day cancel, Fort My-
   er, Va. *(285,800)* 1.00
a. Yellow & black omitted 1,000. 900.00
b. Blue omitted 1,000. 5,000.
c. Black omitted 1,000. 850.00

Paul
Revere
PC36

Issued to honor Paul Revere, Revolutionary War patriot.

Designed by Howard C. Mildner after statue near Old North
Church, Boston

1971, May 15
Precanceled with 3 printed brown lines
UX58 PC36 6c **brown** .30 *1.00*
   First day cancel, Boston,
   Mass. 1.00
a. Double impression 300.00
First day cancellation was applied to 340,000 of Nos. UX58
and UY22.

Map Type of 1963
For International Use

1971, June 10
UX59 PC27 10c **blue & red** 4.50 *60.00*
   First day cancel, New York, NY 1.00
First day cancellation was applied to 297,000 of Nos. UX59
and UXC11.

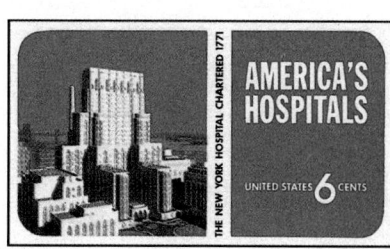
New York Hospital, New York City — PC37

Issued as a tribute to America's hospitals in connection with
the 200th anniversary of New York Hospital.

Designed by Dean Ellis

1971, Sept. 16
UX60 PC37 6c **blue & multicolored** .30 *1.00*
   First day cancel, New York,
   NY *(218,200)* 1.00
a. Blue & yellow omitted 1,000.
b. Yellow omitted 500.00
c. Red & black omitted —
d. Red omitted —
e. Tagging omitted 150.00
f. Black omitted 3,500.
No. UX60f is significantly miscut, with only a small portion of
the indicia present at the center top. The black vertical inscription line at the center is missing.

U.S.F. Constellation — PC38

Monument Valley — PC39

Gloucester, Mass. — PC40

Tourism Year of the Americas.

Designed by Melbourne Brindle

1972, June 29
Size: 152½x108½mm

UX61 PC38 6c **black,** U.S.F. Constellation, *buff* (Yosemite, Mt. Rushmore, Niagara Falls, Williamsburg on back) .85 10.00
First day cancel, any city 1.25
a. Address side blank 300.00
b. Reverse blank — 750.00
c. Tagging omitted 200.00
UX62 PC39 6c **black,** Monument Valley, *buff* (Monterey, Redwoods, Gloucester, U.S.F. Constellation on back) .40 10.00
First day cancel, any city 1.25
a. Black omitted on back —
b. Orange omitted on back —
c. Reverse blank 350.00
d. Tagging omitted 200.00
UX63 PC40 6c **black,** Gloucester, *buff* (Rodeo, Mississippi Riverboat, Grand Canyon, Monument Valley on back) .40 6.00
First day cancel, any city 1.25
a. Black inverted —
b. Reverse blank 500.00
c. Tagging omitted 200.00
Nos. UX61-UX63,UXC12-UXC13 (5) 3.15 251.00

Nos. UX61-UX63, UXC12-UXC13 went on sale throughout the United States. They were sold as souvenirs without postal validity at Belgica Philatelic Exhibition in Brussels and were displayed at the American Embassies in Paris and Rome. This is reflected in the first day cancel.
Varieties of the pictorial back printing include: black omitted (UX62), black and pale salmon omitted (UX63), and back inverted in relation to address side (UX63).
Used value for No. UX61b is for a copy that is canceled but unaddressed.

John Hanson — PC41

Designed by Thomas Kronen after statue by Richard Edwin Brooks in Maryland Capitol

1972, Sept. 1
Precanceled with 3 printed blue lines.

UX64 PC41 6c **blue** .50 1.00
First day cancel, Baltimore, MD 1.00
a. Coarse paper .60 1.25

Liberty Type of 1873

Centenary of first U.S. postal card.

1973, Sept. 14

UX65 PC1 6c **magenta** .25 1.00
First day cancel, Washington, D.C. (289,950) 1.00
a. Tagging omitted —

Samuel Adams — PC42

Designed by Howard C. Mildner

1973, Dec. 16
Precanceled with 3 printed orange lines

UX66 PC42 8c **orange** .50 1.00
First day cancel, Boston, Mass. (147,522) 1.00
a. Coarse paper .75 1.00
b. Double impression 1,200.

Ship's Figurehead, 1883 — PC43

Design is after a watercolor by Elizabeth Moutal of the oak figurehead by John Rogerson from the barque Edinburgh.

1974, Jan. 4
For International Use

UX67 PC43 12c **multicolored** .35 45.00
First day cancel, Miami, Fla. (138,500) 1.00
a. Yellow omitted 650.00

Charles Thomson — PC44

John Witherspoon — PC45

Caesar Rodney — PC46

Designed by Howard C. Mildner

1975-76
Precanceled with 3 printed emerald lines

UX68 PC44 7c **emerald,** *Sept. 14, 1975* .30 10
First day cancel, Bryn Mawr, Pa. 1
Precanceled with 3 printed brown lines
UX69 PC45 9c **yellow brown,** *Nov. 10, 1975* .30 1.
First day cancel, Princeton, N.J. 1
Precanceled with 3 printed blue lines
UX70 PC46 9c **blue,** *July 1, 1976* .30 1.
First day cancel, Dover, Del. 1.
a. Double impression 4,500.

First day cancellation applied to 231,919 of Nos. UX68 a UY25; 254,239 of Nos. UX69 and UY26; 304,061 of Nos. UX and UY27.

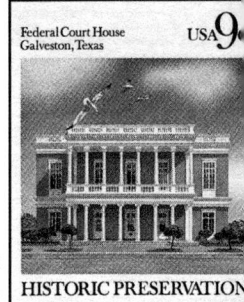

Federal Court House, Galveston, Texas — PC47

The Court House, completed in 1861, is on the Nation Register of Historic Places.

Designed by Donald Moss

1977, July 20

UX71 PC47 9c **multicolored** .25 1.
First day cancel, Galveston, Tex. (245,535) 1.0
a. Black Omitted 6,000.
b. Tagging omitted 150.00

Nathan Hale PC48

Designed by Howard C. Mildner

1977, Oct. 14
Precanceled with 3 printed green lines

UX72 PC48 9c **green** .25 1.0
First day cancel, Coventry, Conn. 1.0
a. Cent sign missing after "9" 125.00
b. Double impression 275.00

First day cancellation applied to 304,592 of Nos. UX72 an UY28.
Approximately 400 examples are recorded of No. UX72a The variety also exists on fluorescent stock (18 recorded) Value thus is 7 times the listed value.

Cincinnati Music Hall — PC49

Centenary of Cincinnati Music Hall, Cincinnati, Ohio.

Designed by Clinton Orlemann

1978, May 12

UX73 PC49 10c **multicolored** .30 *1.00*
    First day cancel,
    Cincinnati, O.
    (300,000) 1.75

John Hancock — PC50

Designed by Howard Behrens

1978

Precanceled with 3 printed brown orange lines.

UX74 PC50 (10c) **brown orange,** *May 19* .30 *1.00*
    First day cancel, Quincy, Mass.
    (299,623) 1.00

Inscribed "U.S. Postage 10¢"

UX75 PC50 10c **brown orange,** *June 20* .30 *1.00*
    First day cancel, Quincy, Mass.
    (187,120) 1.00

US Coast Guard Eagle USA 14c

Coast Guard Cutter Eagle — PC51

Designed by Carl G. Evers

For International Use

1978, Aug. 4

UX76 PC51 14c **multicolored** .40 *30.00*
    First day cancel, Seattle, Wash.
    (196,400) 1.00

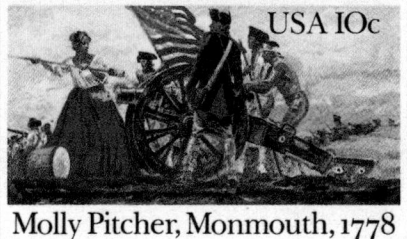

Molly Pitcher Firing Cannon at Monmouth — PC52

Bicentennial of Battle of Monmouth, June 28, 1778, and to honor Molly Pitcher (Mary Ludwig Hays).

Designed by David Blossom

1978, Sept. 8 **Litho.**

UX77 PC52 10c **multicolored** .30 *1.60*
    First day cancel, Freehold, N.J.
    (180,280) 1.00

Clark and his Frontiersmen Approaching Fort Sackville — PC53

Bicentenary of capture of Fort Sackville from the British by George Rogers Clark.

Designed by David Blossom

1979, Feb. 23 **Litho.**

UX78 PC53 10c **multicolored** .30 *1.50*
    First day cancel, Vincennes, Ind. 1.00
  a. Yellow omitted —

Gen. Casimir Pulaski — PC54

Bicentenary of the death of Gen. Casimir Pulaski (1748-1779), Polish nobleman who served in American Revolutionary Army.

1979, Oct. 11 **Litho.**

UX79 PC54 10c **multicolored** .30 *1.50*
    First day cancel, Savannah. GA
    (210,000) 1.00

Olympic Games Issue

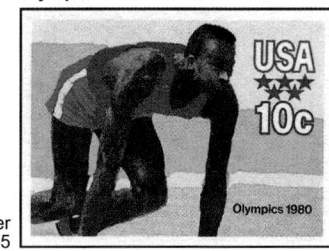

Sprinter
PC55

22nd Olympic Games, Moscow, July 19-Aug. 3, 1980.

Designed by Robert M. Cunningham

1979, Sept. 17 **Litho.**

UX80 PC55 10c **multicolored** .60 *1.50*
    First day cancel, Eugene,
    Ore. 1.00
  a. Tagging omitted 200.00

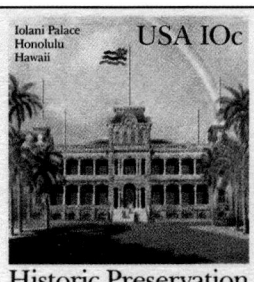

Iolani Palace, Honolulu — PC56

1979, Oct. 1 **Litho.**

UX81 PC56 10c **multicolored** .30 *1.50*
    First day cancel, Honolulu, HI
    (242,804) 1.00
  a. Tagging omitted — —

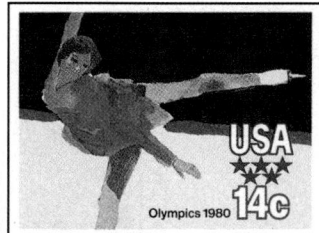

Women's Figure Skating PC57

13th Winter Olympic Games, Lake Placid, N.Y., Feb. 12-24.

Designed by Robert M. Cunningham

For International Use

1980, Jan. 15 **Litho.**

UX82 PC57 14c **multicolored** .60 *20.00*
    First day cancel, Atlanta, GA
    (160,977) 1.00

Salt Lake Temple, Salt Lake City — PC58

1980, Apr. 5 **Litho.**

UX83 PC58 10c **multicolored** .25 *1.50*
    First day cancel, Salt Lake
    City, UT *(325,260)* 1.00
  a. Tagging omitted 300.00

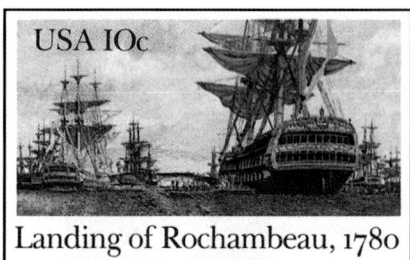

Rochambeau's Fleet — PC59

Count Jean-Baptiste de Rochambeau's landing at Newport, R.I. (American Revolution) bicentenary.

Designed by David Blossom

1980, July 11 **Litho.**

UX84 PC59 10c **multicolored** .25 *1.50*
    First day cancel, New-
    port, R.I. *(180,567)* 1.00
  a. Front normal, black & yellow on
    back *4,000.*
  b. Magenta & blue omitted —

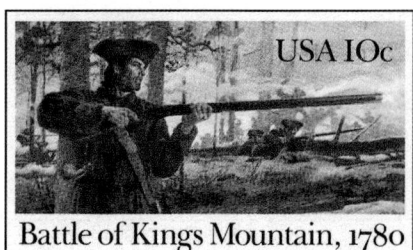

Whig Infantrymen — PC60

Bicentenary of the Battle of Kings Mountain (American Revolution).

Designed by David Blossom

1980, Oct. 7 **Litho.**

UX85 PC60 10c **multicolored** .25 *1.50*
    First day cancel, Kings Mountain,
    NC *(136,130)* 1.00

Golden
Hinde — PC61

Drake's Golden Hinde 1580

300th anniv. of Sir Francis Drake's circumnavigation (1578-1580).

Designed by Charles J. Lundgren

For International Use

1980, Nov. 21
UX86 PC61 19c **multicolored**   .70 35.00
    First day cancel, San Rafael,
    CA *(290,547)*   1.00

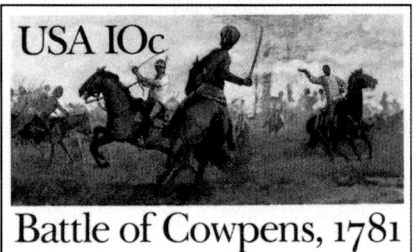

Cols. Washington and Tarleton — PC62

Bicentenary of the Battle of Cowpens (American Revolution).

Designed by David Blossom

1981, Jan. 17
UX87 PC62 10c **multicolored**   .25 17.50
    First day cancel, Cowpens, SC
    (160,000)   1.00

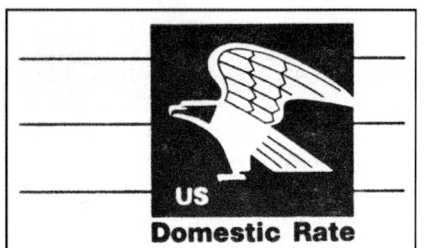

Eagle — PC63

1981, Mar. 15
Precanceled with 3 printed violet lines
UX88 PC63 (12c) **violet**   .30   .65
    First day cancel, Memphis, TN   1.00
    See No. 1818, FDC section.

Isaiah Thomas — PC64

Designed by Chet Jezierski

1981, May 5   Precanceled with 3 printed lines
UX89 PC64 12c **light blue**   .30   .60
    First day cancel, Worcester, MA
    (185,610)   1.00

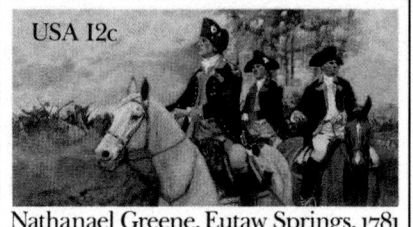

Nathanael Greene, Eutaw Springs, 1781

PC65

Bicentenary of the Battle at Eutaw Springs (American Revolution)

Designed by David Blossom

1981, Sept. 8   Litho.
UX90 PC65 12c **multicolored**   .30   15.00
    First day cancel, Eutaw
    Springs, SC *(115,755)*   1.00
  a.   Red & yellow omitted   2,900.

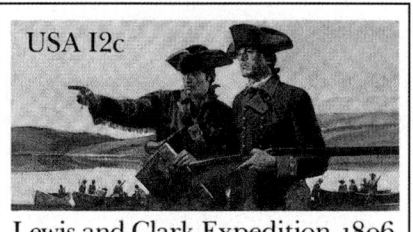

Lewis and Clark Expedition, 1806

PC66

Designed by David Blossom

1981, Sept. 23
UX91 PC66 12c **multicolored**   .30   25.00
    First day cancel, Saint Louis,
    MO   1.00

Robert Morris — PC67

1981
    Precanceled with 3 printed lines
UX92 PC67 (13c) **buff**, *Oct. 11*   .30   .60
    First day cancel, Memphis,
    TN   1.00
    See No. 1946, FDC section.

    Inscribed: U.S. Postage 13¢
UX93 PC67 13c **buff**, *Nov. 10*   .30   .60
    First day cancel, Philadel-
    phia, PA   1.00
  a.   Buff omitted   500.00
On No. UX93a, the copyright symbol and "1981" in buff is present at the lower left corner of the card.

"Swamp Fox" Francis Marion, 1782

General Francis Marion (1732?-1795) — PC68

Designed by David Blossom

1982, Apr. 3   Litho.
UX94 PC68 13c **multicolored**   .30   1.00
    First day cancel, Marion, SC
    (141,162)   1.00

La Salle claims Louisiana, 1682

Rene Robert Cavelier, Sieur de la Salle (1643-1687) — PC69

Designed by David Blossom

1982, Apr. 7   Lith•
UX95 PC69 13c **multicolored**   .30   1.•
    First day cancel, New Orleans,
    LA   1.•

PC70

Designed by Melbourne Brindle

1982, June 18   Litho•
UX96 PC70 13c **brown, red & cream**, *buff*   .30   1.0
    First day cancel, Philadel-
    phia, PA   1.0
  a.   Brown & cream omitted   750.00

Historic Preservation PC71

Designed by Clint Orlemann

1982, Oct. 14   Litho
UX97 PC71 13c **multicolored**   .30   1.00
    First day cancel, St. Louis, MO   1.00

Landing of Oglethorpe, Georgia, 1733

Gen. Oglethorpe Meeting Chief Tomo-Chi-Chi of the Yamacraw — PC72

Designed by David Blossom

1983, Feb. 12   Litho.
UX98 PC72 13c **multicolored**   .30   1.00
    First day cancel, Savannah, GA
    (165,750)   1.00

PC73

Old Post Office, Washington, D.C.

Designed by Walter Brooks

1983, Apr. 19 **Litho.**
UX99 PC73 13c **multicolored** .30 1.00
    First day cancel, Washington,
    DC (125,056) 1.00

Olympics 84, Yachting — PC74

Designed by Bob Peak

1983, Aug. 5 **Litho.**
UX100 PC74 13c **multicolored** .30 1.00
    First day cancel, Long
    Beach, CA (132,232) 1.00
    a. Yellow & red omitted 5,500. —
      Preprinted 5,000.

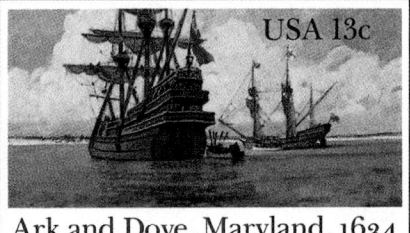

The Ark and the Dove — PC75

Designed by David Blossom

1984, Mar. 25 **Litho.**
UX101 PC75 13c **multicolored** .30 1.00
    First day cancel, St. Clement's
    Island, MD (131,222) 1.00

Runner Carrying Olympic Torch — PC76

Designed by Robert Peak

1984, Apr. 30 **Litho.**
UX102 PC76 13c **multicolored** .30 1.25
    First day cancel, Los Ange-
    les, CA (110,627) 1.00
    a. Black & yellow inverted —
    b. Tagging omitted 350.00

Father Baraga and Indian Guide in Canoe — PC77

Designed by David Blossom

1984, June 29 **Litho.**
UX103 PC77 13c **multicolored** .30 1.00
    First day cancel, Marquette, MI
    (100,156) 1.00

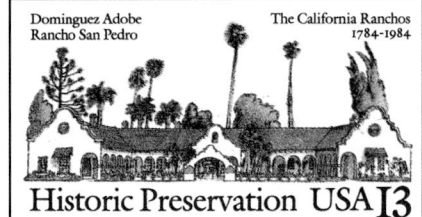

Dominguez Adobe at Rancho San Pedro — PC78

Designed by Earl Thollander

1984, Sept. 16 **Litho.**
UX104 PC78 13c **multicolored** .30 1.00
    First day cancel,
    Compton, CA
    (100,545) 1.00
    a. Black & blue omitted 1,500.
    b. Tagging omitted —

Charles Carroll (1737-1832) — PC79

Designed by Richard Sparks

1985
    Precanceled with 3 printed lines
UX105 PC79 (14c) **pale green,** *Feb. 1* .45 .60
    First day cancel, New Carroll-
    ton, MD (135,642) 1.00
    Inscribed: USA 14
UX106 PC79 14c **pale green,** *Mar. 6* .45 .50
    First day cancel, Annapolis,
    MD (111,122) 1.00

Clipper Flying Cloud — PC80

Designed by Richard Schlecht

    For International Use
1985, Feb. 27 **Litho.**
UX107 PC80 25c **multicolored** .70 22.50
    First day cancel, Salem, MA
    (95,559) 1.25
No. UX107 was sold by the USPS at CUP-PEX 87, Perth,
Western Australia, with a cachet honoring CUP-PEX 87 and the
America's Cup race. Value $2.

George Wythe (1726-1806) — PC81

Designed by Chet Jezierski from a portrait by John
Fergusson.

1985, June 20
    Precanceled with 3 printed lines
UX108 PC81 14c **bright apple green** .30 .75
    First day cancel, Williamsburg,
    VA (133,334) 1.00
    a. Indicia missing —
On No. UX108a, the left precancel, "George Wythe" and the
copyright symbol are normal.

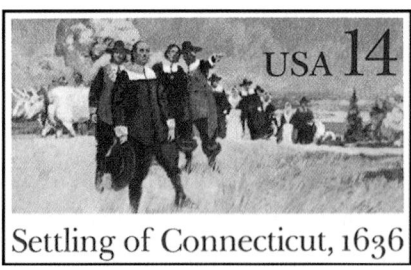

Arrival of Thomas Hooker and Hartford
Congregation — PC82

Settlement of Connecticut, 350th Anniv.

Designed by David Blossom

1986, Apr. 18 **Litho.**
UX109 PC82 14c **multicolored** .30 1.50
    First day cancel, Hartford, CT
    (76,875) 1.00

Stamp Collecting — PC83

Designed by Ray Ameijide

1986, May 23 **Litho.**
UX110 PC83 14c **multicolored** .30 1.25
    First day cancel, Chicago, IL
    (75,548) 1.00
No. UX110 was sold by the USPS at "najubria 86" with a
show cachet. Value $6.

Francis Vigo (1747-1836) — PC84

Designed by David Blossom

1986, May 24 **Litho.**
UX111 PC84 14c **multicolored** .30 1.25
    First day cancel, Vincennes, IN
    (100,141) 1.00

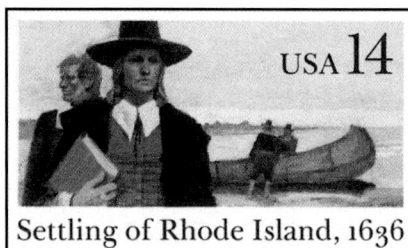

Roger Williams (1603-1683), Clergyman, Landing at
Providence — PC85

Settling of Rhode Island, 350th Anniv.

Designed by David Blossom

1986, June 26   **Litho.**
UX112 PC85 14c **multicolored**   .30 *1.50*
    First day cancel, Providence, RI
    (54,559)   1.00

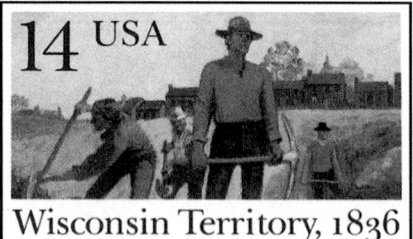

Miners, Shake Rag Street Housing — PC86

Wisconsin Territory Sesquicentennial.

Designed by David Blossom

1986, July 3   **Litho.**
UX113 PC86 14c **multicolored**   .30 *1.00*
    First day cancel, Mineral
    Point, WI *(41,224)*   1.00
  a.   Tagging omitted   200.00

The First Muster, by Don Troiani — PC87

Designed by Bradbury Thompson

1986, Dec. 12   **Litho.**
UX114 PC87 14c **multicolored**   .30 *1.25*
    First day cancel, Boston, MA
    (72,316)   1.00

PC88

The self-scouring steel plow invented by blacksmith John
Deere in 1837 pictured at lower left.

Designed by William H. Bond

1987, May 22   **Litho.**
UX115 PC88 14c **multicolored**   .30 *1.25*
    First day cancel, Moline, IL
    (160,009)   1.00

Convening of the Constitutional Convention,
1787 — PC89

George Mason, Gouverneur Morris, James Madison, Alexander Hamilton and Charles C. Pinckney are listed in the lower left
corner of the card.

Designed by David K. Stone

1987, May 25   **Litho.**
UX116 PC89 14c **multicolored**   .30   *.75*
    First day cancel, Philadel-
    phia, PA *(138,207)*   1.00
  a.   Double black and blue, with first
      day cancel   650.00

Stars and
Stripes — PC90

Designed by Steven Dohanos

1987, June 14   **Litho.**
UX117 PC90 14c **black, blue & red**   .30   *.60*
    First day cancel, Baltimore, MD   1.00

No. UX117 was sold by the USPS at Cologne, Germany, with
a cachet for Philatelia'87. Value $2.

Take Pride in America — PC91

Designed by Lou Nolan

1987, Sept. 22   **Litho.**
UX118 PC91 14c **multicolored**   .30 *1.25*
    First day cancel, Jackson, WY
    (47,281)   1.00

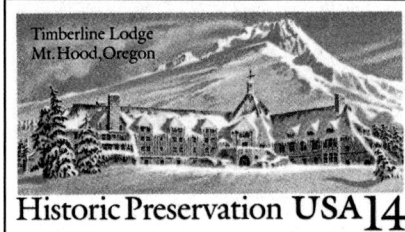

Timberline Lodge, 50th Anniversary — PC92

Designed by Walter DuBois Richards

1987, Sept. 28   **Litho.**
UX119 PC92 14c **multicolored**   .30 *1.25*
    First day cancel, Timberline, OR
    (63,595)   1.25

American Buffalo and Prairie — PC93

Designed by Bart Forbes

1988, Mar. 28   **Lith.**
UX120 PC93 15c **multicolored**   .30
    First day cancel, Buffalo,
    WY *(52,075)*   1
  a.   Black omitted   1,750.
  b.   Printed on both sides   450.00
  c.   Front normal, blue & black on back 650.00
  d.   Black & magenta omitted   1,500.
  e.   Black, yellow, blue & tagging omit-
      ted   1,000.
  f.   Black, blue & tagging omitted   1,250.
  g.   Black, magenta, yellow & tagging
      omitted   1,250.
  h.   Double black impression   —
  i.   Triple black impression   —
  j.   Double black and blue impression   —
  k.   Double magenta & blue, and triple
      black impression   —

Tagged
Postal cards from No. UX57 onward are eith
tagged or printed with luminescent ink unless ot
erwise noted.

PC94

Designed by Pierre Mion

1988, May 4   **Litho**
UX121 PC94 15c **multicolored**   .30   *.7*
    First day cancel, Washington,
    DC *(52,188)*   1.0

Yorkshire, Squarerigged Packet — PC95

Inscribed: Yorkshire, Black Ball Line, Packet Ship, circa 185(
at lower left.

Designed by Richard Schlect

For International Use
1988, June 29   **Litho**
UX122 PC95 28c **multicolored**   .60 *20.0(*
    First day cancel, Mystic, CT
    (46,505)   1.0(
  a.   Black & blue omitted   850.00
  b.   Black, blue, yellow & tagging omitted 1,250.
  c.   Black, magenta & tagging omitted   1,000.
  d.   Black, magenta, yellow & tagging
      omitted   1,000.
  e.   Black & tagging omitted   2,000.

Iowa Territory, 1838 **USA 15**

Harvesting Corn Fields — PC96

Iowa Territory Sesquicentennial.

Designed by Greg Hargreaves

1988, July 2 | | **Litho.**
UX123 PC96 15c **multicolored** .30 .75
    First day cancel, Burlington, IA
    (45,565) 1.00

Settling of Ohio, Northwest Territory, 1788 **USA 15**

Flatboat Ferry Transporting Settlers Down the Ohio
River — PC97

Bicentenary of the settlement of Ohio, the Northwest Territory. Design at lower left shows map of the eastern United States with Northwest Territory highlighted.

Designed by James M. Gurney and Susan Sanford

1988, July 15 | | **Litho.**
UX124 PC97 15c **multicolored** .30 .75
    First day cancel, Marietta, OH
    (28,778) 1.00
    a. Black, blue, yellow & tagging omitted *1,150.*
    b. Black, magenta & tagging omitted *750.00*
    c. Blue, black & tagging omitted *1,000.*
    d. Black & tagging omitted *2,000.*

Hearst Castle San Simeon California **USA 15**

PC98

Designed by Robert Reynolds

1988, Sept. 20 | | **Litho.**
UX125 PC98 15c **multicolored** .30 .75
    First day cancel, San Simeon, CA *(84,786)* 1.00
    a. Black, magenta & tagging omitted *750.00*
    b. Black, blue, yellow & tagging omitted *2,000.*
    c. Black, magenta, yellow & tagging
        omitted *1,000.*
    d. Black & tagging omitted *2,000.*
    e. Black, blue & tagging omitted —

The Federalist Papers, 1787-88 **USA 15**

Pressman, New Yorker Reading Newspaper,
1787 — PC99

Designed by Roy Andersen

1988, Oct. 27 | | **Litho.**
UX126 PC99 15c **multicolored** .30 .75
    First day cancel, New York, NY
    (37,661) 1.00

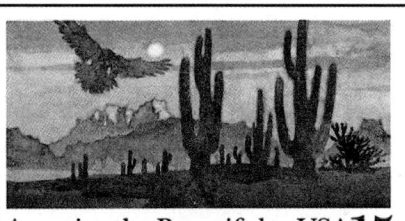

America the Beautiful **USA 15**

Red-tailed Hawk and Sonora Desert at
Sunset — PC100

Designed by Bart Forbes

1989, Jan. 13 | | **Litho.**
UX127 PC100 15c **multicolored** .30 .75
    First day cancel, Tucson, AZ
    (51,891) 1.00

USA 15

Healy Hall, Georgetown University — PC101

Designed by John Morrell. Inscription at lower left: "Healy Hall
/ Georgetown / Washington, DC / HISTORIC PRESERVATION."

1989, Jan. 23 | | **Litho.**
UX128 PC101 15c **multicolored** .30 .75
    First day cancel, Washington,
    DC *(54,897)* 1.00

America the Beautiful **USA 15**

Great Blue Heron, Marsh — PC102

Designed by Bart Forbes

1989, Mar. 17 | | **Litho.**
UX129 PC102 15c **multicolored** .30 .75
    First day cancel, Okefenokee,
    GA *(58,208)* 1.25

Settling of Oklahoma **15 USA**

Settling of Oklahoma — PC103

Designed by Bradbury Thompson

1989, Apr. 22 | | **Litho.**
UX130 PC103 15c **multicolored** .30 .75
    First day cancel, Guthrie, OK
    (68,689) 1.00

Used values are for contemporaneous usage
without additional postage applied. Used values
for international-rate cards are for proper usage.

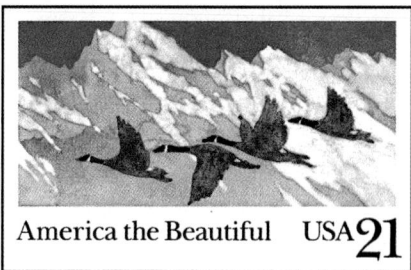

America the Beautiful **USA 21**

Canada Geese and Mountains — PC104

Designed by Bart Forbes

1989, May 5 **Litho.** **For Use to Canada**
UX131 PC104 21c **multicolored** .40 17.50
    First day cancel, Denver, CO
    (59,303) 1.25

America the Beautiful **USA 15**

Seashore — PC105

Designed by Bart Forbes

1989, June 17 | | **Litho.**
UX132 PC105 15c **multicolored** .30 .75
    First day cancel, Cape Hatter-
    as, NC *(67,073)* 1.25

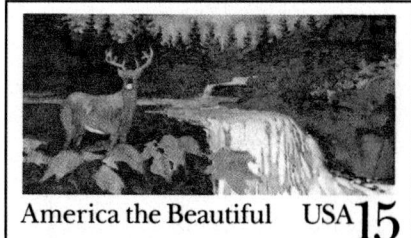

America the Beautiful **USA 15**

PC106

Designed by Bart Forbes

1989, Aug. 26 | | **Litho.**
UX133 PC106 15c **multicolored** .30 .75
    First day cancel, Cherokee,
    NC *(67,878)* 1.25

USA 15

Jane Addams' Hull House Community Center 1889,
Chicago — PC107

Designed by Michael Hagel

1989, Sept. 16 | | **Litho.**
UX134 PC107 15c **multicolored** .30 .75
    First day cancel, Chicago, IL
    (53,773) 1.00

Aerial View of Independence Hall,
Philadelphia — PC108

Designed by Bart Forbes

1989, Sept. 25   **Litho.**
UX135 PC108 15c **multicolored**   .30 .75
    First day cancel, Philadelphia,
    PA *(61,659)*   1.00
     See No. UX139.

Inner Harbor, Baltimore — PC109

Designed by Bart Forbes

1989, Oct. 7   **Litho.**
UX136 PC109 15c **multicolored**   .30 .75
    First day cancel, Baltimore,
    MD *(58,746)*   1.00
     See No. UX140.

59th Street Bridge, New York City — PC110

Designed by Bart Forbes

1989, Nov. 8   **Litho.**
UX137 PC110 15c **multicolored**   .30 .75
    First day cancel, New York, NY
    (48,044)   1.00
     See No. UX141.

West Face of the Capitol, Washington D.C. — PC111

Designed by Bart Forbes

1989, Nov. 26   **Litho.**
UX138 PC111 15c **multicolored**   .30 .75
    First day cancel, Washington,
    DC   1.00
     See No. UX142.

1989, Dec. 1   **Litho.**

Designed by Bart Forbes. Issued in sheets of 4 + 2 inscribed labels picturing 20th UPU Congress or World Stamp Expo '89 emblems, and rouletted 9½ on 2 or 3 sides.

UX139 PC108 15c **multicolored**   3.25 *4.00*
    First day cancel, Washington, DC   1.00
UX140 PC109 15c **multicolored**   3.25 *4.00*
    First day cancel, Washington, DC   1.00
UX141 PC110 15c **multicolored**   3.25 *4.00*
    First day cancel, Washington, DC   1.00
UX142 PC111 15c **multicolored**   3.25 *4.00*
    First day cancel, Washington, DC   1.00
    a.   Sheet of 4, #UX139-UX142   14.00
     Nos. UX135-UX142 (8)   14.20 *19.00*

Unlike Nos. UX135-UX138, Nos. UX139-UX142 do not contain inscription and copyright symbol at lower left. Order on sheet is Nos. UX140, UX139, UX142, UX141.

Most copies of No. UX142a and UX139 are bent at the upper right corner.

The White House — PC112

Jefferson Memorial — PC113

Designed by Pierre Mion. Space for message at left.

1989   **Litho.**
UX143 PC112 15c **multicolored,** *Nov. 30*   1.50 *2.50*
    First day cancel, Washington, DC   2.00
UX144 PC113 15c **multicolored,** *Dec. 2*   1.50 *2.00*
    First day cancel, Washington, DC   2.00

Nos. UX143-UX144 sold for 50c each. Illustrations of the buildings without denominations are shown on the back of the card

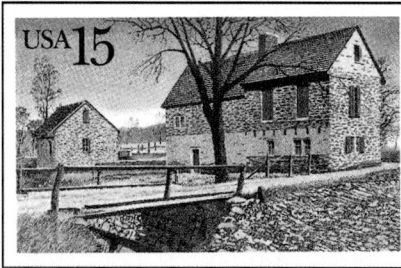

Rittenhouse Paper Mill, Germantown, PA — PC114

Designed by Harry Devlin.

1990, Mar. 13   **Litho.**
UX145 PC114 15c **multicolored**   .30 .40
    First day cancel, New York, NY
    (9,866)   1.00

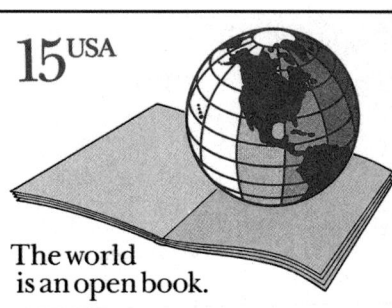

World Literacy Year — PC115

Designed by Joe Brockert.

1990, Mar. 22   **Lith**
UX146 PC115 15c **multicolored**   .30
    First day cancel, Washington,
    DC *(11,163)*   1

PC116

Designed by Bradbury Thompson. Inscription in upper le corner: "Fur Traders Descending the Missouri / George Cale Bingham, 1845 / Metropolitan Museum of Art".

1990, May 4   **Lith**
UX147 PC116 15c **multicolored**   1.50 2.
    First day cancel, St. Louis, MO
    (13,632)   2.

No. UX147 sold for 50c and shows more of the painti without the denomination on the back.

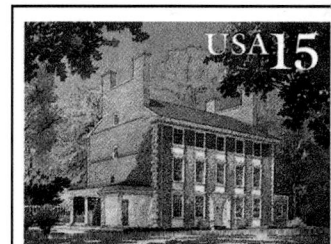

PC117

Designed by Frank Constantino. Inscription at lower lef "HISTORIC PRESERVATION SERIES / Isaac Royall House 1700s / Medford, Massachusetts / National Historic Landmark

1990, June 16   **Litho**
UX148 PC117 15c **multicolored**   .30 .7
    First day cancel, Medford, MA
    (21,708)   1.0

Quadrangle, Stanford University — PC119

Designed by Jim M'Guinness.

1990, Sept. 30   **Litho.**
UX150 PC119 15c **multicolored**   .30 .75
    First day cancel, Stanford, CA
    (28,430)   1.00

Constitution Hall, Washington, DC — PC120

Designed by Pierre Mion. Inscription at upper left: "Washington: Constitution Hall (at right)/ Memorial Continental Hall (reverse side) / Centennial, Daughters of the American Revolution".

1990, Oct. 11 **Litho.**
UX151 PC120 15c **multicolored** 1.50 2.00
First day cancel, Washington, DC *(33,254)* 2.00

No. UX151 sold for 50c.

Chicago Orchestra Hall — PC121

Designed by Michael Hagel. Inscription at lower left: "Chicago: Orchestra Hall / HISTORIC PRESERVATION / Chicago Symphony Orchestra / Centennial, 1891-1991".

1990, Oct. 19 **Litho.**
UX152 PC121 15c **multicolored** .30 .75
First day cancel, Chicago, IL *(28,546)* 1.00

PC122

Designed by Richard Sheaff.

1991, Jan. 24 **Litho.**
UX153 PC122 19c **rose, ultramarine & black** .40 .75
First day cancel, Washington, DC *(26,690)* 1.00

PC123

Designed by Howard Koslow.

1991, Apr. 1 **Litho.**
UX154 PC123 19c **multicolored** .40 .75
First day cancel, New York, NY *(27,063)* 1.00

Old Red, University of Texas Medical Branch, Galveston, Cent. — PC124

Designed by Don Adair.

1991, June 14 **Litho.**
UX155 PC124 19c **multicolored** .40 .75
First day cancel, Galveston, TX *(24,308)* 1.00

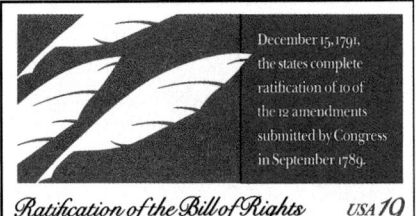

Ratification of the Bill of Rights, Bicent. — PC125

Designed by Mark Zaref.

1991, Sept. 25 **Litho.**
UX156 PC125 19c **red, blue & black** .40 .75
First day cancel, Richmond, VA *(27,457)* 1.00

Main Building, University of Notre Dame PC126

Designed by Frank Costantino. Inscription at lower left: Notre Dame / Sesquicentennial / 1842-1992.

1991, Oct. 15 **Litho.**
UX157 PC126 19c **multicolored** .40 .75
First day cancel, Notre Dame, IN *(34,325)* 1.00

Niagara Falls — PC127

Designed by Wendell Minor.

1991, Aug. 21 **Litho.**
For Use to Canada & Mexico
UX158 PC127 30c **multicolored** .75 9.00
First day cover, Niagara Falls, NY *(29,762)* 1.25

Tagged
Postal cards from No. UX57 onward are either tagged or printed with luminescent ink unless otherwise noted.

The Old Mill — PC128

Designed by Harry Devlin. Inscription at lower left: The Old Mill / University of Vermont / Bicentennial.

1991, Oct. 29 **Litho.**
UX159 PC128 19c **multicolored** .40 .75
First day cancel, Burlington, VT *(23,965)* 1.00

Wadsworth Atheneum, Hartford, CT — PC129

Designed by Frank Costantino. Inscription at lower left: Wadsworth Atheneum / Hartford, Connecticut / 150th Anniversary / 1842-1992.

1992, Jan. 16 **Litho.**
UX160 PC129 19c **multicolored** .40 .75
First day cancel, Hartford, CT *(41,499)* 1.00

Cobb Hall, University of Chicago — PC130

Designed by Michael P. Hagel. Inscription at lower left: Cobb Hall / The University of Chicago / Centennial Year, 1991-1992.

1992, Jan. 23 **Litho.**
UX161 PC130 19c **multicolored** .40 .75
First day cancel, Chicago, IL *(27,150)* 1.00

Waller Hall, Willamette University — PC131

Designed by Bradbury Thompson. Inscription at lower left: Waller Hall / Salem, Oregon / Willamette University / Sesquicentennial / 1842-1992.

1992, Feb. 1 **Litho.**
UX162 PC131 19c **multicolored** .40 .75
First day cancel, Salem, OR *(28,463)* 1.00

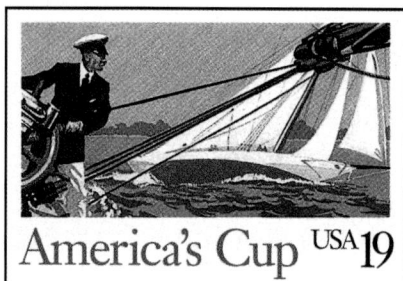

PC132

Designed by Dennis Simon. Space for message at left. Inscription at upper left: "At right: The Reliance, USA 1903 / Reverse: The Ranger, USA 1937."

1992, May 6   **Litho.**
UX163 PC132 19c **multicolored**   1.75 *3.00*
         First day cancel, San Diego,
         CA *(19,944)*   2.00
    No. UX163 sold for 50 cents.

PC133

Designed by Ken Hodges.

1992, May 9   **Litho.**
UX164 PC133 19c **multicolored**   .40 *.75*
         First day cancel, Stevenson,
         WA *(32,344)*   1.00

Ellis Island Immigration Museum — PC134

Designed by Howard Koslow. Inscription at lower left: "Ellis Island / Centennial 1992."

1992, May 11   **Litho.**
UX165 PC134 19c **multicolored**   .40 *.75*
         First day cancel, Ellis Island,
         NY *(38,482)*   1.00

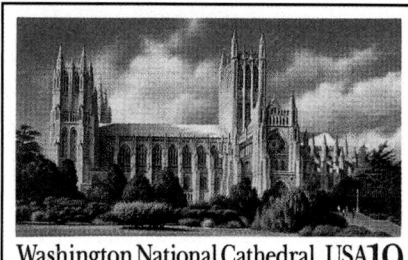

PC135

Designed by Howard Koslow.

1993, Jan. 6   **Litho.**
UX166 PC135 19c **multicolored**   .40 *.75*
         First day cancel, Washington,
         DC *(8,315)*   1.00

PC136

Designed by Pierre Mion.

1993, Feb. 8   **Litho.**
UX167 PC136 19c **multicolored**   .40 *.75*
         First day cancel, Williamsburg,
         VA *(9,758)*   1.00

Opening of Holocaust Memorial Museum — PC137

Designed by Tom Engeman. Space for message at left. Inscription at upper left: "Washington, DC: / United States / Holocaust Memorial Museum."

1993, Mar. 23   **Litho.**
UX168 PC137 19c **multicolored**   1.75 *3.00*
         First day cancel, Washington,
         DC *(8,234)*   2.00
    No. UX168 sold for 50c, and shows aerial view of museum on the back.

PC138

Designed by Michael Hagel.

1993, June 13   **Litho.**
UX169 PC138 19c **multicolored**   .40 *.75*
         First day cancel, Fort Recov-
         ery, OH *(8,254)*   1.00

University of North Carolina Bicentennial

PC139

Designed by Robert Timberlake.

1993, Sept. 14   **Litho.**
UX170 PC139 19c **multicolored**   .40 *.75*
         First day cancel, Chapel Hill,
         NC *(7,796)*   1.00

PC140

Designed by Frank Constantino.

1993, Sept. 17   **Lith**
UX171 PC140 19c **multicolored**   .40
         First day cancel, Worcester,
         MA *(4,680)*   1.

PC141

Designed by Michael Hagel.

1993, Oct. 9   **Litho**
UX172 PC141 19c **multicolored**   .40 *.7*
         First day cancel, Jacksonville,
         IL *(5,269)*   1.0

PC142

Designed by Harry Devlin.

1993, Oct. 14   **Litho.**
UX173 PC142 19c **multicolored**   .40 *.7*
         First day cancel, Brunswick,
         ME *(33,750 est.)*   1.0

PC143

Designed by Michael Hagel.

1994, Feb. 12   **Litho.**
UX174 PC143 19c **multicolored**   .40 *.75*
         First day cancel, Springfield, IL
         (26,164)   1.00

PC144

Designed by Michael Hagel.

					Litho.
	94, Mar. 11				**Litho.**
175	PC144	19c	**multicolored**	.40	.75
	First day cancel, Springfield, OH (20,230)				1.00

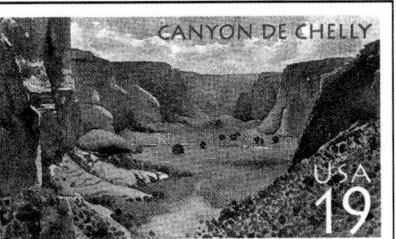

PC145

Designed by William Matthews.

	94, Aug. 11				**Litho.**
X176	PC145	19c	**multicolored**	.40	.75
	First day cancel, Chinle, AZ (19,826)				1.00

St. Louis Union Station — PC146

Designed by Harry Devlin.

	994, Sept. 3				**Litho.**
X177	PC146	19c	**multicolored**	.40	.75
	First day cancel, St. Louis, MO (38,881)				1.00

Legends of the West Type

Designed by Mark Hess.

	994, Oct. 18				**Litho.**
JX178	A2197	19c	Home on the Range	1.10	3.00
JX179	A2197	19c	Buffalo Bill	1.10	3.00
JX180	A2197	19c	Jim Bridger	1.10	3.00
JX181	A2197	19c	Annie Oakley	1.10	3.00
JX182	A2197	19c	Native American Culture	1.10	3.00
JX183	A2197	19c	Chief Joseph	1.10	3.00
JX184	A2197	19c	Bill Pickett (revised)	1.10	3.00
JX185	A2197	19c	Bat Masterson	1.10	3.00
JX186	A2197	19c	John Fremont	1.10	3.00
JX187	A2197	19c	Wyatt Earp	1.10	3.00
JX188	A2197	19c	Nellie Cashman	1.10	3.00
JX189	A2197	19c	Charles Goodnight	1.10	3.00
JX190	A2197	19c	Geronimo	1.10	3.00
JX191	A2197	19c	Kit Carson	1.10	3.00
JX192	A2197	19c	Wild Bill Hickok	1.10	3.00
JX193	A2197	19c	Western Wildlife	1.10	3.00
JX194	A2197	19c	Jim Beckwourth	1.10	3.00
JX195	A2197	19c	Bill Tilghman	1.10	3.00
JX196	A2197	19c	Sacagawea	1.10	3.00
JX197	A2197	19c	Overland Mail	1.10	3.00
	Nos. UX178-UX197 (20)			22.00	
	First day cancel, #UX178-UX197, any card, Tucson, AZ, Lawton, OK or Laramie, WY (10,000 USPS est.)				1.50

Nos. UX178-UX197 sold in packages of 20 different for $7.95.

Red Barn — PC147

Designed by Wendell Minor.

	1995, Jan. 3				**Litho.**
UX198	PC147	20c	**multicolored**	.40	.60
	First day cancel, Williamsburg, PA				1.00

First day cancellation was applied to 54,102 of Nos. U632, UX198.

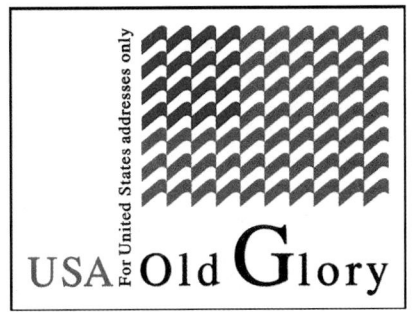

PC148

	1995				**Litho.**
UX199	PC148	(20c)	**black, blue & red**	3.25	2.50

No. UX199 was only available through the Philatelic Fulfillment Center after its announcement 1/12/95. Cards submitted for first day cancels received a 12/13/94 cancel, even though they were not available on that date.

Civil War Types

Designed by Mark Hess.

	1995, June 29				**Litho.**
UX200	A2289	20c	Monitor & Virginia	1.75	3.00
UX201	A2289	20c	Robert E. Lee	1.75	3.00
UX202	A2289	20c	Clara Barton	1.75	3.00
UX203	A2289	20c	Ulysses S. Grant	1.75	3.00
UX204	A2289	20c	Battle of Shiloh	1.75	3.00
UX205	A2289	20c	Jefferson Davis	1.75	3.00
UX206	A2289	20c	David Farragut	1.75	3.00
UX207	A2289	20c	Frederick Douglass	1.75	3.00
UX208	A2289	20c	Raphael Semmes	1.75	3.00
UX209	A2289	20c	Abraham Lincoln	1.75	3.00
UX210	A2289	20c	Harriet Tubman	1.75	3.00
UX211	A2289	20c	Stand Watie	1.75	3.00
UX212	A2289	20c	Joseph E. Johnston	1.75	3.00
UX213	A2289	20c	Winfield Hancock	1.75	3.00
UX214	A2289	20c	Mary Chesnut	1.75	3.00
UX215	A2289	20c	Battle of Chancellorsville	1.75	3.00
UX216	A2289	20c	William T. Sherman	1.75	3.00
UX217	A2289	20c	Phoebe Pember	1.75	3.00
UX218	A2289	20c	Stonewall Jackson	1.75	3.00
UX219	A2289	20c	Battle of Gettysburg	1.75	3.00
	Nos. UX200-UX219 (20)			35.00	
	First day cancel, any card, Gettysburg, PA				1.50
	First day cancel, any card, any other city				1.50

Nos. UX200-UX219 sold in packages of 20 different for $7.95.

PC148a

For International Use

	1995, Aug. 24				**Litho.**
UX219A	PC148a	50c	**multicolored**	1.25	9.00
	First day cancel, St. Louis, MO (6,008)				1.25

PC149

Designed by Richard Sheaff.

	1995, Sept. 3				**Litho.**
UX220	PC149	20c	**multicolored**	.40	.75
	First day cancel, Hunt Valley, MD (5,281)				1.00

Comic Strip Types

Designed by Carl Herrman.

	1995, Oct. 1				**Litho.**
UX221	A2313	20c	The Yellow Kid	2.50	3.00
UX222	A2313	20c	Katzenjammer Kids	2.50	3.00
UX223	A2313	20c	Little Nemo in Slumberland	2.50	3.00
UX224	A2313	20c	Bringing Up Father	2.50	3.00
UX225	A2313	20c	Krazy Kat	2.50	3.00
UX226	A2313	20c	Rube Goldberg's Inventions	2.50	3.00
UX227	A2313	20c	Toonerville Folks	2.50	3.00
UX228	A2313	20c	Gasoline Alley	2.50	3.00
UX229	A2313	20c	Barney Google	2.50	3.00
UX230	A2313	20c	Little Orphan Annie	2.50	3.00
UX231	A2313	20c	Popeye	2.50	3.00
UX232	A2313	20c	Blondie	2.50	3.00
UX233	A2313	20c	Dick Tracy	2.50	3.00
UX234	A2313	20c	Alley Oop	2.50	3.00
UX235	A2313	20c	Nancy	2.50	3.00
UX236	A2313	20c	Flash Gordon	2.50	3.00
UX237	A2313	20c	Li'l Abner	2.50	3.00
UX238	A2313	20c	Terry and the Pirates	2.50	3.00
UX239	A2313	20c	Prince Valiant	2.50	3.00
UX240	A2313	20c	Brenda Starr Reporter	2.50	3.00
	Nos. UX221-UX240 (20)			50.00	
	First day cancel, any card, Boca Raton, FL				1.50

Nos. UX221-UX240 sold in packages of 20 different for $7.95.

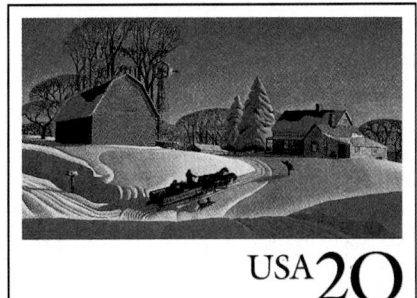

Winter Scene — PC150

	1996, Feb. 23				**Litho.**
UX241	PC150	20c	**multicolored**	.40	.40
	First day cancel, Watertown, NY (11,764)				1.00

Summer Olympics Type

Designed by Richard Waldrep.

	1996, May 2				**Litho.**
	Size: 150x108mm				
UX242	A2368	20c	Men's cycling	2.75	3.00
UX243	A2368	20c	Women's diving	2.75	3.00
UX244	A2368	20c	Women's running	2.75	3.00
UX245	A2368	20c	Men's canoeing	2.75	3.00
a.	Tagging omitted			—	
UX246	A2368	20c	Decathlon (javelin)	2.75	3.00
a.	Inverted impression of entire address side, men's cycling picture on reverse			500.00	
UX247	A2368	20c	Women's soccer	2.75	3.00
UX248	A2368	20c	Men's shot put	2.75	3.00
UX249	A2368	20c	Women's sailboarding	2.75	3.00
UX250	A2368	20c	Women's gymnastics	2.75	3.00
UX251	A2368	20c	Freestyle wrestling	2.75	3.00
UX252	A2368	20c	Women's softball	2.75	3.00
UX253	A2368	20c	Women's swimming	2.75	3.00
UX254	A2368	20c	Men's sprints	2.75	3.00
UX255	A2368	20c	Men's rowing	2.75	3.00
UX256	A2368	20c	Beach volleyball	2.75	3.00
UX257	A2368	20c	Men's basketball	2.75	3.00
UX258	A2368	20c	Equestrian	2.75	3.00
UX259	A2368	20c	Men's gymnastics	2.75	3.00
UX260	A2368	20c	Men's swimming	2.75	3.00

UX261 A2368 20c Men's hurdles   2.75 *3.00*
  a. Booklet of 20 postal cards, #UX242-
      UX261   55.00
      First day cancel, any card,
      Washington, DC   1.50

First day cancels of Nos. UX242-UX261 were available as sets from the US Postal Service. Unused sets of Nos. UX242-UX261 were not available from the US Philatelic Fullfillment Center for several months after the "official" first day.

St. John's College, Annapolis, Maryland

PC151

Designed by Harry Devlin.

1996, June 1   **Litho.**
UX262 PC151 20c **multicolored**   .50 .75
      First day cancel, Annapolis,
      MD *(8,793)*   1.00

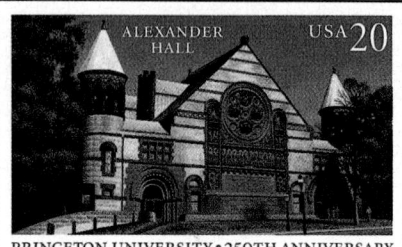

PC152

Designed by Howard Koslow.

1996, Sept. 20   **Litho.**
UX263 PC152 20c **multicolored**   .50 .75
      First day cancel, Princeton, NJ
      (11,621)   1.00

Endangered Species Type
Designed by James Balog.

1996, Oct. 2   **Litho.**
UX264 A2403 20c Florida panther   3.50 1.75
UX265 A2403 20c Black-footed ferret   3.50 1.75
UX266 A2403 20c American crocodile   3.50 1.75
UX267 A2403 20c Piping plover   3.50 1.75
UX268 A2403 20c Gila trout   3.50 1.75
UX269 A2403 20c Florida manatee   3.50 1.75
UX270 A2403 20c Schaus swallowtail butterfly   3.50 1.75
UX271 A2403 20c Woodland caribou   3.50 1.75
UX272 A2403 20c Thick-billed parrot   3.50 1.75
UX273 A2403 20c San Francisco garter snake   3.50 1.75
UX274 A2403 20c Ocelot   3.50 1.75
UX275 A2403 20c Wyoming toad   3.50 1.75
UX276 A2403 20c California condor   3.50 1.75
UX277 A2403 20c Hawaiian monk seal   3.50 1.75
UX278 A2403 20c Brown pelican   3.50 1.75
  a. Booklet of 15 cards, #UX264-UX278   55.00
      First day cancel, #UX264-UX278, any
      card, San Diego, CA *(5,000)*   1.75

Nos. UX264-UX278 were issued bound three-to-a-page in a souvenir booklet that was sold for $11.95.

Love (Swans) Type
Designed by Supon Design.

1997, Feb. 4   **Litho.**
UX279 A2415 20c multicolored   .80 1.10

Stamp Designs Depicted on Reverse of Card
      Scott 2814   2.50 1.10
      Scott 2815   2.50 1.10
      Scott 3123   2.50 1.10
      Scott 3124   2.50 1.10
      Sheet of 4, #2814-2815, 3123-3124   10.00
      Scott 2202   7.50 1.10
      Scott 2248   7.50 1.10
      Scott 2440   7.50 1.10
      Scott 2813   7.50 1.10
      Sheet of 4, #2202, 2248, 2440, 2813 30.00

No. UX279 was sold in sets of 3 sheets of 4 picture postal cards with 8 different designs for $6.95 (two sheets of #2814-2815, 3123-3124 and one sheet of #2202, 2248, 2440, 2813). The cards are separated by microperfs. The picture side of each card depicted a previously released Love stamp design without the inscriptions and value.

First day cancels were not available on Feb. 4. It was announced after Feb. 4 that collectors could purchase the cards and send them to the U.S.P.S. for First Day cancels.

PC153

Designed by Howard Koslow.

1997, May 7   **Litho.**
UX280 PC153 20c **multicolored**   .50 .75
      First day cancel, New York,
      NY *(9,576)*   1.00

Bugs Bunny Type
Designed by Warner Bros.

1997, May 22   **Litho.**
UX281 A2425 20c **multicolored**   1.25 *2.00*
      First day cancel, Burbank, CA   1.75
  a. Booklet of 10 cards   12.50

No. UX281a sold for $5.95.
First day cancellations applied to 378,142 of Nos. UX281 and 3138.

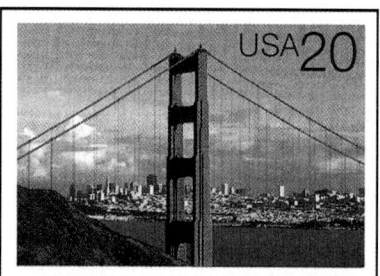

Golden Gate in Daylight — PC154

Golden Gate at Sunset — PC155

Designed by Carol Simowitz.

1997, June 2   **Litho.**
UX282 PC154 20c **multicolored**, *June 2*   .40 *.80*
      First day cancel, San Francis-
      co, CA   1.25

For International Use
UX283 PC155 50c **multicolored**, *June 3*   1.10 2.50
      First day cancel, San Francis-
      co, CA   2.00

First day cancellation was applied to 21,189 of Nos. UX282-UX283.

PC156

Designed by Richard Sheaff.

1997, Sept. 7   **Lith**
UX284 PC156 20c **multicolored**   .40
      First day cancel, Baltimore,
      MD *(9,611)*   1

Similar to Types A2451-A2455 with 20c Denomination
Designed by Derry Noyes.

1997, Sept. 30   **Lith**
UX285 A2451 20c Phantom of the Opera   1.50 1
UX286 A2452 20c Dracula   1.50 1
UX287 A2453 20c Frankenstein's Monster   1.50 1.
UX288 A2454 20c The Mummy   1.50 1.
UX289 A2455 20c The Wolf Man   1.50 1.
  a. Booklet of 20 cards, 4 each #UX285-
      UX289   30.00
      First day cancel, #UX285-
      UX289, any card, Universal
      City, CA   1.

Nos. UX285-UX289 were issued bound in a booklet of cards containing four of each card. Booklet was sold in packa for $5.95.

The Lyceum, University of Mississippi, Oxford

PC157

Designed by Howard Paine.

1998, Apr. 20   **Lithc**
UX290 PC157 20c **multicolored**   .50 .7
      First day cancel, University,
      MS *(22,276)*   1.0

Similar to Sylvester & Tweety with 20c Denomination
Designed by Brenda Guttman.

1998, Apr. 27   **Litho**
UX291 A2487 20c **multicolored**   1.40 *2.0*
      First day cancel, New York,
      NY   1.7*
  a. Booklet of 10 cards   14.00

No. UX291a sold for $5.95.
First day cancellations applied to 231,839 of Nos. UX291 3204 and 3205.

Girard College Philadelphia, PA 1848-1998

PC158

Designed by Phil Jordan.

1998, May 1   **Litho.**
UX292 PC158 20c **multicolored**   .50 *.75*
      First day cancel, Philadelphia,
      PA *(13,853)*   1.00

Similar to Tropical Birds with 20c Denomination and No Inscription

Designed by Phil Jordan.

1998, July 29 — **Litho.**

X293	A2503 20c Antillean euphonia	1.00	1.75
X294	A2504 20c Green-throated carib	1.00	1.75
X295	A2505 20c Crested honeycreeper	1.00	1.75
X296	A2506 20c Cardinal honeyeater	1.00	1.75
a.	Booklet of 20 cards, 5 ea #UX293-UX296	20.00	
	First day cancel, #UX293-UX296, any card, Ponce PR		1.75

Nos. UX293-UX296 were issued bound in a booklet of 20 cards containing five of each card. Illustration of the stamp without denomination is shown on the back of each card. Booklet was sold in packages for $6.95.

American Ballet Type

Designed by Derry Noyes.

1998, Sept. 16 — **Litho.**

X297	A2517 20c multicolored	1.25	1.40
a.	Booklet of 10 cards	12.50	
	First day cancel, New York, NY		1.75

No. UX297a was sold for $5.95.

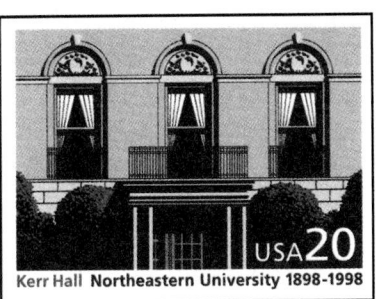
PC159

Designed by Richard Sheaff.

1998, Oct. 3 — **Litho.**

UX298	PC159 20c multicolored	.50	.75
	First day cancel, Boston, MA (14,812)		1.00

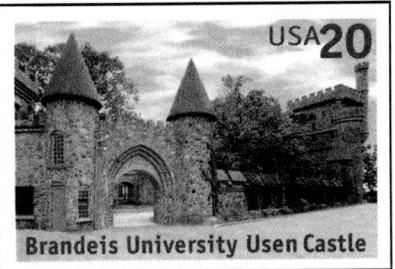
PC160

Designed by Richard Sheaff.

1998, Oct. 17 — **Litho.**

UX299	PC160 20c multicolored	.50	.75
	First day cancel, Waltham, MA (14,137)		1.00

Love Type

Designed by John Grossman, Holly Sudduth.

1999, Jan. 28 — **Litho.**

UX300	A2537 20c multicolored	1.25	1.50
	First day cancel, Loveland, CO	1.00	

No. UX300 was sold in packs containing 5 sheets of 4 cards for $6.95.

University of Wisconsin-Madison • Bascom Hill
PC161

Designed by Carl Herrman.

1999, Feb. 5 — **Litho.**

UX301	PC161 20c multicolored	.50	.50
	First day cancel, Madison, WI (12,582)		1.00

PC162

Designed by Derry Noyes.

1999, Feb. 11

UX302	PC162 20c multicolored	.50	.50
	First day cancel, Lexington, VA (17,556)		1.00

PC163

Designed by Richard Sheaff.

1999, Mar. 11

UX303	PC163 20c red & black	.50	.50
	First day cancel, Newport, RI (13,649)		1.00

Daffy Duck Type

Designed by Ed Wieczyk.

1999, Apr. 16 — **Litho.**

UX304	A2554 20c multicolored	1.40	1.40
	First day cancel, Los Angeles, CA		1.40
a.	Booklet of 10 cards	14.00	

No. UX304a sold for $6.95.
First day cancellation was applied to 177,988 of UX304, 3306 and 3307.

PC164

Designed by Richard Sheaff.

1999, May 14 — **Litho.**

UX305	PC164 20c multicolored	.50	.50
	First day cancel, Mount Vernon, VA (14,642)		1.00

Block Island Lighthouse — PC165

Designed by Derry Noyes.

1999, July 24 — **Litho.**

UX306	PC165 20c multicolored	.40	.45
	First day cancel, Block Island, RI (12,694)		1.25

Famous Trains Type

Designed by Howard Paine.

1999, Aug. 26 — **Litho.**

UX307	A2583 20c Super Chief	1.25	1.00
UX308	A2582 20c Hiawatha	1.25	1.00
UX309	A2579 20c Daylight	1.25	1.00
UX310	A2580 20c Congressional	1.25	1.00
UX311	A2581 20c 20th Century Limited	1.25	1.00
a.	Booklet of 20 cards, 4 ea #UX307-UX311	22.50	
	First day cancel, #UX307-UX311, any card, Cleveland, OH		1.75
	First day cancel, #UX307-UX311, any card, any other city		1.75

Nos. UX307-UX311 were issued bound in a booklet of 20 cards containing four of each card. Booklet sold for $6.95.

PC166

Designed by Ethel Kessler.

2000, Feb. 28 — **Litho.**

UX312	PC166 20c multicolored	.40	.50
	First day cancel, Salt Lake City, UT (14,230)		1.00

PC167 — Ryman Auditorium, Nashville, Tennessee

Designed by Richard Sheaff.

2000, Mar. 18 — **Litho.**

UX313	PC167 20c multicolored	.40	.50
	First day cancel, Nashville, TN (12,690)		1.00

Road Runner & Wile E. Coyote Type

Designed by Ed Wleczyk, Warner Bros.

2000, Apr. 26 — **Litho.**

UX314	A2622 20c multicolored	1.40	1.40
	First day cancel, Phoenix, AZ		1.40
a.	Booklet of 10 cards	14.00	

No. UX314a sold for $6.95.
First day cancellation was applied to 154,903 of UX314 and 3391.

Adoption Type

Designed by Greg Berger.

2000, May 10   **Litho.**
UX315 A2628 20c **multicolored**   1.40 1.50
  First day cancel, Beverly Hills,
  CA   1.40
 a. Booklet of 10 cards   14.00

No. UX315a sold for $6.95. The design, without denominations, is shown on the back of the card.
 First day cancellation was applied to 137,903 of UX315 and 3398.

PC168

Designed by Howard Paine.

2000, May 19   **Litho.**
UX316 PC168 20c **multicolored**   .40 *.50*
  First day cancel, Middlebury,
  VT (13,586)   1.00

Stars and Stripes Type
Designed by Richard Sheaff.

2000, June 14   **Litho.**
UX317 A2633 20c Sons of Liberty Flag, 1775   1.50 1.25
UX318 A2633 20c New England Flag, 1775   1.50 1.25
UX319 A2633 20c Forster Flag, 1775   1.50 1.25
UX320 A2633 20c Continental Colors, 1776   1.50 1.25
 a. Sheet of 4 cards, #UX317-UX320 6.50
UX321 A2633 20c Francis Hopkinson Flag,
  1777   1.50 1.25
UX322 A2633 20c Brandywine Flag, 1777   1.50 1.25
UX323 A2633 20c John Paul Jones Flag, 1779   1.50 1.25
UX324 A2633 20c Pierre L'Enfant Flag, 1783   1.50 1.25
 a. Sheet of 4 cards, #UX321-UX324 6.50
UX325 A2633 20c Indian Peace Flag, 1803   1.50 1.25
UX326 A2633 20c Easton Flag, 1814   1.50 1.25
UX327 A2633 20c Star-Spangled Banner, 1814   1.50 1.25
UX328 A2633 20c Bennington Flag, c. 1820   1.50 1.25
 a. Sheet of 4 cards, #UX325-UX328 6.50
UX329 A2633 20c Great Star Flag, 1837   1.50 1.25
UX330 A2633 20c 29-Star Flag, 1847   1.50 1.25
UX331 A2633 20c Fort Sumter Flag, 1861   1.50 1.25
UX332 A2633 20c Centennial Flag, 1876   1.50 1.25
 a. Sheet of 4 cards, #UX329-UX332 6.50
UX333 A2633 20c 38-Star Flag, 1877   1.50 1.25
UX334 A2633 20c Peace Flag, 1891   1.50 1.25
UX335 A2633 20c 48-Star Flag, 1912   1.50 1.25
UX336 A2633 20c 50-Star Flag, 1960   1.50 1.25
 a. Sheet of 4 cards, #UX333-UX336 6.50
  First day cancel, any card,
  Baltimore, MD   .90
  Nos. UX317-UX336 (20)   30.00 25.00

Nos. UX320a, UX324a, UX328a, UX332a and UX336a were sold together in a package for $8.95. Microperforations are between individual cards on each sheet. Illustrations of the flags, without denominations, are shown on the back of the cards.

Legends of Baseball Type
Designed by Phil Jordan.

2000, July 6   **Litho.**
UX337 A2638 20c Jackie Robinson   1.50 1.25
UX338 A2638 20c Eddie Collins   1.50 1.25
UX339 A2638 20c Christy Mathewson   1.50 1.25
UX340 A2638 20c Ty Cobb   1.50 1.25
UX341 A2638 20c George Sisler   1.50 1.25
UX342 A2638 20c Rogers Hornsby   1.50 1.25
UX343 A2638 20c Mickey Cochrane   1.50 1.25
UX344 A2638 20c Babe Ruth   1.50 1.25
UX345 A2638 20c Walter Johnson   1.50 1.25
UX346 A2638 20c Roberto Clemente   1.50 1.25
UX347 A2638 20c Lefty Grove   1.50 1.25
UX348 A2638 20c Tris Speaker   1.50 1.25
UX349 A2638 20c Cy Young   1.50 1.25
UX350 A2638 20c Jimmie Foxx   1.50 1.25
UX351 A2638 20c Pie Traynor   1.50 1.25
UX352 A2638 20c Satchel Paige   1.50 1.25
UX353 A2638 20c Honus Wagner   1.50 1.25
UX354 A2638 20c Josh Gibson   1.50 1.25
UX355 A2638 20c Dizzy Dean   1.50 1.25
UX356 A2638 20c Lou Gehrig   1.50 1.25
 a. Booklet of 20 cards, #UX337-UX356 30.00
  First day cancel, any card,
  Atlanta, GA   .90

No. UX356a sold for $8.95.

Christmas Deer Type of 1999
Designed by Tom Nikosey.

2000, Oct. 12 **Litho.** *Rouletted on 2 sides*
UX357 A2600 20c **gold & blue**   1.25 1.25
UX358 A2600 20c **gold & red**   1.25 1.25
UX359 A2600 20c **gold & purple**   1.25 1.25
UX360 A2600 20c **gold & green**   1.25 1.25
 a. Sheet of 4, #UX357-UX360 5.00
  First day cancel, any card,
  Rudolph, WI   1.75

Nos. UX357-UX360 were sold in packs containing five No. UX360a for $8.95.

PC169

Designed by Derry Noyes.

2001, Mar. 30   **Litho.**
UX361 PC169 20c **multicolored**   .40 .60
  First day cancel, New Haven, CT   1.00

PC170

Designed by Ethel Kessler.

2001, Apr. 26   **Litho.**
UX362 PC170 20c **multicolored**   .40 .75
  First day cancel, Columbia, SC   1.00

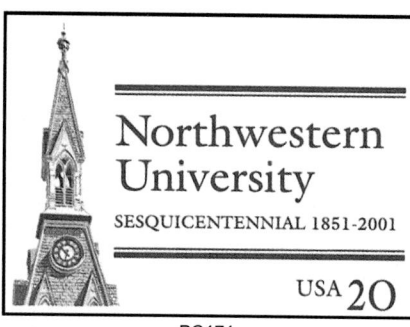

PC171

Designed by Howard Paine.

2001, Apr. 28   **Litho.**
UX363 PC171 20c **multicolored**   .40 .75
  First day cancel, Evanston, IL   1.00

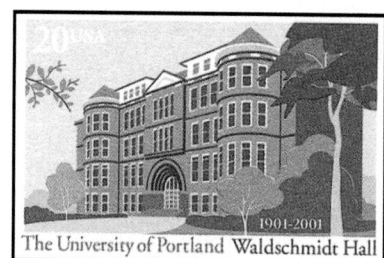

PC172

Designed by Richard Sheaff.

2001, May 1   **Litho.**
UX364 PC172 20c **multicolored**   .40 .65
  First day cancel, Portland, OR   1.00

Legendary Playing Fields Type with 21c Denomination
Designed by Phil Jordan.

2001, June 27   **Lith.**
UX365 A2712 21c Ebbets Field   1.75 1.
UX366 A2713 21c Tiger Stadium   1.75 1.
UX367 A2714 21c Crosley Field   1.75 1.
UX368 A2715 21c Yankee Stadium   1.75 1.
UX369 A2716 21c Polo Grounds   1.75 1.
UX370 A2717 21c Forbes Field   1.75 1.
UX371 A2718 21c Fenway Park   1.75 1.
UX372 A2719 21c Comiskey Park   1.75 1.
UX373 A2720 21c Shibe Park   1.75 1.
UX374 A2721 21c Wrigley Field   1.75 1.
 a. Booklet of 10 cards, #UX365-UX374 22.50

No. UX374a sold for $6.95.

White Barn — PC173

Designed by Derry Noyes.

2001, Sept. 20   **Lith.**
UX375 PC173 21c **multicolored**   .45 .
  First day cancel, Washington, DC   1.0

That's All Folks! Type
Designed by Ed Wleczyk, Warner Bros.

2001, Oct. 1   **Litho.**
UX376 A2736 21c **multicolored**   1.50 1.5
  First day cancel, Beverly Hills, CA   1.5
 a. Booklet of 10 cards   15.00

No. UX376a sold for $7.25.

Christmas Type
Designed by Richard Sheaff.

2001, Oct. 10 **Litho.** *Rouletted on 2 Sides*
UX377 A2740 21c **multicolored**   1.25 1.00
  First day cancel, Santa Claus, IN   1.25
UX378 A2741 21c **multicolored**   1.25 1.00
  First day cancel, Santa Claus, IN   1.25
UX379 A2738 21c **multicolored**   1.25 1.00
  First day cancel, Santa Claus, IN   1.25
UX380 A2739 21c **multicolored**   1.25 1.00
  First day cancel, Santa Claus, IN   1.25
 a. Sheet of 4, #UX377-UX380   5.00

Packages of 5 No. UX380a sold for $9.25.

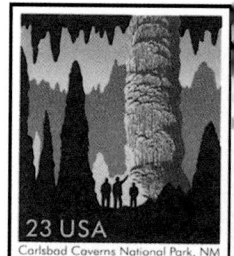

Carlsbad Caverns
National Park — PC174

Designed by Carl Herrman.

2002, June 7   **Litho.**
UX381 PC174 23c **multicolored**   .50 .50
  First day cancel, Carlsbad, NM   1.00
  First day cancel, any other city   1.00

Teddy Bears Type
Designed by Margaret Bauer.

2002, Aug. 15 **Litho.** *Rouletted on 2 Sides*
UX382 A2827 23c Ideal Bear, c. 1905   1.10 1.00
  First day cancel, Atlantic City, NJ   1.00
UX383 A2826 23c Gund Bear, c. 1948   1.10 1.00
  First day cancel, Atlantic City, NJ   1.00
UX384 A2824 23c Bruin Bear, c. 1907   1.10 1.00
  First day cancel, Atlantic City, NJ

85 A2825 23c "Stick" Bear, 1920s   1.10 1.00
    First day cancel, Atlantic City, NJ   1.00
a.   Sheet of 4, #UX382-UX385   5.00

Packages of 5 No. UX385a sold for $9.25.

Christmas Snowmen Type
Designed by Derry Noyes.

02, Oct. 28   Litho.   *Rouletted on 2 Sides*
Design Size: 28x38mm
386 A2844 23c **multicolored**   1.25 1.00
    First day cancel, Houghton, MI   1.00
387 A2845 23c **multicolored**   1.25 1.00
    First day cancel, Houghton, MI   1.00
388 A2846 23c **multicolored**   1.25 1.00
    First day cancel, Houghton, MI   1.00
389 A2847 23c **multicolored**   1.25 1.00
    First day cancel, Houghton, MI   1.00
a.   Sheet of 4, #UX386-UX389   5.00

Packages of 5 #UX389a sold for $9.75.

Old Glory Type
Designed by Richard Sheaff.

03, Apr. 3   Litho.   *Rouletted on 1 Side*
390 A2883 23c **multicolored**   1.10 1.00
    First day cancel, New York, NY   1.00
391 A2884 23c **multicolored**   1.10 1.00
    First day cancel, New York, NY   1.00
392 A2885 23c **multicolored**   1.10 1.00
    First day cancel, New York, NY   1.00
393 A2886 23c **multicolored**   1.10 1.00
    First day cancel, New York, NY   1.00
394 A2887 23c **multicolored**   1.10 1.00
    First day cancel, New York, NY   1.00
a.   Booklet of 20 cards, 4 each #UX390-UX394   22.50

No. UX394a sold for $9.75.

Southeastern Lighthouses Type
Designed by Howard E. Paine.

03, June 13   Litho.   *Rouletted on 1 Side*
395 A2893 23c **multicolored**   1.10 1.00
    First day cancel, Tybee Island, GA   1.00
396 A2894 23c **multicolored**   1.10 1.00
    First day cancel, Tybee Island, GA   1.00
397 A2895 23c **multicolored**   1.10 1.00
    First day cancel, Tybee Island, GA   1.00
398 A2896 23c **multicolored**   1.10 1.00
    First day cancel, Tybee Island, GA   1.00
399 A2897 23c **multicolored**   1.10 1.00
    First day cancel, Tybee Island, GA   1.00
a.   Booklet of 20 cards, 4 each #UX395-UX399   22.50

No. UX399a sold for $9.75.

Ohio University, 200th Anniv. — PC175

Designed by Tom Engemann.

003, Oct. 10   Litho.
X400 PC175 23c **multicolored**   .50 .50
    First day cancel, Athens, OH   1.00

Christmas Music Makers Type
Designed by Ethel Kessler.

003, Oct. 23   Litho.   *Rouletted on 2 Sides*
X401 A2917 23c **multicolored**   1.00 1.00
    First day cancel, New York, NY   1.00
JX402 A2918 23c **multicolored**   1.00 1.00
    First day cancel, New York, NY   1.00
JX403 A2919 23c **multicolored**   1.00 1.00
    First day cancel, New York, NY   1.00
JX404 A2920 23c **multicolored**   1.00 1.00
    First day cancel, New York, NY   1.00
a.   Sheet of 4, #UX401-UX404   4.00

Packages of 5 #UX404a sold for $9.75.

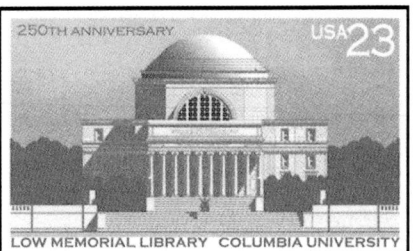

Columbia University, 250th Anniv. — PC176

Designed by Tom Engeman.

2004, Mar. 25   Litho.
UX405 PC176 23c **multicolored**   .50 .50
    First day cancel, New York, NY   1.00

Harriton House, Bryn Mawr, PA, Bicent. PC177

Designed by Carl T. Herrman.

2004, June 10   Litho.
UX406 PC177 23c **multicolored**   .50 .50
    First day cancel, Bryn Mawr, PA   1.00

Disney Type of 2004
Designed by David Pacheco.

2004, June 23   Litho.
UX407 A2950 23c **multicolored**   1.00 1.00
    First day cancel, Anaheim, CA   1.00
UX408 A2951 23c **multicolored**   1.00 1.00
    First day cancel, Anaheim, CA   1.00
UX409 A2949 23c **multicolored**   1.00 1.00
    First day cancel, Anaheim, CA   1.00
UX410 A2952 23c **multicolored**   1.00 1.00
    First day cancel, Anaheim, CA   1.00
a.   Booklet of 20 cards, 5 each #UX407-UX410   20.00

No. UX410a sold for $9.75.

Art of the American Indian Type of 2003
Designed by Richard Sheaff.

2004, Aug. 21   Litho.   *Rouletted on 1 Side*
UX411 A2957 23c Mimbres bowl   1.00 1.00
    First day cancel, Santa Fe, NM   1.00
UX412 A2957 23c Kutenai parfleche   1.00 1.00
    First day cancel, Santa Fe, NM   1.00
UX413 A2957 23c Tlingit sculptures   1.00 1.00
    First day cancel, Santa Fe, NM   1.00
UX414 A2957 23c Ho-Chunk bag   1.00 1.00
    First day cancel, Santa Fe, NM   1.00
UX415 A2957 23c Seminole doll   1.00 1.00
    First day cancel, Santa Fe, NM   1.00
UX416 A2957 23c Mississippian effigy   1.00 1.00
    First day cancel, Santa Fe, NM   1.00
UX417 A2957 23c Acoma pot   1.00 1.00
    First day cancel, Santa Fe, NM   1.00
UX418 A2957 23c Navajo weaving   1.00 1.00
    First day cancel, Santa Fe, NM   1.00
UX419 A2957 23c Seneca carving   1.00 1.00
    First day cancel, Santa Fe, NM   1.00
UX420 A2957 23c Luiseño basket   1.00 1.00
    First day cancel, Santa Fe, NM   1.00
a.   Booklet of 20 cards, 2 each #UX411-UX420   20.00

No. UX420a sold for $9.75.

Cloudscapes Type
Designed by Howard E. Paine.

2004, Oct. 4   Litho.   *Rouletted at Left*
UX421 A2960 23c Cirrus radiatus   1.00 1.00
    First day cancel, Milton, MA   1.00
UX422 A2960 23c Cirrostratus fibratus   1.00 1.00

    First day cancel, Milton, MA   1.00
UX423 A2960 23c Cirrocumulus undulatus   1.00 1.00
    First day cancel, Milton, MA   1.00
UX424 A2960 23c Cumulonimbus mammatus   1.00 1.00
    First day cancel, Milton, MA   1.00
UX425 A2960 23c Cumulonimbus incus   1.00 1.00
    First day cancel, Milton, MA   1.00
UX426 A2960 23c Altocumulus stratiformis   1.00 1.00
    First day cancel, Milton, MA   1.00
UX427 A2960 23c Altostratus translucidus   1.00 1.00
    First day cancel, Milton, MA   1.00
UX428 A2960 23c Altocumulus undulatus   1.00 1.00
    First day cancel, Milton, MA   1.00
UX429 A2960 23c Altocumulus castellanus   1.00 1.00
    First day cancel, Milton, MA   1.00
UX430 A2960 23c Altocumulus lenticularis   1.00 1.00
    First day cancel, Milton, MA   1.00
UX431 A2960 23c Stratocumulus undulatus   1.00 1.00
    First day cancel, Milton, MA   1.00
UX432 A2960 23c Stratus opacus   1.00 1.00
    First day cancel, Milton, MA   1.00
UX433 A2960 23c Cumulus humilis   1.00 1.00
    First day cancel, Milton, MA   1.00
UX434 A2960 23c Cumulus congestus   1.00 1.00
    First day cancel, Milton, MA   1.00
UX435 A2960 23c Cumulonimbus with tornado   1.00 1.00
    First day cancel, Milton, MA   1.00
a.   Booklet of 20, #UX421-UX422, UX425, UX427, UX429, UX431-UX435, 2 each #UX423-UX424, UX426, UX428, UX430   20.00

No. UX435a sold for $9.75.

Disney Type of 2005
Designed by David Pacheco.

2005, June 30   Litho.
UX436 A2989 23c **multicolored**   1.00 1.00
    First day cancel, Anaheim, CA   1.00
UX437 A2990 23c **multicolored**   1.00 1.00
    First day cancel, Anaheim, CA   1.00
UX438 A2991 23c **multicolored**   1.00 1.00
    First day cancel, Anaheim, CA   1.00
UX439 A2992 23c **multicolored**   1.00 1.00
    First day cancel, Anaheim, CA   1.00
a.   Booklet of 20 cards, 5 each #UX436-UX439   20.00

No. UX439a sold for $9.75.

Sporty Cars Type of 2005
Designed by Art M. Fitzpatrick.

2005, Aug. 20   Litho.   *Rouletted at Left*
UX440 A3012 23c 1955 Ford Thunderbird   1.00 1.00
    First day cancel, Detroit, MI   1.75
UX441 A3011 23c 1952 Nash Healey   1.00 1.00
    First day cancel, Detroit, MI   1.75
UX442 A3010 23c 1953 Chevrolet Corvette   1.00 1.00
    First day cancel, Detroit, MI   1.75
UX443 A3008 23c 1953 Studebaker Starliner   1.00 1.00
    First day cancel, Detroit, MI   1.75
UX444 A3009 23c 1954 Kaiser Darrin   1.00 1.00
    First day cancel, Detroit, MI   1.75
a.   Booklet of 20 cards, 4 each #UX440-UX444   20.00

No. UX444a sold for $9.75.

Let's Dance Type
Designed by Ethel Kessler.

2005, Sept. 17   Litho.   *Rouletted at Left*
UX445 A3018 23c Cha cha cha   1.00 1.00
    First day cancel, New York, NY   1.75
    First day cancel, Miami, FL   1.75
UX446 A3019 23c Mambo   1.00 1.00
    First day cancel, New York, NY   1.75
    First day cancel, Miami, FL   1.75
UX447 A3017 23c Salsa   1.00 1.00
    First day cancel, New York, NY   1.75
    First day cancel, Miami, FL   1.75
UX448 A3016 23c Merengue   1.00 1.00
    First day cancel, New York, NY   1.75
    First day cancel, Miami, FL   1.75
a.   Booklet of 20, 5 each #UX445-UX448   20.00

No. UX448a sold for $9.75.

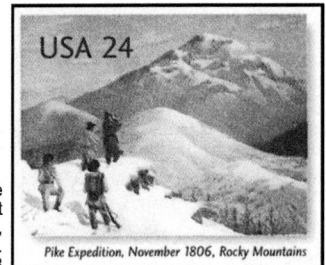

Zebulon Pike Expedition at Pikes Peak, Bicent. PC178

Designed by Carl Herrman.

2006, Jan. 9   **Litho.**
UX449 PC178 24c **multicolored**   .55   .55
  First day cancel, Washington,
  DC   1.75
  First day cancel, any other
  city   1.75

Disney Type of 2006
Designed by David Pacheco.

2006, Apr. 21   **Litho.**   *Rouletted at Left*
UX450 A3066 24c **multicolored**   1.00 1.00
  First day cancel, Orlando, FL   1.75
UX451 A3067 24c **multicolored**   1.00 1.00
  First day cancel, Orlando, FL   1.75
UX452 A3069 24c **multicolored**   1.00 1.00
  First day cancel, Orlando, FL   1.75
UX453 A3068 24c **multicolored**   1.00 1.00
  First day cancel, Orlando, FL   1.75
  a. Booklet of 20, 5 each #UX450-UX453B 20.00
  No. UX453a sold for $9.75.

Baseball Sluggers Type of 2006
Designed by Phil Jordan.

2006, July 15   **Litho.**   *Rouletted at Left*
UX454 A3121 24c Mickey Mantle   1.00 1.00
  First day cancel, Bronx, NY   1.75
UX455 A3118 24c Roy Campanella   1.00 1.00
  First day cancel, Bronx, NY   1.75
UX456 A3119 24c Hank Greenberg   1.00 1.00
  First day cancel, Bronx, NY   1.75
UX457 A3120 24c Mel Ott   1.00 1.00
  First day cancel, Bronx, NY   1.75
  a. Booklet of 20 cards, 5 each #UX454-UX457 20.00
  No. UX457a sold for $9.95.

DC Comics Superheroes Type of 2006
Designed by Carl T. Herrman.

2006, July 20   **Litho.**   *Rouletted at Left*
UX458 A3122 24c Superman cover   1.00 1.00
  First day cancel, San Diego, CA   1.75
UX459 A3122 24c Superman   1.00 1.00
  First day cancel, San Diego, CA   1.75
UX460 A3122 24c Batman cover   1.00 1.00
  First day cancel, San Diego, CA   1.75
UX461 A3122 24c Batman   1.00 1.00
  First day cancel, San Diego, CA   1.75
UX462 A3122 24c Wonder Woman cover   1.00 1.00
  First day cancel, San Diego, CA   1.75
UX463 A3122 24c Wonder Woman   1.00 1.00
  First day cancel, San Diego, CA   1.75
UX464 A3122 24c Green Lantern cover   1.00 1.00
  First day cancel, San Diego, CA   1.75
UX465 A3122 24c Green Lantern   1.00 1.00
  First day cancel, San Diego, CA   1.75
UX466 A3122 24c Green Arrow cover   1.00 1.00
  First day cancel, San Diego, CA   1.75
UX467 A3122 24c Green Arrow   1.00 1.00
  First day cancel, San Diego, CA   1.75
UX468 A3122 24c The Flash cover   1.00 1.00
  First day cancel, San Diego, CA   1.75
UX469 A3122 24c The Flash   1.00 1.00
  First day cancel, San Diego, CA   1.75
UX470 A3122 24c Plastic Man cover   1.00 1.00
  First day cancel, San Diego, CA   1.75
UX471 A3122 24c Plastic Man   1.00 1.00
  First day cancel, San Diego, CA   1.75
UX472 A3122 24c Aquaman cover   1.00 1.00
  First day cancel, San Diego, CA   1.75
UX473 A3122 24c Aquaman   1.00 1.00
  First day cancel, San Diego, CA   1.75
UX474 A3122 24c Supergirl cover   1.00 1.00
  First day cancel, San Diego, CA   1.75
UX475 A3122 24c Supergirl   1.00 1.00
  First day cancel, San Diego, CA   1.75
UX476 A3122 24c Hawkman cover   1.00 1.00
  First day cancel, San Diego, CA   1.75
UX477 A3122 24c Hawkman   1.00 1.00
  First day cancel, San Diego, CA   1.75
  a. Booklet of 20 cards, #UX458-UX477 20.00
  No. UX477a sold for $9.95.

PAID REPLY POSTAL CARDS

These are sold to the public as two unsevered cards, one for message and one for reply. These are listed first as unsevered cards and then as severed cards. Values are for:

Unused cards (both unsevered and severed) without printed or written address or message.

Unsevered cards sell for a premium if never folded.

Used unsevered cards, Message Card with Post Office cancellation and Reply Card uncanceled (from 1968 value is for a single used severed card); and used severed cards with cancellation when current.

Used values for International Paid Reply Cards are for proper usage. Those domestically used or with postage added sell for less than the unused value.

"Preprinted," unused cards (both unsevered and severed) with printed or written address or message. Used value applies after 1952.

First day cancel values are for cards without cachets.

Head of Grant, card framed.
PR1 inscribed "REPLY CARD."

1892, Oct. 25   **Size: 140x89mm**
UY1 PM1+PR1 1c +1c **black**, *buff*, unsevered   37.50 9.00
  Preprinted   15.00
  a. Message card printed on both sides, reply card blank 250.00
  b. Message card blank, reply card printed on both sides 300.00
  c. Cards joined at bottom 200.00 100.00
    Preprinted 100.00
  m. PM1 Message card detached 6.00 1.75
    Preprinted 3.00
  r. PR1 Reply card detached 6.00 1.75
    Preprinted 3.00

For other postal cards of types PM1 and PR1 see No. UY3.

Liberty — PM2

PR2 inscribed "REPLY CARD."

1893, Mar. 1   **For International Use**
UY2 PM2+PR2 2c +2c **blue**, *grayish white*, unsevered 20.00 20.00
  Preprinted 12.50
  a. 2c+2c **dark blue**, *grayish white*, unsevered 20.00 20.00
    Preprinted 12.50
  b. Message card printed on both sides, reply card blank 500.00
  c. Message card blank, reply card printed on both sides —
  d. Message card normal, reply card blank 300.00
  m. PM2 Message card detached 5.00 6.00
    Preprinted 2.50
  r. PR2 Reply card detached 5.00 6.00
    Preprinted 2.50

For other postal cards of types PM2 and PR2 see No. UY11.

Design same as PM1 and PR1, without frame around card
1898, Sept.   **Size: 140x82mm**
UY3 PM1+PR1 1c +1c **black**, *buff*, unsevered 62.50 12.50
  Preprinted 12.50
  a. Message card normal, reply card blank 400.00
  b. Message card printed on both sides, reply card blank 450.00
  c. Message card blank, reply card printed on both sides 400.00
  d. Message card without "Detach annexed card/for answer" 250.00 150.00
    Preprinted —
  e. Message card blank, reply card normal 250.00
  f. Message card normal, reply card double impression, preprinted 825.00
  m. PM1 Message card detached 12.50 2.50

PM3

PR3 pictures Sherman.

1904, Mar. 31
UY4 PM3+PR3 1c +1c **black**, *buff*, unsevered 52.50 6
  Preprinted 9.00
  a. Message card normal, reply card blank 275.00
  b. Message card printed on both sides, reply card blank 950.00
  c. Message card blank, reply card normal 275.00
  d. Message card blank, reply card printed on both sides — 175
    Preprinted 200.00
  m. PM3 Message card detached 9.00 1
    Preprinted 4.00
  r. PR3 Reply card detached 9.00 1
    Preprinted 4.00

PM4

PR4 pictures Martha Washington.

Double frame line around instructions
1910, Sept. 14
UY5 PM4+PR4 1c +1c **blue**, *bluish*, unsevered 160.00 25.
  Preprinted 40.00
  a. Message card normal, reply card blank 325.00
  m. PM4 Message card detached 15.00 3.
    Preprinted 9.00
  r. PR4 Reply card detached 15.00 3.
    Preprinted 9.00

1911, Oct. 27
UY6 PM4+PR4 1c +1c **green**, *cream*, unsevered 160.00 25.0
  Preprinted 60.00
  a. Message card normal, reply card blank —
  m. PM4 Message card detached 22.50 6.5
    Preprinted 12.50
  r. PR4 Reply card detached 22.50 6.5
    Preprinted 12.50

Single frame line around instructions
1915, Sept. 18
UY7 PM4+PR4 1c +1c **green**, *cream*, unsevered 1.25 .5
  Preprinted .60
  a. 1c+1c **dark green**, *buff*, unsevered 1.25 .5
    Preprinted .60
  b. Message card normal, reply card blank —
  m. PM4 Message card detached .30 .2
    Preprinted .20
  r. PR4 Reply card detached .30 .2
    Preprinted .20
  s. As "a," missing Reply indicia 2,000.
  See No. UY13.

PR5

PM5 pictures George Washington.

18, Aug. 2

8	PM5+PR5 2c +2c **red**, *buff*, unsevered		82.50	40.00
	Preprinted		30.00	
1.	PM5 Message card detached		20.00	7.50
	Preprinted		10.00	
r.	PR5 Reply card detached		20.00	7.50
	Preprinted		10.00	

Same Surcharged

Fifteen canceling machine types

20, Apr.

Y9	PM5+PR5 1c on 2c+1c on 2c **red**, *buff*, unsevered		20.00	11.00
	Preprinted		10.00	
a.	Message card normal, reply card no surcharge		85.00	—
	Preprinted		—	
b.	Message card normal, reply card double surcharge		85.00	—
	Preprinted		—	
c.	Message card double surcharge, reply card normal		85.00	—
	Preprinted		—	
d.	Message card no surcharge, reply card normal		85.00	—
	Preprinted		—	
e.	Message card no surcharge, reply card double surcharge		85.00	
m.	PM5 Message card detached		5.00	4.00
	Preprinted		3.00	
r.	PR5 Reply card detached		5.00	4.00
	Preprinted		3.00	

One press printed type

Y10	PM5+PR5 1c on 2c+1c on 2c **red**, *buff*, unsevered		350.00	200.00
	Preprinted		150.00	
a.	Message card no surcharge, reply card normal		—	
	Preprinted		—	
b.	Surcharge double on message card, reply card normal		950.00	
m.	PM5 Message card detached		75.00	45.00
	Preprinted		40.00	
r.	PR5 Reply card detached		75.00	45.00
	Preprinted		40.00	

Designs same as PM2 and PR2

924, Mar. 18   For International Use
Size: 139x89mm

Y11	PM2+PR2 2c +2c **red**, *cream*, unsevered		2.00	35.00
	Preprinted		1.50	
m.	PM2 Message card detached		.50	12.50
	Preprinted		.40	
r.	PR2 Reply card detached		.50	12.50
	Preprinted		.40	

PM6

PR6 inscribed "REPLY CARD."

For International Use

1926, Feb. 1

UY12	PM6+PR6 3c +3c **red**, *buff*, unsevered		10.00	25.00
	Preprinted		6.00	
a.	3c +3c **red**, *yellow*, unsevered		10.00	25.00
	Preprinted		6.00	
	First day cancel		—	
m.	PM6 Message card detached		3.00	6.00
	Preprinted		1.50	
r.	PR6 Reply card detached		3.00	6.00
	Preprinted		1.50	

Type of 1910
Single frame line around instructions

1951, Dec. 29

UY13	PM4+PR4 2c +2c **carmine**, *buff*, unsevered		1.25	2.00
	Preprinted		.65	
	First day cancel, Washington, D.C.			1.25
m.	PM4 Message card detached		.35	1.00
	Preprinted		.25	
r.	PR4 Reply card detached		.35	1.00
	Preprinted		.25	

No. UY7a Surcharged Below Stamp in Green by Canceling Machine

1952, Jan. 1

UY14	PM4+PR4 2c on 1c+2c on 1c **green**, *buff*, unsevered		1.00	2.00
	Preprinted		.50	
a.	Surcharge vertical at left of stamps		12.50	7.50
	Preprinted		7.50	
b.	Surcharge horizontal at left of stamps		15.00	12.50
	Preprinted		8.50	
c.	Inverted surcharge horizontal at left of stamps		140.00	90.00
	Preprinted		75.00	
d.	Message card normal, reply card no surcharge		40.00	40.00
	Preprinted		—	
e.	Message card normal, reply card double surcharge		40.00	40.00
	Preprinted		—	
f.	Message card no surcharge, reply card normal		40.00	40.00
	Preprinted		—	
g.	Message card double surcharge, reply card normal		40.00	40.00
	Preprinted		—	
h.	Both cards, dbl. surch.		50.00	50.00
	Preprinted		—	
m.	PM4 Message card detached		.40	1.00
	Preprinted		.30	
r.	PR4 Reply card detached		.40	1.00
	Preprinted		.30	

No. UY7a with Similar Surcharge (horizontal) Typographed at Left of Stamp in Dark Green

1952

UY15	PM4+PR4 2c on 1c+2c on 1c **green**, *buff*, unsevered		110.00	45.00
	Preprinted		35.00	
a.	Surcharge on message card only		150.00	
m.	PM4 Message card detached		17.50	10.00
	Preprinted		9.00	
r.	PR4 Reply card detached		17.50	10.00
	Preprinted		9.00	

On No. UY15a, the surcharge also appears on blank side of card.

Liberty Type
For International Use

1956, Nov. 16

UY16	PC24 4c +4c **carmine & dark violet blue**, *buff*, unsevered		1.25	75.00
	First day cancel, New York, N. Y. (127,874)			1.00
a.	Message card printed on both halves		125.00	—
b.	Reply card printed on both halves		125.00	—
c.	Double scarlet on reply card		200.00	
d.	Double scarlet on message side		200.00	
e.	Double violet blue on message side		—	
f.	Double violet blue on both sides		—	
g.	Message side blank, reply side normal		—	
m.	Message card detached		.40	45.00
r.	Reply card detached		.40	45.00

Liberty Type of 1956

1958, July 31

UY17	PC25 3c +3c **purple**, *buff*, unsevered		3.00	2.00
	First day cancel, Boise, Idaho (136,768)			1.00
a.	One card blank		625.00	

Both halves of No. UY17 are identical, inscribed as No. UX46, "This side of card is for address."

Lincoln Type

1962, Nov. 19
Precanceled with 3 printed red violet lines

UY18	PC26 4c +4c **red violet**, unsevered		3.00	2.50
	First day cancel, Springfield, Ill. (107,746)			1.00
a.	Tagged, *Mar. 7, 1967*		6.50	3.00
	First day cancel, Dayton, OH			30.00

Both halves of No. UY18 are identical, inscribed as No. UX48, "This side of card is for address."
No. UY18a was printed with luminescent ink.

Map Type

1963, Aug. 30   For International Use

UY19	PC27 7c +7c **blue & red**, unsevered		2.50	60.00
	First day cancel, New York			1.00
a.	Message card normal, reply card blank		400.00	100.00
b.	Message card blank, reply card normal		400.00	
c.	Additional message card on back of reply card		550.00	
d.	Double red on message side			

---

e.	Double red & blue on message side		—	
m.	Message card detached		.85	40.00
r.	Reply card detached		.85	40.00

Message card inscribed "Postal Card With Paid Reply" in English and French. Reply card inscribed "Reply Postal Card Carte Postale Reponse".

Map Type of 1963

1967, Dec. 4   For International Use

UY20	PC27 8c +8c **blue & red**, unsevered		2.50	60.00
	First day cancel, Washington, D.C.			1.00
m.	Message card detached		.85	40.00
r.	Reply card detached		.85	40.00
s.	Message card normal, reply card blank		—	

Message card inscribed "Postal Card With Paid Reply" in English and French. Reply card inscribed "Reply Postal Card Carte Postale Résponse."

Tagged
Paid Reply Postal cards from No. UY21 onward are either tagged or printed with luminescent ink unless otherwise noted.

Lincoln Type

1968, Jan. 4

UY21	PC33 5c +5c **emerald**, unsevered		1.25	2.00
	First day cancel, Hodgenville, Ky.			1.50
a.	Printed on one side only		—	

Paul Revere Type

1971, May 15
Precanceled with 3 printed brown lines.

UY22	PC36 6c +6c **brown**, unsevered		.85	2.00
	First day cancel, Boston, Mass.			1.00

John Hanson Type

1972, Sept. 1
Precanceled with 3 printed blue lines.

UY23	PC41 6c +6c **blue**, unsevered		1.00	2.00
	First day cancel, Baltimore, Md.			1.00

Samuel Adams Type

1973, Dec. 16
Precanceled with 3 printed orange lines

UY24	PC42 8c +8c **orange**, unsevered		.75	2.00
	First day cancel, Boston, Mass. (105,369)			1.00
a.	Coarse paper		1.25	2.00
b.	Printed on one side only, preprinted		750.00	

Thomson, Witherspoon, Rodney, Hale & Hancock Types

1975-78
Precanceled with 3 printed emerald lines

UY25	PC44 7c +7c **emerald**, unsevered, *Sept. 14, 1975*		.75	8.00
	First day cancel, Bryn Mawr, Pa.			1.00

Precanceled with 3 printed yellow brown lines

UY26	PC45 9c +9c **yellow brown**, unsevered, *Nov. 10, 1975*		.75	2.00
	First day cancel, Princeton, N.J.			1.00

Precanceled with 3 printed blue lines

UY27	PC46 9c +9c **blue**, unsevered, *July 1, 1976*		1.00	2.00
	First day cancel, Dover, Del.			1.00

Precanceled with 3 printed green lines

UY28	PC48 9c +9c **green**, unsevered, *Oct. 14, 1977*		1.00	2.00
	First day cancel, Coventry, Conn.			1.00

Inscribed "U.S. Domestic Rate"
Precanceled with 3 printed brown orange lines

UY29	PC50 (10c +10c) **brown orange**, unsevered, *May 19, 1978*		9.00	9.00
	First day cancel, Quincy, Mass.			1.75

Precanceled with 3 printed brown orange lines

UY30	PC50 10c +10c **brown orange**, unsevered, *June 20, 1978*		1.00	.25
	First day cancel, Quincy, Mass.			1.00
a.	One card "Domestic Rate," other "Postage 10¢"		—	
b.	Printed on one side only		800.00	
	Nos. UY25-UY30 (6)		13.50	

Eagle Type
Inscribed "U. S. Domestic Rate"

1981, Mar. 15
Precanceled with 3 printed violet lines

UY31	PC63 (12c +12) **violet**, unsevered		1.00	2.00
	First day cancel, Memphis, TN			1.00

Isaiah Thomas Type

1981, May 5
Precanceled with 3 printed lines
UY32 PC64 12c +12c **light blue**, unsevered   5.00 2.00
    First day cancel, Worcester, MA   1.00
a. Small die on one side   3.00 —

Morris Type
Inscribed "U.S. Domestic Rate"

1981
Precanceled with 3 printed lines
UY33 PC67 (13c +13c) **buff**, *Oct. 11*, unsev-
    ered   1.50 2.00
    First day cancel, Memphis, TN   1.25
Inscribed "U.S. Postage 13¢"
UY34 PC67 13c +13c **buff**, *Nov. 10*, unsevered   .85 .20
    First day cancel, Philadelphia,
    PA   1.25
a. Message card normal, reply card blank 200.00
b. Extra copyright symbol and "USPS
    1981" on back of reply card   —

Charles Carroll Type
Inscribed: U.S. Domestic Rate

1985
Precanceled with 3 printed lines
UY35 PC79 (14c +14c) **pale green**, *Feb. 1*,
    unsevered   2.50 2.00
    First day cancel, New Car-
    rollton, MD   1.25
Inscribed: USA
UY36 PC79 14c +14c **pale green**, *Mar. 6*,
    unsevered   1.00 2.00
    First day cancel, Annapolis,
    MD   1.25
a. One card blank   425.00

George Wythe Type

1985, June 20
Precanceled with 3 printed lines
UY37 PC81 14c +14c **bright apple green**,
    unsevered   .75 2.00
    First day cancel, Williams-
    burg, VA   1.25
a. One card blank, preprinted   225.00

Flag Type

1987, Sept. 1
UY38 PC90 14c +14c **black, blue & red**, unsev-
    ered   .75 2.00
    First day cancel, Washington, DC
    (22,314)   1.25

America the Beautiful Type

1988, July 11
UY39 PC93 15c +15c **multicolored**, unsevered   .75 1.00
    First day cancel, Buffalo, WY
    (24,338)   1.25

Flag Type

1991, Mar. 27
UY40 PC122 19c +19c **rose, ultramarine &**
    black, unsevered   .80 1.00
    First day cancel, Washing-
    ton, DC *(25,562)*   1.25
a. Printed on one side only   750.00

Red Barn Type

1995, Feb. 1   Litho.
UY41 PC147 20c +20c **multi**, unsevered   .80 1.25
    First day cancel, Williams-
    burg, PA   1.50
a. One card blank   —

Block Island Lighthouse Type

1999, Nov. 10   Litho.
UY42 PC165 20c +20c **multi**, unsevered   .85 1.25
    First day cancel, Block Island,
    RI   1.75

White Barn Type

2001, Sept. 20   Litho.
UY43 PC173 21c +21c **multi**, unsevered   .90 1.25
    First day cancel, Washington,
    DC   1.50

Carlsbad Caverns Type

2002, June 7   Litho.
UY44 PC174 23c+23c **multi**, unsevered   1.00 1.25
    First day cancel, Carlsbad,
    NM   1.50
    First day cancel, any other
    city   1.50

Pikes Peak Type of 2006

2006, Jan. 9   Litho.
UY45 PC178 24c+24c **multicolored**, unsevered   1.10 1.25
    First day cancel, Washing-
    ton, DC   1.50
    First day cancel, any other
    city   1.50

AIR POST POSTAL CARDS

Eagle in Flight — APC1

1949, Jan.10   Typo.
UXC1 APC1 4c **red orange**, *buff*   .50 .75
    Preprinted   .35
    First day cancel, Washington,
    D.C. *(236,620)*   3.00
a. 4c **deep red**, *buff*   600.00 450.00
    First day cancel, Washington,
    D.C.   250.00

Expertization is recommended for No. UXC1a.

Type of Air Post Stamp, 1954
1958, July 31
UXC2 AP31 5c **red**, *buff*   1.75 .75
    First day cancel, Wichita, Kans.
    (156,474)   1.00

Type of 1958 Redrawn
1960, June 18   Lithographed (Offset)
UXC3 AP31 5c **red**, *buff*, bicolored border   6.50 2.00
    First day cancel, Minneapolis,
    Minn. *(228,500)*   1.50
a. Red omitted   —

Size of stamp of No. UXC3: 18½x21mm; on No. UXC2: 19x22mm. White cloud around eagle enlarged and finer detail of design on No. UXC3. Inscription "AIR MAIL-POSTAL CARD" has been omitted and blue and red border added on No. UXC3.

Bald Eagle — APC2

1963, Feb. 15
Precanceled with 3 printed red lines
UXC4 APC2 6c **red**, bicolored border   1.10 2.50
    First day cancel, Maitland, Fla.
    (216,203)   1.50

Emblem of Commerce Department's Travel
Service — APC3

Issued at the Sixth International Philatelic Exhibition (SIPEX), Washington, D.C., May 21-30.

1966, May 27   For International Use
UXC5 APC3 11c **blue & red**   .65 20.00
    First day cancel, Washington,
    D.C. *(272,813)*   1.00

Four photographs at left on address side show: Mt. Rainier, New York skyline, Indian on horseback and Miami Beach. The card has blue and red border.
See Nos. UXC8, UXC11.

Virgin Islands and Territorial Flag — APC4

50th anniv. of the purchase of the Virgin Islands.

Designed by Burt Pringle

1967, Mar. 31   Lith.
UXC6 APC4 6c **multicolored**   .75 10.
    First day cancel, Charlotte
    Amalie, V. I. *(346,906)*   1.
a. Red & yellow omitted   1,700.
b. Orange red (instead of red)   6.00

The orange red in No. UXC6b is most easily seen in the t lines at the bottom of the card.

Borah Peak, Lost River Range, Idaho, and Scout
Emblem — APC5

12th Boy Scout World Jamboree, Farragut State Park, Idah Aug. 1-9.

Designed by Stevan Dohanos

1967, Aug. 4   Litho
UXC7 APC5 6c **blue, yellow, black &**
    red   .75 15.0
    First day cancel, Far-
    ragut State Park, ID
    (471,585)   1.0
a. Blue omitted   —
b. Blue & black omitted   11,000.
c. Red & yellow omitted   11,000.

Travel Service Type of 1966

Issued in connection with the American Air Mail Society Con vention, Detroit, Mich.

1967, Sept. 8   For International Us
UXC8 APC3 13c **blue & red**   1.50 25.0
    First day cancel, Detroit, Mich.
    (178,189)   1.0

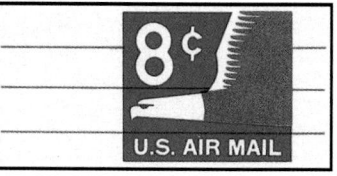

Stylized
Eagle
APC6

Designed by Muriel R. Chamberlain

1968, Mar. 1
Precanceled with 3 printed red lines
UXC9 APC6 8c **blue & red**   .75 2.5(
    First day cancel, New York,
    N.Y. *(179,923)*   1.00
a. Tagged, *Mar. 19, 1969*   2.50 3.00
    Tagged, first day cancel   15.00
b. **Blue & pale pink**, tagged   1,250.

No. UXC9a is known with tagging omitted. It can be distinguished from No. UXC9, as No. UXC9a was printed on fluorescent stock. Believed to be unique. Value $2,500.

Tagged
Air Post Postal Cards from No. UXC10 onward are either tagged or printed with luminescent ink unless otherwise noted.

1971, May 15
Precanceled with 3 printed blue lines
UXC10 APC6 9c **red & blue**   .50 1.25
    First day cancel, Kitty Hawk,
    N.C.   1.00

Travel Service Type of 1966

1, June 10

For International Use

C11 APC3 15c **blue & red** 1.75 *45.00*
First day cancel, New York, N.Y. 1.00

Grand Canyon APC7

U.S. AIR MAIL 9 CENTS

U.S. AIR MAIL 15 CENTS

Niagara Falls APC8

Tourism Year of the Americas 1972.

Designed by Melbourne Brindle

72, June 29 **Size: 152½x108½mm** Litho.

C12 APC7 9c **black**, Grand Canyon, *buff* (Statue of Liberty, Hawaii, Alaska, San Francisco on back) .75 *150.00*
First day cancel, any city 1.50
a. Red and blue lozenges omitted 2,250. —
b. Red lozenges omitted —
c. Tagging omitted —

For International Use

C13 APC8 15c **black**, Niagara Falls, *buff* (Mt. Vernon, Washington, D.C., Lincoln, Liberty Bell on back) .75 *75.00*
First day cancel, any city 1.50
a. Address side blank 400.00
b. Double blue lozenges 6,000.
c. Tagging omitted 2,500.
d. Red and blue lozenges omitted —

See note after No. UX63.

Stylized Eagle — APC9

11c Mail early in the day USAirmail

USAirmail 18c

Eagle Weather Vane — APC10

Designed by David G. Foote (11c) & Stevan Dohanos (18c)

974, Jan. 4 Litho.

UXC14 APC9 11c **ultramarine & red** 1.10 *20.00*
First day cancel, State College, Pa. *(160,500)* 1.00
a. Double tagging 500.00

For International Use

UXC15 APC10 18c **multicolored** 1.10 *20.00*
First day cancel, Miami, Fla. *(132,114)* 1.00
a. Tagging omitted 350.00
b. Black and yellow omitted 7,500.

All following issues are for international use.

Angel Gabriel Weather Vane — APC11

Visit USA Bicentennial Era USAirmail 21c

Designed by Stevan Dohanos

1975, Dec. 17 Litho.

UXC16 APC11 21c **multicolored** .85 *20.00*
First day cancel, Kitty Hawk, N.C. 1.00
a. Blue & red omitted 7,500.
b. Tagging omitted 350.00

USAirmail 21c

Curtiss (JN4H) Jenny — APC12

Designed by Keith Ferris

1978, Sept. 16 Litho.

UXC17 APC12 21c **multicolored** 1.00 *20.00*
First day cancel, San Diego, Cal. *(174,886)* 1.25

USA Airmail 21c

Gymnast APC13

22nd Olympic Games, Moscow, July 19-Aug. 3, 1980.

Designed by Robert M. Cunningham

1979, Dec. 1 Litho.

UXC18 APC13 21c **multicolored** 1.25 *20.00*
First day cancel, Fort Worth, Tex. 1.00

First Transpacific Flight · 1931

Sabishiro Beach, Japan to Wenatchee, Washington
Clyde Pangborn & Hugh Herndon Jr.
USAirmail 28c

Pangborn, Herndon and Miss Veedol — APC14

First non-stop transpacific flight by Clyde Pangborn and Hugh Herndon, Jr., 50th anniv.

Designed by Ken Dallison

1981, Jan. 2 Litho.

UXC19 APC14 28c **multicolored** 1.00 *20.00*
First day cancel, Wenatchee, WA 1.25

USAirmail 28c

Gliders — APC15

Designed by Robert E. Cunningham

1982, Mar. 5 Litho.

UXC20 APC15 28c **magenta, yellow, blue & black** 1.00 *20.00*
First day cancel, Houston, TX *(106,932)* 1.25

Olympics 84 USA 28c Airmail

Speedskater — APC16

Designed by Robert Peak

1983, Dec. 29 Litho.

UXC21 APC16 28c **multicolored** 1.00 *20.00*
First day cancel, Milwaukee, WI *(108,397)* 1.25

China Clipper USAirmail 33

Martin M-130 China Clipper Seaplane — APC17

Designed by Chuck Hodgson

1985, Feb. 15 Litho.

UXC22 APC17 33c **multicolored** 1.00 *20.00*
First day cancel, San Francisco, CA 1.50

First day cancellation was applied to 269,229 of Nos. UXC22 and C115.

USAirmail 33 AMERIPEX 86 Chicago, Illinois

Chicago Skyline — APC18

AMERIPEX '86, Chicago, May 22-June 1.

Designed by Ray Ameijide

1986, Feb. 1 Litho.

UXC23 APC18 33c **multicolored** 1.00 *20.00*
First day cancel, Chicago, IL *(84,480)* 1.25

No. UXC23 was sold at Sudposta '87 by the U.S.P.S. with a show cachet.

DC-3 — APC19

Designed by Chuck Hodgson

1988, May 14   Litho.
UXC24 APC19 36c **multicolored**   85 20.00
   First day cancel, San Die-
   go, CA   1.25

No. UXC24 was sold at SYDPEX '88 by the USPS with a
cachet for Australia's bicentennial and SYDPEX '88.
  First day cancellations applied to 167,575 of Nos. UXC24 and
C118.

Yankee Clipper — APC20

Designed by Chuck Hodgson.

1991, June 28   Litho.
UXC25 APC20 40c **multicolored**   .90 20.00
   First day cancel, Flushing,
   NY (24,865)   1.50

Mt. Rainier — APC22

Designed by Ethel Kessler.

1999, May 15   Litho.
UXC27 APC22 55c **multicolored**   1.25 20.00
   First day cancel, Denver, CO   1.50

First day cancellation was applied to 19,658 of Nos. UXC27
and UC65.
  See note before No. C133.

Badlands Natl. Park, South Dakota — APC23

Designed by Ethel Kessler.

2001, Feb. 22   Litho.
UXC28 APC23 70c **multicolored**   1.40 10.00
   First day cancel, Wall, SD   1.50

OFFICIAL POSTAL CARDS

PO1

1913, July
      Size: 126x76mm
UZ1 PO1 1c **black**   600.00 160.00

All No. UZ1 cards have printed address and printed form on
message side.

**Used values are for contemporaneous usage
without additional postage applied.**

Great Seal — PO2

1983-85
UZ2 PO2 13c **blue,** *Jan. 12*   .75 90.00
   First day cancel, Washington, DC   1.00
UZ3 PO2 14c **blue,** *Feb. 26, 1985*   .75 80.00
   First day cancel, Washington, DC
   (62,396)   1.25

PO3

Designed by Bradbury Thompson

1988, June 10   Litho.
UZ4 PO3 15c **multicolored**   .75 90.00
   First day cancel, New York
   (133,498)   1.25

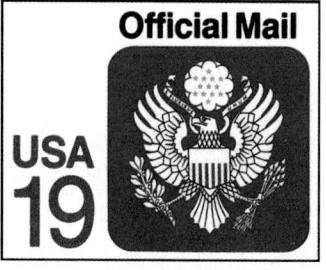

PO4

Designed by Bradbury Thompson

1991, May 24   Litho.
UZ5 PO4 19c **multicolored**   .75 90.00
   First day cancel, Seattle, WA
   (23,097)   1.25

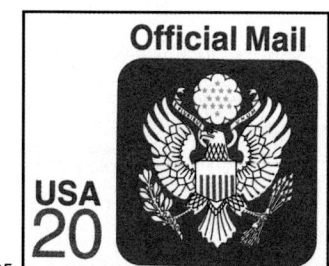

PO5

1995, May 9   Lit
UZ6 PO5 20c **multicolored**   .90 9
   First day cancel, Washington, DC

REVENUE STAMPS

The Commissioner of Internal Revenue advertised for bids for revenue stamps in August, 1862, and the contract was awarded to Butler & Carpenter Philadelphia.

Nos. R1-R102 were used to pay taxes on documents and proprietary articles including playing cards. Until December 25, 1862, the law stated that a amp could be used only for payment of the tax upon the particular instrument or article specified on its face. After that date, stamps, except the oprietary, could be used indiscriminately.

Most stamps of the first issue appeared in the latter part of 1862 or early in 1863. The 5c and 10c Proprietary were issued in the fall of 1864, and the Proprietary on April 13, 1871.

Plate numbers and imprints are usually found at the bottom of the plate on all denominations except 25c and $1 to $3.50. On these it is nearly always the left of the plate. The imprint reads "Engraved by Butler & Carpenter, Philadelphia" or "Jos. R. Carpenter."

Plates were of various sizes: 1c and 2c, 210 subjects (14x15); 3c to 20c, 170 subjects (17x10); 25c to 30c, 102 subjects (17x6); 50c to 70c, 85 ibjects (17x5); $1 to $1.90, 90 subjects (15x6); $2 to $10, 72 subjects (12x6); $15 to $50, 54 subjects (9x6); $200, 8 subjects (2x4). No. R132, one abject.

The paper varies, the first employed being thin, hard and brittle until September, 1869, from which time it acquired a softer texture and varied from edium to very thick. Early printings of some revenue stamps occur on paper which appears to have laid lines. Some are found on experimental silk aper, first employed about August, 1870.

Some of the stamps were in use eight years and were printed several times. Many color variations occurred, particularly if unstable pigments were sed and the color was intended to be purple or violet, such as the 4c Proprietary, 30c and $2.50 stamps. Before 1868 dull colors predominate on ese and the early red stamps. In later printings of the 4c Proprietary, 30c and $2.50 stamps, red predominates in the mixture and on the dollar values red is brighter. The early $1.90 stamp is dull purple, imperforate or perforated. In a later printing, perforated only, the purple is darker.

In the first issue, canceling usually was done with pen and ink and all values quoted are for stamps canceled in that way. Handstamped cancellations a rule sell for more than pen. Printed cancellations are scarce and command much higher prices. Herringbone, punched or other types of ancellation which break the surface of the paper adversely affect prices.

Many, but not all, of the pre-1898 revenue stamps exist unused with original gum. These are not valued in the listings, but they sell for more than used xamples in the marketplace.

1862-72 revenue stamps from the first three issues were often used on large folded documents. As a result, multiples (blocks and strips of four or ore) are not often found in sound condition. In addition, part perforate pairs of all but the most common varieties generally are off center. Catalogue alues of the noted multiples are for items in fine condition or for very fine appearing examples with small faults. Examples of such multiples in a true ry fine grade without any faults are scarce to rare and will sell for well above catalogue value.

Where a stamp is known in a given form or variety but insufficient information is available on which to base a value, its existence is indicated by a ash.

Part perforate stamps are understood to be imperforate horizontally unless otherwise stated.

Part perforate stamps with an asterisk (*) exist imperforate horizontally or vertically.

Part perforate PAIRS should be imperforate between the stamps as well as imperforate at opposite ends. See illustration **Type A** under "Information or Collectors-Perforations."

All imperforate or part perforate stamps listed are known in pairs or larger multiples. Certain unlisted varieties of this nature exist as singles and pecialists believe them genuine. Exceptions are Nos. R13a, R22a and R60b, which have not been reported in multiples but are regarded as legitimate y most students.

Documentary revenue stamps were no longer required after December 31, 1967.

First Issue

George Washington

R1	R2

862-71 **Engr.** **Perf. 12**

		a. Imperf.	b. Part Perf.	c. Old Paper	d. Silk Paper
R1	R1 1c	Express, red	65.00	40.00*	1.40	110.00
		Pair	150.00	180.00	3.25	
		Block of 4	600.00	600.00	12.50	
		Dble. transfer			45.00	
		Short transfer, No. 156	—	—	85.00	
e.		Vert. pair, imperf. btwn.			200.00	
R2	R1 1c	Playing Cards, red	1,500.	1,400.	160.00	
		Pair	3,250.	3,500.	350.00	
		Block of 4			900.00	
		Cracked plate	—		225.00	
R3	R1 1c	Proprietary, red	1,000.	225.00*	.50	40.00
		Pair	2,100.	600.00	1.25	100.00
		Block of 4		3,000.	3.25	
R4	R1 1c	Telegraph, red	550.00		12.00	
		Pair	1,500.		30.00	
		Block of 4			110.00	

Double transfer (T5)

			a. Imperf.	b. Part Perf.	Perforated c. Old Paper	d. Silk Paper
R5	R2 2c	Bank Check, blue	1.00	2.00*	.25	
		Pair	17.50	9.00	.50	
		Block of 4	175.00	80.00	2.00	
		Double transfer (T5)	100.00	120.00	50.00	
		Cracked plate		22.50	10.00	
e.		Double impression			800.00	
f.		Vert. pair, imperf. btwn.			400.00	
R6	R2 2c	Bank Check, orange		55.00*	.25	250.00
		Pair		—	.50	
		Block of 4			1.40	
		Double transfer (T5)			300.00	
e.		2c orange,green			600.00	
f.		As No. R6, vert. half used as 1c on document				

Double transfer (T7)

			a. Imperf.	b. Part Perf.	Perforated c. Old Paper	d. Silk Paper
R7	R2 2c	Certificate, blue	14.00		30.00	
		Pair	45.00		75.00	
		Block of 4	180.00		300.00	
		Double transfer (T7)	350.00		300.00	

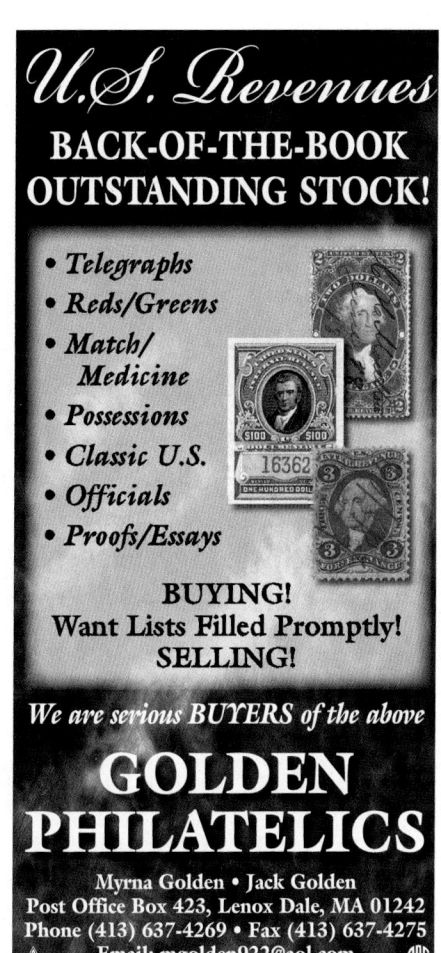

R8   R2   2c   **Certificate, orange**

		Imperf/Part Perf/Perf
Cracked plate		37.50
Certificate		30.00
Pair		180.00
Block of 4		825.00
Double transfer (T7)		450.00

R9   R2   2c   **Express, blue**   14.00   25.00*   .40
- Pair   50.00   120.00   1.25
- Block of 4   160.00   300.00   4.25
- Dble. transfer   60.00   17.50
- Cracked plate   20.00

R10   R2   2c   **Express, orange**   750.00   8.50   110.00
- Pair   20.00
- Block of 4   45.00
- Dble. transfer   22.50

R11   R2   2c   **Playing Cards, blue**   250.00   4.00
- Pair   600.00   13.00
- Block of 4   50.00
- Cracked plate   30.00

R12   R2   2c   **Playing Cards, orange**   45.00
- Pair   400.00

Double transfer (T13)

Double transfer (T13a)

---

	a. Imperf.	b. Part Perf.	c. Old Paper (Perforated)	d. Silk Paper
R13 R2 2c **Proprietary, blue**	600.	225.	.40	90.00
Pair		600.	.90	
Block of 4	1,400.		5.00	
Double transfer (T13)			150.00	
Complete double transfer (T13a)			200.00	
Cracked plate			25.00	
e. 2c **ultra**			250.00	
Pair			600.00	
Block of 4			—	
Dble. transfer (T13)				
Complete dble. transfer (T13a)			750.00	
f. As No. R13, horiz. half used as 1c on document			—	
R14 R2 2c **Proprietary, orange**			45.00	
Pair			275.00	
Block of 4				
Double transfer (T13)			250.00	
Complete double transfer (T13a)			400.00	

Double transfer (T15)

Double transfer (T15a)

	—	Perf	c. Old Paper	d. Silk Paper
R15 R2 2c **U. S. Internal Revenue, orange ('64)**	—		.20	
Pair	—	—	.20	1
Block of 4			.40	
Double transfer (T15)			60.00	
Double transfer (T15a)			45.00	
Dble. transfer			12.00	
Triple transfer			40.00	
Cracked plate			10.00	
e. 2c **orange, green**			700.00	
f. As No. R15, half used as 1c on document			—	

R3

	Imperf.	Perf.	Old Paper	Silk Paper
R16 R3 3c **Foreign Exchange, green**	450.00		4.50	90.
Pair	1,275.		10.50	
Block of 4			75.00	
Dble. transfer			—	
R17 R3 3c **Playing Cards, green ('63)**	20,000.		150.00	
Pair	50,000.		350.00	
Block of 4			900.00	
R18 R3 3c **Proprietary, green**	450.00		5.00	60.0
Pair	1,000.		12.00	135.0
Block of 4			35.00	
Dble. transfer			9.00	
Cracked plate			—	
e. Double impression			1,000.	
f. Printed on both sides			3,500.	
R19 R3 3c **Telegraph, green**	80.00	27.50	2.75	
Pair	450.00	82.50	8.75	
Block of 4	1,200.	300.00	80.00	
R20 R3 4c **Inland Exchange, brown ('63)**			2.00	100.0
Pair			5.25	
Block of 4			22.50	
Double transfer at top			7.50	
R21 R3 4c **Playing Cards, slate ('63)**			600.00	
Pair			1,250.	
Block of 4			2,600.	
R22 R3 4c **Proprietary, purple**	—	400.00	7.50	140.0
Pair		900.00	17.50	300.0
Block of 4	1,900.		55.00	—
Double transfer at top			17.50	
Double transfer at bottom			12.50	

There are shade and color variations of Nos. R21-R22. See foreword of Revenue Stamps section.

	Imperf.	Perf.	Old Paper	Silk Paper
R23 R3 5c **Agreement, red**			.35	2.00
			.70	4.25
Block of 4			1.50	17.50
Dble. transfer in numerals			25.00	
R24 R3 5c **Certificate, red**	3.50	13.00	.50	.55
Pair	35.00	150.00	1.25	1.25
Block of 4	250.00	400.00	3.00	6.00
Double transfer in upper label			10.00	
Dble. transfer throughout			200.00	
Triple transfer (No. 121)			35.00	

No.			Description	Imperf	Part Perf	Old Paper	Silk Paper
			e. Half used as 2c on document	—		—	
			f. Impression of #R3 on back				2,750.
25	R3	5c	**Express, red**	6.00	7.00*	.40	
			Pair	20.00	100.00	.90	
			Block of 4	200.00	300.00	2.25	
			Double transfer			5.00	
26	R3	5c	**Foreign Exchange, red**		—	.50	375.00
			Pair		—	1.25	
			Block of 4			15.00	
			Double transfer at top			20.00	
			Double transfer at bottom			10.00	
27	R3	5c	**Inland Exchange, red**	8.25	5.50	.40	17.50
			Pair	37.50	40.00	1.00	40.00
			Block of 4	120.00	100.00	2.50	
			Double transfer at top	77.50	47.50	27.50	
			Cracked plate	95.00	90.00	32.50	
			e. Double impression			—	
28	R3	5c	**Playing Cards, red** ('63)			25.00	
			Pair			55.00	
			Block of 4			110.00	
			e. Double impression			750.00	
29	R3	5c	**Proprietary, red** ('64)			25.00	200.00
			Pair			55.00	
			Block of 4			150.00	
30	R3	6c	**Inland Exchange, orange** ('63)			2.00	125.00
			Pair			18.50	
			Block of 4			100.00	
31	R3	6c	**Proprietary, orange** ('71)			1,800.	

Nearly all copies of No. R31 are faulty and poorly centered. The Catalogue value is for a fine centered copy with minor faults which do not detract from its appearance.

No.			Description	Imperf	Part Perf	Old Paper	Silk Paper
32	R3	10c	**Bill of Lading, blue**	50.00	375.00	1.50	
			Pair	220.00	850.00	4.00	
			Block of 4	700.00		10.00	
			Dble. transfer (#33 & 143)			—	
			Half used as 5c on document			200.00	
33	R3	10c	**Certificate, blue**	200.00	650.00*	.35	6.00
			Pair	600.00	1,500.	.75	17.50
			Block of 4	1,400.	—	2.25	90.00
			Dble. transfer			7.50	
			Cracked plate			15.00	
			e. Half used as 5c on document			200.00	
34	R3	10c	**Contract, blue**	400.00		.50	2.25
			Pair	1,000.		1.25	6.00
			Block of 4	—		4.75	60.00
			Complete double transfer			70.00	
			e. 10c **ultra**	550.00		1.00	
			Pair			2.50	
			Block of 4			17.50	
			f. As No. 34, vertical half used as 5c on document			200.00	
35	R3	10c	**Foreign Exchange, blue**			10.00	—
			Pair			25.00	
			Block of 4			85.00	
			e. 10c **ultra**			12.50	
			Pair			37.50	
			Block of 4			95.00	

No.			Description	Imperf	Part Perf	Old Paper	Silk Paper
36	R3	10c	**Inland Exchange, blue**	350.00	4.00*	.30	60.00
			Pair	900.00	15.00	.60	140.00
			Block of 4	3,000.	80.00	1.75	—
			e. Half used as 5c on document			200.00	
37	R3	10c	**Power of Attorney, blue**	800.00	27.50	1.00	
			Pair	2,000.	100.00	2.25	
			Block of 4	4,500.	300.00	8.00	
			e. Half used as 5c on document			200.00	
38	R3	10c	**Proprietary, blue** ('64)			17.50	
			Pair			40.00	
			Block of 4			110.00	
39	R3	15c	**Foreign Exchange, brown** ('63)			15.00	
			Pair			50.00	
			Block of 4			250.00	
			e. Double impression			500.00	
40	R3	15c	**Inland Exchange, brown**	37.50	12.50	1.25	
			Pair	250.00	50.00	2.85	
			Block of 4	850.00	400.00	10.25	
			Dble. transfer			6.25	
			Cracked plate	60.00	37.50	14.00	
			e. Double impression		1,200.	550.00	
41	R3	20c	**Foreign Exchange, red**	65.00		50.00	
			Pair	300.00		125.00	
			Block of 4	900.00		325.00	
42	R3	20c	**Inland Exchange, red**	15.00	20.00	.45	—
			Pair	50.00	60.00	1.00	
			Block of 4	300.00	300.00	14.00	
			e. Half used as 10c on document			200.00	

R4

R5

				a. Imperf.	b. Part Perf.	Perforated c. Old Paper	d. Silk Paper
43	R4	25c	**Bond, red**	250.00	6.00	3.50	
			Pair	700.00	60.00	8.00	
			Block of 4	5,000.	400.00	60.00	

No.			Description	a. Imperf.	b. Part Perf.	Perforated c. Old Paper	d. Silk Paper
44	R4	25c	**Certificate, red**	10.00	6.00*	.25	2.75
			Pair	50.00	40.00	.55	8.25
			Block of 4	450.00	200.00	4.00	27.50
			Double transfer, top or bottom			2.00	
			Triple transfer			—	
			e. Printed on both sides			4,500	
			f. Impression of No. R48 on back			—	
45	R4	25c	**Entry of Goods, red**	20.00	100.00*	1.25	55.00
			Pair	70.00	700.00	47.50	
			Block of 4	500.00		125.00	
			Top frame line double	72.50	105.00	11.00	
46	R4	25c	**Insurance, red**	11.00	14.00	.30	5.50
			Pair	42.50	30.00	.75	13.00
			Block of 4	700.00	210.00	5.50	
			Cracked plate			17.50	
			e. Double impression			500.00	
47	R4	25c	**Life Insurance, red**	40.00	475.00	9.50	
			Pair	135.00	1,200.	50.00	
			Block of 4	600.00		240.00	
48	R4	25c	**Power of Attorney, red**	8.00	30.00	.60	

	a. Imperf.	b. Part Perf.	Perforated c. Old Paper	d. Silk Paper
Pair	50.00	125.00	1.75	
Block of 4	500.00	600.00	10.00	
Dble. transfer			1.10	
Bottom frame line double			5.50	
R49 R4 25c Protest, red	30.00	600.00	7.50	
Pair	200.00	1,400.	29.00	
Block of 4	700.00		115.00	
R50 R4 25c Warehouse Receipt, red	47.50	500.00	40.00	
Pair	250.00	1,100.	95.00	
Block of 4	1,200.		325.00	
R51 R4 30c Foreign Exchange, lilac	110.00	1,750.	55.00	—
Pair	500.00	3,750.	225.00	
Block of 4	3,500.		—	
Dble. transfer			100.00	
Top frame line double			—	
R52 R4 30c Inland Exchange, lilac	65.00	75.00	8.00	—
Pair	300.00	400.00	40.00	
Block of 4	1,000.	—	140.00	
Dble. transfer			30.00	

There are shade and color variations of Nos. R51-R52. See foreword of "Revenues" section.

	a. Imperf.	b. Part Perf.	Perforated c. Old Paper	d. Silk Paper
R53 R4 40c Inland Exchange, brown	1,000.	8.00	7.50	—
Pair	5,000.	50.00	16.00	
Block of 4		210.00	140.00	
Dble. transfer		50.00	30.00	
f. Double impression			—	
R54 R5 50c Conveyance, blue	17.00	2.25	.35	3.00
Pair	100.00	40.00	.70	6.50
Block of 4	600.00	150.00	2.50	
Dble. transfer			6.00	
Cracked plate			15.00	
Scatched plate			—	
e. 50c ultra			.50	
Pair			1.25	
Block of 4			10.00	

	a. Imperf.	b. Part Perf.	Perforated c. Old Paper	d. Silk Paper
R55 R5 50c Entry of Goods, blue			15.00	.45 75.00
Pair		300.00	1.75	175.00
Block of 4		650.00	25.00	
Dble. transfer			5.00	
Cracked plate			20.00	
R56 R5 50c Foreign Exchange, blue	60.00	90.00	7.00	
Pair	200.00	475.00	42.50	
Block of 4			140.00	
Double transfer at left			11.00	
e. Double impression			500.00	
f. Half used as 25c on document			200.00	
R57 R5 50c Lease, blue	27.50	125.00	9.00	
Pair	200.00	525.00	67.50	
Block of 4	1,000.	1,250.	225.00	
R58 R5 50c Life Insurance, blue	40.00	75.00	1.00	
Pair	160.00		7.50	
Block of 4	850.00		45.00	
Dble. transfer	47.50		11.00	
e. Double impression			800.00	

Cracked Plate (C59)

	a. Imperf.	b. Part Perf.	Perforated c. Old Paper	d. Silk Paper
R59 R5 50c Mortgage, blue	20.00	4.50	.65	—
Pair	100.00	225.00	1.50	
Block of 4	400.00	500.00	7.50	
Cracked plate (C59)		37.50	12.50	
Scratched plate, diagonal	35.00	25.00	12.50	
Dble. transfer			3.50	
e. Double impression	—		—	

Scratch is across three stamps. Value is for a single.

	a. Imperf.	b. Part Perf.	Perforated c. Old Paper	d. Silk Paper
R60 R5 50c Original Process, blue	4.00	600.00	.75	2.00
Pair	75.00		1.75	8.00
Block of 4	900.00		6.00	100.00
Double transfer at top			5.00	
Double transfer at bottom			8.00	
Scratched plate			10.00	
e. Half used as 25c on document			—	
R61 R5 50c Passage Ticket, blue	80.00	275.00	2.00	
Pair	250.00	1,100.	12.50	
Block of 4	900.00		225.00	
Cracked plate			—	

	a. Imperf.	b. Part Perf.	Perforated c. Old Paper	d. Silk Paper
R62 R5 50c Probate of Will, blue	50.00	140.00	20.00	
Pair	200.00	700.00	50.00	
Block of 4	850.00	1,500.	350.00	
Scratched plate			—	
R63 R5 50c Surety Bond, blue	275.00	2.50	.30	
Pair	1,200.	15.00	1.75	
Block of 4		100.00	10.00	
e. 50c ultra			.75	
Pair			5.50	
Block of 4			55.00	
R64 R5 60c Inland Exchange, orange	100.00	65.00	8.00	50
Pair	300.00	200.00	17.50	110.
Block of 4	750.00	500.00	100.00	
R65 R5 70c Foreign Exchange, green	600.00	160.00	12.00	80
Pair	2,500.	850.00	40.00	160
Block of 4		1,900.	250.00	
Cracked plate			30.00	

Pairs and blocks of No. R65b are valued in the grade of fine

R6   R7

	a. Imperf.	b. Part Perf.	Perforated c. Old Paper	d. Silk Paper
R66 R6 $1 Conveyance, red	22.50	600.00	25.00	125.0
Pair	85.00	2,000.	65.00	
Block of 4	600.00		160.00	
Dble. transfer	35.00		37.50	
Right frame line double	90.00		77.50	
Top frame line double	—		60.00	
R67 R6 $1 Entry of Goods, red	42.50		2.50	100.0
Pair	150.00		6.50	
Block of 4	500.00		55.00	
R68 R6 $1 Foreign Exchange, red	80.00		.75	85.0
Pair	250.00		1.75	
Block of 4	1,475.		11.00	
Dble. transfer			5.50	
Left frame line double	180.00		19.00	
e. Diagonal half used as 50c on document				200.0
R69 R6 $1 Inland Exchange, red	15.00	400.00*	.70	3.75
Pair	75.00	3,500.	2.00	9.00
Block of 4	800.00	—	9.50	35.00

	e.	Double impression		1,400.	

There are many shade and color variations of Nos. R84c and R84d. See foreword of "Revenues" section.

No.	Ill.	Val.	Description	Price	Price	Price
R85	R8	$3	Charter Party, green	175.00	10.00	150.00
			Pair	400.00	65.00	325.00
			Block of 4	2,000.	250.00	
			Double transfer at top	—		
			Double transfer at bottom	12.00		
	e.		Printed on both sides	2,300.		
	f.		Half used as $1.50 on document	—		
	g.		Impression of No. RS208 on back	4,000.		
R86	R8	$3	Manifest, green	175.00	50.00	
			Pair	400.00	125.00	
			Block of 4	3,000.	300.00	
			Dble. transfer	210.00		
R87	R8	$3.50	Inland Exchange, blue ('63)	6,500.	65.00	
			Pair	18,000.	180.00	
			Block of 4		450.00	
	e.		Printed on both sides	4,000.		

R9

R10

	b. Part	c. Old	d. Silk
	Perf.	Paper	Paper
a. Imperf			Perforated

No.	Ill.	Val.	Description	Price	Price	Price
R88	R9	$5	Charter Party, red	300.00	9.00	80.00
			Pair	625.00	65.00	
			Block of 4	1,400.	200.00	
			Right frame line double	325.00	70.00	
			Top frame line double	325.00	60.00	
R89	R9	$5	Conveyance, red	40.00	10.00	110.00
			Pair	180.00	22.50	250.00
			Block of 4	900.00	110.00	
R90	R9	$5	Manifest, red	185.00	90.00	
			Pair	400.00	250.00	
			Block of 4	1,100.	550.00	
			Left frame line double	210.00	150.00	
R91	R9	$5	Mortgage, red	150.00	22.50	
			Pair	800.00	87.50	
			Block of 4	—	—	
R92	R9	$5	Probate of Will, red	700.00	25.00	
			Pair	1,450.	100.00	
			Block of 4	3,000.	375.00	
R93	R9	$10	Charter Party, green	750.00	32.50	
			Pair	1,600.	95.00	
			Block of 4	—	450.00	
			Dble. transfer		85.00	
R94	R9	$10	Conveyance, green	125.00	70.00	
			Pair	300.00	175.00	
			Block of 4	850.00	700.00	
			Double transfer at top	150.00	125.00	
			Right frame line double		150.00	
R95	R9	$10	Mortgage, green	600.00	35.00	
			Pair	1,500.	120.00	
			Block of 4	4,000.	—	
			Top frame line double	525.00	52.50	
R96	R9	$10	Probate of Will, green	1,800.	40.00	
			Pair	5,000.	87.50	
			Block of 4		400.00	
			Double transfer at top		57.50	
R97	R10	$15	Mortgage, blue	2,500.	225.00	
			Pair	6,000.	500.00	
			Block of 4	14,000.	2,750.	
	e.		$15 ultra		250.00	
			Pair		750.00	
			Block of 4		—	
	f.		$15 milky blue		250.00	
R98	R10	$20	Conveyance, orange	150.00	110.00	175.00
			Pair	400.00	250.00	350.00
			Block of 4	1,000.	800.00	
R99	R10	$20	Probate of Will, orange	2,000.	2,000.	
			Pair	4,250.	4,250.	
			Block of 4	9,000.	9,000.	
R100	R10	$25	Mortgage, red ('63)	1,400.	175.00	250.00
			Pair	3,000.	375.00	

	a. Imperf	b. Part Perf	c. Old Paper	d. Pa[...]
				Perforate[d]
Block	8,000.		1,250.	
e. Horiz. pair, imperf. between			1,100.	
R101 R10 $50 U.S. Internal Revenue, green ('63)	250.00		140.00	
Pair	600.00		300.00	
Block of 4	2,000.		650.00	
Cracked plate			160.00	

R11

R102	R11	$200	U.S. Internal Revenue, grn & red ('64)	2,500.	900.00
			Pair	5,500.	2,000.
			Block of 4	12,000.	5,000.

DOCUMENTARY STAMPS
Second Issue

After release of the First Issue revenue stamps, the Bureau of Internal Revenue received many reports of fraudulent cleaning and re-use. The Bureau ordered a Second Issue with new designs and colors, using patented "chameleon" paper which is usually violet or pinkish, with silk fibers.

While designs are different from those of the first issue, stamp sizes and make up of the plates are the same as for corresponding denominations.

George Washington
R12   R12a

Engraved and printed by Jos. R. Carpenter, Philadelphia.

Various Frames and Numeral Arrangements

1871   **Perf. [...]**

No.	Ill.	Val.	Description	Price
R103	R12	1c	blue & black	60.
			Cut cancel	20.
			Pair	150.
			Block of 4	375.
a.			Inverted center	1,50
			Pair	3,10
			Block of 4	—
R104	R12	2c	blue & black	2.7
			Cut cancel	.2
			Pair	6.2
			Block of 4	40.0
a.			Inverted center	6,00
R105	R12a	3c	blue & black	30.0
			Cut cancel	10.0
			Pair	70.0
			Block of 4	210.0
R106	R12a	4c	blue & black	90.0
			Cut cancel	30.0
			Pair	200.0
			Block of 4	375.0
a.			Horiz. half used as 2c on document	250.0
b.			Vert. half used as 2c on document	250.0
R107	R12a	5c	blue & black	2.0
			Cut cancel	.5
			Pair	6.0
			Block of 4	22.5
a.			Inverted center	2,75[0]

08 R12a 6c **blue & black**	160.00
Cut cancel	55.00
Pair	325.00
Block of 4	850.00
09 R12a 10c **blue & black**	1.50
Cut cancel	.20
Pair	9.50
Block of 4	25.00
a. Inverted center	*2,000.*
Pair	*4,500.*
b. Double impression of center	—
c. Half used as 5c on document	*250.00*

No. R109a is valued in the grade of fine.

10 R12a 15c **blue & black**	47.50
Cut cancel	17.50
Pair	100.00
Block of 4	190.00
11 R12a 20c **blue & black**	7.50
Cut cancel	2.75
Pair	22.50
Block of 4	87.50
a. Inverted center	*8,000.*
Pair	—

Nos. R109a and R111a are valued in the grade of fine.

R13   R13a

112 R13 25c **blue & black**	1.25
Cut cancel	.20
Pair	2.75
Block of 4	9.50
Double transfer, position 57	15.00
a. Inverted center	*10,000.*
b. Sewing machine perf.	110.00
Cut cancel	65.00
Pair	300.00
Block of 4	1,150.
c. Perf. 8	275.00
113 R13 30c **blue & black**	110.00
Cut cancel	42.50
Pair	200.00
Block of 4	525.00
114 R13 40c **blue & black**	90.00
Cut cancel	22.50
Pair	175.00
115 R13a 50c **blue & black**	1.00
Cut cancel	.20
Pair	2.25
Block of 4	8.75
Double transfer	25.00
a. Sewing machine perf.	75.00
Pair	200.00
Block of 4	900.00
b. Inverted center	1,000.
Pair	2,250.
Inverted center, punch cancellation	275.00
Pair	650.00
116 R13a 60c **blue & black**	150.00
Cut cancel	50.00
Pair	275.00
Foreign entry, design of 70c	185.00
117 R13a 70c **blue & black**	60.00
Cut cancel	20.00
Pair	130.00
a. Inverted center	*3,500.*
Cut cancel	*2,000.*

R13b

R13c

R118 R13b $1 **blue & black**	8.00
Cut cancel	1.75
Pair	20.00
Block of 4	50.00
a. Inverted center	*5,000.*
Punch cancel	*900.00*
R119 R13b $1.30 **blue & black**	550.00
Cut cancel	150.00
Pair	1,150.
R120 R13b $1.50 **blue & black**	19.00
Cut cancel	8.00
Pair	65.00
Block of 4	—
Foreign entry, design of $1	350.00
a. Sewing machine perf.	450.00
Pair	—
R121 R13b $1.60 **blue & black**	575.00
Cut cancel	300.00
Pair	1,200.
R122 R13b $1.90 **blue & black**	400.00
Cut cancel	120.00
Pair	850.00
Block of 4	—
R123 R13c $2 **blue & black**	20.00
Cut cancel	7.50
Pair	55.00
Block of 4	180.00
Double transfer	20.00
R124 R13c $2.50 **blue & black**	35.00
Cut cancel	16.00
Pair	95.00
Block of 4	750.00
R125 R13c $3 **blue & black**	45.00
Cut cancel	17.50
Pair	110.00
Block of 4	550.00
Double transfer	
R126 R13c $3.50 **blue & black**	300.00
Cut cancel	100.00
Pair	700.00

R13d

R13e

R127 R13d $5 **blue & black**	27.50
Cut cancel	9.00
Pair	100.00
Block of 4	275.00
a. Inverted center	*3,250.*
Punch cancel	*950.00*
R128 R13d $10 **blue & black**	200.00
Cut cancel	70.00
Pair	450.00
Block of 4	*950.00*
R129 R13e $20 **blue & black**	650.00
Cut cancel	260.00
Pair	1,400.
R130 R13e $25 **blue & black**	650.00
Cut cancel	275.00
Pair	1,400.
R131 R13e $50 **blue & black**	650.00
Cut cancel	275.00
Pair	1,400.

R13f

R132 R13f $200 **red, blue & black**   6,500.
    Cut cancel   2,800.

Printed in sheets of one.

R13g

R133 R13g $500 **red orange, green &**
            black   13,000.

Printed in sheets of one.

Value for No. R133 is for a very fine appearing example with a light circular cut cancel or with minor flaws.

Inverted Centers: Fraudulently produced inverted centers exist, some excellently made.

Confusion resulting from the fact that all 1c through $50 denominations of the Second Issue were uniform in color, caused the ordering of a new printing with values in distinctive colors.

Plates used were those of the preceding issue.

Third Issue
Engraved and printed by Jos. R. Carpenter, Philadelphia.
Various Frames and Numeral Arrangements.
Violet "Chameleon" Paper with Silk Fibers.

1871-72   **Perf. 12**
R134 R12   1c **claret & black** ('72)   40.00
    Cut cancel   19.00
    Pair   90.00
    Block of 4   310.00

R135 R12   2c **orange & black**   .40
    Cut cancel   .20
    Pair   .80
    Block of 4   1.75
    Double transfer   —
    Double impression of frame   1,500.
    Frame printed on both sides   1,600.
    Double impression of center   150.00
   a.   2c vermilion & black (error)   650.00
   b.   Inverted center   400.00
    Pair   —
    Block of 4   1,200.
   c.   Imperf., pair   —
R136 R12a   4c **brown & black** ('72)   65.00
    Cut cancel   21.00
    Pair   150.00
R137 R12a   5c **orange & black**   .35
    Cut cancel   .20
    Pair   .75
    Block of 4   1.60
   a.   Inverted center   3,500.
    "Block" of 3   —

    No. R137a is valued in the grade of fine.

R138 R12a   6c **orange & black** ('72)   75.00
    Cut cancel   25.00
    Pair   160.00
    Block of 4   450.00
R139 R12a   15c **brown & black** ('72)   17.50
    Cut cancel   5.00
    Pair   40.00
    Block of 4   130.00
   a.   Inverted center   15,000.
R140 R13   30c **orange & black** ('72)   25.00
    Cut cancel   7.50
    Pair   65.00
    Block of 4   250.00
    Double transfer   —
   a.   Inverted center   3,000.
    Cut cancel   1,750.
R141 R13   40c **brown & black** ('72)   60.00
    Cut cancel   20.00
    Pair   140.00
    Block of 4   325.00
R142 R13a   60c **orange & black** ('72)   90.00
    Cut cancel   32.50
    Pair   250.00
    Block of 4   550.00
    Foreign entry, design of 70c   125.00
R143 R13a   70c **green & black** ('72)   75.00
    Cut cancel   22.50
    Pair   175.00
    Block of 4   450.00
R144 R13b $1 **green & black** ('72)   2.00
    Cut cancel   .55
    Pair   8.50
    Block of 4   75.00
   a.   Inverted center   5,500.
R145 R13c $2 **vermilion & black** ('72)   30.00
    Cut cancel   14.00
    Pair   65.00
    Block of 4   155.00
    Double transfer   30.00
R146 R13c $2.50 **claret & black** ('72)   55.00
    Cut cancel   22.00
    Pair   120.00
    Block of 4   210.00
   a.   Inverted center   25,000.
R147 R13c $3 **green & black** ('72)   55.00
    Cut cancel   21.00
    Pair   120.00
    Block of 4   250.00
    Double transfer   —
R148 R13d $5 **vermilion & black** ('72)   35.00
    Cut cancel   12.50
    Pair   75.00
    Block of 4   150.00
R149 R13d $10 **green & black** ('72)   175.00
    Cut cancel   45.00
    Pair   375.00
    Block of 4   850.00
R150 R13e $20 **orange & black** ('72)   625.00
    Pair   1,300.
    Block of 4   3,000.
   a. $20 vermilion & black (error)   800.00

   (See note on Inverted Centers after No. R133.)

1874   **Perf. 12**
R151 R12   2c **orange & black**, *green*   .20
    Cut cancel   .20
    Pair   .40
    Block of 4   .90
   a.   Inverted center   400.00

Liberty — R14

1875-78

            Silk
          Paper   Wmkd. 191R
         a. Perf.   b. Perf.   c. Roul
R152 R14 2c **blue**, *blue*   .25   .25   32
    Pair   .50   .50   125
    "L" shaped   600
     strip of 3
    Block of 4   1.40   1.50
    Double   5.50   5.50
     transfer
   d.   Vert. pair,   525.00
     imperf.
     horiz.
   e.   Imperf., pair   275.00

   The watermarked paper came into use in 1878.

   Nos. 279, 267a, 267, 279Bg, 279B, 272-274
     Overprinted in Red or Blue:

I. R.   I. R
a —   a — Squar
Rectangular   Periods
Periods

I.R.   I.R
b   b — Small
                 Period

Overprint "a" exists in two (or possibly more) settings, w upright rectangular periods or with changed leg of "R" a square periods, both illustrated. Overprint "b" has 4 stamps w small period in each pane of 100 (pos. 41, 46, 91 & 96).

1898   **Wmk. 191**   **Perf.**

For Nos. R153-R160, values in the first column are f unused examples, values in the second column are for use

R153 A87 (a)   1c **green**, red overprint   4.00   2.
    Block of 4   22.50   12.
    P# strip of 3, Impt.   27.50
    P# block of 6, Impt.   75.00
R154 A87 (b)   1c **green**, red overprint   .35   .
    Block of 4   1.50   1.
    P# strip of 3, Impt.   10.50
    P# block of 6, Impt.   57.50
   a.   Overprint inverted   21.00   18.
    Block of 4   110.00
    P# strip of 3, Impt.   115.00
    P# block of 6, Impt.   275.00
   b.   Overprint on back instead of face, inverted   —
   c.   Pair, one without overprint   —
R155 A88 (b)   2c **pink**, type III, blue over-
        print, *July 1, 1898*   .30   .
    Block of 4   1.25   1.
    P# strip of 3, Impt.   11.50
    P# block of 6, Impt.   55.00
    Dot in "S" of "CENTS"   1.10
       P# strip of 3, Impt.   18.00
   b.   2c **carmine**, type III, blue over-
        print, *July 1, 1898*   .35   .
    Block of 4   1.40   1.
    P# strip of 3, Impt.   13.00
    P# block of 6, Impt.   57.50
    Dot in "S" of "CENTS"   1.40
       P# strip of 3, Impt.   24.00
   c.   As No. R155, overprint inverted, *July 1898*   3.75   3.0
    Block of 4   16.00   13.0
    P# strip of 3, Impt.   42.50
    P# block of 6, Impt.   110.00
   d.   Vertical pair, one without overprint   750.00
   e.   Horiz. pair, one without overprint   —
   f.   As No. R155, overprint on back instead of face, inverted   —

NOTE: Old No. R155 is now Nos. R155b, R155Ag; old No R155a is Nos. R155c, R155Ah; old No. R155b is Nos. R155c R155e; old No. R155c is No. R155f.

R155A A88 (b)   2c **pink**, type IV, blue over-
        print *July 1, 1898*   .25   .
    Block of 4   1.25   1.1
    P# strip of 3, Impt.   10.50
    P# block of 6, Impt.   52.50
   g.   2c **carmine**, type IV, blue over-
        print, *July 1, 1898*   .25   .
    Block of 4   1.40   1.1
    P# strip of 3, Impt.   11.50
    P# block of 6, Impt.   55.00
   h.   As No. R155A, overprint inverted, *July 1898*   2.75   2.0
    Block of 4   13.00   9.2
    P# strip of 3, Impt.   32.50
    P# block of 6, Impt.   77.50

   Handstamped Type "b" in Magenta
R156 A93   8c **violet brown**   5,250
R157 A94   10c **dark green**   4,000
    Block of 6   —
R158 A95   15c **dark blue**   6,500

Nos. R156-R158 were emergency provisionals, privately prepared, not officially issued.

Privately Prepared Provisionals

No. 285 Overprinted in Red

I. R.
L. H. C.

	Wmk. 191	Perf. 12
⌐8		
58A A100 1c **dark yellow green**	12,500.	10,000.

Same Overprinted "I.R./P.I.D. & Son" in Red

| 58B A100 1c **dark yellow green** | 25,000. | 22,500. |

No. R158B is valued with small faults as each of the four ⌐orded examples have faults.

⌐os. R158A-R158B were overprinted with federal govern-⌐nt permission by the Purvis Printing Co. upon order of Capt. ⌐H. Chapman of the Chapman Steamboat Line. Both the ⌐apman Line and P. I. Daprix & Son operated freight-carrying ⌐amboats on the Erie Canal. The Chapman Line touched at ⌐acuse, Utica, Little Falls and Fort Plain; the Daprix boat ran ⌐ween Utica and Rome. Overprintings of 250 of each stamp ⌐e made.

⌐r. Kilmer & Co. provisional overprints are listed under "Pri-⌐e Die Medicine Stamps," Nos. RS307-RS315.

Newspaper Stamp No. ⌐121 Surcharged in Red

		Perf. 12
⌐98		
⌐59 N18 $5 **dark blue,** surcharge read-		
ing down	500.00	200.00
Block of 4	2,100.	950.00
P# strip of 3, Impt.	—	
⌐60 N18 $5 **dark blue,** surcharge read-		
ing up	140.00	110.00
Block of 4	550.00	750.00
P# strip of 3, Impt.	2,000.	

Battleship — R15

There are two styles of rouletting for the proprietary and ⌐cumentary stamps of the 1898 issue, an ordinary rouletting ⌐2 and one by which small rectangles of the paper are cut out, ⌐ually called hyphen-hole perforation 7. Several stamps are ⌐own with an apparent roulette 14 caused by slippage of a ⌐phen-hole 7 rouletting wheel.

	Wmk. 191R		
⌐398			

Rouletted 5½, Hyphen Hole Perf 7

			Roul. 5½		p. Hyphen Hole Perf. 7	
			Unused	Used	Unused	Used
⌐161 R15 ½c		**orange**	3.50	15.00		
		Block of 4	12.50	110.00		
⌐162 R15 ½c		**dark gray**	.30	.25		
		Block of 4	1.60	1.10		
		Double transfer		7.75		
	a.	Vert. pair, imperf. horiz.	90.00			
⌐163 R15 1c		**pale blue**	.20	.20	.30	.25
		Block of 4	.40	.25	1.60	1.50
		Double transfer	10.00			
	a.	Vert. pair, imperf. horiz.	8.00			
	b.	Imperf., pair	450.00			
⌐164 R15 2c		**carmine rose**	.30	.30	.35	.25
		Block of 4	1.50	1.50	2.75	1.10
		Double transfer	1.10	.30		

			Roul. 5½		p. Hyphen Hole Perf. 7	
			Unused	Used	Unused	Used
	a.	Vert. pair, imperf. horiz.	90.00			
	b.	Imperf., pair	250.00			
	c.	Horiz. pair, imperf. vert.	—			
R165 R15 3c		**dark blue**	3.00	.25	30.00	1.10
		Block of 4	11.50	1.25	125.00	5.00
		Double transfer	—			
R166 R15 4c		**pale rose**	2.00	.25	11.00	1.60
		Block of 4	9.00	1.25	45.00	7.75
	a.	Vert. pair, imperf. horiz.	155.00			
R167 R15 5c		**lilac**	.55	.25	11.00	.25
		Block of 4	2.75	1.25	45.00	1.40
	a.	Pair, imperf. horiz. or vert.	250.00	160.00		
	b.	Horiz. pair, imperf. between		550.00		
R168 R15 10c		**dark brown**	1.75	.25	7.50	.25
		Block of 4	10.50	1.25	32.50	1.25
	a.	Vert. pair, imperf. horiz.	35.00	30.00		
	b.	Horiz. pair, imperf. vert.	—			
R169 R15 25c		**purple brown**	4.00	.50	12.50	.30
		Block of 4	19.00	2.25	55.00	1.40
		Double transfer	—			
R170 R15 40c		**blue lilac**	125.00	1.10	175.00	37.50
		Block of 4	600.00	52.50	875.00	275.00
		Cut cancel		.35		12.50
R171 R15 50c		**slate violet**	25.00	.25	55.00	.80
		Block of 4	110.00	2.25	250.00	6.25
	a.	Imperf., pair	300.00			
	b.	Horiz. pair, imperf. between			—	250.00
R172 R15 80c		**bister**	100.00	.30	210.00	50.00
		Block of 4	500.00	32.50	1,050.	240.00
		Cut cancel		.20		20.00

Numerous double transfers exist on this issue.

Commerce — R16

R173 R16 $1		**dark green**	17.50	.20	25.00	.65
		Block of 4	72.50	.50		3.25
		Cut cancel		.20		.30
	a.	Vert. pair, imperf. horiz.	—			
	b.	Horiz. pair, imperf. vert.		325.00	—	
R174 R16 $3		**dark brown**	37.50	1.00	60.00	2.40

		Block of 4	—	5.25		12.00
		Cut cancel		.25		.30
	a.	Horiz. pair, imperf. vert.	500.00			
R175 R16 $5		**orange red**	60.00	1.90		
		Block of 4		9.50		
		Cut cancel		.25		
R176 R16 $10		**black**	125.00	3.25		
		Block of 4		16.00		
		Cut cancel		.55		
	a.	Horiz. pair, imperf. vert.				
R177 R16 $30		**red**	400.00	135.00		
		Block of 4		525.00		
		Cut cancel		47.50		
R178 R16 $50		**gray brown**	200.00	5.75		
		Block of 4		29.00		
		Cut cancel		2.10		

John Marshall — R17

Alexander Hamilton — R18

James Madison — R19

Various Portraits in Various Frames, Each Inscribed "Series of 1898"

1899				Imperf.
		Without Gum		
R179 R17 $100 **yellow brown & black**			225.00	37.50
	Cut cancel			21.00
	Vertical strip of 4		—	175.00
	Vertical strip of 4, cut cancel			90.00
R180 R18 $500 **carmine lake & black**			1,400.	800.00
	Cut cancel			300.
	Vertical strip of 4		—	2,250.
	Vertical strip of 4, cut cancel			1,000.

R181 R19 $1000 green & black 1,000. 375.00
Cut cancel 150.00
Vertical strip of 4 1,750.
Vertical strip of 4, cut cancel 600.00

1900   *Hyphen-hole perf. 7*
Allegorical Figure of Commerce
R182 R16 $1 carmine 30.00 .55
Cut cancel .30
Block of 4 130.00 2.50
Block of 4, cut cancel 1.25
R183 R16 $3 lake (fugitive ink) 200.00 52.50
Cut cancel 9.00
Block of 4 900.00 275.00
Block of 4, cut cancel 40.00

Warning: The ink on No. R183 will run in water.

Surcharged in Black with Open Numerals of Value

R184 R16 $1 gray 25.00 .30
Cut cancel .25
Block of 4 — 1.25
Block of 4, cut cancel 1.10
a. Horiz. pair, imperf. vert
b. Surcharge omitted 125.00
Surcharge omitted, cut cancel 82.50
R185 R16 $2 gray 25.00 .25
Cut cancel .25
Block of 4 85.00 1.25
Block of 4, cut cancel 1.10
R186 R16 $3 gray 100.00 11.50
Cut cancel 4.25
Block of 4 — 50.00
Block of 4, cut cancel 18.00
R187 R16 $5 gray 67.50 9.00
Cut cancel 1.40
Block of 4 — 35.00
Block of 4, cut cancel 7.00
R188 R16 $10 gray 150.00 20.00
Cut cancel 3.25
Block of 4 — 92.50
Block of 4, cut cancel 15.00
R189 R16 $50 gray 1,100. 500.00
Cut cancel 125.00
Block of 4 2,250.
Block of 4, cut cancel 500.00

Surcharged in Black with Ornamental Numerals of Value

Warning: If Nos. R190-R194 are soaked, the center part of the surcharged numeral may wash off. Before the surcharging, a square of soluble varnish was applied to the middle of some stamps.

1902
R190 R16 $1 green 35.00 2.75
Cut cancel .25
Block of 4 — 12.00
Block of 4, cut cancel 1.10
a. Inverted surcharge 190.00
R191 R16 $2 green 35.00 1.75
Cut cancel .30
Block of 4 — 7.50
Block of 4, cut cancel 1.40
a. Surcharged as No. R185 110.00 75.00
b. Surcharged as No. R185, in violet 1,350. —
c. As "a," double surcharge 140.00
d. As "a," triple surcharge
R192 R16 $5 green 190.00 30.00
Cut cancel 4.25
Block of 4 — 115.00
Block of 4, cut cancel 19.00
a. Surcharge omitted 225.00
b. Pair, one without surcharge 400.00

R193 R16 $10 green 400.00 125.00
Cut cancel 47.50
Block of 4 550.00
Block of 4, cut cancel 210.00
R194 R16 $50 green 1,150. 1,000.
Cut cancel 250.00
Block of 4 —
Block of 4, cut cancel 1,050.

R20   Wmk. 190

Inscribed "Series of 1914"
1914   Wmk. 190   Offset Printing   *Perf. 10*
R195 R20 ½c rose 12.00 4.50
Block of 4 50.00 19.00
R196 R20 1c rose 2.50 .30
Block of 4 11.00 1.25
R197 R20 2c rose 3.00 .30
Block of 4 13.00 1.25
Double impression —
R198 R20 3c rose 70.00 30.00
Block of 4 300.00 40.00
R199 R20 4c rose 22.50 2.25
Block of 4 92.50 9.50
Recut U. L. corner 300.00
R200 R20 5c rose 7.50 .35
Block of 4 32.50 1.50
R201 R20 10c rose 6.00 .25
Block of 4 25.00 .45
R202 R20 25c rose 45.00 .55
Block of 4 200.00 2.25
R203 R20 40c rose 27.50 2.50
Block of 4 110.00 11.00
R204 R20 50c rose 10.00 .25
Block of 4 42.00 1.00
R205 R20 80c rose 175.00 15.00
Block of 4 725.00 65.00

Wmk. 191R
R206 R20 ½c rose 1.60 .50
Block of 4 7.00 2.50
R207 R20 1c rose .25 .20
Block of 4 .70 .25
Double impression 300.00
R208 R20 2c rose .30 .25
Block of 4 1.25 1.10
R209 R20 3c rose 1.50 .25
Block of 4 6.50 1.10
R210 R20 4c rose 4.00 .50
Block of 4 19.00 2.25
R211 R20 5c rose 1.75 .30
Block of 4 8.00 1.25
R212 R20 10c rose .80 .20
Block of 4 3.75 .35
R213 R20 25c rose 6.00 1.50
Block of 4 25.00 7.00
R214 R20 40c rose 110.00 14.00
Cut cancel .45
Block of 4 525.00 57.50
R215 R20 50c rose 22.50 .25
Cut cancel .20
Block of 4 100.00 1.10
R216 R20 80c rose 175.00 27.50
Cut cancel 1.00
Block of 4 750.00 210.00

Liberty — R21

Inscribed "Series 1914"
Engr.
R217 R21 $1 green 50.00 .45
Cut cancel .25
Block of 4 — 2.75
Block of 4, cut cancel 1.10
a. $1 yellow green 45.00 .25
R218 R21 $2 carmine 70.00 .75
Cut cancel .20
Block of 4 300.00 3.25
Block of 4, cut cancel .25
R219 R21 $3 purple 90.00 3.75
Cut cancel .50
Block of 4 400.00 13.50
Block of 4, cut cancel 2.10
R220 R21 $5 blue 80.00 4.00
Cut cancel .55
Block of 4 350.00 17.00
Block of 4, cut cancel 2.75

R221 R21 $10 yellow orange 185.00
Cut cancel
Block of 4 — 2.
Block of 4, cut cancel
R222 R21 $30 vermilion 550.00 1.
Cut cancel
Block of 4 — 6.
Block of 4, cut cancel 1.
R223 R21 $50 violet 1,600. 1,.
Cut cancel 35.
Block of 4 4,.

Portrait Types of 1899 Inscribed "Series of 1915" (#R224), or "Series of 1914"
1914-15   Without Gum   *Perf.*
R224 R19 $60 brown (Lincoln) 200.00 140.
Vertical strip of 4
Cut cancel 6.
Vertical strip of 4, cut cancel 30.
R225 R17 $100 green (Washington) 67.50 4.
Vertical strip of 4 19.
Cut cancel 1.
Vertical strip of 4, cut cancel 7.
R226 R18 $500 blue (Hamilton) — 60.
Cut cancel 25.
Vertical strip of 4, cut cancel 1,0.
R227 R19 $1000 orange (Madison) — 52.
Cut cancel 27.
Vert. strip of 4, cut cancel 1,.

The stamps of types R17, R18 and R19 in this and subsequent issues are issued in vertical strips of 4 which are imperforate at the top, bottom and right side; therefore, single copies are always imperforate on one or two sides.

R22

Two types of design R22 are known.
Type I — With dot in centers of periods before and a... "CENTS."
Type II — Without such dots.
First printings were done by commercial companies, la... printings by the Bureau of Engraving and Printing.

1917   Offset Printing   Wmk. 191R   *Perf.*
R228 R22 1c carmine rose .25
Block of 4 1.10
Double impression 20.00 4.
R229 R22 2c carmine rose .20
Block of 4 .50
Double impression 20.00 5.
R230 R22 3c carmine rose 1.50
Block of 4 6.25
Double impression
R231 R22 4c carmine rose .75
Block of 4 3.50 1.
Double impression
R232 R22 5c carmine rose .30
Block of 4 1.25
R233 R22 8c carmine rose 2.50
Block of 4 11.50 1.
R234 R22 10c carmine rose .40
Block of 4 1.90
Double impression 5.
R235 R22 20c carmine rose .75
Block of 4 3.50 1.
Double impression
R236 R22 25c carmine rose 1.50
Block of 4 6.25 1.
Double impression
R237 R22 40c carmine rose 2.25
Block of 4 10.50 2.
Double impression 8.00 5.
R238 R22 50c carmine rose 2.25
Block of 4 9.50
Double impression —
R239 R22 80c carmine rose 7.50
Block of 4 32.50 1.
Double impression

No. R234 is known used provisionally as a playing card revenue stamp in August 1932. Value for this use, authenticate... $300.

Liberty Type of 1914 without "Series 1914"
1917-33   Eng...
R240 R21 $1 yellow green 7.50
Block of 4 32.50 1.
a. $1 green 12.50
R241 R21 $2 rose 11.50
Block of 4 52.50 .
R242 R21 $3 violet 45.00
Cut cancel
Block of 4 — 4.5
R243 R21 $4 yellow brown ('33) 30.00 1.9
Cut cancel
Block of 4 — 8.7
Block of 4, cut cancel 1.0
R244 R21 $5 dark blue 20.00
Cut cancel
Block of 4 — 1.5
R245 R21 $10 orange 40.00 1.2
Cut cancel
Block of 4 — 6.2
Block of 4, cut cancel 1.1

Portrait Types of 1899 without "Series of" and Date

			Without Gum	Perf. 12

6	R17	$30 **deep orange, green numerals** (Grant)	50.00	13.00
		Cut cancel		2.25
		Vertical strip of 4		—
		Cut cancel		3.50
a.		As "b," imperf. pair		750.00
b.		Numerals in blue	80.00	2.25
		Cut cancel		1.40
7	R19	$60 **brown** (Lincoln)	60.00	8.00
		Cut cancel		.85
		Vertical strip of 4		—
		Cut cancel		5.00
8	R17	$100 **green** (Washington)	37.50	1.25
		Cut cancel		.40
		Vertical strip of 4		—
		Cut cancel		2.50
9	R18	$500 **blue, red numerals** (Hamilton)	325.00	40.00
		Cut cancel		12.50
		Vertical strip of 4		150.00
		Cut cancel		57.50
		Double transfer	—	52.50
a.		Numerals in orange	375.00	52.50
		Double transfer	—	—
50	R19	$1000 **orange** (Madison)	150.00	12.50
		Cut cancel		4.25
		Vertical strip of 4		75.00
		Cut cancel		17.50
a.		Imperf., pair		1,250.

See note after No. R227.

			Offset Printing	Perf. 10
28-29				

51	R22	1c **carmine rose**	2.10	1.60
		Block of 4	9.50	7.50
52	R22	2c **carmine rose**	.60	.30
		Block of 4	3.00	1.50
53	R22	4c **carmine rose**	7.00	4.00
		Block of 4	32.50	19.00
54	R22	5c **carmine rose**	1.60	.55
		Block of 4	7.75	2.50
55	R22	10c **carmine rose**	2.40	1.25
		Block of 4	11.00	5.50
56	R22	20c **carmine rose**	5.50	4.50
		Block of 4	25.00	20.00
		Double impression	—	—

Engr.

57	R21	$1 **green**	160.00	40.00
		Block of 4	—	—
		Cut cancel		5.00
58	R21	$2 **rose**	70.00	3.75
		Block of 4	—	16.50
59	R21	$10 **orange**	225.00	50.00
		Block of 4	—	—
		Cut cancel		26.00

			Offset Printing	Perf. 11x10
29				

60	R22	2c **carmine rose** ('30)	3.00	2.75
		Block of 4	13.00	12.00
		Double impression	—	—
61	R22	5c **carmine rose** ('30)	2.00	1.90
		Block of 4	10.00	8.75
62	R22	10c **carmine rose**	9.25	6.75
		Block of 4	45.00	32.50
63	R22	20c **carmine rose**	15.00	8.25
		Block of 4	70.00	42.50

Types of 1917-33 Overprinted in Black
SERIES 1940

			Wmk. 191R	Offset Printing	Perf. 11
40					

64	R22	1c **rose pink**	3.50	2.40
		Cut cancel		.35
		Perf. initial		.25
65	R22	2c **rose pink**	4.00	1.90
		Cut cancel		.40
		Perf. initial		.35
66	R22	3c **rose pink**	10.00	4.25
		Cut cancel		.75
		Perf. initial		.50
67	R22	4c **rose pink**	4.50	.60
		Cut cancel		.20
		Perf. initial		.25
68	R22	5c **rose pink**	4.50	.95
		Cut cancel		.30
		Perf. initial		.20
69	R22	8c **rose pink**	20.00	16.00
		Cut cancel		3.00
		Perf. initial		2.00
70	R22	10c **rose pink**	2.25	.65
		Cut cancel		.25
		Perf. initial		.25
71	R22	20c **rose pink**	3.00	.70
		Cut cancel		.20
		Perf. initial		.25
72	R22	25c **rose pink**	7.50	1.40
		Cut cancel		.25
		Perf. initial		.25
73	R22	40c **rose pink**	6.25	.90
		Cut cancel		.25
		Perf. initial		.25
74	R22	50c **rose pink**	8.00	.55
		Cut cancel		.25
		Perf. initial		.25
75	R22	80c **rose pink**	13.00	1.50
		Cut cancel		.25
		Perf. initial		.25

Engr.

R276	R21	$1 **green**	60.00	1.00
		Cut cancel		.25
		Perf. initial		.25
R277	R21	$2 **rose**	60.00	1.75
		Cut cancel		.25
		Perf. initial		.25
R278	R21	$3 **violet**	80.00	30.00
		Cut cancel		3.50
		Perf. initial		1.60
R279	R21	$4 **yellow brown**	140.00	35.00
		Cut cancel		5.50
		Perf. initial		2.10
R280	R21	$5 **dark blue**	70.00	15.00
		Cut cancel		1.25
		Perf. initial		.55
R281	R21	$10 **orange**	175.00	40.00
		Cut cancel		2.75
		Perf. initial		.55

Types of 1917 Handstamped "Series 1940" like R264-R281 in Green (Nos. R282-R284, R286) or Violet (No. R285)

			Wmk. 191R	Perf. 12
1940			Without Gum	

R282	R17	$30 **vermilion**		800.
		Cut cancel		425.
		Perf. initial		325.
a.		With black 2-line handstamp in larger type		12,500.
R283	R19	$60 **brown**		1,100.
		Cut cancel		700.
		Perf. initial		500.
a.		As #R282a, cut cancel		—
R284	R17	$100 **green**		2,500.
		Cut cancel		1,150.
		Perf. initial		800.
R285	R18	$500 **blue**		2,000.
		Cut cancel		1,250.
		Perf. initial		1,000.
		Double transfer		1,850.
a.		As #R282a	3,250.	3,500.
		Cut cancel		2,750.
		Double transfer	—	2,650.
b.		Blue handstamp; double transfer		—
R286	R19	$1000 **orange**		700.
		Cut cancel		400.
		Perf. initial		275.
a.		Double overprint, cut cancel		—

Alexander Hamilton — R23

Levi Woodbury — R24

Overprinted in Black **SERIES 1940**

Various Portraits: 2c, Oliver Wolcott, Jr. 3c, Samuel Dexter. 4c, Albert Gallatin. 5c. G. W. Campbell. 8c, Alexander Dallas. 10c, William H. Crawford. 20c, Richard Rush. 25c, S. D. Ingham. 40c. Louis McLane. 50c, William J. Duane. 80c, Roger B. Taney. $2, Thomas Ewing. $3, Walter Forward. $4, J. C. Spencer. $5, G. M. Bibb. $10, R. J. Walker. $20, William M. Meredith. The "sensitive ink" varieties are in a bluish-purple overprint showing minute flecks of gold.

			Engr.	Wmk. 191R	Perf. 11
1940					

Plates of 400 subjects, issued in panes of 100

R288	R23	1c **carmine**	5.00	3.50
		Cut cancel		1.40
		Perf. initial		.70
		Sensitive ink	8.25	4.25
R289	R23	2c **carmine**	6.50	3.25
		Cut cancel		1.40
		Perf. initial		.85
		Sensitive ink	8.25	4.25
R290	R23	3c **carmine**	25.00	10.50
		Cut cancel		3.50
		Perf. initial		2.40
		Sensitive ink	24.00	9.25
R291	R23	4c **carmine**	57.50	25.00
		Cut cancel		4.75
		Perf. initial		4.00
R292	R23	5c **carmine**	4.50	.70
		Cut cancel		.30
		Perf. initial		.25
R293	R23	8c **carmine**	80.00	60.00
		Cut cancel		18.00
		Perf. initial		13.00
R294	R23	10c **carmine**	4.00	.55
		Cut cancel		.25
		Perf. initial		.25
R295	R23	20c **carmine**	5.00	3.75
		Cut cancel		1.10
		Perf. initial		.80

R296	R23	25c **carmine**	4.25	.60
		Cut cancel		.25
		Perf. initial		.25
R297	R23	40c **carmine**	60.00	25.00
		Cut cancel		5.25
		Perf. initial		2.40
R298	R23	50c **carmine**	6.25	.45
		Cut cancel		.25
		Perf. initial		.20
R299	R23	80c **carmine**	150.00	90.00
		Cut cancel		26.00
		Perf. initial		18.00
a.		Imperf, pair, without gum	475.00	
		Block of 4	1,400.	

Plates of 200 subjects, issued in panes of 50

R300	R24	$1 **carmine**	37.50	.55
		Cut cancel		.20
		Perf. initial		.20
		Sensitive ink	52.50	21.00
R301	R24	$2 **carmine**	60.00	.75
		Cut cancel		.20
		Perf. initial		.20
		Sensitive ink	55.00	10.50
R302	R24	$3 **carmine**	160.00	87.50
		Cut cancel		10.50
		Perf. initial		7.25
		Sensitive ink	160.00	87.50
a.		Imperf, pair, without gum	1,400.	
		Block of 4	3,000.	
R303	R24	$4 **carmine**	95.00	32.50
		Cut cancel		6.25
		Perf. initial		1.60
R304	R24	$5 **carmine**	60.00	2.00
		Cut cancel		.45
		Perf. initial		.25
R305	R24	$10 **carmine**	100.00	6.25
		Cut cancel		1.00
		Perf. initial		.40
R305A	R24	$20 **carmine**	2,500.	900.00
		Cut cancel		550.00
		Perf. initial		425.00
b.		Imperf, pair, without gum	700.00	
		Block of 4	1,500.	

Thomas Corwin — R25

Overprint: "SERIES 1940"

Various Frames and Portraits: $50, James Guthrie. $60, Howell Cobb. $100, P. F. Thomas. $500, J. A. Dix, $1,000, S. P. Chase.

Perf. 12
Plates of 16 subjects, issued in strips of 4
Without Gum

R306	R25	$30 **carmine**	160.00	42.50
		Cut cancel		14.00
		Perf. initial		10.50
R306A	R25	$50 **carmine**	—	3,250.
		Cut cancel		1,600.
		Perf. initial		800.00
R307	R25	$60 **carmine**	300.00	62.50
		Cut cancel		40.00
		Perf. initial		21.00
a.		Vert. pair, imperf. btwn.	2,750.	1,450.
R308	R25	$100 **carmine**	225.00	67.50
		Cut cancel		37.50
		Perf. initial		13.00
R309	R25	$500 **carmine**	—	3,750.
		Cut cancel		1,600.
		Perf. initial		800.00
R310	R25	$1000 **carmine**	—	450.00
		Cut cancel		210.00
		Perf. initial		150.00

The $30 to $1,000 denominations in this and following similar issues, and the $2,500, $5,000 and $10,000 stamps of 1952-58 have straight edges on one or two sides. They were issued without gum through No. R723.

Nos. R288-R310 Overprinted: **SERIES 1941**

			Wmk. 191R	Perf. 11
1941				

R311	R23	1c **carmine**	4.25	2.40
		Cut cancel		.75
		Perf. initial		.65
R312	R23	2c **carmine**	4.25	.95
		Cut cancel		.45
		Perf. initial		.40
R313	R23	3c **carmine**	8.25	3.75
		Cut cancel		1.40
		Perf. initial		.90

R314 R23 4c **carmine** 5.50 1.40
Cut cancel .35
Perf. initial .25
R315 R23 5c **carmine** 1.10 .30
Cut cancel .25
Perf. initial .30
R316 R23 8c **carmine** 17.50 7.75
Cut cancel 3.25
Perf. initial 2.75
R317 R23 10c **carmine** 1.40 .25
Cut cancel .25
Perf. initial .25
R318 R23 20c **carmine** 3.25 .50
Cut cancel .25
Perf. initial .30
R319 R23 25c **carmine** 1.90 .55
Cut cancel .25
Perf. initial .25
R320 R23 40c **carmine** 14.00 2.75
Cut cancel 1.10
Perf. initial .65
R321 R23 50c **carmine** 2.75 .25
Cut cancel .20
Perf. initial .20
R322 R23 80c **carmine** 65.00 10.50
Cut cancel 3.00
Perf. initial 2.40
R323 R24 $1 **carmine** 12.50 .25
Cut cancel .20
Perf. initial .20
R324 R24 $2 **carmine** 15.00 .45
Cut cancel .25
Perf. initial .25
R325 R24 $3 **carmine** 25.00 2.75
Cut cancel .35
Perf. initial .30
R326 R24 $4 **carmine** 40.00 27.50
Cut cancel .90
Perf. initial .70
R327 R24 $5 **carmine** 50.00 .95
Cut cancel .20
Perf. initial .20
R328 R24 $10 **carmine** 75.00 3.75
Cut cancel .30
Perf. initial .25
R329 R24 $20 **carmine** 800.00 300.00
Cut cancel 67.50
Perf. initial 42.50

Without Gum *Perf. 12*
R330 R25 $30 **carmine** 150.00 45.00
Cut cancel 16.00
Perf. initial 10.50
R331 R25 $50 **carmine** 450.00 375.00
Cut cancel 100.00
Perf. initial 52.50
R332 R25 $60 **carmine** 200.00 70.00
Cut cancel 26.00
Perf. initial 13.00
R333 R25 $100 **carmine** 90.00 32.50
Cut cancel 7.75
Perf. initial 5.00
R334 R25 $500 **carmine** — 275.00
Cut cancel 140.00
Perf. initial 55.00
R335 R25 $1000 **carmine** — 175.00
Cut cancel 40.00
Perf. initial 29.00

Nos. R288-R310 Overprinted: SERIES 1942

1942 **Wmk. 191R** *Perf. 11*
R336 R23 1c **carmine** .55 .50
Cut cancel .25
Perf. initial .25
R337 R23 2c **carmine** .50 .50
Cut cancel .25
Perf. initial .25
R338 R23 3c **carmine** .75 .65
Cut cancel .30
Perf. initial .25
R339 R23 4c **carmine** 1.40 .95
Cut cancel .30
Perf. initial .25
R340 R23 5c **carmine** .50 .25
Cut cancel .25
Perf. initial .20
R341 R23 8c **carmine** 7.00 4.50
Cut cancel 1.25
Perf. initial 1.10
R342 R23 10c **carmine** 1.40 .25
Cut cancel .25
Perf. initial .25
R343 R23 20c **carmine** 1.40 .50
Cut cancel .25
Perf. initial .25
R344 R23 25c **carmine** 2.25 .45
Cut cancel .25
Perf. initial .25
R345 R23 40c **carmine** 5.25 1.40
Cut cancel .55
Perf. initial .35
R346 R23 50c **carmine** 3.25 .25
Cut cancel .20
Perf. initial .20
R347 R23 80c **carmine** 22.50 10.50
Cut cancel 3.00
Perf. initial 2.00
R348 R24 $1 **carmine** 11.00 .25
Cut cancel .20
Perf. initial .20
R349 R24 $2 **carmine** 12.50 .20
Cut cancel .20
Perf. initial .20
R350 R24 $3 **carmine** 22.50 2.75
Cut cancel .35
Perf. initial .20

R351 R24 $4 **carmine** 30.00 6.00
Cut cancel .50
Perf. initial .30
R352 R24 $5 **carmine** 32.50 1.25
Cut cancel .25
Perf. initial .20
R353 R24 $10 **carmine** 75.00 2.75
Cut cancel .25
Perf. initial .20
R354 R24 $20 **carmine** 145.00 40.00
Cut cancel 18.00
Perf. initial 11.50

Without Gum *Perf. 12*
R355 R25 $30 **carmine** 80.00 40.00
Cut cancel 13.00
Perf. initial 6.25
R356 R25 $50 **carmine** 1,400. 800.00
Cut cancel 275.00
Perf. initial 150.00
R357 R25 $60 **carmine** 2,500. 850.00
Cut cancel 350.00
Perf. initial 150.00
R358 R25 $100 **carmine** 190.00 130.00
Cut cancel 52.50
Perf. initial 40.00
R359 R25 $500 **carmine** *1,600.* 240.00
Cut cancel 140.00
Perf. initial 77.50
R360 R25 $1000 **carmine** — 120.00
Cut cancel 52.50
Perf. initial 42.50

Nos. R288-R310 Overprinted: SERIES 1943

1943 **Wmk. 191R** *Perf. 11*
R361 R23 1c **carmine** .65 .55
Cut cancel .25
Perf. initial .25
R362 R23 2c **carmine** .50 .45
Cut cancel .25
Perf. initial .25
R363 R23 3c **carmine** 3.25 3.00
Cut cancel .55
Perf. initial .35
R364 R23 4c **carmine** 1.40 1.25
Cut cancel .35
Perf. initial .30
R365 R23 5c **carmine** .55 .35
Cut cancel .25
Perf. initial .25
R366 R23 8c **carmine** 4.75 3.25
Cut cancel 1.60
Perf. initial 1.10
R367 R23 10c **carmine** .75 .25
Cut cancel .25
Perf. initial .20
R368 R23 20c **carmine** 2.10 .70
Cut cancel .35
Perf. initial .30
R369 R23 25c **carmine** 2.25 .40
Cut cancel .25
Perf. initial .25
R370 R23 40c **carmine** 5.50 2.75
Cut cancel 1.25
Perf. initial .65
R371 R23 50c **carmine** 1.60 .25
Cut cancel .20
Perf. initial .20
R372 R23 80c **carmine** 22.50 5.75
Cut cancel 2.10
Perf. initial 1.10
R373 R24 $1 **carmine** 7.50 .35
Cut cancel .25
Perf. initial .25
R374 R24 $2 **carmine** 15.00 .25
Cut cancel .25
Perf. initial .20
R375 R24 $3 **carmine** 25.00 2.40
Cut cancel .35
Perf. initial .20
R376 R24 $4 **carmine** 40.00 5.00
Cut cancel .45
Perf. initial .35
R377 R24 $5 **carmine** 45.00 .65
Cut cancel .35
Perf. initial .20
R378 R24 $10 **carmine** 70.00 4.25
Cut cancel 1.60
Perf. initial .65
R379 R24 $20 **carmine** 140.00 35.00
Cut cancel 5.25
Perf. initial 3.25

Without Gum *Perf. 12*
R380 R25 $30 **carmine** 70.00 20.00
Cut cancel 5.00
Perf. initial 4.50
R381 R25 $50 **carmine** 140.00 35.00
Cut cancel 13.00
Perf. initial 5.25
R382 R25 $60 **carmine** 300.00 100.00
Cut cancel 35.00
Perf. initial 11.50
R383 R25 $100 **carmine** 30.00 19.00
Cut cancel 5.75
Perf. initial 3.75
R384 R25 $500 **carmine** *375.00* 225.00
Cut cancel 110.00
Perf. initial 87.50
R385 R25 $1000 **carmine** *350.00* 185.00
Cut cancel 52.50
Perf. initial 40.00

Nos. R288-R310 Overprinted: Series 1944

1944 **Wmk. 191R** *Perf*
R386 R23 1c **carmine** .45
Cut cancel
Perf. initial
R387 R23 2c **carmine** .50
Cut cancel
Perf. initial
R388 R23 3c **carmine** .55
Cut cancel
Perf. initial
R389 R23 4c **carmine** .60
Cut cancel
Perf. initial
R390 R23 5c **carmine** .35
Cut cancel
Perf. initial
R391 R23 8c **carmine** 2.00
Cut cancel
Perf. initial
R392 R23 10c **carmine** .45
Cut cancel
Perf. initial
R393 R23 20c **carmine** .80
Cut cancel
Perf. initial
R394 R23 25c **carmine** 1.50
Cut cancel
Perf. initial
R395 R23 40c **carmine** 3.00
Cut cancel
Perf. initial
R396 R23 50c **carmine** 3.25
Cut cancel
Perf. initial
R397 R23 80c **carmine** 19.00
Cut cancel
Perf. initial
R398 R24 $1 **carmine** 9.00
Cut cancel
Perf. initial
R399 R24 $2 **carmine** 12.50
Cut cancel
Perf. initial
R400 R24 $3 **carmine** 20.00 2
Cut cancel
Perf. initial
R401 R24 $4 **carmine** 27.50 1(
Cut cancel
Perf. initial
R402 R24 $5 **carmine** 30.00
Cut cancel
Perf. initial
R403 R24 $10 **carmine** 60.00
Cut cancel
Perf. initial
R404 R24 $20 **carmine** 125.00 16
Cut cancel 3
Perf. initial 2

Without Gum *Perf.*
R405 R25 $30 **carmine** 90.00 32
Cut cancel 7
Perf. initial 6
R406 R25 $50 **carmine** 40.00 20
Cut cancel 6
Perf. initial 4
R407 R25 $60 **carmine** 250.00 70
Cut cancel 26
Perf. initial 9
R408 R25 $100 **carmine** 50.00 12
Cut cancel 5
Perf. initial 3
R409 R25 $500 **carmine** — 2,6
Cut cancel 1,2
Perf. initial 775
R410 R25 $1000 **carmine** — 325
Cut cancel 110
Perf. initial 57

Nos. R288-R310 Overprinted: Series 19

1945 **Wmk. 191R** *Perf.*
R411 R23 1c **carmine** .30
Cut cancel
Perf. initial
R412 R23 2c **carmine** .30
Cut cancel
Perf. initial
R413 R23 3c **carmine** .55
Cut cancel
Perf. initial
R414 R23 4c **carmine** .35
Cut cancel
Perf. initial
R415 R23 5c **carmine** .40
Cut cancel
Perf. initial
R416 R23 8c **carmine** 5.00 2.
Cut cancel
Perf. initial
R417 R23 10c **carmine** 1.00
Cut cancel
Perf. initial
R418 R23 20c **carmine** 6.25 .
Cut cancel
Perf. initial
R419 R23 25c **carmine** 1.50
Cut cancel
Perf. initial
R420 R23 40c **carmine** 8.00 1.
Cut cancel
Perf. initial
R421 R23 50c **carmine** 3.50
Cut cancel
Perf. initial

422 R23	80c **carmine**		24.00	10.00
	Cut cancel			3.25
	Perf. initial			2.10
423 R24	$1 **carmine**		12.50	.25
	Cut cancel			.20
	Perf. initial			.20
424 R24	$2 **carmine**		12.50	.35
	Cut cancel			.20
	Perf. initial			.25
425 R24	$3 **carmine**		22.50	2.40
	Cut cancel			.85
	Perf. initial			.65
426 R24	$4 **carmine**		30.00	3.75
	Cut cancel			.55
	Perf. initial			.35
427 R24	$5 **carmine**		30.00	.45
	Cut cancel			.25
	Perf. initial			.25
428 R24	$10 **carmine**		60.00	2.00
	Cut cancel			.30
	Perf. initial			.25
429 R24	$20 **carmine**		125.00	14.00
	Cut cancel			3.25
	Perf. initial			2.75

Without Gum — **Perf. 12**

430 R25	$30 **carmine**		160.00	37.50
	Cut cancel			8.75
	Perf. initial			5.75
431 R25	$50 **carmine**		175.00	40.00
	Cut cancel			18.00
	Perf. initial			10.50
432 R25	$60 **carmine**		325.00	65.00
	Cut cancel			29.00
	Perf. initial			13.00
433 R25	$100 **carmine**		30.00	17.50
	Cut cancel			8.25
	Perf. initial			5.50
434 R25	$500 **carmine**		375.00	200.00
	Cut cancel			72.50
	Perf. initial			52.50
435 R25	$1000 **carmine**		250.00	100.00
	Cut cancel			29.00
	Perf. initial			17.50

Nos. R288-R310 Overprinted: **Series 1946**

1946 — **Wmk. 191R** — **Perf. 11**

436 R23	1c **carmine**		.25	.30
	Cut cancel			.25
	Perf. initial			.25
437 R23	2c **carmine**		.40	.35
	Cut cancel			.25
	Perf. initial			.25
438 R23	3c **carmine**		.40	.35
	Cut cancel			.25
	Perf. initial			.25
439 R23	4c **carmine**		.65	.55
	Cut cancel			.25
	Perf. initial			.25
440 R23	5c **carmine**		.40	.25
	Cut cancel			.25
	Perf. initial			.25
441 R23	8c **carmine**		1.90	1.50
	Cut cancel			.30
	Perf. initial			.25
442 R23	10c **carmine**		.95	.25
	Cut cancel			.25
	Perf. initial			.25
443 R23	20c **carmine**		1.50	.45
	Cut cancel			.25
	Perf. initial			.25
444 R23	25c **carmine**		5.00	.30
	Cut cancel			.20
	Perf. initial			.20
445 R23	40c **carmine**		3.00	.75
	Cut cancel			.35
	Perf. initial			.25
446 R23	50c **carmine**		5.00	.25
	Cut cancel			.20
	Perf. initial			.20
447 R23	80c **carmine**		15.00	4.50
	Cut cancel			.65
	Perf. initial			.50
448 R24	$1 **carmine**		14.00	.25
	Cut cancel			.20
	Perf. initial			.20
449 R24	$2 **carmine**		16.00	.25
	Cut cancel			.20
	Perf. initial			.20
450 R24	$3 **carmine**		22.50	5.00
	Cut cancel			.90
	Perf. initial			.40
451 R24	$4 **carmine**		32.50	10.50
	Cut cancel			2.10
	Perf. initial			1.00
452 R24	$5 **carmine**		32.50	.45
	Cut cancel			.25
	Perf. initial			.25
453 R24	$10 **carmine**		60.00	1.60
	Cut cancel			.35
	Perf. initial			.30
454 R24	$20 **carmine**		120.00	13.00
	Cut cancel			2.75
	Perf. initial			1.60

Without Gum — **Perf. 12**

455 R25	$30 **carmine**		55.00	15.00
	Cut cancel			4.75
	Perf. initial			3.25
456 R25	$50 **carmine**		45.00	11.00
	Cut cancel			4.25
	Perf. initial			2.75
457 R25	$60 **carmine**		85.00	20.00
	Cut cancel			12.50
	Perf. initial			7.75

R458 R25	$100 **carmine**		60.00	11.00
	Cut cancel			3.75
	Perf. initial			3.00
R459 R25	$500 **carmine**		275.00	125.00
	Cut cancel			40.00
	Perf. initial			26.00
R460 R25	$1000 **carmine**		325.00	140.00
	Cut cancel			27.50
	Perf. initial			18.00

Nos. R288-R310 Overprinted: **Series 1947**

1947 — **Wmk. 191R** — **Perf. 11**

R461 R23	1c **carmine**		.75	.50
	Cut cancel			.25
	Perf. initial			.25
R462 R23	2c **carmine**		.60	.55
	Cut cancel			.25
	Perf. initial			.25
R463 R23	3c **carmine**		.75	.50
	Cut cancel			.25
	Perf. initial			.25
R464 R23	4c **carmine**		.75	.65
	Cut cancel			.25
	Perf. initial			.25
R465 R23	5c **carmine**		.40	.35
	Cut cancel			.25
	Perf. initial			.25
R466 R23	8c **carmine**		1.40	.75
	Cut cancel			.25
	Perf. initial			.25
R467 R23	10c **carmine**		1.25	.25
	Cut cancel			.25
	Perf. initial			.25
R468 R23	20c **carmine**		2.00	.50
	Cut cancel			.25
	Perf. initial			.25
R469 R23	25c **carmine**		2.60	.65
	Cut cancel			.25
	Perf. initial			.25
R470 R23	40c **carmine**		4.50	.95
	Cut cancel			.25
	Perf. initial			.25
R471 R23	50c **carmine**		3.50	.35
	Cut cancel			.25
	Perf. initial			.25
R472 R23	80c **carmine**		10.00	6.00
	Cut cancel			.65
	Perf. initial			.25
R473 R24	$1 **carmine**		7.50	.30
	Cut cancel			.25
	Perf. initial			.20
R474 R24	$2 **carmine**		12.00	.60
	Cut cancel			.25
	Perf. initial			.20
R475 R24	$3 **carmine**		15.00	5.00
	Cut cancel			1.10
	Perf. initial			.80
R476 R24	$4 **carmine**		16.50	4.50
	Cut cancel			.45
	Perf. initial			.35
R477 R24	$5 **carmine**		25.00	.55
	Cut cancel			.25
	Perf. initial			.25
R478 R24	$10 **carmine**		60.00	2.25
	Cut cancel			.65
	Perf. initial			.25
R479 R24	$20 **carmine**		90.00	11.50
	Cut cancel			1.10
	Perf. initial			.75

Without Gum — **Perf. 12**

R480 R25	$30 **carmine**		125.00	24.00
	Cut cancel			5.25
	Perf. initial			2.75
R481 R25	$50 **carmine**		65.00	16.00
	Cut cancel			5.00
	Perf. initial			3.25
R482 R25	$60 **carmine**		160.00	50.00
	Cut cancel			21.00
	Perf. initial			9.25
R483 R25	$100 **carmine**		60.00	12.50
	Cut cancel			4.25
	Perf. initial			2.10
R484 R25	$500 **carmine**		450.00	160.00
	Cut cancel			62.50
	Perf. initial			37.50
R485 R25	$1000 **carmine**		250.00	90.00
	Cut cancel			35.00
	Perf. initial			24.00

Nos. R288-R310 Overprinted: **Series 1948**

1948 — **Wmk. 191R** — **Perf. 11**

R486 R23	1c **carmine**		.30	.30
	Cut cancel			.25
	Perf. initial			.25
R487 R23	2c **carmine**		.40	.40
	Cut cancel			.25
	Perf. initial			.25
R488 R23	3c **carmine**		.50	.35
	Cut cancel			.25
	Perf. initial			.25
R489 R23	4c **carmine**		.45	.35
	Cut cancel			.25
	Perf. initial			.25
R490 R23	5c **carmine**		.40	.25
	Cut cancel			.25
	Perf. initial			.25
R491 R23	8c **carmine**		.80	.35
	Cut cancel			.25
	Perf. initial			.25
R492 R23	10c **carmine**		.75	.25
	Cut cancel			.25
	Perf. initial			.20

R493 R23	20c **carmine**		1.90	.35
	Cut cancel			.25
	Perf. initial			.25
R494 R23	25c **carmine**		1.60	.25
	Cut cancel			.25
	Perf. initial			.25
R495 R23	40c **carmine**		5.00	1.75
	Cut cancel			.35
	Perf. initial			.25
R496 R23	50c **carmine**		2.25	.20
	Cut cancel			.20
	Perf. initial			.25
R497 R23	80c **carmine**		9.00	5.00
	Cut cancel			2.00
	Perf. initial			.55
R498 R24	$1 **carmine**		9.00	.25
	Cut cancel			.25
	Perf. initial			.25
R499 R24	$2 **carmine**		15.00	.30
	Cut cancel			.25
	Perf. initial			.25
R500 R24	$3 **carmine**		20.00	2.75
	Cut cancel			.40
	Perf. initial			.30
R501 R24	$4 **carmine**		30.00	3.25
	Cut cancel			.80
	Perf. initial			.55
R502 R24	$5 **carmine**		25.00	.50
	Cut cancel			.30
	Perf. initial			.25
R503 R24	$10 **carmine**		55.00	1.50
	Cut cancel			.30
a.	Pair, one dated "1946"			.30
R504 R24	$20 **carmine**		110.00	15.00
	Cut cancel			3.50
	Perf. initial			1.75

Without Gum — **Perf. 12**

R505 R25	$30 **carmine**		80.00	25.00
	Cut cancel			6.25
	Perf. initial			3.75
R506 R25	$50 **carmine**		82.50	24.00
	Cut cancel			10.50
	Perf. initial			3.25
a.	Vert. pair, imperf. btwn.		2,750.	
R507 R25	$60 **carmine**		160.00	42.50
	Cut cancel			18.00
	Perf. initial			7.25
a.	Vert. pair, imperf. btwn.		2,750.	
R508 R25	$100 **carmine**		65.00	11.00
	Cut cancel			5.00
	Perf. initial			3.25
a.	Vert. pair, imperf. btwn.		2,000.	
R509 R25	$500 **carmine**		425.00	140.00
	Cut cancel			52.50
	Perf. initial			29.00
R510 R25	$1000 **carmine**		225.00	82.50
	Cut cancel			35.00
	Perf. initial			20.00

Nos. R288-R310 Overprinted: **Series 1949**

1949 — **Wmk. 191R** — **Perf. 11**

R511 R23	1c **carmine**		.30	.30
	Cut cancel			.25
	Perf. initial			.25
R512 R23	2c **carmine**		.60	.40
	Cut cancel			.25
	Perf. initial			.25
R513 R23	3c **carmine**		.45	.40
	Cut cancel			.25
	Perf. initial			.25
R514 R23	4c **carmine**		.65	.55
	Cut cancel			.25
	Perf. initial			.25
R515 R23	5c **carmine**		.40	.25
	Cut cancel			.25
	Perf. initial			.25
R516 R23	8c **carmine**		.75	.65
	Cut cancel			.25
	Perf. initial			.25
R517 R23	10c **carmine**		.45	.30
	Cut cancel			.25
	Perf. initial			.25
R518 R23	20c **carmine**		1.40	.65
	Cut cancel			.35
	Perf. initial			.30
R519 R23	25c **carmine**		2.00	.75
	Cut cancel			.30
	Perf. initial			.30
R520 R23	40c **carmine**		5.50	2.50
	Cut cancel			.45
	Perf. initial			.35
R521 R23	50c **carmine**		4.00	.35
	Cut cancel			.25
	Perf. initial			.25
R522 R23	80c **carmine**		12.50	6.00
	Cut cancel			1.60
	Perf. initial			.80
R523 R24	$1 **carmine**		11.00	.75
	Cut cancel			.25
	Perf. initial			.30
R524 R24	$2 **carmine**		14.00	2.25
	Cut cancel			.45
	Perf. initial			.30
R525 R24	$3 **carmine**		22.50	7.00
	Cut cancel			2.75
	Perf. initial			1.10
R526 R24	$4 **carmine**		25.00	7.00
	Cut cancel			3.00
	Perf. initial			1.60
R527 R24	$5 **carmine**		26.00	3.75
	Cut cancel			.65
	Perf. initial			.45

R528	R24	$10 carmine	60.00	4.75
		Cut cancel		1.10
		Perf. initial		.90
R529	R24	$20 carmine	125.00	12.00
		Cut cancel		2.10
		Perf. initial		1.40

Without Gum — **Perf. 12**

R530	R25	$30 carmine	100.00	29.00
		Cut cancel		7.25
		Perf. initial		4.25
R531	R25	$50 carmine	120.00	50.00
		Cut cancel		14.50
		Perf. initial		7.50
R532	R25	$60 carmine	225.00	55.00
		Cut cancel		24.00
		Perf. initial		11.50
R533	R25	$100 carmine	60.00	19.00
		Cut cancel		4.00
		Perf. initial		2.75
R534	R25	$500 carmine	450.00	225.00
		Cut cancel		110.00
		Perf. initial		57.50
R535	R25	$1000 carmine	325.00	150.00
		Cut cancel		42.50
		Perf. initial		22.50

Nos. R288-R310 Overprinted: Series 1950

1950 — **Wmk. 191R** — **Perf. 11**

R536	R23	1c carmine	.30	.25
		Cut cancel		.25
		Perf. initial		.25
R537	R23	2c carmine	.35	.30
		Cut cancel		.25
		Perf. initial		.25
R538	R23	3c carmine	.40	.35
		Cut cancel		.25
		Perf. initial		.25
R539	R23	4c carmine	.55	.45
		Cut cancel		.25
		Perf. initial		.25
R540	R23	5c carmine	.35	.25
		Cut cancel		.25
		Perf. initial		.25
R541	R23	8c carmine	1.40	.70
		Cut cancel		.25
		Perf. initial		.25
R542	R23	10c carmine	.65	.25
		Cut cancel		.25
		Perf. initial		.25
R543	R23	20c carmine	1.10	.40
		Cut cancel		.30
		Perf. initial		.30
R544	R23	25c carmine	1.60	.40
		Cut cancel		.30
		Perf. initial		.30
R545	R23	40c carmine	4.00	1.90
		Cut cancel		.45
		Perf. initial		.30
R546	R23	50c carmine	6.00	.25
		Cut cancel		.25
		Perf. initial		.25
R547	R23	80c carmine	11.00	8.00
		Cut cancel		.90
		Perf. initial		.55
R548	R24	$1 carmine	11.50	.35
		Cut cancel		.30
		Perf. initial		.25
R549	R24	$2 carmine	14.00	2.50
		Cut cancel		.40
		Perf. initial		.20
R550	R24	$3 carmine	16.00	6.00
		Cut cancel		1.40
		Perf. initial		.80
R551	R24	$4 carmine	22.50	7.50
		Cut cancel		2.75
		Perf. initial		1.40
R552	R24	$5 carmine	26.00	1.00
		Cut cancel		.30
		Perf. initial		.25
R553	R24	$10 carmine	60.00	10.00
		Cut cancel		.85
		Perf. initial		.55
R554	R24	$20 carmine	125.00	12.50
		Cut cancel		2.75
		Perf. initial		1.90

Without Gum — **Perf. 12**

R555	R25	$30 carmine	85.00	60.00
		Cut cancel		14.50
		Perf. initial		10.50
R556	R25	$50 carmine	80.00	20.00
		Cut cancel		8.50
		Perf. initial		5.75
a.		Vert. pair, imperf. horiz.		—
R557	R25	$60 carmine	175.00	65.00
		Cut cancel		21.00
		Perf. initial		9.75
R558	R25	$100 carmine	70.00	20.00
		Cut cancel		5.25
		Perf. initial		3.25
R559	R25	$500 carmine	250.00	110.00
		Cut cancel		50.00
		Perf. initial		32.50
R560	R25	$1000 carmine	250.00	85.00
		Cut cancel		26.00
		Perf. initial		19.00

Nos. R288-R310 Overprinted: **Series 1951**

1951 — **Wmk. 191R** — **Perf. 11**

R561	R23	1c carmine	.30	.25
		Cut cancel		.25
		Perf. initial		.25
R562	R23	2c carmine	.35	.30
		Cut cancel		.25
		Perf. initial		.25
R563	R23	3c carmine	.30	.30
		Cut cancel		.25
		Perf. initial		.25
R564	R23	4c carmine	.35	.30
		Cut cancel		.25
		Perf. initial		.25
R565	R23	5c carmine	.35	.30
		Cut cancel		.25
		Perf. initial		.25
R566	R23	8c carmine	1.10	.40
		Cut cancel		.25
		Perf. initial		.25
R567	R23	10c carmine	.60	.30
		Cut cancel		.25
		Perf. initial		.25
R568	R23	20c carmine	1.40	.50
		Cut cancel		.30
		Perf. initial		.25
R569	R23	25c carmine	1.60	.45
		Cut cancel		.30
		Perf. initial		.25
R570	R23	40c carmine	4.50	1.40
		Cut cancel		.45
		Perf. initial		.30
R571	R23	50c carmine	3.50	.40
		Cut cancel		.25
		Perf. initial		.25
R572	R23	80c carmine	7.50	2.75
		Cut cancel		1.60
		Perf. initial		.80
R573	R24	$1 carmine	12.50	.25
		Cut cancel		.20
		Perf. initial		.20
R574	R24	$2 carmine	17.50	.50
		Cut cancel		.25
		Perf. initial		.30
R575	R24	$3 carmine	27.50	3.50
		Cut cancel		1.90
		Perf. initial		1.10
R576	R24	$4 carmine	32.50	7.00
		Cut cancel		2.75
		Perf. initial		1.40
R577	R24	$5 carmine	22.50	.70
		Cut cancel		.35
		Perf. initial		.25
R578	R24	$10 carmine	55.00	2.25
		Cut cancel		1.10
		Perf. initial		.80
R579	R24	$20 carmine	115.00	14.00
		Cut cancel		4.25
		Perf. initial		3.25

Without Gum — **Perf. 12**

R580	R25	$30 carmine	85.00	15.00
		Cut cancel		5.25
		Perf. initial		3.75
a.		Imperf., pair	2,000.	775.00
R581	R25	$50 carmine	110.00	26.00
		Cut cancel		7.75
		Perf. initial		4.50
R582	R25	$60 carmine	160.00	55.00
		Cut cancel		21.00
		Perf. initial		16.00
R583	R25	$100 carmine	60.00	14.00
		Cut cancel		7.00
		Perf. initial		5.00
R584	R25	$500 carmine	325.00	125.00
		Cut cancel		62.50
		Perf. initial		26.00
R585	R25	$1000 carmine	300.00	110.00
		Cut cancel		40.00
		Perf. initial		29.00

No. R583 is known imperf horizontally. It exists as a reconstructed used vertical strip of 4 that was separated into single stamps.

Documentary Stamps and Types of 1940 Overprinted in Black

Series 1952

Designs: 55c, $1.10, $1.65, $2.20, $2.75, $3.30, L. J. Gage; $2500, William Windom; $5000, C. J. Folger; $10,000, W. Q. Gresham.

1952 — **Wmk. 191R** — **Perf. 11**

R586	R23	1c carmine	.30	.30
		Cut cancel		.25
		Perf. initial		.25
R587	R23	2c carmine	.40	.30
		Cut cancel		.25
		Perf. initial		.25
R588	R23	3c carmine	.35	.30
		Cut cancel		.25
		Perf. initial		.25
R589	R23	4c carmine	.40	.30
		Cut cancel		.25
		Perf. initial		.25
R590	R23	5c carmine	.30	.30
		Cut cancel		.25
		Perf. initial		.25
R591	R23	8c carmine	.80	.50
		Cut cancel		.25
		Perf. initial		.25
R592	R23	10c carmine	.45	.25
		Cut cancel		.25
		Perf. initial		.20

Column 3 (right edge of second price column partly cut off)

R593	R23	20c carmine	1.10	
		Cut cancel		
		Perf. initial		
R594	R23	25c carmine	2.00	
		Cut cancel		
		Perf. initial		
R595	R23	40c carmine	4.50	1.
		Cut cancel		
		Perf. initial		
R596	R23	50c carmine	3.25	
		Cut cancel		
		Perf. initial		
R597	R23	55c carmine	25.00	12.
		Cut cancel		1.
		Perf. initial		1.
R598	R23	80c carmine	17.50	4.
		Cut cancel		
		Perf. initial		
R599	R24	$1 carmine	6.00	1.
		Cut cancel		
		Perf. initial		
R600	R24	$1.10 carmine	55.00	25.
		Cut cancel		10.
		Perf. initial		6.
R601	R24	$1.65 carmine	175.00	55.
		Cut cancel		32.
		Perf. initial		21.
R602	R24	$2 carmine	15.00	
		Cut cancel		
		Perf. initial		
R603	R24	$2.20 carmine	150.00	65.
		Cut cancel		32.
		Perf. initial		16.
R604	R24	$2.75 carmine	175.00	65.
		Cut cancel		32.
		Perf. initial		16.
R605	R24	$3 carmine	27.50	6.
		Cut cancel		1.
		Perf. initial		1.
a.		Horiz. pair, imperf. btwn.	1,300.	
R606	R24	$3.30 carmine	150.00	65.
		Cut cancel		32.
		Perf. initial		16.
R607	R24	$4 carmine	35.00	6.
		Cut cancel		2.
		Perf. initial		1.
R608	R24	$5 carmine	30.00	1.
		Cut cancel		
		Perf. initial		
R609	R24	$10 carmine	55.00	1.
		Cut cancel		
		Perf. initial		
R610	R24	$20 carmine	85.00	14.
		Cut cancel		3.
		Perf. initial		3.

Without Gum — **Perf. 1**

R611	R25	$30 carmine	60.00	25.0
		Cut cancel		5.
		Perf. initial		4.2
R612	R25	$50 carmine	55.00	22.5
		Cut cancel		6.2
		Perf. initial		5.2
R613	R25	$60 carmine	375.00	60.0
		Cut cancel		16.0
		Perf. initial		10.5
R614	R25	$100 carmine	50.00	9.0
		Cut cancel		3.2
		Perf. initial		2.1
R615	R25	$500 carmine	750.00	110.0
		Cut cancel		60.0
		Perf. initial		35.0
R616	R25	$1000 carmine	225.00	35.0
		Cut cancel		16.0
		Perf. initial		10.5
R617	R25	$2500 carmine	375.00	200.0
		Cut cancel		150.0
		Perf. initial		110.0
R618	R25	$5000 carmine	—	3,250
		Cut cancel		1,500
		Perf. initial		900.0
R619	R25	$10,000 carmine	—	1,300
		Cut cancel		825.0
		Perf. initial		675.0

Documentary Stamps and Types of 1940 Overprinted in Black

Series 1953

1953 — **Wmk. 191R** — **Perf. 1**

R620	R23	1c carmine	.30	.30
		Cut cancel		.25
		Perf. initial		.25
R621	R23	2c carmine	.30	.30
		Cut cancel		.25
		Perf. initial		.25
R622	R23	3c carmine	.35	.30
		Cut cancel		.25
		Perf. initial		.25
R623	R23	4c carmine	.55	.40
		Cut cancel		.25
		Perf. initial		.25
R624	R23	5c carmine	.40	.25
		Cut cancel		.25
		Perf. initial		.25
a.		Vert. pair, imperf. horiz.		650.00
R625	R23	8c carmine	.95	.75
		Cut cancel		.25
		Perf. initial		.25
R626	R23	10c carmine	.55	.30
		Cut cancel		.25
		Perf. initial		.25
R627	R23	20c carmine	1.25	.45
		Cut cancel		.25
		Perf. initial		.25

No.	Type	Denom.	Color	Unused	Used
628	R23	25c	carmine	1.50	.55
		Cut cancel			.30
		Perf. initial			.25
629	R23	40c	carmine	2.25	.80
		Cut cancel			.45
		Perf. initial			.35
630	R23	50c	carmine	2.75	.30
		Cut cancel			.25
		Perf. initial			.25
631	R23	55c	carmine	5.50	2.00
		Cut cancel			.80
		Perf. initial			.55
a.		Horiz. pair, imperf. vert.		375.00	
632	R23	80c	carmine	8.50	2.10
		Cut cancel			1.50
		Perf. initial			1.40
633	R24	$1	carmine	4.75	.30
		Cut cancel			.25
		Perf. initial			.25
634	R24	$1.10	carmine	10.00	2.50
		Cut cancel			2.10
		Perf. initial			1.60
a.		Horiz. pair, imperf. vert.		700.00	
b.		Imperf. pair		600.00	
635	R24	$1.65	carmine	10.00	4.50
		Cut cancel			3.25
		Perf. initial			2.10
636	R24	$2	carmine	7.50	.70
		Cut cancel			.30
		Perf. initial			.25
637	R24	$2.20	carmine	17.50	6.00
		Cut cancel			2.75
		Perf. initial			2.10
638	R24	$2.75	carmine	25.00	7.00
		Cut cancel			3.75
		Perf. initial			2.75
639	R24	$3	carmine	15.00	3.50
		Cut cancel			1.60
		Perf. initial			1.40
640	R24	$3.30	carmine	32.50	8.00
		Cut cancel			5.25
		Perf. initial			3.50
641	R24	$4	carmine	30.00	9.00
		Cut cancel			2.40
		Perf. initial			2.10
642	R24	$5	carmine	25.00	1.25
		Cut cancel			.55
		Perf. initial			.35
643	R24	$10	carmine	55.00	2.25
		Cut cancel			1.10
		Perf. initial			.90
644	R24	$20	carmine	110.00	20.00
		Cut cancel			3.25
		Perf. initial			2.40

Without Gum — Perf. 12

No.	Type	Denom.	Color	Unused	Used
645	R25	$30	carmine	85.00	17.50
		Cut cancel			6.75
		Perf. initial			4.25
646	R25	$50	carmine	150.00	37.50
		Cut cancel			13.00
		Perf. initial			6.25
647	R25	$60	carmine	550.00	300.00
		Cut cancel			125.00
		Perf. initial			67.50
648	R25	$100	carmine	50.00	15.00
		Cut cancel			5.75
		Perf. initial			3.75
649	R25	$500	carmine	650.00	160.00
		Cut cancel			62.50
		Perf. initial			29.00
650	R25	$1000	carmine	400.00	75.00
		Cut cancel			24.00
		Perf. initial			16.00
651	R25	$2500	carmine	2,000.	1,250.
		Cut cancel			475.00
		Perf. initial			325.00
652	R25	$5000	carmine	—	4,000.
		Cut cancel			2,500.
		Perf. initial			1,100.
653	R25	$10,000	carmine	—	3,500.
		Cut cancel			1,600.
		Perf. initial			750.00

Types of 1940
Without Overprint

1954 — Wmk. 191R — Perf. 11

No.	Type	Denom.	Color	Unused	Used
654	R23	1c	carmine	.30	.25
		Cut cancel			.25
		Perf. initial			.20
a.		Horiz. pair, imperf. vert.		—	
655	R23	2c	carmine	.30	.30
		Cut cancel			.25
		Perf. initial			.20
656	R23	3c	carmine	.30	.30
		Cut cancel			.25
		Perf. initial			.20
657	R23	4c	carmine	.30	.30
		Cut cancel			.25
		Perf. initial			.20
658	R23	5c	carmine	.30	.25
		Cut cancel			.20
		Perf. initial			.20
659	R23	8c	carmine	.30	.25
		Cut cancel			.25
		Perf. initial			.20
660	R23	10c	carmine	.30	.25
		Cut cancel			.25
		Perf. initial			.25
661	R23	20c	carmine	.55	.40
		Cut cancel			.30
		Perf. initial			.25
662	R23	25c	carmine	.65	.45
		Cut cancel			.30
		Perf. initial			.25

No.	Type	Denom.	Color	Unused	Used
663	R23	40c	carmine	1.40	.60
		Cut cancel			.45
		Perf. initial			.35
664	R23	50c	carmine	1.90	.25
		Cut cancel			.20
		Perf. initial			.20
a.		Horiz. pair, imperf. vert.		250.00	
665	R23	55c	carmine	1.60	1.25
		Cut cancel			.55
		Perf. initial			.45
666	R23	80c	carmine	2.50	1.90
		Cut cancel			1.25
		Perf. initial			1.10
667	R24	$1	carmine	1.60	.30
		Cut cancel			.30
		Perf. initial			.25
668	R24	$1.10	carmine	3.50	2.50
		Cut cancel			1.60
		Perf. initial			1.10
669	R24	$1.65	carmine	110.00	70.00
		Cut cancel			50.00
		Perf. initial			22.50
670	R24	$2	carmine	1.90	.45
		Cut cancel			.25
		Perf. initial			.25
671	R24	$2.20	carmine	5.00	3.75
		Cut cancel			2.75
		Perf. initial			1.60
672	R24	$2.75	carmine	110.00	65.00
		Cut cancel			37.50
		Perf. initial			21.00
673	R24	$3	carmine	3.25	3.00
		Cut cancel			1.10
		Perf. initial			.80
674	R24	$3.30	carmine	7.25	5.00
		Cut cancel			3.25
		Perf. initial			2.10
675	R24	$4	carmine	4.50	4.00
		Cut cancel			2.10
		Perf. initial			1.60
676	R24	$5	carmine	6.00	.50
		Cut cancel			.35
		Perf. initial			.20
677	R24	$10	carmine	11.00	1.50
		Cut cancel			.85
		Perf. initial			.70
678	R24	$20	carmine	40.00	6.50
		Cut cancel			3.25
		Perf. initial			1.90

Documentary Stamps and Type of 1940 Overprinted in Black
Series 1954

1954 — Wmk. 191R — Perf. 12
Without Gum

No.	Type	Denom.	Color	Unused	Used
679	R25	$30	carmine	65.00	16.00
		Cut cancel			4.75
		Perf. initial			3.25
680	R25	$50	carmine	80.00	24.00
		Cut cancel			9.25
		Perf. initial			5.75
681	R25	$60	carmine	120.00	25.00
		Cut cancel			13.00
		Perf. initial			9.25
682	R25	$100	carmine	60.00	7.50
		Cut cancel			5.25
		Perf. initial			4.00
683	R25	$500	carmine	300.00	77.50
		Cut cancel			30.00
		Perf. initial			25.00
684	R25	$1000	carmine	200.00	65.00
		Cut cancel			19.00
		Perf. initial			16.00
		With complete receipt tab		225.00	
a.		Booklet pane of 4		900.00	
		Complete booklet, 1 #R684a		1,100.	
685	R25	$2500	carmine	225.00	240.00
		Cut cancel			92.50
		Perf. initial			62.50
		With complete receipt tab		250.00	
a.		Booklet pane of 4		1,000.	
		Complete booklet, 10 #R685a		10,000.	
686	R25	$5000	carmine	—	1,000.
		Cut cancel			550.00
		Perf. initial			475.00
		With complete receipt tab		1,250.	
a.		Booklet pane of 4		5,000.	
687	R25	$10,000	carmine	—	1,200.
		Cut cancel			350.00
		Perf. initial			210.00
		With complete receipt tab		1,250.	
a.		Booklet pane of 4		5,000.	

Documentary Stamps and Type of 1940 Overprinted in Black
Series 1955

1955 — Wmk. 191R — Perf. 12
Without Gum

No.	Type	Denom.	Color	Unused	Used
688	R25	$30	carmine	80.00	15.00
		Cut cancel			6.25
		Perf. initial			3.75
689	R25	$50	carmine	85.00	20.00
		Cut cancel			9.25
		Perf. initial			6.50
690	R25	$60	carmine	140.00	37.50
		Cut cancel			14.50
		Perf. initial			5.25

No.	Type	Denom.	Color	Unused	Used
691	R25	$100	carmine	70.00	8.50
		Cut cancel			5.00
		Perf. initial			3.75
692	R25	$500	carmine	750.00	140.00
		Cut cancel			37.50
		Perf. initial			21.00
693	R25	$1000	carmine	240.00	45.00
		Cut cancel			18.00
		Perf. initial			13.00
694	R25	$2500	carmine	450.00	175.00
		Cut cancel			82.50
		Perf. initial			52.50
695	R25	$5000	carmine	2,500.	1,300.
		Cut cancel			600.00
		Perf. initial			400.00
696	R25	$10,000	carmine	—	1,100.
		Cut cancel			500.00
		Perf. initial			190.00

Documentary Stamps and Type of 1940 Overprinted in Black "Series 1956"

1956 — Wmk. 191R — Without Gum — Perf. 12

No.	Type	Denom.	Color	Unused	Used
697	R25	$30	carmine	110.00	17.50
		Cut cancel			9.25
		Perf. initial			4.75
698	R25	$50	carmine	120.00	25.00
		Cut cancel			13.00
		Perf. initial			6.25
699	R25	$60	carmine	150.00	50.00
		Cut cancel			16.00
		Perf. initial			7.25
700	R25	$100	carmine	100.00	15.00
		Cut cancel			6.00
		Perf. initial			5.00
701	R25	$500	carmine	325.00	100.00
		Cut cancel			26.00
		Perf. initial			16.00
702	R25	$1000	carmine	600.00	75.00
		Cut cancel			21.00
		Perf. initial			13.00
703	R25	$2500	carmine	—	600.00
		Cut cancel			210.00
		Perf. initial			125.00
704	R25	$5000	carmine	—	1,900.
		Cut cancel			1,075.
		Perf. initial			700.00
705	R25	$10,000	carmine	—	750.00
		Cut cancel			250.00
		Perf. initial			150.00

Documentary Stamps and Type of 1940 Overprinted in Black "Series 1957"

1957 — Wmk. 191R — Perf. 12 — Without Gum

No.	Type	Denom.	Color	Unused	Used
706	R25	$30	carmine	140.00	40.00
		Cut cancel			13.00
		Perf. initial			6.25
707	R25	$50	carmine	110.00	42.50
		Cut cancel			13.00
		Perf. initial			5.75
708	R25	$60	carmine	400.00	225.00
		Cut cancel			110.00
		Perf. initial			55.00
709	R25	$100	carmine	95.00	17.50
		Cut cancel			8.00
		Perf. initial			4.50
710	R25	$500	carmine	400.00	125.00
		Cut cancel			57.50
		Perf. initial			35.00
711	R25	$1000	carmine	250.00	90.00
		Cut cancel			32.50
		Perf. initial			21.00
712	R25	$2500	carmine	—	800.00
		Cut cancel			450.00
		Perf. initial			300.00
713	R25	$5000	carmine	2,250.	1,250.
		Cut cancel			600.00
		Perf. initial			210.00
714	R25	$10,000	carmine	—	500.00
		Cut cancel			175.00
		Perf. initial			150.00

Documentary Stamps and Type of 1940 Overprinted in Black "Series 1958"

1958 — Wmk. 191R — Perf. 12 — Without Gum

No.	Type	Denom.	Color	Unused	Used
715	R25	$30	carmine	95.00	24.00
		Cut cancel			16.00
		Perf. initial			8.25
716	R25	$50	carmine	80.00	24.00
		Cut cancel			14.50
		Perf. initial			6.25
717	R25	$60	carmine	140.00	37.50
		Cut cancel			16.00
		Perf. initial			10.50
718	R25	$100	carmine	70.00	12.50
		Cut cancel			5.75
		Perf. initial			2.10
719	R25	$500	carmine	300.00	82.50
		Cut cancel			37.50
		Perf. initial			21.00
720	R25	$1000	carmine	350.00	80.00
		Cut cancel			32.50
		Perf. initial			25.00
721	R25	$2500	carmine	—	1,000.
		Cut cancel			525.00
		Perf. initial			350.00
722	R25	$5000	carmine	—	3,250.
		Cut cancel			2,000.
		Perf. initial			1,750.
723	R25	$10,000	carmine	—	1,750.
		Cut cancel			1,100.
		Perf. initial			650.00

Documentary Stamps and Type of 1940 Without Overprint

1958		Wmk. 191R WITH GUM		Perf. 12
R724	R25	$30 **carmine**	45.00	7.00
		Cut cancel		6.00
		Perf. initial		4.25
a.		Vert. pair, imperf. horiz.	2,250.	
R725	R25	$50 **carmine**	50.00	7.00
		Cut cancel		4.00
		Perf. initial		3.25
a.		Vert. pair, imperf. horiz.		
R726	R25	$60 **carmine**	100.00	21.00
		Cut cancel		10.50
		Perf. initial		5.25
R727	R25	$100 **carmine**	25.00	4.75
		Cut cancel		3.25
		Perf. initial		2.00
R728	R25	$500 **carmine**	95.00	26.00
		Cut cancel		10.50
		Perf. initial		7.75
R729	R25	$1000 **carmine**	60.00	21.00
		Cut cancel		10.50
		Perf. initial		7.75
a.		Vert. pair, imperf. horiz.	1,750.	
R730	R25	$2500 **carmine**	175.00	175.00
		Cut cancel		90.00
		Perf. initial		55.00

		With complete receipt tab	—	
a.		Booklet pane of 4	850.00	
		Complete booklet, 10 #R730a	—	
R731	R25	$5000 **carmine**	—	175.00
		Cut cancel		90.00
		Perf. initial		65.00
		With complete receipt tab	—	
a.		Booklet pane of 4	—	
		Complete booklet, 10 #R731a	—	
R732	R25	$10,000 **carmine**	275.00	140.00
		Cut cancel		55.00
		Perf. initial		25.00
		With complete receipt tab	—	
a.		Booklet pane of 4	1,200.	
		Complete booklet, 10 #R732a	—	

Internal Revenue Building, Washington, D.C. — R26

Centenary of the Internal Revenue Service.

Giori Press Printing

1962, July 2		Unwmk.		Perf.
R733	R26	10c **violet blue & bright green**		1.00
		Never hinged		1.25
		Cut cancel		
		Perf. initial		
		P# block of 4		15.00

1963

"Established 1862" Removed

R734	R26	10c **violet blue & bright green**		3.00
		Never hinged		5.00
		Cut cancel		
		Perf. initial		
		P# block of 4		30.00

Documentary revenue stamps were no longer required aft Dec. 31, 1967.

PROPRIETARY STAMPS

Stamps for use on proprietary articles were included in the first general issue of 1862-71. They are R3, R13, R14, R18, R22, R29, R31 and R38

Several varieties of "violet" paper were used in printing Nos. RB1-RB10. One is grayish with a slight greenish tinge, called "intermediate" paper b specialists. It should not be confused with the "green" paper, which is truly green.

All values prior to 1898 are for used copies. Printed cancellations on proprietary stamps command sizable premiums.

George Washington — RB1a
RB1
Engraved and printed by Jos. R. Carpenter, Philadelphia.

1871-74				Perf. 12

a. Violet Paper **b. Green Paper** (1871) (1874)

RB1	RB1c	**green** 6.50		
		& **black**	11.00	
		Pair 12.00	26.00	
		Block 27.50 of 4	65.00	
	c.	Imperf.	80.00	
		Imperf. pair	175.00	
		Imperf. block of 4	475.00	
	d.	Inverted center	3,000.	
RB2	RB2c	**green** 6.75		
		& **black**	25.00	
		Pair 15.00	57.50	
		Block 34.00 of 4	125.00	
		Double transfer 18.00		
		Vert. half used as 1c on document	—	
	c.	Inverted center	40,000.	
			9,000.	

No. RB2bc is valued with fine centering and small faults. Only two examples recorded of the inverted center on violet paper, No. RB2ac.

RB3	RB3a	**green** 25.00		
		& **black**	60.00	
		Pair 60.00	140.00	
		Block 125.00 of 4	290.00	
		Double transfer		

a. Violet Paper **b. Green Paper** (1871) (1874)

	c.	Sewing machine perf.	275.00	
	d.	Inverted center	16,000.	

No. RB3ad is valued with small faults as 6 of the 7 recorded examples have faults.

RB4	RB4a	**green** 14.00		
		& **black**	22.50	
		Pair 32.50	55.00	
		Block 90.00 of 4	120.00	
		Double transfer		
		Vert. half used as 2c on document	—	
	c.	Inverted center	19,000.	

No. RB4ac is valued with small faults as 6 of the 7 recorded examples have faults.

RB5	RB5a	**green** 150.00		
		& **black**	160.00	
		Pair 325.00	375.00	
		Block 675.00 of 4	800.00	
	c.	Inverted center	130,000.	

No. RB5ac is unique. Value represents price realized in 2000 auction sale.

RB6	RB6a	**green** 60.00		
		& **black**	120.00	
		Pair 110.00	280.00	
		Block 300.00 of 4	625.00	
		Double transfer		
RB7	RB10c	**green** 225.00		
		& **black** ('73)	60.00	
		Pair 550.00	140.00	
		Block — of 4	325.00	
		Double transfer		

(See note on Inverted Centers after No. R133.)

RB1b

			a. Violet Paper	b. Green Paper (1874)
RB8	RB1b	50c **green & black** ('73)	725.	1,000
		Pair	1,500.	
RB9	RB1b	$1 **green & black** ('73)	2,500.	10,000
		Pair	—	

— RB1c

RB4

Inscribed "Series of 1914"

		Silk Paper	Wmkd. 191R	
		a. Perf.	b. Perf.	c. Roul. 6
RB15	RB2a	4c	**red**		4.50	200.00
		Pair		10.00	475.00
		Block of 4		25.00	
RB16	RB2a	5c	**black**	125.00	100.00	1,500.
		Pair	275.00	240.00	
		Block of 4		—	
RB17	RB2a	6c	**violet blue**	25.00	20.00	350.00
		Pair	62.50	50.00	875.00
		Block of 4	175.00	140.00	
RB18	RB2a	6c	**violet**		30.00	—
		Pair		80.00	
		Block of 4		225.00	
RB19	RB2a	10c	**blue** ('81)		300.00	
		Pair		700.00	
		Block of 4		—	

Many fraudulent roulettes exist.

Battleship — RB3

Inscribed "Series of 1898." and "Proprietary."
See note on rouletting preceding No. R161.

1898   Wmk. 191R   Engr.

				Roul. 5½		p. Hyphen Hole Perf. 7	
				Unused	Used	Unused	Used
RB20	⅛c	**yellow green**		.20	.20	.20	.20
		Block of 4		.50	.50	.75	.70
		Double transfer		—			
	a.	Vert. pair, imperf. horiz.		—			
RB21	¼c	**brown**		.20	.20	.20	.20
	a.	¼c red brown		.20	.20		
	b.	¼c yellow brown		.20	.20	.20	.20
	c.	¼c orange brown		.20	.20	.20	.20
	d.	¼c bister		.20	.20		
		Block of 4		.50	.25	.55	1.00
		Double transfer		—	—		
	e.	Vert. pair, imperf. horiz.		—			
	f.	Printed on both sides		—			
RB22	⅜c	**deep orange**		.25	.25	.30	.25
		Block of 4		1.10	1.00	1.40	
	a.	Horiz. pair, imperf. vert.		10.50			
	b.	Vert. pair, imperf. horiz.		—			
RB23	⅝c	**deep ultra**		.25	.25	.30	.25
		Block of 4		1.25	1.10	1.50	1.25
		Double transfer		1.50			
	a.	Vert. pair, imperf. horiz.		77.50	—		
	b.	Horiz. pair, imperf. vert.		325.00			
RB24	1c	**dark green**		2.10	.25	26.00	13.00
		Block of 4		10.50	1.10	140.00	67.50
	a.	Vert. pair, imperf. horiz.		325.00			
RB25	1¼c	**violet**		.25	.25	.30	.25
		Block of 4		1.10	1.00	1.40	1.25
	a.	1¼c brown violet		.25	.20	.25	.25
	b.	Vertical pair, imperf. between		—			
RB26	1⅞c	**dull blue**		12.00	1.60	32.50	7.75
		Block of 4		57.50	—	160.00	—
		Double transfer		—			
RB27	2c	**violet brown**		1.10	.25	6.25	.80
		Block of 4		5.00	—	27.50	—
		Double transfer		—			
	a.	Horiz. pair, imperf. vert.		52.50			
RB28	2½c	**lake**		4.25	.25	5.25	.30
		Block of 4		20.00	1.10	29.00	—
	a.	Vert. pair, imperf. horiz.		190.00			
RB29	3¾c	**olive gray**		42.50	10.50	72.50	21.00
		Block of 4		210.00	—	350.00	110.00
RB30	4c	**purple**		13.00	1.10	62.50	18.00
		Block of 4		62.50	5.50	325.00	90.00
		Double transfer		—			
RB31	5c	**brown orange**		13.00	1.10	67.50	21.00
		Block of 4		62.50	5.75	350.00	175.00
	a.	Vert. pair, imperf. horiz.		—	325.00		
	b.	Horiz. pair, imperf. vert.		—	425.00		

See note after No. RS315 regarding St. Louis Provisional Labels of 1898.

1914   Wmk. 190   Offset Printing   Perf. 10

				Unused	Used
RB32	RB4	⅛c	**black**	.25	.25
			Block of 4	1.25	1.10
RB33	RB4	¼c	**black**	2.25	1.20
			Block of 4	11.00	
RB34	RB4	⅜c	**black**	.25	.25
			Block of 4	1.25	1.10
RB35	RB4	⅝c	**black**	5.00	2.00
			Block of 4	22.50	
RB36	RB4	1¼c	**black**	3.50	1.20
			Block of 4	17.50	
RB37	RB4	1⅞c	**black**	47.50	17.50
			Block of 4	210.00	
RB38	RB4	2½c	**black**	10.00	3.00
			Block of 4	50.00	11.00
RB39	RB4	3⅛c	**black**	100.00	57.50
			Block of 4	450.00	
RB40	RB4	3¾c	**black**	45.00	22.50
			Block of 4	250.00	
RB41	RB4	4c	**black**	65.00	30.00
			Block of 4	325.00	
RB42	RB4	4⅜c	**black**	1,600.	—
			Block of 4	10,000.	
RB43	RB4	5c	**black**	130.00	80.00
			Block of 4	—	

Wmk. 191R

				Unused	Used
RB44	RB4	⅛c	**black**	.25	.25
			Block of 4	1.25	1.10
RB45	RB4	¼c	**black**	.25	.25
			Block of 4	1.25	1.10
			Double impression	25.00	
RB46	RB4	⅜c	**black**	.65	.35
			Block of 4	3.25	1.75
RB47	RB4	½c	**black**	3.50	3.00
			Block of 4	14.50	
RB48	RB4	⅝c	**black**	.25	.25
			Block of 4	1.25	1.10
RB49	RB4	1c	**black**	4.50	4.25
			Block of 4	19.00	17.50
RB50	RB4	1¼c	**black**	.40	.30
			Block of 4	1.75	1.25
RB51	RB4	1½c	**black**	3.25	2.50
			Block of 4	15.00	11.00
RB52	RB4	1⅞c	**black**	1.10	.65
			Block of 4	4.75	2.40
RB53	RB4	2c	**black**	5.25	4.25
			Block of 4	24.00	
RB54	RB4	2½c	**black**	1.40	1.10
			Block of 4	6.25	5.00
RB55	RB4	3c	**black**	4.25	3.00
			Block of 4	19.00	
RB56	RB4	3⅛c	**black**	5.25	3.25
			Block of 4	24.00	
RB57	RB4	3¾c	**black**	11.50	7.75
			Block of 4	50.00	
RB58	RB4	4c	**black**	.35	.25
			Block of 4	1.75	1.25
			Double impression	—	
RB59	RB4	4⅜c	**black**	16.00	8.25
			Block of 4	70.00	
RB60	RB4	5c	**black**	3.25	2.75
			Block of 4	15.00	
RB61	RB4	6c	**black**	57.50	42.50
			Block of 4	275.00	
RB62	RB4	8c	**black**	18.00	11.50
			Block of 4	77.50	
RB63	RB4	10c	**black**	11.50	7.25
			Block of 4	55.00	
RB64	RB4	20c	**black**	24.00	18.00
			Block of 4	100.00	

RB5

1919   Offset Printing   Perf. 11

				Unused	Used
RB65	RB5	1c	**dark blue**	.25	.25
			Block of 4	1.25	1.10
			Double impression	30.00	20.00
RB66	RB5	2c	**dark blue**	.25	.25
			Block of 4	1.25	1.10
			Double impression	70.00	
RB67	RB5	3c	**dark blue**	1.10	.65
			Block of 4	5.00	3.00
			Double impression	70.00	
RB68	RB5	4c	**dark blue**	1.60	.55
			Block of 4	7.25	
RB69	RB5	5c	**dark blue**	1.40	.65
			Block of 4	6.25	3.00
RB70	RB5	8c	**dark blue**	14.50	9.25
			Block of 4	65.00	

				a. Violet Paper	b. Green Paper (1874)
RB10	RB1c	$5	**green & black** ('73)	8,000.	40,000.
			Pair	17,500.	

No. RB10b is valued with small faults.

When the Carpenter contract expired Aug. 31, 1875, the proprietary stamps remaining unissued were delivered to the Bureau of Internal Revenue. Until the taxes expired, June 30, 1883, the B.I.R. issued 34,315 of the 50c, 6,585 of the $1 and 2,109 of the $5, Nos. RB8-RB10. No. RB19, the 10c blue, replaced No. RB7b, the 10c on green paper, after 336,000 copies were issued, exhausting the supply in 1881.

RB2   George Washington
                        — RB2a

Plates prepared and printed by both the National Bank Note Co. and the Bureau of Engraving and Printing. No. RB11, and possibly others, also printed by the American Bank Note Co. All silk paper printings were by National, plus early printings of Nos. RB11b-RB14b, RB16b, RB17b. All rouletted stamps printed by the BEP plus Nos. RB15b, RB18b, RB19b. Otherwise, which company printed the stamps can be told only by guide lines (BEP) or full marginal inscriptions. ABN used National plates with A. B. Co. added on the second stamp to the left of the National inscription.

1875-81

				Silk Paper	Wmkd. 191R	
				a. Perf.	b. Perf.	c. Roul. 6
RB11	RB2	1c	**green**	1.90	.40	100.00
			Pair	4.50	1.10	250.00
			Block of 4	12.00	2.75	600.00
			Dble. transfer	—		
	d.		Vert. pair, imperf between		250.00	
RB12	RB2	2c	**brown**	2.50	1.40	125.00
			Pair	6.25	3.40	275.00
			Block of 4	62.50	8.00	650.00
RB13	RB2a	3c	**orange**	12.50	3.00	110.00
			Pair	27.50	6.75	250.00
			Block of 4	60.00	15.00	575.00
	d.		Horizontal pair, imperf. between			—
RB14	RB2a	4c	**red brown**	6.75	5.50	
			Pair	15.00	15.00	
			Block of 4	32.50	25.00	

RB71	RB5	10c	**dark blue**	5.25	2.10
			Block of 4	24.00	9.00
RB72	RB5	20c	**dark blue**	7.75	3.25

			Block of 4	37.50	
RB73	RB5	40c	**dark blue**	47.50	10.50

Block of 4	210.00

FUTURE DELIVERY STAMPS

Issued to facilitate the collection of a tax upon each sale, agreement of sale or agreement to sell any products or merchandise at any exchange o board of trade, or other similar place for future delivery.

Documentary Stamps of 1917 Overprinted in Black or Red

Type I

1918-34   Wmk. 191R   Offset Printing   Perf. 11
Overprint Horizontal (Lines 8mm apart)
Left Value — Unused
Right Value — Used

RC1	R22	2c **carmine rose**		7.50	.25
		Block of 4		32.50	1.10
RC2	R22	3c **carmine rose** ('34)		35.00	24.00
		Cut cancel			13.00
RC3	R22	4c **carmine rose**		12.50	.25
		Cut cancel			.20
		Block of 4		57.50	1.10
		Double impression of stamp			10.00
RC3A	R22	5c **carmine rose** ('33)		85.00	6.00
		Block of 4		—	30.00
RC4	R22	10c **carmine rose**		20.00	.25
		Block of 4		97.50	1.10
a.		Double overprint			5.25
b.		"FUTURE" omitted		—	210.00
c.		"DELIVERY FUTURE"			37.50
RC5	R22	20c **carmine rose**		30.00	.25
		Cut cancel			.20
		Block of 4		150.00	1.10
a.		Double overprint			21.00
RC6	R22	25c **carmine rose**		60.00	.45
		Cut cancel			.25
		Block of 4		275.00	2.25
		Block of 4, cut cancel			1.10
RC7	R22	40c **carmine rose**		70.00	.80
		Cut cancel			.25
		Block of 4		325.00	4.00
		Block of 4, cut cancel			1.10
RC8	R22	50c **carmine rose**		15.00	.25
		Cut cancel			.20
		Block of 4		72.50	1.10
a.		"DELIVERY" omitted		—	110.00
RC9	R22	80c **carmine rose**		125.00	10.50
		Cut cancel			1.10
		Block of 4		600.00	52.50
		Block of 4, cut cancel			5.00
a.		Double overprint			37.50
		Double overprint, cut cancel			6.25

Engr.
Overprint Vertical, Reading Up (Lines 2mm apart)

RC10	R21	$1 **green** (R)		50.00	.30
		Cut cancel			.20
		Block of 4		230.00	1.40
a.		Overprint reading down			300.00
b.		Black overprint		—	
		Cut cancel			125.00
RC11	R21	$2 **rose**		55.00	.30
		Cut cancel			.20
		Block of 4		250.00	1.40
RC12	R21	$3 **violet** (R)		125.00	2.75
		Cut cancel			.25
		Block of 4		—	12.50
		Block of 4, cut cancel			1.10
a.		Overprint reading down		—	52.50
RC13	R21	$5 **dark blue** (R)		100.00	.40
		Cut cancel			.25
		Block of 4		—	1.75
		Block of 4, cut cancel			1.10
RC14	R21	$10 **orange**		125.00	.80
		Cut cancel			.25
		Block of 4		575.00	3.25
		Block of 4, cut cancel			1.10
a.		"DELIVERY FUTURE"			110.00
RC15	R21	$20 **olive bister**		225.00	6.25
		Cut cancel			.55
		Perf initial			.30
		Block of 4			32.50
		Block of 4, cut cancel			2.50

Overprint Horizontal (Lines 11⅔mm apart)
Perf. 12
Without Gum

RC16	R17	$30 **vermilion**, green numerals		82.50	3.75
		Cut cancel			1.40
		Perf initial			1.00
		Vertical strip of 4			24.00
		Vertical strip of 4, cut cancel			6.50

a.		Numerals in blue		72.50	3.75
		Cut cancel			1.60
		Perf initial			1.25
b.		Imperf., blue numerals			*110.00*
RC17	R19	$50 **olive green** (*Cleveland*)		55.00	1.40
		Cut cancel			.65
		Vertical strip of 4			13.00
		Vertical strip of 4, cut cancel			2.75
a.		$50 olive bister		55.00	2.10
		Cut cancel			.45
		Perf initial			.35
RC18	R19	$60 **brown**		82.50	2.40
		Cut cancel			.80
		Perf initial			.70
		Vertical strip of 4			16.00
		Vertical strip of 4, cut cancel			3.75
a.		Vert. pair, imperf. horiz.			*425.00*
RC19	R17	$100 **yellow green** ('34)		140.00	32.50
		Cut cancel			7.00
		Perf initial			6.00
		Vertical strip of 4		—	*160.00*
		Vertical strip of 4, cut cancel			30.00
RC20	R18	$500 **blue**, red numerals (R)		92.50	11.50
		Cut cancel			4.75
		Perf initial			4.00
		Vertical strip of 4			*62.50*
		Vertical strip of 4, cut cancel			21.00
		Double transfer			15.00
a.		Numerals in orange		—	50.00
		Cut cancel			11.50
		Perf initial			10.00
		Double transfer			75.00
RC21	R19	$1000 **orange**		125.00	5.75
		Cut cancel			1.60
		Perf initial			1.25
		Vertical strip of 4			29.00
		Vertical strip of 4, cut cancel			8.00
a.		Vert. pair, imperf. horiz.			*1,100.*

See note after No. R227.

1923-24   Offset Printing   Perf. 11
Overprint Horizontal (Lines 2mm apart)

RC22	R22	1c **carmine rose**		1.10	.25
		Block of 4		5.50	1.25
RC23	R22	80c **carmine rose**		125.00	1.90
		Cut cancel			.40
		Block of 4		—	8.50
		Block of 4, cut cancel			1.75

Type II

1925-34   Engr.

RC25	R21	$1 **green** (R)		50.00	.80
		Cut cancel			.20
		Block of 4		—	3.00
		Block of 4, cut cancel			.30
RC26	R21	$10 **orange** (Bk) ('34)		140.00	16.00
		Cut cancel			10.50
		Perf initial			9.00

Overprint Type I

1928-29   Offset Printing   Perf. 10

RC27	R22	10c **carmine rose**	*2,500.*
RC28	R22	20c **carmine rose**	*2,500.*

STOCK TRANSFER STAMPS

Issued to facilitate the collection of a tax on all sales or agreements to sell, or memoranda of sales or delivery of, or transfers of legal title to shares or certificates of stock.

Documentary Stamps of 1917 Overprinted in Black or Red

1918-22 Offset Printing Wmk. 191R Perf. 11
Overprint Horizontal (Lines 8mm apart)

RD1	R22	1c carmine rose	.90	.25
		Block of 4	3.75	1.10
a.		Double overprint	—	
RD2	R22	2c carmine rose	.20	.20
		Block of 4	1.10	.20
a.		Double overprint	—	5.00
		Double overprint, cut cancel		2.50
		Double impression of stamp	—	
RD3	R22	4c carmine rose	.25	.25
		Block of 4	1.25	1.10
a.		Double overprint	—	4.25
		Double overprint, cut cancel		2.10
b.		"STOCK" omitted		10.50
d.		Ovpt. lines 10mm apart	—	
		Double impression of stamp		6.00
RD4	R22	5c carmine rose	.30	.25
		Block of 4	1.40	1.10
RD5	R22	10c carmine rose	.30	.25
		Block of 4	1.40	1.10
a.		Double overprint	—	5.25
b.		"STOCK" omitted		2.75
		Double impression of stamp	—	
RD6	R22	20c carmine rose	.55	.25
		Perf initial		.20
		Block of 4	2.25	1.10
a.		Double overprint		6.25
b.		"STOCK" double	—	
		Double impression of stamp		6.00
RD7	R22	25c carmine rose	1.60	.25
		Cut cancel		.20
		Block of 4	7.50	1.10
RD8	R22	40c carmine rose ('22)	1.40	.25
		Block of 4	6.75	1.10
RD9	R22	50c carmine rose	.70	.25
		Block of 4	3.25	1.10
a.		Double overprint	—	
		Double impression of stamp		—
RD10	R22	80c carmine rose	3.25	.35
		Cut cancel		.20
		Block of 4	15.00	1.60

Engr.
Overprint Vertical, Reading Up (Lines 2mm apart)

RD11	R21	$1 green (R)	95.00	21.00
		Cut cancel		3.00
		Block of 4	—	
		Block of 4, cut cancel		14.00
a.		Overprint reading down	140.00	21.00
		Overprint reading down, cut cancel		7.50
RD12	R21	$1 green (Bk)	2.75	.30
		Block of 4	12.00	1.40
a.		Pair, one without overprint	—	160.00
b.		Overprinted on back instead of face, inverted	—	110.00
c.		Overprint reading down	—	6.00
d.		$1 yellow green	3.00	.25
RD13	R21	$2 rose	2.75	.25
		Perf initial		.20
		Block of 4	12.00	1.10
a.		Overprint reading down		10.50
		Overprint reading down, cut cancel		1.50
b.		Vert. pair, imperf. horiz.	500.00	
RD14	R21	$3 violet (R)	20.00	4.50
		Cut cancel		.20
		Perf initial		.20
		Block of 4	90.00	—
		Block of 4, cut cancel		1.00
RD15	R21	$4 yellow brown	11.00	.25
		Cut cancel		.20
		Block of 4	47.50	1.10
RD16	R21	$5 dark blue (R)	7.00	.25
		Cut cancel		.20
		Block of 4	35.00	1.10
		Block of 4, cut cancel		.20
a.		Overprint reading down	21.00	1.10
		Overprint reading down, cut cancel		.20
RD17	R21	$10 orange	17.50	.35
		Cut cancel		.20
		Block of 4	80.00	1.50
		Block of 4, cut cancel		.20
RD18	R21	$20 olive bister ('21)	95.00	18.00
		Cut cancel		3.25
		Perf initial		2.50
		Block of 4	425.00	82.50
		Block of 4, cut cancel		16.00

Shifted overprints on the $2, and $10 result in "TRANSFER STOCK," "TRANSFER" omitted, and possibly other varieties.

Overprint Horizontal (Lines 11½mm apart)
1918 Without Gum Perf. 12

RD19	R17	$30 vermilion, green numerals	18.00	4.75
		Cut cancel		1.10
		Perf initial		1.00
		Vertical strip of 4		21.00
		Vertical strip of 4, cut cancel		6.50
a.		Numerals in blue		57.50
RD20	R19	$50 olive green (Cleveland)	110.00	57.50
		Cut cancel		21.00
		Perf initial		22.50
		Vertical strip of 4		260.00
		Vertical strip of 4, cut cancel		85.00
RD21	R19	$60 brown	125.00	21.00
		Cut cancel		9.25
		Perf initial		6.00
		Vertical strip of 4		90.00
		Vertical strip of 4, cut cancel		42.50
RD22	R17	$100 green	24.00	5.75
		Cut cancel		2.40
		Perf initial		2.00
		Vertical strip of 4		26.00
		Vertical strip of 4, cut cancel		11.00
RD23	R18	$500 blue (R)	325.00	110.00
		Cut cancel		50.00
		Perf initial		50.00
		Vertical strip of 4		65.00
		Vertical strip of 4, cut cancel		275.00
		Double transfer	500.00	175.00
a.		Numerals in orange		150.00
		Numerals in orange, double transfer		190.00
RD24	R19	$1,000 orange	175.00	75.00
		Cut cancel		26.00
		Perf initial		20.00
		Vertical strip of 4		350.00
		Vertical strip of 4, cut cancel		125.00

See note after No. R227.

1928 Offset Printing Perf. 10
Overprint Horizontal (Lines 8mm apart)

RD25	R22	2c carmine rose	2.75	.30
		Block of 4	12.00	1.40
RD26	R22	4c carmine rose	2.75	.30
		Block of 4	12.00	1.40
RD27	R22	10c carmine rose	2.10	.30
		Block of 4	9.50	1.40
a.		Inverted overprint		1,000.
RD28	R22	20c carmine rose	3.25	.30
		Perf initial		.20
		Block of 4	15.00	1.40
		Double impression of stamp	—	
RD29	R22	50c carmine rose	3.75	.30
		Block of 4	17.50	1.40

Engr.
Overprint Vertical, Reading Up (Lines 2mm apart)

RD30	R21	$1 green	35.00	.20
		Cut cancel		.20
		Block of 4	—	.90
a.		$1 yellow green	35.00	.45
RD31	R21	$2 carmine rose	35.00	.25
		Perf initial		.20
		Block of 4	—	1.10
a.		Pair, one without overprint	225.00	190.00
RD32	R21	$10 orange	37.50	.40
		Cut cancel		.20
		Perf initial		.20
		Block of 4	—	1.90
		Perf. 11 at top or bottom	—	

Overprinted Horizontally in Black

1920 Offset Printing Perf. 11

RD33	R22	2c carmine rose	7.75	.75
		Block of 4	37.50	3.75

RD34	R22	10c carmine rose	2.75	.35
		Block of 4	13.00	1.50
b.		Inverted overprint	1,550.	
RD35	R22	20c carmine rose	5.25	.25
		Block of 4	24.00	1.10
a.		Horiz. pair, one without overprint	175.00	
d.		Inverted overprint (perf. initials)	—	
RD36	R22	50c carmine rose	3.25	.25
		Block of 4	15.00	1.10

Shifted overprints on the 10c, 20c and 50c result in "TRANSFER STOCK," "TRANFSER" omitted, "STOCK" omitted, pairs, and other varieties.

Engr.

RD37	R21	$1 green	55.00	9.75
		Cut cancel		.25
		Block of 4	250.00	45.00
		Block of 4, cut cancel		1.25
RD38	R21	$2 rose	50.00	8.25
		Cut cancel		.25
		Block of 4	225.00	42.50
		Block of 4, cut cancel		1.10

Offset Printing
Perf. 10

RD39	R22	2c carmine rose	6.75	.95
		Block of 4	35.00	4.25
		Double impression of stamp	—	
RD40	R22	10c carmine rose	1.60	.55
		Block of 4	7.50	2.50
RD41	R22	20c carmine rose	2.75	.25
		Cut cancel		.20
		Block of 4	13.50	1.10

Documentary Stamps of 1917-33 Overprinted in Black

1940 Offset Printing Wmk. 191R Perf. 11

RD42	R22	1c rose pink	3.25	.50
		Cut cancel		.20
		Perf. initial		.25
a.		"Series 1940" inverted	—	275.00
		Cut cancel		100.00

No. RD42a always comes with a natural straight edge at left.

RD43	R22	2c rose pink	3.25	.55
		Cut cancel		.20
		Perf. initial		.25
RD45	R22	4c rose pink	3.25	.35
		Cut cancel		.25
		Perf. initial		.25
RD46	R22	5c rose pink	3.75	.25
		Cut cancel		.20
		Perf. initial		.20
RD48	R22	10c rose pink	4.75	.25
		Cut cancel		.20
		Perf. initial		.20
RD49	R22	20c rose pink	7.75	.25
		Cut cancel		.20
		Perf. initial		.20
RD50	R22	25c rose pink	7.75	.65
		Cut cancel		.25
		Perf. initial		.25
RD51	R22	40c rose pink	5.25	.80
		Cut cancel		.25
		Perf. initial		.25
RD52	R22	50c rose pink	6.25	.30
		Cut cancel		.25
		Perf. initial		.25
RD53	R22	80c rose pink	97.50	60.00
		Cut cancel		35.00
		Perf. initial		24.00

Engr.

RD54	R21	$1 green	35.00	.40
		Cut cancel		.25
		Perf. initial		.25
RD55	R21	$2 rose	35.00	.65
		Cut cancel		.25
		Perf. initial		.25
RD56	R21	$3 violet	175.00	13.00
		Cut cancel		.35
		Perf. initial		.25
RD57	R21	$4 yellow brown	70.00	1.25
		Cut cancel		.30
		Perf. initial		.25
RD58	R21	$5 dark blue	60.00	1.40
		Cut cancel		.35
		Perf. initial		.25
RD59	R21	$10 orange	140.00	8.25
		Cut cancel		.80
		Perf. initial		.65
RD60	R21	$20 olive bister	300.00	100.00
		Cut cancel		16.00
		Perf. initial		10.50

Nos. RD19-RD24 Handstamped in Blue "Series 1940"

1940		**Wmk. 191R**	**Perf. 12**
		Without Gum	
RD61	R17	$30 **vermilion**	925. 700.
		Cut cancel	325.
		Perf. initial	160.
RD62	R19	$50 **olive green**	1,500. 2,000.
		Cut cancel	900.
		Perf. initial	400.
a.		Double ovpt., perf. initial	1,000.
RD63	R19	$60 **brown**	2,400. 2,200.
		Cut cancel	675.
		Perf. initial	350.
RD64	R17	$100 **green**	1,250. 625.
		Cut cancel	225.
		Perf. initial	87.50
RD65	R18	$500 **blue**	2,250.
		Cut cancel	1,400.
		Perf. initial	775.
		Double transfer	2,300.
RD66	R19	$1,000 **orange**	3,000.
		Cut cancel	2,250.
		Perf. initial	1,750.

Alexander Hamilton — ST1

Levi Woodbury — ST2

Overprinted in Black   SERIES 1940

Same Portraits as Nos. R288-R310.

1940	**Engr.**	**Wmk. 191R**	**Perf. 11**
RD67	ST1	1c **bright green**	12.00 3.25
		Cut cancel	.65
		Perf. initial	.40
RD68	ST1	2c **bright green**	7.75 1.75
		Cut cancel	.30
		Perf. initial	.30
RD70	ST1	4c **bright green**	14.00 4.50
		Cut cancel	.65
		Perf. initial	.35
RD71	ST1	5c **bright green**	8.75 1.75
		Cut cancel	.25
		Perf. initial	.25
a.		Without overprint, cut cancel	275.00
RD73	ST1	10c **bright green**	12.00 2.10
		Cut cancel	.25
		Perf. initial	.25
RD74	ST1	20c **bright green**	14.00 2.40
		Cut cancel	.25
		Perf. initial	.25
RD75	ST1	25c **bright green**	40.00 9.25
		Cut cancel	.75
		Perf. initial	.45
RD76	ST1	40c **bright green**	72.50 35.00
		Cut cancel	2.40
		Perf. initial	1.00
RD77	ST1	50c **bright green**	12.00 2.10
		Cut cancel	.45
		Perf. initial	.30
RD78	ST1	80c **bright green**	95.00 57.50
		Cut cancel	24.00
		Perf. initial	3.50
RD79	ST2	$1 **bright green**	42.50 4.25
		Cut cancel	.55
		Perf. initial	.30
a.		Without overprint, perf. initial	240.00
RD80	ST2	$2 **bright green**	47.50 10.50
		Cut cancel	.60
		Perf. initial	.30
RD81	ST2	$3 **bright green**	72.50 13.00
		Cut cancel	.70
		Perf. initial	.25
RD82	ST2	$4 **bright green**	300.00 210.00
		Cut cancel	92.50
		Perf. initial	50.00
RD83	ST2	$5 **bright green**	67.50 14.50
		Cut cancel	1.75
		Perf. initial	.30
RD84	ST2	$10 **bright green**	160.00 42.50
		Cut cancel	5.25
		Perf. initial	3.00
RD85	ST2	$20 **bright green**	900.00 82.50
		Cut cancel	13.00
		Perf. initial	5.75

Nos. RD67-RD85 exist imperforate, without overprint. Value, set of pairs, $1,100.

Thomas Corwin — ST3

Overprinted "SERIES 1940"
Various frames and portraits as Nos. R306-R310.

		Without Gum	**Perf. 12**
RD86	ST3	$30 **bright green**	650.00 160.00
		Cut cancel	72.50
		Perf. initial	37.50
RD87	ST3	$50 **bright green**	725.00 475.00
		Cut cancel	200.00
		Perf. initial	92.50
RD88	ST3	$60 **bright green**	3,000. 1,100.
		Cut cancel	450.00
		Perf. initial	120.00
RD89	ST3	$100 **bright green**	— 325.00
		Cut cancel	125.00
		Perf. initial	67.50
RD90	ST3	$500 **bright green**	— 2,000.
		Cut cancel	1,150.
		Perf. initial	700.
RD91	ST3	$1,000 **bright green**	— 2,000.
		Cut cancel	1,050.
		Perf. initial	650.00

Nos. RD86-RD91 exist as unfinished imperforates with complete receipt tabs, without overprints or serial numbers. Known in singles, pairs, panes of four with plate number, uncut sheets of four panes (with two plate numbers), cross gutter blocks of eight, and blocks of four with vertical gutter between and plate number.

Nos. RD67-RD91 Overprint Instead: SERIES 1941

1941		**Wmk. 191R**	**Perf. 11**
RD92	ST1	1c **bright green**	.70 .55
		Cut cancel	.25
		Perf. initial	.25
RD93	ST1	2c **bright green**	.50 .30
		Cut cancel	.25
		Perf. initial	.25
RD95	ST1	4c **bright green**	.55 .25
		Cut cancel	.20
		Perf. initial	.20
RD96	ST1	5c **bright green**	.50 .25
		Cut cancel	.20
		Perf. initial	.20
RD98	ST1	10c **bright green**	.80 .25
		Cut cancel	.20
		Perf. initial	.20
RD99	ST1	20c **bright green**	1.90 .30
		Cut cancel	.25
		Perf. initial	.20
RD100	ST1	25c **bright green**	1.90 .45
		Cut cancel	.30
		Perf. initial	.30
RD101	ST1	40c **bright green**	2.75 .75
		Cut cancel	.30
		Perf. initial	.20
RD102	ST1	50c **bright green**	4.00 .35
		Cut cancel	.25
		Perf. initial	.25
RD103	ST1	80c **bright green**	25.00 7.75
		Cut cancel	.55
		Perf. initial	.50
RD104	ST2	$1 **bright green**	17.00 .20
		Cut cancel	.20
		Perf. initial	.20
RD105	ST2	$2 **bright green**	17.50 .30
		Cut cancel	.20
		Perf. initial	.20
RD106	ST2	$3 **bright green**	26.00 1.50
		Cut cancel	.35
		Perf. initial	.25
RD107	ST2	$4 **bright green**	47.50 7.75
		Cut cancel	.45
		Perf. initial	.30
RD108	ST2	$5 **bright green**	47.50 .65
		Cut cancel	.30
		Perf. initial	.25
RD109	ST2	$10 **bright green**	100.00 4.25
		Cut cancel	.75
		Perf. initial	.25
RD110	ST2	$20 **bright green**	275.00 67.50
		Cut cancel	18.00
		Perf. initial	4.25

Perf. 12
Without Gum

RD111	ST3	$30 **bright green**	250.00 240.00
		Cut cancel	77.50
		Perf. initial	29.00
RD112	ST3	$50 **bright green**	800.00 425.00
		Cut cancel	125.00
		Perf. initial	55.00

RD113	ST3	$60 **bright green**	1,350. 325.
		Cut cancel	190.
		Perf. initial	125.
RD114	ST3	$100 **bright green**	— 175.
		Cut cancel	57.
		Perf. initial	24.
RD115	ST3	$500 **bright green**	1,900. 1,55
		Cut cancel	975.
		Perf. initial	525.
RD116	ST3	$1,000 **bright green**	— 1,50
		Cut cancel	850.0
		Perf. initial	575.0

Nos. RD67-RD91 Overprint Instead: SERIES 194

1942		**Wmk. 191R**	**Perf. 1**
RD117	ST1	1c **bright green**	.55 .3
		Cut cancel	.2
		Perf. initial	.2
RD118	ST1	2c **bright green**	.45 .3
		Cut cancel	.2
		Perf. initial	.1
RD119	ST1	4c **bright green**	3.25 1.1
		Cut cancel	.5
		Perf. initial	.4
RD120	ST1	5c **bright green**	.45 .2
		Cut cancel	.2
		Perf. initial	.2
a.		Overprint inverted, cut cancel	240.0
			200.0
RD121	ST1	10c **bright green**	1.90 .2
		Cut cancel	.2
		Perf. initial	.2
RD122	ST1	20c **bright green**	2.25 .2
		Cut cancel	.2
		Perf. initial	.2
RD123	ST1	25c **bright green**	2.25 .2
		Cut cancel	.2
		Perf. initial	.2
RD124	ST1	40c **bright green**	4.75 .4
		Cut cancel	.2
		Perf. initial	.2
RD125	ST1	50c **bright green**	5.75 .2
		Cut cancel	.20
		Perf. initial	.20
RD126	ST1	80c **bright green**	25.00 6.0
		Cut cancel	1.5
		Perf. initial	.3
RD127	ST2	$1 **bright green**	17.00 .4
		Cut cancel	.2
		Perf. initial	.20
RD128	ST2	$2 **bright green**	27.50 .40
		Cut cancel	.25
		Perf. initial	.20
RD129	ST2	$3 **bright green**	32.50 1.10
		Cut cancel	.30
		Perf. initial	.20
RD130	ST2	$4 **bright green**	47.50 21.00
		Cut cancel	.40
		Perf. initial	.25
RD131	ST2	$5 **bright green**	42.50 .40
		Cut cancel	.25
		Perf. initial	.25
a.		Double overprint, perf. initial	
RD132	ST2	$10 **bright green**	77.50 8.25
		Cut cancel	1.40
		Perf. initial	1.10
RD133	ST2	$20 **bright green**	175.00 37.50
		Cut cancel	7.75
		Perf. initial	3.50

Perf. 12
Without Gum

RD134	ST3	$30 **bright green**	225.00 62.50
		Cut cancel	24.00
		Perf. initial	16.00
RD135	ST3	$50 **bright green**	375.00 140.00
		Cut cancel	47.50
		Perf. initial	21.00
RD136	ST3	$60 **bright green**	450.00 200.00
		Cut cancel	80.00
		Perf. initial	52.50
RD137	ST3	$100 **bright green**	550.00 80.00
		Cut cancel	29.00
		Perf. initial	16.00
RD138	ST3	$500 **bright green**	— 12,500.
		Cut cancel	9,500.
		Perf. initial	8,000.
RD139	ST3	$1,000 **bright green**	— 575.00
		Cut cancel	275.00
		Perf. initial	160.00

Nos. RD67-RD91 Overprint Instead: SERIES 1943

1943		**Wmk. 191R**	**Perf. 11**
RD140	ST1	1c **bright green**	.45 .30
		Cut cancel	.25
		Perf. initial	.25
RD141	ST1	2c **bright green**	.55 .40
		Cut cancel	.20
		Perf. initial	.20
RD142	ST1	4c **bright green**	1.90 .20
		Cut cancel	.20
		Perf. initial	.20
RD143	ST1	5c **bright green**	.55 .20
		Cut cancel	.20
		Perf. initial	.20
RD144	ST1	10c **bright green**	1.10 .20
		Cut cancel	.20
		Perf. initial	.20
RD145	ST1	20c **bright green**	1.90 .20
		Cut cancel	.20
		Perf. initial	.20
RD146	ST1	25c **bright green**	5.00 .35
		Cut cancel	.25
		Perf. initial	.20

No.	Type	Denom	Color	Unused	Used
D147	ST1	40c	bright green	4.25	.25
			Cut cancel		.20
			Perf. initial		.20
D148	ST1	50c	bright green	4.25	.20
			Cut cancel		.20
			Perf. initial		.20
D149	ST1	80c	bright green	17.00	4.75
			Cut cancel		1.60
			Perf. initial		1.10
D150	ST2	$1	bright green	17.00	.20
			Cut cancel		.20
			Perf. initial		.20
D151	ST2	$2	bright green	19.00	.35
			Cut cancel		.20
			Perf. initial		.25
D152	ST2	$3	bright green	22.50	1.40
			Cut cancel		.30
			Perf. initial		.25
D153	ST2	$4	bright green	47.50	16.00
			Cut cancel		1.10
			Perf. initial		.30
D154	ST2	$5	bright green	72.50	.40
			Cut cancel		.25
			Perf. initial		.25
D155	ST2	$10	bright green	95.00	4.75
			Cut cancel		.80
			Perf. initial		.30
D156	ST2	$20	bright green	160.00	40.00
			Cut cancel		14.50
			Perf. initial		3.75

Perf. 12
Without Gum

No.	Type	Denom	Color	Unused	Used
D157	ST3	$30	bright green	350.00	150.00
			Cut cancel		52.50
			Perf. initial		24.00
D158	ST3	$50	bright green	725.00	140.00
			Cut cancel		29.00
			Perf. initial		14.50
RD159	ST3	$60	bright green	—	1,000.
			Cut cancel		350.00
			Perf. initial		120.00
RD160	ST3	$100	bright green	125.00	62.50
			Cut cancel		18.00
			Perf. initial		13.00
RD161	ST3	$500	bright green	—	1,100.
			Cut cancel		400.00
			Perf. initial		210.00
RD162	ST3	$1,000	bright green	—	260.00
			Cut cancel		175.00
			Perf. initial		140.00

Nos. RD67-RD91 Overprint Instead: **Series 1944**

1944		**Wmk. 191R**			**Perf. 11**
RD163	ST1	1c	bright green	.70	.65
			Cut cancel		.25
			Perf. initial		.25
RD164	ST1	2c	bright green	.50	.25
			Cut cancel		.20
			Perf. initial		.20
RD165	ST1	4c	bright green	.65	.25
			Cut cancel		.20
			Perf. initial		.20
RD166	ST1	5c	bright green	.55	.20
			Cut cancel		.20
			Perf. initial		.20
RD167	ST1	10c	bright green	.80	.20
			Cut cancel		.20
			Perf. initial		.20
RD168	ST1	20c	bright green	1.40	.20
			Cut cancel		.20
			Perf. initial		.20
RD169	ST1	25c	bright green	2.25	.30
			Cut cancel		.25
			Perf. initial		.25
RD170	ST1	40c	bright green	8.75	5.25
			Cut cancel		2.40
			Perf. initial		1.60
RD171	ST1	50c	bright green	5.00	.20
			Cut cancel		.20
			Perf. initial		.20
RD172	ST1	80c	bright green	10.00	4.75
			Cut cancel		2.10
			Perf. initial		1.60
RD173	ST2	$1	bright green	11.00	.45
			Cut cancel		.25
			Perf. initial		.25
RD174	ST2	$2	bright green	42.50	.65
			Cut cancel		.25
			Perf. initial		.25
RD175	ST2	$3	bright green	37.50	1.40
			Cut cancel		.30
			Perf. initial		.25
RD176	ST2	$4	bright green	45.00	5.25
			Cut cancel		.25
			Perf. initial		.25
RD177	ST2	$5	bright green	42.50	1.10
			Cut cancel		.35
			Perf. initial		.25
RD178	ST2	$10	bright green	82.50	4.75
			Cut cancel		.50
			Perf. initial		.35
RD179	ST2	$20	bright green	140.00	9.25
			Cut cancel		4.25
			Perf. initial		3.50

Perf. 12
Without Gum

Designs: $2,500, William Windom. $5,000, C. J. Folger. $10,000, W. Q. Gresham.

No.	Type	Denom	Color	Unused	Used
RD180	ST3	$30	bright green	225.00	77.50
			Cut cancel		29.00
			Perf. initial		12.50

No.	Type	Denom	Color	Unused	Used
RD181	ST3	$50	bright green	150.00	62.50
			Cut cancel		16.00
			Perf. initial		11.50
RD182	ST3	$60	bright green	260.00	150.00
			Cut cancel		67.50
			Perf. initial		50.00
RD183	ST3	$100	bright green	225.00	62.50
			Cut cancel		24.00
			Perf. initial		11.50
RD184	ST3	$500	bright green	—	525.00
			Cut cancel		325.00
			Perf. initial		240.00
RD185	ST3	$1,000	bright green	2,500.	825.00
			Cut cancel		325.00
			Perf. initial		190.00
RD185A	ST3	$2,500	bright green		—
RD185B	ST3	$5,000	bright green		—
RD185C	ST3	$10,000	bright green, cut cancel		25,000.

Nos. RD185A-R185C exist as unfinished imperforates with complete receipt tabs, without overprints or serial numbers. Known in singles, pairs, panes of four with plate number, uncut sheets of four panes (with two plate numbers), cross gutter blocks of eight, and blocks of four with vertical gutter between and plate number.

Nos. RD67-RD91 Overprint Instead: **Series 1945**

1945		**Wmk. 191R**			**Perf. 11**
RD186	ST1	1c	bright green	.30	.25
			Cut cancel		.20
			Perf. initial		.20
RD187	ST1	2c	bright green	.30	.30
			Cut cancel		.20
			Perf. initial		.20
RD188	ST1	4c	bright green	.30	.20
			Cut cancel		.20
			Perf. initial		.20
RD189	ST1	5c	bright green	.30	.20
			Cut cancel		.20
			Perf. initial		.20
RD190	ST1	10c	bright green	.80	.35
			Cut cancel		.25
			Perf. initial		.25
RD191	ST1	20c	bright green	1.40	.35
			Cut cancel		.25
			Perf. initial		.25
RD192	ST1	25c	bright green	2.25	.35
			Cut cancel		.30
			Perf. initial		.25
RD193	ST1	40c	bright green	3.25	.25
			Cut cancel		.20
			Perf. initial		.20
RD194	ST1	50c	bright green	8.75	.30
			Cut cancel		.20
			Perf. initial		.25
RD195	ST1	80c	bright green	8.25	3.25
			Cut cancel		.80
			Perf. initial		.70
RD196	ST2	$1	bright green	16.00	.30
			Cut cancel		.20
			Perf. initial		.25
RD197	ST2	$2	bright green	25.00	.50
			Cut cancel		.20
			Perf. initial		.25
RD198	ST2	$3	bright green	40.00	.95
			Cut cancel		.25
			Perf. initial		.25
RD199	ST2	$4	bright green	40.00	2.75
			Cut cancel		.80
			Perf. initial		.55
RD200	ST2	$5	bright green	26.00	.55
			Cut cancel		.20
			Perf. initial		.25
RD201	ST2	$10	bright green	60.00	6.75
			Cut cancel		.80
			Perf. initial		.75
RD202	ST2	$20	bright green	140.00	13.00
			Cut cancel		2.10
			Perf. initial		1.25

Perf. 12
Without Gum

No.	Type	Denom	Color	Unused	Used
RD203	ST3	$30	bright green	150.00	72.50
			Cut cancel		29.00
			Perf. initial		19.00
RD204	ST3	$50	bright green	72.50	26.00
			Cut cancel		6.50
			Perf. initial		5.25
RD205	ST3	$60	bright green	260.00	150.00
			Cut cancel		62.50
			Perf. initial		29.00
RD206	ST3	$100	bright green	95.00	42.50
			Cut cancel		17.00
			Perf. initial		8.75
RD207	ST3	$500	bright green	—	925.00
			Cut cancel		425.00
			Perf. initial		240.00
RD208	ST3	$1,000	bright green	1,650.	1,000.
			Cut cancel		450.00
			Perf. initial		240.00
RD208A	ST3	$2,500	bright green		
			Cut cancel		30,000.
			Perf. initial		20,000.
RD208B	ST3	$5,000	bright green		20,000.
RD208C	ST3	$10,000	bright green		
			Cut cancel		20,000.

Stock Transfer Stamps and Type of 1940 Overprinted in Black
Series 1946

1946		**Wmk. 191R**			**Perf. 11**
RD209	ST1	1c	bright green	.25	.25
			Cut cancel		.20
			Perf. initial		.20
a.		Pair, one dated "1945"		475.00	
RD210	ST1	2c	bright green	.40	.20
			Cut cancel		.20
			Perf. initial		.20
RD211	ST1	4c	bright green	.35	.20
			Cut cancel		.20
			Perf. initial		.20
RD212	ST1	5c	bright green	.40	.20
			Cut cancel		.20
			Perf. initial		.20
RD213	ST1	10c	bright green	.80	.20
			Cut cancel		.20
			Perf. initial		.20
RD214	ST1	20c	bright green	1.60	.20
			Cut cancel		.20
			Perf. initial		.20
RD215	ST1	25c	bright green	1.90	.30
			Cut cancel		.25
			Perf. initial		.25
RD216	ST1	40c	bright green	3.75	.65
			Cut cancel		.25
			Perf. initial		.25
RD217	ST1	50c	bright green	5.00	.25
			Cut cancel		.20
			Perf. initial		.20
RD218	ST1	80c	bright green	12.00	6.25
			Cut cancel		2.10
			Perf. initial		1.40
RD219	ST2	$1	bright green	11.00	.50
			Cut cancel		.20
			Perf. initial		.20
RD220	ST2	$2	bright green	12.00	.55
			Cut cancel		.25
			Perf. initial		.25
RD221	ST2	$3	bright green	22.50	1.40
			Cut cancel		.35
			Perf. initial		.25
RD222	ST2	$4	bright green	22.50	6.50
			Cut cancel		2.40
			Perf. initial		1.00
RD223	ST2	$5	bright green	35.00	1.40
			Cut cancel		.30
			Perf. initial		.25
RD224	ST2	$10	bright green	67.50	2.50
			Cut cancel		.80
			Perf. initial		.25
RD225	ST2	$20	bright green	160.00	47.50
			Cut cancel		13.00
			Perf. initial		7.25

Without Gum
Perf. 12

No.	Type	Denom	Color	Unused	Used
RD226	ST3	$30	bright green	140.00	45.00
			Cut cancel		18.00
			Perf. initial		16.00
RD227	ST3	$50	bright green	100.00	50.00
			Cut cancel		21.00
			Perf. initial		11.50
RD228	ST3	$60	bright green	225.00	100.00
			Cut cancel		37.50
			Perf. initial		13.00
RD229	ST3	$100	bright green	140.00	57.50
			Cut cancel		21.00
			Perf. initial		14.50
RD230	ST3	$500	bright green	—	175.00
			Cut cancel		110.00
			Perf. initial		85.00
RD231	ST3	$1,000	bright green	—	200.00
			Cut cancel		125.00
			Perf. initial		85.00
RD232	ST3	$2,500	bright green	20,000.	13,500.
RD233	ST3	$5,000	bright green		20,000.
RD234	ST3	$10,000	bright green		
			Cut cancel		15,000.

Stock Transfer Stamps and Type of 1940 Overprinted in Black
Series 1947

1947		**Wmk. 191R**			**Perf. 11**
RD235	ST1	1c	bright green	1.40	.60
			Cut cancel		.25
			Perf. initial		.25
RD236	ST1	2c	bright green	1.40	.55
			Cut cancel		.25
			Perf. initial		.25
RD237	ST1	4c	bright green	1.10	.45
			Cut cancel		.25
			Perf. initial		.25
RD238	ST1	5c	bright green	1.10	.35
			Cut cancel		.25
			Perf. initial		.25
RD239	ST1	10c	bright green	1.40	.55
			Cut cancel		.25
			Perf. initial		.25
RD240	ST1	20c	bright green	2.25	.55
			Cut cancel		.25
			Perf. initial		.25
RD241	ST1	25c	bright green	3.25	.65
			Cut cancel		.25
			Perf. initial		.25
RD242	ST1	40c	bright green	3.75	.80
			Cut cancel		.30
			Perf. initial		.25
RD243	ST1	50c	bright green	4.50	.30
			Cut cancel		.25
			Perf. initial		.20
RD244	ST1	80c	bright green	22.50	10.50
			Cut cancel		4.25
			Perf. initial		3.75

Scott	Type	Denom.	Color	Un	U
RD245	ST2	$1	bright green	12.00	.55
		Cut cancel			.25
		Perf. initial			.25
RD246	ST2	$2	bright green	19.00	.80
		Cut cancel			.25
		Perf. initial			.25
RD247	ST2	$3	bright green	35.00	1.60
		Cut cancel			.40
		Perf. initial			.35
RD248	ST2	$4	bright green	45.00	6.25
		Cut cancel			1.25
		Perf. initial			.75
RD249	ST2	$5	bright green	37.50	1.60
		Cut cancel			.35
		Perf. initial			.25
RD250	ST2	$10	bright green	60.00	5.25
		Cut cancel			2.10
		Perf. initial			1.40
RD251	ST2	$20	bright green	110.00	32.50
		Cut cancel			7.50
		Perf. initial			6.25

Without Gum   **Perf. 12**

Scott	Type	Denom.	Color	Un	U
RD252	ST3	$30	bright green	110.00	52.50
		Cut cancel			16.00
		Perf. initial			10.50
RD253	ST3	$50	bright green	225.00	125.00
		Cut cancel			47.50
		Perf. initial			21.00
RD254	ST3	$60	bright green	325.00	150.00
		Cut cancel			52.50
		Perf. initial			37.50
RD255	ST3	$100	bright green	125.00	45.00
		Cut cancel			18.00
		Perf. initial			16.00
RD256	ST3	$500	bright green	—	400.00
		Cut cancel			160.00
		Perf. initial			100.00
RD257	ST3	$1,000	bright green	—	110.00
		Cut cancel			52.50
		Perf. initial			32.50
RD258	ST3	$2,500	bright green	—	
		Cut cancel			450.00
RD259	ST3	$5,000	bright green	—	
		Cut cancel			325.00
RD260	ST3	$10,000	bright green	—	
		Cut cancel			55.00
		Perf. initial			—
a.		Horiz. pair, imperf. vert., cut cancel			—

Nos. RD67-RD91 Overprint Instead: **Series 1948**

1948   **Wmk. 191R**   **Perf. 11**

Scott	Type	Denom.	Color	Un	U
RD261	ST1	1c	bright green	.30	.25
		Cut cancel			.20
		Perf. initial			.20
RD262	ST1	2c	bright green	.30	.30
		Cut cancel			.25
		Perf. initial			.20
RD263	ST1	4c	bright green	.50	.35
		Cut cancel			.25
		Perf. initial			.25
RD264	ST1	5c	bright green	.35	.25
		Cut cancel			.20
		Perf. initial			.20
RD265	ST1	10c	bright green	.35	.25
		Cut cancel			.20
		Perf. initial			.20
RD266	ST1	20c	bright green	1.50	.35
		Cut cancel			.20
		Perf. initial			.20
RD267	ST1	25c	bright green	1.50	.40
		Cut cancel			.25
		Perf. initial			.25
RD268	ST1	40c	bright green	2.50	.80
		Cut cancel			.30
		Perf. initial			.25
RD269	ST1	50c	bright green	4.75	.30
		Cut cancel			.20
		Perf. initial			.20
RD270	ST1	80c	bright green	19.00	6.25
		Cut cancel			2.40
		Perf. initial			2.10
RD271	ST2	$1	bright green	13.00	.40
		Cut cancel			.20
		Perf. initial			.20
RD272	ST2	$2	bright green	22.50	.65
		Cut cancel			.25
		Perf. initial			.25
RD273	ST2	$3	bright green	27.50	4.00
		Cut cancel			1.75
		Perf. initial			1.40
RD274	ST2	$4	bright green	30.00	11.50
		Cut cancel			3.25
		Perf. initial			2.10
RD275	ST2	$5	bright green	35.00	2.75
		Cut cancel			.30
		Perf. initial			.25
RD276	ST2	$10	bright green	60.00	4.75
		Cut cancel			.80
		Perf. initial			.65
RD277	ST2	$20	bright green	110.00	19.00
		Cut cancel			6.25
		Perf. initial			4.25

Perf. 12
Without Gum

Scott	Type	Denom.	Color	Un	U
RD278	ST3	$30	bright green	160.00	62.50
		Cut cancel			26.00
		Perf. initial			16.00
RD279	ST3	$50	bright green	110.00	62.50
		Cut cancel			26.00
		Perf. initial			13.00
RD280	ST3	$60	bright green	275.00	140.00
		Cut cancel			55.00
		Perf. initial			21.00
RD281	ST3	$100	bright green	95.00	24.00
		Cut cancel			7.75
		Perf. initial			5.75
RD282	ST3	$500	bright green	—	240.00
		Cut cancel			140.00
		Perf. initial			47.50
RD283	ST3	$1,000	bright green	—	140.00
		Cut cancel			47.50
		Perf. initial			29.00
RD284	ST3	$2,500	bright green	725.00	375.00
		Cut cancel			190.00
		Perf. initial			140.00
RD285	ST3	$5,000	bright green	—	300.00
		Cut cancel			175.00
		Perf. initial			140.00
RD286	ST3	$10,000	bright green	—	
		Cut cancel			52.50
		Perf. initial			

Nos. RD67-RD91 Overprint Instead: **Series 1949**

1949   **Wmk. 191R**   **Perf. 11**

Scott	Type	Denom.	Color	Un	U
RD287	ST1	1c	bright green	1.60	.50
		Cut cancel			.25
		Perf. initial			.25
RD288	ST1	2c	bright green	1.60	.50
		Cut cancel			.25
		Perf. initial			.25
RD289	ST1	4c	bright green	1.90	.55
		Cut cancel			.25
		Perf. initial			.25
RD290	ST1	5c	bright green	1.90	.55
		Cut cancel			.25
		Perf. initial			.25
RD291	ST1	10c	bright green	3.25	.80
		Cut cancel			.25
		Perf. initial			.25
RD292	ST1	20c	bright green	5.50	.65
		Cut cancel			.25
		Perf. initial			.25
RD293	ST1	25c	bright green	6.50	.90
		Cut cancel			.25
		Perf. initial			.25
RD294	ST1	40c	bright green	14.00	1.60
		Cut cancel			.25
		Perf. initial			.25
RD295	ST1	50c	bright green	17.00	.30
		Cut cancel			.25
		Perf. initial			.25
RD296	ST1	80c	bright green	22.50	6.75
		Cut cancel			3.00
		Perf. initial			2.75
RD297	ST2	$1	bright green	19.00	.80
		Cut cancel			.30
		Perf. initial			.25
RD298	ST2	$2	bright green	27.50	.95
		Cut cancel			.25
		Perf. initial			.25
RD299	ST2	$3	bright green	45.00	4.75
		Cut cancel			1.40
		Perf. initial			.95
RD300	ST2	$4	bright green	42.50	7.75
		Cut cancel			2.10
		Perf. initial			1.60
RD301	ST2	$5	bright green	52.50	2.10
		Cut cancel			.30
		Perf. initial			.25
RD302	ST2	$10	bright green	72.50	4.25
		Cut cancel			1.40
		Perf. initial			1.25
RD303	ST2	$20	bright green	150.00	16.00
		Cut cancel			6.25
		Perf. initial			5.25

Perf. 12
Without Gum

Scott	Type	Denom.	Color	Un	U
RD304	ST3	$30	bright green	190.00	87.50
		Cut cancel			35.00
		Perf. initial			16.00
RD305	ST3	$50	bright green	250.00	140.00
		Cut cancel			50.00
		Perf. initial			24.00
RD306	ST3	$60	bright green	425.00	250.00
		Cut cancel			110.00
		Perf. initial			47.50
RD307	ST3	$100	bright green	160.00	70.00
		Cut cancel			26.00
		Perf. initial			16.00
RD308	ST3	$500	bright green	—	250.00
		Cut cancel			92.50
		Perf. initial			57.50
RD309	ST3	$1,000	bright green	—	100.00
		Cut cancel			45.00
		Perf. initial			29.00
RD310	ST3	$2,500	bright green	—	
		Cut cancel			475.00
		Perf. initial			—
RD311	ST3	$5,000	bright green	—	
		Cut cancel			475.00
		Perf. initial			350.00
RD312	ST3	$10,000	bright green	—	425.00
		Cut cancel			45.00
		Perf. initial			—
a.		Pair, one without ovpt., cut cancel			8,000.

No. RD312a is unique.

Nos. RD67-RD91 Overprint Instead: **Series 1950**

1950   **Wmk. 191R**   **Perf.**

Scott	Type	Denom.	Color	Un	U
RD313	ST1	1c	bright green	.65	
		Cut cancel			
		Perf. initial			
RD314	ST1	2c	bright green	.55	
		Cut cancel			
		Perf. initial			
RD315	ST1	4c	bright green	.45	
		Cut cancel			
		Perf. initial			
RD316	ST1	5c	bright green	.55	
		Cut cancel			
		Perf. initial			
RD317	ST1	10c	bright green	2.75	
		Cut cancel			
		Perf. initial			
RD318	ST1	20c	bright green	4.00	
		Cut cancel			
		Perf. initial			
RD319	ST1	25c	bright green	5.50	
		Cut cancel			
		Perf. initial			
RD320	ST1	40c	bright green	8.25	1.
		Cut cancel			
		Perf. initial			
RD321	ST1	50c	bright green	9.00	
		Cut cancel			
		Perf. initial			
RD322	ST1	80c	bright green	17.00	5.
		Cut cancel			2.
		Perf. initial			1.
RD323	ST2	$1	bright green	17.00	
		Cut cancel			
		Perf. initial			
RD324	ST2	$2	bright green	30.00	
		Cut cancel			
		Perf. initial			
RD325	ST2	$3	bright green	40.00	4.
		Cut cancel			
		Perf. initial			
RD326	ST2	$4	bright green	47.50	9.
		Cut cancel			3.
		Perf. initial			2.
RD327	ST2	$5	bright green	47.50	1.9
		Cut cancel			
		Perf. initial			
RD328	ST2	$10	bright green	150.00	5.
		Cut cancel			1.6
		Perf. initial			.8
RD329	ST2	$20	bright green	150.00	26.0
		Cut cancel			17.0
		Perf. initial			4.7

Perf. 12
Without Gum

Scott	Type	Denom.	Color	Un	U
RD330	ST3	$30	bright green	150.00	72.5
		Cut cancel			32.5
		Perf. initial			16.0
a.		Booklet pane of 4		3,300.	
RD331	ST3	$50	bright green	190.00	92.5
		Cut cancel			47.5
		Perf. initial			26.0
a.		Booklet pane of 4		3,300.	
RD332	ST3	$60	bright green	275.00	150.0
		Cut cancel			67.5
		Perf. initial			42.5
a.		Booklet pane of 4		4,750.	
RD333	ST3	$100	bright green	110.00	50.0
		Cut cancel			24.0
		Perf. initial			13.0
a.		Vert. pair, imperf. btwn.		2,250.	1,750
RD334	ST3	$500	bright green	—	250.0
		Cut cancel			125.0
		Perf. initial			92.5
RD335	ST3	$1,000	bright green	—	75.0
		Cut cancel			32.5
		Perf. initial			20.0
RD336	ST3	$2,500	bright green	—	1,250
		Cut cancel			900.0
		Perf. initial			
a.		Booklet pane of 4		10,000.	
RD337	ST3	$5,000	bright green	—	750.0
		Cut cancel			425.0
		Perf. initial			
a.		Booklet pane of 4		10,000.	
RD338	ST3	$10,000	bright green	—	825.0
		Cut cancel			97.5
		Perf. initial			
a.		Booklet pane of 4		10,000.	

Nos. RD67-RD91 Overprint Instead: **Series 1951**

1951   **Wmk. 191R**   **Perf. 11**

Scott	Type	Denom.	Color	Un	U
RD339	ST1	1c	bright green	2.25	.40
		Cut cancel			.25
		Perf. initial			.25
RD340	ST1	2c	bright green	1.90	.35
		Cut cancel			.25
		Perf. initial			.25
RD341	ST1	4c	bright green	2.25	.55
		Cut cancel			.25
		Perf. initial			.25
RD342	ST1	5c	bright green	1.60	.40
		Cut cancel			.25
		Perf. initial			.20
RD343	ST1	10c	bright green	2.25	.35
		Cut cancel			.25
		Perf. initial			.20
RD344	ST1	20c	bright green	5.50	.95
		Cut cancel			.25
		Perf. initial			.25
RD345	ST1	25c	bright green	8.25	.95
		Cut cancel			.25
		Perf. initial			.25
RD346	ST1	40c	bright green	32.50	9.25
		Cut cancel			3.00
		Perf. initial			1.60

0347	ST1	50c **bright green**	14.00	.95
	Cut cancel			.25
	Perf. initial			.25
0348	ST1	80c **bright green**	27.50	10.50
	Cut cancel			4.25
	Perf. initial			2.10
0349	ST2	$1 **bright green**	29.00	.85
	Cut cancel			.25
	Perf. initial			.25
0350	ST2	$2 **bright green**	35.00	1.40
	Cut cancel			.25
	Perf. initial			.25
0351	ST2	$3 **bright green**	47.50	10.50
	Cut cancel			3.75
	Perf. initial			1.60
0352	ST2	$4 **bright green**	55.00	12.50
	Cut cancel			5.00
	Perf. initial			2.10
0353	ST2	$5 **bright green**	65.00	2.75
	Cut cancel			.30
	Perf. initial			.25
0354	ST2	$10 **bright green**	110.00	8.75
	Cut cancel			2.10
	Perf. initial			1.60
0355	ST2	$20 **bright green**	175.00	18.00
	Cut cancel			7.25
	Perf. initial			5.25

Perf. 12
Without Gum

RD356	ST3	$30 **bright green**	175.00	77.50
	Cut cancel			35.00
	Perf. initial			18.00
RD357	ST3	$50 **bright green**	160.00	67.50
	Cut cancel			26.00
	Perf. initial			18.00
RD358	ST3	$60 **bright green**	—	1,400.
	Cut cancel			525.00
	Perf. initial			240.00
RD359	ST3	$100 **bright green**	160.00	67.50
	Cut cancel			24.00
	Perf. initial			11.50
RD360	ST3	$500 **bright green**	—	375.00
	Cut cancel			160.00
	Perf. initial			110.00
RD361	ST3	$1,000 **bright green**	—	100.00
	Cut cancel			67.50
	Perf. initial			52.50
RD362	ST3	$2,500 **bright green**	—	3,500.
	Cut cancel			1,200.
	Perf. initial			500.00
RD363	ST3	$5,000 **bright green**	—	1,450.
	Cut cancel			825.00
	Perf. initial			600.00
RD364	ST3	$10,000 **bright green**	1,650.	160.00
	Cut cancel			67.50
	Perf. initial			50.00

Nos. RD67-RD91 Overprint Instead: **Series 1952**

1952		Wmk. 191R		*Perf. 11*
RD365	ST1	1c **bright green**	37.50	18.00
	Cut cancel			4.25
	Perf. initial			2.10
RD366	ST1	10c **bright green**	37.50	18.00
	Cut cancel			4.25
	Perf. initial			2.10
RD367	ST1	20c **bright green**	450.00	—
	Cut cancel			—
	Perf. initial			—
RD368	ST1	25c **bright green**	600.00	—
	Cut cancel			—
	Perf. initial			—
RD369	ST1	40c **bright green**	125.00	42.50
	Cut cancel			14.50
	Perf. initial			10.50
RD370	ST2	$4 **bright green**	1,500.	575.00
RD371	ST2	$10 **bright green**	3,000.	—
	Cut cancel			—
	Perf. initial			—
RD372	ST2	$20 **bright green**	5,750.	—
	Cut cancel			—
	Perf. initial			—

Stock Transfer Stamps were discontinued in 1952.

CORDIALS, WINES, ETC. STAMPS

RE1

Inscribed "Series of 1914"

1914		Wmk. 190	Offset Printing	*Perf. 10*
RE1	RE1	¼c **green**	.95	.55
RE2	RE1	½c **green**	.50	.50
RE3	RE1	1c **green**	.50	.35
RE4	RE1	1½c **green**	2.40	1.60
RE5	RE1	2c **green**	4.00	3.75
RE6	RE1	3c **green**	3.25	1.40
RE7	RE1	4c **green**	2.75	1.60
RE8	RE1	5c **green**	1.10	.80
RE9	RE1	6c **green**	7.50	4.00
a.		Double impression	—	
RE10	RE1	8c **green**	5.75	1.60
RE11	RE1	10c **green**	3.75	3.00
RE12	RE1	20c **green**	4.50	1.90
RE13	RE1	24c **green**	14.50	8.75
RE14	RE1	40c **green**	3.50	.90

RE1a

		Without Gum		*Imperf.*
RE15	RE1a	$2 **green**	7.75	.25
a.		Double impression	125.00	

1914		Wmk. 191R		*Perf. 10*
RE16	RE1	¼c **green**	6.25	5.25
RE17	RE1	½c **green**	4.75	3.25
RE18	RE1	1c **green**	.30	.20
RE19	RE1	1½c **green**	60.00	37.50
RE20	RE1	2c **green**	.25	.25
a.		Double impression	—	
RE21	RE1	3c **green**	2.75	2.10
RE22	RE1	4c **green**	.90	1.10
RE23	RE1	5c **green**	15.00	11.50
a.		Double impression	—	
RE24	RE1	6c **green**	.65	.30
RE25	RE1	8c **green**	2.10	.50
RE26	RE1	10c **green**	.70	.20
RE27	RE1	20c **green**	.80	.40

Column 2 (middle lower)

RE28	RE1	24c **green**	14.50	.80
RE29	RE1	40c **green**	32.50	11.50

Imperf
Without Gum

RE30	RE1a	$2 **green**	40.00	3.25

Perf. 11

RE31	RE1	2c **green**	82.50	92.50

WINE STAMPS
Issued Without Gum

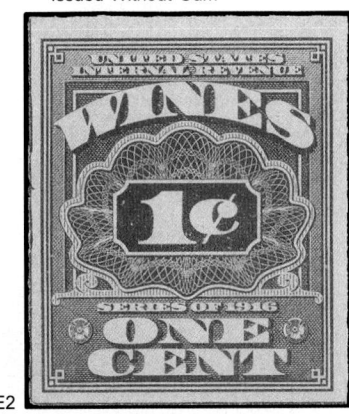

RE2

Inscribed: "Series of 1916"

1916	Wmk. 191R	Offset Printing	*Rouletted 3½*

Plates of 100 subjects

RE32	RE2	1c **green**	.40	.35
a.		Double impression	200.00	
RE33	RE2	3c **green**	5.50	4.25
RE34	RE2	4c **green**	.30	.35
a.		Double impression	—	
RE35	RE2	6c **green**	2.10	.80
RE36	RE2	7½c **green**	7.75	4.25
RE37	RE2	10c **green**	1.25	.40
RE38	RE2	12c **green**	3.00	4.25
RE39	RE2	15c **green**	1.75	1.90
RE40	RE2	18c **green**	24.00	24.00
RE41	RE2	20c **green**	.30	.25
RE42	RE2	24c **green**	5.25	3.75
a.		Double impression	150.00	
RE43	RE2	30c **green**	3.25	3.00
a.		Double impression	—	
RE44	RE2	36c **green**	21.00	16.00
RE45	RE2	50c **green**	.80	.40
RE46	RE2	60c **green**	4.25	2.10
RE47	RE2	72c **green**	35.00	29.00
RE48	RE2	80c **green**	1.40	.60
RE49	RE2	$1.20 **green**	7.00	6.25
RE50	RE2	$1.44 **green**	9.25	3.25
RE51	RE2	$1.60 **green**	25.00	22.50
RE52	RE2	$2 **green**	1.75	1.60

For rouletted 7 see Nos. RE60-RE80, RE102-RE105.

Column 3 (right lower)

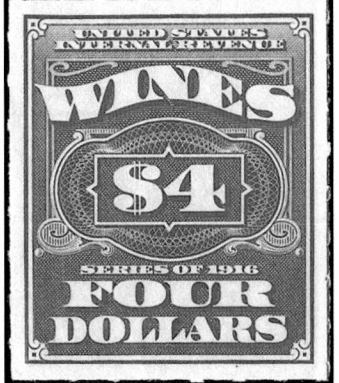

RE3

Engr.
Plates of 50 subjects

RE53	RE3	$4 **green**	1.00	.25
RE54	RE3	$4.80 **green**	3.50	3.25
RE55	RE3	$9.60 **green**	1.40	.35

Nos. RE32-RE55 exist in many shades. Size variations of 1c-$2 are believed due to offset printing. For rouletted 7 see Nos. RE81-RE83, RE106-RE107.

RE4

Illustration reduced.

Plates of 6 subjects
Perf. 12 at left

RE56	RE4	$20 **green**	90.00	42.50
RE57	RE4	$40 **green**	175.00	52.50
RE58	RE4	$50 **green**	62.50	47.50
RE59	RE4	$100 **green**	250.00	140.00

Stamps of design RE4 have an adjoining tablet at right for affixing additional stamps. Values are for examples with the tablets attached. Examples with the tablets removed sell for much less. Used stamps with additional stamps tied on the tablet with cancels sell for about double the values given. See Nos. RE107A-RE107D.

Same designs as Issue of 1916

		1933	Wmk. 191R	Offset Printing	Rouletted 7		
RE60	RE2	1c light green				3.25	.45
a.		Double impression				7.50	2.50
RE61	RE2	3c light green				7.50	2.50
RE62	RE2	4c light green				2.00	.45
RE63	RE2	6c light green				11.00	5.50
RE64	RE2	7½c light green				5.25	1.10
RE65	RE2	10c light green				2.10	.20
a.		Double impression				—	—
RE66	RE2	12c light green				9.00	5.75
RE67	RE2	15c light green				4.25	.30
RE69	RE2	20c light green				5.25	.25
a.		Double impression				—	—
RE70	RE2	24c light green				5.25	.20
a.		Double impression				—	160.00
RE71	RE2	30c light green				5.25	.20
a.		Double impression				—	—
RE72	RE2	36c light green				11.50	.65
RE73	RE2	50c light green				4.50	.25
RE74	RE2	60c light green				8.75	.20
RE75	RE2	72c light green				13.00	.35
RE76	RE2	80c light green				13.00	.35
RE77	RE2	$1.20 light green				10.50	1.50
RE78	RE2	$1.44 light green				13.00	4.25
RE79	RE2	$1.60 light green				350.00	190.00
RE80	RE2	$2 light green				35.00	4.00

Engr.

RE81	RE3	$4 light green	35.00	7.25
RE82	RE3	$4.80 light green	35.00	17.00
RE83	RE3	$9.60 light green	160.00	85.00

RE5

Offset Printing
1934-40   Wmk. 191R   Rouletted 7
Inscribed: "Series of 1934"
Plates of 200 and 224 subjects
Issued With and Without Gum

RE83A	RE5	⅕c green ('40)	.75	.20
RE84	RE5	½c green	.55	.20
RE85	RE5	1c green	.70	.20
RE86	RE5	1¼c green	1.00	.80
RE87	RE5	1½c green	6.00	6.75
RE88	RE5	2c green	1.75	.80
RE89	RE5	2½c green	1.75	.60
RE90	RE5	3c green	5.00	4.00
RE91	RE5	4c green	2.75	.25
RE92	RE5	5c green	.60	.20
RE93	RE5	6c green	1.75	.50
RE94	RE5	7½c green	2.40	.20
RE95	RE5	10c green	.50	.20
RE96	RE5	12c green	1.60	.25
RE96A	RE5	14⅖c green ('40)	150.00	3.25
RE97	RE5	15c green	.80	.20
RE98	RE5	18c green	1.60	.20
RE99	RE5	20c green	1.25	.20
RE100	RE5	24c green	2.00	.20
RE101	RE5	30c green	1.50	.20

Nos. RE83A-RE101 unused are valued without gum. Examples with gum sell for substantially more.
Nos. RE83A, RE86, RE96A were printed from plates of 200 only and all were issued without gum.

Plates of 100 subjects
Issued Without Gum

RE102	RE2	40c green	3.50	.25
RE102A	RE2	43½c green ('40)	14.50	2.75
RE103	RE2	48c green	14.50	1.90
RE104	RE2	$1 green	21.00	11.00
RE105	RE2	$1.50 green	32.50	15.00
		Perforated initials		5.75

Engr.
Plates of 50 subjects.

RE106	RE3	$2.50 green	42.50	18.00
		Perforated initials		9.00
RE107	RE3	$5 green	32.50	7.50
		Perforated initials		2.50

Stamps of types RE5 and RE2 overprinted "Rectified Spirits / Puerto Rico" are listed under Puerto Rico.

Nos. RE102-RE204 issued without gum.

Inscribed: "Series of 1916"
Plates of 6 subjects

		1934		Perf. 12 at left
RE107A	RE4	$20 yellow green		1,800.
RE107B	RE4	$40 yellow green		3,250.

RE107C	RE4	$50 yellow green	—	2,000.
RE107D	RE4	$100 yellow green	1,050.	375.00

The serial numbers of Nos. RE107A-RE107D are much thinner than on Nos. RE56-RE59. See valuing note after No. RE59.

RE6

Offset Printing
Inscribed "Series of 1941"

		1942	Wmk. 191R	Rouletted 7		
RE108	RE6	⅕c green & black			.80	.55
RE109	RE6	¼c green & black			2.50	2.50
RE110	RE6	½c green & black			3.25	2.10
a.		Horiz. pair, imperf. vertically			200.00	
RE111	RE6	1c green & black			1.25	1.25
RE112	RE6	2c green & black			6.00	5.25
RE113	RE6	3c green & black			6.00	4.50
RE114	RE6	3½c green & black			—	12,750.
RE115	RE6	3¾c green & black			11.50	7.25
RE116	RE6	4c green & black			4.25	3.25
RE117	RE6	5c green & black			3.00	2.40
RE118	RE6	6c green & black			3.75	2.75
RE119	RE6	7c green & black			7.50	5.50
RE120	RE6	7½c green & black			11.00	6.00
RE121	RE6	8c green & black			5.50	4.25
RE122	RE6	9c green & black			15.00	9.50
RE123	RE6	10c green & black			5.50	1.10
RE124	RE6	11¼c green & black			6.00	6.00
RE125	RE6	12c green & black			8.50	6.00
RE126	RE6	14c green & black			37.50	26.00
RE127	RE6	15c green & black			6.00	3.00
a.		Horiz. pair, imperf. vertically			925.00	
RE128	RE6	16c green & black			14.00	9.00
RE129	RE6	19½c green & black			175.00	7.75
RE130	RE6	20c green & black			7.50	2.10
RE131	RE6	24c green & black			5.50	.25
RE132	RE6	28c green & black			2,100.	1,500.
RE133	RE6	30c green & black			1.50	.20
RE134	RE6	32c green & black			175.00	7.50
RE135	RE6	36c green & black			3.50	.25
RE136	RE6	40c green & black			3.00	.20
RE137	RE6	45c green & black			8.75	.25
RE138	RE6	48c green & black			21.00	9.25
RE139	RE6	50c green & black			12.00	7.50
RE140	RE6	60c green & black			4.25	.20
RE141	RE6	72c green & black			12.50	1.50
RE142	RE6	80c green & black			300.00	10.50
RE143	RE6	84c green & black			—	77.50
RE144	RE6	90c green & black			25.00	.20
RE145	RE6	96c green & black			15.00	.30

See Nos. RE182D-RE194.

Denomination Spelled Out in Two Lines — RE7

Engraved, Offset (denominations)

		1942			
RE146	RE7	$1.20 yel grn & blk		7.50	.25
RE147	RE7	$1.44 yel grn & blk		1.75	.30
a.		Denomination missing (FO)		—	—
		Pair, one with denomination missing (FO)		—	—
RE148	RE7	$1.50 yel grn & blk		130.00	67.50
RE149	RE7	$1.60 yel grn & blk		10.00	1.40
RE150	RE7	$1.68 yel grn & blk		120.00	50.00
		Perforated initials			35.00
RE151	RE7	$1.80 yel grn & blk		4.00	.20
a.		Pair, one with denomination missing (FO)			

No. RE151a may be collected as a vertical pair or a horizontal pair.

RE152	RE7	$1.92 yel grn & blk		72.50	72.50
RE153	RE7	$2.40 yel grn & blk		12.50	1.25
RE154	RE7	$3 yel grn & blk		87.50	42.50

RE155	RE7	$3.36 yel grn & blk		92.50	29
RE156	RE7	$3.60 yel grn & blk		160.00	6
RE157	RE7	$4 yel grn & blk		32.50	5
RE158	RE7	$4.80 yel grn & blk		160.00	3
RE159	RE7	$5 yel grn & blk		17.50	10
RE159A	RE7	$7.14 yel grn & blk		150.00	
RE160	RE7	$7.20 yel grn & blk		20.00	
RE161	RE7	$10 yel grn & blk		240.00	200
RE162	RE7	$20 yel grn & blk		130.00	77
RE163	RE7	$50 yel grn & blk		125.00	77
		Perforated initials			21
RE164	RE7	$100 yel grn & blk		325.00	30
		Perforated initials			21
RE165	RE7	$200 yel grn & blk		190.00	24
		Perforated initials			8.
RE165A	RE7	$300 yel grn & blk		150.00	
RE165B	RE7	$400 yel grn & blk		8,000.	12,0
RE166	RE7	$500 yel grn & blk		175.00	150.
		Perforated initials			35.
RE167	RC7	$600 yel grn & blk		175.00	125
RE167A	RE7	$700 yel grn & blk		160.00	
RE167B	RE7	$800 yel grn & blk		150.00	
RE168	RE7	$900 yel grn & blk		3,250.	4,0
		Perforated initials			1,5
RE169	RE7	$1,000 yel grn & blk		150.00	200.
RE170	RE7	$2,000 yel grn & blk		4,000.	2,2
RE171	RE7	$3,000 yel grn & blk		175.00	200.
RE172	RE7	$4,000 yel grn & blk		1,250.	800.

Denomination Repeated, Spelled Out in One Line
1949

RE173	RE7	$1 yellow green & black		4.25	1.
RE174	RE7	$2 yellow green & black		7.25	2.
RE175	RE7	$4 yellow green & black		925.00	425.
		Perforated initials			175.
RE176	RE7	$5 yellow green & black		150.00	82.5
RE177	RE7	$6 yellow green & black		700.00	500.
RE178	RE7	$7 yellow green & black			47.
RE179	RE7	$8 yellow green & black		1,250.	450.
		Perforated initials			85.
RE179A	RE7	$9 yel grn & blk		150.00	
RE180	RE7	$10 yellow green & black		10.00	5.2
		Perforated initials			2.1
RE180A	RE7	$12 yel grn & blk		150.00	
RE181	RE7	$20 yel grn & blk		25.00	5.2
		Perforated initials			1.9
RE182	RE7	$30 yellow green & black		1,500.	750.0
RE182A	RE7	$40 yel grn & blk		150.00	
RE182B	RE7	$60 yel grn & blk		150.00	
RE182C	RE7	$70 yel grn & blk		150.00	
RE182D	RE7	$80 yel grn & blk		150.00	
RE182E	RE7	$90 yel grn & blk		150.00	

The $90 denomination, No. RE182E, was printed but was no delivered to the Internal Revenue Service for use.

Types of 1942-49

		1951-54		Offset Printin	
RE182F	RE6	1⁷⁄₁₀c green & black		22,500.	25,000
RE183	RE6	3⅖c green & black		55.00	52.5
RE183A	RE6	6⁷⁄₁₀c green & black		—	
RE184	RE6	8½c green & black		30.00	20.0
RE184A	RE6	10⅕c green & black		—	
RE185	RE6	13⅖c green & black		100.00	82.5
RE186	RE6	17c green & black		16.00	15.0
RE187	RE6	20⅖c green & black		110.00	62.5
RE188	RE6	33⅓c green & black		90.00	92.5
RE189	RE6	38¼c green & black		125.00	90.0
RE190	RE6	40⅘c green & black		3.75	.8
RE191	RE6	51c green & black		4.00	1.4
RE192	RE6	67c green & black		12.50	4.2
RE193	RE6	68c green & black		3.75	.7
RE194	RE6	80⅘c green & black		140.00	110.0

The 6⁷⁄₁₀c and 10⅕c denominations, Nos. RE183A and RE184A, were printed but were not delivered to the Interna Revenue Service for use.

Engr.
Denomination Spelled Out in Two Lines in Small Letters

Two types of $1.60⅘:
I — The "4" slants sharply. Loop of "5" almost closes to form oval. Each numeral 2mm high.
II — The "4" is less slanted. Loop of "5" more open and nearly circular. Each numeral 2½mm high.

RE195	RE7	$1.50¾ yel grn & blk		50.00	47.50
RE196	RE7	$1.60⅘ yel grn & blk (I)		4.25	1.00
a.		"DOLLLAR"		52.50	15.00
		Perforated initials			10.00
b.		As "a," horiz. pair, one with denomination missing		2,600.	
c.		Type II		750.00	250.00
RE197	RE7	$1.88⁹⁄₁₀ yel grn & blk		300.00	85.00
		Perforated initials			35.00

Denomination Spelled Out in Two Lines in Slightly Larger Letters Same as Nos. RE146-RE172

RE198	RE7	$1.60⅘ yel grn & blk		32.50	6.25
a.		First line larger letters, second line small letters		—	3,000.
b.		Type I ('53)		75.00	25.00
RE199	RE7	$2.01 yel grn & blk		3.50	1.00
RE200	RE7	$2.68 yel grn & blk		3.50	1.40
RE201	RE7	$4.08 yel grn & blk		95.00	35.00
RE202	RE7	$5.76 yel grn & blk		275.00	115.00
RE203	RE7	$8.16 yel grn & blk		17.50	7.00
RE204	RE7	$9.60 yel grn & blk		1,750.	5,000.

Wine stamps were discontinued on Dec. 31, 1954.

BEER STAMPS

Basic stamps were printed by the Bureau of Engraving and Printing, unless otherwise noted.
All stamps are imperforate, unless otherwise noted.
Values for Nos. REA1-REA13 are for stamps with small faults, due to the fragile nature of the thin paper. Values for Nos. REA14-REA199 are for canceled stamps with small faults.
All copies of Nos. REA1-REA13 contain a circular pattern of 31 perforations in the design, 27 or 28½mm in diameter, often poorly punched.
Values for cut squares of Nos. REA1-REA13 are for margins clear of the design. Die cut and cut to shape stamps are valued for margins clear to slightly cutting into the design.
Eric Jackson, Michael Aldrich, Henry Tolman II and Thomas W. Priester helped the editors extensively in compiling the listings.
An excellent study of beer stamps by Frank Applegate appeared in *Weekly Philatelic Gossip* from Oct. 1-Nov. 26, 1927.
A List of the Beer Stamps of the United States of America by Ernest R. Vanderhoof appeared in the *American Philatelist* in June 1934. This was printed in pamphlet form.
United States Beer Stamps by Thomas W. Priester, published in 1979, comprised an illustrated and priced catalogue, illustrations of all known provisional surcharges, background notes on the stamps and tax laws, and a census of over 27,500 stamps. The catalogue and census portions were updated in the 1990 edition.

Printed by the Treasury Department. Tax rate $1 per barrel (bbl.).

½c = ⅛ barrel	$1 = 1 barrel
⅝c = ⅛ barrel	$2 = 1 hogshead
25c = ¼ barrel	$5 = 5 barrels
33⅓c = ⅓ barrel	$10 = 10 barrels
50c = ½ barrel	$25 = 25 barrels

1866   Engr.

REA1	12½c **orange**	400.	600.
	Cut to shape		110.
a.	Die cut	300.	300.
b.	Silk paper		1,500.
REA2	16⅝c **dark green**	150.	225.
	Cut to shape		30.
a.	Die cut		85.
REA3	25c **blue**	75.	135.
	Cut to shape		25.
a.	Die cut		50.
b.	Silk paper		2,000.
	Double transfer		—
REA4	50c **orange brown**	30.	50.
	Printed cancellation, "A.S. 1869"		150.
	Cut to shape		10.
a.	Die cut		75.
REA5	$1 **black**	375.	275.
	Cut to shape		75.
a.	Die cut		225.
REA6	$2 **red**	1,200.	1,500.
	Cut to shape		175.
a.	Die cut		475.

Printed by the Treasury Department. See individual rates before No. REA1.

1867   Engr.

REA7	12½c **orange**	2,400.	1,850.
	Cut to shape		750.
a.	Die cut		1,250.
REA8	16⅝c **dark green**	2,600.	2,100.
	Cut to shape		525.
a.	Die cut		1,500.
REA9	25c **blue**	250.	300.
	Cut to shape		50.
a.	Die cut		250.
REA10	33⅓c **violet brown**		5,500.
	Cut to shape		2,500.
b.	Silk paper		3,500.
c.	33⅓c **ocher red**, cut to shape		3,500.
d.	33⅓c **ocher red**, die cut		14,500.
REA11	50c **orange brown**	75.	125.
	Printed cancellation, "A.S. 1869"		350.
	Cut to shape		35.
a.	Die cut		150.
REA12	$1 **black**		1,300.
	Cut to shape		350.
a.	Die cut		750.
REA13	$2 **red**		1,300.
	Cut to shape		500.
a.	Die cut		1,100.

See individual rates before No. REA1.

Silk Paper

1870   Engr.   Lilac Security Lines

REA14	12½c **brown**		220.
a.	Yellow security lines		1,100.
REA15	16⅝c **yellow orange**		275.
a.	Yellow security lines		1,100.
b.	Gray-green and yellow security lines		1,750.
c.	16⅝c **yellow ocher**, lilac security lines		750.
REA16	25c **green**		45.
a.	Yellow security lines		225.
REA17	50c **red**	300.	110.
a.	Yellow security lines		500.
b.	Gray-green and yellow security lines		1,100.
c.	50c **brick red**, lilac security lines		800.
d.	50c **brick red**, yellow security lines		2,500.
REA18	$1 **blue**		800.
a.	Yellow security lines		250.
b.	Gray-green and yellow security lines		1,500.
REA19	$2 **black**	1,000.	650.
a.	Yellow security lines		2,500.
b.	Gray-green and yellow security lines		3,250.

The security lines were printed across the center of the stamp where the cancel was to be placed.

Andrew Jackson

Designs: 16⅝c, Abraham Lincoln. 25c, Daniel Webster. 33⅓c, David G. Farragut. 50c, William T. Sherman. $1, Hugh McCulloch. $2, Alexander Hamilton.
Centers printed by the Bureau of Engraving and Printing. Frames printed by the National Bank Co.
See individual rates before No. REA1.

1871   Engr.
Centers, Plate Letters and Position Numbers in Black

REA20	12½c **blue**, white silk paper	125.
a.	Pinkish gray silk paper	200.
b.	Gray silk paper	65.
c.	Green silk paper	150.
REA21	16⅝c **vermilion**, white silk paper	300.
a.	Pinkish gray silk paper	325.
b.	Gray silk paper	325.
c.	Green silk paper	325.
REA22	25c **green**, white silk paper	25.
a.	Pinkish gray silk paper	110.
b.	Gray silk paper	25.
c.	Green silk paper	25.
REA23	33⅓c **orange**, green silk paper	5,000.
b.	Gray silk paper	11,000.
REA24	33⅓c **violet brown**, white silk paper	6,250.
REA25	50c **brown**, gray silk paper	20.
a.	Pinkish gray silk paper	60.
c.	Green silk paper	75.
REA26	50c **red**, white silk paper	55.
REA27	$1 **yellow orange**, white silk paper	225.
a.	Pinkish gray silk paper	1,100.
b.	Gray silk paper	150.
REA28	$1 **scarlet**, gray silk paper	150.
a.	Pinkish gray silk paper	750.
c.	Green silk paper	300.
REA29	$2 **red brown**, white silk paper	175.
a.	Pinkish gray silk paper	1,250.
b.	Gray silk paper	250.
c.	Green silk paper	1,000.

Bacchus Serving the First Fermented Brew to Man

Printed by the National Bank Note Co. See individual rates before No. REA1.

1875   Typo. & Engr.
Center in Black

REA30	12½c **blue**	25.00
REA31	16⅔c **red brown**	150.00
REA32	25c **green**	20.00
a.	Inverted center	—
REA33	33⅓c **violet**	1,000.
REA34	50c **orange**	75.00
REA35	$1 **red**	175.00
REA36	$2 **brown**	300.00
a.	Inverted center	—

Designs: 12½c, Washington. 16⅔c, Corwin. 25c, Benton. 33⅓c, Thomas. 50c, Jefferson. $1, Johnson. $2, Wright.
Stamps on pale green paper have short greenish blue fibers. Plate designations for center consist of plate letter or number at left and position number at right.
See individual rates before No. REA1.

1878   Typo. & Engr.   Wmk. USIR
Center, Plate Letters and Position Numbers in Black

REA37	12½c **blue**, *green*	7.50
b.	Green silk paper, unwmkd.	1,250.
c.	Pale green paper	200.00
	With plate number and position number	*1,250.*
d.	Light blue paper, with plate number (and position number)	35.00
e.	Blue paper, no plate letter or number or position number	30.00
f.	Dark blue paper, no plate letter or number or position number	45.00
REA38	16⅔c **light brown**, *green*	7.50
	One line under Cents	75.00
b.	Green silk paper, unwmkd., one line under Cents	125.00
c.	Pale green paper	75.00
	With plate number	500.00
d.	Light blue paper, with plate number (and position number)	40.00
e.	Blue paper, no plate letter or number or position number	150.00
	With plate number 1979	250.00
f.	Dark blue paper, no plate letter or number or position number	75.00
REA39	25c **green**, *green*	5.00
a.	Inverted center	—
b.	Green silk paper, unwmkd.	200.00
c.	Pale green paper	90.00
	With plate number	35.00
d.	Light blue paper, with plate number (and position number)	7.50
e.	Blue paper, no plate letter or number or position number	25.00

f.	Dark blue paper, no plate letter or number or position number	27.50
REA40	33⅓c **violet**, *green*	75.00
b.	Green silk paper, unwmkd.	2,000.
c.	Pale green paper	1,250.
d.	Light blue paper, with plate number (and position number)	110.00
e.	Blue paper, no plate letter or number or position number	120.00
f.	Dark blue paper, no plate letter or number or position number	250.00
REA41	50c **orange**, *green*	11.00
	One line under Cents	100.00
b.	Green silk paper, unwmkd.	210.00
c.	Pale green paper	90.00
	With plate number	350.00
d.	Light blue paper, with plate number (and position number)	30.00
e.	Blue paper, no plate letter or number or position number	17.50
f.	Dark blue paper, no plate letter or position number	20.00
REA42	$1 **red**, *green*	27.50
	One line under Dollar	75.00
c.	Pale green paper	200.00
	One line under Dollar	400.00
d.	Light blue paper, with plate number (and position number)	175.00
e.	Blue paper, no plate letter or number or position number	125.00
	One line under Dollar	200.00
f.	Dark blue paper, no plate letter or number or position number	100.00
REA43	$2 **brown**, *green*	75.00
	One line under Dollar	100.00
b.	Green silk paper, unwmkd.	500.00
	One line under dollar	—
c.	Pale green paper	650.00
	One line under dollar	*1,000.*
e.	Blue paper, no plate letter or number or position number	175.00
f.	Dark blue paper, no plate letter or number or position number	150.00

See Nos. REA58-REA64, REA65-REA71, REA75-REA81.

Stamps of 1878 Surcharged in Various Ways

TAX $2 PER BBL.

SERIES OF 1898

Type A

Four general surcharge types:

A — Bureau of Engraving and Printing surcharge "TAX $2 PER BBL./SERIES OF 1898" printed diagonally in red, letters 4¼mm high.

B — same, but letters 5½mm high.

C — handstamped provisional surcharge with similiar wording in 1-3 lines, more than 30 styles.

D — printed provisional 2-line surcharges, horizontal in various colors.

Tax rate $2 per bbl.

25c = ⅛ barrel		$1 = ½ barrel
33⅓c = ⅙ barrel		$2 = 1 barrel
50c = ¼ barrel		$4 = 1 hogshead
66⅔c = ⅓ barrel		

1898   Type A

REA44	(25c) on 12½c #REA37f	350.00
a.	Type C surcharge	250.00
b.	Type D surcharge	750.00
REA45	(33⅓c) on 16⅔c #REA38e	75.00
a.	on #REA38f	175.00
b.	As "a," type C surcharge	250.00
c.	As "a," type D surcharge	400.00
d.	on #REA38d	750.00
REA46	(50c) on 25c #REA39f	90.00
a.	Type C surcharge	150.00
b.	Type D surcharge	750.00
c.	on #REA39e	175.00
d.	on #REA39, type C surcharge	4,000.
REA47	(66⅔c) on 33⅓c #REA40	500.00
REA48	($1) on 50c #REA41f	35.00
a.	Type C surcharge	150.00
b.	Type D surcharge	450.00
REA49	($2) on $1 #REA42f	125.00
a.	Type C surcharge	175.00
b.	Type D surcharge	750.00
c.	on #REA42e, type C surcharge	1,250.
REA50	($4) on $2 #REA43f	500.00
a.	Type C surcharge	500.00
b.	Type D surcharge	2,000.

c.	on #REA43e, type C surcharge	2,
	Type B	
REA51	(25c) on 12½c #REA37f	9
a.	on #REA37e	10
b.	As "a," type C surcharge	2,
REA52	(33⅓c) on 16⅔c #REA38d	50
a.	on #REA38f	50
b.	on #REA38e	70
REA53	(50c) on 25c #REA39f	2
a.	on #REA39e	2
REA54	(66⅔c) on 33⅓c #REA40f	2,
a.	Type D surcharge	7,
b.	On #REA40	3,
REA55	($1) on 50c #REA41f	1
REA56	($2) on $1 #REA42f	5
REA57	($4) on $2 #REA43f	27

Counterfeit type C and D overprints exist.

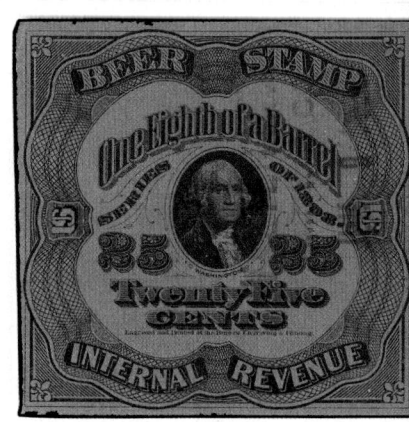

Designs: 25c, Washington. 33⅓c, Corwin. 50c, Benton. 66⅔c, Thomas. $1, Jefferson. $2, Johnson. $4, Wright.
See individual rates before No. REA44.

1898   Typo. & Engr.   Wmk. USI
Center in Black, Dark Blue Paper

REA58	25c blue	9
REA59	33⅓c brown	
REA60	50c green	
REA61	66⅔c violet	10,5(
REA62	$1 yellow	
REA63	$2 red	
REA64	$4 dark brown	22

> **Used values for 1901-51 issues are for stamps canceled by perforated company name (or abbreviation) and date.**

Designs: 20c, Washington. 26⅔c, Corwin. 40c, Benton. 53⅓c, Thomas. 80c, Jefferson. $1.60, Johnson. $3.20, Wright.
Tax rate $1.60 per bbl.

20c = ⅛ barrel		80c = ½ barrel
26⅔c = ⅙ barrel		$1.60 = 1 barrel
40c = ¼ barrel		$3.20 = 1 hogshead
53⅓c = ⅓ barrel		

Engr. (center) & Typo. (frame)
1901   Wmk. USIR
Dark Blue Paper

REA65	20c blue	75
REA66	26⅔c yellow orange	75
REA67	40c green	17.50
REA68	53⅓c violet	7,000.
REA69	80c brown	17.50
REA70	$1.60 red	75
REA71	$3.20 dark brown	275.

amps of 1901 Provisionally Surcharged by Bureau
of Engraving & Printing diagonally in red "TAX $1
PER BBL./SERIES OF 1902."

02		
A72	(16⅔c) on 26⅔c #REA66	125.
A73	(33⅓c) on 53⅓c #REA68	*4,500.*
A74	($2) on $3.20 #REA71	600.

Designs: 12½c, Washington. 16⅔c, Corwin. 25c, Benton.
⅓c, Thomas. 50c, Jefferson. $1, Johnson. $2, Wright.
Stamps on pale green paper have short greenish blue fibers.
See individual rates before No. REA1.

	02 Typo. & Engr.	**Wmk. USIR**
	Center in Black	
EA75	12½c **blue**	
a.	Dark blue paper	75.00
b.	Pale green paper	350.00
c.	Light blue paper	110.00
d.	Bright blue paper	50.00
EA76	16⅔c **yellow orange**	
a.	Dark blue paper	225.00
b.	Pale green paper	350.00
c.	Light blue paper	200.00
d.	Bright blue paper	400.00
EA77	25c **green**	
a.	Dark blue paper	25.00
b.	Pale green paper	80.00
c.	Light blue paper	25.00
d.	Bright blue paper	30.00
EA78	33⅓c **violet**	
a.	Dark blue paper	200.00
c.	Light blue paper	450.00
d.	Bright blue paper	450.00
EA79	50c **brown**	
a.	Dark blue paper	20.00
b.	Pale green paper	30.00
c.	Light blue paper	25.00
d.	Bright blue paper	20.00
EA80	$1 **red**	
a.	Dark blue paper	110.00
b.	Pale green paper	300.00
c.	Light blue paper	75.00
d.	Bright blue paper	75.00
EA81	$2 **dark brown**	
a.	Dark blue paper	750.00
b.	Pale green paper	900.00
c.	Light blue paper	500.00
d.	Bright blue paper	500.00

For surcharges see Nos. REA99a, REA100a, REA100b,
EA141.

**In the 1911-33 issues, the 5-25 barrel sizes
were generally available only as center cutouts
of the stamp. Values for these are for cutout
portions that show enough of the denomination
(or surcharge) to identify the item.**

See individual rates before No. REA1.

1909-11	**Engr.**		**Wmk. USIR**
	Paper of Various Shades of Blue		
REA82	12½c **black**		500.00
REA83	16⅔c **black**	150.00	90.00
REA84	25c **black**		375.00
REA85	33⅓c **black**		*20,000.*
REA86	50c **black**		6.00
REA87	$1 **black**		750.00
REA88	$2 **black**		*4,500.*
	Center Cutout Only		
REA89	$5 **black,** 1911		*150.00*
REA90	$10 **black,** 1911		*125.00*
REA91	$25 **black,** 1911		*100.00*

For surcharges see Nos. REA97, REA99-REA100, REA103-
REA105, REA128.

1910	**Engr.**	**Wmk. USIR**
	Paper of Various Shades of Blue	
REA92	12½c **red brown**	75.00
REA93	25c **green**	10.00
REA94	$1 **carmine**	75.00
REA95	$2 **orange**	125.00

For surcharges see Nos. REA96, REA98, REA101-REA102,
REA126.

1914 Provisional Issue

Stamps of of 1902-11 with printed provisional BEP diagonal
surcharge "EMERGENCY/TAX/UNDER ACT OF 1914" in red,
black or yellow, or handstamped surcharge of value spelled out
in full and separate "Roscoe Irwin" handstamped facsimile
signature.
Tax rate $1.50 per bbl.

18¾c = ⅛ barrel		$1.50 = 1 barrel
25c = ⅙ barrel		$3 = 1 hogshead
37½c = ¼ barrel		$7.5 = 5 barrels
50c = ⅓ barrel		$15 = 10 barrels
75c = ½ barrel		$37.50 = 25 barrels

1914		**Entire Stamps**
REA96	(18¾c) on 12½ #REA92	65.00
REA97	(25c) on 16⅔c #REA83	60.00
REA98	(37½c) on 25c #REA93	7.50
a.	37½c handstamped; 50mm signature	350.00
REA99	(50c) on 33⅓c #REA85	225.00
a.	(50c) on 33⅓c #REA78d	750.00
REA100	(75c) on 50c #REA86	7.50
a.	(75c) On 50c #REA79c	1,000.
b.	(75c) On 50c #REA79b	*5,500.*
c.	75c handstamped on #REA86; 50mm signature	175.00
d.	As "c", 65mm signature	325.00
REA101	($1.50) on $1 #REA94	50.00
a.	$1.50 handstamped; 50mm signature	350.00
b.	As "a", 65mm signature	*2,250.*
REA102	($3.00) on $2 #REA95	75.00
a.	$3 handstamped; 76mm signature	*2,750.*
	Center Cutout Only	
REA103	($7.50) on $5 #REA89	17.50
REA104	($15) on $10 #REA90	150.00
REA105	($37.50) on $25 #REA91	225.00

For surcharges see Nos. REA119, REA123, REA133,
REA140, REA140a.

See individual rates before No. REA96.

1914	**Engr.**		**Wmk. USIR**
	Paper of Various Shades of Blue		
	Entire Stamp		
REA106	18¾c **red brown**		85.00
REA107	25c **black**		175.00
a.	25c **violet blue**		*2,000.*
REA108	37½c **green**		17.50
a.	37½c **black**		*32,500.*
REA108B	50c **black**		—
REA109	75c **black**		6.00
REA110	$1.50 **red orange**		30.00
REA111	$3 **orange**		200.00
	Center Cutout Only		
REA112	$7.50 **black**		10.00
REA113	$15 **black**		15.00
REA114	$37.50 **black**		7.50

For surcharges see Nos. REA118, REA120, REA120a,
REA121, REA124-REA125, REA127, REA129-REA131,
REA134, REA134a, REA137, REA144, REA146-REA149.

See individual rates before No. REA96.

1916	**Engr.**	**Wmk. USIR**
	Paper of Various Shades of Greenish Blue	
	Entire Stamp	
REA115	37½c **green**	110.00
REA116	75c **black**	40.00

For surcharges see Nos. REA122, REA124, REA138.
Surcharge also exists in manuscript on No. REA115.

Stamps of 1914-16 Provisionally Surcharged Types
A, B & C

ACT OF
1917

Type C

Surcharge types:
A — "ACT OF 1917" handstamped in 1-3 lines in more than
30 styles.
B — "ACT OF 1917" locally printed horizontally in black or
red.
C — "ACT OF 1917" printed in black or red by BEP, horizon-
tally on ⅛ bbl-1 hhd and reading down on 5-25 bbl.
Surcharge also exists in manuscript on some values. Tax rate
$3 per bbl.

37½c = ⅛ barrel		$3 = 1 barrel
50c = ⅙ barrel		$6 = 1 hogshead

75c	= ¼ barrel	$15 = 5 barrels	
$1	= ⅓ barrel	$30 = 10 barrels	
$1.50	= ½ barrel	$75 = 25 barrels	

1917   Type A Surcharge
Entire Stamp

REA117	(37½c) on #REA96		—
REA118	(37½c) on #REA106		200.
b.	Type B surcharge		
c.	Type C surcharge		500.00
REA119	(50c) on #REA97		150.
REA120	(50c) on #REA107a		300.
a.	On #107		500.00
REA121	(75c) on #REA108		110.
REA122	(75c) on #REA115		50.
b.	Type B surcharge		1,750.
c.	Type C surcharge		90.
REA123	($1) on #REA99		175.
REA124	($1.50) on #REA110		40.
b.	Type B surcharge		1,750.
c.	Type C surcharge		7.50
d.	As "c," inverted surcharge	1,000.	

$1.50 surcharge exists in manuscript on #REA109.

REA125	($3) on #REA110		100.
c.	Type C surcharge		40.
REA126	($6) on #REA102		2,000.
REA127	($6) on #REA111		500.

Center Cutout Only

REA128	($15) on #REA103		500.
REA129	($15) on #REA112, entire stamp, type C surcharge		3,000.
REA130	($30) on #REA113		100.
c.	Type C surcharge		45.
REA131	($75) on #REA114		225.
c.	Type C surcharge		12.50

For surcharges see Nos. REA132, REA132a, REA135-REA136, REA139-REA139b, REA142-REA143, REA145, REA150-REA151.

Stamps of 1914-17 provisionally surcharged "ACT OF 1918" or "Revenue Act of 1918" with rubber stamp in various colors in more than 20 styles.

A subtype has the incorrect date of 1919 due to the effective date of the act (at least five styles).
Tax rate $6 per bbl.

75c	= ⅛ barrel	$6 = 1 barrel	
$1	= ⅙ barrel	$12 = 1 hogshead	
$1.50	= ¼ barrel	$30 = 5 barrels	
$2	= ⅓ barrel	$60 = 10 barrels	
$3	= ½ barrel	$150 = 25 barrels	

1918   Entire Stamp

REA132	(75c) on #REA118		500.
a.	On #REA118c		750.
REA133	($1) on #REA97		900.
REA134	($1) on #REA107		2,000.
a.	On #REA107a		2,750.

Exists with additional overprint "Non-Intoxicating, containing not to/exceed 2¾% of Alcohol by weight." Value, *$1,750.*

REA135	($1) on #REA119		2,500.
REA136	($1) on #REA120		2,500.
REA137	($1.50) on #REA108		600.
a.	Surcharge dated "1919"		1,500.
REA138	($1.50) on #REA115		1,250.
REA139	($1.50) on #REA122c		75.
a.	Surcharge dated "1919"		60.
b.	On #REA122		350.
REA140	($2) on #REA99		800.
a.	On #REA99a		1,100.
REA141	($2) on #REA99a		2,500.

No. REA141 bears additional 1917 provisional surcharge, as well as the 1914 surcharge, but was not issued in that form without 1918 surcharge.

REA142	($2) on #REA123		3,000.
REA143	($3) on #REA124c		75.
a.	Surcharge dated "1919"		600.
REA144	($6) on #REA110		500.
REA145	($6) on #REA125c		50.
a.	Surcharge dated "1919"		500.
REA146	($12) on #REA111		500.
REA147	($12) on #REA111		75.

No. REA147 bears additional 1917 Type C provisional surcharge but was not issued in that form without 1918 surcharge.

Center Cutout Only

REA148	($30) on #REA112		75.
REA149	($60) on #REA113		75.
REA150	($60) on #REA130c		300.
a.	Entire stamp		3,500.
REA151	($150) on #REA131c		35.
a.	Entire stamp		4,000.

REA152-REA158

REA159-REA161

Tax rate $5 per barrel through Jan. 11, 1934. $6 rate also effective Dec. 5, 1933. Provisional handstamp "Surcharged $6.00 Rate" in 1-3 lines (seven styles).

1933   Engr.   Wmk. USIR
Paper of Various Shades of Greenish Blue to Blue
Type A
Entire Stamp

REA152	⅛ bbl., **violet red**		17.50
a.	Provisional surcharge, $6 rate		1,500.
REA153	⅙ bbl., **purple**		450.00
REA154	¼ bbl., **green**		6.00
REA155	⅓ bbl., **brown orange**		1,000.
REA156	½ bbl., **orange**		4.00
a.	Provisional surcharge, $6 rate		750.00
REA157	1 bbl., **blue**		25.00
a.	Provisional surcharge, $6 rate		3,000.
REA158	1 hhd., **black**		5,000.
REA159	5 bbl., **black**, center cutout only		250.00
REA160	10 bbl., **black**, with cut-out center, rouletted 7 at left		7,500.
a.	Center cutout only		250.00
REA161	25 bbl., **black**, with cut-out center, rouletted 7 at left		7,500.
a.	Center cutout only		250.00

Center cutout portions of Nos. REA159-REA161 are on greenish blue paper. See Nos. REA177-REA178A for copies on bright blue paper.

Nos. REA152-REA159, REA161 Surcharged in Black

Type B

A — additional provisional handstamped surcharge.
B — additional manuscript and handstamped surcharges.
Tax rate same as Nos. REA152-REA161.

1933   Engr.   Wmk. US
Entire Stamp

REA162	⅛ bbl., **violet red**		8
REA163	⅙ bbl., **purple**		175
REA164	¼ bbl., **green**		15
a.	With 1918 provisional handstamped surcharge, $6 rate		2,2
b.	Type A surcharge, $6 rate		2,7
REA165	⅓ bbl., **brown orange**		6,0
REA166	½ bbl., **orange**		15.
a.	Type A surcharge, $6 rate		3,0
b.	Type B surcharge, $6 rate		1,5
REA167	1 bbl., **blue**		25.
REA168	1 hhd., **black**		9,0
REA169	5 bbl., **black**, center cutout only		500.
REA170	25 bbl., **black**, center cutout only		450.

REA171-REA176

REA177-REA178A

Tax rate same as previous issue. Provisional handstamp reads "SOLD AT $5.00 RATE" or "$5.00 RATE."

1933   Engr.   Wmk. USIR
Entire Stamp

REA171	⅛ bbl., **violet red**		35.00
REA172	⅙ bbl., **purple**		500.00
REA173	¼ bbl., **green**		6.00
a.	Provisional surcharge, $5 rate		3,000.
REA174	½ bbl., **brown orange**		5.00
a.	Provisional surcharge, $5 rate		800.00
REA175	1 bbl., **blue**		100.00
REA176	1 hhd., **black**		5,000.

Bright Blue Paper

REA177	5 bbl., **black**		1,000.
a.	Entire stamp with cut-out center		7.50
b.	Center cutout only		1.00
REA178	10 bbl., **black**	650.00	500.00
a.	Entire stamp with cut-out center		10.00
b.	Center cutout only		1.00
REA178A	25 bbl., **black**		500.00
b.	Entire stamp with cut-out center		4.50
c.	Center cutout only		1.00
d.	Rouletted 7 at left		

For surcharge see No. REA199.

Nos. REA173-REA174 with BEP Printed Surcharge, "Act of March 22, 1933"

Additional provisional handstamped surcharge, $6 rate as previous issue.

1933

Entire Stamp

REA179	¼ bbl., **green**		27.50
a.	Handstamped "Surcharged $6 rate"		750.00
REA180	½ bbl., **brown orange**		12.50
a.	Handstamped "Surcharged $6 rate"		1,250.

REA181-REA187

REA188-REA189

Tax rates $5 per bbl; $6 from July 1, 1940; $7 from Nov. 1, 42; $8 from Apr. 1, 1944.

34-45	Engr.	Wmk. USIR	
With Black Control Numbers			
A181	⅛ bbl., **violet red**		7.50
a.	With cutout center		2.00
b.	Ovptd. "NOT LESS THAN 3⅝ GAL- LONS," uncut		—
A182	⅛ bbl., **purple**		150.00
a.	With cutout center		100.00
b.	Ovptd. "NOT LESS THAN 4⅝ GAL- LONS," uncut		—
A183	¼ bbl., **green**		4.00
a.	With cutout center		2.50
b.	Ovptd. "NOT LESS THAN 7¼ GAL- LONS," uncut		—

REA184	⅓ bbl., **brown orange**		20,000.
REA185	½ bbl., **orange**		3.00
a.	With cutout center		2.00
REA186	1 bbl., **blue**		7.50
a.	With cutout center		7.50
REA187	1 hhd., **black**		500.00
REA188	100 bbl., **carmine**, *1942*		200.00
a.	With cutout center		10.00
REA189	500 bbl., **dark brown**, with cutout center, *1945*		500.00

Most values also exist as center cutout portions only.

REA190-REA193

REA194-REA198

Tax rates $8 per bbl, $9 from Nov. 1, 1951.

1947			Litho.
Black Control Numbers			
REA190	⅛ bbl., **carmine**	125.00	60.00
a.	With cutout center		15.00
REA190B	⅛ bbl., **purple**	160.00	
REA191	¼ bbl., **green**	75.00	20.00
a.	With cutout center		22.50
REA192	½ bbl., **orange**	30.00	10.00
a.	With cutout center		12.50
REA193	1 bbl., **blue**	100.00	150.00
a.	With cutout center		15.00
Blue Paper			
REA194	5 bbl., **black**	100.00	200.00
a.	With cutout center		12.50
REA195	10 bbl., **black**	200.00	300.00
a.	With cutout center		27.50
REA196	25 bbl., **black**	*1,250.*	*3,200.*
a.	With cutout center		*3,000.*
White Paper			
REA197	100 bbl., **carmine**	150.00	250.00
a.	With cutout center		10.00
REA198	500 bbl., **dark brown**	500.00	600.00
a.	With cutout center		60.00

All values except No. REA190B also exist as center cutouts only.

No. REA190B was not officially issued.

No. REA158 Provisionally Handstamp Surcharged "Value increased under / Revenue Act of 1951" in black or purple.

Tax rate $9 per bbl.

1951			
REA199	($225) on 25 bbl., #REA178A, un- cut		20,000.

Also exists as center cutout only, showing portion of hand-stamped surcharge. Value, $150.

FERMENTED FRUIT JUICE STAMPS

Fermented fruit juice stamps were issued pending the ratification of the Repeal Amendment (Dec. 5, 1933) that made full-strength beer and wine legal again.

Congress, as a temporary measure, redefined intoxicating beverages by changing the legal definition from .5% to 3.2%, thus permitting the sale of 3.2 beer and wine beginning April 7, 1933.

Regular wine stamps were available to pay the Internal Revenue taxes. However, these Fermented Fruit Juice stamps were authorized for placement on individual bottles or containers of fermented fruit juice. Use was discontinued at the end of 1933.

Stamps are valued in the grade of very fine. Most stamps are found in average to fine condition. Unused stamps are valued with original gum.

REF1

Plates of 220 subjects in two panes of 110.

1933		Wmk. USIR	Engr.	Perf. 11
REF1	REF1	4 oz **gray**		85.00
REF3	REF1	8 oz **light green**		70.00
REF4	REF1	12 oz **light blue**	15.00	6.00
REF5	REF1	13 oz **olive green**		55.00
REF6	REF1	16 oz **lavender**		160.00
REF7	REF1	24 oz **orange**		110.00
REF8	REF1	29 oz **brown**		160.00
REF9	REF1	32 oz **red**	90.00	70.00

A dark blue 7-ounce stamp was issued, but the only recorded examples currently are in the National Postal Museum collection.

No. REF4 stamps canceled "H. B. Co." (Hoffman Beverage Company) or "M. D. C." (Mission Dry Corporation) command a premium of 10-100 percent. Specialists collect them by date (H. B. Co. and M. D. C.) and control number (M. D. C.). Earliest known use: May 28, 1933.

Beer Stamp No. REA154 Overprinted "WINE OR FERMENTED FRUIT JUICE" in Red

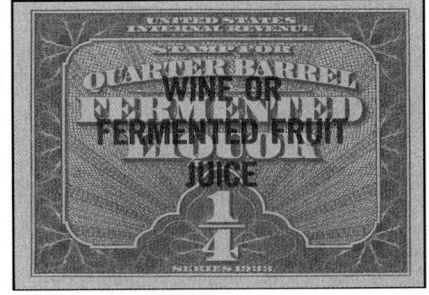

REF10

1933		Engr.	Imperf.
REF10	¼ bbl., **green**, *blue*		

The ½ barrel and 1 barrel stamps Beer Stamps, Nos. REA156-REA157, also were issued with this overprint, but no examples are currently recorded.

PLAYING CARDS

Stamps for use on packs of playing cards were included in the first general issue of 1862-71. They are Nos. R2, R11, R12, R17, R21 and R. The tax on playing cards was repealed effective June 22, 1965.

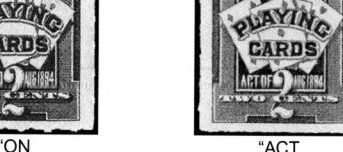

"ON
HAND . . ." — RF1

"ACT
OF . . ." — RF2

1894	Engr.	Unwmk.	Rouletted 5½	
RF1	RF1	2c **lake**	.75	.45
a.	Horizontal pair, imperf. between		450.00	—
b.	Horiz. pair, imperf. vert.			
RF2	RF2	2c **ultramarine**	21.00	2.75
a.	2c **blue**		30.00	3.75
b.	Imperf., pair		500.00	
c.	Imperf. horizontally		160.00	160.00
d.	Rouletted 12½		100.00	100.00
e.	Imperf. horizontally, rouletted 12½ vertically, pair		200.00	200.00

No vertical pairs of No. RF2e are known. Pairs will be horizontal. Singles are valued at 50% of the pair value.

1896-99	Wmk. 191R	Rouletted 5½, 7	
RF3	RF2	2c **blue**	7.75	.65
a.	2c **ultramarine** ('99)	7.50	2.00
b.	Imperf., pair	125.00	

No. RF3 surcharged " VIRGIN / ISLANDS / 4 CTS" are listed under Danish West Indies.

1902		Perf. 12
RF4	RF2	2c **deep blue**	55.00

No. RF4 is known with cancel date "1899" but that is due to the use of an old canceling plate. The stamp was first used in 1902.

ACT OF 1917
7
CENTS
Stamp of 1899 Surcharged in Rose

1917	Wmk. 191R	Rouletted 7	
RF5	RF2	7c on 2c **ultramarine**	750.00	600.00
a.	Inverted surcharge	—	

The surcharge on No. RF5 was handstamped at the Internal Revenue Office in New York City. Different handstamps were used at other Internal Revenue Offices as well, values $250 to $300.

17
Surcharged in Black

1917			
RF6	RF2	(7c) on 2c **blue**	57.50
a.	Inverted surcharge		57.50

The "17" indicated that the 7 cent tax had been paid according to the Act of 1917.
Used by N. Y. Consolidated Card Co.
Cancellations are in red.

7
Surcharged in Black

RF7	RF2	7c on 2c **blue**	950.00
a.	Inverted surcharge		600.00

Used by Standard Playing Card Co.

The surcharges on Nos. RF7-RF10, RF13, RF15, RF18 were applied by the manufacturers, together with their initials, dates, etc., thus forming a combination of surcharge and precancellation. The surcharge on No. RF16 was made by the Bureau of Engraving and Printing. After it appeared the use of some combinations was continued but only as cancellations.

7 CTS.

Surcharged Vertically Reading Up in Red or Violet

RF8	RF2	7c on 2c **blue**	1,350.
a.	Double surcharge	1,900.
b.	Reading down	2,100.

Used by Russell Playing Card Co.

Surcharged Vertically, Reading Up in Black, Violet or Red

RF9	RF2	7c on 2c **blue**	9.75
a.	Double surcharge (violet)	100.00
b.	Numeral omitted (black)	90.00
c.	Surcharge reading down	11.50
d.	As "c," numeral omitted (black)	77.50
e.	As "c," double surcharge (violet)	275.00
f.	Double surcharge, one down (red)	300.00
g.	Surcharge and "A.D." in violet	375.00
h.	Surcharge and "A.D." in red, "U.S.P.C. Co." in black	1,050.
i.	Surcharge and "A.D." in red reading up, "U.S.P.C. Co." in black reading down	775.00
j.	As "g," reading down	—
k.	Double surcharge (black)	1,000.
l.	Double surcharge (red)	400.00
m.	Double surcharge and "A.D.," both reading down (red)	—

"A.D." (Andrew Dougherty Co.) printed in red, "S. P. C. Co." (Standard Playing Card Co.) printed in violet, "U.S.P.C. Co." printed in black. The first two became divisions of United States Playing Card Co.
See No. RF13.

Surcharged in Carmine

RF10	RF2	7c on 2c **blue**	85.00
a.	Inverted surcharge	47.50
b.	Double surcharge	550.00
c.	Double surcharge, inverted	550.00
d.	Triple surcharge	—

Used by Russell Playing Card Co.

RF3

1918	Size: 21x40mm	Imp
RF11	RF3	blue	45.00	3
	Block of 4	190.00	15

Private Roulette 14

RF12	RF3	blue	
a.	Rouletted 13 in red	1,
b.	Rouletted 6½	1,900.
c.	Perf. 12 horiz., imperf. vert.	
d.	Perf. 12 on 4 sides	1,

Nos. RF11-RF12 served as 7c stamps when used be April 1, 1919, and as 8c stamps when used after that date.
No. RF11 is known handstamped "7" or "8," or both "7" "8," as well as "Act of 1918" in black and magenta, either by user to indicate the value when applied to the pack or by IRS district offices at the time of sale.
No. RF12 was used by N. Y. Consolidated Card Co., N RF12a, RF12b were used by Russell Playing Card Co., N RF12, RF12d were used by Logan Printing House.

Surcharged like No. RF9 (but somewhat smalle in Violet, Red or Black
Private Roulette 9½

RF13	RF3	7c **blue**	52
a.	Inverted surcharge	52
b.	Double surcharge	275
c.	Double surcharge, inverted	325

REVENUE A
OF   19
8
CENTS

Stamp of 1899 Surcharged in
Magenta or Rose

1919		Rouletted
RF14	RF2	8c on 2c **ultramarine**	110
a.	Double surcharge	300
b.	Inverted surcharge	325

The surcharge on No. RF14 was handstamped at the Inter Revenue Office in New York City. A handstamp in black known.
Exists in pair, one double surcharge, also in pair, one w inverted surcharge.

Inverted Surcharge in Carmine   8c

RF15	RF2	8c on 2c **blue**	625.
a.	Double surcharge	1,00

No. RF15 is surcharged only with large "8c" inverted, a overprinted with date and initials (also inverted). No. RF16 often found with additional impression of large "8c," as on N RF15, but in this usage the large "8c" is a cancellation.
Used by Russell Playing Card Co.

Surcharged in Carmine or Vermilion   8 Cts

RF16	RF2	8c on 2c **blue**	150.00	.9
a.	Inverted surcharge		

See note after No. RF15.

RF4

1922	Size: 19x22mm	Rouletted
RF17	RF4	(8c) **blue**	22.50	1.5
	Block of 4	110.00	

No. RF17, rouletted 7 and perforated 11, surcharged " VIR GIN / ISLANDS / 4 cts." are listed under Danish West Indies.

Surcharged in Carmine, Blue or Black

18	RF4	8c on (8c) blue	62.50
a.		Inverted surcharge	62.50

Used by Pyramid Playing Card Co.

RF5

Rouletted 7

19	RF5	10c blue	15.00	.45
		Block of 4	80.00	

ROTARY PRESS COIL STAMP

Perf. 10 Vertically

20	RF5	10c blue		.30
		Pair		3.25
		Joint line pair		6.50

No. RF20 exists only precanceled. **Bureau precancels:** 11 erent.

FLAT PLATE PRINTING

Perf. 11

21	RF5	10c blue	30.00	5.25
		Block of 4	140.00	

Perf. 10

22	RF5	10c blue	19.00	4.25
		Block of 4	87.50	—

RF6

ROTARY PRESS COIL STAMP

1929 **Perf. 10 Horizontally**

RF23	RF6	10c light blue	.25
		Pair	2.50
		Joint line pair	5.00

No. RF23 exists only precanceled. **Bureau precancels:** 16 different.

FLAT PLATE PRINTING

1930 **Perf. 10**

RF24	RF6	10c blue	19.00	1.40
		Block of 4	87.50	11.00
a.		Horiz. pair, imperf. vert.	175.00	

1931 **Perf. 11**

RF25	RF6	10c blue	15.00	1.40
		Block of 4	70.00	—

No. R234 is known used provisionally as a playing card revenue stamp August 6 and 8, 1932. Value for this use, authenticated, $300.

RF7

ROTARY PRESS COIL STAMP

1940 **Perf. 10 Vertically**

RF26	RF7	blue, wet printing	—	.45
		Pair		2.25
		Joint line pair		4.50
		Dry printing, unwatermarked	25.00	.40

See note after No. 1029.
Bureau precancels: 11 different.

RF8

ROTARY PRESS COIL STAMP

1940 **Wmk. 191R** **Perf. 10 Horizontally**

RF27	RF8	blue, wet printing	3.00	.25
		Pair	7.50	
		Joint line pair	12.50	
		Dry printing, unwatermarked		3.25

Bureau precancels: 10 different.

FLAT PLATE PRINTING

Perf. 11

RF28	RF8	blue, wet printing	5.25	.80
		Block of 4	26.00	
		Dry printing (rotary press)	5.25	4.25
		Dry printing (rotary press), unwatermarked		5.25
		Block of 4		—

ROTARY PRESS PRINTING

Perf. 10x11

RF29	RF8	blue	175.00	92.50
		Block of 4	750.00	—
a.		Imperforate (P.C. Co.)		900.00

SILVER TAX STAMPS

The Silver Purchase Act of 1934 imposed a 50 per cent tax on the net profit realized on a transfer of silver bullion occurring after May 15, 1934. The tax was paid by affixing stamps to the transfer memorandum. Congress authorized the Silver Tax stamps on June 19, 1934. They were discontinued on June 4, 1963.

Documentary Stamps of
1917 Overprinted

1934 **Offset Printing** **Wmk. 191R** **Perf. 11**

G1	R22	1c carmine rose	1.40	.95
G2	R22	2c carmine rose	1.50	.65
		Double impression of stamp	—	
RG3	R22	3c carmine rose	1.75	.80
RG4	R22	4c carmine rose	1.90	1.60
RG5	R22	5c carmine rose	3.25	1.40
RG6	R22	8c carmine rose	4.25	3.25
RG7	R22	10c carmine rose	4.50	3.00
RG8	R22	20c carmine rose	6.25	3.75
RG9	R22	25c carmine rose	5.75	4.25
RG10	R22	40c carmine rose	6.75	6.00
RG11	R22	50c carmine rose	9.00	7.50
RG12	R22	80c carmine rose	16.00	10.50

Engr.

RG13	R21	$1 green	30.00	16.00
RG14	R21	$2 rose	37.50	25.00
RG15	R21	$3 violet	72.50	35.00
RG16	R21	$4 yellow brown	57.50	24.00
RG17	R21	$5 dark blue	72.50	27.50
RG18	R21	$10 orange	92.50	22.50

Perf. 12
Without Gum

RG19	R17	$30 vermilion	190.00	55.00
		Cut cancel		20.00
RG20	R19	$60 brown	210.00	82.50
		Cut cancel		27.50
		Vertical strip of 4	375.00	
RG21	R17	$100 green	250.00	35.00
		Vertical strip of 4		150.00

RG22	R18	$500 blue	550.00	250.00
		Cut cancel		110.00
		Vertical strip of 4		
RG23	R19	$1000 orange	—	110.00
		Cut cancel		60.00
		Vertical strip of 4		

See note after No. R227.

Same Overprint, spacing 11mm between words
"SILVER TAX"
Without Gum

1936 **Perf. 12**

RG26	R17	$100 green	475.00	82.50
		Vertical strip of 4		
RG27	R19	$1000 orange	800.00	

Documentary Stamps of 1917 Handstamped
"SILVER TAX" in Violet, Large Block Letters, in Two
Lines

1939 **Wmk. 191R** **Offset Printing** **Perf. 10**

RG28	R22	1c rose pink	12,500.

Perf. 11

RG29	R22	3c rose pink	—
RG30	R22	5c rose pink	17,500.
RG31	R22	10c rose pink	10,000.
RG32	R22	80c rose pink	8,000.

Other handstamps exist on various values. One has letters 4mm high, 2mm wide with "SILVER" and "TAX" applied in separate operations. Another has "Silver Tax" in two lines in a box, but it is believed this handstamp was privately applied.

Overprint Typewritten in Black ($2, $3) or Red
($5)

1934-35 **Engr.** **Perf. 11**

RG34	R21	$2 carmine	
RG35	R21	$3 violet	2,600.
RG36	R21	$5 dark blue	—

Typewritten overprints also exist on 2c, 3c, 4c, 20c and 50c.

Type of Documentary
Stamps 1917, Overprinted in
Black

1940 **Offset Printing** **Perf. 11**

RG37	R22	1c rose pink	25.00	—
RG38	R22	2c rose pink	25.00	—
RG39	R22	3c rose pink	25.00	—
RG40	R22	4c rose pink	27.50	—
RG41	R22	5c rose pink	17.50	—
RG42	R22	8c rose pink	27.50	—
RG43	R22	10c rose pink	25.00	—
RG44	R22	20c rose pink	27.50	—
RG45	R22	25c rose pink	25.00	—
RG46	R22	40c rose pink	42.50	—
RG47	R22	50c rose pink	42.50	—
RG48	R22	80c rose pink	42.50	—

Engr.

RG49	R21	$1 green	160.00	—
RG50	R21	$2 rose	250.00	—
RG51	R21	$3 violet	325.00	—
RG52	R21	$4 yellow brown	650.00	—
RG53	R21	$5 dark blue	775.00	—
RG54	R21	$10 orange	875.00	—

Nos. RG19-RG20, RG26 Handstamped in Blue "Series 1940"

1940			Without Gum	Perf. 12	
RG55	R17	$30	vermilion	—	6,250.
RG56	R19	$60	brown	—	15,000.
RG57	R17	$100	green	—	4,500.

Alexander Hamilton — RG1

Levi Woodbury — RG2

Thomas Corwin — RG3

Overprinted in Black   **SERIES 1941**

1941		Wmk. 191R	Engr.	Perf. 11	
RG58	RG1	1c	gray	6.00	2.40
a.		Imperf, pair, without gum		75.00	
RG59	RG1	2c	gray (Oliver Wolcott, Jr.)	6.00	3.00
a.		Imperf, pair, without gum		75.00	
RG60	RG1	3c	gray (Samuel Dexter)	6.00	3.00
a.		Imperf, pair, without gum		75.00	
RG61	RG1	4c	gray (Albert Gallatin)	8.50	5.25
a.		Imperf, pair, without gum		75.00	

RG62	RG1	5c	gray (G.W. Campbell)	11.00	9.25
a.		Imperf, pair, without gum		75.00	
RG63	RG1	8c	gray (A.J. Dallas)	12.00	—
a.		Imperf, pair, without gum		75.00	
RG64	RG1	10c	gray (Wm. H. Crawford)	15.00	8.50
a.		Imperf, pair, without gum		75.00	
RG65	RG1	20c	gray (Richard Rush)	25.00	7.75
a.		Imperf, pair, without gum		75.00	
RG66	RG1	25c	gray (S.D. Ingham)	29.00	—
a.		Imperf, pair, without gum		75.00	
RG67	RG1	40c	gray (Louis McLane)	50.00	37.50
a.		Imperf, pair, without gum		75.00	
RG68	RG1	50c	gray (Wm. J. Duane)	60.00	32.50
a.		Imperf, pair, without gum		75.00	
RG69	RG1	80c	gray (Roger B. Taney)	100.00	32.50
a.		Imperf, pair, without gum		125.00	
RG70	RG2	$1	gray	125.00	45.00
a.		Imperf, pair, without gum		600.00	
RG71	RG2	$2	gray (Thomas Ewing)	300.00	72.50
a.		Imperf, pair, without gum		600.00	
RG72	RG2	$3	gray (Walter Forward)	250.00	97.50
a.		Imperf, pair, without gum		600.00	
RG73	RG2	$4	gray (J.C. Spencer)	375.00	80.00
a.		Imperf, pair, without gum		600.00	
RG74	RG2	$5	gray (G.M. Bibb)	300.00	95.00
a.		Imperf, pair, without gum		600.00	
RG75	RG2	$10	gray (R.J. Walker)	575.00	97.50
a.		Imperf, pair, without gum		650.00	
RG76	RG2	$20	gray (Wm. M. Meredith)	825.00	300.00
a.		Imperf, pair, without gum		2,000.	

Perf. 12   Without Gum

RG77	RG3	$30	gray	400.	250.
		Cut cancel			110.
a.		Imperf, pair, without gum		—	
RG78	RG3	$50	gray (James Guthrie)	4,500.	4,000.
a.		Imperf, pair, without gum		—	
RG79	RG3	$60	gray (Howell Cobb)	1,800.	275.
		Cut cancel			125.
a.		Imperf, pair, without gum		—	
RG80	RG3	$100	gray (P.F. Thomas)	7,500.	425.00
		Cut cancel			150.
		Vertical strip of 4		—	
a.		Imperf, pair, without gum		—	
RG81	RG3	$500	gray (J.A. Dix)	—	18,000.
a.		Imperf, pair, without gum		—	
RG82	RG3	$1000	gray (S.P. Chase)	—	2,500.
		Cut cancel			1,000.
a.		Imperf, pair, without gum		—	

Nos. RG58-RG82 Overprinted Instead: **SERIES 1942**

1942		Wmk. 191R		Perf. 11	
RG83	RG1	1c	gray	2.50	—
RG84	RG1	2c	gray	2.50	—
RG85	RG1	3c	gray	2.50	—
RG86	RG1	4c	gray	2.50	—
RG87	RG1	5c	gray	2.10	—
RG88	RG1	8c	gray	5.00	—
RG89	RG1	10c	gray	6.00	—
RG90	RG1	20c	gray	12.00	—
RG91	RG1	25c	gray	21.00	—
RG92	RG1	40c	gray	30.00	—
RG93	RG1	50c	gray	35.00	—
RG94	RG1	80c	gray	90.00	—
RG95	RG2	$1	gray	125.00	72.50
a.		Overprint "SERIES 5942"		500.00	
RG96	RG2	$2	gray	125.00	72.50
a.		Overprint "SERIES 5942"		950.00	
RG97	RG2	$3	gray	240.00	140.00
a.		Overprint "SERIES 5942"		1,000.	
RG98	RG2	$4	gray	250.00	140.00
a.		Overprint "SERIES 5942"		1,000.	

RG99	RG2	$5	gray	250.00	17.
a.		Overprint "SERIES 5942"		950.00	
RG100	RG2	$10	gray	650.00	42.
RG101	RG2	$20	gray	825.00	
a.		Overprint "SERIES 5942"		—	

Perf. 12   Without Gum

RG102	RG3	$30	gray	—	
		Cut cancel			2,
RG103	RG3	$50	gray	10,000.	
RG104	RG3	$60	gray	—	
		Cut cancel			1,
RG105	RG3	$100	gray	—	
		Cut cancel			
RG106	RG3	$500	gray	—	6,
		Cut cancel			3,
RG107	RG3	$1000	gray	—	5,
		Cut cancel			4,

Silver Purchase Stamps of 1941 without Overpri...

1944		Wmk. 191R		Perf.	
RG108	RG1	1c	gray	.85	
RG109	RG1	2c	gray	.85	
RG110	RG1	3c	gray	1.10	
RG111	RG1	4c	gray	1.40	
RG112	RG1	5c	gray	2.75	
RG113	RG1	8c	gray	4.50	
RG114	RG1	10c	gray	5.00	
RG115	RG1	20c	gray	8.25	
RG116	RG1	25c	gray	14.00	
RG117	RG1	40c	gray	20.00	1
RG118	RG1	50c	gray	22.50	14
RG119	RG1	80c	gray	30.00	20
RG120	RG2	$1	gray	60.00	21
RG121	RG2	$2	gray	87.50	47
RG122	RG2	$3	gray	100.00	37
RG123	RG2	$4	gray	125.00	85
RG124	RG2	$5	gray	125.00	47
RG125	RG2	$10	gray	175.00	35
		Cut cancel			19
RG126	RG2	$20	gray	700.00	500
		Cut cancel			250

Perf. 12   Without Gum

RG127	RG3	$30	gray	350.00	160
		Cut cancel			72
		Vertical strip of 4			
a.		Booklet pane of 4		7,250.	
RG128	RG3	$50	gray	775.00	625
		Cut cancel			325
		Vertical strip of 4			
a.		Booklet pane of 4		9,500.	
RG129	RG3	$60	gray	—	525
		Cut cancel			225
a.		Booklet pane of 4		10,000.	
RG130	RG3	$100	gray	—	35
		Cut cancel			15
		Vertical strip of 4			
RG131	RG3	$500	gray	—	500
		Cut cancel			250.
		With complete receipt tab		1,050.	
a.		Booklet pane of 4		5,500.	
		Complete booklet, 2 #RG131a		11,500.	
RG132	RG3	$1000	gray	—	160
		Cut cancel			80.
		Vertical strip of 4			
		With complete receipt tab		800.00	
a.		Booklet pane of 4			
		Complete booklet, 1 #RG132a		5,000.	

CIGARETTE TUBES STAMPS

These stamps were for a tax on the hollow tubes of cigarette paper, with or without thin cardboard mouthpieces attached. They were sold i... packages so buyers could add loose tobacco to make cigarettes.

Documentary Stamp of 1917 Overprinted

RH1

1919		Offset Printing	Wmk. 191R	Perf. 11	
RH1	R22	1c	carmine rose	1.00	.50
		Block of 4		5.00	2.50
		On package		20.00	
		Pair on package		40.00	
a.		Without period		15.00	9.00
		On package		—	

1929				Perf. 10	
RH2	R22	1c	carmine rose	50.00	10.00
		On package		—	

1933		Without Gum	Wmk. 191R	Perf. 11	
RH3	RH1	1c	rose (shades)	3.00	2.25
		Block of 4		17.50	
		On package		21.00	
RH4	RH1	2c	rose (shades)	10.00	4.00
		Pair		12.50	
		On package		100.00	

Cigarette tube on-package values for Nos. RH1 and RH3 are for fine undamaged stamps affixed to an empty package of Himyar Tobacco cigarette tubes manufactured by the Axton-Fisher Tobacco Co. Unopened packages containing cigarette

tubes command a 50 to 100 percent premium. No. RH1 pair... are unseparated stamps. The listing for No. RH1 pair on pack... age is not on a Himyar package.

Specialists have questioned whether Nos. RH1a or RH2 ar... known on packages. The editors would like to see evidence o... the existence of these listings.

POTATO TAX STAMPS

These stamps were required by the Potato Act of 1935, an amendment to the Agricultural Adjustment Act that became effective Dec. 1, 1935. Potato growers were given allotments for which they were provided Tax Exempt Potato stamps. Growers exceeding their allotments would have paid the excess with Tax Paid Potato stamps at the rate of ¾ cent per pound.

On Jan. 6, 1936, the U. S. Supreme Court declared the Agricultural Adjustment Act unconstitutional. Officially the Potato Act was in effect until Feb. 1936, when it was repealed by Congress but, in essence, the law was ignored once the Supreme Court ruling was issued. Because of the Act's short life, Tax Paid stamps were never used.

oung Woman from he Bouquet — RI1

RI2

Tax Paid Potatoes

35		Engr.	Unwmk.	Perf. 11
	RI1	¾c carmine rose		.35
	RI1	1½c black brown		.50
	RI1	2¼c yellow green		.50
	RI1	3c light violet		.60
	RI1	3¾c olive bister		.75
	RI1	7½c orange brown		2.50
	RI1	11½c deep orange		2.50
	RI1	18¾c violet brown		6.00
	RI1	37½c red orange		6.00
0	RI1	75c blue		7.50
1	RI1	93¾c rose lake		9.00

RI12	RI1	$1.12½ green	17.50	
RI13	RI1	$1.50 yellow brown	17.50	
		Nos. RI1-RI13 (13)	71.20	

Tax Exempt Potatoes

1935		Engr.	Unwmk.	Perf. 11x10½
RI14	RI2	2 lb black brown	1.00	10.50
a.		Booklet pane of 12	14.00	250.00
		Provisional booklet of 24, purple on pink cover	35.00	
		Provisional booklet of 96, purple on buff cover	100.00	
		Provisional booklet of 192, purple on white cover	300.00	
		Definitive booklet of 96, black on buff cover	100.00	
		Definitive booklet of 192, black on white cover	200.00	
RI15	RI2	5 lb black brown	22.50	
a.		Booklet pane of 12	375.00	
		Provisional booklet of 192, purple on white cover	—	
RI16	RI2	10 lb black brown	22.50	
a.		Booklet pane of 12	375.00	
		Provisional booklet of 192, purple on white cover	—	
RI17	RI2	25 lb black brown		
a.		Booklet pane of 12	6,000.	
RI18	RI2	50 lb black brown	1.10	40.00
a.		Booklet pane of 12	21.00	
		Provisional booklet of 24, purple on pink cover	50.00	
		Provisional booklet of 96, purple on buff cover	150.00	

	Provisional booklet of 192, purple on white cover	300.00
	Definitive booklet of 96, black on buff cover	100.00
	Definitive booklet of 192, black on white cover	200.00
	Nos. RI14-RI16,RI18 (4)	47.10

The booklet panes are arranged 4x3 with a tab at top. Edges are imperforate at left, right and bottom, yielding four stamps fully perforated, six stamps imperf. on one side and two stamps imperf. on two sides per pane.

These stamps were printed from 360-subject rotary booklet plates and cut into 30 panes of 12. The panes were stapled into booklets of 24 (2 panes, pink covers), 96 (8 panes, buff covers) and 196 (16 panes, white covers), with handstamped covers (provisionals) and later with covers printed with the Dept. of Agriculture seal in the center (definitives). Both types of cover were prepared by the Bureau of Engraving and Printing.

Values for booklets are for examples containing panes that have very good to fine centering, because the overwhelming majority of booklets are in this grade. It should be noted that Scott values for individual panes (listed above) are for very fine panes. For this reason, individual panes are valued higher than the per-pane value of panes in booklets. For example, a pane of No. RI14a is valued at $20, but the No. RI14 definitive booklet of 96 (8 panes) is valued at $100, or $12.50 per pane, which is a little more than what a collector would pay for an individual very good to fine pane. Booklets containing very fine panes will command a premium over the values given.

All recorded examples of No. RI17 were in three unbroken panes of 12. One pane appears to have been broken up and sold. A 100 lb Tax Exempt stamp was printed, but all are believed to have been destroyed.

TOBACCO SALE TAX STAMPS

These stamps were required to pay the tax on the sale of tobacco in excess of quotas set by the Secretary of Agriculture. The tax was 25 per cent of e price for which the excess tobacco was sold. It was intended to affect tobacco harvested after June 28, 1934 and sold before May 1, 1936. The tax is stopped when the Agricultural Adjustment Act was declared unconstitutional by the Supreme Court on Dec. 1, 1935. Values for unused stamps are for copies with original gum.

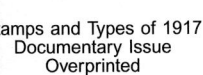

tamps and Types of 1917
Documentary Issue
Overprinted

34	Offset Printing	Wmk. 191R	Perf. 11	
1	R22	1c carmine rose	.30	.20
2	R22	2c carmine rose	.40	.20
3	R22	5c carmine rose	1.25	.45
4	R22	10c carmine rose	1.60	.40
a.		Inverted overprint	13.00	15.00
5	R22	25c carmine rose	4.25	1.60
6	R22	50c carmine rose	4.25	1.60
		Engr.		
J7	R21	$1 green	10.00	1.75
J8	R21	$2 rose	19.00	1.90
J9	R21	$5 dark blue	24.00	4.25
J10	R21	$10 orange	37.50	10.00
J11	R21	$20 olive bister	90.00	12.50
		Nos. RJ1-RJ11 (11)	192.55	34.85

On No. RJ11 the overprint is vertical, reading up. The right serif on the "T" of "TOBACCO" exists both normal d split. Both varieties exist within the same sheet, and the antities of each type are approximately equal.

No. RJ2 is known with a counterfeit inverted overprint.

NARCOTIC TAX STAMPS

The Revenue Act of 1918 imposed a tax of 1 cent per ounce or fraction thereof on opium, coca leaves and their derivatives. The tax was paid affixing Narcotic stamps to the drug containers. The tax lasted from Feb. 25, 1919, through Apr. 30, 1971.
Members of the American Revenue Association helped compile the listings in this section.

Documentary Stamps of 1914 Handstamped "NARCOTIC" in Magenta or Black

1919	**Wmk. 191R**	**Offset Printing**		**Perf. 10**
RJA1	R20	1c **rose**	85.00	75.00

The overprint was applied by District Collectors of Internal Revenue.

It is always in capital letters and exists in various type faces and sizes, including: 21½x2½mm, serif; 21x2¼mm, sans-serif boldface; 15½x 2½mm, sans-serif; 13x2mm, sans-serif.

The ½c, 2c, 3c, 4c, 5c, 10c, 25c and 50c with similar handstamp in serif capitals measuring about 20x2¼mm are bogus.

Documentary Stamps of 1917 Handstamped "NARCOTIC," "Narcotic," "NARCOTICS" or "ACT/NARCOTIC/1918" in Magenta, Black, Blue, Violet or Red

1919	**Wmk. 191R**	**Offset Printing**		**Perf. 11**
RJA9	R22	1c **carmine rose**	2.40	1.90
RJA10	R22	2c **carmine rose**	5.25	4.00
RJA11	R22	3c **carmine rose**	30.00	32.50
RJA12	R22	4c **carmine rose**	11.50	10.00
RJA13	R22	5c **carmine rose**	17.00	16.00
RJA14	R22	8c **carmine rose**	14.00	12.50
RJA15	R22	10c **carmine rose**	45.00	20.00
RJA16	R22	20c **carmine rose**	67.50	60.00
RJA17	R22	25c **carmine rose**	40.00	32.50
RJA18	R22	40c **carmine rose**	125.00	100.00
RJA19	R22	50c **carmine rose**	17.00	*19.00*
RJA20	R22	80c **carmine rose**	110.00	100.00

		Engr.	
RJA21	R21	$1 **green**	100.00 52.50
RJA22	R21	$2 **rose**	*1,000.*
RJA23	R21	$3 **violet**	*1,200.*
RJA24	R21	$5 **dark blue**	*1,000.*
RJA25	R21	$10 **orange**	*1,200.*

Drug manufacturer cancels have enabled experts to identify conclusively the origin of only six of the handstamped overprints. Four of these read simply "Narcotic." A 3-line handstamp, "Act / Narcotic / 1918," was used in Seattle; "Narcotics" in Kansas City, Missouri. Perhaps as many as 20 other styles and sizes have been recorded, although these occur only on mint stamps.

Many fake overprints exist.

No. R228 Overprinted in Black: "NARCOTIC / E.L. CO. / 3-19-19"

1919	**Wmk. 191R**		**Perf. 11**
"NARCOTIC" 14½mm wide			
RJA26	R22	1c **carmine rose**	*2,600.*

Overprinted by Eli Lilly Co., Indianapolis, for that firm's use.

No. R228 Overprinted in Black: "J W & B / NARCOTIC"

1919	**Wmk. 191R**		**Perf. 11**
"NARCOTIC" 14½mm wide			
RJA27	R22	1c **carmine rose**	—
RJA27A	R22	2c **carmine rose**	*3,250.*

Overprinted by John Wyeth & Brother, Philadelphia, for that firm's use.

Nos. R228, R231-R232 Handstamped in Blue: "P-W-R-Co. / NARCOTIC"

1919	**Wmk. 191R**		**Perf. 11**
RJA28	R22	1c **carmine rose**	625.00
RJA28A	R22	4c **carmine rose**	*1,200.*
RJA29	R22	5c **carmine rose**	—
RJA29A	R22	25c **carmine rose**	—
RJA29B	R21	$1 **green** (violet handstamp)	—

The handstamp was applied by the Powers-Weightmann-Rosengarten Co., Philadelphia, for that firm's use.

Proprietary Stamps of 1919 Handstamped "NARCOTIC" in Blue

1919	**Wmk. 191R**	**Offset Printing**		**Perf. 11**
RJA30	RB5	1c **dark blue**	—	—
RJA31	RB5	2c **dark blue**	—	
RJA32	RB5	4c **dark blue**	—	

No. RB65 is known with "Narcotic" applied in red ms.

Documentary Stamps of 1917 Overprinted in Black, "Narcotic" 17½mm wide

---

1919	**Wmk. 191R**	**Offset Printing**		**Perf. 11**
RJA33	R22	1c **carmine rose** *(6,900,000)*	1.00	.80
RJA34	R22	2c **carmine rose** *(3,650,000)*	2.00	1.10
RJA35	R22	3c **carmine rose** *(388,400)*	32.50	21.00
RJA36	R22	4c **carmine rose** *(2,400,000)*	5.25	4.75
RJA37	R22	5c **carmine rose** *(2,400,000)*	13.50	10.50
RJA38	R22	8c **carmine rose** *(1,200,000)*	21.00	18.00
RJA39	R22	10c **carmine rose** *(3,400,000)*	3.25	2.75
RJA40	R22	25c **carmine rose** *(700,000)*	21.00	16.00

Overprint Reading Up			
Engr.			
RJA41	R21	$1 **green** *(270,000)*	47.50 19.00

The overprint on Nos. RJA33-RJA41 was produced by the Bureau of Engraving & Printing. Fake overprints exist on Nos. RJA33-RJA41. In the genuine the C's are not slanted.

NT1

NT2

Imperf., Rouletted

1919-64	**Offset Printing**		**Wmk. 191R**
Left Value — "a" Imperf.			
Right Value — "b" Rouletted 7			
RJA42	NT1	1c **violet**	5.25 .25
d.		1c **purple**	— 7.50
RJA43	NT2	1c **violet**	.55 .30
d.		1c **purple**	5.00 5.25
RJA44	NT2	2c **violet**	1.40 .55
d.		2c **purple**	5.25
RJA45	NT2	3c **violet** ('64)	125.00

NT3

NT4

Left Value — "a" Imperf.			
Right Value — "b" Rouletted 7			
RJA46	NT3	1c **violet**	2.75
d.		1c **purple**	9.
RJA47	NT3	2c **violet**	1.60
d.		2c **purple**	8.
RJA48	NT3	3c **violet**	750.00
RJA49	NT3	4c **violet** ('42)	— 10.
d.		4c **purple**	— 30.
RJA50	NT3	5c **violet**	42.50 3.
d.		5c **purple**	13.
RJA51	NT3	6c **violet**	9.
d.		6c **purple**	9.
RJA52	NT3	8c **violet**	57.50 3.
d.		8c **purple**	26.
RJA53	NT3	9c **violet** ('53)	67.50 21.
RJA54	NT3	10c **violet**	32.50
d.		10c **purple**	7.
RJA55	NT3	16c **violet**	52.50 4.
d.		16c **purple**	14.
RJA56	NT3	18c **violet** ('61)	110.00 10.
RJA57	NT3	19c **violet** ('61)	125.00 26.
RJA58	NT3	20c **violet**	375.00 200.

Nos. RJA47-RJA58 have "CENTS" below the value.

Left Value — "a" Imperf.			
Right Value — "b" Rouletted 7			
RJA59	NT4	1c **violet**	47.50 10.
c.		Rouletted 3½	4.

60	NT4	2c **violet**	50.00	20.00
61	NT4	3c **violet**	52.50	62.50
62	NT4	5c **violet**		26.00
63	NT4	6c **violet**	62.50	21.00
64	NT4	8c **violet**		47.50
65	NT4	9c **violet** ('61)	26.00	21.00
66	NT4	10c **violet**	15.00	15.00
67	NT4	16c **violet**	16.00	10.00
68	NT4	18c **violet** ('61)	250.00	425.00
69	NT4	19c **violet**	16.00	190.00
70	NT4	20c **violet**	150.00	240.00
71	NT4	25c **violet**	—	21.00
c.		Rouletted 3½		4.25
72	NT4	40c **violet**	400.00	1,250.
c.		Rouletted 3½		67.50
73	NT4	$1 **green**		1.60
74	NT4	$1.28 **green**	32.50	10.50

On Nos. RJA60-RJA74 the value tablet is solid.

Imperf., Rouletted

3(?)-70   **Offset Printing**   **Unwatermarked**
Left Value — "a" Imperf.
Right Value — "b" Rouletted 7

75	NT1	1c **violet**	7.75	2.10+
76	NT2	1c **violet**	1.10	1.10
77	NT2	2c **violet**	5.25	2.10+
78	NT2	3c **violet**		125.00
79	NT3	1c **violet**	5.25	2.10
80	NT3	2c **violet**		2.00
81	NT3	4c **violet**		10.00
82	NT3	5c **violet**	72.50	
83	NT3	6c **violet**	—	10.50+
84	NT3	8c **violet**		5.25
85	NT3	9c **violet**	—	50.00

RJA86	NT3	10c **violet**	—	10.50+
RJA87	NT3	16c **violet**	150.00	4.25
RJA88	NT3	18c **violet**	—	52.50+
RJA89	NT3	20c **violet**	—	325.00+

Nos. RJA80-RJA89 have "CENTS" below the value.
+ Items so marked currently are only known unused with original gum and are valued thus.

Unwatermarked
Left Value — "a" Imperf.
Right Value — "b" Rouletted 7

RJA91	NT4	1c **violet**	67.50	15.00
RJA92	NT4	2c **violet**		52.50+
RJA93	NT4	3c **violet**	85.00	125.00+
RJA94	NT4	6c **violet**	100.00	52.50+
RJA95	NT4	9c **violet**		125.00+
RJA96	NT4	10c **violet**		60.00+
RJA97	NT4	16c **violet**	40.00	21.00
RJA98	NT4	19c **violet**	26.00	400.00
RJA99	NT4	20c **violet**	—	500.00+
RJA100	NT4	25c **violet**	350.00+	250.00
RJA101	NT4	40c **violet**	1,000.	
RJA102	NT4	$1 **green**		32.50+
RJA103	NT4	$1.28 **green**		60.00+
RJA104	NT4	$4 **green** ('70)	1,000.	

On Nos. RJA92-RJA104 the value tablet is solid.
+ Items so marked currently are only known unused with original gum and are valued thus.

NT5

Denomination added in black by rubber plate in an operation similar to precanceling.

1963   **Engr.**   **Unwmk.**   *Imperf.*
Left Value — Unused
Right Value — Used

RJA105	NT5	1c **violet**, type 2	100.00	85.00
a.		Type 1	140.00	140.00

Type 1 was produced with four electric eye markings, one in each corner. Type 2 was produced later and has two electric eye markings, one in each corner on the left side of the stamp. Type 2 is the more common of the two varieties and, therefore, is listed as the major number.
Nos. RAJ105 and RAJ105a were issued in vertical coil strips.

Denomination on Stamp Plate
1964   **Offset Printing**   *Imperf.*

RJA106	NT5	1c **violet**	90.00	5.25

RJA106 was issued in sheet of 80 stamps.

MARIHUANA TAX STAMPS

Act of Congress, 1937, to enforce uniform regulation of cannabis.

Nos. R240, R244, R245 overprinted

37   **Engr.**   *Perf. 10*

M1	R21	$1 **yellow green**	450.00	15,000.
		On document		
		P# block of 6	2,800.	
a.		Imperf, pair	925.00	
M2	R21	$5 **blue**	575.00	
		P# block of 6	3,750.	
a.		Imperf, pair	1,200.	
M3	R21	$10 **yellow orange**	675.00	
		P# block of 6	4,250.	
a.		Imperf, pair	1,450.	

Same overprint on No. R248

№ 1635	
Issued to	
At	
By	
Collector	Dist.
	191

(Illustration reduced)

Without Gum   *Perf. 12*
Control Number in Red

JM4	R17	$100 **green**, with complete receipt tab	900.00	
a.		Booklet pane of 4	3,600.	
		Complete booklet, 4 #RJM4a	15,000.	

Nos. R300, R304, R305 without date inscription overprinted:

1962   *Perf. 11*

RJM5	R24	$1 **carmine**	475.00
RJM6	R24	$5 **carmine**	600.00
RJM7	R24	$10 **carmine**	750.00

No. R306A without date inscription overprinted:

Issued to	
At	
By	
Director located at	
	19

(Illustration reduced)

RJM8	R25	$50 **carmine**, with complete receipt tab, no serial #	1,500.	
a.		Booklet pane of 4	6,000.	

CONSULAR SERVICE FEE STAMPS

Act of Congress, April 5, 1906, effective June 1, 1906, provided that every consular officer should be provided with special adhesive stamps printe[d] denominations determined by the Department of State.

Every document for which a fee was prescribed had to have attached a stamp or stamps representing the amount collected, and such stamps w[ere] used to show payment of these prescribed fees.

These stamps were usually affixed close to the signature, or at the lower left corner of the document. If no document was issued, the stamp [or] stamps were attached to a receipt for the amount of the fee and canceled either with pen and ink or rubber stamp showing the date of cancellation [and] bearing the initials of the canceling officer or name of the Consular Office. These stamps were not sold to the public uncanceled. Their use [was] discontinued Sept. 30, 1955.

CSF1

CSF2

Perf. 11			
RK14	CSF1	25c dark green	90.00
RK15	CSF1	50c carmine	150.00
RK16	CSF1	$1 dark violet	2.00
a.		Diagonal half used as 50c, on document	375.00
RK17	CSF1	$2 brown	2.40
RK18	CSF1	$2.50 dark blue	.95
RK19	CSF1	$5 brown red	5.00
a.		Diagonal half used as $2.50, on document	50.00
RK20	CSF1	$9 gray	22.50
RK21	CSF1	$10 orange	45.00
a.		Diagonal half used as $5, on document	62.50

1924			Perf. 11
RK22	CSF2	$1 violet	110.00
RK23	CSF2	$2 brown	125.00
RK24	CSF2	$2.50 blue	20.00
RK25	CSF2	$5 brown red	95.00
RK26	CSF2	$9 gray	325.00
		Nos. RK22-RK26 (5)	675.00

1906		Unwmk. Engr.	Perf. 12
RK1	CSF1	25c dark green	80.00
RK2	CSF1	50c carmine	100.00
RK3	CSF1	$1 dark violet	9.00
a.		Diagonal half used as 50c with 2 #RK3, paying $2.50 fee, on document	325.00
RK4	CSF1	$2 brown	6.00
RK5	CSF1	$2.50 dark blue	1.90
RK6	CSF1	$5 brown red	27.50
a.		Horizontal or diagonal half used as $2.50, on document	250.00
RK7	CSF1	$10 orange	95.00
		Perf. 10	
RK8	CSF1	25c dark green	85.00
RK9	CSF1	50c carmine	100.00
RK10	CSF1	$1 dark violet	475.00
RK11	CSF1	$2 brown	110.00
a.		Diagonal half used as $1, on document	—
RK12	CSF1	$2.50 dark blue	25.00
RK13	CSF1	$5 brown red	190.00

1925-52			Perf
RK27	C3F3	$1 violet	3
RK28	CSF3	$2 brown	8
RK29	CSF3	$2.50 ultramarine	
RK30	CSF3	$5 carmine	1
RK31	CSF3	$9 gray	5
		Perf. 11	
RK32	CSF3	25c green ('37)	9
RK33	CSF3	50c orange ('34)	9
RK34	CSF3	$1 violet	
a.		Diagonal half used as 50c, on document	
RK35	CSF3	$2 brown	
RK36	CSF3	$2.50 blue	
a.		$2.50 ultramarine	
RK37	CSF3	$5 carmine	
RK38	CSF3	$9 gray	2
RK39	CSF3	$10 blue gray ('37)	11
RK40	CSF3	$20 violet ('52)	12
		Nos. RK27-RK40 (14)	64

CSF3

Consular Fee

The "Consular Fee stamp" on revenue stamp[ed] paper (previously listed as No. RN-Y1 but si[nce] deleted) was found to be nothing more than an illus[tra]tion. Two identical copies are known.

CUSTOMS FEE STAMPS

New York Custom House

Issued to indicate the collection of miscellaneous customs fees. Use was discontinued on February 28, 1918. The stamps were not utilized in t[he] collection of customs duties.

Silas Wright
CF1

Size: 48x34mm

1887		Engr.	Rouletted 5½	
RL1	CF1	20c dull rose	110.00	1.00
a.		20c red, perf. 10		—
b.		Vert. half used as 10c, on document		250.00
c.		20c red, rouletted 7		200.00
RL2	CF1	30c orange	150.00	2.00
RL3	CF1	40c green	175.00	3.50
RL4	CF1	50c dark blue	175.00	5.50
RL5	CF1	60c red violet	140.00	2.00
RL6	CF1	70c brown violet	140.00	30.00
RL7	CF1	80c brown	200.00	77.50
RL8	CF1	90c black	250.00	90.00
		Nos. RL1-RL8 (8)	1,340.	211.50

Each of these stamps has its own distinctive background.

EMBOSSED REVENUE STAMPED PAPER

Some of the American colonies of Great Britain used embossed stamps in raising revenue, as Britain had done from 1694. The British government also imposed stamp taxes on the colonies, and in the early 19th century the U.S. government and some of the states enacted similar taxes.

Under one statute or another, these stamps were required on such documents as promissory notes, bills of exchange, insurance policies, bills of lading, bonds, protests, powers of attorney, stock certificates, letters patent, writs, conveyances, leases, mortgages, charter parties, commissions and liquor licenses.

A few of these stamps were printed, but most were colorless impressions resembling a notary public's seal.

The scant literature of these stamps includes E.B. Sterling's revenue catalogue of 1888, *The Stamps that Caused the American Revolution: The Stamps of the British Stamp Act for America,* by Adolph Koeppel, published in 1976 by the Town of North Hempstead (New York) American Revolution Bicentennial Commission, *New Discovery from British Archives on the 1765 Tax Stamps for America,* edited by Adolph Koeppel and published in 1962 by the American Revenue Association, *First Federal Issue 1798-1801 U.S. Embossed Revenue Stamped Paper,* by W.V. Combs, published in 1979 by the American Philatelic Society, *Second Federal Issue, 1801-1802,* by W.V. Combs, published in 1988 by the American Revenue Association, and *Third Federal Issue, 1814-1817,* by W.V. Combs, published in 1993 by the American Revenue Association.

Values are for stamps of clear impression on entire documents of the most common usage in good condition. The document may be folded. Unusual or rare usages may sell for much more. Parts of documents, cut squares or poor impressions sell for much less.

Colin MacR. Makepeace originally compiled the listings in this section.

INCLUDING COLONIAL EMBOSSED REVENUES
I. COLONIAL ISSUES
A. MASSACHUSETTS
Act of January 8, 1755
In effect May 1, 1755-April 30, 1757

ERP1   ERP2

ERP3   ERP4

Die 2 — ERP2

Typo.

M1	ERP1	½p **red**	2,300.

Embossed

M2	ERP2	2p	400.
M3	ERP3	3p	200.
M4	ERP4	4p	600.

A second die of ERP2 with no fin on the under side of the codfish has been seen. There were at least two dies of the ½p.

B. NEW YORK
Act of December 1, 1756
In effect January 1, 1757-December 31, 1760

ERP9

Typo.

M9	ERP9	½p **red**	2,250.

Embossed

RM10	ERP9	1p	525.
RM11	ERP9	2p	300.
RM12	ERP9	3p	450.
RM13	ERP9	4p	375.

II. BRITISH REVENUES FOR USE IN AMERICA
Act of March 22, 1765
In effect November 1, 1765-May 1, 1766.
A. ALMANAC STAMPS

ERP15

Engr.

RM15	ERP15	2p **red**
RM16	ERP15	4p **red**
RM17	ERP15	8p **red**

Proofs of all of these stamps printed in the issued color are known. Full size facsimile reproductions in the color of the originals were made about 1876 of the proof sheets of the 8p stamp, Plates 1 and 2, Dies 1 to 50 inclusive.

B. PAMPHLETS AND NEWSPAPER STAMPS

ERP18

Engr.

RM18	ERP18	½p **red**	
RM19	ERP18	1p **red**	
RM20	ERP18	2p **red**	2,000.

Proofs of all of these stamps printed in the issued color are known. Full size facsimile reproductions in the color of the originals were made about 1876 of the proof sheets of the 1p stamp, Plates 3 and 4, Dies 51 to 100 inclusive.

C. GENERAL ISSUE

ERP24   ERP25

ERP26   ERP27

ERP28   ERP29

ERP30   ERP31

ERP33   ERP34

ERP35

Embossed

RM24	ERP24	3p	3,000.
RM25	ERP25	4p	3,000.
RM26	ERP26	6p	3,000.
RM27	ERP27	1sh	1,750.
RM28	ERP28	1sh6p	1,250.
RM29	ERP29	2sh	3,000.
RM30	ERP30	2sh3p	1,800.
RM31	ERP31	2sh6p	2,000.
a.	Not on document		450.
RM33	ERP33	4sh	1,750.
RM34	ERP34	5sh	2,500.
RM35	ERP35	10sh	3,250.

Proofs exist of similar 1sh, 1sh6p and 2sh6p stamps inscribed "AMERICA CONT.& c."

Various Similar Designs

RM36	£1	—
RM37	£2	—
RM38	£3	—
RM39	£4	—
RM40	£6	—
RM41	£10	—

The £1 to £10 denominations probably exist only as proofs.

D. PLAYING CARDS STAMP

Type similar to EP29, with Arms of George III Encircled by Garter.

RM42	1sh	—

All of these were embossed without color and most of them were embossed directly on the document except the 2sh 6p which was general embossed on a rectangular piece of bluish or brownish stiff paper or cardboard only slightly larger than the stamp which was attached to the document by a small piece of metal. Three dies exist of the 3p; two of the 4p, 6p, 1sh, 1sh 6p, 2sh and 2sh 3p.

All of these stamps have the word "America" somewhere in the design and this is the feature which distinguishes them from the other British revenues. The stamps of the general issue are occasionally found with a design of a British revenue stamp struck over the American design, as a number of them were afterwards re-struck and used elsewhere as British revenues.

These stamps are sometimes called the "Teaparty" or "Tax on Tea" stamps. This, however, is a misnomer, as the act under which these stamps were issued laid no tax on tea. The tax on tea was levied by an act passed two years later, and the duties imposed by that act were not collected by stamps.

It must be remembered that these stamps were issued under an act applicable to all of the British colonies in America which included many which are not now part of the United States. Copies have been seen which were used in Quebec, Nova Scotia and in the West Indies. So great was the popular clamor against taxation by a body in which the colonists had no representation that ships bringing the stamps from England were not allowed to land them in some of the colonies, the stamps were destroyed in others, and in practically all of those which are now a part of the United States the "Stamp Masters" who were to administer the act were forced to resign and to take oath that they would never carry out the duties of the offices. Notwithstanding the very general feeling about these stamps there is evidence that a very small number of them were actually used on ships' documents for one vessel clearing from New York and for a very small number of vessels clearing from the Savannah River. Florida was at this time under British authority and the only known copies of these stamps used in what is now the United States, a 4p (#RM25), a 1sh (#RM27), and two copies of the 5sh (#RM34) were used there.

III. ISSUES OF THE UNITED STATES
A. FIRST FEDERAL ISSUE

Act of July 6, 1797
In effect July 1, 1798-February 28, 1801

The distinguishing feature of the stamps of this issue is the name of a state in the design. These stamps were issued by the Federal Government, however, and not by the United States. The design, with the exception of the name of the state, was the same for each denomination; but different denominations had the shield and the eagle in different positions. The design of only one denomination of these stamps is illustrated.

In addition to the eagle and shield design on the values from four cents to ten dollars there are two other stamps for each state, similar in design to one another, one of which is illustrated. All of these are embossed without color.
Values are for clearly impressed examples.

RM45	4c	Connecticut	45.00
RM46	10c	Connecticut	125.00
RM47	20c	Connecticut	300.00
RM48	25c	Connecticut	45.00
RM49	30c	Connecticut	2,750.
RM50	50c	Connecticut	135.00
RM51	75c	Connecticut	
RM52	$1	Connecticut	1,750.
RM54	$4	Connecticut	1,250.
RM58	4c	Delaware	350.00
RM59	10c	Delaware	350.00
RM60	20c	Delaware	500.00
RM61	25c	Delaware	450.00
RM62	30c	Delaware	
RM63	50c	Delaware	550.00
RM64	75c	Delaware	700.00
RM65	$1	Delaware	
RM71	4c	Georgia	250.00
RM72	10c	Georgia	200.00
RM73	20c	Georgia	
RM74	25c	Georgia	250.00
RM75	30c	Georgia	3,000.
RM76	50c	Georgia	400.00
RM77	75c	Georgia	1,750.
RM78	$1	Georgia	
RM84	4c	Kentucky	20.00
RM85	10c	Kentucky	75.00
RM86	20c	Kentucky	250.00
RM87	25c	Kentucky	40.00
RM88	30c	Kentucky	275.00
RM89	50c	Kentucky	50.00
RM90	75c	Kentucky	125.00
RM91	$1	Kentucky	
RM97	4c	Maryland	75.00
RM98	10c	Maryland	50.00
RM99	20c	Maryland	700.00
RM100	25c	Maryland	75.00
RM101	30c	Maryland	600.00
RM102	50c	Maryland	125.00
RM103	75c	Maryland	50.00
RM104	$1	Maryland	—
RM106	$4	Maryland	—
RM110	4c	Massachusetts	20.00
RM111	10c	Massachusetts	50.00
RM112	20c	Massachusetts	80.00
RM113	25c	Massachusetts	35.00
RM114	30c	Massachusetts	950.00
RM115	50c	Massachusetts	125.00
RM116	75c	Massachusetts	400.00
RM117	$1	Massachusetts	200.00
RM123	4c	New Hampshire	25.00
RM124	10c	New Hampshire	25.00
RM125	20c	New Hampshire	350.00
RM126	25c	New Hampshire	70.00
RM127	30c	New Hampshire	425.00
RM128	50c	New Hampshire	80.00
RM129	75c	New Hampshire	75.00
RM130	$1	New Hampshire	550.00
RM136	4c	New Jersey	400.00
RM137	10c	New Jersey	175.00
RM138	20c	New Jersey	
RM139	25c	New Jersey	110.00
RM140	30c	New Jersey	750.00
RM141	50c	New Jersey	125.00
RM142	75c	New Jersey	
RM143	$1	New Jersey	—
RM147	$10	New Jersey	4,750.
RM149	4c	New York	35.00
RM150	10c	New York	20.00
RM151	20c	New York	25.00
RM152	25c	New York	40.00
RM153	30c	New York	25.00
RM154	50c	New York	30.00
RM155	75c	New York	35.00
RM156	$1	New York	350.00
RM157	$2	New York	
RM159	$5	New York	—
RM160	$10	New York	—
RM162	4c	North Carolina	45.00
RM163	10c	North Carolina	50.00
RM164	20c	North Carolina	950.00
RM165	25c	North Carolina	55.00
RM166	30c	North Carolina	2,500.
RM167	50c	North Carolina	175.00
RM168	75c	North Carolina	325.00
RM169	$1	North Carolina	3,750.
RM175	4c	Pennsylvania	30.00
RM176	10c	Pennsylvania	20.00
RM177	20c	Pennsylvania	27.50
RM178	25c	Pennsylvania	15.00
RM179	30c	Pennsylvania	30.00
RM180	50c	Pennsylvania	25.00
RM181	75c	Pennsylvania	75.00
RM182	$1	Pennsylvania	300.00
RM184	$4	Pennsylvania	13,000.
RM187		Pennsylvania, "Ten cents per centum"	
RM188	4c	Rhode Island	35.00
RM189	10c	Rhode Island	50.00
RM190	20c	Rhode Island	200.00
RM191	25c	Rhode Island	65.00
RM192	30c	Rhode Island	900.00
RM193	50c	Rhode Island	150.00
RM194	75c	Rhode Island	1,000.
RM195	$1	Rhode Island	1,750.
RM201	4c	South Carolina	90.00
RM202	10c	South Carolina	200.00
RM203	20c	South Carolina	350.00
RM204	25c	South Carolina	125.00
RM205	30c	South Carolina	
RM206	50c	South Carolina	175.00
RM207	75c	South Carolina	4,000.
RM208	$1	South Carolina	6,000.

RM211	$5	South Carolina	
RM214	4c	Tennessee	35
RM215	10c	Tennessee	20
RM216	20c	Tennessee	
RM217	25c	Tennessee	27
RM218	30c	Tennessee	
RM219	50c	Tennessee	90
RM220	75c	Tennessee	
RM221	$1	Tennessee	
RM227	4c	Vermont	7
RM228	10c	Vermont	3
RM229	20c	Vermont	35
RM230	25c	Vermont	10
RM231	30c	Vermont	1,
RM232	50c	Vermont	13
RM233	75c	Vermont	3,
RM234	$1	Vermont	
RM238	$10	Vermont	
RM240	4c	Virginia	1
RM241	10c	Virginia	2
RM242	20c	Virginia	125
RM243	25c	Virginia	20
RM244	30c	Virginia	500
RM245	50c	Virginia	2
RM246	75c	Virginia	50
RM247	$1	Virginia	1,

The Act calls for a $2, $4, $5 and $10 stamp for each st only the listed ones have been seen.

The Act also calls for a "Ten cents per centum" and a mills per dollar" stamp for each state, none of which has b seen except No. RM187.

A press and a set of dies, one die for each denominat were prepared and sent to each state where it was the dut the Supervisors of the Revenue to stamp all docume presented to them upon payment of the proper tax. The Sup visors were also to have on hand for sale blank paper stamp with the different rates of duty to be sold to the public u which the purchaser would later write or print the proper typ instrument corresponding with the value of the sta impressed thereon. So far as is now known there was no tinctive watermark for the paper sold by the government. Vermont set of dies is in the Vermont Historical Society Montpelier.

B. SECOND FEDERAL ISSUE

Act of April 23, 1800
In effect March 1, 1801-June 30, 1802

RM260 RM261

		(a)Government watermark in italics; laid paper	(b)Government watermark in Roman; wove paper	(c)No Government watermark
RM260	4c	15.00	15.00	50.00
RM261	10c	20.00	20.00	50.00
RM262	20c	65.00	75.00	85.00
RM263	25c	15.00	15.00	17.50
RM264	30c	75.00	75.00	400.00
RM265	50c	65.00	45.00	85.00
RM266	75c	30.00	50.00	100.00
RM267	$1	200.00	150.00	175.00
RM269	$4			500.00
RM271	$10		3,250.	

The distinguishing feature of the stamps of this issue is th counter stamp, the left stamp shown in the illustration whi usually appears on a document below the other stamp. In th right stamp the design of the eagle and the shield are similar their design in the same denomination of the First Federal Iss but the name of the state is omitted and the denominatio appears below instead of above the eagle and the shield. All these stamps were embossed without color.

All the paper which was furnished by the government co tained the watermark vertically along the edge of the shee "GEN STAMP OFFICE," either in Roman capitals on wov paper or in italic capitals on laid paper. The wove paper als had in the center of each half sheet either the watermark "W. & Co." or "Delaware." William Young & Co. who owned th Delaware Mills made the government paper. The laid pap omitted the watermark "Delaware." The two stamps were sep rately impressed. The design of the eagle and shield differed each value.

All the stamping was done in Washington, the right stam being put on in the General Stamp Office and the left one a counter stamp in the office of the Commissioner of the Revenu as a check on the stamping done in the General Stamp Offic The "Com. Rev. C. S." in the design of the counter stam stands for "Commissioner of the Revenue, Counter Stamp."

The Second Federal issue was intended to include $2 and $ stamps, but these denominations have not been seen.

C. THIRD FEDERAL ISSUE
Act of August 2, 1813
In effect January 1, 1814-December 31, 1817

RM276

		a. Watermark	b. Unwmkd.
1275	5c	10.00	15.00
1276	10c	10.00	10.00
1277	25c	15.00	15.00
1278	50c	10.00	10.00
1279	75c	13.00	17.50
1280	$1	13.00	27.50
1281	$1.50	13.00	65.00
1282	$2	27.50	50.00
1283	$2.50	27.50	110.00
1284	$3.50	175.00	100.00
1285	$4		350.00
1286	$5	100.00	125.00

he distinguishing features of the stamps of this issue are the ence of the name of a state in the design and the absence he counter stamp. Different values show different positions he eagle.

ll stamps of this issue were embossed without color at shington. The paper with the watermark "Stamp U. S." was d by the government. Unwatermarked paper may be either e or laid.

IV. ISSUES BY VARIOUS STATES
DELAWARE
Act of June 19, 1793
In effect October 1, 1793-February 7, 1794

ERP50

ERP51

ERP53

RM291	EP50	5c	1,700.
RM292	EP51	20c	1,350.
RM294	EP53	50c	

In some cases a reddish ink was used in impressing the amp and in other cases the impressions are colorless. Besides the denominations listed, 3c, 33c, and $1 stamps ere called for by the taxing act. Stamps of these denomina-ns have not been seen.

VIRGINIA
Act of February 20, 1813
In effect May 1, 1813-April 30, 1815
Act of December 21, 1814
In effect May 1, 1815-February 27, 1816

ERP60

ERP61

			a. Die cut	b. On Document
RM305	EP61	4c	17.50	90.00
RM306	EP60	6c	17.50	200.00
RM307	EP61	10c		200.00
RM308	EP60	12c	25.00	200.00
RM309	EP61	20c	40.00	500.00
RM310	EP61	25c	17.50	225.00
RM311	EP61	37c	17.50	300.00
RM312	EP61	45c	40.00	200.00
RM313	EP61	50c	17.50	225.00
RM314	EP61	70c	40.00	
RM315	EP61	75c	22.50	90.00
RM316	EP61	95c	40.00	300.00
RM317	EP61	100c	40.00	300.00
RM318	EP61	120c		225.00
RM319	EP61	125c	17.50	
RM323	EP60	175c	17.50	
RM325	EP61	200c	17.50	475.00

All of these stamps are colorless impressions and with some exceptions as noted below those issued under the 1813 Act cannot be distinguished from those issued under the 1814 Act. The 10c, 20c, 45c, 70c, 95c, 120c, 145c, 150c, 170c and 190c were issued only under the 1813 Act, the 6c, 12c, and 37c only under the 1814 Act.

No. RM311 has the large lettering of EP60 but the 37 is to the left and the XXXVII to the right as in EP61. The design of the dogwood branch and berries is similar but not identical in all values.

When the tax on the document exceeded "two hundred cents," two or more stamps were impressed or attached to the document. For instance a document has been seen with 45c and 200c to make up the $2.45 rate, and another with 75c and 200c.

Since both the Virginia and the Third Federal Acts to some extent taxed the same kind of document, and since during the period from Jan. 1, 1814 to Feb. 27, 1816, both Acts were in effect in Virginia, some instruments have both stamps on them.

The circular die cut Virginia stamps about 29mm in diameter were cut out of previously stamped paper which after the Act was repealed, was presented for redemption at the office of the Auditor of Public Accounts. They were threaded on fine twine and until about 1940 preserved in his office as required by law. Watermarked die cut Virginia stamps are all cut out of Third Federal watermarked paper.

Not seen yet, the 145c, 150c, and 170c stamps were called for by the 1813 Act, and 195c by both the 1813 and 1814 Acts.

MARYLAND
1. Act of February 11, 1818
In effect May 1, 1818-March 7, 1819

ERP70

RM362	EP70	30c **red** (printed), unused		400.
		Sheet of 4, unused		2,500.

The Act called for six other denominations, none of which has been seen. The Act imposing this tax was held unconstitutional by the United States Supreme Court in the case of McCulloch vs. Maryland.

2. Act of March 10, 1845
In effect May 10, 1845-March 10, 1856

ERP71

RM370	EP71	10c	12.50
RM371	EP71	15c	10.00
RM372	EP71	25c	10.00
RM373	EP71	50c	12.50
RM374	EP71	75c	10.00
RM375	EP71	$1	10.00
RM376	EP71	$1.50	12.50
RM377	EP71	$2	45.00
RM378	EP71	$2.50	17.50
RM379	EP71	$3.50	55.00

RM380	EP71	$4	90.00
RM381	EP71	$5.50	50.00
RM382	EP71	$6	100.00

Nos. RM370-RM382 are embossed without color with a similar design for each value. They vary in size from 20mm in diameter for the 10c to 33mm for the $6.

V. FEDERAL LICENSES TO SELL LIQUOR, ETC.
1. Act of June 5, 1794
In effect September 30, 1794-June 30, 1802

ERP80

RM400	EP80	$5	550.00

Provisionals are in existence using the second issue Connecticut Supervisors' stamp with the words "Five Dollars" written or printed over it or the second issue of the New Hampshire Supervisors' stamp without the words "Five Dollars."

2. Act of August 2, 1813
In effect January 1, 1814-December 31, 1817

ERP81

RM451	EP81	$10	725.00
RM452	EP81	$12	700.00
RM453	EP81	$15	350.00
RM454	EP81	$18	900.00
RM455	EP81	$20	1,400.
RM456	EP81	$22.50	650.00
RM457	EP81	$25	425.00
RM458	EP81	$30	1,500.
RM459	EP81	$37.50	550.00

The Act of December 23, 1814, increased the basic rates of $10, $12, $15, $20 and $25 by 50 per cent, effective February 1, 1815. This increase applied to the unexpired portions of the year so far as licenses then in effect were concerned and these licenses were required to be brought in and to have the payment of the additional tax endorsed on them.

VI. FEDERAL LICENSES TO WORK A STILL
Act of July 24, 1813
In effect January 1, 1814-December 31, 1817

(Embossed) ERP82   (Printed) ERP83

		a. Embossed	b. Printed
RM466	4 ½c		1,900.
RM468	9c	1,250.	1,800.
RM471	18c	—	1,400.
RM477	36c		2,100.
RM480	52c	2,000.	
RM484	70c	2,100.	
RM488	$1.08	2,000.	

The statute under which these were issued provided for additional rates of 2½c, 5c, 10c, 16c, 21c, 25c, 26c, 32c, 35c, 42c, 50c, 54c, 60c, 64c, 84c, $1.04, $1.05, $1.20, $1.35, $1.40, $2.10, $2.16 and $2.70 per gallon of the capacity of the still. Stamps of these denominations have not been seen.

VII. SUPERVISORS' AND CUSTOM HOUSE SEALS

1. Supervisors' Seals Act of March 3, 1791.
In effect July 1, 1791-March 2, 1799.

ERP90

		Check Letter	State	
RM501	EP90	"B"	South Carolina	50.00
RM503	EP90	"D"	Virginia	1,350.
RM505	EP90	"F"	Delaware	—
RM506	EP90	"G"	Pennsylvania	75.00
RM508	EP90	"I"	New York	22.50
RM509	EP90	"K"	Connecticut	30.00
RM510	EP90	"L"	Rhode Island	90.00
RM511	EP90	"M"	Massachusetts	22.50
RM512	EP90	"N"	New Hampshire	700.00
RM514	EP90	"P"	Kentucky	—

2. Supervisors' Seals Act of March 2, 1799
In effect from March 2, 1799

ERP91

RM552	EP91	North Carolina	500.00	
RM553	EP91	Virginia	—	
RM554	EP91	Maryland	200.00	
RM556	EP91	Pennsylvania	250.00	
RM558	EP91	New York	20.00	
RM559	EP91	Connecticut	30.00	
RM560	EP91	Rhode Island	35.00	
RM561	EP91	Massachusetts	25.00	
RM562	EP91	New Hampshire	90.00	

3. Custom House Seals

ERP92

RM575	EP92	Custom House, Philadelphia	5(..
RM576	EP92	Custom House, Perth Amboy, N.J.	35..

Although no value is expressed in the Supervisors' and C[...] tom House seals, and they do not evidence the payment [...] tax in the same way that the other stamps do, some collec[...] of stamped paper include them in their collections if they are[...] instruments evidencing the payment of a tax.

They were all embossed without color and, as to Supervis[...] seals issued under the Act of 1791, the only difference in des[...] is that at the left of the eagle there was a different check le[...] for each state. Custom House seals used in the other cities [...] in existence, but, in view of the doubtful status of Custom Ho[...] seals as revenue stamps, it is not proposed to list them.

REVENUE STAMPED PAPER

These stamps were printed in various denominations and designs on a variety of financial documents, including checks, drafts, receipts, specie cle[...] statements, insurance policies, bonds and stock certificates.

They were authorized by Act of Congress of July 1, 1862, effective October 1, 1862, although regular delivery of stamped paper did not begin un[...] July 1, 1865. The 2-cent tax on receipts ended Oct. 1, 1870. The 2-cent tax on checks and sight drafts ended July 1, 1883. All other taxes ended Oct. [...] 1872. The use of stamped paper was revived by the War Revenue Act of 1898, approved June 13, 1898. Type X was used July 1, 1898 through Ju[...] 30, 1902.

Most of these stamps were typographed; some, types H, I and J, were engraved. They were printed by private firms under supervision [...] government representatives from dies loaned by the Bureau of Internal Revenue. Types A-F, P-W were printed by the American Phototype Co., Ne[...] York (1865-75); type G, Graphic Co., New York (1875-83); types H-L, Joseph R. Carpenter, Philadelphia (1866-75); types M-N, A. Trochsler, Bost[...] (1873-75); type O, Morey and Sherwood, Chicago (1874). Type X was printed by numerous regional printers under contract with the government.

Samples of these stamps are known for types B-G, P and Q with a section of the design removed and replaced by the word "Sample." Types G, P-[...] U-W exist with a redemption clause added by typography or rubber stamp. Redeemed type X's have a 5mm punched hole.

Multiples or single impressions on various plain papers are usually considered proofs or printers' waste.

For further information see "Handbook for United States Revenue Stamped Paper," published (1979) by the American Revenue Association.

Illustration size varies, with actual size quoted for each type.

Values for types A-O are for clear impressions on plain entire checks and receipts. Attractive documents with vignettes sell for more. Th[...] value of individual examples is also affected by the place of use. For example, territorial usage generally sells for more than a similar ite[...] from New York City.

Values for types P-W are for stamps on documents with attractive engravings, usually stock certificates, bonds and insurance policies.

Examples on plain documents and cut squares sell for less.

Type A

Size: 22x25mm

RN-A1	2c	black	90.	75.
a.	Printed on both sides			30.
RN-A2	2c	orange		125.
RN-A3	2c	gray		
RN-A4	2c	blue		8,000.
RN-A5	2c	brown		
RN-A8	2c	purple		2,000.
RN-A9	2c	green		1,250.
a.	Inverted			—

No. RN-A4 is unique. The unique example of No. RN-A9a is on a partial document. The catalogue value for RN-A8 is for an impression on William Moller & Son stationery; a second more violet shade is on Carter, Kirkland & Co. receipts. Value of latter is $3,250.

Same Type with 1 Entire and 53 or 56 Partial Impressions in Vertical Format ("Tapeworm")
Left Col. — Full Document
Right Col. — Strip with Bank Names

RN-A10	2c **orange**, 1 full plus 56 partial impressions	750.	100.
	Cut square (full strip without bank names)		45.
RN-A11	2c **orange**, 1 full plus 53 partial impressions	1,250.	250.

Nos. RN-A10 and RN-A11 were used by the Mechanics' National Bank of New York on a bank specie clerk's statement. It was designed so that the full stamp or one of the repeated bottom segments fell on each line opposite the name of a bank.

The three additional banks were added at the bottom of the form. No. RN-A11 must show white space below the "First National Bank" line.

Eagle Type B

Size: 31x48mm

RN-B1	2c	**orange**	5.00	3.0
		yellow orange	5.00	3.0
		deep orange	5.00	3.0
a.	Printed on both sides		200.00	20.0
b.	Double impression		350.00	
c.	Printed on back			
d.	With 10 centimes blue French handstamp, right		400.00	
e.	Inverted			600.0

The unique example of No. RN-B1e is on a partial document[...]

All examples of the previously-listed "yellow" have some re[...] in them.

-B2	2c **black**	125.00	40.00
-B3	2c **blue**	125.00	40.00
	light blue	125.00	40.00
-B4	2c **brown**	125.00	40.00
-B5	2c **bronze**	125.00	40.00
-B6	2c **green** (shades)	110.00	15.00
-	2c **red** (shades)		
0		200.00	22.50
1	2c **purple**		
		100.00	125.00
1	2c **violet** (shades)		
3		125.00	40.00
	a. 2c **violet brown**	110.00	45.00

"Good only for checks and drafts payable at sight." in Rectangular Tablet at Base

N-	2c **orange**		
6		45.00	12.50
	a. With 2c orange red Nevada	325.00	225.00

"Good only for checks and drafts payable at sight." in Octagonal Tablet at Base

N-	2c **orange**		
7		42.50	10.00
	a. Tablet inverted		1,250.
	b. With 2c orange red Nevada	85.00	35.00
	c. With 2c green Nevada	100.00	35.00
	d. With 2c dull violet Nevada		1,500.
	e. With 2c brownish violet Nevada		2,500.

"Good when issued for the payment of money." in Octagonal Tablet at Base

N-	2c **orange**		
20		70.00	12.50
	a. Printed on both sides	30.00	10.00
	b. As "a," one stamp inverted		1,500.
	c. Tablet inverted		3,750.

"Good when issued for the payment of money" in two lines at base in orange

N-	2c **orange**		
23			900.00

"Good when the amount does not exceed $100." in Octagonal Tablet at Base

N-	2c **orange**		
24		200.00	90.00

Washington Type C

Size: 108x49mm

RN-C1	2c **orange**	7.00	4.00
	red orange	7.00	4.00
	yellow orange	7.00	4.00
	salmon	8.00	4.00
	brown orange	8.00	4.00
	a. "Good when used..." vert. at left		
	black		22.50

All examples of the previously-listed "yellow" have some red in them.

RN-C2	2c **brown**	30.00	12.00
	a. 2c **buff**	30.00	12.00
RN-C5	2c **pale red** (shades)	50.00	25.00
RN-C8	2c **green**	—	

"Good only for Sight Draft" in two lines in color of stamp

RN-C9	2c **orange**, legend at lower right	85.00	50.00
RN-C11	2c **brown**, legend at lower left	125.00	110.00
RN-C13	2c **orange**, legend at lower left	45.00	20.00

"Good only for Receipt for Money Paid" in two lines in color of stamp

RN-C15	2c **orange**, legend at lower right	2,500.	—
RN-C16	2c **orange**, legend at lower left		350.00

"Good when issued for the payment of money" in one line at base in color of stamp

RN-C17	2c **orange** (shades)		600.00

"Good when issued for the/Payment of Money" in two tablets at lower left and right

RN-C19	2c **orange**		550.00
	a. Printed on both sides		35.00

"Good/only for Bank/Check" in 3-part Band

RN-C21	2c **orange**	50.00	12.50
	salmon		12.50
	yellow orange		20.00
	a. Inverted		550.00
	b. With 2c red orange Nevada	140.00	65.00
	c. Printed on back		2,900.
RN-C22	2c **brown**	300.00	25.00
	a. Printed on back		500.00

"Good when the amount does not exceed $100" in tablet at lower right

RN-C26	2c **orange**		200.00

Franklin Type D

Size: 80x43mm

RN-D1	2c **orange** (shades)	5.00	2.00
	a. Double impression		—
	b. Printed on back	700.00	400.00
	c. Inverted		425.00

All examples of the previously-listed "yellow" have some red in them and are included in the "shades."

RN-D3	2c **brown**	—	500.00
RN-D4	2c **buff** (shades)	9.00	5.00
RN-D5	2c **red**		2,000.

"Good only for/Bank Check" in panels within circles at left and right

RN-D7	2c **orange**	25.00	10.00
	a. Printed on back		2,100.

"Good only for/Bank Check" in two lines at lower right in color of stamp

RN-D8	2c **orange**		750.00

"Good only for Sight Draft" in two lines at lower left in color of stamp

RN-D9	2c **orange**	175.00	75.00

Franklin Type E

Size: 28x50mm

RN-E2	2c **brown**		1,200.
RN-E4	2c **orange**	12.50	5.00
	Broken die, lower right or left	40.00	20.00
	a. Double impression		925.00

"Good only for sight draft" in two lines at base in orange

RN-E5	2c **orange**	75.00	30.00

"Good only for Bank / Check" in two lines at base in orange

RN-E6	2c **orange**		

"Good only for / Bank Check" in colorless letters in two lines above and below portrait

RN-E7	2c **orange**	75.00	17.50
	a. Double impression		—

Franklin Type F

Size: 56x34mm

RN-F1	2c **orange**	10.00	5.00
	a. Inverted		—

All examples of the previously-listed "yellow" have some red in them

Liberty Type G

Size: 80x48mm

RN-G1	2c **orange**	2.00	1.00
	a. Printed on back	65.00	40.00
	b. Printed on back, inverted	125.00	50.00

All examples of the previously-listed "yellow" have some red in them

Imprint: "Graphic Co., New York" at left and right in minute type

RN-G3	2c **orange**	110.00	100.00

Eagle Type H

Size: 32x50mm

RN-H3	2c **orange**	15.00	5.00
	a. Inverted		—
	b. Double impression		600.00
	c. "Good when used. . ." added in 2 lines at base, black		400.00
	d. As "c," legend added in 1 line upward at left, black		1,500.
	e. As "c," legend added in 1 line horiz., black	800.00	600.00
	f. As "c," legend in yellow		1,500.
	g. As "c," legend in red		500.00
	h. "Good for bank check . . ." added in black		150.00
	i. As "e," inverted legend		—

"Good for check or sight draft only" at left and right in color of stamp

RN-H5	2c **orange**		

Experts claim that No. RN-H5 exists only as a proof.

Type I
Design R2 of 1862-72 adhesive revenues
Size: 20x23mm
"BANK CHECK"

RN-I1	2c **orange**		225.00

"U.S. INTER. REV."

RN-I2	2c **orange**	650.00	350.00

Washington Type J

Size: 105x40mm
Background of medallion crosshatched, filling oval except for bust

RN-J4	2c **orange**	20.00	10.00
	pale orange	20.00	10.00
	deep orange	50.00	12.50
a.	Double impression		
b.	"Good only for . . ." added vertically at left in red orange		750.00
RN-J5	2c **red**	50.00	12.00
a.	Double impression		—

"Good for check or sight draft only" curved, below

RN-J9	2c **red**	—	2,000.

Background shaded below bust and at left.

RN-J11	2c **orange**	60.00	15.00

Washington Type K

Size: 84x33mm

RN-K1	2c **blue**		—
RN-K4	2c **gray**	45.00	15.00
	pale gray	45.00	10.00
RN-K5	2c **brown**	175.00	125.00
RN-K6	2c **orange**	15.00	7.50
RN-K8	2c **red** (shades)	600.00	350.00
RN-K11	2c **olive**	200.00	175.00
	pale olive		110.00

Washington Type L

Size: 50x33mm

RN-L1	2c **blue** (shades)	200.00	—
RN-L2	2c **turquoise**	250.00	200.00
RN-L3	2c **gray**	35.00	20.00
	pale gray	35.00	20.00
RN-L4	2c **green**	900.00	600.00
	light green	600.00	400.00
RN-L5	2c **orange**	15.00	10.00
RN-L6	2c **olive**		55.00
	gray olive		30.00
RN-L10	2c **red**	15.00	10.00
a.	2c violet red	15.00	10.00
RN-L13	2c **brown**	—	300.00

Washington Type M

Size: 68x37mm

RN-M2	2c **orange**	50.	10.
a.	Printed on back, inverted		1,600.

All examples of the previously-listed "yellow" have some red in them.

RN-M3	2c **green**		475.
RN-M4	2c **gray**		1,250.

Eagle, Numeral and Monitor Type N

Size: 107x48mm

RN-N3	2c **orange**	60.00	15.00
a.	Printed on back	300.00	225.00
b.	Inverted		900.00
RN-N4	2c **light brown**		150.00

Liberty Type O

Size: 75x35mm

RN-O2	2c **orange**	1,750.	600.

Values for types P-W
are for stamps on documents with attractive engravings, usually stock certificates, bonds and insurance policies. Examples on plain documents sell for less.

Lincoln Type P

Size: 32x49mm

RN-P2	5c **brown**		350.00
	Cut square		90.00
RN-P3	5c **green**		—
RN-P4	5c **pink**		—
RN-P5	5c **orange**	55.00	40.00
	Cut square		7.00

All examples of the previously listed "yellow" have some orange in them.

RN-P6	5c **red** (shades)	—	225.00
	Cut square		40.00

No. RN-P3 only exists in combination with a 25c green or 50c green. No. RN-P4 is unique and only exists in combination with a $1 pink. See Nos. RN-T2, RN-V1, RN-W6.

Madison Type Q (See note before No. RN-P2)

Size: 28x56mm

RN-Q1	5c **orange**	175.	15
	Cut square		2
	brownish orange	175.	15
RN-Q2	5c **brown**		2,75
	Cut square		50

Type R
Frame as Type B, Lincoln in center
Size: 32x49mm

RN-R1	10c **brown**		2,50
RN-R2	10c **pale red**	—	67
	Cut square		10
RN-R3	10c **orange**		50
	Cut square		5

"Good when the premium does not exceed $10" in tablet at base

RN-R6	10c **orange**	—	40
	Cut square		5

Motto Without Tablet

RN-R7	10c **orange**		
	Cut square		50

Washington Type S
(See note before No. RN-P2)

Size: 33x54mm

RN-S1	10c **orange**		3,750

"Good when the premium does not exceed $10" in tablet at base

RN-S2	10c **orange**		4,750
	Cut square		400

Eagle Type T
(See note before No. RN-P2)

For type T design with Lincoln in center see type V, Nos. RN-V1 to RN-V10.

Size: 33x40mm

N-T1	25c **black**	—	
	Cut square		
N-T2	25c **green**		*7,500.*
N-T3	25c **red**	175.00	*100.00*
	Cut square		9.00
N-T4	25c **orange**	150.00	75.00
	Cut square		7.50
	light orange	150.00	75.00
	light orange, cut square		7.50
	brown orange		75.00
	brown orange, cut square		8.00

No. RN-T2 includes No. RN-P3, and a 25c green, type T, literating a No. RN-V4.

"Good when the premium does not exceed $50" in tablet at base

N-T6	25c **orange**	450.	350.
	Cut square		50.
N-T7	25c **orange**, motto without tablet		1,500.
	Cut square		400.

"Good when the amount insured shall not exceed $1000" in tablet at base

N-T8	25c **deep orange**	800.	700.
	Cut square		75.
N-T9	25c **orange**, motto without tablet		
	Cut square		600.

Franklin Type U (See note before No. RN-P2)

Size: 126x65mm

N-U1	25c **orange**	35.00	35.00
	Cut square		5.00
N-U2	25c **brown**	45.00	35.00
	Cut square		5.00

"Good when the premium does not exceed $50" in tablet at lower right

RN-U3	25c **orange**		*2,500.*
	Cut square		400.

Tablet at lower left

RN-U5	25c **red**	800.	
	Cut square		250.
RN-U6	25c **orange**	500.	450.
	Cut square		65.

All examples of the previously-listed "yellow" have some red a them.

Tablet at base

RN-U7	25c **brown**		*1,750.*
	Cut square		300.
RN-U9	25c **orange**		*1,000.*
	Cut square		400.

Lincoln Type V

Size: 32x41mm

RN-V1	50c **green**		175.00
	Cut square		52.50
RN-V2	50c **brown**	—	400.00
	Cut square		125.00
RN-V4	50c **orange**	175.00	90.00
	Cut square		17.50
	deep orange	175.00	90.00
	deep orange, cut square		17.50
RN-V5	50c **red**	700.00	
	Cut square		250.00

No. RN-V1 includes a 50c green, type V, and a No. RN-P3, obliterating a No. RN-W2.

"Good when the amount insured shall not exceed $5000" in tablet at base

RN-V6	50c **orange**	450.00	400.00
	Cut square		60.00

RN-V9	50c **red**	—	
	Cut square		500.00

Motto Without Tablet

RN-V10	50c **orange**		
	Cut square		500.00

Washington Type W
(See note before No. RN-P2)

Size: 34x73mm

RN-W2	$1 **orange** (shades)	150.00	90.00
	Cut square		15.00
RN-W5	$1 **brown**		*4,500.*
RN-W6	$1 **pink**		*3,750.*

The former light brown is now included with the orange shades.

No. RN-W6 used with No. RN-P4 is unique. Two examples of No. RN-W6 exist used alone.

SPANISH-AMERICAN WAR SERIES

Many of these stamps were used for parlor car tax and often were torn in two or more parts.

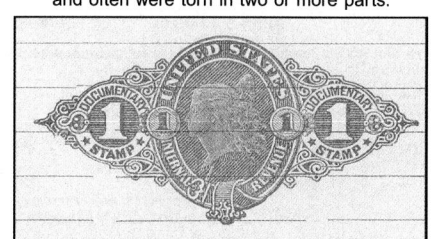

Liberty Type X

1898		Size: 68x38mm	
RN-X1	1c **rose**	800.00	
	Partial		65.00
	dark red, partial		65.00
RN-X4	1c **orange**	165.00	
	a. On pullman ticket	600.00	—
	Partial		25.00
	b. As "a," printed on back		
	As "a," printed on back, partial		65.00
RN-X5	1c **green**	65.00	30.00
	Partial		25.00
	a. On parlor car ticket	65.00	15.00
	b. On pullman ticket	500.00	
	On pullman ticket, partial		15.00
RN-X6	2c **yellow**	2.00	1.00
	pale olive		*900.00*
RN-X7	2c **orange**	1.50	1.00
	pale orange	1.50	1.00
	a. Printed on back only	400.00	400.00
	c. Printed on front and back	—	—
	d. Vertical		85.00
	e. Double impression		
	f. On pullman ticket	1,000.	200.00
	g. Inverted		550.00

The substantial reduction recently in catalogue value for No. RN-X7g is due to a new discovery of 25 additional examples.

No. RN-X1 exists only as a four-part unused pullman ticket, used as an unsevered auditor's and passenger's parts of the four-part ticket, or partial as a used half of a two-part ticket. Nos. RN-X4a and RN-X5b exist as unused two-part tickets and as used half portions. No. RN-X7f exists as an unused four-part ticket and as a used two-piece portion with nearly complete stamp design.

PRIVATE DIE PROPRIETARY STAMPS

The extraordinary demands of the Civil War upon the Federal Treasury resulted in Congress devising and passing the Revenue Act of 1862. The Government provided revenue stamps to be affixed to boxes or packages of matches, and to proprietary medicines, perfumery, playing cards — as well as to documents, etc.

But manufacturers were permitted, at their expense, to have dies engraved and plates made for their exclusive use. Many were only too willing to do this because a discount or premium of from 5% to 10% was allowed on orders from the dies which often made it possible for them to undersell their competitors and too, the considerable advertising value of the stamps could not be overlooked. These are now known as Private Die Proprietary stamps.

The face value of the stamp used on matches was determined by the number, i.e., 1c for each 100 matches or fraction thereof. Medicines and perfumery were taxed at the rate of 1c for each 25 cents of the retail value or fraction thereof up to $1 and 2c for each 50 cents or fraction above that amount. Playing cards were first taxed at the same rate but subsequently the tax was 5c for a deck of 52 cards and 10c for a greater number of cards or double decks.

The stamp tax was repealed on March 3, 1883, effective July 1, 1883.

The various papers were:

a. Old paper, 1862-71. First Issue. Hard and brittle varying from thick to thin.

b. Silk paper, 1871-77. Second Issue. Soft and porous with threads of silk, mostly red, blue and black, up to ¼ inch in length.

c. Pink paper, 1877-78. Third Issue. Soft paper colored pink ranging from pale to deep shades.

d. Watermarked paper, 1878-83. Fourth Issue. Soft porous paper showing part of "USIR." Roulettes on unwatermarked paper are rouletted 6.

e. Experimental silk paper. Medium smooth paper, containing minute fragments of silk threads either blue alone or blue and red (infrequent), widely scattered, sometimes but a single fiber on a stamp.

Early printings of some private die revenue stamps are on paper which appears to have laid lines.

These stamps were usually torn in opening the box or container. **Values quoted are for examples which are somewhat faulty but reasonably attractive, with the faults usually not readily apparent on the face.** Nos. RS278-RS306 are valued in the grade of very fine. Sound examples of these stamps (other than Nos. RS278-RS306) at a grade of fine-very fine can sell for 50% to 300% more than catalogue value. Outstanding examples of stamps in this section with a lower catalogue value can bring up to 10 times catalogue value.

	a. Old Paper	b. Silk Paper	c. Pink Paper	d. Wmkd. USIR (191R)

PRIVATE DIE MATCH STAMPS

1864   ——— A ———   *Perf. 12*

Akron Match Company — RO1

Akron Match Company

RO1	1c	blue	250.00

Alexander's Matches — RO2   J.J. Allen's Sons — RO4

Alexander's Matches

RO2	1c	orange	25.00	90.00
RO3	1c	blue		4,000.

J. J. Allen's Sons

RO4	1c	blue			14.00

Thos. Allen — RO5

Thos. Allen

RO5	1c	green	125.00

Allen & Powers — RO6

Allen & Powers

As No. RO141, inscribed "Allen & Powers" instead of "Orono Match Co."

RO6	1c	blue	7.00	25.00	10.00

Alligator Match Company

RO7	1c	blue			20.00
		Dbl. transfer			—
RO8	1c	bl, roulette			85.00

American Fusee Company — RO9

American Fusee Company

RO9	1c	black	7.50	10.00	7.50
		Dbl. transfer	100.00		

American Match Company — RO10

American Match Co.

RO10	1c	black	115.00		30.00
	e.	Experimental silk paper	—		
RO11	3c	black	425.00	125.00	
		Dbl. transfer		200.00	
	e.	Experimental silk paper	1,000.		

American Match Co. — RO12   American Match Co. — RO13

RO12	1c	black	55.00
RO13	3c	green, Rock Island	8,500.

Arnold & Co. — RO14

Arnold & Co.

RO14	1c	black	50.00

——— B ———

Bagley & Dunham — RO15

Bagley & Dunham

RO15	1c	green	27.50

Geo. & O. C. Barber

As No. RO17, inscribed "Geo. & O. C. Barber" instead of "Barber Match Co."

RO16	1c	blue	65.00

Barber Match Co. — RO17

Barber Match Co.

RO17	1c	blue	22.50	1.00	16.00	1.50
		Dbl. transfer	77.50	30.00	77.50	30.00
e.		Experimental silk paper	95.00			
u.	1c	ultra	350.00			
RO18	1c	bl, roulette				3,500.
RO19	3c	black	175.00	125.00		
e.		Experimental silk paper	375.00			

Barber & Peckham — RO20

Barber & Peckham

RO20	1c	blue	60.00	
RO21	3c	black	175.00	

Bauer & Beudel

RO22	1c	blue	65.00	140.00
u.	1c	ultra	175.00	

A.B. & S. (A. Beecher & Son) — RO23

A. B. & S. (A. Beecher & Son)

As No. RO175, inscribed "A. B. & S." instead of "C. B. C. S." in the four corners.

RO23	1c	orange	15.00	57.50
		Dbl. transfer	—	—
e.		Experimental silk paper	110.00	
		As "e," dbl. transfer	—	

B. Bendel & Co. — RO25

Illustration reduced.

B. Bendel & Co.

RO24	1c	brown	2.50	500.00
		Dbl. transfer	—	
RO25	12c	brown	250.00	

H. Bendel — RO26

H. Bendel

Nos. RO26-RO27 are RO24-RO25 altered to read "H. Bendel doing business as B. Bendel & Co."

RO26	1c	brown	4.50	2.25	1.75
RO27	12c	brown	450.00		

H. & M. Bentz — RO28   Bent & Lea — RO29

H. & M. Bentz

RO28	1c	blue	37.50

Bent & Lea

RO29	1c	black	35.000
		Double transfer at left	110.00
e.		Experimental silk paper	35.00
		Double transfer	500.00

B. J. & Co. — RO30   Bock, Schneider & Co. — RO31

B. J. & Co. (Barber, Jones & Co.)

As No. RO100 with "B. J. & Co." added above eagle.

RO30	1c	green	95.00
		Dbl. transfer	140.00

Bock, Schneider & Co.

RO31	1c	black	17.50

Wm. Bond & Co. — RO32/RO33   Bousfield & Poole — RO34/RO35

Wm. Bond & Co.

RO32	4c	black	250.00	
RO33	4c	green	160.00	175.00	16.00

Bousfield & Poole

RO34	1c	lilac	140.00	
		Dbl. transfer	135.00	
RO35	1c	black	16.00	11.00
		Dbl. transfer	62.50	82.50
e.		Experimental silk paper	55.00	
RO36	3c	lilac	2,500.	

For illustration of No. RO37, see large stamp illustration pages.

RO37	3c	black	175.00	140.00
		Dbl. transfer		110.00

		Experimental silk paper	375.00

Boutell & Maynard — RO38

Boutell & Maynard

RO38	1c	black	225.00

Bowers & Dunham

As No. RO15, inscribed "Bowers & Dunham" instead of "Bagley & Dunham."

RO39	1c	green	250.00
RO40	1c	blue	85.00

B. & N. (Brocket & Newton)

RO41	1c	lake, die I	40.00
RO42	1c	lake, die II	7.50

The initials "B. & N." measure 5¼mm across the top in Die I, and 4¾mm in Die II.

Brown & Durling

RO43

RO43	1c	black	1,750.
RO44	1c	green	75.00

L. W. Buck & Co. — RO45

L. W. Buck & Co.

RO45	1c	black	2,500.
e.		Experimental silk paper	900.00

D. Burhans & Co. — RO46

D. Burhans & Co.

RO46	1c	**black**	140.00	6,000.
		Dbl. transfer	250.00	
	e.	Experimental silk paper	750.00	

Charles Busch — RO47

Charles Busch

| RO47 | 1c | **black** | 32.50 |

Byam, Carlton & Co. — RO48

2 heads to left, 41x75mm.

Byam, Carlton & Co.

| RO48 | 1c | **black**, imperf | 3,500. |

Byam, Carlton & Co. — RO49

RO49	1c	**black,** 19x23mm	25.00	7.00		1.25
		Dbl. transfer		125.00		
	e.	Experimental silk paper	85.00			
	i.	Vert. pair, imperf horiz.		125.00		
RO50	1c	**black**	2,500.			

2 heads to left, buff wrapper, 131x99mm.

For illustrations of Nos. RO51, RO52, RO54, RO55 and RO56, see large stamp illustration pages.

| RO51 | 1c | **black** | 225.00 |

As #RO50, 131x89mm.

| RO52 | 1c | **black** | 55.00 |

1 head to right, white wrapper, 94x54mm.

| RO53 | 1c | **black** | 150.00 |

As #RO52, buff wrapper.

| RO54 | 1c | **black** | 9.00 |
| | h. | Up | 50.00 |

2 heads to right, buff wrapper, 81x50mm.
#RO54h has right block reading up.

| RO55 | 1c | **black** | 30.00 |

1 head to left, white wrapper, 94x56mm.

| RO56 | 1c | **black** | 7.50 |

As #RO50, 95x57mm.

--- **C** ---

Cannon Match Co. — RO57

Cannon Match Co.

As No. RO68, "Cannon Match Co." instead of "W. D. Curtis."

| RO57 | 1c | **green** | 45.00 |

Cardinal Match Co. — RO58

Cardinal Match Co.

| RO58 | 1c | **lake** | 27.50 |

F. E. C. (Frank E. Clark)

As No. RO41, "F.E.C." instead of "B. & N."

| RO59 | 1c | **lake** | 75.00 | 75.00 |
| | e. | Experimental silk paper | 100.00 | |

Chicago Match Co. — RO60

Henry A. Clark — RO61

Chicago Match Co.

| RO60 | 3c | **black** | 400.00 |

Henry A. Clark

| RO61 | 1c | **green** | 90.00 |

Jas. L. Clark — RO62/RO63

Clark Match Co. — RO64

Jas. L. Clark

RO62	1c	**green**	2.50	25.00		1.50
		Dbl. transfer				60.00
RO63	1c	**green**, rouletted				800.00

The Clark Match Co.

| RO64 | 1c | **lake** | 10.00 |

Cramer & Kemp — RO65/RO66

Crown Match Co. — RO67

Cramer & Kemp

RO65	1c	**black**	45.00	
RO66	1c	**blue,**	110.00	7.00
	e.	Experimental silk paper	210.00	
	u.	1c **ultra**	375.00	

Crown Match Co.

| RO67 | 1c | **black** | 22.50 |

W. D. Curtis Matches — RO68

W. D. Curtis Matches

| RO68 | 1c | **green** | 140.00 | 125.00 |
| | e. | Experimental silk paper | 175.00 | |

--- **D** ---

G. W. H. Davis — RO69/RO70

G. W. H. Davis

| RO69 | 1c | **black** | 47.50 | |
| RO70 | 1c | **carmine** | | 80.0 |

W.E. Doolittle — RO71

W. E. Doolittle

| RO71 | 1c | **blue** | 400.00 |

E. P. Dunham

| RO72 | 1c | **green** | | 80.0 |

--- **E** ---

Jas. Eaton — RO73   Jas. Eaton — RO74

Jas. Eaton

RO73	1c	**black**	50.00	1.25	17.50	1.5
	e.	Experimental silk paper	150.00			
RO74	1c	**black**, rouletted			55.00	

B. Eddy — RO75   E.B. Eddy — RO75A

E. B. Eddy

O75	1c	car, die I		22.50	
O75A	1c	car, die II		35.00	

Die II shows eagle strongly recut; ribbon across bottom is narrower; color is deeper.

Aug. Eichele

Aug. Eichele — RO76

O76	1c	black	125.00	

P. Eichele & Co. — RO77

P. Eichele & Co.

As No. RO78, "P. Eichele & Co." at top.

O77	1c	blue	60.00	7.50
	e.	Experimental silk paper	150.00	
	u.	1c ultra	350.00	

Eichele & Co. — RO78/RO79   J.W. Eisenhart's — RO80

Eichele & Co.

O78	1c	blue	4.50	17.50	4.00
O79	1c	blue, rouletted			250.00

J. W. Eisenhart's Matches

O80	1c	blue	50.00	95.00	37.50

Excelsior Match Co. (Watertown) — RO81/RO82

Excelsior Match Co.

O81	1c	black, Watertown, N.Y.	95.00	
O82	1c	black, Syracuse, N.Y.	9.00	16.00	9.00
		Dbl. transfer			47.50

Excelsior Match, Baltimore — RO83

Excelsior Match, Baltimore, Md.

RO83	1c	blue	85.00	115.00
	u.	1c ultra	725.00	

F

G. Farr & Co. — RO84   L. Frank — RO85

G. Farr & Co.

RO84	1c	black	125.00

L. Frank

RO85	1c	brown	100.00

G

Gardner, Beer & Co. — RO86   Wm. Gates — RO88

Gardner, Beer & Co.

RO86	1c	black	225.00

Wm. Gates

RO87	1c	black, die I	8.00	5.50
RO88	1c	black, die II	45.00	5.00
		Dbl. transfer		30.00
	e.	Experimental silk paper	175.00	

The shirt collar is colorless in Die I and shaded in Die II. The colorless circle surrounding the portrait appears about twice as wide on Die I as it does on Die II.

For illustration of No. RO89, see large stamp illustration pages.

RO89	3c	black	55.00	47.50
		Dbl. transfer	82.50	80.00
	e.	Experimental silk paper	180.00	
RO90	6c	black	180.00	
RO91	3c	black, 3 1c stamps	140.00	

William Gates' Sons — RO92

William Gates' Sons

The 1c is as No. RO87, 3c as No. RO91, "William Gates' Sons" replaces "Wm. Gates."

For illustration of No. RO94, see large stamp illustration pages.

RO92	1c	black	30.00	10.00	2.00
RO93	1c	black, rouletted			2,750.
RO94	3c	black, 3 1c stamps	125.00	175.00	85.00

A. Goldback & Co. — RO95

A. Goldback & Co.

RO95	1c	green	50.00

A. Goldback

As No. RO95, "A. Goldback" instead of "A. Goldback & Co."

RO96	1c	green	125.00	12,500.

T. Gorman & Bro.

As No. RO99, "T. Gorham & Bro." instead of "Thomas Gorham."

RO97	1c	black	800.00	
		Dbl. transfer	—	
RO98	1c	green	30.00	35.00
		Dbl. transfer	—	

Thomas Gorman

RO99	1c	green	4.00	35.00	75.00

Greenleaf & Co. — RO101/RO102   Griggs & Goodwill — RO103/RO104

Greenleaf & Co.

RO100	1c	green	90.00	125.00
	e.	Experimental silk paper	575.00	
RO101	3c	carmine	85.00	160.00
	e.	Experimental silk paper	950.00	
RO102	5c	orange	160.00	3,000.
	e.	Experimental silk paper	400.00	

Griggs & Goodwill

RO103	1c	black	55.00
RO104	1c	green	30.00
		Dbl. transfer	150.00

Griggs & Scott

As No. RO69, inscribed "Griggs & Scott" instead of "G. W. H. Davis."

RO105	1c	black	11.00	37.50
	e.	Experimental silk paper	50.00	

Bousfield & Poole – RO37

Byam, Carlton & Co. – RO51

Byam, Carlton & Co. – RO52

Byam, Carlton & Co. – RO54

Byam, Carlton & Co. – RO55

Byam, Carlton & Co. – RO56

Wm. Gates – RO89

William Gates' Sons – RO94

P.T. Ives – RO118

H

Charles S. Hale — RO106

Charles S. Hale
RO106 1c green   275.00

Henning & Bonhack
RO107 1c blue   250.00

W. E. Henry & Co. — RO108

W. E. Henry & Co.
RO108 1c red   30.00
RO109 1c black   15.00

J. G.   L. G.
Hotchkiss — RO110   Hunt — RO113

The J. G. Hotchkiss Match Co.
RO110 1c green   15.00   45.00   11.00

B. & H. D. Howard
RO111 1c lake   95.00
RO112 1c blue   11.00
       u. 1c ultra   225.00

L. G. Hunt
RO113 1c black   225.00   1,500.
       e. Experi-   175.00
           mental
           silk pa-
           per

D. F. Hutchinson Jr.
RO114 1c lake   20.00

I

Ives Matches
As No. RO116, "Ives Matches" instead of "P. T. Ives."
RO115 1c blue   7.00   6.00
       Dbl.   —
       transfer
       u. 1c ultra   260.00

P. T. Ives —   Ives &
RO116/RO117   Judd — RO119

P. T. Ives
For illustration of No. RO118, see large stamp illustration pages.

RO116 1c blue   7.00   40.00   4.50
RO117 1c blue, rouletted   500.00

RO118 8c blue   210.00
       e. Experimental 850.
           silk
           paper
       u. 8c ultra   3,000.

Ives & Judd
RO119 1c green   25.00   60.00   140.00

Ives & Judd Match
Co. — RO120

The Ives & Judd Match Co.
RO120 1c green   125.00
       Dbl. transfer   250.00

K

Kirby & Sons

Kirby & Sons — RO121

RO121 1c green   70.00

W. S. Kyle
RO122 1c black   20.00   15.00
       Dbl.   75.00
       transfer
       e. Experi-   —
           mental
           silk pa-
           per

L

Lacour's Matches
RO123 1c black   17.50   55.00
       Dbl.   100.00
       transfer
       e. Experi-   80.00
           mental
           silk pa-
           per

Leeds, Robinson &
Co. — RO124

Leeds, Robinson & Co.
RO124 1c green   75.00

H. Leigh
RO125 1c blue   10.00

Leigh & Palmer
As No. RO125, "Leigh & Palmer" replaces "H. Leigh."
RO126 1c black   22.50   70.00   42.50

John Loehr — RO127

John Loehr
RO127 1c blue   25.00

Joseph Loehr
As No. RO127, "Joseph" replaces "John."
RO128 1c blue   3.25   17.50   5.00

M

John J.
Macklin &
Co. — RO129

John J. Macklin & Co.
RO129 1c blk, rou-   10,000.
           lette

F. Mansfield &   Maryland Match
Co. — RO130   Co. — RO131

F. Mansfield & Co.
RO130 1c blue   6.50   12.50   12

Maryland Match Co.
RO131 1c blue   125.00   25,0

"Matches" — RO132   A.
                              Messinger — RO1

"Matches"
RO132 1c blue   7.00   5.00
       Dbl.   95.00
       transfer
       e. Experi-   135.00
           mental
           silk pa-
           per
       u. 1c ultra   950.00
           See Nos. RO168-RO169.

A. Messinger
RO133 1c black   4.00   16.00   3

N

National Match
Co. — RO134

F. P.
Newton — RO135

National Match Co.

RO134	1c	blue	75.00	

Newbauer & Co. (N. & C.) follows No. RO139.

National Union Match Co. items are bogus.

F. P. Newton

RO135	1c	lake	3.00	12.00	4.00

See No. RO64 for another "The Clark Match Co." design.

N.Y. Match Co. — RO136

N.Y. Match Co.

No. RO136 is as No. RO22, "N.Y. Match Co." instead of "Bauer & Beudel."

RO136	1c	blue,	500.00	8.00
		shield		

No. RO137 is as No. RO111, "N.Y. Match Co." instead of "B. H. D. Howard."

RO137	1c	ver, eagle	85.00	6,000.
e.		Experimental silk paper	150.00	
		As "e," dbl. transfer	240.00	

RO139

New York Match Company

RO138	1c	green, 22x60mm	55.00	10.00
e.		Experimental silk paper	75.00	
RO139	5c	blue, 22x60mm	2,500.	

N. & C. (Newbauer & Co.)

RO140	4c	green	5.00	125.00	6.00

O

Orono Match Co.

RO141	1c	blue	35.00	35.00
e.		Experimental silk paper	275.00	

---

u.	1c ultra	500.00	

P

Park City Match Co. — RO142

Park City Match Co.

RO142	1c	green	50.00	47.50
e.		Experimental silk paper	275.00	
RO143	3c	orange	55.00	—
e.		Experimental silk paper		

Penn Match Co. Limited

RO144	1c	blue	45.00

Pierce Match Co. — RO145

Pierce Match Co.

RO145	1c	green	2,500.

P. M. Co. (Portland M. Co.)

RO146	1c	black	25.00

Portland Match Co.

RO147	1c	black, wrapper	100.00

The value of No. RO147 applies to commonest date (Dec. 1866); all others are much rarer.

RO148

V.R. Powell — RO149-
RO151

V. R. Powell

RO148	1c	blue	8.00	11.00
		Dbl. transfer	100.00	

---

e.		Experimental silk paper	135.00	
u.	1c ultra		350.00	
RO149	1c	black	6,500.	
		Buff wrapper, uncut.		
RO150	1c	black	2,500.	
		Buff wrapper, cut to shape.		
RO151	1c	black	2,750.	
		White wrapper, cut to shape.		

R

Reading Match Company

RO152	1c	black	9.00

Reed & Thompson — RO153

Reed & Thompson

RO153	1c	black	20.00

D.M. Richardson
RO155

D.M. Richardson
RO156

D. M. Richardson

RO154	1c	red	140.00	
RO155	1c	black	3.75	3.00
		Dbl. transfer		40.00
e.		Experimental silk paper	55.00	
RO156	3c	ver	165.00	
RO157	3c	blue	7.00	4.50
		Dbl. transfer		27.50
e.		Experimental silk paper	67.50	

The Richardson
Match Co. — RO158

H. & W.
Roeber — RO160

The Richardson Match Co.

The 1c is as No. RO154, 3c as No. RO156, inscribed "The Richardson Match Co." instead of "D. M. Richardson."

RO158	1c	black	2.00	6.00	8.00
RO159	3c	blue	85.00		

H. & W. Roeber

RO160	1c	blue	7.25	2.75
		Dbl. transfer	175.00	
e.		Experimental silk paper	400.00	
u.	1c ultra		225.00	

J.C. Ayer & Co. – RS4

Barham Pile Cure Co. – RS14

**D.S. Barnes
RS16**

**D.S. Barnes
RS17**

**Demas
Barnes
RS23**

Demas Barnes & Co. – RS24

T.H. Barr & Co. RS27

**Fred Brown Co.
RS37**

**Dr.
John
Bull
RS42**

John I. Brown & Son RS39

J.W. Campion & Co. – RS47

Cannon & Co. – RS49

Dr. A.W. Chase, Son & Co. – RS55

Oliver Crook & Co. – RS65

Jeremiah Curtis & Son – RS67

Dalley's
Galvanic Horse
Salve – RS73

Dalley's Magical Pain Extractor – RS74

L. Pills – RS90

The Father Mathew
Temperance &
Manufacturing
Company – RS85

(Dr.) S.B. Hartman & Co. – RS100

John F. Henry
RS114

Hiscox
& Co.
RS123

Herrick's Pills
RS117

William Roeber — RO161

William Roeber

As No. RO160, "William Roeber" instead of "H. & W. Roeber."

RO161	1c	blue		2.50	8.00	3.75
RO162	1c	bl, roulette				110.00

E. T. Russell — RO163

E. T. Russell

RO163	1c	black	8.50	17.50
	e.	Experimental silk paper	42.50	

R. C. & W. (Ryder, Crouse & Welch)

RO164	1c	lake	85.00

— S —

San Francisco Match Co. — RO165

Illustration reduced.

San Francisco Match Company

RO165	12c	blue	500.00

Schmitt & Schmittdiel — RO166/RO167

Schmitt & Schmittdiel

RO166	1c	ver	5.00	90.00	5.00
RO167	3c	blue	60.00		

E. K. Smith — RO168/RO169

Standard Match Co. — RO170

E. K. Smith

RO168	1c	blue	12.50	50.00	17.50
RO169	1c	blue, roulette			6,000.

See No. RO132.

The Standard Match Company

RO170	1c	black	32.50

H. Stanton — RO171

H. Stanton

RO171	1c	black	15.00	10.00	20.00	9.00
	e.	Experimental silk paper	75.00			

Star Match — RO172

Star Match

RO172	1c	black	5.00	1.00	1.75	.75
		Dbl. transfer		—		17.50
	e.	Experimental silk paper	30.00			

Swift & Courtney — RO173

Swift & Courtney

As No. RO174, "Swift & Courtney" in one line.

RO173	1c	blue	3.00	3.00	
		Dbl. transfer		—	
	e.	Experimental silk paper	30.00		
	u.	1c ultra	75.00		

RO174	RO175
Swift & Courtney & Beecher Co.	Swift & Courtney & Beecher

Swift & Courtney & Beecher Co.

RO174	1c	blue	3.00	5.00	2.00
		Dbl. transfer			—
RO175	1c	black			90.00

— T —

Trenton Match Co. — RO176

Trenton Match Co.

RO176	1c	blue	11.00

E. R. T. (E. R. Tyler)

As No. RO120, inscribed "E. R. T." instead of "The Ives Judd Match Co."

RO177	1c	green	15.00	4.00
		Dbl. transfer		—
	e.	Experimental silk paper	80.00	

— U —

Alex. Underwood & Co.

RO178	1c	green	85.00	140.00
	e.	Experimental silk paper	325.00	

Union Match Co. — RO179

U.S.M. Co. — RO180

Union Match Co.

RO179	1c	black	55.

U. S. M. Co. (Universal Safety Match Co.)

RO180	1c	black	4.00	27.50
	e.	Experimental silk paper	70.00	

— W —

Washington Match Co. — RO181

Wilmington Parlor Match Co. — RO182

Washington Match Co.

RO181	1c	black	50.00

Wilmington Parlor Match Co.

RO182	1c	black	160.00	6,000.
	e.	Experimental silk paper	225.00	

Wise & Co. — RO183

Wise & Co.

RO183	1c	black	1,750.

— Z —

F. Zaiss & Co. — RO184

F. Zaiss & Co.

RO184	1c	black	2.00	8.00	2.50

Zisemann, Griesheim & Co.

RO185	1c	green	1,750.	
RO186	1c	blue	140.00	22.50
	u.	1c ultra	800.00	

PRIVATE DIE CANNED FRUIT STAMP

a.	b.	c.	d.
Old Paper	Silk Paper	Pink Paper	Wmkd. USIR (191R)

T. Kensett & Co. — RP1

67   *Perf. 12*

T. Kensett & Co.

P1   1c   **green**   2,250.

a.	b.	c.	d.
Old Paper	Silk Paper	Pink Paper	Wmkd. USIR (191R)

PRIVATE DIE MEDICINE STAMPS

62   *Perf. 12*

———— **A** ————

Anglo American Drug Co. — RS1

Anglo American Drug Co.

RS1   1c   **black**   70.00

J. C. Ayer & Co.

or illustration of No. RS4, see large stamp illustration pages.

RS2	1c	**brn car,** imperf	10,000.			
RS3	1c	**green,** imperf	17,500.			
RS4	1c	**black,** imperf, type 1	150.00	125.00		75.00
		Type 2 Dbl. transfer	150.00	125.00	1,500.	70.00
	e.	Experimental silk paper	—			

Type 1: long, full-pointed "y" in "Ayers;" Type 2: short, truncated "y" in "Ayers."

RS5	1c	**blue,** imperf	10,000.
RS6	1c	**org,** imperf	17,500.
RS6F	1c	**red,** imperf	—
RS7	1c	**gray lilac,** imperf	17,500.

J.C. Ayer & Co. RS8, RS9, RS11/RS13

J.C. Ayer & Co. RS10

RS8	4c	**red,** die cut	10,000.		
RS9	4c	**blue,** die cut	8.50	8.50	8.50
	e.	Experimental silk paper	—		
	u.	**4c ultra** (die cut)	525.00		
RS10	4c	**blue,** imperf	350.00	250.00	325.00
RS11	4c	**purple,** die cut	17,500.		
RS12	4c	**green,** die cut	15,000.		
RS13	4c	**ver,** die cut	10,000.		

The 4c in black was printed and sent to Ayer & Co. It may exist but has not been seen by collectors.

———— **B** ————

Barham Pile Cure Co.

For illustration of No. RS14, see large stamp illustration pages.

RS14   4c   **green,** wmkd. lozenges   85.00

D. S. Barnes

The 1c, 2c and 4c are about 184mm, 242mm and 304mm tall. The products mentioned differ. "D. S. Barnes" is in manscript.

For illustration of No. RS16 and RS17, see larger stamp illustration pages.

RS15	1c	**ver**	200.00
RS16	2c	**ver**	350.00
RS17	4c	**ver**	1,000.
RS18	1c	**black**	27.50
RS19	2c	**black**	55.00
RS20	4c	**black**	75.00

Demas Barnes

Same as above but with "Demas Barnes" in serifed letters.

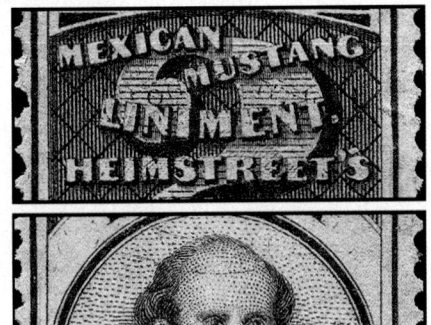

RS22 Foreign entry

For illustration of No. RS23, see large stamp illustration pages.

RS21	1c	**black**	25.00
RS22	2c	**black**	67.50
		Foreign entry of 1c (No. RS15 or RS21)	2,500.
RS23	4c	**black**	30.00

Demas Barnes & Co.

For illustration of No. RS24, see large stamp illustration pages.

RS24	1c	**black**	17.50	600.00
RS25	2c	**black**	17.50	450.00
	e.	Experimental silk paper	210.00	
RS26	4c	**black**	17.50	

T. H. Barr & Co.

For illustration of No. RS27, see larger stamp illustration pages.

RS27	4c	**black**	27.50	
		Dbl. transfer	200.00	
	e.	Experimental silk paper	275.00	

Barry's — RS28/RS29

Barry's

RS28	2c	**green,** Tricopherous	11.00	20.00	
RS29	2c	**grn,** Proprietary Dbl. transfer	6.50 250.00	175.00	5.50

D. M. Bennett — RS30

D. M. Bennett

RS30	1c	**lake**	17.50
	e.	Experimental silk paper	100.00

W. T. Blow — RS31

W. T. Blow

RS31	1c	**green**	300.00	70.00	300.00	85.00
	e.	Experimental silk paper	1,750.		

B. Brandreth — RS33   R. Brandreth — RS35

B. Brandreth

RS32	1c	**black,** perf	550.00	675.00
RS33	1c	**black,** imperf	2.50	1.50
	e.	Experimental silk paper	35.00	

Nos. RS32-RS33 inscribed "United States Certificate of Genuineness" around vignette.

RS34	1c	**blk,** 41x50mm, imperf	250.00		
RS35	1c	**blk,** 24x30mm, imperf	1.75	10.00	2.00
	p.	Perf	500.00		

The Home Bitters Co. – RS128

S.D. Howe – RS137

T.J. Husband – RS140

James A. Jackson & Co. – RS143

Dr. D. Jayne & Son – RS149

Lyon Manufg. Co. – RS167

**J.B. Kelly & Co.
RS153**

Dr. Jas. C. Kerr – RS159

Jacob Lippman & Bro. – RS163

T.W. Marsden – RS175

T.W. Marsden – RS176

Mercado & Seully – RS177

Mette & Kanne – RS180

Mishler Herb Bitters Co. – RS181

Moody, Michel & Co. – RS182

Morehead's – RS186

**New York Pharmacal Association
RS187**

Dr. M. Perl & Co. – RS188

Bennett Pieters & Co. – RS191

Bennett Pieters & Co. – RS192

**R. V.
Pierce
RS190**

Radway & Co. – RS193

M., P.J. & H.M. Sands – RS209

Dr. C.F. Brown — RS36

Dr. C. F. Brown

RS36	1c	**blue**	275.00	75.00	90.00

Fred Brown Co.

For illustration of No. RS37, see larger stamp illustration pages.

RS37	2c	**black,** imperf, die I	125.00	42.50	3,000.	35.00
	e.	Experimental silk paper	450.00			
RS38	2c	**black,** imperf, die II	75.00			

Die I has "E" of "Fred" incomplete. Die II shows recutting in the "E" of "Fred" and "Genuine."

John I. Brown & Son.

For illustration of No. RS39, see larger stamp illustration pages.

RS39	1c	**black**	10.00	40.00		9.00
RS40	2c	**green**	10.00	17.50	350.00	350.00
		Dbl. transfer	—			
	e.	Experimental silk paper	100.00			
RS41	4c	**brown**	350.00	100.00		2,000.

Dr. John Bull

For illustration of No. RS42, see larger stamp illustration pages.

RS42	1c	**black**	165.00	20.00	750.00	20.00
	e.	Experimental silk paper	325.00			
RS43	4c	**blue**	200.00	12.00	550.00	11.00
	e.	Experimental silk paper	400.00			
	u.	4c **ultra**	1,250.			

J. S. Burdsal & Co.

"J. S. Burdsal & Co./Sole Proprietors" added under United States Proprietary Medicine Co. design, as on Nos. RS245-RS247.

RS44	1c	**blk,** wrapper, white paper	55.00		35.00
RS45	1c	**blk,** wrapper, orange paper	4,000.		800.00

Joseph Burnett & Co. — RS46

Joseph Burnett & Co.

RS46	4c	**black**	100.00	14.50	350.00	7.00

C

J. W. Campion & Co.

For illustration of No. RS47, see large stamp illustration pages.

RS47	4c	**black,** imperf	525.00		375.00
	p.	Pair, perf horiz.			2,500.
RS48	4c	**black,** die cut	140.00	350.00	110.00

Cannon & Co.

For illustration of No. RS49, see larger stamp illustration pages.

RS49	4c	**green,** imperf	115.00	275.00	70.00

The Centaur Co. — RS50/RS52

The Centaur Co.

RS50	1c	**ver**	65.00	10.00
RS51	2c	**black**	14.00	3.75
RS52	4c	**black**	60.00	

Dr. A. W. Chase, Son & Co.

For illustration of No. RS55, see large stamp illustration pages.

RS53	1c	**black**	100.00	3,000.
RS54	2c	**black**	140.00	
RS55	4c	**black**	140.00	

Wm. E. Clarke
RS56   RS57

Wm. E Clarke

RS56	3c	**blue**	200.00
RS57	6c	**black**	95.00

R. C. & C. S. Clark — RS58

R. C. & C. S. Clark

RS58	4c	**black**	20.00		25.00

Collins Bros. — RS59

W. H. Comstock — RS60

Collins Bros.

RS59	1c	**black**	26.00	325.00

W. H. Comstock

RS60	1c	**black**	5.00

Cook & Bernheimer

RS61	4c	**blue**	110.00

Charles N. Crittenton —
RS62/RS64

Charles N. Crittenton

RS62	1c	**black**	10.00		
RS63	1c	**blue**		12.50	6.5
RS64	2c	**black**	85.00	50.00	5.

Oliver Crook & Co.

For illustration of No. RS65, see larger stamp illustration pages.

RS65	4c	**black**	110.00	25.00
	e.	Experimental silk paper	60.00	

Jeremiah Curtis & Son

For illustration of No. RS67, see larger stamp illustration pages.

RS66	1c	**black**	125.00	
		Die I, small "1s."		
RS67	1c	**black**		110.0
		Die II, large "1s."		
RS68	2c	**black**	10.00	10.00	—	160.00	275.00
		Dbl. transfer		

Die II numerals nearly fill the circles.

Curtis & Brown RS69

Curtis & Brown

RS69	1c	**black**	5.75	4.00
	e.	Experimental silk paper		
RS70	2c	**black**	150.00	

Curtis & Brown Mfg. Co. RS71

Curtis & Brown Mfg. Co.

These are identical to RS69-RS70 with "Mfg. Co. Limtd." instead of the right hand "TWO CENTS."

RS71	1c	**black**		250.00	9.00
RS72	2c	**black**	2,200.		1,000.

D

Dalley's Galvanic Horse Salve

For illustration of No. RS73, see larger stamp illustration pages.

RS73	2c	**green**	110.00	200.00	275.00

Dalley's Magical Pain Extractor

For illustration of No. RS74, see larger stamp illustration pages.

RS74	1c	**black**	14.00	11.00	8.50
	h.	$100	375.00		20.00

#RS74h reads "$100" instead of "$1.00."

Perry Davis & Son —
RS75/RS81

Perry Davis & Son

75	1c	blue	9.00	3.75	350.00	2.50
e.		Experimental silk paper	135.00			
u.		1c ultra	200.00			
76	2c	brown red	175.00			
77	2c	black	80.00			
78	2c	dull pur		10.00		
78A	2c	slate		12.50		6.50
79	2c	dull red		95.00		
80	2c	brown		5,500.		
81	4c	brown	13.00	4.00		3.00

P. H. Drake & Co.

82	2c	black	4,500.		
83	4c	black	60.00	70.00	
e.		Experimental silk paper	175.00		

--------- F ---------

B. A. Fahnestock — RS84

B. A. Fahnestock

S84	1c	lake, imperf	160.00	125.00

he Father Mathew Temperance & Manufacturing Company

For illustration of No. RS85, see large stamp illustration ges.

S85	4c	black	10.00

A. H. Flanders, M. D. — RS87

A. H. Flanders, M. D.

S86	1c	green, perf		14.00	13.00
S87	1c	green, part perf	25.00	2.00	40.00 3.00

Fleming Bros. — RS88/RS90

Fleming Bros.
Vermifuge

RS88	1c	black, imperf	14.00	22.50	60.00
e.		Experimental silk paper	95.00		

L. Pills

For illustration of No. RS90, see large stamp illustration ages.

RS89	1c	black, imperf	4,500.		
RS90	1c	blue, imperf	7.00	8.00	10.00
		Dbl. transfer		70.00	70.00
e.		Experimental silk paper	—		
u.		1c ultra	1,000.		

Seth W. Fowle & Son — RS91

Seth W. Fowle & Son, J. P. Dinsmore

RS91	4c	black	20.00	3.00	3.00

--------- G ---------

G. G. Green — RS92/RS93

G. G. Green

RS92	3c	black			7.00
h.		Tete beche pair	550.00		
RS93	3c	blk, rouletted	160.00		

--------- H ---------

Reuben P. Hall & Co.

RS94	4c	black	20.00	20.00	22.50
e.		Experimental silk paper	500.		

Hall & Ruckel — RS95

Hall & Ruckel — RS96

Hall & Ruckel as agents for Xavier Bazin — RS95h/RS96h

Hall & Ruckel

RS95	1c	green	1.75	1.75	30.00	1.75
e.		Experimental silk paper	35.00			
h.		Hand-stamped "X.B." (Xavier Bazin) and obliteration			—	
RS96	3c	black	3.25	3.00	60.00	3.00
h.		Hand-stamped "X.B." (Xavier Bazin) and obliteration			—	

Dr. Harter & Co.

RS97	1c	black	25.00	16.00

Dr. Harter — RS98

Dr. Harter

As No. RS97, inscribed "Dr. Harter" instead of "Dr. Harter & Co."

RS98	1c	black	4.00	14.00	5.00
		Dbl. impression	3,000.		

(Dr.) S. B. Hartman & Co.

For illustration of No. RS100, see large stamp illustration pages.

RS99	4c	black	1,500.	75.00	1,250. 1,750.
RS100	6c	black	550.00	350.00	

E. T. Hazeltine — RS101/RS103

E. T. Hazeltine

RS101	1c	black			19.00
RS102	2c	blue		37.50	
RS103	4c	black	600.00	25.00	18.00
e.		Experimental silk paper	2,000.		
i.		Imperf, pair	950.00		

E. H. (Edward Heaton) — RS105

E. H. (Edward Heaton)

RS104	3c	black		50.00
RS105	3c	brown		17.50

Helmbold's — RS106/RS109

Helmbold's

RS106	2c	blue	1.50	350.00
		Dbl. transfer	—	
RS107	3c	green	50.00	35.00
RS108	4c	black	4.50	200.00
		Dbl. transfer	160.00	
RS109	6c	black	2.00	3.50
e.		Experimental silk paper	37.50	

A. L. Helmbold's

Same as "Helmbold's" but inscribed "A. L. Helmbold's."

RS110	2c	blue	125.00	180.00	100.00
RS111	4c	black	27.50	160.00	10.00

e. Experimental silk paper 175.00

Scheetz's Celebrated Bitter Cordial – RS210

Schenck's Mandrake Pills – RS212

Schenck's Pulmonic Syrup – RS213

J.E. Schwartz & Co. – RS215

Dr. D.H. Seelye & Co. RS222

Jas. Swaim RS231

Wm. Swaim RS234

George Tallcot RS240

**United States Proprietary
Medicine Co. – RS243**

S.R. Van Duzer – RS249

**United States Proprietary
Medicine Co. – RS247**

**World's Dispensary
Medical Association
RS272**

**World's
Dispensary
Medical
Association
RS273**

West India Manufacturing Co. – RS264

Hostetter Co. – RS285

**X. Bazin
RT1**

**E.W. Hoyt & Co.
RT7**

**E.W. Hoyt & Co.
RT8**

E.W. Hoyt & Co. – RT11

RS112

John F. Henry

RS112	2c	violet	550.00			
RS113	4c	bister	1,000.			

For illustration of No. RS114, see large stamp illustration pages.

RS114	1c	black	60.00	1.00	10.00	1.50
	e.	Experimental silk paper	175.00			
RS115	2c	blue	35.00	6.50	140.00	6.00
	u.	ultra	550.00			
RS116	4c	red	180.00	1.50	35.00	2.50
	e.	Experimental silk paper	95.00			

Herrick's Pills

For illustration of No. RS117, see large stamp illustration pages.

RS117	1c	black	90.00	40.00	100.00	45.00
	e.	Experimental silk paper	200.00			
	i.	Imperf, pair	3,500.			

Horiz. pairs imperf between were issued of No. RS114d. All known pairs were originally separated, and some have been matched and rejoined. Three rejoined pairs are reported.
No. RS117i is valued in sound condition.
Most pairs are faulty and sell for much less.

Herrick's Pills &
Plasters — RS118

Herrick's Pills & Plasters

RS118	1c	red	2.50	5.00	75.00	2.50
	e.	Experimental silk paper	—			

J.E. Hetherington — RS121

J. E. Hetherington

RS119	1c	black		17.50
RS120	2c	black		575.00
RS121	3c	black		22.50
	i.	Imperf, pair		1,000.

Hiscox & Co.

For illustration of No. RS123, see large stamp illustration pages.

RS122	2c	black		15.00	
RS123	4c	black	110.00	300.00	2,000.

Holloway's Pills and Ointment — RS124/RS125

Holloway's Pills and Ointment

RS124	1c	blue, perf	10.00
RS125	1c	blue, imperf	350.00

Holman Liver Pad Co. —
RS126/RS127

Holman Liver Pad Co.

RS126	1c	green	20.00
RS127	4c	green	10.00

The Home Bitters Co.

For illustration of No. RS128, see large stamp illustration pages.

RS128	2c	blue			225.00
		Dbl. transfer			—
RS129	3c	green	125.00	160.00	100.00
RS130	4c	green	250.00		250.00

Hop Bitters Co. — RS131

Hop Bitters Co.

RS131	4c	black				7.00

Hostetter & Smith

RS132	4c	blk, imperf	75.00	40.00	100.00	30.00
		Dbl. transfer	—	50.00	87.50	37.50
	e.	Experimental silk paper	—			
RS133	6c	blk, imperf	90.00			
	e.	Experimental silk paper	300.00			

S. D. Howe

For illustration of No. RS137, see large stamp illustration pages.

RS134	4c	black, Duponco's Pills	125.00	225.00
RS135	4c	red, Duponco's Pills		425.00
RS136	4c	green, Duponco's Pills		425.00

Nos. RS135 and RS136 were never used.

RS137	4c	blue, Arabian Milk	8.00	160.00

C.E. Hull & Co. — RS138

C. E. Hull & Co.

RS138	1c	black	125.00	5.75	55.00	5.75

T. J. Husband

For illustration of No. RS140, see large stamp illustration pages.

RS139	2c	vio, imperf	1,500.	
RS140	2c	ver, imperf	15.00	10.00

Hutchings & Hillyer

RS141	4c	grn, imperf	20.00	30.00
	e.	Experimental silk paper	190.00	

—————— I ——————

H. A. Ingham & Co.

RS142	1c	black		55

—————— J ——————

James A. Jackson & Co.

For illustration of No. RS143, see large stamp illustration pages.

RS143	4c	green	1,500.	250.00
		Dbl. transfer	—	

Dr. D. Jayne & Son

For illustration of No. RS149, see large stamp illustration pages.

RS144	1c	blue, imperf		1,500.		550
	p.	Perf	800.00			3,2.
RS145	2c	blk, imperf	3,250.	5,500.		1,3.
	p.	Perf	3,500.			
RS146	4c	grn, imperf	4,000.	2,000.	1,400.	500.
	p.	Perf	4,000.			
RS146F	4c	red, imperf	—			
RS146G	4c	org, imperf	—			
RS147	1c	bl, die cut	6.00	5.00	225.00	5.
	e.	Experimental silk paper	—			
	p.	Perf and die cut	150.00	250.00		
		On horiz. laid paper	57.50			
RS148	2c	blk, die cut	10.00	8.00	100.00	5.
		Dbl. transfer	55.00	55.00	110.00	75.
	e.	Experimental silk paper	160.			
	p.	Perf & die cut	40.00	225.00	—	
RS149	4c	grn, die cut	7.00	5.00	90.00	8.5
		Dbl. transfer	—			
	e.	Experimental silk paper	110.			
	p.	Perf & die cut	45.00	210.00		
		On vertically laid paper	30.00			

I. S. Johnson & Co. — RS150

Johnston Holloway & Co. — RS151/RS152

I. S. Johnson & Co.

RS150	1c	ver	1.25	14.00		.90
		Dbl. transfer	20.00	55.00		25.00

Johnston Holloway & Co.

RS151	1c	black	3.50			2.75

S152 2c green   3.50   3.00

K

J. B. Kelly & Co.
For illustration of No. RS153, see large stamp illustration pages.

S153 4c blk,   1,750.
          imperf
      e. Experimental 1,900.
          silk
          paper

B. J. Kendall & Co.
S154 4c blue   30.00

Dr. Kennedy — RS155   Dr. Kennedy — RS156

Dr. Kennedy
S155 2c green   55.00   8.00   35.00   6.00
          Dbl.
          transfer
      e. Experi-   —
          mental
          silk pa-
          per
S156 6c black   8.00   75.00   8.00

Kennedy & Co. RS157

Kennedy & Co.
S157 2c black   7.00   110.00   8.50

K & Co. (Kennedy & Co.)
S158 1c green   7.50

Dr. Jas. C. Kerr
For illustration of No. RS159, see large stamp illustration pages.

S159 4c blue   5,500.   325.00   180.00
S160 6c black   750.00

L

Lawrence & Martin
S161 4c black   45.00

Lee & Osgood
S162 1c blue   14.00   20.00   15.00

Jacob Lippman & Bro.
For illustration of No. RS163, see large stamp illustration pages.

S163 4c blue   1,750.   2,250.
      e. Experi- 3,500.
          mental
          silk pa-
          per

Alvah Littlefield — RS165

Alvah Littlefield
RS164 1c black   1.50   1.00   20.00
           Dbl.   90.00 75.00
           transfer

---

      e. Experi-   125.00
          mental
          silk pa-
          per
          On   500.00
          horiz.
          laid pa-
          per
RS165 4c green   1,750.   225.00

Prof. Low — RS166

Prof. Low
RS166 1c black   3.00   17.50   3.00
           Dbl. transfer   —   55.00   40.00

Lyon Manufg. Co.
As No. RS24, inscribed "Lyon Manufg. Co." instead of "Demas Barnes & Co."

For illustration of No. RS167, see large stamp illustration pages.

RS167 1c black   20.00   375.00   14.00
RS168 2c black   9.50   175.00   9.00
      i.   Vert. pair, imperf   2,000.
           btwn.

M

J. McCullough
As No. RS137, inscribed "J. McCullough" instead of "S. D. Howe."

RS169 4c black   125.00   110.00

Manhattan Medicine Co. — RS171/RS172

J. H. McLean — RS170

Dr. J. H. McLean
RS170 1c black   2.50   1.50   15.00   1.50
           Dbl.   50.00 65.00   —   35.00
           transfer
      e.   Experi- 100.00
           mental
           silk pa-
           per
      i.   Vert.   —
           pair,
           imperf
           horiz.

Manhattan Medicine Co.
RS171 1c violet   37.50
      u.   1c purple   60.00
RS172 2c black   27.50   37.50   14.00

Mansfield & Higbee
As No. RS174, inscribed "Mansfield & Higbee Memphis, Tenn."

RS173 1c blue   16.00
      i.   Pair, imperf btwn.   150.00
      j.   Block of 4, imperf   175.00
           btwn.

S. Mansfield & Co. — RS174   Merchant's Gargling Oil — RS178/RS179

S. Mansfield & Co.
RS174 1c blue   27.50   190.00   15.00
      i.   Pair, imperf btwn.   175.00   375.00   275.00
      j.   Block of 4, imperf   135.00   900.00   225.00
           btwn.

Nos. RS173-RS174 are perf on 4 sides. The i. and j. varieties served as 2c or 4c stamps. Straight edged copies from severed pairs or blocks are worth much less.

T. W. Marsden
For illustrations of No. RS175-RS176, see large stamp illustration pages.

RS175 2c blue   9,000.
RS176 4c black   475.00

Mercado & Seully
For illustration of No. RS177, see large stamp illustration pages.

RS177 2c blk, im-   7,000.
           perf

Merchant's Gargling Oil
RS178 1c black   250.00   40.00   500.00   30.00
      e.   Experi- 3,000.
           mental
           silk pa-
           per
RS179 2c green   250.00   30.00   1,350.   25.00
           Foreign   2,750.   3,500.
           entry
      e.   Experi- 3,000.
           mental
           silk pa-
           per

Foreign entry is over design of #RO11.

Mette & Kanne
For illustration of No. RS180, see large stamp illustration pages.

RS180 3c black   350.00

Mishler Herb Bitters Co.
For illustration of No. RS181, see large stamp illustration pages.

RS181 4c black   150.00
      p.   Imperf at ends   200.00

Moody, Michel & Co.
For illustration of No. RS182, see large stamp illustration pages.

RS182 4c blk, imperf   180.00

Dr. C. C. Moore — RS183

Dr. C. C. Moore
RS183 1c ver, Pilules   6.00
RS184 2c black, Sure Cure   75.00   6,000.   27.50

Morehead's
For illustration of No. RS186, see large stamp illustration pages.

RS185 1c black,   27.50
           Magetic
           Plaster
RS186 4c black,   2,500.
           Neurodyne

N

New York Pharmacal Association
For illustration of No. RS187, see larger stamp illustration pages.

RS187 4c black   15.00   37.50   9.00

P

Dr. M. Perl & Co.
For illustration of No. RS188, see large stamp illustration pages.

RS188 6c black,   1,500.
           cut to
           shape

R. V. Pierce

For illustration of No. RS190, see large stamp illustration pages.

RS189	1c	**green**		22.50	140.00	25.00
RS190	2c	**black**	27.50	7.50	30.00	7.00
		Dbl. transfer		—		
	e.	Experi-mental silk pa-per	110.00			

Bennett Pieters & Co.

For illustration of No. RS191, see large stamp illustration pages.

RS191	4c	**black**	550.00	2,500.
	e.	Experi-mental silk pa-per	2,500.	
RS192	6c	**black**	1,500.	
	i.	Imperf	*1,400.*	

— R —

Radway & Co.

For illustration of No. RS193, see large stamp illustration pages.

RS193	2c	**black**	4.50	3.00	11.00	5.00
		Dbl. transfer	65.00	100.00	75.00	
	e.	Experi-mental silk pa-per	60.00			

D. Ransom & Co.

RS194	1c	**blue**	4.50	2.75	
		Dbl. transfer		—	
	e.	Experi-mental silk pa-per	125.00		
RS195	2c	**black**	25.00	30.00	
	e.	Experi-mental silk pa-per	125.00		

D. Ransom, Son & Co. — RS197

D. Ransom, Son & Co.

As Nos. RS194-RS195 with "Son" added.

RS196	1c	**blue**	4.00	15.00	6.00
		Dbl. transfer		—	
RS197	2c	**black**	16.00	75.00	10.00

Redding's Russia Salve — RS198

Redding's Russia Salve

RS198	1c	**black**		8.00		8.00
		Dbl. transfer	125.00			

Ring's Vegetable Ambrosia — RS199/RS200

Ring's Vegetable Ambrosia

RS199	2c	**blue,** imperf		3,000.
	p.	Perf		*3,250.*
RS200	4c	**blk,** im-perf	4,000.	4,000.

Ring's Vegetable Ambrosia — RS201/RS202

RS201	2c	**bl,** die cut		22.50	
RS202	4c	**black,** die cut	16.00	16.00	22.50
	e.	Experi-mental silk pa-per	110.00		
RS203	4c	**black,** perf		1,500.	2,400.
	k.	Perf & die cut			1,000.
	p.	Part perf		1,600.	—

J. B. Rose & Co. — RS204/RS205

J. B. Rose & Co.

RS204	2c	**black**		6.00	32.50
		Dbl. transfer		140.00	200.00
RS205	4c	**black**	*8,000.*	140.00	
		Dbl. transfer		—	

Rumford Chemical Works

RS206	2c	**green**		4.50
RS207	2c	**grn,** im-perf		25.00

— S —

A. B. & D. Sands

RS208	1c	**green**	10.00	20.00	
	e.	Experi-mental silk pa-per	70.00		

M., P. J. & H. M. Sands

The #RS208 die was altered to make #RS209.

For illustration of No. RS209, see large stamp illustration pages.

RS209	2c	**green**	17.50	110.00	15.00

Scheetz's Celebrated Bitter Cordial

For illustration of No. RS210, see large stamp illustration pages.

RS210	4c	**black,** perf		650.00
RS211	4c	**blk,** imperf		*5,000.*

Schenck's Mandrake Pills

For illustration of No. RS212, see large stamp illustration pages.

RS212	1c	**grn,** imperf	5.00	10.00	125.00	5.00
		Dbl. transfer		30.00		—
	e.	Experimental silk paper	280.			
	p.	Perf				—

Schenck's Pulmonic Syrup

For illustration of No. RS213, see larger stamp illustration pages.

RS213	6c	**blk,** im-perf	7.50	5.00	100.00	145.00
		Dbl. transfer		57.50		—
	e.	Experi-mental silk pa-per	140.00			

	p.	Perf	210.00

J. H. Schenck & Son — RS214

J. H. Schenck & Son

RS214	4c	**black**		1(

J. E. Schwartz & Co.

As No. RS84, inscribed "J. E. Schwartz & Co." instead of A. Fahnestock."

For illustration of No. RS215, see large stamp illustration pages.

RS215	1c	**lake,** imperf	140.00	750.00	110

"A. L. Scovill" follows No. RS219.

Seabury & Johnson — RS216

Seabury & Johnson — RS218

Seabury & Johnson

RS216	1c	**black**		75.
RS217	1c	**black,** printed obliteration over "porous"		5.
	h.	"Porous" obliterated by pen		5.
RS218	1c	**lake**		3,2

"Dr. D. H. Seelye & Co." follows No. RS221.

Dr. S. Brown Sigesmond

RS219	4c	**blue**		87.

A. L. Scovill & Co. — RS220/RS221

A. L. Scovill & Co.

RS220	1c	**black**	1.75	2.50	
		Dbl. transfer		—	
	e.	Experi-mental silk pa-per	67.50		
	r.	Printed on both sides		*2,250.*	
RS221	4c	**green**	2.00	5.00	
	e.	Experi-mental silk pa-per	125.00		

Dr. D. H. Seelye & Co.

For illustration of No. RS222, see larger stamp illustration pages.

RS222	8c	**blk,** im-perf	25.00	

Dr. M. A. Simmons

RS223	1c	**black,** luka, Miss.	110.00		*9,500*
RS224	1c	**black,** St. Louis, Mo.			110.0(

S. N. Smith & Co.

As No. RS65, inscribed "S. N. Smith & Co." instead of "Olive Crook & Co."

RS225	4c	**black**		50.00	50.0(

For illustration of No. RS225, see larger stamp illustration pages.

Dr. E. L. Soule & Co.
N.Y. Wrapper

RS226	1c	**blue**	75.00	

For. en-
try   —

Syracuse Wrapper

227	1c	blue	75.00	35.00	
	For. entry		—		
u.	ultra		700.00		
	For. entry		—		

For Nos. RS226, RS227, the foreign entry is the design of RT1 (pos. 1).

H. R. Stevens —
RS228/RS229

H. R.
Stevens — RS230

H. R. Stevens

S228	1c	brown		16.00
S229	2c	choc		6.00
S230	6c	black	110.00	6.00

Jas. Swaim

For illustration of No. RS231, see large stamp illustration ages.

S231	6c	org	5,000.	
		Die cut, ms signature.		
S232	8c	org, imperf	2,750.	
h.		Ms.	10,000.	10,000.
S233	8c	org, die cut	350.00	
e.		Experimental silk paper		
h.		Ms.	4,000.	

No. RS232h, RS233h have manuscript signature.

Wm. Swaim

For illustration of No. RS234, see large stamp illustration ages.

S234	8c	org,imperf	9,000.	4,500.	2,000.
k.		None	10,000.	10,000.	

No. RS234k is without signature. No. RS234d is found with signature "Suaim" or "Swaim." Also, No. RS234b is found with a period under the raised "m" of "Wm" and the right leg of "w" of "waim" retouched, both by pen.

S235	8c	org, die cut	1,500.	190.00	225.00
h.		Ms.	950.00		
k.		Invt.		6,000.	

Nos. RS235h has manuscript signature. No. RS235k has gnature inverted.

RS237

Dr. G. W. Swett

RS236	4c	blk, die cut	15.00

RS237	4c	green, perf	225.00		2,250.
RS238	4c	green, perf and die cut	400.00		2,750.

T

George Tallcot

For illustration of No. RS240, see large stamp illustration ages.

RS239	2c	ver			15.00
RS240	4c	black	85.00	7,500.	20.00

Tarrant & Co.
RS241

John L. Thompson
RS242

Tarrant & Company

RS241	4c	red	3.00	90.00	2.00

John L. Thompson

RS242	1c	black	6.00	7.50	6.00
		Dbl. transfer		—	
e.		Experimental silk paper	110.00		

U

United States Proprietary Medicine Co.

For illustration of No. RS243, see large stamp illustration pages.

RS243	4c	black	45.00	95.00
e.		Experimental silk paper	175.00	
RS244	6c	black	1,500.	

U. S. Proprietary Medicine Co.
Wrappers

For illustration of No. RS247, see larger stamp illustration pages.

RS245	1c	black, white	45.00	45.00
e.		Experimental silk paper	450.00	
RS246	1c	black, yel	120.00	220.00
RS247	1c	black, org	250.00	6,500.
RS248	1c	black, org red	2,000.	10,000.

V

S. R. Van Duzer

For illustration of No. RS249, see large stamp illustration pages.

RS249	4c	black	40.00	35.00	190.00
RS250	6c	black			75.00

A. Vogeler &
Co. — RS251

Vogeler, Meyer &
Co. — RS252

A. Vogeler & Co.

RS251	1c	black	1.50	2.00

Vogeler, Meyer & Co.

RS252	1c	ver	4.00	1.25

W

Dr. J. Walker

RS253	4c	black	40.00	20.00	20.00
		Dbl. transfer	50.00		40.00
e.		Experimental silk paper	200.00		

H. H. Warner & Co. —
RS254/RS255

H. H. W. & Co. (H. H. Warner & Co.)

RS254	1c	brown	6.00
RS255	6c	brown, 19x26mm	80.00

RS256	2c	brown, 88x11mm	30.00
RS257	4c	brown, 95x18mm	30.00
RS258	6c	brown	7.00
		Dbl. transfer	47.50

Weeks & Potter — RS259

RS261

RS262

Weeks & Potter

RS259	1c	black		7.00	5.00
RS260	2c	black		100.00	
RS261	4c	black	27.50	27.50	7.00
RS262	2c	red		35.00	7.00

Wells, Richardson
& Co. — RS263

Edward Wilder —
RS265/RS269

Wells, Richardson & Co.

RS263	4c	black	27.50

West India Manufacturing Co.

For illustration of No. RS264, see large stamp illustration pages.

RS264	4c	blk, die I	225.00	275.00	400.00
RS264A	4c	blk, die II			350.00

Die II shows evidence of retouching, particularly in the central disk.

Edward Wilder

RS265	1c	grn, imperf	2,000.	300.00	275.00
e.		Experimental silk paper	3,500.		
RS266	1c	grn, die cut	50.00	45.00	22.50
e.		Experimental silk paper	200.		
RS266A	4c	ver, imperf			
e.		Experimental silk paper	7,500.		
RS267	4c	ver, die cut	175.00	1,500.	
e.		Experimental silk paper	100.		
RS268	4c	lake, imperf		190.00	2,000.
RS269	4c	lake, die cut	1,750.	12.50	12.50

Rev. E. A. Wilson

RS270	12c blue		75.00	400.00

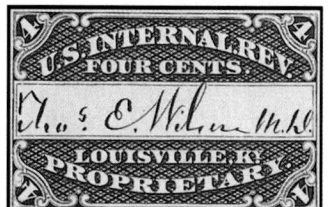

Thos. E.
Wilson, M.D.
RS271

Thos. E. Wilson, M. D.

RS271	4c black	25,000.	

World's Dispensary Medical Assocn.

For illustration of No. RS273, see larger stamp illustration pages.

RS272	1c	green	25.00
RS273	2c	black, 56x256mm	8.00

Wright's Indian Vegetable
Pills — RS274

Wright's Indian Vegetable Pills

RS274	1c	green	2.00	1.50	35.00	3.00
		Dbl. transfer			
	e.	Experimental silk paper	100.		

— Z —

J.H. Zeilin & Co. —
RS275/RS277

J.H. Zeilin & Co.

RS275	2c	red	1,000.
RS276	2c	green, perf	40.00
RS277	2c	grn, imperf	175.00	7.50	125.00	5.00

	Roul. 5½		p. Hyphen Hole Perf. 7	
	Unused	Used	Unused	Used

1898-1900
See rouletting note preceding No. R161.

The Antikamnia
Chemical
Co. — RS278

The Antikamnia Chemical Co.

RS278	2½c car	3.00	3.00

Fernet Branca (Branca Bros.)

RS279	4c	black	8.50	8.50	8.50	8.50

	Roul. 5½		p. Hyphen Hole Perf. 7	
	Unused	Used	Unused	Used

Emerson Drug Co. — RS281

Emerson Drug Co.

RS280	¼c	car	6.00	2.50
RS281	⅝c	green	6.00	3.00
RS282	1¼c	vio brn	8.00	6.50
RS283	2½c	brn org	7.50	4.50

Chas. H. Fletcher — RS284

Chas. H. Fletcher

RS284	1¼c	black	.30	.30	.30	.30

Hostetter Co.

For illustration of No. RS285, see large stamp illustration pages.

RS285	2½c	black, imperf	.40	.40

Johnson &
Johnson — RS286

Johnson & Johnson

RS286	⅝c	car	.30	.30	.30	.30

Lanman &
Kemp — RS287

Lanman & Kemp

RS287	⅝c	green	7.50	5.50	10.00	4.00
RS288	1¼c	brown	10.00	6.00	15.00	11.00
RS289	1⅞c	blue	10.00	7.50	20.00	10.00

J. Ellwood Lee Co. — RS290

J. Ellwood Lee Co.

RS290	⅛c	dk bl	2.50	2.50
RS291	⅝c	car	2.00	1.50
RS292	1¼c	dk grn	1.50	1.50
RS293	2½c	org	2.00	2.00
RS294	5c	chocolate	2.25	2.25

Charles Marchand — RS295

Charles Marchand

RS295	⅝c	black	7.50	7.50	8.00	
RS296	1¼c	black	1.25	1.25	1.25	
RS297	1⅞c	black	2.00	2.00	2.50	
RS298	2½c	black	2.50	2.50	2.50	
RS299	3⅛c	black	7.50	7.50	7.50	
RS300	4⅝c	black	15.00	15.00	15.00	15
RS301	7½c	black	10.00	10.00	10.00	10

Od Chem. Co.

RS302	2½c	car

The Piso Company — RS303

The Piso Company (E. T. Hazletine)

RS303	⅝c	blue	.30	.30	.30	

Radway & Co. — RS304

Radway & Co.

RS304	⅝c	blue	1.00	1.00	1.00	1

Warner's Safe Cure Co. — RS305

Warner's Safe Cure Co.

RS305	3⅛c	brown	1.00	1.00	1.00	1.

Dr. Williams Medicine
Co. — RS306

Dr. Williams Medicine Co.

RS306	1¼c	pink	2.00	2.0

Dr. Kilmer & Co., Provisionals

Postage Stamps of 1895, 1897-1903, Nos. 267a, 279, 279Bg and 268, Precancel Overprinted in Black:

Dr. K. & Co.

I. R.

7-5-'98.

a

b

c

98 **Wmk. 191** *Perf. 12*

Overprint "a," Large "I.R." Dated July 5, 1898.

S307	A87	1c **deep green**	150.00
	a.	Red (trial) plus black ovpts.	—
S308	A88	2c **pink,** type III	145.00
S308A	A88	2c **pink,** type IV	150.00
	b.	Dark blue (trial) ovpt.	—
S309	A89	3c **purple**	140.00
	a.	Red (trial) ovpt.	—
	b.	Inverted ovpt.	—

A trial overprint in dark blue on the 2c stamp is known used July 5.

Overprint "b," Small "I.R.,"
"Dr. K. & Co." with Serifs
Dated July 6, 7, 9, 11 to 14, 1898

S310	A87	1c **deep green**	125.00
S311	A88	2c **pink,** type III	135.00
S311A	A88	2c **pink,** type IV	70.00
S312	A89	3c **purple**	60.00
	a.	Inverted ovpt.	—

Overprint "c," Small "I.R.,"
"Dr. K. & Co." without Serifs
Dated July 7, 9, 11 to 14, 1898

S313	A87	1c **deep green**	130.00
S314	A88	2c **pink,** type III	135.00
S314A	A88	2c **pink,** type IV	90.00
S315	A89	3c **purple**	105.00
	a.	Inverted ovpt.	—

Nos. RS307a, RS308Ab and RS309a were all overprinted on y 5, the first day of overprinting. Though called "trials," there every reason to believe they were used in the regular course business, as they represented money spent by Dr. Kilmer & . and there was no reason not to use them. Four examples e recorded of No. RS307a, three of No. RS308Ab and one of . RS309a.

r the inverted overprints, four examples are recorded of No. S309b, 16 of No. RS312a and three of No. RS315a. Forger-s exist of No. RS312a, all dated July 6. The height of "I.R." shorter on the forgeries, and the periods after these letters are circular rather than diamond shaped.

Many varieties of the Kilmer overprints exist. For the complete listing see "The Case of Dr. Kilmer's," by Morton Dean Joyce, 1954 (also serialized in "The Bureau Specialist," Mar.-Nov. 1957).

St. Louis Provisional Labels, 1898

> **INTERNAL REVENUE TAX.**
> **II 1-4 CENTS.**
> Stamps not being obtainable at time of sale and shipment of this package, the tax will be paid on sworn returns thereof to Collector of Internal Reve-nue, 1st Dist. Mo.
> Meyer Brothers Drug Co., St. Louis.

Ten proprietary drug companies of St. Louis (Antikamnia hemical Co., W. R. Holmes, Lambert Pharmacal Co., Meyer rothers Drug Co., Jno. T. Milliken & Co., Phenique Chemical o., Prickly Ash Bitters Co., T. M. Sayman, Van Dyke Bitters o. and Walker Pharmacal Co.) prepared and used labels to enote payment of July 1, 1898, Proprietary Revenue tax ecause the government issue of "Battleship" stamps (Nos. B20-RB31) was not available on the effective date.

An illustrated descriptive list of these labels, compiled by Morton Dean Joyce, appeared in the December, 1970, issue of cott's Monthly Journal.

a.	b.	c.	d.
Old Paper	Silk Paper	Pink Paper	Wmkd. USIR (191R)

PRIVATE DIE PERFUMERY STAMPS
1864 *Perf. 12*
X. Bazin

For illustration of No. RT1, see large stamp illustration pages.

RT1	2c	**blue,** die cut	1,250.

This stamp was never placed in use.

Corning & Tappan — RT2/RT4

Corning & Tappan

RT2	1c	**black,** imperf	1,750.
	h.	Die cut, 19mm diameter	110.00
	k.	Die cut, 21mm diameter	150.00
RT3	1c	**black,** perf	650.00
RT4	1c	**blue,** perf	4.00

Fetridge & Co. — RT5

Fetridge & Co.

RT5	2c	**ver,** cut to shape	110.00

E. W. Hoyt & Co. — RT6

E. W. Hoyt & Co.

For illustrations of Nos. RT7, RT8 and RT11, see large stamp illustration pages.

RT6	1c	**black,** imperf	*4,500.*	4,500.	140.00
RT7	1c	**black,** die cut	30.00	30.00	15.00
RT8	2c	**black,** imperf			650.00
RT9	2c	**black,** die cut			90.00
RT10	4c	**black,** imperf	2,500.	325.00	1,500.
RT11	4c	**black,** die cut	100.00	70.00	70.00

The 2c is larger than the 1c, 4c larger than 2c.

Kidder & Laird

RT12	1c	**vermilion**	15.00
RT13	2c	**vermilion**	15.00

George W. Laird — RT14/RT15

George W. Laird

RT14	3c	**blk,** imperf	900.00	1,000.	900.00
		Double transfer	1,000.	1,400.	1,000.
	p.	Perf	1,500.	3,750.	
		As "p," double transfer	1,600.		
RT15	3c	**black,** die cut	2,500.	100.00	3,000. 100.00
		Double transfer		250.00	900.00 300.00
	e.	Experi-mental silk pa-per, double transfer	—		
	p.	Perf and die cut	1,000.		

Lanman & Kemp — RT16/RT18   Tetlow's Perfumery — RT19

Lanman & Kemp

RT16	1c	**black**	7.50	300.00	7.50
		Dbl. transfer	—		
RT17	2c	**brown**	30.00		10.00
RT18	3c	**green**	8.00		7.50
		Dbl. transfer	150.00		70.00

Tetlow's Perfumery

RT19	1c	**vermilion**	3.50

C. B. Woodworth &   R. & G. A. Wright —
Son — RT20/RT21   RT22/RT25

C. B. Woodworth & Son
RT20	1c	green	5.50	17.50	7.00
		Dbl. transfer	60.00	75.00	60.00
RT21	2c	blue	140.00	3,500.	9.00

R. & G. A. Wright
RT22	1c	blue	6.00	8.00	60.00
	e.	Experimental silk paper	85.00		
RT23	2c	black	11.00	20.00	200.00
RT24	3c	lake	30.00	110.00	290.00
RT25	4c	green	90.00	125.00	275.00

Young, Ladd & Coffin —
RT26/RT33

Young, Ladd & Coffin
RT26	1c	green, imperf	90.00	85.00	90.00
RT27	1c	green, perf	22.50	15.00	15.00
RT28	2c	blue, imperf	125.00	110.00	75.00
RT29	2c	blue, perf	55.00	85.00	15.00
RT30	3c	ver, imperf	110.00	130.00	80.00
RT31	3c	ver, perf	35.00	7.50	7.00
RT32	4c	brown, imperf	6,000.	145.00	50.00
RT33	4c	brown, perf	40.00	12.50	5.00

	a. Old Paper	b. Silk Paper	c. Pink Paper	d. Wmkd. USIR (191R)

PRIVATE DIE PLAYING CARD STAMPS
1864

Caterson Brotz & Co.
RU1	5c	brown		10,000.

This stamp was never placed in use.

A. Dougherty —   A.
RU2/RU6   Dougherty — RU5

A. Dougherty
RU2	2c	orange	70.00		
RU3	4c	black	45.00		
RU4	5c	blue, 20x26mm	1.50	1.50	12.50
		Double transfer		—	
	e.	Experimental silk paper		—	
		As "e," inverted dbl. transfer		—	
	u.	5c ultra	125.00		

RU5	5c	blue, 18x23mm			1.50
RU6	10c	blue	40.00		

The 2c, 4c and 5c have numerals in all four corners.

Eagle Card Co. — RU7

Eagle Card Co.
RU7	5c	black		85.00

Goodall — RU8   Samuel Hart & Co. — RU9

Goodall (London, New York)

As No. RU13, "London Goodall New York" replaces both "American Playing Cards" and Victor E. Mauger and Petrie New York."

RU8	5c	black	150.00	4.00
	e.	Experimental silk paper	2,500.	

Samuel Hart & Co.
RU9	5c	black	6.00	6.00
	e.	Experimental silk paper	2,500.	

Lawrence & Cohen —
RU10/RU11

Lawrence & Cohen
RU10	2c	blue	80.00	
RU11	5c	green	5.00	7.00
	e.	Experimental silk paper	85.00	

Jn. J. Levy
RU12	5c	black	25.00	27.50
	e.	Experimental silk paper	95.00	

Victor E. Mauger &   New York
Petrie — RU13   Consolidated Card
                           Co. — RU14

Victor E. Mauger and Petrie
RU13	5c	blue	2.00	2.00	1.00

New York Consolidated Card Co.
RU14	5c	black	5.00	15.00	4.50

Paper   Russell, Morgan
Fabrique — RU15   Co. — RU16

Paper Fabrique Company
RU15	5c	black	9.00	20.00	

Russell, Morgan & Co.
RU16	5c	black			20

MOTOR VEHICLE USE REVENUE STAMPS

When affixed to a motor vehicle, permitted use of that vehicle for a stated period.

RV1

Daniel Manning — RV2

1943

RV12	RV1	$2.50	rose red	(January)	52.50 16.00
RV13	RV1	$2.09	rose red	(February)	35.00 11.00
RV14	RV1	$1.67	rose red	(March)	30.00 12.50
RV15	RV1	$1.25	rose red	(April)	30.00 9.00
RV16	RV1	84c	rose red	(May)	30.00 9.00
RV17	RV1	42c	rose red	(June)	30.00 10.00
RV18	RV1	$5	yellow	(July)	3.75 .80
RV19	RV1	$4.59	yellow	(August)	55.00 17.00
RV20	RV1	$4.17	yellow	(September)	70.00 21.00
RV21	RV1	$3.75	yellow	(October)	70.00 21.00
RV22	RV1	$3.34	yellow	(November)	77.50 22.00
RV23	RV1	$2.92	yellow	(December)	90.00 25.00
			Nos. RV12-RV23 (12)		573.75 174.30

1944

RV24	RV1	$2.50	yellow	(January)	95.00 25.00
RV25	RV1	$2.09	yellow	(February)	60.00 19.00
RV26	RV1	$1.67	yellow	(March)	52.50 16.00
RV27	RV1	$1.25	yellow	(April)	52.50 17.00
RV28	RV1	84c	yellow	(May)	45.00 16.00
RV29	RV1	42c	yellow	(June)	45.00 16.00

Gum on Face

Control Number and Inscriptions on Back

RV30	RV1	$5	violet	(July)	2.40 .55
RV31	RV1	$4.59	violet	(August)	80.00 21.00
RV32	RV1	$4.17	violet	(September)	57.50 19.00
RV33	RV1	$3.75	violet	(October)	57.50 19.00
RV34	RV1	$3.34	violet	(November)	52.50 12.50
RV35	RV1	$2.92	violet	(December)	52.50 12.50
			Nos. RV24-RV35 (12)		652.40 193.55

1945

RV36	RV1	$2.50	violet	(January)	45.00 12.00
RV37	RV1	$2.09	violet	(February)	40.00 12.00
RV38	RV1	$1.67	violet	(March)	40.00 10.50
RV39	RV1	$1.25	violet	(April)	40.00 10.50
RV40	RV1	84c	violet	(May)	32.50 9.00
RV41	RV1	42c	violet	(June)	26.00 7.25

Gum on Face

Control Number and Inscriptions on Back

1945	Wmk. 191R	Offset Printing	*Perf. 11*	

Bright Blue Green & Yellow Green

RV42	RV2	$5	(July)	3.25 .55
RV43	RV2	$4.59	(August)	57.50 19.00
RV44	RV2	$4.17	(Sept.)	57.50 19.50
RV45	RV2	$3.75	(October)	52.50 12.50
RV46	RV2	$3.34	(November)	42.50 12.00
RV47	RV2	$2.92	(December)	37.50 9.00
			Nos. RV36-RV47 (12)	474.25 133.80

1946

Bright Blue Green & Yellow Green

RV48	RV2	$2.50	(January)	40.00 12.50
RV49	RV2	$2.09	(February)	40.00 12.00
RV50	RV2	$1.67	(March)	32.50 9.00
RV51	RV2	$1.25	(April)	25.00 9.00
RV52	RV2	84c	(May)	25.00 9.00
RV53	RV2	42c	(June)	19.00 1.20
			Nos. RV48-RV53 (6)	181.50 52.70

1942   Wmk. 191R   OFFSET PRINTING   *Perf. 11*

With Gum on Back

1	RV1	$2.09	light green	(February)	1.60 .40

With Gum on Face

Inscriptions on Back

2	RV1	$1.67	light green	(March)	26.00 8.50
3	RV1	$1.25	light green	(April)	19.00 7.50
4	RV1	84c	light green	(May)	21.00 7.25
5	RV1	42c	light green	(June)	21.00 7.25

With Gum and Control Number on Face

Inscriptions on Back

6	RV1	$5	rose red	(July)	3.25 1.10
7	RV1	$4.59	rose red	(August)	45.00 13.00
8	RV1	$4.17	rose red	(September)	50.00 16.00
9	RV1	$3.75	rose red	(October)	45.00 12.50
10	RV1	$3.34	rose red	(November)	45.00 12.50
11	RV1	$2.92	rose red	(December)	45.00 12.50
			Nos. RV1-RV11 (11)		321.85 98.50

BOATING STAMPS

Required on applications for the certificate of number for motorboats of more than 10 horsepower, starting April 1, 1960. The pictorial upper part of the $3 stamp was attached to the temporary certificate and kept by the boat owner. The lower part (stub), showing number only, was affixed to the application and sent by the post office to the U.S. Coast Guard, which issues permanent certificates. The $3 fee was for three years. The $1 stamp covered charges for reissue of a lost or destroyed certificate of number. These stamps were used in the 12 states and the District of Columbia that had not passed laws in conformity with the Boating Act of 1958.

Catalogue value for unused stamps in this section are for Never Hinged items.

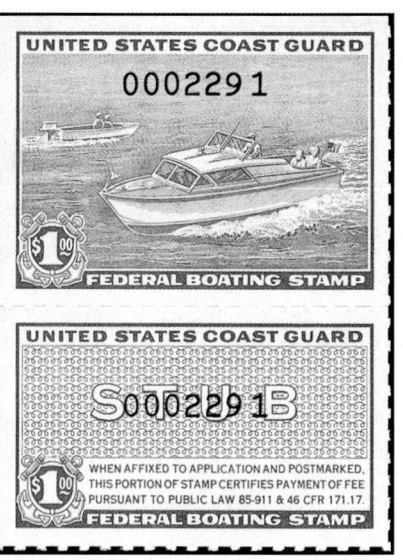

Outboard and Inboard Motorboats — RVB1

Offset Printing, Number Typographed

1960, Apr. 1   Unwmk.   *Rouletted*

RVB1	RVB1	$1	rose red, black number	37.50 750.00
			P# block of 4	160.00
			On license	—
RVB2	RVB1	$3	blue, red number	42.50 27.50
			P# block of 4	180.00
			On license	40.00
			First day license	1,000.

Nos. RVB1 and RVB2 unused stamp values are for MNH complete two-part stamps. Used values are for stamps, without the stubs, bearing a complete cancel dated between April 1, 1960, and January 31, 1964. On-license values are for clean licenses with undamaged stamps and a complete cancel. A license fold can be expected. Mute oval cancels are usually favor cancels.

CAMP STAMPS

The Camp Stamp program of the Department of Agriculture's National Forest Service was introduced in 1985. The public was offered the option of prepaying their recreation fees through the purchase of camp stamps. The fees varied but were typically $3 to $4.

The stamps were supplied in rolls with the backing rouletted 9 horizontally. The letter preceding the serial number indicated the face value and printer (A-D, Denver; E-J, Washington). The stamps were designed so that any attempt to remove them from the fee envelope would cause them to come apart.

The program ended in the summer of 1988. The envelopes containing the stamps were destroyed by the National Forerst Service after use. No used examples have been reported.

Catalogue value for unused stamps in this section are for Never Hinged items.

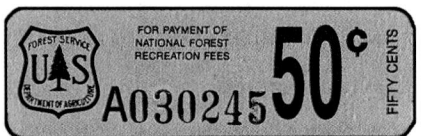

National Forest Service Logo — RVC1

Printed in Denver, CO.

1985   Typo.   Die Cut
Self-Adhesive, Coated Paper

RVC1	RVC1	50c **black,** *pink,* "A"	50.00
RVC2	RVC1	$1 **black,** *red,* "B"	50.00
RVC3	RVC1	$2 **black,** *yellow,* "C"	50.00
RVC4	RVC1	$3 **black,** *green,* "D"	50.00

RVC2

Printed by the Government Printing Office, Washington, DC (?).

1986		Typo.	Die C
		Self-Adhesive, Coated Paper	
RVC5	RVC2	50c **black,** *pink,* "E"	80.00
RVC6	RVC2	$1 **black,** *red,* "F"	80.00
RVC7	RVC2	$2 **black,** *yellow,* "G"	80.00
RVC8	RVC2	$3 **black,** *green,* "H"	80.00
RVC9	RVC2	$5 **black,** *silver,* "I"	275.00
RVC10	RVC2	$10 **black,** *bronze,* "J"	—

TRAILER PERMIT STAMPS

Issued by the National Park Service of the Department of the Interior. Required to be affixed to "License to Operate Motor Vehicle" starting July 1939, when a house trailer was attached to a motor vehicle entering a national park or national monument.

Issued to rangers in booklets of 50 (five 2x5 panes).

Use was continued at least until 1952.

Unused stamps may have a ranger's handwritten control number.

Trailer and Automobile RVT1

1939		Unwmk.	Offset Printing	*Perf. 11*	
RVT1	RVT1	50c **bright blue**		1,100.	700.00
		On license			1,250.
RVT2	RVT1	$1 **carmine**		500.00	175.00
		On license			400.00

Earliest known use: July 1939.

DISTILLED SPIRITS EXCISE TAX STAMPS

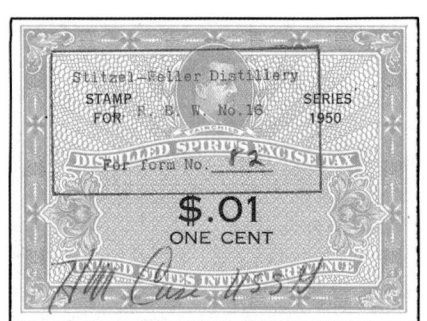

Charles S. Fairchild, Secretary of Treasury 1887-89 — DS1

Actual size: 89½x63½mm

Inscribed "STAMP FOR SERIES 1950"

1950   Wmk. 191R   Offset Printing   *Rouletted 7*
Left Value — Used
Right Value — Punched Cancel

RX1	DS1	1c **yellow green & black**	25.00	21.00
RX2	DS1	3c **yellow green & black**	100.00	92.50
RX3	DS1	5c **yellow green & black**	20.00	17.50
RX4	DS1	10c **yellow green & black**	17.50	15.00
RX5	DS1	25c **yellow green & black**	9.00	7.25
RX6	DS1	50c **yellow green & black**	9.00	7.25
RX7	DS1	$1 **yellow green & black**	2.00	1.25

RX8	DS1	$3 **yellow green & black**	20.00	15.00
RX9	DS1	$5 **yellow green & black**	5.00	3.75
RX10	DS1	$10 **yellow green & black**	3.00	1.50
RX11	DS1	$25 **yellow green & black**	12.50	9.25
RX12	DS1	$50 **yellow green & black**	6.00	5.00
RX13	DS1	$100 **yellow green & black**	4.00	2.75
RX14	DS1	$300 **yellow green & black**	25.00	21.00
RX15	DS1	$500 **yellow green & black**	15.00	10.00
RX16	DS1	$1,000 **yellow green & black**	9.00	7.50
RX17	DS1	$1,500 **yellow green & black**	50.00	40.00
RX18	DS1	$2,000 **yellow green & black**	4.50	3.50
RX19	DS1	$3,000 **yellow green & black**	21.00	15.00
RX20	DS1	$5,000 **yellow green & black**	21.00	16.00
RX21	DS1	$10,000 **yellow green & black**	27.50	22.50
RX22	DS1	$20,000 **yellow green & black**	32.50	30.00
RX23	DS1	$30,000 **yellow green & black**	70.00	50.00
RX24	DS1	$40,000 **yellow green & black**	750.00	400.00
RX25	DS1	$50,000 **yellow green & black**	87.50	75.00

Inscription "STAMP FOR SERIES 1950" omitted

1952

Left Value — Used
Right Value — Punched Cancel

RX28	DS1	5c **yellow green & black**		40.00
RX29	DS1	10c **yellow green & black**	30.00	4.00
RX30	DS1	25c **yellow green & black**	25.00	15.00
RX31	DS1	50c **yellow green & black**	30.00	12.00
RX32	DS1	$1 **yellow green & black**	20.00	2.50
RX33	DS1	$3 **yellow green & black**	35.00	22.50
RX34	DS1	$5 **yellow green & black**	37.50	25.00
RX35	DS1	$10 **yellow green & black**	20.00	2.50
RX36	DS1	$25 **yellow green & black**	25.00	10.00
RX37	DS1	$50 **yellow green & black**	65.00	25.00
RX38	DS1	$100 **yellow green & black**	20.00	2.50
RX39	DS1	$300 **yellow green & black**	25.00	7.00
RX40	DS1	$500 **yellow green & black**		30.00

RX41	DS1	$1,000 **yellow green & black**	75.00	6.
RX43	DS1	$2,000 **yellow green & black**		70.
RX44	DS1	$3,000 **yellow green & black**	800.00	500.
RX45	DS1	$5,000 **yellow green & black**		50.
RX46	DS1	$10,000 **yellow green & black**		80.

Seven other denominations with "Stamp for Series 195_ omitted were prepared but are not known to have been put in use: 1c, 3c, $1,500, $20,000, $30,000, $40,000 and $50,00
Copies listed as used have staple holes.
Distilled Spirits Excise Tax stamps were discontinued in 195_

FIREARMS TRANSFER TAX STAMPS

Documentary Stamp of 1917
Overprinted Vertically in Black.
Reading Up

	Engr.	Wmk. 191R	Perf. 11
	Without Gum		
1934 R21	$1 **green**		350.00 —
	On license		

RY1

RY2

Eagle, Shield and Stars from U.S. Seal

Two types of $200:
I — Serial number with serifs, not preceded by zeros. Tips of 6 lines project into left margin.
II — Gothic serial number preceded by zeros. Five line tips in left margin.

1934	**Wmk. 191R**	**Size: 28x42mm**
	Without Gum	
RY2 RY1	$200 **dark blue & red**, type I, #1-1500	1,350. 750.00 900.00

Issued in vertical strips of 4 which are imperforate at top, bottom and right side.
See Nos. RY4, RY6-RY8.

1938	**Size: 28x33½mm**	**Perf. 11**
RY3 RY2	$1 **green**	85.00 —
	On license	—

See No. RY5.

1950 (?)	**Wmk. 191R**	**Size: 29x43mm**
RY4 RY1	$200 **dull blue & red**, type II, #1501-3000	600.00 450.00
	On license	500.00

No. RY4 has a clear impression and is printed on white paper. No. RY2 has a "muddy" impression in much darker blue ink and is printed on off-white paper.

1960, July 1	**Size: 29x34mm**	**Perf. 11**
RY5 RY2	$5 **red**	25.00 40.00
	On license	200.00

No. RY5 was issued in sheets of 50 (10x5) with straight edge on four sides of sheet.
The watermark is hard to see on many copies of #RY2-RY5.

1974	**Unwmk.**	**Size: 29x43mm**
RY6 RY1	$200 **dull blue & red**, type II, #3001-up	225.00 110.00
	On license	140.00

		Panes of 32	
1990(?)	**Litho.**	**Without Gum**	**Imperf.**
RY7 RY1	$200 **dull blue**		500.00
	On license		750.00
1990			**Perf. 12½**
RY8 RY1	$200 **dull blue**		75.00
	On license		90.00
RY9 RY2	$5 **red**, *1994*		125.00
	On license		200.00

Nos. RY7 and RY8 do not have a printed serial number or the tabs at left. Because the stamps do not have a serial number mint copies were not sold to the public.
WARNING: Nos. RY7-RY9 are usually taped or glued to the transfer of title documents. The glue used is NOT water soluble. Attempts to soak the stamps may result in damage.

2001(?)	**Serpentine Die Cut 11.5**	
	Self-Adhesive	
RY10 RY2	$5 **dull red**	—
	On license	250.00

RECTIFICATION TAX STAMPS

Used to indicate payment of the tax on distilled spirits that were condensed and purified for additional blending through repeated distillations.

RZ1

Actual size: 89½x64mm

1946	**Offset Printing**	**Wmk. 191R**	**Rouletted 7**	
RZ1	RZ1	1c **blue & black**	7.50	4.00
		Punched cancel		2.00
RZ2	RZ1	3c **blue & black**	25.00	8.00
		Punched cancel		7.50
RZ3	RZ1	5c **blue & black**	15.00	2.50
		Punched cancel		1.25
RZ4	RZ1	10c **blue & black**	15.00	2.75
		Punched cancel		1.25
RZ5	RZ1	25c **blue & black**	15.00	3.00
		Punched cancel		2.00
RZ6	RZ1	50c **blue & black**	20.00	5.00
		Punched cancel		3.50
RZ7	RZ1	$1 **blue & black**	20.00	4.00
		Punched cancel		2.50
RZ8	RZ1	$3 **blue & black**	100.00	18.00
		Punched cancel		9.00
RZ9	RZ1	$5 **blue & black**	30.00	10.00
		Punched cancel		6.00
RZ10	RZ1	$10 **blue & black**	25.00	3.00
		Punched cancel		1.25
RZ11	RZ1	$25 **blue & black**	100.00	10.00
		Punched cancel		3.00
RZ12	RZ1	$50 **blue & black**	100.00	7.50
		Punched cancel		3.00
RZ13	RZ1	$100 **blue & black**	—	9.50
		Punched cancel		3.50

RZ14	RZ1	$300 **blue & black**	250.00	10.00
		Punched cancel		7.50
RZ15	RZ1	$500 **blue & black**	—	10.00
		Punched cancel		7.00
RZ16	RZ1	$1000 **blue & black**	—	18.00
		Punched cancel		15.00
RZ17	RZ1	$1500 **blue & black**	—	52.50
		Punched cancel		37.50
RZ18	RZ1	$2000 **blue & black**	—	80.00
		Punched cancel		60.00

Copies listed as used have staple holes.

HUNTING PERMIT STAMPS

Authorized by an Act of Congress, approved March 16, 1934, to license hunters. Receipts go to maintain waterfowl life in the United States. Sales collectors were made legal June 15, 1935.

No. RW1 used is valued with handstamp or manuscript cancel, though technically it was against postal regulations to deface the stamp or to apply postal cancellation. Beginning with No. RW2, the used values are for stamps with signatures.

Plate number blocks of six have selvage on two sides.

Hunting permit stamps are valid from July 1 - June 30. Stamps have been made available prior to the date of validity, and stamps are sold through philatelic agency after the period of validity has passed.

All hunting permit stamps through No. RW68A were printed by the Bureau of Engraving & Printing.

Catalogue values for all unused stamps in this section are for stamps with never-hinged original gum. Minor natural gum skips and bends are normal c Nos. RW1-RW20. No-gum stamps are without signature or other cancel.

Department of Agriculture

Mallards Alighting — HP1

Engraved: Flat Plate Printing
Issued in panes of 28 subjects.

1934		Unwmk.		Perf. 11	
Inscribed "Void after June 30, 1935"					
RW1	HP1	$1	blue	800.	140.
			Hinged	400.	
			No gum	160.	
			P# block of 6	16,500.	
a.			Imperf., vertical pair	—	
b.			Vert. pair, imperf. horiz.	—	

Used value is for stamp with handstamp or manuscript cancel.

It is almost certain that No. RW1a is No. RW1b with vertical perfs trimmed off. No horizontal pairs of No. RW1a are known.

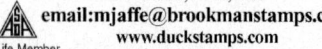
All recorded pairs are vertical, with narrow side margins. Both varieties probably are printer's waste since copies exist with gum on front or without gum.

Canvasbacks Taking to Flight — HP2

1935		Inscribed "Void after June 30, 1936"			
RW2	HP2	$1	rose lake	700.	160.
			Hinged	350.	
			No gum	200.	
			P# block of 6	11,500.	

Canada Geese in Flight — HP3

1936		Inscribed "Void after June 30, 1937"			
RW3	HP3	$1	brown black	350.	75.00
			Hinged	175.	
			No gum	115.	
			P# block of 6	4,000.	

Scaup Ducks Taking to Flight — HP4

1937		Inscribed "Void after June 30, 1938"			
RW4	HP4	$1	light green	350.	60.00
			Hinged	150.	
			No gum	80.	
			P# block of 6	3,000.	

Pintail Drake and Hen Alighting — HP5

1938		Inscribed "Void after June 30, 193			
RW5	HP5	$1	light violet	450.	60
			Hinged	210.	
			No gum	80.	
			P# block of 6	4,250.	

Department of the Interior

Green-winged Teal — HP6

1939		Inscribed "Void after June 30, 194			
RW6	HP6	$1	chocolate	275.	45.
			Hinged	125.	
			No gum	60.	
			P# block of 6	2,500.	

Black Mallards — HP7

1940		Inscribed "Void after June 30, 1941			
RW7	HP7	$1	sepia	250.	45.0
			Hinged	120.	
			No gum	60.	
			P# block of 6	2,500.	

Family of Ruddy Ducks — HP8

41   **Inscribed "Void after June 30, 1942"**
8 HP8 $1 **brown carmine**   250.   45.00
     Hinged   110.
     No gum   60.
     P# block of 6   2,500.

Baldpates — HP9

42   **Inscribed "Void after June 30, 1943"**
9 HP9 $1 **violet brown**   250.   45.00
     Hinged   110.
     No gum   60.
     P# block of 6   2,500.

Wood Ducks — HP10

43   **Inscribed "Void After June 30, 1944"**
10 HP10 $1 **deep rose**   110.00   35.00
     Hinged   50.00
     No gum   40.00
     P# block of 6   650.00

White-fronted Geese — HP11

44   **Inscribed "Void after June 30, 1945"**
W11 HP11 $1 **red orange**   110.00   30.00
     Hinged   57.50
     No gum   42.50
     P# block of 6   650.00

Shoveller Ducks in Flight — HP12

1945   **Inscribed "Void after June 30, 1946"**
RW12 HP12 $1 **black**   95.00   25.00
     Hinged   50.00
     No gum   30.00
     P# block of 6   450.00

> Beginning with No. RW13, there is a message printed on the back of the sheet stamps telling hunters to sign their names on the face of the stamp. On Nos. RW13-RW17, offset plate no. 47510 for the printing on the backs of the stamps appears on the back of the selvage opposite the stamp in position 24 on the upper right panes. These are collected as plate blocks of six with side and bottom selvage bearing the plate number on the back of the selvage opposite the center margin stamp. Value, mint never hinged $550 each for Nos. RW13-RW16, $1,500 for No. RW17.

Redhead Ducks — HP13

1946   **Inscribed "Void after June 30, 1947"**
RW13 HP13 $1 **red brown**   50.00   16.00
     No gum   18.00
     P# block of 6   300.00
  a. $1 **bright rose pink**   *35,000.*

Snow Geese — HP14

1947   **Inscribed "Void after June 30, 1948"**
RW14 HP14 $1 **black**   50.00   16.00
     No gum   18.00
     P# block of 6   350.00

Buffleheads in Flight — HP15

1948   **Inscribed "Void after June 30, 1949"**
RW15 HP15 $1 **bright blue**   55.00   16.00
     No gum   21.00
     P# block of 6   400.00

Goldeneye Ducks — HP16

1949   **Inscribed "Void after June 30, 1950"**
RW16 HP16 $2 **bright green**   65.00   15.00
     No gum   22.50
     P# block of 6   450.00

Trumpeter Swans in Flight — HP17

1950   **Inscribed "Void after June 30, 1951"**
RW17 HP17 $2 **violet**   85.00   12.00
     No gum   22.50
     P# block of 6   575.00

Gadwall Ducks — HP18

1951   **Inscribed "Void after June 30, 1952"**
RW18 HP18 $2 **gray black**   85.00   12.00
     No gum   22.50
     P# block of 6   575.00

Harlequin Ducks — HP19

1952   **Inscribed "Void after June 30, 1953"**
RW19 HP19 $2 **deep ultramarine**   85.00   12.00
     No gum   22.50
     P# block of 6   575.00

Blue-winged Teal — HP20

1953   **Inscribed "Void after June 30, 1954"**
RW20 HP20 $2 **deep brown rose**   85.00   12.00
     No gum   22.50
     P# block of 6   575.00

> No. RW21 and following issues are printed on dry, pregummed paper and the back inscription is printed on top of the gum, except for the self-adhesive stamp issues starting in 1998.

Ring-necked Ducks — HP21

1954   **Inscribed "Void after June 30, 1955"**
RW21 HP21 $2 **black**   85.00   10.50
     No gum   22.50
     P# block of 6   575.00

Blue Geese — HP22

1955   **Inscribed "Void after June 30, 1956"**
RW22 HP22 $2 **dark blue**   85.00   10.50
     No gum   22.50
     P# block of 6   575.00
     a.   Back inscription inverted   5,500.   —

American Merganser — HP23

1956   **Inscribed "Void after June 30, 1957"**
RW23 HP23 $2 **black**   85.00   10.50
     No gum   22.50
     P# block of 6   575.00

American Eiders — HP24

1957   **Inscribed "Void after June 30, 19**
RW24 HP24 $2 **emerald**   85.00   1
     No gum   22.50
     P# block of 6   575.00
     a.   Back inscription inverted   5,000.

Canada Geese — HP25

1958   **Inscribed "Void after June 30, 19**
RW25 HP25 $2 **black**   85.00   1(
     No gum   22.50
     P# block of 6   575.00

Labrador Retriever Carrying Mallard Drake — HP2

Giori Press Printing
Issued in panes of 30 subjects
1959   **Inscribed "Void after June 30, 196**
RW26 HP26 $3 **blue, ocher & black**   120.00   11
     No gum   40.00
     P# block of 4   550.00
     a.   Back inscription inverted   35,000.

Redhead Ducks — HP27

1960   **Inscribed "Void after June 30, 196**
RW27 HP27 $3 **red brown, dark blue &**
       bister   90.00   10.
     No gum   37.50
     P# block of 4   450.00

Mallard Hen and Ducklings — HP28

61 Inscribed "Void after June 30, 1962"
V28 HP28 $3 **multicolored** 110.00 10.50
No gum 50.00
P# block of 4 525.00

Pintail
Drakes
coming
in for
landing
HP29

62 Inscribed "Void after June 30, 1963"
V29 HP29 $3 **dark blue, dark red brown**
& black 125.00 10.50
No gum 60.00
P# block of 4 600.00
a. Back inscription omitted —

Pair of Brant Landing — HP30

963 Inscribed "Void after June 30, 1964"
W30 HP30 $3 **multicolored** 110.00 10.50
No gum 55.00
P# block of 4 500.00

Hawaiian Nene Geese — HP31

964 Inscribed "Void after June 30, 1965"
RW31 HP31 $3 **multicolored** 110.00 10.50
No gum 55.00
P# block of 6 2,200.

Three Canvasback Drakes — HP32

1965 Inscribed "Void after June 30, 1966"
RW32 HP32 $3 **multicolored** 110.00 10.50
No gum 55.00
P# block of 4 550.00

Whistling Swans — HP33

1966 Inscribed "Void after June 30, 1967"
RW33 HP33 $3 **multicolored** 110.00 10.50
No gum 55.00
P# block of 4 550.00

Old Squaw Ducks — HP34

1967 Inscribed "Void after June 30, 1968"
RW34 HP34 $3 **multicolored** 125.00 10.50
No gum 60.00
P# block of 4 600.00

Hooded Mergansers — HP35

1968 Inscribed "Void after June 30, 1969"
RW35 HP35 $3 **multicolored** 65.00 10.50
No gum 25.00
P# block of 4 325.00
a. Back inscription omitted —

White-winged Scoters — HP36

1969 Inscribed "Void after June 30, 1970"
RW36 HP36 $3 **multicolored** 65.00 8.00
No gum 25.00
P# block of 4 300.00

Ross's Geese — HP37

1970 Engraved & Lithographed
Inscribed "Void after June 30, 1971"
RW37 HP37 $3 **multicolored** 65.00 8.00
No gum 24.00
P# block of 4 300.00

Three Cinnamon Teal — HP38

1971 Inscribed "Void after June 30, 1972"
RW38 HP38 $3 **multicolored** 42.50 7.75
No gum 21.00
P# block of 4 200.00

Emperor Geese — HP39

1972 Inscribed "Void after June 30, 1973"
RW39 HP39 $5 **multicolored** 25.00 7.00
No gum 12.50
P# block of 4 110.00

Steller's Eiders — HP40

1973 Inscribed "Void after June 30, 1974"
RW40 HP40 $5 **multicolored** 18.00 7.00
No gum 11.50
P# block of 4 90.00

Wood Ducks — HP41

1974   Inscribed "Void after June 30, 1975"
RW41 HP41 $5 **multicolored**   18.00   6.00
       No gum   9.50
       P# block of 4   75.00

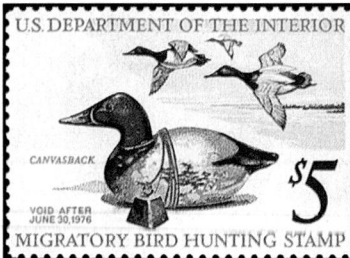

Canvasback Ducks and Decoy — HP42

1975   Inscribed "Void after June 30, 1976"
RW42 HP42 $5 **multicolored**   15.00   6.00
       No gum   8.50
       P# block of 4   60.00

Family of Canada Geese — HP43

1976   **Engr.**
     Inscribed "Void after June 30, 1977"
RW43 HP43 $5 **green & black**   15.00   6.00
       No gum   8.50
       P# block of 4   55.00

Pair of Ross's Geese — HP44

1977   **Litho. & Engr.**
     Inscribed "Void after June 30, 1978"
RW44 HP44 $5 **multicolored**   15.00   6.00
       No gum   8.50
       P# block of 4   55.00

Hooded Merganser Drake — HP45

1978   Inscribed "Void after June 30, 1979"
RW45 HP45 $5 **multicolored**   12.50   6.00
       No gum   7.00
       P# block of 4   55.00

Green-winged Teal — HP46

1979   Inscribed "Void after June 30, 1980"
RW46 HP46 $7.50 **multicolored**   14.00   7.00
       No gum   9.00
       P# block of 4   55.00

Mallards — HP47

1980   Inscribed "Void after June 30, 1981"
RW47 HP47 $7.50 **multicolored**   14.00   7.00
       No gum   9.00
       P# block of 4   55.00

Ruddy Ducks — HP48

1981   Inscribed "Void after June 30, 1982"
RW48 HP48 $7.50 **multicolored**   14.00   7.00
       No gum   9.00
       P# block of 4   55.00

Canvasbacks — HP49

1982   Inscribed "Void after June 30, 1983"
RW49 HP49 $7.50 **multicolored**   15.00   7.00
       No gum   9.00
       P# block of 4   55.00
   a.   Orange and violet omitted   7,500.

A certificate from a recognized expertization committee is required for No. RW49a.

Pintails — HP50

1983   Inscribed "Void after June 30, 198▢"
RW50 HP50 $7.50 **multicolored**   15.00   7▢
       No gum   9.00
       P# block of 4   60.00

Widgeons — HP51

1984   Inscribed "Void after June 30, 198▢"
RW51 HP51 $7.50 **multicolored**   15.00   7.▢
       No gum   9.00
       P# block of 4   62.50

See Special Printings section that follows.

Cinnamon Teal — HP52

1985   Inscribed "Void after June 30, 198▢"
RW52 HP52 $7.50 **multicolored**   15.00   8.▢
       No gum   9.00
       P# block of 4   60.00
   a.   Light blue (litho.) omitted   22,500.

The omitted color on No. RW52a coincides with a doub▢ paper splice affecting the top row of five stamps from the she▢ and top ⅓ of stamps in the second row. There is also a col▢ changeling of the brownish red ducks and their reflections in t▢ water to yellow and yellow orange, respectively, on the err▢ stamps. This error currently exists as three vertical strips of ▢ (top stamp the error) and a plate number block of 12 (2x6, t▢ two stamps the error.

Fulvous Whistling Duck — HP53

1986   Inscribed "Void after June 30, 1987"
RW53 HP53 $7.50 **multicolored**   15.00   7.0▢
       No gum   9.50
       P# block of 4   60.00
   a.   Black omitted   3,750.

Redheads — HP54

87 **Perf. 11¹⁄₂x11**
Inscribed "Void after June 30, 1988"
54 HP54 $10 multicolored 17.50 9.50
No gum 10.00
P# block of 4 65.00

Snow Goose — HP55

88 Inscribed "Void after June 30, 1989"
V55 HP55 $10 multicolored 17.00 10.00
No gum 11.00
P# block of 4 75.00

Lesser Scaup — HP56

989 Inscribed "Void after June 30, 1990"
W56 HP56 $12.50 multicolored 19.00 10.00
No gum 12.00
P# block of 4 82.50

Black Bellied Whistling Duck — HP57

990 Inscribed "Void after June 30, 1991"
RW57 HP57 $12.50 multicolored 19.00 10.00
No gum 12.00
P# block of 4 82.50
a. Back inscription omitted 375.00
b. Black inscription printed on the
stamp paper rather than the gum —

The back inscription is normally on top of the gum so beware of copies with gum removed offered as No. RW57a. Full original gum must be intact on No. RW57a. Used examples of No. RW57a cannot exist.

King
Eiders
HP58

1991 Inscribed "Void after June 30, 1992"
RW58 HP58 $15 multicolored 27.50 11.00
No gum 15.00
P# block of 4 120.00
a. Black (engr.) omitted 20,000.

Spectacled Eider — HP59

1992 Inscribed "Void after June 30, 1993"
RW59 HP59 $15 multicolored 27.50 11.00
No gum 15.00
P# block of 4 120.00

Canvasbacks — HP60

1993 Inscribed "Void after June 30, 1994"
RW60 HP60 $15 multicolored 30.00 11.00
No gum 16.00
P# block of 4 130.00
a. Black (engr.) omitted 3,000.

Red-breasted Mergansers — HP61

1994 **Perf. 11¹⁄₄x11**
Inscribed "Void after June 30, 1995"
RW61 HP61 $15 multicolored 30.00 11.00
No gum 16.00
P# block of 4 130.00

Mallards — HP62

1995 Inscribed "Void after June 30, 1996"
RW62 HP62 $15 multicolored 27.50 11.00
No gum 15.00
P# block of 4 120.00

Surf Scoters — HP63

1996 Inscribed "Void after June 30, 1997"
RW63 HP63 $15 multicolored 25.00 11.00
No gum 14.00
P# block of 4 110.00

Canada Goose — HP64

"Long breast feather" plate flaw

"Short breast feather" plate flaw

1997   **Inscribed "Void after June 30, 1998"**
RW64   HP64 $15 **multicolored**   30.00 11.00
      No gum   16.00
      P# block of 4   110.00
      "Long breast feather" plate
        flaw, pos. 28   85.00 —
      In pair with normal stamp   125.00
      "Short breast feather" plate
        flaw, pos. 28   65.00 —
      In pair with normal stamp   85.00

Barrow's Goldeneye — HP65

1998   **Perf. 11¼**
Inscribed "Void after June 30, 1999"
RW65   HP65 $15 **multicolored**   30.00 11.00
      No gum   16.00
      P# block of 4   140.00
Self-Adhesive
Die Cut Perf. 10
RW65A HP65 $15 *Barrow's Goldeneye*   25.00 11.00
      No gum   15.00

> Nos. RW65 and later issues were sold in panes of 30 (RW65 and RW66) or 20 (RW67 and later issues), with four plate numbers per pane. The self-adhesives starting with No. RW65A were sold in panes of 1. The self-adhesives are valued unused as complete panes and used as single stamps.

Greater Scaup — HP66

1999   **Perf. 11¼**
Inscribed "Void after June 30, 2000"
RW66   HP66 $15 **multicolored**   25.00 11.00
      No gum   15.00
      P# block of 4   110.00
Self-Adhesive
Die Cut Perf. 10
RW66A HP66 $15 **multicolored**   25.00 10.00
      No gum   15.00

Mottled Duck — HP67

2000   **Perf. 11¼**
Inscribed "Void after June 30, 2001"
RW67   HP67 $15 **multicolored**   25.00 11.00
      No gum   15.00
      P# block of 4   110.00
Self-Adhesive
Die Cut 10
RW67A HP67 $15 **multicolored**   22.50 10.00
      No gum   15.00

Northern Pintail — HP68

2001   **Perf. 11¼**
Inscribed "Void after June 30, 2002"
RW68   HP68 $15 **multicolored**   25.00 11.00
      No gum   15.00
      P# block of 4   100.00
Self-Adhesive
Die Cut Perf. 10
RW68A HP68 $15 **multicolored**   22.50 10.00
      No gum   15.00

Black Scoters — HP69

Printed by Banknote Corporation of America.

2002   **Perf. 11¼**
Inscribed "Void after June 30, 2003"
RW69   HP69 $15 **multicolored**   25.00 11.00
      No gum   15.00
      P# block of 4   100.00
Self-Adhesive
Serpentine Die Cut 11x10¾
RW69A HP69 $15 **multicolored**   22.50 10.00
      No gum   15.00

Snow Geese — HP70

Printed by Ashton-Potter (USA) Ltd.

2003   **Perf.**
Inscribed "Void after June 30, 2004"
RW70   HP70 $15 **multicolored**   25.00 11
      No gum   15.00
      P# block of 4   100.00
     b.   Imperf, pair   7,500.
     c.   Back inscription omitted   4,500.
Self-Adhesive
Serpentine Die Cut 11x10¾
RW70A HP70 $15 **multicolored**   22.50 10
      No gum   15.00

Redheads — HP71

Printed by Banknote Corporation of America for Senn Security Products.

2004   **Perf.**
Inscribed "Void after June 30, 2005"
RW71 $15 **multicolored**   25.00 10.
      No gum   15.00
      P# block of 4   100.00
Self-Adhesive
Serpentine Die Cut 11x10¾
RW71A HP71 $15   22.50 10
      No gum   15.00

   No. RW71 was sold in panes of 20. No. RW71A was sold panes of 1. No. RW71A is valued unused as a complete pa and used as a single stamp.

Hooded Mergansers — HP72

Printed by Banknote Corporation of America for Senne Security Products
   Two types of RW72: I, No framelines at top, right or botto (from left two panes of the press sheet); II, Gray framelines top, right and bottom (from right two panes of the press sheet

2005   **Litho. & Engr.**   **Perf. 1**
Inscribed "Void after June 30, 2006"
RW72   HP72 $15 **multicolored, type I**   22.50 11.0
      No gum   15.00
      P# block of 4   100.00
     b.   Souvenir sheet of 1   2,000.
     c.   Type II,   22.50 11.0
      No gum   15.00
      P# block of 4   100.00
Self-Adhesive
Litho. & Debossed
Serpentine Die Cut 11x10¾
RW72A HP72 $15 **multicolored**   22.50 11.0
      No gum   15.00

   One hundred press sheets containing four panes of 20 of No RW72 and one hundred press sheets containing 18 of No RW72A were offered for sale by the U.S. Fish and Wildlif Service.
   No. RW72b sold for $20. 1,000 No. RW72b were issued Approximately 750 were signed by the artist in black, value $2,000 as shown. Approximately 150 were signed in blue ink value $2,500. Approximately 100 were signed in gold ink, value $3,000. Most examples of No. RW72b are in the grade of F-VF Catalogue values are for Very Fine examples.
   The Duck Stamp Office never announced the existence c No. RW72b to the public through a press release or a website announcement during the time the sheet was on sale, appar ently because it was not clear beforehand that the souveni sheet could be produced successfully and on time. No. RW72 sold out before a public announcement of the item's existence could be made.

Ross's Goose — HP73

Printed by Banknote Corporation of America for Sennett Security Products

2006   **Litho. & Engr.**   **Perf. 11**

Inscribed "Void after June 30, 2007"

RW73	HP73 $15 **multicolored**		22.50	11.00
	No gum		15.00	
	P# block of 4		100.00	
b.	Souvenir sheet of 1		*250.00*	

Self-Adhesive

Serpentine Die Cut 11x10¾

RW73A	HP73 $15 **multicolored**		22.50	11.00
	No gum		20.00	

Two hundred fifty press sheets containing four panes of 20 of No. RW73 and two hundred fifty press sheets containing 18 of No. RW73A were offered for sale by the U.S. Fish and Wildlife Service.

No. RW73b sold for $25. All examples of No. RW73b have a black signature of the artist on a designated line in the sheet margin. Ten thousand were issued.

The sheet margin of No. RW73b has a line designated for the signature of the engraver, Piotr Naszarkowski, but no sheets were sold with his signature. Naszarkowski signed approximately 2,500 sheets during three days at the Washington 2006 World Philatelic Exhibition. Value thus, $350.

SPECIAL PRINTING

After No. RW51 became void, fifteen uncut sheets of 120 (4 panes of 30 separated by gutters) were overprinted "1934-84" and "50th ANNIVERSARY" in the margins and auctioned by the U.S. Fish and Wildlife Service.

Bids were accepted from September 1 through November 1, 1985. Minimum bid for each sheet was $2,000. The face value of each sheet, had they still been valid, was $900. Each sheet also had the sheet number and pane position printed in the corner of each pane ("01 of 15-1," "01 of 15-2," etc.). Fourteen of the sheets were sold at this and one subsequent auction and one was donated to the Smithsonian.

An individual sheet could be broken up to create these identifiable collectibles: 4 margin overprint blocks of 10; cross gutter block of 4; 6 horizontal pairs with gutter between; 8 vertical pairs with gutter between.

Single stamps from the sheet cannot be distinguished from No. RW51. No used examples can exist.

RW51x $7.50   *Widgeons*

DESIGNERS

1934 —	RW1	J.N. Darling
1935 —	RW2	Frank W. Benson
1936 —	RW3	Richard E. Bishop
1937 —	RW4	J.D. Knap
1938 —	RW5	Roland Clark
1939 —	RW6	Lynn Bogue Hunt
1940 —	RW7	Francis L. Jaques
1941 —	RW8	E.R. Kalmbach
1942 —	RW9	A. Lassell Ripley
1943 —	RW10	Walter E. Bohl
1944 —	RW11	Walter A. Weber
1945 —	RW12	Owen J. Bromme
1946 —	RW13	Robert W. Hines
1947 —	RW14	Jack Murray
1948 —	RW15	Maynard Reece
1949 —	RW16	"Roge" E. Preuss
1950 —	RW17	Walter A. Weber
1951 —	RW18	Maynard Reece
1952 —	RW19	John H. Dick
1953 —	RW20	Clayton B. Seagears
1954 —	RW21	Harvey D. Sandstrom
1955 —	RW22	Stanley Searns
1956 —	RW23	Edward J. Bierly
1957 —	RW24	Jackson Miles Abbott,
1958 —	RW25	Leslie C. Kouba
1959 —	RW26	Maynard Reece
1960 —	RW27	John A. Ruthven,
1961 —	RW28	Edward A. Morris
1962 —	RW29	Edward A. Morris
1963 —	RW30	Edward J. Bierly
1964 —	RW31	Stanley Searns
1965 —	RW32	Ron Jenkins
1966 —	RW33	Stanley Searns
1967 —	RW34	Leslie C. Kouba
1968 —	RW35	C.G. Pritchard
1969 —	RW36	Maynard Reece
1970 —	RW37	Edward J. Bierly
1971 —	RW38	Maynard Reece
1972 —	RW39	Arthur M. Cook
1973 —	RW40	Lee LeBlanc
1974 —	RW41	David A. Maass
1975 —	RW42	James L. Fisher
1976 —	RW43	Alderson Magee
1977 —	RW44	Martin R. Murk
1978 —	RW45	Albert Earl Gilbert
1979 —	RW46	Kenneth L. Michaelsen
1980 —	RW47	Richard W. Plasschaert
1981 —	RW48	John S. Wilson
1982 —	RW49	David A. Maass
1983 —	RW50	Phil Scholer
1984 —	RW51	William C. Morris
1985 —	RW52	Gerald Mobley
1986 —	RW53	Burton E. Moore, Jr.
1987 —	RW54	Arthur G. Anderson
1988 —	RW55	Daniel Smith
1989 —	RW56	Neal R. Anderson
1990 —	RW57	Jim Hautman
1991 —	RW58	Nancy Howe
1992 —	RW59	Joe Hautman
1993 —	RW60	Bruce Miller
1994 —	RW61	Neal R. Anderson
1995 —	RW62	Jim Hautman
1996 —	RW63	Wilhelm Goebel
1997 —	RW64	Robert Hautman
1998 —	RW65	Robert Steiner
1999 —	RW66	Jim Hautman
2000 —	RW67	Adam Grimm
2001 —	RW68	Robert Hautman
2002 —	RW69	Joe Hautman
2003 —	RW70	Ron Louque
2004 —	RW71	Scot Storm
2005 —	RW72	Mark Anderson
2006 —	RW73	Sherrie Russell Meline

QUANTITIES SOLD

(Quantities from No. RW65 on are quantities ordered. Quantities sold of these numbers were much less.)

RW1	635,001	RW43	2,170,194
RW2	448,204	RW44	2,196,774
RW3	603,623	RW45	2,216,621
RW4	783,039	RW46	2,090,155
RW5	1,002,715	RW47	2,045,114
RW6	1,111,561	RW48	1,907,120
RW7	1,260,810	RW49	1,926,253
RW8	1,439,967	RW50	1,867,998
RW9	1,383,629	RW51	1,913,861
RW10	1,169,352	RW52	1,780,636
RW11	1,487,029	RW53	1,794,484
RW12	1,725,505	RW54	1,663,270
RW13	2,016,841	RW55	1,402,096
RW14	1,722,677	RW56	1,415,882
RW15	2,127,603	RW57	1,408,373
RW16	1,954,734	RW58	1,423,374
RW17	1,903,644	RW59	1,347,393
RW18	2,167,767	RW60	1,402,569
RW19	2,296,628	RW61	1,471,751
RW20	2,268,446	RW62	1,539,622
RW21	2,184,550	RW63	1,560,123
RW22	2,369,940	RW64	1,697,590
RW23	2,332,014	RW65	1,195,000
RW24	2,355,190	RW65A	2,805,000
RW25	2,176,425	RW66	1,194,000
RW26	1,626,115	RW66A	2,799,600
RW27	1,725,634	RW67	1,200,000
RW28	1,344,236	RW67A	2,800,000
RW29	1,147,212	RW68	1,194,000
RW30	1,448,191	RW68A	2,806,000
RW31	1,573,155	RW69	1,194,000
RW32	1,558,197	RW69A	2,806,000
RW33	1,805,341	RW70	1,000,000
RW34	1,934,697	RW70A	3,000,000
RW35	1,837,139	RW71	1,000,000
RW36	2,072,108	RW71A	3,000,000
RW37	2,420,244		
RW38	2,445,977		
RW39	2,184,343		
RW40	2,094,414		
RW41	2,214,056		
RW42	2,237,126		

JUNIOR DUCK STAMPS

As a courtesy to Duck stamp collectors, we list here the Duck stamps issued under the Federal Junior Duck Stamp program, run by the U.S. Fish and Wildlife Service branch of the Department of the Interior and the Federal Duck Stamp Office. The purpose of this program is to teach youth through the medium of art the importance of conserving wetlands and migratory birds.

Students in kindergarden to 12th grade from all 50 states, the District of Columbia, American Samoa and the U.S. Virgin Islands are invited to participate in an annual art competition. The winning entry from each state, district or territory competes

for the national championship. The national winner's art appears on that year's Junior Duck stamp, which is sold to raise funds to support the Junior Duck Stamp art and educational program. The United States Postal Service, through its Stamp Fulfillment Services unit, acts as a sales agent for these stamps.

These stamps are not valid for hunting, nor is it required that hunters buy the stamps in order to hunt.

A precursor sheet of nine stamps was released in 1992 as a part of a pilot program instituted before the formal, annual Junior Duck Stamp art competition was begun. The sheet shows stamps from Arkansas, California (2), Florida (2), Illinois (2), Kansas and Vermont. Value, $30.

All issues were printed in panes of 30 with four control/plate numbers. Imperforate examples of Nos. JDS1, JDS2 and JDS3 exist and are believed to be printer's waste.

Catalogue values for all stamps in this section are for stamps with never-hinged original gum.

JD1

1993   **Artist: Jason Parsons (IL)**
JDS1   JD1 $5 *Redhead*   75.00

1994   **Artist: Clark Weaver (PA)**
JDS2   JD1 $5 *Hooded mergansers*   75.00

1995   **Artist: Jie Huang (MT)**
JDS3   JD1 $5 *Pintail*   190.00

1996   **Artist: Clark Weaver (PA)**
JDS4   JD1 $5 *Canvasbacks*   190.00

1997   **Artist: Scott Russell (CA)**
JDS5   JD1 $5 *Canada geese*   225.00

1998   **Artist: Eric Peterson (MI)**
JDS6   JD1 $5 *Black ducks*   350.00

1999   **Artist: Ryan Kirby (IL)**
JDS7   JD1 $5 *Wood ducks*   350.00

2000   **Artist: Bonnie Latham (MN)**
JDS8   JD1 $5 *Pintails*   350.00

2001   **Artist: Aremy McCann (MN)**
JDS9   JD1 $5 *Trumpeter swan*   65.00

2002   **Artist: Nathan Closson (MT)**
JDS10 JD1 $5 *Mallards*   30.00

2003   **Artist: Nathan Bauman (PA)**
JDS11 JD1 $5 *Green-winged teals*   20.00

2004   **Artist: Adam Nisbett (MO)**
JDS12 JD1 $5 *Fulvous whistling ducks*   15.00

2005   **Artist: Kerissa Nelson (WI)**
JDS13 JD1 $5 *Ring-necked ducks*   10.00

2006   **Artist: Rebekah Nastav (MO)**
JDS14 JD1 $5 *Redhead*   10.00

collecting **accessorie**

2.5" Crystal View Magnifier

Form and function come together with this attractive, high quality 4x mager. Dome-shaped magnifier "draws light like a magnet," illuminating the intricate details of stamps or coins. Magre availfits in handsome solid ring and slides easily across any flat surface.

ITEM	DESCRIPTION	RETAIL
MG25	Crystal View Magnifier	$39.99

Lighted 4x and 10X Magnifier

An inexpensive tool for anyone who needs illuminated magnification. Spring-loaded lens hidden within the body of the magnifer

ITEM	DESCRIPTION	RETAIL
MG4XL	Red 4x	$13.99
MG10XL	Black 10x	$17.99

5X-20X Folding Pocket Magnifier

This folding pocket magnifier contains three separate glass lenses housed in a durable plastic swing-away case. Seven different powers of magnification from 5x to 20x can be created when the lenses are used in combination. Depending on magnification, the focal distance is between .5" and 2".

ITEM	DESCRIPTION	RETAIL
MG520	5X-20X Magnifier	$29.99

Scott/Linn's Multi Gauge

"The best peforation gauge in the world just got better!" The gauge used by the Scott Editorial staff to perf stamps for the Catalogue has been improved. Not only is the Scott/Linn's gauge graduated in tenths, each division is marked by thin lines to assist collectors in gauging stamp to the tenth. The Scott/Linn's Multi-Gauge is a perforation gauge, cancellation gauge, zero-center ruler and millimeter ruler in one easy-to-use instrument. It's greate for measuring multiples and stamps on cover.

ITEM	DESCRIPTION	RETAIL
LIN01	Multi-Gauge	$6.95

Rotary Mount Cutter

German engineered mount cutter delivers precise and accurate cuts. The metal base features cm-measurements across the to and down both sides. The rotary cutter has an exchangeable, s sharpening blade that rotates within a plastic casing, safely insu ing perfectly straight and rectangular cuts.

ITEM	DESCRIPTION	RETAIL
980RMC	Mount Cutter	$69.00

These accessories and others are available from your favorite stamp dealer or direct from:

SCOTT

AMOS
HOBBY PUBLISHING

STATE HUNTING PERMIT STAMPS

These stamps are used on licenses for hunting waterfowl (ducks, geese, swans) by states and Indian reservations. Stamps which include waterfowl along with a variety of other animals are listed here. Stamps for hunting birds that exclude waterfowl are not listed.

A number of states print stamps in sheets as well as in booklets. The booklets are sent to agents for issuing to hunters. Both varieties are listed. The major listing is given to the sheet stamp since it generally is available in larger quantities and has been the more popularly collected item. In some cases the stamp removed from a booklet, with no tabs or selvage, is identical to a single sheet stamp (see Rhode Island). In these cases the identifiable booklet stamp with tabs and selvage receives an unlettered listing. If the single booklet stamp can be identified by type of perforation or the existence of one or more straight edges, the item receives a lettered listing (see Oregon).

Governor's editions are sold at a premium over the license fee with proceeds intended to help waterfowl habitats. Only those which differ from the regular stamp are listed.

After the period of validity, a number of these stamps were sold at less than face value. This explains the low values on stamps such as Montana Nos. 30, 33, and Flathead Indian Reservation Nos. 2-10.

When used, most stamps are affixed to licenses and signed by the hunter. Values for used stamps are for copies off licenses and without tabs. Although used examples may be extremely scarce, they will always sell for somewhat less than unused examples (two-thirds of the unused value would be the upper limit).

ALABAMA

Printed in sheets of 10.
Stamps are numbered serially.

Catalogue values for all unused stamps in this section are for Never Hinged items.

Artists: Barbara Keel, #1; Wayne Spradley, #2; Jack Deloney, #3; Joe Michelet, #4; John Lee, #5, 25; William Morris, #6, 14; Larry Martin, #7; Danny W. Dorning, #8; Robert C. Knutson, #9, 20; John Warr, #10; Elaine Byrd, #11; Steven Garst, #12; Larry Chandler, #13, 24; James Brantley, #15; Neil Blackwell, #17; Judith Huey, #18; E. Hatcher, #19; Eddie LeRoy, #21; David Sellers, #22, 26, 27; H. Andrew McNeely, #23.

1979-2004

	$5 Wood ducks, rouletted	10.00	3.00
	$5 Mallards, 1980	10.00	3.00
	$5 Canada geese, 1981	10.00	3.00
	$5 Green-winged teal, 1982	10.00	3.00
	$5 Widgeons, 1983	10.00	3.00
	$5 Buffleheads, 1984	10.00	3.00
	$5 Wood ducks, 1985	14.00	3.00
	$5 Canada geese, 1986	14.00	3.00
	$5 Pintails, 1987	15.00	3.00
0	$5 Canvasbacks, 1988	10.00	3.00
1	$5 Hooded mergansers, 1989	12.00	3.00
2	$5 Wood ducks, 1990		
3	$5 Redheads, 1991	10.00	2.50
4	$5 Cinnamon teal, 1992	10.00	2.50
5	$5 Green-winged teal, 1993	10.00	2.50
6	$5 Canvasbacks, 1994	10.00	2.50
7	$5 Canada geese, 1995	10.00	2.50
8	$5 Wood ducks, 1996	10.00	2.50
9	$5 Snow goose, 1997	10.00	2.50
0	$5 Barrow's goldeneye, 1998	10.00	2.50
1	$5 Redheads, 1999	10.00	2.50
2	$5 Buffleheads, 2000	9.00	2.50
3	$5 Ruddy duck, 2001	9.00	2.50
4	$5 Pintail, 2002	8.00	2.50
5	$5 Wood ducks, 2003	9.00	2.50
6	$5 Ring-necked ducks, 2004	8.00	2.50
7	$5 Canada geese, 2005	8.00	2.50

ALASKA

Printed in sheets of 30.
Stamps are numbered serially on reverse. Booklet pane stamps printed in panes of 5.

Catalogue values for all unused stamps in this section are for Never Hinged items.

1985 Alaska Waterfowl Stamp

Artist: Daniel Smith, #1; James Meger, #2; Carl Branson, #3; Jim Beaudoin, #4; Richard Timm, #5; Louis Frisino, #6; Ronald Louque, #7; Fred Thomas, #8; Ed Tussey, #9; George Lockwood, #10, 13; Cynthia Fisher, #11, 20; Wilhelm Goebel, #12; Robert Steiner, #14, 18; Sherrie Russell Meline, #15; Adam Grimm, #16, 19; Greg Alexander, #17; Don Moore, #21.

1985-2004

1	$5 Emperor geese	10.00	3.00
2	$5 Steller's eiders, 1986	10.00	3.00
3	$5 Spectacled eiders, perforated, 1987	10.00	
a.	Bklt. single, rouletted, with tab	10.00	2.50
4	$5 Trumpeter swans, perforated, 1988	10.00	
a.	Bklt. single, rouletted, with tab	10.00	2.50
5	$5 Barrow's goldeneyes, perforated, 1989	10.00	
a.	Bklt. single, rouletted, with tab	10.00	2.50
b.	Governor's edition	140.00	

No. 5b was sold in full panes through a sealed bid auction.

6	$5 Old squaws, perforated, 1990	9.00	
a.	Bklt. single, rouletted, with tab	9.50	2.50
7	$5 Snow geese, perforated, 1991	8.25	
a.	Bklt. single, rouletted, with tab	9.50	2.50
8	$5 Canvasbacks, perforated, 1992	8.25	
a.	Bklt. single, rouletted, with tab	9.00	2.50
9	$5 Tule white front geese, perforated, 1993	14.00	
a.	Bklt. single, rouletted, with tab	14.00	2.50
10	$5 Harlequin ducks, perforated, 1994	20.00	
a.	Bklt. single, rouletted, with tab	15.00	2.50
b.	Governor's edition	90.00	
11	$5 Pacific brant, perforated, 1995	22.00	
a.	Bklt. single, rouletted, with tab	15.00	2.50
12	$5 Canada geese, 1996	25.00	
a.	Bklt. single, rouletted, with tab	20.00	2.50
13	$5 King eiders, 1997	20.00	
a.	Bklt. single, rouletted, with tab	16.00	2.50
14	$5 Barrow's goldeneye, 1998	12.00	
a.	Bklt. single, with tab	12.00	2.50
15	$5 Pintail, 1999	11.00	
a.	Bklt. single, with tab	11.00	2.50
16	$5 Common eider, 2000	10.00	
a.	Bklt. single, with tab	10.00	2.50
17	$5 American wigeon, 2001	10.00	
a.	Bklt. single, with tab	10.00	2.50
18	$5 Black scoters, 2002	10.00	
a.	Bklt. single, with tab	10.00	2.50
19	$5 Lesser Canada geese, 2003	12.00	
a.	Bklt. single, with tab	12.00	2.50
20	$5 Lesser scaup, 2004	10.00	
a.	Bklt. single, with tab	10.00	2.50
21	$5 Hooded merganser, 2005	7.50	
a.	Bklt. single, with tab	8.50	2.50

ARIZONA

Printed in booklet panes of 5 with tab and in sheets of 30.
Stamps are numbered serially.

Catalogue values for all unused stamps in this section are for Never Hinged items.

Artists: Daniel Smith, #1; Sherrie Russell Meline, #2, 6-7, 9, 11-18; Robert Steiner, #3; Ted Blaylock, #4; Brian Jarvi, #5; Harry Adamson, #8; Larry Hayden, #10; Tom Finley, #19.

1987-2004

1	$5.50 Pintails, perf. 4 sides	11.00	
a.	Bklt. single, perf. 3 sides, with tab	11.00	3.00
2	$5.50 Green-winged teal, perf. 4 sides, 1988	12.00	
a.	Bklt. single, perf. 3 sides, with tab	12.00	3.00
3	$5.50 Cinnamon teal, perf. 4 sides, 1989	11.00	
a.	Bklt. single, perf. 3 sides, with tab	11.00	2.50
b.	$5.50 +$50 Governor's edition	75.00	
4	$5.50 Canada geese, perf. 4 sides, 1990	12.00	
a.	Bklt. single, perf. 3 sides, with tab	12.00	2.50
b.	$5.50 +$50 Governor's edition	75.00	
5	$5.50 Blue-winged teal, perf. 4 sides, 1991	10.00	
a.	Bklt. single, perf. 3 sides, with tab	11.00	2.50
b.	$55.50 Governor's edition	75.00	
6	$5.50 Buffleheads, perf. 4 sides, 1992	10.00	
a.	Bklt. single, perf. 3 sides, with tab	11.00	2.50
b.	$55.50 Governor's edition	75.00	
7	$5.50 Mexican ducks, perf. 4 sides, 1993	12.00	
a.	Bklt. single, perf. 3 sides, with tab	12.00	2.50
b.	$55.50 Governor's edition	75.00	
8	$5.50 Mallards, perf. 4 sides, 1994	12.00	
a.	Bklt. single, perf. 3 sides, with tab	12.00	2.50
b.	$55.50 Governor's edition	75.00	
9	$5.50 Widgeon, perf. 4 sides, 1995	12.00	
a.	Bklt. single, perf. 3 sides, with tab	12.00	2.50
b.	$55.50 Governor's edition	75.00	

10	$5.50 Canvasbacks, perf. 4 sides, *1996*	10.00	
a.	Bklt. single, perf 3 sides, with tab	10.00	2.50
b.	$55.50 Governor's edition	75.00	
11	$5.50 Gadwalls, *1997*	12.00	
a.	Bklt. single, perf 3 sides, with tab	12.00	2.50
b.	$55.50 Governor's edition	75.00	
12	$5.50 Wood duck, *1998*	12.00	
a.	Bklt. single, perf 3 sides, with tab	12.00	2.50
b.	$55.50 Governor's edition	—	
13	$5.50 Snow goose, *1999*	12.00	
a.	Bklt. single, perf. 3 sides, with tab	12.00	2.50
b.	$55.50 Governor's edition	75.00	
14	$7.50 Ruddy duck, *2000*	11.00	
a.	Bklt. single, perf 3 sides, with tab	11.00	2.50
b.	$55.50 Governor's edition	75.00	
15	$7.50 Redheads, *2001*	10.50	
a.	Bklt. single, perf 3 sides, with tab	10.50	2.50
b.	$55.50 Governor's edition	75.00	
16	$7.50 Ring-necked ducks, *2002*	10.00	
a.	Bklt. single, perf. 2 sides, with tabs	10.50	2.60
b.	$55.50 Governor's edition	75.00	
17	$7.50 Northern shovelers, *2003*	14.00	
a.	Bklt. single, perf. 2 sides, with tabs	14.00	2.50
b.	$55.50 Governor's edition	75.00	
18	$7.50 Lesser scaup, *2004*	12.00	
a.	Bklt. single, perf. 3 sides, with tab	12.00	2.50
b.	$55.50 Governor's edition	75.00	—
19	$7.50 Pintails, *2005*	9.50	
a.	Bklt. single, perf. 3 sides, with tabs	10.50	2.50

ARKANSAS

Imperforate varieties of these stamps exist in large quantities. Imperforate copies of Nos. 1 and 2 were sold by the state for $1 each.

No. 1 printed in sheets and booklet panes of 30, others in sheets and booklet panes of 10.

Stamps are numbered serially on reverse.

> **Catalogue values for all unused stamps in this section are for Never Hinged items.**

Artists: Lee LeBlanc, #1; Maynard Reece, #2, 8; David Maass, #3, 10, 21; Larry Hayden, #4, 15; Ken Carlson, #5, 13; John P. Cowan, #6; Robert Bateman. #7; Phillip Crowe, #9, 16, 22; Daniel Smith, #11, 14; Jim Hautman, #12, 19; L. Chandler, #17, 20, 26, 27; John Dearman, #18; Zettie Jones, #23; Ralph McDonald, #24-25.

1981-2003

1	$5.50 Mallards	55.00	12.00
	Booklet single with top tab, Nos. 110,001-200,000 on back	60.00	
2	$5.50 Wood ducks, *1982*	40.00	9.00
3	$5.50 Green-winged teal, *1983*	65.00	12.00
4	$5.50 Pintails, *1984*	22.50	5.00
5	$5.50 Mallards, *1985*	13.00	2.50
6	$5.50 Black swamp mallards, *1986*	11.00	2.50
7	$7 Wood ducks, *1987*	11.00	2.50

Stamps like Nos. 7 and 8 with $5.50 face values were sold following an order of the state Supreme Court restoring the fee level of 1986. The stamps were sold after the 1988 season had ended. Value, $11 each.

8	$7 Pintails, *1988*	10.00	2.50

See footnote following No. 7.

9	$7 Mallards, *1989*	10.00	2.50
10	$7 Black ducks & mallards, *1990*	12.00	2.50
11	$7 Sulphur river widgeons, *1991*	10.00	2.50
12	$7 Shirey Bay shovelers, *1992*	12.00	2.50
13	$7 Grand prairie mallards, *1993*	12.00	2.50
14	$7 Canada goose, *1994*	14.00	2.50
15	$7 White River mallards, *1995*	14.00	2.50
16	$7 Mallards, black labrador, *1996*	14.00	2.00
17	$7 Labrador retriever, mallards, *1997*	15.00	2.00
18	$7 Labrador retriever, mallards, *1998*	12.00	2.00
19	$7 Wood duck, *1999*	12.00	2.00
20	$7 Mallards and golden retriever, *2000*	11.00	2.00
21	$7 Canvasbacks, *2001*	11.00	2.00
22	$7 Mallards, *2002*	11.00	2.00
23	$7 Mallards & Chesapeake retriever, *2003*	14.00	2.00
24	$7 Mallards, *2004*	11.00	2.00
25	$20 Mallards, *2004*	25.00	2.00
26	$7 Mallards, Labrador retriever *2004*	9.00	2.00
27	$20 Mallards, Labrador retriever *2004*	25.00	2.00

Resident and non-resident fees begin in 2004.

CALIFORNIA

Honey Lake Waterfowl Stamps

Required to hunt waterfowl at Honey Lake. Valid for a full season. Stamps are rouletted. Used values are for signed copies. Unsigned stamps without gum probably were used. Values for these stamps are higher than used values, but lower than values shown for gummed unused stamps.

1956-86

A1	$5 black, *1956-1957*		—
A2	$5 black, *blue green, 1957-1958*		—
A3	$5 black, *dark yellow, 1958-1959*		—
A4	$5 black, *dark yellow, 1959-1960*	1,350.	550.00
A5	$5 black, *1960-1961*		1,250.
A6	$5 black, *bluish green, 1961-1962*	—	1,200.
A7	$5 black, *dark yellow, 1962-1963*		600.00
A8	$5 black, *1963-1964*		375.00
A9	$6.50 black, *pink, 1964-1965*	1,500.	350.00
A10	$6.50 black, *1965-1966*		300.00
A11	$6.50 black, *yellow, Nos. 1-700, printer's information at bottom right, 1966-1967*		325.00
a.	Serial Nos. 701-1050, no printer's information		7,500.
A12	$10 black, *pink, 1967-1968*	—	300.00
A13	$10 black, *blue, 1968-1969*		375.00
A14	$10 black, *green, 1969-1970*	—	400.00
A15	$15 black, *dark yellow, 1970-1971*	—	550.00
A16	$15 black, *pink, 1971-1972*		1,950.
A17	$15 black, *blue, 1972-1973*		2,750.
A18	$15 black, *blue, 1973-1974*	—	
A19	$15 black, *pink, 1974-1975*	50.00	25.00
A20	$15 black, *green, 1975-1976*	150.00	35.00
A21	$15 black, *light yellow, 1976-1977*	150.00	35.00
A22	$20 black, *blue, 1977-1978*	150.00	35.00
A23	$20 blk, *light yel brown, 1978-1979*	150.00	35.00
A24	$20 black, *light yellow, 1979-1980*	150.00	35.00
A25	$15 black, *light blue, 1980-1981*	110.00	30.00
A26	$20 black, *light yellow, 1981-1982*	—	
A27	$20 black, *pink, 1982-1983*	95.00	30.00
A28	$20 black, *light green, 1983-1984*	45.00	25.00
A29	$20 black, *dark yellow, 1984-1985*	42.50	25.00
A30	$20 black, *light blue, 1985-1986*	37.50	20.00

Eighteen $5 black on dark yellow permit stamps were sold for hunting at the state-owned and operated Madeline Plains waterfowl management area for the 1956-57 season. No examples have been recorded.

Statewide Hunting License Validation Stamps

Fees are for resident, junior and non-resident hunters. "No fee" stamps were for disabled veterans. Stamps with special serial numbers for state officials are known for some years. Nos. 2A1-2A3 imperf on 3 sides, rouletted at top. Others die cut.

Stamps are numbered serially.

Used values are for written-upon copies. Starting with No. 2A4, unused values are for stamps on backing paper.

1962-1963

2A1	$4 black	450.00	7
a.	Ovptd. "NO FEE"	475.00	300
2A2	$1 black, *yellow*	1,350.	75
2A3	$25 black, *green*	2,500.	150

No. 2A25

1963-1964

2A4	$4 black, *green*		3
a.	Ovptd. "NO FEE"	—	20
2A5	$1 black, *gray*		20
2A6	$25 black, *yellow orange*		300.

1964-1965

2A7	$4 black, *pink*	30.00	1.
a.	Ovptd. "NO FEE"	550.00	275.
2A8	$1 black, *yellow brown*	225.00	25.
2A9	$25 black, *dark gray*		70.

1965-1966

2A10	$4 black, *gray*	25.00	1.
a.	Ovptd. "NO FEE"		
2A11	$1 black, *yellow gray*		25.
2A12	$25 black, *ivory*		75.

1966-1967

2A13	$4 black, *salmon*	25.00	1.
a.	Ovptd. "NO FEE"		650.
2A14	$1 black, *lt blue*	75.00	10.
2A15	$25 black, *burgundy*		65.

1967-1968

2A16	$4 black, *yellow*	20.00	1.
a.	Ovptd. "NO FEE"		600.
2A17	$1 black, *green*	45.00	5.
a.	black, *yellow gray*		
2A18	$25 black, *brown*	75.00	25.

1968-1969

2A19	$4 black, *pink*	55.00	1.
a.	Ovptd. "NO FEE"		650.
2A20	$1 black, *blue gray*	175.00	20.
2A21	$25 black, *light orange*		85.

1969-1970

2A22	$4 black	55.00	1.
a.	Ovptd. "NO FEE"		575.
2A23	$1 black, *dark pink*	175.00	20.
2A24	$25 black, *light yellow*	70.00	25.

1970-1971

2A25	$4 black, *manila*	70.00	2.
a.	Ovptd. "NO FEE"	1,350.	1,00
2A26	$1 black, *blue gray*	75.00	10.
2A27	$25 black, *gray brown*	100.00	25.

1971-1972

2A28	$4 black, *green*	45.00	1.
a.	Ovptd. "NO FEE"		600.
b.	Ovptd. "DISABLED VETERANS/NO FEE"		750.
2A29	$1 black, *lavender*		20.
2A30	$25 black, *peach*	275.00	35.

1972-1973

2A31	$6 black, *pink*		1.
a.	Ovptd. "DISABLED VETERANS/NO FEE"		750.
2A32	$2 black, *light yellow*		30.
2A33	$35 black, *lavender*	225.00	

1973-1974

2A34	$6 black, *blue*		1.
a.	Ovptd. "DISABLED VETERANS/NO FEE"		750.
2A35	$2 black, *lavender*	175.00	20.
2A36	$35 black, *gray*	275.00	35.

1974-1975

2A37	$6 black, *green*	35.00	1.
a.	Ovptd. "DISABLED VETERANS/NO FEE"		800.
2A38	$2 black, *orange*		20.
2A39	$35 black, *reddish purple*	175.00	25.

1975-1976

2A40	$10 red brown, *brown*	40.00	1.
a.	Ovptd. "DISABLED VETERANS/NO FEE"		800.
2A41	$2 black, *dark red*	80.00	20.
2A42	$35 black, *yellow*	85.00	25.

1976-1977

2A43	$10 black, *blue*	30.00	1.00
a.	Ovptd. "DISABLED VETERANS/NO FEE"		900.

14    $2 black, *gray violet*   100.00   20.00
a.   Inscibed "Deer Tag No." instead of "Bear Tag No."   —
45    $35 black, *lavender*   85.00   25.00

1977-1978
46    $10 black, *red orange*   30.00   1.00
a.   Ovptd. "DISABLED VETERANS/NO FEE"   850.00
47    $2 black, *yellow green*   95.00   25.00
48    $35 black, *pink*   95.00

1978-1979
49    $10 black, *yellow*   40.00   1.50
a.   Ovptd. "DISABLED VETERANS/NO FEE"   800.00
50    $2 black, *red*   80.00   20.00
51    $35 black, *light brown*   85.00

1979-1980
52    $10 black, *red*   30.00   1.00
a.   Ovptd. "DISABLED VETERANS/NO FEE"   900.00
53    $2 black, *yellow green*   80.00   20.00
54    $35 black, *dark blue*   85.00

1980-1981
55    $10.25 black, *blue*   30.00   1.00
a.   Ovptd. "DISABLED VETERANS/NO FEE"   1,200.
56    $2 black, *light brown*   75.00   15.00
57    $36.25 black, *tan*   75.00   25.00

1981-1982
58    $11.50 black, *dark green*   30.00   1.00
59    $2.25 black, *blue*   75.00   20.00
60    $40 black, *gray*   200.00

1982-1983
61    $12.50 black, *pink*   30.00   1.00
62    $2.50 black, *brown*   75.00   20.00
63    $43.50 black, *orange*   140.00

1983-1984
64    $13.25 black, *blue*   50.00   1.00
65    $2.75 black, *purple*   150.00   20.00
66    $46.50 black, *green*   175.00

1984-1985
67    $13.25 black, *yellow*   50.00   1.00
68    $2.75 black, *green*   150.00   20.00
69    $49.25 black, *brown*   175.00

1985-1986
70    $14 black, *blue*   50.00   1.00
71    $3.50 black, *yellow*   150.00   20.00
72    $51.75 black, *purple*   175.00

1986-1987
73    $18.50 black, *green*   1.00
74    $4.50 black, *dark blue*   15.00

1987-1988
76    $17.50 black, *dark blue*   1.00
77    $4.50 black, *purple*   15.00

1988-1989
79    $19.25 black, *tan*   1.00
80    $5 black, *yellow*   15.00

1989-1990
82    $19.75 black, *blue gray*   1.00
83    $5 black, *dark green*   15.00

1990-1991
85    $21.50 black, *reddish gray*   1.00
86    $5.50 black, *yellow*   15.00
87    $73 black, *pink*   25.00

1991-1992
88    $23.10 black, *lime green*   1.00
89    $5.50 black, *bluish purple*   15.00
90    $79.80 black, *brown*   25.00

1992-1993
91    $24.15 black, *yellow*   —   1.00
92    $5.80 black, *greenish gold*   15.00
93    $83.75 black, *mauve*   —   25.00

1993-1994 CALIFORNIA JUNIOR HUNTING LICENSE $5.80 NONREFUNDABLE — H372223-07 — 1st Deer Tag No. — 2nd Deer Tag No. — DATE ISSUED Exp. June 30, 1994

1993-1994
2A94 $24.40 black & white, *green*   1.00
2A95 $5.80 black & white, *light blue*   15.00

1994-1995
2A97 $24.95 black & white, *pale yellow*   1.00
2A98 $6.05 black & white, *lavender*   15.00
2A99 $86.90 black & white, *gray*   25.00

1996-1997
2A100 $25.45 black, *gray brown*   1.00
2A101 $6.30 black, *pink*   15.00
2A102 $88.70 black, *pale blue*   25.00

Statewide Waterfowl Issues

Nos. 1-24 printed in booklet panes of five, No. 25 in pane of 4.
Issues through 1978 are die cut and self-adhesive. Starting with the 1979 issue, stamps are rouletted. Stamps are numbered serially.

> **Catalogue values for all unused stamps in this section are for Never Hinged items.**

Artists: Paul Johnson, #1-8; Ken Michaelson, #9; Walter Wolfe, #10-11; Robert Steiner, #12, 18-20, 26-35; Robert Richert, #13; Charles Allen, #14; Robert Montanucci, #15; Richard Wilson, #16; Sherrie Russell Meline, #17, 23; Ronald Louque, #21; Larry Hayden, #22; Richard Clifton, #24-25; Richard Radigonda, #36.

Stamps valued with original backing paper. Caution should be used when buying especially Nos. 1 and 2. Both these issues have wider rouletting on the backing paper than Nos. 3-9.

1971-2004
1   $1 Pintails   600.00   65.00
2   $1 Canvasbacks, *1972*   2,000.   150.00
3   $1 Mallards, *1973*   14.50   2.50
4   $1 White-fronted geese, *1974*   3.00   2.50
5   $1 Green-winged teal, backing paper with red wavy lines, *1975*   35.00   8.00
   Waxy backing paper without lines   140.00

The gum bleeds through the stamp with red wavy lines resulting in a spotted or blotchy effect. Little or no gum bleeds through on stamps with waxy backing paper.

6   $1 Widgeons, *1976*   20.00   2.50
7   $1 Cinnamon teal, *1977*   45.00   9.00
8   $5 Cinnamon teal, *1977*   125.00   2.50
9   $5 Hooded mergansers, *1978*   100.00   15.00
10   $5 Wood ducks, *1979*   9.00   2.50
11   $5 Pintails, *1980*   9.00   2.50
12   $5 Canvasabacks, *1981*   9.00   2.50
13   $5 Widgeons, *1982*   9.00   2.50
14   $5 Green-winged teal, *1983*   12.00   2.50
15   $7.50 Mallard decoy, *1984*   11.00   2.50
16   $7.50 Ring-necked ducks, *1985*   11.00   2.50
17   $7.50 Canada goose, *1986*   11.00   3.00
18   $7.50 Redheads, *1987*   11.00   3.00
19   $7.50 Mallards, *1988*   11.00   3.00
20   $7.50 Cinnamon teal, *1989*   11.00   3.00
21   $7.50 Canada goose, *1990*   11.00   3.00
22   $7.50 Gadwalls, *1991*   11.00   3.00
23   $7.90 White-fronted goose, *1992*   12.00   3.00
24   $10.50 Pintails, *1993*   15.00   4.00

Rouletted Horiz.
25   $10.50 Wood duck, *1994*   15.00   4.00

Perf. Vertically
Birds in flight, denomination at: b, UL. c, UR. d, LL. e, LR.

26   $10.50 Snow geese, booklet pane of 4, #b.-e., *1995*   60.00
a.   Souvenir sheet of 4, #b.-e. (decorative border)   125.00
b.-   Booklet single, each
e.   14.00   4.00

Stamps in No. 26a are perfed on all four sides.

Perf. Horizontally
27   $10.50 Mallards, *1996*   15.00   2.50

Issued in panes of 4.

28   $10.50 Pintails, *1997*   15.00   2.50
29   $10.50 Green-winged teal, pair, *1998*   29.00
a.-   a, Female, b, Male, each
b.   14.00   2.50

No. 29 issued in strips of 4 stamps.

30   $10.50 Wood duck, pair, *1999*   29.00
a.-   a, Male, b, Male and female, each
b.   13.00   2.50

No. 30 issued in strips of 2 pairs.

31   $10.50 Canada geese, mallard, widgeon *2000*   15.00   2.50
32   $10.50 Canvasbacks, *2001*   15.00   2.50
33   $10.50 Pintails, *2002*   15.00   2.50
34   $10.50 Mallards, *2003*   15.00   2.50
35   $13.90 Cinnamon teal, *2004*   17.00   2.50

Perf. Vertically
36   $14.20 Pintails, *2005*   17.50   2.50

COLORADO

North Central Goose Stamp

Used in an area extending from Ft. Collins to approximately 50 miles east of the city.

Illustration reduced.

1973
A1 $2 black   —   —

No. A1 is die cut and self-adhesive. Unused copies have glassine backing.

Statewide Issues

Printed in booklet panes of 5 and panes of 30.
Stamps are numbered serially.
Imperforate varieties of these stamps are printer's proofs.

> **Catalogue values for all unused stamps in this section are for Never Hinged items.**

Artists: Robert Steiner, #1-2; Charles Allen, #3; Dan Andrews, #4; Sarah Woods, #5; Cynthie Fisher, #6, 9-14; Bill Border, #7; Gerald G. Putt, #8; Jeffrey Klinefelter, #15-16.

1990-2004

1	$5 Canada geese	12.00	
	Bklt. single, with tab, Nos. 80,001-150,000	12.50	3.00
a.	$5 +$50 Governor's edition	60.00	
2	$5 Mallards, 1991	16.00	
	Bklt. single, with tab, Nos. 80,001-150,000	16.00	3.00
a.	$5 +$50 Governor's edition	60.00	
3	$5 Pintails, 1992	10.00	
	Bklt. single, with tab, Nos. 80,001-150,000	10.00	3.00
a.	$5 +$50 Governor's edition	60.00	
4	$5 Green-winged teal, 1993	12.00	
	Bklt. single, with tab, Nos. 80,001-150,000	12.00	3.00
a.	$5 +$50 Governor's edition	60.00	
5	$5 Wood ducks, 1994	12.00	
	Bklt. single, with tab	12.00	2.50
6	$5 Buffleheads, 1995	12.00	
	Bklt. single, with tab	12.00	2.50
7	$5 Cinnamon teal, 1996	12.00	
	Bklt. single, with tab and top selvage	12.00	2.50
8	$5 Widgeons, gold text, 1997	10.00	
a.	Bklt. single, with tab and top selvage, text in black & white	10.00	2.50
9	$5 Redheads, 1998	10.00	
	Bklt. single, with tab and top selvage	10.00	2.50
10	$5 Blue-winged teal, 1999	10.00	
a.	Blkt. single, with tab and top selvage	10.00	2.50
11	$5 Gadwalls, 2000	10.00	
a.	Bklt. single, with tab and top selvage	10.00	2.50
12	$5 Ruddy ducks, 2001	10.00	2.50
13	$5 Common goldeneyes, 2002	10.00	2.50
14	$5 Canvasbacks, 2003	10.00	2.50
15	$5 Snow geese, 2004	10.00	2.50
16	$5 Shovelers, 2005	10.00	2.50

CONNECTICUT

Printed in booklet panes of 10 and sheets of 30.
Stamps are numbered serially.
Imperforate varieties are proofs.

> **Catalogue values for all unused stamps in this section are for Never Hinged items.**

Artists: Thomas Hirata, #1; Robert Leslie, #2, 9; Phillip Crowe, #3; Keith Mueller, #4, 7; Robert Steiner, #5; Joe Hautman, #6; George Lockwood, #8; Robert Richert, #10; Paul Fusco, #11-13.

1993-2004

1	$5 Black ducks	12.00	3.00
	Booklet pane pair with L & R selvage, Nos. 51,001-81,000	24.00	
a.	Sheet of 4	70.00	
b.	$5 +$50 Governor's edition	75.00	
2	$5 Canvasbacks, 1994	10.00	3.00
	Booklet pair with L & R selvage, Nos. 53,000-up	20.00	
a.	Sheet of 4	42.50	
3	$5 Mallards, 1995	15.00	3.00
	Booklet pair with L & R selvage	30.00	
4	$5 Old squaw ducks, 1996	15.00	3.00
	Booklet pair with L & R selvage	30.00	
5	$5 Green-winged teal, 1997	10.00	3.00
a.	$5 +$50 Governor's edition	150.00	
6	$5 Mallards, 1998	10.00	3.00
7	$5 Canada geese, 1999	15.00	3.00
a.	$5 +$50 Governor's edition	450.00	

8	$5 Wood duck, 2000	10.00	3.00
a.	$5 +$50 Governor's edition	425.00	
9	$5 Buffleheads, 2001	9.00	3.00
a.	$5 +$50 Governor's edition	425.00	
10	$5 Greater scaups, 2002	12.00	3.00
a.	$5 +$50 Governor's edition	450.00	

11	$5 Black Duck, 2003	9.00	3.00
12	$5 Wood duck, 2004	9.00	3.00
13	$10 Mallards, 2005	16.00	3.00

DELAWARE

Printed in sheets of 10.
Starting in 1991, a portion of the printing is numbered serially on the reverse.

> **Catalogue values for all unused stamps in this section are for Never Hinged items.**

Artists: Ned Mayne, #1; Charles Rowe, #2; Lois Butler, #3; John Green, #4; Nolan Haan, #5; Don Breyfogle, #6; Robert Leslie, #7, 10; Bruce Langton, #8; Jim Hautman, #9; Francis Sweet, #11; Ronald Louque, #12; Richard Clifton, #13, 17, 19; Robert Metropulos, #14; Louis Frisino, #15; Michael Ashman, #16, 21; Jeffrey Klinefelter, #18, 24; Russ Duerksen, #20; Brian Blight, #22; George Lockwood, #23; Bonnie Field, #25; Joanna Rivera, #26.

1980-2004

1	$5 Black ducks	85.00	20.00
2	$5 Snow geese, 1981	70.00	20.00
3	$5 Canada geese, 1982	70.00	20.00
4	$5 Canvasbacks, 1983	40.00	10.00
5	$5 Mallards, 1984	15.00	5.00
6	$5 Pintail, 1985	12.00	3.00
7	$5 Widgeons, 1986	11.00	3.00
8	$5 Redheads, 1987	11.00	3.00
9	$5 Wood ducks, 1988	9.00	3.00
10	$5 Buffleheads, 1989	9.00	3.00
11	$5 Green-winged teal, 1990	10.00	3.00
a.	$5 +$50 Governor's edition	85.00	
12	$5 Hooded merganser, no serial number on reverse, 1991	10.00	
	With serial number on reverse	11.00	3.00
13	$5 Blue-winged teal, no serial number on reverse, 1992	10.00	
	With serial number on reverse	10.00	2.50
14	$5 Goldeneye, no serial number on reverse, 1993	10.00	
	With serial number on reverse	10.00	2.50
15	$5 Blue goose, no serial number on reverse, 1994	10.00	
	With serial number on reverse	10.00	2.50
16	($6)Scaup, no serial number on reverse, 1995	10.00	
	With serial number on reverse	10.00	2.50
17	$6 Gadwall, no serial number on reverse, 1996	12.00	
	With serial number on reverse	12.00	2.50
18	$6 White-winged scoter, no serial number on reverse, 1997	12.00	
	With serial number on reverse	12.00	2.50
19	$6 Blue-winged teal, 1998	9.00	2.50
20	$6 Tundra swan, 1999	9.00	
21	$6 American brant, 2000	12.00	2.50
22	$6 Oldsquaw, 2001	9.00	2.50
23	$6 Ruddy ducks, 2002	9.00	2.50
24	$9 Ring-necked ducks, 2003	12.00	3.00
25	$9 Black scoters and lighthouse, 2004	12.00	3.00
a.	$9 +$50 Governor's edition	95.00	
26	$9 Common mergansers and lighthouse, 2005	12.00	3.00
a.	$9 +$50 Governor's edition	75.00	

FLORIDA

#1-7 issued in booklet panes of 5. Nos. 8-19 in sheets of 10. No. 20 in sheet of 12.
Stamps are numbered serially and rouletted. Serial numbers for stamps with survey tabs attached end ...-04.

> **Catalogue values for all unused stamps in this section are for Never Hinged items.**

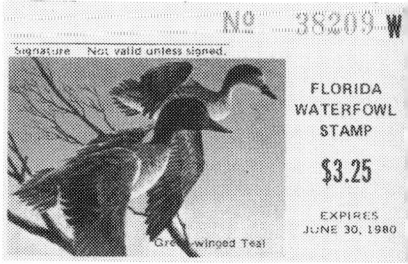

Illustration reduced.

Artists: Bob Binks, #1, 7; Ernest Simmons, #2; Clark Sullivan, #3; Lee Cable, #4; Heiner Hertling, #5; John Taylor, #6; Robert Steiner, #8; Ronald Louque, #9-10; J. Byron Test, #11; Byron Test, #12; Richard Hansen, #13; Richard Clifton, #14; John Mogus, #15; Antonie Rossini, #16; Kenneth Nanney, #17; Wayne Makuchal, #18; M. Frase, #19; Brian Blight, #20; John Harris, #21, 23; Jeffrey Klinefelter, #22; John Nelson Harris, #24.

1979-2003

1	$3.25 Green-winged teal	160.00	20.
	With tab	200.00	
2	$3.25 Pintails, 1980	15.00	5.
	With tab	20.00	

3	$3.25 Widgeon, 1981	15.00	5.0
	With tab	45.00	
4	$3.25 Ring-necked ducks, 1982	22.50	5.
	With tab	30.00	
5	$3.25 Buffleheads, 1983	45.00	5.0
	With tab	60.00	
6	$3.25 Hooded merganser, 1984	11.00	3.5
	With tab	35.00	
7	$3.25 Wood ducks, 1985	11.00	3.5
	With tab	30.00	
8	$3 Canvasbacks, 1986	11.00	3.5
	With small tab at top	11.00	
	With larger survey tab at side and small tab at top	25.00	
9	$3.50 Mallards, 1987	10.00	3.5
	With small tab at top	10.00	
	With larger survey tab at side and small tab at top	25.00	
10	$3.50 Redheads, 1988	9.00	2.5
	With small tab at top	9.00	
	With larger survey tab at side and small tab at top	20.00	
11	$3.50 Blue-winged teal, 1989	8.00	2.5
	With small tab at top	8.00	
	With larger survey tab at side and small tab at top	35.00	
12	$3.50 Wood ducks, 1990	8.00	2.5
	With small tab at top	8.00	
	With larger survey tab at side and small tab at top	35.00	
13	$3.50 Northern Pintails, 1991	9.00	2.5
	With small tab at top	9.00	
	With larger survey tab at side and small tab at top	30.00	
14	$3.50 Ruddy duck, 1992	8.00	2.5
	With small tab at top	7.00	
	With larger survey tab at side and small tab at top	12.00	
15	$3.50 American widgeon, 1993	8.00	2.5
	With small tab at top	8.00	
	With larger survey tab at side and small tab at top	25.00	
16	$3.50 Mottled duck, 1994	9.00	2.5
	With small tab at top	9.00	
	With larger survey tab at side and small tab at top	25.00	

	$3.50 Fulvous whistling duck, *1995*	10.00	2.50
	With small tab at top	10.00	
	With larger survey tab at side and small tab at top	25.00	
	$3.50 Goldeneyes, *1996*	15.00	2.50
	With small tab at top	15.00	
	With larger survey tab at side and small tab at top	25.00	
	($3.00) Hooded merganser, *1997*	12.00	2.50
	With small tab at top	12.00	
	With larger survey tab at side and small tab at top	25.00	

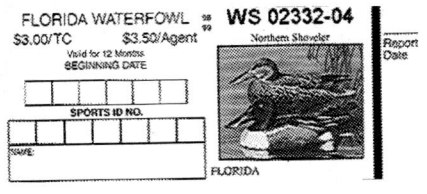

Self-Adhesive

	$3 Shoveler, *1998*	20.00	2.50
	Sold for $3.50 through agents.		
	$3 Pintail, *1999*	12.00	2.50
	Sold for $3.50 through agents.		
2	$3 Ring-necked duck, *2000*	8.00	2.50
	Sold for $3.50 through agents.		
3	$3 Canvasback, *2001*	8.00	2.50
	Sold for $3.50 through agents.		
4	$3 Mottled duck, *2002*	8.00	2.50

Sold for $3.50 through agents. No. 24 with rouletting and with duck facing right come from a special limited reprinting demanded by the artist to correct the appearance of his work.

The 2003 stamp was sold by Florida officials only to the stamp's artist.

GEORGIA

Not required to hunt waterfowl until 1989.
Nos. 1-4 printed in sheets of 30, others in sheets of 20.
Starting with No 5, stamps are numbered serially.

> **Catalogue values for all unused stamps in this section are for Never Hinged items.**

Artists: Daniel Smith, #1; Jim Killen, #2, 14; James Partee, Jr., #3; Paul Bridgeford, #4; Ralph J. McDonald, #5; Guy Coheleach, #6; Phillip Crowe, #7-8, 11; Jerry Raedeke, #9, 13, 15; Herb Booth, #10; David Lanier, #12.

1985-99

1	$5.50 Wood ducks	15.00	
2	$5.50 Mallards, *1986*	9.00	
3	$5.50 Canada geese, *1987*	9.00	
4	$5.50 Ring-necked ducks, *1988*	9.00	
5	$5.50 Duckling & golden retriever puppy, *1989*	13.00	2.50
6	$5.50 Wood ducks, *1990*	9.00	2.50

7	$5.50 Green-winged teal, *1991*	9.50	2.50
8	$5.50 Buffleheads, *1992*	15.00	2.50
9	$5.50 Mallards, *1993*	15.00	2.50
10	$5.50 Ring-necked ducks, *1994*	15.00	2.50
11	$5.50 Widgeons, Labrador retreiver, *1995*	30.00	2.50
12	$5.50 Black ducks, *1996*	22.00	2.50
13	$5.50 Lesser scaup, Cockspur Island lighthouse, *1997*	35.00	2.50
14	$5.50 Labrador retreiver, ring-necked ducks, *1998*	25.00	2.50
15	$5.50 Pintails, *1999*	20.00	2.50

HAWAII

Required for the hunting of small game. Hunting birds was illegal in Hawaii until 2003. Game bird hunting was permitted beginning July 1, 2003. Game birds that can be hunted include pheasants, francolins, partridges, quail, sand grouses, doves and wild turkeys.

Artists: Patrick Ching, #1, D. Van Zyle, #2; Michael Furuya, #3; Norman Nagai, #4, 7, 10; Marion Berger, #5; Daniel Wang, #6; Joy Keown, #8, 9.

1996-2004

1	$5 Nene goose	10.00	
a.	$5 +$50 Governor's edition	75.00	
b.	As No. 1, sheet of 4	45.00	
	No. 1b exists imperf.		
2	$5 Hawaiian duck, *1997*	10.00	
	With tab	10.00	
a.	As No. 2, sheet of 4	45.00	
	No. 2a exists imperf.		
3	$5 Wild turkey, *1998*	10.00	
	With tab	10.00	
4	$5 Ring-necked pheasant, *1999*	14.00	
	With tab	14.00	
5	$5 Erckel's francolin, *2000*	12.00	
	With tab	12.00	
6	$5 Green pheasant, *2001*	12.00	
	With tab	12.00	2.50
7	$10 Chukar partridge, *2002*	15.00	
8	$10 Nene geese, *2003*	15.00	
9	$10 Nene geese, *2004*	15.00	
10	$10 California quail, *2005*	15.00	

IDAHO

Printed in booklet panes of 5 and sheets of 30, except No. 5, which was issued in booklets of 10.
Numbered serially except for No. 11.

> **Catalogue values for all unused stamps in this section are for Never Hinged items.**

Artists: Robert Leslie, #1; Jim Killen, #2; Daniel Smith, #3; Francis E. Sweet, #4; Richard Clifton, #6, 11; Richard Plasschaert, #7; Sherrie Russell Meline, #8; Bill Moore, #9; David Gressard, #12; T. Smith, #12; Maynard Reece, #13.

1987-98

1	$5.50 Cinnamon teal, perforated	14.00	
a.	Bklt. single, rouletted, with 2-part tab	11.00	3.00
2	$5.50 Green-winged teal, perforated, *1988*	13.00	
a.	Bklt. single, rouletted, with 2-part tab	11.00	3.00

3	$6 Blue-winged teal, perforated, *1989*	10.00	
a.	Bklt. single, rouletted, with 2-part tab	10.00	3.00
4	$6 Trumpeter swans, perforated, *1990*	20.00	
a.	Bklt. single, rouletted, with 2-part tab	20.00	3.00

Die cut self-adhesive

5	$6 green, *1991*	150.00	*35.00*

No. 5 was used provisionally in 1991 when the regular stamps were delayed. Unused value is for stamp, remittance tab and selvage pieces on backing paper.

Designs like No. 1

6	$6 Widgeons, perforated, *1991*	10.00	
a.	Bklt. single, rouletted, with 2-part tab	10.00	2.50
7	$6 Canada geese, perforated, *1992*	10.00	
a.	Bklt. single, rouletted, with 2-part tab	10.00	2.50
8	$6.00 Common goldeneye, perforated, *1993*	12.00	
a.	Bklt. single, rouletted, with 2-part tab	12.00	2.50
9	$6 Harlequin ducks, perforated, *1994*	12.00	
a.	Bklt. single, rouletted, with 2-part tab	12.00	2.50
10	$6 Wood ducks, perforated, *1995*	12.00	
a.	Bklt. single, rouletted, with 2-part tab	12.00	2.50
11	$6.50 Mallard, *1996*	16.00	2.50
12	$6.50 Shovelers, *1997*	20.00	2.50
13	$6.50 Canada geese, *1998*	10.00	2.50

ILLINOIS

Daily Usage Stamps for State-operated Waterfowl Areas.

Date and fee overprinted in black. $2 and $3 stamps were for hunting ducks, $5 stamps for hunting geese and pheasants. 1953-58 had separate pheasant stamps. No duck stamp was printed in 1971.
Some unused stamps have dry gum.
Used stamps have no gum or have staple holes.
Black printing.
Stamps are numbered serially.

1953-1972

A1	$2 orange, *blue*	—	—
A4	$2 green, *manila, 1956*	12,500.	7,500.
A5	$2 orange, *light blue green, 1957*	1,050.	500.
A6	$2 green, *manila, 1958*	950.	450.
A7	$3 green, *manila, 1959*	900.	450.
A8	$5 red brown, *light blue green, 1959*	950.	450.
A9	$3 red brown, *light blue green, 1960*	950.	450.
A10	$5 green, *manila, 1960*	950.	450.
A11	$3 green, *manila, 1961*	950.	450.
A12	$5 red brown, *light blue green, 1961*	900.	450.
A13	$3 green, *manila, 1962*	900.	450.
A14	$5 red brown, *light blue green, 1962*	900.	450.
A15	$3 orange, *light blue green, 1963*	900.	450.
A16	$5 green, *manila, 1963*	900.	450.
A17	$3 green, *manila, 1964*	900.	450.
A18	$5 red, *light blue green, 1964*	900.	350.
A19	$3 orange, *light blue green, 1965*	900.	450.
A20	$5 green, *manila, 1965*	900.	450.
A21	$3 green, *manila, 1966*	900.	450.
A22	$5 orange, *light blue green, 1966*	900.	450.
A23	$3 orange, *light blue green, 1967*	900.	450.
A24	$5 green, *yellow, 1967*	900.	450.
A25	$3 green, *yellow, 1968*	900.	450.
A26	$5 orange, *light blue, 1968*	900.	450.
A27	$3 orange, *light blue, 1969*	900.	450.
A28	$5 green, *manila, 1969*	900.	450.

A29	$3 green, *manila,* 1970	1,500.	900.
A30	$5 orange, *light blue,* 1970	1,750.	900.
A31	$5 green, *manila,* 1971	1,950.	1,000.
A32	$3 orange, *light blue green,* 1972	4,250.	
A33	$5 orange, *light blue green,* 1972	4,250.	2,250.

> Catalogue values for unused stamps in this section, from this point to the end, are for Never Hinged items.

No. A34

No. A35

1977-91(?)

A34	black, *light blue,* duck, *1991*	—	—
A35	black, *manila,* goose	—	—

Nos. A34-A35 do not show year or denomination and were used until 1994. No. A34 used before 1991 should exist but has not been reported yet. Separate pheasant and controlled quail and pheasant stamps of a similar design have also been used.

No. A36

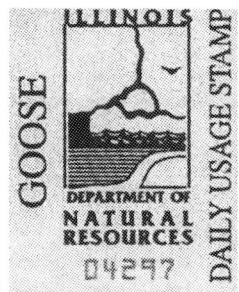

No. A37

1996

A36	black, *light blue,* duck	—	—
A37	black, *manila,* goose	—	—

Nos. A36-A37 do not show year or denomination.

Statewide Issues

Nos. 1-10 in sheets of 10. Starting with No. 11, in booklet panes of 5; starting with No. 22, in panes of 10.

Stamps are numbered serially and rouletted.

> Catalogue values for all unused stamps in this section are for Never Hinged items.

Artists: Robert Eschenfeldt, #1; Robert G. Larson, #2; Richard Lynch, #3; Everett Staffeldt, #4; John Eggert, #5; Bart Kassabaum, #6, 9, 11, 13; Jim Trindel, #7; Arthur Sinden, #8, 12, 14; George Kieffer, #10; Charles McKay Freeman, #15; John Henson, #16; Phillip Crowe, #17-21; Thomas Hirata, #22-24; Jim Killen, #25-29; Gerald Putt, #30-31.

1975-2004

1	$5 Mallard		575.00	85.00
2	$5 Wood ducks, *1976*		250.00	50.00
3	$5 Canada goose, *1977*		150.00	35.00
4	$5 Canvasbacks, *1978*		125.00	22.50
5	$5 Pintail, *1979*		115.00	16.00
6	$5 Green-winged teal, *1980*		100.00	16.00
7	$5 Widgeons, *1981*		115.00	16.00
a.	"Green-winged teal"		500.00	
8	$5 Black ducks, *1982*		60.00	12.50
9	$5 Lesser scaup, *1983*		75.00	10.00
10	$5 Blue-winged teal, *1984*		60.00	10.00
11	$5 Redheads, *1985*		16.00	3.00
	With 2-part tab		22.50	
12	$5 Gadwalls, *1986*		12.00	3.00
	With 2-part tab		20.00	
13	$5 Buffleheads, *1987*		12.00	3.00
	With 2-part tab		15.00	
14	$5 Common goldeneyes, *1988*		12.00	2.50
	With 2-part tab		15.00	
15	$5 Ring-necked ducks, *1989*		10.00	2.50
	With 2-part tab		10.00	
16	$10 Lesser snow geese, *1990*		16.00	3.00
	With 2-part tab		17.00	
17	$10 Labrador retriever & Canada goose, *1991*		16.00	3.00
	With 2-part tab		16.00	
a.	Governor's edition with tab		85.00	
18	$10 Retriever & mallards, *1992*		22.00	3.00
	With 2-part tab		22.00	
19	$10 Pintail decoys and puppy, *1993*		30.00	3.00
	With 2-part tab		30.00	
20	$10 Canvasbacks & retrievers, *1994*		30.00	3.00
	With 2-part tab		30.00	
21	$10 Retriever, green-winged teal, decoys, *1995*		30.00	3.00
	With 2-part tab		30.00	
22	$10 Wood ducks, *1996*		20.00	2.50
23	$10 Canvasbacks, *1997*		16.00	2.50
24	$10 Canada goose, *1998*		16.00	2.50
25	$10 Canada geese, black Labrador retriever, *1999*		18.00	2.50
a.	Anniversary edition, perforated		92.50	
b.	Governor's edition, perforated		92.50	
c.	Silver edition, perforated		92.50	

Nos. 25a-25c were sold as a set of three.

26	$10 Mallards, golden retriever, *2000*		20.00	2.50
27	$10 Pintails, yellow Labrador retriever, *2001*		20.00	2.50
28	$10 Canvasbacks, Chesapeake retriever, *2002*		20.00	2.50
29	$10 Green-winged teal, Labrador retriever, *2003*		15.00	2.50
30	$10 Wood ducks, *2004*		15.00	2.50
31	$10 Green-winged teals, *2005*		15.00	2.50

INDIANA

Issued in booklet panes of 4 (Nos. 1-10) and booklet panes of 2, starting with No. 11.

Stamps are numbered serially and rouletted.

> Catalogue values for all unused stamps in this section are for Never Hinged items.

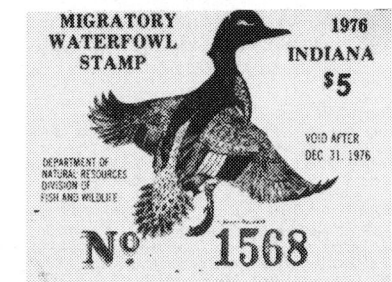

Artists: Justin H. (Sonny) Bashore, #1-2; Carl (Spike) Kn[u], #3; Daniel Renn Pierce, #4; Dean Barrick, #5; Rodney Cro[...]man, #6; George Metz, #7; Kieth Freeman, #8; Lyn Briggs, [...] Rick Pas, #10; Ronald Louque, #11; Susan Hastings Bat[...] #12.

Bruce Langton, #13, 17; Ann Dahoney, #14; Ken Buckl[e] #15, 20, 22, 24, 29; Richard Hansen, #16; Jeffrey Klinefel[...] #18, 26, 28, 30; Jeffrey Mobley, #19; Charles Riggles, #21, [...] George Lockwood, #25; Biran Blight, 27.

1976-2004

1	$5 Green-winged teal		12.00	2
2	$5 Pintail, *1977*		10.00	2
3	$5 Canada geese, *1978*		8.00	2
4	$5 Canvasbacks, *1979*		8.00	2
5	$5 Mallard ducklings, *1980*		8.00	2.
6	$5 Hooded mergansers, *1981*		8.00	2.
7	$5 Blue-winged teal, *1982*		8.00	2
8	$5 Snow geese, *1983*		8.00	2.
9	$5 Redheads, *1984*		8.00	2.
10	$5 Pintail, *1985*		10.00	2.
	With tab		10.50	
11	$5 Wood duck, *1986*		8.00	2.
	With tab		10.00	
12	$5 Canvasbacks, *1987*		8.00	2.
	With tab		10.00	
13	$6.75 Redheads, *1988*		10.00	2.
	With tab		10.50	
14	$6.75 Canada goose, *1989*		10.00	2.
	With tab		10.50	
15	$6.75 Blue-winged teal, *1990*		10.00	2.
	With tab		10.50	
16	$6.75 Mallards, *1991*		10.00	2.
	With tab		10.50	
17	$6.75 Green-winged teal, *1992*		10.00	2.
	With tab		10.50	
18	$6.75 Wood ducks, *1993*		10.00	2.
	With tab		10.50	
19	$6.75 Pintail, *1994*		10.00	2.
	With tab		10.50	
20	$6.75 Goldeneyes, *1995*		10.00	2.
	With tab		10.50	
21	$6.75 Black ducks, *1996*		10.00	2.
	With tab		10.50	
22	$6.75 Canada geese, *1997*		10.00	2.
	With tab		10.50	
23	$6.75 Widgeon, *1998*		10.00	2.
	With tab		10.50	
24	$6.75 Bluebills, *1999*		9.00	2.
	With tab		10.00	
25	$6.75 Ring-necked duck, *2000*		9.00	2.
	With tab		10.00	
26	$6.75 Hooded mergansers, *2001*		9.00	2.
	With tab		10.00	
27	$6.75 Green-winged teal, *2002*		9.00	2.
	With tab		10.00	
28	$6.75 Northern shovelers, *2003*		9.00	2.
	With tab		10.00	
29	$6.75 Wood duck, *2004*		9.00	2.
	With tab		10.00	
30	$6.75 Buffleheads, *2005*		9.00	2.
	With tab		10.00	

IOWA

> Catalogue values for all unused stamps in this section are for Never Hinged items.

Issued in booklet pane of 5 (No. 1), 10 (others) and sheets o[f] 10 (No. 19).

Artists: Maynard Reece, #1, 6, 22; Thomas Murphy, #2; James Landenberger, #3; Mark Reece, #4; Nick Klepinger, #5, 7; Andrew Peters, #8; Paul Brigford, #9, 12, 15; Brad Reece, #10; Tom Walker, #11; Larry Zach, #13.

Jack C. Hahn, #14, 18; John Heidersbach, #16; Mark Cary, #17; Patrick Murillo, #19; Jerry Raedeke, #20; Charlotte Edwards, #21, 26; Dietmar Krumrey, #23, 25, 33; Cynthia Fisher, #24; Sherrie Russell Meline, #27, 29; Mark Anderson, #28; Darren Maurer, #30, 31; Neal Anderson, #32, 34.

1972-98

1	$1 Mallards		150.00	25.00
2	$1 Pintails, *1973*		35.00	7.50
3	$1 Gadwalls, rouletted, *1974*		85.00	7.00
4	$1 Canada geese, *1975*		95.00	9.00
5	$1 Canvasbacks, *1976*		25.00	2.50
6	$1 Lesser scaup, rouletted, *1977*		21.00	2.50
7	$1 Wood ducks, rouletted, *1978*		50.00	5.00
8	$5 Buffleheads, *1979*		375.00	25.00
9	$5 Redheads, *1980*		27.50	6.00
10	$5 Green-winged teal, rouletted, *1981*		27.50	4.00
11	$5 Snow geese, rouletted, *1982*		18.00	2.50
12	$5 Widgeons, *1983*		18.00	2.75

$5	Wood ducks, *1984*	35.00	3.00
$5	Mallard & mallard decoy, *1985*	20.00	2.50
$5	Blue-winged teal, *1986*	15.00	2.50
$5	Canada goose, *1987*	15.00	2.50
$5	Pintails, *1988*	15.00	2.50
$5	Blue-winged teal, *1989*	15.00	2.50
$5	Canvasbacks, *1990*	9.00	2.50
$5	Mallards, *1991*	9.00	2.50
$5	Labrador retriever & ducks, *1992*	10.00	2.50
$5	Mallards, *1993*	9.00	2.50
$5	Green-winged teal, *1994*	9.00	2.50
$5	Canada geese, *1995*	9.00	2.50
$5	Canvasbacks, *1996*	9.00	2.50
$5	Canada geese, *1997*	10.00	2.50
$5	Pintails, *1998*	12.00	2.50

DEPARTMENT OF NATURAL RESOURCES

:99

28   Trumpeter swan, *1999*   12.00   2.50

No. 28 not required for hunting. The Department of Natural Resources sent customers No. 28 upon receipt of a postcard given to the customer after paying license fee of $5.

IOWA DEPT. OF NATURAL RESOURCES

:000

29   Hooded merganser, *2000*   10.00   2.50

No. 29 not required for hunting. The Department of Natural Resources sent customers No. 29 upon receipt of a postcard given to the customer after paying license fee of $5.

IOWA DEPT. OF NATURAL RESOURCES

:001

30   Snow goose, *2001*   10.00   2.50

No. 30 not required for hunting. The Department of Natural Resources sent customers No. 30 upon receipt of a postcard given to the customer after paying license fee of $5.

WATERFOWL STAMP

IOWA DEPT. OF NATURAL RESOURCES

2002

31   Shovelers, *2002*   15.00   4.00

No. 31 not required for hunting. The Department of Natural Resources sent customers No. 31 upon receipt of a postcard given to the customer after paying license fee of $8.50.

2003

32   Ruddy duck, *2003*   13.00   4.00

No. 32 not required for hunting. The Department of Natural Resources sent customers No. 32 upon receipt of a postcard given to the customer after paying license fee of $8.50.

2004

33   Wood ducks, *2004*   13.00   4.00

No. 33 not required for hunting. The Department of Natural Resources sent customers No. 33 upon receipt of a postcard given to the customer after paying license fee of $8.50.

2005

34   Green-winged teals, *2005*   13.00   4.00

No. 34 not required for hunting. The Department of Natural Resources sent customers No. 34 upon receipt of a postcard given to the customer after paying license fee of $8.50.

KANSAS

Marion County Resident Duck Stamps
Wording, type face, border and perforation/roulette differs.
Used values are for stamps without gum.

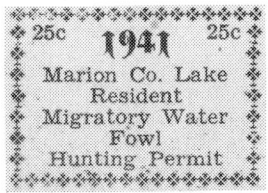

25c   **1941**   25c
Marion Co. Lake
Resident
Migratory Water
Fowl
Hunting Permit

1941-42

A1	25c black	—	
A2	25c black, *1942*	—	

Remainders from 1941 were rubber stamped "1942" in purple and initialed "J.E.M." by the Park and Lake Supervisor.

25c   25
RESIDENT
DUCK STAMP
1943
Marion County
Park & Lake
25c   25

1943-73

A3	25c black, *pink*	—	
A4	25c black, *green, 1944*	—	
A5	25c green, *1945*	—	
A6	25c black, *yellow, 1946*	15,000.	
A7	25c black, *pink, 1947*	9,500.	
A8	50c black, *blue, 1948*	18,000.	
A9	50c black, *1949*	—	
A10	50c black, *blue, 1950*	—	
A11	50c black, *1951*	—	
A13	50c black, *blue, 1953*	—	
A14	50c black, *pink, 1954*	140.	65.
A15	50c black, *green, 1955*	125.	65.
A16	50c black, *1956*	150.	100.
A17	50c black, *blue, 1957*	125.	65.
a.	"1" instead of "I" in "RESIDENT," pos. 3	2,250.	1,500.
b.	1st 2 lines reversed, pos. 6	2,750.	1,900.
A18	50c black, *light yellow, 1958*	475.	240.
A19	50c black, *1959*	85.	65.

A20	50c black, *pink, 1960*	160.	110.
a.	Missing ornamental ball, pos. 9	2,900.	
A21	50c black, *1961*	175.	150.
A22	50c black, *1962*	275.	150.
A23	50c black, *pink, 1963*	800.	500.
A24	50c black, *pink, 1964*	800.	500.
a.	2nd & 3rd lines reversed, pos. 10	15,000.	
A25	50c black, *green, 1965*	550.	400.
A26	50c black, *yellow, 1966*	—	9,500.
A27	50c black, *green, 1967*	3,500.	2,000.
A28	50c black, *pink, 1968*	300.	250.
A29	50c black, *yellow, 1969*	325.	225.
a.	"Dusk" instead of "Duck," pos. 8	17,000.	
A30	50c black, *1970*	500.	400.
A31	50c black, *pink, 1971*	2,750.	2,000.
A32	50c black, *blue, 1972*	2,750.	2,000.
A33	50c black, *pink, 1972*	5,500.	4,750.

Statewide Issues
Issued in booklet panes of 10 (Nos. 1-5) and sheets of 30 (starting with No. 2). Starting with No. 11, issued in sheets of 10. No. 1 issued in booklets with one pane of 10 (serial number has prefix "DD") and booklets with two panes of 10 (serial number has prefix "SS").
Nos. 1-4 numbered serially.

> **Catalogue values for all unused stamps in this section are for Never Hinged items.**

1987 KANSAS Waterfowl Habitat Stamp $3
50th Year-DUCKS UNLIMITED
Exp. 6-30-88

Artists: Guy Coheleach, #1; Ann Dahoney, #2, 8; Leon Parson, #3; Wes Dewey, #4; J. Byron Test, #5; Jerry Thomas, #6, 10; Jerry Roedeke, #7; Neal Anderson, #9; Dustin Teasley, #14-18.

1987-96

1	$3 Green-winged teal	10.00	2.50
	Pair from booklet pane with L & R selvage	20.00	
2	$3 Canada geese, *1988*	8.00	2.50
	Pair from booklet pane with L & R selvage	16.00	
a.	Serial number missing	—	
3	$3 Mallards, *1989*	8.00	2.50
	Pair from booklet pane with L & R selvage	16.00	
4	$3 Wood ducks, *1990*	8.00	2.50
	Pair from booklet pane with L & R selvage	16.00	
5	$3 Pintail, rouletted, *1991*	8.00	2.50
	Pair from booklet pane with selvage at L & straight edge at R	16.00	
6	$3 Canvasbacks, *1992*	8.00	2.50
7	$3 Mallards, *1993*	9.00	2.50
8	$3 Blue-winged teal, *1994*	9.00	2.50
9	$3 Barrow's goldeneye, *1995*	9.00	2.50
10	$3 American widgeon, *1996*	10.00	2.50

No. 2a resulted from a drastic misregistration of the serial numbers during printing. Only one example is documented.

1997   Expires 6-30-98 $3
Waterfowl
Habitat Stamp
Kansas Department of Wildlife and Parks
KANSAS

Artist: Dustin Teasley.

1997-2004	**Self-Adhesive**	*Die Cut*	
11	$3 blue	9.00	2.50
12	$3 green, *1998*	9.00	2.50
13	$3 red, *1999*	8.00	2.50
14	$3 red lilac, *2000*	8.00	2.50
15	$3 orange, *2001*	8.00	2.50
16	$5 blue, *2002*	8.75	2.50
17	$5 green, *2003*	8.75	2.50
18	$5 red, *2004*	8.75	2.50

KENTUCKY

Printed in booklet panes of 5, starting with No. 12 in panes of 30.
Stamps are numbered serially.

Catalogue values for all unused stamps in this section are for Never Hinged items.

Artists: Ray Harm, #1, 7; David Chapple, #2; Ralph J. McDonald, #3, 10; Lynn Kaatz, #4, 15; Phillip Crowe, #5, 9; Jim Oliver, #6; Phillip Powell, #8, 13; Jim Killen, #11; Laurie Parsons Yarnes, #12; Harold Roe, #14, 17; Tim Donovan, #16; Larry Chandler, #18; Ben Burney, #19; Chris Walden, #20-21.

1985-2004

1	$5.25	Mallards, rouletted	15.00	3.00
		With tab	15.00	
2	$5.25	Wood ducks, rouletted, 1986	10.00	2.50
		With tab	10.00	
3	$5.25	Black ducks, 1987	9.00	2.50
		With tab	10.00	
4	$5.25	Canada geese, 1988	9.00	2.50
		With tab	10.00	
5	$5.25	Retriever & canvasbacks, 1989	15.00	2.50
		With tab	15.00	
6	$5.25	Widgeons, 1990	9.00	2.50
		With tab	10.00	
7	$5.25	Pintails, 1991	9.00	2.50
		With tab	10.00	
8	$5.25	Green-winged teal, 1992	13.00	2.50
		With tab	13.00	
9	$5.25	Canvasback & decoy, 1993	20.00	2.50
		With tab	20.00	
10	$5.25	Canada goose, 1994	16.00	2.50
		With tab	18.00	
11	$7.50	Retriever, decoy, ringnecks, 1995	25.00	3.00
		With tab	25.00	
12	$7.50	Blue-winged teal, 1996	13.00	3.00
13	$7.50	Shovelers, 1997	13.00	3.00
14	$7.50	Gadwalls, 1998	15.00	3.00
15	$7.50	Common goldeneyes, 1999	14.00	3.00
16	$7.50	Hooded mergansers, 2000	11.00	3.00
17	$7.50	Mallards, 2001	11.00	3.00
18	$7.50	Pintails, 2002	10.00	3.00
19	$7.50	Snow geese, 2003	10.00	3.00
20	$7.50	Black ducks, 2004	9.50	3.00
21	$7.50	Canada geese, 2005	9.50	3.00

Nos. 19-21 not required for hunting.

LOUISIANA

Printed in sheets of 30.
Stamps are numbered serially. Stamps without numbers are artist presentation copies.
Two fees: resident and non-resident.

Catalogue values for all unused stamps in this section are for Never Hinged items.

Artists: David Noll, #1-2; Elton Louviere, #3-4; Brett J. Smith, #5-6; Bruce Heard, #7-8; Ronald Louque, #9-10, 15-16, 21-22; Don Edwards, #11-12; John Bertrand, #13-14; R. Hall, #17-18; R. C. Davis, #19-20; Jude Brunet, #23-24; Edward Butler, #25-26; Reggie McLeroy, #27-28; Dale Pousson, #29-30; Jeffrey Klinefelter, #31-32; Ken Michaelsen, #33-34.

1989-2004

1	$5	Blue-winged teal	12.00	2.50
a.		Governor's edition	100.00	
2	$7.50	Blue-winged teal	13.00	2.50
a.		Governor's edition	150.00	

Nos. 1a and 2a were available only through a sealed bid auction where sheets of 30 of each denomination with matching serial numbers were sold as a unit.

3	$5	Green-winged teal, 1990	9.50	2.50
4	$7.50	Green-winged teal, 1990	12.00	2.50
5	$5	Wood ducks, 1991	9.00	2.50
6	$7.50	Wood ducks, 1991	12.00	2.50
7	$5	Pintails, 1992	9.00	2.50
8	$7.50	Pintails, 1992	12.00	2.50
9	$5	American widgeon, 1993	12.00	2.50
10	$7.50	American widgeon, 1993	13.00	2.50
11	$5	Mottled duck, 1994	12.00	2.50
12	$7.50	Mottled duck, 1994	13.00	2.50
13	$5	Speckle bellied goose, 1995	12.00	2.50
14	$7.50	Speckle bellied goose, 1995	13.00	2.50
15	$5	Gadwall, 1996	12.00	2.50
16	$7.50	Gadwall, 1996	13.00	2.50
17	$5	Ring-necked ducks, 1997	8.00	2.50
18	$13.50	Ring-necked ducks, 1997	20.00	2.50
19	$5.50	Mallards, 1998	9.00	2.50
a.		Governor's edition	150.00	
20	$13.50	Mallards, 1998	20.00	2.50
a.		Governor's edition	200.00	
21	$5.50	Snow geese, 1999	9.00	2.50
22	$13.50	Snow geese, 1999	20.00	2.50
23	$5.50	Lesser scaup, 2000	9.00	2.50
24	$13.50	Lesser scaup, 2000	30.00	2.50

No. 24 sold for $25 as stamps were printed before fee increase was finalized.

25	$5.50	Shovelers, 2001	10.00	2.50
26	$25	Shovelers, 2001	30.00	2.50
27	$5.50	Canvasbacks, 2002	10.00	2.50
28	$25	Canvasbacks, 2002	30.00	2.50
29	$5.50	Redheads, 2003	10.00	2.50
30	$25	Redheads, 2003	30.00	2.50
31	$5.50	Hooded mergansers, 2004	8.00	2.50
32	$25	Hooded mergansers, 2004	30.00	2.50
33	$5.50	Pintails, Labrador retriever, 2005	8.00	2.50
34	$25	Pintails, Labrador retriever, 2005	30.00	2.50

Nos. 29-34 not required for hunting.

MAINE

Printed in sheets of 10. Nos. 1-10 are numbered serially.

Catalogue values for all unused stamps in this section are for Never Hinged items.

Artists: David Maass, #1-3; Ron Van Gilder, #4; Rick Allen, #5; Jeannine Staples, #6, 10, 15, 18, 20; Thea Flanagan, #7; Patricia D. Carter, #8; Persis Weirs, #9; Susan Jordan, #11; Richard Alley, #12, 19, 16, 21; Paul Fillion, #13; T. Kemp, #14; Darby Mumford, #17; Daniel Cake, #22.

1984-2004

1	$2.50	Black ducks	22.50	5.00
2	$2.50	Common eiders, 1985	45.00	5.00
3	$2.50	Wood ducks, 1986	9.00	2.50
4	$2.50	Buffleheads, 1987	8.00	2.50
5	$2.50	Green-winged teal, 1988	8.00	2.50
6	$2.50	Common goldeneyes, 1989	8.00	2.50
7	$2.50	Canada geese, 1990	8.00	2.50
8	$2.50	Ring-necked duck, 1991	8.00	2.50
9	$2.50	Old squaw, 1992	8.00	2.50
10	$2.50	Hooded merganser, 1993	8.00	2.50
11	$2.50	Mallards, 1994	8.00	2.50
12	$2.50	White-winged scoters, 1995	12.00	2.50
13	$2.50	Blue-winged teal, 1996	12.00	2.50
14	$2.50	Greater scaup, 1997	12.00	2.50
15	$2.50	Surf scoters, 1998	8.00	2.50
16	$2.50	Black duck, 1999	8.00	2.50
17	$2.50	Common eider, 2000	8.00	2.50
18	$2.50	Wood duck, 2001	8.00	2.50
19	$2.50	Buffleheads, 2002	8.00	2.50
20	$5.50	Green-winged teal, 2003	9.00	2.50
21	$8.50	Barrow's goldeneye, 2004	12.50	2.50
22	$8.50	Canada goose, 2005	12.50	2.50

MARYLAND

Nos. 1-19 printed in sheets of 10. Starting with No. 20, printed in sheets of 5 with numbered tab at bottom and selvage at top.
Each stamp has tab. Unused value is for stamp with tab. Many used copies have tab attached.

Catalogue values for all unused stamps in this section are for Never Hinged items.

Artists: John Taylor, #1, 6, 24; Stanley Stearns, #2, 5; Louis Frisino, #3, 13, 20; Jack Schroeder, #4, 7; Arthur Eakin, ; Roger Bucklin, #9; Roger Lent, #10, 16; Carla Huber, #11, ; David Turnbaugh, #12, 18, 23, 27, 31; Francis Sweet, # ; Christopher White, #15; Will Wilson, #19; Robert Bealle, #2 , 30; Charles Schauck, #22; Paul Makuchal, #25; Wa Makuchal, #26; Wilhelm Goebel, #28, 32; James Kinnett, #2

1974-2004

1	$1.10	Mallards	11.00	2.
2	$1.10	Canada geese, rouletted, 1975	10.00	2
3	$1.10	Canvasbacks, rouletted, 1976	10.00	2
4	$1.10	Greater scaup, 1977	10.00	2
5	$1.10	Redheads, 1978	10.00	2.
6	$1.10	Wood ducks, rouletted, 1979	10.00	2.
7	$1.10	Pintail decoy, rouletted, 1980	10.00	2.
8	$3	Widgeon, rouletted, 1981	9.00	2
9	$3	Canvasback, 1982	8.00	2.
10	$3	Wood duck, 1983	10.00	2.
11	$6	Black ducks, 1984	10.00	2.
12	$6	Canada geese, 1985	9.50	2.
13	$6	Hooded mergansers, 1986	9.50	2.
14	$6	Redheads, 1987	12.00	2.
15	$6	Ruddy ducks, 1988	9.50	2.
16	$6	Blue-winged teal, 1989	10.00	2.
17	$6	Lesser scaup, 1990	8.00	2.
18	$6	Shovelers, 1991	8.50	2.
19	$6	Bufflehead, 1992	8.50	2.
20	$6	Canvasbacks, 1993	8.50	2.
21	$6	Redheads, 1994	8.50	2.
22	$6	Mallards, 1995	12.00	2.
23	$6	Canada geese, 1996	15.00	2.
24	$6	Canvasbacks, 1997	10.00	2.
25	$6	Pintails, 1998	10.00	2.
26	$6	Wood ducks, 1999	10.00	2.
27	$6	Oldsquaws, 2000	14.00	2.
28	$6	Wigeons, 2001	9.00	2.
29	$9	Black scoters, 2002	12.00	2.
30	$9	Lesser scaup, 2003	12.00	2.
31	$9	Pintails, 2004	12.00	2.
32	$9	Ruddy duck, 2005	12.00	2.

Public Lands Hunting Stamps

Required to hunt waterfowl in state-managed wildlife areas.
Issued in booklet panes of 10.

1975-79

A1	$2	purple	1,000.	75
A2	$2	black, pink, 1976	950.	45
A3	$2	black, yellow, 1977	850.	45
A4	$2	black, 1978	1,900.	125
A5	$2	black, yellow, 1979	750.	35

MASSACHUSETTS

Printed in sheets of 12.

Catalogue values for all unused stamps in this section are for Never Hinged items.

Artists: Milton Weiler, #1; Tom Hennessey, #2; William Tyner, #5; Randy Julius, #6, 8, 10, 12, 19, 27; John Eggert, #7, 9, Joseph Cibula, #11; Robert Piscatori, #13, 15, 25, 30; Peter ...edita, #14, 29; Lou Barnicle, #16; Warren Racket Shreve, ...7; Benjamin Smith, #18; Donald Little, #20, 32; Sergio Roffo, ..1; David Brega, #22; Christine Wilkinson, #23; Stephen ...dlam; Barry Julius, #28; Larry Denton, #31.

...74-2004

	$1.25 Wood duck decoy, rouletted	15.00	3.00
	$1.25 Pintail decoy, 1975	13.00	3.00
	$1.25 Canada goose decoy, 1976	13.00	3.00
	$1.25 Goldeneye decoy, 1977	13.00	3.00
	$1.25 Black duck decoy, 1978	13.00	3.00
	$1.25 Ruddy turnstone duck decoy, 1979	15.00	3.00
	Imperf, pair	160.00	
	$1.25 Old squaw decoy, 1980	15.00	3.00
	$1.25 Red-breasted merganser decoy, 1981	15.00	3.00
	$1.25 Greater yellowlegs decoy, 1982	15.00	3.00
	$1.25 Redhead decoy, 1983	15.00	3.00
	$1.25 White-winged scoter decoy, 1984	15.00	3.00
	$1.25 Ruddy duck decoy, 1985	12.00	3.00
	$1.25 Preening bluebill decoy, 1986	12.00	2.50
	$1.25 American widgeon decoy, 1987	12.00	2.50
	$1.25 Mallard decoy, 1988	12.00	2.50
	$1.25 Brant decoy, 1989	12.00	2.50
	$1.25 Whistler hen decoy, 1990	10.00	2.50
	$5 Canvasback decoy, 1991	10.00	2.50
	$5 Black-bellied plover decoy, 1992	10.00	2.50
	$5 Red-breasted merganser decoy, 1993	10.00	2.50
	$5 White-winged scoter decoy, 1994	10.00	2.50
	$5 Female hooded merganser decoy, 1995	10.00	2.50
	$5 Eider decoy, 1996	10.00	2.50
	$5 Curlew decoy, 1997	10.00	2.50
	$5 Canada goose decoy, 1998	10.00	2.50
	$5 Oldsquaw decoy, 1999	10.00	2.50
	$5 Merganser hen decoy, 2000	10.00	2.50
	$5 Black duck decoy, 2001	10.00	2.50
	$5 Bufflehead decoy, 2002	10.00	2.50
	$5 Greenwing teal decoy, 2003	10.00	2.50
	$5 Wood duck drake decoy, 2004	8.00	2.50
	$5 Oldsquaw drake decoy, 2005	8.00	2.50

MICHIGAN

Nos. 1-5 printed in sheets of 10 with center gutter, rouletted. Printed in sheets of 10 die cut self-...dhesives on backing paper (Nos. 6-19), or sheets of 15 (starting with No. 20).
Nos. 1, 3-19 are serially numbered.

> Catalogue values for all unused stamps in this section are for Never Hinged items.

Artist: Oscar Warbach.

1976

1	$2.10 Wood duck	5.00	2.50

Artists: Larry Hayden, #2, 5, 12; Richard Timm, #3; Andrew Kurzmann, #4; Dietmar Krumrey, #6, 14, 23-24; Gijsbert van Frankenhuyzen, #7; Rod Lawrence, #8, 15, 20, 25, 27; Larry Cory, #9, 16; Robert Steiner, #10; Russell Cobane, #11; John Martens, #13; Heiner Hertling, #17; Clark Sullivan, #18; David Bollman, #19; Rusty Fretner, #21; M. Monroe, #22; Kim Diment, #26; Dietmar Krumrey, #28; Tim McDonald, #29; Christopher Smith, 30.

1977-2004

2	$2.10 Canvasbacks	275.00	35.00
	With numbered tab	400.00	
3	$2.10 Mallards, 1978	20.00	5.00
	With tab	47.50	
4	$2.10 Canada geese, 1979	60.00	5.00
	With tab	75.00	
5	$3.75 Lesser scaup, 1980	15.00	4.00
	With tab	25.00	
6	$3.75 Buffleheads, 1981	25.00	4.00
7	$3.75 Redheads, 1982	25.00	4.00

Unused value is for stamp with sufficient margin to show printed spaces for date and time the stamp was sold.

8	$3.75 Wood ducks, 1983	25.00	4.00
9	$3.75 on $3.25 Pintails, 1984	25.00	3.00

No. 9 not issued without surcharge.

10	$3.75 Ring-necked ducks, 1985	25.00	3.00
11	$3.75 Common goldeneyes, 1986	22.00	2.50
12	$3.85 Green-winged teal, 1987	10.00	2.50
13	$3.85 Canada geese, 1988	10.00	2.50
14	$3.85 Widgeons, 1989	10.00	2.50
15	$3.85 Wood ducks, 1990	10.00	2.50
16	$3.85 Blue-winged teal, 1991	9.00	2.50
17	$3.85 Red-breasted merganser, 1992	9.00	2.50
18	$3.85 Hooded merganser, 1993	9.00	2.50
19	$3.85 Black duck, 1994	9.00	2.50
20	$4.35 Blue winged teal, 1995	9.00	3.00
21	$4.35 Canada geese, 1996	9.00	3.00
22	$5 Canvasbacks, 1997	15.00	3.00
23	$5 Pintail, 1998	9.00	3.00
24	$5 Shoveler, 1999	9.00	3.00
25	$5 Mallards, 2000	20.00	3.00

Self-Adhesive Die Cut

26	$5 Ruddy ducks, 2001	10.00	3.00
27	$5 Wigeons, 2002	8.00	3.00
28	$5 Redheads, 2003	8.00	3.00

Rouletted

29	$5 Wood duck, 2004	8.00	3.00
30	$5 Blue-winged teals, 2005	8.00	3.00

Nos. 24-30 not required for hunting.

MINNESOTA

License Surcharge Stamps

No. A1 printed in sheets of 10. These stamps served as a $1 surcharge to cover the cost of a license increase.
Nos. A1-A2 issued to raise funds for acquisition and development of wildlife lands.

1957 — Perf. 12½

A1	$1 Mallards & Pheasant	125.00	8.00

1971 — Rouletted 9½

A2	$1 black, *dark yellow*	2,900.	25.00

Regular Issues
Printed in sheets of 10.

> Catalogue values for all unused stamps in this section are for Never Hinged items.

Artists: David Maass, #1, 3; Leslie Kouba, #2; James Meger, #4; Terry Redlin, #5, 9, Phil Scholer, #6, 17; Gary Moss, #7; Thomas Gross, #8; Brian Jarvi, #10; Ron Van Gilder, #11; Robert Hautman #12, 16, 25; Jim Hautman, #13, 20; Kevin Daniel, #14, 21; Daniel Smith, #15; Edward DuRose, #18; Bruce Miller, #19; Thomas Moen, #22; John House, #23; Kim Norlien, #24; John Freiberg, #26; Mark Kness, #27; Scot Storm, #28; David Chapman, #29.

1977-2004

1	$3 Mallards	15.00	2.50
2	$3 Lesser scaup, 1978	12.00	2.50
3	$3 Pintails, 1979	12.00	2.50
4	$3 Canvasbacks, 1980	12.00	2.50
5	$3 Canada geese, 1981	9.50	2.50
6	$3 Redheads, 1982	11.00	2.50
7	$3 Blue geese & snow goose, 1983	11.00	2.50
8	$3 Wood ducks, 1984	11.00	2.50
9	$3 White-fronted geese, 1985	9.00	2.50
10	$5 Lesser scaup, 1986	10.00	2.50

Beginning with this issue, left side of sheet has an agent's tab, detachable from the numbered tab.

11	$5 Common goldeneyes, 1987	11.00	2.50
	With numbered tab	11.00	
	With agent's and numbered tabs	15.00	
12	$5 Buffleheads, 1988	11.00	2.50
	With numbered tab	11.00	
	With agent's and numbered tabs	15.00	
13	$5 Widgeons, 1989	11.00	2.50
	With numbered tab	11.00	
	With agent's and numbered tabs	15.00	
14	$5 Hooded mergansers, 1990	25.00	2.50
	With numbered tab	25.00	
	With agent's and numbered tabs	40.00	
15	$5 Ross's geese, 1991	10.00	2.50
	With numbered tab	10.00	
	With agent's and numbered tabs	13.00	
16	$5 Barrow's goldeneyes, 1992	10.00	2.50
	With numbered tab	10.00	
	With agent's and numbered tabs	13.00	
17	$5 Blue-winged teal, 1993	10.00	2.50
	With numbered tab	10.00	
	With agent's and numbered tabs	13.00	
18	$5 Ringneck duck, 1994	10.00	2.50
	With numbered tab	10.00	
	With agent's and numbered tabs	13.00	
19	$5 Gadwall, 1995	10.00	2.50
	With numbered tab	10.00	
	With agent's and numbered tabs	13.00	
20	$5 Greater scaup, 1996	10.00	2.50
	With numbered tab	10.00	
	With agent's and numbered tabs	13.00	
21	$5 Shovelers, 1997	11.00	2.50
	With numbered tab	11.00	
	With agent's and numbered tabs	15.00	
22	$5 Harlequins, 1998	11.00	2.50
	With numbered tab	11.00	
	With agent's and numbered tabs	15.00	
23	$5 Green-winged teal, 1999	11.00	2.50
	With numbered tab	11.00	
	With agent's and numbered tabs	15.00	

Self-Adhesive Die Cut

24	$5 Red-breasted merganser, 2000	10.00	2.50

No. 24 is on backing paper affixed to back of license form.

25	$5 Black duck, 2001	12.50	2.50

No. 25 is on backing paper affixed to back of license form.

26	$5 Ruddy duck, 2002	12.50	2.50
27	$5 Oldsquaws, 2003	12.50	2.50

28	$7.50 Common mergansers, *2004*	11.50	2.50
29	$7.50 White-winged scoters, lighthouse, *2005*	11.50	2.50

Nos. 26-29 are on backing paper affixed to mailing envelopes.

MISSISSIPPI

Starting with No. 2, stamps are printed in sheets of 10. Nos. 2-14 are rouletted. All stamps are numbered serially.

Catalogue values for all unused stamps in this section are for Never Hinged items.

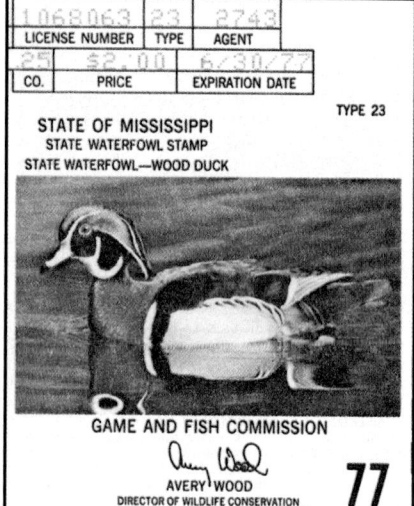

TYPE 23

STATE OF MISSISSIPPI
STATE WATERFOWL STAMP
STATE WATERFOWL—WOOD DUCK

GAME AND FISH COMMISSION

AVERY WOOD
DIRECTOR OF WILDLIFE CONSERVATION
77
NOT VALID UNLESS SIGNED IN INK ACROSS THE FACE OF THIS LICENSE
NOT VALID UNLESS PUNCHED

Illustration reduced.

Artists: Carroll & Gwen Perkins, #1; Allen Hughes, #2; John C. A. Reimers, #3, 6; Carole Pigott Hardy, #4; Bob Tompkins, #5, 13; Jerry Johnson, #7; Jerrie Glasper, #8; Tommy Goodman, #9; Lottie Fulton, #10; Joe Lattl, #11, 17, 22-23; Robert Garner, #12; Debra Aven Swartzendruber, #14; Kathy Dickson, #15; Phillip Crowe, #16; Eddie Suthoff, #18; Emitt Thames, #19-20; James Josey, #21; John Mac Hudspeth, #24, 25; Joe Mac Hudspeth, #26-30.

1976　　　　　　　　　　　　　Without Gum
1	$2 Wood duck	18.00	5.00
a.	Complete 2-part data processing card	25.00	

1977-2004
2	$2 Mallards	9.00	2.50
3	$2 Green-winged teal, *1978*	9.00	2.50
4	$2 Canvasbacks, *1979*	9.00	2.50
5	$2 Pintails, *1980*	9.00	2.50
6	$2 Redheads, *1981*	9.00	2.50
7	$2 Canada geese, *1982*	9.00	2.50
8	$2 Lesser scaup, *1983*	9.00	2.50
9	$2 Black ducks, *1984*	9.00	2.50
10	$2 Mallards, *1985*	9.00	2.50
a.	Vert. serial No., imperf btwn. serial No. and stamp	150.00	
b.	Horiz. serial No., no vert. silver bar	650.00	
11	$2 Widgeons, *1986*	9.00	2.50
12	$2 Ring-necked ducks, *1987*	9.00	2.50
13	$2 Snow geese, *1988*	9.00	2.50
14	$2 Wood ducks, *1989*	7.00	2.50
15	$2 Snow geese, *1990*	12.50	2.50
16	$2 Labrador retriever & canvasbacks, *1991*	7.50	2.50
17	$2 Green-winged teal, *1992*	7.50	2.50
18	$5 Mallards, *1993*	9.00	2.50
19	$5 Canvasbacks, *1994*	9.00	2.50
20	$5 Blue-winged teal, *1995*	15.00	2.50
21	$5 Hooded merganser, *1996*	15.00	2.50
22	$5 Pintail, *1997*	20.00	2.50
23	$5 Pintails, *1998*	13.00	2.50
24	$5 Ring-necked duck, *1999*	10.00	2.50
25	$5 Mallards, *2000*	10.00	2.50
26	$5 Gadwall, *2001*	13.00	2.50
27	$10 Wood duck, *2002*	14.00	2.50
28	$10 Pintail, *2003*	14.00	2.50
29	$10 Wood ducks, *2004*	14.00	2.50
30	$10 Blue-winged teal, *2005*	14.00	2.50

MISSOURI

Issued in booklet panes of five with tab. Nos. 1-8 are rouletted. No. 18 issued in pane of 30.

Catalogue values for all unused stamps in this section are for Never Hinged items.

Artists: Charles Schwartz, #1; David Plank, #2; Tom Crain, #3, 0; Gary Lucy, #4; Doug Ross, #5; Glenn Chambers, #6; Ron Clayton, #7; Ron Ferkol, #9, 13, 18; Bruce Bollman, #10; Kathy Dickson, #11; Eileen Melton, #12; Kevin Guinn, #14; Thomas Bates, #15; Keith Alexander, #16; Ryan Peterson, #17.

1979-96
1	$3.40 Canada geese	550.00	75.00
	With tab	650.00	
2	$3.40 Wood ducks, *1980*	120.00	18.00
	With tab	150.00	
3	$3 Lesser scaup, *1981*	60.00	9.00
	With tab	75.00	
4	$3 Buffleheads, *1982*	60.00	8.00
	With tab	75.00	
5	$3 Blue-winged teal, *1983*	45.00	8.00
	With tab	55.00	
6	$3 Mallards, *1984*	40.00	7.00
	With tab	50.00	
7	$3 American widgeons, *1985*	22.50	3.00
	With tab	25.00	
8	$3 Hooded mergansers, *1986*	12.00	3.00
	With tab	15.00	
9	$3 Pintails, *1987*	9.00	3.00
	With tab	13.00	
10	$3 Canvasback, *1988*	8.00	2.50
	With tab	11.00	
11	$3 Ring-necked ducks, *1989*	8.00	2.50
	With tab	9.25	

All copies of Nos. 12b, 13b, 14b, 15b, 16b, 17b are signed by the governor.

12	$5 Redheads, *1990*	8.00	2.50
	With two part tab	10.00	
a.	$50 Governor's edition with tab	75.00	
b.	$100 Governor's edition with tab	—	
13	$5 Snow geese, *1991*	8.00	2.50
	With two part tab	9.00	
a.	$50 Governor's edition with tab	72.50	
b.	$100 Governor's edition with tab	—	
14	$5 Gadwalls, *1992*	8.00	2.50
	With tab	9.00	
a.	$50 Governor's edition with tab	75.00	
b.	$100 Governor's edition with tab	—	
15	$5 Green-winged teal, *1993*	8.00	2.50
	With tab	9.00	
a.	$50 Governor's edition with tab	75.00	
b.	$100 Governor's edition with tab	—	
16	$5 White-fronted goose, *1994*	8.00	2.50
	With 2-part tab	9.00	
a.	$50 Governor's edition with tab	75.00	
b.	$100 Governor's edition with tab	—	
17	$5 Goldeneyes, *1995*	8.00	2.50
	With 2-part tab	9.00	
a.	$50 Governor's edition with tab	75.00	
b.	$100 Governor's edition with tab	—	
18	$5 Black ducks, *1996*	8.00	2.50

MONTANA

Bird License Stamps
Required to hunt waterfowl.
Resident ($2, $4, $6), youth ($1, $2), and non-resident ($25, $30, $53) bird licenses. Licenses were no longer produced for youth, beginning in 1985, and non-resident, beginning in 1989.
Nos. 1-33 rouletted.

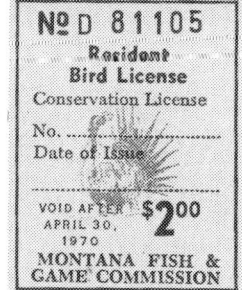

1969
A1	$2 Sage grouse	575.00	15.
A2	$1 Sage grouse	575.00	50.
A3	$25 Sage grouse	575.00	75.

1970
A4	$2 Sage grouse	575.00	10.
a.	Missing "1" in "1971," pos. 10		500.
A5	$1 Sage grouse	1,450.	150.
A6	$25 Sage grouse	—	275.

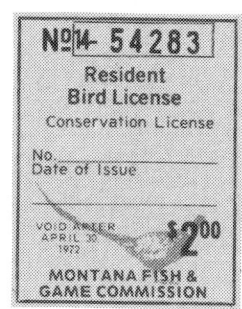

1971
A7	$2 Pheasant	575.00	10.0
A8	$1 Pheasant	575.00	35.0
A9	$25 Pheasant	575.00	50.0

1972
A10	$2 Pheasant	575.00	10.0
A11	$1 Pheasant	575.00	35.0
A12	$25 Pheasant	575.00	50.0

1973
A13	$2 Pheasant	575.00	10.0
A14	$1 Pheasant	575.00	35.0
A15	$25 Pheasant	575.00	50.0

1974
A16	$2 Pheasant	575.00	10.00
A17	$1 Pheasant	575.00	35.00
A18	$25 Pheasant	575.00	50.00

1975
A19	$2 Pheasant	575.00	10.00
A20	$1 Pheasant	575.00	35.00
A21	$25 Pheasant	575.00	50.00

1976
A22	$4 Pheasant	575.00	10.00
A23	$2 Pheasant	575.00	35.00
A24	$30 Pheasant	575.00	50.00

1977
A25	$4 Pheasant	575.00	10.00
A26	$2 Pheasant	575.00	35.00
A27	$30 Pheasant	575.00	50.00

'78			
	$4 Sage grouse	8.00	2.00
	$2 Sage grouse	8.00	5.00
	$30 Sage grouse	8.00	5.50

'79			
	$4 Snow geese	8.00	2.00
	$2 Snow geese	8.00	5.00
	$30 Snow geese	8.00	5.50

'80			
6	$30 black, *gray green*	35.00	

'82			
0	$4 black, *yellow*	5.00	

'83			
3	$4 black, *yellow gray*	225.00	5.00
4	$2 black, *gray*	225.00	
5	$30 black, *light blue*	225.00	

'84			
6	$4 black, *light blue green*	185.00	5.00
7	$2 black, *light violet*	275.00	
8	$30 black, *gray*	185.00	

'85			
9	$4 black, *light blue*	275.00	5.00
50	$30 black, *lavender*	185.00	

'986			
51	$4 black, *orange*	275.00	5.00
52	$30 black, *light blue*	275.00	

'987			
53	$4 black, *orange brown*	160.00	3.00
54	$30 black, *tan*	225.00	

'988			
55	$6 black, *light blue*	140.00	3.00
56	$53 black, *purple*	225.00	

'989-99			
57	$6 black, *rose*	100.00	2.00
58	$6 black, *lavender, 1990*	90.00	2.00
59	$6 black, *pale blue, 1991*	80.00	2.00
60	$6 black, *brown, 1992*	70.00	2.00
61	$6 black, *blue, 1993*	60.00	1.50
62	$6 black, *red orange, 1994*	55.00	1.50
63	$6 black, *blue, 1995*	42.50	1.50
64	$6 black, *purple, 1996*	25.00	1.00
65	$6 black, *mauve, 1997*	15.00	1.00
66	$6 black, *gray, 1998*	13.00	1.00
67	$6 black, *green, 1999*	13.00	1.00

Waterfowl Stamps

Issued in booklet panes of 10 and sheets of 30.
Stamps are numbered serially.
Stamps with serial numbers above 31,000 (1986) and above 21,000 (other years) are from booklet panes.

Artist: Joe Thornbrugh, #34, 38, 39, 45, 46, 48; Roger Cruwys, #35, 37, 42; Dave Samuelson, #36; Craig Philips, #40; Darrell Davis, #41; Wayne Dowdy, #43; Jim Borgreen, #44, 50, 51; Cliff Rossberg, #47, 49.

1986-2003

34	$5 Canada geese	12.00	3.00
	Pair from booklet pane with L & R selvage	1,850.	
	Top pair from booklet pane with agent tabs and L & R selvage	—	
35	$5 Redheads, *1987*	15.00	3.00
	Pair from booklet pane with L & R selvage	30.00	
	Top pair from booklet pane with agent tabs and L & R selvage	55.00	
36	$5 Mallards, *1988*	11.00	3.00
	Pair from booklet pane with L & R selvage	25.00	
	Top pair from booklet pane with agent tabs and L & R selvage	40.00	
37	$5 Black Labrador retriever & pintail, *1989*	11.00	3.00
	Pair from booklet pane with L & R selvage	25.00	
	Top pair from booklet pane with agent tabs and L & R selvage	40.00	
a.	Governor's edition	140.00	

No. 37a was available only in full sheets only through a sealed bid auction.

38	$5 Blue-winged & cinnamon teal, *1990*	9.00	2.50
	Pair from booklet pane with L & R selvage	20.00	
	Top pair from booklet pane with agent tabs and L & R selvage	25.00	
39	$5 Snow geese, *1991*	9.00	2.50
	Pair from booklet pane with L & R selvage	20.00	
	Top pair from booklet pane with agent tabs and L & R selvage	25.00	
40	$5 Wood ducks, *1992*	9.00	2.50
	Pair from booklet pane with L & R selvage	20.00	
	Top pair from booklet pane with agent tabs and L & R selvage	25.00	
41	$5 Harlequin ducks, *1993*	10.00	2.50
	Pair from booklet pane with L & R selvage	22.00	
	Top pair from booklet pane with agent tabs and L & R selvage	25.00	
42	$5 Widgeons, *1994*	11.00	2.50
	Pair from booklet pane with L & R selvage	25.00	
	Top pair from booklet pane with agent tabs and L & R selvage	25.00	
43	$5 Tundra swans, *1995*	11.00	2.50
	Pair from booklet pane with L & R selvage	25.00	
	Top pair from booklet pane with agent tabs and L & R selvage	25.00	
44	$5 Canvasbacks, *1996*	11.00	2.50
	Pair from booklet pane with L & R selvage	25.00	
	Top pair from booklet pane with agent tabs and L & R selvage	30.00	
45	$5 Golden retriever, mallard, *1997*	11.00	2.50
	Pair from booklet pane with L & R selvage	25.00	
	Top pair from booklet pane with agent tabs and L & R selvage	30.00	
46	$5 Gadwalls, *1998*	11.00	2.50
	Pair from booklet pane with L & R selvage	25.00	
	Top pair from booklet pane with agent tabs and L & R selvage	30.00	
47	$5 Barrow's goldeneye, *1999*	11.00	2.50
	Pair from booklet pane with L & R selvage	25.00	
	Top pair from booklet pane with agent tabs and L & R selvage	30.00	
48	$5 Mallard decoy, Chesapeake retriever, *2000*	12.00	2.50
	Pair from booklet pane with L & R selvage	25.00	
	Top pair from booklet pane with agent tabs and L & R selvage	30.00	
49	$5 Canada geese, *2001*	11.00	2.50
	Pair from booklet pane with L & R selvage	25.00	
	Top pair from booklet pane with agent tabs and L & R selvage	30.00	
50	($5) Sandhill crane, *2002*	7.50	2.50
51	$5 Mallards, *2003*	7.50	2.50

No. 51 is not required for hunting.

NEBRASKA

Habitat Stamps
Required to hunt waterfowl.
Printed in sheets of 20.

1977-98

A1	$7.50 Ring-necked pheasant		12.00	1.50
A2	$7.50 White-tailed deer, *1978*		12.00	1.50
A3	$7.50 Bobwhite quail, *1979*		12.00	1.50
A4	$7.50 Pheasant, *1980*		12.00	1.50
A5	$7.50 Cottontail rabbit, *1981*		12.00	1.50
A6	$7.50 Coyote, *1982*		12.00	1.50
A7	$7.50 Wild turkey, *1983*		12.00	1.50
A8	$7.50 Canada goose, *1984*		12.00	1.50
A9	$7.50 Cardinal, *1985*		12.00	1.50
A10	$7.50 Sharp-tailed grouse, *1986*		12.00	1.50
A11	$7.50 Sandhill crane, *1987*		12.00	1.50
A12	$7.50 Snow geese, *1988*		12.00	1.50
A13	$7.50 Mallards, *1989*		12.00	1.50
A14	$7.50 Pheasants, *1990*		12.00	1.50
A15	$7.50 Canada geese, *1991*		12.00	1.50
A16	$10.00 Raccoon, *1992*		14.00	1.50
A17	$10.00 Fox squirrel, *1993*		14.00	1.50
A18	$10.00 Hungarian partridge, *1994*		14.00	1.50
A19	$10.00 Prairie pronghorns, *1995*		14.00	1.50
A20	$10.00 Ring-necked pheasant, *1996*		14.00	1.50
A21	$10.00 White-tailed deer, *1997*		14.00	1.50
A22	$10.00 Mourning doves, *1998*		14.00	1.50

Pictorial Labels
These stamps are not valid for any hunting fees.
Printed in sheets of 10.
Stamps are numbered serially.

Artist: Neal Anderson.

1991-95

Artist: Neal Anderson

1	$6 Canada geese	11.00
2	$6 Pintails, *1992*	11.00
3	$6 Canvasbacks, *1993*	11.00
4	$6 Mallards, *1994*	11.00
5	$6 Wood ducks, *1995*	11.00

NEVADA

Printed in booklet panes of 4.
Stamps are rouletted and selvage is found above and below stamps on the pane. The tab portion of the panes is imperforate.
Starting with No. 4 stamps are numbered serially.

Artists: Larry Hayden, #1; Dick Morill, #2; Phil Scholer, #3; Richard Timm, #4; Charles Allen, #5; Robert Steiner, #6; Richard Wilson, #7; Nolan Haan. #8, 12; Sherrie Russell Meline, #9, 21; Jim Hautman, #10; Robert Hautman, #11; Tak Nakamura, #13, 17; Richard Clifton, #14; Steve Hopkins, #15; Mark Mueller, #16; Jeffrey Klinefelter, #18, 23; B. Blight, #19; Janie Kreutzjans, #20; Jeff Hoff, #24; David Brevick, #25; Louis Frisino, #26; Adam Oswald, #27.

1979-2004

1	$2 Canvasbacks and decoy	45.00	12.00
	With numbered tab	50.00	

Copies with tabs without numbers are printer's waste.

2	$2 Cinnamon teal, 1980	8.00	3.00
	With tab	10.00	
3	$2 Whistling swans, 1981	10.00	3.00
	With tab	12.00	
4	$2 Shovelers, 1982	10.00	3.00
	With tab	12.00	
5	$2 Gadwalls, 1983	10.50	3.00
	With tab	11.00	
6	$2 Pintails, 1984	11.00	3.00
	With tab	12.00	
7	$2 Canada geese, 1985	20.00	3.00
	With tab	22.00	
8	$2 Redheads, 1986	16.00	2.50
	With tab	18.00	
9	$2 Buffleheads, 1987	14.00	2.50
	With tab	15.00	
10	$2 Canvasbacks, 1988	11.00	2.50
	With tab	12.00	
11	$2 Ross's geese, 1989	10.00	2.50
	With tab	11.00	
12	$5 Green-winged teal, 1990	10.00	2.50
	With tab	11.00	
13	$5 White-faced ibis, 1991	10.00	2.50
	With tab	11.00	
14	$5 American widgeon, 1992	10.00	2.50
	With tab	11.00	
15	$5 Common goldeneye, 1993	10.00	2.50
	With tab	11.00	
16	$5 Mallards, 1994	10.00	2.50
	With tab	11.00	
17	$5 Wood duck, 1995	10.00	2.50
	With tab	11.00	
18	$5 Ring-necked ducks, 1996	10.00	2.50
	With tab	11.00	
19	$5 Ruddy ducks, 1997	10.00	2.50
	With tab	11.00	
20	$5 Hooded merganser, 1998	10.00	2.50
	With tab	11.00	
21	$5 Canvasback decoy, 1999	10.00	2.50
22	$5 Canvasbacks, 2000	10.00	2.50
23	$5 Lesser Scaups, 2001	10.00	2.50
	With tab	11.00	
24	$5 Cinnamon teal, 2002	10.00	2.50
25	$5 Green-winged teal, 2003	10.00	2.50
	With tab	11.00	
26	$10 Redheads, 2004	15.00	2.50
	With tab	16.00	
27	$10 Gadwalls, 2005	15.00	2.50
	With tab	16.00	

NEW HAMPSHIRE

Printed in booklet panes of 1 with 2-part tab and in sheets of 30. Sheet stamps are perf on four sides.
Stamps are numbered serially.

Catalogue values for all unused stamps in this section are for Never Hinged items.

Artists: Richard Plasschaert, #1; Phillip Crowe, #2; Thomas Hirata, #3; Durrant Bell, #4; Robert Steiner, #5-9; Richard Clifton, #10-11, 15; Louis Frisino, #12; Matthew Scharle, #13; Jeffrey Klinefelter, #14; Jim Collins, #16, 20, 23; Bruce Holloway, #17, 21; Susan Knowles Jordan, #18; Charles Freeman, #19; Lindsey Rothe, #22.

1983-2004

1	$4 Wood ducks	135.00	
a.	Booklet single with 2-part tab	95.00	25.00
2	$4 Mallards, 1984	90.00	
a.	Booklet single with 2-part tab	175.00	20.00
3	$4 Blue-winged teal, 1985	80.00	
a.	Booklet single with 2-part tab	100.00	20.00
4	$4 Hooded mergansers, 1986	20.00	
a.	Booklet single with 2-part tab	30.00	6.00
5	$4 Canada geese, 1987	12.00	
a.	Booklet single with 2-part tab	14.00	4.00
b.	$50 Governor's edition	400.00	
6	$4 Buffleheads, 1988	12.00	
a.	Booklet single with 2-part tab	14.00	3.00
b.	$4 +$46 Governor's edition	60.00	
7	$4 Black ducks, 1989	11.00	
a.	Booklet single with 2-part tab	12.00	3.00
b.	$4 +$50 Governor's edition	67.50	
8	$4 Green-winged teal, 1990	11.00	
a.	Booklet single with 2-part tab	12.00	3.00
b.	$4 +$50 Governor's edition	62.50	
9	$4 Golden retriever & mallards, 1991	15.00	
a.	Booklet single with 2-part tab	17.00	3.00
b.	$4 +$50 Governor's edition	80.00	

Governor's Editions that follow are so inscribed.

10	$4 Ring-necked ducks, 1992	10.00	
a.	Booklet single with 2-part tab	12.00	3.00
b.	Governor's edition	625.00	
11	$4 Hooded mergansers, 1993	10.00	
a.	Booklet single with 2-part tab	12.00	3.00
b.	Governor's edition	650.00	
12	$4 Common goldeneyes, 1994	10.00	
a.	Bklt. single with 2-part tab	12.00	2.50
b.	Governor's edition	175.00	
13	$4 Northern pintails, 1995	10.00	
a.	Bklt. single with 2-part tab	12.00	2.50
b.	Governor's edition	150.00	
14	$4 Surf scooters, 1996	10.00	
a.	Bklt. single with 2-part tab	12.00	2.50
b.	Governor's edition	150.00	
15	$4 Wood ducks, 1997	10.00	
a.	Bklt. single with 2-part tab	12.00	2.50
b.	Governor's edition	125.00	
16	$4 Canada geese, 1998	10.00	
a.	Bklt. single with 2-part tab	12.00	2.50
b.	Governor's edition	130.00	
17	$4 Mallards, 1999	11.00	
a.	Bklt. single with 2-part tab	12.00	2.50
b.	Governor's edition	130.00	
18	$4 Black ducks, 2000	11.00	
a.	Bklt. single with 2-part tab	12.00	2.50
b.	Governor's edition	—	
19	$4 Blue-winged teal, 2001	11.00	
a.	Bklt. single with 2-part tab	12.00	2.50
b.	Governor's edition	—	
20	$4 Pintails, 2002	8.00	
a.	Bklt. single with 2-part tab	10.00	2.50
b.	Governor's edition	150.00	
21	$4 Wood ducks, 2003	8.00	
a.	Bklt. single with 2-part tab	10.00	2.50
b.	Governor's edition	125.00	
22	$4 Wood duck, 2004	8.00	
a.	Bklt. single with 2-part tab	10.00	2.50
b.	Governor's edition	125.00	
23	$4 Oldsquaw, lighthouse, 2005	8.00	
a.	Bklt. single with 2-part tab	10.00	
b.	Governor's edition	125.00	

NEW JERSEY

Resident and non-resident fees.
Printed in sheets of 30 (starting with No. 1) and booklet panes of 10 (all but Nos. 2, 4, 6, 17b, 18b).
Sheet stamps are perf on 4 sides.
Stamps are numbered serially.

Catalogue values for all unused stamps in this section are for Never Hinged items.

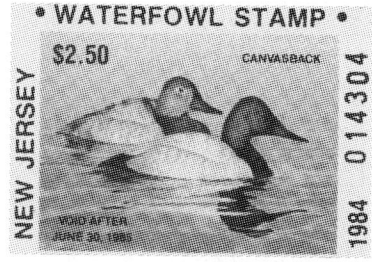

Artists: Thomas Hirata, #1-2, 17-18; David Maass, #3-4; Ronald Louque, #5-6; Louis Frisino, #7-8; Robert Leslie, #9-10, 19-20, 29-30; Daniel Smith, #11-12; Richard Plasschaert, #13-14; Bruce Miller, #21-22; Wilhelm Goebel, #23-24, 27-28; Joe

---

Hautman, #25-26, 35-36; Phillip Crowe, #31-32, 43-46; Ric Clifton, #33-34; Bob Hautman, #37-40; Jim Killen, #41-42.

1984-2004

1	$2.50 Canvasbacks	45.00	
a.	Booklet single, #51,000-102,000	70.00	1
2	$5 Canvasbacks	60.00	1
3	$2.50 Mallards, 1985	15.00	
a.	Booklet single, #51,000-102,000	25.00	
4	$5 Mallards, 1985	18.00	
5	$2.50 Pintails, 1986	15.00	
a.	Booklet single, #51,000-102,000	15.00	
6	$5 Pintails, 1986	13.00	
7	$2.50 Canada geese, 1987	15.00	
a.	Booklet single, #51,000-102,000	15.00	
8	$5 Canada geese, 1987	15.00	
a.	Booklet single, #45,001-60,000	15.00	
9	$2.50 Green-winged teal, 1988	12.00	
a.	Booklet single, #51,000-102,000	12.00	
10	$5 Green-winged teal, 1988	12.00	
a.	Booklet single, #45,001-60,000	12.00	1
11	$2.50 Snow geese, 1989	11.00	
a.	Booklet single, #45,001-60,000	11.00	1
b.	Governor's edition	72.50	
12	$5 Snow geese, 1989	11.00	
a.	Booklet single, #45,001-60,000	11.00	1
b.	Governor's edition	140.00	3

Nos. 11b and 12b were available only in sets of sheets of stamps with matching serial numbers through a sealed auction.

13	$2.50 Wood ducks, 1990	12.00	
a.	Booklet single, #45,001-60,000	12.00	3
14	$5 Wood ducks, 1990	12.00	
a.	Booklet single, #45,001-60,000	12.00	3
17	$2.50 Atlantic brant, 1991	9.00	
a.	Booklet single, #45,001-60,000	9.00	3
b.	Atlantic "brandt"	18.00	
18	$5 Atlantic brant, 1991	12.00	
a.	Booklet single, #45,001-60,000	12.00	3
b.	Atlantic "brandt"	32.50	

Matching serial number sets of Nos. 17b and 18b were available for sale only with the purchase of matching serial number sets of Nos. 17 and 18.

19	$2.50 Bluebills, 1992	9.00	
a.	Booklet single, #27,691-78,690	9.00	2
20	$5 Bluebills, 1992	10.00	
a.	Booklet single, #27,691-57,690	10.00	2
21	$2.50 Buffleheads, 1993	9.00	
a.	Booklet single, #27,691-78,690	9.00	2
b.	Sheet of 4	22.00	
c.	Governor's edition, signed by Florio or Whitman	42.50	
22	$5 Buffleheads, 1993	9.00	
a.	Booklet single, #27,691-57,690	10.00	2
b.	Sheet of 4	40.00	
c.	Governor's edition, signed by Florio or Whitman	82.50	

Nos. 21b and 22b were available only in sets of sheets with matching serial numbers. The set of sheets sold for $35.
Nos. 21c and 22c were available only in sets with matching serial numbers.

23	$2.50 Black ducks, 1994	12.00	
a.	Bklt. single, perf. 2 or 3 sides	12.00	2.
24	$5 Black ducks, 1994	14.00	
a.	Bklt. single, perf. 2 or 3 sides	14.00	2.
25	$2.50 Widgeon, lighthouse, 1995	12.00	
a.	Bklt. single, perf. 3 sides	12.00	2.5
26	$5 Widgeon, lighthouse, 1995	14.00	
a.	Bklt. single, perf. 3 sides	14.00	2.5
27	$5 Goldeneyes, lighthouse, 1996	12.00	
a.	Bklt. single, perf. 2 or 3 sides	12.00	2.5
28	$10 Goldeneyes, lighthouse, 1996	15.00	
a.	Bklt. single, perf. 2 or 3 sides	15.00	2.5

The $2.50 was printed but not used as the rate no longer existed. Later they were sold to collectors. Value, unused $5

29	$5 Old squaws, schooner, 1997	12.00	
a.	Bklt. single, perf. 2 or 3 sides	12.00	2.5
30	$10 Old squaws, schooner, 1997	15.00	
a.	Bklt. single, perf. 2 or 3 sides	15.00	2.5
31	$5 Mallards, 1998	12.00	
a.	Bklt. single, perf. 2 or 3 sides	12.00	2.5
32	$10 Mallards, 1998	15.00	
a.	Bklt. single, perf. 2 or 3 sides	15.00	2.5
33	$5 Redheads, perf. 4 sides, 1999	12.00	
a.	Bklt. single, perf. 2 or 3 sides	12.00	2.5
34	$10 Redheads, perf. 4 sides, 1999	15.00	
a.	Bklt. single, perf. 2 or 3 sides	15.00	2.5
35	$5 Canvasbacks, perf. 4 sides, 2000	12.00	
a.	Bklt. single, perf. 2 or 3 sides	12.00	2.5
36	$10 Canvasbacks, perf. 4 sides, 2000	15.00	
a.	Bklt. single, perf. 2 or 3 sides	15.00	2.5
37	$5 Tundra swans, perf. 4 sides, 2001	10.00	
a.	Bklt. single, perf. 2 or 3 sides	10.00	2.5
38	$10 Tundra swans, perf. 4 sides, 2001	14.00	
a.	Bklt. single, perf. 2 or 3 sides	14.00	2.5
39	$5 Wood ducks, perf. 4 sides, 2002	10.00	
a.	Bklt. single, perf. 2 or 3 sides	10.00	2.5
40	$10 Wood ducks, perf. 4 sides, 2002	14.00	
a.	Bklt. single, perf. 2 or 3 sides	14.00	2.5
41	$5 Pintails, Labrador retriever perf. 4 sides, 2003	10.00	
a.	Bklt. single, perf. 2 or 3 sides	10.00	2.5
42	$10 Pintails, Labrador retriever, perf. 4 sides, 2003	14.00	
a.	Bklt. single, perf. 2 or 3 sides	14.00	2.5
43	$5 Hooded merganser decoy, Labrador retriever, perf. 4 sides, 2004	7.50	
a.	Bklt. single, perf. 2 or 3 sides	7.50	2.5
44	$10 Hooded merganser decoy, Labrador retriever, perf. 4 sides, 2004	12.50	
a.	Bklt. single, perf. 2 or 3 sides	13.00	2.5
45	$5 Canvasback decoys, Chesapeake Bay retriever, perf. 4 sides, 2005	7.50	
a.	Bklt. single, perf. 2 or 3 sides	7.50	2.5

$10 Canvasback decoys, Chesapeake
    Bay retriever, perf. 4 sides, 2005   12.50
Bklt. single, perf. 2 or 3 sides   13.00   2.50

NEW MEXICO

Printed in booklet panes of 5 and sheets of 30.
Stamps are numbered serially.

**Catalogue values for all unused stamps in this
section are for Never Hinged items.**

Artist: Robert Steiner.

91-94

	$7.50 Pintails	13.00	
	Booklet single, with large tab and selvage	13.00	5.00
	$7.50 +$50 Governor's edition	72.50	
	$7.50 American widgeon, 1992	13.00	
	Booklet single, with large tab and selvage	13.00	4.00
	$7.50 +$50 Governor's edition	65.00	
	$7.50 Mallard, 1993	13.00	
	Booklet single, with large tab and selvage	13.00	4.00
	Sheet of 4	50.00	
	$7.50 +$50 Governor's edition	65.00	

No. 3a exists imperf.

No. 4: b, Three birds in flight. c, Two birds in flight. d, Two
birds flying over land. e, Bird's head close-up.

	$7.50 Green-winged teal, sheet of 4, #b.-e., 1994	80.00	
	Souvenir sheet of 4, #b.-e. (decorative border)	40.00	
	Bklt. single with large tab and selvage, each	10.00	4.00
	Bklt. pane of 4, #b.-e.	40.00	

Stamps in Nos. 4-4a are printed with continuous design and
have serial numbers reading down. Stamps in No. 4f have
framelines around each design, inscriptions at the top and
serial numbers reading up.

NEW YORK

Not required to hunt. Printed in sheets of 30.

**Catalogue values for all unused stamps in this
section are for Never Hinged items.**

Artists: Larry Barton, #1; David Maass, #2; Lee LeBlanc, #3;
Richard Plasschaert, #4; Robert Bateman, #5; John Seerey-
Lester, #6; Terry Isaac, #7; Anton Ashak, #8; Ron Kleiber, #9;
Jerome Hageman, #10; Frederick Szatkowski, #11; Len Rusin,
#12; R. Easton, #13; Barbara Woods, #14; Richard Clifton, #15;
Rob Leslie, #16; Bruce Miller, #17; Adam Grimm, #18.

1985-2002

1	$5.50 Canada geese	13.00
2	$5.50 Mallards, 1986	9.00
3	$5.50 Wood ducks, 1987	9.00
4	$5.50 Pintails, 1988	9.00
5	$5.50 Greater scaup, 1989	9.00
6	$5.50 Canvasbacks, 1990	9.00
7	$5.50 Redheads, 1991	11.00
8	$5.50 Wood ducks, 1992	11.00
9	$5.50 Blue-winged teal, 1993	9.00

10	$5.50 Canada geese, 1994	12.00	
11	$5.50 Common goldeneye, 1995	11.00	
12	$5.50 Common loon, 1996	11.00	
13	$5.50 Hooded merganser, 1997	9.00	
14	$5.50 Osprey, 1998	9.00	
15	$5.50 Buffleheads, 1999	13.00	
16	$5.50 Wood ducks, 2000	11.00	
17	$5.50 Pintails, 2001	7.50	
18	$5.50 Canvasbacks, 2002	7.50	3.00

NORTH CAROLINA

Not required to hunt until 1988. Printed in sheets of
30. Starting with No. 6, stamps are numbered
serially.

**Catalogue values for all unused stamps in this
section are for Never Hinged items.**

Artists: Richard Plasschaert, #1, 10; Jim Killen, #2, 13;
Thomas Hirata, #3-4, 17-18; Larry Barton, #5; Ronald Louque,
#6, 21-22, 23-26; Louis Frisino, #7; Robert Leslie, #8, 14; Phillip
Crowe, #9, 12; Bruce Miller, #11; Wilhelm Goebel, #15-16, 27-
28; Robert Flowers, #19-20; Gerald Putt, #29-32.

1983-2004

1	$5.50 Mallards	65.00	
2	$5.50 Wood ducks, 1984	45.00	
3	$5.50 Canvasbacks, 1985	25.00	
4	$5.50 Canada geese, 1986	20.00	
5	$5.50 Pintails, 1987	13.00	
6	$5 Green-winged teal, 1988	10.00	3.00
7	$5 Snow geese, 1989	14.00	3.00
8	$5 Redheads, 1990	14.00	3.00
9	$5 Blue-winged teal, 1991	14.00	3.00
10	$5 American widgeon, 1992	14.00	3.00
11	$5 Tundra swans, 1993	14.00	3.00
12	$5 Buffleheads, 1994	14.00	3.00
13	$5 Brant, lighthouse, 1995	14.00	3.00
14	$5 Pintails, 1996	14.00	3.00
15	$5 Wood ducks, perf., 1997	12.00	3.00
16	$5 As #15, self-adhesive, die cut, 1997	30.00	
17	$5 Canada geese, perf., 1998	12.00	3.00
18	$5 As #17, self-adhesive, die cut, 1998	20.00	
19	$5 Green-winged teal, perf., 1999	12.00	3.00
20	$5 As #19, self-adhesive, die cut, 1999	20.00	
21	$10 Green-winged teal, perf., 2000	20.00	3.00
22	$10 Green-winged teal, self-adhesive, die cut, 2000	20.00	
23	$10 Black duck, perf., 2001	15.00	3.00
24	$10 Black duck, self-adhesive, die cut, 2001	20.00	
25	$10 Pintails, hunters, dog, perf., 2002	15.00	3.00
26	$10 Pintails, hunters, dog, self-adhesive, die cut, 2002	20.00	
27	$10 Ring-necked ducks, hunters, dog, perf., 2003	15.00	3.00
28	$10 Ring-necked ducks, hunters, dog, self-adhesive, die cut, 2003	20.00	
29	$10 Mallards, perf., 2004	14.00	3.00
30	$10 Mallards, self-adhesive, die cut, 2004	20.00	
31	$10 Green-winged teals, perf., 2004	14.00	3.00
32	$10 Green-winged teals, self-adhesive, die cut, 2004	14.00	

Nos. 27-32 not required for hunting.

NORTH DAKOTA

Small Game Stamps

Required to hunt small game and waterfowl
statewide. Resident and non-resident fees.
Values for 1967-70 non-resident stamps are for
copies with staple holes.
Used values are for signed copies. Unused values
for Nos. 12, 16, 18, 20, 22, 24, 26 and 28 are for
stamps on backing.

1967-80

1	$2 black, green	850.00	60.00
2	$25 black, green	3,250.	350.00
3	$2 black, pink, 1968	200.00	20.00
4	$25 black, yellow, 1968	450.00	
5	$2 black, green, 1969	190.00	20.00
6	$35 black, 1969	400.00	
7	$2 blue, 1970	160.00	15.00
8	$35 black, pink, 1970	250.00	50.00
9	$2 black, yellow, 1971	125.00	10.00
10	$35 black, 1971		150.00
11	$3 black, pink, 1972	65.00	5.00
12	$35 red, 1972	450.00	75.00
13	$3 black, yellow, 1973	65.00	5.00
14	$35 green, 1973	1,750.	125.00
15	$3 black, blue, 1974	125.00	15.00
16	$35 red, 1974	400.00	50.00
17	$3 black, 1975	95.00	10.00
18	$35 green, 1975	300.00	40.00
19	$3 black, dark yellow, 1976	55.00	5.00
20	$35 red, 1976	140.00	25.00
21	$3 black, 1977	90.00	10.00
22	$35 red, 1977	125.00	25.00
23	$5 black, 1978	45.00	5.00
24	$40 red, 1978	85.00	20.00
25	$5 black, 1979	35.00	5.00
26	$40 red, 1979	45.00	15.00
27	$5 black, 1980	35.00	5.00
28	$40 green, 1980	45.00	15.00

Small Game and Habitat Stamps

Required to hunt small game and waterfowl
statewide.
Resident ($9), youth ($6) and non-resident ($53)
fees.

Resident stamps issued in booklet panes of 5 numbered 20,001-150,000 (1982-86 issues) or 20,001-
140,000 (starting with 1987 issue) or sheets of 30
numbered 150,001 and up (1982-86 issues) or
140,001 and up (starting with 1987 issue).
Starting with 1984, resident booklet stamps have
straight edges at sides.
Nos. 31, 34, 37, 40 are die cut self adhesives.
Unused values are for stamps on backing.
All youth stamps were issued in booklet panes of 5.
Non-resident stamps for 1981, 1982, 1996 and following years were issued in booklet panes of 5.
The 1984-95 non-resident stamps were issued se-
tenant with non-resident waterfowl and non-resident
general game stamps (rouletted on three sides). The
1994 and 1995 non-resident stamps also were issued
se-tenant with only the non-resident general game
stamp (rouletted at sides), as well as in booklet panes
of 5 (rouletted top and bottom).

**Catalogue values for all unused stamps in this
section, from this point to the end, are for Never
Hinged items.**

A1

1981

29	A1	$9 black	35.00	3.00
30	A1	$6 black, *blue green*	175.00	25.00
31	A1	$53 blue	110.00	20.00

A2

Artists: Richard Plaschaert, #32, 73; Terry Radlin, #35; David Maass, #38; Leslie Kouba, #41; Mario Fernandez, #44; Ronald Louque, #47, 75; Louis Frisino, #50; Robert Leslie, #53; Roger Cruwys, #56; Thomas Hirata, #59; Phillip Crowe, #62, 77, 81; Bruce Miller, #65; Darrell Davis, #67; Richard Clifton, #69; Wilhelm Goebel, #71; Jeffrey Klinefelter, #79.

1982

32	A2	$9 Canada geese	125.	
		Booklet single with L & R salvage	1,250.	25.00

Serial numbers 1-20,000 are from sheets of 10. Stamps without selvage from booklets sell for considerably less.

33	A1	$6 black, *blue*	175.00	25.00
34	A1	$53 black	35.00	15.00

1983

35	A2	$9 Mallards	75.00	
		Booklet single with L & R salvage	2,750.	25.00

Serial numbers 1-20,000 are from sheets. Stamps without selvage from booklets sell for considerably less.

36	A1	$6 black, *orange*		25.00
37	A1	$53 black		40.00

1984

38	A2	$9 Canvasbacks	30.00	
a.		Booklet single, perforated horiz. on 1 or 2 sides	3,000.	25.00
39	A1	$6 black, *light blue*		25.00
40	A1	$53 black		40.00

1985

41	A2	$9 Bluebills	20.00	
a.		Booklet single, perforated horiz. on 1 or 2 sides	4,000.	25.00
42	A1	$6 black, *light blue*		25.00
43	A1	$53 black		40.00

1986

44	A2	$9 Pintails	20.00	
a.		Booklet single, perforated horiz. on 1 or 2 sides	625.00	20.00
45	A1	$6 black, *light blue*		20.00
46	A1	$53 black		35.00

1987

47	A2	$9 Snow geese	18.00	
a.		Booklet single, perforated horiz. on 1 or 2 sides	60.00	18.00
48	A1	$6 black, *light blue*	—	25.00
49	A1	$53 black		30.00

1988

50	A2	$9 White-winged scoters	14.00	
a.		Booklet single, perforated horiz. on 1 or 2 sides	30.00	12.00
51	A1	$6 black, *light blue*		25.00
52	A1	$53 black		30.00

Stamps Inscribed "Small Game"
Resident ($6), youth ($3) and non-resident ($50, $75) fees.

1989

53	A2	$6 Redheads	12.00	
a.		Booklet single, perforated horiz. on 1 or 2 sides	15.00	8.00
54	A1	$3 black, *light blue*	—	25.00
55	A1	$50 black		30.00

1990

56	A2	$6 Labrador retriever & mallard	15.00	
a.		Booklet single, perforated horiz. on 1 or 2 sides	15.00	8.00
57	A1	$3 black, *light blue*	200.00	25.00
58	A1	$50 black		25.00

1991

59	A2	$6 Green-winged teal	12.50	
a.		Booklet single, perforated horiz. on 1 or 2 sides	13.00	6.00
60	A1	$3 black, *light blue*	200.00	25.00
61	A1	$50 black	350.00	25.00

1992

62	A2	$6 Blue-winged teal	12.50	
a.		Booklet single, perforated horiz. on 1 or 2 sides	13.00	6.00
63	A1	$3 black, *light blue*	325.00	
64	A1	$50 black		25.00

When supplies of No. 64 ran out, copies of No. 58 were used with the date changed by hand. Unused copies exist. Value, $300.

1993

65	A2	$6 Wood ducks	12.50	
a.		Booklet single, perforated horiz. on 1 or 2 sides	13.00	6.00
66	A1	$50 black	550.00	25.00

1994

67	A2	$6 Canada geese	10.00	
a.		Booklet single, perforated horiz. on 1 or 2 sides	10.00	6.00
68	A1	$75 black, rouletted on 2 adjacent sides	400.00	20.00
a.		Booklet single, rouletted top and bottom	—	

1995

69	A2	$6 Widgeon	10.00	
a.		Booklet single, perforated horiz. on 1 or 2 sides	10.00	5.00
70	A1	$75 black, rouletted on 2 adjacent sides	350.00	20.00
a.		Booklet single, rouletted top and bottom	—	

1996

71	A2	$6 Mallards	10.00	
a.		Booklet single, perforated horiz. on 1 or 2 sides	10.00	2.50
72	A1	$75 black, rouletted at top and bottom	—	

1997

73	A2	$6 White-fronted geese	10.00	
a.		Booklet single, perforated horiz. on 1 or 2 sides	10.00	2.50
74	A1	$75 black, rouletted at top and bottom	—	

1998

75	A2	$6 Blue-winged teal	10.00	
a.		Bklt. single, perforated horiz. on 1 or 2 sides	10.00	2.50
76	A1	$75 black, rouletted at top and bottom	—	

1999

77	A2	$6 Gadwalls	10.00	
a.		Bklt. single, perforated horiz. on 1 or 2 sides	10.00	2.50
78	A1	$75 black, rouletted at top and bottom	—	

2000

79		$6 Pintails, *2000*	10.00	
a.		Bklt. single, perforated horiz. on 1 or 2 sides	10.00	2.50
81	A2	$6 Canada geese, *2001*	10.00	
a.		Bklt. single, perforated horiz. on 1 or 2 sides	10.00	2.50

Expires June 30, 2003
State of North Dakota
Resident Small Game
$6.00

Nº 105573

N.D. Game and Fish Dept.
NON-TRANSFERABLE

A3

83	A3	$6 black, *green, 2002*	10.00
84	A3	$6 black, *green, 2003*	10.00
85	A3	$6 black, *green*	10.00
86	A3	$6 black, *green*	10.00

Non-Resident Waterfowl Stamps
Required by non-residents to hunt waterfowl only.
Unused copies of Nos. A1a, A13a-A19a have no serial number. Used copies have number written in. Nos. A1-A10 are self-adhesive, die cut. Others are rouletted.

Catalogue values for all unused stamps in this section are for Never Hinged items.

17	18	19	20	21	22	23	24	25	26	27	28	29	30	31
☐ SEPT.			1975 - Zone_____			$5					1975			
☐ OCT.			State of N. Dak.											
☐ NOV.			NR. Waterfowl Stamp											
☐ DEC.			**NON-TRANSFERABLE**											
			N. Dak. Game & Fish Dept.											
1	2	3	4	5	6	7	8	9	10	11	12	13	14	15	16

Illustration reduced.

1975-99

A1		$5 green		15
a.		No serial number	175.00	
A2		$5 red, *1976*	500.00	10
A3		$5 red, *1977*	325.00	7
A4		$5 red, *1978*	110.00	2
A5		$5 red, *1979*	85.00	2
A6		$5 green, *1980*	90.00	2
A7		$8 blue, *1981*	175.00	2
A8		$8 black, *1982*	27.50	1
A9		$8 black, *1983*		5
A10		$8 black, *1984*		5
A11		$8 black, *1985*		4
A12		$8 black, *1986*		4
A13		$8 black, *1987*		4
a.		No serial number	400.00	4
A14		$8 black, *1988*		3
a.		No serial number	350.00	5
A15		$8 black, *1989*		2
a.		No serial number, light green paper	350.00	5
A16		$8 black, *1990*		2
a.		No serial number	300.00	5
A17		$8 black, *1991*	400.00	2
a.		No serial number	250.00	3
A18		$8 black, *1992*		2
a.		No serial number	200.00	35

When supplies of No. A18 ran out copies of No. A16 were used with the date changed by hand. Values, unused $2 used $50.

A19		$10 black, *1993*	275.00	20
a.		No serial number	175.00	30
A20		$10 black, rouletted on 2 adjacent sides, *1994*	250.00	20
a.		No serial number, rouletted top and bottom	175.00	30
A21		$10 black, rouletted on 2 adjacent sides, *1995*	225.00	20
a.		No serial number, rouletted top and bottom	100.00	25
A22		$10 black, rouletted top and bottom, *1996*	95.00	20
A23		$10 black, rouletted top and bottom, *1997*	85.00	14
A24		$10 black, rouletted top and bottom, *1998*	75.00	12
A25		$10 black, rouletted top and bottom, *1999*	65.00	12.

Resident Sportsmen's Stamps
Required to hunt a variety of game, including waterfowl.

Catalogue values for all unused stamps in this section are for Never Hinged items.

1992-93 Resident
ND Sportsmens License
$25.00
Fishing - Small Game
General Game & Habitat
Furbearer

Nº 12969
NON-TRANSFERABLE

1992-98

2A1	$25 black & purple, *1992-1993*	3,500.	75.0
2A2	$25 black & purple, *1993-1994*	1,650.	35.0
2A3	$25 black & purple, *1994-1995*	375.00	25.0
2A4	$25 black & purple, *1995-1996*	250.00	20.0
2A5	$25 black & purple, *1996-1997*	200.00	15.0
2A6	$27 black & purple, *1997-1998*	125.00	12.0

OHIO

Pymatuning Lake Waterfowl Hunting Stamps

Pymatuning Hunting License
Valid when attached to Resident Hunters and Trappers License.
Authority H. B. 668.
YEAR 1938 $1.00 NO FEE

1938-45

A1	$1 black, *light yellow*		—
A2	$1 black, *gray, 1939*		—
A3	$1 black, *blue, 1940*		—
A4	$1 black, *pink, 1941*		—
A5	$1 black, *green, 1942*		—
A6	$1 black, *1943*		—
A7	$1 black, *manila, 1944*		—
A8	$1 black, *manila, 1945*		—

Statewide Issues

s. 1-18 printed in sheets of 16. Starting with No.
9, stamps are printed in souvenir sheets of 1.

Catalogue values for all unused stamps in this
ction are for Never Hinged items.

Artists: John Ruthven, #1; Harry Antis, #2; Harold Roe, #3, 6,
17; Ronald Louque, #4; Lynn Kaatz, #5, 8; Cynthia Fisher,
Jon Henson, #9; Gregory Clair, #10; Samuel Timm, #11;
neth Nanney, #12; Richard Clifton, #13; Ron Kleiber, #14;
. Cleland-Hura, #16: Timothy Donovan, #18; Mark Ander-
, #19; Brian Bright, #20, 22; Jeffrey Klinefelter, #21; Robert
topulos, #23; Adam Grimm, #24.

2-2004

	$5.75 Wood ducks	75.00	10.00
	$5.75 Mallards, 1983	65.00	10.00
	$5.75 Green-winged teal, 1984	65.00	6.00
	$5.75 Redheads, 1985	35.00	6.00
	$5.75 Canvasback, 1986	30.00	5.00
	$6 Blue-winged teal, 1987	12.00	4.00
	$6 Common goldeneyes, 1988	12.00	4.00
	$6 Canada geese, 1989	12.00	3.00
	$9 Black ducks, 1990	16.00	3.00
	$9 Lesser scaup, 1991	14.00	3.00
	$9 Wood duck, 1992	16.00	3.00
	$9 Buffleheads, 1993	16.00	3.00
	$11 Mallards, 1994	18.00	2.50
	$11 Pintails, 1995	18.00	2.50
	$11 Hooded mergansers, 1996	18.00	2.50
	$11 Widgeons, 1997	20.00	2.50
	$11 Gadwall, 1998	20.00	2.50
	$11 Mallard, 1999	18.00	2.50
	$11 Buffleheads, 2000	15.00	2.50
	$11 Canvasback, 2001	18.00	2.50

Souvenir Sheet
Rouletted

	$11 Ring-necked ducks, 2002	15.00	2.50
	$11 Hooded mergansers, 2003	15.00	2.50
	$15 Tundra swans, 2004	19.00	2.50
	$15 Wood duck, 2005	19.00	2.50

Nos. 19-24 not required for hunting.

OKLAHOMA

Printed in booklet panes of 10 (Nos. 1-3) and
booklet panes of 5 (Starting with No. 4). No. 10 was
the first to be printed in a sheet of 30, No. 17 in a
sheet of 24.

Catalogue values for all unused stamps in this
section are for Never Hinged items.

Artists: Patrick Sawyer, #1; Hoyt Smith, #2, 5, 7, 20; Jeffrey
rey, #3; Gerald Mobley, #4, 6; Rayburn Foster, #8, 12; Jim
aar, #9; Wanda Mumm, #10; Ronald Louque, #11; Jeffrey
obley, #13; Jerome Hageman, #14; Richard Kirkman, #15;
ichard Clifton, #16; Greg Everhart, #17; M. Anderson, #18, 24;
effrey Klinefelter, #19, 26; Paul Makuchal, #21; Daniel Brevick,
22; Brian Blight, #23; Scot Storm, #25.

980-2004

	$4 Pintails	55.00	10.00
	$4 Canada goose, 1981	25.00	8.00
	$4 Green-winged teal, 1982	10.00	4.00

4	$4 Wood ducks, 1983	10.00	10.00
5	$4 Ring-necked ducks, 1984	10.00	3.00
	With tab	10.00	
6	$4 Mallards, 1985	8.00	3.00
	With tab	10.00	
7	$4 Snow geese, 1986	10.00	3.00
	With tab	10.00	
8	$4 Canvasbacks, 1987	8.00	3.00
	With tab	8.00	
9	$4 Widgeons, 1988	8.00	3.00
	With tab	8.00	
10	$4 Redheads, 1989	8.00	3.00
	Booklet single, with tab & selvage at L, selvage at R	8.00	
a.	Governor's edition	125.00	

No. 10a was available only in sheets of 30 through a sealed
bid auction.

11	$4 Hooded merganser, 1990	7.50	3.00
	Booklet single, with tab & selvage at L, selvage at R	7.50	
12	$4 Gadwalls, 1991	7.50	3.00
	Booklet single, with tab & selvage at L, selvage at R	7.50	
13	$4 Lesser scaup, 1992	7.50	3.00
	Booklet single, with tab & selvage at L, selvage at R	7.50	
14	$4 White-fronted geese, 1993	7.50	3.00
	Booklet single, with tab & selvage at L, selvage at R	7.50	
15	$4 Blue-winged teal, 1994	7.50	3.00
	Booklet single, with tab & selvage at L, selvage at R	7.50	
16	$4 Ruddy ducks, 1995	7.50	3.00
	Booklet single, with tab & selvage at L, selvage at R	7.50	
17	$4 Bufflehead, 1996	7.50	3.00
	Booklet single, with selvage at L & R	7.50	
18	$4 Goldeneyes, 1997	7.50	3.00
	Bklt. single, with selvage at L & R	7.50	
19	$4 Shovelers, 1998	7.50	3.00
	Bklt. single, with selvage at L & R	7.50	
20	$4 Canvasbacks, 1999	7.50	3.00
21	$4 Pintails, 2000	7.50	3.00
22	$4 Canada goose, 2001	7.50	3.00
23	$4 Green-winged teal, 2002	7.50	3.00
24	$10 Wood duck, 2003	14.00	3.00
25	$10 Mallard, 2004	14.00	3.00
26	$10 Snow geese, 2005	14.00	3.00

OREGON

Non-resident fees begin in 1994.
Issued in sheets of 30, except for No. 6. Nos. 2-4
also exist from booklet panes of 5.
Stamps are numbered serially. Nos. 11b, 11c have
serial numbers on sheet selvage.
Nos. 10 and 11 were issued on computer form.
Unused values are for stamps on form.

Catalogue values for all unused stamps in this
section are for Never Hinged items.

1984 Oregon Waterfowl Stamp

Artists: Michael Sieve, #1-3; Dorothy M. Smith, #4; Darrell
Davis, #5; Phillip Crowe, #7; Roger Cruwys, #8; Louis Frisino,
#9; Kip Richmond, #10; R. Bruce Horsfall, #11; Richard Plass-
chaert, #12-13; Robert Steiner, #14-29.

1984-88

1	$5 Canada geese	22.50	7.00
2	$5 Lesser snow goose, 1985	35.00	10.00
	Booklet single, with 3 tabs (2 at left)	450.00	
3	$5 Pacific brant, perf. 4 sides, 1986	15.00	
a.	Booklet single, with 2-part tab	15.00	4.00
4	$5 White-fronted geese, perf. 4 sides, 1987	15.00	
a.	Booklet single, with 2-part tab	15.00	3.00
5	$5 Great Basin Canada geese, 1988	15.00	3.00
a.	Booklet pane of 1	15.00	

1989-2004	Die cut self-adhesive		
6	($5) Red Nos., 16,001 and up	15.00	6.00
a.	Black Nos., 001-16,000	30.00	12.50

This provisional stamp was used in early 1989, when the
regular stamps were delayed. Unused value is for stamp and
adjacent label with serial number on backing paper.

Designs like No. 1

7	$5 Black Labrador retriever & pintails, 1989	15.00	2.50
a.	Booklet pane of 1	15.00	
8	$5 Mallards & golden retriever, 1990	15.00	2.50
a.	Booklet pane of 1	15.00	
9	$5 Buffleheads & Chesapeake Bay retriever, perf, 1991	15.00	2.50
a.	Rouletted at L	15.00	

No. 9a is straight edged on 3 sides and stamp is attached to
paper by selvage. Unused value is for stamp attached to paper.

10	$5 Green-winged teal, 1992	15.00	
a.	Die cut, self-adhesive	15.00	2.50
11	$5 Mallards, vert., 1993	15.00	
a.	Die cut self-adhesive	15.00	2.50
b.	Sheet of 2	20.00	
c.	$50 Governor's edition sheet of 1	75.00	

No. 11b contains No. 11 and the Oregon upland bird stamp.
Nos. 11b, 11c exist imperf.

12	$5 Pintails, perf. 4 sides, 1994	15.00	
a.	Die cut self-adhesive	15.00	2.50
13	$25 Pintails, diff., die cut self-adhesive, 1994	35.00	—
14	$5 Wood ducks, 1995	15.00	
a.	Booklet pane of 1	15.00	2.50
15	$25 Columbian sharp-tailed grouse, bklt. pane of 1, 1995	50.00	—
16	$5 Mallards, 1996	15.00	
a.	Booklet pane of 1	15.00	2.50
17	$25 Common snipe, booklet pane of 1, 1996	45.00	—
18	$5 Canvasbacks, 1997	15.00	
a.	Booklet pane of 1	15.00	2.50
19	$25 Canvasbacks, booklet pane of 1, 1997	40.00	
20	$5 Pintails, 1998	15.00	
a.	Booklet pane of 1	15.00	2.50
21	$25 Pintails, booklet pane of 1, 1998	37.50	
22	$5 Canada geese, 1999	15.00	
a.	Booklet pane of 1	15.00	2.50
23	$25 Canada geese, booklet pane of 1, 1999	30.00	
24	$7.50 Canada geese, mallard, widgeon, 2000	15.00	2.50
a.	Booklet pane of 1, no cover	—	
25	$7.50 Redheads, 2001	15.00	2.50
a.	Booklet pane of 1, no cover	—	
26	$7.50 American wigeon, 2002	12.00	2.50
a.	Booklet pane of 1, no cover	—	
27	$7.50 Wood duck, 2003	12.00	2.50
a.	Booklet pane of 1, no cover	—	
28	$7.50 Ross's goose, 2004	12.00	2.50
a.	Booklet pane of 1, no cover	12.00	
29	$7.50 Hooded merganser, 2005	12.00	2.50
a.	Booklet pane of 1, no cover	12.00	

Nos. 27-29 not required for hunting.

PENNSYLVANIA

Not required to hunt.
Printed in sheets of 10.

Catalogue values for all unused stamps in this
section are for Never Hinged items.

1983 Pennsylvania
Save Our Wetlands
$5.50
Void After August 31, 1984
Waterfowl Management Stamp

Artists: Ned Smith, #1, 3; Jim Killen, #2; Robert Knutson, #4; Robert Leslie, #5; John Heldersbach, #6; Ronald Louque, #7; Thomas Hirata, #8, 12; Gerald W. Putt, #9, 14, 16, 18, 20, 23; Robert Sopchick, #10; Glen Reichard, #11; Mark Bray, #13; Clark Weaver, #15, 17, 19; Jocelyn Beatty, #21; Carl Clark, #22.

1983-2004

1	$5.50 Wood ducks	15.00	
2	$5.50 Canada geese, *1984*	12.00	
3	$5.50 Mallards, *1985*	10.00	
4	$5.50 Blue-winged teal, *1986*	10.00	
5	$5.50 Pintails, *1987*	10.00	
6	$5.50 Wood ducks, *1988*	10.00	
7	$5.50 Hooded mergansers, *1989*	9.00	
8	$5.50 Canvasbacks, *1990*	9.00	
9	$5.50 Widgeons, *1991*	9.00	
10	$5.50 Canada geese, *1992*	9.00	
11	$5.50 Northern shovelers, *1993*	9.00	
12	$3.30 Pintails, *1994*	9.00	
13	$5.50 Buffleheads, *1995*	9.00	
14	$5.50 Black ducks, *1996*	9.00	
15	$5.50 Hooded merganser, *1997*	9.00	
16	$5.50 Wood ducks, *1998*	9.00	
17	$5.50 Ring-necked ducks, *1999*	9.00	
18	$5.50 Green-winged teal, *2000*	9.00	
19	($5.50) Pintails, *2001*	8.00	
20	$5.50 Snow geese, *2002*	8.00	2.50
21	$5.50 Canvasbacks, *2003*	8.00	2.50
22	$5.50 Hooded mergansers, *2004*	8.00	2.50
23	$5.50 Red-breasted mergansers, *2005*	8.00	2.50

RHODE ISLAND

Issued in booklet panes of 5 and sheets of 30. Starting with No. 8, the spacing of the reverse text of the booklet stamp differs from the sheet stamp. Stamps are numbered serially.

Catalogue values for all unused stamps in this section are for Never Hinged items.

Artists: Robert Steiner, #1-7, 9-10, 16; Charles Allen, #8; Keith Mueller, #11-15, 17.

1989-2004

1	$7.50 Canvasbacks	12.00	3.00
	Booklet single, with tab	15.00	
a.	$7.50 +$50 Governor's edition	92.50	

No. 1a exists without serial number.

2	$7.50 Canada geese, *1990*	12.00	3.00
	Booklet single, with tab	15.00	
a.	$7.50 +$50 Governor's edition	72.50	

No. 2a exists without serial number.

3	$7.50 Wood ducks & Labrador retriever, *1991*	20.00	3.00
	Booklet single, with tab	20.00	
a.	$7.50 +$50 Governor's edition	60.00	

No. 3a exists without serial number.

4	$7.50 Blue-winged teal, *1992*	15.00	3.00
	Booklet single, with tab	15.00	
a.	$7.50 +$50 Governor's edition	60.00	

No. 4a exists without serial number.

5	$7.50 Pintails, *1993*	13.00	3.00
	Booklet single, with tab	13.00	
a.	Sheet of 4	55.00	

No. 5a imperf. is printer's waste.

6	$7.50 Wood ducks, *1994*	15.00	2.50
	Booklet single, with tab and selvage	15.00	
7	$7.50 Hooded mergansers, *1995*	12.00	2.50
	Booklet single, with tab and selvage	12.00	
a.	Governor's edition	110.00	

No. 7a inscribed "Governor's edition."

8	$7.50 Harlequin, *1996*	20.00	2.50
	Booklet single, with tab and selvage	20.00	
a.	Governor's edition	125.00	

No. 8a inscribed "Governor's edition" and has serial number with "G" prefix.

9	$7.50 Greater scaup, *1997*	12.00	2.50
	Booklet single, with tab and selvage	12.00	
a.	Governor's edition	110.00	

No. 9a inscribed "Governor's edition" and has serial number with "G" prefix.

10	$7.50 Black ducks, *1998*	12.00	2.50
	Booklet single, with tab and selvage	12.00	
a.	Governor's edition	125.00	

No. 11-14 do not have a serial number.

Rouletted

11	$7.50 Common eiders, *1999*	15.00	2.50
	Horiz. pair from booklet pane	30.00	

Booklet pane contains 10 stamps.

12	$7.50 Canvasbacks, *2000*	14.00	2.50
a.	Inscribed "Hunter"	14.00	
a.	Governor's edition	—	
13	$7.50 Mallard, black duck, *2001*	14.00	2.50
a.	Inscribed "Hunter"	14.00	
a.	Governor's edition	125.00	
14	$7.50 White-winged scoter, lighthouse, *2002*	12.00	2.50
a.	Inscribed "Hunter"	12.00	
b.	Governor's edition	130.00	
15	$7.50 Oldsquaws, *2003*	11.00	2.50
a.	Inscribed "Hunter"	11.00	
b.	Governor's edition	130.00	—
16	$7.50 Canvasbacks, *2004*	10.00	2.50
a.	Inscribed "Hunter"	10.00	
b.	Governor's edition	130.00	—
17	$7.50 Black ducks, lighthouse, *2005*	9.50	2.50
a.	Inscribed "Hunter"	9.50	

Nos. 15-17 have no serial number.

SOUTH CAROLINA

Issued in sheets of 30. Stamps with serial numbers were to be issued to hunters.

Catalogue values for all unused stamps in this section are for Never Hinged items.

Artists: Lee LeBlanc, #1; Bob Binks, #2; Jim Killen, #3, 8, 11; Al Dornish, #4; Rosemary Millette, #5; Daniel Smith, #6; Steve Dillard, #7; Lee Cable, #9; John Wilson, #10; Russell Cobane, #12; Bob Bolin, #13; Joe Hautman, #14; Rodney Huckaby, #15, 17, 22, 25; D. J. Cleland-Hura, #16, 18; Denise Nelson, #19; Mark Constantine, #20; Jeffrey Klinefelter, #21; James Hublick, #23; Eddie LeRoy, #24.

1981-2004

1	$5.50 Wood ducks	60.00	15.00

No. 2-22 do not have a serial number.

2	$5.50 Mallards, *1982*	95.00	
a.	Serial number on reverse	495.00	25.00
3	$5.50 Pintails, *1983*	95.00	
a.	Serial number on reverse	450.00	25.00
4	$5.50 Canada geese, *1984*	65.00	
a.	Serial number on reverse	190.00	15.00
5	$5.50 Green-winged teal, *1985*	60.00	
a.	Serial number on reverse	100.00	15.00
6	$5.50 Canvasbacks, *1986*	25.00	
a.	Serial number on reverse	42.50	10.00
7	$5.50 Black ducks, *1987*	20.00	
a.	Serial number on reverse	22.50	5.00
8	$5.50 Widgeon & spaniel, *1988*	20.00	
a.	Serial number on reverse	30.00	5.00
9	$5.50 Blue-winged teal, *1989*	11.00	
a.	Serial number on reverse	14.00	4.00
10	$5.50 Wood ducks, *1990*	10.00	
a.	Serial number on reverse	10.00	4.00
b.	$5.50 +$44.50 Governor's edition	82.50	
c.	$5.50 +$94.50 Governor's edition	225.00	

All copies of No. 10c are signed by the governor.

11	$5.50 Labrador retriever, pintails & decoy, *1991*	10.00	
a.	Serial number on reverse	10.00	4.00
12	$5.50 Buffleheads, *1992*	12.00	
a.	Serial number on front	12.00	3.00
13	$5.50 Lesser scaup, *1993*	12.00	
a.	Serial number on front	12.00	3.00
14	$5.50 Canvasbacks, *1994*	12.00	
a.	Serial number on front	12.00	2.50
15	$5.50 Shovelers, lighthouse, *1995*	12.00	
a.	Serial number on front	12.00	2.50
16	$5.50 Redheads, lighthouse, *1996*	15.00	
a.	Serial number on front	15.00	2.50
17	$5.50 Old squaws, *1997*	15.00	
a.	Serial number on front	15.00	2.50

18	$5.50 Green-winged teal, *1998*	15.00	
a.	Serial number on front	15.00	
19	$5.50 Barrow's goldeneye, *1999*	15.00	
20	$5.50 Wood ducks, boykin spaniel, *2000*	12.00	
21	$5.50 Mallard, decoy, yellow Labrador retriever, *2001*	12.00	
22	$5.50 Wigeons, chocolate Labrador retriever, *2002*	10.00	
23	$5.50 Green-winged teal, *2003*	10.00	
24	$5.50 Pintails, Labrador retriever, *2004*	10.00	
25	$5.50 Canvasbacks, *2005*	8.00	

Nos. 23-25 have no serial number.

SOUTH DAKOTA

Resident Waterfowl Stamps

Vertical safety paper (words read up)

1949-50

1	$1 blk, *grn*, vert. safety paper	950.00	8(
a.	Horizontal safety paper	—	15(
2	$1 blk, *lt brn*, vert. safety paper	800.00	65
a.	Horizontal safety paper	—	17:

Safety paper design of Nos. 1 and 2 washes out if stam soaked. Washed out copies sell for considerably less. U values are for copies showing safety paper design.

Printed in booklet panes of 5. Stamps are numbered serially.

Catalogue values for all unused stamps in th section, from this point to the end of the Res dent Waterfowl stamps, are for Never Hinge items.

Artists: Robert Kusserow, #3; Don Steinbeck, #4; Jo Moisan, #5; John Wilson, #6, 12; Rosemary Millett, #7; Marion Toillion, #8; John Green, #10, 17; Russell Duerkse #11, 15-16, 19-20; Mark Anderson, #13, 18, 21, 22; Jeff Reut #14; Joshua Spies, #23.

1976-2004

3	$1 Mallards	35.00	3.
a.	Serial number 4mm high	65.00	10.
4	$1 Pintails, *1977*	27.50	2.
5	$1 Canvasbacks, *1978*	13.00	2.
6	$2 Canada geese, *1988*	8.50	2.!
7	$2 Blue geese, *1987*	7.00	2.!
8	$2 White-fronted geese, *1988*	6.00	2.!
9	$2 Mallards, *1989*	6.00	2.!
10	$2 Blue-winged teal, *1990*	6.00	2.!
11	$2 Pintails, *1991*	6.00	2.!
12	$2 Canvasbacks, *1992*	6.00	2.!
13	$2 Lesser scaup, *1993*	6.00	2.!
14	$2 Redheads, *1994*	6.00	2.!
15	$2 Wood ducks, *1995*	6.00	2.!
16	$2 Canada geese, *1996*	6.00	2.!
17	$2 Widgeons, *1997*	6.00	2.!
18	$2 Green-winged teal, *1998*	6.00	2.!

Migratory Bird Certification Stamps

$3 Tundra swan, *1999*		5.50	2.50
$3 Buffleheads, *2000*		5.50	2.50
$3 Mallards, *2001*		5.50	2.50
$3 Canvasbacks, *2002*		5.50	2.50
$3 Pintails, *2003*		5.50	2.50
$3 purple		5.50	2.50
$5 magenta		9.00	2.50

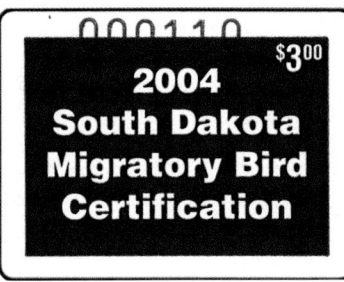

...04			
$3 purple		5.50	2.50

Non-resident Waterfowl Stamps

...os. A1-A7, A9 have serial No. in red. Nos. A1-A18 ...sued in booklet panes of 5. Type faces and designs of Nos. A1-A18 vary.
Unused values are for unpunched copies. Used values are for signed and punched copies.

Illustration reduced.

...970-86			
...1	$30 black, *pink*	20.00	
a.	Missing serial number	5,000.	
...2	$30 black, *pink, 1971*	9.00	
a.	Overprinted "3"		275.00
...3	$30 black, *1972*	3.75	
...4	$30 black, *blue, 1973*	8.00	
a.	Overprinted "2"	2,750.	
...5	$30 black, *green, 1974*	5.50	
a.	Overprinted "1"	25.00	
b.	Overprinted "2"	30.00	
c.	Overprinted "4"	30.00	
...6	$30 black, *yellow, 1975*	6.50	
a.	Overprinted "UNIT 1"	45.00	
b.	Overprinted "UNIT 4"	35.00	
c.	Overprinted "UNIT 3"		—
...7	$30 black, *yellow, 1976*	5.00	
a.	Overprinted "1"	18.00	
b.	Overprinted "2"	30.00	20.00
c.	Serial No. 4mm high	18.00	
d.	As "c," overprinted "1"	35.00	
e.	As "c," overprinted "2"	85.00	
...8	$30 black, *red, 1977*	7.00	
a.	Overprinted "1"	20.00	
b.	Overprinted "2"	30.00	
c.	Overprinted "3"	35.00	
d.	Overprinted "4"	30.00	
e.	Overprinted "5"	150.00	
...9	$30 black, *yellow, 1978*	7.00	
a.	Overprinted "1" and 3 strikes of "UNIT 2"	125.00	
b.	Overprinted "1"	150.00	
...10	$30 black, *red, 1979*	2.50	
...11	$30 black, *light manila, 1980*	4.50	
a.	Overprinted "1"	6.00	
b.	Overprinted "2"	10.00	

A12	$30 black, *light yellow, 1981*	4.50	
a.	Overprinted "UNIT 1"	6.00	
b.	Overprinted "UNIT 2"	10.00	5.00
A13	$30 black, *blue, 1982*	6.50	
A14	$50 black, *dark yellow, 1982*	7.00	
a.	Overprinted "UNIT 2"		—
A15	$50 black, *red, 1983*	8.00	
a.	Overprinted "AREA 1"	50.00	
b.	Overprinted "AREA 2"	65.00	
c.	Serial No. with serifs	750.00	
A16	$50 black, *light manila, 1984*	16.00	
a.	Overprinted "A"	275.00	
b.	Overprinted "B"	110.00	
A17	$50 black, *red, 1985*	3,500.	750.00
A18	$50 black, *1986*	9.00	5.00

Bennett County Canada Goose Stamps

Type faces and designs vary. Nos. 2A1-2A2 imperf. Nos. 2A3-2A12 printed in booklet panes of 5, perforated horizontally. Some show vertical perforations.
Nos. 2A1-2A4 were free. No. 2A5 cost $5. Stamps were issued to hunters by means of a drawing.
Used values are for signed stamps.

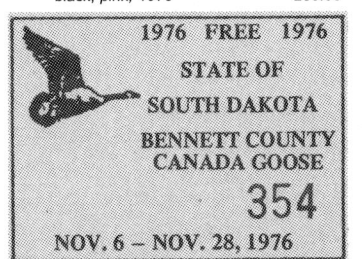

Illustration reduced.

1974-78				
2A1		black	75.00	35.00
2A2		black, *pink, 1975*	250.00	

2A3		black, *blue, 1976*	47.50	25.00
2A4		black, *yellow, 1977*	42.50	25.00
2A5		black, *greenish blue, 1978*	750.00	

West River Unit Canada Goose

Counties handstamped.
Used values are for signed stamps.

1979				
2A6	$2 black, *yellow*		400.00	
a.	Bennettt County		450.00	275.00
b.	Haakon County		250.00	
c.	Jackson County		250.00	
d.	Pennington County		200.00	100.00

Stamps overprinted for Perkins County exist but may not have been regularly issued.

1980				
2A7	$2 black, *blue*		75.00	
a.	Bennett County		200.00	75.00
b.	Haakon County		100.00	
c.	Jackson County		110.00	
d.	As "c," missing serial number		5,000.	
e.	Pennington County		90.00	45.00
f.	Perkins County		110.00	

Prairie Canada Geese

Counties or Units handstamped.
Used values are for signed stamps.

1981				
Perf. 12				
2A8	$2 black, *red*		8.00	
a.	Bennett County		80.00	35.00
b.	Haakon County		60.00	20.00
c.	Jackson County		60.00	20.00
d.	Pennington County		60.00	
e.	Perkins County		60.00	
1982				
2A9	$2 black, *blue*		125.00	
a.	Bennett County		750.00	250.00
b.	Haakon County		475.00	
c.	Jackson County		475.00	
d.	Pennington County		475.00	
e.	Perkins County		475.00	
1983				
Perf. 12				
2A10	$2 black, *yellow*		60.00	
a.	UNIT 2A		70.00	
b.	UNIT 31		70.00	35.00
c.	UNIT 39		70.00	35.00
d.	UNIT 49		70.00	35.00
e.	UNIT 53		70.00	35.00
f.	UNIT 11, 3mm type		100.00	50.00
g.	UNIT 23		100.00	
Rouletted top and bottom				
2A11	$2 black, *yellow*		11.00	
a.	UNIT 2A		65.00	
b.	UNIT 6		45.00	
c.	UNIT 11, 3mm type		60.00	
d.	UNIT 11, 4½mm type		45.00	
e.	UNIT 23		45.00	
f.	UNIT 31		65.00	
g.	UNIT 32		45.00	
h.	UNIT 39		65.00	
i.	UNIT 42		45.00	
j.	UNIT 49		65.00	
k.	UNIT 53, 3mm type		45.00	
l.	UNIT 53, 4½mm type		50.00	
1984				
Perf. 12				
2A12	$2 black, *green*		45.00	
a.	UNIT 6		75.00	
b.	UNIT 11, 3mm type		85.00	
c.	UNIT 11, 4½mm type		75.00	
d.	UNIT 23, 3mm type		85.00	
e.	UNIT 23, 4½mm type		75.00	30.00
f.	UNIT 32		85.00	
g.	UNIT 42		75.00	
h.	UNIT 47, 3mm type		85.00	
i.	UNIT 53, 3mm type		75.00	
j.	UNIT 47, 4½mm type			65.00
k.	UNIT 53, 4½mm type			65.00
1985				
Rouletted two adjacent sides				
2A13	$2 black, *red*			
a.	UNIT 47			90.00
b.	UNIT 53			90.00
c.	UNIT 23			100.00
d.	UNIT 32			140.00
e.	UNIT 42			100.00
f.	UNIT 11			140.00
1986				
No fee printed on stamp				
Imperf. on 3 sides, rouletted at top				
2A14	black			
a.	UNIT 11			95.00
b.	UNIT 47			95.00
c.	UNIT 53			95.00
d.	UNIT 23			125.00

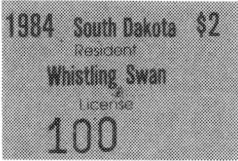

105 stamps for hunting whistling swans during the 1984 season exist. The season was canceled. Value, unused $400.

Pheasant Restoration Stamps

Required to hunt all small game, including waterfowl. Printed in booklet panes of 5. No. 3A4 rouletted, others perforated. Stamps are numbered serially.

> Catalogue values for all unused stamps in this section, from this point to the end of the Wildlife Habitat stamps, are for Never Hinged items.

1977-88

3A1	$5 Pheasants	12.00	2.50
a.	Rubber-stamped serial number		
3A2	$5 Pheasants, *1978*	12.00	1.50
3A3	$5 Pheasants, *1979*	12.00	1.50
3A4	$5 Pheasants, *1980*	10.00	2.00
a.	Serial number omitted	—	
3A5	$5 Pheasants, *1981*	10.00	1.50
3A6	$5 Pheasants, *1982*	10.00	1.50
a.	Pair, imperf. between	—	
3A7	$5 Pheasant, *1983*	10.00	1.00
3A8	$5 Pheasant, *1984*	10.00	2.00
3A9	$5 Pheasant, *1985*	10.00	2.00
3A10	$5 Pheasants, *1986*	10.00	2.50
3A11	$5 Pheasants, *1987*	10.00	2.00
3A12	$5 Pheasants, *1988*	10.00	2.00

Wildlife Habitat Stamps

Required to hunt all small game, including waterfowl. Printed in booklet panes of 5. Starting with No. 3A18 stamps are rouletted, others are perforated. Stamps are numbered serially.

1989-99

3A13	$8 Pheasants	12.00	2.00
3A14	$8 White-tailed deer, *1990*	12.00	2.00
3A15	$8 Greater prairie chicken, *1991*	12.00	2.00
3A16	$8 Mule Deer, *1992*	12.00	2.50
3A17	$8 Sharp-tailed grouse, *1993*	12.00	2.00
a.	Pair, imperf. between	—	
3A18	$8 Turkey, *1994*	12.00	2.00
3A19	$8 Elk, *1995*	12.00	2.00
3A20	$8 Pheasants, *1996*	10.00	2.00
3A21	$8 Antelope, *1997*	10.00	2.00
3A22	$8 Buffalo, *1998*	10.00	2.00
3A23	$8 Buffalo, *1999*	10.00	2.00

Resident Small Game Stamps

Required by residents wishing to hunt small game, including waterfowl. Nos. 4A1, 4A2 issued panes of 10. Others issued in booklet panes of 5. Stamps are numbered serially in red from 1960 to 1967 and 1978.

> Catalogue values for all unused stamps in this section are for Never Hinged items.

1960-79

4A1	$2 black, *pink*	12.00	2.00
4A2	$2 black, *blue, 1961*	25.00	3.00
4A3	$2 black, *dark yellow, 1962*	35.00	3.00
4A4	$2 black, *light yellow, 1963*	25.00	3.00
4A5	$2 black, *green, 1964*	25.00	3.00
4A6	$2 black, *1965*	25.00	3.00
4A7	$2 black, *yellow, 1966*	10.00	2.00
4A8	$2 black, *light green, 1967*	25.00	2.00
4A9	$2 black, *light yellow, 1968*	10.00	2.00
4A10	$3 black, *blue, 1969*	25.00	2.00
4A11	$3 black, *light yellow, 1970*	10.00	2.00
4A12	$3 black, *green, 1971*		3.00
4A13	$3 black, *light yellow, 1972*	10.00	2.00
4A14	$3 black, *light yellow, 1973*	9.00	2.00
4A15	$3 black, *1974*	10.00	2.00
4A16	$3 black, *pink, 1975*	8.00	2.00
4A17	$3 black, *gray, 1976*	6.00	1.00
4A18	$3 black, *red, 1977*	5.00	1.00
4A19	$3 black, *1978*	6.00	1.00
4A20	$3 black, *red, 1979*	7.00	1.00

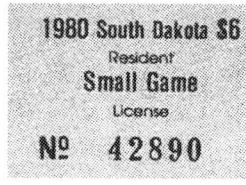

1980-98

4A21	$6 black	8.00	1.00
4A22	$6 black, *light yellow, 1981*	9.00	1.00
4A23	$6 black, *blue, 1982*	5.00	.50
4A24	$6 black, *green, 1983*	10.00	1.00
4A25	$6 black, *light blue, 1984*	*20.00*	1.00
4A26	$6 black, *light blue, 1985*	12.00	1.00
4A27	$6 black, *light blue green, 1986*		2.00
4A28	$6 black, *1987*		2.00
4A29	$6 black, *light green, 1988*	5.00	.50
4A30	$6 black, *1989*		1.00
4A31	$6 black, *light green, 1990*	8.00	.50
4A32	$6 black, *light blue green, 1991*	5.00	.50
4A33	$6 black, *light green, 1992*		1.00
4A34	$6 black, *light pink, 1993*	5.00	.50
4A35	$6 black, *light blue, 1994*	5.00	.50
4A36	$6 black, *yellow, 1995*		1.00
4A37	$6 black, *pink, 1996*	5.00	.50
4A38	$6 black, *light blue, 1997*		.50
4A39	$6 black, *pink, 1998*	8.00	.50

TENNESSEE

Stamps are die cut self-adhesives and are numbered serially.
Cards include both license cost and a fee of 30c (Nos. 1-5), 50c (Nos. 6-13) or $1 (starting with No. 14).
Nos. 3, 5, 7-15 come as 3-part card.
Starting with No. 12, cards come in four parts as well.
1979 and 1980 issues are for resident and non-resident fees.
Unused values are for stamps on original computer card stub.

> Catalogue values for all unused stamps in this section are for Never Hinged items.

Artists: Dick Elliott, #1-2; Phillip Crowe, #3-4, 7, 17; Gillespie, #5; Ken Schulz, #6; Allen Hughes, #8; Jimmy Stew #9; Ralph J. McDonald, #10, 18; Thomas Hirata, #11, 16; Lamb, #12; Roger Cruwys, #13; Tom Freeman, #14; Rich Clifton, #15, 19; Bob Leslie, #20; Bethany Carter, #21; B Ann McMurray, #22; Nick Williamson, #23, 24.; J. Mefford, # Joshua Lester, #26-27.

1979-2004

1	$2 Mallards	140.00	25
2	$5 Mallards	*900.00*	150
3	$2 Canvasbacks, *1980*	60.00	15
	3-part card	725.00	
4	$5 Canvasbacks, *1980*	*350.00*	75
5	$2 Wood ducks, *1981*	45.00	10
	3-part card	—	
6	$6 Canada geese, *1982*	55.00	15
7	$6 Pintails, *1983*	50.00	15
	3-part card	75.00	
8	$6 Black ducks, *1984*	50.00	12
	3-part card	75.00	
9	$6 Blue-winged teal, *1985*	20.00	7
	3-part card	50.00	
10	$6 Mallard, *1986*	15.00	5
	3-part card	60.00	
11	$6 Canada geese, *1987*	12.00	5
	3-part card	25.00	

Card exists with 2/28/88 expiration date rather than corr 2/29 date.

12	$6 Canvasbacks, *1988*	12.00	4
	3-part card	20.00	
	4-part card	20.00	
13	$6 Green-winged teal, *1989*	12.00	4
	3-part card	20.00	
	4-part card	20.00	
14	$12 Redheads, *1990*	18.00	4.
	3-part card	25.00	
	4-part card	25.00	
15	$12 Mergansers, *1991*	18.00	4.
	3-part card	22.00	
	4-part card	22.00	
16	$13 Wood ducks, *1992*	18.00	4.
	4-part card	22.00	
17	$13 Pintails & decoy, *1993*	20.00	4.
	4-part card	25.00	
18	$15 Mallard, *1994*	25.00	5.
	4-part card	30.00	
19	$16 Ring-necked duck, *1995*	25.00	5.
	4-part card	30.00	
20	$17 Black ducks, *1996*	35.00	5.
	4-part card	40.00	

Starting with No. 21 stamps are perforated. Not required for hunting.

21	$10 Mallard, *1999*	15.00	2.5
22	$10 Bufflehead, *2000*	15.00	2.5
23	$10 Wood ducks, *2001*	15.00	2.5
24	$10 Green-winged teal, *2002*	12.00	2.5
25	$10 Canada geese, *2003*	12.00	2.5
26	$10 Wood ducks, *2004*	12.00	2.5
27	$10 Mallards, *2005*	12.00	2.5

TEXAS

Printed in sheets of 10.
Nos. 1-4 are rouletted.
Stamps are numbered serially.

> Catalogue values for all unused stamps in this section are for Never Hinged items.

Artists: Larry Hayden, #1, 12; Ken Carlson, #2, 14; Maynard ...ece, #3; David Maass, #4, 9, 15; John Cowan, #5, 8; Herb ...oth, #6, 25; Gary Moss, #7; Robert Bateman, #10; Daniel ...ith, #11, 16; Jim Hautman, #13, 17, 22; Phillip Crowe, #18; ...ert Hautman, #19; Sherrie Russell Meline, #20, 23; John ...arman, #21; Scott and Stuart Gentling, #24.

...81-2004

	$5 Mallards	45.00	8.00
	$5 Pintails, 1982	25.00	5.00
	$5 Widgeons, 1983	140.00	18.00
	$5 Wood ducks, 1984	25.00	5.00
	$5 Snow geese, 1985	10.00	3.00
	$5 Green-winged teal, 1986	10.00	2.50
	$5 White-fronted geese, 1987	10.00	2.50
	$5 Pintails, 1988	10.00	2.50
	$5 Mallards, 1989	10.00	2.50
	$5 American widgeons, 1990	10.00	2.50
	$7 Wood duck, 1991	10.00	2.50
	$7 Canada geese, 1992	10.00	2.50
	$7 Blue-winged teal, 1993	10.00	2.50
	$7 Shovelers, 1994	10.00	2.50
	$7 Buffleheads, 1995	10.00	2.50

Beginning with No. 16, these stamps were sold ...ly in booklets with seven other wildlife stamps ...d were not valid for hunting.

$3 Gadwalls, 1996	75.00	
$3 Cinnamon teal, 1997	65.00	
$3 Pintail, labrador retriever, 1998	55.00	
$3 Canvasbacks, 1999	40.00	
$3 Hooded merganser, 2000	30.00	
$3 Snow geese, 2001	20.00	
$3 Redheads, 2002	20.00	
$3 Mottled duck, 2003	20.00	
$3 American goldeneye, 2004	12.00	
$7 Mallards, 2005	13.00	

No. 23 was issued in booklets with seven other wildlife ...mps and was not valid for hunting.
No. 25 was issued in booklets with five other wildlife stamps ...d was not valid for hunting.

UTAH

Game Bird Stamps

...or hunting game birds, including waterfowl. In 1951 ...o. A1 or No. 2A1 were required, in 1952 No. A3 or ...A2. No. A1 printed in booklet panes of 25, others in booklet panes of 10. Perforated.

A1　　　　　　　　A2

...951

1	A1	$3 brown, resident	50.00	7.00
2	A1	$15 red, non-resident	250.00	50.00

...952

3	A2	$3 red, resident	135.00	
4	A2	$15 blue, non-resident	325.00	50.00

Resident Fishing and Hunting Stamps

...or hunting game birds, including waterfowl. Printed in sheets of 40. No. 2A1 printed on linen. Unused values are for stamps with deer tags attached at left.

No. 2A1 — UT-2A1

No. 2A2 — UT-2A2

1951-52

2A1	$5 blue	3.00	.50
2A2	$5 green, 1952	3.00	.50

Waterfowl Issues

Printed in sheets of 30 or in booklet panes of 5 (starting in 1990). No. 11 issued in sheets of 9. Stamps are numbered serially.

Catalogue values for all unused stamps in this section are for Never Hinged items.

FIRST OF STATE *1986* Exp. 6-30-87

Artists: Leon Parsons, #1; Arthur Anderson, #2; David Chapple, #3; Jim Morgan, #4; Daniel Smith, #5; Robert Steiner, #6-12.

1986-97

1		$3.30 Whistling swans	10.00	3.00
2		$3.30 Pintails, 1987	8.00	3.00
3		$3.30 Mallards, 1988	8.00	2.50
4		$3.30 Canada geese, 1989	8.00	2.50
5		$3.30 Canvasbacks, perf. 4 sides, 1990	8.00	
a.		Booklet single, with 2-part tab	8.00	2.50
6		$3.30 Tundra swans, perf. 4 sides, 1991	12.00	
a.		Booklet single, with 2-part tab	12.00	2.50
7		$3.30 Pintails, perf. 4 sides, 1992	10.00	
a.		Booklet single, with 2-part tab	10.00	2.50
8		$3.30 Canvasbacks, perf. 4 sides, 1993	10.00	
a.		Booklet single, with 2-part tab	10.00	2.50
9		$3.30 Chesapeake Retriever and ducks, perf. 4 sides, 1994	85.00	
a.		Booklet single, with 2-part tab	85.00	2.50
10		$3.30 Green-winged teal, 1995	12.00	
a.		Booklet single, with 2-part tab	12.00	2.50
b.		Governor's edition	130.00	
11		$7.50 White-fronted goose, 1996	12.00	2.50
a.		$97.50 Governor's edition	125.00	

Redheads: a, Male, serial # at UL. b, Female, serial # at LL.

12	Pair, 1997	30.00	
a.-b.	$7.50 Any single	11.00	2.50
c.	$97.50 Governor's Edition	110.00	

No. 12c is No. 12 without the central perforations. The denomination appears only in the upper right corner. The bottom inscription has Governor's Edition plus a serial number.

VERMONT

Printed in sheets of 30.

Catalogue values for all unused stamps in this section are for Never Hinged items.

Artists: Jim Killen, #1-4; Richard Plasschaert, #5-8; Reed Prescott, #9, 11; Robert Mullen, #10; J. Collins, #12; George Lockwood, #13-17; Richard E. Bishop, #18-20.

1986-2004

1		$5 Wood ducks	11.00	4.00
2		$5 Common goldeneyes, 1987	10.00	3.00
3		$5 Black ducks, 1988	10.00	2.50
4		$5 Canada geese, 1989	10.00	2.50
5		$5 Green-winged teal, 1990	10.00	2.50
6		$5 Hooded mergansers, 1991	10.00	2.50
7		$5 Snow geese, 1992	10.00	2.50
8		$5 Mallards, 1993	12.00	2.50
9		$5 Ring-necked duck, 1994	12.00	2.50
10		$5 Bufflehead, 1995	12.00	2.50
11		$5 Lesser scaup, 1996	10.00	2.50
12		$5 Pintails, 1997	10.00	2.50
13		$5 Blue-winged teal, 1998	12.00	2.50
14		$5 Canvasbacks, 1999	12.00	2.50
15		$5 Widgeons, 2000	8.00	2.50
16		$5 Oldsquaws, 2001	8.00	2.50
17		$5 Greater scaups, 2002	7.00	2.50
18		$5 Mallards, 2003	7.00	2.50
19		$5 Pintails, 2004	7.00	2.50
20		$5 Canvasbacks, 2005	7.00	2.50

VIRGINIA

Printed in booklet panes of 10 and/or sheets of 30. Stamps are numbered serially.

Catalogue values for all unused stamps in this section are for Never Hinged items.

Artists: Ronald Louque, #1; Arthur LeMay, #2; Louis Frisino, #3; Robert Leslie, #4, 11; Carl Knuth, #5, 12, 17; Bruce Miller, #6; Francis Sweet, #7; Richard Clifton, #8; Wilhelm Goebel, #9; Roger Cruwys, #10; Tim Donovan, #13-14; Jim Wilson, #15-16; Guy Crittenden, #18-20.

1988-2004

1		$5 Mallards, serial Nos. 1-40,000	13.00	2.50
		Booklet pair with L & R salvage, serial Nos. above 40,000	26.00	
2		$5 Canada geese, serial Nos. 1-40,000, 1989	12.00	2.50
		Booklet pair with L & R salvage, serial Nos. above 40,000	24.00	
3		$5 Wood ducks, serial Nos. 1-20,000, 1990	10.00	2.50
		Booklet pair with L & R salvage, serial Nos. above 20,000	20.00	
4		$5 Canvasbacks, serial Nos. 1-20,000, 1991	10.00	2.50
		Booklet pair with L & R salvage, serial Nos. above 20,000	20.00	
5		$5 Buffleheads, serial Nos. 1-20,000, 1992	10.00	2.50
		Booklet pair with L & R salvage, serial Nos. above 20,000	20.00	
6		$5 Black ducks, serial Nos. 1-20,000, 1993	10.00	2.50
		Booklet pair with L & R salvage, serial Nos. above 20,000	20.00	
7		$5 Lesser scaup, 1994	10.00	2.50
		Booklet pair with L & R salvage	20.00	
8		$5 Snow geese, 1995	10.00	2.50
		Booklet pair with L & R salvage	20.00	
9		$5 Hooded mergansers, 1996	10.00	2.50
10		($5) Pintail, Labrador retriever, 1997	12.00	2.50
11		$5 Mallards, 1998	10.00	2.50
12		$5 Green-winged teal, 1999	10.00	2.50
13		$5 Mallards, 2000	10.00	2.50
14		$5 Blue-winged teal, 2001	10.00	2.50
15		$5 Canvasbacks, 2002	10.00	2.50
16		$5 Tundra Swan, 2003	10.00	2.50
17		$5 American goldeneye, 2004	7.50	2.50
18		$9.75 Wood ducks, perf. 2005	13.00	2.50
19		$9.75 Wood ducks, rouletted, with tab 2005	13.00	2.50
20		$9.75 Wood ducks, self-adhesive, die cut 2005	13.00	2.50

Starting with 2005, Virginia stamps are mandatory for hunting.

WASHINGTON

Printed in booklet panes of 1 and sheets of 30.
Stamps are numbered serially.
Booklet panes starting with No. 7 without staple
holes were sold to collectors.

Catalogue values for all unused stamps in this
section are for Never Hinged items.

Artists: Keith Warrick, #1; Ray Nichol, #2; Robert Bateman,
#3; Maynard Reece, #4; Thomas Quinn, #5; Ronald Louque,
#6-7; Phillip Crowe, #8; Fred Thomas, #9; David Hagenbaumer,
#10; Cynthie Fisher, #11; Greg Beecham, #12; A. Young, #13;
Robert Steiner, #14-16; Adam Grimm, #17; Don Nicholson
Miller, #18-19; Dan Smith, #20-21.

1986-2004

1	$5 Mallards, Nos. 1-60,000		9.00	
	Booklet pane of 1, Nos. 60,001-160,000		12.50	4.00
2	$5 Canvasbacks, Nos. 1-24,000, 1987		12.00	
	Booklet pane of 1, Nos. 24,001-124,000		12.00	3.00
3	$5 Harlequin, Nos. 1-60,000, 1988		9.00	
	Booklet pane of 1, Nos. 60,001-160,000		10.00	3.00
4	$5 American widgeons, Nos. 1-60,000, 1989		9.00	
	Booklet pane of 1, Nos. 60,001-160,000		10.00	2.50
5	$5 Pintails & sour duck, Nos. 1-60,000, 1990		9.00	
	Booklet pane of 1, Nos. 60,001-160,000		10.00	2.50
6	$5 Wood duck, Nos. 1-30,000, 1991		12.00	
	Booklet pane of 1, Nos. above 30,000		12.00	4.00
7	$6 Wood duck, Nos. 100,000-130,000, 1991		10.00	
	Booklet pane of 1, Nos. above 130,000		10.00	2.50
8	$6 Labrador puppy & Canada geese, Nos. 1-30,000, 1992		14.00	
	Booklet pane of 1, Nos. above 30,000		14.00	2.50
9	$6 Snow geese, Nos. 1-30,000, 1993		10.00	
	Booklet pane of 1, Nos. above 30,000		10.00	2.50
10	$6 Black brant, Nos. 1-30,000, 1994		14.00	
	Booklet pane of 1, Nos. above 30,000		14.00	2.50
11	$6 Mallards, Nos. 1-30,000, 1995		12.00	
	Booklet pane of 1, Nos. above 30,000		12.00	2.50
12	$6 Redheads, Nos. 1-25,050, 1996		20.00	
	Booklet pane of 1, Nos. above 25,050		15.00	2.50
13	$6 Canada geese, Nos. 9600001-9625050, 1997		10.00	
	Bklt. pane of 1, Nos. above 9625050		10.00	2.50
14	$6 Barrow's goldeneye Nos. 1-25,050, 1998		13.00	
	Bklt. pane of 1, Nos. 25,051-27,050		13.00	2.50
15	$6 Bufflehead, 1999		15.00	
a.	Bklt. pane of 1		15.00	2.50
16	$6 Canada geese, mallard, widgeon, 2000		20.00	
a.	Bklt. pane of 1		15.00	2.50
17	$6 Mallards, 2001		12.00	
a.	Bklt. pane of 1		12.00	2.50
18	$10 Green-winged teal, 2002		15.00	
a.	Souvenir sheet of 1		15.00	2.50
19	$10 Pintails, 2003		20.00	
a.	Souvenir sheet of 1		15.00	2.50
20	$10 Canada goose, 2004		13.50	
a.	Souvenir sheet of 1		15.00	2.50
21	$10 Barrow's goldeneyes, 2005		13.50	
a.	Souvenir sheet of 1		15.00	2.50

Nos. 19-21 not required for hunting.

WEST VIRGINIA

Printed in sheets of 30 and booklet panes of 5.
All booklet stamps have straight edges at sides.
Starting in 1990, booklet stamps are numbered
serially. Some, but not all, of the 1988 booklet
stamps are numbered serially. Stamps from sheets
are not numbered serially.

Catalogue values for all unused stamps in this
section are for Never Hinged items.

Artists: Daniel Smith, #1-2; Steven Dillard, #3-4; Ronald
Louque, #5-6; Louis Frisino, #7-8; Robert Leslie, #9-10;
Thomas Hirata, #11-12; Phillip Crowe, #13-14; Richard Clifton,
#15-16; Fran Sweet, #17-18; Karl Badgley, #19-20.

1987-96

1	$5 Canada geese, resident		15.00	8.00
	Booklet single with tab at top		75.00	
2	$5 Canada geese, non-resident		15.00	8.00
	Booklet single with tab at top		75.00	
3	$5 Wood ducks, resident, 1988		10.00	4.00
	Booklet single with tab at top, no serial number		40.00	
a.	Booklet single with serial number on reverse		45.00	4.00
4	$5 Wood ducks, non-resident, 1988		12.00	4.00
	Booklet single with tab at top, no serial number		40.00	
a.	Booklet single with serial number on reverse		45.00	4.00
5	$5 Decoys, resident, 1989		12.00	3.00
	Booklet single with tab at top		35.00	
a.	Governor's edition		80.00	
6	$5 Decoys, non-resident, 1989		16.00	3.00
	Booklet single with tab at top		35.00	
a.	Governor's edition		80.00	

Nos. 5a and 6a were available only in sheets of 30 through a
sealed bid auction.

7	$5 Labrador retriever & decoy, resident, 1990		20.00	
a.	Booklet single		15.00	3.00
8	$5 Labrador retriever & decoy, non-resident, 1990		22.00	
a.	Booklet single		15.00	3.00
9	$5 Mallards, resident, 1991		12.00	
a.	Booklet single		12.00	2.50
10	$5 Mallards, non-resident, 1991		12.00	
a.	Booklet single		12.00	2.50
b.	Sheet, 3 each #9-10		50.00	

No. 10b is numbered serially; exists imperf. without serial
numbers.

11	$5 Canada geese, resident, 1992		12.00	
a.	Booklet single		12.00	2.50
12	$5 Canada geese, non-resident, 1992		12.00	
a.	Booklet single		12.00	2.50
13	$5 Pintails, resident, 1993		12.00	
a.	Booklet single		12.00	2.50
14	$5 Pintails, non-resident, 1993		12.00	
a.	Booklet single		12.00	2.50
15	$5 Green-winged teal, resident, 1994		12.00	
a.	Booklet single		12.00	2.50
16	$5 Green-winged teal, non-resident, 1994		12.00	
a.	Booklet single		12.00	2.50
17	$5 Mallards, resident, 1995		12.00	
a.	Booklet single		12.00	2.50
18	$5 Mallards, non-resident, 1995		12.00	
a.	Booklet single		12.00	2.50
19	$5 Widgeons, resident, 1996		12.00	
a.	Booklet single		12.00	2.50
20	$5 Widgeons, non-resident, 1996		12.00	
a.	Booklet single		12.00	2.50

WISCONSIN

Printed in sheets of 10. Starting in 1980 the left side
of the sheet has an agent tab and a numbered tab,
the right side a numbered tab.

Catalogue values for all unused stamps in this
section are for Never Hinged items.

Artists: Owen Gromme, #1; Rockne (Rocky) Knuth, #2, 6;
Martin Murk, #3; Timothy Schultz, #4; William Koelpin, #5;

Michael James Riddet, #7, 15, 26; Greg Alexander, #8, 20;
Moore, #9, 17, 23; Al Kraayvanger, #10; Richard Timm,
Rick Kelley, #12; Daniel Renn Pierce, #13; Terry Doughty,
25, 28; Frank Middlestadt, #16, 22; Les Didler, #18, 21, 24;
Timm, #19; Arthur Anderson, #27.

1978-2004

1	$3.25 Wood ducks		100.00	
2	$3.25 Buffleheads, rouletted, 1979		20.00	
3	$3.25 Widgeons, 1980		12.00	
	With tab		15.00	
4	$3.25 Lesser Scaup, 1981		10.00	
	With tab		13.00	
5	$3.25 Pintails, 1982		9.00	
	With numbered tab		9.00	
	With agent's and numbered tab		10.00	
6	$3.25 Blue-winged teal, 1983		9.00	
	With numbered tab		9.00	
	With agent's and numbered tab		10.00	
7	$3.25 Hooded merganser, 1984		9.00	
	With numbered tab		9.00	
	With agent's and numbered tab		10.00	
8	$3.25 Lesser scaup, 1985		10.00	
	With numbered tab		10.00	
	With agent's and numbered tab		11.00	
9	$3.25 Canvasbacks, 1986		12.00	
	With numbered tab		12.00	
	With agent's and numbered tab		14.00	
10	$3.25 Canada geese, 1987		9.00	
	With numbered tab		9.00	
	With agent's and numbered tab		10.00	
11	$3.25 Hooded merganser, 1988		9.00	
	With numbered tab		9.00	
	With agent's and numbered tab		10.00	
12	$3.25 Common goldeneye, 1989		9.00	
	With numbered tab		9.00	
	With agent's and numbered tab		10.00	
13	$3.25 Redheads, 1990		9.00	
	With numbered tab		9.00	
	With agent's and numbered tab		10.00	
14	$5.25 Green-winged teal, 1991		9.00	
	With numbered tab		9.00	
	With agent's and numbered tab		10.00	
15	$5.25 Tundra swans, 1992		10.00	
	With numbered tab		10.00	
	With agent's and numbered tab		12.00	
16	$5.25 Wood ducks, 1993		10.00	
	With numbered tab		10.00	
	With agent's and numbered tab		12.00	
17	$5.25 Pintails, 1994		10.00	
	With numbered tab		10.00	
	With agent's and numbered tabs		12.00	
18	$5.25 Mallards, 1995		10.00	
	With numbered tab		10.00	
	With agent's and numbered tabs		12.00	
19	($5.25) Green-winged teal, 1996		10.00	
	With numbered tab		10.00	
	With agent's and numbered tabs		12.00	
20	($7) Canada geese, 1997		15.00	
	With numbered tab		15.00	
	With agent's and numbered tabs		16.00	
21	$7 Snow goose, 1998		15.00	
	With numbered tab		15.00	
	With agent's and numbered tabs		16.00	
22	$7 Greater scaups, 1999		11.00	2.
23	$7 Canvasbacks, 2000		11.00	2.
24	$7 Common goldeneyes, 2001		11.00	2
25	$7 Shovelers, 2002		11.00	2
26	$7 Ring-necked ducks, 2003		11.00	2.
27	$7 Pintail, 2004		11.00	2.
28	$7 Wood ducks, 2005		9.00	2.

Nos. 26-28 not required for hunting.

WYOMING

Issued in panes of 5. Required to fish as well as to
hunt all small and big game, including waterfowl.
Stamps are numbered serially.

Catalogue values for all unused stamps in this
section are for Never Hinged items.

Artists: From photo by Luroy Parker, #1; Robert Kusserow
#2; Dan Andrews, #3; Ted Feeley, #4; Clark Ostergaard, #5
Dave Wade, #6, 8, 10, 13, 17; Connie J. Robinson, #7; Sara

...rs, #9; James Brooks, #11; Peter Eades, #12; D. Enright, ...Garth Hegeson, #15; Nick Reitzel, #16; Brent Todd, #18; ...Kay, #19; R. Piskorski, #20; Dustin Van Wechel, #21; Ron ...r, #22.

...o. 1 is in vertical format. All others are horizontal.

...4-2004

	$5 Meadowlark	60.00	6.00
	$5 Canada geese, *1985*	50.00	5.00
	$5 Antelope, *1986*	85.00	8.00

4	$5 Grouse, *1987*		85.00	8.00
5	$5 Trout, *1988*		100.00	12.00
6	$5 Mule deer, *1989*		175.00	15.00
7	$5 Bear, *1990*		50.00	5.00
8	$5 Rams, *1991*		45.00	3.50
9	$5 Bald eagle, *1992*		40.00	3.50
10	$5 Elk, *1993*		25.00	3.50
11	$5 Bobcat, *1994*		22.00	3.50
12	$5 Moose, *1995*		22.00	3.50
13	$5 Turkey, *1996*		22.00	3.00

14	$5 Mountain goats, *1997*		20.00	3.00
15	$5 Trumpeter swan, *1998*		20.00	3.00
16	$5 Brown trout, *1999*		20.00	3.00
17	$5 Buffalo, *2000*		20.00	3.00
18	$10 White-tailed deer, *2001*		20.00	5.00
19	$10 River otters, *2002*		20.00	5.00
20	$10 Mountain bluebirds, *2003*		19.00	5.00
21	$10 Mountain lion, *2004*		19.00	5.00
22	$10.50 Burrowing owls, *2005*		20.00	5.00

INDIAN RESERVATIONS

...tamps for other reservations exist and will be listed ...r more information is received about them.

CHEYENNE RIVER INDIAN RESERVATION

South Dakota
Birds and Small Game Stamps

...os. A1-A2 issued in booklet panes of 6, rouletted. Nos. A3-...ssued in booklet panes of 5, perforated, self-adhesive. Nos. ...A6 issued in booklet panes of 5, perforated.

A1

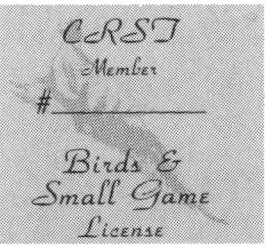

A2

A1	black, *light yellow*, member	2,750.	350.00
A1	black, *yellow*, non-member	750.	150.00

Nos. A1-A2 probably issued starting in 1984.

Catalogue values for all unused stamps in this section, from this point to the end, are for Never Hinged items.

A2	black, *yellow*, member	25.00	10.00
A2	black, *yellow*, non-member	45.00	15.00
A2	black, *light yellow*, member	13.00	5.00
A2	black, *light yellow*, non-member	27.50	10.00

Nos. A3-A4 issued starting in 1989. Nos. A5-A6 issued start-...in 1992.

Waterfowl Stamps

...Issued starting in 1993 in panes of 5. Perforated.

Catalogue values for all unused stamps in this section are for Never Hinged items.

	black, *light yellow*, member	15.00	5.00
	black *light yellow*, non-member	27.50	10.00

COLVILLE INDIAN RESERVATION

Washington
Bird Stamps

Required by non-tribal members to hunt birds, including waterfowl. Stamps are die cut, self-adhesive. No. 2 is numbered serially in red.

Catalogue values for all unused stamps in this section are for Never Hinged items.

A1

A2

1990-91

1	A1	black, *yellow*		—
2	A2 $20	black, *yellow*, *1992*		—

CROW INDIAN RESERVATION

Montana
Waterfowl Stamps

Issued in panes of 5 stamps (4 each No. 1, 1 No. 1a). Die cut, self-adhesive. Numbered serially in red.

Catalogue values for all unused stamps in this section are for Never Hinged items.

1992

1	blue	95.00	25.00
a.	Inscribed "Apr. 30, 199_"	300.00	75.00

Stamps without serial numbers exist. Some may have been issue to hunters during an abbreviated 1993 season.

CROW CREEK SIOUX INDIAN RESERVATION

South Dakota
Non-Indian Small Game Hunting Stamps

Issued 1961-64. The 1961 fee was $2.50. No example is recorded. The 1962 stamps were changed by hand for use in 1963 and 1964. No example of the 1964 stamp is recorded.

1962-63

2	$5 black		16,500.	—
3	$5 black, *1963*		—	—

Waterfowl Stamps

Fees: $10, reservation resident, non-tribal member; $30, South Dakota resident; $65, non-South Dakota resident.

Catalogue values for all unused stamps in this section, from this point to the end, are for Never Hinged items.

1989

5	$10 black		500.	*150.*
6	$30 black		10,500.	*1,000.*

7	$65 black	*1,500.*	*350.*

1990

8	$10 black	*350.*	*100.*
9	$30 black	*250.*	
10	$65 black	*1,250.*	*300.*

Fees: $5, tribal member; $15, affiliate, reservation resident; $30 ($35), South Dakota resident/non-resident daily use; $75 ($100), South Dakota resident/non-resident season.

1994

11	$5 green	75.00	15.00
12	$15 blue	100.00	
13	$30 red	125.00	
a.	$25 red (error)	—	
14	$75 red	200.00	65.00

1995

15	$5 green	35.00	10.00
16	$15 blue	55.00	
17	$30 red	95.00	
18	$75 red	150.00	40.00

1996

19	$5 green	27.50	10.00
20	$15 blue	45.00	
21	$35 red	75.00	
22	$100 red	125.00	35.00

1997

23	$5 green	12.00	
24	$15 blue	35.00	
25	$35 red	85.00	
26	$75 red	190.00	

No. 25 is inscribed $75, but sold for $35.

1998

27	$5 green	12.00	
28	$15 blue	35.00	
29	$35 red	85.00	
30	$75 red	190.00	

1999

31	$5 green	12.00	
32	$15 blue	35.00	
33	$35 red	85.00	
34	$75 red	190.00	

Sportsmen's Stamps
For hunting game including waterfowl.

Fees: $10, tribal member; $25, reservation resident, non-tribal member; $100, South Dakota resident; $250, non-South Dakota resident.
Used values are for signed stamps.

Catalogue values for all unused stamps in this section are for Never Hinged items.

1989

A1	$10 black	450.	100.
A2	$25 black	1,150.	300.
A3	$100 black	450.	75.
A4	$250 black	450.	150.

1990

A5	$10 black	500.	100.
A6	$25 black	650.	150.
A7	$100 black	275.	125.
A8	$250 black	400.	150.

FLATHEAD INDIAN RESERVATION

Montana
Bird or Fish Stamps

The 1988 stamp was printed in booklet panes of 10. Starting in 1989, printed in booklet panes of 5 stamps se-tenant with 5 stamps marked "Duplicate." Numbered serially in red. Rouletted.

Catalogue values for all unused stamps in this section are for Never Hinged items.

1987-90

1	$10 black	*1,450.*	350.00
1A	$10 black, *1988*	*1,350.*	275.00
2	$10 blue, *1989*	16.00	5.00
3	$10 blue, *1990*	16.00	5.00

Joint Bird License Stamps

Printed in booklet panes of 10. Die cut, self-adhesive. Numbered serially.

1991

4	$10 black, *green*	10.50	5.00

Bird License Stamps

Printed in booklet panes of 10. Die cut, self-adhesive. Numbered serially.

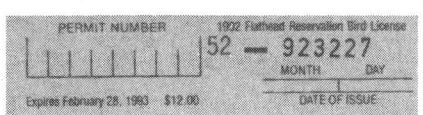

1992-2000

5	$12 black, *rose,* season	10.50	5.00
6	$12 black, *salmon,* 3-day	9.50	5.00
7	$12 black, *dark green,* season, *1993*	8.00	4.00
8	$12 black, *dark blue,* 3-day, *1993*	7.50	4.00
9	$12 black, *blue,* season, *1994*	8.00	4.00
10	$12 black, *orange,* 3-day, *1994*	7.00	3.00
11	$12 black, *yellow,* resident, *1995*	8.00	3.00
12	$55 black, *pale blue green,* non-resident, *1995*	17.50	9.00
13	$12 black, *turquoise,* resident, *1996*	11.00	3.00
14	$55 black, *pale orange,* non-resident, *1996*	18.00	15.00
15	$12 black, *pale yellow,* resident, *1997*	10.00	3.00
16	$55 black, *pale blue green,* non-resident, *1997*	11.00	
17	$13 black, *turquoise,* resident, *1998*	12.00	3.00
18	$56 black, *blue,* non-resident, *1998*	12.00	3.00
19	$13 black, *orange,* resident, *1999*	10.00	3.00
20	$56 black, *red,* non-resident, *1999*	10.00	3.00
21	$13 black, *yellow,* reservation, *2000*	12.00	3.00
22	$14 black, *green,* resident, *2000*	12.00	3.00
23	$110 black, *pink,* out-of-state, *2000*	12.00	3.00

FORT BERTHOLD INDIAN RESERVATION

North Dakota
Small Game Stamps

Stamps issued before 1990 may exist.
Issued in booklet panes of 6 stamps and 6 tabs. Required for hunting small game including waterfowl.
Values are for stamps with tabs. Fees varied, usually $6 for tribe members and $20-30 for non-members.
Stamps are numbered serially.

Catalogue values for all unused stamps in this section are for Never Hinged items.

1990-98

		Rouletted	
A6	black, *pink*	85.00	
A7	black, *green, 1991*	80.00	
A8	black, *pink, 1992*	80.00	
A9	black, *blue, 1993*	175.00	
A10	black, *pink, 1994*	70.00	
A11	black, *pink, 1995*	100.00	
A12	black, *green, 1996*	57.50	
A13	black, *light green, 1997*	50.00	
A14	black, *green, 1998*	30.00	

Waterfowl Stamps

Stamps issued before 1990 may exist.
Issued in booklet panes of 6 stamps and 6 tabs.
Required for non-member waterfowl hunters only.
Values are for stamps with tabs.
Fees varied, usually $20-30.
Stamps are numbered serially.

Catalogue values for all unused stamps in th[is] section are for Never Hinged items.

1990-2000

		Rouletted	
2A6	black	2,750.	
2A7	black, *blue, 1991*	950.00	
2A8	black, *yellow, #1-60, 1992*	4,000.	
2A9	black, *yellow, #61-120, 1993*	650.00	
2A10	black, *green, #1-60, 1994*	625.00	
2A11	black, *green, #61-120, 1995*	275.00	
2A12	black, *green, #121-198, 1996*	225.00	
2A13	black, *light green, #199-276, 1997*	250.00	
2A14	black, *light green, #277-, 1998*	300.00	
2A15	black, *light green, #355-432, 1999*	300.00	
2A16	black, *light green, #433-588, 2000*	250.00	

FORT PECK INDIAN RESERVATION

Montana
Stamps issued before 1975 may exist.

1975-78

		Rouletted	
2	$4 black	1,650.	
3	$4 black, *1976*	100.	
a.	Double impression	9,500.	
4	$4 black, *1977*		
5	$5 black, *orange, 1978*	325.	

JICARILLA APACHE INDIAN RESERVATION

New Mexico
Wildlife Stamp

Believed to have been issued starting in 1988. Issued in booklet panes of 4. Numbered serially. Rouletted.

Catalogue values for all unused stamps in this section are for Never Hinged items.

JICARILLA WILDLIFE STAMP
$5.00

$5 black & gold, *blue*   12.00

LAKE TRAVERSE (SISSETON-WAHPETON) INDIAN RESERVATION

South Dakota-North Dakota
Waterfowl Stamps

No examples are recorded of stamps from 1987-1990. No. 1 die cut. Nos. 6, 8-9 are die cut, self-adhesive. No. 7 issued in booklet panes of 5, rouletted, numbered serially in red.

A1

A2

A3

A4

986-2000

A1   green   250.00   75.00

Catalogue values for all unused stamps in this section, from this point to the end, are for Never Hinged items.

A2	black, *bright green, 1991*		125.00	
A3	Wood duck, *1992*		15.00	
A2	black, *bright red, 1993*		25.00	
A4	black, *yellow orange, 1994*		7.50	4.00

Inscribed SWST

0 A4	black, *red orange, 1995*		12.00	4.00
1 A4	black, *blue, 1996*		10.00	4.00
2 A4	black, *bright green, 1997*		11.00	3.00
3 A4	black, *red, 1998*		40.00	
4 A4	black, *orange, 1999*		10.00	
5 A4	black, *orange, 2000*		35.00	

LOWER BRULE INDIAN RESERVATION

South Dakota
Waterfowl Stamps

Serial Nos. are in red. Year and fee are written by hand or typewritten on each stamp. The $5 fee was for for non-members

---

and non-Indians. There was a $2.50 fee for tribal members but no examples of these stamps are recorded.

Numbers have been reserved for the $2.50 stamps.

Since no year is on an unused copy, they are listed under the first year only.

1962-70

2	$5 black	—	—
4	$5 black, *1963*		
6	$5 black, *1964*		2,900.
8	$5 black, *1965*		2,900.
10	$5 black, *1966*		2,750.
12	$5 black, *1967*		2,500.
14	$5 black, *1968*		2,400.
18	$5 black, *1969*		4,250.

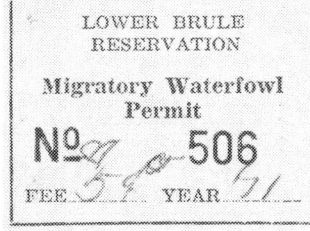

1969-71

20	$5 black		4,750.
24	$5 black, *1971*		
26	$5 black, *1972*		—

Migratory Bird Hunting and Conservation Stamps
Issued in panes of 20.
All stamps have serial number on reverse.

Catalogue values for all unused stamps in this section, from this point to the end, are for Never Hinged items.

1995

27	$5 green, tribal member		7.00
28	$5 orange brown, resident deeded land owner / operator		7.00
29	$5 blue, resident government employee		7.00
30	$10 red, non-tribal S.D. resident		12.00
31	$10 purple, non-resident, out of state		12.00
	1996		
32	$5 multi, tribal / resident		7.00
33	$10 multi, non-tribal S.D. resident		12.00
34	$10 multi, non-resident, out of state		12.00
	1997		
35	$5 multi, tribal / resident		7.00
36	$10 multi, non-tribal S.D. resident		12.00
37	$10 multi, non-resident, out of state		12.00

Nos. 38-40 have been reserved for 1998 stamps which were printed, but use of which has not yet been verified.

	1999		
41	$5 multi, tribal / resident		7.00
42	$10 multi, non-tribal S. D. resident		14.00
43	$10 multi, non-resident, out of state		14.00

PINE RIDGE (OGLALA SIOUX) INDIAN RESERVATION

South Dakota
Waterfowl Stamps

Nos. 1-3 issued in booklet panes of 5, numbered serially in red.

No. 2 perforated, others rouletted.

A1

A2

A3

1	A1 $4 black		350.00

Earliest known use of No. 1 is 1988.

Catalogue values for all unused stamps in this section, from this point to the end, are for Never Hinged items.

2	A2 $4 black, perforated		15.00
3	A3 $4 Canada geese, *1992*		11.00

$6 stamps picturing Canada geese were produced and sold for the 1993 season. The same stamp was rubber hand-stamped for the 1994 season. However, there was no hunting season those years. Value, each $15.

ROSEBUD INDIAN RESERVATION

South Dakota
Tribal Game Bird Stamps

Nos. 1, 3-4 have red serial number. Stamps for 1960, 1963-69 may exist.

Since no year is on an unused copy, they are listed under the first year only.

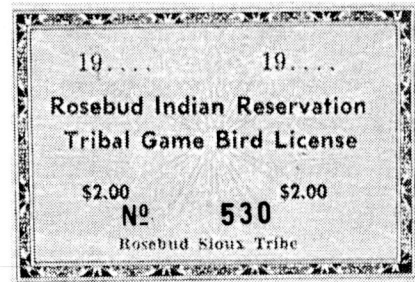

1959-62

1	$2 green		—
3	$2 green, *1961*		6,500.
4	$2 green, *1962*		7,500.

Small Game Stamps

No. 12

No. 13

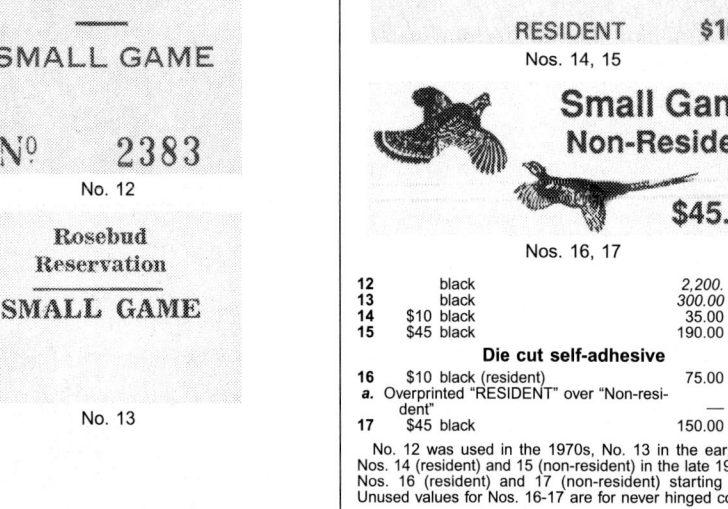

RESIDENT $10.00
Nos. 14, 15

Small Game
Non-Resident

$45.00
Nos. 16, 17

12		black	2,200.
13		black	300.00
14	$10	black	35.00	20.00
15	$45	black	190.00

Die cut self-adhesive

16	$10	black (resident)	75.00	15.00
a.		Overprinted "RESIDENT" over "Non-resident"	
17	$45	black	150.00	50.00

No. 12 was used in the 1970s, No. 13 in the early 1980s, Nos. 14 (resident) and 15 (non-resident) in the late 1980s, and Nos. 16 (resident) and 17 (non-resident) starting in 1990. Unused values for Nos. 16-17 are for never hinged copies.

STANDING ROCK INDIAN RESERVATION

**South Dakota-North Dakota
Waterfowl Stamps**
Die cut, self-adhesive.

Catalogue values for all unused stamps in this section are for Never Hinged items.

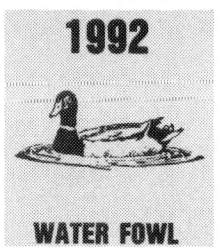

1992-98

1	black	16.00	5.
2	black, 1993	10.00	4.
3	black, inscribed "SRST," 1994	8.50	3.
4	black, 1995	15.00	5.
5	black, 1996	13.00	4.
6	black, 1997	9.00	4.
7	black, 1998	15.00	4.

SAVINGS STAMPS

"Savings Stamps" is a general philatelic category that includes four slightly different types of stamps issued at different times by either the U.S. Post Office Department or the U.S. Treasury Department. Their common feature was that they all effectively acted as a means for ordinary citizens to save and/or invest incrementally, a little bit at a time. At the same time, the investments effectively were loans to the federal government.

The four types of Savings Stamps are Postal Savings Stamps (issued from 1911-41) and Savings Stamps (1954-61), both issued by the Post Office Department; and War Savings Stamps (1917-45) and a Treasury Savings Stamp (1920), both issued by the Treasury Department.

Postal Savings Stamps were issued in 10c to $5.00 denominations and were redeemable in the form of credits to postal savings accounts. The 1911 10c stamps were available either as stamps or as a stamp imprint on a card to which other stamps could be added. The postal savings system was discontinued March 28, 1966.

Savings Stamps, also issued in 10c to $5.00 denominations, are the savings stamps most familiar to older philatelists. These collectors may remember buying these stamps at school and placing them in booklets. When full, the booklets were redeemable in the form of United States savings bonds. Sale of Savings Stamps was discontinued June 30, 1970.

War Savings Stamps were issued in 25c and $5 denominations (1917-20) and 10c to $5 denominations (1942-45). They were redeemable in the form of United States treasury war certificates, defense bonds or war bonds.

One Treasury Savings Stamp with a $1.00 denomination was issued in 1920. These stamps were redeemable in the form of either war savings stamps or treasury savings certificates.

POSTAL SAVINGS STAMPS

PS1

Plates of 400 subjects in four panes of 100 each
FLAT PLATE PRINTING

1911, Jan. 3   Wmk. 191   Engr.   Perf. 12
Size of design: 18x21½mm

PS1	PS1	10c orange	8.50	1.40
		Never hinged	15.00	
		Block of 4, 2mm spacing	37.50	
		Block of 4, 3mm spacing	40.00	
		P# strip of 3, Impt. open star	57.50	
		P# block of 6, Impt. open star	525.00	

Plate Nos. 5504-5507.

1911, Jan. 3   Unwmk.
Imprinted on Deposit Card
Size of design: 137x79mm

PS2	PS1	10c orange	175.00	40.00

A 10c deep blue with head of Washington in circle imprinted on deposit card (design 136x79mm) exists, but there is no evidence that it was ever placed in use.

1911, Aug. 14   Wmk. 190   Perf. 12

PS4	PS1	10c deep blue	5.00	1.00
		Never hinged	8.50	
		Block of 4, 2mm spacing	22.50	
		Block of 4, 3mm spacing	25.00	
		P# strip of 3, Impt. open star	30.00	
		P# block of 6, Impt. open star	175.00	

Plate Nos. 5504-5507.

1911   Unwmk.
Imprinted on Deposit Card
Size of design: 133x78mm

PS5	PS1	10c deep blue	150.00	22.50

Catalogue values for unused stamps in this section, from this point to the end, are for Never Hinged items.

1936   Unwmk.   Perf. 11

PS6	PS1	10c deep blue	5.50	1.25
		violet blue	5.50	1.25
		Block of 4	25.00	
		P# block of 6, Impt. solid star	135.00	

Plate Nos. 21485, 21486.

PS2

Plates of 400 subjects in four panes of 100 each
FLAT PLATE PRINTING

1940   Unwmk.   Engr.   Perf. 1
Size of design: 19x22mm

PS7	PS2	10c deep ultramarine, Apr. 3	25.00	6.
		Block of 4	105.00	
		P# block of 6	290.00	

Plate Nos. 22540, 22541.

PS8	PS2	25c dark car rose, Apr. 1	30.00	9.
		Block of 4	125.00	
		P# block of 6	325.00	

Plate Nos. 22542, 22543.

PS9	PS2	50c dark blue green, Apr. 1	75.00	17.5
		Block of 4	320.00	
		P# block of 6	1,100.	

Plate No. 22544.

PS10	PS2	$1 gray black, Apr. 1	210.00	17.5
		Block of 4	475.00	
		P# block of 6	2,300.	

Plate No. 22545.
Nos. PS11-PS15 redeemable in the form of United States Treasury Defense, War or Savings Bonds.

Minute Man — PS3

E.E. Plates of 400 subjects in four panes of 100 each

ROTARY PRESS PRINTING

1, May 1   Unwmk.   Perf. 11x10½
Size of design: 19x22½mm

1	PS3	10c **rose red**		.60
a.		10c carmine rose		.60
		Block of 4		2.40
		P# block of 4		7.25
b.		Bklt. pane of 10, *July 30*, trimmed horizontal edges		50.00
		As "b," with Electric Eye marks at left		55.00
c.		Booklet pane of 10, perf. horizontal edges		100.00
		As "c," with Electric Eye marks at left		115.00

Plate Nos., sheet stamps, 22714-22715, 22722-22723, 148245-148246.
Plate Nos., booklet panes, 147084, 147086, 148241-148242.

2	PS3	25c **blue green**		2.00
		Block of 4		8.25
		P# block of 4		22.50
b.		Bklt. pane of 10, *July 30*		60.00
		Booklet pane with Electric Eye marks at left		65.00

Plate Nos., sheet stamps, 22716-22717, 22724-22725, 148247-148248.
Plate Nos., booklet panes, 147087-147088, 148243-148244.

3	PS3	50c **ultramarine**		7.50
		Block of 4		32.50
		P# block of 4		50.00

Plate Nos. 22718-22719, 22726-22727.

4	PS3	$1 **gray black**		12.50
		Block of 4		52.50
		P# block of 4		75.00

Plate Nos. 22720, 22728.

FLAT PLATE PRINTING
Plates of 100 subjects in four panes of 25 each

Size: 36x46mm   Perf. 11

5	PS3	$5 **sepia**		42.50
		Block of 4		175.00
		P# block of 6 at top or bottom		475.00

Plate Nos. 22730-22737, 22740.

SAVINGS STAMPS

> Catalogue values for unused stamps in this section are for Never Hinged items.

Minute Man — S1

E.E. Plates of 400 subjects in four panes of 100 each

ROTARY PRESS PRINTING

1954-57   Unwmk.   Perf. 11x10½
Size of design: 19x22½mm

1	S1	10c **rose red,** wet printing, *Nov. 30, 1954*		.50
		Block of 4		2.00
		P# block of 4		3.50
a.		Booklet pane of 10, *Apr. 22, 1955*		150.00
		Booklet pane with Electric Eye marks at left		165.00
b.		Dry printing		.50

		Block of 4		2.00
		P# block of 4		3.50
c.		As "b," booklet pane of 10		150.00
		Booklet pane with Electric Eye marks at left		165.00

Plate Nos., sheet stamps, 164991-164992 (wet), 165917-165918, 166643-166644, 167089-167090, 168765-168766 (dry).
Plate Nos., booklet panes, 165218-165219 (wet), 165954-165955, 167001-167002 (dry).

S2	S1	25c **blue green,** wet printing, *Dec. 30, 1954*		7.50
		Block of 4		30.00
		P# block of 4		35.00
a.		Booklet pane of 10, *Apr. 15, 1955*		800.00
		Booklet pane with Electric Eye marks at left		825.00
b.		Dry printing		7.50
		Block of 4		30.00
		P# block of 4		35.00
c.		As "b," booklet pane of 10		800.00
		Booklet pane with Electric Eye marks at left		825.00

Plate Nos., sheet stamps, 165007-165008 (wet), 165919-165920 (dry), booklet panes, 165220-165221 (wet), 165956-165957 (dry).

S3	S1	50c **ultramarine,** wet printing, *Dec. 31, 1956*		9.00
		Block of 4		37.50
		P# block of 4		50.00
a.		Dry printing		9.00
		Block of 4		37.50
		P# block of 4		50.00

Plate Nos. 165050-165051 (wet), 166741-166742, 166941-166942 (dry).

S4	S1	$1 **gray black,** *Mar. 13, 1957*		25.00
		Block of 4		100.00
		P# block of 4		125.00

Plate Nos. 166097-166098, 166683-166684.

FLAT PLATE PRINTING
Plates of 100 subjects in four panes of 25 each

Size: 36x46mm   Perf. 11

S5	S1	$5 **sepia,** *Nov. 30, 1956*		95.00
		Block of 4		400.00
		P# block of 6 at top or bottom		725.00

Plate No. 166068.

Minute Man and 48-Star Flag — S2

GIORI PRESS PRINTING
Plates of 400 subjects in four panes of 100 each

1958, Nov. 18   Unwmk.   Perf. 11

S6	S2	25c **dark blue & carmine**		2.00
		Block of 4		8.00
		P# block of 4		10.00
a.		Booklet pane of 10		75.00

Plate Nos.: sheet stamps, 166921, 166925, 166946; booklet panes, 166913, 166916.

Minute Man and 50-Star Flag — S3

Plates of 400 subjects in four panes of 100 each.

1961   Unwmk.   Perf. 11

S7	S3	25c **dark blue & carmine**		1.50
		Block of 4		6.00
		P# block of 4		11.00
a.		Booklet pane of 10		300.00

Plate Nos.: sheet stamps, 167473, 167476, 167486, 167489, 169089; booklet panes, 167495, 167502, 167508, 167516.

WAR SAVINGS STAMPS

Unused values of War Savings stamps are for copies with full original gum. Used values are for stamps without gum that generally have been removed from

---

savings certificates or booklets. **Caution:** beware of used stamps that have been regummed to appear unused.

WS1

Plates of 300 subjects in six panes of 50 each
FLAT PLATE PRINTING

1917, Dec. 1   Unwmk.   Engr.   Perf. 11
Size of design: 28x18½mm

WS1	WS1	25c **deep green**	16.00	2.25
		Never hinged	25.00	
		Block of 4	70.00	
		Margin strip of 3, P#	80.00	
		P# block of 6	1,200.	

Plate Nos. 56800, 56810-56811, 56817, 57074-57077, 57149-57152, 57336, 57382, 57395-57396, 57399, 57443, 58801-58804, 59044-59045, 59156, 61207-61210.

George Washington — WS2

Plates of 80 subjects in four panes of 20 each
FLAT PLATE PRINTING

1917   Unwmk.   Engr.   Perf. 11
Size of design: 39x55mm

WS2	WS2	$5 **deep green,** *Nov. 17*	85.00	35.00
		Never hinged	140.00	
		Block of 4	325.00	
		Margin copy with P#	90.00	
		P# block of 6	1,600.	
b.		Vert. pair, imperf. horiz.		

Plate Nos. 56914-56917, 57066-57073, 57145-57148, 57169-57176, 57333-57334, 57343-57348, 58431, 58433-58438, 58726-58729, 59071, 60257-60260, 60659-60662, 60665-60668, 60846-60852, 60899, 61203-61206, 61265-61268, 61360-61367, 61388, 61435, 61502.

Rouletted 7

WS3	WS2	$5 **deep green**	1,200.	650.
		Never hinged	2,250.	
		Block of 4	5,000.	
		Margin copy with P#	1,500.	

Benjamin Franklin — WS3

Plates of 150 subjects in six panes of 25 each
FLAT PLATE PRINTING

1919, July 3   Unwmk.   Engr.   Perf. 11
Size of design: 27x36mm

WS4	WS3	$5 **deep blue**	325.	160.
		Never hinged	550.	
		Block of 4	1,350.	

Margin copy with P#   350.
Margin copy with inverted
P#   375.

Plate Nos. 61882-61885, 61910-61913, 61970-61972,
61997-61998, 62007-62013.

George
Washington
WS4

Plates of 100 subjects in four panes of 25 each
FLAT PLATE PRINTING

1919, Dec. 11   Unwmk.   Engr.   Perf. 11
Size of design: 36x41½mm
WS5 WS4 $5 carmine   800.   350.
Never hinged   1,400.
Block of 4   3,500.
Margin copy with P#   850.

Plate Nos. 67545-67552, 69349-69352, 69673-69675,
69677-69680, 69829.

Abraham
Lincoln — WS5

Plates of 100 subjects in four panes of 25 each
FLAT PLATE PRINTING

1920, Dec. 21   Unwmk.   Engr.   Perf. 11
Size of design: 39½x42mm
WS6 WS5 $5 orange, green   3,500.   1,350.
Never hinged   6,500.
Block of 4   15,000.
Margin copy with P#   3,750.

Plate Nos. 73129-73136.

> Catalogue values for unused stamps in this section, from this point to the end, are for Never Hinged items.

Minute Man — WS6

Plates of 400 subjects in four panes of 100 each
ROTARY PRESS PRINTING

1942   Unwmk.   Perf. 11x10½
Size of design: 19x22½mm
WS7 WS6 10c rose red, Oct. 29   .50   .20
a.   10c carmine rose   .50
Block of 4   2.00
P# block of 4   5.00
b.   Booklet pane of 10, Oct. 27   50.00
Booklet pane with Electric
Eye marks at left   55.00

Plate Nos., sheet stamps, 149492-149495, 150206-150207,
150706-150707, 155311-155312.
Plate Nos., booklet panes, 149655-149657, 150664.

WS8 WS6 25c dark blue green, Oct. 15   1.10   .25
Block of 4   5.00
P# block of 4   8.25
b.   Booklet pane of 10, Nov. 6   50.00
Booklet pane with Electric
Eye marks at left   55.00

Plate Nos., sheet stamps, 149587-149590, 150320-150321,
150708-150709, 155313-155314, 155812-155813, 156517-
156518, booklet panes, 149658-149660, 150666.

WS9 WS6 50c deep ultra, Nov. 12   4.00   1.25
Block of 4   16.00
P# block of 4   22.50

Plate Nos. 149591-149594.

WS10 WS6 $1 gray black, Nov. 17   12.50   3.50
Block of 4   52.50
P# block of 4   70.00

Plate Nos. 149595-149598.

Type of 1942
FLAT PLATE PRINTING
Plates of 100 subjects in four panes of 25 each

1945   Unwmk.   Size: 36x46mm   Perf.
WS11 WS6 $5 violet brown   55.00   1
Block of 4   240.00
P# block of 6 at top or
bottom   500.00

Plate Nos. 150131-150134, 150291.

Type of 1942
Coil Stamps

1943, Aug. 5   Unwmk.   Perf. 10 Vertic
WS12 WS6 10c rose red   2.75
Pair   6.00
Line pair   10.50

Plate Nos. 153200-153207.

WS13 WS6 25c dark blue green   5.00
Pair   10.50
Line pair   22.50

Plate Nos. 153289-153290.

TREASURY SAVINGS STAMP

Alexander
Hamilton — TS1

FLAT PLATE PRINTING

1920, Dec. 21   Unwmk.   Engr.   Perf.
Size of design: 33½x33½mm
TS1 TS1 $1 red, green   3,500.   1,2
Never hinged   6,500.
Block of 4   15,000.
Margin copy with P#   3,750.

Plate Nos. 73196-73203.

TELEGRAPH STAMPS

These stamps were issued by the individual companies for use on their own telegrams, and can usually be divided into three classes: Free franki privileges issued to various railroad, newspaper and express company officials, etc., whose companies were large users of the lines; those issued part cost to the lesser officials of the same type companies; and those bearing values which were usually sold to the general public. Occasionally, son of the companies granted the franking privilege to stockholders and minor State (not Federal) officials. Most Telegraph Stamps were issued in book form and will be found with one or more straight edges.

Serial numbers may show evidence of doubling, often of a different number. Such doubling is not scarce.

American Rapid Telegraph Company

Organized Feb. 21, 1879, in New York State. Its wires extended as far north as Boston, Mass., and west to Cleveland, Ohio. It was amalgamated with the Bankers and Merchants Telegraph Co., but when that company was unable to pay the fixed charges, the properties of the American Rapid Telegraph Company were sold on Mar. 11, 1891, to a purchasing committee comprised of James W. Converse and others. This purchasing committee deeded the property and franchise of the American Rapid Telegraph Company to the Western Union Telegraph Company on June 25, 1894. Issued three types of stamps: Telegram, Collect and Duplicate. Telegram stamps were issued in sheets of 100 and were used to prepay messages which could be dropped in convenient boxes for collection. Collect and duplicate stamps were issued in alternate rows on the same sheet of 100 subjects. Collect stamps were attached to telegrams sent collect, the receiver of which paid the amount shown by the stamps, while the Duplicate stamps were retained by the Company as vouchers. **Remainders with punched cancellations were bought up by a New York dealer.**

T1   T2

"Prepaid Telegram" Stamps
Engraved and Printed by the American Bank Note Co.

1881   Perf. 12
1T1 T1 1c black   10.00   3.00
Punched   .20
Block of 4   45.00
Punched   1.00
1T2 T1 3c orange   40.00 32.50

Punched   1.
Block of 4, punched   10.
1T3 T1 5c bister brown   2.50
Punched
Block of 4   11.00
Punched   1.
a.   5c brown   2.50
Punched
Block of 4   11.00
Punched   1.
1T4 T1 10c purple   14.00   5.
Punched
Block of 4   62.50
Punched   1.
1T5 T1 15c green   4.50   1.
Punched
Block of 4   20.00
Punched   1.
1T6 T1 20c red   4.50   1.
Punched
Block of 4, punched
1T7 T1 25c rose   6.00   1.
Punched
Block of 4   21.00
Punched   1.

8	T1	50c **blue**	27.50	12.50
		Punched		1.50
		Block of 4, punched		8.00

"Collect" Stamps

9	T2	1c **brown**	4.00	3.50
		Punched		.20
10	T2	5c **blue**	3.25	2.50
		Punched		.20
11	T2	15c **red brown**	3.50	2.00
		Punched		.25
12	T2	20c **olive green**	3.50	2.50
		Punched		.20

T3

"Office Coupon" Stamps

13	T3	1c **brown**	7.50	2.75
		Punched		.20
a.		Pair, #1T9, 1T13, punched	2.00	
		As "a," block of 4, punched	4.50	
14	T3	5c **blue**	6.50	3.25
		Punched		.20
a.		Pair, #1T10, 1T14	32.50	
		Punched		3.00
		As "a," block of 4	70.00	
		Punched		7.00
15	T3	15c **red brown**	11.00	3.00
		Punched		.25
a.		Pair, #1T11, 1T15	27.50	
		Punched		2.50
		As "a," block of 4	65.00	
		Punched		5.50
16	T3	20c **olive green**	11.00	3.00
		Punched		.20
a.		Pair, #1T12, 1T16, punched	2.75	
		As "a," block of 4, punched	6.00	

Atlantic Telegraph Company

Organized 1884 at Portland, Me., to Boston, Mass., and terminated in the office of the Baltimore and Ohio Telegraph Company at Boston. Later bought out by the Baltimore and Ohio Telegraph Co. Stamps issued by the Atlantic Telegraph Company could also be used for messages destined to any point on the Baltimore and Ohio system. Stamps were printed in panes of six and a full book sold for $10. **Remainders of these stamps, without control numbers, were purchased by a Boston dealer and put on the market about 1932.**

T4

1888			**Perf. 13**	
1	T4	1c **green**	5.00	—
		Remainders		2.25
		Pane of 6	—	
		Remainders		14.00
2	T4	5c **blue**	7.50	—
		Remainders		2.25
		Pane of 6	—	
		Remainders		14.00
a.		Horiz. pair, imperf. vert.		
b.		Vert. pair, imperf. horiz.	25.00	—
3	T4	10c **purple brown**	9.00	—
		Remainders		2.25
		Pane of 6	—	
		Remainders		14.00
a.		Horiz. pair, imperf. between	40.00	
4	T4	25c **carmine**	6.00	—
		Remainders		2.25
		Pane of 6, remainders		16.00

Baltimore & Ohio Telegraph Companies

"The Baltimore & Ohio Telegraph Co. of the State of New York" was incorporated May 17, 1882. Organization took place under similar charter in 26 other states. It absorbed the National Telegraph Co. and several others. Extended generally along the lines of the Baltimore & Ohio Railroad, but acquired interests in other states. Company absorbed in 1887 by the Western Union Telegraph Co. Stamps were issued in booklet form and sold for $5 and $10, containing all denominations.

T5

T6

Engraved by the American Bank Note Co.

1885			**Perf. 12**	
3T1	T5	1c **vermilion**	70.00	25.00
		Pane of 6	450.00	
3T2	T5	5c **blue**	70.00	35.00
3T3	T5	10c **red brown**	35.00	12.50
		Pane of 6	225.00	
3T4	T5	25c **orange**	55.00	25.00
3T5	T6	**brown**		1.75
		Pane of 4		12.50

1886				
3T6	T6	**black**	2.00	25.00
		Pane of 4	22.50	

Imprint of Kendall Bank Note Co.
Thin Paper

1886			**Perf. 14**	
3T7	T5	1c **green**	6.00	3.00
a.		Thick paper	10.00	.85
b.		Imperf., pair	90.00	
3T8	T5	5c **blue**	4.00	1.25
a.		Thick paper	9.00	4.00
b.		Imperf., pair		55.00
3T9	T5	10c **brown**	6.00	.75
a.		Thick paper	10.00	1.50
3T10	T5	25c **deep orange**	35.00	.75
a.		Thick paper	40.00	1.50

Used copies of Nos. 3T7-3T20 normally have heavy grid cancellations. Lightly canceled copies command a premium.

Litho. by A. Hoen & Co.
Imprint of firm

1886			**Perf. 12**	
3T11	T5	1c **green**	3.00	.65
		Pane of 6	22.50	
3T12	T5	5c **blue**	7.50	.65
		Pane of 6	50.00	
a.		Imperf., pair	90.00	
3T13	T5	10c **dark brown**	7.50	.75
		Pane of 6	45.00	
a.		Vert. pair, imperf. between	60.00	

Wmk. "A HOEN AND CO. BALTIMORE" in double lined capitals in sheet
Perf. 12

3T14	T5	1c **green**	12.50	1.25
		Pane of 6	75.00	
3T15	T5	5c **blue**	20.00	1.50
		Pane of 6	130.00	
a.		Imperf., pair	52.50	
3T16	T5	10c **dark brown**	15.00	1.25
		Pane of 6	100.00	

Lithographed by Forbes Co., Boston
Imprint of firm

1887			**Perf. 12½**	
3T17	T5	1c **green**	35.00	2.75
3T18	T5	5c **blue**	55.00	6.00
3T19	T5	10c **brown**	55.00	5.50
3T20	T5	25c **yellow**	55.00	8.25
a.		25c **orange**	55.00	5.50

Baltimore & Ohio-Connecticut River Telegraph Companies

The Connecticut River Telegraph Co. ran from New Haven to Hartford. An agreement was entered wherein the Baltimore & Ohio System had mutual use of their lines. This agreement terminated when the Baltimore & Ohio System was absorbed by the Western Union. The Connecticut River Telegraph Company then joined the United Lines. In 1885 stamps (black on yellow) were issued and sold in booklets for $10. In 1887 the Connecticut River Telegraph Co. had extended its lines to New Boston, Mass., and new books of stamps (black on blue) were issued for use on this extension. **Remainders were canceled with bars and sold to a New York dealer.**

T7

1885			**Perf. 11**	
4T1	T7	1c **black,** *yellow*	6.50	6.00
		Remainders		1.25
		Pane of 10	70.00	
		Remainders		6.00
a.		Imperf., pair	40.00	
b.		Vert. pair, imperf. horiz., remainders		—
4T2	T7	5c **black,** *yellow*	4.00	10.00
		Remainders		1.00
		Pane of 10	45.00	
		Remainders		6.00
a.		Horizontal pair, imperf. between, remainders		
b.		Vert. pair, imperf. between, remainders		35.00
c.		Imperf., pair, remainders		35.00
4T3	T7	1c **black,** *blue*	10.00	
		Remainders		4.00
		Pane of 10	110.00	
		Remainders		35.00
4T4	T7	5c **black,** *blue*	12.50	9.00
		Remainders		4.00
		Pane of 10	135.00	
		Remainders		52.50

California State Telegraph Company

Incorporated June 17, 1854 as the California Telegraph Company and constructed a line from Nevada through Grass Valley to Auburn. Extended to run from San Francisco to Marysville via San Jose and Stockton. Later absorbed Northern Telegraph Co. and thus extended to Eureka. It was incorporated as the California State Telegraph Company on April 6, 1861. At the time of its lease to the Western Union on May 16, 1867 the California State consisted of the following companies which had been previously absorbed:

Alta California Telegraph Co., Atlantic and Pacific States Telegraph Co., National Telegraph Co., Northern California Telegraph Co., Overland Telegraph Co., Placerville and Humboldt Telegraph Co., Tuolumne Telegraph Co. Stamps were issued in booklets, six to a pane. **Remainders of Nos. 5T1 and 5T4 are without frank numbers.**

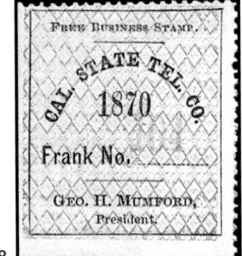

T8

1870   *Perf. 13½*

5T1	T8	black & blue	600.	—
		Pane of 6	3,750.	
		Without number	200.	

T9   T10

1870   *Perf. 12, 13*

5T2	T9	black & red, without number	250.00	175.00

1871   *Dated "1871"*

5T3	T9	black & red, without number	600.00	
a.		Imperf., pair		
5T4	T10	black & salmon, blue number	600.00	240.00
		Pane of 6	3,750.	
		Without number	200.00	

1872

5T5	T10	green & red, red number (no year date)	300.00	—
		Pane of 6	—	

1873   *Dated "1873"*

5T6	T10	red & salmon, blue number	400.00	300.00

1874   *Dated "1874"*

5T7	T10	blue & salmon, black number	450.00	—
		Pane of 6	—	

1875   *Dated "1875"*

5T8	T10	brown & green, black number	375.00	—
		Pane of 6	—	

City & Suburban Telegraph Company
(New York City and Suburban Printing Telegraph Company)

Organized 1855. Extended only through New York City and Brooklyn. Sold out to the American Telegraph Co. Stamps were sold to the public for prepayment of messages, which could be dropped in convenient boxes for collection. Stamps were issued in sheets of 60 having a face value of $1. These were arranged in six vertical rows of ten, the horizontal rows having the following denominations: 2c, 1c, 1c, 1c, 2c, 3c.

Counterfeits are known both in black and blue, mostly on pelure or hard white paper. Originals are on soft wove paper, somewhat yellowish. Scalloped edge is more sharply etched on the counterfeits.

T11

			Typo.	**Imperf.**
6T1	T11	1c black	400.	225.
		Pair	—	
		Block of 4	—	
6T2	T11	2c black	500.	300.
		Pair	—	
		Pair, 2c + 1c	750.	
6T3	T11	3c black	650.	400.
		Pair	—	
		Strip of 3, 1c, 2c & 3c	3,750.	

Colusa, Lake & Mendocino Telegraph Company

Was organized in California early in 1873. First known as the Princeton, Colusa and Grand Island Telegraph Co. In May, 1873 they completed their line from Princeton through Colusa, at which point it was connected with the Western Union office, to Grand Island. On Feb. 10, 1875 it was incorporated as the Colusa, Lake & Mendocino Telegraph Co. Its lines were

extended into the counties of Colusa, Lake, Mendocino and Napa. Eventually reached a length of 260 miles. Went out of business in 1892. Stamps were issued for prepayment of messages and were sold in books. When sold they were stamped "P.L.W." (the superintendent's initials) in blue. The 5c value was printed 10 to a pane, being two horizontal rows of five. Of the 10c and 25c nothing definite is known about the settings.

T11a

1876   *Perf. 12*

7T1	T11a	5c black	900.	—
		Block of 4	4,000.	
		Pane of 10	10,000.	
		Without "P.L.W."	1,000.	
7T2	T11a	10c black	9,000.	—
7T3	T11a	25c red	9,000.	

Commercial Union Telegraph Company

Incorporated in New York State on March 31, 1886. Its lines ran from Albany through Troy to Berlin, N.Y., thence to North Adams, Mass. The lines of this Company, which was controlled by the Postal Telegraph Company, were later extended throughout Northern New York and the States of Massachusetts, Vermont, New Hampshire and Maine. Stamps issued in panes of four.

T12

T13

T14

1891   **Lithographed by A. C. Goodwin**   *Perf. 12*

8T1	T12	25c yellow	22.50	—
		Pane of 4	95.00	
8T2	T13	25c green	22.50	10.00
		Pane of 4	95.00	
a.		Horiz. pair, imperf. vert.	60.00	
8T3	T14	lilac rose	55.00	

Mutual Union Telegraph Company

Incorporated October 4, 1880. Extended over 22 states. Absorbed about 1883 by the Western Union Telegraph Co. Franks issued for use of stockholders, in books, four to a pane.

T15

Engr. by Van Campen Engraving Co., New Yor[k]

1882-83   *Perf.*

9T1	T15	blue	45.00	20
		Pane of 4	200.00	
a.		Vert. pair, imperf. horizontal	110.00	
b.		Imperf., pair	120.00	
9T2	T15	carmine	45.00	
		Pane of 4	200.00	

North American Telegraph Company

Incorporated October 15, 1885 to run from Chicago to Min[ne]apolis, later being extended into North and South Dako[ta]. Absorbed in 1929 by the Postal System.

Apparently these stamps were not canceled when used. Issued in panes of four.

T15a

1899-1907   *Perf.*

10T1	T15a	violet (1899)	225.00
		Pane of 4	950.00
10T2	T15a	green (1901)	225.00
10T3	T15a	dark brown (1902)	400.00
10T4	T15a	blue (1903)	400.00
10T5	T15a	violet (1904)	160.00
		Pane of 4	725.00
a.		Horiz. pair, imperf. vertically	375.00
10T6	T15a	red brown (1905)	240.00
10T7	T15a	rose (1906)	275.00
10T8	T15a	green (1907)	1,600.

Nos. 10T1 to 10T8 are known imperforate.

Northern Mutual Telegraph Company

Incorporated in New York State as the Northern Mutual Te[le]graph and Telephone Company on June 20, 1882. Its lin[e] which consisted of a single wire, extended from Syracuse [to] Ogdensburg via Oswego, Watertown and Clayton, a distance [of] 170 miles. It was sold to the Bankers and Merchants Telegra[ph] Company in 1883. Stamps were in use for a few days only [in] April, 1883. Issued in panes of 35 having a face value of $[ ]. Seven horizontal rows of five covering all denominations [as] follows: 2 rows of 25c, 1 of 20c, 2 of 10c, 2 of 5c. **The remain[n]ders and plates were purchased by a New York dealer [in] 1887.**

T16

1883   *Perf. 1[2]*

11T1	T16	5c yellow brown	6.50
		Block of 4	30.00
11T2	T16	10c yellow brown	8.50
		Block of 4	37.50
11T3	T16	20c yellow brown	20.00
		Horizontal pair	45.00
11T4	T16	25c yellow brown	5.50
		Block of 4	30.00
		Pane of 35	375.00

The first reprints are lighter in color than the originals, perf. 1[2] and the gum is yellowish instead of white. The pane makeu[p] differs in the reprints. The second reprints are darker than th[e] original, perf. 12. Value $1 each.

Northern New York Telegraph Company

rganized about 1892. Extended from Malone, N.Y. to Mas-
a, N.Y. Re-incorporated as the New York Union Telegraph
on April 2, 1896.

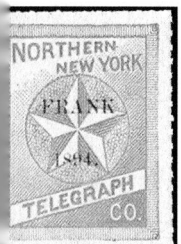

T16a

Typo. by Charles H. Smith, Brushton, N.Y.

4-95 *Rouletted*

1	T16a	**green** (overprinted in red "Frank 1894")	45.
		Pane of 6	290.
a.		Imperf., pair	50.
2	T16a	**red** (overprinted in black "Frank 1895")	160.
		Pane of 6	1,500.
a.		Imperf., pair	50.
3	T16a	1c **yellow** (overprinted in black "One")	80.
		Pane of 6	525.
a.		Imperf., pair	50.
4	T16a	10c **blue** (overprinted in red "10")	150.
		Pane of 6	950.
a.		Imperf., pair	50.

Some specialists believe that Nos. 12T1-12T4 were not
ued and probably are essays. However, one Northern New
k stamp is recorded tied to a piece of a telegraph form by a
ch cancel.

Pacific Mutual Telegraph Company

ncorporated in Missouri on June 21, 1883. Operated
ween St. Louis and Kansas City, Mo., during the years 1884
d 1885. It had 15 offices, 425 miles of poles and 850 miles of
e. The controlling interests were held by the Bankers and
rchants Telegraph Company. The name was changed on
t. 10, 1910 to Postal Telegraph-Cable Company of Missouri.
mps were issued in booklets having a face value of $10 and
taining 131 stamps as follows: 50-1c, 20-5c, 45-10c, 16-25c.
ey are not known used.

T17

83 *Perf. 12*

1	T17	1c **black**	22.50
2	T17	1c **slate**	.35
		Block of 4	1.50
a.		1c gray	.35
		Block of 4	1.50
3	T17	5c **black,** *buff*	1.00
		Block of 4	4.50
4	T17	10c **black,** *green*	.35
		Block of 4	1.75
a.		Horiz. pair, imperf. between	—
5	T17	25c **black,** *salmon buff*	1.00
		Block of 4	4.50

Pacific Postal Telegraph-Cable Company

The Pacific Postal Telegraph-Cable Company was the Pacific
ast Department of the Postal Telegraph-Cable Company,
d was organized in 1886. Its first wire ran from San Francisco
New Westminster, B.C., where it touched the lines of the
nadian Pacific Railway Company, then the only connection
tween the Eastern and Western Postal systems. Later the
stal's own wires spanned the continent and the two compa-
es were united.
Stamps issued in booklet form in vertical panes of five.

T17a

Perf. 12 Horiz.

14T1	T17a	10c **brown**	75.00	60.00
		Pane of 5	400.00	
14T2	T17a	15c **black**	80.00	55.00
		Pane of 5	425.00	
14T3	T17a	25c **rose red**	80.00	55.00
		Pane of 5	425.00	
14T4	T17a	40c **green**	75.00	65.00
		Pane of 5	400.00	
14T5	T17a	50c **blue**	65.00	60.00
		Pane of 5	350.00	

These stamps were issued with three sizes of frank numbers;
large closely spaced, small closely spaced and small widely
spaced figures. They also exist without frank numbers.

Postal Telegraph Company

Organized in New York in 1881. Reorganized in 1891 as the
Postal Telegraph-Cable Co. The Postal Telegraph Co stamps of
1885 were issued in sheets of 100. **Some years after the
reorganization a New York dealer purchased the remainders which were canceled with a purple star.** The Postal
Telegraph-Cable Co. issued frank stamps in booklets, usually
four stamps to a pane. This company was merged with the
Western Union Telegraph Company in 1943.

T18

T19

T20

T21

Engraved by Hamilton Bank Note Co.

1885 *Perf. 14*

15T1	T18	10c **green**	3.50	—
		Remainders		.25
		Block of 4	15.00	
		Remainders		1.25
a.		Horiz. pair, imperf. btwn., remainders		20.00
b.		10c **deep green**	3.50	—
		Remainders		.25
		Block of 4	15.00	
		Remainders		1.25
15T2	T19	15c **orange red**	3.50	—
		Remainders		.60
		Block of 4	15.00	
		Remainders		3.00
a.		Horizontal pair, imperf. between	37.50	
15T3	T20	25c **blue**	2.00	5.00
		Remainders		.20
		Block of 4	9.00	
		Remainders		.75
a.		Horizontal pair, imperf. between	37.50	
15T4	T21	50c **brown**	1.75	—
		Remainders		.60
		Block of 4	8.00	
		Remainders		3.00

The 25c in ultramarine and the 50c in black were printed and
perforated 16 but are not known to have been issued. Value
about $7.50 each.

T22

T22a

Typographed by Moss Engraving Co.

1892-1920 *Perf. 14*

Signature of A.B. Chandler

15T5	T22	**blue gray** (1892)	35.00
a.		Imperf., pair	85.00

Perf. 13 to 14½ and Compound

15T6	T22	**gray lilac** (1892)	40.00	
15T7	T22	**red** (1893)	17.50	10.00
		Pane of 4	75.00	
15T8	T22	**red brown** (1893)	6.00	4.00

Perf. 12

15T9	T22	**violet brown** (1894)	6.75
15T10	T22	**gray green** (1894)	4.50
a.		Imperf., pair	10.00
15T11	T22	**blue** (1895)	35.00
15T12	T22	**rose** (1895)	275.00

Nos. 15T11 and 15T12 are from a new die resembling T22
but without shading under "Postal Telegraph Co."

15T13	T22a	**slate green** (1896)	5.50
		Pane of 4	25.00
15T14	T22a	**brown** (1896)	225.00

Signature of Albert B. Chandler

15T15	T22a	**lilac brown** (1897)	1.50	10.00
		Pane of 4	6.50	
15T16	T22a	**orange** (1897)	175.00	

Typographed by Knapp & Co.

15T17	T22a	**pale blue** (1898)	2.25
		Pane of 4	10.00
15T18	T22a	**rose** (1898)	210.00

Typographed by Moss Engraving Co.

Perf. 12

15T19	T22a	**orange brown** (1899)	1.75
		Pane of 4	8.25

Perf. 11

15T20	T22a	**blue** (1900)	3.00	3.00
a.		"I" of "Complimentary" omitted	.75	1.00
		Pane of 4	3.25	

The variety 15T20a represents a different die with many variations in the design.

Perf. 14

15T21	T22a	**sea green** (1901)	.60	.60
		Pane of 4	2.50	
a.		Horiz. pair, imperf. between	—	

Signature of John W. Mackay

15T22	T22a	**chocolate** (1902)	1.25	.65
		Pane of 4	5.50	
a.		Horiz. pair, imperf. vert.	—	

Signature of Clarence H. Mackay

15T23	T22a	**blue** (1903)	2.75	2.50
		Pane of 4	12.50	

Perf. 12

15T24	T22a	**blue,** *blue* (1904)	4.00	3.00
		Pane of 4	17.50	
15T25	T22a	**blue,** *yellow* (1905)	5.00	
		Pane of 4	22.50	
15T26	T22a	**blue,** *light blue* (1906)	5.00	5.00
		Pane of 4	22.50	
a.		Horiz. pair, imperf. vert.	—	

T22b

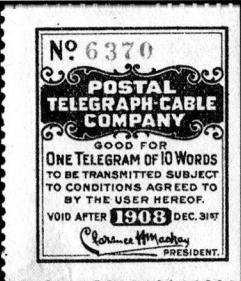

T22c

Perf. 12

15T27	T22b	**black,** *yellow* (laid paper) (1907)	60.00	
		Pane of 4	250.00	
15T28	T22b	**blue,** *pink* (laid paper) (1907)	35.00	
		Pane of 4	150.00	

"One Telegram of 10 Words"

15T29	T22c	**blue** (1908)	55.00	
		Pane of 4	240.00	
15T30	T22c	**yellow** (1908)	225.00	
		Pane of 4	950.00	
15T31	T22c	**black** (1908)	45.00	
		Pane of 4	200.00	
15T32	T22c	**brown** (1909)	35.00	
		Pane of 4	150.00	
a.		Date reads "1908"	*2,000.*	
15T33	T22c	**olive green** (1909)	20.00	
		Pane of 4	90.00	
15T34	T22c	**dark blue** (1910)	30.00	
15T35	T22c	**dark brown** (1910)	30.00	
		Pane of 4	130.00	
15T36	T22c	**violet** (1911)	300.00	
15T37	T22c	**blue** (1912)	575.00	
15T38	T22c	**violet** (1913)	700.00	

Perf. 14

15T39	T22c	**violet** (not dated) (1914)	200.00	
a.		Red violet	175.00	
		Pane of 4	850.00	

"One Telegram"
Perf. 12

15T40	T22c	**blue** (1908)	50.00	
		Pane of 4	220.00	
a.		Horiz. pair, imperf. between	350.00	
15T41	T22c	**lilac** (1909)	20.00	
		Pane of 4	87.50	
15T42	T22c	**black,** *yellow* (laid paper) (1910)	600.00	
a.		Date reads "1909"	—	
15T43	T22c	**violet** (1910)	15.00	
a.		Red violet	15.00	
		Pane of 4		
		Pane of 8	140.00	
15T44	T22c	**dark blue** (1911)	50.00	
		Pane of 4	220.00	
a.		Vert. pair, imperf between	400.00	
15T45	T22c	**light violet** (1912)	32.50	
		Pane of 4	150.00	

Perf. 14

15T46	T22c	**dark blue** (1913)	140.00	
		Pane of 8	1,150.	
a.		Imperf. vertically, pair	225.00	
b.		Perf. 12	75.00	
		Pane of 4	300.00	
15T47	T22c	**dark blue** (not dated) (1914)	.25	
		Pane of 4	2.50	
		Pane of 8	5.00	

In panes of four the stamps are 4½mm apart horizontally, panes of eight 5½mm. There are two types of design T22c, one with and one without spurs on colored curved lines above "O" of "Postal" and below "M" of "Company". No. 15T47 comes in both types.

Nos. 15T39 and 15T47 handstamped with date in double line numerals, all four numerals complete on each stamp.

15T47A	T22c	**violet** (1916)	2,750.	
15T48	T22c	**dark blue** (1917)	1,500.	
15T49	T22c	**dark blue** (1918)	2,000.	
15T49A	T22c	**dark blue** (1919)	90.00	
		Pane of 8	800.00	
15T49B	T22c	**dark blue** (1920)	70.00	
		Pane of 8	650.00	

No. 15T49B is handstamped "1920" in small single line numerals.

T22d

T22e

1907				**Perf. 12**	
15T50	T22d	1c	**dark brown**	30.00	20.00
			Pane of 4	125.00	
15T51	T22d	2c	**dull violet**	25.00	20.00
			Pane of 4	110.00	
15T52	T22d	5c	**green**	30.00	22.50
			Pane of 4	125.00	
15T53	T22d	25c	**light red**	32.50	20.00
			Pane of 4	140.00	

1931				**Perf. 14**	
15T54	T22e	25c	**gray blue** (1931)	.25	
			Pane of 6	2.00	

1932

No. 15T54 overprinted "1932" and control number in red

15T55	T22e	25c	**gray blue**	75.00	
			Pane of 6	500.00	

Many varieties between Nos. 15T5 and 15T55 are known without frank numbers.

OFFICIAL

1900-14		Inscribed "Supts."	**Perf. 11, 12**	
15TO1	T22c	**black,** *magenta*	2.00	2.00

For Use of Railroad Superintendents
Perf. 12
"C. G. W." (Chicago, Great Western Railroad) at top

15TO2	T22c	**carmine** (1908)	45.00	
		Pane of 4	200.00	
15TO3	T22c	**carmine** (1909)	175.00	
15TO4	T22c	**carmine** (1910)	140.00	
15TO5	T22c	**carmine** (1911)	115.00	
15TO6	T22c	**carmine** (1912)	125.00	

Perf. 14

15TO7	T22c	**carmine** (1913)	180.00	
a.		Perf. 12	—	
15TO8	T22c	**dull red** (not dated) (1914)	.50	
		Pane of 8	5.00	

Perf. 12
"E. P." (El Paso and Northeastern Railroad) at top

15TO9	T22c	**orange** (1908)	200.00	

"I. C." (Illinois Central Railroad) at top

15TO10	T22c	**green** (1908)	55.00	
		Pane of 4	250.00	
15TO11	T22c	**yellow green** (1909)	15.00	
		Pane of 4	—	
		Pane of 8	130.00	
15TO12	T22c	**dark green** (1910)	140.00	
15TO13	T22c	**dark green** (1911)	85.00	
		Pane of 4	375.00	
		Pane of 8	725.00	
15TO14	T22c	**dark green** (1912)	1,000.	
15TO15	T22c	**dark green** (1913)	1,000.	

Perf. 14

15TO16	T22c	**dark green** (not dated) (1914)	2.50	
		Pane of 4	11.00	
		Pane of 8	22.50	
a.		Green (spurs)	1.25	
		Pane of 4	7.50	
b.		Line under "PRESIDENT" (no spurs)	1.00	
		Pane of 8	12.50	

(See note after No. 15T47.)
Both types of design T22c are known of 15TO16.

Perf. 12
"O. D." (Old Dominion Steamship Co.) at top

15TO17	T22c	**violet** (1908)	1,800.	

"P. R." (Pennsylvania Railroad) at top

15TO18	T22c	**orange brown** (1908)	30.00	
		Pane of 4	130.00	
		Pane of 8	260.00	
15TO19	T22c	**orange brown** (1909)	35.00	
		Pane of 4	150.00	
		Pane of 8	325.00	
15TO20	T22c	**orange brown** (1910)	35.00	
		Pane of 4	150.00	
		Pane of 8	325.00	
15TO21	T22c	**orange brown** (1911)	125.00	
15TO22	T22c	**orange brown** (1912)	75.00	
		Pane of 4	*500.00*	

Perf. 14

15TO23	T22c	**orange brown** (1913)	35.00	
		Pane of 8	300.00	
a.		Perf. 12	125.00	

"P. R. R." (Pennsylvania Rail Road) at top

15TO24	T22c	**orange** (not dated) (1914)	25.00	
		Pane of 4	115.00	
		Pane of 8	225.00	

Perf. 12
"S. W." (El Paso Southwestern Railroad) at top

15TO25	T22c	**yellow** (1909)	275.00	
15TO26	T22c	**yellow** (1910)	1,100.	
15TO27	T22c	**yellow** (1911)	350.00	
15TO28	T22c	**yellow** (1912)	350.00	
		Pane of 4	1,500.	

Nos. 15TO1-15TO17 and 15TO25-15TO28 are without fr_ numbers.

TO1

1942			**Litho.**	**Unwn**	
15TO29	TO1	5c	**pink**	6.50	3
			Pane of 8	55.00	
15TO30	TO1	25c	**pale blue**	7.75	4
			Pane of 8	65.00	

The stamps were issued in booklets to all Postal Telegra_ employees in the Armed Forces for use in the United Stat_ They were discontinued Oct. 8, 1943. Used copies norm_ bear manuscript cancellations.

Western Union Telegraph Company

Organized by consolidation in 1856. Now extends through_ the United States. Frank stamps have been issued regul_ since 1871 in booklet form. The large size, early issues, were_ panes of four, 1871-1913; the medium size, later issues, w_ in panes of six, 1914-32; and the recent small size issues ar_ panes of nine, 1933 to 1946.

T23

T24

Engraved by the National Bank Note Co.

1871-94				**Perf.**	
		Signature of William Orton			
16T1	T23	**green** (not dated) (1871)	32.50	22.
16T2	T23	**red** (not dated) (1872)	35.00	20.
		Pane of 4	160.00	
16T3	T23	**blue** (not dated) (1873)	37.50	22.
		Pane of 4	170.00	
16T4	T23	**brown** (not dated) (1874)	30.00	22.
		Pane of 4	135.00	
16T5	T24	**deep green** (1875)	32.50	21.
16T6	T24	**red** (1876)	35.00	
		Pane of 4	160.00	
16T7	T24	**violet** (1877)	37.50	28.
16T8	T24	**gray brown** (1878)	35.00	
		Signature of Norvin Green			
16T9	T24	**blue** (1879)	35.00	28.
		Pane of 4	160.00	

Engraved by the American Bank Note Co.

16T10	T24	**lilac rose** (1880)	25.00	
		Pane of 4	110.00	
16T11	T24	**green** (1881)	22.50	
		Pane of 4	97.50	

12	T24	blue (1882)		12.50	
		Pane of 4		57.50	
13	T24	yellow brown (1883)		25.00	
		Pane of 4		110.00	
14	T24	gray violet (1884)		.60	.30
		Pane of 4		3.00	
15	T24	green (1885)		3.25	1.75
		Pane of 4		15.00	
16	T24	brown violet (1886)		3.25	2.00
		Pane of 4		15.00	
17	T24	red brown (1887)		4.50	
		Pane of 4		22.50	
18	T24	blue (1888)		3.25	
		Pane of 4		15.00	
19	T24	olive green (1889)		1.75	.80
		Pane of 4		8.00	
20	T24	purple (1890)		.75	.40
		Pane of 4		3.25	
21	T24	brown (1891)		1.50	
		Pane of 4		6.50	
22	T24	vermilion (1892)		1.75	
		Pane of 4		8.00	
23	T24	blue (1893)		1.40	.40
		Pane of 4		6.25	

Signature of Thos. T. Eckert

24	T24	green (1894)	.60	.40
		Pane of 4	3.00	

T25

Engraved by the International Bank Note Co.
95-1913 *Perf. 14*

Signature of Thos. T. Eckert

25	T25	dark brown (1895)	.50	.40
		Pane of 4	2.50	
26	T25	violet (1896)	.50	.40
		Pane of 4	2.50	
27	T25	rose red (1897)	.50	.40
		Pane of 4	2.50	
28	T25	yellow green (1898)	.50	.40
		Pane of 4	2.50	
a.		Vertical pair, imperf. between	—	
29	T25	olive green (1899)	.50	.40
		Pane of 4	2.25	
30	T25	red violet, perf. 13 (1900)	.50	.45
		Pane of 4	3.00	
31	T25	brown, perf. 13 (1901)	.50	.40
		Pane of 4	2.50	
32	T25	blue (1902)	8.00	
		Pane of 4	40.00	

Signature of R.C. Clowry

33	T25	blue (1902)	8.00	
		Pane of 4	40.00	
34	T25	green (1903)	.60	.40
		Pane of 4	4.00	
35	T25	red violet (1904)	.60	
		Pane of 4	2.75	
36	T25	carmine rose (1905)	.60	.50
		Pane of 4	2.75	
37	T25	blue (1906)	.80	.40
		Pane of 4	4.00	
a.		Vertical pair, imperf. between	200.00	
38	T25	orange brown (1907)	1.75	.90
		Pane of 4	10.00	
39	T25	violet (1908)	2.00	1.00
		Pane of 4	9.00	
40	T25	olive green (1909)	2.00	
		Pane of 4	10.00	

Perf. 12

41	T25	buff (1910)	.75	.50
		Pane of 4	3.25	

Engraved by the American Bank Note Co.

Signature of Theo. N. Vail

42	T24	green (1911)	14.00	
		Pane of 4	65.00	
43	T24	violet (1912)	9.00	
		Pane of 4	42.50	

Imprint of Kihn Brothers Bank Note Company
Perf. 14

44	T24	brown (1913)	10.00	
		Pane of 4	50.00	
a.		Vert. pair, imperf. between	35.00	
b.		Horiz. pair, imperf. between	40.00	

T26 · · · T27

Engraved by the E.A. Wright Bank Note Co.
1914-15 Signature of Theo. N. Vail *Perf. 12*

16T45	T26	5c brown (1914)	1.10	
		Pane of 6	8.00	
a.		Vert. pair, imperf. between	—	
b.		Horiz. pair, imperf. between	—	
16T46	T26	25c slate (1914)	7.00	5.00
		Pane of 6	45.00	

Signature of Newcomb Carlton

16T47	T26	5c orange (1915)	1.50	
		Pane of 6	10.00	
		orange yellow	5.00	
16T48	T26	25c olive green (1915)	4.00	
		Pane of 6	30.00	
a.		Vert. pair, imperf. horizontally	45.00	

Engraved by the American Bank Note Co.
1916-32

16T49	T27	5c light blue (1916)	1.50	
		Pane of 6	11.00	
16T50	T27	25c carmine lake (1916)	1.75	
		Pane of 6	11.00	

Engraved by the Security Bank Note Co.
Perf. 11

16T51	T27	5c yellow brown (1917)	1.00	
		Pane of 6	7.50	
16T52	T27	25c deep green (1917)	3.00	
		Pane of 6	20.00	
16T53	T27	5c olive green (1918)	.60	
		Pane of 6	4.50	
16T54	T27	25c dark violet (1918)	1.75	
		Pane of 6	14.00	
16T55	T27	5c brown (1919)	1.25	
		Pane of 6	9.00	
16T56	T27	25c blue (1919)	3.25	
		Pane of 6	22.50	

Engraved by the E.A. Wright Bank Note Co.
Perf. 12

16T57	T27	5c dark green (1920)	.65	
		Pane of 6	4.25	
a.		Vert. pair, imperf. between	300.00	
16T58	T27	25c olive green (1920)	.75	
		Pane of 6	5.00	

Engraved by the Security Bank Note Co.

16T59	T27	5c carmine rose (1921)	.55	
		Pane of 6	4.25	
16T60	T27	25c deep blue (1921)	1.30	
		Pane of 6	8.50	
16T61	T27	5c yellow brown (1922)	.55	
		Pane of 6	3.75	
a.		Horizontal pair, imperf. between	16.00	
16T62	T27	25c claret (1922)	1.65	
		Pane of 6	11.50	
16T63	T27	5c olive green (1923)	.65	
		Pane of 6	4.25	
16T64	T27	25c dull violet (1923)	1.35	
		Pane of 6	9.00	
16T65	T27	5c brown (1924)	1.75	
		Pane of 6	12.00	
16T66	T27	25c ultramarine (1924)	4.00	
		Pane of 6	30.00	
16T67	T27	5c olive green (1925)	.65	
		Pane of 6	4.25	
16T68	T27	25c carmine rose (1925)	1.10	
		Pane of 6	7.00	
16T69	T27	5c blue (1926)	1.00	
		Pane of 6	6.50	
16T70	T27	25c light brown (1926)	2.25	
		Pane of 6	14.00	
16T71	T27	5c carmine (1927)	.85	
		Pane of 6	5.75	
16T72	T27	25c green (1927)	7.25	
		Pane of 6	47.50	

Engraved by the E. A. Wright Bank Note Co.
Without Imprint

16T73	T27	5c yellow brown (1928)	.75	
		Pane of 6	4.50	
16T74	T27	25c dark blue (1928)	1.00	
		Pane of 6	6.25	

Engraved by the Security Bank Note Co.
Without Imprint

16T75	T27	5c dark green (1929)	.30	.25
		Pane of 6	2.00	
16T76	T27	25c red violet (1929)	.85	.50
		Pane of 6	5.50	
16T77	T27	5c olive green (1930)	.25	.20
		Pane of 6	1.75	
16T78	T27	25c carmine (1930)	.25	.25
		Pane of 6	2.00	
a.		Horiz. pair, imperf. vertically	35.00	

16T79	T27	5c brown (1931)	.20	.20
		Pane of 6	1.25	
16T80	T27	25c blue (1931)	.20	.20
		Pane of 6	1.50	
16T81	T27	5c green (1932)	.20	.20
		Pane of 6	1.50	
16T82	T27	25c rose carmine (1932)	.20	.20
		Pane of 6	1.50	

T28

1933-40
Lithographed by Oberly & Newell Co.
Without Imprint
Perf. 14x12½

16T83	T28	5c pale brown (1933)	.25	
		Pane of 9	3.25	
16T84	T28	25c green (1933)	.25	
		Pane of 9	3.25	

Lithographed by Security Bank Note Co.
Without Imprint
Perf. 12, 12½

Signature of R. B. White

16T85	T28	5c lake (1934)	.20	
		Pane of 9	2.00	
16T86	T28	25c dark blue (1934)	.20	
		Pane of 9	2.50	
16T87	T28	5c yellow brown (1935)	.20	
		Pane of 9	2.00	
16T88	T28	25c lake (1935)	.20	
		Pane of 9	2.00	
16T89	T28	5c blue (1936)	.25	.20
		Pane of 9	2.75	
16T90	T28	25c apple green (1936)	.20	.20
		Pane of 9	2.50	
16T91	T28	5c bister brown (1937)	.20	
		Pane of 9	2.50	
16T92	T28	25c carmine rose (1937)	.20	
		Pane of 9	2.00	
16T93	T28	5c green (1938)	.25	.20
		Pane of 9	3.00	
16T94	T28	25c blue (1938)	.30	.20
		Pane of 9	3.50	
16T95	T28	5c dull vermilion (1939)	1.00	
		Pane of 9	11.50	
a.		Horiz. pair, imperf. between	—	
16T96	T28	25c bright violet (1939)	.50	
		Pane of 9	6.00	
16T97	T28	5c light blue (1940)	.55	
		Pane of 9	5.75	
16T98	T28	25c bright green (1940)	.50	
		Pane of 9	5.50	

Samuel F. B. Morse
T29

Plates of 90 stamps.
Stamp designed by Nathaniel Yontiff.
Unlike the frank stamps, Nos. 16T99 to 16T103 were sold to the public in booklet form for use in prepayment of telegraph services.

Engraved by Security Bank Note Co. of Philadelphia
1940 Unwmk. *Perf. 12, 12½x12, 12x12½*

16T99	T29	1c yellow green	1.25	
		Pane of 5	6.50	
a.		Imperf., pair	50.00	
16T100	T29	2c chestnut	1.75	1.00
		Pane of 5	15.00	
a.		Imperf., pair	50.00	
16T101	T29	5c deep blue	3.00	
		Pane of 5	18.00	
a.		Vert. pair, imperf. btwn.	65.00	
b.		Imperf., pair	50.00	
16T102	T29	10c orange	5.00	
		Pane of 5	27.50	
a.		Imperf., pair	50.00	
16T103	T29	25c bright carmine	4.00	
		Pane of 5	24.00	
a.		Imperf., pair	50.00	

Type of 1933-40
1941 Litho. *Perf. 12½*
Without Imprint
Signature of R.B. White

16T104	T28	5c dull rose lilac	.25	
		Pane of 9	2.50	
16T105	T28	25c vermilion	.60	
		Pane of 9	6.00	

1942   Signature of A.N. Williams
16T106	T28	5c	brown	.30
			Pane of 9	3.50
16T107	T28	25c	ultramarine	.30
			Pane of 9	3.50

1943
16T108	T28	5c	salmon	.30
			Pane of 9	3.50
16T109	T28	25c	red violet	.30
			Pane of 9	3.50

1944
16T110	T28	5c	light green	.65
			Pane of 9	7.25
16T111	T28	25c	buff	.35
			Pane of 9	3.75

1945
16T112	T28	5c	light blue	.40
			Pane of 9	5.00
a.			Pair, imperf. between	—
16T113	T28	25c	light green	.35
			Pane of 9	3.75

1946
16T114	T28	5c	light bister brown	1.25
			Pane of 9	15.00
16T115	T28	25c	rose pink	1.00
			Pane of 9	12.00

Many of the stamps between 16T1 and 16T98 and 16T104 to 16T115 are known without frank numbers. Several of them are also known with more than one color used in the frank number and with handstamped and manuscript numbers. The numbers are also found in combination with various letters: O, A, B, C, D, etc.

Western Union discontinued the use of Telegraph stamps with the 1946 issue.

United States
Telegraph-Cable-Radio Carriers

Booklets issued to accredited representatives to the World Telecommunications Conferences, Atlantic City, New Jersey, 1947. Valid for messages to points outside the United States. Issued by All America Cables & Radio, Inc., The Commercial Cable Company, Globe Wireless, Limited, Mackay Radio and Telegraph Company, Inc., R C A Communications, Inc., Tropical Radio Telegraph Company and The Western Union Telegraph Company.

 TX1

1947		Litho.	Unwmk.	Perf. 12½
17T1	TX1	5c	olive bister	7.00
			Pane of 9	70.00
			Pane of 9, 8 5c + 1 10c	700.00
17T2	TX1	10c	olive bister	750.00
17T3	TX1	50c	olive bister	9.00
			Pane of 9	90.00

UNLISTED ISSUES

Several telegraph or wireless companies other than those listed above have issued stamps or franks, but as evidence of actual use is lacking, they are not listed. Among these are:
American District Telegraph Co.
American Telegraph Typewriter Co.
Continental Telegraph Co.
Los Angeles and San Gabriel Valley Railroad
Marconi Wireless Telegraph Co.
Mercantile Telegraph Co.
Telepost Co.
Tropical Radio Telegraph Co.
United Fruit Co. Wireless Service.
United Wireless Telegraph Co.

ESSAYS

An essay is a proposed design that differs in some way from the issued stamp.

During approximately 1845-1890, when private banknote engravers competed for contracts to print U.S. postage stamps, essays were produced primarily as examples of the quality of the firms' work and as suggestions as to what their finished product would look like. In most cases, dies were prepared, often with stock vignettes used in making banknotes. These dies were used to print essays for the Post Office Department. Rarely did the competitors go so far as to have essay plates made.

From 1894 onward, virtually all stamps were engraved and printed by the Bureau of Engraving and Printing (BEP). This usually required two types of essays. The first was a model design which was approved — or disapproved — by the Postmaster General. Sometimes preliminary drawings were made by the BEP designers, often in an enlarged size, subsequently photographically reduced to stamp size. An accepted stamp design usually became the engraver's model.

Occasionally during the course of engraving the die, a "progressive proof" was pulled to check the progress of the engraver's work. Because these were produced from an incompletely engraved die, they differ from the final design and are listed here as essays.

During approximately 1867-1870, various experiments were conducted to prevent the reuse of postage stamps. These included experimental grill types, safety papers, water-sensitive papers and inks, coupon essays, and others. These also differed in some way from issued stamps, even if the design was identical. A preliminary listing has been made here.

Because the essays in all their various colors have not been examined by the editors, traditional color names have been retained. Some color names have been taken from *Color Standards and Color Nomenclature,* by Robert Ridgway.

Only essays in private hands have been listed. Others exist but are not available to collectors. Some essays were produced after the respective stamps were issued. Year dates are given where information is available.

Essay papers and cards are white, unless described otherwise.

Values are for full-size essays, where they are known. Measurements are given where such information is available. Essays are valued in the grade of very fine, where such exist. Cut-down or faulty examples sell for less, often much less. A number of essays are unique or are reported in very limited quantities. Such items are valued in the conditions in which they exist.

The listings are by manufacturer. Basic stamps may appear in two or more places.

This listing is not complete. Other designs, papers and colors exist. The editors would appreciate reports of unlisted items, as well as photos of items listed herein without illustrations.

POSTMASTERS' PROVISIONALS

NON-CONTIGUOUS LISTINGS
Because many listings are grouped by manufacturer, some catalogue numbers are separated.

No. 5-E1 to 5-E2	follow 11-E16
No. 11-E17 to 72-E5	follow 5-E2
No. 65-E5 to 72-E8	follow 72-E5
No. 63-E13 to 113-E2	follow 72-E8
No. 112-E2 to 129-E2	follow 113-E2
No. 120-E1 to 122-E5	follow 129-E2
No. 115-E3a to 129-E6	follow 122-E5
No. 115-E11 to 116-E8	follow 129-E6
No. 115-E17 to 148-E1	follow 116-E8
No. 145-E2 to 179-E2	follow 148-E1
No. 156-E2 to 191-E2	follow 179-E3
No. 184-E8	follows 191-E2
No. 182-E4 to 190-E3	follow 184-E8
No. 184-E17 to 293-E11	follow 190-E3
No. 285-E10 to 856-E2	follow 293-E11

Albany, N.Y.
Gavit & Co.

1Xa-E1

Design size: 23½x25½mm
Die size: 58x48mm

Benjamin Franklin. With crosshatching about 2mm outside border (usually cut off).

1847
Xa-E1   5c
  a. Die on India die sunk on large card,
    printed through a mat to eliminate cross-
    hatching

brownish black	600.
scarlet	600.
red brown	600.
blue	600.
green	600.

  b. Die on India; some mounted on small card

bluish black	325.
scarlet	325.
brown	325.
yellow green	325.
gray blue	325.

  c. Die on India cut close

black	250.
blue	250.
red brown	250.
scarlet	250.
green	250.
yellow green	250.
brown violet	250.
rose red	250.

  d. Die on bond (1858)

bluish black	375.
scarlet	375.
brown	375.
blue	375.
blue green	375.
violet	375.

  e. Die on white glazed paper (1905)

black	900.
dark brown	900.
scarlet	900.
blue	900.

New York, N.Y.
Rawdon, Wright & Hatch

9X1-E1

Design 22mm wide
Die size: 50x102mm

Vignette of Washington. Two transfers laid down vertically on the die 22mm apart; top one retouched, with frame around it (this is a proof). Values are for combined transfers. Vignette essay exists cut apart from proof, value $200 each.

1845
9X1-E1   5c
  a. Die on India (1879)

black	450.
violet black	450.
gray black	450.
scarlet	450.
dull scarlet	450.
orange	450.
brown	450.
dull brown	450.
green	450.
dull green	450.
ultramarine	450.
dull blue	450.
red violet	450.

  b. Die on white bond (1879)

gray black	550.
dull scarlet	550.
dull brown	550.
dull green	550.
dull blue	550.

  c. Die on white glazed paper, die sunk (1879)

gray black	700.

POSTAGE STAMPS

1847 ISSUE
Rawdon, Wright, Hatch & Edson

The original model for No. 1 exists, engraved vignette of Franklin mounted on frame, part of frame engraved, rest in pencil, ink and a gray wash. Formerly

No. 1-E1, now in the National Postal Museum collection.

  Engraved vignette only, matted.
1-E2   5c Die on India (1895), brown   *2,500.*

1-E3

Engraved frame only, matted from complete die.

1-E3 5c Die on India (1895), brown   2,500.

The 1895 dates are suppositional.

The original model for No. 2 exists, engraved vignette of Washington mounted (replaced) on frame, "POST OFFICE" and "FIVE CENTS" engraved on former No. 1-E1, "U" and "S" at top and "X" in bottom corners in black ink, rest in pencil and a gray wash. Formerly No. 2-E1, now in the National Postal Museum collection.

2-E2

2-E3

Engraved vignette only.

2-E2 10c Die on India (1895)
black	2,500.
brownish black	2,500.
brown	2,500.

Engraved frame only.

2-E3 10c Die on India (1895)
black	2,500.
brown orange	2,500.

The 1895 dates are in suppositional.

1851 ISSUE
Attributed to
Rawdon, Wright, Hatch & Edson

11-E1

11-E2

Design size: 18½x23mm
Large 3 in vignette.

11-E1 3c Die on India
black	3,000.
blue	10,000.

Design size: 19x24mm
Vignette of Washington.

11-E2 3c
a. Die on India
black	4,500.

b. Die on proof paper, die sunk on 40x51mm card
black	4,500.

Attributed to
Gavit & Co.

11-E3   11-E4

Design size: 19x23mm

Vignette of Franklin. Three states of die. Second state has double line dash above P of POSTAGE, third state has single dash above P and dot in O of POSTAGE.

11-E3 3c
a. Die on India, die sunk on card
warm black	750.
scarlet	750.
red brown	750.
blue green	750.

b. Die on India, 41x43mm or smaller
black	300.
greenish black	300.
carmine	300.
scarlet	300.
yellow green	300.
brown	300.
blue green	300.
dull blue	300.
dark blue	300.

c. Die on India, cut to shape
warm black	225.
cool black	225.
black	225.
carmine	225.
orange	225.
brown	225.
dark green	225.
yellow green	225.
olive	225.
light blue	225.
dark blue	225.
violet	225.
scarlet	225.

d. Die on bond
cool black	225.
scarlet	225.
orange brown	225.
brown	225.
green	225.
blue	225.

e. Die on white glazed paper
black	750.
dark brown	750.
scarlet	750.
blue	750.

f. Die on thin card, dusky blue, cut to shape   200.
g. Die on Francis Patent experimental paper with trial cancel
black	1,250.
dark blue	1,250.
brown	1,250.

Design size: 19x22mm
Die size: 47x75mm
Vignette of Washington. Two states of die. Second state has small diagonal dash in top of left vertical border below arch.

11-E4 3c
a. Die on India, die sunk on card
black	750.
scarlet	750.
brown red	750.
blue green	750.

b. Die on India, about 30x40mm or smaller
orange	400.
orange brown	400.
brown	400.
dusky yellow brown	400.
yellow green	400.
blue green	400.
dull blue	400.
red violet	400.
deep red orange	400.
black	400.

c. Die on bond (1858)
black	400.
scarlet	400.
brown	400.
green	400.
blue	400.

d. Die on white glazed paper (1858)
black	750.
dark brown	750.
scarlet	750.
blue	750.

e. Die on proof paper (1858)
cool black	475.
dull red	475.
dull brown	475.
dull blue green	475.
dull blue	475.

Bradbury, Wilkinson & Co., England

11-E5

Design size: 20½x23½mm
Vignette of Washington.

11-E5 3c
a. On stiff stamp paper about stamp size
black	1,250.
violet red	1,250.
deep carmine	1,250.
dusky carmine	1,250.

---

deep scarlet	1,2..
orange brown	1,2..
deep green	1,2..
blue	1,2..
ultramarine	1,2..
brown	1,2..

b. On card
violet black	1,2..
dull scarlet	1,2..
blue	1,2..
green	1,2..
brown	1,2..

c. On stiff bond
brown	1,2
blue	1,2
violet black	1,2

Draper, Welsh & Co.

11-E6

11-E7

Design size: 18x23mm
Vignette of Washington.

11-E6 3c Surface printed on card, black   7£

Design size: 17½x24mm
Die size: 44x106mm
Engraved vignette of Washington.

11-E7 3c
a. Die on India, about 44x105mm, die sunk on card, in vert. pair with No. 11-E8
black	1,50
scarlet	1,50
brown red	1,50
green	1,50

b. Die on India, about 40x45mm or smaller
warm black	40
cool black	40
dark carmine	40
scarlet	40
brown red	40
orange brown	40
brown	40
yellow green	40
blue green	40
blue	40
dull blue	40
brown violet	40

c. Die on India, stamp size
rose	35
scarlet	35
red brown	35
brown	35
green	35
cool black	35
warm black	35
yellow green	35
brown violet	35
ultramarine blue	35

d. Die on bond
black	40
scarlet	40
brown	40
blue green	40
blue	40

e. Die on white glazed paper
black	75
dark brown	75
scarlet	75
blue	75

11-E8

Design size: 19½x24mm
Die size: 44x106mm
On same die 30mm below No. 11-E7
Vignette of Washington.

11-E8 3c
a. Die on India, 28x32mm or smaller
black	300
dark carmine	300
scarlet	300
brown red	300
red brown	300
orange brown	300
brown	300
yellow green	300
green	300
blue green	300
blue	300

b. Die on bond, about 32x40mm
black	225.
scarlet	225.
brown	225.
green	225.
blue	225.

c. Die on white glazed paper
black	750.
dark brown	750.
scarlet	750.
blue	750.

11-E8D

11-E9

Design size: 18x23mm
Vignette of Washington.
Washington vignette only. Same head as No. 11-E6 through 11-E8, but with more bust. No gridwork in background.

11-E8D 3c Die on proof paper, mounted on
card, black 750.

Design size (No. 11-E9a): 18x33mm
Vignette design size (Nos. 11-E9b, 11-E9c): 18x22mm
As No. 11-E8D, gridwork added to background oval.

11-E9 3c
a. Die on India
black	350.
scarlet	350.

b. Die on India, single line frame
black	300.
blue	300.
dark carmine	300.
orange red	300.
lilac	300.
brown	300.
scarlet	300.
rose violet	300.
deep yellow green	300.

c. Die on India, imprint of Jocelyn, Draper,
Welsh & Co., New York
black	300.
blue	300.
dark carmine	300.
orange red	300.
lilac	300.
brown	300.
scarlet	300.
rose violet	300.
deep yellow green	300.

Danforth, Bald & Co.

11-E10

11-E11

Vignette size: 18x22mm
Design size: 20x26mm
Die size: 57x74mm
Vignette of Washington. Double line frame.

11-E10 3c
a. Die on India, die sunk on card
black	750.
scarlet	750.
red brown	750.
green	750.

b. Die on India, off card, about 33x38mm
black	175.
scarlet	175.
brown	175.
blue	175.
green	175.
dull violet	175.
dull blue	175.
red brown	175.
rose	175.

c. Die on bond, black 350.
d. Die on white glazed paper
black	750.
dark brown	750.
scarlet	750.
blue	750.

Washington vignette only.

11-E11 3c Die on India
black	325.
dull rose	325.
scarlet	325.
orange	325.
brown orange	325.

brown	325.
green	325.
dark blue	325.
dull violet	325.
rose violet	325.

11-E12

Design size: 20x26mm
Die size: 62x66mm
Vignette of Washington. Single line frame. Two states of die. Second state shows scars in lathe lines in front of neck over T, and small dot below design. A third printing has more scars in front of neck.

11-E12 3c
a. Die on India, die sunk on card
black	750.
scarlet	750.
brown red	750.
dusky brown yellow	750.
brown	750.
green	750.
blue	750.
dull blue	750.

b. Die on India, about 43x45mm
black	300.
scarlet	300.
deep scarlet	300.
brown	300.
yellow brown	300.
green	300.
yellow green	300.
blue	300.
dull blue	300.
dark blue	300.
ultramarine blue	300.
orange	300.
red	300.

c. Die on bond
dusky brown yellow	275.
blue	275.

d. Die on white glazed paper
black	750.
dark brown	750.

scarlet	750.
blue	750.

e. Plate on thick buff wove
rose	125.
violet brown	125.
orange	125.
dark orange	125.
pink orange	125.

f. Plate on India, dark red orange 150.
g. Plate on white wove (head more completely engraved, ruled lines between designs)
black	125.
dark carmine	125.
yellow	125.
blue	125.

11-E13

Design size: 20x26mm
Die size: 62x66mm
Vignette of Washington. No. 11-E12 reengraved: more dark dots in forehead next to hair, thus line between forehead and hair more distinct.

11-E13 3c
a. Die on India, die sunk on card
black	750.
scarlet	750.
brown red	750.
brown	750.
green	750.

b. Die on white glazed paper
black	750.
dark brown	750.
scarlet	750.
blue	750.

Bald, Cousland & Co.

11-E14　　　　　　　11-E15

Design size: 22x28mm
Die size: 95x43mm
Vignette of Washington. On same die with Nos. 11 E16 and incomplete 11-E14.

11-E14　3c
  a. Die on India
    black　　　　　　　　　　　450.
    scarlet　　　　　　　　　　450.
    red brown　　　　　　　　　450.
    brown　　　　　　　　　　　450.
    yellow green　　　　　　　　450.
    green　　　　　　　　　　　450.
    blue green　　　　　　　　　450.
    orange brown　　　　　　　　450.
    rose pink　　　　　　　　　450.
    dull blue　　　　　　　　　450.
    violet　　　　　　　　　　　450.
  b. Die on bond
    black　　　　　　　　　　　250.
    scarlet　　　　　　　　　　250.
    brown　　　　　　　　　　　250.
    blue green　　　　　　　　　250.
    blue　　　　　　　　　　　250.

Design size: 28x22½mm
POSTAGE / 3 / CENTS in scalloped frame.

11-E15　3c
  a. Die on India, die sunk on card
    black　　　　　　　　　　　750.
    scarlet　　　　　　　　　　750.
    red brown　　　　　　　　　750.
    green　　　　　　　　　　　750.
    slate　　　　　　　　　　　750.
  b. Die on bond, about 40x30mm
    black　　　　　　　　　　　175.
    scarlet　　　　　　　　　　175.
    brown　　　　　　　　　　　175.
    green　　　　　　　　　　　175.
    blue　　　　　　　　　　　175.
    slate　　　　　　　　　　　275.
  c. Die on white glazed paper
    black　　　　　　　　　　　750.
    dark brown　　　　　　　　750.
    scarlet　　　　　　　　　　750.
    blue　　　　　　　　　　　750.

11-E16

Design size: 28x22½mm
U.S. at sides of 3.

11-E16　3c
  a. Die on India, cut small
    black　　　　　　　　　　　275.
    light red　　　　　　　　　275.
    red brown　　　　　　　　　275.
    brown　　　　　　　　　　　275.
    yellow green　　　　　　　　275.
    blue green　　　　　　　　　275.
    green　　　　　　　　　　　275.
    blue　　　　　　　　　　　275.
    red violet　　　　　　　　　275.
  b. Die on bond, about 40x30mm
    black　　　　　　　　　　　175.
    scarlet　　　　　　　　　　175.
    brown　　　　　　　　　　　175.
    red brown　　　　　　　　　175.
    green　　　　　　　　　　　175.
    blue green　　　　　　　　　175.
    blue　　　　　　　　　　　175.
    violet　　　　　　　　　　　175.
    slate　　　　　　　　　　　175.
  c. Die on India, Nos. 11-E14 and 11-E16
    with albino 11-E14
    black　　　　　　　　　　1,000.
    scarlet　　　　　　　　　1,000.
    brown　　　　　　　　　　1,000.
    green　　　　　　　　　　1,000.
    blue　　　　　　　　　　1,000.
    red violet　　　　　　　　1,000.
  d. Die on bond
    black　　　　　　　　　　　225.
    scarlet　　　　　　　　　　225.
    brown　　　　　　　　　　　225.
    green　　　　　　　　　　　225.
    blue green　　　　　　　　　225.
    gray blue　　　　　　　　　225.
  e. Die on white glazed paper, 64x78mm,
    black　　　　　　　　　　　650.

---

  f. Die on India, die sunk on card
    black　　　　　　　　　　　900.
    scarlet　　　　　　　　　　900.

Toppan, Carpenter, Casilear & Co.

5-E1　　　　　　　　5-E1E

5-E1f

Design size: 20½x26mm
Franklin vignette.

5-E1　1c
  a. Die on old proof paper, master die short-
    ened to 18½x22½mm, black　　　1,500.
  b. Die on thick old proof paper, black　　1,500.
  c. Pair, Nos. 5-E1b, 11-E23, black　　2,000.

Design size: 20x24mm
Similar to No. 5-E1 but with no additional shaded oval border.

5-E1E　1c Die on thin card, black blue　　—
  f. Block of 4 in combination with pair of No.
    11-E23, on old proof paper, black　　3,500.

5-E2

Complete design, but with SIX CENTS in value tablet.
5-E2　1c Die on India, black, cut to shape　　2,750.

11-E17　　　　　　11-E18

Design size: 21½x25mm
Die size: 50½x60mm
Vignette of Washington.

11-E17　3c
  a. Die on India, 22x26mm, rose carmine　　2,500.
  b. Die on old ivory paper, rose carmine　　2,500.
  c. Die on proof paper, printed through a
    mat (1903)
    black　　　　　　　　　　　175.
    bright carmine　　　　　　　175.
    dull carmine　　　　　　　　175.
    dark violet red　　　　　　　175.
    dull scarlet　　　　　　　　175.
    dull violet　　　　　　　　175.
    dull red violet　　　　　　　175.
    deep yellow　　　　　　　　175.
    deep orange　　　　　　　　175.
    orange brown　　　　　　　　175.
    dull brown olive　　　　　　175.
    deep green　　　　　　　　　175.
    dark blue green　　　　　　　175.
    ultramarine　　　　　　　　175.
    dark blue　　　　　　　　　175.
    brown　　　　　　　　　　　175.
  d. Die on colored card (1903)

---

    deep orange, *ivory*　　　　　　2
    dark blue, *pale green*　　　　　2
    orange brown, *light blue*　　　　2
    See note above No. 63-E1.

Design size: 20½x22½mm
Washington. Vignette has solid color background. Cr
between N and T of CENTS.

11-E18　3c Die on India, card mounted,
    24½x25mm
    black　　　　　　　　　　　2,0
    carmine　　　　　　　　　　2,0

Design size: 20½x22½mm
Washington. Like No. 11-E18 except background of vigne
is clearly engraved horizontal and vertical lines. Crack betwe
N and T of CENTS.

11-E18A　3c Die on India, die sunk on
    60x50mm card, carmine　　7,000.
  b. As No. 11-E18A, cut down to stamp's
    size, black　　　　　　　　2,000.
  c. As No. 11-E18A, on old ivory paper,
    cut down to stamp size, rose car-
    mine　　　　　　　　　　2,000.

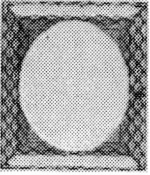

11-E19　　　　　　　11-E20

No. 11-E19
Design size: 20½x22½mm
Similar to No. 11-E18, with a slightly modified desig
vignette background engraved horiz. and vert. lines. In pair w
No. 11-E20.

No. 11-E20
Design size: 20x22½mm
Blank curved top and bottom labels. In pair with 11-E19. Als
found in pair with 11-E21.

11-E19　3c Die on India, Nos. 11-E19, 11-E20
    mounted on card, black　　　6,00

11-E21

Straight labels. Similar to No. 11-E19 but labels erased an
vignette cut out. In pair with No. 11-E20.

11-E21　3c Die on India, Nos. 11-E20, 11-E21
    mounted on card, black　　　4,50

11-E22　　　　　　　11-E23

Die size: 37½x46mm
Similar to issued stamp except lathework impinges on color
less oval.

11-E22　3c Die on India
    dusky blue　　　　　　　　5,000
    black　　　　　　　　　　5,000

Some students consider No. 11-E22 to be proof strikes of the
die used to make the "Roosevelt" and Panama-Pacific small die
proofs, as the lathework impinges on the colorless oval of Nos
11P2 and 11P2a as well.

Design size: 18x22mm
Washington vignette only. From master die (21½mm high)
with more robe and dark background.

11-E23　3c
  a. Master die impression, old proof paper,
    black　　　　　　　　　　900
  b. Block of 4, 2mm between ovals, thick old
    ivory paper, black　　　　　3,000

13-E1   13-E2

Design as adopted but top label has pencil lettering only, also lines in leaf ornaments around Xs in top corners.

-E1   10c Die on India, black   3,000.

Similar to No. 13-E1 but vert. shading around Xs and lines ded in leaf ornaments. No lettering in top label.

-E2   10c Die on India, black   3,000.

17-E1   17-E2

Design size: 19x21½mm
Block sinkage size: 57x49mm
Engine engraved frame without labels or interior shadow lines m straight bands and left side rosettes. No small equilateral sses in central row of diamonds. Original vignette cut out d replaced by engraved vignette of Washington as adopted.

-E1   12c Die on India, cut close, mounted on
            block sunk card, 77x57mm, black   6,000.

Similar to adopted design but no small vertical equilateral sses in center rows of diamond networks at top, sides and ttom.

-E2   12c Die on India, brown violet, cut close   750.

37-E1   37-E2

Design size: 19½x25½mm
Die size: 46x49mm or larger
Probably not the die used to make the plates. No exterior yout lines. Oval outline recut at bottom of jabot and vignette ackground etched much darker. Light horizontal lines on stock elow chin.

7-E1   24c Die on India, black   2,500.

Incomplete essay for frame only as adopted: no outer frame-
e and lathework not retouched. Also known with 37TC1 truck above it on same piece.

7-E2   24c Die on India, black   —

38-E1

Design size: 19x24mm
Incomplete engraving of entire design. Scrolls at each side of 0 have only one outer shading line.

38-E1   30c Die on India, black, cut to stamp
            size, black   2,500.

1861 ISSUE
Toppan, Carpenter & Co.

Examples on 1861 paper and in 1861 colors are rare. Most of the following listed on proof paper, colored card and bond paper are 1903 reprints. Ten sets of reprints on proof paper (and fewer on colored card, bond and pelure papers) supposedly were made for Ernest Schernikow, who

bought the original dies about 1903. Similar reprints in similar colors on the same papers also were made of Nos. LO1-E2, 11-E18 and the Philadelphia sanitary fair stamps, plus several master dies of vignettes.

63-E1   63-E2b

Vignette size: 18½x21½mm
Die size: 49x51mm
Franklin vignette only.

63-E1   1c
a. Die on proof paper (1903)
   black   75.
   carmine   75.
   dark carmine   75.
   scarlet   75.
   red brown   75.
   orange   75.
   yellow brown   75.
   dark brown   75.
   violet brown   75.
   light green   75.
   green   75.
   dark blue   75.
   ultramarine   75.
   red violet   75.
   dark violet   75.
   dusky olive green   75.
b. Die on colored card (1903)
   orange red, *pale yellow*   125.
   orange, *pale pink*   125.
   yellow brown, *buff*   125.
   dark blue, *pink*   125.
   dark violet, *pale olive*   125.
   dull violet, *blue*   125.
   deep green, *pale blue*   125.
   violet, *light green*   125.
c. Die on green bond (1903)
   black   125.
   dismal red   125.
   green   125.

Franklin vignette with U S POSTAGE at top and ONE CENT at bottom.

63-E2   1c
a. Die on proof paper (1903)
   black   100.
   carmine   100.
   dark carmine   100.
   scarlet   100.
   red brown   100.
   orange   100.
   yellow brown   100.
   violet brown   100.
   gray brown   100.
   light green   100.
   green   100.
   blue   100.
   red violet   100.
   ultramarine   100.
   dusky olive   100.
b. Die on old proof paper, outer line at sides
      of oval missing (1861), black   1,000.
c. Die on green bond (1903)
   orange   150.
   orange brown   150.
   violet   150.
d. Die on colored card (1903)
   deep green, *pale blue*   150.
   violet, *light green*   150.
   dark orange red, *pale dull green*   150.
   olive, *ivory*   150.
   brown, *pink*   150.
   scarlet, *yellow*   150.

63-E3

Side ornaments added.

63-E3   1c
a. Die on old proof paper (1861)
   black   1,250.
   blue   1,250.
b. Die on stiff old ivory paper (1861)
   black   1,250.
   blue   1,750.
c. Die on colored card (1903)
   black, *ivory*   150.
   brown, *pale pink*   150.
   blue, *blue*   150.
   orange brown, *pale pink*   150.

gray olive, *ivory*   150.
gray olive, *buff*   150.
scarlet, *pale yellow*   150.
d. Die on proof paper (1903)
   black   85.
   carmine   85.
   dark carmine   85.
   scarlet   85.
   red brown   85.
   orange   85.
   yellow brown   85.
   violet brown   85.
   light green   85.
   green   85.
   blue   85.
   violet   85.
   red violet   85.
   orange brown   85.
   dusky olive   85.
   ultramarine   85.
e. Die on green bond (1903)
   carmine   150.
   orange   150.
   violet   150.
f. Die on glazed card, black   —

63-E4   63-E4E

With upper and lower right corners incomplete. Serifs of 1s point to right.

63-E4   1c Die on old proof paper (1861), black   2,250.

As No. 63-E4 but with pencil shading in upper right corner.

63-E4E   1c Die on old proof paper (1861),
            black   3,500.

63-E5   63-E6

With four corners and numerals in pencil (ornaments differ in each corner).

63-E5   1c Die on old proof paper (1861), blue   2,750.

As No. 63-E5 but ornaments different.

63-E6   1c Die on old proof paper (1861), blue   3,500.

63-E7

As Nos. 63-E5 and 63-E6 but ornaments different.

63-E7   1c Die on old proof paper (1861), blue   3,250.

Die proof of No. 5 with lower corners cut out of India paper and resketched in pencil on card beneath.

63-E8   1c Die on India, on card (1861), black   2,000.

63-E9

Completely engraved design.
63-E9 1c
　　a. Die on India, cut to shape (1861)
　　　　black, on brown toned paper   1,000.
　　　　blue   600.
　　b. Die on India, about 58x57mm, die sunk
　　　　　on card (1861)
　　　　blue   2,000.
　　c. Die on old proof paper, about 48x55mm
　　　　　(1861)
　　　　black   2,000.
　　d. Die on large old white ivory paper (1861)
　　　　black   2,000.
　　　　blue   2,000.
　　e. Die on proof paper, printed through mat
　　　　　(1903)
　　　　black   100.
　　　　carmine   100.
　　　　dark carmine   100.
　　　　scarlet   100.
　　　　orange   100.
　　　　orange brown   100.
　　　　yellow brown   100.
　　　　light green   100.
　　　　green   100.
　　　　black blue   100.
　　　　violet   100.
　　　　red violet   100.
　　　　violet brown   100.
　　　　gray   100.
　　　　blue   100.
　　　　ultramarine   100.
　　f. Die on bond (1903)
　　　　orange   125.
　　　　dismal blue green   125.
　　g. Die on bond, Walls of Troy wmk. (1903)
　　　　carmine   200.
　　　　orange red   200.
　　　　orange   200.
　　　　orange brown   200.
　　　　dark green   200.
　　　　light ultramarine   200.
　　h. Die on bond, double line of scallops wmk.
　　　　　(1903)
　　　　orange red   200.
　　　　dark green   200.
　　i. Die on green bond (1903)
　　　　dismal carmine   125.
　　　　dismal violet brown   125.
　　　　dull dark green   125.
　　j. Die on pinkish pelure (1903)
　　　　orange red   300.
　　　　brown red   300.
　　　　brown orange   300.
　　　　dull blue green   300.
　　　　violet   300.
　　k. Die on colored card (1903)
　　　　black, *pale blue*   225.
　　　　carmine, *pale yellow*   225.
　　　　carmine, *pale pink*   225.
　　　　brown red, *pale pink*   225.
　　　　chestnut, *pale olive*   225.
　　　　dismal olive, *buff*   225.
　　　　ultramarine, *ivory*   225.
　　l. Die on stiff card (1903), green   250.

65-E1   65-E2

Vignette size: 16½x19mm
Die size: 49x50mm
1851 master die of Washington vignette only.

65-E1 3c
　　a. Die on proof paper (1903)
　　　　black   75.
　　　　carmine   75.
　　　　dark carmine   75.
　　　　scarlet   75.
　　　　red brown   75.
　　　　orange   75.
　　　　brown orange   75.
　　　　violet brown   75.
　　　　dusky olive   75.
　　　　light green   75.
　　　　green   75.
　　　　dark blue   75.
　　　　ultramarine   75.
　　　　lilac   75.
　　　　red violet   75.
　　b. Die on green bond (1903)
　　　　red   125.
　　　　brown   125.
　　　　blue   125.
　　　　olive   125.
　　c. Die on colored card (1903)
　　　　carmine, *pale green*   125.
　　　　scarlet, *yellow*   125.
　　　　orange, *ivory*   125.
　　　　olive brown, *blue*   125.
　　　　dark blue, *pink*   125.
　　　　violet, *buff*   125.
　　　　dark green, *pink*   125.

With tessellated frame, bottom label and diamond blocks.
Without rosettes, top label and diamond blocks.
65-E2 3c
　　a. Die on old proof paper (1861)
　　　　black   1,000.
　　　　red   1,000.
　　b. Die on proof paper, printed through a mat
　　　　　(1903)
　　　　black   85.
　　　　carmine   85.
　　　　dark carmine   85.
　　　　scarlet   85.
　　　　orange   85.
　　　　yellow   85.
　　　　yellow brown   85.
　　　　dusky gray   85.
　　　　light green   85.
　　　　green   85.
　　　　black blue   85.
　　　　ultramarine   85.
　　　　lilac   85.
　　　　dark lilac   85.
　　　　red violet   85.
　　c. Die on green bond (1903)
　　　　black   150.
　　　　dull orange red   150.
　　　　orange   150.
　　　　orange brown   150.
　　　　blue violet   150.
　　　　black blue   150.
　　　　dusky green   150.
　　d. Die on dull pale gray blue thin wove
　　　　　(1903)
　　　　dull red   300.
　　　　orange   300.
　　　　yellow brown   300.
　　　　dusky green   300.
　　　　black blue   300.
　　e. Die on colored card (1903)
　　　　black, *light blue*   150.
　　　　orange red, *yellow*   150.
　　　　red brown, *ivory*   150.
　　　　light green, *pink*   150.
　　　　green, *light green*   150.
　　　　blue, *buff*   150.
　　f. Die on India
　　　　black   —
　　　　rose   —

65-E3   65-E4

With top label and diamond blocks.
65-E3 3c
　　a. Die on old proof paper (1861)
　　　　brown red   1,500.
　　　　black   1,500.
　　b. Same as No. 65-E3 with numerals in pen-
　　　　　cil, Die on old proof paper (1861), black   3,500.
　　c. Die on proof paper, no numerals, printed
　　　　　through a mat (1903)
　　　　black   90.
　　　　carmine   90.
　　　　dark carmine   90.
　　　　scarlet   90.
　　　　orange   90.
　　　　yellow   90.
　　　　yellow brown   90.
　　　　dusky olive   90.
　　　　light green   90.
　　　　green   90.
　　　　black blue   90.
　　　　violet blue   90.
　　　　violet brown   90.
　　　　lilac   90.
　　　　red violet   90.
　　d. Die on green bond (1903)
　　　　dull scarlet   150.
　　　　dim red   150.
　　　　orange   150.
　　　　yellow brown   150.
　　　　green   150.
　　　　dusky blue   150.
　　　　violet   150.
　　　　black   150.
　　e. Die on colored card (1903)
　　　　black, *buff*   150.
　　　　scarlet, *ivory*   150.
　　　　orange, *light yellow*   150.
　　　　brown, *light blue*   150.
　　　　violet blue, *light pink*   150.
　　　　violet, *light green*   150.
　　f. Die on pink thin wove (1903)
　　　　dull yellow   300.
　　　　dismal red   300.
　　　　yellow brown   300.
　　　　dusky blue green   300.
　　　　dusky blue   300.

Complete die, with numerals in rosette circles.
65-E4 3c
　　a. Die on India, 75x76mm die sinkage
　　　　　(1861)

　　　　black   1,
　　　　carmine   1,
　　b. Die on old proof paper (1861)
　　　　black   1,
　　　　dark red   1,
　　c. Die on India, cut to shape (1861)
　　　　black   1,
　　　　carmine   1,

67-E1 — Die   67-E1 — Die
      I   II

Vignette size: 13½x16mm
Jefferson vignette only. Two dies: die I incomplete, light ba
ground in vignette; die II background essentially complete.

67-E1 5c
　　a. Die I on proof paper, black   6
　　b. Die II on proof paper (1903)
　　　　black
　　　　carmine
　　　　dark carmine
　　　　scarlet
　　　　red brown
　　　　orange brown
　　　　brown
　　　　dusky olive
　　　　green
　　　　dark green
　　　　black blue
　　　　ultramarine
　　　　violet brown
　　　　red violet
　　　　lilac
　　c. Die II on colored card (1903)
　　　　olive, *buff*   1
　　　　carmine, *pale yellow*   1
　　　　scarlet, *green*   1
　　　　brown, *pink*   1
　　　　black, *ivory*   1
　　　　ultramarine, *pale blue*   1
　　d. Die II on green bond (1903)
　　　　orange brown   1
　　　　dismal red brown   1
　　　　dark green   1
　　　　violet   1
　　　　black blue   1
　　e. Die II on old thin ivory paper (1903)
　　　　green   1
　　　　dark carmine   1
　　f. Die I on old thin ivory paper (1861), dark
　　　　　blue   1,00
　　g. Die I on old proof paper (1861)
　　　　black   75
　　　　dusky ultramarine   1,50
　　h. Die II on old ivory paper (1861), navy
　　　　　blue   75

67-E2

Vignette die II framed, with spaces for numerals.
67-E2 5c
　　a. Die II on proof paper (1903)
　　　　black   9
　　　　carmine   9
　　　　dark carmine   9
　　　　scarlet   9
　　　　red brown   9
　　　　orange   9
　　　　yellow brown   9
　　　　dusky olive   9
　　　　violet brown   9
　　　　light green   9
　　　　green   9
　　　　blue   9
　　　　ultramarine   9
　　　　red violet   9
　　　　lilac   95
　　b. Die II on colored card (1903)
　　　　orange brown, *light yellow*   175
　　　　deep blue, *light pink*   175
　　　　dusky olive, *light buff*   175
　　　　dark green, *pale blue*   175
　　　　red violet, *ivory*   175
　　c. Die II on green bond (1903)
　　　　orange brown   160
　　　　olive green   160
　　　　violet   160
　　　　blue   160
　　　　ultramarine   160

67-E3

67-E4

With numerals.

E3 5c
a. Die I on proof paper, printed through a
    mat (1903)
black	125.
carmine	125.
dark carmine	125.
scarlet	125.
red brown	125.
yellow brown	125.
dark brown	125.
violet brown	125.
light green	125.
green	125.
dark blue	125.
lilac	125.
ultramarine	125.
red violet	125.
dusky olive	125.

b. Die I on soft laid paper (1861)
black	750.
dark brown	750.
orange brown	750.

c. Die I on old proof paper, pencil designs
    drawn in corners (1861), black — 1,500.
d. Die I on old proof paper, outer lines on
    corner curves missing (1861), black — 500.
e. Die I on colored card (1903)
orange red, *buff*	175.
orange red, *light yellow*	175.
olive green, *pale green*	175.
deep green, *ivory*	175.
dark blue, *light pink*	175.
violet brown, *light blue*	175.

f. Die I on green bond (1903)
black	160.
scarlet	160.
brown	160.
green	160.

g. Die I on yellow pelure (1903)
scarlet	350.
brown red	350.
brown	350.
dark green	350.
violet	350.
blue	350.

h. Die I on bond, Walls of Troy wmk. (1903)
dark orange	250.
blue	250.
carmine	250.

i. Die I on bond, two line scalloped border
    wmk. (1903)
dark blue green	250.
scarlet	250.

Complete die II design with corner ornaments.

67-E4 5c
a. Die II on India, cut to shape (1861), black — 500.
b. Die II on brown toned paper (1861)
black	1,000.
brown	1,000.

c. Die II on old proof paper (1861)
orange brown	1,000.
black	1,000.

d. Die II on old ivory paper (1861), black — 1,000.
e. Die II on old proof paper, additional
    frameline drawn on curved corners and
    small circle drawn in each corner
    (1861), black — 1,500.
f. Die II on proof paper, printed through a
    mat (1903)
black	125.
carmine	125.
dark carmine	125.
scarlet	125.
orange	125.
brown	125.
yellow brown	125.
dusky olive	125.
light green	125.
green	125.
blue	125.
black blue	125.
violet brown	125.
red violet	125.
lilac	125.
ultramarine	125.

g. Die II on colored card (1903)
red, *light yellow*	150.
brown, *buff*	150.
olive green, *light pink*	150.
dark violet	150.
violet brown, *pale green*	150.
dusky yellow green, *dull pale*	150.
blue green	150.
brown, *ivory*	150.

h. Die II on green bond (1903)
black	125.
dull dark orange	125.
violet	125.

i. Die II on bond, Walls of Troy wmk. (1903)

---

scarlet	250.
deep red	250.
dark green	250.

j. Die II on bond, two-line scalloped border
    wmk. (1903)
deep orange	250.
blue	250.

k. Die II on greenish pelure (1903)
orange	350.
olive brown	350.
dark green	350.

l. Die II on bluish pelure (1903), red brown — 450.

69-E1

69-E2

Vignette size: 15x17mm

Washington vignette only. Two dies: die I incomplete, horiz.
background lines irregularly spaced, space occurring about
every 2mm; die II more engraving on face, horiz. background
lines regularly spaced, outer oval border smudged. Die II known
only as 1851 master die.

69-E1 12c
a. Die II on old proof paper (1851), black — 650.
b. Die I on proof paper (1903)
black	60.
carmine	60.
dark carmine	60.
scarlet	60.
red brown	60.
orange	60.
yellow brown	60.
violet brown	60.
gray brown	60.
light green	60.
green	60.
blue	60.
black blue	60.
red violet	60.
lilac	60.
ultramarine	60.

c. Die I on green bond (1903)
black	150.
red brown	150.
brown	150.

d. Die I on colored card (1903)
dark carmine, *ivory*	150.
dark carmine, *light blue*	150.
dark olive, *buff*	150.
dark green, *light yellow*	150.
dark blue, *pale green*	150.
violet brown, *light pink*	150.

Die II with curved labels at top and bottom.

69-E2 12c
a. Die II on proof paper, some printed
    through a mat (1903)
black	75.
carmine	75.
dark carmine	75.
scarlet	75.
orange	75.
yellow	75.
yellow brown	75.
violet brown	75.
gray brown	75.
light green	75.
green	75.
light blue	75.
black blue	75.
red violet	75.
lilac	75.
ultramarine	75.

b. Die II on old proof paper (1861)
dim red violet	500.
red violet	500.

c. Die II on dull light green bond (1903)
black	150.
dull red	150.
dim orange	150.
yellow brown	150.
dusky green	150.
dusky blue	150.
red violet	150.

d. Die I on pale yellow thin wove (1903)
dim red	200.
deep orange red	200.
yellow brown	200.
dusky blue	200.
red violet	200.

e. Die I on colored card (1903)
dull red, *light pink*	150.
orange red, *buff*	150.
brown, *light blue*	150.
dark olive, *light yellow*	150.
dull dark blue, *ivory*	150.
violet, *pale green*	150.

69-E3

Frame incomplete: all four rosettes blank.

69-E3 12c
a. Die on proof paper (1903)
black	125.
carmine	125.
dark carmine	125.
scarlet	125.
red brown	125.
orange	125.
orange brown	125.
violet brown	125.
light green	125.
green	125.
light blue	125.
black blue	125.
red violet	125.
lilac	125.
ultramarine	125.

b. Die on old proof paper (1861)
black	750.
olive gray	750.

c. Die on old ivory, top border and half of
    rosettes missing (1861), black — 750.
d. Die on stiff old ivory, top border missing
    (1861), bluish black — 750.
e. Die on colored card, top border missing
    (1903)
orange brown, *light blue*	175.
deep green, *light yellow*	175.
deep blue, *light pink*	175.
violet, *ivory*	175.
deep yellow orange, *pale yellow green*	175.
brown, *buff*	175.

f. Die on green bond, top border missing
    (1903)
orange	175.
green	175.
violet	175.

g. Die on old proof paper, 1851 die with bor-
    der lines complete, upper right rosette
    blank (1861)
orange	750.
dark green	750.
ultramarine	750.
violet	750.

h. Die I on old proof paper, vignette back-
    ground incomplete or worn, stock on
    neck unfinished (1861)
i. Die I on old proof paper, as 69-E3h but
    both upper rosettes blank (1861), ul-
    tramarine — 1,000.

69-E3j

69-E3k

j. Die I on old proof paper, as No. 69-E3h
    but both upper plus lower left rosettes
    blank (1861), ultramarine — 1,000.
k. Die I on old proof paper, as No. 69-E3h
    but both lower plus upper left rosettes
    blank, corner borders removed around
    blank rosettes (1861), ultramarine — 1,000.
l. Die I on old proof paper, as No. 69-E3h
    but all rosettes blank, border lines com-
    plete (1861)
dim scarlet	750.
orange	750.
green	750.
ultramarine	750.
violet	750.

m. Die I on white wove, as No. 69-E3l
    (1861), scarlet — 750.
n. Die I on old proof paper, complete design
    (1861)
orange	750.
dark red	750.
orange red	750.
ultramarine	750.

o. Die I on pale yellow thin wove (1903),
    dark red — 750.
p. Die I on pink thin wove (1903), blue — 750.
q. Die I on pale pink (1903), blue — 750.

69-E4

Original complete design with numerals in corners.

69-E4 12c
- **a.** Die on India, card mounted (1861)
  - black
  - gray black   750.
  -   750.
- **b.** Die on India, cut to shape (1861), black   500.
- **c.** Die on old proof paper (1861), black   500.
- **d.** Die on old proof paper, corners drawn in pencil (1861), black   1,500.
- **e.** Die on old proof paper, as No. 69-E3a but numerals sketched in diagonally and vert. (1861), black   3,000.
- **f.** Die on stiff old ivory paper, as No. 69-E4e but without top border (1861), bluish black   1,500.
- **g.** Die on thin card, black   —

70-E1

70-E2

Vignette size: 7x16mm
Washington die II vignette only.

70-E1 24c
- **a.** Die II on proof paper (1903)
  - black   60.
  - carmine   60.
  - dark carmine   60.
  - scarlet   60.
  - orange   60.
  - yellow   60.
  - yellow brown   60.
  - violet brown   60.
  - gray olive   60.
  - light green   60.
  - green   60.
  - light blue   60.
  - black blue   60.
  - red violet   60.
  - lilac   60.
- **b.** Die II on green bond (1903)
  - black   150.
  - red brown   150.
  - violet   150.
  - orange   150.
- **c.** Die II on colored card (1903)
  - dull red, *ivory*   150.
  - brown red, *buff*   150.
  - brown orange, *light pink*   150.
  - dark green, *light yellow*   150.
  - blue, *pale green*   150.
  - violet, *blue*   150.

Washington vignette with oval label. Background complete, eyes retouched.

70-E2 24c
- **a.** Die II on proof paper (1903)
  - black   60.
  - carmine   60.
  - dark carmine   60.
  - scarlet   60.
  - orange   60.
  - yellow   60.
  - yellow brown   60.
  - violet brown   60.
  - light green   60.
  - green   60.
  - light blue   60.
  - black blue   60.
  - red violet   60.
  - lilac   60.
  - gray olive   60.
  - ultramarine   60.
- **b.** Die I on old proof paper, background lines incomplete (1861)
  - black   750.
  - dim red violet   750.
- **c.** Die I on colored card (1903)
  - black, *light pink*   150.
  - orange, *buff*   150.
  - orange, *light blue*   150.
  - dark green, *pale green*   150.
  - violet blue, *light yellow*   150.
  - violet, *ivory*   150.
- **d.** Die I on green bond (1903), brown   150.
- **e.** Die I on dull light blue green bond (1903)
  - black   150.
  - orange red   150.
  - orange   150.
  - yellow brown   150.
  - dusky green   150.
  - dull blue   150.
  - red violet   150.

- **f.** Die I on dull pale green blue thin wove (1903)
  - orange red   300.
  - orange   300.
  - yellow brown   300.
  - dusky green   300.
  - dull blue   300.

70-E3   70-E4

With frame. Blank areas in corners for numerals.

70-E3 24c
- **a.** Die on proof paper (1903)
  - black   100.
  - carmine   100.
  - dark carmine   100.
  - scarlet   100.
  - orange   100.
  - yellow brown   100.
  - orange brown   100.
  - violet brown   100.
  - gray olive   100.
  - light green   100.
  - green   100.
  - light blue   100.
  - black blue   100.
  - red violet   100.
  - lilac   100.
  - ultramarine   100.
- **b.** Die on old proof paper (1861), dusky red violet   1,000.
- **c.** Die on colored card (1903)
  - carmine, *light blue*   175.
  - blue, *pale green*   175.
  - scarlet, *buff*   175.
  - yellow brown, *cream*   175.
  - dull violet, *pink*   175.
  - dusky green, *light yellow*   175.
  - gray olive, *ivory*   175.
- **d.** Die on green bond (1903)
  - black   175.
  - orange brown   175.
  - green   175.

Complete design with numerals in corners.

70-E4 24c
- **a.** Die on old proof paper, cut to shape (1861)
  - lilac   400.
  - black   400.
  - red violet   400.
- **b.** Die on India, cut close (1861)
  - black   400.
  - lilac   400.
  - brown lilac   400.
- **c.** Die on India (1861), dark blue   750.
- **d.** Die on India, mounted on 80x115mm card (1861), lilac   750.
- **e.** On stiff old ivory paper (1861)
  - black   1,000.
  - lilac   1,000.
- **f.** Die on proof paper, printed through a mat (1903)
  - black   125.
  - carmine   125.
  - dark carmine   125.
  - scarlet   125.
  - red borwn   125.
  - yellow brown   125.
  - brown   125.
  - violet brown   125.
  - gray olive   125.
  - light green   125.
  - green   125.
  - light blue   125.
  - black blue   125.
  - red violet   125.
  - lilac   125.
  - ultramarine   125.
- **g.** Die on blue pelure (1903)
  - dark carmine   300.
  - scarlet   300.
  - orange   300.
  - brown   300.
  - dusky green   300.
- **h.** Die on bond (1903)
  - black   175.
  - scarlet   175.
  - orange   175.
  - dark green   175.
  - blue   175.
- **i.** Die on green bond (1903)
  - black   250.
  - dark red   250.
  - green   250.
- **j.** Die on bond, Walls of Troy wmk. (1903), dark green   300.
- **k.** Die on bond, double line of scallops wmk. (1903)
  - deep orange red   300.
  - scarlet   300.
  - orange   300.
  - light blue   300.

- **l.** Die on colored card, printed through a mat
  - dark orange, *ivory*
  - dark orange, *light pink*
  - brown, *light blue*
  - dull dark blue, *pale green*
  - violet, *light yellow*
  - violet brown, *buff*

72-E1   72-E2

Vignette size: 16x17½mm
Washington vignette only.

72-E1 90c
- **a.** Die on proof paper (1903)
  - black
  - carmine
  - dark carmine
  - scarlet
  - red brown
  - orange
  - orange brown
  - violet brown
  - gray olive
  - light green
  - green
  - dark blue
  - lilac
  - red violet
  - yellow brown
  - ultramarine
- **b.** Die on colored card (1903)
  - black, *light yellow*
  - red brown, *light pink*
  - carmine, *buff*
  - brown, *pale green*
  - dark brown, *light blue*
  - ultramarine, *ivory*
- **c.** Die on dull light blue green bond (1903)
  - violet brown
  - dusky green
  - dusky blue
  - red violet

Vignette with blank top and bottom labels.

72-E2 90c
- **a.** Die on proof paper (1903)
  - black
  - carmine
  - dark carmine
  - scarlet
  - orange
  - yellow brown
  - brown
  - violet brown
  - gray olive
  - light green
  - green
  - dark blue
  - red violet
  - lilac
  - ultramarine
- **b.** Die on green bond (1903)
  - dull orange
  - dull orange brown
  - red violet
- **c.** Die on colored card (1903)
  - black, *buff*
  - orange red, *light yellow*
  - brown, *ivory*
  - olive green, *light pink*
  - green, *light blue*
  - violet brown, *pale green*

72-E3   72-E5

U.S. POSTAGE in top label.

72-E3 90c
- **a.** Die on proof paper (1903)
  - black   125.
  - carmine   125.
  - dark carmine   125.
  - scarlet   125.
  - yellow   125.
  - yellow brown   125.
  - brown   125.

violet brown	125.
gray olive	125.
light green	125.
green	125.
dark blue	125.
lilac	125.
red violet	125.
ultramarine	125.

b. Die on colored card (1903)

orange, *light blue*	185.
orange red, *light yellow*	185.
dark blue, *buff*	185.
violet, *pale green*	185.
violet brown, *ivory*	185.
orange brown, *pale pink*	185.

c. Die on green bond (1903)

black	175.
brown	175.
green	175.

Lower corners of vignette cut out, "NINETY 90 CENTS" in
~ncil in bottom label.

~E4 90c Die on India (1861), black 2,000.

Complete design.

~E5 90c

a. Die on India, cut to shape (1861)

black	300.
dark blue	300.

b. Die on India, die sunk on card (1861),
   blue 2,000.

c. Die on India, cut close (1861)

black	300.
blue	300.

d. Die on proof paper, printed through a mat
   (1903)

black	175.
carmine	175.
dark carmine	175.
scarlet	175.
orange	175.
yellow brown	175.
brown	175.
violet brown	175.
gray olive	175.
light green	175.
green	175.
dark blue	175.
lilac	175.
red violet	175.
ultramarine	175.

e. Die on colored card (1903)

carmine, *light blue*	250.
dismal brown, *light pink*	250.
orange brown, *buff*	250.
blue, *ivory*	250.
violet, *pale green*	250.
green, *pale yellow*	250.

f. Die on green bond (1903)

dark carmine	225.
red brown	225.
green	225.

g. Die on bond (1903), orange brown 250.

h. Die on bond, "Bond No. 1" wmk. (1903),
   orange brown 350.

i. Die on bond, "Bond No 2" wmk. (1903),
   orange brown 350.

j. Die on bond, Walls of Troy wmk. (1903)

carmine	300.
scarlet	300.
orange	300.
dark green	300.
ultramarine	300.

k. Die on pink pelure (1903)

brown red	350.
dull yellow	350.
very dark green	350.
dark blue	350.
dull violet	350.

American Bank Note Co.

65-E5   65-E6

Design size: 19x23½mm
Engraved frame with pencil border, center cut out, mounted
over 22x27mm engraved vignette of Washington.

65-E5 3c Die on India, black 2,500.

Design size: 19x24½mm
Engraved frame with pencil border, center cut out, mounted
over engraved ruled background with engraved Washington
vignette mounted on it.

65-E6 Three Cents Die on India, on card
   about 23x27½mm, black 2,500.

65-E7   65-E8

Master die No. 80 of frame only.

65-E7 3c Die on India, card mounted

deep orange	2,000.
dark brown	2,000.
green	2,000.
dark blue	2,000.
black	2,000.

Design size: 19½x24½mm
Engraved lathework frame with Bald, Cousland & Co.
engraved Washington vignette and engraved lettered labels and
numerals mounted on it.

65-E8 3c Die on India, on 22x27mm card,
   black 11,000.

65-E9   65-E10

Master die No. 81 of frame only.

65-E9 3c Die on India

black	2,750.
brown yellow	2,750.
dark green	2,750.
orange red	2,750.

Engraved lathework frame with Bald, Cousland & Co.
engraved Washington vignette and engraved lettered labels and
numerals mounted on it.

65-E10 3c Die on India, on 28x35mm card,
   black 7,000.

67-E5

Design size: 21x25mm
Engraved frame used for the 1860 Nova Scotia 5c stamp cut
to shape, with engraved lettered labels and Washington
vignette No. 209-E7 mounted on it.

67-E5 Five Cents Die on India, on 23x27mm
   card, black 2,500.

67-E6   67-E7

Design size: 19x24
Engraved lathework background with Bald, Cousland & Co.
engraved Washington vignette and engraved lettered labels and
numerals mounted on it.

67-E6 5c Die on India, mounted on 22x26mm
   card, black 7,000.

Design size: 19x24mm
Engraved lathework background with Bald, Cousland & Co.
engraved Washington vignette and engraved lettered labels and
numerals mounted on it.

67-E7 5c Die on India, mounted on
   21x26½mm card, black 7,000.

National Bank Note Co.

The following essays include those formerly listed as
Nos. 55-57, 59 and 62 in the Postage section, and the corresponding die and plate essays formerly listed in the Proof
section. Former No. 58 is now No. 62B. Former Nos. 60 and
61 are now Nos. 70eTC and 71bTC in the Trial Color Proofs
section.

63-E10

Frame essay with blank areas for Franklin vignette, labels,
numerals, U and S.

63-E10 1c Die on India, black 2,000.

63-E11   63-E12

Die size: 58x56mm
"Premiere Gravure" die No. 440.

63-E11 1c

a. "Premiere Gravure" die essay on India
   (formerly Nos. 55P1, 55TC1)

black	4,000.
indigo	1,500.
ultramarine	2,250.

b. "Premiere Gravure" small die essay on
   white wove, 28x31mm (**formerly No.
   55P2**), indigo 325.

c. "Premiere Gravure" plate essay on India
   (**formerly Nos. 55P3, 55TC3**)

indigo	250.
blue	—
ultramarine	300.
violet ultramarine	—

d. "Premiere Gravure" plate essay on
   semitransparent stamp paper (**formerly No. 55TC4**), ultramarine 400.

e. Finished "Premiere Gravure" plate essay on semitransparent stamp paper,
   perf. 12, gummed (**formerly No. 55**),
   indigo 30,000.

No. 63-E11e is valued with perfs cutting slightly into design at
top.

Die size: 47x55mm
Apparently complete die except value numerals have been
cut out.

63-E12 1c Die on India, die sunk on card,
   black 1,500.

65-E11   65-E12

Die size: 64x76½mm
Incomplete engraving of Washington head only.

65-E11 3c

a. Die on India, on card, carmine 750.
b. Die on white glazed paper

black	750.
scarlet	750.
brown violet	750.

Die size: 78x55mm
Incomplete engraved design, no scrolls outside framelines,
no silhouette under chin, no ornaments on 3s, U and S.

65-E12 3c Die on India, die sunk on card

black	1,000.
blue	1,000.

65-E13

65-E14

As No. 65-E12 but ornaments on 3s, U and S. Shows traces of first border design erased. With imprint and No. 441 below design.

65-E13	3c Die on India, card mounted	
	scarlet	1,000.
	brown red	1,000.
	ultramarine	1,000.

Die size: 59x55mm
As No. 65-E13 but with ornaments outside frame.

65-E14 3c Die on India, die sunk on card

black	750.
scarlet	750.
pink	1,250.
brown orange	750.
deep orange red	750.
deep red	750.

As No. 65-E14 but top of head silhouetted, lines added or strengthened in hair at top of head, around eye, on chin, in hair behind ear. The three lines on bottom edge of bust extended to back. No imprint or die number.

65-E15

65-E15 3c
a. Die on India, card mounted, deep orange red — 1,000.
b. "Premiere Gravure" die essay on semitransparent stamp paper, 20x25mm-30x37mm

deep orange red	750.
deep red orange	750.
dim red	750.
dim deep red	750.
dim orange red	750.
dull pink	750.
dull violet red	750.

c. "Premiere Gravure" die essay on India **(formerly Nos. 56P1, 56TC1)**

red	1,350.
black	2,000.
scarlet	2,000.
pink	2,850.
orange red	2,000.
dark orange red	2,000.

d. Small die essay on white wove, 28x31mm altered laydown die of complete design but with outer scrolls removed and replaced by ones similar to "Premiere Gravure" design (1903) **(formerly No. 56P2)**, dim deep red — 325.
e. As "c," small die essay on pale cream soft wove, 24x29mm (1915) **(formerly No. 56P2a)**, deep red — 1,250.
f. "Premiere Gravure" plate No. 2 essay on India **(formerly Nos. 56P3, 56TC3)**

| red | 250. |
| scarlet | 350. |

g. "Premiere Gravure" plate essay on semitransparent stamp paper **(formerly Nos. 56aP4, 56TC4)**

| red, pair with gum | 1,750. |
| black | 400. |

h. Finished "Premiere Gravure" plate essay on semitransparent stamp paper, perf. 12, gummed **(formerly No. 56)**

brown rose	550.
P# block of 8, Impt.	20,000.
orange red	475.
bright orange red	475.
dark orange red	475.
dim deep red	475.
pink	475.
deep pink	475.

67-E8

67-E9

Incomplete impression from die No. 442, border lines and corner scrolls missing.

67-E8 5c Die on India, mounted on 34x50mm card, black — 1,750.

Size of die: 58x59mm
"Premiere Gravure" design, with corner scrolls but without leaflets.

67-E9 5c
a. "Premiere Gravure" die essay on India, card mounted (formerly No. 57TC1)

| black | 1,750. |
| scarlet | 1,750. |

b. Small die essay on white wove, 28x31mm, altered laydown die of complete design but with scrolls removed from corners to resemble "Premiere Gravure" (1903) **(formerly No. 57P2), brown** — 325.
c. As "b," die essay on pale cream soft wove, 24x29mm (1915) **(formerly No. 57P2a)**, brown — 1,350.
d. "Premiere Gravure" plate No. 3 essay on India **(formerly Nos. 57P3, 57TC3)**

brown	250.
light brown	300.
dark brown	300.
red brown	300.

e. Finished "Premiere Gravure" plate essay on semitransparent stamp paper, perf. 12, gummed **(formerly No. 57)**, brown — 15,000.

68-E1

68-E2

Design size: 14x17½mm
Die size: 26x31mm
Washington vignette only.

68-E1 10c
a. Die on ivory paper, black — 1,000.
b. Die on India — 1,000.

Incomplete die No. 443.

68-E2 10c Die on India, 22x26mm, dark green — 2,500.

Incomplete die of No. 68P1, thin lines missing on top of frame

68-E3

68-E3 10c Die on India

| yellowish green | 1,000. |
| dark green | 1,000. |

69-E5

69-E6

Design size: 12½x16mm

Die size: about 62x65mm
Washington vignette only.

69-E5 12c
a. Die on India, die sunk on card

black	4
dark red	4
orange red	4

b. Die on ivory paper, about 24x28mm

black	5
scarlet	5
black brown	5
blue	5

Incomplete die No. 444, without corner ornaments.

69-E6 12c
a. "Premiere Gravure" die essay on India, mounted on card (formerly Nos. 59P1, 59TC1)

black	1,3
scarlet	1,7
dark green	1,5

b. "Premiere Gravure" small die essay on white wove, 28x31mm (1903) **(formerly No. 59P2)**, black — 4
c. "Premiere Gravure" small die essay on pale cream soft wove, 24x29mm (1915) **(formerly No. 59P3)**, black — 1,7
d. "Premiere Gravure" plate No. 5 essay on India **(formerly No. 59P3)**, black — 3
e. Finished "Premiere Gravure" plate essay on semitransparent stamp paper, perf. 12, gummed **(formerly No. 59)**, black — 60,00

70-E5

70-E6

Washington vignette in incomplete frame.

70-E5 24c Die on India, black — 3,25

Die size: 56½x56mm
Incomplete die (No. 445): silhouette unfinished, especially scrolls around numerals; shadows over numerals not ac etched.

70-E6 24c Die on India, die sunk on card

black	90
violet	90
gray violet	90
dark violet	90
scarlet	90
green	900
orange	900
red brown	900
orange brown	900
orange yellow	900
rose red	900
gray	900
steel blue	900
blue	900

For finished "Premiere Gravure" trial color plate proof o semitransparent stamp paper, perf 12, gummed (formerly No 60), see 70eTC in the Trial Color Proof section.

71-E1

71-E2

Die size: 46x60mm
Incomplete die (No. 446): additional ornaments at top and bottom in pencil, as later engraved.

71-E1 30c Die on India, black — 1,750.

"Premiere Gravure" die: left side of frame and silhouette at lower right unfinished.

71-E2 30c
a. "Premiere Gravure" die essay on India, die sunk on card **(formerly No. 61TC1)**

black	1,750.
green	1,750.
dull gray blue	1,750.
violet brown	1,750.
scarlet	1,750.
dull rose	1,750.

b. "Premiere Gravure" plate essay on India **(formerly No. 61P3)**, deep red orange — 500.
c. "Premiere Gravure" plate essay on card

| black (split thin) | 500. |
| blue | 750. |

d. "Premiere Gravure" plate essay on card,
black 12x2mm SPECIMEN overprint,
blue 750.
e. "Premiere Gravure" plate essay on semi-
transparent stamp paper
deep red orange 1,250.
yellow orange 1,250.
lemon yellow 1,250.
dark orange yellow 1,250.
dull orange yellow 1,250.

or finished "Premiere Gravure" trial color proof on semi-
sparent stamp paper, perf 12, gummed (formerly No. 61),
No. 71bTC in the Trial Color Proof section.

72-E6   72-E7

Die size: 54x63mm
ncomplete die: without thin lines at bottom of frame and in
per left triangle between label and frame, and without leaves
left of U and right of S.

-E6   90c Die on India, blue (shades)   1,000.

Similar to 72-E6 but lines added in upper left triangle, leaves
ded at left of U and at right of S. Exists with and without
print and Die No. 447 added below design.

-E7   90c
a. Die on India, die sunk on card, black   1,750.
b. "Premiere Gravure" die essay on India,
thin line under bottom center frame
(formerly Nos. 62P1, 62TC1)
blue   1,350.
black   1,750.
c. "Premiere Gravure" small die essay on
white wove, 28x31mm (1903) **(formerly No. 62P2)**, blue   500.
d. "Premiere Gravure" small die essay on
pale cream soft wove, 24x29mm
(1915) **(formerly No. 62P2a)**, blue   1,750.
e. "Premiere Gravure" plate essay on India,
blue   350.
f. "Premiere Gravure" plate essay on card,
black (split thin)   500.
g. "Premiere Gravure" plate essay on semi-
transparent stamp paper **(formerly
Nos. 62aP4, 62TC4)**
blue, pair, gummed   5,500.
blue green   275.
h. Finished "Premiere Gravure" plate essay
on semitransparent stamp paper, perf.
12, gummed **(formerly No. 62)**, blue   32,500.

Die size: 54x63mm
Similar to Nos. 72-E6 and 72-E7 but leaf at left of "U" only, no
hading around "U" and "S," leaf and some shading missing at
ottom right above "S," shading missing in top label, etc., faint
ns. "8" at bottom of backing card.

2-E8   90c Die on India, die sunk on 3¼x3½-
inch card, dark blue   —

63-E13

Design size: 20x47mm
Die size: 57x95mm
Bowlsby patent coupon at top of 1c stamp design.

63-E13   1c
a. Die on India, die sunk on card
black   1,600.
red   1,600.
scarlet   1,600.
orange   1,600.
orange brown   1,600.
brown   1,600.
yellow brown   1,600.
blue green   1,600.
blue   1,600.

violet   1,600.
red violet   1,600.
gray   1,600.
gray brown   1,600.
dull orange yellow   1,600.
b. Die on white glazed paper
black   1,600.
dark brown   1,600.
scarlet   1,600.
blue   1,600.
c. Plate on pelure paper, gummed, red   250.
d. Plate on white paper, red   200.
e. Plate on white paper, with 13x16mm
points-up grill, red   350.
Split grill   600.
f. Plate on white paper, perf. all around
and between stamp and coupon
red   150.
blue   150.
g. Plate on white paper, perf. all around,
imperf. between stamp and coupon
red   150.
blue   150.
h. Plate on white paper, perf. all around,
rouletted between stamp and coupon
red   300.
blue   300.

1861-66 Essays
Authors Unknown

73-E2   73-E3

Design size: 21x26mm

73-E2   2c Pencil and watercolor on thick card,
bright green   3,750.

Design size: 21x26mm
Indian vignette. Typographed printings from woodcuts. Plates
of three rows of three, one row each of Nos. 73-E3, 73-E4, 73-
E5. Listings are of singles.

73-E3   2c
a. Plate on white wove
red   30.
scarlet   30.
violet   30.
black   30.
blue   30.
green   30.
b. Plate on mauve wove
red   50.
violet   50.
black   50.
blue   50.
green   50.
c. Plate on yellow wove
red   50.
violet   50.
black   50.
blue   50.
green   50.
d. Plate on yellow laid
red   50.
violet   50.
black   50.
blue   50.
green   50.
e. Plate on pink laid
red   50.
violet   50.
black   50.
blue   50.
green   50.
f. Plate on green laid
red   50.
violet   50.
black   50.
blue   50.
green   50.
g. Plate on cream laid
red   50.
violet   50.
black   50.
blue   50.
green   50.
h. Plate on pale yellow wove
red   50.
green   50.
blue   50.
i. Plate on yellow-surfaced card, violet   50.

73-E4   73-E5

Design size: 23x26½mm
Small head of Liberty in shield. Typographed printings from
woodcuts. On plate with Nos. 73-E3 and 73-E5. Listings are of
singles.

73-E4   3c
a. Plate on white wove
red   30.
scarlet   30.
violet   30.
black   30.
blue   30.
green   30.
b. Plate on mauve wove, violet   50.
c. Plate on yellow wove
red   50.
violet   50.
black   50.
blue   50.
green   50.
d. Plate on yellow laid
red   50.
violet   50.
black   50.
blue   50.
green   50.
e. Plate on pink laid
carmine   50.
violet   50.
black   50.
blue   50.
green   50.
f. Plate on green laid
carmine   50.
green   50.
dull violet   50.
blue   50.
g. Plate on cream laid
red   50.
violet   50.
black   50.
blue   50.
green   50.
h. Plate on pale yellow wove
red   50.
green   50.
blue   50.
i. Plate on yellow-surfaced card, violet   50.
j. Plate on fawn wove, green   50.

Design size: 22½x25½mm
Large head of Liberty. Typographed impressions from woodcut. On plate with Nos. 73-E3 and 73-E4. Listings are of singles.

73-E5   5c
a. Plate on white wove
red   30.
scarlet   30.
violet   30.
black   30.
blue   30.
green   30.
b. Plate on mauve wove, violet   50.
c. Plate on yellow wove
red   50.
violet   50.
black   50.
blue   50.
green   50.
d. Plate on yellow laid
red   50.
violet   50.
black   50.
blue   50.
green   50.
e. Plate on pink laid
red   50.
black   50.
blue   50.
green   50.
f. Plate on green laid
red   50.
violet   50.
black   50.
blue   50.
green   50.
g. Plate on cream laid
red   50.
black   50.
blue   50.
green   50.
h. Plate on pale yellow wove
red   50.
blue   50.
green   50.
i. Plate on yellow-surfaced card, violet   50.

73-E6

Size of design: 21x27mm
Indian vignette. Typographed impressions from woodcut.

73-E6 10c
- **a.** Die on proof paper
  - black — 200.
  - gray black — 200.
  - carmine — 200.
  - dusky red — 200.
  - brown — 200.
  - green — 200.
  - blue — 200.
  - violet — 200.
- **b.** Plate on white paper (pane of 4)
  - red — 600.
  - violet — 600.
  - brown — 600.
  - black — 600.
  - blue — 600.
  - green — 600.
- **c.** Plate on soft cream card (pane of 4)
  - black — 600.
  - red — 600.
  - blue — 600.
  - green — 600.
  - red violet — 600.

1867 Essays
Re-use Prevention
Authors Unknown

Unfolded — 79-E1

Folded — 79-E1

Design size (folded): 18x23mm
Design size (unfolded): 18x58mm
Folded and scored four times, horiz. crease at center. Bronze overprint U 2 S, (2 punched out). Lower ⅔ gummed below second fold so top ⅓ could be torn off for canceling.

79-E1 2c On white paper, dull red violet — 5,000.

79-E2

Similar to No. 79-E1 but larger and not folded. Pierced with S-shaped cuts as well as punched out 2.

79-E2 2c
- **a.** On white paper, US 7½mm high, bronze, US in dull black — 5,000.
- **b.** On white paper, US 10mm high, bronze, US in violet — 5,000.

79-E3   Cuts as on back

U.S. No. 73 as issued but pierced with S-shaped cuts, ovptd. in metallic color.

79-E3 2c Essay on 2c stamp, gold overprint — 7,500.

79-E4   79-E6

Similar to No. 79-E1 but with punched out 3.

79-E4 3c
- **a.** On white paper, U 3 S black above, bronze below and on face beneath folds — 5,000.
- **b.** On green paper, 3 not punched out, 3 black, POSTAGE blue — 5,000.

Similar to No. 79-E4, with "3 U.S. 3 / Three Cents / Void if detached."

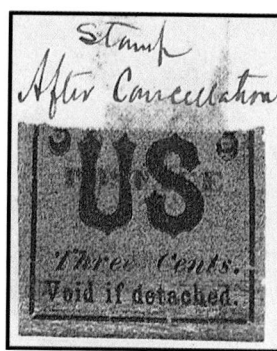

79-E5

79-E5 3c On green paper, black — 3,000.

Similar to No. 79-E2 but with punched out 3, gummed.

79-E6 3c
- **a.** On white paper, bronze over viole — 3,000.
- **b.** On white paper, U S black, rest bronze — 3,000.

79-E7

Vignette map of U.S.

79-E7 3c On thick white paper, rouletted, green, gold 3 on map — 2,500.

1867 Essays
Henry Lowenberg

79-E8   79-E9

Washington vignette. Printed in reverse on back of transparent paper, reads correctly from front. Plate essays from sheet of 25.

79-E8 3c
- **a.** Plate on onionskin paper, imperf., gummed
  - brown
  - orange brown
  - deep orange brown
  - orange
  - green
  - light green
  - blue green
  - pale green
  - red
  - light red
  - dark red
  - violet red
  - violet
  - light violet
  - dull pale violet
  - blue
  - dark blue
  - deep blue
  - pale blue
  - dull blue
  - gold
  - gray
  - black
  - carmine
- **b.** Plate on onionskin paper, perf. 12, gummed
  - gray black — 2
  - gray — 2
  - gray violet — 2
  - dull violet — 2
  - brown red — 2
- **c.** Plate on more opaque onionskin paper, imperf.
  - black — 2
  - red violet — 2
  - dull violet — 2
- **d.** Plate on thick transparent paper
  - gray — 2
  - black — 2

Washington vignette. Printed with design reversed on front various opaque papers, Plate essays are from sheets of 25.

79-E9 3c
- **a.** Plate on white wove, imperf., gummed
  - blue — 1
  - red — 1
  - gray — 1
  - brown — 1
  - orange — 1
  - green — 1
  - yellow green — 1
- **b.** Plate on clear white paper, imperf.
  - orange — 1
  - blue — 1
  - gray — 1
  - dark gray — 1
- **c.** Plate on thick wove, fugitive ink, perf., gummed
  - carmine — 10
  - violet carmine — 10
  - pale dull red — 10
  - gray — 10
  - pale gray — 10.
  - pale dull tan — 10.
  - green — 10.
- **d.** As "c," strip of 3, signed Henry Lowenberg, pale tan — 400.
- **e.** Plate on white chemically treated paper (turns blue if wet), imperf.
  - carmine — 10.
  - Prussian blue — 10.
  - orange — 10.
  - green — 10.
  - brown — 10.
  - black — 10.
- **f.** As "e," perf.
  - carmine — 10.
  - scarlet — 10.
  - orange — 10.
  - blue — 10.
  - green — 10.
  - brown — 10.
- **g.** Plate on India
  - violet brown — 10.
  - green — 10.
  - blue — 10.
  - dark blue — 10.
- **h.** Plate on India, signed D.H. Craig, red — 350.
- **i.** On white card, 62x72mm, design deeply indented, green — 15.
- **j.** On blue wove, red — 15.

k. On orange laid
    black   15.
    gray   15.
l. On blue laid, scarlet   15.
m. On white laid, blue   15.
n. On pink laid, blue   15.
o. On linen cloth
    green   50.
    red   50.
    blue   50.
p. On glazed white paper, blue   20.

1867 Essays
John M. Sturgeon

79-E10

Liberty vignette. Curved labels top and bottom. Self-cancel-
ng: CANCELLED in colorless sensitive ink, becomes colored
hen wet. Patented 1867, 1868.

9-E10   10c
a. Die on stiff card, cut close, clearly en-
    graved, not canceled, both labels com-
    pletely blank, dark carmine   350.
b. Die on wove, rough impression, CAN-
    CELLED diagonally each way, dark
    carmine   450.
c. Die on thick white or tinted paper,
    gummed, rough impression, about
    21x26mm, two lines in upper label,
    one line in lower label
    carmine   200.
    dark carmine   200.
    very dark carmine   200.
    green   200.
    dark green   200.
    dull red violet   200.
d. As "c," on thick pinkish paper, dark
    green   250.
g. Single centered in 6-inch wide strip of
    thick white paper, almost always cut in
    at top and bottom, dark carmine   400.
h. Horiz. row of five designs on thick white
    paper, 10mm apart
    dark carmine   1,200.
    dark purple   1,200.
    black   1,200.
i. Single on blue card, ovptd. seal BRIT-
    ISH CONSULATE, V.R. in center,
    black   1,250.

American Bank Note Co.

79-E11

Design size: 18x21mm
Vignette of Columbia. Probably submitted by Charles F.
Steel.

79-E11   2c and 3c
a. Engraved plate on thick yellowish wove,
    imperf. (usually found in upper left
    margin blocks)
    rose scarlet   300.
    Block of 4   1,250.
    blue green   300.
    Block of 4   1,250.
b. Engraved plate on stamp paper, perf.
    12, gummed
    black   175.
    rose scarlet   175.
    blue green   175.
    blue   175.

Author Unknown

79-E12

Design size: 20x26mm
Vignette of Liberty in circle of stars. Vertical color lines
outside design to 24x28mm. Curved labels blank. Lithographed.

79-E12   No denomination
a. Die on white paper, dull violet   2,750.
b. Die on bluish paper, blue   2,750.

1867 Grill Essays
National Bank Note Co.

79-E13

Grill essays patented by Charles F. Steel.

79-E13
a. Wove paper, 80x140mm, impressed with
    four diff. seals, crossed lines and
    square dots down, circles 11 or 12mm   9,000.

79-E13b

b. Grills in odd shapes on white wove,
    each about 20x25mm
    cross   1,500.
    star in square   1,500.
    horizontal lined oval in square   1,500.
    diagonal lined oval in square   1,500.
c. White wove, gummed, 15mm circle with
    points down grill, surrounded by 24
    perforated holes   1,000.
d. White wove, quadrille batonne water-
    mark, 12mm colored circle with points
    down grill around 3, roughly grilled
    colorless 3 below, carmine   1,250.

79-E13e

e. Colorless 12mm grilled circle as on "d,"
    on tan wove, perf. 12   200.
f. As "e," yellow wove   200.
g. As "e," white wove, block of 6 with ms.
    "Subject to a half hour pressure after
    embossing"   3,500.
h. Colorless 15mm points down grilled cir-
    cle on white wove, perf. 12   200.

79-E14a

79-E14b

Allover grill.

79-E14
a. White wove, about 55x30mm, points
    down grill, stamped with red 6-digit
    number   450.
b. Wove paper in various colors, about
    85x40mm, points up grill as adopted
    white   200.
    pale pink   200.
    salmon   200.
    light yellow   200.
    light gray green   200.
    light blue   200.
    pale lilac   200.
    light gray   200.

79-E15

Experimental grills on perf. or imperf. stamps or stamp-size
pieces of paper.

79-E15
a. Allover grill of small squares, points
    down (points do not break paper as
    on issued stamp, No. 79)
    on 3c rose, gummed (No. 65)   250.
    on 3c lake, imperf. pair, gummed (No.
    66aP4)   250.
b. As "a" but points up, on 3c stamp, perf.
    12, gummed
    black   200.
    rose   200.
c. As "a" but points up, imperf pair,
    gummed
    3c rose **(formerly No. 79P4)**   400.
    3c lake **(formerly No. 66aP4)**   400.

79-E15d

d. Allover pinpoint grill (so-called "Music
Box" grill), points up, on No. 65 (plates
11, 34, 52)   75.
e. As "d" but points down, on 3c rose (plate
11)   125.
f. 15x16mm grill on stamp size white wove
paper, perf. 12, gummed   125.
g. C grill, 13x16mm, points down on stamp
size wove paper, perf. 12, gummed
  white   100.
  yellowish   100.
  pinkish   100.
h. As "g" but points up, on white wove   100.
i. C grill on 1c stamp (No. 63), points
  down   4,000.
j. C grill on 3c stamp (No. 65)
  points up   4,000.
  points down   4,000.

The 3c C grill essay is almost identical to the issued
stamp. There are slight differences in the essay grill which match those
on No. 79-E15i and Nos. 79-E15k through 79-E15n.

k. C grill on 5c stamp (No. 76)
  points up   4,000.
  points down   4,000.
l. C grill on 10c stamp (No. 68)
  points up   4,000.
  points down   4,000.
m. C grill on 12c stamp (No. 69)
  points up   4,000.
  points down   4,000.
n. C grill on 30c stamp (No. 71)
  points up   4,000.
  points down   4,000.
o. E grill, 11x13mm, points up, on stamp
size white wove paper, perf. 12,
gummed   100.
p. As "o," points down   100.

79-E15q

q. Z grill, 11x14mm, points down on stamp
size wove paper, perf. 12, partly
gummed
  white   125.
  salmon   125.
  yellow   125.
  greenish   125.
  dull violet   125.
  pale lilac   125.

These were made on fully perforated sheet selvage from
other essays.

79-E15r

r. As "q," in sheet of white wove stamp paper, imperf., gummed   175.

Continental Bank Note Co.

White wove paper about 6x9 inches with 7x9½mm grills
spaced as they would fall on centers of stamps in a sheet.

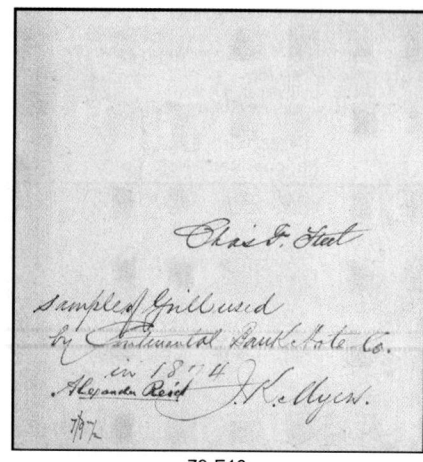

79-E16

79-E16
a. End roller grill at left, ms. "Chas. F.
Steel-Sample of Grill used by Continental Bank Note Co. in 1874. Alexan-
der Reid. J.K. Myers."   1,250.
b. Without end roller grill, ms. "Grill of Continental Bank Note Co. Chas. F.
Steel."   1,750.
c. End roller grill at right, same inscription
as "b"   250.
d. On soft card, six grills   450.

Wilbur I. Trafton

79-E17

Coarse grill in 15mm circle with 7 points up in 11mm, found
on 1873 1c, some with 18mm circular cancel, stuck down on
printed ad circular along with black, red and albino grill impressions (two each) on paper labeled "The Security Impression
from the plates."
79-E17   Entire ad circular with grill examples   750.

Natonal Bank Note Co.

79-E18

Albino 3 in points down shield-shaped grill in lithographed
frame of 3c 1861 stamp.
79-E18   3c
a. Die on thick white paper, gummed
  black   1,000.
  deep pink   1,000.
b. As "a," with Washington, D.C. Feb. 21
pmk.
  black   1,750.
  deep pink   1,750.

79-E18c

c. As "a" but grill with points up, black   1,000.
d. As "a," perf. 12, gummed, black   1,000.
e. Die on yellow wove, gummed

  black   1,
  red   1,
f. Die on orange wove
  black   1,0
  carmine   1,0
g. Die on yellow laid, black   1,0
h. Numeral handcolored, dull carmine   1,5
i. Frame only, no grill, on grayish wove
with pencil "McDonald P.O. Dept.
Steel Nature(?)", pale orange brown   1,5

79-E18j   **79-E18k**

Albino 3 in 13x14mm shield made up of embossed narr
spaced horiz. lines.

j. White wove stamp paper, 22x27mm,
perf. 12, gummed   45

Albino 3 in 13x14mm shield slightly different from No. 7
E18j.

k. As "j," different shield   35

79-E1

Illustration reduced.

Typographed impression of frame, lettering and numerals o
3c 1861
stamp with 3 in double lined shield in center. In strip of thre
about
20mm apart, impression of 3 and shield progressively lighte
on
impressions two and three.

79-E19   3c
a. Engraved (die No. 1570), green   3,00
b. Typographed in color on white paper
  blue green   2,75
  dark red brown   2,75
c. As "b," colored and colorless parts interchanged, on thick paper
  blue green   2,75
  dark red brown   2,75

79-E21

Lathework frame with shield shaped vignette cut out, albino 3
in circular grill in center.
79-E21   3c
a. Thick paper, perf. 12
  blue   500.
  carmine   500.
b. At left in strip of 3 with 2 No. 79-E13f,
latter black cancels, blue   3,500.
c. Lathework frame on thin wove, allover
diagonal grill, imperf., gummed, blue   500.

Lathework frame similar to No. 79-E21 but vignette of 6 horiz.
bars with 3 in center printed in glossy ink.

79-E22

79-E22   3c On pink lilac paper, blue   3,000.

79-E23

Design of 3c 1861 stamp typographed in relief for surface printing. Single impression lightly block sunk 63x62mm in color. Design has 21x26½mm border inside 23x28½mm colorless rectangle.

79-E23 3c
- **a.** Die on 64x75mm ivory paper, black .... 325.
- **b.** Die on India, dull violet-red red .... 325.
- **c.** Die on 59x54mm stiff white card, color about 40mm wide (not extending to edges)
  - light red violet .... 325.
  - carmine .... 325.
  - blue .... 325.
- **d.** Washington head only, lines on face around eye, on soft card
  - dim blue-green blue .... 250.
  - dim orange-orange red .... 250.

On 17x21mm plain colored rectangle printed through a mat, surrounded by 55x62mm colorless rectangle, vert. 4½mm wide color bands at sides inside 64x62mm die sinkage.

- **e.** Washington head with dots around eye, on 17x42mm solid color, on 77x45mm stiff white paper, dull violet-red .... 250.
- **f.** India paper on soft white card block sunk 63x62mm, dull violet-red-red with solid color margins .... 250.

Colored India generally cut away outside colorless rectangle 23x28½mm, design heavily embossed through to card beneath.

- **g.** As "f," trimmed to shape
  - dark carmine .... 350.
  - orange .... 350.
  - blue green .... 350.
  - red violet .... 350.
- **h.** Complete design on India, sunk on card, trimmed to shape
  - blue .... 100.
  - dull green blue .... 100.
- **i.** Plate typographed on white wove, imperf., gummed
  - dim red .... 50.
  - dim light orange red .... 50.
  - dim blue green .... 50.
  - dim pale blue .... 50.
  - dim dark blue .... 50.
  - dusky violet red .... 50.

Color outside design generally fills rectangle, design impression shows on back.

- **j.** Complete design on glossy sticky paper, deep violet red .... 150.
- **k.** As "j," on pelure, perf. 12, gummed, rose .... 175.
- **l.** As "k," allover grill, dim red .... 150.
- **m.** As "k," 13x16mm grill, gray black .... 150.

79-E24   79-E24c

Block sinkage: 65x76mm
Washington head only.

79-E24 3c
- **a.** Lithographed, face dotted, on 65x76mm solid color background
  - black .... 750.
  - red violet .... 750.
  - olive black .... 750.
- **b.** Typographed, background irregular edge, on card, gray black .... 750.
- **c.** Face lined, on 64x72mm solid color background
  - black .... 750.
  - scarlet .... 750.

79-E25

Plate essays of complete 1861 3c design.

79-E25 3c
- **a.** Plate on hard white transparent wove, dark red
- **b.** Plate on more opaque white wove, dim red .... 50.
- **c.** Plate on Gibson patent starch coated opaque white paper, generally crinkled, lathework design usually poorly printed
  - orange red .... 25.
  - deep orange red .... 25.
  - pink .... 25.
  - dull yellow .... 25.
  - yellow orange .... 25.
  - dull yellow orange .... 25.
  - brown yellow .... 25.
  - brown .... 25.
  - green .... 25.
  - blue green .... 25.
  - blue .... 25.
  - light blue .... 25.
- **d.** Plate on semitransparent white wove
  - dull pale blue .... 20.
  - green .... 20.
  - dull yellow orange .... 20.
- **e.** Plate on pale green paper, clearly printed, dark g-b green .... 40.
- **f.** Plate on white wove, 13x16mm points down grill, gummed, dark blue .... 40.
- **g.** Plate on lilac gray paper, 13x16mm grill, gummed
  - dark blue .... 40.
  - dull red .... 40.
  - black .... 40.
- **h.** Plate on white paper (ungrilled), perf. 12, gummed
  - red .... 25.
  - light red .... 25.
  - pale red .... 25.
  - light orange red .... 25.
  - deep yellow orange .... 25.
  - brown .... 25.
  - dark green .... 25.
  - deep blue .... 25.
  - dull g-b blue .... 25.
  - gray black .... 25.
- **i.** As "h," ms. A or B in UL corner, red .... 50.
- **j.** Plate on white paper, 13x16mm points down grill, perf. 12, gummed
  - black .... 25.
  - gray black .... 25.
  - pale red .... 25.
  - light red .... 25.
  - orange red .... 25.
  - deep orange yellow .... 25.
  - brown .... 25.
  - dark brown .... 25.
  - green .... 25.
  - blue .... 25.
  - dark blue .... 25.
- **k.** As "j," ms. "s No. 6" on back
  - red .... 50.
  - gray black .... 50.
  - dark blue .... 50.
- **l.** As "j," but grill points up
  - red .... 40.
  - pink .... 40.
  - pale rose .... 40.
  - brown .... 40.
  - orange yellow .... 40.
  - deep red orange .... 40.
  - green .... 40.
  - dull blue .... 40.
  - dull light blue .... 40.
- **m.** As "l," pair with blue oval "American Bank Note Co. April 17, '79", pink .... 150.
- **n.** Plate on greenish gray chemical paper, 13x16mm grill, perf. 12
  - black .... 50.
  - green .... 50.
  - dark blue .... 50.
  - orange red .... 50.
  - light yellow gray .... 50.
  - light red gray .... 50.
- **o.** As "n," without grill
  - red .... 50.
  - rose .... 50.
- **p.** Plate on pelure, without grill, imperf., gummed, dim red .... 50.
- **q.** As "p," perf. 12, dim red .... 50.

79-E26

Plate impressions of 1861 3c stamp overprinted with various safety network designs. Inks probably fugitive.

79-E26 3c
- **a.** Vert. pair on 58x80mm India, overprint die 54x71mm or more, small ONE repeated in 41 vert. lines per 40mm, rose pink, overprint deep orange yellow .... 2,000.
- **b.** As "a," block of 6 inscribed "J. Sangster Pat. 190376, Jan. 6, 1877" .... 3,500.
- **c.** 65TC3, "VEINTE" overprint, in miniature sheet of 12, perf. 12, black, overprint orange .... 7,500.

3c 1861 printed in various colors in miniature sheets of 12 with safety ovpts. (Apparently only one sheet printed of each color combination, except two Type D combinations known both perf. and imperf.)

- **d.** Type A
  - perf. 12, dull violet, overprint gray .... 425.
  - perf. 12, rose red, overprint gray blue .... 425.
  - perf. 12, violet, overprint gray tan .... 425.
  - imperf., pale olive, overprint gray tan .... 425.
  - imperf., green, overprint gray tan .... 425.
- **e.** Type B
  - perf. 12, green, overprint pale tan .... 425.
  - perf. 12, violet, overprint gray tan .... 425.
  - perf. 12, dull red brown, ovpt. pale brown .... 425.
  - perf. 12, dark dull red brown, overprint pale brown .... 425.

Type C   Type D

- **f.** Type C
  - perf. 12, dull violet, overprint gray tan .... 550.
  - perf. 12, dull red, overprint gray blue .... 550.
  - perf. 12, rose red, overprint gray blue .... 550.
  - perf. 12, green, overprint gray tan .... 550.
  - imperf., rose red, overprint pale tan .... 550.
  - imperf., pale rose red, overprint pale tan .... 550.
  - imperf., yellow brown, overprint tan .... 550.
- **g.** Type D
  - perf. 12, dull violet, overprint gray blue .... 550.
  - perf. 12, rose red, overprint gray blue .... 550.
  - perf. 12, light red brown, overprint pale brown .... 550.
  - perf. 12, dark green, overprint dull blue .... 550.
  - imperf., pale olive, overprint tan .... 550.
  - imperf., ultramarine, overprint tan .... 550.
  - imperf., dull violet, overprint gray blue .... 550.
  - imperf., dull violet, overprint pale green .... 550.
  - imperf., dark green, overprint dull blue .... 550.

79-E27

Design size: 20½x26½mm
Engraved in relief for surface printing, large 2 vignette, on same die with No. 79-E28, 20mm apart. Also essayed for envelopes on thick papers.

79-E27 2c
  a. Untrimmed die, 30x42mm, on paper with "US" monogram, pale rose ... 850.
  b. Die on stiff glazed paper, 63x50mm, black ... 600.
  c. Trimmed die on India, on thick soft card, colorless parts in relief
      black ... 450.
      red ... 450.
      orange ... 450.
      violet red ... 450.
  d. Die on 35x40mm white wove, imperf., gummed
      blue ... 450.
      albino ... 450.
  e. Die on white wove, perf. 12, gummed, smoky violet red ... 450.
  f. Untrimmed die on white wove, 61x42mm, black ... 550.

79-E28

79-E28g

Design size: 21x25½mm
Engraved in relief for surface printing, large 3 in shield vignette, on same die with No. 79-E27, 20mm apart. Also essayed for envelopes on thick papers.

79-E28 3c
  a. Untrimmed die on stiff ivory paper, showing color 30x42mm
      black ... 700.
      rose ... 700.
      orange ... 700.
      blue ... 700.
  b. Untrimmed die on India with No. 79-E27, both embossed, yellow orange ... 1,000.
  c. Trimmed die heavily struck on India, card mounted, colorless parts in relief
      black ... 500.
      red ... 500.
      orange ... 500.
  d. Die on wide laid paper, "US" monogram, perf. 12, gummed
      pale rose ... 250.
      dull brown yellow ... 250.
  e. Die on greenish wove, 10x12mm points down grill, imperf., gummed, dull brown ... 250.
  f. Die on white paper, perf. 12, gummed
      smoky violet red ... 250.
      green ... 250.
  g. Underprinted design only on thin white wove
      light blue ... 350.
      albino ... 350.

79-E28H

Illustration reduced.
Design size: 68x38mm
Two compound surface-printed designs, "3" within ornate frame.

79-E28H 3c Untrimmed die on wove paper, green ... 1,250.

79-E29

1861 1c frame only.
79-E29 1c
  a. Die on thin crisp paper, safely design underprint, black on dull olive green ... 2,750.
  b. Die on pink paper, 18x13mm points down grill, imperf., gummed, red brown ... 1,250.
  c. Die on pink "laid" paper, red ... 1,250.
  d. Die on pale pink paper, red brown ... 1,250.
  e. Die on transparent white paper, red brown ... 1,250.
  f. Die on thick yellow paper, red brown ... 1,250.
  g. Die on thin transparent white paper, 11x13mm points down grill, perf. 12, gummed, red brown ... 1,250.
  h. As "g," imperf. ... 2,000.

79-E29i

As No. 79-E29 but with monogram in vignette.
  i. Die on transparent white stamp paper, perf. 12, gummed, red brown ... 11,000.

79-E30

Design size: 20x26mm
Block size: 64x76½mm
Vignette of Liberty. Typographed.
79-E30 3c
  a. Head only on solid color (die size: 67x76mm), on 32x37mm stiff yellowish wove
      black ... 750.
      blue green ... 750.
  b. Vignette only, on 66x100mm card
      black ... 750.
      blue green ... 750.
      blue ... 750.
  c. Vignette only, on proof paper
      bright blue ... 600.
      black ... 600.
  d. Complete design, untrimmed block, colorless 22x27 rectangle around design, broad outer edge in color, on stiff yellowish wove
      black ... 750.
      blue green ... 750.
      violet brown ... 750.
      bright violet red ... 750.
      red violet ... 750.
      buff ... 750.
  e. As "d," on proof paper
      buff ... 750.
      deep blue green ... 750.

red brown
carmine
black
  f. Die on proof paper, perf. 12, vignette oval perf. 16, carmine
  g. Die on stiff ivory paper about 28x32mm
      black
      carmine
      yellow
      dark blue green
      rose violet
  h. Die on stiff ivory paper, no color outside design, block of 4, carmine
      Block of 8 with vert. pairs in orange, dull yellow green, dark green and dark violet
  i. Die on deep orange-surfaced white paper, carmine
  j. As "i," perf. 12, gummed, carmine
  k. Die on yellow-surfaced wove, carmine

79-E30l

  l. Die with outer color removed, on 64x90mm white wove stamp paper with imprint below, imperf., gummed
      carmine ... 15
      scarlet ... 15
      dim orange red ... 15
      orange ... 15
      dull yellow orange ... 15
      pale dull yellow ... 15
      brown ... 15
      lemon ... 15
      yellow green ... 15
      dull olive green ... 15
      dull greenish gray ... 15
      dim blue green ... 15
      dull blue ... 15
      dull red violet ... 15
      pale red violet ... 15
  m. As "l," tete-beche pairs, each with imprint
      carmine, orange ... 35
      buff, pale lilac ... 35
      dark orange brown, yellow ... 35
      dull green gray ... 35

79-E30n

  n. As "l," perf. 12, vignette oval perf. 16 (also found without paper outside perfs.
      carmine ... 150
      pale rose ... 150
      dim scarlet ... 150
      dull scarlet ... 150
      dim orange red ... 150
      light red brown ... 150
      dark brown ... 150
      orange ... 150
      dull orange ... 150
      dismal orange ... 150
      dull brown orange ... 150
      pale dull yellow ... 150
      dull brown ... 150
      yellow brown ... 150
      dull olive green ... 150
      dim dark yellow orange ... 150
      light yellow green ... 150
      green ... 150
      dim blue green ... 150
      dark blue green ... 150
      dull greenish gray ... 150
      dull yellowish gray ... 150
      dull blue ... 150.
      dim red violet ... 150.
      dull red violet ... 150.
      pale red violet ... 150.
      red violet ... 150.

79-E30o

o. Plate essay on wove, designs 7mm apart, in two colors shading into each other, imperf.

red brown to dark orange	150.
dark orange to brown red	150.
brown olive to red brown	150.
red brown to yellow green	150.
yellow green to dull carmine	150.
dull carmine to yellow green	150.
blue green to dull carmine	150.
brown olive to dull carmine	150.
dull carmine to orange	150.
orange to deep blue	150.
deep blue to orange brown	150.
orange brown to dull orange	150.
dull carmine to deep blue	150.

79-E30p Block

Illustration reduced.

p. As "o," on transparent wove, imperf.

red violet to deep violet	150.
deep violet to carmine	150.
dull scarlet to gold	150.
gold to carmine	150.
dark violet to blue green	150.
blue green to dark violet red	150.
violet to yellow green	150.
yellow green to red violet	150.

q. Plate on stiff yellowish wove, imperf.

dull carmine to orange	150.
orange to deep blue	150.
brown olive to brown red	150.
brown red to yellow green	150.
blue green to dull carmine	150.
dull carmine to deep blue	150.
deep blue to dark brown	150.
dark brown to orange	150.

r. As "q," outside edge perf. 12

blue green to dull carmine	150.
dull carmine to deep blue	150.
deep blue to dark brown	150.
dark brown to dull orange	150.
dull carmine to dull orange	150.
dull orange to deep blue	150.
yellow green to dull carmine	150.
dull carmine to yellow green	150.
brown olive to brown red	150.
brown red to yellow green	150.

s. Plate in single color, outside edge perf. 12, gummed

carmine	150.
dull orange	150.
orange brown	150.
dark brown	150.
brown olive	150.
dark blue green	150.
violet	150.

t. As "s," imperf., gummed

brown	125.
brown orange	125.
dull blue green	125.
deep blue	125.
carmine	125.

u. As "t," one color directly over another (gives effect of one color), black on scarlet   275.

v. As "b," heavily stamped on white card, only faint traces of vignette, albino   125.

w. As "v," printed design at right, very dark blue green   250.

79-E31a

79-E31b

79-E31d

79-E31e

79-E13f

79-E31g

Same design as No. 79-E30, black green on white wove safety paper, underprinted with different designs in various colors, imperf.

79-E31   3c

a.	Red horiz. diamonds	1,400.
b.	Dull yellow green with ONE repeated	1,400.
c.	Red with 2 in circles	1,400.
d.	Red with 2 in circular stars	1,400.
e.	Red with 2 in ovals	1,400.
f.	Red with 3 in diamonds	1,400.
g.	Black with 5 in hexagons	1,400.
h.	Red with X repeated	1,400.

79-E32

Similar to No. 79-E30f, but perf. vignette removed and frame mounted over 18x23mm Washington vignette.

79-E32   3c Die on 34x40mm white wove, black vignette, blueframe   8,000.

1868 Essays
Experiments for bicolor printing

1c 1861 design, color reversed as adopted. Typographed frame with 43x60mm solid color border.

79-E33   1c Die on thin white paper, frame pink, vignette dark blue over pink   750.

79-E35a

79-E35c

Frame lithographed, colored and colorless parts interchanged, vignette engraved and printed in another color.
Die I: colorless vignette oval (Nos. 79-E35a, 79-E35b)
Die II: vignette with horiz. lines (Nos. 79-E35d through 79-E35f)

79-E35   5c
a. Untrimmed die on thin white paper, 40x60mm (values for cut to stamp size)

frame buff, vignette black	2,000.
frame buff, vignette blue	2,000.
frame buff, vignette red brown	2,000.
frame buff, vignette dark brown	2,000.
frame buff, vignette orange	2,000.
frame buff, vignette carmine	2,000.
frame blue green, vignette dark brown	2,000.
frame blue green, vignette red brown	2,000.
frame blue green, vignette orange	2,000.
frame carmine, vignette blue	2,000.
frame carmine, vignette red brown	2,000.
frame violet, vignette orange	2,000.
frame light red, vignette deep orange red	2,000.
frame light red, vignette yellow orange	2,000.

b. Die on stiff wove, frame brown, vignette scarlet   2,000.

c. 45x65mm die impression of lithographed frame only, on ivory paper

black	2,000.
blue green	2,000.

d. Die on thin white paper

frame violet, vignette carmine	2,000.
frame violet, vignette brown	2,000.
frame violet, vignette red brown	2,000.
frame carmine, vignette black	2,000.

e. Vignette only on white glazed paper

black	2,000.
blue	2,000.
scarlet	2,000.
dark brown	2,000.

f. As "e," without thin outer frameline, on India

lake	2,000.
red	2,000.
deep red orange	2,000.
scarlet	2,000.
deep green	2,000.
ultramarine	2,000.

79-E36

Die II vignette as No. 79-E35e, with gothic "United States" above.

79-E36   5c
a. Die on white glazed paper

black	450.
scarlet	450.
dark brown	450.
green	450.
blue	450.

79-E37

Die size: 51x63½
5c 1861 design, color reversed as adopted, vignette mounted on typographed frame.

79-E37   5c
a. Die on white card, frame light blue, vignette black   1,000.
b. Vignette only, die on India, black   350.
c. Vignette only, die on white glazed paper

blue	350.
black	350.
green	350.

100-E1

Design size: 20½x24½mm

Engraved circular Franklin vignette mounted on 43x75mm white card, engraved Washington head mounted thereon; background, silhouette, etc., retouched in black ink. With engraved frame of No. 71-E1 (vignette cut out) mounted over the double vignette.

100-E1   30c Die on India, 30x34mm, black   *6,000.*

1869 ISSUE
George T. Jones

    112-E1   113-E1

Design size: 24x30mm
U.S. Grant vignette in frame with blank labels, ovals, etc. Paper overprinted with network of fine colored wavy lines in fugitive inks as on beer stamps.

112-E1   No Denomination
   a. Die on India cut to stamp size, 1 color
      black   *2,250.*
      blue   *2,250.*
   b. Die on India cut to stamp size, 2 colors
      (head in black)
      blue, light gray overprint   *3,250.*
      red, light gray overprint   *3,250.*
      black, light violet overprint   *3,250.*
      black brown, pale red violet ovpt.   *3,250.*
      carmine, gray overprint   *3,250.*
      blue, yellow overprint   *3,250.*

Design size: 24x30mm
U.S. Treasury Dept. seal in vignette oval.

113-E1   2c
   a. Die on India cut to stamp size, 1 color
      carmine   *2,500.*
      blue   *2,500.*
   b. Die on India cut to stamp size, 3 colors,
      black on pale red violet wavy lines and
      blue green lined vignette   *3,750.*

Frame as 112-E1 but with Washington vignette and 2c denomination. Another Washington vignette below but in horiz. lined oval frame.

113-E2   2c Die on 1⅝x3½inch India, black   *5,000.*

National Bank Note Co.

All values originally essayed with numerals smaller than adopted. All designs are same size as issued stamps. Sheets of 150 of 1c-12c, sheets of 50 of 24c-90c. Many colors of plate essays exist from one sheet only, some colors from two sheets and a few from three. Some plate essays exist privately perforated.

   112-E2   112-E3

Die size: 40x65mm
Vignette size: 17mm diameter
Vignette of Franklin.

112-E2   1c Die of vignette only on India
      orange   *900.*
      violet brown   *900.*
      black   *900.*

Circle of pearls added to vignette, suggestion for frame and 1 in circle at bottom penciled in.

112-E3   1c Die on India, black   *1,500.*

   112-E4   112-E5

Complete design as issued but with small value numeral.

112-E4   1c
   a. Die on India, die sunk on card
      black   *1,250.*
      violet brown   *1,250.*
      dark brown   *1,250.*
      yellow brown   *1,250.*
      scarlet   *1,250.*
      carmine   *1,250.*
      deep violet   *1,250.*
      blue   *1,250.*
      green   *1,250.*
      yellow   *1,250.*
   b. Plate on stamp paper, imperf., gummed
      buff   *100.*
      deep orange brown   *100.*
      orange brown   *100.*
   c. Plate on stamp paper, perf. 12, gummed
      buff   *100.*
      orange brown   *100.*
      orange   *125.*
   d. As "c," with 9x9mm grill
      buff   *110.*
      orange brown   *85.*
      red brown   *85.*
      chocolate   *85.*
      black brown   *85.*
      dull red   *85.*
      violet   *110.*
      dark violet   *110.*
      blue   *110.*
      deep blue   *110.*
      green   *110.*
      yellow   *110.*
      orange   *110.*
      rose red   *110.*

Design size: 23x31mm
Die size: 51x55mm
Design as issued but surrounded by fancy frame with flags and shield. Also essayed for envelopes and wrappers on thick paper.

112-E5   1c
   a. Die on stamp paper, perf. 12, gummed,
      gray   *3,000.*
   b. Die on white ivory paper
      black   *2,000.*
      black brown   *2,000.*
      scarlet   *2,000.*
      blue   *2,000.*
   c. Die on India
      blue   *2,000.*
      blue green   *2,000.*
   d. Die on India, cut to shape
      carmine   *750.*
      yellow   *750.*

         113-E3

Die size: 41x50mm
Design as issued but with small value numeral. Nos. 113-E3a and 113-Eb have incomplete shading around "UNITED STATES."

113-E3   2c
   a. Die on India, die sunk on card
      black   *1,500.*
      yellow   *1,500.*
      red orange   *1,500.*
      deep scarlet   *1,500.*
      brown   *1,500.*
      green   *1,500.*
      dusky blue   *1,500.*
      deep blue   *1,500.*
   b. Die on India, cut to stamp size
      deep orange red   *400.*
      deep orange yellow   *400.*
      blue green   *400.*
      gray black   *400.*
      light blue   *400.*
      rose   *400.*
   c. Complete die on India, die sunk on card
      brown   *1,500.*
      rose   *1,500.*
      mauve   *1,500.*
      green   *1,500.*
      dark chocolate   *1,500.*
      red brown   *1,500.*
   d. Plate on stamp paper, perf. 12, gummed
      brown   *425.*
      dark brown   *425.*
      yellow   *425.*
   e. As "d," with 9x9mm grill
      brown   *80.*
      dark brown   *80.*
      orange brown   *80.*
      dark orange brown   *80.*
      rose   *80.*
      brown rose   *80.*
      copper red   *80.*
      deep copper red   *80.*
      green   *80.*
      deep green   *80.*
      blue green   *80.*
      yellow   *80.*
      orange   *80.*

---

      dull yellow orange
      blue
      light violet
      violet
      dark violet
   f. As "e," double grill, orange

           113-E4

Original sketch of postrider, printed "NATIONAL BANK N[...] COMPANY. BUSINESS DEPARTMENT. 1868" at top, p[...] instructions at bottom, "Reduce to this length" and "2 copie[...] one plate. Daguerrotype."

113-E4   2c Drawing on paper, black

   114-E3   114-E4

Die size: 53x47mm
Design nearly as issued: larger motive above and be[...] "POSTAGE" erased, no shading on numeral shield, top lea[...] and corner leaves do not touch, no dots in lower corners[...] scrolls beside bottom of shield, no vert. shading lines in "POS[...] AGE" label. Small value numeral.

114-E3   3c Die on 30x30mm ivory paper, black   *1,5[...]*

Similar to 114-E3, but smaller motive around "POSTAG[...] shield shaded.

114-E4   3c
   a. Die on India, die sunk on card
      black   *1,5[...]*
      carmine   *1,5[...]*
      scarlet   *1,5[...]*
      orange red   *1,5[...]*
      yellow orange   *1,5[...]*
      dull yellow   *1,5[...]*
      red sepia   *1,5[...]*
      blue green   *1,5[...]*
      blue   *1,5[...]*
      dull red   *1,5[...]*
      orange brown   *1,5[...]*
   b. Die on India, cut to stamp size
      black   *5[...]*
      rose   *5[...]*
      scarlet   *5[...]*
      chocolate   *5[...]*
      dull dusky orange   *5[...]*
      red violet   *5[...]*
      blackish slate   *5[...]*

Similar to No. 114-E4 but vert. shading lines added to "POS[...] AGE" frame.

114-E5   3c Die on India, dusky yellow orange   *1,75[...]*

   114-E6   114-E7

Completed small numeral die essay: leaves at top and side[...] touch, dots in lower corners added, vert. shading lines in fram[...] around "POSTAGE," shield shaded darker at bottom, scroll[...] added to bottom of shield.

114-E6   3c
   a. Die on India, card mounted
      black   *1,75[...]*
      blue   *1,75[...]*
      deep orange red   *1,75[...]*
   b. Plate on stamp paper, imperf., gummed
      ultramarine   *12[...]*
      dark ultramarine   *12[...]*
      light brown   *85[...]*
      red brown   *85[...]*
      dark red brown   *85[...]*
      pale rose   *85[...]*
      rose   *85[...]*
      brown rose   *85[...]*
   c. Plate on stamp paper, perf. 12, gummed
      ultramarine   *500[...]*

dark ultramarine	500.

d. As "c," with 9x9mm grill
blue	80.
deep blue	80.
orange brown	80.
black brown	80.
deep black brown	80.
rose red	80.
green	80.
yellow	80.
orange	80.
deep orange	80.
dull violet	80.
deep violet	80.
red violet	80.

Same design and color as issued stamp, but with allover array grill of squares up.

E7 3c
a. Imperf., gummed, ultramarine ... 700.
b. As "a," 23mm "NATIONAL BANK NOTE CO. N.Y. SEP 27, 1869" circular pmk., ultramarine ... 1,100.
c. On thick paper, imperf., gummed, horiz. line defacement, ultramarine ... 700.
d. Perf. 12, horiz. line defacement, ultramarine ... 700.

115-E1

115-E2

Die size: 40x60mm
Vignette of Washington. Design as issued 6c stamp but with 5c denomination. Large lettering, large U and S in corners. Also essayed for envelopes on thick paper.

115-E1 6c
a. Die on India, no frameline, solid vignette background, corner spandrels short at centers
black	700.
carmine	700.
dismal red brown	700.
smoky dusky brown	700.
gray violet	700.

b. Completed die on India, die sunk on card
black	600.
carmine	600.
deep rose	600.
red violet	600.
red brown	600.
deep yellow brown	600.
black brown	600.
dull yellow	600.
orange	600.
dusky blue	600.
dusky slate blue	600.
green	600.
blue green	600.
scarlet	600.

c. Die on proof paper, about 40x65mm
black	600.
carmine	600.
scarlet	600.
red orange	600.
orange	600.
dull yellow	600.
orange brown	600.
olive brown	600.
dusky green	600.
dusky yellow green	600.
light blue	600.
deep blue	600.
red violet	600.

d. Die on pink bond
orange	600.
brown	600.
blue	600.

e. Die on light yellow green bond, black ... 600.
f. Die on pale olive buff bond
black	600.
carmine	600.
orange	600.
red orange	600.
brown	600.

g. Die on cream wove
black	600.
orange	600.
brown	600.
blue	600.

h. Die on clear white bond
black	600.
blue	600.
orange	600.
red orange brown	600.

i. Die on thick cloudy bond
black	600.
red	600.
orange	600.
orange brown	600.
blue	600.
reddish brown	600.

j. Die on pale lilac bond
dark red orange	700.
orange	700.

blue	700.

k. Die on glazed paper
black	550.
scarlet	550.
yellow	550.
dark brown	550.
blue	550.

l. Die on marbled white card
green on red violet veined	1,750.
black on green veined	1,750.
red violet on green veined	1,750.

m. Die on ivory card
black	1,500.
blue	1,500.

n. Die on white card, cut to stamp size, red orange ... 250.

Die size: 43x63mm
Similar to No. 115-E1 but lettering, U and S smaller.

115-E2 6c
a. Incomplete die on India (incomplete spandrel points, hair on top of head, etc.)
black	750.
dull red brown	750.

b. Complete die on India, die sunk on card
black	750.
blue	750.
dull dusky violet	750.
scarlet	750.
dark orange red	750.
dim dusky red orange	750.
dusky green	750.
dusky green blue green	750.
dusky blue green	750.

c. Plate essay on wove, imperf., gummed
deep ultramarine	150.
orange	150.
dull red violet	80.
deep red violet	80.
red brown	80.
dull red brown	80.
buff	80.
green	80.

d. Plate essay on wove, perf. 12, gummed
orange	200.
blue	200.

115-E3

Vignette of Washington as used on stamp but with longer shirt front.

115-E3 6c Die on india, affixed to card, 35x37mm, black ... —

116-E1

Die size: 14x18mm
Vignette of Lincoln as on No. 77.
116-E1 10c Die on India, on card, black ... —

116-E1a

Design size:14x14½mm
Vignette of Lincoln as on No. 77, reduced.
116-E1a Die on India, on card, black ... 1,500.

116-E1b

Design size: about 19½x19½mm
Die size: 64x68½mm
Head as on No. 77 but less bust, large unshaded collar, no cross shading in triangles between labels and fasces, no shading on diamonds at end of value label.

116-E1b Incomplete die on India, on card, black ... 800.00

116-E1c

Small collar, shading on diamonds at end of value label. Also essayed for envelopes on yellow laid paper.

116-E1c Complete die on India, die sunk on card
black	1,000.
brown black	1,000.
gray black	1,000.
carmine	1,000.
scarlet	1,000.
brown red	1,000.
orange	1,000.
deep orange	1,000.
deep red	1,000.
yellow brown	1,000.
yellow	1,000.
green	1,000.
blue green	1,000.
deep blue	1,000.
red violet	1,000.
brown	1,000.

d. Die on proof paper
black	1,000.
carmine	1,000.
bright red	1,000.
orange red	1,000.
orange	1,000.
dark chocolate	1,000.
dusky yellow brown	1,000.
green	1,000.
blue	1,000.
red violet	1,000.

e. Die on ivory paper
black	1,000.
scarlet	1,000.
black brown	1,000.
blue	1,000.

f. Die on clear white thin bond, about 30x35mm
black	1,000.
red orange	1,000.
red brown	1,000.
orange	1,000.
yellow	1,000.
blue	1,000.

g. Die on cloudy cream bond, about 30x35mm
black	1,000.
light red brown	1,000.
red orange	1,000.
blue	1,000.

h. Die on pink bond, about 39x45mm
red orange	1,000.
red brown	1,000.
yellow	1,000.

i. Die on pale greenish gray bond, about 33x37mm
black	1,000.
deep carmine	1,000.
dull scarlet	1,000.
dark brown	1,000.
blue	1,000.

j. Die on marbled white ivory card, about 38x62mm
black on green veined	1,900.
orange red on green veined	1,900.
red orange on green veined	1,900.
dark orange brown on red violet veined	1,900.

k. Plate on stamp paper, imperf., gummed
deep green	150.
blue	125.
ultramarine	125.
dark ultramarine	125.
light ultramarine	125.

l. Plate on stamp paper, perf. 12, gummed, orange ... 200.

116-E2

Die size: 101x62mm
Vignette of signing the Declaration of Independence as
adopted for 24c.

116-E2 10c
   a. Die on India, die sunk on card
     black   2,500.
     carmine   2,500.
     dim rose   2,500.
     dull scarlet   2,500.
     red orange   2,500.
     orange yellow   2,500.
     red brown   2,500.
     orange brown   2,500.
     green   2,500.
     blue   2,500.
     gray   2,500.
   b. Die on India, cut to stamp size
     black   800.
     red orange   800.
     blue green   800.
     dim rose   800.
     brown   800.
     buff   800.
     dull scarlet   800.
        Other colors reported to exist.

116-E3   116-E4

Die size: 63x75mm
Design as adopted for issued stamp, but incomplete shading
on bottom ribbon, thin shading lines behind "States," and center
of "0" of "10" not filled in.

116-E3 10c Die on India on 61x53mm card,
     black   2,500.

Similar to No. 116-E3 except shading lines added behind
"Ten Cents" and center of "0" of "10" filled in.

116-E4 10c Die on India, die sunk on card
     black   2,500.
     orange   2,500.
     blue   2,500.

117-E1   117-E2

Die size: 47x51mm
Design as issued but with smaller value numerals.

117-E1 12c
   a. Die on card, black   1,600.
   b. Vignette die on India, pencil "Adriatic",
     black   1,600.
   c. Complete die on India, die sunk on card
     black   1,350.
     rose   1,350.
     yellow   1,350.
     scarlet   1,350.
     dark red brown   1,350.
     blue green   1,350.
     blue   1,350.
     dull violet   1,350.
     gray black   1,350.
     orange brown   1,350.
     yellow brown   1,350.
     dull orange red   1,350.
   d. Die on India, cut to stamp size
     black   600.
     dusky red orange   600.
     deep orange red   600.
     dim blue   600.
   e. Plate on stamp paper, 9x9mm grill, perf.
     12, gummed
     green   125.
     rose red   125.
     pale rose red   125.
     yellow brown   125.
     red brown   125.
     orange   125.

---

     blue   125.
     dull violet   125.
     dull red violet   125.
     yellow orange   125.

Similar to No. 117-E1, but small numeral not printed, large 12
drawn in pencil.

117-E2 12c Die on India, black   2,750.

117-E3   117-E4

Typographed small numeral design similar to No. 117-E1,
relief engraved for surface printing. Heavier lines, upper label
with solid background, letters of "UNITED STATES POSTAGE"
colorless. Nos. 117-E3a through 117-E3c from untrimmed die,
heavily struck with uncolored areas in relief, color covering borders beyond white line exterior of frame. Untrimmed die size:
58x45mm.

117-E3 12c
   a. Untrimmed die on card
     brown red   750.
     green   750.
     black   750.
     red brown   750.
   b. Untrimmed die on thin pinkish wove
     gray black   450.
     dull deep red orange   450.
     dark red orange   450.
   c. Untrimmed die on thick white wove
     carmine   600.
     green   600.
   d. Die on white paper, stamp size
     carmine   400.
     orange   400.
     brown   400.
     lilac   400.
     green   400.
   e. Die on thin white wove
     carmine   400.
     gray black   400.
     dull deep red orange   400.
     deep orange red   400.
   g. Die on pinkish wove, perf. 12, gummed,
     red brown   400.
   h. Die on yellow wove, imperf.
     gray black   400.
     carmine   400.
     red brown   400.
     dark red violet   400.
   i. Die on yellow wove, 11x13mm grill, im-
     perf., red brown   400.
   j. Die on white laid
     gray   400.
     gray black   400.
     brown   400.
     red brown   400.
   k. Die on yellow laid
     red brown   400.
     brown   400.
     dull red violet   400.
     carmine   400.
   l. Die on salmon laid, red brown   400.
   m. Die on pinkish laid
     red brown   400.
     gray   400.
   n. Die on pinkish laid, 11x13mm grill,
     gummed, red brown   400.
   o. Die on dull red violet laid, gray   400.

Vignette size: 15x11mm
Untrimmed die size: 63x32mm
Vignette only, similar to No. 117-E3 but lithographed instead
of typographed.

117-E4 12c
   a. Die on white ivory paper, black   1,000.
   b. Complete impression from untrimmed
     stone in solid color about 63x63mm,
     on white ivory paper, black   750.
   c. Die on glossy-surfaced thin white wove,
     trimmed to stamp size
     carmine   750.
     rose pink   750.
     yellow   750.
     blue green   750.
     dim red violet   750.
     pale red violet   750.
     deep red orange   750.
     dull dark red orange   750.
     dull dark yellow orange   750.
     dark violet red   750.
     pale gray   750.
   d. Die on thick white wove
     yellow   750.
     violet red   750.
     deep red violet   750.

118-E1a

Die size: 62x49mm
Type I design as issued but with smaller value numerals

118-E1 15c
   a. Die of vignette only on India, mounted
     on 62x62mm India, die sunk on card,
     dark blue   3,
   b. Incomplete die (no outer frameline or
     shading outside frame scrolls) on In-
     dia, black   4,

118-E1c

   c. Complete die on India, die sunk on card
     black   5,0
     scarlet   5,0
     orange brown   5,0
     green   5,0
     dull violet   5,0
     red brown   5,0

119-E1a

Type II design with large value numerals as issued.

119-E1 15c
   a. Type II frame only, die on India
     black   3,0
     red brown   3,0
   b. Vignette only, die on India, blue

119-E1c

   c. Type II frame with vignette mounted in
     place, die on India, red brown frame,
     blue vignette   3,00
   d. Type II frame with vignette mounted at
     right, die on India, red brown frame,
     blue vignette

129-E1   129-E2

Die size: 65x49
Type III design as adopted, except in various single color
large "15" overprint in diff. color.

129-E1 15c
   a. Die on India, die sunk on card
     orange brown, red overprint   3,50
     blue green, red overprint   3,50
     ultramarine, red overprint   3,50
     violet, red overprint   3,50
     red brown, red overprint   3,50
   b. Die on India, die sunk on card
     rose red, ultramarine overprint   3,50
     dull scarlet, ultramarine overprint   3,50
     dark red brown, ultramarine ovpt.   3,50
   c. Die on India, die sunk on card
     scarlet, blue green overprint   3,500
     orange brown, blue green overprint   3,500
     dark red brown, blue green overprint   3,500

Type III frame only.

129-E2 15c
   a. Die on India, red brown   2,75
   b. Die on India, with vignette mounted in
     place, blue frame, yellow vignette   3,50

120-E1

120-E2

Die size: 102x63mm
Design nearly as issued, but shading under leaves at top of frame and ribbon over "TWENTY" are unfinished. Small value numerals. Single color.

120-E1 24c Die on India, black ..... 4,000.

Completed small numeral design in single color. No. 120-E2a has 8mm-high bands of shaded colored lines 31mm long overprinted above and below vignette, printed in various single colors with bands in contrasting color.

120-E2 24c
  a. Die on India
    black with carmine bands ..... 4,000.
    black with violet brown bands ..... 4,000.
    black with brown orange bands ..... 4,000.
    orange brown with deep dull violet
      bands ..... 4,000.
    orange brown with blue green bands ..... 4,000.
  b. Die on India
    black ..... 2,250.
    scarlet ..... 2,250.
    dark red brown ..... 2,250.
    blue ..... 2,250.
    violet ..... 2,250.
  c. Plate on red salmon tinted paper, black ..... 200.
  d. Plate on orange buff tinted paper, black ..... 250.
  e. Plate on dull yellowish tinted paper,
    black ..... 250.
  f. Plate on blue tinted paper, black ..... 250.
  g. Plate on gray tinted paper, black ..... 500.
  h. Plate on India, black ..... 300.
  j. Plate on card, imperf., black ..... 250.

120-E3a

120-E3b

No. 120-E3a bicolor design as issued, except vignette printed separately and mounted in place; No. 120-E3b frame only with border lines around vignette space; No. 120-E3c frame only with 2 border lines around vignette space as issued.

120-E3 24c
  a. Die on India, card mounted
    dull violet frame, green vignette ..... 2,500.
    violet frame, red vignette ..... 2,500.
    green frame, violet vignette ..... 2,500.
    rose frame, green vignette ..... 2,500.
  b. Frame die on India, card mounted
    black ..... 5,000.
    light green ..... 2,500.
    dark green ..... 2,500.
  c. Frame die on India, block sunk on India,
    green ..... 2,500.

121-E1

Design size: 21½x22mm
Die Size: 71x51mm
Vignette of Surrender of Gen. Burgoyne in ornate frame.

121-E1 30c
  a. Die on India, die sunk on card
    black ..... 800.
    carmine ..... 800.
    rose red ..... 800.
    light brown red ..... 800.
    red brown ..... 800.
    brown orange ..... 800.
    orange ..... 800.
    red orange ..... 800.
    yellow green ..... 800.
    blue ..... 800.
    dull dark violet ..... 800.
    yellow brown ..... 800.
    scarlet ..... 800.
  b. Die on stiff ivory paper
    black ..... 650.
  c. Die on India, cut to stamp size
    dim deep orange red ..... 250.

deep yellow orange ..... 250.
dim deep blue green ..... 250.
dim dusky blue ..... 250.
  d. Die on India die sunk on 78x58mm
    white card
    dusky blue ..... 1,000.
  e. Die on white card, cut to stamp size
    dim orange ..... 500.
  f. Die on proof paper, about 70x50mm
    black ..... 500.
    carmine ..... 500.
    scarlet ..... 500.
    red orange ..... 500.
    green ..... 500.
    violet ..... 500.
  g. Die on ivory paper, about 64x50mm
    black ..... 750.
    dark brown ..... 750.
    scarlet ..... 750.
    blue ..... 750.
  h. Die on ivory card
    black ..... 1,000.
    carmine ..... 1.000.
  i. Die on clear white bond, about
    33x33mm
    black ..... 600.
    blue ..... 600.
    light red brown ..... 600.
    orange ..... 600.
  j. Die on yellowish cloudy bond, about
    34x34mm
    black ..... 600.
    orange ..... 600.
    light red brown ..... 600.
    blue ..... 600.
  k. Die on smoky yellow greenish bond
    black ..... 600.
    carmine ..... 600.
    orange ..... 600.
  l. Die on pink bond, about 40x40mm
    blue ..... 600.
    dim orange red ..... 600.
    orange ..... 600.
  m. Die on pale olive buff paper
    black ..... 600.
    dim orange red ..... 600.
    orange ..... 600.
  n. Die on thick yellowish wove, dim green
    blue ..... 600.
  o. Die on marbled white ivory card, about
    40x60mm
    black on green veined ..... 2,250.
    black on red violet veined ..... 2,250.
  p. Plate essay in black on thin surface-
    tinted paper
    pale gray ..... 275.
    salmon red ..... 175.
    yellow ..... 175.
    orange ..... 275.
    orange buff ..... 275.
    pink ..... 275.
    pale pink ..... 275.
    blue ..... 275.
    light blue ..... 275.
    pale green ..... 275.
    brown violet ..... 275.
  q. Plate essay in black on India ..... 300.
  r. Plate on thick rough pitted card, black ..... 300.

121-E1s

  s. Plate on bond, red bands overprinted
    top and bottom as on No. 120-E2a,
    dull red violet ..... 350.

121-E2

121-E3

Flags, stars and rays only as adopted for issued stamp. Black essay shows traces of vignette also.

121-E2 30c Die on India, mounted on India,
    block sunk on card
    black ..... 7,500.
    light ultramarine ..... 6,000.
    dark blue ..... 6,000.

Eagle, shield and value only as adopted for issued stamp.

121-E3 30c Die on India, card mounted, black ..... 8,500.

122-E1

Die size: 62x69mm
Vignette of Washington in frame similar to that of issued stamp but no shading over U and S in lower corners, small value numerals.

122-E1 90c Die on India, black ..... 3,250.

Similar to No. 122-E1 but shading over U and S.

122-E2

122-E2 90c
  a. Die on India, die sunk on card
    black ..... 2,500.
    carmine ..... 2,500.
    scarlet ..... 2,500.
    red brown ..... 2,500.
    blue green ..... 2,500.
    violet ..... 2,500.
  b. Plate essay with black vignette on stamp
    paper, imperf.
    dull violet ..... 275.
    red brown ..... 275.
    orange red ..... 275.
    pale orange red ..... 275.
    blue ..... 275.

122-E3

122-E4

Frame as No. 122-E2, vignette oval with narrow-spaced horiz. lines in same color as frame, but no head.

122-E3 90c Plate on stamp paper, imperf.
    red brown ..... 225.
    blue ..... 225.
    dark blue ..... 225.
    red violet ..... 225.
    dull violet ..... 225.
    dark violet ..... 225.
    rose red ..... 225.
    deep rose red ..... 225.
    yellow ..... 225.
    orange brown ..... 225.
    dark navy blue ..... 225.
    blue green ..... 225.
    deep blue green ..... 225.
    dark blue green ..... 225.
    orange ..... 225.

Small numeral frame but with Lincoln vignette from No. 77 mounted in place.

122-E4 90c
  a. Die on India
    yellow ..... 2,000.
    deep blue green ..... 2,000.
    dark navy blue ..... 2,000.
  b. Plate of Lincoln vignette only, on rough
    pitted thick gray paper, black ..... 600.
    Block of 4 ..... 2,500.
  c. Die on India, Lincoln vignette as used
    on No. 77, black ..... 2,500.

122-E5

Similar to No. 122-E1, with Washington vignette but with large numerals as on issued stamp.

122-E5 90c
- *a.* Die on India, die sunk on card
  - black — *5,000.*
  - carmine — *2,500.*
- *b.* Plate of frame only, 2 lines at top, 3 lines at bottom, on India, mounted on block sunk card, rose red — *1,250.*
- *c.* As "b," 3 lines at top, 2 lines at bottom
  - rose red — *4,500.*
  - red brown — *1,250.*

Safety essays: die essays on thin wove, underprinted with various engraved safety paper designs in another color, probably with fugitive ink.
Found on 5c (No. 115-E1), 10c (No. 116-E1), 15c (No. 129-E1 without overprint) and 30c (No. 121-E1). Stamp color given first.

115-E3a

Design 1: wavy lines
115-E3
- *a.* 5c
  - carmine on scarlet — *3,250.*
  - orange on scarlet — *3,250.*
- *b.* 10c blue on scarlet — *5,000.*
- *c.* 30c carmine on scarlet — *3,500.*

115-E4

Design 2: banknote type
115-E4
- *a.* 5c
  - carmine on violet — *3,250.*
  - orange on violet — *3,250.*
- *b.* 10c carmine on violet — *5,000.*
- *c.* 30c
  - carmine on violet — *3,500.*
  - orange on violet — *3,500.*
  - orange on gray — *3,500.*

115-E5

Design 3: banknote type
115-E5
- *a.* 5c
  - carmine on orange and red — *3,250.*
  - carmine on brown — *3,250.*
  - orange on brown — *3,250.*
- *b.* 10c
  - carmine on orange and red — *5,000.*
  - blue on orange and red — *5,000.*
- *c.* 30c
  - carmine on orange and red — *3,500.*
  - orange on brown — *3,500.*

115-E6

Design 4: continuous wavy lines
115-E6
- *a.* 5c orange on scarlet — *3,250.*
- *b.* 10c
  - blue on scarlet — *5,000.*
  - carmine on scarlet — *5,000.*
- *c.* 30c black on scarlet — *3,500.*

115-E7

Design 5: wavy lines
115-E7
- *a.* 5c
  - orange on scarlet — *3,250.*
  - orange on black — *3,250.*
- *b.* 10c
  - dark brown on black — *5,000.*
  - orange red on black — *5,000.*
  - carmine on scarlet — *5,000.*
- *c.* 30c
  - carmine on black — *3,500.*
  - carmine on scarlet — *3,500.*

115-E8

Design 6: wavy lines
115-E8
- *a.* 5c orange on black — *3,250.*
- *b.* 10c blue on black — *5,000.*
- *c.* 30c
  - carmine on black — *3,500.*
  - orange on black — *3,500.*

115-E9

Design 7: crossed wavy lines
115-E9
- *a.* 5c
  - carmine on black — *3,250.*
  - orange on black — *3,250.*
- *b.* 10c blue on black — *5,000.*
- *c.* 30c orange on black — *5,000.*

115-E10

Design 8: wavy lines
115-E10
- *a.* 5c carmine on scarlet — *3,250.*
- *b.* 10c
  - blue on scarlet — *5,000.*
  - carmine on scarlet — *5,000.*
  - orange red on scarlet — *5,000.*

129-E3

Design 9: wavy lines
129-E3 15c
- orange brown on orange, vert. — *3,500.*
- blue green on orange, horiz. — *3,500.*
- dark blue on orange, horiz. — *3,500.*

129-E4

Design 10: banknote type
129-E4 15c
- orange brown on scarlet — *3,5*
- blue green on scarlet — *3,5*
- dark blue on scarlet — *3,5*

129-E5

Design 11: banknote type
129-E5 15c
- orange brown on light scarlet — *3,5*
- blue green on light scarlet, vert. — *3,5*
- dark blue on light scarlet — *3,5*

129-E6

Design 12: banknote type
129-E6 15c
- orange brown on deep scarlet — *3,50*
- blue green on deep scarlet — *3,50*
- dark blue on deep scarlet — *3,50*

115-E11

Design 13: banknote type
115-E11
- *a.* 5c orange on brown — *3,25*
- *b.* 10c
  - carmine on brown — *5,50*
  - orange red on brown — *5,50*
  - blue on brown (horiz. underprinting) — *5,50*
  - blue on brown (vert. underprinting) — *5,50*
- *c.* 30c carmine on brown — *3,50*

115-E12

Design 14: banknote type
115-E12
- *a.* 5c
  - carmine on scarlet (horiz.) — *4,000*
  - black on scarlet (vert.) — *4,000*
- *b.* 10c
  - carmine on scarlet — *5,500*
  - orange on scarlet — *5,500*
  - sepia on scarlet — *5,500*
  - blue on scarlet — *5,500*
- *c.* 30c black on scarlet — *3,500*

115-E13

Design 15: banknote type
115-E13
- *a.* 5c carmine on orange brown — *3,250.*
- *b.* 30c carmine on deep orange — *3,500.*

115-E14

Design 16: multiple rosettes
115-E14
    a. 5c orange on scarlet   3,250.
    b. 10c
        carmine on scarlet   5,500.
        orange red on scarlet   5,500.
        sepia on scarlet   5,500.
        blue on scarlet   5,500.

115-E15

Design 17: multiple oval rosettes
115-E15
    a. 5c carmine on scarlet   3,250.
    b. 10c
        carmine on scarlet   3,500.
        orange on scarlet   3,500.

115-E16

Design 18: negative stars in diagonal lines
115-E16
    a. 5c
        black on scarlet   3,250.
        carmine on scarlet   3,250.
    b. 10c
        carmine on scarlet   5,500.
        sepia on scarlet   5,500.
    c. 30c carmine on scarlet   3,500.

116-E6

Design 19: multiple 6-point stars in lathework
116-E6
    a. 10c blue on blue green   5,500.
    b. 30c carmine on blue green 3,500.

116-E7

Design 20: banknote type
116-E7
    a. 10c
        brown on orange   5,500.
        blue on orange   5,500.
    b. 30c carmine on orange   3,500.

116-E8

Design 21: multiple "ONE"
116-E8   10c blue on scarlet   5,500.

115-E17

Design 22: multiple "TWO"
115-E17
    a. 5c orange on scarlet   3,250.
    b. 10c carmine on scarlet   5,500.

115-E18

Design 23: multiple "5"s in oval rosettes
115-E18   5c black on carmine   3,250.

115-E19

Design 24: multiple "TEN 10"
115-E19
    a. 5c
        orange on scarlet   3,250.
        carmine on scarlet   3,250.
    b. 10c
        carmine on scarlet   5,500.
        orange red on scarlet   5,500.
        blue on scarlet   5,500.
    c. 30c
        carmine on scarlet   3,500.
        orange red on scarlet   3,500.
        brown on scarlet   3,500.
        blue on scarlet   3,500.

115-E20

Design 25: multiple "50"
115-E20   5c
        black on black   3,250.
        orange on black   3,250.

1870 ISSUE
Continental Banknote Co.

145-E1

Vignette of Washington in large ornate "1."
145-E1   One Cent
    a. Die on India, die sunk on card
        black   1,500.
        scarlet   1,500.
        green   1,500.
        ultramarine   1,500.
        blue   1,500.
    b. On proof paper, about 25x30mm
        black   1,000.
        green   1,000.

146-E1   147-E1

Blank vignette in large ornate "2."
146-E1   2c Engraved die on India, die sunk on
           card
        black   1,500.
        scarlet   1,500.
        ultramarine   1,500.
        blue   1,500.
        green   1,500.

Design size: 20x25mm
Die size: 43x48mm
Vignette of Lincoln in large ornate "3" with rounded top.
147-E1   3c Engraved die on proof paper
        black   2,250.
        scarlet   1,750.
        ultramarine   1,750.
        green   1,750.

147-E1A   147-E1B

Design size: 11½x15½mm
Die size: 25x32mm
Vignette only of Columbia. Imprint and die number below design.
147-E1A   3c Engraved die on India, black   —

Design size: 21x25mm
Blank vignette in frame of large ornate "3" with upper and lower labels not yet engraved.
147-E1B   3c Engraved die on India, die sunk
              on card
        black   2,250.
        green   2,000.

147-E1C

Design size: 21x25mm
No. 147-E1A cut to shape and mounted in frame of large ornate "3" with upper and lower labels not yet engraved.
147-E1C   3c Engraved die on India, die sunk
              on card
        black   2,250.
        green   2,000.

147-E2

Design size: 21x25mm
Blank vignette in frame only as No. 147-E1B but with upper and lower labels engraved.

147-E2 3c Engraved die on India, die sunk on card
    black   2,250.
    green   2,000.

Vignette of Columbia mounted in place on No. 147-E2.

147-E3 3c Engraved die on India, die sunk on card
    black   2,250.
    green   2,000.

147-E4

Complete design with Columbia vignette in large ornate "3" surrounded by foliate ornamentation.

147-E4 3c Engraved die on India, die sunk on card
    black   2,250.
    green   2,000.

147-E5

Design size: 22x27mm
Blank vignette in large ornate "3" surrounded by scrolled ornamentation.

147-E5 3c Engraved die on India, die sunk on card
    black   2,250.
    green   2,000.

147-E6

Vignette of Columbia mounted in place on No. 147-E5B.

147-E6 3c Engraved die on India, die sunk on card
    black   2,250.
    green   2,000.

148-E1

Blank vignette in large ornate "6."

148-E1 6c
  a. Engraved die on India, die sunk on card
      black   2,000.
      scarlet   2,000.
      green   2,000.
      dark green   2,000.
      ultramarine   2,000.
  b. Engraved die on India, cut close
      black   1,750.
      scarlet   1,750.
      blue   1,750.
      green   1,750.

National Banknote Co.

145-E2   145-E3

Die size: 64x74mm
Engraved vignette of Franklin facing right.

145-E2 1c Die on India, die sunk on card
    black (with pencil lines on bust0   700.
    dull dark orange   700.

Engraved incomplete Franklin vignette facing right mounted over pencil sketch of frame.

145-E3 1c Die on thin white card, 55x66mm,
    black   2,850.

145-E4   145-E5

Incomplete Franklin vignette mounted on more complete pencil sketch of frame.

145-E4 1c Die on thin white card, orange
    brown   2,000.

Design size: 20x26mm
Engraved vignette mounted on pencil and watercolor frame design.

145-E5 1c Die on thin white card, 45x51mm,
    dull dark orange   2,000.

145-E6

Incomplete engraving of entire design; lower edge of bust vert. shading only.

145-E6 1c
  a. Die on 64x71mm India, die sunk on card
      ultramarine   475.
      red   475.
      orange brown   475.
      red brown   475.
      blue green   475.
      mauve   475.
      dull lilac   475.
      black   475.
      gray   475.
      carmine   475.
      carmine rose   475.
      dull rose   475.
      dull yellow brown   475.
      brown violet   475.
      light green   475.
      green   475.
      gray olive   475.
      yellow   475.
  b. Die on bond, die sunk on card, dark yellow   750.

145-E8

Completed die: additional shading lines in background, f horiz. shading lines at top of lower edge of bust.

145-E0 1c
  a. Die on India, die sunk on card
      black   4
      blue green   4
      carmine   4
      yellow   4
      orange brown   4
      orange   4
      gray green   4
      dull red violet   4
      dark blue   4
  b. Die on white glazed paper, 65x72mm
      black   4
      black brown   4
      scarlet   4
      blue   4
  c. Completed die on thick wove, dismal dusky yellow   4

145-E9   145-E10

Die size: 50½x64mm
Engraved vignette of Franklin facing left, no shading lines top of bust, etc.

145-E9 1c
  a. Die on white glazed paper, black   47
  b. Die on India, mounted on card stamped "J.I. PEASE.", black   45

Engraved Franklin vignette with 1 and value label.

145-E10 1c Die on India, on card (1873),
    black   2,00

    May be essay for Official stamps.

146-E2   146-E3

Die size: 62x76mm
Vignette only of Jackson in high stiff collar.

146-E2 2c Die on India, die sunk on card
    black   90
    orange brown   90
    dull violet   90

Engraved Jackson vignette mounted on watercolor frame.

146-E3 2c Die on thin white card, 46x89mm,
    black vignette, dark gray frame   5,000

146-E4   146-E5

Engraved Jackson vignette, mounted on watercolor frame (diff. from No. 146-E3).

146-E4 2c Die on thin white card, 46x89mm,
    black vignette, gray frame   5,000

milar to No. 146-E4 but with pencil border around frame.

-E5 2c Die on thin white card, 45x50mm,
dark orange 5,000.

complete die: without shading lines under value ribbon, lines in colorless strips, and broken horiz. lines at top and om of frame.

146-E6

-E6 2c Die on thin white card, dark orange 1,250.

146-E7

Die size: 64½x73mm
Completed die of unadopted design.

-E7 2c
a. Die on India
carmine 1,000.
deep rose 1,000.
scarlet 1,000.
dim dusky orange orange red 1,000.
deep yellow orange 1,000.
bone brown 1,000.
orange brown 1,000.
brown 1,000.
canary yellow 1,000.
yellow brown 1,000.
dark olive green 1,000.
green 1,000.
dim dusky blue green 1,000.
dark blue 1,000.
deep ultramarine 1,000.
bright blue 1,000.
dull violet 1,000.
smoky deep red violet red 1,000.
gray 1,000.
black 1,000.
b. Die on ivory paper, about 64x77mm
black 1,000.
brown black 1,000.
scarlet 1,000.
blue 1,000.
c. Die on thin wove, dark yellow 1,000.

146-E8

Die size: 62x76mm
Incomplete vignette of Jackson as on issued stamp: incomplete shading in eye and hair in front of ear, right neck tendon n chest not shaded.
46-E8 2c
a. Die on India, on 55x66mm card
black 750.
orange 750.
deep yellow orange 750.
red brown 750.
orange brown 750.
dark blue green 750.
red violet 750.

Also known on 87x143mm card showing full die sinkage, encil inscribed "2c" above and "Jackson" below sinkage area. alue, $750.

b. Die on glazed paper, die sinkage
50x63mm, black 1,000.

Completed Jackson vignette.

146-E9

146-E9 2c Die on glazed paper, black 750.

146-E10   146-E11

Engraved Jackson vignette with 2 and value label.
146-E10 2c Die on glazed paper (1873), black 1,750.
May be essay for Official stamps.

Engraved vignette with pencil and watercolor frame design, labels blank.
146-E11 2c Die on thin white card, 50x60mm,
dim dusky bright blue green
vignette, dark green frame 6,250.

146-E12

Die size: 62x75mm
Incomplete engraving of entire design: no leaves on wide bands at sides below vignette, neck tendon and hair in front of ear changed, top of head incomplete, ear hole too dark. This design essayed for envelopes on thick papers.
146-E12 2c Die on India, die sunk on card
carmine 1,250.
orange 1,250.
brown orange 1,250.
brown 1,250.
blue 1,250.
violet 1,250.
green 1,250.

147-E7

Incomplete engraved vignette of Lincoln (horiz. line background), mounted on pencil and watercolor frame design.
147-E7 3c Die on thin white card, black
vignette, gray black frame 3,500.

147-E8   147-E9

Design size: 20x25mm

Die Size: 62x72½mm
Incomplete engraving of head only of Washington.
147-E8 3c Die on white glazed paper, black 550.

Engraved Washington vignette only as adopted.
147-E9 3c Die on white glazed paper, black 650.
Nos. 147-E8 and 147-E9 may have been made from completed dies of No. 147 to produce Nos. 184-E9 and 184-E10.

147-E10   147-E11

Washington vignette, 3 and value label.
147-E10 3c Die on India, card mounted
(1873), black 1,600.
May be essay for Official stamps.

Design size: 20x25½mm
Incomplete engraved vignette (horiz. lined background), mounted on pencil and watercolor frame design.
147-E11 3c Die on thin white card, 45x54mm,
carmine vignette, dim light red
violet red frame 5,000.

Incomplete engraving of entire design: no horizontal lines on nose, parts of hair, chin, collar, forehead unfinished.

147-E12

147-E12 3c Die on India, die sunk on card
black 575.
deep red 575.
carmine 575.
yellow orange 575.
brown 575.
red brown 575.
dark red brown 575.
yellow brown 575.
ultramarine 575.
dark blue 575.
dark violet blue 575.
blue green 575.
dark red violet 575.

Issued stamp, No. 147, in trial colors, underprinted network in fugitive ink.
147-E13 3c
a. On thick paper, perf. 12, gummed
gray blue, underprinting gray brown 150.
gray blue, underprinting olive gray 150.
green, underprinting olive gray 150.
dim red, underprinting olive gray 150.
dull orange, underprinting olive gray 150.
brown, underprinting olive gray 150.
b. As "a," faint 6mm-high horiz. bar trial
cancel
dim red 450.
dull orange 450.
c. As "a," underprinting omitted
gray blue —
dim red —
dull orange —
brown —
d. As "a," imperf, green, underprinting olive gray 325.
Pair 700.
e. As "d," underprinting omitted 325.
Pair 700.
P# block of 10 —

Multiples of the No. 147-E13 varieties can be found with fully or partially underprinted stamps in conjunction with underprinting-omitted stamps.

148-E2

148-E3

Design size: 19½x25½mm
Die size: 63x76mm
Engraved Lincoln vignette only, hair brushed back, horiz. line background.

148-E2 6c Die on India, die sunk on card
black 700.
blue 700.

Incomplete engraved Lincoln vignette (horiz. lined background) mounted on pencil and watercolor frame with blank labels.

148-E3 6c Die on thin white card, 45x52mm, dim blue vignette, dim dark blue frame 4,000.

148-E4

Incomplete engraving of entire design: horiz. line background in vignette, lines on cheek and hair unfinished.

148-E4 6c Die on India, on card, about 50x52mm
carmine 600.
rose 600.
dull rose 600.
red violet 600.
dull violet 600.
deep ultramarine 600.
dark black blue 600.
yellow 600.
green 600.
dark green 600.
dark red brown 600.
deep yellow brown 600.
yellow brown 600.
orange brown 600.

Incomplete engraving of entire design: horiz. line background in vignette, no shading directly under value label, shadows on "SIX CENTS" and shading on ornaments in upper corners unfinished.

148-E5 6c Die on India, on card, ultramarine 900.

148-E6

Similar to No. 148-E5 but with diagonal lines added to vignette background. (Essay in orange brown has pencil notations for changes.)

148-E6 6c Die on India, die sunk on card
black 1,000.
dull carmine 1,000.
dark rose 1,000.
yellowish black 1,000.
brown 1,000.
gray brown 1,000.
black brown 1,000.
yellow 1,000.
gray olive green 1,000.
dark green 1,000.
ultramarine 1,000.
deep ultramarine 1,000.
dull ultramarine 1,000.
violet 1,000.
dark violet 1,000.
red violet 1,000.
orange brown 1,000.

148-E7

Similar to No. 148-E6 but with dots added to top of hair.

148-E7 6c Die on India, on card
dark carmine 1,000.
dull rose 1,000.
orange 1,000.
yellow brown 1,000.
dark brown 1,000.
black brown 1,000.
yellow green 1,000.
blue green 1,000.
ultramarine 1,000.
dark red violet 1,000.

Completed die with lines on cheek softened to dots only.

148-E8

148-E8 6c Die on India
yellow green 250.
brown 250.
rose 250.

All known examples are much reduced.

Incomplete engraving of entire design, similar to No. 148-E10 but with hair brushed forward as on adopted design but shadow under hair in front of ear is round at bottom, not pointed as on approved design. Shading on cheek behind nostril is dotted instead of lined on completed design.

148-E9

148-E9 6c Die on India, on card, red violet 750.

148-E10

Die size: 64x75mm
Frame as adopted, vignette similar to No. 148-E6 but with hair brushed back; lines on cheek.

148-E10 6c
a. Die on India, die sunk on card, deep blue 850.
b. Die on India, about 30x35mm, carmine 600.
c. As "a," but no panels above top label, carmine 850.

Similar to No. 148-E10a but dots (not lines) on cheek and on lower lip. Shadow under hair in front of ear is rounded at bottom, not pointed as on approved design.

148-E11

148-E11 6c Die on India, on card
rose pink
deep rose
pale rose
brown rose
rose carmine
deep carmine
brown
yellow brown
blue
red violet

Die of completed vignette only with hair brushed forward

148-E12 6c Die on white glazed paper, black 1,5

148-E13

Completed vignette with 6 and value label.

148-E13 6c Die on India, on card (1873), black 1,5

May be essay for Official stamps.

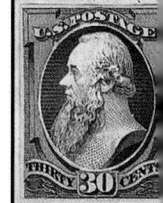

149-E4

149-E4a

Die size: 62x75mm
Vignette of Stanton.

149-E4 7c Die on India, on card, black 1,0

Engraved frame of adopted 30c design but with vignette out and mounted over Stanton vignette on India No. 149-E4

149-E4a Stanton vignette with 30c frame on thin, stiff paper mounted on top, black 5(

The status of No. 149-E4a has been questioned.

149-E5

Die size: 62x76mm
Completed vignette with 7 and value label.

149-E5 7c
a. Die on India, on card (1873), black 1,00
b. Die on white glazed paper, black 1,00

May be essay for Official stamps.

149-E6

Design as issued but shading under ear incomplete.

-E6 7c Die on India, die sunk on card

black	500.
dark red	500.
light red	500.
gray green	500.
gray black	500.
yellow brown	500.
dark brown	500.
dull yellow brown	500.
dull red brown	500.
blue green	500.
ultramarine	500.
dim blue	500.
lilac	500.
red orange	500.
yellow orange	500.

Similar to No. 149-E6 but with dots added on forehead.

-E7 7c Die on India, brown 1,000.

150-E1 150-E2

Design size: 20x25½mm
Incomplete engraved vignette of Jefferson (horiz. line background) mounted on pencil and watercolor frame design with blank labels.

-E1 10c Die on thin white card, 45x51mm,
black vignette, gray frame 3,000.

Design size: 19½x25½mm
Die size: 62x75mm
Jefferson vignette with incomplete engraving of frame: unfinished shading under "TEN" ribbon, under oval at ends of "U.S. POSTAGE," and under shield over ends of value label ribbons.

-E2 10c Die on India, on card, deep blue
green 2,500.

Similar to No. 150-E2 but showing horizontal shading lines only.

-E2A 10c Die on India, die sunk on
152x225mm card

blue green	750.
red violet	750.

150-E3

Completed engraving of unadopted design.

50-E3 10c
a. Die on India, die sunk on card

carmine	750.
rose	750.
gray brown rose	750.
yellow	750.
yellow brown	750.
orange	750.
orange brown	750.
brown	750.
chocolate	750.
green	750.
blue green	750.
greenish gray	750.
blue	750.
dull violet	750.
dull red violet	750.
dark navy blue	750.
ultramarine	750.
deep ultramarine	750.

dull dusky blue	750.
navy blue	750.
slate	750.
b. Die on bond	
dull dusky brown	500.
brown gray	500.

All known examples of No. 153-E3b are reduced.

150-E4 150-E5

Three separate designs. Left one dark blue green, similar to No. 150-E3 but shows engraved attempt to remove coat collar to obtain nude neck (some coat still shows under chin). Middle one brown orange (No. 150-E2) with coat collar and top of hair cut out, neck and bust drawn in. Right one black vignette of head finally adopted (No. 150-E7).

150-E4 10c Dies on India, on card 2,500.

Design size: 19½x25½mm
Same frame as No. 150-E2, but Jefferson vignette has hair arranged differently and bust has no clothing.

150-E5 10c
a. Die on India, die sunk on card

black	600.
scarlet	600.
brown	600.
blue	600.
green	600.
b. Die on glazed paper, 66x75mm	
black	500.
black brown	500.
scarlet	500.
blue	500.
c. Die on thin wove, dark yellow	500.

150-E6 150-E7

Frame of No. 150-E5 with vignette cut out and replaced by black vignette as adopted.

150-E6 10c Die on India

deep orange brown	1,500.
black	1,500.

Die size: 62x76mm
Vignette of Jefferson as adopted.

150-E7 10c Die on India, die sunk on card

dark ultramarine	700.
yellow	700.
brown	700.

151-E1 151-E2

Design size: 20x25½mm
Engraved vignette of Washington (No. 79-E37b) mounted on incomplete pencil drawing of frame design.

151-E1 12c Die on India, on 38x47½mm card,
black vignette, pencil frame 2,500.

Design size: 20x25½mm
Engraved vignette of Washington (No. 79-E37b) mounted on pencil and watercolor frame design with blank labels.

151-E2 12c Die on card, 46x89mm, black
vignette, gray frame 3,000.

151-E3 151-E4

Design size: 20x25½mm
Engraved vignette of Washington (No. 79-E37b) mounted on pencil and watercolor frame design with ribbons and blank labels.

151-E3 12c Die on card, 46x89mm, black
vignette, gray frame 3,000.

Design size: 20x25½mm
Engraved vignette of Washington (No. 79-E37b) mounted on pencil and watercolor frame design with "U, S, 12" and blank labels.

151-E4 12c Die on card, 46x89mm, black
vignette, gray frame 3,000.

151-E5 151-E6

Design size: 19½x25½mm
Die size: 62x74mm
Vignette of Henry Clay only.

151-E5 12c Die on India, die sunk on card

black	600.
deep carmine	600.
yellow	600.
yellow brown	600.
brown orange	600.
dark orange brown	600.
black brown	600.
ultramarine	600.
dark blue green	600.
red violet	600.

Incomplete Clay vignette mounted on watercolor shield-like frame design on gray background, pencil notation "background of stars to be gray."

151-E6 12c Die on card, 53x75mm, blue black
vignette, blue frame 3,250.

151-E7

Die sinkage size: 63x77mm
Completed die of unadopted design similar to No. 151-E6. This design essayed for envelopes on thick paper.

151-E7 12c
a. Die on India, on card

deep orange brown	900.
green	900.
deep ultramarine	900.
violet	900.
deep red	900.
deep orange red	900.
dusky red	900.
b. Die on wove	
carmine	700.
orange	700.
brown	700.
orange brown	700.
ultramarine	700.
c. Die on card colored yellow, black	700.

Engraved vignette of Washington mounted on partly complete pencil drawing of frame, pencil notation "new border for clay 12c."

151-E8

151-E8 12c Die on card, black, pencil frame   2,750.

151-E9   151-E10

Die size: 55x63mm
Incomplete engraving of entire adopted design, without 3 vert. shading lines at left side of lower triangle.

151-E9 12c
 a. Die on India, die sunk on card
  black   650.
  carmine   650.
  blue green   650.
  blue   650.
  light blue   650.
  orange   650.
  orange brown   650.
  dull red   650.
  brown red   650.
 b. Die on proof paper, about 38x45mm
  carmine   650.
  dull carmine   650.
  orange brown   650.
  dull red   650.
  ultramarine   650.
 c. Die on India, on card, about 30x35mm,
  dark blue   650.

Completed Clay vignette with 12 and value label.
151-E10 12c Die on white glazed paper
  (1873), black   1,250.

May be essay for Official stamps.

152-E1   152-E2

Design size: 19½x25mm
Incomplete vignette of Webster with side whiskers bolder than as adopted, mounted on watercolor frame design with 15 and blank labels.

152-E1 15c Die on white card, 40x61mm, dim
  red vignette, light red violet frame   2,250.

Design size: 19½x25mm
Die size: 63x76mm
Incomplete engraving of vignette only: missing shading under ear and at back of neck.
152-E2 15c Die on India, die sunk on card,
  black   750.

152-E3   152-E4

Vignette similar to No. 152-E2 but with shading under ear, more shading at back of neck.

152-E3 15c Die on India, die sunk on card
  black   700.
  dark orange   700.
  orange   700.

yellow   700.
red violet   700.
ultramarine   700.
brown   700.

Vignette of Webster with 15 below.
152-E4 15c Die on white glazed paper (1873),
  black   1,000.

May be essay for Official stamps.

152-E5

Incomplete engraved design: shading on corner panel bevels incomplete, side whiskers bolder than as adopted. Also essayed for envelopes on thick paper.
152-E5 15c Die on India, die sunk on card, or-
  ange brown   750.

Similar to No. 152-E5 but with pencil marks suggesting shading on corner panels.
152-E6 15c Die on India, orange brown   750.

Similar to No. 152-E5 with engraved shading added to corner panels but white areas incomplete.

152-E7

152-E7 15c Die on India
  orange   650.
  orange yellow   650.
  orange brown   650.
  green   650.
  red violet   650.
  rose carmine   650.

Similar to No. 152-E7 but shading on corner panels complete.

152-E8

152-E8 15c Die on India, on card, black   1,000.

153-E1   153-E2

Design size: 18x23mm
Incomplete engraved vignette of Scott mounted on pencil sketch of partial frame design.
153-E1 24c Die on white card, 33x39mm, dull
  red violet vignette, pencil frame   1,750.

Design size: 19½x25mm
Complete engraved vignette mounted on pencil and water-color frame design with "U.S. POSTAGE" in ink.
153-E2 24c Die on white card, 73x110mm, dim
  blue green   3,250.

153-E3   153-E4

Die size: 62x76mm
Incomplete engraved vignette only.

153-E3 24c Die on India, die sunk on card
  black   6
  yellow   6
  yellow brown   6
  dark orange brown   6
  ultramarine   6
  dark ultramarine   6
  red violet   6

Die size: 62x77mm
Incomplete design as adopted: upper corners not squa outside scrolls, no periods after U and S in stars.
153-E4 24c Die on India, die sunk on card
  carmine   6
  orange   6
  brown orange   6
  yellow brown   6
  deep brown   6
  ultramarine   6
  dark red violet   6
  green   6

Value off card, cut down, $275.

Previous No. 154-E1 is now No. 149-E4a.

154-E2

Pencil drawing of entire design, labeled "Scott."
154-E2 30c Pencil drawing on white card,
  53x92mm   2,4

Engraved vignette of Hamilton mounted on pencil drawing frame.
154-E3 30c Die on card, yellow brown vignette,
  pencil frame   1,5

154-E4

Incomplete engraved vignette of Hamilton.
154-E4 30c Die on India, die sunk on card
  yellow brown   70
  dark ultramarine blue   70
  orange   70

Vignette of Hamilton with more engraving on forehead, nos neck, etc.

154-E5

154-E5 30c Die on India, die sunk on card
  dark red brown   70
  dull carmine   70
  ultramarine   70

154-E6

completed vignette with 30 below.

E6 30c Die on white glazed paper (1873),
    black   1,750.

May be essay for Official stamps.

155-E1   155-E2

Pencil drawing of entire design, labeled "Perry."

E1 90c Pencil drawing on white card,
    53x92mm   2,000.

Design size: 19½x25mm
Engraved vignette of Perry mounted on pencil and watercolor
line design.

E2 90c Die on white card, 73x110mm, dull
    dark violet vignette, dull red violet
    frame   3,250.

155-E3

Die size: 58x79mm
Incomplete engraving of Perry vignette as adopted.

E3 90c
  a. Die on India, die sunk on card
    deep yellow orange   600.
    orange brown   600.
    dark brown   600.
    dull carmine   600.
    ultramarine blue   600.
    dark blue green   600.
    dark red violet   600.
  b. Die on white ivory paper, black   600.

Similar to No. 155-E3 but more lines in hair above forehead.

155-E4

5-E4 90c Die on India, on card, black   600.

155-E5

Incomplete engraving of design as adopted: rope above
vignette unfinished. Also essayed for envelopes on thick paper.

5-E5 90c Die on India, die sunk on card
    black   750.
    carmine, off card   325.
    orange   750.
    dark orange   750.

---

    yellow brown   750.
    brown   750.
    deep orange brown   750.
    deep ultramarine   750.
    blue green   750.
    red violet   750.

Value off card, cut down, $250.

1873 ISSUE
Continental Bank Note Co.

179-E1   179-E2

Die size: 20x25mm
Vignette of Taylor by Bureau of Engraving and Printing, in
engraved frame.
179-E1 Five Cents, Die on India
    black   4,500.
    blue   4,500.

Design size: 24x29mm
Vignette of Taylor by Bureau of Engraving and Printing, in
ornate wash drawing of frame ("FIVE CENTS" black, on shaded
ribbon).
179-E2 5c Die on card, black   4,000.

Incomplete vignette: hair, coat, background, etc., unfinished.

179-E3

179-E3 5c Die on India, violet   2,000.

George W. Bowlsby 1873 essay similar in concept to his No.
63-E13 but without coupon attached. It consisted of an unused
1c stamp (No. 156) with horiz. sewing machine perfs. through
center, gummed on upper half only, as described in his Dec. 26,
1865 patent. Stamp was meant to be torn in half by postal clerk
as cancellation, to prevent reuse.
156-E1 1c blue   250.

1876 Experimental Ink and Paper Essays

Plate designs of 1873-75 issues in normal colors, printed
on paper tinted with sensitive inks and on heavily laid
(horiz.) colored papers (unless otherwise noted).

156-E2 1c Blue on:
    carmine   150.
    pale rose   150.
    deep yellow   150.
    pale violet   150.

158-E1 3c Green on:
    pale rose   150.
    deep yellow   150.
    pale violet   150.

158-E2 3c Green on paper covered with pink
    varnish which vanishes with the
    color   100.

158-E3 3c Green on thick white blotting paper
    which absorbs canceling ink   100.

161-E1 10c Brown on:
    pale rose   150.
    deep yellow   150.
    pale violet   150.

163-E1 15c Yellow orange on:
    pale rose   200.
    deep yellow   200.
    pale violet   200.

165-E1 30c Gray black on:
    pale rose   200.
    deep yellow   200.
    pale violet   200.

166-E1 90c Rose carmine on:
    pale rose   200.
    deep yellow   200.
    pale violet   200.

178-E1 2c Vermilion on:
    pale rose   150.
    deep yellow   150.
    pale violet   150.

179-E4

179-E4 5c Blue on:
    pale rose   300.
    deep yellow   300.
    pale violet   300.

See No. 147-E13.

1877 Essays
Philadelphia Bank Note Co.

Die essays for this section were all engraved. The frame-only
dies for all values of this series were engraved with two values
appearing per die, except the 3c (No. 184-E1) which was
engraved alone. In each case the listing is under the lower
denomination. The Washington vignette associated with each
value of the frames is from engraved master die No. 14. (No.
182-E1).

Except as noted, plate essays in this section are all lithographed from a composite stone plate of two panes. The left
pane ("plate 1") consists of horiz. rows of four of the 1c, 3c, 7c,
24c and 90c. The right pane ("plate 2") consists of horiz. rows of
four 2c, 6c, 12c and 30c. "Printed by Philadelphia Bank Note
Co. Patented June 16, 1876" imprint below 2nd and 3rd designs
on each row.

See note above No. 63-E1.

182-E1

Vignette master die "No. 14": two slightly diff. vignettes of Washington, one above the other, bottom one with truncated queue, bust and shading in front of neck.

182-E1
- **a.** Die on old white glazed paper, black — 500.
- **b.** Die on proof paper (1903)
  - black — 100.
  - carmine — 100.
  - dull carmine — 100.
  - dusky carmine — 100.
  - yellow — 100.
  - dull scarlet — 100.
  - dull orange — 100.
  - brown orange — 100.
  - brown — 100.
  - gray olive — 100.
  - blue green — 100.
  - dark green — 100.
  - black blue — 100.
  - ultramarine — 100.
  - violet — 100.
  - red violet — 100.

182-E2

Design size: 20x25mm
Die size: 98x53mm
Frames of 1c and 2c side by side.

182-E2 1c + 2c
- **a.** Die on white pelure
  - dark carmine — 250.
  - orange — 250.
  - brown — 250.
  - blue green — 250.
  - blue — 250.
- **b.** Die with vertical line between designs (die size 85x54mm), on India, die sunk on card
  - dusky red — 400.
  - deep orange — 400.
  - orange brown — 400.
  - dark green — 400.
  - dark blue — 400.
- **c.** Die on stiff glazed paper, black — 400.
- **d.** Die on proof paper, printed through a mat (1903)
  - black — 100.
  - bright carmine — 100.
  - dull carmine — 100.
  - dim scarlet — 100.
  - dark orange — 100.
  - dull yellow — 100.
  - dark orange brown — 100.
  - black olive — 100.
  - dark blue green — 100.
  - dark blue — 100.
  - ultramarine — 100.
  - dark navy blue — 100.
  - blue violet — 100.
  - dull violet — 100.
  - red violet — 100.
- **e.** Plate sheet of 1c, 2c, 3c, 12c, 24c, 30c, 90c frames only, on card, pale green blue — 1,500.

182-E3

Complete 1c design, lithographed.
182-E3 1c
- **a.** Plate on stamp paper, imperf., gummed
  - black — 75.
  - blue green — 75.
  - bright ultramarine — 75.
  - yellow — 75.
- **b.** Plate on stamp paper, perf. 12, gummed
  - dark red orange — 50.
  - orange brown — 50.
  - red brown — 50.
  - red violet — 50.
  - violet blue — 50.
  - ultramarine — 50.
- **c.** Plate 1 "sheet" of 20, complete designs, without imprint, on old glazed paper, imperf., deep brown orange — 800.
- **d.** As "c," with imprint, on old glazed paper, imperf., gummed
  - dull deep violet red — 800.
  - ultramarine — 800.
  - scarlet — 800.
  - orange — 800.
  - carmine — 800.
  - dark carmine — 800.
  - green — 800.
  - bluish green — 800.
- **e.** As "d," perf. 12, gummed
  - dull deep violet red — 700.
  - ultramarine — 700.
  - red brown — 700.
  - violet blue — 700.

Concerning plate 1 sheets of 20, note that composite stone plates also contained the plate 2 sheets of 20 listed as Nos. 183-E2c to 183-E2e. Many such composite sheets remain intact. All separated plate 1 or plate 2 sheets originally were part of a composite sheet.

183-E2b

Complete 2c design, lithographed.
183-E2 2c
- **a.** Plate on stamp paper, imperf.
  - blue green — 60.
  - bright ultramarine — 60.
  - brown — 60.
- **b.** Plate on stamp paper, perf. 12, gummed
  - bright red orange — 35.
  - dull red orange — 35.
  - dark red orange — 35.
  - red brown — 35.
  - dark red brown — 35.
  - dark orange brown — 35.
  - yellow brown — 35.
  - dull yellow green — 35.
  - green — 35.
  - dull ultramarine — 35.
  - bright ultramarine — 35.
  - blue violet — 35.
  - red violet — 35.
  - light red violet — 35.
  - violet red — 35.
- **c.** Plate 2 "sheet" of 16, complete designs, without imprint, on old glazed paper, imperf., deep brown orange — 600.
- **d.** As "c," with imprint, on old glazed paper, imperf., gummed, dull deep violet red — 600.
- **e.** As "d," perf. 12, gummed, dull deep violet red — 500.

See note following No. 182-E3e.

Design size: 20x25mm
Die size: 54x55mm
Engraved frame of 3c alone on die.

184-E1 3c
- **a.** Die on pelure paper
  - dark carmine — 250.
  - dark orange — 250.
  - orange brown — 250.
  - bright blue — 250.
  - bright blue — 250.
  - green — 250.
  - dark green — 250.
- **b.** Die on proof paper (1903)

black
bright carmine
dull carmine
dim scarlet
dark orange
dull yellow
dark orange brown
black olive
dark rose
green
yellow green
dark blue green
dark blue
deep ultramarine
dark navy blue
blue violet
dull violet
red violet

Built-up model of engraved frame cut to shape inside and mounted atop engraved vignette of the same color. Warr[...] fraudulent models combining engraved and lithographed ma[...]ials exist.

184-E2 3c
- **a.** Die on proof paper, cut close
  - dark scarlet
  - blue green
  - deep blue
- **b.** Four examples mounted 2½mm apart on stiff white card, 80x87mm
  - red — 1,[...]
  - orange brown — 1,[...]
  - green — 1,[...]
  - blue — 1,[...]
  - violet — 1,[...]
  - green frame, light blue vignette — 1,[...]

Built-up model as No. 184-E2, vignette as No. 184-E5[...] dark background.
184-E3 3c Die on proof paper, scarlet — [...]

184-E4

Complete 3c design, vignette with light background.
184-E4 3c
- **c.** Plate lithographed on stamp paper, imperf.
  - black
  - green
  - dark green
  - bright ultramarine
  - orange

No. 184-E4c exists in two plates of 9 tete-beche, in [...] colors, on same piece of paper. Value, $800 sheet of 18.
- **d.** Plate lithographed on stamp paper, perf. 12, gummed
  - dark red orange
  - red brown
  - red voilet
  - brown orange
  - ultramarine
  - violet blue
- **e.** Plate sheet of 9 (3x3), imprint below, on stiff white wove
  - carmine — 3[...]
  - blue green — 3[...]
- **f.** Plate sheet of 9 (3x3), on glazed thin wove
  - carmine — 3[...]
  - blue green — 3[...]
  - blue — 3[...]
  - orange — 3[...]
- **g.** Plate sheet of 9 (3x3), on yellowish wove
  - carmine — 3[...]
  - blue green — 3[...]
  - blue — 3[...]
- **h.** Die of complete design on old stiff glazed paper (die size: 55x66mm), black — 3[...]
- **i.** Complete die on glazed wove
  - deep carmine — 2[...]
  - scarlet — 2[...]
  - ultramarine — 2[...]
- **j.** Complete die on India, light orange red — 2[...]
- **k.** Complete die on proof paper (1903)
  - black
  - bright carmine
  - dull carmine
  - dim scarlet
  - dark orange
  - dull yellow
  - dark orange brown
  - black olive
  - green
  - dark blue green
  - deep ultramarine
  - dark navy blue
  - blue violet
  - dull violet
  - red violet

I. Complete die on large colored card
(1903)
black, *light green*	150.
deep scarlet, *ivory*	150.
red violet, *light blue*	150.
carmine, *pink*	150.

184-E5

design size: 19x24½mm
e No. 1 size: about 63x94mm Vignette of Washington
tly diff. from rest of series but with quite diff. frame design.

E5 3c
a. Die on glazed paper, about 50x75mm,
black	350.

b. Die on proof paper (with and without
printing through mats) (1903)
black	100.
dark carmine	100.
carmine	100.
bright carmine	100.
brown	100.
red brown	100.
yellow	100.
orange	100.
violet	100.
red violet	100.
violet brown	100.
blue	100.
steel blue	100.
light green	100.
dark green	100.
dull olive	100.

c. Die on colored card, 61x93mm (1903)
scarlet, *yellow*	150.
olive gray, *pale pink*	150.
dull violet, *buff*	150.

late proofs printed in sheets of 25 (plate size: 140x164mm).
oriz. crack extends through upper 3s from 2mm back of
d on position 11 to vignette on position 12.
l plate essay items valued as singles except No. 184-E5d.

d. Engraved plate of 25 on India, mounted
on large card, red brown 750.
e. Plate on proof paper (1903)
black	15.
blue black	15.
greenish black	15.
dull red violet	15.
dark red violet	15.
dull violet	15.
violet brown	15.
light red brown	15.
orange brown	15.
brown carmine	15.
brown	15.
dim orange	15.
yellow	15.
dull yellow	15.
carmine	15.
light carmine	15.
dark carmine	15.
dull carmine	15.
dull scarlet	15.
dark green	15.
light green	15.
dull olive green	15.
deep ultramarine	15.

f. Plate on proof paper, perf. 12, lithographed
carmine	100.
rose lilac	100.
red orange	100.

g. Plate on green bond, "Crane & Co.
1887" wmk. (1903)
black	25.
carmine	25.
dull carmine	25.
scarlet	25.
brown	25.
brown red	25.
orange brown	25.
red violet	25.
yellow	25.
orange	25.
dark green	25.
light green	25.
yellow green	25.
deep ultramarine	25.
dark navy blue	25.

h. Plate (printed before plate crack developed) on semiglazed yellowish wove,
laid watermark
carmine	30.
dull red	30.
bright orange red	30.
deep orange red	30.
scarlet	30.
deep orange	30.
yellow orange	30.
orange brown	30.
orange yellow	30.
dark yellow green	30.
dusky blue green	30.

dull green blue	30.
violet blue	30.
red violet	30.
black	30.

i. Plate in sheets of 100 with imprint on
yellowish glazed chemically prepared
wove, lithographed
black	20.
brown	20.
scarlet	20.
light red	20.
rose pink	20.
carmine	20.
deep carmine	20.
violet rose	20.
deep violet rose	20.
violet red	20.
red violet	20.
violet	20.
blue	20.
pale blue	20.
pale dull blue	20.
yellow	20.
dull brown yellow	20.
orange	20.
red orange	20.

184-E6

Illustration with card margins reduced.
Similar to No. 184-E1 but engraved vignette of Lincoln on
India facing ¾ to right. Each design has vignette attached to
frame from behind.

184-E6 3c Four copies mounted on 80x89mm
card to resemble block of 4
blue	3,500.
green	3,500.

Frame of No. 184-E5 with engraved vignette of Lincoln
mounted in place.

184-E7 3c Die on card, brown —

There is some doubt whether No. 184-E7 exists as a genuine
essay. The editors would like to see authenticated evidence of
its existence.

Design size: 20x25mm
Die size: 92x50mm
Frames of 6c and 7c side by side (6c at right).

186-E1 6c + 7c
a. Die on white pelure, orange 375.
b. Die on proof paper, printed through a
mat (1903)
black	100.
bright carmine	100.
dull carmine	100.
dim scarlet	100.
dark orange	100.
dull yellow	100.
dark orange brown	100.
black olive	100.
green	100.
dark blue green	100.
dark blue	100.
deep ultramarine	100.
dark navy blue	100.
blue violet	100.
dull violet	100.
red violet	100.

c. Die on white pelure, both 7s reversed on
7c frame, orange 750.
d. Die on old stiff glazed, black 400.

186-E2

Complete 6c design, lithographed.
186-E2 6c
a. Plate on stamp paper, perf. 12, gummed
bright red orange	35.
dull red orange	35.
dark red orange	35.
red brown	35.
dark red brown	35.
dark orange brown	35.
yellow brown	35.
dull yellow green	35.
green	35.
dull ultramarine	35.
bright ultramarine	35.
blue violet	35.
red violet	35.
light violet red	35.
violet red	35.

b. Plate on stamp paper, gummed
ultramarine	60.
lilac	60.
scarlet	60.
orange	60.
carmine	60.
dark carmine	60.
blue green	60.

186a-E2

Complete 7c design, lithographed.
186a-E2 7c
a. Plate on stamp paper, imperf.
black	75.
carmine	75.
red orange	75.
yellow orange	75.
green	75.
dark green	75.
dark blue	75.

b. Plate on stamp paper, perf. 12,
gummed
red brown	50.
dark red orange	50.
brown orange	50.
red violet	50.
ultramarine	50.
violet blue	50.

Design size: 20x25mm
Die size: 78½x64mm
Frames of 12c and 24c side by side (12c on right).

188a-E1 12c + 24c
a. Die on white pelure
deep carmine	300.
brown orange	300.
orange brown	300.
blue green	300.
blue	300.

b. Die on proof paper, printed through a
mat (1903)
black	100.
bright carmine	100.
dull carmine	100.
dim scarlet	100.
dark orange	100.
dull yellow	100.
dark orange brown	100.
black olive	100.
green	100.
dark blue green	100.
dark blue	100.
deep ultramarine	100.
dark navy blue	100.
blue violet	100.
dull violet	100.
red violet	100.

c. Die on old stiff glazed, black 400.

188a-E2

Complete 12c design, lithographed.

188a-E2   12c
   a. Plate on stamp paper, perf. 12,
      gummed
      bright red orange   35.
      dull red orange   35.
      dark red orange   35.
      red brown   35.
      dark red brown   35.
      dark orange brown   35.
      yellow brown   35.
      dull yellow green   35.
      green   35.
      dull ultramarine   35.
      bright ultramarine   35.
      blue violet   35.
      red violet   35.
      light red violet   35.
      violet red   35.
   b. Plate on stamp paper, gummed
      ultramarine   60.
      lilac   60.
      scarlet   60.
      orange   60.
      carmine   60.
      dark carmine   60.
      blue green   60.

189a-E2

Complete 24c design, lithographed.

189a-E2   24c
   a. Plate on stamp paper, perf. 12,
      gummed
      red brown   50.
      dark red orange   50.
      brown orange   50.
      ultramarine   50.
      violet blue   50.
      red violet   50.
   b. Plate on stamp paper, gummed
      ultramarine   75.
      lilac   75.
      scarlet   75.
      orange   75.
      carmine   75.
      dark carmine   75.
      green   75.

Design size: 20x25mm
Die size: 79x64mm
Frames of 30c and 90c side by side.

190-E1   30c + 90c
   a. Die on white pelure
      dark carmine   300.
      dark red orange   300.
      dark orange brown   300.
      brown   300.
      blue green   300.
      bright blue   300.
   b. Die on stiff glazed paper, blue black   500.
   c. Die on proof paper, printed through a
      mat (1903)
      black   100.
      bright carmine   100.
      dull carmine   100.
      dim scarlet   100.
      dark orange   100.
      dull yellow   100.
      dark orange brown   100.
      black olive   100.
      green   100.
      dark blue green   100.
      dark blue   100.
      deep ultramarine   100.
      dark navy blue   100.
      blue violet   100.
      dull violet   100.
      red violet   100.

190-E2

191-E2

Complete 30c design, lithographed.

190-E2   30c
   a. Plate on stamp paper, perf. 12, gummed
      bright red orange   35.
      dull red orange   35.
      dark red orange   35.
      red brown   35.
      dark red brown   35.
      dark orange brown   35.
      yellow brown   35.
      dull yellow green   35.
      green   35.
      dull ultramarine   35.
      bright ultramarine   35.
      blue violet   35.
      red violet   35.
      light red violet   35.
      violet red   35.
   b. Plate on stamp paper, gummed
      ultramarine   60.
      lilac   60.
      scarlet   60.
      orange   60.
      carmine   60.
      dark carmine   60.
      blue green   60.

Complete 90c design, lithographed.

191-E2   90c
   a. Plate on stamp paper, perf. 12, gummed
      black   50.
      red brown   50.
      dark red orange   50.
      brown orange   50.
      ultramarine   50.
      violet blue   50.
      red violet   50.
      violet red   50.
      dark blue green   50.
      orange brown   50.
   b. Plate on stamp paper, gummed
      ultramarine   75.
      lilac   75.
      scarlet   75.
      orange   75.
      carmine   75.
      dark carmine   75.
      green   75.

1879 Coupon Essay
Azariah B. Harris

184-E8

Size of coupon design: 25x7½mm
A proposed $300 30-year Postal Revenue Bond with 3.65%
interest. Daily coupons 3c each, "Receivable for Postage in all
parts of the U.S>" after date thereon. Entire bond contained six
pages of coupons with 16 rows of four (one for each day of two
months); 20% bear month and day, others blank.

184-E8   3c
   a. Coupon on bond (dated Jan. or Feb.),
      imperf., black   350.
   b. Engraved die on old ivory paper (undat-
      ed), black   900.
   c. Single coupon on bond (dated), perf. 12,
      gummed, blue green   125.
   d. Single coupon on bond (undated), perf.
      12, gummed, blue green   50.

Continental Bank Note Co.

182-E4

Design size: 18x22mm
Die size: 59x67mm

Engraved vignette of Franklin on white backgroun[d]
unadopted frame.

182-E4   1c
   a. Die on India, blue
   b. Die on proof paper
      black
      dull scarlet
      dull brown
      dull green
      dull blue
   c. Die on white glazed paper
      black
      black brown
      scarlet
      blue

All known examples of "b" have reduced margins

184-E9

184-E10

Die size: 61½x76½mm
Vignette of Washington on white background in incom[plete]
frame as adopted: no veins in trifoliate ornaments in u[pper]
corners.

184-E9   3c Die on India, on card
      black
      green

Similar to No. 184-E9 but completed frame with veins in tr[ifoli-]
ate ornaments.

184-E10   3c
   a. Die on India, die sunk on card, green
   b. Die on proof paper, about 35x40mm
      gray black
      dull red
      dull blue
      dull green
      dull brown
   c. Die on white glazed paper
      black
      black brown
      scarlet
      blue

Nos. 147-E8 and 147-E9 may have been made from c[om-]
pleted dies of No. 147 to produce Nos. 184-E9 and 184-E[10.]

184-E11

Design size: 17½x21½mm
Die size: 60x75mm
Complete unadopted design with vignette of Liberty on w[hite]
background.

184-E11   3c
   a. Die on India
      black
      brown red
      orange
      green
      blue
      scarlet
   b. Die on proof paper
      brown
      green
      gray black
      dull red
      dull blue
   c. Die on white glazed paper
      black
      black brown
      scarlet
      blue

All known examples of Nos. 184-E11a, 184-E11b ha[ve]
reduced margins.

184-E12

Design size: 19½x24½mm
Die size: 61x71mm
Complete unadopted design with vignette of Washington on
the background in frame similar to No. 184-E11 but with
numerals of value.

184-E12   3c
   a. Die on India, die sunk on card
black	650.
dull scarlet	650.
brown	650.
green	650.

   b. Die on white glazed paper
black	500.
black brown	500.
scarlet	500.
blue	500.

   c. Plate on India (some adhering to origi-
      nal card backing), imperf.
black	100.
scarlet	100.
orange red	100.
green	100.

   d. Plate on white paper, perf. 12, gummed
black	75.
green	75.
blue	75.
brown	75.
red brown	75.
orange	75.
dull scarlet	75.
orange brown	75.

   e. Plate on Francis Patent bluish chemical
      paper, perf. 12, gummed
black	150.
scarlet	150.
red brown	150.
brown	150.
yellow	150.
green	150.
gray	150.

   f. Plate on brown chemical paper, perf.
      12, gummed
blue	150.
ultramarine	150.

   g. Hybrid die on India, mounted on India,
      block sunk on card, green | 400.

184-E13

184-E14

Design size: 18x22mm
Die size: about 61x62mm
Similar to No. 184-E12 but slightly different frame.

184-E13   3c
   a. Die on India, die sunk on card
black	650.
scarlet	650.
green	650.
blue	650.
black brown	650.
blue green	650.

   b. Die on white glazed paper
black	750.
black brown	750.
scarlet	750.
blue	750.

   c. Plate on India, imperf.
black	100.
deep scarlet	100.
green	100.
dark green	100.
dark yellow brown	100.
olive brown	100.
violet brown	100.
orange	100.

   d. Plate on stamp paper, perf. 12,
      gummed
black	75.
dull scarlet	75.
blue green	75.
brown	75.
red brown	75.
dull blue	75.
dark blue	75.
orange	75.
yellow	75.
yellow brown	75.
gray	

Design size: 19x24½mm
Die size: about 67x71mm
Similar to No. 184-E13 but value label with "THREE" above
"CENTS."

184-E14   3c
   a. Hybrid die on India mounted on India,
      block sunk on card
brown red	400.
green	400.

   b. Die on white glazed paper
black	500.
black brown	500.
scarlet	500.
blue	500.

   c. Die on proof paper, about 35x35mm
black	300.
dull scarlet	300.
dull brown	300.
dull green	300.
dull blue	300.
brown red	300.
red brown	300.

184-E15

184-E16

Design size: 20x25½mm
Die size: 60x73mm
Vignette of Indian maiden in headdress, "PORTAGE" error in
top label.

184-E15   3c
   a. Hybrid die on India, cut close, mounted
      on India, block sunk on card
black	900.
dark green	900.

   b. Die on proof paper, about 28x35mm
black	600.
dull scarlet	500.
dull brown	500.
dull blue	500.
dull green	500.

   c. Die on white glazed paper
black	750.
black brown	750.
scarlet	750.
blue	750.

   d. Die on India, scarlet | —

Similar to No. 184-E15 but with spelling corrected to
"POSTAGE."

184-E16   3c Die on India, cut close, mounted
         on India, block sunk on card
black	1,250.
blue	1,250.
steel blue	1,250.
carmine	1,250.
scarlet	1,250.
brown	1,250.
dark green	1,250.

190-E3

Die size: 44½x71½mm
Vignette of Hamilton on white background in frame as
adopted.

190-E3   30c
   a. Die on proof paper, about 35x48mm
gray black	500.
dull red	500.
dull green	500.
dull brown	500.
dull blue	500.

   b. Die on white glazed paper
black	750.
black brown	750.
scarlet	750.
blue	750.

American Bank Note Co.

184-E17

Design size: 22x30mm
Silver photo print of engraved vignette of Washington
mounted on pencil and ink frame design.

184-E17   3c
   a. Die on white card, 38x49mm
      light brown vignette, black frame | 1,250.
   b. Die on white card, 38x50mm
      light brown vignette, black frame | 1,250.

Frame ornaments extend beyond framelines, lettering less
complete than on No. 184-E17a.

1881-82 ISSUE
American Bank Note Co.

205-E1

Die size: 59x74mm
Vignette of Garfield in lined oval.

205-E1   5c Die on India, die sunk on card,
      black | 500.

205-E2

205-E3

Die No. C-47 size: 70x83mm
Vignette of Garfield in beaded oval, in plain border of horiz.
lines. Found with and without imprint and die number.

205-E2   5c Die on India, die sunk on card
gray brown	250.
gray black	250.

      No. 205-E2 may not be a stamp essay.

Die size: 78x78mm
Vignette of Garfield in beaded oval with cutout at bottom for
top of star.

205-E3   5c
   a. Die on India, die sunk on card
black	750.
deep red orange	750.
red brown	750.
blue	750.
green	750.

   b. Die on white glazed paper
black	750.
green	750.
blue	750.
scarlet	750.
red brown	750.

   c. Negative impression, solid color outside
      design, die on India, bright red orange | 1,000.

205-E4

Vignette of Garfield as No. 205-E1 in lined oval and finished frame as adopted.

205-E4 5c Die on India, 24x30mm, black 900.

E206-E1

Image of unadopted frame, printed on 40x60mm India paper with text and right "1" cut out.

206-E1 5c Black on India 2,500.

206-E1B

Image of frame with "DOS CENTAVOS" in upper label and "ONE CENT" pasted on bottom label, affixed to 57x71mm card with additional pencil sketch at right.

206-E1B 5c Black image affixed to card 2,500.

206-E1C 206-E2

Design size: 21x26mm
Engraved frame of unadopted design.
206-E1C 1c
  a. Die on white glazed paper, 42x74mm,
    black 1,000.
  b. Die on surface-tinted glazed paper, cut
    close
    green, *buff* 600.
    black, *orange* 600.
    brown orange, *blue* 600.

Engraved frame almost identical to No. 206-E1C with small typographed vignette of Peace.
206-E2 1c Die on blue surface-tinted ivory pa-
    per, cut close, buff vignette, car-
    mine frame 800.

206-E3

Vignette of Peace only.
206-E3 1c
  a. Engraved vignette
    black 350.
    dull red violet 350.
  b. Typographed vignette 350.

206-E4

Engraved frame (No. 206-E1) with typographed vignette of Lincoln mounted on it. Four diff. colors (dull carmine, dull scarlet, dark brown, green) on cream white ivory paper, 22x27mm each, mounted together on 92x114mm thick white card, ms. "American Bank Note Co. N.Y." at lower right.
206-E4 1c Four designs on cream white ivory
    on card 2,500.

Design size: 18x23½mm
Typographed vignette of Lincoln only.

206-E5

206-E5 1c Die on white ivory paper
    dull carmine 400.
    dark yellowish brown 400.
    dull purple 400.
    dull dark blue 400.
    orange 400.

206-E6

Incomplete engraving of complete design as issued: no shading in upper arabesques.
206-E6 1c
  a. Die on India
    gray blue 750.
    green blue 750.
  b. Die on India, cut close, on India block
    sunk on card, deep gray blue 350.

207-E1 207-E2

Design size: 20½x25½mm
Die size: 49x54½mm
Engraved unadopted frame design with 3's at sides and large 3 at top.
207-E1 3c
  a. Die on India
    yellow brown 750.
    dull brown 750.
    dull blue 750.
    green 750.
  b. Die on white glazed paper, 32x38mm
    black 650.
    dull dark yellow 650.
  c. Die on surface-tinted ivory paper, cut
    close
    black, *orange* 500.
    green, *buff* 500.
    violet blue, *orange* 500.

Engraved frame as No. 207-E1, with typographed vignette of Peace.
207-E2 3c Die on blue surface-tinted ivory pa-
    per, cut close, buff vignette, car-
    mine frame 850.

Engraved frame (No. 207-E1) with typographed vignette of Peace mounted on it. Four diff. color combinations (orange vignette, dull carmine frame; dull carmine vignette, dull brown frame; yellow brown vignette and frame; blue green vignette and frame) on cream white ivory paper, 22x27mm each, mounted together on 92x114mm thick white card, "American Bank Note Co. N.Y." at lower right.
207-E3 3c 4 designs on cream white ivory on
    card 2,

208-E1

Incomplete engraving of design as adopted: unfinished shading on top label and bottom ribbon, four lines between frame sinkage at right and left edges, horiz. line at bottom.
208-E1 6c Die on India, on card, black 1,5

This is a new die engraved by the Bureau of Engraving Printing for "Roosevelt" proof albums.

209-E1

Design size: 20x25mm
Die size: 58x76mm
Engraving of unadopted frame only, no horiz. lines background.
209-E1 10c Die on thick white card, about
    25x33mm
    blue 8
    green 8

Similar to No. 209-E1 but with horiz. lines added background.

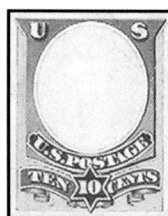

209-E2

209-E2 10c
  a. Die on thick white card
    black 7
    red 7
    green 7
    blue 7
  b. Die on India, on 50x70mm card, black 8
  c. Die on white glazed paper, black 8

209-E3

Engraved frame similar to No. 209-E2 with typographed vignette of Peace.
209-E3 10c
  a. Die on blue surface-tinted glazed paper,
    cut close, buff vignette, carmine frame 65
  b. Die on orange surface-tinted glazed pa-
    per
    dull carmine vignette, violet frame 65
    dull yellow vignette, violet frame 65
    yellow vignette, green frame 65

209-E4   209-E5

ignette diameter: 17mm
ngraved Franklin vignette.

-E4   10c
  a. Die on India
      black   575.
      dusky carmine   575.
      dull scarlet   575.
      dim orange   575.
      orange brown   575.
      yellow green   575.
      dim blue green   575.
      deep blue   575.
      red brown on blue ground   575.
      dark red violet   575.
  b. Die sunk on glazed paper, approx.
      51x69mm
      dusky carmine   775.
      dim scarlet   775.
      dim orange   775.
      deep blue   775.
      dim blue green   775.

Design size: 21x26mm
ngraved frame with typographed vignette mounted on it.
r diff. color combinations (dull scarlet vignette, dull carmine
ne; dull orange vignette, brown orange frame; yellow brown
nette, dark brown frame; blue green vignette and frame) on
am white ivory paper, 22x27mm each, mounted together on
114mm thick white card, ms. "American Bank Note Co.
." at lower right.

9-E5   10c Four designs on cream white ivory
              on card   2,500.

209-E6   209-E7

vignette diameter: 18mm
Engraved Washington vignette.

9-E6   10c
  a. Die on India
      black   600.
      dim deep carmine   600.
      dim deep scarlet   600.
      dull orange   600.
      dull brown   600.
      dim blue green   600.
      blue   600.
      dusky red violet   600.
  b. Die sunk on white ivory paper, 55x67mm
      dusky carmine   800.
      dull orange   800.
      dull blue green   800.
      scarlet   800.
      dull brown   800.
      red violet   800.

Design size: 21x26mm
Engraved frame with typographed vignette mounted on it.
ur diff. color combinations (dull carmine vignette and frame;
ll orange vignette, brown orange frame; yellow brown
gnette, dark brown frame; blue green vignette and frame) on
eam white ivory paper, 22x27mm each, mounted together on
2x114mm thick white card, ms. "American Bank Note Co.
Y." at lower right.

09-E7   10c
  a. Four designs on cream white ivory on
      card   2,500.
  b. Single composite off card, dull carmine
      vignette, blue green frame   400.

Issued stamp, No. 209, in trial color, overprinted network in
gitive ink.

09-E8   10c On thick paper, perf. 12, gummed,
              sepia, overprint olive gray   150.

1883 ISSUE
American Bank Note Co.

210-E1   210-E2

Design size: 20x25½mm
Engraved vignette of Washington (from proof on India of No.
207) with watercolor frame design nearly as adopted but with
"TWO" and "CENTS" at an angle, rubber stamp "Feb. 17, 1883"
on back.

210-E1   2c Die on white card, 80x90mm, black
              vignette, gray and white frame   3,000.

Design size: 20x25mm
Engraved vignette of Washington (from proof on India of No.
207) mounted on unadopted watercolor and ink frame design.
backstamped "American Bank Note Co. Feb. 27, 1883."

210-E2   2c Die on thick white card,
              87x100mm, black and white   3,000.

210-E3   210-E4

Design size: 20x25½mm
Engraved vignette of Washington (from proof on India of No.
207) mounted on watercolor frame design as adopted, ms. "2
March 1883 No. 1."

210-E3   2c Die on white card, 80x90mm, black
              vignette, gray & white frame   3,000.

Design size: 20x25mm
Engraved vignette of Washington on white background
mounted on a brush and pen watercolor drawing of unadopted
fancy frame design, backstamped "American Bank Note Co.
Mar. 2, 1883" and pencil "No. 2."

210-E4   2c Die on white card, 88x101mm,
              dusky blue green   3,000.

210-E5

Design size: 20x25mm
Engraved vignette of Washington (from revenue stamp No.
RB17) mounted on wash drawing of unadopted ornate frame
design, backstamped "American Bank Note Co. Mar. 2, 1883"
and pencil "No. 3."

210-E5   2c Die on white card, 88x101mm,
              blue violet vignette, black frame   2,500.

211-E1

Design size: 20x25½mm
Engraved vignette of Jackson mounted on unadopted watercolor frame design.

211-E1   4c Die on white card, 70x70mm, blue
              green vignette and frame   3,500.

Engraved head of Jackson only.

211-E2   4c Die on India, die sunk on card,
              black   1,000.

211-E3

Incomplete engraved vignette of Jackson: lower edge of bust
incomplete.

211-E3   4c Die on India, die sunk on card
      black   2,500.
      green   2,500.
      red brown   2,500.

Complete engraved vignette of Jackson.

211-E4   4c Die on India, die sunk on card,
              blue green   2,500.

211-E6

Die size: 60x62mm
Complete design as adopted but with pencil sketch of pedestal top under bust.

211-E5   4c Die on India, die sunk on card,
              gray black   5,750.

Similar to No. 211-E5 but with incomplete shading engraved
on pedestal.

211-E6   4c Die on India, die sunk on card,
              blue green   2,500.

1887 ISSUE
American Bank Note Co.

212-E1

Die size: 55x63mm
Incomplete engraved vignette of Franklin facing right: horiz.
background lines only.

212-E1   1c Die on 32½x35mm card, India
              mounted, die sunk on card
      black   600.
      ultramarine   600.

Die size: 62x62mm
Franklin vignette similar to No. 212-E1 but diagonal lines (in
one direction only) added to background.

212-E2

212-E2   1c Die on India, die sunk on card
      black   600.
      ultramarine   600.

Die size: 55x64mm
Similar to No. 212-E2 but diagonal lines in both directions.

212-E3   1c Die on India, die sunk on card,
              black   500.

212-E4

Complete design as issued except Franklin facing right.

212-E4   1c
  a. Die on India, die sunk on card
     black   600.
     ultramarine   600.
  b. Die on white glazed paper, about
        64x76mm
     black   750.
     black brown   750.
     scarlet   750.
     blue   750.

Die size: 62x62mm
Incomplete vignette of Franklin facing left as adopted.

212-E5   1c Die on India, die sunk on card, ul-
           tramarine   450.

212-E6   212-E7

Die size: 56x64½mm
Incomplete design as adopted except three lines below value
label and taller numeral, shadow on edge of bust and in background below chin too dark.

212-E6   1c Die on India, die sunk on card
     ultramarine   750.
     green   750.

Similar to No. 212-E6 but with shadows lightened.

212-E7   1c Die on India, die sunk on card, ul-
           tramarine   750.

1890 ISSUE
American Bank Note Co.

219-E1

Design size: 19x22½mm
Die size: 58x64mm
Engraved die of frame only with blank labels quite similar to
adopted design.

219-E1   1c Die on ivory paper, 64x72mm,
           black   700.

219-E2   219-E3

Design size: 19x22mm
Engraved Franklin vignette cut down from 1887 1c stamp (No.
212) mounted on watercolor frame design.

219-E2   1c Die on thick light buff card, ul-
           tramarine frame   3,500.

Die size: 62x62mm
Engraved Franklin vignette with lettered label above.

219-E3   1c Die on India, die sunk on card,
           blue   800.

220-E1   220-E2

Design size: 19x22mm
Engraved Washington vignette from 3c stamp (from proof on
India of No. 184) mounted on watercolor frame design.
220-E1   2c Die on thick white card, 62x66mm,
           light carmine frame   3,750.

Design size: 19x23mm
Engraved Washington vignette cut from 1887 2c stamp (No.
213) mounted on shield-like watercolor frame design.
220-E2   2c Die on thick light buff card, gray
           frame   3,000.

220-E3   220-E4

Design size: 19x23mm
Engraved Washington vignette cut from 1887 2c stamp (No.
213) mounted on watercolor frame design.
220-E3   2c Die on white card, 105x135mm,
           gray black frame   3,000.

Design size: 19x22mm
Die size: 56x63mm
Engraved unadopted frame only.
220-E4   2c Die on white ivory paper, black   1,250.

220-E5   220-E6

Die size: 62x62mm
Engraved vignette of Washington in oval line frame.
220-E5   2c Die on India, die sunk on card,
           dark carmine   800.

Engraved Washington vignette with lettered label above.
220-E6   2c Die on India, dusky carmine   1,250.

220-E7   220-E8

Design size: 19x22½mm
Engraved Washington vignette and lettered top label
mounted on pencil drawing of frame design adopted, ms.
"J.J.M. — engraved background only without figures or words;"
backstamped "Nov. 15, 1889 American Bank Note Co."
220-E7   2c Die on 50x55mm white card,
           mounted on thick white card,
           119x122mm, black vignette, pen-
           cil frame   3,000.

Design size: 19x22mm
Die size: 56x63mm
Engraved frame only as adopted with numerals, blank curved
top label.
220-E8   2c
  a. Die on ivory paper, 64x71mm, black   900.
  b. Die on India, 51x62mm
     black   700.
     brown black   700.
     dark brown   700.
     dull scarlet   700.
     dark blue green   700.

dark blue
red violet
red orange

220-E9

Incomplete engraving of entire design as adopted: no do
rectangular spaces between shading lines on cheek under
in front of ear and on back of neck.
220-E9   2c Die on India, die sunk on card,
           lake   1,

(Probably by) The Times, Philadelphia

220-E11

Surface-printed essay for proposed business advertising
stamps.
220-E11   2c Die on India, on card, bright
            green blue

American Bank Note Co.

221-E1   221-E2

Engraved 3c frame as adopted with vignette cut out, moun
over photo of James Madison.
221-E1   3c Die on India, cut close, dark green   2,5

Engraved vignette of Jackson with lettered label above.
221-E2   3c Die on India, die sunk on card,
           purple   7

Design size: 19x22mm
Incomplete engraved design as adopted except Lincoln f
ing ¾ left: unfinished shading under collar.
222-E1   4c Die on India, die sunk on card,
           black brown   1,2

222-E2   222-E3

Die No. C-226 size: 62½x62½mm
Completed design with die no. and impt., Lincoln facing
left.
222-E2   4c Die on India, on 25x32mm card,
           black brown   1,00

Incomplete engraving as adopted: no wart on face, no line
on shirt.
222-E3   4c Die on India, die sunk on card,
           black brown   1,00

223-E1

design size: 19x21½mm
...oto of Seward vignette mounted on watercolor frame
...gn.

E1 5c Die on light buff paper in upper
right corner of short envelope,
gray & white   1,750.

223-E2   223-E3

design size: 19x26½mm
...ie size: 63x62mm
...complete engraved design as adopted except Grant facing
...eft: hair neatly combed.

-E2 5c Die on India, die sunk on card
black   700.
orange brown   700.

design size: 19x26½mm
...ie size: 63x62mm
...complete engraving of complete bearded left-facing design:
pupils not solid color, light shading on right side of face,
...y one diagonal shading line on left coat shoulder.

-E3 5c Die on India, die sunk on card,
chocolate   700.

...imilar to No. 223-E3 but more complete. Left beard has no
...gonal lines and is light at top center.

-E4 5c Die on India, die sunk on card,
chocolate   700.

...hird state of die: no horiz. lines on left moustache or under
...er lip.

-E5 5c Die on India, die sunk on card,
chocolate   700.

223-E6   223-E7

...Completed left-facing design: shows lines omitted from No.
...3-E5, several diagonal shading lines on left shoulder of coat.

-E6 5c Die on India, die sunk on card
black   700.
chocolate   700.

Design size: 19x26½mm
Die size: 62x62mm
...Left-facing design with slightly diff. portrait, hair neatly
...mbed. Horiz. shading lines on left coat shoulder, no wash-
...ched shadows on coat, beard and tie.

-3-E7 5c
a. Die on India, die sunk on card
black   700.
dark brown   700.
b. Die on glazed paper, impt. and "ESSAY
MARCH 1890"
black   750.
black brown   750.
scarlet   750.
blue   750.

Design size: 19x26½mm
...Die similar to No. 223-E7 but diagonal shading lines on left
...oat shoulder, wash-etched shadows on coat, beard and tie.

23-E8 5c Die on India, on card, brown   700.

223-E9   223-E10

Die size: 62x63mm
...Engraving of right-facing Grant design diff. than adopted: light
...val line around vignette, three diagonal lines on shirtfront
...nder tie. Incomplete engraving: right collar unshaded.

23-E9 5c Die on India, dark orange brown   700.

Similar to No. 223-E9 but engraving completed: right collar
shaded.

223-E10 5c
a. Die on India, die sunk on card, dark
orange brown   700.
b. Die on ivory paper, impt. and "ESSAY
MARCH 1890"
black   750.
black brown   750.
scarlet   750.
blue   750.

Ferrotype plate 39x51mm of Grant facing ¾ right, outlines
engraved, filled with red.

223-E11 5c Metal plate   650.

223-E12

Printing from ferrotype plate, No. 223-E11.
223-E12 5c Die on card, 43x56mm, red   650.

226-E1   226-E2

Design size: 19x22½mm
Incomplete engraved vignette of Webster with curved label
above, mounted on pencil drawing of frame design (includes
additional pencil drawings of lower part of frame, value lettering), backstamped "D.S. Ronaldson," frame engraver.

226-E1 10c Die on white card, 51x55mm,
black   13,500.

Design size: 19x22½mm
Engraving of unadopted frame design.
226-E2 10c Die on white glazed paper, black   1,000.

226-E3   226-E4

Design size: 19x22mm
Engraved 10c frame as adopted, vignette cut out and
mounted over photo of John Adams.
226-E3 10c Die on India, cut close, dark green   2,500.

Design size: 19x22mm
Engraved 10c frame as adopted, vignette cut out and
mounted over photo of William T. Sherman.
226-E4 10c Die on India, cut close, dark green   2,500.

227-E1

Design size: 19x22½mm
Engraved vignette of Henry Clay with curved label above,
mounted on wash drawing of frame design (includes additional
enlarged pencil and wash drawing of frame).

227-E1 15c Die on white card, mounted at left
on light buff card, 110x123mm
(frame drawing at right), black   1,750.

228-E1

Design size: 19x22½mm
Die size: 62x61mm
Incomplete engraved vignette of Jefferson with curved let-
tered label at top: hair shading incomplete.

228-E1 30c Die on India, die sunk on card,
black   750.

Similar to No. 228-E1 but more shading on hair, vert. shading
lines on chin.

228-E2 30c Die on India, die sunk on card,
black   750.

229-E1

Design size: 19x22½mm
Die size: 62x62mm
Engraved vignette of Perry with curved lettered label at top.

229-E1 90c Die on India, die sunk on card, red
orange   750.

COLUMBIAN ISSUE
Lyman H. Bagg

230-E1   237-E1

Design sizes: 22x22mm
Left: No. 230-E1 — pencil drawing of Columbus in armor, on
paper. "I do not know whether these designs will be of any use
to you or not — they are so rough. L.H.B." written at top, "My
idea illustrated" at bottom.
Right: No. 237-E1 — pencil drawing of North American continent, on paper.

230-E1 One Cent, Ten Cents, Drawings on
114x72mm white wove, Nos. 230-E1,
237-E1   6,000.

American Bank Note Co.

230-E2

230-E3

230-E4

Design size: 33x22mm
Silver print photo vignette of Columbus head mounted on watercolor drawing of unadopted frame design.

230-E2 1c Die on stiff white drawing paper, red violet
230-E3 1c Die on stiff white drawing paper, blue green ... 4,500.
230-E4 1c Die on stiff white drawing paper, light red ... 4,500.

230-E5

Ferrotype metal plate with outline of adopted vignette (reversed) and drawings of Indian man and woman at sides in single line frame 39mm long.

230-E5 1c Metal plate, 57x38mm ... 1,250.

230-E6

Vignette size: 16x15mm
Engraved vignette only as adopted.

230-E6 1c Die on 53x39mm India, on card
              yellow brown ... 2,000.
              black ... 2,000.

230-E7

Incomplete engraving of vignette, lettering, value numerals and tablet as issued: without palm tree, incomplete shading on and behind Indian and maiden, on Columbus' head, no shading on scrollwork, etc.

230-E7 1c Die on 39x28mm stiff wove, deep blue ... 2,000.

230-E8

Incomplete engraving of entire design as issued: maiden's skirt only lightly engraved, chief's torso and shoulder incompletely engraved, incomplete shading in frame design at top, etc.

230-E8 1c Die on India, die sunk on 99x84mm card, deep blue ... 1,500.

231-E1

Design size: 34x22mm
Silver print photo of vignette as adopted, mounted on watercolor drawing of unadopted frame design.

231-E1 2c Die on stiff white drawing paper, red violet ... 8,500.

Die size: 74x61½mm
Incomplete engraving of adopted vignette only.

231-E2 2c Die on India, die sunk on card
              black ... 1,500.
              sepia ... 1,500.

231-E3

Design size: 35½x22mm
Engraved vignette of Columbus asking aid of Isabella as adopted for 5c, mounted on watercolor drawing of frame design similar to that adopted for 2c.

231-E3 2c Die on stiff white drawing paper, dark brown ... 4,000.

231-E4

Vignette size: 29x15mm
Die size: 74x61½mm
Incomplete engraving of vignette as adopted (probably first state of die): cape on back of central figure incomplete, etc.

231-E4 2c Die on India, die sunk on card, black ... 2,500.

231-E5

Incomplete engraving of vignette as adopted (probably second state of die): more shading on top right face, etc.; also pencil sketches for lengthening vignette.

231-E5 2c Die on India, die sunk on card, black ... 3,250.

231-E6

Vignette size: 31½x15mm
Die size: 74x61½mm
Incomplete engraving of vignette, longer than Nos. 231-E4 and 231-E5, later shortened as adopted: Columbus' legs, central figure's cape, etc., are incomplete.

231-E6 2c Die on India, die sunk on card, black ... 2,500.

231-E7

Design size: 33x22mm
Die size: 74x61½mm
Incomplete engraving of entire design almost as ado figures of value narrower, unfinished crosset shadows in corners.

Ridgway numbers used for colors of No. 231-E7.

231-E7 2c
  a. ie on India, die sunk on card
         13m/4 smoky dusky o-yellow-orange ... 1
  b. Die on thin white wove card
         69o/5 black
         1m/0 dusky red
         3k/2 dull dark orange-red
         5i/0 deep o-orange-red
         5j/1 deep v-deep o-orange-red
         6i/0 deep m. red-orange
         9i/0 deep o-yellow-orange
         9m/0 dusky o-red-orange
         9m/3 dismal dusky o red-orange
         9m/4 smoky ducky o-red-orange
         9n/2 dull v. dusky o-red-orange
         10k/0 m. dark orange
         11i/0 deep orange
         11k/1 dim dark orange
         13m/1 dim dusky o-yellow-orange
         13m/4 smoky dusky o-yellow-orange
         33m/2 dull dusky g-yellow-green
         37m/1 dim dusky g-blue-green
         43m/2 dull dusky green-blue
         49m/0 dusky blue
         49m/1 dim dusky blue
         55m/2 dull dusky blue-violet
         59m/2 dull dusky violet
         65m/2 dull dusky r-red-violet
         70i/0 deep violet-red-red

231-E8

Design size: 33x22mm
Incomplete engraving of entire design as adopted: va numerals same as on issued stamp but without thick shac bars at ends of outer frame rectangles, etc.

231-E8 2c Die on India, card mounted, sepia ... 1,5

232-E1

Design size: 33½x22mm
Silver print photo of vignette unadopted for any value (Colu bus embarking on voyage of discovery), mounted on waterco drawing of unadopted frame design.

232-E1 3c Die on stiff white drawing paper, 41x29mm, orange brown ... 4,0

Ferrotype metal plate showing 19x15mm outline of Sar Maria (reversed) in 33x15mm vignette frame, outline engrav and filled with red ink.

232-E2 3c Metal plate, 51x30mm ... 1,2

232-E3

Printing from ferrotype plate No. 232-E3.

232-E3 3c Die on stiff white card with rounded corners, 55x42mm, red ... 1,25

232-E4

Vignette size: 30x15mm
Die size: 74x61mm

complete engraving of vignette as adopted: sky composed horiz. ruled lines, no clouds.

-E4 3c Die on India, die sunk on card
black 1,250.
dark yellow-orange 1,250.
sepia 1,750.

232-E5

ngraved vignette similar to No. 232-E4 but with "1492 TED STATES OF AMERICA 1892" and scrolls around nerals engraved in outline only, pencil outline of frame.

-E5 3c Die on thick artist's card with beveled edges, 50x38mm, dark yellow orange 3,000.

233-E1

Design size: 33½x22mm
Silver print photo of wash drawing of vignette as adopted, unted on watercolor drawing of frame design as adopted but ed "COLUMBUS ON VOYAGE OF DISCOVERY. SHIPS AT A."

-E1 4c Die on stiff white drawing paper, 41x29mm, brown red 4,750.

233-E2

Design size: 33x22mm
Die size: 74x61½mm
Incomplete engraving of complete design as adopted: unfined crosset shadows in lower corners.

Ridgway numbers used for some colors of No. 233-E2.

3-E2 4c
a. Die on India, die sunk on card
black 1,250.
dark yellow orange 1,250.
b. Die on thin white wove card, die sunk on card
1m/0 dusky red 800.
3i/1 dim deep orange-red 800.
3k/2 dull dark orange-red 800.
5i/0 deep o-orange-red 800.
9i/0 deep o-red-orange 800.
9m/1 dim dusky o-red-orange 800.
11i/0 deep orange 800.
11k/1 dim dark orange 800.
11m/2 dull dusky orange 800.
13k/1 dim dark o-yellow-orange 800.
13m/2 dull dusky o-yellow-orange 800.
13k/3 dismal dark o-yellow-orange 800.
13k/4 smoky dark o-yellow-orange 800.
13m/4 smoky dusky o-yellow-orange 800.
15m/2 dull dusky yellow-orange 800.
33m/2 dull dusky g-yellow-green 800.
35m/5 gloomy dusky green 800.
37m/1 dim dusky g-blue-green 800.
39m/1 dim dusky blue-green 800.
41m/1 dim dusky b-blue-green 800.
47m/0 dusky green-blue-blue 800.
55m/2 dull dusky blue-violet 800.
63m/2 dull dusky red-violet 800.
69m/1 dull dusky red-violet-red 800.
69k/3 dismal dark red-violet-red 800.
71i/0 deep violet-red-red 800.
71m/0 dusky violet-red-red 800.
71o/5 black 800.
ultramarine 800.
violet 800.
red violet 800.
brown violet 800.
orange brown 800.
dark brown 800.

234-E1

Design size: 38½x22mm
Engraved vignette as adopted, mounted on watercolor drawing of frame design similar to but longer than adopted. Vignette also used on No. 231-E3.

234-E1 5c Die on thick artist's card, block sunk as die essay, black brown 4,000.

234-E2

Design size: 34x22½mm
Die size: 67x63mm
Engraved vignette as adopted, mounted on watercolor drawing of frame design as adopted, pencil "Oct. 5/92," approval monogram of J.D. Macdonough and ⅞x1 1/32 inches. Vignette also used on No. 231-E3.

234-E2 5c Die on thick artist's card, die sunk, black brown & white 4,000.

234-E3

Vignette size: 29½x15mm
Die size: 74x61½mm
Engraved vignette only as adopted.

234-E3 5c Die on India, die sunk on card, sepia 1,250.

234-E4

Incomplete engraving of entire design: bench at left has horiz. shading only, incomplete shading in Columbus' face, etc.

234-E4 5c Die on 74x60mm India, on card
sepia 1,000.
blue 1,000.

Ferrotype metal plate with engraved outline design (reversed) of vignette as used on 6c, engraved lines filled with red ink.

235-E1 6c Metal plate, 38x38mm 1,100.

235-E2

Printing from ferrotype plate No. 235-E1.

235-E2 6c Die on stiff white card with rounded corners, 55x42mm, red 1,250.

235-E3

Incomplete engraving of frame as adopted: unfinished crosset shadows in lower corners.

235-E3 6c Die on India, black 2,000.

235-E4

Design size: 34x22mm
Die size: 73x60mm
Incomplete engraving of entire design as adopted: neck and shoulder of horse, side figures in niches, crosset shadows in lower corners all unfinished.

235-E4 6c Die on India, die sunk on card, blue violet 1,500.

236-E1

Design size: 33½x22mm
Die size: 73x62mm
Design as adopted but frame incompletely engraved: unfinished crosset shadows in lower corners.

236-E1 8c Die on India, on card, black 2,500.

236-E2

Design as adopted but frame incompletely engraved: unfinished crosset shadows in lower corners, incomplete gown at left and faces at right.

236-E2 8c Die on India, on card, black 1,000.

237-E2

Ferrotype metal plate with engraved outline design (reversed) of vignette as used on 10c, engraved lines filled with red ink.

237-E2 10c Metal plate, 43x28mm 1,000.

237-E3

Printing from ferrotype plate No. 237-E2.

237-E3 10c Die on stiff white card with rounded corners, 55x42mm, red 1,000.

237-E4

Design size: 33x22mm
Die size: 74x62mm
Incomplete engraving of entire design as adopted: surround-
ings of Columbus, floor, etc., three figures behind King Ferdinand, crosset shadows in lower corners all unfinished.

237-E4   10c Die on India, card mounted
black brown   1,000.
rose carmine   1,000.

Similar to No. 237-E4 but more completely engraved: missing
lines on ankle bracelet of Indian, many details in vignette and
crosset shadows in lower corners.

237-E5   10c Die on India, die sunk on card
black brown   1,500.
carmine   1,500.

238-E1

Design size: 33½x22mm
Silver print photo of vignette unadopted for any value (Columbus relating incidents of voyage to Ferdinand and Isabella),
mounted on watercolor drawing of frame design similar to that
adopted.

238-E1   15c Die on stiff white drawing paper,
42x30mm, bright ultramarine   5,000.

238-E2

Vignette size: 30x15mm
Die size: 71x59mm
Incomplete engraving of vignette only as adopted: shading on
Columbus' tunic and arms, Isabella's sholder, Ferdinand's robe,
seated Indian's robe, robe of kneeling figure in lower left corner,
etc., all unfinished.

238-E2   15c Die on India, die sunk on card,
black brown   1,500.

Complete engraving of vignette adopted.

238-E3   15c Die on India, black brown   1,500.

238-E4

Design size: 33½x22mm
Die size: 73½x62mm
Incomplete engraving of complete design as adopted: shading on Isabella's shoulder, Ferdinand's robe, seated Indian's
blanket and crosset shadows in lower corners all unfinished.

238-E4   15c Die on India, on card
black brown   1,500.
blue green   1,500.

239-E1

Design size: 34½x22½mm

Silver print photo of vignette adopted for 15c, mounted on
watercolor and ink drawing of unadopted frame design, titled
"COLUMBUS PRESENTING NATIVES TO FERDINAND AND
ISABELLA."

239-E1   30c Die on stiff white drawing paper,
42x30mm, bluish gray   5,000.

239-E2

Ferrotype metal plate with engraved outline design (reversed)
of vignette as used on 30c, engraved lines filled with red ink.

239-E2   30c Metal plate, 39x29mm   1,000.

239-E3

Printing from ferrotype plate No. 239-E2.

239-E3   30c Die on stiff white card with rounded corners, 55x43mm, red   1,000.

239-E4

Vignette size: 30x15mm
Die size: 74x62mm
Incomplete engraving of adopted vignette only: table cloth
dark at top; horiz. lines on front edge of octagonal footstool,
horiz. dots in shadow below windowsill at left, dots on top of
head of man standing next to Columbus, etc., all missing.

239-E4   30c Die on India, die sunk on card,
black   1,750.

Similar to No. 239-E4 but further engraved: has horiz. lines
on front of footstool, etc. Eight pencil instructions for finishing
vignette engraving written on large card backing, e.g., "Too
much color on table cloth near top."

239-E5   30c Die on India, die sunk on
177x117mm card
black   2,000.
black brown   2,000.

239-E6

Design size: 33½x22mm
Die size: 74x63mm
Incomplete engraving of entire design as adopted: table cloth
dark at top, diagonal dashes in one direction only between
horiz. lines at lower left of vignette, etc.

239-E6   30c Die on India, die sunk on card
black   2,000.
black brown   2,000.

Similar to No. 239-E6 but diagonal dashes in two directions,
more dots on head and hand of man seated at near end of
table.

239-E7   30c Die on India, die sunk on card
black brown   1,750.
orange   1,750.

Incomplete engraving of entire design: window frame, horiz.
shading lines on shoulder of man at right, vert. lines on front of

table cloth below Columbus all missing. Lighter shading a
of table cloth as on issued stamp.

239-E8   30c Die on India, on card, orange   2

240-E1

Design size: 34x22mm
Die size: Incomplete engraving of entire design as adop
unfinished shadows between right arm and body of mar
donkey, distant object in front of bowing man's head darker
on issued stamp.

240-E1   50c Die on India, on card, slate blue   1,

240-E2

Incomplete engraving of entire design: missing dots on c
key's flank and long lines on wrist of bowing man, no etching
two riders or their mounts.

240-E2   50c Die on India, on card, slate blue   1,5

240-E3

Incomplete engraving of entire design: additional engrav.
on donkey's hindquarters and face of figure to left of Columb

240-E3   50c Die on India, on card, slate blue   1,5

241-E1

Ferrotype metal plate with engraved outline design (reverse
of vignette as used on $1, engraved lines filled with red ink.

241-E1 $1 Metal plate, 45x29mm   1,00

241-E2

Printing from ferrotype plate No. 241-E1.

241-E2 $1 Die on stiff white card with round-
ed corners, 55½x43mm, red   1,00

241-E3

Vignette size: 31x15mm
Die size: 72x59mm

ncomplete engraving of vignette only as adopted (very early
e of die): very little shading on Isabella, floor, walls, etc.

-E3 $1 Die on India, die sunk on card,
           black brown   2,000.

241-E4

ncomplete engraving of entire design as adopted: shadow on
le cloth, woman in front of table, crosslet shadows at lower
rners all unfinished.

-E4 $1 Die on India, on card, black brown   2,000.

241-E5

Later state of complete design: horiz. lines in rectangle above
abella missing.

1-E5 $1 Die on India, die sunk on
           86x69mm card, black brown   2,000.

242-E1

Design size: 33½x22mm
Die size: 75x62mm
Incomplete engraving of entire design as adopted: about 12
oriz. lines missing on back of cape of tall man at right, some
rt. dashes missing on corselet of soldier at right, incomplete
liage over "C" of "COLUMBUS," etc.

42-E1 $2 Die on India, die sunk on card
           dull yellow orange   2,000.
           olive brown   2,000.

243-E1

Ferrotype metal plate with engraved outline design (reversed)
of vignette as used on $3, engraved lines filled with red wax.

243-E1 $3 Metal plate, 45x29mm   1,250.

243-E2

Printing from ferrotype plate No. 243-E1.

243-E2 $3 Die on stiff white card with round-
             ed corners, 55x43mm, red   1,250.

243-E3

Design size: 33½x22mm
Incomplete engraving of entire design as adopted: unshaded
crossets in lower corners, shading lines on crossets and frame
above title label too light. Pencil marks correct these.

243-E3 $3 Die on India, die sunk on card,
             dark yellow green   1,500.

243-E4

Incomplete engraving of entire design as adopted, before
etching of shadows on Columbus, Ferdinand, backs of chairs,
etc.

243-E4 $3 Die on India, on card, dark red   2,000.

Ferrotype metal plate with engraved outline design (reversed)
of Queen Isabella vignette as used on $4, engraved lines filled
with red wax.

244-E1 $4 Metal plate, 33x44mm   1,500.

244-E2

Printing from ferrotype plate No. 244-E1.

244-E2 $4 Die on stiff white card with round-
             ed corners, 43x55mm, red   1,500.

244-E3

Vignette diameter: 14mm
Incomplete engraving of Isabella head with background of
uniform ruled horiz. lines only, blank circle for Columbus
vignette at right adjoining.

244-E3 $4 Die on India, on card, black   3,000.

Similar to No. 244-E3 but background has diagonal shading
also.

244-E4 $4 Die on India, on card, black   3,000.

244-E5

Design size: about 34x21½mm
Die size: 74½x61½mm
Incomplete engraving of vignettes and lettering only: no diago-
nal shading lines in background of Columbus vignette.

244-E5 $4 Die on India, die sunk on card
             black   3,500.
             dark red   4,000.

244-E6

Design size: 34x22mm
Same engraving as No. 244-E5 but with wash drawing of
frame design as adopted.

244-E6 $4 Die on thick artist's card with bev-
             eled edges, 50x39mm, gray black   3,000.

244-E7

Incomplete engraving of entire design as adopted: shadow at
top of vert. bar and lines on leaves at bottom between vignettes
unfinished; no circular line bordering vignette at Isabella's right
shoulder.

244-E7 $4 Die on India, on card, black brown   2,000.

244-E8

More complete engraving than No. 244-E7 but still missing
circular line at Isabella's shoulder; only light shading on Columbus' collar.

244-E8 $4 Die on India, on card
             black brown   2,000.
             dark red   —

245-E1

Design size: 34½x22½mm
Incomplete engraved vignette as adopted for 1c: missing sky,
etc., with pencil drawing of part of frame design.

245-E1 $5 Die on 50x38mm artist's card-
             board, on thicker card, 55x43mm,
             black   4,000.

Design size: 34x22½mm
Die size: 74½x61½mm
Incomplete engraving of vignette, lettering and frame as
adopted (side panels blank): shading unfinished on Columbus'
neck, hair and background, and with white and black wash
touches.

245-E2 $5 Die on India, die sunk on card,
             black   3,000.

245-E3

Similar to No. 245-E2 but further engraved: shading lines on neck, diagonal lines in background, etc.

245-E3 $5 Die on India, on card, 49x38mm, black   3,000.

Model with photos of female figures mounted each side of vignette, pencil "Design approved subject to inspection of engraved proof, color to be black. A.D.H. Dec. 6 '92" (A.D. Hazen, 3rd asst. PMG).

245-E4 $5 Die on thick white card, on 117x116mm card, black   3,000.

245-E5

Engraving of No. 245-E3 with retouched photos of side subjects mounted in place.

245-E5 $5 Die on white artist's cardboard, 56½x46mm, die sunk on card, black   2,000.

Design size: 33½x22mm
Incomplete engraving of entire design: one line under "POSTAGE FIVE DOLLARS", no lines outside and no diagonal lines in sky to upper right and upper left of vignette, etc.

245-E6 $5 Die on India, on card, black   2,000.

245-E7

Similar to No. 245-E2 but with pencil marks to show engraver where to place diagonal shading lines behind head and in front of bust.

245-E7 $5 Die on 65x55mm India, card mounted, black   3,000.

245-E8

Similar to No. 245-E6 but with pencil marks and white ink suggestions for further engraving.

245-E8 $5 Die on India, die sunk on 83x68mm card, black   2,000.

245-E9

Similar to No. 245-E6 but further engraved: with diagonal shading above side figures, below numerals and around vignette circle, but still incomplete in arched band above vignette.

245-E9 $5 Die on India, die sunk on 110x83mm card, black   2,000.

245-E10

Similar to No. 245-E9 but further engraved: with shading lines in arched band above vignette but no shading on pole of liberty cap, object below shield has dotted shading only, spear tip shading incomplete.

245-E10 $5 Die on India, die sunk on 85x70mm card, black   2,000.

1894 ISSUE
Bureau of Engraving and Printing

The 1c-15c designs of the 1890 issue engraved by the American Bank Note Co. were worked over by the BEP, including the addition of triangles in the upper corners. The 1890 30c was changed to a 50c and the 90c to a $1. Some 1894 essays have American Bank Note Co. imprints below the design.

247-E1

Design size: 18½x22mm
Die size: 61x62mm
Large die engraving of 1890 1c with pencil drawing of UL triangle 3½mm high with straight side next to curved upper label, freehand horiz. ink line at UR.

247-E1   1c Die on India, die sunk on card, black   2,000.

247-E2

Experimental laydown die with 1890 1c proof 4mm to left of similar design with 15-line high type I triangle in UR corner. Same laydown die also contains two 2c designs 18mm below, 5½mm apart, either uninked or lightly inked in color of 1c (sometimes found separated from 1c designs). No. 247-E2b nearly always found cracked horiz. through designs.

247-E2   1c
  a. Die on semiglazed white wove with pencil notations
    blue   1,750.
    ultramarine   1,750.
  b. Die on white card with pencil notations re color
    "1-1 Antwerp, 4 Ultra."   1,500.
    "2--little lighter--"   1,500.
    "1 Antwerp blue, 1 Ultra." (not cracked)   1,750.
    "4 Cobalt and Indigo"   1,500.
    "No 5"   1,500.
    "No. 6--Antwerp blue"   1,500.
    "No. 6--with little Antwerp blue"   1,500.

Die impression of 1890 1c with 15-line high type I triangle in UR corner.

247-E3   1c Die on India, 50x52mm, dusky green   2,000.

Experimental die impression of single 1890 1c with 2c 18mm below, triangles added in ink to upper corners of both designs, ms. "Approved" notations.

247-E4   1c +2c, Die on India, mounted on 57x102mm card, mounted on another card, 144x195mm
    green   2,500.
    dull violet (without added triangles)   2,400.

247-E5   247-E6

Large die engraving of 1890 1c with 18-line high triangle in UL corner (inner lines very thick).

247-E5   1c Die on India, die sunk on card, dusky blue green   1,250.

Similar to No. 247-E5 but inner line of triangle almost as thin as outer line.

247-E6   1c Die on India, die sunk on card, dusky blue green   1,250.

247-E7

Similar to No. 247-E6 but inner line of triangle same thickn as adopted.

247-E7   1c Die on India, die sunk on card, dusky blue green   1,2

Incomplete engraving of entire design as adopted includ triangles, coat collar, scroll under "U," horiz. lines on frame, line of vignette, etc., all unfinished; vignette background not etched.

247-E8   1c Die on India, die sunk on card
    ultramarine   1,0
    blue ("Cobalt 2--Indigo 4")   1,2

Design size: 18½x22mm
Die size: 61x62½mm
Large die engraving of 1890 2c with pencil drawing of triangle 2½mm high.

250-E1   2c Die on India, die sunk on card, black   2,0

Die width: 92mm
Experimental laydown die with 1890 2c proof 5½mm to left similar design with 14-line high type I triangles in upper corne (found cut apart from No. 247-E2 and used for trial colors noted thereon in pencil).

250-E2   2c Die on white card
    "1 R&D Lake, 1½P. white"   1,75
    "M3 1 white, 7 Gem Lake, ¼ Car. Lake"   1,75
    "2 White, 4 Ger. Lake No. 1, ½ R&D Lake"   1,75
    "Opal Red"   1,75
    "Opal Orange"   1,75
    "Opal Maroon"   1,75

250-E3

Die size: 61½x62½mm
American Banknote Co. die No. C-224 annealed, with 18-lin high type I triangles engraved in upper corners, ms "No. 1" lower left of card backing.

250-E3   2c Die on India, die sunk on card
    medium deep red   1,00(
    deep red   1,00(
    dusky red   1,00(
    dim red   1,00(
    medium deep orange-red   1,00(
    deep o-orange-red   1,00(
    dusky g-blue-green   1,00(
    dark medium violet-red-red   1,00(

Incomplete engraving of entire design: shadows on frame no etched; lines on foliage, front collar and oval line at vignette bottom not recut; dots instead of lines over corner of eye; onl one line on truncated scroll at left of right 2 and no line o similar scroll at right of left 2; shadows of TWO CENTS no etched.

250-E4   2c Die on India, die sunk on card
    bright red   1,000
    light red   1,000
    dark red   1,000
    deep orange red   1,000

Similar to No. 250-E4 but line added to scroll at right of left 2, ms. "A.B.N.Co. Die worked over and ornaments put in" at top, ms. "No. 1" at lower left.

250-E5   2c medium deep red   1,250.

Incomplete engraving of entire design: two lines on truncated scroll at left of right 2 (one later removed), scroll at left of right 2 unfinished, profile of nose and forehead darker than on issued stamp, shadows of "TWO CENTS" not etched, short dashes on inside of outer edge of white oval at lower right, veins on scrolls around 2s not recut. Pencil notations incl. "Old A.B.N.Co. annealed & triangles engraved and rehardened to take up roll for plate."

250-E6   2c Die on India, die sunk on card, medium deep red   1,250.

Incomplete engraving of entire design: bottom of ear still angular and not yet rounded, dots on lobe not yet gathered into two lines, dot shading under corner of eye not yet gathered into four lines, shadows of "TWO CENTS" have been etched.

250-E7   2c Die on India, die sunk on card, medium deep red   1,000.

die size: 57x76mm
incomplete engraving of entire design with type II triangles: of head not silhouetted. Pencil notation "2/ Transfer from roll n from No. 1 so as to change portrait and make cameo ct. Unfinished."

-E1   2c Die on India, die sunk on card,
       dark violet red   1,250.

imilar to No. 251-E1 but hair in front of ear unfinished, head and hair lightened.

-E2   2c Die on India, die sunk on card,
       dusky gray   1,500.

252-E1

Die size: 57x81mm
Incomplete engraving of entire design with type III triangles: of head not silhouetted, unfinished shadow over eye, etc.

2-E1   2c Die on India, die sunk on card,
       medium deep red   1,000.

ncomplete engraving of entire design with type III triangles: finished shadow over eye, etc.

2-E2   2c Die on India, die sunk on card
       dusky blue green   1,500.
       dark violet red   1,000.

252-E3

Design size: 19x22mm
Die size: 56x80½mm
Discarded die, vignette overengraved: too much shading on ont hair, cheek, nose, below eye; background too dark; hair in ont of ear very prominent.

52-E3   2c Die on India, die sunk on card
        light carmine   1,750.
        green   2,250.

253-E1

Die size: 60x63mm
Complete engraved design as adopted but with type II riangles.

253-E1   3c
     a. Die on India, die sunk on card
        dusky blue green   1,500.
        dark red violet   1,000.
        dusky red violet   1,000.
     b. Die printed directly on card, die sunk on
        card, violet   1,250.

254-E1

Design size: about 19x22mm
Die size: 61x63mm
Incomplete engraving of entire design: line under collar wings missing, oval line around vignette not recut; hair, beard, forehead, neck, collar, shirt, etc., all incomplete.

254-E1   4c Die on India, die sunk on card,
         dark yellow brown   1,500.

Entire design engraved further than No. 254-E1 but still incomplete: shadows in lettering, etc., not etched, faint lines under collar incomplete, oval around vignette not recut.

254-E2   4c Die on India, die sunk on card,
         dark yellow brown   1,500.

Entire design engraved further than No. 254-E2 but still incomplete: beard, collar and necktie, etc., unfinished. Some veins recut on foliage under oval label.

254-E3   4c Die on India, die sunk on card,
         dark brown   1,250.

255-E1

Design size: 19x22mm
Engraved frame of American Bank Note Co. die No. C-227 with triangles, vignette cut out, mounted over engraved vignette of Washington.

255-E1   5c Die on 41x53mm India, on white
         wove, 48x75mm, black   3,250.

Washington vignette only as on No. 255-E1.

255-E2   5c Die on India, green   2,000.

255-E3   255-E4

Design size: 19x22mm
Engraved frame as adopted with William H. Seward photo mounted on it.

255-E3   5c Die on India, cut close, mounted
         on 74x84mm white card, black   3,250.

Design size: about 19x22mm
Die size: 62½x75mm
Incomplete engraving of entire design as adopted: no oval border line around vignette.

255-E4   5c Die on India, die sunk on card, or-
         ange brown   1,250.

256-E1

Design size: about 19x22mm
Die size: 62½x61½mm
Incomplete engraving of entire design as adopted: white spot on eye and shadows not darkened, diagonal lines missing on beard under mouth, lines on coat unfinished.

256-E1   6c Die on India, die sunk on card,
         dark red   1,250.

256-E2

Entire design engraved further than No. 256-E1 but still incomplete: diagonal lines on beard under mouth incomplete, lines on coat not as dark as on issued stamp.

256-E2   6c Die on India, die sunk on card,
         dim dusky red   1,000.

257-E1

Design size: about 19x22mm
Die size: 58½x60mm
Incomplete engraving of entire design as adopted: lines on coat not recut darker, vignette background not etched darker.

257-E1   8c Die on India, die sunk on card,
         dusky red violet   1,000.

258-E1

Design size: about 19x22mm
Die size: 61½x61½mm
Incomplete engraving of entire design as adopted: shading unfinished on cheek, in ear, etc.

258-E1   10c Die on India, die sunk on card,
         dark brown   1,500.

Entire design engraved further than No. 258-E1 but still incomplete: unfinished shading on cheek under eye.

258-E2   10c Die on India, die sunk on card, red
         brown   1,500.

261-E1

Design size: 19x22mm
Die size: 50x101mm
Large die engraving of 1890 90c with value label and figure circles blank, no triangles.

261-E1 $1 Die on India, die sunk on card,
         black   3,000.

Similar to No. 261-E1 but head further re-engraved and background shadows etched deeper.

261-E2 $1 Die on India, die sunk on card,
         blue green   3,000.

261-E3   261-E4

Design size: 19x22mm
Model of engraved Perry vignette mounted on 1890 engraved frame with penciled in triangles, values painted in white and black. Ms. "O.K. July 14/94 TFM" below.

261-E3 $1 Die on India, cut close, mounted
         on 63x101mm white card, green
         vignette, black frame   3,250

Similar to No. 261-E3 but with value lettering and circles added, background of circles unfinished, no triangles.

261-E4 $1 Die on India, die sunk on card,
         dark indigo blue   2,750.

Incomplete engraving of entire design: hair on top and back of head, whiskers and back of neck, and shading in value circles all unfinished. Triangles are engraved.

261-E5 $1 Die on India, die sunk on card,
         black   1,600.

261-E6

Similar to No. 261-E5 but hair at back of head and whiskers darker, face in front of whiskers darker as on issued stamp. Circular lines extend into colorless vignette oval.

261-E6 $1 Die on India, die sunk on card
  black   *1,500.*
  blue green   *2,000.*

261-E7

Design size: 19x21½mm
Die size: 49x100mm
Incomplete engraving of unadopted dollar value design with portrait of Sen. James B. Beck: value label and numerals blank.

261-E7 $1 Die on India, die sunk on card,
  black   *4,000.*

262-E1

262-E2

Design size: 19x22mm
Die size: 50x101mm
Incomplete engraving of frame only nearly as adopted: smaller $2's.

262-E1 $2 Die on India, die sunk on card,
  blue green   *3,500.*

Design size: 19x22mm
Die size: 51x112mm
Incomplete engraving of entire design: left value circle blank, right circle engraved $2 outline only.

262-E2 $2 Die on India, die sunk on card,
  black   *3,250.*

Die size: 51x112mm
Incomplete engraving of entire design: vignette shading unfinished, no veins in leaves around value circles.

262-E3 $2 Die on India, die sunk on card,
  black   *2,850.*

262-E4

Incomplete engraving of entire design: inside of right border line above $2 unfinished.

262-E4 $2 Die on India, die sunk on card,
  black   *2,750.*

Similar to No. 262-E4 but border line complete.

262-E5 $2 Die on India, die sunk on card,
  black   *2,500.*

263-E1

Die size: 50x112½mm
Incomplete engraving of entire design: only one line in each scroll at right and left of $5, inner line of right border above $5 unfinished, etc., veins on leaves around right value circle unfinished.

263-E1 $5 Die on India, die sunk on card,
  black   *2,750.*

Similar to No. 263-E1 but horiz. lines cut into oval line at top and inner oval line above L and R of DOLLARS required retouching as indicated by pencil instructions. Two lines in scrolls around value circles as adopted.

263-E2 $5 Die on India, die sunk on card,
  black   *3,250.*

The bicolored essays commonly offered as No. 285-293 bicolored proofs can be found under the following listings: Nos. 285-E8, 286 E8, 287-E9, 288-E5, 289-E4, 290-E4, 291-E0, 292 E6, 293 E7. Values are for full-size cards (approximately 8x6 inches).

TRANS-MISSISSIPPI ISSUE

Die size: 79x68mm
Incomplete engraving of vignette only: initial state of die, no lines in sky or water.

285-E1 1c Die on India, die sunk on card,
  black   *2,500.*

Vignette further engraved: lines in sky and water.

285-E2 1c Die on India, die sunk on card,
  black   *2,500.*

Vignette further engraved: more background lines added.

285-E3 1c Die on India, die sunk on card,
  black   *2,500.*

285-E4

Vignette further engraved: Indian at right darker, robe shadow etched.

285-E4 1c Die on India, die sunk on card,
  black   *2,500.*

Vignette further engraved: rock in water more complete.

285-E5 1c Die on India, die sunk on card,
  black   *2,500.*

Design size: 34x22mm
Die size: 73x62mm
Incomplete bicolor engraving of entire design: no second inner line in numerals.

285-E6 1c Die on India, die sunk on card, orange red & black   *2,500.*

Die size: 83x68mm
Incomplete engraving of entire design: vignette unfinished and unetched, frame has second inner line in numerals.

285-E7 1c Die on India, die sunk on card,
  black   *3,500.*

285-E8

Die size: 63x51mm
Complete bicolor engraving of entire design.

285-E8 1c Die with black vignette on India,
  die sunk on card
  dark yellow green ("normal" bicolor)   *300.*
  dusky green   *2,000.*
  dusky blue green   *2,000.*
  brown   *2,000.*

Incomplete engraving of entire design: corn husks and panels in ends of cartouche unfinished, lines under MARQUETTE and MISSISSIPPI not as thick as on completed die.

285-E9 1c Die on India, die sunk on card,
  dusky green   *2,500.*

285-E10

Unfinished frame in red brown missing second inner lin[e] numerals, with black unfinished "Cattle in the Storm" vignette used on the $1 value, foreground snow at left incomplete.

285-E10 1c Die on India, red brown & black   *3,5[..]*

Die size: 78x68mm
Incomplete engraving of Mississippi River Bridge vign[ette] (originally intended for 2c but eventually used on $2): in[itial] state of die, very lightly engraved.

286-E1 2c Die on India, die sunk on card,
  black   *3,7[..]*

Vignette further engraved but no lines on bridge beside [the] trolley cars.

286-E2 2c Die on India, die sunk on card,
  black   *5,0[..]*

286-E3

Vignette further engraved but foreground between bridge a[nd] boat and foretopdeck incomplete, horse truck visible (la[ter] removed).

286-E3 2c Die on India, die sunk on card,
  black   *3,0[0]*

Complete engraving of vignette only.

286-E4 2c Die on India, die sunk on card,
  black   *3,0[0]*

286-E5

Design size: 137x88½mm
Pencil sketch by R. Ostrander Smith of 2c frame design a[s] adopted except titled "ST. LOUIS BRIDGE."

286-E5 2c Sketch on tracing paper,
  120x178mm   *1,50[0]*

286-E6

Complete pencil drawing by R.O. Smith of frame design ("P" [part] of "POSTAGE" in ink), titled "ST. LOUIS BRIDGE."

286-E6 2c Drawing on Whatman drawing
  board, 1889 wmk., 237x184mm   *1,500.*

286-E7

Pencil drawing by R.O. Smith, no title.

| 6-E7 | 2c | Drawing on 72x61mm tracing paper | 1,500. |

286-E7A

Ink and wash drawing of frame, stamp size, similar to adopted design.

| 86-E7A | 2c | Drawing on hard, thick paper, black | 11,000. |

286-E8

Die size: 63x51mm
Complete bicolor engraving of 2c design but with Mississippi River Bridge vignette as used on $2.

Ridgway numbers used for colors of No. 286-E8.

286-E8	2c Die with black vignette on India, die sunk on card	
	dark red ("normal" bicolor)	300.
	3k/0 dark orange red	2,000.
	5k/0 dark o-orange-red	2,000.
	5m/1 dim dusky o-orange-red	2,000.
	7i/0 deep red orange	2,000.
	7m/0 dusky red orange	2,000.
	9m/0 dusky o-red-orange	2,000.
	9k/2 dull dark o-red-orange	2,000.
	13m/3 dismal dusky o-yellow-orange	2,000.
	35m/1 dim dusky green	2,000.
	49m/1 dim v. dusky blue	2,000.
	63m/1 dim dusky red violet	2,000.
	71-/0 deep violet-red-red	2,000.

286-E10

Die size: 82x68mm
Complete engraving with "FARMING IN THE WEST" vignette as adopted but from a die not used for the stamp: horses at left vignette border engraved dark up to border line which is solid complete line at both left and right.

286-E10	2c Die on India, die sunk on card (marked "Proof from 1st die.")	
	black	2,500.
	dark orange red	2,500.

Design size: 34x22mm
Die No. 259 size: 63x51mm

Initial state of die, very lightly engraved.

| 287-E1 | 4c Die on India, die sunk on card, black | 3,000. |

Vignette further engraved: sky lines ruled in.

| 287-E2 | 4c Die on India, die sunk on card, black | 3,000. |

287-E3

Vignette further engraved: more lines added, no right forefoot on bison.

| 287-E3 | 4c Die on India, die sunk on card, black | 4,500. |

Shadow under bison incomplete.

| 287-E4 | 4c Die on India, die sunk on card, black | 3,750. |

Shadow under bison and foreground penciled in.

| 287-E5 | 4c Die on India, die sunk on card, black | 3,750. |

Vignette further engraved: right forefoot added, shadow under bison engraved but not etched.

| 287-E6 | 4c Die on India, die sunk on card, black | 3,750. |

287-E7

Die size: 83x67mm
Incomplete engraving of entire design: no lines in sky, frame shadow etching unfinished.

287-E7	4c Die on India, die sunk on card	
	black	3,500.
	deep orange	3,500.

287-E8

Die size: 63x51mm
Incomplete engraving of entire design: corn husks at lower sides of frame unfinished.

Ridgway numbers used for colors of No. 287-E8.

287-E8	4c Die with black vignette on India, die sunk on card	
	5k/0 dark o-orange-red	2,000.
	5m/0 dusky o-orange-red	2,000.
	7m/0 dusky red orange	2,000.
	11o/2 dull v. dusky orange	2,000.
	13m/3 dismal dusky o-yellow-orange	2,000.
	35m/1 dim dusky green	2,000.
	39m/1 dim dusky blue green	2,000.
	49o/1 dim v. dusky blue	2,000.
	61k/1 dim dark violet-red violet	2,000.
	63m/1 dim dusky red violet	2,000.
	71m/0 dusky violet-red-red	2,000.

Complete bicolor engraving.

287-E9	4c Die with black vignette on India, die sunk on card	
	red orange ("normal" bicolor)	300.
	deep red orange ("normal" bicolor)	300.

Die size: 77x69mm
Initial state of die, very lightly engraved.

| 288-E1 | 5c Die on India, die sunk on card, black | 3,500. |

Vignette further engraved: lower clouds at right darkened.

288-E2

| 288-E2 | 5c Die on India, die sunk on card, black | 5,500. |

Vignette further engraved: shading penciled in on figures at right, etc.

| 288-E3 | 5c Die on India, die sunk on card, black | 3,750. |

288-E4

Vignette further engraved but dots in sky at left of flag unfinished.

| 288-E4 | 5c Die on India, die sunk on card, black | 3,750. |

288-E5

Design size: 34x22mm
Die size: 63x51mm
Incomplete bicolor engraving of entire design: unfinished crosshatching at left of "FREMONT," lines against bottom label and frame unfinished, no etching on flag.

Ridgway numbers used for colors of No. 288-E5.

288-E5	5c Die with black vignette on India, die sunk on card	
	49m/1 dim dusky blue ("normal" bicolor)	300.
	49k/1 dim dark blue ("normal" bicolor)	300.
	3k/0 dark orange red	2,000.
	3m/0 dusky orange red	2,000.
	7m/0 dusky red orange	2,000.
	7m/1 dim dusky red orange	2,000.
	9m/0 dusky o-red-orange	2,000.
	11o/2 dull v. dusky orange	2,000.
	37m/1 dim dusky g-blue-green	2,000.
	39m/1 dim dusky blue green	2,000.
	49o/1 dim v. dusky blue	2,000.
	63m/1 dim dusky red violet	2,000.
	71n/0 medium deep violet-red-red	2,000.
	35m/1 dim dusky green	2,000.

Die size: 82x68½mm
Incomplete engraving of entire design: cornhusks, panels at ends of cartouche, mountains, foreground at sides of title label, sky, etc., all unfinished, figures and mountains not etched dark.

| 288-E7 | 5c Die on India, die sunk on card, black | 3,250. |

Incomplete engraving of vignette: no dots on mountain tops next to right border, unfinished crosshatching at left end of title label.

| 288-E8 | 5c Die on India, die sunk on card, black | 3,750. |

289-E1

Engraved vignette only of mounted Indian, not used for any value.

| 289-E1 | 8c Die on India, on card, black | 7,500. |

Incomplete engraving of vignette only as adopted: blank area for label wider than completed bicolor vignette, knee of kneeling soldier unfinished, etc.

| 289-E2 | 8c Die on India, die sunk on card, black | 3,000. |

289-E3

Design size: about 33½x21½mm
Incomplete engraving of frame only: shading of sunken center of cartouche at right of vignette unfinished.

289-E3 8c Die on India, 26x37mm, black 3,000.

289-E4

Incomplete engraving of entire design: top row of distant shrubbery under "ERICA" missing, crosshatching on distant mountains at left, blades of grass at left end of label, some dots against top label all unfinished.

Ridgway numbers used for colors of No. 289-E4.

289-E4 8c Die with black vignette on India,
die sunk on card

dark red ("normal" bicolor)	375.
dusky red ("normal" bicolor)	375.
3m/0 dusky orange red	2,750.
5m/0 dusky o-orange-red	2,750.
7i/0 deep red orange	2,750.
7m/0 dusky red orange	2,750.
9m/0 dusky o-red-orange	2,750.
11o/2 dull v. dusky orange	2,750.
35m/1 dim dusky green	2,750.
39m/1 dim dusky blue-green	2,750.
49o/1 dim v. dusky blue	2,750.
63m/1 dim dusky red violet	2,750.
71-/0 deep violet-red-red	2,750.

Die size: 77x64mm
Incomplete engraving of vignette only: two rows of dots in sky over wagon.

290-E1

290-E1 10c Die on India, die sunk on card,
black 8,500.

290-E2

Vignette further engraved: three rows of dots in sky over wagon.

290-E2 10c Die on India, die sunk on card,
black 3,750.

Vignette further engraved: front of wagon canvas crosshatched.

290-E3 10c Die on India, die sunk on card,
black 3,750.

290-E4

Incomplete bicolor engraving of entire design: cornhusks unfinished, blades of grass to right of girl's feet and some to right of dark horse's feet are missing. Five lines of dots in sky over wagon.

Ridgway numbers used for colors of No. 290-E4.

290-E4 10c Die with black vignette on India,
die sunk on card

dull dusky violet blue ("normal" bicolor)	350.
dusky blue violet ("normal" bicolor)	350.
1i/0 deep red	2,500.
3k/0 dark orange red	2,500.
5k/0 dark o-orange-red	2,500.
5m/0 dusky o-orange-red	2,500.
7i/0 deep red orange	2,500.
9m/0 dusky o-red-orange	2,500.
11o/2 dull v. dusky orange	2,500.
35m/1 dim dusky green	2,500.
39m/1 dim dusky blue green	2,500.
49o/1 dim v. dusky blue	2,500.
55m/2 smoky dark v.-blue violet	2,500.
63m/1 dim dusky red violet	2,500.
71-/0 deep violet-red-red	2,500.

Incomplete engraving of entire design: cornhusks unfinished, vignette from No. 290-E4 trimmed by engraving to fit frame.

290-E6 10c Die on India, die sunk on card,
dark red orange 3,000.

Incomplete engraving of entire design: cornhusks and panels at ends of cartouche and both sides and botton of vignette next to border unfinished.

290-E7 10c Die on India, die sunk on card, dull
red violet 3,000.

Incomplete engraving of entire design: cornhusks and both sides and bottom of vignette next to border are unfinished, vert. lines on cartouche frame at right of vignette missing.

290-E8 10c Die on India, dull red violet 3,000.

291-E1

Die size: 62x52mm
Incomplete engraving of vignette only: without sky or mountains.

291-E1 50c Die on India, die sunk on card,
black 3,750.

Vignette further engraved: sky ruled in.

291-E2 50c Die on India, die sunk on card,
black 3,750.

Vignette further engraved but no shading on distant mountains.

291-E3

291-E3 50c Die on India, die sunk on card,
black 3,750.

Vignette further engraved: light shading on distant mountains.

291-E4 50c Die on India, die sunk on card,
black 3,750.

Vignette further engraved: more shading on distant mountains.

291-E5 50c Die on India, die sunk on card,
black 3,750.

291-E6

Vignette further engraved: shadows on miner's hat darker (etched).

291-E6 50c Die on India, die sunk on card,
black 3,750.

291-E7

Vignette further engraved: girth under donkey darkened.

291-E7 50c Die on India, die sunk on card,
black 9,0

291-E8

Design size: 34x22mm
Die size: 89x71mm
Incomplete bicolor engraving of entire design: shading lin on scroll in LR corner of frame and shrubbery in UL corner vignette unfinished, sky incomplete.

Ridgway numbers used for colors of No. 291-E8.

291-E8 50c Die with black vignette on India,
die sunk on card

dull dusky b-blue-green ("normal" bicolor; die size: 63x51mm)	3
dull dusky g-blue-green ("normal" bicolor; die size: 63x51mm)	3
1i/0 deep red	2,50
3k/0 dark orange red	2,50
5m/0 dusky o-orange-red	2,50
7m/0 dusky red orange	2,50
9i/0 deep o-yellow-orange	2,50
9m/0 dusky o-red-orange	2,5
11m/2 dull dusky orange	2,5
13m/3 dismal dusky o-yellow-orange	2,5
35m/1 dim dusky green	2,5
39m/1 dim dusky blue green	2,5
47n/2 dull v. dusky green-blue blue	2,5
49o/1 dim v. dusky blue	2,50
61k/1 dim dark violet-red-violet	2,50
71m/0 dusky violet-red-red	2,50

Incomplete engraving of entire design: vignette against t frame unfinished.

291-E9 50c Die on India, die sunk on card
black 3,00
deep red orange 3,00

Incomplete engraving of entire design: engraving on botto of miner's pan dots only, not lines as on issued stamp.

291-E10 50c Die on wove, sage green 3,00

Incomplete engraving of vignette only: initial state of di lightly engraved.

292-E1

292-E1 $1 Die on India, die sunk on card,
black 4,50

292-E2

Vignette further engraved: light shield-shaped vignette outline (later removed.)

292-E2 $1 Die on India, die sunk on card,
black 4,500

Vignette further engraved: left front hoof of lead bull darker.

292-E3 $1 Die on India, die sunk on card,
black 3,750.

Vignette similar to No. 292-E3 but with penciled modeling in snow and among cattle.

292-E4 $1 Die on India, die sunk on card,
black 3,750.

Vignette further engraved: foreground snow at left darkened, shield outline removed.

292-E5

2-E5 $1 Die on India, die sunk on card,
        black   10,000.

292-E6

Incomplete engraving of entire bicolored design: right
ornhusk and sky against top of frame unfinished, bull's right
refoot does not touch frame, foreground at right end of label
nfinished.

**Ridgway numbers used for colors of No. 292-E6, where
vailable.**

2-E6 $1 Die with black vignette on India,
        die sunk on card
        dull violet blue ("normal" bicolor)   450.
        dull blue ("normal" bicolor)   450.
        dull violet ("normal" bicolor)   3,000.
        3k/0 dark orange red   3,000.
        5m/0 dusky-o-orange-red   3,000.
        7m/0 dusky red orange   3,000.
        9m/0 dusky o-red-orange   3,000.
        9n/3 dismal v. dusky o-red-orange   3,000.
        13n/3 dismal v. dusky o-yellow-orange   3,000.
        35m/1 dim dusky green   3,000.
        43m/1 dim dusky green blue   3,000.
        49m/1 dim dusky blue   3,000.
        57k/4 smoky dark violet-blue violet   3,000.
        63m/1 dim dusky red violet   3,000.
        71-/0 violet-red-red   3,000.
        47n/2 dull dusky green blue   3,000.
        dark brown   3,000.

Incomplete engraving of entire design: left frameline,
cornhusks and shading in frame over cornhusks all unfinished.

2-E7 $1 Die on India, die sunk on card,
        dusky red orange   3,000.

293-E1

Design size: 34x22mm
Die size: 73x63mm
Vignette of Western mining prospector as used on 50c, but
labeled HARVESTING IN THE WEST, frame shows $ same
size as numeral 2.

293-E1 $2 Die on India, on card, dusky violet
        & black   3,500.

293-E2

Die size: 77x66mm
Incomplete engraving of Farming in the West vignette (originally intended for $2 but eventually used on 2c): initial state of
die, very lightly engraved.

293-E2 $2 Die on India, die sunk on card,
        black   3,000.

Vignette further engraved: four horses shaded.

293-E3 $2 Die on India, die sunk on card,
        black   3,000.

Vignette further engraved: shading added to background
figures and horses, pencil shading above and below half horse
at left.

293-E4 $2 Die on India, die sunk on card,
        black   3,000.

Vignette further engraved: foreground and shadows under
horse teams darkened, no shading dots above half horse at left,
etc.

293-E5 $2 Die on India, die sunk on card,
        black   3,000.

293-E6

Vignette further engraved but foreground in front of plow
wheel still unfinished.

293-E6 $2 Die on India, die sunk on card,
        black   3,000.

293-E7

Die size: 62x51mm
Incomlpete engraving of entire bicolor design: only one plow-
share shown, label longer, less foreground than on issued
stamp.

Ridgway numbers used for colors of No. 293-E7.

293-E7 $2 Die with black vignette on India,
        die sunk on card
        dusky orange red ("normal" bicolor;
        die size: 63x61mm)   450.
        dark red orange ("normal" bicolor; die
        size: 63x61mm)   450.
        1-/0 red   3,000.
        3k/0 dark orange red   3,000.
        7m/0 dusky red orange   3,000.
        35m/1 dim dusky green   3,000.
        39m/1 dim dusky blue green   3,000.
        45o/1 dim v. dusky blue-green blue   3,000.
        45m/2 dull dusky blue-green blue   3,000.
        63m/1 dim dusky red violet   3,000.
        71i/0 deep violet-red-red   3,000.
        47n/2 dull dusky green blue   3,000.

Incomplete engraving of entire design as adopted: black
wash over engraving on side of bridge and foreground (engraving under wash unfinished).

293-E9 $2 Die on India, die sunk on card,
        black   3,500.

Complete design, vignette further engraved: engraving completed between title label and steamboat and city next to right
frame, near side of bridge and smoke shadow on water lighter
than on issued stamp.

293-E10 $2 Die on India, die sunk on card,
        black   3,500.

Incomplete engraving of entire design: circles in upper corners of vignette next to value ovals, water next to right end of
value label, panels at ends of cartouche all unfinished.

293-E11 $2 Die on India, die sunk on card,
        black   3,500.

Edward Rosewater

Rosewater, of St. Louis, was asked by the Post Office Dept. in
1897 to submit proposed designs for the Trans-Mississippi
Exposition issue. For that reason, they are listed here.
All are drawings on tracing paper, on 91x142mm buff card.

285-E11

Design size: 62x97mm
Wash drawing of cattle.

285-E11   1c dull orange   12,500.

286-E11

Design size: 57x98mm
Wash drawing of mounted Indian saluting wagon train.

286-E11   2c deep orange red   12,500.

288-E9

Design size: 61x100mm
Wash drawing of man plowing field.
288-E9   5c dark yellow   *12,500.*

290-E9

Design size: 62x99mm
Wash drawing of train coming around mountain.
290-E9   Ten Cents, dusky blue   *12,500.*

292-E9

Design size: 60x98mm
Wash drawing of woman holding light, standing on globe.
292-E9 $1 deep orange yellow   *12,500.*

PAN-AMERICAN ISSUE
Bureau of Engraving and Printing

294-E1

Design size: 108x82mm
Preliminary pencil drawing for frame design as adopted.
294-E1   1c Drawing on tracing paper, black   *750.*

294-E2

Design size: 114x82½mm
Final ink drawing for frame design as adopted.
294-E2   1c Drawing on white card, about
              6½x5 inches, black   *750.*

294-E3

Die size: 87x68½mm
Incomplete engraving of vignette only.
294-E3   1c Die on India, die sunk on card,
              black   *1,5*

295-E1

Design size: 108x82mm
Preliminary pencil drawing of frame similar to that adopt(
(side ornaments, etc., different); UR corner, etc., unfinished.
295-E1   2c Drawing on tracing paper, black   *75*

295-E2

Design size: 114x83mm
Preliminary pencil drawing of frame similar to No. 295-E
(minor differences) but with UR corner complete.
295-E2   2c Drawing on tracing paper, black   *75(*

295-E3

Design size: 108x82mm
Preliminary pencil drawing of frame design similar to No. 295
E2 but with minor differences at top, in lettering, etc.
295-E3   2c Drawing on tracing paper, black   *750*

295-E4

Design size: 95x70mm
Ink and wash drawing model of frame design as adopted,
side torchbearers engraved on India as on U.S. Series of 1901
$10 note.
295-E4   2c Die on white card, about
              108x82mm, black   *750.*

295-E4A

Design size: 88x69mm
Incomplete engraving of vignette only.
295-E4A 2c Die on India, die sunk on card,
black 3,500.

295-E5 295-E6

Design size: 27x19½mm
Die size: 88x68mm
Complete engraving of frame only as adopted.
295-E5 2c Die on India, die sunk on card,
carmine 3,750.

Die size: 88½x69mm
Engraving of entire design with vignette incomplete near
frame and on cars.
295-E6 2c Die on India, die sunk on card,
carmine & black 4,750.

296-E1

Preliminary pencil drawing of unadopted frame design.
296-E1 4c Drawing on tracing paper, black 750.

296-E2

Design size: 114x82½mm
Final ink drawing for frame design as adopted.
296-E2 4c Drawing on white card, about
6½x5 inches, black 750.

296-E3

Design size: 27x19mm
Die size: 88x67mm
Incomplete engraving of entire design as adopted: lines missing at base of capitol dome, above driver's head.
296-E3 4c Die on India, die sunk on card,
deep red brown & black 1,750.

297-E1

Photo reproduction of pencil sketch of unadopted frame
design on photosensitive tan paper, reduced to stamp size.
Incomplete preliminary pencil drawing of frame design as
adopted.
297-E1 5c Photo reproduction on tan paper 750.

297-E2

Design size: 114x83mm
Incomplete preliminary pencil drawing of frame design as
adopted.
297-E2 5c Drawing on tracing paper, black 750.

297-E3

Design size: 114x82½mm
Final ink drawing for frame design as adopted.
297-E3 5c Drawing on white card, about
6½x5 inches, black 750.

297-E4

Photo reproduction of sketch of adopted frame design on
photosensitive paper, reduced to stamp size.
297-E4 5c Photo reproduction on tan paper 750.

297-E5 297-E6

Die size: 87x68mm
Incomplete engraving of vignette only.
297-E5 5c Die on India, die sunk on card,
black 1,500.

Die size: 87x68mm
As No. 297-E5, but more completely engraved.
297-E6 5c Die on India, die sunk on card,
black 1,500.

297-E7

Design size: 27x19½mm
Die size: 87x68mm
Incomplete engraving of entire design as adopted: shading at
bottom of battleaxes and scrolls at ends of title frame
unfinished.
297-E7 5c Die on India, die sunk on card,
blue & black 1,750.

298-E1

Design size:108x82mm
Preliminary pencil drawing of unadopted frame design.
298-E1 8c Drawing on tracing paper, black 750.

298-E2

Design size: 114x83mm
Incomplete preliminary pencil drawing of unadopted frame
design.
298-E2 8c Drawing on tracing paper, black 750.

298-E3

Design size: 114x83mm
Preliminary pencil drawing of unadopted frame design.

298-E3 8c Drawing on tracing paper, black 750.

298-E4

Design size: 114x83mm
Preliminary pencil drawing of frame design as adopted.

298-E4 8c Drawing on tracing paper, black 750.

298-E5

Design size: 114x82½mm
Final ink drawing for frame design as adopted. No. 298-E5 has an example of No. 298 mounted in the vignette area.

298-E5 8c Drawing on white card, about
6½x5 inches, black 750.

298-E6

Photo reproduction of sketch of adopted frame design on photosensitive paper, reduced to stamp size.

298-E6 8c Photo reproduction on tan paper 750.

298-E7

Design size: 27x20mm
Die size: 87x69mm
Incomplete engraving of entire design: shading lines of ornaments, scrolls and ribbons at top unfinished, vignette incomplete at right, no etching on building in left foreground.

298-E7 8c Die on India, die sunk on card, bicolored 1,750.

299-E1

Design size: 114x83mm
Preliminary pencil drawing of unadopted frame design (small blank oval at center).

299-E1 10c Drawing on tracing paper, black 750.

299-E2

Design size: 114x82½mm
Similar to No. 299-E1 but with outline of eagle and shield in center oval.

299-E2 10c Drawing on tracing paper, black 750.

299-E3

Design size: 114x83mm
Preliminary pencil drawing for frame design as adopted.

299-E3 10c Drawing on tracing paper, black 750.

299-E4

Design size: 114x82½mm
Final ink drawing for frame design as adopted.

299-E4 10c Drawing on white card, about
6½x9 inches, black 750.

299-E5

Photo reproduction of sketch of adopted frame design photosensitive paper, reduced to stamp size.

299-E5 10c Photo reproduction on tan paper 7

299-E6

Die size: 87x68mm
Incomplete engraving of entire design: frame complete b
lines later engraved in the mast, smokestack and sky.

200 E6 10c Die on India, die sunk on card, bicolored 1,75

1902 ISSUE

300-E1   300-E2

Incomplete engraving of vignette and lower part of frame.

300-E1 1c Die on India, die sunk on card,
black 4,00

Design size: 19x22mm
Die size: 74½x88½mm
Incomplete engraving of entire design: vignette backgroun
has horiz. lines only, neckpiece, men at sides, etc., a
unfinished.

300-E2 1c Die on India, die sunk on card,
black 3,50

300-E3

Design size: 136x190mm

Preliminary ink drawing for 5c frame design but later adopted 1c.

0-E3   1c Drawing on manila paper, black & blue green   2,000.

300-E4

Design size: 116x135mm
Preliminary pencil and ink drawing for frame design as opted.

0-E4   1c Drawing on white card, black   3,000.

301-E1

Design size: 164x181mm
Paper size: 169x214mm
Preliminary pencil drawing of frame design (Raymond strander Smith). Not adopted.

01-E1   2c Drawing on yellowed transparent tracing paper, black   1,500.

301-E1A

Preliminary pencil and ink drawing of unadopted frame design, on 77x82mm yellowish wove paper, folded vertically and with ink tracing of frame on reverse.

301-E1A   2c Drawing on woven paper, black   2,000.

301-E1B

Design size: 145x168mm
Preliminary pencil drawing of frame design as adopted.

301-E1B   2c Drawing on tracing paper, black   3,500.

301-E2   301-E3

Model with vignette of Houdon bust of Washington, on wash drawing over photo reduced to stamp size for approval by PMG.

301-E2   2c Model mounted on card, black   750.

Design size: 19x22mm
Die size: 75x87½mm
Incomplete engraving of entire design: head unfinished, horiz. background lines only, frame unfinished, lettering either blank or unfinished.

301-E3   2c Die on India, die sunk on card, black   4,000.

301-E4

Design size: 60x88mm
Preliminary pencil drawing of right numeral 2 design as adopted.

301-E4   2c Drawing on tracing paper, black   500.

301-E5

Design size: 176x120mm
Preliminary pencil drawing of lower left and upper right design.

301-E5   2c Drawing on tracing paper, black   700.00

301-E6

Design size: 19x22mm
Die size: 74x89mm
Incomplete engraving of entire design: head unfinished, horiz. background lines only, frame almost finished, lettering complete. No. 62057 on back.

301-E6   2c Die on India, die sunk on 153x202mm card, black   3,000.

302-E1   303-E1

Design size: 19x22mm
Die size: 74½x88mm
Incomplete engraving of entire design: vignette unfinished, horiz. background lines only, atlantes at sides unfinished. No. 66218 on back.

302-E1   3c Die on India, die sunk on card, black   3,250.

Design size: 19x22mm
Die size: 75x88mm
Incomplete engraving of entire design: vignette unfinished on eyes, hair, beard, etc. No. 58920 on back.

303-E1   4c Die on India, die sunk on card, black   3,250.

Design size: 19x22mm
Incomplete engraving of entire design, shading lines in top of frame unfinished. No. 60085 on back.

303-E2   4c Die on India, die sunk on card, black   2,000.

Photograph of unaccepted design, stamp size, with white wash inside vignette and eagles in corners drawn in pen over protions of photo.

303-E3   4c Retouched photo-sensitive paper, black   900.

Photograph of unaccepted design with additional overlay photo of top portion of frame with eagles similar to those on No. 303-E3.

303-E4   4c Photo-sensitive paper mounted on paper, black   1,100.

304-E1

Design size: 19x22mm

Die size: 74x87½mm
Rejected die: figure at right poorly draped, blank triangles
below "UNITED STATES," no shading in frame around "POST-
AGE/FIVE CENTS" except at extreme ends.

304-E1 5c Die on India, die sunk on card,
blue   2,300.

Incomplete engraving of entire design: shading on side
figures unfinished.

304-E2 5c Die on India, die sunk on card,
blue   1,250.

304-E3

Design size: 107x110mm
Paper size: 141x128mm
Preliminary pencil and ink drawing of unadopted frame
design.

304-E3 5c Drawing on onion skin paper, black   —

Incomplete engraving of entire design as adopted.

305-E1 6c Die on India, lake   1,250.

305-E2

Design size: 123x210mm
Preliminary ink drawing for unadopted frame design.

305-E2 6c Drawing on kraft paper, black &
blue green   1,500.

Nos. 305-E2, 306-E3 and 308-E2, are all on same piece of
kraft paper, with No. 306-E3 on one side and the other two on
the other side. Value for entire unit is $4,500.

306-E1

Design size: 7x3½ inches
Preliminary pencil drawing of left side of frame design as
adopted.

306-E1 8c Drawing on tracing paper, black   2,200.

306-E2

Die size: 76x89mm
Incomplete engraving of vignette and numerals only: head
drapery unfinished, horiz. background lines only.

306-E2 8c Die on India, die sunk on card,
black   5,000.

306-E3

Design size: 165x175mm
Preliminary ink drawing for unadopted frame design.

306-E3 8c Drawing on kraft paper, black, blue
& green   1,500.

307-E1

Design size: 135x174mm
Preliminary ink drawing for unadopted frame design.

307-E1 10c Drawing on kraft paper, black, blue
& green   8●

308-E1

Design size: 19x22mm
Die size: 69x85½mm
Incomplete engraving of entire design: hair, beard, rig
cheek, eyes and right shoulder all unfinished, horiz. backgrou
lines only, name panel blank, ribbon shading unfinished, e
No. 57796 on back.

308-E1 13c Die on India, die sunk on card,
black   3,75

Design size: 177x220mm
Preliminary ink drawing of 3c frame design but later adopte
for 13c.

308-E2 13c Drawing on kraft paper, black &
blue green   1,500

310-E1

Design size: 19x22mm
Die size: 74x87½mm
Incomplete engraving of entire design: hair and right cheek finished, horiz. background lines only, top of frame and ~gles unfinished.

0-E1   50c Die on India, die sunk on card,
       black   4,000.

310-E2

Incomplete engraving of entire design, further engraved than ~. 310-E1: oval line outside top label thinner at bottom ends ~an on issued stamp.

~0-E2 50c Die on India, die sunk on card,
       black   4,000.

312-E1   313-E1

Design size: 19x22mm
Die size: 76x88mm
Incomplete engraving of entire design: hair, neckpiece, etc., ~nfinished, horiz. background lines only; top of frame, leaves ~nd numeral surrounds all unfinished.

~12-E1 $2 Die on India, die sunk on card,
        black   4,500.

Design size: 19x22mm
Die size: 75½x87½mm
Incomplete engraving of entire design: eyes, cheeks, hair, ~eckpiece all unfinished, horiz. background lines only, frame ~ngraved in outlines only.

~3-E1 $5 Die on India, die sunk on card,
        dark green   8,000.

319-E1

Design size: 19½x22mm
Die size: 75x87½mm
Incomplete engraving of entire design from rejected die (cen~ral star between UNITED and STATES, four lines above small ~ettering, bottom of shield curved): name and date ribbon blank.

~19-E1 2c Die on India, die sunk on card,
        carmine   5,250.

319-E2   319-E3

Incomplete engraving of entire design from rejected die: ~shading on leaves and vignette completed, lettering added to ~ottom ribbon and started on label above vignette. Blue pencil ~ote on card backing, "May 1903. This die was abandoned at

this stage because of crowded condition of lettering above portrait. G.F.C.S." No. 83909 on back.

319-E2   2c Die on India, die sunk on card, carmine   5,250.

Design size: 19½x22mm
Die I size: 75½x88mm
Incomplete engraving of entire design as adopted (no star between UNITED and STATES, bottom of shield straight): small label above vignette is blank.

319-E3   2c Die on India, die sunk on card, black   5,250.

LOUISIANA PURCHASE ISSUE

324-E1

Incomplete engraving of entire design: head, hair, eyes, chin, coat all unfinished, horiz. background lines only, bottom label and upper corner labels blank, frame shading unfinished.

324-E1   2c Die on India, die sunk on card,
         black   2,500.

325-E1

Incomplete engraving of entire design: head only lightly engraved, horiz. background lines only, laurel leaves unshaded, leaves' background and numeral shields blank.

325-E1   3c Die on India, die sunk on card,
         black   2,500.

326-E1

Incomplete engraving of entire design: vignette unfinished, horiz. background lines only, much of frame blank or incomplete.

326-E1   5c Die on India, die sunk on card,
         black blue   2,500.

JAMESTOWN ISSUE

328-E1

Incomplete engraving of entire design: vignette, shading on heads in upper corners, numerals and numeral shields all unfinished.

328-E1   1c Die on pale cream soft wove,
         30x24mm, dusky green   1,250.

Incomplete engraving of entire design: vignette, shading on heads in upper corners, and value tablets unfinished, pencil note "unfinished" at bottom of card.

328-E2   1c Die on India, die sunk on card,
         109x94mm, green   2,500.

330-E1   330-E2

Incomplete engraving of vignette only: collar, hat, corselet, etc., unfinished. No. 245910 on back.

330-E1   5c Die on India, die sunk on card,
         123x132mm, black   2,250.

Incomplete engraving of entire design: no shading in frame background.

330-E2   5c Die on India, die sunk on card,
         109x95mm, blue   6,000.

330-E3

Incomplete engraving of entire design: shading on corselet and arm of Pocahontas unfinished, horiz. background lines only, shading around date and name ribbon unfinished. No. 247606 on back.

330-E3   5c Die on card, 123x175mm, die
         sunk, blue   4,250.

Incomplete engraving of entire design: shading on ribbons unfinished.

330-E4   5c Die on India, die sunk on card,
         108x98mm, black   5,000.

1908 ISSUE

331-E1

Photograph of wash drawing of entire design, head and vignette background retouched with black wash. Ms. "GVLM-Sept. 26th-1908" (PMG) in LR corner of backing card.

331-E1   1c Retouched photo on thick gray
         cardboard, 83x100mm, black   5,000.

332-E1   332-E2

Design size: 6⅛x7¼ inches
Wash drawing of frame design with vignette cut out, mounted over retouched glossy black photo of Houdon bust of Washington.

332-E1   Two Cents, Design on drawing pa-
         per, black   1,250.

Design size: 19x22mm
Photograph of wash drawing of entire design, almost completely retouched with black ink and wash. Pencil "GVLM" (PMG) at top of backing card.

332-E2   Two Cents, Retouched photo on
         thick gray cardboard, 81x100mm,
         black   2,000.

332-E3

Design size: 19x22mm

Incomplete engraving of entire design: shading on leaves at right unfinished. Pencil "Oct 15 - 1908" at LR of backing card.

332-E3   Two Cents, Die on India, die sunk
             on card, carmine   1,250.

333-E1   333-E2

Design size: 18½x22mm
Engraving of design as adopted except "THREE CENTS" at bottom.

333-E1   Three Cents, Die printed directly
             on card, deep violet   1,250.

Design size: 19x22mm
Photograph of wash drawing of entire design with "3 CENTS 3" drawn in black and white wash. Ms. "Nov. 24/08. J.E.R." (BEP director) in LR corner of backing card.

333-E2   3c Retouched photo on thick gray
             cardboard, 80x100mm, black   2,000.

334-E1   334-E2

Design size: 18½x22mm
Engraving of design as adopted except "FOUR CENTS" at bottom.

334-E1   Four Cents, Die printed directly on
             card, orange brown   1,250.

Design size: 19x22mm
Photograph of wash drawing of entire design with "4 CENTS 4" drawn in black and white wash. Ms. "Nov. 24/08. J.E.R." (BEP director) in LR corner of backing card.

334-E2   4c Retouched photo on thick gray
             cardboard, 80x100mm, black   2,000.

335-E1   335-E2

Design size: 18½x22mm
Engraving of design as adopted except "FIVE CENTS" at bottom.

335-E1   Five Cents, Die printed directly on
             card, blue   1,500.

Design size: 19x22mm
Photograph of wash drawing of entire design with "5 CENTS 5" drawn in black and white wash. Ms. "Nov. 24/08. J.E.R." (BEP director) in LR corner of backing card.

335-E2   5c Retouched photo on thick gray
             cardboard, 80x100mm, black   2,000.

Design size: 18½x22mm
Incomplete engraving of design with "SIX CENTS" at bottom.

336-E1   Six Cents, Die on India, on card,
             red orange   1,250.

336-E2

Design size: 19x22mm

Photograph of wash drawing of entire design with "6 CENTS 6" drawn in black and white wash. Ms. "Nov. 24/08. J.E.R." (BEP director) in LR corner of backing card.

336-E2   6c Retouched photo on thick gray
             cardboard, 80x100mm, black   2,000.

337-E1   338-E1

Design size: 19x22mm
Photograph of wash drawing of entire design with "8 CENTS 8" drawn in black and white wash. Ms. "Nov. 24/08. J.E.R." (BEP director) in LR corner of backing card.

337-E1   8c Retouched photo on thick gray
             cardboard, 80x100mm, black   2,000.

Design size: 19x22mm
Photograph of wash drawing of entire design with "10 CENTS 10" drawn in black and white wash. Ms. "Nov. 24/08. J.E.R." (BEP director) in LR corner of backing card.

338-E1   10c Retouched photo on thick gray
             cardboard, 80x100mm, black   2,000.

338a-E1

Design size: 18½x22mm
Complete engraving of entire adopted design but a value not issued: "12 CENTS 12" at bottom. Virtually all are stamp size, imperf.

Ridgway numbers used for colors of No. 338a-E1.

338a-E1 12c
  a. Die on bluish white wove
       41n/1 dim v. dusky b-blue-green   900.
  b. Die on 1f/1 dim pale red wove
  c. Die on 7d/1 dim light red orange wove
       47m/1 dim dusky g-b. blue   900.
  d. Die on 17b/1 dim bright o-y. yellow
       wove
       1i/0 deep red   900.
       5i/0 deep o-orange-red   900.
       27m/0 dusky green yellow   900.
       37m/0 dusky g-blue-green   900.
       41m/0 dusky b-blue-green   900.
       55m/1 dim dusky blue violet   900.
       59m/1 dim dusky violet   900.
       69m/3 dismal dusky r-violet-red   900.
  e. Die on 19f/0 pale y-orange yellow wove
       1i/0 deep red   900.
       15i/1 dim deep yellow orange   900.
       35m/0 dusky green   900.
       43d/1 dim light green blue   900.
       61m/3 dismal dusky v-red-violet   900.
       690/5 black   900.
  f. Die on 31f/2 dull pale yellow green
       wove
       69o/5 black   900.
  g. Die on 42d/1 dim bright green blue
       wove
       41m/1 dim dusky b-blue-green   900.
  h. Die on 44-/1 dim medium green blue
       wove
       9k/2 dull dark o-r-orange   900.
  i. Die on 45l/1 dim v. dark b-green-blue
       wove
       5i/0 deep o-orange-red   900.
       27m/2 dull dusky green yellow   900.
  j. Die on 69g/0 pale r-v. red wove   900.
  k. Die on dark blue bond, 69o/5 black   900.

339-E1   340-E1

Design size: 19x22mm
Photograph of wash drawing of entire design with "13 CENTS 13" drawn in black and white wash. Ms. "Oct. 7-08. J.E.R.-GVLM" (BEP director, PMG) in LL corner of backing card.

339-E1   13c Retouched photo on thick gray
             cardboard, 80x100mm, black   2,000.

Design size: 19x22mm
Photograph of wash drawing of entire design with "15 CEN 15" drawn in black and white wash. Ms. "Oct. 7-08. J.E. GVLM" (BEP director, PMG) at bottom of backing card.

340-E1   15c Retouched photo on thick gray
             cardboard, 80x100mm, black   2,0

341-E1   342-E1

Design size: 19x22mm
Photograph of wash drawing of entire design with "50 CENT 50" drawn in black and white wash. Ms. "Oct. 7-08. J.E. GVLM" (BEP director, PMG) at bottom of backing card.

341-E1   50c Retouched photo on thick gray
             cardboard, 80x100mm, black   2,00

Design size: 19x22mm
Photograph of wash drawing of entire design with "1 DOLLA 1" drawn in black and white wash. Ms. "Oct. 7-08. J.E.R.-GVLM" (BEP director, PMG) at bottom of backing card.

342-E1 $1 Retouched photo on thick gray
             cardboard, 80x100mm, black   2,00

LINCOLN MEMORIAL ISSUE

Design size: 7x8 inches
Photostat of 1980 2c frame design with wash drawing ribbons and vignette photo of Lincoln's head.

367-E1   Two Cents, Model of Lincoln de-
             sign, black   1,50

Photo of No. 367-E1 reduced to stamp size, retouched highlight hair and beard.

367-E2   Two Cents, Retouched photo,
             black   1,50

367-E3

Design size: 19x22mm
Incomplete engraving of entire design: head, background name/date ribbon all unfinished.

367-E3   Two Cents, Die on India, die sunk
             on card, 148x201mm, carmine   3,50

ALASKA-YUKON-PACIFIC EXPOSITION ISSUE

Design size: 18½x22mm
Wash drawing of frame similar to 1908 2c design with phot of wash drawing of seal on ice cake as vignette. Ms. "#1" at U corner of backing card.

370-E1   2c Model on card, about 3x4 inches,
             black   1,50C

370-E2

Design size: 18½x22mm
Engraved frame similar to 1908 2c but with wash drawing o "1870 1909" in ribbons and "2 CENTS 2" at bottom, vignette cu out, mounted over engraved vignette of Wm. H. Seward from snuff stamp. Ms. "#2" at UL corner of backing card.

370-E2   2c Model on card, about 3x4 inches,
             black   1,500

370-E3

Design size: 27½x20½mm

Photo of seal on ice cake vignette as originally approved, ...unted on ink and wash drawing of frame design as approved. ... "#3" at UL corner of backing card, engraved Seward ...nette pasted on at bottom, "Approved April 3, 1909 FH Hitch-...k Postmaster-General" at right.

0-E3　2c Model on glazed card, 93x70mm,
　　　　black, white and gray　　　　　　　　　　2,250.

370-E4

Design size: 27½x20mm
Photo of wash drawing of frame and arched ribbon as ...pted, vignette cut out, mounted over photo of engraved ...ward vignette, background retouched with black wash. Ms. ...proved subject to addition of the name Seward, as indicated ...letter of Director, Bureau of Engraving and Printing, dated ...ril 24, 1909. F.H. Hitchcock Postmaster General."

0-E4　2c Model on 93x75mm thick gray
　　　　card, black　　　　　　　　　　　　　　2,250.

370-E5

Design size: 27x20mm
Retouched photo of wash drawing of adopted frame with seal ... ice cake vignette but pencil "WILLIAM H. SEWARD" on white ...sh ribbon below. Ms. "April 26/09 Approved J.E.R." (BEP ...ector) at LR corner of backing card.

0-E5　2c Retouched photo and pencil on
　　　　94x66mm thick gray card, black　　　　2,000.

Incomplete engraving of entire design: no shading on head or ...gnette background, no shading lines on ribbons.

0-E6　2c Die on India, die sunk on 8x6 inch
　　　　card, carmine　　　　　　　　　　　　　2,000.

370-E7

Design size: 26½x19½mm
Similar to No. 370-E6 but further engraved: face and collar ...htly engraved, horiz. background lines only, no shading lines ...n ribbons.

70-E7　2c Die on wove, 32x26½mm, carmine　　2,000.

372-E1

Wash drawing of adopted vignette design.

72-E1　2c Drawing on artist's cardboard,
　　　　11¼x6¾ inches, black　　　　　　　　1,500.

372-E2

Wash drawing of frame design as adopted except "HUDSON-FULTON CENTENARY" at top.

372-E2　2c Drawing on artist's cardboard,
　　　　7¾x6¾ inches, black　　　　　　　　1,500.

Design size: 33x21½mm
Wash drawing of frame design as adopted with dates "1609-1807" and photo of No. 372-E1 reduced to fit and worked over with wash.

372-E3　2c Model on card, 4x3 inches, black　　2,000.

Design size: 33x21½mm
Wash drawing of frame with vignette cut out, mounted over photo of No. 372-E1. Typed/ms. "Approved August 17, 1909 F.H. Hitchcock Postmaster General" and "August 19, 1909 Amend by substituting word 'Celebration' for 'Centenary.' F.H. Hitchcock Postmaster General." Pencil "P.O. 488" in LR corner.

372-E4　2c Model on white card, 129x103mm,
　　　　black　　　　　　　　　　　　　　　2,000.

372-E5

Incomplete engraving of entire design: lettering on flag at masthead of *Clermont* has "N" reversed and no "T."

372-E5　2c Die on wove, 38x27mm, carmine　　2,000.

PANAMA-PACIFIC ISSUE

397-E1

Design size: 27x20mm
Photo of incomplete frame with overlay of circular photo vignette as adopted, with wash drawing of palm trees on each side and "1 CENT 1" in wash. Ms. "Approved July 16, 1912 Frank H. Hitchcock Postmaster General" on backing card.

397-E1　1c Model on card, about 89x77mm,
　　　　black　　　　　　　　　　　　　　　1,500.

Design size: 27x20mm
Photo of incomplete frame with overlay circular photo vignette as adopted, with wash drawing of palm trees on each side and "1 CENT 1" in wash, with "Approved" and signed by the BEP Director J.E. Ralph, but "Opening of Panama Canal 1913" later changed for stamp to "San Francisco 1913."

397-E2　1c Model on thick gray card,
　　　　106x86mm, black　　　　　　　　　1,500.

398-E1

Design size: about 29½x20mm
Ink and wash drawing of frame design longer than adopted with photo of wash drawing of Golden Gate as eventually used (reduced) on 5c. Backstamp "STAMP DIVISION FEB. 12, 1912 P.O. DEPT" on backing card.

398-E1　2c Model on card, about 4x3 inches,
　　　　black　　　　　　　　　　　　　　　1,500.

398-E2

Design size: 27x20mm
Photo of incomplete frame with photo of wash drawing of vignette as adopted with title "GATUN LOCKS," wash drawing of value numerals. Ms. "Approved Aug. 27, 1912 Frank H. Hitch-cock Postmaster General" on backing card.

398-E2　2c Model on thick gray card,
　　　　99x72¾, black　　　　　　　　　1,500.

Very similar to No. 398-E2 with slightly different wash touch-up and "2"s, with "Approved" and signed by BEP Director J.E. Ralph.

398-E2A　2c Model on thick gray card,
　　　　107x86mm, black　　　　　　　　1,500.

398-E3

Completely engraved design as adopted except titled "GATUN LOCKS" in error (design pictures Pedro Miguel locks).

398-E3　2c
　　a. Large die on India, die sunk on card,
　　　202x152mm, carmine　　　　　　　10,000.
　　b. Small die on India (formerly
　　　#398AP2), carmine　　　　　　　　6,000.

398-E4

Design size: 27x20mm
Photo of incomplete engraving (no sky in vignette) with "GATUN LOCKS" in error, ms. "Approved Dec. 17, 1912 Frank Hitchcock Postmaster General" on backing card.

398-E4　2c Model on thick gray card,
　　　　97x74mm, black　　　　　　　　1,500.

399-E1

Design size: 27x20mm
Photo of wash drawing of frame design as adopted with photo of wash drawing of adopted vignette mounted in place, with additional hand touch-up done in wash on vignette, ms. "Approved July 16, 1912 Frank H., Hitchcock Postmaster General" on backing card.

399-E1　5c Model on 30x22mm white paper,
　　　　mounted on card, 97x73mm,
　　　　black　　　　　　　　　　　　1,500.

Very similar to No. 399-E1 with slightly different wash touch-up and no steamship below sun, with "Approved" and signed by BEP Director J.E. Ralph.

399-E2　5c Model on thick gray card,
　　　　106x86mm, black　　　　　　　1,500.

400-E1

Design size: 27x20mm
Photo of wash drawing of frame design as adopted with photo of painting adopted for vignette mounted in place, ms. printed "Approved" and dated and signed " Aug. 22, 1912, Frank H. Hitchcock Postmaster General" on backing card.

400-E1　10c Model on 31x34mm white paper,
　　　　on thick gray card, 98x73mm,
　　　　black　　　　　　　　　　　　1,500.

Very similar to No. 400-E1 with more extensive touching-up of the vignette and frame, with "Approved" and signed by BEP Director J.E. Ralph.

400-E1A　10c Model on thick gray card,
　　　　107x86mm, black　　　　　　　1,500.

Design size: 27x20mm

Photo of wash drawing of frame design as adopted with photo of wash drawing of two galleons at anchor in bay, titled "CABRILLO 1542" mounted in place. Backing card marked "II."

400-E2 10c Model on white paper, on
91x85mm thick gray card, black   *1,500.*

400-E3

Design size: 27x20mm
Photo of wash drawing of frame design as adopted with photo of Liberty standing among palm fronds, wash touch-up on vignette and "10" denominations drawn in black and white wash, two battleships in bay. Backing card marked "III."

400-E3 10c Model on white paper, on thick
gray card, 90x84mm, black   *1,500.*

400-E4

Design size: 27x20mm
Similar to No. 400-E3 but steamships replace battleships. Backing card marked "IV."

400-E4 10c Model on white paper, on thick
gray card, 90x83mm, black   *1,500.*

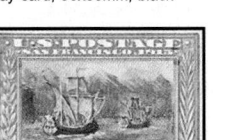

400-E5

Design size: 27x20mm
Similar to No. 400-E2 but different hand drawn vignette picturing two galleons under full sail in front of snowclad mountains. Backing card marked "V."

400-E5 10c Model on white paper, on thick
gray card, 89x83mm, black   *1,500.*

1912 ISSUE

Incomplete engraving of entire design: wash drawing of "1 CENT 1" at bottom. Ms. "Approved. July 17, 1911 Frank H. Hitchcock. P.M. Gen." on backing card.

405-E1 1c Model on 3½x3¾-inch card, black   *5,750.*

406-E1

Incomplete engraving of , except value tablet area which is "2 CENTS 2" at bottom drawn in wash. Ms. "Approved. July 17, 1911 Frank H. Hitchcock P. M. Gen." on backing card.

406-E1 2c Model on 3⅜x3¹¹⁄₁₆-inch card, black   —

Wash drawing of design as adopted, worked over partial photo with 8 in lower corners drawn in wash. Ms. "Approved. July 17, 1911 Frank H. Hitchcock Postmaster General" on backing card.

414-E1 8c Model on 3½x3¾-inch card, black   —

414-E2

Vignette of head only without background gridwork, control #490311 on back of card.

414-E2 8c Die on India, die sunk on
152x202mm, olive green   *2,250.*

416-E1   418-E1

Design size: 19x22mm
Photo of wash drawing of generic design with 10 in lower corners drawn in black ink. Ms. "July 17, 1911. (May, 1911 erased) Approved: Frank H. Hitchcock PM Gen" on backing card, backstamped "STAMP DIVISION P.O. DEPT. MAY 15, 1911."

416-E1 10c Model on 87x113mm thick gray
card, black   *1,000.*

Design size: 19x22mm
Photo of wash drawing of generic design with background of frame between oval and outer colorless line in dark gray wash and some colorless retouching, 15 in lower corners drawn in black ink. Ms. "July 17, 1911. (May, 1911 erased) Approved: Frank H. Hitchcock PM Gen" on backing card, backstamped "STAMP DIVISION P.O. DEPT. MAY 15, 1911."

418-E1 15c Model on 87x113mm thick gray
card, black   *1,000.*

421-E1   423-E1

Design size: 19x22mm
Photo of wash drawing of generic design with 50 in lower corners drawn in black ink. Ms. "July 17, 1911. (May, 1911 erased) Approved: Frank H. Hitchcock PM Gen" on backing card, backstamped "STAMP DIVISION P.O. DEPT. MAY 15, 1911."

421-E1 50c Model on 77x112mm thick gray
card, black   *1,000.*

Design size: 19x22mm
Photo of wash drawing of generic design with entire value label drawn in black ink. Ms. "July 17, 1911. (May, 1911 erased) Approved: Frank H. Hitchcock PM Gen" on backing card, backstamped "STAMP DIVISION P.O. DEPT. MAY 15, 1911."

423-E1 $1 Model on 87x113mm thick gray
card, black   *1,000.*

1916 PRECANCEL ESSAYS

499-E1

Design size: 19x22mm
Die size: 90x88mm
"NEW YORK/N.Y." precancel engraved directly onto type I die, printed in one color. Ms. "8/16/22 J.S." in LR corner of backing card on No. 499-E1a. Although dated 1922, records indicate an original proof was pulled in 1916.

499-E1 2c
  a. Die on India, die sunk on card, lake   —
  b. Die on bond paper, 33x36mm, dark carmine   —

1918 ISSUE

Complete engraving of Franklin head only as on $2 and $5 values, no shading around head, control #834424 on back of card.

523-E2 $2 Die on India, die sunk on
151x103mm card, black   *1,750.*

523-E3

Design size: 16x18¾mm
Complete engraving of vignette only including shading. Pe[...] control # "837660 May 1917" on back of India paper, pe[...] "Schofield" at bottom of backing card (#523-E3a), or con[...] #837662 (1917) on back of card (No. 523-E3b).

523-E3 $2
  a. Die on 32x33mm India, card mounted,
    black   *1,0[...]*
  b. Die on wove, die sunk on card,
    203x151mm, black   *1,0[...]*

PEACE ISSUE

537-E1   537-E2

Design size: 21½x18½mm
Stamp never issued due to World War I.

537-E1 2c
  a. Die on India, die sunk on card, deep red   *1,5[...]*
  b. Die on wove, die sunk on card,
    201x138mm, signed on card by Harry
    S. New   *4,0[...]*

Die size: 22x19mm
Stamp never issued due to World War I.

537-E2 5c
  a. Die on India, die sunk on card, dim
    dusky g-b-blue   *1,5[...]*
  b. Die on wove, die sunk on card,
    201x138mm, signed on card by Harry
    S. New   *4,0[...]*

SAMUEL F.B. MORSE ISSUE

537-E3

Design size: 21½x18½mm
Incomplete engraving of entire design: vignette and letteri[...] finished but blank spaces beside vignette. Backstampe[...] "932944" and "Jan. 1, 1919" or "932945" and "Jan. 7, 191[...] Frame design subsequently used for 3c Victory issue, No. 53[...] though lettering and value numerals made slightly smaller.

537-E3 3c Die on India, die sunk on card,
    141x173mm (#932944) or
    151x202mm (#932945), black   *3,00[...]*

VICTORY ISSUE

537-E4

Design size: 21½x18½mm
Die size: 85½x75½mm
Incomplete engraving of entire design: no shading in bord[...] and some flags unfinished. Backstamped "936356 Jan. 2[...] 1919."

537-E4 3c Die on India, die sunk on card,
    black   *1,50[...]*

PILGRIM ISSUE

548-E1

Design size: 26x19mm
Incomplete engraving of entire design: sky blank, sail[...] unshaded.

548-E1 1c Die on India, die sunk on card,
    201x151mm, green   *1,60[...]*

PILGRIM ISSUE

Almost complete engraving of entire design as adopted, but crosshatching behind the "1" denominations.

...-E2 1c Die on India, die sunk on card,
203x151mm, green — *1,600.*

549-E1

Incomplete engraving of frame only: "CENTS" engraved but numeral circles blank (probably an essay for the 2c and 5c).

...-E1 Die on India, die sunk on card
black — *1,600.*
green — *1,600.*

549-E2

Design size: 26x19mm
Incomplete engraving of entire design: vignette unfinished, control #1063097 on back of card.

...-E2 2c Die on India, die sunk on card,
202x151mm, black — *1,600.*

Incomplete engraving of entire design, virtually complete but crosshatching behind the numeral "2" denominations.

...-E3 2c
a. Die on India, die sunk on card,
202x151mm, control #1063875 on
back, black — *1,600.*
b. Die on India, die sunk on card,
202x151mm, control #1064174 or
#1064271 on back, carmine rose — *1,600.*

1922 ISSUE

551-E1

Design size: 19x22mm
Incomplete engraving of entire design as adopted: name panel blank, vignette unfinished. Ms. "Approved--Harry S. New" backing card on olive brown essay; others not signed but with notation of denomination of stamp for color used ("1c" for green, etc.)

...-E1 ½c Die on India, die sunk on
151x202mm card
olive brown — *3,000.*
green — *2,000.*
carmine — *2,000.*
orange — *2,000.*
rose — *2,000.*
yellow — *2,000.*
blue green — *2,000.*
yellow green — *2,000.*
carmine rose — *2,000.*

Incomplete engraving of entire design but further engraved than No. 551-E1: no lines in white oval over ends of title ribbon and ribbon foldunders not etched as darkly as on issued stamp.

551-E2 ½c Die on India, die sunk on
149x201mm card, olive brown — *1,000.*

555-E2

Complete engraving with horizontal lines surrounding bust of Lincoln.

555-E2 3c Die on India, affixed to card,
26x30mm, violet — *2,750.*

560-E1

Complete engraving with horizontal lines surrounding slightly larger bust of Grant.

560-E1 8c Die on India, die sunk on
97x111mm card, dark olive
green — *2,000.*

567-E2

568-E2

Design size: 19x22mm
Engraving of unadopted vignette with unadopted engraved frame cut away.

567-E2 20c Die on India, die sunk on
151x201mm card, cobalt blue — *1,750.*

Design size: 19x15mm
Die size: 88x75mm
Engraving of adopted vignette with engraved frame cut away.

568-E2 25c Die on India, die sunk on
202x151mm card, green — *1,750.*

Pencil drawings for unadopted frame design.

555-E1	3c black	*1,150.*
557-E1	5c black	*1,150.*
557-E2	5c black	*1,150.*
566-E1	15c black	*1,150.*
571-E1	$1 black	*1,150.*

573-E1

Engraving of accepted vignette.

573-E1 $5 Die on India, affixed to card,
73x87mm, blue — *3,750.*

HUGUENOT-WALLOON TERCENTENARY ISSUE

614-E1

Design size: 8 ½x7 ¼ inches
Preliminary pencil drawing of *Nieu Nederland* in circular frame. Pencil note: "Reverse--Sailing to America, not away from America--J. B. Stoudt" originally on drawing has been removed.

614-E1 1c black — *1,000.*

Incomplete engraving of entire design, background of vignette incomplete and central figures only roughed in.

615-E1 2c Die on India, 82x69mm, black — *4,500.*

616-E1

Design size: 5 ½x3 ⅛ inches
Wash drawing of design adopted for vignette.

616-E1 5c black — *1,500.*

Almost complete engraving of entire design, lacking strong shading in the foreground of the vignette.

617-E1 5c Die on India, die sunk on card,
126x115mm, green — *1,500.*

618-E1

Design size: 36x21mm
Incomplete engraving of entire design as adopted: spaces between letters of "BIRTH OF LIBERTY" not solid color.

618-E1 2c Die on India, die sunk on card,
carmine — *1,250.*

Design size: 36x21mm
Incomplete engraving of entire design as adopted: numeral circles blank, many shading lines missing in vignette, no shading around "TWO CENTS," etc.

618-E2 2c Die on India, die sunk on
91x71mm card, black — *1,500.*

Design size: 36x21mm
Engraving of frame only, without vignette or value tablets, control #1317765 on back of card.

618-E3 2c Die on India, die sunk on card,
202x118mm, carmine — *1,500.*

ERICSSON MEMORIAL ISSUE

Wash drawing of design as adopted, stamp size.

628-E1 5c black — *750.*

BATTLE OF WHITE PLAINS ISSUE

629-E1

Design size: 8 ⅜x9 inches
Preliminary ink and watercolor drawing of entire design quite similar to that adopted.

629-E1 2c black & red — *750.*

BURGOYNE CAMPAIGN ISSUE

644-E1

Design size: 22x19mm
Essay size: 25x22mm
Card size: 78x98mm
Photo of wash drawing of unadopted design, on white paper mounted on thick gray card with "Approved" in ink and "May 7, 1927" in pencil subsequently crossed out with "X's."

644-E1   2c black   1,500.

683-E1

Design size: 13x17 inches
Preliminary ink drawing of design nearly as adopted.

683-E1   2c Drawing on artist's cardboard,
             black   500.

American flag and pencil touch-up of outer frame on photo of artist's model with vignette as adopted but entirely different frame.

690-E1   2c black   400.

702-E1

Engraving of entire design without red cross, engraved cross shows faintly, control #70015 on back of card.

702-E1   2c Die on India, die sunk on
             120x142mm card, black   5,000.

704-E1

Design size: 119x150mm
Preliminary pencil sketch of unadopted ½c design.

704-E1   ½c Drawing on tracing paper, mounted
             on 195x192mm manila paper,
             black   1,250.

718-E1

Design size: 6x7 inches
Watercolor drawing of unadopted design with 2c denomination.

718-E1   2c Drawing on thick artist's card, red   1,250.

719-E1

Design size: 6x7 inches
Watercolor drawing of entire design similar to that eventually adopted for 5c but with 2c denomination.

719-E1   2c Drawing on thick artist's card,
             150x175mm, blue   1,250.

Engraving of vignette as adopted, within frame, but reversed from final design, without denomination or inscriptions.

742-E1   3c Die on white card, 88x69mm, black   1,750.

Unadopted engraving of entire design without denomination, portraits as adopted but rest of design different from accepted design, control #70027 on back of card.

786-E1   2c Die on wove, die sunk on card,
             202x153mm, carmine   1,500.

Engravings of Decatur and MacDonough as adopted, widely spaced.

791-E1   2c Die on wove, die sunk on card,
             202x153mm, carmine   1,500.

Engraving of incomplete design without central vignette, control #491747 (1936) on back of card.

791-E2   2c Die on wove, die sunk on card,
             198x136mm, carmine   1,500.

Unfinished engravings of three portraits only, control #70031 on back.

793-E1   4c Die on wove, die sunk on card,
             202x153mm, red brown   1,500.

Engraving of entire design, lacks crosshatching in the shading of background.

899-E1   1c Die on wove, die sunk on card,
             140x162mm, green   1,000.

Engraving of frame as adopted, with "84075" at top and "United States of America" at bottom of die impression, stamped "For Approval" at top of card, signed and dated by four individuals on card.

909-921-E1   5c Die on India, die sunk on
                 card, 227x151mm, violet   3,000.

Unadopted design showing steamship under sail, with denomination or background shading, handstamp "Engrav[er's] Stock Proof/Authorized by," initials, "Brooks" (the engrav[er]) pencil and control #818347A all on back of stamp.

923-E1   3c Die on wove, die sunk on card,
             201x152mm, violet   1,

Unfinished engraving of adopted design, lacking smoke f[rom] the smokestack and background shading. "Modeling" ha[ndstamp and control #818995A on back of card.

**923E-   3c Die on wove, die sunk on card,
E2**   201x150mm, violet   1,

Engraved vignette as adopted, "Engraver's St[ock] Proof/Authorized by," initials, "Brooks" (the engraver) in pe[ncil] and control #867263A all on back of stamp.

930-933-E2   Die on wove, die sunk on card,
                 202x151mm, black   1,6

PANAMA CANAL ISSUE

856-E1

Design size: 37x21½mm
Essay size: 99x81mm
Card size: 141x117mm
Engraving of unadopted design: "3 CENTS 3" and "2[5th] ANNIVERSARY PANAMA CANAL" changed for final des[ign.] "W. O. Marks" at lower right corner, "Engraver's Stock P[roof] 594256 / Authorized by 'OML'" on reverse.

856-E1   3c Die on India, die sunk on card,
             deep violet

1016-E1

Engraving of adopted design, except "c" cut in design at ri[ght] where cross should be printed (held in place by tape on bac[k]), "Engraver's Stock Proof, Authorized by," initials and b[lue] "103120B" control number on back.

1016-E1   3c Die on wove, die sunk on card,
              202x152mm, deep blue   2,5

Drawing, similar to issued design but with different symbo[ls at] left and different signature of Benjamin Franklin, signed [by] Frank V. Conley (designer of Credo issue).

1140-E1   4c Drawing on tracing paper, red,
              blue and white ink   6

AIR POST STAMPS

1918 ISSUE

Complete engraving of frame only as adopted. Backstamp[ed] "626646A ENGRAVER'S STOCK PROOF AUTHORIZED B[Y]" (signature), plus pencil "663" and "Weeks" (?).

C3-E1   24c Die on India, die sunk on card,
            deep carmine   5,00

Incomplete engraving of entire design as adopted: unfinish[ed] plumes above value numerals and no serial number on bipla[ne.]

C3-E2   24c Die on wove, 40x37mm, black
            vignette, blue frame

Engraving of adopted design except without denominatio[n,] "C" punch where denominations go, control #722657A (194[?]) on back of card.

C25-C31-E1   Die on wove, die sunk on card,
                 201x150mm, black   5,50

SPECIAL DELIVERY STAMPS

1885 ISSUE
American Bank Note Co.

E1-E1

Incomplete engraving of entire design as adopted: ornaments missing at each side of "SPECIAL," line under messenger is in pencil, shading on left side of messenger tablet missing, leaves in vert. background lines unfinished (latter shaded over with pencil).

E1   10c Die on India, dim dusky g-b. green   2,500.

1888 ISSUE

No. E1P1 with "AT ANY OFFICE" drawn in wash on small piece of thin paper and mounted over "AT A SPECIAL / DELIV-RY / OFFICE." Pencil "any post office" and ms. "At once O.K. / J.M. 14 Aug. 86" (?) on backing card.

E1   10c Die on India, on card, black   2,500.

1908 ISSUE
Bureau of Engraving and Printing

E7-E1

Design size: about 8½x7⅛ inches
Preliminary ink and pencil drawing of entire design somewhat similar to that adopted: ("V.S." for U.S. and other minor changes).

E7-E1   10c Drawing on vellum, black   750.

E7-E2

Design size: about 8½x7⅛ inches
Preliminary ink and pencil drawing of entire design nearly as adopted: ("V.S." for U.S.)

E7-E2   10c Drawing on white drawing paper, black   750.

E7-E3

Design size: 213½x179mm
Similar to No. E7-E2 but with "U.S."

E7-E3   10c Drawing on white drawing paper, black   750.

E7-E4   E7-E5

Design size: 26x21½mm
Woodblock size: 45x42mm
Woodblock of entire design as adopted with about 5mm colorless border outside design, solid color beyond, engraved on wood by Giraldon of Paris. (One exists with ms. "Wood cut made in Paris by Mr. Whitney Warren -- The cuts and the impression therefrom were turned over to the Director of the Bureau of Engraving & Printing, and by him turned over to the Custodian of Dies, Rolls and Plates and given No. 446. They are now held by the Custodian." Another has typewritten "Prints made in Paris, France, from a wood-cut engraving by an unknown engraver from a design made by Mr. Whitney Warren, architect, of New York City." with ms. "Compliments J.E. Ralph" director of B.E.P. and pencil date "9/7/1917.")

Ridgeway numbers used for colors of Nos. E7-E4 and E7-E5.

E7-E4   10c
    a. Woodcut on 19g/2 yellowish wove
          43k/1 dim dark green blue   450.
          44m/2 dull dusky m. g-blue   450.
          45j/1 dim v. dark b-g-blue   450.
          45m/1 dim dusky b-g-blue   450.
    b. Woodcut on 19f/2 dull faint y-o-yellow wove
          43k/1 dim dark g-blue   450.
          43m/1 dim dusky g-blue   450.
          44k/1 dim dark m. g-blue   450.
          44k/2 dull dark m. g-blue   450.
          45m/1 dim dusky b-g-blue   450.
          45m/2 dull dusky b-g-blue   450.
    c. Woodcut on 19g/2 dull v. faint y-o-yellow wove
          43k/1 dim dark g-blue   450.
          43m/1 dim dusky g-blue   450.

Design size: 26x21½mm
Complete engraving of entire design fairly similar to that adopted but with minor differences.

E7-E5   10c
    a. Die on India, die sunk on card, 37m/0 dusky g-b. green blue   750.
    b. Die on soft white wove, 30x35mm, 37m/0 dusky g-blue-green   750.

REGISTRATION STAMP

F1-E1

Design size: 19x22½mm
Retouched circular photo of vignette mounted on wash drawing of frame design as adopted. Ms. "Approved July 8/11 — Frank H. Hitchcock — Postmaster General" on backing card.

F1-E1   10c Model on white paper, mounted on thick gray cardboard, 81x92mm, black   1,250.

POSTAGE DUE STAMPS

1879 ISSUE
American Bank Note Co.

J1-E1

Design size: 19½x25½mm
Die size: 54x66½mm
Complete engraving of entire design as adopted except "UNPAID POSTAGE" instead of "POSTAGE DUE" above vignette oval.

J1-E1   1c
    a. Die on India, die sunk on card
          orange brown   850.
          slate gray   850.
          dark red violet   850.
          dull yellow   850.
          light orange   850.
          red brown   850.
    b. Die on India, cut small (1-4mm)
          gray black   400.
          dull red   400.
          dull brown   400.
          dull green   400.
          dull blue   400.
    c. Die on India, cut close (0-1mm)
          orange brown   400.
          slate gray   400.
          dark red violet   400.
          dull yellow   400.
    d. Die on white ivory paper, die sunk
          black   700.
          black brown   700.
          scarlet   700.
          blue   700.

Design size: 19½x25½mm
Die size: 53½x53½mm
Complete engraving of entire design as adopted except "UNPAID POSTAGE" instead of "POSTAGE DUE" above vignette oval.

J2-E1   2c
    a. Die on India, die sunk on card
          dark red violet   850.
          black   850.
    b. Die on India, cut small
          gray black   400.
          dull red   400.
          dull brown   400.
          dull green   400.
          dull blue   400.
    c. Die on India, cut close
          orange brown   400.
          dark red violet   400.
          slate gray   400.
    d. Die on white ivory paper, die sunk
          black   700.
          black brown   700.
          scarlet   700.
          blue   700.

Design size: 19½x25½mm
Die size: 53x53mm
Complete engraving of entire design as adopted except "UNPAID POSTAGE" instead of "POSTAGE DUE" above vignette oval.

J3-E1   3c
    a. Die on India, die sunk on card, dull yellow   850.
    b. Die on India, cut small
          gray black   400.
          dull red   400.
          dull brown   400.
          dull green   400.
          dull blue   400.
    c. Die on India, cut close, dull yellow   400.
    d. Die on white ivory paper, die sunk
          black   700.
          black brown   700.
          scarlet   700.
          blue   700.

Design size: 19½x25½mm
Complete engraving of entire design as adopted except "UNPAID POSTAGE" instead of "POSTAGE DUE" above vignette oval.

J4-E1   5c
    a. Die on India, die sunk on card, slate gray   850.
    b. Die on India, cut small
          gray black   400.
          dull red   400.
          dull brown   400.
          dull green   400.
          dull blue   400.
    c. Die on India, cut close
          orange brown   400.
          slate gray   400.
          dark red violet   400.
          dull yellow   400.
    d. Die on white ivory paper, die sunk
          black   700.
          black brown   700.
          scarlet   700.
          blue   700.

1894 ISSUE
Bureau of Engraving and Printing

J31-E1

J31-E2

Design size: 18½x22½mm
Die size: 50x99mm
Incomplete engraving of entire design: no engraved lines on numeral, lathework unfinished on two inclined spots at each side of numeral.

J31-E1 1c Die on India, die sunk on card,
deep claret   1,000.

Design size: 18½x22½mm
Die size: 50x99mm
Incomplete engraving of entire design: engraved lines on numeral but lathework still unfinished on two inclined spots at each side of numeral.

J31-E2 1c Die on India, die sunk on card,
claret   1,000.

J33-E1

J33-E2

Incomplete engraving of entire design: blank space for numeral with "3" drawn in pencil.

J33-E1 3c Die on India, die sunk on card,
black   1,000.

Incomplete engraving of entire design: no engraved lines on numeral, bottom lettering in pencil only, no hand retouching of lathework around numeral.

J33-E2 3c Die on India, die sunk on card,
black   1,000.

J33-E3

Incomplete engraving of entire design: no engraved lines on numeral.

J33-E3 3c Die on India, die sunk on card,
claret   1,000.

J35-E1

J36-E1

Incomplete engraving of entire design: no engraved lines on numerals.

J35-E1 10c Die on India, die sunk on card,
black   1,000.

Incomplete engraving of entire design: no engraved lines on numerals.

J36-E1 30c Die on India, die sunk on card,
claret   1,000.

J37-E1

J37-E2

Incomplete engraving of entire design: 9x9mm blank space for numerals.

J37-E1 50c Die on India, die sunk on card
black   1,000.
claret   1,000.

Incomplete engraving of entire design: numerals engraved but hand engraving to retouch lathework around numerals missing.

J37-E2 50c Die on India, die sunk on card,
black   1,000.

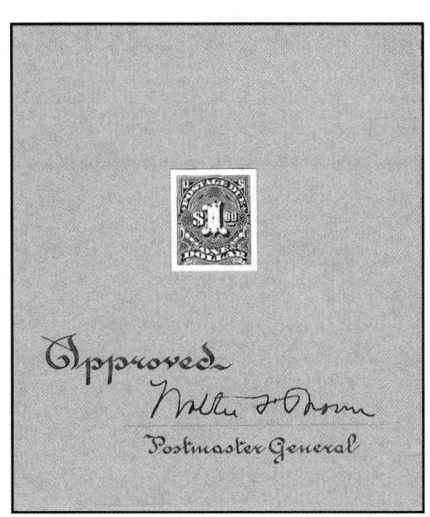

J67-E1

Complete engraving of unissued 1917 denomination, "Approved / Walter F. Brown (signature) / Postmaster General" below design.

J67-E1 $1 Die on white card, mounted on
gray card, black   4,500.

OFFICIAL STAMPS

Continental Bank Note Co.
AGRICULTURE

O2-E1

Design size: 20x25mm
Engraved vignette, numeral and value label from 1873 2c (No. 146-E10) mounted on pencil and wash drawing for frame design as adopted for Agriculture set. Pencil signature "J. Claxton" on backing card. Frame differs for each dept.

O2-E1 2c Model on yellowish card, 23x30mm,
on 90x118mm white card, black
vignette, gray black frame   6,500.

EXECUTIVE

O12-E1

O12-E2

Design size: 20x25mm
See design note for No. O2-E1.
O12-E1 3c Model on yellowish card,
23x30mm, on 90x118mm white
card, black   6,

Design size: 19½x25mm
Die size: 64x76mm
Engraving of complete design of No. O12-E1 with "DEP" top label.
O12-E2 3c
a. Die on India, die sunk on card, green   2,
b. Die on India, cut close
black   2,
green   2,

INTERIOR

O17-E1

Design size: 20x25mm
See design note for No. O2-E1.
O17-E1 3c Model on yellowish card,
23x30mm, on 90x118mm white
card, black   9,0

JUSTICE

O27-E1

Design size: 20x25mm
See design note for No. O2-E1.
O27-E1 3c Model on yellowish card,
23x30mm, on 90x118mm
white card, black   10,0

NAVY

O37-E1

Design size: 20x25mm
See design note for No. O2-E1.
O37-E1 3c Model on yellowish card,
23x30mm, on 90x118mm white
card, black   4,7

POST OFFICE

O47-E1

Design size: 19½x25mm
Complete engraving of entire design as adopted except wit Franklin vignette instead of large numeral.

O47-E1 1c
a. Die on India, mounted on white ivory
card
blue   1,75
b. Die on proof paper
gray black   1,25

dull scarlet	1,250.
dull brown	1,250.
dull green	1,250.
dull blue	1,250.

c. Die on white ivory paper
brown black	1,750.
orange red	1,750.
blue	1,750.

O48-E1

Design size: 19½x25mm
Complete engraving of entire design as adopted except with ...kson vignette instead of large numeral.

.8-E1   2c
a. Die on India, mounted on white ivory card
| orange brown | 1,500. |

b. Die on proof paper
gray black	1,250.
dull scarlet	1,250.
dull brown	1,250.
dull green	1,250.
dull blue	1,250.

c. Die on white ivory paper
brown black	1,750.
orange red	1,750.
blue	1,750.

O49-E1   O49-E2

Design size: 20x25mm
Engraved vignette, numeral and value label from 1873 3c ...o. 147-E10) mounted on pencil and wash drawing for frame ...sign not adopted for Post Office set.

.9-E1   3c Model on yellowish card, 23x30mm, on 90x118mm white card, black 5,750.

.9-E2   3c Model on yellowish card, 23x30mm, on 90x118mm white card, black 5,750.

O49-E3

Design size: 20x25mm
See design note for No. O2-E1.

.49-E3 3c Model on yellowish card, 23x30mm, on 90x118mm white card, black 5,750.

O49-E4

Design size: 19½x25mm
Complete engraving of entire design as adopted except with Washington vignette instead of large numeral.

.49-E4 3c
a. Die on India, mounted on white ivory card
| green | 1,500. |

---

b. Die on proof paper
gray black	1,250.
dull scarlet	1,250.
dull brown	1,250.
dull green	1,250.
dull blue	1,250.

c. Die on white ivory paper
brown black	1,750.
orange red	1,750.
blue	1,750.

O49-E5

1870 1c stamp (No. 145) with vignette cut out, "OFFICIAL 3 STAMP" drawn in pencil on envelope on which stamp is mounted. Blue pencil notations on backing envelope "1st design of official stamp for POD" and "Design by Mr. J. Barber for P O Official."

O49-E5 1c Stamp frame mounted on envelope, ultramarine frame, black vignette 7,500.

O49-E6   O49-E8

Model of engraved frame from No. O49-E4 with hollow oval engraved lathework band with "OFFICIAL / STAMP" drawn in wash mounted in place, numeral drawn in pencil and wash. Ms. "No. 1" on backing card.

O49-E6 3c Model on stiff white card, 50x75mm, green 7,500.

Like No. O49-E6, Ms. "No. 3" on backing card.

O49-E8 3c Model on stiff white card, 50x75mm, black 7,500.

O50-E1

Incomplete engraving of design with Lincoln vignette, without rectangular frame design.

O50-E1 6c Die on white ivory paper, black 4,250.

O56-E1

Design size: 19½x25mm
Complete engraving of entire design as adopted except with Perry vignette instead of large numeral.

O56-E1 90c
a. Die on India, mounted on white ivory card
brown	1,500.
blue	1,500.
orange red	1,500.

b. Die on proof paper
| gray black | 1,500. |
| dull scarlet | 1,500. |

---

dull brown	1,500.
dull green	1,500.
dull blue	1,500.

c. Die on white ivory paper
brown black	1,750.
orange red	1,750.
blue	1,750.

STATE

O59-E1   O68-E1

Design size: 20x25mm
Engraved vignette, numeral and value label from 1873 3c (No. 147-E10) mounted on pencil and wash drawing for frame design as adopted for State set. Pencil signature "J. Claxton" on backing card.

O59-E1 3c Model on yellowish card, 23x30mm, on 90x118mm white card, black 4,750.

Design size: 25½x40mm
Engraved vignette of Seward mounted in watercolor drawing of adopted frame design. Ms. signatures of J. Claxton and Chas. Skinner on backing card.

O68-E1 Two Dollars, Model on 29x43mm grayish white card, mounted on 96x120mm white card, black 7,500.

O68-E2

Complete engraving of adopted frame only with "TWO DOLLARS." in value label at bottom. With "FIVE DOLLARS." and "TEN DOLLARS." value labels outside design at left and "TWENTY DOLLs." value tablet at right.

O68-E2 Two Dollars, Die on India, black 8,750.

O68-E3

Plate engraved frame only (three examples in a block of four with complete bicolor plate proof of $2 at upper left in block).

O68-E3 Two Dollars, Plate essay on India, green 10,000.

O71-E1

Plate engraving of top half of frame only, paired with $20 plate proof.

O71-E1   Die on India, mounted on card, green   9,000.

WAR

O85-E1

Design size: 20x25mm
Engraved vignette, numeral and value label from 1873 3c (No. 147-E10) mounted on pencil and wash drawing for frame design as adopted for War set. Pencil signature "J. Claxton" on backing card.

O85-E1   3c Model on yellowish card,
             23x30mm, on 90x118mm white
             card, black   2,500.

NEWSPAPER AND PERIODICALS

1865 ISSUE
National Bank Note Co.

PR1-E1

Design size: 51x89mm
Typographed design somewhat similar to that adopted but with large Franklin vignette facing left, "PACKAGE" at bottom, other minor differences.

PR1-E1   5c Die on stiff white ivory paper
             deep orange red   2,000.
             dusky g-b. blue   2,000.
             bright blue   2,000.
          a. Die on paper with blue ruled lines
             deep orange red   2,000.
             carmine   2,000.

1875 ISSUE
National Bank Note Co.

PR5-E1

Design size: 52x96½mm

Typographed design as issued but lacking "National Bank Note Company, New York" imprint at bottom.

PR5-E1   5c Die on wove paper, blue

1875 ISSUE
Continental Bank Note Co.

PR9-E1   PR9-E2

Design size: 19½x25mm
Engraved vignette and numerals (25's) with pencil sketch unadopted frame design.

PR9-E1   25c Die on India, on card, black   2,7

Design size: 19½x25mm
Complete engraving of unadopted design with "U S" at and "25 CENTS 25" at bottom.

PR9-E2   25c
          a. Die on India, on card
             black   1,3
             scarlet   1,3
             blue   1,3
          b. Die on white ivory paper
             black   1,3
             black brown   1,3
             scarlet   1,3
             blue   1,3

PR14-E1   PR23-E1

Design size: 25x35mm
Wash drawing of complete design as adopted. Backing ca signed by both designers, Chas. Skinner and Jos. Claxton.

PR14-E1 9c Drawing on 26x36mm card, on
             56x74mm card, black   9

Design size: 24x35½mm
Wash drawing similar to that adopted, backing card signed designers Skinner and Claxton, also has pencil "$12" and n "Continental Bank Note Co."

PR23-E1 96c Drawing on 88x121mm card,
             black   9

PR27-E1   PR28-E1

Design size: 24½x35mm
Incomplete engraving of entire design: unshaded (shadi pencilled in) inside left, right and bottom framelines, value labe top of "9." Upper corners unfinished.

PR27-E1 $9 Die on India, die sunk on
             76x82mm card, black   1,35

Design size: 24½x35mm
Incomplete engraving of entire design: no shading on doll signs and numerals. No shading on frame around numerals an around value tablet.

PR28-E1 $12 Die on India, die sunk on
             66x80mm card, black   1,35

ESSAYS

693

...omplete engraving of entire design, shading pencilled in
...d bottom value tablet and top right and left dollar signs
...numerals.

...-E2 $12 Die on India, die sunk on card,
75x90mm, black —

PR29-E1

...sign size: 24x35½mm
...ash drawing similar to that adopted but with "U S" in six-
...ed stars instead of at top. Backing card signed by design-
...Skinner and Claxton, also pencil "31/32" and "8 13/32,"
...il "Alter" with lines to stars.

...9-E1 $24 Drawing on 88x121mm card,
black 750.

R31-E1 PR31-E2

...gnette size: 13½x26mm
...ngraved vignette only as adopted.

...1-E1 $48 Die on India, die sunk on card,
black 750.

...sign size: 24x36mm
...ash drawing similar to that adopted, backing card signed by
...gners Skinner and Claxton, also has pencil "$48" above
...n value numeral.

...1-E2 $48 Drawing on 88x121mm card,
black 1,350.

PR32-E1

...esign size: 24½x35½mm
...ash drawing similar to that adopted, backing card signed by
...igners Skinner and Claxton.

...2-E1 $60 Drawing on 88x121mm card,
black 750.

1885 ISSUE
American Bank Note Co.

PR81-E1

Design size: 23x25mm
Complete engraving of entire design as adopted for 12c-96c.

PR81-E1 1c
a. Die on India, die sunk on card
black 1,350.
b. Die on white ivory paper
black 600.
black brown 600.
scarlet 600.
blue 600.

1895 ISSUE
Bureau of Engraving and Printing

Incomplete engraving of entire design: background at upper
ends of value label, shading on side lettering and numerals
missing.

PR102-E2 1c Die on India, die sunk on card
black 900.
green 900.

Incomplete engraving of entire design but further engraved
than No. PR102-E2: shading on PA is light, no shading on PE of
NEWSPAPERS or IO of PERIODICALS and shading on OD is
light.

PR102-E3 1c Die on India, die sunk on card,
black 900.

Incomplete engraving of entire design but further engraved
than No. PR102-E3: shading on PERIODICALS is finished but
not on PAPE.

PR102-E4 1c Die on India, die sunk on card,
black 900.

PR103-E1 PR103-E2

Design size: 21½x34½mm
Die size: 56x75½mm
Incomplete engraving of entire design: spaces for numerals
and value label blank but with pencil outline of lettering.

PR103-E1 2c Die on India, die sunk on card,
black 1,500.

Incomplete engraving of entire design but further engraved
than No. PR103-E1: shading on leaves at ends of value label
unfinished, numerals unshaded, unfinished shading on APE of
NEWSPAPERS and RIO of PERIODICALS.

PR103-E2 2c Die on India, black 1,250.

Incomplete engraving of entire design but further engraved
than No. PR103-E2: no shading on PE of NEWSPAPERS,
unfinished shading on PA of NEWSPAPERS and RIO of
PERIODICALS.

PR103-E3 2c Die on India, die sunk on card,
black 1,250.

PR104-E1

Design size: 21½x34½mm
Die size: 57x73mm
Incomplete engraving of entire design: spaces for numerals
and value label blank but with pencil outline of lettering.

PR104-E1 5c Die on India, die sunk on card,
black 1,250.

PR105-E1 PR105-E2

Design size: 21½x34½mm
Die size: 56x75mm
Incomplete engraving of entire design: spaces for numerals
and value label blank but with pencil outline of lettering.

PR105-E1 10c Die on India, die sunk on card,
black 1,250.

Incomplete engraving of entire design but further engraved
than No. PR105-E1: numerals unfinished, lower corners blank.

PR105-E2 10c Die on India, die sunk on card,
black 1,500.

Incomplete engraving of entire design but further engraved
than No. PR105-E2: lower right corner blank.

PR105-E3 10c Die on India, die sunk on card,
black 1,250.

Incomplete engraving of entire design but further engraved
than No. PR105-E3: numerals blank, no inner lines.

PR105-E4 10c Die on India, die sunk on card,
black 1,250.

PR105-E5

Design size: 21½x34½mm
Die size: 56x75mm
Incomplete engraving of entire design (early state of die similar to No. PR105-E1) with "10" pencilled in upper right corner
and "TEN CENTS" pencilled in at bottom. Pencil notes on India
include "Make top of 1 a little larger and put on spur," "Work up
Vignette" and "Use same scrolls as marked on 5c-."

PR105-E5 10c Die on India, die sunk on card,
black 2,750.

PR106-E1 PR106-E2

Vignette size: 13x25½mm
Die size: 56x72mm
Incomplete engraving of vignette only (transfer of Continental
Banknote Co. die for 72c with left side cut off): eagle crest faces
front and its right wing is not pointed, shading on left thigh near
sword hilt incomplete, bottom of vignette straight instead of
curved.

PR106-E1 25c Die on India, die sunk on card
black 2,250.
deep red 2,250.

Design size: about 21x34½mm
Die size: 57½x75mm
Entire design with frame incompletely engraved: vert. lines
around CENTS label missing, no shading on TWENTY FIVE,
colorless beads under E and FI of same.

PR106-E2 25c Die on India, die sunk on card
black 2,250.
deep red 2,250.

An impression from No. PR106-E2 with pencil shading on TWENTY FIVE and vert. ink lines in spaces around CENTS label, colorless beads also blacked out in ink. Below engraving are three diff. pencil sketches for shape and shading to be engraved.

PR106-E3 25c Die on India, die sunk on card,
black 2,250.

An impression from No. PR106-E2 but with shading suggestions from No. PR106-E3 partly engraved except colorless beads have pencil shading only. Below engraving is pencil sketch for corner of CENTS label.

PR106-E4 25c Die on India, die sunk on card
black 2,250.
deep red 2,000.

PR106-E5

Design size: 21½x34½mm
Die size: 55x72mm
Large die proof of PR107 with bottom value label cut out and "TWENTY-FIVE CENTS" pencilled in on backing card.

PR106-E5 25c Die on India, die sunk on card,
black 1,250.

PR107-E1   PR107-E3

Incomplete engraving of entire design: eagle's head and much of bottom of stamp's design unfinished, top of frame unfinished, value lettering sketched in pencil.

PR107-E1 50c Die on India, die sunk on card,
black 1,750.

Incomplete engraving of entire design: top of frame and scrolls below FIFTY CENTS unfinished.

PR107-E3 50c Die on India, die sunk on card,
black 1,300.

PR108-E1   PR108-E2

Design size: 24½x37mm
Die size: 75x76mm
Incomplete engraving of entire design: vignette and spaces around numerals incomplete, pencil sketch instructions for engraver at top and side for these spaces.

PR108-E1 $2 Die on India, die sunk on card,
black 1,650.

Design size: 24½x37mm
Die size: 75x76mm
Incomplete engraving of entire design but further engraved than No. PR108-E1: space for ornaments under POSTAGE blank, numerals unshaded.

PR108-E2 $2 Die on India, die sunk on card,
scarlet 1,500.

Further engraved than No. PR108-E2: scrolls under POSTAGE engraved but unfinished.

PR108-E3 $2 Die on India, die sunk on card,
black 1,500.

Incomplete engraving of design, no frame line under "Postage" and other small differences from final design.

PR110-E1 $10 Die on India, green 1,500.

PR111-E1   PR112-E1

Design size (incomplete): 24½x30mm
Die size: 75x84mm
Incomplete engraving of partial design: spaces for stars and 0s of numerals blank, design missing below bottom of vignette.

PR111-E1 $20 Die on India, die sunk on card,
black 1,850.

Design size: 24½x35½mm
Die size: 72½x76mm
Incomplete engraving of entire design: upper corners around value numerals unfinished, etc.

PR112-E1 $50 Die on India, on card, black 1,850.

PR113-E1

Design size: 24½x35½mm
Die size: 75x74mm
Incomplete engraving of entire design: spaces at lower inner corners of value shields blank, shading on numerals and letters at top unfinished.

PR113-E1 $100 Die on India, on card, black 1,350.

Further engraved than No. PR113-E1: vignette completed but numerals not shaded, shadows on frame not etched dark.

PR113-E2 $100 Die on India
black 1,350.
red-violet 1,350.

Further engraved than No. PR113-E2: numerals shaded, shadows on frame not finally etched, especially above POSTAGE.

PR113-E3 $100 Die on India, black 1,350.

PARCEL POST STAMPS

Q1-E1

Design size: 35½x23mm
Photo of wash drawing of frame design with numerals, CENT and POST OFFICE CLERK in black ink, vignette in black wash. Ms. "Changed from 15c" and "Approved Nov. 15, 1912 — Frank H. Hitchcock — Postmaster General" on backing card.

Q1-E1 1c Model on thick gray card,
106x91mm, black 3,000.

Q2-E1

Design size: 35x23½mm
Photo of wash drawing of frame only as adopted. "Approved Oct. 10, 1912, for border and size of stamps. Er ing to be ⅞ by 1⅜ inches. Frank H Hitchcock Postm General" on backing card.

Q2-E1 2c Model on thick gray cardboard,
122x110mm, black

Q2-E2

Design size: 35x23mm
Photo of wash drawing of frame design and retouched p of ship vignette as eventually used for 10c, numerals STEAMSHIP AND MAIL TENDER in black ink. Ms. "Chang 10c" and "Approved Oct. 11, 1912. Frank H. Hitchcock. I master General" on backing card.

Q2-E2 2c Model on thick gray cardboard,
110x83mm, black 2,

Q2-E3

Design size: 34x22mm
Photo of wash drawing of entire design with adopted vign numerals in white wash and CITY CARRIER in black ink. "Changed from 5c" and "Approved Nov. 14, 1912. Fran Hitchcock. Postmaster General" on backing card.

Q2-E3 2c Model on thick gray cardboard,
111x92mm, black 2,

Design size: 34½x22mm
Engraving of adopted design with blank value tablets "CITY CARRIER" inscription, mail carrier unfinished.

Q2-E4 2c Die on India, sunk on 118x89mm
card, black

Q3-E1

Design size: 35x23mm
Complete engraving of unadopted design: vignette sh mail truck backing up to railroad mail train with clerk abou handle pouches.

Q3-E1 3c Die on white wove, about
43x31mm, carmine 2,(

Q3-E2

Design size: 35x22mm
Photo of wash drawing of entire design with adopted vign (retouched around door to mail car). Ms. "Approved Feb.

. Frank H. Hitchcock. Postmaster General" on backing
.

2   3c Model on thick gray cardboard,
     black   2,500.

Q3-E3

Design size: 35x22mm
most complete engraving of adopted design with subtle
rences (most evident in shading on windows), on
x76mm card, affixed with tape to 125x98mm card, small
ut in design, blue control No. 578444 on back.

E3   3c Die sunk on card, affixed to card,
      carmine   2,500.

Q4-E1

esign size: 33½x22mm
hoto of wash drawing of entire design with adopted vignette,
nerals drawn in white and RURAL CARRIER in black ink.
"Changed from 10c" and "Approved Nov. 14, 1912. Frank
Hitchcock. Postmaster General" on backing card.

E1   4c Model on thick gray cardboard,
      116x92mm, black   2,500.

Q5-E1

Design size: 35x23mm
Photo of wash drawing of entire design with vignette
touched) eventually used for 2c, numerals and CITY LET-
R CARRIER in black ink and white wash. Ms. "Changed to
—City Carrier" and "Approved Oct. 10, 1912. Frank H. Hitch-
k. Postmaster General" on backing card.

E1   5c Model on thick gray cardboard,
      110x84mm, black   2,500.

Q5-E2

Design size: 33½x21½mm
Photo of wash drawing of entire design with numerals in gray,
adopted vignette with MAIL TRAIN in black ink, first car
touched with wash. Ms. "Approved . . . 1912 / . . . Postmaster
neral" on backing card.

-E2   5c Model on thick gray cardboard,
      104½x92mm, black   2,500.

Q5-E3

Design size: 33½x22mm

Photo of wash drawing of entire design with numerals in gray,
MAIL TRAIN in black ink, first car retouched with wash. Ms.
"Approved . . . 1912 / . . . Postmaster General" on backing card.

Q5-E3   5c Model on thick gray cardboard,
         104½x92mm, black   2,500.

Q5-E4

Design size: 33½x22mm
Photo of wash drawing of entire design with numerals in white
with black background, MAIL TRAIN and pouch catcher in black
ink. Ms. "Approved Nov. 19, 1912 Frank H. Hitchcock Postmaster General" on backing card.

Q5-E4   5c Model on thick gray cardboard,
         94x90mm, black   2,500.

Q6-E1

Design size: 35½x23mm
Photo of wash drawing of entire design with vignette
(retouched) eventually used for 4c, numerals and RURAL
DELIVERY in black ink and white wash. Ms. "Changed to 4c."
and "Approved Oct. 10, 1912. Frank H. Hitchcock. Postmaster
General" on backing card.

Q6-E1   10c Model on thick gray cardboard,
         111x83mm, black   2,500.

Q6-E2

Design size: 35x23mm
Photo of wash drawing of entire design with adopted vignette,
numerals and STEAMSHIP AND MAIL TENDER in black ink
and white wash. Ms. "Changed from 2c." and "Approved Nov. 8,
1912. Frank H. Hitchcock. Postmaster General" on backing
card.

Q6-E2   10c Model on thick gray cardboard,
         116x92mm, black   2,500.

Q7-E1

Design size: 33½x22mm
Photo of wash drawing of entire design (redrawn in front of
autocar and U S MAIL and STATION A) with AUTOMOBILE
SERVICE in black ink. Ms. "Approved . . . 1912 / . . . Postmaster
General" on backing card.

Q7-E1   15c Model on thick gray cardboard,
         115x93mm, black   1,500.

Design size:
Complete engraving of entire design with unadopted title
label "COLLECTION SERVICE" instead of the adopted "AUTO-
MOBILE SERVICE."

Q7-E2   15c Die on white wove, card mounted,
         carmine   1,500.

Q8-E1

Design size: 35x22mm
Incomplete engraved design nearly as adopted: aviator wears
football helmet, head tilted far forward and one leg dangling
over edge of plane, mail bag "No. 1" at his right while another
sack hangs loosely out of plane.

Q8-E1   20c Die on white wove, about
         37x24mm, carmine   1,500.

Q8-E2

Design size: 35x22mm
Photo of incomplete engraved design as adopted. Ms.
"Approved Nov. 19, 1912. Frank H. Hitchcock. Postmaster Gen-
eral" on backing card.

Q8-E2   20c Model on thick gray cardboard,
         98x95mm, black   2,500.

Q9-E1

Design size: 34½x22½mm
Photo of wash drawing of entire design with numerals and
smoke at right painted in. Ms. "Changed from $1.00." and
"Approved Nov. 14, 1912. Frank H. Hitchcock. Postmaster General" on backing card.

Q9-E1   25c Model on thick gray cardboard,
         112x92mm, black   2,500.

Q10-E1

Design size: 35x23mm
Photo of drawing of entire design with vignette eventually
used for 25c with roof, smokestacks and smoke drawn in. Typed
label "Stamp Division / Feb / 21 / 1912 / P.O. Dept" on back of
backing paper.

Q10-E1   50c Model on thick white paper, black   1,500.

Q10-E2

Design size: 33x21½mm
Photo of wash drawing of frame design with vignette cut out,
mounted over photo of wash drawing of unadopted vignette
design, retouched with wash on cows, etc., with DAIRYING in
black ink. Pencil "Original" and ms. "Approved . . . 1912 / . . .
Postmaster General" on backing card.

Q10-E2   50c Model on thick gray cardboard,
          98x93mm, black   1,500.

Q10-E3

Design size: 35x23mm
Complete engraving of entire design with unadopted vignette: silo and barns placed closer to front of design.

Q10-E3 50c Die on white wove, about
43x31mm, carmine   *1,500.*

Q10-E4

Design size: 35x22mm
Photo of incomplete engraved design: no vert. lines on frame around corner foliate spandrels or in numeral circles. Ms. "Approved Jan. 8, 1913. Frank H. Hitchcock. Postmaster General" on backing card.

Q10-E4 50c Model on thick gray cardboard,
99x94mm, black   *2,500.*

Q11-E1

Design size: 33½x21½mm
Photo of wash drawing of entire design with central horses and thresher retouched. Ms. "Approved Dec. 12, 1912. Frank H. Hitchcock. Postmaster General" on backing card.

Q11-E1 75c Model on thick gray cardboard,
108x89mm, black   *2,500.*

Q12-E1

Photo of wash drawing of entire design with vignette much retouched in black ink, numerals, MANUFACTURING and DOLLAR drawn in black ink and white wash. Ms. "Changed to 25c" and "Approved Oct. 22, 1912. Frank H. Hitchcock. Postmaster General" on backing card.

Q12-E1 $1 Model on thick gray cardboard,
114x86mm, black   *2,500.*

Q12-E2

Design size: 35x22mm
Photo of wash drawing of complete design with DOLLAR painted in white and black and FRUIT GROWING in black ink, vignette retouched with wash on fruit pickers. Ms. "Approved . . . 1912 . . . Postmaster General" on backing card.

Q12-E2 $1 Model on thick gray cardboard,
105x94mm, black   *1,500.*

Q12-E3

Design size: 36x23½mm
Incomplete engraving of entire design: no shading lines in sky. This may be from a rejected die.

Q12-E3 $1 Die on white wove, about
43x31mm, carmine   *1,500.*

Q12a-E1

Engraving of entire design as adopted for 1917 offset Documentary Revenues, etc., but with "U.S. PARCEL POST" around value oval.

Q12a-E1	1c	Die on card, green	*1,000.*
Q12b-E1	2c	Die on card, carmine	*1,000.*
Q12c-E1	3c	Die on card, deep violet	*1,000.*
Q12d-E1	4c	Die on card, brown	*1,000.*
Q12e-E1	5c	Die on card, blue	*1,000.*
Q12f-E1	10c	Die on card, orange yellow	*1,000.*
Q12g-E1	15c	Die on card, gray	*1,000.*
Q12h-E1	20c	Die on wove, carmine rose, affixed to card	*1,500.*

PARCEL POST POSTAGE DUE

Retouched photo of design as adopted, officially dated and approved.

QJQ5-E1a 25c Model, black   *1,500.*

CARRIER'S STAMPS

Essays by Toppan, Carpenter, Casilear & Co. in 1851

LO1-E1

Unfinished die with lathework impinging on white oval and framelines complete at top and bottom, plus uncleaned horizontal and vertical layout lines.

1851
LO1-E1   (1c) Die on 34x42mm,
white bond, black   *10,000.*

LO1-E1A

Die size: 57x50mm

Unfinished die distinguished by having top and bottom f lines, lathework impinging on white oval, and rosettes in l right corner.

LO1-E1A   (1c) Die on 62x54mm,
pale green bond,
red   4,

Essays by Schernikow in 1903 from a new s steel die made from the original 1851 transf roll.
See note above No. 63-E1.

LO1-E2   LO1-E3

Die size: 50x50mm
Engraving of Franklin vignette only.

1903
LO1-E2   (1c)
  a. Die on proof paper
    black
    carmine
    red
    light red
    orange
    orange brown
    yellow
    olive
    green
    dark green
    dark blue
    violet
    violet brown
  b. Die on colored card, about
    75x75mm
    deep red, *pinkish white*
    yellow brown, *pale blue*
    violet brown, *pale green*
    dark green, *pale pink*
    dark blue, *pale pink*
    violet, *pale yellow*
  c. Die on green bond (die size:
    49x50mm)
    dull scarlet
    dull olive
    dark ultramarine

Design size: 19½x25mm
Die size: 50x50mm
Design as No. LO1-E1, but distinguished by addition of and right inner frame lines.

1903
LO1-E3   (1c)
  a. Die on proof paper
    black
    carmine
    dark carmine
    scarlet
    orange
    yellow
    yellow brown
    olive
    light green
    green
    steel blue
    violet
    red violet
    violet brown
    ultramarine
  b. Die on colored card
    dull carmine, *pale olive*
    brown orange, *pink*
    brown, *pale buff*
    brown, *pale blue*
    gray green, *buff*
    gray green, *yellow*
    violet, *ivory*
    dull carmine, *pale blue*
  c. Die on blue pelure
    carmine
    scarlet
    orange
    brown
    dark green
  d. Die on green bond
    scarlet
    orange
    green
    dull violet

Essays by Clarence Brazer in 1952 using the Schernikow complete die with addition of two diagonal lines in upper right corner.

Die size: 50x50mm

2

(1c) Die on glazed card

scarlet	500.
brown	500.
green	500.
red	500.

POST OFFICE SEALS

Registry Seals
1872 ISSUE
National Bank Note Co.

esign size: 72x40mm
ock size: 100x56½mm

pographed design similar to that adopted but inscription
MP HERE DATE AND PLACE OF MAILING around central
lar disk is in colorless capitals, remainder of lettering in
colors without shading lines. The word REGISTERED
erates other words where it touches them.

¹-E1
  a. Block impression on white card,
    brown   2,000.
  b. Die on India, dark brown   —

imilar to No. OXF1-E1 except REGISTERED appears to be
er other words it touches and does not obliterate them, as in
gn adopted.

¹-E2
  a. Block impression on white paper,
    card mounted, brown   2,000.
  b. Block impression on large card
    brown   2,000.
    red   2,000.
    yellow   2,000.

imilar to adopted type but circular disk in center has a
und of concentric circles, REGISTERED without colorless
ding and obliterates other words where it touches them.

F1-E3   Block impression on white card,
    red violet   —

LO1-E4 — OXF1-E4

Similar to adopted design except REGISTERED obliterates
er words where it touches them; colored shading as
pted.

F1-E4
  a. Block on India, on card
    carmine   1,000.
    yellow   1,000.
    blue   1,000.
    green   1,000.
    red brown   1,000.
    rose   1,000.
    brown orange   1,000.
  b. Block on India, printed in two colors
    top dark green, bottom light green   1,000.
    left half blue, right half green   1,000.
  c. Block sunk on white card, colored
    border around stamp (full size
    57x100mm)
    deep carmine   1,000.
    brown orange   1,000.
    brown   1,000.
    light green   1,000.
    blue   1,000.
  d. Block sunk on white wove, colorless
    border, stamp size, imperf., dim
    dusky blue   1,000.
  e. As "d," perf. 12, gummed, dim dusky
    blue   1,000.

OXF1-E5

Block size: 80x128mm

Engraving of entire design as adopted but in reverse for making typographed block.

OXF1-E5   Die on white wove, chocolate   1,000.

Post Office Seals
1877 ISSUE

OX1-E3

Design size: 45x27½mm
Incomplete engraving of entire design: no shading lines on 2mm-wide border frame, no cap or background in vignette.

OX1-E3   Die on India, on card, orange brown   1,000.

DIE AND PLATE PROOFS

PROOFS are known in many styles other than those noted in this section. For the present, however, listings are restricted to die proofs, large small, and plate proofs on India paper and card, and occasionally on stamp paper. The listing of normal color proofs includes several that d somewhat from the types and colors of the issued stamps.

Large Die Proofs are so termed because of the relatively large piece of paper on which they are printed which is about the size of the die bl 40mm by 50mm or larger. The margins of this group of proofs usually are from 15mm to 20mm in width though abnormal examples prevent acceptance of these measurements as a complete means of identification.

These proofs were prepared in most cases by the original contracting companies and 19th century issues often show the imprint thereof and let and numbers of identification. They are listed under "DIE-Large (1)." The India paper on which these proofs are printed is of an uneven texture an some respects resembles hand-made paper. These large die proofs were usually mounted on cards though many are found removed from the c Large Die Proofs autographed by the engraver or officially approved are worth much more, except for those of the 1922-29 period, which are gene approved and signed proofs.

Values for Large Die Proofs are for the full die proots mounted on cards unless noted otherwise. Full large die proofs measure 5 6" x 7 8". Cut-dc Large Die Proofs sell for less. Values for die proofs of the bicolored 1869 issue are for examples which are completely printed. Occasionally the vign has been cut out and affixed to an impression of the border.

Die Proofs of all United States stamps of later issues exist. Only those known outside of government ownership are listed.

Small Die Proofs are so called because of the small piece of paper on which they are printed. Proofs of stamps issued prior to 1904, are repri and not in all cases from the same dies as the large die proofs.

Small Die Proofs (Roosevelt Album, "DIE-Small (2)") — These 302 small die proofs are from sets prepared for 85 ("Roosevelt presentatic albums in 1903 by the Bureau of Engraving and Printing but bear no imprint to this effect. The white wove paper on which they are printed is of a fibre nature. The margins are small, seldom being more than from 3-5mm in width. Values are for proofs affixed to the original gray card backing from Roosevelt album. Proofs without the card backing sell for less.

Small Die Proofs (Panama-Pacific Issue, "DIE-Small (2a)") — A special printing of 413 different small die proofs was made in 1915 for Panama-Pacific Exposition. These have small margins (2½-3mm) and are on soft yellowish wove paper. They are extremely scarce as only 3-5 of e are known and a few exist only in this special printing. 6-10 exist of No. E6 in two slightly different colors.

Plate Proofs are, quite obviously, impressions taken from finished plates and differ from the stamps themselves chiefly in their excellence impression and the paper on which they are printed. Some of the colors vary.

Hybrids are plate proofs of all issues before 1894 which have been cut to shape, mounted and pressed on large cards to resemble large proc These sell for somewhat less than the corresponding large die proofs.

India Paper is a thin, soft, opaque paper which wrinkles when wet. It varies in thickness and shows particles of bamboo.

Card is a plain, clear white card of good quality, which is found in varying thicknesses for different printings. Plate proofs on card were made in printings in 1879-94. Quantities range from 500 to 3,200 of the card proofs listed between Scott 3P and 245P.

Margin blocks with full imprint and plate number are indicated by the abbreviation "P# blk. of -."

Numbers have been assigned to all proofs consisting of the number of the regular stamp with the suffix letter "P" to denote Proof.

Proofs in other than accepted or approved colors exist in a large variety of shades, colors and papers produced at various times by various people many different reasons. The field is large. The task of listing has been begun under "Trial Colors" following the regular proofs.

Some proofs are not identical to the issued stamps. Some of these are now listed in the Essay section. Others have been left in the proof sectior keep sets together at this time.

Values are for items in very fine condition. Most "Panama-Pacific" small die proofs are toned. Values are for moderately toned examples. **Plate pro pairs on stamp paper are valued with original gum unless otherwise noted.**

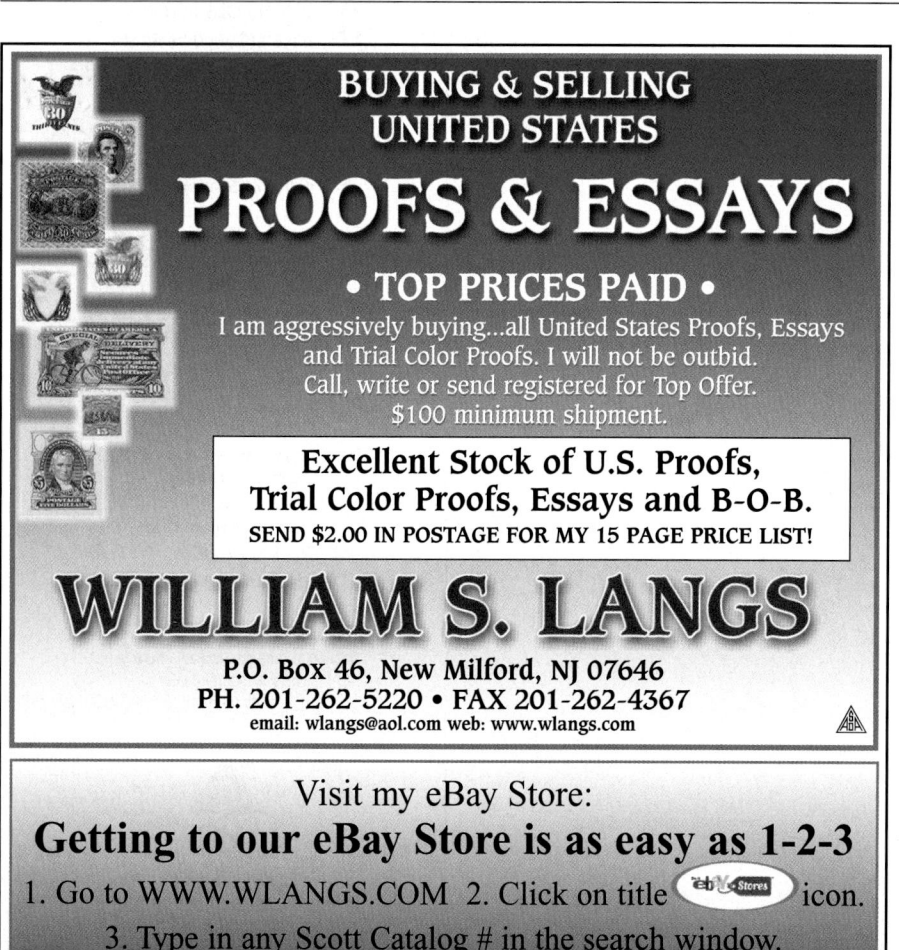
NORMAL COLORS

1845   New Y

			DIE		PLAT
		(1)	(2)		(3)
		Large	Small	(2a)	India C
9X1P	5c black on India paper	750.	350.		—
a.	With scar on neck		300.		
b.	Dot in "P" of "POST" and scar on neck	525.	300.		
c.	As "b," on Bond	525.	300.		
d.	As "b," on glazed paper	525.			
e.	As "a," on Bond	525.			

The above listed Large Die varieties have an additio impression of the portrait medallion. Some experts question existance of plate proofs from the sheets of 40. Plate pro from the sheet of 9 exist on white and bluish bond paper. Va $125.

Providence, R.I.

10X1P	5c black		3
10X2P	10c black		5
	Sheet of 12		3,2

General Issues

1847

1P	5c red brown on India paper	800.	600.
a.	White bond paper	800.	
b.	Colored bond paper	1,000.	
c.	White laid paper	800.	
d.	Bluish laid paper	800.	
e.	Yellowish wove paper	800.	
f.	Bluish wove paper	800.	
g.	White wove paper	800.	
h.	Card	1,000.	
i.	Glazed paper	1,000.	
2P	10c black on India paper Double transfer (31R1)	800.	900.
a.	White bond paper	800.	
b.	Colored bond paper	1,000.	
c.	White laid paper	800.	
d.	Bluish laid paper	800.	
e.	Yellowish wove paper	800.	
g.	White wove paper	800.	
h.	Card	1,000.	
i.	Glazed paper	1,000.	

Original die proofs are generally found cut to stamp size; f size die proofs sell at higher prices. Reprint proofs with cros hatching are valued as full size; cut down examples sell for les Plate proofs overprinted "Specimen" sell for about half th above figures.

Reproductions of 1847 Issue

ually, official imitations made about 1875 from new dies lates by order of the Post Office Department.

		(1)	(2)	(2a)	(3)	(4)

5c red brown 900. 425. 2,750. 225. 200.
Block of 4 1,200. 750.
a. On bond paper 650.
10c black 900. 425. 2,750. 225. 200.
Block of 4 1,200. 750.
a. On bond paper 650.

-60

1c blue, type I 5,000.
3c red, type I 5,000.
brush obliteration 1,000.
Block of 4 5,000.
P# block of 8 20,000.
5c brn, type I 7,500. 2,000.
10c grn, type I 5,000.
12c black 10,000.
1c blue, type V (pl. 9) 1,250.
Pair 3,000.
3c red, type II (pl. 20) 1,250.
Pair 3,000.
5c brn, type II 1,250.
10c grn, type V 1,250.
12c black, plate III (broken frame lines) 1,250.
Block of 4 5,500.
d. On stamp paper —
Pair —
Block of 4 —
24c lilac — 1,250.
Pair 3,000.
c. On stamp paper 1,500.
Pair 15,500.
30c orange — — 1,250.
Pair 3,000.
a. On stamp paper 2,500.
Pair 7,750.
90c blue — — 1,250.
Pair 3,000.
a. On stamp paper 2,750.
Pair 37,500.

ate proofs of 24P to 39P are from the original plates. They be distinguished from the 40P to 47P by the type in the e of the 1c, 3c, 10c and 12c, and by the color in the case of 5c, 24c, 30c and 90c.

he 3c plate proofs (No. 11) are on proof paper and all known ies have a vertical brush stroke obliteration.

ie proofs of the 30c show full spear point in corners of gn.

		DIE			PLATE	
		(1) Large	(2) Small	(2a)	(3) India	(4) Card

Reprints of 1857-60 Issue

P 1c bright blue, type I (new plate) 325. 350. 1,750. 80. 75.
Block of 4 400. 300.
a. On stamp paper 750.
P 3c scarlet, type I (new plate) 325. 350. 1,750. 80. 50.
Block of 4 400. 250.
Orange brown 2,500.
P 5c orange brown type II (plate II) 325. 350. 80. 50.
Block of 4 400. 250.
P# blk. of 8 1,050. —
P 10c blue green, type I (new plate) 325. 350. 1,750. 80. 50.
Block of 4 400. 250.
P 12c greenish black (new plate, frame line complete) 325. 350. 2,500. 110. 50.
Block of 4 550. 250.
24c blksh vio (pl. I) 325. 350. 1,750. 80. 50.
Block of 4 400. 250.
P# blk. of 8 1,050.
30c yel org (pl. I) 325. 350. 1,750. 80. 50.
Block of 4 400. 250.
P# blk. of 8 1,050. —
90c deep blue (pl. I) 325. 350. 1,750. 110. 75.
Block of 4 550. 375.
P# blk. of 8 1,150. 1,050.

Nos. 42P2-44P2 were printed from original dies, and the 5c ows type I projections at top and bottom.
Nos. 40P-47P, large die, exist only as hybrids.

SECOND DESIGNS (Regular Issue)

For "First Designs" see Essay section (former Nos. 55-57, 59,), Proofs and Trial Color Proofs (former No. 58) and Trial lor Proofs (former Nos. 60-61).

1861

62BP 10c dark green 325. 325.
63P 1c blue 700. 225. 2,000. 55. 40.
Block of 4 225. 250.
P# blk. of 8 1,100.
Indigo 2,000.
64P 3c pink 3,500. —
65P 3c rose 1,000. — 1,750. 100. 130.
Block of 4 550.
P# blk. of 8 1,400.
a. 3c dull red 100.
c. On stamp paper, pair 1,000.
P# blk. of 8 —
67P 5c buff 5,000. 1,750.
76P 5c brown 700. 225. 1,750. 45. 30.
Block of 4 225. 140.
P# blk. of 8 875.
68P 10c green 650. 225. 1,750. 65. 30.
Block of 4 300. 140.
P# blk. of 8 950.
69P 12c black 700. 225. 2,000. 65. 30.
Block of 4 300. 140.
P# blk. of 8 950.
70P 24c red lilac — 2,750. 500.
78P 24c lilac 225. 2,750. 80. 75.
Block of 4 400. 375.
P# blk. of 8 1,200.
71P 30c orange 500. 225. 2,750. 50. 30.
Block of 4 250. 140.
P# blk. of 8 1,100.
72P 90c blue 500. 225. 2,750. 50. 30.
Block of 4 225. 140.
P# blk. of 8 1,100.

1861-67

73P 2c black, die I 10,000. 150.
Block of 4 750.
P# blk. of 8 2,000. —
a. Die II 2,500. 1,350. 8,750. 110. 75.
Block of 4 550. 400.
P# blk. of 8 1,500.
77P 15c black 1,250. 500. 2,750. 55. 45.
Block of 4 250. 200.
P# blk. of 8 950.
79P 3c rose, A grill, on stamp paper, pair 1,500.
Block of 4 4,000.
P# blk. of 8 10,000.
83P 3c rose, C grill, on stamp paper, pair 1,850.
94P 3c red, F grill, on stamp paper, pair 1,500.

The listed plate proofs of the 1c (63P), 5c (76P), 10c (68P) and 12c (69P) are from the 100 subject re-issue plates of 1875. Single proofs of these denominations from the regular issue plates cannot be told apart from the reprints. As the reprint plates had wider spacing between the subjects, multiples can be differentiated. Values are for proofs from the reprint plates. The 2c Die II has a small dot on the left cheek.

1869

112P 1c buff 750. 350. 2,000. 55. 65.
Block of 4 250. 300.
P# blk. of 10 750.
113P 2c brown 750. 350. 2,000. 40. 50.
Block of 4 175. 225.
P# blk. of 10 600. —
114P 3c ultra. 900. 575. 2,000. 45. 85.
Block of 4 190. 375.
P# blk. of 10 800. —
115P 6c ultra. 900. 350. 2,000. 45. 85.
Block of 4 190. 375.
P# blk. of 10 800. —
116P 10c yellow 900. 350. 2,000. 45. 55.
Block of 4 190. 250.
P# blk. of 10 800. —
117P 12c green 900. 350. 2,000. 45. 55.
Block of 4 190. 265.
P# blk. of 10 875. —
119P 15c brown & blue (type II) 550. 450. 2,000. 120.
Block of 4 600.
P# blk. of 8 1,450.
129P 15c Reissue (type III) 550. 450. 2,000. 250. 140.
Block of 4 1,200. 725.
P# blk. of 8 3,000. —
a. Center inverted (100) 2,500.
Block of 4 11,000.
P# blk. of 8 37,500.
120P 24c green & violet 550. 450. 2,000. 140. 140.
Block of 4 625. 650.
P# blk. of 8 1,450.
a. Center inverted (100) 2,750.
Block of 4 12,000.
P# blk. of 8 37,500.
121P 30c ultra & carmine 1,250. 450. 2,000. 140. 170.
Block of 4 625. 875.
P# blk. of 8 1,450.
a. Flags inverted (100) 2,750.
Block of 4 12,000.
P# blk. of 8 37,500.

122P 90c carmine & black 550. 450. 2,000. 180. 170.
Block of 4 825. 875.
P# blk. of 8 1,750. —
a. Center inverted (100) 2,750.
Block of 4 14,000.
P# blk. of 8 37,500.

Large die proofs of Nos. 119, 129, 120 and 122 exist only as hybrids.

1880

133P 1c dark buff 1,000. 100.
Block of 4 450.
P# blk. of 10 1,250.

1870-71 National Bank Note Co.

136P 3c green, grill, on stamp paper, pair 1,200.
P# blk. of 12 —
145P 1c ultra 250. 175. 1,200. 20.
Block of 4 90.
P# blk. of 12 385.
146P 2c red brown 250. 20.
Block of 4 90.
P# blk. of 12 385.
147P 3c green 300. 20.
Block of 4 90.
P# blk. of 12 —

The former No. 147Pc4 is now listed in the Essay section as No. 147-E13e.

148P 6c carmine 450. 35.
Block of 4 150.
P# blk. of 12 650.
149P 7c vermilion 200. 15.
Block of 4 70.
P# blk. of 12 360.
150P 10c brown 300. 40.
Block of 4 165.
P# blk. of 12 750.
151P 12c violet 200. 16.
Block of 4 70.
P# blk. of 12 385.
152P 15c orange 250. 30.
Block of 4 135.
P# blk. of 12 550.
153P 24c purple 250. 30.
Block of 4 135.
P# blk. of 12 550.
154P 30c black 250. 40.
Block of 4 170.
P# blk. of 12 750.
155P 90c carmine 250. 45.
Block of 4 195.

P# blk. of 12   800.

Secret Marks on 24, 30 and 90c Dies of the Bank Note Issues

National 24c — Rays of lower star normal.   Continental 24c — Rays of lower star strengthened.

National 30c — Lower line does not join point of shield.

Continental and American 30c — Lower line joins point of shield and bottom line of shield thicker.

National 90c — Rays of star in upper right normal.   Continental and American 90c — Rays of star in upper right strengthened.

1873   Continental Bank Note Co.

			(1) Large	DIE (2) Small	(2a)	PLATE (3) India	(4) Card
156P	1c	ultra	450.			55.	150.
		Block of 4				250.	
		P# blk. of 14				1,150.	
157P	2c	brown	350.	175.	1,200.	35.	15.
		Block of 4				165.	80.
		P# blk. of 12				650.	—
a.		On stamp paper					—
158P	3c	green	350.	175.	1,200.	55.	150.
		Block of 4				250.	
		P# blk. of 14				1,150.	
f.		On stamp paper, pair					750.
g.		On stamp paper, grill, pair					650.
159P	6c	pink	750.	250.	1,400.	110.	200.
		Block of 4				525.	
		P# blk. of 12				2,000.	
160P	7c	orange vermilion	250.	175.	1,200.	35.	10.
		Block of 4				165.	50.
		P# blk. of 14				825.	—
161P	10c	brown	450.	200.	1,200.	60.	150.
		Block of 4				300.	
		P# blk. of 14				1,300.	
162P	12c	blackish violet	200.	175.	1,200.	38.	20.
		Block of 4				190.	100.
		P# blk. of 14				975.	—
a.		On stamp paper					—
163P	15c	yellow orange	400.	175.	1,200.	65.	20.
		Block of 4				250.	100.
		P# blk. of 12				1,000.	—
a.		On stamp paper					—
164P	24c	violet	400.	175.	1,200.	50.	30.
		Block of 4				225.	140.
		P# blk. of 12				975.	
165P	30c	gray black	400.	175.	1,200.	40.	20.
		Block of 4				200.	90.

			(1) Large	DIE (2) Small	(2a)	PLATE (3) India	(4) Card
		P# blk. of 12				825.	
166P	90c	rose carmine	400.	175.	1,200.	55.	40.
		Block of 4				250.	190.
		P# blk. of 12				1,000.	

Die proofs of the 24c, 30c and 90c show secret marks, as illustrated, but as plates of these denominations were not made from these dies, plate proofs can be identified only by color.

178P	2c	vermilion	—				
a.		On stamp paper, pair					600.
		P# blk. of 12					—
179P	5c	blue	—				

1879   American Bank Note Co.

182P	1c	gray blue	525.			60.	
		Block of 4				275.	
		P# blk. of 12				1,000.	
183P	2c	vermilion	300.	190.	1,200.	35.	20.
		Block of 4				160.	100.
		P# blk. of 12				600.	—
184P	3c	green on stamp paper, pair					400.
		P# blk. of 12					—
185P	5c	blue	450.	225.	1,200.	70.	25.
		Block of 4				325.	110.
		P# blk. of 12				1,300.	—
190P	30c	full black				—	150.
		Block of 4				—	600.
		P# blk. of 12					2,000.
191P	90c	carmine on stamp paper, pair					2,500.
		P# strip of 5					—

1881-82   American Bank Note Co.

205P	5c	yellow brown	250.	190.	1,200.	40.	15.
		Block of 4				175.	75.
		P# blk. of 12				600.	—
206P	1c	blue	375.	190.	1,200.	40.	20.
		Block of 4				175.	90.
		P# blk. of 12				600.	—
207P	3c	blue green	375.	190.	1,200.	40.	20.
		Block of 4				175.	90.
		P# blk. of 12				600.	—
208P	6c	rose	800.	190.	1,200.	90.	60.
		Block of 4				425.	210.
		P# blk. of 12					—
a.		6c brown red				1,200. 100.	50.
209P	10c	brown	800.	190.	1,200.	90.	25.
		Block of 4				170.	110.
		P# blk. of 12				650.	—

1883

210P	2c	red brown	400.	190.	1,200.	32.	20.
		Block of 4				145.	85.
		P# blk. of 12				600.	—
a.		On stamp paper, pair					—
211P	4c	green	500.	190.	1,200.	40.	25.
		Block of 4				165.	110.
		P# blk. of 12				750.	—
a.		On stamp paper, pair					—

1887-88

212P	1c	ultra	650.	190.	1,200.	125.	2,000.
		Block of 4				600.	
		P# blk. of 12				2,250.	
a.		On stamp paper, pair					1,000.

Copies of No. 212P3 mounted on card are frequently offered as No. 212P4.

213P	2c	green	450.	190.	1,200.	75.	50.
		Block of 4				325.	225.
		P# blk. of 12				1,150.	—
a.		On stamp paper, pair					750.
214P	3c	vermilion	475.	190.	1,200.	75.	50.
		Block of 4				325.	225.
		P# blk. of 12				—	—

Nos. 207P1 & 214P1 inscribed: "Worked over by new company, June 29th, 1881."

215P	4c	carmine	600.	190.	1,200.	95.	50.
		Block of 4				475.	225.
		P# blk. of 12					—
216P	5c	indigo	600.	190.	1,200.	75.	50.
		Block of 4				325.	225.
		P# blk. of 12					—
b.		On stamp paper, pair					1,400.
217P	30c	orange brown	625.	190.	1,200.	75.	50.
		Block of 4				325.	225.
		P# blk. of 10					—
a.		On stamp paper, pair					1,750.
218P	90c	purple	625.	190.	1,200.	90.	50.
		Block of 4				400.	225.
		P# blk. of 10					—
a.		On stamp paper, pair					—

1890-93

219P	1c	ultra	225.	190.	1,100.	25.	40.
		Block of 4				110.	180.
		P# blk. of 12				500.	650.
c.		On stamp paper, pair					190.

219DP	2c	lake	550.	190.	1,100.	80.	
		Block of 4					385.
		P# blk. of 12					1,650.
e.		On stamp paper, pair					
220P	2c	carmine	450.	190.		300.	
		Block of 4					1,250.
		P# blk. of 12					3,850.
d.		On stamp paper, pair					
		As "d," without gum					
		P# blk. of 12					
221P	3c	purple	225.	190.	1,100.	35.	
		Block of 4					160.
		P# blk. of 12					650.
a.		On stamp paper, pair					
222P	4c	dark brown	225.	190.	1,100.	35.	
		Block of 4					160.
		P# blk. of 12					650.
a.		On stamp paper, pair					
223P	5c	chocolate	225.	190.	1,100.	32.	
		Block of 4					135.
		P# blk. of 12					600.
b.		Yellow brown, on stamp paper, pair					
224P	6c	brown red	225.	190.	1,100.	35.	
		Block of 4					135.
		P# blk. of 12					600.
a.		On stamp paper, pair					
225P	8c	lilac	600.	190.	1,100.	55.	
		Block of 4					250.
		P# blk. of 12					1,100.
a.		On stamp paper, pair					
226P	10c	green	225.	190.	1,100.	45.	
		Block of 4					200.
		P# blk. of 12					700.
a.		On stamp paper, pair					
227P	15c	indigo	300.	190.	1,100.	45.	
		Block of 4					190.
		P# blk. of 12					825.
a.		On stamp paper, pair					
228P	30c	black	300.	190.	1,100.	45.	
		Block of 4					190.
		P# blk. of 12					825.
a.		On stamp paper, pair					
229P	90c	orange	300.	190.	1,100.	60.	
		Block of 4					275.
		P# blk. of 12					1,100.
a.		On stamp paper, pair					

COLUMBIAN ISSUE

1893

230P	1c	blue	700.	325.	1,400.	40.	
		Block of 4					175.
		P# blk. of 8					400.
231P	2c	violet	800.	350.	1,750.	225.	
		Block of 4					1,000.
		P# blk. of 8					2,250.
b.		On stamp paper, pair					
c.		"Broken hat" variety					

Almost all examples of No. 231Pb are faulty. Value is for with minimal faults.

232P	3c	green	700.	325.	2,000.	60.	
		Block of 4					260.
		P# blk. of 8					675.
233P	4c	ultra.	700.	325.	2,000.	60.	
		Block of 4					260.
		P# blk. of 8					675.
233aP	4c	blue (error) on thin card	2,750.				
234P	5c	chocolate	700.	325.	2,000.	60.	
		Block of 4					260.
		P# blk. of 8					675.
235P	6c	purple	700.	325.	2,000.	60.	
		Block of 4					260.
		P# blk. of 8					675.
236P	8c	magenta	700.	325.	2,000.	60.	
		Block of 4					260.
		P# blk. of 8					675.
237P	10c	black brown	700.	325.	2,000.	60.	
		Block of 4					260.
		P# blk. of 8					675.
238P	15c	dark green	700.	325.	2,000.	60.	
		Block of 4					260.
		P# blk. of 8					675.
239P	30c	orange brown	700.	325.	2,000.	90.	
		Block of 4					400.
		P# blk. of 8					1,250.
240P	50c	slate blue	700.	325.	2,000.	135.	
		Block of 4					575.
		P# blk. of 8					1,500.
241P	$1	salmon	900.	450.	2,000.	160.	
		Block of 4					775.
		P# blk. of 8					1,900.
242P	$2	brown red	900.	450.	2,000.	180.	
		Block of 4					750.
		P# blk. of 8					2,050.
243P	$3	yellow green	900.	450.	2,000.	225.	
		Block of 4					1,000.
		P# blk. of 8					2,700.
244P	$4	crimson lake	900.	450.	2,000.	275.	
		Block of 4					1,200.
		P# blk. of 8					3,000.

5P	$5	black	900. 450. 2,000.	325.	225.
		Block of 4		1,425. 1,000.
		P# blk. of 8		3,500. 3,000.

This set also exists as Large Die proofs, not die sunk, but printed directly on thin card. Set value $4,725. 1c through 50c, $5 each; $1 through $5, $450 each.
Nos. 234P1, 234P2 differ from issued stamp.

Bureau of Engraving and Printing

94

46P	1c	ultra	450.		
47P	1c	blue	250. 250. 1,100.		100.
		Block of 4			450.
		P# blk. of 6			950.
48P	2c	pink, type I			100.
		Block of 4			475.
		P# blk. of 6			950.
50P	2c	car, type I	250. 250.	
51P	2c	car, type II	250.	

The existence of No. 251P2 has been questioned by specialists. The editors would like to see evidence that the item exists.

52P	2c	car, type III	350.	
		Block of 4	1,200.	
53P	3c	purple (triangle I)	750.	
a.		On stamp paper, pair		300.
		Block of 4		625.
		P# blk. of 6		—
53AP	3c	purple (triangle II)	325. 250. 1,100.
54P	4c	dark brown	250. 250. 1,100.
a.		On stamp paper, pair		300.
		Block of 4		625.
		P# blk. of 6		—
55P	5c	chocolate	250. 250. 1,100.
b.		On stamp paper, pair		300.
		Block of 4		625.
		P# blk. of 6		—
56P	6c	brown	250. 250. 1,100.	450.
		Block of 4		1,900.
		P# blk. of 6		3,750.
57P	8c	violet brown	275. 250. 1,100.
58P	10c	green	275. 250. 1,100.
a.		On stamp paper, pair		500.
		Block of 4		1,100.
		P# blk. of 6		—
59P	15c	dark blue	300. 250. 1,100.
60P	50c	orange	450. 210. 1,100.
61AP	$1	black	475. 350. 1,100.	450.
62P	$2	dark blue	475. 350. 1,100.	2,250.
		Block of 4		2,750.
		Margin block of 4, arrow		
		P# blk. of 6		6,250.
63P	$5	dark green	650. 375. 1,100.	450.
		Block of 4		2,250.
		Margin block of 4, arrow		2,750.
		P# blk. of 6		6,250.

895

Imperf, with gum

264P	1c	blue, on stamp paper, pair		275.
		Block of 4		600.
		P# blk. of 6		—
b.		Horiz. P# strip of 3, perf horiz., imperf. vert.		7,500.
267P	2c	carmine, type III, on stamp paper, pair		225.
		Block of 4		475.
		P# blk. of 6		—
268P	3c	purple, on stamp paper, pair		275.
		Block of 4		600.
		P# blk. of 6		—
269P	4c	dark brown, on stamp paper, pair		275.
		Block of 4		600.
		P# blk. of 6		—
270P	5c	chocolate, on stamp paper, pair		275.
		Block of 4		600.
271P	6c	dull brown, on stamp paper, pair		300.
		Block of 4		650.
272P	8c	violet brown, on stamp paper, pair		450.
		Block of 4		1,000.
		P# blk. of 6		—
273P	10c	dark green, on stamp paper, pair		350.
		Block of 4		750.
274P	15c	dark blue, on stamp paper, pair		1,100.
		Block of 4		2,500.
275P	50c	orange, on stamp paper, pair		1,250.
		Block of 4		2,750.
276P	$1	black, type I, on stamp paper, pair		1,600.
		Block of 4		3,500.
277P	$2	bright blue, on stamp paper, pair		3,500.
		Block of 4		7,500.
278P	$5	dark green, on stamp paper, pair		3,500.
		Block of 4		7,500.

No. 264Pb exists only as a bottom margin P#24 and imprint strip of 3.

1897-1903

279P	1c	green	700. 375. 1,100.
279BdP	2c	orange red, type IV	1,100.
279BfP	2c	car, type IV	400. 1,100.
280P	4c	rose brown	700. 1,100.
281P	5c	blue	700. 375. 1,100.
282P	6c	lake	700. 1,100.
283P	10c	orange brown, type II	800. 375. 1,100.
283aP	10c	brown, type II	800.
284P	15c	olive green, type II	800. 375. 1,100.

TRANS-MISSISSIPPI ISSUE

1898

285P	1c	green	650. 650. 1,250.
286P	2c	copper red	650. 650. 1,250.	4,000.
287P	4c	orange	650. 650. 1,250.
288P	5c	dull blue	650. 650. 1,250.
289P	8c	violet brown	650. 650. 1,250.
290P	10c	gray violet	650. 650. 1,250.
291P	50c	sage green	650. 650. 1,250.
292P	$1	black	750. 650. 1,250.
293P	$2	orange brown	750. 650. 1,250.	6,000.
		Block of 4		30,000.
		P# block of 4		35,000.

The bicolored items commonly offered as No. 285-293 bicolored proofs can be found under the following essay listings: No. 285-E8a, 286-E8a, 287-E9a, 288-E5a, 289-E4a, 290-E4a, 291-E8a, 292-E6a, 293-E7a.

PAN-AMERICAN ISSUE

1901

294P	1c	green & black	575. 575. 2,000.
295P	2c	carmine & black	575. 575. 2,000.
296P	4c	chocolate & black	575. 575. 2,000.
297P	5c	ultra & black	575. 575. 2,000.
298P	8c	brown violet & black	575. 575. 2,000.
299P	10c	yel brn & blk	575. 575. 2,000.

1902-03

300P	1c	green	1,500. 300. 2,500.
301P	2c	carmine	1,500. 300. 2,500.
302P	3c	purple	1,500. 300. 2,500.
303P	4c	orange brown	1,500. 300. 2,500.
304P	5c	blue	1,500. 300. 2,500.
305P	6c	lake	1,500. 300. 2,500.
306P	8c	violet black	1,500. 300. 2,500.
307P	10c	orange brown	1,500. 300. 2,500.
308P	13c	deep vio brn	1,500. 300. 2,500.
309P	15c	olive green	1,500. 300. 2,500.
310P	50c	orange	1,500. 300. 2,500.
311P	$1	black	1,500. 300. 2,500.
312P	$2	blue	2,000. 300. 2,500.
313P	$5	green	2,500. 375. 2,500.

1903

319P	2c	carmine, Type I	1,500.
319aP	2c	lake, Type I	—
319iP	2c	carmine, Type II	2,000. 1,000. 3,500.

LOUISIANA PURCHASE ISSUE

1904

323P	1c	green	1,400. 750. 1,250.
324P	2c	carmine	1,400. 750. 1,250.
325P	3c	violet	1,400. 750. 1,250.
326P	5c	dark blue	1,400. 750. 1,250.
327P	10c	brown	1,400. 750. 1,250.

JAMESTOWN EXPOSITION ISSUE

1907

328P	1c	green	1,000. 900. 1,250.
329P	2c	carmine	1,000. 900. 1,250.
330P	5c	blue	1,000. 900. 1,250.

1908-09

331P	1c	green	1,250. 725. 1,200.
332P	2c	carmine	1,250. 725. 1,200.
		carmine, amber	—
		carmine, lt blue	—
333P	3c	deep violet	1,250. 725. 1,200.
334P	4c	brown	1,250. 725. 1,200.
335P	5c	blue	1,250. 725. 1,200.
		blue, salmon	—
336P	6c	red orange	1,250. 725. 1,200.
337P	8c	olive green	1,250. 725. 1,200.
		olive green, yellow	—
338P	10c	yellow	1,250. 725. 1,200.
339P	13c	blue green	1,250. 725. 1,200.
340P	15c	pale ultramarine	1,250. 725. 1,200.
341P	50c	violet	1,250. 725. 1,200.
		violet, pale lilac	—
		violet, yellow	—
		violet, greenish	—
342P	$1	violet black	1,500. 725. 1,200.

LINCOLN MEMORIAL ISSUE

1909

367P	2c	carmine	1,100. 1,000. 1,750.

ALASKA-YUKON ISSUE

1909

370P	2c	carmine	1,100. 1,000. 1,750.

HUDSON-FULTON ISSUE

1909

372P	2c	carmine	1,250. 1,000. 1,750.

PANAMA-PACIFIC ISSUE

1912-13

397P	1c	green	1,750. 1,500. 1,250.
398P	2c	carmine	1,750. 1,500. 1,250.
399P	5c	blue	1,750. 1,500. 1,250.
400P	10c	org. yellow	1,750. 1,500. 1,250.
400AP	10c	orange	1,750. 1,500. 1,250.

No. 398P inscribed "Gatun Locks" is listed in the Essay section as No. 398-E3.

1912-19

				DIE		
				(1) Large	(2) Small	(2a)
405P	1c	green		1,400.	650.	1,200.
406P	2c	carmine		1,400.	650.	1,200.
407P	7c	black		1,400.	650.	1,200.
414P	8c	olive green		1,400.	650.	1,200.
415P	9c	salmon red		1,400.	650.	1,200.
416P	10c	orange yellow		1,400.	650.	1,200.
434P	11c	dark green		1,500.		
417P	12c	claret brown		1,400.	650.	1,200.
513P	13c	apple green		1,500.		
418P	15c	gray		1,400.	650.	1,200.
419P	20c	ultramarine		1,400.	650.	1,200.
420P	30c	orange red		1,400.	650.	1,200.
421P	50c	violet		1,400.	650.	1,200.
423P	$1	violet black		1,400.	650.	1,200.

1918-20

524P	$5	deep green & black	1,500.
547P	$2	carmine & black	1,500.

VICTORY ISSUE

1919

537P	3c	violet	1,100. 850.

PILGRIM ISSUE

1920

548P	1c	green	1,250. 1,200.
549P	2c	carmine rose	1,250. 1,200.
550P	5c	deep blue	1,250. 1,200.

1922-26

			LARGE DIE		PLATE	
			(1) India	(1a) White Wove	(3) White Wove	(4) Card
551P	½c	olive brown	1,500.	—	—	—
552P	1c	deep green	1,000.	700.	—
553P	1½c	yel brn	1,500.		
554P	2c	carmine	1,000.	700.	—
555P	3c	violet	1,250.	1,000.	—
556P	4c	yel brn	1,200.	700.	—
557P	5c	dark blue	1,000.	700.	—
558P	6c	red orange	1,000.	700.	—
559P	7c	black	1,000.	700.	—
560P	8c	olive green	1,000.	700.	—
561P	9c	rose	1,000.	700.	—
562P	10c	orange	1,000.	700.	—
563P	11c	light blue	1,500.	700.	—
564P	12c	brn vio	1,000.	700.	—
622P	13c	green	1,000.	700.	—
565P	14c	dark blue	1,250.	700.	—
566P	15c	gray	1,250.	700.	—
623P	17c	black	1,000.		
567P	20c	car rose	1,000.	700.	—
568P	25c	deep green	1,000.	700.	—
569P	30c	olive brown	1,000.	700.	—
570P	50c	lilac	1,250.	700.	—
571P	$1	vio brn	1,500.	700.	—
572P	$2	deep blue	2,500.	700.	—
572P	$2	deep blue, small die on India	—		
573P	$5	carmine & dark blue	5,000.		

1923-26

			LARGE DIE		SMALL DIE (2)
			(1) India	(1a) White Wove	White or Yellowish Wove
610P		Harding, 2c black	1,400.	1,400.	1,000.
614P		Huguenot Walloon, 1c	750.	700.	700.
615P		Huguenot Walloon, 2c	750.	700.	700.
616P		Huguenot Walloon, 5c	750.	700.	700.
617P		Lexington Concord, 1c	750.	700.	700.
618P		Lexington Concord, 2c	750.	700.	700.
619P		Lexington Concord, 5c	750.	700.	700.
620P		Norse American, 2c	850.	850.	850.
621P		Norse American, 5c	850.	850.	850.
627P		Sesquicentennial, 2c	800.	750.	750.
628P		Ericsson, 5c	800.	750.	750.
629P		White Plains, 2c	800.	750.	750.

1927-29

643P		Vermont, 2c	800.	750.	750.
644P		Burgoyne, 2c	800.	750.	750.
645P		Valley Forge, 2c	800.	750.	750.
649P		Aeronautics, 2c	1,250.	900.	900.
650P		Aeronautics, 5c	1,250.	900.	900.
651P		Clark, 2c	900.	800.	750.
654P		Edison, 2c	900.	800.	750.
657P		Sullivan, 2c	850.	800.	750.
680P		Fallen Timbers, 2c	850.	800.	750.
681P		Ohio River Canalization, 2c	850.	800.	750.

1930-31

682P		Massachusetts Bay, 2c	850.	800.	750.
683P		Carolina Charleston, 2c	850.	800.	750.
684P		1½c brown	650.		
685P		4c brown	650.		
688P		Braddock's Field, 2c	850.	800.	750.
689P		von Steuben, 2c	850.	800.	750.
690P		Pulaski, 2c	850.	800.	750.

702P	Red Cross, 2c black & red		900.	900.
703P	Yorktown, 2c	1,250.	800.	750.

1932

Washington Bicentennial

704P	½c olive brown	1,000.	800.	750.
705P	1c green	1,000.	800.	750.
706P	1½c brown	1,000.	800.	750.
707P	2c carmine rose	1,000.	800.	750.
708P	3c deep violet	1,000.	800.	750.
709P	4c light brown	1,000.	800.	750.
710P	5c blue	1,000.	800.	750.
711P	6c red orange	1,000.	800.	750.
712P	7c black	1,000.	800.	750.
713P	8c olive bister	1,000.	800.	750.
714P	9c pale red	1,000.	800.	750.
715P	10c orange yellow	1,000.	800.	750.
716P	Winter Games, 2c	1,100.	950.	900.
717P	Arbor Day, 2c	900.	900.	800.
718P	Olympic Games, 3c violet	10,000.	950.	900.
719P	Olympic Games, 5c blue	15,000.	950.	900.
720P	3c deep violet	1,000.		
724P	Penn, 3c violet	800.	850.	750.
725P	Webster, 3c violet	800.	850.	750.

1933-34

726P	Georgia, 3c violet	700.	800.	650.
727P	Peace, 3c violet	700.	800.	650.
728P	Century of Progress, 1c	700.	800.	650.
729P	Century of Progress, 3c	700.	800.	650.
732P	N.R.A., 3c violet		900.	650.
733P	Byrd Antarctic, 3c	1,150.	900.	650.
734P	Kosciuszko, 5c blue	1,150.	800.	650.
736P	Maryland, 3c carmine rose	1,150.	800.	650.
737P	Mothers Day, 3c	800.	800.	650.
739P	Wisconsin, 3c deep violet		800.	650.
740P	Parks, 1c green		800.	650.
741P	Parks, 2c red			650.
742P	Parks, 3c violet		800.	650.
743P	Parks, 4c brown			650.
744P	Parks, 5c blue			650.
745P	Parks, 6c dark blue			650.
746P	Parks, 7c black		800.	650.
747P	Parks, 8c sage green			650.
748P	Parks, 9c red orange	800.		650.
749P	Parks, 10c gray black			650.

1935-37

772P	Conn., 3c violet	1,150.		650.
773P	San Diego, 3c purple			650.
774P	Boulder Dam, 3c purple			650.
775P	Michigan, 3c purple			650.
776P	Texas, 3c purple			650.
777P	Rhode Is., 3c purple			650.
782P	Arkansas, 3c pur.	800.	800.	650.
783P	Oregon, 3c purple	—	800.	650.
784P	Anthony, 3c violet			650.
785P	Army, 1c green		800.	800.
786P	Army, 2c carmine			800.
787P	Army, 3c purple	800.	800.	800.
788P	Army, 4c gray			800.
789P	Army, 5c ultramarine	1,350.	800.	800.
790P	Navy, 1c green			800.
791P	Navy, 2c car.	800.		800.
792P	Navy, 3c purple			800.
793P	Navy, 4c gray			800.
794P	Navy, 5c ultramarine			800.
795P	Ordinance, 3c red violet			650.
796P	Virginia Dare, 5c	800.		650.
797P	S.P.A. Sheet, 10c			650.
798P	Constitution, 3c red violet	800.		650.
799P	Hawaii, 3c violet	800.		650.
800P	Alaska, 3c violet			750.
801P	Puerto Rico, 3c	800.		650.
802P	Virgin Is., 3c light violet	—		650.

PRESIDENTIAL ISSUE

1938

803P	½c deep orange	2,000.		650.
804P	1c green			650.
805P	1½c bister brown			650.
806P	2c rose carmine		1,800.	650.
807P	3c deep violet			650.
a.	On glazed card	—		
808P	4c red violet			650.
809P	4½c dark gray	1,500.		650.
810P	5c bright blue	1,500.		650.
811P	6c red orange			650.
812P	7c sepia	1,500.		650.
813P	8c olive green		1,800.	650.
814P	9c olive green	1,800.	1,800.	650.
815P	10c brown red	2,500.		650.
816P	11c ultramarine			650.
817P	12c bright violet	1,500.		650.
818P	13c blue green			650.
819P	14c blue			650.
820P	15c blue gray	1,800.	1,800.	650.
821P	16c black	1,500.		650.
822P	17c rose red			650.
823P	18c brown carmine			650.
824P	19c bright violet	1,800.	1,800.	650.
825P	20c bright blue green	1,800.	1,800.	650.
826P	21c dull blue			650.
827P	22c vermilion			650.
828P	24c gray black	1,800.		650.
829P	25c deep red lilac			650.
830P	30c deep ultramarine			650.
831P	50c light red violet	1,250.		650.
832P	$1 purple & black			650.
833P	$2 yellow green & black			800.
834P	$5 carmine & black			800.

1938

835P	Constitution, 3c	—		600.
836P	Swedes & Finns, 3c	—		600.

837P	N.W. Territory, 3c		600.	
838P	Iowa, 3c violet	1,250.	600.	

1939

852P	Golden Gate, 3c	1,800.	600.	
853P	World's Fair, 3c	1,250.	700.	
854P	Inauguration, 3c	1,250.	650.	
855P	Baseball, 3c violet	1,500.	2,000.	600.
856P	Panama Canal, 3c		600.	
857P	Printing, 3c violet		600.	
858P	Statehood, 3c rose violet		600.	

FAMOUS AMERICANS ISSUE

1940

859P	Authors, 1c bright blue green		800.	
860P	Authors, 2c rose carmine		800.	
861P	Authors, 3c bright red violet		800.	
862P	Authors, 5c ultramarine	800.	800.	
863P	Authors, 10c dark brown	2,500.	800.	
864P	Poets, 1c bright blue green	1,300.	800.	
865P	Poets, 2c rose carmine		800.	
866P	Poets, 3c bright red violet		800.	
867P	Poets, 5c ultramarine	—	800.	
868P	Poets, 10c dark brown	1,450.	800.	
869P	Educators, 1c bright blue green		800.	
870P	Educators, 2c rose carmine		800.	
871P	Educators, 3c bright red violet		800.	
872P	Educators, 5c ultramarine	800.	800.	
873P	Educators, 10c dark brown	900.	800.	
874P	Scientists, 1c bright blue green	1,450.	800.	
875P	Scientists, 2c rose carmine	800.	800.	
876P	Scientists, 3c bright red violet	800.	800.	
877P	Scientists, 5c ultramarine		800.	
878P	Scientists, 10c dark brown	1,300.	800.	
879P	Composers, 1c bright blue green		800.	
880P	Composers, 2c rose carmine	900.	800.	
881P	Composers, 3c bright red violet		800.	
882P	Composers, 5c ultramarine	800.	800.	
883P	Composers, 10c dark brown		800.	
884P	Artists, 1c bright blue green		800.	
885P	Artists, 2c rose carmine		800.	
886P	Artists, 3c bright red violet		800.	
887P	Artists, 5c ultramarine	800.	800.	
888P	Artists, 10c dark brown	800.	800.	
889P	Inventors, 1c bright blue green		800.	
890P	Inventors, 2c rose carmine	1,275.	800.	
891P	Inventors, 3c bright red violet	800.	800.	
892P	Inventors, 5c ultramarine		800.	
893P	Inventors, 10c dark brown		800.	

1940

894P	Pony Express, 3c henna brown	1,100.	600.	
895P	Pan American, 3c light violet		600.	
896P	Idaho, 3c bright violet	800.	600.	
897P	Wyoming, 3c brown violet		600.	
898P	Coronado, 3c violet	1,100.	600.	
899P	Defense, 1c bright blue green	800.	600.	
900P	Defense, 2c rose carmine	800.	600.	
901P	Defense, 3c bright violet	800.	600.	
902P	Emancipation, 3c deep violet	800.	750.	

1941-44

903P	Vermont, 3c light violet		600.	
904P	Kentucky, 3c violet	750.	600.	
905P	Win the War, 3c violet		600.	
906P	China, 5c bright blue		600.	
907P	Allied Nations, 2c rose carmine		600.	
908P	Four Freedoms, 1c br blue green	800.	600.	
922P	Railroad, 3c violet	800.	600.	
923P	Steamship, 3c violet	1,500.	600.	
924P	Telegraph, 3c br red violet	800.	600.	
925P	Corregidor, 3c deep violet	1,275.	600.	
926P	Motion Picture, 3c deep violet	800.	600.	

1945-46

927P	Florida, 3c br red violet	1,100.	600.	
928P	United Nations, 5c ultramarine		600.	
929P	Iwo Jima, 3c yellow green		600.	
930P	Roosevelt, 1c blue green		600.	
931P	Roosevelt, 2c carmine rose	800.	600.	
932P	Roosevelt, 3c purple	1,400.	600.	
933P	Roosevelt, 5c bright blue	—		
934P	Army, 3c olive	1,250.	600.	
935P	Navy, 3c blue	800.	600.	
939P	Merchant Marine, 3c blue green			
941P	Tennessee, 3c dark violet	800.		
942P	Iowa, 3c deep blue	800.		
944P	Kearny, 3c brown violet	800.		

1947-50

945P	Edison, 3c br red violet	700.	
946P	Pulitzer, 3c purple	1,100.	
947P	Stamp Centenary, 3c deep blue		
949P	Doctors, 3c brown violet	1,325.	
951P	Constitution, 3c blue green	700.	
955P	Mississippi, 3c brown violet	—	
956P	Four Chaplains, 3c gray black	—	
958P	Wisconsin, 5c deep blue	700.	
959P	Women, 3c dark violet	700.	
960P	White, 3c br red violet	900.	
962P	Key, 3c rose pink	700.	
965P	Stone, 3c bright violet	700.	
967P	Barton, 3c rose pink	1,900.	
971P	Volunteer Firemen, bright rose carmine	—	
972P	Indian Centennial, 3c dark brown	900.	
973P	Rough Riders, 3c violet brown	700.	
975P	Rogers, 3c br red violet	—	
976P	Fort Bliss, 3c henna brown	—	
977P	Michael, 3c rose pink	1,150.	
981P	Minnesota Terr., 3c blue green	725.	—
983P	Puerto Rico, 3c green	1,000.	
985P	G.A.R., 3c br rose carmine	725.	
988P	Gompers, 3c br red violet	825.	
989P	Statue of Freedom, 3c br blue	1,325.	
991P	Supreme Court, 3c light violet	700.	
992P	Capitol, 3c br red violet	700.	

1951-53

999P	Nevada, 3c lt olive green	1,000.	
1000P	Cadillac, 3c blue	800.	
1001P	Colorado, 3c blue violet	700.	
1002P	Chemical, 3c violet brown	700.	
1003P	Brooklyn, 3c violet	1,325.	
1004P	Betsy Ross, 3c carmine rose	800.	
1005P	4H Clubs, 3c blue green	700.	
1006P	B. & O. Railroad, 3c br blue	1,750.	
1007P	A.A.A., 3c deep blue	700.	—
1009P	Grand Coulee Dam, 3c blue green	700.	
1010P	Lafayette, 3c br blue	800.	
1011P	Mt. Rushmore, 3c blue green	700.	—
1012P	Engineering, 3c violet blue	—	
1013P	Service Women, 3c deep blue	800.	
1016P	Red Cross, 3c dp blue * carmine	—	
1017P	National Guard, 3c br blue	700.	
1018P	Ohio Statehood, 3c chocolate		
1019P	Washington, 3c green	700.	
1020P	Louisiana, 3c violet brown	800.	
1021P	Japan, 5c green	1,650.	
1022P	American Bar, 3c rose violet	700.	
1025P	Trucking, 3c violet	950.	
1026P	Gen. Patton, 3c blue violet	700.	—

1954

1029P	Columbia, 3c blue	700.	

LIBERTY ISSUE

1030P	Franklin, ½c red orange	1,500.	
1031P	Washington, 1c dark green	700.	
1032P	Mount Vernon, 1½c brown carmine	900.	
1033P	Jefferson, 2c carmine rose	—	—
1036P	Lincoln, 4c red violet	700.	
1038P	Monroe, 5c dp blue	700.	
1039P	Roosevelt, 6c carmine	—	
1044P	Independence Hall, 10c rose lake	—	
1047P	Monticello, 20c ultramarine	1,100.	
1049P	Lee, 30c black	700.	
1050P	Marshall, 40c brown red	700.	
1051P	Anthony, 50c br purple	1,000.	
1052P	Henry, $1 purple	700.	
1053P	Hamilton, $5 black	1,200.	

1954-61

1060P	Nebraska, 3c violet	950.	
1062P	Eastman, 3c brown orange	900.	
1063P	Lewis & Clark, 3c violet brown	825.	
1064P	Academy of Fine Arts, 3c rose brown	800.	
1067P	Armed Forces Reserve, 3c purple	1,275.	
1068P	New Hampshire, 3c green	700.	
1069P	Soo Locks, 3c blue	825.	
1071P	Fort Ticonderoga, 3c lt brown	825.	
1073P	Franklin, 3c br carmine	700.	
1074P	Washington, 3c dp blue	700.	
1076P	FIPEX, 3c & 8c S/S	700.	—
1077P	Turkey, 3c rose lake	800.	
1078P	Antelope, 3c brown	700.	
1079P	Salmon, 3c bl green	700.	
1080P	Pure Food & Drug Act, 3c dk bl green	800.	
1081P	Wheatland, 3c black brown	700.	
1082P	Labor Day, 3c dp blue	700.	

83P	Nassau Hall, 3c black, orange	700.		
85P	Children, 3c dk blue	800.		
86P	Hamilton, 3c rose red	700.	—	
87P	Polio, 3c red lilac	800.		
88P	Coast & Geodetic Survey, 3c dk blue	—		
90P	Steel, 3c br ultramarine	700.		
92P	Oklahoma, 3c dk blue	—		
78P	Ft. Sumter, lt green	1,250.		
93P	Project Mercury, dark blue & yellow	—		

AIR POST

1918

			DIE	
			(1) Large	(2) Small
1P	6c	orange	8,500.	
2P	16c	green	7,000.	
3P	24c	carmine rose & blue	8,500.	

1923

4P	8c	dark green	4,750.	6,500.
5P	16c	dark blue	4,750.	6,500.
6P	24c	carmine	4,750.	6,500.

1926-27

7P	10c	dark blue	3,000.	
8P	15c	olive brown	3,000.	—
9P	20c	yellow green	3,000.	

LINDBERGH ISSUE

1927

C10P	10c	dark blue	6,000.	6,000.

1928

C11P	5c	carmine & blue	6,000.	

1930

C12P	5c	violet	3,000.	

ZEPPELIN ISSUE

1930

C13P	65c	green	15,000.	8,250.
a.		on wove, gummed	15,000.	
C14P	$1.30	brown	15,000.	8,500.
a.		on wove, gummed	15,000.	
C15P	$2.60	blue	15,000.	8,500.
a.		on wove, gummed	15,000.	

1932

C17P	8c	olive bister	4,000.	

CENTURY OF PROGRESS ISSUE

1933

C18P	50c	green	12,500.	8,250.

1935-39

C20P	25c	blue on wove		2,750.
C21P	20c	green on wove		2,750.
C22P	50c	carmine on wove		2,750.
C23P	6c	dark blue & carm. on wove		2,750.
C24P	30c	dull blue	3,500.	2,750.

1941-53

C25P	6c	carmine on wove		3,000.
C26P	8c	olive green on wove		3,000.
C27P	10c	violet on wove	5,000.	3,000.
C28P	15c	brown carmine on wove		3,000.
C29P	20c	bright green on wove		3,000.
C30P	30c	blue on wove		3,000.
C31P	50c	orange on wove		3,000.
C33P	5c	carmine	—	
C40P	6c	carmine	5,000.	
C44P	25c	rose carmine	5,000.	2,750.
C45P	6c	magenta	5,500.	5,000.
C46P	80c	bright red violet	5,000.	
C47P	6c	carmine	5,000.	—
C48P	4c	bright blue	—	

AIR POST SPECIAL DELIVERY

1934

CE1P	16c	dark blue on wove	3,000.
CE2P	16c	red & blue on wove	3,000.

SPECIAL DELIVERY

1885

				DIE		PLATE	
			(1) Large	(2) Small	(2a)	(3) India	(4) Card
E1P	10c	blue	600.	250.	2,250.	35.	30.
		Block of 4				175.	150.
		P# blk. of 8					

1888

E2P	10c	blue	750.	250.	2,250.	35.	30.
		Block of 4				200.	150.
		P# blk. of 8				525.	—

1893

E3P	10c	orange	1,100.	300.	2,250.	65.	70.
		Block of 4				280.	310.
		P# blk. of 8					875.

1894-95

E4P	10c	blue	500.	250.	2,250.		
a.		On stamp paper, pair					5,500.
E5P	10c	blue, on stamp paper, pair					4,500.

1902

E6P	10c	ultra	900.	250.	1,250.

1908

E7P	10c	green	2,250.	1,500.	2,250.

1922

			LARGE DIE		DIE
			(1) India	(1a) White Wove	(2) Small
E12P	10c	deep ultra	1,850.	1,100.	

1925-54

E13P	15c	deep orange	1,750.	
E14P	20c	black	1,750.	
E17P	13c	blue		—
E20P	20c	deep blue	1,500.	

REGISTRATION

1911

			DIE			PLATE	
			(1) Large	(2) Small	(2a)	(3) India	(4) Card
F1P	10c	ultra	2,500.	1,000.	1,100.		

POSTAGE DUE

1879

J1P	1c	brown	250.	100.	500.	22.	10.
		Block of 4				105.	65.
		P# blk. of 12				450.	
J2P	2c	brown	250.	100.	500.	20.	10.
		Block of 4				90.	65.
		P# blk. of 12				425.	
		2c dark brown	—				
J3P	3c	brown	250.	100.	500.	20.	10.
		Block of 4				90.	65.
		P# blk. of 12				425.	
		3c dark brown	—	—			
J4P	5c	brown	250.	100.	500.	20.	10.
		Block of 4				90.	65.
		P# blk. of 12				425.	
		5c dark brown	—				
J5P	10c	brown	250.	100.	500.		10.
		10c dark brown	—			32.	
		Block of 4				145.	65.
		P# blk. of 12				675.	
J6P	30c	brown	250.	100.	500.		10.
		30c dark brown	—			32.	
		Block of 4				145.	65.
		P# blk. of 12				675.	
J7P	50c	brown	250.	100.	500.		10.
		50c dark brown	—			32.	
		Block of 4				145.	65.
		P# blk. of 12				675.	

1887

J15P	1c	red brown			500.		15.
		Block of 4					
		P# blk. of 12					
J16P	2c	red brown			500.		15.
		Block of 4					
		P# blk. of 12					
J17P	3c	red brown			500.		20.
		Block of 4					
		P# blk. of 12					
J18P	5c	red brown			500.		15.
		Block of 4					
		P# blk. of 12					
J19P	10c	red brown			500.	19.	25.
		Block of 4				90.	
		P# blk. of 12				360.	
J20P	30c	red brown			500.	19.	18.
		Block of 4				90.	

					360.	
		P# blk. of 12				
J21P	50c	red brown		500.	45.	25.
		Block of 4			210.	
		P# blk. of 12			900.	

1891-93

J22P	1c	bright claret	140.	125.	500.	12.	17.
		Block of 4				65.	80.
		P# blk. of 12					—
a.		On stamp paper, pair					425.
J23P	2c	bright claret	140.	125.	500.	12.	17.
		Block of 4				65.	80.
		P# blk. of 12					—
a.		On stamp paper, pair					425.
J24P	3c	bright claret	140.	125.	500.	12.	17.
		Block of 4				65.	80.
		P# blk. of 12					—
a.		On stamp paper, pair					425.
J25P	5c	bright claret	140.	125.	500.	12.	17.
		Block of 4				65.	80.
		P# blk. of 12					—
a.		On stamp paper, pair					425.
J26P	10c	bright claret	140.	125.	500.	12.	17.
		Block of 4				65.	80.
		P# blk. of 12					—
a.		On stamp paper, pair					425.
J27P	30c	bright claret	140.	125.	500.	28.	17.
		Block of 4				140.	80.
		P# blk. of 12					—
a.		On stamp paper, pair					500.
J28P	50c	bright claret	140.	125.	500.	19.	17.
		Block of 4				90.	80.
		P# blk. of 12					—
a.		On stamp paper, pair					500.

Values for J22Pa-J28Pa are for pairs with original gum and minor faults.

1894

J31P	1c	claret	165.	120.	500.		
a.		On stamp paper, pair					225.
		Block of 4					500.
J32P	2c	claret	165.	120.	500.		100.
		Block of 4					475.
		P# blk. of 6					3,000.
J33P	3c	claret	165.	120.	500.		
J34P	5c	claret	165.	120.	500.		
J35P	10c	claret	165.	120.	500.		
J36P	30c	claret	165.	120.	500.		
J37P	50c	claret	165.	120.	500.		

1925

J68P	½c	dull red	5,750.

1930-31

J69P	½c	deep car	450.
J70P	1c	deep car	450.
J71P	2c	deep car	450.
J72P	3c	deep car	450.
J73P	5c	deep car	450.
J74P	10c	deep car	450.
J75P	30c	deep car	450.
J76P	50c	deep car	450.
J77P	$1	deep car	1,400.
J78P	$5	deep car	1,400.

PARCEL POST POSTAGE DUE

1912

			DIE			PLATE	
			(1) Large	(2) Small	(2a)	(3) India	(4) Card
JQ1P	1c	dark green	600.	500.	700.		
JQ2P	2c	dark green	600.	500.	700.		
JQ3P	5c	dark green	600.	500.	700.		
JQ4P	10c	dark green	600.	500.	700.		
JQ5P	25c	dark green	600.	500.	700.		

CARRIERS

1851

LO1P	1c	blue (Franklin)	800.	300.	1,500.	50.	30.
		Block of 4				210.	125.
		Cracked plate				—	
LO2P	1c	blue (Eagle)	800.	300.	1,500.	50.	30.
		Block of 4				210.	125.
		P # blk. of 8				675.	

Nos. LO1P (1) and LO2P (1) exist only as hybrids.

OFFICIAL

AGRICULTURE

1873

O1P	1c	yellow	80.	100.	500.	15.	8.
		Block of 4				65.	50.
		P# blk. of 12					225.
O2P	2c	yellow	80.	100.	500.	15.	8.
		Block of 4				65.	50.
		P# blk. of 10					225.
O3P	3c	yellow	80.	100.	500.	15.	8.
		Block of 4				65.	50.
		P# blk. of 12					225.
O4P	6c	yellow	80.	100.	500.	15.	8.
		Block of 4				65.	50.
		P# blk. of 12					225.
O5P	10c	yellow	80.	100.	500.	15.	8.
		Block of 4				65.	50.
		P# blk. of 12					225.
O6P	12c	yellow	80.	100.	500.	15.	8.
		Block of 4				65.	50.
		P# blk. of 12					225.
O7P	15c	yellow	80.	100.	500.	15.	8.
		Block of 4				65.	50.
		P# blk. of 12					225.
O8P	24c	yellow	80.	100.	500.	15.	8.
		Block of 4				65.	50.
		P# blk. of 12					225.
O9P	30c	yellow	80.	100.	500.	15.	8.
		Block of 4				65.	50.
		P# blk. of 12					225.

EXECUTIVE

O10P	1c	carmine	100.	100.	500.	15.	10.
		Block of 4				65.	50.
		P# blk. of 14					225.
O11P	2c	carmine	100.	100.	500.	15.	10.
		Block of 4				65.	50.
		P# blk. of 12					225.
		Foreign entry of 6c Agriculture					—
O12P	3c	carmine	100.	100.	500.	15.	10.
		Block of 4				65.	50.
		P# blk. of 12					225.
O13P	6c	carmine	100.	100.	500.	25.	15.
		Block of 4				125.	85.
		P# blk. of 10					350.
O14P	10c	carmine	100.	100.	500.	15.	10.
		Block of 4				65.	50.
		P# blk. of 12					225.

INTERIOR

O15P	1c	vermilion	80.	100.	500.	15.	8.
		Block of 4				65.	50.
		P# blk. of 12					225.
O16P	2c	vermilion	80.	100.	500.	15.	8.
		Block of 4				65.	50.
		P# blk. of 10					200.
O17P	3c	vermilion	80.	100.	500.	15.	8.
		Block of 4				65.	50.
		P# blk. of 10					225.
O18P	6c	vermilion	80.	100.	500.	20.	10.
		Block of 4				90.	50.
		P# blk. of 12					250.
O19P	10c	vermilion	80.	100.	500.	15.	8.
		Block of 4				65.	45.
		P# blk. of 12					225.
O20P	12c	vermilion	80.	100.	500.	15.	8.
		Block of 4				65.	45.
		P# blk. of 10					225.
O21P	15c	vermilion	80.	100.	500.	15.	8.
		Block of 4				65.	45.
		P# blk. of 12					225.
O22P	24c	vermilion	80.	100.	500.	15.	8.
		Block of 4				65.	45.
		P# blk. of 12					225.
O23P	30c	vermilion	80.	100.	500.	15.	8.
		Block of 4				65.	45.
		P# blk. of 12					225.
O24P	90c	vermilion	80.	100.	500.	15.	8.
		Block of 4				65.	45.
		P# blk. of 12					225.

JUSTICE

O25P	1c	purple	80.	100.	500.	15.	8.
		Block of 4				65.	50.
		P# blk. of 12					225.
O26P	2c	purple	80.	100.	500.	15.	8.
		Block of 4				65.	50.
		P# blk. of 12					225.
O27P	3c	purple	80.	100.	500.	15.	8.
		Block of 4				65.	50.
		P# blk. of 12					225.
		Plate Scratches					—
O28P	6c	purple	80.	100.	500.	15.	8.
		Block of 4				65.	50.
		P# blk. of 12					225.
O29P	10c	purple	80.	100.	500.	15.	8.
		Block of 4				65.	50.
		P# blk. of 10					225.
O30P	12c	purple	80.	100.	500.	15.	8.
		Block of 4				65.	50.
		P# blk. of 12					225.
O31P	15c	purple	80.	100.	500.	15.	8.
		Block of 4				65.	50.
		P# blk. of 10					225.
O32P	24c	purple	80.	100.	500.	15.	8.
		Block of 4				65.	50.
		P# blk. of 12					225.
		Short transfer (pos. 98)					—
O33P	30c	purple	80.	100.	500.	15.	8.
		Block of 4				65.	50.
		P# blk. of 12					225.
O34P	90c	purple	80.	100.	500.	15.	8.
		Block of 4				65.	50.

NAVY

		P# blk. of 10					225.
O35P	1c	ultramarine	80.	100.	500.	15.	8.
		Block of 4				65.	50.
		P# blk. of 12					225.
O36P	2c	ultramarine	80.	100.	500.	15.	8.
		Block of 4				65.	50.
		P# blk. of 12					225.
O37P	3c	ultramarine	80.	100.	500.	15.	8.
		Block of 4				65.	50.
		P# blk. of 10					225.
O38P	6c	ultramarine	80.	100.	500.	20.	15.
		Block of 4				90.	75.
		P# blk. of 10					350.
O39P	7c	ultramarine	80.	100.	500.	15.	8.
		Block of 4				65.	50.
		P# blk. of 10					225.
O40P	10c	ultramarine	80.	100.	500.	15.	8.
		Block of 4				65.	50.
		P# blk. of 12					225.
O41P	12c	ultramarine	80.	100.	500.	15.	8.
		Block of 4				65.	50.
		P# blk. of 12					225.
O42P	15c	ultramarine	80.	100.	500.	15.	8.
		Block of 4				65.	50.
		P# blk. of 12					225.
O43P	24c	ultramarine	80.	100.	500.	15.	8.
		Block of 4				65.	50.
		P# blk. of 12					225.
O44P	30c	ultramarine	80.	100.	500.	15.	8.
		Block of 4				65.	50.
		P# blk. of 12					225.
O45P	90c	ultramarine	80.	100.	500.	15.	8.
		Block of 4				65.	50.
		P# blk. of 12					225.
		Short transfer at upper left (106, pos. 1, 5)					—

POST OFFICE

O47P	1c	black	80.	100.	500.	15.	8.
		Block of 4				65.	50.
		P# blk. of 10					225.
O48P	2c	black	80.	100.	500.	15.	8.
		Block of 4				65.	50.
		P# blk. of 14					225.
O49P	3c	black	80.	100.	500.	15.	8.
		Block of 4				65.	50.
		P# blk. of 12					225.
O50P	6c	black	80.	100.	500.	15.	8.
		Block of 4				65.	50.
		P# blk. of 12					225.
O51P	10c	black	80.	100.	500.	15.	8.
		Block of 4				65.	50.
		P# blk. of 12					225.
O52P	12c	black	80.	100.	500.	15.	8.
		Block of 4				65.	50.
		P# blk. of 12					225.
O53P	15c	black	80.	100.	500.	15.	8.
		Block of 4				65.	50.
		P# blk. of 12					225.
O54P	24c	black	80.	100.	500.	15.	8.
		Block of 4				65.	50.
		P# blk. of 12					225.
O55P	30c	black	80.	100.	500.	15.	8.
		Block of 4				65.	50.
		P# blk. of 12					225.
O56P	90c	black	80.	100.	500.	15.	8.
		Block of 4				65.	50.
		P# blk. of 12					225.

STATE

O57P	1c	green	80.	100.	600.	15.	8.
		Block of 4				65.	50.
		P# blk. of 12					225.
O58P	2c	green	80.	100.	600.	15.	8.
		Block of 4				65.	50.
		P# blk. of 10					225.
O59P	3c	green	80.	100.	600.	15.	8.
		Block of 4				65.	50.
		P# blk. of 10					225.
O60P	6c	green	80.	100.	600.	25.	16.
		Block of 4				120.	85.
		P# blk. of 12					375.
O61P	7c	green	80.	100.	600.	15.	8.
		Block of 4				65.	50.
		P# blk. of 12					225.
O62P	10c	green	80.	100.	600.	15.	8.
		Block of 4				65.	50.
		P# blk. of 12					225.
O63P	12c	green	80.	100.	600.	15.	8.
		Block of 4				65.	50.
		P# blk. of 10					225.
O64P	15c	green	80.	100.	600.	15.	8.
		Block of 4				65.	50.
		P# blk. of 12					225.
O65P	24c	green	80.	100.	600.	15.	8.
		Block of 4				65.	50.
		P# blk. of 12					225.
O66P	30c	green	80.	100.	600.	15.	8.
		Block of 4				65.	50.
		P# blk. of 12					225.
O67P	90c	green	80.	100.	600.	15.	8.
		Block of 4				65.	50.
		P# blk. of 12					225.
O68P	$2	green & black	150.	125.	750.	85.	35.
		Block of 4				375.	175.
		Sheet of 10					4,000.
a.		Invtd. center					7,000.
		Half sheet of 5				31,500.	
O69P	$5	green & black	150.	125.	750.	85.	35.
		Block of 4				375.	175.
		Sheet of 10					4,000.
a.		Invtd. center					7,000.
		Half sheet of 5				31,500.	
		Sheet of 10					40,000.
O70P	$10	green & black	150.	125.	800.	85.	
		Block of 4				375.	
		Sheet of 10					4,[
O71P	$20	green & black	150.	125.	800.	85.	
		Block of 4				375.	
		Sheet of 10					4,[
a.		Invtd. center					7,[
		Block of 4					21,[
		Half sheet of 5				31,500.	

O68P to O71P Large Dies exist as hybrids only.

TREASURY

O72P	1c	brown	80.	100.	500.	15.	
		Block of 4				65.	
		P# blk. of 12					2[
O73P	2c	brown	80.	100.	500.	15.	
		Block of 4				65.	
		P# blk. of 12					2[
O74P	3c	brown	80.	100.	500.	15.	
		Block of 4				65.	
		P# blk. of 14					2[
O75P	6c	brown	80.	100.	500.	20.	
		Block of 4				100.	
		P# blk. of 12					3[
O76P	7c	brown	80.	100.	500.	15.	
		Block of 4				65.	
		P# blk. of 12					2[
O77P	10c	brown	80.	100.	500.	15.	
		Block of 4				65.	
		P# blk. of 12					2[
O78P	12c	brown	80.	100.	500.	15.	
		Block of 4				65.	
		P# blk. of 12					2[
O79P	15c	brown	80.	100.	500.	15.	
		Block of 4				65.	
		P# blk. of 12					2[
O80P	24c	brown	80.	100.	500.	15.	
		Block of 4				65.	
		P# blk. of 12					2[
O81P	30c	brown	80.	100.	500.	15.	
		Block of 4				65.	
		P# blk. of 12					2[
O82P	90c	brown	80.	100.	500.	15.	
		Block of 4				65.	
		P# blk. of 12					2[

WAR

O83P	1c	rose	80.	100.	500.	15.	
		Block of 4				65.	
		P# blk. of 12					22[
O84P	2c	rose	80.	100.	500.	15.	
		Block of 4				65.	
O85P	3c	rose	80.	100.	500.	15.	
		Block of 4				65.	
		Plate flaw at upper left (32R20)					
O86P	6c	rose	80.	100.	500.	15.	
		Block of 4				65.	
		P# blk. of 12					22
O87P	7c	rose	80.	100.	500.	15.	
		Block of 4				65.	
		P# blk. of 10					22
O88P	10c	rose	80.	100.	500.	15.	
		Block of 4				65.	
		P# blk. of 10					22
O89P	12c	rose	80.	100.	500.	15.	
		Block of 4				65.	
		P# blk. of 12					22
O90P	15c	rose	80.	100.	500.	15.	
		Block of 4				65.	
		P# blk. of 12					22
O91P	24c	rose	80.	100.	500.	15.	
		Block of 4				65.	
		P# blk. of 10					22
O92P	30c	rose	80.	100.	500.	15.	
		Block of 4				65.	
		P# blk. of 10					22
O93P	90c	rose	80.	100.	500.	15.	
		Block of 4				65.	
		P# blk. of 12					22[

O83-O93 exist in a plum shade.

POSTAL SAVINGS MAIL

1911

O124P	1c	dark violet	450.	275.	1,000.
O121P	2c	black	450.	275.	1,000.
O126P	10c	carmine	450.	275.	1,000.
O122P	50c	dark green	450.	275.	1,000.
O123P	$1	ultramarine	450.	275.	1,000.

NEWSPAPERS

1865

			DIE			PLATE	
			(1) Large	(2) Small	(2a)	(3) Wove Paper	(4) Card
PR2P	10c	green	575.	225.		40.	60.
		Block of 4				200.	300.
		P# blk. of 6					
PR3P	25c	orange red	575.	225.		45.	60.
		Block of 4				225.	300.
		P# blk. of 6					
PR4P	5c	blue	575.	225.		40.	60.
		Block of 4				200.	300.
		P# blk. of 6					

5

No.	Denom	Color					
PR5P	5c	dark blue			1,750.		60.
PR6P	10c	deep green			1,750.		60.
PR7P	25c	dark car red			1,750.		60.
PR9P	2c	black	80.	40.	250.	15.	12.
		Block of 4				65.	55.
		P# blk. of 8					—
PR10P	3c	black	80.	40.	250.	15.	12.
		Block of 4				65.	55.
		P# blk. of 8					—
PR11P	4c	black	80.	40.	250.	15.	12.
		Block of 4				65.	55.
		P# blk. of 8					—
PR12P	6c	black	80.	40.	250.	15.	12.
		Block of 4				65.	55.
		P# blk. of 8					—
PR13P	8c	black	80.	40.	250.	15.	12.
		Block of 4				65.	55.
		P# blk. of 8					—
PR14P	9c	black	80.	40.	250.	15.	12.
		Block of 4				65.	55.
		P# blk. of 8					—
PR15P	10c	black	80.	40.	250.	15.	12.
		Block of 4				65.	55.
		P# blk. of 8					—
PR16P	12c	rose	80.	40.	250.	15.	12.
		Block of 4				65.	55.
		P# blk. of 8					—
PR17P	24c	rose	80.	40.	250.	15.	12.
		Block of 4				65.	55.
		P# blk. of 8					—
PR18P	36c	rose	80.	40.	250.	15.	12.
		Block of 4				65.	55.
		P# blk. of 8					—
PR19P	48c	rose	80.	40.	250.	15.	12.
		Block of 4				65.	55.
		P# blk. of 8					—
PR20P	60c	rose	80.	40.	250.	15.	12.
		Block of 4				65.	55.
		P# blk. of 8					—
PR21P	72c	rose	80.	40.	250.	15.	12.
		Block of 4				65.	55.
		P# blk. of 8					—
PR22P	84c	rose	80.	40.	250.	15.	12.
		Block of 4				65.	55.
		P# blk. of 8					—
PR23P	96c	rose	80.	40.	250.	15.	12.
		Block of 4				65.	55.
		P# blk. of 8					—
PR24P	$1.92	dark brown	80.	40.	250.	18.	15.
		Block of 4				80.	70.
		P# blk. of 8					—
PR25P	$3	vermilion	80.	40.	250.	18.	15.
		Block of 4				80.	70.
		P# blk. of 8					—
PR26P	$6	ultra	80.	40.	250.	18.	15.
		Block of 4				80.	70.
		P# blk. of 8					—
PR27P	$9	yellow	80.	40.	250.	18.	15.
		Block of 4				80.	70.
		P# blk. of 8					—
PR28P	$12	blue green	80.	40.	250.	18.	15.
		Block of 4				80.	70.
		P# blk. of 8					—
PR29P	$24	dark gray violet	80.	40.	250.	18.	15.
		Block of 4				80.	70.
		P# blk. of 8					—
PR30P	$36	brown rose	80.	40.	250.	21.	15.
		Block of 4				90.	70.
		P# blk. of 8					—
PR31P	$48	red brown	80.	40.	250.	23.	15.
		Block of 4				100.	70.
		P# blk. of 8					—
PR32P	$60	violet	80.	40.	250.	25.	18.
		Block of 4				110.	85.
		P# blk. of 8					—

1879

No.	Denom	Color			
PR57P	2c	deep black	80.	12.	4.
		Block of 4		60.	24.
	a.	On stamp paper, pair			—
PR58P	3c	deep black	80.	12.	4.
		Block of 4		60.	24.
	a.	On stamp paper, pair			—
PR59P	4c	deep black	90.	12.	4.
		Block of 4		60.	24.
	a.	On stamp paper, pair			—
PR60P	6c	deep black	90.	12.	4.
		Block of 4		60.	24.
	a.	On stamp paper, pair			—
PR61P	8c	deep black	90.	12.	4.
		Block of 4		60.	24.
	a.	On stamp paper, pair			—
PR62P	10c	deep black	90.	12.	4.
		Block of 4		60.	24.
	a.	On stamp paper, pair			—
PR63P	12c	red	90.	12.	6.
		Block of 4		60.	32.
PR64P	24c	red	90.	12.	6.
		Block of 4		60.	32.
PR65P	36c	red	90.	12.	6.
		Block of 4		60.	32.
PR66P	48c	red	90.	12.	6.
		Block of 4		60.	32.
PR67P	60c	red	90.	12.	6.
		Block of 4		60.	32.
PR68P	72c	red	90.	12.	6.
		Block of 4		60.	32.
PR69P	84c	red	90.	12.	6.
		Block of 4		60.	32.
PR70P	96c	red	90.	12.	6.
		Block of 4		60.	32.

No.	Denom	Color			
PR71P	$1.92	pale brown	90.	15.	8.
		Block of 4		75.	45.
	a.	On stamp paper, pair			—
PR72P	$3	red verm.	90.	15.	8.
		Block of 4		75.	45.
	a.	On stamp paper, pair			—
PR73P	$6	blue	90.	15.	8.
		Block of 4		75.	45.
	a.	On stamp paper, pair			—
PR74P	$9	orange	90.	15.	8.
		Block of 4		75.	45.
	a.	On stamp paper, pair			—
PR75P	$12	yel. green	90.	15.	8.
		Block of 4		75.	45.
	a.	On stamp paper, pair			—
PR76P	$24	dark violet	90.	18.	8.
		Block of 4		90.	45.
	a.	On stamp paper, pair			—
PR77P	$36	Indian red	90.	20.	8.
		Block of 4		100.	45.
	a.	On stamp paper, pair			—
PR78P	$48	yellow brown	90.	24.	8.
		Block of 4		120.	45.
	a.	On stamp paper, pair			—
PR79P	$60	purple	90.	24.	8.
		Block of 4		120.	45.
	a.	On stamp paper, pair			—

1885

No.	Denom	Color					
PR81P	1c	black	100.	60.	250.	10.	8.
		Block of 4				50.	40.
		P# blk. of 8					200.
	a.	On stamp paper, pair					—
PR82P	12c	carmine		80.	250.	17.	8.
		Block of 4				85.	
	a.	On stamp paper, pair					—
PR83P	24c	carmine		80.	250.	17.	8.
		Block of 4				85.	
	a.	On stamp paper, pair					—
PR84P	36c	carmine		80.	250.	17.	8.
		Block of 4				85.	
	a.	On stamp paper, pair					—
PR85P	48c	carmine		80.	250.	17.	8.
		Block of 4				85.	
	a.	On stamp paper, pair					—
PR86P	60c	carmine		80.	250.	17.	8.
		Block of 4				85.	
	a.	On stamp paper, pair					—
PR87P	72c	carmine		80.	250.	17.	8.
		Block of 4				85.	
	a.	On stamp paper, pair					—
PR88P	84c	carmine		80.	250.	17.	8.
		Block of 4				85.	
	a.	On stamp paper, pair					—
PR89P	96c	carmine		80.	250.	17.	8.
		Block of 4				85.	
	a.	On stamp paper, pair					—

1895

No.	Denom	Color			
PR102P	1c	black	125.	100.	275.
PR103P	2c	black	125.	100.	275.
PR104P	5c	black	125.	100.	275.
PR105P	10c	black	125.	100.	275.
PR106P	25c	carmine	125.	100.	275.
PR107P	50c	carmine	125.	100.	275.
PR108P	$2	scarlet	125.	100.	275.
PR109P	$5	blue	125.	100.	275.
PR110P	$10	green	125.	100.	275.
PR111P	$20	slate	125.	100.	275.
PR112P	$50	carmine	125.	100.	275.
PR113P	$100	purple	125.	100.	275.

PARCEL POST

1912-13

No.	Denom	Color	DIE ON INDIA (1) Large	(2) Small	(2a)	PLATE (3) India	(4) Card
Q1P	1c	car rose	1,400.	1,200.	1,200.		
Q2P	2c	car rose	1,400.	1,200.	1,200.		
Q3P	3c	car rose	1,400.	1,200.	1,200.		
Q4P	4c	car rose	1,400.	1,200.	1,200.		
Q5P	5c	car rose	1,400.	1,200.	1,200.		
Q6P	10c	car rose	1,400.	1,200.	1,200.		
Q7P	15c	car rose	1,400.	1,200.	1,200.		
Q8P	20c	car rose	1,400.	1,200.	1,200.		
Q9P	25c	car rose	1,400.	1,200.	1,200.		
Q10P	50c	car rose	1,400.	1,200.	1,200.		
Q11P	75c	car rose	1,400.	1,200.	1,200.		
Q12P	$1	car rose	1,400.	1,200.	1,200.		

SPECIAL HANDLING

1925-28

No.	Denom	Color	
QE1P	10c	yel grn	900.
QE2P	15c	yel grn	900.
QE3P	20c	yel grn	900.
QE4P	25c	yel grn	1,500.
QE4aP	25c	deep grn	900.

LOCAL

1844

No.	Denom	Color	
5L1P	5c	black	2,250.

TELEGRAPH

AMERICAN RAPID TELEGRAPH CO.

1881

No.	Denom	Color	DIE (2) Small	PLATE (3) India
1T1P	1c	black	80.	32.
		Pair		68.
1T2P	3c	orange		32.
		Pair		68.
1T3P	5c	bister brown	80.	32.
		Pair		68.
1T4P	10c	purple		32.
		Pair		68.
1T5P	15c	green	80.	32.
		Pair		68.
1T6P	20c	red	80.	32.
		Pair		68.
1T7P	25c	rose	80.	32.
		Pair		68.
1T8P	50c	blue		32.
		Pair		68.

"Collect"

No.	Denom	Color		Plate
1T9P	1c	brown		32.
		Pair, Nos. 1T9P, 1T13P		68.
		Same, block of 4		145.
1T10P	5c	blue		32.
		Pair, Nos. 1T10P, 1T14P		68.
		Same, block of 4		145.
1T11P	15c	red brown		32.
		Pair, Nos. 1T11P, 1T15P		68.
		Same, block of 4		145.
1T12P	20c	olive green		32.
		Pair, Nos. 1T12P, 1T16P		68.
		Same, block of 4		145.

Office Coupon

No.	Denom	Color	Plate
1T13P	1c	brown	32.
1T14P	5c	blue	32.
1T15P	15c	red brown	32.
1T16P	20c	olive green	32.

BALTIMORE & OHIO TELEGRAPH CO.

1885

No.	Denom	Color	Plate
3T1P	1c	vermilion	32.
		Pair	68.
3T2P	5c	blue	32.
		Pair	68.
3T3P	10c	red brown	32.
		Pair	68.
3T4P	25c	orange	32.
		Pair	68.

1886

No.	Denom	Color	Plate
3T6P		black	32.
		Pair	68.
3T7P	1c	green	32.
3T8P	5c	blue	32.
3T9P	10c	brown	32.
3T10P	25c	orange	32.

POSTAL TELEGRAPH CO.

1885

No.	Denom	Color	DIE (1) Large	(2) Small	PLATE (3) India
15T1P	10c	green		55.	32.
15T2P	15c	orange red			32.
15T3P	25c	blue	65.		32.
15T4P	50c	brown		65.	32.

WESTERN UNION TELEGRAPH CO.

No.		Color	Plate
16T1P	(1871)	green	17.
		Pair	35.
16T2P	(1872)	red	17.
		Pair	35.
16T3P	(1873)	blue	17.
		Pair	35.
16T4P	(1874)	brown	17.
		Pair	35.
16T5P	(1875)	deep green	17.
16T6P	(1876)	red	17.
16T7P	(1877)	violet	—
16T8P	(1878)	gray brown	20.
16T9P	(1879)	blue	14.
16T10P	(1880)	lilac rose	16.
16T11P	(1881)	green	16.
16T12P	(1882)	blue	20.

16T13P (1883)	yellow brown		16.
16T14P (1884)	gray violet		20.
16T15P (1885)	green		20.
16T16P (1886)	brown violet		13.
	Pair		28.
16T17P (1887)	red brown		13.
	Pair		28.
16T18P (1888)	blue		13.
	Pair		28.
16T19P (1889)	olive green		16.
16T22P (1892)	vermilion		16.
16T30P (1900)	red violet		28.
16T44P (1913)	brown	— —	—

REVENUE

NORMAL COLORS
1862-68 by Butler & Carpenter, Philadelphia.
1868-75 by Joseph R. Carpenter, Philadelphia.

In the following listing the so-called small die proofs on India paper may be, in fact probably are, plate proofs. The editors shall consider them die proofs, however, until they see them in pairs or blocks. Many revenue proofs on India are mounted on card.

FIRST ISSUE

1862-71

			DIE ON INDIA (1) Large	(2) Small	PLATE (3) India	(4) Card
R1P	1c	Express, red			70.	65.
		Block of 4				275.
R2P	1c	Playing Cards, red	600.		60.	65.
		Block of 4			250.	275.
R3P	1c	Proprietary, red			140.	45.
		Block of 4				200.
R4P	1c	Telegraph, red				28.
		Block of 4				125.
R5P	2c	Bank Check, blue		525.		33.
		Block of 4				140.
R6P	2c	Bank Check, orange			60.	
		Block of 4			250.	
R7P	2c	Certificate, blue				28.
		Block of 4				125.
R8P	2c	Certificate, orange			82.	
		Block of 4			350.	
R9P	2c	Express, blue				28.
		Block of 4				125.
R10P	2c	Express, orange	600.		60.	
		Pair			250.	
R11P	2c	Playing Cards, blue				38.
		Block of 4				160.
R13P	2c	Proprietary, blue		400.		28.
		Block of 4				125.
R15P	2c	U.S.I.R., orange			1,250.	
R16P	3c	Foreign Exchange, green	600.		225.	38.
		Block of 4				160.
		R16P1 + R19P1 composite	—			
R17P	3c	Playing Cards, green	700.	400.		100.
		Block of 4				425.
R18P	3c	Proprietary, green			60.	28.
		Block of 4			250.	125.
R19P	3c	Telegraph, green	600.		225.	28.
		Block of 4				125.
R20P	4c	Inland Exchange, brown			225.	28.
		Block of 4				125.
R21P	4c	Playing Cards, violet		400.		95.
		Block of 4				400.
R22P	4c	Proprietary, violet	600.		110.	60.
		Block of 4			475.	250.
R23P	5c	Agreement, red				33.
		Block of 4				140.
R24P	5c	Certificate, red			95.	110.
		Block of 4			400.	
		R24P1 + R25P1 composite	—			
R25P	5c	Express, red		250.		33.
		Block of 4				145.
R26P	5c	Foreign Exchange, red				300.
R27P	5c	Inland Exchange, red		250.		28.
		Block of 4				125.
R28P	5c	Playing Cards, red	—	105.		325.
		Block of 4				440.

			DIE ON INDIA (1) Large	(2) Small	PLATE (3) India	(4) Card
R29P	5c	Proprietary, red on blue wove, gummed				—
R30P	6c	Inland Exchange, orange			60.	33.
		Block of 4			250.	140.
R32P	10c	Bill of Lading, blue				33.
		Block of 4				140.
R33P	10c	Certificate, blue			140.	33.
		Block of 4				140.
R34P	10c	Contract, blue				33.
		Block of 4				140.
R35P	10c	Foreign Exchange, blue				33.
		Block of 4				140.
R36P	10c	Inland Exchange, blue				33.
		Block of 4				140.
R37P	10c	Power of Attorney, blue				33.
		Block of 4				140.
R38P	10c	Proprietary, blue	700.		70.	
		Block of 4			300.	
R39P	15c	Foreign Exchange, brown			90.	325.
		Block of 4			375.	1,600.
R40P	15c	Inland Exchange, brown			120.	33.
		Block of 4				140.
R41P	20c	Foreign Exchange, red	600.		90.	100.
		Block of 4			375.	425.
		R41P1 + R42P1 composite	—			
R42P	20c	Inland Exchange, red	600.	250.	260.	33.
		Block of 4				140.
R43P	25c	Bond, red				500.
		Block of 4				2,500.
R44P	25c	Certificate, red				33.
		Block of 4				140.
R45P	25c	Entry of Goods, red				550.
R46P	25c	Insurance, red			60.	33.
		Block of 4			250.	140.
R47P	25c	Life Insurance, red				33.
		Block of 4				140.
R48P	25c	Power of Attorney, red				33.
		Block of 4				140.
R49P	25c	Protest, red				33.
		Block of 4				140.
R50P	25c	Warehouse Receipt, red				33.
		Block of 4				140.
R51P	30c	Foreign Exchange, lilac			110.	100.
		Block of 4			475.	425.
R52P	30c	Inland Exchange, lilac			65.	55.
		Block of 4			275.	230.
R53P	40c	Inland Exchange, brown			150.	75.
		Block of 4				325.
R54P	50c	Conveyance, blue		250.		33.
		Block of 4				140.
R55P	50c	Entry of Goods, blue			65.	45.
		Block of 4			275.	190.
R56P	50c	Foreign Exchange, blue			65.	45.
		Block of 4			275.	190.
R57P	50c	Lease, blue			65.	38.
		Block of 4			275.	160.
R58P	50c	Life Insurance, blue			65.	38.
		Block of 4			275.	160.
R59P	50c	Mortgage, blue				110.
		Block of 4			475.	
R60P	50c	Original Process, blue			65.	38.
		Block of 4			275.	160.
R61P	50c	Passage Ticket, blue				55.
		Block of 4				230.
R62P	50c	Probate of Will, blue			65.	55.
		Block of 4			275.	230.
R63P	50c	Surety Bond, blue				55.
		Block of 4				230.

			DIE ON INDIA (1) Large	(2) Small	PLATE (3) India	(4) Card
R64P	60c	Inland Exchange, orange			55.	
		Block of 4				
R65P	70c	Foreign Exchange, green			120.	
		Block of 4				
R66P	$1	Conveyance, red				
		Block of 4				
R67P	$1	Entry of Goods, red		525.		
		Block of 4				
R68P	$1	Foreign Exchange red				
		Block of 4				
R69P	$1	Inland Exchange, red				
		Block of 4				
R70P	$1	Lease, red				
R71P	$1	Life Insurance, red				
		Block of 4				
R72P	$1	Manifest, red			55.	—
		Block of 4				
R73P	$1	Mortgage, red				
		Block of 4				
R74P	$1	Passage Ticket, red				
		Block of 4				1,8..
R75P	$1	Power of Attorney, red				
		Block of 4				4..
R76P	$1	Probate of Will, red				
		Block of 4				
R77P	$1.30	Foreign Exchange, orange	700.		140.	
		Block of 4			575.	4..
R78P	$1.50	Inland Exchange, blue			110.	
		Block of 4			475.	1..
R79P	$1.60	Foreign Exchange green			140.	
		Block of 4				
R80P	$1.90	Foreign Exchange, violet			140.	
		Block of 4			575.	4..
R81P	$2	Conveyance, red			120.	
		Block of 4				1..
R82P	$2	Mortgage, red			120.	
		Block of 4				1..
R83P	$2	Probate of Will, red				
		Block of 4				
R84P	$2.50	Inland Exchange, violet			250.	2..
		Block of 4				
R85P	$3	Charter Party, green			120.	6..
		Block of 4			500.	27..
R86P	$3	Manifest, green	—	350.	180.	27..
		Block of 4				27..
R87P	$3.50	Inland Exchange, blue			180.	14..
		Block of 4				57..
R88P	$5	Charter Party, red			70.	5..
		Block of 4			300.	23..
R89P	$5	Conveyance, red			450.	5..
		Block of 4				23..
R90P	$5	Manifest, red		300.		5..
		Block of 4				23..
R91P	$5	Mortgage, red			650.	5..
		Block of 4				23..
R92P	$5	Probate of Will, red		300.		5..
		Block of 4				23..
R93P	$10	Charter Party, green			120.	5..
		Block of 4				23..
R94P	$10	Conveyance, green				5..
		Block of 4				23..
R95P	$10	Mortgage, green				5..
		Block of 4				23..
R96P	$10	Probate of Will, green	700.	300.		7..
		Block of 4				32..
R97P	$15	Mortgage, dark blue			—	18..
R97eP	$15	Mortgage, ultramarine			—	800.. / 35..
	$15	Mortgage, milky blue			290.	
R98P	$20	Conveyance, orange			220.	100..
		Block of 4			900.	425..

			DIE ON INDIA (1) Large	(2) Small	PLATE (3) India	(4) Card
9P	$20	Probate of Will, orange				220.
00P	$25	Mortgage, red			220.	160.
		Block of 4				675.
01P	$50	U.S.I.R., green			220.	230.
		Block of 4				950.
02P	$200	U.S.I.R., green & orange red			1,400.	

SECOND ISSUE
71-72

			DIE ON INDIA (1) Large	(2) Small	PLATE (3) India	(4) Card
05P	3c	blue & black			20.	15.
		Block of 4			90.	65.
09P	10c	blue & black			20.	15.
		Block of 4			90.	65.
11P	20c	blue & black			20.	15.
		Block of 4			90.	65.
12P	25c	blue & black			20.	15.
		Block of 4			90.	65.
15P	50c	blue & black			50.	15.
		Block of 4			225.	65.
19P	$1.30	blue & black			50.	38.
		Block of 4			225.	160.
20P	$1.50	blue & black			28.	22.
		Block of 4			120.	100.
		Double transfer, design of $1				—
21P	$1.60	blue & black			60.	60.
		Block of 4			260.	260.
22P	$1.90	blue & black			50.	38.
		Block of 4			225.	170.
26P	$3.50	blue & black			90.	100.
		Block of 4			400.	425.
30P	$25	blue & black			150.	110.
		Block of 4			650.	500.
31P	$50	blue & black			160.	140.
		Block of 4			700.	625.

The "small die proofs" formerly listed under Nos. R103P-31P are plate proofs from the sheets listed under "Trial Color Proofs."

132P	$200	red, blue & black	3,500.	2,750.	2,500.
		Red (frame) inverted			—
133P	$500	red orange, green & black	3,750.		
133AP	$5000	red orange, dark green & black	7,500.		

No. R133AP was approved in these colors but never issued. Shade differences of the red orange and dark green colors will be found. It comes both with and without manufacturer's imprints to the left and right of the design. One example exists on bond paper mounted on card with "853½" printed on the lower right card margin.

Due to the unusual manufacturing process of printing these 3-color stamps from single impression plates, proofs with imprints could also be considered to be plate proofs. All are extremely scarce or unique, and are valued in the grade, condition and scarcity in which they exist. For other colors see the trial color proofs listings under No. R133ATC.

THIRD ISSUE
371-72

			PLATE (3) India	(4) Card
R134P	1c	claret & black		15.
		Block of 4		70.
R135P	2c	orange & black	16.	15.
		Block of 4	70.	70.
R136P	4c	brown & black	20.	15.
		Block of 4	85.	70.
R137P	5c	orange & black	20.	15.
		Block of 4	85.	70.
R138P	6c	orange & black	20.	15.
		Block of 4	85.	70.
R139P	15c	brown & black	20.	15.
		Block of 4	85.	70.
R140P	30c	orange & black	25.	18.
		Block of 4	105.	80.
R141P	40c	brown & black	25.	18.
		Block of 4	105.	80.
R142P	60c	orange & black	65.	50.
		Block of 4	270.	225.
		Foreign entry, design of 70c	200.	150.
a.		Center inverted		1,500.
		Block of 4		6,500.
		Foreign entry, design of 70c		—
R143P	70c	green & black	45.	38.
		Block of 4	190.	170.
R144P	$1	green & black	40.	38.
		Block of 4	170.	170.
R145P	$2	vermilion & black	80.	105.
		Block of 4	335.	450.
R146P	$2.50	claret & black	50.	40.
		Block of 4	210.	170.
R147P	$3	green & black	65.	70.
		Block of 4	270.	300.
R148P	$5	vermilion & black	65.	55.
		Block of 4	270.	240.

			PLATE (3) India	(4) Card
R149P	$10	green & black	80.	55.
		Block of 4	335.	240.
R150P	$20	orange & black	115.	150.
		Block of 4	500.	635.

The "small die proofs" formerly listed under Nos. R134P-R150P are plate proofs from the sheets listed under "Trial Color Proofs."

1875   National Bank Note Co., New York City

			DIE ON INDIA (1) Large	(2) Small	PLATE (3) India
R152P	2c	blue (Liberty)	450.		110.
		Block of 4			475.

DOCUMENTARY
1898

			PLATE (3) India
R173P	$1	dark green	600.
R174P	$3	dark brown	600.
R175P	$5	orange red	600.
R176P	$10	black	600.
R177P	$30	red	600.
R178P	$50	gray brown	600.

1899

R180P	$500	car lake & blk	1,650.

1914

R197P	2c	rose	—

1914-15

R226P	$500	blue	675.

1917

R246P	$30	deep orange (without serial No.)	650.

1940

R298P	50c	car (without ovpt.)	700.
R305P	$10	carmine	825.
		Without overprint	—
R306AP	$50	carmine	825.
		Without overprint	—

1952

R597P	55c	carmine	675.

PROPRIETARY

1871-75   Joseph R. Carpenter, Philadelphia

			DIE ON INDIA (2) Small	(3) India	PLATE (4) Card	(5) Bond
RB1P	1c	grn & blk		—	12.	12.
		Block of 4			52.	52.
RB2P	2c	grn & blk		175.	12.	
		Block of 4			52.	
RB3P	3c	grn & blk		22.	12.	
		Block of 4		100.	52.	
RB4P	4c	grn & blk		22.	12.	
		Block of 4		100.	52.	
RB5P	5c	grn & blk		22.	12.	
		Block of 4		100.	52.	
RB6P	6c	grn & blk		22.	12.	
		Block of 4		100.	52.	
RB7P	10c	grn & blk		22.	12.	
		Block of 4		100.	52.	
RB8P	50c	grn & blk		1,000.	850.	
RB9P	$1	grn & blk		1,000.	1,250.	
RB10P	$5	grn & blk		2,000.	1,750.	2,000.

The "small die proofs" formerly listed under Nos. RB1P-RB7P are from the composite plate proofs listed under "Trial Color Proofs."

National Bank Note Co., New York City
1875-83

			DIE ON INDIA (1) Large	(2) Small	PLATE (3) India	(4) Card
RB11P	1c	green	600.		65.	—
		Block of 4			325.	
RB12P	2c	brown	600.		65.	—
		Pair			160.	
RB13P	3c	orange	600.		65.	—
		Pair			160.	
		Block of 4				—
RB14P	4c	red brown	600.		65.	—
		Pair			160.	
		Block of 4				—
RB15P	4c	red	600.			—
RB16P	5c	black	600.		65.	—
		Pair			160.	
RB17P	6c	violet blue	600.		65.	—
		Pair			160.	

			DIE ON INDIA (1) Large	(2) Small	PLATE (3) India	(4) Card
RB18P	6c	blue	600.		175.	
		Pair				400.
RB19P	10c	blue	600.			

No. RB19P was produced by the Bureau of Engraving and Printing.

Battleship Type
1898

RB20P	1/8c	yellow green	2,000.
RB21P	1/4c	brown	2,000.
RB22P	3/8c	deep orange	2,000.
RB23P	5/8c	deep ultramarine	2,000.
RB24P	1c	dark green	2,000.
RB25P	1 1/4c	violet	2,000.
RB26P	1 7/8c	dull blue	2,000.
RB27P	2c	violet brown	2,000.
RB28P	2 1/2c	lake	2,000.
RB29P	3 3/4c	olive gray	2,000.
RB30P	4c	purple	2,000.
RB31P	5c	brown orange	2,000.

Wines
1916

RE56P	$20	green	5,000.

PLAYING CARDS

1896   Bureau of Engraving & Printing

RF2P	2c	ultramarine	550.
a.		2c blue	1,100.

PRIVATE DIE PROPRIETARY

The editors are indebted to Eric Jackson and Philip T. Bansner for the compilation of the following listing of Private Die Proprietary die and plate proofs as well as the corresponding trial color proofs. The large die proofs range in size and format from die impressions on India die sunk on cards generally up to 6x9 inches, through die impressions on India on or off card in medium to stamp size. Many individual listings are known in more than one size and format. Values reflect the size and format most commonly seen.

PRIVATE DIE MATCH STAMPS
1864

			DIE ON INDIA (1) Large	PLATE (3) India	(4) Card
RO1P	1c	blue	225.		
RO2P	1c	orange	500.	90.	
RO3P	1c	blue	225.		
RO4P	1c	blue	500.		
RO5P	1c	green	500.		
RO6P	1c	Blue	175.		
RO7P	1c	blue	175.		
RO9P	1c	black	175.		
RO10P	1c	black	175.		
RO11P	3c	Black	250.		
RO12P	1c	black	225.		
RO12/185P	1c	black	750.		
RO13P	3c	green	1000.		
RO14P	1c	black	175.		
RO15P	1c	green	300.		
RO16P	1c	black	225.	60.	
RO17P	1c	blue	175.		
RO17/19P	1c/3c	blue	1000.		
RO17/19P	1c/3c	black	750.		
RO19P	3c	black	375.		
RO20P	1c	blue	175.		
RO21P	3c	black	250.		
RO23P	1c	orange	225.		
RO24P	1c	brown	225.		
RO28P	1c	blue	300.	90.	
RO29P	1c	black	175.		
RO30P	1c	green	175.		
RO31P	1c	black	175.		
RO32P	4c	black	300.		
RO33P	4c	green	225.		
RO35P	1c	black	175.		
RO37P	3c	black	225.		
RO38P	1c	black	350.		
RO39P	1c	blue	175.		
RO40P	1c	green	500.		
RO41P	1c	lake	225.		
RO42P	1c	lake	225.		
RO43P	1c	black	225.		
RO44P	1c	green	300.		
RO45P	1c	black	225.		
RO46P	1c	black	300.		
RO47P	1c	black	225.	90.	75.
RO48P	1c	black	500.		
RO49P	1c	black	175.		
RO50P	1c	black	375.		
RO55P	1c	black	250.		
RO56P	1c	black	250.		
RO57P	1c	green	300.		
RO58P	1c	lake	225.	75.	
RO60P	3c	black	300.		

No.	Value	Color	DIE ON INDIA (1) Large	PLATE (3) India	(4) Card
RO61P	1c	green	300.		
RO62P	1c	green	175.		
RO64P	1c	lake	225.		
RO65P	1c	black	225.		
RO66P	1c	blue	175.		
RO67P	1c	black	175.		
RO68P	1c	green	225.		
RO69P	1c	black	175.		
RO72P	1c	green	500.		
RO73P	1c	black	175.		
RO75P	1c	carmine	450.		
RO76P	1c	black	175.		
RO77P	1c	blue	225.		
RO78P	1c	blue	225.		
RO80P	1c	blue	300.		
RO81P	1c	black	175.		
RO82P	1c	black	175.		
RO83P	1c	blue	175.		
RO84P	1c	black	175.		
RO85P	1c	brown	300.	100.	
RO86P	1c	black	250.	125.	
RO87P	1c	black	500.	50.	
RO88P	1c	black	175.		
RO89P	3c	black	175.		
RO90P	6c	black	175.	125.	
RO91P	3c	black	225.	125.	
RO92P	1c	black	175.		
RO94P	3c	black	175.	175.	
RO95P	1c	green	225.		
RO96P	1c	green	300.		
RO97P	1c	black	175.		
RO98P	1c	green	225.		
RO99P	1c	green	300.		
RO100P	1c	green	225.	65.	
RO101P	3c	carmine		75.	
RO102P	5c	orange		75.	
RO103P	1c	black	175.		
RO104P	1c	green	175.		
RO105P	1c	black	175.	100.	
RO106P	1c	green	300.		
RO107P	1c	blue	225.		
RO108P	1c	red	750.		
RO109P	1c	black	300.		
RO110P	1c	green	175.		
RO112P	1c	blue	225.	100.	
RO113P	1c	black	175.		
RO114P	1c	lake	750.		
RO115P	1c	blue	175.		
RO116P	1c	blue	175.		
RO118P	8c	blue	500.		
RO119P	1c	green	300.		
RO121P	1c	green	500.		
RO122P	1c	black	175.		
RO123P	1c	black	175.		
RO124P	1c	green	750.		
RO125P	1c	blue	300.		
RO126P	1c	black	175.		
RO127P	1c	blue	175.		
RO128P	1c	blue	225.		
RO130P	1c	blue	500.		
RO131P	1c	blue	300.		
RO132P	1c	blue	225.	125.	
RO133P	1c	black	225.		
RO134P	1c	blue	175.	75.	
RO135P	1c	lake	500.		
RO136P	1c	blue	175.		
RO138P	1c	green	175.		
RO139P	5c	blue	225.		
RO140P	4c	green	225.		
RO141P	1c	blue	175.		
RO142P	1c	green	225.		
RO143P	3c	orange	225.		
RO144P	1c	blue	400.		
RO146P	1c	black	175.		
RO148P	1c	blue	225.	100.	
RO152P	1c	black	175.	75.	
RO153P	1c	black	175.	75.	
RO155P	1c	black	175.	65.	
RO157P	3c	blue	225.	80.	
RO158P	1c	black	175.		
RO159P	3c	blue	175.		
RO160P	1c	blue	175.		
RO161P	1c	blue	500.		
RO163P	1c	black	175.		
RO164P	1c	lake	500.		
RO165P	12c	blue	750.		
RO166P	1c	vermilion	225.		
RO167P	3c	blue	175.		
RO168P	1c	blue	175.		
RO170P	1c	black	450.		
RO171P	1c	black	175.		
RO172P	1c	black	175.		
RO173P	1c	blue	225.	75.	
RO174P	1c	blue	175.		
RO175P	1c	black	225.		
RO176P	1c	blue	500.		
RO177P	1c	green	175.		
RO178P	1c	green	500.		
RO179P	1c	black	175.	75.	75.
RO180P	1c	black	175.	80.	
RO181P	1c	black	175.		
RO182P	1c	black	175.		
RO183P	1c	black	500.		
RO184P	1c	black	225.	75.	
RO186P	1c	black	225.		

PRIVATE DIE CANNED FRUIT STAMP

No.	Value	Color	Large	India	Card
RP1P	1c	green	375.		

PRIVATE DIE MEDICINE STAMPS

No.	Value	Color	DIE ON INDIA (1) Large	PLATE (3) India	(4) Card
RS1P	1c	black	175.		
RS4P	1c	black	225.	125.	150.
RS5P	1c	blue	500.		
RS10P	4c	blue	225.	125.	150.
RS14P	4c	green	500.	10.	
RS16P	2c	vermilion	500.		
RS18P	1c	black	500.		125.
RS19P	2c	black			125.
RS20P	4c	black			125.
RS21P	1c	black	175.	125.	
RS22P	2c	black	225.	125.	
RS23P	4c	black	225.	125.	
RS24P	1c	black	175.		
RS25P	2c	black	175.		
RS26P	4c	black	175.		
RS27P	4c	black	175.		
RS28P	2c	green	175.		
RS29P	2c	green	225.		
RS29/RO120P	2c/1c	green	1250.		
RS30P	1c	lake	300.		
RS31P	1c	green	175.	100.	100.
RS33P	1c	black	175.	50.	50.
RS34P	1c	black	225.		
RS35P	1c	black	175.		
RS36P	1c	blue	175.		
RS37P	2c	black	450.		
RS38P	2c	black	300.		
RS39P	1c	black	175.	100.	100.
RS40P	2c	green	500.	100.	100.
RS41P	4c	brown		125.	125.
RS42P	1c	black	175.		
RS43P	4c	blue	225.		
RS44P	1c	black	600.		
RS46P	4c	black	175.		
RS47P	4c	black	175.	125.	
RS49P	4c	green	175.		
RS50P	1c	vermilion	225.		
RS51P	2c	black	175.		
RS52P	4c	black	175.		
RS53P	1c	black	175.	125.	
RS54P	2c	black	175.	125.	
RS55P	4c	black	175.	125.	
RS56P	3c	blue	350.	125.	
RS57P	6c	black	175.	100.	
RS58P	4c	black	175.		
RS59P	1c	black	175.		
RS60P	1c	black	175.	65.	
RS61P	4c	blue	500.		
RS62P	1c	black	225.	125.	
RS63P	1c	blue	175.		
RS64P	2c	black	175.	125.	
RS65P	4c	black	175.		
RS66P	1c	black	500.		85.
RS67P	1c	black	175.		
RS68P	2c	black	175.	90.	
RS69P	1c	black	175.		
RS70P	2c	black	225.		
RS71P	1c	black	175.		
RS72P	2c	black	175.		
RS73P	2c	green	500.		
RS74P	1c	black	225.		
RS74hP	1c	black	175.		
RS75P	1c	blue	175.		
RS77P	2c	black	225.		
RS78P	2c	dull pur	750.		
RS81P	4c	brown	225.		
RS82P	2c	black	175.		
RS83P	4c	black	225.		
RS84P	1c	lake	500.	—	110.
RS85P	4c	black	250.	—	
RS86P	1c	green	175.		
RS88P	1c	black	225.	100.	100.
RS89P	1c	black	500.		
RS90P	1c	blue	225.	125.	125.
RS91P	4c	black	175.		
RS92P	3c	black	175.	—	
RS94P	4c	black	175.		
RS95P	1c	green	225.	90.	
RS96P	3c	black	175.	50.	
RS97P	1c	black	175.		
RS98P	1c	black	175.		
RS99P	4c	black	175.		
RS100P	6c	black	175.		
RS101P	1c	black	175.		
RS102P	2c	blue	175.		
RS103P	4c	black	175.		
RS104P	3c	black	750.		
RS105P	3c	brown	600.		
RS106P	2c	blue	225.	60.	
RS107P	3c	black	225.		
RS107/109P	3c/6c	black	1000.		
RS108P	4c	black	175.	45.	
RS109P	6c	black	225.		
RS110P	2c	blue	175.		
RS111P	4c	black	175.		
RS114P	1c	black	225.		
RS114/115P	1c/2c	black	1000.		
RS115P	2c	blue	225.		
RS116P	4c	red	225.		
RS117P	1c	black	250.		
RS118P	1c	red	300.	55.	50.
RS119P	1c	black	225.		
RS120P	2c	black	175.		
RS121P	3c	black	225.	75.	
RS122P	2c	black	175.	100.	
RS123P	4c	black	175.	125.	
RS124P	1c	black	300.	90.	65.
RS126P	1c	green	175.		
RS127P	4c	green	175.	65.	
RS128P	2c	blue	275.	150.	
RS130P	4c	green	275.		
RS131P	4c	black	175.	75.	
RS132P	4c	black	175.		75.
RS133P	6c	black	175.	125.	
RS134P	4c	blue	225.		

No.	Value	Color	DIE ON INDIA (1) Large	PLATE (3) India	(4) Card
RS137P	4c	blue	500.		
RS138P	1c	black	175.		
RS141P	4c	green	300.	125.	
RS142P	1c	black	175.		
RS143P	4c	green	225.		
RS144P	1c	blue	175.	100.	
RS145P	2c	black	175.	100.	
RS146P	4c	green	225.	100.	
RS150P	1c	vermilion	225.	100.	
RS151P	1c	black	175.		
RS152P	2c	green	175.		
RS153P	4c	black	450.	175.	
RS154P	4c	blue	500.		
RS155P	2c	green	175.		
RS156P	6c	black	175.		
R3137P	2c	black	175.		
RS158P	1c	green	500.		
RS159P	4c	blue	225.		
RS160P	6c	black	225.		
RS161P	4c	black	300.	150.	
RS162P	1c	blue	300.		
RS163P	4c	blue	600.		
RS164P	1c	black	175.		
RS165P	4c	green	500.		
RS166P	1c	black	175.		
RS169P	4c	black	175.		
RS170P	1c	black	175.		
RS171P	1c	violet	175.		
RS171uP	1c	purple	500.		
RS172P	2c	black	175.	100.	
RS173P	1c	blue	175.		
RS174P	1c	blue	175.		
RS176P	4c	black	250.		
RS177P	2c	black	350.		
RS178P	1c	black	225.		
RS179P	2c	green	225.		
RS180P	3c	black	275.	125.	
RS181P	4c	black	225.		
RS182P	4c	black	175.		
RS183P	1c	vermilion	225.	85.	
RS184P	2c	black	175.	100.	
RS185P	1c	black	175.	100.	
RS186P	4c	black	175.		
RS187P	4c	black	175.	100.	
RS188P	6c	black	300.		
RS189P	1c	green	225.		
RS190P	2c	black	175.		
RS191P	4c	black	250.		
RS192P	6c	black	250.	125.	
RS193P	2	black	175.		
RS194P	1c	blue	175.		
RS195P	2c	black	175.		
RS196P	1c	blue	175.		
RS197P	2c	black	175.		
RS198P	1c	black	225.		
RS199P	1c	black	175.		
RS204P	2c	black	175.		
RS205P	4c	black	175.		
RS208P	1c	green	175.	100.	
RS209P	2c	green	225.		
RS210P	4c	black	225.		
RS212P	1c	green	225.	100.	
RS213P	6c	black	175.	100.	1..
RS214P	4c	black	175.	65.	
RS215P	1c	lake	300.		
RS216P	1c	black	175.	75.	
RS219P	4c	blue	300.		
RS220P	1c	black	175.	50.	
RS221P	4c	green	225.	50.	
RS222P	8c	black	175.		
RS223P	1c	black	175.	—	
RS224P	1c	black	175.	—	
RS225P	4c	black	175.		
RS226P	1c	blue	175.		350.
RS228P	1c	brown	225.	—	
RS229P	2c	chocolate	175.	75.	
RS230P	6c	black	175.	—	
RS231P	6c	orange	750.		75.
RS232P	8c	orange	750.		
RS236P	4c	black	175.		
RS239P	2c	vermilion	225.	100.	
RS240P	4c	black	175.	125.	5..

"USIR" & "4 cents" obliterated on #RS240P4.

No.	Value	Color	Large	India	Card
RS241P	4	red	225.		
RS242P	1c	black	175.	80.	7..
RS243P	4c	black	175.		
RS244P	6c	black	175.		
RS245P	1c	black	250.		
RS250P	6c	black	175.	100.	
RS251P	1c	black	175.		
RS252P	1c	ver	175.	100.	
RS253P	4c	black	175.		
RS258P	6c	brown	175.		
RS259P	1c	black	175.	90.	
RS260P	2c	black	225.	90.	
RS261P	4c	black	175.	100.	
RS262P	2c	black	175.		
RS263P	4c	black	225.	90.	
RS264P	4c	black	225.		
RS264AP	4c	black	300.		
RS265P	1c	green	225.		
RS267P	4c	lake	225.		
RS270P	12c	blue	175.		
RS271P	4c	black	2500.		
RS272P	1c	green	225.		
RS273P	2c	green	175.		
RS274P	1c	green	225.	65.	6..
RS276P	2c	green	225.		
RS300P	4⅜c	black	1,000.		
RS306P	1¼c	pink	1,000.		

PRIVATE DIE PERFUMERY STAMPS

			DIE ON INDIA (1) Large	(3) India	PLATE (4) Card
RT1P	2c	blue		125.	125.
RT2P	1c	black	250.	95.	
RT4P	1c	blue	225.		
RT5P	2c	ver			100.
RT6P	1c	black	250.	150.	
RT8P	2c	black	500.		
RT10P	4c	black	250.	150.	
RT12P	1c	ver	225.		
RT14P	3c	black	500.		
RT16P	1c	black	175.		
RT17P	2c	brown	175.		
RT18P	3c	green	175.		
RT19P	1c	ver	225.		
RT20P	1c	green	225.		
RT21P	2c	blue	175.		
RT22P	1c	blue	225.		
RT23P	2c	black	175.		
RT25P	4c	green	175.		
RT26P	1c	green	175.		
RT27P	1c	green			100.
RT28P	2c	blue	175.		
RT30P	3c	ver	225.		
RT32P	4c	brown	175.		

PRIVATE DIE PLAYING CARD STAMPS

			DIE ON INDIA (1) Large	(3) India	PLATE (4) Card
RU1P	5c	black	2500.		
RU3P	4c	black	175.	100.	
RU4P	5c	blue	175.		
RU5P	5c	blue	175.		
RU6P	10c	blue	500.	100.	
RU7P	5c	black	250.	100.	
RU8P	5c	black	175.		
RU9P	5c	black	175.		
RU10P	2c	blue	175.		
RU11P	5c	green	225.		
RU12P	5c	black	175.		
RU13P	5c	blue	300.		
RU14P	5c	black	175.		—
RU15P	5c	black	175.		
RU16P	5c	black	500.		

HUNTING PERMIT

				DIE (Wove) (1) Large	(2) Small
RW1P	1934	$1	blue	—	2,750.
RW2P	1935	$1	rose lake		2,750.
RW3P	1936	$1	brown black	5,000.	2,750.
RW4P	1937	$1	light green	—	2,750.
RW5P	1938	$1	light violet	—	2,750.
RW6P	1939	$1	chocolate		2,750.
RW7P	1940	$1	sepia		2,750.
RW8P	1941	$1	brown carmine	5,500.	2,750.
RW9P	1942	$1	violet brown		2,750.
RW10P	1943	$1	deep rose	5,500.	2,750.
RW11P	1944	$1	red orange		2,750.
RW12P	1945	$1	black	3,850.	2,750.
RW13P	1946	$1	red brown	3,850.	
RW14P	1947	$1	black	3,850.	
RW15P	1948	$1	bright blue	3,850.	
RW19P	1952	$2	deep ultra.	3,850.	
RW23P	1956	$2	black		

POSTAL SAVINGS

1911

			DIE (1) Large	(2) Small	(2a)
PS1P	10c	orange	1,000.	750.	
PS4P	10c	deep blue		750.	

1940

PS7P	10c	deep ultra. on wove		1,200.
PS8P	25c	dk. car. rose on wove		1,200.
PS9P	50c	dk. bl. green on wove		1,200.
PS10P	$1	gray black on wove		1,200.

1941

PS11P	10c	rose red on wove		1,000.
PS12P	25c	blue green on wove		1,000.
PS13P	50c	ultramarine on wove		1,000.
PS14P	$1	gray black on wove		1,000.
PS15P	$5	sepia on wove		1,000.

WAR SAVINGS STAMP

1942

WS7P	10c	rose red	1,400.

POST OFFICE SEALS

1872

		DIE Large	PLATE India
OXF1P	green		275.
a.	Wove paper		950.
b.	Glazed paper		190.

1877

		DIE Large	PLATE India
OX1P	brown	1,750.	18.
	Block of 4		200.

1879

		DIE Large	PLATE India
OX2aP	brown	2,500.	15.
	Block of 4		65.

1888-94

		DIE Large	PLATE India
OX5P	chocolate		750.

1901-03

		DIE Large	PLATE India
OX11P	red brown		650.

No. OX11P is a hybrid proof sunk on card.

1972

OX41P	Pane of 5, blue line proof		—

TRIAL COLOR PROOFS

Values are for items in very fine condition. The listings of trial color proofs include several that are similar to the colors of the issued stamps.

New York

All on India paper unless otherwise stated.
Original Die

1845

			DIE (1) Lg.	(2) Sm.	PLATE (5) Bond
9X1TC	5c	dull dark violet		300.	
9X1TC	5c	brown violet		300.	
9X1TC	5c	deep rose violet		300.	
9X1TC	5c	deep blue		300.	200.
9X1TC	5c	dark green		300.	200.
9X1TC	5c	orange yellow		300.	
9X1TC	5c	brown		300.	200.
9X1TC	5c	scarlet			200.

With "Scar" on Neck

			DIE (1) Lg.	(2) Sm.	PLATE (5) Bond
9X1TC	5c	dull blue			175.
9X1TC	5c	vermilion			175.

With "Scar" and dot in "P" of "POST"

			DIE (1) Lg.	(2) Sm.	PLATE (5) Bond
9X1TC	5c	dull gray blue			300.
9X1TC	5c	deep blue on Bond			250.
9X1TC	5c	deep ultramarine on thin glazed card		450.	
9X1TC	5c	deep green			300.
9X1TC	5c	deep green on Bond			250.
9X1TC	5c	dull dark green			300.
9X1TC	5c	orange vermilion on thin glazed card		450.	
9X1TC	5c	dull brown red on Bond			250.
9X1TC	5c	dark brown red			300.
9X1TC	5c	dull dark brown			300.
9X1TC	5c	dull dark brown on Bond			250.
9X1TC	5c	brown black on thin glazed card		450.	

Large die trial color proofs with additional impression of the portrait medallion are listed in the Essay section as Nos. 9X1-E1.

Plate proofs are from the small sheet of 9.

Providence, R. I.

1846

			Plate on Card
10X1TC	5c	gray blue	250.
10X1TC	5c	green	250.
10X1TC	5c	brown carmine	250.
10X1TC	5c	brown	250.
10X2TC	10c	gray blue	450.
10X2TC	10c	green	450.
10X2TC	10c	brown carmine	450.
10X2TC	10c	brown	450.
		Sheet of 12, any color	3,750.

General Issues

1847

			LARGE DIE India	Bond	Wove	Thin Glazed Card
1TC	5c	violet	1,000.			
1TC	5c	dull blue	1,000.			
1TC	5c	deep blue		800.	800.	
		Small, India				625.
1TC	5c	deep ultra				850.
1TC	5c	blue green	1,000.			
		Small, India				625.
1TC	5c	dull blue green		800.		
1TC	5c	dull green	1,000.			
		Small, bond		600.		
1TC	5c	dark green	1,000.			
1TC	5c	yellow green, small India				625.
1TC	5c	orange yellow	1,000.	800.	800.	
		Small, India				625.
1TC	5c	deep yellow			800.	
1TC	5c	orange vermilion	1,000.	800.	800.	
1TC	5c	scarlet vermilion	1,000.	800.		850.
1TC	5c	rose lake	1,000.			
		Small, bond				625.
1TC	5c	black brown		800.		850.
1TC	5c	dull rose lake, small bond				625.
1TC	5c	brown red	1,000.			
1TC	5c	black	1,000.	800.		850.
		Small, India				675.
2TC	10c	violet	1,000.			
2TC	10c	dull blue				
2TC	10c	deep blue	1,000.	800.	800.	850.
		Small, India				675.
2TC	10c	dull gray blue, small India				625.
2TC	10c	blue green		800.		
2TC	10c	dull blue green		800.		
2TC	10c	dull green		800.		
2TC	10c	dark green	1,000.			
2TC	10c	yel green, small India				675.
2TC	10c	dull yellow			800.	
2TC	10c	orange yellow	1,000.	800.		
2TC	10c	orange vermilion	1,000.	800.	800.	
		Small, India				625.
2TC	10c	scarlet vermilion				850.
2TC	10c	golden brown	1,000.	800.		850.
2TC	10c	light brown	1,000.			
2TC	10c	dark brown	1,000.	800.		
2TC	10c	red brown				675.
2TC	10c	dull red				675.
2TC	10c	rose lake	1,000.			

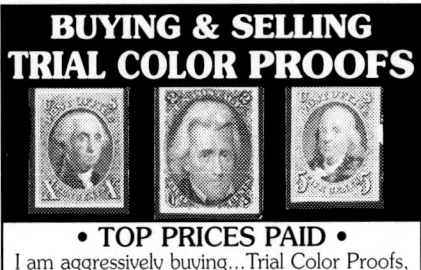

			India	Bond	Wove	Thin Glazed Card
				LARGE DIE		
2TC	10c	dull rose lake, small India				625.
2TC	10c	black brown				850.
2TC	10c	yellow green on blue pelure paper		1,000.		

Original die proofs are often cut down and reduced in size; full-size die proofs sell at higher prices. Reprint proofs with cross-hatching are valued as full-size; cut down examples sell for less.

			DIE		PLATE	
			(1) Lg.	(2) Sm.	(3) India	(4) Card
1TC	5c	orange			600.	
1TC	5c	black			600.	
		Double transfer (80R1)			—	
		Double transfer (90R1)			—	
2TC	10c	orange			600.	
2TC	10c	deep brown			600.	

Nos. 1TC3-2TC3 exist with and without "specimen" overprint. Values are for examples without the overprint. Examples with the overprint are equally as scarce but sell for slightly less.

1875

3TC	5c	dull rose lake			600.
3TC	5c	black	900.		
3TC	5c	green	900.		
4TC	10c	green	900.		750.

1851-60

			DIE		PLATE	
			(1) Lg.	(2) Sm.	(3) India	(5) Wove Paper
5TC	1c	black			—	
7TC	1c	black on stamp paper				3,750.
11TC	3c	black on stamp paper				3,000.
12TC	5c	pale brown				300.
12TC	5c	rose brown				300.
12TC	5c	deep red brown				1,500.
12TC	5c	dark olive bister				300.
12TC	5c	olive brown				300.
12TC	5c	olive green				300.
12TC	5c	deep orange				300.
12TC	5c	black	6,500.			5,000.
13TC	10c	black	5,000.			1,500.
37TC	24c	claret brown				600.
37TC	24c	red brown				600.
37TC	24c	orange				600.
37TC	24c	deep yellow				600.
37TC	24c	yellow				600.
37TC	24c	deep blue				600.
37TC	24c	black	7,000.			—
37TC	24c	violet black				600.
37TC	24c	red lilac on stamp paper, perf. 15½, gummed (formerly No. 37b)				1,000.
		Block of 4				6,000.
38TC	30c	black	5,000.	1,250.	1,400.	600.
		Block of 4			9,000.	
39TC	90c	rose lake				625.
39TC	90c	henna brown				625.
39TC	90c	orange red				625.
39TC	90c	brown orange	5,000.			625.
39TC	90c	sepia				625.
39TC	90c	dark green				625.
39TC	90c	dark violet brown				625.
39TC	90c	black	5,000.	1,250.		675.

Former Nos. 55-57, 59, 62 are now in the Essay section. Former Nos. 60-61 will be found below as Nos. 70TCe and 71TCb, respectively.

1875

				PLATE (5) Wove Paper, Imperf.
40TC	1c	orange vermilion		275.
40TC	1c	orange		275.
40TC	1c	yellow orange		275.
40TC	1c	orange brown		275.
40TC	1c	dark brown		275.
40TC	1c	dull violet		275.
40TC	1c	violet		275.
40TC	1c	red violet		275.
40TC	1c	gray		275.
41TC	3c	red		—

1861

			PLATE	
			(5) Wove Paper, Imperf.	(6) Wove Paper, Perf.
63TC	1c	rose	40.	50.
63TC	1c	deep orange red	40.	50.
63TC	1c	deep red orange	40.	50.
63TC	1c	dark orange	40.	50.
63TC	1c	yellow orange	40.	50.
63TC	1c	orange brown	40.	50.
63TC	1c	dark brown	40.	50.
63TC	1c	yellow green	40.	50.
63TC	1c	green	40.	50.
63TC	1c	blue green	40.	50.
63TC	1c	gray lilac	40.	50.
63TC	1c	gray black	40.	50.

			PLATE	
			(5) Wove Paper, Imperf.	(6) Wove Paper, Perf.
63TC	1c	slate black	40.	50.
63TC	1c	blue	40.	50.
63TC	1c	light blue	40.	50.
63TC	1c	deep blue	100.	50.

The perforated 1861 1c trial colors are valued with perfs cutting the design on two sides. Well centered items are extremely scarce and sell for more.

There are many trial color impressions of the issues of 1861 to 1883 made for experimentation with various patent papers, grills, eTC. Some are fully perforated, gummed and with grill.

1861-62

			DIE			PLATE
			(1) Lg.	(2) Sm.	(2a)	India (3)
62BTC	10c	black	1,750.			
62BTC	10c	green				300.
62BTC	10c	light green				300.
63TC	1c	black	2,000.	750.		
63TC	1c	red		750.		
63TC	1c	brown		750.		
63TC	1c	green		—		
63TC	1c	orange		—		
64TC	3c	carmine pink on thin stamp paper, perf 12, gummed				—
65TC	3c	black	1,400.			
65TC	3c	black on glazed	1,400.			
65TC	3c	blue green	1,400.			
65TC	3c	orange	1,400.			
65TC	3c	brown	1,400.			
65TC	3c	dark blue	1,400.			
65TC	3c	ocher	1,400.			
65TC	3c	green	1,400.			
65TC	3c	dull red	1,400.			
65TC	3c	slate	1,400.			
65TC	3c	red brown	1,400.			
65TC	3c	deep pink	1,400.			
65TC	3c	rose pink	1,400.			
65TC	3c	dark rose	1,400.			
67TC	5c	black	1,750.		—	
67TC	5c	dark orange	1,500.			
67TC	5c	green	1,500.			
67TC	5c	ultramarine	1,500.			
67TC	5c	gray	1,500.			
67TC	5c	rose brown			—	
68TC	10c	orange	1,400.			
68TC	10c	red brown	1,400.			
68TC	10c	dull pink	1,400.			
68TC	10c	scarlet	1,400.			
68TC	10c	black	1,750.	550.		
69TC	12c	scarlet verm.	1,400.			
69TC	12c	brown	1,400.			
69TC	12c	red brown	1,400.			
69TC	12c	green	1,400.			
69TC	12c	orange yellow	1,400.			
69TC	12c	black		550.		
70TC	24c	scarlet	2,250.			
70TC	24c	green	2,250.			
70TC	24c	orange	2,250.			
70TC	24c	red brown	2,250.			
70TC	24c	orange brown	2,250.			
70TC	24c	orange yellow	2,250.			
70TC	24c	rose red	2,250.			
70TC	24c	gray	2,250.			
70TC	24c	gray on bluish gray stamp paper				—
70TC	24c	steel blue	2,250.			
70TC	24c	blue	2,250.			
70TC	24c	violet	2,250.	500.		
70TC	24c	violet	1,250.	375.	2,250.	250.
		Block of 4				1,125.
e.		dark violet, semitransparent stamp paper, perf. 12, gummed **(formerly #60)**				8,000.
71TC	30c	rose	1,750.			
71TC	30c	black		600.		
71TC	30c	red orange	1,750.	375.	1,250.	
		Block of 4				
b.		red orange, semitransparent stamp paper, perf. 12, gummed **(formerly #61)**			25,000.	
72TC	90c	black	1,750.	600.		
72TC	90c	ultramarine	1,750.			
72TC	90c	bluish gray	1,750.			
72TC	90c	violet gray	1,750.			
72TC	90c	red brown	1,750.			
72TC	90c	orange	1,750.			
72TC	90c	yellow orange	1,750.			
72TC	90c	scarlet	1,750.			
72TC	90c	green	1,750.			

1861

			STAMP PAPER	
			Unused	Used
66TC	3c	lake, perf. 12, gummed	2,000.	
		Pair	4,500.	
		Block of 4	9,250.	
		P# strip of 4	10,000.	
		Double transfer	2,250.	
a.		Imperf, pair, gummed	1,850.	
		P# blk. of 8		

John N. Luff recorded the plate number for No. 66TC as 34.

			STAMP PAPER	
			Unused	Used
74TC	3c	scarlet, perf. 12, gummed	7,000.	
		Block of 4	29,000.	
		With 4 horiz. black pen strokes		5,0..
a.		Imperf, pair, gummed	4,000.	

John N. Luff recorded the plate number for No. 74TC as 19..

1861

			DIE			PLATE	
			(1) Large	(2) Small	(2a)	(3) India	(4) Car..
66TC	3c	lake	250.	1,100.		125.	
		Block of 4				725.	
		P# blk. of 8				1,850.	
74TC	3c	scarlet	2,250.	375.	1,100.	100.	10..
		Block of 4				500.	45..
		P# blk. of 8					

1863

			DIE		PLATE	
			(1) Lg.	(2) Sm.	(3) India	(4 Ca..
73TC	2c	light blue			250.	
73TC	2c	dull chalky blue	8,000.		500.	
73TC	2c	green	8,000.		250.	
73TC	2c	olive green			250.	
73TC	2c	blue green			400.	
73TC	2c	dull yellow	8,000.			
73TC	2c	dark orange	8,000.			
73TC	2c	vermilion			250.	
73TC	2c	scarlet	8,000.		250.	
73TC	2c	dull red			250.	
73TC	2c	dull rose	8,000.		250.	
73TC	2c	brown	8,000.			
73TC	2c	gray black			250.	
73TC	2c	ultramarine	8,000.			

1866

			DIE		PLATE	
				Lg.	Sm.	India
77TC	15c	deep blue	2,500.		335.	
		Block of 4			1,650.	
77TC	15c	dark red	2,500.			
77TC	15c	orange red	2,500.			
77TC	15c	dark orange	2,500.			
77TC	15c	yellow orange	2,500.			
77TC	15c	yellow	2,500.			
77TC	15c	orange brown	2,500.			
77TC	15c	red brown	2,500.			
77TC	15c	blue green	2,500.			
77TC	15c	dusky blue	2,500.			
77TC	15c	gray black	2,500.			

1869

112TC	1c	black	2,500.
113TC	2c	black	2,500.
114TC	3c	black	2,500.
115TC	6c	deep dull blue	2,500.
115TC	6c	black	2,500.
116TC	10c	black	2,500.
116TC	10c	dull dark violet	2,500.
116TC	10c	deep green	2,500.
116TC	10c	dull dark orange	2,500.
116TC	10c	dull rose	2,500.
116TC	10c	copper red	2,500.
116TC	10c	chocolate	2,500.
116TC	10c	dk Prussian bl	2,500.
117TC	12c	black	2,500.
118TC	15c	dull dark violet	2,500.
118TC	15c	deep blue	2,500.
118TC	15c	dull red brown	2,500.
118TC	15c	black	2,500.
118TC	15c	dark blue gray	2,500.
120TC	24c	black	3,500.
121TC	30c	deep blue & deep green	3,500.
121TC	30c	deep brown & blue	3,500.
121TC	30c	golden brown & carmine lake	3,500.
121TC	30c	carmine lake & dull violet	3,500.
121TC	30c	car lake & green	3,500.
121TC	30c	car lake & brown	3,500.
121TC	30c	car lake & black	3,500.
121TC	30c	dull orange red & deep green	3,500.
121TC	30c	deep ocher & golden brown	3,500.
121TC	30c	dull violet & golden brown	3,500.
121TC	30c	black & deep green	3,500.
122TC	90c	brown & deep green	3,500.
122TC	90c	green & black		1,500..

1870-71

			DIE		PLATE	
			(1) Lg.	(2) Sm.	(3) India	(4) Card
145TC	1c	yellow orange			600.	
145TC	1c	red brown			600.	
145TC	1c	red violet			600.	
145TC	1c	black			—	—
145TC	1c	green			600.	
146TC	2c	black			600.	
147TC	3c	brown			—	125.
147TC	3c	dark brown				125.

No.			DIE (1) Lg.	(2) Sm.	PLATE (3) India	(4) Card
147TC	3c	red brown	—			125.
147TC	3c	orange brown	—			125.
147TC	3c	dark red	—			125.
147TC	3c	deep red brown, wove paper				125.
147TC	3c	light ultramarine	—			125.
147TC	3c	yellow brown	—			125.
147TC	3c	dull red violet	—			125.
147TC	3c	dull grayish red	—			
147TC	3c	yellow orange	—			125.
147TC	3c	red violet	—			125.
147TC	3c	black	600.			

Former Nos. 147aTC and 147bTC are now listed in the Essay section as No. 147-E13c.

No.			Lg.			
148TC	6c	deep magenta	600.			
148TC	6c	ultramarine	600.			
148TC	6c	carmine	600.			
148TC	6c	maroon	600.			
149TC	7c	black	550.			
150TC	10c	blue	550.			
150TC	10c	dull pale blue	550.			
150TC	10c	ultramarine	550.			
150TC	10c	blue green	550.			
150TC	10c	carmine	550.			
150TC	10c	bister	550.			
150TC	10c	dull red	550.			
150TC	10c	red orange	550.			
150TC	10c	yellow brown	550.			
150TC	10c	brown orange	550.			
151TC	12c	orange	550.			
151TC	12c	orange brown	550.			
151TC	12c	brown red	550.			
151TC	12c	dull red	550.			
151TC	12c	carmine	550.			
151TC	12c	blue	550.			
151TC	12c	light blue	550.			
151TC	12c	ultramarine	550.			
151TC	12c	green	550.			
153TC	24c	dark brown	550.			
155TC	90c	carmine	550.			
155TC	90c	ultramarine	550.			
155TC	90c	black	550.			

1873

No.			Lg.	Sm.	India	Card
156TC	1c	black			15.	30.
		Block of 4			65.	140.
156TC	1c	scarlet			—	
157TC	2c	black		850.	15.	
		Block of 4			65.	
157TC	2c	dull blue		850.		
157TC	2c	rose		850.		
157TC	2c	deep rose		850.		
158TC	3c	black		750.	12.	
		Block of 4			55.	
158TC	3c	orange red		—		
159TC	6c	black		300.	30.	
		Block of 4			150.	
159TC	6c	deep green		300.		
159TC	6c	deep brown		300.		
159TC	6c	dull red		300.		
159TC	6c	dull gray blue		300.		
160TC	7c	black		300.	75.	
		Block of 4			325.	
160TC	7c	deep green		300.		
160TC	7c	deep brown		300.		
160TC	7c	dull gray blue		300.		
160TC	7c	dull red		300.		
161TC	10c	black		300.		
161TC	10c	deep green		300.		
161TC	10c	deep brown		300.		
161TC	10c	dull gray blue		300.		
161TC	10c	dull red		300.		
162TC	12c	black		300.		
162TC	12c	deep green		300.		
162TC	12c	dull gray blue		300.		
162TC	12c	deep brown		300.		
162TC	12c	dull red		300.		
163TC	15c	black		300.		
163TC	15c	deep green		300.		
163TC	15c	dull gray blue		300.		
163TC	15c	deep brown		300.		
163TC	15c	dull red		300.		
164TC	24c	black		300.		
164TC	24c	deep green		300.		
164TC	24c	dull gray blue		300.		
164TC	24c	deep brown		300.		
164TC	24c	dull red		300.		
165TC	30c	black		300.		
165TC	30c	deep green		300.		
165TC	30c	dull gray blue		300.		
165TC	30c	deep brown		300.		
165TC	30c	dull red		300.		
166TC	90c	black		300.		
166TC	90c	deep green		300.		
166TC	90c	dull gray blue		300.		
166TC	90c	deep brown		300.		
166TC	90c	dull red		300.		

1875

No.			Lg.	Sm.	India	Card
179TC	5c	black	650.	300.	25.	45.
		Block of 4			125.	200.
179TC	5c	deep green		300.		
179TC	5c	dull gray blue		300.		
179TC	5c	deep brown		300.		
179TC	5c	dull red		300.		
179TC	5c	scarlet	1,000.			

Small die proofs of 1873-75 issues are "Goodall" prints.

1879   On stamp paper, gummed   Perf. 12

182TC	1c	ultramarine				300.
182TC	1c	green				300.

No.						
182TC	1c	deep green				300.
182TC	1c	vermilion				300.
182TC	1c	brown				300.
183TC	2c	ultramarine				300.
183TC	2c	blue				300.
183TC	2c	green				300.
184TC	3c	ultramarine				300.
184TC	3c	blue				300.
184TC	3c	vermilion				300.
		Block of 4				1,100.
184TC	3c	brown				300.
185TC	5c	ultramarine				300.
185TC	5c	green				300.
185TC	5c	vermilion				300.
186TC	6c	ultramarine				300.
186TC	6c	blue				300.
186TC	6c	vermilion				300.
187TC	10c	ultramarine				300.
187TC	10c	blue				300.
187TC	10c	vermilion				300.
189TC	15c	ultramarine				300.
189TC	15c	green				300.
189TC	15c	vermilion				300.
189TC	15c	brown				300.
189TC	15c	dull red				300.
190TC	30c	ultramarine				300.
190TC	30c	blue				300.
190TC	30c	green				300.

See Specimens for No. 189 in deep blue (No. 189S L), No. 209 in green (No. 209S L), No. 210 in pale rose lake (No. 210S L).

1881-82

No.			Lg.	Sm.	India	Card
206TC	1c	deep green	600.		125.	
206TC	1c	black	600.		125.	
206TC	1c	ultramarine	600.			
206TC	1c	dark yellow green	600.			

1882-87

No.			LARGE DIE (1) India	(2) Card	PLATE (3) India	(4) Card
212TC	1c	indigo	1,000.			
212TC	1c	carmine	1,000.			
212TC	1c	green	1,000.		450.	
212TC	1c	deep green	1,000.		450.	
212TC	1c	copper brown	1,000.		450.	
212TC	1c	chestnut brown	1,000.			
210TC	2c	brown red	1,000.		450.	
210TC	2c	deep dull orange	1,000.			
210TC	2c	chestnut brown	1,000.		450.	
210TC	2c	violet rose	1,000.		450.	
210TC	2c	indigo	1,000.		450.	
210TC	2c	black	1,000.			
210TC	2c	pale ultramarine	1,000.			
210TC	2c	olive green	1,000.		450.	
210TC	2c	olive brown			450.	
210TC	2c	lake				140.
210TC	2c	rose lake				140.
210TC	2c	dark carmine				140.
210TC	2c	deep red				140.
214TC	3c	green	1,000.		450.	
214TC	3c	dark green			—	
214TC	3c	dark brown	1,000.		450.	
214TC	3c	chestnut brown	1,000.		450.	
214TC	3c	dull red brown	1,000.		450.	
214TC	3c	deep dull orange	—		—	

All of 214TC above bear inscription "Worked over by new company, June 29th, 1881."

211TC	4c	green	1,000.		450.	
211TC	4c	chestnut brown	1,000.		450.	
211TC	4c	orange brown	1,000.		450.	
211TC	4c	pale ultra.	1,000.		450.	
211TC	4c	dark brown	1,000.			
211TC	4c	black	1,000.		450.	
205TC	5c	chestnut brown	1,000.		—	
205TC	5c	deep dull orange	1,000.			
205TC	5c	pale ultra	1,000.		—	
205TC	5c	deep green	1,000.			
205TC	5c	green	1,000.		200.	
205TC	5c	carmine	1,000.		450.	
205TC	5c	carmine lake	1,000.		225.	
205TC	5c	blue black	1,000.			
205TC	5c	black on glazed	1,000.			
208TC	6c	indigo	1,000.			
208TC	6c	deep dull orange	1,000.		450.	
208TC	6c	orange vermilion	1,000.		450.	
208TC	6c	dark violet	1,000.			
208TC	6c	chestnut brown	1,000.		450.	
208TC	6c	carmine	1,000.			
209TC	10c	carmine	1,000.			
209TC	10c	orange brown	1,000.		450.	125.
209TC	10c	orange	1,000.			
209TC	10c	deep dull orange	1,000.		450.	
209TC	10c	chestnut brown	1,000.		450.	
209TC	10c	indigo	1,000.		450.	
209TC	10c	pale ultra	1,000.		450.	
209TC	10c	green				125.
209TC	10c	black (glazed)	1,000.			
189TC	15c	orange vermilion	1,000.		450.	
189TC	15c	orange brown	1,000.		450.	
189TC	15c	chestnut brown	1,000.		450.	
189TC	15c	dark brown	1,000.		450.	
189TC	15c	deep green	1,000.		450.	
189TC	15c	black	1,000.		450.	
190TC	30c	black	1,000.			
190TC	30c	orange vermilion	1,000.		450.	
190TC	30c	dark brown	1,000.		450.	
190TC	30c	deep green	1,000.			
190TC	30c	dull red brown	1,000.		450.	
190TC	30c	green	1,000.		450.	
191TC	90c	carmine	1,000.		450.	
191TC	90c	dark brown	1,000.		450.	

No.			LARGE DIE (1) India	(2) Card	PLATE (3) India	(4) Card
191TC	90c	deep dull orange	1,000.	450.		
191TC	90c	indigo	1,000.	450.		
191TC	90c	dull red brown	1,000.	450.		
191TC	90c	black	1,000.	450.		

1890-93

No.			DIE (1) India	(2) Card	PLATE (3) India	(4) Card
219TC	1c	green	400.			
219TC	1c	dull violet	400.			
220TC	2c	dull violet	400.			
220TC	2c	blue green	400.			
220TC	2c	slate black	400.			
222TC	4c	orange brown on wove				—
222TC	4c	yellow brown on wove				—
222TC	4c	green	400.			
223TC	5c	blue on glossy wove	400.			
223TC	5c	dark brown on glossy wove	400.			
223TC	5c	bister on wove				—
223TC	5c	sepia on wove				—
223TC	5c	blk brown on wove				—
224TC	6c	deep orange red	400.			
224TC	6c	orange red on wove				120.
224TC	6c	vio. blk. on wove				120.
224TC	6c	yellow on wove				120.
224TC	6c	olive grn. on wove				120.
224TC	6c	purple on wove				120.
224TC	6c	red org. on wove				120.
224TC	6c	brown on wove				120.
224TC	6c	red brn. on wove				120.
224TC	6c	org. brn. on wove				120.
224TC	6c	blk. brn. on wove				120.
224TC	6c	slate grn. on wove				120.
224TC	6c	brn. olive on wove				120.
225TC	8c	dark violet red		400.		
225TC	8c	metallic green		400.		
225TC	8c	salmon		400.		
225TC	8c	yellow orange		—		
225TC	8c	orange brown		400.		
225TC	8c	green		—		
225TC	8c	light green		400.		
225TC	8c	blue		400.		
225TC	8c	steel blue		400.		

1893

No.			LARGE DIE (1) India	(2) Card	PLATE (3) India	(4) Card
231TC	2c	sepia	850.	850.		
231TC	2c	orange brown	850.			
231TC	2c	deep orange	850.			
231TC	2c	light brown	850.			
231TC	2c	blue green	850.			
231TC	2c	bright rose red	850.			
231TC	2c	rose violet	850.			
232TC	3c	sepia	850.			
232TC	3c	blackish green	850.		800.	
232TC	3c	black	850.			
233TC	4c	sepia	850.			
233TC	4c	deep orange	850.			
233TC	4c	light brown	850.			
233TC	4c	blue green	850.			
233TC	4c	rose red	850.			
233TC	4c	rose violet	850.			
234TC	5c	black	850.		850.	
234TC	5c	dark violet	850.		850.	
234TC	5c	rose violet	850.		850.	
234TC	5c	red violet	850.			
234TC	5c	brown violet	850.			
234TC	5c	deep blue	850.			
234TC	5c	deep ultra	850.			
234TC	5c	green	850.			
234TC	5c	deep green	850.			

234TC	5c	blue green	—	850.
234TC	5c	dark olive green	850.	—
234TC	5c	deep orange	850.	
234TC	5c	orange red	850.	
234TC	5c	orange brown	850.	850.
234TC	5c	bright rose red	850.	
234TC	5c	claret	850.	
234TC	5c	brown rose	850.	
234TC	5c	dull rose brown		850.
234TC	5c	sepia	850.	850.
234TC	5c	black brown	—	850.

The 5c trial color proofs differ from the issued stamp.

237TC	10c	bright rose red	1,250.	
237TC	10c	claret	1,250.	
239TC	30c	sepia	1,000.	
239TC	30c	black		350.
240TC	50c	sepia	1,000.	
242TC	$2	blackish brown		1,000.
242TC	$2	sepia		
242TC	$2	red brown	—	

1894

			DIE		PLATE	
			(1) Lg.	(2) Sm.	(3) India	(4) Card
246TC	1c	dusky blue green	—			
246TC	1c	dark blue	—			
253TC	3c	light red violet	—			
253TC	3c	dark red violet	—			
255TC	5c	black	1,250.			
256TC	6c	dark brown	1,000.			
257TC	8c	black	1,250.			
258TC	10c	olive	1,250.			
259TC	15c	red violet	1,250.			
259TC	15c	dark red orange	1,250.			
261ATC	$1	lake	1,500.			
262TC	$2	black	1,500.			
262TC	$2	dull violet	1,500.			
262TC	$2	violet	1,500.			
262TC	$2	turquoise blue	1,500.			
262TC	$2	orange brown	1,500.			
262TC	$2	olive green	1,500.			
262TC	$2	sepia	1,500.			
262TC	$2	greenish black	1,500.			
263TC	$5	black	1,500.			
263TC	$5	dark yellow	1,500.			
263TC	$5	orange brown	1,500.			
263TC	$5	olive green	1,500.			
263TC	$5	dull violet	1,500.			
263TC	$5	sepia	1,500.			
263TC	$5	brown red	1,500.			

1898

283TC	10c	orange	1,250.	
283TC	10c	sepia	1,250.	
284TC	15c	yellowish olive	—	
284TC	15c	red violet	2,000.	

1898

285TC	1c	black	—	
286TC	2c	purple		1,750.
286TC	2c	black	—	1,750.
286TC	2c	blue		1,750.
286TC	2c	brown		1,750.
286TC	2c	deep carmine rose		1,750.
287TC	4c	black	—	
288TC	5c	black	—	
288TC	5c	orange brown	2,500.	
289TC	8c	black	—	
290TC	10c	black	1,500.	1,250.
291TC	50c	black	1,500.	1,250.
292TC	$1	black	—	
293TC	$2	black	5,000.	

1901

298TC	8c	violet & black on wove paper	2,500.

1902-03

308TC	13c	gray violet, type I	1,000.
319TC	2c	black, type I	3,250.

1904

326TC	5c	black on glazed card	—

1907

330TC	5c	ultramarine	1,600.
330TC	5c	black	1,700.

1908

332TC	2c	dull violet	750.
332TC	2c	light ultra.	750.
332TC	2c	bright ultra.	750.
332TC	2c	light green	750.
332TC	2c	dark olive green	750.
332TC	2c	golden yellow	750.
332TC	2c	dull orange	750.
332TC	2c	rose carmine	750.
332TC	2c	ultramarine	750.
332TC	2c	black	—
332TC	2c	dark blue	—
332TC	2c	blue	850.
332TC	2c	lilac brown	850.
332TC	2c	lilac	850.
332TC	2c	blue black	850.
332TC	2c	sage green	850.
332TC	2c	lilac black	850.
332TC	2c	brown	850.
332TC	2c	brown black	850.
332TC	2c	purple	—
332TC	2c	orange brown	850.

332TC	2c	ultra. on orange brown	750.
332TC	2c	ultra. on green	750.
332TC	2c	green on pink	750.
332TC	2c	green on rose	750.
332TC	2c	dark green on grn	750.
332TC	2c	green on orange brown	750.
332TC	2c	purple on orange brown	750.
332TC	2c	blue on yellow	750.
332TC	2c	green on yellow	750.
332TC	2c	brown on orange brown	750.
332TC	2c	brown on yellow	750.
332TC	2c	green on amber yel	—
335TC	5c	green on pink	—
336TC	6c	brown	—
337TC	8c	green (shades) on yellow	—
337TC	8c	orange (shades) on yellow	—
337TC	8c	blue on buff	—
337TC	8c	blue on yellow	—
338TC	10c	carmine on pale yellow green	—
338TC	10c	brown on yellow	—
338TC	10c	green on pink	—
338TC	10c	orange on greenish blue	—
338TC	10c	brown on gray lavender	—
338TC	10c	orange on orange	—
338TC	10c	black on pink	—
338TC	10c	orange on yellow	—
338TC	10c	brown	—
338TC	10c	carmine	—
338TC	10c	blue on pink	—
338TC	10c	brown on pink	—
338TC	10c	black	—
339TC	13c	blue on yellow	—
339TC	13c	sea green on deep yellow	—
339TC	13c	sea green on pale blue	—
339TC	13c	deep violet on yellow	—
340TC	15c	blue on pale lilac	—
340TC	15c	blue on greenish blue	—
340TC	15c	blue on pink	—
340TC	15c	blue on yellow	—
340TC	15c	dark blue on buff	—
340TC	15c	orange brown on yellow	—
340TC	15c	dark purple on yel	—
340TC	15c	orange on yellow	—
340TC	15c	violet on yellow	—
340TC	15c	black on orange	—
341TC	50c	lilac on light blue	—
341TC	50c	dark violet on yellow	—
341TC	50c	violet on yellow	—
341TC	50c	orange on yellow	—
341TC	50c	orange brown on yellow	—
342TC	$1	brown on blue	—

1909

342TC	$1	carmine lake	1,200.	1,100.
342TC	$1	pink	1,200.	1,100.
342TC	$1	brown on blue green	—	
342TC	$1	violet brown on pink	—	
342TC	$1	violet brown on gray	—	

1912-13

400TC	10c	brown red	1,750.	1,100.
414TC	8c	black	1,750.	

1918

524TC	$5	carmine & black	1,350.

1919

513TC	13c	violet	650.
513TC	13c	lilac	650.
513TC	13c	violet brown	650.
513TC	13c	light ultra	650.
513TC	13c	ultramarine	650.
513TC	13c	deep ultra	650.
513TC	13c	green	650.
513TC	13c	dark green	650.
513TC	13c	olive green	650.
513TC	13c	orange yellow	650.
513TC	13c	orange	650.
513TC	13c	red orange	650.
513TC	13c	ocher	650.
513TC	13c	salmon red	650.
513TC	13c	brown carmine	650.
513TC	13c	claret brown	650.
513TC	13c	brown	650.
513TC	13c	black brown	650.
513TC	13c	gray	650.
513TC	13c	black	650.

1920

547TC	$2	green & black	1,500.

1922-25

554TC	2c	black (bond paper)	1,250.
561TC	9c	red orange	2,250.
563TC	11c	deep green	2,250.
565TC	14c	dark brown	2,250.
566TC	15c	black	2,250.

1923

610TC	2c	Harding, green	4,000.

1925

618TC	2c	Lexington Concord, black	1,650.

1926

622TC	13c	black	2,250.
628TC	5c	Ericsson, dull dusky blue	1,000.
628TC		gray blue	1,000.

1932

718TC	3c	Olympic, carmine	10,000.
720TC	3c	black (bond paper)	750.

1935

772TC	3c	Connecticut Tercentenary, black (thin glazed card)	1,500.
773TC	3c	San Diego, org. red (yel. glazed card)	1,500.

1936-43

785TC	1c	Army, black (bond paper)		750.
788TC	4c	Army, dark brown	1,000.	
789TC	5c	Army, blue	1,000.	
793TC	4c	Navy, dark brown	1,000.	
798TC	3c	Constitution, black (bond paper)		750.
799TC	3c	Hawaii, black (bond paper)		750.
800TC	3c	Alaska, black (bond paper)		750.
800TC		(India paper)		750.
801TC	3c	Puerto Rico, black (bond paper)	900.	750.
801TC		(India paper)	900.	
802TC	3c	Virgin Islands, black (bond paper)		750.
803TC	½c	black	3,000.	
815TC	10c	sepia	900.	
829TC	25c	green	2,000.	
836TC	3c	Swedes & Finns, purple	900.	
837TC	3c	Northwest Terr., dark purple	900.	
854TC	3c	Inauguration, purple	900.	
855TC	3c	Baseball, red violet	2,250.	
862TC	5c	Authors, dull blue	900.	
866TC	3c	Poets, dark blue violet	900.	
897TC	3c	Wyoming, red violet	—	
929TC	3c	Iwo Jima, bright purple	2,300.	
959TC	3c	Progress of Women, brt. violet	1,500.	
963TC	3c	Youth, violet	900.	
964TC	3c	Oregon, dull violet	900.	
968TC	3c	Poultry, red brown	900.	

1923-47

AIR POST

			DIE		PLATE	
			(1) Lg.	(2) Sm.	(3) India	(4) Card
C5TC	16c	dark green	5,000.			
C8TC	15c	orange	4,500.			
C32TC	5c	blue	4,500.			
C35TC	15c	brown violet	4,500.			

1934

AIR POST SPECIAL DELIVERY

CE1TC	16c	black	3,500.

1885-1902

SPECIAL DELIVERY

E1TC	10c	black	2,500.	
E1TC	10c	dark brown	2,500.	
E1TC	10c	org. yellow (wove paper)		2,000.
E2TC	10c	black	2,500.	
E2TC	10c	green	2,500.	
E2TC	10c	olive yellow		800.
E6TC	10c	orange	2,500.	
E6TC	10c	black	2,500.	
E6TC	10c	rose red	4,000.	

1922-25

E12TC	10c	black	1,500.

1911

REGISTRATION

F1TC	10c	black (glazed card)	1,500.

1851

CARRIERS

LO1TC	deep green	250.	
	Block of 4	1,250.	
	a. orange (wove paper)		350
LO2TC	deep green	250.	
	Block of 4	1,250.	
	a. orange (wove paper)		350

79

POSTAGE DUE

		DIE		PLATE	
		(1) Lg.	(2) Sm.	(3) India	(4) Card
1TC	1c	black	500.		50.
1TC	1c	gray black	500.		
1TC	1c	ultramarine	500.		
1TC	1c	blue	500.		
1TC	1c	blue green	500.		
1TC	1c	orange	500.	100.	
1TC	1c	red orange	500.		
1TC	1c	olive bister	500.		
2TC	2c	black	500.		
2TC	2c	gray black	500.		
2TC	2c	ultramarine	500.		
2TC	2c	blue	500.		
2TC	2c	blue green	500.		
2TC	2c	orange	500.	100.	
2TC	2c	red orange	500.		
2TC	2c	sepia	500.		
3TC	3c	black	500.		
3TC	3c	gray black		100.	
3TC	3c	ultramarine	500.		
3TC	3c	blue	500.		
3TC	3c	blue green	500.		
3TC	3c	orange	500.	100.	
3TC	3c	red orange	500.		
3TC	3c	light brown	500.		
4TC	5c	black	500.		
4TC	5c	gray black	500.		
4TC	5c	ultramarine	500.		
4TC	5c	blue	500.		
4TC	5c	blue green	500.		
4TC	5c	orange	500.	100.	
4TC	5c	red orange	500.		
5TC	10c	black	500.		
5TC	10c	gray black	500.		
5TC	10c	olive yellow	500.		
5TC	10c	blue green	500.		
5TC	10c	orange	500.	100.	
5TC	10c	red orange	500.		
5TC	10c	olive bister	500.		
5TC	10c	sepia	500.		
5TC	10c	gray	500.		
6TC	30c	black	500.		
6TC	30c	gray black	500.		
6TC	30c	blue		100.	
6TC	30c	olive yellow		100.	
6TC	30c	blue green	500.		
6TC	30c	orange	500.	100.	
6TC	30c	red orange	500.		
6TC	30c	olive bister	500.		
6TC	30c	sepia		100.	
7TC	50c	black	500.		
7TC	50c	gray black	500.		
7TC	50c	blue	500.	100.	
7TC	50c	olive yellow		100.	
7TC	50c	blue green	500.		
7TC	50c	orange	500.	100.	
7TC	50c	red orange	500.		
7TC	50c	olive bister	500.		
7TC	50c	sepia	500.		
7TC	50c	gray	500.		

OFFICIAL
Agriculture

O1TC	1c	black	500.	75.
O2TC	2c	black	500.	75.
O3TC	3c	black	500.	
O3TC	3c	deep green	500.	
O4TC	6c	black	500.	150.
O5TC	10c	black	500.	
O6TC	12c	black	500.	75.
O9TC	30c	black	500.	

Executive

O11TC	2c	black	500.	75.
O11TC	2c	deep brown	500.	
O11TC	2c	brown carmine		75.
O12TC	3c	black	500.	75.
O12TC	3c	deep green	500.	
O13TC	6c	black		90.
O14TC	10c	black		90.

Interior

O16TC	2c	black	500.	
O16TC	2c	deep brown	500.	
O17TC	3c	black	500.	90.
O17TC	3c	deep green	500.	

Justice

O27TC	3c	black	500.	90.
O27TC	3c	deep green	500.	
O27TC	3c	bister yellow		90.
O27TC	3c	dull orange		90.
O27TC	3c	black violet		90.

Navy

O35TC	1c	black		90.
O36TC	2c	black	500.	
O36TC	2c	deep brown	500.	
O36TC	2c	black on wove paper, perf.		250.
O36TC	2c	deep green on wove paper, perf.		250.
O36TC	2c	deep green on wove paper, imperf.		250.
O37TC	3c	black	500.	90.
O37TC	3c	deep green	500.	

Post Office

O48TC	2c	deep brown	500.
O49TC	3c	deep green	500.
O50TC	6c	deep brown	500.
O50TC	6c	brown carmine	500.

State

O57TC	1c	black	500.
O57TC	1c	light ultramarine	500.
O58TC	2c	black	500.
O58TC	2c	deep brown	500.
O59TC	3c	black	500.
O67TC	90c	black	500.
O68TC	$2	violet & black	2,500.
O68TC	$2	brown red & black	2,500.
O68TC	$2	orange red & slate blue	2,500.

Treasury

O72TC	1c	black	500.
O72TC	1c	light ultramarine	500.
O73TC	2c	black	500.
O74TC	3c	black	500.
O74TC	3c	deep green	500.
O75TC	6c	black	500.
O77TC	10c	black	500.
O78TC	12c	black	500.
O79TC	15c	black	500.
O80TC	24c	black	500.
O81TC	30c	black	500.
O82TC	90c	black	500.

War

O83TC	1c	black	500.	80.	
O83TC	1c	light ultramarine	500.		
O84TC	2c	black	500.	80.	75.
O84TC	2c	deep brown	500.		
O85TC	3c	black	500.		
O85TC	3c	deep green	500.		
O85TC	3c	chocolate	675.		
O86TC	6c	black		80.	
O89TC	12c	black		80.	

1910

POSTAL SAVINGS MAIL

O121TC	2c	lake	500.
O126TC	10c	black (on wove)	1,250.

The so-called "Goodall" set of Small Die proofs on India Paper of Official Stamps in five colors

Agriculture

		(a) Black	(b) Deep green	(c) Dull gray blue	(d) Deep brown	(e) Dull red
O1TC	1c	150.	140.	140.	140.	140.
O2TC	2c	150.	140.	140.	140.	140.
O3TC	3c	150.	140.	140.	140.	140.
O4TC	6c	150.	140.	140.	140.	140.
O5TC	10c	150.	140.	140.	140.	140.
O6TC	12c	150.	140.	140.	140.	140.
O7TC	15c	150.	140.	140.	140.	140.
O8TC	24c	150.	140.	140.	140.	140.
O9TC	30c	150.	140.	140.	140.	140.

Executive

O10TC	1c	150.	140.	140.	140.	140.
O11TC	2c	150.	140.	140.	140.	140.
O12TC	3c	150.	140.	140.	140.	140.
O13TC	6c	150.	140.	140.	140.	140.
O14TC	10c	150.	140.	140.	140.	140.

Interior

O15TC	1c	150.	140.	140.	140.	140.
O16TC	2c	150.	140.	140.	140.	140.
O17TC	3c	150.	140.	140.	140.	140.
O18TC	6c	150.	140.	140.	140.	140.
O19TC	10c	150.	140.	140.	140.	140.
O20TC	12c	150.	140.	140.	140.	140.
O21TC	15c	150.	140.	140.	140.	140.
O22TC	24c	150.	140.	140.	140.	140.
O23TC	30c	150.	140.	140.	140.	140.
O24TC	90c	150.	140.	140.	140.	140.

Justice

O25TC	1c	150.	140.	140.	140.	140.
O26TC	2c	150.	140.	140.	140.	140.
O27TC	3c	150.	140.	140.	140.	140.
O28TC	6c	150.	140.	140.	140.	140.
O29TC	10c	150.	140.	140.	140.	140.
O30TC	12c	150.	140.	140.	140.	140.
O31TC	15c	150.	140.	140.	140.	140.
O32TC	24c	150.	140.	140.	140.	140.
O33TC	30c	150.	140.	140.	140.	140.
O34TC	90c	150.	140.	140.	140.	140.

Navy

O35TC	1c	150.	140.	140.	140.	140.
O36TC	2c	150.	140.	140.	140.	140.
O37TC	3c	150.	140.	140.	140.	140.
O38TC	6c	150.	140.	140.	140.	140.
O39TC	7c	150.	140.	140.	140.	140.
O40TC	10c	150.	140.	140.	140.	140.
O41TC	12c	150.	140.	140.	140.	140.
O42TC	15c	150.	140.	140.	140.	140.
O43TC	24c	150.	140.	140.	140.	140.
O44TC	30c	150.	140.	140.	140.	140.
O45TC	90c	150.	140.	140.	140.	140.

Post Office

O47TC	1c	150.	140.	140.	140.	140.
O48TC	2c	150.	140.	140.	140.	140.
O49TC	3c	150.	140.	140.	140.	140.
O50TC	6c	150.	140.	140.	140.	140.
O51TC	10c	150.	140.	140.	140.	140.
O52TC	12c	150.	140.	140.	140.	140.
O53TC	15c	150.	140.	140.	140.	140.
O54TC	24c	150.	140.	140.	140.	140.
O55TC	30c	150.	140.	140.	140.	140.
O56TC	90c	150.	140.	140.	140.	140.

State

O57TC	1c	150.	140.	140.	140.	140.
O58TC	2c	150.	140.	140.	140.	140.

		(a) Black	(b) Deep green	(c) Dull gray blue	(d) Deep brown	(e) Dull red
O59TC	3c	150.	140.	140.	140.	140.
O60TC	6c	150.	140.	140.	140.	140.
O61TC	7c	150.	140.	140.	140.	140.
O62TC	10c	150.	140.	140.	140.	140.
O63TC	12c	150.	140.	140.	140.	140.
O64TC	15c	150.	140.	140.	140.	140.
O65TC	24c	150.	140.	140.	140.	140.
O66TC	30c	150.	140.	140.	140.	140.
O67TC	90c	150.	140.	140.	140.	140.

O68TC	$2	scarlet frame, green center				2,000.
O68TC	$2	scarlet frame, black center				2,000.
O68TC	$2	scarlet frame, blue center				2,000.
O68TC	$2	scarlet frame, brown center				2,500.
O68TC	$2	violet frame, black center				2,000.
O68TC	$2	green frame, brown center				2,000.
O68TC	$2	brown frame, green center				2,000.
O68TC	$2	brown frame, black center				2,000.
O68TC	$2	red brown frame, green center				2,000.

Treasury

O72TC	1c	150.	140.	140.	140.	140.
O73TC	2c	150.	140.	140.	140.	140.
O74TC	3c	150.	140.	140.	140.	140.
O75TC	6c	150.	140.	140.	140.	140.
O76TC	7c	150.	140.	140.	140.	140.
O77TC	10c	150.	140.	140.	140.	140.
O78TC	12c	150.	140.	140.	140.	140.
O79TC	15c	150.	140.	140.	140.	140.
O80TC	24c	150.	140.	140.	140.	140.
O81TC	30c	150.	140.	140.	140.	140.
O82TC	90c	150.	140.	140.	140.	140.

War

O83TC	1c	150.	140.	140.	140.	140.
O84TC	2c	150.	140.	140.	140.	140.
O85TC	3c	150.	140.	140.	140.	140.
O86TC	6c	150.	140.	140.	140.	140.
O87TC	7c	150.	140.	140.	140.	140.
O88TC	10c	150.	140.	140.	140.	140.
O89TC	12c	150.	140.	140.	140.	140.
O90TC	15c	150.	140.	140.	140.	140.
O91TC	24c	150.	140.	140.	140.	140.
O92TC	30c	150.	140.	140.	140.	140.
O93TC	90c	150.	140.	140.	140.	140.

OFFICIAL SEALS

1872

OXF1TC	ultra	Die on India	1,000.
OXF1TC	blue	Die on card, colored border	1,000.
OXF1TC	dp bl	Die on card, colored border	1,000.
OXF1TC	green	Die on card, colored border	1,000.
OXF1TC	choc	Die on glossy bond	1,000.
OXF1TC	choc	Die on card, colored border	1,000.
OXF1TC	car	Die on India	1,000.
OXF1TC	brown	Die on India	1,000.
OXF1TC	red vio	Die on India	1,000.

1877

OX1TC	blue	Die on India	500.
OX1TC	green	Die on India	500.
OX1TC	green	Plate on bond	500.
OX1TC	green	Plate on bond, perforated and gummed	—
OX1TC	orange	Die on India	500.
OX1TC	red orange	Die on India	500.
OX1TC	black	Die on India	500.

1879

OX2TC	black	Die on India	—

POSTAL NOTE STAMPS

PN1TC	1c bister	imperf. on white wove	—

NEWSPAPERS

1865

		(1) Die on India	(5) Thick cream wove paper
PR1TC	5c	bright red	500.	
PR1TC	5c	deep reddish brown	2,000.	
PR1TC	5c	dark orange	2,000.	
PR1TC	5c	green	2,000.	
PR2TC	10c	brown	500.	
PR2TC	10c	dull red	500.	
PR2TC	10c	blue	500.	
PR2TC	10c	black		70.
PR2TC	10c	lake		70.
PR2TC	10c	blue green		70.
PR2TC	10c	blue		70.
PR3TC	25c	black		70.
PR3TC	25c	lake		70.
PR3TC	25c	blue green		70.
PR3TC	25c	blue		70.
PR3TC	25c	ocher	500.	
PR3TC	25c	brown	500.	
PR3TC	25c	brick red	500.	
PR4TC	5c	black		70.
PR4TC	5c	lake		70.
PR4TC	5c	blue green		70.

			(1) Die on India	(5) Thick cream wove paper
PR4TC	5c	blue		70.

1875

			(1) Die on India	(3) Plate on India
PR9TC	2c	dark carmine		35.
PR9TC	2c	brown rose		35.
PR9TC	2c	scarlet		35.
PR9TC	2c	orange brown	250.	35.
PR9TC	2c	black brown	250.	
PR9TC	2c	sepia		35.
PR9TC	2c	orange yellow		35.
PR9TC	2c	dull orange		35.
PR9TC	2c	green		35.
PR9TC	2c	blue green	250.	
PR9TC	2c	light ultramarine		35.
PR9TC	2c	light blue		35.
PR9TC	2c	dark violet		35.
PR9TC	2c	violet black		35.
PR10TC	3c	rose lake	250.	
PR16TC	12c	dark carmine		35.
PR16TC	12c	brown rose	250.	35.
PR16TC	12c	scarlet	250.	35.
PR16TC	12c	orange brown		35.
PR16TC	12c	sepia	250.	35.
PR16TC	12c	orange yellow		35.
PR16TC	12c	dull orange		35.
PR16TC	12c	green	250.	35.
PR16TC	12c	light ultramarine	250.	35.
PR16TC	12c	light blue		35.
PR16TC	12c	dark violet	250.	35.
PR16TC	12c	violet black	250.	35.
PR16TC	12c	black	250.	35.
PR17TC	24c	sepia		
PR17TC	24c	green	250.	
PR17TC	24c	black	250.	35.
PR18TC	36c	black	250.	35.
PR18TC	36c	sepia	250.	
PR18TC	36c	green	250.	
PR19TC	48c	black	250.	35.
PR19TC	48c	sepia	250.	
PR19TC	48c	green	250.	
PR20TC	60c	black	250.	35.
PR21TC	72c	black	250.	35.
PR22TC	84c	black	250.	35.
PR23TC	96c	black		35.
PR24TC	$1.92	dark carmine		35.
PR24TC	$1.92	brown rose		35.
PR24TC	$1.92	scarlet		35.
PR24TC	$1.92	orange brown	250.	35.
PR24TC	$1.92	sepia		35.
PR24TC	$1.92	orange yellow		35.
PR24TC	$1.92	dull orange		35.
PR24TC	$1.92	green	250.	35.
PR24TC	$1.92	light ultramarine		35.
PR24TC	$1.92	dark violet		35.
PR24TC	$1.92	violet black		35.
PR24TC	$1.92	black		35.
PR25TC	$3	dark carmine	250.	35.
PR25TC	$3	brown rose		35.
PR25TC	$3	scarlet		35.
PR25TC	$3	orange brown		35.
PR25TC	$3	sepia		35.
PR25TC	$3	orange yellow	250.	35.
PR25TC	$3	dull orange	250.	35.
PR25TC	$3	green	250.	35.
PR25TC	$3	light ultramarine	250.	35.
PR25TC	$3	light blue		35.
PR25TC	$3	dark violet		35.
PR25TC	$3	violet black		35.
PR25TC	$3	black		35.
PR26TC	$6	dark carmine	250.	35.
PR26TC	$6	brown rose	250.	35.
PR26TC	$6	scarlet		35.
PR26TC	$6	orange brown		35.
PR26TC	$6	dark brown		35.
PR26TC	$6	sepia	250.	35.
PR26TC	$6	orange yellow	250.	35.
PR26TC	$6	dull orange	250.	35.
PR26TC	$6	green	250.	35.
PR26TC	$6	light ultramarine		35.
PR26TC	$6	light blue	250.	35.
PR26TC	$6	dark violet		35.
PR26TC	$6	violet black		35.
PR26TC	$6	black		35.
PR27TC	$9	dark carmine		35.
PR27TC	$9	brown rose		35.
PR27TC	$9	scarlet	250.	35.
PR27TC	$9	orange brown		35.
PR27TC	$9	sepia	250.	35.
PR27TC	$9	orange yellow	250.	35.
PR27TC	$9	dull orange	250.	35.
PR27TC	$9	green	250.	35.
PR27TC	$9	light ultramarine	250.	35.
PR27TC	$9	light blue		35.
PR27TC	$9	dark violet	250.	35.
PR27TC	$9	violet black	250.	35.
PR27TC	$9	black	250.	35.
PR28TC	$12	black	250.	
PR28TC	$12	sepia	250.	
PR28TC	$12	orange brown	250.	
PR29TC	$24	black	250.	35.
PR29TC	$24	black brown	250.	
PR29TC	$24	orange brown	250.	
PR29TC	$24	green	250.	
PR30TC	$36	dark carmine	250.	
PR30TC	$36	black	250.	35.
PR30TC	$36	black brown	250.	
PR30TC	$36	orange brown	250.	
PR30TC	$36	sepia	250.	
PR30TC	$36	violet	250.	
PR30TC	$36	green	250.	

			(1) Die on India	(3) Plate on India
PR31TC	$48	violet brown	250.	35.
PR31TC	$48	black	250.	35.
PR31TC	$48	sepia	250.	
PR31TC	$48	green	250.	
PR32TC	$60	dark carmine	250.	40.
PR32TC	$60	scarlet	250.	40.
PR32TC	$60	sepia	250.	40.
PR32TC	$60	green	250.	40.
PR32TC	$60	light ultramarine	250.	40.
PR32TC	$60	black	250.	40.
PR32TC	$60	violet black	250.	
PR32TC	$60	orange brown	250.	
PR32TC	$60	orange yellow	250.	
PR32TC	$60	dull orange	250.	
PR32TC	$60	brown rose	250.	

1885

			(1) Die on India	(3) Plate on India
PR81TC	1c	salmon	250.	
PR81TC	1c	scarlet		120.
PR81TC	1c	dark brown		120.
PR81TC	1c	violet brown		120.
PR81TC	1c	dull orange		120.
PR81TC	1c	green		120.
PR81TC	1c	light blue		120.

1894

			(3) Plate on India
PR106TC	25c	deep carmine	250.
PR106TC	25c	dark carmine	250.
PR107TC	50c	black	250.
PR108TC	$2	deep scarlet	250.
PR108TC	$2	dark scarlet	250.
PR109TC	$5	light ultramarine	250.
PR109TC	$5	dark ultramarine	250.
PR110TC	$10	black	250.
PR112TC	$50	black	250.
PR112TC	$50	deep rose	250.
PR112TC	$50	dark rose	250.
PR113TC	$100	black	250.

The so-called "Goodall" set of Small Die proofs on India Paper of Newspaper Stamps in five colors

		(a) Black	(b) Deep green	(c) Dull gray blue	(d) Deep brown	(e) Dull red
PR9TC	2c	150.	125.	125.	125.	125.
PR10TC	3c	150.	125.	125.	125.	125.
PR11TC	4c	150.	125.	125.	125.	125.
PR12TC	6c	150.	125.	125.	125.	125.
PR13TC	8c	150.	125.	125.	125.	125.
PR14TC	9c	150.	125.	125.	125.	125.
PR15TC	10c	150.	125.	125.	125.	125.
PR16TC	12c	150.	125.	125.	125.	125.
PR17TC	24c	150.	125.	125.	125.	125.
PR18TC	36c	150.	125.	125.	125.	125.
PR19TC	48c	150.	125.	125.	125.	125.
PR20TC	60c	150.	125.	125.	125.	125.
PR21TC	72c	150.	125.	125.	125.	125.
PR22TC	84c	150.	125.	125.	125.	125.
PR23TC	96c	150.	125.	125.	125.	125.
PR24TC	$1.92	150.	125.	125.	125.	125.
PR25TC	$3	150.	125.	125.	125.	125.
PR26TC	$6	150.	125.	125.	125.	125.
PR27TC	$9	150.	125.	125.	125.	125.
PR28TC	$12	150.	125.	125.	125.	125.
PR29TC	$24	150.	125.	125.	125.	125.
PR30TC	$36	150.	125.	125.	125.	125.
PR31TC	$48	150.	125.	125.	125.	125.
PR32TC	$60	150.	125.	125.	125.	125.

1925

SPECIAL HANDLING

QE4TC	25c	apple green	700.
QE4TC	25c	olive green	700.
QE4TC	25c	light blue green	700.
QE4TC	25c	dark blue	700.
QE4TC	25c	orange yellow	700.
QE4TC	25c	orange	700.
QE4TC	25c	dull rose	700.
QE4TC	25c	carmine lake	700.
QE4TC	25c	brown	700.
QE4TC	25c	gray brown	700.
QE4TC	25c	dark violet brown	700.
QE4TC	25c	gray black	700.
QE4TC	25c	black	700.

THE "ATLANTA" SET OF PLATE PROOFS

A set in five colors on thin card reprinted in 1881 for display at the International Cotton Exhibition in Atlanta, Ga.

1847 Designs (Reproductions)

		Black	Scarlet	Brown	Green	Blue
3TC	5c	300.	300.	300.	300.	300.
4TC	10c	300.	300.	300.	300.	300.

1851-60 Designs

		Black	Scarlet	Brown	Green	Blue
40TC	1c	120.	100.	100.	100.	100.
41TC	3c	120.	100.	100.	100.	100.
42TC	5c	120.	100.	100.	100.	100.
43TC	10c	120.	100.	100.	100.	100.
44TC	12c	120.	100.	100.	100.	100.
45TC	24c	120.	100.	100.	100.	100.
46TC	30c	120.	100.	100.	100.	100.
47TC	90c	120.	100.	100.	100.	100.

		Black	Scarlet	Brown	Green	Bl
1861-66 Designs						
102TC	1c	100.	90.	90.	90.	
103TC	2c	175.	175.	175.	175.	1
104TC	3c	100.	90.	90.	90.	
105TC	5c	100.	90.	90.	90.	
106TC	10c	100.	90.	90.	90.	
107TC	12c	100.	90.	90.	90.	
108TC	15c	100.	90.	90.	90.	
109TC	24c	100.	90.	90.	90.	
110TC	30c	100.	90.	90.	90.	
111TC	90c	100.	90.	90.	90.	
1869 Designs						
123TC	1c	175.	150.	150.	150.	1
124TC	2c	175.	150.	150.	150.	1
125TC	3c	175.	150.	150.	150.	1
126TC	6c	175.	150.	150.	150.	1
127TC	10c	175.	150.	150.	150.	1
128TC	12c	175.	150.	150.	150.	1
129TC	15c black frame, scarlet center					37
129TC	15c black frame, green center					37
129TC	15c scarlet frame, black center					37
129TC	15c scarlet frame, blue center					37
129TC	15c brown frame, black center					37
129TC	15c brown frame, green center					37
129TC	15c brown frame, blue center					37
129TC	15c green frame, black center					37
129TC	15c green frame, blue center					37
129TC	15c blue frame, black center					37
129TC	15c blue frame, brown center					37
129TC	15c blue frame, green center					37
130TC	24c black frame, scarlet center					37
130TC	24c black frame, green center					37
130TC	24c black frame, blue center					37
130TC	24c scarlet frame, black center					37
130TC	24c scarlet frame, blue center					37
130TC	24c brown frame, black center					37
130TC	24c brown frame, blue center					37
130TC	24c green frame, black center					37
130TC	24c green frame, brown center					37
130TC	24c blue frame, black center					37
130TC	24c blue frame, brown center					37
130TC	24c blue frame, green center					37
131TC	30c black frame, scarlet center					37
131TC	30c black frame, green center					37
131TC	30c black frame, blue center					37
131TC	30c scarlet frame, black center					37
131TC	30c scarlet frame, green center					37
131TC	30c scarlet frame, blue center					37
131TC	30c brown frame, black center					37
131TC	30c brown frame, scarlet center					37
131TC	30c brown frame, blue center					37
131TC	30c green frame, black center					37
131TC	30c green frame, brown center					37
131TC	30c blue frame, scarlet center					37
131TC	30c blue frame, brown center					37
131TC	30c blue frame, green center					37
132TC	90c black frame, scarlet center					55
132TC	90c black frame, brown center					55
132TC	90c black frame, green center					55
132TC	90c scarlet frame, blue center					55
132TC	90c brown frame, black center					55
132TC	90c brown frame, blue center					55
132TC	90c green frame, black center					55
132TC	90c green frame, blue center					55
132TC	90c blue frame, brown center					55
132TC	90c blue frame, green center					55

1873-75 Designs

		Black	Scarlet	Brown	Green	Blue
156TC	1c	55.	50.	50.	50.	5
157TC	2c	55.	50.	50.	50.	5
158TC	3c	60.	55.	55.	55.	5
159TC	6c	65.	60.	60.	60.	6
160TC	7c	55.	50.	50.	50.	5
161TC	10c	55.	50.	50.	50.	5
162TC	12c	55.	50.	50.	50.	5
163TC	15c	55.	50.	50.	50.	5
164TC	24c	55.	50.	50.	50.	5
165TC	30c	60.	55.	55.	55.	5
166TC	90c	55.	50.	50.	50.	5
179TC	5c	80.	75.	75.	75.	75

POSTAGE DUE

		Black	Scarlet	Brown	Green	Blue
J1TC	1c	55.	50.	50.	50.	5
J2TC	2c	55.	50.	50.	50.	5
J3TC	3c	55.	50.	50.	50.	5
J4TC	5c	55.	50.	50.	50.	5
J5TC	10c	55.	50.	50.	50.	5
J6TC	30c	55.	50.	50.	50.	5
J7TC	50c	55.	50.	50.	50.	5

OFFICIALS
Agriculture

		Black	Scarlet	Brown	Green	Blue
O1TC	1c	43.	37.	37.	37.	37
O2TC	2c	43.	37.	37.	37.	37
O3TC	3c	43.	37.	37.	37.	37
O4TC	6c	55.	50.	50.	50.	50
O5TC	10c	43.	37.	37.	37.	37
O6TC	12c	43.	37.	37.	37.	37
O7TC	15c	43.	37.	37.	37.	37
O8TC	24c	43.	37.	37.	37.	37
O9TC	30c	43.	37.	37.	37.	

Executive

		Black	Scarlet	Brown	Green	Blue
O10TC	1c	43.	37.	37.	37.	37
O11TC	2c	43.	37.	37.	37.	37
O12TC	3c	43.	37.	37.	37.	37
O13TC	6c	55.	50.	50.	50.	50
O14TC	10c	43.	37.	37.	37.	37

Interior

		Black	Scarlet	Brown	Green	Blue
O15TC	1c	43.	37.	37.	37.	37
O16TC	2c	43.	37.	37.	37.	37
O17TC	3c	43.	37.	37.	37.	37

		Black	Scarlet	Brown	Green	Blue
O18TC	6c	55.	50.	50.	50.	50.
O19TC	10c	43.	37.	37.	37.	37.
O20TC	12c	43.	37.	37.	37.	37.
O21TC	15c	43.	37.	37.	37.	37.
O22TC	24c	43.	37.	37.	37.	37.
O23TC	30c	60.	55.	55.	55.	55.
O24TC	90c	43.	37.	37.	37.	37.

Justice

O25TC	1c	43.	37.	37.	37.	37.
O26TC	2c	43.	37.	37.	37.	37.
O27TC	3c	43.	37.	37.	37.	37.
O28TC	6c	55.	50.	50.	50.	50.
O29TC	10c	43.	37.	37.	37.	37.
O30TC	12c	43.	37.	37.	37.	37.
O31TC	15c	43.	37.	37.	37.	37.
O32TC	24c	43.	37.	37.	37.	37.
O33TC	30c	60.	55.	55.	55.	55.
O34TC	90c	43.	37.	37.	37.	37.

Navy

O35TC	1c	43.	37.	37.	37.	37.
O36TC	2c	43.	37.	37.	37.	37.
O37TC	3c	43.	37.	37.	37.	37.
O38TC	6c	55.	50.	50.	50.	50.
O39TC	7c	43.	37.	37.	37.	37.
O40TC	10c	43.	37.	37.	37.	37.
O41TC	12c	43.	37.	37.	37.	37.
O42TC	15c	43.	37.	37.	37.	37.
O43TC	24c	43.	37.	37.	37.	37.
O44TC	30c	60.	55.	55.	55.	55.
O45TC	90c	43.	37.	37.	37.	37.

Post Office

O48TC	2c	43.	37.	37.	37.	37.
O49TC	3c	43.	37.	37.	37.	37.
O50TC	6c	43.	37.	37.	37.	37.
O51TC	10c	43.	37.	37.	37.	37.
O52TC	12c	43.	37.	37.	37.	37.
O53TC	15c	43.	37.	37.	37.	37.
O54TC	24c	43.	37.	37.	37.	37.
O55TC	30c	60.	55.	55.	55.	55.
O56TC	90c	43.	37.	37.	37.	37.

State

O57TC	1c	43.	37.	37.	37.	37.
O58TC	2c	43.	37.	37.	37.	37.
O59TC	3c	43.	37.	37.	37.	37.
O60TC	6c	55.	50.	50.	50.	50.
O61TC	7c	43.	37.	37.	37.	37.
O62TC	10c	43.	37.	37.	37.	37.
O63TC	12c	43.	37.	37.	37.	37.
O64TC	15c	43.	37.	37.	37.	37.
O65TC	24c	43.	37.	37.	37.	37.
O66TC	30c	60.	55.	55.	55.	55.
O67TC	90c	43.	37.	37.	37.	

O68TC	$2	scarlet frame, black center	1,000.
O68TC	$2	scarlet frame, blue center	1,000.
O68TC	$2	brown frame, black center	1,000.
O68TC	$2	brown frame, blue center	1,000.
O68TC	$2	green frame, brown center	1,000.
O68TC	$2	blue frame, brown center	1,000.
O68TC	$2	blue frame, green center	1,000.
O69TC	$5	scarlet frame, black center	1,000.
O69TC	$5	scarlet frame, blue center	1,000.
O69TC	$5	brown frame, black center	1,000.
O69TC	$5	brown frame, blue center	1,000.
O69TC	$5	green frame, brown center	1,000.
O69TC	$5	blue frame, brown center	1,000.
O69TC	$5	blue frame, green center	1,000.
O70TC	$10	scarlet frame, black center	1,000.
O70TC	$10	scarlet frame, blue center	1,000.
O70TC	$10	brown frame, black center	1,000.
O70TC	$10	brown frame, blue center	1,000.
O70TC	$10	green frame, brown center	1,000.
O70TC	$10	blue frame, brown center	1,000.
O70TC	$10	blue frame, green center	1,000.
O71TC	$20	scarlet frame, black center	1,000.
O71TC	$20	scarlet frame, blue center	1,000.
O71TC	$20	brown frame, blue center	1,000.
O71TC	$20	green frame, brown center	1,000.
O71TC	$20	blue frame, brown center	1,000.
O71TC	$20	blue frame, green center	1,000.

Treasury

		Black	Scarlet	Brown	Green	Blue
O72TC	1c	43.	37.	37.	37.	37.
O73TC	2c	43.	37.	37.	37.	37.
O74TC	3c	43.	37.	37.	37.	37.
O75TC	6c	55.	50.	50.	50.	50.
O76TC	7c	43.	37.	37.	37.	37.
O77TC	10c	43.	37.	37.	37.	37.
O78TC	12c	43.	37.	37.	37.	37.
O79TC	15c	43.	37.	37.	37.	37.
O80TC	24c	43.	37.	37.	37.	37.
O81TC	30c	60.	55.	55.	55.	55.
O82TC	90c	43.	37.	37.	37.	37.

War

O83TC	1c	43.	37.	37.	37.	37.
O84TC	2c	43.	37.	37.	37.	37.
O85TC	3c	43.	37.	37.	37.	
	Plate flaw at upper left (32R20)			—		
O86TC	6c	55.	50.	50.	50.	50.
O87TC	7c	43.	37.	37.	37.	37.
O88TC	10c	43.	37.	37.	37.	37.
O89TC	12c	43.	37.	37.	37.	37.
O90TC	15c	43.	37.	37.	37.	37.
O91TC	24c	43.	37.	37.	37.	37.
O92TC	30c	60.	55.	55.	55.	55.
O93TC	90c	43.	37.	37.	37.	37.

NEWSPAPERS

		Black	Scarlet	Brown	Green	Blue
PR9TC	2c	55.	40.	40.	40.	40.
PR10TC	3c	55.	40.	40.	40.	40.
PR11TC	4c	55.	40.	40.	40.	40.
PR12TC	6c	55.	40.	40.	40.	40.
PR13TC	8c	55.	40.	40.	40.	40.
PR14TC	9c	55.	40.	40.	40.	40.
PR15TC	10c	55.	40.	40.	40.	40.
PR16TC	12c	55.	40.	40.	40.	40.
PR17TC	24c	55.	40.	40.	40.	40.
PR18TC	36c	55.	40.	40.	40.	40.
PR19TC	48c	55.	40.	40.	40.	40.
PR20TC	60c	55.	40.	40.	40.	40.
PR21TC	72c	55.	40.	40.	40.	40.
PR22TC	84c	55.	40.	40.	40.	40.
PR23TC	96c	55.	40.	40.	40.	40.
PR24TC	$1.92	55.	40.	40.	40.	40.
PR25TC	$3	55.	40.	40.	40.	40.
PR26TC	$6	55.	40.	40.	40.	40.
PR27TC	$9	55.	40.	40.	40.	40.
PR28TC	$12	55.	40.	40.	40.	40.
PR29TC	$24	55.	40.	40.	40.	40.
PR30TC	$36	55.	40.	40.	40.	40.
PR31TC	$48	55.	40.	40.	40.	40.
PR32TC	$60	55.	40.	40.	40.	40.

CARRIERS

		Black	Scarlet	Brown	Green	Blue
LO1TC	1c Franklin	120.	110.	110.	110.	110.
LO2TC	1c Eagle	120.	110.	110.	110.	110.

TELEGRAPH

American Rapid Telegraph Co.

			DIE (2) Small	PLATE (3) India	PLATE (4) Card
1T1TC	1c	green		55.	
1T1TC	1c	brown		55.	
1T1TC	1c	red		55.	
1T1TC	1c	blue		55.	
1T1TC	1c	bluish green		55.	
1T3TC	5c	green		55.	
1T3TC	5c	black		55.	
1T3TC	5c	red		55.	
1T3TC	5c	blue		55.	
1T3TC	5c	bluish green		55.	
1T5TC	15c	red		55.	
1T5TC	15c	black		55.	
1T5TC	15c	brown		55.	
1T5TC	15c	bluish green		55.	
1T6TC	20c	green		55.	
1T6TC	20c	black		55.	
1T6TC	20c	brown		55.	
1T6TC	20c	blue		55.	
1T6TC	20c	bluish green		55.	

Collect

			DIE (1) Large	DIE (2) Small	PLATE (3) India	PLATE (4) Card
1T10TC	5c	red			55.	
1T10TC	5c	black			55.	
1T10TC	5c	brown			55.	
1T10TC	5c	green			55.	
1T10TC	5c	bluish green			55.	
1T11TC	15c	red			55.	
1T11TC	15c	black			55.	
1T11TC	15c	brown			55.	
1T11TC	15c	green			55.	
1T11TC	15c	bluish green			55.	

Office Coupon

1T14TC	5c	red		55.	
1T14TC	5c	black		55.	
1T14TC	5c	brown		55.	
1T14TC	5c	green		55.	
1T14TC	5c	bluish green		55.	
1T15TC	15c	red		55.	
1T15TC	15c	black		55.	
1T15TC	15c	brown		55.	
1T15TC	15c	green		55.	
1T15TC	15c	blue		55.	
1T15TC	15c	bluish green		55.	

Baltimore & Ohio Telegraph Co.

3T2TC	5c	dark olive	65.	
3T4TC	25c	dark olive	65.	

Postal Telegraph Co.

			Small	India	Card
15T1TC	10c	brown red		65.	
15T1TC	10c	red	65.		
15T1TC	10c	blue	65.		
15T1TC	10c	black	65.		
15T1TC	10c	orange		65.	
15T2TC	15c	black	65.	55.	
15T2TC	15c	red	65.	55.	
15T2TC	15c	blue	65.	55.	
15T2TC	25c	brown red		65.	
15T3TC	25c	black	65.		
15T3TC	25c	red	65.		
15T3TC	25c	ultramarine		40.	
15T3TC	25c	brown	65.	40.	
15T4TC	50c	dull blue	65.		
15T4TC	50c	black	65.	40.	
15T4TC	50c	red	65.		
15T4TC	50c	blue	65.		
15T6TC		red brown		40.	

Western Union Telegraph Co.

16T1TC	lilac (1871)		20.	20.
	Pair		45.	45.
16T1TC	orange		20.	20.
	Pair		45.	45.
16T1TC	black		20.	20.

	Pair		45.	45.
16T1TC	violet brown		20.	
	Pair		45.	
16T1TC	light olive		20.	
	Pair		45.	
16T1TC	brown		20.	
	Pair		45.	
16T1TC	orange brown		20.	
	Pair		45.	
16T1TC	blue green		20.	
	Pair		45.	
16T6TC	violet blue (1876)	20.	20.	
16T7TC	orange yellow (1877)		20.	
	Pair		45.	
16T7TC	dark brown		20.	
	Pair		45.	
16T7TC	black		20.	
	Pane of 4		—	
16T8TC	dark brown (1878)		—	
16T9TC	blue (1879)		—	
16T10TC	violet brown (1880)		—	
16T10TC	rose		—	
16T22TC	black (1892)		—	

Die Proof Printed Directly on Card

16T44TC	dull red	—
16T44TC	orange	—
16T44TC	rose red	—
16T44TC	orange brown	—
16T44TC	ocher	—
16T44TC	dark blue	—
16T44TC	dark ultramarine	—
16T44TC	green	—
16T44TC	brown lake	—
16T44TC	reddish brown	—
16T44TC	sepia	—
16T44TC	sepia, unsurfaced card	—
16T44TC	dull violet	—
16T44TC	slate green	—
16T44TC	slate blue	—
16T44TC	black	—
16T44TC	black, unsurfaced card	—

On India

16T44TC	deep rose	—
16T44TC	carmine lake	—
16T44TC	rose lake	—
16T44TC	deep ultramarine	—

Plate Proofs, Sheets of 16 on India or Bond

16T44TC	deep rose, on India	—
16T44TC	deep rose, on Bond	—
16T44TC	orange, on India	—
16T44TC	orange, on Bond	—
16T44TC	dark blue, on India	—
16T44TC	dark blue, on Bond	—
16T44TC	slate green, on India	—
16T44TC	slate green, on Bond	—
16T44TC	rose lake, on India	—
16T44TC	rose lake, on Bond	—
16T44TC	sepia, on Bond	—

REVENUES

Several lists of revenue proofs in trial colors have been published, but the accuracy of some of them is questionable. The following listings are limited to items seen by the editors. The list is not complete.

1862-71   **FIRST ISSUE**

R3TC	1c	**Proprietary,** black	Plate on India	80.
R3TC		carmine	Plate on Card	125.
R3TC		dull red	Plate on Bond	125.
R3TC		orange red	Plate on Bond	125.
R3TC		dull yel.	Plate on Bond	125.
R3TC		violet rose	Plate on Bond	125.
R3TC		deep blue	Plate on Bond	125.
R3TC		red on blue	Plate on Bond	125.
R3TC		blue, perf. & gum	Plate on Bond	125.
R3TC		green	Plate on buff wove	—
R3TC		black	Die on India	*950.*
R7TC	2c	**Certificate,** ultra.	Plate on Card	65.
R11TC	2c	**Playing Cards,** black	Die on India	500.
R13TC	2c	**Proprietary,** black	Plate on India	75.
R13TC		black	Die on India	650.
R13TC		carmine	Die on India	650.
R15TC	2c	**U.S.I.R.,** violet rose	Plate on Bond	110.
R15TC		light green	Plate on Bond	110.
R15TC		pale blue	Plate on Bond	110.
R15TC		pale rose	Plate on Bond	200.
R15TC		orange	Plate on blue Bond	—
R15TC		black	Plate on India	110.
R15TC		pale orange, perf. & gum	Plate on Bond	110.
R16TC	3c	**Foreign Exchange,** green on blue	Plate on Bond	140.
R16TC		blue	Plate on Goldbeater's Skin	110.
R18TC	3c	**Proprietary,** black	Die on India	300.
R21TC	4c	**Playing Cards,** black	Die (?) on India	300.
R22TC	4c	**Proprietary,** black	Plate on India	110.
R22TC		black	Die on India	350.
R22TC		deep red lilac	Die on India	400.
R22TC		red lilac	Plate on Card	110.

R24TC	5c	Certificate, carmine	Plate on India	110.
R25TC	5c	Express, pale olive	Plate on Wove	—
R26TC	5c	Foreign Exchange, orange	Plate on India	110.
R28TC	5c	Playing Cards, black	Die (?) on India	300.
R29TC	5c	Proprietary, red	Plate on blue Bond	—
R30TC	6c	Inland Exchange, black	Die on India	350.
R31TC	6c	Proprietary, black	Die on India	350.
R32TC	10c	Bill of Lading, greenish blue	Die on India	350.
R32TC+R37TC		composite, dark green	Large Die on India	—
R35TC	10c	Foreign Exchange, black	Die (?) on India	350.
R37TC	10c	Power of Attorney, greenish blue	Die on India	350.
R38TC	10c	Proprietary, black	Die on India	350.
R43TC	25c	Bond, carmine	Plate on Card	90.
R44TC	25c	Certificate, blue	Plate on Bond	300.
R44TC		green	Plate on Bond	300.
R44TC		orange	Plate on Bond	300.
R45TC	25c	Entry of Goods, black	Hybrid Die on India	—
R46TC	25c	Insurance, dull red	Plate on Bond	150.
R46TC		dull red	Plate on Goldbeater's Skin	210.
R46TC		vermilion	Plate on Goldbeater's Skin	210.
R46TC		vermilion	Plate on Bond	170.
R46TC		blue	Plate on Bond	170.
R46TC		blue	Plate on Goldbeater's Skin	215.
R46TC		dark blue	Plate on Bond	155.
R46TC		dark blue	Plate on Goldbeater's Skin	215.
R46TC		green	Plate on Goldbeater's Skin	215.
R51TC	30c	Foreign Exchange, violet	Plate on India	130.
R51TC		violet gray	Plate on India	130.
R51TC		deep red lilac	Plate on India	155.
R51TC		slate blue	Plate on India	155.
R51TC		black	Plate on India	155.
R51TC		red	Plate on India	155.
R52TC		Inland Exchange, deep red lilac	Plate on India	155.
R53TC	40c	Inland Exchange, black	Hybrid Die on India	—
R55TC	50c	Entry of Goods, orange	Plate on Bond	275.
R55TC		green	Plate on Bond	275.
R55TC		red	Plate on Bond	340.
R55TC		deep blue	Plate on Bond	—
R58TC	50c	Life Insurance, ultramarine	Plate on India	85.
R60TC	50c	Original Process, black	Die (?) on India	280.
R64TC	60c	Inland Exchange, green	Die (?) on India	—
R65TC	70c	Foreign Exchange, orange	Die (?) on India	—
R65TC		black	Die (?) on India	285.
R66TC	$1	Conveyance, carmine	Plate on India	85.
R67TC	$1	Entry of Goods, carmine	Plate on India	60.
R68TC	$1	Foreign Exchange, carmine	Plate on India	60.
R69TC	$1	Inland Exchange, carmine	Plate on India	60.
R70TC	$1	Lease, carmine	Plate on India	130.
R71TC	$1	Life Insurance, carmine	Plate on India	75.
R72TC	$1	Manifest, carmine	Plate on India	80.
R73TC	$1	Mortgage, carmine	Plate on India	85.
R73TC		black	Hybrid Die on India	—
R74TC	$1	Passage Ticket, carmine	Plate on India	120.
R75TC	$1	Power of Attorney, carmine	Plate on India	120.

R76TC	$1	Probate of Will, carmine	Plate on India	60.
R78TC	$1.50	Inland Exchange, black	Die on India	475.
R80TC	$1.90	Foreign Exchange, black	Plate on India	155.
R81TC	$2	Conveyance, carmine	Plate on Card	85.
R82TC	$2	Mortgage, carmine	Plate on Card	85.
R83TC	$2	Probate of Will, black	Hybrid Die on India	—
R84TC	$2.50	Inland Exchange, black	Die (?) on India	120.
R85TC	$3	Charter Party, dark green	Plate on Thin Card	—
R87TC	$3.50	Inland Exchange, black	Die on India	400.
R88TC	$5	Charter Party, carmine	Plate on India	85.
R88TC		black	Hybrid Die on India	—
R89TC	$5	Conveyance, carmine	Plate on India	90.
R91TC	$5	Mortgage, carmine	Plate on India	90.
R95TC	$10	Mortgage, yellow green	Plate on Thin Card	—
R98TC	$20	Conveyance, red orange	Plate on Card	120.
R98TC		red orange	Plate on India	220.
R99TC	$20	Probate of Will, red orange	Plate on Card	275.
R99TC		black	Plate on Card	275.
R101TC	$50	U.S.I.R., orange	Plate on Bond	275.
R101TC		deep blue	Plate on Bond	275.
R101TC		black	Hybrid Die on India	—
R102TC	$200	black & red	Plate on Card	1,600.
R102TC		gray brown & red	Plate on India	1,600.
R102TC		green & brown red	Plate on India	1,600.
R102TC		black	Plate on India	—

SECOND ISSUE

R104TC	2c	pale blue & black	Plate on Bond	60.
R132TC	$200	red, green & black	India	2,500.
R132TC		orange (master die)	India	2,500.
R132TC		blue (master die)	India	2,500.
R132TC		green (master die)	India	2,500.
R133TC	$500	black (master die)	India	7,000.
R133TC		yellow, green & black	India	5,000.
R133TC		bright green, orange brown & black	India	5,000.
R133TC		red, green & black	Bond	5,000.
R133TC		light green, light brown & black	Bond	5,000.
R133TC		blue, scarlet & black	Bond	5,000.
R133ATC	$5000	yel org, green & black	India	7,500.
R133ATC		olive brown, green & black	India	8,000.
R133ATC		org red, dark green & black	India	8,000.
R133ATC		org red, dark blue & black	India	8,000.

The master die is the completed stamp design prior to its division into separate color dies.
See note after No. R133AP in Die and Plate Proofs section.

THIRD ISSUE

R134TC	1c	brown & black	Plate on Card	60.

1875 National Bank Note Co., New York City

R152TC	2c	(Liberty), green	Die on India	600.
R152TC		(Liberty), brown	Die on India	600.
R152TC		(Liberty), black	Die on India	600.

1898

R161TC	½c	green	Lg. die on India	750.
R163TC	1c	green	Lg. die on India	750.
R163TC		black	Lg. die on India	750.
R165TC	3c	green	Sm. die on India	650.
R169TC	25c	green	Lg. die on India	650.
R170TC	40c	black	Lg. die on India	650.
R172TC	80c	green	Lg. die on India	650.

1898

R174TC	$3	black	Die on India	65
R176TC	$10	green	Die on India	65

1899

R179TC	$100	dark green & black	Die on India	1,25
R181TC	$1000	dark blue & black	Die on India	1,25

1914

R195TC	½c	black	Small die on Wove	
R196TC	1c	blue green	Small die on Wove	
R198TC	3c	ultramarine	Small die on Wove	
R199TC	4c	brown	Small die on Wove	
R200TC	5c	blue	Small die on Wove	
R201TC	10c	yellow	Small die on Wove	
R202TC	25c	dull violet	Small die on Wove	
R203TC	40c	blue green	Small die on Wove	
R204TC	50c	red brown	Small die on Wove	
R205TC	80c	orange	Small die on Wove	

PROPRIETARY

1871-75

RB1TC	1c	blue & black	Plate on Bond	7
RB1TC		scarlet & black	Plate on Bond	7
RB1TC		orange & black	Plate on Bond	7
RB1TC		orange & ultramarine	Plate on Granite Bond	6
RB3TC	3c	blue & black, with gum	Plate on Bond	6
RB3TC		blue & black	Plate on Gray Bond	6
RB3TC		blue & black	Plate on wove	—
RB8TC	50c	green & brown	Die on India	67
RB8TC		green & purple	Die on India	67½
RB8TC		green & brown red	Die on India	67
RB8TC		green & violet	Die on India	67
RB8TC		green & dark carmine	Die on India	67½
RB8TC		ultramarine & red	Die on India	67½
RB9TC	$1	green & brown	Die on India	67
RB9TC		green & purple	Die on India	67½
RB9TC		green & violet brown	Die on India	67½
RB9TC		green & brown red	Die on India	67½
RB9TC		green & violet	Die on India	67
RB9TC		green & dark carmine	Die on India	67½

1875-83

RB11TC	1c	brown	Die on India	50
RB11TC		red brown	Die on India	50
RB11TC		blue	Die on India	50
RB11TC		black	Die on India	500
RB12TC	2c	green	Die on India	500
RB12TC		black	Die on India	500
RB12TC		brown	Die on India	500
RB12TC		orange brown	Die on India	500
RB12TC		blue	Die on India	500
RB13TC	3c	brown	Die on India	500
RB13TC		green	Die on India	500
RB13TC		blue	Die on India	500
RB13TC		black	Plate on India	150
RB14TC	4c	dark brown	Die on India	450
RB14TC		green	Die on India	450
RB14TC		black	Die on India	450
RB14TC		blue	Die on India	450
RB14TC		black	Plate on India	150
RB16TC	5c	green	Die on India	450
RB16TC		dark slate	Die on India	450
RB16TC		blue	Die on India	450
RB17TC	6c	green	Plate on India	150
RB17TC		black	Plate on India	150
RB17TC		black	Die on India	500
RB17TC		blue	Die on India	500
RB17TC		purple	Die on India	500
RB17TC		dull violet	Die on India	500
RB17TC		violet	Die on India	500
RB17TC		violet brown	Die on India	500
RB17TC		dark brown	Die on India	500
RB19TC	10c	black	Die on India	550

SECOND, THIRD AND PROPRIETARY ISSUES

Stamps Nos. R103 to R131, R134 to R150 and RB1 to RB7.

A special composite plate was made and impressions taken in various colors and shades. Although all varieties must have been made, only those seen by the editors are listed.

PLATE PROOFS ON INDIA PAPER
CENTERS IN BLACK

1871-75

R103TC   1c

a.	dark purple	60
b.	dull purple	60
d.	brown	60
e.	black brown	60
g.	light blue	60

(continued)
- h. dark blue 70.
- i. ultramarine 70.
- k. yellow green 70.
- n. green 65.
- o. dark green 65.
- p. blue green 65.
- q. light orange 65.
- r. dark orange 65.
- s. deep orange 65.
- t. scarlet 65.
- u. carmine 65.
- x. dark brown red 65.
- y. dark brown orange, goldbeater's skin 90.

?4TC 2c
- a. dark purple 60.
- b. dull purple 60.
- d. brown 60.
- e. black brown 60.
- g. light blue 60.
- h. dark blue 70.
- i. ultramarine 70.
- k. yellow green 70.
- l. dark yellow green 70.
- n. green 65.
- o. dark green 65.
- p. blue green 65.
- q. light orange 65.
- r. dark orange 65.
- s. deep orange 65.
- t. scarlet 65.
- u. carmine 65.
- x. dark brown red 65.
- y. dark brown orange, goldbeater's skin 90.

?5TC 3c
- a. dark purple 60.
- b. dull purple 60.
- d. brown 60.
- e. black brown 60.
- g. light blue 60.
- h. dark blue 70.
- i. ultramarine 70.
- k. yellow green 70.
- n. green 65.
- o. dark green 65.
- p. blue green 65.
- q. light orange 65.
- r. dark orange 65.
- s. deep orange 65.
- t. scarlet 65.
- u. carmine 65.
- x. dark brown red 65.
- y. dark brown orange, goldbeater's skin 90.

?06TC 4c
- a. dark purple 60.
- b. dull purple 60.
- d. brown 60.
- e. black brown 60.
- f. orange brown 65.
- g. light blue 60.
- h. dark blue 70.
- i. ultramarine 70.
- k. yellow green 70.
- n. green 65.
- o. dark green 65.
- p. blue green 65.
- q. light orange 65.
- r. dark orange 65.
- s. deep orange 65.
- t. scarlet 65.
- u. carmine 65.
- x. dark brown red 65.
- y. dark brown orange, goldbeater's skin 90.

?07TC 5c
- a. dark purple 60.
- b. dull purple 60.
- d. brown 60.
- e. black brown 60.
- f. orange brown 65.
- g. light blue 60.
- h. dark blue 70.
- i. ultramarine 70.
- k. yellow green 70.
- n. green 65.
- o. dark green 65.
- p. blue green 65.
- q. light orange 65.
- r. dark orange 65.
- s. deep orange 65.
- t. scarlet 65.
- u. carmine 65.
- v. dark carmine 65.
- w. purplish carmine 65.
- x. dark brown red 65.
- y. dark brown orange, goldbeater's skin 90.

?08TC 6c
- a. dark purple 60.
- b. dull purple 60.
- d. brown 60.
- e. black brown 60.
- f. orange brown 65.
- g. light blue 60.
- h. dark blue 70.
- i. ultramarine 70.
- k. yellow green 70.
- n. green 65.
- o. dark green 65.
- p. blue green 65.
- q. light orange 65.
- r. dark orange 65.
- s. deep orange 65.
- t. scarlet 65.
- u. carmine 65.
- v. dark carmine 65.
- w. purplish carmine 65.
- x. dark brown red 65.
- y. dark brown orange, goldbeater's skin 90.

R109TC 10c
- a. dark purple 60.
- b. dull purple 60.
- d. brown 60.
- e. black brown 60.
- g. light blue 60.
- h. dark blue 70.
- i. ultramarine 70.
- k. yellow green 70.
- n. green 65.
- o. dark green 65.
- p. blue green 65.
- q. light orange 65.
- r. dark orange 65.
- s. deep orange 65.
- t. scarlet 65.
- u. carmine 65.
- x. dark brown red 65.

R110TC 15c
- a. dark purple 60.
- b. dull purple 60.
- d. brown 60.
- e. black brown 60.
- f. orange brown 65.
- g. light blue 60.
- h. dark blue 70.
- i. ultramarine 70.
- k. yellow green 70.
- n. green 65.
- o. dark green 65.
- p. blue green 65.
- q. light orange 65.
- r. dark orange 65.
- s. deep orange 65.
- t. scarlet 65.
- u. carmine 65.
- w. purplish carmine 65.
- x. dark brown red 65.

R111TC 20c
- a. dark purple 60.
- b. dull purple 60.
- d. brown 60.
- e. black brown 60.
- g. light blue 60.
- h. dark blue 70.
- i. ultramarine 70.
- k. yellow green 70.
- n. green 65.
- o. dark green 65.
- p. blue green 65.
- q. light orange 65.
- r. dark orange 65.
- s. deep orange 65.
- t. scarlet 65.
- u. carmine 65.
- w. purplish carmine 65.
- x. dark brown red 65.
- y. dark brown orange, goldbeater's skin 90.

R112TC 25c
- a. dark purple 60.
- b. dull purple 60.
- d. brown 60.
- e. black brown 60.
- g. light blue 60.
- h. dark blue 70.
- i. ultramarine 70.
- k. yellow green 70.
- l. dark yellow green 70.
- n. green 65.
- o. dark green 65.
- p. blue green 65.
- q. light orange 65.
- r. dark orange 65.
- s. deep orange 65.
- t. scarlet 65.
- u. carmine 65.
- x. dark brown red 65.
- y. dark brown orange, goldbeater's skin 90.

R113TC 30c
- a. dark purple 60.
- b. dull purple 60.
- d. brown 60.
- e. black brown 60.
- g. light blue 60.
- h. dark blue 70.
- i. ultramarine 70.
- k. yellow green 70.
- n. green 65.
- o. dark green 65.
- p. blue green 65.
- q. light orange 65.
- r. dark orange 65.
- s. deep orange 65.
- t. scarlet 65.
- u. carmine 65.
- v. dark carmine 65.
- w. purplish carmine 65.
- x. dark brown red 65.
- y. dark brown orange, goldbeater's skin 90.

R114TC 40c
- a. dark purple 60.
- b. dull purple 60.
- d. brown 60.
- e. black brown 60.
- f. orange brown 65.
- g. light blue 60.
- h. dark blue 70.
- i. ultramarine 70.
- k. yellow green 70.
- n. green 65.
- o. dark green 65.
- p. blue green 65.
- q. light orange 65.
- r. dark orange 65.
- s. deep orange 65.
- t. scarlet 65.
- u. carmine 65.
- x. dark brown red 65.

R115TC 50c
- a. dark purple 60.
- b. dull purple 60.
- d. brown 60.
- e. black brown 60.
- g. light blue 60.
- h. dark blue 70.
- i. ultramarine 70.
- k. yellow green 70.
- n. green 65.
- o. dark green 65.
- p. blue green 65.
- q. light orange 65.
- r. dark orange 65.
- s. deep orange 65.
- t. scarlet 65.
- u. carmine 65.
- x. dark brown red 65.

R116TC 60c
- a. dark purple 60.
- b. dull purple 60.
- d. brown 60.
- e. black brown 60.
- g. light blue 60.
- h. dark blue 70.
- i. ultramarine 70.
- k. yellow green 70.
- n. green 65.
- o. dark green 65.
- p. blue green 65.
- q. light orange 65.
- r. dark orange 65.
- s. deep orange 65.
- t. scarlet 65.
- u. carmine 65.
- v. dark carmine 65.
- x. dark brown red 65.
- y. dark brown orange, goldbeater's skin 90.

R117TC 70c
- a. dark purple 60.
- b. dull purple 60.
- d. brown 60.
- e. black brown 60.
- g. light blue 60.
- h. dark blue 70.
- i. ultramarine 70.
- k. yellow green 70.
- n. green 65.
- o. dark green 65.
- p. blue green 65.
- q. light orange 65.
- r. dark orange 65.
- s. deep orange 65.
- t. scarlet 65.
- u. carmine 65.
- x. dark brown red 65.

R118TC $1
- a. dark purple 70.
- b. dull purple 70.
- d. brown 70.
- e. black brown 70.
- g. light blue 80.
- h. dark blue 85.
- i. ultramarine 85.
- k. yellow green 80.
- n. green 75.
- o. dark green 75.
- p. blue green 75.
- q. light orange 75.
- r. dark orange 75.
- s. deep orange 75.
- t. scarlet 80.
- u. carmine 80.
- w. purplish carmine 80.
- x. dark brown red 80.
- y. dark brown orange, goldbeater's skin 90.

R119TC $1.30
- a. dark purple 70.
- b. dull purple 70.
- d. brown 70.
- e. black brown 70.
- g. light blue 80.
- h. dark blue 85.
- i. ultramarine 85.
- k. yellow green 80.
- n. green 75.
- o. dark green 75.
- p. blue green 75.
- q. light orange 75.
- r. dark orange 75.
- s. deep orange 75.
- t. scarlet 80.
- u. carmine 80.
- x. dark brown red 80.

R120TC $1.50
- a. dark purple 70.
- b. dull purple 70.
- d. brown 70.
- e. black brown 70.
- g. light blue 80.
- h. dark blue 85.
- i. ultramarine 85.
- j. bright yellow green, on card 75.
- k. yellow green 80.
- n. green 75.
- o. dark green 75.
- p. blue green 75.
- q. light orange 75.
- r. dark orange 75.
- s. deep orange 75.

t. scarlet	80.	
u. carmine	80.	
x. dark brown red	80.	

R121TC $1.60

a. dark purple	70.
b. dull purple	70.
d. brown	70.
e. black brown	70.
g. light blue	80.
h. dark blue	85.
i. ultramarine	85.
k. yellow green	80.
n. green	75.
o. dark green	75.
p. blue green	75.
q. light orange	75.
r. dark orange	75.
s. deep orange	75.
t. scarlet	80.
u. carmine	80.
x. dark brown red	80.

R122TC $1.90

a. dark purple	70.
b. dull purple	70.
d. brown	70.
e. black brown	70.
g. light blue	80.
h. dark blue	85.
i. ultramarine	85.
j. bright yellow green, on card	75.
k. yellow green	80.
n. green	75.
o. dark green	75.
p. blue green	75.
q. light orange	75.
r. dark orange	75.
s. deep orange	75.
t. scarlet	80.
u. carmine	80.
x. dark brown red	80.

R123TC $2

a. dark purple	70.
b. dull purple	70.
d. brown	70.
e. black brown	70.
g. light blue	80.
h. dark blue	85.
i. ultramarine	85.
j. bright yellow green, on card	75.
k. yellow green	80.
n. green	75.
o. dark green	75.
p. blue green	75.
q. light orange	75.
r. dark orange	75.
s. deep orange	75.
t. scarlet	80.
u. carmine	80.
w. purplish carmine	80.
x. dark brown red	80.
y. dark brown orange, goldbeater's skin	90.

R124TC $2.50

a. dark purple	70.
b. dull purple	70.
d. brown	70.
e. black brown	70.
g. light blue	80.
h. dark blue	85.
i. ultramarine	85.
k. yellow green	80.
n. green	75.
o. dark green	75.
p. blue green	75.
q. light orange	75.
r. dark orange	75.
s. deep orange	75.
t. scarlet	80.
u. carmine	80.
v. dark carmine	80.
x. dark brown red	80.

R125TC $3

a. dark purple	70.
b. dull purple	70.
d. brown	70.
e. black brown	70.
g. light blue	80.
h. dark blue	85.
i. ultramarine	85.
j. bright yellow green, on card	75.
k. yellow green	80.
n. green	75.
o. dark green	75.
p. blue green	75.
q. light orange	75.
r. dark orange	75.
s. deep orange	75.
t. scarlet	80.
u. carmine	80.
x. dark brown red	80.

R126TC $3.50

a. dark purple	70.
b. dull purple	70.
c. red purple	75.
d. brown	70.
e. black brown	70.
g. light blue	80.
h. dark blue	85.
i. ultramarine	85.
k. yellow green	80.
n. green	75.
o. dark green	75.
p. blue green	75.
q. light orange	75.
r. dark orange	75.
s. deep orange	75.

t. scarlet	90.	
u. carmine	80.	
x. dark brown red	80.	

R127TC $5

a. dark purple	70.
b. dull purple	70.
d. brown	70.
e. black brown	70.
g. light blue	80.
h. dark blue	85.
i. ultramarine	85.
k. yellow green	80.
n. green	75.
o. dark green	75.
p. blue green	75.
q. light orange	75.
r. dark orange	75.
s. deep orange	75.
t. scarlet	75.
u. carmine	75.
w. purplish carmine	75.
x. dark brown red	80.
y. dark brown orange, goldbeater's skin	100.

R128TC $10

a. dark purple	70.
b. dull purple	70.
d. brown	70.
e. black brown	70.
g. light blue	80.
h. dark blue	85.
i. ultramarine	85.
j. bright yellow green, on card	75.
k. yellow green	75.
n. green	75.
o. dark green	75.
p. blue green	75.
q. light orange	75.
r. dark orange	75.
s. deep orange	75.
t. scarlet	75.
u. carmine	80.
x. dark brown red	80.

R129TC $20

a. dark purple	95.
b. dull purple	95.
d. brown	95.
e. black brown	95.
g. light blue	90.
h. dark blue	90.
i. ultramarine	90.
k. yellow green	85.
m. emerald green	85.
n. green	75.
o. dark green	75.
p. blue green	75.
q. light orange	75.
r. dark orange	85.
s. deep orange	85.
t. scarlet	90.
u. carmine	80.
v. dark carmine	90.
x. dark brown red	80.

R130TC $25

a. dark purple	100.
b. dull purple	100.
d. brown	100.
e. black brown	100.
g. light blue	90.
h. dark blue	90.
i. ultramarine	90.
k. yellow green	85.
m. emerald green	85.
n. green	75.
o. dark green	75.
p. blue green	75.
q. light orange	75.
r. dark orange	85.
s. deep orange	85.
t. scarlet	90.
u. carmine	80.
w. purplish carmine	90.
x. dark brown red	300.
y. dark brown orange, goldbeater's skin	100.

R131TC $50

a. dark purple	95.
b. dull purple	95.
d. brown	95.
e. black brown	95.
g. light blue	90.
h. dark blue	90.
i. ultramarine	90.
j. bright yellow green, on card	85.
k. yellow green	85.
m. emerald green	85.
n. green	75.
o. dark green	75.
p. blue green	75.
q. light orange	75.
r. dark orange	85.
s. deep orange	85.
t. scarlet	90.
u. carmine	80.
x. dark brown red	80.

RB1TC   1c

a. dark purple	70.
b. dull purple	70.
d. brown	65.
e. black brown	65.
g. light blue	75.
h. dark blue	75.
i. ultramarine	70.
k. yellow green	70.
l. dark yellow green	70.
n. green	65.
o. dark green	65.

p. blue green	70.
q. light orange	70.
r. dark orange	70.
s. deep orange	70.
t. scarlet	70.
u. carmine	70.
x. dark brown red	70.

RB2TC   2c

a. dark purple	
b. dull purple	
d. brown	
e. black brown	
g. light blue	
h. dark blue	
i. ultramarine	
j. bright yellow green, on card	
k. yellow green	
n. green	
o. dark green	
p. blue green	
q. light orange	
r. dark orange	
s. deep orange	
t. scarlet	
u. carmine	
x. dark brown red	

RB3TC   3c

a. dark purple	
b. dull purple	
d. brown	
e. black brown	
g. light blue	
h. dark blue	
i. ultramarine	
k. yellow green	
l. dark yellow green	
n. green	
o. dark green	
p. blue green	
q. light orange	
r. dark orange	
s. deep orange	
t. scarlet	
u. carmine	
x. dark brown red	

RB4TC   4c

a. dark purple	
b. dull purple	
d. brown	
e. black brown	
g. light blue	
h. dark blue	
i. ultramarine	
k. yellow green	
n. green	
o. dark green	
p. blue green	
q. light orange	
r. dark orange	
s. deep orange	
t. scarlet	
u. carmine	
x. dark brown red	

RB5TC   5c

a. dark purple	
b. dull purple	
d. brown	
e. black brown	
g. light blue	
h. dark blue	
i. ultramarine	
j. bright yellow green, on card	
k. yellow green	
l. dark yellow green	
n. green	
o. dark green	
p. blue green	
q. light orange	
r. dark orange	
s. deep orange	
t. scarlet	
u. carmine	
x. dark brown red	

RB6TC   6c

a. dark purple	
b. dull purple	
d. brown	
e. black brown	
g. light blue	
h. dark blue	
i. ultramarine	
k. yellow green	
l. dark yellow green	
n. green	
o. dark green	
p. blue green	
q. light orange	
r. dark orange	
s. deep orange	
t. scarlet	
u. carmine	
x. dark brown red	

RB7TC   10c

a. dark purple	
b. dull purple	
d. brown	
e. black brown	
g. light blue	
h. dark blue	
i. ultramarine	
k. yellow green	
l. dark yellow green	
n. green	
o. dark green	
p. blue green	

q.	light orange		65.
r.	dark orange		65.
s.	deep orange		65.
t.	scarlet		65.
u.	carmine		65.
x.	dark brown red		65.

R8

R20TC	⅛c	light blue	Large die on card	1,000.
R21TC	¼c	dull green	Large die on India	1,300.
R22TC	⅜c	dull green	Large die on India	750.
R24TC	1c	dull green	Large die on India	750.
R26TC	1⅞c	dull green	Large die on India	750.
R26TC	1⅞c	black	Large die on India	750.
R27TC	2c	dull green	Large die on India	500.
R31TC	5c	dull green	Large die on India	500.

R18-29

Stock Transfer

R20TC	$50	black	Die on India	2,250.
R20TC	$50	blue	Die on India	2,250.

R4

Playing Cards

R1TC	2c	black (On hand)	Die on India	1,500.
R2TC	2c	lake (Act of)	Die on India	1,000.

PRIVATE DIE MATCH STAMPS

For important valuing information see the note before Private Die Proprietary die and plate proofs.

R64

			DIE ON INDIA (1) Large (3) India	PLATE (4) Card
RO1TC	1c	black	175.	
RO1TC	1c	green	300.	
RO2TC	1c	black	225.	
RO2TC	1c	green	300.	
RO5TC	1c	black	275.	
RO5TC	1c	blue	500.	
RO6TC	1c	black	300.	
RO6TC	1c	green	500.	
RO7TC	1c	black	300.	
RO7TC	1c	dull green	300.	
RO7TC	1c	green	500.	
RO9TC	1c	blue	225.	
RO9TC	1c	brown	275.	
RO9TC	1c	dark green	500.	
RO9TC	1c	green	300.	
RO10TC	1c	blue	300.	
RO10TC	1c	green	500.	
RO11TC	3c	blue	500.	
RO11TC	3c	green	500.	
RO12TC	1c	blue	225.	
RO12TC	1c	green	500.	
RO13TC	3c	black	500.	
RO13TC	3c	blue	1,000.	
RO14TC	1c	blue	225.	
RO14TC	1c	green	500.	
RO15TC	1c	black	225.	
RO15TC	1c	blue	225.	
RO16TC	1c	black	225.	
RO16TC	1c	green	300.	
RO17/19TC	1c/3c	green	1,250.	
RO17TC	1c	black	225.	
RO17TC	1c	green	500.	
RO19TC	3c	blue	250.	
RO19TC	3c	green	600.	
RO20TC	1c	black	175.	
RO20TC	1c	green	500.	
RO21TC	3c	blue	375.	
RO21TC	3c	green	375.	
RO22TC	1c	black	300.	
RO23TC	1c	black	225.	
RO23TC	1c	blue	225.	
RO23TC	1c	green	500.	
RO24TC	1c	black	225.	
RO24TC	1c	blue	225.	
RO24TC	1c	green	500.	
RO25TC	12c	black	400.	
RO25TC	12c	blue	750.	
RO25TC	12c	green	750.	
RO26TC	1c	black	225.	
RO26TC	1c	blue	225.	
RO26TC	1c	dark brn	225.	
RO26TC	1c	green	300.	
RO26TC	1c	light brn	300.	
RO27TC	12c	black	400.	
RO27TC	12c	blue	500.	
RO27TC	12c	green	750.	
RO28TC	1c	black	175.	
RO28TC	1c	brown	300.	
RO28TC	1c	green	300.	
RO29TC	1c	blue	300.	
RO29TC	1c	green	300.	
RO30TC	1c	black	175.	
RO30TC	1c	blue	225.	
RO30TC	1c	green	300.	
RO30TC	1c	red	500.	
RO31TC	1c	blue	300.	
RO31TC	1c	green	225.	
RO31TC	1c	red	500.	
RO32TC	4c	blue	500.	
RO32TC	4c	brown	500.	
RO32TC	4c	orange	500.	
RO32TC	4c	vermilion	500.	
RO35TC	1c	blue	300.	
RO35TC	1c	green	500.	
RO37TC	3c	blue	400.	

			DIE ON INDIA (1) Large (3) India	PLATE (4) Card
RO37TC	3c	green	400.	
RO38TC	1c	blue	350.	
RO38TC	1c	dk bl	500.	
RO38TC	1c	green	375.	
RO38TC	1c	red	600.	
RO39TC	1c	black	300.	
RO41TC	1c	black	225.	
RO41TC	1c	green	300.	
RO42TC	1c	black	300.	
RO42TC	1c	blue	300.	
RO42TC	1c	green	500.	
RO43TC	1c	blue	500.	
RO45TC	1c	blue	350.	
RO45TC	1c	green	750.	
RO46TC	1c	blue	350.	
RO46TC	1c	dk bl	500.	
RO46TC	1c	green	500.	
RO46TC	1c	orange	300.	
RO47TC	1c	blue	300.	
RO47TC	1c	green	500.	
RO49TC	1c	blue	225.	
RO49TC	1c	brown	500.	
RO49TC	1c	brn red	300.	
RO49TC	1c	dk bl	500.	
RO49TC	1c	green	500.	
RO49TC	1c	red brn	500.	
RO55TC	1c	blue	375.	
RO56TC	1c	blue	750.	
RO56TC	1c	green	300.	
RO57TC	1c	black	175.	
RO57TC	1c	blue	225.	
RO58TC	1c	black	300.	
RO58TC	1c	blue	225.	
RO58TC	1c	dark rose	500.	
RO58TC	1c	green	500.	
RO58TC	1c	rose	300.	
RO59TC	1c	black	225.	
RO60TC	3c	blue	500.	
RO60TC	3c	green	500.	
RO61TC	1c	black	175.	
RO61TC	1c	blue	300.	
RO62TC	1c	black	175.	
RO62TC	1c	blue	175.	
RO64TC	1c	black	225.	
RO64TC	1c	blue	300.	
RO64TC	1c	green	300.	
RO65TC	1c	green	300.	
RO67TC	1c	blue	225.	
RO67TC	1c	green	300.	
RO67TC	1c	red	500.	
RO67TC	1c	rose	500.	
RO68TC	1c	black	225.	
RO68TC	1c	black	225.	
RO69TC	1c	blue	300.	
RO69TC	1c	green	500.	
RO71TC	1c	black	250.	
RO71TC	1c	green	400.	
RO72TC	1c	black	500.	
RO73TC	1c	blue	225.	
RO73TC	1c	green	300.	
RO73TC	1c	red	500.	
RO73TC	1c	red brn	225.	
RO76TC	1c	blue	500.	
RO76TC	1c	green	300.	
RO77TC	1c	black	225.	
RO77TC	1c	green	500.	
RO78TC	1c	black	225.	
RO78TC	1c	dk bl	500.	
RO78TC	1c	green	500.	
RO80TC	1c	black	225.	
RO80TC	1c	green	500.	
RO81TC	1c	blue	175.	
RO81TC	1c	dark green	500.	
RO81TC	1c	green	225.	
RO81TC	1c	lake	500.	
RO81TC	1c	red	300.	
RO82TC	1c	blue	175.	
RO82TC	1c	green	500.	
RO83TC	1c	black	175.	
RO83TC	1c	green	300.	
RO83TC	1c	red	500.	
RO84TC	1c	blue	300.	
RO84TC	1c	green	500.	
RO85TC	1c	black	250.	
RO85TC	1c	blue	300.	
RO85TC	1c	green	350.	
RO85TC	1c	orange	500.	
RO85TC	1c	vermilion	500.	
RO86TC	1c	blue	500.	
RO86TC	1c	brown	500.	
RO86TC	1c	green	400.	
RO86TC	1c	orange	500.	
RO86TC	1c	red	500.	
RO87TC	1c	dull rose	500.	
RO87TC	1c	orange	500.	
RO88TC	1c	blue	300.	
RO88TC	1c	green	500.	
RO89TC	3c	blue	300.	
RO89TC	3c	green	300.	
RO90TC	6c	blue	225.	
RO90TC	6c	brown	500.	
RO90TC	6c	green	500.	
RO90TC	6c	orange	500.	
RO91TC	3c	blue	225.	
RO91TC	3c	brown	500.	
RO91TC	3c	green	500.	
RO91TC	3c	orange	500.	
RO91TC	3c	red	500.	
RO92TC	1c	blue	300.	
RO92TC	1c	green	500.	
RO94TC	3c	blue	225.	
RO94TC	3c	brown	300.	

			DIE ON INDIA (1) Large (3) India	PLATE (4) Card
RO94TC	3c	green	225.	
RO94TC	3c	orange	300.	
RO94TC	3c	red	500.	
RO94TC	3c	vermilion	500.	
RO95TC	1c	black	175.	
RO95TC	1c	blue	175.	
RO95TC	1c	brown	225.	
RO95TC	1c	dk bl	500.	
RO96TC	1c	black	175.	
RO96TC	1c	blue	225.	
RO97TC	1c	blue	300.	
RO99TC	1c	black	175.	
RO99TC	1c	blue	500.	
RO100TC	1c	blue	500.	
RO101TC	3c	black	175.	
RO101TC	3c	green	300.	
RO101TC	3c	orange		75.
RO102TC	5c	black	175.	
RO102TC	5c	blue	500.	
RO102TC	5c	green	500.	
RO103TC	1c	blue	225.	
RO103TC	1c	rose	300.	
RO105TC	1c	blue	300.	
RO105TC	1c	green	500.	
RO106TC	1c	black	175.	
RO106TC	1c	blue	225.	
RO107TC	1c	black	175.	
RO107TC	1c	green	300.	
RO110TC	1c	black	175.	
RO110TC	1c	blue	175.	
RO110TC	1c	orange	500.	
RO110TC	1c	red	225.	
RO112TC	1c	black	175.	
RO112TC	1c	green	500.	
RO113TC	1c	blue	300.	
RO113TC	1c	green	500.	
RO113TC	1c	orange	500.	
RO114TC	1c	black	750.	
RO115TC	1c	black	175.	
RO115TC	1c	green	500.	
RO116TC	1c	black	225.	
RO116TC	1c	green	300.	
RO118TC	8c	black	225.	
RO118TC	8c	dk bl	500.	
RO118TC	8c	green	500.	
RO119TC	1c	black	225.	
RO119TC	1c	blue	225.	
RO120TC	1c	black	500.	
RO121TC	1c	black	175.	
RO122TC	1c	blue	300.	
RO122TC	1c	green	500.	
RO123TC	1c	blue	500.	
RO125TC	1c	black	225.	
RO126TC	1c	blue	300.	
RO126TC	1c	green	500.	
RO127TC	1c	black	300.	
RO127TC	1c	green	225.	
RO128TC	1c	black	225.	
RO128TC	1c	green	500.	
RO130TC	1c	black	225.	
RO130TC	1c	green	300.	
RO131TC	1c	black	175.	
RO131TC	1c	green	225.	
RO131TC	1c	red	225.	
RO132TC	1c	black	225.	
RO132TC	1c	green	500.	
RO133TC	1c	blue	500.	
RO133TC	1c	green	300.	
RO134TC	1c	black	300.	150.
RO134TC	1c	green	300.	
RO135TC	1c	black	500.	
RO135TC	1c	blue	300.	
RO135TC	1c	green	300.	
RO135TC	1c	rose	225.	
RO136TC	1c	black	225.	
RO136TC	1c	green	300.	
RO137TC	1c	black	175.	
RO137TC	1c	blue	175.	
RO137TC	1c	green	500.	
RO138TC	1c	black	175.	
RO138TC	1c	blue	500.	
RO139TC	5c	black	175.	
RO139TC	5c	green	500.	
RO140TC	4c	black	225.	
RO140TC	4c	blue	300.	
RO141TC	1c	black	175.	
RO141TC	1c	dk bl	300.	
RO141TC	1c	green	500.	
RO141TC	1c	yellow green	300.	
RO141TC	1c	green	500.	
RO142TC	1c	black	175.	
RO142TC	1c	blue	225.	
RO143TC	3c	black	175.	
RO143TC	3c	blue	225.	
RO143TC	3c	green	300.	
RO144TC	1c	black	500.	
RO145TC	1c	black	500.	
RO145TC	1c	blue	500.	
RO146TC	1c	blue	500.	
RO146TC	1c	green	300.	
RO148TC	1c	black	175.	
RO148TC	1c	green	300.	
RO148TC	1c	red	300.	
RO152TC	1c	blue	300.	
RO152TC	1c	green	500.	
RO153TC	1c	blue	225.	
RO153TC	1c	brown	300.	
RO153TC	1c	green	225.	
RO153TC	1c	orange	300.	
RO153TC	1c	red	300.	
RO155TC	1c	blue	225.	
RO155TC	1c	green	500.	
RO157TC	3c	black	175.	

			DIE ON INDIA (1) Large	PLATE (3) India (4) Card
RO157TC	3c	green	300.	
RO158TC	1c	blue	300.	
RO158TC	1c	green	500.	
RO159TC	3c	black	225.	
RO159TC	3c	green	500.	
RO160TC	1c	black	225.	
RO160TC	1c	brown	500.	
RO160TC	1c	green	300.	
RO161TC	1c	black	225.	
RO161TC	1c	green	300.	
RO163TC	1c	blue	300.	
RO163TC	1c	green	500.	
RO164TC	1c	black	500.	
RO165TC	12c	black	750.	
RO165TC	12c	green	1,000.	
RO166TC	12c	red	1,000.	
RO166TC	1c	black	300.	
RO166TC	1c	blue	225.	
RO166TC	1c	green	500.	
RO166TC	1c	red	175.	
RO167TC	3c	black	175.	
RO167TC	3c	green	300.	
RO167TC	3c	red	300.	
RO167TC	3c	ultramarine	300.	
RO168TC	1c	black	500.	
RO168TC	1c	green	300.	
RO171TC	1c	blue	300.	
RO171TC	1c	green	300.	
RO172TC	1c	blue	225.	
RO172TC	1c	green	500.	
RO173TC	1c	black	225.	
RO173TC	1c	green	300.	
RO174TC	1c	black	300.	
RO174TC	1c	green	300.	
RO175TC	1c	blue	275.	
RO175TC	1c	green	350.	
RO175TC	1c	red	500.	
RO177TC	1c	black	175.	
RO177TC	1c	blue	225.	
RO177TC	1c	green	500.	
RO178TC	1c	black	175.	
RO178TC	1c	blue	300.	
RO179TC	1c	blue	500.	
RO179TC	1c	green	500.	
RO180TC	1c	blue	225.	
RO180TC	1c	green	500.	
RO181TC	1c	blue	500.	
RO181TC	1c	green	300.	
RO182TC	1c	blue	300.	
RO182TC	1c	green	300.	
RO183TC	1c	blue	650.	
RO183TC	1c	green	650.	
RO184TC	1c	blue	225.	
RO184TC	1c	brown	300.	
RO184TC	1c	green	225.	
RO184TC	1c	orange	300.	
RO184TC	1c	red	300.	
RO186TC	1c	black	175.	

PRIVATE DIE CANNED FRUIT STAMP

| RP1TC | 1c | black | 375. | |

PRIVATE DIE MEDICINE STAMPS

			DIE ON INDIA (1) Large	PLATE (3) India (4) Card
RS1TC	1c	blue	300.	
RS1TC	1c	green	300.	
RS4TC	1c	green	500.	
RS10TC	4c	black	300.	
RS10TC	4c	green	500.	
RS14TC	4c	black	300.	
RS14TC	4c	blue	300.	
RS16TC	2c	green	500.	
RS21TC	1c	blue	500.	
RS21TC	1c	green	500.	
RS22TC	2c	blue	500.	
RS22TC	2c	green	500.	
RS23TC	4c	green	500.	
RS24TC	1c	blue	500.	
RS24TC	1c	green	500.	
RS25TC	2c	blue	500.	
RS25TC	2c	green	500.	
RS26TC	4c	blue	500.	
RS26TC	4c	green	500.	
RS27TC	4c	blue	225.	
RS27TC	4c	green	500.	
RS28TC	2c	black	225.	
RS28TC	2c	blue	225.	
RS29TC	1c	black	175.	
RS29/RO120TC	2c/1c	black	750.	
RS29TC	2c	blue	175.	
RS29TC	2c	dk bl	500.	
RS29TC	2c	green	500.	
RS29TC	2c	red	300.	
RS30TC	1c	black	175.	
RS30TC	1c	blue	500.	
RS30TC	1c	green	500.	
RS30TC	1c	red	500.	
RS31TC	1c	black	500.	
RS31TC	1c	blue	225.	
RS31TC	1c	red	500.	
RS33TC	1c	blue	175.	
RS33TC	1c	green	225.	
RS33TC	1c	red	500.	
RS34TC	1c	blue	500.	
RS34TC	1c	green	500.	
RS35TC	1c	blue	300.	
RS35TC	1c	green	500.	
RS36TC	1c	black	500.	
RS36TC	1c	dk bl	500.	
RS36TC	1c	green	500.	
RS36TC	1c	ultramarine	500.	

			DIE ON INDIA (1) Large	PLATE (3) India (4) Card
RS36TC	1c	yellow green	225.	
RS38TC	2c	blue	750.	
RS38TC	2c	green	750.	
RS39TC	1c	blue	300.	
RS39TC	1c	green	300.	
RS39TC	1c	orange	500.	
RS40TC	2c	black	225.	
RS40TC	2c	blue	300.	
RS41TC	4c	black	225.	
RS41TC	4c	blue	500.	
RS41TC	4c	green	500.	
RS42TC	1c	green	500.	
RS43TC	4c	black	225.	
RS43TC	4c	green	500.	
RS44TC	1c	green	750.	
RS46TC	4c	blue	225.	
RS46TC	4c	green	300.	
RS47TC	4c	blue	300.	
RS47TC	4c	brown	500.	
RS47TC	4c	green	300.	
RS47TC	4c	orange	500.	
RS47TC	4c	red	500.	
RS49TC	4c	black	225.	
RS49TC	4c	blue	300.	
RS50TC	1c	black	300.	
RS50TC	1c	blue	300.	
RS50TC	1c	green	500.	
RS51TC	2c	blue	500.	
RS51TC	2c	green	500.	
RS52TC	4c	blue	500.	
RS52TC	4c	green	500.	
RS53TC	1c	blue	225.	
RS53TC	1c	brown	300.	
RS53TC	1c	green	225.	
RS53TC	1c	orange	300.	
RS53TC	1c	red	300.	
RS54TC	2c	blue	225.	
RS54TC	2c	brown	300.	
RS54TC	2c	green	225.	
RS54TC	2c	orange	300.	
RS54TC	2c	red	500.	
RS55TC	4c	blue	225.	
RS55TC	4c	green	225.	
RS55TC	4c	orange	225.	
RS55TC	4c	red	500.	
RS56TC	3c	black	350.	
RS56TC	1c	green	500.	
RS57TC	6c	blue	225.	
RS57TC	6c	brown	300.	
RS57TC	6c	green	225.	
RS57TC	6c	orange	300.	
RS57TC	6c	red	300.	
RS58TC	4c	blue	225.	
RS58TC	4c	blue green	500.	
RS58TC	4c	dk bl	500.	
RS58TC	4c	green	225.	
RS58TC	4c	light blue	500.	
RS58TC	4c	red	225.	
RS59TC	1c	blue	300.	
RS59TC	1c	green	500.	
RS60TC	1c	blue	500.	
RS62TC	1c	brown	300.	
RS62TC	1c	green	225.	
RS62TC	1c	orange	300.	
RS62TC	1c	red	500.	
RS62TC	1c	vermilion	500.	
RS64TC	2c	blue	225.	
RS64TC	2c	brown	300.	
RS64TC	2c	green	225.	
RS64TC	2c	orange	300.	
RS64TC	2c	red	500.	
RS64TC	1c	vermilion	500.	
RS65TC	4c	blue	500.	
RS65TC	4c	green	500.	
RS66TC	1c	blue	300.	
RS66TC	1c	green	500.	
RS66TC	1c	light green	500.	
RS66TC	1c	orange	500.	
RS66TC	1c	rose red	500.	
RS67TC	1c	green	500.	
RS69TC	1c	blue	500.	
RS69TC	1c	green	500.	
RS70TC	2c	blue	500.	
RS70TC	2c	green	500.	
RS71TC	1c	blue	500.	
RS71TC	1c	green	500.	
RS72TC	2c	blue	500.	
RS72TC	2c	green	500.	
RS73TC	2c	black	500.	
RS73TC	2c	blue	750.	
RS73TC	2c	red	1,000.	
RS74TC	1c	blue	500.	
RS74TC	1c	green	500.	
RS74hTC	1c	blue	500.	
RS74hTC	1c	green	500.	
RS75TC	1c	black	300.	
RS75TC	1c	green	500.	
RS76TC	2c	blue	300.	
RS76TC	2c	green	300.	
RS81TC	4c	black	225.	
RS81TC	4c	blue	500.	
RS81TC	4c	green	500.	
RS83TC	4c	blue	500.	
RS83TC	4c	green	500.	
RS84TC	1c	black	250.	
RS84TC	1c	blue	350.	
RS84TC	1c	green	250.	
RS84TC	1c	orange	650.	
RS84TC	1c	red	650.	
RS84TC	1c	slate	650.	

			DIE ON INDIA (1) Large	PLATE (3) India (4) C
RS85TC	4c	blue	275.	
RS85TC	4c	brown	275.	
RS85TC	4c	green	300.	
RS85TC	4c	orange	375.	
RS86TC	1c	black	225.	
RS86TC	1c	blue	225.	
RS88TC	1c	blue	500.	
RS88TC	1c	green	500.	
RS89TC	1c	green	300.	
RS91TC	4c	blue	225.	
RS91TC	4c	green	500.	
RS92TC	3c	blue	225.	
RS92TC	3c	brown	300.	
RS92TC	3c	green	225.	
RS92TC	3c	orange	300.	
RS92TC	3c	red	500.	
RS92TC	3c	vermilion	600.	
RS94TC	4c	blue	500.	
RS94TC	4c	green	500.	
RS95TC	1c	black	300.	
RS95TC	1c	blue	225.	
RS95TC	1c	dk bl	90.	
RS96TC	3c	blue	225.	
RS96TC	3c	green	500.	
RS97TC	1c	blue	300.	
RS97TC	1c	green	500.	
RS98TC	1c	blue	225.	
RS98TC	1c	green	175.	
RS98TC	1c	red	500.	
RS99TC	4c	blue	500.	
RS100TC	6c	green	500.	
RS101TC	1c	blue	500.	
RS101TC	1c	green	500.	
RS102TC	2c	black	175.	
RS102TC	2c	green	225.	
RS102TC	2c	rose	225.	
RS103TC	4c	blue	500.	
RS103TC	4c	green	500.	
RS106TC	2c	black	500.	
RS106TC	2c	green	300.	
RS107/109TC	3c/6c	green	1,250.	
RS107TC	3c	blue	300.	
RS108TC	4c	blue	300.	
RS108TC	4c	green	500.	
RS109TC	6c	blue	300.	
RS110TC	2c	black	300.	
RS110TC	2c	green	300.	
RS111TC	4c	blue	300.	
RS111TC	4c	green	500.	
RS114TC	1c	green	300.	
RS116TC	4c	black	225.	
RS116TC	4c	blue	300.	
RS116TC	4c	brown	500.	
RS116TC	4c	green	500.	
RS116TC	4c	vermilion	500.	
RS117TC	1c	blue	350.	
RS117TC	1c	green	750.	
RS118TC	1c	black	175.	
RS118TC	1c	blue	225.	
RS118TC	1c	brn red	300.	
RS118TC	1c	green	300.	
RS120TC	2c	blue	225.	
RS120TC	2c	brown	300.	
RS120TC	2c	green	225.	
RS120TC	2c	orange	300.	
RS120TC	2c	red	500.	
RS120TC	2c	vermilion	500.	
RS121TC	3c	blue	500.	
RS121TC	3c	green	500.	
RS122TC	2c	blue	500.	
RS122TC	2c	green	500.	
RS123TC	4c	blue	225.	
RS123TC	4c	brown	300.	
RS123TC	4c	green	225.	
RS123TC	4c	orange	300.	
RS123TC	4c	red	500.	
RS123TC	4c	vermilion	500.	
RS124TC	1c	black	175.	
RS124TC	1c	blue green	300.	
RS124TC	1c	green	500.	
RS124TC	1c	orange	500.	
RS124TC	1c	red	225.	
RS126TC	1c	black	225.	
RS126TC	1c	blue	225.	
RS126TC	1c	brown	300.	
RS126TC	1c	orange	300.	
RS126TC	1c	red	500.	
RS126TC	1c	vermilion	500.	
RS127TC	4c	black	225.	
RS127TC	4c	blue	225.	
RS127TC	4c	brown	225.	
RS127TC	4c	orange	300.	
RS127TC	4c	red	500.	
RS127TC	4c	vermilion	500.	
RS128TC	2c	black	600.	
RS128TC	2c	green	400.	
RS128TC	2c	pale blue	500.	
RS130TC	4c	black	275.	
RS130TC	4c	blue	350.	
RS131TC	4c	blue	225.	
RS131TC	4c	brown	500.	
RS131TC	4c	green	300.	
RS131TC	4c	orange	300.	
RS131TC	4c	red	500.	
RS131TC	4c	vermilion	500.	
RS132TC	4c	blue	500.	
RS132TC	4c	orange	500.	
RS133TC	6c	blue	500.	
RS133TC	6c	green	500.	
RS134TC	4c	black	300.	
RS134TC	4c	green	300.	
RS134TC	4c	red	500.	

No.	Denom	Color	(1) Large	(3) India	(4) Card
RS138TC	1c	blue	300.		
RS138TC	1c	green	500.		
RS138TC	1c	red	500.		
RS138TC	1c	yel grn	500.		
RS139TC	2c	black	225.		
RS139TC	2c	blackish violet			90.
RS139TC	2c	blue	500.		
RS139TC	2c	green	500.		
RS139TC	2c	red	225.		
RS139TC	2c	rose	500.		
RS141TC	4c	black	225.		
RS141TC	4c	blue	300.		
RS142TC	1c	blue	225.		
RS142TC	1c	brown	300.		
RS142TC	1c	green	225.		
RS142TC	1c	orange	300.		
RS142TC	1c	red	500.		
RS142TC	1c	vermilion	500.		
RS143TC	4c	black	225.		
RS143TC	4c	blue	225.		
RS144TC	1c	black	500.		
RS144TC	1c	green	500.		
RS145TC	2c	blue	500.		
RS146TC	4c	black	300.		
RS146TC	4c	blue	300.		
RS150TC	1c	black	300.		
RS150TC	1c	blue	175.		
RS150TC	1c	carmine	500.		
RS150TC	1c	green	225.		
RS151TC	1c	blue	500.		
RS151TC	1c	green	500.		
RS152TC	2c	black	175.		
RS152TC	2c	blue	300.		
RS153TC	4c	blue	750.		
RS153TC	4c	green	750.		
RS154TC	4c	black	500.		
RS155TC	2c	black	300.		
RS155TC	2c	black	300.		
RS155TC	2c	blue	225.		
RS155TC	2c	red	500.		
RS156TC	6c	blue	225.		
RS156TC	6c	green	225.		
RS156TC	6c	red	225.		
RS157TC	2c	blue	225.		
RS157TC	2c	green	225.		
RS157TC	2c	red	500.		
RS157TC	2c	vermilion	300.		
RS158TC	1c	black	500.		
RS159TC	4c	black	375.		
RS160TC	6c	blue	300.		
RS160TC	6c	green	500.		
RS161TC	4c	blue	500.		
RS161TC	4c	green	750.		
RS162TC	1c	black	175.		
RS162TC	1c	green	300.		
RS162TC	1c	red	500.		
RS163TC	4c	black	300.		
RS163TC	4c	green	600.		
RS163TC	4c	yellow green	600.		
RS164TC	1c	blue	225.		
RS164TC	1c	green	500.		
RS165TC	4c	black	175.		
RS165TC	4c	blue	225.		
RS166TC	1c	blue	300.		
RS166TC	1c	green	500.		
RS169TC	4c	blue	225.		
RS169TC	4c	green	500.		
RS169TC	4c	red	225.		
RS170TC	1c	blue	300.		
RS170TC	1c	green	500.		
RS171TC	1c	black	225.		
RS171TC	1c	blue	225.		
RS171TC	1c	brown	300.		
RS171TC	1c	dull blue	500.		
RS171TC	1c	green	225.		
RS171TC	1c	orange	300.		
RS171TC	1c	red	500.		
RS171TC	1c	vermilion	500.		
RS172TC	2c	blue	225.		
RS172TC	2c	brown	300.		
RS172TC	2c	green	225.		
RS172TC	2c	orange	225.		
RS172TC	2c	red	500.		
RS172TC	2c	vermilion	500.		
RS173TC	1c	black	225.		
RS173TC	1c	green	225.		
RS173TC	1c	red	300.		
RS174TC	1c	black	225.		
RS174TC	1c	dk bl	500.		
RS174TC	1c	green	300.		
RS175TC	2c	black	250.		
RS175TC	2c	blue	500.		
RS175TC	2c	green	500.		
RS176TC	4c	blue	375.		
RS176TC	4c	green	500.		
RS177TC	2c	blue	750.		
RS177TC	2c	green	1,000.		
RS178TC	6c	blue	300.		
RS178TC	6c	green	500.		
RS179TC	2c	black	300.		
RS179TC	2c	blue	375.		
RS180TC	3c	blue	300.		
RS180TC	3c	green	300.		
RS181TC	4c	blue	225.		
RS181TC	4c	green	500.		
RS182TC	4c	blue	225.		
RS182TC	4c	green	225.		
RS182TC	4c	rose	300.		
RS183TC	1c	black	500.		
RS183TC	1c	blue	300.		
RS183TC	1c	green	500.		
RS183TC	1c	red	225.		
RS184TC	2c	blue	300.		
RS184TC	2c	brown	225.		
RS184TC	2c	green	225.		
RS184TC	2c	orange	300.		
RS184TC	2c	vermilion	300.		
RS185TC	1c	blue	300.		
RS186TC	4c	blue	225.		
RS186TC	4c	green	500.		
RS187TC	4c	blue	225.		
RS187TC	4c	brown	300.		
RS187TC	4c	green	300.		
RS187TC	4c	orange	500.		
RS187TC	4c	red	500.		
RS187TC	4c	vermilion	500.		
RS188TC	1c	blue	500.		
RS188TC	1c	green	500.		
RS189TC	1c	black	175.		
RS189TC	1c	blue	225.		
RS189TC	1c	red	225.		
RS190TC	2c	blue	500.		
RS190TC	2c	green	500.		
RS191TC	4c	blue	400.		
RS191TC	4c	green	400.		
RS192TC	6c	blue	400.		
RS192TC	6c	green	400.		
RS192TC	6c	rose	500.		
RS193TC	2c	blue	500.		
RS193TC	2c	green	500.		
RS194TC	1c	green	175.		
RS195TC	2c	blue	500.		
RS195TC	2c	green	500.		
RS196TC	1c	black	500.		
RS196TC	1c	green	225.		
RS197TC	2c	blue	300.		
RS198TC	1c	green	300.		
RS198TC	1c	red	500.		
RS199TC	2c	blue	225.		
RS199TC	2c	green	500.		
RS204TC	2c	blue	500.		
RS204TC	2c	green	500.		
RS205TC	4c	blue	225.		
RS205TC	4c	green	500.		
RS208TC	1c	black	225.		
RS208TC	1c	blue	225.		
RS208TC	1c	orange	300.		
RS209TC	2c	black	500.		
RS209TC	2c	blue	500.		
RS210TC	4c	blue	225.		
RS210TC	4c	green	225.		
RS210TC	4c	red	225.		
RS212TC	1c	black	225.		
RS212TC	1c	blue	300.		
RS212TC	1c	green	500.		
RS213TC	6c	blue	500.		
RS213TC	6c	green	500.		
RS214TC	4c	blue	300.		
RS214TC	4c	brown	300.		
RS214TC	4c	green	225.		
RS214TC	4c	orange	300.		
RS214TC	4c	red	500.		
RS214TC	4c	vermilion	500.		
RS215TC	1c	black	300.		
RS215TC	1c	blue	450.		
RS215TC	1c	dark red	500.		
RS215TC	1c	green	500.		
RS216TC	1c	blue	500.		
RS216TC	1c	green	500.		
RS220TC	1c	blue	300.		
RS221TC	4c	black	175.		
RS221TC	4c	blue	225.		
RS222TC	8c	green	500.		
RS223TC	1c	blue	300.		
RS223TC	1c	brown	300.		
RS223TC	1c	green	225.		
RS223TC	1c	orange	300.		
RS223TC	1c	vermilion	300.		
RS224TC	1c	blue	500.		
RS224TC	1c	brown	300.		
RS224TC	1c	green	225.		
RS224TC	1c	orange	300.		
RS224TC	1c	red	500.		
RS225TC	4c	blue	500.		
RS225TC	4c	green	500.		
RS226TC	1c	black	350.		
RS228TC	1c	black	175.		
RS228TC	1c	blue	225.		
RS228TC	1c	brown	500.		
RS228TC	1c	green	225.		
RS228TC	1c	orange	500.		
RS228TC	1c	red	500.		
RS228TC	1c	vermilion	500.		
RS229TC	2c	black	225.		
RS229TC	2c	blue	225.		
RS229TC	2c	brown	300.		
RS229TC	2c	green	225.		
RS229TC	2c	orange	225.		
RS229TC	2c	red	300.		
RS229TC	2c	vermilion	500.		
RS230TC	6c	blue	225.		
RS230TC	6c	brown	300.		
RS230TC	6c	green	225.		
RS230TC	6c	orange	300.		
RS230TC	6c	vermilion	225.		
RS231TC	6c	black	1,000.		
RS231TC	6c	blue	1,000.		
RS231TC	6c	green	1,000.		
RS231TC	6c	red	750.		
RS236TC	4c	blue	500.		
RS239TC	2c	black	225.		
RS239TC	2c	blue	300.		
RS239TC	2c	brown	500.		
RS239TC	2c	green	225.		
RS239TC	2c	orange	300.		
RS239TC	2c	vermilion	500.		
RS240TC	4c	red	500.		
RS240TC	4c	blue	175.		
RS240TC	4c	blue green	500.		
RS240TC	4c	brown	500.		
RS240TC	4c	green	225.		
RS240TC	4c	orange	225.		
RS240TC	4c	vermilion	225.		
RS241TC	4c	green	500.		
RS242TC	1c	blue	225.		
RS242TC	1c	green	500.		
RS243TC	4c	blue	500.		
RS243TC	4c	green	500.		
RS244TC	6c	blue	500.		
RS244TC	6c	green	500.		
RS245TC	1c	blue	500.		
RS250TC	6c	blue	500.		
RS250TC	6c	green	500.		
RS251TC	1c	blue	225.		
RS251TC	1c	brown	225.		
RS251TC	1c	green	225.		
RS252TC	1c	black	225.		
RS252TC	1c	blue	225.		
RS252TC	1c	brown	300.		
RS252TC	1c	green	225.		
RS252TC	1c	orange	500.		
RS252TC	1c	red	500.		
RS252TC	1c	rose	225.		
RS253TC	4c	blue	500.		
RS253TC	4c	green	500.		
RS258TC	6c	black	500.		
RS259TC	1c	blue	225.		
RS259TC	1c	brown	300.		
RS259TC	1c	green	225.		
RS259TC	1c	orange	300.		
RS259TC	1c	red	500.		
RS259TC	1c	vermilion	500.		
RS260TC	2c	blue	175.		
RS260TC	2c	brown	300.		
RS260TC	2c	green	225.		
RS260TC	2c	orange	300.		
RS260TC	2c	red	500.		
RS260TC	2c	rose	500.		
RS260TC	2c	vermilion	225.		
RS261TC	4c	blue	225.		
RS261TC	4c	brown	300.		
RS261TC	4c	green	225.		
RS261TC	4c	orange	300.		
RS261TC	4c	red	500.		
RS261TC	4c	vermilion	500.		
RS262TC	2c	blue	500.		
RS262TC	2c	green	500.		
RS264TC	4c	blue	300.		
RS264TC	4c	green	300.		
RS265TC	1c	black	225.		
RS265TC	1c	blue	500.		
RS267TC	4c	black	225.		
RS267TC	4c	blue	500.		
RS267TC	4c	green	300.		
RS270TC	12c	black	300.		
RS270TC	12c	blue green	500.		
RS270TC	12c	green	300.		
RS270TC	12c	red	225.		
RS271TC	4c	blue	2,500.		
RS272TC	1c	black	300.		
RS272TC	1c	blue	300.		
RS273TC	2c	blue	500.		
RS274TC	1c	black	225.		
RS274TC	2c	blue	300.		
RS276TC	2c	black	225.		
RS276TC	2c	blue	300.		
RS278TC	2½c	black	1,000.		
RS280TC	¼c	black	1,000.		
RS302TC	2½c	black	1,000.		
RS303TC	⅝c	black	1,000.		

PRIVATE DIE PERFUMERY STAMPS

No.	Denom	Color	(1) Large	(3) India	(4) Card
RT2TC	1c	brown	500.		
RT2TC	1c	green	400.		
RT2TC	1c	orange	300.		
RT2TC	1c	red	500.		
RT5TC	2c	black	175.		
RT5TC	2c	blue	225.		
RT5TC	2c	green	500.		
RT5TC	2c	orange	500.		125.
RT6TC	1c	blue	375.		
RT6TC	1c	brown	500.		
RT6TC	1c	green	375.		
RT6TC	1c	orange	500.		
RT6TC	1c	red	500.		
RT10TC	4c	blue	375.		
RT10TC	4c	brown	500.		
RT10TC	4c	green	400.		
RT10TC	4c	orange	500.		
RT10TC	4c	red	500.		
RT12TC	1c	black	225.		90.
RT12TC	1c	blue	225.		
RT12TC	1c	green	500.		
RT13TC	2c	black	225.		75.
RT13TC	2c	blue	300.		
RT13TC	2c	green	300.		
RT13TC	2c	red	225.		
RT14TC	3c	blue	1,000.		
RT16TC	1c	blue	175.		
RT16TC	1c	green	225.		
RT17TC	2c	black	300.		
RT17TC	2c	blue	300.		
RT17TC	2c	green	300.		
RT17TC	2c	orange	500.		

			DIE ON INDIA (1) Large	(3) India	PLATE (4) Card
RT18TC	3c	black	175.		
RT18TC	3c	blue	175.		
RT18TC	3c	green	500.		
RT18TC	3c	orange	500.		
RT18TC	3c	red	300.		
RT19TC	1c	black	500.		
RT20TC	1c	black	225.		
RT20TC	1c	blue	300.		
RT20TC	1c	green	175.		
RT21TC	2c	black	500.		
RT21TC	2c	green	500.		
RT22TC	1c	black	175.		
RT22TC	1c	blue	300.		
RT22TC	1c	green	300.		
RT22TC	1c	red brn	300.		
RT22TC	1c	ultramarine	500.		
RT23TC	2c	blue	225.		
RT23TC	2c	green	500.		
RT24TC	3c	black	175.		
RT24TC	3c	blue	225.		
RT24TC	3c	green	300.		
RT24TC	3c	red	225.		
RT25TC	4c	black	175.		
RT25TC	4c	blue	225.		
RT26TC	1c	black	175.		
RT26TC	1c	blue	225.		
RT26TC	1c	brown	300.		
RT26TC	1c	green	500.		
RT26TC	1c	orange	300.		
RT26TC	1c	red	500.		
RT28TC	2c	black	225.		
RT28TC	2c	brown	300.		
RT28TC	2c	green	225.		
RT28TC	2c	orange	300.		
RT28TC	2c	red	300.		

			DIE ON INDIA (1) Large	(3) India	PLATE (4) Card
RT30TC	3c	black	225.		
RT30TC	3c	blue	225.		
RT30TC	3c	brown	300.		
RT30TC	3c	green	225.		
RT30TC	3c	orange	300.		
RT30TC	3c	red	175.		
RT32TC	4c	black	225.		
RT32TC	4c	blue	225.		
RT32TC	4c	brown	500.		
RT32TC	4c	green	225.		
RT32TC	4c	orange	225.		
RT32TC	4c	red	300.		

PRIVATE DIE PLAYING CARD STAMPS

			DIE ON INDIA (1) Large	(3) India	PLATE (4) Card
RU2TC	2c	black	175.		
RU2TC	2c	blue	225.		
RU2TC	2c	green	300.		
RU3TC	4c	blue	225.		
RU3TC	4c	green	225.		
RU4TC	5c	black	225.		
RU4TC	5c	green	300.		
RU5TC	5c	black	225.		
RU5TC	5c	brown	300.		
RU5TC	5c	green	300.		
RU5TC	5c	light brn	500.		
RU5TC	5c	orange	500.		
RU5TC	5c	red	500.		
RU6TC	10c	black	175.		
RU6TC	10c	green	300.		

			DIE ON INDIA (1) Large	(3) India	PLATE (4) C
RU7TC	5c	blue	375.		
RU7TC	5c	green	375.		
RU8TC	5c	blue	225.		
RU8TC	5c	green	225.		
RU8TC	5c	orange	300.		
RU9TC	5c	blue	225.		
RU9TC	5c	green	500.		
RU10TC	2c	black	175.		
RU10TC	2c	brown	500.		
RU10TC	2c	green	500.		
RU11TC	5c	black	225.		
RU11TC	5c	blue	225.		
RU11TC	5c	brown	300.		
RU12TC	5c	blue	300.		
RU12TC	5c	green	300.		
RU13TC	5c	green	175.		
RU14TC	5c	blue	225.		
RU14TC	5c	brown	300.		
RU14TC	5c	green	300.		
RU14TC	5c	light brn	500.		
RU14TC	5c	orange	500.		
RU14TC	5c	red	300.		
RU15TC	5c	blue	300.		
RU15TC	5c	green	300.		

HUNTING PERMIT

			DIE ON INDIA (1) Large
RW4TC	$1	light violet	5,500.

SPECIMEN STAMPS

These are regular stamps overprinted "Specimen." Each number has a suffix letter "S" to denote "specimen." The Scott number is that of the stam as shown in the regular listings and the second letter "A," etc., indicates the type of overprint. Values are for items of a grade of fine-very fine, with least part original gum.

𝔖𝔭𝔢𝔠𝔦𝔪𝔢𝔫
Type A;
12mm
long

𝔖𝔭𝔢𝔠𝔦𝔪𝔢𝔫.
Type B; 15mm
long

𝔖𝔭𝔢𝔠𝔦𝔪𝔢𝔫.
Type C; 30mm long

SPECIMEN
Type D;
Capital
Letters

Specimen.
Type E;
Initial
Capital

𝔖𝔭𝔢𝔠𝔦𝔪𝔢𝔫.
Type F; 22mm long

SPECIMEN
Type G;
14mm long

SPECIMEN
Type H;
16mm long

Type I; 20mm long

Specimen
(script)

Overprinted in Black

𝔖𝔭𝔢𝔠𝔦𝔪𝔢𝔫

1851-56
7S	A	1c blue, type II	2,500.
11S	A	3c dull red, type I	6,500.

1857-60
21S	A	1c blue, type III	1,500.
24S	A	1c blue, type V	1,000.
26S	A	3c dull red, type II	1,000.
30S	A	5c orange brown, type II	1,000.
35S	A	10c green, type V	1,250.
36bS	A	12c black	1,000.
37S	A	24c lilac	1,000.
38S	A	30c orange	1,000.
26S	F	3c dull red, type II	2,000.
26S	I	3c dull red, type II	4,000.

1861
63S	A	1c blue	750.
65S	A	3c rose	750.
68S	A	10c dark green	750.
70S	A	24c red lilac	750.

72S	A	90c blue	750.
73S	A	2c black	1,750.
76S	A	5c brown	750.

𝔖𝔭𝔢𝔠𝔦𝔪𝔢𝔫.

Overprint Black, Except As Noted

1861-66
63S	B	1c blue (1300)	120.
		P# block of 8, Impt.	1,750.
		Without period	—
65S	B	3c rose (1500)	120.
68S	B	10c dark green (1600)	120.
		P# block of 8, Impt.	—
69S	B	12c black (orange) (1300)	120.
71S	B	30c orange (1400)	120.
		P# block of 8, Impt.	15,000.
72S	B	90c blue (1394)	120.
		P# block of 8, Impt.	—
73S	B	2c black (vermilion) (1306)	250.
		Block of 4	1,100.
		Without period	500.
		Block of 4, one stamp without period	1,500.
76S	B	5c brown (1306)	120.
		P# block of 8, Impt.	—
77S	B	15c black (vermilion) (1208)	200.
		Block of 4	900.
78S	B	24c lilac (1300)	200.

1867-68
86S	A	1c blue	1,000.
85ES	A	12c black	1,000.
93S	A	2c black	1,100.
94S	A	3c rose	1,000.
95S	A	5c brown	1,100.
97S	A	12c black	—
98S	A	15c black	1,000.
99S	A	24c gray lilac	1,250.
		Split grill	—
100S	A	30c orange	1,250.

1869
112S	A	1c buff	1,750.
113S	A	2c brown	1,500.
115S	A	6c ultramarine	1,250.
116S	A	10c yellow	1,250.
117S	A	12c green	1,250.
119S	A	15c brown & blue	1,500.
120S	A	24c green & violet	1,750.
a.		Without grill	—
121S	A	30c blue & carmine	1,750.
a.		Without grill	—
122S	A	90c carmine & black	2,000.
a.		Without grill	—
123S	B	1c buff	3,500.
124S	B	2c brown	3,500.
125S	B	3c blue (blue)	3,500.

126S	B	6c blue (blue)	3,5(
127S	B	10c yellow (blue)	—
129S	B	10c brown & blue (blue)	5,25

1870-71
145S	A	1c ultramarine	6(
146S	A	2c red brown	6(
146S	B	2c red brown	6(
147S	A	3c green	6(
148S	A	6c carmine	6(
149S	A	7c vermilion	6(
150S	A	10c brown	6(
151S	A	12c dull violet	6(
152S	A	15c bright orange	6(
155S	A	90c carmine	6(
155S	B	90c carmine (blue)	6(

1873
158S	B	3c green (blue)	75
159S	B	6c dull pink	70
160S	B	7c orange vermilion (blue)	70
162S	B	12c blackish violet (blue)	70
165S	B	30c greenish black (blue)	70
166S	B	90c carmine (blue)	75

Overprinted in Red   SPECIME

1879

Type D
189S	D	15c red orange	8
190S	D	30c full black	8
191S	D	90c carmine	8
a.		Overprint in black brown	8

1881-82
205S	D	5c yellow brown	8
206S	D	1c gray blue	8
207S	D	3c blue green	8
208S	D	6c brown red	8
209S	D	10c brown	8

1883
210S	D	2c red brown	10
211S	D	4c blue green	10

Handstamped in Dull Purple   Specime

1890-93

Type E
219S	E	1c dull blue	15
220S	E	2c carmine	15
221S	E	3c purple	15
222S	E	4c dark brown	15
223S	E	5c chocolate	15
224S	E	6c dull red	15
225S	E	8c lilac	15

6S	E	10c green	150.
7S	E	15c blue	150.
8S	E	30c black	150.
9S	E	90c orange	175.

COLUMBIAN ISSUE

93

0S	E	1c deep blue	400.
		Double overprint	—
1S	E	2c violet	400.
2S	E	3c green	400.
3S	E	4c ultramarine	400.
4S	E	5c chocolate	400.
5S	E	6c purple	400.
6S	E	8c magenta	400.
7S	E	10c black brown	400.
8S	E	15c dark green	400.
9S	E	30c orange brown	400.
0S	E	50c slate blue	400.
1S	E	$1 salmon	500.
2S	E	$2 brown red	500.
3S	E	$3 yellow green	550.
4S	E	$4 crimson lake	575.
5S	E	$5 black	675.

Overprinted in Magenta **Specimen.**

Type F

0S	F	1c deep blue	550.
2S	F	3c green	550.
3S	F	4c ultramarine	550.
4S	F	5c chocolate	550.
5S	F	6c purple	550.
7S	F	10c black brown	550.
43S	F	$3 yellow green	700.

Overprinted Type H in Black or Red

1S	H	2c violet (Bk)	625.
3S	H	4c ultramarine (R)	625.
4S	H	5c chocolate (R)	625.

Overprinted Type I in Black or Red

1S	I	2c violet (R)	625.
2S	I	3c green (R)	625.
3S	I	4c ultramarine (R)	625.
4S	I	5c chocolate (Bk)	625.
5S	I	6c purple (R)	625.
6S	I	8c magenta (Bk)	625.
7S	I	10c black brown (R)	625.
8S	I	15c dark green (R)	625.
9S	I	30c orange brown (Bk)	625.
0S	I	50c slate blue (R)	625.

895

Handstamped Type E in Purple

4S	E	1c blue	90.
7S	E	2c carmine, type III	90.
7aS	E	2c pink, type III	90.
8S	E	3c purple	90.
9S	E	4c dark brown	100.
0S	E	5c chocolate	90.
1S	E	6c dull brown	90.
2S	E	8c violet brown	90.
3S	E	10c dark green	90.
4S	E	15c dark blue	90.
5S	E	50c orange	90.
6S	E	$1 black, type I	325.
6AS	E	$1 black, type II	2,000.
7S	E	$2 dark blue	300.
8S	E	$5 dark green	400.

897-1903

9S	E	1c deep green	90.
9BS	E	2c light red, type IV	90.
9BeS	E	2c Booklet pane of 6, light red, type IV (Bk)	525.
		Never hinged	750.
		With plate number	1,100.
		Never hinged	1,500.
a.		As No. 279BeS, inverted overprint	—
b.		As No. 279BeS, double impression of overprint on bottom two stamps	—
80S	E	4c rose brown	160.
81S	E	5c dark blue	80.
82S	E	6c lake	80.
82CS	E	10c brown, type I	80.
83S	E	10c brown, type II	80.
84S	E	15c olive green	80.

Special Printing

In March 1900 one pane of 100 stamps of each of Nos. 279, 279B, 268, 280-282, 272, 282C, 284 and 275-278 were specially handstamped type E "Specimen" in black for displays at the Paris Exposition (1900) and Pan American Exposition (1901). The 2c pane was light red, type IV.

These examples were handstamped by H. G. Mandel and mounted by him in separate displays for the two Expositions. Examples from the panes in addition to those displayed were handstamped "Specimen," but most were destroyed after the Expositions. Examples of all issues that were handstamped are known.

Additional copies, not from the mounted display panes, do exist with a black "Specimen" handstamp, but it is believed Mandel applied such handstamps to regularly issued stamps from his personal collection. These include Nos. 267, 267a and 279B in pale red.

TRANS-MISSISSIPPI ISSUE

1898

Type F

285S	F	1c dark yellow green	250.

Type E

285S	E	1c dark yellow green	250.
286S	E	2c copper red	250.
287S	E	4c orange	250.
288S	E	5c dull blue	250.
289S	E	8c violet brown	250.
290S	E	10c gray violet	250.
291S	E	50c sage green	300.
292S	E	$1 black	600.
293S	E	$2 orange brown	750.

PAN-AMERICAN ISSUE

1901

294S	E	1c green & black	235.
295S	E	2c carmine	235.
296S	E	4c chocolate & black	235.
a.		Center inverted	6,500.
297S	E	5c ultramarine & black	235.
298S	E	8c brown violet & black	235.
299S	E	10c yellow brown & black	235.

1902

300S	E	1c blue green	125.
301S	E	2c carmine	125.
302S	E	3c bright violet	125.
303S	E	4c brown	125.
304S	E	5c blue	125.
305S	E	6c claret	125.
306S	E	8c violet black	125.
307S	E	10c pale red brown	125.
308S	E	13c purple black	125.
309S	E	15c olive green	125.
310S	E	50c orange	125.
311S	E	$1 black	250.
312S	E	$2 dark blue	375.
313S	E	$5 dark green	500.

1903

319S	E	2c carmine	110.

LOUISIANA PURCHASE ISSUE

1904

323S	E	1c green	350.
324S	E	2c carmine	350.
325S	E	3c violet	350.
326S	E	5c dark blue	350.
327S	E	10c red brown	350.

SPECIAL DELIVERY STAMPS

Overprinted in Red **SPECIMEN**

1885

Type D

E1S	D	10c blue	140.

Handstamped in Dull Purple **Specimen.**

1888

Type E

E2S	E	10c blue	150.

1893

E3S	E	10c orange	200.

1894

E4S	E	10c blue	300.

1895

E5S	E	10c blue	175.

1902

E6S	E	10c ultramarine	175.

POSTAGE DUE STAMPS

Overprinted in Red **SPECIMEN**

1879

Type D

J1S	D	1c brown	250.00
J2S	D	2c brown	250.00
J3S	D	3c brown	250.00
J4S	D	5c brown	250.00

1884

J15S	D	1c red brown	45.00
J16S	D	2c red brown	45.00
J17S	D	3c red brown	45.00
J18S	D	5c red brown	45.00
J19S	D	10c red brown	45.00
J20S	D	30c red brown	45.00
J21S	D	50c red brown	45.00

Handstamped in Dull Purple **Specimen.**

1895

Type E

J38S	E	1c deep claret	85.00
J39S	E	2c deep claret	85.00
J40S	E	3c deep claret	85.00
J41S	E	5c deep claret	85.00
J42S	E	10c deep claret	85.00
J43S	E	30c deep claret	85.00
J44S	E	50c deep claret	85.00

OFFICIAL STAMPS

Special printings of Official stamps were made in 1875 at the time the other Reprints, Re-issues and Special Printings were printed. The Official stamps reprints received specimen overprints, but philatelists believe they most properly should be considered to be part of the special printings. See Official section after No. O120.

NEWSPAPER STAMPS

Overprinted in Red **Specimen.**

1865-75

Type C — Overprint 30mm Long

PR5S	C	5c dark blue	400.00
a.		Triple overprint	900.00
PR2S	C	10c blue green	400.00
PR3S	C	25c carmine red	400.00

Handstamped in Black **Specimen**

1875

Type A

PR9S	A	2c black	300.00
PR11S	A	4c black	300.00
PR12S	A	6c black	300.00
PR16S	A	12c rose	300.00

Overprinted in Black, except as noted **Specimen.**

1875

Type B

Overprint 15mm Long

PR9S	B	2c black	45.00
PR10S	B	3c black	45.00
PR11S	B	4c black	45.00
PR12S	B	6c black	45.00
PR13S	B	8c black	45.00
PR14S	B	9c black	45.00
a.		Overprint in blue	—
PR15S	B	10c black	45.00
PR16S	B	12c rose	45.00
PR17S	B	24c rose	45.00
PR18S	B	36c rose	45.00
PR19S	B	48c rose	45.00
a.		Overprint in blue	62.50
PR20S	B	60c rose	45.00
PR21S	B	72c rose	45.00
a.		Overprint in blue	62.50
PR22S	B	84c rose	45.00
a.		Overprint in blue	—
PR23S	B	96c rose	45.00
a.		Overprint in blue	—
PR24S	B	$1.92 dark brown	45.00
PR25S	B	$3 vermilion	45.00
a.		Overprint in blue	62.50
PR26S	B	$6 ultramarine	45.00
a.		Overprint in blue	250.00
PR27S	B	$9 yellow	45.00
a.		Overprint in blue	250.00
PR28S	B	$12 dark green	45.00
a.		Overprint in blue	250.00
PR29S	B	$24 dark gray violet	45.00
a.		Overprint in blue	60.00
PR30S	B	$36 brown rose	62.00
PR31S	B	$48 red brown	62.00
PR32S	B	$60 violet	62.00

Overprinted in Red **SPECIMEN**

1875

Type D

PR14S	D	9c black	30.00

1879

PR57S	D	2c black	50.00
PR58S	D	3c black	50.00
PR59S	D	4c black	50.00
PR60S	D	6c black	50.00
PR61S	D	8c black	50.00
PR62S	D	10c black	50.00
a.		Double overprint	2,000.

PR63S	D	12c red	50.00
PR64S	D	24c red	50.00
PR65S	D	36c red	50.00
PR66S	D	48c red	50.00
PR67S	D	60c red	50.00
PR68S	D	72c red	50.00
PR69S	D	84c red	50.00
PR70S	D	96c red	50.00
PR71S	D	$1.92 pale brown	50.00
PR72S	D	$3 red vermilion	50.00
PR73S	D	$6 blue	50.00
PR74S	D	$9 orange	50.00
PR75S	D	$12 yellow green	50.00
PR76S	D	$24 dark violet	50.00
PR77S	D	$36 Indian red	50.00
PR78S	D	$48 yellow brown	50.00
PR79S	D	$60 purple	50.00

1885

PR81S	D	1c black	25.00

Handstamped in Dull Purple   *Specimen.*

1879

Type E

PR57S	E	2c black	22.50
PR58S	E	3c black	22.50
PR59S	E	4c black	22.50
PR60S	E	6c black	22.50
PR61S	E	8c black	22.50
PR62S	E	10c black	22.50
PR63S	E	12c red	22.50
PR64S	E	24c red	22.50
PR65S	E	36c red	22.50
PR66S	E	48c red	22.50
PR67S	E	60c red	22.50
PR68S	E	72c red	22.50
PR69S	E	84c red	22.50
PR70S	E	96c red	22.50
PR71S	E	$1.92 pale brown	22.50
PR72S	E	$3 red vermilion	22.50
PR73S	E	$6 blue	22.50
PR74S	E	$9 orange	22.50
PR75S	E	$12 yellow green	22.50
PR76S	E	$24 dark violet	22.50
PR77S	E	$36 Indian red	22.50
PR78S	E	$48 yellow brown	22.50
PR79S	E	$60 purple	22.50

1885

PR81S	E	1c black	22.50

1895   Wmk. 191

PR114S	E	1c black	100.00
PR115S	E	2c black	100.00
PR116S	E	5c black	100.00
PR117S	E	10c black	100.00
PR118S	E	25c carmine	100.00
PR119S	E	50c carmine	100.00
PR120S	E	$2 scarlet	100.00
PR121S	E	$5 dark blue	100.00
PR122S	E	$10 green	100.00
PR123S	E	$20 slate	100.00
PR124S	E	$50 dull rose	100.00
PR125S	E	$100 purple	100.00

REVENUE STAMPS

SPECIMEN

1862

Overprint 14mm Long

R5S	G	2c Bank Check, blue (red)	375.00
R15S	A	2c U. S. I. R., orange	—

SPECIMEN

Overprint 16mm Long

R23S	H	5c Agreement, red	375.00
R34S	H	10c Contract, blue (red)	375.00
R35eS	H	10c Foreign Exchange, ultra (red)	375.00
R36S	H	10c Inland Exchange, blue (red)	375.00
R46S	H	25c Insurance, red	375.00
R52S	H	30c Inland Exchange, lilac (red)	375.00
R53S	H	40c Inland Exchange, brown (red)	375.00
R68S	H	$1 Foreign Exchange, red	375.00

Type I   *Specimen*

1898   Overprint 20mm Long

R153S	I	1c green (red)	475.00

1875

RB11S	H	1c green (red)	300.00

PRIVATE DIE MATCH STAMP

Overprinted with Type G in Red   SPECIMEN

RO133dS	G	1c black, A. Messinger	*500.00*

SAVINGS STAMPS

Overprinted Vertically Reading Down in Red   SPECIMEN

1911

PS4S		10c deep blue	—

1917-18   Handstamped "SPECIMEN" in Violet

WS1S		25c deep green	—
WS2S		$5 deep green	—

VARIOUS OVERPRINTS

Overprinted with control numbers in carmine   *7890*

1861

Type J

63S	J A24	1c pale blue (overprint 9012)	200.00
65S	J A25	3c brown red (overprint 7890)	200.00
		Block of 4	*900.*
68S	J A27	10c green (overprint 5678)	200.00
69S	J A28	12c gray black (overprint 4567)	200.00
71S	J A30	30c orange (overprint 2345)	200.00
		Block of 4	*900.*
72S	J A31	90c pale blue (overprint 1234)	200.00
a.		Pair, one without overprint	—

1863-66

73S	J A32	2c black (overprint 8901)	300.00
		Block of 4	*1,400.*
76S	J A26	5c brown (overprint 6789)	200.00
77S	J A33	15c black (overprint 235)	250.00
		Block of 4	*1,150.*
78S	J A29	24c gray lilac (overprint 3456)	200.00

Special Printings Overprinted in Red or Blue   SAMPLE.

1889

Type K

212S	K A59	1c ultramarine (red)	75.00
210S	K A57	2c red brown (blue)	75.00
210S	K A57	2c lake (blue)	75.00
210S	K A57	2c rose lake (blue)	75.00
210S	K A57	2c scarlet (blue)	75.00
214S	K A46b	3c vermilion (blue)	75.00
211S	K A58	4c blue green (red)	75.00
205S	K A56	5c gray brown (red)	75.00
208S	K A47b	6c brown red (blue)	75.00
209S	K A49b	10c brown (red)	75.00
		Without overprint	80.00
189S	K A51a	15c orange (blue)	75.00
190S	K A53	30c full black (red)	75.00
191S	K A54	90c carmine (blue)	75.00

Special Printings Overprinted in Red or Blue   SAMPLE A.

Type L

212S	L A59	1c ultramarine (red)	75.00
210S	L A57	2c rose lake (blue)	75.00
		Without overprint	—
214S	L A46b	3c purple (red)	75.00
211S	L A58	4c dark brown (red)	75.00
205S	L A56	5c yellow brown (blue)	75.00
		Without overprint	—
208S	L A47b	6c vermilion (blue)	75.00
209S	L A49b	10c green (red)	75.00
		Without overprint	100.00
189S	L A51a	15c blue (red)	75.00
		Without overprint	100.00
190S	L A53	30c full black (red)	75.00
191S	L A54	90c orange (blue)	75.00

Overprinted with Type K Together with "A" in Black Manuscript

191S	M A54	90c carmine (blue)	140.
209S	M A49b	10c brown (red)	140.
211S	M A58	4c blue green (red)	140.

"SAMPLE A" in Manuscript (red or black)

216S	N A56	5c indigo	160.

UNIVERSAL POSTAL CONGRESS

Regular Issues Overprinted in Blue or Red

125 sets were distributed to delegates to the Universal Postal Congress held in Washington, D. C., May 5 to June 15, 189[?]

1897   Type [O]

264S	O A87	1c blue	110.
267S	O A88	2c carmine, type III	110.
268S	O A89	3c purple	110.
269S	O A90	4c dark brown	110.
270S	O A91	5c chestnut	110.
271S	O A92	6c claret brown	110.
272S	O A93	8c violet brown	110.
273S	O A94	10c dark green	110.
274S	O A95	15c dark blue	110.
275S	O A96	50c red orange	110.
276S	O A97	$1 black, type I	350.
276AS	O A97	$1 black, type II	300.
277S	O A98	$2 dark blue	250.
278S	O A99	$5 dark green	350.

SPECIAL DELIVERY

E5S	O SD3	10c blue (R)	250.

POSTAGE DUE

J38S	O D2	1c deep claret	125.
J39S	O D2	2c deep claret	125.
J40S	O D2	3c deep claret	125.
J41S	O D2	5c deep claret	125.
J42S	O D2	10c deep claret	125.
J43S	O D2	30c deep claret	125.
J44S	O D2	50c deep claret	125.

NEWSPAPERS

PR114S	O N15	1c black	150.
PR115S	O N15	2c black	150.
PR116S	O N15	5c black	150.
PR117S	O N15	10c black	150.
PR118S	O N16	25c carmine	150.
PR119S	O N16	50c carmine	150.
PR120S	O N17	$2 scarlet	150.
PR121S	O N18	$5 dark blue	150.
PR122S	O N19	$10 green	150.
PR123S	O N20	$20 slate	150.
PR124S	O N21	$50 dull rose	150.
PR125S	O N22	$100 purple	150.

ENVELOPES

Overprinted   UNIVERSAL POSTAL CONGRESS

Type P

U294S	P	1c blue	100.0
U296S	P	1c blue, amber	100.0
U300S	P	1c blue, manila	100.0
W301S	P	1c blue, manila	100.0
U304S	P	1c blue, amber manila	100.0
U311S	P	2c green, Die 2	100.0
U312S	P	2c green, Die 2, amber	100.0
U313S	P	2c green, Die 2, oriental buff	100.0
U314S	P	2c green, Die 2, blue	100.0
a.		Double impression of overprint	—
U315S	P	2c green, Die 2, manila	100.0
W316S	P	2c green, Die 2, manila	100.0
U317S	P	2c green, Die 2, amber manila	100.0
U324S	P	4c carmine	100.0
U325S	P	4c carmine, amber	120.0
U330S	P	5c blue, Die 1	110.0
U331S	P	5c blue, Die 1, amber	110.0

Two settings of type P overprint are found.
See the July\August 1949 issue of the Scott Monthly Stamp Journal for others.

POSTAL CARDS

Overprinted   UNIVERSAL POSTAL CONGRESS

Type Q

UX12S	Q	1c black, buff	650.0
UX13S	Q	2c blue, cream	650.0

PAID REPLY POSTAL CARDS

Overprinted with Type Q

UY1S	Q	1c black, buff	650.0
UY2S	Q	2c blue, grayish white	650.0

As Nos. UY1S-UY2S were made by overprinting unsevered reply cards, values are for unsevered cards.

SOUVENIR CARDS

hese cards were issued as souvenirs of the philatelic and numismatic gatherings at which they were distributed by the United States Postal Service PS), its predecessor the United States Post Office Department (POD), or the Bureau of Engraving and Printing (BEP). They were not valid for age.

ost of the cards bear reproductions of United States stamps with the design enlarged, altered by removal of denomination, country name and tage" or "Air Mail" or defaced by diagonal bars. The cards are not perforated.

umismatic cards are listed following the philatelic cards.

forerunner of the souvenir cards is the 1939 Philatelic Truck souvenir sheet which the Post Office Department issued and distributed in various s visited by the Philatelic Truck. It shows the White House, printed in blue on white paper. Issued with and without gum. Value, with gum, $50; out gum, $8.

Standard abbreviations:

PS — American Philatelic Society
SDA — American Stamp Dealers Association

INTERNATIONALE BRIEFMARKEN AUSSTELLUNG
IBRA 73

MÜNCHEN   11.-20. MAI 1973

Diese Andenkenkarte wird zu Ehren der Internationalen Briefmarkenausstellung IBRA 73 in München ausgegeben. Auf der Karte ist die 65 cent-Luftpostmarke, die in einer Sonderserie anläßlich des ersten Fluges des Luftschiffs "Graf Zeppelin" von Europa nach Nord- und Südamerika im Mai 1930 herausgegeben wurde, abgebildet. Die Briefmarke zeigt 'Graf Zeppelin' auf seinem Rückflug über den Atlantik.

L. T. Klassen
Postmaster General

THE COPYING OF THIS PRINT IS SUFFICIENT TO STYLE IT IN U. S. IS KNOWN PROHIBITS THE UNAUTHORIZED REPRODUCTION, IN WHOLE OR IN PART, OF CURRENCY, POSTAGE STAMPS, OR OTHER SECURITIES OF THE UNITED STATES.

No. SC28

4	Postage Stamp Design Exhibition, Natl. Philatelic Museum, Mar. 13, 1954, Philadelphia. Card of 4 monochrome views of Washington. Inscribed: "Souvenir sheet designed, engraved and printed by members, Bureau, Engraving and Printing. Reissued by popular request."	1,500.
0	Barcelona, 1st Intl. Philatelic Congress, Mar. 26-Apr. 5, 1960. Vignette, Landing of Columbus from #231. (POD)	250.00
6	SIPEX, 6th Intl. Philatelic Exhibition, May 21-30, 1966, Washington. Card of 3 multicolored views of Washington.	100.00
8	EFIMEX, Intl. Philatelic Exhibition, Nov. 1-9, 1968, Mexico City. #292. Spanish text. (POD)	1.50
9	SANDIPEX, San Diego Philatelic Exhibition, July 16-20, 1969, San Diego, Cal. Card of 3 multicolored views of Washington. (BEP)	40.00
	ASDA Natl. Postage Stamp Show, Nov. 21-23, 1969, New York. Card of 4 #E4. (BEP)	15.00
0	INTERPEX, Mar. 13-15, 1970, New York. Card of 4, #1027, 1035, C35, C38. (BEP)	40.00
	COMPEX, Combined Philatelic Exhibition of Chicagoland, May 29-31, 1970. Card of 4 #C18. (BEP)	10.00
	PHILYMPIA, London Intl. Stamp Exhibition, Sept. 18-26 1970. Card of 3, #548-550. (POD)	1.25
0	HAPEX, APS Convention, Nov. 5-8, 1970, Honolulu. Card of 3, #799, C46, C55. (BEP)	8.00
1	INTERPEX, Mar. 12-14, 1971, New York. Card of 4 #1193. Background includes #1331-1332, 1371, C76. (BEP)	1.40
2	WESTPEX, Western Philatelic Exhibition, Apr. 23-25, 1971, San Francisco. Card of 4, #740, 852, 966, 997. (BEP)	1.40
3	NAPEX 71, Natl. Philatelic Exhibition, May 21-23, 1971, Washington. Card of 3, #990, 991, 992. (BEP)	1.50
4	TEXANEX 71, Texas Philatelic Association and APS conventions, Aug. 26-29, 1971, San Antonio, Tex. Card of 3, #938, 1043, 1242. (BEP)	1.50
5	EXFILIMA 71, 3rd Inter-American Philatelic Exhibition, Nov. 6-14, 1971, Lima, Peru. Card of 3, #1111, 1126, Peru #360. Spanish text. (USPS)	1.00
6	ASDA Natl. Postage Stamp Show, Nov. 19-21, 1971, New York. Card of 3, #C13-C15. (BEP)	2.00
7	ANPHILEX '71, Anniv. Philatelic Exhibition, Nov. 26-Dec. 1, 1971, New York. Card of 2, #1-2. (BEP)	1.00

1972

SC18	INTERPEX, Mar. 17-19, 1972, New York. Card of 4 #1173. Background includes #976, 1434-1435, C69. (BEP)	1.00
SC19	NOPEX, Apr. 6-9, 1972, New Orleans. Card of 4 #1020. Background includes #323-327. (BEP)	1.00
SC20	BELGICA 72, Brussels Intl. Philatelic Exhibition, June 24-July 9, 1972, Brussels, Belgium. Card of 3, #914, 1026, 1104. Flemish and French text. (USPS)	.75
SC21	Olympia Philatelie Munchen 72, Aug. 18-Sept. 10, 1972, Munich, Germany. Card of 4, #1460-1462, C85. German text. (USPS)	.75
SC22	EXFILBRA 72, 4th Inter-American Philatelic Exhibition, Aug. 26-Sept. 2, 1972, Rio de Janeiro, Brazil. Card of 3 #C14, Brazil #C18-C19. Portuguese text. (USPS)	.75
SC23	Natl. Postal Forum VI, Aug. 28-30, 1972, Washington. Card of 4 #1396.	.75
SC24	SEPAD '72, Oct. 20-22, 1972, Philadelphia. Card of 4 #1044. (BEP)	1.00
SC25	ASDA Natl. Postage Stamp Show, Nov. 17-19, 1972, New York. Card of 4, #883, 863, 868, 888. (BEP)	1.00
SC26	STAMP EXPO, Nov. 24-26, 1972, San Francisco. Card of 4 #C36. (BEP)	1.50

1973

SC27	INTERPEX, Mar. 9-11, 1973, New York. Card of 4 #976. (BEP)	1.00
SC28	IBRA 73 Intl. Philatelic Exhibition, Munich, May 11-20, 1973. #C13. (USPS)	1.10
SC29	COMPEX 73, May 25-27, 1973, Chicago. Card of 4 #245. (BEP)	2.00
SC30	APEX 73, Intl. Airmail Exhibition, Manchester, England, July 4-7, 1973. Card of 3, #C3a, Newfoundland #C4, Honduras #C12. (USPS)	1.10
SC31	POLSKA 73, World Philatelic Exhibition, Poznan, Poland, Aug. 19-Sept. 2, 1973. Card of 3, #1488, Poland #1944-1945. Polish text. (USPS)	1.10
SC32	NAPEX 73, Sept. 14-16, 1973, Washington. Card of 4 #C3. Background includes montage of #C4-C6. (BEP)	1.75
SC33	ASDA Natl. Postage Stamp Show, Nov. 16-18, 1973, New York. Card of 4 #908. Foreground includes #1139-1144. (BEP)	.75
SC34	STAMP EXPO NORTH, Dec. 7-9, 1973, San Francisco. Card of 4 #C20. (BEP)	1.50

A card of 10, Nos. 1489-1498, was distributed to postal employees. Not available to public. Size: about 14x11 inches.

1974

SC35	Natl. Hobby Industry Trade Show, Feb. 3-6, 1974, Chicago. Card of 4, #1456-1459. Reproductions of silversmith (#1457) and glassmaker (#1456). (USPS)	1.40
SC36	MILCOPEX 1974, Mar. 8-10, 1974, Milwaukee. Card of 4 #C43. (BEP)	1.10
SC37	INTERNABA 1974, June 6, 1974, Basel, Switzerland. Card of 8, #1530-1537. German, French, and Italian text. (USPS)	2.25
SC38	STOCKHOLMIA 74, Intl. Philatelic Exhibition, Sept. 21-29, 1974, Stockholm. Card of 3, #836, Sweden #300, 767. Swedish text. (USPS)	2.25
SC39	EXFILMEX 74, Interamerican Philatelic Exposition, Oct. 26-Nov. 3, 1974, Mexico City. Card of 2, #1157, Mexico #910. Spanish text. (USPS)	2.25

1975

SC40	ESPANA 75, World Stamp Exhibition, Apr. 4-13, 1975, Madrid. Card of 3, #233, #1271, Spain #1312. Spanish text. (USPS)	1.10
SC41	NAPEX 75, May 9-11, 1975, Washington. Card of 4 #708. (BEP)	4.00
SC42	ARPHILA 75, June 6-16, 1975, Paris. Card of 3. Designs of #1187, #1207, France #1117. French text. (USPS)	1.75
SC43	Intl. Women's Year, 1975. Card of 3 #872, 878, 959. Reproduction of 1886 dollar bill. (BEP)	15.00

SC44	ASDA Natl. Postage Stamp Show, Nov. 21-23, 1975. Bicentennial series. Card of 4 #1003. (BEP)	13.00

1976

SC45	WERABA 76, 3rd Intl. Space Stamp Exhibition, Apr. 1-4, 1976, Zurich, Switzerland. Card of 2, #1434-1435. (USPS)	2.25
SC46	INTERPHIL 76, 7th Intl. Philatelic Exhibition, May 29-June 6, 1976. Philadelphia. Bicentennial series. Card of 4 #120. (BEP)	4.00

An Interphil '76 card issued by the American Revolution Bicentennial Administration was bound into the Interphil program. It shows an altered #1044 in black brown, the Bicentennial emblem and a view of Independence Hall. Printed by BEP

SC48	Bicentennial Exposition on Science and Technology, May 30-Sept. 6, 1976, Kennedy Space Center, Fla. #C76. (USPS)	2.50
SC49	STAMP EXPO 76, June 11-13, 1976, Los Angeles. Bicentennial series. Card of 4, #1351, 1352, 1345, 1348. (BEP)	4.50
SC50	Colorado Statehood Centennial, Aug. 1, 1976. Card of 3, #743, 288, 1670. (USPS)	2.25
SC51	HAFNIA 76, Intl. Stamp Exhibition, Copenhagen. Aug. 20-29, 1976. Card of 2, #5, Denmark #2. Danish and English text. (USPS)	2.25
SC52	ITALIA 76, Intl. Philatelic Exhibition, Oct. 14-24, Milan. Card of 3, #1168, Italy #578, 601. Italian text. (USPS)	2.25
SC53	NORDPOSTA 76, North German Stamp Exhibition, Oct. 30-31, Hamburg. Card of 3, #689, Germany #B366, B417. German text. (USPS)	2.00

1977

SC54	MILCOPEX, Milwaukee Philatelic Society, Mar. 4-6, Milwaukee. Card of 2, #733, 1128. (BEP)	1.75
SC55	ROMPEX 77, Rocky Mountain Philatelic Exhibition, May 20-22, Denver. Card of 4 #1001. (BEP)	1.50
SC56	AMPHILEX 77, Intl. Philatelic Exhibition, May 26-June 5, Amsterdam. Card of 3, #1027, Netherlands #41, 294. Dutch text. (USPS)	2.25
SC57	SAN MARINO 77, Intl. Philatelic Exhibition, San Marino, Aug. 28-Sept. 4. Card of 3, #1-2, San Marino #1. Italian text. (USPS)	2.25

SC58	PURIPEX 77, Silver Anniv. Philatelic Exhibit, Sept. 2-5, San Juan, P. R. Card of 4 #801. (BEP)	2.00
SC59	ASDA Natl. Postage Stamp Show, Nov. 15-20, New York. Card of 4 #C45. (BEP)	2.25

1978

SC60	ROCPEX 78, Intl. Philatelic Exhibition, Mar. 20-29, Taipei. Card of 6, #1706-1709, China #1812, 1816. Chinese text. (USPS)	2.50
SC61	NAPOSTA '78 Philatelic Exhibition, May 20-25, Frankfurt. Card of 3, #555, 563, Germany #1216. German text. (USPS)	2.25
SC62	CENJEX 78, Federated Stamp Clubs of New Jersey, 30th annual exhibition, June 23-25, Freehold, NJ. Card of 9, #646, 680, 689, 1086, 1716; 4 #785. (BEP)	2.00

1979

SC63	BRASILIANA 79, Intl. Philatelic Exhibition, Sept. 15-23, Rio de Janeiro. Card of 3, #C91-C92, Brazil #1295. Portuguese text. (USPS)	2.75
SC64	JAPEX 79, Intl. Philatelic Exhibition, Nov. 2-4, Tokyo. Card of 2, #1158, Japan #1024. Japanese text. (USPS)	3.00

1980

SC65	LONDON 1980, Intl. Philatelic Exhibition, May 6-14, London. #329. (USPS)	3.00
SC66	NORWEX 80, Intl. Stamp Exhibition, June 13-22, Oslo. Card of 3, #620-621, Norway #658. Norwegian text. (USPS)	3.00
SC67	NAPEX 80, July 4-6, Washington. Card of 4 #573. (BEP)	8.00
SC68	ASDA Stamp Festival, Sept. 25-28, 1980, New York. Card of 4 #962. (BEP)	9.50
SC69	ESSEN 80, 3rd Intl. Stamp Fair, Nov. 15-19, Essen. Card of 2, #1014, Germany #723. German text. (USPS)	3.00

1981

SC70	STAMP EXPO '81 SOUTH, Mar. 20-22, Anaheim, Calif. Card of 6, #1331-1332, 4 #1287. (BEP)	11.00
SC71	WIPA 1981, Intl. Stamp Exhibition, May 22-31, Vienna. Card of 2, #1252, Austria #789. German text. (USPS)	3.00
SC72	Natl. Stamp Collecting Month, Oct., 1981. Card of 2, #245, 1918. (USPS)	3.00
SC73	PHILATOKYO '81, Intl. Stamp Exhibition, Oct. 9-18. Tokyo. Card of 2, #1531, Japan #800. Japanese text. (USPS)	3.00
SC74	NORDPOSTA 81, North German Stamp Exhibition, Nov. 7-8. Hamburg. Card of 2, #923, Germany #B538. German text. (USPS)	3.00

1982

SC75	MILCOPEX '82, Milwaukee Philatelic Association Exhibition, Mar. 5-7. Card of 4 #1137. (BEP)	10.00
SC76	CANADA 82, Intl. Philatelic Youth Exhibition, May 20-24, Toronto. Card of 2, #116, Canada #15. French and English text. (USPS)	3.00
SC77	PHILEXFRANCE '82, Intl. Philatelic Exhibition, June 11-21, Paris. Card of 2, #1753, France #1480. French text. (USPS)	3.00
SC78	Natl. Stamp Collecting Month, Oct. #C3a. (USPS)	3.00
SC79	ESPAMER '82, Intl. Philatelic Exhibition, Oct. 12-17, San Juan, P.R. Card of 4 #244. English and Spanish text. (BEP)	18.00
SC80	ESPAMER '82, Intl. Philatelic Exhibition, Oct. 12-17, San Juan, P.R. Card of 3, #801, 1437, 2024. Spanish and English text. (USPS)	3.00

1983

SC81	Joint stamp issues, Sweden and US. Mar. 24. Card of 3, #958, 2036, Sweden #1453. Swedish and English text. (USPS)	3.00
SC82	Joint stamp issues, Germany and US. Apr. 29. Card of 2, #2040, Germany #1397. German and English text. (USPS)	3.00
SC83	TEMBAL 83, Intl. Philatelic Exhibition, Mar. 21-29, Basel. Card of 2, #C71, Basel #3L1. German text. (USPS)	3.00
SC84	TEXANEX-TOPEX '83 Exhibition, June 17-19, San Antonio. Card of 5, #1660, 4 #776. (BEP)	15.00
SC85	BRASILIANA 83, Intl. Philatelic Exhibition, July 29-Aug. 7, Rio de Janeiro. Card of 2, #2, Brazil #1. Portuguese text. (USPS)	3.00
SC86	BANGKOK 83, Intl. Philatelic Exhibition, Aug. 4-13, Bangkok. Card of 2, #210, Thailand #1. Thai text. (USPS)	3.00
SC87	Intl. Philatelic Memento, 1983-84. #1387. (USPS)	2.75
SC88	Natl. Stamp Collecting Month, Oct. #293 bicolored. (USPS)	3.75
SC89	Philatelic Show '83, Boston, Oct. 21-23. Card of 2, #718-719. (BEP)	9.00
SC90	ASDA 1983, Natl. Postage Stamp Show, New York, Nov. 17-20. Card of 4 #881. (BEP)	9.00

1984

SC91	ESPANA 84, World Exhibition of Philately. Madrid, Apr. 27-May 6. Card of 4 #241. Enlarged vignette, Landing of Columbus, from #231. English and Spanish text. (BEP)	15.00
SC92	ESPANA 84, Intl. Philatelic Exhibition, Madrid, Apr. 27-May 6. Card of 2, #233, Spain #428. Spanish text. (USPS)	3.00
SC93	Stamp Expo '84 South, Anaheim, CA, Apr. 27-29. Card of 4, #1791-1794. (BEP)	12.00
SC94	COMPEX '84, Rosemont, IL, May 25-27. Card of 4 #728. (BEP)	15.00
SC95	HAMBURG '84, Intl. Exhibition for 19th UPU Congress, Hamburg, June 19-26. Card of 2, #C66, Germany #669. English, French and German text. (USPS)	3.00
SC96	St. Lawrence Seaway, 25th anniv., June 26. Card of 2, #1131, Canada #387. English and French text. (USPS)	3.25
SC97	AUSIPEX '84, Australia's 1st intl. exhibition, Melbourne, Sept. 21-30. Card of 2, #290, Western Australia #1. (USPS)	3.00
SC98	Natl. Stamp Collecting Month, Oct. #2104, tricolored. (USPS)	2.75
SC99	PHILAKOREA '84, Seoul, Oct. 22-31. Card of 2, #741, Korea #994. Korean and English text. (USPS)	3.00
SC100	ASDA 1984, Natl. Postage Stamp Show, New York, Nov. 15-18. Card of 4 #1470. (BEP)	10.00

1985

SC101	Intl. Philatelic Memento, 1985. #2. (USPS)	3.00
SC102	OLYMPHILEX '85. Intl. Philatelic Exhibition, Lausanne. Mar. 18-24. Card of 2, #C106, Switzerland #746. French and English text. (USPS)	3.00
SC103	ISRAPHIL '85. Intl. Philatelic Exhibition, Tel Aviv, May 14-22. Card of 2, #566, Israel #33. Hebrew and English text. (USPS)	3.00
SC104	LONG BEACH '85, Numismatic and Philatelic Exposition, Long Beach, CA, Jan. 31-Feb. 3. Card of 4 #954, plus a Series 1865 $20 Gold Certificate. (BEP)	10.00
SC105	MILCOPEX '85, Milwaukee Philatelic Society annual stamp show, Mar. 1-3. Card of 4 #880. (BEP)	10.50
SC106	NAPEX '85, Natl. Philatelic Exhibition, Arlington, VA, June 7-9. Card of 4 #2014. (BEP)	9.00
SC107	ARGENTINA '85, Intl. Philatelic Exhibition, Buenos Aires, July 5-14. Card of 2, #1737, Argentina #B27. Spanish text. (USPS)	3.00
SC108	MOPHILA '85, Intl. Philatelic Exhibition, Hamburg, Sept. 11-15. Card of 2, #296, Germany #B595. German text. (USPS)	3.00
SC109	ITALIA '85, Intl. Philatelic Exhibition, Rome, Oct. 25-Nov. 3. Card of 2, #1107, Italy #830. Italian text. (USPS)	3.00

1986

SC110	Statue of Liberty Centennial, Natl. Philatelic Memento, 1986. #C87. (USPS)	4.50
SC111	Garfield Perry Stamp Club, Natl. Stamp Show, Cleveland, Mar. 21-23. Card of 4 #306. (BEP)	9.50
SC112	AMERIPEX '86, Intl. Philatelic Exhibition, Chicago, May 22-June 1. Card of 3, #134, 2052, 1474.(BEP)	8.50
SC113	STOCKHOLMIA '86, Intl. Philatelic Exhibition, Stockholm, Aug. 28-Sept. 7. Card of 2, #113, Sweden #253. Swedish text. (USPS)	4.50
SC114	HOUPEX '86, Natl. Stamp Show, Houston. Sept. 5-7. Card of 3, #1035, 1042, 1044A. (BEP)	10.00
SC115	LOBEX '86, Numismatic and Philatelic Exhibition, Long Beach, CA, Oct. 2-5. Long Beach Stamp Club 60th anniv. Card of 4, #291, plus a series 1907 $10 Gold Certificate. (BEP)	15.00
SC116	DCSE '86, Dallas Coin and Stamp Exhibition, Dallas, Dec. 11-14. Card of 4 #550, plus $10,000 Federal Reserve Note. (BEP)	15.00

1987

SC117	CAPEX '87, Intl. Philatelic Exhibition, Toronto, June 13-21. Card of 2, #569, Canada #883. English and French text. (USPS)	4.00
SC118	HAFNIA '87, Intl. Philatelic Exhibition, Copenhagen, Oct. 16-25. Card of 2, #299, Denmark #B52. English and Danish text. (USPS)	4.00
SC119	SESCAL '87, Stamp Exhibition of Southern California, Los Angeles, Oct. 16-18. #798. (BEP)	11.00
SC120	HSNA '87, Hawaii State Numismatic Association Exhibition, Honolulu, Nov. 12-15. #799 and a Series 1923 $5 Silver Certificate. (BEP)	17.50
SC121	MONTE CARLO, Intl. Philatelic Exhibition, Monte Carlo, Nov. 13-17. Card of 3, #2287, 2300, Monaco #1589. French and English text. (USPS)	4.00

1988

SC122	FINLANDIA '88, Intl. Philatelic Exhibition, Helsinki, June 1-12. Card of 2, #836, Finland #768. English and Finnish text. (USPS)	
SC123	STAMPSHOW '88, APS natl. stamp show, Detroit, Aug. 25-28. #835.	
SC124	MIDAPHIL '88, Kansas City, Nov. 18-20. #627. (BEP)	

1989

SC125	PHILEXFRANCE '89 intl. philatelic exhibition, Paris, July 7-17. Card of 2, #C120, France #2144. English and French text. (USPS)	
SC126	STAMPSHOW '89, APS natl. stamp show, Anaheim, CA, Aug. 24-27. #565. Various reproductions of the portrait of Chief Hollow Horn Bear from which the stamp was designed. (BEP)	
SC127	WORLD STAMP EXPO '89, Washington, Nov. 17-Dec. 3. Card of 4, #2433a-2433d. Embossed reproductions of Supreme Court, Washington Monument, Capitol and Jefferson Memorial. (USPS)	

1990

SC128	ARIPEX 90, Arizona Philatelic Exhibition, Phoenix, Apr. 20-22. Card of 2, #285 and #285 with black vignette. (BEP)	
SC129	STAMPSHOW '90, APS natl. stamp show, Cincinnati, Aug. 23-26. Card of 2, #286 and essay with frame of #286 in red with vignette of #293 in black. (BEP)	
SC130	STAMP WORLD LONDON 90, London, England, May 3-13. Card of 2, #1, Great Britain #1. (USPS)	

1991

SC131	STAMPSHOW '91, APS natl. stamp show, Philadelphia, Aug. 22-25. Card of 3, #537, Essays #537a-E1, 537b-E1. Embossed figure of "Freedom." (BEP)	

1992

SC132	World Columbian Stamp Expo, Chicago, May 22-31. Card of 2, #118, 119b. (BEP)	
SC133	Savings Bond, produced as gift to BEP employees, available to public. 1954 Savings stamp, Series E War Savings bond. (BEP)	
SC134	STAMPSHOW '92. Oakland, CA (BEP)	

1993

SC135	Combined Federal Campaign, produced as gift to BEP employees, available to public. #1016. Photos of 6 other stamps. (BEP)	
SC136	ASDA stamp show, New York, May 1993. Card of 7 #859, 864, 869, 874, 879, 884, 889 (BEP)	
SC137	Savings Bonds, produced as gift to BEP employees, available to the public Aug. 1993. $200 War Savings Bond, #WS8 (BEP)	
SC138	Omaha Stamp Show, Sept. 1993. Card of 4, #E7, PR2, JQ5, QE4 (BEP)	
SC139	ASDA New York Stamp Show, Oct. 1993. Card of 2, #499-E1a and similar with negative New York precancel (BEP)	

1994

SC140	Sandical, San Diego, CA, Feb. 1994. Card of 4 #E4 (BEP)	
SC140A	Centennial of U.S. Stamp Production, July 1994, BEP Intaglio Print. Card of 13 Types A87-A99 in black	10
SC141	Savings Bonds, produced as a gift to BEP employees, available to the public Aug. 1, 1994. #WS7-WS11.	1
SC142	STAMPSHOW '94, APS National Stamp Show Pittsburgh, PA. Card of 3, 1c, 2c and 10c Type D2	
SC143	American Stamp Dealers Association, Nov. 1994, New York, NY. Card of 4, 2c, 12c, $3, $6 Types N4-N5, N7-N8	1

1995

SC144	Natl. Exhibition of the Columbus Philatelic Club, Apr. 1995, Columbus, OH. Block of 4 of #261.	
	No. 144 was issued folded in half.	
SC145	Centennial of U.S. Stamp Production, June 1995, BEP Intaglio Print. Card of 13 of Types A87-A99 in blue	7
SC146	Savings Bonds, produced as a gift to BEP employees, available to the public Aug. 1, 1995. Card of 3 #905, 907, 940	1
SC147	American Stamp Dealers Association, Nov. 1995, New York, NY. Block of 4, #292	
	No. SC147 issued folded in half.	

1996

SC148	CAPEX '96, Toronto, Canada, June 1996. Block of 4, #291	
SC149	Olymphilex '96, Atlanta, GA, July-August, 1996, Block of 4, #718	

60	Billings Stamp Club, Billings, MT, Oct. 1996, Block of 4, #1130	9.50
61	Long Beach Coin & Collectibles Expo, Feb. 1997, Lock Seal revenue stamp	11.00
62	PACIFIC 97, May 1997, Process or renovated butter revenue stamp	10.00
63	Milcopex, Milwaukee, WI, Sept. 1997, Newspaper Types N15, N16 and N19	10.00
64	OKPEX 98, Oklahoma City, OK, May 1998, Block of 4, #922	10.00
65	Centennial of Trans-Mississippi Exposition Issue, Sept. 1998, BEP Engraved Print. Card of 9 die impressions in green of designs A100-A108	40.00
66	Philadelphia National Stamp Exhibition, Oct. 1999, Card of 4, #RS281, RS284, RS290, RS306	12.00
67	ANA Coin, Stamp and Collectibles Show, Las Vegas, Oct. 2005, Card of 7, #999, 1248, RF1, RF11, RF26, 7c essay of #RF11, 5c essay of #RF26	45.00

NUMISMATIC SOUVENIR CARDS

...cluded in this section are cards issued by the ...eau of Engraving and Printing showing fractional ...ency, paper money or parts thereof, for numis-...c shows. Not included are press samples sold or ...n away only at the shows and other special print-... Cards showing both money and stamps are listed ...e preceeding section.

Standard abbreviations:
...NA- American Numismatic Association
...MS- International Paper Money Show
...UN- Florida United Numismatists

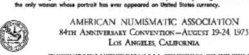

No. NSC8

69-84

C1	ANA	45.00
C2	Fresno Numismatic Fair	225.00
C3	ANA ('70)	55.00
C4	ANA ('71)	6.00
C5	ANA ('72)	6.00
C6	ANA ('73)	7.00
C7	ANA ('74)	8.00
C8	ANA ('75)	8.50
C9	ANA ('76)	7.00
C10	ANA ('77)	11.00
C11	IPMS ('78)	3.50
C12	ANA ('80)	16.00
C13	IPMS ('80)	22.00
C14	IPMS ('81)	16.00
C15	ANA ('81)	12.00
C16	IPMS ('82)	12.00
C17	ANA ('82)	10.50
C18	FUN ('83)	18.00
C19	ANA ('83)	15.00
C20	FUN ('84)	18.00
C21	IPMS ('84)	22.00
C22	ANA ('84)	15.00

85

C23	International Coin Club of El Paso	15.00
C24	Pacific Northwest Numismatic Assoc.	15.00
C25	IPMS	18.00
C26	ANA	16.00
C27	International Paper Money Convention (IPMC)	13.50

86

C28	FUN	15.00
C29	ANA Midwinter	14.00
C30	IPMS	11.00
C31	ANA	10.00
C32	National World Paper Money Convention (NWPMC)	10.50

87

C33	FUN	15.00
C34	ANA Midwinter	14.00
C35	BEP Fort Worth	18.00

NSC36	IPMS	18.00
NSC37	ANA	12.00
NSC38	Great Eastern Numismatic Association	15.00

1988

NSC39	FUN	11.00
NSC40	ANA Midwinter	16.00
NSC41	IPMS	16.00
NSC42	ANA	17.00
NSC43	Illinois Numismatic Association	13.00

1989

NSC44	FUN	13.00
NSC45	ANA Midwinter	13.00
NSC46	TNA	13.00
NSC47	IPMS	14.00
NSC48	ANA	15.00

1990

NSC49	FUN	13.00
NSC50	ANA Midwinter	12.00
NSC51	Central States Numismatic Society	15.00
NSC52	Dallas Coin and Stamp Exposition	14.00
NSC53	ANA, Seattle, WA	22.00
NSC54	Westex	14.00
NSC55	Honolulu State Numismatic Association	15.00

1991

NSC56	FUN	14.00
NSC57	ANA Midwinter, Dallas, Texas	14.00
NSC58	IPMS	14.00
NSC59	ANA Convention, Chicago, IL	20.00

1992

NSC60	FUN	13.00
NSC61	Central States Numismatics Society	20.00
NSC62	IPMS, Memphis, TN	14.00
NSC63	ANA Convention, Orlando, FL	14.00

1993

NSC64	FUN	15.00
NSC65	ANA Convention, Colorado Springs, CO	16.00
NSC66	Texas Numismatic Association Show	16.00
NSC67	Georgia Numismatic Association Show	15.00
NSC68	ANA Convention, Baltimore, MD	15.00
NSC69	IPMS, Memphis, TN	18.00

1994

NSC70	FUN	15.00
NSC71	ANA Convention, New Orleans, LA	20.00
NSC72	European Paper Money Bourse, Netherlands	16.00
NSC73	IPMS, Memphis, TN	14.00
NSC74	ANA Convention, Detroit, MI	14.00

Nos. NSC75-NSC79 were issued folded in half.

1995

NSC75	FUN	15.00
NSC76	New York Intl. Numismatic Convention	18.00
NSC77	IPMS, Memphis, TN	15.00
NSC78	ANA Convention, Anaheim, CA	18.00
NSC79	Long Beach Numismatic/Philatelic Exposition, Long Beach, CA	18.00

1996

NSC80	FUN	15.00
NSC81	Suburban Washington/Baltimore Coin Show	16.00
NSC82	Central States Numismatic Association	15.00
NSC83	ANA Convention, Denver, CO	15.00

1997

NSC84	FUN	17.00
NSC85	Bay State Coin Show	14.00
NSC86	IPMS, Memphis, TN	18.00
NSC87	ANA Convention, New York, NY	15.00

1998

NSC88	FUN	14.00
NSC89	IPMS, Memphis, TN	14.00
NSC90	ANA Convention, Portland, OR	14.00
NSC91	Long Beach Coin & Collectibles Expo, Long Beach, CA	15.00

1999

NSC92	FUN	18.00
NSC93	Bay State Coin Club	16.00
NSC94	IPMS, Memphis, TN	18.00
NSC95	ANA Convention, Rosemont, IL	16.00

2001

NSC96	FUN	18.00
NSC97	Intl. Paper Money Show, Memphis, TN	16.00
NSC98	ANA Convention, Atlanta, GA	16.00
NSC99	Long Beach Coin & Collectibles Expo, Long Beach, CA	16.00

2002

NSC100	FUN	18.00
NSC101	Texas Numismatic Association, Fort Worth	20.00
NSC102	ANA Convention, New York, NY	18.00
NSC103	Long Beach Coin & Collectibles Expo, Long Beach, CA	18.00

2003

NSC104	FUN	45.00
NSC105	Georgia Numismatic Association, Dalton, GA (card of one #C45 in blue gray, without denomination and some inscriptions)	45.00

2002

NSC106	ANA Convention, Baltimore, MD	45.00

2003

NSC107	Natl. & World Paper Money Convention, St. Louis, MO	45.00

2004

NSC108	ANA Convention, Portland, OR	45.00
NSC109	ANA Convention, Pittsburgh, PA	45.00

2005

NSC110	FUN	40.00
NSC111	Money Show of the Southwest, Houston, TX	40.00
NSC112	Long Beach Coin & Stamp Expo, Long Beach, CA	40.00
NSC113	ANA National Money Show, Kansas City, MO	40.00
NSC114	ANA World's Fair of Money, San Francisco, CA	40.00

2006

NSC115	ANA National Money Show, Atlanta, GA	35.00

COMMEMORATIVE PANELS

The U.S. Postal Service began issuing commemorative panels September 20, 1972, with the Wildlife Conservation issue (Scott Nos. 1464-14
Each panel is devoted to a separate issue. It includes unused examples of the stamp or stamps (usually a block of four), reproduction of s
engravings, and background information on the subject of the issue. Values are for panels without protective sleeves. Values for panels with prote
sleeves are 10% to 25% higher.

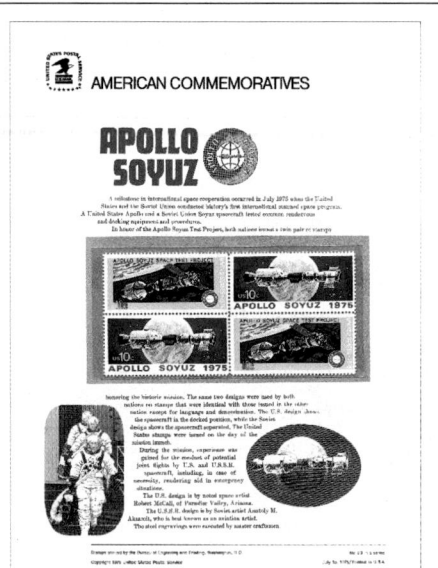

No. CP53

1972

CP1	Wildlife Conservation, #1467a	4.75
CP2	Mail Order, #1468	4.75
CP3	Osteopathic Medicine, #1469	6.50
CP4	Tom Sawyer, #1470	5.00
CP5	Pharmacy, #1473	6.00
CP6	Christmas (angel), #1471	8.00
CP7	Santa Claus, #1472	8.00
CP8	Stamp Collecting, #1474	5.50

1973

CP9	Love, #1475	6.75
CP10	Pamphleteers, #1476	5.50
CP11	George Gershwin, #1484	6.00
CP12	Posting a Broadside, #1477	5.50
CP13	Copernicus, #1488	5.50
CP14	Postal Service Employees, #1489-1498	5.25
CP15	Harry S Truman, #1499	6.50
CP16	Postrider, #1478	6.00
CP17	Boston Tea Party, #1483a	15.00
CP18	Electronics Progress, #1500-1502, C86	5.50
CP19	Robinson Jeffers, #1485	4.75
CP20	Lyndon B. Johnson, #1503	6.50
CP21	Henry O. Tanner, #1486	5.50
CP22	Willa Cather, #1487	5.00
CP23	Drummer, #1479	8.25
CP24	Angus and Longhorn Cattle, #1504	5.50
CP25	Christmas (Madonna), #1507	7.75
CP26	Christmas Tree, needlepoint, #1508	7.75

1974

CP27	Veterans of Foreign Wars, #1525	5.25
CP28	Robert Frost, #1526	5.25
CP29	EXPO '74, #1527	6.00
CP30	Horse Racing, #1528	8.00
CP31	Skylab, #1529	8.50
CP32	Universal Postal Union, #1537a	6.00
CP33	Mineral Heritage, #1541a	7.00
CP34	Kentucky Settlement (Ft. Harrod), #1542	5.25
CP35	First Continental Congress, #1546a	7.00
CP36	Chautauqua, #1505	5.75
CP37	Kansas Wheat, #1506	5.75
CP38	Energy Conservation, #1547	5.00
CP39	Sleepy Hollow Legend, #1548	5.75
CP40	Retarded Children, #1549	5.00
CP41	Christmas (Currier-Ives), #1551	7.50
CP42	Christmas (angel), #1550	7.50

1975

CP43	Benjamin West, #1553	5.50
CP44	Pioneer 10, #1556	8.50
CP45	Collective Bargaining, #1558	4.75
CP46	Contributors to the Cause, #1559-1562	6.25
CP47	Mariner 10, #1557	9.00
CP48	Lexington-Concord Battle, #1563	5.50
CP49	Paul Laurence Dunbar, #1554	6.00
CP50	D. W. Griffith, #1555	5.75
CP51	Battle of Bunker Hill, #1564	5.75
CP52	Military Services (uniforms), #1568a	5.00
CP53	Apollo Soyuz, #1569a	8.25
CP54	World Peace through Law, #1576	5.00
CP55	International Women's Year, #1571	5.75
CP56	Postal Service 200 Years, #1575a	5.50
CP57	Banking and Commerce, #1577a	6.25
CP58	Early Christmas Card, #1580	7.00

CP59	Christmas (Madonna), #1579	7.00

1976

CP60	Spirit of '76, #1631a	8.00
CP61	Interphil '76, #1632	7.00
CP62	State Flags, block of 4 from #1633-1682	15.00
CP63	Telephone Centenary, #1683	6.75
CP64	Commercial Aviation, #1684	9.25
CP65	Chemistry, #1685	7.00
CP66	Benjamin Franklin, #1690	7.00
CP67	Declaration of Independence, #1694a	7.00
CP68	12th Winter Olympics, #1698a	7.50
CP69	Clara Maass, #1699	8.00
CP70	Adolph S. Ochs, #1700	9.00
CP71	Christmas (Currier print), #1702	8.00
CP72	Christmas (Copley Nativity), #1701	8.75

1977

CP73	Washington at Princeton, #1704	9.00
CP74	Sound Recording, #1705	16.00
CP75	Pueblo Art, #1709a	45.00
CP76	Lindbergh Flight, #1710	45.00
CP77	Colorado Statehood, #1711	11.00
CP78	Butterflies, #1715a	12.00
CP79	Lafayette, #1716	10.50
CP80	Skilled Hands for Independence, #1720a	10.50
CP81	Peace Bridge, #1721	10.50
CP82	Battle of Oriskany, #1722	10.50
CP83	Energy Conservation-Development, #1723a	12.00
CP84	Alta California, #1725	11.00
CP85	Articles of Confederation, #1726	15.00
CP86	Talking Pictures, #1727	13.50
CP87	Surrender at Saratoga, #1728	15.00
CP88	Christmas (Washington at Valley Forge), #1729	18.00
CP89	Christmas (rural mailbox), #1730	24.00

1978

CP90	Carl Sandburg, #1731	6.50
CP91	Captain Cook, #1732a	12.00
CP92	Harriet Tubman, #1744	9.50
CP93	American Quilts, #1748a	14.00
CP94	American Dance, #1752a	10.00
CP95	French Alliance, #1753	10.00
CP96	Pap Test, #1754	8.25
CP97	Jimmie Rodgers, #1755	11.00
CP98	Photography, #1758	8.00
CP99	George M. Cohan, #1756	12.50
CP100	Viking Missions, #1759	27.50
CP101	American Owls, #1763a	27.50
CP102	American Trees, #1767a	26.00
CP103	Christmas (Madonna), #1768	10.50
CP104	Christmas (hobby-horse), #1769	10.50

1979

CP105	Robert F. Kennedy, #1770	7.25
CP106	Martin Luther King, Jr., #1771	7.50
CP107	Year of the Child, #1772	6.50
CP108	John Steinbeck, #1773	6.00
CP109	Albert Einstein, #1774	7.25
CP110	Pennsylvania Toleware, #1778a	6.75
CP111	American Architecture, #1782a	7.50
CP112	Endangered Flora, #1786a	7.00
CP113	Seeing Eye Dogs, #1787	6.25
CP114	Special Olympics, #1788	7.50
CP115	John Paul Jones, #1789	7.00
CP116	Olympic Games, #1794a	8.50
CP117	Christmas (Madonna), #1799	8.50
CP118	Christmas (Santa Claus), #1800	8.50
CP119	Will Rogers, #1801	7.00
CP120	Viet Nam Veterans, #1802	9.50
CP121	10c, 31c Olympics, #1790, C97	8.50

1980

CP122	Winter Olympics, #1798a	7.50
CP123	W.C Fields, #1803	7.50
CP124	Benjamin Banneker, #1804	7.25
CP125	Frances Perkins, #1821	5.50
CP126	Emily Bissell, #1823	6.00
CP127	Helen Keller, #1824	5.50
CP128	Veterans Administration, #1825	6.00
CP129	Galvez, #1826	5.25
CP130	Coral Reefs, #1830a	8.00
CP131	Organized Labor, #1831	5.50
CP132	Edith Wharton, #1832	5.25
CP133	Education, #1833	5.50
CP134	Indian Masks, #1837a	8.00
CP135	Architecture, #1841a	6.75
CP136	Christmas Window, #1842	8.00
CP137	Christmas Toys, #1843	8.00

1981

CP138	Dirksen, #1874	6.50
CP139	Young, #1875	7.00
CP140	Flowers, #1879a	7.00
CP141	Red Cross, #1910	7.00
CP142	Savings and Loan, #1911	6.75
CP143	Space Achievements, #1919a	11.00
CP144	Management, #1920	5.50
CP145	Wildlife, #1924a	8.00
CP146	Disabled, #1925	5.50
CP147	Millay, #1926	6.00
CP148	Architecture, #1931a	6.50
CP149	Zaharias, Jones, #1932, 1933	20.00
CP150	Remington, #1934	6.75

CP151	18c, 20c Hoban, #1935, 1936	
CP152	Yorktown, Va. Capes, #1938a	
CP153	Madonna and Child, #1939	
CP154	Teddy Bear, #1940	
CP155	John Hanson, #1941	
CP156	Desert Plants, #1945a	

1982

CP157	FDR, #1950	
CP158	Love, #1951	
CP159	Washington, #1952	
CP160	Birds and Flowers, block of 4 from #1953-2002	
CP161	US-Netherlands, #2003	
CP162	Library of Congress, #2004	
CP163	Knoxville World's Fair, #2009a	
CP164	Horatio Alger, #2010	
CP165	Aging, #2011	
CP166	Barrymores, #2012	
CP167	Dr. Mary Walker, #2013	
CP168	Peace Garden, #2014	
CP169	Libraries, #2015	
CP170	Jackie Robinson, #2016	
CP171	Touro Synagogue, #2017	
CP172	Wolf Trap Farm, #2018	
CP173	Architecture, #2022a	
CP174	Francis of Assisi, #2023	
CP175	Ponce de Leon, #2024	
CP176	Puppy, Kitten, #2025	
CP177	Madonna and Child, #2026	
CP178	Children Playing, #2030a	

1983

CP179	Science, #2031	
CP180	Ballooning, #2035a	
CP181	US-Sweden, #2036	
CP182	CCC, #2037	
CP183	Priestley, #2038	
CP184	Voluntarism, #2039	
CP185	German Immigration, #2040	
CP186	Brooklyn Bridge, #2041	
CP187	TVA, #2042	
CP188	Fitness, #2043	
CP189	Scott Joplin, #2044	
CP190	Medal of Honor, #2045	
CP191	Babe Ruth, #2046	
CP192	Hawthorne, #2047	
CP193	13c Olympics, #2051a	
CP194	28c Olympics, #C104a	
CP195	40c Olympics, #C108a	
CP196	35c Olympics, #C112a	
CP197	Treaty of Paris, #2052	
CP198	Civil Service, #2053	
CP199	Metropolitan Opera, #2054	
CP200	Inventors, #2058a	
CP201	Streetcars, #2062a	
CP202	Madonna and Child, #2063	
CP203	Santa Claus, #2064	
CP204	Martin Luther, #2065	

1984

CP205	Alaska, #2066	
CP206	Winter Olympics, #2070a	
CP207	FDIC, #2071	
CP208	Love, #2072	
CP209	Woodson, #2073	
CP210	Conservation, #2074	
CP211	Credit Union, #2075	
CP212	Orchids, #2079a	
CP213	Hawaii, #2080	
CP214	National Archives, #2081	
CP215	Olympics, #2085a	
CP216	World Expo, #2086	
CP217	Health Research, #2087	
CP218	Fairbanks, #2088	
CP219	Thorpe, #2089	
CP220	McCormack, #2090	
CP221	St. Lawrence Seaway, #2091	
CP222	Waterfowl, #2092	
CP223	Roanoke Voyages, #2093	
CP224	Melville, #2094	
CP225	Horace Moses, #2095	
CP226	Smokey Bear, #2096	15
CP227	Roberto Clemente, #2097	25
CP228	Dogs, #2101a	
CP229	Crime Prevention, #2102	
CP230	Hispanic Americans, #2103	
CP231	Family Unity, #2104	
CP232	Eleanor Roosevelt, #2105	
CP233	Readers, #2106	
CP234	Madonna and Child, #2107	
CP235	Child's Santa, #2108	
CP236	Vietnam Memorial, #2109	

1985

CP237	Jerome Kern, #2110	
CP238	Bethune, #2137	
CP239	Duck Decoys, #2141a	10
CP240	Winter Special Olympics, #2142	
CP241	Love, #2143	
CP242	REA, #2144	
CP243	AMERIPEX '86, #2145	
CP244	Abigail Adams, #2146	
CP245	Bartholdi, #2147	
CP246	Korean Veterans, #2152	
CP247	Social Security, #2153	
CP248	World War I Veterans, #2154	
CP249	Horses, #2158a	

No.	Description	Value
CP250	Education, #2159	5.00
CP251	Youth Year, #2163a	8.25
CP252	Hunger, #2164	5.00
CP253	Madonna and Child, #2165	7.00
CP254	Poinsettias, #2166	7.00

1986

No.	Description	Value
CP255	Arkansas, #2167	5.25
CP256	Stamp Collecting booklet pane, #2201a	6.75
CP257	Love, #2202	6.00
CP258	Sojourner Truth, #2203	7.50
CP259	Texas Republic, #2204	7.50
CP260	Fish booklet pane, #2209a	6.75
CP261	Hospitals, #2210	4.75
CP262	Duke Ellington, #2211	7.50
CP263	Presidents Souvenir Sheet No. 1, #2216	6.25
CP264	Presidents Souvenir Sheet No. 2, #2217	6.25
CP265	Presidents Souvenir Sheet No. 3, #2218	6.25
CP266	Presidents Souvenir Sheet No. 4, #2219	6.25
CP267	Arctic Explorers, #2223a	6.75
CP268	Statue of Liberty, #2224	7.50
CP269	Navajo Art, #2238a	8.00
CP270	T.S. Eliot, #2239	6.25
CP271	Woodcarved Figurines, #2243a	6.75
CP272	Madonna and Child, #2244	5.75
CP273	Village Scene, #2245	5.75

1987

No.	Description	Value
CP274	Michigan, #2246	5.75
CP275	Pan American Games, #2247	3.50
CP276	Love, #2248	5.75
CP277	du Sable, #2249	5.75
CP278	Caruso, #2250	5.50
CP279	Girl Scouts, #2251	7.50
CP280	Special Occasions booklet pane, #2274a	5.50
CP281	United Way, #2275	4.75
CP282	Wildlife, #2286, 2287, 2296, 2297, 2306, 2307, 2316, 2317, 2326, 2327	6.50
CP283	Wildlife, #2288, 2289, 2298, 2299, 2308, 2309, 2318, 2319, 2328, 2329	6.50
CP284	Wildlife, #2290, 2291, 2300, 2301, 2310, 2311, 2320, 2321, 2330, 2331	6.50
CP285	Wildlife, #2292, 2293, 2302, 2303, 2312, 2313, 2322, 2323, 2332, 2333	6.50
CP286	Wildlife, #2294, 2295, 2304, 2305, 2314, 2315, 2324, 2325, 2334, 2335	6.50

1987-90

No.	Description	Value
CP287	Delaware, #2336	5.75
CP288	Pennsylvania, #2337	5.25
CP289	New Jersey, #2338	5.25
CP290	Georgia, #2339	5.25
CP291	Connecticut, #2340	5.25
CP292	Massachusetts, #2341	5.25
CP293	Maryland, #2342	5.25
CP294	South Carolina, #2343	5.25
CP295	New Hampshire, #2344	5.25
CP296	Virginia, #2345	5.25
CP297	New York, #2346	5.25
CP298	North Carolina, #2347	5.25
CP299	Rhode Island, #2348	5.25

1987

No.	Description	Value
CP300	U.S.-Morocco, #2349	4.75
CP301	William Faulkner, #2350	4.75
CP302	Lacemaking, #2354a	5.50
CP303	Drafting of the Constitution booklet pane, #2359a	5.00
CP304	Signing of the Constitution, #2360	5.00
CP305	Certified Public Accounting, #2361	20.00
CP306	Locomotives booklet pane, #2366a	7.50
CP307	Madonna and Child, #2367	6.25
CP308	Christmas Ornaments, #2368	5.50

1988

No.	Description	Value
CP309	Winter Olympics, #2369	6.25
CP310	Australia Bicentennial, #2370	5.75
CP311	James Weldon Johnson, #2371	5.00
CP312	Cats, #2375a	6.50
CP313	Knute Rockne, #2376	9.00
CP314	New Sweden, #C117	5.75
CP315	Francis Ouimet, #2377	14.00
CP316	25c, 45c Love, #2378 and #2379	6.50
CP317	Summer Olympics, #2380	6.25
CP318	Classic Automobiles booklet pane, #2385a	7.00
CP319	Antarctic Explorers, #2389a	6.25
CP320	Carousel Animals, #2393a	7.00
CP321	Special Occasions booklet singles, #2395-2398	6.50
CP322	Madonna and Child, Sleigh, #2399, 2400	6.50

1989

No.	Description	Value
CP323	Montana, #2401	6.25
CP324	A. Philip Randolph, #2402	8.00
CP325	North Dakota, #2403	6.25
CP326	Washington Statehood, #2404	6.25
CP327	Steamboats booklet pane, #2409a	7.50
CP328	World Stamp Expo, #2410	5.50
CP329	Arturo Toscanini, #2411	6.25

1989-90

No.	Description	Value
CP330	House of Representatives, #2412	6.25
CP331	Senate, #2413	6.25
CP332	Executive Branch, #2414	6.25
CP333	Supreme Court, #2415	6.00

1989

No.	Description	Value
CP334	South Dakota, #2416	6.25
CP335	Lou Gehrig, #2417	25.00
CP336	French Revolution, #C120	6.50
CP337	Ernest Hemingway, #2418	8.75
CP338	Letter Carriers, #2420	6.50
CP339	Bill of Rights, #2421	6.50

No.	Description	Value
CP340	Dinosaurs, #2425a	13.50
CP341	Pre-Columbian Artifacts, #2426, C121	7.25
CP342	Madonna, Sleigh with Presents, #2427, 2428	8.50
CP343	Traditional Mail Delivery, #2437a	6.50
CP344	Futuristic Mail Delivery, #C125a	8.00

1990

No.	Description	Value
CP345	Idaho, #2439	5.50
CP346	Love, #2440	7.25
CP347	Ida B. Wells, #2442	12.50
CP348	Wyoming, #2444	6.25
CP349	Classic Films, #2448a	13.00
CP350	Marianne Moore, #2449	5.50
CP351	Lighthouses booklet pane, #2474a	10.00
CP352	Olympians, #2500a	8.50
CP353	Indian Headdresses booklet pane, #2505c	10.00
CP354	Micronesia, Marshall Islands, #2507a	7.00
CP355	Sea Creatures, #2511a	11.50
CP356	Grand Canyon & Tropical Coastline, #2512, C127	7.50
CP357	Eisenhower, #2513	8.25
CP358	Madonna and Child, Christmas Tree, #2514-2515	8.00

1991

No.	Description	Value
CP359	Switzerland, #2532	8.00
CP360	Vermont Statehood, #2533	6.00
CP361	Savings Bonds, #2534	6.25
CP362	Love, #2535-2536	8.00
CP363	William Saroyan, #2538	8.50
CP364	Fishing Flies, #2549a	10.00
CP365	Cole Porter, #2550	6.00
CP366	Antarctic Treaty, C130	5.50
CP367	Operations Desert Shield & Desert Storm, #2551	25.00
CP368	Summer Olympics, #2557a	7.50
CP369	Numismatics, #2558	6.50
CP370	World War II, #2559	12.00
CP371	Basketball, #2560	12.50
CP372	District of Columbia, #2561	7.00
CP373	Comedians, #2566c	9.50
CP374	Jan E. Matzeliger, #2567	7.50
CP375	Space Exploration, #2577a	11.50
CP376	Bering Land Bridge, #C131	6.50
CP377	Madonna and Child, Santa in Chimney, #2578-2579	9.50

1992

No.	Description	Value
CP378	Winter Olympics, #2615a	8.50
CP379	World Columbian Stamp Expo '92, #2616	8.75
CP380	W.E.B. DuBois, #2617	10.00
CP381	Love, #2618	8.75
CP382	Olympic Baseball, #2619	30.00
CP383	Voyages of Columbus, #2623a	10.00
CP384	Columbus, #2624-2625	40.00
CP385	Columbus, #2626, 2629	40.00
CP386	Columbus, #2627-2628	40.00
CP387	New York Stock Exchange, #2630	11.00
CP388	Space Accomplishments, #2634a	10.00
CP389	Alaska Highway, #2635	7.50
CP390	Kentucky Statehood, #2636	6.50
CP391	Summer Olympics, #2641a	8.00
CP392	Hummingbirds, #2646a	10.00
CP393	World War II, #2697	10.00
CP394	Wildflowers, #2647, 2648, 2657, 2658, 2667, 2668, 2677, 2678, 2687, 2688	27.50
CP395	Wildflowers, #2649, 2650, 2659, 2660, 2669, 2670, 2679, 2680, 2689, 2690	27.50
CP396	Wildflowers, #2651, 2652, 2661, 2662, 2671, 2672, 2681, 2682, 2691, 2692	27.50
CP397	Wildflowers, #2653, 2654, 2663, 2664, 2673, 2674, 2683, 2684, 2693, 2694	27.50
CP398	Wildflowers, #2655, 2656, 2665, 2666, 2675, 2676, 2685, 2686, 2695, 2696	27.50
CP399	Dorothy Parker, #2698	6.50
CP400	Dr. Theodore von Karman, #2699	10.00
CP401	Minerals, #2703a	9.50
CP402	Juan Rodriguez Cabrillo, #2704	10.50
CP403	Wild Animals, #2709a	10.00
CP404	Madonna and Child, wheeled toys, #2710, 2714a	10.50
CP405	Chinese New Year, #2720	15.00

1993

No.	Description	Value
CP406	Elvis Presley, #2721	20.00
CP407	Space Fantasy, #2745a	11.00
CP408	Percy Lavon Julian, #2746	10.00
CP409	Oregon Trail, #2747	9.00
CP410	World University Games, #2748	9.00
CP411	Grace Kelly, #2749	17.50
CP412	Oklahoma!, #2722	8.50
CP413	Circus, #2753a	9.00
CP414	Cherokee Strip, #2754	8.50
CP415	Dean Acheson, #2755	10.50
CP416	Sports horses, #2759a	10.00
CP417	Garden flowers, #2764a	8.50
CP418	World War II, #2765	12.00
CP419	Hank Williams, #2723	15.00
CP420	Rock & Roll/Rhythm & Blues, #2737b	20.00
CP421	Joe Louis, #2766	27.50
CP422	Broadway Musicals, #2770a	11.00
CP423	National Postal Museum, #2782a	9.00
CP424	American Sign Language, #2784a	9.00
CP425	Country & Western Music, #2778a	17.50
CP426	Christmas, #2789, 2794a	10.00
CP427	Youth Classics, #2788a	10.00
CP428	Mariana Islands, #2804	8.75
CP429	Columbus' Landing in Puerto Rico, #2805	10.50
CP430	AIDS Awareness, #2806	10.00

Starting with No. CP431, panels are shrink wrapped in plastic with cardboard backing. Values are for items with plastic intact.

1994

No.	Description	Value
CP431	Winter Olympics, #2807-2811	15.00
CP432	Edward R. Murrow, #2812	9.00
CP434	Love, #2814	9.50
CP436	Dr. Allison Davis, #2816	10.00
CP437	Chinese New Year, #2817	14.00
CP438	Buffalo Soldiers, #2818	13.00
CP439	Silent Screen Stars, #2828a	14.00
CP440	Garden Flowers, #2829-2833	11.00
CP441	World Cup Soccer, #2837	12.00
CP442	World War II, #2838	15.00
CP443	Norman Rockwell, #2839	19.00
CP444	Moon Landing, #2841	16.00
CP445	Locomotives, #2843-2847	12.00
CP446	George Meany, #2848	8.00
CP447	Popular Singers, #2853a	12.50
CP448	Jazz/Blues Singers, block of 10, 2854-2861	15.00

Block of 10 on No. CP448 may contain different combination of stamps.

No.	Description	Value
CP449	James Thurber, #2862	8.00
CP450	Wonders of the Sea, #2866a	11.00
CP451	Cranes, block of 2 #2868a	11.00
CP453	Christmas Madonna and Child, #2871	8.00
CP454	Christmas stocking, #2872	8.00
CP455	Chinese New Year, #2876	13.00

1995

No.	Description	Value
CP456	Florida Statehood, #2950	10.00
CP457	Earth Day, #2954a	10.00
CP458	Richard M. Nixon, #2955	15.00
CP459	Bessie Coleman, #2956	14.00
CP460	Love, #2957-2958	14.00
CP461	Recreational Sports, #2965a	14.00
CP462	Prisoners of War/Missing in Action, #2966	12.50
CP463	Marilyn Monroe, #2967	22.50
CP464	Texas Statehood, #2968	12.50
CP465	Great Lakes Lighthouses, #2973a	14.00
CP466	United Nations, #2974	11.00
CP467	Carousel Horses, #2979a	14.00
CP468	Woman Suffrage, #2980	11.00
CP469	World War II, #2981	15.00
CP470	Louis Armstrong, #2982	16.00
CP471	Jazz Musicians, #2992a	17.50
CP472	Garden Flowers, #2993-2997	11.00
CP473	Republic of Palau, #2999	11.00
CP474	Naval Academy, #3001	14.00
CP475	Tennessee Williams, #3002	12.50
CP476	Christmas, Madonna and Child, #3003	14.00
CP477	Santa Claus, Children with toys, #3007a	14.00
CP478	James K. Polk, #2587	10.00
CP479	Antique Automobiles, 3023a	17.50

1996

No.	Description	Value
CP480	Utah Statehood, #3024	10.00
CP481	Garden Flowers, #3029a	10.00
CP482	Ernest E. Just, #3058	12.50
CP483	Smithsonian Institution, #3059	10.00
CP484	Chinese New Year, #3060	17.50
CP485	Pioneers of Communication, #3064a	14.00
CP486	Fulbright Scholarships, #3065	10.00
CP487	Summer Olympic Games, #3068, 2 pages	30.00

Beginning with No. CP487, some items contain two pages. One has text and engraved illustrations, the second has the stamp(s).

No.	Description	Value
CP488	Marathon, #3067	13.50
CP489	Georgia O'Keeffe, #3069	10.00
CP490	Tennessee Statehood, #3070	10.00
CP491	Indian Dances, #3076a	17.50
CP492	Prehistoric Animals, #3080a	17.50
CP493	Breast Cancer Awareness, #3081	11.00
CP494	James Dean, #3082	17.50
CP495	Folk Heroes, #3086a	17.50
CP496	Olympic Games, Cent., #3087	11.50
CP497	Iowa Statehood, #3088	10.00
CP498	Rural Free Delivery, #3090	10.00
CP499	Riverboats, #3095a	17.50
CP500	Big Band Leaders, #3099a	17.50
CP501	Songwriters, #3103a	17.50
CP502	F. Scott Fitzgerald, #3104	19.00
CP503	Endangered Species, #3105, 2 pages	27.50
CP504	Computer Technology, #3106	19.00
CP505	Madonna & Child, #3107	13.50
CP506	Family Scenes, #3111a	14.00
CP507	Hanukkah, #3118	15.00
CP507A	Cycling, #3119	15.00

1997

No.	Description	Value
CP508	Chinese New Year, #3120	19.00
CP509	Benjamin O. Davis, Sr., #3121	14.00
CP510	Love Swans, #3123-3124	12.00
CP511	Helping Children Learn, #3125	10.50
CP512	PACIFIC 97 Stagecoach & Ship, #3131a	14.00
CP513	Thornton Wilder, #3134	12.00
CP514	Raoul Wallenberg, #3135	12.00
CP515	Dinosaurs, #3136	20.00
CP516	Bugs Bunny, #3137c	16.00
CP517	PACIFIC 97 Franklin, #3139	40.00
CP518	PACIFIC 97 Washington, #3140	40.00
CP519	Marshall Plan, #3141	10.00
CP520	Classic American Aircraft, #3142, 2 pages	27.50
CP521	Football Coaches, #3146a	17.50

CP522	American Dolls, #3151	25.00
CP523	Humphrey Bogart, #3152	14.00
CP524	"The Stars & Stripes Forever!," #3153	13.00
CP525	Opera Singers, #3157a	14.00
CP526	Composers & Conductors, #3165a	14.00
CP527	Padre Felix Varela, #3166	13.00
CP528	Department of the Air Force, #3167	13.50
CP529	Movie Monsters, #3172a	16.00
CP530	Supersonic Flight, #3173	16.00
CP531	Women in Military Service, #3174	13.00
CP532	Kwanzaa, #3175	14.00
CP533	Madonna & Child, #3176a	18.00
CP534	Holly, #3177a	18.00

1998

CP535	Chinese New Year, #3179	13.00
CP536	Alpine Skiing, #3180	13.00
CP537	Madam C.J. Walker, #3181	13.00

1998-2000

Celebrate the Century

CP537A	1900s, #3182, 2 pages	20.00
CP537B	1910s, #3183, 2 pages	20.00
CP537C	1920s, #3184, 2 pages	20.00
CP537D	1930s, #3185, 2 pages	20.00
CP537E	1940s, #3186, 2 pages	20.00
CP537F	1950s, #3187, 2 pages	20.00
CP537G	1960s, #3188, 2 pages	20.00
CP537H	1970s, #3189, 2 pages	20.00
CP537I	1980s, #3190, 2 pages	20.00
CP537J	1990s, #3191, 2 pages	20.00

1998

CP538	Remember the Maine, inscribed "Key West, Florida" #3192	13.00
	a. Inscribed "Scottsdale, Arizona."	20.00
CP539	Flowering Trees, #3197a	16.00
CP540	Alexander Calder, #3202a	16.00
CP541	Cinco de Mayo, #3203	13.00
CP542	Sylvester & Tweety, #3204c	17.00
CP543	Wisconsin Statehood, #3206	13.00
CP544	Trans-Mississippi, #3209-3210, 2 pages	20.00
CP545	Berlin Airlift, #3211	13.00
CP546	Folk Musicians, #3215a	14.00
CP547	Gospel Singers, #3219a	13.00
CP548	Spanish Settlement, #3220	14.00
CP549	Stephen Vincent Benét, #3221	13.00
CP550	Tropical Birds, #3225a	13.00
CP551	Alfred Hitchcock, #3226	13.00
CP552	Organ & Tissue Donation, #3227	13.50
CP553	Bright Eyes, #3234a	13.00
CP554	Klondike Gold Rush, #3235	13.00
CP555	American Art, #3236	20.00
CP556	American Ballet, #3237	13.00
CP557	Space Discovery, #3242a	13.50
CP558	Giving & Sharing, #3243	13.00
CP559	Madonna & Child, #3244a	18.00
CP560	Wreaths, #3252a	13.00
CP561	Breast Cancer Awareness, #B1	17.50

1999

CP562	Chinese New Year, #3272	15.00
CP563	Malcolm X, #3273	15.00
CP564	Love, #3274a	20.00
CP565	Love, #3275	15.00
CP566	Hospice Care, #3276	15.00
CP567	Irish Immigration, #3286	15.00
CP568	Lunt & Fontanne, #3287	15.00
CP569	Arctic Animals, #3292a	15.00
CP570	Sonoran Desert, #3293, 2 pages	22.50
CP571	Daffy Duck, #3306c	22.50
CP572	Ayn Rand, #3308	15.00
CP573	Cinco de Mayo, #3309	15.00
CP574	John & William Bartram, #3314	15.00
CP575	Prostate Cancer, #3315	15.00
CP576	California Gold Rush, #3316	15.00
CP577	Aquarium Fish, #3320a	15.00
CP578	Extreme Sports, #3324a	15.00
CP579	American Glass, #3328a	15.00
CP580	James Cagney, #3329	15.00
CP581	Honoring Those Who Served, #3331	15.00
CP582	Famous Trains, #3337a	16.00
CP583	Frederick Law Olmsted, #3338	15.00
CP584	Hollywood Composers, #3344a	16.00
CP585	Broadway Songwriters, #3350a	16.00
CP586	Insects & Spiders, #3351, 2 pages	22.50
CP587	Hanukkah, #3352	15.00
CP588	NATO, #3354	15.00
CP589	Madonna & Child, #3355	15.00
CP590	Deer, #3359a	15.00
CP591	Kwanzaa, #3368	15.00
CP592	Year 2000, #3369	16.00

2000

CP593	Chinese New Year, #3370	15.00
CP594	Patricia Roberts Harris, #3371	15.00
CP595	Los Angeles Class Submarine, #3372	10.00
CP596	Pacific Coast Rain Forest, #3378, 2 pages	25.00
CP597	Louise Nevelson, #3383a	10.00
CP598	Hubble Space Telescope Images, #3388a	10.00
CP599	American Samoa, #3389	10.00
CP600	Library of Congress, #3390	10.00
CP601	Road Runner & Wile E. Coyote, #3391c	10.00
CP602	Distinguished Soldiers, #3396a	10.00
CP603	Summer Sports, #3397	10.00
CP604	Adoption, #3398	10.00
CP605	Youth Team Sports, #3402a	10.00
CP606	The Stars and Stripes, #3403, 2 pages	25.00
CP607	Legends of Baseball, #3408, 2 pages	25.00
CP608	Stampin' the Future, #3417a	10.00
CP609	California Statehood, #3438	10.00
CP610	Deep Sea Creatures, #3443a	10.00
CP611	Thomas Wolfe, #3444	10.00

CP612	White House, #3445	10.00
CP613	Edward G. Robinson, #3446	10.00
CP614	Non-denominated Love Letters, #3496	12.00
CP615	34c Love, #3497	12.00
CP615A	55c Love, #3499	12.00
CP616	Chinese New Year, #3500	12.00
CP617	Roy Wilkins, #3501	12.00
CP618	Nine-Mile Prairie, #C136	12.00
CP618A	American Illustrators, #3502, 2 pages	30.00
CP619	Diabetes Awareness, #3503	16.00
CP620	Nobel Prize, #3504	12.00
CP621	Pan-American Inverts, #3505, 2 pages	30.00
CP622	Mt. McKinley, #C137	12.00
CP623	Great Plains Prairie, #3506, 2 pages	30.00

2001

CP624	Peanuts Comic Strip, #3507	12.00
CP625	Honoring Veterans, #3508	12.00
CP626	Frida Kahlo, #3509	12.00
CP627	Legendary Playing Fields, #3510-3519	30.00

No. CP627 consists of 2 pages. One has text and engraved illustrations. The other consists of the pane of stamps.

CP628	Leonard Bernstein, #3521	12.00
CP629	Lucille Ball, #3523	12.00
CP630	Amish Quilts, #3527a	12.00
CP631	Carnivorous Plants, #3531a	12.00
CP632	Eid, #3532	12.00
CP633	Enrico Fermi, #3533	12.00
CP634	That's All Folks!, #3535c	12.00
CP635	Madonna & Child, #3536	12.00
CP636	Santas, #3540b	12.00
CP637	James Madison, #3545	12.00
CP638	Thanksgiving, #3546	12.00
CP639	Hanukkah, #3547	12.00
CP640	Kwanzaa, #3548	12.00
CP641	57c Love, #3551	12.00
CP648	Greetings from America, #3610a	40.00
CP649	Longleaf Pine Forest, #3611	30.00

Nos. CP648 and CP649 each consist of 2 pages. One has text and engraved illustrations. The other contains the pane of stamps.

2002

CP642	Winter Olympics, #3555a	12.00
CP643	Mentoring a Child, #3556	12.00
CP644	Langston Hughes, #3557	12.00
CP645	Happy Birthday, #3558	12.00
CP646	Chinese New Year, #3559	12.00
CP647	U.S. Military Academy Bicentennial, #3560	12.00
CP650	Heroes of 2001, #B2	12.00
CP651	Masters of American Photography, #3649	30.00

No. CP651 consists of 2 pages. One has text and engraved illustrations. The other consists of the pane of stamps.

CP652	John James Audubon, #3650	12.00
CP653	Harry Houdini, #3651	12.00
CP654	Andy Warhol, #3652	12.00
CP655	Teddy Bears, #3653-3656	12.00
CP656	37c Love, #3657	12.00
CP657	60c Love, #3658	12.00
CP658	Ogden Nash, #3659	12.00
CP659	Duke Kahanamoku, #3660	12.00
CP660	American Bats, #3664a	12.00
CP661	Women in Journalism, #3668a	12.00
CP662	Irving Berlin, #3669	12.00
CP663	Neuter or Spay, #3671a	12.00
CP664	Hanukkah, #3672	12.00
CP665	Kwanzaa, #3673	12.00
CP666	Eid, #3674	12.00
CP667	Madonna & Child, #3675	12.00
CP668	Christmas Snowmen, #3679a	12.00
CP669	Cary Grant, #3692	12.00
CP670	Hawaiian Missionary Stamps, #3694	30.00

No. CP670 consists of 2 pages. One has text and engraved illustrations. The other contains the pane of stamps.

CP671	Happy Birthday, #3695	12.00
CP672	Greetings from America, #3745a	42.50

No. CP672 consists of 2 pages. One has text and engraved illustrations. The other contains the pane of stamps.

2003

CP673	Thurgood Marshall, #3746	12.00
CP674	Chinese New Year, #3747	12.00
CP675	Zora Neale Hurston, #3748	12.00
CP676	Special Olympics, #3771	12.00
CP677	American Filmmaking: Behind the Scenes, #3772	30.00

No. CP677 consists of 2 pages. One has text and engraved illustrations. The other contains the pane of stamps.

CP678	Ohio Statehood, Bicent., #3773	12.00
CP679	Pelican Island National Wildlife Refuge, #3774	12.00
CP680	Old Glory, #3780b	12.00
CP681	Cesar E. Chavez, #3781	12.00
CP682	Louisiana Purchase, #3782	12.00
CP683	First Flight of Wright Brothers, #3783b	12.00
CP684	Audrey Hepburn, #3786	12.00
CP685	Southeastern Lighthouses, #3791a	12.00
CP686	Arctic Tundra, #3802	30.00
CP687	Korean War Veterans Memorial, #3803	12.00
CP688	Mary Cassatt Paintings, #3807a	12.00
CP689	Early Football Heroes, #3811a	12.00
CP690	Roy Acuff, #3812	12.00

CP691	District of Columbia, #3813	
CP692	Reptiles and Amphibians, #3818a	
CP693	Stop Family Violence, #B3	
CP694	Madonna and Child, #3820	
CP695	Christmas Holiday Music Makers, #3824a	

2004

CP696	Pacific Coral Reef, #3831	

No. CP696 consists of 2 pages. One has text and engraved illustrations. The other contains the pane of stamps.

CP697	Chinese New Year, #3832	
CP698	Love, #3833	
CP699	Paul Robeson, #3834	
CP700	Theodor Seuss Geisel (Dr. Seuss), #3835	
CP701	Love (White Lilacs and Pink Roses), #3836	
CP702	Love (Five Varieties of Pink Roses), #3837	
CP703	U.S. Air Force Academy, #3838	
CP704	Henry Mancini, #3839	
CP705	American Choreographers, #3843a	
CP706	Lewis and Clark, #3854	
CP707	Lewis and Clark booklet pane, #3856b	
CP708	Isamu Noguchi, #3861a	
CP709	National World War II Memorial, #3862	
CP710	Summer Olympics, Athens, Greece, #3863	
CP711	Art of Disney, #3868a	
CP712	USS Constellation, #3869	
CP713	R. Buckminster Fuller, #3870	
CP714	James Baldwin, #3871	
CP715	Martin Johnson Heade, #3872	
CP716	Art of the American Indian, #3873	

No. CP716 consists of 2 pages. One has text and engraved illustrations. The other contains the pane of stamps.

CP717	John Wayne, #3876	
CP718	Sickle Cell Disease, #3877	
CP719	Cloudscapes, #3878	

No. CP719 consists of 2 pages. One has text and engraved illustrations. The other contains the pane of stamps.

CP720	Christmas Madonna, #3879	
CP722	Kwanzaa, #3881	
CP723	Moss Hart, #3882	
CP724	Christmas Ornaments, #3886a	

2005

CP725	Chinese New Year, #3895	

No. CP725 consists of two pages. One has text and engraved illustrations. The other contains the pane of stamps.

CP726	Marian Anderson, #3896	
CP727	Ronald Reagan, #3897	
CP728	Love, #3898	
CP729	Northeast Deciduous Forest, #3899	

No. CP729 consists of 2 pages. One has text and engraved illustrations. The other contains the pane of stamps.

CP730	Spring Flowers, #3903a	
CP731	Robert Penn Warren, #3904	
CP732	Yip Harburg, #3905	
CP733	American Scientists, #3909a	
CP734	Modern American Architecture, #3910	

No. CP734 consists of two pages. One has text and engraved illustrations. The other contains the pane of stamps.

CP735	Henry Fonda, #3911	
CP736	Disney Characters, #3915a	
CP737	Advances in Aviation, #3916-3925	

No. CP737 consists of two pages. One has text and illustrations. The other contains the pane of stamps.

CP738	Rio Grande Blankets, #3929a	
CP739	Presidential Libraries, #3930	
CP740	Sporty Cars of the 1950s, #3935b	
CP741	Arthur Ashe, #3936	
CP742	To Form a More Perfect Union, #3937	

No. CP742 consists of two pages. One has text and illustrations. The other contains the pane of stamps.

CP743	Child Health, #3938	
CP744	Let's Dance, #3942a	
CP745	Greta Garbo, #3943	
CP746	Jim Henson and the Muppets, #3944	

No. CP746 consists of two pages. One has text and engraved illustrations. The other contains the pane of stamps.

CP747	Constellations, #3948a	
CP748	Christmas, #3952a	
CP749	Distinguished Marines, #3964a	

2006

CP750	Love, #3976	
CP751	Children's Book Animals, #3994a	

No. CP751 consists of two pages. One has text and illustrations. The other contains the pane of stamps.

CP752	2006 Winter Olympics, #3995	
CP753	Hattie McDaniel, #3996	

SOUVENIR PAGES

hese are post office new-issue announcement bulletins, including an illustration of the stamp's design and informative text. They bear a copy of the
p, tied by a first day of issue cancellation. Varieties of bulletin watermarks and text changes, etc., are beyond the scope of this catalogue.
lues for Scott Nos. SP1-SP295 are for folded copies. Values for Official Souvenir Pages (Nos. SP296 on) are for copies that never have been
ed.

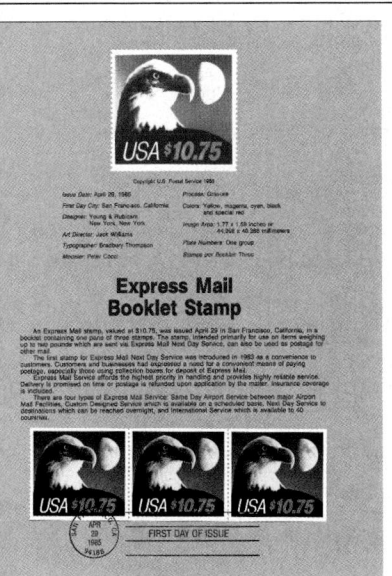

No. SP674a

UNOFFICIAL SOUVENIR PAGES
Liberty Issue

0-65		
	1¼c Palace of Governors, sheet, coil, #1031A, 1054A	50.00
	8c Pershing, #1042A	30.00
	11c Statue of Liberty, #1044A	27.50
	25c Revere coil, #1059A	6.00
9		
	4c 49 Star Flag, #1132	—
	7c Hawaii Statehood, #C55	—
	4c Soil Conservation, #1133	—
	10c Pan American Games, #C56	—
	4c Petroleum, #1134	—
0	4c Dental Health, #1135	—
1	4c, 8c Reuter, #1136, 1137	—
2	4c McDowell, #1138	—
0-61		
3	4c Washington Credo, #1139	75.00
4	4c Franklin Credo, #1140	75.00
5	4c Jefferson Credo, #1141	75.00
6	4c F.S. Key Credo, #1142	75.00
7	4c Lincoln Credo, #1143	65.00
8	4c P. Henry Credo, #1144	35.00
1		
9	4c Boy Scout, #1145	75.00
0	4c Winter Olympics, #1146	75.00
1	4c, 8c Masaryk, #1147, 1148	75.00
2	4c Refugee Year, #1149	35.00
3	4c Water Consevation, #1150	20.00
4	4c SEATO, #1151	20.00
5	4c American Women, #1152	20.00
6	10c Liberty Bell, #C57	—
7	15c Statue of Liberty, #C58	—
8	25c Lincoln, #C59	—
9	4c 50 Star Flag, #1153	50.00
0	4c Pony Express, #1154	50.00
1	7c Jet, carmine, #C60	12.50
2	7c Booklet pane of 6, #C60a	30.00
3	7c Jet coil, #C61	17.50
4	4c Handicapped, #1155	50.00
5	4c Forestry Congress, #1156	50.00
6	4c Mexican Independence, #1157	35.00
7	4c U.S., Japan Treaty, #1158	20.00
8	4c, 8c Paderewski, #1159-1160	37.50
9	4c Sen. Taft, #1161	45.00
0	4c Wheels of Freedom, #1162	45.00
1	4c Boys' Clubs, #1163	45.00
2	4c Automated Post Office, #1164	45.00
3	4c, 8c Mannerheim, #1165-1166	45.00
4	4c Camp Fire Girls, #1167	45.00
5	4c, 8c Garibaldi, #1168-1169	45.00
6	4c Sen. George, #1170	45.00
7	4c Carnegie, #1171	45.00
8	4c Dulles, #1172	45.00
9	4c Echo I, #1173	20.00
1		
0	4c, 8c Gandhi, #1174-1175	20.00
1	4c Range Conservation, #1176	20.00
2	4c Greeley, #1177	20.00

1961-65		
SP53	4c Ft. Sumter, #1178	20.00
SP54	4c Shiloh, #1179	27.50
SP55	5c Gettysburg, #1180	6.00
SP56	5c Wilderness, #1181	6.50
SP57	5c Appomattox, #1182	6.50
1961		
SP58	4c Kansas, #1183	12.00
SP59	13c Liberty Bell, #C62	20.00
SP60	4c Sen. Norris, #1184	11.50
SP61	4c Naval Aviation, #1185	20.00
SP62	4c Workmen's Compensation, #1186	20.00
SP63	4c Remington, #1187	12.00
SP64	4c Sun Yat sen, #1188	20.00
SP65	4c Basketball, #1189	20.00
SP66	4c Nursing, #1190	15.00
1962		
SP67	4c New Mexico, #1191	12.50
SP68	4c Arizona, #1192	12.50
SP69	4c Project Mercury, #1193	10.00
SP70	4c Malaria, #1194	12.50
SP71	4c Hughes, #1195	21.00
SP72	4c Seattle World's Fair, #1196	17.50
SP73	4c Louisiana, #1197	17.50
SP74	4c Homestead Act, #1198	17.50
SP75	4c Girl Scouts, #1199	20.00
SP76	4c McMahon, #1200	17.50
SP77	4c Apprenticeship, #1201	17.50
SP78	4c Rayburn, #1202	17.50
SP79	4c Hammarskjold, #1203	17.50
SP80	4c Hammarskjold, yellow inverted, #1204	40.00
SP81	4c Christmas, #1205	50.00
SP82	4c Higher Education, #1206	10.00
SP83	8c Capitol, #C64	9.00
SP83a	8c Capitol sheet, booklet, coil, #C64, C64b, C65	20.00
SP84	8c Capitol, tagged, #C64a	30.00
SP85	8c Capitol booklet single, #C64b	25.00
SP86	8c Capitol coil, #C65	15.00
SP87	4c Winslow Homer, #1207	15.00
SP88	5c Flag, #1208	12.50
SP89	1c Jackson, #1209	12.50
SP90	5c Washington, #1213	17.50
SP91	5c Washington booklet pane of 5 + label, #1213a	30.00
SP92	1c Jackson coil, #1225	17.50
SP93	5c Washington coil, #1229	17.50
SP94	15c Montgomery Blair, #C66	—
1963		
SP96	5c Food for Peace, #1231	7.00
SP97	5c West Virginia, #1232	6.00
SP97A	6c Eagle, #C67	8.50
SP97B	8c Amelia Earhart, #C68	18.00
SP98	5c Emancipation Proclamation, #1233	12.50
SP99	5c Alliance for Progress, #1234	7.50
SP100	5c Cordell Hull, #1235	7.50
SP101	5c Eleanor Roosevelt, #1236	6.25
SP102	5c Science, #1237	6.00
SP103	5c City Mail Delivery, #1238	7.50
SP104	5c Red Cross, #1239	6.00
SP105	5c Christmas, #1240	7.50
SP106	5c Audubon, #1241	8.00
1964		
SP107	5c Sam Houston, #1242	12.00
SP108	5c C.M. Russell, #1243	9.00
SP109	5c N.Y. World's Fair, #1244	7.50
SP110	5c John Muir, #1245	12.00
SP111	5c Kennedy (Boston, Mass.) (At least 4 other cities known), #1246	12.50
SP112	5c New Jersey, #1247	7.50
SP113	5c Nevada, #1248	7.50
SP114	5c Register and Vote, #1249	7.50
SP115	5c Shakespeare, #1250	7.50
SP116	5c Mayo Brothers, #1251	8.50
SP117	8c Goddard, #C69	5.00
SP118	5c Music, #1252	7.50
SP119	5c Homemakers, #1253	7.50
SP120	5c Christmas Plants, #1257b	17.50
SP121	5c Christmas, tagged, #1257c	90.00
SP122	5c Verrazano Narrows Bridge, #1258	7.50
SP123	5c Fine Arts, #1259	7.50
SP124	5c Amateur Radio, #1260	7.00
1965		
SP125	5c New Orleans, #1261	6.00
SP126	5c Sokols, #1262	6.75
SP127	5c Cancer, #1263	6.00
SP128	5c Churchill, #1264	7.50
SP129	5c Magna Carta, #1265	6.00
SP130	5c I.C.Y., #1266	6.00
SP131	5c Salvation Army, #1267	6.50
SP132	5c Dante, #1268	6.00
SP133	5c Hoover, #1269	6.00
SP134	5c Fulton, #1270	6.00
SP135	5c Florida, #1271	7.50
SP136	5c Traffic Safety, #1272	6.00
SP137	5c Copley, #1273	7.50
SP138	11c I.T.U., #1274	7.50

SP139	5c Stevenson, #1275	6.00
SP140	5c Christmas, #1276	7.50
	Prominent Americans	
1965-73		
SP141	1c Jefferson, #1278	7.50
SP141a	1c Jefferson sheet, booklet, coil, #1278, 1278a 1299	7.00
SP142	1c Jefferson booklet pane of 8, #1278a	8.25
SP143	1¼c Gallatin, #1279	7.50
SP144	2c Wright, #1280	5.25
SP145	2c Wright booklet pane of 5 + label, #1280a	9.50
SP146	3c Parkman, #1281	7.50
SP147	4c Lincoln, #1282	6.00
SP148	5c Washington, #1283	6.00
SP149	5c Washington, redrawn, #1283B	6.50
SP150	6c Roosevelt, #1284	6.00
SP151	6c Roosevelt booklet pane of 8, #1284b	13.00
SP151a	6c Roosevelt booklet, vert. coil, #1284b, 1298	5.00
SP151b	6c Roosevelt booklet, horiz. coil, #1284b, 1305	5.00
SP152	8c Einstein, #1285	10.00
SP153	10c Jackson, #1286	6.00
SP154	12c Ford, #1286A	9.00
SP155	13c Kennedy, #1287	20.00
SP156	15c Holmes, #1288	7.50
SP157	20c Marshall, #1289	9.00
SP158	25c Douglass, #1290	9.00
SP159	30c Dewey, #1291	30.00
SP160	40c Paine, #1292	40.00
SP161	50c Stone, #1293	35.00
SP162	$1 O'Neill, #1294	55.00
SP163	$5 Moore, #1295	125.00
SP164	6c Roosevelt, vert. coil, #1298	5.25
SP165	1c Jefferson, coil, #1299	5.75
SP166	4c Lincoln, coil, #1303	7.50
SP167	5c Washington, coil, #1304	7.00
SP168	6c Roosevelt, horiz. coil, #1305	6.50

Nos. 1297, 1305C and 1305E are known on unofficial pages.
They are not listed here. For official pages of these issues, see
Nos. SP296-SP298.

1966		
SP169	5c Migratory Bird Treaty, #1306	7.00
SP170	5c ASPCA, #1307	7.00
SP171	5c Indiana, #1308	7.00
SP172	5c Circus, #1309	6.00
SP173	5c SIPEX, #1310	7.00
SP174	5c SIPEX Souvenir Sheet, #1311	7.25
SP175	5c Bill of Rights, #1312	7.50
SP176	5c Poland, #1313	7.50
SP177	5c National Park Service, #1314	7.50
SP178	5c Marine Corps Reserve, #1315	7.50
SP179	5c Women's Clubs, #1316	7.50
SP180	5c Johnny Appleseed, #1317	7.50
SP181	5c Beautifcation of America, #1318	7.50
SP182	5c Great River Road, #1319	7.50
SP183	5c Savings Bonds Servicemen, #1320	7.50
SP184	5c Christmas, #1321	6.00
SP185	5c Mary Cassatt, #1322	6.00
1967		
SP186	8c Alaska, #C70	10.00
SP187	5c Grange, #1323	6.00
SP188	20c Audubon, #C71	4.00
SP189	5c Canada, #1324	5.25
SP190	5c Erie Canal, #1325	5.25
SP191	5c Search for Peace, #1326	6.50
SP192	5c Thoreau, #1327	5.50
SP193	5c Nebraska, #1328	5.25
SP194	5c VOA, #1329	5.25
SP195	5c Crockett, #1330	7.00
SP196	5c Space, #1332b	21.00
SP197	5c Urban Planning, #1333	5.25
SP198	5c Finland, #1334	6.00
SP199	5c Eakins, #1335	6.00
SP200	5c Christmas, #1336	7.00
SP201	5c Mississippi, #1337	5.50
1968-71		
SP202	6c Flags, Giori Press, #1338	6.00
SP203	6c Flag, Huck Press, #1338D	5.00
SP204	8c Flag, #1338F	5.50
SP205	6c Flag coil, #1338A	5.75
1968		
SP206	10c 50 star Runway, #C72	5.00
SP207	10c sheet, coil, booklet pane of 8, #C72, C72b, C73	25.00
SP207a	10c sheet, booklet single, coil, #C72, C72b, C73	7.00
SP208	10c 50 star Runway coil, #C73	9.00
SP209	6c Illinois, #1339	5.50
SP210	6c HemisFair, #1340	7.50
SP211	$1 Airlift, #1341	60.00
SP212	6c Youth, #1342	6.00
SP213	10c Air Mail Service, #C74	7.25
SP214	6c Law and Order, #1343	6.00

SP215	6c	Register and Vote, #1344	6.00
SP216	6c	Historic Flags, #1345-1354	70.00
SP217	6c	Disney, #1355	10.00
SP218	6c	Marquette, #1356	7.50
SP219	6c	Daniel Boone, #1357	7.50
SP220	6c	Arkansas River Navigation, #1358	7.50
SP221	6c	Leif Erikson, #1359	15.00
SP222	6c	Cherokee Strip, #1360	7.50
SP223	6c	John Trumbull, #1361	6.00
SP224	6c	Waterfowl, #1362	7.50
SP225	6c	Christmas, #1363	7.50
SP226	6c	Chief Joseph, #1364	6.00
SP227	20c	USA, #C75	5.00

1969

SP228	6c	Beautification, #1368a	18.00
SP229	6c	American Legion, #1369	7.50
SP230	6c	Grandma Moses, #1370	6.00
SP231	6c	Apollo 8, #1371	15.00
SP232	6c	W.C. Handy, #1372	10.00
SP233	6c	California, #1373	6.00
SP234	6c	Powell, #1374	6.00
SP235	6c	Alabama, #1375	7.50
SP236	6c	Botanical Congress, #1379a	20.00
SP237	10c	Man on the Moon, #C76	14.00
SP238	6c	Dartmouth, #1380	7.50
SP239	6c	Baseball, #1381	40.00
SP240	6c	Football, #1382	10.00
SP241	6c	Eisenhower, #1383	6.00
SP242	6c	Christmas, #1384	7.50
SP243	6c	Hope, #1385	6.00
SP244	45c	Special Delivery, #E22	25.00
SP245	6c	Harnett, #1386	6.00

1970

SP246	6c	Natural History, #1390a	30.00
SP247	6c	Maine, #1391	7.50
SP248	6c	Wildlife Conservation, #1392	7.50

Regular Issue

1970-71

SP249	6c	Eisenhower, #1393	6.00
SP249a	6c	sheet, booklet, coil stamps, #1393, 1393a, 1401	7.00
SP249b	6c	sheet, coil stamps, #1393, 1401	6.00
SP250	6c	Eisenhower booklet pane of 8, #1393a	12.50
SP250a	6c	booklet, coil, #1393a, 1401	6.00
SP251	6c	Eisenhower booklet pane of 5 + label, #1393b	6.00
SP252	8c	Eisenhower, #1394	6.00
SP252a	8c	sheet, booklet, coil, #1394-1395, 1402	6.00
SP253	8c	Eisenhower booklet pane of 8, #1395a	15.00
SP254	8c	Eisenhower booklet pane of 8, #1395b	15.00
SP255	8c	U.S.P.S., #1396	10.00
SP256	16c	Pyle, #1398	6.00
SP257	6c	Eisenhower coil, #1401	6.00
SP258	8c	Eisenhower coil, #1402	5.00

1970

SP259	6c	Masters, #1405	7.50
SP260	6c	Suffrage, #1406	6.00
SP261	6c	So. Carolina, #1407	6.00
SP262	6c	Stone Mountain, #1408	6.00
SP263	6c	Ft. Snelling, #1409	6.00
SP264	6c	Anti pollution, #1413a	20.00
SP265	6c	Christmas Nativity, #1414	13.00
SP266	6c	Christmas Toys, #1418b	6.75
SP267	6c	Toys, precanceled, #1418c	35.00
SP268	6c	U.N., #1419	9.00
SP269	6c	Mayflower, #1420	7.50
SP270	6c	DAV, Servicemen, #1422a	27.50

1971

SP271	6c	Wool, #1423	7.50
SP272	6c	MacArthur, #1424	7.50
SP273	6c	Blood Donors, #1425	7.50
SP274	8c	Missouri, #1426	7.50
SP275	9c	Delta Wing, #C77	5.00
SP276	11c	Jet, #C78	3.50
SP276a	11c	sheet, booklet, coil, #C78, C78a, C82	5.00
SP277	11c	Jet booklet pane, #C78a	12.00
SP278	60c	Special Delivery, #E23	24.00
SP279	8c	Wildlife, #1430a	12.50
SP280	8c	Antarctic Treaty, #1431	10.00
SP281	8c	Bicentennial Emblem, #1432	12.50
SP282	17c	Statue of Liberty, #C80	15.00
SP283	21c	USA, #C81	20.00
SP284	11c	Jet coil, #C82	3.25
SP285	8c	Sloan, #1433	10.00
SP286	8c	Space, #1435b	15.00
SP287	8c	Dickenson, #1436	10.00
SP288	8c	San Juan, #1437	10.00
SP289	8c	Drug Abuse, #1438	10.00
SP290	8c	CARE, #1439	10.00
SP291	8c	Historic Preservation, #1443a	12.50
SP292	8c	Adoration, #1444	10.00
SP293	8c	Patridge, #1445	10.00

1972

SP294	8c	Lanier, #1446	10.00
SP295	8c	Peace Corps, #1447	10.00

OFFICIAL SOUVENIR PAGES

In 1972 the USPS began issuing "official" Souvenir pages by subscription. A few more "unofficials" were produced.

Prominent Americans

1970-78

SP296	3c	Parkman, coil, #1297	2.50
SP297	$1	O'Neill, coil, #1305C	10.00
SP298	15c	Holmes, coil, #1305E	3.50
SP299	7c	Franklin, #1393D	4.75

SP300	14c	LaGuardia, #1397	65.00
SP301	18c	Blackwell, #1399	2.00
SP302	21c	Giannini, #1400	3.50

1972

SP303	2c	Cape Hatteras, #1451a	65.00
SP304	6c	Wolf Trap Farm, #1452	22.50
SP305	8c	Yellowstone, #1453	80.00
SP306	11c	City of Refuge, #C84	70.00
SP307	15c	Mt. McKinley, #1454	17.50
SP308	8c	Family Planning, #1455	400.00

Unofficials exist, value $150.

SP309	8c	Colonial Craftsmen, #1459a	12.50
SP310		Olympics, #1460-1462, C85	9.00
SP311	8c	PTA, #1463	4.50
SP312	8c	Wildlife, #1467a	6.00
SP313	8c	Mail Order, #1468	4.50
SP314	8c	Osteopathic, #1469	4.50
SP315	8c	Tom Sawyer, #1470	6.00
SP316	8c	Christmas, #1471-1472	5.50
SP317	8c	Pharmacy, #1473	6.00
SP318	8c	Stamp Collecting, #1474	4.50

1973

SP319	8c	Love, #1475	5.50
SP320	8c	Printing, #1476	3.50
SP321	8c	Broadside, #1477	4.50
SP322	8c	Postrider, #1478	4.50
SP323	8c	Drummer, #1479	3.25
SP324	8c	Tea Party, #1483a	4.75
SP325	8c	Gershwin, #1484	4.50
SP326	8c	Jeffers, #1485	3.50
SP327	8c	Tanner, #1486	4.00
SP328	8c	Cather, #1487	3.25
SP329	8c	Copernicus, #1488	4.25
SP330	8c	Postal People, #1489-1498	4.75
SP331	8c	Truman, #1499	3.75
SP332		Electronics, #1500-1502, C86	5.75
SP333	8c	L.B. Johnson, #1503	2.75

1973-74

SP334	8c	Cattle, #1504	2.75
SP335	10c	Chautauqua, #1505	2.50
SP336	10c	Kansas Winter Wheat, #1506	1.90

1973

SP337	8c	Christmas, #1507	5.00

Regular Issues

1973-74

SP338	10c	Crossed Flags, #1509	2.25
SP339	10c	Jefferson Memorial, #1510	2.25
SP340	10c	ZIP, #1511	3.25
SP341	6.3c	Liberty Bell coil, #1518	2.25
SP341A	13c	Winged Envelope, #C79	2.00
SP341B	13c	Airmail, coil, #C83	2.50

1974

SP342	18c	Statue of Liberty, #C87	4.50
SP343	26c	Mt. Rushmore, #C88	4.00
SP344	10c	VFW, #1525	2.50
SP345	10c	Robert Frost, #1526	3.50
SP346	10c	EXPO '74, #1527	4.00
SP347	10c	Horse Racing, #1528	4.00
SP348	10c	Skylab, #1529	4.50
SP349	10c	UPU, #1537a	4.75
SP350	10c	Minerals, #1541a	4.75
SP351	10c	Ft. Harrod, #1542	2.25
SP352	10c	Continental Congress, #1546a	3.50
SP353	10c	Energy, #1547	2.00
SP354	10c	Sleepy Hollow, #1548	3.00
SP355	10c	Retarded Children, #1549	2.00
SP356	10c	Christmas, #1550-1552	4.25

1975

SP357	10c	Benjamin West, #1553	2.25
SP358	10c	Dunbar, #1554	3.00
SP359	10c	D.W. Griffith, #1555	2.50
SP360	10c	Pioneer, #1556	5.00
SP361	10c	Mariner, #1557	4.25
SP362	10c	Collective Bargaining, #1558	2.25
SP363	8c	Sybil Ludington, #1559	2.25
SP364	10c	Salem Poor, #1560	3.00
SP365	10c	Haym Salomon, #1561	2.25
SP366	15c	Peter Francisco, #1562	2.25
SP367	10c	Lexington & Concord, #1563	2.50
SP368	10c	Bunker Hill, #1564	2.50
SP369	10c	Military Uniforms, #1568a	5.00
SP370	10c	Apollo Soyuz, #1570a	5.00
SP371	10c	Women's Year, #1571	2.00
SP372	10c	Postal Service, #1575	3.00
SP373	10c	Peace through Law, #1576	2.00
SP374	10c	Banking and Commerce, #1578a	3.00
SP375	10c	Christmas, #1579-1580	3.00

Americana Issue

1975-81

SP376	1c, 2c, 3c, 4c	Americana, #1581-1585	2.00
SP377	9c	Capitol Dome, #1591	2.25
SP378	10c	Justice, #1592	2.25
SP379	11c	Printing Press, #1593	1.75
SP380	12c	Torch sheet, coil, #1594, 1816	2.25
SP381	13c	Eagle and Shield, #1596	2.50
SP382	15c	Flag sheet, coil, #1597, 1618C	2.00
SP383	16c	Statue of Liberty sheet, coil, #1599, 1619	1.90
SP384	24c	Old North Church, #1603	1.90
SP385	28c	Ft. Nisqually, #1604	2.00
SP386	29c	Lighthouse, #1605	1.90
SP387	30c	Schoolhouse, #1606	2.50

SP388	50c	"Betty" Lamp, #1608	
SP389	$1	Candle Holder, #1610	
SP390	$2	Kerosene Lamp, #1611	
SP391	$5	R. R. Lantern, #1612	
SP392	1c	Inkwell, coil, #1811	
SP393	3.1c	Guitar, coil, #1613	
SP394	3.5c	Violin, coil, #1813	
SP395	7.7c	Saxhorns, coil, #1614	
SP396	7.9c	Drum, coil, #1615	
SP397	8.4c	Piano, coil, #1615C	
SP398	9c	Capitol Dome, coil, #1616	
SP398A	10c	Justice, coil, #1617	
SP399	13c	Liberty Bell, coil, #1618	
SP400	13c	13 star Flag sheet, coil, #1622, 1625	
SP401	9c, 13c	Booklet pane, perf. 10, #1623Bc	

1976

SP402	13c	Spririt of '76, #1631a	
SP403	25c, 31c	Plane and Globes, #C89-C90	
SP404	13c	Interphil 76, #1632	
SP405	13c	State Flags, #1633-1642	
SP406	13c	State Flags, #1643-1652	
SP407	13c	State Flags, #1653-1662	
SP408	13c	State Flags, #1663-1672	
SP409	13c	State Flags, #1673-1682	
SP410	13c	Telephone, #1683	
SP411	13c	Aviation, #1684	
SP412	13c	Chemistry, #1685	
SP413	13c	Bicentennial Souvenir Sheet, #1686	
SP414	18c	Bicentennial Souvenir Sheet, #1687	
SP415	24c	Bicentennial Souvenir Sheet, #1688	
SP416	31c	Bicentennial Souvenir Sheet, #1689	
SP417	13c	Franklin, #1690	
SP418	13c	Declaration of Independence, #1694a	
SP419	13c	Olympics, #1698a	
SP420	13c	Clara Maass, #1699	
SP421	13c	Adolph Ochs, #1700	
SP422	13c	Christmas, #1701-1703	

1977

SP423	13c	Washington at Princeton, #1704	
SP424	13c	Sound Recording, #1705	
SP425	13c	Pueblo Pottery, #1709a	
SP426	13c	Lindbergh Flight, #1710	
SP427	13c	Colorado, #1711	
SP428	13c	Butterflies, #1715a	
SP429	13c	Lafayette, #1716	
SP430	13c	Skilled Hands, #1720a	
SP431	13c	Peace Bridge, #1721	
SP432	13c	Oriskany, #1722	
SP433	13c	Energy, #1724a	
SP434	13c	Alta California, #1725	
SP435	13c	Articles of Confederation, #1726	
SP436	13c	Talking Pictures, #1727	
SP437	13c	Saratoga, #1728	
SP438	13c	Christmas, #1729-1730	

1978

SP439	13c	Sandburg, #1731	
SP440	13c	Capt. Cook, #1732, 1733	
SP441	13c	Indian Head Penny, #1734	
SP442	15c	A Sheet, coil, #1735, 1743	
SP443	15c	Roses booklet single, #1737	
SP444	15c	Windmills booklet pane of 10, #1742a	
SP445	13c	Tubman, #1744	
SP446	13c	Quilts, #1748a	
SP447	13c	American Dance, #1752a	
SP448	13c	French Alliance, #1753	
SP449	13c	Cancer Detection, #1754	
SP450	13c	Jimmie Rodgers, #1755	
SP451	15c	George M. Cohan, #1756	
SP452	13c	CAPEX '78 Souvenir Sheet, #1757	
SP453	15c	Photography, #1758	
SP454	15c	Viking Missions, #1759	
SP455	15c	Owls, #1763a	
SP456	31c	Wright Brothers, #C92a	
SP457	15c	Trees, #1767a	
SP458	15c	Madonna and Child, #1768	
SP459	15c	Hobby Horse, #1769	

1979

SP460	15c	Robert F. Kennedy, #1770	
SP461	15c	Martin Luther King Jr., #1771	
SP462	15c	Year of the Child, #1772	
SP463	15c	John Steinbeck, #1773	
SP464	15c	Einstein, #1774	
SP465	21c	Chanute, #C94a	
SP466	15c	Toleware, #1778a	
SP467	15c	Architecture, #1782a	
SP468	15c	Endangered Flora, #1786a	
SP469	15c	Seeing Eye Dogs, #1787	
SP470	15c	Special Olympics, #1788	
SP471	15c	John Paul Jones, #1789	
SP472	10c	Olympics, #1790	
SP473	15c	Olympics, #1794a	
SP474	31c	Olympics, #C97	

1980

SP475	15c	Winter Olympics, #1798a	

1979

SP476	15c	Madonna and Child, #1799	
SP477	15c	Santa Claus, #1800	
SP478	15c	Will Rogers, #1801	
SP479	15c	Vietnam Veterans, #1802	
SP480	25c	Wiley Post, #C96a	

1980

SP480		
SP481	15c W.C. Fields, #1803	2.75
SP482	15c Benjamin Banneker, #1804	2.75
SP483	15c Letter Writing Week, #1805-1810	2.00
SP484	18c B sheet, coil, 1818, 1820	2.00
SP485	18c B booklet pane of 8, #1819a	2.00
SP486	15c Frances Perkins, #1821	1.50
SP487	15c Dolley Madison, #1822	2.25
SP488	15c Emily Bissell, #1823	1.90
SP489	15c Helen Keller, #1824	1.75
SP490	15c Veterans Administration, #1825	1.50
SP491	15c Galvez, #1826	1.75
SP492	15c Coral Reefs, #1830a	2.75
SP493	15c Organized Labor, #1831	2.25
SP494	15c Edith Wharton, #1832	2.25
SP495	15c Education, #1833	2.25
SP496	15c Indian Masks, #1837a	2.50
SP497	15c Architecture, #1841a	2.00
SP498	40c Mazzei, #C98	2.00
SP499	15c Christmas Window, #1842	2.00
SP500	15c Christmas Toys, #1843	2.25
SP501	28c Blanche Stuart Scott, #C99	1.60
SP502	35c Curtiss, #C100	1.60

Great Americans

1980-85

SP503	1c Dix, #1844	2.25
SP504	2c Stravinsky, #1845	2.00
SP505	3c Clay, #1846	1.50
SP506	4c Schurz, #1847	1.50
SP507	5c Buck, #1848	1.50
SP508	6c Lippmann, #1849	1.50
SP509	7c Baldwin, #1850	1.75
SP510	8c Knox, #1851	1.50
SP511	9c Thayer, #1852	1.75
SP512	10c Russell, #1853	1.50
SP513	11c Partridge, #1854	1.50
SP514	13c Crazy Horse, #1855	1.75
SP515	14c Lewis, #1856	1.50
SP516	17c Carson, #1857	1.50
SP517	18c Mason, #1858	1.50
SP518	19c Sequoyah, #1859	1.50
SP519	20c Bunche, #1860	4.00
SP520	20c Gallaudet, #1861	1.75
SP521	20c Truman, #1862	1.50
SP522	22c Audubon, #1863	1.75
SP523	30c Laubach, #1864	1.50
SP524	35c Drew, #1865	1.75
SP525	37c Millikan, #1866	1.50
SP526	39c Clark, #1867	1.50
SP527	40c Gilbreth, #1868	1.50
SP528	50c Nimitz, #1869	1.75

1981

SP529	15c Dirksen, #1874	1.50
SP530	15c Young, #1875	2.75
SP531	18c Flowers, #1879a	2.00
SP532	18c Animals, #1889a	3.50
SP533	18c Flag sheet, coil, #1890-1891	2.00
SP534	6c, 18c Booklet pane, #1893a	2.00
SP535	20c Flag sheet, coil, #1894-1895	3.00
SP536	20c Flag booklet pane of 6, #1896a	2.50

1982

SP537	20c Flag booklet pane of 10, #1896b	2.50

Transportation Coils

1981-84

SP538	1c Omnibus, #1897	1.75
SP539	2c Locomotive, #1897A	2.25
SP540	3c Handcar, #1898	2.00
SP541	4c Stagecoach, #1898A	2.50
SP542	5c Motorcycle, #1899	3.75
SP543	5.2c Sleigh, #1900	2.75
SP544	5.9c Bicycle, #1901	4.75
SP545	7.4c Baby Buggy, #1902	2.50
SP546	9.3c Mail Wagon, #1903	2.50
SP547	10.9c Hansom Cab, #1904	2.75
SP548	11c Caboose, #1905	2.25
SP549	17c Electric Auto, #1906	1.75
SP550	18c Surrey, #1907	1.75
SP551	20c Fire Pumper, #1908	3.25

1983

SP552	$9.35 Express Mail single, #1909	75.00
SP552a	$9.35 Express Mail booklet pane of 3, #1909a	125.00

1981

SP553	18c Red Cross, #1910	1.50
SP554	18c Savings and Loan, #1911	1.50
SP555	18c Space Achievements, #1919a	6.75
SP556	18c Management, #1920	1.50
SP557	18c Wildlife, #1924a	2.00
SP558	18c Disabled, #1925	1.50
SP559	18c Millay, #1926	1.75
SP560	18c Alcoholism, #1927	2.25
SP561	18c Architecture, #1931a	2.50
SP562	18c Zaharias, #1932	7.00
SP563	18c Jones, #1933	8.00
SP564	18c Remington, #1934	2.25
SP565	18c, 20c Hoban, #1935-1936	1.50
SP566	18c Yorktown, Va. Capes, #1938a	2.00
SP567	20c Madonna and Child, #1939	2.00
SP568	20c Teddy Bear, #1940	2.25
SP569	20c John Hanson, #1941	1.50
SP570	20c Desert Plants, #1945a	2.00
SP571	20c C sheet, coil, #1946	2.50
SP572	20c C Booklet pane of 10, #1948a	2.50

1982

SP573	20c Bighorn Sheep, #1949a	3.00
SP574	20c FDR, #1950	1.50
SP575	20c Love, #1951	1.50
SP576	20c Washington, #1952	2.25
SP577	20c Birds and Flowers, #1953-1962	7.00
SP578	20c Birds and Flowers, #1963-1972	7.00
SP579	20c Birds and Flowers, #1973-1982	7.00
SP580	20c Birds and Flowers, #1983-1992	7.00
SP581	20c Birds and Flowers, #1993-2002	7.00
SP582	20c US Netherlands, #2003	1.50
SP583	20c Library of Congress, #2004	1.50
SP584	20c Consumer Education, #2005	2.25
SP585	20c Knoxville World's Fair, #2009a	1.50
SP586	20c Horatio Alger, #2010	1.25
SP587	20c Aging, #2011	1.25
SP588	20c Barrymores, #2012	2.50
SP589	20c Dr. Mary Walker, #2013	1.50
SP590	20c Peace Garden, #2014	1.50
SP591	20c Libraries, #2015	1.50
SP592	20c Jackie Robinson, #2016	12.50
SP593	20c Touro Synagogue, #2017	1.75
SP594	20c Wolf Trap Farm, #2018	1.50
SP595	20c Architecture, #2022a	1.75
SP596	20c Francis of Assisi, #2023	1.40
SP597	20c Ponce de Leon, #2024	1.40
SP598	13c Puppy, Kitten, #2025	2.00
SP599	20c Madonna and Child, #2026	2.25
SP600	20c Children Playing, #2030a	2.25

1983

SP601	1c, 4c, Official Mail, #O127-O129 13c	2.50
SP602	17c Official Mail, #O130	2.25
SP603	$1 Official Mail, #O132	4.00
SP604	$5 Official Mail, #O133	9.50
SP605	20c Official Mail coil, #O135	3.25
SP606	20c Science, #2031	1.50
SP607	20c Ballooning, #2035a	1.75
SP608	20c US Sweden, #2036	1.50
SP609	20c CCC, #2037	1.25
SP610	20c Priestley, #2038	1.50
SP611	20c Voluntarism, #2039	1.25
SP612	20c German Immigration, #2040	1.50
SP613	20c Brooklyn Bridge, #2041	2.00
SP614	20c TVA, #2042	1.50
SP615	20c Fitness, #2043	1.50
SP616	20c Scott Joplin, #2044	2.50
SP617	20c Medal of Honor, #2045	3.25
SP618	20c Babe Ruth, #2046	10.00
SP619	20c Hawthorne, #2047	1.50
SP620	13c Olympics, #2051a	3.00
SP621	28c Olympics, #C104a	3.00
SP622	40c Olympics, #C108a	2.75
SP623	35c Olympics, #C112a	2.75
SP624	20c Treaty of Paris, #2052	1.25
SP625	20c Civil Service, #2053	1.25
SP626	20c Metropolitan Opera, #2054	1.75
SP627	20c Inventors, #2058a	1.75
SP628	20c Streetcars, #2062a	2.25
SP629	20c Madonna and Child, #2063	1.50
SP630	20c Santa Claus, #2064	1.50
SP631	20c Martin Luther, #2065	2.25

1984-85

SP632	20c Alaska, #2066	1.50
SP633	20c Winter Olympics, #2070a	2.25
SP634	20c FDIC, #2071	1.50
SP635	20c Love, #2072	1.50
SP636	20c Woodson, #2073	2.25
SP637	14c, 22c D sheet, coil, #O138-O139	1.50
SP638	20c Conservation, #2074	1.25
SP639	20c Credit Union, #2075	1.50
SP640	20c Orchids, #2079a	2.25
SP641	20c Hawaii, #2080	2.00
SP642	20c National Archives, #2081	1.25
SP643	20c Olympics, #2085a	2.75
SP644	20c World Expo, #2086	1.25
SP645	20c Health Research, #2087	1.25
SP646	20c Fairbanks, #2088	3.00
SP647	20c Thorpe, #2089	7.00
SP648	20c McCormack, #2090	3.00
SP649	20c St. Lawrence Seaway, #2091	1.25
SP650	20c Waterfowl, #2092	3.00
SP651	20c Roanoke Voyages, #2093	1.25
SP652	20c Melville, #2094	1.50
SP653	20c Horace Moses, #2095	1.25
SP654	20c Smokey Bear, #2096	7.00
SP655	20c Clemente, #2097	11.00
SP656	20c Dogs, #2101a	3.00
SP657	20c Crime Prevention, #2102	1.50
SP658	20c Hispanic Americans, #2103	1.25
SP659	20c Family Unity, #2104	2.25
SP660	20c Eleanor Roosevelt, #2105	2.50
SP661	20c Readers, #2106	2.00
SP662	20c Madonna and Child, #2107	2.00
SP663	20c Child's Santa, #2108	2.00
SP664	20c Vietnam Memorial, #2109	3.25

1985-87

SP665	20c Jerome Kern, #2110	2.00
SP666	22c D coil, sheet, #2111-2112	1.50
SP667	22c D booklet pane of 10, #2113a	3.00
SP668	33c Verville, #C113	1.25
SP669	39c Sperry, #C114	1.75
SP670	44c Transpacific, #C115	1.50
SP671	22c Flags sheet, coil, #2114-2115	2.00
SP671a	22c Flag "T" coil, #2115b	2.25
SP672	22c Flag booklet pane of 5, #2116a	2.50
SP673	22c Seashells, #2121a	3.50
SP674	$10.75 Express Mail single, #2122	30.00
SP674a	$10.75 Express Mail booklet pane of 3, #2122a	65.00

Transportation Coils

1985-89

SP675	3.4c School Bus, #2123	3.00
SP676	4.9c Buckboard, #2124	2.75
SP677	5.5c Star Route Truck, #2125	3.00
SP678	6c Tricycle, #2126	2.50
SP679	7.1c Tractor, #2127	2.25
SP679a	7.1c Tractor, Zip+4 precancel, #2127b	2.50
SP680	8.3c Ambulance, #2128	2.75
SP681	8.5c Tow Truck, #2129	1.50
SP682	10.1c Oil Wagon, #2130	2.25
SP682a	10.1c Red precancel, #2130a	2.00
SP683	11c Stutz Bearcat, #2131	2.50
SP684	12c Stanley Steamer, #2132	2.75
SP685	12.5c Pushcart, #2133	2.50
SP686	14c Iceboat, #2134	3.25
SP687	17c Dog Sled, #2135	3.00
SP688	25c Bread Wagon, #2136	3.00

1985

SP689	22c Bethune, #2137	2.75
SP690	22c Duck Decoys, #2141a	3.25
SP691	22c Winter Special Olympics, #2142	1.25
SP692	22c Love, #2143	1.25
SP693	22c REA, #2144	1.25
SP694	14c, 22c Official Mail, #O129A, O136	2.00
SP695	22c AMERIPEX '86, #2145	1.25
SP696	22c Abigail Adams, #2146	1.25
SP697	22c Bartholdi, #2147	2.25
SP698	18c Washington coil, #2149	2.25
SP699	21.1c Letters coil, #2150	2.25
SP700	22c Korean Veterans, #2152	2.00
SP701	22c Social Security, #2153	1.50
SP702	44c Serra, #C116	1.50
SP703	22c World War I Veterans, #2154	1.75
SP704	22c Horses, #2158a	3.25
SP705	22c Education, #2159	1.50
SP706	22c Youth Year, #2163a	2.50
SP707	22c Hunger, #2164	1.60
SP708	22c Madonna and Child, #2165	1.50
SP709	22c Poinsettias, #2166	2.50

1986

SP710	22c Arkansas, #2167	1.50

Great Americans

1986-94

SP711	1c Mitchell, #2168	2.50
SP712	2c Lyon, #2169	1.50
SP713	3c White, #2170	1.50
SP714	4c Flanagan, #2171	1.60
SP715	5c Black, #2172	2.25
SP716	5c Munoz Marin, #2173	2.00
SP717	10c Red Cloud, #2175	1.75
SP718	14c Howe, #2176	1.50
SP719	15c Cody, #2177	1.75
SP720	17c Lockwood, #2178	1.50
SP721	20c Apgar, #2179	4.50
SP722	21c Carlson, #2180	1.50
SP723	23c Cassatt, #2181	1.50
SP724	25c London, #2182	1.50
SP724a	25c London, pane of 10, #2182a	4.25
SP725	28c Sitting Bull, #2183	1.75
SP726	29c Warren, #2184	3.00
SP727	29c Jefferson, #2185	2.75
SP728	35c Chavez, #2186	2.75
SP729	40c Chennault, #2187	2.50
SP730	45c Cushing, #2188	1.50
SP731	52c Humphrey, #2189	2.00
SP732	56c Harvard, #2190	2.00
SP733	65c Arnold, #2191	2.25
SP734	75c Willkie, #2192	2.25
SP735	$1 Revel, #2193	1.75
SP736	$1 Hopkins, #2194	2.25
SP737	$2 Bryan, #2195	3.25
SP739	$5 Harte, #2196	8.00
SP740	25c London, #2197a	2.25

1986

SP741	22c Stamp Collecting, #2201a	3.00
SP742	22c Love, #2202	2.00
SP743	22c Sojourner Truth, #2203	2.50
SP744	22c Texas Republic, #2204	1.75
SP745	22c Fish booklet pane of 5, #2209a	3.00
SP746	22c Hospitals, #2210	1.50
SP747	22c Duke Ellington, #2211	3.25
SP748	22c Presidents Sheet #1, #2216	3.75
SP749	22c Presidents Sheet #2, #2217	3.75
SP750	22c Presidents Sheet #3, #2218	3.75
SP751	22c Presidents Sheet #4, #2219	3.75
SP752	22c Arctic Explorers, #2223a	2.75
SP753	22c Statue of Liberty, #2224	2.25

1987

SP754	2c Locomotive, reengraved, #2226	2.25

1986

SP755	22c Navajo Art, #2238a	2.75
SP756	22c T.S. Eliot, #2239	2.50
SP757	22c Woodcarved Figurines, #2243a	2.75
SP758	22c Madonna and Child, #2244	1.75
SP759	22c Village Scene, #2245	1.75

1987

SP760	22c Michigan, #2246	2.50
SP761	22c Pan American Games, #2247	2.50

SP762	22c Love, #2248	2.00
SP763	22c du Sable, #2249	4.00
SP764	22c Caruso, #2250	2.25
SP765	22c Girl Scouts, #2251	3.50

Transportation Coils

1987-88

SP766	3c Conestoga Wagon, #2252	2.50
SP767	5c, Milk Wagon, Racing Car, 17.5c #2253, 2262	2.75
SP768	5.3c Elevator, #2254	2.25
SP769	7.6c Carreta, #2255	2.25
SP770	8.4c Wheelchair, #2256	2.50
SP771	10c Canal Boat, #2257	1.75
SP772	13c Patrol Wagon, #2258	2.75
SP773	13.2c Coal Car, #2259	2.75
SP774	15c Tugboat, #2260	2.50
SP775	16.7c Popcorn Wagon, #2261	2.50
SP776	20c Cable Car, #2263	2.50
SP777	20.5c Fire Engine, #2264	3.00
SP778	21c Mail Car, #2265	3.00
SP779	24.1c Tandem Bicycle, #2266	2.50

1987

SP780	22c Special Occasions, #2274a	3.75
SP781	22c United Way, #2275	1.50

1987-89

SP782	22c Flag and Fireworks, #2276	1.50
SP783	22c Flag, pair from booklet, #2276a	2.25
SP784	(25c) "E" sheet, coil, #2277, 2279	2.75
SP785	(25c) "E" booklet pane of 10, #2282a	3.25
SP786	25c Flag with Clouds, #2278	1.50
SP787	25c Flag with Clouds booklet pane of 6, #2285c	3.00
SP788	25c Flag over Yosemite coil, block tagging, #2280	1.75
SP788a	25c Flag over Yosemite, prephosphored uncoated paper (mottled tagging), #2280a	1.75
SP789	25c Honeybee coil, #2281	3.00
SP790	25c Pheasant, #2283a	3.25
SP791	25c Owl and Grosbeak, #2285b	3.00
SP792	(25c) "E" Official coil, #O140	2.25
SP793	20c Official coil, #O138B	1.75
SP794	15c, 25c Official coils, #O138A, O141	2.25

1987

SP795	22c Wildlife, #2286-2295	4.00
SP796	22c Wildlife, #2296-2305	4.00
SP797	22c Wildlife, #2306-2315	4.00
SP798	22c Wildlife, #2316-2325	4.00
SP799	22c Wildlife, #2326-2335	4.00

Ratification of the Constitution

1987-90

SP800	22c Delaware, #2336	2.00
SP801	22c Pennsylvania, #2337	1.50
SP802	22c New Jersey, #2338	1.75
SP803	22c Georgia, #2339	1.75
SP804	22c Connecticut, #2340	1.75
SP805	22c Massachusetts, #2341	2.25
SP806	22c Maryland, #2342	2.25
SP807	25c South Carolina, #2343	1.50
SP808	25c New Hampshire, #2344	1.75
SP809	25c Virginia, #2345	2.00
SP810	25c New York, #2346	2.00
SP811	25c North Carolina, #2347	2.00
SP812	25c Rhode Island, #2348	2.00

1987

SP813	22c U.S./Morocco, #2349	1.50
SP814	22c William Faulkner, #2350	1.50
SP815	22c Lacemaking, #2354a	3.50
SP816	22c Constitution, #2359a	2.50
SP817	22c Signing of Constitution, #2360	1.50
SP818	22c Certified Public Accounting, #2361	3.25
SP819	22c Locomotives, #2366a	6.75
SP820	22c Madonna and Child, #2367	1.50
SP821	22c Christmas Ornament, #2368	1.50

1988

SP822	22c Winter Olympics, #2369	1.50
SP823	22c Australia Bicentennial, #2370	1.75
SP824	22c James Weldon Johnson, #2371	2.75
SP825	22c Cats, #2375a	3.75
SP826	22c Knute Rockne, #2376	5.00
SP827	44c New Sweden, #C117	1.75
SP828	45c Samuel P. Langley, #C118	1.75
SP829	25c Francis Ouimet, #2377	4.00
SP830	36c Igor Sikorsky, #C119	2.00
SP831	25c Love, #2378	2.00
SP832	45c Love, #2379	1.75
SP833	25c Summer Olympics, #2380	1.75
SP834	25c Classic Automobiles, #2385a	3.75
SP835	25c Antarctic Explorers, #2389a	2.75
SP836	25c Carousel Animals, #2393a	3.00
SP837	$8.75 Express Mail, #2394	15.00
SP838	25c Special Occasions, #2396a	14.00
SP839	25c Special Occasions, #2398a	9.25
SP840	25c Madonna and Child, #2399	1.50
SP841	25c Village Scene, #2400	1.50

1989

SP842	25c Montana, #2401	1.75
SP843	25c A. Philip Randolph, #2402	3.00
SP844	25c North Dakota, #2403	1.50
SP845	25c Washington Statehood, #2404	1.50
SP846	25c Steamboats, #2409a	3.50
SP847	25c World Stamp Expo, #2410	1.50
SP848	25c Toscanini, #2411	2.00

Branches of Government

1989-90

SP849	25c House of Representatives, #2412	1.50
SP850	25c Senate, #2413	1.50
SP851	25c Executive, #2414	1.50
SP852	25c Supreme Court, #2415	1.50

1989

SP853	25c South Dakota, #2416	1.50
SP854	25c Lou Gehrig, #2417	10.00
SP855	1c Official, litho., #O143	2.25
SP856	45c French Revolution, #C120	2.25
SP857	25c Ernest Hemingway, #2418	2.50
SP858	$2.40 Moon Landing, #2419	11.00
SP859	25c Letter Carriers, #2420	1.50
SP860	25c Bill of Rights, #2421	1.50
SP861	25c Dinosaurs, #2425a	5.50
SP862	25c, 45c Pre-Columbian Artifacts, #2426, C121	2.00
SP863	25c Madonna sheet single, booklet pane of 10, #2427, 2427a	4.25
SP864	25c Sleigh single, booklet pane of 10, #2428, 2429a	4.25
SP865	25c Eagle & Shield, #2431	1.75
SP866	90c World Stamp Expo '89, #2433	7.00
SP867	25c Traditional Mail Delivery, #2437a	2.75
SP868	45c Futuristic Mail Delivery, #C126	3.25
SP869	45c Futuristic Mail Delivery, #C125a	3.25
SP870	25c Traditional Mail Delivery, #2438	3.50

1990

SP871	25c Idaho, #2439	1.50
SP872	25c Love, single booklet pane of 10, #2440, 2441a	3.00
SP873	25c Ida B. Wells, #2442	3.00
SP874	15c Beach Umbrella, #2443a	3.00
SP875	25c Wyoming, #2444	2.25
SP876	25c Classic Films, #2448a	4.25
SP877	25c Marianne Moore, #2449	1.50

Transportation Coils

1990-92

SP879	4c Steam Carriage, #2451	2.25
SP880	5c Circus Wagon, #2452	2.75
SP880A	5c Circus Wagon, #2452B	3.25
SP880B	5c Circus Wagon with cent sign, #2452D	5.00
SP881	5c, 10c Canoe, engr., Tractor Trailer, #2453, 2457	2.25
SP882	5c Canoe, photo., #2454	3.00
SP883	10c Tractor trailer, photo., #2458	5.00
SP891	20c Cog Railway, #2463	4.00
SP892	23c Lunch Wagon, #2464	2.25
SP893	32c Ferry Boat, #2466	5.00
SP895	$1 Seaplane, #2468	5.00

1990-94

SP897	25c Lighthouses, booklet pane of 5, #2474a	5.00
SP898	25c Flag, #2475	2.75

Flora and Fauna Series

SP899	1c, 3c, Kestrel, Bluebird, Cardinal, 30c #2476, 2478, 2480	2.25
SP900	1c Kestrel with cent sign, #2477	6.00
SP901	19c Fawn, #2479	2.25
SP902	45c Pumpkinseed Sunfish, #2481	2.75
SP903	$2 Bobcat, #2482	4.00
SP904	20c Blue jay, #2483	6.00
SP905	29c Wood Ducks booklet panes of 10, #2484a, 2485a	9.50
SP906	29c African Violets bklt. pane of 10, #2486a	4.25
SP907	32c Peach & Pear, #2488b, 2493-2494	4.50
SP908	29c Red Squirrel, #2489	2.75
SP909	29c Red Rose, #2490	2.50
SP910	29c Pine Cone, #2491	2.50
SP911	32c Pink rose, #2492	5.00
SP919	25c Olympians, #2496-2500	4.75
SP920	25c Indian Headdresses, #2505a	5.50
SP921	25c Micronesia, Marshall Islands, #2507a	2.25
SP922	25c Sea Creatures, #2511a	4.75
SP923	25c, 45c Grand Canyon, Tropical Coastline, #2512, C127	2.25
SP924	25c Eisenhower, #2513	2.50
SP925	25c Madonna sheet single, booklet pane of 10, #2514, 2514a	5.00
SP926	25c Christmas Tree sheet single, booklet pane of 10, #2515, 2516a	5.00

1991-95

SP927	(29c) "F" Flower single, coil pair, #2517, 2518	2.50
SP928	(29c) "F" Flower booklet panes of 10, #2519a, 2520a	8.00
SP929	(4c) Make-up Rate, #2521	2.00
SP930	(29c) "F" Flag, #2522	2.25
SP931	(29c) "F" Official coil, #O144	2.50
SP932	29c Mt. Rushmore, #2523	2.50
SP933	29c Mt. Rushmore, photo., #2523A	2.25
SP934	29c Flower single, booklet pane of 10, #2524, 2527a	5.00
SP935	29c Flower coil, #2525	1.75
SP936	29c Flower coil, #2526	2.25
SP937	4c Official, #O146	2.00

SP938	29c Flag, Olympic Rings, #2528a	5
SP939	19c Fishing Boat coil, #2529	2
SP939A	19c Fishing Boat coil reissue, #2529C	3
SP940	19c Ballooning, #2530a	4
SP941	29c Flags on Parade, #2531	2
SP942	29c Liberty Torch, #2531A	2
SP943	50c Switzerland, #2532	2
SP944	20c Vermont Statehood, #2533	2
SP945	50c Harriet Quimby, #C128	2
SP946	29c Savings Bonds, #2534	2
SP947	29c, 52c Love, #2535, 2536a, 2537	6
SP948	40c William T. Piper, #C129	2
SP949	29c William Saroyan, #2538	2
SP950	Official 19c, 23c, 29c, #O145, O147-O148	2
SP951	$1.00 USPS/Olympic Rings, #2539	3
SP952	$2.90 Eagle, #2540	7
SP953	$9.95 Eagle, #2541	22
SP955	$14 Eagle, #2542	30
SP955	$2.90 Futuristic Space Shuttle, #2543	8
SP956	$3 Challenger Shuttle, #2544	10
SP956A	$10.75 Endeavour Shuttle, #2544A	22
SP957	29c Fishing Flies, #2549a	5
SP958	29c Cole Porter, #2550	2
SP959	50c Antarctic Treaty, #C130	2
SP960	29c Desert Shield, Desert Storm, #2551	5
SP961	29c 1992 Summer Olympics, #2553-2557	4
SP962	29c Numismatics, #2558	2
SP963	29c World War II, #2559	6
SP964	29c Basketball, #2560	5
SP965	29c District of Columbia, #2561	2
SP966	29c Comedians, #2566a	5
SP967	29c Jan E. Matzeliger, #2567	4
SP968	29c Space Exploration, #2577a	6
SP969	50c Bering Land Bridge, #C131	2
SP970	29c Madonna and Child sheet single, booklet pane of 10, #2578, 2578a	7
SP971	29c Santa Claus sheet and booklet singles, #2579, 2580 or 2581, 2582-2585	11
SP973	32c James K. Polk, #2587	7
SP976	$1 Surrender of Gen. Burgoyne, #2590	4
SP978	$5 Washington and Jackson, #2592	10
SP980	29c Pledge of Allegiance, #2593a	7
SP982	29c Eagle & Shield self-adhesives, #2595-2597	4.0
SP983	29c Eagle self-adhesive, #2598	3.5
SP984	29c Statue of Liberty, #2599	3.5
SP990	(10c) Eagle and Shield coil, #2602	3.7
SP991	(10c) Eagle and Shield coils, #2603-2604	3.7
SP993	23c Stars and Stripes coil, #2605	2.5
SP994	23c USA coil, #2606	2.7
SP994A	23c USA coil, #2607	2.7
SP994B	23c USA coil, #2608	2.5
SP995	29c Flag over White House, #2609	2.5

1992

SP997	29c Winter Olympics, #2611-2615	3.7
SP998	29c World Columbian Stamp Expo '92, #2616	2.5
SP999	29c W.E.B. DuBois, #2617	3.7
SP1000	29c Love, #2618	2.5
SP1001	29c Olympic Baseball, #2619	10.0
SP1002	29c First Voyage of Columbus, #2623a	3.7
SP1003	1c, 4c, First Sighting of Land souvenir sheet, #2624 ($1)	7.5
SP1004	2c, 3c, Claiming a New World souvenir sheet, #2625 ($4)	7.5
SP1005	5c, 30c, Seeking Royal Support souvenir sheet, #2626 (50c)	7.5
SP1006	6c, 8c, Royal Favor Restored souvenir sheet, #2627 ($3)	7.5
SP1007	10c, Reporting Discoveries souvenir sheet, #2628 (15c, $2)	7.5
SP1008	$5 Columbus souvenir sheet, #2629	7.5
SP1009	29c New York Stock Exchange, #2630	2.5
SP1010	29c Space Accomplishments, #2634a	4.0
SP1011	29c Alaska Highway, #2635	2.5
SP1012	29c Kentucky Statehood, #2636	2.5
SP1013	29c Summer Olympics, #2637-2641	3.75
SP1014	29c Hummingbirds, #2646a	5.00
SP1015	29c Wildflowers, #2647-2656	6.50
SP1016	29c Wildflowers, #2657-2666	6.50
SP1017	29c Wildflowers, #2667-2676	6.50
SP1018	29c Wildflowers, #2677-2686	6.50
SP1019	29c Wildflowers, #2687-2696	6.50
SP1020	29c World War II, #2697	6.00
SP1021	29c Dorothy Parker, #2698	2.75
SP1022	29c Dr. Theodore von Karman, #2699	3.50
SP1023	29c Minerals strip of 4, #2703a	4.00
SP1024	29c Juan Rodriguez Cabrillo, #2704	2.50
SP1025	29c Wild Animals, #2709a	5.00
SP1026	29c Madonna and Child sheet single, booklet pane of 10, #2710, 2710a	7.50
SP1027	29c Christmas Toys block of 4, booklet pane of 4 and booklet single, #2714a, 2718a, 2719	5.50
SP1028	29c Chinese New Year, #2720	7.75

...93		
...1029	29c Elvis Presley, #2721	10.00
...1030	29c Oklahoma!, #2722	2.25
...1030A	29c Hank Williams sheet stamp, #2723	5.00
...1030B	29c Rock & Roll/Rhythm & Blues sheet single, booklet pane of 8, #2737b	10.00

No. SP1030B exists with any one of #2724-2730 affixed along with #2737b.

...1034	29c Space Fantasy, #2745a	6.00
...1035	29c Percy Lavon Julian, #2746	3.50
...1036	29c Oregon Trail, #2747	2.75
...1037	29c World University Games, #2748	2.75
...1038	29c Grace Kelly, #2749	6.00
...1039	29c Circus, #2753a	4.50
...1040	29c Cherokee Strip, #2754	3.50
...1041	29c Dean Acheson, #2755	3.00
...1042	29c Sporting Horses, #2759a	5.50
...1043	29c Garden Flowers, #2764a	3.50
...1044	29c World War II, #2765	5.50
...1045	29c Joe Louis, #2766	7.50
...1046	29c Broadway Musicals, #2770a	4.50
...1047	29c National Postal Museum strip of 4, #2782a	3.25
...1048	29c American Sign Language, #2784a	2.75
...1049	29c Country & Western Music sheet stamp and booklet pane of 4, #2778a	9.25

No. SP1049 exists with any one of #2771-2774 affixed along with #2778a.

...1050	10c Official Mail, #O146A	2.75
...1052	29c Classic Books strip of 4, #2788a	3.25
...1053	29c Traditional Christmas sheet stamp, booklet pane of 4, #2789, 2790a	4.75
...1054	29c Contemporary Christmas booklet pane of 10, sheet and self-adhesive single stamps, #2803	8.50

No. SP1054 exists with any one of #2791-2794, 2798a, 2798b, 2799-2802 affixed along with #2803.

...1055	29c Mariana Islands, #2804	2.75
...1056	29c Columbus' Landing in Puerto Rico, #2805	3.25
...1057	29c AIDS Awareness, #2806, 2806b	4.75
...994		
...1058	29c Winter Olympics, #2811a	5.00
...1059	29c Edward R. Murrow, #2812	3.25
...1060	29c Love self-adhesive, #2813	3.25
...1061	29c, 52c Love booklet pane of 10, single sheet stamp, #2814a, 2815	6.50
...1062	29c Love sheet stamp, #2814C	3.25
...1063	29c Dr. Allison Davis, #2816	4.50
...1064	29c Chinese New Year, #2817	4.00
...1065	29c Buffalo Soldiers, #2818	5.00
...1066	29c Silent Screen Stars, #2819-2828	6.00
...1067	29c Garden Flowers, #2833a	6.00
...1068	29c, World Cup Soccer, #2834-2836 40c, 50c	6.00
...1069	World Cup Soccer, #2837	6.00
...1070	29c World War II, #2838	5.50
...1071	29c, 50c Norman Rockwell stamp, souvenir sheet, #2839-2840	9.00
...1072	29c, Moon Landing, #2841-2842 $9.95	15.00
...1073	29c Locomotives, #2847a	6.50
...1074	29c George Meany, #2848	3.25
...1075	29c Popular Singers, #2853a	6.00
...1076	29c Jazz and Blues Singers block of 10, #2854-2861	9.00

Block of 10 on No. SP1076 may contain different combinations of stamps.

SP1077	29c James Thurber, #2862	4.00
SP1078	29c Wonders of the Sea, #2866a	5.00
SP1079	29c Cranes, #2868a	3.25
SP1079A	Legends of the West, #2869	12.00
SP1080	29c Traditional Christmas sheet stamp, booklet pane of 10, #2871, 2871b	8.50
SP1081	29c Contemporary Christmas sheet stamp, block of 4 from booklet pane, #2872	6.50
SP1082	29c Contemporary Christmas self-adhesive stamps, #2873--2874	7.00
SP1083	$2 Bureau of Engraving and Printing Souvenir Sheet, #2875	15.00

1995-96

SP1084	29c Chinese New Year, #2876	5.50
SP1085	G make-up rate, G stamps, #2877, 2884, 2890, 2893	4.00
SP1086	G make-up rate, G stamps, #2878, 2880, 2882, 2885, 2888, 2892	4.00
SP1087	G stamps, official G stamp, #2879, 2881, 2883, 2889, O152	4.00
SP1088	G self-adhesive stamps, #2886-2887	8.00
SP1091	32c Flag over Porch, #2897, 2913, 2915-2916	5.50

SP1096	(5c) Butte coil, #2902	5.00
SP1097	(5c) Mountain coil, #2903, 2904	4.50
SP1099	Butte, Mountain, Juke Box, Auto Tail Fin, Auto, Flag over porch, #2902B, 2904A, 2906, 2910, 2912A, 2915B	5.50
SP1099A	Mountain, Juke Box, Flag Over Porch coil and booklet stamps, #2904B, 2912B, 2915D, 2921b	9.00
SP1100	(10c) Auto coil, #2905	4.50
SP1102	Eagle & shield, Flag over porch, #2907, 2920D, 2921	4.50
SP1103	(15c) Auto Tail Fin, #2908-2909	4.50
SP1105	(25c) Juke Box, #2911-2912	3.00
SP1110	32c Flag over Field self-adhesive, #2919	2.75
SP1114	(32c) Non-denominated Love, #2948-2949	3.00
SP1115	32c Florida Statehood, #2950	2.75

Great Americans Series

1995-99

SP1126	32c Milton Hershey, #2933	2.75
SP1127	32c Cal Farley, #2934	3.25
SP1128	32c Henry R. Luce, #2935	5.50
SP1129	32c Lila & DeWitt Wallace, #2936	5.50
SP1131	46c Ruth Benedict, #2938	3.25
SP1133	55c Alice Hamilton, #2940	2.75
SP1134	55c Justin S. Morrill, #2941	5.50
SP1135	77c Mary Breckinridge, #2942	4.50
SP1136	78c Alice Paul, #2943	2.75

1995

SP1141	32c Kids Care, #2954a	3.50
SP1142	32c Richard Nixon, #2955	3.50
SP1143	32c Bessie Coleman, #2956	4.50
SP1144	1-32c Official, #O153-O156	3.00
SP1145	32c, 55c Love (with denominations), #2957-2960	3.50
SP1146	32c Recreational Sports, #2965a	9.00
SP1147	32c Prisoners of War/Missing in Action, #2966	4.50
SP1148	32c Marilyn Monroe, #2967	12.00
SP1149	32c Texas Statehood, #2968	4.00
SP1150	32c Great Lakes Lighthouses, #2973a	9.00
SP1151	32c United Nations, #2974	2.75
SP1152	32c Civil War, #2975	14.50
SP1153	32c Carousel Horses, #2979a	5.25
SP1154	32c Woman Suffrage, #2980	2.75
SP1155	32c World War II, #2981	6.00
SP1156	32c Louis Armstrong, #2982	4.50
SP1157	32c Jazz Musicians, #2992a	7.00
SP1158	32c Garden Flowers, #2997a	6.00
SP1159	60c Eddie Rickenbacker, #2998	4.50
SP1160	32c Republic of Palau, #2999	3.50
SP1161	32c Comic Strip Classics, #3000	15.00
SP1162	32c Naval Academy, #3001	4.50
SP1163	32c Tennessee Williams, #3002	4.50
SP1164	32c Traditional Christmas sheet stamp, booklet pane of 10, #3003, 3003b	5.50
SP1165	32c Contemporary Christmas block of 4, self-adhesive stamps, #3007a, 3010-3011	5.00

No. SP1165 may include different combinations of Nos. 3008-3011.

SP1166	32c Midnight Angel, #3012	4.75
SP1167	32c Children Sledding, #3013	4.75
SP1168	32c Antique Automobiles, #3023a	6.00

1996

SP1169	32c Utah Statehood, #3024	3.50
SP1170	32c Garden Flowers, #3029a	6.00
SP1171	1, 32c Flag Over Porch, Love self-adhesives, Kestrel coil, #2920e, 3030, 3044	16.00

1996-99

Flora and Fauna Series

SP1171A	1c Kestrel, self-adhesive, #3031	6.50
SP1172	2c Woodpecker, #3032	3.75
SP1173	3c Bluebird, #3033	3.75
SP1184	$1 Red Fox, #3036	7.00
SP1185	2c Woodpecker coil, #3045	6.00
SP1187	20c Bluejay self-adhesive coil, booklet stamps, #3048, 3053	5.00
SP1188	32c Yellow Rose, #3049	6.00
SP1189	20c Ring-necked Pheasant, #3050, 3055	7.00
SP1191A	33c Coral Pink Rose, serpentine die cut 10¾x10½, #3052E	7.00
SP1191	33c Coral Pink Rose, #3052	7.00
SP1192	32c Yellow Rose coil, #3054	7.00

1996

SP1197	32c Ernest E. Just, #3058	5.00
SP1198	32c Smithsonian Institution, #3059	3.75
SP1199	32c Chinese New Year, #3060	6.00
SP1200	32c Pioneers of Communication, #3064a	7.00
SP1201	32c Fulbright Scholarships, #3065	3.75
SP1202	50c Jacqueline Cochran, #3066	3.75
SP1203	32c Marathon, #3067	3.75
SP1204	32c Olympic Games, #3068	15.00

SP1205	32c Georgia O'Keeffe, #3069	4.75
SP1206	32c Tennessee Statehood, #3070	3.75
SP1207	32c American Indian Dances, #3076a	4.75
SP1208	32c Prehistoric Animals, #3080a	4.75
SP1209	32c Breast Cancer Awareness, #3081	4.75
SP1210	32c James Dean, #3082	6.00
SP1211	32c Folk Heroes, #3086a	5.00
SP1212	32c Centennial Olympic Games, #3087	5.00
SP1213	32c Iowa Statehood, #3088-3089	5.00
SP1214	32c Rural Free Delivery, #3090	4.00
SP1215	32c Riverboats, #3095a	5.50
SP1216	32c Big Band Leaders, #3099a	6.00
SP1217	32c Songwriters, #3103a	6.00
SP1218	23c F. Scott Fitzgerald, #3104	4.00
SP1219	32c Endangered Species, #3105	15.00
SP1220	32c Computer Technology, #3106	4.00
SP1221	32c Madonna & Child sheet & booklet stamps, #3107, 3112	6.00
SP1222	32c Contemporary Christmas block of 4, self-adhesive stamp, #3111a, 3113	6.00

#SP1222 may contain #3114-3116 instead of #3113.

SP1223	32c Skaters, #3117	6.00
SP1224	32c Hanukkah, #3118	5.00
SP1225	32c Cycling souvenir sheet, #3119	6.00

1997

SP1226	32c Chinese New Year, #3120	6.00
SP1227	32c Benjamin O. Davis, Sr., #3121	6.00
SP1228	32c Statue of Liberty, #3122	5.50
SP1229	32, 55c Love Swans, #3123-3124	5.50
SP1230	32c Helping Children Learn, #3125	5.00
SP1231	32c Merian Botanical Prints, #3126-3129	5.50
SP1232	32c PACIFIC 97 Triangles, #3131a	6.00
SP1233	(25c), Flag Over Porch, Juke Box 32c linerless coils, #3132-3133	5.50
SP1234	32c Thornton Wilder, #3134	5.00
SP1235	32c Raoul Wallenberg, #3135	5.00
SP1236	32c Dinosaurs, #3136	12.50
SP1237	32c Bugs Bunny, #3137	10.00
SP1238	50c PACIFIC 97 Franklin, #3139	10.00
SP1239	60c PACIFIC 97 Washington, #3140	10.00
SP1240	32c Marshall Plan, #3141	5.00
SP1241	32c Classic American Aircraft, #3142	12.50
SP1242	32c Football Coaches, #3146a	10.00
SP1242A	32c Vince Lombardi, #3147	8.00
SP1242B	32c Bear Bryant, #3148	8.00
SP1242C	32c Pop Warner, #3149	8.00
SP1242D	32c George Halas, #3150	8.00
SP1243	32c Classic American Dolls, #3151	10.00
SP1244	32c Humphrey Bogart, #3152	6.00
SP1245	32c The Stars and Stripes Forever!, #3153	6.00
SP1246	32c Opera Singers, #3157a	6.00
SP1247	32c Composers & Conductors, #3165a	9.00
SP1248	32c Padre Felix Varela, #3155	6.00
SP1249	32c Department of the Air Force, #3167	8.00
SP1250	32c Movie Monsters, #3172a	10.00
SP1251	32c Supersonic Flight, #3173	8.00
SP1252	32c Women in Military Service, #3174	6.00
SP1253	32c Kwanzaa, #3175	7.50
SP1254	32c Madonna and Child, #3176	7.50
SP1255	32c Holly, #3177	7.50
SP1256	$3 Mars Pathfinder, #3178	12.00

1998

SP1257	32c Chinese New Year, #3179	6.00
SP1258	32c Alpine Skiing, #3180	6.00
SP1259	32c Madam C.J. Walker, #3181	6.00

1998-2000

Celebrate the Century

SP1259A	32c 1900s, #3182	10.00
SP1259B	32c 1910s, #3183	10.00
SP1259C	32c 1920s, #3184	10.00
SP1259D	32c 1930s, #3185	10.00
SP1259E	32c 1940s, #3186	10.00
SP1259F	33c 1950s, #3187	10.00
SP1259G	33c 1960s, #3188	10.00
SP1259H	33c 1970s, #3189	10.00
SP1259I	33c 1980s, #3190	10.00
SP1259J	33c 1990s, #3191	10.00

1998

SP1260	32c "Remember the Maine," #3192	6.00
SP1261	32c Flowering Trees, #3197a	8.00
SP1262	32c Alexander Calder, #3202a	8.00
SP1263	32c Cinco de Mayo, #3203	6.00
SP1264	32c Sylvester & Tweety, #3204a	6.00
SP1265	32c Wisconsin Statehood, #3206	6.00
SP1266	(5c), Wetlands, Diner Coils, (25c) #3207-3208	5.50
SP1266A	(25c) Diner coil, #3208A	5.50
SP1267	1c-$2 Trans-Mississippi, #3209	10.00
SP1268	$1 Trans-Mississippi, #3209h	6.00
SP1269	32c Berlin Airlift, #3211	5.50
SP1270	32c Folk Musicians, #3215a	8.00

SP1271	32c Gospel Singers, #3219a	7.50
SP1272	32c Spanish Settlement, #3220	6.00
SP1273	32c Stephen Vincent Benét, #3221	6.00
SP1274	32c Tropical Birds, #3225a	8.00
SP1275	32c Alfred Hitchcock, #3226	6.00
SP1276	32c Organ & Tissue Donation, #3227	6.00
SP1277	(10c) Modern Bicycle, #3229	6.00
SP1278	32c Bright Eyes, #3234a	7.50
SP1279	32c Klondike Gold Rush, #3235	6.00
SP1280	32c American Art, #3236	10.00
SP1281	32c Ballet, #3237	6.00
SP1282	32c Space Discovery, #3242a	7.50
SP1283	32c Giving & Sharing, #3243	6.00
SP1284	32c Madonna & Child, #3244	6.00
SP1285	32c Wreaths, #3248a, 3252a	7.50
SP1286	(32+8c) Breast Cancer Awareness, #B1	6.00
SP1287	(1c), Weather Vane, Uncle (33c) Sam's Hat, #3257-3258, 3260	7.00
SP1288	22c Uncle Sam, #3259, 3263	6.00
SP1289	$3.20 Space Shuttle Landing, #3261	9.00
SP1290	$11.75 Piggyback Space Shuttle, #3262	17.50
SP1291	(33c) Uncle Sam's Hat, #3267-3269	7.50
SP1292	(33c) Uncle Sam's Hat, #3264, 3266	7.50
SP1293	(5c), Wetlands, Eagle & Shield, (10c) #3207A, 3270-3271	6.50

1999

SP1294	33c Chinese New Year, #3272	6.00
SP1295	33x Malcolm X, #3273	6.00
SP1296	33c Love, #3274	7.50
SP1297	55c Love, #3275	6.50
SP1298	33c Hospice Care, #3276	6.00
SP1299	33c Flag and City, #3279-3280, 3282	6.50
SP1300	33c Flag Over Chalkboard, #3283	6.00
SP1301	33c Irish Immigration, #3286	6.00
SP1302	33c Lunt & Fontanne, #3287	6.00
SP1303	33c Arctic Animals, #3292a	7.50
SP1304	33c Sonoran Desert, #3293	10.00
SP1305	33c Berries, #3294-3297	7.50
SP1306	33c Daffy Duck, #3306a	8.00
SP1307	33c Ayn Rand, #3308	6.50
SP1308	33c Cinco de Mayo, #3309	6.00
SP1309	33c Tropical Flowers, #3310-3313	7.50
SP1310	48c Niagara Falls, #C133	6.50
SP1311	33c John & William Bartram, #3314	6.00
SP1312	33c Prostate Cancer, #3315	6.00
SP1313	33c California Gold Rush, #3316	6.00
SP1314	33c Aquarium Fish, #3317-3320	7.50
SP1315	33c Extreme Sports, #3321-3324	7.50
SP1316	33c American Glass, #3328a	7.50
SP1317	33c James Cagney, #3329	7.50
SP1318	55c Billy Mitchell, #3330	7.50
SP1319	40c Rio Grande, #C134	6.00
SP1320	33c Honoring Those Who Served, #3331	6.00
SP1321	45c Universal Postal Union, #3332	6.00
SP1322	33c Famous Trains, #3337a	7.50
SP1323	33c Frederick Law Olmsted, #3338	6.00
SP1324	33c Hollywood Composers, #3344a	7.50
SP1325	33c Broadway Songwriters, #3350a	7.50
SP1326	33c Insects & Spiders, #3351	10.00
SP1327	33c Hanukkah, #3352	6.00
SP1328	22c Uncle Sam, #3353	6.00
SP1329	33c Official coil, #O157	6.00
SP1330	33c NATO, #3354	6.00
SP1331	33c Madonna & Child, #3355	6.00
SP1332	33c Christmas Deer, #3359a	7.50
SP1333	33c Kwanzaa, #3368	6.00
SP1334	33c Year 2000, #3369	6.00

2000

SP1335	33c Chinese New Year, #3370	6.00
SP1336	60c Grand Canyon, #C135	6.00
SP1337	33c Patricia Roberts Harris, #3371	6.00
SP1338	33c Berries, dated 2000, #3294a-3296a, 3297c	6.00
SP1339	33c Los Angeles Class Submarine (sheet stamp), #3372	6.00
SP1340	33c Pacific Coast Rain Forest, #3378	10.00
SP1341	33c Louise Nevelson, #3383a	7.50
SP1342	33c Hubble Space Telescope Images, #3388a	7.50
SP1343	33c American Samoa, #3389	6.00
SP1344	33c Library of Congress, #3390	6.00
SP1345	33c Road Runner & Wile E. Coyote, #3391a	7.50
SP1346	33c Distinguished Soldiers, 3396a	8.00
SP1347	33c Summer Sports, #3397	6.00
SP1348	33c Adoption, #3398	6.00
SP1349	33c Youth Team Sports, #3402a	6.50
SP1350	33c The Stars and Stripes, #3403	10.00
SP1351	33c Legends of Baseball, #3408	10.00
SP1352	33c Stampin' the Future, #3417a	6.50

Distinguished Americans Series

2000-04

SP1355	10c Gen. Joseph W. Stilwell, #3420	6.00
SP1357	23c Wilma Rudolph, #3422, 3436	6.00
SP1361	33c Claude Pepper, #3426	6.00
SP1366	76c Hattie Caraway, #3431	6.00
SP1367	83c Edna Ferber, #3432	7.50

2000

SP1373	33c California Statehood, #3438	6.00
SP1374	33c Deep Sea Creatures, #3443a	7.50
SP1375	33c Thomas Wolfe, #3444	6.00
SP1376	33c White House, #3445	6.00
SP1377	33c Edward G. Robinson, #3446	6.00
SP1378	(10c) New York Public Library Lion, #3447	6.00
SP1379	(34c) Flag Over Farm, #3448-3450	6.00
SP1380	(34c) Statue of Liberty, #3451-3453	6.00
SP1381	(34c) Flowers, #3454-3457	6.00

2001

SP1382	34c Statue of Liberty self-adhesive coil, #3466	6.00
SP1382A	21c American Buffalo, #3467, 3484	6.00
SP1383	21c American Buffalo, #3468, 3475	6.00
SP1383A	23c George Washington, #3468A, 3475A	6.00
SP1384	34c Flag over Farm, #3469	6.00
SP1385	34c Flag over Farm self-adhesive, #3470	6.00
SP1386	55c Eagle, #3471	6.00
SP1386A	57c Eagle, #3471A	7.50
SP1387	$3.50 US Capitol, #3472	10.00
SP1388	$12.25 Washington Monument, #3473	20.00
SP1389	34c Statue of Liberty, #3476, 3477, 3485	7.50
SP1390	34c Flowers, #3478-3481	7.50
SP1391	20c George Washington, #3482	6.00
SP1392	34c Apple and Orange, #3491, 3492	6.00
SP1393	34c Flag over Farm self-adhesive booklet, #3495	6.00
SP1394	(34c) Love, #3496	6.00
SP1395	34c, 55c Love, #3497, 3499	7.50
SP1396	34c Chinese New Year, #3500	6.00
SP1397	34c Roy Wilkins, #3501	6.00
SP1398	34c American Illustrators, #3502	10.00
SP1399	34c Official, #O158	6.00
SP1400	70c Nine-Mile Prairie, #C136	6.00
SP1401	34c Diabetes Awareness, #3503	6.00
SP1402	34c Nobel Prize, #3504	6.00
SP1403	1c-80c Pan-American Inverts, #3505	10.00
SP1404	80c Mt. McKinley, #C137	7.50
SP1405	34c Great Plains Prairie, #3506	10.00
SP1406	34c Peanuts Comic Strip, #3507	6.00
SP1407	34c Honoring Veterans, #3508	6.00
SP1408	60c Acadia National Park, #C138	7.50
SP1409	34c Frida Kahlo, #3509	6.00
SP1410	34c Legendary Playing Fields, #3510-3519	12.50
SP1411	(10c) Atlas Statue, #3520	6.00
SP1412	34c Leonard Bernstein, #3521	6.00
SP1413	(15c) Woody Wagon, #3522	6.00
SP1414	34c Lucille Ball, #3523	6.00
SP1415	34c Amish Quilts, #3524-3527	7.50
SP1416	34c Carnivorous Plants, #3528-3531	7.50
SP1417	34c Eid, #3532	6.00
SP1418	34c Enrico Fermi, #3533	6.00
SP1419	34c That's All Folks!, #3534a	6.00
SP1420	34c Christmas Madonna, #3536	6.00
SP1421	34c Christmas Santas, #3537-3540	7.50
SP1422	34c James Madison, #3545	6.00
SP1423	34c Thanksgiving, #3546	6.00
SP1424	34c Hanukkah, #3547	6.00
SP1425	34c Kwanzaa, #3548	6.00
SP1426	34c United We Stand booklet and coil, #3549, 3550	7.50
SP1427	57c Love, #3551	6.00

2002

SP1428	34c Winter Olympics, #3552-3555	7.50
SP1429	34c Mentoring a Child, #3556	6.00
SP1430	34c Langston Hughes, #3557	6.00
SP1431	34c Happy Birthday, #3558	6.00
SP1432	34c Chinese New Year, #3559	6.00
SP1433	34c US Military Academy, Bicent., #3560	6.00
SP1434	34c Greetings from America, #3561-3610	37.50
SP1435	34c Longleaf Pine Forest, #3611	10.00
SP1436	5c Toleware Coffeepot, #3612	6.00
SP1437	3c Star, #3613-3615	6.00
SP1438	23c George Washington, #3616-3618	7.50
SP1439	(37c) Flag, #3620-3623	7.50
SP1440	(37c) Toy coils, #3626-3629	7.50

2003

SP1440A	37c Flag, perf. 11¼, #3629F	6.00

2002

SP1441	37c Flag, #3630-3631, 3633, 3635	7.50

2003

SP1441A	37c Flag, self-adhesive booklet stamp, #3637	6.

2002

SP1442	37c Toy coils, #3638-3641	7

2003

SP1442A	37c Antique Toys booklet stamps, #3642a, 3643a, 3644a, 3644f	7

2002

SP1443	60c Coverlet Eagle, #3646	6
SP1444	$3.85 Jefferson Memorial, #3647	10
SP1445	$13.65 Capitol Dome, #3648	21
SP1446	(34c+11c) Heroes of 2001, #B2	6
SP1447	37c Masters of American Photography, #3649	10
SP1448	37c John James Audubon, #3650	6
SP1449	37c Harry Houdini, #3651	6
SP1450	37c Official coil, #O159	6
SP1451	37c Andy Warhol, #3652	6
SP1452	37c Teddy Bears, #3653-3656	7
SP1453	37c,60c Love, #3657-3658	7
SP1454	37c Ogden Nash, #3659	6
SP1455	37c Duke Kahanamoku, #3660	6
SP1456	37c American Bats, #3661-3664	7.
SP1457	37c Women in Journalism, #3665-3668	7.
SP1458	37c Irving Berlin, #3669	6.
SP1459	37c Neuter and Spay, #3670-3671	7.
SP1460	37c Hanukkah, #3672	6.
SP1461	37c Kwanzaa, #3673	6.
SP1462	37c Eid #3674	6.
SP1463	37c Christmas Madonna, #3675	6.
SP1464	37c Christmas Snowmen, #3676-3679	7.
SP1465	37c Cary Grant, #3692	6.
SP1466	(5c) Sea Coast, #3693	6.
SP1467	37c Hawaiian Missionary Stamps, #3694	7.
SP1468	37c Happy Birthday, #3695	6.
SP1469	37c Greetings from America, #3696-3745	37.

2003

SP1470	37c Thurgood Marshall, #3746	6.
SP1471	37c Chinese New Year, #3747	6.
SP1472	37c Zora Neale Hurston, #3748	6.0

2004

SP1473	2c Navajo Necklace, #3749	6.0
SP1473A	2c Navajo Necklace, #3749A-3749B, 2005	6.0
SP1474	4c Chippendale Chair, #3750	6.0
SP1474A	5c Toleware, #3750A	6.0

2003

SP1475	10c American Clock, #3751	6.0
SP1481	1c Tiffany Lamp coil, #3757	6.0
SP1483	3c Silver Coffeepot coil, #3759, 2005	6.0
SP1490	$1 Wisdom, #3766	7.5
SP1493	(10c) New York Public Library Lion, perf. 10 vert, #3769	6.0

2004

SP1494	(10c) Atlas Statue, #3770	6.0

2003

SP1495	80c Special Olympics, #3771	7.5
SP1496	37c American Filmmaking: Behind the Scenes, #3772	10.0
SP1497	37c Ohio Statehood, Bicent., #3773	6.0
SP1498	37c Pelican Island National Wildlife Refuge, #3774	6.0
SP1499	(5c) Sea Coast perforated coil, #3775	6.0
SP1500	37c Old Glory, #3776-3780	7.5
SP1501	37c Cesar E. Chavez, #3781	6.0
SP1502	37c Louisiana Purchase, #3782	6.0
SP1503	37c First Flight of Wright Brothers, #3783	6.0
SP1504	37c Purple Heart, #3784	6.0
SP1505	37c Purple Heart, #3784A	6.0
SP1506	37c Audrey Hepburn, #3786	6.0
SP1507	37c Southeastern Lighthouses #3787-3791	7.5
SP1508	(25c) Eagles, two different stamps from #3792-3801	6.0
SP1508A	(25c) Eagles, #3792-3801	10.0
SP1508Ab	(25c) Eagles, dated 2005, #3792a-3801b	10.0
SP1509	37c Arctic Tundra, #3802	10.0
SP1510	37c Korean War Veterans Memorial, #3803	6.0
SP1511	37c Mary Cassatt Paintings, #3804-3807	7.5
SP1512	37c Early Football Heroes, #3808-3811	7.5
SP1513	37c Roy Acuff, #3812	6.0
SP1514	37c District of Columbia, #3813	6.0
SP1515	37c Reptiles And Amphibians, #3814-3818	7.5
SP1516	(37c+8c) Stop Family Violence, #B3	6.00
SP1517	37c Christmas Madonna, #3820	6.00
SP1518	37c Christmas Holiday Music Makers, 2 sets of #3821-3824	7.50
SP1519	37c Snowy Egret coil, #3829	6.00

520	37c	Snowy Egret booklet stamp, #3830	6.00
521	37c	Pacific Coral Reef, #3831	10.00
522	37c	Chinese New Year, #3832	6.00
523	37c	Love, #3833	6.00
524	37c	Paul Robeson, #3834	6.00
525	37c	Theodor Seuss Geisel (Dr. Seuss), #3835	6.00
526	37c	Love (White Lilacs and Pink Roses), #3836	6.00
527	60c	Love (Five Varieties of Pink Roses), #3837	6.00
528	37c	US Air Force Academy, #3838	6.00
529	(5c)	Sea Coast coil reprint, serpentine die cut 9½x10, #3785	6.00

souvenir page containing the original printing of No. 3785 not prepared as there was no first day cancel applied to stamp.

530	37c	Henry Mancini, #3839	6.00
531	37c	American Choreographers, #3840-3843	7.50
532	(25c)	Eagles, perforated, #3844-3853	10.00
533	37c	Lewis and Clark sheet stamp, #3854 (11 cancels)	10.00
534	37c	Lewis and Clark booklet stamps, #3855-3856 (11 cancels)	10.00
535	37c	Isamu Noguchi, #3857-3861	7.50
536	37c	National World War II Memorial, #3862	6.00
537	37c	Summer Olympic Games, Athens, #3863	6.00
538	(5c)	Sea Coast coil, perf. 9¾ vert., #3864	6.00
539	37c	Disney Characters, #3865-3868	7.50
540	37c	USS Constellation, #3869	6.00
541	37c	R. Buckminster Fuller, #3870	6.00
542	37c	James Baldwin, #3871	6.00
543	37c	Martin Johnson Heade, #3872	6.00

SP1544	37c	Art of the American Indian, #3873	10.00
SP1547	37c	John Wayne, #3876	6.00
SP1548	37c	Sickle Cell Disease Awareness, #3877	6.00
SP1549	37c	Cloudscapes, #3878	10.00
SP1550	37c	Christmas Madonna, #3879	6.00
SP1551	37c	Hanukkah, #3880	6.00
SP1552	37c	Kwanzaa, #3881	6.00
SP1553	37c	Moss Hart, #3882	6.00
SP1554	37c	Christmas Santa Claus Ornaments, #3883-3894	10.00

2005

SP1555	37c	Chinese New Year double-sided sheet, #3895	18.00

No. SP1555 was sold in a shrink-wrapped package containing the announcement page, a stamp mount, a cardboard backing and one pane of No. 3895 canceled on both sides.

SP1556	37c	Marian Anderson, #3896	6.00
SP1557	37c	Ronald Reagan, #3897	6.00
SP1558	37c	Love, #3898	6.00
SP1559	37c	Northeast Deciduous Forest, #3899	10.00
SP1560	37c	Spring Flowers, #3900-3903	7.50
SP1561	37c	Robert Penn Warren, #3904	6.00
SP1562	37c	Yip Harburg, #3905	6.00
SP1563	37c	American Scientists, #3906-3909	7.50
SP1564	37c	Modern American Architecture, #3910	10.00
SP1565	37c	Henry Fonda, #3911	6.00
SP1566	37c	Disney Characters, #3912-3915	7.50
SP1567	37c	Advances in Aviation, pane of #3916-3925	15.00
SP1568	37c	Rio Grande Blankets, #3926-3929	7.50
SP1568A	37c	Presidential Libraries, #3930	10.00
SP1569	37c	Sporty Cars, #3931-3935	7.50

SP1570	37c	Arthur Ashe, #3936	6.00
SP1571	37c	To Form a More Perfect Union, #3937	10.00
SP1572	37c	Child Health, #3938	6.00
SP1573	37c	Let's Dance, #3939-3942	7.50
SP1574	37c	Greta Garbo, #3943	6.00
SP1575	37c	Jim Henson and the Muppets, #3944	10.00
SP1576	37c	Constellations, #3945-3948	7.50
SP1577	37c	Christmas, #3949-3960	10.00
SP1578	37c	Distinguished Marines, #3961-3964	7.50
SP1579	(37c)	Flag and Statue of Liberty, #3965-3967, 3970, 3972, 3974, 3975	10.00

No. SP1579 consists of two sheets.

2006

SP1580	(39c)	Love, #3976	6.00
SP1584	39c	Flag and Statue of Liberty Coil serpentine die cut 11 vert., #3980	6.00
SP1591	39c	Children's Book Animals, #3987-3994	10.00

COMPUTER VENDED POSTAGE

1992

SPCVP1	29c	Postage and Mailing Center (PMC) coil strip of 3, #31	3.50

1994

SPCVP2	29c	Postage and Mailing Center (PMC) horiz. coil strip of 3, #32	4.25

1996

SPCVP3	32c	Postage and Mailing Center (PMC) horiz. strip of 3, #33	4.75

INTERNATIONAL REPLY COUPONS

Coupons produced by the Universal Postal Union for member countries to provide for payment of postage on a return letter from a foreign country. Exchangeable for a stamp representing single-rate ordinary postage (and starting with the use of Type D3, airmail postage) to a foreign country under the terms of contract as printed on the face of the coupon in French and the language of the issuing country and on the reverse in four, five or six other languages.

Postmasters are instructed to apply a postmark indicating date of sale to the left circle on the coupon. When offered for exchange for stamps, the receiving postmaster is instructed to cancel the right circle.

Coupons with no postmark are not valid for exchange. Coupons with two postmarks have been redeemed and normally are kept by the post office making the exchange. **Coupons with one postmark are valued here.** Some coupons with a stamp added to pay an increased rate are listed in footnotes.

The following is a list of all varieties issued by the Universal Postal Union for any or all member countries.

Dates are those when the rate went into effect. The date that any item was put on sale in the United States can be very different.

Type A — Face

Wmk. "25c Union Postale Universelle 25c"

1907-20

A1	Face	Name of country in letters 1½mm high.
	Reverse	Printed rules between paragraphs German text contains four lines.

1907-20

A2	Face	Same as A1.
	Reverse	Same as A1 but without rules between paragraphs.

1910-20

A3	Face	Same as A1 and A2.
	Reverse	Same as A2 except German text has but three lines.

1912-20

A4	Face	Name of country in bold face type; letters 2mm to 2½mm high.
	Reverse	Same as A3.

1922-25

A5	Face	French words "le mois d'émission écoulé, deux mois encore."
	Reverse	As A3 and A4 but overprinted with new contract in red; last line of red German text has five words.

Wmk. "50c Union Postale Universelle 50c"

1925-26

A6	Face	Same as A5.
	Reverse	Four paragraphs of five lines each.

1926-29

A7	Face	French words "il est valable pendant un délai de six mois."
	Reverse	As A6 but overprinted with new contract in red; last line of red German text has two words.

Wmk. "40c Union Postale Universelle 40c"

1926-29

A8	Face	Design redrawn. Without lines in hemispheres.
	Reverse	Four paragraphs of four lines each.

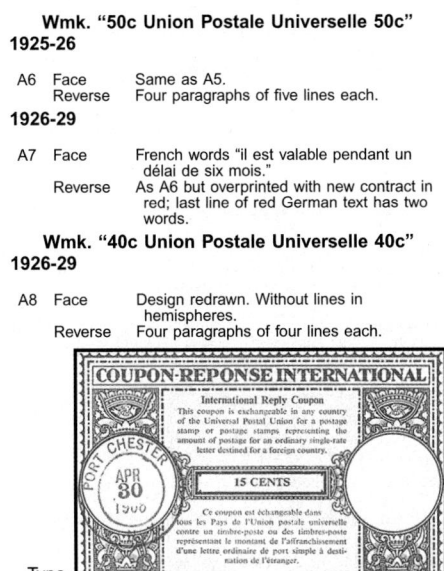

Type B — Face

1931-35   **Wmk. Double-lined "UPU"**

B1	Face	French words "d'une lettre simple."
	Reverse	Four paragraphs of three lines each.

1935-36

B2	Face	French words "d'une lettre ordinaire de port simple."
	Reverse	Last line of German text contains two words.

1936-37

B3	Face	Same as B2.
	Reverse	Last line of German text contains one word.

1937-40

B4	Face	Same as B2 and B3. "Any Country of the Union."
	Reverse	German text is in German Gothic type.

1945

B5	Face	"Any Country of the Universal Postal Union."
	Reverse	Each paragraph reads "Universal Postal Union."

Type B5 exists without central printing on face.

1950

B6	Face	Same as B5.
	Reverse	Five paragraphs (English, Arabic, Chinese, Spanish, Russian).

1954

B7	Face	Same as B5.
	Reverse	Six paragraphs (German, English, Arabic, Chinese, Spanish, Russian.)

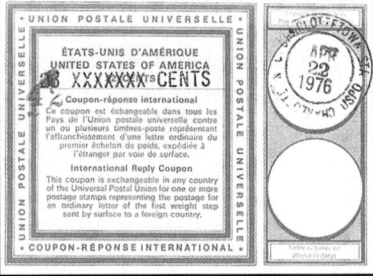

Type C — Face

1968   **Wmk. Single-lined "UPU" Multiple**

C1   Face   French words "d'une lettre ordinaire de port
                  simple."
       Reverse   Six paragraphs (German, English, Arabic,
                  Chinese, Spanish, Russian).

Foreign coupons, but not U.S., of type C1 are known with
large double-lined "UPU" watermark, as on type B coupons.

1971

C2   Face   French words "d'une lettre ordinaire du
                  premier échelon de poids."
       Reverse   Six paragraphs (German, English, Arabic,
                  Chinese, Spanish, Russian).

Type D — Face

1975   **Wmk. Single-lined "UPU" Multiple**

D1   Face   French words "d'une lettre ordinaire,
                  expédiée à l'étranger par voie de surface."
       Reverse   Six paragraphs (German, English, Arabic,
                  Chinese, Spanish, Russian).
D2   Face   Left box does not have third line of French
                  and dotted circle.
       Reverse   Same as D1.

On D1 and D2 the watermark runs horizontally or vertically.

D3   Face   ...aerienne. Left box as D2 with (facultative)
                  added.
       Reverse   As D1, all references are to air service.
D4   Face   As D3, "CN 01 / (ancien C22)" replaces
                  "C22."

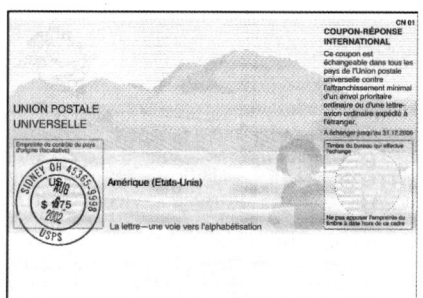

Type E — Face

**Wmk. "UPU" in cross & 8-pointed star horiz.
across sheet**

2002
E1   Face   Shown
       Reverse   Six paragraphs (German, English,
                  Arabic, Chinese, Spanish, Russian),
                  repeating expiration date paragraph
                  in same languages, bar code.

Coupons exist without the validating origination
markings. Type E coupons have a bar code on the
reverse that identifies the originating country and the
date of printing.

**REPLY COUPONS ISSUED FOR THE UNITED
STATES**

1907, Oct. 1
IRC2   A2   6c   **slate green & gray green**   27.50
                  Rules omitted on reverse.
       Earliest documented use: Oct. 10, 1907.

1912
IRC3   A4   6c   **slate green & gray green**   32.50
                  Three line English paragraph on face.

1922, Jan. 1
IRC4   A5   11c   **slate green & gray green,**
                  name 81 ½mm long   25.00
   a.   Name 88 ½mm long   25.00
Five line English paragraph on face. Red overprint on reverse.

1925-26
IRC5   A6   11c   **slate green & gray green**   22.50
Five line English paragraph on face. No overprint on reverse.
IRC6   A6   9c   **slate green & gray green,** *Oct.*
                  1, 1925   22.50

1926
IRC7   A7   9c   **slate green & gray green**   32.50
   Four line English paragraph on face. Red overprint on
reverse.
IRC8   A8   9c   **slate green & gray green**   25.00
                  Without lines in hemispheres.

1935
IRC9   B2   9c   **blue & yellow**   11.00
   On reverse, last line of German text contains two words.

1936
IRC10   B3   9c   blue and yellow   11.00
   On reverse, last line of German text contains one word.

1937
IRC11   B4   9c   **blue & yellow**   8.00
   On reverse, German text in German Gothic type.

1945
IRC12   B5   9c   **blue & yellow,** Italian text on re-
                  verse in 4 lines   6.00
   a.   Italian text on reverse in 3 lines   7.50

1948, Oct. 15
IRC13   B5   11c   **blue & yellow**   5.00
   On face, "Universal Postal Union" replaces "Union."

1950
IRC14   B6   11c   **blue & yellow**   6.00
   On reverse, text in English, Arabic, Chinese, Spanish,
Russian.

1954, July 1
IRC15   B7   13c   **blue & yellow**   6.00
   On reverse, text in German, English, Arabic, Chinese, Spanish, Russian.
   Varieties: period under "u" of "amount" in English text on
reverse, and period under "n" of "amount." Also, country name
either 47mm or 50mm long.

No. IRC15 Surcharged in Various Manners
1959, May 2
IRC16   B7   15c on 13c   **blue & yellow**   6.00
   Individual post offices were instructed to surcharge the 13c
coupon, resulting in many types of surcharge in various inks.
For example, "REVALUED 15 CENTS," reading vertically; "15,"
etc.

1959, May 2
IRC17   B7   15c   **blue & yellow**   5.00

1964
IRC18   B7   15c   **blue & yellow**   5.00
   a.   Reverse printing 60mm deep instead of
                  65mm (smaller Arabic characters)   5.00
   On face, box at lower left: "Empreinte de contrôle / du Pays
d'origine / (date facultative)" replaces "Timbre du / Bureau /
d'Emission."

1969
IRC19   C1   15c   **blue & yellow**   4.50

1971, July 1
IRC20   C2   22c   **blue & yellow**   4.50

No. IRC20 Surcharged in Various Manners
1974, Jan. 5
IRC21   C2   26c on 22c   **blue & yellow**   6.50
                  See note after No. IRC16.

1975, Jan. 2
IRC22   D1   26c   **blue & yellow**   4.00

No. IRC22 Surcharged in Various Manners
1976, Jan. 3
IRC23   D1   42c on 26c   **blue & yellow**   6.50
   See note after No. IRC16. Several post offices are known to
have surcharged No. IRC21 (42c on 26c on 22c).

Provisional surcharges on Nos. IRC24-IRC27
not permitted.

1976, Jan. 3
IRC24   D1   42c   blue & yellow

Many foreign countries use non-denominated IR
The U.S. has never ordered or used these "gen
items.

1981, July 1
IRC26   D1   65c   blue & yellow

1986, Jan. 1
IRC27   D2   80c   blue & yellow

1988, Apr. 3
IRC28   D2   95c   blue & yellow
IRC29   D3   95c   blue & yellow
   a.   "9.1992" in lower left corner

   Post offices were authorized on July 11, 1995 to rev
remaining stock of 95c IRCs to $1.05 by applying 10c in sta
until new stock (No. 30) arrived. All 95c varieties are kn
revalued thus.
   The date of issue of No. 29 is not known. Earliest d
mented use: Jan. 2, 1992.
   No. 28 exists with inverted watermark (tops of letters fa
right).

1995
IRC30   D4 $1.05   blue & yellow, "4.95" in lower
                  left corner
   a.   "10.98" in lower left corner
   b.   As "a," with "United States of America" in
                  left box

   "1.05" comes 1 ½mm or 3mm high. 3mm height has nume
more widely spaced.
   Earliest documented use: July 12, 1995.
   Post offices were authorized on Jan. 7, 2001, to rev
remaining stock of $1.05 IRCs to $1.75 by applying 70
stamps until new stock arrived. All $1.05 varieties are kn
revalued thus. Value $7.

2002, Jan. 1
IRC31   E1 $1.75   multicolored

   Effective Jan. 8, 2006, the rate increased to $1.85. F
offices were authorized to revalue remaining stock of $1
IRCs to $1.85 by applying 10c in stamps.

POST OFFICE SEALS

fficial Seals began to appear in 1872. They do not express any value, having no franking power.
he first seal issued was designed to prevent tampering with registered letters while in transit. It was intended to be affixed over the juncture of the
s of the large official envelopes in which registered mail letters were enclosed or stamp requisitions were shipped to postmasters and was so used
lusively. Beginning in 1877 (No. OX1 and later), Post Office Seals were used to repair damaged letters, reseal those opened by mistake or by
toms inspectors, and to seal letters received by the Post Office unsealed.

alues for unused Post Office Seals are for those without creases. Uncanceled seals without gum will sell for less.

sed Post Office Seals will usually have creases from being applied over the edges of damaged or accidentally opened covers but will
e either cancels, precancels or a signature or notation indicating use on the seal. Creased, uncanceled seals without gum are considered
d and will sell for less than either an unused or a canceled used seal.

overs with Post Office Seals are almost always damaged except in cases when the seal was applied to a cover marked "Received
sealed." The values shown are for covers where the damage is consistent with the application of the seal.

ost Office Seals must be tied or exhibit some auxiliary marking or docketing to qualify for "on cover" values. No. OXF1 must bear a
cular date stamp cancel and the cover to which it is affixed must bear the identical cancel to qualify for the "on cover" value.

REGISTRY SEALS

RGS1

National Bank Note Co.
Typographed from a copper plate of 30 subjects
(3x10) in two panes of 15 (3x5)

		White Wove Paper	Perf. 12	
'72		**Unwmk.**		
F1	RGS1	**green**	30.00	7.50
		On cover, Barber signature		40.00
		On cover, Terrell signature		75.00
		Block of 4	500.00	
		Pane of 15	2,500.	
a.		**Yellow green,** pelure paper	75.00	40.00
b.		Imperf., pair	1,500.	
c.		Horizontally laid paper	500.00	
d.		Printed on both sides	500.00	
e.		Printed on both sides, back inverted	800.00	
f.		Double impression	750.00	—
g.		Double impression, one inverted	—	750.00

e second impression of Nos. OXF1d-OXF1g, is very faint.
lso issued as a pane of 9 (3x3) (attributed to Continental
k Note Co.).

Cancellations

Black	7.50
Blue	+5.00
Red	+15.00
Green	+50.00
Magenta	+50.00
Carrier	+25.00
Panama	—
Shanghai	—

Special Printings

Continental Bank Note Co.
Plate of 30 subjects (5x6)

		Hard White Wove Paper	Perf. 12
'75(?)		**Without Gum**	
F2	RGS1	bluish green	1,000.

American Bank Note Co.
Plate of 15 subjects (5x3)

		Soft Porous Paper	Perf. 12
80 (?)		**Without Gum**	
F3	RGS1	bluish green	1,000.

POSTAGE STAMP AGENCY SEALS

Used to seal registered pouches containing stamps
r distribution to Post Offices.

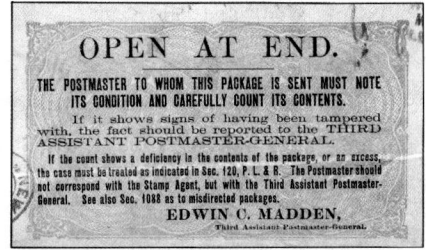

PSA1

Background size: 102x52mm.

1875-93		Litho.	Unwmk.	Die Cut
		Barber Signature		
OXF4	PSA1	brown & black		20.00
		On cover		50.00
		Hazen Signature, Text 87mm Wide		
OXF5	PSA1	brown & black, *1877*		15.00
		On cover		50.00
		Hazen Signature		
OXF6	PSA1	pink & red, *1886*		50.00
		On cover		350.00
a.		Salmon & red		60.00
		On cover		400.00
		Harris Signature		
OXF7	PSA1	pink & red, *1887*		20.00
		On cover		75.00
a.		Salmon & red, on cover		150.00
		Hazen Signature, Text 90½mm Wide		
OXF8	PSA1	pink & red, *1889*		20.00
		On cover		75.00
		Craige Signature		
OXF9	PSA1	pink & red, *1893*		35.00
		On cover		90.00

PSA2

Background size: 120½x67mm.

1894		Litho.	Unwmk.	Die Cut
		Craige Signature, "3rd Asst. P.M.G."		
OXF10	PSA2	pink & red		25.00
		On cover		85.00
		Craige Signature, "Third Assistant Postmaster General"		
OXF11	PSA2	pale pink & red		25.00
		On cover		85.00
a.		Deep pink & red		25.00
		On cover		85.00

**"John A. Merritt" in Sans-Serif Capitals at Left.
Two Horizontal Lines Obliterating "Kerr Craige."**

1897				
OXF12	PSA2	pale pink & red		40.00
		On cover		

Design of 1894

1897-1910(?)				
		Merritt Signature		
OXF13	PSA2	rose & black		20.00
		On cover		75.00
		Madden Signature		
OXF14	PSA2	rose & black		25.00
		On cover		100.00
		"Section 878"		
OXF15	PSA2	rose & black		25.00
		On cover		125.00
		"Section 970"		
OXF16	PSA2	rose & black, *1910*		22.50
		On cover		125.00

DEAD LETTER OFFICE SEALS

No. OX1 supposedly was issued as a Dead Letter
Office Seal. Most on-cover examples are normal Post
Office usages from larger East Coast cities. New York
and Philadelphia predominate. Very few examples with

Dead Letter Office markings are recorded. For that
reason, No. OX1 is listed with the other Post Office
Seals.

"Hazen" — DLO1

1884		Litho.	Unwmk.	Perf. 10½, 12
OXA1	DLO1	black		32.50
		On cover		125.00

"Baird" — DLO2

1889				Perf. 12
OXA2	DLO2	black		45.00
		On cover		250.00

"Superintendent" — DLO3

1891				Perf. 10½, 12
OXA3	DLO3	black		25.00
		On cover		90.00

"5-2807" — DLO4

1892			Perf. 12
OXA4	DLO4	black	25.00
		On cover	90.00

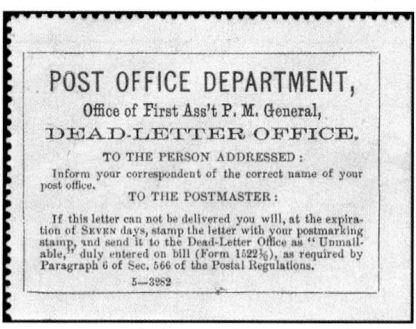

"5-3282" — DLO5

1895			Perf. 12
OXA5	DLO5	black	22.50
		On cover	75.00

1898(?)			Hyphen hole perf. 7
OXA6	DLO5	black	40.00
		On cover	200.00

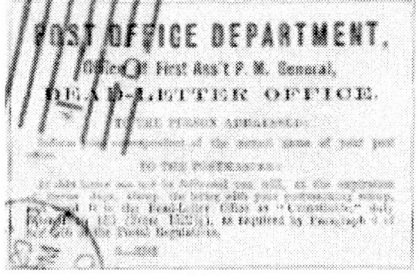

DLO6

Similar to DLO5 but smaller type used for instructions to the postmasters.

1900			Perf. 12
OXA7	DLO6	black	20.00
		On cover	75.00

"5-3282" at Right — DLO7

1902(?) 12			Perf. 12
OXA8	DLO7	black	25.00
		On cover	85.00

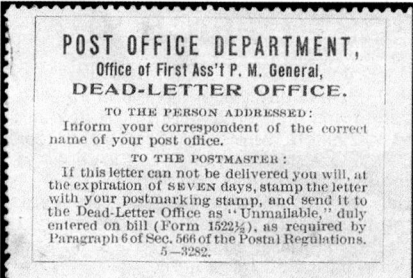

"5-3282" at Center — DLO8

1902(?)			Perf. 12
OXA9	DLO8	black	25.00
		On cover	85.00

POST OFFICE SEALS

See introduction.
No. OX1 was prepared for use in the Dead Letter Office but was distributed to other offices and used in the same way as the later seals.

POS1

("Post Obitum" in background.)
National Bank Note Co.
Plate of 100 subjects (10x10)
Silk Paper

1877			Engr.		Perf. 12
OX1	POS1	brown		45.00	25.00
		On cover			1,200.
		Block of 4	500.00		

POS2

American Bank Note Co.
Plate of 100 subjects (10x10) in two panes of 50 bearing imprint of American Bank Note Co.
(Also plates of 50 (10x5) subjects)

1879			Engr.		Perf. 12
		Thin, crisp, semi-translucent paper, yellowish gum			
OX2	POS2	red brown		3.00	1.00
		On cover			85.00
		Block of 4		15.00	
		Margin block with imprint		25.00	
a.		Brown		10.00	5.00
		On cover			200.00
		Block of 4		60.00	
		Margin block with imprint		85.00	

Seal impression can be clearly seen when viewed from the back.

Plate of 50 subjects (5x10). Four imprints of the American Bank Note Co. centered on each side of the pane with a reversed "2" to the right of the top imprint.

1879(?)				
		Thick, opaque paper, clear transparent gum		
OX3	POS2	yellow brown	150.00	150.00

1881(?)				
		Thin, hard porous paper, clear transparent gum		
OX4	POS2	deep brown		75.00
		Block of 4		350.00
		Margin block of 4 with imprint (side)		400.00

	Margin block of 6 with imprint (bottom)		550.00
	Margin block of 4 with imprint & reversed "2" (top)		575.00

No. OX4 is the so-called "Special Printing." It was proc from a new plate prepared from the original die. It receive usage, but at least two full panes are known to have exis

Colors

Beginning with OX5, many Official Seals exhi wide variety of shades. Minimal care was exercis their printing. It is not uncommon for seals wit single pane to vary in shade from dark to very ligh attempt is being made here to list all of the var shades separately.

POS3

Typographed
Without words in lower label.
Outer frame line at top and left is thick and hea (compare with POS4).
Plate of 72 subjects (8x9)

1888			Rough perf
		Medium thick, crisp paper	
OX5	POS3	chocolate (shades)	.75
		On cover	5
		On cover with typeset seal No. LOX8	
		Block of 4	5.00
a.		Imperf, pair	50.00
		Sheet of 72, imperf	—

Imperforates
Imperforates of Nos. OX6, OX7, OX10 and OX13 believed to be printer's waste. No seals were iss imperforate, though some may have been sent to p offices.

Plate of 42 subjects (7x6)

1889			Rough perf.
		Thick to extremely thick paper	
OX6	POS3	chocolate (shades)	.75
		On cover	4
		Block of 4	5.00

1889(?)			Perf.
OX7	POS3	bister brown (shades)	.75
		On cover	4
		Block of 4	5.00
a.		Rose brown	4.00
		On cover	2
		Block of 4	22.50
b.		Yellow brown	2.00
		On cover	2
		Block of 4	10.00
c.		Imperf. vertically, pair	25.00
d.		Imperf. horizontally, pair	25.00
e.		Vertical pair, imperf. between	20.00
f.		Horizontal pair, imperf. between	75.00
g.		Double impression	
		Cancellation	
		Puerto Rico	+75

Examples of No. OX7 with multiple impressions wid spaced or at angles to each other, are found on normal pa and various documents. These are printer's waste.

1892			Rouletted
OX8	POS3	light brown (shades)	20.00 15
		On cover	1,2
		Block of 4	300.00

1895 (?)			Hyphen Hole Perf
OX9	POS3	gray brown	7.50 5
		On cover	500.
		Block of 4	200.00

Earliest documented use: Feb. 3, 1897.

1898(?)			Perf.
		Thin soft paper	
OX10	POS3	brown (shades)	1.50 1
		On cover	250.
		Block of 4	8.00

POS4

Plate of 143 (11x13)

Outer frame line at top and left is thin.
Otherwise similar to POS3.

1900			**Perf. 12**	
X11	POS4	**red brown**	.50	.25
		On cover		30.00
		Block of 4	2.50	
a.		**Gray brown**	2.00	1.25
		On cover		45.00
		Block of 4	15.00	
b.		**Dark brown**	2.50	*4.50*
		On cover		85.00
		Block of 4	15.00	
c.		**Orange brown**	.75	*2.00*
		On cover		75.00
		Block of 4	4.00	

Most imperfs and part perfs are printers waste. Some genuine perforation errors may have been issued to post offices.

Watermarks

Watermarks cover only a portion of the panes. Many stamps in each pane did not receive any of the watermark. Values for watermarked panes are for examples with at least 50% of the watermark present.

Similar to POS4 but smaller.
Design: 38x23mm
Issued in panes of 20 (5x4)

1907		**Typo.**		**Perf. 12**
OX12	POS4	**bright royal blue**	2.00	2.00
		On cover		45.00
		Pane of 20	60.00	

Earliest documented use: June 1, 1907.

OX13	POS4	**blue** (shades)	.20	.20
		On cover		25.00
		Pane of 20	20.00	
a.		Wmkd. Seal of U.S. in sheet (2 types)	1.50	1.50
		Pane of 20	50.00	
b.		Wmkd. "Rolleston Mills" in sheet	1.00	1.00
		Pane of 20	40.00	
c.		Wmkd. "Birchwood Superfine" in sheet	—	—
		Pane of 20	—	
d.		Pelure paper	20.00	20.00
e.		Toned paper	25.00	25.00
f.		Printed on both sides		

Numerous varieties such as imperf., part perf., tete beche, and double impressions exist. These seem to be from printer's waste. Some genuine perforation errors may have been issued to post offices.

1912			**Hyphen Hole 6½**	
OX14	POS4	**blue**	1.75	1.50
		On cover		75.00
		Pane of 20	45.00	
a.		Wmkd. Seal of U.S. in sheet	10.00	10.00
		Pane of 20	300.00	
b.		Wmkd. "Rolleston Mills" in sheet	2.50	2.50
		Pane of 20	80.00	

Panes of 10 were made from panes of 20 for use in smaller post offices. Complete booklets with covers exist.

1913			**Perf. 12 x Hyphen Hole 6½**	
OX15	POS4	**blue**	3.50	3.00
		On cover		100.00
		Pane of 20	110.00	
a.		Hyphen-hole perf 6½ (right) x Perf. 12 (left, top, bottom)	15.00	—
		Pane of 20	150.00	
b.		Wmkd. Seal of U.S. in sheet	4.50	4.00
		Pane of 20	125.00	
c.		As "a" and "b"	20.00	—

No. OX15a comes from panes that are perfed between the left selvage and the seals.

1913			**Hyphen Hole 6½ x Perf. 12**	
OX16	POS4	**blue**	5.25	5.25
		On cover		250.00
		Pane of 20	250.00	
a.		Wmkd. Seal of U.S. in sheet	6.50	6.50
		Pane of 20	300.00	
b.		Wmkd. "Rolleston Mills" in sheet	—	—
		Pane of 20	—	

1916			**Perf. 12**	
OX17	POS4	**black,** *pink*	1.25	1.25
		On cover		150.00
		Pane of 20	75.00	
a.		Vert. pair, imperf. horizontal	—	

Three complete panes of No. OX17a have been reported.

1917			**Perf. 12**	
OX18	POS4	**gray black**	.40	.40
		On cover		27.50
		Pane of 20	40.00	
a.		**Black**	.50	.50
		On cover		30.00
		Pane of 20	45.00	
b.		Vert. pair, imperf horizontally	25.00	
c.		Horiz. pair, imperf vertically	20.00	
d.		Vertical pair, imperf between	60.00	
e.		Horizontal pair, imperf between	35.00	
f.		Imperf, pair	50.00	

POS5

Quartermaster General's Office
Issued in panes of 10 (2x5) without selvage.

1919			**Perf. 12**	
OX19	POS5	**indigo**	300.	
		Block of 4	1,600.	
		Pane of 10	3,600.	

			Rouletted 7	
OX20	POS5	**indigo**	—	3,250.

The pane format of No. OX20 is not known. One of the few reported examples is rouletted on four sides.
Nos. OX19-OX20 were used on mail to and from the Procurement Division of the Quartermaster General's Office. After five weeks of use the seals were withdrawn when the Mail and Records Section became a full branch of the Quartermaster General's Office.

POS6

Issued in panes of 20 (5x4) and 16 (4x4).
Panes of 10 were made from panes of 20 for use in smaller post offices.

1919			**Perf. 12 (sometimes rough)**	
			Thin, white, crisp paper	
OX21	POS6	**black** (shades)	.20	.20
		On cover		10.00
		Pane of 20	10.00	
a.		Imperf, pair	15.00	
		On cover		—
b.		Vert. pair, imperf horiz.	10.00	
c.		Horiz. pair, imperf vert.	10.00	
d.		Vert. pair, imperf btwn.	25.00	
e.		Horiz. pair, imperf btwn.	25.00	
f.		Wmkd. eagle and star in sheet (1936?)	2.00	2.00
		Pane of 20	70.00	
g.		As "f," imperf, pair	35.00	
h.		As "f," vert. pair, imperf horiz.	27.50	
i.		As "f," vert. pair, imperf btwn.	27.50	
j.		Wmkd. "Certificate Bond" in sheet (1936?)	10.00	10.00
		Pane of 20	300.00	

The paper used for Nos. OX21-OX27 is thin enough to allow reading text on the envelope.

Earliest documented use: 1920.

1936(?)			**Perf. 12x9**	
OX22	POS6	**black** (shades)	7.50	7.50
		On cover		85.00
		Pane of 20	200.00	
a.		Vert. pair, imperf horiz.	50.00	
b.		Horiz. pair, imperf vert.	50.00	
c.		Wmkd. eagle and star in sheet	7.50	7.50
		Pane of 20	200.00	
d.		As "c." vert. pair, imperf horiz.	50.00	
e.		As "c," horiz. pair, imperf vert.	50.00	

Earliest documented use: Oct. 1936 (No. OX22 or OX23.)

1936(?)			**Perf. 12x8½**	
OX23	POS6	**black** (shades)	2.50	2.50
		On cover		40.00
		Pane of 20	75.00	
a.		Wmkd. eagle and star in sheet	4.00	4.00
		Pane of 20	110.00	

1936(?)			**Perf. 12½**	
OX24	POS6	**gray black,** pane of 20	—	

1936(?)			**Perf. 8½**	
OX25	POS6	**gray black**	—	
a.		Wmkd. eagle and star in sheet	—	

1936(?)			**Perf. 12x9½**	
OX26	POS6	**gray black,** pane of 20	—	

1936(?)			**Perf. 11½**	
OX27	POS6	**gray black**	—	
		On cover		—

Medium to thick, opaque, egg or cream colored paper

1946(?)			**Perf. 12**	
OX28	POS6	**gray black**	.40	.40
		On cover		25.00
		Pane of 20	22.50	
a.		Vert. pair, imperf btwn.	15.00	

1946(?)			**Perf. 12½**	
OX29	POS6	**gray black**	.50	.50
		On cover		25.00
		Pane of 20	25.00	

1947(?)			**Perf. 12½x8½**	
OX30	POS6	**gray black**	1.50	1.50
		On cover		45.00
		Pane of 20	50.00	

1947(?)			**Perf. 8½**	
OX31	POS6	**gray black**	1.50	1.50
		On cover		45.00
		Pane of 20	50.00	

1947(?)			**Perf. 8½x12**	
OX32	POS6	**gray black**	—	

1947(?)			**Perf. 8½x8**	
OX33	POS6	**gray black,** on cover	—	

1947(?)			**Perf. 8x8½**	
OX33A	POS6	**gray black,** on cover	—	

Thick, gray, very soft paper

1948			**Perf. 12½ (sometimes rough)**	
OX34	POS6	**gray black**	1.00	1.00
		On cover		35.00
		Pane of 16	45.00	

1948(?)			**Perf. 8½**	
OX35	POS6	**gray black**	5.00	5.00
		On cover		60.00
		Pane of 16	—	

1948(?)			**Perf. 12½x8½**	
OX36	POS6	**gray black**	—	
		Pane of 10	—	
		Pane of 20	—	

1948(?)			**Perf. 8½x12½**	
OX37	POS6	**gray black**	—	

1948			**Hyphen Hole Perf. 9½**	
OX38	POS6	**gray black**	15.00	15.00
		On cover		100.00
		Pane of 5, imperf at sides	—	
		Pane of 16	350.00	

Pane of 5, tab inscribed "16-56146-1 GPO."

1950(?)			**Hyphen Hole Perf. 9½ x Imperf**	
		Medium thick, cream paper		
		Design width: 37½mm		
OX39	POS6	**gray black,** imperf at sides	.25	.20
		On cover		12.50
		Pane of 5, imperf at sides	1.25	
a.		Vert. pair, imperf between	10.00	
b.		Pane of 5, imperf	15.00	
c.		Pane of 5, imperf at top & btwn. rows 2 & 3, 4 & 5	20.00	

Pane of 5 tab inscribed, "16-56164-1 GPO."
Earliest documented use: Jan. 23, 1950.

1969(?)			**Hyphen Hole Perf. 9½ x Imperf**	
		Medium thick, white paper		
		Design width: 38½mm		
OX40	POS6	**gray black**	.25	.20
		On cover		30.00
		Pane of 5, imperf at sides	2.25	
a.		Vert. pair, imperf. btwn.	10.00	
b.		Pane of 5, Imperf	20.00	

Tab inscribed, "c43-16-56164-1 GPO"

Earliest documented use: Feb. 11, 1969.

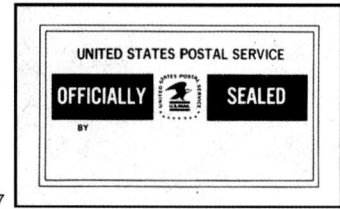

POS7

On Nos. OX41-OX50, tab is inscribed, "LABEL 21, JULY 1971."

1972 **Litho.** *Rouletted 9½ x Imperf*
OX41	POS7	black	.20	.20
		On cover		12.50
		Pane of 5	2.00	
a.		Imperf, pair	10.00	

1972(?) *Rouletted 6½ x Imperf*
OX42	POS7	black	.20	.20
		On cover		5.00
		Pane of 5	2.75	

1973(?) **Litho.** *Hyphen Hole 7 x Imperf*
OX43	POS7	black	.30	.20
		On cover		7.50
		Pane of 5	9.00	

1976(?) **Litho.** *Rouletted 8½ x Imperf*
OX44	POS7	black	.20	.20
		On cover		7.50
		Pane of 5	2.00	

1979(?) **Litho.** *Perf. 12½ x Imperf*
OX45	POS7	black	.20	.20
		On cover		7.50
		Pane of 5	2.25	
		Small holes	.20	.20
		On cover		7.50
		Pane of 5	2.25	

1988(?) **Litho.** *Die Cut*
Self-Adhesive
OX46	POS7	black, 38x21mm, tagged, fluorescent paper	.25	.25
		On cover		7.50
		Pane of 5	3.50	
OX47	POS7	bluish black, 38x21mm, untagged, non-fluorescent paper	.25	.25
		On cover		7.50
		Pane of 5	3.50	
OX48	POS7	gray (shades), 37x21mm	.25	.25
		On cover		7.50
		Pane of 5	3.50	
OX49	POS7	black, 40x21mm	.50	.50
		On cover		15.00
		Pane of 5	10.00	
OX50	POS7	purple, 37x21mm	—	—
		On cover		

No. OX47 is on a creamier, thicker paper than No. OX46.
On No. OX49, BY is 2x1mm, P of POSTAL is left of P in POSTAL of Emblem. Tab inscribed as No. OX41, but 1's have no bottom serif.
Earliest documented use: No. OX50, Dec. 12, 1995.

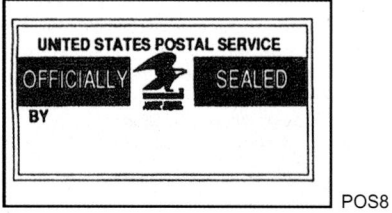

POS8

Tab inscribed "LABEL 21, JAN. 1992."

1992 **Size: 44x22mm** *Die Cut*
Self-adhesive
OX51	POS8	black	1.00	1.00
		On cover		25.00
		Pane of 5	10.00	

Earliest documented use: Mar. 1992.

1992? *Die Cut*
Self-Adhesive
Size: 41x21mm
OX52	POS8	black	.25	.25
		On cover		7.50
		Pane of 5	3.50	

No. OX52 exists on both white and brown backing paper. Those on brown backing paper are worth more.

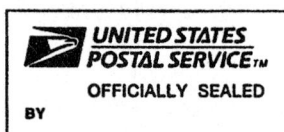

POS9

Tab inscribed "LABEL 21, April 1994."

1994 *Die Cut*
Self-Adhesive
OX53	POS9	black	.25	.25
		On cover		7.50
		Pane of 5	3.50	

POS10

Tab inscribed "LABEL 21, August 1996."

1996 *Die Cut*
Self-Adhesive
OX54	POS10	black	.25	.25
		On cover		7.50
		Pane of 5	2.00	
a.		"OFFICALLY"	1.00	—
		On cover		20.00
		Pane of 5	8.00	

TYPESET SEALS

These seals were privately printed for sale mostly to Fourth Class Post Offices. Many are extremely rare. Unquestioned varieties are listed. Many others exist.

All are imperf or die cut except Nos. LOX7-LOX11 and LOX36.

TSS1

| LOX1 | TSS1 | black | 500.00 | 500.00 |
| | | On cover | | — |

TSS2

LOX2	TSS2	black, 15 diamonds vertically in frame	1,500.	1,500.
a.		14 diamonds vertically		750.
b.		14 diamonds vertically, no period after "DEPARTMENT"		750.
c.		"OFFICALLY" misspelling, 14 diamonds vertically	1,500.	
		On cover		—

TSS3

| LOX3 | TSS3 | black | — |
| | | On cover | |

TSS4

| LOX4 | TSS4 | black, pink | 1,25 |

No. LOX4 used is valued with minor flaws.

TSS5

| LOX5 | TSS5 | black | 500.00 |
| LOX5A | TSS5 | black, pink | — |

TSS6

| LOX6 | TSS6 | black | |

TSS7

Rouletted 9½ horizontally
| LOX7 | TSS7 | black | 500.00 |

TSS8

Printed and distributed by Morrill Bros., P.O. Supply Printers, Fulton, N.Y., in panes of 4, two tete beche pairs.

Rouletted 11½, 12½, 16½ in black at top & side

OX8	TSS8	black	50.00	50.00
		On cover		750.00
a.		Tete beche pair	100.00	
		Sheet of 4	600.00	

TSS9

Solid lines above and below "OFFICIALLY SEALED."

Rouletted 12½, 16½ in black between

OX9	TSS9	black	500.00	500.00
		On cover		

TSS10

Dotted lines above and below "OFFICIALLY SEALED."

Rouletted 11½, 12½ or 16½ in black

OX10	TSS10	black, *pink*	500.00	—
OX11	TSS10	black	1.50	
		On cover		1,000.
a.		Tete beche pair	3.00	
		Pane of 4	6.00	
c.		Dot after "OFFICIALLY"	2.50	
		On cover		—
d.		Pair, Nos. LOX11, LOX11c	4.00	
e.		As "d," in tete beche pair	4.50	
f.		Pane of 4, one stamp with dot	37.50	
g.		As "c," blue, rouletted 12½ horiz.		750.00
h.		Pane of 2, both stamps with dot	—	
i.		Double impression, one inverted	—	

TSS11

Printed and distributed by The Lemoyne Supply Co., Lemoyne, Pa.

No. LOX13 has thin lines above and below 37¼mm long "OFFICIALLY SEALED"

LOX12	TSS11	black	250.00	
		On cover		—
LOX13	TSS11	blue	750.00	

U. S. Postoffice Dept.
OFFICIALLY SEALED
Opened through mistake by

TSS12

LOX14	TSS12	blue	1,750.	1,750.

TSS13

LOX15	TSS13	black	1,250.	—
		On cover		2,000.

No. LOX15 unused is valued with small faults and crease. See No. LOX29 for a similar design in blue.

TSS14

LOX16	TSS14	blue	1,500.	1,000.

No. LOX16 used is valued with usual crease, thin spots and small tear.

TSS15

LOX17	TSS15	dark blue	100.00	200.00
		On cover		1,000.
a.		Printed on both sides	1,250.	
b.		2mm between "y" & "S," no period after "d"	200.00	
LOX18	TSS15	black	400.00	—
		On cover		1,000.

U. S. Post Office.
OFFICIALLY SEALED
Opened Through Mistake by

TSS16

LOX19	TSS16	black	600.00	—

U. S. Post Office.
PLYMOUTH, MICHIGAN
OFFICIALLY SEALED
Opened Through Mistake by

TSS16a

LOX19A	TSS16a	black	2,750.	

No. LOX19A is unique. Valued based on 2000 auction sale.

Type I — TSS17

Type II — Bottom line in heavy type face. Period after "Office."

LOX20	TSS17	black, *light green* (Type I)	—	—

At least two different types or settings are known. The illustrated type has a dotted line above "BY" that does not show in the illustration.

LOX20A	TSS17	black, *light green* (Type II)	2,000.	

No. LOX20A is valued with major thin at top center.

POST OFFICE DEPARTMENT
Officially Sealed
BERKELEY, CAL.

TSS18

LOX21	TSS18	black	750.00	

POST OFFICE DEPARTMENT
Officially Sealed
BERKELEY, CAL.

TSS18a

LOX21A	TSS18a	black	—	1,500.
		On cover		1,500.

No. LOX21A unused is valued with crease and small faults.

U. S. Postoffice
PETALUMA, CAL.
Officially Sealed
Opened by Mistake by

TSS19

LOX22	TSS19	black, *blue*	2,000.	

No. LOX22 is unique. It is creased and is valued as such.

TSS20

LOX23	TSS20	black	—	

TSS21

LOX24 TSS21 **black,** on cover 3,000.

TSS22

LOX25 TSS22 **black** 1,350.

At least three examples of No. LOX25 exist. All have faults. Value is for the finest example.

TSS23

LOX26 TSS23 **black** 1,100.

No. LOX26 used is valued with small fault.

TSS24

LOX27 TSS24 **black,** *dark brown red* 1,250.

No. LOX27 is valued with crease and small flaws.

TSS25

LOX28 TSS25 **black,** on cover 2,000.

No. LOX28 is unique. The seal was torn in half when the envelope was opened. Value is based on 2000 auction sale.

TSS26

LOX29 TSS26 **blue,** on cover 3,750.

No. LOX29 is unique.

TSS27

LOX30 TSS27 **black,** pair on cover 2,500.

No. LOX30 is unique. The seals were torn in half when the envelope was opened.

TSS28

LOX31 TSS28 **red,** *cream* 1,000.

No. LOX31 is unique. It has a thin spot and crease and is valued as such.

TSS29

LOX32 TSS29 **black** 1,250.

TSS30

LOX33 TSS30 **black**

TSS31

LOX34 TSS31 **red,** *rose* 1,25
On cover 1,50

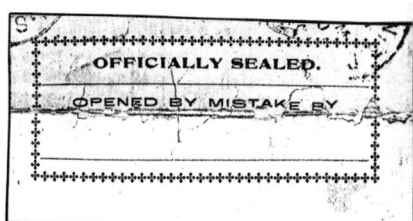

TSS32

LOX35 TSS32 **black,** on cover

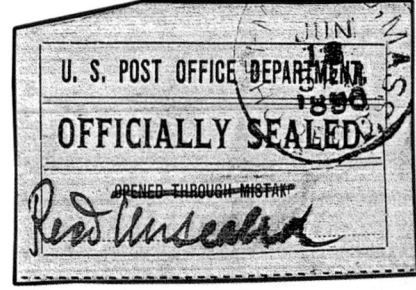

TSS33

Rouletted (at least one side)
LOX36 TSS33 **black**

TSS34

LOX37 TSS34 **green**

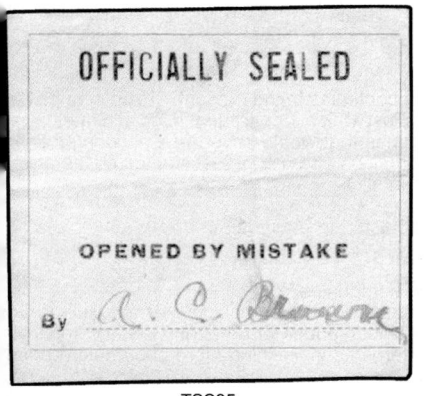

TSS35

OX38　TSS35　**black,** *tan*　　　　1,250.

TSS36

OX39　TSS36　**black,** *tan*　　　　1,750.

TSS37

LOX40　TSS37　**black,** *tan*　　　　1,750.

TSS38

LOX41　TSS38　**black**　　　　—

Akron, N. Y. Post Office.

Officially Sealed.

Opened through mistake by

TSS39

LOX42　TSS39　**black,** on cover　　　　—

STOCKBOOKS

Stockbooks are a classic and convenient storage alternative for many collectors. These German-made stockbooks feature heavyweight archival quality paper with 9 pockets on each page. The 8½" x 11⅝" pages are bound inside a handsome leatherette grain cover and include glassine interleaving between the pages for added protection. The Value Priced Stockbooks are available in two page styles, the white page stockbooks feature glassine pockets while the black page variety includes clear acetate pockets

Black Page Stockbooks
Acetate Pockets

ITEM	COLOR	PAGES	RETAIL
ST16RD	Red	16 pages	$10.95
ST16GR	Green	16 pages	$10.95
ST16BL	Blue	16 pages	$10.95
ST16BK	Black	16 pages	$10.95
ST32RD	Red	32 pages	$16.95
ST32GR	Green	32 pages	$16.95
ST32BL	Blue	32 pages	$16.95
ST32BK	Black	32 pages	$16.95
ST64RD	Red	64 pages	$29.95
ST64GR	Green	64 pages	$29.95
ST64BL	Blue	64 pages	$29.95
ST64BK	Black	64 pages	$29.95

Available from your favorite dealer or direct from:

P.O. Box 828
Sidney OH 45365-0828
www.amosadvantage.com
1-800-572-6885

TEST STAMPS

Test stamps, also called "dummy stamps," came into being in the late 19th century, and their production continues to the present. These stamps hav been printed by both the Bureau of Engraving and Printing and by private companies for use when the Post Office Department, United States Post Service and other companies wanted to use test stamps rather than accountable paper (i.e., actual stamps that would have to be accounted for).

With the growth of automation and the development of vending equipment in the 20th century, the production and use of test stamps proliferated. majority are very scarce, as these items generally were not made available to the general public or philatelists.

The test stamps listed here were produced for several purposes:
1. To develop and test production equipment, including printing presses and stamp and booklet manufacturing equipment.
2. To design stamp vending equipment by private companies.
3. To test, adjust and promote stamp affixing equipment by commercial vendors.
4. To test and adjust stamp vending equipment at dispensing sites by the Postal Service and private companies.

The test stamp listing have been arranged into two sections, the first being sheet and coil stamps, and the second being booklets. These listings we formed by Steven R. Unkrich, in consultation with other leading collectors of test stamps. Thanks to Dan Undersander for preparing the accompanyir Special Feature article and for supplying much of the information in this section's introduction. Those interested in learning more about test (dumm stamps are invited to join the Dummy Stamps Study Group. Contact Terry Scott at trs@napanet.net.

Blank Design — TE9

Produced by Continental Bank Note or American Bank Note Company.

1878-79   Soft Paper   Unwmk.   Perf. 12
TD9 TE9   blank   —
           Block of 4   —

See Nos. TD44-TD50, TD75-TD76, TD79-TD82, TD83-TD86, TD106, TD113-TD114, TD122 for other blank design stamps.

Burt and Toby's Stamp Battery — TE9a

1890   Perf. 12
TD9A TE9a   light green   —

Perf. 12¼x12
TD9B TE9a   lavender   —

Blank Design Type of 1878-79
Produced by Bureau of Engraving and Printing.

1907   Wmk. 191   Perf. 12
Brownish Gum
TD10 TE9   blank   —

TE10

Schermack Coil — TE11

Mailometer Coil — TE12

1906-09   Unwmk.   Perf. 12
TD12 TE10   **orange**, on cover   —

Schermack Type III Perforations
TD13 TE11	**red**	—
	Pair	—
	Pasteup pair	—
TD14 TE12	**brown**	—
	On cover	—
	Pair	—
	Guide line pair	—
	Pasteup pair	—
a.	Imperf.	100.00
	Pair	200.00

Mailometer Type I Perforations
TD15 TE12	**brown**	—
	Pair	—
	Pasteup pair	—

Mailometer Type II Perforations
TD16 TE12	**brown**	—
	Pair	—
	Guide line pair	—
	Pasteup pair	—

Mailometer Type III Perforations
TD17 TE12	**brown**	—
	Pair	—

See Vending and Affixing Machines Perforations section for illustrations of perforation types.

Bureau of Engraving and Printing Test Stamps for Rotary Press Development

Numerals and Oval — TE13

Numerals and Alexander Hamilton — TE14

Nos. TD18-TD23 were the first test stamps used by the BEP during efforts to develop rotary press printing as a less costly method of stamp production than flat plate printing. Experiments were conducted with intaglio (engraving), letterpress (typography) and offest lithography printing. Engraving was the selected technique. The rotary press was developed under the direction of BEP Director Joseph E. Ralph, but is generally named the Stickney Press after its inventor and patent holder, Benjamin F. Stickeny.

1909-10   Engr.   Imperf.
Design: 19x22mm
Ungummed Soft Wove Paper
TD18 TE13	**deep red**	900.00
	Block of 4	—
	Block of 12 with pencil inscription on back	8,000.

Inscription on block of 12 reads "first impression printed from an experimental press designed by J. E. Ralph & B. F. Stickney from intaglio roll JER."

Design: 19½x22½mm
TD19 TE14	**red**	100.00
	Block of 4	—

No. TD19 portrait has facial shading composed of fine lines and dots. Subjects spaced 3½mm horizontally and 2mm vertically. Large die proofs exist with "400894" on back. Value, $2,000.

Coil Stamps (Nos. TD20-TD21, TD23)
Typo.
Design: 19x22½mm
Perf. 12 Vert.
Ungummed Soft Wove Paper
TD20 TE14	**deep red**, *1910*	1,00

Three different die proofs are known for No. TD20. The first black on thick glazed card, measuring 73x83mm, with inscription "first die proof impression of experimental surface die fro surface print. JER April 25/10," with "420279" on back. Valu $2,000.

The second is deep red on thick glazed card, measurir 73x83mm, with inscription "Sample of surface printing from di done by Bureau E&P 5/20/1910," with "420270" on back. Valu $1,500.

The third is deep red cut to design size on thick card wi number stamps on back. Value, $1,000.

Perf. 12 Horiz.
Soft Wove Paper
TD21 TE14	**deep red**, *1910*	3,10

Perf. 12
TD22 TE14	**deep red**, *1910*	

The portrait on Nos. TD21-TD22 has facial shading com posed of fine lines and small squares, open-centered whe large.

Offset (Litho.)
Design: 19x21½mm
Perf. 10½ Horiz.
TD23 TE14	**deep red**, *1910*	75.0
	Pair	150.00
	Pair, on cover	1,00

The portrait of No. TD23 has facial shading composed of do and short lines providing a coarse appearance.

Automatic Vending Co. Coil — TE15

1909   Imperf
TD24	TE15	**dark red**	
		Horiz. pair	—
a.		Vert. pair, U.S. Automatic Vending Co. Type I separations	—
		On cover	—
b.		Vert. pair, imperf. horiz.	—

Rosback perf 11.75 Vert.
TD24C	TE15	**red**	
		Horiz. pair	—
d.		Vert. pair, imperf. horiz.	—

Imperf
TD24E	TE15	**green**	
		Vert. pair	—

Simplex Mfg. Co. — TE16

909-10   *Imperf.*
Solid Background
D25 TE16   red   60.00
Horizontal Lines in Background
D26 TE16   green   60.00

Simplex Stamp Affixer — TE17

909-10   *Imperf.*
D27 TE17   red   —

BEP Test Stamps for Offset Printing

Minerva Facing Right — TE18

Minerva Facing Left (Text Reversed) — TE19

Nos. TD28-TD29 were made to test the Harris offset press at the Bureau of Engraving and Printing. The offset method was not adopted in 1910 but several Harris presses were used to print revenue stamps and the offset postage issues of 1918-20.

1910   Litho.   *Imperf.*
Design: 30½x34mm
Ungummed White Wove Paper
TD28 TE18   red   650.00
    Pair   1,300.
    Block of 4   —
Design: 30x33½mm
TD29 TE19   red   650.00
    Pair   1,300.
    Block of 4   —

Blank Design — TE20

1910 ?   *Rouletted 13¼ Vert.*
Stamp Size: 25.5x25.75mm
Shiny Gum
TD30 TE20   blank, *tan*   20.00
    Pair   40.00

Standard Stamp Affixer Coils

Inscribed "Boston, Mass." — TE21   Inscribed "Everett, Mass." — TE22

Inscribed "Somerville, Mass." — TE23

1910s   *Perf. 10½ Vert.*
TD31 TE21   green   —
    Pair   —
TD32 TE21   red   —
    Pair   —
TD33 TE22   green   —
    Pair   —
TD33A TE22   red   —
    Pair   —
Alternating Perf. 8¼ and 8½ Vert.
TD34 TE23   green   —
    Pair   —
Perf. 8½ Vert.
TD35 TE23   light green   —
    Pair   —
Perf. 10½ Vert.
TD36 TE23   green   —
    Pair   —
TD36A TE23   red   —
    Pair   —

Multipost Co. Coil — TE24a

TE24 Detail

TE24a Detail

1910-20   *Perf. 9¾ Vert.*
TD37 TE24   red   20.00
    Pair   50.00
Perf. 10¼ Vert.
TD38 TE24a   carmine   20.00
    Pair   50.00

No. TD37 has full shading lines, and No. TD38 has shorter shading lines.

Extensive Manufacturing Co. Coils — TE25

1911-13   *Perf. 8½ Horiz.*
TD39 TE25   red & blue   —
    Pair   —
Perf. 10¼ Vert.
TD40 TE25   carmine & black   —
    Pair   —
Perf. 10¾ Vert.
TD41 TE25   carmine & black   —
    Pair   —

Standard Mailing Machine Co. Coils — TE26

1913   *Perf. 10½ Vert.*
TD42 TE26   red   —
    Pair   —
TD43 TE26   light purple   40.00
    Pair   80.00

Blank Designs Type of 1878-79
1910-27   *Imperf.*
Smooth Gum
TD44 TE9   blank   —
    Pair   —
Perf. 10½ Vert.
TD45 TE9   blank   —
    Pair   —
Schermack Type III Perforations
TD46 TE9   blank   —
    Pair   —
    Paste up pair   —
Mailometer Type I Perforations
TD47 TE9   blank   —
    Pair   —
    Paste up pair   —
Mailometer Type II Perforations
TD48 TE9   blank   —
    Pair   —
    Paste up pair   —
Mailometer Type III Perforations
TD49 TE9   blank   —
    Pair   —
    Paste up pair   —
Perf. 11 Vert. Schermack Type I 7-hole Perforations
TD50 TE9   blank   —
    Pair   —

Expertization is recommended for No. TD44.

George Washington — TE27

1912   *Imperf.*
Without Gum
TD51 TE27   brown   100.00
    Pair   200.00

No. TD51 tested a photo-etching process by Bruckmann A. G. of Munich, Germany.

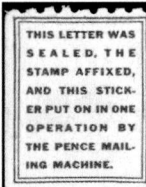

Pence Mailing Machine —
TE27a

1914 *Perf 8½ Horiz.*
TD51A TE27a **red** 100.00
Pair —

New Jersey Vending Machine
Co. Coil — TE28

1914-16 *Perf. 10½ Vert.*
TD52 TE28 **red** —
Pair —

National Envelope Sealing
and Stamp Manufacturing
Coils — TE29

1915 *Perf. 8½ Horiz.*
TD53 TE29 **red & blue** —
Pair —
TD54 TE29 **red** —
Pair —

Mailometer Coils — TE30

1922 *Nine small perforation holes*
TD55 TE30 **red** —
Pair —

Perf. 10¼ Vert. (10 small holes)
TD56 TE30 **deep purple** —
Pair —

Perf. 12 Vert. (8 small holes)
TD57 TE30 **deep purple** —
Pair —

Perf. 12 Vert. (9 small holes)
TD57A TE30 **deep purple** —
Pair —

Perf. 10¼ Vert.
TD58 TE30 **red** —
Pair —
On cover —

Inscribed "10,000 Envelopes Per Hour"
Perf. 10½ Vert.
TD59 TE30 **red** —
Pair —

TE30a

Perf. 10.5 Vert.
TD60 TE30a **red** —
Pair —

TE30b

Perf. 10.5 Vert.
TD60A TE30b **red** —
Pair —

Wizard Label Affixer
Coil — TE31

1912-14 *Perf. 10¼ Vert.*
TD61 TE31 **red** —
Pair —

Wizard Label Affixer
Coil — TE31a

1920s *Schermack Type III Perforations*
TD61A TE31a **red & blue** —

Wizard Stamp Affixer
Coil — TE32

1920s *Perf. 10 Vert.*
TD62 TE32 **red & blue** —
Pair —

Postage Stamp Machine Co.
Coil — TE33

1920s *Perf. 8½ Vert.*
TD63 TE33 *red* —
Pair —

Natural Method Stamp Affixer
— TE33a

1910-30 *Perf. 11¾ Vert.*
TD63A TE33a **red,** *tan* —
Pair —

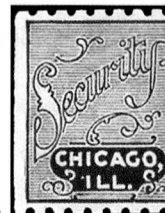

Security Coil — TE33b

1910-30 *Perf. 8½ Hori.*
TD63B TE33b **red** —

Licensed Sanitary
Postage Coil — TE34

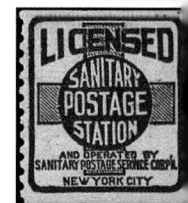

TE34a

1920s *Perf. 10½ Hori.*
TD64 TE34 **red** —
Pair —

Perf. 10¾ Vert.
TD65a TE34 **red** 20.0
Pair 50.0

Postcraft Stamp Affixer
Coil — TE35

1920s *Perf. 10 Ver.*
TD66 TE35 **color unknown** —
Pair —

Vidaver Mailing Machine
Co. Inc. Coil — TE36

1920s *Perf. 10½ Vert.*
TD67 TE36 **red** 90.0
Pair 180.0

Agnew Auto Mailing — TE37

1920s *Perf.*
TD68 TE37 **red brown** 45.00

Royalty Stamp — TE38

1925 ? *Perf.*
TD69 TE38 **red** —

Stearns-Daniels Co.
Coil — TE39

0s-30s   *Perf. 10 Vert.*
TE39   **green**   —
     Pair   —

RO-TA-RE Stamp Affixer
ervice Machines Company
—TE39a

0-30   *Perf. Vert.*
0A TE39a   **blue**   —

Edison Dictating Machine
Coil — TE40

0s-30s   *Perf. 10¼ Vert.*
1 TE40   **red**   60.00
     Pair   125.00

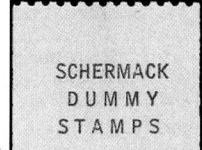

SCHERMACK DUMMY STAMPS

Schermack Dummy
Coil — TE41

0s-30s   *Perf. 10½ Horiz.*
2 TE41   **red**   —
     Pair   —

National Postal Meter Co.,
Inc. Coil — TE42

20s-30s   *Perf. 9¾ Vert.*
3 TE42   **red**   —
     Pair   —

Stampmasters Inc.
Coil — TE43

20s-30s   *Perf. 9¾ Vert.*
74 TE43   **violet**   15.00
     Pair   30.00

Blank Design Types of 1878-79
Produced by Bureau of Engraving & Printing.

27-30   *Perf. 9¾ Vert.*
Horiz. Ribbed Gum
75 TE9   blank, *cream*   .60
     Pair   1.25

With Red Horizontal Lines 13½ mm Apart
TD76 TE9   blank, *1930-40*   .60
     Pair   1.25
     Pair with gap in lines   4.00
     Strip of 10 with wide and narrow line
     gaps   15.00
     Gaps appear every six stamps.

Central Machine & Supply Co.
Coil — TE44

1930s   *Perf. Vert.*
TD77 TE44   **red**   —
     Pair   —

Puritan Mailing Machine Co.
Coil — TE45

1930s   *Perf. 8½ Vert.*
TD78 TE45   **red & black**   —
     Pair   —

The Postamper Co. Coil —
TE45a

1930s   *Perf. 10½ Vert.*
TD78A TE45a   **red**   —
     Pair   —

Peerless Stamp Affixer Coil —
TE45b

1930s   *Perf. 10½ Vert.*
TD78B TE45b   **red**   —
     Pair   —

Blank Design Types of 1878-79
Produced by Electric Vendors (Zeigle), Inc.

1930s   *Perf. 10½ Vert.*
Shiny Smooth Gum

TD79 TE9   blank   15.00
     Pair   35.00
TD80 TE9   *blue*   15.00
     Pair   35.00
TD81 TE9   *green*   15.00
     Pair   35.00
TD82 TE9   *yellow*   15.00
     Pair   35.00

Blank Design Types of 1878-79
Produced by Bureau of Engraving & Printing.

1920s-1950s   *Perf. 10*
With Gum Breaker Ridges 5½mm Apart
TD83 TE9   blank, *1920s*   25.00
     Block of 4   100.00
     Vert. pair with horiz. gutter between
With Gum Breaker Ridges 11mm Apart
     Perf. 11x10½
TD84 TE9   blank, *1936*   25.00
     Block of 4   100.00
     Vert. pair with horiz. gutter between   80.00

Stamp Size:40x25mm
With Gum Breaker Ridges
Brownish Gum
Perf. 11¼x10½
TD85 TE9   blank   50.00
     Block of 4   200.00
Produced by American Bank Note Co.
Perf. 12
TD86 TE9   blank pane of 50 with manuscript
     marginal markings, *1943*   —
No. TD86 was produced as a test for the Overrun Countries stamps.

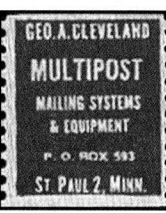

Multipost Mailing System &
Equipment Coil — TE46

1930s-40s   *Perf. 9½ Vert.*
TD87 TE46   **red**   —
     Pair   —

Multipost Co. Walter I. Plant
Agent Coil — TE46a

1930s   *Perf. 11¾ Vert.*
TD87A TE46a   **red**   —
     On cover   —
     Pair   —

Multipost Agents The Office
Appliance Co. Coil — TE46b

1930s   *Perf. 11¾ Vert.*
TD87B TE46b   **red**   —
     Pair   —

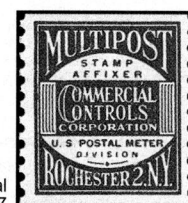

Multipost Commercial
Controls Coil — TE47

1944-49   *Perf. 9¾ Vert.*
TD88 TE47   **blue**   20.00
     Pair   50.00
TD89 TE47   **black**   20.00
     Pair   50.00
     On cover   75.00
TD90 TE47   **blue black**   20.00
     Pair   50.00

Multipost Commercial
Controls Multipost
Mailmaster
Coil — TE48

Multipost Friden
Multipost Mailmaster
Coil — TE49

1944-49 — Perf. 9¾ Vert.

TD91	TE48	**purple**	20.00
		Pair	50.00
TD92	TE48	**carmine**	30.00
		Pair	80.00
TD93	TE49	**carmine**	20.00
		Pair	50.00

Framed Rectangle — TE50

Printed by Bureau of Engraving & Printing.

1954 — Perf. 11.2x10.5

TD94	TE50	**carmine**	100.00
		Block of 4	400.00
		P# block of 4, P#141730 or 141731	—

Imperf

TD94A	TE50	**carmine**	100.00
		Pair	200.00
		Block of 4	400.00
		P# block of 4, P#141730 or 141731	750.00

Coil Stamps
Perf. 9¾ Vert.

TD95	TE50	**purple,** large holes	3.00
		Pair	8.00
		Joint line pair	20.00
		On cover with "Parade of Postal Progress" cancel	85.00
		Small holes, *1959*	6.00
		Pair	15.00
		Joint line pair	35.00
a.		Imperf., pair	35.00
		Joint line pair	85.00

Examples of No. TD95 with poor centering are common and sell for less.

TD96	TE50	**red violet,** small holes	2.00
		Pair	5.00
		Joint line pair	12.00
		Large holes	5.00
		Pair	12.00
		Joint line pair	125.00
		On cover with "Parade of Postal Progress" cancel	85.00
a.		Imperf., pair	80.00
		Joint line pair	—
b.		Block of 8 with joint line, sheet margin and P#165939 or 165940, unslit horiz.	—

See "large hole" and "small hole" illustrations after No. 1053 in Postage section.

TD97	TE50	**carmine**	200.00
		Pair	400.00
		Joint line pair	600.00
a.		Imperf., horiz. pair	300.00
		Joint line pair	—
b.		Vert. pair, unslit horiz.	—
		Block of 4 with joint line, unslit horiz.	—

Expertization is recommended for Nos. TD97, TD97a and TD97b.

Kansas Territorial Centennial Experimental TE51

Printed by Bureau of Engraving and Printing.

1954 — Perf. 12x11¾

TD98	TE51	**brown, red & yellow**	200.00
		Block of 4	800.00

Nebraska Territorial Centennial Experimental — TE52

1954 — Imperf.
Size: 25x40mm

TD99	TE52	**brown**	200.00
		Block of 4	800.00
a.		**brown,** *tan*	—
TD100	TE52	**black**	200.00
		Block of 4	800.00
TD101	TE52	**blue**	200.00
		Block of 4	800.00

Pitney Bowes Co. — TE53

1958-59 — Imperf.
Helecon Paper

TD102	TE53	**rose carmine**	—
a.		Lumogen paper	—
TD103	TE53	**black**	—

Helecon paper glows reddish orange under shortwave UV light. Lumogen paper glows bright yellow-green under shortwave UV light.

Stamp-E-Z Postage Stamp Affixer Coil — TE54

1960s — Imperf.

TD104	TE54	**light purple**	—
		Pair	—

Perf. 9¾ Vert.

TD105	TE54	**red**	—
		Pair	—

Blank Design Type of 1878-79

Produced by Bureau of Engraving and Printing

1960-70s — Overall Tagging — Perf. 9¾ Vert.
Dull Gum

TD106	TE9	**blank**	12.50
		Pair	25.00
		Joint line pair	100.00

No. TD106 was printed on an inked press. The ink was wiped, but some stamps have wiping marks and black joint lines.

For Testing Purposes Only Coil — TE55

Produced by Bureau of Engraving and Printing.

1962-88 — Engr. — Perf. 9¾ Vert.
Design Size: Approximately 19½mm Wide

TD107	TE55	**black,** untagged, shiny gum	.50
		Pair	1.00
		Joint line pair	5.00
a.		Tagged, shiny gum	.50
		Pair	1.00
		Joint line pair	5.00
b.		Tagged, pebble-surfaced gum	1.50

		Pair	
		Joint line pair	
c.	As "b," imperf. pair		
	Joint line pair		2
d.	Tagged, dull gum		
		Pair	
		Joint line pair	
e.	Untagged, dull gum		
		Pair	
		Joint line pair	

No. TD107 is known on hi-brite fluorescent paper.
No. TD107b has been found with red, dark red, rose blue, blue green, green, orange, violet, brown, black black, gray black, gray and silver defacement lines, which in number and thickness and which have been known to been forged. Some defacement line colors may all be forg
No. TD107e is known on fluorescent and non-fluore papers, as well as on papers with diagonal gum striatic wavy, intermittent gum striations

TD108	TE55	**carmine,** tagged, *1970*	5
		Pair	
		Joint line pair	

The tagging on Nos. TD108 and TD114 is orange re other stamps glow yellow green.

TD109	TE55	**green,** untagged, dull gum, *1970*	1
		Pair	
		Joint line pair	
		Block of 12 with joint line, P# 36111 and 36112	
a.		Imperf., pair	4
		Joint line pair	2
b.		Vert. pair, imperf. horiz.	2
c.		Tagged, gray paper, shiny gum	1
		Pair	
		Joint line pair	
d.		As "c," imperf, pair	5
		Joint line pair	
e.		As "c," vert. pair, imperf. horiz.	

No. TD109 was sent to Germany in large imperf. an perforate sheets to test coil production equipment.

TD110	TE55	**orange,** *gray,* tagged, *1975*	
		Pair	
		Joint line pair	
TD111	TE55	**brown,** untagged, *1978*	
		Pair	
		Joint line pair	

Design Size: Approximately 19mm Wide

TD112	TE55	**black,** untagged, dull gum *1978*	
		Pair	

No. TD107 was printed on the Cottrell press. No. TD11 printed on the B press.
See Nos. TD121, TD126-TD127, TD133, TD136-TD13

Blank Design Type of 1878-79

Produced by Bureau of Printing and Printing, with ta added by Pitney Bowes.

1964 — Pe

TD113	TE9	blank, yellow green tagging	2
		Block of 4	
TD114	TE9	blank, orange red tagging	
		Block of 4	

Nos. TD113-TD114 was produced as a test for Nos. 1257.

Flag Coil — TE56

Produced by Avery Products Corp.

1970s — Die

Self-Adhesive

TD115	TE56	**blue,** on rouletted backing paper	2
a.		On imperforate backing paper	

Proclaim Liberty TE57

1970s — Perf. 12

TD116	TE57	**blue, red & green**	

Christmas
Test Stamp
TE58

Printed by Bureau of Engraving and Printing for Avery Prod-
Corp. to add die cutting.

3   *Die Cut*
Self-Adhesive
17 TE58	**black,** rouletted backing paper	2.00
	Block of 4 with intact matrix	8.00
	Pane of 50	110.00
	Press sheet of 200	750.00
a.	With imperforate backing paper	—

No. TD117 was produced as a test for No. 1552.

XPERIMENTAL   Octagons — TE59

rinted by Bureau of Engraving and Printing.

60s   *Imperf.*
18 TE59	**multicolored**	140.00
	Block of 4	400.00
	P# block of 4, P#173404	—

Flag and Eagle Over Trees
Coil — TE60

rinted by Stamp Venturers.

89   *Perf. 10 Vert.*
19 TE60	**gray**	.25
	Pair	.50

Rouletted
20 TE60	**gray**	.25
	Pair	.50

similar design, in multicolor, with "Sennett Security Prod-
s" at lower left was a souvenir distributed at World Stamp
o 2000.

For Testing Purposes Only Type of 1962-88
rinted by Martin Marietta Corp.

90s	**Photo.**	**Untagged**	*Imperf.*
21 TE55	black		75.00
	Pair		150.00
	Block of 4		400.00

Blank Design Type of 1878-79
roduced by Bureau of Engraving and Printing.

90s	**Untagged**	*Perf. 9¾ Vert.*
22 TE9	blank, shiny gum	10.00
	Pair	30.00
	Dull gum	10.00
	Pair	30.00

Stylized Eagle Coil — TE61

Printed by 3M Corp.

Linerless Self-Adhesive
1992			*Imperf.*
TD123 TE61	**multicolored**		20.00
	Pair		40.00
	P# strip of 5, #1111		400.00

Stamps have simulated perforations.

Rectangle With Thick Lines
Coil — TE62

Printed by Bureau of Engraving and Printing.

1996		*Perf. 9¾ Vert.*
TD124 TE62	**blue,** shiny gum	50.00
	Pair	100.00
	Strip of 5 with one stamp with	
	crudely etched reversed "2"	1,500.
	Strip of 5 with one stamp with	
	crudely etched reversed "12"	1,500.

Reversed numbers appear in the center of every 24th stamp.

TD125 TE62	**gray black,** dull gum	125.00
	Pair	250.00

For Testing Purposes Only Type of 1962-88
Printed by Bureau of Engraving and Printing (#TD126),
Avery-Dennison (#TD127).

1996		*Die Cut*
	Self-Adhesive	
TD126 TE55	**black,** *blue*	.25
	Pair	.50
	P# strip of 5, #1111	5.00

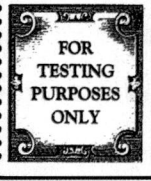

TE55a

Serpentine Die Cut 11.2 Vert.
TD127 TE55a	**black**	.25
	Pair	.50
	P# strip of 5, #V1	15.00

Design T55a has printed perforation "holes" in addition to
serpentine die cutting.

Polar Bear Ice Skating —
TE62a

Printed by Ashton-Potter (USA) Ltd.

1995	*Serpentine Die Cut 11x10.9*
	Design Size: 21x35mm
	Self-Adhesive
TD127A TE62a	**multicolored** —
	Block of 4 —
	Sheetlet of 25 —

The sheetlet of 25 has vertical and horizontal gutters between
the stamps with the matrix removed.

	Serpentine Die Cut 11x11.5
TD127B TE62a	**multicolored** —
	Block of 4 —
	Sheetlet of 25 —

The sheetlet of 25 has no vertical or horizontal gutters
between the stamps.

BCA PERF TEST   Parrot — TE63

Printed by Banknote Corporation of America.

1996	*Serpentine Die Cut 11¾x11½*
	Design Size: 22x31mm
	Self-Adhesive (#TD128)
TD128 TE63	**multicolored** —
	Design Size: 25x40mm
	Perf. 11½
TD129 TE63	**multicolored** —

No. TD129 has hidden lettering "c 1995 GSSC" across bottom, and "Scrambled Indicia" vertically up the right side. Used
to test luminescent inks.

Rectangle With Thin Lines
Coil — TE64

Printed by Bureau of Engraving and Printing.

1998	*Serpentine Die Cut 9¾ Vert.*
	Self-Adhesive
TD130 TE64	**blue** 125.00
	Pair 250.00
	Strip of 3 with one stamp with "3"	
	printed horizontally —

NOT FOR POSTAGE

00 USA   Star Spangled Banner/Not for
Postage Coil — TE64a

1998	*Serpentine Die Cut 11¼ Vert.*
	Self-Adhesive
TD130A TE64a	**multicolored** —
	Pair —

Octagons — TE64b

1998   *Serpentine Die Cut 12.6*
                            Self-Adhesive
TD130B TE64b   **multicolored**   —

RENA Test Stamp
Coil — TE65

1999   *Die Cut*
                            Self-Adhesive
TD131 TE65   **blue**   10.00
               Pair   25.00

Mailbox Coil — TE66

Printed by Avery Dennison.

2000   *Imperf.*
                    Linerless Self-Adhesive
TD132 TE66   **red**   100.00
               Pair   200.00
  a.   Pair with "xxxx" on one stamp   —

Pairs have 1-2mm slit marks between stamps in right margin.

For Testing Purposes Only Type of 1962-88
Printed by Bureau of Engraving and Printing.

2000   *Serpentine Die Cut 9¾ Vert.*
                            Self-Adhesive
TD133 TE55   **black,** *blue*   .25
               Pair   .50
               P# strip of 5, #1111   7.00

Stamps are printed on white backing paper with 2mm gap between perforation tips. A four digit counting number is on the back of the backing paper on every 20th stamp.

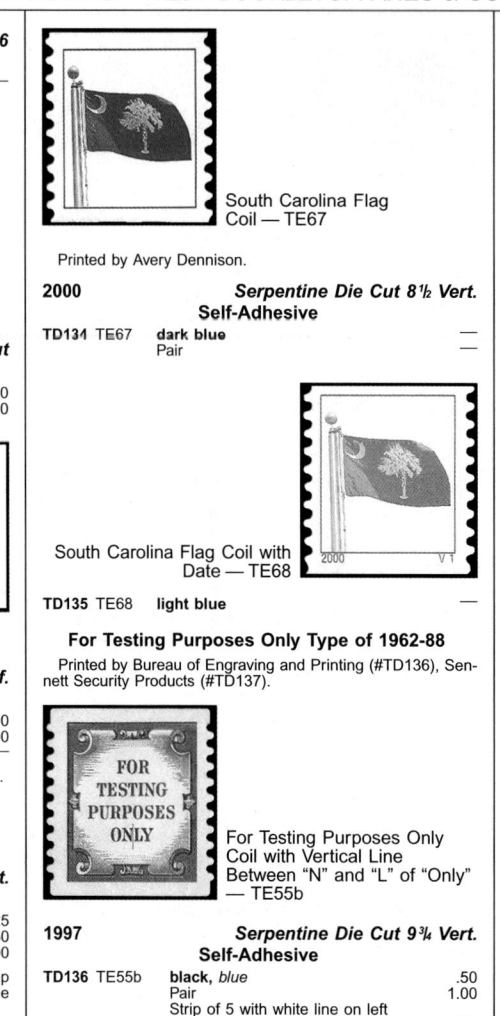

South Carolina Flag
Coil — TE67

Printed by Avery Dennison.

2000   *Serpentine Die Cut 8½ Vert.*
                            Self-Adhesive
TD134 TE67   **dark blue**   —
               Pair   —

South Carolina Flag Coil with
Date — TE68

TD135 TE68   **light blue**   —

For Testing Purposes Only Type of 1962-88
Printed by Bureau of Engraving and Printing (#TD136), Sennett Security Products (#TD137).

For Testing Purposes Only
Coil with Vertical Line
Between "N" and "L" of "Only"
— TE55b

1997   *Serpentine Die Cut 9¾ Vert.*
                            Self-Adhesive
TD136 TE55b   **black,** *blue*   .50
               Pair   1.00
               Strip of 5 with white line on left
                 or right margin of center stamp 7.00

Stamps with white lines appear every 21st stamp.

                    Serpentine Die Cut 11¼ Vert.
TD137 TE55b   **black**
               Pair
               P# strip of 5, #S1

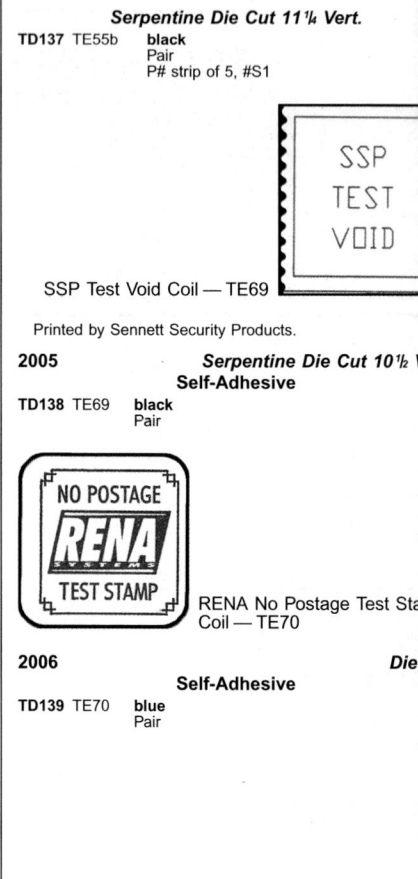

SSP Test Void Coil — TE69

Printed by Sennett Security Products.

2005   *Serpentine Die Cut 10½ V*
                            Self-Adhesive
TD138 TE69   **black**
               Pair

RENA No Postage Test Sta
Coil — TE70

2006   *Die*
                            Self-Adhesive
TD139 TE70   **blue**
               Pair

TEST BOOKLETS: PANES & COVERS

Test booklets normally are collected as complete booklets, and the major listings are for complete booklets. Very often the booklet panes in differ booklets are the same or similar. Booklet panes are presented as lettered minor listings. Where similar booklet panes can be differentiated by g breaker measurements, size measurements, or other factors, they are given separate minor listings. Single stamps from these booklets are not gi minor listings.

This test booklet section is divided into four categories: stapled booklets, folded and glued booklets with water- activated gum, and folded and glu booklets with self-adhesive gum, and ATM sheetlets.

STAPLED BOOKLETS

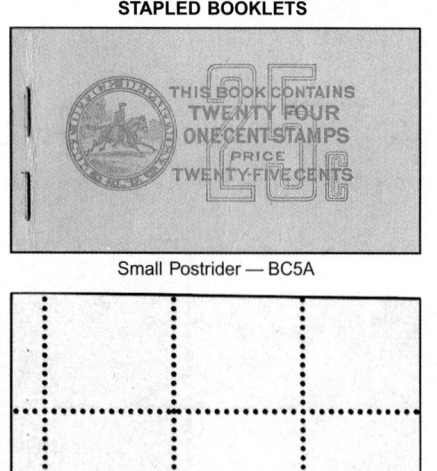

Small Postrider — BC5A

Blank Stamps — TDP1

1927-30   *Perf. 11¼x10½*
TDB1 BC5A 25c **green,** *green,* 4 #TDB1a   —
  a.   TDP1 Pane of 6

Horiz. gum breakers are 22mm apart on No. TDB1a. No. TDB1 has 5 waxed glassine interleaves, 1 in front of the first pane and 1 behind each pane.

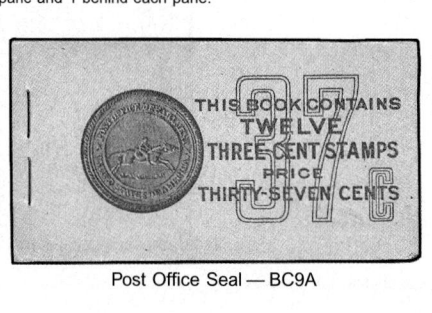

Post Office Seal — BC9A

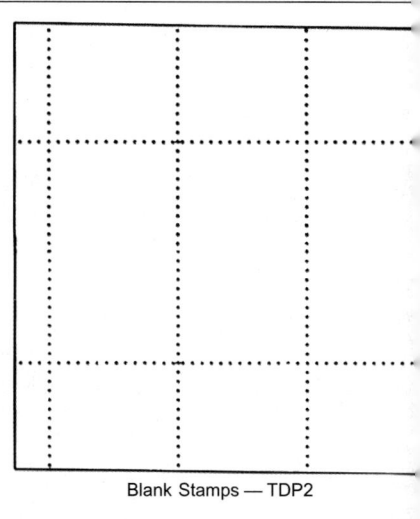

Blank Stamps — TDP2

'0s

2 BC9A 37c **violet,** *buff,* 2 #TDB2a —
   a. TDP2 Pane of 9, 6 definitive and 3 commemorative sized stamps —

Jo. TDB2 has a cover composed of two BC9A items
parated horizontally. No. TDB2 has 2 waxed glassine inter-
ves, 1 behind each pane.

Framed Rectangles — TDP3

'0

3 BC9A 37c **violet,** *buff,* 2 #TDB3a 600.00
   a. TDP3 **purple,** pane of 6 250.00

loriz. gum breakers are 11mm apart on No. TDB3a. No.
B3 has 2 waxed glassine interleaves, 1 behind each pane.

Type of 1940

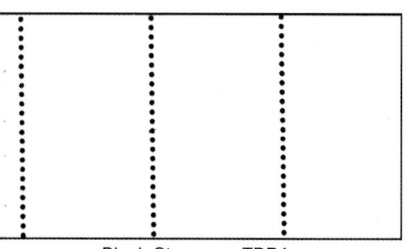

Blank Stamps — TDP4

'0s

B4 BC9A 37c **violet,** *buff,* #TDB4a, TDB4b 450.00
   a. TDP1 Pane of 6 —
   b. TDP4 Pane of 3, perf. 10 vert. —

loriz. gum breakers are 6mm apart on Nos. TDB4a and
B4b. No. TDB4 has 2 waxed glassine interleaves, 1 behind
ch pane.

Post Office Seal — BC9H

'59

B5 BC9H 97c **blue,** *pink,* 4 #TDB5a 175.00
   a. TDP1 Pane of 6 —
   b. As #TDB5, with silicone interleaves 325.00

loriz. gum breakers are 5½mm apart, and vert. gum break-
s are 21mm apart on No. TDB5a. No. TDB5 has 4 waxed
assine interleaves, and No. TDB5a has 4 silicone interleaves,
behind each pane. Some panes may show a joint line and/or
E markings.

U.S. Airmail Wings — BC11C

'59

B6 BC11C 97c **blue,** 4 #TDB6a 175.00
   a. TDP1 Pane of 6 —

Horiz. gum breakers are 5½mm apart on No. TDB6a. Some
nes may exhibit faint vertical gum breakers. Nos. TDB6 has 2
axed glassine interleaves, 1 behind each pane.

Post Office Seal Type of 1959

Misperforated and Miscut Framed
Rectangles — TDP5

1960-62

TDB7 BC9H 97c **blue,** *pink,* 4 #TDB7a 900.00
   a. TDP5 **red violet,** pane of 6 200.00

Horiz. gum breakers are 4½-6½mm apart and vert. gum
breakers are 22½mm apart on No. TDB7a. Panes were made
from coil sheet stock and therefore are always miscut and misperforated. No. TDB7 has 4 glassine interleaves, 1 behind each
pane.

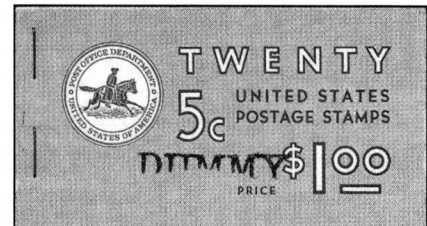

Small Postrider With "DUMMY"
Handstamp — TBC12A

For Testing Purposes Only — TDP6

No. TDP6 panes were made from coil stock and therefore are
always miscut and misperforated.

1962-67 **Untagged**

TDB8 TBC12A $1 **blue,** 4 #TDB8a 200.00
   a. TDP6 **black,** pane of 6 stamps of type
   TE55 35.00

Horiz. gum breakers are 5½mm apart and alternating vert.
gum breakers are 22½mm and 8½mm apart on No. TDB8a.
No. TDB8 has 4 silicone interleaves, 1 behind each pane, and
staples at left. Some panes may show a joint line and/or EE
markings.

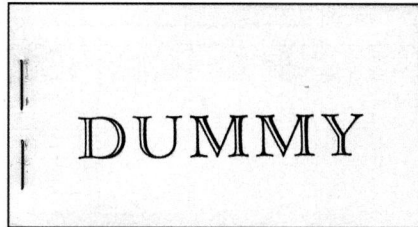

"DUMMY" — TDBC1

1962-67

TDB9 TDBC1 **black** 2 #TDB9a 90.00
   a. TDP1 Pane of 6 —
TDB10 TDBC1 **red** 2 #TDB9a 200.00

Horiz. gum breakers are 11½mm apart, and alternating vert.
gum breakers are 14mm and 8½mm apart on No. TDB9a. Nos.
TDB9 and TDB10 have 2 glassine interleaves, 1 behind each
pane.

Mr. Zip With "DUMMY" — TBC13A

1963-66

Black or Violet "Dummy" Handstamp
TDB11 TBC13A $1 **blue,** 4 #TDB9a 125.00
   a. TDP1 Pane of 6 10.00
   b. As #TDB11, with 4 #TDB11a 125.00

55x7½mm Red "Dummy" Overprint
TDB12 TBC13A $1 **blue,** 4 #TDB9a 50.00
   a. As #TDB12, with different inside front
   cover 15.00

Alternating horiz. gum breakers are 4½mm and 6½mm apart,
and alternating vert. gum breakers are 14mm and 8½mm apart
on No. TDB11a.
No. TDB12 has inside front cover reading "Domestic Postage
Rates." No. TDB12a has inside front cover reading "Minute Man
— Buy — HOLD US Savings Bonds."
Nos. TDB11-TDB12a have 4 silicone interleaves, 1 behind
each pane.

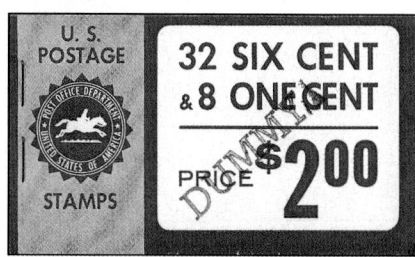

Post Office Seal With Violet "DUMMY"
Handstamp — TBC14A

For Testing Purposes Only — TDP7

No. TDP7 panes were made from coil stock and therefore are
always miscut and misperforated.

1967-68 **Tagged** **Perf. 11¼x10½**
TDB13 TBC14A $2 **brown,** 5 #TDB13a 200.00
   a. TDP7 **black,** pane of 8 stamps of
   type TE55 35.00

Horiz. gum breakers are 11mm apart and alternating vert.
gum breakers are 14mm and 8½mm apart on No. TDB13a. No.
TDB13 has 5 silicone interleaves, 1 behind each pane, and
staples at left. Some booklets and panes have felt pen markings
along the top and bottom edges placed by the technicians for
machine adjustments.

On Nos. TDB14, TDB15, TDB16 and TDB17, the
perforation gauge is measured with the staple position
at left, and the gum breakers are measured with the
staple position at top.

Stamp Silhouette With Violet "DUMMY"
Handstamp — TBC15

1960s-72   Tagged   Perf. 10½x11¼

TDB14   TBC15 $1 **brown,** 4 #TDB14a   150.00
   a.   TDP6 **black,** pane of 6 stamps of
     type TE55, staple position at top   35.00

Horiz. gum breakers are 11mm apart and vert. gum breakers are 22mm apart on No. TDB14a. No. TDB14 has 4 silicone interleaves, 1 behind each pane, and staples at left. "Dummy" handstamp is 34½x6½mm. Some booklets and panes have felt pen markings on the front and/or back covers.

TDP6A

TDB15   TBC15 $1 **blue,** 4 #TDB15a   150.00
   a.   TDP6A **black,** pane of 6 stamps of type TE55, staple position at top   35.00

Horiz. gum breakers are 11mm apart on No. TDB15a. No. TDB15 has 4 silicone interleaves, 1 behind each pane, and staples at left. "Dummy" handstamp is 34½x6½mm. Panes are upside down relative to covers. Some booklets and panes have felt pen markings on the front and/or back covers.

TBC15A

TDB16A   TBC15A $1 **claret,** 3 #TDB16a   250.00
   a.   TDP6A **black,** pane of 6 stamps of
     type TE55, staple position at top   35.00
   b.   As #TDB16, with 34½x6½mm
     "Dummy" handstamp   250.00

Horiz. gum breakers are 11mm apart on No. TDB16a. No. TDB16 has 3 silicone interleaves, 1 behind each pane, and staples at left. "Dummy" handstamp is 29½x4½mm on No. TDB16.

TBC15B

TDB17   TBC15B $1 **red,** 2 #TDB17a   175.00
   a.   TDP6B or TDP6A **black,** pane of 6
     stamps of type TE55, staple posi-
     tion at top   35.00
   b.   As #TDB17, with 34½x6½mm
     "Dummy" handstamp   175.00

Horiz. gum breakers are 11mm apart, and alternating vert. gum breakers are 14 and 8½mm apart on No. TDB17a. Some panes do not show vertical gum breakers. No. TDB17 has 2 silicone interleaves, 1 behind each pane, and staples at left. "Dummy" handstamp is 29½x4½mm on No. TDB17. Some booklets and panes have felt pen markings on the front and/or back covers.

Eisenhower With Violet "DUMMY"
Handstamp — TBC16

1970-71   Tagged   Perf. 11¼x10½

TDB18   TBC16 $2 **blue,** 5 #TDB18a   200.00
   a.   TDP7 **black,** pane of 8 stamps of
     type TE55   35.00
   b.   As #TDB18, with 34½x6½mm "Dum-
     my" handstamp   200.00

Horiz. gum breakers are 11mm apart and vert. gum breakers are 22mm apart on No. TDB18a. No. TDB18 has 5 silicone interleaves, 1 behind each pane, and staples at left. "Dummy" handstamp is 29½x4½mm on No. TDB18.

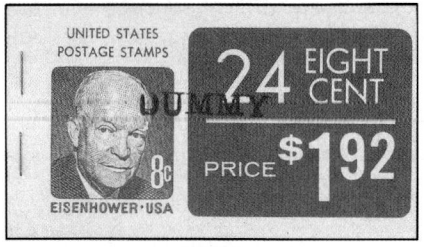

TBC17

With Red "Dummy" Handstamp

TDB19   TBC17 $1.92 **claret,** 3 #TDB13a   150.00
   a.   TDP7 **black,** pane of 8 stamps of type
     TE55   35.00
   b.   As #TDB19, with violet 34½x6½mm
     "Dummy" handstamp   150.00

No. TDB19 has 3 silicone interleaves, 1 behind each pane, and staples at left. "Dummy" handstamp is 29½x4½mm on No. TDB19.

FOLDED AND GLUED BOOKLETS

Blank Cover
TBC20

Blank Pane of 8 — TDP10

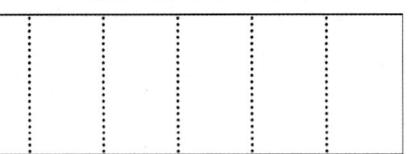

Blank Pane of 10 — TDP11

Blank Pane of 5 — TDP12

Produced by Bureau of Engraving and Printing.

1970s-80s   Untagged   Perf. 11x1

TDB25   TBC20   blank, #TDB25a
   a.   TDP10 Pane of 8

Perf. 10x9¾

TDB26   TBC20   blank, 2 #TDB26a   8(
   a.   TDP11 Pane of 10, 43x137mm

Perf. 10 Horiz.

TDB27   TBC20   blank, 2 #TDB27a   5(
   a.   TDP12 Pane of 5, 43x137mm, dull
     gum
TDB28   TBC20   blank, 2 #TDB28a   3(
   a.   TDP12 Pane of 5, 43x135mm, dull
     gum
   b.   As #TDB28, with 2 #TDB28a, shiny
     gum

Produced by KCS Industries
Imperf

TDB29   TBC20   blank, 2 #TDB29a   5(
   a.   TDP12 Pane of 5, 43x135mm, dull
     gum

Panes in No. TDB29 are fastened to each other and to booklet cover at the top tab with 3 glue spots. The booklet co of No. TDB29 is not scored at the pane fold location.

Perf. 11 Horiz.

TDB30   TBC20   blank, 2 #TDB30a
   a.   TDP12 Pane of 5, 43x137mm, dull
     gum
   b.   As #TDB30, with inverted pane (perfs
     unaligned with cover fold)

Panes in No. TDB30 are fastened to each other with 3 g spots and bottom pane is fastened to booklet cover with a 1 wide glue line. Covers are known with handstamps "A1" (bla "A2" (orange), "B1" (red), or "B2" (violet) on the front and b cover panels.

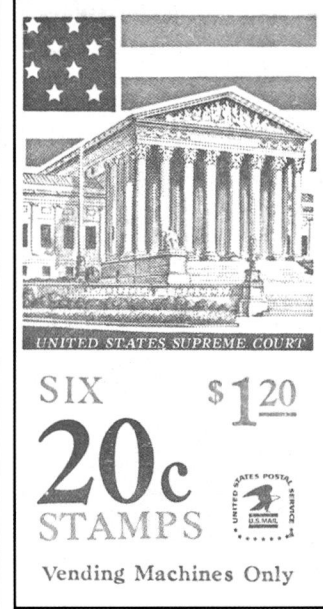

Flag Over
Supreme
Court
BC29

Printed by Bureau of Engraving & Printing.

1985   Untagged   Perf. 10 Hor

TDB31   BC29 $1.20 **red & blue,** #TDB31a   450.
   a.   TDP12 Pane of 5, 43x133mm, dull
     gum

Tab selvage is 9mm high.

Flag Over
Capitol
BC33C

Printed by Bureau of Engraving & Printing.

85	**Untagged**		*Perf. 10 Horiz.*
332	BC33C **$1.10 red & blue**, #TDB32a		20.00
a.	TDP12 Pane of 5, 43x130mm, dull gum		—

Tab selvage is 9 or 12mm high.

Seashells — BC33A

Seashells Without Text — TBC21

Printed by Bureau of Engraving & Printing.

85	**Untagged**		*Perf. 10x9¾*
B33	BC33A **$4.40 multicolored**, 2 #TDB33a		250.00
a.	TDP11 Pane of 10, 43x135mm, dull gum		—

Tab selvage is 11mm high. Panes are scored at all horizontal perforation rows. Some booklet covers have red felt pen marks on the outside front cover.

B34	TBC21	**multicolored**, 2 #TDB33a	250.00
B35	TBC21	**multicolored**, 2 #TDB28a	250.00

Scoring on No. TDB35 varies. Seven adjacent booklet covers e needed to show the complete design of all 25 seashells for s. TDB33-TDB35.

Jack London — TBC22

Rectangles and Numeral — TDP13

Printed by Bureau of Engraving & Printing.

1988	**Untagged**		*Perf. 11x9¾*
TDB36	TBC22 **$5 multicolored**, 2 #TDB36a		—
a.	TDP13 **blue**, pane of 10, 43x135mm, shiny gum		—

Tab selvage is 11½mm high. Panes are scored at all horizontal perforation rows. No. TDB36 booklet covers have a small printed number in the lower right corner that matches the large number on the booklet panes on the inside. Some booklet covers have red felt pen marks on the outside front cover. Numeral on No. TDB36a is "3." An unpublished quote from George Washington is printed on inside front cover and unissued "American Garden" printed on inside back cover.

Hummingbird
BC80

Printed by American Bank Note Company.

1994	**Untagged**		*Perf. 11 Horiz.*
TDB37	BC80 **$5.80 multicolored**, 2 #TDB37a		—
a.	TDP12 Pane of 5, 41x137mm, glossy gum		—

Outside front covers have 2 green felt pen marks.

Flag
BC106

Printed by American Bank Note Company.

1994	**Untagged**		*Perf. 10*
TDB38	BC106 **G multicolored**, 2 #TDB38a		—
a.	TDP12 Pane of 5, 43x137mm, glossy gum		—

Front covers have felt pen marks.

Daffodils —
TBC22

Rectangles — TDP14

Rectangles — TBP14a

Rectangles (Large Stamps) — TDP15

Printed by Bureau of Engraving and Printing.

1990s	**Untagged**		*Perf. 11x9¾*
TDB39	TBC22 **multicolored**, 2 #TDB39a		—
a.	TDP14 **blue,** pane of 10, 43x135mm, shiny gum		—
TDB40	TBC22 **multicolored**, 4 #TDB40a		—
a.	TDP13 **blue,** pane of 10, 43x135mm, shiny gum		—
TDB41	TBC22 **multicolored**, 4 #TDB41a		—
a.	TDP14 **dark blue,** pane of 10, 43x135mm, shiny gum		—
TDB42	TBC22 **multicolored**, 2 #TDB42a		—
a.	TDP14a **dark blue,** pane of 10, 43x135mm, shiny gum		—
TDB43	TBC22 **multicolored**, 2 #TDB42a		—
a.	TDP15 **black,** pane of 10, 66x137mm, shiny gum		—

Tab selvage is 12mm high on Nos. TDB39-TDB43. Numerals shown on Nos. TDB40a, TDB42a are "11." Nos. TDB42 and TDB43 lack printing on inside covers found on Nos. TDB39-TDB41. Booklet cover of No. TDB43 is larger and shows a 3mm tall "6" in the lower right corner of the outside front cover. Other covers of type TBC22 show a 3mm "12" there.

SELF-ADHESIVE FOLDED & GLUED BOOKLETS
Blank Cover and Pane Types

1990s ?   **Untagged**   *Perf. 11 Horiz.*
TDB60 TBC20   blank, 2 #TDB60a   —
   a.   TDP12 blank, pane of 2, self-adhesive,
        44x132mm   —

Blank
Convertible
Booklet
Cover
TBC30

Serpentine Die Cut 10½x11, 11

1999   **Overall Tagging**
TDB61 TBC30   blank, self-adhesive blank pane
            of 10   150.00

Stamps in pane have same arrangement as that of the 1999
20c Pheasant booklet, No. BK242A.

ATM TEST SHEETLETS

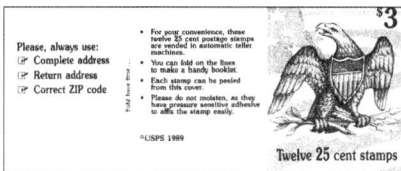

Eagle and Flag Pane Cover — TBC40

Stamp Layout — TBC40R

1989   *Imperf.*
Self-Adhesive
TDB80 TBC40 $3 **multicolored**, *blue,* pane of
          12 (TBC40R)   1,500.
   a.   With "Paper Corp" handwritten in right
       margin   1,500.

Shiny, Water-Activated Gum
TDB81 TBC40R $3 **multicolored**, *blue,* pane of
          12 (TBC40R)   1,500.

The backing paper serves as a booklet cover on No. TDB80.
Sizes: No. TDB80, 61x157mm; No. TDB80a, 62½x178mm; No.
TDB81, 66x160mm. No. TDB80 exists not fully trimmed, and
measuring 62½x159mm. No. TDB81 does not have a cover,
and does not require a backing paper.

Statue of Liberty Torch Pane Cover — TBC41

Stamp Layout — TBC41R

Printed by Avery Dennison.

1990   **Untagged**   *Die Cut*
                      Self-Adhesive
TDB82 TBC41   **green,** pane of 18 (TBC41R)   15.00

No. 2475a Overprinted in Black "SPECIMEN /
FOR ATM TEST" on Each Stamp

Statue of Liberty Torch Pane Cover — TBC41AR

Printed by Avery Dennison.

1990   **Untagged**   *Die Cut*
              Self-Adhesive
          Printed on Plastic
TDB83 TBC41AR 25c **dark red & dark blue,**
          pane of 12   —

Representation of Stamp Layout — TBC42R

Produced by Dittler Brothers.

1992   **Untagged**   *Misaligned Die C*
                 Self-Adhesive
TDB84   blank, pane of 18 (TBC42R)   50C

1992   *No Die C*
TDB85   **blue,** pane of 18 (TBC42R)   30C

Nos. TDB84 and TDB85 were printed on thick paper sim
to regular postage No. 2596a and were used for testing Po
Buddy machines. Backing paper of Nos. TDB84 and TD
reads "SELF-ADHESIVE * DO NOT WET." A detailed illus
tion of No. TBC42R is difficult to reproduce.

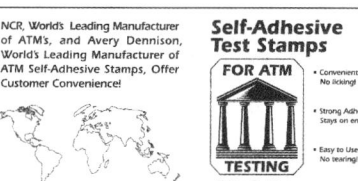

Temple Pane Cover — TBC43

Stamp Layout — TBC43R

Printed by Avery Dennison.

97			Die Cut

Self-Adhesive

B86 TBC43 **dark blue,** pane of 18 (TBC43R), Plate #V1 ... 250.00

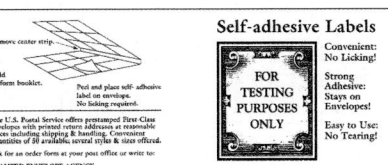

For Testing Purposes Only Pane Cover — TBC44

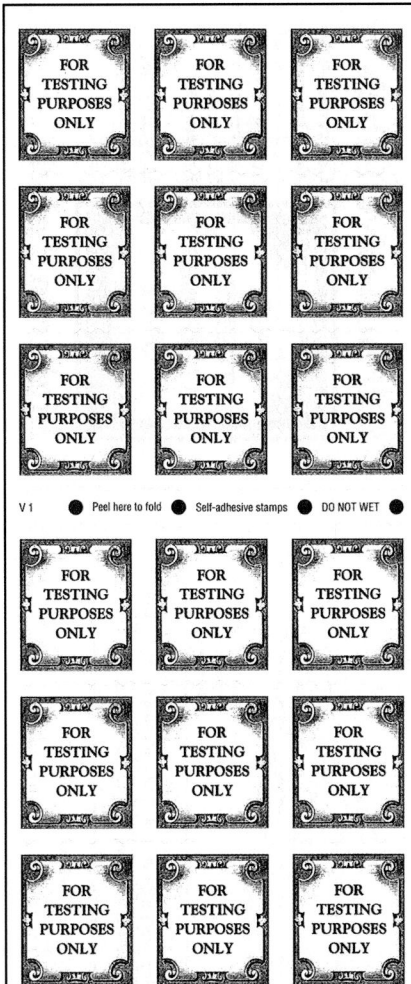

Stamp Layout — TBC44R

Printed by Avery Dennison.

1997			Die Cut

Self-Adhesive

TDB87 TBC44 **black,** pane of 18 black labels (TBC44R), Plate #V1 ... 150.00

Serpentine Die Cut 7¾

TDB88 TBC44 **black,** pane of 18 black labels (TBC44R), Plate #V1 ... 15.00
TDB89 TBC44 **blue,** pane of 12 magenta labels (TBC44R), Plate #V1 ... 250.00

George Clinton — TBC46R

1998		*Serpentine Die Cut 11.2x11.6*

Self-Adhesive

TDB89A TBC46R **blue gray** ... —

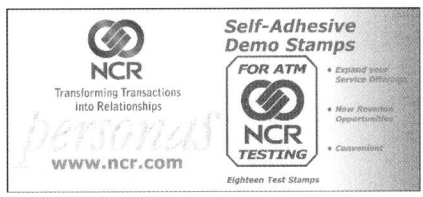

NCR Logo Pane Cover — TBC45

Stamp Layout — TBC45R

Printed by NCR.

2000			Imperf.

Without Gum

TDB90 TBC45 **multicolored,** pane of 18 black labels (TBC45R), Plate #V1 ... 50.00

CHRISTMAS SEALS

Issued by the American National Red Cross (1907-1919), the National Tuberculosis Association (1920-1967), the National Tuberculosis a Respiratory Disease Association (1968-1972) and the American Lung Association (1973-).

While the Christmas Seal is not a postage stamp, it has long been associated with the postal service because of its use on letters and package

Einar Holboell, an employee of the Danish Post Office, created the Christmas Seal. He believed that seal sales could raise money for charity. T post offices of Denmark, Iceland and Sweden began to sell such seals in the 1904 Christmas season. In the United States, Christmas Seals were fi issued in 1907 under the guidance of Emily P. Bissell, following the suggestion of Jacob Riis, social service worker.

Until 1975, all seals (except those of 1907 and 1908 type I) were issued in sheets of 100. The grilled gum (1908) has small square depressions like waffle. The broken gum (1922), devised to prevent paper curling, consists of depressed lines in the gum, ½mm. apart, forming squares. The verti and horizontal broken gum (1922, 1923, 1925, 1927-1932) forms diamonds. The perf. 12.00 (1917-1919, 1923, 1925, 1931) has two larger and wid spaced holes between every 11 smaller holes.

Values are for seals with original gum.

SEALS ISSUED BY THE DELAWARE CHAPTER OF THE AMERICAN NATIONAL RED CROSS

CS1 (Type II)

Designer — Emily P. Bissell.
Nearly $4,000 worth of seals were sold, $3,000 cleared.

Type I — "Merry Christmas" only.
Type II — "Merry Christmas" and "Happy New Year."

1907 **Perf. 14**
WX1 CS1 Type I 17.50
WX2 CS1 Type II 15.00

Types I and II litho. by Theo. Leonhardt & Son, Philadelphia, Pa. The 1st seals were sold Dec. 7, 1907, in Wilmington, Del. Issued in sheets of 228 (19x12). Type II was issued to extend the sale of seals until New Year's Day, 1908.
Counterfeits of both types exist (perf. 12).

SEALS ISSUED BY THE AMERICAN NATIONAL RED CROSS

CS2 (Type II)

Designer — Howard Pyle. Sales $135,000.

Type I — frame lines with square corners, small "C" in "Christmas."
Type II — frame lines have rounded corners, large "C" in "Christmas," leaves veined.

1908 **Perf. 12, 14**
WX3 CS2 Type I, perf. 14, smooth gum 35.00
  a. Perf. 12, smooth gum 45.00
  c. Perf. 14, grilled gum 75.00
  d. Perf. 12, grilled gum 50.00
  e. As #WX3, bklt. pane of 6 .... 250.00
  f. As "c," bklt. pane of 6 .... 250.00
  g. As #WX3, bklt. pane of 3 .... 250.00
WX4 CS2 Type II, perf. 12 .... 30.00
  a. Booklet pane of 6 .... 175.00
  b. Booklet pane of 3 .... 125.00

Type I litho. by Theo. Leonhardt & Son. Sheets of 250 (14x18), with the 1st space in the 9th and 18th rows left blank. Type II litho. by American Bank Note Co., New York, N.Y. in sheets of 100 (10x10).
Booklet panes have straight edges on 3 sides and perforated on left side where there is a stub, except No. WX4b which is a vert. strip of 3 with stub at top. Panes of 6 were made up in books of 24 and 48 and sold for 25c and 50c, and panes of 3 in books of 9 sold for 10c. The grilled gum has small square depressions like on a waffle.

CS3   CS4

Designer — Carl Wingate. Sales $250,000.

1909 **Perf. 12**
WX5 CS3 One type only 1.25
Litho. by The Strobridge, Cincinnati, Ohio. Seals with a round punched hole of 3½mm are printers' samples.

1910 **Perf. 12**
Designer — Mrs. Guion Thompson. Sales $300,000.
WX6 CS4 One type only 20.00
Lithographed by The Strobridge Lithographing Co.

SEALS ISSUED BY THE AMERICAN NATIONAL RED CROSS
(But sold by the National Association for the Study and Prevention of Tuberculosis)

"The Old Home Among the Cedars" — CS5 (Type II)   CS6

Designer — Anton Rudert under directions of F. D. Millet. Sales $320,000.

Type I — diameter of circle 22mm, solid end in house.
Type II — same circle but thinner, lined end to house.
Type III — diameter of circle 20mm, lined end to house.

1911 **Perf. 12**
WX7 CS5 Type I 50.00
WX8 CS5 Type II 100.00

COIL STAMP
Perf. 8½ Vertically
WX9 CS5 Type III 75.00
Typo. by Eureka, Scranton, Pa. Type I has name and address of printer and union label in red in top margin. Type II has union label only in green on left margin.

1912 **Perf. 12**
Designer — John H. Zeh. Sales $402,256.
WX10 CS6 One type only 10.00
Lithographed by The Strobridge Lithographing Co.

CS7 (Type I)

Designer — C. J. Budd. Sales $449,505.

Type I — with Poinsettia flowers and green circles around crosses at either side.
Type II — the Poinsettia flowers have been removed.
Type III — the Poinsettia flowers and green circles have be removed.

1913 **Perf.**
WX11 CS7 Type I 1,2
WX12 CS7 Type II 7
WX13 CS7 Type III 8
Lithographed by American Bank Note Co.

CS8   CS9

Designer — Benjamin S. Nash. Sales $555,854.

1914 **Perf.**
WX15 CS8 One type only .... 10.
Lithographed by The Strobridge Lithographing Co.

1915
Designer — Benjamin S. Nash. Sales $760,000.
WX16 CS9 Perf. 12½ .... 10.
  a. Perf. 12 .... 65.
Lithographed by Andrew B. Graham Co., Washington, D.C.

CS10   CS11

Designer — T. M. Cleland. Sales $1,040,810.

1916
WX18 CS10 Perf. 12 .... 5.
  a. Perf. 12x12½ .... 6.
  b. Perf. 12½x12 .... 15.
  c. Perf. 12½ .... 14.
Lithographed by the Strobridge Lithographing Co.

Seals of 1917-21 are on coated paper.

1917
Designer — T. M. Cleland. Sales $1,815,110.
WX19 CS11 Perf. 12 .... 2.0
  a. Perf. 12½ 15.0
  b. Perf. 12x12.00 .... 2.0
  c. Perf. 12x12½ 20.0
Typographed by Eureka Specialty Printing Co.
Perf. 12.00 has two larger and wider-spaced holes betwee every eleven smaller holes.
Sheets come with straight edged margins on all four side also with perforated margins at either right or left. Perforate margins have the union label imprint in green.

SEALS ISSUED BY THE AMERICAN NATIONAL RED CROSS
(Distributed by the National Tuberculosis Association)

CS12 CS13 (Type II)

Designer — Charles A. Winter.
These seals were given to members and others in lots of 10, Natl. Tuberculosis Assoc. being subsidized by a gift of 100,000 from the American National Red Cross.

Type I — "American Red Cross" 15mm long, heavy circles between date.
Type II — "American Red Cross" 15½mm long, periods between date.

1918

CS21	CS12 Type I, perf. 11½x12.00	7.50
a.	Perf. 12	8.50
b.	Perf. 12.00, booklet pane of 10	2.00
c.	Perf. 12x12.00, booklet pane of 10	2.00
d.	Perf. 12, booklet pane of 10	2.00
e.	Perf. 12.00x12, booklet pane of 10	65.00
CS22	CS12 Type II, from booklet pane, perf. 12½xRoulette 9½	.60
a.	Perf. 12½, booklet pane of 10	1.50
b.	Perf. 12½x12, bklt. pane of 10	—
d.	Roulette 9½xPerf. 12½, bklt. pane of 10	—
e.	Perf. 12½xRoulette 9½, bklt. pane of 10	20.00
f.	Perf. 12½x12, bklt. pane of 10	20.00
h.	Roulette 9½xPerf. 12½, bklt. pane of 10	20.00
i.	Roulette 9½xPerf. 12½ and Roulette 12½, booklet pane of 10	—
j.	Perf. 12½, booklet pane of 10	50.00
k.	Perf. 12½x12½ and 12, bklt. pane of 10	—
l.	Roulette 9½xPerf. 12½, booklet pane of 10	—
m.	As "m," stub at bottom, bklt. pane of 10	50.00

For perf 12.00, see note following No. WX19.
Type I typographed by Eureka Specialty Printing Co. Booklet panes of 10 (2x5) normally have straight edges on all sides. They were cut from the sheets of 100 and can be plated by certain flaws which occur on both. Sheets have union label imprint on top margin in brown.
Type II lithographed by Strobridge Lithographing Co. Booklet panes are the same but normally have a perforated margin at top and stub attached. These too can be plated by flaws. One or both vert. sides are rouletted on #WX22e; perforated on #WX22f and WX22h. #WX22i is rouletted 12½ on left, perf. 12½ on right. #WX22j, WX22k and WX22l are panes of 10 (2x5). #WX22m has a perforated margin at left.
Nos. WX21-WX21a are from sheet of 100, no straight edges. The seal with "American Red Cross" 17¼mm long is believed to be an essay.

1919

Designer — Ernest Hamlin Baker. Sales $3,872,534.
Type I — plume at right side of Santa's cap.
Type II — no plume but a white dot in center of band.

WX24	CS13 Type I, perf. 12	.40
a.	Perf. 12x12.00	.60
b.	Perf. 12½x12	.50
c.	Perf. 12½x12.00	2.75
WX25	CS13 Type II, perf. 12½	.40

For perf. 12.00, see note following No. WX19.
This is the first time the double barred cross, the emblem of the National Tuberculosis Association, appeared in the design of the seals. It is also the last time the red cross emblem of the American National Red Cross was used on seals.
Type I typo. by Eureka, and has union label on margin at left in dark blue. Type II litho. by Strobridge.

SEALS ISSUED BY THE NATIONAL TUBERCULOSIS ASSOCIATION

CS14 CS15

Designer — Ernest Hamlin Baker. Sales $3,667,834.

Type I — size of seal 18x22mm.
Type II — seal 18½x23½mm, letters larger & numerals heavier.

1920

WX26	CS14 Type I, perf. 12x12½	.50
a.	Perf. 12	.40
b.	Perf. 12½x12	13.50
c.	Perf. 12½	15.00
WX27	CS14 Type II, perf. 12½	.50

Type I typo. by Eureka, and has union label imprint and rings on margin at left in dark blue. Type II litho. & offset by Strobridge.

1921

Designer — George V. Curtis. Sales $3,520,303.
Type I — dots in the chimney shading and faces are in diagonal lines, dots on chimney are separate except between the 2 top rows of bricks where they are solid.
Type II — dots in the chimney shading and faces are in horiz. lines.
Type III — as Type I except red dots on chimney are mostly joined forming lines, dots between the 2 top rows of bricks are not a solid mass.

WX28	CS15 Type I, perf. 12½	.65
WX29	CS15 Type II, perf. 12½	.40
WX29A	CS15 Type III, perf. 12	.50

Type I typo. by Eureka. Type II offset by Strobridge. Type III typo. by Zeese-Wilkinson Co., Long Island City, N.Y.

CS16 CS17

Designer — T. M. Cleland. Sales $3,857,086.

1922

WX30	CS16 Perf. 12½, broken gum	.80
a.	Perf. 12, broken gum	3.00
b.	Perf. 12x12½, broken gum	7.50
c.	Perf. 12, smooth gum	3.00
d.	Perf. 12½, vertical broken gum	3.00

Typographed by Eureka Specialty Printing Co.
The broken gum, which was devised to prevent curling of paper, consists of depressed lines in the gum ½mm apart, forming squares, or vertical broken gum forming diamonds.

1923

Designer — Rudolph Ruzicka. Sales $4,259,660.

WX31	CS17 Perf. 12½, vertical broken gum	.30
a.	Perf. 12, horizontal broken gum	3.00
b.	Perf. 12x12.00, vertical broken gum	3.50
c.	Perf. 12½x12, vertical broken gum	6.50
d.	Perf. 12, vertical broken gum	.90
e.	Perf. 12.00x12, vertical broken gum	3.00

For perf 12.00, see note following No. WX19.
Typographed by Eureka Specialty Printing Co.
The broken gum on this and issues following printed by Eureka consists of very fine depressed lines forming diamonds.

CS18 CS19 (Type II)

Designer — George V. Curtis. Sales $4,479,656.

1924

WX32	CS18 One type only	.30

Offset by Strobridge, E.&D., and U.S.P.& L.

1925 Perf. 12½

Designer — Robert G. Eberhard. Sales $4,937,786.
Type I — red lines at each side of "1925" do not join red tablet below.
Type II — red lines, as in type I, join red tablet below.
Type III — as type I but shorter rays around flames and "ea" of "Health" smaller.

WX35	CS19 Type I, vert. broken gum	.30
a.	Perf. 12, vertical broken gum	3.50
b.	Perf. 12x12½ vertical broken gum	.60
c.	Perf. 12.00x12½ vert. broken gum	—
WX36	CS19 Type II	.30
WX37	CS19 Type III	.75

For perf 12.00, see note following No. WX19.
Type I typo. by Eureka. Type II offset by E.&D. Type III litho. by Gugler Lithographing Co., Milwaukee.

CS20 CS21

Designer — George V. Curtis. Sales $5,121,872.

1926 Perf. 12½

WX38	CS20 One type only	.25

Offset by E.&D. and U.S.P.&L.
Printers' marks: E.&D. has a red dot at upper right on seal 91 on some sheets. U.S.P.&L. has a black dot at upper left on seal 56 on some sheets.

1927

Designer — John W. Evans. Sales $5,419,959.

WX39	CS21 Perf. 12, horizontal broken gum	.20
a.	Smooth gum (see footnote)	1.00
WX40	CS21 Perf. 12½, no dot	.20
WX41	CS21 Perf. 12½, one larger red dot in background 1mm above right post of dashboard on sleigh	.20

"Bonne Sante" added to design and #WX39a but with body of sleigh myrtle green instead of green were used in Canada.
Offset: #WX39, WX39a by Eureka. #WX40 by E.&D. #WX41 by U.S.P.&L.
Printer's marks: Eureka has no mark but can be identified by the perf. 12. E.&D. has red dot to left of knee of 1st reindeer on seal 92. U.S.P.&L. has 2 red dots in white gutter, one at lower left of seal 46 (and sometimes 41) and the other at upper right of seal 55. The perforations often strike out one of these dots.

The Gallant Ship
"Argosy" — CS22

CS23

Designer — John W. Evans. Sales $5,465,738.

Type I — shading on sails broken, dots in flag regular.
Type II — shading on sails broken, dots in flag spotty.
Type III — shading on sails unbroken, dots in flag regular.

1928   *Perf. 12½*

WX44	CS22	Type I, vertical broken gum	.20
WX45	CS22	Type II	.20
WX46	CS22	Type III	.20

Seals inscribed "Bonne Annee 1929" or the same as type II
but green in water, and black lines of ship heavier and deeper
color were used in Canada.
Offset: Type I by Eureka, Type II by Strobridge, Type III by
E.&D.
Printers' marks: Type I comes with and without a blue dash
above seal 10, also with a blue and a black dash. Type II has 2
blue dashes below seal 100. Type III has red dot in crest of 1st
wave on seal 92.

1929   *Perf. 12½*

Designer — George V. Curtis. Sales $5,546,147.

WX49	CS23	Vertical broken gum	.20
a.		Perf. 12, vertical broken gum	.50
b.		Perf. 12½x12, vertical broken gum	1.25
WX50	CS23	Smooth gum	.20

Seals inscribed "Bonne Sante 1929" or "Christmas Greetings
1929" were used in Canada.
Offset: #WX49-WX49b by Eureka, #WX50 by E.&D.,
U.S.P.&L., and R.R. Heywood Co., Inc., New York, N.Y.
Printers' marks: Eureka is without mark but identified by bro-
ken gum. E.&D. has a black dot in lower left corner of seal 92.
U.S.P.&L. has blue dot above bell on seal 56. Heywood has a
blue dot at lower right corner of seal 100.

CS24

CS25

Designer — Ernest Hamlin Baker, and redrawn by John W.
Evans. Sales $5,309,352.

1930   *Perf. 12½*

WX55	CS24	Vertical broken gum	.20
a.		Perf. 12, vert. broken gum	.50
b.		Perf. 12.00x12, vert. broken gum	.25
c.		Perf. 12½x12, vertical broken gum	2.50
d.		Perf. 12, booklet pane of 10, horiz. bro-	
		ken gum	.50
WX56	CS24	Smooth gum	.20

Seals inscribed "Bonne Sante" or "Merry Christmas" on red
border of seal were used in Canada.
Offset: #WX55-WX55d by Eureka, #WX56 by Strobridge,
E.&D. and U.S.P.&L.
Printers' marks: Eureka has a dot between the left foot and
middle of "M" of "Merry" on seal 1. Strobridge has 2 dashes
below "ALL" on seal 100. E.&D. printed on Nashua paper has
dot on coat just under elbow on seal 92, and on Gummed
Products Co. paper has the dot on seals 91, 92. U.S.P.&L. has
a dash which joins tree to top frame line just under "MA" of
"Christmas" on seal 55.
The plate for booklet panes was made up from the left half of
the regular plate and can be plated by certain flaws which occur
on both.

1931   *Perf. 12½*

Designer — John W. Evans. Sales $4,526,189.

WX61	CS25	Horiz. broken gum (see footnote)	2.00
WX62	CS25	Horizontal broken gum	.20
a.		Perf. 12x12½, horiz. broken gum	.35
b.		Perf. 12.00x12½, horizontal broken gum	2.50
c.		Perf. 12, horizontal broken gum	1.00
g.		Perf. 12, vertical broken gum, booklet	
		pane of 10	.50
h.		Perf. 12x12.00, vertical broken gum,	
		booklet pane of 10	.60
WX63	CS25	Smooth gum	.20

For perf 12.00, see note following No. WX19.
Offset: #WX61-WX62h by Eureka, #WX63 by Strobridge.
#WX61 has a green dash across inner green frame line at
bottom center on each seal in sheet except those in 1st and last
vertical rows and the 2 rows at bottom.

Printers' marks: Eureka has none. Strobridge has the usual 2
dashes under seal 100.
The plate for booklet panes was made up from transfers of 60
seals (12x5). The panes can be plated by minor flaws.

CS26

CS27

Designer — Edward F. Volkmann. Sales $3,470,637.

1932

WX64	CS26	Perf. 12½x12¾	.20
a.		Vertical broken gum	.50
WX65	CS26	Perf. 12	.20
WX66	CS26	Perf. 12½	.20
WX67	CS26	Perf. 12½	.20

Offset: #WX64 by Eureka, #WX65 by E.&D., #WX66 by
U.S.P.&L., #WX67 by Columbian Bank Note Co., Chicago.
#WX64, WX67 have a little red spur on bottom inner frame line
of each seal, at left corner.
Printers' marks: Eureka has a red dash, in each corner of the
sheet, which joins the red border to the red inner frame line.
E.&D. has a blue dot in snow at lower left on seal 91. U.S.P.&L.
has a blue dot on top of post on seal 56. Columbian Bank Note
has small "C" in lower part of girl's coat on seal 82.

1933

Designer — Hans Axel Walleen. Sales $3,429,311.

| WX68 | CS27 | Perf. 12 | .20 |
| WX69 | CS27 | Perf. 12½ | .20 |

Offset: #WX68 by Eureka, #WX69 by Strobridge, U.S.P.&L.,
and the Columbian Bank Note Co.
Printers' marks; Eureka has rope joining elbow of figure to left
on seals 11, 20, 91, 100. Strobridge has the usual 2 dashes
under seal 100. U.S.P.&L. has green dot on tail of "s" of "Greetings" on seal 55. Columbian has white "c" on margin, under
cross, on seal 93.

CS28

CS29

Designer — Herman D. Giesen. Sales $3,701,344.

1934

WX72	CS28	Perf. 12½x12¼	.20
WX73	CS28	Perf. 12½ (see footnote)	.20
WX74	CS28	Perf. 12½ (see footnote)	.20
WX75	CS28	Perf. 12½ (see footnote)	.20

Offset: #WX72 by Eureka, #WX73 by Strobridge, #WX74 by
E.&D. and #WX75 by U.S.P.&L.
Cutting of blue plate for the under color: #WX72, WX73 (early
printing) and WX74 have lettering and date cut slightly larger
than ultramarine color. #WX73 (later printing) has square cutting around letters and date, like top part of letter "T". #WX75
has cutting around letters and date cut slightly larger.
Printers' marks: Eureka has 5 stars to right of cross on seal
10. Strobridge has 2 blue dashes in lower left corner of seal 91
or in lower right corner of seal 100. E.&D. has a red dot in lower
left corner of seal 99. U.S.P.&L. has 5 stars to left of cross on
seal 56.
Great Britain issued seals of this design which can be distinguished by the thinner and whiter paper. Sheets have perforated margins on all 4 sides but without any lettering on bottom
margin, perf. 12½.

1935

Designer — Ernest Hamlin Baker. Sales $3,946,498.

| WX76 | CS29 | Perf. 12½x12¼ | .20 |
| WX77 | CS29 | Perf. 12½ | .20 |

Offset: #WX76 by Eureka, #WX77 by Strobridge, U.S.P.&L.
and Columbian Bank Note Co.
Eureka recut their blue plate and eliminated the faint blue
shading around cross, girl's head and at both sides of the upper
part of post. U.S.P.& L. eliminated the 2 brown spurs which
pointed to the base of cross, in all 4 corners of the sheet.
Printers' marks: Eureka has an extra vertical line of shading
on girl's skirt on seal 60. Strobridge has 2 brown dashes in
lower right corner of position 100 but sheets from an early
printing are without this mark. U.S.P.&L. has a blue dot under
post on seal 55. Columbian has a blue "c" under post on seal
99.
The corner seals carry slogans: "Help Fight Tuberculosis,"
"Protect Your Home from Tuberculosis," "Tuberculosis Is Preventable," "Tuberculosis Is Curable."

Printers' marks appear on seal 56 on sheets of
unless otherwise noted:
  E Eureka Specialty Printing Co.
  S Strobridge Lithographing Co. (1930-1958).
  S Specialty Printers of America (1975-).
  D Edwards & Deutsch Lithographing Co. (E.&D
  U United States Printing & Lithographing
(U.S.P.&L.)
  F Fleming-Potter Co., Inc.
  W Western Lithograph Co.
  B Berlin Lithographing Co. (1956-1969); I. S. B
Press (1970-1976); Barton-Cotton (1977-).
  R Bradford-Robinson Printing Co.
  N Sale-Niagara, Inc.
Seals from 1936 onward are printed by offset.
Seals with tropical gum (dull), starting in 1966, w
used in Puerto Rico.

CS30

CS31

Designer — Walter I. Sasse. Sales $4,522,269.

1936

| WX80 | CS30 | Perf. 12½x12 (E) | |
| WX81 | CS30 | Perf. 12½ (S,D,U) | |

Seals with red background and green cap-band alternate
seals showing green background and red cap-band. The co
seals carry the same slogans as those of 1935.
Two of the three Strobridge printings show vertical g
dashes in margin below seal 100, besides "S" on seal 56.

1937

Designer — A. Robert Nelson. Sales $4,985,697.

| WX88 | CS31 | Perf. 12x12½ (E) | |
| WX89 | CS31 | Perf. 12½ (S,D,U) | |

Positions 23, 28, 73 and 78, carry slogans: "Health for
"Protect your home," "Preventable" and "Curable."
The "U" printer's mark of U.S.P.&L. appears on seal 55.
omitted on some sheets.

CS32

CS33

Designer — Lloyd Coe. Sales $5,239,526.

1938

WX92	CS32	Perf. 12½x12 (E)	
WX93	CS32	Perf. 12½ (S,D,U)	
a.		Miniature sheet, imperf.	2

The corner seals bear portraits of Rene T. H. Laennec, R
ert Koch, Edward Livingston Trudeau and Einar Holboll.
No. WX93a contains the 4 corner seals, with the regular s
in the center. It sold for 25 cents.

1939

Designer — Rockwell Kent. Sales $5,593,399.

WX96	CS33	Perf. 12½x12 (E)	
a.		Booklet pane of 20, perf. 12	
WX97	CS33	Perf. 12½ (S,D,U)	

The center seals, positions 45, 46, 55, 56, carry sloga
"Health to All," "Protect Your Home." "Tuberculosis Preventa
Curable" and "Holiday Greetings."
Printers' marks appear on seal 57.

CS34

CS35

Designer — Felix L. Martini. Sales $6,305,979.

1940			
100	CS34	Perf. 12½x12 (E)	.20
101	CS34	Perf. 12½x13 (E)	.20
103	CS34	Perf. 12½ (S,D,U)	.20

Seals 23, 32 and 34 carry the slogan "Protect Us from Tuberculosis." Each slogan seal shows one of the 3 children.

1941

Designer — Stevan Dohanos. Sales $7,530,496.

104	CS35	Perf. 12½x12 (E)	.20
105	CS35	Perf. 12½ (S,D,U)	.20

"S" and "U" printers' marks exist on same sheet.

CS36

CS37

Designer — Dale Nichols. Sales $9,390,117.

1942			
108	CS36	Perf. 12x12½ (E)	.20
109	CS36	Perf. 12½ (S,D,U)	.20

1943

Designer — Andre Dugo. Sales $12,521,494.

		Pair	
112	CS37	Perf. 12½x12 (E)	.20
113	CS37	Perf. 12½ (S,D,U)	.20

On alternate seals, the vert. frame colors (blue & red) are transposed as are the horiz. frame colors (buff & black). Seals where "Joyeux Noel" replaces "Greetings 1943" and "1943" added on curtain or the same as #WX113 but darker colors were used in Canada.

CS38

CS39

Designer — Spence Wildey. Sales $14,966,227.

1944			
X118	CS38	Perf. 12½x12 (E)	.20
X119	CS38	Perf. 12½ (S,D,U)	.20

Seals with "USA" omitted are for Canada.

1945   **"USA" at Lower Right Corner**

Designer — Park Phipps. Sales $15,638,755.

X124	CS39	Perf. 12½x12 (E)	.20
X125	CS39	Perf. 12½ (S,D,U)	.20

Seals with "USA" omitted are for Canada.

CS40

CS41

Designer — Mary Louise Estes and Lloyd Coe. Sales $17,075,608.

1946		**"USA" at Left of Red Cross**	
WX130	CS40	Perf. 12½x12 (E)	.20
WX131	CS40	Perf. 12½ (S,D,U)	.20

Seals with "USA" omitted are for Canada and Bermuda. Printers' marks are on seal 86.
The center seals (45, 46, 55, 56) bear portraits of Jacob Riis, Emily P. Bissell, E. A. Van Valkenburg and Leigh Mitchell Hodges.

1947

Designer — Raymond H. Lufkin. Sales $18,665,523.

WX135	CS41	Perf. 12½x12½ (E)	.20
WX136	CS41	Perf. 12½ (S,D,U)	.20

Seals with "USA" omitted are for Canada and Great Britain. The "U" printer's mark of U.S.P.&L. appears on seal 46.

CS42

CS43

Designer — Jean Barry Bart. Sales $20,153,834.

1948			
WX140	CS42	Perf. 12x12½ (E)	.20
WX141	CS42	Perf. 12½ (S,D,U)	.20

Seals with "USA" omitted are for Canada and Great Britain.

1949

Designer — Herbert Meyers. Sales $20,226,794.

WX145	CS43	Perf. 12x12½ (E)	.20
WX146	CS43	Perf. 12½ (S,D,U)	.20

Seals with "USA" omitted are for Canada & Great Britain.

CS44

CS45

Designer — Andre Dugo. Sales $20,981,540.

1950			
WX150	CS44	Perf. 12½x12 (E)	.20
WX151	CS44	Perf. 12½ (S,D,U,F)	.20

Seals with "USA" omitted are for Canada & Great Britain.

1951

Designer — Robert K. Stephens. Sales $21,717,953.

WX155	CS45	Perf. 12½x12 (E)	.20
WX156	CS45	Perf. 12½ (S,D,U,F)	.20

Seals with "USA" omitted are for Canada.

CS46

CS47

Designer — Tom Darling. Sales $23,238,148.

1952			
WX159	CS46	Perf. 12½x12 (E)	.20
WX160	CS46	Perf. 12½ (S,D,U,F)	.20

Overprinted "Ryukyus" (in Japanese characters)

WX163	CS46	Perf. 12½x12, 12½ (U)	1.50

1953

Designers — Elmer Jacobs and E. Willis Jones. Sales $23,889,044.

WX164	CS47	Perf. 13 (E)	.20
WX165	CS47	Perf. 12½ (S,D,U,F)	.20

CS48

Designer — Jorgen Hansen. Sales $24,670,202.

1954			**Block of 4**
WX168	CS48	Perf. 13 (E)	.40
WX169	CS48	Perf. 12½ (S,U,F,W)	.40
WX170	CS48	Perf. 11 (D)	.50

CS49

Designer — Jean Simpson. Sales $25,780,365.

1955			**Pair**
WX173	CS49	Perf. 13 (E)	.25
WX174	CS49	Perf. 12½ (S,U,F,W)	.25
WX175	CS49	Perf. 11 (D)	.25

CS50

Designer — Heidi Brandt. Sales $26,310,491.

1956			**Block of 4**
WX178	CS50	Perf. 12½x12 (E)	.40
WX179	CS50	Perf. 12½ (E,S,U,F,W)	.50
WX180	CS50	Perf. 11 (D,B)	.40
WX183	CS50	"Puerto Rico," perf. 12½	3.00

CS51

Designer — Clinton Bradley. Sales $25,959,998.

1957			Block of 4
WX184	CS51	Perf. 13 (E)	.40
WX185	CS51	Perf. 12½ (S,U,F,W,R)	.40
WX186	CS51	Perf. 11 (D,B)	.50
WX187	CS51	Perf. 10½x11 (D)	.75
WX188	CS51	Perf. 10½ (D)	3.00
WX190	CS51	"Puerto Rico," perf. 13	3.00

CS52

Designer — Alfred Guerra. Sales $25,955,390.

1958			Pair
WX191	CS52	Perf. 13 (E)	.25
WX192	CS52	Perf. 12½ (S,U,F,W,R)	.25
WX193	CS52	Perf. 10½x11 (B,D)	.50
WX194	CS52	Perf. 11 (B,D)	.35
WX196	CS52	"Puerto Rico," perf. 13	1.50

CS53

Designer — Katherine Rowe. Sales $26,740,906.

1959			Pair
WX197	CS53	Perf. 13 (E)	.25
WX198	CS53	Perf. 12½ (F,R,W)	.25
a.		Horiz. pair, imperf. btwn. (D)	1.50
WX199	CS53	Perf. 10½x11 (B)	.40
WX200	CS53	Perf. 11 (B,D)	.25
WX201	CS53	Perf. 10½ (B)	2.00
WX203	CS53	"Puerto Rico," perf. 13	1.25

E.&D. omitted every other vertical row of perforation on a number of sheets which were widely distributed as an experiment. #WX198a (shown above in illustration) is from these sheets.

CS54

Designer — Philip Richard Costigan. Sales $26,259,030.

1960			Block of 4
WX204	CS54	Perf. 12½ (E,F,R,W)	.35
WX205	CS54	Perf. 12½x12 (E)	1.00
WX206	CS54	Perf. 11x10½ (B)	.35
WX207	CS54	Perf. 11 (D)	.35

Puerto Rico used No. WX204 (E).

CS55

Designer — Heidi Brandt. Sales $26,529,517.

1961			Block of 4
WX209	CS55	Perf. 12½ (E,F,R,W)	.35
WX209A	CS55	Perf. 12½x12 (E)	2.00
WX210	CS55	Perf. 11x10½ (B)	.35
WX211	CS55	Perf. 11 (D)	.35

Puerto Rico used No. WX209 (E).

CS56

Designer — Paul Dohanos. Sales $27,429,202.

1962			Block of 4
WX213	CS56	Perf. 12½ (F,R,W)	.35
WX214	CS56	Perf. 13 (E)	.35
WX215	CS56	Perf. 10½x11 (B)	.35
WX216	CS56	Perf. 11 (D,B)	.35

Puerto Rico used No. WX214.

CS57

Designer — Judith Campbell Piussi. Sales $27,411,806.

1963			Block of 4
WX218	CS57	Perf. 12½ (E,F,R,W)	.35
WX219	CS57	Perf. 11 (B,D)	.35

Puerto Rico used No. WX218 (E).

CS58

Designer — Gaetano di Palma. Sales $28,784,043.

1964			Block
WX220	CS58	Perf. 12½ (E,F,R,W)	
WX221	CS58	Perf. 11 (B,D)	

Puerto Rico used No. WX221 (B).

CS59

Designer — Frede Salomonsen. Sales $29,721,878.

1965			Block o
WX222	CS59	Perf. 12½ (F,W)	
WX223	CS59	Perf. 11 (B,D)	
WX224	CS59	Perf. 13 (E)	

Puerto Rico used No. WX223 (B).

CS60

Designer — Heidi Brandt. Sales $30,776,586.

1966			Block of
WX225	CS60	Perf. 12½ (E,F,W)	
WX226	CS60	Perf. 10½x11 (B)	
WX227	CS60	Perf. 11 (D)	

Blocks of four seals with yellow green and white backgroun alternate in sheet in checkerboard style.
Puerto Rico used No. WX226.

Holiday Train — CS61

Designer — L. Gerald Snyder. Sales $31,876,773.

he seals come in 10 designs showing a train filled with ristmas gifts and symbols. The direction of the train is ersed in alternating rows as are the inscriptions "Christmas 7" and "Greetings 1967." The illustration shows first 2 seals op row.

			Block of 20 (10x2)
228	CS61	Perf. 13 (E)	.65
229	CS61	Perf. 12½ (F,W)	.65
230	CS61	Perf. 10½ (B)	1.50
231	CS61	Perf. 11 (D)	.75
232	CS61	Perf. 11x10½ (B)	.75

Puerto Rico used No. WX229 (F).

SEALS ISSUED BY NATIONAL TUBERCULOSIS AND RESPIRATORY DISEASE ASSOCIATION

CS62

Designer — William Eisele. Sales $33,059,107.

			Block of 4
68			
X233	CS62	Perf. 13 (E)	.50
X234	CS62	Perf. 10½x11 (B)	.50
X234A	CS62	Perf. 10½ (B)	.50
X235	CS62	Perf. 11 (D)	.50
X236	CS62	Perf. 12½ (F,W)	.50

Pairs of seals with bluish green and yellow backgrounds alternate in sheet in checkerboard style.
Puerto Rico used No. WX236 (F).

CS63

Designer — Bernice Kochan. Sales $34,437,591.

			Block of 4
969			
X237	CS63	Perf. 13 (E)	.35
X238	CS63	Perf. 12½ (F,W)	.35
X239	CS63	Perf. 10½x11 (B)	.50
X240	CS63	Perf. 11 (B)	.50

Puerto Rico used No. WX238 (F).

CS64

Designer — L. Gerald Snyder. Sales $36,237,977.
Sheets contain 100 different designs, Christmas symbols, oys, decorated windows; inscribed alternately "Christmas 1970" and "Greetings 1970." The illustration shows 6 seals from he center of the sheet.

			Sheet of 100 (10x10)
1970			
WX242	CS64	Perf. 12½ (E,F,W)	1.25
WX243	CS64	Perf. 11 (B)	1.25
WX244	CS64	Perf. 11x10½ (B)	1.25

Puerto Rico used No. WX242 (F).

CS65

Designer — James Clarke. Sales $36,120,000.

1971			Block of 8 (2x4)
WX245	CS65	Perf. 12½ (E,F)	.50
WX246	CS65	Perf. 11 (B)	.50

The 4 illustrated seals each come in a 2nd design arrangement: cross at left, inscriptions transposed, and reversed bugler, candle and tree ornaments. Each sheet of 100 has 6 horiz. rows as shown and 4 rows with 2nd designs.
Puerto Rico used No. WX245 (F).
Eureka printings are found with large "E," small "E" and without "E."

CS66

Designer — Linda Layman. Sales $38,000,557.
The seals come in 10 designs showing various holiday scenes with decorated country and city houses, carolers, Christmas trees and snowman. Inscribed alternately "1972 Christmas" and "Greetings 1972." Shown are seals from center of row.

1972			Strip of 10
WX247	CS66	Perf. 13 (E)	.50
WX248	CS66	Perf. 12½ (F)	.75
WX249	CS66	Perf. 11 (B)	.50

Seal 100 has designer's name. Puerto Rico used No. WX248 (F).

SEALS ISSUED BY AMERICAN LUNG ASSOCIATION

CS67

Designer — Cheri Johnson. Sales $36,902,439.
The seals are in 12 designs representing "The 12 Days of Christmas." Inscribed alternately "Christmas 1973" and "Greetings 1973." Shown is block from center of top 2 rows.

1973			Block of 12
WX250	CS67	Perf. 12½ (F), 18x22mm	.50
a.		Size 16½x20½mm (E)	.50
WX251	CS67	Perf. 11 (B,W)	.50

Seal 100 has designer's name. Puerto Rico used #WX250 (F).

CS68

Designer — Rubidoux. Sales $37,761,745.

1974			Block of 4
WX252	CS68	Perf. 12½ (E,F)	.35
WX253	CS68	Perf. 11 (B)	.35

Seal 99 has designer's name. Puerto Rico used #WX252 (F).

CS69

Children's paintings of holiday scenes. Different design for each state or territory. Paintings by elementary school children were selected in a nationwide campaign ending in Jan., 1974.
Sales $34,710,107.

1975			Sheet of 54 (6x9)
WX254	CS69	Perf. 12½ (S,F)	1.25
WX255	CS69	Perf. 11 (B)	1.25

Printers' marks are on seal 28 (New Mexico). Specialty Printers' seals (S) carry union labels: "Scranton 4," "Scranton 7," "E. Stroudsburg."
Puerto Rico used No. WX254 (F).

CS70

Continuous village picture covers sheet with Christmas activities and Santa crossing the sky with sleigh and reindeer. No inscription on 34 seals. Others inscribed "Christmas 1976," "Greetings 1976," and (on 9 bottom-row seals) "American Lung Association." Illustration shows seals 11-12, 20-21.
Sales $36,489,207.

1976   **Sheet of 54 (9x6)**
WX256 CS70   Perf. 12½ (F,N)   1.25
WX257 CS70   Perf. 11 (B)   1.25
WX258 CS70   Perf. 13 (S)   1.25

Printers' marks (N, B, S) on seal 32 and (F) on seal 23.
Puerto Rico used No. WX256 (F).

CS71

Children's paintings of holiday scenes. Different design for
each state or territory.

Sales $37,583,883.

1977   **Sheet of 54 (6x9)**
WX259 CS71   Perf. 12½ (F)   1.25
WX260 CS71   Perf. 11 (B)   1.25
WX261 CS71   Perf. 13 (S)   1.50

Printers' marks on seal 28 (Georgia).
Puerto Rico used No. WX259.

CS72

Children's paintings of holiday scenes. Different design
each state or territory.
Sales $37,621,466.

1978   **Sheet of 54 (6**
WX262 CS72   Perf. 12½ (F)
WX263 CS72   Perf. 11 (B)
WX264 CS72   Perf. 13 (S)

Printers' marks on seal 29 (New Hampshire).
Puerto Rico used No. WX262.

Type of 1978 Inscribed 1979

1979   **Sheet of 54 (6**
WX265 CS72   Perf. 12½ (F)
WX266 CS72   Perf. 11 (B)
WX267 CS72   Perf. 13 (S)

Printer's marks on seal 22 (Virgin Islands). Puerto Rico us
No. WX265.

Beginning in 1979 there is no longer one national iss
Additional designs are issued on a limited basis as test seals
determine the designs to be used the following year.

SANITARY FAIR

The United States Sanitary Commission was authorized by the Secretary of War on June 9, 1861, and approved by President Lincoln on June 1
1861. It was a committee of inquiry, advice and aid dealing with the health and general comfort of Union troops, supported by public contribution
   Many Sanitary Fairs were held to raise funds for the Commission, and eight issued stamps. The first took place in 1863 at Chicago, where no stam
was issued. Some Sanitary Fairs advertised on envelopes.
   Sanitary Fair stamps occupy a position midway between United States semi-official carrier stamps and the private local posts. Although Sanitary Fa
stamps were not valid for U.S. postal service, they were prepared for, sold and used at the fair post offices, usually with the approval and participation
the local postmaster.
   The Commission undertook to forward soldiers' unpaid and postage due letters. These letters were handstamped "Forwarded by the U.S. Sanita
Commission."
   Details about the Sanitary Fair stamps may be found in the following publications:
American Journal of Philately, Jan. 1889, by J. W. Scott
The Collector's Journal, Aug.-Sept. 1909, by C. E. Severn
Scott's Monthly Journal, Jan. 1927 (reprint, Apr. 1973), by Elliott Perry
Stamps, April 24th, 1937, by Harry M. Konwiser
Pat Paragraphs, July, 1939, by Elliott Perry
Covers, Aug. 1952, by George B. Wray
Sanitary Fairs, 1992, by Alvin and Marjorie Kantor
   The listings were compiled originally by H. M. Konwiser and Dorsey F. Wheless.

SF1

SF2

Albany, New York
Army Relief Bazaar
Setting A: narrow spacing, pane of 12.
Setting B: wider spacing, sheet of 25.
1864, Feb. 22-Mar. 30   **Litho.**   **Imperf.**
Thin White Paper

WV1   SF1 10c rose   125.
              Used on cover (tied "Alba-
                ny")   9,500.
              Block of 4, setting A   1,200.
              Pane of 12, setting A   4,800.
              Block of 4, setting B   500.
              Sheet of 25, setting B   2,500.
WV2   SF1 10c black   700.
              Block of 5   4,500.

The No. WV1 tied by Albany cancel on cover is unique. One
other cover exists in private hands with the stamp uncanceled
and slightly damaged.
   Imitations are typographed in red, blue, black or green on a
thin white or ordinary white paper, also on colored papers and
are:
   (a) Eagle with topknot, printed in sheets of 30 (6x5).
   (b) Eagle without shading around it.
   (c) Eagle with shading around it, but with a period instead of
a circle in "C" of "Cents," and "Ten Cents" is smaller.

Boston, Mass.
National Sailors' Fair
1864, Nov. 9-22   **Litho.**
Die Cut
WV3   SF2 10c **green**   350.

Brooklyn, N.Y.
Brooklyn Sanitary Fair

SF3

1864, Feb. 22-Mar. 8   **Litho.**   **Imperf.**
WV4   SF3 (15c) **green**   1,250.   3,600.
              On cover, Fair postmark on
                envelope   3,000.
              Block of 4   6,500.
              Block of 6   10,000.
WV5   SF3 (25c) **black**   4,750.
              On cover, with 1c local
                #28L2, Fair postmark on
                envelope   36,000.

No. WV4 used is valued canceled by the Fair postmark. One
or more examples also exist with a manuscript cancel. No. WV5
unused is unique as is the usage on cover.
   Imitations: (a) Typographed and shows "Sanitary" with a
heavy cross bar to "T" and second "A" with a long left leg. (b) Is
a rough typograph print without shading in letters of "Fair."

SF4

SF5

1863, Dec.   **Typeset**   **Imper**
WV6 SF4   5c **black,** *rosy buff*   750.   20
WV7 SF5 10c **green**   1,150.
              Tete beche pair   6,500.

No. WV6 used is believed to be unique. It has a manuscrip
cancel and is faulty. It is valued thus.

SF6

SF7

New York, N.Y.
Metropolitan Fair
			Engr.	Imperf.
4, Apr. 4-27			**Engr.**	*Imperf.*

Thin White Paper

3	SF6	10c **blue**		250.
		Sheet of 4		1,500.
9	SF6	10c **red**		1,500.
		Pair		3,500.
10	SF6	10c **black**		*14,000.*

Engraved and printed by John E. Gavit of Albany, N.Y. from a
al plate composed of four stamps, 2x2. Can be plated by the
tions of scrolls and dots around "Ten Cents."
o. WV10 is unique.

Philadelphia, Pa.
Great Central Fair
		Engr.	Perf. 12
4, June 7-28		**Engr.**	*Perf. 12*

**Printed by Butler & Carpenter, Philadelphia
Sheets of 126 (14x9)**

11	SF7	10c **blue**	40.00	525.00
		On cover tied with Fair post-mark		2,250.
		On cover with 3c #65, Fair and Philadelphia postmarks		36,000.
		On cover with 3c #65, New York postmark		42,500.
		Block of 4	250.00	
12	SF7	20c **green**	27.50	500.00
		On cover tied with Fair post-mark		1,500.
		Block of 4	135.00	
		Block of 12	475.00	
13	SF7	30c **black**	35.00	400.00
		On cover tied with Fair post-mark		1,500.
		Nos. WV11-WV13 on single cover, Fair postmark		7,500.
		Block of 4	160.00	
		Block of 6	240.00	

mprint "Engraved by Butler & Carpenter, Philadelphia" on
t margin adjoining three stamps.
Used examples of Nos. WV11-WV13 have Fair cancellation.
he No. WV11 covers used with 3c #65 are each unique. The
w York usage is on a Metropolitan Fair illustrated envelope. The
mitation of No. WV13 comes typographed in blue or green
thick paper.
White and amber envelopes were sold by the fair inscribed
eat Central Fair for the Sanitary Commission," showing pic-
e in several colors of wounded soldier, doctors and ambu-
ce marked "U.S. Sanitary Commission." Same design and
cription are known on U.S. envelope No. U46.

SF8

SF9

Springfield, Mass.
Soldiers' Fair
		Typo.	Imperf.
4, Dec. 19-24		**Typo.**	*Imperf.*

V14	SF8	10c **lilac**		210.00
		On unaddressed cover, Fair postmark on envelope		750.00
		Horizontal strip of 4		950.00

Design by Thomas Chubbuck, engraver of the postmaster
ovisional stamp of Brattleboro, Vt.
One cover exists pencil-addressed to Wm. Ingersoll, Spring-
ld Armory; value slightly more than an unaddressed cover.
Imitations: (a) Without designer's name in lower right corner,
lilac on laid paper. (b) With designer's name, but roughly
pographed, in lilac on white wove paper. Originals show 5
uttons on uniform.

Stamford, Conn.
Soldiers' Fair
Sheets of 8
864, July 27-29				
V15	SF9	15c **pale brown**	2,000.	4,000.

Originals have tassels at ends of ribbon inscribed
SOLDIERS FAIR." Imitations have leaning "S" in "CENTS" and
ome in lilac, brown, green, also black on white paper, green on
nkish paper and other colors.

ESSAY
Great Central Fair, Philadelphia
864		
VV11-E1	Design as issued but value tablets blank, greenish black on glazed paper (unique)	—

PROOFS
Metropolitan Fair, New York
1864			
WV10P	10c **black**, plate on India, mounted on card		900.

Great Central Fair, Philadelphia
1864			
WV11P	10c **blue**, card	32.50	
	Block of 4	150.00	
WV11TC/WV13TC	10c and 30c **grnsh blk**, se-tenant, glazed paper, large die	—	
WV12P	20c **green**, card	35.00	
	Block of 4	175.00	
WV12TC	20c **carmine**, wove, perf.	35.00	
	Block of 4	175.00	
WV12TC	20c **vermilion**, India on card, large die	275.00	
WV12TC	20c **vermilion**, wove, im-perf.	22.50	
	Block of 4	115.00	
WV12TC	20c **vermilion**, wove, perf.	35.00	
	Block of 4	175.00	
WV12TC	20c **orange**, wove, imperf.	22.50	
	Block of 4	115.00	
WV12TC	20c **brown orange**, opaque paper	22.50	
	Block of 4	115.00	
WV12TC	20c **red brown**, wove, perf.	35.00	
	Block of 4	175.00	
WV12TC	20c **black brown**, wove, imperf.	25.00	
	Block of 4	125.00	
WV12TC	20c **olive**, wove, imperf.	22.50	
	Block of 4	100.00	
WV12TC	20c **yellow green**, wove, imperf.	22.50	
	Block of 4	125.00	
WV12TC	20c **light green**, wove, perf.	35.00	
	Block of 4	175.00	
WV12TC	20c **blue**, India on card, large die	275.00	
WV12TC	20c **blue**, wove, perf.	175.00	
WV12TC	20c **bright blue**, wove, im-perf.	22.50	
	Block of 4	125.00	
WV12TC	20c **bright blue**, wove, perf.	35.00	
	Block of 4	175.00	
WV12TC	20c **lt. ultramarine**, wove, imperf.	22.50	
	Block of 4	125.00	
WV12TC	20c **purple**, wove, imperf.	22.50	
	Block of 4	125.00	
WV12TC	20c **claret**, wove, imperf.	35.00	
	Block of 4	200.00	
WV12TC	20c **brown black**, wove, perf.	35.00	
	Block of 4	175.00	
WV12TC	20c **greenish black**, glazed paper, large die	225.00	
WV12TC	20c **gray black**, opaque paper, wove, imperf.	22.50	
	Block of 4	125.00	
WV12TC	20c **gray black**, wove, perf.	35.00	
	Block of 4	175.00	
WV12TC	20c **black**, experimental double paper, wove, imperf.	25.00	
	Block of 4	140.00	
WV13P	30c **black**, card	35.00	
	Block of 4	175.00	
WV13TC	30c **blue**, imperf	35.00	

*Reprints (1903?) exist of WV11TC-WV13TC, se-tenant verti-
cally, large die on glazed white, pink or yellow card and small
die on India paper (mounted se-tenant) in carmine, red carmine, vermilion, orange, brown, yellow brown, olive, yellow
green, blue green, gray blue, ultramarine, light violet, violet,
claret and gray black.
There also exist large die essay reprints on India paper,
green bond paper and glazed cardboard without denomination
or with 20c. The 20c value has an added line below the center
shield.*

ENCASED POSTAGE STAMPS

In early 1862, months after the beginning of the American Civil War, people were conserving resources in anticipation of hard times and shorta ahead. Coins were one of the most hoarded resources, and as a result of this hoarding, coins began to command a premium over paper money. public was reluctant to spend their coins, fearing the premiums for coins might increase, and a loss might result. Many millions of dollars in gold a silver coins, even copper-nickel cents, disappeared into private hands.

The U.S. Mint began coining copper-nickel cents almost exclusively, but could not meet demand. In response, the public turned to postage stamp meet small obligations, and shopkeepers were forced to accept stamps as change. Envelopes stating the amount of stamps contained within and ca bearing stamps were sometimes used to keep the stamps from sticking and becoming destroyed, and printers sold advertisements on large number these envelopes. By July 1862, the government had authorized the monetizing of postage stamps and began printing stamp impressions on bank n paper.

On August 12, 1862, John Gault was issued a patent for a "Design for Encasing Government Stamps" to be used as the equivalent of curren Gault's plans called for a postage stamp to have its corners wrapped around a cardboard circle and show through a thin mica covering. An outer me frame would hold these items secure, and a heavier brass backing would complete the piece. The brass backing would be suitable for advertis purposes. The resulting piece was about the size of a quarter, but much lighter in weight. The stamps placed in the new encased postage were the 3c, 5c, 10c, 12c, 24c, 30c and 90c stamps of the 1861 issue. Of course, Gault sold his encased postage at a small markup over the value of the sta enclosed and the cost of production.

On August 21, 1862, the government issued postage currency in 5c, 10c, 25c and 50c denominations, and fractional currency was issued in 18 These policies, plus the increased production of brass and copper-nickel coinage in 1863, effectively ended Gault's enterprise. Still, encased posta proved very popular, because it solved the major problems of stamp damage and the necessity of opening stamp envelopes to count the contents. least 30 companies took advantage of the advertising possibilities and had their ads stamped on the brass backing. Perhaps $50,000 or a little more encased postage eventually was sold and circulated, not nearly enough by itself to solve the nation's small change crisis. Of the approximately 750,0 pieces sold, only 3,500-7,000 are believed to have survived for collectors.

Values are for very fine specimens with mica intact, although signs of circulation and handling are to be expected.

Grading encompasses three areas: 1. Case will show signs of wear or handling and signs of original toning. 2. Mica will be intact with no piec missing. 3. Stamp will be fresh with no signs of toning or wrinkling.

Examples that came with silvered cases and still have some or all of the original silvering will sell for more than the values shown.

Aerated Bread Co., New York

EP1	1c	5,000.
EP1A	5c	10,000.

No. EP1A is unique.

Ayer's Cathartic Pills, Lowell, Mass.

Varieties with long and short arrows below legend occur on all denominations.

EP2	1c	400.
EP3	3c	350.
EP4	5c	800.
EP5	10c	800.
EP6	12c	2,200.
EP7	24c	3,000.

Take Ayer's Pills

EP8	1c	400.
EP9	3c	400.
EP10	5c	1,000.
a.	Ribbed frame	3,000.
EP11	10c	1,250.
a.	Ribbed frame	4,850.
EP12	12c	2,500.
EP12A	30c	4,850.

Nos. EP11a and EP12A each are unique.

Ayer's Sarsaparilla

Three varieties: "AYER'S" small, medium or large.
Example illustrated is the medium variety.

EP13	1c medium "Ayer's"	500.
a.	Small	750.
EP15	3c medium "Ayer's"	400.
a.	Small	650.
b.	Large	450.
c.	Ribbed frame, medium	2,000.
EP16	5c medium "Ayer's"	2,000.
a.	Large	1,500.
EP17	10c medium "Ayer's"	475.
a.	Ribbed frame, medium	1,750.
b.	Small	1,250.
c.	Large	1,000.
EP18	12c medium "Ayer's"	2,000.
a.	Small	2,500.
EP19	24c medium "Ayer's"	1,750.
EP20	30c medium "Ayer's"	4,250.

Bailey & Co., Philadelphia

EP21	1c	1,000.
EP22	3c	1,100.
EP23	5c	2,000.
EP24	10c	2,000.
EP25	12c	2,750.

"FANCYGOODS" as
one word

"FANCY GOODS" as
two words

EP30 Obverse

Joseph L. Bates, Boston

EP26	1c one word	4
a.	Two words	6
EP27	3c one word	1,5
a.	Two words	7
EP28	5c two words	7
a.	One word	8
b.	Ribbed frame, one word	2,2
EP29	10c two words	1,5
a.	One word	6
b.	Ribbed frame, one word	2,5
EP30	12c two words	4,0

EP33 Obverse

Brown's Bronchial Troches

EP31	1c	2,00
EP32	3c	65
EP33	5c	40
EP34	10c	90
EP35	12c	2,50
EP36	24c	3,00
EP37	30c	4,00

F. Buhl & Co., Detroit

EP38	1c	2,50
EP39	3c	9,00
EP40	5c	2,00
EP41	10c	1,75
EP42	12c	6,00
EP43	24c	5,75

No. EP39 is unique.

Burnett's Cocoaine Kalliston

44	1c	600.
45	3c	600.
46	5c	525.
47	10c	575.
48	12c	3,750.
49	24c	5,000.
50	30c	4,000.
51	90c	7,500.

Burnett's Cooking Extracts

52	1c	450.
53	3c	500.
54	5c	500.
55	10c	700.
a.	Ribbed frame	4,000.
56	12c	2,000.
57	24c	5,000.
58	30c	5,500.
58A	90c	5,500.

No. EP58A is unique.

A. M. Claflin, Hopkinton, Mass.

P59	1c	11,000.
P60	3c	
P61	5c	15,000.
P62	10c	7,500.
P63	12c	16,000.

No. EP60 is unique.

H. A. Cook, Evansville, Ind.

P64	5c	3,500.
P65	10c	3,000.

EP97 Obverse

Dougan, Hatter, New York

EP66	1c	2,500.
EP67	3c	2,250.
EP68	5c	3,750.
EP69	10c	3,750.

Drake's Plantation Bitters

EP70	1c	450.
EP71	3c	450.
EP72	5c	600.
a.	Ribbed frame	2,500.
EP73	10c	650.
a.	Ribbed frame	2,500.
EP74	12c	2,000.
EP75	24c	3,000.
EP76	30c	3,000.
EP77	90c	11,000.

Ellis, McAlpin & Co., Cincinnati

EP78	1c	—
EP79	3c	2,250.
EP80	5c	1,250.
EP81	10c	1,000.
EP82	12c	2,750.
EP83	24c	2,250.

Specialists have questioned the existence of No. EP78. The editors would like to see authenticated evidence of this listing.

G. G. Evans, Philadelphia

EP84	1c	1,250.
EP85	3c	1,500.
EP86	5c	—
EP87	10c	7,000.

Gage Bros. & Drake, Tremont House, Chicago

EP88	1c	1,200.
EP89	3c	600.
EP90	5c	750.
EP91	10c	900.
a.	Ribbed frame	4,000.
EP92	12c	3,000.

Only one example of No. EP91a is available to collectors.

EP99 Obverse

J. Gault

EP93	1c	600.
a.	Ribbed frame	
EP95	3c	500.
a.	Ribbed frame	1,400.
EP96	5c	350.
a.	Ribbed frame	600.
EP97	10c	750.
a.	Ribbed frame	650.
EP98	12c	900.
a.	Ribbed frame	2,500.
EP99	24c	1,700.
a.	Ribbed frame	2,750.
EP100	30c	2,750.
a.	Ribbed frame	3,750.
EP101	90c	6,500.

L. C. Hopkins & Co., Cincinnati

EP102	1c	2,500.
EP103	3c	5,000.
EP104	5c	6,000.
EP105	10c	5,500.

Hunt & Nash, Irving House, New York

EP106	1c	2,000.
EP107	3c	2,000.
a.	Ribbed frame	3,000.
EP108	5c	900.
a.	Ribbed frame	950.
EP109	10c	1,200.
a.	Ribbed frame	800.
EP110	12c	1,750.
a.	Ribbed frame	2,750.
EP111	24c	2,500.
a.	Ribbed frame	3,250.
EP112	30c	5,000.

No. EP112 is unique.

EP119 Obverse

Kirkpatrick & Gault, New York

EP113	1c	500.
EP114	3c	700.
EP115	5c	500.
EP116	10c	500.
EP117	12c	1,250.
EP118	24c	1,750.
EP119	30c	2,750.
EP120	90c	10,000.

Lord & Taylor, New York

EP121	1c	1,250.
EP122	3c	1,500.
EP123	5c	1,100.
EP124	10c	1,250.
EP125	12c	2,500.
EP126	24c	2,750.
EP127	30c	3,750.
EP128	90c	10,000.

Mendum's Family Wine Emporium, New York

EP129	1c	800.
EP130	3c	900.
EP131	5c	1,200.
EP132	10c	2,500.
a.	Ribbed frame	2,250.
EP133	12c	2,750.

B. F. Miles, Peoria

EP134	1c	25,000.
EP135	5c	15,000.

John W. Norris, Chicago

EP136	1c	3,000.
EP137	3c	3,000.
EP138	5c	2,500.
EP139	10c	2,750.

"INSURANCE" Curved   "INSURANCE" Straight

EP141 Obverse

North America Life Insurance Co., N. Y.

EP140	1c	Curved	475.
a.		Straight	525.
EP141	3c	Straight	800.
a.		Curved	1,750.
EP142	5c	Straight	675.
a.		Straight, ribbed frame	1,100.
b.		Curved	3,000.
EP143	10c	Straight	900.
a.		Straight, ribbed frame	3,250.
b.		Curved	1,750.
c.		Curved, ribbed frame	2,250.
EP144	12c	Straight	2,500.
a.		Curved	3,500.

No. EP142b is unique. Nos. EP143a and EP144a each may be unique.

Pearce, Tolle & Holton, Cincinnati

EP145	1c	3,250.
EP146	3c	3,000.
EP147	5c	3,000.
EP148	10c	7,000.
EP149	12c	4,250.
EP150	24c	—

No. EP149 is unique.
The existence of No. EP150 has been questioned by specialists. The editors would like to see authenticated evidence of its existence.

Sands Ale

EP151	5c	3,750.
EP152	10c	4,500.
EP153	12c	—
EP154	30c	—

No. EP154 is unique. The case of the known example has been opened. It is possible that the 30c stamp has been substituted for the original stamp and/or the mica has been replaced.

Schapker & Bussing, Evansville, Ind.

EP155	1c	2,000.
EP156	3c	1,750.
EP157	5c	650.
EP158	10c	700.
EP159	12c	5,000.

John Shillito & Co., Cincinnati

EP160	1c	2,250.
EP161	3c	1,000.
EP162	5c	600.
EP163	10c	700.
EP164	12c	5,500.

EP165 Obverse

S. Steinfeld, New York

EP165	1c	3,5
EP166	5c	7,0
EP167	10c	6,0
EP168	12c	6,0

N. G. Taylor & Co., Philadelphia

EP169	1c	3,7
EP170	3c	3,5
EP171	5c	3,2
EP172	10c	3,5
EP173	12c	3,7

No. EP173 is unique.

Weir and Larminie, Montreal

EP174	1c	4,00
EP175	3c	15,00
EP176	5c	4,25
EP177	10c	3,00

White, the Hatter, New York

EP178	1c	3,70
EP179	3c	2,65
EP180	5c	3,75
EP181	10c	3,75

POSTAGE CURRENCY

Small coins disappeared from circulation in 1861-62 as cash was hoarded. To ease business transactions, merchants issued notes of credit, promises to pay, tokens, store cards, etc. U.S. Treasurer Francis E. Spinner made a substitute for small currency by affixing postage stamps, singly and multiples, to Treasury paper. He arranged with the Post office to replace worn stamps with new when necessary.

The next step was to print the stamps on Treasury paper. On July 17, 1862, Congress authorized the issue of such "Postage Currency." It remained use until May 27, 1863. It was not money, but a means of making stamps negotiable.

On Oct. 10, 1863 a second issue was released. These, and the later three issues, did not show stamps and are called Fractional Currency. In 1876 Congress authorized the minting of silver coins to redeem the outstanding fractional currency.

Values quoted are for notes in crisp, new condition, not creased or worn.
Creased or worn copies sell for 25 to 75 percent less.
Items valued with a dash are believed to be unique.

Front Engraved and Printed by the National Bank Note Co.
Back Engraved and Printed in Black by The American Bank Note Co.
"A B Co." on Back

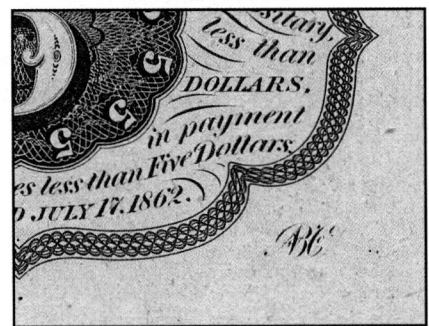

"ABCo." imprint, lower right corner of back (#1-8)

1862, Aug. 21

Perforated Edges-Perf. 12

PC1	5c Bust of Jefferson on 5c stamp, brown	85.00
a.	Inverted back	*575.00*
PC2	10c Bust of Washington on 10c stamp, green	60.00
PC3	25c Five 5c stamps, brown	85.00
PC4	50c Five 10c stamps, green	90.00
a.	Inverted back	*575.00*

Imperforate Edges

PC5	5c Bust of Jefferson on 5c stamp	30.00
a.	Inverted back	*225.00*
PC6	10c Bust of Washington on 10c stamp	30.00
a.	Inverted back	*400.00*
PC7	25c Five 5c stamps	50.00
a.	Inverted back	*350.00*
PC8	50c Five 10c stamps	90.00
a.	Inverted back	*450.00*

No. PC8 exists perforated 14, privately produced.

Front and Back Engraved and Printed by the the National Bank Note Co.

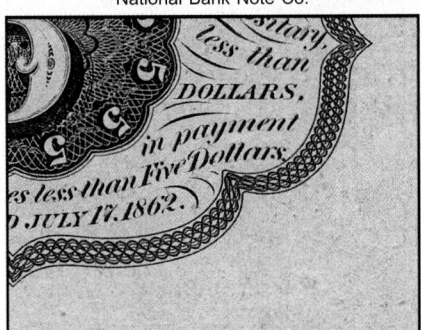

Without "A B Co." on Back

Perforated Edges-Perf. 12

PC9	5c Bust of Jefferson on 5c stamp	85.00
a.	Inverted back	—
PC10	10c Bust of Washington on 10c stamp	85.00
a.	Inverted back	—
PC11	25c Five 5c stamps	175.00
a.	Inverted back	*825.00*
PC12	50c Five 10c stamps	190.00
a.	Inverted back	—

Imperforate Edges

PC13	5c Bust of Jefferson on 5c stamp	85.00
a.	Inverted back	—
PC14	10c Bust of Washington on 10c stamp	140.00
a.	Inverted back	*825.00*
PC15	25c Five 5c stamps	190.00
PC16	50c Five 10c stamps	600.00
a.	Inverted back	—

CONFEDERATE STATES OF AMERICA

3¢ 1861 POSTMASTERS' PROVISIONALS

With the secession of South Carolina from the Union on Dec. 20, 1860, a new era began in U.S. history as well as its postal history. Other South states quickly followed South Carolina's lead, which in turn led to the formation of the provisional government of the Confederate States of America Feb. 4, 1861.

President Jefferson Davis' cabinet was completed Mar. 6, 1861, with the acceptance of the position of Postmaster General by John H. Reagan Texas. The provisional government had already passed regulations that required payment for postage in cash and that effectively carried over the U 3c rate until the new Confederate Post Office Department took over control of the system.

Soon after entering on his duties, Reagan directed the postmasters in the Confederate States and in the newly seceded states to "continue performance of their duties as such, and render all accounts and pay all moneys (sic) to the order of the Government of the U.S. as they h heretofore done, until the Government of the Confederate States shall be prepared to assume control of its postal affairs."

As coinage was becoming scarce, postal patrons began having problems buying individual stamps or paying for letters individually, especially stamp stocks started to run short in certain areas. Even though the U.S. Post Office Department was technically in control of the postal system a southern postmasters were operating under Federal authority, the U.S.P.O. was hesitant in re-supplying seceded states with additional stamps a stamped envelopes.

The U.S. government had made the issuance of postmasters' provisionals illegal many years before, but the southern postmasters had to do w they felt was necessary to allow patrons to pay for postage and make the system work. Therefore, a few postmasters took it upon themselves to is: provisional stamps in the 3c rate then in effect. Interestingly, these were stamps and envelopes that the U.S. government did not recognize as legal, they did do postal duty unchallenged in the Confederate States. Yet the proceeds were to be remitted to the U.S. government in Washington! authenticated postmasters' provisionals in the 3c rate have been recorded.

On May 13, 1861, Postmaster General Reagan issued his proclamation "assuming control and direction of postal service within the limits of Confederate States of America on and after the first day of June," with new postage rates and regulations. The Federal government suspend operations in the Confederate States (except for western Virginia and the seceding state of Tennessee) by a proclamation issued by Postmas General Montgomery Blair on May 27, 1861, effective from May 31, 1861, and June 10 for western and middle Tennessee. As Tennessee did not the Confederacy until July 2, 1861, the unissued 3c Nashville provisional was produced in a state that was in the process of seceding, while the oth provisionals were used in the Confederacy before the June 1 assumption of control of postal service by the Confederate States of America.

HILLSBORO, N.C.

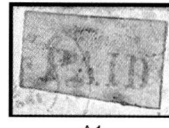

A1

Handstamped Adhesive

1AX1   A1   3c **bluish black,** on cover   —

No. 1AX1 is unique. This is the same handstamp as used for No. 39X1. 3c usage is determined from the May 27, 1861 circular date stamp.

Cancellation: black town.

JACKSON, MISS.

E1

Handstamped Envelope

2AXU1   E1   3c **black**   2,500.

See Nos. 43XU1-43XU4.

MADISON COURT HOUSE, FLA.

A1   "CNETS"

Typeset Adhesive

3AX1   A1   3c **gold**   —   10,000.
         On cover   65,000.
    a.   "CNETS"   14,000.

No. 3AX1 on cover and No. 3AX1a are each unique.

Cancellations: black town, oblong paid, ms "Paid in Money," manuscript.

See No. 137XU1.

NASHVILLE, TENN.

A1

Typeset Adhesive (5 varieties)

4AX1   A1   3c **carmine**   150.
       Horizontal strip of 5 showing
       all varieties   900.

No. 4AX1 was prepared by Postmaster McNish with the U rate, but the stamp was never issued.
See Nos. 61X2-61XU2.

SELMA, ALA.

E1

Handstamped Envelope

5AXU1   E1   3c **black**   1,8

See Nos. 77XU1-77XU3.

TUSCUMBIA, ALA.

E1

Handstamped Envelope, impression at upper right

6AXU1   E1   3c **dull red,** *buff*   16,50

No. 6AXU1 also exists with a 3c 1857 stamp affixed at upp right over the provisional handstamp, tied by black circul "TUSCUMBIA, ALA." town postmark. Value $15,000.
See Nos. 84XU1-84XU3.

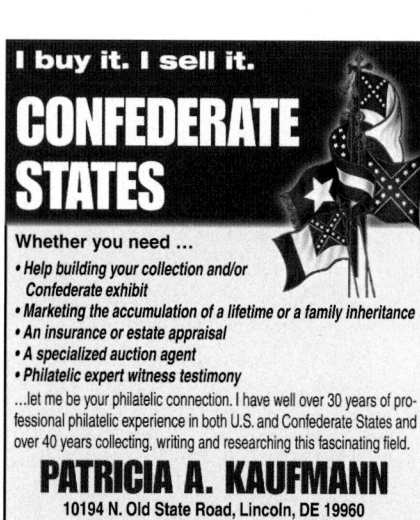

CONFEDERATE POSTMASTERS' PROVISIONALS

These stamps and envelopes were issued by individual postmasters generally during the interim between June 1, 1861, when the use of United States stamps stopped in the Confederacy, and October 16, 1861, when the first Confederate Government stamps were issued. They were occasionally issued at later periods, especially in Texas, when regular issues of government stamps were unavailable.

Canceling stamps of the post offices were often used to produce envelopes, some of which were supplied in advance by private citizens. These envelopes and other stationery therefore may be found in a wide variety of papers, colors, sizes and shapes, including patriotic and semi-official types. It is often difficult to determine whether the impression made by the canceling stamp indicates provisional usage or merely postage paid at the time the letter was deposited in the post office. Occasionally the same mark was used for both purposes.

The *press-printed* **provisional envelopes are in a different category. They were produced in quantity, using envelopes procured in advance** by the postmaster, such as those of Charleston, Lynchburg, Memphis, etc. *The* **press-printed** *envelopes are listed and valued on all known* covers.

The **handstamped** *provisional envelopes are listed and valued according to type and variety of handstamp, but not according to paper. Many exist in such a variety of papers that they defy accurate, complete listing. The value of a handstamped provisional envelope is determined primarily by the rarity of the markings and its overall condition and attractiveness, rather than the type of paper.*

All handstamped provisional envelopes, when used, should also show the postmark of the town of issue.

Most handstamps are impressed at top right, although they exist from some towns in other positions.

Many illustrations in this section are reduced in size.

Values for envelopes are for entires. Values for stamps of provisional issues are for copies with little or no gum; original gum over a large portion of the stamp will increase the value substantially.

ABERDEEN, MISS.

E1

Handstamped Envelopes

1XU1	E1	5c **black**		6,000.
1XU2	E1	10c (ms.) on 5c **black**		12,500.

No. 1XU2 is unique.

ABINGDON, VA.

E1

Handstamped Envelopes

2XU1	E1	2c **black**		11,000.
2XU2	E1	5c **black**		1,250.
		On patriotic cover		3,000.
2XU3	E1	10c **black**	2,200.	3,500.

The unused No. 2XU3 is a unique mint example, and the value represents the price realized in a 1997 auction sale. No. 2XU3 used also is unique.

ALBANY, GA.

E1

E2

Handstamped Envelopes

3XU1	E1	5c **greenish blue**	900.
		On patriotic cover	
3XU2	E1	10c **greenish blue**	2,000.

3XU3	E1	10c on 5c **greenish blue**	3,500.
3XU5	E2	5c **greenish blue**	
3XU6	E2	10c **greenish blue**	2,500.

The "10" in the No. 3XU2 marking is larger than the "10" in the No. 3XU3 marking.

Only one example each recorded of Nos. 3XU2, 3XU3 and 3XU6.

The existence of No. 3XU5 is in question. The editors would like to see an authenticated example of this marking.

ANDERSON COURT HOUSE, S.C.

E1

Handstamped Envelopes

4XU1	E1	5c **black**	500.	2,250.
4XU2	E1	10c (ms.) **black**		3,000.

ATHENS, GA

A1 (Type I)

A1 (Type II)

Typographed Adhesives
(from woodcuts of two types)

Pairs, both horizontal and vertical, always show one of each type.

5X1	A1	5c **purple** (shades)	1,000.	1,500.
		Pair	—	3,250.
		On cover		2,500.
		Pair on cover		4,750.
		Strip of 4 on cover (horiz.)		10,000.
a.		Tete beche pair (vertical)		7,500.
		Tete beche pair on cover		27,500.
5X2	A1	5c **red**	—	4,750.
		On cover		15,000.
		Pair on cover	—	

Cancellations in black: grid, town, "PAID."

The colorless ornaments in the four corners of No. 5X2 were recut making them wider than those in No. 5X1.

Dangerous fakes exist of No. 5X1 type II. Certificates of authenticity from recognized committees are strongly recommended.

The existence of a pair on cover of No. 5X2 is in question. The editors would like to see an example of this usage.

ATLANTA, GA.

E1

E2

Handstamped Envelopes

6XU1	E1	5c **red**		3,500.
6XU2	E1	5c **black**	175.	700.
		On patriotic cover		3,500.
6XU3	E1	10c on 5c **black**		1,500.
		On patriotic cover		—
6XU4	E2	2c **black**		3,000.
6XU5	E2	5c **black**		1,500.
		On patriotic cover		3,500.

6XU6 E2 10c **black**		950.
On patriotic cover		
6XU7 E2 10c on 5c **black**		2,500.

Only one example recorded of No. 6XU1.

E3

Handstamped Envelopes

6XU8 E3 5c **black**		3,500.
6XU9 E3 10c **black** ("10" upright)		2,750.

Only one example recorded of No. 6XU8.

AUGUSTA, GA.

E1

Handstamped Envelope

7XU1 E1 5c **black**

Provisional status questioned. Indistinguishable from a hand-stamp paid cover when used. The only known example purported to be a Postmaster Provisional has a general CSA issue used over the marking.

The editors intend to delist this item unless evidence of a certified unused envelope with the marking is furnished.

AUSTIN, MISS.

E1

Press-printed Envelope (typeset)

8XU1 E1 5c **red,** *amber*		75,000.

One example recorded.

Cancellation: black "Paid."

AUSTIN, TEX.

E1a

Handstamped Adhesive

9X1 E1a10c **black**		—
On cover, uncanceled		1,500.
On cover, tied		

Only one example of No. 9X1 tied on cover is recorded.

Handstamped Envelope

9XU1 E1a10c **black**		1,750.

Cancellation on Nos. 9X1 and 9XU1: black town.

AUTAUGAVILLE, ALA.

E1   E2

Handstamped Envelopes

10XU1 E1 5c **black**		10,000.
10XU2 E2 5c **black**		12,500.

No. 10XU2 is unique.

BALCONY FALLS, VA.

E1

Handstamped Envelope

122XU1 E1 10c **blue**		1,750.

BARNWELL COURT HOUSE, S. C.

E1

Handstamped Envelope

123XU1 E1 5c **black**		1,750.

These are two separate handstamps.

BATON ROUGE, LA.

A1   A2

Typeset Adhesives
Ten varieties of each

11X1 A1 2c **green**		5,250.	5,000.
On cover			20,000.
a. "McCcrmick"		14,000.	8,500.
On cover			—
11X2 A2 5c **green & carmine** (Maltese cross border)		1,500.	1,400.
On cover			2,750.
Strip of 3			5,000.
Strip of 5			22,500.
Canceled in New Orleans, on cover			20,000.
a. "McCcrmick"		—	2,000.
On cover			7,000.

Only one example each is recorded of No. 11X1a unused, used and on cover.

The "Canceled in New Orleans" examples entered the mails in New Orleans after having been placed (uncanceled) on riverboats in Baton Rouge. Two such covers are recorded.

A3

A4

Ten varieties of each

11X3 A3 5c **green & carmine** (crisscross border)		4,500.	2,750.
On cover			10,000.
a. "McCcrmick"			3,500.
11X4 A4 10c **blue**			6,000.
On cover			75,000.

No. 11X4 on cover is unique.

Cancellation on Nos. 11X1-11X4: black town.

BEAUMONT, TEX.

A1   A2

Typeset Adhesives
Several varieties of each

12X1 A1 10c **black,** *yellow*			12,؟
On cover			55,؟
12X2 A1 10c **black,** *pink*			12,؟
On cover			30,؟
12X3 A2 10c **black,** *yellow,* on cover			90,؟

One example recorded of No. 12X3.

Cancellations: black pen; black town.

BLUFFTON, S. C.

E1

Handstamped Envelope

124XU1 E1 5c **black**		3,؟

Only one example recorded of No. 124XU1.

BRIDGEVILLE, ALA.

A1

Handstamped Adhesive in black within red pen-ruled squares

13X1 A1 5c **black & red,** pair on cover		20,0؟

Cancellation is black pen.

CAMDEN, S. C.

E1

E2

Handstamped Envelopes

125XU1 E1 5c **black**		4,50؟
125XU2 E2 10c **black**		450.

No. 125XU2 unused was privately carried and is addresse؟ but has no postal markings. No. 125XU2 is indistinguishab؟ from a handstamp paid cover when used.

CANTON, MISS.

E1

" in star is initial of Postmaster William Priestly.

Handstamped Envelopes

U1	E1	5c **black**	2,750.
U2	E1	10c (ms.) on 5c **black**	5,000.

CAROLINA CITY, N. C.

E1

Handstamped Envelope

XU1	E1	5c **black**	3,500.

CARTERSVILLE, GA.

E1

Handstamped Envelope

XU1	E1	(5c) **red**	1,250.

CHAPEL HILL, N. C.

E1

Handstamped Envelope

XU1	E1	5c **black**	3,250.
		On patriotic cover	5,000.

CHARLESTON, S. C.

A1

E1

E2

Lithographed Adhesive

X1	A1	5c **blue**	1,200.	850.
		Pair	2,500.	2,200.
		On cover		2,500.

On patriotic cover	5,000.	
Pair, on cover	5,000.	
On cover with No. 112XU1	—	
Used on cover with C.S.A. 5c		
#6 to make 10c rate	—	

Values are for copies showing parts of the outer frame lines on at least 3 sides.

Cancellation: black town (two types).

Press-printed Envelopes
(typographed from woodcut)

16XU1	E1	5c **blue**	1,250.	4,000.
16XU2	E1	5c **blue**, *amber*	1,250.	4,000.
16XU3	E1	5c **blue**, *orange*	1,250.	4,000.
16XU4	E1	5c **blue**, *buff*	1,250.	4,000.
16XU5	E1	5c **blue**, *blue*	1,250.	4,000.
16XU6	E2	10c **blue**, *orange*		77,500.

The No. 16XU6 used entire is unique; value based on 1997 auction sale.

Handstamped Cut Square

16XU7	E2	10c **black**	3,000.

There is only one copy of No. 16XU7. It is a cutout, not an entire. It may not have been mailed from Charleston, and it may not have paid postage.

CHARLOTTESVILLE, VA.

E1

Handstamped Envelopes, Manuscript Initials

127XU1	E1	5c **blue**	—
127XU2	E1	10c **blue**	—

CHATTANOOGA, TENN.

E1

Handstamped Envelopes

17XU2	E1	5c **black**	1,500.
17XU3	E1	5c on 2c **black**	3,250.

CHRISTIANSBURG, VA.

E1

Handstamped Envelopes
Impressed at top right

99XU1	E1	5c **black**, *blue*	2,250.
99XU2	E1	5c **blue**	2,000.
99XU3	E1	5c **black**, *orange*	2,250.
99XU4	E1	5c **green** on U.S. envelope No. U27	4,500.
99XU5	E1	10c **blue**	3,500.

COLAPARCHEE, GA.

E1   Control

Handstamped Envelope

119XU1	E1	5c **black**	3,500.

There are only two recorded examples of No. 119XU1, and both are used with general issue stamp from Savannah.

COLUMBIA, S. C.

E1

E2   PAID

Handstamped Envelopes

18XU1	E1	5c **blue**	550.	1,000.
		Used on cover with C.S.A. 5c		
		#1 or #1c to make 10c rate	3,000.	
		Used on cover with C.S.A. 5c		
		#7 to make 10c rate	7,500.	
18XU2	E1	5c **black**	600.	1,000.
18XU3	E1	10c on 5c **blue**		3,500.

Three types of "PAID," one in circle

18XU4	E2	5c **blue**, seal on front	2,500.
a.		Seal on back	1,250.
18XU5	E2	10c **blue**, seal on back	2,750.

Three types of "PAID" for Nos. 18XU4-18XU5, one in circle.

Circular Seal similar to E2, 27mm diameter

18XU6	E2	5c **blue** (seal on back)	4,000.

COLUMBIA, TENN.

E1

Handstamped Envelope

113XU1	E1	5c **red**	3,500.

COLUMBUS, GA.

E1

Handstamped Envelopes

19XU1	E1	5c **blue**	800.
19XU2	E1	10c **red**	2,250.

COURTLAND, ALA.

E1

Handstamped Envelopes (from woodcut)

103XU1	E1	5c **black**	—
103XU2	E1	5c **red**	10,000.

Provisional status of No. 103XU1 questioned.

DALTON, GA.

E1

Handstamped Envelopes

20XU1	E1	5c black		600.
a.		Denomination omitted (5c rate)		725.
20XU2	E1	10c black		800.
20XU3	E1	10c (ms.) on 5c black		1,500.

DANVILLE, VA.

A1

E2   E3

WBP

PAID 10

E4

Typeset Adhesive
Wove Paper

21X1	A1	5c red		5,500.
		On cover		4,000.
		Cut to shape		4,000.
		On cover, cut to shape		6,000.

Two varieties known.

Only four rectangular-cut examples are recorded, one of which is reported to be on laid paper.

Cancellation: blue town.

Press-printed Envelopes (typographed)
Two types: "SOUTHERN" in straight or curved line
Impressed (usually) at top left

21XU1	E1	5c black	5,500.
21XU2	E1	5c black, amber	5,500.
21XU3	E1	5c black, dark buff	5,250.

Unissued 10c envelopes (type E1, in red) are known. All recorded examples are envelopes on which added stamps paid the postage.

Handstamped Envelopes

21XU3A	E4	5c black (ms "WBP" initials)	1,000.
21XU4	E2	10c black	2,000.
21XU5	E2	10c blue	
21XU6	E3	10c black	2,750.
21XU7	E4	10c black (ms "WBP" initials)	—

Types E2 and E3 both exist on one cover. The existence of No. 21XU5 has been questioned.

DEMOPOLIS, ALA.

 PAID *J. Y. Hall.*

E1

Handstamped Envelopes, Signature in ms.

22XU1	E1	5c black ("Jno. Y. Hall")	3,500.
22XU2	E1	5c black ("J. Y. Hall")	3,500.
22XU3	E1	5c (ms.) black ("J. Y. Hall")	4,000.

EATONTON, GA.

E1

E2

Handstamped Envelopes

23XU1	E1	5c black	3,000.
23XU2	E2	5c + 5c black	4,500.

EMORY, VA.

A1

Handstamped Adhesives ("PAID" and "5" in circle on selvage of U.S. 1c 1857 issue)
Perf. 15 on three sides

24X1	A1	5c blue, on cover, ms. tied	15,000.

Also known with "5" above "PAID."

Cancellation: blue town.

E1   E2

Handstamped Envelopes

24XU1	E1	5c blue	2,000.
24XU2	E2	10c blue	10,000.

Only one example recorded of No. 24XU2.

FINCASTLE, VA.

E1

Press-printed Envelope (typeset)
Impressed at top right

104XU1	E1	10c black		20,

One example recorded.

FORSYTH, GA.

E1

Handstamped Envelope

120XU1	E1	10c black	1

Only one example recorded of No. 120XU1.

FRANKLIN, N. C.

E1

Press-printed Envelope (typeset)
Impressed at top right

25XU1	E1	5c blue, buff	30,

The one known envelope shows black circular Franklin mark with manuscript date.

FRAZIERSVILLE, S. C.

E1

Handstamped Envelope, "5" manuscript

128XU1	E1	5c black	2,2

Only one example recorded of No. 128XU1.

FREDERICKSBURG, VA.

A1

Sheets of 20, two panes of 10 varieties each

Typeset Adhesives
Thin bluish paper

26X1	A1	5c blue, bluish	300.	8
		Block of 4	1,750.	
		Sheet of 20	10,000.	
		On cover		5,0
		Pair on cover		12,0
26X2	A1	10c red, bluish	1,000.	
		Brown red, bluish	1,000.	
		Block of 4	—	

Cancellation: black town.

GAINESVILLE, ALA.

E1   E2

Handstamped Envelopes

27XU1	E1	5c black		5,0
27XU2	E2	10c ("01") black		6,0

Postmark spells town name "Gainsville."

GALVESTON, TEX.

E1

Handstamped Envelopes

XU1	E1	5c	**black**	500.	1,500.
XU2	E1	10c	**black**		2,000.

E2

Handstamped Envelopes

XU3	E2	10c	**black**	550.	2,400.
XU4	E2	20c	**black**		3,500.

GASTON, N. C.

E1

Handstamped Envelope

9XU1	E1	5c	**black**		4,500.

Only one example recorded of No. 129XU1.

GEORGETOWN, S. C.

E1   Control

Handstamped Envelope

3XU1	E1	5c	**black**		850.

GOLIAD, TEX.

A1   A2

Typeset Adhesives

9X1	A1	5c	**black**		7,000.
9X2	A1	5c	**black,** *gray*		6,500.
9X3	A1	5c	**black,** *rose*		7,000.
			On cover front		50,000.
9X4	A1	10c	**black**	—	7,000.
9X5	A1	10c	**black,** *rose*		7,000.

Type A1 stamps are signed "Clarke-P.M." vertically in black or red.

9X6	A2	5c	**black,** *gray*		10,000.
a.			"GOILAD"		12,000.
			Pair, left stamp the error		
9X7	A2	10c	**black,** *gray*		7,500.
			On cover		25,000.
a.			"GOILAD"		8,000.
			On cover		30,000.
9X8	A2	5c	**black,** *dark blue,* on cover		7,000.
9X9	A2	10c	**black,** *dark blue*	—	

Cancellations in black: pen, town, "Paid"

GONZALES, TEX.

Colman & Law were booksellers when John B. Law (of the firm) was appointed Postmaster. The firm used a small lithographed label on drugs and on the front or inside of books they sold.

A1

Lithographed Adhesives
on colored glazed paper

30X1	A1	(5c)	**gold,** *dark blue,* pair on cover, *1861*		15,000.
30X2	A1	(10c)	**gold,** *garnet,* on cover, *1864*		12,500.
30X3	A1	(10c)	**gold,** *black,* on cover, *1865*	—	

Cancellations: black town, black pen. No. 30X1 must bear double-circle town cancel as validating control. The control was applied to the labels in the sheet before their sale as stamps. When used, the stamps bear an additional Gonzales double-circle postmark.

GREENSBORO, ALA.

E1

E2

Handstamped Envelopes

31XU1	E1	5c	**black**		3,000.
31XU2	E1	10c	**black**		2,750.
31XU3	E2	10c	**black**		4,250.

GREENSBORO, N. C.

E1

Handstamped Envelope

32XU1	E1	10c	**red**		1,250.

GREENVILLE, ALA.

A1   A2

Typeset Adhesives
On pinkish surface-colored glazed paper.

33X1	A1	5c	**blue & red**	25,000.	
			On cover		40,000.
33X2	A2	10c	**red & blue**	—	
			On cover		40,000.

Two used examples each are known of Nos. 33X1-33X2, and all are on covers. Covers bear a postmark but it was not used to cancel the stamps.
The former No. 33X1a has been identified as a counterfeit.

GREENVILLE COURT HOUSE, S. C.

PAID 5

E1   Control

Handstamped Envelopes (Several types)

34XU1	E1	5c	**black**		2,000.
34XU2	E1	10c	**black**		2,250.
34XU3	E1	20c	(ms.) on 10c **black**		3,000.

Envelopes must bear the black control on the back.

GREENWOOD DEPOT, VA.

A1

"PAID" Handstamped Adhesive ("PAID" with value and signature in ms.)
Laid Paper

35X1	A1	10c	**black,** *gray blue,* uncanceled, on cover		20,000.
			On cover, tied	—	

Six examples recorded of No. 35X1, all on covers. One of these is in the British Library collection. Of the remaining five, only one has the stamp tied to the cover.

Cancellation: black town.

GRIFFIN, GA.

E1

Handstamped Envelope

102XU1	E1	5c	**black**		2,250.

GROVE HILL, ALA.

A1

Handstamped Adhesive (from woodcut)

36X1	A1	5c	**black**	—	
			On cover, tied		75,000.

Two examples are recorded. One is on cover tied by the postmark. The other is canceled by magenta pen on a cover front.

Cancellations: black town, magenta pen.

HALLETTSVILLE, TEX.

A1

Handstamped Adhesive
Ruled Letter Paper

37X1	A1	10c	**black,** *gray blue,* on cover		15,000.
			One example known.		

Cancellation: black ms.

HAMBURGH, S. C.

E1

Handstamped Envelope

112XU1 E1 5c **black**   2,250.
On cover with #16X1 (forwarded)   —

HARRISBURGH (Harrisburg), TEX.

E1

Handstamped Envelope

130XU1 E1 5c **black**   —
No. 130XU1 is indistinguishable from a handstamp paid cover when used.

HELENA, TEX.

A1

Typeset Adhesives
Several varieties
38X1 A1 5c **black,** *buff*   7,500. 6,000.
38X2 A1 10c **black,** *gray*   5,000.
On 10c "Helena" is in upper and lower case italics.
Used examples are valued with small faults or repairs, as all recorded have faults.

Cancellation: black town.

HILLSBORO, N. C.

A1

Handstamped Adhesive

39X1 A1 5c **black,** on cover   15,000.
No. 39X1 is unique.
See 3c 1861 Postmasters' Provisional No. 1AX1.

Cancellation: black town.

Ms./Handstamped Envelope
39XU1 10c "paid 10" in manuscript with undated blue town cancel as control on face   —

HOLLANDALE, TEX.

E1

Handstamped Envelope

132XU1 E1 5c **black**   —

HOUSTON, TEX.

E1

Handstamped Envelopes

40XU1 E1 5c **red**   — 750.
On patriotic cover   —
40XU2 E1 10c **red**   — 1,500.
40XU3 E1 10c **black**   2,250.
40XU4 E1 5c +10c **red**   2,500.
40XU5 E1 10c +10c **red**   2,500.
40XU6 E1 10c (ms.) on 5c **red**   3,000.
Nos. 40XU2-40XU5 show "TEX" instead of "TXS."

HUNTSVILLE, TEX.

PAID
5
E1

Control

Handstamped Envelope

92XU1 E1 5c **black**   5,000.
No. 92XU1 exists with "5" outside or within control circle.

INDEPENDENCE, TEX.

A1

Handstamped Adhesives

41X1 A1 10c **black,** *buff,* on cover, uncanceled, cut to shape   20,000.
41X2 A1 10c **black,** *dull rose,* on cover

With small "10" and "Pd" in manuscript
41X3 A1 10c **black,** *buff,* on cover, uncanceled, cut to shape   32,500.
On cover, uncanceled, cut
square   —

No. 41X1 is unique.
All known examples of Nos. 41X1-41X3 are uncanceled on covers with black "INDEPENDANCE TEX." (sic) postmark.
The existence of No. 41X2 has been questioned by specialists. The editors would like to see authenticated evidence of the existence of this item.

ISABELLA, GA.

E1

Handstamped Envelope, "5" Manuscript
133XU1 E1 5c **black**   2,000.
Only one example recorded of No. 133XU1.

IUKA, MISS.

E1

Handstamped Envelope

42XU1 E1 5c **black**   1,?
On patriotic cover   4,0

JACKSON, MISS.

E1

Handstamped Envelopes
Two types of numeral
43XU1 E1 5c **black**   5
On patriotic cover   3,0
43XU2 E1 10c **black**   2,0
43XU3 E1 10c on 5c **black**   2,7
43XU4 E1 10c on 5c **blue**   2,7
The 5c also exists on a lettersheet.
See 3c 1861 Postmasters' Provisional No. 2AXU1.

JACKSONVILLE, ALA.

E1

Handstamped Envelope

110XU1 E1 5c **black**   — 3,0

JACKSONVILLE, FLA.

PAID
5
E1

Handstamped Envelope

134XU1 E1 5c **black**
Undated double circle postmark control on reverse.

JETERSVILLE, VA.

A1

Handstamped Adhesive
("5" with ms. "AHA." initials)
Laid Paper
44X1 A1 5c **black,** vertical pair on cover,
uncanceled   16,00

Initials are those of Postmaster A. H. Atwood.

Cancellation: black town.

JONESBORO, TENN.

E1

Handstamped Envelopes
45XU1 E1 5c **black**   3,75
45XU2 E1 5c **dark blue**   7,00

KINGSTON, GA.

E1

PAID
5
CENTS
E2

E3

E4

Typeset Envelopes

(Design types E1-E2, E4 are handstamps; typeset design E3 probably impressed by hand but possibly press printed)

XU1	E1	5c	**black**	— 2,250.
XU2	E2	5c	**black**	— 3,250.
XU4	E3	5c	**black**	
XU5	E4	5c	**black**	2,000.

There is only one recorded example of No. 46XU4.

KNOXVILLE, TENN.

A1 — Knxvle1

Typographed Adhesives
(stereotype from woodcut)
Grayish Laid Paper

X1	A1	5c	**brick red**	1,400.	1,400.
			Manuscript cancel		350.
			Horizontal pair	4,000.	3,000.
			Vertical pair	3,100.	
			Vertical strip of 3	6,500.	
			On cover, tied by handstamp		7,500.
			On cover, manuscript cancel		2,100.
			Pair on cover		7,500.
X2	A1	5c	**carmine**	1,900.	2,250.
			Manuscript cancel		1,000.
			Vertical strip of 3		
			On cover, tied by handstamp		7,500.
			On cover, manuscript cancel		2,100.
X3	A1	10c	**green**, on cover		57,750.

The #47X3 cover is unique. Value is based on 1997 auction sale.

Cancellations in black: town, bars, pen or pencil.

E1

E2

Press-printed Envelopes (typographed)

7XU1	E1	5c	**blue**	750. 2,000.
7XU2	E1	5c	**blue**, *orange*	750. 2,250.
7XU3	E1	10c	**red** (cut to shape)	3,000.
7XU4	E1	10c	**red**, *orange* (cut to shape)	3,000.

Only one example each recorded of Nos. 47XU3 and 47XU4.

Handstamped Envelopes

47XU5	E2	5c	**black**	750.	1,500.
		On patriotic cover			3,000.
47XU6	E2	10c on 5c	**black**		3,500.

Type E2 exists with "5" above or below "PAID."

LA GRANGE, TEX.

E1

Handstamped Envelopes

48XU1	E1	5c	**black**	—	2,250.
48XU2	E1	10c	**black**		3,000.

LAKE CITY, FLA.

E1　　　　　　　　　　Control

Handstamped Envelope

96XU1	E1	5c	**black**	2,000.

Envelopes have black circle control mark, or printed name of E. R. Ives, postmaster, on face or back.

LAURENS COURT HOUSE, S. C.

E1

Handstamped Envelope

116XU1	E1	5c	**black**	1,750.

LENOIR, N. C.

A1

E1

Handstamped Adhesive (from woodcut)
White wove paper with cross-ruled orange lines

49X1	A1	5c	**blue & orange**	3,250.	2,750.
			On cover, pen canceled		7,000.
			On cover, tied by handstamp		20,000.

Cancellations: blue town, blue "Paid" in circle, black pen.

Handstamped Envelopes

49XU1	A1	5c	**blue**	3,500.
49XU2	A1	10c (5c+5c)	**blue**	25,000.
49XU3	E1	5c	**blue**	4,500.
49XU4	E1	5c	**black**	

No. 49XU2 is unique. The existence of No. 49XU4 has been questioned.

LEXINGTON, MISS.

E1

Handstamped Envelopes

50XU1	E1	5c	**black**	5,000.
50XU2	E1	10c	**black**	5,000.

LEXINGTON, VA.

E1

Handstamped Envelopes

135XU1	E1	5c	**blue**	500.
			Used with 5c #6 to make 10c rate	500.
135XU2	E1	10c	**blue**	750.

Nos. 135XU1-135XU2 by themselves are indistinguishable from a handstamp paid cover when used.

LIBERTY, VA. (and Salem, Va.)

PAID
5cts.
A1

Typeset Adhesive (probably impressed by hand)
Laid Paper

74X1	A1	5c	**black**, on cover, uncanceled, with Liberty postmark	35,000.
			On cover, uncanceled, with Salem postmark	40,000.

Two known on covers with Liberty, Va. postmark; one cover known with the nearby Salem, Va. office postmark.

LIMESTONE SPRINGS, S. C.

A1

Handstamped Adhesive

121X1	A1	5c	**black**, on cover	10,000.
			Two on cover	15,000.

Stamps are cut round or rectangular, on white or colored paper. Covers are not postmarked.

LIVINGSTON, ALA.

A1

Lithographed Adhesive

51X1	A1	5c	blue	8,000.
		On cover		60,000.
		Pair on cover		120,000.

The pair on cover is unique.

Cancellation: black town.

LYNCHBURG, VA.

A1   E1

Typographed Adhesive
(stereotype from woodcut)

52X1	A1	5c	blue (shades)	1,750.	1,250.
		Pair			2,750.
		On cover			5,000.
		Pair on cover			20,000.

Cancellations: black town, blue town.

Press-printed Envelopes (typographed)
Impressed at top right or left

52XU1	E1	5c	black		3,000.
52XU2	E1	5c	black, amber	650.	3,000.
52XU3	E1	5c	black, buff		3,000.
52XU4	E1	5c	black, brown	900.	3,000.
		On patriotic cover			—

MACON, GA.

A1   A2

A3   A4

Typeset Adhesives
Several varieties of type A1, 10 of A2, 5 of A3
Wove Paper

53X1	A1	5c	black, light blue green		
		(shades)		900.	700.
		On cover			4,000.
		Pair on cover			9,000.
		Comma after "OFFICE"		950.	1,100.
		Comma after "OFFICE," on			
		cover			7,500.

Warning: Dangerous forgeries exist of the normal variety and the Comma after "OFFICE" variety. Certificates of authenticity from recognized committees are strongly recommended.

53X3	A2	5c	black, yellow	2,500.	850.
		On cover			4,750.
		On patriotic cover			9,000.
		Pair on cover			8,000.
53X4	A3	5c	black, yellow (shades)	2,750.	1,400.
		On cover			6,000.
		Pair on cover			10,000.
a.		Vertical tête bêche pair			—
53X5	A4	2c	black, gray green		
		On cover			60,000.

Laid Paper

53X6	A2	5c	black, yellow	3,000.	3,500.
		On cover			6,000.
53X7	A3	5c	black, yellow	6,000.	
		On cover			9,000.
53X8	A1	5c	black, light blue green	1,750.	2,250.
		On cover			4,500.

No. 53X4a is unique.

Cancellations: black town, black "PAID" (2 types).

E1

Handstamped Envelope
Two types: "PAID" over "5," "5" over "PAID"

53XU1	E1	5c	black	250.	575.
		On patriotic cover			1,900.

Values are for "PAID" over "5" variety. "5" over "PAID" is much scarcer.

MADISON, GA.

E1

Handstamped Envelope

136XU1	E1	5c	red	500.

No. 136XU1 is indistinguishable from a handstamp paid cover when used.

MADISON COURT HOUSE, FLA.

E1

Typeset Envelope

137XU1	E1	5c	black, yellow	23,000.

No. 137XU1 is unique.
See 3c 1861 Postmasters' Provisional No. 3AX1.

MARIETTA, GA.

E1   E2

Handstamped Envelopes

54XU1	E1	5c	black	400.
54XU2	E1	10c on 5c black		1,750.

With Double Circle Control

54XU3	E2	10c black		
54XU4	E2	5c	black	2,000.

The existence of No. 54XU3 has been questioned by specialists. The editors would like to see authenticated evidence of this listing.

MARION, VA.

A1

Adhesives with Typeset frame and Handstamp
numeral in center

55X1	A1	5c	black	6,5
		On cover		20,0
55X2	A1	10c	black	16,500. 10,0
		On cover		60,0
55X3	A1	5c	black, bluish, laid paper	—

The 2c, 3c, 15c and 20c are believed to be bogus items printed later using the original typeset frame.

Cancellations: black town, black "PAID."

MEMPHIS, TENN.

A1   A2

Typographed Adhesives
(stereotyped from woodcut)

Plate of 50 (5x10) for the 2c. The stereotypes for the stamps were set in 5 vertical rows of 8, with at least 2 rows sideways to the right (see Thomas H. Pratt's monograph, "T Postmaster's Provisionals of Memphis").

56X1	A1	2c	blue (shades)	100.	1,2
		Block of 4		550.	
		On cover			10,0
		Cracked plate (16, 17, 18)		160.	1,3

The "cracking off" (breaking off) of the plate at right ed caused incomplete printing of stamps in positions 5, 10, 15, and 50. Poor make-ready also caused incomplete printing position 50.

56X2	A2	5c	red (shades)	150.	1
		Pair		340.	4
		Block of 4		1,000.	
		On cover			1,7
		Pair on cover			3,5
		Strip of 4 on cover			7,0
		On patriotic cover			4,0
a.		Tête bêche pair			1,5
		Pair on cover			10,0
b.		Pair, one sideways		750.	
c.		Pelure paper			—

Cancellation on Nos. 56X1-56X2: black town.

Press-printed Envelopes (typographed)

56XU1	A2	5c	red		2,50
		Used with 5c #56X2 to make			
		10c rate			5,00
56XU2	A2	5c	red, amber		4,00
		Used with C.S.A. 5c #1 to			
		make 10c rate			6,50
56XU3	A2	5c	red, orange		2,50
		On patriotic cover			4,00

MICANOPY, FLA.

E1

Handstamped Envelope

105XU1	E1	5c	black	11,50

One example recorded.

MILLEDGEVILLE, GA.

E1

E2 E3

Handstamped Envelopes

J1	E1	5c	black		375.
a.		Wide spacing between "I" and "D" of "PAID"			500.
J2	E1	5c	blue		800.
J3	E1	10c on 5c	black		1,000.
J4	E2	10c	black	375.	1,000.
a.		Wide spacing between "I" and "D" of "PAID"			1,000.
U5	E3	10c	black		800.

n No. 57XU4, the "PAID/10" virtually always falls outside the
dgeville control marking (as in illustration E1).
o types of No. 57XU5; with tall, thin "1" of "10" and with
t, fat "1." The latter is about twice as scarce.
e existence of No. 57XU2 as a provisional has been ques-
ed by specialists. The editors would like to see authenti-
d evidence of provisional use of this marking.

MILTON, N. C.

E1

Handstamped Envelope, "5" Manuscript

| XU1 | E1 | 5c | black | 2,000. |

MOBILE, ALA.

A1

Lithographed Adhesives

1	A1	2c	black	2,250.	1,100.
		Pair		—	2,100.
		On cover			3,500.
		Pair on cover			16,500.
		Three singles on one cover			7,500.
		Five copies on one cover			20,000.
2	A1	5c	blue	350.	400.
		Pair		900.	950.
		On cover			1,800.
		On cover, canceled in Clai-borne, Ala.			—
		On cover, canceled in Mont-gomery, Ala.			—
		Pair on cover			2,400.
		Strip of 3 on cover			14,000.
		Strip of 4 on cover			—
		Strip of 5 on cover			—

Cancellations: black town, express company.
he existence of a strip of 5 of No. 58X2 has been ques-
ed by specialists. The editors would like to see authenti-
ed evidence of the existence of this strip either on or off
er.

MONTGOMERY, ALA.

E1

Handstamped Envelopes

XU1	E1	5c	red		1,100.
XU2	E1	5c	blue	400.	900.
XU3	E1	10c	red		850.
XU4	E1	10c	blue		1,500.
XU5	E1	10c	black		850.
XU6	E1	10c on 5c	red		2,750.

The 10c design is larger than the 5c.

E2 E3

59XU7	E2	2c	red	2,500.
59XU7A	E2	2c	blue	3,500.
59XU8	E2	5c	black	2,250.
59XU9	E3	10c	black	2,750.
59XU10	E3	10c	red	1,750.

MT. LEBANON, LA.

A1

Woodcut Adhesive (mirror image of design)

| 60X1 | A1 | 5c | red brown, on cover | 385,000. |

One example known.

Cancellation: black pen.

NASHVILLE, TENN.

A2

Typographed Adhesives
(stereotyped from woodcut)
Gray Blue Ribbed Paper

61X2	A2	5c	carmine (shades)	850.	600.
		Pair			1,450.
		On cover			3,000.
		On patriotic cover			4,500.
		Pair on cover			6,000.
		On cover with U.S. 3c 1857 (express)			25,000.
a.		Vertical tête bêche pair		3,000.
		On cover		30,000.
61X3	A2	5c	brick red	850.	550.
		Pair			1,250.
		On cover			3,500.
		On patriotic cover			6,000.
		Pair on cover			7,500.
		On U.S. #U26 (express)			35,000.
		On U.S. #U27 with #26 (ex-press)			25,000.
61X4	A2	5c	gray (shades)	950.	750.
		On cover			5,500.
		Pair on cover			7,250.
		Strip of 5 on cover front			8,500.
61X5	A2	5c	violet brown	750.	600.
		Block of 4			—
		On cover			4,500.
		On patriotic cover			—
		Pair on cover			6,000.
a.		Vertical tete beche pair		3,500.	2,500.
		On cover			—
61X6	A2	10c	green	3,000.	3,000.
		On cover			15,000.
		On cover with U.S. 3c 1857 (express)			75,000.
		On U.S. #U26 (express)			100,000.
		On cover with No. 61X2			17,500.

Cancellations

Blue "Paid"
Blue "Postage Paid"
Blue town
Blue numeral "5"
Blue numeral "10"
Blue express company
Black express company

For the former 61X1, see No. 4AX1 in the 3c 1861 Postmasters' Provisional section.

E1

Handstamped Envelopes

61XU1	E1	5c	blue	900.
		On patriotic envelope		1,900.
61XU2	E1	5c +10c	blue	2,750.

NEW ORLEANS, LA.

A1 A2

Typographed Adhesives
(stereotyped from woodcut)
Plate of 40

62X1	A1	2c	blue, July 14, 1861	175.	500.
		Pair		550.	1,150.
		Block of 4		6,500.	
		On cover			4,250.
		On patriotic cover			8,000.
		Pair on cover			10,000.
		Three singles on one cover			20,000.
		Strip of 5 on cover			30,000.
a.		Printed on both sides			—
		On cover			7,500.
62X2	A1	2c	red (shades), Jan. 6, 1862	150.	1,000.
		Pair		350.	
		Block of 4		1,600.	
		On cover			25,000.
62X3	A2	5c	brown, white, June 12, 1861	275.	200.
		Pair		575.	425.
		Block of 4		1,750.	
		On cover			450.
		On cover from town other than N.O.			5,000.
		On patriotic cover			5,500.
		Pair on cover			850.
		Strip of 5 on cover			5,000.
		On cover with U.S. #26 (Southern Letter Unpaid)			150,000.
		On cover with U.S. No. 30A			—
a.		Printed on both sides			2,250.
		On cover			7,500.
b.		5c ocher, June 18, 1861		700.	625.
		Pair			1,500.
		On cover			2,750.
		On patriotic cover			6,000.
		Pair on cover			3,500.
c.		chocolate brown, white, June 20, 1861			1,500.
62X4	A2	5c	red brn, bluish, Aug. 22, 1861	300.	200.
		Pair		675.	475.
		Horizontal strip of 6			3,500.
		Block of 4			2,200.
		On cover			425.
		On patriotic cover			5,500.
		Pair on cover			700.
		Block of 4 on cover			5,000.
		Used on cover with C.S.A. 5c #1 to make 10c rate			7,500.
a.		Printed on both sides			2,750.
62X5	A2	5c	yel brn, off-white, Dec. 3, 1861	140.	240.
		Pair		300.	525.
		Block of 4		650.	
		On cover			850.
		On patriotic cover			3,000.
		Pair on cover			1,000.
		Strip of 5 on cover			—
62X6	A2	5c	red	—	7,500.
62X7	A2	5c	red, bluish		15,000.

Cancellations

Black town (single or double circle New Orle-ans)
Red town (double circle New Orleans)
Town other than New Orleans
Postmaster's handstamp
Black "Paid"
Express Company
Packet boat, cover "STEAM"

PD 5 CTS N O.P.O

E1

These provisional handstamps were applied at the riverfront postal station.

Handstamped Envelopes

62XU1	E1	5c **black**		4,500.
62XU2	E1	10c **black**		12,500.

"J. L. RIDDELL, P. M." omitted

62XU3	E1	2c **black**		9,500.

NEW SMYRNA, FLA.

A1

Handstamped Adhesive
On white paper with blue ruled lines

63X1	A1	10c ("O1") on 5c **black**		45,000.

One example known. It is uncanceled on a postmarked patriotic cover.

NORFOLK, VA.

E1

Handstamped Envelopes
Ms Signature on Front or Back

139XU1	E1	5c **blue**	—	1,250.
139XU2	E1	10c **blue**		1,750.

OAKWAY, S. C.

A1

Handstamped Adhesive (from woodcut)

115X1	A1	5c **black**, on cover		66,000.

Two used examples of No. 115X1 are recorded, both on cover. Value represents 1997 auction realization for the cover on which the stamp is tied by manuscript "Paid."

PENSACOLA, FLA.

E1

Handstamped Envelopes

106XU1	E1	5c **black**		3,750.
106XU2	E1	10c (ms.) on 5c **black**		4,250.
		On patriotic cover		13,500.

PETERSBURG, VA.

A1

Typeset Adhesive
Ten varieties
Thick white paper

65X1	A1	5c **red**	1,750.	600.
		Pair	4,000.	1,500.
		Block of 4	9,000.	
		On cover		2,000.
		On patriotic cover		—
		Pair on cover		8,000.
		Used on cover with C.S.A. 5c #1 to make 10c rate		57,500.

Cancellation: blue town.

PITTSYLVANIA COURT HOUSE, VA.

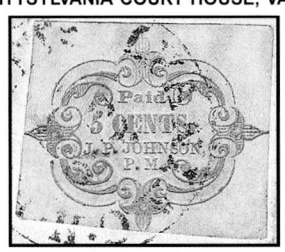

A1

Typeset Adhesives

66X1	A1	5c **dull red**, wove paper	6,000.	5,000.
		Octagonally cut		3,000.
		On cover		55,000.
		On cover, octagonally cut		20,000.
66X2	A1	5c **dull red**, laid paper		6,500.
		Octagonally cut		5,500.
		On cover		55,000.
		On cover, octagonally cut		40,000.

Cancellation: black town.

PLAINS OF DURA, GA.

E1

Handstamped Envelopes, Ms. Initials

140XU1	E1	5c **black**		—
140XU2	E1	10c **black**		

PLEASANT SHADE, VA.

A1

Typeset Adhesive
Five varieties

67X1	A1	5c **blue**	2,750.	20,000.
		On cover		27,500.
		Pair	8,000.	
		Pair on cover		55,000.
		Block of 6	25,000.	

Cancellation: blue town.

PLUM CREEK, TEX.

E1

Manuscript Adhesive

141X1	E1	10c **black**, *blue*, on cover	

The ruled lines and "10" are done by hand. Size and sha[pe] the stamp varies.

PORT GIBSON, MISS.

E1

Handstamped Envelope, Ms Signature

142XU1	E1	5c **black**	

PORT LAVACA, TEX.

A1

Typeset Adhesive

107X1	A1	10c **black**, on cover	25,

One example known. It is uncanceled on a postmarked co[ver]

RALEIGH, N. C.

E1

Handstamped Envelopes

68XU1	E1	5c **red**	
		On patriotic cover	4,
68XU2	E1	5c **blue**	3,

RHEATOWN, TENN.

A1

Typeset Adhesive
Three varieties

69X1	A1	5c **red**	2,000.	2,7
		On cover, ms. cancel		15,0
		On cover, tied by handstamp		35,0
		Pair	5,000.	

Stamps normally were canceled in manuscript. One cove[r] known with stamp tied by red town postmark.

Cancellations: red town or black pen.

RICHMOND, TEX.

E1

Handstamped Envelopes or Letter Sheets

70XU1	E1	5c **red**	1,5
70XU2	E1	10c **red**	1,0
70XU3	E1	10c on 5c **red**	5,0
70XU4	E1	15c (ms.) on 10c **red**	5,0

RINGGOLD, GA.

E1

Handstamped Envelope

XU1	E1	5c **blue black**	3,000.

RUTHERFORDTON, N. C.

A1

Handstamped Adhesive, Ms. "Paid 5cts"

X1	A1	5c **black**, cut round, on cover (uncanceled)	25,000.

No. 72X1 is unique.

SALEM, N. C.

E1

E2

Handstamped Envelopes

XU1	E1	5c **black**	1,750.
XU2	E1	10c **black**	2,250.
XU3	E2	5c **black**	2,250.
XU4	E2	10c on 5c **black**	2,800.

Reprints exist on various papers. They either lack the "Paid" d value or have them counterfeited.

Salem, Va.
See No. 74X1 under Liberty, Va.

SALISBURY, N. C.

E1

Press-printed Envelope (typeset)
Impressed at top left

XU1	E1	5c **black**, *greenish*	5,000.

One example known. Part of envelope is torn away, leaving art of design missing. Illustration E1 partly suppositional.

SAN ANTONIO, TEX.

E1   E2

Control

Handstamped Envelopes

76XU1	E1	10c **black**	275.	2,000.
76XU1A	E2	5c **black**		1,500.
76XU2	E2	10c **black**		2,500.

Black circle control mark is on front or back.

SAVANNAH, GA.

E1

Control

E2

Handstamped Envelopes

101XU1	E1	5c **black**	400.
		On patriotic cover	—
101XU2	E2	5c **black**	600.
101XU3	E1	10c **black**	750.
101XU4	E2	10c **black**	750.
101XU5	E1	10c on 5c **black**	1,500.
101XU6	E2	20c on 5c **black**	2,000.

Envelopes must have octagonal control mark. One example is known of No.101XU6.

SELMA, ALA.

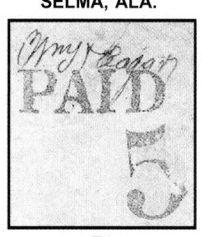

E1

Handstamped Envelopes; Signature in Ms.

77XU1	E1	5c **black**	1,250.
77XU2	E1	10c **black**	2,500.
77XU3	E1	10c on 5c **black**	3,000.

Signature is that of Postmaster William H. Eagar.
See 3c 1861 Postmasters' Provisional No. 5AX1.

SPARTA, GA.

E1

Handstamped Envelopes

93XU1	E1	5c **red**	—	1,750.
93XU2	E1	10c **red**		2,500.

Only one example recorded of No. 93XU2.

SPARTANBURG, S. C.

A1

A2

Handstamped Adhesives
(on ruled or plain wove paper)

78X1	A1	5c **black**	3,500.
		On cover	25,000.
		Pair on cover	30,000.
		On patriotic cover	30,000.
a.		"5" omitted (on cover)	—
78X2	A2	5c **black**, *bluish*	4,000.
		On cover	15,000.
78X3	A2	5c **black**, *brown*	4,000.
		On cover	18,000.

Most examples of Nos. 78X1-78X3 are cut round. Cut square examples in sound condition are worth much more. The only recorded pair of No. 78X1 is on cover. The stamps are cut round, but are still connected.

Cancellations: black "PAID," black town.

STATESVILLE, N. C.

E1

Handstamped Envelopes

79XU1	E1	5c **black**	250.	675.
79XU2	E1	10c on 5c **black**		2,250.

Fakes exist of No. 79XU1 unused.

SUMTER, S. C.

E1

Handstamped Envelopes

80XU1	E1	5c **black**	400.
80XU2	E1	10c **black**	500.
80XU3	E1	10c on 5c **black**	800.
80XU4	E1	2c (ms.) on 10c **black**	1,100.

Used examples of Nos. 80XU1-80XU2 are indistinguishable from handstamped "Paid" covers.

TALBOTTON, GA.

E1

Handstamped Envelopes
94XU1	E1	5c black	1,000.
94XU2	E1	10c black	1,000.
94XU3	E1	10c on 5c black	2,000.

TALLADEGA, ALA.

E1

Handstamped Envelopes
143XU1	E1	5c black	— —
143XU2	E1	10c black	

TELLICO PLAINS, TENN.

A1

Typeset Adhesives
Settings of two 5c and one 10c
Laid Paper

81X1	A1	5c red	1,250.	—
		On cover		50,000.
81X2	A1	10c red	2,500.	
		Se-tenant with 5c	4,000.	
		Strip of 3 (5c+5c+10c)	8,000.	

Cancellation: black pen.

THOMASVILLE, GA.

E1

Control

Handstamped Envelopes
82XU1	E1	5c black	500.
		On patriotic cover	—

On No. 82XU1, the control is on the reverse of the cover. The dated control is known with four different dates.

E2

82XU2	E2	5c black	900.

TULLAHOMA, TENN.

E1

Control

Handstamped Envelope
111XU1	E1	10o black	3,000.

TUSCALOOSA, ALA.

PAID

5

E1

Handstamped Envelopes
83XU1	E1	5c black	250.
83XU2	E1	10c black	250.

Used examples of Nos. 83XU1-83XU2 are indistinguishable from handstamped "Paid" covers. Some authorities question the use of E1 to produce provisional envelopes.

TUSCUMBIA, ALA.

E1

Handstamped Envelopes
84XU1	E1	5c black	2,250.
		On patriotic cover	—
84XU2	E1	5c red	3,000.
84XU3	E1	10c black	3,500.

See 3c 1861 Postmasters' Provisional No. 6AXU1.

Union City, Tenn.

E1

The use of E1 to produce provisional envelopes is doubtful.

UNIONTOWN, ALA.

A1

Typeset Adhesives
(settings of 4 (2x2), 4 varieties of each value)
Laid Paper

86X1	A1	2c dark blue, gray blue, on cover		—
86X2	A1	2c dark blue, sheet of 4	57,500.	
86X3	A1	5c green, gray blue	3,000.	2,000.
		Pair		—
		On cover		6,500.
86X4	A1	5c green	3,000.	2,000.
		On cover		7,000.

86X5	A1	10c red, gray blue		18,
		On cover		37,

Two examples known of No. 86X1, both on cover (droppers), one uncanceled and one pen canceled.
The only recorded examples of No. 86X2 are in a un[it] sheet of 4.
The item listed as No. 86X5 used is an uncanceled stam[p] a large piece with part of addressee's name in manuscript

Cancellation on Nos. 86X3-86X5: black town.

UNIONVILLE, S. C.

A1

Handstamped Adhesive
"PAID" and "5" applied separately
Paper with Blue Ruled Lines

87X1	A1	5c black, grayish		
		On cover, uncanceled		17,5
		On cover, tied		
		Pair on patriotic cover		32,5

The pair on patriotic cover is the only pair recorded.

Cancellation: black town.

VALDOSTA, GA.

E1   Control

Handstamped Envelopes
100XU1	E1	10c black	2,0
100XU2	E1	5c +5c black	

The black circle control must appear on front of the [No.] 100XU2 envelope and on the back of the No. 100X[U1] envelope.
There is one recorded cover each of Nos. 100XU1-100X[U2].

VICTORIA, TEX.

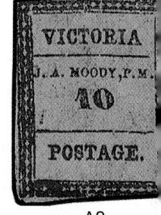

A1   A2

Typeset Adhesives
Surface colored paper

88X1	A1	5c red brown, green	9,000.	
88X2	A1	10c red brown, green	10,000.	5,5
		On cover		115,0
88X3	A2	10c red brown, green, pelure paper	10,000.	10,0

WALTERBOROUGH, S. C.

E1

Handstamped Envelopes
108XU1	E1	10c black, buff	4,25
108XU2	E1	10c carmine	4,25

WARRENTON, GA.

E1

Handstamped Envelopes

XU1	E1	5c **black**	1,250.
U2	E1	10c (ms.) on 5c **black**	1,000.

akes of the Warrenton provisional marking based on the ration shown are known on addressed but postally unused rs.

WASHINGTON, GA.

PAID 10

E1

Handstamped Envelope

XU1	E1	10c **black**	2,000.

nvelopes must have black circle postmark control on back. Examples with the undated control on the front are not sidered provisional unless a dated postmark is also present.

WEATHERFORD, TEX.

E1

Handstamped Envelopes
(woodcut with "PAID" inserted in type)

KU1	E1	5c **black**	2,000.
KU2	E1	5c +5c **black**	11,000.

One example is known of No. 109XU2.

WINNSBOROUGH, S. C.

E1   Control

Handstamped Envelopes

97XU1	E1	5c **black**	1,500.
97XU2	E1	10c **black**	3,500.

Envelopes must have black circle control on front or back.

WYTHEVILLE, VA.

  5 PAID

E1   Control

Handstamped Envelope

114XU1	E1	5c **black**	900.

For later additions, listed out of numerical sequence, see:
#74X1, Liberty, Va.
#92XU1, Huntsville, Tex.

#93XU1, Sparta, Ga.
#94XU1, Talbotton, Ga.
#96XU1, Lake City, Fla.
#97XU1, Winnsborough, S. C.
#98XU1, Galveston, Tex.
#99XU1, Christiansburg, Va.
#100XU1, Valdosta, Ga.
#101XU1, Savannah, Ga.
#102XU1, Griffin, Ga.
#103XU1, Courtland, Ala.
#104XU1, Fincastle, Va.
#105XU1, Micanopy, Fla.
#106XU1, Pensacola, Fla.
#107X1, Port Lavaca, Tex.
#108XU1, Walterborough, S. C.
#109XU1, Weatherford, Tex.
#110XU1, Jacksonville, Ala.
#111XU1, Tullahoma, Tenn.
#112XU1, Hamburgh, S. C.
#113XU1, Columbia, Tenn.
#114XU1, Wytheville, Va.
#115X1, Oakway, S. C.
#116XU1, Laurens Court House, S. C.
#117XU1, Washington, Ga.
#118XU1, Carolina City, N.C.
#119XU1, Colaparchee, Ga.
#120XU1, Forsyth, Ga.
#121XU1, Limestone Springs, S.C.
#122XU1, Balcony Falls, Va.
#123XU1, Barnwell Court House, S.C.
#124XU1, Bluffton, S.C.
#125XU1, Camden, S.C.
#126XU1, Cartersville, Ga.
#127XU1, Charlottesville, Va.
#128XU1, Fraziersville, S.C.
#129XU1, Gaston, N.C.
#130XU1, Harrisburgh, Tex.
#132XU1, Hollandale, Tex.
#133XU1, Isabella, Ga.
#134XU1, Jacksonville, Fla.
#135XU1, Lexington, Va.
#136XU1, Madison, Ga.
#137XU1, Madison Court House, Fla.
#138XU1, Milton, N.C.
#139XU1, Norfolk, Va.
#140XU1, Plains of Dura, Ga.
#141X1, Plum Creek, Tex.
#142XU1, Port Gibson, Miss.
#143XU1, Talladega, Ala.

CONFEDERATE STATES OF AMERICA, GENERAL ISSUES

The general issues are valued in the very fine grade, and unused stamps are valued both with and without original gum. As noted in the catalogue roduction, "original gum" for this era is defined as at least a majority part original gum, that is, at least 51% original gum. Stamps with substantially re than 51% original gum may be expected to sell for more than the values given, and stamps with less than a majority part original gum will sell for mewhat less.
For explanations of various terms used see the notes at the end of the postage listings.

Jefferson Davis — A1

61   Litho.   Soft Porous Paper   Imperf.

ll 5c Lithographs were printed by Hoyer & Ludwig, of Richnd, Va.

Stones A or B — First stones used. Earliest dated cancellation October 16, 1861. Plating not completed hence size of eets unknown. These stones had imprints. Stamps from nes A or B are nearly all in the olive green shade. Sharp, ar impressions. Distinctive marks are few and minute.
Stone 1 — Earliest dated cancellation October 18, 1861. ting completed. Sheet consists of four groups of fifty varies arranged in two panes of one hundred each without rint. The first small printing was in olive green and later all printings appeared in light and dark green; the typical ade, however, is an intermediate shade of bright green. The ressions are clear though not as sharp as those from nes A or B. Distinctive marks are discernible.
Stone 2 — Earliest dated cancellation December 2, 1861. ting completed. Sheet consists of four groups of fifty varies arranged in two panes of one hundred each without rint. All shades other than olive green are known from this

stone, the most common being a dull green. Poor impressions. Many noticeable distinctive marks.

Stone 2

1	A1	5c **green**	275.	175.
		No gum	175.	
		bright green	300.	175.
		dull green	275.	175.
a.		5c **light green**	275.	175.
		No gum	175.	
b.		5c **dark green**	550.	200.
		No gum	225.	
		On cover		275.
		Single on cover (overpaid drop letter)		375.
		On wallpaper cover		1,500.
		On prisoner's cover		—
		On prisoner's cover with U.S. #65		—
		On prisoner's cover with U.S. #U34		—
		On patriotic cover		1,250.
		Pair	600.	425.
		Pair on cover		450.
		Block of 4	1,450.	1,300.
		Pair with full horiz. gutter between		

VARIETIES

	Spur on upper left scroll (Pos. 21)	425.	275.
	Side margin copy showing initials (Pos. 41 or 50)	1,100.	625.
	Misplaced transfer (clear twin impressions of lower left scrolls — pos. 1 entered over pos. 10)		—
	Rouletted unofficially	350.	700.

	On cover		1,750.
	Pair on cover		3,750.

Cancellations

Blue town	+10.
Red town	+125.
Green town	+175.
Orange town	+225.
Texas town	+35.
Arkansas town	+90.
Florida town	+110.
Kentucky town	+300.
Blue gridiron	+5.
Red gridiron	+50.
Blue concentric	+5.
Star or flowers	+100.
Numeral	+50.
"Paid"	+50.
"Steamboat"	+150.
Express Co.	+350.
Railroad	+300.
Pen	60.

Stone 1

1	A1	5c **green**	300.	175.
		No gum	200.	
		bright green	300.	175.
		dull green	275.	175.
a.		5c **light green**	275.	175.
		No gum	175.	
b.		5c **dark green**	325.	200.
		No gum	210.	
c.		5c **olive green**	375.	200.
		No gum	250.	
		On cover		275.
		On patriotic cover		1,250.
		Pair	750.	475.
		Pair on cover		575.

Block of 4	1,650.	1,250.

VARIETIES

Acid flaw	350.	190.
Arrow between panes	600.	325.
Flaw on "at" of "States" (Pos. 38)	325.	225.

Cancellations

Blue town	+10.
Red town	+80.
Green town	+225.
Texas town	+35.
Arkansas town	+90.
Florida town	+110.
Kentucky town	+300.
October, 1861, year date	+40.
Blue gridiron	+5.
Red gridiron	+75.
Blue concentric	+5.
Numeral	+50.
"Paid"	+50.
"Steam"	+150.
"Steamboat"	+150.
Express Company	+350.
Railroad	+300.
Pen	70.

Stones A or B

1c A1 5c **olive green**		400.	200.
No gum		260.	
On cover			325.
On patriotic cover			1,400.
Pair		850.	450.
Pair on cover			700.
Block of 4		2,250.	1,300.

VARIETIES

White curl back of head	425.	275.
Imprint	775.	475.

Cancellations

Blue town	+10.
Red town	+150.
October, 1861, year date	+50.
Blue gridiron	+5.
Blue concentric	+5.
Numeral	+60.
"Paid"	+50.
"Steam"	+150.
Express Co.	+400.
Pen	100.

Thomas Jefferson — A2

1861-62   Litho.   Soft Porous Paper

Hoyer & Ludwig — First stone used. Earliest dated cancellation November 8, 1861. Sheet believed to consist of four groups of fifty varieties each arranged in two panes of one hundred each with imprint at bottom of each pane. Two different imprints are known. Hoyer & Ludwig printings are always in a uniform shade of dark blue. Impressions are clear and distinct, especially so in the early printings. Plating marks are distinct.

J. T. Paterson & Co. — Earliest dated cancellation July 25, 1862. Sheet consists of four groups of fifty varieties each arranged in two panes of one hundred each with imprint at bottom of each pane. Two different imprints are known and at least one pane is known without an imprint. Wide range of shades. Impressions are less clear than those from the Hoyer & Ludwig stone. Paterson stamps show small vertical colored dash below the lowest point of the upper left triangle.

Stone "Y" — Supposedly made by J. T. Paterson & Co., as it shows the distinctive mark of that firm. Plating not completed hence size of sheet unknown. No imprint found. Color is either a light milky blue or a greenish blue. Impressions are very poor and have a blurred appearance. Stone Y stamps invariably show a large flaw back of the head as well as small vertical colored dash beneath the upper left triangle.

Paterson

2 A2 10c **blue**		300.	200.
No gum		200.	
a. 10c **light blue**		300.	200.
No gum		200.	
b. 10c **dark blue**		600.	250.
No gum		425.	
c. 10c **indigo**		3,000.	2,500.
No gum		2,000.	
On cover			260.
On wallpaper cover			700.
On patriotic cover			1,400.
On prisoner's cover with U.S. #65			—
Pair		750.	475.
Pair on cover			950.
Strip of 3 on cover			—
Block of 4		1,850.	
Horiz. pair, gutter btwn.		1,500.	
d. Printed on both sides			—

VARIETIES

Malformed "O" of "POSTAGE" (Pos. 25)	425.	240.
J. T. Paterson & Co. imprint	1,000.	1,150.

Cancellations

Blue town	+
Red town	+
Green town	+
Violet town	+
Texas town	+
Arkansas town	+
Florida town	+
July, 1862, date	+
Straight line town	+
Blue gridiron	+
Red gridiron	+
Blue concentric	+
Numeral	+
"Paid"	+
Star or flower	+
Railroad	+
Express Co.	+
Pen	+

Hoyer

2b A2 10c **dark blue**		600.	
No gum		425.	
On cover			
On wallpaper cover			
On patriotic cover			2,
On prisoner's cover with U.S. #65			
Pair		1,300.	
Pair on cover			1,
Strip of 3 on cover			3,
Block of 4		2,900.	
d. Printed on both sides			—

VARIETIES

Malformed "T" of "TEN" (Pos. 4)	625.	
"G" and "E" of "POSTAGE" joined (Pos. 10)	625.	
Circular flaw, upper left star (Pos. 11)	625.	
Third spiked ornament at right, white (Pos. 45)	625.	
Hoyer & Ludwig imprint	875.	
Rouletted unofficially, on cover		3,

Cancellations

Blue town	+
Red town	+
Texas town	+
Arkansas town	+
Florida town	+
Kentucky town	+
Nov., 1861, date	+
Straight line town	+
Blue gridiron	
Red gridiron	
Blue concentric	
Numeral	
"Paid"	
Railroad	+
Express Company	+
Pen	

Stone Y

2e A2 10c **greenish blue**		700.	
No gum		475.	
light milky blue		800.	
No gum		575.	
On cover			
On patriotic cover			2,
Pair		1,700.	
Block of 4			2,

Cancellations

Blue town	+
Red town	+
Violet town	+
Green town	+
Texas town	+
Arkansas town	+
Florida town	
Straight line town	+
Blue gridiron	
Red gridiron	
Blue concentric	
Numeral	+
"Paid"	+
Pen	

Andrew Jackson — A3

Sheet consists of four groups of fifty varieties arranged in panes of 100 each.

One stone only was used. Printed by Hoyer & Ludwig, Richmond, Va. Issued to prepay drop letter and circular rate. Strips of five used to prepay regular 10c rate, which was changed from 5c on July 1, 1862. Earliest known cancellation March 21, 1862.

1862 (March?)   Soft Porous Paper   Lith

3 A3 2c **green**		800.	6
light green		800.	6
dark green		800.	7
No gum		525.	

dull yellow green	875.	800.
No gum	625.	
On cover		2,750.
Pair on cover (double circular rate)		3,250.
Strip of 5 on cover		13,500.
On patriotic cover		10,000.
Pair	1,750.	—
Block of 4	4,000.	3,500.
Block of 5	5,000.	4,250.
2c **bright yellow green**	1,750.	—
No gum	1,400.	
On cover		—

VARIETIES

Diagonal half used as 1c with unsevered pair, on cover	—	—
Horiz. pair, vert. gutter between	—	—
Pair, mark between stamps (btwn. Pos. 4 and 5)	1,900.	1,900.
Mark above upper right corner (Pos. 30)	950.	850.
Mark above upper left corner (Pos. 31)	950.	850.
Acid flaw	900.	700.

Cancellations

Blue town	+500.
Red town	+800.
Arkansas town	—
Texas town	+1,250.
Blue gridiron	+250.
"Paid"	—
Express Company	—
Railroad	+3,000.
Pen	400.

...62   Soft Porous Paper   Litho.

...tone 2 — First stone used for printing in blue. Plating is the ...ne as Stone 2 in green. Earliest dated cancellation Feb. 26, ...2. Printings from Stone 2 are found in all shades of blue. ...ugh, coarse impressions are typical of printings from Stone

...tone 3 — A new stone used for printings in blue only. ...rliest dated cancellation April 10, 1862. Sheet consists of four ...ups of fifty varieties each arranged in two panes of one ...dred each without imprint. Impressions are clear and sharp, ...n having a proof-like appearance, especially in the deep ...e printing. Plating marks, while not so large as on Stone 2 ... distinct and clearly defined.

Stone 2

A1 5c **blue**	200.	125.
No gum	130.	
light blue	225.	140.
No gum	150.	
5c **dark blue**	250.	175.
No gum	170.	
5c **light milky blue**	290.	200.
No gum	190.	
Pair	450.	450.
Block of 4	1,100.	2,000.
Horiz. pair, wide gutter between	1,250.	—
Vert. pair, narrow gutter between	—	—
On cover		260.
Single on cover (overpaid drop letter)		325.
Pair on cover		450.
On wallpaper cover		575.
On patriotic cover		1,800.
On prisoner's cover		2,000.
On prisoner's cover with U.S. #65		—

VARIETIES

Spur on upper left scroll (Pos. 21)	225.	150.
Thin hard paper	—	140.
Misplaced transfer (faint twin impression of second lower left scroll at left — pos. 2 entered over pos. 10)	—	—

Cancellations

Blue town	+20.
Red town	+100.
Texas town	+300.
Arkansas town	+325.
Florida town	+200.
Straight line town	+300.
Blue gridiron	+10.
Red gridiron	+85.
Star or Flowers	+125.
Numeral	+85.
Railroad	—
"Paid"	+25.
"Steamboat"	+400.
Express Company	—
"Way"	+250.
Pen	65.

Stone 3

A1 5c **blue**	750.	250.
No gum	550.	
. 5c **dark blue**	800.	275.
No gum	550.	
. 5c **light milky blue**	750.	250.
No gum	550.	
Pair	1750.	550.
Block of 4	4,500.	2,000.
On cover		500.
Pair on cover		625.
On patriotic cover		2,000.
Horiz. pair, wide gutter btwn.	—	—
Vert. pair, narrow gutter between	—	—

Stone 3 stamps can be positively identified by plating only. ...olor or shade is not a determinant.

VARIETIES

Tops of "C" and "E" of "cents" joined by flaw (Pos. 33)	850.	325.
"Flying bird" above lower left corner ornament (Pos. 19)	850.	325.

Cancellations

Blue town	+40.
Red town	+100.
Texas town	+300.
Arkansas town	+325.
Straight line town	+325.
Blue gridiron	+10.
Star or Flowers	+125.
"Paid"	+50.
Pen	80.

1862 (March?)   Soft Porous Paper   Litho.

Settings of fifty varieties repeated.
Printed by Hoyer & Ludwig, of Richmond, Va. One stone used, being the same as that used for the Hoyer & Ludwig 10c value in blue. Color change occured probably in March, 1862.
There are many shades of this stamp. The carmine is a very dark, bright color and should not be confused with the deeper shade of rose.
Earliest known cancellation, March 10, 1862. The earliest date of usage of the carmine shade is May 1, 1862.

5	A2 10c **rose**	1,500.	500.
	No gum	1,000.	
	dull rose	1,350.	500.
	brown rose	1,850.	1,000.
	deep rose	1,400.	650.
	carmine rose	1,600.	875.
	On cover		800.
	On wallpaper cover		2,000.
	On patriotic cover		3,000.
	On prisoner's cover		5,500.
	On prisoner's cover with U.S. #65		—
	Pair	3,350.	2,250.
	Strip of 3		4,000.
	Block of 4	11,000.	6,500.
a.	**10c carmine**	3,500.	1,900.
	No gum	2,250.	
	On cover		4,500.

VARIETIES

Malformed "T" of "TEN" (Pos. 4)	1,850.	600.
"G" and "E" of "POSTAGE" joined (Pos. 10)	1,850.	600.
Circular flaw, upper left star (Pos. 11)	1,950.	675.
Third spiked ornament at right, white (Pos. 45)	1,950.	675.
Scratched stone (occurring on Pos. 40, 39, 49 and 48, one pane)	1,950.	925.
Imprint		1,750.
Horiz. pair, vert. gutter between		—
Side margin copy, initials (Pos. 41)		1,500.

Cancellations

Blue town	+50.
Red town	+125.
Green town	+350.
Texas town	+150.
Arkansas town	—
Straight line town	+500.
April, 1862, year date	—
Blue gridiron	+50.
Black concentric	+50.
Blue concentric	+50.
"Paid"	—
Railroad	—
Express Company	—
Pen	200.

Jefferson Davis — A4

Plate of 400 in four panes of 100 each. No imprint.
No. 6 represents London printings from De La Rue & Co., a number of sheets being sent over by blockade runners. Fine clear impressions. The gum is light and evenly distributed. Exact date of issue unknown. Earliest known cancellation, April 16, 1862.

Typographed by De La Rue & Co. in London, England

1862 (April)   **Hard Medium Paper**

6	A4 5c **light blue**	10.00	27.50
	No gum	6.50	
	Single on cover used before July 1, 1862		125.00
	Single on cover (overpaid drop letter)		240.00
	Single on patriotic cover used before July 1, 1862		900.00
	Single on prisoner's cover used before July 1, 1862		—
	On wallpaper cover		350.00
	On patriotic cover		1,100.
	On prisoner's cover		1,250.

On prisoner's cover with U.S. #65			1,250.
Pair	21.00		75.00
Pair on cover			100.00
Pair on patriotic cover			1,300.
Block of 4	45.00		290.00
Block of 4 on cover			900.00

Cancellations

Blue town	+2.00
Red town	+55.00
Green town	+75.00
Texas town	+65.00
Arkansas town	+85.00
Straight line town	+150.00
Blue gridiron	+2.00
Red gridiron	+35.00
Blue concentric	+2.00
Express Company	+350.00
Railroad	+250.00
"Paid"	+50.00

1862 (August)   Typo.   Thin to Thick Paper

Plate of 400 in four panes of 100 each. No imprint.
Locally printed by Archer & Daly of Richmond, Va., from plates made in London, England, by De La Rue & Co. Printed on both imported English and local papers. Earliest known cancellation, August 15, 1862.
No. 7 shows coarser impressions than No. 6, and the color is duller and often blurred. Gum is light or dark and unevenly distributed.

7	A4 5c **blue**	13.00	20.00
	No gum	8.50	
a.	5c **deep blue**	16.00	35.00
	No gum	10.50	
	Single on cover (overpaid drop letter)		200.00
	On wallpaper cover		500.00
	On patriotic cover		1.000.
	On prisoner's cover		1,250.

On prisoner's cover with U.S. #65		—
Pair	30.00	47.50
Pair on cover		95.00
Block of 4	70.00	340.00
Block of 4 on cover		800.00
Eight on cover (Trans-Miss. rate)		—
b. Printed on both sides	2,500.	950.00
Pair		2,100.
Pair on cover		3,250.

VARIETIES

White tie (U.R. 30)	150.00	150.00
White tie on cover		350.00
De La Rue paper (thin)	27.50	45.00
No gum	20.00	
White tie, De La Rue paper	200.00	250.00
Thick paper	22.50	30.00
Horiz. pair, vert. gutter between	200.00	

Cancellations

Blue town	+2.00
Red town	+75.00
Brown town	+30.00
Violet town	+110.00
Green town	+150.00
Texas town	+90.00
Arkansas town	+110.00
Florida town	+140.00
Straight line town	+140.00
Blue gridiron	+2.00
Red gridiron	+60.00
Blue concentric	+2.00
Railroad	+250.00
Express Company	+400.00
Design (stars, etc.)	+75.00
"Paid"	+50.00

The unissued 10c design A4 was privately printed in various colors for philatelic purposes. (See note below No. 14.)
Counterfeits of the 10c exist.

Andrew Jackson — A5

Sheet of 200 (two panes of 100 each).
One plate. Printed by Archer & Daly of Richmond, Va. Earliest known cancellation. Apr. 21, 1863. Issued to prepay drop letter and circular rates. Strips of five used to prepay regular 10c rate.

1863 (April)	**Soft Porous Paper**		**Engraved**
8 A5 2c **brown red**		70.	350.
No gum		52.50	
a. 2c **pale red**		90.	450.
No gum		65.	
Single on cover			1,500.
On prisoner's cover			3,000.
On prisoner's cover with U.S. #65			4,000.
Pair		150.	1,000.
Pair on cover			3,250.
On wallpaper cover			—
Block of 4		350.	—
Block of 5			—
Strip of 5 on cover			5,000.
Strip of 5 on wallpaper cover			—
Strip of 10 on cover			13,000.
Double transfer		125.	450.
Horiz. pair, vert. gutter between		325.	

Cancellations

Blue town	+35.
Red town	+225.
Violet town	+300.
Army of Tenn.	—
Blue gridiron	+35.
Black numeral	—
Railroad	+325.

Jefferson Davis "TEN CENTS" — A6

One plate of 200 subjects all of which were probably recut as every copy examined to date shows distinct recutting. Plating not completed.
Printed by Archer & Daly of Richmond, Va. First printings in milky blue. First issued in April, 1863. Earliest known cancellation, April 23, 1863.

1863, Apr.	**Soft Porous Paper**		**Engraved**
9 A6 10c **blue**		900.	550.
No gum		600.	
a. 10c **milky blue** (first printing)		900.	550.

No gum		600.
b. 10c **gray blue**		950.	650.
No gum		650.	
On cover			1,600.
On wallpaper cover			3,000.
On patriotic cover			3,500.
On prisoner's cover			4,250.
On prisoner's cover with U.S. #65			—
Pair		2,000.	2,200.
Pair on cover			3,000.
Block of 4		5,250.	
Four stamps on one cover (Trans-Mississippi rate)			13,500.
Curved lines outside the labels at top and bottom are broken in the middle (Pos. 63R)		1,050.	775.
Double transfer		1,100.	1,000.
Damaged plate		1,200.	1,100.

Cancellations

Blue town	+25.
Red town	+150.
Green town	+600.
Violet town	—
Straight line town	+500.
April, 1863, year date	—
Black gridiron	+25.
Blue gridiron	+50.
Red gridiron	+200.
Railroad	+400.
Circle of wedges	+1,250.
Pen	350.

Frame Line "10 CENTS" — A6a

Printed by Archer & Daly of Richmond, Va.
One copper plate of 100 subjects, all but one of which were recut. Earliest known use April 19, 1863.
Stamp design same as Die A (Pos. 11).
Values are for copies showing parts of lines on at least 3 of 4 sides. Used stamps showing 4 complete lines sell for 200%-300% of the values given. Unused stamps showing 4 complete lines are exceedingly rare and will sell for many multiples of the values given.

1863, Apr.	**Soft Porous Paper**		**Engraved**
10 A6a 10c **blue**		5,000.	1,700.
No gum		3,750.	
a. 10c **milky blue**		5,000.	1,700.
No gum		3,750.	
b. 10c **greenish blue**		5,500.	1,800.
No gum		4,000.	
c. 10c **dark blue**		5,500.	1,800.
No gum		4,000.	
On cover			2,750.
On wallpaper cover			4,750.
On patriotic cover			6,000.
On prisoner's cover			7,000.
On prisoner's cover with U.S. #65			—
Pair		11,500.	5,750.
Pair on cover			6,750.
Block of 4		27,500.	
Strip of 4		26,000.	
Strip of 6		—	16,000.
Strip of 7		42,500.	
Double transfer (Pos. 74)		5,500.	1,900.

Cancellations

Blue town	+100.
Red town	+500.
Straight line town	+750.
April, 1863, year date	—
Blue gridiron	+100.
Pen	800.

No Frame Line "10 CENTS"
(Die A) — A7

There are many slight differences between A7 (Die A) and A8 (Die B), the most noticeable being the additional line outside the ornaments at the four corners of A8 (Die B).
Stamps were first printed by Archer & Daly, of Richmond, Va. In 1864 the plates were transferred to the firm of Keatinge & Ball in Columbia, S. C., who made further printings from them. Two plates, each with two panes of 100, numbered 1 and 2. First state shows numbers only, later states show various styles of Archer & Daly imprints, and latest show Keatinge & Ball imprints. Archer & Daly stamps show uniformly clear impressions and a good quality of gum evenly distributed (Earliest known cancellation, April 21, 1863); Keatinge & Ball stamps generally show filled in impressions in a deep blue, and the gum is brown and unevenly distributed. (Earliest known cancellation,

---

Oct. 4, 1864). The so-called laid paper is probably due to streaky gum. (These notes also apply to No. 12.)

1863-64	**Thick or Thin Paper**		**Engrav**
11 A7 10c **blue**		10.00	2
No gum		7.00	
a. 10c **milky blue**		25.00	4
No gum		16.00	
b. 10c **dark blue**		22.50	2
No gum		14.00	
c. 10c **greenish blue**		20.00	2
No gum		12.50	
d. 10c **green**		85.00	7
No gum		57.50	
deep blue, Keatinge & Ball ('64)		10.00	3
On cover			5
Single on cover (overpaid drop letter)			15C
On wallpaper cover			40C
On patriotic cover			65C
On prisoner's cover			45C
On prisoner's cover with U.S. #65			1,
On cover, dp. blue (K. & B.) ('64)			12
On wallpaper cover (K. & B.)			87
On prisoner's cover (K. & B.) with U.S. #65 ('64)			
Pair		22.50	4
Pair on cover			17
Block of 4		47.50	29
Strip of 4 on cover (Trans-Mississippi rate)			
Margin block of 12, Archer & Daly impt. & P#		375.00	
Margin block of 12, Keatinge & Ball impt. & P#		350.00	
Horiz. pair, vert. gutter between		110.00	
e. Officially perforated 12½		300.00	275
On cover			50C
On wallpaper cover			
Pair		650.00	60C
Pair on cover			2,7
Block of 4		1,500.	2,2

VARIETIES

Double transfer		75.00	10C
Rouletted unofficially			50C
On cover			80C

Cancellations

Blue town	+5
Red town	+35
Orange town	+110
Brown town	+60
Green town	+15C
Violet town	+10C
Texas town	+60
Arkansas town	+125
Florida town	+200
Straight line town	+300
Army of Tenn.	+300
April, 1863 year date	+75
"FREE"	+250
Blue gridiron	+5
Black concentric circles	+10
Star	+100
Crossroads	+150
"Paid"	+100
Numeral	+100
Railroad	+175
Steamboat	+1,5

Jefferson Davis (Die B) — A8

Plates bore Nos. 3 and 4, otherwise notes on No. 11 app
Earliest known use: Archer & Daly — May 1, 1863; Keatin & Ball — Sept. 4, 1864.

1863-64	**Thick or Thin Paper**		**Engrav**
12 A8 10c **blue**		11.00	20
No gum		7.50	
a. 10c **milky blue**		25.00	37
No gum		17.00	
b. 10c **light blue**		11.00	20.
No gum		7.50	
c. 10c **greenish blue**		20.00	45.
No gum		12.50	
d. 10c **dark blue**		11.00	22.
No gum		7.50	
e. 10c **green**		200.00	150.
No gum		130.00	
deep blue, Keatinge & Ball ('64)		11.00	40.
On cover			75.
Single on cover (overpaid drop letter)			150.
On wallpaper cover			375.
On patriotic cover			700.
On prisoner's cover			450.
On prisoner's cover with U.S. #65			1,75
On cover, dp. blue (K. & B.) ('64)			130.

Pair		27.50	52.50
Pair on cover			200.00
Block of 4		60.00	290.00
Strip of 4 on cover (Trans-Mississippi rate)			—
Margin block of 12, Archer & Daly impt. & P#		400.00	
Margin block of 12, Keatinge & Ball impt. & P#		350.00	
Horiz. pair, vert. gutter between		125.00	
f. Officially perforated 12½		325.00	300.00
On cover			500.00
Pair		700.00	600.00
Pair on cover			—
Block of 4		1,750.	

VARIETIES

Double transfer	95.00	110.00
Rouletted unofficially		375.00
On cover		850.00

Cancellations

Blue town	+5.00
Red town	+35.00
Brown town	+90.00
Green town	+120.00
Violet town	+85.00
Texas town	+125.00
Arkansas town	+150.00
Florida town	+200.00
Straight line town	+350.00
Army of Tenn.	+350.00
May, 1863, year date	+60.00
Blue gridiron	+5.00
Black concentric circles	+10.00
Railroad	+175.00

George Washington — A9

63 (June?) **Engraved by Archer & Daly**

One plate which consisted of two panes of 100 each. First ...ntings were from plates with imprint in Old English type under ...ch pane, which was later removed. Printed on paper of vary-... thickness and in many shades of green. This stamp was ...o used as currency. Earliest known cancellation, June 1, ...63. Forged cancellations exist.

A9 20c **green**		40.00	400.
No gum		27.50	
a. 20c **yellow green**		70.00	450.
No gum		50.00	
b. 20c **dark green**		65.00	500.
No gum		45.00	
On cover			1,250.
On wallpaper cover			1,750.
On prisoner's cover			4,000.
On prisoner's cover with U.S. #65			5,000.
Pair		85.00	900.
Horizontal pair with gutter between		350.00	
Pair on cover (non-Trans-Mississippi rate)			4,500.
Pair on cover (Trans-Mississippi rate)			—
Block of 4		200.00	3,500.
Strip of 4 with imprint		425.00	
Block of 8 with imprint		1,050.	
c. Diagonal half used as 10c on cover			2,000.
Diagonal half on prisoner's cover			—
d. Horizontal half used as 10c on cover			3,500.

VARIETIES

Double transfer, 20 doubled (Pos. 24L and 35R)	300.	—
"20" on forehead	3,000.	
Rouletted unofficially		1,100.
On cover		3,750.

Cancellations

Blue town	+50.
Red town	+200.
Violet town	—
Texas town	+100.
Arkansas town	+400.
Tennessee town	+1,000.
Railroad	—

John C. Calhoun — A10

Typographed by De La Rue & Co., London, England

1862

14	A10	1c **orange**		110.00
		No gum		70.00
		Pair		230.00
		Block of 4		475.00
a.		1c **deep orange**		130.00
		No gum		90.00

This stamp was never put in use.

Upon orders from the Confederate Government, De La Rue & Co. of London, England, prepared Two Cents and Ten Cents typographed plates by altering the One Cent (No. 14) and the Five Cents (Nos. 6-7) designs previously made by them. Stamps were never officially printed from these plates although privately made prints exist in various colors.

Explanatory Notes

The following notes by Lawrence L. Shenfield explain the various routes, rates and usages of the general issue Confederate stamps.

"Across the Lines"
Letters Carried by Private Express Companies

Adams Express Co. and American Letter Express Company Handstamps Used on "Across the Lines" Letters

B. Whitesides Label

About two months after the outbreak of the Civil War, in June, 1861, postal service between North and South and vice versa was carried on largely by Adams Express Company, and the American Letter Express Company. Northern terminus for the traffic was Louisville, Ky.; Southern terminus was Nashville, Tenn. Letters for transmission were delivered to any office of the express company, together with a fee, usually 20c or 25c per ½ ounce to cover carriage. The express company messengers carried letters across the lines and delivered them to their office on the other side, where they were deposited in the Government mail for transmission to addressees, postage paid out of the fee charged. Letters from North to South, always enclosed in 3c U.S. envelopes, usually bear the handstamp of the Louisville office of the express company, and in addition the postmark and "Paid 5" of Nashville, Tenn., indicating its acceptance for delivery at the Nashville Post Office. Letters from South to North sometimes bear the origin postmark of a Southern post office, but more often merely the handstamp of the Louisville express company office applied as the letters cleared through Louisville. The B. Whitesides South to North cover bears a "Private Letter Mail" label. In addition, these covers bear the 3c 1857 U.S. adhesive stamp, cancelled with the postmark and grid of Louisville, Ky., where they went into the Government mail for delivery. Some across-the-lines letters show the handstamp of various express company offices, according to the

---

particular routing the letters followed. On August 26, 1861, the traffic ceased by order of the U.S. Post Office Dept. (Values are for full covers bearing the usual Louisville, Ky., or Nashville, Tenn., handstamps of the express company. Unusual express office markings are rarer and worth more.)

North to South 3c U.S. Envelope, Adams Exp. Co. Louisville, Ky., handstamp	1,500.
North to South 3c U.S. Envelope, American Letter Express Co., Ky., handstamp	2,100.
South to North 3c 1857, Adams Exp. Co., Louisville, Ky., handstamp	1,750.
South to North 3c 1857, American Letter Exp. 250, Nashville, Tenn., handstamp	2,500.
South to North 3c 1861, Adams Exp. Co., Louisville, Ky., handstamp	3,250.
South to North 3c 1857, B. Whitesides, Franklin, Ky., label	16,500.

Blockade-Run Letters from Europe to the Confederate States

Charleston "STEAM-SHIP" in Oval Handstamp

As the Federal Fleet gradually extended its blockade of the Confederate States coastal regions, the South was forced to resort to blockade runners to carry letters to and from outside ports. These letters were all private-ship letters and never bore a foreign stamp if from Europe, nor a Confederate stamp if to Europe. The usual route from Europe was via a West Indies port, Nassau, Bahamas; Hamilton, Bermuda, or Havana, into the Southern ports of Wilmington, N.C. and Charleston, S.C. More rarely such letters came in to Savannah, Mobile and New Orleans. Letters from Europe are the only ones which are surely identified by their markings. They bore either the postmark of Wilmington, N.C., straightline "SHIP" and "12", "22", "32", etc., in manuscript; or the postmark of Charleston, S. C., "STEAMSHIP" in oval, and "12", "22", "32", etc., in manuscript. Very rarely Charleston used a straightline "SHIP" instead of "STEAMSHIP" in oval. All such letters were postage due; the single letter rate of 12c being made up of 2c for the private ship captain plus 10c for the regular single letter Confederate States rate. Over-weight letters were 22c (due), 32c, 42c, etc. A few examples are known on which Confederate General Issue stamps were used, usually as payment for forwarding postage. Covers with such stamps, or with the higher rate markings, 22c, 32, etc., are worth more.

Values are for full covers in fine condition.

Charleston, S.C. "6" handstamp	3,250.
Charleston, S.C., postmark, "STEAMSHIP," and "12" in ms.	2,750.
Charleston, S.C., postmark, "SHIP," and "12" in ms.	1,750.
Wilmington, N.C., postmark, "SHIP," and "12" in ms.	2,500.
Savannah, Ga., postmark "SHIP," and "7" in ms. (*)	4,000.
New Orleans, La. postmark, "SHIP" and "10" in ms.	5,000.

(* 7c rate: 5c postage before July 1, 1862, plus 2c for ship captain.)

Express Company Mail in the Confederacy

Southern Express Company Handstamps

Shortly after the outbreak of war in 1861, the Adams Express Company divisions operating in the South were forced to suspend operations and turned their Southern lines over to a new company organized under the title Southern Express Company. This express did the bulk of the express business in the Confederacy despite the continued opposition of the Post Office Dept. of the C.S.A. and the ravages of the contending armies upon railroads. Other companies operating in the Confederacy were: South Western

Express Co. (New Orleans), Pioneer Express Company, White's Southern Express (only one example known) and some local expresses of limited operation. The first three used handstamps of various designs usually bearing the city name of the office. Postal regulation necessitated the payment of regular Confederate postal rates on letters carried by express companies, express charges being paid in addition. Important letters, particularly money letters, were entrusted to these express companies as well as goods and wares of all kinds. The express rates charged for letters are not known; probably they varied depending upon the difficulty and risk of transmittal. Covers bearing stamps and express company handstamps are very rare.

Prisoner-of-War and Flag-of-Truce Letters

Prison Censor Handstamps

By agreement between the United States and the Confederate States, military prisoners and imprisoned civilians of both sides were permitted to send censored letters to their respective countries. Such letters, if from North to South, usually bore a U.S. 3c 1861 adhesive, postmarked at a city near the prison, to pay the postage to the exchange ground near Old Point Comfort, Va.; and a 10c Confederate stamp, canceled at Richmond, Va. (or "due" handstamp) to pay the Confederate postage to destination. If from South to North, letters usually bore a 10c Confederate stamp canceled at a Southern city (or "paid" handstamp) and a U. S. 3c 1861 adhesive (or "due 3" marking) and the postmark of Old Point Comfort, Va. In addition, prison censor markings, handstamped or manuscript, the name and rank of the soldier, and "Flag of Truce, via Fortress Monroe" in manuscript usually appear on these covers. Federal prison censor handstamps of various designs are known from these prisons:

- Camp Chase, Columbus, O.
- David's Island, Pelham, N.Y.
- Fort Delaware, Delaware City, Del.
- Camp Douglas, Chicago, Ill.
- Elmira Prison, Elmira, N.Y.
- Johnson's Island, Sandusky, O.
- Fort McHenry, Baltimore, Md.
- Camp Morton, Indianapolis, Ind.
- Fort Oglethorpe, Macon, Ga.
- Old Capitol Prison, Washington, D.C.
- Point Lookout Prison, Point Lookout, Md.
- Fort Pulaski, Savannah, Ga.
- Rock Island Prison, Rock Island, Ill.
- Ship Island, New Orleans, La.
- West's Hospital, Baltimore, Md.
- U.S. General Hospital, Gettysburg, Pa.

Several other Federal prisons used manuscript censor markings.

Southern prison censor markings are always in manuscript, and do not identify the prison. The principal Southern prisons were at Richmond and Danville, Va.; Andersonville and Savannah, Ga.; Charleston, Columbia and Florence S.C.; Salisbury, N.C.; Hempstead and Tyler, Tex.

Civilians residing in both the North and the South were also, under exceptional circumstances, permitted to send Flag of Truce letters across the lines. Such covers bore no censor marking nor prison markings, but were always endorsed "via Flag of Truce".

Values will be found under various individual stamps for "on prisoner's cover" and are for the larger prisons. Prisoners' letters from the smaller prisons are much rarer. Only a very small percentage of prisoners' covers bore *both* a U.S. stamp and a Confederate stamp.

The "SOUTHERN LETTER UNPAID" Marking On Northbound Letters of Confederate Origin

DUE 3

SOUTHᴺ LETTER UNPAID.

By mid-May, 1861, correspondence between the North and South was difficult. In the South, postmasters were resigning and closing their accounts with Washington as the Confederacy prepared to organize its own postal system by June 1. From that date on, town marks and "paid" handstamps (and later postmasters' provisional stamps) were used in all post offices of the seceded states. The three most important Southern cities for clearing mail to the North were Memphis, Nashville and Richmond. The Richmond-Washington route was closed in April; Memphis was closed by June 1st, and mail attempting to cross the lines at these points generally ended up at the dead letter office. However, at Louisville, Kentucky, mail from the South via Nashville continued to arrive in June, July and August. On June 24, 1861, the Post Office Department advised the Louisville post office, "You will forward letters from the South for the Loyal States as unpaid, after removing postage stamps, but foreign letters in which prepayment is compulsory must come to the Dead Letter Office." However, Louisville avoided the task of "removing postage stamps," and instead prepared the "Southern Letter Unpaid" handstamp and special "due 3" markers for use. These markings were applied in the greenish-blue color of the Louisville office to letters of Southern origin that had accumulated, in addition to the usual town mark and grid of Louisville. The letters were delivered in the North as unpaid. Probably Louisville continued to forward such unpaid mail until about July 15. The marking is very rare. Other Southern mail was forwarded from Louisville as late as Aug. 27.

For listings see under U.S. 1857-61 issue, Nos. 26, 35-38. Values shown there are generally for this marking on off-cover stamps. Complete covers bearing stamps showing the full markings are valued from $7,500 upward depending upon the stamps, other postal markings and unusual usages, and condition. Fraudulent covers exist.

Trans-Mississippi Express Mail-the 40c Rate

From the fall of New Orleans on April 24, 1862, the entire reach of the Mississippi River was threatened by the Federal fleets. Late in 1862 the Confederacy experienced difficulty in maintaining regular mail routes trans-Mississippi to the Western states. Private express companies began to carry some mail, but by early 1863 when the Meridian-Jackson-Vicksburg-Shreveport route was seriously menaced, the Post Office Department of the Confederate States was forced to inaugurate an express mail service by contracting with a private company the name of which remains undisclosed. The eastern termini were at Meridian and Brandon, Miss.; the western at Shreveport and Alexandria, La. Letters, usually endorsed "via Meridian (or Brandon)" if going West; "via Shreveport (or Alexandria)" if going East were deposited in any Confederate post office. The rate was 40c per ½ ounce or less. Such Trans-Mississippi Express Mail upon arrival at a terminus was carried by couriers in a devious route across the Mississippi and returned to the regular mails at the nearest terminus on the other side of the river. The precise date of the beginning of the Trans-Mississippi service is not known. The earliest date of use so far seen is November 2, 1863 and the latest use February 9, 1865. These covers can be identified by the written endorsement of the route, but particularly by the rate since many bore no route endorsements.

Strips of four of 10c engraved stamps, pairs of the 20c stamp and various combinations of 10c stamps and the 5c London or Local prints are known; also handstamped Paid 40c marking. No identifying handstamps were used, merely the postmark of the office which received the letter originally. Values for Trans-Mississippi Express covers will be found under various stamps of the General Issues.

A 50c Preferred Mail Express rate, announced in April, 1863, preceded the Trans-Mississippi Express Mail 40c rate. One cover showing this rate is known.

Packet and Steamboat Covers and Markings

Letters carried on Confederate packets operating coastal routes or up and down the inland waterw were usually handstamped with the name of packet or marked STEAM or STEAMBOAT. Eit United States stamps of the 1857 issue or stam envelopes of the 1853 or 1860 issues have been fou so used, as well as Confederate Postmasters' Pro sional and General Issue stamps. Some speci designed pictorial or imprinted packet boat covers a exist. All are scarce and command values from $7 upward for handstamped United States envelopes a from $1,250 up for covers bearing Confeder stamps.

TABLE OF SECESSION

	Ordinance of Secession	Admitted to Confederacy	Period for Use of U.S. Stamps As Independent State	Total to 5/31/1861*
SC	12/20/1860	2/4/1861	46 days	163 days
MS	1/9/1861	2/4/1861	26 days	143 days
FL	1/10/1861	2/4/1861	25 days	142 days
AL	1/11/1861	2/4/1861	24 days	141 days
GA	1/19/1861	2/4/1861	16 days	133 days
LA	1/26/1861	2/4/1861	9 days	126 days
TX	2/1/1861	3/6/1861	33 days	120 days
VA	4/17/1861	5/7/1861	20 days	45 days
AR	5/6/1861	5/18/1861	12 days	26 days
TN	5/6/1861	7/2/1861	57 days	26 days
NC	5/20/1861	5/27/1861	7 days	26 days

* The use of United States stamps in the seceded States v prohibited after May 31, 1861.

TX — Ordinance of Secession adopted Feb. 1. Popular v to secede Feb. 23, effective Mar. 2, 1861.

VA — Ordinance of Secession adopted. Admitted to Conf eracy May 7. Scheduled election of May 23 ratified the O nance of Secession.

TN — Ordinance passed to "submit to vote of the people Declaration of Independence, and for other purposes." Adop May 6. Election took place June 8. General Assembly ratif election June 24.

The Confederate postal laws did not provide f franking privilege for any mail except official cor spondence of the Post Office Department. Such l ters could be sent free only when enclosed in officia imprinted envelopes individually signed by the offic using them. These envelopes were prepared a issued for Post Office Department use.

The imprints were on United States envelopes 1853-61 issue, and also on commercial envelopes various sizes and colors. When officially signed a mailed, they were postmarked, usually at Richmon Va., with printed or handstamped "FREE". Envelop are occasionally found unused and unsigned, a more rarely, signed but unused. When such offic envelopes were used on other than official Post Offi Department business, Confederate stamps were use

Semi-official envelopes also exist bearing imprints other government departments, offices, armie states, etc. Regular postage was required to ca such envelopes through the mails.

CONFEDERATE STATES OF AMERICA

POST OFFICE DEPARTMEN
OFFICIAL BUSINES

John H. Reagan

POSTMASTER GENERAL

Confederate States of America

POST OFFICE DEPARTMENT
OFFICIAL BUSINES

CHIEF CLERK P. O. DEPARTMEN

Typical Imprints of Official Envelopes of the Post Office Department. (Many variations of type, style and wording exist.)

Office	Signature
Postmaster General	John H. Reaga
Chief of the Contract Bureau	H. St. Geo. Off
Chief of the Appointment Bureau	B. N. Clements
Chief of the Finance Bureau	Jno. L. Harrell
Chief of the Finance Bureau	J. L. Lancaster
Chief of the Finance Bureau	A. Dimitry
Dead Letter Office	A. Dimitry
Dead Letter Office	Jno. L. Harrell
Chief Clerk, P. O. Department	B. Fuller
Chief Clerk	W. D. Miller
Auditor's Office	W. W. Lester
Auditor's Office	B. Baker
Auditor's Office	J. W. Robertson
First Auditor's Office, Treasury Department	J. W. Robertson
First Auditor's Office, Treasury Department	B. Baker
Third Auditor's Office	A. Moise
Third Auditor's Office	I. W. M. Harris

	Office	Signature
...ency, Post Office Dept. Trans-Miss.		Jas. H. Starr

PROOFS

(1) — Die on Glazed Card
(1a) — Die on Wove Paper
(5) — Plate on Wove Paper
(6) — Plate on Thin Card
(7) — Plate on Thick Ribbed Paper

...1			
	(5)	5c **green,** plate on wove paper	1,500.
	(5)	10c **blue,** plate on wove paper	1,500.
...c	(5)	10c **black,** plate on wove paper (stone Y)	3,000.
...62			
	(1)	5c **light blue,** die on glazed card	600.
14P	(1)	5c **blue & 1c orange,** composite die proof, 20x90mm card	6,000.
	(5)	5c **light blue,** plate on wove paper	150.
		Pair with gutter between	375.
...c	(1a)	5c **dark blue,** die on woven paper	600.
...c	(5)	5c **gray blue,** plate on wove paper	600.
...c	(1)	5c **black,** die on glazed card	900.
...c	(5)	5c **black,** plate on wove paper	1,000.
...c	(1)	5c **pink,** die on glazed card	900.
...c	(5)	5c **carmine,** plate on wove paper	850.
...c	(6)	5c **carmine,** plate on thin card	750.
...63			
...c	(1a)	2c **black,** die on wove paper	1,750.
...c	(1a)	10c **black,** die on wove paper	1,500.
...TC	(1a)	10c **black,** die on wove paper	1,100.
...P	(7)	10c **deep blue,** plate on thick ribbed paper	750.
...P	(1a)	20c **green,** die on wove paper	4,000.
...TC	(1a)	20c **red brown,** die on wove paper	4,000.
...62			
...P	(1)	1c **orange,** die on glazed card	2,000.
TC	(1)	1c **black,** die on glazed card	2,500.
TC	(5)	1c **light yellow brown,** plate on wove paper	800.

Essay Die Proofs
...In working up the final dies, proofs of incomplete ...signs in various stages were made. Usually dated ...typeset lines, they are very rare. Others, of the 10c ...o. 12) and the 20c (No. 13) were proofs made as ...says from the dies. They are deeply engraved and ...nted in deep shades of the issued colors, but show ...ly small differences from the stamps as finally ...ued. All are very rare.

Specimen Overprints
The De La Rue typographed 5c and 1c are known ...h "SPECIMEN" overprinted diagonally, also hori- ...ntally for 1c.

Counterfeits
In 1935 a set of 12 lithographed imitations, later ...own as the "Springfield facsimiles," appeared in ...ate form. They are in approximately normal colors ... yellowish soft wove paper of modern manufacture.

SCHAUFIX MOUNTS

Made from archival quality materials, Schaufix mounts feature a rubberized base film and a crystal clear covering film for optimum protection and flexibility.

PRE-CUT SIZES

Item	WxH MM		Mounts	Retail	*AA
HM701B	40 x 25	U.S. Standard Water-Activated Horizontal Commemoratives	20	99¢	75¢
HM702B	25 x 40	U.S. Standard Water-Activated Vertical Commemoratives	20	99¢	75¢
HM703B	22 x 25	U.S. Standard Water-Activated Horizontal Definitives	20	99¢	75¢
HM704B	25 x 22	U.S. Standard Water-Activated Vertical Definitives	20	99¢	75¢
HM705B	41 x 31	U.S. Horizontal Semi-Jumbo Commemoratives	20	99¢	75¢
HM706B	40 x 26	U.S. Standard SELF-ADHESIVE Horizontal Commemoratives	20	99¢	75¢
HM707B	25 x 41	U.S. Standard SELF-ADHESIVE Vertical Commemoratives	20	99¢	75¢
HM708B	22 x 26	U.S. Standard SELF-ADHESIVE Vertical Definitives	20	99¢	75¢

STRIPS 210 MM LONG

Item	WxH MM		Mounts	Retail	*AA
HM721B	24	U.S., Canada, Great Britain;	5	$1.49	99¢
HM722B	25	U.S. Water-Activated Horizontal Commemorative & Definitives	5	$1.49	99¢
HM723B	26	U.S. Standard SELF-ADHESIVE Horizontal Commemoratives & Definitives, Germany	5	$1.49	99¢
HM724B	27	U.S. Famous Americans	5	$1.49	99¢
HM725B	28	U.S. 19th Century, Liechtenstein	5	$1.49	99¢
HM726B	29	Various Foreign Stamps			
HM727B	30	U.S. Hunting Permit (Ducks), Canada	5	$1.49	99¢
HM728B	30	U.S. Horizontal Jumbo & Semi-Jumbo	5	$1.49	99¢
HM729B	33	U.S. Stampin' the Future	5	$1.49	99¢
HM730B	36	U.S. Hunting Permit (Ducks), Canada	5	$1.49	99¢
HM731B	39	U.S. Early 20th Century			
HM732B	40	U.S. Standard Water-Activated Vertical Commemoratives	5	$1.49	99¢
HM733B	41	U.S. Semi-Jumbo Vertical Commemoratives (Lafayette, Pottery, etc.) Self-Adhesive Vertical Commemoratives	5	$1.49	99¢
HM734B	44	U.S. Vertical Coil Pairs, Booklet Panes (Garden Flowers);	5	$1.49	99¢
HM735B	63	U.S. Jumbo Commemoratives, Horizontal Blocks of 4	5	$1.49	99¢

CANAL ZONE

The Canal Zone, a strip of territory with an area of about 552 square miles following generally the line of the Canal, was under the jurisdiction of the United States, 1904-1979, and under the joint jurisdiction of the United States and Panama, 1979-1999, when the Canal, in its entirety, reverted to Panama.

The Canal organization underwent two distinct and fundamental changes. The construction of the Canal and the general administration of civil affairs were performed by the Isthmian Canal Commission under the provisions of the Spooner Act. This was supplanted in April, 1914, by the Panama Canal Act which established the organization known as The Panama Canal. This was an independent government agency which included both the operation and maintenance of the waterway and civil government in the Canal Zone. Most of the quasi-business enterprises relating to the Canal operation were conducted by the Panama Railroad, an adjunct of The Panama Canal.

A basic change in the mode of operations took effect July 1, 1951, under provisions of Public Law 841 of the 81st Congress. This in effect transferred the Canal operations to the Panama Railroad Co., which had been made a federal government corporation in 1948, and changed its name to the Panama Canal Co. Simultaneously the civil government functions of The Panama Canal, including the postal service, were renamed the Canal Zone Government. The organization therefore consisted of two units — the Panama Canal Co. and Canal Zone Government — headed by an individual who was president of the company and governor of the Canal Zone. His appointment as governor was made by the president of the United States, subject to confirmation by the Senate, and he was ex-officio president of the company.

The Canal Zone Government functioned as an independent government agency, and was under direct supervision of the president of the United States who delegated this authority to the Secretary of the Army.

The Panama Canal is 50 miles long from deep water in the Atlantic to deep water in the Pacific. It runs from northwest to southeast with the Atlantic entrance being 33.5 miles north and 27 miles west of the Pacific entrance. The airline distance between the two entrances is 43 miles. It requires about eight hours for an average ship to transit the Canal. Transportation between the Atlantic and Pacific sides of the Isthmus is available by railway, highway or air.

The Canal Zone Postal Service began operating June 24, 1904, when nine post offices were opened in connection with the construction of the Panama Canal. It ceased Sept. 30, 1979, and the Panama Postal Service took over.

Italicized numbers in parentheses indicate quantity issued.

100 CENTAVOS = 1 PESO
100 CENTESIMOS = 1 BALBOA
100 CENTS = 1 DOLLAR

Catalogue values for unused stamps are for Never Hinged items beginning with No. 118 in the regular postage section and No. C6 in the airpost section.

Map of Panama — A1

Violet to Violet Blue Handstamp on Panama Nos. 72, 72a-72c, 78, 79.

On the 2c "PANAMA" is normally 13mm long. On the 5c and 10c it measures about 15mm.

On the 2c, "PANAMA" reads up on the upper half of the sheet and down on the lower half.

On the 5c and 10c, "PANAMA" reads up at left and down at right on each stamp.

On the 2c only, varieties exist with inverted "V" for "A," accent on "A," inverted "N," etc., in "PANAMA."

1904, June 24   Engr.   Unwmk.   Perf. 12

1	A1	2c rose, both "PANAMA" reading up or down *(2600)*	600.	425.
		Single on post card		*1,650.*
		Strip of 3 on cover		*1,500.*
		Block of 4	2,750.	2,100.
		"PANAMA" 15mm long *(260)*	650.	600.

		"P NAMA"	650.	600.
a.		"CANAL ZONE" inverted *(100)*	1,000.	850.
b.		"CANAL ZONE" double	3,250.	2,000.
c.		"CANAL ZONE" double, both inverted	20,000.	
d.		"PANAMA" reading down and up *(52)*	750.	650.
e.		As "d," "CANAL ZONE" invtd.	9,000.	7,000.
f.		Vert. pair, "PANAMA" reading up on top 2c, down on other	2,100.	2,100.
g.		As "f," "CANAL ZONE" inverted	20,000.	
2	A1	5c blue *(7800)*	250.	175.
		On cover		240.
		First day cover		7,500.
		Block of 4	1,200.	950.
		Left "PANAMA" 2¼mm below bar *(156)*	525.	500.
		Colon between right "PANA-MA" and bar *(156)*	525.	500.
a.		"CANAL ZONE" inverted	725.	600.
		On cover		800.
b.		"CANAL ZONE" double	2,250.	1,500.
c.		Pair, one without "CANAL ZONE" overprint	5,000.	5,000.
d.		"CANAL ZONE" overprint diagonal, reading down to right	750.	700.
3	A1	10c yellow *(4946)*	350.	250.
		On cover		325.
		First day cover		5,000.
		Block of 4	1,500.	1,150.
		Left "PANAMA" 2¼mm below bar *(100)*	625.	575.
		Colon between right "PANA-MA" and bar *(100)*	600.	550.
a.		"CANAL ZONE" inverted *(200)*	725.	600.
		On cover		800.
b.		"CANAL ZONE" double		15,000.
c.		Pair, one without "CANAL ZONE" overprint	6,000.	5,000.

Cancellations consist of town and/or bars in magenta or black, or a mixture of both colors.

Nos. 1-3 were withdrawn July 17, 1904.

Forgeries of the "Canal Zone" overprint and cancellations are numerous.

United States Nos. 300, 319, 304, 306 and 307 Overprinted in Black

1904, July 18   Wmk. 191

4	A115	1c blue green *(43,738)*	35.00	22.50
		green	35.00	22.50
		On cover		75.00
		Block of 4	150.00	140.00
		P# strip of 3, Impt.	140.00	
		P# block of 6, Impt.	875.00	
5	A129	2c carmine *(68,414)*	30.00	25.00
		On cover		75.00
		Block of 4	125.00	125.00
		P# strip of 3, Impt.	125.00	
		P# block of 6, Impt.	950.00	
a.		2c scarlet	35.00	30.00

6	A119	5c blue *(20,858)*	110.00	65
		On cover		250
		Block of 4	525.00	325
		P# strip of 3, Impt.	475.00	
		P# block of 6, Impt.	1,450.	
7	A121	8c violet black *(7932)*	175.00	85
		On cover		
		Block of 4	800.00	450
		P# strip of 3, Impt.	725.00	
		P# block of 6, Impt.	3,500.	
8	A122	10c pale red brown *(7856)*	150.00	90
		On cover		
		Block of 4	675.00	475.
		P# strip of 3, Impt.	650.00	
		P# block of 6, Impt.	2,750.	
		Nos. 4-8 (5)	500.00	287

Nos. 4-8 frequently show minor broken letters.

Cancellations consist of circular town and/or bars in black, blue or magenta.

Beware of fake overprints.

A2

REPÚBLICA DE PANAMA
ANTILLAS
CANAL ZONE PACIFICO
1 CENTAVO

A3

CANAL ZONE

REPÚBLICA DE PANAMA
ANTILLAS
CANAL ZONE
5 CENTAVOS

CANAL ZONE
Regular Type

CANAL ZONE
Antique Type

The Canal Zone overprint on stamps Nos. 9-15 and 18-20 was made with a plate which had six different stages, each with its peculiar faults and errors. Stage 1: Broken CA-L, broken A-L spaced, on Nos. 9, 10, 12-15. Stage 2: broken L, Z, N, E, on Nos. 9, 10, 12-14. Stage 3: same as 2 with additional antique ZONE, on Nos. 9, 11-14, 18. Stage 4: same as 3 with additional antique CANAL on Nos. 9, 12, 13. Stage 5: broken E and letters L, Z, N, and words CANAL and ZONE in antique type on Nos. 12-14, 19, 20. Stage 6: same as 5 except for additional antique Z on stamp which had antique L, on No. 12. The Panama overprints can be distinguished by the different shades of the red overprint, the width of the bar, and the word PANAMA. No. 11 has two different Panama overprints; No. 12 has six; No. 13 five; No. 14 two; and Nos. 15, 18-20, one each. In the "8c" surcharge of Nos. 14 and 15, there are three varieties of the

...e "8." The bar is sometimes misplaced so that it appears on ...ottom of the stamp instead of the top.

4-06			**Unwmk.**
Black Overprint on Stamps of Panama			
A2	1c **green** (319,800) Dec. 12, 1904	2.75	2.25
	On cover		12.50
	Block of 4	12.00	12.00
	Spaced "A L" in "CANAL" (700)	110.00	100.00
	"ON" of "ZONE" dropped	300.00	275.00
	"CANAL" in antique type (500)	100.00	100.00
	"ZONE" in antique type (1500)	70.00	70.00
	Inverted overprint	5,000.	3,750.
	Double overprint	2,750.	2,000.
A2	2c **rose** (367,500) Dec. 12, 1904	4.50	3.00
	On cover		17.50
	Block of 4	21.00	17.50
	Spaced "A L" of "CANAL" (1700)	85.00	85.00
	"ON" of "ZONE" dropped	400.00	400.00
	Inverted overprint	225.00	275.00
	"L" of "CANAL" sideways	2,500.	2,500.

...ANAMA" (15mm long) reading up at left, down at right

...overprint "CANAL ZONE" in Black, "PANAMA" and Bar in Red

A3	2c **rose** (150,000) Dec. 9, 1905	7.50	5.00
	On cover		50.00
	Block of 4	35.00	27.50
	Inverted "M" in "PANAMA" (3,000)	45.00	40.00
	"PANAMA" 16mm long (3000)	45.00	40.00
	"ZONE" in antique type (1500)	200.00	200.00
	"PANAMA" overprint inverted, bar at bottom (200)	475.00	475.00
A3	5c **blue** (400,000) Dec. 12, 1904	8.00	3.75
	On cover		100.00
	Block of 4	35.00	25.00
	Spaced "A L" in "CANAL" (300)	90.00	80.00
	"PAMANA" reading up (2800)	75.00	70.00
	"PANAMA" reading down (400)	200.00	180.00
	"PANAMA" 16mm long (1300)	40.00	37.50
	Inverted "M" in "PANAMA" (1300)	40.00	37.50
	Right "PANAMA" 5mm below bar (600)	75.00	70.00
	"PANAM"	70.00	65.00
	"PANAAM" at right	950.00	900.00
	"PAN MA"	75.00	70.00
	"ANAMA"	80.00	75.00
	"CANAL" in antique type (2750)	75.00	65.00
	"ZONE" in antique type (2950)	75.00	65.00
	"CANAL ZONE" double (200)	750.00	750.00
	"PANAMA" double (120)	1,050.	1,000.
	"PANAMA" inverted, bar at bottom		1,750.
A3	10c **yellow** (64,900) Dec. 12, 1904	22.50	12.50
	On cover		125.00
	Block of 4	110.00	62.50
	Spaced "A L" in "CANAL" (200)	200.00	180.00
	"PANAMA" 16mm long (400)	75.00	65.00
	"PAMANA" reading down (200)	200.00	180.00
	Invtd. "M" in "PANAMA" (400)	100.00	90.00
	Right "PANAMA" 5mm below bar (398)	150.00	140.00
	Left "PANAMA" touches bar (400)	200.00	160.00
	"CANAL" in antique type (200)	200.00	200.00
	"ZONE" in antique type (400)	175.00	160.00
	"PANAMA" ovpt. double (80)	650.00	650.00
	"PANAMA" overprint in red brown (5000)	27.50	27.50
	"PANAMA" ovpt. in orange red	32.50	32.50

With Added Surcharge in Red

a

...here are three varieties of "8" in the surcharge on #14-15.

A3	8c on 50c **bister brown** (27,900) Dec. 12, 1904	32.50	22.50
	On cover		175.00
	Block of 4	190.00	140.00
	Spaced "A L" in "CANAL" (194)	175.00	160.00
	Right "PANAMA" 5mm below bar (438)	200.00	175.00
.	"ZONE" in antique type (25)	1,150.	1,150.
.	"CANAL ZONE" inverted (200)	450.00	425.00
.	"PANAMA" overprint in rose brown (6000)	40.00	40.00
.	As "c," "CANAL" in antique type (10)	2,000.	

e.	As "c," "ZONE" in antique type (10)	2,000.	
f.	As "c," "8 cts" double (30)	1,100.	
g.	As "c," "8" omitted	4,250.	

Nos. 11-14 are overprinted or surcharged on Panama Nos. 77, 77e, 78, 78c, 78d, 78f, 78g, 78h, 79 79c, 79e, 79g and 81 respectively.

Panama No. 74a, 74b Overprinted "CANAL ZONE" in Regular Type in Black and Surcharged Type "a" in Red
Both "PANAMA" (13mm long) Reading Up

15	A3(a)	8c on 50c **bister brown** (435) Dec. 12, 1904	2,600.	4,750.
		On cover		10,000.
		Block of 4	11,500.	
		"PANAMA" 15mm long (50)	2,750.	5,000.
		"P NAMA"	5,000.	
		Spaced "A L" in "CANAL" (5)	5,000.	
a.		"PANAMA" reading down and up (10)	7,500.	—

On No. 15 with original gum the gum is almost always disturbed.

Map of Panama — A4

Panama Nos. 19 and 21 Surcharged in Black:

a   b

c   d

e   f

1906

There were three printings of each denomination, differing principally in the relative position of the various parts of the surcharges. Varieties occur with inverted "V" for the final "A" in "PANAMA," "CA" spaced, "ZO" spaced, "2c" spaced, accents in various positions, and with bars shifted so that two bars appear on top or bottom of the stamp (either with or without the corresponding bar on top or bottom) and sometimes with only one bar at top or bottom.

16	A4	1c on 20c **violet**, type a (100,000) Mar.	2.00	1.60
		On cover		10.00
		Block of 4	9.00	7.50
a.		Type b (100,000) May	2.00	1.60
		On cover		10.00
		Block of 4	9.00	7.50
b.		Type c (300,000) Sept.	2.00	1.60
		On cover		10.00
		Block of 4	10.50	7.50
		Spaced C A	13.00	12.00
c.		As No. 16, double surcharge		2,000.
17	A4	2c on 1p **lake**, type d (200,000) Mar.	2.75	2.75
		On cover		12.00
		Block of 4	14.00	12.50
a.		Type e (200,000) May	2.75	2.50
		On cover		12.00
		Block of 4	14.00	12.50
b.		Type f (50,000) Sept.	20.00	20.00
		On cover		75.00
		Block of 4	90.00	90.00

Panama Nos. 74, 74a and 74b Overprinted "CANAL ZONE" in Regular Type in Black and Surcharged in Red

8 cts   **8 cts**
b   c

1905-06

Both "PANAMA" Reading Up

18	A3(b)	8c on 50c **bister brown** (17,500) Nov. 1905	55.00	50.00
		On cover		225.00
		Block of 4	250.00	230.00
		"PANAMA" 15mm long (1750)	90.00	80.00
		"P NAMA"	125.00	110.00
a.		"ZONE" in antique type (175)	200.00	180.00
b.		"PANAMA" reading down and up (350)	175.00	160.00
19	A3(c)	8c on 50c **bister brown** (19,000) Apr. 23, 1906	55.00	45.00
		On cover		250.00
		Block of 4	250.00	200.00
		"PANAMA" 15mm long (1900)	85.00	70.00
		"P NAMA"	90.00	
a.		"CANAL" in antique type (190)	210.00	180.00
b.		"ZONE" in antique type (190)	210.00	180.00
c.		"8 cts" double	1,100.	1,100.
d.		"PANAMA" reading down and up (380)	110.00	90.00

On Nos. 18-19 with original gum, the gum is usually disturbed.

Panama No. 81 Overprinted "CANAL ZONE" in Regular Type in Black and Surcharged in Red Type "c" plus Period
"PANAMA" reading up and down

20	A3(c)	8c on 50c **bister brown** (19,600) Sept. 1906	45.00	40.00
		On cover		200.00
		Block of 4	190.00	175.00
		"PANAMA" reading up (392)	120.00	110.00
a.		"CANAL" antique type (196)	200.00	180.00
b.		"ZONE" in antique type (196)	200.00	180.00
c.		"8 cts" omitted (50)	800.00	800.00
d.		"8 cts" double	1,500.	
e.		"cts 8"		

Nos. 14 and 18-20 exist without CANAL ZONE overprint but were not regularly issued and are considered printer's waste. Forgeries of the overprint varieties of Nos. 9-15 and 18-20 are known.

Vasco Núñez de
Balboa — A5

Fernández de
Córdoba — A6

Justo
Arosemena — A7

Manuel J.
Hurtado — A8

José de Obaldía — A9

Engraved by Hamilton Bank Note Co.
**Overprinted in Black by Isthmian Canal
Commission Press.**

1906-07   Unwmk.   *Perf. 12*
Overprint Reading Up

21	A6	2c **red & black** (50,000) Oct. 29, 1906	25.00 25.00
		On cover	50.00
		Block of 4	125.00 175.00
a.		"CANAL" only	4,000.

Overprint Reading Down

22	A5	1c **green & black** (2,000,000) Jan. 14, 1907	2.25 1.25
		dull green & black	2.25 1.25
		On cover	5.00
		Block of 4	10.00 8.00
		"ANA" for "CANAL" (1000)	70.00 70.00
		"CAN L" for "CANAL"	80.00 80.00
		"ONE" for "ZONE" (3000)	80.00 80.00
a.		Horiz. pair, imperf. btwn. (50)	1,300. 1,300.
b.		Vert. pair, imperf. btwn. (20)	1,850. 1,750.
c.		Vert. pair, imperf. horiz. (20)	2,250. 1,750.
d.		Inverted overprint reading up (100)	550.00 550.00
e.		Double overprint (300)	275.00 275.00

f.	Double overprint, one inverted		1,500.	1,350.
g.	Invtd. center, ovpt. reading up		3,500.	3,500.
	Pair on cover			10,000.
h.	Horiz. pair, imperf vert.		—	
23	A6	2c **red & black** (2,370,000) Nov. 25, 1906	3.25	1.40
		scarlet & black, 1907	3.25	1.40
		On cover		6.00
		Block of 4	14.00	9.00
		"CAN L" for "CANAL"	45.00	
a.		Horizontal pair, imperf. between (20)	2,000.	1,750.
b.		Vertical pair, one without overprint	2,500.	2,500.
c.		Double overprint (100)	525.00	525.00
d.		Double overprint, one diagonal	800.00	800.00
e.		Double overprint, one diagonal, in pair with normal	2,500.	
f.		2c carmine red & black, Sept. 9, 1907	5.00	2.75
g.		As "f," inverted center and overprint reading up		6,000.
		On cover		12,000.
h.		As "d," one "ZONE CANAL"	4,000.	
i.		"CANAL" double	4,000.	
24	A7	5c **ultramarine & black** (1,390,000) Dec. 1906	6.50	2.25
		light ultramarine & black	6.50	2.25
		blue & black, Sept. 16, 1907	6.50	2.25
		dark blue & black	6.50	2.25
		dull blue & black	6.50	2.25
		light blue & black	6.50	2.25
		On cover		40.00
		Block of 4	27.50	20.00
		"CAN L" for "CANAL"	60.00	
c.		Double overprint (200)	450.00	350.00
d.		"CANAL" only (10)	4,000.	
e.		"ZONE CANAL"	4,500.	
25	A8	8c **purple & black** (170,000) Dec. 1906	22.50	8.00
		On cover		100.00
		Block of 4	125.00	55.00
a.		Horizontal pair, imperf. between and at left margin (34)	2,000.	4,000.
26	A9	10c **violet & black** (250,000) Dec. 1906	20.00	8.00
		On cover		100.00
		Block of 4	110.00	50.00
a.		Dbl. ovpt., one reading up (10)	5,000.	
b.		Overprint reading up	5,500.	
		Nos. 22-26 (5)	54.50	20.90

The early printings of this series were issued on soft, thick, porous-textured paper, while later printings of all except No. 25 appear on hard, thin, smooth-textured paper.

Normal spacing of the early printings is 7¼mm between the words; later printings, 6¾mm. Nos. 22 and 26 exist imperf. between stamp and sheet margin. Nos. 22-25 occur with "CA" of "CANAL" spaced ½mm further apart on position No. 50 of the setting.

The used pair of No. 25a is unique.

Córdoba — A11

Arosemena — A12

Hurtado — A13

José de
Obaldía — A14

Engraved by American Bank Note Co.

1909
Overprint Reading Down

27	A11	2c **vermilion & black** (500,000) May 11, 1909	12.50	5.50
		On cover		15.00
		First day cover		750.00
		Block of 4	57.50	30.00
a.		Horizontal pair, one without overprint	2,600.	
b.		Vert. pair, one without ovpt.	3,500.	
28	A12	5c **deep blue & black** (200,000) May 28, 1909	45.00	12.50
		On cover		60.00
		Block of 4	200.00	60.00
29	A13	8c **violet & black** (50,000) May 25, 1909	40.00	14.00
		On cover		90.00
		Block of 4	200.00	82.50
30	A14	10c **violet & black** (100,000) Jan. 19, 1909	40.00	15.00
		On cover		85.00

	Block of 4	200.00	8
a.	Horizontal pair, one with "ZONE" omitted	2,400.	
b.	Vertical pair, one without overprint	3,000.	

Nos. 27-30 occur with "CA" spaced (position 50).
Do not confuse No. 27 with Nos. 39d or 53a.
On No. 30a, the stamp with "ZONE" omitted is also mis most of "CANAL."

Vasco Núñez de
Balboa — A15

Engraved, Printed and Overprinted by America
Bank Note Co.
Black Overprint Reading Up

Type I

Type I Overprint: "C" with serifs both top and bottom. "L, and "E" with slanting serifs.
Compare Type I overprint with Types II to V illustrated be Nos. 38, 46, 52 and 55. Illustrations of Types I to V are con erably enlarged and do not show actual spacing between l of overprint.

1909-10

31	A15	1c **dark green & black** (4,000,000) Nov. 8, 1909	4.00	
		On cover		
		Block of 4	17.50	
a.		Inverted center and overprint reading down		22,
c.		Bklt. pane of 6, handmade, perf. margins	575.00	
32	A11	2c **vermilion & black** (4,000,000) Nov. 8, 1909	4.50	
		On cover		
		Block of 4	20.00	8
a.		Vert. pair, imperf. horiz.	1,000.	1,
c.		Bklt. pane of 6, handmade, perf. margins	750.00	
d.		Double overprint		
33	A12	5c **deep blue & black** (2,000,000) Nov. 8, 1909	17.00	4
		On cover		40
		Block of 4	80.00	20
a.		Double overprint (200)	375.00	375
		On cover		1,
34	A13	8c **violet & black** (200,000) Mar. 18, 1910	11.00	4
		On cover		75
		Block of 4	50.00	27
a.		Vertical pair, one without overprint (10)	1,750.	
35	A14	10c **violet & black** (100,000) Nov. 8, 1909	50.00	20
		On cover		100
		Block of 4	225.00	100
		Nos. 31-35 (5)	86.50	32

Normal spacing between words of overprint on No. 31 10mm and on Nos. 32 to 35, 8½mm. Minor spacing variati are known.

A16

A17

1911, Jan. 14

36	A16	10c on 13c **gray** (476,700)	6.00	2
		On cover		50
		Block of 4	30.00	15
a.		"10 cts" inverted	350.00	300
b.		"10 cts" omitted	350.00	

The "10 cts" surcharge was applied by the Isthmian Ca Commission Press after the overprinted stamps were receiv from the American Bank Note Co.

ny used stamps offered as No. 36b are merely No. 36 from
h the surcharge has been removed with chemicals.

4, Jan. 6

17 10c **gray** (200,000)		55.00	12.50
On cover			85.00
Block of 4		230.00	65.00

Black Overprint Reading Up

Type II

pe II Overprint: "C" with serif at top only. "L" and "E" with
cal serifs. "O" tilts to left.

2-16

A15 1c **green & black** (3,000,000)			
July 1913		11.00	3.00
On cover			5.50
Block of 4		50.00	20.00
Vertical pair, one without overprint		1,750.	1,750.
On cover			2,250.
Booklet pane of 6, imperf. margins (120,000)		625.00	
Booklet pane of 6, handmade, perf. margins		*1,000.*	
A11 2c **vermilion & black**			
(7,500,000) *Dec. 1912*		8.50	1.40
orange vermilion & black, *1916*		8.50	1.40
On cover			5.00
Block of 4		42.50	8.00
Horiz. pair, right stamp without overprint (20)		*1,250.*	
Horiz. pair, left stamp without overprint (10)		*1,750.*	
Booklet pane of 6, imperf. margins (194,868)		550.00	
Overprint reading down		175.00	
As "d," inverted center		600.00	*750.00*
As "e," booklet pane of 6, handmade, perf. margins		*10,000.*	
As "c," handmade, perf. margins		*1,000.*	
As No. 39, "CANAL" only			*1,100.*
A12 5c **deep blue & black**			
(2,300,000) *Dec. 1912*		22.50	3.25
On cover			35.00
Block of 4		105.00	15.00
With Cordoba portrait of 2c			*10,000.*
A14 10c **violet & black** (200,000)			
Feb. 1916		47.50	8.50
On cover			80.00
Block of 4		240.00	40.00

ormal spacing between words of overprint on the first print-
of Nos. 38-40 is 8½mm and on the second printing 9¼mm.
e spacing of the single printing of No. 41 and the imperf.
rgin booklet pane printings of Nos. 38 and 39 is 7¾mm.
or spacing variations are known.

ap of Panama
Canal — A18

Balboa Taking
Possession of
the Pacific
Ocean — A19

Gatun
Locks — A20

Culebra
Cut — A21

Engraved, Printed and Overprinted by American Bank Note Co.

1915, Mar. 1

Blue Overprint, Type II

42 A18 1c **dark green & black**		8.50	6.50
(100,000)			
On cover			17.50
Block of 4		37.50	30.00
First day cover			200.00
43 A19 2c **carmine & black**		10.00	4.25
(100,000)			
vermilion & black		10.00	4.25
On cover			25.00
First day cover			150.00
Block of 4		42.50	21.00
44 A20 5c **blue & black** (100,000)		11.00	5.75
On cover			55.00
Block of 4		50.00	29.00
First day cover			500.00
45 A21 10c **orange & black** (50,000)		22.50	11.00
On cover			70.00
Block of 4		95.00	55.00
First day cover			500.00

Normal spacing between words of overprint is 9¼mm on all
four values except position No. 61 which is 10mm.

Black Overprint Reading Up

Type III

Type III Overprint: Similar to Type I but letters appear thinner,
particularly the lower bar of "L," "Z" and "E." Impressions are
often light, rough and irregular, and not centered.

**Engraved and Printed by American Bank Note Co.
Overprint applied by
Panama Canal Press, Mount Hope, C.Z.**

1915-20

46 A15 1c **green & black,** *Dec. 1915*		160.00	125.00
light green & black, *1920*		225.00	180.00
On cover			160.00
Pair on cover			*500.00*
Block of 4		725.00	650.00
a. Overprint reading down (200)		375.00	
b. Double overprint (180)		350.00	
c. "ZONE" double (2)		*4,250.*	
d. Double overprint, one reads "ZONE CANAL" (18)		*1,750.*	
47 A11 2c **orange vermilion & black,** *Aug. 1920*		3,250.	100.00
On cover			375.00
Block of 4		*13,500.*	800.00
48 A12 5c **deep blue & black,** *Dec. 1915*		500.00	175.00
On cover			750.00
Block of 4		*2,400.*	850.00

Normal spacing between words of overprint on Nos. 46-48 is
9¼mm. This should not be confused with an abnormal 9¼mm
spacing of the 2c and 5c values of type I, which are fairly
common in singles, particularly used. Blocks of the abnormal
spacing are rare.

A22

S. S. "Panama"
in Culebra
Cut — A23

S. S. "Cristobal"
in Gatun
Locks — A24

Engraved, Printed and Overprinted by American Bank Note Co.

1917, Jan. 23

Blue Overprint, Type II

49 A22 12c **purple & black** (314,914)		17.50	5.50
On cover			50.00
First day cover			—
Block of 4		87.50	30.00
50 A23 15c **bright blue & black**		55.00	25.00
On cover			135.00
Block of 4		250.00	125.00
51 A24 24c **yellow brown & black**		45.00	15.00
On cover			325.00
Block of 4		200.00	90.00

Normal spacing between words of overprint is 11¼mm.

Black Overprint Reading Up

Type IV

Type IV Overprint: "C" thick at bottom, "E" with center bar
same length as top and bottom bars.

Engraved, Printed and Overprinted by American Bank Note Co.

1918-20

52 A15 1c **green & black** (2,000,000) *Jan. 1918*		32.50	11.00
On cover			12.50
Block of 4		150.00	47.50
a. Overprint reading down (60,000)		175.00	
b. Booklet pane of 6		650.00	
c. Booklet pane of 6, left vertical row of 3 without overprint		*7,500.*	

d. Booklet pane of 6, right vertical row of 3
　　 with double overprint　　　　　　　7,500.
e. Horiz. bklt. pair, left stamp without over-
　　 print　　　　　　　　　　　　　　3,000.
f. Horiz. bklt. pair, right stamp with double
　　 overprint　　　　　　　　　　　　3,000.
g. Double overprint, booklet single　　　3,000.
53 A11　2c **vermilion & black** *(2,000,000)*
　　　　　　　　Nov. 1918　　　110.00　7.00
　　　　　On cover　　　　　　　　　　10.00
　　　　　Block of 4　　　　　500.00　35.00
a. Overprint reading down　　150.00　150.00
b. Horiz. pair, right stamp without ovpt.　2,000.
c. Booklet pane of 6 *(34,000)*　　1,050.
d. Booklet pane of 6, left vertical row of 3
　　 without overprint　　　　　　　15,000.
e. Horiz. bklt. pair, left stamp without over-
　　 print　　　　　　　　　　　　　　3,000.
　　　　　On cover (unique)　　　　　　4,500.
54 A12　5c **deep blue & black** *(500,000)*
　　　　　　　　Apr. 1920　　　150.00　35.00
　　　　　On cover　　　　　　　　　200.00
　　　　　Block of 4　　　　　825.00　160.00

Normal spacing between words of overprint on Nos. 52 and 53 is 9¼mm. On No. 54 and the booklet printings of Nos. 52 and 53, the normal spacing is 9mm. Minor spacing varieties are known.

Black Overprint Reading Up

Type V

Type V Overprint: Smaller block type 1¾mm high. "A" with flat top.

1920-21
55 A15　1c **light green & black,** *Apr. 1921*　22.50　3.50
　　　　　On cover　　　　　　　　　　8.00
　　　　　Block of 4　　　　　100.00　17.50
a. Overprint reading down　　300.00　225.00
b. Horiz. pair, right stamp without ovpt.
　　 (10)　　　　　　　　　　　　　1,750.
c. Horiz. pair, left stamp without ovpt. (21)　1,000.
d. "ZONE" only　　　　　　　　4,250.　—
e. Booklet pane of 6　　　　　　2,250.
f. As No. 55, "CANAL" double (10)　1,750.
56 A11　2c **orange vermilion & black,**
　　　　　　　　Sept. 1920　　　8.50　2.25
　　　　　On cover　　　　　　　　　　7.00
　　　　　Block of 4　　　　　37.50　10.50
a. Double overprint *(100)*　　600.00
b. Double overprint, one reading down
　　 (100)　　　　　　　　　　　650.00
c. Horiz. pair, right stamp without overprint
　　 (11)　　　　　　　　　　　1,500.
d. Horiz. pair, left stamp without overprint
　　 (20)　　　　　　　　　　　1,250.
e. Vertical pair, one without overprint　1,500.
f. "ZONE" double　　　　　　　1,250.
g. Booklet pane of 6　　　　　850.00
h. As No. 56, "CANAL" double　1,000.
57 A12　5c **deep blue & black,** *Apr. 1921*　300.00　55.00
　　　　　On cover　　　　　　　　　225.00
　　　　　Block of 4　　　　　1,350.　250.00
a. Horiz. pair, right stamp without overprint
　　 (10)　　　　　　　　　　　2,500.
b. Horiz. pair, left stamp without overprint
　　 (10)　　　　　　　　　　　2,500.

Normal spacing between words of overprint on Nos. 55-57 is 9½mm. On booklet printings of Nos. 55 and 56 the normal spacing is 9¼mm.

Drydock at
Balboa — A25

U.S.S. "Nereus" in
Pedro Miguel
Locks — A26

1920, Sept.
Black Overprint Type V
58 A25　50c **orange & black**　　275.00　160.00
　　　　　On cover　　　　　　　　1,000.
　　　　　Block of 4　　　　1,375.　800.00
59 A26　1b **dark violet & black** *(23,014)*　175.00　65.00
　　　　　On cover　　　　　　　　1,000.
　　　　　Block of 4　　　　825.00　325.00

José Vallarino — A27

"Land Gate" — A28

Bolívar's
Tribute — A29

Municipal Building in
1821 and 1921 — A30

Statue of
Balboa — A31

Tomás Herrera — A32

José de
Fábrega — A33

Engraved, Printed and Overprinted by American
Bank Note Co.
Type V overprinted in black, reading up, on all values except the 5c which is overprinted with larger type in red

1921, Nov. 13
60 A27　1c **green**　　　　　　3.75　1.40
　　　　　On cover　　　　　　　　　6.00
　　　　　Block of 4　　　　17.50　6.75
a. "CANAL" double　　　　　　2,500.
b. Booklet pane of 6　　　　　1,000.
61 A28　2c **carmine**　　　　3.00　1.50
　　　　　On cover　　　　　　　　15.00
　　　　　Block of 4　　　　13.50　6.50
a. Overprint reading down　200.00　225.00
b. Double overprint　　　　　900.00
c. Vertical pair, one without overprint　3,500.
d. "CANAL" double　　　　　1,900.
f. Booklet pane of 6　　　　2,100.
62 A29　5c **blue** (R)　　　11.00　4.50
　　　　　On cover　　　　　　　　30.00
　　　　　Block of 4　　　　50.00　25.00
a. Overprint reading down (R)　60.00
63 A30　10c **violet**　　　　18.00　7.50
　　　　　On cover　　　　　　　　60.00
　　　　　Block of 4　　　　100.00　35.00
a. Overprint, reading down　90.00
64 A31　15c **light blue**　　47.50　17.50
　　　　　On cover　　　　　　　　175.00
　　　　　Block of 4　　　　225.00　95.00
65 A32　24c **black brown**　70.00　22.50
　　　　　On cover　　　　　　　　600.00
　　　　　Block of 4　　　　375.00　125.00
66 A33　50c **black**　　　　150.00　100.00
　　　　　On cover　　　　　　　　600.00
　　　　　Block of 4　　　　725.00　475.00
　　　　　Nos. 60-66 (7)　　303.25　154.90

Experts question the status of the 5c with a small type V overprint in red or black.

Type III overprint in black, reading up, applie[d] the Panama Canal Press, Mount Hope, C. [Z.]
Engraved and printed by the American Bank No[te] Co.

1924, Jan. 28
67 A27　1c **green**　　　　　　500.
　　　　　On cover
　　　　　Block of 4　　　　　2,250.
a. "ZONE CANAL" reading down　850.
b. "ZONE" only, reading down　1,900.
c. Se-tenant pair, #67a and 67b　2,750.

Arms of Panama — A34

1924, Feb.
68 A34　1c **dark green**　　　11.00
　　　　　On cover
　　　　　Block of 4　　　　52.50　2[ ]
69 A34　2c **carmine**　　　　8.25
　　　　　carmine rose　　　　　8.25
　　　　　On cover
　　　　　Block of 4　　　　35.00　1[ ]

The following were prepared for use, but not issued.

A34　5c **dark blue** *(600)*　　　350.
　　　Block of 4　　　　　　1,750.
A34　10c **dark violet** *(600)*　　350.
　　　Block of 4　　　　　　1,750.
A34　12c **olive green** *(600)*　　350.
　　　Block of 4　　　　　　1,750.
A34　15c **ultramarine** *(600)*　　350.
　　　Block of 4　　　　　　1,750.
A34　24c **yellow brown** *(600)*　350.
　　　Block of 4　　　　　　1,750.
A34　50c **orange** *(600)*　　　350.
　　　Block of 4　　　　　　1,750.
A34　1b **black** *(600)*　　　　350.
　　　Block of 4　　　　　　1,750.

The 5c to 1b values were prepared for use but never iss[ued] due to abrogation of the Taft Agreement which required [the] Canal Zone to use overprinted Panama stamps. Six hundr[ed] each denomination were not destroyed, as they were forwar[ded] to the Director General of Posts of Panama for transmissio[n to] the UPU which then required about 400 sets. Only a s[mall] number of sets appear to have reached the public market.

All Panama stamps overprinted "CANAL ZONE" were w[ith-] drawn from sale June 30, 1924, and were no longer valid [for] postage after Aug. 31, 1924.

United States Nos. 551-554,
557, 562, 564-566, 569, 570
and 571 Overprinted in Red
(No. 70) or Black (all others)

Printed and Overprinted by the U.S. Bureau of
Engraving and Printing.
Type A
Letters "A" with Flat Tops

1924-25　　　　　**Unwmk.**　　　*Perf.*
70 A154　½c **olive brown** *(399,500)* Apr. 15,
　　　　　1925　　　　　　　1.25
　　　　　Never hinged　　　　2.00
　　　　　On cover　　　　　　　　　　4
　　　　　First day cover　　　　　　　75
　　　　　Block of 4　　　　5.50　3[ ]
　　　　　P# block of 6　　　18.00
71 A155　1c **deep green** *(1,985,000)* July 1,
　　　　　1924　　　　　　　1.40　1
　　　　　Never hinged　　　　2.25
　　　　　On cover　　　　　　　　　　4
　　　　　Block of 4　　　　6.00　4[ ]
　　　　　P# block of 6　　　30.00
a. Inverted overprint　　500.00　500[ ]
b. "ZONE" inverted　　　350.00　325[ ]
c. "CANAL" only *(20)*　　1,750.
d. "ZONE CANAL" *(180)*　500.00
e. Booklet pane of 6 *(43,152)*　80.00
72 A156　1½c **yellow brown** *(180,599)* Apr.
　　　　　15, 1925　　　　　　1.90　1
　　　　　brown　　　　　　　1.90　1
　　　　　Never hinged　　　　3.00
　　　　　First day cover, Nos. 70, 72　　80
　　　　　Block of 4　　　　8.25　9[ ]
　　　　　P# block of 6　　　35.00
73 A157　2c **carmine** *(2,975,000)* July 1,
　　　　　1924　　　　　　　7.50　1[ ]
　　　　　Never hinged　　　　11.00
　　　　　First day cover　　　　　　　80
　　　　　Block of 4　　　　35.00　1[ ]
　　　　　P# block of 6　　　175.00
a. Booklet pane of 6 *(140,000)*　175.00

A160	5c **dark blue** (500,000) July 1, 1924		19.00	7.50
	Never hinged		29.00	
	On cover			20.00
	Block of 4		80.00	37.50
	P# block of 6		325.00	
A165	10c **orange** (60,000) July 1, 1924		45.00	25.00
	Never hinged		67.50	
	On cover			45.00
	First day cover			500.00
	Block of 4		200.00	115.00
	P# block of 6		850.00	
A167	12c **brown violet** (80,000) July 1, 1924		35.00	32.50
	Never hinged		52.50	
	First day cover			600.00
	Block of 4		150.00	140.00
	P# block of 6		475.00	
	"ZONE" inverted		3,750.	3,000.
A168	14c **dark blue** (100,000) June 27, 1925		30.00	22.50
	Never hinged		45.00	
	On cover			50.00
	Block of 4		130.00	140.00
	P# block of 6		425.00	
A169	15c **gray** (55,000) July 1, 1924		50.00	37.50
	Never hinged		75.00	
	On cover			52.50
	Block of 4		225.00	190.00
	P# block of 6		850.00	
A172	30c **olive brown** (40,000) July 1, 1924		35.00	22.50
	Never hinged		52.50	
	On cover			50.00
	Block of 4		160.00	110.00
	P# block of 6		550.00	
A173	50c **lilac** (25,000) July 1, 1924		77.50	45.00
	Never hinged		115.00	
	On cover			500.00
	Block of 4		340.00	225.00
	P# block of 6		2,750.	
A174	$1 **violet brown** (10,000) July 1, 1924		225.00	95.00
	Never hinged		350.00	
	On cover			1,000.
	Block of 4		1,000.	500.00
	Margin block of 4, arrow, top or bottom		1,250.	
	P# block of 6		4,250.	
	Nos. 70-81 (12)		528.55	292.65

Normal spacing between words of the overprint is 9¼mm. ...nor spacing variations are known. The overprint of the early ...ntings used on all values of this series except No. 77 is a ...arp, clear impression. The overprint of the late printings, used ...ly on Nos. 70, 71, 73, 76, 77, 78 and 80 is heavy and ...udged, with many of the letters, particularly the "A" practi-...lly filled.

Booklet panes Nos. 71e, 73a, 84d, 97b, 101a, 106a and 117a ...re made from 360 subject plates. The handmade booklet ...nes Nos. 102a, 115c and a provisional lot of 117b were made ...m Post Office panes from regular 400-subject plates.

United States Nos. 554, 555, ...67, 562, 564-567, 569, 570, ...71, 623 Overprinted in Red (No. 91) or Black (all others)

Type B
Letters "A" with Sharp Pointed Tops

925-28 **Perf. 11**

...4 A157	2c **carmine** (1,110,000) May 1926		30.00	8.00
	Never hinged		45.00	
	On cover			11.00
	Block of 4		125.00	37.50
	P# block of 6		375.00	
	P# block of 6 & large 5 point star, side only		2,000.	
...	"CANAL" only (20)		2,250.	
...	"ZONE CANAL" (180)		500.00	
...	Horizontal pair, one without overprint		3,500.	
...	Booklet pane of 6 (82,000)		175.00	
...	Vertical pair, "a" and "b" se-tenant		2,750.	
...5 A158	3c **violet** (199,200) June 27, 1925		4.00	3.25
	Never hinged		6.00	
	On cover			6.00
	Block of 4		17.50	13.50
	P# block of 6		175.00	
...	"ZONE ZONE"		600.00	550.00
...6 A160	5c **dark blue** (1,343,147) Jan. 7, 1926		4.00	2.50
	Never hinged		6.00	
	On cover			17.50
	Block of 4		17.50	11.00
	P# block of 6		165.00	
	Double transfer (15571 UL 86)		—	—
...	"ZONE ZONE" (LR18)		1,250.	
...	"CANAL" inverted (LR7)		950.00	
...	Inverted overprint (80)		500.00	
...	Horizontal pair, one without overprint		3,250.	
...	Overprinted "ZONE CANAL" (90)		350.00	
...	"ZONE" only (10)		2,000.	
...	Vertical pair; one without overprint, other overprint inverted (10)		2,500.	
...	"CANAL" only		2,250.	

87 A165	10c **orange** (99,510) Aug. 1925		35.00	13.00
	Never hinged		52.50	
	On cover			40.00
	Block of 4		160.00	75.00
	P# block of 6		500.00	
a.	"ZONE ZONE" (LR18)		3,000.	
88 A167	12c **brown violet** (58,062) Feb. 1926		22.50	14.00
	Never hinged		34.00	
	On cover			45.00
	Block of 4		110.00	62.50
	P# block of 6		375.00	
a.	"ZONE ZONE" (LR18)		5,250.	
89 A168	14c **dark blue** (55,700) Dec. 1928		27.50	16.00
	Never hinged		42.50	
	On cover			50.00
	Block of 4		125.00	75.00
	P# block of 6		350.00	
90 A169	15c **gray** (204,138) Nov. 1925		7.50	4.50
	Never hinged		10.50	
	On cover			15.00
	Block of 4		35.00	21.00
	P# block of 6		200.00	
	P# block of 4, large 5 point star, side only		3,000.	
a.	"ZONE ZONE" (LR18)		5,500.	

It is believed that the three recorded P# blocks of 4 with large 5-point star are the largest known P# multiples from the plate that shows the star.

91 A187	17c **black** (199,500) Apr. 5, 1926		4.50	3.00
	Never hinged		6.50	
	On cover			12.50
	Block of 4		19.00	14.00
	P# block of 6		190.00	
a.	"ZONE" only (20)		900.00	
b.	"CANAL" only		1,700.	
c.	"ZONE CANAL" (270)		200.00	
92 A170	20c **carmine rose** (259,807) Apr. 5, 1926		7.25	3.25
	Never hinged		11.00	
	On cover			32.50
	Block of 4		32.50	14.00
	P# block of 6		175.00	
a.	"CANAL" inverted (UR48)		4,000.	
b.	"ZONE" inverted (LL76)		4,250.	
c.	"ZONE CANAL" (LL91)		3,600.	
93 A172	30c **olive brown** (154,700) Dec. 1925		5.75	4.00
	Never hinged		8.00	
	On cover			60.00
	Block of 4		25.00	20.00
	P# block of 6		250.00	
94 A173	50c **lilac** (13,533) July 1928		240.00	165.00
	Never hinged		350.00	
	On cover			500.00
	Block of 4		1,200.	750.00
	P# block of 6		2,500.	
95 A174	$1 **violet brown** (20,000) Apr. 1926		125.00	60.00
	Never hinged		190.00	
	On cover			1,000.
	Block of 4		550.00	265.00
	Margin block of 4, arrow, top or bottom		575.00	
	P# block of 6		2,000.	
	Nos. 84-95 (12)		513.00	296.50

Nos. 85-88, 90 and 93-95 exist with wrong-font "CANAL" and "ZONE." Positions are: Nos. 85-88 and 90, UL51 (CANAL) and UL82 (ZONE); Nos. 93-95, U51 (CANAL) and U82 (ZONE).

Normal spacing between words of the overprint is 11mm on No. 84; 9mm on Nos. 85-88, 90, first printing of No. 91 and the first, third and fourth printing of No. 92; 7mm on the second printings of Nos. 91-92. Minor spacing varieties exist on Nos. 84-88, 90-92.

Overprint Type B on U.S. Sesquicentennial Stamp No. 627

1926

96 A188	2c **carmine rose** (300,000) July 6, 1926		5.00	3.75
	Never hinged		7.25	
	First day cover			60.00
	Block of 4		22.50	18.00
	P# block of 6		85.00	

On this stamp there is a space of 5mm instead of 9mm between the two words of the overprint.

The authorized date, July 4, fell on a Sunday with the next day also a holiday, so No. 96 was not regularly issued until July 6. But the postmaster sold some copies and canceled some covers on July 4 for a few favored collectors.

Overprint Type B in Black on U.S. Nos. 583, 584, 591

1926-27	**Rotary Press Printings**		**Perf. 10**	
97 A157	2c **carmine** (1,290,000) Dec. 1926		62.50	11.00
	Never hinged		100.00	
	On cover			14.00
	Block of 4		290.00	50.00
	P# block of 4		475.00	
a.	Pair, one without overprint (10)		3,250.	
b.	Booklet pane of 6 (58,000)		525.00	
c.	"CANAL" only (10)		2,000.	
d.	"ZONE" only		2,750.	
98 A158	3c **violet** (239,600) May 9, 1927		8.00	4.25
	Never hinged		12.00	
	On cover			12.00
	Block of 4		35.00	19.00
	P# block of 4		120.00	
99 A165	10c **orange** (128,400) May 9, 1927		18.00	7.50
	Never hinged		26.00	

	On cover			35.00
	Block of 4		82.50	40.00
	P# block of 4		225.00	

No. 97d is valued in the grade of fine. Very fine examples are not known.

Overprint Type B in Black on U.S. Nos. 632, 634 (Type I), 635, 637, 642

1927-31	**Rotary Press Printings**		**Perf. 11x10½**	
100 A155	1c **green** (434,892) June 28, 1927		2.25	1.40
	Never hinged		3.50	
	On cover			3.00
	Block of 4		10.00	6.75
	P# block of 4		20.00	
a.	Vertical pair, one without overprint (10)		5,500.	
101 A157	2c **carmine** (1,628,195) June 28, 1927		2.50	1.00
	Never hinged		3.75	
	On cover			3.00
	Block of 4		11.00	4.75
	P# block of 4		24.00	
a.	Booklet pane of 6 (82,108)		160.00	
102 A158	3c **violet** (1,250,000) Feb., 1931		4.50	2.75
	Never hinged		6.50	
	On cover			5.00
	Block of 4		22.50	13.50
	P# block of 4		90.00	
a.	Booklet pane of 6, handmade, perf. margins		6,500.	
103 A160	5c **dark blue** (60,000) Dec. 13, 1927		30.00	10.00
	Never hinged		47.50	
	On cover			30.00
	Block of 4		130.00	42.50
	P# block of 4		200.00	
104 A165	10c **orange** (119,800) July, 1930		17.50	10.00
	Never hinged		26.00	
	On cover			35.00
	Block of 4		77.50	45.00
	P# block of 4		190.00	
	Nos. 100-104 (5)		56.75	25.15

Wet and Dry Printings

Canal Zone stamps printed by both the "wet" and "dry" process are Nos. 105, 108-109, 111-114, 117, 138-140, C21-C24, C26, J25, J27. Starting with Nos. 147 and C27, the Bureau of Engraving and Printing used the "dry" method exclusively, except for Nos. 152, 157 and 164.

See note on Wet and Dry Printings following U.S. No. 1029.

Maj. Gen. William Crawford Gorgas — A35

Maj. Gen. George Washington Goethals — A36

Gaillard Cut — A37

Maj. Gen. Harry Foote Hodges — A38

Lt. Col. David Du Bose Gaillard — A39

Maj. Gen. William
Luther Sibert — A40

Jackson
Smith — A41

Rear Adm. Harry
Harwood
Rousseau — A42

Col. Sydney Bacon
Williamson — A43

Joseph Clay Styles
Blackburn — A44

Printed by the U. S. Bureau of Engraving and Printing.
Plates of 400 subjects (except 5c), issued in panes of 100.
The 5c was printed from plate of 200 subjects, issued in panes
of 50. The 400-subject sheets were originally cut by knife into
Post Office panes of 100, but beginning in 1948 they were
separated by perforations to eliminate straight edges.

1928-40	**Flat Plate Printing**	**Unwmk.**	**Perf. 11**	
105 A35	1c **green** (22,392,147)		.20	.20
	Never hinged		.25	
	P# block of 6		2.50	—
a.	Wet printing, yel grn, Oct. 3, 1928		.20	.20
	Never hinged		.25	
	First day cover			17.50
	P# block of 6		4.25	—
106 A36	2c **carmine** (7,191,600) Oct. 1, 1928		.20	.20
	Never hinged		.25	
	First day cover			17.50
	P# block of 6		2.75	—
a.	Booklet pane of 6 (284,640)		15.00	20.00
	Never hinged		22.50	
107 A37	5c **blue** (4,187,028) June 25, 1929		1.00	.40
	Never hinged		1.30	
	First day cover			5.00
	P# block of 6		13.00	—
108 A38	10c **orange** (4,559,788)		.20	.20
	Never hinged		.25	
	P# block of 6		4.75	—
a.	Wet printing, Jan. 11, 1932		.40	.25
	Never hinged		.50	
	First day cover			40.00
	P# block of 6		6.00	—
109 A39	12c **brown violet** (844,635)		.75	.60
	Never hinged		1.00	
	P# block of 6		12.00	—
a.	Wet printing, violet brown, July 1, 1929		1.50	1.00
	Never hinged		2.00	
	First day cover			60.00
	P# block of 6		21.00	—
110 A40	14c **blue** (406,131) Sept. 27, 1937		.85	.85
	Never hinged		1.20	
	First day cover			5.00
	P# block of 6		16.00	—
111 A41	15c **gray black** (3,356,500)		.40	.35
	Never hinged		.55	
	P# block of 6		9.00	—
a.	Wet printing, gray, Jan. 11, 1932		.80	.50
	Never hinged		1.10	
	First day cover			45.00
	P# block of 6		12.50	5.00
112 A42	20c **dark brown** (3,619,080)		.60	.20
	Never hinged		.80	
	P# block of 6		9.00	—
a.	Wet printing, olive brown, Jan. 11, 1932		1.00	.30
	Never hinged		1.30	
	First day cover			45.00
	P# block of 6		16.00	—
113 A43	30c **black** (2,376,491)		.80	.70
	Never hinged		1.10	
	P# block of 6		12.00	—
a.	Wet printing, brn blk, Apr. 15, 1940		1.25	1.00
	Never hinged		1.60	
	First day cover			10.00
	P# block of 6		22.50	—
114 A44	50c **rose lilac** (1,500)		1.50	.65
	Never hinged		2.00	
	P# block of 6		18.00	—
a.	Wet printing, lilac, July 1, 1929		2.50	.85

Never hinged		3.50	
First day cover			150.00
P# block of 6		35.00	—
Nos. 105-114 (10)		6.50	4.35

Nos. 105, 108, 112, 113 and 114 exist with both shiny gum
and dull gum.
Coils are listed as Nos. 160-161.

United States Nos. 720 and 695 Overprinted type B

Rotary Press Printing

1933, Jan. 14			**Perf. 11x10½**	
115 A226	3c **deep violet** (3,150,000)		2.75	.25
	Never hinged		4.00	
	First day cover			12.00
	P# block of 4		35.00	—
b.	"CANAL" only		2,600.	
c.	Booklet pane of 6, handmade, perf. margins		175.00	—
116 A168	14c **dark blue** (104,800)		4.50	3.50
	Never hinged		7.00	
	First day cover			20.00
	P# block of 4		60.00	—
a.	"ZONE CANAL" (16)		1,500.	

Maj. Gen. George Washington
Goethals — A45

20th anniversary of the opening of the Panama Canal.

Flat Plate Printing

1934, Aug. 15		**Unwmk.**	**Perf. 11**	
117 A45	3c **red violet**		.20	.20
	Never hinged		.25	
	First day cover			3.00
	P# block of 6		1.00	—
a.	Booklet pane of 6		45.00	32.50
	Never hinged		60.00	
b.	As "a," handmade, perf. margins		160.00	—
c.	Wet printing, violet		.20	.20
	P# block of 6		1.00	—

Coil is listed as No. 153.

> **Catalogue values for unused stamps in this
> section, from this point to the end, are for Never
> Hinged items.**

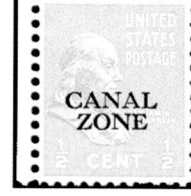

United States Nos. 803 and
805 Overprinted in Black

Rotary Press Printing

1939, Sept. 1		**Unwmk.**	**Perf. 11x10½**	
118 A275	½c **red orange** (1,030,000)		.20	.20
	First day cover			1.00
	P# block of 4		2.75	—
119 A277	1½c **bister brown** (935,000)		.20	.20
	brown		.20	.20
	First day cover			1.00
	P# block of 4		2.25	—

Balboa-Before
A46

Balboa-After
A47

Gaillard Cut-
Before
A48

Gaillard Cut-
After
A49

Bas Obispo-
Before
A50

Bas Obispo-
After
A51

Gatun Locks-
Before
A52

Gatun Locks-
After
A53

Canal Channel-
Before
A54

Canal Channel-
After
A55

Gamboa-Before
A56

Gamboa-After
A57

Pedro Miguel
Locks-Before
A58

Pedro Miguel
Locks-After
A59

Gatun Spillway-
Before
A60

Gatun Spillway-
After
A61

25th anniversary of the opening of the Panama Canal.
Withdrawn Feb. 28, 1941; remainders burned Apr. 12, 1941.

Flat Plate Printing

1939, Aug. 15		Unwmk.		Perf. 11	
20	A46	1c **yellow green** *(1,019,482)*		.65	.30
		First day cover			2.00
		P# block of 6		12.50	—
21	A47	2c **rose carmine** *(227,065)*		.65	.35
		First day cover			2.00
		P# block of 6		12.50	—
22	A48	3c **purple** *(2,523,735)*		.65	.20
		First day cover			2.00
		P# block of 6		12.50	—
23	A49	5c **dark blue** *(460,213)*		1.60	1.25
		First day cover			2.50
		P# block of 6		20.00	—
24	A50	6c **red orange** *(68,290)*		3.00	3.00
		First day cover			6.00
		P# block of 6		45.00	—
25	A51	7c **black** *(71,235)*		3.25	3.00
		First day cover			6.00
		P# block of 6		45.00	—
26	A52	8c **green** *(41,576)*		4.75	3.50
		First day cover			6.00
		P# block of 6		55.00	—
27	A53	10c **ultramarine** *(83,571)*		3.50	5.00
		First day cover			6.00
		P# block of 6		55.00	—
28	A54	11c **blue green** *(34,010)*		8.00	8.00
		First day cover			10.00
		P# block of 6		125.00	—
29	A55	12c **brown carmine** *(66,735)*		8.00	7.50
		First day cover			10.00
		P# block of 6		100.00	—
130	A56	14c **dark violet** *(37,365)*		8.00	7.50
		First day cover			10.00
		P# block of 6		125.00	—

131	A57	15c **olive green** *(105,058)*		11.50	6.00
		First day cover			10.00
		P# block of 6		160.00	—
132	A58	18c **rose pink** *(39,255)*		10.00	8.50
		First day cover			10.00
		P# block of 6		150.00	—
133	A59	20c **brown** *(100,244)*		14.00	7.50
		First day cover			10.00
		P# block of 6		190.00	—
134	A60	25c **orange** *(34,283)*		17.50	17.50
		First day cover			20.00
		P# block of 6		325.00	—
135	A61	50c **violet brown** *(91,576)*		25.00	6.00
		First day cover			20.00
		P# block of 6		350.00	—
		Nos. 120-135 (16)		120.05	85.10

Maj. Gen. George
W. Davis — A62

Gov. Charles E.
Magoon — A63

Theodore
Roosevelt — A64

John F.
Stevens — A65

John F. Wallace — A66

1946-49		Unwmk.		Perf. 11	
		Size: 19x22mm			
136	A62	½c **bright red** *(1,020,000)* Aug. 16, 1948		.40	.25
		First day cover			1.25
		P# block of 6		2.50	—
137	A63	1½c **chocolate** *(603,600)* Aug. 16, 1948		.40	.25
		First day cover			1.25
		P# block of 6		2.50	—
138	A64	2c **light rose carmine** *(6,951,755)*		.20	.20
		P# block of 6		.65	—
a.		Wet printing, rose carmine, Oct. 27, 1949		.20	.20
		First day cover			1.00
		P# block of 6		1.00	—
139	A65	5c **dark blue**		.35	.20
		P# block of 6		2.25	—
a.		Wet printing, deep blue, Apr. 25, 1946		.60	.20
		First day cover			1.00
		P# block of 6		4.00	—
140	A66	25c **green** *(1,520,000)*		.85	.55
		P# block of 6		7.00	—
a.		Wet printing, yel grn, Aug. 16, 1948		3.00	1.00
		First day cover			3.50
		P# block of 6		20.00	—
		Nos. 136-140 (5)		2.20	1.45

See Nos. 155, 162, 164.

Map of
Biological Area
and Coati-
mundi
A67

25th anniversary of the establishment of the Canal Zone Biological Area on Barro Colorado Island.
Withdrawn Mar. 30, 1951, and remainders destroyed Apr. 10,
1951.

1948, Apr. 17		Unwmk.		Perf. 11	
141	A67	10c **black** *(521,200)*		1.25	.80
		First day cover			3.00
		P# block of 6		8.50	—

"Forty-niners"
Arriving at
Chagres — A68

Journeying in
"Bungo" to Las
Cruces — A69

Las Cruces Trail to
Panama — A70

Departure for San
Francisco — A71

Centenary of the California Gold Rush.
Stocks on hand were processed for destruction on Aug. 11,
1952 and destroyed Aug. 13, 1952.

1949, June 1		Unwmk.		Perf. 11	
142	A68	3c **blue** *(500,000)*		.50	.25
		First day cover			1.00
		P# block of 6		6.00	—
143	A69	6c **violet** *(481,600)*		.65	.30
		First day cover			1.00
		P# block of 6		6.50	—
144	A70	12c **bright blue green** *(230,200)*		1.10	.90
		First day cover			2.00
		P# block of 6		18.00	—
145	A71	18c **deep red lilac** *(240,200)*		2.00	1.50
		First day cover			3.25
		P# block of 6		20.00	—
		Nos. 142-145 (4)		4.25	2.95

Workers in Culebra
Cut — A72

Early Railroad
Scene — A73

Contribution of West Indian laborers in the construction of the
Panama Canal.
Entire issue sold, none withdrawn and destroyed.

1951, Aug. 15		Unwmk.		Perf. 11	
146	A72	10c **carmine** *(480,000)*		2.25	1.50
		First day cover			3.00
		P# block of 6		22.50	—

1955, Jan. 28		Unwmk.		Perf. 11	

Centenary of the completion of the Panama Railroad and the
first transcontinental railroad trip in the Americas.

147	A73	3c **violet** *(994,000)*		.60	.50
		First day cover			1.50
		P# block of 6		5.50	—

Gorgas
Hospital and
Ancon
Hill — A74

75th anniversary of Gorgas Hospital.

1957, Nov. 17		Unwmk.		Perf. 11	
148	A74	3c **black**, *dull blue green* *(1,010,000)*		.45	.35
		Light blue green paper		.40	.35
		First day cover			1.00
		P# block of 4		4.25	—

S.S.
Ancon — A75

1958, Aug. 30   Unwmk.   Perf. 11
149 A75   4c **greenish blue** *(1,749,700)*   .40   .30
 First day cover   1.00
 P# block of 4   3.25

Roosevelt
Medal and
Canal Zone
Map — A76

Centenary of the birth of Theodore Roosevelt (1858-1919).

1958, Nov. 15   Unwmk.   Perf. 11
150 A76   4c **brown** *(1,060,000)*   .40   .30
 First day cover   1.00
 P# block of 4   3.00   —

Boy Scout
Badge — A77

Administration Building,
Balboa Heights — A78

50th anniversary of the Boy Scouts of America.

Giori Press Printing
1960, Feb. 8   Unwmk.   Perf. 11
151 A77   4c **dark blue, red & bister**
   (654,933)   .50   .40
 First day cover   1.50
 P# block of 4   4.25   —

1960, Nov. 1   Unwmk.   Perf. 11
152 A78   4c **rose lilac** *(2,486,725)*   .20   .20
 First day cover   1.00
 P# block of 4   .90   —

Types of 1934, 1960 and 1946
Coil Stamps
1960-62   Unwmk.   Perf. 10 Vertically
153 A45   3c **deep violet** *(3,743,959)* Nov. 1,
   1960   .20   .20
 First day cover   1.00
 Pair   .40   .25
 Joint line pair   1.10

Perf. 10 Horizontally
154 A78   4c **dull rose lilac** *(2,776,273)* Nov.
   1, 1960   .20   .20
 First day cover   1.00
 Pair   .40   .25
 Joint line pair   1.10

Perf. 10 Vertically
155 A65   5c **deep blue** *(3,288,264)* Feb. 10,
   1962   .25   .20
 First day cover   1.00
 Pair   .50   .50
 Joint line pair   1.25   —
 Nos. 153-155 (3)   .65   .60

Girl Scout
Badge and
Camp at
Gatun
Lake — A79

50th anniversary of the Girl Scouts.

Giori Press Printing
1962, Mar. 12   Unwmk.   Perf. 11
156 A79   4c **blue, dark green & bister**
   (640,000)   .40   .30
 First day cover *(83,717)*   1.25
 P# block of 4   2.75

Thatcher Ferry
Bridge and
Map of
Western
Hemisphere
A80

Opening of the Thatcher Ferry Bridge, spanning the Panama
Canal.

Giori Press Printing
1962, Oct. 12   Unwmk.   Perf. 11
157 A80   4c **black & silver** *(775,000)*   .35   .25
 First day cover *(65,833)*   1.00
 P# block of 4, 2P#   3.75
 a. Silver (bridge) omitted *(50)*   7,500.
  Hinged   5,500.
  P# block of 6, black P# only   52,500.

Goethals Memorial,
Balboa — A81

Fort San
Lorenzo — A82

1968-71   Giori Press Printing   Perf. 11
158 A81   6c **green & ultra.** *(1,890,000)* Mar.
   15, 1968   .30   .30
 First day cover   1.00
 P# block of 4   2.00   —
159 A82   8c **slate green, blue, dark brown**
   & ocher *(3,460,000)* July 14,
   1971   .35   .20
 First day cover   1.00
 P# block of 4   2.75   —

Types of 1928, 1932 and 1948
Coil Stamps
1975, Feb. 14   Unwmk.   Perf. 10 Vertically
160 A35   1c **green** *(1,090,958)*   .20   .20
 First day cover   1.00
 Pair   .40   .30
 Joint line pair   1.00   —
161 A38   10c **orange** *(590,658)*   .70   .40
 First day cover   1.00
 Pair   1.40   .80
 Joint line pair   5.00   —
162 A66   25c **yellow green** *(129,831)*   2.75   2.75
 First day cover   3.00
 Pair   5.50   5.50
 Joint line pair   20.00
 Nos. 160-162 (3)   3.65   3.35

Dredge
Cascadas
A83

1976, Feb. 23   Giori Press Printing   Perf. 11
163 A83   13c **multicolored** *(3,653,950)*   .35   .20
 First day cover   1.00
 P# block of 4   2.00   —
 a. Booklet pane of 4 *(1,032,400)* Apr. 19   3.00   —

Stevens Type of 1946
1977   Rotary Press Printing   Perf. 11x10½
Size: 19x22½mm
164 A65   5c **deep blue** *(1,009,612)*   .60   .85
 P# block of 4   3.50   —
 a. Tagged, dull gum   12.00 15.00
  P# block of 4   125.00

No. 164 exists with both shiny gum and dull gum.
No. 164a exists even though there was no equipment in the
Canal Zone to detect tagging.

Towing
Locomotive,
Ship in Lock,
by Alwyn
Sprague
A84

1978, Oct. 25   Perf.
165 A84   15c **dp grn & bl grn** *(2,921,083)*   .35
 First day cover *(81,405)*
 P# block of 4   2.00

AIR POST STAMPS

Regular Issue of 1928
Surcharged in Dark Blue

15 Type I — Flag of "5" pointing up

   Type II — Flag of "5" curved **15**

1929-31   Flat Plate Printing   Unwmk.   Perf.
C1 A35   15c on 1c **green,** type I, *Apr. 1,*
   1929   8.00   5
 Never hinged   12.00
 First day cover   25
 Block of 4   35.00 25
 P# block of 6   120.00
C2 A35   15c on 1c **yellow green,** type II,
   Mar. 1931   70.00 47.
 Never hinged   115.00
 On cover   175.
 Block of 4   340.00 340.
 P# block of 6   900.00
C3 A36   25c on 2c **carmine** *(223,880)* Jan.
   11, 1929   3.50   2.
 Never hinged   5.25
 First day cover   17.
 Block of 4   15.00 9.
 P# block of 6   115.00

Nos. 114 and 106 Surcharged
in Black

1929, Dec. 31
C4 A44   10c on 50c **lilac** *(116,666)*   8.00   6.5
 Never hinged   11.00
 First day cover   25.0
 Block of 4   35.00 27.5
 P# block of 6   115.00
C5 A36   20c on 2c **carmine** *(638,395)*   5.00   1.7
 Never hinged   7.50
 First day cover   20.0
 Block of 4   20.00 8.0
 P# block of 6   110.00
 a. Dropped "2" in surcharge *(7,000)*   80.00 60.0

**Catalogue values for unused stamps in this
section, from this point to the end, are for Never
Hinged items.**

Gaillard
Cut — AP1

Printed by the U. S. Bureau of Engraving and Printing.
Plates of 200 subjects, issued in panes of 50.

81-49   Unwmk.   Perf. 11

AP1	4c red violet *(525,000) Jan. 3, 1949*	.75 .70
	First day cover	2.00
	P# block of 6	5.25
AP1	5c yellow green *(9,935,500) Nov. 18, 1931*	.60 .45
	green	.60 .45
	First day cover	10.00
	P# block of 6	4.50
AP1	6c yellow brown *(9,399,500) Feb. 15, 1946*	.75 .35
	First day cover	2.00
	P# block of 6	5.25
AP1	10c orange *(5,079,000) Nov. 18, 1931*	1.00 .35
	First day cover	10.00
	P# block of 6	10.00
AP1	15c blue *(11,072,700) Nov. 18, 1931*	1.25 .30
	pale blue	1.25 .30
	First day cover	15.00
	P# block of 6	11.00
AP1	20c red violet *(3,184,100) Nov. 18, 1931*	2.00 .30
	deep violet	2.00 .30
	First day cover	35.00
	P# block of 6	20.00
AP1	30c rose lake *(1,119,500) July 15, 1941*	3.50 1.00
	dull rose	3.50 1.00
	First day cover	22.50
	P# block of 6	32.50
AP1	40c yellow *(795,600) Nov. 18, 1931*	3.50 1.10
	lemon	3.50 1.10
	First day cover	75.00
	P# block of 6	32.50
AP1	$1 black *(372,500) Nov. 18, 1931*	9.00 1.90
	First day cover	150.00
	P# block of 6	85.00
	Nos. C6-C14 (9)	22.35 6.45

Douglas Plane over Sosa Hill — AP2

Planes and Map of Central America AP3

Pan American Clipper and Scene near Fort Amador — AP4

Pan American Clipper at Cristobal Harbor — AP5

Pan American Clipper over Gaillard Cut — AP6

Pan American Clipper Landing — AP7

10th anniversary of Air Mail service and the 25th anniversary of the opening of the Panama Canal.
Withdrawn Feb. 28, 1941, remainders burned Apr. 12, 1941.

Flat Plate Printing

1939, July 15   Unwmk.   Perf. 11

C15 AP2	5c greenish black *(86,576)*	3.75 2.25
	First day cover	5.00
	P# block of 6	42.50
C16 AP3	10c dull violet *(117,644)*	3.25 3.00
	First day cover	5.00
	P# block of 6	50.00
C17 AP4	15c light brown *(883,742)*	4.75 1.00
	First day cover	3.00
	P# block of 6	55.00
C18 AP5	25c blue *(82,126)*	13.00 8.00
	First day cover	17.50
	P# block of 6	250.00
C19 AP6	30c rose carmine *(121,382)*	13.00 7.75
	First day cover	15.00
	P# block of 6	160.00
C20 AP7	$1 green *(40,051)*	35.00 27.50
	First day cover	60.00
	P# block of 6	525.00
	Nos. C15-C20 (6)	72.75 49.50

Globe and Wing — AP8

Flat Plate Printing

1951, July 16   Unwmk.   Perf. 11

C21 AP8	4c lt red violet *(1,315,000)*	.75 .35
	P# block of 6	7.00
a.	Wet printing, red violet	1.25 .40
	1st day card, Balboa Heights	1.50
	P# block of 6	10.00
C22 AP8	6c lt brown *(22,657,625)*	.50 .25
	P# block of 6	5.00
a.	Wet printing, brown	.95 .35
	1st day cover, Balboa Heights	1.00
	P# block of 6	7.50
C23 AP8	10c lt red orange *(1,049,130)*	.90 .35
	P# block of 6	8.00
a.	Wet printing, red orange	2.00 .50
	1st day cover, Balboa Heights	2.00
	P# block of 6	16.00
C24 AP8	21c lt blue *(1,460,000)*	7.50 4.00
	P# block of 6	70.00
a.	Wet printing, blue	15.00 5.00
	1st day cover, Balboa Heights	7.50
	P# block of 6	125.00
C25 AP8	31c cerise *(375,000)*	7.50 3.75
	1st day cover, Balboa Heights	7.50
	P# block of 6	70.00
a.	Horiz. pair, imperf. vert. *(98)*	1,000.
C26 AP8	80c lt gray black *(827,696)*	4.50 1.50
	P# block of 6	35.00
a.	Wet printing, gray black	12.50 1.65
	1st day cover, Balboa Heights	12.50
	1st day cover, Balboa Heights, #C21-C26	20.00
	P# block of 6	100.00
	Nos. C21-C26 (6)	21.65 10.20

See note after No. 114. Total number of first day covers with one or more of Nos. C21-C26, about 12,000.

Flat Plate Printing

1958, Aug. 16   Unwmk.   Perf. 11

C27 AP8	5c yellow green *(899,923)*	1.00 .60
	First day cover *(2,176)*	4.50
	P# block of 4	6.00
C28 AP8	7c olive *(9,381,797)*	1.00 .45
	First day cover *(2,815)*	4.50
	P# block of 4	6.00
C29 AP8	15c brown violet *(359,923)*	3.75 2.75
	First day cover *(2,040)*	6.00
	P# block of 4	30.00
C30 AP8	25c orange yellow *(600,000)*	10.00 2.75
	First day cover *(2,115)*	9.00
	P# block of 4	95.00
C31 AP8	35c dark blue *(283,032)*	6.25 2.75
	First day cover *(1,868)*	11.00
	P# block of 4	40.00
	Nos. C27-C31 (5)	22.00 9.30
	Nos. C21-C31 (11)	43.65 19.50

Emblem of US Army Caribbean School — AP9

US Army Caribbean School for Latin America at Fort Gulick.

Giori Press Printing

1961, Nov. 21   Unwmk.   Perf. 11

C32 AP9	15c red & blue *(560,000)*	1.25 .75
	First day cover *(25,949)*	1.75
	P# block of 4	10.00

Malaria Eradication Emblem and Mosquito AP10

World Health Organization drive to eradicate malaria.

Giori Press Printing

1962, Sept. 24   Unwmk.   Perf. 11

C33 AP10	7c yellow & black *(862,349)*	.45 .40
	First day cover *(44,433)*	1.00
	P# block of 4	2.75

Globe-Wing Type of 1951

Rotary Press Printing

1963, Jan. 7   Perf. 10½x11

C34 AP8	8c carmine *(5,054,727)*	.40 .30
	First day cover *(19,128)*	1.00
	P# block of 4	2.60

Alliance for Progress Emblem AP11

2nd anniv. of the Alliance for Progress, which aims to stimulate economic growth and raise living standards in Latin America.

Giori Press Printing

1963, Aug. 17   Unwmk.   Perf. 11

C35 AP11	15c gray, grn & dk ultra *(405,000)*	1.10 .85
	First day cover *(29,594)*	1.50
	P# block of 4	10.00

Jet over Cristobal AP12

50th anniversary of the opening of the Panama Canal.
Designs: 8c, Gatun Locks. 15c, Madden Dam. 20c, Gaillard Cut. 30c, Miraflores Locks. 80c, Balboa.

Giori Press Printing

1964, Aug. 15   Unwmk.   Perf. 11

C36 AP12	6c green & black *(257,193)*	.45 .35
	1st day cover, Balboa	1.50
	P# block of 4	2.25
C37 AP12	8c rose red & black *(3,924,283)*	.45 .35
	1st day cover, Balboa	1.00
	P# block of 4	2.25
C38 AP12	15c blue & black *(472,666)*	1.00 .75
	1st day cover, Balboa	1.00
	P# block of 4	6.25
C39 AP12	20c rose lilac & black *(399,784)*	1.50 1.00
	1st day cover, Balboa	2.00
	P# block of 4	8.00
C40 AP12	30c reddish brown & black *(204,524)*	2.25 2.25
	1st day cover, Balboa	3.00
	P# block of 4	15.00
C41 AP12	80c olive bister & black *(186,809)*	3.75 3.00

1st day cover, Balboa		4.00	
1st day cover, Balboa, #C36-C41		10.00	
P# block of 4	20.00		
Nos. C36-C41 (6)		9.40	7.70

There were 57,822 first day covers with one or more of Nos. C36-C41.

Canal Zone Seal and Jet Plane — AP13

Giori Press Printing

1965, July 15   **Unwmk.**   *Perf. 11*

C42	AP13	6c **green & black** *(548,250)*		.35	.30
		First day cover, Balboa			2.00
		P# block of 4		1.90	—
C43	AP13	8c **rose red & black** *(8,357,700)*		.30	.20
		First day cover, Balboa			1.00
		P# block of 4		1.75	—
C44	AP13	15c **blue & black** *(2,385,000)*		.50	.20
		First day cover, Balboa			1.00
		P# block of 4		2.50	—
C45	AP13	20c **lilac & black** *(2,290,699)*		.55	.30
		First day cover, Balboa			1.25
		P# block of 4		2.75	—
C46	AP13	30c **redsh brn & blk** *(2,332,255)*		.80	.30
		First day cover, Balboa			1.25
		P# block of 4		4.00	—
C47	AP13	80c **bister & black** *(1,456,596)*		2.00	.75
		First day cover, Balboa			2.50
		First day cover, Balboa, #C42-C47			7.00
		P# block of 4		12.50	—
		Nos. C42-C47 (6)		4.50	2.05

There were 35,389 first day covers with one or more of Nos. C42-C47.

1968-76

C48	AP13	10c **dull orange & black** *(10,055,000)* Mar. 15, 1968		.25	.20
		First day cover, Balboa *(7,779)*			1.00
		P# block of 4		1.25	—
a.		Booklet pane of 4 *(713,390)* Feb. 18, 1970		4.25	—
		First day cover, Balboa *(5,054)*			5.00
C49	AP13	11c **olive & black** *(3,335,000)* Sept. 24, 1971		.25	.20
		First day cover, Balboa *(10,916)*			1.00
		P# block of 4		1.25	—
a.		Booklet pane of 4 *(1,277,760)* Sept. 24, 1971		3.50	—
		First day cover, Balboa *(2,460)*			5.00
C50	AP13	13c **emerald & black** *(1,865,000)* Feb. 11, 1974		.80	.25
		First day cover, Balboa *(7,646)*			1.00
		P# block of 4		4.75	—
a.		Booklet pane of 4 *(619,200)* Feb. 11, 1974		6.00	—
		First day cover, Balboa *(3,660)*			5.00
C51	AP13	22c **vio & blk** *(363,720)* May 10, 1976		.75	2.00
		First day cover, Balboa			2.50
		P# block of 4		4.00	—
C52	AP13	25c **pale yellow green & black** *(1,640,441)* Mar. 15, 1968		.60	.70
		First day cover, Balboa			1.00
		P# block of 4		2.75	—
C53	AP13	35c **salmon & black** *(573,822)* May 10, 1976		.90	2.00
		First day cover, Balboa			2.50
		P# block of 4		4.75	—
		Nos. C48-C53 (6)		3.55	5.35

There were 5,047 first day covers with one or more of Nos. C51, C53.

AIR POST OFFICIAL STAMPS

Beginning in March 1915, stamps for use on official mail were identified by a large "P" perforated through each stamp. These were replaced by overprinted issues in 1941. The use of official stamps was discontinued December 31, 1951. During their currency, they were not for sale in mint condition and were sold to the public only when canceled with a parcel post rotary canceler reading "Balboa Heights, Canal Zone" between two wavy lines.

After having been withdrawn from use, mint stamps (except Nos. CO8-CO12 and O3, O8) were made available to the public at face value for three months beginning Jan. 2, 1952. **Values for used examples of**

Nos. CO1-CO7, CO14, O1-O2, O4-O9, are for canceled-to-order specimens with original gum, postally used copies being worth more. Sheet margins were removed to facilitate overprinting and plate numbers are, therefore, unknown.

Air Post Stamps of 1931-41 Overprinted in Black

Two types of overprint.

Type I — "PANAMA CANAL" 19-20mm long

1941-42   **Unwmk.**   *Perf. 11*

CO1	AP1	5c **yellow green** *(42,754)* Mar. 31, 1941		5.50	1.50
		green		5.50	1.50
		On cover			50.00
		Block of 4		25.00	6.00
CO2	AP1	10c **orange** *(49,723)* Mar. 31, 1941		8.50	2.00
		On cover			25.00
		Block of 4		37.50	9.00
CO3	AP1	15c **blue** *(56,898)* Mar. 31, 1941		11.00	2.00
		On cover			25.00
		Block of 4		47.50	17.00
CO4	AP1	20c **red violet** *(22,107)* Mar. 31, 1941		12.50	4.00
		deep violet		12.50	4.00
		On cover			110.00
		Block of 4		60.00	22.50
CO5	AP1	30c **rose lake** *(22,100)* June, 4, 1942		17.50	5.00
		dull rose		17.50	4.50
		On cover			40.00
		Block of 4		80.00	22.50
CO6	AP1	40c **yellow** *(22,875)* Mar. 31, 1941		17.50	7.50
		lemon yellow		17.50	7.50
		On cover			75.00
		Block of 4		80.00	37.50
CO7	AP1	$1 **black** *(29,525)* Mar. 31, 1941		20.00	10.00
		On cover			150.00
		Block of 4		90.00	45.00
		Nos. CO1-CO7 (7)		92.50	32.00

Overprint varieties occur on Nos. CO1-CO7 and CO14: "O" of "OFFICIAL" over "N" of "PANAMA" (entire third row). "O" of "OFFICIAL" broken at top (position 31). "O" of "OFFICIAL" over second "A" of "PANAMA" (position 45). First "F" of "OFFICIAL" over second "A" of "PANAMA" (position 50).

1941, Sept. 22

Type II — "PANAMA CANAL" 17mm long

CO8	AP1	5c **yellow green** *(2,000)*		—	160.00
		On cover			500.00
		Block of 4			925.00
CO9	AP1	10c **orange** *(2,000)*		—	275.00
		On cover			400.00
		Block of 4			1,650.
CO10	AP1	20c **red violet** *(2,000)*		—	175.00
		On cover			
		Block of 4			1,050.
CO11	AP1	30c **rose lake** *(5,000)*		1,250.	65.00
		On cover			125.00
		Block of 4			325.00
CO12	AP1	40c **yellow** *(2,000)*		—	180.00
		On cover			500.00
		Block of 4			1,100.
		Nos. CO8-CO12 (5)			855.00

1947, Nov.

Type I — "PANAMA CANAL" 19-20mm long

CO14	AP1	6c **yellow brown** *(33,450)*		12.50	5.00
		On cover			50.00
		Block of 4		57.50	25.00
a.		Inverted overprint *(50)*			2,750.

POSTAGE DUE STAMPS

Prior to 1914, many of the postal issues were handstamped "Postage Due" and used as postage due stamps.

Postage Due Stamps of the United States Nos. J45a, J46a, and J49a Overprinted in Black

1914, Mar.   Wmk. 190   Perf. 12

J1	D2	1c **rose carmine** *(23,533)*		85.	15.
		On cover			275.
		Block of 4 (2mm spacing)		425.	70.
		Block of 4 (3mm spacing)		450.	80.

J2	D2	2c **rose carmine** *(32,312)*		250.	4
		P# block of 6, impt. & star	1,000.		
		On cover			1,250.
		Block of 4			1,250.
		P# block of 6		2,000.	
J3	D2	10c **rose carmine** *(92,493)*		1,000.	
		Block of 4 (2mm spacing)		4,250.	
		Block of 4 (3mm spacing)		4,250.	
		P# block of 6, impt. & star	8,500.		

Many examples of Nos. J1-J3 show one or more letters of overprint out of alignment, principally the "E."

San Geronimo Castle Gate, Portobelo (See footnote) — D1

Statue of Columbus — D2   Pedro J. Sosa — D3

1915, Mar.   Unwmk.   Perf.
Blue Overprint, Type II, on Postage Due Stamp of Panama

J4	D1	1c **olive brown** *(50,000)*		12.50	5
		On cover			150
		Block of 4		55.00	22
J5	D2	2c **olive brown** *(50,000)*		225.00	17
		On cover			400
		Block of 4		975.00	90
J6	D3	10c **olive brown** *(200,000)*		50.00	10
		On cover			175
		Block of 4		225.00	45

Type D1 was intended to show a gate of San Lorenzo Cas Chagres, and is so labeled. By error the stamp actually sho the main gate of San Geronimo Castle, Portobelo.

Surcharged in Red

CANAL 2

1915, Nov.   Unwmk.   Perf.

J7	D1	1c on 1c **olive brown** *(60,614)*		110.00	15.
		On cover			160.
		Block of 4		500.00	70.
J8	D2	2c on 2c **olive brown**		25.00	7.
		On cover			200.
		Block of 4		110.00	35.
J9	D3	10c on 10c **olive brown** *(175,548)*		22.50	5.
		On cover			200.
		Block of 4		100.00	25.

One of the printings of No. J9 shows wider spacing betwee "1" and "0." Both spacings occur on the same sheet.

D4   Capitol, Panama — D5

1919, Dec.
Surcharged in Carmine at Mount Hope

J10	D4	2c on 2c **olive brown**		30.00	12.5
		On cover			110.
		Block of 4		130.00	55.0
J11	D5	4c on 4c **olive brown** *(35,695)*		35.00	15.0
		On cover			190.
		Block of 4		160.00	75.0
a.		"ZONE" omitted		8,250.	
b.		"4" omitted		8,250.	

e Overprint, Type V, on Postage Due Stamp of
Panama

D1   1c   **dark olive brown**   —   10.00
"CANAL ZONE" reading down   200.00

nited States Postage Due
tamps Nos. J61, J62b and
J65b Overprinted

Type A
Letters "A" with Flat Tops

4, July 1   **Perf. 11**
D2   1c   **carmine rose** (10,000)   100.00   27.50
     On cover   100.00
     Block of 4   450.00   125.00
     P# block of 6   1,150.   —
D2   2c   **deep claret** (25,000)   55.00   10.00
     On cover   95.00
     Block of 4   275.00   45.00
     P# block of 6   725.00   —
D2   10c **deep claret** (30,000)   225.00   50.00
     On cover   190.00
     Block of 4 (2mm spacing)   1,150.00   210.00
     Block of 4 (3mm spacing)   1,150.00   210.00
     Margin block of 6, imprint, star
       and P#   3,250.   —

alues for Nos. J12-J29 on cover are for philatelically con-
ed items. Commercial usages on cover are much more
able.

United States Nos. 552, 554 and 562
Overprinted Type A and Additionally
Overprinted at Mount Hope in Red or Blue

25, Feb.   **Perf. 11**
5   A155 1c **deep green** (R) (15,000) 90.00   13.00
     On cover   95.00
     Block of 4   400.00   55.00
     P# block of 6   900.00   —
6   A157 2c **carmine** (Bl) (21,335)   22.50   7.00
     On cover   67.50
     Block of 4   100.00   30.00
     P# block of 6   225.00   —
7   A165 10c **orange** (R) (39,819)   50.00   11.00
     On cover   90.00
     Block of 4   250.00   47.50
     P# block of 6   500.00   —
.   "POSTAGE DUE" double   800.00
.   "E" of "POSTAGE" omitted   750.00
.   As "b," "POSTAGE DUE" double   3,250.00

Overprinted Type B
Letters "A" with Sharp Pointed Tops
On U.S. Postage Due Stamps Nos. J61, J62, J65,
J65a

25, June 24
8   D2   1c **carmine rose** (80,000)   8.00   3.00
     On cover   50.00
     Block of 4   35.00   15.00
     P# block of 6   90.00   —
a.   "ZONE ZONE" (LR18)   1,750.
9   D2   2c **carmine rose** (146,430)   15.00   4.00
     On cover   47.50
     Block of 4   65.00   17.50
     P# block of 6   160.00   —
a.   "ZONE ZONE" (LR18)   1,750.
0   D2   10c **carmine rose** (153,980)   150.00   20.00
     On cover   300.00
     Block of 4, 2mm spacing   650.00   85.00
     Block of 4, 3mm spacing   675.00   90.00
     P# block of 6, Impt. & Star   1,250.
a.   Vert. pair, one without ovpt. (10) 3,500.
     P# block of 6, Impt. & Star   18,000.
b.   10c **rose red**   250.00   150.00
     On cover   —
c.   As "b," double overprint   450.00   —

Nos. J18-J20 exist with wrong font "CANAL" (UL51) and
ONE" (UL82).

Regular Issue
of 1928-29
Surcharged

1929-30
J21 A37   1c on 5c **blue** (35,990) Mar. 20,
                1930   4.50   1.75
     Never hinged   9.00
     On cover   37.50
     P# block of 6   45.00   —
a.   "POSTAGE DUE" omitted (5)   5,500.
J22 A37   2c on 5c **blue** (40,207) Oct. 18,
                1930   7.50   2.50
     Never hinged   15.00
     On cover   32.50
     P# block of 6   75.00   —
J23 A37   5c on 5c **blue** (35,464) Dec. 1, 1930 7.50   2.75
     Never hinged   15.00
     On cover   32.50
     P# block of 6   75.00   —
J24 A37   10c on 5c **blue** (90,504) Dec. 16,
                1929   7.50   2.75
     Never hinged   15.00
     On cover   32.50
     P# block of 6   75.00   —

On No. J23 the three short horizontal bars in the lower corners of the surcharge are omitted.

Canal Zone Seal — D6

Printed by the U.S. Bureau of Engraving and
Printing.
Plates of 400 subjects, issued in panes of 100.

1932-41   **Flat Plate Printing**
J25 D6   1c **claret** (378,300) Jan. 2, 1932   .20   .20
     Never hinged   .25
     On cover   30.00
     P# block of 6   2.00   —
a.   Dry printing, red violet   .25   .20
     Never hinged   .30
     On cover   32.50
     P# block of 6   3.00   —
J26 D6   2c **claret** (413,800) Jan. 2, 1932   .20   .20
     Never hinged   .25
     On cover   22.50
     P# block of 6   3.00   —
J27 D6   5c **claret** Jan. 2, 1932   .35   .20
     Never hinged   .40
     On cover   25.00
     P# block of 6   3.50   —
a.   Dry printing, red violet   1.00   .30
     Never hinged   1.30
     On cover   22.50
     P# block of 6   10.00   —
J28 D6   10c **claret** (400,600) Jan. 2, 1932 1.40   1.50
     Never hinged   2.00
     On cover   32.50
     P# block of 6   15.00   —
J29 D6   15c **claret** Apr. 21, 1941   1.10   1.00
     Never hinged   1.50
     On cover   37.50
     P# block of 6   12.00   —
     Nos. J25-J29 (5)   3.25   3.10

See note after No. 114.

OFFICIAL STAMPS

See note at beginning of Air Post Official Stamps

Regular Issues of 1928-34 Overprinted in Black by
the Panama Canal Press, Mount Hope, C.Z.

Type 1

OFFICIAL
PANAMA CANAL
Type 2

Type 1 — "PANAMA" 10mm long
Type 1a — "PANAMA" 9mm long

1941, Mar. 31   **Unwmk.**   **Perf. 11**
O1   A35   1c **yellow green**, type 1 (87,198)   2.25   .40
     Never hinged   3.00
     On cover   70.00
O2   A45   3c **deep violet**, type 1 (34,958)   4.00   .75
     Never hinged   5.25
     On cover   90.00
O3   A37   5c **blue**, type 2 (19,105)   1,000. 32.50
     On cover   110.00
O4   A38   10c **orange**, type 1 (18,776) 7.50   1.90
     Never hinged   10.00
     On cover   200.00
O5   A41   15c **gray black**, type 1 (16,888)   13.00   2.25
     Never hinged   17.50
     gray   2.25
     On cover   140.00
O6   A42   20c **olive brown**, type 1 (20,264)   15.00   2.75
     Never hinged   22.50
     On cover   100.00
O7   A44   50c **lilac**, type 1 (19,175) 37.50   5.50
     Never hinged   52.50
     rose lilac   5.50
O8   A44   50c **rose lilac**, type 1a (1000)   650.00

No. O3 exists with "O" directly over "N" of "PANAMA."

No. 139 Overprinted in Black

1947, Feb.
O9   A65   5c **deep blue**, type 1 (21,639)   9.00   3.50
     Never hinged   13.50
     On cover   75.00

POST OFFICE SEALS

POS1

Issued in sheets of 8 without gum, imperforate
margins.

1907   **Typo.**   **Unwmk.**   **Perf. 11½**
OX1 POS1   **blue**   40.00
     Block of 4   175.00
a.   Wmkd. seal of U.S. in sheet   55.00   —

No. OX1 clichés are spaced 3½mm apart.

1910
OX2 POS1   **ultramarine**   70.00
     Block of 4, cliches ½mm
       apart   325.00
     Block of 4, cliches 1½mm
       apart horiz., 4mm vert.   800.00
a.   Wmkd. "Rolleston Mills" in sheet   90.00   —
b.   Wmkd. U.S. Seal in sheet   225.00   —
     Block of 4, cliches 1½mm apart
       horiz., 4mm vert.   1,400.

POS2

Printed by the Panama Canal Press, Mount Hope,
C.Z.

Issued in sheets of 25, without gum, imperforate
margins.

*Rouletted 6 horizontally in color of seal, vertically
without color*

1917, Sept. 22
OX3 POS2   **dark blue**   4.00   —
     Block of 4   17.50
a.   Wmkd. double lined letters in sheet
       ("Sylvania")   35.00

1946   *Rouletted 6, without color*
Issued in sheets of 20, without gum, imperforate margins.
OX4 POS2   **slate blue**   9.00   —
     Block of 4   40.00

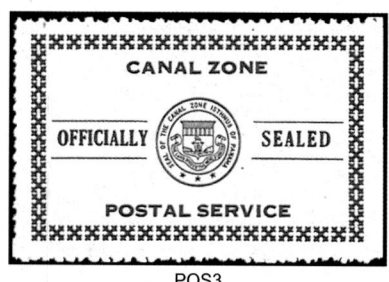

POS3

Typographed by the Panama Canal Press
Issued in sheets of 32, without gum, imperforate
margins
except at top of sheet.
Size: 46x27mm
Seal Diameter: 13mm

1954, Mar. 8	Unwmk.	Perf. 12½
OX5 POS3	**black** (16,000)	5.00 —
a.	Wmkd. Seal of U. S. in sheet	20.00 —

Seal Diameter: 11½mm

1961, May 16		Perf. 12½
OX6 POS3	**black** (48,000)	3.00 —
b.	Wmkd. Seal of U.S. in sheet, perf. 12½	6.00
c.	Double impression	110.00
d.	As "b," double impression	125.00

1974, July 1		Rouletted 5
OX7 POS3	**black**	3.00 —

ENVELOPES

Values for cut squares are for copies with fine margins on all sides. Values for unused entires are for
those without printed or manuscript address. A "full
corner" includes back and side flaps and commands a
premium.

Vasco Núñez de
Balboa — U1

Fernandez de
Córdoba — U2

Envelopes of Panama Lithographed and
Overprinted by American Bank Note Co.

1916, Apr. 24

On White Paper

U1	U1	1c **green & black**	15.00	10.00
		Entire	95.00	35.00
a.		Head and overprint only	—	—
		Entire	2,000.	2,000.
b.		Frame only	—	—
		Entire	1,500.	2,500.
U2	U2	2c **carmine & black**	12.50	5.00
		Entire	90.00	25.00
a.		2c **red & black**	12.50	5.00
		Entire	85.00	45.00
b.		Head and overprint only	—	—
		Entire	1,500.	2,000.
c.		Frame only (red)	—	—
		Entire	1,000.	2,000.
d.		Frame double (carmine)	—	—
		Entire	2,500.	2,250.

José Vallarino — U3

"The Land
Gate" — U4

1921, Nov. 13

On White Paper

U3	U3	1c **green**	140.00	100.00
		Entire	700.00	375.00
U4	U4	2c **red**	35.00	20.00
		Entire	275.00	125.00

Arms of Panama — U5

Typographed and embossed by American Bank
Note Co. with "CANAL ZONE" in color of stamp.

1923, Dec. 15

On White Paper

U5	U5	2c **carmine**	55.00	32.50
		Entire	200.00	125.00

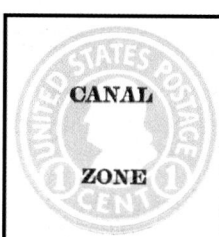

U.S. Nos. U420 and
U429 Overprinted in
Black by Bureau of
Engraving and Printing,
Washington, D.C.

1924, July 1

U6	U92	1c **green** (50,000)	5.00	3.00
		Entire	30.00	19.00
		Entire, 1st day cancel		125.00
U7	U93	2c **carmine** (100,000)	5.00	3.00
		Entire	30.00	19.00
		Entire, 1st day cancel		125.00

Seal of Canal Zone — U6

Printed by the Panama Canal Press, Mount Hope,
C.Z.

1924, Oct.

On White Paper

U8	U6	1c **green** (205,000)	2.00	1.00
		Entire	24.00	15.00
U9	U6	2c **carmine** (1,997,658)	.75	.40
		Entire	27.50	15.00

Gorgas — U7

Goethals — U8

Typographed and Embossed by International
Envelope Corp., Dayton, O.

1932, Apr. 8

U10	U7	1c **green** (1,300,000)	.20	.20
		Entire	3.00	1.10
		Entire, 1st day cancel		35.00
U11	U8	2c **carmine** (400,250)	.25	.20
		Entire	3.50	1.75
		Entire, 1st day cancel		35.00

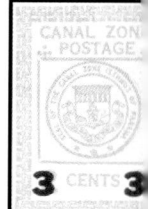

No. U9 Surcharged in Violet by
Panama Canal Press, Mount
Hope, C.Z. Numerals 3mm
high

1932, July 20

U12	U6	3c on 2c **carmine** (20,000)	17.50	
		Entire	225.00	12

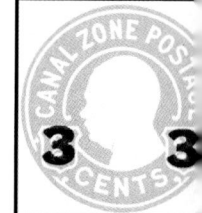

No. U11 Surcharged in
Violet, Numerals 5mm
high

1932, July 20

U13	U8	3c on 2c **carmine** (320,000)	2.00	
		Entire	25.00	1
		Entire, 1st day cancel		7

1934, Jan. 17

Numerals with Serifs

U14	U6	3c on 2c **carmine** (Numerals 4mm high) (8,000)	115.00	6
		Entire	450.00	52
U15	U8	3c on 2c **carmine** (Numerals 5mm high) (23,000)	25.00	1
		Entire	250.00	15

Typographed and Embossed by International
Envelope Corp., Dayton, O.

1934, June 18

U16	U8	3c **purple** (2,450,000)	.20	
		Entire	1.20	

1958, Nov. 1

U17	U8	4c **blue** (596,725)	.20	
		Entire	1.25	1
		Entire, 1st day cancel, Cristobal		2

Surcharged at Left of Stamp in Ultra. as No. UX1

1969, Apr. 28

U18	U8	4c +1c **blue** (93,850)	.20	
		Entire	1.25	1
		Entire, 1st day cancel		1
U19	U8	4c +2c **blue** (23,125)	.50	
		Entire	2.50	4
		Entire, 1st day cancel		1

Ship Passing
through Gaillard
Cut — U9

Typographed and Embossed by United States
Envelope Co., Williamsburg, Pa.

1971, Nov. 17

U20	U9	8c **emerald** (121,500)	.25	
		Entire	.75	
		Entire, 1st day cancel, Balboa (9,650)		1

Surcharged at Left of Stamp in Emerald as #UX1.

1974, Mar. 2

U21	U9	8c +2c **emerald**	.30	
		Entire	1.00	2.
		Entire, 1st day cancel		1.

1976, Feb. 23

U22	U9	13c **violet** (638,350)	.35	
		Entire	.85	
		Entire, 1st day cancel, Balboa (9,181)		1.

Surcharged at Left of Stamp in Violet as No.
UX13

1978, July 5

U23	U9	13c +2c **violet** (245,041)	.35	
		Entire	.85	2.
		Entire, 1st day cancel		1.

AIR POST ENVELOPES

. U9 Overprinted with Horizontal Blue and Red
rs Across Entire Face. Overprinted by Panama
al Press, Mount Hope. Boxed inscription in lower
left with nine lines of instructions. Additional
adhesives required for air post rate.

, May 21
U6   2c **red**, entire *(15,000)*   135.00   65.00
    First day cancel   175.00

U9 with Similar Overprint of Blue and Red Bars,
and "VIA AIR MAIL" in Blue, At Left, no box.

**
U6   2c **red**, entire *(60,200)*   65.00   27.50
.   Inscription centered *(10,000)* Jan. 11   325.00   190.00
    Earliest known use of No. UC2 is Feb. 6.

DC-4
Skymaster
UC1

Typographed and Embossed by International
Envelope Corp., Dayton, O.

9, Jan. 3
 UC1   6c **blue** *(4,400,000)*   .25   .25
    Entire   4.00   3.00
    Entire, 1st day cancel   2.00

8, Nov. 1
 UC1   7c **carmine** *(1,000,000)*   .25   .20
    Entire   4.00   3.50
    Entire, 1st day cancel   1.50

o. U16 Surcharged at
Left of Stamp and
printed "VIA AIR MAIL"
in Dark Blue

urcharged by Panama Canal Press, Mount Hope,
C.Z.

63, June 22
 U8   3c + 5c **purple** *(105,000)*   1.00   1.00
    Entire   6.00   8.00
    Entire, 1st day cancel   5.00
a.   Double surcharge   1,250.

Jet Liner and
Tail Assembly
UC2

Typographed and Embossed by International
Envelope Corp., Dayton, O.

64, Jan. 6
6 UC2   8c **deep carmine** *(600,000)*   .35   .35
    Entire   2.25   2.50
    Entire, 1st day cancel, Bal-
    boa *(3,855)*   2.25

No. U17 Surcharged at Left of Stamp as No. UC5
and Imprinted "VIA AIR MAIL" in Vermilion
Surcharged by Canal Zone Press, La Boca, C.Z.

65, Oct. 15
C7 U8   4c + 4c **blue** *(100,000)*   .50   .40
    Entire   4.50   7.50
    Entire, 1st day cancel   5.00

Jet Liner and Tail
Assembly — UC3

Typographed and Embossed by United States
Envelope Co., Williamsburg, Pa.

1966, Feb.
UC8   UC3   8c **carmine** *(224,000)*   .50   .45
    Entire   5.00   5.00
    Earliest known use: Feb. 23.

No. UC8 Surcharged at Left of Stamp as No. UX13
in Vermilion
Surcharged by Canal Zone Press, La Boca, C.Z.

1968, Jan. 18
UC9   UC3   8c + 2c **carmine** *(376,000)*   .40   .35
    Entire   2.75   5.00
    Entire, 1st day cancel   4.50

No. UC7 with Additional Surcharge at Left
of Stamp as No. UX13 and Imprinted
"VIA AIR MAIL" in Vermilion
Surcharged by Canal Zone Press, La Boca, C.Z.

1968, Feb. 12
UC10   U8   4c + 4c + 2c **blue** *(224,150)*   .60   .50
    Entire   2.25   6.00
    Entire, 1st day cancel   5.00

Type of 1966
Typographed and Engraved by United States
Envelope Co., Williamsburg, Pa.

1969, Apr. 1
Luminescent Ink
UC11 UC3 10c **ultramarine** *(448,000)*   .60   .40
    Entire   4.00   5.00
    Entire, 1st day cancel, Bal-
    boa *(9,583)*   2.00

No. U17 Surcharged at Left of Stamp as Nos. UC5
and UX13, and Imprinted "VIA AIR MAIL"
in Vermilion

1971, May 17
UC12   U8   4c + 5c + 2c **blue** *(55,775)*   .75   .50
    Entire   4.00   6.00
    Entire, 1st day cancel   5.00

No. UC11 Surcharged in Ultra. at Left of Stamp as
No. UX13

1971, May 17
Luminescent Ink
UC13 UC3 10c + 1c **ultramarine** *(152,000)*   .45   .40
    Entire   4.00   7.00
    Entire, 1st day cancel   3.50

Type of 1966
Typographed and Engraved by United States
Envelope Co., Williamsburg, Pa.

1971, Nov. 17
UC14 UC3 11c **rose red** *(258,000)*   .30   .20
    Entire   1.10   1.25
    Entire, 1st day cancel, Bal-
    boa *(3,451)*   1.50
a.   11c **carmine**, stamp tagged,
    (395,000)   .30   .20
    Entire   1.10   1.25
    Entire, 1st day cancel, Bal-
    boa *(5,971)*   1.50

    The red diamonds around the envelope edges are lumines-
cent on both Nos. UC14 and UC14a. No. UC14 is size 10, No.
UC14a size 6¾.

Surcharged at Left of Stamp in Rose Red as No.
UX13

1974, Mar. 2
UC15 UC3 11c + 2c **carmine**, tagged
    (305,000)   .35   .30
    Entire   1.50   3.00
    Entire, 1st day cancel   1.25
a.   11c + 2c **rose red**, untagged,
    (87,000)   .35   .25
    Entire   1.75   2.00

No. U21 with Additional Surcharge in Vermilion
at Left of Stamp as No. UX13 and Imprinted
"VIA AIR MAIL" in Vermilion

1975, May 3
UC16   U9   8c + 2c + 3c **emerald** *(75,000)*   .50   .30
    Entire   1.25   2.50
    Entire, 1st day cancel   1.50

REGISTRATION ENVELOPES

RE1

Panama Registration Envelope surcharged
by Panama Canal Press, Mount Hope, C.Z.

1918, Oct.   **8mm between CANAL & ZONE**
UF1 RE1 10c on 5c **black & red**, *cream*
    (10,000), entire   1,750.   2,000.
a.   9¼mm between CANAL & ZONE
    (25,000), entire ('19)   1,300.   2,000.

    Stamped envelopes inscribed "Diez Centesimos," surcharged
with numerals "5" and with solid blocks printed over "Canal
Zone," were issued by the Republic of Panama after being
rejected by the Canal Zone. Parts of "Canal Zone" are often
legible under the surcharge blocks. These envelopes exist without surcharge.

POSTAL CARDS

Values are for Entires

Map of Panama — PC1

Panama Card Lithographed by American
Bank Note Co., revalued and surcharged in black
by the Isthmian Canal Commission.

1907, Feb. 9
UX1   PC1   1c on 2c **carmine**, "CANAL"
    15mm *(50,000)*   40.   25.
a.   Double surcharge   1,500. 2,000.
b.   Double surcharge, one reading down   2,750.
c.   Triple surcharge, one reading down   3,300.
d.   "CANAL" 13mm *(10,000)*   250.   200.
e.   As "d," double surcharge   2,400.

Balboa — PC2

Panama card lithographed by Hamilton Bank
Note Co. Overprinted in black by Isthmian
Canal Commission.
At least six types of overprint, reading down.

1908, Mar. 3
UX2   PC2   1c **green & black**, "CANAL"
    13mm *(295,000)*   190.   80.
a.   Double overprint   2,000. 2,000.
b.   Triple overprint   1,750.   —
c.   Period after "ZONE" *(40,000)*   200. 125.
d.   "CANAL" 15mm *(30,000)*   200.   125.
e.   "ZONE CANAL", reading up   4,000.

Balboa
PC3   PC4
Lithographed by Hamilton Bank Note Co.
Overprinted in Black by Panama Canal Press, Mount
Hope, C.Z.

1910, Nov. 10
UX3 PC3   1c **green & black** *(40,000)*   190.   70.
  a.   Double overprint   4,250.
  This card, with overprint reading up, is actually the fourth of
seven settings of UX2.

Lithographed and Overprinted by American Bank
Note Co.

1913, Mar. 27
UX4 PC4   1c **green & black** *(634,000)*   160.   60.

Design of Canal Zone Envelopes
Overprinted in black by the American Bank Note Co.

1921, Oct.
UX5 U3   1c **green**   1,100. 450.

Typographed and embossed by American Bank
Note Co. with "CANAL ZONE" in color of stamp.

1924, Jan.
UX6 U5   1c **green**   1,050. *1,100.*

U.S. No. UX27 Overprinted
by U.S. Gov't. Printing
Office at Washington, D.C.

1924, July 1
UX7 PC17 1c **green,** *buff (Jefferson)*
              (50,000)   85.   35.

Design of Canal Zone Envelope
Printed by Panama Canal Press.

1925, Jan.
UX8 U6   1c **green,** *buff (25,000)*   80.   35.
  a.   Background only   1,800.

U.S. No. UX27 Overprinted

1925, May
UX9 PC17 1c **green,** *buff (Jefferson)*
              (850,000)   8.50   5.00

U.S. No. UX27 Overprinted

1935, Oct.
UX10 PC17 1c **green,** *buff (Jefferson)*
              (2,900,000)   1.80 1.80
  a.   Double overprint   1,900.

**Used values are for contemporaneous usage
without additional postage applied.**

Same on U.S. No. UX38
1952, May 1
UX11 PC22 2c **carmine rose,** *buff (Franklin)*
              (800,000)   2.00 2.00
              1st day cancel, Balboa Heights   3.50

                                        Ship in
                                        Lock   PC5

Printed by Bureau of Engraving & Printing,
Washington, D.C.

1958, Nov. 1
UX12 PC5   3c **dark blue,** *buff (335,116)*   1.90 3.00
              First day cancel, Cristobal   1.25

No. UX12 Surcharged at Left of
Stamp in Green by Panama Canal
Press, Mount Hope, C.Z.

1963, July 27
UX13 PC5   3c + 1c **dark blue,** *buff (78,000)* 4.00 6.00
              First day cancel   3.50

Ship Passing through
Panama Canal — PC6

Printed by Panama Canal Press, Mount Hope, C.Z.

1964, Dec. 1
UX14 PC6   4c **violet blue,** *buff (74,200)*   3.75 7.50
              1st day cancel, Cristobal
              (19,260)   3.50

                                        Ship in Lock
                                        (Towing
                                        locomotive at
                                        right
                                        redrawn) — PC7

Printed by Bureau of Engraving & Printing,
Washington, D.C.

1965, Aug. 12
UX15 PC7   4c **emerald** *(95,500)*   1.10 2.00
              1st day cancel, Cristobal
              (20,366)   1.00

No. UX15 Surcharged at Left of Stamp in Green
as No. UX13 by Panama Canal Press, La Boca, C.Z.
1968, Feb. 12
UX16 PC7   4c + 1c **emerald** *(94,775)*   1.10 4.00
              First day cancel   1.00

Ship-in-Lock Type of 1965
1969, Apr. 1
UX17 PC7   5c **light ultramarine** *(63,000)*   1.00 2.50
              1st day cancel, Balboa *(11,835)*   1.00

No. UX17 Surcharged at Left of Stamp in Light
Ultramarine as No. UX13
1971, May 24
UX18 PC7   5c + 1c **light ultramarine** *(100,500)* .90 3.50
              First day cancel   1.00

Ship-in-Lock Type of 1965
Printed by Bureau of Engraving & Printing,
Washington, D.C.
1974, Feb. 11
UX19 PC7   8c **brown** *(90,895)*   .90 2.00
              1st day cancel, Balboa *(10,375)*   1.00

No. UX19 Surcharged at Left of Stamp in Brown
No. UX13
1976, June 1
UX20 PC7   8c + 1c **brown** *(60,249)*   .65
              First day cancel

No. UX19 Surcharged at Left of Stamp in Brown
No. UX13
1978, July 5
UX21 PC7   8c + 2c **brown** *(74,847)*   .85
              First day cancel

AIR POST POSTAL CARDS

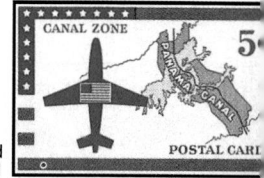

Plane, Flag and
Map — APC1

Printed by Bureau of Engraving & Printing,
Washington, D.C.
1958, Nov. 1
UXC1 APC1   5c **blue & carmine rose**
              (104,957)   3.75
              1st day cancel, Balboa

No. UXC1 Surcharged at Left of Stamp in Green
as No. UX13 by Panama Canal Press,
Mount Hope, C.Z.
1963, July 27
UXC2 APC1   5c + 1c **blue & carmine rose**
              (48,000)   9.50
  a.   Inverted surcharge   1,500.
              First day cancel

No. UX15 Surcharged at Left of Stamp as
No. UX13 and Imprinted "AIR MAIL" in Vermilio
1965, Aug. 18
UXC3 PC7   4c + 2c **emerald** *(41,700)*   4.00   2
              First day cancel

No. UX15 Surcharged at Left of Stamp as No. U
and Imprinted "AIR MAIL" in Vermilion
by Canal Zone Press, La Boca, C.Z.
1968, Feb. 12
UXC4 PC7   4c + 4c **emerald** *(60,100)*   2.75   1
              First day cancel

No. UX17 Surcharged at Left of Stamp as No. U
and Imprinted "AIR MAIL" in Vermilion
1971, May 24
UXC5 PC7   5c + 4c **light ultramarine**
              (68,000)   1.00   1
              First day cancel

PROOFS

1928-40

Column (1) — Large Die
Column (2) — Small Die

106TC	2c **black**		1,300.	
113P	30c **brown black**			9

1934
117P	3c **deep violet** *(8)*		475.	

1939
120P	1c **yellow green**		1,300.	8
121P	2c **rose carmine**			8
122P	3c **purple**		1,300.	8
123P	5c **dark blue**		1,300.	8
124P	6c **red orange**			8
125P	7c **black**			8
126P	8c **green**		1,300.	8
127P	10c **ultramarine**		1,300.	8
128P	11c **blue green**		1,300.	8
129P	12c **brown carmine**		1,300.	8
130P	14c **dark violet**			8
131P	15c **olive green**			8
132P	18c **rose pink**			8
133P	20c **brown**		1,300.	8
134P	25c **orange**		1,300.	8
135P	50c **violet brown**		1,300.	8

1946-48
136P	½c **bright red**		1,300.	
137P	1½c **chocolate**		1,300.	
139P	5c **deep blue**		1,300.	
140P	25c **yellow green**		1,300.	
141P	10c **black**		825.	

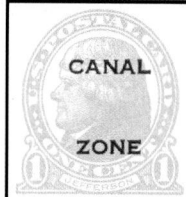

3c	blue	1,150.
6c	violet	1,150.
12c	bright blue green	1,150.
18c	deep red lilac	1,150.
10c	carmine	1,500.
3c	violet	1,500.

Air Post

1931-49

C6P	4c	red violet	1,600.
C7P	5c	light green	1,600.
C8P	6c	yellow brown	1,600.
C13TC	40c	orange	1,600.

1939

C15P	5c	greenish black		925.
C15TC	5c	scarlet	1,300.	
C16P	10c	dull violet	1,300.	925.

C17P	15c	light brown	1,300.	925.
C18P	25c	blue		925.
C19P	30c	rose carmine	1,300.	925.
C20P	$1	green	1,300.	925.

1951

C21P	4c	red violet	1,300.

The Small Die proofs listed are on soft yellowish wove paper. Only No. 117P has more than two copies reported in private collections.

CUBA

After the U.S. battleship "Maine" was destroyed in Havana harbor with a loss of 266 lives in February, 1898, the United States demanded the withdrawal of Spanish troops from Cuba. The Spanish-American War followed. With the peace treaty of Dec. 10, 1898, Spain relinquished Cuba to the United States in trust for its inhabitants. On Jan. 1, 1899, Spanish authority was succeeded by U.S. military rule which lasted until May 20, 1902, when Cuba, as a republic, assumed self-government.

The listings in this catalogue cover the U.S. Administration issue of 1899, the Republic's 1899-1902 issues under U.S. military rule and the Puerto Principe issue of provincial provisionals.

Values for Nos. 176-220 are for stamps in the grade of fine and in sound condition where such exist. Values for Nos. 221-UX2b are for very fine examples.

100 CENTS = 1 DOLLAR

Puerto Principe Issue

In December, 1898, Puerto Principe, a provincial capital now called Camagüey, ran short of 1c, 2c, 3c, 5c and 10c stamps. The Postmaster ordered Cuban stamps to be surcharged on Dec. 19, 1898.

The surcharging was done to horizontal strips of five stamps, vertical pairs and blocks do not exist. Five types are found in each setting, and five printings were made. Counterfeits are plentiful.

First Printing
Black Surcharge, 17½mm high

The surcharge measures 17½mm high and is roughly printed in dull black ink.

HABILITADO HABILITADO HABILITADO

2 **2** **2**
cents. **cents.** **cents.**
Position 1 Position 2 Position 3

HABILITADO HABILITADO

2 **2**
cents. **cents.**
Position 4 Position 5

Position 1	— No serif at right of "t"
Position 2	— Thin numeral except on 1c on 1m No. 176
Position 3	— Broken right foot of "n"
Position 4	— Up-stroke of "t" broken
Position 5	— Broken "DO"

This printing consisted of the following stamps:

178	1c on 1m orange brown, Pos. 1, 2, 3, 4 and 5
180	2c on 2m orange brown, Pos. 1, 3, 4 and 5
181	2c on 2m orange brown, Pos. 2
184	3c on 3m orange brown, Pos. 1, 3, 4 and 5
185	3c on 3m orange brown, Pos. 2
190	5c on 5m orange brown, Pos. 1, 3, 4 and 5
191	5c on 5m orange brown, Pos. 2

Second Printing
Black Surcharge, 17½mm high

This printing was from the same setting as used for the first printing, but the impression is much clearer and the ink quite shiny.

The printing consisted of the following stamps:

189F	3c on 2m orange brown, Pos. 1, 3, 4 and 5
189G	3c on 2m orange brown, Pos. 2
183	5c on 1m orange brown, Pos. 1, 3, 4 and 5
184	5c on 1m orange brown, Pos. 2
185	5c on 2m orange brown, Pos. 1, 3, 4 and 5
186	5c on 3m orange brown, Pos. 1, 3, 4 and 5
187	5c on 3m orange brown, Pos. 2
188	5c on 5m orange brown, Pos. 1, 3, 4 and 5
189	5c on 5m orange brown, Pos. 2
190	5c on ½m blue green, Pos. 1, 3, 4 and 5
191	5c on ½m blue green, Pos. 2

Third Printing
Red Surcharge, 20mm high

The same setting as for the first and second was used for the third printing. The 10c denomination first appeared in this printing and position 2 of that value has numerals same as on positions 1, 3, 4 and 5, while position 4 has broken "1" in "10."

The printing consisted of the following stamps:

196	3c on 1c black violet, Pos. 1, 3, 4 and 5
197	3c on 1c black violet, Pos. 2
198	5c on 1c black violet, Pos. 1, 3, 4 and 5
199	5c on 1c black violet, Pos. 2
200	10c on 1c black violet, Pos. 1, 2, 3 and 5
200a	10c on 1c black violet, Pos. 4

Fourth Printing
Black Surcharge, 19½mm high

The same type as before but spaced between so that the surcharge is 2mm taller. Clear impression, shiny ink.

HABILITADO HABILITADO HABILITADO

1 **1** **1**
cents. **cents.** **cents.**
Position 1 Position 2 Position 3

HABILITADO HABILITADO

1 **1**
cents. **cents.**
Position 4 Position 5

Position 1	— No serif at right of "t"
Position 2	— Broken "1" on No. 177
Position 2	— Thin numerals on 5c stamps
Position 3	— Broken right foot of "n"
Position 4	— Up-stroke of "t" broken
Position 4	— Thin numeral on 3c stamps
Position 5	— Broken "DO"

This printing consisted of the following stamps:

177	1c on 1m orange brn, Pos. 1, 3, 4 and 5
177a	1c on 1m orange brn, Pos. 2
179B	3c on 1m orange brn, Pos. 1, 2, 3 and 5
179D	3c on 1m orange brn, Pos. 4
183B	5c on 1m orange brn, Pos. 1, 3, 4 and 5
189C	5c on 5m orange brn, Pos. 1, 3, 4 and 5
192	5c on ½m blue green, Pos. 1, 3, 4 and 5
193	5c on ½m blue green, Pos. 2

Fifth Printing
Black Surcharge, 19½mm high

HABILITADO HABILITADO HABILITADO

3 **3** **3**
cents. **cents.** **eents.**
Position 1 Position 2 Position 3

HABILITADO HABILITADO

3 **3**
cents. **cents.**
Position 4 Position 5

Position 1	— Nick in bottom of "e"and lower serif of "s"
Position 2	— Normal surcharge
Position 3	— "eents"
Position 4	— Thin numeral
Position 5	— Nick in upper part of right stroke of "n"

This printing consisted of the following stamps:

201	3c on 1m blue green, Pos. 1, 2 and 5
201b	3c on 1m blue green, Pos. 3
202	3c on 1m blue green, Pos. 4
203	3c on 2m blue green, Pos. 1, 2 and 5
203a	3c on 2m blue green, Pos. 3
204	3c on 2m blue green, Pos. 4
205	3c on 3m blue green, Pos. 1, 2 and 5
205b	3c on 3m blue green, Pos. 3
206	3c on 3m blue green, Pos. 4
211	5c on 1m blue green, Pos. 1, 2 and 5
211a	5c on 1m blue green, Pos. 3
212	5c on 1m blue green, Pos. 4
213	5c on 2m blue green, Pos. 1, 2 and 5
213a	5c on 2m blue green, Pos. 3
214	5c on 2m blue green, Pos. 4
215	5c on 3m blue green, Pos. 1, 2 and 5
215a	5c on 3m blue green, Pos. 3
216	5c on 3m blue green, Pos. 4
217	5c on 4m blue green, Pos. 1, 2 and 5
217a	5c on 4m blue green, Pos. 3
218	5c on 4m blue green, Pos. 4
219	5c on 8m blue green, Pos. 1, 2 and 5
219b	5c on 8m blue green, Pos. 3
220	5c on 8m blue green, Pos. 4

Counterfeits exist of all Puerto Principe surcharges. Illustrations have been altered to discourage further counterfeiting.

Regular Issues of Cuba of 1896 and 1898 Surcharged:

HABILITADO HABILITADO

1 **1**
cent. **cents.**
a b

Numeral in ( ) after color indicates printing.

1898-99

Black Surcharge on Nos. 156-158, 160

176	(a)	1 cent on 1m **orange brn** (1)	50.00	30.00
177	(b)	1 cents on 1m **org brn** (4)	45.00	35.00
a.		Broken figure "1"	75.00	65.00
b.		Inverted surcharge		200.00
d.		Same as "a" inverted		250.00

HABILITADO
2
cents.
c

HABILITADO
2
cents.
d

178 (c) 2c on 2m **orange brown** (1) — 24.00 / 18.00
a. Inverted surcharge — 250.00 / 50.00
179 (d) 2c on 2m **orange brown** (1) — 40.00 / 35.00
a. Inverted surcharge — 350.00 / 100.00

HABILITADO
3
cents.
k

HABILITADO
3
cents.
l

179B (k) 3c on 1m **orange brown** (4) — 300. / 175.
c. Double surcharge — 1,500. / 750.
An unused copy is known with "cents" omitted.

179D (l) 3c on 1m **orange brown** (4) — 1,500. / 750.
e. Double surcharge — — / 750.

HABILITADO
3
cents.
e

HABILITADO
3
cents.
f

179F (e) 3c on 2m **orange brown** (2) — 1,500.
Value is for copy with minor faults.

179G (f) 3c on 2m **orange brown** (2) — — / 2,000.
Value is for copy with minor faults.

180 (e) 3c on 3m **orange brown** (1) — 30. / 30.
a. Inverted surcharge — 110.
181 (f) 3c on 3m **orange brown** (1) — 75. / 75.
a. Inverted surcharge — 200.

HABILITADO
5
cents.
g

HABILITADO
5
cents.
h

HABILITADO
5
cents.
i

HABILITADO
5
cents.
j

182 (g) 5c on 1m **orange brown** (2) — 700. / 200.
a. Inverted surcharge — 500.
183 (h) 5c on 1m **orange brown** (2) — 1,300. / 500.
a. Inverted surcharge — 700.
184 (g) 5c on 2m **orange brown** (2) — 750. / 250.
185 (h) 5c on 2m **orange brown** (2) — 1,500. / 500.
186 (g) 5c on 3m **orange brown** (2) — 650. / 175.
a. Inverted surcharge — 1,200. / 700.
187 (h) 5c an 3m **orange brown** (2) — 400.
a. Inverted surcharge — 1,000.
188 (g) 5c on 5m **orange brown** (1) (2) — 80. / 60.
a. Inverted surcharge — 400. / 200.
b. Double surcharge — — / —
189 (h) 5c on 5m **orange brown** (1) (2) — 350. / 250.
a. Inverted surcharge — 400.
b. Double surcharge — — / —
189C (i) 5c on 5m **orange brown** (4) — 7,500.

Values for Nos. 188, 189 are for the first printing.

Black Surcharge on No. P25
190 (g) 5c on ½m **blue green** (2) — 250. / 75.
a. Inverted surcharge — 500. / 150.
b. Pair, one without surcharge — 500.
191 (h) 5c on ½m **blue green** (2) — 300. / 90.
a. Inverted surcharge — 200.
192 (i) 5c on ½m **blue green** (4) — 550. / 200.
a. Double surcharge, one diagonal — 11,500.

Value for No. 190b is for pair with unsurcharged copy at right. One pair with unsurcharged copy at left is known.
No. 192a is unique.

193 (j) 5c on ½m **blue green** (4) — 800. / 300.

Red Surcharge on No. 161
196 (k) 3c on 1c **black violet** (3) — 65. / 35.
a. Inverted surcharge — 325.
197 (l) 3c on 1c **black violet** (3) — 125. / 55.
a. Inverted surcharge — 400.
198 (i) 3c on 1c **black violet** (3) — 25. / 30.
a. Inverted surcharge — 125.
b. Vertical surcharge — 3,500.
c. Double surcharge — 400. / 600.
d. Double inverted surcharge — —
199 (j) 5c on 1c **black violet** (3) — 55. / 55.
a. Inverted surcharge — 250.
b. Vertical surcharge — 2,000.
c. Double surcharge — 1,000. / 600.

Value for No. 198b is for surcharge reading up. One copy is known with surcharge reading down.

HABILITADO
10
cents.
m

200 (m) 10c on 1c **black violet** (3) — 20. / 50.
a. Broken figure "1" — 40. / 100.

Black Surcharge on Nos. P26-P30
201 (k) 3c on 1m **blue green** (5) — 350. / 350.
a. Inverted surcharge — 450.
b. "EENTS" — 550. / 450.
c. As "b," inverted — 850.
202 (l) 3c on 1m **blue green** (5) — 550. / 400.
a. Inverted surcharge — 850.
203 (k) 3c on 2m **blue green** (5) — 850. / 400.
a. Inverted surcharge — 1,250. / 500.
b. "EENTS" — 850.
c. As "a," inverted — 950.
204 (l) 3c on 2m **blue green** (5) — 1,250. / 600.
a. Inverted surcharge — 750.
205 (k) 3c on 3m **blue green** (5) — 900. / 400.
a. Inverted surcharge — 500.
b. "EENTS" — 1,250. / 450.
c. As "b," inverted — 700.
206 (l) 3c on 3m **blue green** (5) — 1,200. / 550.
a. Inverted surcharge — 700.
211 (i) 5c on 1m **blue green** (5) — 1,800.
a. "EENTS" — 2,500.
212 (i) 5c on 1m **blue green** (5) — 2,250.
213 (i) 5c on 2m **blue green** (5) — 1,800.
a. "EENTS" — 1,900.
214 (j) 5c on 2m **blue green** (5) — 1,750.
215 (i) 5c on 3m **blue green** (5) — 550.
a. "EENTS" — 1,000.
216 (j) 5c on 3m **blue green** (5) — — / 1,000.
217 (i) 5c on 4m **blue green** (5) — 2,500. / 900.
a. "EENTS" — 3,000. / 1,500.
b. Inverted surcharge — 2,000.
c. As "a," inverted — 2,000.
218 (j) 5c on 4m **blue green** (5) — 1,500.
a. Inverted surcharge — 2,000.
219 (i) 5c on 8m **blue green** (5) — 2,500. / 1,250.
a. Inverted surcharge — 1,500.
b. "EENTS" — — / 1,800.
c. As "b," inverted — 2,500.
220 (j) 5c on 8m **blue green** (5) — 2,000. / 2,000.
a. Inverted surcharge — 2,500.

Puerto Principe pairs, strips and stamps properly canceled on cover are scarce and command high premiums.
Most copies of all but the most common varieties are faulty or have tropical toning. Values are for sound copies where they exist.

United States Stamps Nos. 279, 267, 267b, 279Bf, 279Bh, 268, 281, 282C and 283 Surcharged in Black

1899   Wmk. 191   Perf. 12
221 A87 1c on 1c **yellow green** — 5.25 / .40
On cover — 15.00
Block of 4 — 27.50 / 4.50
P# strip of 3, Impt. — 57.50
P# block of 6, Impt. — 300.00
222 A88 2c on 2c **reddish carmine,** type III, *Feb.* — 10.00 / .75
On cover — 22.50
Block of 4 — 55.00 / 8.00
P# strip of 3, Impt. — 115.00
P# block of 6, Impt. — 650.00
b. 2c on 2c **vermilion,** type III, *Feb.* — 10.00 / .75
222A A88 2c on 2c **reddish carmine,** type IV, *Feb.* — 6.00 / .40
On cover — 12.50
Block of 4 — 30.00 / 4.50
P# strip of 3, Impt. — 65.00
P# block of 6, Impt. — 425.00
"CUBA" at bottom — 600.00

"CUPA" (broken letter. pos. 99) — 175.00
c. 2c on 2c **vermilion,** type IV, *Feb.* — 6.00
d. As No. 222A, inverted surcharge — 5,500. / 5...
223 A88 2½c on 2c **reddish carmine,** type III, *Jan. 2* — 5.00
On cover
Block of 4 — 27.50
P# strip of 3, Impt. — 90.00
P# block of 6, Impt. — 350.00
b. 2½ on 2c **vermilion,** type III, *Jan. 2* — 5.00
223A A88 2½c on 2c **reddish carmine,** type IV, *Jan. 2* — 3.50
On cover
Block of 4 — 20.00
P# strip of 3, Impt. — 62.50
P# block of 6, Impt. — 250.00
c. 2½c on 2c **vermilion,** type IV, *Jan. 2* — 3.50

All 2½c stamps were sold and used as 2 centavo stamps.

224 A89 3c on 3c **purple** — 14.00
On cover
Block of 4 — 65.00
P# strip of 3, Impt. — 110.00
P# block of 6, Impt. — 675.00
a. Period between "B" and "A" — 37.50

Two types of surcharge
I — "3" directly over "P"
II — "3" to left over "P"

225 A91 5c on 5c **blue** — 14.00
On cover
Block of 4 — 65.00
P# strip of 3, Impt. — 190.00
P# block of 6, Impt. — 800.00
"CUBA" at bottom — —
"CUPA" (broken letter) — 80.00
226 A94 10c on 10c **brown,** type I — 25.00
On cover
Block of 4 — 115.00
P# strip of 3, Impt. — 260.00
P# block of 6, Impt. — 1,000.
"CUBA" at bottom — 400.00
b. "CUBA" omitted — 5,500.
226A A94 10c on 10c **brown,** type II — 6,500.
Block of 4
Nos. 221-226 (8) — 82.75

No. 226A exists only in the special printing.
The No. 225 "CUPA" variety always has a straight edge at right.

Special Printing
In March 1900, one pane of 100 each of Nos. 2... 225, 226A, J1-J4 and two panes of 50 of No. E1, w... specially overprinted for displays at the Paris Exp... tion (1900) and Pan American Exposition (1901). ... 2c pane was light red, type IV. Copies were ha... stamped type E "Specimen" in black ink by H. ... Mandel and mounted by him in separate displays... the two Expositions. Additional copies from each pa... were also handstamped "specimen," but most w... destroyed after the Expositions. Nearly all cop... remaining bear impression of a dealer's handsta... reading "Special Surcharge" in red ink on the ba... Value: Nos. 221-225, J1-J4, each $625; No. ... $1,000.

Issues of the Republic under US Military Rule

Statue of
Columbus — A20

Royal Palms — A...

Allegory,
"Cuba" — A22

Ocean Liner — A2...

Cane Field — A24

Re-engraved

The re-engraved stamps issued by the Republic of Cuba in [19]05-07 may be distinguished from the Issue of 1899 as [follo]ws:

[N]os. 227-231 are watermarked U S-C.
[T]he re-engraved stamps are unwatermarked.

[1]c: The ends of the label inscribed "Centavo" are rounded [inst]ead of square.
[2]c: The foliate ornaments, inside the oval disks bearing the [num]erals of value, have been removed.
[3]c: Two lines forming a right angle have been added in the [low]er corners of the label bearing the word "Cuba."
[1]0c: A small ball has been added to each of the square ends [of t]he label bearing the word "Cuba."

No. 227 — Re-engraved

No. 228 — Re-engraved

No. 230 — Re-engraved

No. 231 — Re-engraved

[P]rinted by the U.S. Bureau of Engraving and Printing

[18]99			Wmk. US-C (191C)	Perf. 12	
[2]27	A20	1c	yellow green	3.50	.20
			On cover		2.00
			Block of 4	15.00	1.00
			P# block of 10, Impt., type VII	225.00	—
[2]28	A21	2c	carmine	3.50	.20
			On cover		2.00
			Block of 4	15.00	1.00
			P# block of 10, Impt., type VII	180.00	—
a.			2c scarlet	3.50	.20
b.			Booklet pane of 6	3,750.	
[2]29	A22	3c	purple	3.50	.20
			On cover		4.00
			Block of 4	15.00	2.50
			P# block of 10, Impt., type VII	275.00	—
[2]30	A23	5c	blue	4.50	.20
			On cover		4.00
			Block of 4	21.00	2.50
			P# block of 10, Impt., type VII	450.00	—
[2]31	A24	10c	brown	11.00	.50
			On cover		6.50
			Block of 4	52.50	5.50
			P# block of 10, Impt., type VII	1,200.	—
			Nos. 227-231 (5)	26.00	1.30

SPECIAL DELIVERY STAMPS

Issued under Administration of the United States

Special
Delivery Stamp
of the United
States No. E5
Surcharged in
Red

1899		Wmk. 191		Perf. 12	
E1	SD3	10c on 10c **blue**		130.	100.
		On cover			450.
		Block of 4		575.	
		Margin block of 4, arrow		650.	
		P# strip of 3, Impt.		1,000.	
		P# block of 6, Impt.		6,000.	
		Five dots in curved frame above messenger's head (Pl. 882)		—	
a.		No period after "CUBA"		575.	400.

Issue of the Republic under US Military Rule

Special
Delivery
Messenger
SD2

Printed by the US Bureau of Engraving and Printing

1899		Wmk. US-C (191C)		
		Inscribed: "Immediata"		
E2	SD2	10c **orange**	50.00	15.00
		On cover		150.00
		Block of 4	250.00	—
		P# strip of 3, Impt., type VII	300.00	
		P# block of 6, Impt., type VII	1,000.	

Re-engraved

In 1902 the Republic of Cuba issued a stamp of design SD2 re-engraved with word correctly spelled "Inmediata." The corrected die was made in 1899 (See No. E3P). It was printed by the U.S. Bureau of Engraving and Printing.

POSTAGE DUE STAMPS

Issued under Administration of the United States
Postage Due Stamps of the United States Nos. J38, J39, J41 and J42 Surcharged in Black Like Regular Issue of Same Date

1899		Wmk. 191		Perf. 12	
J1	D2	1c on 1c **deep claret**		45.00	5.25
		Block of 4		210.00	45.00
		P# block of 6, Impt.		900.00	
J2	D2	2c on 2c **deep claret**		45.00	5.25
		Block of 4		200.00	30.00
		P# block of 6, Impt.		900.00	
a.		Inverted surcharge			4,000.
J3	D2	5c on 5c **deep claret**		45.00	5.25
		Block of 4		220.00	45.00
		P# block of 6, Impt.		900.00	
		"CUPA" (broken letter)		150.00	140.00
J4	D2	10c on 10c **deep claret**		27.50	2.50
		Block of 4		125.00	27.50
		P# block of 6, Impt.		800.00	

The No. J3 "CUPA" variety always has a straight edge at right.

ENVELOPES

Values are for Cut Squares
US Envelopes of 1887-99 Surcharged

a

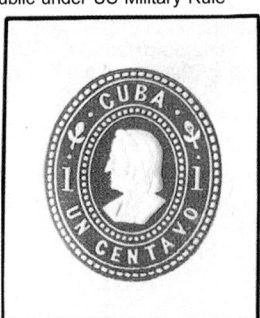

b

1899					
U1	U77 (a)	1c on 1c **green**, *oriental buff* (No. U354)		5.00	3.50
		Entire		12.00	15.00
U2	U77 (a)	1c on 1c **green**, *blue* (No. U355)		3.25	2.50
		Entire		5.00	6.50
a.		Double surcharge, entire		5,250.	
U3	U71 (b)	2c on 2c **green** (No. U311)		1.50	1.10
		Entire		3.00	3.50
a.		Double surcharge, entire		4,500.	6,500.
U4	U71 (b)	2c on 2c **green**, *amber* (No. U312)		2.75	1.65
		Entire		5.25	6.00
a.		Double surcharge, entire		5,250.	
U5	U71 (a)	2c on 2c **green**, *oriental buff* (No. U313)		17.50	8.00
		Entire		47.50	47.50
U6	U79 (a)	2c on 2c **carmine**, *amber* (No. U363)		17.50	17.50
		Entire		47.50	47.50
U7	U79 (a)	2c on 2c **carmine**, *oriental buff* (No. U364)		25.00	25.00
		Entire		100.00	80.00
U8	U79 (a)	2c on 2c **carmine**, *blue* (No. U365)		3.00	2.00
		Entire		7.00	8.00
a.		Double surcharge, entire		6,750.	
		Nos. U1-U8 (8)		75.50	61.25

In addition to the envelopes listed above, several others are known but were not regularly issued. They are:
1c on 1c green
1c on 1c green, *manila*
2c on 2c carmine
4c on 4c brown
5c on 5c blue

Issue of the Republic under US Military Rule

Columbus — E1

Similar envelopes without watermark on white and amber papers, were issued by the Republic after Military Rule ended in 1902.

1899		Wmk. "US POD '99" in Monogram		
U9	E1	1c **green**	.75	.65
		Entire	4.00	4.00
U10	E1	1c **green**, *amber*	1.00	.65
		Entire	4.00	4.00
U11	E1	1c **green**, *buff*	17.50	13.00
		Entire	85.00	42.50
U12	E1	1c **green**, *blue*	25.00	15.00
		Entire	85.00	42.50
U13	E1	2c **carmine**	1.00	.70
		Entire	3.75	3.00
U14	E1	2c **carmine**, *amber*	1.00	.70
		Entire	3.75	3.00
U15	E1	2c **carmine**, *buff*	9.00	7.75
		Entire	35.00	21.00
U16	E1	2c **carmine**, *blue*	25.00	18.00
		Entire	60.00	52.50
U17	E1	5c **blue**	3.25	2.25
		Entire	5.00	2.75
U18	E1	5c **blue**, *amber*	6.00	4.00
		Entire	9.00	5.75
		Nos. U9-U18 (10)	89.50	62.70

WRAPPERS
Issue of the Republic under US Military Rule
1899

W1	E1	1c **green,** *manila*	4.00	10.00
		Entire	11.00	50.00
W2	E1	2c **carmine,** *manila*	12.00	10.00
		Entire	25.00	50.00

POSTAL CARDS

Values are for Entires

CUBA.—1c. de Peso.

U.S. Postal
Cards Nos.
UX14, UX16
Surcharged

UX1	PC8	1c on 1c **black,** *buff,* Jefferson		
		(1,000,000)	15.00	16.50
a.		No period after "1c"	40.00	75.00
b.		No period after "Peso"	35.00	
c.		Surcharge "2c" (error)	6,500.	

UX2	PC3	2c on 2c **black,** *buff,* Liberty		
		(583,000)	15.00	16.50
a.		No period after "Peso"	40.00	75.00
b.		Double surcharge	—	

In 1904 the Republic of Cuba revalued remaining stocks of
No. UX2 by means of a perforated numeral "1."

PROOFS
1899

Column (1) — Large Die
Column (2) — Small Die

227P	1c yellow green	160.	160.
227TC	1c blue green	375.	
227TC	1c black	625.	
228P	2c carmine	160.	160.
228TC	2c black	625.	
229P	3c purple	160.	160.
229TC	3c black	375.	
230P	5c blue	160.	160.
230TC	5c black	625.	
231P	10c nrown	160.	160.
231TC	10c gray	625.	
231TC	10c black	625.	

Special Delivery

E2TC	10c blue	1,500.	
E3P	10c orange	375.	325.

SPECIMEN STAMPS

Handstamped U.S. Type E in
Purple

1899

221S	E	1c on 1c **yellow green**	
222AS	E	2c on 2c **reddish carmine,** type IV	
223AS	E	2 ½c on 2c **reddish carmine,** type IV	
224S	E	3c on 3c **purple**	
225S	E	5c on 5c **blue**	
226S	E	10c on 10c **brown,** type I	
226AS	E	10c on 10c **brown,** type II	4,

See note after No. 226A for Special Printings with b
"Specimen" overprints.

1899

227S	E	1c **yellow green**	
228S	E	2c **carmine**	
229S	E	3c **purple**	
230S	E	5c **blue**	
231S	E	10c **brown**	

Special Delivery
1899

E1S	E	10c on 10c **blue**	5
a.		Five dots in curved frame above messenger's head	1,7
E2S	E	10c **orange**	1,0

Postage Due
1899

J1S	E	1c on 1c **deep claret**	2
J2S	E	2c on 2c **deep claret**	2
J3S	E	5c on 5c **deep claret**	2
J4S	E	10c on 10c **deep claret**	2

Black "Specimen" overprint known on all stamps of the S
cial Printing.

DANISH WEST INDIES

Formerly a Danish colony, these islands were purchased by the United States on March 31, 1917 and have since been known as the U.S. Virg
Islands. They lie east of Puerto Rico, have an area of 132 square miles and had a population of 27,086 in 1911. The capital is Charlotte Amalie (al
called St. Thomas). Stamps of Danish West Indies were replaced by those of the United States in 1917. However, for the first six months of U.
ownership, until September 30, 1917, a postal transition period existed. During this period, either U.S., D.W.I. or mixed frankings could be used. Th
domestic printed matter or postcard rate was 5 bits or 1 cent, and the foreign printed matter or postcard rate was 10 bits, 2 cents, or 5 bits + 1 cent. Th
domestic minimum weight letter rate was 10 bits, 2 cents, or 5 bits + 1 cent, while the foreign minimum letter rate was 25 bits, 5 cents, or a
combination of U.S. and D.W.I. stamps that together totalled 25 bits or 5 cents.

Letters posted to foreign destinations during the transition period are rare because of World War I. Values for covers listed here are for the perio
before the transition. Transition-period covers, including those with mixed franking, sell for much more.

100 CENTS = 1 DOLLAR
100 BIT = 1 FRANC (1905)

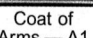

POST
K·GL·FRIM·
3 CENTS

Coat of
Arms — A1

Wmk. 111 —
Small Crown

1856   Typo.   Wmk. 111   Imperf.
Yellowish Paper
Yellow Wavy-line Burelage, UL to LR

1	A1	3c **dark carmine,** brown gum	190.	210.
		On cover		3,000.
		Block of 4	1,250.	
a.		3c **dark carmine,** yellow gum	200.	210.
		On cover		3,000.
		Block of 4	2,750.	
b.		3c **carmine,** white gum	4,000.	—
		On cover		—

The brown and yellow gums were applied locally.
*Reprint: 1981, carmine, back-printed across two stamps
("Reprint by Dansk Post og Telegrafmuseum 1978"), value, pair,
$10.*

1866

White Paper
Yellow Wavy-line Burelage UR to LL

2	A1	3c **rose**	40.	67.50
		On cover		3,000.
		Block of 4	200.	325.
		Rouletted 4 ½ privately	350.	175.
		On cover, rouletted 4 ½		—
		Rouletted 9	450.	200.

The value for used blocks is for favor cancel (CTO).

*No. 2 reprints, unwatermarked: 1930, carmine, value $75.
1942, rose carmine, back-printed across each row ("Nytryk
1942 G. A. Hagemann Danmark og Dansk Vestindiens
Frimaerker Bind 2"), value $50.*

1872   Perf. 12½

3	A1	3c **rose**	85.	225.
		On cover		7,500.
		Block of 4	525.	

1873

Without Burelage

4	A1	4c **dull blue**	200.	400.
		On cover		—
		Block of 4	1,200.	
a.		Imperf., pair	750.	
b.		Horiz. pair, imperf. vert.	550.	

*The 1930 reprint of No. 4 is ultramarine, unwatermarked and
imperf., value $85.
The 1942 4c reprint is blue, unwatermarked, imperf. and has
printing on back (see note below No. 2), value $50.*

Numeral of Value — A2

DANSK·VESTINDISKE·1·OERE·
1 CENT

NORMAL
FRAME

INVERTE[
FRAME

The arabesques in the corners have a main stem and
branch. When the frame is in normal position, in the upper le
corner the branch leaves the main stem half way between tw
little leaflets. In the lower right corner the branch starts at th
foot of the second leaflet. When the frame is inverted th
corner designs are, of course, transposed.
The central element in the fan-shaped scrollwork at th
outside of the lower left corner of Nos. 5a, 6a, 7b and 11a loo
like an elongated diamond.

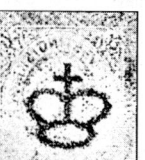

Wmk. 112 — Crown

1874-79   Wmk. 112   Perf. 14x13
White Wove Paper, Printings 1-3 Thin, 4-7 Medium, 8-9 Thick

1c	Nine printings
3c	Eight printings
4c	Two printings
5c	Six printings
7c	Two printings
10c	Seven printings
12c	Two printings

4c One printing
0c Two printings

'alues for inverted frames, covers and blocks are for the apest variety.

A2	1c	**green & brown red**		15.00	*22.50*
		On cover			*250.00*
		Block of 4		75.00	*225.00*
	1c	**green & rose lilac**, thin paper		75.00	*125.00*
	1c	**green & red violet**, medium paper		40.00	*65.00*
	1c	**green & claret**, thick paper		15.00	*22.50*
		As "c," inverted frame		15.00	*22.50*
		As "a," inverted frame		425.00	

No. 5 exists with "b" surcharge, "10 CENTS 1895." See note ow No. 15.

A2	3c	**blue & carmine**		20.00	*16.00*
		On cover			*225.00*
		Block of 4		90.00	—
		White "wedge" flaw		50.00	*50.00*
	3c	**light blue & rose carmine**, thin paper		65.00	*50.00*
	3c	**deep blue & dark carmine**, medium paper		35.00	*16.00*
	3c	**greenish blue & lake**, thick paper		20.00	*16.00*
		Imperf., pair		325.00	
		Inverted frame, thick paper		19.00	*14.00*
		As "a," inverted frame		350.00	
A2	4c	**brown & dull blue**		14.00	*16.00*
		On cover			*225.00*
		Block of 4		70.00	—
	4c	**brown & ultramarine**, thin paper		160.00	*200.00*
		Diagonal half used as 2c on cover			*125.00*
		As "b," inverted frame		750.00	*1,250.*
A2	5c	**green & gray**		20.00	*17.50*
		On cover			*250.00*
		Block of 4		100.00	—
	5c	**yellow green & dark gray**, thin paper		45.00	*30.00*
		Inverted frame, thick paper		20.00	*17.50*
A2	7c	**lilac & orange**		25.00	*85.00*
		On cover			*1,100.*
		Block of 4		150.00	—
	7c	**lilac & yellow**		80.00	*77.50*
		Inverted frame		52.50	*125.00*
A2	10c	**blue & brown**		22.50	*25.00*
		On cover			*300.00*
		Block of 4		105.00	—
	10c	**dark blue & black brown**, thin paper		70.00	*45.00*
		Period between "t" & "s" of "cents"		30.00	*30.00*
		Inverted frame		22.50	*25.00*
A2	12c	**red lilac & yellow green**		40.00	*140.00*
		On cover			*1,750.*
		Block of 4		230.00	—
	12c	**lilac & deep green**		130.00	*150.00*
A2	14c	**lilac & green**		500.00	*850.00*
		On cover			—
		Block of 4		*3,250.*	
		Inverted frame		*2,000.*	*2,750.*
A2	50c	**violet**, thin paper		175.00	*260.00*
		On cover			*2,500.*
		Block of 4		*1,250.*	
	50c	**gray violet**, thick paper		225.00	*350.00*

Issue dates: 1c, 3c, 4c, 14c, Jan. 15, 1874. 7c, July 22, 74. 5c, 10c, 1876; 12c, 1877; 50c, 1879. Colors of major mbers are generally those of the least expensive of two or ore shades, and do not indicate the shade of the first printing.

Nos. 9 and 13 Surcharged in Black:

a

b

887

4	A2 (a)	1c on 7c **lilac & orange**		77.50	*190.00*
		On cover			*3,000.*
		Block of 4		350.00	—
.		1c on 7c **lilac & yellow**		82.50	*210.00*
.		Double surcharge		225.00	*450.00*
.		Inverted frame		95.00	*300.00*

895

5	A2 (b)	10c on 50c **violet**, thin paper		37.50	*62.50*
		On cover			*275.00*
		Block of 4		250.00	—

The "b" surcharge also exists on No. 5, with "10" found in two zes. These are essays.

896-1901   **Perf. 13**

6	A2	1c **green & red violet**, inverted frame ('98)		12.00	*18.00*
		On cover			*150.00*
		Block of 4		60.00	—
.		Normal frame		225.00	*325.00*
7	A2	3c **blue & lake**, inverted frame ('98)		10.00	*13.00*
		On cover			*150.00*
		Block of 4		50.00	—
.		Normal frame		200.00	*325.00*
		White "wedge" flaw		35.00	*45.00*
8	A2	4c **bister & dull blue** ('01)		15.00	*12.50*
		On cover			*150.00*

		Block of 4		70.00	—
a.		Diagonal half used as 2c on cover		50.00	*90.00*
b.		Inverted frame		50.00	*80.00*
		On cover			*250.00*
c.		As "b," diagonal half used as 2c on cover			*300.00*
19	A2	5c **green & gray**, inverted frame		32.50	*30.00*
		On cover			*325.00*
		Block of 4		150.00	
a.		Normal frame		600.00	*850.00*
20	A2	10c **blue & brown** ('01)		70.00	*120.00*
		On cover			*1,150.*
		Block of 4		425.00	—
a.		Inverted frame		750.00	*1,300.*
b.		Period between "t" and "s" of "cents"		160.00	*150.00*
		Nos. 16-20 (5)		*139.50*	*193.50*

Two printings each of Nos. 18-19.

Arms — A5

1900

21	A5	1c **light green**		2.75	*2.75*
		On cover, pair			*80.00*
		On cover, single franking			*300.00*
		Block of 4		11.50	*11.50*
22	A5	5c **light blue**		15.00	*20.00*
		On cover			*300.00*
		Block of 4		75.00	—

Nos. 6, 17 and 20 Surcharged
in Black — c

1902   **Perf. 14x13½**

23	A2	2c on 3c **blue & carmine**, inverted frame		450.00	*500.00*
		On cover			*4,000.*
		Block of 4		*2,250.*	
a.		"2" in date with straight tail		475.00	*525.00*
b.		Normal frame		*3,500.*	

Perf. 13

24	A2	2c on 3c **blue & lake**, inverted frame		9.00	*20.00*
		On cover			*160.00*
		Block of 4		40.00	—
		White "wedge" flaw		55.00	*55.00*
a.		"2" in date with straight tail		11.50	*22.50*
b.		Dated "1901"		450.00	*500.00*
c.		Normal frame		150.00	*225.00*
d.		Dark green surcharge		*1,750.*	
e.		As "d" & "a"		—	—
f.		As "d" & "c"		—	—

One example recorded of No. 24f.

25	A2	8c on 10c **blue & brown**		20.00	*32.50*
		On cover			*225.00*
		Block of 4		82.50	—
a.		"2" with straight tail		25.00	*37.50*
b.		On No. 20b		27.50	*40.00*
c.		Inverted frame		200.00	*325.00*

Nos. 17 and 20 Surcharged in
Black — d

1902   **Perf. 13**

27	A2	2c on 3c **blue & lake**, inverted frame		11.00	*30.00*
		On cover			*500.00*
		Block of 4		47.50	
		White "wedge" flaw		40.00	*50.00*
a.		Normal frame		225.00	*375.00*
28	A2	8c on 10c **blue & brown**		11.00	*11.00*
		On cover			*175.00*
		Block of 4		47.50	
a.		On No. 20b		17.50	*20.00*
b.		Inverted frame		175.00	*350.00*

Wmk. 113 — Crown

1903   **Wmk. 113**

29	A5	2c **carmine**		6.00	*17.50*
		On cover			*125.00*
		Block of 4		25.00	—
30	A5	8c **brown**		22.50	*42.50*
		On cover			*250.00*
		Block of 4		95.00	—

King Christian
IX — A8

St. Thomas Harbor — A9

1905   Typo.   **Perf. 12½**

31	A8	5b **green**		3.50	*3.00*
		On cover			*35.00*
		Block of 4		16.00	—
32	A8	10b **red**		3.50	*3.00*
		On cover			*35.00*
		Block of 4		15.00	—
33	A8	20b **green & blue**		8.00	*7.50*
		On cover			*150.00*
		Block of 4		37.50	—
34	A8	25b **ultramarine**		8.00	*9.50*
		On cover			*85.00*
		Block of 4		37.50	—
35	A8	40b **red & gray**		8.00	*7.50*
		On cover			*225.00*
		Block of 4		35.00	—
36	A8	50b **yellow & gray**		9.00	*11.00*
		On cover			*250.00*
		Block of 4		37.50	—

Perf. 12
Wmk. Two Crowns (113)
Frame Typographed, Center Engraved

37	A9	1fr **green & blue**	17.50	40.00
		On cover		625.00
		Block of 4	75.00	
38	A9	2fr **orange red & brown**	30.00	55.00
		On cover		1,100.
		Block of 4	150.00	
39	A9	5fr **yellow & brown**	70.00	225.00
		On cover		1,750.
		Block of 4	350.00	
		Nos. 31-39 (9)	157.50	361.50

On cover values are for commercial usages, usually parcel address cards. Philatelic covers are valued at approximately 25% of these figures.

Nos. 18, 22 and 30 Surcharged in Black

1905   Wmk. 112   Perf. 13

40	A2	5b on 4c **bister & dull blue**	15.00	40.00
		On cover		250.00
		Block of 4	72.50	
a.		Inverted frame	40.00	75.00
41	A5	5b on 5c **light blue**	12.50	32.50
		On cover		250.00
		Block of 4	55.00	

Wmk. 113

42	A5	5b on 8c **brown**	12.50	32.50
		On cover		250.00
		Block of 4	50.00	

Favor cancels exist on Nos. 40-42. Value 25% less.

King Frederik VIII — A10

Frame Typographed, Center Engraved
1908   Wmk. 113   Perf. 13

43	A10	5b **green**	1.75	1.75
		On cover		22.50
		Block of 4	8.75	
		Number block of 6	17.50	
44	A10	10b **red**	1.75	1.75
		On cover		22.50
		Block of 4	8.75	
		Number block of 6	17.50	
45	A10	15b **violet & brown**	3.50	3.75
		On cover		125.00
		Block of 4	17.50	
		Number block of 6	50.00	
46	A10	20b **green & blue**	30.00	25.00
		On cover		110.00
		Block of 4	130.00	
		Number block of 6	375.00	
47	A10	25b **blue & dark blue**	1.75	2.25
		On cover		35.00
		Block of 4	7.25	
		Number block of 6	17.50	
48	A10	30b **claret & slate**	45.00	45.00
		On cover		350.00
		Block of 4	190.00	190.00
		Number block of 6	500.00	
49	A10	40b **vermilion & gray**	5.25	8.50
		On cover		210.00
		Block of 4	22.50	
		Number block of 6	50.00	
50	A10	50b **yellow & brown**	5.25	12.00
		On cover		210.00
		Block of 4	22.50	
		Number block of 6	67.50	
		Nos. 43-50 (8)	94.25	100.00

Printing numbers appear in the selvage, once per pane, in Roman or Arabic numerals.

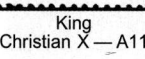

King
Christian X — A11

Wmk. 114 — Multiple
Crosses

Frame Typographed, Center Engraved
1915   Wmk. 114   Perf. 14x14½

51	A11	5b **yellow green**	3.50	3.50
		On cover		45.00
		Block of 4	15.00	
		Number block of 4	35.00	
52	A11	10b **red**	3.50	35.00
		On cover		100.00
		Block of 4	15.00	
		Number block of 4	35.00	
53	A11	15b **lilac & red brown**	3.50	40.00
		On cover		300.00
		Block of 4	15.00	
		Number block of 4	35.00	
54	A11	20b **green & blue**	3.50	40.00
		On cover		350.00
		Block of 4	15.00	
		Number block of 4	35.00	
55	A11	25b **blue & dark blue**	3.50	10.00
		On cover		100.00
		Block of 4	15.00	
		Number block of 4	35.00	
56	A11	30b **claret & black**	3.50	70.00
		On cover		900.00
		Block of 4	15.00	
		Number block of 4	35.00	
57	A11	40b **orange & black**	3.50	70.00
		On cover		550.00
		Block of 4	16.50	
		Number block of 4	35.00	
58	A11	50b **yellow & brown**	3.50	70.00
		On cover		650.00
		Block of 4	16.50	
		Number block of 4	35.00	
		Nos. 51-58 (8)	28.00	338.50

Forged and favor cancellations exist.

Plate identifications 11-D, 50-D or 50-O are located in the selvage in all four corners of the pane. The 50-D is on all denominations, 11-D, all but the 50b, 50-O, all but 15b, 20b, 25b.

POSTAGE DUE STAMPS

Royal Cipher
"Christian
Rex" — D1

Numeral of
Value — D2

1902   Litho.   Unwmk.   Perf. 11½

J1	D1	1c **dark blue**	4.00	15.00
		On cover		400.00
		Block of 4	20.00	
J2	D1	4c **dark blue**	9.00	20.00
		On cover		350.00
		Block of 4	40.00	
J3	D1	6c **dark blue**	17.50	55.00
		On cover		450.00
		Block of 4	85.00	
J4	D1	10c **dark blue**	15.00	60.00
		On cover		400.00
		Block of 4	75.00	

There are five types of each value. On the 4c they may be distinguished by differences in the figure "4"; on the other values differences are minute.

Used values of Nos. J1-J8 are for canceled copies. Uncanceled examples without gum have probably been used. Value 60% of unused. On cover values are for copies tied by cancellation.

Excellent counterfeits of Nos. J1-J4 exist.

1905-13   Perf. 13

J5	D2	5b **red & gray**	4.00	6.25
		On cover		450.00
		Block of 4	18.00	
J6	D2	20b **red & gray**	7.00	12.50
		On cover		450.00
		Block of 4	30.00	
J7	D2	30b **red & gray**	6.00	12.50
		On cover		450.00
		Block of 4	27.50	
J8	D2	50b **red & gray**	5.50	32.50
		On cover		900.00
		Block of 4	25.00	
a.		Perf. 14x14½ ('13)	35.00	125.00
		Block of 4	160.00	
b.		Perf. 11½	300.00	

Nos. J5-J8 are known imperforate but were not regularly issued. Excellent counterfeits exist.
See notes following No. J4 for canceled copies.

ENVELOPES

E1

1877-78   On White Pap

U1	E1	2c **light blue** ('78)	5.50	14
		Entire	22.50	68
a.		2c **ultramarine**	20.00	200
		Entire	100.00	800
U2	E1	3c **orange**	5.50	12
		Entire	22.50	65
a.		3c **red orange**	5.50	12
		Entire	22.50	65

Three different Crown watermarks are found on entires of U1, four on entires of No. U2. Envelope watermarks do show on cut squares.

POSTAL CARDS

Values are for entire cards.
Italicized numbers in parentheses indicate quantiti issued.

Designs of Adhesive Stamps
"BREV-KORT" at top

1877

Inscription in Three Lines

UX1	A2	6c **violet**	40.00	1,4

Used value is for card to foreign destination postmark before April 1, 1879.

1878-85

Inscription in Four Lines

UX2	A2	2c **light blue** (8,800)	22.50	50.
UX3	A2	3c **carmine rose** (17,700)	17.50	35.

1888

Inscription in Five Lines

UX4	A2	2c **light blue** (30,500)	20.00	32.
UX5	A2	3c **red** (26,500)	12.50	22.

Card No. UX5 Locally Surcharged with type "c" bu with date "1901"

1901

UX6	A2	1c on 3c **red** (2,000)	50.00	200.

1902

Card No. UX4 Locally Surcharged with type "c"

UX7	A2	1c on 2c **light blue** (3,000)	37.50	160.

Card No. UX5 Surcharged similar to type "c" but heavy letters

1902

UX8	A2	1c on 3c **red** (7,175)	12.50	150.

1903

UX9	A5	1c **light green** (10,000)	12.50	30.
UX10	A5	2c **carmine** (10,000)	19.00	70.

1905

UX11	A8	5b **green** (16,000)	12.50	22.
UX12	A8	10b **red** (14,000)	12.50	35.

1907-08   Unwm

UX13	A10	5b **green** ('08) (30,750)	9.50	30.
UX14	A10	10b **red** (19,750)	12.50	40.

1913   Wmk. Wood-grai

UX15	A10	5b **green** (10,000)	90.00	210.
UX16	A10	10b **red** (10,000)	100.00	325.

1915-16   Wmk. Wood-grai

UX17	A11	5b **yellow green** (8,200)	80.00	250.
UX18	A11	10b **red** ('16) (2,000)	100.00	

PAID REPLY POSTAL CARDS

Designs similar to Nos. UX2 and UX3 with added inscriptions in Danish and French:
Message Card-Four lines at lower left.
Reply Card-Fifth line centered, "Svar. Réponse."
Italicized numbers in parentheses indicate quantities issued.

1883

UY1	A2	2c +2c **light blue**, unsevered (2,600)	25.00	250.
m.		Message card, detached	12.50	35.
r.		Reply card, detached	12.50	35.

A2	3c +3c **carmine rose,** unsevered	21.00 *150.00*
m.	Message card, detached	12.50 *20.00*
r.	Reply card, detached	12.50 *25.00*

Designs similar to Nos. UX4 and UX5 with added inscription in fifth line, centered in French:
Message Card-"Carte postale avec réponse payée."
Reply Card-"Carte postale-réponse."

A2	2c +2c **light blue,** unsevered (26,000)	25.00 *125.00*
m.	Message card, detached	10.00 *20.00*
r.	Reply card, detached	10.00 *100.00*
A2	3c +3c **carmine rose,** unsevered (5,000)	22.50 *175.00*
m.	Message card, detached	11.00 *35.00*
r.	Reply card, detached	11.00 *125.00*

UY4 Locally Surcharged with type "c" but with date "1901"

A2	1c on 3c+1c on 3c **carmine rose,** unsevered (1,000)	35.00 *300.00*
m.	Message card, detached	12.50 *50.00*
r.	Reply card, detached	14.00 *75.00*

No. UY4 Surcharged in Copenhagen with type similar to "c" but heavy letters

A2	1c on 3c+1c on 3c **carmine rose,** unsevered (975)	50.00 *350.00*
m.	Message card, detached	20.00 *60.00*
r.	Reply card, detached	20.00 *75.00*

Designs similar to Nos. UX9 and UX10 with added inscriptions in Danish and English

A5	1c +1c **light green,** unsevered (5,000)	35.00 *75.00*
m.	Message card, detached	11.00 *20.00*
r.	Reply card, detached	11.00 *25.00*
A5	2c +2c **carmine,** unsevered (5,000)	40.00 *400.00*
m.	Message card, detached	15.00 *50.00*
r.	Reply card, detached	15.00 *75.00*

Designs similar to Nos. UX11 and UX12 with added inscriptions

1905

UY9	A8	5b +5b **green,** unsevered (5,000)	21.00 *75.00*
	m.	Message card, detached	10.00 *20.00*
	r.	Reply card, detached	10.00 *30.00*
UY10	A8	10b +10b **red,** unsevered (4,000)	30.00 *90.00*
	m.	Message card	12.50 *25.00*
	r.	Reply card, detached	15.00 *35.00*

Designs similar to Nos. UX13, UX14 and UX15 with added inscriptions

1908 **Unwmk.**

UY11	A10	5b +5b **green,** unsevered (7,150)	25.00 *100.00*
	m.	Message card, detached	11.00 *30.00*
	r.	Reply card, detached	11.00 *35.00*
UY12	A10	10b +10b **red,** unsevered (6,750)	25.00 *100.00*
	m.	Message card, detached	12.50 *30.00*
	r.	Reply card, detached	11.00 *40.00*

1913 **Wmk. Wood-grain**

UY13	A10	5b +5b **green,** unsevered (5,000)	—
	m.	Message card, detached	—
	r.	Reply card, detached	—

The 10b + 10b red type A10 with wood-grain watermark was authorized and possibly printed, but no example is known.

REVENUES STAMPS

PLAYING CARDS

These stamps were overprinted by the Bureau of Engraving and Printing. Shipments of 10,000 each of Nos. RFV1-RFV3 were sent to the Virgin Islands on June 17, 1920, Jan. 16, 1926, and Mar. 5, 1934, respectively.

U.S. Playing Card Stamp No. RF3 Overprinted in Carmine

1920 **Engr.** **Wmk. 191R** *Rouletted 7*
RFV1 RF2 4c on 2c **blue** 225.00

U.S. Playing Card Stamp No. RF17 Overprinted in Carmine

1926 *Rouletted 7*
RFV2 RF4 4c on (8c) **blue** 60.00
RFV2 was surcharged with new value in "Bits" for use in collecting a tobacco tax.

Same Overprint on U.S. Type RF4
1934 *Perf. 11*
RFV3 RF4 4c on (8c) **light blue** 225.00 *125.00*
The above stamp with perforation 11 was not issued in the United States without the overprint.

GUAM

A former Spanish island possession in the Pacific Ocean, one of the Mariana group, about 1,450 miles east of the Philippines. Captured June 20, 98, and ceded to the United States by treaty after the Spanish-American War. Stamps overprinted "Guam" were used while the post office was under jurisdiction of the Navy Department from July 7, 1899, until March 29, 1901, when a Postal Agent was appointed by the Post Office Department and postal service passed under that Department's control. From this date on Guam was supplied with regular United States postage stamps, although overprints remained in use for several more years.
Italicized numbers in parentheses indicate quantities issued.
Population 9,000 (est. 1899).

100 CENTS = 1 DOLLAR

United States Nos. 279, 279B, 279Bc, 268, 280a, 1, 282, 272, 282C, 283, 284, 275, 275a, 276 and 276A Overprinted

[GUAM overprinted stamp illustration]

99 **Wmk. 191** **Perf. 12**
Black Overprint

A87	1c **deep green** (25,000)	20.00	25.00
	Never hinged	40.00	
	On cover		200.00
	Block of 4	90.00	140.00
	P# strip of 3, Impt.	90.00	
	P# block of 6, Impt.	350.00	
	A bogus inverted overprint exists.		
A88	2c **red,** type IV, *Dec.* (105,000)	17.50	25.00
	light red, type IV	17.50	25.00
	On cover		200.00
	Never hinged	35.00	
	Block of 4	85.00	140.00
	P# strip of 3, Impt.	75.00	
	P# block of 6, Impt.	300.00	
	2c **rose carmine,** type IV, *Aug. 15*	30.00	30.00
	Never hinged	60.00	
	On cover		225.00
	Block of 4	125.00	175.00
	P# strip of 3, Impt.	100.00	
	P# block of 6, Impt.	375.00	
A89	3c **purple** (5000)	140.00	175.00
	Never hinged	275.00	

	On cover		400.00
	Block of 4	600.00	850.00
	P# strip of 3, Impt.	575.00	
	P# block of 6, Impt.	1,600.	
4	A90 4c **lilac brown** (5000)	135.00	175.00
	Never hinged	270.00	
	On cover		450.00
	Block of 4	600.00	825.00
	P# strip of 3, Impt.	550.00	
	P# block of 6, Impt.	2,000.	
	Extra frame line at top (Plate 793 R62)	—	
5	A91 5c **blue** (20,000)	32.50	45.00
	Never hinged	65.00	
	On cover		200.00
	Block of 4	140.00	250.00
	P# strip of 3, Impt.	140.00	
	P# block of 6, Impt.	775.00	
6	A92 6c **lake** (5000)	125.00	200.00
	Never hinged	250.00	
	On cover		450.00
	Block of 4	550.00	1,000.
	P# strip of 3, Impt.	500.00	
	P# block of 6, Impt.	1,600.	
7	A93 8c **violet brown** (5000)	140.00	200.00
	Never hinged	275.00	
	On cover		450.00
	Block of 4	600.00	1,000.
	P# strip of 3, Impt.	600.00	
	P# block of 6, Impt.	1,700.	
8	A94 10c **brown,** type I (10,000)	47.50	55.00
	Never hinged	95.00	
	On cover		275.00
	Block of 4	210.00	300.00
	P# strip of 3, Impt.	225.00	
	P# block of 6, Impt.	1,000.	
9	A94 10c **brown,** type II	4,000.	—
	Never hinged	—	
	Pair	—	
10	A95 15c **olive green** (5000)	150.00	175.00
	Never hinged	300.00	
	On cover		900.00
	Block of 4	650.00	875.00
	P# strip of 3, Impt.	600.00	
	P# block of 6, Impt.	2,200.	

11	A96 50c **orange** (4000)	350.00	425.00
	Never hinged	700.00	
	On cover		1,500.
	Block of 4	1,600.	2,000.
	P# strip of 3, Impt.	1,600.	
	P# block of 6, Impt.	4,500.	
a.	50c **red orange**	550.00	—
	Red Overprint		
12	A97 $1 **black,** type I (3000)	350.00	400.00
	Never hinged	700.00	
	On cover		3,000.
	Block of 4	1,750.	1,750.
	P# strip of 3, Impt.	1,750.	
	P# block of 6, Impt.	16,000.	
13	A97 $1 **black,** type II	4,500.	
	Never hinged	—	
	Block of 4	—	
	Nos. 1-8,10-12 (11)	1,507.	1,900.

Counterfeits of overprint exist.
No. 13 exists only in the special printing.

Special Printing

In March 1900, one pane of 100 stamps of each of Nos. 1-8, 10-12 and two panes of 50 stamps of No. E1 were specially overprinted for displays at the Paris Exposition (1900) and Pan American Exposition (1901). The 2c pane was light red, type IV.

Copies were handstamped type E "Specimen" in black ink by H. G. Mandel and mounted by him in separate displays for the two Expositions. Additional copies from each pane were also handstamped "Specimen" but most were destroyed after the Expositions.

J. M. Bartels, a stamp dealer, signed some copies from these panes "Special Surcharge" in pencil on the gum to authenticate them as coming from the "Mandel" Special Printing panes. In 1904 or later, he handstamped additional surviving copies "Special Surcharge" in red ink on the back as his guarantee. Some of these guaranteed stamps had Mandel's "Specimen" handstamp on the face while others did not. Value (with or without "Specimen" handstamp): Nos. 1-8, 10, each $1,000; Nos. 11, E1, each $1,250; No. 12, $2,000.

SPECIAL DELIVERY STAMP

Special Delivery Stamp of the United States, No. E5 Overprinted diagonally in Red

1899   **Wmk. 191**   **Perf. 12**
E1 SD3 10c **blue** *(5000)*   150.   200.
        Never hinged   275.
        On cover   1,250.
        Block of 4   650.
        Margin block of 4, arrow   750.
        P# strip of 3, Impt.   900.
        P# block of 6, Impt.   4,000.
        Dots in curved frame above messenger
          (Plate 882)   200.
        P# block of 6, Impt. (Plate 882) 4,250.

Counterfeits of overprint exist.
The special stamps for Guam were replaced by the regular issues of the United States.

GUAM GUARD MAIL
LOCAL POSTAL SERVICE

Inaugurated April 8, 1930, by Commander Willis W. Bradley, Jr., U.S.N., Governor of Guam, for the conveyance of mail between Agaña and the other smaller towns.

Philippines Nos. 290 and 291 Overprinted

1930, Apr. 8   **Unwmk.**   **Perf. 11**
M1 A40 2c **green** *(2,000)*   400.   300.
        Never hinged   575.
        On cover   600.
        Block of 4   1,700.
        P# block of 6   —
M2 A40 4c **carmine** *(3,000)*   225.   150.
        Never hinged   325.
        On cover   400.
        Block of 4   950.
        P# block of 6   —

Counterfeits of overprint exist.

Seal of Guam — A1

1930, July   **Unwmk.**   **Perf. 12**
Without Gum
M3 A1 1c **red & black** *(1,000)*   125.00 150.00
        On cover   225.00
        Block of 4   525.00
M4 A1 2c **black & red** *(4,000)*   75.00   95.00
        On cover   250.00
        Block of 4   325.00
 a. Block of 4 with extra impression of
       vignette covering the intersection of
       the block   8,000.

Copies are often found showing parts of watermark "CLEVELAND BOND."

Philippines Nos. 290 and 291 Overprinted in Black

1930, Aug. 10   **Unwmk.**   **Perf. 11**
M5 A40 2c **green** *(20,000)*   2.75   4.50
        Never hinged   4.00
        On cover   75.00
        Block of 4   12.00
        P# block of 6   125.00
 a. 2c **yellow green**   2.50   4.50
M6 A40 4c **carmine** *(80,000)*   .50   1.75
        Never hinged   .75
        On cover   75.00
        Block of 4   2.25
        P# block of 6   90.00

Same Overprint in Red on Philippines Nos. 290, 291, 292, 293a, and 294

1930, Dec.
M7 A40 2c **green** *(50,000)*   .80   2.00
        Never hinged   1.20
        On cover   50.00
        Block of 4   3.50
        P# block of 6   125.00
 a. GRAUD (Pos. 63) *(500)*   425.00
 b. MIAL (Pos. 84) *(500)*   425.00
M8 A40 4c **carmine** *(50,000)*   .85   1.50
        Never hinged   1.30
        On cover   50.00
        Block of 4   3.50
        P# block of 6   90.00
M9 A40 6c **deep violet** *(25,000)*   2.50   4.50
        Never hinged   3.75
        On cover   60.00
        Block of 4   11.00
        P# block of 10, Impt.   250.00
M10 A40 8c **orange brown** *(25,000)* 2.50   4.50
        Never hinged   3.75
        On cover   60.00
        Block of 4   11.00
        P# block of 10, Impt.   300.00
M11 A40 10c **deep blue** *(25,000)*   2.75   4.50
        Never hinged   4.00
        On cover   60.00
        Block of 4   11.00
        P# block of 10, Impt.   350.00

The local postal service was discontinued April 8th, 1931, and replaced by the service of the United States Post Office Department.

SPECIMEN STAMPS

Handstamped U.S. Type E in Purple   **Specimen.**

1899
1S   E 1c **deep green**   175.00
2aS E 2c **rose carmine**, type IV   175.00
3S   E 3c **purple**   175.00
4S   E 4c **lilac brown**   175.00
5S   E 5c **blue**   175.00
6S   E 6c **lake**   175.00
7S   E 8c **violet brown**   175.00
8S   E 10c **brown**, type I   175.00
10S E 15c **olive green**   175.00
11S E 50c **orange**   350.00
12S E $1 **black**, type I   350.00
13S E $1 **black**, type II   —

Special Delivery
1899
E1S E 10c **blue**   500.00

Values for specimen stamps are for fine-very fine appearing copies with minor faults.
See note after No. 13 for Special Printings with black "Specimen" overprints.

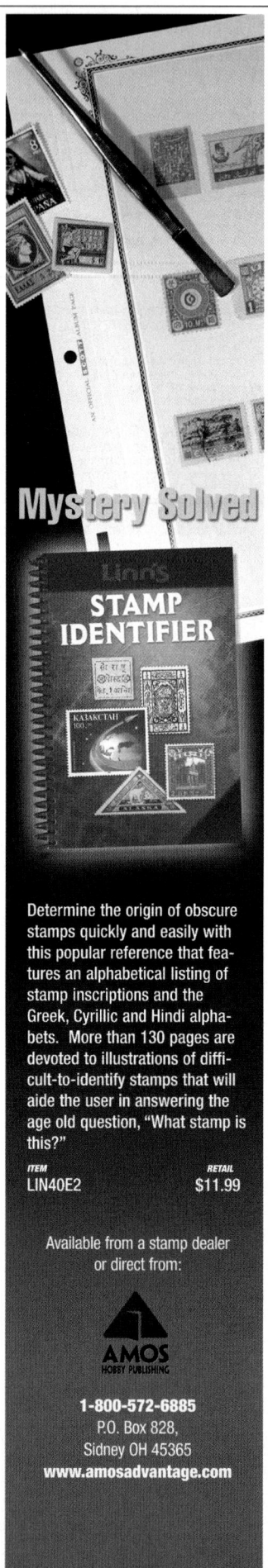

HAWAII

Until 1893, Hawaii was an independent kingdom. From 1893-1898 it was a republic. The United States annexed Hawaii in 1898, and it became a territory on April 30, 1900. Hawaiian stamps remained in use through June 13, 1900, and were replaced by U.S. stamps on June 14. In 1959 Hawaii became the 50th State of the Union. Hawaii consists of about 20 islands in the mid-Pacific, about 2,300 miles southwest of San Francisco. The area is 6,434 square miles and the population was estimated at 150,000 in 1899. Honolulu is the capital.

100 CENTS = 1 DOLLAR

Values of Hawaii stamps vary considerably according to condition. Quotations for Nos. 5-82 are for very fine copies. Extremely fine to superb examples sell at much higher prices, and inferior or poor copies sell at reduced prices, depending on the condition of the individual specimen.

A1

A2

A3

1-52		Unwmk.	Typeset	Pelure Paper	*Imperf.*
A1	2c	blue		660,000.	250,000.
		On cover			2,100,000.
A1	5c	blue		50,000.	30,000.
		On cover			75,000.
A2	13c	blue		27,500.	22,500.
		On cover			70,000.
A3	13c	blue		47,500.	32,500.
		On cover			75,000.

Nos. 1-4 are known as the "Missionaries." Two varieties of each. Nos. 1-4, off cover, are almost invariably damaged. Values are for examples with minor damage which has been skillfully repaired.

No. 1 unused and on cover are each unique; the on-cover value is based on a 1995 auction sale.

A4

King Kamehameha III — A5

Printed in Sheets of 20 (4x5)

1853		Thick White Wove Paper			Engr.
A4	5c	blue		1,500.	1,100.
		On cover			3,750.
		On cover with U.S. #17			12,000.
		Pair		3,250.	3,500.
a.		Line through "Honolulu" (Pos. 2)		2,850.	2,500.
A5	13c	dark red		600.	1,100.
		On cover			27,500.
		On cover with U.S. #11 (pair)			25,000.
		On cover with U.S. #17			35,000.
		On cover with #5 and U.S. #17			35,000.
		On cover with #8 and U.S. #36b			38,500.
		Pair		1,750.	4,000.
		Block of 4			3,500.

Black Manuscript Surcharge on Scott 6

1857					
7	A6	5c on 13c **dark red**		6,750.	9,000.
		On cover with pair U.S. #7 and 15			57,500.
		On cover with pair U.S. #11, 14			55,000.
		On cover with U.S. #14			50,000.
		On cover with U.S. #17			37,500.

1857					
		Thin White Wove Paper			
8	A4	5c **blue**		650.	625.
		On cover			1,500.
		On cover with U.S. #11			—
		On cover with U.S. #7, 15			—
		On cover with U.S. #17			10,000.
		On cover with U.S. #26			—
		On cover with U.S. #35			11,000.
		On cover with U.S. #36			10,000.
		On cover with U.S. #69			12,500.
		On cover with U.S. #76			—
		Pair		1,600.	
		Pair on cover			15,000.
a.		Line through "Honolulu" (Pos. 2)		1,250.	1,250.
		On cover with U.S. #17			6,500.
b.		Double impression		3,500.	3,500.

1861					
		Thin Bluish Wove Paper			
9	A4	5c **blue**		350.	250.
		On cover			3,750.
		On cover with U.S. #36b			3,250.
		On cover with U.S. #65			3,000.
		On cover with U.S. #65, 73			6,500.
		On cover with U.S. #68			4,250.
		On cover with U.S. #76			7,000.
		Block of 4		2,000.	
a.		Line through "Honolulu" (Pos. 2)		750.	900.

1868					
		RE-ISSUE			
		Ordinary White Wove Paper			
10	A4	5c **blue**			25.
		Block of 4			125.
a.		Line through "Honolulu" (Pos. 2)			55.
11	A5	13c **dull rose**			250.
		Block of 4			1,150.

Remainders of Nos. 10 and 11 were overprinted "SPECIMEN." See Nos. 10S-11Sb.

Nos. 10 and 11 were never placed in use but copies (both with and without overprint) were sold at face value at the Honolulu post office.

REPRINTS (Official Imitations) 1889

5c Originals have two small dots near the left side of the square in the upper right corner. These dots are missing in the reprints.

13c The bottom of the 3 of 13 in the upper left corner is flattened in the originals and rounded in the reprints. The "t" of "Cts" on the left side is as tall as the "C" in the reprints, but shorter in the originals.

10R	A4	5c **blue**			60.
		Block of 4			275.
11R	A5	13c **orange red**			250.
		Block of 4			1,100.

On August 19, 1892, the remaining supply of reprints was overprinted in black "REPRINT." The reprints (both with and without overprint) were sold at face value.

Quantities sold (including overprints) were 5c-3634 and 13c-1696. See Nos. 10R-S and 11R-S.

Values for the Numeral stamps, Nos. 12-26, are for four-margin examples. Unused values are for stamps without gum.

A7

A8

A9

1859-62		**Typeset from settings of 10 varieties**			
12	A7	1c **light blue**, *bluish white*		12,000.	9,000.
		Pair			22,500.
a.		"1 Ce" omitted			17,500.
b.		"nt" omitted			—
13	A7	2c **light blue**, *bluish white*		6,250.	4,250.
		On cover			10,500.
		Block of 4		27,500.	
a.		2c **dark blue**, *grayish white*		6,750.	4,000.
		On cover			11,500.
b.		Comma after "Cents"		—	6,250.
		On cover			11,500.
c.		No period after "LETA"		—	11,500.
14	A7	2c **black**, *greenish blue* ('62)		8,000.	4,750.
		On cover			7,750.
a.		"2-Cents."		—	—

1862-63					
15	A7	1c **black**, *grayish* ('63)		650.	1,500.
		Block of 4		3,250.	
a.		Tête bêche pair		9,000.	
b.		"NTER"		—	—
c.		Period omitted after "Postage"		850.	
16	A7	2c **black**, *grayish*		1,000.	700.
		On cover			5,000.
		Pair		—	—
a.		"2" at top of rectangle		3,750.	3,750.
b.		Printed on both sides		—	21,000.
c.		"NTER"		3,250.	3,250.
d.		2c **black**, *grayish white*		1,000.	725.
e.		Period omitted after "Cents"		—	—
f.		Overlapping impressions		—	—
g.		"TAGE"		—	—
17	A7	2c **dark blue**, *bluish* ('63)		12,000.	8,000.
		Pair		25,000.	
a.		"ISL"		—	—
18	A7	2c **black**, *blue gray* ('63)		3,500.	4,750.
		On cover			18,000.
		Pair			11,000.
		Thick paper		—	—

1864-65					
19	A7	1c **black**		500.	2,000.
		Pair		1,050.	
		Block of 4		2,400.	
20	A7	2c **black**		725.	1,250.
		On cover			16,500.
		Pair		1,550.	
		Block of 4		4,000.	
21	A8	5c **blue**, *blue* ('65)		850.	575.
		On cover (pair)			13,000.
		On cover with U.S. #65			—
		On cover with U.S. #68			—
		On cover with U.S. #76			8,250.
		Block of 4		3,400.	
a.		Tête bêche pair		10,500.	
b.		5c **bluish black**, *grayish white*		12,500.	

No. 21b is unique. Value based on 1995 auction sale.

22	A9	5c **blue**, *blue* ('65)		550.	875.
		On cover with U.S. #76			9,250.
		On cover with U.S. #63 and 76			—
		Block of 4		2,500.	
a.		Tête bêche pair		20,000.	
b.		5c **blue**, *grayish white*		—	—
c.		Overlapping impressions		—	—

1864

Laid Paper

23	A7	1c **black**		275.	*2,100.*
		On cover with U.S. #76			—
		Block of 4		1,150.	
a.		"HA" instead of "HAWAIIAN"		*3,750.*	
b.		Tête bêche pair		*6,250.*	
c.		Tête bêche pair, Nos. 23, 23a		*18,000.*	
24	A7	2c **black**		300.	*1,050.*
		Block of 4		1,250.	
a.		"NTER"		*3,750.*	
b.		"S" of "POSTAGE" omitted		*1,500.*	
c.		Tête bêche pair		*5,500.*	

A10

King Kamehameha
IV — A11

1865

Wove Paper

25	A10	1c **dark blue**		300.
		Block of 4		1,350.
a.		Double impression		—
b.		With inverted impression of No. 21 on face		*18,500.*
26	A10	2c **dark blue**		300.
		Block of 4		1,350.

Nos. 12 to 26 were typeset and were printed in sheets of 50 (5 settings of 10 varieties each). The sheets were cut into panes of 25 (5x5) before distribution to the post offices.

1861-63   **Litho.**

Horizontally Laid Paper

27	A11	2c **pale rose**		300.	275.
		On cover			*1,000.*
		Pair			—
a.		2c **carmine rose** ('63)		3,000.	2,500.

Vertically Laid Paper

28	A11	2c **pale rose**		300.	275.
		On cover			*1,500.*
		Block of 4		1,600.	1,500.
a.		2c **carmine rose** ('63)		275.	350.
		On cover			*2,000.*
		Block of 4		1,500.	

RE-ISSUE

1869   **Engr.**   **Thin Wove Paper**

29	A11	2c **red**		45.00
		Block of 4		225.00

No. 29 was not issued for postal purposes although canceled copies are known. It was sold only at the Honolulu post office, at first without overprint and later with overprint "CANCELLED." See No. 29S.

See note following No. 51.

Princess Victoria
Kamamalu — A12

King Kamehameha
IV — A13

King Kamehameha
V — A14

Kamehameha
V — A15

Mataio Kekuanaoa — A16

1864-86   **Engr.**   **Wove Paper**   **Perf. 12**

30	A12	1c **purple** ('86)		9.00	7.50
		On cover			150.00
		Block of 4		50.00	
a.		1c **mauve** ('71)		60.00	20.00
		Block of 4		300.00	
b.		1c **violet** ('78)		20.00	10.00
		Block of 4		160.00	200.00
31	A13	2c **rose vermilion**		50.00	9.00
		On cover			200.00
		On cover with U.S. #76			*1,000.*
		Block of 4		225.00	400.00
a.		2c **vermilion** ('86)		35.00	20.00
		On cover			150.00
b.		Half used as 1c on cover with #32			*8,500.*
		As "b," with U.S. #117			*18,000.*
32	A14	5c **blue** ('66)		175.00	30.00
		On cover			250.00
		On cover with any U.S. issues of 1861-67			*4,000.*
		On cover with U.S. #116			*17,500.*
		On cover with U.S. #116 and 69			*25,000.*
		Block of 4		800.00	175.00
33	A15	6c **yellow green** ('71)		40.00	9.00
		On cover			300.00
a.		6c **bluish green** ('78)		25.00	9.00
		On cover			300.00
		On cover with U.S. #179			*1,500.*
		On cover with U.S. #185			800.00
		Block of 4		140.00	500.00
34	A16	18c **dull rose** ('71)		85.00	35.00
		On cover			350.00
		On cover with No. 36			—
		On cover with No. 36 and U.S. No. 179			*2,000.*
		On cover with U.S. No. 161			—
		On cover with U.S. No. 163			—
		On cover with U.S. No. 185			*10,000.*
		Block of 4		375.00	—
		Nos. 30-34 (5)		*359.00*	*90.50*

Half of No. 31 was used with a 5c stamp to make up the 6-cent rate to the United States.

No. 32 has traces of rectangular frame lines surrounding the design. Nos. 39 and 52C have no such frame lines.

King David
Kalakaua — A17

Prince William Pitt
Leleiohoku — A18

1875

35	A17	2c **brown**		7.50	3.00
		On cover			200.00
		Block of 4		37.50	40.00
36	A18	12c **black**		55.00	27.50
		On cover			400.00
		On cover with U.S. No. 161			—
		On cover with U.S. No. 179b			—
		Block of 4		325.00	

Princess
Likelike — A19

King David
Kalakaua — A20

Queen
Kapiolani — A21

King William
Lunalilo — A23

Statue of King
Kamehameha
I — A22

Queen Emma
Kaleleonalani —

1882

37	A19	1c **blue**	10.00	
		On cover		6
		Block of 4	50.00	5
38	A17	2c **lilac rose**	125.00	4
		On cover		15
		Block of 4	625.00	
39	A14	5c **ultramarine**	15.00	
		On cover		2
		Block of 4	75.00	6
a.		Vert. pair, imperf. horiz.	5,000.	4,
40	A20	10c **black**	35.00	
		On cover		15
		Block of 4	160.00	13
41	A21	15c **red brown**	55.00	2
		On cover		20
		Block of 4	260.00	20
		Nos. 37-41 (5)	*240.00*	*9*

1883-86

42	A19	1c **green**	2.75	
		On cover		2
		Block of 4	14.00	1
43	A17	2c **rose** ('86)	4.00	
		On cover		2
		Block of 4	20.00	1
a.		2c **dull red**	62.50	2
		Block of 4	310.00	
44	A20	10c **red brown** ('84)	30.00	1
		On cover		12
		Block of 4	150.00	10
45	A20	10c **vermilion**	32.50	1.
		On cover		12
		Block of 4	175.00	8
46	A18	12c **red lilac**	75.00	3
		On cover		42
		Block of 4	400.00	24
47	A22	25c **dark violet**	140.00	6
		On cover		37
		Block of 4	650.00	35
48	A23	50c **red**	160.00	8
		On cover		52
		Block of 4	850.00	
49	A24	$1 **rose red**	240.00	25
		On cover		8,
		Block of 4	1,250.	
		Maltese cross cancellation		10
		Nos. 42-49 (8)	*684.25*	*452*

Other fiscal cancellations exist on No. 49.

Nos. 48-49 are valued used with postal cancels. Canceled order cancels exist and are worth less.

REPRODUCTION and REPRINT
Yellowish Wove Paper

1886-89   **Engr.**   **Imp**

50	A11	2c **orange vermilion**	160.00	
		Block of 4	800.00	
51	A11	2c **carmine** ('89)	25.00	
		Block of 4	125.00	

In 1885 the Postmaster General wished to have on sale co plete sets of Hawaii's portrait stamps, but was unable to either the stone from which Nos. 27 and 28, or the plate fr which No. 29 was printed. He therefore sent a copy of No. 29 the American Bank Note Company, with an order to engra new plate like it and print 10,000 stamps therefrom, of wh 5000 were overprinted "SPECIMEN" in blue.

The original No. 29 was printed in sheets of fifteen (5x3), the plate of these "Official Imitations" was made up of stamps (10x5). Later, in 1887, the original die for No. 29 v discovered, and, after retouching, a new plate was made 37,500 stamps were printed (No. 51). These, like the origina were printed in sheets of fifteen. They were delivered dur 1889 and 1890. In 1892 all remaining unsold in the Post Off were overprinted "Reprint".

No. 29 is red in color, and printed on very thin white w paper. No. 50 is orange vermilion in color, on medium, whit buff paper. In No. 50 the vertical line on the left side of portrait touches the horizontal line over the label "Elua Kene

while in the other two varieties, Nos. 29 and 51, it does not touch the horizontal line by half a millimeter. In No. 51 there are three parallel lines on the left side of the King's nose, while in No. 29 and No. 50 there are no such lines. No. 51 is carmine in color and printed on thick, yellowish to buff, wove paper.

It is claimed that both Nos. 50 and 51 were available for postage, although not made to fill a postal requirement. They exist with favor cancellation. No. 51 also is known postally used. See Nos. 50S-51S.

Queen Liliuokalani — A25

1890-91   **Perf. 12**
52	A25	2c **dull violet** ('91)	4.50	1.50
		On cover		25.00
		Block of 4	21.00	12.00
a.		Vert. pair, imperf. horiz.	4,000.	
52C	A14	5c **deep indigo**	110.00	140.00
		On cover		500.00
		Block of 4	525.00	

Stamps of 1864-91
Overprinted in Red

Three categories of double overprints:
I. Both overprints heavy.
II. One overprint heavy, one of moderate strength.
III. One overprint heavy, one of light or weak strength.

1893
53	A12	1c **purple**	7.50	12.50
		On cover		35.00
		Block of 4	37.50	70.00
a.		"189" instead of "1893"	575.00	—
b.		No period after "GOVT"	210.00	210.00
f.		Double overprint (III)	600.00	
54	A19	1c **blue**	7.50	12.50
		On cover		40.00
		Block of 4	40.00	67.50
b.		No period after "GOVT"	140.00	140.00
e.		Double overprint (II)	1,500.	
f.		Double overprint (III)	400.00	
55	A19	1c **green**	1.50	3.00
		On cover		25.00
		Block of 4	7.50	15.00
d.		Double overprint (I)	625.00	450.00
f.		Double overprint (III)	200.00	250.00
g.		Pair, one without ovpt.	10,000.	
56	A17	2c **brown**	10.00	20.00
		On cover		60.00
		Block of 4	50.00	120.00
b.		No period after "GOVT"	300.00	—

57	A25	2c **dull violet**	1.50	1.25
		On cover		25.00
		Block of 4	6.50	6.50
a.		"18 3" instead of "1893"	750.00	500.00
d.		Double overprint (I)	1,300.	650.00
f.		Double overprint (III)	160.00	110.00
g.		Inverted overprint	4,000.	4,500.
58	A14	5c **deep indigo**	10.00	25.00
		On cover		100.00
		Block of 4	50.00	140.00
b.		No period after "GOVT"	225.00	250.00
f.		Double overprint (III)	1,250.	
59	A14	5c **ultramarine**	6.00	2.50
		On cover		40.00
		Block of 4	30.00	20.00
d.		Double overprint (I)	6,500.	
e.		Double overprint (II)	4,000.	4,000.
f.		Double overprint (III)		600.00
g.		Inverted overprint	1,500.	1,500.
60	A15	6c **green**	15.00	25.00
		On cover		140.00
		Block of 4	75.00	125.00
e.		Double overprint (II)	1,000.	
61	A20	10c **black**	9.00	15.00
		On cover		125.00
		Block of 4	45.00	82.50
e.		Double overprint (II)	750.00	650.00
f.		Double overprint (III)	200.00	
61B	A20	10c **red brown**	14,000.	29,000.
		Block of 4	60,000.	
		Strip of 5, plate imprint	75,000.	
62	A18	12c **black**	9.00	17.50
		On cover		150.00
		Block of 4	50.00	110.00
d.		Double overprint (I)	2,000.	
e.		Double overprint (II)	1,750.	
63	A18	12c **red lilac**	150.00	250.00
		On cover		550.00
		Block of 4	900.00	—
64	A22	25c **dark violet**	26.00	40.00
		On cover		225.00
		Block of 4	125.00	200.00
b.		No period after "GOVT"	325.00	325.00
f.		Double overprint (III)	1,000.	
		Nos. 53-61,62-64 (12)	253.00	424.25

Virtually all known copies of No. 61B are cut in at the top.

Overprinted in Black
65	A13	2c **vermilion**	67.50	75.00
		On cover		450.00
		Block of 4	325.00	400.00
b.		No period after "GOVT"	250.00	250.00
66	A17	2c **rose**	1.25	2.25
		On cover		25.00
		Block of 4	6.50	11.00
b.		No period after "GOVT"	50.00	60.00
d.		Double overprint (I)	4,000.	
e.		Double overprint (II)	2,750.	
f.		Double overprint (III)	300.00	
66C	A15	6c **green**	14,000.	29,000.
		On cover		—
		Block of 4	60,000.	
67	A20	10c **vermilion**	15.00	30.00
		On cover		125.00
		Block of 4	80.00	180.00
f.		Double overprint (III)	1,250.	
68	A20	10c **red brown**	7.50	12.50
		On cover		100.00
		Block of 4	37.50	75.00
f.		Double overprint (III)	4,000.	
69	A18	12c **red lilac**	275.00	500.00
		On cover		950.00
		Block of 4	1,250.	2,400.
70	A21	15c **red brown**	20.00	30.00
		On cover		300.00
		Block of 4	110.00	150.00
e.		Double overprint (II)	2,000.	
71	A16	18c **dull rose**	25.00	35.00
		On cover		225.00
		Block of 4	125.00	175.00
a.		"18 3" instead of "1893"	475.00	475.00
b.		No period after "GOVT"	300.00	300.00
d.		Double overprint (I)	600.00	
f.		Double overprint (III)	225.00	—
g.		Pair, one without ovpt.	3,500.	
h.		As "b," double overprint (II)	1,750.	
72	A23	50c **red**	60.00	90.00
		On cover		600.00
		Block of 4	300.00	500.00
b.		No period after "GOVT"	400.00	400.00
f.		Double overprint (III)	1,000.	
73	A24	$1 **rose red**	110.00	175.00
		On cover		775.00
		Block of 4	500.00	875.00
b.		No period after "GOVT"	450.00	425.00
		Nos. 65-66,67-73 (9)	581.25	949.75

Coat of Arms — A26

View of Honolulu — A27

Statue of
Kamehameha
I — A28

S. S. "Arawa" — A30

Stars and
Palms — A29

Pres. Sanford Ballard
Dole — A31

"CENTS" Added — A32

1894
74	A26	1c **yellow**	2.00	
		On cover		2
		Block of 4	8.50	
75	A27	2c **brown**	2.25	
		On cover		2
		Block of 4	9.00	
		"Flying goose" flaw (48 LR 2)	600.00	400
		Double transfer	5.00	5
76	A28	5c **rose lake**	4.00	
		On cover		25
		Block of 4	20.00	15
77	A29	10c **yellow green**	6.00	
		On cover		45
		Block of 4	30.00	25
78	A30	12c **blue**	12.50	1
		On cover		150
		Block of 4	55.00	80
		Double transfer	22.50	25
79	A31	25c **deep blue**	17.50	12
		On cover		100
		Block of 4	90.00	
		Nos. 74-79 (6)	44.25	37

Numerous double transfers exist on Nos. 75 and 81.

1899
80	A26	1c **dark green**	1.50	1
		On cover		25
		Block of 4	7.00	7
81	A27	2c **rose**	1.40	1
		On cover		20
		Block of 4	6.00	6
		Double transfer		
		"Flying goose" flaw (48 LR 2)	325.00	300
a.		2c **salmon**	1.50	1
b.		Vert. pair, imperf. horiz.	4,500.	
82	A32	5c **blue**	6.50	3
		On cover		25
		Block of 4	32.50	52

OFFICIAL STAMPS

Lorrin Andrews
Thurston — O1

96		Engr.	Unwmk.		*Perf. 12*
O1	2c	**green**		40.00	17.50
		On cover			400.00
		Block of 4		175.00	
O1	5c	**black brown**		40.00	17.50
		On cover			450.00
		Block of 4		175.00	
O1	6c	**deep ultramarine**		40.00	17.50
		On cover			
		Block of 4		175.00	
O1	10c	**bright rose**		40.00	17.50
		On cover			500.00
		Block of 4		175.00	
O1	12c	**orange**		40.00	17.50
		On cover			—
		Block of 4		175.00	
O1	25c	**gray violet**		40.00	17.50
		On cover			—
		Block of 4		175.00	
		Nos. O1-O6 (6)		240.00	105.00

Used values for Nos. O1-O6 are for copies canceled-to-order ...OREIGN OFFICE/HONOLULU H.I." in double circle without ...e. Values of postally used copies: Nos. O1-O2, O4, $35, No. ...$100, No. O5, $125, No. O6, $150.

ENVELOPES

...alicized numbers in parentheses indicate quantities issued.
All printed by American Bank Note Co., N.Y.

View of Honolulu Harbor — E1

Envelopes of White Paper, Outside and Inside

...84					
E1	1c	**light green** *(109,000)*		2.50	3.00
		Entire		6.00	15.00
a.		1c **green** *(10,000)*		6.00	15.00
		Entire		15.00	90.00
b.		1c **dark green**		10.00	10.00
		Entire		25.00	75.00
?	E1	2c **carmine** *(386,000 including*			
		U2a, U2b)		2.50	4.00
		Entire		5.00	17.50
a.		2c **red**		2.50	4.00
		Entire		5.00	17.50
b.		2c **rose**		2.50	4.00
		Entire		5.00	17.50
c.		2c **pale pink** *(5,000)*		10.00	12.50
		Entire		35.00	60.00
3	E1	4c **red** *(18,000)*		14.00	17.50
		Entire		30.00	90.00
4	E1	5c **blue** *(90,775)*		6.50	7.50
		Entire		17.50	30.00
5	E1	10c **black** *(3,500 plus)*		20.00	25.00
		Entire		50.00	100.00

Envelopes White Outside, Blue Inside

6	E1	2c **rose**		150.00	200.00
		Entire		400.00	1,500.
7	E1	4c **red**		150.00	200.00
		Entire		400.00	—
8	E1	5c **blue**		150.00	200.00
		Entire		400.00	1,250.
9	E1	10c **black**		250.00	400.00
		Entire		450.00	—
		Nos. U1-U9 (9)		745.50	1,057.

Nos. U1, U2, U4 & U5 Overprinted Locally
"Provisional Government 1893" in Red or Black

893					
10	E1	1c **light green** (R) *(16,000)*		3.50	7.00
		Entire		7.00	20.00
a.		Double overprint		1,750.	

	Entire		6,000.	
U11 E1	2c **carmine** (Bk) *(37,000)*		2.50	3.50
	Entire		4.50	15.00
a.	Double overprint		500.00	
	Entire		1,100.	1,250.
b.	Double overprint, one inverted, entire	1,500.		

No. U11 is known as an unused entire with a triple overprint, two of the overprints being at the bottom right portion of the envelope. Unique. Value, $9,500.

U12 E1	5c **blue** (R) *(34,891)*		4.25	5.00
	Entire		10.00	15.00
a.	Double overprint		375.00	400.00
	Entire		600.00	3,000.
b.	Triple overprint, entire			7,500.
U13 E1	10c **black** (R) *(17,707 incl. No. U14)*	12.50	16.00
	Entire		20.00	90.00
a.	Double overprint, entire		1,800.	2,000.

Envelope No. U9 with same overprint

U14 E1	10c **black** (R)		300.	725.00
	Entire		1,000.	—

SPECIAL DELIVERY ENVELOPE
Value is for Entire.
Envelope No. U5 with added inscription "Special Despatch Letter" etc. in red at top left corner

1885

UE1 E1	10c **black** *(2,000)*		175.

Envelope No. UE1 was prepared for use but never issued for postal purposes. Postally used examples exist, but no special delivery service was performed. Favor cancellations exist.

POSTAL CARDS

All printed by American Bank Note Co., N.Y.
Values are for entires.

Queen
Liliuokalani — PC1

View of Diamond
Head — PC2

Royal
Emblems — PC3

1882-92					**Engr.**
UX1	PC1	1c **red**, *buff (125,000)*		30.00	75.00
UX2	PC2	2c **black** *(45,000)*		50.00	90.00
a.		Lithographed ('92)		150.00	250.00
UX3	PC3	3c **blue green** *(21,426)*		60.00	125.00

1889					**Litho.**
UX4	PC1	1c **red**, *buff (171,240)*		25.00	50.00

Cards Nos. UX4, UX2a and UX3 overprinted locally "Provisional Government 1893" in red or black

1893					
UX5	PC1	1c **red**, *buff* (Bk) *(28,760)*		30.00	75.00
a.		Double overprint		4,000.	3,500.
UX6	PC2	2c **black** (R) *(10,000)*		55.00	95.00

No. UX6 is known unused with double overprint, one inverted at lower left of card. Unique. Value, $16,000.

UX7	PC3	3c **blue green** (R) *(8,574)*		65.00	250.00
a.		Double overprint		1,750.	

Iolani
Palace — PC4

Map of Pacific Ocean, Mercator's Projection — PC5

1894-97				**Litho.**
Border Frame 131½x72½mm				
UX8	PC4	1c **red**, *buff (100,000)*	20.00	40.00
a.		Border frame 132½x74mm ('97)		
		(200,000)	20.00	40.00
UX9	PC5	2c **green** *(60,000)*	45.00	80.00
a.		Border frame 132½x74mm ('97)		
		(190,000)	45.00	80.00

PAID REPLY POSTAL CARDS
Double cards, same designs as postal cards with added inscriptions on reply cards.

1883				**Litho.**
UY1	PC1	1c +1c **purple**, *buff,* unsevered		
		(5,000)	400.00	450.00
m.		Message card, detached	35.00	100.00
r.		Reply card, detached	35.00	100.00
UY2	PC2	2c +2c **dark blue**, unsevered		
		(5,000)	450.00	500.00
m.		Message card, detached	55.00	140.00
r.		Reply card, detached	55.00	140.00

1889				
UY3	PC1	1c +1c **gray violet**, *buff,* unsev-		
		ered *(5,000)*	400.00	450.00
m.		Message card, detached	35.00	100.00
r.		Reply card, detached	35.00	100.00

UY4 PC2 2c +2c **sapphire,** unsevered
    (5,000)   400.00 *450.00*
  m.   Message card, detached   35.00 *80.00*
  r.   Reply card, detached   35.00 *80.00*

Values for unused unsevered Paid Reply Postal Cards are for cards which have not been folded. Folded cards sell for about 33% of these values.

Detached card used values are for canceled cards with printed messages on the back.

REVENUE STAMPS

R1

R2

R3

R4

R5

R6

Printed by the American Bank Note Co.
Sheets of 70

1877		Engr.	Unwmk.	Rouletted 8
R1	R1	25c **green** *(160,000)*		12.50 15.00
R2	R2	50c **yellow orange** *(190,000)*		30.00 12.50
R3	R3	$1 **black** *(580,000)*		30.00 6.50
a.		$1 gray		30.00 6.50

Denominations Typo.

R4	R4	$5 **vermilion & violet blue** *(21,000)*		125.00 40.00
R5	R5	$10 **reddish brown & green** *(14,000)*		125.00 40.00
R6	R6	$50 **slate blue & carmine** *(3,500)*		*1,000.* 350.00

No. R6 unused is valued without gum, as all known examples come thus.

Unused values for all revenues except No. R6 are for stamps with original gum. Apparently unused copies without gum sell for less.

No. R1 Surcharged in Black or Gold

a

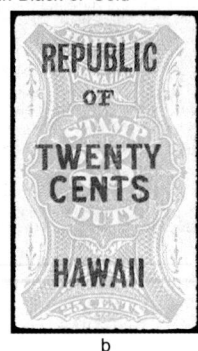
b

1893-94

R7	R1 (a)	20c on 25c **green**	27.50	17.50
a.		Inverted surcharge	*1,250.*	*900.00*
R8	R1 (b)	20c on 25c **green** (G)	55.00	50.00
a.		Inverted surcharge	—	—
b.		Double surcharge	—	—
c.		Double surcharge, one black, one gold	—	*1,500.*
d.		Double surcharge, one gold, one red in different font	—	
e.		Double surcharge, with a single added letter "c"	—	
f.		Double surcharge with two "c" letters added	—	

On No. R8b, one surcharge is always diagonal. On No. R8c, the black surcharge is 20mm wide, while the normal gold surcharge is 15mm wide.

R7

Kamehameha I — R8

Sheets of 50

1894   **Litho.**   **Perf. 14**

R9	R7	20c **red** *(10,000)*	210.00	210.00
a.		Imperf. *(25,000)*	400.00	400.00
		Pair	950.00	

No. R9a is known in an unused pair on paper with "DENNIS" papermaker's watermark.

R10	R7	25c **violet brown**	850.00	800.00
a.		Imperf.	*1,400.*	
		Pair	*3,250.*	
b.		As "a," tete beche pair	—	

Printed by the American Bank Note Co.
Sheets of 100

1897   **Engr.**   **Perf. 12**

R11	R8	$1 **dark blue** *(60,000)*	10.00	8.00

R9

1901   **Rouletted 8**

R12	R9	$50 **slate blue & carmine** *(7,000)*	50.00	60.00

Types of 1877
Printed by the American Bank Note Co.
Sheets of 70

1910-13   **Engr.**   **Perf.**

R13	R2	50c **yellow orange** ('13) *(70,000)*	15.00	2
R14	R3	$1 **black** ('13) *(35,000)*	20.00	3
R15	R4	$5 **vermilion & violet blue** *(14,000)*	40.00	5
a.		Denomination inverted		
R16	R5	$10 **reddish brown & green** *(14,000)*	40.00	5

PROOFS and TRIAL COLOR PROOFS

The large die proofs range in size and format from die impressions on India sunk on cards generally up to 6x9 inches, through impressions on India on or off card in medium stamp size. Many individual listings are known in m than one size and format. Values reflect the size format most commonly seen.

			DIE (1) Large	PLATE (3) India (4) C
1853				
5TC	5c	**black** on wove		*6,000.*
6TC	13c	**black** on wove		*6,000.*
1868-89				
10TC	5c	**orange red**	*875.*	
11TC	13c	**orange red**	*875.*	*475.*
11RP	13c	**orange red**	*2,500.*	*575.*
1861-63				
27TC	2c	**black**		*875.*
1864-71				
30P	1c	**purple**	*650.*	*190.*
		Block of 4		*750.*
31P	2c	**rose vermilion**	*650.*	*190.* 2
		Block of 4		—
31TC	2c	**green**	*1,700.*	
32P	5c	**blue**	*625.*	*230.* 2
32TC	5c	**black**	*1,250.*	
32TC	5c	**dark red**		*250.*
32TC	5c	**orange red**		*250.*
32TC	5c	**orange**		*250.*
32TC	5c	**red brown**		*250.*
		Block of 4		*1,250.*
32TC	5c	**green**		*250.*
		Block of 4		*1,250.*
32TC	5c	**dark violet**		*250.*
		Block of 4		*1,250.*
33P	6c	**green**	*650.*	*250.*
		Block of 4		*1,250.*
34P	18c	**dull rose**	*650.*	*250.* 2
		Block of 4		*1,250.*
34TC	18c	**orange red**	*875.*	*650.*
34TC	18c	**dark orange**	*875.*	
1875				
35P	2c	**brown**	*650.*	*190.*
		Block of 4		*800.*
35TC	2c	**black**	*2,600.*	
36P	12c	**black**	*650.*	*190.* 2
36TC	12c	**violet blue**	*875.*	
1882				
37P	1c	**blue**		*190.*
		Block of 4		*800.*
37TC	1c	**black**	*3,750.*	
39P	5c	**ultramarine**	*575.*	*190.*
40P	10c	**black**	*575.*	*230.*
		Block of 4		*950.*
41P	15c	**red brown**		*190.* 2
		Block of 4		*800.*
1883-86				
42P	1c	**green**		*190.* 2.
		Block of 4		*800.*
43P	2c	**rose**		*150.* 2:
		Block of 4		*700.*
47P	25c	**dark violet**	*550.*	*190.*
		Block of 4		*800.*
47TC	25c	**black**	*875.*	
48P	50c	**red**	*550.*	*230.*
		Block of 4		*1,300.*
48TC	50c	**lake**	*1,150.*	*375.*
49P	$1	**rose red**	*1,750.*	*190.* 2:
		Block of 4		*800.*
49TC	$1	**black**		*190.*
49TC	$1	**orange red**	*875.*	*375.*
49TC	$1	**carmine**		*375.*
49TC	$1	**vermilion**		*375.*
		Block of 4		*1,600.*
1886-89				
50P	2c	**orange vermilion**	*875.*	*250.*
51P	2c	**carmine**	*875.*	
1890-91				
52P	2c	**dull violet**	*3,750.*	*250.* 2:
52CP	5c	**deep indigo**		*175.*
1894				
74P	1c	**yellow**	*700.*	*150.* 2:
75P	2c	**brown**	*700.*	*150.*
75TC	2c	**dark green**	*650.*	
76P	5c	**rose lake**	*700.*	*150.* 2:
77P	10c	**yellow green**	*700.*	*150.* 2:
		Block of 4		*625.*

10c	deep blue green	700.		
12c	blue	700.	150.	225.
25c	deep blue	700.	150.	225.
5c	blue		190.	225.
	Block of 4		800.	

Official

2c		875.	300.	190.
5c	black brown	875.	300.	190.
6c	deep ultramarine	875.	300.	190.
10c	bright rose	875.	300.	190.
	Block of 4		—	
10c	black	875.		
12c	orange	875.	300.	190.
12c	black	875.		
25c	gray violet	875.	300.	190.
25c	black	875.		

Envelopes

Uncleared indicia only

1c	green	725.
1c	black	725.
1c	orange	725.
2c	carmine	725.
2c	black	725.
2c	blue	725.
4c	red	725.
4c	black	725.
5c	blue	725.
5c	black	725.
10c	black	725.

Postal Cards

...e die proofs are of indicia only, India proofs are entire card.

...-95

	1c	red	3,500.	1,700.
TC	1c	green		1,950.
	2c	black		1,700.
	3c	blue green		3,000.
TC	1c	orange		3,000.
TC	1c	brown		3,000.

Revenues

		DIE (1) Large	PLATE (3) India (4) Card

...-97

25c	green		300.	300.
	Block of 4		1,300.	
25c	blue green	1,150.		
25c	black	1,150.		
25c	brown red	1,150.		
25c	brown	1,150.		
25c	grayish blue	1,150.		
50c	yellow orange		300.	350.
	Block of 4		1,300.	
50c	blue green	1,150.		
50c	black	1,150.		
50c	brown red	1,150.		
50c	brown	1,150.		
50c	grayish blue	1,150.		
$1	black	1,150.		350.
	Block of 4		1,300.	
$1	blue green	1,150.		
$1	brown red	1,150.		

			DIE (1) Large	PLATE (3) India (4) Card
R3TC	$1	brown	1,150.	
R3TC	$1	grayish blue	1,150.	
R4P	$5	vermilion & violet blue		350.
		Block of 4		1,200.
R5P	$10	reddish brown & green	300.	350.
		Block of 4		1,200.
R6P	$50	slate blue & carmine		350.
		Block of 4		1,200.
R11P	$1	dark blue	1,250. / 300.	350.

SPECIMEN STAMPS

Overprinted in Black or Red — Type A

1868

10S	A	5c	blue (R)	20.
		Block of 4		100.
a.		Line through "Honolulu" (Pos. 2)		75.
11S	A	13c	dull rose	20.
		Block of 4		100.

Overprinted in Black — Type B

11S	B	13c	dull rose	275.
		Block of 4		1,250.
a.		Double overprint, one as #11S A, one as #11S B		4,000.
b.		Period omitted (Pos. 18, 20)		575.

Overprinted in Black — Type C

1889

10RS	C	5c	blue	60.
		Block of 4		250.
11RS	C	13c	orange red	225.
		Block of 4		950.

Overprinted in Black — Type D

1869

29S	D	2c	red	50.
		Block of 4		250.

Overprinted in Blue — Type E

1886

50S	E	2c	orange vermilion	60.
		Block of 4		250.

Overprinted in Black — Type C

1889

51S	C	2c	carmine	25.
		Block of 4		125.

PHILIPPINES

Issued under U.S. Administration

...llowing the American occupation of the Philippines, May 1, 1898, after Admiral Dewey's fleet entered Manila Bay, an order was issued by the U. S. ...master General (No. 201, May 24, 1898) establishing postal facilities with rates similar to the domestic rates.

...itary postal stations were established as branch post offices, each such station being placed within the jurisdiction of the nearest regular post ...e. Supplies were issued to these military stations through the regular post office of which they were branches.

...veral post office clerks were sent to the Philippines and the San Francisco post office was made the nearest regular office for the early Philippine ...and the postmarks of the period point out this fact.

...S. stamps overprinted "PHILIPPINES" were placed on sale in Manila June 30, 1899. Regular U.S. stamps had been in use from early March, and ...e Manila post office Spanish stamps were also acceptable.

...e first regular post office was established at Cavite on July 30, 1898, as a branch of the San Francisco post office. The first cancellation was a ...d handstamp with "PHILIPPINE STATION" and "SAN FRANCISCO, CAL."

...n May 1, 1899, the entire Philippine postal service was separated from San Francisco and numerous varieties of postmarks resulted. Many of the ...used stamps show postmarks and cancellations of the Military Station, Camp or R.P.O. types, together with "Killers" of the types employed in the ...at the time.

...e Philippines became a commonwealth of the United States on November 15, 1935, the High Commissioner of the United States taking office on ...ame day. The official name of the government was "Commonwealth of the Philippines" as provided by Article 17 of the Constitution. Upon the ...and complete withdrawal of sovereignty of the United States and the proclamation of Philippine independence on July 4, 1946, the Commonwealth ...e Philippines became the "Republic of the Philippines."

...licized numbers in parenthesis indicate quantities issued.

Authority for dates of issue, stamps from 1899 to 1911, and some quantities issued-"The Postal Issues of the Philippines," by F. L. Palmer (New 1912). Authority for quantities issued — "NAPP's Numbers, Volume 2," by Joseph M. Napp (2001).

100 CENTS = 1 DOLLAR
100 CENTAVOS = 1 PESO (1906)

Regular Issues of the United States Overprinted in Black

Printed and overprinted by the U.S. Bureau of Engraving and Printing.

1899, June 30   **Unwmk.**   **Perf. 12**
On U.S. Stamp No. 260

212	A96	50c **orange**	350.	225.
		On cover		
		Block of 4	1,650.	—
		P# strip of 3, Impt.	1,550.	
		P# block of 6, Impt.	12,500.	

On U.S. Stamps
Nos. 279, 279B, 279Bd, 279Be, 279Bf, 279Bc, 268, 281, 282C, 283, 284, 275, 275a

Wmk. Double-lined USPS (191)

213	A87	1c **yellow green**		
		(5,500,000)	4.00	.60
		On cover		10.00
		Block of 4	20.00	5.00
		P# strip of 3, Impt.	40.00	
		P# block of 6, Impt.	225.00	
a.		Inverted overprint	32,500.	
214	A88	2c **red**, type IV (6,970,000)	1.60	.60
		light red	1.60	.60
		On cover		10.00
		Block of 4	7.00	4.00
		P# strip of 3, Impt.	25.00	
		P# block of 6, Impt.	175.00	
a.		2c **orange red**, type IV, 1901	1.60	.60
		pale orange red	1.60	60

		deep orange red, 1903	1.60	.60
b.		Booklet pane of 6, **red**, type IV		
		1900	250.00	200.00
		orange red, 1901	250.00	200.00
c.		2c **reddish carmine**, type IV	2.50	.90
		On cover		12.50
		Block of 4	11.00	7.50
		P# strip of 3, Impt.	35.00	
		P# block of 6, Impt.	225.00	
d.		2c **rose carmine**, type IV	3.00	1.10
		On cover		15.00
		Block of 4	14.00	8.50
		P# strip of 3, Impt.	40.00	
		P# block of 6, Impt.	260.00	
215	A89	3c **purple** (673,814)	9.00	1.25
		On cover		30.00
		Block of 4	42.50	13.50
		P# strip of 3, Impt.	85.00	
		P# block of 6, Impt.	475.00	
216	A91	5c **blue** (1,700,000)	9.00	.90
		On cover		20.00
		Block of 4	42.50	9.00
		P# strip of 3, Impt.	85.00	
		P# block of 6, Impt.	500.00	
a.		Inverted overprint		3,750.

No. 216a is valued in the grade of fine.

217	A94	10c **brown**, type I		
		(750,000)+	35.00	4.00
		On cover		60.00
		Block of 4	160.00	55.00
		P# strip of 3, Impt.	175.00	
		P# block of 6, Impt.	700.00	

(+ Quantity includes Nos. 217, 217A)

217A	A94	10c **orange brown**, type II (200,000)	125.00	25.00
		On cover		160.00
		Block of 4	625.00	175.00
		P# strip of 3, Impt.	925.	
		P# block of 6, Impt.	2,750.	
218	A95	15c **olive green** (200,000)	40.00	8.00
		light olive green	37.50	8.50
		On cover		110.00
		Block of 4	175.00	52.50
		P# strip of 3, Impt.	200.00	
		P# block of 6, Impt.	1,250.	
219	A96	50c **orange** (50,000)+	125.00	37.50
		On cover		400.00
		Block of 4	575.00	250.00
		P# strip of 3, Impt.	575.00	
		P# block of 6, Impt.	5,000.	
a.		50 **red orange**	250.00	
		Block of 4	1,700.	
		Nos. 213-219 (8)	348.60	77.85

(+ Quantity includes Nos. 212, 219, 219a)

Special Printing

In March 1900 one pane of 100 stamps of each of Nos. 213-217, 218, 219 and J1-J5 were specially overprinted for displays at the Paris Exposition (1900) and Pan American Exposition (1901). The 2c pane was light red, type IV.

Copies were handstampd type E "Specimen" in black ink on the face by H. G. Mandel and mounted by him in separate displays for the two Expositions. Additional copies from each pane were also handstamped "Specimen" but most were destroyed after the Expositions.

J. M. Bartels, a stamp dealer, signed some copies from these panes "Special Surcharge" in pencil on the gum to authenticate them as coming from the "Mandel" Special Printing panes. In 1904 or later, he handstamped additional surviving copies "Special Surcharge" in red ink on the back as his guarantee. Some of these guaranteed stamps had Mandel's "Specimen" handstamp on the face while others did not. Value, each $775.

Regular Issue

1901, Aug. 30
Same Overprint in Black On U.S. Stamps Nos. 280b, 282 and 272

220	A90	4c **orange brown**		
		(404,907)	27.50	5.00
		On cover		50.00
		Block of 4	125.00	50.00
		P# strip of 3, Impt.	140.00	
		P# block of 6, Impt.	700.00	
221	A92	6c **lake** (223,465)	35.00	7.00
		On cover		65.00
		Block of 4	175.00	50.00
		P# strip of 3, Impt.	175.00	
		P# block of 6, Impt.	900.00	
222	A93	8c **violet brown** (248,000)	35.00	7.50
		On cover		50.00
		Block of 4	175.00	55.00
		P# strip of 3, Impt.	175.00	
		P# block of 6, Impt.	900.00	

Same Overprint in Red On U.S. Stamps Nos. 276A, 277a and 278

223	A97	$1 **black**, type I (3,000)+	475.00	2
		On cover		8
		Block of 4	2,000.	
		P# strip of 3, Impt.	2,100.	
		P# block of 6, Impt.		
		Horiz. pair, types I & II	3,750.	

(+ Quantity includes Nos. 223, 223A)

223A	A97	$1 **black**, type II	2,400.	7
		On cover		
		Block of 4	10,500.	
		P# strip of 3, Impt., one stamp No. 223	8,500.	
		P# block of 6, Impt., two stamps No. 223	—	
224	A98	$2 **dark blue** (1800)	475.00	3
		On cover		
		Block of 4	2,000.	
		P# strip of 3, Impt.	2,600.	
		P# block of 6, Impt.		
225	A99	$5 **dark green** (782)	825.00	9
		On cover		12
		Block of 4	3,350.	
		P# strip of 3, Impt.	4,000.	
		P# block of 6, Impt.		

Special Printing

Special printings exist of Nos. 227, 221, 223-225, made defaced plates. These were made for display at the St. Exposition. All but a few copies were destroyed. Most e existing copies have the handstamp "Special Printing" c back. Value: Nos. 227, 221, each $775; No. 223, $1,200 224, $1,650; No. 225, $2,500.

Regular Issue

1903-04
Same Overprint in Black On U.S. Stamps N 300 to 310 and shades

226	A115	1c **blue green** (9,631,172)	6.50	
		On cover		
		Block of 4	30.00	
		P# strip of 3, Impt.	22.50	
		P# block of 6, Impt.	250.00	
227	A116	2c **carmine** (850,000)	9.00	
		On cover		
		Block of 4	42.50	
		P# strip of 3, Impt.	42.50	
		P# block of 6, Impt.	325.00	
228	A117	3c **bright violet** (14,500)	67.50	
		On cover		
		Block of 4	275.00	
		P# strip of 3, Impt.	275.00	
		P# block of 6, Impt.	1,650.	
229	A118	4c **brown** (13,000)	75.00	
a.		4c **orange brown**	75.00	
		On cover		
		Block of 4	325.00	1
		P# strip of 3, Impt.	300.00	
		P# block of 6, Impt.	1,850.	
230	A119	5c **blue** (1,211,844)	16.00	
		On cover		
		Block of 4	75.00	
		P# strip of 3, Impt.	65.00	
		P# block of 6, Impt.	450.00	
231	A120	6c **brownish lake** (11,500)	80.00	
		On cover		6
		Block of 4	325.00	1
		P# strip of 3, Impt.	325.00	
		P# block of 6, Impt.	1,950.	
232	A121	8c **violet black** (49,033)	45.00	
		On cover		3
		Block of 4	225.00	1
		P# strip of 3, Impt.	250.00	
		P# block of 6, Impt.	1,400.	
233	A122	10c **pale red brown** (300,179)	35.00	
		On cover		2
		Block of 4	160.00	2
		P# strip of 3, Impt.	175.00	
		P# block of 6, Impt.	1,000.	
a.		10c **red brown**	30.00	
		On cover		3
		Block of 4	140.00	3
		P# strip of 3, Impt.	150.00	
		P# block of 6, Impt.	1,200.	
b.		Pair, one without overprint		1,
234	A123	13c **purple black** (91,341)	35.00	1
a.		13c **brown violet**	35.00	1
		On cover		5
		Block of 4	150.00	11
		P# strip of 3, Impt.	175.00	
		P# block of 6, Impt.	1,350.	
235	A124	15c **olive green** (183,965)	60.00	1
		On cover		10
		Block of 4	275.00	10
		P# strip of 3, Impt.	300.00	
		P# block of 6, Impt.	2,000.	
236	A125	50c **orange** (57,641)	125.00	3
		On cover		30
		Block of 4	575.00	27
		P# strip of 3, Impt.	575.00	
		P# block of 6, Impt.	17,500.	
		Nos. 226-236 (11)	554.00	14

me Overprint in Red On U.S. Stamps Nos. 311, 312 and 313

A126	$1 black *(5617)*		475.00	275.00
	On cover			750.00
	Block of 4		2,100.	1,850.
	P# strip of 3, Impt.		2,100.	
	P# block of 6, Impt.		8,500.	
A127	$2 dark blue *(695)*		800.00	850.00
	Block of 4		3,400.	—
	P# strip of 3, Impt.		3,600.	
	P# block of 6, Impt.		16,000.	
A128	$5 dark green *(746)*		1,000.	5,000.
	Block of 4		4,250.	—
	P# strip of 3, Impt.		4,750.	
	P# block of 6, Impt.			

me Overprint in Black On U.S. Stamp No. 319

A129	2c carmine *(862,245)*		6.00	2.25
	On cover			3.50
	Block of 4		27.50	15.00
	P# strip of 3, Impt.		37.50	
	P# block of 6, Impt.		300.00	
a.	Booklet pane of 6		1,100.	
b.	2c scarlet		6.25	2.75
	On cover			4.00
	Block of 4		27.50	17.50
	P# strip of 3, Impt.		40.00	
	P# block of 6, Impt.		325.00	
c.	As "b," booklet pane of 6			

Dates of issue:
ept. 20, 1903, Nos. 226, 227, 236.
an. 4, 1904, Nos. 230, 234, 235, 237, 240a.
ov. 1, 1904, Nos. 228, 229, 231, 232, 233, 238, 239, 240.
os. 212 to 240 became obsolete on Sept. 8, 1906, the
ainders being destroyed.

Special Printing

wo sets of special printings exist of the 1903-04 issue. The
consists of Nos. 226, 230, 234, 235, 236, 237 and 240.
w were made for display at the St. Louis Exposition. All but
w copies were destroyed. Most of the existing copies have
handstamp "Special Surcharge" on the back. Value: No.
, $1,550; others $900; J6, J7, $1,150:
1907 the entire set Nos. 226, 228 to 240, J1 to J7 were
cially printed for the Bureau of Insular Affairs on very white
er. They are difficult to distinguish from the ordinary stamps
pt the Special Delivery stamp which is on U.S. No. E6 (see
ippines No. E2A). Value: No. 237, $1,300; No. 238, $2,600;
239, $3,500; others, $775.

Regular Issue

José Rizal — A40

Printed by the U.S. Bureau of Engraving and
Printing.

Plates of 400 subjects in four panes of 100 each.

ooklet panes Nos. 240a, 241b, 242b, 261a, 262b, 276a,
a, 285a, 286a, 290e, 291b and 292c were made from plates
80 subjects. No. 214b came from plates of 360 subjects.

esigns: 4c, McKinley. 6c, Ferdinand Magellan. 8c, Miguel
ez de Legaspi. 10c, Gen. Henry W. Lawton. 12c, Lincoln.
, Adm. William T. Sampson. 20c, Washington. 26c, Fran-
co Carriedo. 30c, Franklin. 1p-10p, Arms of City of Manila.

Wmk. Double-lined PIPS (191)

				Perf. 12	
	A40	2c deep green *(51,000,019)*		.25	.20
		Block of 4		1.10	.20
a.		2c yellow green ('10)		.40	.20
		Double transfer			40.00
b.		Booklet pane of 6 *(720,120)*		750.00	
2	A40	4c carmine *(11,000,019)*		.40	.20
		Block of 4		1.75	.20
a.		4c carmine lake ('10)		.80	.20
b.		Booklet pane of 6*(300,600)*		650.00	
3	A40	6c violet *(1,980,019)*		2.00	.20
		Block of 4		9.00	.85
4	A40	8c brown *(770,019)*		3.00	.70
		Block of 4		13.50	4.75
5	A40	10c blue *(5,500,019)*		2.25	.20
a.		10c dark blue		2.25	.20
		Block of 4		10.00	.85
6	A40	12c brown lake *(670,019)*		7.50	2.00
		Block of 4		35.00	13.50
7	A40	16c violet black *(1,300,019)*		5.00	.20
		Block of 4		25.00	1.40
8	A40	20c orange brown *(2,100,019)*		6.00	.30
		Block of 4		30.00	2.00
9	A40	26c violet brown *(428,000)*		8.00	2.25
		Block of 4		40.00	15.00
0	A40	30c olive green *(1,256,019)*		6.00	1.50
		Block of 4		30.00	7.50
1	A40	1p orange *(200,019)*		40.00	7.00
		Block of 4		180.00	37.50
2	A40	2p black *(100,000)*		50.00	1.25
		Block of 4		225.00	10.00
3	A40	4p dark blue *(10,000)*		150.00	17.50
		Block of 4		650.00	80.00
4	A40	10p dark green *(6,019)*		275.00	80.00
		Block of 4		1,250.	400.00
		Nos. 241-254 (14)		555.40	113.50

1909

		Change of Colors		
255	A40	12c red orange *(300,000)*	10.00	2.50
		Block of 4	47.50	12.50
256	A40	16c olive green *(500,000)*	5.00	.75
		Block of 4	22.50	3.50
257	A40	20c yellow *(800,000)*	8.00	1.25
		Block of 4	37.50	7.50
258	A40	26c blue green *(250,000)*	3.00	.75
		Block of 4	13.50	4.00
259	A40	30c ultramarine *(600,000)*	12.00	3.25
		Block of 4	55.00	20.00
260	A40	1p pale violet *(100,000)*	40.00	5.00
		Block of 4	200.00	32.50
260A	A40	2p violet brown *(50,000)*	95.00	2.75
		Block of 4	450.00	19.00
		Nos. 255-260A (7)	173.00	16.25

1911   Wmk. Single-lined PIPS (190)   *Perf. 12*

261	A40	2c green *(44,000,000)*	.65	.20
		Block of 4	4.25	.35
a.		Booklet pane of 6 *(896,160)*	800.00	
262	A40	4c carmine lake *(6,000,000)*	2.50	.20
		Block of 4	11.50	.35
a.		4c carmine	—	—
b.		Booklet pane of 6 *(100,020)*	600.00	
263	A40	6c deep violet *(3,200,000)*	2.50	.20
		Block of 4	11.00	.30
264	A40	8c brown *(1,400,000)*	8.50	.45
		Block of 4	40.00	2.00
265	A40	10c blue *(3,700,000)*	3.75	.20
		Block of 4	17.00	.30
266	A40	12c orange *(1,320,000)*	3.00	.45
		Block of 4	13.00	2.10
267	A40	16c olive green *(1,000,000)*	3.00	.20
a.		16c pale olive green	3.00	.20
		Block of 4	13.00	.65
268	A40	20c yellow *(3,000,000)*	3.00	.20
		Block of 4	13.00	.65
a.		20c orange	3.00	.20
		Block of 4	13.00	.75
269	A40	26c blue green *(249,900)*	4.00	.20
		Block of 4	17.50	1.00
270	A40	30c ultramarine *(1,000,000)*	5.00	.40
		Block of 4	22.50	2.00
271	A40	1p pale violet *(694,000)*	25.00	.55
		Block of 4	120.00	2.75
272	A40	2p violet brown *(100,000)*	35.00	.75
		Block of 4	160.00	4.75
273	A40	4p deep blue *(10,000)*	700.00	100.00
		Block of 4	3,250.	500.00
274	A40	10p deep green *(20,000)*	250.00	30.00
		Block of 4	1,100.	150.00
		Nos. 261-274 (14)	1,045.	134.00

1914

275	A40	30c gray *(700,000)*	10.00	.40
		Block of 4	47.50	2.40

1914   *Perf. 10*

276	A40	2c green *(60,000,000)*	2.00	.20
		Block of 4	8.50	.45
a.		Booklet pane of 6 *(400,080)*	750.00	
277	A40	4c carmine *(2,500,000)*	2.00	.20
		Block of 4	8.50	.55
a.		Booklet pane of 6 *(56,040)*	750.00	
278	A40	6c light violet *(700,000)*	40.00	9.50
		Block of 4	190.00	55.00
a.		6c deep violet	45.00	6.25
		Block of 4	200.00	35.00
279	A40	8c brown *(200,000)*	45.00	10.50
		Block of 4	200.00	57.50
280	A40	10c dark blue *(2,000,000)*	27.50	.20
		Block of 4	120.00	1.00
281	A40	16c olive green *(700,000)*	100.00	4.75
		Block of 4	450.00	26.00
282	A40	20c orange *(2,000,000)*	30.00	.90
		Block of 4	135.00	5.50
283	A40	30c gray *(1,300,000)*	60.00	4.00
		Block of 4	275.00	17.50
284	A40	1p pale violet *(198,000)*	130.00	3.25
		Block of 4	575.00	19.00
		Nos. 276-284 (9)	436.50	33.50

1918   *Perf. 11*

285	A40	2c green *(40,000,000)*	21.00	4.25
		Block of 4	92.50	18.00
a.		Booklet pane of 6 *(50,040)*	750.00	
286	A40	4c carmine *(3,000,000)*	26.00	2.50
		Block of 4	115.00	12.50
a.		Booklet pane of 6	1,350.	
287	A40	6c deep violet *(1,000,000)*	37.50	1.75
		Block of 4	150.00	8.50
287A	A40	8c light brown *(200,000)*	210.00	25.00
		Block of 4	875.00	160.00
288	A40	10c dark blue *(2,000,000)*	55.00	1.50
		Block of 4	240.00	8.00
289	A40	16c olive green *(700,000)*	100.00	7.50
		Block of 4	475.00	32.50
289A	A40	20c orange *(1,000,000)*	75.00	8.50
		Block of 4	350.00	42.50
289C	A40	30c gray *(500,000)*	70.00	12.50
		Block of 4	310.00	60.00
289D	A40	1p pale violet *(200,000)*	85.00	16.00
		Block of 4	375.00	80.00
		Nos. 285-289D (9)	679.50	79.00

1917   Unwmk.   *Perf. 11*

290	A40	2c yellow green *(444,746,800)*	.20	.20
		Block of 4	.30	.20
a.		2c dark green	.20	.20
		green	.20	.20
		Double transfer	—	—
b.		Vert. pair, imperf. horiz.	1,500.	
c.		Horiz. pair, imperf. between	1,500.	—

d.		Vertical pair, imperf. btwn.	1,750.	1,000.
e.		Booklet pane of 6 *(3,251,080)*	27.50	
291	A40	4c carmine *(50,579,100)*	.20	.20
a.		4c light rose	.20	.20
		Block of 4	.30	.20
b.		Booklet pane of 6 *(500,820)*	17.50	—
292	A40	6c deep violet *(8,803,600)*	.30	.20
		Block of 4	1.30	.30
a.		6c lilac	.35	.20
b.		6c red violet	.35	.20
c.		Booklet pane of 6 *(75)*	550.00	—
293	A40	8c yellow brown *(6,036,700)*	.35	.20
a.		8c orange brown	.35	.20
		Block of 4	1.75	.35
294	A40	10c deep blue *(15,848,800)*	.20	.20
		Block of 4	.85	.25
295	A40	12c red orange *(3,396,500)*	.30	.20
		Block of 4	1.25	.50
296	A40	16c light olive green *(3,249,600)*	60.00	.25
		Block of 4	275.00	1.25
a.		16c olive green	60.00	.40
297	A40	20c orange yellow *(10,814,600)*	.30	.20
		Block of 4	1.90	.30
298	A40	26c green *(1,595,400)*	.45	.45
		Block of 4	2.00	2.10
a.		26c blue green	.55	.25
299	A40	30c gray *(6,031,300)*	.55	.20
		Block of 4	2.60	.35
		Dark gray	.55	.20
300	A40	1p pale violet *(1,173,200)*	40.00	1.00
		Block of 4	175.00	4.50
a.		1p red lilac	40.00	1.00
b.		1p pale rose lilac	40.00	1.10
301	A40	2p violet brown *(475,300)*	27.50	.75
		Block of 4	125.00	3.50
302	A40	4p blue *(541,800)*	25.00	.45
		Block of 4	110.00	2.00
a.		4p dark blue	25.00	.45
		Nos. 290-302 (13)	155.35	4.50

1923-26

303	A40	16c olive bister *(Adm. George Dewey) (13,524,300)*	.90	.20
		Block of 4	4.25	.45
a.		16c olive green	1.25	.20
304	A40	10p deep green ('26) *(32,400)*	45.00	5.00
		Block of 4	190.00	22.50

Legislative Palace Issue

Issued to commemorate the opening of the
Legislative Palace.

Legislative
Palace — A42

Printed by the Philippine Bureau of Printing.

1926, Dec. 20   Unwmk.   *Perf. 12*

319	A42	2c green & black *(502,300)*	.40	.20
		First day cover		3.50
		Block of 4	1.75	1.10
a.		Horiz. pair, imperf. between	300.00	
b.		Vert. pair, imperf. between	575.00	
320	A42	4c carmine & black *(304,150)*	.40	.35
		First day cover		3.50
		Block of 4	1.75	1.40
a.		Horiz. pair, imperf. between	325.00	
b.		Vert. pair, imperf. between	600.00	
321	A42	16c olive green & black *(203,500)*	.75	.65
		First day cover		10.00
		Block of 4	3.75	3.00
a.		Horiz. pair, imperf. between	350.00	
b.		Vert. pair, imperf. between	625.00	
c.		Double impression of center	675.00	
322	A42	18c light brown & black *(103,700)*	.85	.50
		First day cover		10.00
		Block of 4	3.75	2.25
a.		Double impression of center *(150)*	1,250.	
b.		Vertical pair, imperf. between	675.00	
323	A42	20c orange & black *(103,200)*	1.25	.80
		Block of 4	5.50	4.00
a.		20c orange & brown *(100)*	600.00	—
b.		As No. 323, imperf., pair *(50)*	575.00	575.00
c.		As "a," imperf., pair *(100)*	1,750.	
d.		Vert. pair, imperf. between	700.00	
324	A42	24c gray & black *(103,100)*	.85	.55
		Block of 4	3.75	2.50
a.		Vert. pair, imperf. between	700.00	
325	A42	1p rose lilac & black *(10,800)*	45.00	30.00
		Block of 4	190.00	140.00
a.		Vert. pair, imperf. between	700.00	
		First day cover, #319-325		400.00
		Nos. 319-325 (7)	49.50	33.10

No. 322a is valued in the grade of fine.

Coil Stamp
Rizal Type of 1906
Printed by the U.S. Bureau of Engraving and
Printing.

1928   Unwmk.   *Perf. 11 Vertically*

326	A40	2c green *(110,000)*	7.50	15.00
		Pair	17.50	37.50
		Line pair	55.00	100.00

Types of 1906-1923

1925-31		Unwmk.			Imperf.
340	A40	2c **yellow green** ('31) *(99,986)*		.30	.20
		Block of 4		1.25	.25
a.		2c **green** ('25) *(51,000)*		.75	.50
341	A40	4c **carmine rose** ('31) *(49,855)*		.35	.20
		Block of 4		1.50	.40
a.		4c **carmine** ('25) *(25,500)*		1.00	.60
342	A40	6c **violet** ('31) *(10,000)*		1.25	1.00
		Block of 4		5.25	4.25
a.		6c **deep violet** ('25) *(5,200)*		12.00	6.00
343	A40	8c **brown** ('31) *(10,000)*		1.00	.90
		Block of 4		4.25	3.75
a.		8c **yellow brown** ('25) *(5,200)*		12.00	6.00
344	A40	10c **blue** ('31) *(7,000)*		2.50	1.40
		Block of 4		10.50	5.50
a.		10c **deep blue** ('25) *(2,200)*		40.00	12.00
345	A40	12c **deep orange** ('31) *(7,000)*		4.00	2.10
		Block of 4		17.00	8.75
a.		12c **red orange** ('25) *(2,200)*		50.00	20.00
346	A40	16c **olive green** *(Dewey)* ('31)			
		(7,000)		2.50	1.50
		Block of 4		11.00	6.75
a.		16c **bister green** ('25) *(2,200)*		35.00	10.00
347	A40	20c **deep yellow orange** ('31)			
		(7,000)		2.75	1.50
		Block of 4		12.00	6.75
a.		20c **yellow orange** ('25) *(2,200)*		37.50	12.00
348	A40	26c **green** ('31) *(7,000)*		2.75	1.50
		Block of 4		12.00	6.75
a.		26c **blue green** ('25) *(2,200)*		40.00	14.00
349	A40	30c **light gray** ('31) *(7,000)*		3.00	1.75
		Block of 4		13.00	7.25
a.		30c **gray** ('25) *(2,200)*		40.00	14.00
350	A40	1p **light violet** ('31) *(6,395)*		5.50	4.00
		Block of 4		25.00	16.50
a.		1p **violet** ('25) *(2,100)*		160.00	70.00
351	A40	2p **brown violet** ('31) *(3,612)*		13.00	10.00
		Block of 4		55.00	42.50
a.		2p **violet brown** ('25) *(600)*		325.00	150.00
352	A40	4p **blue** ('31) *(2,570)*		50.00	30.00
		Block of 4		225.00	—
a.		4p **deep blue** ('25) *(300)*		1,800.	750.00
353	A40	10p **green** ('31) *(2,208)*		130.00	100.00
		Block of 4		550.00	
a.		10p **deep green** ('25) *(200)*		2,750.	1,350.
		Nos. 340-353 (14)		218.90	156.05

Nos. 340a-353a were the original post office issue. These were reprinted twice in 1931 for sale to collectors (Nos. 340-353).

Mount Mayon, Luzon — A43

Post Office, Manila — A44

Pier No. 7, Manila Bay — A45

Vernal Falls, Yosemite Park, California (See Footnote) — A46

Rice Planting — A47

Rice Terraces — A48

Baguio Zigzag — A49

1932, May 3		Unwmk.		Perf. 11	
354	A43	2c **yellow green** *(5,432,000)*		.50	.20
		First day cover			2.00
		Block of 4		2.50	1.00
355	A44	4c **rose carmine** *(1,602,800)*		.45	.25
		First day cover			2.00
		Block of 4		2.00	1.20
356	A45	12c **orange** *(483,000)*		.60	.50
		First day cover			6.50
		Block of 4		2.75	2.00
357	A46	18c **red orange** *(983,400)*		30.00	9.00
		First day cover			16.00
		Block of 4		130.00	40.00
358	A47	20c **yellow** *(441,000)*		.75	.55
		First day cover			6.50
		Block of 4		3.25	2.25
359	A48	24c **deep violet** *(425,000)*		1.20	.65
		First day cover			6.50
		Block of 4		5.00	3.75
360	A49	32c **olive brown** *(510,600)*		1.20	.70
		First day cover			6.50
		Block of 4		5.00	3.75
		First day cover, #354-360			50.00
		Nos. 354-360 (7)		34.70	11.85

The 18c vignette was intended to show Pagsanjan Falls in Laguna, central Luzon, and is so labeled. Through error the stamp pictures Vernal Falls in Yosemite National Park, California.

Nos. 302, 302a Surcharged in Orange or Red

1932					
368	A40	1p on 4p **blue** (O) *(134,000)*		4.00	.45
		On cover			.60
		Block of 4		17.50	2.10
a.		1p on 4p **dark blue** (O)		4.00	1.25
369	A40	2p on 4p **dark blue** (R) *(80,000)*		6.00	.75
a.		2p on 4p **blue** (R)		6.00	.75
		On cover			.90
		Block of 4		27.50	3.50

Far Eastern Championship
Issued in commemoration of the Tenth Far Eastern Championship Games.

Baseball Players — A50

Tennis Player — A51

Basketball Players — A52

Printed by the Philippine Bureau of Printing.

1934, Apr. 14		Unwmk.		Perf.	
380	A50	2c **yellow brown** *(999,985)*		1.50	
		brown		1.50	
		First day cover			
		"T" of "Eastern" malformed		2.00	
381	A51	6c **ultramarine** *(800,000)*		.25	
		pale ultramarine		.25	
		First day cover			
a.		Vertical pair, imperf. between		1,250.	
382	A52	16c **violet brown** *(500,000)*		.50	
		dark violet		.50	
		First day cover			
a.		Imperf. horizontally, pair		1,250.	
		Nos. 380-382 (3)		2.25	

José Rizal — A53

Woman and Carabao — A54

La Filipina — A55

Pearl Fishing — A56

Fort Santiago — A5[?]

Salt Spring — A58

Magellan's Landing, 1521 — A59

"Juan de la Cruz" — A60

Rice Terraces — A61

guel Lopez de Legaspi and Chief Sikatuna Signing "Blood Compact," 1565 — A62

Barasoain Church, Malolos A63

Battle of Manila Bay, 1898 — A64

Montalban Gorge — A65

George Washington — A66

Printed by U.S. Bureau of Engraving and Printing.

		1935, Feb. 15	Unwmk.	Perf. 11	
383	A53	2c **rose** (62,183,400)		.20	.20
		First day cover			1.00
384	A54	4c **yellow green** (14,238,193)		.20	.20
		Light yellow green		.20	.20
		First day cover			1.00
385	A55	6c **dark brown** (1,958,928)		.20	.20
		First day cover			1.00
386	A56	8c **violet** (792,000)		.20	.20
		First day cover			1.60
387	A57	10c **rose carmine** (341,400)		.20	.20
		First day cover			1.60
388	A58	12c **black** (319,500)		.30	.20
		First day cover			1.60
389	A59	16c **dark blue** (2,422,778)		.30	.20
		First day cover			1.60
390	A60	20c **light olive green** (1,061,400)		.30	.20
		First day cover			2.25
391	A61	26c **indigo** (212,000)		.35	.25
		First day cover			3.00
392	A62	30c **orange red** (171,200)		.35	.25
		First day cover			3.00
393	A63	1p **red orange & black** (80,000)		1.90	1.25
		First day cover			8.25
394	A64	2p **bister brown & black** (61,100)		5.25	1.25
		First day cover			14.00
395	A65	4p **blue & black** (59,000)		6.50	3.00
		First day cover			20.00
396	A66	5p **green & black** (54,000)		15.00	3.00
		First day cover			27.50
		Nos. 383-396 (14)		31.25	10.60

USED VALUES

Used values in italics are for postally used examples with cancels of the proper function during the correct period of use.

Issues of the Commonwealth
Commonwealth Inauguration Issue
Issued to commemorate the inauguration of the Philippine Commonwealth, Nov. 15, 1935.

"The Temples of Human Progress" A67

		1935, Nov. 15	Unwmk.	Perf. 11	
397	A67	2c **carmine rose** (1,531,000)		.20	.20
		First day cover			1.00
398	A67	6c **deep violet** (523,000)		.20	.20
		First day cover			1.00
399	A67	16c **blue** (313,500)		.20	.20
		First day cover			1.00
400	A67	36c **yellow green** (261,000)		.35	.30
		First day cover			1.40
401	A67	50c **brown** (218,500)		.55	.55
		First day cover			2.00
		Nos. 397-401 (5)		1.50	1.45

Jose Rizal Issue
75th anniversary of the birth of Jose Rizal (1861-1896), national hero of the Filipinos.

Jose Rizal — A68

Printed by the Philippine Bureau of Printing.

		1936, June 19	Unwmk.	Perf. 12	
402	A68	2c **yellow brown** (500,000)		.20	.20
		light yellow brown		.20	.20
		First day cover			1.00
403	A68	6c **slate blue** (300,000)		.20	.20
		light slate green		.20	.20
		First day cover			1.00
a.		Imperf. vertically, pair		1,350.	
404	A68	36c **red brown** (200,000)		.50	.45
		light red brown		.50	.45
		First day cover			2.25
		Nos. 402-404 (3)		.90	.85

Commonwealth Anniversary Issue
Issued in commemoration of the first anniversary of the Commonwealth.

President Manuel L. Quezon — A69

Printed by U.S. Bureau of Engraving and Printing.

		1936, Nov. 15	Unwmk.	Perf. 11	
408	A69	2c **orange brown** (4,946,816)		.20	.20
		First day cover			1.00
409	A69	6c **yellow green** (1,019,900)		.20	.20
		First day cover			1.00
410	A69	12c **ultramarine** (527,600)		.20	.20
		First day cover			1.50
		Nos. 408-410 (3)		.60	.60

Stamps of 1935 Overprinted in Black

a

b

		1936-37	Unwmk.	Perf. 11	
411	A53(a)	2c **rose**, Dec. 28, 1936 (84,092,400)		.20	.20
		First day cover			35.00
a.		Bklt. pane of 6, Jan. 15 1937 (239,492)		2.50	2.00
		First day cover			40.00
412	A54(b)	4c **yellow green**, Mar. 29, 1937 (100,000)		.50	4.00
413	A55(a)	6c **dark brown**, Oct. 7, 1936 (2,230,394)		.20	.20
		On cover			.20
414	A56(b)	8c **violet**, Mar. 29, 1937 (627,500)		.25	.20
		On cover			.25
415	A57(b)	10c **rose carmine**, Dec. 28, 1936 (1,687,550)		.20	.20
		First day cover			35.00
a.		"COMMONWEALT"			—
416	A58(b)	12c **black**, Mar. 29, 1937 (2,118,600)		.20	.20
		On cover			.20
417	A59(b)	16c **dark blue**, Oct. 7, 1936 (597,300)		.25	.20
		On cover			.20
418	A60(a)	20c **lt olive green**, Mar. 29, 1937 (100,000)		.75	.40
		On cover			.45
419	A61(b)	26c **indigo**, Mar. 29, 1937 (100,000)		.50	.35
		On cover			.40
420	A62(b)	30c **orange red**, Dec. 28, 1936 (836,252)		.45	.20
		First day cover			35.00
421	A63(b)	1p **red org & blk**, Oct. 7, 1936 (319,250)		.75	.20
		On cover			.35
422	A64(b)	2p **bis brn & blk**, Mar. 29, 1937 (50,000)		6.75	2.75
		On cover			3.00
423	A65(b)	4p **blue & blk**, Mar. 29, 1937 (30,000)		30.00	6.00
		On cover			50.00

424	A66(b)	5p **green & blk**, *Mar. 29, 1937* (60,500)	7.50	2.00
		On cover		35.00
		Nos. 411-424 (14)	48.50	17.10

Eucharistic Congress Issue
Issued to commemorate the 33rd International Eucharistic Congress held at Manila, Feb. 3-7, 1937.

Map, Symbolical of the Eucharistic Congress Spreading Light of Christianity — A70

FLAT PLATE PRINTING
Plates of 256 subjects in four panes of 64 each.

1937, Feb. 3   Unwmk.   *Perf. 11*

425	A70	2c **yellow green** (4,102,848)	.20	.20
		First day cover		1.00
426	A70	6c **light brown** (2,626,240)	.20	.20
		First day cover		1.00
427	A70	12c **sapphire** (2,165,440)	.20	.20
		First day cover		1.00
428	A70	20c **deep orange** (1,640,640)	.25	.20
		First day cover		1.00
429	A70	36c **deep violet** (1,115,840)	.50	.40
		First day cover		1.40
430	A70	50c **carmine** (1,115,840)	.65	.35
		First day cover		2.00
		Nos. 425-430 (6)	2.00	1.55

Arms of City of Manila — A71

1937, Aug. 27   Unwmk.   *Perf. 11*

431	A71	10p **gray** (70,000)	5.00	2.00
432	A71	20p **henna brown** (90,600)	3.00	1.40
		First day cover, #431-432		50.00

Stamps of 1935 Overprinted in Black:

a

b

1938-40   Unwmk.   *Perf. 11*

433	A53(a)	2c **rose**, *1939* (103,549,959)	.20	.20
a.		Booklet pane of 6 (157,176)	3.50	2.50
b.		As "a," lower left-hand stamp overprinted "WEALTH COMMON-" (24)	4,000.	
c.		Hyphen omitted	—	—
434	A54(b)	4c **yellow green**, *1940* (72,500)	2.50	30.00
435	A55(a)	6c **dark brown**, *May 12, 1939* (4,013,440)	.20	.20
		First day cover		35.00
a.		6c golden brown	.20	.20
436	A56(b)	8c **violet**, *1939* (1,583,357)	.20	.20
a.		"COMMONWEALT" (LR 31)	90.00	
437	A57(b)	10c **rose carmine**, *May 12, 1939* (2,695,242)	.20	.20
a.		"COMMONWEALT" (LR 31)	—	
438	A58(b)	12c **black**, *1940* (3,765,000)	.20	.20
439	A59(b)	16c **dark blue** (1,415,700)	.20	.20
440	A60(a)	20c **light olive green**, *1939* (1,663,799)	.20	.20
441	A61(b)	26c **indigo**, *1940* (597,500)	.20	.20
442	A62(b)	30c **orange red**, *May 23, 1939* (643,100)	1.50	.70
443	A63(b)	1p **red org & blk**, *Aug. 29, 1938* (1,065,629)	.50	.20
		First day cover		40.00
444	A64(b)	2p **bister brown & black**, *1939* (98,000)	5.00	.75
445	A65(b)	4p **blue & black**, *1940* (6,500)	350.00	350.00

		On cover		500.00
446	A66(b)	5p **green & black**, *1940* (31,500)	10.00	3.25
		Nos. 433-446 (14)	371.10	386.50

Overprint *"b"* measures 18½x1¾mm.
No. 433b occurs in booklet pane, No. 433a, position 5; all copies are straight-edged, left and bottom.

First Foreign Trade Week Issue
Nos. 384, 298a and 432 Surcharged in Red, Violet or Black:

a

b

c

1939, July 5

449	A54(a)	2c on 4c **yellow green** (R) (500,000)	.20	.20
		First day cover		1.40
450	A40(b)	6c on 26c **blue green** (V) (166,700)	.20	.20
		First day cover		2.00
a.		6c on 26c **green**	1.00	.30
451	A71(c)	50c on 20p **henna brown** (Bk) (60,000)	1.00	1.00
		First day cover		5.00

Commonwealth 4th Anniversary Issue (#452-460)

Triumphal Arch — A72

Printed by U.S. Bureau of Engraving and Printing.

1939, Nov. 15   Unwmk.   *Perf. 11*

452	A72	2c **yellow green** (1,562,352)	.20	.20
		First day cover		1.00
453	A72	6c **carmine** (1,267,717)	.20	.20
		First day cover		1.00
454	A72	12c **bright blue** (971,724)	.20	.20
		First day cover		1.40
		Nos. 452-454 (3)	.60	.60

Malacañan Palace — A73

1939, Nov. 15   Unwmk.   *Perf. 11*

455	A73	2c **green** (1,578,600)	.20	.20
		First day cover		1.00
456	A73	6c **orange** (1,252,859)	.20	.20
		First day cover		1.00
457	A73	12c **carmine** (935,800)	.20	.20
		First day cover		1.40
		Nos. 455-457 (3)	.60	.60

President Quezon Taking Oath of Office — A74

1940, Feb. 8   Unwmk.   *Perf.*

458	A74	2c **dark orange** (1,572,400)	.20
		First day cover	
459	A74	6c **dark green** (1,257,900)	.20
		First day cover	
460	A74	12c **purple** (980,779)	.25
		First day cover	
		Nos. 458-460 (3)	.65

José Rizal — A75

ROTARY PRESS PRINTING

1941, Apr. 14   Unwmk.   *Perf. 11x*
Size: 19x22½mm

461	A75	2c **apple green** (59,915,600)	.20
		First day cover	
		P# block of 4	1.00

FLAT PLATE PRINTING

1941-43   Unwmk.   Size: 18¾x22mm   *Perf*

462	A75	2c **apple green**	.20
a.		2c pale apple green ('41)	.20
b.		As No. 462, booklet pane of 6 (24,000)	1.25
c.		As "a," booklet pane of 6 ('41) (114,960)	2.50

This stamp was issued only in booklet panes and all co have one or two straight edges.
Further printings were made in 1942 and 1943 in diffe shades from the first supply of stamps sent to the islands.

Stamps of 1935-41 Handstamped in Violet

1944   Unwmk.   *Perf. 11, 11x1*

463	A53	2c **rose** (On 411), *Dec. 3* (168)	325.00	16
a.		Booklet pane of 6 (28)	12,500.	
463B	A53	2c **rose** (On 433), *Dec. 14* (41)	1,400.	1,
464	A75	2c **apple green** (On 461), *Nov. 8* (24,400)	3.75	1
		On cover		
465	A54	4c **yellow green** (On 384), *Nov. 8* (807)	42.50	4
		On cover		
466	A55	6c **dark brown** (On 385), *Dec. 14* (64)	3,250.	2,0
		On cover		
467	A69	6c **yellow green** (On 409), *Dec. 3*	150.00	110
		On cover		
468	A55	6c **dark brown** (On 413), *Dec. 28* (206)	3,500.	825
		On cover		
469	A72	6c **carmine** (On 453), *Nov. 8* (235)	350.00	125
		On cover		
470	A73	6c **orange** (On 456), *Dec. 14* (141)	1,750.	725
		On cover		
471	A74	6c **dark green** (On 459), *Nov. 8*	225.00	200
		On cover		
472	A56	8c **violet** (On 436), *Nov. 8* (1,643)	17.50	24
		On cover		
473	A57	10c **carmine rose** (On 415), *Nov. 8* (450)	200.00	90
		On cover		
474	A57	10c **carmine rose** (On 437), *Nov. 8* (358)	175.00	140
		On cover		
475	A69	12c **ultramarine** (On 410), *Dec. 3*	1,100.	400
		On cover		
476	A72	12c **bright blue** (On 454), *Nov. 8* (36)	5,500.	2,2
		On cover		
477	A74	12c **purple** (On 460), *Nov. 8*	275.00	190
		On cover		
478	A59	16c **dark blue** (On 389), *Dec. 3* (122)	2,000.	
479	A59	16c **dark blue** (On 417), *Nov. 8* (200)	650.00	550
		On cover		
480	A59	16c **dark blue** (On 439), *Nov. 8* (500)	500.00	200
		On cover		
481	A60	20c **light olive green** (On 440), *Nov. 8* (1,401)	110.00	35
		On cover		
482	A62	30c **orange red** (On 420), *Dec. 3* (248)	350.00	325
		On cover		
483	A62	30c **orange red** (On 442), *Dec. 3* (200)	750.00	375

On cover —
A63 1p **red orange & black** (On 443)
Dec. 3 (21)   6,250. 4,500.
On cover —

s. 463-484 are valued in the grade of fine to very fine.
. 463 comes only from the booklet pane. All copies have
or two straight edges.

Types of 1935-37 Overprinted

a

b

c

		Unwmk.	Perf. 11	
45				
	A53(a)	2c **rose**, *Jan. 19 (65,816,000)*	.20	.20
		First day cover		2.50
	A54(b)	4c **yellow green**, *Jan. 19 (4,986,800)*	.20	.20
		First day cover		2.50
A55(a)		6c **golden brown**, *Jan. 19 (4,381,440)*	.20	.20
		First day cover		2.50
A56(b)		8c **violet**, *Jan. 19 (535,000)*	.20	.20
		First day cover		3.00
A57(b)		10c **rose carmine**, *Jan. 19 (1,060,000)*	.20	.20
		First day cover		3.00
A58(b)		12c **black**, *Jan. 19 (3,214,200)*	.20	.20
		First day cover		3.50
A59(b)		16c **dark blue**, *Jan. 19 (1,060,000)*	.25	.20
		First day cover		4.00
A60(a)		20c **light olive green**, *Jan. 19 (976,800)*	.30	.20
		First day cover		4.25
A62(b)		30c **orange red**, *May 1 (535,000)*	.40	.35
		First day cover		2.50
A63(b)		1p **red orange & black**, *Jan. 19 (1,434,400)*	1.10	.25
		First day cover		6.50
A71(c)		10p **gray**, *May 1 (22,000)*	40.00	13.50
		First day cover		20.00
A71(c)		20p **henna brown**, *May 1 (42,500)*	35.00	15.00
		First day cover		25.00
		Nos. 485-496 (12)	78.25	30.70

José Rizal — A76

ROTARY PRESS PRINTING
46, May 28   Unwmk.   Perf. 11x10½
7 A76   2c **sepia** (53,560,000)   .20   .20
P# block of 4   .50

Later issues, released by the Philippine Republic on
y 4, 1946, and thereafter, are listed in Scott's Stan-
rd Postage Stamp Catalogue, Vol. 5.

AIR POST STAMPS

Madrid-Manila Flight Issue
Issued to commemorate the flight of Spanish aviators
Gallarza and Loriga from Madrid to Manila.

Regular Issue of 1917-26
Overprinted in Red or Violet by
the Philippine Bureau of
Printing

		1926, May 13 Unwmk.	Perf. 11	
C1	A40	2c **green** (R) *(9,900)*	16.50	15.00
		First day cover		26.00
		Block of 4	72.50	67.50
C2	A40	4c **carmine** (V) *(8,900)*	18.50	17.50
		First day cover		26.00
		Block of 4	85.00	80.00
a.		Inverted overprint *(100)*	3,500.	—
C3	A40	6c **lilac** (R) *(5,000)*	55.00	55.00
		First day cover		40.00
		Block of 4	240.00	
C4	A40	8c **orange brown** (V) *(5,000)*	57.50	57.50
		First day cover		40.00
		Block of 4	250.00	
C5	A40	10c **deep blue** (R) *(5,000)*	57.50	57.50
		First day cover		40.00
		Block of 4	250.00	
C6	A40	12c **red orange** (V) *(4,000)*	57.50	57.50
		First day cover		42.50
		Block of 4	250.00	
C7	A40	16c **light olive green** (Sampson) (V) *(300)*	3,250.	1,600.
		Block of 4	—	
C8	A40	16c **olive bister** (Sampson) (R) *(100)*	5,000.	3,000.
		Block of 4	—	
C9	A40	16c **olive green** (Dewey) (V) *(3,600)*	70.00	30.00
		First day cover		42.50
		Block of 4	325.00	
C10	A40	20c **orange yellow** (V) *(4,000)*	70.00	70.00
		First day cover		42.50
		Block of 4	325.00	
C11	A40	26c **blue green** (V) *(3,900)*	70.00	70.00
		First day cover		45.00
		Block of 4	325.00	
C12	A40	30c **gray** (V) *(4,000)*	70.00	70.00
		First day cover		45.00
		Block of 4	325.00	
C13	A40	2p **violet brown** (R) *(900)*	550.00	300.00
		On cover		300.00
		Block of 4	—	
C14	A40	4p **dark blue** (R) *(700)*	750.00	500.00
		On cover		475.00
		Block of 4	—	
C15	A40	10p **deep green** (V) *(500)*	1,350.	700.00
		On cover		675.00
		Block of 4	—	

Same Overprint on No. 269
Wmk. Single-lined PIPS (190)
Perf. 12
C16 A40 26c **blue green** (V) *(100)*   6,250.
Block of 4 —

Same Overprint on No. 284
Perf. 10
C17	A40	1p **pale violet** (V) *(2,000)*	210.00	175.00
		On cover		200.00
		First day cover		225.00
		Block of 4	900.00	

Overprintings of Nos. C1-C6, C9-C15 and C17 were made
from two plates. Position No. 89 of the first printing shows
broken left blade of propeller.

London-Orient Flight Issue
Issued Nov. 9, 1928, to celebrate the arrival of a
British squadron of hydroplanes.

Regular Issue of 1917-25
Overprinted in Red

		1928, Nov. 9 Unwmk.	Perf. 11	
C18	A40	2c **green** *(101,200)*	.60	.30
		First day cover		7.75
C19	A40	4c **carmine** *(50,500)*	.75	.50
		First day cover		9.50
C20	A40	6c **violet** *(12,600)*	2.75	1.75
		On cover		1.90
C21	A40	8c **orange brown** *(10,000)*	3.00	1.90
		On cover		2.25
C22	A40	10c **deep blue** *(10,000)*	3.00	1.90
		On cover		2.25

C23	A40	12c **red orange** *(8,000)*	3.75	2.75
		On cover		3.25
C24	A40	16c **olive green** (No. 303a) *(12,600)*	3.25	1.90
		On cover		2.40
C25	A40	20c **orange yellow** *(8,000)*	4.25	2.75
		On cover		3.25
C26	A40	26c **blue green** *(7,000)*	11.00	6.50
		On cover		8.50
C27	A40	30c **gray** *(7,000)*	11.00	6.50
		On cover		8.50

Same Overprint on No. 271
Wmk. Single-lined PIPS (190)
Perf. 12
C28	A40	1p **pale violet** *(6,000)*	55.00	25.00
		On cover		27.50
		Nos. C18-C28 (11)	98.35	51.75

Von Gronau Issue
Issued commemoration of the visit of Capt. Wolfgang
von Gronau's airplane on its round-the-world flight.

Nos. 354-360
Overprinted by
the Philippine
Bureau of
Printing

		1932, Sept. 27 Unwmk.	Perf. 11	
C29	A43	2c **yellow green** *(100,000)*	.75	.30
		First day cover		2.00
C30	A44	4c **rose carmine** *(80,000)*	.75	.30
		First day cover		2.00
C31	A45	12c **orange** *(55,000)*	1.00	.50
		First day cover		1.00
C32	A46	18c **red orange** *(25,305)*	5.00	3.25
		First day cover		3.50
C33	A47	20c **yellow** *(30,000)*	3.00	1.50
		On cover		1.60
C34	A48	24c **deep violet** *(30,000)*	3.00	1.50
		On cover		1.60
C35	A49	32c **olive brown** *(30,000)*	2.00	1.50
		On cover		1.60
		First day cover, #C29-C35		35.00
		Nos. C29-C35 (7)	15.50	8.85

Rein Issue
Commemorating the flight from Madrid to Manila of
the Spanish aviator Fernando Rein y Loring.

Regular Issue of 1917-25
Overprinted in Black

		1933, Apr. 11		
C36	A40	2c **green** *(95,000)*	.45	.35
		First day cover		1.60
C37	A40	4c **carmine** *(75,000)*	.50	.35
		First day cover		1.60
C38	A40	6c **deep violet** *(65,000)*	.90	.75
		First day cover		3.00
C39	A40	8c **orange brown** *(35,000)*	2.75	1.50
C40	A40	10c **dark blue** *(35,000)*	2.75	1.00
C41	A40	12c **orange** *(35,000)*	2.50	1.00
C42	A40	16c **olive green** (Dewey) *(35,000)*	2.50	1.00
C43	A40	20c **yellow** *(35,000)*	2.50	1.00
C44	A40	26c **green** *(35,000)*	2.75	1.50
a.		26c blue green	3.50	1.75
C45	A40	30c **gray** *(30,000)*	3.50	1.75
		First day cover, #C36-C45		40.00
		Nos. C36-C45 (10)	21.10	10.20

Stamp of 1917 Overprinted by
the Philippine Bureau of
Printing

		1933, May 26 Unwmk.	Perf. 11	
C46	A40	2c **green** *(500,000)*	.60	.40

Regular Issue
of 1932
Overprinted

C47	A44	4c **rose carmine** *(799,878)*	.25	.20
C48	A45	12c **orange** *(500,000)*	.40	.20
C49	A47	20c **yellow** *(500,000)*	.40	.20
C50	A48	24c **deep violet** *(500,000)*	.50	.25
C51	A49	32c **olive brown** *(500,000)*	.75	.35
		First day cover, #C46-C51		36.00
		Nos. C46-C51 (6)	2.90	1.60

Transpacific Issue
Issued to commemorate the China Clipper flight from
Manila to San Francisco, Dec. 2-5, 1935.

Nos. 387, 392
Overprinted in
Gold

1935, Dec. 2		**Unwmk.**	**Perf. 11**	
C52	A57	10c **rose carmine** *(500,000)*	.30	.20
		First day cover		2.00
C53	A62	30c **orange red** *(300,000)*	.50	.35
		First day cover		3.00

Manila-Madrid Flight Issue
Issued to commemorate the Manila-Madrid flight by
aviators Antonio Arnaiz and Juan Calvo.

Nos. 291, 295, 298a, 298
Surcharged in Various Colors
by Philippine Bureau of Printing

1936, Sept. 6				
C54	A40	2c on 4c **carmine** (Bl)		
		(2,000,000)	.20	.20
		First day cover		1.00
C55	A40	6c on 12c **red orange** (V)		
		(500,000)	.20	.20
		First day cover		3.00
C56	A40	16c on 26c **blue green** (Bk)		
		(300,000)	.25	.20
		First day cover		5.00
a.		16c on 26c **green**	2.00	.70
		Nos. C54-C56 (3)	.65	.60

Air Mail Exhibition Issue
Issued to commemorate the first Air Mail Exhibition,
held Feb. 17-19, 1939.

Nos. 298a, 298, 431
Surcharged in Black or Red by
Philippine Bureau of Printing

1939, Feb. 17				
C57	A40	8c on 26c **blue green** (Bk)		
		(200,000)	.75	.40
		First day cover		3.50
a.		8c on 26c **green** (Bk)	3.50	.55
C58	A71	1p on 10p **gray** (R) *(30,000)*	3.00	2.25
		First day cover		8.00

Moro Vinta and
Clipper — AP1

Printed by the US Bureau of Engraving and Printing.

1941, June 30		**Unwmk.**	**Perf. 11**	
C59	AP1	8c **carmine** *(210,000)*	2.00	.60
		First day cover		2.00
C60	AP1	20c **ultramarine** *(25,000)*	2.50	.45
		First day cover		2.50
C61	AP1	60c **blue green** *(50,000)*	2.00	1.00
		First day cover		3.50
C62	AP1	1p **sepia** *(1,110,000)*	.70	.50
		First day cover		2.25
		Nos. C59-C62 (4)	7.20	2.55

No. C47
Handstamped
in Violet

1944, Dec. 3		**Unwmk.**	**Perf. 11**	
C63	A44	4c **rose carmine** *(122)*	2,750.	2,750.
		On cover		—

SPECIAL DELIVERY STAMPS

U.S. No. E5 Overprinted in Red

a

Printed by U.S. Bureau of Engraving & Printing
Wmk. Double-lined USPS (191)

1901, Oct. 15			**Perf. 12**	
E1	SD3	10c **dark blue** *(14,998)*	110.	85.
		On cover		350.
		Block of 4	500.	
		P# strip of 3, Impt.	500.	
		P# block of 6, Impt.	5,000.	
		Dots in curved frame above		
		messenger (Pl. 882)	175.	160.
		P# block of 6, Impt. (Pl. 882)	5,250.	

Special Delivery
Messenger
SD2

Wmk. Double-lined PIPS (191)

1906, Sept. 8			**Perf. 12**	
E2	SD2	20c **deep ultramarine** *(40,019)*	40.00	7.50
		On cover		17.50
		Block of 4	175.00	
b.		20c **pale ultramarine**	30.00	7.50
		On cover		17.50
		Block of 4	125.00	

SPECIAL PRINTING
U.S. No. E6 Overprinted Type "a" in Red

1907		**Wmk. Double-lined USPS (191)**	**Perf. 12**
E2A	SD4	10c **ultramarine**	2,750.
		Block of 4	11,500.
		P# block of 6, Impt.	38,500.

This stamp was part of the set specially printed for the
Bureau of Insular Affairs in 1907. See note following No. 240.
There is only one intact plate block of No. E2A. It is fine and is
valued thus.

1911, Apr.		**Wmk. Single-lined PIPS (190)**	**Perf. 12**	
E3	SD2	20c **deep ultramarine** *(200,000)*	22.00	1.75
		On cover		12.50
		Block of 4	90.00	

1916			**Perf. 10**	
E4	SD2	20c **deep ultramarine** *(200,000)*	175.00	75.00
		On cover		100.00
		Block of 4	825.00	
		pale ultramarine		

Early in 1919 the supply of Special Delivery stamps in the
Manila area was exhausted. A Government decree permitted
the use of regular issue postage stamps for payment of the

---

special delivery fee when so noted on the cover. This u[...]
was permitted until the new supply of Special Delivery sta[...]
arrived.

1919		**Unwmk.**	**Per[...]**	
E5	SD2	20c **ultramarine** *(4,195,862)*	.60	
		On cover		2.50
		Block of 4	2.50	
a.		20c **pale blue**	.75	
		On cover		3.00
		Block of 4	3.00	
b.		20c **dull violet**	.60	
		On cover		2.50
		Block of 4	2.50	

Type of 1906 Issue

1925-31		**Unwmk.**	**Imp[...]**	
E6	SD2	20c **dull violet** ('31) *(6,500)*	25.00	5[...]
		On cover		25[...]
		Block of 4	110.00	
		P# block of 6	400.00	
a.		20c **violet blue** ('25) *(2,100)*	50.00	
		On cover		
		Block of 4	250.00	
		P# block of 6	750.00	

Type of 1919
Overprinted in
Black

1939, Apr. 27		**Unwmk.**	**Perf[...]**	
E7	SD2	20c **blue violet** *(1,253,250)*	.25	
		First day cover		3[...]

Nos. E5b and
E7
Handstamped
in Violet

1944		**Unwmk.**	**Perf.**	
E8	SD2	20c **dull violet** (On E5b) *(138)*	1,400.	550[...]
E9	SD2	20c **blue violet** (On E7), Nov. 8		
		(600)	500.00	225[...]
		On cover		

Type SD2 Overprinted "VICTORY" As No. 486

1945, May 1		**Unwmk.**	**Perf.**	
E10	SD2	20c **blue violet** *(578,600)*	.70	
		First day cover		10[...]
a.		"IC" close together	3.25	2[...]

SPECIAL DELIVERY OFFICIAL STAMP

Type of 1906
Issue
Overprinted

1931		**Unwmk.**	**Perf.**	
EO1	SD2	20c **dull violet** *(46,750)*	2.00	75[...]
a.		No period after "B"	35.00	
b.		Double overprint		

It is strongly recommended that expert opinion be acqui[...]
for No. EO1 used.

POSTAGE DUE STAMPS

U.S. Nos. J38-J44 Overprinted
in Black

Printed by the U.S. Bureau of Engraving and Printing.
Wmk. Double-lined USPS (191)

9, Aug. 16			**Perf. 12**	
D2	1c	**deep claret** *(340,892)*	7.50	2.50
		On cover		30.00
		On cover, used as regular postage		110.00
		P# strip of 3, Impt.	125.00	
		P# block of 6, Impt.	*650.00*	
D2	2c	**deep claret** *(306,983)*	7.50	2.50
		On cover		37.50
		P# strip of 3, Impt.	125.00	
		P# block of 6, Impt.	*650.00*	
D2	5c	**deep claret** *(34,565)*	15.00	2.50
		On cover		70.00
		P# strip of 3, Impt.	200.00	
		P# block of 6, Impt.	*1,500.*	
D2	10c	**deep claret** *(15,848)*	19.00	5.50
		On cover		100.00
		P# strip of 3, Impt.	175.00	
		P# block of 6, Impt.	*1,100.*	
D2	50c	**deep claret** *(6,168)*	200.00	100.00
		On cover		—
		P# strip of 3, Impt.	*1,100.*	
		P# block of 6, Impt.	*4,000.*	

. J1 was used to pay regular postage Sept. 5-19, 1902.

1, Aug. 31				
D2	3c	**deep claret** *(14,885)*	17.50	7.00
		On cover		60.00
		P# strip of 3, Impt.	175.00	
		P# block of 6, Impt.	*875.00*	
D2	30c	**deep claret** *(2,140)*	250.00	110.00
		On cover		—
		P# strip of 3, Impt.	*1,000.*	
		P# block of 6, Impt.	*4,000.*	
		Nos. J1-J7 (7)	516.50	230.00

Post Office Clerk — D3

28, Aug. 21		**Unwmk.**	**Perf. 11**	
D3	4c	**brown red** *(948,054)*	.25	.20
D3	6c	**brown red** *(255,490)*	.25	.20
D3	8c	**brown red** *(508,621)*	.25	.20
D3	10c	**brown red** *(254,195)*	.25	.20
D3	12c	**brown red** *(407,457)*	.25	.20
D3	16c	**brown red** *(253,215)*	.25	.20
D3	20c	**brown red** *(259,665)*	.25	.20
		Nos. J8-J14 (7)	1.75	1.40

No. J8 Surcharged in Blue

37, July 29		**Unwmk.**	**Perf. 11**	
5 D3	3c on 4c **brown red**		.25	.20
	First day cover			35.00

See note after No. NJ1.

Nos. J8-J14 Handstamped in Violet

VICTORY

44, Dec. 3		**Unwmk.**	**Perf. 11**	
6 D3	4c	**brown red** *(306)*	140.00	—
7 D3	6c	**brown red** *(390)*	90.00	—
8 D3	8c	**brown red** *(379)*	95.00	—
9 D3	10c	**brown red** *(405)*	90.00	—
0 D3	12c	**brown red** *(423)*	90.00	—
1 D3	16c	**brown red** *(425)*	95.00	—
2 D3	20c	**brown red** *(375)*	95.00	—
		Nos. J16-J22 (7)	695.00	

OFFICIAL STAMPS

Official Handstamped Overprints

"Officers purchasing stamps for government business may, if ey so desire, surcharge them with the letters O.B. either in riting with black ink or by rubber stamps but in such a manner s not to obliterate the stamp that postmasters will be unable to etermine whether the stamps have been previously used." — .M. Cotterman, Director of Posts, December 26, 1905.

Beginning with January 1, 1906, all branches of the Insular overnment, used postage stamps to prepay postage instead

---

of franking them as before. Some officials used manuscript, some utilized the typewriting machines but by far the larger number provided themselves with rubber stamps. The majority of these read "O.B." but other forms were: "OFFICIAL BUSINESS" or "OFFICIAL MAIL" in two lines, with variations on many of these.

These "O.B." overprints are known on U.S. 1899-1901 stamps; on 1903-06 stamps in red and blue; on 1906 stamps in red, blue, black, yellow and green.

"O.B." overprints were also made on the centavo and peso stamps of the Philippines, per order of May 25, 1907.

Beginning in 1926 the Bureau of Posts issued press-printed official stamps, but many government offices continued to hand-stamp ordinary postage stamps "O.B."

During the Japanese occupation period 1942-45, the same system of handstamped official overprints prevailed, but the handstamp usually consisted of "K.P.", initials of the Tagalog words, "Kagamitang Pampamahalaan" (Official Business), and the two Japanese characters used in the printed overprint on Nos. NO1 to NO4.

Legislative Palace Issue of 1926 Overprinted in Red

Printed and overprinted by the Philippine Bureau of Printing.

1926, Dec. 20		**Unwmk.**	**Perf. 12**	
O1	A42	2c **green & black** *(90,500)*	2.75	1.00
		On cover		2.00
		Block of 4	12.00	5.50
O2	A42	4c **carmine & black** *(90,450)*	2.75	1.25
		On cover		2.00
		First day cover		10.00
		Block of 4	12.00	5.50
a.		Vertical pair, imperf. between	750.00	
O3	A42	18c **light brown & black** *(70,000)*	7.75	4.00
		On cover		6.50
		Block of 4	35.00	20.00
O4	A42	20c **orange & black** *(70,250)*	7.50	1.75
		On cover		2.25
		Block of 4	35.00	8.25
		First day cover, #O1-O4		50.00
		Nos. O1-O4 (4)	20.75	8.00

Regular Issue of 1917-25 Overprinted

Printed and overprinted by the U.S. Bureau of Engraving and Printing.

1931		**Unwmk.**	**Perf. 11**	
O5	A40	2c **green** *(22,940,100)*	.40	.20
a.		No period after "B"	15.00	5.00
b.		No period after "O"	—	
O6	A40	4c **carmine** *(5,377,000)*	.40	.20
a.		No period after "B"	20.00	5.00
O7	A40	6c **deep violet** *(616,500)*	.60	.20
O8	A40	8c **yellow brown** *(706,700)*	.60	.20
O9	A40	10c **deep blue** *(1,006,800)*	1.00	.20
O10	A40	12c **red orange** *(158,050)*	1.25	.20
a.		No period after "B"	60.00	
O11	A40	16c **light olive green** *(Dewey)* *(824,400)*	.90	.20
a.		16c olive bister	2.000	.20
O12	A40	20c **orange yellow** *(509,050)*	1.00	.20
a.		No period after "B"	50.00	15.00
O13	A40	26c **green** *(68,600)*	1.50	.30
a.		26c blue green	2.00	.65
O14	A40	30c **gray** *(199,400)*	1.50	.25
		Nos. O5-O14 (10)	9.15	2.15

Regular Issue of 1935 Overprinted in Black

1935		**Unwmk.**	**Perf. 11**	
O15	A53	2c **rose** *(7,927,800)*	.20	.20
a.		No period after "B"	15.00	5.00
O16	A54	4c **yellow green** *(5,079,266)*	.20	.20
a.		No period after "B"	15.00	8.50
O17	A55	6c **dark brown** *(786,896)*	.20	.20
a.		No period after "B"	35.00	17.50
O18	A56	8c **violet** *(656,200)*	.20	.20
O19	A57	10c **rose carmine** *(756,100)*	.20	.20
O20	A58	12c **black** *(104,500)*	.20	.20

O21	A59	16c **dark blue** *(254,800)*	.20	.20
O22	A60	20c **light olive green** *(203,079)*	.20	.20
O23	A61	26c **indigo** *(67,750)*	.25	.25
O24	A62	30c **orange red** *(83,500)*	.30	.20
		Nos. O15-O24 (10)	2.15	2.05

Nos. 411 and 418 with Additional Overprint in Black

1937-38		**Unwmk.**	**Perf. 11**	
O25	A53	2c **rose**, *Apr. 10, 1937* *(11,580,800)*	.20	.20
		First day cover		50.00
a.		No period after "B"	15.00	2.25
b.		Period after "B" raised (UL 4)	150.00	
O26	A60	20c **light olive green**, *Apr. 26, 1938* *(174,929)*	.65	.50

Regular Issue of 1935 Overprinted In Black:

a

b

1938-40		**Unwmk.**	**Perf. 11**	
O27	A53(a)	2c **rose** *(23,239,872)*	.20	.20
a.		Hyphen omitted	20.00	20.00
b.		No period after "B"	25.00	25.00
O28	A54(b)	4c **yellow green** *(85,000)*	.20	.20
O29	A55(a)	6c **dark brown** *(393,549)*	.20	.20
O30	A56(b)	8c **violet** *(82,000)*	.20	.20
O31	A57(b)	10c **rose carmine** *(1,188,735)*	.20	.20
a.		No period after "O"	40.00	30.00
O32	A58(b)	12c **black** *(340,000)*	.20	.20
O33	A59(b)	16c **dark blue** *(490,000)*	.20	.20
O34	A60(a)	20c **light olive green** *('40)* *(162,000)*	.25	.25
O35	A61(b)	26c **indigo** *(77,000)*	.30	.30
O36	A62(b)	30c **orange red** *(82,000)*	.25	.25
		Nos. O27-O36 (10)	2.20	2.20

No. 461 Overprinted in Black

c

ROTARY PRESS PRINTING

1941, Apr. 14		**Unwmk.**	**Perf. 11x10½**	
O37	A75	2c **apple green** *(21,087,900)*	.20	.20
		First day cover		3.50
		Margin block of 4, P#	.25	

Nos. O27, O37, O16, O29, O31, O22 and O26 Handstamped in Violet

1944		**Unwmk.**	**Perf. 11, 11x10½**	
O38	A53	2c **rose** (On O27) *(128)*	375.00	150.00
O39	A75	2c **apple green** (On O37) *(13,100)*	6.50	3.00
		On cover		10.00

		Block of 4	32.50	—	
O40	A54	4c **yellow green** (On O16)			
		(2,634)	42.50	30.00	
		Block of 4	190.00		
O40A	A55	6c **dark brown** (On O29)	6,500.	—	
O41	A57	10c **rose carmine** (On O31) (665)	500.00		
		Block of 4	2,100.		
a.		No period after "O"	4,000.		
O42	A60	20c **light olive green** (On O22)	6,000.		
O43	A60	20c **light olive green** (On O26)	1,750.		

No. 497 Overprinted Type "c" in Black

1946, June 19	**Unwmk.**	**Perf. 11x10½**
O44 A76 2c **sepia** (10,470,000)	.20	.20
Margin block of 4, P#	.40	

POST OFFICE SEALS

POS1

1906	**Litho.**	**Unwmk.**	**Perf. 12**
OX1 POS1 **light brown**			65.00 65.00

Wmk. "PIRS" in Double-lined Capitals

1907		**Perf. 12**
OX2 POS1 **light brown**		85.00 85.00

	Hyphen-hole Perf. 7
OX3 POS1 **orange brown**	40.00 45.00

1911		**Hyphen-hole Perf. 7**
OX4 POS1 **yellow brown**		37.50 40.00
OX5 POS1 **olive bister**		75.00 75.00
a. Unwatermarked		—
OX6 POS1 **yellow**		85.00 85.00

1913	**Unwmk.**	**Hyphen-hole Perf. 7**
OX7 POS1 **lemon yellow**		2.00 3.00

	Perf. 12
OX8 POS1 **yellow**	100.00 50.00

Wmk. "USPS" in Single-lined Capitals
Hyphen-hole Perf. 7

OX9 POS1 **yellow**	100.00 75.00

1934	**Unwmk.**	**Rouletted**
OX10 POS1 **dark blue**		1.00 1.50

POS2

OX11 POS2 **dark blue**	1.00 1.50

POS3

1938		**Hyphen-hole Perf. 7**
OX12 POS3 **dark blue**		5.50 5.50

ENVELOPES

U.S. Envelopes of 1899 Issue Overprinted
below stamp in color of the stamp, except where
noted

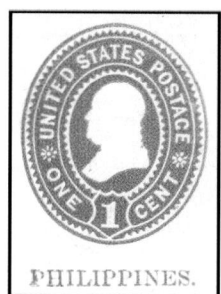

1899-1900

Note: Many envelopes for which there was no obvious need were issued in small quantities. Anyone residing in the Islands could, by depositing with his postmaster the required amount, order any envelopes in quantities of 500, or multiples thereof, provided it was on the schedule of U.S. envelopes.

Such special orders are indicated by an plus sign after the quantity.

U1	U77	1c **green** (#U352) (370,000)	3.00	2.00
		Entire	8.75	9.50
U2	U77	1c **green**, *amber* (#U353) (1,000)+	18.00	14.00
		Entire	40.00	40.00
U3	U77	1c **green**, *amber* (#U353) red overprint (500)+	22.50	20.00
		Entire	60.00	57.50
U4	U77	1c **green**, *oriental buff* (#U354) (1,000)+	14.00	14.00
		Entire	30.00	30.00
U5	U77	1c **green**, *oriental buff* (#U354) red overprint (500)+	35.00	35.00
		Entire	72.50	72.50
U6	U77	1c **green**, *blue* (#U355) (1,000)+	9.00	9.00
		Entire	30.00	30.00
U7	U77	1c **green**, *blue* (#U355) red over-print (500)+	20.00	19.00
		Entire	72.50	67.50
U8	U79	2c **carmine** (#U362) (1,180,000)	1.50	1.50
		Entire	4.00	3.00
U9	U79	2c **carmine**, *amber* (#U363) (21,000)	5.25	5.00
		Entire	15.00	12.50
U10	U79	2c **carmine**, *oriental buff* (#U364) (10,000)	5.25	4.75
		Entire	17.00	13.50
U11	U79	2c **carmine**, *blue* (#U365) (10,000)	4.75	6.25
		Entire	12.50	12.00
U12	U81	4c **brown**, *amber* (#U372) (500)+	40.00	35.00
		Entire	85.00	92.50
a.		Double overprint	—	
		Entire	4,000.	
U13	U83	4c **brown** (#U374) (10,500)	12.50	9.00
		Entire	30.00	40.00
U14	U83	4c **brown**, *amber* (#U375) (500)+	55.00	50.00
		Entire	175.00	125.00
U15	U84	5c **blue** (#U377) (20,000)	6.25	6.00
		Entire	13.00	13.00
U16	U84	5c **blue**, *amber* (#U378) (500)+	35.00	35.00
		Entire	87.50	110.00
		Nos. U1-U16 (16)	287.00	265.50

1903	**Same Overprint on U.S. Issue of 1903**
U17	U85	1c **green** (#U379) (300,000)	1.50	1.25
		Entire	4.25	4.25
U18	U85	1c **green**, *amber* (#U380) (1,000)+	12.50	12.00
		Entire	22.50	25.00

U19	U85	1c **green**, *oriental buff* (#U381) (1,000)	14.50	
		Entire	26.00	
U20	U85	1c **green**, *blue* (#U382) (1,500)+	12.00	
		Entire	26.00	
U21	U85	1c **green**, *manila* (#U383) (500)+	20.00	
		Entire	45.00	
U22	U86	2c **carmine** (#U385) (150,500)	5.00	
		Entire	7.50	
U23	U86	2c **carmine**, *amber* (#U386) (500)+	17.50	
		Entire	35.00	
U24	U86	2c **carmine**, *oriental buff* (#U387) (500)+	17.50	
		Entire	45.00	
U25	U86	2c **carmine**, *blue* (#U388) (500)+	17.50	
		Entire	40.00	
U26	U87	4c **chocolate**, *amber* (#U391) (500)+	55.00	
		Entire	140.00	
a.		Double overprint, entire	7,000.	
U27	U88	5c **blue**, *amber* (#U394) (500)+	55.00	
		Entire	125.00	
		Nos. U17-U27 (11)	228.00	

1906
Same Overprint on Re-cut U.S. issue of 1904

U28	U89	2c **carmine** (#U395)	42.50	
		Entire	150.00	
U29	U89	2c **carmine**, *Oriental buff* (#U397)	67.50	
		Entire	225.00	

Rizal — E1

E2, McKinley.

1908

U30	E1	2c **green**	.50	
		Entire	.85	
U31	E1	2c **green**, *amber*	4.00	
		Entire	9.00	
U32	E1	2c **green**, *oriental buff*	5.00	
		Entire	9.00	
U33	E1	2c **green**, *blue*	5.00	
		Entire	9.00	
U34	E1	2c **green**, *manila* (500)	7.25	
		Entire	15.00	
U35	E2	4c **carmine**	.50	
		Entire	1.40	
U36	E2	4c **carmine**, *amber*	4.00	
		Entire	9.00	
U37	E2	4c **carmine**, *oriental buff*	4.25	
		Entire	9.00	
U38	E2	4c **carmine**, *blue*	4.00	
		Entire	8.50	
U39	E2	4c **carmine**, *manila* (500)	9.00	
		Entire	20.00	
		Nos. U30-U39 (10)	43.50	

Rizal — E3   "Juan de la Cruz" — E

1927, Apr. 5

U40	E3	2c **green**	11.50	9.
		Entire	30.00	25.
		Entire, 1st day cancel		37.

1935, June 19

U41	E4	2c **carmine**	.35	
		Entire	1.25	
U42	E4	4c **olive green**	.50	
		Entire	1.65	1.

For surcharges see Nos. NU1-NU2.

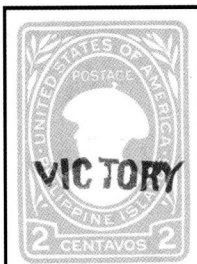

s. U30, U35, U41 and
Handstamped in Violet

E1	2c **green** (On U30), Entire		—	
E4	2c **carmine** (On U41)	17.50	14.00
	Entire	47.50	77.00
E2	4c **carmine**, *McKinley* (On U35)		—	
	Entire	950.00	950.00
E4	4c **olive green** (On U42)	82.50	70.00
	Entire	140.00	175.00

WRAPPERS

U.S. Wrappers
Overprinted in Color of
Stamp

1				
U77	1c **green**, *manila* (No. W357)		1.50	1.25
	(320,000)			
	Entire		5.00	10.00
5				
U85	1c **green**, *manila* (No. W384)		9.00	9.00
	Entire		22.50	25.00
	Double overprint, entire		4,500.	
U86	2c **carmine**, *manila* (No. W389)		11.00	10.50
	Entire		22.50	27.50

Design of Philippine Envelopes

8				
E1	2c **green**, *manila*		2.00	2.00
	Entire		11.00	15.00

POSTAL CARDS

Values are for Entires.
U.S. Cards Overprinted in Black below Stamp

a   **PHILIPPINES**.

0, Feb.				
1	(a)	1c **black** (Jefferson) (UX14)	17.50	15.00
		(100,000)		
a.	Without period	47.50	75.00
2	(a)	2c **black** (Liberty) (UX16)	40.00	30.00
		(20,000)		

b

PHILIPPINES

03, Sept. 15				
3	(b)	1c **black** (McKinley) (UX18)	1,350.	1,150.
4	(b)	2c **black** (Liberty) (UX16)	800.	700.

c   PHILIPPINES.

1903, Nov. 10				
UX5	(c)	1c **black** (McKinley) (UX18)	47.50	40.00
UX6	(c)	2c **black** (Liberty) (UX16)	60.00	55.00

d   **PHILIPPINES**

1906				
UX7	(d)	1c **black** (McKinley) (UX18)	*275.*	*300.*
UX8	(d)	2c **black** (Liberty) (UX16)	*2,000.*	*1,500.*

Designs same as postage issue of 1906

1907				
UX9	A40	2c **black**, *buff* (Rizal)	10.00	8.00
UX10	A40	4c **black**, *buff* (McKinley)	25.00	20.00

Color changes

1911				
UX11	A40	2c **blue**, *light blue* (Rizal)	8.00	8.00
a.		2c blue on white	20.00	20.00
UX12	A40	4c **blue**, *light blue* (McKinley)	25.00	25.00

An impression of No. UX11 exists on the back of a U.S. No. UX21.

1915				
UX13	A40	2c **green**, *buff* (Rizal)	3.00	2.00
UX14	A40	2c **yellow green**, *amber*	3.50	1.50
UX15	A40	4c **green**, *buff* (McKinley)	20.00	15.00

Design of postage issue of 1935

1935				
UX16	A53	2c **red**, *pale buff* (Rizal)	2.50	1.60

No. UX16 Overprinted at left of
Stamp   **COMMONWEALTH**

1938				
UX17	A53	2c **red**, *pale buff*	2.50	1.60

No. UX16 Overprinted   **COMMONWEALTH**

UX18	A53	2c **red**, *pale buff*	45.00	45.00

No. UX16 Overprinted   **COMMONWEALTH**

UX19	A53	2c **red**, *pale buff*	4.00	4.00

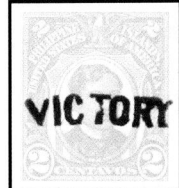

Nos. UX13, UX18 and UX19
Handstamped in Violet

1944				
UX20	A40	2c **green**, *buff*, Rizal (On UX13)	180.00	225.00
UX21	A53	2c **red**, *pale buff* (On UX18)	650.00	—
UX22	A53	2c **red**, *pale buff* (On UX19)	285.00	550.00

Overprinted in Black at left   **VICTORY**

1945, Jan. 19				
UX23	A76	2c **gray brown**, *pale buff*	1.25	.75
		First day cancel		3.25
a.		"IC" of "Victory" very close	5.00	3.00

This card was not issued without overprint.

PAID REPLY POSTAL CARDS
U.S. Paid Reply Cards of 1892-93 issues
Overprinted with type "a" in blue

1900, Feb.				
UY1		2c +2c **blue**, unsevered	160.00	500.00
		(5,000)		
m.		PM2 Message card, detached	27.50	50.00
r.		PR2 Reply card, detached	27.50	50.00

Overprinted type "c" in black

1903				
UY2		1c + 1c **black**, *buff,* unsevered	150.00	375.00
		(20,000)		
m.		PM1 Message card, detached	22.50	25.00
r.		PR1 Reply card, detached	22.50	25.00
UY3		2c + 2c **blue**, unsevered	300.00	700.00
		(20,000)		
m.		PM2, Message card, detached	55.00	50.00
r.		PR2, Reply card, detached	55.00	50.00

OFFICIAL CARDS

Overprinted at left of stamp

1925		**On postal card No. UX13**		
UZ1	A40	2c **green**, *buff* (Rizal)	35.00	35.00
1935		**On postal card No. UX16**		
UZ2	A53	2c **red**, *pale buff*	14.00	*17.50*

Overprinted at Left of Stamp   **O. B.**

1938		**On postal card No. UX19**		
UZ3	A53	2c **red**, *pale buff*	13.00	*17.50*

Overprinted Below Stamp   **O. B.**

1941		**Design of postage issue of 1941**		
UZ4	A75	2c **light green**, *pale buff*	160.00	*200.00*

This card was not issued without overprint.

Postal Card No. UX19 Overprinted at Left of Stamp   **O. B.**

1941				
UZ5	A53	2c **red**, *pale buff*	20.00	*25.00*

OCCUPATION STAMPS

Issued Under Japanese Occupation
Nos. 461, 438 and 439 Overprinted with Bars in Black

1942-43		**Unwmk.** *Perf. 11x10½, 11*		
N1	A75	2c **apple green**, *Mar. 4, 1942*	.20	.20
		(3,000,000)		
		P# block of 4	.25	
a.		Pair, one without overprint	—	
N2	A58	12c **black**, *Apr. 30, 1943*	.20	.20
		(310,000)		
N3	A59	16c **dark blue**, *Mar. 4, 1942*	5.00	3.75
		(160,000)		

Nos. 435a, 435, 442, 443, and 423 Surcharged in Black

1942-43 *Perf. 11*

N4	A55(a)	5(c) on 6c **golden brown** *Sept.*		
		1, 1942 (800,000)	.20	.20
		First day cover, Manila		4.00
a.		Top bar shorter and thinner *(200,000)*	.20	.20
b.		5(c) on 6c **dark brown**	.20	.20
c.		As "b," top bar shorter and thinner	.20	.20
N5	A62(b)	16(c) on 30c **orange red,** *Jan.*		
		11, 1943 (210,000)	.25	.25
		First day cover		5.00
N6	A63(c)	50c on 1p **red orange & black,**		
		Apr. 30, 1943 (20,000)	.60	.60
a.		Double surcharge		300.00
N7	A65(d)	1p on 4p **blue & black,** *Apr.*		
		30, 1943 (19,975)	100.00	200.00
		Inverted "S" in "PESO;" position 4	150.00	225.00

On Nos. N4 and N4b, the top bar measures 1½x22½mm. On Nos. N4a and N4c, the top bar measures 1x21mm and the "5" is smaller and thinner.

The used value for No. N7 is for postal cancellation. Used stamps exist with first day cancellations. They are worth somewhat less.

1942, May 18

N8	A54	2(c) on 4c **yellow green**		
		(100,000)	6.00	6.00
		First day cover		6.00

Issued to commemorate Japan's capture of Bataan and Corregidor. The American-Filipino forces finally surrendered May 7, 1942. No. N8 exists with "R" for "B" in BATAAN.

No. 384 Surcharged in Black

1942, Dec. 8

N9	A54	5(c) on 4c **yellow green**		
		(400,000)	.50	.50
		First day cover		3.00

1st anniversary of the "Greater East Asia War."

Nos. C59 and C62 Surcharged in Black

1943, Jan. 23

N10	AP1	2(c) on 8c **carmine** *(400,000)*	.25	.25
N11	AP1	5c on 1p **sepia** *(300,000)*	.50	.50
		First day cover, #N10-N11		4.00

1st anniv. of the Philippine Executive Commission.

Nipa Hut — OS1

Rice Planting — OS2

Mt. Mayon and Mt. Fuji — OS3

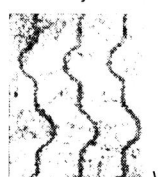

Moro Vinta — OS4

Wmk. 257

The "c" currency is indicated by four Japanese characters, "p" currency by two.

Engraved; Typographed (2c, 6c, 25c)

1943-44 **Wmk. 257** *Perf. 13*

N12	OS1	1c **deep orange,** *June 7,*		
		1943	.20	.20
N13	OS2	2c **bright green,** *Apr. 1, 1943*	.20	.20
N14	OS1	4c **slate green,** *June 7, 1943*	.20	.20
N15	OS3	5c **orange brown,** *Apr. 1,*		
		1943	.20	.20
N16	OS2	6c **red,** *July 14, 1943*	.20	.20
N17	OS3	10c **blue green,** *July 14, 1943*	.20	.20
N18	OS4	12c **steel blue,** *July 14, 1943*	1.00	1.00
N19	OS4	16c **dark brown,** *July 14, 1943*	.20	.20
N20	OS1	20c **rose violet,** *Aug. 16, 1943*	1.25	1.25
N21	OS3	21c **violet,** *Aug. 16, 1943*	.20	.20
N22	OS3	25c **pale brown,** *Aug. 16, 1943*	.20	.20
N23	OS3	1p **deep carmine,** *June 7,*		
		1943	.75	.75
N24	OS4	2p **dull violet,** *Sept. 16, 1943*	5.50	5.50
		First day cover		14.00
N25	OS4	5p **dark olive,** *Apr. 10, 1944*	14.00	9.00
		First day cover		14.00
		Nos. N12-N25 (14)	24.30	19.30

Map of Manila Bay Showing Bataan and Corregidor — OS5

1943, May 7 **Photo.** **Unwmk.**

N26	OS5	2c **carmine red**	.20	.20
N27	OS5	5c **bright green**	.25	.25
		Colorless dot after left "5"	1.10	—
		First day cover, #N26-N27, Manila		4.00

1st anniversary of the fall of Bataan and Corregidor.

No. 440 Surcharged in Black

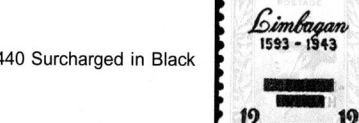

1943, June 20 **Engr.** *Perf. 11*

N28	A60	12(c) on 20c **light olive green**		
		(350,000)	.20	.20
		First day cover		6.00
a.		Double surcharge		—

350th anniversary of the printing press in the Philippines. "Limbagan" is Tagalog for "printing press."

Rizal Monument, Filipina and Philipp Flag — OS6

1943, Oct. 14 **Photo.** **Unwmk.** *Per*

N29	OS6	5c **light blue**		.20
a.		Imperf.		.20
N30	OS6	12c **orange**		.20
a.		Imperf.		.20
N31	OS6	17c **rose pink**		.20
		First day cover, #N29-N31, Manila		
a.		Imperf.		.20
		First day cover, #N29a-N31a, Manila		
		Nos. N29-N31 (3)		.60

"Independence of the Philippines." Japan granted "ind dence" Oct. 14, 1943, when the puppet republic was fou The imperforate stamps were issued without gum.

José Rizal — OS7

Rev. Jos Burgos — C

Apolinario Mabini — OS9

1944, Feb. 17 **Litho.** **Unwmk.** *Per*

N32	OS7	5c **blue**		.20
a.		Imperf.		.20
N33	OS8	12c **carmine**		.20
a.		Imperf.		.20
N34	OS9	17c **deep orange**		.20
		First day cover, #N32-N34, Manila		
a.		Imperf.		.20
		First day cover, #N32a-N34a, *Apr. 17,* Manila		
		Nos. N32-N34 (3)		.60

Nos. C60 and C61 Surcharged in Black

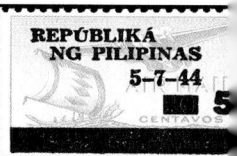

1944, May 7 **Unwmk.** *Perf.*

N35	AP1	5(c) on 20c **ultramarine**		.50
N36	AP1	12(c) on 60c **blue green** *(165,000)*		1.25
		First day cover, #N35-N36		

2nd anniversary of the fall of Bataan and Corregidor.

José P. Laurel — OS10

1945, Jan. 12 **Litho.** **Unwmk.** *Imp* **Without Gum**

N37	OS10	5c **dull violet brown**		.20
N38	OS10	7c **blue green**		.20
N39	OS10	20c **chalky blue**		.20
		First day cover, #N37-N39		
		Nos. N37-N39 (3)		.60

Issued belatedly on Jan. 12, 1945, to commemorate the anniversary of the puppet Philippine Republic, Oct. 14, 19 "S" stands for "sentimos."

The special cancellation devices prepared for use on Oct. 1944, were employed on "First Day" covers Jan. 12, 1945.

OCCUPATION SEMI-POSTAL STAMPS

Woman, Farming and
Cannery — OSP1

|2, Nov. 12   Litho.   Unwmk.   Perf. 12

1 OSP1	2c + 1c **pale violet**	.20	.20
2 OSP1	5c + 1c **bright green**	.25	.20
3 OSP1	16c + 2c **orange**	32.50	32.50
	First day cover, #NB1-NB3		37.50
	Nos. NB1-NB3 (3)	32.95	32.90

ssued to promote the campaign to produce and conserve
d. The surtax aided the Red Cross.

Souvenir Sheet

OSP2

Illustration reduced.

943, Oct. 14   Without Gum   Imperf.

⬛4 OSP2	Sheet of 3	75.00	—
	Sheet with first day cancel and		
	cachet, Manila	15.00	
	First day cover, Manila		

"Independence of the Philippines."
No. NB4 contains one each of Nos. N29a-N31a. Marginal
scription is from Rizal's "Last Farewell." Sold for 2.50p.

Nos. N18, N20 and N21
Surcharged in Black

943, Dec. 8   Wmk. 257   Perf. 13

⬛B5 OS4	12c + 21c **steel blue**	.20	.20
⬛B6 OS1	20c + 36c **rose violet**	.20	.20
⬛B7 OS3	21c + 40c **violet**	.20	.20
	First day cover, #NB5-NB7		2.50
	Nos. NB5-NB7 (3)	.60	.60

The surtax was for the benefit of victims of a Luzon flood.
Baha" is Tagalog for "flood."

Souvenir Sheet

REPUBLIKA NG PILIPINAS
MAYNILA

Sa kapahintulutan ng Kgg. QUINTIN PAREDES, Kagawad
ng mga Gawaing-Bayan at Pahatiran

Sa pagsilang ng makabayang
damdamin sa Pilipinas

OSP3

Illustration reduced.

1944, Feb. 9   Litho.   Unwmk.   Imperf.
Without Gum

NB8 OSP3	Sheet of 3	6.00	3.50
	First day cover		4.00

No. NB8 contains one each of Nos. N32a-N34a.
The sheet sold for 1p, the surtax going to a fund for the care
of heroes' monuments. Size: 101x143mm. No. NB8 exists with
5c inverted.

OCCUPATION POSTAGE DUE

No. J15 Overprinted with Bar in Blue

1942, Oct. 14   Unwmk.   Perf. 11

NJ1 D3	3c on 4c **brown red** (40,000)	35.00	20.00
	First day cover		35.00
	Double bar		

On copies of No. J15, two lines were drawn in India ink with a
ruling pen across "United States of America" by employees of
the Short Paid Section of the Manila Post Office to make a
provisional 3c postage due stamp which was used from Sept. 1,
1942 (when the letter rate was raised from 2c to 5c) until Oct. 14
when No. NJ1 went on sale. Value on cover, $125.

OCCUPATION OFFICIAL STAMPS

Nos. 461, 413, 435, 435a and
442 Overprinted or Surcharged
in Black with Bars and

1943-44   Unwmk.   Perf. 11x10½, 11

NO1 A75	2c **apple green,** *Apr. 7, 1943*		
	(200,000)	.20	.20
	P# block of 4	.25	
a.	Double overprint	500.00	
	On cover (double over-		
	print)		1,250.
NO2 A55	5(c) on 6c **dark brown** (On		
	No. 413), *June 26, 1944*		
	(23,049)	45.00	45.00
	First day cover		125.00
NO3 A55	5(c) on 6c **golden brown** (On		
	No. 435a), *Apr. 7, 1943*		
	(250,000)	.20	.20
a.	Narrower spacing between bars		
	(249,951)	.20	.20
b.	5(c) on 6c **dark brown** (On No. 435)	.20	.20
c.	As "b," narrower spacing between		
	bars	.20	.20
d.	Double overprint		
NO4 A62	16(c) on 30c **orange red,** *Apr.*		
	7, 1943 (100,000)	.30	.30
a.	Wider spacing between bars	.30	.30
	First day cover, Nos. NO1,		
	NO3-NO4		35.00

On Nos. NO3 and NO3b the bar deleting "United States of
America" is 9¾ to 10mm above the bar deleting "Common." On
Nos. NO3a and NO3c, the spacing is 8 to 8½mm.

On No. NO4, the center bar is 19mm long, 3½mm below the
top bar and 6mm above the Japanese characters. On No.
NO4a, the center bar is 20½mm long, 9mm below the top bar
and 1mm above the Japanese characters.
"K.P." stands for Kagamitang Pampamahalaan, "Official Business" in Tagalog.

Nos. 435 and 435a
Surcharged in Black

1944, Aug. 28   Unwmk.   Perf. 11

NO5 A55	(5c) on 6c **golden brown**		
	(500,000)	.20	.20
a.	5(c) on 6c **dark brown**	.20	.20

Nos. O34 and C62 Overprinted in Black

a

b

NO6 A60(a)	20c **light olive green** (200,000)	.25	.25
NO7 AP1(b)	1p **sepia** (100,000)	.65	.65
	First day cover, #NO5-NO7		4.00
	Nos. NO5-NO7 (3)	1.10	1.10

OCCUPATION ENVELOPES

5   **5**   No. U41 Surcharged in Black

1943, Apr. 1

NU1 E4	5c on 2c **carmine**	.50	.30
	Entire	1.90	1.25
	Entire, 1st day cancel		4.00

No. U41 Surcharged in Black

1944, Feb. 17

NU2 E4	5c on 2c **carmine**	.75	.50
	Entire	3.00	5.00
	Entire, 1st day cancel		7.50
a.	Inverted surcharged	—	
b.	Double surcharge	—	
c.	Both 5's missing	—	

OCCUPATION POSTAL CARDS

Values are for entire cards.
Nos. UX19 and UZ4 Overprinted with Bars in Black

1942
NUX1	A53	2c	**red,** *pale buff, Mar. 4, 1942*	15.00	15.00
		First day cancel			85.00
a.		Vertical obliteration bars reversed		*140.00*	
NUX2	A75	2c	**light green,** *pale buff, Dec.*		
		12, 1942		2.50	2.00
		First day cancel			6.00

Rice Planting — A77

1943, May 17
NUX3	A77	2c	**green**	1.00	*1.00*
		First day cancel, Manila		*2.00*

OCCUPATION OFFICIAL CARDS

Nos. UX19, UX17 and UX18 Overprinted in 公 用 Black with Bars and (K. P.)

1943, Apr. 7
NUZ1	A53	2c	**red,** *pale buff*	4.00	3.00
		First day cancel		100.00
a.	On No. UX17		—	—
b.	On No. UX18		—	—

No. NUX3 Overprinted in Black

REPUBLIKA NG PILIPINAS (K. P.)

1944, Aug. 28
NUZ2	A77	2c	**green**	1.50	*1.00*
		First day cancel		*2.00*
a.	Double overprint		—	

FILIPINO REVOLUTIONARY GOVERNMENT

Following the defeat of the Spanish fleet by U.S. Commodore Dewey in Manila on May 1, 1898, which essentially ended the Spanish-American War in the Philippines, postal services were disrupted throughout the Philippines. Postal service was reestablished through U.S. Army military stations, beginning in June 1898 near Manila, continuing province by province until culminating at Zamboanga and other cities in the southern areas in late 1899.

Provisional stamps were prepared for use in the central part of the island of Luzon at Malolos in late 1898 under the leadership of General Emilio Aguinaldo, who had proclaimed the Philippine Republic on June 12, 1898. Later, other provisional stamps were prepared by local Filipino insurgents at Iloilo (Panay Island), Bohol, Cebu and Negros, and Spanish period stamps were overprinted and/or surcharged for use by postal officials at Zamboanga and La Union.

The most familiar of these provisionals were the "Aguinaldo" issues of the Filipino Revolutionary Government in central Luzon near Manila. The letters "KKK," the initials of the revolutionary society, "Kataas-taasang, Kagalang-galang Katipunan nang Mañga Anak nang Bayan," meaning "Sovereign Worshipful Association of the Sons of the Country," readily identify the Aguinaldo provisionals. Hostilities broke out between the Aguinaldo regime and the occupying American administration in February 1899, and the Filipino-American War continued until the American capture of Aguinaldo on March 23, 1901.

The Aguinaldo regular postage, registration, revenue, newspaper and telegraph stamps were in use in Luzon as early as November 10, 1898, and continued in use through early 1901. Although the postal regulations specified that these stamps be used for their inscribed purpose, they were commonly used interchangeably.

POSTAGE ISSUES

A1

A2

Coat of Arms — A3

1898-99   Unwmk.   Perf. 11½
Y1	A1	2c	**red**	175.00	125.00
		On cover			*1,500.*
a.		Double impression		*225.00*	
Y2	A2	2c	**red**	.20	.25
		On cover			450.00
b.		Double impression		—	
d.		Horiz. pair, imperf. between		—	
e.		Vert. pair, imperf. between		200.00	
Y3	A3	2c	**red**	150.00	*200.00*
		On cover			*2,000.*

Imperf pairs and pairs, imperf horizontally, have been created from No. Y2e.

RS1

N1

REGISTRATION STAMP
YF1	RS1	8c	**green**	2.50	*10.00*
		On cover with #Y2			*3,500.*
a.	Imperf., pair		400.00	
b.	Imperf. vertically, pair		—	

NEWSPAPER STAMP
YP1	N1	1m	**black**	1.00
a.	Imperf., pair		1.00

PROOFS

1906

				DIE	
				(1) Large	*(2)* Small	*(2a)*
241P	2c	yellow green			500.	750.
242P	4c	carmine lake		600.	500.	750.
243P	6c	violet		600.	500.	750.
244P	8c	brown		600.	500.	750.
245P	10c	dark blue			500.	750.
246P	12c	brown lake			500.	750.
247P	16c	violet black		600.	500.	750.
248P	20c	orange brown			500.	750.
249P	26c	violet brown			500.	750.
250P	30c	olive green		600.	500.	750.
251P	1p	orange			500.	750.
252P	2p	black			500.	750.
253P	4p	dark blue			500.	750.
254P	10p	dark green			500.	750.

1909-13
255P	12c	red orange			600.	625.
256P	16c	olive green			600.	625.
257P	20c	yellow			600.	625.
258P	26c	blue green			600.	625.
259P	30c	ultramarine			600.	625.
260P	1p	pale violet			600.	625.
260AP	2p	violet brown			600.	625.
275P	30c	gray			600.	625.

1923
303P	16c	olive bister		450.
303TC	16c	olive green		450.

1926
322P	18c	light brown & black, plate, glazed card		350.

1932
357P	18c	red orange	450.
357TC	18c	orange red	450.
360TC	32c	green	450.
360TC	18c	olive green	450.

1935
383P	2c	rose	600.
384P	4c	yellow green	600.
385P	6c	dark brown	600.
386P	8c	violet	600.
387P	10c	rose carmine	600.
388P	12c	black	600.
389P	16c	dark blue	600.
390P	20c	light olive green	600.
390TC	20c	black	600.
391P	2cc	indigo	000.
392P	30c	orange red	600.
393P	1p	red orange & black	600.
394P	2p	bister brown & black	600.
395P	4p	blue & black	600.
396P	5p	green & black	600.

1936
408P	2c	orange brown	450.
408TC	2c	yellow green	450.

1937
425P	2c	yellow green	500.

1939
452P	2c	yellow green	500.
453P	6c	carmine	500.
454P	12c	bright blue	500.

1939
455P	2c	green	750.	500.
456P	6c	orange		500.
457P	12c	carmine		500.

1940
458P	2c	dark orange	1,000.	600.
459P	6c	dark green		600.
460P	12c	purple		600.

1941
461P	2c	apple green	600.

1946
497P	2c	sepia	—

AIR POST

1941
C59P	8c	carmine	500.
C60P	20c	ultramarine	500.
C61P	60c	blue green	500.
C62P	1p	sepia	500.

SPECIAL DELIVERY

1906
E2P	20c	ultramarine	1,000.	1,000.	85
E2TC	20c	green		1,000.

POSTAGE DUE

1899
J1P	1c	deep claret	1,100.
J2P	2c	deep claret	1,100.
J3P	5c	deep claret	1,100.
J4P	10c	deep claret	1,100.
J5P	50c	deep claret	1,100.

1901
J6P	3c	deep claret	1,100.
J7P	30c	deep claret	1,100.

SPECIMEN STAMPS

Handstamped US Type E in Purple   *Specimen*

1899
213S E	1c yellow green	175.0
214dS E	2c rose carmine, type IV	175.0
215S E	3c purple	175.0
216S E	5c blue	175.0
217S E	10c brown, type I	175.0
218S E	15c olive brown	175.0
219S E	50c orange	175.0

See note after No. 219 for Special Printings with black "Specimen" overprints.

Overprinted US Type R in Black   *Specimen*

1917-25
290S R	2c green	40.0
291S R	4c carmine	40.00
292S R	6c deep violet	40.00
293S R	8c yellow brown	40.00
294S R	10c deep blue	40.00
295S R	12c red orange	40.00
297S R	20c orange yellow	40.00
298S R	26c green	40.00
299S R	30c gray	40.00

; R	1p pale violet	40.00	
; R	2p violet brown	40.00	
; R	4p blue	40.00	

3-26			
; R	16c olive bister	25.00	
; R	10p deep green	25.00	

Overprinted Type R in Red

; R	2c green & black	65.00	
; R	4c carmine & black	65.00	
; R	16c olive green & black	65.00	
; R	18c light brown & black	65.00	
; R	20c orange & black	65.00	
; R	24c gray & black	65.00	
; R	1p rose lilac & black	65.00	

Overprinted US Type S in Red   *Cancelled*

6			
S S	2c green & black	65.00	
S S	4c carmine & black	65.00	
S S	16c olive green & black	65.00	
S S	18c light brown & black	65.00	
S S	20c orange & black	65.00	
S S	24c gray & black	65.00	
S S	1p rose lilac & black	65.00	

mperforate copies of this set, on glazed cards with centers in
wn, are known with the "Cancelled" overprint. Value, $2,250
set.

Handstamped "SPECIMEN" in Red Capitals, 13x3mm

1925		
340S S	2c green	75.00
341S S	4c carmine	75.00
342S S	6c deep violet	75.00
343S S	8c yellow brown	100.00
344S S	10c deep blue	100.00
345S S	12c red orange	100.00
346S S	16c olive bister	100.00
347S S	20c yellow	100.00
348S S	26c blue green	100.00
349S S	30c gray	100.00
350S S	1p violet	100.00
351S S	2p violet brown	100.00
352S S	4p deep blue	150.00
353S S	10p deep green	250.00

SPECIAL DELIVERY

1919		**Overprinted Type R in Black**	
E5S R	20c ultramarine		200.00
E5bS R	20c dull violet		

Handstamped "SPECIMEN" in Red Capitals, 13x3mm

1925		
E6aS	20c violet blue	300.00

POSTAGE DUE

1899		**Overprinted Type E in Black**	
J1S E	1c deep claret		225.00
J2S E	2c deep claret		225.00
J3S E	5c deep claret		225.00
J4S E	10c deep claret		225.00
J5S E	50c deep claret		225.00

OFFICIAL

1926		**Overprinted Type R in Red**	
O1S R	2c green & black		30.00
O2S R	4c carmine & black		30.00
O3S R	18c light brown & black		30.00
O4S R	20c orange & black		30.00

1926		**Overprinted Type S in Red**	
O1S S	2c green & black		30.00
O2S S	4c carmine & black		30.00
O3S S	18c light brown & black		30.00
O4S S	20c orange & black		30.00

PUERTO RICO

(Porto Rico)

Jnited States troops landed at Guanica Bay, Puerto Rico, on July 25, 1898, and mail service between various points in Puerto Rico began soon after
der the authority of General Wilson, acting governor of the conquered territory, who authorized a provisional service early in August, 1898. The first
itary Postal Station was opened at La Playa de Ponce on August 3, 1898. Control of the island passed formally to the United States on October 18,
98. Twenty-one military stations operating under the administration of the Military Postal Service, were authorized in Puerto Rico after the Spanish-
nerican war. After the overprinted provisional issue of 1900, unoverprinted stamps of the United States replaced those of Puerto Rico.
Name changed to Puerto Rico by Act of Congress, approved May 17, 1932.
talicized numbers in parentheses indicate quantities issued.

100 CENTS = 1 DOLLAR.

PROVISIONAL ISSUES
Ponce Issue

A11

98		Unwmk.	Handstamped	*Imperf.*	
0 A11	5c violet, *yellowish*			7,500.	—

The only way No. 200 is known used is handstamped on
velopes. Both unused stamps and used envelopes have a
let control mark.
Uses on 2c U.S. stamps on cover were strictly as a cancella-
n, not as provisional postage.
Dangerous counterfeits exist.

Coamo Issue

A12

Types of "5":
I — Curved flag. Pos. 2, 3, 4, 5.
II — Flag turns down at right. Pos. 1, 9, 10.
III — Fancy outlined "5." Pos. 6, 7.
IV — Flag curls into ball at right. Pos. 8.

Typeset, setting of 10

898, Aug.		Unwmk.	*Imperf.*	
01 A12	5c black, Type I	650.	1,050.	
	Type II	700.	1,100.	
	Type III	775.	1,200.	
	Type IV	850.	1,350.	
	Irregular "block" of 4 showing one of each type	3,750.		

Sheet of 10		10,000.	
On cover		*32,500.*	
Pair on cover		—	

Blocks not showing all four types and pairs normally sell for
10-20% over the value of the individual stamps.
The stamps bear the control mark "F. Santiago" in violet.
About 500 were issued.
Dangerous counterfeits exist.

Regular Issue

United States Nos. 279, 279Bf,
281, 272 and 282C
Overprinted in Black at 36
degree Angle

1899		**Wmk. 191**		*Perf. 12*	
210 A87	1c yellow green, *Mar. 15*			5.00	1.40
	On cover				22.00
	First day cover				
	Block of 4			25.00	10.00
	P# strip of 3, Impt.			45.00	
	P# block of 6, Impt.			275.00	
a.	Overprint at 25 degree angle			7.50	2.25
	Pair, 36 degree and 25 degree angles			25.00	
	"PORTO RICU"			30.00	—
211 A88	2c reddish carmine, type IV, *Mar. 15*			4.25	1.25
	On cover				15.00
	Block of 4			22.50	10.00
	P# strip of 3, Impt.			37.50	
	P# block of 6, Impt.			350.00	
	"FORTO RICO" (pos. 77)				—
a.	Overprint at 25 degree angle, *Mar. 15*			5.50	2.25
	On cover				20.00
	First day cover				
	Block of 4			27.50	17.50
	P# strip of 3, Impt.			45.00	
	P# block of 6, Impt.			275.00	
	Pair, 36 degree and 25 degree angles			25.00	
	P# strip of 3, Impt.			95.00	
	P# block of 6, Impt.			700.00	
	"PORTU RICO" (pos. 46)			50.00	20.00
	"PORTO RICU" (pos. 3)			—	
	"PURTO RICO"			—	
	"FURTU RICO"			—	

212 A91	5c blue			12.50	2.50
	On cover				40.00
	Block of 4			55.00	27.50
	P# strip of 3, Impt.			70.00	
	P# block of 6, Impt.			350.00	
213 A93	8c violet brown			35.00	17.50
	On cover				125.00
	Block of 4			160.00	110.00
	P# strip of 3, Impt.			250.00	
	P# block of 6, Impt.			2,250.	
	"FORTO RICO"			90.00	60.00
a.	Overprint at 25 degree angle			40.00	19.00
	Pair, 36 degree and 25 degree angles			100.00	
c.	"PORTO RIC"			150.00	110.00
214 A94	10c brown, type I			25.00	6.00
	On cover				120.00
	Block of 4			110.00	45.00
	P# strip of 3, Impt.			160.00	
	P# block of 6, Impt.			1,250.	
	"FORTO RICO"			85.00	70.00
	Nos. 210-214 (5)			81.75	28.65

Misspellings of the overprint on Nos. 210-214 (PORTO RICU,
PORTU RICO, FORTO RICO) are actually broken letters.

United States Nos. 279 and
279B Overprinted in Black

1900				
215 A87	1c yellow green		6.50	1.40
	On cover			17.50
	Block of 4		27.50	10.00
	P# strip of 3, Impt.		30.00	
	P# block of 6, Impt.		175.00	
216 A88	2c red, type IV, *Apr. 2*		4.75	2.00
	On cover			15.00
	Block of 4		22.50	15.00
	P# strip of 3, Impt.		32.50	
	P# block of 6, Impt.		175.00	
b.	Inverted overprint		*8,250.*	

Special Printing

In March 1900 one pane of 100 stamps of each of the 1c (No. 215), 2c (No. 216) and 5c, 8c and 10c values, as well as 1c, 2c and 10c postage due stamps were specially overprinted for displays at the Paris Exposition (1900) and Pan American Exposition (1901). These last six items were never regularly issued with the PUERTO RICO overprint and therefore have no Scott catalogue number. The 2c pane was light red, type IV.

Copies were handstampd type E "Specimen" in black ink by H. G. Mandel and mounted by him in separate displays for the two Expositions. Additional copies from each pane were also handstamped "Specimen," but most were destroyed after the Expositions.

J. M. Bartels, a stamp dealer, signed some copies from these panes "Special Surcharge" in pencil on the gum to authenticate them as coming from the "Mandel" Special Printing panes. In 1904 or later, he handstamped additional surviving copies "Special Surcharge" in red ink on the back as his guarantee. Some of these guaranteed stamps had Mandel's "Specimen" handstamp on the face while others did not. Value, each $1,750.

No Special Printing panes overprinted "Porto Rico" were produced by the government. Copies do exist with a black type E "Specimen" handstamp, but it is believed that H. G. Mandel applied such handstamps to regularly issued overprinted "Porto Rico" stamps from his personal collection. Copies are known of the 2c type IV, in reddish carmine, 25 degree angle.

AIR POST

In 1938 a series of eight labels, two of which were surcharged, was offered to the public as "Semi-Official Air Post Stamps", the claim being that they had been authorized by the "Puerto Rican postal officials." These labels, printed by the Ever Ready Label Co. of New York, were a private issue of Aerovias Nacionales Puerto Rico, operating a passenger and air express service. Instead of having been authorized by the postal officials, they were at first forbidden but later tolerated by the Post Office Department at Washington.

In 1941 a further set of eight triangular labels was prepared and offered to collectors, and again the Post Office Department officials at Washington objected and forbade their use after September 16, 1941.

These labels represent only the charge for service rendered by a private enterprise for transporting matter outside the mails by plane. Their use did not and does not eliminate the payment of postage on letters carried by air express, which must in every instance be paid by United States postage stamps.

POSTAGE DUE STAMPS

United States Nos. J38, J39 and J42 Overprinted in Black at 36 degree Angle

1899   Wmk. 191   Perf. 12

J1	D2	1c **deep claret**		22.50	5.50
		On cover			125.00
		Block of 4		100.00	35.00
		P# strip of 3, Impt.		120.00	
		P# block of 6, Impt.		625.00	
a.		Overprint at 25 degree angle		22.50	7.50
		Pair, 36 degree and 25 degree angles		65.00	
		P# strip of 3, Impt.		150.00	
		P# block of 6, Impt.		750.00	
J2	D2	2c **deep claret**		20.00	6.00
		On cover			250.00
		Block of 4		80.00	37.50
		P# strip of 3, Impt.		120.00	
		P# block of 6, Impt.		800.00	
a.		Overprint at 25 degree angle		20.00	7.00
		Pair, 36 degree and 25 degree angles		60.00	
		P# strip of 3, Impt.		140.00	
		P# block of 6, Impt.		900.00	
J3	D2	10c **deep claret**		190.00	60.00
		On cover		800.00	—
		Block of 4		800.00	
		P# strip of 3, Impt.		1,250.	
		P# block of 6, Impt.		3,750.	
a.		Overprint at 25 degree angle		175.00	85.00
		Pair, 36 degree and 25 degree angles		650.00	

ENVELOPES

U.S. Envelopes of 1887 Issue Overprinted in Black

PORTO RICO.

20mm long

1899-1900

Note: Some envelopes for which there was no obvious need were issued in small quantities. Anyone residing in Puerto Rico could, by depositing with his postmaster the required amount, order any envelope in quantities of 500, or multiples thereof, provided it was on the schedule of U.S. envelopes. Such special orders are indicated by a plus sign, i. e., Nos. U15 and U18, and half the quantities of Nos. U16 and U17.

U1	U71	2c **green** (No. U311) *(3,000)*	16.00	20.00
		Entire	40.00	350.00
a.		Double overprint, entire	3,500.	
U2	U74	5c **blue** (No. U330) *(1,000)*	20.00	20.00
		Entire	55.00	350.00
a.		Double overprint, entire		

U.S. Envelopes of 1899 Overprinted in color of the stamp

PORTO RICO.

21mm long

U3	U79	2c **carmine** (No. U362) *(100,000)*	3.00	3.00
		Entire	10.00	12.00
U4	U84	5c **blue** (No. U377) *(10,000)*	8.00	9.00
		Entire	17.50	32.50

Overprinted in Black   **PORTO RICO.**

19mm long

U5	U77	1c **green**, *blue* (No. U355) *(1,000)*		750.
		Entire		1,900.
U6	U79	2c **carmine**, *amber* (No. U363), Die 2 *(500)*	450.	500.
		Entire	1,100.	1,250.
U7	U79	2c **carmine**, *oriental buff* (No. U364), Die 2 *(500)*		500.
		Entire		1,250.
U8	U80	2c **carmine**, *oriental buff* (No. U369), Die 3 *(500)*		600.
		Entire		1,300.
U9	U79	2c **carmine**, *blue* (No. U365), Die 2		4,000.
U10	U83	4c **brown** (No. U374), Die 3 *(500)*	200.	500.
		Entire	500.	900.

U.S. Envelopes of 1899 Issue Overprinted

PUERTO RICO.

23mm long

U11	U79	2c **carmine** (No. U362) red overprint *(100,000)*	4.00	3.00
		Entire	10.00	11.00
U12	U79	2c **carmine**, *oriental buff* (No. U364), Die 2, black overprint *(1,000)*	—	325.00
		Entire	1,200.	1,300.
U13	U80	2c **carmine**, *oriental buff* (No. U369), Die 3, black overprint *(1,000)*		375.00
		Entire		1,750.
U14	U84	5c **blue** (No. U377) blue overprint *(10,000)*	14.00	14.00
		Entire	42.50	50.00

Overprinted in Black   **PUERTO RICO.**

U15	U77	1c **green**, *oriental buff* (No. U354) *(500)+*	20.00	50.00
		Entire	75.00	80.00
U16	U77	1c **green**, *blue* (No. U355) *(1,000)+*	25.00	50.00
		Entire	95.00	125.00
U17	U79	2c **carmine**, *oriental buff* (No. U364) *(1,000)+*	20.00	50.00
		Entire	95.00	135.00
U18	U79	2c **carmine**, *blue* (No. U365) *(500)+*	20.00	50.00
		Entire	75.00	135.00

There were two settings of the overprint, with minor differences, which are found on Nos. U16 and U17.

WRAPPER

U.S. Wrapper of 1899 Issue Overprinted in Green

PORTO RICO.

21mm long

W1	U77	1c **green**, *manila* (No. W357) *(15,000)*	8.00	35.00
		Entire	17.00	110.00

POSTAL CARDS

Values are for Entires.

Imprinted below stamp   **PORTO RI**

1899-1900   U.S. Postal Card No. U

UX1	PC8 1c **black**, *buff*, imprint 21mm long	165.	
b.	Double imprint	2,250.	

Imprinted below stamp   **PORTO RI**

UX1A	PC8 1c **black**, *buff*, imprint 20mm long	1,200. 1,

Imprinted below stamp   **PORTO RIC**

UX2	PC8 1c **black**, *buff*, imprint 26mm long	165.

Imprinted below stamp   **PUERTO RI**

UX3	PC8 1c **black**, *buff*	150.

REVENUE STAMPS

U.S. Revenue Stamps Nos. R163, R168-R169, R and Type of 1898 Surcharged in Black or Dark B

PORTO RICO

PORTO RICO
10 c.
Excise Revenue
a

$1
EXCISE REVEN
b

1901   Wmk. 191R   *Hyphen-hole Roulett*

R1	R15(a)	1c on 1c **pale blue** (Bk)	10.00	8
R2	R15(a)	10c on 10c **dark brown**	12.50	1
R3	R15(a)	25c on 25c **purple brown**	15.00	1
R4	R15(a)	50c on 50c **slate violet**	25.00	18
R5	R16(b)	$1 on $1 **pale greenish gray**	62.50	22
R6	R16(b)	$3 on $3 **pale greenish gray**	70.00	32
R7	R16(b)	$5 on $5 **pale greenish gray**	85.00	37
R8	R16(b)	$10 on $10 **pale greenish gray**	120.00	7C
R9	R16(b)	$50 on $50 **pale greenish gray**	325.00	16C
		Nos. R1-R9 (9)	725.00	369

Lines of 1c surcharge spaced farther apart; total depth surcharge 15¾mm instead of 11mm.

RECTIFIED SPIRITS

U.S. Wine Stamps of 1933-34 Overprinted in Red or Carmine

RECTIFIE

SPIRIT

1934   Offset Printing   Wmk. 191R   *Roulettec*
Overprint Lines 14mm Apart, Second Line 25m Long

RE1	RE5	2c **green**	15
RE2	RE5	3c **green**	55
RE3	RE5	4c **green**	17.
RE4	RE5	5c **green**	15.
RE5	RE5	6c **green**	17.

Overprint Lines 21½mm Apart, Second Line 23½mm Long

RE6	RE2	50c **green**	27.
RE7	RE2	60c **green**	25.

Handstamped overprints are also found on U.S. Wine stam of 1933-34.

U.S. Wine Stamps of 1933-34 Overprinted in Black

RECTIFIE

RECTIFIED

SPIRITS   **SPIRITS**
a   b

1934   Offset Printing   Wmk. 191R   *Rouletted*

RE8	RE5(a)	1c **green**	22.5
RE9	RE5(a)	2c **green**	12.5
RE10	RE5(a)	3c **green**	60.0

11	RE5(a)	5c green		12.50
12	RE5(a)	6c green		15.00
13	RE2(b)	50c green		17.50
14	RE2(b)	60c green		15.00
15	RE2(b)	72c green		75.00
16	RE2(b)	80c green		40.00

RECTIFIED SPIRITS

U.S. Wine Stamps of 1933-34
Overprinted in Black

PUERTO RICO

34	Offset Printing	Wmk. 191R	Rouletted 7	
17	RE5	½c green		2.50
18	RE5	1c green	50.00	.60
19	RE5	2c green	50.00	.50
20	RE5	3c green	100.00	3.50
21	RE5	4c green		.75
22	RE5	5c green	50.00	1.00
23	RE5	6c green	50.00	1.25
24	RE5	10c green	100.00	3.50
25	RE5	30c green		30.00

Overprint Lines 12½mm Apart

26	RE2	36c green		6.00
27	RE2	40c green	150.00	5.00
28	RE2	50c green	150.00	2.50
29	RE2	60c green	125.00	.50
a.		Inverted overprint		—
30	RE2	72c green	150.00	3.00
31	RE2	80c green	150.00	4.00
32	RE2	$1 green	175.00	7.50

George Sewall
Boutwell — R1

Engr. (8c & 58c); Litho.

1942-57		Wmk. 191	Rouletted 7	
		Without Gum		
RE33	R1	½c carmine	3.50	1.25
RE34	R1	1c sepia	8.25	3.50
RE35	R1	2c bright yellow green	1.10	.20
RE36	R1	3c lilac	70.00	35.00
RE37	R1	4c olive	2.25	.50
RE38	R1	5c orange	5.50	1.00
RE39	R1	6c red brown	4.00	1.25
RE40	R1	8c bright pink ('57)	8.25	3.50
RE41	R1	10c bright purple	12.50	5.00
RE41A	R1	30c vermilion	175.00	
RE42	R1	36c dull yellow	250.00	70.00
RE43	R1	40c deep claret	20.00	7.00
RE44	R1	50c green	11.00	4.00
RE45	R1	58c red orange	87.50	7.00
RE46	R1	60c brown	1.40	.20
RE47	R1	62c black	3.50	.70
RE48	R1	72c blue	40.00	1.00

RE49	R1	77½c olive gray	11.00	3.50
RE50	R1	80c brownish black	14.00	6.00
RE51	R1	$1 violet	87.50	25.00
		Nos. RE33-RE51 (20)	816.25	175.60

The 30c is believed not to have been placed in use.

SPECIMEN STAMPS

Handstamped U.S. Type E in Purple   **Specimen.**

1899			
210S	E	1c yellow green	180.00
211S	E	2c reddish carmine, type IV	180.00
212S	E	5c blue	180.00
213S	E	8c violet brown	180.00
214S	E	10c brown	180.00

See note after No. 216 for Special Printings with **black** "Specimen" overprint.

Postage Due

1899			
J1S	E	1c deep claret	225.00
J2S	E	2c deep claret	225.00
J3S	E	10c deep claret	225.00

Revenue

R1S	E	1c on 1c pale blue	40.00
R2S	E	10c on 10c dark brown	40.00
R3S	E	25c on 25c purple brown	40.00
R4S	E	50c on 50c state violet	40.00
R5S	E	$1 on $1 pale greenish gray	40.00
R6S	E	$3 on $3 pale greenish gray	40.00
R7S	E	$5 on $5 pale greenish gray	40.00
R8S	E	$10 on $10 pale greenish gray	40.00
R9S	E	$50 on $50 pale greenish gray	40.00

RYUKYU ISLANDS

LOCATION — Chain of 63 islands between Japan and Formosa, separating the East China Sea from the Pacific Ocean.
GOVT. — Semi-autonomous under United States administration.
AREA — 848 sq. mi.
POP. — 945,465 (1970)
CAPITAL — Naha, Okinawa
The Ryukyus were part of Japan until American forces occupied them in 1945. The islands reverted to Japan May 15, 1972.

100 Sen = 1 Yen
100 Cents = 1 Dollar (1958).

In the Provisional Issues and Postal Stationery sections, italicized numbers in parentheses indicate quantity sold.
Values for First Day Covers are for unaddressed, cacheted covers. Values are for official cachets for Scott 1-26, C1-C3 and E1; and for commercial cachets for all others. Early cachets from the Japanese Philatelic Society command substantial premiums.

Catalogue values for unused stamps are for Never Hinged items beginning with Scott 1 in the regular postage section, Scott C1 in the air post section, Scott E1 in the special delivery section, Scott R1 in the revenue section, Scott 91S in the specimen section and Scott RQ1 in the unemployment insurance section.

Cycad — A1

Sailing Ship — A3

Lily — A2

Farmer — A4

Wmk. 257

1948-49		Typo.	Wmk. 257	Perf. 13	
		Second Printing, July 18, 1949			
1	A1	5s magenta		2.50	2.50
		Imprint block of 10		37.50	
2	A2	10s yellow green		6.00	5.50
		Imprint block of 10		90.00	
3	A1	20s yellow green		3.50	3.50
		Imprint block of 10		55.00	
4	A3	30s vermilion		1.50	1.50
		Imprint block of 10		30.00	
5	A2	40s magenta		1.50	1.50
		Imprint block of 10		25.00	
6	A3	50s ultramarine		6.00	*4.00*
		Imprint block of 10		90.00	
7	A4	1y ultramarine		6.00	5.50
		Imprint block of 10		90.00	
		Nos. 1-7 (7)		27.00	24.00
		First Printing, July 1, 1948			
1a	A1	5s magenta		3.00	*3.50*
		First day cover			250.00
		Imprint block of 10		45.00	
2a	A2	10s yellow green		2.00	*2.00*
		First day cover			250.00
		Imprint block of 10		30.00	
3a	A1	20s yellow green		2.00	*2.00*
		First day cover			250.00
		Imprint block of 10		30.00	
4a	A3	30s vermilion		4.00	*3.50*
		First day cover			250.00
		Imprint block of 10		45.00	
5a	A2	40s magenta		60.00	60.00
		First day cover			250.00
		Imprint block of 10		900.00	
6a	A3	50s ultramarine		4.00	4.00
		First day cover			250.00
		Imprint block of 10		55.00	
7a	A4	1y ultramarine		475.00	350.00

	First day cover			250.00
	Imprint block of 10		*7,000.*	
	Nos. 1a-7a (7)		550.00	425.00

First printing: thick yellow gum, dull colors, rough perforations, grayish paper. Second printing: white gum, sharp colors, cleancut perforations, white paper.

A5

Ryukyu University — A6

Designs: 50s, Tile rooftop & Shishi. 1y, Ryukyu girl. 2y, Shuri Castle. 3y, Guardian dragon. 4y, Two women. 5y, Sea shells.

1950, Jan. 21		Photo.	Unwmk.	Perf. 13x13½	
		Off-white Paper			
8	A5	50s dark carmine rose		.20	.20
		First day cover			20.00
		Imprint block of 6		2.00	
a.		White paper, third printing, *Sept. 6, 1958*		.50	.50
		First day cover			27.50
		Imprint block of 10		6.50	
b.		"White Sky" variety (pos. 76)		3.50	3.50
9	A5	1y deep blue		4.00	3.00
		First day cover			20.00
		Imprint block of 6		35.00	
10	A5	2y rose violet		12.00	6.00
		First day cover			20.00

		Imprint block of 6	100.00		
11	A5	**3y carmine rose**	30.00	11.00	
		First day cover			20.00
		Imprint block of 6	275.00		
12	A5	**4y greenish gray**	15.00	11.00	
		First day cover			20.00
		Imprint block of 6	110.00		
13	A5	**5y blue green**	8.00	6.00	
		First day cover			20.00
		Imprint block of 6	60.00		
		First day cover, #8-13			200.00
		Nos. 8-13 (6)	69.20	37.20	

No. 8a has colorless gum and an 8-character imprint in the sheet margin. The original 1950 first two printings on off-white paper have yellowish gum and a 5-character imprint.

For No. 8b, a defect in pos. 76 of the plates used for the first two printings resulted in the sky above the tile roof being predominantly white. A new master negative and plate was made for the third printing, so pos. 76 for this printing does not have the "white sky" variety.

For surcharges see Nos. 16-17.

1951, Feb. 12   **Perf. 13½x13**

14	A6	**3y red brown**	60.00	25.00
		First day cover		60.00
		Imprint block of 6	450.00	

Opening of Ryukyu University, Feb. 12.

Pine Tree — A7

1951, Feb. 19   **Perf. 13**

15	A7	**3y dark green**	55.00	25.00
		First day cover		60.00
		Imprint block of 6	450.00	

Reforestation Week, Feb. 18-24.

No. 8 surcharged in Black

16 Type II   16A Type I   16B Type III

There are three types of 10y surcharge:
Type I: narrow-spaced rules, "10" normal spacing, "Kai Tei" characters in 9-point type. First printing, Jan. 1, 1952.
Type II: wide-spaced rules, "10" normal spacing, "Kai Tei" characters in 9-point type. Second printing, June 5, 1952.
Type III: rules and "10" both wide-spaced, "Kai Tei" characters in 8-point type. Third printing, Dec. 8, 1952.

9 Point Kai Tei   8 Point Kai Tei

Both eight and nine point type were used in overprinting Nos. 16-17. In the varieties listed below, the first number indicates the size of the "Kai" character, and the second number is the size of the "Tei" character.

1952   **Perf. 13½x13**

16	A5	**10y on 50s dark carmine rose** (II)	10.00	10.00
		Imprint block of 6	90.00	
		Top imprint block of 4, *Higa Seal* (pos. 8, 9, 18, 19)	75.00	
c.		8/8 point Kai Tei	10.00	10.00
d.		9/8 point Kai Tei	90.00	90.00
		9/9-9/8-8/8 se-tenant (horiz. strip of all 3 varieties)	150.00	150.00
		8/8-9/9 horiz. se-tenant pair	30.00	30.00
		9/9-8/8 horiz. se-tenant pair	30.00	30.00
e.		Surcharge transposed	900.00	—
f.		Legend of surcharge only (no obliteration bars)	1,200.	
g.		Wrong font for "0" (pos. 59)	150.00	150.00
h.		Wrong font for "Yen" symbol (pos. 69)	150.00	150.00
i.		Surcharge on "white sky" variety (No. 8b) (pos. 76)	150.00	150.00

On No. 16e, the entire obliteration-bars portion of the surcharge normally under the 10 Yen must be visible at the top of the stamp. Ten examples of No. 16e exist (pos. 91-100) with the full obliteration bars also in the bottom selvage.

Forgeries to defraud the Postal Agency of revenue are known, used only, at the Gusikawa Post Office. Two types. Value, $500 each.

16A	A5	**10y on 50s dark carmine rose** (I)	40.00	40.00
		Imprint block of 6	300.00	
a.		8/8 point Kai Tei	40.00	40.00
		8/8-9/9 horiz. se-tenant pair (pos. 23-24)	250.00	250.00
		9/9-8/8 horiz. se-tenant pair	110.00	110.00
b.		Bottom two bars inverted (pos. 17)	150.00	150.00
c.		Wrong font for "0" (pos. 73)	250.00	250.00
d.		Surcharge on "white sky" variety (No. 8b) (pos. 76)	250.00	250.00
e.		Wide spaced obliterating bars (pos. 72)	150.00	150.00
f.		Wide spaced bottom obliterating bars (pos. 86, 95)	80.00	80.00
16B	A5	**10y on 50s dark carmine rose** (III)	50.00	40.00
		Imprint block of 6	400.00	
a.		Wrong font for "Yen" symbol (pos. 25, 35, 85)	200.00	200.00
b.		Wrong font for "Tei" (pos. 26)	350.00	350.00
c.		Asterisk missing (pos. 54)	—	
d.		"Kai Tei" 1.25mm above asterisk (pos. 54)	350.00	350.00
e.		"Kai" omitted (pos. 71)	—	
f.		Narrow spaced "10" (pos. 96)	350.00	350.00
		Strip of 3, narrow spaced "10" in center (pos. 95-97)	450.00	
g.		Surcharge on "white sky" variety (No. 8b)	350.00	350.00
h.		Extra wide spaced "10" (pos. 60)	200.00	200.00
i.		Asterisk within 2.0mm of "Kai Tei" (pos. 87)	200.00	200.00

The Kai Tei of the third printing measures the same as the 8-point type in the earlier printings but has differing characteristics. The Top curved line of the Kai is shorter and the lower curved line is also much shorter.

No. 10 surcharged 100y in black

17	A5	**100y on 2y rose violet,** Kai Tei characters in 9/9-point type, June 16, 1952	2,200.	1,6
		Hinged	1,600.	
		Imprint block of 6	18,500.	
		Top imprint block of 4, *Higa Seal* (pos. 7, 8, 17, 18)	10,000.	
a.		8/8 point Kai Tei	2,200.	1,6
b.		9/8 point Kai Tei	3,500.	3,5
		9/9-9/8-8/8 se-tenant (horiz. strip of all 3 varieties)	9,750.	9,7
		8/8-9/9 horiz. se-tenant pair	5,000.	5,0
		9/9-8/8 horiz. se-tenant pair	7,000.	7,0
c.		Center "0" in wrong font, stamp with 9/9 Kai Tei (pos. 42)	5,000.	5,0
d.		Center "0" in wrong font, stamp with 8/8 Kai Tei (pos. 67, 86)	3,500.	3,5
e.		Center "0" in wrong font, stamp with 9/8 Kai Tei (pos. 53)	5,000.	5,0
f.		Wrong font for last "0" (pos. 59)	5,000.	5,0
g.		Wrong font for "yen" symbol (pos. 69)	5,000.	5,0

Varieties of shifted and damaged surcharge characters exist, most notably a damaged ("clipped") Kai.

See note after 16B to differentiate between 8-point and point charaters.

Surcharge forgeries are known. Authentication by competent experts is recommended.

Dove, Bean Sprout and Map — A8   Madanbashi Bridge — A9

1952, Apr. 1   **Perf. 13½x1**

18	A8	**3y deep plum**	120.00	40.
		First day cover		80.
		Imprint block of 10	1,800.	

Establishment of the Government of the Ryukyu Islands (GRI), April 1, 1952.

1952-53

Designs: 2y, Main Hall, Shuri Castle. 3y, Shurei Gate. 6y, Stone Gate, Soenji Temple, Naha. 10y, Benzaiten-do Temple. 30y, Sonohan Utaki (altar) at Shuri Castle. 50y, Tamaudun (royal mausoleum). Shuri. 100y, Stone Bridge, Hosho Pond, Enkaku Temple.

19	A9	**1y red,** *Nov. 20, 1952*	.30	.3
		Imprint block of 10	4.50	
20	A9	**2y green,** *Nov. 20, 1952*	.40	.4
		Imprint block of 10	6.00	
21	A9	**3y aquamarine,** *Nov. 20, 1952*	.50	.5
		First day cover, #19-21		40.00
		Imprint block of 10	7.50	
22	A9	**6y blue,** *Jan. 20, 1953*	3.00	3.00
		First day cover		27.5
		Imprint block of 10	45.00	
23	A9	**10y crimson rose,** *Jan. 20, 1953*	4.00	1.5
		First day cover		47.5
		Imprint block of 10	60.00	
24	A9	**30y olive green,** *Jan. 20, 1953*	15.00	10.0
		First day cover		75.0
		Imprint block of 10	225.00	
a.		30y light olive green, *1958*	60.00	
		Imprint block of 10	850.00	
25	A9	**50y rose violet,** *Jan. 20, 1953*	20.00	12.0
		First day cover		125.0
		Imprint block of 10	250.00	
26	A9	**100y claret,** *Jan. 20, 1953*	25.00	6.5
		First day cover		190.0
		Imprint block of 10	325.00	
		First day cover, #22-26		550.0
		Nos. 19-26 (8)	68.20	34.2

Issued: 1y, 2y and 3y, Nov. 20, 1952. Others, Jan. 20, 1953.

Reception at Shuri Castle — A10

Perry and American
et — A11

53, May 26 ***Perf. 13½x13, 13x13½***

A10	3y	**deep magenta**	14.00	6.50
		Imprint block of 6	120.00	
A11	6y	**dull blue**	1.50	1.50
		First day cover, #27-28		15.00
		Imprint block of 6	12.00	

Centenary of the arrival of Commodore Matthew Calbraith
ry at Naha, Okinawa.

hofu Ota and Pencil-
haped Matrix — A12

Shigo Toma and Pen — A13

53, Oct. 1 ***Perf. 13½x13***

A12	4y	**yellow brown**	12.00	5.00
		First day cover		20.00
		Imprint block of 10	150.00	

Third Newspaper Week.

54, Oct. 1

A13	4y	**blue**	14.00	7.50
		First day cover		25.00
		Imprint block of 10	175.00	

Fourth Newspaper Week.

Ryukyu Pottery — A14

Noguni Shrine and Sweet Potato Plant — A15

Designs: 15y, Lacquerware. 20y, Textile design.

954-55 **Photo.** ***Perf. 13***

1	A14	4y	**brown,** *June 25, 1954*	1.00	.60
			First day cover		10.00
			Imprint block of 10	11.00	
2	A14	15y	**vermilion,** *June 20, 1955*	5.00	4.00
			First day cover		12.50
			Imprint block of 10	65.00	
3	A14	20y	**yellow orange,** *June 20, 1955*	3.00	2.50
			First day cover		12.50
			Imprint block of 10	45.00	

First day cover, #32-33		35.00
Nos. 31-33 (3)	9.00	7.10

For surcharges see Nos. C19, C21, C23.

1955, Nov. 26

34	A15	4y	**blue**	14.00	7.00
			First day cover		22.50
			Imprint block of 10	175.00	

350th anniv. of the introduction of the sweet potato to the Ryukyu Islands.

Stylized Trees — A16

Willow Dance — A17

1956, Feb. 18 **Unwmk.**

35	A16	4y	**bluish green**	12.00	6.00
			First day cover		20.00
			Imprint block of 6	95.00	

Arbor Week, Feb. 18-24.

1956, May 1 ***Perf. 13***

8y, Straw hat dance. 14y, Dancer in warrior costume with fan.

36	A17	5y	**rose lilac**	1.00	.60
			First day cover		6.50
			Imprint block of 10	15.00	
37	A17	8y	**violet blue**	2.50	2.00
			First day cover		6.50
			Imprint block of 10	37.50	
38	A17	14y	**reddish brown**	4.00	3.00
			First day cover		6.50
			Imprint block of 10	55.00	
			First day cover, #36-38		35.00
			Nos. 36-38 (3)	7.50	5.60

For surcharges see Nos. C20, C22.

Telephone A18

1956, June 8

39	A18	4y	**violet blue**	15.00	8.00
			First day cover		20.00
			Imprint block of 6	120.00	

Establishment of dial telephone system.

Garland of Pine, Bamboo and Plum — A19

Map of Okinawa and Pencil Rocket — A20

1956, Dec. 1 ***Perf. 13½x13***

40	A19	2y	**multicolored**	2.00	2.00
			First day cover		3.50
			Imprint block of 10	27.50	

New Year, 1957.

1957, Oct. 1 **Photo.** ***Perf. 13½x13***

41	A20	4y	**deep violet blue**	1.00	1.00
			First day cover		6.00
			Imprint block of 10	12.50	

7th annual Newspaper Week, Oct. 1-7.

Phoenix — A21

1957, Dec. 1 **Unwmk.** ***Perf. 13***

42	A21	2y	**multicolored**	.25	.25
			First day cover		1.50
			Imprint block of 10	3.50	

New Year, 1958.

Ryukyu Stamps — A22

1958, July 1 ***Perf. 13½***

43	A22	4y	**multicolored**	.80	.80
			First day cover		1.25
			Imprint block of 4	4.00	

10th anniv. of 1st Ryukyu stamps.

Yen Symbol and Dollar
Sign — A23

Perf. 10.3, 10.8, 11.1 & Compound
1958, Sept. 16　　　　　　　　**Typo.**
Without Gum

44	A23	½c **orange**	.90	.90
		Imprint block of 6	8.00	
a.		Imperf., pair	1,750.	
b.		Horiz. pair, imperf. between	150.00	
c.		Vert. pair, imperf. between	200.00	
d.		Vert. strip of 4, imperf. between	800.00	
45	A23	1c **yellow green**	1.40	1.40
		Imprint block of 6	11.00	
a.		Horiz. pair, imperf. between	200.00	
b.		Vert. pair, imperf. between	150.00	
c.		Vert. strip of 3, imperf. between	700.00	
d.		Vert. strip of 4, imperf. between	800.00	
e.		Block of 4, imperf. btwn. vert. & horiz.	10,000.	
46	A23	2c **dark blue**	2.25	2.25
		Imprint block of 6	17.50	
a.		Horiz. pair, imperf. between	200.00	
b.		Vert. pair, imperf. between	2,000.	
c.		Horiz. strip of 3, imperf. between	450.00	
d.		Horiz. strip of 4, imperf. between	800.00	
47	A23	3c **deep carmine**	1.75	1.50
		Imprint block of 6	14.00	
a.		Horiz. pair, imperf. between	200.00	
b.		Vert. pair, imperf. between	150.00	
c.		Vert. strip of 3, imperf. between	450.00	
d.		Vert. strip of 4, imperf. between	800.00	
e.		Block of 4, imperf. btwn. vert. & horiz.	10,000.	
48	A23	4c **bright green**	2.25	2.25
		Imprint block of 6	17.50	
a.		Horiz. pair, imperf. between	500.00	
b.		Vert. pair, imperf. between	200.00	
49	A23	5c **orange**	4.25	3.75
		Imprint block of 6	35.00	
a.		Horiz. pair, imperf. between	225.00	
b.		Vert. pair, imperf. between	850.00	
50	A23	10c **aquamarine**	5.75	4.75
		Imprint block of 6	42.50	
a.		Horiz. pair, imperf. between	300.00	
b.		Vert. pair, imperf. between	200.00	
c.		Vert. strip of 3, imperf. between	800.00	
51	A23	25c **bright violet blue**	8.00	6.00
		Imprint block of 6	62.50	
a.		Gummed paper, perf. 10.3 ('61)	15.00	10.00
		Imprint block of 6	95.00	
b.		Horiz. pair, imperf. between	2,000.	
c.		Vert. pair, imperf. between	5,000.	
d.		Vert. strip of 3, imperf. between	900.00	
52	A23	50c **gray**	17.50	10.00
		Imprint block of 6	140.00	
a.		Gummed paper, perf. 10.3 ('61)	15.00	15.00

		Imprint block of 6	150.00	
		First day cover, #51a-52a		35.00
b.		Horiz. pair, imperf. between	1,750.	
53	A23	$1 **rose lilac**	12.50	5.50
		Imprint block of 6	100.00	
a.		Horiz. pair, imperf. between	500.00	
b.		Vert. pair, imperf. between	2,500.	
		Nos. 44-53 (10)	56.55	38.30

Printed locally. Perforation, paper and shade varieties exist. Nos. 51a and 52a are on off-white paper and perf 10.3.
First day covers come with various combinations of stamps: Nos. 44-48, 49-53, 44-53 etc. Values $20 for short set of low values (Nos. 44-48) to $60 for full set on one cover.

Gate of Courtesy — A24

1958, Oct. 15　　**Photo.**　　**Perf. 13½**
54	A24	3c **multicolored**	1.25	1.25
		First day cover		1.50
		Imprint block of 4	6.25	

Restoration of Shureimon, Gate of Courtesy, on road leading to Shuri City.
Imitations of this stamp were distributed in 1972 to discourage speculation in Ryukyuan stamps. The imitations were printed without gum and have a lengthy message in light blue printed on the back. A second type exists, with printed black perforations and three Japanese characters on the back ("Mozo Hin" - imitation) in black. Value, sheet of 10 $15.

Lion Dance — A25

Trees and
Mountains — A26

1958, Dec. 10　　**Unwmk.**　　**Perf. 1**
55	A25	1½c **multicolored**		.30
		First day cover		
		Imprint block of 6	2.00	

New Year, 1959.

1959, Apr. 30　　**Litho.**　　**Perf. 13½**
56	A26	3c **blue, yellow green, green & red**		.70
		First day cover		
		Imprint block of 6	5.50	

"Make the Ryukyus Green" movement.

Yonaguni
Moth — A27

1959, July 23　　**Photo.**　　**Perf.**
57	A27	3c **multicolored**	1.20	1
		First day cover		1
		Imprint block of 6	9.00	

Meeting of the Japanese Biological Education Society Okinawa.

Perforation and Paper Varieties of Ryukyu Islands Scott 44-53

Perforation	Perf. ID#	1/2¢ (No. 44) Paper Type				1¢ (No. 45) Paper Type				2¢ (No. 46) Paper Type				3¢ (No. 47) Paper Type				4¢ (No. 48) Paper Type				5¢ (No. 49) Paper Type				10¢ (No. 50) Paper Type				25¢ (No. 51) Paper Type				50¢ (No. 52) Paper Type				$1 (No. 53) Paper Type			
		1	2	3	4	1	2	3	4	1	2	3	4	1	2	3	4	1	2	3	4	1	2	3	4	1	2	3	4	1	2	3	4	1	2	3	4	1	2	3	4
11.1 x 11.1	M	*		*		*				*				*		*		*		*		*				*		*		*		*		*				*		*	
11.1 x 10.8	N	*				*	*			*	*			*				*		*	∞	*	?			*				*		*		*				*		*	
11.1 x 10.3	O	*			*	?	*			*				*		*		*	*			*				*		*		*		*		*				*			
10.8 x 11.1	P	*			*	*	*			*		*		*				*	*			*				*		*		*				*				*		*	
10.8 x 10.8	Q	*				*		*		*		*		*				?	*			*		*		*				*		*		*		*		*		*	
10.8 x 10.3	R	*			*	*		*		*				*	?	*		*	*			*		*		*		*		*				*				*			
10.3 x 11.1	S	*				*		*		*		*		*				?	*			*		*		*				*				*				*			
10.3 x 10.8	T	*				*		*		*				*		*		*	*			*		*		?	*	*		*				*		*		*			
10.3 x 10.3	U	*				?	*			*			*	?	*			*		*		*		*		?	*			\		*		\							

Paper Legend: 1= off-white; 2= white; 3= ivory; 4= thick

Specialists use a shorthand to refer to perf. and paper types: e.g., 50M3 =10¢ stamp, perf. 11.1 x 11.1, ivory paper.

Notes:
　* = Verified variety
　? = Reported in literature, but unverified variety.
　∞ = 48N4 is unknown; however, a single example of 48N exists on a thick white paper unknown used for any other issue.
　\ = These particular perf/paper combinations are known only in stamps of the Second (1961) Printing (51a and 52a)

The following are known unused only: 45R1, 45T2, 47O1, 48N4, 53O1.
The following are known used only: 47N4, 47T4, 50M3, 50Q2, 50R2, 50T2, 51P3, 51S1, 53T3.
Chart classifications and data supplied by courtesy of the Ryukyu Philatelic Specialist Society.

Hibiscus — A28   Toy (Yakaji) — A29

Designs: 3c, Fish (Moorish idol). 8c, Sea shell (Phalium _datum). 13c, Butterfly (Kallinia Inachus Eucerca), denomi-_on at left, butterfly going up. 17c, Jellyfish (Dactylometra _ifera Goette).

Inscribed:

琉球郵便

_59, Aug. 10			Perf. 13x13½	
	A28	½c multicolored	.25	.20
		Imprint block of 10	3.50	
	A28	3c multicolored	.75	.40
		Imprint block of 10	9.00	
	A28	8c light ultramarine, black & ocher	15.00	5.50
		Imprint block of 10	225.00	
	A28	13c light blue, gray & orange	2.50	1.75
		Imprint block of 10	32.50	
	A28	17c violet blue, red & yellow	25.00	9.00
		Imprint block of 10	375.00	
		First day cover, #58-62		17.50
		Nos. 58-62 (5)	43.50	16.85

_our-character inscription measures 10x2mm on ½c; _3mm on 3c, 8c; 8½x2mm on 13c, 17c. See Nos. 76-80.

_59, Dec. 1			Litho.	
	A29	1½c gold & multicolored	.55	.45
		First day cover		1.50
		Imprint block of 10	8.00	

New Year, 1960.

University Badge A30

_60, May 22		Photo.	Perf. 13	
	A30	3c multicolored	.95	.75
		First day cover		1.25
		Imprint block of 6	7.25	

10th anniv. opening of Ryukyu University.

Dancer — A31

Designs: Various Ryukyu Dances.

_960, Nov. 1		Photo.	Perf. 13	
Dark Gray Background				
_	A31	1c yellow, red & violet	1.50	.80
		Imprint block of 10	18.00	
_	A31	2½c crimson, blue & yellow	3.00	1.00
		Imprint block of 10	37.50	
_	A31	5c dark blue, yellow & red	.70	.50
		Imprint block of 10	10.00	
_	A31	10c dark blue, yellow & red	.90	.70
		Imprint block of 10	12.00	
		First day cover, #65-68		5.50
		Nos. 65-68 (4)	6.10	3.00

See Nos. 81-87, 220.

Torch and Nago Bay — A32

Runners at Starting Line — A33

1960, Nov. 8				
72	A32	3c light blue, green & red	6.00	3.00
		First day cover		3.50
		Imprint block of 6	45.00	
73	A33	8c orange & slate green	1.00	.75
		First day cover		1.50
		Imprint block of 6	7.50	
		First day cover, #72-73		5.00

8th Kyushu Inter-Prefectural Athletic Meet, Nago, Northern Okinawa, Nov. 6-7.

Little Egret and Rising Sun — A34

1960, Dec. 1		Unwmk.	Perf. 13	
74	A34	3c reddish brown	5.50	3.50
		First day cover		4.00
		Imprint block of 6	42.50	

National census.

Okinawa Bull Fight — A35

1960, Dec. 10			Perf. 13½	
75	A35	1½c bister, dark blue & red brown	1.75	1.50
		First day cover		2.00
		Imprint block of 6	12.50	

New Year, 1961.

Type of 1959 With Japanese Inscription Redrawn:

A28a

1960-61		Photo.	Perf. 13x13½	
76	A28a	½c multicolored, Oct. 1961	.45	.45
		Imprint block of 10	5.50	
77	A28a	3c multicolored, Aug. 23, 1961	.90	.35
		First day cover		1.50
		Imprint block of 10	12.50	
78	A28a	8c light ultramarine, black & ocher, July 1, 1960	.90	.80
		Imprint block of 10	12.50	
79	A28a	13c blue, brown & red, July 1, 1960	1.10	.90
		Imprint block of 10	15.00	

80	A28a	17c violet blue, red & yellow, July 1, 1960	15.00	6.00
		Imprint block of 10	190.00	
		First day cover, #78-80		15.00
		Nos. 76-80 (5)	18.35	8.50

Size of Japanese inscription on Nos. 78-80 is 10½x1½mm. On No. 79 the denomination is at right, butterfly going down.

Dancer Type of 1960 with "RYUKYUS" Added in English

1961-64			Perf. 13	
81	A31	1c multicolored, Dec. 5, 1961	.20	.20
		First day cover		1.00
		Imprint block of 10	2.00	
82	A31	2½c multicolored, June 20, 1962	.20	.20
		Imprint block of 10	2.25	
83	A31	5c multicolored, June 20, 1962	.25	.25
		Imprint block of 10	3.00	
84	A31	10c multicolored, June 20, 1962	.45	.40
		First day cover, #82-84		1.50
		Imprint block of 10	5.75	
84A	A31	20c multicolored, Jan. 20, 1964	3.25	1.40
		First day cover		2.50
		Imprint block of 10	37.50	
85	A31	25c multicolored, Feb. 1, 1962	1.00	.90
		First day cover		2.00
		Imprint block of 10	13.00	
86	A31	50c multicolored, Sept. 1, 1961	2.50	1.40
		Imprint block of 10	32.50	
87	A31	$1 multicolored, Sept. 1, 1961	6.00	.25
		Imprint block of 10	70.00	
		First day cover, #86-87		35.00
		Nos. 81-87 (8)	13.85	5.00

Pine Tree — A36

1961, May 1		Photo.	Perf. 13	
88	A36	3c yellow green & red	1.80	1.25
		First day cover		1.50
		Imprint block of 6	15.00	

"Make the Ryukyus Green" movement.

Naha, Steamer and Sailboat A37

1961, May 20				
89	A37	3c aquamarine	2.25	1.50
		First day cover		1.75
		Imprint block of 6	18.00	

40th anniv. of Naha.

White Silver Temple — A38   Books and Bird — A39

1961, Oct. 1		Typo.	Unwmk.	Perf. 11	
90	A38	3c red brown	2.50	2.00	
		First day cover		2.00	
		Imprint block of 6	18.00		
a.		Horiz. pair, imperf. between		850.00	
b.		Vert. pair, imperf. between		700.00	

Merger of townships Takamine, Kanegushiku and Miwa with Itoman.

A 3-cent stamp to commemorate the merger of two cities, Shimoji-cho and Hirara-shi of Miyako Island, was scheduled to be issued on Oct. 30, 1961. However, the merger was called off and the stamp never issued. It features a white chaplet on Kiyako linen on a blue background.

1961, Nov. 12   **Litho.**   *Perf. 13*
91   A39   3c **multicolored**   1.10   .90
    First day cover   1.25
    Imprint block of 6   10.00

Book Week.

Rising Sun and Eagles — A40

Symbolic Steps, Trees and Government Building — A41

1961, Dec. 10   **Photo.**   *Perf. 13½*
92   A40   1½c **gold, vermilion & black**   2.00   2.00
    First day cover   3.00
    Imprint block of 6   16.00

New Year, 1962.

1962, Apr. 1   **Unwmk.**   *Perf. 13½*
Design: 3c, Government Building.
93   A41   1½c **multicolored**   .60   .60
    Imprint block of 6   4.75
94   A41   3c **bright green, red & gray**   .80   .80
    Imprint block of 6   6.50
    First day cover, #93-94   2.00

10th anniv. of the Government of the Ryukyu Islands (GRI).

Anopheles Hyrcanus Sinensis — A42

Design: 8c, Malaria eradication emblem and Shurei gate.

1962, Apr. 7   *Perf. 13½x13*
95   A42   3c **multicolored**   .60   .60
    Imprint block of 6   4.50
96   A42   8c **multicolored**   .90   .75
    Imprint block of 6   7.50
    First day cover, #95-96   2.25

World Health Organization drive to eradicate malaria.

Dolls and Toys — A43

Linden or Sea Hibiscus — A44

1962, May 5   **Litho.**   *Perf. 13½*
97   A43   3c **red, black, blue & buff**   1.10   1.00
    First day cover   1.50
    Imprint block of 6   9.00

Children's Day, 1962.

1962, June 1   **Photo.**
Flowers: 3c, Indian coral tree. 8c, Iju (Schima liukiuensis Nakal). 13c, Touch-me-not (garden balsam). 17c, Shell flower (Alpinia speciosa).

98   A44   ½c **multicolored**   .20   .20
    Imprint block of 10   1.75
99   A44   3c **multicolored**   .35   .20
    Imprint block of 10   4.75
100 A44   8c **multicolored**   .50   .45
    Imprint block of 10   6.50
101 A44   13c **multicolored**   .70   .60
    Imprint block of 10   9.00
102 A44   17c **multicolored**   1.25   .80
    Imprint block of 10   15.00
    First day cover, #98-102   3.75
    Nos. 98-102 (5)   3.00   2.25

See Nos. 107 and 114 for 1½c and 15c flower stamps. For surcharge see No. 190.

Earthenware A45

1962, July 5   *Perf. 13½x13*
103 A45   3c **multicolored**   3.50   2.50
    First day cover   2.75
    Imprint block of 6   26.00

Philatelic Week.

Japanese Fencing (Kendo) A46

1962, July 25   *Perf. 13*
104 A46   3c **multicolored**   4.00   3.00
    First day cover   3.50
    Imprint block of 6   30.00

All-Japan Kendo Meeting in Okinawa, July 25, 1962.

Rabbit Playing near Water, Bingata Cloth Design — A47

Young Man and Woman, Stone Relief — A48

1962, Dec. 10   *Perf. 13x1*
105 A47   1½c **gold & multicolored**   1.00
    First day cover
    Imprint block of 10   12.50

New Year, 1963.

1963, Jan. 15   **Photo.**   *Perf. 1*
106 A48   3c **gold, black & blue**   .90
    First day cover
    Imprint block of 6   6.75

Gooseneck Cactus — A49

Trees and Wood Hills — A50

1963, Apr. 5   *Perf. 13x1*
107 A49   1½c **dark blue green, yellow & pink**   .20
    First day cover
    Imprint block of 10   1.50

1963, Mar. 25   *Perf. 13½x*
108 A50   3c **ultramarine, green & red brown**   1.00
    First day cover
    Imprint block of 6   7.00

"Make the Ryukyus Green" movement.

Map of Okinawa — A51

Hawks over Islands — A52

1963, Apr. 30   **Unwmk.**   *Perf. 13*
109 A51   3c **multicolored**   1.25   1.
    First day cover   1.
    Imprint block of 6   9.00

Opening of the Round Road on Okinawa.

1963, May 10   **Photo**
110 A52   3c **multicolored**   1.10   .
    First day cover   1.
    Imprint block of 6   9.00

Bird Day, May 10.

Shioya Bridge — A53

63, June 5
A53 3c multicolored 1.10 .95
First day cover 1.40
Imprint block of 6 8.25

Opening of Shioya Bridge over Shioya Bay.

Tsuikin-wan Lacquerware Bowl — A54

63, July 1 Unwmk. Perf. 13½
2 A54 3c multicolored 3.00 2.50
First day cover 2.75
Imprint block of 6 22.50

Map of Far East and JCI Emblem — A55

63, Sept. 16 Photo. Perf. 13½
3 A55 3c multicolored .70 .70
First day cover 1.25
Imprint block of 6 6.00

Meeting of the International Junior Chamber of Commerce
CI), Naha, Okinawa, Sept. 16-19.

Mamaomoto — A56

Site of Nakagusuku Castle — A57

63, Oct. 15 Perf. 13x13½
4 A56 15c multicolored 2.00 .80
First day cover 1.25
Imprint block of 10 25.00

963, Nov. 1 Perf. 13½x13
5 A57 3c multicolored .70 .60
First day cover 1.25
Imprint block of 6 5.25

Protection of national cultural treasures.

Flame — A58

Dragon (Bingata Pattern) — A59

1963, Dec. 10 Perf. 13½
116 A58 3c red, dark blue & yellow .70 .60
First day cover 1.25
Imprint block of 6 5.25

15th anniv. of the Universal Declaration of Human Rights.

1963, Dec. 10 Photo.
117 A59 1½c multicolored .60 .50
First day cover 1.50
Imprint block of 10 7.50

New Year, 1964.

Carnation — A60

Pineapples and Sugar Cane — A61

1964, May 10 Perf. 13½
118 A60 3c blue, yellow, black & carmine .40 .35
First day cover 1.25
Imprint block of 6 3.00

Mothers Day.

1964, June 1
119 A61 3c multicolored .40 .35
First day cover 1.25
Imprint block of 6 3.00

Agricultural census.

Minsah Obi (Sash Woven of Kapok) — A62

1964, July 1 Unwmk. Perf. 13½
120 A62 3c deep blue, rose pink & ocher .55 .50
First day cover 2.25
Imprint block of 6 4.50
a. 3c deep blue, deep carmine & ocher .70 .65
First day cover 2.75
Imprint block of 6 5.25

Philatelic Week.

Girl Scout and Emblem — A63

1964, Aug. 31 Photo.
121 A63 3c multicolored .40 .35
First day cover 1.25
Imprint block of 6 3.00

10th anniv. of Ryukyuan Girl Scouts.

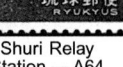

Shuri Relay Station — A64

Parabolic Antenna and Map — A65

1964, Sept. 1 Unwmk. Perf. 13½
Black Overprint
122 A64 3c deep green .65 .65
Imprint block of 6 5.50
a. Figure "1" inverted 35.00 35.00
b. Overprint inverted 1,500.
c. Overprint missing 3,500.
123 A65 8c ultramarine 1.25 1.25
Imprint block of 6 10.00
First day cover, #122-123 4.75
a. Overprint missing 3,500.

Opening of the Ryukyu Islands-Japan microwave system carrying telephone and telegraph messages. The overprints indicate the system was not actually opened until 1964.
Many of the stamps with overprint errors listed above are damaged. The values listed here are for stamps in very fine condition.
A number of different overprint shifts also exist with the shifts to greater and lesser degrees.

Gate of Courtesy, Olympic Torch and Emblem — A66

1964, Sept. 7 Photo. Perf. 13½x13
124 A66 3c ultramarine, yellow & red .30 .20
First day cover (Sept. 7) 1.25
First day cover (Sept. 6 & 7) 25.00
Imprint block of 6 2.50

Relaying the Olympic torch on Okinawa en route to Tokyo. Torch arrival was scheduled for Sept. 6. A typhoon delayed arrival until Sept. 7. A small number of covers received both Sept. 6 and 7 cancels.

"Naihanchi," Karate Stance — A67

"Makiwara," Strengthening Hands and Feet — A68

"Kumite," Simulated
Combat — A69

1964-65　　　　　**Photo.**　　　　**Perf. 13½**
125 A67 3c **dull claret, yel & blk,** *Oct. 5,*
　　　　　1964　　　　　　　　.50　　.45
　　First day cover　　　　　　　　　　1.25
　　Imprint block of 6　　　　　3.25
126 A68 3c **yel & multi,** *Feb. 5, 1965*　.40　　.40
　　First day cover　　　　　　　　　　1.25
　　Imprint block of 6　　　　　3.00
　　Incomplete vertical stroke in
　　"$" sign　　　　　　　　　17.50 17.50
　　　First day cover　　　　　　　　25.00
127 A69 3c **gray, red & blk,** *June 5, 1965*　.40　.40
　　First day cover　　　　　　　　　　1.25
　　Imprint block of 6　　　　　3.00
　　Nos. 125-127 (3)　　　　1.30　　1.25

　　Karate, Ryukyuan self-defense sport.

Miyara
Dunchi — A70

Snake and Iris
(Bingata) — A71

1964, Nov. 1　　　　　　**Perf. 13½**
128 A70 3c **multicolored**　　　　.30　　.25
　　First day cover　　　　　　　　　　1.25
　　Imprint block of 6　　　　　2.25

　　Protection of national cultural treasures. Miyara Dunchi was
built as a residence by Miyara-pechin Toen in 1819.

1964, Dec. 10　　　　　　**Photo.**
129 A71 1½c **multicolored**　　　.30　　.25
　　First day cover　　　　　　　　　　2.00
　　Imprint block of 10　　　　4.00

　　　　　　New Year, 1965.

Boy Scouts — A72

1965, Feb. 6　　　　　　**Perf. 13½**
130 A72 3c **light blue & multi**　　.45　　.40
　　First day cover　　　　　　　　　　1.50
　　Imprint block of 6　　　　　4.00

　　10th anniv. of Ryukyuan Boy Scouts.

Main
Stadium,
Onoyama
A73

1965, July 1　　　　　　**Perf. 13x13½**
131 A73 3c **multicolored**　　　　.25　　.25
　　First day cover　　　　　　　　　　1.00
　　Imprint block of 6　　　　　2.00

　　Inauguration of the main stadium of the Onoyama athletic
facilities.

Samisen of King
Shoko — A74

1965, July 1　　　　**Photo.**　　　**Perf. 13½**
132 A74 3c **buff & multicolored**　　.45　　.40
　　First day cover　　　　　　　　　　1.25
　　Imprint block of 6　　　　　3.25

　　　　Philatelic Week.

Kin Power Plant — A75

ICY Emblem, Ryukyu
Map — A76

1965, July 1
133 A75 3c **green & multicolored**　　.25　　.25
　　First day cover　　　　　　　　　　1.00
　　Imprint block of 6　　　　　2.00

　　Completion of Kin power plant.

1965, Aug. 24　　　　**Photo.**　　　**Perf. 13½**
134 A76 3c **multicolored**　　　　.20　　.20
　　First day cover　　　　　　　　　　1.00
　　Imprint block of 6　　　　　1.75

　　20th anniv. of the UN and International Cooperation Year,
1964-65.

Naha City
Hall — A77

1965, Sept. 18　　　**Unwmk.**　　　**Perf. 13½**
135 A77 3c **blue & multicolored**　　.20　　.20
　　First day cover　　　　　　　　　　1.00
　　Imprint block of 6　　　　　1.75

　　Completion of Naha City Hall.

Chinese Box
Turtle — A78

Horse (Bingata) — A79

　　Turtles: No. 137, Hawksbill turtle (denomination at top, country name at bottom). No. 138, Asian terrapin (denomination country name on top).

1965-66　　　　　**Photo.**　　　　**Perf. 1**
136 A78 3c **golden brown & multi,** *Oct. 20,*
　　　　　1965　　　　　　　　　.30
　　First day cover　　　　　　　　　　2.50
　　Imprint block of 6　　　　　2.50
137 A78 3c **black, yel & brown,** *Jan. 20, 1966*　.30
　　First day cover　　　　　　　　　　2.50
　　Imprint block of 6　　　　　2.50
138 A78 3c **gray & multicolored,** *Apr. 20,*
　　　　　1966　　　　　　　　　.30
　　First day cover　　　　　　　　　　2.50
　　Imprint block of 6　　　　　2.50
　　Nos. 136-138 (3)　　　　　　.90

1965, Dec. 10　　　　　**Photo.**　　　**Perf. 1**
139 A79 1½c **multicolored**　　　　.20
　　First day cover
　　Imprint block of 10　　　　2.25
　　a.　　Gold omitted　　　　　*1,200.*

　　　　　New Year, 1966.
　　There are 92 unused and 2 used examples of No. 1
known.

NATURE CONSERVATION ISSUE

Noguchi's Okinawa
Woodpecker — A80

Sika Deer — A81

　　Design: No. 142, Dugong.

1966　　　　　**Photo.**　　　　**Perf. 13**
140 A80 3c **blue green & multi,** *Feb. 15*　.20
　　First day cover　　　　　　　　　　1.
　　Imprint block of 6　　　　　1.65
141 A81 3c **blue, red, black, brown & green,**
　　　　　Mar. 15　　　　　　.25
　　First day cover　　　　　　　　　　1.
　　Imprint block of 6　　　　　1.75
142 A81 3c **blue, yellow green, black & red,**
　　　　　Apr. 20　　　　　　.25
　　First day cover　　　　　　　　　　1.
　　Imprint block of 6　　　　　1.75
　　Nos. 140-142 (3)　　　　　　.70

Ryukyu Bungalow
Swallow — A82

66, May 10 Photo. Perf. 13½
A82 3c **sky blue, black & brown** .20 .20
First day cover 1.00
Imprint block of 6 1.10
4th Bird Week, May 10-16.

Lilies and Ruins A83

66, June 23 Perf. 13x13½
A83 3c **multicolored** .20 .20
First day cover 1.00
Imprint block of 6 1.00
Memorial Day, end of the Battle of Okinawa, June 23, 1945.

University of the Ryukyus A84

66, July 1
A84 3c **multicolored** .20 .20
First day cover 1.00
Imprint block of 6 1.00
Transfer of the University of the Ryukyus from U.S. authority to the Ryukyu Government.

Lacquerware, 18th Century — A85

Tile-Roofed House and UNESCO Emblem — A86

66, Aug. 1 Perf. 13½
A85 3c **gray & multicolored** .20 .20
First day cover 1.50
Imprint block of 6 1.30
Philatelic Week.

66, Sept. 20 Photo. Perf. 13½
A86 3c **multicolored** .20 .20
First day cover 1.00
Imprint block of 6 1.10
20th anniv. of UNESCO.

Government Museum and Dragon Statue — A87

66, Oct. 6
A87 3c **multicolored** .20 .20
First day cover 1.00
Imprint block of 6 1.00
Completion of the GRI (Government of the Ryukyu Islands) Museum, Shuri.

Tomb of Nakasone-Tuimya Genga, Ruler of Miyako — A88

1966, Nov. 1 Photo. Perf. 13½
149 A88 3c **multicolored** .20 .20
First day cover 1.00
Imprint block of 6 1.00
Protection of national cultural treasures.

Ram in Iris Wreath — A89

Clown Fish — A90

1966, Dec. 10 Photo. Perf. 13½
150 A89 1½c **dark blue & multicolored** .20 .20
First day cover 1.50
Imprint block of 10 1.10
New Year, 1967.

1966-67
Fish: No. 152, Young boxfish (white numeral at lower left). No. 153, Forceps fish (pale buff numeral at lower right). No. 154, Spotted triggerfish (orange numeral). No. 155, Saddleback butterflyfish (carmine numeral, lower left).

151 A90 3c **orange red & multi,** Dec. 20, 1966 .20 .20
First day cover 1.00
Imprint block of 6 1.75
152 A90 3c **orange yellow & multi,** Jan. 10, 1967 .25 .20
First day cover 1.00
Imprint block of 6 1.75
153 A90 3c **multicolored,** Apr. 10, 1967 .40 .25
First day cover 1.00
Imprint block of 6 2.75
154 A90 3c **multicolored,** May 25, 1967 .35 .25
First day cover 1.00
Imprint block of 6 2.25
155 A90 3c **multicolored,** June 10, 1967 .30 .25
First day cover 1.00
Imprint block of 6 1.90
Nos. 151-155 (5) 1.50 1.15

A 3-cent stamp to commemorate Japanese-American-Ryukyuan Joint Arbor Day was scheduled for release on March 16, 1967. However, it was not released. The stamp in light blue and white features American and Japanese flags joined by a shield containing a tree.

Tsuboya Urn — A91

Episcopal Miter — A92

1967, Apr. 20
156 A91 3c **yellow & multicolored** .20 .20
First day cover 1.25
Imprint block of 6 1.65
Philatelic Week.

1967-68 Photo. Perf. 13½
Seashells: No. 158, Venus comb murex. No. 159, Chiragra spider. No. 160, Green truban. No. 161, Euprotomus bulla.

157 A92 3c **light green & multi,** July 20, 1967 .20 .20
First day cover 1.00
Imprint block of 6 1.25
158 A92 3c **greenish blue & multi,** Aug. 30, 1968 .25 .20
First day cover 1.00
Imprint block of 6 1.75
159 A92 3c **emerald & multi,** Jan. 18, 1968 .25 .20
First day cover 1.00
Imprint block of 6 1.65
160 A92 3c **light blue & multi,** Feb. 20, 1968 .30 .25
First day cover 1.00
Imprint block of 6 1.65
161 A92 3c **bright blue & multi,** June 5, 1968 .60 .50
First day cover 1.00
Imprint block of 6 4.00
Nos. 157-161 (5) 1.60 1.35

Red-tiled Roofs and ITY Emblem — A93

1967, Sept. 11 Photo. Perf. 13½
162 A93 3c **multicolored** .20 .20
First day cover 1.00
Imprint block of 6 1.25
International Tourist Year.

Mobile TB Clinic — A94

1967, Oct. 13 Photo. Perf. 13½
163 A94 3c **lilac & multicolored** .20 .20
First day cover 1.00
Imprint block of 6 1.25
15th anniv. of the Anti-Tuberculosis Society.

Hojo Bridge, Enkaku Temple, 1498 — A95

1967, Nov. 1
164 A95 3c **blue green & multicolored** .20 .20
First day cover 1.00
Imprint block of 6 1.50
Protection of national cultural treasures.

Monkcy (Bingata) — A96

TV Tower and Map — A97

1967, Dec. 11   **Photo.**   **Perf. 13½**
165 A96 1½c **silver & multicolored**   .25   .20
    First day cover   1.50
    Imprint block of 10   3.00

New Year, 1968.

1967, Dec. 22
166 A97   3c **multicolored**   .25   .25
    First day cover   1.00
    Imprint block of 6   1.50

Opening of Miyako and Yaeyama television stations.

Dr. Kijin Nakachi and Helper — A98

Pill Box (Inro) — A99

1968, Mar. 15   **Photo.**   **Perf. 13½**
167 A98   3c **multicolored**   .30   .25
    First day cover   1.00
    Imprint block of 6   1.75

120th anniv. of the first vaccination in the Ryukyu Islands, by Dr. Kijin Nakachi.

1968, Apr. 18
168 A99   3c **gray & multicolored**   .45   .45
    First day cover   1.25
    Imprint block of 6   3.50

Philatelic Week.

Young Man, Library, Book and Map of Ryukyu Islands — A100

1968, May 13
169 A100 3c **multicolored**   .30   .25
    First day cover   1.00
    Imprint block of 6   1.75

10th International Library Week.

Mailmen's Uniforms and Stamp of 1948 A101

1968, July 1   **Photo.**   **Perf. 13x13½**
170 A101 3c **multicolored**   .30   .25
    First day cover   1.00
    Imprint block of 6   1.75

First Ryukyuan postage stamps, 20th anniv.

Main Gate, Enkaku Temple — A102

1968, July 15   **Photo. & Engr.**   **Perf. 13½**
171 A102 3c **multicolored**   .30   .25
    First day cover   1.00
    Imprint block of 6   1.75

Restoration of the main gate Enkaku Temple, built 1492-1495, destroyed during World War II.

Old Man's Dance — A103

Mictyris Longicarpus — A104

1968, Sept. 15   **Photo.**   **Perf. 13½**
172 A103 3c **gold & multicolored**   .30   .25
    First day cover   1.00
    Imprint block of 6   2.00

Old People's Day.

1968-69   **Photo.**   **Perf. 13½**
Crabs: No. 174, Uca dubia stimpson. No. 175, Baptozius vinosus. No. 176, Cardisoma carnifex. No. 177, Ocypode ceratophthalma pallas.
173 A104 3c **blue, ocher & black,** *Oct. 10,*   .30   .25
    1968
    First day cover   1.25
    Imprint block of 6   2.50
174 A104 3c **light blue green & multi,** *Feb. 5,*   .35   .30
    1969
    First day cover   1.25
    Imprint block of 6   2.75
175 A104 3c **light green & multi,** *Mar. 5, 1969*   .35   .30
    First day cover   1.25
    Imprint block of 6   2.75
176 A104 3c **light ultra & multi,** *May 15, 1969*   .45   .40
    First day cover   1.25
    Imprint block of 6   3.25
177 A104 3c **light ultra & multi,** *June 2, 1969*   .45   .40
    First day cover   1.25
    Imprint block of 6   3.25
    Nos. 173-177 (5)   1.90   1.65

Saraswati Pavilion — A105

1968, Nov. 1   **Photo.**   **Perf. 13½**
178 A105 3c **multicolored**   .30   .25
    First day cover   1.00
    Imprint block of 6   2.00

Restoration of the Sarawati Pavilion (in front of Enkaku Temple), destroyed during World War II.

Tennis Player — A106

Cock and Iris (Bingata) — A107

1968, Nov. 23   **Photo.**   **Perf. 1**
179 A106 3c **green & multicolored**   .40
    First day cover
    Imprint block of 6   3.25

35th All-Japan East-West Men's Soft-ball Tennis Tournam Naha City, Nov. 23-24.

1968, Dec. 10
180 A107 1½c **orange & multicolored**   .25
    First day cover
    Imprint block of 10   3.50

New Year, 1969.

Boxer — A108

Ink Slab Screen — A109

1969, Jan. 3
181 A108 3c **gray & multicolored**   .40
    First day cover
    Imprint block of 6   2.75

20th All-Japan Amateur Boxing Championships held at University of the Ryukyus, Jan. 3-5.

1969, Apr. 17   **Photo.**   **Perf. 1**
182 A109 3c **salmon, indigo & red**   .40
    First day cover   1
    Imprint block of 6   2.75

Philatelic Week.

Box Antennas and Map of Radio Link — A110

Gate of Courtesy an Emblems — A111

1969, July 1   **Photo.**   **Perf. 13**
183 A110 3c **multicolored**   .30
    First day cover
    Imprint block of 6   2.25

Opening of the UHF (radio) circuit system between Okina and the outlying Miyako-Yaeyama Islands.

1969, Aug. 1   **Photo.**   **Perf. 13**
184 A111 3c **Prussian blue, gold & vermil-ion**   .30
    First day cover   1.
    Imprint block of 6   2.25

22nd All-Japan Formative Education Study Conf., Naha, Au 1-3.

FOLKLORE ISSUE

Tug of War Festival
A112

Hari Boat Race
A113

Izaiho Ceremony, Kudaka Island
A114

Mortardrum Dance
A115

Sea God Dance
A116

969-70		**Photo.**		**Perf. 13**
85 A112	3c **multicolored,** *Aug. 1, 1969*		.30	.25
	First day cover			1.50
	Imprint block of 6		2.25	
86 A113	3c **multicolored,** *Sept. 5, 1969*		.35	.30
	First day cover			1.50
	Imprint block of 6		2.25	
87 A114	3c **multicolored,** *Oct. 3, 1969*		.35	.30
	First day cover			1.50
	Imprint block of 6		2.25	
88 A115	3c **multicolored,** *Jan. 20, 1970*		.50	.45
	First day cover			1.50
	Imprint block of 6		3.50	
89 A116	3c **multicolored,** *Feb. 27, 1970*		.50	.45
	First day cover			1.50
	Imprint block of 6		3.50	
	Nos. 185-189 (5)		2.00	1.75

No. 99 Surcharged

1969, Oct. 15   **Photo.**   **Perf. 13½**
90 A44   ½c on 3c **multicolored**   1.00   1.00
    First day cover   3.00
    Imprint block of 10   13.50
  a. "1/2c" only surcharge   750.00

No. 190a are right margin stamps from a pane with a leftward misregistration of the surcharging plate.

Nakamura-ke Farm House, Built 1713-51 — A117

1969, Nov. 1   **Photo.**   **Perf. 13½**
191 A117   3c **multicolored**   .25   .20
    First day cover   1.00
    Imprint block of 6   1.50

Protection of national cultural treasures.

Statue of Kyuzo Toyama, Maps of Hawaiian and Ryukyu Islands — A118

1969, Dec. 5   **Photo.**   **Perf. 13½**
192 A118   3c **light ultra & multi**   .50   .50
    First day cover   1.50
    Imprint block of 6   3.75
  a.   Without overprint   2,500.
  b.   Wide-spaced bars   725.00

70th anniv. of Ryukyu-Hawaii emigration led by Kyuzo Toyama.
The overprint "1969" at lower left and bars across "1970" at upper right was applied before No. 192 was issued.

Dog and Flowers (Bingata) — A119

Sake Flask Made from Coconut — A120

1969, Dec. 10
193 A119   1½c **pink & multicolored**   .20   .20
    First day cover   1.50
    Imprint block of 10   2.75

New Year, 1970.

1970, Apr. 15   **Photo.**   **Perf. 13½**
194 A120   3c **multicolored**   .25   .25
    First day cover   1.25
    Imprint block of 6   1.75

Philatelic Week, 1970.

CLASSIC OPERA ISSUE

"The Bell" (Shushin Kaneiri) — A121

Child and Kidnapper (Chunusudu)
A122

Robe of Feathers (Mekarushi)
A123

Vengeance of Two Young Sons (Nidotichiuchi)
A124

The Virgin and the Dragon (Kokonomaki)
A125

1970		**Photo.**		**Perf. 13½**
195 A121	3c **dull blue & multi,** *Apr. 28*		.40	.40
	First day cover			1.75
	Imprint block of 6		3.00	
a.	Souvenir sheet of 4		5.00	5.00
	First day cover			5.00
196 A122	3c **light blue & multi,** *May 29*		.40	.40
	First day cover			1.75
	Imprint block of 6		3.00	
a.	Souvenir sheet of 4		5.00	5.00
	First day cover			5.00
197 A123	3c **bluish green & multi,** *June 30*		.40	.40
	First day cover			1.75
	Imprint block of 6		3.00	
a.	Souvenir sheet of 4		5.00	5.00
	First day cover			5.00
198 A124	3c **dull blue green & multi,** *July 30*		.40	.40
	First day cover			1.75
	Imprint block of 6		3.00	
a.	Souvenir sheet of 4		5.00	5.00
	First day cover			5.00
199 A125	3c **multicolored,** *Aug. 25*		.40	.40
	First day cover			1.75
	Imprint block of 6		3.00	
a.	Souvenir sheet of 4		5.00	5.00
	First day cover			5.00
	Nos. 195-199 (5)		2.00	2.00
	Nos. 195a-199a (5)		25.00	25.00

Underwater Observatory and Tropical Fish — A126

1970, May 22
200 A126   3c **blue green & multi**   .30   .25
    First day cover   1.25
    Imprint block of 6   2.00

Completion of the underwater observatory of Busena-Misaki, Nago.

Noboru Jahana (1865-1908), Politician — A127

Map of Okinawa and People — A128

Portraits: No. 202, Saion Gushichan Bunjaku (1682-1761), statesman. No. 203, Choho Giwan (1823-1876), regent and poet.

1970-71		Engr.		Perf. 13½
201 A127	3c	rose claret, *Sept. 25, 1970*	.50	.45
		First day cover		2.50
		Imprint block of 6	3.50	
202 A127	3c	dull blue green, *Dec. 22, 1970*	.75	.65
		First day cover		2.50
		Imprint block of 6	6.00	
203 A127	3c	black, *Jan. 22, 1971*	.50	.45
		First day cover		2.50
		Imprint block of 6	3.50	

1970, Oct. 1				Photo.
204 A128	3c	red & multicolored	.25	.25
		First day cover		1.00
		Imprint block of 6	1.75	

Oct. 1, 1970 census.

Great Cycad of Une — A129

1970, Nov. 2		Photo.		Perf. 13½
205 A129	3c	gold & multicolored	.25	.25
		First day cover		1.00
		Imprint block of 6	1.75	

Protection of national treasures.

Japanese Flag, Diet and Map of Ryukyus — A130

Wild Boar and Cherry Blossoms (Bingata) — A131

1970, Nov. 15		Photo.		Perf. 13½
206 A130	3c	ultramarine & multicolored	.80	.75
		First day cover		2.00
		Imprint block of 6	6.00	

Citizen's participation in national administration to Japanese law of Apr. 24, 1970.

1970, Dec. 10				
207 A131	1½c	multicolored	.20	.20
		First day cover		1.50
		Imprint block of 10	2.40	

New Year, 1971.

Low Hand Loom (Jibata) — A132

Farmer Wearing Palm Bark Raincoat and Kuba Leaf Hat — A133

Fisherman's Wooden Box and Scoop — A134

Designs: No. 209, Woman running a filature (reel). No. 211, Woman hulling rice with cylindrical "Shiri-ushi."

1971		Photo.		Perf. 13½
208 A132	3c	light blue & multi, *Feb. 16*	.30	.25
		First day cover		1.25
		Imprint block of 6	2.00	
209 A132	3c	pale green & multi, *Mar. 16*	.30	.25
		First day cover		1.25
		Imprint block of 6	2.00	
210 A133	3c	light blue & multi, *Apr. 30*	.35	.30
		First day cover		1.25
		Imprint block of 6	2.25	
211 A132	3c	yellow & multi, *May 20*	.40	.35
		First day cover		1.25
		Imprint block of 6	3.00	
212 A134	3c	gray & multi, *June 15*	.35	.30
		First day cover		1.25
		Imprint block of 6	2.25	
		Nos. 208-212 (5)	1.70	1.45

Water Carrier (Taku) — A135

1971, Apr. 15		Photo.		Perf. 13½
213 A135	3c	blue green & multicolored	.35	.30
		First day cover		1.50
		Imprint block of 6	2.75	

Philatelic Week, 1971.

Old and New Naha, and City Emblem A136

1971, May 20				Perf. 13
214 A136	3c	ultramarine & multicolored	.25	.20
		First day cover		1.00
		Imprint block of 6	1.75	

50th anniv. of Naha as a municipality.

Caesalpinia Pulcherrima — A137

Design: 2c, Madder (Sandanka).

1971		Photo.		Perf.
215 A137	2c	gray & multicolored, *Sept. 30*	.25	1.
		First day cover		
		Imprint block of 10	3.00	
216 A137	3c	gray & multicolored, *May 10*	.25	1.
		First day cover		
		Imprint block of 10	3.00	

GOVERNMENT PARK SERIES

View from Mabur Hill — A138

Mt. Arashi from Haneji Sea — A139

Yabuchi Island from Yakena Port — A140

1971-72				
217 A138	3c	green & multi, *July 30, 1971*	.20	.2
		First day cover		1.2
		Imprint block of 6	1.50	
218 A139	3c	blue & multi, *Aug. 30, 1971*	.20	.2
		First day cover		1.2
		Imprint block of 6	1.50	
219 A140	4c	multicolored, *Jan. 20, 1972*	.25	.2
		First day cover		1.2
		Imprint block of 6	1.75	
		Nos. 217-219 (3)	.65	.6

For the 4-cent unissued "stamp" picturing Iriomo Park, originally planned for issue in 1971 but neve released, see the note after No. R31.

Dancer — A141

Deva King, Torinji Temple — A142

1971, Nov. 1		Photo.		Perf. 1
220 A141	4c	Prussian blue & multicolored	.20	.2
		First day cover		1.0
		Imprint block of 10	2.50	

1, Dec. 1

A142   4c   **deep blue & multicolored**   .20   .20
              First day cover   1.00
              Imprint block of 6   1.50

Protection of national cultural treasures.

Rat and
Chrysanthemums
A143

Student Nurse
A144

1, Dec. 10

A143   2c   **brown orange & multi**   .20   .20
              First day cover   1.50
              Imprint block of 10   2.50

New Year, 1972.

1, Dec. 24

A144   4c   **lilac & multicolored**   .20   .20
              First day cover   1.00
              Imprint block of 6   1.50

Nurses' training, 25th anniversary.

A145

A147

Coral
Reef — A146

72   **Photo.**   **Perf. 13**
A145   5c   **bright blue & multi**, *Apr. 14*   .40   .35
              First day cover   1.25
              Imprint block of 6   2.75
A146   5c   **gray & multi**, *Mar. 30*   .40   .35
              First day cover   1.25
              Imprint block of 6   2.75
A147   5c   **ocher & multi**, *Mar. 21*   .40   .35
              First day cover   1.25
              Imprint block of 6   2.75
              Nos. 224-226 (3)   1.20   1.05

Dove, U.S. and
Japanese
Flags — A148

72, Apr. 17   **Photo.**   **Perf. 13**
A148   5c   **bright blue & multi**   .80   .80
              First day cover   1.50
              Imprint block of 6   5.50

Antique Sake Pot
(Yushibin) — A149

1972, Apr. 20

228   A149   5c   **ultramarine & multicolored**   .60   .60
                     First day cover   1.25
                     Imprint block of 6   4.50

Ryukyu stamps were replaced by those of Japan after May 15, 1972.

AIR POST STAMPS

Catalogue values for all unused stamps in this section are for Never Hinged items.

Dove and Map of
Ryukyus — AP1

1950, Feb. 15   Photo.   Unwmk.   Perf. 13x13½
C1   AP1   8y   **bright blue**   150.00   60.00
                  First day cover   35.00
                  Imprint block of 6   1,250.
C2   AP1   12y   **green**   35.00   30.00
                   First day cover   35.00
                   Imprint block of 6   275.00
C3   AP1   16y   **rose carmine**   20.00   20.00
                   First day cover   35.00
                   Imprint block of 6   125.00
                   First day cover, #C1-C3   200.00
                   Nos. C1-C3 (3)   205.00   110.00

Heavenly
Maiden
AP2

1951-54
C4   AP2   13y   **blue**, *Oct. 1, 1951*   3.00   2.00
                   First day cover   60.00
                   Imprint block of 6, 5-charac-
                   ter   300.00
                   Imprint block of 6, 8-charac-
                   ter   37.50
C5   AP2   18y   **green**, *Oct. 1, 1951*   4.00   3.00
                   First day cover   60.00
                   Imprint block of 6, 5-charac-
                   ter   55.00
                   Imprint block of 6, 8-charac-
                   ter   45.00
C6   AP2   30y   **cerise**, *Oct. 1, 1951*   6.00   1.50
                   First day cover   60.00
                   First day cover, #C4-C6   250.00
                   Imprint block of 6, 5-charac-
                   ter   70.00
                   Imprint block of 6, 8-charac-
                   ter   150.00
C7   AP2   40y   **red violet**, *Aug. 16, 1954*   8.00   7.00
                   First day cover   35.00
                   Imprint block of 6   90.00
C8   AP2   50y   **yellow orange**, *Aug. 16,
                   1954*   9.00   8.00
                   First day cover   35.00
                   Imprint block of 6   100.00
                   First day cover, #C7-C8   125.00
                   Nos. C4-C8 (5)   30.00   21.50

Heavenly Maiden
Playing
Flute — AP3

1957, Aug. 1   Engr.   Perf. 13½
C9   AP3   15y   **blue green**   9.00   4.00
                   Imprint block of 6   65.00
C10   AP3   20y   **rose carmine**   15.00   7.00
                   Imprint block of 6   100.00
C11   AP3   35y   **yellow green**   17.00   8.00
                   Imprint block of 6   130.00
a.   35y   *light yellow green, 1958*   150.00
C12   AP3   45y   **reddish brown**   20.00   10.00
                   Imprint block of 6   150.00
C13   AP3   60y   **gray**   24.00   12.00
                   Imprint block of 6   210.00
                   First day cover, #C9-C13   45.00
                   Nos. C9-C13 (5)   85.00   41.00

On one printing of No. C10, position 49 shows an added spur on the right side of the second character from the left. Value unused, $150.

Same Surcharged
in Brown Red or
Light Ultramarine

1959, Dec. 20
C14   AP3   9c on 15y   **blue green** (BrR)   3.00   2.00
                         Imprint block of 6   22.50
a.   Inverted surcharge   950.00
             Imprint block of 6   6,750.
C15   AP3   14c on 20y   **rose carmine** (L.U.)   4.00   4.00
                          Imprint block of 6   30.00
C16   AP3   19c on 35y   **light yellow green**
                          (BrR)   8.00   6.00
                          Imprint block of 6   57.50
C17   AP3   27c on 45y   **reddish brown** (L.U.)   19.00   6.00
                          Imprint block of 6   150.00
C18   AP3   35c on 60y   **gray** (BrR)   16.00   9.00
                          Imprint block of 6   125.00
                          First day cover, #C14-C18   35.00
                          Nos. C14-C18 (5)   50.00   27.00

No. C15 is found with the variety described below No. C13. Value unused, $100.

Nos. 31-33, 36 and 38
Surcharged in Black, Brown,
Red, Blue or Green

1960, Aug. 3   Photo.   Perf. 13
C19   A14   9c on 4y   **brown**   4.00   1.00
                        Imprint block of 10   50.00
a.   Surcharge inverted and transposed   15,000.   15,000.
b.   Inverted surcharge (legend only)   12,000.
c.   Surcharge transposed   1,500.
d.   Legend of surcharge only   4,000.
e.   Vert. pair, one without surcharge   —

Nos. C19c and C19d are from a single sheet of 100 with surcharge shifted downward. Ten examples of No. C19c exist with "9c" also in bottom selvage. No. C19d is from the top row of the sheet.
No. C19e is unique, pos. 100, caused by paper foldover.

C20   A17   14c on 5y   **rose lilac** (Br)   5.00   3.00
                         Imprint block of 10   65.00
C21   A14   19c on 15y   **vermilion** (R)   3.50   3.00
                          Imprint block of 10   45.00
C22   A17   27c on 14y   **reddish brown** (Bl)   10.50   2.50
                          Imprint block of 10   150.00
C23   A14   35c on 20y   **yellow orange** (G)   7.50   5.00
                          Imprint block of 10   90.00
                          First day cover, #C19-C23   25.00
                          Nos. C19-C23 (5)   30.50   14.50

Wind God — AP4

Designs: 9c, Heavenly Maiden (as on AP2). 14c, Heavenly Maiden (as on AP3). 27c, Wind God at right. 35c, Heavenly Maiden over treetops.

1961, Sept. 21   Unwmk.   Perf. 13½

C24	AP4	9c multicolored	.30	.20
		Imprint block of 6	2.25	
C25	AP4	14c multicolored	.80	.80
		Imprint block of 6	6.00	
C26	AP4	19c multicolored	.90	.90
		Imprint block of 6	6.50	
C27	AP4	27c multicolored	3.50	.60
		Imprint block of 6	27.50	
C28	AP4	35c multicolored	2.50	1.25
		Imprint block of 6	20.00	
		First day cover, #C24-C28		35.00
		Nos. C24-C28 (5)	8.00	3.75

AP5

AP6

1963, Aug. 28   Perf. 13x13½

C29	AP5	5½c multicolored	.25	.25
		First day cover		1.00
		Imprint block of 10	3.00	
C30	AP6	7c multicolored	.30	.30
		First day cover		1.00
		First day cover, #C29-C30		2.50
		Imprint block of 10	3.50	

SPECIAL DELIVERY STAMPS

Catalogue value for the unused stamp in this section is for a Never Hinged item.

Sea Horse and Map of Ryukyus — SD1

1950, Feb. 15   Unwmk.   Photo.   Perf. 13x13½

E1	SD1	5y bright blue	35.00	20.00
		First day cover		100.00
		Imprint block of 6	350.00	

QUANTITIES ISSUED
Regular Postage and Commemorative Stamps

Cat. No.	Quantity	Cat. No.	Quantity
1	90,214	87	3,019,000
2	55,901	88	298,966
3	94,663	89	298,966
4	55,413	90	398,901
5	76,387	91	398,992
6	117,321	92	1,498,970
7	291,403	93	598,989
1a	61,000	94	398,998
2a-4a	181,000	95	398,993
5a	29,936	96	298,993
6a	99,300	97	398,997
7a	46,000	98	9,699,000
8	2,559,000	99	10,991,500
8a	300,000	100	1,549,000
9	1,198,989	101	799,000
10	589,000	102	1,299,000
11	479,000	103	398,995
12	598,999	104	298,892
13	397,855	105	1,598,949
14	499,000	106	348,989
15	498,960	107	10,099,000
16	199,197	108	348,865
16A	199,900	109	348,937
16B	39,900	110	348,962
17	9,800	111	348,974
18	299,500	112	398,974

Cat. No.	Quantity	Cat. No.	Quantity
19	3,014,427	113	398,911
20	3,141,777	114	1,199,000
21	2,970,827	115	398,948
22	191,917	116	398,943
23	1,118,617	117	1,698,912
24	276,218	118	550,000
24a	ca. 1,300	119	549,000
25	231,717	120	749,000
26	220,130	121	799,000
27	398,993	122	389,000
28	386,421	123	319,000
29	498,854	124	1,999,000
30	298,994	125-127	999,000
31	4,768,413	128	799,000
32	1,202,297	129	1,699,000
33	500,059	130-131	799,000
34	298,994	132	849,000
35	199,000	133	799,000
36	455,896	134	1,299,000
37	160,518	135	1,099,000
38	198,720	136	1,299,000
39	198,199	137-138	1,598,000
40	599,000	139	3,098,000
41	598,075	140-142	1,598,000
42	1,198,179	143-148	2,498,000
43	1,625,406	149	2,298,000
44	994,880	150	3,798,000
45	997,759	151	2,298,000
46	996,759	152-156	1,998,000
47	2,705,955	157-158	1,698,000
48	997,542	159-160	1,298,000
49	996,609	161	898,000
50	996,928	162	1,498,000
51	499,000	163-164	1,298,000
52	249,000	165	3,998,000
52a	78,415	166-167	1,298,000
53	248,700	168	998,000
54	1,498,991	169-179	898,000
55	2,498,897	180	3,198,000
56	1,098,972	181-189	898,000
57	998,918	190	1,773,050
58	2,699,000	191	898,000
59	2,499,000	192	864,960
60	199,000	193	3,198,000
61	499,000	194	898,000
62	199,000	195-199	598,000
63	1,498,931	195a-199a	124,500
64	798,953	200-206	898,000
65-68	999,000	207	3,198,000
72	598,912	208-210	1,098,000
73	398,990	211-212	1,298,000
74	598,936	213	1,098,000
75	1,998,992	214	1,298,000
76	1,000,000	215-216	4,998,000
77	2,000,000	217	1,498,000
78	500,000	218-219	1,798,000
79-80	400,000	220	2,998,000
81	12,599,000	221	1,798,000
82	11,979,000	222	4,998,000
83	6,850,000	223	1,798,000
84	5,099,000	224-226	2,498,000
84A	1,699,000	227	2,998,000
85	4,749,000	228	3,998,000
86	2,099,000		

AIR POST STAMPS

Cat. No.	Quantity	Cat. No.	Quantity
C1-C3	198,000	C18	96,650
C4	1,952,348	C19	1,033,900
C5	331,360	C19a	100
C6	762,530	C20	230,000
C7	76,166	C21	185,000
C8	122,816	C22	191,000
C9	708,319	C23	190,000
C10	108,824	C24	17,199,000
C11	164,147	C25	1,999,000
C12	50,335	C26	1,250,000
C13	69,092	C27	3,499,000
C14	597,103	C28	1,699,000
C15	77,951	C29	1,199,000
C16	97,635	C30	1,949,000
C17	98,353		

SPECIAL DELIVERY STAMP

E1	198,804

PROVISIONAL ISSUES

Stamps of Japan Overprinted by Postmasters in Four Island Districts

Trading Ship — A82

Rice Harvest — A83

Gen. Maresuke Nogi — A84

Garambi Lighthouse, Taiwan — A88

Plane and Map of Japan — A92

Mount Fuji and Cherry Blossoms — A94

Miyajima Torii, Itsukushima Shrine — A96

Great Budda, Kamakura — A98

War Factory Girl — A144

Admiral Heihachiro T — A86

Meiji Shrin Tokyo — A

Kasuga Shr Nara — A

Horyu Temp Nara — A

Golden Pavil Kyoto — A

Kamatari Fujiwara — A

Hyuga Monument & Fuji — A14

...ar Worker &
...nes — A147

...iator Saluting
...apanese Flag
— A150

...Mt. Fuji and
...erry Blossoms
— A152

...Garambi
Lighthouse,
...iwan — A154

...unrise at Sea
Plane — A162

...sukuni Shrine
— A164

Palms and Map
of "Greater East
Asia" — A148

Torii of Yasukuni
Shrine — A151

Torii of Miyajima
— A153

Sun & Cherry
Blossoms —
A161

Coal Miners —
A163

"Thunderstorm
below Fuji," by
Hokusai — A167

KUME ISLAND

Values are for unused stamps. Used copies sell for considerably more, should be expertized and are preferred on cover or document.

A1

Mimeographed
Seal Handstamped in Vermilion

1945, Oct. 1   Without Gum   Unwmk.   Imperf.

1X1	A1	7s **black**, *cream (2,400)*	3,200.	—
a.		"7" & "SEN" one letter space to left	3,500.	

Printed on legal-size U.S. military mimeograph paper and validated by the official seal of the Kume Island postmaster, Norifume Kikuzato. Valid until May 4, 1946.
Cancellations "20.10.1" (Oct. 1, 1945) or "20.10.6" (Oct. 6, 1945) are by favor. See proofs section for copies on white watermarked U.S. official bond paper.

AMAMI DISTRICT

Inspection Seal ("Ken," abbreviation for *kensa zumi*, inspected or examined; five types)

Stamps of Japan 1937-46 Handstamped in Black, Blue, Purple, Vermilion or Red
Typographed, Lithographed, Engraved

1947-48   Wmk. 257   Perf. 13, Imperf

2X1	A82	½s **purple**, #257	1,000.	
2X2	A83	1s **fawn**, #258		
2X3	A144	1s **orange brown**, #325	*1,750.*	
2X4	A84	2s **crimson**, #259	600.	
a.		2s **vermilion**, #259c		
2X5	A84	2s **rose red**, imperf., #351	2,000.	
2X6	A85	3s **green**, #260	*1,700.*	
2X7	A84	3s **brown**, #329		
2X8	A161	3s **rose carmine**, imperf., #352	*1,800.*	
2X9	A146	4s **emerald**, #330	700.	
2X10	A86	5s **brown lake**, #331	700.	
2X11	A162	5s **green**, imperf., #353	*1,500.*	
2X12	A147	6s **light ultramarine**, #332		
2X13	A86	7s **orange vermilion**, #333	*1,250.*	
2X14	A90	8s **dark purple & pale violet**, #265	*1,500.*	
2X15	A148	10s **crimson & dull rose**, #344	600.	
2X16	A152	10s **red orange**, imperf., #355 (48)	*2,500.*	
2X17	A93	14s **rose lake & pale rose**, #268	—	
2X18	A150	15s **dull blue**, #336	600.	
2X19	A151	17s **gray violet**, #337	*1,750.*	
2X20	A94	20s **ultramarine**, #269	*1,750.*	
2X21	A152	20s **blue**, #338	600.	
2X22	A152	20s **ultramarine**, imperf., #356 (48)	*1,750.*	
2X23	A95	25s **dark brown & pale brown**, #270	900.	
2X24	A151	27s **rose brown**, #339	—	
2X25	A153	30s **bluish green**, #340		
2X26	A153	30s **bright blue**, imperf., #357	2,000.	
2X27	A88	40s **dull violet**, #341	*1,750.*	
2X28	A154	40s **dark violet**, #342	*1,750.*	
2X29	A97	50s **olive & pale olive**, #272	—	
2X30	A163	50s **dark brown**, imperf., #358 (48)	2,000.	
2X31	A164	1y **deep olive green**, imperf., #359	*2,500.*	
2X32	A167	1y **deep ultramarine**, imperf., #364	—	
2X33	A99	5y **deep gray green**, #274	—	
2X34	A99	5y **deep gray green**, imperf., #360	—	

Nos. 2X5, 2X8, 2X11, 2X16, 2X22, 2X26, 2X30, 2X31, 2X32 and 2X34 were issued without gum.

MIYAKO DISTRICT

Personal Seal of Postmaster Jojin Tomiyama

Stamps of Japan 1937-46 Handstamped in Vermilion or Red
Typographed, Lithographed, Engraved

1946-47   Wmk. 257   Perf. 13

3X1	A144	1s **orange brown**, #325	175.	
3X2	A84	2s **crimson**, #259	125.	—
a.		2s **vermilion** #259c ('47)	150.	
b.		2s **pink** #259b ('47)	550.	
3X3	A84	3s **brown**, #329	100.	
3X4	A86	4s **dark green**, #261	100.	
3X5	A86	5s **brown lake**, #331	550.	
		On cover with #3X17		
3X6	A88	6s **orange**, #263	100.	
3X7	A90	8s **dark purple & pale violet**, #265	100.	
3X8	A148	10s **crimson & dull rose**, #334	100.	—

		On cover with #3X15		
3X9	A152	10s **red orange**, imperf., #355 ('47) *(1,000)*	150.	—
3X10	A92	12s **indigo**, #267	100.	—
3X11	A93	14s **rose lake & pale rose**, #268	100.	—
3X12	A150	15s **dull blue**, #336	100.	—
3X13	A151	17s **gray violet**, #337	100.	—
3X14	A94	20s **ultramarine**, #269	—	—
3X15	A152	20s **blue**, #338	100.	—
3X16	A152	20s **ultramarine**, imperf., #356 ('47)	200.	
3X17	A95	25s **dark brown & pale brown**, #270	100.	
3X18	A153	30s **bluish green**, #340	100.	
3X19	A88	40s **dull violet**, #341	250.	
3X20	A154	40s **dark violet**, #342	100.	
3X21	A97	50s **olive & pale olive**, #272	100.	
3X22	A163	50s **dark brown**, #358 ('47) *(750)*	250.	
3X23	A98	1y **brown & pale brown**, #273	9,000.	
3X24	A167	1y **deep ultramarine**, #364 ('47) *(500)*	1,500.	600.

Nos. 3X9, 3X16, 3X22 and 3X24 were issued without gum.
Nos. 3X22 and 3X24 have sewing machine perf.; No. 3X16 exists with that perf. also.

Nos. 3X1-3X2, 3X2a, 3X3-3X5, 3X8 Handstamp Surcharged with 2 Japanese Characters

1946-47

3X25	A144	1y on 1s **orange brown**	140.	—
3X26	A84	1y on 2s **crimson**	3,000.	
3X27	A84	1y on 3s **brown** ('47)	3,000.	
3X28	A84	2y on 2s **crimson**	175.	—
a.		2y on 2s **vermilion** ('47)	175.	—
3X29	A86	4y on 4s **dark green**	140.	—
3X30	A86	5y on 5s **brown lake**	140.	—
3X31	A148	10y on 10s **crimson & dull rose**	140.	—

The overwhelming majority of used examples of Miyako District stamps were used on Bulk Mailing Records documents and Letter Content Certification Records documents. Stamps affixed to such documents command a substantial premium above off-document used stamps.
Cancellation: black Miyako cds.

OKINAWA DISTRICT

Personal Seal of Postmaster Shiichi Hirata

R1

Japan Nos. 355-356, 358, 364 Overprinted in Black

1947, Nov. 1   Wmk. 257   Litho.   Imperf.
Without Gum

4X1	A152	10s **red orange** *(13,997)*	1,200.	*1,000.*
		On cover, strip of 3		*9,500.*
		On cover with #4X2		*7,500.*
4X2	A152	20s **ultramarine** *(13,611)*	600.	*1,000.*
4X3	A163	50s **dark brown** *(6,276)*	900.	*700.*
4X4	A167	1y **deep ultramarine** *(1,947)*	1,750.	*1,000.*

On Revenue Stamp of Japan

4X5	R1	30s **brown** *(14,000)*	3,500.	*3,500.*
		On cover		*7,500.*

No. 4X5 is on Japan's current 30s revenue stamp. The Hirata seal validated it for postal use.
Nos. 4X1-4X5 are known with rough sewing machine perforations, full or partial.

YAEYAMA DISTRICT

Personal Seal of Postmaster Kenpuku Miyara

Stamps of Japan 1937-46 Handstamped in Black
Typographed, Engraved, Lithographed

1948   Wmk. 257   Perf. 13

5X1	A86	4s **dark green**, #261	1,200.	
5X2	A86	5s **brown lake**, #331	1,200.	
5X3	A86	7s **orange vermilion**, #333	800.	
5X4	A148	10s **crimson & dull rose**, #334	5,000.	
5X5	A94	20s **ultramarine**, #269	150.	
		On cover with 2 #5X8		—
5X6	A96	30s **peacock blue**, #271	1,000.	
5X7	A88	40s **dull violet**, #341	80.	
5X8	A97	50s **olive & pale olive**, #272	100.	

5X9 A163 50s **dark brown,** imperf., #358
(250) 1,350.
5X10 A99 5y **deep gray green,** #274 2,000.

No. 5X9 was issued without gum.
This handstamp exists double, triple, inverted and in pair, one stamp without overprint.

Provisional postal stationery of the four districts also exists.

LETTER SHEETS

Values are for entires.

Stylized Deigo
Blossom — US1

Banyan
Tree — US2

Typographed by Japan Printing Bureau.
Stamp is in upper left corner.
Designer: Shutaro Higa

1948-49
U1 US1 50s **vermilion,** cream, July 18,
1949 (250,000) 50.00 60.00
First day cancel —
a. 50s **orange red,** gray, July 1, 1948
(1,000) 1,500. —

Designer: Ken Yabu

1950, Jan. 21
U2 US2 1y **carmine red,** cream (250,000) 40.00 50.00
First day cancel —

AIR LETTER SHEETS

DC-4 Skymaster and
Shurei Gate — UC1

UC2

Designer: Chosho Ashitomi
"PAR AVION" (Bilingual) below Stamp
Litho. & Typo. by Japan Printing Bureau
1952-53
UC1 UC1 12y **light rose,** pale blue green,
Mar. 9, 1953 (76,000) 20.00 12.50
a. 12y **dull rose,** pale blue green, Nov.
1, 1952 (50,000) 30.00 15.00
First day cancel, No. UC1a 80.00

No. UC1a is on tinted paper with colorless overall inscription "RYUKYU FOREIGN AIRMAIL," repeated in parallel vertical lines, light and indistinct. Dull rose ink of imprinted design and legend "AIR LETTER" appears to bleed. No. UC1 has overall inscription darker and more distinct. Light rose ink of design and legend does not bleed. Model: U.S. No. UC16.

Litho. & Typo. by Nippon Toppan K.K.
"AEROGRAMME" below Stamp
1955, Sept. 10
UC2 UC2 15y **violet blue & bright red,**
pale yellow green (89,300) 30.00 15.00
First day cancel 60.00
a. 15y **violet blue & dull red,** pale blue
green, Oct. 1957 (33,742) 45.00 25.00

Printing on the envelope stamp is heavier on No. UC2a than on No. UC2.

No. UC2 surcharged in Red

"13" & "¢" aligned at bot.;
2 thick bars — a

"¢" raised; 2 thick bars —
b

"13" & "¢" as in "a"; 4 thin
bars — c

"¢" raised; 4 thin bars —
d

Printers: Type "a," Nakamura Printing Co., "b" and "d," Okinawa Printing Co., "c," Sun Printing Co.
1958-60
UC3 UC2 13c on 15y type "a," Sept. 16,
1958 (60,000) 20.00 18.00
First day cancel 60.00
a. Type "b," on No. UC2, June 1, 1959
(2,000) 40.00 30.00
b. Type "b," on No. UC2a (7,000) 50.00 30.00
c. Type "c," on No. UC2, Sept. 22, 1959
(1,000) 80.00 80.00
d. As "c," small wrong font "¢" sign 1,000. —
e. Type "c," on No. UC2a (1,000) 80.00 80.00
f. As "e," double surcharge, one on reverse 2,000.
g. Type "b" and No. 46 on No. UC2a,
Aug. 22, 1960 (1,000) 500.00 —
h. Type "d" and Nos. 55, 58 on No.
UC2, Oct. 1, 1960 (1,000) 450.00 450.00
i. Type "d" and Nos. 55, 58 on No.
UC2a (2,000) 300.00 300.00

For Nos. UC3g, UC3h and UC3i, additional stamps have been affixed to make up the 15c rate.

UC3

Lithographed by Japan Printing Bureau
1959, Nov. 10
UC4 UC3 15c **dark blue,** pale blue
(560,000) 4.00 2.50
First day cancel 10.00

POSTAL CARDS

Values are for entire cards.
Nos. UX1-UX9 are typo., others litho.
Printed by Japan Printing Bureau unless otherwise stated.
Quantities in parentheses; "E" means estimated.
Deigo Blossom Type
Designer: Shutaro Higa

1948, July 1
UX1 US1 10s **dull red,** grayish tan (100,000) 50.00 60.00

1949, July 1
UX2 US1 15s **orange red,** gray (E 175,000) 40.00 70.00
First day cancel —
a. 15s **vermilion,** tan (E 50,000) 110.00 125.00

Banyan Tree Type
Designer: Ken Yabu

1950, Jan. 21
UX3 US2 50s **carmine red,** light tan (E
200,000) 10.00 1
First day cancel 6
a. Grayish tan card (E 25,000) 25.00 5

Nos. UX2, UX2a Handstamp Surcharged in Vermilion

19-21x23-25mm —
a

22-23x26-27mm —

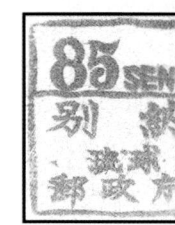

20-21x24-24½mm
— c

22-23½x25-26mm

1951
UX4 US1 (c) 15s + 85s on #UX2 (E
35,000) 100.
a. Type "c" on #UX2a (E 5,000) 150.
b. Type "a" on #UX2 (E 39,000) 75.
c. Type "a" on #UX2a 1,000.
d. Type "b" on #UX2 1,000. 1,
e. Type "d" on #UX2 (E 4,000) 150.
f. Type "d" on #UX2a (E 1,000) 250.

Type "a" exists on the 15s cherry blossom postal card Japan. Value $75.

Crown, Leaf Ornaments

Naha die 21x22mm
PC3

Tokyo die
18½x19mm
PC4

Designer: Masayoshi Adaniya Koshun Printing Co.

1952
UX5 PC3 1y **vermilion,** tan, Feb. 8
(400,600) 50.00 30
UX6 PC4 1y **vermilion,** off-white, Oct. 6
(1,295,000) 25.00 14
a. Tan card, coarse (50,000) 30.00 20
b. Tan card, smooth (16,000) 500.00 150

Naminoue Shrine

PC5	PC6
Naha die 23x25 ½mm	Tokyo die 22x24 ½mm

Designer: Gensei Agena

-57

PC5 2y **green**, *off-white, Dec. 2, 1953*
   (1,799,400) 60.00 20.00
   First day cancel 80.00
   Printed both sides 500.00
PC6 2y **green**, *off-white, 1955*
   (2,799,400) 15.00 6.00
   2y **deep blue green**, *1956 (300,000)* ... 30.00 16.50
   2y **yellow green**, *1957 (2,400,000)* ... 12.50 3.50
   As "a," printed on both sides ... 500.00
   As "b," printed on both sides ... 500.00

Stylized Pine,
Bamboo, Plum
Blossoms — PC7

1956 New Year Card

Designer: Koya Oshiro Kotsura and Koshun Printing
   ...anies

, Dec. 1

PC7 2y **red**, *cream* 100.00 45.00
   First day cancel 125.00

   UX9 was printed on rough card (43,400) and smooth-
   ...card (356,600)

Sun — PC8	Temple Lion — PC9

1957 New Year Card

Designer: Seikichi Tamanaha Kobundo Printing Co.

, Dec. 1

) PC8 2y **brown carmine & yellow**, *off-
   white (600,000)* 6.00 3.75
   First day cancel 10.00

1958 New Year Card

Designer: Shin Isagawa Fukuryu Printing Co.

7, Dec. 1

1 PC9 2y **lilac rose**, *off-white
   (1,000,000)* 1.75 2.25
   First day cancel 4.00
. "1" omitted in right date 75.00 75.00
. Printed on both sides 250.00 300.00

**...os. UX8, UX8a and UX8b "Revalued" in Red,
Cherry or Pink by Three Naha Printeries**

a	b

---

c

1958-59

UX12 PC6 1 ½c on 2y **green**, type "a,"
   Sept. 16 (600,000) 5.00 5.00
   First day cancel 10.00
a.   Shrine stamp omitted .... 750.00 1,000.
b.   Bar of ½ omitted, top of 2 broken 75.00 100.00
c.   Type "b," *Nov. (1,000,000)* 10.00 12.50
d.   Type "c," *1959 (200,000)* 15.00 22.50
e.   Wrong font "¢," type "c" 30.00 45.00
f.   "¢" omitted, type "c" .... 1,500. 1,500.
g.   Double surcharge, type "c" .... 1,000. —

Multicolor Yarn Ball PC10	Toy Pony 19½x23mm PC11

1959 New Year Card

Designer: Masayoshi Adaniya Kobundo Printing Co.

1958, Dec. 10

UX13 PC10 1 ½c **black, red, yellow & gray
   blue**, *off-white (1,514,000)* ... 1.50 1.90
   First day cancel 2.00
a.   Black omitted .... —

1959, June 20

Designer: Seikichi Tamanaha Kobundo Printing Co.

UX14 PC11 1 ½c **dark blue & brown**
   (1,140,000) 1.50 1.25
   First day cancel 1.50
a.   Dark blue omitted 500.00

Toy Carp and Boy — PC12	Toy Pony 21x25mm — PC13

1960 New Year Card

Designer: Masayoshi Adaniya

1959, Dec. 1

UX15 PC12 1 ½c **violet blue, red & black,**
   cream (2,000,000) 1.25 1.50
   First day cancel 1.75

1959, Dec. 30

UX16 PC13 1 ½c **gray violet & brown**, *cream
   (3,500,000)* .... 3.00 .75
   First day cancel 2.75

Household Altar — PC14	Coral Head — PC15

1961 New Year Card

Designer: Shin Isagawa

1960, Nov. 20

UX17 PC14 1 ½c **gray, carmine, yellow &
   black**, *off-white (2,647,591)* ... 1.50 1.50
   First day cancel 1.50

Summer Greeting Card

Designer: Shinzan Yamada Kidekuni Printing Co.

1961, July 5

UX18 PC15 1 ½c **ultramarine & cerise,** *off-
   white (264,900)* 2.25 3.75
   First day cancel 4.00

Tiger — PC16	Inscribed "RYUKYUS" — PC17

1962 New Year Card

Designer: Shin Isagawa

1961, Nov. 15

UX19 PC16 1 ½c **ocher, black & red,** *off-
   white (2,891,626)* 1.50 2.50
   First day cancel 1.65
a.   Red omitted .... 750.00 —
b.   Red inverted .... 500.00 —
c.   Red omitted on face, inverted on back ... 500.00 —
d.   Double impression of red, one invert-
       ed .... 500.00 —
e.   Double impression of ocher & black,
       red inverted .... 500.00 —
f.   Double impression of ocher & black,
       one inverted .... 500.00 —

1961-67

Designer: Seikichi Tamanaha

UX20 PC17 1 ½c **gray violet & brown**, *white
   ('67) (18,600,000)* .... 1.00 .50
a.   Off-white card ('66) (4,000,000) ... 1.50 .75
b.   Cream card, *Dec. 23 (12,500,000)* ... 1.00 .50
   First day cancel 1.35

Ie Island — PC18	New Year Offerings — PC19

Summer Greeting Card

Designer: Shinzan Yamada Sakai Printing Co.

1962, July 10

UX21 PC18 1 ½c **bright blue, yellow &
   brown**, *off-white (221,500)* ... 1.50 2.50
   First day cancel 3.00
   Square notch at left 40.00 45.00

1963 New Year Card; Precanceled

Designer: Shin Isagawa Sakai Printing Co.

1962, Nov. 15

UX22 PC19 1 ½c **olive brown, carmine & black**
   (3,000,000) 1.50 3.00
   First day cancel 2.25
a.   Yellow brown background .... —
b.   Brown ocher background .... —

Ryukyu Temple
Dog and Wine
Flask Silhouette
PC20

Water Strider — PC21

International Postal Card

Designer: Shin Isagawa

1063, Feb. 15
UX23 PC20   5c **vermilion, emerald &
black,** *pale yellow
(150,000)*   1.75   2.75
First day cancel   1.65
a.   Black & emerald omitted   450.00

Summer Greeting Card

Designer: Seikichi Tamanaha

1963, June 20
UX24 PC21 1½c **Prussian green & black,** *off-
white (250,000)*   4.00   4.25
First day cancel   3.50

Princess   Bitter Melon
Doll — PC22   Vine — PC23

1964 New Year Card; Precanceled

Designer: Koya Oshiro

1963, Nov. 15
UX25 PC22 1½c **orange red, yellow & ultra,**
off-white (3,200,000)   2.00   2.00
First day cancel   2.00

Summer Greeting Card

Designer: Shinzan Yamada

1964, June 20
UX26 PC23 1½c **multicolored,** *off-white
(285,410)*   1.40   2.25
First day cancel   1.75

Fighting Kite with   Palm-leaf Fan — PC25
Rider — PC24

1965 New Year Card; Precanceled

Designer: Koya Oshiro

1964, Nov. 15
UX27 PC24 1½c **multicolored,** *off-white
(4,876,618)*   1.25   1.75
First day cancel   2.00

Summer Greeting Card

Designer: Koya Oshiro

1965, June 20
UX28 PC25 1½c **multicolored,** *off-white
(340,604)*   1.40   2.50
First day cancel   1.65

Toy Pony   Fan Palm
Rider — PC26   Dipper — PC27

1966 New Year Card; Precanceled

Designer: Seikichi Tamanaha

1965, Nov. 15
UX29 PC26 1½c **multicolored,** *off-white
(5,224,622)*   1.25   1.75
First day cancel   1.40
a.   Silver (background) omitted   250.00

Summer Greeting Card

Designer: Seikichi Tamanaha

1966, June 20
UX30 PC27 1½c **multicolored,** *off-white
(339,880)*   1.25   2.00
First day cancel   1.40

Toy Dove — PC28   Cycad Insect Cage and
                      Praying Mantis — PC29

1967 New Year Card; Precanceled

Designer: Seikichi Tamanaha

1966, Nov. 15
UX31 PC28 1½c **multicolored,** *off-white
(5,500,000)*   1.25   1.75
First day cancel   1.65
a.   Silver (background) omitted   500.00
b.   Gray blue & green omitted   750.00

Summer Greeting Card

Designer: Shin Isagawa

1967, June 20
UX32 PC29 1½c **multicolored,** *off-white
(350.000)*   1.50   2.50
First day cancel   1.75

Paper Doll   Pandanus
Royalty — PC30   Drupe — PC31

1968 New Year Card; Precanceled

Designer: Shin Isagawa

1967, Nov. 15
UX33 PC30 1½c **multicolored,** *off-white
(6,200,000)*   1.10   1.50
First day cancel   1.75
a.   Gold omitted   500.00

Summer Greeting Card

Designer: Seikan Omine

1968, June 20
UX34 PC31 1½c **multicolored,** *off-white
(350,000)*   1.25   2.25
First day cancel   1.75

Toy Lion — PC32   Ryukyu Trading
                      Ship — PC33

1969 New Year Card; Precanceled

Designer: Teruyoshi Kinjo

1968, Nov. 15
UX35 PC32 1½c **multicolored,** *off-white
(7,000,000)*   1.10
First day cancel

Summer Greeting Card

Designer: Seikichi Tamanaha

1969, June 20
UX36 PC33 1½c **multicolored,** *(349,800)*   1.25
First day cancel

Toy Devil   Ripe Litchis — P
Mask — PC34

1970 New Year Card; Precanceled

Designer: Teruyoshi Kinjo

1969, Nov. 15
UX37 PC34 1½c **multicolored** *97,200,000)*   1.10
First day cancel

Summer Greeting Card

Designer: Kensei Miyagi

1970, June 20
UX38 PC35 1½c **multicolored** *(400,000)*   1.40
First day cancel

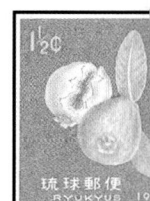

Thread-winding   Ripe
Implements for   Guavas — PC3
Dance — PC36

1971 New Year Card; Precanceled

Designer: Yoshinori Arakai

1970, Nov. 16
UX39 PC36 1½c **multicolored** *(7,500,000)*   1.10
First day cancel

Summer Greeting Card

Designer: Kensei Miyagi

1971, July 10
UX40 PC37 1½c **multicolored** *(400,000)*   1.25
First day cancel

Pony Type of 1961
Zip Code Boxes in Vermilion

1971, July 10
UX41 PC17 1½c **gray violet & brown**
(3,000,000)   1.25
First day cancel

No. UX41 Surcharged below
Stamp in Vermilion

"Revalued 2¢" applied by Nakamura Printing Co.

, Sept. 1
PC17 2c on 1½c **gray violet & brown**
(1,699,569) 1.10 2.25
First day cancel 2.00
Inverted surcharge *500.00*
Double surcharge *500.00*
Surcharge on back *500.00*
Surcharge on back, inverted *500.00*

1972 New Year Card; Precanceled

asseled Castanets — PC38

Zip Code Boxes in Vermilion
esigner: Yoshinori Arakaki

, Nov. 15
PC38 2c **multicolored** (8,000,000) 1.00 *1.50*
First day cancel 1.25

Type of 1961
Zip Code Boxes in Vermilion

, Dec. 15
PC17 2c **gray violet & brown** (3,500,000) 1.25 *1.75*
First day cancel 1.65

PAID REPLY POSTAL CARDS

old as two attached cards, one for message, one
reply. The major listings are of unsevered cards
ept Nos. UY4-UY6.

 Message   Reply

8, July 1
US1 10s + 10s **dull red,** *grayish tan*
(1,000) 2,000. —
m. Message card 600. 1,000.
r. Reply card 600. 1,000.

9, July 18
US1 15s + 15s **vermilion,** *tan (E 150,000)* 30.00 40.00
a. Gray card (E 75,000) 75.00 —
First day cancel —
m. Message card 8.00 16.50
r. Reply card 8.00 16.50

0, Jan. 21
US2 50s + 50s **carmine red,** *gray cream (E 130,000)* 25.00 40.00
a. Double impression of message card — —
b. Light tan card (E 96,000) 15.00 —
First day cancel
m. Message card 3.50 13.50
r. Reply card 3.50 13.50

o. UY2a Handstamp Surcharged in Vermilion
51
US1 1y (15s+85s) message, type
"b" (E 3,000) 350. 350.
a. Reply, type "b" (E 3,000) 350. 350.
b. Message, type "a" (E 300) 600. —
c. Reply, type "a" (E 300) 600. —
d. Message, type "d" (E 200) 500. —
e. Reply, type "d" (E 200) 500. —
f. Message, UY2, type "a" (E 3,000) 150. 225.
g. Reply, UY2, type "a" (E 3,000) 150. 225.
h. Message, UY2, type "b" (E 2,500) 275. 275.
i. Reply, UY2, type "b" (E 2,500) 275. 275.
j. Message, UY2, type "d" (E 2,800) 150. 250.
k. Reply, UY2, type "d" (E 2,800) 150. 250.
l. 1y + 1y unsevered, type "b" 850.
m. 1y + 1y unsevered, type "a" 1,450.
n. 1y + 1y unsevered, type "d" 1,200.
o. 1y + 1y unsevered, UY2, type "a" 360.
p. 1y + 1y unsevered, UY2, type "b" 650.

q. 1y + 1y unsevered, UY2, type "d" 360.
r. 1y + 1y unsevered, UY2, type "c" 3, 500.
s. Message, UY2, type "c," —
t. Reply, UY2, type "c" —
u. Message, type "c" —
v. Reply, type "c" —

Types are illustrated above No. UX4.

e f

g h

Typographed Surcharge in Vermilion on No. UY2a
UY5 US1 1y (15s+85s) message, type
"f" (E 20,000) 125. 125.
a. Reply, type "f" (E 20,000) 125. 125.
b. Message, type "e" (E 12,500) 225. 225.
c. Reply, type "e" (E 12,500) 225. 225.
d. Message, type "g" (E 500) 1,000. 1,000.
e. Reply, type "g" (E 500) 1,000. 1,000.
f. Message, UY2, type "e" (E 15,000) 125. 125.
g. Reply, UY2, type "e" (E 15,000) 125. 125.
h. Message, UY2, type "f" (E 9,000) 125. 125.
i. Reply, UY2, type "f" (E 9,000) 125. 125.
j. Message, UY2, type "g" (E 500) 1,000. 1,000.
k. Reply, UY2, type "g" (E 500) 1,000. 1,000.
l. 1y + 1y unsevered, type "e" 675.
m. 1y + 1y unsevered, UY2, type "e" 375.

Typographed Surcharge Type "h" in Vermilion on No. UY3
UY6 US2 1y (50s+50s) message (E 35,000) 125.00 150.00
a. Reply (E 35,000) 125.00 150.00
b. Message, UY3b (E 10,000) 125.00 150.00
c. Reply, UY3b (E 10,000) 125.00 150.00

No. UY6 is unknown as a joined card.

Smooth or Coarse Card
1952, Feb. 8
UY7 PC3 1y + 1y **vermilion,** *gray tan*
(60,000) 120.00 140.00
First day cancel 250.00
m. Message card 25.00 50.00
r. Reply card 25.00 50.00

1953
UY8 PC4 1y + 1y **vermilion,** *tan (22,900)* 30.00 40.00
First day cancel
a. Off-white card (13,800) 40.00 50.00
m. Message card 7.50 19.00
r. Reply card 7.50 26.50

Off-white or Light Cream Card
1953, Dec. 2
UY9 PC5 2y + 2y **green** (50,000) 100.00 90.00
First day cancel 150.00
m. Message card 15.00 25.00
r. Reply card 15.00 35.00

1955, May
UY10 PC6 2y + 2y **green,** *off-white*
(280,000) 10.00 —
a. Reply card blank 500.00
m. Message card 3.25 11.00
r. Reply card 3.25 15.00

No. UY10 Surcharged in Red
1958, Sept. 16
UY11 PC6 1½c on 2y, 1½c on 2y (95,000) 8.00 —
First day cancel 22.50
a. Surcharge on reply card only 500.00
b. Surcharge on message card only 500.00
c. Reply card double surcharge 750.00
d. Reply card stamp omitted (surcharge only) 1,000.
m. Message card 2.75 10.00
r. Reply card 2.75 16.50

Surcharge varieties include: "1" omitted; wrong font "2".

Pony Types
1959, June 20
UY12 PC11 1½c + 1½c **dark blue & brown** (366,000) 3.50 —
First day cancel 4.00
m. Message card .65 *3.50*
r. Reply card .65 *3.50*

1960, Mar. 10
UY13 PC13 1½c + 1½c **gray violet & brown,** (150,000) 7.00 —
First day cancel 5.00
m. Message card 1.50 *5.00*
r. Reply card 1.50 *5.00*

International Type
1963, Feb. 15
UY14 PC20 5c + 5c **vermilion, emerald & black,** *pale yellow* (70,000) 2.50 —
First day cancel 3.00
m. Message card .75 *3.75*
r. Reply card .75 *3.75*

Pony ("RYUKYUS") Type
1963-69
UY15 PC17 1½c + 1½c **gray violet & brown,** *cream, Mar. 15,* (800,000) 2.00 —
First day cancel 2.50
a. Off-white card, *Mar. 13, 1967* (100,000) 2.25
b. White card, *Nov. 22, 1969* (700,000) 1.75
m. Message card detached .40 *4.00*
r. Reply card detached .40 *4.00*

No. UY14 Surcharged below Stamp in Vermilion
1971, Sept. 1
UY16 PC17 2c on 1½c + 2c on 1½c **gray violet & brown** (80,000) 2.00 —
First day cancel 2.25
m. Message card .50 *2.50*
r. Reply card .50 *2.50*

Pony ("RYUKYUS") Type
Zip Code Boxes in Vermilion
1971, Nov. 1
UY17 PC17 2c + 2c **gray violet & brown** (150,000) 2.00 —
First day cancel 2.50
m. Message card .50 *2.50*
r. Reply card .50 *2.50*

OFFICIAL STAMPS ELECTION POSTAL CARDS

Official election free-mail postal cards were authorized by the United States Civil Administration of the Ryukyus, Ordinance 57, Dec. 18, 1951, as a measure to insure equal access to voters for each candidate standing in district or general elections in the islands. Under the terms of the ordinance and the local enabling legislation, each candidate, on request, could receive a fixed number of cards per election, which were serviced with no mailing costs to the candidate.

Until the issuance of No. UZE15 in 1960, cards were processed without canceling; beginning with that issue, they were treated as regular postal cards and canceled.

With the exception of pieces bearing emergency handstamp or machine-cancel indicia, the cards were special-order printings (incorporating the election indicium) of designs and types of postal cards concurrently in use as regular postal cards (though at times in different colors).

ELECTION INDICIA

Type I Type II

Type I: Typographed, Size: 18x45mm
Type II: Typographed, Size: 17½x48-49mm

Type III

Type IV

Type III: Typographed, Size: 17 ½x49-51mm
Type IV: Typographed, Size: 16 ½x62mm

Type IVa   Type V

Type IVa: Like Type IV but with second character from bottom ("SEN") having one stroke at upper left instead of two
Type V: Typographed, Size: 16-17x61-63mm (similar to Type IV, but with different bottom character)

Type VI   Type VII

Type VI: Typographed, Size: 17 ½x51-52mm
Type VII: Typographed, Size: 17 ½x51-52mm (similar to Type VI, but with different bottom character)

Type VIII   Type IX

Type VIII: Typographed, Size: 17 ¼-17 ½x 52mm (similar to Type VII but with second character from bottom ("SEN") having one stroke at upper left instead of two)
Type IX: Handstamped, Size: 17 ½x51mm

Type X   Type XI

Type X: Typographed, Size: 17 ½x51-51 ½mm (similar to Type VIII, but with different appearance of five smaller characters at top)
Type XI: Typographed, Size: 10x31 ½mm

Type XII   Type XIII

Type XII: Handstamped, Size: 17 ½-18x49 ½-51 ½mm, Thick characters
Type XIII: Handstamped, Size: 17 ½-18x50 ¼-51mm, Thin characters

Type XIIIa   Type XIV

Type XIIIa: Handstamped, Size: 17 ½-18x50 ¼x51mm, characters, with shorter lvertical line at lower left.
Type XIV: Typographed, Size: 18x50-50 ½mm

Type XV   Type XVI

Type XV: Typographed, Size: 18x50-50 ½mm
Type XVI: Machine cancel, Circle diameter: 20mm, Heigh legend box: 23 ½mm

Type XVIa   Type XVII

Type XVIa: Machine cancel, Circle diameter: 20mm, Heigh legend box: 20 ½-22mm
Type XVII: Typographed, Size: 18 ½x48 ½-50mm

Type XVIII

Type XVIII: Machine cancel, Circle diameter: 20mm, Height of end box: 20½-22 mm

UZE1

952, Feb. 2   First General Election
E1 PC3 1y **vermilion,** *tan* coarse (Naha
          die) + Type I *(345,000)*   300.00   —
  a. Postmarked (error)   —

952, July 26   1st District Special Election
E2 PC3 1y **vermilion,** *tan* coarse (Naha die)
          + Type II *(est. 25,000)*   50.00   —
  a. 2nd character from bottom in indicium
        (SEN) inverted   —   —

Used copies or unused with campaign messages must have
erence to the 1st District (Kasari, Amami Gunto) election.

953, Mar. 3   4th District Special Election
   PC4 1y **vermilion,** *tan* coarse (Tokyo die) +
          Type II *(est. 10,000)*   —
  a. Postmarked (error)   —

Identifiable only when postmarked (in error, with dates
tween Mar. 3-Mar.31, 1953) and/or with campaign message
reference to 4th District election (Motobu, Okinawa Gunto).

953, Mar. 27   3rd District Special Election
ZE4 PC4 1y **vermilion,** *tan* coarse (Tokyo die) +
          Type II *(est. 10,000)*   —
  a. Postmarked (error)   —

Identifiable only when postmarked (in error, with dates
tween Mar. 27-Apr. 1953) and/or with campaign message in
ference to 3rd District election (Yagaji, Okinawa Gunto).

UZE5

1954, Feb. 23   Second General Election
UZE5 PC5 2y **rose red,** *off white* (Naha die) +
          Type III *(70,000)*   50.00   —
  a. Postmarked (error)   —

1954, Nov. 19   18th District Special Election
UZE6   PC6 2y **red,** *off white* (Tokyo die) +
          Type IV   500.00   —
  a. Postmarked (error)   —
UZE6A PC6 2y **red,** *off white* (Tokyo die) +
          Type V   500.00   —
  a. Postmarked (error)   —

Postal records show receipt of 4,000 total cards of Nos. UZE6
and UZE6A, undefined as to type.

1955, Feb. 15   20th District Special Election
UZE7 PC6 2y **dark purple,** *off white* (Tokyo
          die) + Type IV *(2,000)*   500.00   —

1955, Mar. 8   23rd District Special Election
UZE8 PC6 2y **turquoise blue,** *off white* (Tokyo
          die) + Type V *(2,000)*   500.00   —
  a. Postmarked (error)   —

1955, June 28   22nd District Special Election
UZE9 PC6 2y **dull brown,** *gray cream* (Tokyo
          die) + Type V *(3,030)*   400.00   —
  a. Postmarked (error)   —

1956, Feb. 20   Third General Election
UZE10   PC6 2y **pale blue green,** *off white*
          (Tokyo die) + Type VI   75.00 150.00
  a. Postmarked (error)   —
UZE10A PC6 2y **pale blue green,** *off white*
          (Tokyo die) + Type VII   75.00 150.00
  a. Postmarked (error)   —

Postal records show receipt of 65,000 total cards of Nos.
UZE10 and UZE10A, undefined as to type.

1956, Oct. 26   25th District Special Election
UZE11   PC6 2y **brown red,** *off white* (Tokyo
          die) + Type IV   300.00   —
UZE11A PC6 2y **brown red,** *off white* (Tokyo
          die) + Type V   180.00 350.00

Postal records show a total quantity of 3,030 examples of
Nos. UZE11 and UZE11A prepared, unidentified as to type, of
which 2,000 were issued.

1957, Aug. 5   18th District Special Election
UZE12 PC6 2y **lilac,** *off white* (Tokyo die) +
          Type IVa *(3,030)*   250.00   —

1958, Feb. 25   Fourth General Election
UZE13   PC6 2y **deep blue,** *off white* (Tokyo
          die) + Type VI (bold face
          print)   130.00 70.00
UZE13A PC6 2y **deep blue,** *off white* (Tokyo
          die) + Type VI (light face
          print)   130.00 70.00
UZE13B PC6 2y **deep blue,** *off white* (Tokyo
          die) + Type VII (bold face
          print)   130.00 70.00
UZE13C PC6 2y **deep blue,** *off white* (Tokyo
          die) + Type VII (light face
          print)   90.00 70.00

Postal records show a total of 140,300 cards of Nos. UZE13-
UZE13C prepared in two printings, undefined as to types.

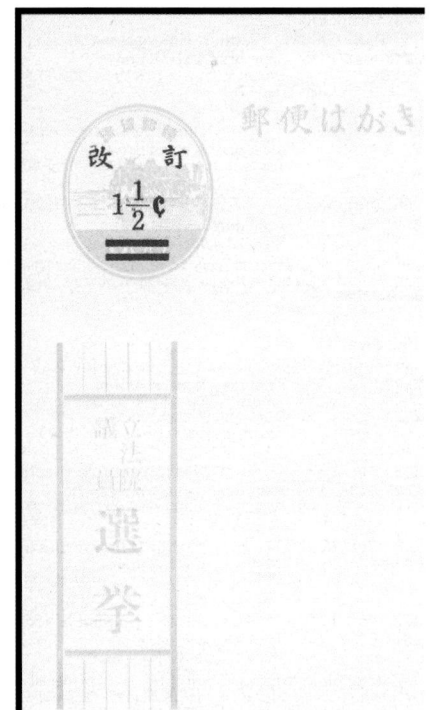

UZE14

1959, July 23   26th District Special Election
UZE14 PC6 1½c on 2y **lemon,** *white* (Tokyo
          die) + Type VIII *(4,100)*   450.00   —

UZE15

1960, Oct. 24   Fifth General Election
UZE15 PC11 1½c **indigo & claret brown,**
          white (Naha die) + Type
          VIII *(150,000)*   70.00 70.00
UZE16 PC13 1½c **violet gray & claret brown,**
          cream (Tokyo die) + Type
          IX in LL corner *(10,000)*   —   —

1962, Oct. 22   Sixth General Election
UZE17   PC17 1½c **violet gray & claret
          brown,** *cream* + Type VIII 50.00   —
UZE17A PC17 1½c **violet gray & claret
          brown,** *cream* + Type X   50.00   —

Postal records show a total of 116,000 cards of Nos. UZE17-
UZE17A prepared, undefined as to type.

1962, Oct. 22
Sixth General Election Emergency Issue
UZE18 PC17 1½c **violet gray & claret brown,**
  cream + Type IX *(6,000)* 250.00 —
 a. Indicium inverted — —

1965, Oct. 25 Seventh General Election
UZE19 PC17 1½c **violet gray & claret brown,**
  cream + Type XI *(134,000)* 20.00 90.00

1966, Aug. 1 3rd District Special Election
UZE20 PC17 1½c **violet gray & claret brown,**
  cream + Type XI *(est. 3,800)*

No. UZE20 is a remainder copy of No. UZE19, identifiable only when canceled at the Nakijin Post Office between Aug. 1-Aug. 20, 1966.

1966, Aug. 11
3rd District Special Election Emergency Issue
UZE21 PC17 1½c **violet gray & claret brown,**
  cream + Type XII *(est. 200)* — —
UZE22 PC17 1½c **violet gray & claret brown,**
  cream + Type XIII 225.00 —

1968, Oct. 21 First Chief Executive Election
UZE23 PC17 1½c **violet gray & claret brown,**
  white + Type XIV *(300,000)* 30.00 25.00

1968, Oct. 21 Eighth General Election
UZE24 PC17 1½c **violet gray & claret brown,**
  white + Type XV *(142,000)* 30.00 35.00

1970, Oct. 12 1st District Special Election
UZE25 PC17 1½c **violet gray & claret brown,**
  white + Type XV *(4,000)* —

No. UZE25 is a remainder copy of No. UZE24, identifiable only when canceled at the Higashi, Kunigami, Ogimi or Oku Post Offices between Oct. 12-Oct. 31, 1970.

UZE26A

1970, Oct. 23
First General Election for Coucilors and Representatives to the Japanese Diet
UZE26 PC17 1½c **violet gray & claret brown,** *white* + Type XVI *(300,000)* 250.00 30.00
UZE26A PC17 1½c **violet gray & claret brown,** *white* + Type XVIa *(300,000)* 250.00 30.00

Postal records show a total of 171,000 copies of Nos. UZE26-UZE26A prepared, undefined as to type.

Emergency Commercial Card Issue for First General Japanese Diet Election
UZE27 *white or light gray blue* + Type XVI — 30.00
UZE27A *white or light gray blue* + Type XVIa — 30.00

Postal records show a total of 79,000 commercial cards were acquired for official issue as Nos. UZE27-UZE27A after validating. Some of the cards show an imprinted black square, while others show nothing.

1970, Nov. 16 21st District Special Election
UZE28 PC17 1½c **violet gray & claret brown,**
  white + Type XVII *(8,000)* — 180.00

島本「ケン」は言う
「政治は相互の理解と協調と和の中にあり、抵抗や反抗はいたずらに憎悪の感情を増し、混乱を招くだけである」と、常に現実を踏へて、前向きに誠実で勇気をもつて実践する人、島本「ケン」こそは新沖縄建設に必要な人であります。善意に満ちた、豊かな明るい清らかな新沖縄建設の為に第二十二区から立候補しました島本「ケン」に絶大なる御支持、御支援を賜りります様お願い申し上げると共に絶対自信をもつて「ケン」を推薦致します。

昭和四十五年十一月
日

那覇市古波蔵二四四
島本ケン選挙本部
推薦者 伊⚫⚫⚫⚫

推薦状

UZE29

1970, Nov. 16 22nd District Special Election
UZE29 PC17 1½c **violet gray & claret brown,** *white* + Type XVII *(2,000)* — 350.00

No. UZE29 is a remainder copy of No. UZE28, identifiable only with the imprinted message shown above of candidate Shimamoto Ken.

UZE30 PC17 1½c **violet gray & claret brown,** *white* + Type XIII — —
UZE30A PC17 1½c **violet gray & claret brown,** *white* + Type XIIIa — —

Postal records show a total of 2,000 of Nos. UZE30-UZE30A prepared, undefined as to type.

1971, Feb. 15 7th District Special Election
UZE31 PC17 1½c **violet gray & claret brown,**
  white + Type XV *(4,000)* — —

1971, June 4
Second General Election for Coucilors and Representatives to the Japanese Diet
UZE32 PC17 1½c **violet gray & claret brown,** *white* + Type XVIII *(25,000)* — 45.00
Emergency Commercial Card Issue for Second General Japanese Diet Election
UZE33 *white* + Type XVIII, 100x148mm *(25,000)* — 20.00
 a. Double strike of election indicia, one inverted in LR corner
UZE33A *white* + Type XVIII, 104x150mm *(25,000)* — 50.00

REVENUE STAMPS

Upon its establishment Apr. 1, 1952, the government of the Ryukyu Islands assumed responsibility for the issuing and the profit from revenue stamps. The various series served indiscriminately as evidence of payment of the required fees for various legal, realty and general commercial transactions.

1 yen — R1

参	五	拾	五拾
3	5	10	50

百	五百	千
100	500	1000

Litho. by Japan Printing Bureau.
Designer: Eizo Yonamine

1952-54			Wmk. 257	Perf. 13x1
R1	R1	1y **brown**	16.00	1
R2	R1	3y **carmine**	20.00	1
R3	R1	5y **green**	25.00	1
R4	R1	10y **blue**	30.00	2
R5	R1	50y **purple**	35.00	2
R6	R1	100y **yellow brown**	80.00	3
R7	R1	500y **dark green**	350.00	1
R8	R1	1,000y **carmine**	300.00	15
		Nos. R1-R8 (8)	855.00	362

Issued: #R1-R6, July 15, 1952; #R7-R8, Apr. 16, 1954.

Denomination Vertical

"Cent"

"Dollar"

Litho. by Kobundo Printing Co., Naha
Perf. 10, 10½, 11 and combinations

1958, Sept. 16		Without Gum		Unwm
R9	R1	1c **red brown**	30.00	25
a.		Horiz. pair, imperf. between	500.00	
R10	R1	3c **red**	40.00	35
a.		Horiz. pair, imperf. between	500.00	
R11	R1	5c **green**	50.00	45
R12	R1	10c **blue**	70.00	65
a.		Horiz. pair, imperf. between	500.00	
R13	R1	50c **purple**	135.00	120
R14	R1	$1 **sepia**	200.00	175
R15	R1	$5 **dark green**	400.00	350
R16	R1	$10 **carmine**	450.00	400
		Nos. R9-R16 (8)	1,375.	1,2

R2

R3

R4

Litho. by Japan Printing Bureau.

1959-69		Wmk. 257	Perf. 13x13
R17	R2	1c **brown**	3.00	1.9
R18	R2	3c **red**	3.00	1.
R19	R2	5c **purple**	5.50	3.
R20	R2	10c **green**	10.00	6.0
R21	R2	20c **sepia** ('69)	80.00	55.

| R2 | 30c **light olive** ('69) | 100.00 | 65.00 |
| R2 | 50c **blue** | 40.00 | 14.00 |

Engr.

R3	$1 **olive**	45.00	12.50
R3	$2 **vermilion** ('69)	250.00	50.00
R3	$3 **purple** ('69)	450.00	60.00
R3	$5 **orange**	120.00	45.00
R3	$10 **dark green**	180.00	60.00
R4	$20 **carmine** ('69)	2,000.	200.00
R4	$30 **blue** ('69)	2,500.	—
R4	$50 **black** ('69)	3,000.	—
	Nos. R17-R28 (12)	1,286.	373.75

UNEMPLOYMENT INSURANCE

These stamps, when affixed in an official booklet and canceled, certified a one-day contract for a day laborer. They were available to employers at certain post offices on various islands.

Dove — RQ1   Shield — RQ2

Lithographed in Naha

1961, Jan. 10   Without Gum   Unwmk.   *Rouletted*

| 1 | RQ1 | 2c **pale red** | 800.00 | — |
| 2 | RQ2 | 4c **violet** | 50.00 | 50.00 |

Redrawn

Lithographed by Japan Printing Bureau

1966, Feb.   Unwmk.   *Perf. 13x13½*

| 3 | RQ1 | 2c **pale red** | | |
| 4 | RQ2 | 4c **violet** | 30.00 | 30.00 |

Redrawn stamps have bolder numerals and inscriptions, and over, stronger lines of shading in background.

Cycad — RQ3

Lithographed by Japan Printing Bureau

1968, Apr. 19   Wmk. 257   *Perf. 13x13½*

| 5 | RQ3 | 8c **brown** | 35.00 | 35.00 |

Nos. RQ3-RQ4 Surcharged with New Values and 2 Bars

1967-72

26	RQ1	8c on 2c **pale red**	70.00	70.00
27	RQ2	8c on 4c **violet** ('72)	35.00	35.00
28	RQ2	12c on 4c **violet** ('71)	30.00	30.00

A 4-cent "stamp" picturing Iriomote Park was originally planned for postage in 1971. Its use was changed, and it became a label that was used on the "Ryukyu Islands Emergency Conversion Confirmation Certificate." Value, $125 unused, $200 on document.

PROVISIONAL ISSUES MIYAKO

Stamps of Japan 1938-42 Handstamped in Black, Red or Orange

1948   Typo., Litho., Engr.   Wmk. 257   *Perf. 13*

3XR1	A84	3s **brown,** #329	75.00	—
3XR2	A86	5s **brown lake,** #331	75.00	—
3XR3	A152	20s **blue,** #338 (R)	60.00	—
3XR4	A95	25s **dark brown & pale brown,** #270 (R)	60.00	—
a.		Black overprint	600.00	
3XR5	A96	30s **peacock blue,** #271 (R)	60.00	—
3XR6	A154	40s **dark violet,** #342 (R)	60.00	—
3XR7	A97	50s **olive & pale olive,** #272 (R)	135.00	—
a.		Orange overprint	500.00	

Doubled handstamps are known on all values and pairs with one stamp without handstamp exist on the 5s and 20s.

PROVISIONAL ISSUES YAEYAMA

In addition to the continued use of the then-current Japanese revenue stamps in stock from the wartime period, the varying authorities of the Yaeyama Gunto issued three district-specific revenue series, with a total of 28 values. Only those values at present verified by surviving copies are indicated. Numbers are reserved for other values believed to have been issued, but as yet not seen and verified.

No. 5XR2 — R5   No.
                                      5XR3 — R6

No. 5XR5 — R7   No. 5XR27 — R8

1946 (?)   Without Gum   *Imperf.*

Value printed, frame handstamped

| 5XR1 | R5 | 3s **vermilion & black** | — | — |
| 5XR2 | R5 | 10s **vermilion & black** | — | — |

Validating handstamp below

| 5XR3 | R6 | 1y **vermilion & black** | — | — |

Civil Administration Issues

1947 (?)   Without Gum   *Imperf.*

Value printed, frame handstamped

Cream Paper

| 5XR5 | R7 | 10s **vermilion & black** | — | — |
| 5XR6 | R7 | 50s **vermilion & black** | — | — |

Gunto Government Issues

1950 (?)   Without Gum   *Imperf.*

Value printed, frame handstamped

Cream Paper

5XR17	R8	10s **vermilion & black**	—	
5XR18	R8	50s **vermilion & black**	—	
a.		50s **vermilion & blue**	—	
5XR20	R8	1.50y **vermilion & black**	—	
5XR22	R8	5y **vermilion & black**	—	
5XR24	R8	20y **vermilion & black**	—	
5XR27	R8	100y **vermilion & black**	—	

Nos. 5XR17-5XR27 are known with rough perforations, full or partial.

SPECIMEN STAMPS

Regular stamps and postal cards of 1958-65 overprinted with three cursive syllabics *mi-ho-n* ("specimen").

Type A

1961-64

Overprinted in Black

91S	3c **multicolored** *(1,000)*	250.00	
118S	3c **multicolored** *(1,100)*	450.00	
119S	3c **multicolored** *(1,100)*	400.00	

Type B

1964-65

Overprinted in Red or Black

120aS	3c **deep blue, deep carmine & ocher** (R) *(1,500)*	200.00	
121S	3c **multicolored** (R) *(1,500)*	175.00	
124S	3c **ultra, yel & red** (R) *(5,000)*	35.00	
125S	3s **dull claret, yel & black** *(1,500)*	70.00	
126S	3c **yellow & multi** *(2,000)*	60.00	
127S	3c **gray, red & black** *(2,000)*	60.00	
128S	3c **multicolored** *(1,500)*	70.00	
129S	1½c **multicolored** (R) *(1,500)*	70.00	
130S	3c **light blue & multi** (R) *(1,500)*	200.00	
131S	3c **multicolored** (R) *(1,500)*	60.00	
132S	3c **buff & multicolored** *(2,000)*	60.00	
133S	3c **green & multi** *(2,000)*	50.00	
134S	3c **multicolored** *(2,000)*	50.00	
135S	3c **blue & multicolored** *(2,000)*	50.00	
136S	3c **golden brown & multi** *(2,000)*	50.00	
139S	1½c **multicolored** (R) *(2,500)*	50.00	

Postal Cards

1964-65

Overprinted Type A or B in Black or Red

UX26S	A	1½c **multicolored** *(1,000)*	500.00	
UX27S	B	1½c **multicolored** *(1,000)*	350.00	
UX28S	A	1½c **multicolored** *(1,000)*	300.00	
UX29S	A	1½c **multicolored** *(1,100)*	250.00	

See also Nos. 46TCS and 48TCS following Proofs and Trial Color Proofs.

PROOFS AND TRIAL COLOR PROOFS

1948

Salmon Paper, Imperf.

1aP	5s **magenta**	—
2aP	10s **yellow green**	—
3aP	20s **yellow green**	—
5aP	40s **magenta**	—
6aP	50s **ultramarine**	—
7aP	1y **ultramarine**	—

Between the printing of Nos. 1a-7a and Nos. 1-7 essay sheets of the series were prepared in Tokyo and overprinted with a swirl-pattern of blue or red dots. These essays sell for about $800 each.

Except for No. 12TC 4y olive, the trial color proofs of Nos. 8-13, 18, C1-C3 and E1 are from blocks of 9.

1950

Soft White Paper, Imperf.
Proofs are Gummed, Trial Color Proofs are Without Gum

8P	50s **dark carmine rose**	1,500.
8TC	50s **rose**	1,750.
8TC	50s **green**	1,750.
9P	1y **deep blue**	1,500.
9TC	1y **rose**	1,750.
9TC	1y **green**	1,750.
10P	2y **rose violet**	1,500.
10TC	2y **rose**	1,750.
10TC	2y **green**	1,750.
11P	3y **carmine rose**	1,500.
11TC	3y **rose**	1,750.
11TC	3y **green**	1,750.
12P	4y **greenish gray**	1,500.
12TC	4y **rose**	1,750.
12TC	4y **olive**	1,750.
13P	5y **blue green**	1,500.
13TC	5y **rose**	1,750.
13TC	5y **green**	1,750.

1951

Soft White Paper, Imperf., Without Gum

| 14P | 3y **red brown** | 1,000. |
| 15P | 3y **dark green** | 800. |

1952

Whitish Paper, Imperf., With Gum

18TC	3y **pale salmon**	1,750.
18TC	3y **scarlet**	1,750.
18TC	3y **red orange**	1,900.

Perforated, gummed proof sheets of Nos. 18, 27 and 28 with oversized, untrimmed selvage were printed for display purposes.

1958

Off White Paper, Imperf., Without Gum

46TC	2c **black** (100)	800.
48TC	4c **black** (100)	800.

AIR POST

1950

Soft White Paper, Imperf.

Proofs are Gummed, Trial Color Proofs are Without Gum

C1P	8y **bright blue**	1,500.
C1TC	8y **rose**	1,750.
C1TC	8y **light green**	1,750.

C2P	12y **green**	1,500.
C2TC	12y **rose**	1,750.
C2TC	12y **light green**	1,750.
C3P	16y **rose carmine**	1,500.
C3TC	16y **rose**	1,750.

1951

Soft White Paper, Imperf., Without Gum

C4P	13y **blue**	1,000.
C5P	18y **green**	1,000.
C6P	30y **cerise**	800.

SPECIAL DELIVERY

1950

Soft White Paper, Imperf.

Proofs are Gummed, Trial Color Proofs are Without Gum

E1P	5y **bright blue**	1,500.
E1TC	5y **rose**	1,750.
E1TC	5y **green**	1,750.

Official proof folders contain one each of Nos. 8P-13P, 12TC in olive, C1P-C3P and E1P. The stamps are securely adhered to the folder. Value, $9,000.

Similar folders exist containing die proofs in black of the s[...] issues and mockups of Nos. U2, UX3 and UY3.

KUME ISLAND

1945

U.S. Official Watermarked White Bond Pape[r]

Seal Handstamped in Vermilion

Without Gum

1X1P	7s **black**	3,
a.	"7" and "SEN" one letter space to left, pos. 8	4,

SPECIMEN OVERPRINTS ON TRIAL COLOR[ ] PROOFS

1961

Overprinted in Vermillion

46TCS	2c **black** (100)	1,
48TCS	4c **black** (100)	1,

Cursive type used for these two trial color proofs is diffe[...] from the mihon overprints.

UNITED NATIONS

United Nations stamps are used on UN official mail sent from UN Headquarters in New York City, the UN European Office in Geneva, Switzerland, from the Donaupark Vienna International Center or Atomic Energy Agency in Vienna, Austria to points throughout the world. They may be used [...] private correspondence sent through the UN post offices.

UN mail is carried by the US, Swiss and Austrian postal systems.

See Switzerland official stamp listings in the Scott *Standard Postage Stamp Catalogue* for stamps issued by the Swiss Government for official use [...] the UN European Office and other UN affiliated organizations. See France official stamp listings for stamps issued by the French Government for offic[...] use of UNESCO.

+: When following the quantity, this indicates the total printed to date. Unless otherwise noted, these are the initial printing order. Final quantiti[...] frequently are not given for definitives and air post stamps. The total printed is shown here.

Blocks of four generally sell for four times the single stamp value.

Values for first day covers are for cacheted and unaddressed covers. Addressed covers sell for much less, and addressed and uncacheted first c[...] covers sell for very little.

For imperforate stamps, see the Proofs section following U.N. Souvenir Cards.

> **Catalogue values for all unused stamps in this section are for Never Hinged items.**

Peoples of the World — A1

UN Headquarters Building — A2

"Peace, Justice, Security" — A3

UN Flag — A4

UN International Children's Emergency Fund — A5

World Unity — A6

Printed by Thomas De La Rue & Co., Ltd., London (1c, [...] 10c, 15c, 20c, 25c), and Joh. Enschedé and Sons, Haarle[...] Netherlands (1½c, 2c, 5c, 50c, $1). The 3c, 15c and 25c ha[...] frame engraved, center photogravure; other denominations a[...] engraved. Panes of 50. Designed by O. C. Meronti (A1), Le[...] Helguera (A2), J. F. Doeve (A3), Ole Hamann (A4), S. L. Ha[...] (5c) and Hubert Woyty-Wimmer (20c).

Perf. 13x12½, 12½x13

1951		Engr. and Photo.	Unwm[ ]	
1	A1	1c **magenta**, *Oct. 24*	.20	.[ ]
		(8,000,000)		
		First day cover		1.[ ]
		Margin block of 4, UN seal	.20	
2	A2	1½c **blue green**, *Oct. 24*	.20	.[ ]
		(7,450,000)		
		First day cover		1.[ ]
		Margin block of 4, UN seal	.20	
		Precanceled (361,700)		55.[ ]
3	A3	2c **purple**, *Nov. 16* (8,470,000)	.20	.[ ]
		First day cover		1.[ ]
		Margin block of 4, UN seal	.25	
4	A4	3c **magenta & blue**, *Oct. 24*	.20	.[ ]
		(8,250,000)		
		First day cover		1.[ ]
		Margin block of 4, UN seal	.25	
5	A5	5c **blue**, *Oct. 24* (6,000,000)	.20	.[ ]
		First day cover		1.7[ ]
		Margin block of 4, UN seal	.40	
6	A1	10c **chocolate**, *Nov. 16*	.35	.[ ]
		(2,600,000)		
		First day cover		2.[ ]
		Margin block of 4, UN seal	1.50	
7	A4	15c **violet & blue**, *Nov. 16*	.35	.[ ]
		(2,300,000)		
		First day cover		2.0[ ]
		Margin block of 4, UN seal	1.50	
8	A6	20c **dark brown**, *Nov. 16*	.55	.[ ]
		(2,100,000)		
		First day cover		2.0[ ]
		Margin block of 4, UN seal	2.40	

A4	25c	**olive gray & blue,** Oct. 24		
		(2,100,000)	.60	.30
		First day cover		2.00
		Margin block of 4, UN seal	2.75	
A2	50c	**indigo,** Nov. 16 (1,785,000)	6.00	2.50
		First day cover		8.00
		Margin block of 4, UN seal	27.50	
A3	$1	**red,** Oct. 24 (2,252,500)	2.50	1.50
		First day cover		8.00
		Margin block of 4, UN seal	11.50	
		Nos. 1-11 (11)	11.35	6.10

st day covers of Nos. 1-11 and C1-C4 total 1,113,216.
e various printings of Nos. 1-11 vary in sheet marginal
ration. Some were perforated through left or right margins,
th; some through all margins.

eets of this issue carry a marginal inscription consisting of
N seal and "First UN/Issue 1951." This inscription appears
times on each sheet. The listing "Margin block of 4, UN
" or "Inscription block of 4" in this and following issues refers
corner block.

he 1½c, 2c, 50c and $1 have a cut-out of different
e in one margin. The printer trimmed this off entirely on
t of the 1½c third printing, and partially on the 1½c fourth
ing and $1 fifth and sixth printings.

he UN Offices in Geneva Nos. 4, 14.
rgeries of the 1½c precancel abound. Examination by a
petent authority is necessary.

Veterans' War Memorial Building, San Francisco A7

ssued to mark the 7th anniversary of the signing of the
ed Nations Charter.
ngraved and printed by the American Bank Note Co., New
k. Panes of 50. Designed by Jean Van Noten.

52, Oct. 24				**Perf. 12**
A7	5c	**blue** (1,274,670)	.80	.35
		First day cover (160,117)		1.00
		Inscription block of 4	3.25	—

Globe and Encircled Flame — A8

4th anniversary of the adoption of the Universal Declaration of Human Rights.
Engraved and printed by Thomas De La Rue & Co., Ltd., London. Panes of 50. Designed by Hubert Woyty-Wimmer.

1952, Dec. 10				**Perf. 13½x14**
13	A8	3c **deep green** (1,554,312)	.40	.35
		First day cover		1.50
		Inscription block of 4	1.60	
14	A8	5c **blue** (1,126,371)	.45	.40
		First day cover		2.00
		First day cover, #13-14		5.75
		Inscription block of 4	1.90	

First day covers of Nos. 13 and 14 total 299,309.

Refugee Family — A9

Issued to publicize "Protection for Refugees."
Engraved and printed by Thomas De La Rue & Co., Ltd., London. Panes of 50. Designed by Olav Mathiesen.

1953, Apr. 24				**Perf. 12½x13**
15	A9	3c **dark red brown & rose brown** (1,299,793)	.25	.25
		First day cover		2.25
		Inscription block of 4	1.00	
16	A9	5c **indigo & blue** (969,224)	.50	.40

Envelope, UN Emblem and Map — A10

Issued to honor the Universal Postal Union.
Engraved and printed by Thomas De La Rue & Co., Ltd., London. Panes of 50. Designed by Hubert Woyty-Wimmer.

		First day cover		3.25
		First day cover, #15-16		7.50
		Inscription block of 4	2.40	—

First day covers of Nos. 15 and 16 total 234,082.

1953, June 12				**Perf. 13**
17	A10	3c **black brown** (1,259,689)	.40	.40
		First day cover		5.00
		Inscription block of 4	1.60	
18	A10	5c **dark blue** (907,312)	1.10	1.00
		First day cover		4.50
		First day cover, #17-18		9.00
		Inscription block of 4	4.50	

First day covers of Nos. 17 and 18 total 231,627.
Plate number ("1A" or "1B") in color of stamp appears below 47th stamp of sheet.

Gearwheels and UN Emblem — A11

Hands Reaching Toward
Flame — A12

Issued to publicize United Nations activities in the field of technical assistance.
Engraved and printed by Thomas De La Rue & Co. Ltd. London. Panes of 50. Designed by Olav Mathiesen.

1953, Oct. 24   *Perf. 13x12½*
19 A11   3c dark gray *(1,184,348)*   .30   .25
           First day cover   2.00
           Inscription block of 4   1.25   —
20 A11   5c dark green *(968,182)*   .50   .45
           First day cover   5.00
           First day cover, #19-20   9.00
           Inscription block of 4   2.25   —

First day covers of Nos. 19 and 20 total 229,211.

1953, Dec. 10   *Perf. 12½x13*
Issued to publicize Human Rights Day.
Engraved and printed by Thomas De La Rue & Co., Ltd., London. Panes of 50. Designed by León Helguera.

21 A12   3c bright blue *(1,456,928)*   .35   .30
           First day cover   2.00
           Inscription block of 4   1.50   —
22 A12   5c rose red *(983,831)*   1.50 1.00
           First day cover   4.00
           First day cover, #21-22   8.00
           Inscription block of 4   6.00   —

First day covers of Nos. 21 and 22 total 265,186.

Ear of Wheat — A13

UN Emblem and Anvil
Inscribed "ILO" — A14

Issued to honor the Food and Agriculture Organization and printed by Thomas De La Rue & Co., Ltd., London. Panes of 50. Designed by Dirk Van Gelder.

1954, Feb. 11   *Perf. 12½x13*
23 A13   3c dark green & yellow
           (1,250,000)   .30   .20
           First day cover   2.00
           Inscription block of 4   1.75   —
24 A13   8c indigo & yellow *(949,718)*   .75   .50
           First day cover   4.00
           First day cover, #23-24   5.00
           Inscription block of 4   3.75   —

First day covers of Nos. 23 and 24 total 272,312.

1954, May 10   *Perf. 12½x13*
Design: 8c, inscribed "OIT."
Issued to honor the International Labor Organization.
Engraved and printed by Thomas De La Rue & Co., Ltd., London. Panes of 50. Designed by José Renau.

25 A14   3c brown *(1,085,651)*   .20   .20
           First day cover   2.00
           Inscription block of 4   .50   —
26 A14   8c magenta *(903,561)*   1.25   .85
           First day cover   4.00
           First day cover, #25-26   4.75
           Inscription block of 4   5.25   —

First day covers of Nos. 25 and 26 total 252,796.

UN European
Office,
Geneva — A15

Issued on the occasion of United Nations Day.
Engraved and printed by Thomas De La Rue & Co., Ltd., London. Panes of 50. Designed by Earl W. Purdy.

1954, Oct. 25   *Perf. 14*
27 A15   3c dark blue violet *(1,000,000)* 1.75 1.25
           First day cover   1.75
           Inscription block of 4   8.50   —
28 A15   8c red *(1,000,000)*   .35   .30
           First day cover   2.25
           First day cover, #27-28   3.50
           Inscription block of 4   1.50   —

First day covers of Nos. 27 and 28 total 233,544.

Mother and Child — A16

Issued to publicize Human Rights Day.
Engraved and printed by Thomas De La Rue & Co., Ltd. London. Panes of 50. Designed by Leonard C. Mitchell.

1954, Dec. 10   *Perf. 14*
29 A16   3c red orange *(1,000,000)*   12.00 5.00
           First day cover   2.75
           Inscription block of 4   55.00   —
30 A16   8c olive green *(1,000,000)*   .75   .35
           First day cover   3.75
           First day cover, #29-30   8.00
           Inscription block of 4   4.50   —

First day covers of Nos. 29 and 30 total 276,333.

Symbol of
Flight — A17

Design: 8c, inscribed "OACI."
Issued to honor the International Civil Aviation Organization.
Engraved and printed by Waterlow & Sons, Ltd., London. Panes of 50. Designed by Angel Medina Medina.

1955, Feb. 9   *Perf. 13*
31 A17   3c blue *(1,000,000)*   1.50
           First day cover
           Inscription block of 4   7.00
32 A17   8c rose carmine *(1,000,000)*   .85
           First day cover
           First day cover, #31-32
           Inscription block of 4   3.50

First day covers of Nos. 31 and 32 total 237,131.

UNESCO
Emblem — A18

Issued to honor the UN Educational, Scientific and Cultural Organization.
Engraved and printed by Waterlow & Sons, Ltd., London. Panes of 50. Designed by George Hamori.

1955, May 11   *Perf. 13½*
33 A18   3c lilac rose *(1,000,000)*   .45
           First day cover
           Inscription block of 4   2.50
34 A18   8c light blue *(1,000,000)*   .40
           First day cover
           First day cover, #33-34
           Inscription block of 4   1.75

First day covers of Nos. 33 and 34 total 255,326.

United Nations
Charter — A19

Design: 4c, Spanish inscription. 8c, French inscription.
10th anniversary of the United Nations.
Engraved and printed by Waterlow & Sons, Ltd., London. Panes of 50. Designed by Claude Bottiau.

1955, Oct. 24   *Perf. 13½*
35 A19   3c deep plum *(1,000,000)*   1.00
           First day cover
           Inscription block of 4   4.00
36 A19   4c dull green *(1,000,000)*   .55
           First day cover
           Inscription block of 4   2.25
37 A19   8c bluish black *(1,000,000)*   .40
           First day cover
           First day cover, #35-37   1.
           Inscription block of 4   1.75
           Nos. 35-37 (3)   1.95

Wmk. 309 —
Wavy Lines

Souvenir Sheet
1955, Oct. 24   **Wmk. 309**   *Impe.*
38 A19   Sheet of 3 *(250,000)*   120.00 20
           Hinged   65.00
a.   3c deep plum   3.00
b.   4c dull green   3.00
c.   8c bluish black   3.00
           First day cover   20.
           Sheet with retouch on 8c   135.00 42.

No. 38 measures 108x83mm and has marginal inscriptions deep plum.
Two printings were made of No. 38. The first (200,000) m be distinguished by the broken line of background shading the 8c. It leaves a small white spot below the left leg of the "n" "Unies." For the second printing (50,000), the broken line w retouched, eliminating the white spot. The 4c was al retouched.
First day covers of Nos. 35-38 total 455,791.
Copies of No. 38 are known with the 4c and 8c stam misaligned.

Hand Holding
Torch — A20

Issued in honor of Human Rights Day.
Engraved and printed by Waterlow & Sons, Ltd., London.
...s of 50. Designed by Hubert Woyty-Wimmer.

			Dec. 9	Unwmk.	Perf. 14x13½
...20	3c	ultramarine (1,250,000)		.30	.30
		First day cover			1.25
		Inscription block of 4		1.25	
...20	8c	green (1,000,000)		.35	.30
		First day cover			1.25
		First day cover, #39-40			2.50
		Inscription block of 4		1.50	

First day covers of Nos. 39 and 40 total 298,038.

Symbols of Telecommunication — A21

Design: 8c, inscribed "UIT."
...sued in honor of the International Telecommunication
...n.
...ngraved and printed by Thomas De La Rue & Co., Ltd.,
...don. Panes of 50. Designed by Hubert Woyty-Wimmer.

			Feb. 17		Perf. 14
..A21	3c	turquoise blue (1,000,000)		.25	.25
		First day cover			1.50
		Inscription block of 4		1.10	
..A21	8c	deep carmine (1,000,000)		.30	.30
		First day cover			2.25
		First day cover, #41-42			3.50
		Inscription block of 4		1.40	

...ate number ("1A" or "1B") in color of stamp appears below
... stamp of sheet.

Globe and
Caduceus — A22

Design: 8c, inscribed "OMS."
...ssued in honor of the World Health Organization.
...Engraved and printed by Thomas De La Rue & Co., Ltd.,
...don. Panes of 50. Designed by Olav Mathiesen.

			Apr. 6		Perf. 14
..A22	3c	bright greenish blue (1,250,000)		.20	.20
		First day cover			1.00
		Inscription block of 4		.50	
..A22	8c	golden brown (1,000,000)		.20	.25
		First day cover			1.50
		First day cover, #43-44			14.00
		Inscription block of 4		1.25	

First day covers of Nos. 43 and 44 total 260,853.

General
Assembly
A23

Design: 8c, French inscription.
Issued to commemorate United Nations Day.
Engraved and printed by Thomas De La Rue & Co., Ltd.,
London. Panes of 50. Designed by Kurt Plowitz.

			1956, Oct. 24		Perf. 14
45	A23	3c	dark blue (2,000,000)	.20	.20
			First day cover		1.00
			Inscription block of 4	.30	
46	A23	8c	gray olive (1,500,000)	.20	.20
			First day cover		1.00
			First day cover, #45-46		7.50
			Inscription block of 4	.80	

First day covers of Nos. 45 and 46 total 303,560.

Flame and
Globe — A24

Issued to publicize Human Rights Day
Engraved and printed by Thomas De La Rue & Co., Ltd.,
London. Panes of 50. Designed by Rashid-ud Din.

			1956, Dec. 10		Perf. 14
47	A24	3c	plum (5,000,000)	.20	.20
			First day cover		1.00
			Inscription block of 4	.30	
48	A24	8c	dark blue (4,000,000)	.20	.20
			First day cover		1.00
			First day cover, #47-48		2.00
			Inscription block of 4	.60	

First day covers of Nos. 47 and 48 total 416,120.

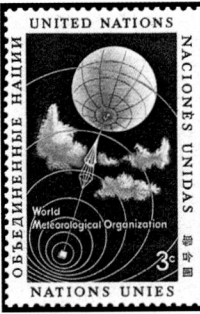

Weather Balloon — A25

Design: 8c, Agency name in French.
Issued to honor the World Meterological Organization.
Engraved and printed by Thomas De La Rue & Co., Ltd.,
London. Panes of 50. Designed by A. L. Pollock.

			1957, Jan. 28		Perf. 14
49	A25	3c	violet blue (5,000,000)	.20	.20
			First day cover		1.00
			Inscription block of 4	.25	
50	A25	8c	dark carmine rose (3,448,985)	.20	.25
			First day cover		1.00
			First day cover, #49-50		2.25
			Inscription block of 4	.65	

First day covers of Nos. 49 and 50 total 376,110.

Badge of UN
Emergency
Force — A26

1957, Apr. 8   **Perf. 14x12½**

Issued in honor of the UN Emergency Force.

Engraved and printed by Thomas De La Rue & Co., Ltd.,
London. Panes of 50. Designed by Ole Hamann.

					Perf. 14x12½
51	A26	3c	light blue (4,000,000)	.20	.20
			First day cover		1.00
			Inscription block of 4	.30	
52	A26	8c	rose carmine (3,000,000)	.20	.20
			First day cover		1.00
			First day cover, #51-52		1.75
			Inscription block of 4	.70	

First day covers of Nos. 51 and 52 total 461,772.

Nos. 51-52 Re-engraved

1957, Apr.-May					**Perf. 14x12½**
53	A26	3c	blue (2,736,206)	.20	.20
			Inscription block of 4	.40	—
54	A26	8c	rose carmine (1,000,000)	.35	.20
			Inscription block of 4	1.40	—

On Nos. 53-54 the background within and around the circles
is shaded lightly, giving a halo effect. The lettering is more
distinct with a line around each letter.

UN Emblem and
Globe — A27

Design: 8c, French inscription.
Issued to honor the Security Council.
Engraved and printed by Thomas De La Rue & Co., Ltd.,
London. Panes of 50. Designed by Rashid-ud Din.

			1957, Oct. 24		Perf. 12½x13
55	A27	3c	orange brown (3,674,968)	.20	.20
			First day cover		1.00
			Inscription block of 4	.25	—
56	A27	8c	dark blue green (2,885,938)	.20	.20
			First day cover		1.00
			First day cover, #55-56		2.25
			Inscription block of 4	.70	—

First day covers of Nos. 55 and 56 total 460,627.

Flaming
Torch — A28

Issued in honor of Human Rights Day.
Engraved and printed by Thomas De La Rue & Co., Ltd.,
London. Panes of 50. Designed by Olav Mathiesen.

			1957, Dec. 10		Perf. 14
57	A28	3c	red brown (3,368,405)	.20	.20
			First day cover		1.00
			Inscription block of 4	.25	—
58	A28	8c	black (2,717,310)	.20	.20
			First day cover		1.00
			First day cover, #57-58		1.25
			Inscription block of 4	.65	—

First day covers of Nos. 57 and 58 total 553,669.

UN Emblem
Shedding Light on
Atom — A29

Design: 8c, French inscription.
Issued in honor of the International Atomic Energy Agency.
Engraved and printed by the American Bank Note Co., New
York. Panes of 50. Designed by Robert Perrot.

			1958, Feb. 10		Perf. 12
59	A29	3c	olive (3,663,305)	.20	.20
			First day cover		1.00
			Inscription block of 4	.25	—
60	A29	8c	blue (3,043,622)	.20	.20

First day cover 1.00
First day cover, #59-60 1.00
Inscription block of 4 .65

First day covers of Nos. 59 and 60 total 504,832.

Central Hall,
Westminster — A30

UN Seal — A31

Design: 8c, French inscription.
Central Hall, Westminster, London, was the site of the first session of the United Nations General Assembly, 1946.
Engraved and printed by the American Bank Note Co., New York. Panes of 50. Designed by Olav Mathiesen.

1958, Apr. 14   **Perf. 12**
61 A30   3c **violet blue** (3,353,716)   .20   .20
            First day cover   1.00
            Inscription block of 4   .25
62 A30   8c **rose claret** (2,836,747)   .20   .20
            First day cover   1.00
            First day cover, #61-62   2.00
            Inscription block of 4   .60

First day covers of Nos. 61 and 62 total 449,401.

1958, Oct. 24   **Perf. 13½x14**

Engraved and printed by Bradbury, Wilkinson & Co., Ltd., England. Panes of 50. Designed by Herbert M. Sanborn.

63 A31   4c **red orange** (9,000,000)   .20   .20
            First day cover   1.00
            First day cover of #63 also
              bearing #64   75.00
            Inscription block of 4   .20

1958, June 2   **Perf. 13x14**
64 A31   8c **bright blue** (5,000,000)   .20   .20
            First day cover (219,422)   1.00
            Inscription block of 4   .55
            Margin block of 4, Bradbury,
              Wilkinson imprint   3.00

Gearwheels — A32

Hands Upholding
Globe — A33

Design: 8c, French inscription.
Issued to honor the Economic and Social Council.
Engraved and printed by the American Bank Note Co., New York. Panes of 50. Designed by Ole Hamann.

1958, Oct. 24   **Unwmk.**   **Perf. 12**
65 A32   4c **dark blue green** (2,556,784)   .20   .20
            First day cover   1.00
            Inscription block of 4   .30
66 A32   8c **vermilion** (2,175,117)   .20   .20
            First day cover   1.00
            First day cover, #65-66   1.00
            Inscription block of 4   .60

First day covers of Nos. 63, 65 and 66 total 626,236.

1958, Dec. 10   **Unwmk.**   **Perf. 12**

Issued for Human Rights Day and to commemorate the 10th anniversary of the signing of the Universal Declaration of Human Rights.

Engraved and printed by the American Bank Note Co., New York. Panes of 50. Designed by Leonard C. Mitchell.

67 A33   4c **yellow green** (2,644,340)   .20   .20
            First day cover   1.00
            Inscription block of 4   .40
68 A33   8c **red brown** (2,216,838)   .20   .20
            First day cover   1.00
            First day cover, #67-68   1.00
            Inscription block of 4   .75

First day covers of Nos. 67 and 68 total 618,124.

New York City
Building,
Flushing
Meadows
A34

Design: 8c, French inscription.
New York City Building at Flushing Meadows, New York, was the site of many General Assembly meetings, 1946-50.
Engraved and printed by Canadian Bank Note Company, Ltd., Ottawa. Panes of 50. Designed by Robert Perrot.

1959, Mar. 30   **Unwmk.**   **Perf. 12**
69 A34   4c **light lilac rose** (2,035,011)   .20   .20
            First day cover   1.00
            Inscription block of 4   .30
70 A34   8c **aquamarine** (1,627,281)   .20   .20
            First day cover   1.00
            First day cover, #69 70   1.75
            Inscription block of 4   .70

First day covers of Nos. 69 and 70 total 440,955.

A35

A36

Design: UN emblem and symbols of agriculture, industry and trade.
Issued to honor the Economic Commission for Europe.
Engraved and printed by Canadian Bank Note Company, Ltd., Ottawa. Panes of 50. Designed by Ole Hamann.

1959, May 18   **Unwmk.**   **Perf. 12**
71 A35   4c **blue** (1,743,502)   .20   .20
            First day cover   1.00
            Inscription block of 4   .60
72 A35   8c **red orange** (1,482,898)   .20   .20
            First day cover   1.00
            First day cover, #71-72   1.25
            Inscription block of 4   .75

First day covers of Nos. 71 and 72 total 433,549.

1959, Oct. 23   **Unwmk.**   **Perf. 12**

Designs: 4c, Figure Adapted from Rodin's "Age of Bronze." 8c, same, French inscription.
Issued to honor the Trusteeship Council.
Engraved and printed by Canadian Bank Note Co., Ltd., Ottawa. Panes of 50. Designed by León Helguera; lettering by Ole Hamann.

73 A36   4c **bright red** (1,929,677)   .20   .20
            First day cover   1.00
            Inscription block of 4   .30
74 A36   8c **dark olive green** (1,587,647)   .20   .20
            First day cover   1.00
            First day cover, #73-74   1.50
            Inscription block of 4   1.00

First day covers of Nos. 73 and 74 total 466,053.

World Refugee Year
Emblem — A37

Chaillot Palace,
Paris — A38

Design: 8c, French inscription.
Issued to publicize World Refugee Year, July 1, 1959 30, 1960.
Engraved and printed by Canadian Bank Note Co. Ottawa. Panes of 50. Designed by Olav Mathiesen.

1959, Dec. 10   **Unwmk.**   **Per**
75 A37   4c **olive & red** (2,168,963)   .20
            First day cover
            Inscription block of 4   .35
76 A37   8c **olive & bright greenish blue**
               (1,843,886)   .20
            First day cover
            First day cover, #75-76
            Inscription block of 4   .75

First day covers of Nos. 75 and 76 total 502,262.

1960, Feb. 29   **Unwmk.**   **Per**

Design: 8c, French inscription.
Chaillot Palace in Paris was the site of General Asse meetings in 1948 and 1951.
Engraved and printed by Thomas De La Rue & Co., London. Panes of 50. Designed by Hubert Woyty-Wimme

77 A38   4c **rose lilac & blue** (2,276,678)   .20
            First day cover
            Inscription block of 4
78 A38   8c **dull green & brown** (1,930,869)   .20
            First day cover
            First day cover, #77-78
            Inscription block of 4   .70

First day covers of Nos. 77 and 78 total 446,815.

Map of Far
East and S
Beam — A3

Design: 8c, French inscription.
Issued to honor the Economic Commission for Asia and Far East (ECAFE).
Printed by the Government Printing Bureau, Tokyo. Pane 50. Designed by Hubert Woyty-Wimmer.

1960, Apr. 11   Photo.   Unwmk.   Perf. 13x1
79 A39   4c **deep claret, blue green & dull yellow**
               (2,195,945)   .20
            First day cover
            Inscription block of 4   .20
80 A39   8c **olive green, blue & rose** (1,897,902) .20
            First day cover
            First day cover, #79-80
            Inscription block of 4   .75

First day covers of Nos. 79 and 80 total 415,127.

Tree, FAO and UN
Emblems — A40

UN Headquarters and Preamble to UN Charter — A41

Design: 8c, French inscription.
Issued to commemorate the Fifth World Forestry Congress, Seattle, Washington, Aug. 29-Sept. 10.
Printed by the Government Printing Bureau, Tokyo. Panes of 50. Designed by Ole Hamann.

60, Aug. 29	**Photo.**	**Unwmk.**	**Perf. 13½**	
A40 4c **dark blue, green & orange**				
(2,188,293)			.20	.20
First day cover				1.00
Inscription block of 4			.35	—
A40 8c **yellow green, black & orange**				
(1,837,778)			.20	.20
First day cover				1.00
First day cover, #81-82				2.00
Inscription block of 4			.65	—

First day covers of Nos. 81 and 82 total 434,129.

60, Oct. 24   Unwmk.   Perf. 11

Design: 8c, French inscription.
Issued to commemorate the 15th anniversary of the United Nations.
Engraved and printed by the British American Bank Note Co., Ltd., Ottawa, Canada. Panes of 50. Designed by Robert Perrot.

A41 4c **blue** (2,631,593)		.20	.20
First day cover			1.00
Inscription block of 4		.35	—
A41 8c **gray** (2,278,022)		.20	.20
First day cover			1.00
First day cover, #83-84			1.50
Inscription block of 4		.65	—

Souvenir Sheet
Imperf

Sheet of 2 (1,000,000)		1.25	1.25
. A41 4c blue		.55	.55
. A41 8c gray		.55	.55
First day cover (256,699)			.50

No. 85 has dark gray marginal inscription. Size: 92x71mm. Broken "I" and "V" flaws occur in "ANNIVERSARY" in marginal inscription. Copies are known with the two stamps misaligned.

Block and Tackle — A42

Scales of Justice from Raphael's Stanze — A43

Design: 8c, French inscription.
Issued to honor the International Bank for Reconstruction and Development.
Printed by the Government Printing Bureau, Tokyo. Panes of 50. Designed by Angel Medina Medina.

60, Dec. 9	**Photo.**	**Unwmk.**	**Perf. 13½x13**	
6 A42 4c **multicolored** (2,286,117)			.20	.20
First day cover				1.00
Inscription block of 4			.35	—
7 A42 8c **multicolored** (1,882,019)			.20	.20
First day cover				1.00
First day cover, #86-87				1.25
Inscription block of 4			.65	—

First day covers of Nos. 86 and 87 total 559,708.

961, Feb. 13   Photo.   Unwmk.   Perf. 13½x13

Design: 8c, French inscription.
Issued to honor the International Court of Justice.
Printed by the Government Printing Bureau, Tokyo, Japan. Panes of 50. Designed by Kurt Plowitz.

8 A43 4c **yellow, orange brown & black** (2,234,588)		.20	.20
First day cover			1.00
Inscription block of 4		.35	—
89 A43 8c **yellow, green & black** (2,023,968)		.20	.20
First day cover			1.00
First day cover, #88-89			1.00
Inscription block of 4		.65	—

First day covers of Nos. 88 and 89 total 447,467.

Seal of International Monetary Fund — A44

Design: 7c, French inscription.
Issued to honor the International Monetary Fund.
Printed by the Government Printing Bureau, Tokyo, Japan. Panes of 50. Designed by Roy E. Carlson and Hordur Karlsson, Iceland.

1961, Apr. 17	**Photo.**	**Unwmk.**	**Perf. 13x13½**	
90 A44 4c **bright bluish green** (2,305,010)			.20	.20
First day cover				1.00
Inscription block of 4			.35	—
91 A44 7c **terra cotta & yellow** (2,147,201)			.20	.20
First day cover				1.00
First day cover, #90-91				1.00
Inscription block of 4			.65	—

First day covers of Nos. 90 and 91 total 448,729.

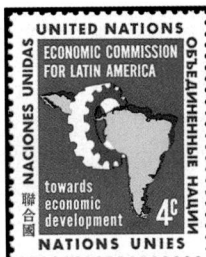

Abstract Group of Flags — A45

Printed by Courvoisier S.A., La Chaux-de-Fonds, Switzerland. Panes of 50. Designed by Herbert M. Sanborn.

1961, June 5	**Photo.**	**Unwmk.**	**Perf. 11½**	
92 A45 30c **multicolored** (3,370,000)			.45	.20
First day cover (182,949)				1.00
Inscription block of 4			2.00	—

See UN Offices in Geneva No. 10.

Cogwheel and Map of Latin America — A46

Design: 11c, Spanish inscription.
Issued to honor the Economic Commission for Latin America.
Printed by the Government Printing Bureau, Tokyo. Panes of 50. Designed by Robert Perrot.

1961, Sept. 18	**Photo.**	**Unwmk.**	**Perf. 13½**	
93 A46 4c **blue, red & citron** (2,037,912)			.20	.20
First day cover				1.00
Inscription block of 4			.45	—
94 A46 11c **green, lilac & orange vermilion**				
(1,835,097)			.25	.20
First day cover				1.00
First day cover, #93-94				1.00
Inscription block of 4			1.25	—

First day covers of Nos. 93 and 94 total 435,820.

Africa House, Addis Ababa, and Map — A47

Design: 11c, English inscription.
Issued to honor the Economic Commission for Africa.
Printed by Courvoisier S.A., La Chaux-de-Fonds, Switzerland. Panes of 50. Designed by Robert Perrot.

1961, Oct. 24	**Photo.**	**Unwmk.**	**Perf. 11½**	
95 A47 4c **ultramarine, orange, yellow & brown** (2,044,842)			.20	.20
First day cover				1.00
Inscription block of 4			.30	—

96 A47 11c **emerald, orange, yellow & brown**			
(1,790,894)		.25	.20
First day cover			1.00
First day cover, #95-96			1.00
Inscription block of 4		1.10	—

First day covers of Nos. 95 and 96 total 435,131.

Mother Bird Feeding Young and UNICEF Seal — A48

Designs: 3c, Spanish inscription. 13c, French inscription.
15th anniversary of the United Nations Children's Fund.
Printed by Courvoisier S.A., La Chaux-de-Fonds, Switzerland. Panes of 50. Designed by Minoru Hisano.

1961, Dec. 4	**Photo.**	**Unwmk.**	**Perf. 11½**	
97 A48 3c **brown, gold, orange & yellow**				
(2,867,456)			.20	.20
First day cover				1.00
Inscription block of 4			.25	—
98 A48 4c **brown, gold, blue & emerald**				
(2,735,899)			.20	.20
First day cover				1.00
Inscription block of 4			.35	—
99 A48 13c **deep green, gold, purple & pink**				
(1,951,715)			.20	.20
First day cover				1.00
First day cover, #97-99				1.40
Inscription block of 4			1.25	—
Nos. 97-99 (3)			.60	.60

First day covers of Nos. 97-99 total 752,979.

Family and Symbolic Buildings A49

Design: 7c, inscribed "Services Collectifs".
Issued to publicize the UN program for housing and urban development, and in connection with the expert committee meeting at UN headquarters, Feb. 7-21.
Printed by Harrison and Sons, Ltd., London, England. Panes of 50. Designed by Olav Mathiesen.

1962, Feb. 28	**Photo.**	**Unwmk.**	**Perf. 14½x14**	
	Central design multicolored			
100 A49 4c **bright blue** (2,204,190)			.20	.20
First day cover				1.00
Inscription block of 4			.35	—
a.	Black omitted		200.00	
b.	Yellow omitted			
c.	Brown omitted			
101 A49 7c **orange brown** (1,845,821)			.20	.20
First day cover				1.00
First day cover, #100-101				1.25
Inscription block of 4			.65	—
a.	Red omitted			
b.	Black omitted			
c.	Gold omitted			

First day covers of Nos. 100-101 total 466,178.

"The World Against Malaria" — A50

Issued in honor of the World Health Organization and to call attention to the international campaign to eradicate malaria from the world.

Printed by Harrison and Sons, Ltd., London, England. Panes of 50. Designed by Rashid-ud Din.

1962, Mar. 30   Photo.   Unwmk.   Perf. 14x14½
Word frame in gray
102 A50 4c orange, yellow, brown, green &
           black *(2,047,000)* .20 .20
         First day cover 1.00
         Inscription block of 4 .35 —
103 A50 11c green, yellow, brown & indigo
           (1,683,766) .25 .20
         First day cover 1.00
         First day cover, #102-103 1.50
         Inscription block of 4 1.10 —
    First day covers of Nos. 102-103 total 522,450.

"Peace" — A51

UN Flag — A52

Hands Combining "UN" and Globe — A53

UN Emblem over Globe — A54

Printed by Harrison & Sons, Ltd. London, England (1c, 3c and 11c), and by Canadian Bank Note Co., Ltd., Ottawa (5c). Panes of 50. Designed by Kurt Plowitz (1c), Ole Hamann (3c), Renato Ferrini (5c) and Olav Mathiesen (11c).

Photo.; Engr. (5c)
1962, May 25   Unwmk.   Perf. 14x14½
104 A51 1c vermilion, blue, black & gray
           (5,000,000) .20 .20
         First day cover 1.00
         Inscription block of 4 .25 —
105 A52 3c light green, Prussian blue, yellow
           & gray *(5,000,000)* .20 .20
         First day cover 1.00
         Inscription block of 4 .25 —
Perf. 12
106 A53 5c dark carmine rose *(4,000,000)* .20 .20
         First day cover 1.00
         Inscription block of 4 .65 —
Perf. 12½
107 A54 11c dark & light blue & gold
           (4,400,000) .25 .20
         First day cover 1.00
         First day cover, #104-107 6.00
         Inscription block of 4 1.10 —
         Nos. 104-107 (4) .85 .80
    First day covers of Nos. 104-107 total 738,985.
Size of 5c, No. 106: 36½x23½mm.
See No. 167. See UN Offices in Geneva Nos. 2 and 6.

Flag at Half-mast and UN Headquarters — A55

World Map Showing Congo — A56

Issued on the 1st anniversary of the death of Dag Hammarskjold, Secretary General of the United Nations 1953-61, in memory of those who died in the service of the United Nations.
    Printed by Courvoisier S. A., La Chaux-de-Fonds, Switzerland. Panes of 50. Designed by Ole Hamann.

1962, Sept. 17   Photo.   Unwmk.   Perf. 11½
108 A55 5c black, light blue & blue *(2,195,707)* .20 .20
         First day cover 1.00
         Inscription block of 4 .50 —
109 A55 15c black, gray olive & blue
           (1,155,047) .20 .20
         First day cover 1.00
         First day cover, #108-109 2.00
         Inscription block of 4 .85 —
    First day covers of Nos. 108-109 total 513,963.

1962, Oct. 24   Photo.   Unwmk.   Perf. 11½
Design: 11c inscribed "Operation des Nations Unies au Congo."
    Issued to commemorate the United Nations Operation in the Congo.
    Printed by Courvoisier S. A., La Chaux-de-Fonds, Switzerland. Panes of 50. Designed by George Hamori.
110 A56 4c olive, orange, black & yellow
           (1,477,958) .20 .20
         First day cover 1.00
         Inscription block of 4 .50 —
111 A56 11c blue green, orange, black & yellow
           (1,171,255) .20 .20
         First day cover 1.00
         First day cover, #110-111 1.75
         Inscription block of 4 .95 —
    First day covers of Nos. 110-111 total 460,675.

Globe in Universe and Palm Frond — A57

Development Decade Emblem — A58

Design: 4c, English inscription.
    Issued to honor the Committee on Peaceful Uses of Outer Space.
    Printed by Bradbury, Wilkinson and Co., Ltd., England. Panes of 50. Designed by Kurt Plowitz.

1962, Dec. 3   Engr.   Unwmk.   Perf. 14x13½
112 A57 4c violet blue *(2,263,876)* .20 .20
         First day cover 1.00
         Inscription block of 4 .35 —
113 A57 11c rose claret *(1,681,584)* .25 .20
         First day cover 1.00
         First day cover, #112-113 2.00
         Inscription block of 4 1.25 —
    First day covers of Nos. 112-113 total 529,780.

1963, Feb. 4   Photo.   Unwmk.   Perf. 11½
Design: 11c, French inscription.
    UN Development Decade and UN Conference on the Application of Science and Technology for the Benefit of the Less Developed Areas, Geneva, Feb. 4-20.
    Printed by Courvoisier S. A., La Chaux-de-Fonds, Switzerland. Panes of 50. Designed by Rashid-ud Din.
114 A58 5c pale green, maroon, dark blue &
           Prussian blue *(1,802,406)* .20 .20
         First day cover 1.00
         Inscription block of 4 .35 —

115 A58 11c yellow, maroon, dark blue & Prus-
           sian blue *(1,530,190)* .20
         First day cover 1.00
         First day cover, #114-115
         Inscription block of 4 .90
    First day covers of Nos. 114-115 total 460,877.

Stalks of Wheat — A59

Design: 11c, French inscription.
    Issued for the "Freedom from Hunger" campaign of the Food and Agriculture Organization.
    Printed by Courvoisier S. A., La Chaux-de-Fonds, Switzerland. Panes of 50. Designed by Ole Hamann.

1963, Mar. 22   Photo.   Unwmk.   Perf. 11
116 A59 5c vermilion, green & yellow
           (1,666,178) .20
         First day cover
         Inscription block of 4 .35
117 A59 11c vermilion, deep claret & yellow
           (1,563,023) .25
         First day cover
         First day cover, #116-117
         Inscription block of 4 1.10
    First day covers of Nos. 116-117 total 461,868.

Bridge over Map of New Guinea — A60

1st anniversary of the United Nations Temporary Executive Authority (UNTEA) in West New Guinea (West Irian).
    Printed by Courvoisier S.A., La Chaux-de-Fonds, Switzerland. Panes of 50. Designed by Henry Bencsath.

1963, Oct. 1   Photo.   Unwmk.   Perf. 11
118 A60 25c blue, green & gray *(1,427,747)* .45
         First day cover *(222,280)* 1.
         Inscription block of 4 2.00

General Assembly Building, New York — A61

Design: 11c, French inscription.
    Since October 1955 all sessions of the General Assembly have been held in the General Assembly Hall, UN Headquarters, NY.
    Printed by the Government Printing Bureau, Tokyo. Panes of 50. Designed by Kurt Plowitz.

1963, Nov. 4   Photo.   Unwmk.   Perf. 11
119 A61 5c violet blue, blue, yellow green &
           red *(1,892,539)* .20 .2
         First day cover 1.0
         Inscription block of 4 .35
120 A61 11c green, yellow green, blue, yellow
           & red *(1,435,079)* .20 .2
         First day cover 1.0
         First day cover, #119-120 1.2
         Inscription block of 4 .85
    First day covers of Nos. 119-120 total 410,306.

Flame — A62

esign: 11c inscribed "15e Anniversaire."
5th anniversary of the signing of the Universal Declaration of
an Rights.
inted by the Government Printing Bureau, Tokyo. Panes of
Designed by Rashid-ud Din.

3, Dec. 10   Photo.   Unwmk.   Perf. 13
A62	5c **green, gold, red & yellow**	.20	.20
	(2,208,008)		
	First day cover		1.00
	Inscription block of 4	.55	—
A62	11c **carmine, gold, blue & yellow**	.20	.20
	(1,501,125)		
	First day cover		1.00
	First day cover, #121-122		1.00
	Inscription block of 4	.70	—

First day covers of Nos. 121-122 total 567,907.

Ships at Sea and
IMCO
Emblem — A63

esign: 11c, inscribed "OMCI."
ssued to honor the Intergovernmental Maritime Consultative
anization.
inted by Courvoisier S.A., La Chaux-de-Fonds, Switzer-
d. Panes of 50. Designed by Henry Bencsath; emblem by
v Mathiesen.

64, Jan. 13   Photo.   Unwmk.   Perf. 11½
A63	5c **blue, olive, ocher & yellow**	.20	.20
	(1,805,750)		
	First day cover		1.00
	Inscription block of 4	.35	—
A63	11c **dark blue, dark green, emerald &**	.20	.20
	yellow (1,583,848)		
	First day cover		1.00
	First day cover, #123-124		1.00
	Inscription block of 4	.85	—

First day covers of Nos. 123-124 total 442,696.

World Map,
Sinusoidal
Projection — A64

UN Emblem — A65

Three Men United Before
Globe — A66

Stylized Globe and
Weather
Vane — A67

Printed by Thomas De La Rue & Co. Ltd., London (2c) and
ourvoisier S.A., La Chaux-de-Fonds, Switzerland (7c, 10c and
0c). Panes of 50.
Designed by Ole Hamann (2c), George Hamori (7c, 10c) and
atim El Mekki (50c).

964-71   Photo.   Unwmk.   Perf. 14
25	A64	2c **light & dark blue, orange & yellow**	.20	.20
		green (3,800,000)		
		First day cover		1.00
		Inscription block of 4	.20	—
a.		Perf. 13x13½, Feb. 24, 1971 (1,500,000)	.20	.20

Perf. 11½
26	A65	7c **dark blue, orange brown & black**	.20	.20
		(2,700,000)		
		First day cover		1.00

	Inscription block of 4	.80	—
127 A66	10c **blue green, olive green & black**	.20	.25
	(3,200,000)		
	First day cover		1.00
	First day cover, #125-127		5.00
	Inscription block of 4	.80	—
128 A67	50c **multicolored** (2,520,000)	.75	.45
	First day cover (210,713)		1.00
	Inscription block of 4	3.75	—
	Nos. 125-128 (4)	1.35	1.10

Issue dates: 50c, Mar. 6; 2c, 7c, 10c, May 29, 1964.
First day covers of 2c, 7c and 10c total 524,073.
See UN Offices in Geneva Nos. 3 and 12.

Arrows
Showing
Global Flow of
Trade — A68

Design: 5c, English inscription.
Issued to commemorate the UN Conference on Trade and
Development, Geneva, Mar. 23-June 15.
Printed by Thomas De La Rue & Co., Ltd., London. Panes of
50. Designed by Herbert M. Sanborn and Ole Hamann.

1964, June 15   Photo.   Unwmk.   Perf. 13
129 A68	5c **black, red & yellow** (1,791,211)	.20	.20
	First day cover		1.00
	Inscription block of 4	.35	—
130 A68	11c **black, olive & yellow** (1,529,526)	.20	.20
	First day cover		1.00
	First day cover, #129-130		1.50
	Inscription block of 4	.85	—

First day covers of Nos. 129-130 total 422,358.

Poppy
Capsule and
Reaching
Hands — A69

Design: 11c, Inscribed "Echec au Stupéfiants."
Issued to honor international efforts and achievements in the
control of narcotics.
Printed by the Canadian Bank Note Co., Ottawa. Panes of 50.
Designed by Kurt Plowitz.

1964, Sept. 21   Engr.   Unwmk.   Perf. 12
131 A69	5c **rose red & black** (1,508,999)	.20	.20
	First day cover		1.00
	Inscription block of 4	.45	—
132 A69	11c **emerald & black** (1,340,691)	.20	.20
	First day cover		1.00
	First day cover, #131-132		1.75
	Inscription block of 4	1.10	—

First day covers of Nos. 131-132 total 445,274.

Padlocked Atomic
Blast — A70

Education for
Progress — A71

Signing of the nuclear test ban treaty pledging an end to
nuclear explosions in the atmosphere, outer space and under
water.
Printed by Artia, Prague, Czechoslovakia.   Panes of 50.
Designed by Ole Hamann.

Litho. and Engr.
1964, Oct. 23   Unwmk.   Perf. 11x11½
133 A70	5c **dark red & dark brown** (2,422,789)	.20	.20
	First day cover (298,652)		1.00
	Inscription block of 4	.45	—

1964, Dec. 7   Photo.   Unwmk.   Perf. 12½

Design: 11c, French inscription.
Issued to publicize the UNESCO world campaign for universal literacy and for free compulsory primary education.
Printed by Courvoisier, S. A., La Chaux-de-Fonds, Switzerland. Panes of 50. Designed by Kurt Plowitz.

134 A71	4c **orange, red, bister, green & blue**	.20	.20
	(2,375,181)		
	First day cover		1.00
	Inscription block of 4	.25	—
135 A71	5c **bister, red, dark & light blue**	.20	.20
	(2,496,877)		
	First day cover		1.00
	Inscription block of 4	.35	—
136 A71	11c **green, light blue, black & rose**	.20	.20
	(1,773,645)		
	First day cover		1.00
	First day cover, #134-136		1.25
	Inscription block of 4	.75	—
	Nos. 134-136 (3)	.60	.60

First day covers of Nos. 134-136 total 727,875.

Progress Chart of
Special Fund, Key
and Globe — A72

UN Emblem, Stylized
Leaves and View of
Cyprus — A73

Design: 11c, French inscription.
Issued to publicize the Special Fund program to speed economic growth and social advancement in low-income countries.
Printed by the Government Printing Bureau, Tokyo. Panes of
50. Designed by Rashid-ud Din, Pakistan.

1965, Jan. 25   Photo.   Unwmk.   Perf. 13½x13
137 A72	5c **dull blue, dark blue, yellow & red**	.20	.20
	(1,949,274)		
	First day cover		1.00
	Inscription block of 4	.40	—
138 A72	11c **yellow green, dark blue, yellow &**	.20	.20
	red (1,690,908)		
	First day cover		1.00
	First day cover, #137-138		1.25
	Inscription block of 4	.85	—
a.	Black omitted (UN emblem on key)		

First day covers of Nos. 137-138 total 490,608.

1965, Mar. 4   Photo.   Unwmk.   Perf. 11½

Design: 11c, French inscription.
Issued to honor the United Nations Peace-keeping Force on
Cyprus.
Printed by Courvoisier S.A., Switzerland. Panes of 50.
Designed by George Hamori, Australia.

139 A73	5c **orange, olive & black** (1,887,042)	.20	.20
	First day cover		1.00
	Inscription block of 4	.40	—
140 A73	11c **yellow green, blue green & black**	.20	.20
	(1,691,767)		
	First day cover		1.00
	First day cover, #139-140		1.25
	Inscription block of 4	.80	—

First day covers of Nos. 139-140 total 438,059.

"From Semaphore
to Satellite" — A74

Design: 11c, French inscription.
Centenary of the International Telecommunication Union.
Printed by Courvoisier S.A., Switzerland. Panes of 50.
Designed by Kurt Plowitz, United States.

1965, May 17   Photo.   Unwmk.   Perf. 11½
141 A74 5c **aquamarine, orange, blue & purple**
                  (2,432,407)   .20   .20
           First day cover   1.00
           Inscription block of 4   .40   —
142 A74 11c **light violet, red orange, bister &**
                  bright green *(1,731,070)*   .20   .20
           First day cover   1.00
           First day cover, #141-142   1.25
           Inscription block of 4   .80   —

       First day covers of Nos. 141-142 total 434,393.

ICY Emblem — A75

Design: 15c, French inscription.
20th anniversary of the United Nations and International
Cooperation Year.
Printed by Bradbury, Wilkinson and Co., Ltd., England. Panes
of 50. Designed by Olav Mathiesen, Denmark.

1965, June 26   Engr.   Unwmk.   Perf. 14x13½
143 A75 5c **dark blue** *(2,282,452)*   .20   .20
           First day cover   1.00
           Inscription block of 4   .40   —
144 A75 15c **lilac rose** *(1,993,562)*   .20   .20
           First day cover   1.00
           First day cover, #143-144   1.00
           Inscription block of 4   1.00 —

                      Souvenir Sheet
145 A75 Sheet of two *(1,928,366)*   .35   .35
           First day cover   1.00

No. 145 contains one each of Nos. 143-144 with dark blue
and ocher marginal inscription, ocher edging. Size: 92x70mm.
First day covers of Nos. 143-145 total: New York, 748,876;
San Francisco, 301,435.

"Peace" — A76

Opening Words, UN
Charter — A77

UN Headquarters and
Emblem — A78

UN Emblem — A79

UN Emblem
Encircled — A80

Printed by Government Printing Bureau, Tokyo (1c); Govern-
ment Printing Office, Austria (15c, 20c); Government Printing
Office (Bundesdruckerei), Berlin (25c), and Courvoisier S.A.,
Switzerland ($1). Panes of 50.

Designed by Kurt Plowitz US (1c); Olav S. Mathiesen, Denmark (15c); Vergniaud Pierre-Noel, US (20c); Rashid-ud Din,
Pakistan (25c), and Ole Hamann, Denmark ($1).

1965-66   Photo.   Unwmk.   Perf. 13½x13
146 A76 1c **vermilion, blue, black & gray**
                  (7,000,000)   .20   .20
           First day cover   1.00
           Inscription block of 4   .20
                      Perf. 14
147 A77 15c **olive bister, dull yellow, black &**
                  deep claret *(2,500,000)*   .25   .20
           First day cover   1.00
           Inscription block of 4   1.10
                      Perf. 12
148 A78 20c **dark blue, blue, red & yellow**
                  (3,000,000)   .30   .25
           First day cover   1.00
           First day cover, #147-148   1.25
           Inscription block of 4   1.25
    a.   Yellow omitted
              Litho. and Embossed
                      Perf. 14
149 A79 25c **light & dark blue** *(3,200,000)*   .35   .30
           First day cover   1.25
           First day cover, #146, 149   1.50
           Inscription block of 4   1.50
           Inscription block of 6,
              "Bundesdruckerei Berlin" imprint 20.00
           First day cover, "Bundesdrucker-
              ei," margin block of 6   32.50
    a.   Tagged (Berlin printing)   20.00 20.00
                      Photo.
                      Perf. 11½
150 A80 $1 **aquamarine & sapphire**
                  (2,570,000)   1.75 1.60
           First day cover *(181,510)*   2.00
           Inscription block of 4   7.75
                  Nos. 146-150 (5)   2.85 2.55

Issued: 1c, 25c, Sept. 20, 1965; 15c, 20c, Oct. 25, 1965; $1,
Mar. 25, 1966.
First day covers of Nos. 146 and 149 total 443,964. Those of
Nos. 147-148 total 457,596.
The 25c has the marginal inscription (UN emblem and
"1965") in two sizes: 1st printing, 6mm in diameter; 2nd printing, 8mm. In 1st printing, "halo" of
UN emblem is larger, overlapping "25c."
See UN Offices in Geneva Nos. 5, 9 and 11.

Fields and
People — A81

Globe and Flags of UN
Members — A82

Design: 11c, French inscription.
Issued to emphasize the importance of the world's population
growth and its problems and to call attention to population
trends and development.
Printed by Government Printing Office, Austria. Panes of 50.
Designed by Olav S. Mathiesen, Denmark.

1965, Nov. 29   Photo.   Unwmk.   Perf. 12
151 A81 4c **multicolored** *(1,966,033)*   .20   .20
           First day cover   1.00
           Inscription block of 4   .25
152 A81 5c **multicolored** *(2,298,731)*   .20   .20
           First day cover   1.00
           Inscription block of 4   .30
153 A81 11c **multicolored** *(1,557,589)*   .20   .20
           First day cover   1.00
           First day cover, #151-153   1.75
           Inscription block of 4   .90
                  Nos. 151-153 (3)   .60   .60

       First day covers of Nos. 151-153 total 710,507.

1966, Jan. 31   Photo.   Unwmk.   Perf. 11½
Design: 15c, French inscription.
Issued to honor the World Federation of United Nations
Associations.

Printed by Courvoisier S.A., Switzerland. Panes of
Designed by Olav S. Mathiesen, Denmark.
154 A82 5c **multicolored** *(2,462,215)*   .20
           First day cover   .35
155 A82 15c **multicolored** *(1,643,661)*   .20
           First day cover
           First day cover, #154-155
           Inscription block of 4   .90

       First day covers of Nos. 154-155 total 474,154.

WHO Headquarte
Geneva — A83

Design: 11c, French inscription.
Issued to commemorate the opening of the World He
Organization Headquarters, Geneva.
Printed by Courvoisier, S.A., Switzerland. Panes of
Designed by Rashid-ud Din.

1966, May 26   Photo.   Perf. 12½
                      Granite Paper
156 A83 5c **lt & dk blue, orange, green & bis-**
                  ter *(2,079,893)*   .20
           First day cover
           Inscription block of 4   .45
157 A83 11c **orange, lt & dark blue, green &**
                  bister *(1,879,879)*   .20
           First day cover
           First day cover, #156-157
           Inscription block of 4   .90

       First day covers of Nos. 156-157 total 466,171.

Coffee — A84

UN Observer — A85

Design: 11c, Spanish inscription.
Issued to commemorate the International Coffee Agreeme
of 1962.
Printed by the Government Printing Bureau, Tokyo. Panes
50. Designed by Rashid-ud Din, Pakistan.

1966, Sept. 19   Photo.   Perf. 13½x
158 A84 5c **orange, lt blue, green, red & dk**
                  brown *(2,020,308)*   .20
           First day cover
           Inscription block of 4   .40
159 A84 11c **lt blue, yellow, green, red & dk**
                  brown *(1,888,682)*   .20
           First day cover   1.
           First day cover, #158-159   1.
           Inscription block of 4   .90

       First day covers of Nos. 158-159 total 435,886.

1966, Oct. 24   Photo.   Perf. 11

Issued to honor the Peace Keeping United Nation Observe
Printed by Courvoisier, S.A. Panes of 50. Designed by Ole
Hamann.

                      Granite Paper
160 A85 15c **steel blue, orange, black & green**
                  (1,889,809)   .25   1.
           First day cover *(255,326)*   1.0
           Inscription block of 4   1.40

Children of Various
Races — A86

Designs: 5c, Children riding in locomotive and tender. 11c, children in open railroad car playing medical team (French inscription).
20th anniversary of the United Nations Children's Fund (UNICEF).
Printed by Thomas De La Rue & Co., Ltd. Panes of 50. Designed by Kurt Plowitz.

1966, Nov. 28   Litho.   Perf. 13x13½
161 A86 4c pink & multi (2,334,989)   .20 .20
   First day cover   1.00
   Inscription block of 4   .30   —
162 A86 5c pale green & multi (2,746,941) .20 .20
   First day cover   1.00
   Inscription block of 4   .35   —
 a. Yellow omitted   —   —
163 A86 11c light ultramarine & multi
            (2,123,841)   .20 .20
   First day cover   1.00
   First day cover, #161-163   1.00
   Inscription block of 4   .85   —
 b. Dark blue omitted   —   —
        Nos. 161-163 (3)   .60 .60
   First day covers of Nos. 161-163 total 987,271.

Hand Rolling up
Sleeve and Chart
Showing
Progress — A87

Design: 11c, French inscription.
United Nations Development Program.
Printed by Courvoisier, S.A. Panes of 50. Designed by Olav S. Mathiesen.

1967, Jan. 23   Photo.   Perf. 12½
164 A87 5c green, yellow, purple & orange
            (2,204,679)   .20 .20
   First day cover   1.00
   Inscription block of 4   .35   —
165 A87 11c blue, chocolate, light green & or-
            ange (1,946,159)   .20 .20
   First day cover   1.00
   First day cover, #164-165   1.00
   Inscription block of 4   1.00 —
   First day covers of Nos. 164-165 total 406,011.

Type of 1962 and

UN Headquarters, NY, and
World Map — A88

Printed by Courvoisier, S.A. Panes of 50. Designed by Jozsef Vertel, Hungary (1½c); Renato Ferrini, Italy (5c).

1967   Photo.   Perf. 11½
166 A88 1½c ultramarine, black, orange &
            ocher (4,000,000)   .20 .20
   First day cover (199,751)   1.00
   Inscription block of 4   .20   —

Size: 33x23mm
167 A53 5c red brown, brown & orange yel-
            low (5,500,000)   .20 .20
   First day cover (212,544)   1.00
   Inscription block of 4   .40   —
   Issue dates: 1½c, Mar. 17; 5c, Jan. 23.
   For 5c of type A88, see UN Offices in Geneva No. 1.

Fireworks — A89

Design: 11c, French inscription.
Issued to honor all nations which gained independence since 1945.
Printed by Harrison & Sons, Ltd. Panes of 50. Designed by Rashid-ud Din.

1967, Mar. 17   Photo.   Perf. 14x14½
168 A89 5c dark blue & multi (2,445,955)   .20 .20
   First day cover   1.00
   Inscription block of 4   .35   —
169 A89 11c brown lake & multi (2,011,004) .20 .20
   First day cover   1.00
   First day cover, #168-169   1.00
   Inscription block of 4   .85   —
   First day covers of Nos. 168-169 total 390,499.

"Peace" — A90

UN Pavilion, EXPO
'67 — A91

Designs: 5c, Justice. 10c, Fraternity. 15c, Truth.
EXPO '67, International Exhibition, Montreal, Apr. 28-Oct. 27, 1967.
Under special agreement with the Canadian Government Nos. 170-174 were valid for postage only on mail posted at the UN pavilion during the Fair. The denominations are expressed in Canadian currency.
Printed by British American Bank Note Co., Ltd., Ottawa. The 8c was designed by Olav S. Mathiesen after a photograph by Michael Drummond. The others were adapted by Ole S. Hamann from reliefs by Ernest Cormier on doors of General Assembly Hall, presented to UN by Canada.

1967, Apr. 28   Engr. & Litho.   Perf. 11
170 A90 4c red & red brown (2,464,813)   .20 .20
   First day cover   1.00
   Inscription block of 4   .20   —
171 A90 5c blue & red brown (2,177,073)   .20 .20
   First day cover   1.00
   Inscription block of 4   .20   —
Litho.
172 A91 8c multicolored (2,285,440)   .20 .20
   First day cover   1.00
   Inscription block of 4   .35   —
Engr. and Litho.
173 A90 10c green & red brown (1,955,352) .20 .20
   First day cover   1.00
   Inscription block of 4   .50   —
174 A90 15c dark brown & red brown
            (1,899,185)   .20 .20
   First day cover   1.00
   First day cover, #170-174   1.25
   Inscription block of 4   .60   —
        Nos. 170-174 (5)   1.00 1.00
   First day covers of Nos. 170-174 total 901,625.

Luggage
Tags and UN
Emblem
A92

Issued to publicize International Tourist Year, 1967.
Printed by Government Printing Office, Berlin. Panes of 50. Designed by David Dewhurst.

1967, June 19   Litho.   Perf. 14
175 A92 5c reddish brown & multi (2,593,782) .20 .20
   First day cover   1.00
   Inscription block of 4   .35   —
176 A92 15c ultramarine & multi (1,940,457) .25 .20
   First day cover   1.00
   First day cover, #175-176   1.25
   Inscription block of 4   1.10 —
   First day covers of Nos. 175-176 total 382,886.

Quotation from
Isaiah 2:4 — A93

Design: 13c, French inscription.
Issued to publicize the UN General Assembly's resolutions on general and complete disarmament and for suspension of nuclear and thermonuclear tests.
Printed by Heraclio Fournier S.A., Spain. Panes of 50. Designed by Ole Hamann.

1967, Oct. 24   Photo.   Perf. 14
177 A93 6c ultramarine, yellow, gray & brown
            (2,462,277)   .20 .20
   First day cover   1.00
   Inscription block of 4   .45   —
178 A93 13c magenta, yellow, gray & brown
            (2,055,541)   .20 .20
   First day cover   1.00
   First day cover, #177-178   1.00
   Inscription block of 4   .95   —
   First day covers of Nos. 177-178 total 403,414.

Art at UN Issue
Miniature Sheet

Stained Glass Memorial Window by Marc Chagall, at
UN Headquarters — A94

"The Kiss of Peace" by
Marc Chagall — A95

Printed by Joh. Enschede and Sons, Netherlands. No. 180 issued in panes of 50. Design adapted by Ole Hamann from photograph by Hans Lippmann.
   Sizes: a, 41x46mm. b, 24x46mm. c, 41x33½mm. d, 36x33½mm. e, 29x33½mm. f, 41½x47mm.

1967, Nov. 17   Litho.   Rouletted 9
179 A94   6c Sheet of 6, #a.-f. (3,178,656)   .40   .40
                First day cover   1.00

Perf. 13x13½
180 A95   6c multicolored (3,438,497)   .20   .20
                First day cover   1.00
                Inscription block of 4   .50   —

No. 179 contains six 6c stamps, each rouletted on 3 sides, imperf. on fourth side. Size: 124x80mm. On Nos. 179a-179c, "United Nations 6c" appears at top; on Nos. 179d-179f, at bottom. No. 179f includes name "Marc Chagall."
First day covers of Nos. 179-180 total 617,225.

Globe and Major UN Organs — A96

Statue by Henrik Starcke — A97

Design: 13c, French inscriptions.
Issued to honor the United Nations Secretariat.
Printed by Courvoisier, S. A., Switzerland. Panes of 50. Designed by Rashid-ud Din.

1968, Jan. 16   Photo.   Perf. 11½
181 A96   6c multicolored (2,772,965)   .20   .20
                First day cover   1.00
                Inscription block of 4   .40   —
182 A96 13c multicolored (2,461,992)   .20   .20
                First day cover   1.00
                First day cover, #181-182   1.00
                Inscription block of 4   .90   —

First day covers of Nos. 181-182 total 411,119.

Art at UN Issue

The 6c is part of the "Art at the UN" series. The 75c belongs to the regular definitive series. The teakwood Starcke statue, which stands in the Trusteeship Council Chamber, represents mankind's search for freedom and happiness.
Printed by Courvoisier, S.A., Switzerland. Panes of 50.

1968, Mar. 1   Photo.   Perf. 11½
183 A97   6c blue & multi (2,537,320)   .20   .20
                First day cover   1.00
                Inscription block of 4   .50   —
184 A97 75c rose lake & multi (2,300,000)   1.10   .90
                First day cover   1.25
                First day cover, #183-184   5.00
                Inscription block of 4   4.00   —

First day covers of Nos. 183-184 total 413,286.
See UN Offices in Geneva No. 13.

Factories and Chart — A98

UN Headquarters — A99

Design: 13c, French inscription ("ONUDI," etc.).
Issued to publicize the UN Industrial Development Organization.
Printed by Canadian Bank Note Co., Ltd., Ottawa. Panes of 50. Designed by Ole Hamann.

1968, Apr. 18   Litho.   Perf. 12
185 A98   6c greenish blue, lt greenish blue,
              black & dull claret (2,439,656) .20   .20
                First day cover   1.00
                Inscription block of 4   .35   —
186 A98 13c dull red brown, light red brown,
              black & ultra (2,192,453)   .20   .20
                First day cover   1.00
                First day cover, #185-186   1.00
                Inscription block of 4   .80   —

First day covers of Nos. 185-186 total 396,447.

1968, May 31   Litho.   Perf. 12x13½
Printed by Aspioti Elka-Chrome Mines, Ltd., Athens. Panes of 50. Designed by Olav S. Mathiesen.

187 A99   6c green, blue, black & gray
              (4,000,000)   .20   .20
                First day cover (241,179)   1.00
                Inscription block of 4   .50   —

Radarscope and Globe — A100

Design: 20c, French inscription.
Issued to publicize World Weather Watch, a new weather system directed by the World Meteorological Organization.
Printed by the Government Printing Bureau, Tokyo. Designed by George A. Gundersen and George Fanais, Canada.

1968, Sept. 19   Photo.   Perf. 13x13½
188 A100   6c green, black, ocher, red & blue
               (2,245,078)   .20   .20
                First day cover   1.00
                Inscription block of 4   .40   —
189 A100 20c lilac, black, ocher, red & blue
               (2,069,966)   .30   .20
                First day cover   1.00
                First day cover, #188-189   1.25
                Inscription block of 4   1.25   —

First day covers of Nos. 188-189 total 620,510.

Human Rights Flame — A101

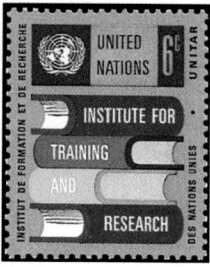

Books and UN Emblem — A102

Design: 13c, French inscription.
Issued for International Human Rights Year, 1968.
Printed by Harrison & Sons, Ltd., England. Designed by Robert Perrot, France.

1968, Nov. 22   Photo.; Foil Embossed   Perf. 12
190 A101   6c bright blue, deep ultra & gold
               (2,394,235)   .20
                First day cover   1.00
                Inscription block of 4   .40
191 A101 13c rose red, dark red & gold
               (2,284,838)   .20
                First day cover   1.00
                First day cover, #190-191   1.00
                Inscription block of 4   .85

First day covers of Nos. 190-191 total 519,012.

1969, Feb. 10   Litho.   Perf. 13
Design: 13c, French inscription in center, denomination panel at bottom.
United Nations Institute for Training and Research (UNITAR).
Printed by the Government Printing Bureau, Tokyo. Panes of 50. Designed by Olav S. Mathiesen.

192 A102   6c yellow green & multi (2,436,559) .20
                First day cover   1.00
                Inscription block of 4   .35
193 A102 13c bluish lilac & multi (1,935,151) .25
                First day cover   1.00
                First day cover, #192-193   1.00
                Inscription block of 4   1.00

First day covers of Nos. 192-193 total 439,606.

UN Building, Santiago, Chile A103

Design: 15c, Spanish inscription.
The UN Building in Santiago, Chile, is the seat of the UN Economic Commission for Latin America and of the Latin American Institute for Economic and Social Planning.
Printed by Government Printing Office, Berlin. Panes of 50. Design by Ole Hamann, adapted from a photograph.

1969, Mar. 14   Litho.   Perf. 11
194 A103   6c light blue, violet blue & light
               green (2,543,992)   .20   .20
                First day cover   1.00
                Inscription block of 4   .35   —
195 A103 15c pink, cream & red brown
               (2,030,733)   .25   .20
                First day cover   1.00
                First day cover, #194-195   1.00
                Inscription block of 4   1.10   —

First day covers of Nos. 194-195 total 398,227.

"UN" and UN Emblem — A104

UN Emblem and Scales of — A105

Printed by Government Printing Bureau, Tokyo. Panes of 50. Designed by Leszek Holdanowicz and Marek Freudenreich, Poland.

69, Mar. 14 **Photo.** *Perf. 13½*

A104	13c	bright blue, black & gold	.20	.20
		(4,000,000)		
		First day cover (177,793)		1.00
		Inscription block of 4	.90	—

See UN Offices in Geneva No. 7.

69, Apr. 21 **Photo.** *Perf. 11½*

Design: 13c, French inscription.
20th anniversary session of the UN International Law Commission.
Printed by Courvoisier S.A., Switzerland. Panes of 50. Designed by Robert Perrot, France.

Granite Paper

A105	6c	bright green, ultra & gold	.20	.20
		(2,501,492)		
		First day cover		1.00
		Inscription block of 4	.40	—
A105	13c	crimson, lilac & gold (1,966,994)	.20	.20
		First day cover		1.00
		First day cover, #197-198		1.00
		Inscription block of 4	.90	—

First day covers of Nos. 197-198 total 439,324.

Allegory of Labor, Emblems of UN and ILO — A106

Design: 20c, French inscription.
Printed by Government Printing Bureau, Tokyo. Panes of 50. Designed by Nejat M. Gur, Turkey.
Issued to publicize "Labor and Development" and to commemorate the 50th anniversary of the International Labor Organization.

69, June 5 **Photo.** *Perf. 13*

9	A106	6c	blue, deep blue, yellow & gold	.20	.20
		(2,078,381)		
		First day cover		1.00
		Inscription block of 4	.40	—
0	A106	20c	orange vermilion, magenta, yellow & gold (1,751,100)	.25	.20
		First day cover		1.00
		First day cover, #199-200		1.25
		Inscription block of 4	1.25	—

First day covers of Nos. 199-200 total 514,155.

Art at UN Issue

Ostrich, Tunisian Mosaic, 3rd Century — A107

Design: 13c, Pheasant; French inscription.
The mosaic "The Four Seasons and the Genius of the Year" was found at Haidra, Tunisia. It is now at the Delegates' North Lounge, UN Headquarters, New York.
Printed by Heraclio Fournier, S. A., Spain. Panes of 50. Designed by Olav S. Mathiesen.

969, Nov. 21 **Photo.** *Perf. 14*

01	A107	6c	blue & multi (2,280,702)	.20	.20
		First day cover		1.00
		Inscription block of 4	.35	—
02	A107	13c	red & multi (1,918,554)	.20	.20
		First day cover		1.00
		First day cover, #201-202		1.00
		Inscription block of 4	.90	—

First day covers of Nos. 201-202 total 612,981.

Art at UN Issue

Peace Bell, Gift of Japanese — A108

Design: 25c, French inscription.
The Peace Bell was a gift of the people of Japan in 1954, cast from donated coins and metals. It is housed in a Japanese cypress structure at UN Headquarters, New York.
Printed by Government Printing Bureau, Tokyo. Panes of 50. Designed by Ole Hamann.

1970, Mar. 13 **Photo.** *Perf. 13½x13*

203	A108	6c	violet blue & multi (2,604,253)	.20	.20
		First day cover		1.00
		Inscription block of 4	.35	—
204	A108	25c	claret & multi (2,090,185)	.35	.25
		First day cover		1.25
		First day cover, #203-204		1.25
		Inscription block of 4	1.60	—

First day covers of Nos. 203-204 total 502,384.

Mekong River, Power Lines and Map of Mekong Delta — A109

Design: 13c, French inscription.
Issued to publicize the Lower Mekong Basin Development project under UN auspices.
Printed by Heraclio Fournier, S.A., Spain. Panes of 50. Designed by Ole Hamann.

1970, Mar. 13 *Perf. 14*

205	A109	6c	dark blue & multi (2,207,309)	.20	.20
		First day cover		1.00
		Inscription block of 4	.35	—
206	A109	13c	deep plum & multi (1,889,023)	.20	.20
		First day cover		1.00
		First day cover, #205-206		1.00
		Inscription block of 4	.90	—

First day covers of Nos. 205-206 total 522,218.

"Fight Cancer" — A110

Design: 13c, French inscription.
Issued to publicize the fight against cancer in connection with the 10th International Cancer Congress of the International Union Against Cancer, Houston, Texas, May 22-29.
Printed by Government Printing Office, Berlin. Panes of 50. Designed by Leonard Mitchell.

1970, May 22 **Litho.** *Perf. 14*

207	A110	6c	blue & black (2,157,742)	.20	.20
		First day cover		1.00
		Inscription block of 4	.35	—
208	A110	13c	olive & black (1,824,714)	.20	.20
		First day cover		1.00
		First day cover, #207-208		1.00
		Inscription block of 4	.85	—

First day covers of Nos. 207-208 total 444,449.

UN Emblem and Olive Branch — A111

UN Emblem — A112

Design: 13c, French inscription.
25th anniv. of the UN. First day covers were postmarked at UN Headquarters, NY, and at San Francisco.
Printed by Courvoisier, S.A., Switzerland. Designed by Ole Hamann and Olav S. Mathiesen (souvenir sheet).

1970, June 26 **Photo.** *Perf. 11½*

209	A111	6c	red, gold, dark & light blue	.20	.20
		(2,365,229)		
		First day cover		1.00
		Inscription block of 4	.35	—
210	A111	13c	dark blue, gold, green & red	.20	.20
		(1,861,613)		
		First day cover		1.00
		Inscription block of 4	.80	—

Perf. 12½

211	A112	25c	dark blue, gold & light blue	.35	.25
		(1,844,669)		
		First day cover		1.25
		First day cover, #209-211		1.50
		Inscription block of 4	1.50	—
		Nos. 209-211 (3)	.75	.65

Souvenir Sheet
Imperf

212		Sheet of 3 (1,923,639)	.75	.75
a.	A111 6c	red, gold & multicolored	.20	.20
b.	A111 13c	violet blue, gold & multi	.20	.20
c.	A112 25c	violet blue, gold & light blue	.35	.35
		First day cover		1.25

No. 212 contains 3 imperf. stamps, gold border and violet blue marginal inscription. Size: 94½x78mm.
First day covers of Nos. 209-212 total: New York, 846,389; San Francisco, 471,100.

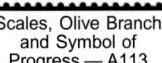

Scales, Olive Branch and Symbol of Progress — A113

Sea Bed, School of Fish and Underwater Research — A114

Design: 13c, French inscription.
Issued to publicize "Peace, Justice and Progress" in connection with the 25th anniversary of the United Nations.
Printed by Government Printing Bureau, Tokyo. Panes of 50. Designed by Ole Hamann.

1970, Nov. 20 **Photo.** *Perf. 13½*

213	A113	6c	gold & multi (1,921,441)	.20	.20
		First day cover		1.00
		Inscription block of 4	.40	—
214	A113	13c	silver & multi (1,663,669)	.20	.20
		First day cover		1.00
		First day cover, #213-214		1.00
		Inscription block of 4	1.00	—

First day covers of Nos. 213-214 total 521,419.

1971, Jan. 25 **Photo. & Engr.** *Perf. 13*

Issued to publicize peaceful uses of the sea bed.
Printed by Setelipaino, Finland. Panes of 50. Designed by Pentti Rahikainen, Finland.

215	A114	6c	blue & multi (2,354,179)	.20	.20
		First day cover (405,554)		1.00
		Inscription block of 4	.50	—

See UN Offices in Geneva No. 15.

Refugees, Sculpture
by Kaare K.
Nygaard — A115

Wheat and Globe — A116

International support for refugees.
Printed by Joh. Enschede and Sons, Netherlands. Panes of
50. Designed by Dr. Kaare K. Nygaard and Martin J. Weber.

1971, Mar. 2   Litho.   Perf. 13x12½
216 A115 6c brown, ocher & black (2,247,232) .20 .20
             First day cover   1.00
             Inscription block of 4   .30   —
217 A115 13c ultramarine, greenish blue &
             black (1,890,048)   .20 .20
             First day cover   1.00
             First day cover, #216-217   1.00
             Inscription block of 4   .90   —

    First day covers of Nos. 216-217 total 564,785.
    See UN Offices in Geneva No. 16.

1971, Apr. 13   Photo.   Perf. 14

Publicizing the UN World Food Program.
Printed by Heraclio Fournier, S.A., Spain. Panes of 50.
Designed by Olav S. Mathiesen.

218 A116 13c red & multicolored (1,968,542) .20 .20
             First day cover (409,404)   1.00
             Inscription block of 4   .90   —

    See UN Offices in Geneva No. 17.

UPU
Headquarters,
Bern — A117

Opening of new Universal Postal Union Headquarters, Bern.
Printed by Courvoisier, S.A. Panes of 50. Designed by Olav
S. Mathiesen.

1971, May 28   Photo.   Perf. 11½
219 A117 20c brown orange & multi (1,857,841) .35 .25
             First day cover (375,119)   1.00
             Inscription block of 4   1.40   —

    See UN Offices in Geneva No. 18.

A118

"Eliminate Racial
Discrimination"
A119

International Year Against Racial Discrimination.
Printed by Government Printing Bureau, Tokyo. Panes of 50.
Designers: Daniel Gonzague (8c); Ole Hamann (13c).

1971, Sept. 21   Photo.   Perf. 13½
220 A118 8c yellow green & multi (2,324,349) .20 .20
             First day cover   1.00
             Inscription block of 4   .60   —
221 A119 13c blue & multi (1,852,093)   .20 .20
             First day cover   1.00
             First day cover, #220-221   1.00
             Inscription block of 4   .90   —

    First day covers of Nos. 220-221 total 461,103.
    See UN Offices in Geneva Nos. 19-20.

UN
Headquarters,
New
York — A120

UN Emblem
and Symbolic
Flags — A121

No. 222 printed by Heraclio Fournier, S.A., Spain. No. 223
printed by Government Printing Bureau, Tokyo. Panes of 50.
Designers: O. S. Mathiesen (8c); Robert Perrot (60c).

1971, Oct. 22   Photo.   Perf. 13½
222 A120 8c violet blue & multi (5,600,000)   .20 .20
             First day cover   1.00
             Inscription block of 4   .60   —
                          Perf. 13
223 A121 60c ultra & multi (3,500,000)+   .80 .80
             First day cover   1.25
             First day cover, #222-223   3.00
             Inscription block of 4   3.50   —

    First day covers of Nos. 222-223 total 336,013.

Maia, by Pablo
Picasso — A122

To publicize the UN International School.
Printed by Courvoisier, S.A. Panes of 50. Designed by Ole
Hamann.

1971, Nov. 19   Photo.   Perf. 11½
224 A122 8c olive & multi (2,668,214)   .20 .20
             First day cover   1.00
             Inscription block of 4   .45   —
225 A122 21c ultra & multi (2,040,754)   .30 .20
             First day cover   1.00
             First day cover, #224-225   1.75
             Inscription block of 4   1.40   —

    First day covers of Nos. 224-225 total 579,594.
    See UN Offices in Geneva No. 21.

Letter
Changing
Hands
A123

Printed by Bundesdruckerei, Berlin. Panes of 50. Design
by Olav S. Mathiesen.

1972, Jan. 5   Litho.   Perf.
226 A123 95c carmine & multi (2,000,000)   1.30
             First day cover (188,193)
             Inscription block of 4   5.50

"No More
Nuclear
Weapons"
A124

To promote non-proliferation of nuclear weapons.
Printed by Heraclio Fournier, S. A., Spain. Panes of
Designed by Arne Johnson, Norway.

1972, Feb. 14   Photo.   Perf. 13½x
227 A124 8c dull rose, black, blue & gray
             (2,311,515)   .20
             First day cover (268,789)
             Inscription block of 4   .55

    See UN Offices in Geneva No. 23.

Proportions of Man, by
Leonardo da
Vinci — A125

"Human
Environment" — A126

World Health Day, Apr. 7.
Printed by Setelipaino, Finland. Panes of 50. Designed
George Hamori.

1972, Apr. 7   Litho. & Engr.   Perf. 13x13
228 A125 15c black & multi (1,788,962)   .25
             First day cover (322,724)   1.
             Inscription block of 4   1.00

    See UN Offices in Geneva No. 24.

1972, June 5   Litho. & Embossed   Perf. 12½x1

UN Conf. on Human Environment, Stockholm, June 5-1
1972.
Printed by Joh. Enschede and Sons, Netherlands. Panes
50. Designed by Robert Perrot.

229 A126 8c red, buff, green & blue
             (2,124,604)   .20
             First day cover   1.
             Inscription block of 4   .50
230 A126 15c blue green, buff, green & blue
             (1,589,943)   .25
             First day cover   1.
             First day cover, #229-230   1.
             Inscription block of 4   1.25

    First day covers of Nos. 229-230 total 437,222.
    See UN Offices in Geneva Nos. 25-26.

"Europe" and UN
Emblem — A127

The Five Continents by
José Maria Sert — A128

Economic Commission for Europe, 25th anniversary.
Printed by Government Printing Bureau, Tokyo. Panes of 50.
Designed by Angel Medina Medina.

1972, Sept. 11   Litho.   Perf. 13x13½
A127 21c **yellow brown & multi** (1,748,675)   .35   .25
   First day cover (271,128)   1.00
   Inscription block of 4   1.60   —

See UN Offices in Geneva No. 27.

Art at UN Issue

Design shows part of ceiling mural of the Council Hall, Palais
Nations, Geneva. It depicts the five continents joining in
peace.
Printed by Courvoisier, S. A. Panes of 50. Designed by Ole
Hamann.

1972, Nov. 17   Photo.   Perf. 12x12½
A128 8c **gold, brown & golden brown**
   (2,573,478)   .20   .20
   First day cover   .50
   Inscription block of 4   .50   —
A128 15c **gold, blue green & brown**
   (1,768,432)   .30   .20
   First day cover   1.00
   First day cover, #232-233   1.00
   Inscription block of 4   1.25   —

First day covers of Nos. 232-233 total 589,817.
See UN Offices in Geneva Nos. 28-29.

Olive Branch and
Broken
Sword — A129

Poppy Capsule and
Skull — A130

Disarmament Decade, 1970-79.
Printed by Ajans-Turk, Turkey. Panes of 50. Designed by Kurt
Schwitz.

1973, Mar. 9   Litho.   Perf. 13½x13
234 A129 8c **blue & multi** (2,272,716)   .20   .20
   First day cover   1.00
   Inscription block of 4   .50   —
235 A129 15c **lilac rose & multi** (1,643,712)   .35   .20
   First day cover   1.00
   First day cover, #234-235   1.00
   Inscription block of 4   1.50   —

First day covers of Nos. 234-235 total 548,336.
See UN Offices in Geneva Nos. 30-31.

1973, Apr. 13   Photo.   Perf. 13½
Fight against drug abuse.
Printed by Heraclio Fournier, S.A., Spain. Panes of 50.
Designed by George Hamori.

236 A130 8c **deep orange & multi** (1,846,780)   .20   .20
   First day cover   1.00
   Inscription block of 4   .60   —
237 A130 15c **pink & multi** (1,466,806)   .35   .25

First day cover   1.00
First day cover, #236-237   1.00
Inscription block of 4   1.50   —

First day covers of Nos. 236-237 total 394,468.
See UN Offices in Geneva No. 32.

Honeycomb — A131

5th anniversary of the United Nations Volunteer Program.
Printed by Heraclio Fournier, S.A., Spain. Panes of 50.
Designed by Courvoisier, S.A.

1973, May 25   Photo.   Perf. 14
238 A131 8c **olive bister & multi** (1,868,176)   .20   .20
   First day cover   1.00
   Inscription block of 4   .50   —
239 A131 21c **gray blue & multi** (1,530,114)   .35   .25
   First day cover   1.00
   First day cover, #238-239   1.25
   Inscription block of 4   1.50   —

First day covers of Nos. 238-239 total 396,517.
See UN Offices in Geneva No. 33.

Map of Africa with
Namibia — A132

To publicize Namibia (South-West Africa) for which the UN
General Assembly ended the mandate of South Africa and
established the UN Council for Namibia to administer the terri-
tory until independence.
Printed by Heraclio Fournier, S.A., Spain. Panes of 50.
Designed by George Hamori.

1973, Oct. 1   Photo.   Perf. 14
240 A132 8c **emerald & multi** (1,775,260)   .20   .20
   First day cover   1.00
   Inscription block of 4   .50   —
241 A132 15c **bright rose & multi** (1,687,782)   .35   .25
   First day cover   1.00
   First day cover, #240-241   1.00
   Inscription block of 4   1.50   —

First day covers of Nos. 240-241 total 385,292.
See UN Offices in Geneva No. 34.

UN Emblem and
Human Rights
Flame — A133

25th anniversary of the adoption and proclamation of the
Universal Declaration of Human Rights.
Printed by Government Printing Bureau, Tokyo. Panes of 50.
Designed by Alfred Guerra.

1973, Nov. 16   Photo.   Perf. 13½
242 A133 8c **deep carmine & multi** (2,026,245)   .20   .20
   First day cover   1.00
   Inscription block of 4   .50   —
243 A133 21c **blue green & multi** (1,558,201)   .35   .25
   First day cover   1.00
   First day cover, #242-243   1.25
   Inscription block of 4   1.50   —

First day covers of Nos. 242-243 total 398,511.
See UN Offices in Geneva Nos. 35-36.

ILO Headquarters,
Geneva — A134

New Headquarters of International Labor Organization.
Printed by Heraclio Fournier, S.A., Spain. Panes of 50.
Designed by Henry Bencsath.

1974, Jan. 11   Photo.   Perf. 14
244 A134 10c **ultra & multi** (1,734,423)   .20   .20
   First day cover   1.00
   Inscription block of 4   .90   —
245 A134 21c **blue green & multi** (1,264,447)   .35   .25
   First day cover   1.00
   First day cover, #244-245   1.25
   Inscription block of 4   1.75   —

First day covers of Nos. 244-245 total 282,284.
See UN Offices in Geneva Nos. 37-38.

UPU Emblem
and Post Horn
Encircling
Globe — A135

Centenary of Universal Postal Union.
Printed by Ashton-Potter Ltd., Canada. Panes of 50.
Designed by Arne Johnson.

1974, Mar. 22   Litho.   Perf. 12½
246 A135 10c **gold & multi** (2,104,919)   .25   .20
   First day cover (342,774)   1.00
   Inscription block of 4   1.10   —

See UN Offices in Geneva Nos. 39-40.

Art at UN Issue

Peace Mural, by
Candido
Portinari — A136

The mural, a gift of Brazil, is in the Delegates' Lobby, General
Assembly Building.
Printed by Heraclio Fournier, S.A., Spain. Panes of 50.
Design adapted by Ole Hamann.

1974, May 6   Photo.   Perf. 14
247 A136 10c **gold & multi** (1,769,342)   .20   .20
   First day cover   1.00
   Inscription block of 4   .75   —
248 A136 18c **ultra & multi** (1,477,500)   .40   .30
   First day cover   1.00
   First day cover, #247-248   1.25
   Inscription block of 4   1.50   —

First day covers of Nos. 247-248 total 271,440.
See UN Offices in Geneva Nos. 41-42.

Dove and UN
Emblem — A137

UN
Headquarters — A138

Globe, UN Emblem,
Flags — A139

Printed by Heraclio Fournier, S.A., Spain. Panes of 50.
Designed by Nejut M. Gur (2c); Olav S. Mathiesen (10c);
Henry Bencsath (18c).

1974, June 10　　　Photo.　　　Perf. 14
249 A137 2c dark & light blue (6,900,000)　.20　.20
　　First day cover　　　　　　　　　　1.00
　　Inscription block of 4　　　　　.25
250 A138 10c multicolored (4,000,000)　.20　.20
　　First day cover　　　　　　　　　　1.00
　　Inscription block of 4　　　　　.70
251 A139 18c multicolored (2,300,000)　.30　.20
　　First day cover　　　　　　　　　　1.00
　　First day cover, #249-251　　　　　1.25
　　Inscription block of 4　　　　1.50
　　Nos. 249-251 (3)　　　　　.70　.60

First day covers of Nos. 249-251 total 307,402.
+ Printing orders to Feb. 1990.

Children of the
World — A140　　　Law of the Sea — A141

World Population Year
Printed by Heraclio Fournier, S.A., Spain. Panes of 50.
Designed by Henry Bencsath.

1974, Oct. 18　　　Photo.　　　Perf. 14
252 A140 10c light blue & multi (1,762,595)　.20　.20
　　First day cover　　　　　　　　　　1.00
　　Inscription block of 4　　　　1.00
253 A140 18c lilac & multi (1,321,574)　.40　.25
　　First day cover　　　　　　　　　　1.00
　　First day cover, #252-253　　　　　1.25
　　Inscription block of 4　　　　1.75

First day covers of Nos. 253-254 total 354,306.
See UN Offices in Geneva Nos. 43-44.

1974, Nov. 22　　　Photo.　　　Perf. 14

Declaration of UN General Assembly that the sea bed is
common heritage of mankind, reserved for peaceful purposes.
Printed by Heraclio Fournier, S.A., Spain. Panes of 50.
Designed by Asher Kalderon.

254 A141 10c green & multi (1,621,328)　.20　.20
　　First day cover　　　　　　　　　　1.00
　　Inscription block of 4　　　　.80
255 A141 26c orange red & multi (1,293,084)　.40　.30
　　First day cover　　　　　　　　　　1.25
　　First day cover, #254-255　　　　　1.40
　　Inscription block of 4　　　　1.90

First day covers of Nos. 254-255 total 280,686.
See UN Offices in Geneva No. 45.

Satellite and
Globe — A142

Peaceful uses (meteorology, industry, fishing, communications) of outer space.
Printed by Setelipaino, Finland. Panes of 50. Designed by Henry Bencsath.

1975, Mar. 14　　　Litho.　　　Perf. 13
256 A142 10c multicolored (1,681,115)　.20　.20
　　First day cover　　　　　　　　　　1.00
　　Inscription block of 4　　　　.85
257 A142 26c multicolored (1,463,130)　.40　.30
　　First day cover　　　　　　　　　　1.25
　　First day cover, #256-257　　　　　1.40
　　Inscription block of 4　　　　1.75

First day covers of Nos. 256-257 total 330,316.
See UN Offices in Geneva Nos. 46-47.

Equality Between
Men and
Women — A143

UN Flag and
"XXX" — A144

International Women's Year
Printed by Questa Colour Security Printers, Ltd., England.
Panes of 50. Designed by Asher Kalderon and Esther Kurti.

1975, May 9　　　Litho.　　　Perf. 15
258 A143 10c multicolored (1,402,542)　.20　.20
　　First day cover　　　　　　　　　　1.00
　　Inscription block of 4　　　　.80
259 A143 18c multicolored (1,182,321)　.40　.30
　　First day cover　　　　　　　　　　1.00
　　First day cover, #258-259　　　　　1.25
　　Inscription block of 4　　　　1.75

First day covers of Nos. 258-259 total 285,466.
See UN Offices in Geneva Nos. 48-49.

1975, June 26　　　Litho.　　　Perf. 13

30th anniversary of the United Nations.
Printed by Ashton-Potter, Ltd., Canada. Nos. 260-261 panes of 50. Stamps designed by Asher Calderon, sheets by Olav S. Mathiesen.

260 A144 10c olive bister & multi (1,904,545)　.20　.20
　　First day cover　　　　　　　　　　1.00
　　Inscription block of 4　　　　.70
261 A144 26c purple & multi (1,547,766)　.50　.35
　　First day cover　　　　　　　　　　1.25
　　First day cover, #260-261　　　　　1.40
　　Inscription block of 4　　　　2.25

Souvenir Sheet
Imperf
262　　Sheet of 2 (1,196,578)　.65　.50
a.　A144 10c olive bister & multicolored　.20　.20
b.　A144 26c purple & multicolored　.40　.25
　　First day cover　　　　　　　　　　1.25

No. 262 has blue and bister margin with inscription and UN emblem.
First day covers of Nos. 260-262 total: New York 477,912; San Francisco, 237,159.
See Offices in Geneva Nos. 50-52.

Hand Reaching up over
Map of Africa and
Namibia — A145　　　Wild Rose Growing from
Barbed Wire — A146

"Namibia-United Nations direct responsibility." See note after No. 241.
Printed by Heraclio Fournier S.A., Spain. Panes of 50. Designed by Henry Bencsath.

1975, Sept. 22　　　Photo.　　　Perf. 13½
263 A145 10c multicolored (1,354,374)　.20　.20
　　First day cover　　　　　　　　　　1.00
　　Inscription block of 4　　　　.80
264 A145 18c multicolored (1,243,157)　.35　.30
　　First day cover　　　　　　　　　　1.00
　　First day cover, #263-264　　　　　1.25
　　Inscription block of 4　　　　1.60

First day covers of Nos. 263-264 total 281,631.
See UN Offices in Geneva Nos. 53-54.

1975, Nov. 21　　　Engr.　　　Perf. 12½

United Nations Peace-keeping Operations
Printed by Setelipaino, Finland. Panes of 50. Designed by Mrs. Eeva Oivo.

265 A146 13c ultramarine (1,628,039)　.25　.20
　　First day cover　　　　　　　　　　1.00
　　Inscription block of 4　　　　1.00
266 A146 26c rose carmine (1,195,580)　.50　.40

First day cover, #265-266
Inscription block of 4　　　　2.00
First day covers of Nos. 265-266 total 303,711.
See UN Offices in Geneva Nos. 55-56.

Symbolic Flags Forming
Dove — A147　　　UN Emblem — A14

People of All
Races
A148

United Nations
Flag — A150　　　Dove and
Rainbow — A151

Printed by Ashton-Potter, Ltd., Canada (3c, 4c, 30c, 50c), Questa Colour Security Printers, Ltd., England (9c). Pane 50.
Designed by Waldemar Andrzesewski (3c); Arne John (4c); George Hamori (9c, 30c); Arthur Congdon (50c).

1976　　　Litho.　　　Perf. 13x13½, 13½x
267 A147 3c multicolored (4,000,000)　　.20
　　First day cover
　　Inscription block of 4　　　.25
268 A148 4c multicolored (4,000,000)　　.20
　　First day cover
　　Inscription block of 4　　　.30
Photo.
Perf. 14
269 A149 9c multicolored (3,270,000)+　　.20
　　First day cover
　　Inscription block of 4　　　.6
Litho.
Perf. 13x13½
270 A150 30c blue, emerald & black (2,500,000)　.40
　　First day cover
　　Inscription block of 4　　　1.75
271 A151 50c yellow green & multi (2,000,000)　.70
　　First day cover
　　First day cover, #267-268, 270-271　　1.25
　　Inscription block of 4　　　3.25
　　Nos. 267-271 (5)　　　1.70　—

Issue dates: 3c, 4c, 30c, 50c, Jan. 6; 9c, Nov. 19.
First day covers of Nos. 267-268, 270-271 total 355,165;
Nos. 269 and 280 total 366,556.
See UN Offices in Vienna No. 8.

c United Nations   Interlocking Bands and UN Emblem — A152

World Federation of United Nations Associations.
Printed by Heraclio Fournier, S.A., Spain. Panes of 50.
Designed by George Hamori.

1976, Mar. 12   Photo.   Perf. 14
A152 13c **blue, green & black** *(1,331,556)* .20 .20
First day cover 1.00
Inscription block of 4 .80
A152 26c **green & multi** *(1,050,145)* .35 .30
First day cover 1.25
First day cover, #272-273 1.25
Inscription block of 4 1.60

First day covers of Nos. 272-273 total 300,775.
See UN Offices in Geneva No. 57.

Cargo, Globe and Graph — A153   Houses Around Globe — A154

UN Conference on Trade and Development (UNCTAD), Nairobi, Kenya, May 1976.
Printed by Courvoisier, S.A. Panes of 50. Designed by Henry Bencsath.

1976, Apr. 23   Photo.   Perf. 11½
A153 13c **deep magenta & multi** *(1,317,900)* .20 .20
First day cover 1.00
Inscription block of 4 .80
A153 31c **dull blue & multi** *(1,216,959)* .40 .30
First day cover 1.25
First day cover, #274-275 1.40
Inscription block of 4 1.90

First day covers of Nos. 274-275 total 234,657.
See UN Offices in Geneva No. 58.

1976, May 28   Photo.   Perf. 14
Habitat, UN Conference on Human Settlements, Vancouver, Canada, May 31-June 11.
Printed by Heraclio Fournier, S.A., Spain. Panes of 50. Designed by Eliezer Weishoff.
A154 13c **red brown & multi** *(1,346,589)* .20 .20
First day cover 1.00
Inscription block of 4 .75
A154 25c **green & multi** *(1,057,924)* .40 .30
First day cover 1.25
First day cover, #276-277 1.40
Inscription block of 4 1.75

First day covers of Nos. 276-277 total 232,754.
See UN Offices in Geneva Nos. 59-60.

Magnifying Glass, Sheet of Stamps, UN Emblem — A155

Grain — A156

United Nations Postal Administration, 25th anniversary.
Printed by Courvoisier, S.A. Designed by Henry Bencsath.

1976, Oct. 8   Photo.   Perf. 11½
278 A155 13c **blue & multi** *(1,996,309)* .20 .20
First day cover 1.00
Inscription block of 4 .90
279 A155 31c **green & multi** *(1,767,465)* 1.40 1.40
First day cover 2.00
First day cover, #278-279 2.50
Inscription block of 4 6.25
Panes of 20, #278-279 32.50

First day covers of Nos. 278-279 total 366,784.
Upper margin blocks are inscribed "XXV ANNIVERSARY"; lower margin blocks "UNITED NATIONS POSTAL ADMINISTRATIONS."
See UN Offices in Geneva Nos. 61-62.

1976, Nov. 19   Litho.   Perf. 14½
World Food Council.
Printed by Questa Colour Security Printers, Ltd., England. Panes of 50. Designed by Eliezer Weishoff.
280 A156 13c **multicolored** *(1,515,573)* .25 .20
First day cover 1.00
Inscription block of 4 1.10

See UN Offices in Geneva No. 63.

WIPO Headquarters, Geneva A157

World Intellectual Property Organization (WIPO).
Printed by Heraclio Fournier, S. A., Spain. Panes of 50. Designed by Eliezer Weishoff.

1977, Mar. 11   Photo.   Perf. 14
281 A157 13c **citron & multi** *(1,330,272)* .20 .20
First day cover 1.00
Inscription block of 4 .75
282 A157 31c **bright green & multi** *(1,115,406)* .45 .35
First day cover 1.25
First day cover, #281-282 1.25
Inscription block of 4 2.00

First day covers of Nos. 281-282 total 364,184.
See UN Offices in Geneva No. 64.

Drops of Water Falling into Funnel — A158

UN Water Conference, Mar del Plata, Argentina, Mar. 14-25.
Printed by Government Printing Bureau, Tokyo. Panes of 50. Designed by Elio Tomei.

1977, Apr. 22   Photo.   Perf. 13½x13
283 A158 13c **yellow & multi** *(1,317,536)* .20 .20
First day cover 1.00
Inscription block of 4 .75
284 A158 25c **salmon & multi** *(1,077,424)* .45 .35
First day cover 1.25
First day cover, #283-284 1.40
Inscription block of 4 2.00

First day covers of Nos. 283-284 total 321,585.
See UN Offices in Geneva Nos. 65-66.

Burning Fuse Severed — A159

UN Security Council.
Printed by Heraclio Fournier, S.A., Spain. Panes of 50. Designed by Witold Janowski and Marek Freudenreich.

1977, May 27   Photo.   Perf. 14
285 A159 13c **purple & multi** *(1,321,527)* .20 .20
First day cover 1.00
Inscription block of 4 .75
286 A159 31c **dark blue & multi** *(1,137,195)* .45 .30
First day cover 1.25
First day cover, #285-286 1.40
Inscription block of 4 2.00

First day covers of Nos. 285-286 total 309,610.
See UN Offices in Geneva Nos. 67-68.

"Combat Racism" — A160

Fight against racial discrimination.
Printed by Setelipaino, Finland. Panes of 50. Designed by Bruno K. Wiese.

1977, Sept. 19   Litho.   Perf. 13½x13
287 A160 13c **black & yellow** *(1,195,739)* .20 .20
First day cover 1.00
Inscription block of 4 .75
288 A160 25c **black & vermilion** *(1,074,639)* .40 .30
First day cover 1.25
First day cover, #287-288 1.40
Inscription block of 4 1.75

First day covers of Nos. 287-288 total 356,193.
See UN Offices in Geneva Nos. 60-70.

Atom, Grain, Fruit and Factory — A161

Peaceful uses of atomic energy.
Printed by Heraclio Fournier, S.A., Spain. Panes of 50. Designed by Henry Bencsath.

1977, Nov. 18   Photo.   Perf. 14
289 A161 13c **yellow bister & multi** *(1,316,473)* .20 .20
First day cover 1.00
Inscription block of 4 .90
290 A161 18c **dull green & multi** *(1,072,246)* .35 .25
First day cover 1.00
First day cover, #289-290 1.25
Inscription block of 4 1.50

First day covers of Nos. 289-290 total 325,348.
See UN Offices in Geneva Nos. 71-72.

Opening Words of UN Charter — A162

"Live Together in Peace" — A163

People of the World — A164

Printed by Questa Colour Security Printers, United Kingdom. Panes of 50. Designed by Salahattin Kanidinc (1c); Elio Tomei (25c); Paula Schmidt ($1).

1978, Jan. 27   **Litho.**   *Perf. 14½*
291 A162 1c **gold, brown & red** *(4,800,000)*+   .20   .20
    First day cover   1.00
    Inscription block of 4   .25
292 A163 25c **multicolored** *(3,000,000)*+   .35   .30
    First day cover   1.25
    Inscription block of 4   1.50
293 A164 $1 **multicolored** *(3,400,000)*+   1.25   1.25
    First day cover   1.50
    First day cover, #291-293   1.75
    Inscription block of 4   5.50
    Nos. 291-293 (3)   1.80   1.75

+ Printing orders to Sept. 1989.
First day covers of Nos. 291-293 total 264,782.
See UN Offices in Geneva No. 73.

Smallpox Virus — A165

Global eradication of smallpox.
Printed by Courvoisier, S.A. Panes of 50. Designed by Herbert Auchli.

1978, Mar. 31   **Photo.**   *Perf. 12x11½*
294 A165 13c **rose & black** *(1,188,239)*   .20   .20
    First day cover   1.00
    Inscription block of 4   .75
295 A165 31c **blue & black** *(1,058,688)*   .45   .40
    First day cover   1.25
    First day cover, #294-295   1.40
    Inscription block of 4   2.00

First day covers of Nos. 294-295 total 306,626.
See UN Offices in Geneva Nos. 74-75.

Open Handcuff — A166

Multicolored Bands and Clouds — A167

Liberation, justice and cooperation for Namibia.
Printed by Government Printing Office, Austria. Panes of 50. Designed by Cafiro Tomei.

1978, May 5   **Photo.**   *Perf. 12*
296 A166 13c **multicolored** *(1,203,079)*   .20   .20
    First day cover   1.00
    Inscription block of 4   1.00
297 A166 18c **multicolored** *(1,066,738)*   .30   .25
    First day cover   1.00
    First day cover, #296-297   1.25
    Inscription block of 4   1.40

First day covers of Nos. 296-297 total 324,471.
See UN Offices in Geneva No. 76.

1978, June 12   **Photo.**   *Perf. 14*
International Civil Aviation Organization for "Safety in the Air." Printed by Heraclio Fournier, S.A., Spain. Panes of 50. Designed by Cemalettin Mutver.
298 A167 13c **multicolored** *(1,295,617)*   .20   .20
    First day cover   1.00
    Inscription block of 4   .85
299 A167 25c **multicolored** *(1,101,256)*   .40   .30
    First day cover   1.25
    First day cover, #298-299   1.40
    Inscription block of 4   1.75

First day covers of Nos. 298-299 total 329,995.
See UN Offices in Geneva Nos. 77-78.

General Assembly — A168

Printed by Government Printing Bureau, Tokyo. Panes of 50. Designed by Jozsef Vertel.

1978, Sept. 15   **Photo.**   *Perf. 13½*
300 A168 13c **multicolored** *(1,093,005)*   .20   .20
    First day cover   1.00
    Inscription block of 4   1.00
301 A168 18c **multicolored** *(1,065,934)*   .35   .30
    First day cover   1.00
    First day cover, #300-301   1.25
    Inscription block of 4   1.50

First day covers of Nos. 300-301 total 283,220.
See UN Offices in Geneva Nos. 79-80.

Hemispheres as Cogwheels A169

Technical Cooperation Among Developing Countries Conference, Buenos Aires, Argentina, Sept. 1978.
Printed by Heraclio Fournier, S.A., Spain. Panes of 50. Designed by Simon Keter and David Pesach.

1978, Nov. 17   **Photo.**   *Perf. 14*
302 A169 13c **multicolored** *(1,251,272)*   .20   .20
    First day cover   1.00
    Inscription block of 4   1.00
303 A169 31c **multicolored** *(1,185,213)*   .50   .40
    First day cover   1.25
    First day cover, #302-303   1.40
    Inscription block of 4   2.25

First day covers of Nos. 302-303 total 272,556.
See UN Offices in Geneva No. 81.

Hand Holding Olive Branch — A170

Various Races Tree — A171

Globe, Dove with Olive Branch — A172

Birds and Globe — A173

Printed by Heraclio Fournier, S.A., Spain. Panes of 50. Designed by Raymon Müller (5c); Alrun Fricke (14c); Eli Weishoff (15c); Young Sun Hahn (20c).

1979, Jan. 19   **Photo.**   *Perf.*
304 A170 5c **multicolored** *(3,000,000)*   .20
    First day cover
    Inscription block of 4   .35
305 A171 14c **multicolored** *(3,000,000)*+   .20
    First day cover
    Inscription block of 4   .90
306 A172 15c **multicolored** *(3,000,000)*+   .30
    First day cover
    Inscription block of 4   1.40
307 A173 20c **multicolored** *(3,400,000)*+   .30
    First day cover
    First day cover, #304-307
    Inscription block of 4   1.40
    Nos. 304-307 (4)   1.00

First day covers of Nos. 304-307 total 295,927.
+ Printing orders to June 1990.

UNDRO Against Fire and Water — A174

Office of the UN Disaster Relief Coordinator (UNDRO). Printed by Heraclio Fournier, S.A., Spain. Panes of Designed by Gidon Sagi.

1979, Mar. 9   **Photo.**   *Perf.*
308 A174 15c **multicolored** *(1,448,600)*   .25
    First day cover   1.00
309 A174 20c **multicolored** *(1,126,295)*   .35
    First day cover
    First day cover, #308-309
    Inscription block of 4   1.50

First day covers of Nos. 308-309 total 266,694.
See UN Offices in Geneva Nos. 82-83.

Child and IYC Emblem — A175

International Year of the Child.
Printed by Heraclio Fournier, S.A., Spain. Panes of 20 (5x Designed by Helena Matuszewska (15c) and Krystyna Tark-ska-Gruszecka (31c).

1979, May 4   **Photo.**   *Perf.*
310 A175 15c **multicolored** *(2,290,329)*   .20
    First day cover   1
    Inscription block of 4   .90
311 A175 31c **multicolored** *(2,192,136)*   .35
    First day cover   1
    First day cover, #310-311   2
    Inscription block of 4   1.50
    Panes of 20, #310-311   11.50

First day covers of Nos. 310-311 total 380,022.
See UN Offices in Geneva Nos. 84-85.

ap of Namibia, Olive
Branch — A176

Scales and Sword of
Justice — A177

or a free and independent Namibia.
rinted by Ashton-Potter Ltd., Canada. Panes of 50.
signed by Eliezer Weishoff.

79, Oct. 5   **Litho.**   **Perf. 13½**

A176 15c **multicolored** *(1,470,231)*	.20	.20
First day cover		1.00
Inscription block of 4	.95	
A176 31c **multicolored** *(1,355,323)*	.40	.35
First day cover		1.25
First day cover, #312-313		1.50
Inscription block of 4	1.75	—

First day covers of Nos. 312-313 total 250,371.
See UN Offices in Geneva No. 86.

79, Nov. 9   **Litho.**   **Perf. 13x13½**

nternational Court of Justice, The Hague, Netherlands.
rinted by Setelipaino, Finland. Panes of 50. Designed by
nning Simon.

A177 15c **multicolored** *(1,244,972)*	.20	.20
First day cover		1.00
Inscription block of 4	.85	
A177 20c **multicolored** *(1,084,483)*	.40	.35
First day cover		1.00
First day cover, #314-315		1.25
Inscription block of 4	1.75	—

First day covers of Nos. 314-315 total 322,901.
See UN Offices in Geneva Nos. 87-88.

Graph of Economic
Trends — A178

Key — A179

New International Economic Order.
rinted by Questa Colour Security Printers, United Kingdom.
nes of 50. Designed by Cemalettin Mutver (15c), George
mori (31c)

80, Jan. 11   **Litho.**   **Perf. 15x14½**

6 A178 15c **multicolored** *(1,163,801)*	.20	.20
First day cover		1.00
Inscription block of 4	.85	
7 A179 31c **multicolored** *(1,103,560)*	.50	.35
First day cover		1.25
First day cover, #316-317		1.40
Inscription block of 4	2.25	—

First day covers of Nos. 316-317 total 211,945.
See UN Offices in Geneva No. 89; Vienna No. 7.

Women's Year
Emblem — A180

United Nations Decade for Women.
Printed by Questa Colour Security Printers, United Kingdom.
nes of 50. Designed by Susanne Rottenfusser.

980, Mar. 7   **Litho.**   **Perf. 14½x15**

8 A180 15c **multicolored** *(1,409,350)*	.20	.20
First day cover		1.00
Inscription block of 4	1.00	—
9 A180 20c **multicolored** *(1,182,016)*	.30	.25

First day cover		1.00
First day cover, #318-319		1.25
Inscription block of 4	2.00	

First day covers of Nos. 318-319 total 289,314.
See UN Offices in Geneva Nos. 90-91; Vienna Nos. 9-10.

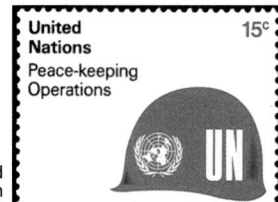

UN Emblem and
"UN" on
Helmet — A181

Arrows and UN
Emblem — A182

United Nations Peace-keeping Operations.
Printed by Joh. Enschede en Zonen, Netherlands. Panes of
50. Designed by Bruno K. Wiese (15c), James Gardiner (31c)

1980, May 16   **Litho.**   **Perf. 14x13**

320 A181 15c **blue & black** *(1,245,521)*	.25	.20
First day cover		1.00
Inscription block of 4	1.00	—
321 A182 31c **multicolored** *(1,191,009)*	.40	.40
First day cover		1.25
First day cover, #320-321		1.40
Inscription block of 4	2.25	—

First day covers of Nos. 320-321 total 208,442.
See UN Offices in Geneva No. 92; Vienna No. 11.

"35" and Flags — A183

Globe and
Laurel — A184

35th Anniversary of the United Nations.
Printed by Ashton-Potter Ltd, Canada. Nos. 322-323, panes
of 50. Designed by Cemalettin Matver (15c), Mian Mohammad
Saeed (31c).

1980, June 26   **Litho.**   **Perf. 13x13½**

322 A183 15c **multicolored** *(1,554,514)*	.20	.20
First day cover		1.00
Inscription block of 4	1.00	—
323 A184 31c **multicolored** *(1,389,606)*	.40	.35
First day cover		1.25
First day cover, #322-323		1.40
Inscription block of 4	2.00	—

Souvenir Sheet
Imperf

324	Sheet of 2 *(1,215,505)*	.70	.60
a.	A183 15c **multicolored**	.20	.20
b.	A184 31c **multicolored**	.40	.40
	First day cover		1.25

First day covers of Nos. 322-324 total: New York, 369,345;
San Francisco, 203,701.
See UN Offices in Geneva Nos. 93-95; Vienna Nos. 12-14.

Flag of
Turkey — A185

Printed by Courvoisier, S.A., Switzerland. Panes of 16.
Designed by Ole Hamann.

Each pane contains 4 blocks of 4 (Nos. 325-328, 329-332,
333-336, 337-340). A se-tenant block of 4 designs centers each
pane.

1980, Sept. 26   **Litho.**   **Perf. 12**
Granite Paper

325 A185 15c shown *(3,490,725)*	.20	.20
326 A185 15c Luxembourg *(3,490,725)*	.20	.20
327 A185 15c Fiji *(3,490,725)*	.20	.20
328 A185 15c Viet Nam *(3,490,725)*	.20	.20
a. Se-tenant block of 4, #325-328	.80	.75
329 A185 15c Guinea *(3,442,633)*	.20	.20
330 A185 15c Surinam *(3,442,633)*	.20	.20
331 A185 15c Bangladesh *(3,442,633)*	.20	.20
332 A185 15c Mali *(3,442,633)*	.20	.20
a. Se-tenant block of 4, #329-332	.80	.75
333 A185 15c Yugoslavia *(3,416,292)*	.20	.20
334 A185 15c France *(3,416,292)*	.20	.20
335 A185 15c Venezuela *(3,416,292)*	.20	.20
336 A185 15c El Salvador *(3,416,292)*	.20	.20
a. Se-tenant block of 4, #333-336	.80	.75
337 A185 15c Madagascar *(3,442,497)*	.20	.20
338 A185 15c Cameroon *(3,442,497)*	.20	.20
339 A185 15c Rwanda *(3,442,497)*	.20	.20
340 A185 15c Hungary *(3,442,497)*	.20	.20
a. Se-tenant block of 4, #337-340	.80	.75
First day covers of Nos. 325-340, each		.75
Set of 4 diff. panes of 16	8.00	
Nos. 325-340 (16)	3.20	3.20

First day covers of Nos. 325-340 total 6,145,595.
See Nos. 350-365, 374-389, 399-414, 425-440, 450-465,
477-492, 499-514, 528-543, 554-569, 690-697, 719-726, 744-
751.

Symbolic
Flowers — A186

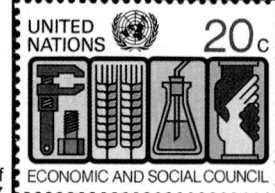

Symbols of
Progress — A187

Printed by Ashton-Potter Ltd., Canada. Panes of 50.
Designed by Eliezer Weishoff (15c), Dietman Kowall (20c).

1980, Nov. 21   **Litho.**   **Perf. 13½x13**

341 A186 15c **multicolored** *(1,192,165)*	.25	.25
First day cover		1.00
Inscription block of 4	1.25	—
342 A187 20c **multicolored** *(1,011,382)*	.40	.35
First day cover		1.00
First day cover, #341-342		1.40
Inscription block of 4	1.75	—

First day covers of Nos. 341-342 total 232,149.
See UN Offices in Geneva, Nos. 96-97; Vienna Nos. 15-16.

Inalienable Rights
of the Palestinian
People — A188

Printed by Courvoisier S.A., Switzerland. Panes of 50.
Designed by David Dewhurst.

1981, Jan. 30   **Photo.**   **Perf. 12x11½**

343 A188 15c **multicolored** *(993,489)*	.25	.20
First day cover *(127,187)*		1.00
Inscription block of 4	1.25	—

See UN Offices in Geneva No. 98; Vienna No. 17.

Interlocking Puzzle
Pieces — A189

Stylized Person — A190

International Year of the Disabled.
Printed by Heraclio Fournier S.A., Spain. Panes of 50.
Designed by Sophia Van Heeswijk (20c) and G.P. Van der Hyde (35c).

1981, Mar. 6　　Photo.　　Perf. 14
344 A189 20c multicolored (1,218,371)　.25　.20
　　First day cover　　　　　1.00
　　Inscription block of 4　　1.25　—
345 A190 35c black & orange (1,107,298)　.50　.45
　　First day cover　　　　　1.25
　　First day cover, #344-345　　1.40
　　Inscription block of 4　　2.25　—
　First day covers of Nos. 344-345 total 204,891.
　See UN Offices in Geneva Nos. 99-100; Vienna Nos. 18-19.

Desislava and
Sebastocrator Kaloyan,
Bulgarian Mural, 1259,
Boyana Church,
Sofia — A191

Art at UN Issue
Printed by Courvoisier. Panes of 50. Designed by Ole Hamann.

1981, Apr. 15　Photo.　Perf. 11½
Granite Paper
346 A191 20c multicolored (1,252,648)　.25　.25
　　First day cover　　　　　1.00
　　Inscription block of 4　　1.40　—
347 A191 31c multicolored (1,061,056)　.45　.45
　　First day cover　　　　　1.25
　　First day cover, #346-347　　1.40
　　Inscription block of 4　　2.00　—
　First day covers of Nos. 346-347 total 210,978.
　See UN Offices in Geneva No. 101; Vienna No. 20.

Solar
Energy — A192

Conference
Emblem — A193

Conference on New and Renewable Sources of Energy, Nairobi, Aug. 10-21.
Printed by Setelipaino, Finland. Panes of 50. Designed by Ulrike Dreyer (20c); Robert Perrot (40c).

1981, May 29　Litho.　Perf. 13
348 A192 20c multicolored (1,132,877)　.30　.25
　　First day cover　　　　　1.00
　　Inscription block of 4　　1.40　—
349 A193 40c multicolored (1,158,319)　.55　.50

First day cover　　　　　1.25
First day cover, #348-349　　1.40
Inscription block of 4　　2.50
　First day covers of Nos. 348-349 total 240,205.
　See UN Offices in Geneva No. 102; Vienna No. 21.

Flag Type of 1980
Printed by Courvoisier, S.A., Switzerland. Panes of 16. Designed by Ole Hamann.
Each pane contains 4 blocks of 4 (Nos. 350-353, 354-357, 358-361, 362-365). A se-tenant block of 4 designs centers each pane.

1981, Sept. 25　　　　　Litho.
Granite Paper
350 A185 20c Djibouti (2,342,224)　.25　.20
351 A185 20c Sri Lanka (2,342,224)　.25　.20
352 A185 20c Bolivia (2,342,224)　.25　.20
353 A185 20c Equatorial Guinea (2,342,224)　.25　.20
　a.　Se-tenant block of 4, #350-353　1.50 1.40
354 A185 20c Malta (2,360,297)　.25　.20
355 A185 20c Czechoslovakia (2,360,297)　.25　.20
356 A185 20c Thailand (2,360,297)　.25　.20
357 A185 20c Trinidad & Tobago (2,360,297)　.25　.20
　a.　Se-tenant block of 4, #354-357　1.50 1.40
358 A185 20c Ukrainian SSR (2,344,755)　.25　.20
359 A185 20c Kuwait (2,344,755)　.25　.20
360 A185 20c Sudan (2,344,755)　.25　.20
361 A185 20c Egypt (2,344,755)　.25　.20
　a.　Se-tenant block of 4, #358-361　1.50 1.40
362 A185 20c US (2,450,537)　.25　.20
363 A185 20c Singapore (2,450,537)　.25　.20
364 A185 20c Panama (2,450,537)　.25　.20
365 A185 20c Costa Rica (2,450,537)　.25　.20
　a.　Se-tenant block of 4, #362-365　1.50 1.40
　　First day covers, #350-365, each　.60
　　Set of 4 diff. panes of 16　14.00
　　Nos. 350-365 (16)　4.00 3.20
　First day covers of Nos. 350-365 total 3,961,237.

Seedling and Tree
Cross-section
A194

"10" and Symbols
of
Progress — A195

United Nations Volunteers Program, 10th anniv.
Printed by Walsall Security Printers, Ltd., United Kingdom. Pane of 50. Designed by Gabriele Nussgen (18c), Angel Medina Medina (28c).

1981, Nov. 13　　　　　Litho.
366 A194 18c multicolored (1,246,833)　.30　.25
　　First day cover　　　　　1.00
　　Inscription block of 4　　1.50　—
367 A195 28c multicolored (1,282,868)　.60　.55
　　First day cover　　　　　1.25
　　First day cover, #366-367　　1.40
　　Inscription block of 4　　2.75　—
　First day covers of Nos. 366-367 total 221,106.
　See UN Offices in Geneva Nos. 103-104; Vienna Nos. 22-23.

A196　　　　A197

A198

Respect for Human Rights (17c), Independence of Colonial Countries and People (28c), Second Disarmament Decade (40c).
Printed by Courvoisier, S.A., Switzerland. Panes of Designed by Rolf Christianson (17c); George Hamori (28 Marek Kwiatkowski (40c).

1982, Jan. 22　　　　Perf. 11½x
368 A196 17c multicolored (3,000,000)+　.30
　　First day cover　　　　　1
　　Inscription block of 4　　1.25
369 A197 28c multicolored (3,000,000)+　.50
　　First day cover　　　　　1
　　Inscription block of 4　　2.25
370 A198 40c multicolored (3,000,000)　.80
　　First day cover　　　　　1
　　First day cover, #368-370　　1
　　Inscription block of 4　　3.50
　　Nos. 368-370 (3)　1.60 1
　First day covers of Nos. 368-370 total 243,073.

Sun and Hand Holding
Seedling — A199

Sun, Plant Land and
Water — A200

10th Anniversary of United Nations Environment Program.
Printed by Joh. Enschede En Zonen, Netherlands. Panes 50. Designed by Philine Hartert (20c); Peer-Ulrich Brem (40c).

1982, Mar. 19　Litho.　Perf. 13½x
371 A199 20c multicolored (1,017,117)　.25　1.
　　First day cover　　　　　1.
　　Inscription block of 4　　1.25
372 A200 40c multicolored (884,798)　.70　1.
　　First day cover　　　　　1.
　　First day cover, #371-372　　1.
　　Inscription block of 4　　3.25
　First day covers of Nos. 371-372 total 288,721.
　See UN Offices in Geneva Nos. 107-108; Vienna Nos. 25-2

UN Emblem and
Olive Branch in
Outer
Space — A201

Exploration and Peaceful Uses of Outer Space.
Printed By Enschede. Panes of 50. Designed by Wiktor C Nerwinski.

1982, June 11　Litho.　Perf. 13x13
373 A201 20c multicolored (1,083,426)　.55　.
　　First day cover (156,965)　　1.
　　Inscription block of 4　　2.40
　See UN Offices in Geneva Nos. 109-110; Vienna No. 27.

Flag Type of 1980
Printed by Courvoisier. Panes of 16. Designed by Ol Hamann.
Issued in 4 panes of 16. Each pane contains 4 blocks of four (Nos. 374-377, 378-381, 383-385, 386-389). A se-tenant block of 4 designs centers each pane.

82, Sept. 24   **Litho.**   *Perf. 12*

Granite Paper

4	A185	20c	Austria (2,314,006)	.25 .20
5	A185	20c	Malaysia (2,314,006)	.25 .20
6	A185	20c	Seychelles (2,314,006)	.25 .20
7	A185	20c	Ireland (2,314,006)	.25 .20
a.			Se-tenant block of 4, #374-377	1.50 1.40
8	A185	20c	Mozambique (2,300,958)	.25 .20
9	A185	20c	Albania (2,300,958)	.25 .20
0	A185	20c	Dominica (2,300,958)	.25 .20
1	A185	20c	Solomon Islnads (2,300,958)	.25 .20
a.			Se-tenant block of 4, #378-381	1.50 1.40
2	A185	20c	Philippines (2,288,589)	.25 .20
3	A185	20c	Swaziland (2,288,589)	.25 .20
4	A185	20c	Nicaragua (2,288,589)	.25 .20
5	A185	20c	Burma (2,288,589)	.25 .20
a.			Se-tenant block of 4, #382-385	1.50 1.40
6	A185	20c	Cape Verde (2,285,848)	.25 .20
7	A185	20c	Guyana (2,285,848)	.25 .20
8	A185	20c	Belgium (2,285,848)	.25 .20
9	A185	20c	Nigeria (2,285,848)	.25 .20
a.			Se-tenant block of 4, #386-389	1.50 1.40
			First day cover, #374-389, each	.75
			Set of 4 diff. panes of 16	16.00
			Nos. 374-389 (16)	4.00 3.20

First day covers of Nos. 374-389 total 3,202,744.

Conservation and Protection of Nature — A202

Printed by Fournier. Panes of 50. Designed by Hamori.

82, Nov. 19   **Photo.**   *Perf. 14*

0	A202	20c	Leaf (1,110,027)	.35 .30
			First day cover	1.00
			margin block of 4, inscription	1.75
1	A202	28c	Butterfly (848,772)	.55 .50
			First day cover	1.25
			First day cover, #390-391	1.40
			Inscription block of 4	2.40 —

First day covers of Nos. 390-391 total 214,148.
See UN Offices in Geneva Nos. 111-112; Vienna Nos. 28-29.

A203

A204

World Communications Year
Printed by Walsall. Panes of 50. Designed by Hanns Lohrer (A203) and Lorena Berengo (A204).

983, Jan. 28   **Litho.**   *Perf. 13*

92	A203	20c	multicolored (1,282,079)	.25 .25
			First day cover	1.00
			Inscription block of 4	1.25 —
93	A204	40c	multicolored (931,903)	.70 .65
			First day cover	1.25
			First day cover, #392-393	1.40
			Inscription block of 4	3.50 —

First day covers of Nos. 392-393 total 183,499.
See UN Offices in Geneva No. 113; Vienna No. 30.

A205

A206

Safety at Sea.
Printed by Questa. Panes of 50. Designed by Jean-Marie Lenfant (A205), Ari Ron (A206).

1983, Mar. 18   **Litho.**   *Perf. 14½*

394	A205	20c	multicolored (1,252,456)	.30 .25
			First day cover	1.00
			Inscription block of 4	1.50 —
395	A206	37c	multicolored (939,910)	.60 .55
			First day cover	1.25
			First day cover, #394-395	1.40
			Inscription block of 4	2.75 —

First day covers of Nos. 394-395 total 199,962.
See UN Offices in Geneva Nos. 114-115; Vienna Nos. 31-32.

World Food Program — A207

Printed by Government Printers Bureau, Japan. Designed by Marek Kwiatkowski.

1983, Apr. 22   **Engr.**   *Perf. 13½*

396	A207	20c	rose lake (1,238,997)	.35 .35
			First day cover (180,704)	1.00
			Inscription block of 4	1.60 —

See UN Offices in Geneva No. 116; Vienna Nos. 33-34.

A208

A209

UN Conference on Trade and Development.
Printed by Carl Uberreuter Druck and Verlag M. Salzer, Austria. Panes of 50. Designed by Dietmar Braklow (A208), Gabriel Genz (A209).

1983, June 6   **Litho.**   *Perf. 14*

397	A208	20c	multicolored (1,060,053)	.35 .35
			First day cover	1.10
			Inscription block of 4	1.50 —
398	A209	28c	multicolored (948,981)	.70 .65
			First day cover	1.40
			First day cover, #397-398	1.50
			Inscription block of 4	2.90 —

First day covers of Nos. 397-398 total 200,131.
See UN Offices in Geneva Nos. 117-118; Vienna Nos. 35-36.

Flag Type of 1980

Printed by Courvoisier. Panes of 16. Designed by Ole Hamann.

Issued in 4 panes of 16. Each pane contains 4 blocks of four (Nos. 399-402, 403-406, 407-410, 411-414). A se-tenant block of 4 designs centers each pane.

1983, Sept. 23   **Photo.**   *Perf. 12*

Granite Paper

399	A185	20c	Great Britain (2,490,599)	.25 .20
400	A185	20c	Barbados (2,490,599)	.25 .20
401	A185	20c	Nepal (2,490,599)	.25 .20
402	A185	20c	Israel (2,490,599)	.25 .20
a.			Se-tenant block of 4, #399-402	1.75 1.50
403	A185	20c	Malawi (2,483,010)	.25 .20
404	A185	20c	Byelorussian SSR (2,483,010)	.25 .20
405	A185	20c	Jamaica (2,483,010)	.25 .20

406	A185	20c	Kenya (2,483,010)	.25 .20
a.			Se-tenant block of 4, #403-406	1.75 1.50
407	A185	20c	People's Republic of China (2,474,140)	.25 .20
408	A185	20c	Peru (2,474,140)	.25 .20
409	A185	20c	Bulgaria (2,474,140)	.25 .20
410	A185	20c	Canada (2,474,140)	.25 .20
a.			Se-tenant block of 4, #407-410	1.75 1.50
411	A185	20c	Somalia (2,482,070)	.25 .20
412	A185	20c	Senegal (2,482,070)	.25 .20
413	A185	20c	Brazil (2,482,070)	.25 .20
414	A185	20c	Sweden (2,482,070)	.25 .20
a.			Se-tenant block of 4, #411-414	1.75 1.50
			First day cover, #399-414, each	.75
			Set of 4 diff. panes of 16	17.00
			Nos. 399-414 (16)	4.00 3.20

First day covers of Nos. 399-414 total 2,214,134.

Window Right — A210

Peace Treaty with Nature — A211

35th Anniversary of the Universal Declaration of Human Rights.
Printed by Government Printing Office, Austria. Panes of 16 (4x4). Designed by Friedensreich Hundertwasser, Austria.

1983, Dec. 9   **Photo. & Engr.**   *Perf. 13½*

415	A210	20c	multicolored (1,591,102)	.30 .25
			First day cover	1.00
			Inscription block of 4	1.25 —
416	A211	40c	multicolored (1,566,789)	.70 .65
			First day cover	1.25
			First day cover, #415-416	1.50
			Inscription block of 4	3.00 —
			Panes of 16, #415-416	16.00

First day covers of Nos. 415-416 total 176,269.
See UN Offices in Geneva Nos. 119-120; Vienna Nos. 37-38.

International Conference on Population — A212

Printed by Bundesdruckerei, Federal Republic of Germany. Panes of 50. Designed by Marina Langer-Rosa and Helmut Langer, Federal Republic of Germany.

1984, Feb. 3   **Litho.**   *Perf. 14*

417	A212	20c	multicolored (905,320)	.30 .25
			First day cover	1.00
			Inscription block of 4	1.40 —
418	A212	40c	multicolored (717,084)	.65 .55
			First day cover	1.25
			First day cover, #417-418	1.40
			Inscription block of 4	2.50 —

First day covers of Nos. 417-418 total 118,068.
See UN Offices in Geneva No. 121; Vienna No. 39.

Tractor
Plowing
A213

Rice Paddy
A214

World Food Day, Oct. 16
Printed by Walsall Security Printers, Ltd., United Kingdom.
Panes of 50. Designed by Adth Vanooijen, Netherlands.

1984, Mar. 15   Litho.   Perf. 14½

419	A213	20c	multicolored (853,641)	.35 .30
		First day cover		1.25
		Inscription block of 4		1.60
420	A214	40c	multicolored (727,165)	.65 .65
		First day cover		1.50
		First day cover, #419-420		1.75
		Inscription block of 4		2.75 —

First day covers of Nos. 419-420 total 116,009.
See UN Offices in Geneva Nos. 122-123; Vienna Nos. 40-41.

Grand
Canyon — A215

Ancient City of
Polonnaruwa, Sri
Lanka — A216

World Heritage
Printed by Harrison and Sons, United Kingdom. Panes of 50.
Designs adapted by Rocco J. Callari, U.S., and Thomas Lee,
China.

1984, Apr. 18   Litho.   Perf. 14

421	A215	20c	multicolored (814,316)	.25 .20
		First day cover		1.00
		Inscription block of 4		1.10
422	A216	50c	multicolored (579,136)	.75 .75
		First day cover		1.25
		First day cover, #421-422		1.40
		Inscription block of 4		3.50 —

First day covers of Nos. 421-422 total 112,036.
See Nos. 601-602, UN Offices in Geneva Nos. 124-125, 211-
212; Vienna Nos. 42-43, 125-126.

A217

A218

Future for Refugees
Printed by Courvoisier. Panes of 50. Designed by Hans Erni,
Switzerland.

1984, May 29   Photo.   Perf. 11½

423	A217	20c	multicolored (956,743)	.40 .35
		First day cover		1.00
		Inscription block of 4		2.00
424	A218	50c	multicolored (729,036)	1.00 .85
		First day cover		1.25
		First day cover, #423-424		1.40
		Inscription block of 4		4.50

First day covers of Nos. 423-424 total 115,789.
See UN Offices in Geneva Nos. 126-127; Vienna Nos. 44-45.

Flag Type of 1980

Printed by Courvoisier. Panes of 16. Designed by Ole
Hamann.
Issued in 4 panes of 16. Each pane contains 4 blocks of four
(Nos. 425-428, 429-432, 433-436, 437-440). A se-tenant block
of 4 designs centers each pane.

1984, Sept. 21   Photo.   Perf. 12
Granite Paper

425	A185	20c	Burundi (1,941,471)	.50 .45
426	A185	20c	Pakistan (1,941,471)	.50 .45
427	A185	20c	Benin (1,941,471)	.50 .45
428	A185	20c	Italy (1,941,471)	.50 .45
a.			Se-tenant block of 4, #425-428	2.75 2.50
429	A185	20c	Tanzania (1,969,051)	.50 .45
430	A185	20c	United Arab Emirates (1,969,051)	.50 .45
431	A185	20c	Ecuador (1,969,051)	.50 .45
432	A185	20c	Bahamas (1,969,051)	.50 .45
a.			Se-tenant block of 4, #429-432	2.75 2.50
433	A185	20c	Poland (2,001,091)	.50 .45
434	A185	20c	Papua New Guinea (2,001,091)	.50 .45
435	A185	20c	Uruguay (2,001,091)	.50 .45
436	A185	20c	Chile (2,001,091)	.50 .45
a.			Se-tenant block of 4, #433-436	2.75 2.50
437	A185	20c	Paraguay (1,969,875)	.50 .45
438	A185	20c	Bhutan (1,969,875)	.50 .45
439	A185	20c	Central African Republic (1,969,875)	.50 .45
440	A185	20c	Australia (1,969,875)	.50 .45
a.			Se-tenant block of 4, #437-440	2.75 2.50
			First day cover, #425-440, each	1.00
			Set of 4 diff. panes of 16	32.50
			Nos. 425-440 (16)	8.00 7.20

First day covers of Nos. 425-440 total 1,914,972.

International Youth
Year — A219

ILO Turin
Center — A220

Printed by Waddingtons Ltd., United Kingdom. Panes of 50.
Designed by Ramon Mueller, Federal Republic of Germany.

1984, Nov. 15   Litho.   Perf. 13½

441	A219	20c	multicolored (884,962)	.40 .35
		First day cover		1.00
		Inscription block of 4		2.00
442	A219	35c	multicolored (740,023)	1.25 1.10
		First day cover		1.25
		First day cover, #441-442		1.40
		Inscription block of 4		5.75 —

First day covers of Nos. 441-442 total 125,315.
See UN Offices in Geneva No. 128; Vienna Nos. 46-47.

1985, Feb. 1   Engr.   Perf. 13½

Printed by the Government Printing Bureau, Japan. Panes of
50. Engraved by Mamoru Iwakuni and Hiroshi Ozaki, Japan.

443	A220	23c	blue (612,942)	.55 .45
		First day cover (76,541)		1.00
		Inscription block of 4		2.50 —

See UN Offices in Geneva Nos. 129-130; Vienna No. 48.

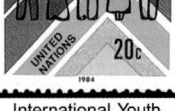

UN University
A221

Printed by Helio Courvoiser, Switzerland. Panes of 50.
Designed by Moshe Pereg, Israel, and Hinedi Geluda, Brazil.

1985, Mar. 15   Photo.   Perf. 13

444	A221	50c	Farmer plowing, discussion group (625,043)	1.10 1.
		First day cover (77,271)		1.
		Inscription block of 4		5.00

See UN Offices in Geneva Nos. 131-132; Vienna No. 49.

Peoples of the
World
United — A222

Painting UN
Emblem — A223

Printed by Carl Ueberreuter Druck and Verlag M. Salze
Austria. Panes of 50. Designed by Fritz Henry Oerter, Feder
Republic of Germany (22c), and Rimondi Rino, Italy ($3).

1985, May 10   Litho.   Perf. 1

445	A222	22c	multicolored (2,000,000)+	.35
		First day cover		1.0
		Inscription block of 4		1.50
446	A223	$3	multicolored (2,000,000)+	4.00 1.0
		First day cover		4.5
		First day cover, #445-446		6.5
		Inscription block of 4		17.00

First day covers of Nos. 445-446 total 88,613.
See UN Offices in Geneva Nos. 133-134; Vienna Nos. 50-5

The Corner,
1947 — A224

Alvaro Raking
Hay,
1953 — A225

UN 40th anniversary. Oil paintings (details) by American art
ist Andrew Wyeth (b. 1917). Printed by Helio Courvoisier, Swit
zerland. Nos. 447-448 panes of 50. Designed by Rocco J. Ca
lari, U.S., and Thomas Lee, China (#449).

1985, June 26   Photo.   Perf. 12 x 11

447	A224	22c	multicolored (944,960)	.45 .3
		First day cover		1.0
		Inscription block of 4		2.25
448	A225	45c	multicolored (680,079)	1.10 .8
		First day cover		1.2
		First day cover, #447-448		1.5
		Inscription block of 4		5.50 —

Souvenir Sheet
Imperf

449		Sheet of 2 (506,004)	1.50 1.4
a.	A224	22c multicolored	.50 .4
b.	A225	45c multicolored	.75 .9
		First day cover	.7

First day covers of Nos. 447-449 total; New York, 210,189
San Francisco, 92,804.
See UN Offices in Geneva Nos. 135-137; Vienna Nos. 52-54

Flag Type of 1980

Printed by Helio Courvoisier, Switzerland. Designed by Ole
Hamann.
Issued in panes of 16; each contains 4 blocks of four (Nos
450-453, 454-457, 458-461, 462-465). A se-tenant block of 4
designs is at the center of each pane.

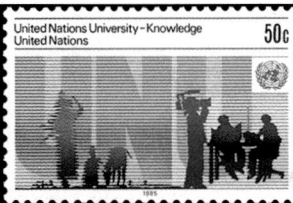

5, Sept. 20   Photo.   Perf. 12
Granite Paper

A185 22c Grenada (1,270,755)		.55	.50
A185 22c Federal Republic of Germany (1,270,755)		.55	.50
A185 22c Saudi Arabia (1,270,755)		.55	.50
A185 22c Mexico (1,270,755)		.55	.50
Se-tenant block of 4, #450-453		3.25	2.75
A185 22c Uganda (1,216,878)		.55	.50
A185 22c St. Thomas & Prince (1,216,878)		.55	.50
A185 22c USSR (1,216,878)		.55	.50
A185 22c India (1,216,878)		.55	.50
Se-tenant block of 4, #454-457		3.25	2.75
A185 22c Liberia (1,213,231)		.55	.50
A185 22c Mauritius (1,213,231)		.55	.50
A185 22c Chad (1,213,231)		.55	.50
A185 22c Dominican Republic (1,213,231)		.55	.50
Se-tenant block of 4, #458-461		3.25	2.75
A185 22c Sultanate of Oman (1,215,533)		.55	.50
A185 22c Ghana (1,215,533)		.55	.50
A185 22c Sierra Leone (1,215,533)		.55	.50
A185 22c Finland (1,215,533)		.55	.50
Se-tenant block of 4, #462-465		3.25	2.75
First day covers, #460-465, each			1.00
Set of 4 diff. panes of 16		37.50	
Nos. 450-465 (16)		8.80	8.00

First day covers of Nos. 450-465 total 1,774,193.

NICEF Child Survival Campaign — A226

Africa in Crisis — A227

rinted by the Government Printing Bureau, Japan. Panes of Designed by Mel Harris, United Kingdom (#466) and Dipok i, India (#467).

85, Nov. 22   Photo. & Engr.   Perf. 13½

A226 22c Asian Toddler (823,724)		.35	.30
First day cover			1.00
Inscription block of 4		1.50	—
A226 33c Breastfeeding (632,753)		.65	.60
First day cover			1.25
First day cover, #466-467			1.75
Inscription block of 4		3.00	—

First day covers of Nos. 466-467 total 206,923.
ee UN Offices in Geneva Nos. 138-139; Vienna Nos. 55-56.

86, Jan. 31   Photo.   Perf. 11½x12

rinted by Helio Courvoisier, Switzerland. Pane of 50. signed by Wosene Kosrof, Ethiopia.

A227 22c multicolored (708,169)		.50	.45
First day cover (80,588)			1.75
Inscription block of 4		2.50	—

ampaign against hunger. See UN Offices in Geneva No. ; Vienna No. 57.

Water Resources A228

rinted by the Government Printing Bureau, Japan. Pane of 2 blocks of 4 horizontal by 5 blocks of 4 vertical. Designed Thomas Lee, China.

86, Mar. 14   Photo.   Perf. 13½

A228 22c Dam (525,839)		1.00	.90
A228 22c Irrigation (525,839)		1.00	.90
A228 22c Hygiene (525,839)		1.00	.90
A228 22c Well (525,839)		1.00	.90
Block of 4, #469-472		4.00	4.00
First day cover, #472a			6.50
First day cover, #469-472, each			2.00
Inscription block of 4, #469-472		7.50	—
Pane of 40, #469-472		45.00	

Development Program. No. 472a has continuous design.
First day covers of Nos. 469-472 total 199,347.
See UN Offices in Geneva Nos. 141-144; Vienna Nos. 58-61.

Human Rights Stamp of 1954 — A229

Stamp collecting: 44c, Engraver. Printed by the Swedish Post Office, Sweden. Panes of 50. Designed by Czeslaw Slania and Ingalill Axelsson, Sweden.

1986, May 22   Engr.   Perf. 12½

473 A229 22c dark violet & bright blue (825,782)		.30	.25
First day cover			1.00
Inscription block of 4		1.50	—
474 A229 44c brown & emerald green (738,552)		.80	.70
First day cover			1.25
First day cover, #473-474			1.50
Inscription block of 4		3.25	—

First day covers of Nos. 473-474 total: New York, 121,143; Chicago, 89,557.
See UN Offices in Geneva Nos. 146-147; Vienna Nos. 62-63.

Bird's Nest in Tree — A230

Peace in Seven Languages A231

Printed by the Government Printing Bureau, Japan. Panes of 50. Designed by Akira Iriguchi, Japan (#475), and Henryk Chylinski, Poland (#476).

1986, June 20   Photo. & Embossed   Perf. 13½

475 A230 22c multicolored (836,160)		.50	.40
First day cover			1.00
Inscription block of 4		2.50	—
476 A231 33c multicolored (663,882)		1.25	1.25
First day cover			2.00
First day cover, #475-476			4.50
Inscription block of 4		6.50	—

International Peace Year.
First day covers of Nos. 475-476 total 149,976.
See UN Offices in Geneva Nos. 148-149; Vienna Nos. 64-65.

Flag Type of 1980

Printed by Helio Courvoisier, Switzerland. Designed by Ole Hamann. Issued in panes of 16; each contains 4 blocks of four (Nos. 477-480, 481-484, 485-488, 489-492). A se-tenant block of 4 designs centers each pane.

1986, Sept. 19   Photo.   Perf. 12
Granite Paper

477 A185 22c New Zealand (1,150,584)		.55	.50
478 A185 22c Lao PDR (1,150,584)		.55	.50
479 A185 22c Burkina Faso (1,150,584)		.55	.50
480 A185 22c Gambia (1,150,584)		.55	.50
a. Se-tenant block of 4, #477-480		3.25	2.75
481 A185 22c Maldives (1,154,870)		.55	.50
482 A185 22c Ethiopia (1,154,870)		.55	.50
483 A185 22c Jordan (1,154,870)		.55	.50
484 A185 22c Zambia (1,154,870)		.55	.50
a. Se-tenant block of 4, #481-484		3.25	2.75
485 A185 22c Iceland (1,152,740)		.55	.50
486 A185 22c Antigua & Barbuda (1,152,740)		.55	.50
487 A185 22c Angola (1,152,740)		.55	.50
488 A185 22c Botswana (1,152,740)		.55	.50
a. Se-tenant block of 4, #485-488		3.25	2.75
489 A185 22c Romania (1,150,412)		.55	.50
490 A185 22c Togo (1,150,412)		.55	.50
491 A185 22c Mauritania (1,150,412)		.55	.50
492 A185 22c Colombia (1,150,412)		.55	.50
a. Se-tenant block of 4, #489-492		3.25	2.75
First day covers, #477-492, each			1.00
Set of 4 diff. panes of 16		35.00	
Nos. 477-492 (16)		8.80	8.00

First day covers of Nos. 477-492 total 1,442,284.

World Federation of UN Associations, 40th anniv. — A232

Printed by Johann Enschede and Sons, Netherlands. Designed by Rocco J. Callari, U.S.
Designs: 22c, Mother Earth, by Edna Hibel, U.S. 33c, Watercolor by Salvador Dali (b. 1904), Spain. 39c, New Dawn, by Dong Kingman, U.S. 44c, Watercolor by Chaim Gross, U.S.

1986, Nov. 14   Litho.   Perf. 13x13½
Souvenir Sheet

493 Sheet of 4 (433,888)		4.25	4.00
a. A232 22c multicolored		.60	.55
b. A232 33c multicolored		.75	.70
c. A232 39c multicolored		1.10	1.00
d. A232 44c multicolored		1.25	1.10
First day cover (106,194)			2.00

No. 493 has inscribed margin picturing UN and WFUNA emblems.
See UN Offices in Geneva No. 150; Vienna No. 66.

Trygve Halvdan Lie (1896-1968), first Secretary-General — A233

1987, Jan. 30   Photo. & Engr.   Perf. 13½

Printed by the Government Printing Office, Austria. Panes of 50. Designed by Rocco J. Callari, U.S., from a portrait by Harald Dal, Norway.

494 A233 22c multicolored (596,440)		.90	.90
First day cover (84,819)			1.75
Inscription block of 4		4.00	—

See Offices in Geneva No. 151; Vienna No. 67.

International Year of Shelter for the Homeless A234

Printed by Johann Enschede and Sons, Netherlands. Panes of 50. Designed by Wladyslaw Brykczynski, Poland.
Designs: 22c, Surveying and blueprinting. 44c, Cutting lumber.

1987, Mar. 13   Litho.   Perf. 13½x12½

495 A234 22c multicolored (620,627)		.40	.35
First day cover			1.60
Inscription block of 4		1.75	—
496 A234 44c multicolored (538,096)		1.25	1.25
First day cover			1.90
First day cover, #495-496			2.75
Inscription block of 4		5.50	—

First day covers of Nos. 495-496 total 94,090.
See Offices in Geneva Nos. 154-155; Vienna Nos. 68-69.

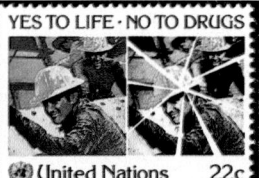

Fight Drug Abuse — A235

Printed by the House of Questa, United Kingdom. Panes of 50. Designed by Susan Borgen and Noel Werrett, U.S. Designs: 22c, Construction. 33c, Education.

1987, June 12   Litho.   Perf. 14½x15

497 A235 22c **multicolored** *(674,563)*	.65	.50
First day cover		1.75
Inscription block of 4	2.75	
498 A235 33c **multicolored** *(643,153)*	1.10	1.00
First day cover		2.00
First day cover, #497-498		2.25
Inscription block of 4	5.25	—

First day covers of Nos. 497-498 total 106,941.
See Offices in Geneva Nos. 156-157; Vienna Nos. 70-71.

Flag Type of 1980

Printed by Courvoisier. Designed by Ole Hamann.
Issued in panes of 16; each contains 4 block of four (Nos. 499-502, 503-506, 507-510, 511-514). A se-tenant block of 4 designs centers each pane.

1987, Sept. 18   Photo.   Perf. 12
Granite Paper

499 A185 22c Comoros *(1,235,828)*	.55	.50
500 A185 22c Yemen PDR *(1,235,828)*	.55	.50
501 A185 22c Mongolia *(1,235,828)*	.55	.50
502 A185 22c Vanuatu *(1,235,828)*	.55	.50
a. Se-tenant block of 4, #499-502	3.25	2.75
503 A185 22c Japan *(1,244,534)*	.55	.50
504 A185 22c Gabon *(1,244,534)*	.55	.50
505 A185 22c Zimbabwe *(1,244,534)*	.55	.50
506 A185 22c Iraq *(1,244,534)*	.55	.50
a. Se-tenant block of 4, #503-506	3.25	2.75
507 A185 22c Argentina *(1,238,065)*	.55	.50
508 A185 22c Congo *(1,238,065)*	.55	.50
509 A185 22c Niger *(1,238,065)*	.55	.50
510 A185 22c St. Lucia *(1,238,065)*	.55	.50
a. Se-tenant block of 4, #507-510	3.25	2.75
511 A185 22c Bahrain *(1,239,323)*	.55	.50
512 A185 22c Haiti *(1,239,323)*	.55	.50
513 A185 22c Afghanistan *(1,239,323)*	.55	.50
514 A185 22c Greece *(1,239,323)*	.55	.50
a. Se-tenant block of 4, #511-514	3.25	2.75
First day covers, #499-514, each		1.00
Set of 4 diff. panes of 16	37.50	
Nos. 499-514 (16)	8.80	8.00

United Nations
Day — A236

Printed by The House of Questa, United Kingdom. Panes of 12. Designed by Elisabeth von Janota-Bzowski (#515) and Fritz Henry Oerter (#516), Federal Republic of Germany.
Designs: Multinational people in various occupations.

1987, Oct. 23   Litho.   Perf. 14½x15

515 A236 22c **multicolored** *(1,119,286)*	.40	.35
First day cover		1.00
Inscription block of 4	2.00	—
516 A236 39c **multicolored** *(1,065,468)*	.60	.65
First day cover		2.00
First day cover, #515-516		1.60
Inscription block of 4	2.50	—
Panes of 12, #515-516	12.00	

See Offices in Geneva Nos. 158-159; Vienna Nos. 74-75.

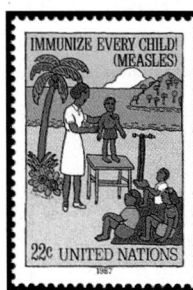

Immunize Every
Child — A237

Printed by The House of Questa, United Kingdom. Panes of 50. Designed by Seymour Chwast, U.S.
Designs: 22c, Measles. 44c, Tetanus.

1987, Nov. 20   Litho.   Perf. 15x14½

517 A237 22c **multicolored** *(660,495)*	1.25	.60
First day cover		2.00
Inscription block of 4	5.00	—
518 A237 44c **multicolored** *(606,049)*	2.25	1.75
First day cover		2.25
First day cover, #517-518		3.50
Inscription block of 4	11.00	—

See Offices in Geneva Nos. 160-161; Vienna Nos. 76-77.

Intl. Fund for
Agricultural
Development
(IFAD)
A238

Printed by CPE Australia Ltd., Australia. Panes of 50. Designed by Santiago Arolas, Switzerland.
Designs: 22c, Fishing. 33c, Farming.

1988, Jan. 29   Litho.   Perf. 13½

519 A238 22c **multicolored** *(392,649)*	.45	.40
First day cover		1.00
Inscription block of 4	2.25	—
520 A238 33c **multicolored** *(475,185)*	.90	.85
First day cover		1.25
First day cover, #519-520		3.00
Inscription block of 4	4.75	—

See Offices in Geneva Nos. 162-163; Vienna Nos. 78-79.

A239

Printed by Heraclio Fournier, S.A., Spain. Panes of 50. Designed by David Ben-Hador, Israel.

1988, Jan. 29   Photo.   Perf. 13½x14

521 A239 3c **multicolored** *(3,000,000)+*	.20	.20
First day cover		1.00
Inscription block of 4	.75	—

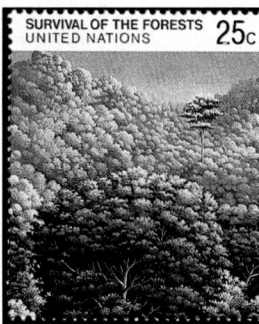

Survival of the
Forests — A240

Printed by The House of Questa, United Kingdom. Panes of six se-tenant pairs. Designed by Braldt Bralds, the Netherlands.
Tropical rain forest: 25c, Treetops. 44c, Ground vegetation and tree trunks. Printed se-tenant in a continuous design.

1988, Mar. 18   Litho.   Perf. 14x15

522 A240 25c **multicolored** *(647,360)*	1.00	1.00
First day cover		4.00
523 A240 44c **multicolored** *(647,360)*	1.75	1.75
First day cover		7.50
a. Pair, #522-523	3.00	3.00
First day cover, #523a		12.00
Inscription block of 4	6.50	
Pane of 12, #522-523	22.50	

See Offices in Geneva Nos. 165-166; Vienna Nos. 80-81.

Intl. Volunteer Day — A241

Printed by Johann Enschede and Sons, the Netherlands. Panes of 50. Designed by James E. Tennison, U.S.
Designs: 25c, Edurahon. 50c, Vocational training, horiz.

1988, May 6   Litho.   Perf. 13x14, 14

524 A241 25c **multicolored** *(688,444)*	.55	
First day cover		
Inscription block of 4	2.50	
525 A241 50c **multicolored** *(447,784)*	1.25	
First day cover		
First day cover, #524-525		
Inscription block of 4	5.00	

See Offices in Geneva Nos. 167-168; Vienna Nos. 82-8

Health in
Sports
A242

Printed by the Government Printing Bureau, Japan. Pane 50. Paintings by LeRoy Neiman, American sports artist.
Designs: 25c, Cycling, vert. 35c, Marathon.

1988, June 17   Litho.   Perf. 13½x13, 13x1

526 A242 25c **multicolored** *(658,991)*	.50	
First day cover		
Inscription block of 4	2.50	
527 A242 38c **multicolored** *(420,421)*	1.10	
First day cover		
First day cover, #526-527		
Inscription block of 4	6.50	

See Offices in Geneva Nos. 169-170; Vienna Nos. 84-85

Flag Type of 1980

Printed by Helio Courvoisier, Switzerland. Designed by Hamann, Denmark. Issued in panes of 16; each contain blocks of four (Nos. 528-531, 532-535, 536-539 and 540-54 A se-tenant block of 4 centers each pane.

1988, Sept. 15   Photo.   Perf.
Granite Paper

528 A185 25c Spain *(1,029,443)*	.60	
529 A185 25c St. Vincent & Grenadines		
(1,029,443)	.60	
530 A185 25c Ivory Coast *(1,029,443)*	.60	
531 A185 25c Lebanon *(1,029,443)*	.60	
a. Se-tenant block of 4, #528-531	3.25	
532 A185 25c Yemen (Arab Republic)		
(1,010,774)	.60	
533 A185 25c Cuba *(1,010,774)*	.60	
534 A185 25c Denmark *(1,010,774)*	.60	
535 A185 25c Libya *(1,010,774)*	.60	
a. Se-tenant block of 4, #532-535	3.25	
536 A185 25c Qatar *(1,016,941)*	.60	
537 A185 25c Zaire *(1,016,941)*	.60	
538 A185 25c Norway *(1,016,941)*	.60	
539 A185 25c German Democratic Republic		
(1,016,941)	.60	
a. Se-tenant block of 4, #536-539	3.25	
540 A185 25c Iran *(1,009,234)*	.60	
541 A185 25c Tunisia *(1,009,234)*	.60	
542 A185 25c Samoa *(1,009,234)*	.60	
543 A185 25c Belize *(1,009,234)*	.60	
a. Se-tenant block of 4, #540-543	3.25	
First day covers, #528-543, each		
Set of 4 diff. panes of 16	35.00	
Nos. 528-543 (16)	9.60	8

Universal Declaration of
Human Rights, 40th.
Anniv. — A243

Printed by Helio Couvoisier, Switzerland. Panes of 5
Designed by Rocco J. Callari, U.S.

1988, Dec. 9   Photo. & Engr.   Perf. 11x11

544 A243 25c **multicolored** *(893,706)*	.50	
First day cover		2
Inscription block of 4	2.40	

Souvenir Sheet

545 A243 $1 **multicolored** *(411,863)*	1.50	1
First day cover		2

No. 545 has multicolored decorative margin inscribed with th preamble to the human rights declaration in English.
See Offices in Geneva Nos. 171-172; Vienna Nos. 86-87.

World Bank — A244   A245

Printed by Johann Enschede and Sons, the Netherlands.
Panes of 50. Designed by Saturnino Lumboy, Philippines.

1989, Jan. 27   Litho.   Perf. 13x14
A244 25c Energy and nature (612,114)   .75 .45
  First day cover   2.00
  Inscription block of 4   3.00
A244 45c Agriculture (528,184)   1.50 1.00
  First day cover   2.50
  First day cover, #546-547   3.00
  Inscription block of 4   7.00

First day covers of Nos. 546-547 total 103,087 (NYC), 56,501 Washington).
See Offices in Geneva Nos. 173-174; Vienna Nos. 88-89.

1989, Mar. 17   Litho.   Perf. 14x13½
UN Peace-Keeping Force, awarded 1988 Nobel Peace Prize.
Printed by CPE Australia, Ltd., Australia. Panes of 50.
Designed by Tom Bland, Australia.
A245 25c multicolored (808,842)   .50 .40
  First day cover (52,115)   2.25
  Inscription block of 4   2.25

See Offices in Geneva No. 175; Vienna No. 90.

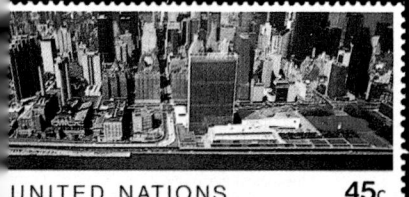

Aerial Photograph of New York
Headquarters — A246

Printed by Johann Enschede and Sons, the Netherlands.
Panes of 25. Designed by Rocco J. Callari, United States, from photograph by Simon Nathan.

1989, Mar. 17   Litho.   Perf. 14½x14
A246 45c multicolored (2,000,000)+   .75 .65
  First day cover (41,610)   2.00
  Inscription block of 4   3.25

World Weather Watch,
25th Anniv. (in 1988) — A247

Printed by Johann Enschede and Sons, the Netherlands.
Panes of 50.
Satellite photographs: 25c, Storm system off the U.S. east coast. 36c, Typhoon Abby in the north-west Pacific.

1989, Apr. 21   Litho.   Perf. 13x14
A247 25c multicolored (849,819)   .70 .60
  First day cover   1.75
  Inscription block of 4   3.00
A247 36c multicolored (826,547)   1.40 1.25
  First day cover   2.50
  First day cover, #550-551   3.00
  Inscription block of 4   7.25

First day covers of Nos. 550-551 total 92,013.
See Offices in Geneva Nos. 176-177; Vienna Nos. 91-92.

Offices in Vienna, 10th Anniv.
A248   A249

Printed by the Government Printing Office, Austria. Panes of 25. Designed by Paul Flora (25c) and Rudolf Hausner (90c), Austria.

Photo. & Engr., Photo. (90c)
1989, Aug. 23   Perf. 14
552 A248 25c multicolored (580,663)   2.75 2.50
  First day cover   2.50
  Inscription block of 4   12.50
553 A249 90c multicolored (505,776)   2.25 2.00
  First day cover   2.50
  First day cover, #552-553   8.50
  Inscription block of 4   9.00
  Panes of 25, #552-553   150.00

First day covers of Nos. 552-553 total 89,068.
See Offices in Geneva Nos. 178-179; Vienna Nos. 93-94.

Flag Type of 1980
Printed by Helio Courvoisier, Switzerland. Designed by Ole Hamann, Denmark. Issued in panes of 16; each contains 4 blocks of 4 (Nos. 554-557, 558-561, 562-565, 566-569). A se-tenant block of 4 designs centers each pane.

1989, Sept. 22   Photo.   Perf. 12
Granite Paper
554 A185 25c Indonesia (959,076)   .60 .55
555 A185 25c Lesotho (959,076)   .60 .55
556 A185 25c Guatemala (959,076)   .60 .55
557 A185 25c Netherlands (959,076)   .60 .55
  a. Se-tenant block of 4, #554-557   3.50 3.00
558 A185 25c South Africa (960,502)   .60 .55
559 A185 25c Portugal (960,502)   .60 .55
560 A185 25c Morocco (960,502)   .60 .55
561 A185 25c Syrian Arab Republic (960,502)   .60 .55
  a. Se-tenant block of 4, #558-561   3.50 3.00
562 A185 25c Honduras (959,814)   .60 .55
563 A185 25c Kampuchea (959,814)   .60 .55
564 A185 25c Guinea-Bissau (959,814)   .60 .55
565 A185 25c Cyprus (959,814)   .60 .55
  a. Se-tenant block of 4, #562-565   3.50 3.00
566 A185 25c Algeria (959,805)   .60 .55
567 A185 25c Brunei (959,805)   .60 .55
568 A185 25c St. Kitts and Nevis (959,805)   .60 .55
569 A185 25c United Nations (959,805)   .60 .55
  a. Se-tenant block of 4, #566-569   3.50 3.00
  First day covers, #554-569, each   1.25
  Set of 4 diff. panes of 16   42.50
  Nos. 554-569 (16)   9.60 8.80

First day covers of Nos. 554-569 total 794,934.

Declaration of
Human Rights, 40th
Anniv. (in 1988) — A250

Printed by Johann Enschede and Sons, the Netherlands.
Panes of 12+12 se-tenant labels containing Articles 1 (25c) or 2 (45c) inscribed in English, French or German. Designed by Rocco J. Callari and Robert Stein, US.
Paintings: 25c, The Table of Universal Brotherhood, by Jose Clemente Orozco. 45c, Study for Composition II, by Vassily Kandinsky.

1989, Nov. 17   Litho.   Perf. 13½
570 A250 25c multicolored (1,934,135)   .40 .30
  First day cover   1.25
  Inscription block of 3 + 3 labels   1.25
571 A250 45c multicolored (1,922,171)   .90 .80
  First day cover   1.25
  First day cover, #570-571   2.00
  Inscription block of 3 + 3 labels   2.75
  Panes of 12, #570-571   17.00

First day covers of Nos. 570-571 total 146,489 (NYC), 46,774 (Washington).
See Nos. 582-583, 599-600, 616-617, 627-628; Offices in Geneva Nos. 180-181, 193-194, 209-210, 224-225, 234-235; Vienna Nos. 95-96, 108-109, 123-124, 139-140, 150-151.

Intl. Trade
Center — A251

Printed by House of Questa, United Kingdom. Panes of 50.
Designed by Richard Bernstein, US.

1990, Feb. 2   Litho.   Perf. 14½x15
572 A251 25c multicolored (429,081)   1.60 1.25
  First day cover (52,614)   2.50
  Inscription block of 4   6.50

See Offices in Geneva No. 182; Vienna No. 97.

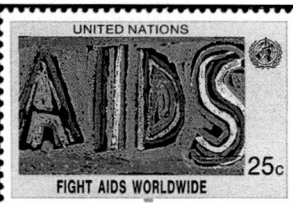

Fight AIDS
Worldwide
A252

Printed by Johann Enschede and Sons, the Netherlands.
Panes of 50. Designed by Jacek Tofil, Poland (25c) and Fritz Henry Oerter, Federal Republic of Germany (40c).
Design: 40c, Shadow over crowd.

1990, Mar. 16   Litho.   Perf. 13½x12½
573 A252 25c multicolored (492,078)   .50 .40
  First day cover   2.00
  Inscription block of 4   2.25
574 A252 40c multicolored (394,149)   1.50 1.25
  First day cover   3.50
  First day cover, #573-574   6.50
  Inscription block of 4   6.25

First day covers of Nos. 573-574 total 95,854.
See Offices in Geneva Nos. 184-185, Vienna Nos. 99-100.

Medicinal Plants — A253

Printed by Helio Courvoisier, Switzerland. Panes of 50.
Designed by Rocco J. Callari & Robert Stein, US from illustrations from "Curtis's Botanical Magazine".

1990, May 4   Photo.   Granite Paper   Perf. 11½
575 A253 25c Catharanthus roseus (796,792)   .75 .65
  First day cover   1.50
  Inscription block of 4   2.75
576 A253 90c Panax quinquefolium (605,617)   1.75 1.50
  First day cover   2.10
  First day cover, #575-576   9.50
  Inscription block of 4   8.00

First day covers of Nos. 575-576 total 100,548.
See Offices in Geneva Nos. 186-187, Vienna Nos. 101-102.

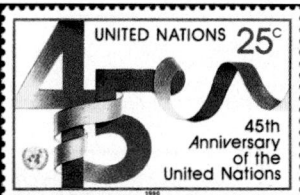

United
Nations, 45th
Anniv.
A254

Printed by Johann Enschede and Sons, the Netherlands.
Panes of 50. Designed by Kris Geysen, Belgium (25c), Nejat M. Gur, Turkey (45c), Robert Stein, US (No. 579).
Design: 45c, "45," emblem.

1990, June 26   Litho.   Perf. 14½x13
577 A254 25c multicolored (581,718)   .75 .70
  First day cover   1.25
  Inscription block of 4   4.00
578 A254 45c multicolored (582,769)   2.50 2.50
  First day cover   1.25

First day cover, #577-578   4.00
Inscription block of 4   12.00

Souvenir Sheet

579   Sheet of 2, #577-578 *(315,946)*   7.00 7.00
First day cover   4.00

First day covers of Nos. 577-579 total 129,011.
See Offices in Geneva Nos. 188-190; Vienna Nos. 103-105.

Crime Prevention — A255

Printed by Heraclio Fournier, S.A. Spain. Panes of 50.
Designed by Josef Ryzec, Czechoslovakia.

1990, Sept. 13   Photo.   Perf. 14
580 A255 25c Crimes of youth *(533,089)*   1.10   1.00
First day cover   2.00
Inscription block of 4   4.75
581 A255 36c Organized crime *(427,215)*   2.50   2.25
First day cover   4.00
First day cover, #580-581   10.00
Inscription block of 4   10.00   —

First day covers of Nos. 580-581 total 68,660.
See Offices in Geneva Nos. 191-192; Vienna Nos. 106-107.

Human Rights Type of 1989

Printed by Johann Enschede and Sons, the Netherlands.
Panes of 12+12 se-tenant labels containing Articles 7 (25c) or 8
(45c) inscribed in English, French or German. Designed by
Rocco J. Callari and Robert Stein, US.
Artwork: 25c, Fragment from the sarcophagus of Plotinus, c.
270 A.D. 45c, Combined Chambers of the High Court of Appeal
by Charles Paul Renouard.

1990, Nov. 16   Litho.   Perf. 13½
582 A250 25c **black, gray & tan** *(1,492,950)*   .45   .35
First day cover   1.25
Inscription block of 3 + 3 labels   1.50
583 A250 45c **black & brown** *(1,490,934)*   .90   .75
First day cover   1.25
Inscription block of 3 + 3 labels   3.75
First day cover, #582-583   4.00
Inscription block of 3 + 3 labels   4.00
Panes of 12, #582-583   17.50

First day covers of Nos. 582-583 total 108,560.
See Offices in Geneva Nos. 193-194; Vienna Nos. 108-109.

Economic
Commission for
Europe — A256

Printed by Heraclio Fournier, S.A., Spain. Panes of 40.
Designed by Carlos Ochagavia, Argentina.

1991, Mar. 15   Litho.   Perf. 14
584 A256 30c Two storks *(590,102)*   1.10   .90
585 A256 30c Woodpecker, ibex *(590,102)*   1.10   .90
586 A256 30c Capercaille, plover *(590,102)*   1.10   .90
587 A256 30c Falcon, marmot *(590,102)*   1.10   .90
a.   Block of 4, #584-587   4.50 4.50
First day cover, #587a   4.00
First day cover, #584-587, any single   3.00
Inscription block of 4, #587a   5.00
Pane of 40, #584-587   45.00

First day covers of Nos. 584-587 total 53,502.
See Offices in Geneva Nos. 195-198; Vienna Nos. 110-113.

Namibian
Independence
A257

Printed by Heraclio Fournier, S.A., Spain. Designed by Rocco
J. Callari, US, from photographs by John Isaac, India.

1991, May 10   Litho.   Perf. 14
588 A257 30c Dunes, Namib Desert *(360,825)*   .80   .65
First day cover   2.50
Inscription block of 4   3.50
589 A257 50c Savanna *(415,648)*   1.75 1.50
First day cover   3.50
First day cover, #588-589   6.50
Inscription block of 4   8.00

First day covers of Nos. 588-589 total 114,258.
See Offices in Geneva Nos. 199-200; Vienna Nos. 114-115.

A258

The Golden Rule by
Norman Rockwell — A259

UN Headquarters, New
York — A260

Printed by Johann Enschede and Sons, the Netherlands
(30c), Helio Courvoisier, S.A., Switzerland (50c), and by Government Printing Bureau, Japan ($2). Panes of 50. Designed by
Rocco J. Callari (30c), Norman Rockwell, US (50c), Rocco J.
Callari and Robert Stein, US ($2).

1991   Litho.   Perf. 13½
590 A258 30c **multi**, *Sept. 11, (2,000,000)+*   .90   .75
First day cover   1.25
Inscription block of 4   3.50   —

Photo.
Perf. 12x11½
591 A259 50c **multi**, *Sept. 11, (2,000,000)+*   1.50 1.25
First day cover   4.00
Inscription block of 4   6.50

Engr.
592 A260 $2 **dark blue**, *May 10, (2,000,000)+*   3.00 2.75
First day cover   5.50
Inscription block of 4   12.50

First day covers of Nos. 590-591 total 66,016, No. 592,
36,022.
See Offices in Geneva Nos. 199-200; Vienna Nos. 114-115.

Rights of the
Child — A261

Printed by The House of Questa, United Kingdom. Panes of
50. Designed by Nicole Delia Legnani, US (30c) and Alissa
Duffy, US (70c).

1991, June 14   Litho.   Perf. 14½
593 A261 30c Children, globe *(440,151)*   1.25 1.00
First day cover   2.00
Inscription block of 4   7.00   —
594 A261 70c House, rainbow *(447,803)*   3.00 2.25
First day cover   5.00
First day cover, #593-594   4.00
Inscription block of 4   15.00   —

First day covers of Nos. 593-594 total 96,324.
See Offices in Geneva Nos. 203-204; Vienna Nos. 117-118.

Banning of
Chemical
Weapons
A262

Printed by Heraclio Fournier, S.A., Spain. Panes of
Designed by Oscar Asboth, Austria (30c), Michael Gran
France (90c).
Design: 90c, Hand holding back chemical drums.

1991, Sept. 11   Litho.   Perf. ?
595 A262 30c **multicolored** *(367,548)*   1.50
First day cover   6.00
Inscription block of 4   4.50
596 A262 90c **multicolored** *(346,161)*   4.50
First day cover
First day cover, #595-596
Inscription block of 4   19.00

First day covers of Nos. 595-596 total 91,552.
See Offices in Geneva Nos. 205-206; Vienna Nos. 119-

UN Postal
Administration, 40th
Anniv. — A263

Printed by The House of Questa, United Kingdom. Panes
25. Designed by Rocco J. Callari, US.

1991, Oct. 24   Litho.   Perf. 14.
597 A263 30c No. 1 *(442,548)*   1.00
First day cover
Inscription block of 4   4.50
598 A263 40c No. 3 *(419,127)*   1.50
First day cover
First day cover, #597-598   2
Inscription block of 4   7.50
Panes of 25, #597-598   70.00

First day covers of Nos. 597-598 total 81,177 (New Yo
58,501 (State College, PA).
See Offices in Geneva Nos. 207-208; Vienna Nos. 121-

Human Rights Type of 1989

Printed by Johann Enschede and Sons, the Netherlan
Panes of 12+12 se-tenant labels containing Articles 13 (30c
14 (50c) inscribed in English, French or German. Designed
Robert Stein, US.
Artwork: 30c, The Last of England, by Ford Madox Bro
40c, The Emigration to the East, by Tito Salas.

1991, Nov. 20   Litho.   Perf. 1.
599 A250 30c **multicolored** *(1,261,198)*   .50
First day cover   1
Inscription block of 3 + 3 labels   2.10
600 A250 50c **multicolored** *(1,255,077)*   1.10 1
First day cover   1
First day cover, #599-600
Inscription block of 3 + 3 labels   4.00
Panes of 12, #599-600   17.50

First day covers of Nos. 599-600 total 136,605.
See Offices in Geneva Nos. 209-210; Vienna Nos. 123-1

World Heritage Type of 1984

Printed by Cartor S.A., France. Panes of 50. Designed
Robert Stein, US.
Designs: 30c, Uluru Natl. Park, Australia. 50c, The Great W
of China.

1992, Jan. 24   Litho.   Perf.
Size: 35x28mm
601 A215 30c **multicolored** *(337,717)*   .70
First day cover   2
Inscription block of 4   3.00
602 A215 50c **multicolored** *(358,000)*   1.10 1
First day cover   3
First day cover, #601-602   4
Inscription block of 4   7.00

First day covers of Nos. 601-602 total 62,733.
See Offices in Geneva Nos. 211-212; Vienna Nos. 125-12

Printed by House of Questa, Ltd., United Kingdom. Designed by Salahattin Kanidinc, US.

1993, May 7	Litho.	Perf. 15x14	
626 A273 5c multicolored (1,500,000)+		.20	.20
First day cover (23,452)			1.25
Inscription block of 4		.85	—

Human Rights Type of 1989

Printed by Johann Enschede and Sons, the Netherlands. Panes of 12 + 12 se-tenant labels containing Articles 25 (29c) and 26 (35c) inscribed in English, French or German. Designed by Robert Stein, US.

Artwork: 29c, Shocking Corn, by Thomas Hart Benton. 35c, The Library, by Jacob Lawrence.

1993, June 11	Litho.	Perf. 13½	
627 A250 29c multicolored (1,049,134)		.80	.65
First day cover			1.25
Inscription block of 3 + 3 labels		3.25	
628 A250 35c multicolored (1,045,346)		1.10	1.00
First day cover			1.75
First day cover, #627-628			6.00
Inscription block of 3 + 3 labels		4.00	—
Panes of 12, #627-628		22.50	

First day covers of Nos. 627-628 total 77,719.
See Offices in Geneva Nos. 234-235; Vienna Nos. 150-151.

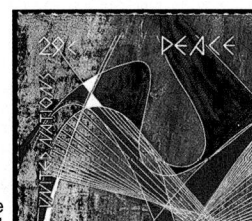

Intl. Peace
Day — A274

Printed by the PTT, Switzerland. Designed by Hans Erni, Switzerland.
Denomination at: #629, UL. #630, UR. #631, LL. #632, LR.

1993, Sept. 21	Litho. & Engr.	Rouletted 12½	
629 A274 29c blue & multi (298,367)		1.75	1.75
630 A274 29c blue & multi (298,367)		1.75	1.75
631 A274 29c blue & multi (298,367)		1.75	1.75
632 A274 29c blue & multi (298,367)		1.75	1.75
a. Block of 4, #629-632		7.00	7.00
First day cover, #629-632, each			3.00
First day cover, #632a			5.00
Inscription block of 4, #632a		9.00	—
Pane of 40, #629-632		80.00	

First day covers of Nos. 629-632a total 41,743.
See Offices in Geneva Nos. 236-239; Vienna Nos. 152-155.

Environment-Climate — A275

Printed by House of Questa, Ltd., United Kingdom. Designed by Braldt Bralds, Netherlands.
Designs: #633, Chameleon. #634, Palm trees, top of funnel cloud. #635, Bottom of funnel cloud, deer, antelope. #636, Bird of paradise.

1993, Oct. 29	Litho.	Perf. 14½	
633 A275 29c multicolored (383,434)		1.00	.90
634 A275 29c multicolored (383,434)		1.00	.90
635 A275 29c multicolored (383,434)		1.00	.90
636 A275 29c multicolored (383,434)		1.00	.90
a. Strip of 4, #633-636		4.50	4.50
First day cover, #636a			4.50
First day cover, #633-636, each			3.00
Inscription block, 2 #636a		9.00	—
Pane of 24, #633-636		22.50	

First day covers of Nos. 633-636a total 38,182.
See Offices in Geneva Nos. 240-243; Vienna Nos. 156-159.

Intl. Year of the
Family — A276

Printed by Cartor S.A., France. Designed by Rocco J. Callari, US.
Designs: 29c, Mother holding child, two children, woman. 45c, People tending crops.

1994, Feb. 4	Litho.	Perf. 13.1	
637 A276 29c green & multi (590,000)+		1.25	1.10
First day cover			1.25
Inscription block of 4		5.75	
638 A276 45c blue & multi (540,000)+		1.75	1.50
First day cover			1.75
First day cover, #637-638			3.50
Inscription block of 4		9.00	

First day covers of Nos. 637-638 total 47,982. See Offices in Geneva Nos. 244-245; Vienna Nos. 160-161.

Endangered Species Type of 1993

Printed by Johann Enschede and Sons, the Netherlands. Designed by Rocco J. Callari, US (frame), and Kerrie Maddeford, Australia (stamps).
Designs: No. 639, Chimpanzee. No. 640, St. Lucia Amazon. No. 641, American crocodile. No. 642, Dama gazelle.

1994, Mar. 18	Litho.	Perf. 12.7	
639 A271 29c multicolored (1,200,000)+		.50	.50
640 A271 29c multicolored (1,200,000)+		.50	.50
641 A271 29c multicolored (1,200,000)+		.50	.50
642 A271 29c multicolored (1,200,000)+		.50	.50
a. Block of 4, #639-642		2.00	2.00
First day cover, #642a			4.50
First day cover, #639-642, each			1.50
Inscription block of 4, #642a		2.50	—
Pane of 16, #639-642		10.00	

First day covers of Nos. 639-642 total 79,599. See Offices in Geneva Nos. 246-249; Vienna Nos. 162-165.

Protection for
Refugees — A277

Printed by Leigh-Mardon Pty. Limited, Australia. Designed by Francoise Peyroux, France.

1994, Apr. 29	Litho.	Perf. 14.3x14.8	
643 A277 50c multicolored (600,000)+		1.25	1.00
First day cover (33,558)			3.00
Inscription block of 4		5.75	

See Offices in Geneva No. 250; Vienna No. 166.

Dove of
Peace — A278

Sleeping Child, by
Stanislaw
Wyspianski — A279

Mourning Owl,
Vanessa Isitt — A

Printed by Cartor S.A., France, and Norges Banks Se
trykkeri, Norway (#646).

1994, Apr. 29	Litho.	Perf.	
644 A278 10c multicolored (1,000,000)+		.20	
First day cover			
Inscription block of 4		1.00	
645 A279 19c multicolored (1,000,000)+		.80	
First day cover			
Inscription block of 4		3.00	

Engr.
Perf. 13.1

646 A280 $1 red brown (1,000,000)+		2.75	
First day cover			
Inscription block of 4		12.00	
Nos. 644-646 (3)		3.75	

First day covers of Nos. 644-646 total 48,946.

Intl. Decade for
Natural Disaster
Reduction — A281

Printed by The House of Questa, UK. Designed by
Koga, Japan.
Earth seen from space, outline map of: #647, North Ame
#648, Eurasia. #649, South America, #650, Australia and S
Asia.

1994, May 27	Litho.	Perf. 13.9x	
647 A281 29c multicolored (630,000)+		1.75	
648 A281 29c multicolored (630,000)+		1.75	
649 A281 29c multicolored (630,000)+		1.75	
650 A281 29c multicolored (630,000)+		1.75	
a. Block of 4, #647-650		7.50	
First day cover, #650a			
First day cover, #647-650, each			
Inscription block of 4, #650a		8.00	
Pane of 40, #647-650		75.00	

First day covers of Nos. 647-650 total 37,135. See Offic
Geneva Nos. 251-254; Vienna Nos. 170-173.

Population
and
Developm
A282

Printed by Johann Enschede and Sons, the Netherla
Designed by Jerry Smath, US.
Designs: 29c, Children playing. 52c, Family with house
other possessions.

1994, Sept. 1	Litho.	Perf. 13.2x	
651 A282 29c multicolored (590,000)+		.75	
First day cover			
Inscription block of 4		3.25	
652 A282 52c multicolored (540,000)+		1.25	
First day cover			
First day cover, #651-652			
Inscription block of 4		5.25	

First day covers of Nos. 651-652 total 45,256.
See Offices in Geneva Nos. 258-259; Vienna Nos. 174

UNCTAD, 30th
Anniv. — A283

[P]rinted by Johann Enschede and Sons, the Netherlands.
[Desi]gned by Luis Sarda, Spain.

[199]4, Oct. 28
A283 29c **multicolored** (590,000)+		.55	.50
First day cover			1.25
Inscription block of 4	2.75		
A283 50c **multi, diff.** (540,000)+		1.00	.70
First day cover			1.75
First day cover, #653-654			2.25
Inscription block of 4	4.50		

[Fir]st day covers of Nos. 653-654 total 42,763. See Offices in
[Gen]eva Nos. 260-261; Vienna Nos. 176-177.

UN, 50th Anniv. — A284

[Pr]inted by Swiss Postal Service. Designed by Rocco J. Cal-
[lo] US.

[199]5, Jan. 1   Litho. & Engr.   Perf. 13.4
A284 32c **multicolored** (938,644)		1.00	1.00
First day cover (39,817)			4.50
Inscription block of 4	4.25		—

See Offices in Geneva No. 262; Vienna No. 178.

Social Summit,
[C]openhagen — A285

[19]95, Feb. 3   Photo. & Engr.   Perf. 13.6x13.9
[P]rinted by Austrian Government Printing Office.
[D]esigned by Friedensreich Hundertwasser.
A285 50c **multicolored** (495,388)		1.10	1.00
First day cover (31,797)			3.00
Inscription block of 4	5.00		—

See Offices in Geneva No. 263; Vienna No. 179.

Endangered Species Type of 1993
[P]rinted by Johann Enschede and Sons, the Netherlands.
[De]signed by Chris Calle, US.
[De]signs: No. 657, Giant armadillo. No. 658, American bald
[eag]le. No. 659, Fijian/Tongan banded iguana. No. 660, Giant
[pan]da.

[19]95, Mar. 24   Litho.   Perf. 13x12½
A271 32c **multicolored** (756,000)+		.55	.55
A271 32c **multicolored** (756,000)+		.55	.55
A271 32c **multicolored** (756,000)+		.55	.55
A271 32c **multicolored** (756,000)+		.55	.55
Block of 4, 657-660		2.25	2.25
First day cover, #660a			3.25
First day cover, #657-660, each			1.75
Inscription block of 4, #660a	2.50		—
Pane of 16, #657-660	12.50		

[Fir]st day covers of Nos. 657-660 total 67,311. See Offices in
[Gen]eva Nos. 264-267; Vienna Nos. 180-183.

Intl. Youth Year,
10th
Anniv. — A286

Printed by The House of Questa (UK). Designed by Gottfried
Kumpf, Austria.
Designs: 32c, Seated child. 55c, Children cycling.

1995, May 26   Litho.   Perf. 14.4x14.7
661 A286 32c **multicolored** (358,695)		1.00	.75
First day cover			1.25
Inscription block of 4	4.00		
662 A286 55c **multicolored** (288,424)		1.60	1.50
First day cover			1.75
First day cover, #661-662			2.25
Inscription block of 4	7.00		—

First day covers of Nos. 661-662 total 42,846. See Offices in
Geneva Nos. 268-269; Vienna Nos. 184-185.

UN, 50th
Anniv. — A287

Printed by Johann Enschede Security Printing, the Nether-
lands. Designed by Paul and Chris Calle, US.
Designs: 32c, Hand with pen signing UN Charter, flags. 50c,
Veterans' War Memorial, Opera House, San Francisco.

1995, June 26   Engr.   Perf. 13.3x13.6
663 A287 32c **black** (501,961)		.75	.60
First day cover			1.50
Inscription block of 4	2.75		
664 A287 50c **maroon** (419,932)		1.50	1.50
First day cover			2.00
First day cover, #663-664			3.75
Inscription block of 4	5.00		—

Souvenir Sheet
Litho. & Engr.
Imperf
665	Sheet of 2, #663-664 (347,963)+	2.75	2.50
a.	A287 32c **black**	1.10	.95
b.	A287 50c **maroon**	1.50	1.40
	First day cover		3.50

First day covers of Nos. 663-665 total: New York, 69,263; San
Francisco, 53,354.
No. 665 exists with gold China 1996 overprint. Value $7.50.
See Offices in Geneva Nos. 270-272; Vienna Nos. 186-188.

4th World
Conference on
Women,
Beijing — A288

Printed by Postage Stamp Printing House, MPT, People's
Republic of China. Designed by Ting Shao Kuang, People's
Republic of China.
Designs: 32c, Mother and child. 40c, Seated woman, cranes
flying above.

1995, Sept. 5   Photo.   Perf. 12
666 A288 32c **multicolored** (561,847)		.80	.60
First day cover			1.25
Inscription block of 4	3.50		—

Size: 28x50mm
667 A288 40c **multicolored** (499,850)		1.25	1.00
First day cover			1.25
First day cover, #666-667			3.50
Inscription block of 4	5.25		—

First day covers of Nos. 666-667 total 103,963. See Offices in
Geneva Nos. 273-274; Vienna Nos. 189-190.

UN
Headquarters
A289

Designed by John B. De Santis, Jr. US.

1995, Sept. 5   Litho.   Perf. 15
668 A289 20c **multicolored**		.40	.30
First day cover (18,326)			2.00
Inscription block of 4	2.00		—

Miniature Sheet

United Nations, 50th Anniv. — A290

Designed by Ben Verkaaik, Netherlands.
Printed by House of Questa, UK.
Designs: #669a-669 l, Various people in continuous design (2
blocks of six stamps with gutter between).

1995, Oct. 24   Litho.   Perf. 14
669	Sheet of 12 (214,639 sheets)	15.00	10.00
	First day cover		20.00
a.-l.	A290 32c any single	1.25	.80
	First day cover, #669a-669l, each		7.00
670	Souvenir booklet (85,256 booklets)	19.00	
a.	A290 32c Booklet pane of 3, vert. strip of 3 from UL of sheet	3.50	3.50
b.	A290 32c Booklet pane of 3, vert. strip of 3 from UR of sheet	3.50	3.50
c.	A290 32c Booklet pane of 3, vert. strip of 3 from LL of sheet	3.50	3.50
d.	A290 32c Booklet pane of 3, vert. strip of 3 from LR of sheet	3.50	3.50
	First day covers, #670a-670d, set booklet tab singles		140.00

First day covers of Nos. 669-670 total 47,632. See Offices in
Geneva Nos. 275-276; Vienna Nos. 191-192.

WFUNA, 50th
Anniv. — A291

Designed by Rudolf Mirer, Switzerland.
Printed by Johann Enschede and Sons, the Netherlands.

1996, Feb. 2   Litho.   Perf. 13x13½
671 A291 32c **multicolored** (580,000)+		.55	.45
First day cover			1.25
Inscription block of 4	2.50		—

See Offices in Geneva No. 277; Vienna No. 193.

Mural, by Fernand
Leger — A292

Designed by Fernand Leger, France.
Printed by House of Questa, UK.

1996, Feb. 2   Litho.   Perf. 14½x15
672 A292 32c **multicolored** (780,000)+		.55	.40
First day cover			1.25
Inscription block of 4	2.50		—
673 A292 60c **multi, diff.** (680,000)+		1.10	.80
First day cover			1.75
First day cover, #672-673			2.25
Inscription block of 4	4.75		—

Endangered Species Type of 1993

Printed by Johann Enschede and Sons, the Netherlands. Designed by Diane Bruyninckx, Belgium.

Designs: No. 674, Masdevallia veitchiana. No. 675, Saguaro cactus. No. 676, West Australian pitcher plant. No. 677, Encephalartos horridus.

1996, Mar. 14 Litho. *Perf. 12½*

674 A271 32c **multicolored** *(640,000)+* .60 .60
675 A271 32c **multicolored** *(640,000)+* .60 .60
676 A271 32c **multicolored** *(640,000)+* .60 .60
677 A271 32c **multicolored** *(640,000)+* .60 .60
a. Block of 4, #674-677 2.40 2.40
First day cover, #677a 3.25
First day cover, #674-677, each 1.75
Inscription block of 4, #677a 3.00 —
Pane of 16, #674-677 12.00

See Offices in Geneva Nos. 280-283; Vienna Nos. 196-199.

City Summit (Habitat II) — A293

Printed by Johann Enschede and Sons, the Netherlands. Designed by Teresa Fasolino, US.

Designs: No. 678, Deer. No. 679, Man, child, dog sitting on hill, overlooking town. No. 680, People walking in park, city skyline. No. 681, Tropical park, Polynesian woman, boy. No. 682, Polynesian village, orchids, bird.

1996, June 3 Litho. *Perf. 14x13½*

678 A293 32c **multicolored** *(475,000)+* 1.25 1.00
679 A293 32c **multicolored** *(475,000)+* 1.25 1.00
680 A293 32c **multicolored** *(475,000)+* 1.25 1.00
681 A293 32c **multicolored** *(475,000)+* 1.25 1.00
682 A293 32c **multicolored** *(475,000)+* 1.25 1.00
a. Strip of 5, #678-682 6.25 5.25
First day cover, #682a 10.00
First day cover, #678-682, each 3.50
Inscription block of 10, 2 #682a 13.50
Sheet of 25 32.50

See Offices in Geneva Nos. 284-288; Vienna Nos. 200-204.

Sport and the Environment — A294

Printed by The House of Questa, UK. Designed by LeRoy Neiman, US.

Designs: 32c, Men's basketball. 50c, Women's volleyball, horiz.

1996, July 19 Litho. *Perf. 14x14½, 14½x14*

683 A294 32c **multicolored** *(680,000)+* 1.00 .75
First day cover 1.25
Inscription block of 4 4.50 —
684 A294 50c **multicolored** *(680,000)+* 1.90 1.50
First day cover 1.50
First day cover, #683-684 2.25
Inscription block of 4 9.00 —

Souvenir Sheet

685 A294 Sheet of 2, #683-684 *(370,000)+* 2.75 2.50
First day cover 5.00

See Offices in Geneva Nos. 289-291; Vienna Nos. 205-207.
1996 Summer Olympic Games, Atlanta, GA.

Plea for Peace — A295

Printed by House of Questa, UK.
Designed by: 32c, Peng Yue, China. 60c, Cao Chenyu, China.

Designs: 32c, Doves. 60c, Stylized dove.

1996, Sept. 17 Litho. *Perf. 14½x15*

686 A295 32c **multicolored** *(580,000)+* .60 .45
First day cover 1.25
Inscription block of 4 3.00 —
687 A295 60c **multicolored** *(580,000)+* 1.10 .90
First day cover 1.50
First day cover, #686-687 2.25
Inscription block of 4 5.50 —

See Offices in Geneva Nos. 292-293; Vienna Nos. 208-209.

UNICEF, 50th Anniv. — A296

Printed by The House of Questa, UK. Designed by The Walt Disney Co.

Fairy Tales: 32c, Yeh-Shen, China. 60c, The Ugly Duckling, by Hans Christian Andersen.

1996, Nov. 20 Litho. *Perf. 14½x15*

688 A296 32c **multicolored** *(1,000,000)+* .60 .50
First day cover 1.25
Pane of 8 + label 5.00
689 A296 60c **multicolored** *(1,000,000)+* 1.40 1.25
First day cover 1.50
First day cover, #688-689 2.50
Pane of 8 + label 15.00

See Offices in Geneva Nos. 294-295; Vienna Nos. 210-211.

Flag Type of 1980

Printed by Helio Courvoisier, S.A., Switzerland. Designed by Oliver Corwin,US, and Robert Stein, UN. Each pane contains 4 blocks of 4 (Nos. 690-693, 694-697). A se-tenant block of 4 designs centers each pane.

1997, Feb. 12 Photo. *Perf. 12*
Granite Paper

690 A185 32c Tadjikistan *(940,000)+* 1.00 .75
691 A185 32c Georgia *(940,000)+* 1.00 .75
692 A185 32c Armenia *(940,000)+* 1.00 .75
693 A185 32c Namibia *(940,000)+* 1.00 .75
a. Block of 4, #690-693 5.00 4.00
694 A185 32c Liechtenstein *(940,000)+* 1.00 .75
695 A185 32c Republic of Korea *(940,000)+* 1.00 .75
696 A185 32c Kazakhstan *(940,000)+* 1.00 .75
697 A185 32c Latvia *(940,000)+* 1.00 .75
a. Block of 4, #694-697 5.00 4.00
First day cover, #690-697, each 3.00
Set of 2 panes of 16 21.00

First day covers of Nos. 690-697 total 136,114.

Cherry Blossoms, UN Headquarters — A297

Peace Rose — A298

Printed by The House of Questa, Ltd., UK.

1997, Feb. 12 Litho. *Perf.*

698 A297 8c **multicolored** *(700,000)+* .30
First day cover
Inscription block of 4 1.50
699 A298 55c **multicolored** *(700,000)+* 1.40
First day cover
First day cover, #698-699
Inscription block of 4 5.75

First day covers of Nos. 698-699 total 34,794.

Endangered Species Type of 1993

Printed by Johann Enschedé and Sons, the Netherla
Designed by Rocco J. Callari, US.
Designs: No. 700, African elephant. No. 701, Major Mitch cockatoo. No. 702, Black-footed ferret. No. 703, Cougar.

1997, Mar. 13 Litho. *Perf.*

700 A271 32c **multicolored** *(532,000)+* .60
701 A271 32c **multicolored** *(532,000)+* .60
702 A271 32c **multicolored** *(532,000)+* .60
703 A271 32c **multicolored** *(532,000)+* .60
a. Block of 4, #700-703 2.40
First day cover, #703a
First day cover, #700-703, each
Inscription block of 4, #703a 3.00
Pane of 16 10.00

First day covers of Nos. 700-703 total 66,863.
See Offices in Geneva Nos. 298-301; Vienna Nos. 214-

Earth Summit, 5 Anniv. — A299

Printed by Helio Courvoisier SA, Switzerland. Designed Peter Max, US.
Designs: No. 704, Sailboat. No. 705, Three sailboats. 706, Two people watching sailboat, sun. No. 707, Per sailboat.
$1, Combined design similar to Nos. 704-707.

1997, May 30 Photo. *Perf. 1*
Granite Paper

704 A299 32c **multicolored** *(328,566)* 1.00
705 A299 32c **multicolored** *(328,566)* 1.00
706 A299 32c **multicolored** *(328,566)* 1.00
707 A299 32c **multicolored** *(328,566)* 1.00
a. Block of 4, #704-707 4.00
First day cover, #707a
First day cover, #704-707, each
Inscription block of 4, #707a 4.50

Souvenir Sheet

708 A299 $1 **multicolored** *(181,667)* 3.25
First day cover
a. Ovptd. in sheet margin *(154,435)* 20.00 2(
First day cover, #708a 2

First day covers of Nos. 704-708 total: New York, 52,528; Francisco, 49,197.
See Offices in Geneva Nos. 302-306; Vienna Nos. 218-
No. 708 contains one 60x43mm stamp. Overprint in sh margin of No. 708a reads "PACIFIC 97 / World Philatelic Exh tion / San Francisco, California / 29 May - 8 June 1997".

Transportation — A300

Printed by The House of Questa, UK. Panes of 20.
Designed by Michael Cockcroft, UK.

..ships: No. 709, Clipper ship. No. 710, Paddle steamer. No.
..Ocean liner. No. 712, Hovercraft. No. 713, Hydrofoil.

..7, Aug. 29		Litho.		Perf. 14x14½	
A300	32c	multicolored (303,767)		.65	.60
A300	32c	multicolored (303,767)		.65	.60
A300	32c	multicolored (303,767)		.65	.60
A300	32c	multicolored (303,767)		.65	.60
A300	32c	multicolored (303,767)		.65	.60
		Strip of 5, #709-713		3.25	2.75
		First day cover, #713a		5.00	
		First day cover, #709-713, each		3.00	
		Inscription block of 10, 2#713a		8.00	
		Sheet of 20		21.00	

First day covers of Nos. 709-713 total 29,287.

..ee Offices in Geneva Nos. 307-311; Vienna Nos. 223-227.
..o. 713a has continuous design.

Philately — A301

Printed by Joh. Enschedé and Sons, the Netherlands. Panes
..0. Designed by Robert Stein, US.
..esigns: 32c, No. 473. 50c, No. 474.

..7, Oct. 14		Litho.		Perf. 13½x14	
.	A301	32c multicolored (363,237)		1.25	1.25
		First day cover			1.25
		Inscription block of 4		6.00	
.	A301	50c multicolored (294,967)		3.00	3.00
		First day cover			1.50
		First day cover, #714-715			2.50
		Inscription block of 4		12.50	—

First day covers of Nos. 714-715 total 43,684.

..ee Offices in Geneva Nos. 312-313; Vienna Nos. 228-229.

World Heritage
Convention, 25th
Anniv. — A302

..Printed by Government Printing Office, Austria. Panes of 20.
..signed by Robert Stein, US, based on photographs by Guo
..umin, People's Republic of China.
..Terracotta warriors of Xian: 32c, Single warrior. 60c, Massed
..rriors. No. 718a, like #716. No. 718b, like #717. No. 718c,
.. Geneva #314. No. 718d, like Geneva #315. No. 718e, like
..nna #230. No. 718f, like Vienna #231.

..7, Nov. 19		Litho.		Perf. 13½	
.6	A302	32c multicolored (549,095)		1.00	.75
		First day cover			1.25
		Inscription block of 4		4.50	—
.7	A302	60c multicolored (505,265)		2.00	1.75
		First day cover			1.75
		First day cover, #716-717			2.75
		Inscription block of 4		8.50	—
.8		Souvenir booklet (304,406 booklets)		8.50	
a.-f.		A302 8c any single		.30	.30
g.		Booklet pane of 4 #718a		.75	.50
h.		Booklet pane of 4 #718b		.75	.50
i.		Booklet pane of 4 #718c		.75	.50
j.		Booklet pane of 4 #718d		.75	.50
k.		Booklet pane of 4 #718e		.75	.50
l.		Booklet pane of 4 #718f		.75	.50

First day covers of Nos. 716-718 total 33,386.
..See Offices in Geneva Nos. 314-316; Vienna Nos. 230-232.

Flag Type of 1980

..Printed by Helio Courvoisier, S.A., Switzerland. Designed by
..ver Corwin, and Robert Stein, US. Each pane contains 4
..ocks of 4 (Nos. 719-722, 723-726). A se-tenant block of 4
..signs centers each pane.

1998, Feb. 13		**Photo.**		**Perf. 12**	
		Granite Paper			
719	A185	32c Micronesia (718,000)+		.90	.50
720	A185	32c Slovakia (718,000)+		.90	.50
721	A185	32c Democratic People's Republic of			
		Korea (718,000)+		.90	.50
722	A185	32c Azerbaijan (718,000)+		.90	.50
a.		Block of 4, #719-722		6.00	5.00
723	A185	32c Uzbekistan (718,000)+		.90	.50
724	A185	32c Monaco (718,000)+		.90	.50
725	A185	32c Czech Republic (718,000)+		.90	.50
726	A185	32c Estonia (718,000)+		.90	.50
a.		Block of 4, #723-726		6.00	5.00
		First day cover, #719-726, each			3.00
		Set of 2 panes of 16		21.00	
		Nos. 719-726 (8)		7.20	4.00

A303

A304

A305

Printed by The House of Questa, UK. Designed by Zhang Le
Lu, China (1c), Robert Stein, US (2c), Gregory Halili, Philippines (21c). Panes of 20.

1998, Feb. 13		**Litho.**		**Perf. 14½x15, 15x14½**	
727	A303	1c multicolored (1,000,000)+		.20	.20
		First day cover			1.00
		Inscription block of 4		.20	
728	A304	2c multicolored (1,000,000)+		.20	.20
		First day cover			1.00
		Inscription block of 4		.20	
729	A305	21c multicolored (1,000,000)+		.45	.35
		First day cover			1.00
		First day cover, #727-729			3.00
		Inscription block of 4		1.75	—
		Nos. 727-729 (3)		.85	.75

Endangered Species Type of 1993

Printed by Johann Enschedé and Sons, the Netherlands.
Designed by Rocco J. Callari, US and Pat Medearis-Altman,
New Zealand.
Designs: No. 730, Lesser galago. No. 731, Hawaiian goose.
No. 732, Golden birdwing. No. 733, Sun bear.

1998, Mar. 13		**Litho.**		**Perf. 12½**	
730	A271	32c multicolored (502,000)+		.60	.50
731	A271	32c multicolored (502,000)+		.60	.50
732	A271	32c multicolored (502,000)+		.60	.50
733	A271	32c multicolored (502,000)+		.60	.50
a.		Block of 4, #730-733		2.40	2.25
		First day cover, #733a			3.50
		First day cover, #730-733, each			2.00
		Inscription block of 4, #733a		3.00	—
		Pane of 16		12.50	

See Offices in Geneva Nos. 318-321; Vienna Nos. 235-238.

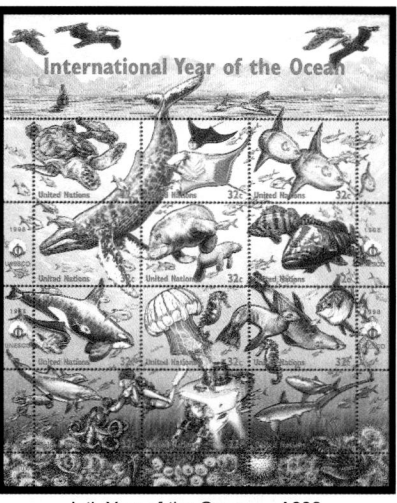

Intl. Year of the Ocean — A306

Printed by Johann Enschedé and Sons, the Netherlands.
Designed by Larry Taugher, US.

1998, May 20		**Litho.**		**Perf. 13x13½**	
734	A306	Sheet of 12 (280,000)+		9.00	7.50
		First day cover			12.50
a.-l.		32c any single		.75	.60
		First day cover, #734a-734l, each			6.00

See Offices in Geneva No. 322; Vienna No. 239.

Rain Forests
A307

Printed by Government Printing Bureau, Japan. Designed by
Rick Garcia, US.

1998, June 19		**Litho.**		**Perf. 13x13½**	
735	A307	32c Jaguar (570,000)+		.65	.65
		First day cover			2.50
		Inscription block of 4		3.50	—
		Souvenir Sheet			
736	A307	$2 like #735 (280,000)+		3.50	1.00
		First day cover			5.00

See Offices in Geneva Nos. 323-324; Vienna Nos. 240-241.

U.N.
Peacekeeping
Forces, 50th
Anniv. — A308

Printed by Helio Courvoisier, S.A. (Switzerland). Designed by
Andrew Davidson, UK.
Designs: 33c, Commander with binoculars. 40c, Two soldiers
on vehicle.

1998, Sept. 15		**Photo.**		**Perf. 12**	
737	A308	33c multicolored (485,000)+		.60	.50
		First day cover			1.25
		Inscription block of 4		3.25	—
738	A308	40c multicolored (445,000)+		1.10	.90
		First day cover			1.25
		First day cover, #737-738			2.00
		Inscription block of 4		5.00	—

See Offices in Geneva Nos. 325-326; Vienna Nos. 242-243.

Universal Declaration of
Human Rights. 50th
Anniv. — A309

Printed by Cartor Security Printing (France). Designed by
Jean-Michel Folon, France.
  Stylized people: 32c, Carrying flag. 55c, Carrying pens.

1998, Oct. 27   Litho. & Photo.   Perf. 13
739 A309 32c multicolored (485,000)+   .60   .50
        First day cover   1.25
        Inscription block of 4   3.25
740 A309 55c multicolored (445,000)+   1.10   .90
        First day cover   1.50
        First day cover, #739-740   2.50
        Inscription block of 4   5.00   —

See Offices in Geneva Nos. 327-328; Vienna Nos. 244-245.

Schönbrunn Palace, Vienna — A310

Printed by the House of Questa, UK. Panes of 20. Designed
by Robert Stein, US.
  Designs: 33c, #743f, The Gloriette. 60c, #743b, Wall painting
on fabric (detail), by Johann Wenzl Bergl, vert. No. 743a, Blue
porcelain vase, vert. No. 743c, Porcelain stove, vert. No. 743d,
Palace. No. 743e, Great Palm House (conservatory).

1998, Dec. 4   Litho.   Perf. 14
741 A310 33c multicolored (485,000)+   .75   .65
        First day cover   1.25
        Inscription block of 4   3.00
742 A310 60c multicolored (445,000)+   1.50   1.25
        First day cover   1.50
        First day cover, #741-742   2.50
        Inscription block of 4   6.00   —

Souvenir Booklet
743   Booklet (110,000)+   9.75
a.-c.   A310 11c any single   .40   .40
d.-f.   A310 15c any single   .50   .50
g.   Booklet pane of 4 #743d   2.00   2.00
h.   Booklet pane of 3 #743a   1.25   1.25
i.   Booklet pane of 3 #743b   1.25   1.25
j.   Booklet pane of 3 #743c   1.25   1.25
k.   Booklet pane of 4 #743e   2.00   2.00
l.   Booklet pane of 4 #743f   2.00   2.00

See Offices in Geneva Nos. 329-331; Vienna Nos. 246-248.

Flag Type of 1980

Printed by Helio Courvoisier S.A., Switzerland. Designed by
Oliver Corwin, Robert Stein and Blake Tarpley, US. Each pane
contains 4 blocks of 4 (Nos. 744-747, 748-751). A se-tenant
block of 4 designs centers each pane.

1999, Feb. 5   Photo.   Perf. 12
744 A185 33c Lithuania (524,000)+   .90   .60
745 A185 33c San Marino (524,000)+   .90   .60
746 A185 33c Turkmenistan (524,000)+   .90   .60
747 A185 33c Marshall Islands (524,000)+   .90   .60
a.   Block of 4, #744-747   6.00   5.00
748 A185 33c Moldova (524,000)+   .90   .60
749 A185 33c Kyrgyzstan (524,000)+   .90   .60
750 A185 33c Bosnia & Herzegovina (524,000)+   .90   .60
751 A185 33c Eritrea (524,000)+   .90   .60
a.   Block of 4, #748-751   6.00   5.00
        First day cover, #744-751, each   2.50
        Set of 2 panes of 16   30.00
        Nos. 744-751 (8)   7.20   4.80

First day covers of Nos. 744-751 total 102,040.

Flags and Globe — A311

Roses — A312

Designed by Blake Tarpley (#752), Rorie Katz, (#753), US.
Printed by Johann Enschedé and Sons, the Netherlands
(#752), Helio Courvoisier SA, Switzerland (#753).

1999, Feb. 5   Litho.   Perf. 14x13½
752 A311 33c multicolored (960,000)+   .65   .50
        First day cover   1.25
        Inscription block of 4   2.75   —

Photo.
Granite Paper
Perf. 11½x12
753 A312 $5 multicolored (420,000)+   8.00   1.00
        First day cover   7.50
        First day cover, #752-753   8.25
        Inscription block of 4   32.50   —

First day covers of Nos. 752-753 total 32,142.

World Heritage
Sites, Australia
— A313

Printed by House of Questa, UK. Panes of 20. Designed by
Passmore Design, Australia.
  Designs: 33c, #756f, Willandra Lakes region. 60c, #756b,
Wet tropics of Queensland. No. 756a, Tasmanian wilderness.
No. 756c, Great Barrier Reef. No. 756d, Uluru-Kata Tjuta Natl.
Park. No. 756e, Kakadu Natl. Park.

1999, Mar. 19   Litho.   Perf. 13
754 A313 33c multicolored (480,000)+   .85   .75
        First day cover   1.25
        Inscription block of 4   3.50   —
755 A313 60c multicolored (440,000)+   1.75   1.50
        First day cover   1.50
        First day cover, #754-755   2.50
        Inscription block of 4   7.00   —

Souvenir Booklet
756   Booklet (97,000)+   7.00
a.-c.   A313 5c any single   .20   .20
d.-f.   A313 15c any single   .35   .35
g.   Booklet pane of 4, #756a   .45   .45
h.   Booklet pane of 4, #756d   1.40   1.40
i.   Booklet pane of 4, #756b   .45   .45
j.   Booklet pane of 4, #756e   1.40   1.40
k.   Booklet pane of 4, #756c   .45   .45
l.   Booklet pane of 4, #756f   1.40   1.40

First day covers of Nos. 754-756 total 42,385.
See Offices in Geneva Nos. 333-335; Vienna Nos. 250-252.

Endangered Species Type of 1993

Printed by Johann Enschedé and Sons, the Netherlands.
Designed by Jimmy Wang, China.
  Designs: No. 757, Tiger. No. 758, Secretary bird. No. 759,
Green tree python. No. 760, Long-tailed chinchilla.

1999, Apr. 22   Litho.   Perf. 12½
757 A271 33c multicolored (494,000)+   .60   .50
758 A271 33c multicolored (494,000)+   .60   .50
759 A271 33c multicolored (494,000)+   .60   .50

760 A271 33c multicolored (494,000)+   .60
a.   Block of 4, #757-760   2.50
        First day cover, #760a
        First day cover, #757-760, each
        Inscription block of 4, #760a   2.75
        Pane of 16   12.00

First day covers of Nos. 757-760 total 49,656.
See Offices in Geneva Nos. 336-339; Vienna Nos. 253-

UNISPACE III, Vienna — A314

Printed by Helio Courvoisier SA, Switzerland. Designed
Attila Hejja, US.
  Designs: No. 761, Probe on planet's surface. No. 762, Pla
tary rover. No. 763, Composite of #761-762.

1999, July 7   Photo.   Roulette
761 A314 33c multicolored (1,000,000)+   .85
762 A314 33c multicolored (1,000,000)+   .85
a.   Pair, #761-762   1.75
        First day cover, #761-762, each
        Inscription block of 4   4.00
        Pane of 10, #761-762   9.00

Souvenir Sheet
Perf. 14½
763 A314 $2 multicolored (530,000)+   4.75
        First day cover
a.   Ovptd. in sheet margin   14.00
        First day cover   1

No. 763a was issued 7/7/00 and is overprinted in violet i
"WORLD STAMP EXPO 2000 / ANAHEIM, CALIFORN
U.S.A./ 7-16 JULY 2000."
  First day covers of Nos. 761-763 total 48,190.
  See Offices in Geneva #340-342; Vienna #257-259.

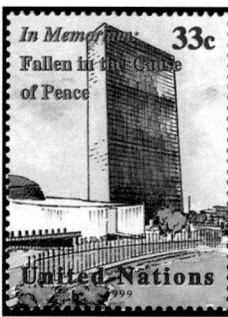

UPU, 125th
Anniv. — A315

Printed by Helio Courvoisier S.A., Switzerland. Panes of
Designed by Mark Hess, US.

Various people, 19th century methods of mail transportat
denomination at: No. 764, UL. No. 765, UR. No. 766, LL.
767, LR.

1999, Aug. 23   Photo.   Perf. 1
764 A315 33c multicolored (378,000)+   .75
765 A315 33c multicolored (378,000)+   .75
766 A315 33c multicolored (378,000)+   .75
767 A315 33c multicolored (378,000)+   .75
a.   Block of 4, #764-767   3.00   2
        Inscription block of 4   3.50
        First day cover, #767a   4
        First day cover, #764-767, each   1
        Sheet of 20   17.00

First day covers of Nos. 764-767 total 25,294.
See Offices in Geneva Nos. 343-346; Vienna Nos. 260-2

In Memoriam — A316

Printed by Walsall Security Printers, Ltd., United Kingdo
Panes of 20. Designed by Robert Stein, US.

Designs: 33c, $1, UN Headquarters. Size of $1 stan
34x63mm.

9, Sept. 21   Litho.   Perf. 14½x14

A316	33c **multicolored** (550,000)+	1.75	1.75
	Inscription block of 4	6.00	—
	First day cover		1.25

Souvenir Sheet
Perf. 14

A316	$1 **multicolored** (235,000)+	2.75	1.00
	First day cover		2.75

First day covers of Nos. 768-769 total 42,130.
See Offices in Geneva #347-348, Vienna #264-265.

Education, Keystone to the 21st Century — A317

Printed by Government Printing Office, Austria. Panes of 20.
Designed by Romero Britto, Brazil.

9, Nov. 18   Litho.   Perf. 13½x13¾

A317	33c Two readers (450,000)+	.65	.30
	First day cover		1.25
	Inscription block of 4	2.50	—
A317	60c Heart (430,000)+	1.25	.60
	First day cover		1.50
	First day cover, #770-771		2.50
	Inscription block of 4	5.00	—

First day covers of Nos. 770-771 total 34,679.
See Offices in Geneva Nos. 349-350, Vienna Nos. 266-267.

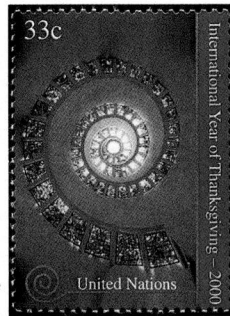

International Year of Thanksgiving — A318

Printed by Cartor Security Printing, France. Panes of 20.
Designed by Rorie Katz, US.

00, Jan. 1   Litho.   Perf. 13¼x13½

2	A318 33c **multicolored** (550,000)+	.90	.75
	First day cover		1.25
	Inscription block of 4	3.75	—

On No. 772 portions of the design were applied by a thermographic process producing a shiny, raised effect. See Offices in Geneva No. 351, Vienna No. 268.

Endangered Species Type of 1993

Printed by Johann Enschedé and Sons, the Netherlands. Designed by Suzanne Duranceau, Canada.
Designs: No. 773, Brown bear. No. 774, Black-bellied bustard. No. 775, Chinese crocodile lizard. No. 776, Pygmy chimpanzee.

00, Apr. 6   Litho.   Perf. 12¾x12½

3	A271 33c **multicolored** (490,000)+	.65	.30
4	A271 33c **multicolored** (490,000)+	.65	.30
5	A271 33c **multicolored** (490,000)+	.65	.30
6	A271 33c **multicolored** (490,000)+	.65	.30
a.	Block of 4, #773-776	2.50	2.25
	First day cover		3.50
	First day cover, #773-776, each		1.75
	Inscription block of 4, #776a	2.75	—
	Pane of 16	10.50	

See Offices in Geneva Nos. 352-355; Vienna Nos. 269-272.

Our World 2000 — A319

Printed by Cartor Security Printing, France. Panes of 20. Designed by Robert Stein, US.
Winning artwork in Millennium painting competition: 33c, Crawling Toward the Millennium, by Sam Yeates, US. 60c, Crossing, by Masakazu Takahata, Japan, vert.

2000, May 30   Litho.   Perf. 13x13½, 13½x13

777	A319 33c **multicolored** (400,000)+	.65	.30
	First day cover		1.25
	Inscription block of 4	2.60	—
778	A319 60c **multicolored** (360,000)+	1.25	.60
	First day cover		1.50
	First day cover, #777-778		2.50
	Inscription block of 4	7.00	—

See Offices in Geneva No. 356-357, Vienna No. 273-274.

UN, 55th Anniv. — A320

Printed by Cartor Security Printing, France. Panes of 20. Designed by Rorie Katz, US.
Designs: 33c, Workmen removing decorative discs in General Assembly Hall, 1956. 55c, UN Building in 1951.

2000, July 7   Litho.   Perf. 13¼x13

779	A320 33c **multicolored** (400,000)+	.65	.30
	First day cover		1.25
	Inscription block of 4	2.60	—
780	A320 55c **multicolored** (360,000)+	1.10	.55
	First day cover		1.50
	First day cover, #779-780		2.25
	Inscription block of 4	4.50	—

Souvenir Sheet

781	A320 Sheet of 2, #779-780 (277,000)+	2.50	2.50
	First day cover		3.00

See Offices in Geneva No. 358-360, Vienna No. 275-277.

International Flag of Peace — A321

Printed by House of Questa, UK. Panes of 20. Designed by Mateja Prunk, Slovenia.

2000, Sept. 15   Litho.   Perf. 14½x14

782	A321 33c **multicolored** (400,000)+	.65	.30
	First day cover		1.25
	Inscription block of 4	2.60	—

The UN in the 21st Century — A322

Printed by Government Printing Office, Austria. Designed by Wilson McLean, UK.

No. 783: a, Farmers, animals in rice paddy. b, Vehicle chassis being lifted. c, People voting. d, Baby receiving inoculation. e, Woman, man at pump. f, Mason, construction workers.

2000, Sept. 15   Litho.   Perf. 14

783	A322 Sheet of 6 (274,000)+	5.00	5.00
	First day cover		7.50
a.-f.	33c any single	.80	.30

See Offices in Geneva No. 361; Vienna No. 278.

World Heritage Sites, Spain — A323

Printed by House of Questa, UK. Panes of 20. Designed by Robert Stein, US.
Designs: Nos. 784, 786a, Alhambra, Generalife and Albayzin, Granada. Nos. 785, 786d, Amphitheater of Mérida. #786b, Walled Town of Cuenca. #786c, Aqueduct of Segovia. #786e, Toledo. #786f, Güell Park, Barcelona.

2000, Oct. 6   Litho.   Perf. 14¾x14½

784	A323 33c **multicolored** (400,000)+	.65	.30
	First day cover		1.25
	Inscription block of 4	2.60	—
785	A323 60c **multicolored** (360,000)+	1.25	.60
	First day cover		1.50
	First day cover, #784-785		2.50
	Inscription block of 4	5.00	—

Souvenir Booklet

786	Booklet (63,000)+	5.50	
a.-c.	A323 5c any single	.20	.20
d.-f.	A323 15c any single	.30	.30
g.	Booklet pane of 4, #786a	.50	.50
h.	Booklet pane of 4, #786d	1.25	1.25
i.	Booklet pane of 4, #786b	.50	.50
j.	Booklet pane of 4, #786e	1.25	1.25
k.	Booklet pane of 4, #786c	.50	.50
l.	Booklet pane of 4, #786f	1.25	1.25

See Offices in Geneva Nos. 362-364, Vienna Nos. 279-281.

Respect for
Refugees — A324

Printed by Johann Enschedé and Sons, the Netherlands.
Panes of 20. Designed by Yuri Gevorgian, Armenia.

2000, Nov. 9   Litho.   Perf. 13¼x12¾
787 A324 33c **multicolored** *(540,000)*+   .75   .30
   First day cover   1.25
   Inscription block of 4   3.00   —

Souvenir Sheet
788 A324 $1 **multicolored** *(225,000)*+   2.25   1.00
   First day cover   2.50

See Offices in Geneva Nos. 365-366, Vienna Nos. 282-283.

Endangered Species Type of 1993

Printed by Johann Enschedé and Sons, the Netherlands.
Designed by Grace DeVito, US.
   Designs: No. 789, Common spotted cuscus. No. 790,
Resplendent quetzal. No. 791, Gila monster. No. 792, Guereza.

2001, Feb. 1   Litho.   Perf. 12¾x12½
789 A271 34c **multicolored** *(430,000)*+   .65   .30
790 A271 34c **multicolored** *(430,000)*+   .65   .30
791 A271 34c **multicolored** *(430,000)*+   .65   .30
792 A271 34c **multicolored** *(430,000)*+   .65   .30
  a. Block of 4, #789-792   2.60   2.25
   First day cover, #792a   3.50
   First day cover, #789-792 each   1.25
   Inscription block of 4, #792a   2.75   —
   Pane of 16   10.50

See Offices in Geneva Nos. 367-370; Vienna Nos. 284-287.

Intl. Volunteers
Year — A325

Printed by Johann Enschedé and Sons, the Netherlands.
Panes of 20. Designed by Rorie Katz and Robert Stein, US.
   Paintings by: 34c, Jose Zaragoza, Brazil. 80c, John Terry,
Australia.

2001, Mar. 29   Litho.   Perf. 13¼
793 A325 34c **multicolored** *(390,000)*+   .65   .30
   First day cover   1.25
   Inscription block of 4   2.60
794 A325 80c **multicolored** *(360,000)*+   1.60   .80
   First day cover   2.40
   First day cover, #793-794   3.00
   Inscription block of 4   6.50

See Offices in Geneva Nos. 371-372; Vienna Nos. 288-289.

Flag Type of 1980

Printed by Helio Courvoisier, Switzerland. Designed by Ole
Hamann. Issued in panes of 16; each contains 4 blocks of 4
(Nos. 795-798, 799-802). A se-tenant block of 4 designs cen-
ters each pane.

2001, May 25   Photo.   Perf. 12
Granite Paper
795 A185 34c Slovenia *(460,000)*+   .80   .30
796 A185 34c Palau *(460,000)*+   .80   .30
797 A185 34c Tonga *(460,000)*+   .80   .30
798 A185 34c Croatia *(460,000)*+   .80   .30
  a. Block of 4, #795-798   6.00   5.00
799 A185 34c Former Yugoslav Republic of
        Macedonia *(460,000)*+   .80   .30
800 A185 34c Kiribati *(460,000)*+   .80   .30
801 A185 34c Andorra *(460,000)*+   .80   .30
802 A185 34c Nauru *(460,000)*+   .80   .30
  a. Block of 4, #799-802   6.00   5.00

   First day cover, #795-802, each   1.25
   Set of 2 panes of 16   21.00
   Nos. 795-802 (8)   6.40   2.40

Sunflower — A326

Rose — A327

Printed by Johann Enschedé and Sons, the Netherlands.
Panes of 20. Designed by Rorie Katz, US.

2001, May 25   Litho.   Perf. 13¼x13¾
803 A326 7c **multicolored** *(550,000)*+   .20   .20
   First day cover   1.25
   Margin block of 4, inscription   .75
804 A327 34c **multicolored** *(650,000)*+   .75   .30
   First day cover   1.25
   First day cover, #803-804   1.40
   Margin block of 4, inscription   3.25   —

World Heritage Sites, Japan — A328

Printed by Johann Enschedé and Sons, the Netherlands.
Panes of 20. Designed by Rorie Katz, US.
   Designs: 34c, #807a, Kyoto. 70c, #807d, Shirakawa-Go and
Gokayama. #807b, Nara. #807c, Himeji-Jo. #807e, Itsukushima
Shinto Shrine. #807f, Nikko.

2001, Aug. 1   Litho.   Perf. 12¾x13¼
805 A328 34c **multicolored** *(380,000)*+   .65   .30
   First day cover   1.25
   Inscription block of 4   2.60   —
806 A328 70c **multicolored** *(360,000)*+   1.40   .70
   First day cover   2.10
   First day cover, #805-806   2.75
   Inscription block of 4   5.75   —

Souvenir Booklet
807   Booklet *(51,000)*+   6.00
a.-c. A328 5c any single   .20   .20
d.-f. A328 20c any single   .40   .40
g.   Booklet pane of 4, #807a   .40   .40
h.   Booklet pane of 4, #807d   1.60   1.60
i.   Booklet pane of 4, #807b   .40   .40
j.   Booklet pane of 4, #807e   1.60   1.60
k.   Booklet pane of 4, #807c   .40   .40
l.   Booklet pane of 4, #807f   1.60   1.60

See Offices in Geneva Nos. 373-375, Vienna Nos. 290-292.

Dag Hammarskjöld (1905-
61), UN Secretary
General — A329

Printed by Banknote Corporation of America, US. Pane
20. Designed by Robert Stein, US.

2001, Sept. 18   Engr.   Perf. 11x1
808 A329 80c **blue** *(530,000)*+   1.60
   First day cover
   Inscription block of 4   6.50

See Offices in Geneva No. 376, Vienna No. 293.

A330

UN Postal Administration, 50th Anniv. — A331

Printed by Johann Enschedé and Sons, the Netherlan
Panes of 20. Designed by Rorie Katz, US.

2001, Oct. 18   Litho.   Perf. 1
809 A330 34c Stamps, streamers *(350,000)*+   .75
   First day cover
   Inscription block of 4   3.00
810 A330 80c Stamps, gifts *(310,000)*+   1.75   1
   First day cover   2.
   First day cover, #809-810   3
   Inscription block of 4   7.00

Souvenir Sheet
811 A331   Sheet of 2 #811a *(180,000)*+   5.00   2.
a. $1 **blue & light blue**, 38mm diameter   2.50   1.
   First day cover   16.

See Offices in Geneva Nos. 377-379, Vienna Nos. 294-296

Climate Change — A332

Printed by Walsall Security Printers Limited, UK. Panes of 2
Designed by Robert Giusti, US.
   Designs: No. 812, Canada geese, greenhouses, butterf.
thistle. No. 813, Canada geese, iceberg, penguins, toma
plant. No. 814, Palm tree, solar collector. No. 815, Hand plan
ing ginkgo cutting.

1, Nov. 16	Litho.	**Perf. 13¼**	
A332 34c **multicolored** *(70,500)+*		.75	.45
A332 34c **multicolored** *(70,500)+*		.75	.45
A332 34c **multicolored** *(70,500)+*		.75	.45
A332 34c **multicolored** *(70,500)+*		.75	.45
Horiz. strip, #812-815		3.00	3.00
Inscription block of 8		6.00	—
First day cover, #815a			3.50
Pane of 24		18.00	—

Offices in Geneva Nos. 380-383, Vienna Nos. 297-300.

arding of Nobel Peace Prize to Secretary General
Kofi Annan and UN — A333

rinted by Cartor S. A., France. Panes of 12. Designed by
ert Stein, US.

1, Dec. 10	Litho.	**Perf. 13¼**	
A333 34c **multicolored** *(840,000)+*		.80	.60
Inscription block of 4		3.50	—
First day cover			1.25
Pane of 12		11.50	—

See Offices in Geneva Nos. 384, Vienna Nos. 301.

Children and
Stamps — A334

rinted by Government Printing Office, Austria. Panes of 20.
signed by Jerry Smath, US.

02, Mar. 1	Litho.	**Perf. 13¾**	
7 A334 80c **multicolored** *(420,000)+*		1.60	.80
First day cover			2.25
Inscription block of 4		6.50	—

Endangered Species Type of 1993

rinted by Johann Enschedé and Sons, the Netherlands.
signed by Teresa Fasolino, US.
Designs: No. 818, Hoffmann's two-toed sloth. No. 819, Big-
rn sheep. No. 820, Cheetah. No. 821, San Esteban Island
uckwalla.

02, Apr. 4	Litho.	**Perf. 12¾x12½**	
8 A271 34c **multicolored** *(414,000)+*		.75	.40
9 A271 34c **multicolored** *(414,000)+*		.75	.40
0 A271 34c **multicolored** *(414,000)+*		.75	.40
1 A271 34c **multicolored** *(414,000)+*		.75	.40
a. Block of 4, #818-821		3.00	2.50
First day cover, #821a			3.50
First day cover, #818-821 each			1.50
Inscription block of 4, #821a		3.25	—
Pane of 16		11.00	—

See Offices in Geneva Nos. 386-389; Vienna 308-311.

Independence of East
Timor — A335

Printed by The House of Questa, UK. Designed by Karen
Kelleher, US. Panes of 20
Designs: 34c, Wooden ritual mask. 57c, Decorative door
panel.

2002, May 20	Litho.	**Perf. 14x14½**	
822 A335 34c **multicolored** *(355,000)+*		.70	.40
First day cover			1.25
Inscription block of 4		3.00	—
823 A335 57c **multicolored** *(325,000)+*		1.20	.70
First day cover			1.90
First day cover, #822-823			2.50
Inscription block of 4		5.00	—

See Offices in Geneva Nos. 390-391; Vienna Nos. 312-313.

Intl. Year of
Mountains
A336

Printed by Cartor Security Printing, France. Designed by
Robert Stein and Rorie Katz, US.
Designs: No. 824, Khan Tengri, Kyrgyzstan. No. 825, Mt.
Kilimanjaro, Tanzania. No. 826, Mt. Foraker, US. No. 827, Paine
Grande, Chile.

2002, May 24	Litho.	**Perf. 13x13¼**	
824 A336 34c **multicolored** *(1,362,000)+*		.75	.40
First day cover			1.25
825 A336 34c **multicolored** *(1,362,000)+*		.75	.40
First day cover			1.25
826 A336 80c **multicolored** *(1,362,000)+*		1.70	1.00
First day cover			2.25
First day cover, #824, 826			3.25
827 A336 80c **multicolored** *(1,362,000)+*		1.70	1.00
a. Vert. strip or block of four, #824-827		5.00	4.00
First day cover			2.25
First day cover, #825, 827			3.25
First day cover, #823-827			5.25
Pane of 12, 3 each #824-827		13.50	—

See Offices in Geneva Nos. 392-395; Vienna Nos. 314-317.

World Summit
on Sustainable
Development,
Johannesburg
A337

Printed by The House of Questa, UK. Designed by Peter
Max, US.
Designs: No. 828, Sun, Earth, planets, stars. No. 829, Three
women. No. 830, Sailboat. No. 831, Three faceless people.

2002, June 27	Litho.	**Perf. 14½x14**	
828 A337 37c **multicolored** *(1,350,000)+*		.75	.40
First day cover			1.25
829 A337 37c **multicolored** *(1,350,000)+*		.75	.40
First day cover			1.25
830 A337 60c **multicolored** *(1,350,000)+*		1.50	.80
First day cover			2.00
First day cover, #828, 830			2.25
831 A337 60c **multicolored** *(1,350,000)+*		1.50	.80
a. Vert. strip or block of four, #828-831		4.50	3.50
First day cover			2.00
First day cover, #829, 831			2.25
First day cover, #828-831			4.50
Pane of 12, 3 each #828-831		12.00	—

See Offices in Geneva Nos. 396-399; Vienna Nos. 318-321.

World Heritage Sites, Italy — A338

Printed by Cartor Security Printing, France. Panes of 20.
Designed by Rorie Katz, US.
Designs: 37c, #834d, Florence. 70c, #834a, Amalfi Coast.
#834b, Aeolian Islands. #834c, Rome. #834e, Pisa. #834f,
Pompeii.

2002, Aug. 30	Litho.	**Perf. 13½x13¼**	
832 A338 37c **multicolored** *(365,000)+*		.75	.40
First day cover			1.25
Inscription block of 4		3.25	—
833 A338 70c **multicolored** *(345,000)+*		1.50	.80
First day cover			2.40
First day cover, #832-833			3.00
Inscription block of 4		6.50	—

Souvenir Booklet

834	Booklet *(52,000)+*	5.00	
a.-c.	A338 5c any single	.20	.20
d.-f.	A338 15c any single	.30	.30
g.	Booklet pane of 4, #834d	1.25	1.25
h.	Booklet pane of 4, #834a	.40	.40
i.	Booklet pane of 4, #834e	1.25	1.25
j.	Booklet pane of 4, #834b	.40	.40
k.	Booklet pane of 4, #834f	1.25	1.25
l.	Booklet pane of 4, #834c	.40	.40

See Offices in Geneva Nos. 400-402, Vienna Nos. 322-324.
See Italy Nos. 2506-2507.

AIDS
Awareness — A339

Printed by Walsall Security Printers Limited, UK. Panes of 20.
Designed by Rorie Katz, US.

2002, Oct. 24	Litho.	**Perf. 13½**	
835 A339 70c **multicolored** *(365,000)+*		1.40	.80
Inscription block of 4		5.75	—
First day cover, #835			2.10
Pane of 20		30.00	—

See No. B1, Offices in Geneva Nos. 403, B1, Vienna Nos.
325, B1.

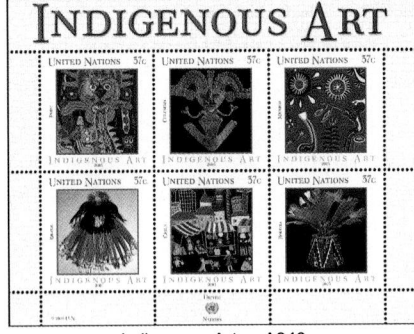

Indigenous Art — A340

Printed by House of Questa, UK.
Designed by Rorie Katz and Robert Stein, US.

No. 836: a, Detail of Paracas textile, Peru. b, Sinu culture
anthropo-zoomorphic pendant, Colombia. c, Hicholi Indian
embroidery, Mexico. d, Rigpaktsa back ornament, Brazil. e,
Wool crafts, Chile. f, Huari feathered woven hat, Bolivia.

2003, Jan. 31   **Litho.**   **Perf. 14¼**
836 A340   Sheet of 6 (165,000)+   4.50 2.50
        First day cover   6.25
a.-f.   37c Any single   .75   .40
        See Offies in Geneva No. 405; Vienna No. 326.

Clasped
Hands — A341

UN
Emblem — A342

UN Headquarters
A343

Printed by House of Questa, UK (23c, 37c); Walsall Security
Printers Ltd., UK (70c). Designed by Rorie Katz, US (23c, 37c),
Robert Stein and Rorie Katz (70c). Panes of 20.

2003, Mar. 28   **Litho.**   **Perf. 14¼**
837 A341   23c multicolored (870,000)+   .45   .30
        First day cover   1.25
        Inscription block of 4   1.80   —

Litho. with Foil Application
838 A342   37c gold & multicolored (870,000)+ .75   .50
        First day cover   1.25
        Inscription block of 4   3.00   —

Litho. with Hologram
839 A343   70c multicolored (910,000)+   1.40   .90
        First day cover   2.50
        First day cover, #837-839   3.25
        Inscription block of 4   5.60   —

Powered Flight, Cent. — A344

Printed by Government Printing Office, Austria. Designed by
Robert Stein, US. Panes of 16 (eight pairs).

2003, Mar. 28   **Litho.**   **Perf. 13½x13¾**
840   23c multicolored (175,000)+   .50   .35
841   70c multicolored (175,000)+   1.50   .90
a.   A344 Tete beche pair, #840-841   2.00 1.25
        First day cover, #841a   2.60
        Inscription block of 4   3.75

Endangered Species Type of 1993

Printed by Johann Enschedé and Sons, the Netherlands.
Designed by Joseph Hautman, US.
   Designs: No. 842, Great hornbill. No. 843, Scarlet ibis. No.
844, Knob-billed goose. No. 845, White-faced whistling duck.

2003, Apr. 3   **Litho.**   **Perf. 12¾x12½**
842 A271   37c multicolored (364,000)+   .75   .40
843 A271   37c multicolored (364,000)+   .75   .40
844 A271   37c multicolored (364,000)+   .75   .40
845 A271   37c multicolored (364,000)+   .75   .40
a.   Block of 4, #842-845   3.00 2.50
        First day cover, #845a   3.75
        First day cover, #842-845 each   1.25
        Inscription block of 4, #845a   3.00   —
        Pane of 16   12.00   —

        See Offices in Geneva Nos. 407-410; Vienna 329-332.

Intl. Year of
Freshwater
A345

Printed by De La Rue Global Services, United Kingdom.
Panes of 20. Designed by Rick Garcia, US.

2003, June 20   **Litho.**   **Perf. 14¼x14½**
846 A345   23c Wildlife, garbage (211,000)+   .60   .35
847 A345   37c Trees, canoe (211,000)+   .90   .40
a.   Horiz. pair, #846-847   1.50   .75
        First day cover, #847a   3.00
        Inscription block of 4   2.50   —

        See Offices in Geneva, Nos. 411-412; Vienna Nos. 333-334.

Ralph Bunche (1903-
71), Diplomat — A346

Printed by Johann Enschedé and Sons, the Netherlands.
Panes of 20. Designed by Rorie Katz, US.

Litho. With Foil Application
2003, Aug. 7   **Perf. 13¼**
848 A346   37c blue & multicolored (405,000)+   .75
        First day cover
        Inscription block of 4   3.00
        Pane of 20   15.00

        See Offices in Geneva No. 413; Vienna No. 336.

In Memoriam of Victi
of Aug. 19 Bombing
UN Complex in
Baghdad, Iraq — A34

Printed by Cartor Security Printing, France. Panes o
Designed by Jenny J. Karia and Robert Stein, US.

2003, Oct. 24   **Litho.**   **Perf. 13¼**
849 A347   60c multicolored (850,000)+   1.25
        First day cover
        Inscription block of 4   5.00
        Pane of 20   25.00

        See Offices in Geneva No. 414, Vienna No. 337.

World
Heritage
Sites,
United
States
A348

Printed by De La Rue Global Services, United Kingo
Panes of 20. Designed by Rorie Katz, US.
   Designs: 37c, #852a, Yosemite National Park. 60c, #8
Hawaii Volcanoes National Park. #852b, Great Smoky Mo
tains National Park. #852c, Olympic National Park. #8
Everglades National Park. #852f, Yellowstone National Par

2003, Oct. 24   **Litho.**   **Perf. 14½x1**
850 A348   37c multicolored (303,000)+   .90
        First day cover
        Inscription block of 4   3.75
851 A348   60c multicolored (193,000)+   1.50
        First day cover
        First day cover, #850-851
        Inscription block of 4   6.50

Souvenir Booklet
852   Booklet (38,500)+   9.00
a.-c.   A348 10c any single   .25
d.-f.   A348 20c any single   .50
g.   Booklet pane of 4 #852a   1.00
h.   Booklet pane of 4 #852d   2.00
i.   Booklet pane of 4 #852b   1.00
j.   Booklet pane of 4 #852e   2.00
k.   Booklet pane of 4 #852c   1.00
l.   Booklet pane of 4 #852f   1.60

        See Offices in Geneva Nos. 415-417, Vienna Nos. 338-34

UN Security Council — A349

UN Emblem — A350

UN General Assembly — A351

Flags — A352

UN Headquarters — A353

, Nov. 26   Litho.   Perf. 13¼

	A349	37c **multicolored** + label	1.60	1.60
	A350	37c **multicolored** + label	1.60	1.60
	A351	37c **multicolored** + label	1.60	1.60
	A352	37c **multicolored** + label	1.60	1.60
	A353	37c **multicolored** + label	1.60	1.60
		Vert. strip of 5, #853-857, + 5 labels	9.00	9.00
		Sheet, 4 #857a	40.00	
		First day cover, #857c		3.75
		First day cover, #853-857, each		3.75

he full sheet sold for $14.95 with or without personalized
ls. The personalization of labels was available only at UN
dquarters, and not through mail order.
ne thousand full sheets with sheet margins inscribed "Hong
g Stamp Expo" were sold only at that venue. Value $95.
o exists with sheet margins inscribed "Essen." Value $45.
sheet containing two strips of five stamps similar to Nos.
–857 but dated "2005" and ten labels sold for $4.95. These
ets were only available canceled.

Endangered Species Type of 1993

rinted by Johann Enschedé and Sons, the Netherlands.
signed by Yuan Lee, U.S.
signs: No. 858, American black bear. No. 859, Musk deer.
860, Golden snub-nosed monkey. No. 861, Wild yak.

4, Jan. 29   Litho.   Perf. 12¾x12½

	A271	37c **multicolored** (316,000)+	.75	.35
	A271	37c **multicolored** (316,000)+	.75	.35
	A271	37c **multicolored** (316,000)+	.75	.35
	A271	37c **multicolored** (316,000)+	.75	.35
		Block of 4, #858-861	3.00	2.50
		First day cover, #861a		3.75
		First day cover, #858-861, each		1.25
		Inscription block of 4, #861a	3.00	
		Pane of 16	12.00	

e Offices in Geneva Nos. 418-421; Vienna Nos. 342-345.

Indigenous Art Type of 2003

rinted by Johann Enschedé and Sons, the Netherlands.
esigned by Rorie Katz and Robert Stein, US.

lo. 862: a, Viking wood carving depicting Saga of Sigurd
rnesbane, Norway. b, Stele, Italy. c, Detail of matador's suit,
ain. d, Amphora, Greece. e, Bronze figurine of bull, Czech
ublic. f, Detail of lacquer box illustration depicting scene
n "On the Seashore," by Alexander Pushkin, Russia.

4, Mar. 4   Litho.   Perf. 13¼

	A340	Sheet of 6 (134,000)+	4.50	2.25
		First day cover		6.25
f.		37c Any single	.75	.35
		First day cover, a.-f., each		3.00

See Offices in Geneva No. 422; Vienna No. 346.

Road
Safety — A354

Printed by Cartor Security Printing. Panes of 20. Designed by
Michel Granger, France.
Road map art with: 37c, Automobile with road signs, city
skyline. 70c, Automobile, hand, vert.

2004, Apr. 7   Litho.   Perf. 13x13¼, 13¼x13

863	A354	37c **multicolored** (266,000)+	.75	.35
		First day cover		1.25
		Inscription block of 4	3.00	
864	A354	70c **multicolored** (196,000)+	1.40	.70
		First day cover		2.40
		First day cover, #863-864		3.00
		Inscription block of 4	5.75	

See Offices in Geneva Nos. 423-424, Vienna Nos. 347-348.

Japanese Peace Bell, 50th Anniv. — A355

Printed by Imprimerie des Timbres-Poste, France. Panes of
20. Designed by Martin Mörck, Norway.

2004, June 20   Litho. & Engr.   Perf. 13¼x13

865	A355	80c **multicolored** (376,000)+	1.60	.80
		First day cover		2.25
		Inscription block of 4	6.50	
		Pane of 20	32.00	

See Offices in Geneva No. 425; Vienna No. 349.

World Heritage Sites, Greece — A356

Printed by Johann Enschedé and Sons, the Netherlands.
Panes of 20. Designed by Rorie Katz, US.
Designs: No. 866, Acropolis, Athens. 60c, No. 868e, Delos.
No. 868a, Delphi. No. 868b, Pythagoreion and Heraion of
Samos. No. 868c, Olympia. No. 868d, Mycenae and Tiryns.

2004, Aug. 12   Litho.   Perf. 14x13¼

866	A356	37c **multicolored** (275,000)+	.75	.35
		First day cover		1.25
		Inscription block of 4	3.25	
a.		Booklet pane of 4	3.00	
867	A356	60c **multicolored** (195,000)+	1.25	.60
		First day cover		2.10
		First day cover, #866-867		2.75
		Inscription block of 4	5.00	

Souvenir Booklet

868		Booklet, #866a, 868f-868j (31,000)+	11.50	
a.-d.	A356	23c any single	.50	.25
e.	A356	37c multi	.80	.80
f.		Booklet pane of 4 #868a	2.00	2.00
g.		Booklet pane of 4 #868b	2.00	2.00
h.		Booklet pane of 4 #868c	2.00	2.00
i.		Booklet pane of 4 #868d	2.00	2.00
j.		Booklet pane of 4 #868e	3.25	3.25

See Offices in Geneva Nos. 426-428, Vienna Nos. 350-352.
No. 868 sold for $7.20.

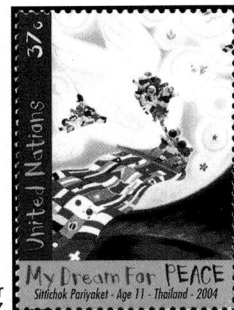

My Dream for
Peace — A357

Printed by Government Printing Office, Austria. Panes of 20.
Winning designs of Lions Club International children's global
peace poster contest by: 37c, Sittichok Pariyaket, Thailand.
80c, Bayan Fais Abu Bial, Israel.

2004, Sept. 21   Litho.   Perf. 14

869	A357	37c **multicolored** (276,000)+	.75	.35
		First day cover		1.25
		Inscription block of 4	3.00	
		Pane of 20	15.00	
870	A357	80c **multicolored** (206,000)+	1.60	.80
		First day cover		2.40
		First day cover, #869-870		3.00
		Inscription block of 4	6.50	
		Pane of 20	32.00	

See Offices in Geneva Nos. 429-430, Vienna Nos. 353-354.

A358

Human
Rights — A359

Printed by Banknote Corportation of America, US. Designed
by Yuri Gervorgian, Armenia.

2004, Oct. 14   Litho.   Perf. 11¼

871	A358	37c **multicolored** (464,000)+	.75	.75
		First day cover		1.25
		Pane of 8	6.00	
872	A359	70c **multicolored** (464,000)+	1.40	1.40
		First day cover		2.40
		First day cover, #871-872		3.00
		Pane of 8	11.50	

See Offices in Geneva Nos. 431-432, Vienna Nos. 355-356.

Disarmament
A360

Printed by Government Printing Office, Austria. Designed by Michel Granger, France.

2004, Oct. 15   **Litho.**   **Perf. 13¾**
873 A360 37c multicolored *(270,000)+*   .75   .75
   First day cover   1.25
   Inscription block of 4   3.00
   Pane of 20   15.00

The U.N. Postal Administration announced that it would begin offering canceled-to-order stamps at the same price as mint stamps, effective Feb. 4, 2005. It has been reliably reported that this did not happen.

United Nations, 60th Anniv. — A361

Printed by Banknote Corporation of America, US. Designed by Czeslaw Slania, Sweden.

2005, Feb. 4   **Litho. & Engr.**   **Perf. 11x11¼**
874 A361 80c multicolored *(395,000)+*   1.60   1.60
   First day cover   2.50
   Inscription block of 4   6.50
   Pane of 20   32.50

Souvenir Sheet
Litho.
Imperf
875 A361 $1 multicolored *(135,000)+*   17.50   15.00
   First day cover   3.25

See Offices in Geneva Nos. 434-435; Vienna Nos. 357-358.

Endangered Species Type of 1993
Printed by Johann Enschedé and Sons, the Netherlands. Designed by Boris Zlotsky, US.

Designs: No. 876, Blue orchid. No. 877, Swan orchid. No. 878, Christmas orchid. No. 879, Aerangis modesta.

2005, Mar. 3   **Litho.**   **Perf. 12¾x12½**
876 A271 37c multicolored *(248,000)+*   .75   .75
877 A271 37c multicolored *(248,000)+*   .75   .75
878 A271 37c multicolored *(248,000)+*   .75   .75
879 A271 37c multicolored *(248,000)+*   .75   .75
a.   Block of 4, #876-879   3.00   3.00
   First day cover, #879a   4.25
   First day cover, #876-879, each   1.75
   Inscription block of 4, #879a   3.00
   Pane of 16   12.00

See Offices in Geneva Nos. 436-439; Vienna Nos. 360-363.

Non-Violence, Sculpture by Carl Fredrik Reuterswärd, New York — A362

Armillary Sphere, Sculpture by Paul Manship, Geneva — A363

Terra Cotta Warriors, Vienna — A364

Single Form, Sculpture by Barbara Hepworth, New York — A365

Sphere Within a Sphere, Sculpture by Arnaldo Pomodoro, New York — A366

2005, Mar. 3   **Litho.**   **Perf. 13¼**
880 A362 80c multicolored + label   3.00   3.00
881 A363 80c multicolored + label   3.00   3.00
882 A364 80c multicolored + label   3.00   3.00
883 A365 80c multicolored + label   3.00   3.00

884 A366 80c multicolored + label   3.00
a.   Vert. strip of 5, #880-884, + 5 labels   15.00
   Sheet, 2 #884a   30.00
   First day cover, #884a
   First day cover, #880-884, each

The full sheet sold for $14.95 with or without persona labels. The personalization of labels was available only a Headquarters, and not through mail order.

The full sheet exists with sheet margins and labels comm orating the Riccione 2005 Philatelic Exhibition. This sheet on sale 8/20/05 and was also sold for $14.95. Value $50.

Nature's Wisdom — A367

Printed by Cartor Security Printing, France. Panes o' Designed by Robert Stein, US.
Designs: 37c, Ice climber, Norway. 80c, Egret, Japan.

2005, Apr. 21   **Litho.**   **Perf. 13½x**
885 A367 37c multicolored *(280,000)+*   .75
   First day cover
   Inscription block of 4   3.00
   Pane of 20   15.00
886 A367 80c multicolored *(200,000)+*   1.60
   First day cover, #885-886
   Inscription block of 4   6.50
   Pane of 20   32.50

See Offices in Geneva Nos. 440-441, Vienna Nos. 364-3

Intl. Year of Sport — A368

Printed by Cartor Security Printing, France. Designed Roland Hirter, Switzerland.

2005, June 3   **Litho.**   **Perf. 13x1**
887 A368 37c Sailing *(255,000)+*   .75
   First day cover
   Inscription block of 4   3.00
   Pane of 20   15.00
888 A368 70c Running *(185,000)+*   1.40
   First day cover
   First day cover, #887-888
   Inscription block of 4   5.60
   Pane of 20   28.00

See Offices in Geneva Nos. 442-443; Vienna Nos. 366-36

World Heritage Sites, Egypt — A369

Printed by Johann Enschedé and Sons, the Netherlar Panes of 20. Designed by Rorie Katz, US.
Designs: Nos. 889, 891a, Memphis and its Necropolis. N 890, 891d, Ancient Thebes. No. 891b, Philae. No. 891c, A Mena. No. 891e, Islamic Cairo. No. 891f, St. Catherine are

2005, Aug. 4   **Litho.**   **Perf. 14x1**
889 A369 37c multicolored *(275,000)+*   .75
   First day cover   1
   Inscription block of 4   3.00
890 A369 80c multicolored *(195,000)+*   1.60
   First day cover   3
   First day cover, #889-890   3
   Inscription block of 4   6.50

Souvenir Booklet

Booklet, #891g-891l *(29,000)+*	15.00		
c. A369 23c any single		.50	.50
f. A369 37c any single		.75	.75
g. Booklet pane of 4 #891a	2.00		—
h. Booklet pane of 4 #891b	2.00		—
i. Booklet pane of 4 #891c	2.00		—
j. Booklet pane of 4 #891d	3.00		—
k. Booklet pane of 4 #891e	3.00		—
l. Booklet pane of 4 #891e	3.00		—

e Offices in Geneva Nos. 444-446, Vienna Nos. 368-370.

My Dream for Peace Type of 2004

rinted by Government Printing Office, Austria. Panes of 20.
Winning designs of Lions Club International children's global
ce poster contest by: 37c, Vittoria Sansebastiano, Italy. 80c,
lan Harris, US.

05, Sept. 21	Litho.	*Perf. 14*	
A357 37c **multicolored** *(270,000)+*		.75	.75
First day cover			1.40
Inscription block of 4	3.00		—
Pane of 20	15.00		—
A357 80c **multicolored** *(200,000)+*		1.60	1.60
First day cover			3.00
First day cover, #892-893			3.50
Inscription block of 4	6.50		—
Pane of 20	32.00		—

e Offices in Geneva Nos. 447-448, Vienna Nos. 371-372.

Food for Life
A370

Printed by Government Printing Office, Austria. Designed by
drew Davidson, United Kingdom.
Designs: 37c, Oats, children and adults. 80c, Wheat, mothers
eastfeeding babies.

05, Oct. 20	Litho.	*Perf. 13¾*	
4 A370 37c **multicolored** *(245,000)+*		.75	.75
First day cover			1.25
Inscription block of 4	3.00		—
Pane of 20	15.00		—
5 A370 80c **multicolored** *(185,000)+*		1.60	1.60
First day cover			2.75
First day cover, #894-895			3.25
Inscription block of 4	6.50		—
Pane of 20	32.00		—

ee Offices in Geneva Nos. 449-450; Vienna Nos. 373-374.

Stylized Flags in Heart and Hands — A371

Printed by Cartor Security Printing, France. Panes of 20.
esigned by Eliezer Weishoff, Israel.

006, Feb. 3	Litho.	*Perf. 13x13¼*	
96 A371 25c **multicolored** *(670,000)+*		.50	.50
First day cover			1.75
Inscription block of 4	2.00		—
Pane of 20	10.00		—

Indigenous Art Type of 2003

Printed by Johann Enschedé and Sons, the Netherlands.
Designed by Robert Stein, US.

No. 897 — Musical instruments: a, Drum, Ivory Coast. b,
Drum, Tunisia. c, Stringed instruments, Morocco. d, Drums,
Sudan. e, Instruments, Cameroun. f, Harp, Congo.

006, Feb. 3	Litho.	*Perf. 13¼*	
897 A340 Sheet of 6 *(88,000)+*	4.50	4.50	
First day cover			6.25
a.-f. 37c Any single		.75	.75

See Offices in Geneva No. 452; Vienna No. 375.

UN Symbols Type of 2003

2006, Mar. 6	Litho.	*Perf. 13¼*	
898 A349 39c **multicolored** + label		1.50	1.50
899 A350 39c **multicolored** + label		1.50	1.50
900 A351 39c **multicolored** + label		1.50	1.50
901 A352 39c **multicolored** + label		1.50	1.50
902 A353 39c **multicolored** + label		1.50	1.50
a. Vert. strip of 5, #898-902, + 5 labels	7.50	7.50	
Sheet, 4 #902a	30.00		—

The full sheet sold for $14.95 with or without personalized
labels. The personalization of labels was available only at UN
Headquarters, and not through mail order.

Sculpture Type of 2005

2006, Mar. 6	Litho.	*Perf. 13¼*	
903 A362 84c **multicolored** + label		3.00	3.00
904 A363 84c **multicolored** + label		3.00	3.00
905 A364 84c **multicolored** + label		3.00	3.00
906 A365 84c **multicolored** + label		3.00	3.00
907 A366 84c **multicolored** + label		3.00	3.00
a. Vert. strip of 5, #903-907, + 5 labels	15.00	15.00	
Sheet, 2 #907a	30.00		—

The full sheet sold for $14.95 with or without personalized
labels. The personalization of labels was available only at UN
Headquarters, and not through mail order.
Full sheets with different margins were sold at the Washington 2006 World Philatelic Exhibition, where the labels could be
personalized.

Endangered Species Type of 1993

Printed by Johann Enschedé and Sons, the Netherlands.
Designed by John D. Dawson, US.
Designs: No. 908, Golden mantella. No. 909, Panther chameleon. No. 910, Peruvian rainbow boa. No. 911, Dyeing poison
frog.

2006, Mar. 16	Litho.	*Perf. 12¾x12½*	
908 A271 39c **multicolored** *(212,000)+*		.80	.80
909 A271 39c **multicolored** *(212,000)+*		.80	.80
910 A271 39c **multicolored** *(212,000)+*		.80	.80
911 A271 39c **multicolored** *(212,000)+*		.80	.80
a. Block of 4, #908-911	3.20	3.20	
First day cover, #911a			4.50
First day cover, #908-911, each			2.00
Inscription block of 4, #911a	3.20		—
Pane of 16	13.00		—

See Offices in Geneva Nos. 453-456; Vienna Nos. 376-379.

Dove Between War and Peace — A372

Designed by Armando Milani, Italy.

2006, Apr. 10	Litho.	*Perf. 13¼*	
912 A372 75c **multicolored** + label		3.00	3.00
Sheet of 10 + 10 labels	30.00		—

The full sheet sold for $14.95 with or without personalized
labels. The personalization of labels was available only at UN
Headquarters, and not through mail order.

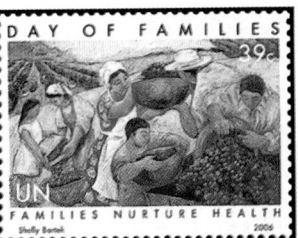

Intl. Day of Families
A373

Printed by Johann Enschedé and Sons, the Netherlands.
Designed by Shelly Bartek, US.
Designs: 39c, Family harvesting grapes. 84c, Children play-
ing with toy sailboats.

2006, May 27	Litho.	*Perf. 14x13½*	
913 A373 39c **multicolored** *(226,000)+*		.80	.80
First day cover			1.50
Inscription block of 4	3.20		—
Pane of 20	16.00		—
914 A373 84c **multicolored** *(186,000)+*		1.75	1.75
First day cover			3.25
First day cover, #913-914			3.75
Inscription block of 4	7.00		—
Pane of 20	35.00		—

See Offices in Geneva Nos. 457-458; Vienna Nos. 380-381.

2006 END-OF-YEAR ISSUES

The UNPA has announced that the following items
will be released in late 2006. Dates and denominations
are tentative.
World Heritage — France, *June 17,* 39c, 84c,
booklet containing twelve 5c and twelve 15c stamps;
Geneva, 1fr, 1.30fr, booklet containing twelve 10c and
twelve 20c stamps; Vienna, 55c, 75c, booklet containing twelve 20c and twelve 25c stamps.
My Dream of Peace One Day, *Sept. 21,* 39c, 84c;
Geneva, 85c, 1.20fr; Vienna, 55c, €1.
Coins and Flags, *Oct. 5,* 39c, sheet of eight
stamps; Geneva, 85c, sheet of eight stamps; Vienna,
55c, sheet of eight stamps.
Listings as of Noon, Aug. 11, 2006.

SEMI-POSTAL STAMPS

Souvenir Sheet

AIDS Awareness — SP1

Printed by Walsall Security Printers Limited, UK. Designed by
Rorie Katz, US.

2002, Oct. 24	Litho.	*Perf. 14½*	
B1 SP1 37c + 6c **multicolored** *(175,000)+*		2.50	2.50
First day cover, #B1			3.00

See Offices in Geneva No. B1, Vienna No. B1.

AIR POST STAMPS

Plane and
Gull — AP1

Swallows and
UN Emblem
AP2

Engraved and printed by Thomas De La Rue & Co., Ltd.,
London. Panes of 50. Designed by Ole Hamann (AP1) and Olav
Mathiesen (AP2).

1951, Dec. 14   Unwmk.   Perf. 14

C1	AP1	6c **henna brown** (2,500,000)	.20	.20
		First day cover		2.00
		Inscription block of 4	.25	—
C2	AP1	10c **bright blue green** (2,750,000)	.30	.20
		First day cover		2.00
		Inscription block of 4	1.25	
C3	AP2	15c **deep ultramarine** (3,250,000)	.40	.25
		First day cover		3.00
		Inscription block of 4	1.75	—
a.		15c **Prussian blue**	75.00	
C4	AP2	25c **gray black** (2,250,000)	.85	.50
		First day cover		7.50
		First day cover, #C1-C4		30.00
		Inscription block of 4	5.00	—
		Nos. C1-C4 (4)	1.75	1.15

First day covers of Nos. 1-11 and C1-C4 total 1,113,216.
Early printings of Nos. C1-C4 have wide, imperforate sheet
margins on three sides. Later printings were perforated through
all margins.

Airplane Wing and
Globe — AP3

Engraved and printed by Thomas De La Rue & Co., Ltd.,
London. Panes of 50. Designed by W. W. Wind.

1957, May 27   Perf. 12½x14

C5	AP3	4c **maroon** (5,000,000)	.20	.20
		First day cover (282,933)		1.00
		Inscription block of 4	.30	—

For 5c see No. C6.

Type of 1957 and

UN Flag and
Plane — AP4

Engraved and printed by Waterlow & Sons, Ltd., London.
Panes of 50. Designed by W. W. Wind (5c) and Olav Mathiesen
(7c).

1959, Feb. 9   Unwmk.   Perf. 12½x13½

C6	AP3	5c **rose red** (4,000,000)	.20	.20
		First day cover		1.00
		Inscription block of 4	.50	—

Perf. 13½x14

C7	AP4	7c **ultramarine** (4,000,000)	.20	.20
		First day cover		1.00
		First day cover, #C6-C7		17.50
		Inscription block of 4	.75	

First day covers of Nos. C6 and C7 total 413,556.

Outer
Space — AP5

UN Emblem — AP6

Bird of Laurel
Leaves — AP7

Printed by Courvoisier S.A., La Chaux-de-Fonds, Switzerland. Panes of 50. Designed by Claude Bottiau (6c), George
Hamori (8c) and Kurt Plowitz (13c).

1963, June 17   Photo.   Unwmk.   Perf. 11½

C8	AP5	6c **black, blue & yellow green** (4,000,000)	.20	.20
		First day cover		1.00
		Inscription block of 4	.45	—
C9	AP6	8c **yellow, olive green & red** (4,000,000)	.20	.20
		First day cover		1.00
		Inscription block of 4	.60	—

Perf. 12½x12

C10	AP7	13c **ultra, aquamarine, gray & carmine** (2,700,000)	.20	.20
		First day cover		1.00
		First day cover, #C8-C10		8.50
		Inscription block of 4	.90	

First day covers of Nos. C8-C10 total 535,824.

"Flight Across the
Globe" — AP8

Jet Plane and
Envelope — AP9

Printed by the Austrian Government Printing Office, Vienna,
Austria. Panes of 50. Designed by Ole Hamann (15c) and
George Hamori (25c).

Perf. 11½x12, 12x11½

1964, May 1		Photo.		Unw
C11	AP8	15c **violet, buff, gray & pale green** (3,000,000)	.30	
		First day cover		
		Inscription block of 4	1.40	
C12	AP9	25c **yellow, orange, gray, blue & red** (2,000,000)	.50	
		First day cover		
		First day cover, #C11-C12		
		Inscription block of 4	2.50	
		Nos. C8-C12 (5)	1.40	

First day covers of Nos. C11-C12 total 353,696.
For 75c in type AP8, see UN Offices in Geneva No. 8.

Jet Plane and U
Emblem — AP1

Printed by Setelipaino, Finland. Panes of 50. Designed
Ole Hamann.

1968, Apr. 18   Litho.   Perf.

C13	AP10	20c **multicolored** (3,000,000)		.35
		First day cover (225,378)		
		Inscription block of 4	1.60	

Wings, Envelopes
and UN
Emblem — AP11

Printed by Setelipaino, Finland. Panes of 50. Designed
Olav S. Mathiesen.

1969, Apr. 21   Litho.   Perf.

C14	AP11	10c **orange vermilion, orange, yellow & black** (4,000,000)	.20	1
		First day cover (132,686)		
		Inscription block of 4	.75	

UN Emblem and Stylized
Wing — AP12

Birds in
Flight — AP13

Clouds
AP14

"UN" and
Plane — AP15

inted by Government Printing Bureau, Japan (9c); Heraclio
nier, S. A., Spain (11c, 17c); Setelipaino, Finland (21c).
es of 50. Designed by Lyell L. Dolan (9c), Arne Johnson
), British American Bank Note Co. (17c) and Asher
eron (21c).

2, May 1	**Litho. & Engr.**	***Perf. 13x13½***	
AP12	9c light blue, dark red & violet		
	blue *(3,000,000)+*	.20	.20
	First day cover		1.00
	Inscription block of 4	.50	—

Photo.
Perf. 14x13½

AP13 11c blue & multicolored
(3,000,000)+ .20 .20
First day cover 1.00
Inscription block of 4 .75 —

Perf. 13½x14

AP14 17c yellow, red & orange
(3,000,000)+ .25 .20
First day cover 1.00
Inscription block of 4 1.10 —

Perf. 13

AP15 21c silver & multi *(3,500,000)* .25 .25
First day cover 1.00
First day cover, #C15-C18 3.50
Inscription block of 4 1.25 —
Nos. C15-C18 (4) .90 .85

First day covers of Nos. C15-C18 total 553,535.

Globe and
Jet — AP16

Pathways
Radiating
from UN
Emblem
AP17

Bird in Flight, UN
Headquarters
AP18

Printed by Setelipaino, Finland. Panes of 50. Designed by
eorge Hamori (13c), Shamir Bros. (18c) and Olav S.
athiesen (26c).

974, Sept. 16	**Litho.**	***Perf. 13, 12½x13 (18c)***	
19 AP16	13c multicolored *(2,500,000)+*	.20	.20
	First day cover		1.00
	Inscription block of 4	.80	—
20 AP17	18c gray olive & multicolored		
	(2,000,000)	.25	.20
	First day cover		1.00
	Inscription block of 4	1.10	—
21 AP18	26c blue & multi *(2,000,000)*	.35	.30
	First day cover		1.25
	First day cover, #C19-C21		2.50
	Inscription block of 4	1.60	—
	Nos. C19-C21 (3)	.80	.70

First day covers of Nos. C19-C21 total 309,610.

Winged Airmail
Letter — AP19

Symbolic Globe
and Plane — AP20

Printed by Heraclio Fournier, S.A. Panes of 50. Designed by
Eliezer Weishoff (25c) and Alan L. Pollock (31c).

1977, June 27	**Photo.**	***Perf. 14***	
C22 AP19	25c greenish blue & multi		
	(2,000,000)+	.40	.25
	First day cover		1.25
	Inscription block of 4	1.75	—
C23 AP20	31c magenta *(2,000,000)*	.45	.30
	First day cover		1.25
	First day cover, #C22-C23		1.50
	Inscription block of 4	2.10	—

First day covers of Nos. C22-C23 total 209,060.

ENVELOPES

Used values for all postal stationery are for non-
philatelic contemporaneous usages.

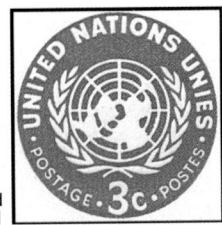

Emblem of United
Nations — U1

Printed by the International Envelope Corp., Dayton, Ohio.
Die engraved by the American Bank Note Co., New York.

1953, Sept. 15		**Embossed**	
U1 U1	3c blue, entire *(555,000)*	.40	.40
	Entire, first day cancel *(102,278)*		1.00

Printed by International Envelope Corp., Dayton,
Ohio.

1958, Sept. 22		**Embossed**	
U2 U1	4c ultramarine, entire *(1,000,000)*	.40	.40
	Entire, first day cancel *(213,621)*		1.00

Stylized Globe
and Weather
Vane — U2

Printed by United States Envelope Co., Springfield, Mass.
Designed by Hatim El Mekki.

1963, Apr. 26		**Litho.**	
U3 U2	5c multicolored, entire *(1,115,888)*	.25	.25
	Entire, first day cancel *(165,188)*		1.00

Printed by Setelipaino, Finland.

1969, Jan. 8		**Litho.**	
U4 U2	6c black, blue, magenta & dull yel-		
	low, entire *(850,000)*	.25	.25
	Entire, first day cancel *(152,593)*		1.00

Headquarters Type of Regular Issue, 1968
Printed by Eureka Co., a division of Litton Industries.

1973, Jan. 12		**Litho.**	
U5 A99	8c sepia, blue & olive, entire		
	(700,000)	.50	.50
	Entire, first day cancel *(145,510)*		1.00

Headquarters Type of Regular Issue, 1974
Printed by United States Envelope Co., Springfield,
Mass.

1975, Jan. 10		**Litho.**	
U6 A138	10c blue, olive bister & multi, entire		
	(547,500)	.40	.40
	Entire, first day cancel *(122,000)*		1.00

Bouquet of Ribbons — U3

Printed by Carl Ueberreuter Druck and Verlag M. Salzer,
Austria. Designed by George Hamori, Australia.

1985, May 10		**Litho.**	
U7 U3	22c multicolored, entire *(250,000)*	8.50	3.50
	Entire, first day cancel *(28,600)*		3.50

New York
Headquarters
U4

Printed by Mercury Walch, Australia. Designed by Rocco J.
Callari, United States.

1989, Mar. 17		**Litho.**	
U8 U4	25c multicolored, entire *(350,000)*	2.75	2.25
	Entire, first day cancel *(28,567)*		6.00

For surcharge see No. U9A.

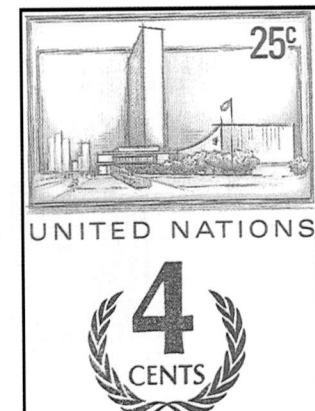

No. U8
Surcharged

1991, Apr. 15		**Litho.**	
U9 U4	25c +4c multicolored, entire *(50,000)+*	2.75	2.75
	Entire, first day cover		5.50

No. U8
Surcharged

1995   **Litho.**
U9A U4 25c +7c **multicolored,** entire   3.00 3.00
     Entire, first day cover   6.00

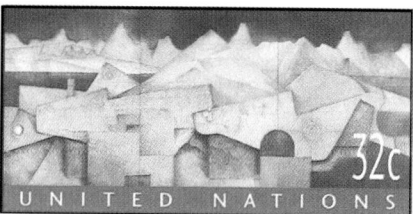

Cripticandina, by Alfredo La Placa — U5

Illustration reduced.
Design sizes: No. U10, 79x38mm. No. U11, 89x44mm.

1997, Feb. 12   **Litho.**
U10 U5 32c **multicolored,** #6¾, entire (65,000)+   3.00 2.00
     Entire, first day cancel   5.50
U11 U5 32c **multicolored,** #10, entire (80,000)+   3.00 2.00
     Entire, first day cancel   5.50

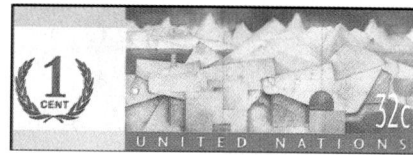

Nos. U10-U11 Surcharged

1999, Jan. 10   **Litho.**
U12 U5 32c +1c **multicolored,** on #U10, entire   2.00 2.00
     First day cancel, entire   2.50
U13 U5 32c +1c **multicolored,** on #U11, entire   2.00 2.00
     First day cancel, entire   2.50

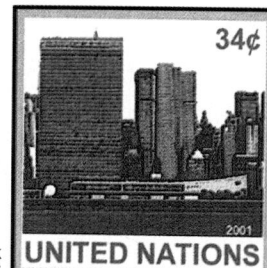

New York
Headquarters — U6

Design sizes: No. U14, 34x34mm. No. U15, 36x36mm.

2001, May 25   **Litho.**
U14 U6 34c **multicolored,** #6¾, entire   .90   .90
     Entire, first day cancel   1.25
U15 U6 34c **multicolored,** #10, entire   .90   .90
     Entire, first day cancel   1.25

Nos. U14-U15 Surcharged

2002, June 30   **Litho.**
U16 U6 34c +3c **multicolored,** entire (#U14)   2.00 2.00
     Entire, first day cancel   2.00
U17 U6 34c +3c **multicolored,** entire (#U15)   2.00 2.00
     Entire, first day cancel   2.00

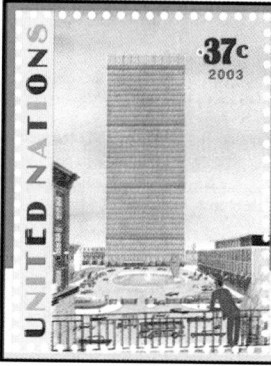

UN Headquarters
U7

Printed by Australia Post Spintpak, Australia.
Design sizes: No. U18, 37x47mm. No. U19, 40x52mm.

2003, Mar. 28   **Litho.**
U18 U7 37c **multicolored,** #6¾, entire (62,000)+ 1.00   .50
     Entire, first day cancel   1.25
U19 U7 37c **multicolored,** #10, entire (72,000)+ 1.00   .50
     Entire, first day cancel   1.25

Nos. U18-U19 Surcharged

2006, Jan. 8   **Litho.**
U20 U7 37c +2c **multicolored,** entire (#U18)   1.00 1.00
     Entire, first day cancel   1.25
U21 U7 37c +2c **multicolored,** entire (#U19)   1.00 1.00
     Entire, first day cancel   1.25

AIR POST ENVELOPES AND AIR LETTER SHEETS

Used values for all postal stationery are for non-
philatelic contemporaneous usages.

Letter Sheet
Type of Air Post Stamp of 1951
Inscribed "Air Letter" at Left
Printed by Dennison & Sons, Long Island City, NY.

1952, Aug. 29   **Litho.**
UC1 AP2 10c **blue,** bluish, entire (187,000)   22.50 20.00
     Entire, 1st day cancel (57,274)   2.50

Designed by C. Mutver.

Letter Sheet
Inscribed "Air Letter" and "Aerogramme" at Le

1954, Sept. 14   **Li**
UC2 AP2 10c **royal blue,** bluish, entire,
     (207,000)   9.50
     Entire, 1st day cancel   20
  a. No white border, 1958 (148,800)   7.00

No. UC2 was printed with a narrow white border (½ to
wide) surrounding the stamp. On No. UC2a, this border
been partly or entirely eliminated.

UN Flag and
Plane — UC1

(UN Emblem Embossed)

Printed by International Envelope Corp., Dayton, O.
Die engraved by American Bank Note Co., New York.

1959, Sept. 21   **Embos**
UC3 UC1 7c **blue,** entire (550,000)   1.00
     Entire, 1st day cancel (172,107)

Letter Sheet
Type of Air Post Stamp of 1959
Printed by Thomas De La Rue & Co., Ltd., Londo

1960, Jan. 18   **Lit**
UC4 AP4 10c **ultramarine,** bluish, entire
     (405,000)   .65
     Entire, 1st day cancel (122,425)

Printed on protective tinted paper containing colorl
inscription "United Nations" in the five official languages of
UN.

Letter Sheet
Type of Air Post Stamp of 1951
Inscribed "Correo Aereo" instead of "Poste Aerienr
Printed by Thomas De La Rue & Co., Ltd., Londo

1961, June 26   **Lit**
UC5 AP1 11c **ultramarine,** bluish, entire
     (550,000)   .50
     Entire, 1st day cancel (128,557)
  a. 11c **dark blue,** green entire, July 16, 1965
     (419,000)   1.25 1

Printed on protective tinted paper containing colorle
inscription "United Nations" in the five official languages of
UN.

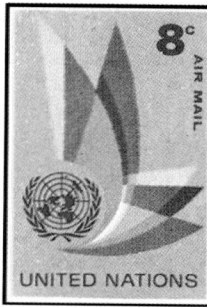

UN Emblem — UC2

Printed by United States Envelope Co., Springfield, Mas
Designed by George Hamori.

1963, Apr. 26   **Lith**
UC6 UC2 8c **multicolored,** entire (880,000)   .30 .3
     Entire, 1st day cancel (165,208)   1.0

Letter Sheet

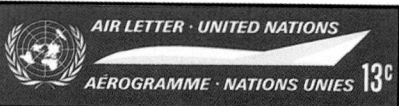

UN Emblem and Stylized Plane — UC3

Printed by Setelipaino, Finland. Designed by Robert Perrot

1968, May 31   **Litho**
UC7 UC3 13c **violet blue & light blue,** entire
     (750,000)   .30 .3
     Entire, 1st day cancel (106,700)   .5

Type of 1963
Printed by Setelipaino, Finland.

9, Jan. 8 Litho.
~ UC2 10c **pink, Prussian blue, orange & se-**
pia, entire *(750,000)* .35 .35
Entire, 1st day cancel *(153,472)* .50

Letter Sheet

UN Emblem, "UN," Globe and Plane — UC4

~rinted by Joh. Enschede and Sons. Designed by Edmondo
~vis, Egypt. Sheet surface printed in greenish blue.

~2, Oct. 16 Litho.
~9 UC4 15c **violet blue & greenish blue,** entire
(500,000) .60 .60
Entire, 1st day cancel *(85,500)* 1.00

Bird Type of Air Post Stamp, 1972
~nted by Eureka Co., a division of Litton Industries

~3, Jan. 12 Litho.
~10 AP13 11c **blue & multicolored,** entire
(700,000) .40 .40
Entire, 1st day cancel *(134,500)* 1.00

Globe and Jet Air Post Type of 1974
~rinted by United States Envelope Co., Springfield,
Mass.

~75, Jan. 10 Litho.
~11 AP16 13c **blue & multicolored,** entire
(555,539) .60 .60
Entire, 1st day cancel *(122,000)* 1.00

Letter Sheet
Headquarters Type of Regular Issue, 1971
~Printed by Joh. Enschede and Sons, Netherlands

~75, Jan. 10 Photo.
~12 A120 18c **blue & multicolored,** entire
(400,000) .60 .60
Entire, 1st day cancel *(70,500)* 1.00

Letter Sheet

"UN"
~mblem and
Birds
UC5

~Printed by Joh. Enschede and Sons. Designed by Angel
~edina Medina.

~977, June 27 Litho.
~C13 UC5 22c **multicolored,** entire *(400,000)* .65 .60
Entire, 1st day cancel *(70,000)* 1.00

Letter Sheet

Paper
Airplane
UC6

~Printed by Joh. Enschede and Sons.
Designed by Margaret-Ann Champion.

~982, Apr. 28 Litho.
~C14 UC6 30c **black,** *pale green,* entire
(400,000) 1.50 1.50
Entire, 1st day cancel *(61,400)* 1.25

Letter Sheet No. UC14 Surcharged

~987, July 7 Litho.
~C15 UC6 30c + 6c **black,** *green,* entire
(43,000) 45.00 45.00
Entire, 1st day cancel 20.00

New York
Headquarters
UC7

Printed by Mercury Walch, Australia. Designed by Thomas
Lee, China.

1989, Mar. 17 Litho.
UC16 UC7 39c **multicolored,** entire *(350,000)* 3.50 3.00
Entire, 1st day cancel *(14,798)* 9.50

No. UC16
Surcharged

1991, Feb. 12 Litho.
UC17 UC7 39c + 6c **multicolored,** entire
(35,563) 16.00 16.00
Entire, first day cancel 8.50

UC8

Designed by Robert Stein. Printed by Mercury-Walch,
Australia.

1992, Sept. 4 Litho.
UC18 UC8 45c **multicolored,** entire, *(185,000)+* 3.00 3.00
First day cancel 10.00

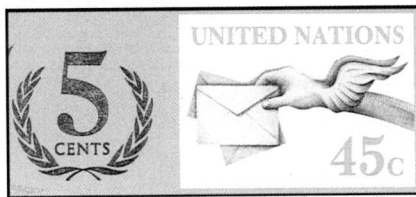

Letter Sheet No. UC18 Surcharged

1995, July 9 Litho.
UC19 UC8 45c +5c **multicolored,** entire 5.00 5.00
First day cover 9.00

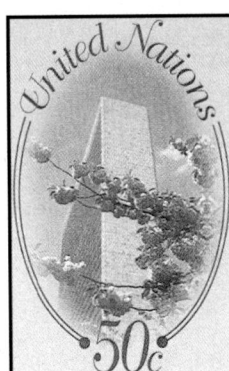

Cherry
Blossoms — UC9

1997, Mar. 13 Litho.
UC20 UC9 50c **multicolored,** entire *(115,000)+* 2.50 2.00
Entire, first day cancel 2.50

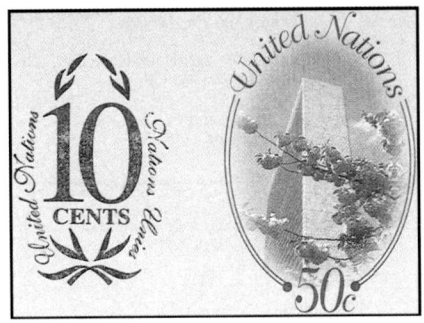

No. UC20 Surcharged

1999, Aug. 23 Litho.
UC21 UC9 50c +10c **multicolored,** entire 1.75 1.75
Entire, first day cancel 2.00

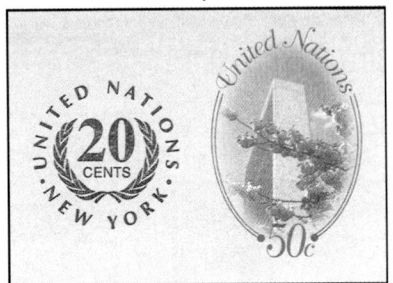

No. UC20 Surcharged

2001, Jan. 9 Litho.
UC22 UC9 50c +20c **multicolored,** entire 1.75 1.75
Entire, first day cancel 2.00

Cherry Blossoms at
New York
Headquarters
UC10

2001, May 25 Litho.
UC23 UC10 70c **multicolored,** entire 1.75 1.75
Entire, first day cancel 1.75

No. UC23 Surcharged

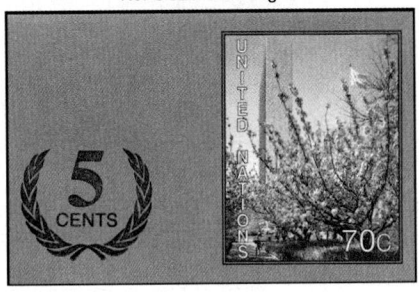

2006, Jan. 8 Litho.
UC24 UC10 70c +5c **multicolored,** entire 1.50 1.50
Entire, first day cancel 1.50

POSTAL CARDS

Values are for entire cards.

Type of Postage Issue of 1951
Printed by Dennison & Sons, Long Island City, N.Y.
1952, July 18   **Litho.**
UX1   A2   2c **blue**, *buff* (899,415)   .20   .20
    First day cancel (116,023)   .50

Printed by British American Bank Note Co., Ltd.,
Ottawa, Canada
1958, Sept. 22   **Litho.**
UX2   A2   3c **gray olive**, *buff* (575,000)   .20   .20
    First day cancel (145,557)   .50

World Map,
Sinusoidal
Projection — PC1

Printed by Eureka Specialty Printing Co., Scranton, Pa.

1963, Apr. 26   **Litho.**
UX3   PC1   4c **light blue, violet blue, orange &**
       bright citron (784,000)   .25   .20
    First day cancel (112,280)   .50
   a. Bright citron omitted   —

UN Emblem and Post   "UN" — PC3
Horn — PC2

Printed by Canadian Bank Note Co., Ltd., Ottawa. Designed
by John Mason.

1969, Jan. 8   **Litho.**
UX4   PC2   5c **blue & black** (500,000)   .25   .20
    First day cancel (95,975)   .50

1973, Jan. 12   **Litho.**
Printed by Government Printing Bureau, Tokyo. Designed by
Asher Kalderon.
UX5   PC3   6c **gray & multicolored** (500,000) .20   .20
    First day cancel (84,500)   .50

Type of 1973
Printed by Setelipaino, Finland.
1975, Jan. 10   **Litho.**
UX6   PC3   8c **light green & multi** (450,000) .60   .60
    First day cancel (72,500)   .50

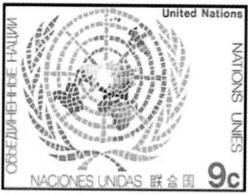

UN Emblem — PC4

Printed by Setelipaino, Finland. Designed by George Hamori.

1977, June 27   **Litho.**
UX7   PC4   9c **multicolored** (350,000)   .60   .60
    First day cancel (70,000)   .50

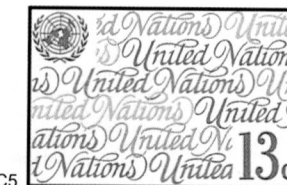

PC5

Printed by Courvoisier. Designed by Salahattin Kanidinc.

1982, Apr. 28   **Photo.**
UX8   PC5   13c **multicolored** (350,000)   .50   .50
    First day cancel (59,200)   1.00

Views of New
York
Headquarters
PC6

Designs: No. UX9, Spring at U.N. Headquarters, vert. No.
UX10, Cherry Blossoms, U.N. Gardens, vert. No. UXC11, Row
of Flags of member states. No. UX12, U.N. General Assembly.
No. UX13, River view, U.N. Headquarters. No. UX14, U.N.
Headquarters, vert. No. UX15, Row of flags of member states,
vert. No. UX16, Night view, U.N. Headquarters, vert. No. UX17,
U.N. Security Council. No. UX18, U.N. Gardens.
  Printed by Johann Enschede and Sons, the Netherlands.
Designed by Thomas Lee, China, from photographs.

1989, Mar. 17   **Litho.**
UX9   PC6   15c **multicolored** (120,000)+   .65   1.00
    First day cancel   2.25
UX10   PC6   15c **multicolored** (120,000)+   .65   1.00
    First day cancel   2.25
UX11   PC6   15c **multicolored** (120,000)+   .65   1.00
    First day cancel   2.25
UX12   PC6   15c **multicolored** (120,000)+   .65   1.00
    First day cancel   2.25
UX13   PC6   15c **multicolored** (120,000)+   .65   1.00
    First day cancel   2.25
UX14   PC6   36c **multicolored** (120,000)+   .90   1.50
    First day cancel   2.50
UX15   PC6   36c **multicolored** (120,000)+   .90   1.50
    First day cancel   2.50
UX16   PC6   36c **multicolored** (120,000)+   .90   1.50
    First day cancel   2.50
UX17   PC6   36c **multicolored** (120,000)+   .90   1.50
    First day cancel   2.50
UX18   PC6   36c **multicolored** (120,000)+   .90   1.50
    First day cancel   2.50
    Nos. UX9-UX18 (10)   7.75 12.50

Nos. UX9-UX13 and UX14-UX18 sold only in sets. Nos. UX9-
UX13 sold for $2 and Nos. UX14-UX18 sold for $3.
First day cancels of Nos. UX9-UX18 total 125,526.

New York Headquarters Type of 1991
Printed by Mercury-Walch, Australia.

1992, Sept. 4   **Litho.**
UX19   A260 40c **blue** (150,000)+   3.50   4.00
    First day cancel (9,603)   12.50

Secretariat Building,
Roses — PC7

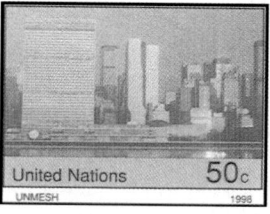

UN
Complex — PC8

Printed by Mercury-Walsh, Australia.

1998, May 20   **Litho.**
UX20   PC7   21c **multicolored** (150,000)+   1.25   1.25
    First day cancel   1.75
UX21   PC8   50c **multicolored** (150,000)+   2.00   2.00
    First day cancel   2.25

Illustrations of the buildings and other scenes are shown on
the back of each card.

New York
Headquarters
PC9

2001, May 25   **Lit...**
UX22   PC9   70c **multicolored**   1.75
    Entire, first day cancel

No. UX20 Surcharged

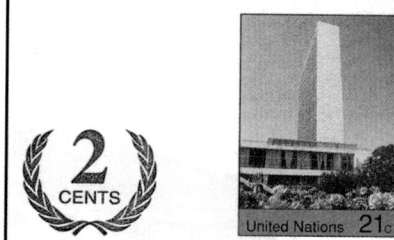

2002, June 30   **Lit...**
UX23   PC7   21c +2c **multicolored**   1.25 1...
    First day cancel

PC10

PC11

PC12

PC13

PC15

PC16   PC17

PC18

Illustrations from *This is the United Nations*, by M. Sasek — PC19

Printed by Banknote Corporation of America, US.

				Litho.
003, Mar. 28				
X24	PC10	23c multicolored (61,500)+	.45	.45
	Entire, first day cancel			1.00
X25	PC11	23c multicolored (61,500)+	.45	.45
	Entire, first day cancel			1.00
X26	PC12	23c multicolored (61,500)+	.45	.45
	Entire, first day cancel			1.00
X27	PC13	23c multicolored (61,500)+	.45	.45
	Entire, first day cancel			1.00
X28	PC14	23c multicolored (61,500)+	.45	.45
	Entire, first day cancel			1.00
X29	PC15	70c multicolored (86,500)+	1.40	1.40
	Entire, first day cancel			1.40
X30	PC16	70c multicolored (86,500)+	1.40	1.40
	Entire, first day cancel			1.40
X31	PC17	70c multicolored (86,500)+	1.40	1.40
	Entire, first day cancel			1.40
X32	PC18	70c multicolored (86,500)+	1.40	1.40
	Entire, first day cancel			1.40
X33	PC19	70c multicolored (86,500)+	1.40	1.40
	Entire, first day cancel			1.40
	Nos. UX24-UX33 (10)		9.25	9.25

Nos. UX24-UX28 and UX29-UX33 were sold only in shrink-wrapped sets.

AIR POST POSTAL CARDS

Values are for entire cards.

Type of Air Post Stamp of 1957

Printed by British American Bank Note Co., Ltd., Ottawa.

			Litho.
1957, May 27			
UXC1 AP3	4c maroon, buff (631,000)	.25	.30
	First day cancel (260,005)		1.00

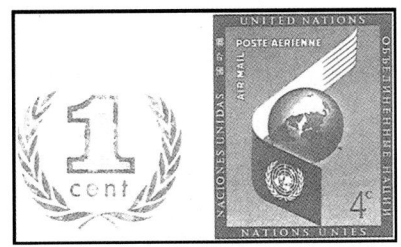

No. UXC1 Surcharged in Maroon at Left of Stamp

			Litho.
1959, June 5			
UXC2 AP3	4c + 1c maroon, buff (1,119,000)	.30	.50
	Cancel first day of public use, June 8		300.00
a.	Double surcharge	—	
b.	Inverted surcharge	—	
c.	Double surcharge, one inverted	—	

This surcharge also exists on a No. U1 envelope. Status uncertain.

Type of Air Post Stamp, 1957

Printed by Eureka Specialty Printing Co., Scranton, Pa.

			Litho.
1959, Sept. 21			
UXC3 AP3	5c crimson, buff (500,000)	.65	.65
	First day cancel (119,479)		.50

Outer Space — APC1

Printed by Eureka Specialty Printing Co., Scranton, Pa.

			Litho.
1963, Apr. 26			
UXC4 APC1	6c black & blue (350,000)	.60	.60
	First day cancel (109,236)		.50

APC2

Printed by Eureka-Carlisle Co., Scranton, Pa. Designed by Olav S. Mathiesen.

			Litho.
1966, June 9			
UXC5 APC2	11c dark red, rose, yellow & brown (764,500)	.30	.30
	First day cancel (162,588)		.50

			Litho.
1968, May 31			
UXC6 APC2	13c dark green, bright green & yellow (829,000)	.40	.40
	First day cancel (106,500)		1.00

UN Emblem and Stylized Planes — APC3

Printed by Canadian Bank Note Co., Ltd., Ottawa. Designed by Lawrence Kurtz.

			Litho.
1969, Jan. 8			
UXC7 APC3	8c gray, dull yellow, lt blue, indigo & red (500,000)	.65	.65
	First day cancel (94,037)		.50

Type of Air Post Stamp of 1972

Printed by Government Printing Bureau, Tokyo. Designed by L. L. Dolan.

			Litho.
1972, Oct. 16			
UXC8 AP12	9c orange, red, gray & green (500,000)	.45	.45
	First day cancel (85,600)		.50

Type of 1969

Printed by Government Printing Bureau, Tokyo

			Litho.
1972, Oct. 16			
UXC9 APC3	15c lilac, light blue, pink & carmine (500,000)	.50	.50
	First day cancel (84,800)		.50

Types of Air Post Stamps, 1972-74

Printed by Setelipaino, Finland.

			Litho.
1975, Jan. 10			
UXC10 AP14	11c greenish blue, blue & dark blue (250,000)	.50	.50
	First day cancel (70,500)		.50
UXC11 AP17	18c gray & multicolored (250,000)	.50	.50
	First day cancel (70,500)		.50

Flying Mailman — APC4

Printed by Courvoisier. Designed by Arieh Glaser.

			Photo.
1982, Apr. 28			
UXC12 APC4	28c multicolored (350,000)	.45	.50
	First day cancel (58,700)		1.40

OFFICES IN GENEVA, SWITZERLAND

For use only on mail posted at the Palais des Nations (UN European Office), Geneva. Inscribed in French unless otherwise stated.

100 Centimes = 1 Franc

Types of United Nations Issues 1961-69 and

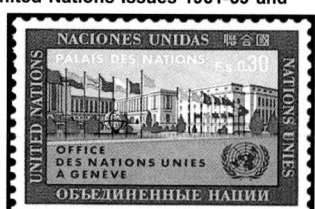

United Nations European Office, Geneva — G1

Printed by Setelipaino, Finland (5c, 70c, 80c, 90c, 2fr, 10fr), Courvoisier, S.A., Switzerland (10c, 20c, 30c, 50c, 60c, 3fr). Government Printing Office, Austria (75c) and Government Printing Office, Federal Republic of Germany (1fr).
Panes of 50. 30c designed by Ole Hamann, others as before.

Designs: 5c, UN Headquarters, New York, and world map. 10c, UN flag. 20c, Opening words of UN Charter. 60c, UN emblem over globe. 70c, "un" and UN emblem. 75c, "Flight Across Globe." 80c, UN Headquarters and emblem. 90c, Abstract group of flags. 1fr, UN emblem. 2fr, Stylized globe and weather vane. 3fr, Statue by Henrik Starcke. 10fr, "Peace, Justice, Security."
The 20c, 80c and 90c are inscribed in French. The 75c and 10fr carry French inscription at top, English at bottom.

1969-70   **Photo.**   **Unwmk.**
Perf. 13 (5c, 70c, 90c); 12½x12 (10c);

1	A88	**5c purple & multi,** *Oct. 4, 1969 (3,300,000)*	.20	.20
		First day cover		1.00
		Inscription block of 4	.25	—
a.		Green omitted	—	
2	A52	**10c salmon & multi,** *Oct. 4, 1969 (4,300,000)+*	.20	.20
		First day cover		1.00
		Inscription block of 4	.25	—

Perf. 11½ (20c-60c, 3fr)

3	A66	**20c black & multi,** *Oct. 4, 1969 (4,500.000)*	.20	.20
		First day cover		1.00
		Inscription block of 4	.45	—
4	G1	**30c dark blue & multi,** *Oct. 4, 1969 (3,000,000)*	.20	.20
		First day cover		1.00
		Inscription block of 4	.60	—
5	A77	**50c ultra & multi,** *Oct. 4, 1969 (3,300,000)*	.30	.30
		First day cover		1.25
		Inscription block of 4	.80	—
6	A54	**60c dark brown, salmon & gold,** *Apr. 17, 1970 (3,300,000)+*	.35	.35
		First day cover		1.00
		Inscription block of 4	1.50	—
7	A104	**70c red, black & gold,** *Sept. 22, 1970 (3,300,000)+*	.40	.40
		First day cover		1.00
		Inscription block of 4	1.75	—

Perf. 11½x12 (75c)

8	AP8	**75c carmine rose & multi,** *Oct. 4, 1969 (3,300,000)+*	.45	.45
		First day cover		1.00
		Inscription block of 4	1.90	—

Perf. 13½x14 (80c)

9	A78	**80c blue green, red & yellow,** *Sept. 22, 1970 (3,300,000)*	.45	.45
		First day cover		1.00
		Inscription block of 4	1.90	—
10	A45	**90c blue & multi,** *Sept. 22, 1970 (3,300,000)*	.50	.50
		First day cover		1.00
		Inscription block of 4	2.10	—

Litho. & Embossed
Perf. 14 (1fr)

11	A79	**1fr light & dark green,** *Oct. 4, 1969 (3,000,000)*	.55	.55
		First day cover		1.00
		Inscription block of 4	2.40	—

Photo.
Perf. 12x11½ (2fr)

12	A67	**2fr blue & multi,** *Sept. 22, 1970 (3,000,000)+*	1.10	1.10
		First day cover		2.00
		Inscription block of 4	4.50	—
13	A97	**3fr olive & multi,** *Oct. 4, 1969 (3,000,000)+*	1.75	1.75
		First day cover		2.25
		Inscription block of 4	7.50	—

Engr.
Perf. 12 (10fr)

14	A3	**10fr dark blue,** *Apr. 17, 1970 (2,250,000)+*	5.75	5.75
		First day cover		8.50
		Inscription block of 4	24.00	—
		Nos. 1-14 (14)	12.40	12.40

+ Printing orders to June 1084.
First day covers of Nos. 1-5, 8, 11, 13 total 607,578; of Nos. 6 and 14, 148,055; of Nos. 7, 9-10 and 12, 226,000.

Sea Bed Type of UN

1971, Jan. 25   **Photo. & Engr.**   **Perf. 13**

15	A114	**30c green & multi** *(1,935,871)*	.20	.20
		First day cover *(152,590)*		1.00
		Inscription block of 4	.65	—

Refugee Type of UN

1971, Mar. 12   **Litho.**   **Perf. 13x12½**

16	A115	**50c deep carmine, deep orange & black** *(1,820,114)*	.25	.25
		First day cover *(148,220)*		1.00
		Inscription block of 4	1.05	—

World Food Program Type of UN

1971, Apr. 13   **Photo.**   **Perf. 14**

17	A116	**50c dark violet & multi** *(1,824,170)*	.25	.25
		First day cover *(151,580)*		1.00
		Inscription block of 4	1.05	—

UPU Headquarters Type of UN

1971, May 28   **Photo.**   **Perf. 11½**

18	A117	**75c green & multi** *(1,821,878)*	.35	.35
		First day cover *(140,679)*		1.00
		Inscription block of 4	1.60	—

Eliminate Racial Discrimination Types of UN

Designed by Daniel Gonzague (30c) and Ole Hamann (50c).

1971, Sept. 21   **Photo.**   **Perf. 13½**

19	A118	**30c blue & multi** *(1,838,474)*	.20	.20
		First day cover		1.00
		Inscription block of 4	.75	—
20	A119	**50c yellow green & multi** *(1,804,126)*	.25	.25
		First day cover		1.00
		First day cover, #19-20		1.25
		Inscription block of 4	1.10	—

First day covers of Nos. 19-20 total 308,420.

Picasso Type of UN

1971, Nov. 19   **Photo.**   **Perf. 11½**

21	A122	**1.10fr multicolored** *(1,467,993)*	.75	.75
		First day cover *(195,215)*		1.25
		Inscription block of 4	3.00	—

Palais des Nations, Geneva — G2

Printed by Courvoisier, S. A. Panes of 50. Designed by Ole Hamann.

1972, Jan. 5   **Photo.**   **Perf. 11½**

22	G2	**40c olive, blue, salmon & dark green** *(3,500,000)+*	.25	.25
		First day cover *(152,300)*		1.00
		Inscription block of 4	1.05	—

+ Initial printing order.

Nuclear Weapons Type of UN

1972, Feb. 14   **Photo.**   **Perf. 13½x14**

23	A124	**40c yellow, green, black, rose & gray** *(1,567,305)*	.25	.25
		First day cover *(151,350)*		1.00
		Inscription block of 4	1.25	—

World Health Day Type of UN

1972, Apr. 7   **Litho. & Engr.**   **Perf. 13x13½**

24	A125	**80c black & multi** *(1,543,368)*	.45	.45
		First day cover *(192,600)*		1.00
		Inscription block of 4	2.00	—

Human Environment Type of UN
Lithographed & Embossed

1972, June 5   **Perf. 12½**

25	A126	**40c olive, lemon, green & blue** *(1,594,089)*	.25	
		First day cover		
		Inscription block of 4	1.00	
26	A126	**80c ultra, pink, green & blue** *(1,568,009)*	.45	
		First day cover		
		First day cover, #25-26		
		Inscription block of 4	1.80	

First day covers of Nos. 25-26 total 296,700.

Economic Commission for Europe Type of U

1972, Sept. 11   **Litho.**   **Perf. 13x**

27	A127	**1.10fr red & multi** *(1,604,082)*	1.00	
		First day cover *(149,630)*		
		Inscription block of 4	4.25	

Art at UN (Sert) Type of UN

1972, Nov. 17   **Photo.**   **Perf. 12x**

28	A128	**40c gold, red & brown** *(1,932,428)*	.30	
		First day cover		
		Inscription block of 4	1.25	
29	A128	**80c gold, brown & olive** *(1,759,600)*	.60	
		First day cover		
		First day cover, #28-29		
		Inscription block of 4	2.50	

First day covers of Nos. 28-29 total 295,470.

Disarmament Decade Type of UN

1973, Mar. 9   **Litho.**   **Perf. 13½**

30	A129	**60c violet & multi** *(1,586,845)*	.40	
		First day cover		
		Inscription block of 4	1.60	
31	A129	**1.10fr olive & multi** *(1,408,169)*	.85	
		First day cover		
		First day cover, #30-31		
		Inscription block of 4	3.50	

First day covers of Nos. 30-31 total 260,680.

Drug Abuse Type of UN

1973, Apr. 13   **Photo.**   **Perf.**

32	A130	**60c blue & multi** *(1,481,432)*	.45	
		First day cover *(144,760)*		
		Inscription block of 4	1.90	

Volunteers Type of UN

1973, May 25   **Photo.**   **Perf.**

33	A131	**80c gray green & multi** *(1,443,519)*	.35	
		First day cover *(143,430)*		
		Inscription block of 4	1.50	

Namibia Type of UN

1973, Oct. 1   **Photo.**   **Perf.**

34	A132	**60c red & multi** *(1,673,898)*	.35	
		First day cover *(148,077)*		
		Inscription block of 4	1.50	

Human Rights Type of UN

1973, Nov. 16   **Photo.**   **Perf.**

35	A133	**40c ultramarine & multi** *(1,480,791)*	.30	
		First day cover		
		Inscription block of 4	1.25	
36	A133	**80c olive & multi** *(1,343,349)*	.50	
		First day cover		
		First day cover, #35-36		
		Inscription block of 4	2.10	

First day covers of Nos. 35-36 total 438,260.

ILO Headquarters Type of UN

1974, Jan. 11   **Photo.**   **Perf.**

37	A134	**60c violet & multi** *(1,212,703)*	.45	
		First day cover		
		Inscription block of 4	1.90	
38	A134	**80c brown & multi** *(1,229,851)*	.65	
		First day cover		
		First day cover, #37-38		
		Inscription block of 4	2.75	

First day covers of Nos. 37-38 total 240,660.

Centenary of UPU Type of UN

1974, Mar. 22   **Litho.**   **Perf.**

39	A135	**30c gold & multi** *(1,567,517)*	.25	
		Inscription block of 4	1.25	
40	A135	**60c gold & multi** *(1,430,839)*	.60	
		First day cover		
		First day cover, #39-40		
		Inscription block of 4	2.50	

First day covers of Nos. 39-40 total 231,840.

Art at UN (Portinari) Type of UN

4, May 6		**Photo.**		***Perf. 14***
A136	60c	**dark red & multi** *(1,202,357)*	.40	.40
		First day cover		1.00
		Inscription block of 4	1.75	—
A136	1fr	**green & multi** *(1,230,045)*	.70	.70
		First day cover		1.20
		First day cover, #41-42		1.50
		Inscription block of 4	3.00	—

First day covers of Nos. 41-42 total 249,130.

World Population Year Type of UN

4, Oct. 18		**Photo.**		***Perf. 14***
A140	60c	**bright green & multi** *(1,292,954)*	.50	.50
		First day cover		1.00
		Inscription block of 4	2.25	—
A140	80c	**brown & multi** *(1,221,288)*	.70	.70
		First day cover		1.00
		First day cover, #43-44		1.25
		Inscription block of 4	3.25	—

First day covers of Nos. 43-44 total 189,597.

Law of the Sea Type of UN

4, Nov. 22		**Photo.**		***Perf. 14***
A141	1.30fr	**blue & multicolored** *(1,266,270)*	1.00	1.00
		First day cover *(181,000)*		1.25
		Inscription block of 4	4.00	—

Outer Space Type of UN

5, Mar. 14		**Litho.**		***Perf. 13***
A142	60c	**multicolored** *(1,339,704)*	.50	.50
		First day cover		1.00
		Inscription block of 4	2.00	—
A142	90c	**multicolored** *(1,383,888)*	.75	.75
		First day cover		1.00
		First day cover, #46-47		1.50
		Inscription block of 4	3.25	—

First day covers of Nos. 46-47 total 250,400.

International Women's Year Type of UN

75, May 9		**Litho.**		***Perf. 15***
A143	60c	**multicolored** *(1,176,080)*	.40	.40
		First day cover		1.00
		Inscription block of 4	1.90	—
A143	90c	**multicolored** *(1,167,863)*	.70	.70
		First day cover		1.00
		First day cover, #48-49		1.50
		Inscription block of 4	3.25	—

First day covers of Nos. 48-49 total 250,660.

30th Anniversary Type of UN

75, June 26		**Litho.**		***Perf. 13***
A144	60c	**green & multi** *(1,442,075)*	.40	.40
		First day cover		1.00
		Inscription block of 4	2.00	—
A144	90c	**violet & multi** *(1,612,411)*	.70	.70
		First day cover		1.00
		First day cover, #50-51		1.25
		Inscription block of 4	3.25	—

Souvenir Sheet
Imperf

	Sheet of 2 *(1,210,148)*	1.00	1.00
A144	60c **green & multicolored**	.30	.30
A144	90c **violet & multicolored**	.60	.60
	First day cover		1.25

No. 52 has blue and bister margin with inscription and UN emblem. Size: 92x70mm.
First day covers of Nos. 50-52 total 402,500.

Namibia Type of UN

75, Sept. 22		**Photo.**		***Perf. 13½***
A145	50c	**multicolored** *(1,261,019)*	.30	.30
		First day cover		1.00
		Inscription block of 4	1.25	—
A145	1.30fr	**multicolored** *(1,241,990)*	.85	.85
		First day cover		1.10
		First day cover, #53-54		1.25
		Inscription block of 4	4.00	—

First day covers of Nos. 53-54 total 226,260.

Peace-keeping Operations Type of UN

75, Nov. 21		**Engr.**		***Perf. 12½***
A146	60c	**greenish blue** *(1,249,305)*	.35	.35
		First day cover		1.00
		Inscription block of 4	1.50	—
A146	70c	**bright violet** *(1,249,935)*	.65	.65
		First day cover		1.00
		First day cover, #55-56		1.25
		Inscription block of 4	2.75	—

First day covers of Nos. 55-56 total 229,245.

WFUNA Type of UN

976, Mar. 12		**Photo.**		***Perf. 14***
A152	90c	**multicolored** *(1,186,563)*	.90	.90
		First day cover		1.00
		Inscription block of 4	4.00	—

First day covers of No. 57 total 121,645.

UNCTAD Type of UN

1976, Apr. 23		**Photo.**		***Perf. 11½***
58	A153	1.10fr **sepia & multi** *(1,167,284)*	.90	.90
		First day cover *(107,030)*		1.25
		Inscription block of 4	4.00	—

Habitat Type of UN

1976, May 28		**Photo.**		***Perf. 14***
59	A154	40c **dull blue & multi** *(1,258,986)*	.20	.20
		First day cover		1.00
		Inscription block of 4	1.00	—
60	A154	1.50fr **violet & multi** *(1,110,507)*	.75	.75
		First day cover		1.25
		First day cover, #59-60		1.60
		Inscription block of 4	3.50	—

First day covers of Nos. 59-60 total 242,530.

UN Emblem, Post Horn and Rainbow — G3

UN Postal Administration, 25th anniversary.
Printed by Courvoisier, S.A. Panes of 20 (5x4). Designed by Hector Viola.

1976, Oct. 8		**Photo.**		***Perf. 11½***
61	G3	80c **tan & multicolored** *(1,794,009)*	.50	.50
		First day cover		2.00
		Inscription block of 4	2.50	—
62	A3	1.10fr **light green & multi** *(1,751,178)*	1.60	1.60
		First day cover		2.00
		Inscription block of 4	8.00	—
		First day cover, #61-62		3.00
		Panes of 20, #61-62	37.50	

Upper margin blocks are inscribed "XXVe ANNIVERSAIRE"; lower margin blocks "ADMINISTRATION POSTALE DES NATIONS UNIES."
First day covers of Nos. 61-62 total 152,450.

World Food Council Type of UN

1976, Nov. 19		**Litho.**		***Perf. 14½***
63	A156	70c **multicolored** *(1,507,630)*	.50	.50
		First day cover *(170,540)*		1.00
		Inscription block of 4	2.25	—

WIPO Type of UN

1977, Mar. 11		**Photo.**		***Perf. 14***
64	A157	80c **red & multi** *(1,232,664)*	.60	.60
		First day cover *(212,470)*		1.00
		Inscription block of 4	2.75	—

Drop of Water and Globe — G4

UN Water Conference, Mar del Plata, Argentina, Mar. 14-25.
Printed by Government Printing Bureau, Tokyo. Panes of 50. Designed by Eliezer Weishoff.

1977, Apr. 22		**Photo.**		***Perf. 13½x13***
65	G4	80c **ultramarine & multi** *(1,146,650)*	.50	.50
		First day cover		1.00
		Inscription block of 4	2.25	—
66	G4	1.10fr **dark carmine & multi** *(1,138,236)*	.80	.80
		First day cover		1.25
		First day cover, #65-66		1.75
		Inscription block of 4	3.50	—

First day covers of Nos. 65-66 total 289,836.

Hands Protecting UN Emblem — G5

UN Security Council.

Printed by Heraclio Fournier, S.A., Spain. Panes of 50. Designed by George Hamori.

1977, May 27		**Photo.**		***Perf. 11***
67	G5	80c **blue & multi** *(1,096,030)*	.50	.50
		First day cover		1.00
		Inscription block of 4	2.25	—
68	G5	1.10fr **emerald & multi** *(1,075,925)*	.80	.80
		First day cover		1.25
		First day cover, #67-68		1.75
		Inscription block of 4	3.50	—

First day covers of Nos. 67-68 total 305,349.

Colors of Five Races Spun into One Firm Rope — G6

Fight against racial discrimination.
Printed by Setelipaino, Finland. Panes of 50. Designed by M. A. Munnawar.

1977, Sept. 19		**Litho.**		***Perf. 13½x13***
69	G6	40c **multicolored** *(1,218,834)*	.25	.25
		First day cover		1.00
		Inscription block of 4	1.10	—
70	G6	1.10fr **multicolored** *(1,138,250)*	.65	.65
		First day cover		1.25
		First day cover, #69-70		1.75
		Inscription block of 4	2.75	—

First day covers of Nos. 69-70 total 308,722.

Atomic Energy Turning Partly into Olive Branch — G7

Peaceful uses of atomic energy.
Printed by Heraclio Fournier, S.A., Spain. Panes of 50. Designed by Witold Janowski and Marek Freudenreich.

1977, Nov. 18		**Photo.**		***Perf. 14***
71	G7	80c **dark carmine & multi** *(1,147,787)*	.55	.55
		First day cover		1.00
		Inscription block of 4	2.50	—
72	G7	1.10fr **Prussian blue & multi** *(1,121,209)*	.75	.75
		First day cover		1.20
		First day cover, #71-72		1.50
		Inscription block of 4	3.50	—

First day covers of Nos. 71-72 total 298,075.

"Tree" of Doves — G8

Printed by Questa Colour Security Printers, United Kingdom. Panes of 50. Designed by M. Hioki.

1978, Jan. 27		**Litho.**		***Perf. 14½***
73	G8	35c **multicolored** *(3,000,000)+*	.20	.20
		First day cover *(259,735)*		1.00
		Inscription block of 4	.75	—

Globes with Smallpox Distribution — G9

Global eradication of smallpox.

Printed by Courvoisier, S.A. Panes of 50. Designed by Eliezer Weishoff.

1978, Mar. 31	Photo.	Perf. 12x11½	
74	G9	80c yellow & multi (1,116,044)	.60	.60
	First day cover	1.00	
	Inscription block of 4	2.50	—
75	G9	1.10fr light green & multi (1,109,946)	.90	.90
	First day cover	1.25	
	First day cover, #74-75	2.00	
	Inscription block of 4	3.75	—

First day covers of Nos. 74-75 total 254,700.

Namibia Type of UN

1978, May 5	Photo.	Perf. 12	
76	A166	80c multicolored (1,183,208)	.85	.85
	First day cover (316,610)	1.00	
	Inscription block of 4	3.50	—

Jets and Flight Patterns — G10

International Civil Aviation Organization for "Safety in the Air." Printed by Heraclio Fournier, S.A., Spain. Panes of 50. Designed by Tomas Savrda.

1978, June 12	Photo.	Perf. 14	
77	G10	70c multicolored (1,275,106)	.40	.40
	First day cover	1.00	
	Inscription block of 4	1.75	—
78	G10	80c multicolored (1,144,339)	.70	.70
	First day cover	1.00	
	First day cover, #77-78	1.60	
	Inscription block of 4	3.00	—

First day covers of Nos. 77-78 total 255,700.

General Assembly, Flags and Globe — G11

Printed by Government Printing Bureau, Tokyo. Panes of 50. Designed by Henry Bencsath.

1978, Sept. 15	Photo.	Perf. 13½	
79	G11	70c multicolored (1,204,441)	.45	.45
	First day cover	1.00	
	Inscription block of 4	2.25	—
80	G11	1.10fr multicolored (1,183,889)	.85	.85
	First day cover	1.25	
	First day cover, #79-80	1.75	
	Inscription block of 4	3.75	—

First day covers of Nos. 79-80 total 245,600.

Technical Cooperation Type of UN

1978, Nov. 17	Photo.	Perf. 14	
81	A169	80c multicolored (1,173,220)	.70	.70
	First day cover (264,700)	1.00	
	Inscription block of 4	3.25	—

Seismograph Recording Earthquake — G12

Office of the UN Disaster Relief Coordinator (UNDRO). Printed by Heraclio Fournier, S.A., Spain. Panes of 50. Designed by Michael Klutmann.

1979, Mar. 9	Photo.	Perf. 14	
82	G12	80c multicolored (1,183,155)	.50	.50
	First day cover	1.00	
	Inscription block of 4	2.00	—
83	G12	1.50fr multicolored (1,168,121)	.80	.80

	First day cover	1.40
	First day cover, #82-83	1.90
	Inscription block of 4	3.50

First day covers of Nos. 82-83 total 162,070.

Children and Rainbow — G13

International Year of the Child. Printed by Heraclio Fournier, S.A., Spain. Panes of 20 (5x4). Designed by Arieh Glaser.

1979, May 4	Photo.	Perf. 14	
84	G13	80c multicolored (2,251,623)	.35	.35
	First day cover	1.25	
	Inscription block of 4	1.60	—
85	G13	1.10fr multicolored (2,220,463)	.65	.65
	First day cover	1.75	
	Inscription block of 4	2.75	—
	First day cover, #84-85	1.25	
	Panes of 20, #84-85	20.00	

First day covers of Nos. 84-85 total 176,120.

Namibia Type of UN

1979, Oct. 5	Litho.	Perf. 13½	
86	A176	1.10fr multicolored (1,229,830)	.60	.60
	First day cover (134,160)	1.25	
	Inscription block of 4	2.25	—

International Court of Justice, Scales — G14

International Court of Justice, The Hague, Netherlands. Printed by Setelipaino, Finland. Panes of 50. Designed by Kyohei Maeno.

1979, Nov. 9	Litho.	Perf. 13x13½	
87	G14	80c multicolored (1,123,193)	.40	.40
	First day cover	1.00	
	Inscription block of 4	1.75	—
88	G14	1.10fr multicolored (1,063,067)	.60	.60
	First day cover	1.25	
	First day cover, #87-88	1.75	
	Inscription block of 4	2.75	—

First day covers of Nos. 87-88 total 158,170.

New Economic Order Type of UN

1980, Jan. 11	Litho.	Perf. 15x14½	
89	A179	80c multicolored (1,315,918)	.85	.85
	First day cover (176,250)	1.00	
	Inscription block of 4	3.50	—

Women's Year Emblem — G15

United Nations Decade for Women. Printed by Questa Colour Security Printers, United Kingdom. Panes of 50. Designed by M.A. Munnawar.

1980, Mar. 7	Litho.	Perf. 14½x15	
90	G15	40c multicolored (1,265,221)	.30	.30
	First day cover	1.00	
	Inscription block of 4	1.40	—
91	G15	70c multicolored (1,240,375)	.70	.70
	First day cover	1.10	
	First day cover, #90-91	1.25	
	Inscription block of 4	3.50	—

First day covers of Nos. 90-91 total 204,350.

Peace-keeping Operations Type of UN

1980, May 16	Litho.	Perf. 14	
92	A181	1.10fr blue & green (1,335,391)	.85	
	First day cover (184,700)		
	Inscription block of 4	3.50	

35th Anniversary Type of UN and Dove and "35" — G16

35th Anniversary of the United Nations. Printed by Ashton-Potter Ltd., Canada. Panes of Designed by Gidon Sagi (40c), Cemalattin Mutver (70c).

1980, June 26	Litho.	Perf. 13x1	
93	G16	40c blue green & black (1,462,005)	.35	
	First day cover		
	Inscription block of 4	1.40	
94	A183	70c multicolored (1,444,639)	.65	
	First day cover		
	First day cover, #93-94	1.75	
	Inscription block of 4	3.00	

Souvenir Sheet
Imperf
95		Sheet of 2 (1,235,200)	1.10	
a.	G16	40c blue green & black	.30	
b.	A183	70c multicolored	.80	
	First day cover		

First day covers of Nos. 93-95 total 379,800.

ECOSOC Type of UN and

Family Climbing Line Graph — G17

Printed by Ashton-Potter Ltd., Canada. Panes of Designed by Eliezer Weishoff (40c), A. Medina Medina (70c).

1980, Nov. 21	Litho.	Perf. 13½x	
96	A186	40c multicolored (986,435)	.30	
	First day cover		1
	Inscription block of 4	1.25	
97	G17	70c multicolored (1,016,462)	.60	
	First day cover		1
	First day cover #96-97		1
	Inscription block of 4	2.50	

Economic and Social Council. First day covers of Nos. 96-97 total 210,460.

Palestinian Rights

Printed by Courvoisier S.A., Switzerland. Panes of 50. Designed by David Dewhurst.

1981, Jan. 30	Photo.	Perf. 12x11	
98	A188	80c multicolored (1,031,737)	.55	
	First day cover (117,480)		1.
	Inscription block of 4	2.75	

International Year of the Disabled.

Printed by Heraclio Fournier S.A., Spain. Panes of 50. Designed by G.P. Van der Hyde (40c) and Sophia van Heeswijk (1.50fr).

1981, Mar. 6	Photo.	Perf. 1	
99	A190	40c black & blue (1,057,909)	.25	
	First day cover		1.
	Inscription block of 4	1.00	
100	V4	1.50fr black & red (994,748)	1.00	1.
	First day cover		1.
	First day cover, #99-100		1.
	Inscription block of 4	4.00	

First day covers of Nos. 99-100 total 202,853.

Art Type of UN

1981, Apr. 15	Photo.	Perf. 11
	Granite Paper	
101	A191	80c multicolored (1,128,782)	.80	
	First day cover (121,383)		1.
	Inscription block of 4	3.75	

Energy Type of 1981

		1, May 29	**Litho.**	*Perf. 13*	
A192	1.10fr	**multicolored** *(1,096,806)*		.75	.75
		First day cover *(113,700)*			1.25
		Inscription block of 4		3.50	—

Volunteers Program Type and

Symbols of Science, Agriculture and Industry — G18

Printed by Walsall Security Printers, Ltd., United Kingdom. ...es of 50.
...Designed by Gabriele Nussgen (40c), Bernd Mirbach (70c).

		31, Nov. 13	**Litho.**		
A194	40c	**multicolored** *(1,032,700)*		.45	.45
		First day cover			1.00
		Inscription block of 4		2.25	—
G18	70c	**multicolored** *(1,123,672)*		.90	.90
		First day cover			1.00
		First day cover, #103-104			1.50
		Inscription block of 4		4.25	—

First day covers of Nos. 103-104 total 190,667.

Fight against Apartheid — G19

Flower of Flags — G20

Printed by Courvoisier, S.A., Switzerland. Panes of 50.
...signed by Tomas Savrda (30c); Dietmar Kowall (1fr).

		82, Jan. 22		*Perf. 11½x12*	
5	G19	30c **multicolored** *(3,000,000)+*		.25	.25
		First day cover			1.00
		Inscription block of 4		1.10	—
6	G20	1fr **multicolored** *(3,000,000)+*		.80	.80
		First day cover			1.00
		First day cover, #105-106			1.25
		Inscription block of 4		3.25	—

First day covers of Nos. 105-106 total 199,347.

Human Environment Type of UN and:

Sun and Leaves — G21

10th Anniversary of United Nations Environment Program.
Printed by Joh. Enschede en Zonen, Netherlands. Panes of
. Designed by Sybille Brunner (40c); Philine Hartert (1.20fr).

		82, Mar. 19	**Litho.**	*Perf. 13½x13*	
7	G21	40c **multicolored** *(948,743)*		.30	.30
		First day cover			1.00
		Inscription block of 4		1.50	—
8	A199	1.20fr **multicolored** *(901,096)*		1.10	1.25
		First day cover			1.10
		First day cover, #107-108			1.40
		Inscription block of 4		5.25	—

First day covers of Nos. 107-108 total 190,155.

Outer Space Type of UN and:

Satellite, Applications of Space Technology G22

Exploration and Peaceful Uses of Outer Space.
Printed by Enschede. Panes of 50. Designed by Wiktor C. Nerwinski (80c) and George Hamori (1fr).

		1982, June 11	**Litho.**	*Perf. 13x13½*	
109	A201	80c **multicolored** *(964,593)*		.60	.60
		First day cover			1.00
		Inscription block of 4		3.00	—
110	G22	1fr **multicolored** *(898,367)*		.80	.80
		First day cover			1.25
		First day cover, #109-110			1.50
		Inscription block of 4		3.75	—

First day covers of Nos. 109-110 total 205,815.

Conservation & Protection of Nature

		1982, Nov. 19	**Photo.**	*Perf. 14*	
111	A202	40c Bird *(928,143)*		.45	.40
		First day cover			1.00
		Inscription block of 4		2.10	—
112	A202	1.50fr Reptile *(847,173)*		1.10	1.10
		First day cover			1.25
		First day cover, #111-112			1.75
		Inscription block of 4		5.25	—

First day covers of Nos. 111-112 total 198,504.

World Communications Year

		1983, Jan. 28	**Litho.**	*Perf. 13*	
113	A204	1.20fr **multicolored** *(894,025)*		1.25	1.25
		First day cover *(131,075)*			1.25
		Inscription block of 4		5.25	—

Safety at Sea Type of UN and

G23

Designed by Valentin Wurnitsch (A22).

		1983, Mar. 18	**Litho.**	*Perf. 14½*	
114	A205	40c **multicolored** *(892,365)*		.40	.40
		First day cover			1.00
		Inscription block of 4		1.75	—
115	G23	80c **multicolored** *(882,720)*		.80	.80
		First day cover			1.00
		First day cover, #114-115			1.50
		Inscription block of 4		3.50	—

First day covers of Nos. 114-115 total 219,592.

World Food Program

		1983, Apr. 22	**Engr.**	*Perf. 13½*	
116	A207	1.50fr **blue** *(876,591)*		1.25	1.25
		First day cover			1.25
		Inscription block of 4		5.25	—

Trade Type of UN and

G24

Designed by Wladyslaw Brykczynski (A23).

		1983, June 6	**Litho.**	*Perf. 14*	
117	A208	80c **multicolored** *(902,495)*		.50	.50
		First day cover			1.00
		Inscription block of 4		2.50	—
118	G24	1.10fr **multicolored** *(921,424)*		.90	.90
		First day cover			1.00
		First day cover, #117-118			1.40
		Inscription block of 4		4.00	—

First day covers of Nos. 117-118 total 146,507.

Homo Humus Humanitas — G25

Right to Create — G26

35th Anniversary of the Universal Declaration of Human Rights.
Printed by Government Printing Office, Austria. Designed by Friedensreich Hundertwasser, Austria. Panes of 16 (4x4).

		1983, Dec. 9	**Photo. & Engr.**	*Perf. 13½*	
119	G25	40c **multicolored** *(1,770,921)*		.45	.45
		First day cover			1.00
		Inscription block of 4		2.00	—
120	G26	1.20fr **multicolored** *(1,746,735)*		.95	.95
		First day cover			1.10
		Inscription block of 4		4.25	—
		First day cover, #119-120			1.40
		Panes of 16, #119-120		22.50	—

First day covers of Nos. 119-120 total 315,052.

International Conference on Population Type

		1984, Feb. 3	**Litho.**	*Perf. 14*	
121	A212	1.20fr **multicolored** *(776,879)*		.90	.90
		First day cover *(105,377)*			1.00
		Inscription block of 4		4.00	—

Fishing G27

Women Farm Workers, Africa — G28

World Food Day, Oct. 16
Printed by Walsall Security Printers, Ltd., United Kingdom. Panes of 50. Designed by Adth Vanooijen, Netherlands.

		1984, Mar. 15	**Litho.**	*Perf. 14½*	
122	G27	50c **multicolored** *(744,506)*		.30	.30
		First day cover			1.00
		Inscription block of 4		1.60	—
123	G28	80c **multicolored** *(784,047)*		.60	.60

First day cover 1.25
First day cover, #122-123 1.75
Inscription block of 4 2.75 —

First day covers of Nos. 122-123 total 155,234.

Valletta,
Malta — G29

Los Glaciares
National Park,
Argentina — G30

World Heritage
Printed by Harrison and Sons, United Kingdom. Panes of 50.
Designs adapted by Rocco J. Callari, US, and Thomas Lee,
China.

1984, Apr. 18   **Litho.**   *Perf. 14*
124 G29   50c **multicolored** *(763,627)*   .60   .60
    First day cover   1.00
    Inscription block of 4   2.50   —
125 G30   70c **multicolored** *(784,489)*   .85   .85
    First day cover   1.25
    First day cover, #124-125   1.75
    Inscription block of 4   4.50   —

First day covers of Nos. 124-125 total 164,498.

G31

G32

Future for Refugees
Printed by Courvoisier. Panes of 50. Designed by Hans Erni,
Switzerland.

1984, May 29   **Photo.**   *Perf. 11½*
126 G31   35c **multicolored** *(880,762)*   .30   .30
    First day cover   1.00
    Inscription block of 4   1.50   —
127 G32   1.50fr **multicolored** *(829,895)*   1.10   1.10
    First day cover   1.25
    First day cover, #126-127   1.75
    Inscription block of 4   5.00   —

First day covers of Nos. 126-127 total 170,306.

International Youth
Year — G33

Printed by Waddingtons Ltd., United Kingdom. Panes of 50.
Designed by Eliezer Weishoff, Israel.

1984, Nov. 15   **Litho.**   *Perf. 13½*
128 G33   1.20fr **multicolored** *(755,622)*   1.25   1.25
    First day cover *(96,680)*   1.00
    Inscription block of 4   5.50   —

ILO Type of UN and

ILO Turin
Center — G34

Printed by the Government Printing Bureau, Japan. Panes of
50. Engraved by Mamoru Iwakuni and Hiroshi Ozaki, Japan
(#129) and adapted from photographs by Rocco J. Callari, US,
and Thomas Lee, China (#130).

1985, Feb. 1   **Engr.**   *Perf. 13½*
129 A220   80c **dull red** *(654,431)*   .70   .70
    First day cover   1.00
    Inscription block of 4   3.00   —
130 G34   1.20fr **U Thant Pavilion** *(609,493)*   1.10   1.10
    First day cover   1.50
    First day cover, #129-130   2.25
    Inscription block of 4   4.75   —

First day covers of Nos. 129-130 total 118,467.

UN University Type

1985, Mar. 15   **Photo.**   *Perf. 13½*
131 A221   50c **Pastoral scene, advanced commu-**
    nications *(625,087)*   .65   .60
    First day cover   1.00
    Inscription block of 4   2.75   —
132 A221   80c **like No. 131** *(712,674)*   1.10   1.00
    First day cover   1.25
    First day cover, #131-132   1.75
    Inscription block of 4   4.50   —

First day covers of Nos. 131-132 total 93,324.

Flying
Postman — G35

NATIONS UNIES   Interlocked Peace
Doves — G36

Printed by Carl Uebereuter Druck and Verlag M. Salzer,
Austria. Panes of 50. Designed by Arieh Glaser, Israel (#133),
and Carol Sliwka, Poland (#134).

1985, May 10   **Litho.**   *Perf. 14*
133 G35   20c **multicolored** *(2,000,000)+*   .25   .25
    First day cover   1.00
    Inscription block of 4   1.25   —
134 G36   1.20fr **multicolored** *(2,000,000)+*   1.50   1.50
    First day cover   1.50
    First day cover, #133-134   2.00
    Inscription block of 4   6.50   —

First day covers of Nos. 133-134 total 103,165.

40th Anniversary Type
Designed by Rocco J. Callari, U.S., and Thomas Lee, C
(No. 137).

1985, June 26   **Photo.**   *Perf. 12 x*
135 A224   50c **multicolored** *(764,924)*   .60
    First day cover
    Inscription block of 4   2.50
136 A225   70c **multicolored** *(779,074)*   .90
    First day cover
    First day cover, #135-136
    Inscription block of 4   4.00

Souvenir Sheet
Imperf
137   Sheet of 2 *(498,041)*   2.25
   a.   A224 50c **multicolored**   .85
   b.   A225 70c **multicolored**   1.10
    First day cover

First day covers of Nos. 135-137 total 252,418.

UNICEF Child Survival Campaign Type
Printed by the Government Printing Bureau, Japan. Pane
50. Designed by Mel Harris, United Kingdom (#138) and
Vanooijen, Netherlands (#139).

1985, Nov. 22   **Photo. & Engr.**   *Perf. 1*
138 A226   50c **Three girls** *(657,409)*   .40
    First day cover
    Inscription block of 4   2.00
139 A226   1.20fr **Infant drinking** *(593,568)*   1.10
    First day cover
    First day cover, #138-139
    Inscription block of 4   4.50

First day covers of Nos. 138-139 total 217,696.

Africa in Crisis Type
Printed by Helio Courvoisier, Switzerland. Panes of
Designed by Alemayehou Gabremedhiu, Ethiopia.

1986, Jan. 31   **Photo.**   *Perf. 11½*
140 A227   1.40fr **Mother, hungry children**
    (590,576)   1.25
    First day cover *(80,159)*
    Inscription block of 4   5.25

UN Development Program Type
Forestry. Printed by the Government Printing Bureau, Jap
Pane of 40, 2 blocks of 4 horizontal and 5 blocks of 4 verti
Designed by Thomas Lee, China.

1986, Mar. 14   **Photo.**   *Perf. 1*
141 A228   35c **Erosion control** *(547,567)*   1.75
142 A228   35c **Logging** *(547,567)*   1.75
143 A228   35c **Lumber transport** *(547,567)*   1.75
144 A228   35c **Nursery** *(547,567)*   1.75
   a.   Block of 4, #141-144   7.50
    First day cover, #144a
    First day cover, #141-144, each
    Inscription block of 4, #144a   8.50
    Pane of 40, #141-144   80.00

No. 144a has a continuous design.
First day covers of Nos. 141-144 total 200,212.

Dove and Sun — G37

Printed by Questa Color Security Printers, Ltd., United Kir
dom. Panes of 50. Designed by Ramon Alcantara Rodrigue
Mexico.

1986, Mar. 14   **Litho.**   *Perf. 15x14*
145 G37   5c **multicolored** *(2,000,000)+*   .20
    First day cover *(58,908)*   1
    Inscription block of 4   .50

Stamp Collecting Type
Designs: 50c, UN Human Rights stamp. 80c, UN stam
Printed by the Swedish Post Office, Sweden. Panes of 5
Designed by Czeslaw Slania and Ingalill Axelsson, Sweden.

1986, May 22   **Engr.**   *Perf. 12*
146 A229   50c **dark green & henna brown**
    (722,015)   1.25 1.
    First day cover   1.
    Inscription block of 4   5.50
147 A229   80c **dark green & yellow orange**
    (750,945)   1.75 1.
    First day cover   1.
    First day cover, #146-147   1.
    Inscription block of 4   7.50

First day covers of Nos. 146-147 total 137,653.

International Peace Year. Printed by the Government Printing Bureau, Japan. Panes of 50. Designed by Renato Ferrini, Italy (148), and Salahattin Kanidinc, US (#149).

Peace in French — G39

1986, June 20   Photo. & Embossed   Perf. 13½
G38 45c multicolored (620,978)   .70 .70
  First day cover   1.00
  Inscription block of 4   3.00
G39 1.40fr multicolored (559,658)   1.50 1.50
  First day cover   1.60
  First day cover, #148-149   3.00
  Inscription block of 4   6.50 —

First day covers of Nos. 148-149 total 123,542.

WFUNA Anniversary Type
Souvenir Sheet

Printed by Johann Enschede and Sons, Netherlands. Designed by Rocco J. Callari, US.
Designs: 35c, Abstract by Benigno Gomez, Honduras. 45c, Abstract by Alexander Calder (1898-1976), US. 50c, Abstract by Joan Miro (b. 1893), Spain. 70c, Sextet with Dove, by Ole Hamann, Denmark.

1986, Nov. 14   Litho.   Perf. 13x13½
  Sheet of 4 (478,833)   3.75 3.75
  A232 35c multicolored   .50 .50
  A232 45c multicolored   .70 .70
  A232 50c multicolored   .90 .90
  A232 70c multicolored   1.25 1.25
  First day cover (58,452)   2.00

No. 150 has inscribed margin picturing UN and WFUNA emblems.

Trygve Lie Type
1987, Jan. 30   Photo. & Engr.   Perf. 13½
A233 1.40fr multicolored (516,605)   1.10 1.10
  First day cover (76,152)   1.50
  Inscription block of 4   5.50 —

Sheaf of Colored Bands, by Georges Mathieu — G40

Armillary Sphere, Palais des Nations — G41

Printed by Helio Courvoisier, Switzerland (#152), and the Government Printing Bureau, Japan (#153). Panes of 50. Designed by Georges Mathieu (#152) and Rocco J. Callari (153), US.

Photo., Photo. & Engr. (#153)
1987, Jan. 30   Perf. 11½x12, 13½
152 G40 90c multicolored (1,600,000)+   .65 .65
  First day cover   1.00
  Inscription block of 4   3.00
153 G41 1.40fr multicolored (1,600,000)+ 1.25 1.25
  First day cover   1.00
  First day cover, #152-153   2.00
  Inscription block of 4   5.00

First day covers of Nos. 152-153 total 85,737.

Shelter for the Homeless Type
Designs: 50c, Cement-making and brick-making. 90c, Interior construction and decorating.

1987, Mar. 13   Litho.   Perf. 13½x12½
154 A234 50c multicolored (564,445)   .50 .50
  First day cover   1.00
  Inscription block of 4   2.50
155 A234 90c multicolored (526,646)   1.00 1.00
  First day cover   1.10
  First day cover, #154-155   2.00
  Inscription block of 4   4.25

First day covers of Nos. 154-155 total 100,366.

Fight Drug Abuse Type
Designs: 80c, Mother and child. 1.20fr, Workers in rice paddy.

1987, June 12   Litho.   Perf. 14½x15
156 A235 80c multicolored (634,776)   .50 .50
  First day cover   1.25
  Inscription block of 4   3.00
157 A235 1.20fr multicolored (609,475) 1.00 1.00
  First day cover   1.75
  First day cover, #156-157   2.50
  Inscription block of 4   4.75

First day covers of Nos. 156-157 total 95,247.

UN Day Type
Designed by Elisabeth von Janota-Bzowski (35c) and Fritz Oerter (50c).
Designs: Multinational people in various occupations.

1987, Oct. 23   Litho.   Perf. 14½x15
158 A236 35c multicolored (1,114,756)   .55 .55
  First day cover   1.60
  Inscription block of 4   2.50
159 A236 50c multicolored (1,117,464)   .80 .80
  First day cover   1.90
  Inscription block of 4   3.50
  First day cover, #158-159   2.50
  Panes of 12, #158-159   15.00

Immunize Every Child Type
Designs: 90c, Whooping cough. 1.70fr, Tuberculosis.

1987, Nov. 20   Litho.   Perf. 15x14½
160 A237 90c multicolored (634,614)   1.50 1.50
  First day cover   1.00
  Inscription block of 4   6.25
161 A237 1.70fr multicolored (607,725) 2.75 2.75
  First day cover   1.25
  First day cover, #160-161   2.50
  Inscription block of 4   11.50

IFAD Type
Designs: 35c, Flocks, dairy products. 1.40fr, Fruit.

1988, Jan. 29   Litho.   Perf. 13½
162 A238 35c multicolored (524,817)   .35 .35
  First day cover   1.00
  Inscription block of 4   1.90
163 A238 1.40fr multicolored (499,103) 1.40 1.40
  First day cover   1.50
  First day cover, #162-163   2.00
  Inscription block of 4   7.00

G42

Printed by Heraclio Fournier, S.A., Spain. Panes of 50. Designed by Bjorn Wiinblad, Denmark.

1988, Jan. 29   Photo.   Perf. 14
164 G42 50c multicolored (1,600,000)+   .80 .80
  First day cover   2.00
  Inscription block of 4   3.75

Survival of the Forests Type
Pine forest: 50c, Treetops, mountains. 1.10fr, Lake, tree trunks. Printed se-tenant in a continuous design.

1988, Mar. 18   Litho.   Perf. 14x15
165 A240 50c multicolored (728,569)   1.25 1.25
  First day cover   4.00
166 A240 1.10fr multicolored (728,569) 3.50 3.50
  First day cover   6.00
a. Pair, #165-166   5.50 5.25
  First day cover, #166a   10.00
  Inscription block of 4, 2 #166a 12.50
  Pane of 12, #165-166   30.00

Intl. Volunteer Day Type
Designed by Christopher Magadini, US.
Designs: 80c, Agriculture, vert. 90c, Veterinary medicine.

1988, May 6   Litho.   Perf. 13x14, 14x13
167 A241 80c multicolored (612,166)   .80 .80
  First day cover   1.50
  Inscription block of 4   4.00
168 A241 90c multicolored (467,334)   1.00 1.00
  First day cover   1.75
  First day cover, #167-168   3.50
  Inscription block of 4   4.25

Health in Sports Type
Paintings by LeRoy Neiman, American sports artist: 50c, Soccer, vert. 1.40fr, Swimming.

1988, June 17   Litho.   Perf. 13½x13, 13x13½
169 A242 50c multicolored (541,421)   .40 .40
  First day cover   1.25
  Inscription block of 4   3.00
170 A242 1.40fr multicolored (475,445) 1.40 1.40
  First day cover   2.40
  First day cover, #169-170   3.00
  Inscription block of 4   10.00

Universal Declaration of Human Rights 40th Anniv. Type
1988, Dec. 9   Photo. & Engr.   Perf. 12
171 A243 90c multicolored (745,508)   .70 .70
  First day cover   2.50
  Inscription block of 4   3.25

Souvenir Sheet
172 A243 2fr multicolored (517,453)   2.75 2.75
  First day cover   4.00

World Bank Type
1989, Jan. 27   Litho.   Perf. 13x14
173 A244 80c Telecommunications (524,056) 1.10 1.10
  First day cover   1.50
  Inscription block of 4   5.50
174 A244 1.40fr Industry (488,058)   2.25 2.25
  First day cover   2.40
  First day cover, #173-174   3.50
  Inscription block of 4   10.50

First day covers of Nos. 173-174 total 111,004.

Peace-Keeping Force Type
1989, Mar. 17   Perf. 14x13½
175 A245 90c multicolored (684,566)   1.25 1.25
  First day cover (52,463)   1.00
  Inscription block of 4   6.75

World Weather Watch Type
Satellite photographs: 90c, Europe under the influence of Arctic air. 1.10fr, Surface temperatures of sea, ice and land surrounding the Kattegat between Denmark and Sweden.

1989, Apr. 21   Litho.   Perf. 13x14
176 A247 90c multicolored (864,409)   1.25 1.25
  First day cover   1.50
  Inscription block of 4   5.50
177 A247 1.10fr multicolored (853,556) 2.00 2.00
  First day cover   1.90
  First day cover, #176-177   3.00
  Inscription block of 4   9.00

First day covers of Nos. 176-177 total 83,343.

Offices in Geneva, 10th Anniv.
G43   G44

Printed by Government Printing Office, Austria. Panes of 25. Designed by Anton Lehmden (50c) and Arik Brauer (2fr), Austria.

Photo., Photo. & Engr. (2fr)
1989, Aug. 23   Perf. 14
178 G43 50c multicolored (605,382)   1.00 1.00
  First day cover   1.25
  Inscription block of 4   5.00

179	G44	2fr **multicolored** (538,140)	3.50	3.50
		First day cover		2.75
		Inscription block of 4	15.00	
		First day cover, #178-179		3.25
		Panes of 25, #178-179	110.00	

First day covers of Nos. 178-179 total 83,304.

Human Rights Type of 1989

Printed by Johann Enschede and Sons, the Netherlands. Panes of 12+12 se-tenant labels containing Articles 3 (35c) or 4 (80c) inscribed in English, French or German. Designed by Rocco J. Callari and Robert Stein, US.
Artwork: 35c, Young Mother Sewing, by Mary Cassatt. 80c, The Unknown Slave, sculpture by Albert Mangones.

1989, Nov. 17   **Litho.**   *Perf. 13½*

180	A250	35c **multicolored** (1,923,810)	.35	.35
		First day cover		1.25
		Inscription block of 3 + 3 labels	1.60	
181	A250	80c **multicolored** (1,917,953)	1.00	1.00
		First day cover		3.00
		Inscription block of 3 + 3 labels	4.50	
		First day cover, #180-181		4.50
		Panes of 12, #180-181	17.50	

First day covers of Nos. 180-181 total 134,469.
See Nos. 193-194, 209-210, 234-235.

Intl. Trade Center Type

1990, Feb. 2   **Litho.**   *Perf. 14½x15*

182	A251	1.50fr **multicolored** (409,561)	2.25	2.25
		First day cover (61,098)		3.50
		Inscription block of 4	11.00	

G45

Printed by Heraclio Fournier, S.A., Spain. Designed by Guy Breniaux, France and Elizabeth White, US.

1990, Feb. 2   **Photo.**   *Perf. 14x13½*

183	G45	5fr **multicolored** (1,600,000)+	4.75	4.75
		First day cover (54,462)		7.00
		Inscription block of 4	21.00	

G46

Fight AIDS Worldwide — G46a

Fight AIDS Type

Designed by Jacek Tofil, Poland (50c) and Lee Keun Moon, Korea (80c).
Designs: 50c, "SIDA." 80c, Proportional drawing of man like the illustration by Leonardo da Vinci.

1990, Mar. 16   **Litho.**   *Perf. 13½x12½*

184	G46	50c **multicolored** (480,625)	1.00	1.00
		First day cover		1.25
		Inscription block of 4	5.00	
185	G46a	80c **multicolored** (602,721)	1.75	1.75
		First day cover		1.50
		First day cover, #184-185		2.00
		Inscription block of 4	7.75	

First day covers of Nos. 184-185 total 108,364.

Medicinal Plants Type

1990, May 4   **Photo.**   **Granite Paper**   *Perf. 11½*

186	A253	90c **Plumeria rubra** (625,522)	1.00	1.00
		First day cover		1.40
		Inscription block of 4	5.00	
187	A253	1.40fr **Cinchona officinalis** (648,619)	2.00	2.00
		First day cover		2.25
		First day cover, #186-187		3.50
		Inscription block of 4	9.50	

First day covers of Nos. 186-187 total 114,062.

UN 45th Anniv. Type

Designed by Fritz Henry Oerter and Ruth Schmidthammer, Federal Republic of Germany (90c), Michiel Mertens, Belgium (1.10fr), Robert Stein, US (No. 190).
"45," emblem and: 90c, Symbols of clean environment, transportation and industry. 1.10fr, Dove in silhouette.

1990, June 26   **Litho.**   *Perf. 14½x13*

188	A254	90c **multicolored** (557,253)	1.10	1.10
		First day cover		1.40
		Inscription block of 4	5.25	
189	A254	1.10fr **multicolored** (519,635)	2.25	2.25
		First day cover		2.00
		First day cover, #188-189		3.00
		Inscription block of 4	9.50	

Souvenir Sheet

190		Sheet of 2, #188-189 (401,027)	6.00	6.00
		First day cover		4.50

First day covers of Nos. 188-190 total 148,975.

Crime Prevention Type

1990, Sept. 13   **Photo.**   *Perf. 14*

191	A255	50c **Official corruption** (494,876)	1.25	1.25
		First day cover		1.40
		Inscription block of 4	5.50	
192	A255	2fr **Environmental crime** (417,033)	3.00	3.00
		First day cover		3.25
		First day cover, #191-192		4.50
		Inscription block of 4	15.00	

First day covers of Nos. 191-192 total 76,605.

Human Rights Type of 1989

Panes of 12+12 se-tenant labels containing Articles 9 (35c) or 10 (90c) inscribed in French, German or English.
Artwork: 35c, The Prison Courtyard by Vincent Van Gogh. 90c, Katho's Son Redeems the Evil Doer From Execution by Albrecht Durer.

1990, Nov. 16   **Litho.**   *Perf. 13½*

193	A250	35c **multicolored** (1,578,828)	.45	.45
		First day cover		2.75
		Inscription block of 3 + 3 labels	1.75	
194	A250	90c **black & brown** (1,540,200)	1.25	1.25
		First day cover		6.00
		Inscription block of 3 + 3 labels	4.50	
		First day cover, #193-194		2.50
		Panes of 12, #193-194	20.00	

First day covers of Nos. 193-194 total 100,282.

Economic Commission for Europe Type

1991, Mar. 15   **Litho.**   *Perf. 14*

195	A256	90c **Owl, gull** (643,143)+	1.25	1.25
		First day cover		3.00
196	A256	90c **Bittern, otter** (643,143)+	1.25	1.25
		First day cover		3.00
197	A256	90c **Swan, lizard** (643,143)+	1.25	1.25
		First day cover		3.00
198	A256	90c **Great crested grebe** (643,143)+	1.25	1.25
		First day cover		3.00
a.		Block of 4, #195-198	5.00	5.00
		First day cover, #198a		5.50
		Inscription block of 4, #198a	6.50	
		Pane of 40, #195-198	52.50	

First day covers of Nos. 195-198a total 75,759.

Namibian Independence Type

1991, May 10   **Litho.**   *Perf. 14*

199	A257	70c **Mountains** (328,014)	1.25	1.25
		First day cover		1.60
		Inscription block of 4	6.25	
200	A257	90c **Baobab tree** (395,362)	2.25	2.25
		First day cover		2.25
		First day cover, #199-200		5.00
		Inscription block of 4	11.50	

First day covers of Nos. 199-200 total 94,201.

Ballots Filling Ballot Box — G47

UN Emblem — G48

Printed by House of Questa, United Kingdom. Designed by Ran Banda Mawilmada, Sri Lanka (80c), Maurice Gouju, France (1.50fr).

1991, May 10   **Litho.**   *Perf. 15x14½*

201	G47	80c **multicolored** (1,600,000)+	1.25	1.25
		First day cover		1.75
		Inscription block of 4	6.50	
202	G48	1.50fr **multicolored** (1,600,000)+	2.75	2.75

		First day cover		
		First day cover, #201-202		
		Inscription block of 4	12.50	

First day covers of Nos. 201-202 total 77,590.

G49

Rights of the Child — G50

Printed by The House of Questa. Panes of 50. Designed Ryuta Nakajima, Japan (80c) and David Popper, Switzerl (1.10fr).

1991, June 14   **Litho.**   *Perf. 1*

203	G49	80c **Hands holding infant** (469,962)	1.25	1
		First day cover		
		Inscription block of 4	6.25	
204	G50	1.10fr **Children, flowers** (494,382)	2.00	2
		First day cover		2
		First day cover, #203-204		3
		Inscription block of 4	9.50	

First day covers of Nos. 203-204 total 97,732.

G51

Banning of Chemical Weapons G52

Printed by Heraclio Fournier S.A. Panes of 50. Designed Oscar Asboth, Austria (80c), Michel Granger, France (1.40fr).

1991, Sept. 11   **Litho.**   *Perf. 13*

205	G51	80c **multicolored** (345,658)	2.50	2.
		First day cover		1.
		Inscription block of 4	10.50	
206	G52	1.40fr **multicolored** (366,076)	4.00	4.
		First day cover		2.
		First day cover, #205-206		3.
		Inscription block of 4	20.00	

First day covers of Nos. 205-206 total 91,887.

UN Postal Administration, 40th Anniv. Type

1991, Oct. 24   *Perf. 14x*

207	A263	50c **UN NY No. 7** (506,839)	1.10	1.
		First day cover		1.
		Inscription block of 4	5.00	
208	A263	1.60fr **UN NY No. 10** (580,493)	2.75	2.
		First day cover		3.
		Inscription block of 4	12.00	
		First day cover, #207-208		3.
		Panes of 25, #207-208	75.00	

First day covers of Nos. 207-208 total 88,784.

Human Rights Type of 1989

Panes of 12+12 se-tenant labels containing Articles 15 (50 or 16 (90c) inscribed in French, German or English.
Artwork: 50c, Early Morning in Ro...1925, by Paul Klee. 90 Marriage of Giovanni (?) Arnolfini and Giovanna Cenami (?), Jan Van Eyck.

1, Nov. 20   Litho.   Perf. 13½
A250 50c multicolored (1,295,172)   .85   .85
   First day cover   3.25
   Inscription block of 3 + 3 labels   2.75
A250 90c multicolored (1,324,091)   1.50 1.40
   First day cover   6.75
   Inscription block of 3 + 3 labels   4.50
   First day cover, #209-210   2.00
   Panes of 12, #209-210   27.50

First day covers of Nos. 209-210 total 139,904.

World Heritage Type of 1984

Designs: 50c, Sagarmatha Natl. Park, Nepal. 1.10fr, Stone-
ge, United Kingdom.

2, Jan. 24   Litho.   Perf. 13
      Size: 35x28mm
G29 50c multicolored (468,647)   1.10 1.10
   First day cover   1.25
   Inscription block of 4   5.25
G29 1.10fr multicolored (369,345)   2.25 2.25
   First day cover   2.25
   First day cover, #211-212   3.00
   Inscription block of 4   11.00

First day covers of Nos. 211-212 total 77,034.

F.S.3,00
NATIONS UNIES   G53

Printed by The House of Questa. Panes of 50. Designed by
tor Jose Martin, Argentina.

2, Jan. 24   Litho.   Perf. 15x14½
G53 3fr multicolored (1,600,000)+   3.50 3.50
   First day cover (36,135)   4.00
   Inscription block of 4   16.00

Clean Oceans Type

2, Mar. 13   Litho.   Perf. 14
A264 80c Ocean surface, diff. (850,699)   .90 .90
A264 80c Ocean bottom, diff. (850,699)   .90 .90
   Pair, #214-215   1.80 2.00
   First day cover, #215a   2.75
   First day cover, #214-215, each   1.75
   Inscription block of 4, 2 #215a   5.00
   Pane of 12, #214-215   11.00

First day covers of Nos. 214-215a total 90,725.

Earth Summit Type

Designs: No. 216, Rainbow. No. 217, Two clouds shaped as
es. No. 218, Two sailboats. No. 219, Woman with parasol,
t, flowers.

2, May 22   Photo.   Perf. 11½
A265 75c multicolored (826,543)   1.25 1.25
A265 75c multicolored (826,543)   1.25 1.25
A265 75c multicolored (826,543)   1.25 1.25
A265 75c multicolored (826,543)   1.25 1.25
   Block of 4, #216-219   5.25 5.25
   First day cover, #219a   4.00
   First day cover, #216-219, each   2.50
   Inscription block of 4, #216-219   5.75
   Pane of 40, #216-219   55.00

First day covers of Nos. 216-219a total 74,629.

Mission to Planet Earth Type

Designs: No. 220, Space station. No. 221, Probes near
iter.

2, Sept. 4   Photo.   Rouletted 8
      Granite Paper
A266 1.10fr multicolored (668,241)   2.50 2.50
A266 1.10fr multicolored (668,241)   2.50 2.50
   Pair, #220-221   5.00 5.00
   First day cover, #221a   5.00
   First day cover, #220-221, each   5.50
   Inscription block of 4, 2 #220-221   11.00
   Pane of 10, #220-221   25.00

First day covers of Nos. 220-221 total 76,060.

Science and Technology Type of 1992

Designs: 90c, Doctor, nurse. 1.60fr, Graduate seated before
mputer.

92, Oct. 2   Litho.   Perf. 14
2 A267 90c multicolored (438,943)   1.50 1.50
   First day cover   1.60
   Inscription block of 4   6.00
3 A267 1.60fr multicolored (400,701)   3.50 3.50

   First day cover   2.50
   First day cover, #222-223   3.25
   Inscription block of 4   14.00

First day covers of Nos. 222-223 total 75,882.

Human Rights Type of 1989

Panes of 12+12 se-tenant labels containing Articles 21 (50c)
and 22 (90c) inscribed in French, German or English.
Artwork: 50c, The Oath of the Tennis Court, by Jacques Louis
David. 90c, Rocking Chair I, by Henry Moore.

1992, Nov. 20   Litho.   Perf. 13½
224 A250 50c multicolored, (1,201,788)   .80 .80
   First day cover   3.00
   Inscription block of 3 + 3 labels   3.00
225 A250 90c multicolored, (1,179,294)   1.50 1.50
   First day cover   6.00
   Inscription block of 3 + 3 labels   5.00
   First day cover, #224-225   1.75
   Panes of 12, #224-225   26.00

First day covers of Nos. 224-225 total 104,491.

Aging With Dignity Type

Designs: 50c, Older man coaching soccer. 1.60fr, Older man
working at computer terminal.

1993, Feb. 5   Litho.   Perf. 13
226 A270 50c multicolored (483,452)   .70 .70
   First day cover   1.00
   Inscription block of 4   3.50
227 A270 1.60fr multicolored (331,008)   2.25 2.25
   First day cover   2.75
   First day cover, #226-227   3.00
   Inscription block of 4   10.50

First day covers of Nos. 226-227 total 61,361.

Endangered Species Type

Designed by Rocco J. Callari, US, and Betina Ogden,
Australia.
Designs: No. 228, Pongidae (gorilla). No. 229, Falco per-
egrinus (peregrine falcon). No. 230, Trichechus inunguis (Ama-
zonian manatee). No. 231, Panthera uncia (snow leopard).

1993, Mar. 2   Litho.   Perf. 13x12½
228 A271 80c multicolored (1,200,000)+   1.10 1.10
229 A271 80c multicolored (1,200,000)+   1.10 1.10
230 A271 80c multicolored (1,200,000)+   1.10 1.10
231 A271 80c multicolored (1,200,000)+   1.10 1.10
a.   Block of 4, #228-231   4.50 4.50
   First day cover, #231a   5.00
   First day cover, #228-231, each   2.00
   Inscription block of 4, #228-231   4.50
   Pane of 16, #228-231   19.00

First day covers of Nos. 228-231a total 75,363.

Healthy Environment Type

1993, May 7   Litho.   Perf. 15x14½
232 A272 60c Neighborhood (456,304)   1.10 1.10
   First day cover   1.25
   Inscription block of 4   4.75
233 A272 1fr Urban skyscrapers (392,015)   2.25 2.25
   First day cover   2.00
   First day cover, #232-233   3.25
   Inscription block of 4   10.00

First day covers of Nos. 232-233 total 59,790.

Human Rights Type of 1989

Printed in panes of 12 + 12 se-tenant labels containing Article
27 (50c) and 28 (90c) inscribed in French, German or English.
Artwork: 50c, Three Musicians, by Pablo Picasso. 90c, Voice
of Space, by Rene Magritte.

1993, June 11   Litho.   Perf. 13½
234 A250 50c multicolored (1,166,286)   .85 .85
   First day cover   2.50
   Inscription block of 3 + 3 labels   2.75
235 A250 90c multicolored (1,122,348)   2.00 2.00
   First day cover   4.50
   Inscription block of 3 + 3 labels   6.25
   First day cover, #234-235   2.00
   Panes of 12, #234-235   26.00

First day covers of Nos. 234-235 total 83,432.

Intl. Peace Day Type

Denomination at: #236, UL. #237, UR. #238, LL. #239, LR.

1993, Sept. 21   Litho. & Engr.   Rouletted 12½
236 A274 60c purple & multi (357,760)   2.00 2.00
237 A274 60c purple & multi (357,760)   2.00 2.00
238 A274 60c purple & multi (357,760)   2.00 2.00
239 A274 60c purple & multi (357,760)   2.00 2.00
a.   Block of 4, #236-239   8.00 8.00
   First day cover, #239a   5.50
   First day cover, #236-239, each   3.00
   Inscription block of 4, #239a   9.50
   Pane of 40, #236-239   75.00

First day covers of Nos. 236-239a total 47,207.

Environment-Climate Type

1993, Oct. 29   Litho.   Perf. 14½
240 A275 1.10fr Polar bears (391,593)   2.00 2.00
241 A275 1.10fr Whale sounding (391,593)   2.00 2.00
242 A275 1.10fr Elephant seal (391,593)   2.00 2.00
243 A275 1.10fr Penguins (391,593)   2.00 2.00
a.   Strip of 4, #240-243   8.00 8.00

   First day cover, #243a   7.25
   First day cover, #240-243, each   6.00
   Inscription block of 8, 2 #243a   22.50
   Pane of 24, #240-243   52.50

First day covers of Nos. 240-243a total 41,819.

Intl. Year of the Family Type of 1993

Designs: 80c, Parents teaching child to walk. 1fr, Two women
and child picking plants.

1994, Feb. 4   Litho.   Perf. 13.1
244 A276 80c rose violet & multi (535,000)+   1.20 1.20
   First day cover   1.75
   Inscription block of 4   5.75
245 A276 1fr brown & multi (535,000)+   1.60 1.60
   First day cover   2.00
   First day cover, #244-245   3.25
   Inscription block of 4   7.25

First day covers of Nos. 244-245 total 50,080.

Endangered Species Type of 1993

Designed by Rocco J. Callari (frame) and Leon Parson, US
(stamps).
Designs: No. 246, Mexican prairie dog. No. 247, Jabiru. No.
248, Blue whale. No. 249, Golden lion tamarin.

1994, Mar. 18   Litho.   Perf. 12.7
246 A271 80c multicolored (1,200,000)+   1.10 1.10
247 A271 80c multicolored (1,200,000)+   1.10 1.10
248 A271 80c multicolored (1,200,000)+   1.10 1.10
249 A271 80c multicolored (1,200,000)+   1.10 1.10
a.   Block of 4, #246-249   4.50 4.50
   First day cover, #249a   5.50
   First day cover, #246-249, each   1.75
   Inscription block of 4, #246-249   4.50
   Pane of 16, #246-249   20.00

First day covers of Nos. 246-249a total 82,043.

Protection for Refugees Type of 1994

Design: 1.20fr, Hand lifting figure over chasm.

1994, Apr. 29   Litho.   Perf. 14.3x14.8
250 A277 1.20fr multicolored (550,000)+   2.50 2.50
   First day cover (33,805)   2.50
   Inscription block of 4   12.00

Intl. Decade for Natural Disaster Reduction Type of 1994

Earth seen from space, outline map of: No. 251, North
America. No. 252, Eurasia. No. 253, South America. No. 254,
Australia and South Pacific region.

1994, May 27   Litho.   Perf. 13.9x14.2
251 A281 60c multicolored (570,000)+   1.75 1.75
252 A281 60c multicolored (570,000)+   1.75 1.75
253 A281 60c multicolored (570,000)+   1.75 1.75
254 A281 60c multicolored (570,000)+   1.75 1.75
a.   Block of 4, #251-254   7.00 7.00
   First day cover, #254a   7.00
   First day cover, #251-254, each   4.00
   Inscription block of 4, #254a   9.50
   Pane of 40, #251-254   75.00

First day covers of Nos. 251-254a total 37,595.

Palais des
Nations,
Geneva — G54

Creation of the
World, by Oili
Maki — G55

Printed by House of Questa, United Kingdom. Designed by
Rocco J. Callari, US.

1994, Sept. 1   Litho.   Perf. 14.3x14.6
255 G54 60c multicolored (1,075,000)+   .75 .75
   First day cover   1.10
   Inscription block of 4   3.50
256 G55 80c multicolored (1,075,000)+   1.00 1.00
   First day cover   1.50
   Inscription block of 4   4.50
257 G54 1.80fr multi, diff. (1,075,000)+   2.25 2.25
   First day cover   2.75
   Inscription block of 4   11.00
   First day cover, #255-257   4.50

First day covers of Nos. 255-257 total 51,637.

Population and Development Type of 1994

Designs: 60c, People shopping at open-air market. 80c, People on vacation crossing bridge.

1994, Sept. 1 Litho. Perf. 13.2x13.6
258 A282 60c multicolored (535,000)+ 1.10 1.10
   First day cover 1.25
   Inscription block of 4 5.00
259 A282 80c multicolored (535,000)+ 1.50 1.50
   First day cover 1.75
   Inscription block of 4 7.50
   First day cover, #258-259 3.00

First day covers of Nos. 258-259 total 50,443.

UNCTAD Type of 1994

1994, Oct. 28
260 A283 80c multi, diff. (535,000)+ 1.25 1.25
   First day cover 1.75
   Inscription block of 4 5.50
261 A283 1fr multi, diff. (535,000)+ 1.75 1.75
   First day cover 2.00
   Inscription block of 4 7.75
   First day cover, #260-261 3.50
a. Grayish green omitted —
   Inscription block of 4 —

First day covers of Nos. 260-261 total 48,122.

UN 50th Anniv. Type of 1995

1995, Jan. 1 Litho. & Engr. Perf. 13.4
262 A284 80c multicolored (823,827) 1.25 1.25
   First day cover (38,988) 3.00
   Inscription block of 4 5.75

Social Summit Type of 1995

1995, Feb. 3 Photo. & Engr. Perf. 13.6x13.9
263 A285 1fr multi, diff. (452,116) 1.50 1.50
   First day cover (35,246) 2.00
   Inscription block of 4 7.00

Endangered Species Type of 1993

Designed by Sibylle Erni, Switzerland.
Designs: No. 264, Crowned lemur, Lemur coronatus. No. 265, Giant Scops owl, Otus gurneyi. No. 266, Zetek's frog, Atelopus varius zeteki. No. 267, Wood bison, Bison bison athabascae.

1995, Mar. 24 Litho. Perf. 13x12½
264 A271 80c multicolored (730,000)+ 1.25 1.25
265 A271 80c multicolored (730,000)+ 1.25 1.25
266 A271 80c multicolored (730,000)+ 1.25 1.25
267 A271 80c multicolored (730,000)+ 1.25 1.25
a. Block of 4, 264-267 5.00 5.00
   First day cover, #267a 4.50
   First day cover, #264-267, each 1.60
   Inscription block of 4, #267a 5.75
   Pane of 16, #264-267 19.00

First day covers of Nos. 264-267a total 71,907.

Intl. Youth Year Type of 1995

Designs: 80c, Farmer on tractor, fields at harvest time. 1fr, Couple standing by fields at night.

1995, May 26 Litho. Perf. 14.4x14.7
268 A286 80c multicolored (294,987) 1.60 1.60
   First day cover 1.75
   Inscription block of 4 7.00
269 A286 1fr multicolored (264,823) 2.75 2.75
   First day cover 2.00
   First day cover, #268-269 4.00
   Inscription block of 4 12.00

First day covers of Nos. 268-269 total 45,665.

UN, 50th Anniv. Type of 1995

Designs: 60c, Like No. 663. 1.80fr, Like No. 664.

1995, June 26 Engr. Perf. 13.3x13.6
270 A287 60c maroon (352,336) 1.00 1.00
   First day cover .90
   Inscription block of 4 4.50
271 A287 1.80fr green (377,391) 3.25 3.25
   First day cover 3.00
   First day cover, #270-271 4.00
   Inscription block of 4 14.00

Souvenir Sheet
Litho. & Engr.
Imperf

272 Sheet of 2, #270-271 (251,272) 4.25 4.25
a. A287 60c maroon 1.00 1.00
b. A287 1.80fr green 3.25 3.25
   First day cover 8.00

First day covers of Nos. 270-272 total 72,666.

Conference on Women Type of 1995

Designs: 60c, Black woman, cranes flying above. 1fr, Women, dove.

1995, Sept. 5 Photo. Perf. 12
273 A288 60c multicolored (342,336) 1.40 1.40
   First day cover 1.25
   Inscription block of 4 6.50

Size: 28x50mm
274 A288 1fr multicolored (345,489) 2.50 2.00
   First day cover 2.25
   First day cover, #273-274 3.25
   Inscription block of 4 11.00

First day covers of Nos. 273-274 total 57,542.

UN People, 50th Anniv. Type of 1995

1995, Oct. 24 Litho. Perf. 14
275 Sheet of 12 (216,832 sheets) 17.00 12.50
   First day cover 20.00
a.-l. A290 30c each 1.30 1.25
   First day cover, #275a-275l, each 5.00
276 Souvenir booklet, (74,151 booklets) 17.00
a. A290 30c Booklet pane of 3, vert. strip of 3 from UL of sheet 4.25 4.25
b. A290 30c Booklet pane of 3, vert. strip of 3 from UR of sheet 4.25 4.25
c. A290 30c Booklet pane of 3, vert. strip of 3 from LL of sheet 4.25 4.25
d. A290 30c Booklet pane of 3, vert. strip of 3 from LR of sheet 4.25 4.25

First day covers of Nos. 275-276d total 53,245.

WFUNA, 50th Anniv. Type

Design: 80c, Fishing boat, fish in net.

1996, Feb. 2 Litho. Perf. 13x13½
277 A291 80c multicolored (550,000)+ 1.25 1.25
   First day cover 2.00
   Inscription block of 4 6.50

The Galloping Horse Treading on a Flying Swallow, Chinese Bronzework, Eastern Han Dynasty (25-220 A.D.) — G56

Palais des Nations, Geneva — G57

Printed by House of Questa, UK.

1996, Feb. 2 Litho. Perf. 14½x15
278 G56 40c multicolored (1,125,000)+ .50 .50
   First day cover 1.25
   Inscription block of 4 3.50
279 G57 70c multicolored (1,125,000+) 1.10 1.10
   First day cover 1.50
   First day cover, #278-279 3.50
   Inscription block of 4 6.00

Endangered Species Type of 1993

Designs: No. 280, Paphiopedilum delenatii. No. 281, Pachypodium baronii. No. 282, Sternbergia lutea. No. 283, Darlingtonia californica.

1996, Mar. 14 Litho. Perf. 12½
280 A271 80c multicolored (680,000)+ 1.10 1.10
281 A271 80c multicolored (680,000)+ 1.10 1.10
282 A271 80c multicolored (680,000)+ 1.10 1.10
283 A271 80c multicolored (680,000)+ 1.10 1.10
a. Block of 4, #280-283 4.50 4.50
   First day cover, #280-283, each 2.00
   First day cover, #283a 4.50
   Inscription block of 4, #283a 4.50
   Pane of 16, #280-283 18.00

City Summit Type of 1996

Designs: No. 284, Asian family. No. 285, Oriental garden. No. 286, Fruit, vegetable vendor, mosque. No. 287, Boys playing ball. No. 288, Couple reading newspaper.

1996, June 3 Litho. Perf. 14x13½
284 A293 70c multicolored (420,000)+ 1.50 1.50
285 A293 70c multicolored (420,000)+ 1.50 1.50
286 A293 70c multicolored (420,000)+ 1.50 1.50
287 A293 70c multicolored (420,000)+ 1.50 1.50
288 A293 70c multicolored (420,000)+ 1.50 1.50
a. Strip of 5, #284-288 7.50 7.50
   First day cover, #288a 11.00
   First day cover, #284-288, each 5.00
   Inscription block of 10, 2 #288a 20.00

Sport and the Environment Type

Designs: 70c, Cycling, vert. 1.10fr, Sprinters.

1996, July 19 Litho. Perf. 14x14½, 14½x14
289 A294 70c multicolored (625,000)+ 1.25 1.25
   First day cover 1.50
   Inscription block of 4 5.75

---

290 A294 1.10fr multicolored(625,000)+ 1.75
   First day cover
   First day cover, #289-290
   Inscription block of 4 8.75

Souvenir Sheet
291 A294 Sheet of 2, #289-290 (345,000)+ 3.00
   First day cover 1

Plea for Peace Type

Designed by: 90c, Chen Yu, China. 1.10fr, Zhou Jing, Ch

Designs: 90c, Tree filled with birds, vert. 1.10fr, Bouque flowers in rocket tail vase, vert.

1996, Sept. 17 Litho. Perf. 15x1
292 A295 90c multicolored (550,000)+ 1.50
   First day cover
   Inscription block of 4 7.50
293 A295 1.10fr multicolored (550,000)+ 2.00
   First day cover
   First day cover, #292-293
   Inscription block of 4 11.00

UNICEF Type

Fairy Tales: 70c, The Sun and the Moon, South Ame 1.80fr, Ananse, Africa.

1996, Nov. 20 Litho. Perf. 14½
294 A296 70c multicolored (1,000,000)+ 1.00
   First day cover
   Pane of 8 + label 8.50
295 A296 1.80fr multicolored (1,000,000)+ 2.40
   First day cover
   First day cover, #294-295
   Pane of 8 + label 21.00

UN Flag — G58

Palais des Natio Under Construction by Massimo Campigli — G59

Printed by The House of Questa, Ltd., UK.

1997, Feb. 12 Litho. Perf. 1
296 G58 10c multicolored (600,000)+ .20
   First day cover 1
   Inscription block of 4 .55
297 G59 1.10fr multicolored (700,000)+ 1.50 1
   First day cover 2
   First day cover, #296-297 3
   Inscription block of 4 6.00

First day covers of Nos. 296-297 total 41,186.

Endangered Species Type of 1993

Designs: No. 298, Ursus maritimus (polar bear). No. 2 Goura cristata (blue-crowned pigeon). No. 300, Amblyrhynch cristatus (marine iguana). No. 301, Lama guanicoe (guanac

1997, Mar. 13 Litho. Perf. 1:
298 A271 80c multicolored (620,000)+ 1.00 1
299 A271 80c multicolored (620,000)+ 1.00 1
300 A271 80c multicolored (620,000)+ 1.00 1
301 A271 80c multicolored (620,000)+ 1.00 1
a. Block of 4, #298-301 4.00 4
   First day cover, #301a 5
   First day cover, #298-301, each 2
   Inscription block of 4, #301a 4.50
   Pane of 16 17.00

First day covers of Nos. 298-301 total 71,905.

Earth Summit Anniv. Type

Designs: No. 302, Person flying over mountain. No. 3 Mountain, person's face. No. 304, Person standing on mou tain, sailboats. No. 305, Person, mountain, trees. 1.10fr, Combined design similar to Nos. 302-305.

1997, May 30 Photo. Perf. 11
Granite Paper
302 A299 45c multicolored (227,187) 1.00 1.
303 A299 45c multicolored (227,187) 1.00 1.
304 A299 45c multicolored (227,187) 1.00 1.
305 A299 45c multicolored (227,187) 1.00 1.
a. Block of 4, #302-305 4.00 4.
   First day cover, #305a 8.
   First day cover, #302-305, each 3.
   Inscription block of 4, #305a 7.25

Souvenir Sheet

A299 1.10fr **multicolored** *(176,386)* — 3.50 3.50
First day cover — 9.00

First day covers of Nos. 302-306 total 55,389.

Transportation Type of 1997

r transportation: No. 307, Zeppelin, Fokker tri-motor. No.
Boeing 314 Clipper, Lockheed Constellation. No. 309,
avilland Comet. No. 310, Boeing 747, Illyushin jet. No. 311,
corde.

7, Aug. 29		**Litho.**	**Perf. 14x14½**	
A300	70c **multicolored** *(271,575)*		1.00	1.00
A300	70c **multicolored** *(271,575)*		1.00	1.00
A300	70c **multicolored** *(271,575)*		1.00	1.00
A300	70c **multicolored** *(271,575)*		1.00	1.00
A300	70c **multicolored** *(271,575)*		1.00	1.00
	Strip of 5, #307-311		5.00	5.00
	First day cover, #311a		7.00	
	First day cover, #307-311, each		3.00	
	Margin block of 10, 2#311a		12.50	

No. 311a has continuous design.
rst day covers of Nos. 307-311 total 33,303.

Philately Type

esigns: 70c, No. 146. 1.10fr, No. 147.

7, Oct. 14		**Litho.**	**Perf. 13½x14**	
A301	70c **multicolored** *(254,406)*		1.50	1.50
	First day cover		1.75	
	Inscription block of 4		8.50	
A301	1.10fr **multicolored** *(303,125)*		2.25	2.25
	First day cover		2.25	
	First day cover, #312-313		6.00	
	Inscription block of 4		11.50	

First day covers of Nos. 312-313 total 47,528.

World Heritage Convention Type

erracotta warriors of Xian: 45c, Single warrior. 70c, Massed
iors. No. 316a, like #716. No. 316b, like #717. No. 316c,
Geneva #314. No. 316d, like Geneva #315. No. 316e, like
nna #230. No. 316f, like Vienna #231.

7, Nov. 19		**Litho.**	**Perf. 13½**	
A302	45c **multicolored** *(409,820)*		1.25	1.25
	First day cover		1.40	
	Inscription block of 4		6.50	
A302	70c **multicolored** *(414,059)*		2.25	2.25
	First day cover		1.50	
	First day cover, #314-315		4.00	
	Inscription block of 4		11.00	
	Souvenir booklet *(275,114 booklets)*		8.50	
-f.	A302 10c any single		.35	.35
g.	Booklet pane of 4 #316a		1.40	1.40
h.	Booklet pane of 4 #316b		1.40	1.40
i.	Booklet pane of 4 #316c		1.40	1.40
j.	Booklet pane of 4 #316d		1.40	1.40
k.	Booklet pane of 4 #316e		1.40	1.40
l.	Booklet pane of 4 #316f		1.40	1.40

First day covers of Nos. 314-316 total 40,366.

Palais des
Nations,
Geneva — G60

rinted by The House of Questa, UK. Designed by UN (2fr).

98, Feb. 13		**Litho.**	**Perf. 14½x15**	
G60	2fr **multicolored** *(550,000)+*		2.50	2.50
	First day cover		6.00	
	Inscription block of 4		12.00	

Endangered Species Type of 1993

esigned by Rocco J. Callari, US and Suzanne Duranceau,
nada.

esigns: No. 318, Macaca thibetana (short-tailed Tibetan
caque). No. 319, Phoenicopterus ruber (Caribbean fla-
ngo). No. 320, Ornithoptera alexandrae (Queen Alexandra's
wing). No. 321, Dama mesopotamica (Persian fallow deer).

98, Mar. 13		**Litho.**	**Perf. 12½**	
A271	80c **multicolored** *(560,000)+*		1.10	1.10
A271	80c **multicolored** *(560,000)+*		1.10	1.10
A271	80c **multicolored** *(560,000)+*		1.10	1.10
A271	80c **multicolored** *(560,000)+*		1.10	1.10
	Block of 4, #318-321		4.50	4.50
	First day cover, #321a		6.00	
	First day cover, #318-321, each		2.50	
	Inscription block of 4, #321a		4.50	
	Pane of 16		17.00	

Intl. Year of the Ocean — G61

Designed by Jon Ellis, US.

1998, May 20		**Litho.**	**Perf. 13x13½**	
322	G61	Sheet of 12 *(270,000)+*	10.00	10.00
	First day cover		14.50	
a.-l.	45c any single		.80	.80
	First day cover, #322a-322l, each		2.00	

Rain Forests Type

1998, June 19			**Perf. 13x13½**	
323	A307 70c **Orangutans** *(430,000)+*		.90	.90
	First day cover		5.00	
	Inscription block of 4		4.00	

Souvenir Sheet

324	A307 3fr like #323 *(250,000)+*		5.00	5.00
	First day cover		10.00	

Peacekeeping Type

Designs: 70c, Soldier with two children. 90c, Two soldiers, children.

1998, Sept. 15		**Photo.**	**Perf. 12**	
325	A308 70c **multicolored** *(400,000)+*		1.10	1.10
	First day cover		1.50	
	Inscription block of 4		6.00	
326	A308 90c **multicolored** *(390,000)+*		2.00	2.00
	First day cover		4.00	
	First day cover, #325-326		5.00	
	Inscription block of 4		8.50	

Declaration of Human Rights Type of 1998

Designs: 90c, Stylized birds. 1.80fr, Stylized birds flying from hand.

1998, Oct. 27		**Litho. & Photo.**	**Perf. 13**	
327	A309 90c **multicolored** *(400,000)+*		1.10	1.10
	First day cover		2.00	
	Inscription block of 4		5.75	
328	A309 1.80fr **multicolored** *(390,000)+*		2.75	2.75
	First day cover		3.50	
	First day cover, #327-328		5.00	
	Inscription block of 4		12.00	

Schönbrunn Palace Type

Designs: 70c, #331b, Great Palm House. 1.10fr, #331d, Blue
porcelain vase, vert. No. 331a, Palace. No. 331c, The Gloriette
(archway). No. 331e, Wall painting on fabric (detail), by Johann
Wenzl Bergl, vert. No. 331f, Porcelain stove, vert.

1998, Dec. 4		**Litho.**	**Perf. 14**	
329	A310 70c **multicolored** *(375,000)+*		1.25	1.25
	First day cover		1.50	
	Inscription block of 4		4.00	
330	A310 1.10fr **multicolored** *(375,000)+*		1.50	1.50
	First day cover		2.25	
	First day cover, #329-330		5.00	
	Inscription block of 4		6.00	

Souvenir Booklet

331		Booklet *(100,000)+*	9.00	
a.-c.	A310 10c any single		.25	.25
d.-f.	A310 30c any single		.75	.75
g.	Booklet pane of 4 #331a		.75	.75
h.	Booklet pane of 3 #331d		2.25	2.25
i.	Booklet pane of 3 #331e		2.25	2.25
j.	Booklet pane of 3 #331f		2.25	2.25
k.	Booklet pane of 4 #331b		.75	.75
l.	Booklet pane of 4 #331c		.75	.75

Palais Wilson,
Geneva — G62

Designed and printed by Helio Courvoisier, SA, Switzerland.

1999, Feb. 5		**Photo.**	**Perf. 11½**	
	Granite Paper			
332	G62 1.70fr **brown red** *(600,000)+*		2.50	2.50
	First day cover *(25,568)*		3.50	
	Inscription block of 4		13.00	

World Heritage, Australia Type

Designs: 90c, #335e, Kakadu Natl. Park. 1.10fr, #335c, Great
Barrier Reef. No. 335a, Tasmanian Wilderness. No. 335b, Wet
tropics of Queensland. No. 335d, Uluru-Kata Tjuta Natl. Park.
No. 335f, Willandra Lakes region.

1999, Mar. 19		**Litho.**	**Perf. 13**	
333	A313 90c **multicolored** *(420,000)+*		1.40	1.40
	First day cover		2.00	
	Inscription block of 4		5.75	
334	A313 1.10fr **multicolored** *(420,000)+*		1.50	1.50
	First day cover		2.25	
	First day cover, #333-334		4.50	
	Inscription block of 4		8.00	

Souvenir Booklet

335		Booklet *(90,000)+*	8.00	
a.-c.	A313 10c any single		.20	.20
d.-f.	A313 20c any single		.50	.50
g.	Booklet pane of 4, #335a		.65	.65
h.	Booklet pane of 4, #335d		2.00	2.00
i.	Booklet pane of 4, #335b		.65	.65
j.	Booklet pane of 4, #335e		2.00	2.00
k.	Booklet pane of 4, #335c		.65	.65
l.	Booklet pane of 4, #335f		2.00	2.00

First day covers of Nos. 333-335 total 44,622.

Endangered Species Type of 1993

Designed by Tim Barrall, US.
Designs: No. 336, Equus hemionus (Asiatic wild ass). No.
337, Anodorhynchus hyacinthinus (hyacinth macaw). No. 338,
Epicrates subflavus (Jamaican boa). No. 339, Dendrolagus
bennettianus (Bennetts' tree kangaroo).

1999, Apr. 22		**Litho.**	**Perf. 12½**	
336	A271 90c **multicolored** *(488,000)+*		1.25	1.25
337	A271 90c **multicolored** *(488,000)+*		1.25	1.25
338	A271 90c **multicolored** *(488,000)+*		1.25	1.25
339	A271 90c **multicolored** *(488,000)+*		1.25	1.25
a.	Block of 4, #336-339		5.00	5.00
	First day cover, #339a		5.75	
	First day cover, #336-339, each		2.00	
	Inscription block of 4, #339a		6.00	
	Pane of 16		19.00	

First day covers of Nos. 336-339 total 52,856.

UNISPACE III Type

Designs: No. 340, Farm, satellite dish. No. 341, City, satellite
in orbit. No. 342, Composite of #340-341.

1999, July 7		**Photo.**	**Rouletted 8**	
340	A314 45c **multicolored** *(925,000)+*		.90	.90
341	A314 45c **multicolored** *(925,000)+*		.90	.90
a.	Pair, #340-341		2.00	2.00
	First day cover, #341a		2.25	
	First day cover, #340-341, each		3.00	
	Inscription block of 4		5.00	
	Pane of 10, #340-341		9.50	

Souvenir Sheet
Perf. 14½

342	A314 2fr **multicolored** *(275,000)+*		4.50	4.50
	First day cover		6.00	
a.	Ovptd. in sheet margin		9.50	9.50
	First day cover		19.00	

No. 342a is ovptd. in violet blue "PHILEXFRANCE 99 / LE
MONDIAL DU TIMBRE / PARIS / 2 AU 11 JUILLET 1999.
First day covers of Nos. 340-342 total 63,412.

UPU Type

Various people, early 20th century methods of mail transportation, denomination at: No. 343, UL. No. 344, UR. No. 345, LL.
No. 346, LR.

1999, Aug. 23		**Photo.**	**Perf. 11¾**	
343	A315 70c **multicolored** *(336,000)+*		1.00	1.00
344	A315 70c **multicolored** *(336,000)+*		1.00	1.00
345	A315 70c **multicolored** *(336,000)+*		1.00	1.00
346	A315 70c **multicolored** *(336,000)+*		1.00	1.00
a.	Block of 4, #343-346		4.00	4.00
	First day cover, #346a		3.50	
	First day cover, #343-346, each		1.50	
	Inscription block of 4, #346a		4.25	

First day covers of Nos. 343-346 total 27,041.

In Memoriam Type

Designs: 1.10fr, 2fr, Armillary sphere, Palais de Nations. Size of 2fr stamp: 34x63mm.

1999, Sept. 21		**Litho.**	**Perf. 14½x14**	
347	A316	1.10fr **multicolored** *(400,000)+*	1.40	1.40
		First day cover		3.00
		Inscription block of 4	6.50	—

Souvenir Sheet
Perf. 14

348	A316	2fr **multicolored** *(225,000)+*	3.00	3.00
		First day cover		3.50

First day covers of Nos. 347-348 total 46,527.

Education Type

1999, Nov. 18		**Litho.**	**Perf. 13½x13¾**	
349	A317	90c Rainbow over globe *(350,000)+*	1.25	1.25
		First day cover		1.75
		Inscription block of 4	5.75	—
350	A317	1.80fr Fish, tree, globe, book *(370,000)+*	2.25	2.25
		First day cover		3.50
		First day cover, #349-350		4.50
		Inscription block of 4	13.50	—

First day covers of Nos. 349-350 total 37,925.

Intl. Year Of Thanksgiving Type

2000, Jan 1		**Litho.**	**Perf. 13¼x13½**	
351	A318	90c **multicolored** *(450,000)+*	1.25	1.25
		First day cover		3.00
		Inscription block of 4	5.75	—

On No. 351 portions of the design were applied by a thermographic process producing a shiny, raised effect.

Endangered Species Type of 1993

Designed by Robert Hynes, US.
Designs: No. 352, Hippopotamus amphibius (hippopotamus). No. 353, Coscoroba coscoroba (Coscoroba swan). No. 354, Varanus prasinus (emerald monitor). No. 355, Enhydra lutris (sea otter).

2000, Apr. 6		**Litho.**	**Perf. 12¾x12½**	
352	A271	90c **multicolored** *(488,000)+*	1.25	1.25
353	A271	90c **multicolored** *(488,000)+*	1.25	1.25
354	A271	90c **multicolored** *(488,000)+*	1.25	1.25
355	A271	90c **multicolored** *(488,000)+*	1.25	1.25
a.		Block of 4, #352-355	5.00	5.00
		First day cover, #355a		5.00
		First day cover, #352-355, each		1.90
		Inscription block of 4, #355a	5.25	—
		Pane of 16	20.00	

Our World 2000 Type

Winning artwork in Millennium painting competition: 90c, The Embrace, by Rita Adaimy, Lebanon. 1.10fr, Living Single, by Richard Kimanthi, Kenya, vert.

2000, May 30		**Litho.**	**Perf. 13x13½, 13½x13**	
356	A319	90c **multicolored** *(330,000)+*	1.25	1.25
		First day cover		1.75
		Inscription block of 4	5.00	—
357	A319	1.10fr **multicolored** *(330,000)+*	1.50	1.50
		First day cover		2.25
		First day cover, #356-357		3.50
		Inscription block of 4	6.00	—

55th Anniversary Type

Designs: 90c, Trygve Lie, Harry S Truman, workers at cornerstone dedication ceremony, 1949. 1.40fr, Window cleaner on Secretariat Building, General Assembly Hall under construction, 1951.

2000, July 7		**Litho.**	**Perf. 13¼x13**	
358	A320	90c **multicolored** *(370,000)+*	1.25	1.25
		First day cover		1.75
		Inscription block of 4	5.00	—
359	A320	1.40fr **multicolored** *(370,000)+*	2.00	2.00
		First day cover		2.60
		First day cover, #358-359		3.75
		Inscription block of 4	8.00	—

Souvenir Sheet

360	A320	Sheet of 2, #358-359 *(235,000)+*	3.25	3.25
		First day cover		5.00

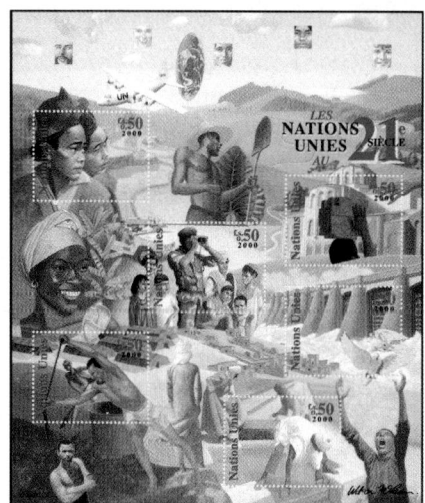

The UN in the 21st Century — G63

Printed by Government Printing Office, Austria. Designed by Wilson McLean, UK.

No. 361: a, Two people, terraced rice paddy. b, Man carrying bricks on head. c, UN Peacekeeper with binoculars. d, Dam, doves. e, Men with shovels. f, People working on irrigation system.

2000, Sept. 15		**Litho.**	**Perf. 14**	
361	G63	Sheet of 6 *(266,000)+*	6.00	6.00
		First day cover		10.00
a.-f.		50c any single	.90	.90

World Heritage, Spain Type

Designs: Nos. 362, 364b, Walled Town of Cuenca. Nos. 363, 364e, Toledo. #364a, Alhambra, Generalife and Albayzin, Granada. #364c, Aqueduct of Segovia. #364d, Amphitheater of Mérida. #364f, Güell Park, Barcelona.

2000, Oct. 6		**Litho.**	**Perf. 14¾x14½**	
362	A323	1fr **multicolored** *(340,000)+*	1.40	1.40
		First day cover		1.90
		Inscription block of 4	5.75	—
363	A323	1.20fr **multicolored** *(340,000)+*	1.60	1.60
		First day cover		2.25
		First day cover, #362-363		3.50
		Inscription block of 4	6.50	—

Souvenir Booklet

364		Booklet *(64,000)+*	5.50	
a.-		A323 10c any single		
c.			.20	.20
d.-		A323 20c any single		
f.			.30	.30
g.		Booklet pane of 4, #364a	.55	.55
h.		Booklet pane of 4, #364d	1.25	1.25
i.		Booklet pane of 4, #364b	.55	.55
j.		Booklet pane of 4, #364e	1.25	1.25
k.		Booklet pane of 4, #364c	.55	.55
l.		Booklet pane of 4, #364f	1.25	1.25

Respect for Refugees Type

Designs: 80c, 1.80fr, Refugee with cane, four other refugees.

2000, Nov. 9		**Litho.**	**Perf. 13¼x12¾**	
365	A324	80c **multicolored** *(400,000)+*	1.25	1.25
		First day cover		1.75
		Inscription block of 4	4.50	—

Souvenir Sheet

366	A324	1.80fr **multicolored** *(215,000)+*	2.50	2.50
		First day cover		3.00

Endangered Species Type of 1993

Printed by Johann Enschedé and Sons, the Netherlands. Designed by Higgins Bond, US.
Designs: No. 367, Felis lynx canadensis (North American lynx). No. 368, Pavo muticus (green peafowl). No. 369, Geochelone elephantopus (Galapagos giant tortoise). No. 370, Lepilemur spp. (sportive lemur).

2001, Feb. 1		**Litho.**	**Perf. 12¾x12½**	
367	A271	90c **multicolored** *(448,000)+*	1.25	1.25
368	A271	90c **multicolored** *(448,000)+*	1.25	1.25
369	A271	90c **multicolored** *(448,000)+*	1.25	1.25
370	A271	90c **multicolored** *(448,000)+*	1.25	1.25
a.		Block of 4, #367-370	5.00	5.00
		First day cover, #370a		5.50
		First day cover, #367-370 each		1.90
		Inscription block of 4, #370a	5.25	—
		Pane of 16	20.00	

Intl. Volunteers Year — G64

Printed by Johann Enschedé and Sons, the Netherla Panes of 20. Designed by Rorie Katz and Robert Stein, U Paintings by: 90c, Ernest Pignon-Ernest, France. 1.30fr, Siché, France.

2001, Mar. 29		**Litho.**	**Perf.**	
371	G64	90c **multicolored** *(350,000)+*	1.10	
		First day cover		
		Inscription block of 4	4.50	
372	G64	1.30fr **multicolored** *(340,000)+*	1.60	
		First day cover		
		First day cover, #371-372		
		Inscription block of 4	6.50	

World Heritage, Japan Type

Designs: 1.10fr, #375b, Nara. 1.30fr, #375e, Itsukush Shinto Shrine. #375a, Kyoto. #375c, Himeji-Jo. #3 Shirakawa-Go and Gokayama. #375f, Nikko.

2001, Aug. 1		**Litho.**	**Perf. 12¾x1**	
373	A328	1.10fr **multicolored** *(350,000)+*	1.30	
		First day cover		
		Inscription block of 4	5.75	
374	A328	1.30fr **multicolored** *(350,000)+*	1.50	
		First day cover		
		First day cover, #373-374		
		Inscription block of 4	6.50	

Souvenir Booklet

375		Booklet *(52,000)+*	7.50	
a.-		A328 10c any single		
c.			.25	
d.-		A328 30c any single		
f.			.40	
g.		Booklet pane of 4, #375a	.75	
h.		Booklet pane of 4, #375d	1.75	
i.		Booklet pane of 4, #375b	.75	
j.		Booklet pane of 4, #375e	1.75	
k.		Booklet pane of 4, #375c	.75	
l.		Booklet pane of 4, #375f	1.75	

Dag Hammarskjöld Type

2001, Sept. 11		**Engr.**	**Perf. 11x1**	
376	A329	2fr **carmine lake** *(380,000)+*	2.50	
		First day cover		
		Inscription block of 4	10.00	

UN Postal Administration, 50th Anniv. Types

2001, Oct. 18		**Litho.**	**Perf. 1**	
377	A330	90c Stamps, globe *(310,000)+*	1.25	
		First day cover		
		Inscription block of 4	5.75	
378	A330	1.30fr Stamps, horns *(310,000)+*	2.25	
		First day cover		
		First day cover, #377-378		
		Inscription block of 4	9.25	

Souvenir Sheet

379	A331	Sheet of 2 *(175,000)+*	4.00	
a.		1.30fr **red & light blue**, 38mm diameter	1.75	
b.		1.80fr **red & light blue**, 38mm diameter	2.25	
		First day cover		

Climate Change Type

Designs: No. 380, Lizard, flowers, shoreline. No. 381, Wi mills, construction workers. No. 382, Non-polluting factory. 383, Solar oven, city, village, picnickers.

2001, Nov. 16		**Litho.**	**Perf. 1**	
380	A332	90c **multicolored** *(73,500)+*	1.10	
381	A332	90c **multicolored** *(73,500)+*	1.10	
382	A332	90c **multicolored** *(73,500)+*	1.10	
383	A332	90c **multicolored** *(73,500)+*	1.10	
a.		Horiz. strip, #380-383	4.50	
		Inscription block of 8	9.00	
		First day cover, #383a		
		Pane of 24	27.00	

Nobel Peace Prize Type

2001, Dec. 10		**Litho.**	**Perf. 1**	
384	A333	90c **multicolored** *(840,000)+*	1.10	
		Inscription block of 4	4.50	
		First day cover		
		Pane of 12	13.50	

Palais des
Nations — G65

...nted by Government Printing Office, Austria. Panes of 20.
...gned by Robert Stein, US.

2, Mar. 1		Litho.		Perf. 13¾	
G65	1.30fr **multicolored** *(630,000)*+			1.75	1.75
	First day cover				2.25
	Inscription block of 4			7.00	—

Endangered Species Type of 1993

...nted by Johann Enschedé and Sons, the Netherlands.
...gned by Lori Anzalone, US.
...signs: No. 386, Cacajao calvus (white uakari). No. 387,
...vora capensis (honey badger). No. 388, Otocolobus manul
...ul). No. 389, Varanus exanthematicus (Bosc's monitor).

2, Apr. 4		Litho.		Perf. 12¾x12½	
A271	90c **multicolored** *(420,000)*+			1.25	1.25
A271	90c **multicolored** *(420,000)*+			1.25	1.25
A271	90c **multicolored** *(420,000)*+			1.25	1.25
A271	90c **multicolored** *(420,000)*+			1.25	1.25
	Block of 4, #386-389			5.00	5.00
	First day cover, #389				5.50
	First day cover, #386-389 each				1.90
	Inscription block of 4, #389a		5.25		—
	Pane of 16			18.00	—

Independence of East Timor Type

...esigns: 90c, Wooden statue of male figure. 1.30fr, Carved
...den container.

2, May 20		Litho.		Perf. 14x14½	
A335	90c **multicolored** *(305,000)*+			1.25	1.25
	First day cover				1.90
	Inscription block of 4			5.00	—
A335	1.30fr **multicolored** *(295,000)*+			1.75	1.75
	First day cover				2.60
	First day cover, #390-391				3.75
	Inscription block of 4			7.00	—

Intl. Year of Mountains Type

...designs: No. 392, Weisshorn, Switzerland. No. 393, Mt. Fuji,
...n. No. 394, Vinson Massif, Antarctica. No. 395, Mt. Kamet,
...a.

2, May 24		Litho.		Perf. 13x13¼	
A336	70c **multicolored** *(1,230,000)*+			.90	.90
	First day cover				1.40
A336	70c **multicolored** *(1,230,000)*+			.90	.90
	First day cover				1.40
A336	1.20fr **multicolored** *(1,230,000)*+			1.60	1.60
	First day cover				2.40
	First day cover, #392, 394				3.25
A336	1.20fr **multicolored** *(1,230,000)*+			1.60	1.60
	Vert. strip or block of four, #392-395			5.00	5.00
	First day cover				2.40
	First day cover, #392, 395				3.25
	First day cover, #392-395				6.00
	Pane of 12, 3 each #392-395		15.00		—

World Summit on Sustainable Development (Peter Max) Type

...esigns: No. 396, Sun, birds, flowers, heart. No. 397, Three
...less people, diff. No. 398, Three women, diff. No. 399,
...boat, mountain.

02, June 27		Litho.		Perf. 14½x14	
A337	90c **multicolored** *(1,215,000)*+			1.25	1.25
	First day cover				1.90
A337	90c **multicolored** *(1,215,000)*+			1.25	1.25
	First day cover				1.90
A337	1.80fr **multicolored** *(1,215,000)*+			2.50	2.50
	First day cover				3.50
	First day cover, #396, 398				4.00
A337	1.80fr **multicolored** *(1,215,000)*+			2.50	2.50
	Vert. strip or block of four, #396-399			7.50	7.50
	First day cover				3.50
	First day cover, #397, 399				4.00
	First day cover, #396-399				8.00
	Pane of 12, 3 each #396-399		22.50		—

World Heritage, Italy Type

...esigns: 90c, #402e, Pisa. 1.30fr, #402b, Aeolian Islands.
...2a, Amalfi Coast. #402c, Rome. #402d, Florence. #402f,
...npeii.

02, Aug. 30		Litho.		Perf. 13½x13¼	
A338	90c **multicolored** *(355,000)*+			1.25	1.25
	First day cover				1.90
	Inscription block of 4		5.00		—
A338	1.30fr **multicolored** *(355,000)*+			2.00	2.00
	First day cover				2.75
	First day cover, #400-401				4.00
	Inscription block of 4			8.25	—

Souvenir Booklet

?	Booklet *(51,000)*+			12.50	
-c.	A338 10c any single			.50	.50
-f.	A338 20c any single			.75	.75
g.	Booklet pane of 4 #402d			3.00	3.00
h.	Booklet pane of 4 #402a			1.00	1.00

i.	Booklet pane of 4, #402e			3.00	3.00
j.	Booklet pane of 4, #402b			1.00	1.00
k.	Booklet pane of 4, #402f			3.00	3.00
l.	Booklet pane of 4, #402c			1.00	1.00

AIDS Awareness Type

2002, Oct. 24		Litho.		Perf. 13½	
403	A339 1.30fr **multicolored** *(305,000)*+			2.00	2.00
	Inscription block of 4			7.75	—
	First day cover, #403				2.60
	Pane of 20			40.00	—

Entry of
Switzerland into
United
Nations — G66

Printed by House of Questa, UK. Panes of 20. Designed by
Thierry Clauson, Switzerland.

2002, Oct. 24		Litho.		Perf. 14½x14¾	
404	G66 3fr **multicolored** *(580,000)*+			4.25	4.25
	Inscription block of 4			17.00	—
	First day cover, #404				5.00
	Pane of 20			85.00	—

Indigenous Art — G67

Printed by House of Questa, UK.
Designed by Rorie Katz and Robert Stein, US.

No. 405: a, Detail of Inca poncho, Peru. b, Bahia culture
seated figure, Brazil. c, Blanket, Ecuador. d, Mayan stone
sculpture, Belize. e, Embroidered fabric, Guatemala. f, Colima
terra-cotta dog sculpture, Mexico.

2003, Jan. 31		Litho.		Perf. 14¼	
405	G67 Sheet of 6 *(168,000)*+			7.75	7.75
	First day cover				9.75
a.-f.	90c Any single			1.25	1.25
	First day cover, a.-f., each				2.50

New Inter-Parliamentary Union Headquarters,
Geneva — G68

Printed by House of Questa, UK. Panes of 20. Designed by
Cyril Wursten, Switzerland.

2003, Feb. 20		Litho.		Perf. 14½x14	
406	G68 90c **multicolored** *(480,000)*+			1.75	1.75
	Inscription block of 4			6.00	—
	First day cover				2.00
	Pane of 20			25.00	—

Endangered Species Type of 1993

Printed by Johann Enschedé and Sons, the Netherlands.
Designed by James Hautman, US.
Designs: No. 407, Branta ruficollis (red-breasted goose). No.
408, Geronticus calvus (bald ibis). No. 409, Dendrocygna
bicolor (fulvous whistling duck). No. 410, Ramphastos vitellinus
(channel-billed toucan).

2003, Apr. 3		Litho.		Perf. 12¾x12½	
407	A271 90c **multicolored** *(368,000)*+			1.25	1.25
408	A271 90c **multicolored** *(368,000)*+			1.25	1.25
409	A271 90c **multicolored** *(368,000)*+			1.25	1.25
410	A271 90c **multicolored** *(368,000)*+			1.25	1.25
a.	Block of 4, #407-410			5.00	5.00
	First day cover, #410a				6.25

	First day cover, #407-410 each				2.10
	Inscription block of 4, #410a			5.60	—
	Pane of 16			22.50	—

International Year of Freshwater Type of 2003

2003, June 20		Litho.		Perf. 14¼x14½	
411	A345 70c Waterfall *(255,000)*+			1.00	1.00
412	A345 1.30fr People, mountain *(255,000)*+			2.00	2.00
a.	Horiz. pair.			3.00	3.00
	First day cover, #412a				3.75
	Inscription block of 4			6.00	—

Ralph Bunche Type

Litho. With Foil Application

2003, Aug. 7				Perf. 13½x14	
413	A346 1.80fr **brown red & multicolored** *(300,000)*+			2.75	2.75
	First day cover				3.50
	Inscription block of 4			11.00	—
	Pane of 20			55.00	—

In Memoriam Type of 2003

2003, Oct. 24		Litho.		Perf. 13¼x13	
414	A347 85c **multicolored** *(700,000)*+			1.50	1.50
	First day cover				2.10
	Inscription block of 4			6.00	—
	Pane of 20			30.00	—

World Heritage Sites, United States Type

Designs: 90c, #417b, Great Smoky Mountains National Park.
1.30fr, #417f, Yellowstone National Park. #417a, Yosemite
National Park. #417c, Olympic National Park. #417d, Hawaii
Volcanoes National Park. #417e, Everglades National Park.

2003, Oct. 24		Litho.		Perf. 14½x14¼	
415	A348 90c **multicolored** *(205,000)*+			1.50	1.40
	First day cover				2.10
	Inscription block of 4			6.00	—
416	A348 1.30fr **multicolored** *(205,000)*+			2.25	2.10
	First day cover				3.25
	First day cover, #415-416				4.50
	Inscription block of 4			9.00	—

Souvenir Booklet

417	Booklet *(39,000)*+			9.00	
a.-c.	A348 10c any single			.20	.20
d.-f.	A348 30c any single			.55	.55
g.	Booklet pane of 4 #417a			.70	.70
h.	Booklet pane of 4 #417d			2.25	2.25
i.	Booklet pane of 4 #417b			.70	.70
j.	Booklet pane of 4 #417e			2.25	2.25
k.	Booklet pane of 4 #417c			.70	.70
l.	Booklet pane of 4 #417f			2.25	2.25

Endangered Species Type of 1993

Printed by Johann Enschedé and Sons, the Netherlands.
Designed by Yuan Lee, US.
Designs: No. 418, Ursus thibetanus (Asiatic black bear). No.
419, Hippocamelus antisensis (Northern Andean deer). No.
420, Macaca silenus (Lion-tailed macaque). No. 421, Bos
gaurus (Gaur).

2004, Jan. 29		Litho.		Perf. 12¾x12½	
418	A271 1fr **multicolored** *(300,000)*+			1.40	1.40
419	A271 1fr **multicolored** *(300,000)*+			1.40	1.40
420	A271 1fr **multicolored** *(300,000)*+			1.40	1.40
421	A271 1fr **multicolored** *(300,000)*+			1.40	1.40
a.	Block of 4, #418-421			5.75	5.75
	First day cover, #421a				7.50
	First day cover, #418-421, each				2.50
	Inscription block of 4, #421a		7.00		—
	Pane of 16			28.00	—

Indigenous Art Type of 2003

Printed by Johann Enschedé and Sons, the Netherlands.
Designed by Rorie Katz and Robert Stein, US.

No. 422: a, Decoration for cows, Switzerland. b, Stone Age
terra cotta sculpture of seated woman, Romania. c, Butter
stamps, France. d, Detail of herald's tabard, United Kingdom. e,
Woodcut print of medieval Cologne, Germany. f, Mesolithic era
terra cotta sculpture of mother and child, Serbia and
Montenegro.

2004, Mar. 4		Litho.		Perf. 13¼	
422	G67 Sheet of 6 *(102,000)*+			9.00	9.00
	First day cover				12.00
a.-f.	1fr Any single			1.50	1.50

Road Safety Type

Road map art with: 85c, Man on hand. 1fr, Person, seat belt,
vert.

2004, Apr. 7		Litho.		Perf. 13x13¼, 13¼x13	
423	A354 85c **multicolored** *(185,000)*+			1.40	1.40
	First day cover				2.10
	Inscription block of 4			6.00	—
424	A354 1fr **multicolored** *(185,000)*+			1.75	1.75
	First day cover				2.50
	First day cover, #423-424				4.00
	Inscription block of 4			7.00	—

See France No. 3011.

Japanese Peace Bell, 50th Anniv. Type

2004, June 20		Litho. & Engr.		Perf. 13¼x13	
425	A355 1.30fr **multicolored** *(230,000)*+			2.00	2.00
	First day cover				3.00
	Inscription block of 4			9.00	—
	Pane of 20			45.00	—

World Heritage Sites, Greece Type

Designs: 1fr, No. 428b, Delphi. 1.30fr, #428e, Pythagoreion and Heraion of Samos. No. 428a, Acropolis, Athens. No. 428c, Olympia. #428d, Delos. #428f, Mycenae and Tiryns.

2004, Aug. 12	Litho.	Perf. 14x13¼	
426 A356	1fr multicolored (180,000)+	1.50	1.50
	First day cover		2.25
	Inscription block of 4	6.50	
427 A356	1.30fr multicolored (180,000)+	2.00	2.00
	First day cover		3.00
	First day cover, #426-427		4.50
	Inscription block of 4	8.50	—

Souvenir Booklet

428	Booklet (33,000)+	12.00	
a.-c.	A356 20c any single	.25	.25
d.-f.	A356 50c any single	.75	.75
g.	Booklet pane of 4 #428a	1.00	1.00
h.	Booklet pane of 4 #428b	1.00	1.00
i.	Booklet pane of 4 #428c	1.00	1.00
j.	Booklet pane of 4 #428d	3.00	3.00
k.	Booklet pane of 4 #428e	3.00	3.00
l.	Booklet pane of 4 #428f	3.00	3.00

My Dream for Peace Type

Winning designs of Lions Club International children's global peace poster contest by: 85c, Anggun Sita Rustinya, Indonesia. 1.20fr, Amanda Nunez, Belize.

2004, Sept. 21	Litho.	Perf. 14	
429 A357	85c multicolored (195,000)+	1.40	1.40
	First day cover		1.90
	Inscription block of 4	5.75	
	Pane of 20	28.00	
430 A357	1.20fr multicolored (195,000)+	2.00	2.00
	First day cover		2.75
	First day cover, #429-430		4.00
	Inscription block of 4	8.00	
	Pane of 20	40.00	

Human Rights — G70

Human Rights — G69

Printed by Banknote Corportation of America, US. Designed by Yuri Gervorgian, Armenia. Panes of 8.

2004, Oct. 14	Litho.	Perf. 11¼	
431 G69	85c multicolored (408,000)+	1.25	1.25
	First day cover		2.10
	Pane of 8	12.00	—
432 G70	1.30fr multicolored (408,000)+	2.25	2.25
	First day cover		3.25
	First day cover, #431-432		4.50
	Pane of 8	20.00	

Sports — G71

Printed by Cartor Security Printing, France. Designed by Roland Hirter, Switzerland. Panes of 20.

2004, Nov. 23	Litho.	Perf. 13x13½	
433 G71	180c multicolored (216,000)+	3.25	3.25
	First day cover		4.00
	Inscription block of 4	13.00	—
	Pane of 20	65.00	—

See Switzerland No. 1196.

United Nations, 60th Anniv. Type of 2005

Printed by Banknote Corporation of America, US. Designed by Czeslaw Slania, Sweden.

2005, Feb. 4	Litho. & Engr.	Perf. 11x11¼	
434 A361	1.30fr multicolored (270,000)+	2.50	2.50
	First day cover		3.50
	Inscription block of 4	10.00	
	Pane of 20	50.00	—

Souvenir Sheet
Litho.
Imperf

435 A361	3fr multicolored (125,000)+	6.00	6.00
	First day cover		6.75

Endangered Species Type of 1993

Printed by Johann Enschedé and Sons, the Netherlands. Designed by Boris Zlotsky, US.

Designs: No. 436, Laelia milleri. No. 437, Psygmorchis pusilla. No. 438, Dendrobium cruentum. No. 439, Orchis purpurea.

2005, Mar. 3	Litho.	Perf. 12¾x12½	
436 A271	1fr multicolored (248,000)+	1.90	1.90
437 A271	1fr multicolored (248,000)+	1.90	1.90
438 A271	1fr multicolored (248,000)+	1.90	1.90
439 A271	1fr multicolored (248,000)+	1.90	1.90
a.	Block of 4, #436-439	7.75	7.75
	First day cover, #439a		8.75
	First day cover, #436-439, each		3.00
	Inscription block of 4, #439a	7.75	—
	Pane of 16	26.00	

Nature's Wisdom — G72

Printed by Cartor Security Printing, France. Panes of 20. Designed by Robert Stein, US.
Designs: 1fr, Children collecting water, India. 80c, Ruby brittle star, Bahamas.

2005, Apr. 21	Litho.	Perf. 13½x13¼	
440 G72	1fr multicolored (180,000)+	2.00	2.00
	First day cover		2.75
	Inscription block of 4	8.00	
	Pane of 20	40.00	—
441 G72	1.30fr multicolored (180,000)+	2.50	2.50
	First day cover		3.75
	First day cover, #440-441		5.50
	Inscription block of 4	10.00	
	Pane of 20	50.00	—

Intl. Year of Sport Type

Printed by Cartor Security Printing, France. Designed by Roland Hirter, Switzerland.

2005, June 3	Litho.	Perf. 13x13¼	
442 A368	1fr Wheelchair racing (185,000)+	2.00	2.00
	First day cover		2.75
	Inscription block of 4	8.00	
	Pane of 20	40.00	—
443 A368	1.30fr Cycling (185,000)+	2.50	2.50
	First day cover		3.75
	First day cover, #442-443		5.50
	Inscription block of 4	10.00	
	Pane of 20	50.00	—

World Heritage Sites, Egypt Type

Printed by Johann Enschedé and Sons, the Netherl Panes of 20. Designed by Rorie Katz, US.
Designs: Nos. 444, 446b, Philae. Nos. 445, 446e, I Cairo. No. 446a, Memphis and its Necropolis. No. 446c Mena. No. 446d, Ancient Thebes. No. 446f, St. Catherine

2005, Aug. 4	Litho.	Perf. 14x	
444 A369	1fr multicolored (180,000)+	2.00	
	First day cover		
	Inscription block of 4	8.00	
445 A369	1.30fr multicolored (180,000)+	2.50	
	First day cover		
	First day cover, #444-445		
	Inscription block of 4	10.00	

Souvenir Booklet

446	Booklet, #446g-446i (31,000)+	16.50	
a.-c.	A369 20c any single	.40	
d.-f.	A369 50c any single	.90	
g.	Booklet pane of 4 #446a	1.60	
h.	Booklet pane of 4 #446b	1.60	
i.	Booklet pane of 4 #446c	1.60	
j.	Booklet pane of 4 #446d	3.75	
k.	Booklet pane of 4 #446e	3.75	
l.	Booklet pane of 4 #446f	3.75	

My Dream for Peace Type

Winning designs of Lions Club International children's g peace poster contest by: 1fr, Marisa Harun, Indonesia. 1 Carlos Javier Parramón Teixidó, Spain.

2005, Sept. 21	Litho.	Per	
447 A357	1fr multicolored (175,000)+	1.90	
	First day cover		
	Inscription block of 4	7.75	
	Pane of 20	38.00	
448 A357	1.30fr multicolored (175,000)+	2.40	
	First day cover		
	First day cover, #447-448		
	Inscription block of 4	9.75	
	Pane of 20	48.00	

Food for Life Type

Printed by Government Printing Office, Austria. Designe Andrew Davidson, United Kingdom.
Designs: 1fr, Rye, airplane dropping parcels, camel cara 1.30fr, Sorghum, people carrying grain sacks, trucks.

2005, Oct. 20	Litho.	Perf.	
449 A370	1fr multicolored (170,000)+	1.90	
	First day cover		
	Inscription block of 4	7.75	
	Pane of 20	38.00	
450 A370	1.30fr multicolored (170,000)+	2.40	
	First day cover		
	First day cover, #449-450		
	Inscription block of 4	9.75	
	Pane of 20	48.00	

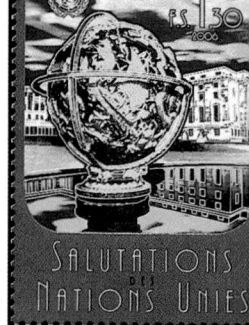

Armillary Sphere, Palais des Nations — G73

Printed by Cartor Security Printing, France. Panes of Designed by Rorie Katz, United States.

Litho. with Hologram

2006, Feb. 3		Perf. 13¼x1	
451 G73	1.30fr multicolored (280,000)+	2.25	
	First day cover		
	Inscription block of 4	9.00	
	Pane of 20	45.00	

Indigenous Art Type of 2003

Printed by Johann Enschedé and Sons, the Netherlands Designed by Robert Stein, US.

No. 452 — Musical instruments: a, Bell, Benin. b, Dr Swaziland. c, Sanza, Congo. d, Stringed instruments, C Verde. e, Caixixi, Ghana. f, Bells, Central Africa.

2006, Feb. 3	Litho.	Perf. 1	
452 G67	Sheet of 6 (91,000)+	12.00	12
	First day cover		14
a.-f.	1.20fr Any single	2.00	2

Endangered Species Type of 1993

Printed by Johann Enschedé and Sons, the Netherlands Designed by John D. Dawson, US.

esigns: No. 453, Dyscophus antongilii. No. 454, Chamaeleo
sis. No. 455, Corallus caninus. No. 456, Phyllobates
us.

6, Mar. 16	Litho.	Perf. 12¾x12½	
A271	1fr multicolored (228,000)+	1.75	1.75
A271	1fr multicolored (228,000)+	1.75	1.75
A271	1fr multicolored (228,000)+	1.75	1.75
A271	1fr multicolored (228,000)+	1.75	1.75
	Block of 4, #453-456	7.00	7.00
	First day cover, #456a		7.75
	First day cover, #453-456, each		2.60
	Inscription block of 4, #456a	7.00	
	Pane of 16	28.00	—

Intl. Day of Families Type

inted by Johann Enschedé and Sons, the Netherlands.
gned by Shelly Bartek, US.
esigns: 1fr, Family reading together. 1.30fr, Family on
orcycle.

6, May 27	Litho.	Perf. 14x13½	
A373	1fr multicolored (150,000)+	1.75	1.75
	First day cover		2.50
	Inscription block of 4	7.00	—
	Pane of 20	35.00	—
A373	1.30fr multicolored (150,000)+	2.25	2.25
	First day cover		3.25
	First day cover, #457-458		5.00
	Inscription block of 4	7.00	—
	Pane of 20	35.00	—

2006 END-OF-YEAR ISSUES

ee end of New York postage listings.

SEMI-POSTAL STAMP

AIDS Awareness Semi-postal Type
Souvenir Sheet

02, Oct. 24	Litho.	Perf. 14½	
SP1	90c + 30c multicolored (171,000)+	2.50	2.50
	First day cover, #B1		3.00

AIR LETTER SHEET

Jsed values for all postal stationery are for non-
latelic contemporaneous usages.

UN Type of 1968
inted by Setelipaino, Finland. Designed by Robert
Perrot.

69, Oct. 4	Litho.		
1 UC3	65c ultra & light blue, entire (350,000)	.50	1.50
	Entire, first day cancel (52,000)		.75

POSTAL CARDS

UN Type of 1969 and Type of Air Post Postal Card, 1966

inted by Courvoisier, S.A., Switzerland. Designed
y John Mason (20c) and Olav S. Mathiesen (30c).

Wmk. Post Horn, Swiss Cross, "S" or "Z"

69, Oct. 4	Litho.		
1 PC2	20c olive green & black, buff (415,000)	.25	.30
	First day cancel (51,500)		.50
2 APC2	30c violet blue, blue, light & dark green, buff (275,000)	.25	.30
	First day cancel (49,000)		.50

No. UX2, although of design APC2, is not inscribed "Poste
rienne" or "Air Mail."

UN Emblem — GPC1

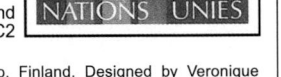

UN Emblem and
Ribbons — GPC2

Printed by Setelipaino, Finland. Designed by Veronique
ombez (40c) and Lieve Baeten (70c).

1977, June 27		Litho.	
UX3 GPC1	40c multicolored (500,000)	.30	.30
	First day cancel (65,000)		1.00
UX4 GPC2	70c multicolored (300,000)	.40	.40
	First day cancel (65,000)		.50

A second printing of No. UX3 was made in 1984. It was
released after the Swiss postal card rate had been increased to
50c so instructions were issued that all cards must have a 10c
stamp affixed before being sold. A few were sold in NY without
the added stamp. The card stock differs from the original
printing.

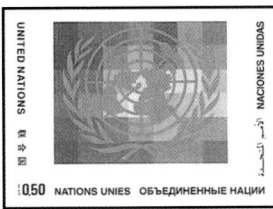

Emblem of the
United
Nations — GPC3

Peace
Dove — GPC4

Printed by Johann Enschede en Zonen, Netherlands.
Designed by George Hamori, Australia (50c) and Ryszard
Dudzicki, Poland (70c).

1985, May 10		Litho.	
UX5 GPC3	50c multicolored (300,000)	1.00	3.50
	First day cancel (34,700)		1.00
UX6 GPC4	70c multicolored (300,000)	3.25	3.25
	First day cancel (34,700)		4.50

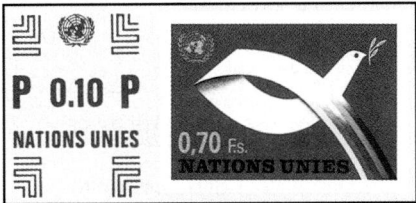

No. UX6 Surcharged in Lake

1986, Jan. 2		Litho.	
UX7 GPC4	70c + 10c multi (90,500)	2.50	2.50
	First day cancel (8,000 est.)		10.00

Type of 1990
Printed by Mercury-Walch, Australia.

1992, Sept. 4		Litho.	
UX8 G45	90c multicolored (150,000)+	1.75	1.75
	First day cancel (12,385)		6.00

No. UX5 Surcharged in Lake like No. UX7

1993, May 7		Litho.	
UX9 GPC3	50c +10c multicolored (47,000)+	1.50	1.50
	First day cancel		20.00

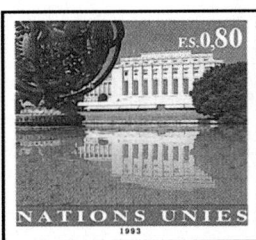

Palais des
Nations — GPC5

Printed by Leigh Mardon Pty. Limited, Australia.

1993, May 7		Litho.	
UX10 GPC5	80c multicolored (200,000)+	3.00	3.00
	First day cancel		7.50

#UX5, UX10 Surcharged in Carmine like #UX7

1996, Mar. 22		Litho.	
UX11 GPC3	50c +20c multi	3.00	3.00
	First day cancel		4.00
UX12 GPC5	80c +30c multi	3.00	3.00
	First day cancel		4.00

Assembly
Hall — GPC6

Palais des
Nations — GPC7

Printed by Mercury-Walsh, Australia.

1998, May 20		Litho.	
UX13 GPC6	70c multicolored (80,000)+	2.00	2.00
	First day cancel		3.00
UX14 GPC7	1.10fr multicolored (80,000)+	3.00	3.00
	First day cancel		3.25

Illustrations of the buildings are shown on the back of each
card.

Type of 2002
Printed by Johann Enschedé and Sons, the Netherlands.

2002, Mar. 1		Litho.	
UX15 G65	1.30fr multicolored (68,000)+	1.75	1.75
	First day cancel		2.00

Nos. UX8, UX13 and UX14 Surcharged Like No. UX7, But With Serifed Numerals

2004, Sept. 21		Litho.	
UX16 GPC6	70c +15c multicolored	1.40	1.40
	First day cancel		1.40
UX17 G45	90c +10c multicolored	1.60	1.60
	First day cancel		1.60
UX18 GPC7	1.10fr +10c multicolored	2.00	2.00
	First day cancel		2.00

OFFICES IN VIENNA, AUSTRIA

For use only on mail posted at the Vienna International Center for the UN and the International Atomic Energy Agency.

100 Groschen = 1 Schilling
100 Cents = 1 Euro (2002)

Type of Geneva, 1978, UN Types of 1961-72 and

Donaupark,
Vienna — V1

Aerial View — V2

Printed by Helio Courvoisier S.A., Switzerland. Panes of 50.
Designed by Henryk Chylinski (4s); Jozsef Vertel (6s).

1979, Aug. 24   Photo.   Perf. 11½
Granite Paper

1	G8	50g multicolored (3,500,000)+	.20	.20
		First day cover		1.00
		Inscription block of 4	.20	
2	A52	1s multicolored (3,800,000)+	.20	.20
		First day cover		1.00
		Inscription block of 4	.40	
3	V1	4s multicolored (3,500,000)+	.25	.25
		First day cover		1.00
		Inscription block of 4	1.10	
4	AP13	5s multicolored (3,500,000)+	.30	.30
		First day cover		1.00
		Inscription block of 4	1.40	
5	V2	6s multicolored (4,500,000)+	.35	.35
		First day cover		1.25
		Inscription block of 4	1.75	
6	A45	10s multicolored (3,500,000)+	.60	.60
		First day cover		2.00
		Inscription block of 4	3.25	
		Nos. 1-6 (6)	1.90	1.90

+ Printing orders to Mar. 1993.
No. 4 is not inscribed "Air Mail," No. 6 has no frame.
First day covers of Nos. 1-6 total 1,026,575.

New Economic Order Type of UN

1980, Jan. 11   Litho.   Perf. 15x14½

7	A178	4s multicolored (1,418,418)	.60	.60
		First day cover		1.25
		Inscription block of 4	9.00	

Value for margin inscription block is for one from bottom of
sheet. One from top is about twice the value shown.

Dove Type of UN

1980, Jan. 11   Litho.   Perf. 14x13½

8	A147	2.50s multicolored (3,500,000)+	.25	.25
		First day cover		1.00
		Inscription block of 4	1.25	

First day covers of Nos. 7-8 total 336,229.

Women's Year
Emblem on World
Map — V3

United Nations Decade for Women.

Printed by Questa Colour Security Printers, United Kingdom.
Panes of 50. Designed by Gunnar Janssen.

1980, Mar. 7   Litho.   Perf. 14½x15

9	V3	4s light green & dark green (1,569,080)	.40	.40
		First day cover		1.00
		Inscription block of 4	1.75	

10	V3	6s bister brown (1,556,016)	.75	.75
		First day cover		1.25
		First day cover, #9-10		1.50
		Inscription block of 4	3.25	

First day covers of Nos. 9-10 total 443,893.

Peace-keeping Operations Type of UN

1980, May 16   Litho.   Perf. 14x13

11	A182	6s multicolored (1,719,852)	.40	.40
		First day cover (323,923)		1.00
		Inscription block of 4	2.00	

35th Anniversary Types of Geneva and UN

1980, June 26   Litho.   Perf. 13x13½

12	G16	4s carmine rose & black (1,626,582)	.35	.35
		First day cover		1.00
		Inscription block of 4	1.60	
13	A184	6s multicolored (1,625,400)	.60	.60
		First day cover		1.25
		Inscription block of 4	2.75	

Souvenir Sheet
Imperf

14		Sheet of 2 (1,675,191)	.90	.90
a.		G16 4s carmine rose & black	.25	.25
b.		A184 6s multicolored	.65	.65
		First day cover		1.00

First day covers of Nos. 12-14 total 657,402.

ECOSOC Types of UN and Geneva

Printed by Ashton-Potter Ltd., Canada. Panes of 50.
Designed by Dietman Kowall (4s), Angel Medina Medina (6s).

1980, Nov. 21   Litho.   Perf. 13½x13

15	A187	4s multicolored (1,811,218)	.30	.30
		First day cover		1.00
		Inscription block of 4	1.50	
16	G17	6s multicolored (1,258,420)	.60	.60
		First day cover		1.00
		First day cover #15-16		1.25
		Inscription block of 4	2.50	

Economic and Social Council (ECOSOC).
First day covers of Nos. 15-16 total 224,631.

Palestinian Rights Type of UN

Printed by Courvoisier S.A., Switzerland. Panes of 50.
Designed by David Dewhurst.

1981, Jan. 30   Photo.   Perf. 12x11½

17	A188	4s multicolored (1,673,310)	.45	.45
		First day cover (208,812)		1.00
		Inscription block of 4	2.00	

Disabled Type of UN and

Interlocking Stitches — V4

International Year of the Disabled.
Printed by Heraclio Fournier S.A., Spain.   Panes of 50.
Designed by Sophia van Heeswijk.

1981, Mar. 6   Photo.   Perf. 14

18	A189	4s multicolored (1,508,719)	.40	.40
		First day cover		1.00
		Inscription block of 4	1.75	
19	V4	6s black & orange (1,569,385)	.60	.60
		First day cover		1.00
		First day cover, #18-19		1.25
		Inscription block of 4	2.75	

First day covers of Nos. 18-19 total 290,603.

Art Type of UN

1981, Apr. 15   Photo.   Perf. 11½
Granite Paper

20	A191	6s multicolored (1,643,527)	.75	.75
		First day cover (196,916)		1.00
		Inscription block of 4	3.25	

Energy Type of UN

1981, May 29   Litho.   Perf

21	A193	7.50s multicolored (1,611,130)	.70
		First day cover (216,197)	
		Inscription block of 4	3.00

Volunteers Program Types

1981, Nov. 13   Li

22	A195	5s multicolored (1,582,780)	.40
		First day cover	
		Inscription block of 4	2.25
23	G18	7s multicolored (1,516,139)	.90
		First day cover	
		First day cover, #22-23	
		Inscription block of 4	4.25

First day covers of Nos. 22-23 total 282,414.

"For a Better World" — V5

Printed by Courvoisier, S.A., Switzerland.   Sheets of
Designed by Eliezer Weishoff.

1982, Jan. 22   Perf. 11½x

24	V5	3s multicolored (3,300,000)+	.35
		First day cover (203,872)	
		Inscription block of 4	1.75

Human Environment Types of UN

10th Anniversary of United Nations Environment Progra
Printed by Joh. Enschede en Zonen, Netherlands. Panes of
Designed by Peer-Ulrich Bremer (5s); Sybille Brunner (7s).

1982, Mar. 19   Litho.   Perf. 13½x

25	A200	5s multicolored (1,312,765)	.40
		First day cover	
		Inscription block of 4	1.90
26	G21	7s multicolored (1,357,513)	.80
		First day cover	
		First day cover, #25-26	
		Inscription block of 4	3.75

First day covers of Nos. 25-26 total 248,576.

Outer Space Type of UN

Exploration and Peaceful Uses of Outer Space. Printed
Enschede. Panes of 50. Designed by George Hamori.

1982, June 11   Litho.   Perf. 13x13

27	G22	5s multicolored (1,339,038)	.60
		First day cover (150,845)	1
		Inscription block of 4	3.00

Conservation & Protection of Nature Type

1982, Nov. 16   Photo.   Perf.

28	A202	5s Fish (1,202,694)	.50
		First day cover	1
		Inscription block of 4	2.50
29	A202	7s Animal (1,194,403)	.70
		First day cover	
		First day cover, #28-29	1
		Inscription block of 4	3.00

First day covers of Nos. 28-29 total 243,548.

World Communications Year Type

1983, Jan. 28   Litho.   Perf.

30	A203	4s multicolored (1,517,443)	.40
		First day cover (150,541)	1.
		Inscription block of 4	2.10

Safety at Sea Type

1983, Mar. 18   Litho.   Perf. 14

31	G23	4s multicolored (1,506,052)	.40
		First day cover	1.
		Inscription block of 4	2.00
32	A206	6s multicolored (1,527,990)	.65
		First day cover	1.
		First day cover, #31-32	1.
		Inscription block of 4	2.75

First day covers of Nos. 31-32 total 219,118.

World Food Program Type

3, Apr. 22	Engr.	Perf. 13½	
A207 5s **green** (1,419,237)		.45	.45
First day cover			1.00
Inscription block of 4		2.25	—
A207 7s **brown** (1,454,227)		.70	.70
First day cover			1.00
First day cover, #33-34			1.25
Inscription block of 4		2.75	—

First day covers of Nos. 33-34 total 212,267.

Conference on Trade and Development Type

3, June 6	Litho.	Perf. 14	
G24 4s **multicolored** (1,544,973)		.30	.30
First day cover			1.00
Inscription block of 4		1.90	—
A209 8.50s **multicolored** (1,423,172)		.75	.75
First day cover			1.00
First day cover, #35-36			1.25
Inscription block of 4		3.25	—

First day covers of Nos. 35-36 total 184,023.

The Second Skin — V6

Right to Think — V7

5th Anniversary of the Universal Declaration of Human Rights

Printed by Government Printing Office, Austria. Designed by edensreich Hundertwasser, Austria. Panes of 16 (4x4).

83, Dec. 9	Photo. & Engr.	Perf. 13½	
V6 5s **multicolored** (2,163,419)		.45	.45
First day cover			1.25
Inscription block of 4		2.25	—
V7 7s **multicolored** (2,163,542)		.70	.70
First day cover			1.25
First day cover, #37-38			2.25
Inscription block of 4		3.25	—
Panes of 16, #37-38		18.00	

First day covers of Nos. 37-38 total 246,440.

International Conference on Population Type

Printed by Bundesdruckerei, Federal Republic of Germany. nes of 50. Designed by Marina Langer-Rosa and Helmut nger, Federal Republic of Germany.

84, Feb. 3	Litho.	Perf. 14	
A212 7s **multicolored** (1,135,791)		.65	.65
First day cover (80,570)			1.50
Inscription block of 4		2.75	—

Field Irrigation V8

Harvesting Machines V9

World Food Day, Oct. 16

Printed by Walsall Security Printers, Ltd., United Kingdom. Panes of 50. Designed by Adth Vanooijen, Netherlands.

1984, Mar. 15	Litho.	Perf. 14½	
40 V8 4.50s **multicolored** (994,106)		.40	.40
First day cover			1.00
Inscription block of 4		2.00	—
41 V9 6s **multicolored** (1,027,115)		.65	.65
First day cover			1.00
First day cover #40-41			2.25
Inscription block of 4		2.50	—

First day covers of Nos. 40-41 total 194,546.

Serengeti Park, Tanzania — V10

Ancient City of Shiban, People's Democratic Rep. of Yemen — V11

World Heritage

Printed by Harrison and Sons, United Kingdom. Panes of 50. Designs adapted by Rocco J. Callari, US, and Thomas Lee, China.

1984, Mar. 15	Litho.	Perf. 14	
42 V10 3.50s **multicolored** (957,518)		.25	.25
First day cover			1.25
Inscription block of 4		1.25	—
43 V11 15s **multicolored** (928,794)		1.25	1.25
First day cover			1.75
First day cover, #42-43			2.50
Inscription block of 4		5.75	—

First day covers of Nos. 42-43 total 193,845.

V12

V13

Future for Refugees

Designed by Hans Erni, Switzerland.
Printed by Courvoisier. Panes of 50.

1984, Mar. 29	Photo.	Perf. 11½	
44 V12 4.50s **multicolored** (1,086,393)		.45	.45
First day cover			1.25
Inscription block of 4		2.25	—
45 V13 8.50s **multicolored** (1,109,865)		1.25	1.25
First day cover			1.75
First day cover, #44-45			2.25
Inscription block of 4		5.75	—

First day covers of Nos. 44-45 total 185,349.

International Youth Year — V14

Printed by Waddingtons Ltd., United Kingdom. Panes of 50. Designed by Ruel A. Mayo, Phillipines.

1984, Nov. 15	Litho.	Perf. 13½	
46 V14 3.50s **multicolored** (1,178,833)		.45	.45
First day cover			1.25
Inscription block of 4		2.10	—
47 V14 6.50s **multicolored** (1,109,337)		.70	.70
First day cover			1.50
First day cover, #46-47			2.25
Inscription block of 4		3.25	—

First day covers of Nos. 46-47 total 165,762.

ILO Type of Geneva

Printed by the Government Printing Bureau, Japan. Panes of 50. Adapted from photographs by Rocco J. Callari, US, and Thomas Lee, China.

1985, Feb. 1	Engr.	Perf. 13½	
48 G34 7.50s U Thant Pavilion (948,317)		.75	.75
First day cover (115,916)			1.75
Inscription block of 4		3.50	—

UN University Type

Printed by Helio Courvoisier, Switzerland. Panes of 50. Designed by Moshe Pereg, Israel, and Hinedi Geluda, Brazil.

1985, Mar. 15	Photo.	Perf. 13½	
49 A221 8.50s Rural scene, lab researcher (863,673)		.75	.75
First day cover (108,479)			1.75
Inscription block of 4		3.75	—

Ship of Peace — V15

Shelter under UN Umbrella — V16

Printed by Carl Ueberreuter Druck and Verlag M. Salzer, Austria. Panes of 50. Designed by Ran Banda Mawilmada, Sri Lanka (4.50s), and Sophia van Heeswijk, Federal Republic of Germany (15s).

1985, May 10	Litho.	Perf. 14	
50 V15 4.50s **multicolored** (2,000,000)+		.30	.30
First day cover			.75
Inscription block of 4		1.50	—
51 V16 15s **multicolored** (2,000,000)+		2.00	2.00
First day cover			2.75
First day cover, #50-51			3.50
Inscription block of 4		9.50	—

First day covers of Nos. 50-51 total 142,687.

40th Anniversary Type

Designed by Rocco J. Callari, U.S., and Thomas Lee, China (No. 54).

1985, June 26	Photo.	Perf. 12 x 11½	
52 A224 6.50s **multicolored** (984,820)		.90	.90
First day cover			1.25
Inscription block of 4		4.25	—
53 A225 8.50s **multicolored** (914,347)		1.40	1.40
First day cover			1.75
First day cover, #52-53			2.50
Inscription block of 4		6.25	—

Souvenir Sheet
Imperf

54		Sheet of 2 (676,648)	2.50	2.50
a.	A224	6.50s **multi**	1.00	1.00
b.	A225	8.50s **multi**	1.40	1.40
		First day cover		2.50

First day covers of Nos. 52-54 total 317,652.

UNICEF Child Survival Campaign Type

Printed by the Government Printing Bureau, Japan. Panes of 50. Designed by Mel Harris, United Kingdom (No. 55) and Vreni Wyss-Fischer, Switzerland (No. 56).

1985, Nov. 22   **Photo. & Engr.**   *Perf. 13½*

55	A226	4s Spoonfeeding children (889,918)	.75	.75
		First day cover		1.50
		Inscription block of 4	3.50	—
56	A226	6s Mother hugging infant (852,958)	1.40	1.40
		First day cover		1.50
		First day cover, #55-56		2.50
		Inscription block of 4	6.00	—

First day covers of Nos. 55-56 total 239,532.

Africa in Crisis Type

Printed by Helio Courvoisier, Switzerland. Panes of 50. Designed by Tesfaye Tessema, Ethiopia.

1986, Jan. 31   **Photo.**   *Perf. 11½x12*

57	A227	8s **multicolored** (809,854)	.80	.80
		First day cover (99,996)		2.75
		Inscription block of 4	3.50	—

UN Development Program Type

Agriculture. Printed by the Government Printing Bureau, Japan. Panes of 40, 2 blocks of 4 horizontal and 5 blocks of 4 vertical. Designed by Thomas Lee, China.

1986, Mar. 14   **Photo.**   *Perf. 13½*

58	A228	4.50s Developing crop strains (730,691)	1.50	1.25
59	A228	4.50s Animal husbandry (730,691)	1.50	1.25
60	A228	4.50s Technical instruction (730,691)	1.50	1.25
61	A228	4.50s Nutrition education (730,691)	1.50	1.25
a.		Block of 4, #58-61	6.25	5.50
		First day cover, #61a		6.00
		First day cover, #58-61, each		2.00
		Inscription block of 4, #58-61	7.00	—
		Pane of 40, #58-61	87.50	

No. 61a has a continuous design.
First day covers of Nos. 58-61 total 227,664.

Stamp Collecting Type

Designs: 3.50s, UN stamps. 6.50s, Engraver. Printed by the Swedish Post Office, Sweden. Panes of 50. Designed by Czeslaw Slania and Ingalill Axelsson, Sweden.

1986, May 22   **Engr.**   *Perf. 12½*

62	A229	3.50s dk ultra & dk brown (874,119)	.40	.40
		First day cover		1.50
		Inscription block of 4	2.25	—
63	A229	6.50s int blue & brt rose (877,284)	.90	.90
		First day cover		1.50
		First day cover, #62-63		2.25
		Inscription block of 4	4.50	—

First day covers of Nos. 62-63 total 150,836.

Olive Branch, Rainbow, Earth — V17

International Peace Year. Printed by the Government Printing Bureau, Japan. Panes of 50. Designed by Milo Schor, Israel (No. 64), and Mohammad Sardar, Pakistan (No. 65).

Photogravure & Embossed

1986, June 20   *Perf. 13½*

64	V17	5s shown (914,699)	.75	.75
		First day cover		1.50
		Inscription block of 4	3.75	—
65	V17	6s Doves, UN emblem (818,386)	1.00	1.00
		First day cover		1.50
		First day cover, #64-65		2.50
		Inscription block of 4	4.50	—

First day covers of Nos. 64-65 total 169,551.

WFUNA Anniversary Type
Souvenir Sheet

Printed by Johann Enschede and Sons, Netherlands. Designed by Rocco J. Callari, US.

Designs: 4s, White stallion by Elisabeth von Janota-Bzowski, Germany. 5s, Surrealistic landscape by Ernst Fuchs, Austria. 6s, Geometric abstract by Victor Vasarely (b. 1908), France. 7s, Mythological abstract by Wolfgang Hutter (b. 1928), Austria.

1986, Nov. 14   **Litho.**   *Perf. 13x13½*

66		Sheet of 4 (668,264)	4.00	4.00
a.	A232	4s **multicolored**	.75	.75
b.	A232	5s **multicolored**	.85	.85
c.	A232	6s **multicolored**	1.00	1.00
d.	A232	7s **multicolored**	1.25	1.25
		First day cover (121,852)		4.00

No. 66 has inscribed margin picturing UN and WFUNA emblems.

Trygve Lie Type
Photogravure & Engraved

1987, Jan. 30   *Perf. 13½*

67	A233	8s **multicolored** (778,010)	.70	.70
		First day cover (94,112)		2.50
		Inscription block of 4	3.50	—

Shelter for the Homeless Type

Designs: 4s, Family and homes. 9.50s, Family entering home.

1987, Mar. 13   **Litho.**   *Perf. 13½x12½*

68	A234	4s **multicolored** (704,922)	.50	.50
		First day cover		1.25
		Inscription block of 4	2.40	—
69	A234	9.50s **multicolored** (671,200)	1.10	1.10
		First day cover		1.75
		First day cover, #68-69		2.75
		Inscription block of 4	4.75	—

First day covers of Nos. 68-69 total 117,941.

Fight Drug Abuse Type

Designs: 5s, Soccer players. 8s, Family.

1987, June 12   **Litho.**   *Perf. 14½x15*

70	A235	5s **multicolored** (869,875)	.40	.40
		First day cover		1.40
		Inscription block of 4	2.40	—
71	A235	8s **multicolored** (797,889)	.90	.90
		First day cover		1.75
		First day cover, #70-71		2.75
		Inscription block of 4	4.00	—

First day covers of Nos. 70-71 total 117,964.

Donaupark, Vienna — V18

Peace Embracing the Earth — V19

Printed by The House of Questa, United Kingdom. Panes of 50. Designed by Henry Bencsath, US (2s), and Eliezer Weishoff, Israel (17s).

1987, June 12   **Litho.**   *Perf. 14½x15*

72	V18	2s **multicolored** (2,000,000)+	.30	.30
		First day cover		1.25
		Inscription block of 4	1.50	—
73	V19	17s **multicolored** (2,000,000)+	1.60	1.60
		First day cover		2.50
		First day cover, #72-73		3.50
		Inscription block of 4	8.00	—

First day covers of Nos. 72-73 total 111,153.

UN Day Type

Designed by Elisabeth von Janota-Bzowski (5s) and Fritz Henry Oerter (6s), Federal Republic of Germany.
Designs: Multinational people in various occupations.

1987, Oct. 23   **Litho.**   *Perf. 14½x15*

74	A236	5s **multicolored** (1,575,731)	.75	.75
		First day cover		1.40
		Inscription block of 4	3.75	—
75	A236	6s **multicolored** (1,540,523)	.90	.90
		First day cover		1.75
		First day cover, #74-75		2.75
		Inscription block of 4	4.25	—
		Panes of 12, #74-75	22.00	

Immunize Every Child Type

Designs: 4s, Poliomyelitis. 9.50s, Diphtheria.

1987, Nov. 20   **Litho.**   *Perf. 15x14½*

76	A237	4s **multicolored** (793,716)	.75	.75
		First day cover		1.00
		Inscription block of 4	4.00	—

77	A237	9.50s **multicolored** (769,288)		2.00
		First day cover		
		First day cover, #76-77		
		Inscription block of 4	8.25	

IFAD Type

Designs: 4s, Grains. 6s, Vegetables.

1988, Jan. 29   **Litho.**   *Perf.*

78	A238	4s **multicolored** (697,307)		.40
		First day cover		
		Inscription block of 4	2.75	
79	A238	6s **multicolored** (701,521)		.90
		First day cover		
		First day cover, #78-79		
		Inscription block of 4	4.25	

Survival of the Forests Type

Deciduous forest in fall: 4s, Treetops, hills and dales. 5s, trunks. Printed se-tenant in a continuous design.

1988, Mar. 18   **Litho.**   *Perf. 14*

80	A240	4s **multicolored** (990,607)		2.25
		First day cover		
81	A240	5s **multicolored** (990,607)		3.00
		First day cover		
a.		Pair, #80-81		5.25
		First day cover, #81a		
		Inscription block of 4, #80-81	12.00	
		Pane of 12, #80-81	30.00	

Intl. Volunteer Day Type

Designed by George Fernandez, U.S.
Designs: 6s, Medical care, vert. 7.50s, Construction.

1988, May 6   **Litho.**   *Perf. 13x14, 14*

82	A241	6s **multicolored** (701,167)		.75
		First day cover		
		Inscription block of 4	4.00	
83	A241	7.50s **multicolored** (638,240)		1.00
		First day cover		
		First day cover, #82-83		
		Inscription block of 4	5.75	

Health in Sports Type

Paintings by LeRoy Neiman, American Sports artist: 6s, ing, vert. 8s, Tennis.

1988, June 17   **Litho.**   *Perf. 13½x13, 13x1*

84	A242	6s **multicolored** (668,902)		.90
		First day cover		
		Inscription block of 4	5.50	
85	A242	8s **multicolored** (647,915)		1.40
		First day cover		
		First day cover #84-85		
		Inscription block of 4	9.50	

Universal Declaration of Human Rights 40th Anniv. Type

1988, Dec. 9   **Photo. & Engr.**   *Perf. 1*

86	A243	5s **multicolored** (1,080,041)		.50
		First day cover		
		Inscription block of 4	3.00	

Souvenir Sheet

87	A243	11s **multicolored** (688,994)	1.25	1
		First day cover		4

No. 87 has multicolored decorative margin inscribed with p amble to the human rights declaration in German.

World Bank Type

1989, Jan. 27   **Litho.**   *Perf. 13x*

88	A244	5.50s Transportation (682,124)	1.10	1
		First day cover		
		Inscription block of 4	5.25	
89	A244	8s Health care, education (628,649)	1.75	1
		First day cover		2
		First day cover, #88-89		3
		Inscription block of 4	8.25	

First day covers of Nos. 88-89 total 135,964.

Peace-Keeping Force Type

1989, Mar. 17   *Perf. 14x13*

90	A245	6s **multicolored** (912,731)		.85
		First day cover (81,837)		2.
		Inscription block of 4	4.00	

World Weather Watch Type

Satellite photograph and radar image: 4s, Helical cloud fc mation over Italy, the eastern Alps, and parts of Yugoslavi 9.50s, Rainfall in Tokyo, Japan.

1989, Apr. 21   **Litho.**   *Perf. 13x1*

91	A247	4s **multicolored** (948,680)	1.00	1.
		First day cover		1.
		Inscription block of 4	4.50	
92	A247	9.50s **multicolored** (880,138)	2.10	2.
		First day cover		2.
		First day cover, #91-92		4.
		Inscription block of 4	10.50	

First day covers of Nos. 91-92 total 116,846.

Offices in Vienna, 10th Anniv.
V20   V21

Printed by the Government Printing Office, Austria. Panes of 50. Designed by Gottfried Kumpf (5s) and Andre Heller (7.50s), Austria.

Photo. & Engr., Photo. (7.50s)

1989, Aug. 23			Perf. 14	
V20	5s multicolored (958,339)		2.25	2.25
	First day cover			1.25
	Inscription block of 4		11.50	—
V21	7.50s multicolored (785,517)		2.25	2.25
	First day cover			3.00
	First day cover, #93-94			4.00
	Inscription block of 4		11.50	—
	Panes of 25, #93-94		100.00	

First day covers of Nos. 93-94 total 210,746.

Human Rights Type of 1989

Panes of 12+12 se-tenant labels containing Articles 5 (4s) or 6 (6s) inscribed in German, English or French.
Paintings: 4s, The Prisoners, by Kathe Kollwitz. 6s, Justice, by Raphael.

1989, Nov. 17			Perf. 13½	
A250	4s multicolored (2,267,450)		.50	.50
	First day cover			2.50
	Inscription block of 3 + 3 labels		1.75	—
A250	6s multicolored (2,264,876)		.75	.75
	First day cover			3.50
	First day cover, #95-96			3.00
	Inscription block of 3 + 3 labels		2.50	—
	Panes of 12, #95-96		15.00	

First day covers of Nos. 95-96 total 183,199.
See Nos. 108-109, 123-124, 150-151.

Intl. Trade Center Type

1990, Feb. 2			Perf. 14½x15	
A251	12s multicolored (559,556)		1.50	1.50
	First day cover (77,928)			4.00
	Inscription block of 4		8.00	—

Painting by Kurt Regschek
V22

Printed by the National Postage Stamps and Fiduciary Print-ing Works, France. Designed by Robert J. Stein, US.

1990, Feb. 2			Perf. 13x13½	
V22	1.50s multicolored (1,000,000)+		.30	.30
	First day cover (64,622)			2.50
	Inscription block of 4		1.40	—

Fight AIDS Type

Designed by Jacek Tofil, Poland (5s), Orlando Pelaez, Colombia (11s).
Designs: 5s, "SIDA." 11s, Stylized figures, ink blot.

1990, Mar. 16			Perf. 13½x12½	
A252	5s multicolored (623,155)		1.00	1.00
	First day cover			1.50
	Inscription block of 4		6.00	—
A252	11s multicolored (588,742)		2.25	2.25
	First day cover			2.50
	First day cover, #99-100			4.75
	Inscription block of 4		11.50	—

First day covers of Nos. 99-100 total 123,657.

Medicinal Plants Type

1990, May 4	Photo.	Granite Paper	Perf. 11½	
A253	4.50s Bixa orellana (709,840)		1.25	1.25
	First day cover			1.50
	Inscription block of 4		6.00	—
A253	9.50s Momordica charantia (732,883)		2.50	2.50
	First day cover			2.50
	First day cover, #101-102			4.75
	Inscription block of 4		11.50	—

First day covers of Nos. 101-102 total 117,545.

UN 45th Anniv. Type

Designed by Talib Nauman, Pakistan (7s), Marleen Bosmans (9s), Robert Stein, US (No. 105).
Designs: 7s, 9s, "45" and emblem.

1990, June 26		Litho.	Perf. 14½x13	
103	A254 7s multicolored (604,878)		1.40	1.40
	First day cover			1.75
	Inscription block of 4		6.50	—
104	A254 9s multicolored, diff. (550,902)		2.40	2.40
	First day cover			2.25
	First day cover, #103-104			4.00
	Inscription block of 4		12.00	—

Souvenir Sheet

105	Sheet of 2, #103-104 (423,370)		6.00	6.00
	First day cover			5.00

First day covers of Nos. 103-105 total 181,174.

Crime Prevention Type

1990, Sept. 13		Photo.	Perf. 14	
106	A255 6s Domestic violence (661,810)		1.00	1.00
	First day cover			1.50
	Inscription block of 4		5.50	—
107	A255 8s Crimes against cultural heritage (607,940)		2.25	2.25
	First day cover			2.25
	First day cover, #106-107			3.00
	Inscription block of 4		11.00	—

First day covers of Nos. 106-107 total 112,193.

Human Rights Type of 1989

Panes of 12+12 se-tenant labels containing Articles 11 (4.50s) or 12 (7s) inscribed in German, English or French.
Paintings: 4.50s, Before the Judge, by Sandor Bihari. 7s, Young Man Greeted by a Woman Writing a Poem, by Suzuki Harunobu.

1990, Nov. 16		Litho.	Perf. 13½	
108	A250 4.50s multicolored (1,684,833)		.30	.30
	First day cover			2.50
	Inscription block of 3 + 3 labels		1.25	—
109	A250 7s multicolored (1,541,022)		.90	.90
	First day cover			3.50
	First day cover, #108-109			2.50
	Inscription block of 3 + 3 labels		4.25	—
	Panes of 12, #108-109		20.00	

First day covers of Nos. 108-109 total 168,831.

Economic Commission for Europe Type

1991, Mar. 15		Litho.	Perf. 14	
110	A256 5s Weasel, hoopoe (727,436)		1.10	1.10
111	A256 5s Warbler, swans (727,436)		1.10	1.10
112	A256 5s Badgers, squirrel (727,436)		1.10	1.10
113	A256 5s Fish (727,436)		1.10	1.10
a.	Block of 4, #110-113		4.50	4.50
	First day cover, No. 113a			5.00
	First day cover, Nos. 110-113, each			3.25
	Inscription block of 4, #110-113		6.00	—
	Pane of 40, #110-113		55.00	

First day covers of Nos. 110-113 total 81,624.

Namibian Independence Type

1991, May 10		Litho.	Perf. 14	
114	A257 6s Mountains, clouds (531,789)		1.25	1.50
	First day cover			2.50
	Inscription block of 4		6.00	—
115	A257 9.50s Dune, Namib Desert (503,735)		2.75	2.75
	First day cover			3.75
	First day cover, #114-115			4.50
	Inscription block of 4		14.50	—

First day covers of Nos. 114-115 total 111,184.

V24

Printed by House of Questa, United Kingdom. Designed by Marina Langer-Rosa, Germany.

1991, May 10		Litho.	Perf. 15x14½	
116	V24 20s multicolored (1,750,000)+		3.50	3.50
	First day cover (60,843)			4.00
	Inscription block of 4		15.00	—

V25

Rights of the Child — V26

Printed by The House of Questa. Panes of 50. Designed by Anna Harmer, Austria (7s) and Emiko Takegawa, Japan (9s).

1991, June 14		Litho.	Perf. 14½	
117	V25 7s Stick drawings (645,145)		1.50	1.50
	First day cover			1.75
	Inscription block of 4		6.75	—
118	V26 9s Child, clock, fruit (568,214)		2.00	2.00
	First day cover			2.25
	First day cover, #117-118			3.50
	Inscription block of 4		10.00	—

First day covers of Nos. 117-118 total 120,619.

V27

Banning of Chemical Weapons
V28

Printed by Heraclio Fournier, S.A. Panes of 50. Designed by Oscar Asboth, Austria (5s), Michel Granger, France (10s).

1991, Sept. 11		Litho.	Perf. 13½	
119	V27 5s multicolored (469,454)		1.40	1.40
	First day cover			1.40
	Inscription block of 4		7.00	—
120	V28 10s multicolored (525,704)		2.75	2.75
	First day cover			2.50
	First day cover, #119-120			3.00
	Inscription block of 4		14.00	—

First day covers of Nos. 119-120 total 116,862.

UN Postal Administration, 40th Anniv. Type

1991, Oct. 24		Litho.	Perf. 14x15	
121	A263 5s UN NY No. 8 (564,450)		.75	.75
	First day cover			1.40
	Inscription block of 4		4.00	—
122	A263 8s UN NY No. 5 (609,830)		1.75	1.75
	First day cover			2.10
	First day cover, #121-122			3.25
	Inscription block of 4		9.00	—
	Panes of 25, #121-122		60.00	

First day covers of Nos. 121-122 total 107,802.

Human Rights Type of 1989

Panes of 12+12 se-tenant labels containing Articles 17 (4.50s) or 18 (7s) inscribed in German, English or French.
Artwork: 4.50s, Pre-columbian Mexican pottery. 7s, Windows, by Robert Delaunay.

1991, Nov. 20		Litho.	Perf. 13½	
123	A250 4.50s black & brown (1,717,097)		.50	.50
	First day cover			2.75
	Inscription block of 3 + 3 labels		3.00	—
124	A250 7s multicolored (1,717,738)		.80	.80
	First day cover			5.00
	First day cover, #123-124			1.75
	Inscription block of 3 + 3 labels		5.00	—
	Panes of 12+12 labels, #123-124		25.00	25.00

First day covers of Nos. 123-124 total 204,854.

World Heritage Type of 1984

Designs: 5s, Iguacu Natl. Park, Brazil. 9s, Abu Simbel, Egypt.

1992, Jan. 24	Litho.	Perf. 13
	Size: 35x28mm	
125 V10 5s multicolored (586,738)	1.25	1.25
First day cancel		1.50
Inscription block of 4	5.75	—
126 V10 9s multicolored (476,965)	2.25	2.25
First day cancel		2.75
First day cancel, #125-126		4.00
Inscription block of 4	9.00	—

First day covers of Nos. 125-126 total 93,016.

Clean Oceans Type

1992, Mar. 13	Litho.	Perf. 14
127 A264 7s Ocean surface, diff. (1,121,870)	1.00	1.00
128 A264 7s Ocean bottom, diff. (1,121,870)	1.00	1.00
a. Pair, #127-128	2.25	2.25
First day cover, #128a		3.25
First day cover, #127-128, any single		2.00
Inscription block of 4, 2 each #127-128	5.00	—
Pane of 12, #127-128	14.00	—

First day covers of Nos. 127-128 total 128,478.

Earth Summit Type

1992, May 22	Photo.	Perf. 11½
129 A265 5.50s Man in space (784,197)	1.30	1.30
130 A265 5.50s Sun (784,197)	1.30	1.30
131 A265 5.50s Man fishing (784,197)	1.30	1.30
132 A265 5.50s Sailboat (784,197)	1.30	1.30
a. Block of 4, #129-132	5.50	5.50
First day cover, #132a		6.00
First day cover, #129-132, any single		4.00
Inscription block of 4, #129-132	7.00	—
Pane of 40, #129-132	60.00	—

First day covers of Nos. 129-132a total 82,920.

Mission to Planet Earth Type

Designs: No. 133, Satellite, person's mouth. No. 134, Satellite, person's ear.

1992, Sept. 4	Photo.	Rouletted 8
	Granite Paper	
133 A266 10s multicolored (881,716)	2.50	2.50
134 A266 10s multicolored (881,716)	2.50	2.50
a. Pair, #133-134	5.00	5.00
First day cover, #134a		4.50
First day cover, #133-134, any single		7.50
Inscription block of 4, #133-134	12.50	—
Pane of 10, #133-134	30.00	—

First day covers of Nos. 133-134 total 99,459.

Science and Technology Type of 1992

Designs: 5.50s, Woman emerging from computer screen. 7s, Green thumb growing flowers.

1992, Oct. 2	Litho.	Perf. 14
135 A267 5.50s multicolored (482,830)	.75	.75
First day cover		1.75
Inscription block of 4	3.75	—
136 A267 7s multicolored (500,517)	1.40	1.40
First day cover		2.00
First day cover, #135-136		4.00
Inscription block of 4	6.75	—

First day covers of Nos. 135-136 total 98,091.

V29

Intl. Center,
Vienna — V30

Printed by Walsall Security Printers, Ltd., UK. Designed by Gundi Groh, Austria (5.50s), Rocco J. Callari, US (7s).

1992, Oct. 2	Litho.	Perf. 13x13½
137 V29 5.50s multicolored (2,100,000)+	.90	.90
First day cover		1.25
Inscription block of 4	5.00	—
	Perf. 13½x13	
138 V30 7s multicolored (2,100,000)+	1.25	1.25
First day cover		2.00
First day cover, #137-138		3.50
Inscription block of 4	7.50	—

First day covers of Nos. 137-138 total 151,788.

Human Rights Type of 1989

Panes of 12+12 se-tenant labels containing Articles 23 (6s) and 24 (10s) inscribed in German, English or French.

Artwork: 6s, Les Constructeurs, by Fernand Leger. 10s, Sunday Afternoon on the Island of Le Grande Jatte, by Georges Seurat.

1992, Nov. 20	Litho.	Perf. 13½
139 A250 6s multicolored, (1,536,516)	.75	.75
First day cover		3.50
Inscription block of 3 + 3 labels	4.00	—
140 A250 10s multicolored, (1,527,861)	1.25	1.25
First day cover		5.00
Inscription block of 3 + 3 labels	7.00	—
First day cover, #139-140		2.00
Panes of 12, #139-140	30.00	30.00

Aging With Dignity Type

Designs: 5.50s, Elderly couple, family working in garden. 7s, Older woman teaching.

1993, Feb. 5	Litho.	Perf. 13
141 A270 5.50s multicolored (428,886)	.75	.75
First day cover		1.60
Inscription block of 4	4.50	—
142 A270 7s multicolored (459,471)	1.40	1.40
First day cover		2.00
First day cover, #141-142		3.00
Inscription block of 4	7.50	—

First day covers of Nos. 141-142 total 87,052.

Endangered Species Type

Designed by Rocco J. Callari and Steve Brennan, US.

Designs: No. 143, Equus grevyi (Grevy's zebra). No. 144, Spheniscus humboldti (Humboldt's penguins). No. 145, Varanus griseus (desert monitor). No. 146, Canis lupus (gray wolf).

1993, Mar. 2	Litho.	Perf. 13x12½
143 A271 7s multicolored (1,200,000)+	1.05	1.05
144 A271 7s multicolored (1,200,000)+	1.05	1.05
145 A271 7s multicolored (1,200,000)+	1.05	1.05
146 A271 7s multicolored (1,200,000)+	1.05	1.05
a. Block of 4, #143-146	4.25	4.25
First day cover, #146a		5.25
First day cover, #143-146, any single		1.75
Inscription block of 4, #146a	5.00	—
Pane of 16, #143-146	18.00	—

First day covers of Nos. 143-146a total 106,211.

Healthy Environment Type

1993, May 7	Litho.	Perf. 15x14½
147 A272 6s Wave in ocean (517,433)	1.25	1.25
First day cover		1.50
Inscription block of 4	6.00	—
148 A272 10s Globe (453,123)	2.00	2.00
First day cover		2.25
First day cover, #147-148		3.50
Inscription block of 4	10.00	—

First day covers of Nos. 147-148 total 79,773.

V31

Designed by Marek Kwiatkowski, Poland. Printed by Helio Courvoisier S.A., Switzerland.

1993, May 7	Photo.	Perf. 11½
	Granite Paper	
149 V31 13s multicolored (1,500,000)+	2.50	2.50
Inscription block of 4	12.50	—

Human Rights Type of 1989

Printed in sheets of 12 + 12 se-tenant labels containing Article 29 (5s) and 30 (6s) inscribed in German, English or French.

Artwork: 5s, Lower Austrian Peasants' Wedding, by Ferdinand G. Waldmuller. 6s, Outback, by Sally Morgan.

1993, June 11	Litho.	Perf.
150 A250 5s multicolored (1,532,531)		1.00
First day cover		
Inscription block of 3 + 3 labels	4.00	
151 A250 6s multicolored (1,542,716)		1.25
First day cover		
Inscription block of 3 + 3 labels	5.00	
Panes of 12, #150-151	28.00	

First day covers of Nos. 150-151 total 128,687.

Intl. Peace Day Type

Denomination at: No. 152, UL. No. 153, UR. No. 154, LL. 155, LR.

1993, Sept. 21	Litho. & Engr.	Rouletted
152 A274 5.50s green & multi (445,699)		1.80
153 A274 5.50s green & multi (445,699)		1.80
154 A274 5.50s green & multi (445,699)		1.80
155 A274 5.50s green & multi (445,699)		1.80
a. Block of 4, #152-155		7.25
First day cover, #155a		
First day cover, #152-155, any single		
Inscription block of 4, #155a		8.75
Pane of 40, #152-155		80.00

First day covers of Nos. 152-155a total 67,075.

Environment-Climate Type

Designs: No. 156, Monkeys. No. 157, Bluebird, industrial lution, volcano. No. 158, Volcano, nuclear power plant, stumps. No. 159, Cactus, tree stumps, owl.

1993, Oct. 29	Litho.	Perf. 1
156 A275 7s multicolored (484,517)		2.00
157 A275 7s multicolored (484,517)		2.00
158 A275 7s multicolored (484,517)		2.00
159 A275 7s multicolored (484,517)		2.00
a. Strip of 4, #156-159		8.00
First day cover, #159a		
First day cover, #156-159, any single		
Inscription block of 8, 2 #159a		21.00
Pane of 24, #156-159		47.50

First day covers of Nos. 156-159a total 61,946.

Intl. Year of the Family Type of 1993

Designs: 5.50s, Adults, children holding hands. 8s, adults, child planting crops.

1994, Feb. 4	Litho.	Perf. 1
160 A276 5.50s blue green & multi (650,000)+	1.20	
First day cover		
Inscription block of 4	5.75	
161 A276 8s red & multi (650,000)+	1.80	
First day cover		
First day cover, #160-161		
Inscription block of 4	8.75	

First day covers of Nos. 160-161 total 78,532.

Endangered Species Type of 1993

Designed by Rocco J. Callari, US (frame), and Pa Margocsy, Australia (stamps).

Designs: No. 162, Ocelot. No. 163, White-breasted silv eye. No. 164, Mediterranean monk seal. No. 165, Asi elephant.

1994, Mar. 18	Litho.	Perf. 1:
162 A271 7s multicolored (1,200,000)+	1.30	
163 A271 7s multicolored (1,200,000)+	1.30	
164 A271 7s multicolored (1,200,000)+	1.30	
165 A271 7s multicolored (1,200,000)+	1.30	
a. Block of 4, #162-165	5.25	
First day cover, #165a		
First day cover, #162-165, each		
Inscription block of 4, #165a	5.75	
Pane of 16, #162-165	21.00	

First day covers of Nos. 162-165a total 104,478.

Protection for Refugees Type

Design: 12s, Protective hands surround group of refugees

1994, Apr. 29	Litho.	Perf. 14.3x14
166 A277 12s multicolored (650,000)+	1.50	1.
First day cover (49,519)		3.
Inscription block of 4	8.00	

V32

V33

V34

Designed by Masatoshi Hioki, Japan (#167), Ramon antara Rodriguez, Mexico (#168), Eliezer Weishoff, Israel 69).
Printed by Cartor, S.A., France.

94, Apr. 29		Litho.		Perf. 12.9	
7 V32	50g	multicolored (1,450,000)+		.20	.20
		First day cover			1.25
		Inscription block of 4		.40	
8 V33	4s	multicolored (1,150,000)+		.50	.50
		First day cover			1.25
		Inscription block of 4		3.50	—
9 V34	30s	multicolored (560,000)+		4.50	4.50
		First day cover			5.00
		Inscription block of 4		22.50	—

First day covers of Nos. 167-169 total 74,558.

Intl. Decade for Natural Disaster Reduction Type

Earth seen from space, outline map of: No. 170, North merica. No. 171, Eurasia. No. 172, South America. No. 173, stralia and South Asia.

94, May 27		Litho.		Perf. 13.9x14.2	
0 A281	6s	multicolored (690,000)+		1.75	1.75
1 A281	6s	multicolored (690,000)+		1.75	1.75
2 A281	6s	multicolored (690,000)+		1.75	1.75
3 A281	6s	multicolored (690,000)+		1.75	1.75
a.		Block of 4, #170-173		7.00	7.00
		First day cover, #173a			6.00
		First day cover, #170-173, each			3.25
		Inscription block of 4, #173a		8.50	—
		Pane of 40, #170-173		82.50	

First day covers of Nos. 170-173a total 52,502.

Population and Development Type

Designs: 5.50s, Women teaching, running machine tool, ming home to family. 7s, Family on tropical island.

94, Sept. 1		Litho.		Perf. 13.2x13.6	
4 A282	5.50s	multicolored (650,000)+		1.50	1.50
		First day cover			2.00
		Inscription block of 4		7.50	—
5 A282	7s	multicolored (650,000)+		2.00	2.00
		First day cover, #174-175			2.00
		Inscription block of 4		9.00	5.00

First day covers of Nos. 174-175 total 67,423.

UNCTAD Type

94, Oct. 28					
6 A283	6s	multi, diff. (650,000)+		1.25	1.25
		First day cover			1.25
		Inscription block of 4		6.50	—
7 A283	7s	multi, diff. (650,000)+		1.50	1.50
		First day cover, #176-177			1.75
		Inscription block of 4		7.50	3.00

First day covers of Nos. 176-177 total 67,064.

UN 50th Anniv. Type

95, Jan. 1		Litho. & Engr.		Perf. 13.4	
8 A284	7s	multicolored (742,052)		1.25	1.25
		First day cover (118,537)			2.00
		Inscription block of 4		7.00	—

Social Summit Type

95, Feb. 3		Photo. & Engr.		Perf. 13.6x13.9	
9 A285	14s	multi, diff. (595,554)		2.25	2.25
		First day cover (51,244)			3.50
		Inscription block of 4		11.00	—

Endangered Species Type of 1993

Designed by Salvatore Catalano, US.
Designs: No. 180, Black rhinoceros, Diceros bicornis. No. 81, Golden conure, Aratinga guarouba. No. 182, Douc langur, ygathrix nemaeus. No. 183, Arabian oryx, Oryx leucoryx.

95, Mar. 24		Litho.		Perf. 13x12½	
80 A271	7s	multicolored (938,000)+		1.00	1.00
81 A271	7s	multicolored (938,000)+		1.00	1.00
82 A271	7s	multicolored (938,000)+		1.00	1.00
83 A271	7s	multicolored (938,000)+		1.00	1.00
a.		Block of 4, #180-183		4.00	4.00
		First day cover, #183a			4.50
		First day cover, #180-183, each			2.00
		Inscription block of 4, #183a		5.00	—
		Pane of 16, #180-183		17.50	

First day covers of Nos. 180-183a total 95,401.

Intl. Youth Year Type

Designs: 6s, Village in winter. 7s, Teepees.

1995, May 26		Litho.		Perf. 14.4x14.7	
184 A286	6s	multicolored (437,462)		1.50	1.50
		First day cover			1.50
		Inscription block of 4		6.00	—
185 A286	7s	multicolored (409,449)		1.75	1.75
		First day cover			2.50
		First day cover, #184-185			4.25
		Inscription block of 4		7.50	—

First day covers of Nos. 184-185 total 60,979.

UN, 50th Anniv. Type

Designs: 7s, Like No. 663. 10s, Like No. 664.

1995, June 26		Engr.		Perf. 13.3x13.6	
186 A287	7s	green (433,922)		1.25	1.25
		First day cover			2.00
		Inscription block of 4		6.50	—
187 A287	10s	black (471,198)		2.00	2.00
		First day cover			1.75
		First day cover, #186-187			4.00
		Inscription block of 4		11.00	—

Souvenir Sheet
Litho. & Engr.
Imperf

188		Sheet of 2, #186-187 (367,773)	4.50	4.50
a.	A287 7s green		1.75	1.75
b.	A287 10s black		2.50	2.50
	First day cover			6.50

First day covers of Nos. 186-188b total 171,765.

Conference on Women Type

Designs: 5.50s, Women amid tropical plants. 6s, Woman reading, swans on lake.

1995, Sept. 5		Photo.		Perf. 12	
189 A288	5.50s	multicolored (549,951)		1.25	1.25
		First day cover			1.50
		Inscription block of 4		5.50	—

Size: 28x50mm

190 A288	6s	multicolored (556,569)		2.25	2.25
		First day cover			1.50
		First day cover, #189-190			3.50
		Inscription block of 4		10.00	—

First day covers of Nos. 189-190 total 71,976.

UN People, 50th Anniv. Type

1995, Oct. 24		Litho.		Perf. 14	
191		Sheet of 12 (280,528 sheets)		16.00	16.00
		First day cover			16.00
a.-l.	A290 3s any single		1.30	1.30
		First day cover, #191a-191 l, each			1.25
192		Souvenir booklet, (95,449 booklets)		19.00	
a.	A290 3s Booklet pane of 3, vert. strip of 3 from UL of sheet		4.75	4.75
b.	A290 3s Booklet pane of 3, vert. strip of 3 from UR of sheet		4.75	4.75
c.	A290 3s Booklet pane of 3, vert. strip of 3 from LL of sheet		4.75	4.75
d.	A290 3s Booklet pane of 3, vert. strip of 3 from LR of sheet		4.75	4.75

First day covers of Nos. 191-192d total 107,436.

WFUNA, 50th Anniv. Type

Design: 7s, Harlequin holding dove.

1996, Feb. 2		Litho.		Perf. 13x13½	
193 A291	7s	multicolored (655,000)+		1.25	1.25
		First day cover			2.00
		Inscription block of 4		6.75	—

UN Flag — V35

Abstract, by Karl Korab — V36

Printed by House of Questa, UK.

1996, Feb. 2		Litho.		Perf. 15x14½	
194 V35	1s	multicolored (1,180,000)+		.20	.20
		First day cover			1.25
		Inscription block of 4		1.00	—
195 V36	10s	multicolored (880,000)+		1.60	1.60
		First day cover			2.75
		First day cover, #194-195			4.50
		Inscription block of 4		10.00	—

Endangered Species Type of 1993

Designs: No. 196, Cypripedium calceolus. No. 197, Aztekium ritteri. No. 198, Euphorbia cremersii. No. 199, Dracula bella.

1996, Mar. 14		Litho.		Perf. 12½	
196 A271	7s	multicolored (846,000)+		1.00	1.00
197 A271	7s	multicolored (846,000)+		1.00	1.00
198 A271	7s	multicolored (846,000)+		1.00	1.00
199 A271	7s	multicolored (846,000)+		1.00	1.00
a.		Block of 4, #196-199		4.00	4.00
		First day cover, #199a			4.50
		First day cover, #196-199, each			2.00
		Inscription block of 4, #199a		5.50	—
		Pane of 16, #196-199		17.50	

City Summit Type

Designs: No. 200, Arab family selling fruits, vegetables. No. 201, Women beside stream, camels. No. 202, Woman carrying bundle on head, city skyline. No. 203, Woman threshing grain, yoke of oxen in field. No. 204, Native village, elephant.

1996, June 3		Litho.		Perf. 14x13½	
200 A293	6s	multicolored (500,000)+		1.50	1.50
201 A293	6s	multicolored (500,000)+		1.50	1.50
202 A293	6s	multicolored (500,000)+		1.50	1.50
203 A293	6s	multicolored (500,000)+		1.50	1.50
204 A293	6s	multicolored (500,000)+		1.50	1.50
a.		Strip of 5, #200-204		7.50	7.50
		First day cover, #204a			11.50
		First day cover, #200-204, each			3.00
		Inscription block of 10, 2 #204a		25.00	—

Sport and the Environment Type

6s, Men's parallel bars (gymnastics), vert. 7s, Hurdles.

1996, July 19		Litho.		Perf. 14x14½, 14½x14	
205 A294	6s	multicolored (730,000)+		1.00	1.00
		Inscription block of 4		5.50	2.75
206 A294	7s	multicolored (730,000)+		1.50	1.50
		First day cover			3.00
		First day cover, #205-206			6.00
		Inscription block of 4		7.75	—

Souvenir Sheet

207 A294		Sheet of 2, #205-206 (500,000)+	2.50	2.50
		First day cover		10.00

Plea for Peace Type

Designed by: 7s, Du Keqing, China. 10s, Xu Kangdeng, China.

Designs: 7s, Dove and butterflies. 10s, Stylized dove, diff.

1996, Sept. 17		Litho.		Perf. 14½x15	
208 A295	7s	multicolored (655,000)+		1.00	1.00
		First day cover			1.50
		Inscription block of 4		7.50	—
209 A295	10s	multicolored (655,000)+		2.00	2.00
		First day cover			2.50
		First day cover, #208-209			5.00
		Inscription block of 4		10.00	—

UNICEF Type

Fairy Tales: 5.50s, Hansel and Gretel, by the Brothers Grimm. 8s, How Maui Stole Fire from the Gods, South Pacific.

1996, Nov. 20		Litho.		Perf. 14½x15	
210 A296	5.50s	multicolored (1,160,000)+		.90	.90
		First day cover			1.25
		Pane of 8 + label		8.00	
211 A296	8s	multicolored (1,160,000)+		1.40	1.40
		First day cover			2.00
		First day cover, #210-211			4.00
		Pane of 8 + label		12.00	

V37

Phoenixes Flying Down (Detail), by Sagenji Yoshida — V38

Printed by The House of Questa, Ltd., UK.

1997, Feb. 12		Litho.		Perf. 14½	
212 V37	5s	multicolored (750,000)+		.80	.80
		First day cover			1.25
		Inscription block of 4		3.40	—
213 V38	6s	multicolored (1,050,000)+		.90	.90
		First day cover			1.50
		First day cover, #212-213			4.00
		Inscription block of 4		4.00	—

First day covers of Nos. 212-213 total 156,021.

Endangered Species Type of 1993

Designs: No. 214, Macaca sylvanus (Barbary macaque). No. 215, Anthropoides paradisea (blue crane). No. 216, Equus przewalskii (Przewalski horse). No. 217, Myrmecophaga tridactyla (giant anteater).

1997, Mar. 13		**Litho.**	**Perf. 12½**	
214	A271	7s **multicolored** *(710,000)+*	1.10	1.10
215	A271	7s **multicolored** *(710,000)+*	1.10	1.10
216	A271	7s **multicolored** *(710,000)+*	1.10	1.10
217	A271	7s **multicolored** *(710,000)+*	1.10	1.10
a.		Block of 4, #214-217	4.50	4.50
		First day cover, #217a	6.00	
		First day cover, #214-217, each	2.50	
		Inscription block of 4, #217a	6.25	
		Pane of 16	25.00	

First day covers of Nos. 214-217 total 86,406.

Earth Summit Anniv. Type

Designs: No. 218, Person running. No. 219, Hills, stream, trees. No. 220, Tree with orange leaves. No. 221, Tree with pink leaves.

11s, Combined design similar to Nos. 218-221.

1997, May 30		**Photo.**	**Perf. 11.5**	
		Granite Paper		
218	A299	3.50s **multicolored** *(282,016)*	1.25	1.25
219	A299	3.50s **multicolored** *(282,016)*	1.25	1.25
220	A299	3.50s **multicolored** *(282,016)*	1.25	1.25
221	A299	3.50s **multicolored** *(282,016)*	1.25	1.25
a.		Block of 4, #218-221	5.00	5.00
		First day cover, #221a	10.00	
		First day cover, #218-221, each	3.50	
		Inscription block of 4, #221a	7.25	
		Souvenir Sheet		
222	A299	11s **multicolored** *(221,434)*	2.50	2.50
		First day cover	12.00	

First day covers of Nos. 218-222 total 62,390.

Transportation Type

Ground transportation: No. 223, 1829 Rocket, 1901 Darraque. No. 224, Steam engine from Vladikawska Railway, trolley. No. 225, Double-decker bus. No. 226, 1950s diesel locomotive, semi-trailer. No. 227, High-speed train, electric car.

1997, Aug. 29		**Litho.**	**Perf. 14x14½**	
223	A300	7s **multicolored** *(356,097)*	1.00	1.00
224	A300	7s **multicolored** *(356,097)*	1.00	1.00
225	A300	7s **multicolored** *(356,097)*	1.00	1.00
226	A300	7s **multicolored** *(356,097)*	1.00	1.00
227	A300	7s **multicolored** *(356,097)*	1.00	1.00
a.		Strip of 5, #223-227	5.00	5.00
		First day cover, #227a	16.00	
		First day cover, #223-227, each	4.75	
		Inscription block of 10, 2#227a	30.00	

No. 227a has continuous design.
First day covers of Nos. 223-227 total 44,877.

Philately Type

Designs: 6.50s, No. 62. 7s, No. 63.

1997, Oct. 14		**Litho.**	**Perf. 13½x14**	
228	A301	6.50s **multicolored** *(379,767)*	1.00	1.00
		First day cover	2.50	
		Inscription block of 4	5.25	—
229	A301	7s **multicolored** *(378,107)*	1.50	1.50
		First day cover	3.50	
		First day cover, #228-229	6.00	
		Inscription block of 4	7.00	—

First day covers of Nos. 228-229 total 57,651.

World Heritage Convention Type

Terracotta warriors of Xian: 3s, Single warrior. 6s, Massed warriors. No. 232a, like #716. No. 232b, like #717. No. 232c, like Geneva #314. No. 232d, like Geneva #315. No. 232e, like Vienna #230. No. 232f, like Vienna #231.

1997, Nov. 19		**Litho.**	**Perf. 13½**	
230	A302	3s **multicolored** *(528,352)*	1.00	1.00
		First day cover	1.50	
		Inscription block of 4	5.00	—
231	A302	6s **multicolored** *(530,947)*	2.00	2.00
		First day cover	2.75	
		First day cover, #230-231	5.00	
		Inscription block of 4	10.00	—
232		**Souvenir booklet** *(298,055 booklets)*	8.00	
a.-f.		A302 1s any single	.30	.30
g.		Booklet pane of 4 #232a	1.25	1.25
h.		Booklet pane of 4 #232b	1.25	1.25
i.		Booklet pane of 4 #232c	1.25	1.25
j.		Booklet pane of 4 #232d	1.25	1.25
k.		Booklet pane of 4 #232e	1.25	1.25
l.		Booklet pane of 4 #232f	1.25	1.25

First day covers of Nos. 230-232 total 71,708.

Japanese Peace Bell, Vienna — V39

Vienna Subway, Vienna Intl. Center — V40

Printed by The House of Questa, UK. Panes of 20.
Designed by Heinz Pfeifer, Austria (6.50s), Pigneter, Austria (9s).

1998, Feb. 13		**Litho.**	**Perf. 15x14½**	
233	V39	6.50s **multicolored** *(670,000)+*	1.00	1.00
		First day cover	3.25	
		Inscription block of 4	4.50	
234	V40	9s **multicolored** *(770,000)+*	1.50	1.50
		First day cover	4.50	
		First day cover, #233-234	3.00	
		Inscription block of 4	6.25	

Endangered Species Type of 1993

Designed by Rocco J. Callari, US and Robert Hynes, US.
Designs: No. 235, Chelonia mydas (green turtle). No. 236, Speotyto cunicularia (burrowing owl). No. 237, Trogonoptera brookiana (Rajah Brooke's birdwing). No. 238, Ailurus fulgens (lesser panda).

1998, Mar. 13		**Litho.**	**Perf. 12½**	
235	A271	7s **multicolored** *(620,000)+*	1.10	1.10
236	A271	7s **multicolored** *(620,000)+*	1.10	1.10
237	A271	7s **multicolored** *(620,000)+*	1.10	1.10
238	A271	7s **multicolored** *(620,000)+*	1.10	1.10
a.		Block of 4, #235-238	4.50	4.50
		First day cover, #238a	5.00	
		First day cover, #235-238, each	2.50	
		Inscription block of 4, #238a	6.25	—
		Pane of 16	25.00	

Intl. Year of the Ocean — V41

Designed by Yuan Lee, China.

1998, May 20		**Litho.**	**Perf. 13x13½**	
239	V41	Sheet of 12 *(345,000)+*	12.00	12.00
a.-l.		3.50s any single	1.00	1.00
		First day cover, 3239	17.00	
		First day cover, #239a-239l, each	2.00	

Rain Forests Type

1998, June 19		**Litho.**	**Perf. 13x13½**	
240	A307	6.50s Ocelot *(590,000)+*	.90	.90
		First day cover	4.00	
		Inscription block of 4	5.00	—
		Souvenir Sheet		
241	A307	22s like #240 *(340,000)+*	3.50	3.50
		First day cover	5.25	

Peacekeeping Type of 1998

Designs: 4s, Soldier passing out relief supplies. 7.50s, UN supervised voting.

1998, Sept. 15		**Photo.**	**Perf. 12**	
242	A308	4s multicolored *(555,000)+*	.70	.70
		First day cover	1.25	
		Inscription block of 4	2.80	—
243	A308	7.50s multicolored *(545,000)+*	1.25	1.25

		First day cover		
		First day cover, #242-243		
		Inscription block of 4	5.25	

Declaration of Human Rights Type

Designs: 4.50s, Stylized person. 7s, Gears.

1998, Oct. 27		**Litho. & Photo.**	**Perf.**	
244	A309	4.50s multicolored *(555,000)+*	.80	
		First day cover		
		Inscription block of 4	3.25	
245	A309	7s multicolored *(545,000)+*	1.25	
		First day cover		
		First day cover, #244-245		
		Inscription block of 4	5.00	

Schönbrunn Palace Type

Designs: 3.50s, #248d, Palace. 7s, #248c, Porcelain stove vert. No. 248a, Blue porcelain vase, vert. No. 248b, Wall paneling on fabric (detail), by Johann Wenzl Bergl, vert. No. 248, Great Palm House (conservatory). No. 248f, The Gloriette (archway).

1998, Dec. 4		**Litho.**	**Perf.**	
246	A310	3.50s **multicolored** *(615,000)+*	.60	
		First day cover		
		Inscription block of 4	2.50	
247	A310	7s **multicolored** *(615,000)+*	1.10	1
		First day cover		
		First day cover, #246-247		
		Inscription block of 4	4.50	
		Souvenir Booklet		
248		Booklet *(158,000)+*	9.00	
a.-c.		A310 1s any single	.25	
d.-f.		A310 2s any single	.55	
g.		Booklet pane of 4 #248d	2.20	2
h.		Booklet pane of 3 #248a	.75	
i.		Booklet pane of 3 #248b	.75	
j.		Booklet pane of 3 #248c	.75	
k.		Booklet pane of 4 #248e	2.20	2
l.		Booklet pane of 4 #248f	2.20	2

Volcanic Landscape — V4

Designed by Peter Pongratz, Austria. Printed by Joha Enschedé and Sons, the Netherlands.

1999, Feb. 5		**Litho.**	**Perf. 13x13**	
249	V42	8s **multicolored** *(660,000)+*	1.50	1
		First day cover *(33,022)*		4.
		Inscription block of 4	9.00	

World Heritage, Australia Type

Designs: 4.50s, #252d, Uluru-Kata Tjuta Natl. Park. 6.5 #252a, Tasmanian Wilderness. No. 252b, Wet tropics Queensland. No. 252c, Great Barrier Reef. No. 252e, Kaka Natl. Park. No. 252f, Willandra Lakes region.

1999, Mar. 19		**Litho.**	**Perf.**	
250	A313	4.50s **multicolored** *(540,000)+*	.75	
		First day cover		1.
		Inscription block of 4	3.00	
251	A313	6.50s **multicolored** *(540,000)+*	1.10	1.
		First day cover		1.
		First day cover, #250-251		4.
		Inscription block of 4	4.50	
		Souvenir Booklet		
252		Booklet *(116,000)+*	7.50	
a.-c.		A313 1s any single	.20	
d.-f.		A313 2s any single	.40	
g.		Booklet pane of 4, #252a	.80	
h.		Booklet pane of 4, #252d	1.60	1.
i.		Booklet pane of 4, #252b	.80	
j.		Booklet pane of 4, #252e	1.60	1.
k.		Booklet pane of 4, #252c	.80	
l.		Booklet pane of 4, #252f	1.60	1.

First day covers of Nos. 250-252 total 65,123.

Endangered Specied Type of 1993

Designed by Jeffrey Terreson, US.

Designs: No. 253, Pongo pygmaeus (oran-utan). No. 25 Pelecanus crispus (Dalmatian pelican). No. 255, Eunecte notaeus (yellow anaconda). No. 256, Caracal.

1999, Apr. 22		**Litho.**	**Perf. 12**	
253	A271	7s **multicolored** *(552,000)+*	1.00	1.0
254	A271	7s **multicolored** *(552,000)+*	1.00	1.0
255	A271	7s **multicolored** *(552,000)+*	1.00	1.0
256	A271	7s **multicolored** *(552,000)+*	1.00	1.0
a.		Block of 4, #253-256	4.00	4.0

First day cover, #256a 6.00
First day cover, #253-256, each 2.25
Inscription block of 4, #256a 4.75 —
Pane of 16 17.00

First day covers of Nos. 253-256 total 66,733.

UNISPACE III Type

Designs: No. 257, Satellite over ships. No. 258, Satellite up
e. No. 259, Composite of #257-258.

99, July 7	Photo.		Rouletted 8
A314 3.50s multicolored (1,200,000)+		.75	.75
A314 3.50s multicolored (1,200,000)+		.75	.75
Pair, #257-258		1.50	1.50
First day cover, #258a		3.00	
First day cover, #257-258, each		2.50	
Inscription block of 4, #257-258	6.00		
Pane of 10, #257-258	9.00	—	

Souvenir Sheet
Perf. 14½

A314 13s multicolored (350,000)+		4.50	4.50
First day cover		5.00	

First day covers of Nos. 257-259 total 72,143.

UPU Type

Various people, late 20th century methods of mail transporta-
, denomination at: No. 260, UL. No. 261, UR. No. 262, LL.
263, LR.

99, Aug. 23	Photo.		Perf. 11¾
A315 6.50s multicolored (417,000)+		1.00	1.00
A315 6.50s multicolored (417,000)+		1.00	1.00
A315 6.50s multicolored (417,000)+		1.00	1.00
A315 6.50s multicolored (417,000)+		1.00	1.00
Block of 4, #260-263		4.00	4.00
First day cover, #263a		4.50	
First day cover, #260-263, each		2.00	
Inscription block of 4	4.50		

First day covers of Nos. 260-263 total 38,453.

In Memoriam Type

Designs: 6.50s, 14s, Donaupark. Size of 14s stamp:
63mm.

99, Sept. 21	Litho.		Perf. 14½x14
A316 6.50s multicolored (530,000)+		.90	.90
First day cover		3.00	
Inscription block of 4	4.50	—	

Souvenir Sheet
Perf. 14

A316 14s multicolored (338,000)+		2.40	2.40
First day cover		4.00	

First day covers of Nos. 264-265 total 61,089.

Education Type

99, Nov. 18	Litho.		Perf. 13½x13¾
A317 7s Boy, girl, book (490,000)+		1.00	1.00
First day cover		1.60	
Inscription block of 4	5.00	—	
A317 13s Group reading (490,000)+		2.00	2.00
First day cover		3.00	
First day cover, #266-267		4.00	
Inscription block of 4	9.00	—	

First day covers of Nos. 266-267 total 48,590.

Intl. Year of Thanksgiving Type

00, Jan. 1	Litho.		Perf. 13¼x13½
A318 7s multicolored (510,000)+		1.00	1.00
First day cover		3.00	
Inscription block of 4	5.00	—	

On No. 268 portions of the design were applied by a thermo-
phic process producing a shiny, raised effect.

Endangered Species Type of 1993

Designed by Lori Anzalone, US.
Designs: No. 269, Panthera pardus (leopard). No. 270,
atalea leucorodia (white spoonbill). No. 271, Hippocamelus
sulcus (huemal). No. 272, Orcinus orca (killer whale).

00, Apr. 6	Litho.		Perf. 12¾x12½
A271 7s multicolored (548,000)+		1.10	1.10
A271 7s multicolored (548,000)+		1.10	1.10
A271 7s multicolored (548,000)+		1.10	1.10
A271 7s multicolored (548,000)+		1.10	1.10
Block of 4, #269-272		4.50	4.50
First day cover, #272a		6.00	
First day cover, #269-272, each		2.00	
Inscription block of 4, #272a	4.75	—	
Pane of 16	18.00		

Our World 2000 Type

Winning artwork in Millennium painting competition: 7s,
morrow's Dream, by Voltaire Perez, Philippines. 8s, Remem-
ance, by Dimitris Nalbandis, Greece, vert.

00, May 30	Litho.	Perf. 13x13½, 13½x13
A319 7s multicolored (430,000)+		1.00	1.00
First day cover		1.75	
Inscription block of 4	4.50	—	
A319 8s multicolored (430,000)+		1.20	1.20
First day cover		2.00	
First day cover, #273-274		3.00	
Inscription block of 4	5.00	—	

55th Anniversary Type

Designs: 7s, Secretariat Building, unfinished dome of General Assembly Hall, 1951. 9s, Trygve Lie and Headquarters
Advisory Committee at topping-out ceremony, 1949.

2000, July 7	Litho.		Perf. 13½x13
275 A320 7s multicolored (440,000)+		.90	.90
First day cover		1.75	
Inscription block of 4	4.50		
276 A320 9s multicolored (440,000)+		1.25	1.25
First day cover		2.25	
First day cover, #275-276		3.00	
Inscription block of 4	6.00	—	

Souvenir Sheet

277 A320	Sheet of 2, #275-276 (300,000)+		2.75	2.75
	First day cover		3.25	

The UN in the 21st Century — V43

Printed by Government Printing Office, Austria. Designed by
Wilson McLean, UK.

No. 278: a, Farm machinery. b, UN Peacekeepers and children. c, Oriental farm workers. d, Peacekeepers searching for
mines. e, Medical research. f, Handicapped people.

2000, Sept. 15	Litho.		Perf. 14
278 V43	Sheet of 6 (330,000)+		4.50	4.50
	First day cover		3.75	
a.-f.	3.50s any single		.75	.75

World Heritage, Spain Type

Designs: Nos. 279, 281c, Aqueduct of Segovia. Nos. 280,
281f, Güell Park, Barcelona. #281a, Alhambra, Generalife and
Albayzin, Granada. #281b, Walled Town of Cuenca. #281d,
Amphitheater of Mérida. #281e, Toledo.

2000, Oct. 6	Litho.		Perf. 14¾x14½
279 A323 4.50s multicolored (430,000)+		.80	.80
First day cover		1.25	
Inscription block of 4	3.00	—	
280 A323 6.50s multicolored (430,000)+		1.20	1.20
First day cover		1.75	
First day cover, #279-280		2.40	
Inscription block of 4	4.00	—	

Souvenir Booklet

281	Booklet (92,000)+		7.00	
a.-c.	A323 1s any single		.20	.20
d.-f.	A323 2s any single		.40	.40
g.	Booklet pane of 4, #281a		.65	.65
h.	Booklet pane of 4, #281d		1.60	1.60
i.	Booklet pane of 4, #281b		.65	.65
j.	Booklet pane of 4, #281e		1.60	1.60
k.	Booklet pane of 4, #281c		.65	.65
l.	Booklet pane of 4, #281f		1.60	1.60

Respect for Refugees Type

Designs: 7s, 25s, Refugee with hat, three other refugees.

2000, Nov. 9	Litho.		Perf. 13¼x12¾
282 A324 7s multicolored (530,000)+		1.10	1.10
First day cover		1.75	
Inscription block of 4	4.50	—	

Souvenir Sheet

283 A324 25s multicolored (273,000)+		3.75	3.75
First day cover		4.50	

Endangered Species Type of 1993

Printed by Johann Enschedé and Sons, the Netherlands.
Designed by Betina Ogden, Australia.
Designs: No. 284, Tremarctos ornatus (spectacled bear). No.
285, Anas laysanensis (Laysan duck). No. 286, Proteles cristatus (aardwolf). No. 287, Trachypithecus cristatus (silvered leaf
monkey).

2001, Feb. 1	Litho.		Perf. 12¾x12½
284 A271 7s multicolored (540,000)+		1.10	1.10
285 A271 7s multicolored (540,000)+		1.10	1.10
286 A271 7s multicolored (540,000)+		1.10	1.10
287 A271 7s multicolored (540,000)+		1.10	1.10
a.	Block of 4, #284-287		4.50	4.50

First day cover, #287a 5.00
First day cover, #284-287 each 1.75
Inscription block of 4, #287a 4.25 —
Pane of 16 16.00

Intl. Volunteers
Year — V44

Printed by Johann Enschedé and Sons, the Netherlands.
Panes of 20. Designed by Rorie Katz and Robert Stein, US.
Paintings by: 10s, Nguyen Thanh Chuong, Viet Nam. 12s,
Ikko Tanaka, Japan.

2001, Mar. 29	Litho.		Perf. 13¼
288 V44 10s multicolored (440,000)+		1.40	1.40
First day cover		2.00	
Inscription block of 4	5.75		
289 V44 12s multicolored (430,000)+		1.75	1.75
First day cover		2.40	
First day cover, #288-289		3.75	
Inscription block of 4	7.00		

World Heritage, Japan Type

Designs: 7s, #290c, Himeji-Jo. 15s, #291f, Nikko. #292a,
Kyoto. #292b, Nara. #292d, Shirakawa-Go and Gokayama.
#292e, Itsukushima Shinto Shrine.

2001, Aug. 1	Litho.		Perf. 12¾x13¼
290 A328 7s multicolored (440,000)+		1.00	1.00
First day cover		1.40	
Inscription block of 4	4.00	—	
291 A328 15s multicolored (440,000)+		2.10	2.10
First day cover		3.00	
First day cover, #290-291		3.75	
Inscription block of 4	8.50		

Souvenir Booklet

292	Booklet (78,000)+		5.00	
a.-c.	A328 1s any single		.20	.20
d.-f.	A328 2s any single		.25	.25
g.	Booklet pane of 4, #292a		.55	.55
h.	Booklet pane of 4, #292d		1.10	1.10
i.	Booklet pane of 4, #292b		.55	.55
j.	Booklet pane of 4, #292e		1.10	1.10
k.	Booklet pane of 4, #292c		.55	.55
l.	Booklet pane of 4, #292f		1.10	1.10

Dag Hammarskjöld Type

2001, Sept. 18	Engr.		Perf. 11x11¼
293 A329 7s green (480,000)+		1.00	1.00
First day cover		1.60	
Inscription block of 4	4.00	—	

UN Postal Administration, 50th Anniv. Types

2001, Oct. 18	Litho.		Perf. 13½
294 A330 7s Stamps, balloons (380,000)+		1.00	1.00
First day cover		1.60	
Inscription block of 4	4.00	—	
295 A330 8s Stamps, cake (380,000)+		1.10	1.10
First day cover		1.75	
First day cover, #294-295		2.75	
Inscription block of 4	4.50	—	

Souvenir Sheet

296 A331	Sheet of 2 (225,000)+		4.00	4.00
a.	7s green & light blue, 38mm diameter		1.00	1.00
b.	21s green & light blue, 38mm diameter		3.00	3.00
	First day cover		4.50	

Climate Change Type

Designs: No. 297, Solar panels, automobile at pump. No.
298, Blimp, bicyclists, horse and rider. No. 299, Balloon, sailboat, lighthouse, train. No. 300, Bird, train, traffic signs.

2001, Nov. 16	Litho.		Perf. 13¼
297 A332 7s multicolored (87,000)+		1.00	1.00
298 A332 7s multicolored (87,000)+		1.00	1.00
299 A332 7s multicolored (87,000)+		1.00	1.00
300 A332 7s multicolored (87,000)+		1.00	1.00
a.	Horiz. strip, #297-300		4.00	4.00
Inscription block of 8	8.00	—	
First day cover, #300a		4.50	
Pane of 24	24.00	—	

Nobel Peace Prize Type

2001, Dec. 10	Litho.		Perf. 13¼
301 A333 7s multicolored (1,260,000)+		1.00	.50
Inscription block of 4	5.00	—	
First day cover		1.60	
Pane of 12	12.00	—	

100 Cents = 1 Euro (€)

Austrian Tourist
Attractions
V45

Printed by House of Questa, UK. Panes of 20. Designed by Rorie Katz, US.

Designs: 7c, Semmering Railway. 51c, Pferdschwemme, Salzburg. 58c, Aggstein an der Donau Ruins. 73c, Hallstatt. 87c, Melk Abbey. €2.03, Kapitelschwemme, Salzburg.

2002, Mar. 1	**Litho.**		**Perf. 14½x14**	
302	V45	7c multicolored (860,000)+	.20	.20
		First day cover		1.25
		Inscription block of 4	.65	
303	V45	51c multicolored (960,000)+	1.00	1.00
		First day cover		1.40
		Inscription block of 4	4.50	
304	V45	58c multicolored (860,000)+	1.10	1.10
		First day cover		1.60
		Inscription block of 4	5.25	
305	V45	73c multicolored (760,000)+	1.40	1.40
		First day cover		2.00
		Inscription block of 4	6.75	
306	V45	87c multicolored (760,000)+	1.75	1.75
		First day cover		2.40
		Inscription block of 4	7.75	
307	V45	€2.03 multicolored (710,000)+	4.00	4.00
		First day cover		5.50
		First day cover, #288-289		10.50
		Inscription block of 4	18.00	
		Nos. 302-307 (6)	9.45	9.45

Endangered Species Type of 1993

Printed by Johann Enschedé and Sons, the Netherlands. Designed by Tim Barrall, US.

Designs: No. 308, Hylobates syndactylus (siamang). No. 309, Spheniscus demersus (jackass penguin). No. 310, Prionodon linsang (banded linsang). No. 311, Bufo retiformis (Sonoran green toad).

2002, Apr. 4	**Litho.**		**Perf. 12¾x12½**	
308	A271	51c multicolored (500,000)+	1.10	1.10
309	A271	51c multicolored (500,000)+	1.10	1.10
310	A271	51c multicolored (500,000)+	1.10	1.10
311	A271	51c multicolored (500,000)+	1.10	1.10
a.		Block of 4, #308-311	4.50	4.50
		First day cover, #311a		4.75
		First day cover, #308-311 each		1.75
		Inscription block of 4, #311a	4.75	
		Pane of 16	18.00	

Independence of East Timor Type

Designs: 51c, Deer horn container with carved wooden stopper. €1.09, Carved wooden tai weaving loom.

2002, May 20	**Litho.**		**Perf. 14x14½**	
312	A335	51c multicolored (384,000)+	1.00	1.00
		First day cover		1.50
		Inscription block of 4	4.50	
313	A335	€1.09 multicolored (374,000)+	2.25	2.25
		First day cover		3.25
		First day cover, #312-313		4.00
		Inscription block of 4	9.50	

Intl. Year of Mountains Type

Designs: No. 314, Mt. Cook, New Zealand. No. 315, Mt. Robson, Canada. No. 316, Mt. Rakaposhi, Pakistan. No. 317, Mt. Everest (Sagarmatha), Nepal.

2002, May 24	**Litho.**		**Perf. 13x13¼**	
314	A336	22c multicolored (1,335,000)+	.50	.50
		First day cover		1.25
315	A336	22c multicolored (1,335,000)+	.50	.50
		First day cover		1.25
316	A336	51c multicolored (1,335,000)+	1.10	1.10
		First day cover		1.50
		First day cover, #314, 316		2.25
317	A336	51c multicolored (1,335,000)+	1.10	1.10
a.		Vert. strip or block of four, #314-317	3.50	3.50
		First day cover		1.50
		First day cover, #315, 317		2.25
		First day cover, #314-317		3.75
		Pane of 12, 3 each #314-317	10.50	

World Summit on Sustainable Development (Peter Max) Type

Designs: No. 318, Rainbow. No. 319, Three women, diff. No. 320, Three faceless people. No. 321, Birds, wave.

2002, June 27	**Litho.**		**Perf. 14½x14**	
318	A337	51c multicolored (1,305,000)+	1.10	1.10
		First day cover		1.50
319	A337	51c multicolored (1,305,000)+	1.10	1.10
		First day cover		1.50
320	A337	58c multicolored (1,305,000)+	1.25	1.25
		First day cover		1.60
		First day cover, #318, 320		2.50
321	A337	58c multicolored (1,305,000)+	1.25	1.25
a.		Vert. strip or block of four, #318-321	4.75	4.75

	First day cover		1.60
	First day cover, #319, 321		2.50
	First day cover, #318-321		3.75
	Pane of 12, 3 each #318-321	14.50	—

World Heritage, Italy Type

Designs: 51c, #324f, Pompeii. 58c, #324c, Rome. #324a, Amalfi Coast. #324b, Aeolian Islands. #324d, Florence. #324e, Pisa.

2002, Aug. 30	**Litho.**		**Perf. 13½x13¼**	
322	A338	51c multicolored (400,000)+	1.10	1.10
		First day cover		1.75
		Inscription block of 4	4.50	—
323	A338	58c multicolored (400,000)+	1.25	1.25
		First day cover		2.00
		First day cover, #322-323		3.00
		Inscription block of 4	5.00	—

Souvenir Booklet

324	Booklet (71,000)+	7.00	
a.-c.	A338 7c any single	.20	.20
d.-f.	A338 15c any single	.40	.40
g.	Booklet pane of 4, #324d	1.60	1.60
h.	Booklet pane of 4, #324a	.65	.65
i.	Booklet pane of 4, #324e	1.60	1.60
j.	Booklet pane of 4, #324b	.65	.65
k.	Booklet pane of 4, #324f	1.60	1.60
l.	Booklet pane of 4, #324c	.65	.65

AIDS Awareness Type

2002, Oct. 24	**Litho.**		**Perf. 13½**	
325	A339	€1.53 multicolored (370,000)+	3.50	3.75
		Inscription block of 4	13.00	
		First day cover, #325		4.00
		Pane of 20	65.00	

EINGEBORENENKUNST

Indigenous Art — V46

Printed by House of Questa, UK.
Designed by Rorie Katz and Robert Stein, US.

No. 326: a, Mola, Panama. b, Mochican llama-shaped spouted vessel, Peru. c, Tarabuco woven cloth, Bolivia. d, Masks, Cuba. e, Aztec priest's feather headdress, Mexico. f, Bird-shaped staff head, Colombia.

2003, Jan. 31	**Litho.**		**Perf. 14¼**	
326	V46	Sheet of 6 (212,000)+	6.00	6.00
		First day cover		8.25
a.-f.		51c Any single	1.00	1.00
		First day cover, a.-f., each		2.75

Austrian Tourist Attractions Type of 2002

Printed by House of Quest, UK. Designed by Rorie Katz, US. Panes of 20.
Designs: 25c, Kunsthistorisches Museum, Vienna. €1, Belvedere Palace, Vienna.

2003, Mar. 28	**Litho.**		**Perf. 14½x14**	
327	V45	25c multicolored (650,000)+	.55	.55
		First day cover		1.25
		Inscription block of 4	2.25	
328	V45	€1 multicolored (650,000)+	2.25	2.25
		First day cover		3.25
		First day cover, #327-328		3.50
		Inscription block of 4	9.00	—

Endangered Species Type of 1993

Printed by Johann Enschedé and Sons, the Netherlands. Designed by Robert Hautman, US.
Designs: No. 329, Anas formosa (Baikal teal). No. 330, Bostrychia hagedash (Hadada ibis). No. 331, Ramphastos toco (toco toucan). No. 332, Alopochen aegyptiacus (Egyptian goose).

2003, Apr. 3	**Litho.**		**Perf. 12¾x12½**	
329	A271	51c multicolored (432,000)+	1.00	1.00
330	A271	51c multicolored (432,000)+	1.00	1.00
331	A271	51c multicolored (432,000)+	1.00	1.00
332	A271	51c multicolored (432,000)+	1.00	1.00
a.		Block of 4, #329-332	4.00	4.00
		First day cover, #332a		5.25
		First day cover, #329-332 each		1.90
		Inscription block of 4, #332a	4.50	—
		Pane of 16	18.00	—

International Year of Freshwater Type of 200

2003, June 20	**Litho.**		**Perf. 14¼x**	
333	A345	55c Bridge, bird (316,000)+		1.40
334	A345	75c Horse, empty river (316,000)+		1.90
a.		Horiz. pair, #333-334		3.00
		First day cover, #334a		
		Inscription block of 4		7.50

Austrian Tourist Attractions Type of 2002

Printed by Johann Enschedé and Sons, the Netherla Panes of 20. Designed by Rorie Katz, US.
Design: 4c, Schloss Eggenberg, Graz.

2003, Aug. 7	**Litho.**		**Perf. 14x**	
335	V45	4c multicolored (650,000)+		.20
		First day cover		
		Inscription block of 4		.35
		Pane of 20		1.60

Ralph Bunche Type
Litho. With Foil Application

2003, Aug. 7			**Perf. 13½**	
336	A346	€2.10 olive green & multicolored (384,000)+		4.50
		First day cover		
		Inscription block of 4		19.00
		Pane of 20		95.00

In Memoriam Type of 2003

2003, Oct. 24	**Litho.**		**Perf. 13¼**	
337	A347	€2.10 multicolored (670,000)+		4.75
		First day cover		
		Inscription block of 4		22.00
		Pane of 20		110.00

World Heritage Sites, United States Type

Designs: 55c, #340c, Olympic National Park. 75c, #34 Everglades National Park. #340a, Yosemite National P #340b, Great Smoky Mountains National Park. #340d, Ha Volcanoes National Park. #340f, Yellowstone National Park

2003, Oct. 24	**Litho.**		**Perf. 14½x1**	
338	A348	55c multicolored (275,000)+		1.50
		First day cover		
		Inscription block of 4		6.00
339	A348	75c multicolored (275,000)+		2.00
		First day cover		
		First day cover, #338-339		
		Inscription block of 4		8.00

Souvenir Booklet

340	Booklet (57,500)+	9.00	
a.-c.	A348 15c any single	.35	
d.-f.	A348 20c any single	.40	
g.	Booklet pane of 4 #340a	1.40	
h.	Booklet pane of 4 #340d	1.60	
i.	Booklet pane of 4 #340b	1.40	
j.	Booklet pane of 4 #340e	1.60	
k.	Booklet pane of 4 #340c	1.40	
l.	Booklet pane of 4 #340f	1.60	

Austrian Tourist Attractions Type of 2002

Printed by Imprimerie de Timbres-Poste, France.
Design: 55c, Schloss Schönbrunn, Vienna.

2004, Jan. 29	**Litho.**		**Perf. 13x1**	
341	V45	55c multicolored (740,000)+	1.50	1
		First day cover		2
		Inscription block of 4	6.00	
		Pane of 20	30.00	

Endangered Species Type of 1993

Printed by Johann Enschedé and Sons, the Netherlan Designed by Yuan Lee, U.S.
Designs: No. 342, Melursus ursinus (Sloth bear). No. 3 Cervus eldi (Eld's deer). No. 344, Cercocebus torqua (Cherry-crowned mangabey). No. 345, Bubalus arnee (W water buffalo).

2004, Jan. 29	**Litho.**		**Perf. 12¾x1**	
342	A271	55c multicolored (376,000)+	1.20	1
343	A271	55c multicolored (376,000)+	1.20	1
344	A271	55c multicolored (376,000)+	1.20	1
345	A271	55c multicolored (376,000)+	1.20	1
a.		Block of 4, #342-345	4.75	4
		First day cover, #345a		6
		First day cover, #342-345, each		
		Inscription block of 4, #345a	6.00	
		Pane of 16	24.00	

Indigenous Art Type of 2003

Printed by Johann Enschedé and Sons, the Netherlands. Designed by Rorie Katz and Robert Stein, US.

No. 346: a, Illuminated illustration from the Book of Ke Ireland. b, Easter eggs, Ukraine. c, Venus of Willendorf, Pal lithic age limestone statue, Austria. d, Flatatunga panel, In land. e, Neolithic era idol, Hungary. f, Illuminated illustrati from medical treatise, Portugal.

2004, Mar. 4	**Litho.**		**Perf. 13**	
346	V46	Sheet of 6 (133,000)+	7.00	7.
		First day cover		10.
a.-f.		55c Any single	1.15	1.
		First day cover, a.-f., each		2.

Road Safety Type

Road map art with: 55c, Automobile, alcohol bottles. 7 Road, clouds in traffic light colors, vert.

4, Apr. 7		**Litho.**	**Perf. 13x13¼, 13¼x13**		
A354	55c	multicolored *(225,000)*+		1.25	1.25
		First day cover			2.10
		Inscription block of 4		6.00	—
A354	75c	multicolored *(225,000)*+		1.75	1.75
		First day cover			2.75
		First day cover, #338-339			4.25
		Inscription block of 4		8.00	—

Japanese Peace Bell, 50th Anniv. Type

4, June 20		**Litho. & Engr.**	**Perf. 13¼x13**		
A355	€2.10	multicolored *(280,000)*+		4.50	4.50
		First day cover			6.25
		Inscription block of 4		22.00	—
		Pane of 20		110.00	—

World Heritage Sites, Greece Type

Designs: 55c, No. 352f, Mycenae and Tiryns. 75c, No. 352e, mpia. No. 352a, Acropolis, Athens. No. 352b, Delos. No. c, Delphi. No. 352d, Pythagoreion and Heraion of Samos.

4, Aug. 12		**Litho.**	**Perf. 14x13¼**		
A356	55c	multicolored *(250,000)*+		1.40	1.40
		First day cover			1.90
		Inscription block of 4		5.75	—
A356	75c	multicolored *(250,000)*+		1.90	1.90
		First day cover			2.75
		First day cover, #350-351			4.00
		Inscription block of 4		7.75	—

Souvenir Booklet

	Booklet *(49,000)*+		14.00	
d.	A356 25c any single		.55	.55
f.	A356 30c either single		.70	.70
g.	Booklet pane of 4 #352a		2.20	2.20
h.	Booklet pane of 4 #352b		2.20	2.20
i.	Booklet pane of 4 #352c		2.20	2.20
j.	Booklet pane of 4 #352d		2.20	2.20
k.	Booklet pane of 4 #352e		2.80	2.80
l.	Booklet pane of 4 #352f		2.80	2.80

My Dream for Peace Type

Winning designs of Lions Club International children's global ce poster contest by: 55c, Henry Ulfe Renteria, Peru. €1, helle Fortaliza, Philippines.

04, Sept. 21		**Litho.**	**Perf. 14**		
A357	55c	multicolored *(235,000)*+		1.40	1.40
		First day cover			1.90
		Inscription block of 4		5.75	—
		Pane of 20		28.00	—
A357	€1	multicolored *(235,000)*+		2.50	2.50
		First day cover			3.50
		First day cover, #353-354			4.50
		Inscription block of 4		10.00	—
		Pane of 20		50.00	—

Vereinte Nationen 2004
Menschenrechte € 0,55
V47

ereinte Nationen 2004
Menschenrechte € 1,25
Human Rights — V48

Printed by Banknote Corportation of America, US. Designed Yuri Gervorgian, Armenia. Panes of 8.

04, Oct. 14		**Litho.**	**Perf. 11¼**		
5	V47	55c	multicolored *(480,000)*+	1.00	1.00
		First day cover			2.00
		Pane of 8		12.00	—

356	V48	€1.25 multicolored *(480,000)*+		3.00	3.00
		First day cover			4.50
		First day cover, #355-356			5.75
		Pane of 8		28.00	—

United Nations, 60th Anniv. Type of 2005

Printed by Banknote Corporation of America, US. Designed by Czeslaw Slania, Sweden.

2005, Feb. 4		**Litho. & Engr.**	**Perf. 11x11¼**		
357	A361	55c	multicolored *(310,000)*+	1.60	1.60
		First day cover			2.60
		Inscription block of 4		6.50	—
		Pane of 20		32.50	—

Souvenir Sheet
Litho.
Imperf

358	A361	€2.10	multicolored *(165,000)*+	5.50	5.50
		First day cover			6.25

GRUSS VON DEN VEREINTEN NATIONEN
€0,75
International Center, Vienna — V49

Printed by Cartor Security Printing, France.

Litho. with Hologram

2005, Feb. 4			**Perf. 13½x13½**	
359	V49	75c multicolored *(360,000)*+	2.25	2.25
		First day cover		3.25
		Inscription block of 4	9.00	—
		Pane of 20	45.00	—

Endangered Species Type of 1993

Designs: No. 360, Ansellia africana. No. 361, Phragmipedium kovachii. No. 362, Cymbidium ensifolium. No. 363, Renanthera imschootiana.

2005, Mar. 3		**Litho.**	**Perf. 12¾x12½**		
360	A271	55c multicolored		1.40	1.40
361	A271	55c multicolored		1.40	1.40
362	A271	55c multicolored		1.40	1.40
363	A271	55c multicolored		1.40	1.40
a.		Block of 4, #360-363		6.50	6.50
		First day cover, #363a			7.00
		First day cover, #360-363, each			2.25
		Inscription block of 4, #363a		6.00	—
		Pane of 16		19.00	—

€0,55 Vereinte Nationen 2005
WEISHEIT DER NATUR
Wüste, China — Foto: W. Wu © UNEP
Nature's Wisdom — V50

Printed by Cartor Security Printing, France. Panes of 20. Designed by Robert Stein, US.
Designs: 55c, Desert landscape, China. 80c, Cheetah family, Africa.

2005, Apr. 21		**Litho.**	**Perf. 13½x13¼**		
364	V50	55c multicolored *(230,000)*+		1.60	1.60
		First day cover			2.40
		Inscription block of 4		6.50	—
		Pane of 20		32.50	—
365	V50	75c multicolored *(230,000)*+		2.25	2.25
		First day cover			3.50
		First day cover, #364-365			4.75
		Inscription block of 4		9.00	—
		Pane of 20		45.00	—

Intl. Year of Sport Type

Printed by Cartor Security Printing, France. Designed by Roland Hirter, Switzerland.

2005, June 3		**Litho.**	**Perf. 13x13¼**		
366	A368	55c Equestrian *(245,000)*+		1.60	1.60
		First day cover			2.25
		Inscription block of 4		6.50	—
		Pane of 20		32.50	—
367	A368	€1.10 Soccer *(245,000)*+		3.25	3.25
		First day cover			4.50

	First day cover, #366-367			6.00
	Inscription block of 4		13.00	—
	Pane of 20		65.00	—

World Heritage Sites, Egypt Type

Printed by Johann Enschedé and Sons, the Netherlands. Panes of 20. Designed by Rorie Katz, US.
Designs: Nos. 368, 370c, Abu Mena. Nos. 369, 370f, St. Catherine area. No. 370a, Memphis and its Necropolis. No. 370b, Philae. No. 370d, Ancient Thebes. No. 370e, Islamic Cairo.

2005, Aug. 4		**Litho.**	**Perf. 14x13¼**		
368	A369	55c multicolored *(250,000)*+		1.60	1.60
		First day cover			2.40
		Inscription block of 4		6.50	—
369	A369	75c multicolored *(250,000)*+		2.25	2.25
		First day cover			3.25
		First day cover, #368-369			4.75
		Inscription block of 4		9.00	—

Souvenir Booklet

370		Booklet, #370g-370l *(45,000)*+	19.50	
a.-		A369 25c any single	.75	.75
c.				
d.-		A369 30c any single	.85	.85
f.				
g.		Booklet pane of 4 #370a	3.00	—
h.		Booklet pane of 4 #370b	3.00	—
i.		Booklet pane of 4 #370c	3.00	—
j.		Booklet pane of 4 #370d	3.50	—
k.		Booklet pane of 4 #370e	3.50	—
l.		Booklet pane of 4 #370f	3.50	—

No. 370 sold for €6.80.

My Dream for Peace Type

Winning designs of Lions Club International children's global peace poster contest by: 55c, Lee Min Gi, Republic of Korea. €1, Natalie Chan, US.

2004, Sept. 21		**Litho.**	**Perf. 14**		
371	A357	55c multicolored *(225,000)*+		1.60	1.60
		First day cover			2.25
		Inscription block of 4		6.50	—
		Pane of 20		32.00	—
372	A357	€1 multicolored *(225,000)*+		2.75	2.75
		First day cover			4.00
		First day cover, #371-372			5.25
		Inscription block of 4		11.00	—
		Pane of 20		55.00	—

Food for Life Type

Printed by Government Printing Office, Austria. Designed by Andrew Davidson, United Kingdom.
Designs: 55c, Corn, people with food bowls, teacher and students. €1.25, Rice, helicopter dropping food, elephant caravan.

2005, Oct. 20		**Litho.**	**Perf. 13¾**		
373	A370	55c multicolored *(210,000)*+		1.60	1.60
		First day cover			2.10
		Inscription block of 4		6.50	—
		Pane of 20		32.00	—
374	A370	€1.25 multicolored *(210,000)*+		3.50	3.50
		First day cover			4.75
		First day cover, #373-374			6.00
		Inscription block of 4		14.00	—
		Pane of 20		70.00	—

Indigenous Art Type of 2003

Printed by Johann Enschedé and Sons, the Netherlands. Designed by Robert Stein, US.

No. 375 — Musical instruments: a, Drum, Guinea. b, Whistle, Congo. c, Horn, Botswana. d, Drums, Burundi. e, Harp, Gabon. f, Bell, Nigeria.

2006, Feb. 3		**Litho.**	**Perf. 13¼**		
375	V46	Sheet of 6 *(117,000)*+		8.50	8.50
		First day cover			10.50
a.-		55c Any single			
f.				1.40	1.40

Endangered Species Type of 1993

Printed by Johann Enschedé and Sons, the Netherlands. Designed by John D. Dawson, US.

Designs: No. 376, Dendrobates pumilio. No. 377, Furcifer lateralis. No. 378, Corallus hortulanus. No. 379, Dendrobates leucomelas.

2006, Mar. 16		**Litho.**	**Perf. 12¾x12½**		
376	A271	55c multicolored *(260,000)*+		1.40	1.40
377	A271	55c multicolored *(260,000)*+		1.40	1.40
378	A271	55c multicolored *(260,000)*+		1.40	1.40
379	A271	55c multicolored *(260,000)*+		1.40	1.40
a.		Block of 4, #376-379		5.75	5.75
		First day cover, #379a			6.75
		First day cover, #376-379, each			2.40
		Inscription block of 4, #379a		5.75	—
		Pane of 16		23.00	—

Intl. Day of Families Type

Printed by Johann Enschedé and Sons, the Netherlands. Designed by Shelly Bartek, US.
Designs: 55c, Family at water pump. €1.25, Family preparing food.

2006, May 27		**Litho.**	**Perf. 14x13½**		
380	A373	55c multicolored *(190,000)*+		1.50	1.50
		First day cover			2.00
		Inscription block of 4		6.00	—

	Pane of 20	30.00	—
381 A373	€1.25 **multicolored** *(190,000)*+	3.25	3.25
	First day cover		4.50
	First day cover, #380-381		5.75
	Inscription block of 4	13.00	
	Pane of 20	65.00	—

2006 END-OF-YEAR ISSUES
See end of New York postage listings.

SEMI-POSTAL STAMP

AIDS Awareness Semi-postal Type
Souvenir Sheet

2002, Oct. 24	**Litho.**		**Perf. 14½**
B1 SP1 51c + 25c **multicolored** *(220,000)*+		2.50	2.50
First day cover, #B1			3.00

ENVELOPES

Used values for all postal stationery are for non-philatelic contemporaneous usages.

Donaupark,
Vienna — VU1

Printed by Mercury-Walch Pty. Ltd. (Australia). Designed by Hannes Margreiter (Austria).
Design: 7s, Landscape. Design at lower left shows Vienna landmarks (6s), river scene (7s).

1995, Feb. 3	**Litho.**		
U1 VU1 6s **multicolored**, entire *(128,000)*+		2.00	2.00
First day cancel *(14,132)*			2.75
U2 VU1 7s **multicolored**, entire *(128,000)*+		2.00	2.00
First day cancel *(9,684)*			3.50

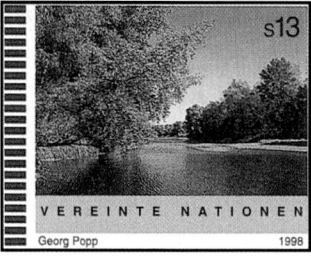

VU2

Printed by Mercury-Walch Pty. Ltd. (Australia).

1998, Mar. 13	**Litho.**		
U3 VU2 13s **multicolored**, entire *(87,000)*+		3.50	3.00
Entire, first day cancel			3.50

VU3

Vienna International Center — VU4

Printed by Australia Post Sprintpak (Australia). Designed by Robert Stein (US).

2002, June 27	**Litho.**		
U4 VU3 51c **multicolored**, entire *(93,000)*+		1.50	1.50
Entire, first day cancel			2.00
U5 VU4 €1.09 **multicolored**, entire *(88,000)*+		2.60	2.60
Entire, first day cancel			3.25

Nos. U4-U5 Surcharged

2003, June 2	**Litho.**		
U6 VU3 51c +4c **multicolored**, entire		3.75	1.10
Entire, first day cancel			3.75
U7 VU4 €1.09 +16c **multicolored**, entire		4.75	2.10
Entire, first day cancel			4.75

UN
Flag — VU5

Dove With Olive
Branch — VU6

Printed by Government Printing Office, Austria. Designed by Rorie Katz, US.

2004, June 3	**Litho.**		
U8 VU5 55c **multicolored**, entire *(53,000)*+		2.10	1.40
Entire, first day cancel			2.50
U9 VU6 €1.25 **multicolored**, entire *(48,000)*+		4.00	2.75
Entire, first day cancel			4.50

AIR LETTER SHEETS

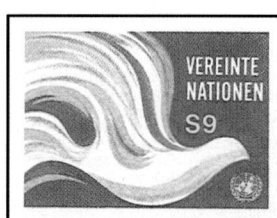

VLS1

Printed by Joh. Enschede and Sons. Designed by Ir Ousland.

1982, Apr. 28	**Lit**
UC1 VLS1 9s **multi**, *light green*, entire *(650,000)*	2.50
First day cancel *(120,650)*	

No. UC1 Surcharged in Lake

1986, Feb. 3	**Lit**
UC2 VLS1 9s +2s **multi**, *light green*, entire *(131,190)*	52.50 5.
First day cancel *(18,500)*	2

Birds in
Flight, UN
Emblem
VLS2

Printed by Mercury-Walch, Australia. Designed by Miec law Wasiliewski, Poland.

1987, Jan. 30	**Lit**
UC3 VLS2 11s **bright blue**, entire *(414,000)*	3.00 3
First day cancel *(48,348)*	4

No. UC3 Surcharged

1992, Jan. 1	**Lit**
UC4 VLS2 11s +1s **bright blue**, entire *(80,000)*	52.50 52
First day cancel	25

Donaupark,
Vienna — VLS3

Designed by Rocco J. Callari. Printed by Mercury-Wa Australia.

1992, Sept. 4	**Lit**
UC5 VLS3 12s **multicolored**, entire *(200,000)*+	5.00 5
First day cancel *(16,261)*	27

POSTAL CARDS

Olive Branch — VPC1

Bird Carrying Olive
Branch — VPC2

Printed by Courvoisier. Designed by Rolf Christianson (3 M.A. Munnawar (5s).

2, Apr. 28 — Photo.
1 VPC1 3s **multicolored,** *cream (500,000)* 1.00 1.00
First day cancel *(93,010)* 1.65
2 VPC2 5s **multicolored** *(500,000)* .75 1.00
First day cancel *(89,502)* 1.65

VEREINTE NATIONEN Emblem of the United
Nations — VPC3

Printed by Johann Enschede en Zonen, Netherlands.
Signed by George Hamori, Australia.

85, May 10 — Litho.
3 VPC3 4s **multicolored** *(350,000)* 1.50 3.50
First day cancel *(53,450)* 3.00

No. UX2 Surcharged Like No. UC4
92, Jan. 1 — Photo.
4 VPC2 5s +1s **multicolored** *(71,700)* 19.00 19.00
First day cancel 17.00

Type of 1990
Printed by Mercury-Walch, Australia.
92, Sept. 4 — Litho.
5 V22 6s **multicolored** *(445,000)+* 2.00 3.00
First day cancel *(16,359)* 10.00
See No. UX9.

Type of 1985
Printed by Leigh Mardon Pty. Limited, Australia.
93, May 7 — Litho.
6 A222 5s **multicolored** *(450,000)* 16.00 16.00
First day cancel 10.00

Donaupark,
Vienna — VPC4

Printed by Leigh Mardon Pty. Limited, Australia.
93, May 7 — Litho.
7 VPC4 6s **multicolored** *(450,000)+* 4.00 4.00
First day cancel 7.50
See No. UX10.

No. UX6 with design of Vienna #1 Added

1994, Jan. 1 — Litho.
UX8 A222+G8 5s +50g **multi** *(350,000)+* 2.50 4.00
First day cancel 4.00

No. UX5 with design of Vienna #167 Added
1997, July 1 — Litho.
UX9 V22+V32 6s +50g **multi** 2.50 2.50
First day cancel 5.00
No. UX7 with design of Vienna #194 Added
UX10 VPC4+V35 6s +1s **multi** 3.00 3.00
First day cancel 5.00

VPC5

Designed by Günter Leidenfrost.

1998, May 20 — Litho.
UX11 VPC5 6.50s **multicolored** *(137,000)+* 1.50 1.50
First day cancel 2.00

The
Gloriette — VPC6

1999, Feb. 5 — Litho.
UX12 VPC6 7s **multicolored** *(136,000)+* 2.00 2.00
First day cancel 2.50

Type of 1983
2000, June 2 — Litho.
UX13 V7 7s **multicolored** 2.25 2.25
First day cancel 2.25

VEREINTE NATIONEN Clock Tower, Graz,
Austria — VPC7

Printed by Johann Enschedé and Sons, the Netherlands.
Designed by Robert Stein, US.
2002, Mar. 1 — Litho.
UX14 VPC7 51c **multicolored** *(83,000)+* 1.00 1.00
First day cancel 1.25

No. UX14 Surcharged

2003, June 2 — Litho.
UX15 VPC7 51c +4c **multicolored** 2.75 .60
First day cancel 2.75

Vienna International
Center — VPC8

Printed by Government Printing Office, Austria. Designed by
Rorie Katz, US.
2004, June 3 — Litho.
UX16 VPC8 55c **multicolored** *(63,000)+* 2.60 1.25
First day cancel 3.00

U.N. SOUVENIR CARDS

No. 39

These cards were issued by the United Nations Postal
Administration and were not valid for postage.

Each card bears reproductions of UN stamps and a statement by the Secretary-General in English.
Values are for mint cards without cancels.

SC1 World Health Day, Apr. 7, 1972.
Card of 5: #43, 102, 156, 207,
228. .65
A second printing shows several minor differences.
SC2 Art on UN Stamps, Nov. 17,
1972. Card of 11: #170, 171,
173, 174, 180, 183, 201, 202,
203, 224, 232. #201, 202 form
a simulated setenant pair .45
SC3 Disarmament Decade, Mar. 9,
1973. Card of 5: #133, 147,
177, 227, 234 .50
SC4 Declaration of Human Rights,
25th Anniversary, Nov. 16,
1973. Card of 10: #13, 22, 29,
39, 47, 58, 68, 121, 190, 242 .75
SC5 UPU centenary, Mar. 22, 1974.
Card of 7: #17, 18, 219, 246;
Geneva 18, 39, 40. .75
SC6 World Population Year, Oct. 18,
1974. Card of 7: #151, 152,
153, 252, 253; Geneva 43, 44. 4.00

SC7 Peaceful Uses of Outer Space,
Mar. 14, 1975. Card of 6: #112,
113, 256, 257; Geneva 46, 47. 2.00
SC8 UN Peace Keeping Operations,
Nov. 21, 1975. Card of 9: #52,
111, 118, 139, 160, 265, 266;
Geneva 55, 56. 2.00
SC9 World Federation of United Nations Associations, Mar. 12,
1976. Card of 5: #154, 155,
272, 273; Geneva 57. 2.00
SC10 World Food Council, Nov. 19,
1976. Card of 6: #116, 117,
218, 280; Geneva 17, 63. 2.50
SC11 World Intellectual Property Organization (WIPO), Mar. 11,
1977. Card of 15: #17, 23, 25,
31, 33, 41, 43, 49, 59, 86, 90,
123, 281, 282; Geneva 64. 2.50
SC12 Combat Racism, Sept. 19, 1977.
Card of 8: #220, 221, 287, 288;
Geneva 19, 20, 69, 70. 2.50
SC13 Namibia, May 5, 1978. Card of
10: #240, 241, 263, 264, 296,
297; Geneva 34, 53, 54, 76. 1.00

SC14	Intl. Civil Aviation Organization, June 12, 1978. Card of 6: #31, 32, 298, 299; Geneva 77, 78.	2.50
SC15	Intl. Year of the Child, May 4, 1979. Card of 9: #5, 97, 161, 162, 163, 310, 311; Geneva 84, 85.	.75
SC16	Intl. Court of Justice, Nov. 9, 1979. Card of 6: #88, 89, 314, 315; Geneva 87, 88.	.75
SC17	UN Decade for Women, Mar. 7, 1980. Card of 4: #258, 318; Geneva 90; Vienna 9.	10.00
SC18	Economic and Social Council, Nov. 7, 1980. Card of 8: #65, 66, 341, 342; Geneva 96, 97; Vienna 15, 16.	.75
SC19	Intl. Year of Disabled Persons, Mar. 6, 1981. Card of 6: #344, 345; Geneva 99, 100; Vienna 18, 19.	.65
SC20	New and Renewable Sources of Energy, May 29, 1981. Card of 4: #348, 349; Geneva 102; Vienna 21.	1.00
SC21	Human Environment, Mar. 19, 1982. Card of 5: #230, 371; Geneva 26, 107; Vienna 25	.75
SC22	Exploration and Peaceful Uses of Outer Space, June 11, 1982. Card of 7: #112, 256, 373; Geneva 46, 109, 110; Vienna 27.	1.40
SC23	Safety at Sea, Mar. 18, 1983. Card of 8: #123, 124, 394, 395; Geneva 114, 115; Vienna 31, 32.	1.10
SC24	Trade and Development, June 6, 1983. Card of 11: #129, 130, 274, 275, 397, 398; Geneva 58, 117, 118; Vienna 31, 32.	1.50
SC25	Intl. Conference on Population, Feb. 3, 1984. Card of 10: #151, 153, 252, 253, 417, 418; Geneva 43, 44, 121; Vienna 39.	2.00
SC26	Intl. Youth Year, Nov. 15, 1984. Card of 5: #441, 442; Geneva 128; Vienna 46, 47.	3.00
SC27	ILO Turin Center, Feb. 1, 1985. Card of 8: #25, 200, 244, 443; Geneva 37, 129, 130; Vienna 48.	2.75
SC28	Child Survival Campaign, Nov. 22, 1985. Card of 6: #466, 467; Geneva 138, 139; Vienna 55, 56.	3.00

SC29	Stamp Collecting, May 22, 1986. Card of 5: #278, 473; Geneva 61, 147; Vienna 63.	8.25

No. 29 with stitch marks has been removed from the Ameripex program. Value is one-half that of unstitched copy.

SC30	Intl. Peace Year, June 20, 1986. Card of 6: #475, 476; Geneva 148, 149; Vienna 64, 65.	4.00
SC31	Shelter for the Homeless, Mar. 13, 1987. Card of 6: #495, 496; Geneva 154, 155; Vienna 68, 69.	2.50
SC32	Immunize Every Child, Nov. 20, 1987. Card of 13: #44, 103, 157, 240, 294, 517, 518; Vienna 76, 77.	3.00
SC33	Intl. Volunteer Day, May 6, 1988. Card of 10: #239, 367, 524, 525; Geneva 103, 167, 168; Vienna 23, 82, 83.	4.00
SC34	Health in Sports, June 17, 1988. Card of 6: #526, 527; Geneva 169, 170; Vienna 84, 85.	5.00
SC35	World Bank, Jan. 27, 1989. Card of 8: #86-87, 546-547; Geneva 173-174; Vienna 88-89.	5.00
SC36	World Weather Watch, Apr. 21, 1989. Card of 10: #49-50, 188-189, 550-551; Geneva 176-177; Vienna 91-92.	5.00
SC37	Fight AIDS Worldwide, Mar. 16, 1990. Card of 6: #573-574; Geneva 184-185; Vienna 99-100	6.50
SC38	Crime Prevention, Sept. 13, 1990. Card of 6: #580-581; Geneva 191-192; Vienna 106-107.	6.00
SC39	Economic Commission for Europe, Mar. 15, 1991. Card of 12: #584-587; Geneva 195-198; Vienna 110-113.	6.00
SC40	Rights of the Child, June 14, 1991. Card of 6: #593-594; Geneva 203-204; Vienna 117-118.	7.00
SC41	Mission to Planet Earth, Sept. 4, 1992, Card of 6: #609-610; Geneva 220-221; Vienna 133-134	17.00
SC42	Science and Technology for Development, Oct. 2, 1992, Card of 6, #611-612; Geneva 222-223; Vienna 135-136	15.00
SC43	Healthy Environment, May 7, 1993, Card of 6, #624-625; Geneva #232-233; Vienna #147-148	17.50

SC44	Peace, Sept. 21, 1993. Card of 12, #629-632; Geneva #236-239; Vienna #152-155	16

No. 44 exists overprinted in gold with Hong Kong '94 emble

SC45	Intl. Year of the Family, Feb. 4, 1994, Card of 6, #637-638; Geneva #244-245; Vienna #160-161	13
SC46	Population & Development, 1994, Card of 9, #151, 651-652; Geneva #43, 258-259; Vienna #39, 174-175	12
SC47	World Summit for Social Development, 1995, Card of 3, #656; Geneva #263; Vienna #179	10
SC48	Intl. Youth Year, 1995, Card of 9, #441, 661-662; Geneva #128, 268-269; Vienna #46, 184-185	16
SC49	WFUNA, 1996, Card of 3, #671; Geneva #277; Vienna #193	14
SC50	UNICEF, 1996, Card of 6, #688-689; Geneva #294-295; Vienna #210-211	7
SC51	Philately, 1997, Card of 6, #714-715; Geneva #312-313; Vienna #228-229	12
SC52	Peacekeeping, #737-738; Geneva #325-326; Vienna #242-243	9
SC53	Universal Declaration of Human Rights, #739-740; Geneva #327-328; Vienna #244-245	9
SC54	UPU, #767a; Geneva #346a; Vienna #263a	5
SC55	Respect for Refugees, #787; Geneva #365; Vienna #282	6
SC56	Intl. Volunteers Year, #793-794; Geneva #371-372; Vienna #288-289	4
SC57	Johannesburg Summit on Sustainable Development, #828-831; Geneva #396-399; Vienna #318-321	5
SC58	International Year of Freshwater, #846-8471; Geneva #411-412; Vienna #333-334	4
SC59	Japanese Peace Bell, 50th Anniv., #865; Geneva #425; Vienna #349	4
SC60	Nature's Wisdom, #885-886; Geneva #440-441; Vienna #364-365	3
SC61	Intl. Day of Families, #913-914, Geneva #457-458, Vienna #380-381	3

U.N. PROOFS

Proofs of United Nations stamps are known in four basic types: Die Proofs, Trial Color Proofs, Progressive Color Proofs, and Imperforate Plate Proof on gummed stamp paper.

Die Proofs (PD suffix) for United Nations stamps show the design of the issued stamp. They are usually imperforate singles printed on stamp pape that are either affixed to a backing paper that is a component of a printer's card, or affixed directly to a printer's card. These cards usually have handstamp denoting the status of the proof (approved, approved with corrections, not approved, etc.). Many cards have signatures of UN Pos Administration officials. Cards with an "approved" handstamp and/or signature do not always contain proofs having the designs of the actual stan produced for sale. As most proof cards have a handstamp, the listings mention specific handstamps only when it is critical to distinguishing items. Iter not affixed to cards that are indistinguishable from imperforate singles of the issued stamps are not listed, even though they may have come from "sto sheet style" proof cards that have approval handstamps. Items affixed to art boards available to the general public are not considered to be proc unless they are identified, usually by handstamps, that they are proofs. Die proofs of sheet layouts showing marginal inscriptions only exist, but a beyond the scope of these listings.

Trial Color Proofs (TC suffix) show the design of the stamp, but with one or more colors differing from that of the actual stamp. Items will be liste as trial color proofs when they differ significantly from the issued color. As evidenced by printer's identification numbers on some trial color proof carc shades of individual items may differ slightly, but two similar yet discrete shades may fall under one color description. Trial colors can sometimes found on cards with die proofs.

Progressive Color Proofs (PP suffix) are a set of color proofs containing the number of items stated in the listing. Values, therefore, are for the s of singles (unless otherwise mentioned in the description), not a single progressive color proof from that set. Numbers in parentheses represent the total number of complete sets that were created. Partial sets are not listed if complete sets are known.

Imperforate Plate Proofs (PI suffix) are usually found on gummed stamp paper. Any exceptions are noted in the listing description. Numbers parentheses represent the total number of imperforate proof stamps created. Many items have inked fingerprints on the reverse as a security devic Values are for pairs unless otherwise stated. Many gutter pairs will have creases. Some gutter pairs will have marginal inscriptions. These are wor more.

Organization of listings Listings have all of the New York, Geneva and Vienna stamps and souvenir cards for any set all together. The first part of a item's catalogue number is the same catalogue number as shown in the listings for stamps and postal stationery. The prefix "G" is before the catalogu number for items from Geneva; prefix "V" for items from Vienna. Items with prefix "SC" are souvenir cards, and catalogue numbers without prefix a from New York. The suffix describing the type of proof follows the catalogue number. Die proofs (suffix PD) are the first proof category in the listing and will be followed by the other categories in the same order as listed above. Each proof category will list New York items first, followed by Genev items, Vienna items, and then souvenir cards.

Often cards of proofs will contain all of the items in an issued set. The catalogue numbers for cards that contain New York, Geneva and Vienna proo are organized by the highest New York catalogue number of the various die proof items in the set. If there are no New York items in the card, then th numbering will be organized by the highest Geneva or Vienna catalogue number in the card of die proofs. Cards that contain both die proofs and tri color proofs are catalogued under the die proofs.

Numbers in parentheses represent the total number of items created. The number of items coming in part or in total from printer's archives are ~roximations. Listings for single proofs affixed to cards do not usually mention that they are affixed to a card. Cards containing more than one proof have a minor letter following the PD suffix, and the listing will detail the component parts, as some cards may in the future be broken down by ~ners into individual proof items. Cutting up cards, however, may destroy their value, as listings are often based on the presence of the handstamp. ~moving proofs from the card may also destroy their value, as it may then be impossible to distinguish them from imperforate singles.

No. 303PDa — A Typical Die Proof Card

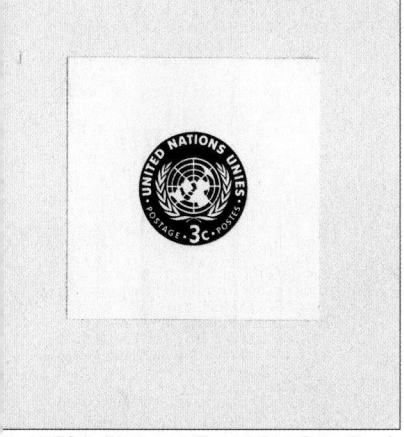

No. U1TC in Black — A Typical Trial Color Proof

~eets of 50 of No. V1PP — A Typical Progressive Proof Set

No. 1PI — A Typical Pair of Imperforate Plate Proofs

New York #1-11
Definitives

1951		
1PD	(1)	600.
2PD	(3)	500.
3PD	(1)	450.
3PDa	Card, #3PD, 3TC blue violet (1)	575.
4PD	(1)	600.
5PD	(1)	575.
5PDa	Card, #5PD, 5TC dark blue violet	1,150.
6PD	(1)	600.
6PDa	Card, #1PD, 6PD (3)	3,100.
7PD	(1)	600.
8PD	(4)	300.
9PD	(1)	600.
9PDa	Card, #4PD, 7PD, 9PD, essays of #7, 9 (1)	1,850.
9PDb	Card, #9PD, 9TC green (1)	825.
10PD	(1)	500.
11PD	(4)	475.
2TC	indigo (1)	—
3TC	red violet (2)	—
3TC	dark red (2)	350.
3TC	red orange (1)	450.
3TC	carmine (3)	—
3TC	orange red (3)	—
3TCa	Card, #3TC carmine, #3TC orange red (1)	700.
5TC	orange red (1)	750.
5TC	brown (1)	750.
5TC	bright blue (1)	—
5TC	light blue (1)	—
5TC	dark blue (1)	—
5TC	black (1)	—
5TC	red orange (1)	—
5TCa	Card, #5TC black, 5TC brown (1)	925.
10TC	black (1)	—
10TC	dark green (1)	—
10TCa	Card, #10TC blue green, #10TC yellow green (1)	—
11TC	dark red, 2 impressions side by side (1)	—
11TC	purple, 2 impressions side by side (1)	—
11TCa	dark blue (2 impressions side by side below two impressions of #5TC (1)	—
1PI	Pair (25)	1,000.
2PI	Pair (5)	—
5PI	Pair (42)	350.
	Vert. pair with horiz. gutter (8)	—
6PI	Pair (25)	375.
8PI	Pair (50)	500.
11PI	Pair (3)	800.

Imperforate printer's waste has impression of No. 6 with stamps of other countries.

New York #12
Signing of UN Charter, 7th Anniv.

1952		
12PD	(3)	—
12TC	dark blue (2)	—
12TC	black (2)	—
12TC	green (2)	—
12TC	light blue (1)	—

New York #13-14
Universal Declaration of Human Rights, 4th Anniv.

1952		
13PDa	Card, #13PD and two #13TC in slightly different shades (1)	975.
14PDa	Card, #14PD and two #14TC in slightly different shades (1)	975.
14PDb	Card, #13PD, 14PD (1)	—

New York #15-16
Protection for Refugees

1953		
15PD	(1)	450.
16PD	(1)	450.
16PDa	Card, #15PD, 16PD (3)	775.
16PDb	Card, #15PD, 16PD, 16TC indigo (1)	875.
16PDc	Card, #16PDb and card, #15PD, 15TC, 16PD (some staining) (1)	575.
15PI	Pair (80)	400.
	Vert. pair with horiz. gutter (20)	—
16PI	Pair (80)	400.
	Vert. pair with horiz. gutter (20)	—

New York #17-18
Universal Postal Union

1953		
17PDa	Card, #17PD, 17TC red brown, 17TC ultramarine, 17TC blue	2,000.
17PDb	Card, #17PD, 17TC violet brown (1)	—
18PDa	Card, #18PD, 18TC bright blue (1)	—
18PDb	Card, #17PDa, 18PDa (1)	—
17PI	Pair (82)	200.
	Horiz. pair with vert. gutter (8)	—
18PI	Pair (84)	200.
	Horiz. pair with vert. gutter (6)	—

Approximately half of PI items are stained and glued on cardboard. Imperforate printer's waste has No. 17 with No. 18 and impressions of other items on the reverse.

New York #19-20
Technical Assistance

1953		
20PDa	Card, #19PD-20PD, #19TC-20TC in slightly different shades (2)	1,250.

New York #21-22
Human Rights Day

1953		
22PDa	Card, #23PD-24PD, two #23TC, two #24TC in slightly different shades (2)	1,600.
21PI	Pair (40)	350.
	Vert. pair with horiz. gutter (10)	—
22PI	Pair (40)	350.
	Vert. pair with horiz. gutter (10)	—

New York #23-24
Food and Agricultural Organization

1954		
24PDa	Card, #23PD-24PD, two #23TC-24TC in slightly different colors (2)	1,600.
23PI	Pair (40)	225.
	Vert. pair with horiz. gutter (10)	—
24PI	Pair (40)	225.
	Vert. pair with horiz. gutter (120)	—

New York #25-26
International Labor Organization

1954		
25PDa	Card, #25PD, two #25TC in slightly different shades, three #26TC in purple shades (2)	2,400.
26PDa	Card, #25PD-26PD, #26TC in slightly different shade (2)	—
25PI	Pair (40)	350.
	Vert. pair with horiz. gutter (10)	—
26PI	Pair (40)	350.
	Vert. pair with horiz. gutter (10)	—

New York #27-28
United Nations Day

1954		
27PI	Pair (40)	300.
	Horiz. pair with vert. gutter (10)	—
28PI	Pair (40)	300.
	Horiz. pair with vert. gutter (10)	—

New York #29-30
Human Rights Day

1954		
29PD	(5)	350.
30PD	(5)	350.
29PI	Pair (40)	350.
	Vert. pair with horiz. gutter (10)	—
30PI	Pair (40)	—
	Vert. pair with horiz. gutter (10)	—

New York #31-32
International Civil Aviation Organization

1955		
31PDa	Card, #31PD, two #31TC in different blue shades (3)	—
32PDa	Card, #32PD, three #32TC in different red shades (3)	1,400.
32PDb	Card, #31PD-32PD, #31TC-#32TC in different shades, three essays of #31-32 (1)	1,650.

31TC	black (1)	—
32TC	black (1)	—
31PI	Pair (171)	225.
	Horiz. pair with vert. gutter (26)	—
32PI	Pair (130)	225.
	Horiz. pair with vert. gutter (20)	—

No. 31PI exists with and without punch holes.

New York #33-34
UN Educational, Scientific and Cultural Organization

1955

33PD	(1)	—
33PDa	Card, #33PD, two #33TC in different shades (3)	700.
34PD	(1)	—
34PDa	Card, #34PD, two #34TC in different shades (3)	700.
33TC	black (1)	—
34TC	black (1)	—
33PI	Pair (128)	—
	Horiz. pair with vert. gutter (16)	—
34PI	Pair (90)	—
	Horiz. pair with vert. gutter (10)	—

No. 33PI exists with and without punch holes.

New York #35-38
UN, 10th Anniv.

1955

35PDa	Card, #35PD, two #35TC in different shades (2)	2,400.
35PDb	Card, #35PD, #35TC in lighter shade (1)	—
36PDa	Card, #36PD, two #36TC in different shades (3)	—
37PDa	Card, #37PD, two #37TC in different shades (3)	—
38PD	Sheet of #38 with security punches (2)	1,950.
38bPD	Watermarked sheet of nine #38b and nine #38c with security punches (1)	4,250.
38cPD	Watermarked sheet of nine #38c with security punches (1)	5,000.
35TC	carmine (1)	—
35TC	black (1)	—
36TC	black (1)	—
37TC	black (1)	—
38PP	4 items (9 souvenir sheets)	—
38PP	Retouch, 2 items (9 souvenir sheets)	—
35PI	Pair (130)	325.
	Horiz. pair with vert. gutter (20)	—
36PI	Pair (130)	325.
	Horiz. pair with vert. gutter (20)	—
37PI	Pair (180)	325.
	Horiz. pair with vert. gutter (30)	—
38PI	Pairs of souvenir sheets (16)	3,000.
	Single with sheet margin (4)	850.
38PI	Retouch Pairs of souvenir sheets (4)	—
	Retouch, single with sheet margin (1)	—

No. 37PI exists with and without punch holes.

New York #39-40
Human Rights Day

1955

39PDa	Card, #39PD, two #39TC in different shades (2)	850.
40PDa	Card, #40PD, two #40TC in different shades (2)	850.
39TC	black (1)	—
40TC	black (1)	—
40TCa	Card, #39TC in aquamarine, #40TC in dark green and two essays (1)	1,250.
39PI	Pair (180)	425.
	Vert. pair with horiz. gutter (20)	—
40PI	Pair (130)	425.
	Vert. pair with horiz. gutter (20)	—

No. 39PI exists with and without punch holes.

New York #41-42
International Telecommunication Union

1956

41PD	(2)	300.
42PD	(2)	300.
41PI	Pair (40)	350.
	Horiz. pair with vert. gutter (10)	—
42PI	Pair (40)	350.
	Horiz. pair with vert. gutter (10)	—

New York #43-44
World Health Organization

1956

43PD	(2)	225.
44PD	(2)	225.
43PI	Pair (40)	250.
	Vert. pair with horiz. gutter (10)	—
44PI	Pair (40)	250.
	Vert. pair with horiz. gutter (10)	—

Nos. 43PI-44PI have "Colour approved" handstamped in margin.

New York #45-46
General Assembly

1956

45PD	(7)	275.
46PD	(7)	275.
45PI	Pair (40)	350.

	Horiz. pair with vert. gutter (10)	—
46PI	Pair (40)	350.
	Horiz. pair with vert. gutter (10)	—

New York #47-48
Human Rights Day

1956

47PD	(2)	.375
48PD	(2)	.375
47TC	red (3)	400.
47TC	carmine (3)	—
48TC	blue (6)	400.
47PI	Pair (40)	300.
	Horiz. pair with vert. gutter (10)	—
48PI	Pair (40)	300.
	Horiz. pair with vert. gutter (10)	—

New York #49-50
World Meteorological Organization

1957

49PD	(2)	275.
50PD	(2)	275.
49TC	blue (3)	250.
50TC	carmine rose (3)	250.
49PI	Pair (40)	—
	Vert. pair with horiz. gutter (10)	—
50PI	Pair (40)	—
	Vert. pair with horiz. gutter (10)	—

Nos. 49PI-50PI have "Colour approved" handstamped in margin.

New York #51-52
UN Emergency Force

1957

51PD	(7)	275.
52PD	(7)	275.
51PI	Pair (40)	—
	Horiz. pair with vert. gutter (10)	—
52PI	Pair (40)	—
	Horiz. pair with vert. gutter (10)	—

New York #55-56
Security Council

1957

55PD	(6)	275.
56PD	(11)	275.
55TC	golden brown (6)	—
55TC	brown (5)	—
55PI	Pair (40)	—
	Vert. pair with horiz. gutter (10)	—
56PI	Pair (40)	—
	Vert. pair with horiz. gutter (10)	—

New York #57-58
Human Rights Day

1957

57PD	(12)	275.
58PD	(9)	275.
57TC	light red brown (1)	300.
58TC	dark blue (3)	—
58TC	gray green (6)	300.
57PI	Pair (50)	—
58PI	Pair (50)	—

Nos. 57TC-58TC have handstamps with "Approved" crossed out.

New York #59-60
International Atomic Energy Agency

1958

59PD	(12)	250.
60PD	(13)	250.
59TC	emerald (7)	—
59TC	black (7)	350.
60TC	black (8)	350.
59PI	With security punch (358 pairs)	—
	Cross gutter block, with security punch (4)	—
	Horiz. pair with vert. gutter, with security punch (52)	—
	Vert. pair with horiz. gutter, with security punch (32)	—
60PI	Pair with security punch (358)	—
	Cross gutter block, with security punch (4)	—
	Horiz. pair with vert. gutter, with security punch (52)	—
	Vert. pair with horiz. gutter, with security punch (32)	—

New York #61-62
Central Hall, Site of First General Assembly Meeting

1958

61PD	(8)	275.
62PD	(8)	275.
61TC	black (3)	275.
62TC	black (3)	275.
61PI	With security punch (358 pairs)	—
	Cross gutter block, with security punch (4)	—
	Horiz. pair with vert. gutter, with security punch (32)	—
	Vert. pair with horiz. gutter, with security punch (52)	—
62PI	Pair with security punch (358)	—
	Cross gutter block, with security punch (4)	—

	Horiz. pair with vert. gutter, with security punch (32)	—
	Vert. pair with horiz. gutter, with security punch (52)	—

New York #63-64
UN Emblem

1958

63PD	(21)	
64PD	(7)	
64PDa	Card, #64PD, #64TC Prussian blue, #64TC ultramarine (2)	
63TC	brown orange (3)	
64TC	light blue (1)	
64TC	ultramarine (1)	
63PI	Pair (80)	
	Vert. pair with horiz. gutter (20)	
64PI	Pair (80)	
	Vert. pair with horiz. gutter (20)	

No. 63TC is affixed to cards inscribed "D."

New York #65-66
Economic and Social Council

1958

65PD	(8)	
66PD	(7)	
65TC	black (2)	
65TC	orange brown (1)	
65TC	green (1)	
65TC	red orange (1)	
66TC	black (2)	
65PI	Pair with security punch (358)	
	Cross gutter block, with security punch (4)	
	Horiz. pair with vert. gutter, with security punch (32)	
	Vert. pair with horiz. gutter, with security punch (52)	
66PI	Pair with security punch (358)	
	Cross gutter block, with security punch (4)	
	Horiz. pair with vert. gutter, with security punch (32)	
	Vert. pair with horiz. gutter, with security punch (52)	

New York #67-68
Human Rights Day

1958

67PD	(5)	
68PD	(5)	
67TC	black (2)	
68TC	black (1)	
67PI	Pair (358)	
	Cross gutter block, with security punch and "SPECIMEN" ovpt. (4)	
	Horiz. pair with vert. gutter, with security punch and "SPECIMEN" ovpt. (52)	
	Vert. pair with horiz. gutter, with security punch and "SPECIMEN" ovpt. (32)	
68PI	Pair (358)	
	Cross gutter block, with security punch and "SPECIMEN" ovpt. (4)	
	Horiz. pair with vert. gutter, with security punch and "SPECIMEN" ovpt. (52)	
	Vert. pair with horiz. gutter, with security punch and "SPECIMEN" ovpt. (32)	

Essays of Nos. 67 and 68 without denominations exist issued colors and black.

New York #69-70
New York City Building, Flushing Meadows

1959

69PD	(7)	
70PD	(7)	
69PI	Pair (216)	
	Cross gutter block (3)	
	Horiz. pair with vert. gutter (54)	
	Vert. pair with horiz. gutter (24)	
70PI	Pair (216)	
	Cross gutter block (3)	
	Horiz. pair with vert. gutter (54)	
	Vert. pair with horiz. gutter (24)	

New York #71-72
Economic Commission for Europe

1959

71PD	(7)	
72PD	(7)	
71PI	Pair (216)	
	Cross gutter block (3)	
	Horiz. pair with vert. gutter (24)	
	Vert. pair with horiz. gutter (54)	
72PI	Pair (216)	
	Cross gutter block (3)	
	Horiz. pair with vert. gutter (24)	
	Vert. pair with horiz. gutter (54)	

New York #73-74
Trusteeship Council

1959

73PD	(5)	
74PD	(5)	
73TC	orange red (2)	
73PI	Pair (216)	
	Cross gutter block (3)	
	Horiz. pair with vert. gutter (24)	
	Vert. pair with horiz. gutter (54)	
74PI	Pair (216)	

Cross gutter block (3) —
Horiz. pair with vert. gutter (24) —
Vert. pair with horiz. gutter (54) —

b. 73TC has handstamps with words "Color and" crossed

New York #75-76
World Refugee Year

1959
(6) 300.
(5) 300.
purple & red (3) —
olive & Prussian blue (2) —
purple & green (3) —
Pair (216) —
Cross gutter block (3) —
Horiz. pair with vert. gutter (54) —
Vert. pair with horiz. gutter (24) —
Pair (216) —
Cross gutter block (3) —
Horiz. pair with vert. gutter (54) —
Vert. pair with horiz. gutter (24) —

New York #77-78
Chaillot Palace

(4) 250.
(4) 250.
brown & blue green(1) 325.
blue & red (1) 325.
Card, #78TC brown & blue green, #78TC blue &red (1) —
Pair (25) —
Pair (25) —

New York #79-80
Economic Commission for Asia and the Far East

(1) —
Card, #79PD, #80PD (1) —
Card, two #79PD, two #80PD (1) 1,250.
Pair (50) —
Pair (50) —

New York #81-82
World Forestry Congress

(2) 425.
Card, #81PD-82PD (3) 350.
Pair (100) —
Pair (100) —

New York #83-85
UN, 15th Anniv.

(5) 325.
(6) 325.
(2) 700.
black (1) —
bright blue (2) —
Pair (144) —
Cross gutter block (2) —
Horiz. pair with vert. gutter (36) —
Vert. pair with horiz. gutter (16) —
Pair (119) —
Cross gutter block (2) —
Horiz. pair with vert. gutter (36) —
Vert. pair with horiz. gutter (16) —
Pair (16) —
Cross gutter block (2) —
Horiz. pair with vert. gutter (8) —
Vert. pair with horiz. gutter (8) —

An essay in blue has diagonal lines in background rather than cross-hatching.

New York #86-87
International Bank for Reconstruction and Development

Da Card, 2 #86PD, 2 #87PD (2) 1,150.
Db Card, #86PD-87PD with simulated perforations (1) —
Pair (100) —
Pair (100) —

New York #88-89
International Court of Justice

Da Card, #88PD-89PD affixed, dated 10/31/61 (2) 450.
Db Card, 2 #88PD, 2 #89PD, disapproved (2) —
Pair (100) —
Pair (100) —

New York #90-91
International Monetary Fund

Da Card with 2 #90PD, 2 #91PD in slightly different shades (1) 1,300.
Pair (100) —
Pair (50) —

New York #92
Abstract Flags

1961
92PI Pair (80) —
Horiz. pair with vert. gutter (20) —

New York #93-94
Economic Commission for Latin America

1961
93PDa Card, 2 #93PD, 2 essays of #94 (2) —
94PDa Card, 2 #94PD (1) 400.

Essays of No. 94 lack serifs in "1's."

New York #95-96
Economic Commission for Africa

1961
96PDa Card with #95PD-96PD affixed (8) 500.
95PP 4 items (100) —
96PP 8 items (100) —
95PI Pair (100) —
96PI Pair (100) —

New York #97-99
UN Children's Fund (UNICEF)

1961
99PDa Card, #97PD-99PD, with approval handstamp (3) 1,050.
99PDb Card, #97PD-99PD, no approval handstamp (5) 600.
97PP 4 items (80) —
Vert. pair with horiz. gutter (10) —
98PP 4 items (80) —
Vert. pair with horiz. gutter (10) —
99PP 4 items (80) —
Vert. pair with horiz. gutter (10) —
97PI Pair (80) —
Vert. pair with horiz. gutter (20) —
98PI Pair (80) —
Vert. pair with horiz. gutter (20) —
99PI Pair (80) —
Vert. pair with horiz. gutter (20) —

New York #100-101
Housing and Urban Development Program

1962
100PD With approval handstamp (3) 200.
101PD With approval handstamp (3) 200.
100PI Pair with oval "Harrison's Photogravure Specimen" handstamp (25) 350.
101PI Pair with oval "Harrison's Photogravure Specimen" handstamp (25) 350.

Three essays each of Nos. 100 and 101 have larger numerals than issued stamps are are on cards marked "disapproved."

New York #102-103
Malaria Eradication Campaign

1962
102PD (5) 400.
103PD (5) 400.

New York #104-107
Definitives

1962
104PD (5) 400.
105PD (7) 425.
106PD With approval handstamp & signature (2) 400.
107PD (3) 500.
104PI Pair with oval "Harrison's Photogravure Specimen" handstamp (25) 250.
105PI Pair with oval "Harrison's Photogravure Specimen" handstamp (25) 250.
107PI Pair with oval "Harrison's Photogravure Specimen" handstamp (25) 250.
Same, without handstamp (25) 400.

Three essays of No. 106 have indistinct line between "U" and "N," and are on cards marked "disapproved."

New York #108-109
Death of Dag Hammarskjold, 1st Anniv.

1962
108PDa Card, #108PD, essay of #109 (1) —
109PDa Card, #109PD, essay of #108 (1) —
109PDb Card, #108PD-#109PD (2) 600.
108PI Pair (80) —
Vert. pair with horiz. gutter (20) —
109PI Pair (80) —
Vert. pair with horiz. gutter (20) —

Essays of Nos 108-109 lack denomination.

New York #110-111
UN Operation in the Congo

1962
111PDa Card, 3 #110PD, 3 #111PD (1) 1,150.
111PDb Card, #111PD, essay of #110 (2) 550.
110PP 4 items (80) —
Horiz. pair with vert. gutter (10) —
111PP 4 items (80) —
Horiz. pair with vert. gutter (10) —
110PI Pair (80) —

111PI Pair (80) —
Horiz. pair with vert. gutter (20) —
Pair (80) —
Horiz. pair with vert. gutter (20) —

Essays of No. 110 have 5c denomination.

New York #112-113
Committee on Peaceful Uses of Outer Space

1962
112PD (2) —
113PD (1) —
113PDa Card, #112PD-113PD (3) 500.

Essays similar to Nos. 112PD-113PD have text in white panel below palm frond.

New York #114-115
UN Development Decade

1963
115PDa Card, #114PD, 2 #115PD (one in slightly different shade) with approval handstamp (3) 875.
115PDb Card, #114PD-115PD (3) 400.
114PP 4 items (80) —
Vert. pair with horiz. gutter (10) —
115PP 4 items (80) —
Vert. pair with horiz. gutter (10) —
114PI Pair (80) —
Vert. pair with horiz. gutter (20) —
115PI Pair (80) —
Vert. pair with horiz. gutter (20) —

New York #116-117
Freedom from Hunger Campaign

1963
116PD (1) —
117PD (1) —
117PDa Card, #116PD-117PD (5) 500.
116PP 3 items (80) —
Horiz. pair with vert. gutter (10) —
117PP 3 items (80) —
Horiz. pair with vert. gutter (10) —
116PI Pair (80) —
Horiz. pair with vert. gutter (20) —
117PI Pair (80) —
Horiz. pair with vert. gutter (20) —

Essays similar to Nos. 116PD-117PD have taller numerals and lettering.

New York #118
UN Temporary Executive Authority in West New Guinea

1963
118PD With approval handstamp (2) 400.
118PDa Card, #118PD (approved), #118TC (not approved) (3) 500.
118TCa Card, 2 #118TC (disapproved or with instructions to printer) (3) 500.
118PP 3 items (100) —
Horiz. pair with vert. gutter (10) —
118PI Pair (100) —
Horiz. pair with vert. gutter (20) —

No. 118TC has right side of map in a lighter shade of green.

New York #119-120
General Assembly Building, New York

1963
120PDa Card, #119PD-120PD (2) 400.

New York #121-122
Universal Declaration of Human Rights, 15th Anniv.

1963
121PD (2) 250.
122PD (2) 250.
121PI Pair (100) —
122PI Pair (100) —

Essays similar to Nos. 121PD-122PD have top line of frame text flush left rather than centered, and are on a disapproved card.

New York #123-124
Intergovernmental Maritime Consultative Organization

1964
124PDa Card, #123PD-124PD (3) 550.
123PP 4 items (80) —
Horiz. pair with vert. gutter (10) —
124PP 4 items (80) —
Horiz. pair with vert. gutter (10) —
123PI Pair (80) —
Horiz. pair with vert. gutter (20) —
124PI Pair (80) —
Horiz. pair with vert. gutter (20) —

New York #125-128
Definitives

1964
125PD (3) 275.
125PDa Card, #125 perforated with approval handstamp (1) —
126PD (3) 240.
127PDa Card, #126PD-127PD with approval handstamp (3) 550.

127PDb Card, #127PD (approved), #127PD (not approved, in slightly different shade, #126PD (disapproved in slightly different shade (3)) 925.
128PD (3) 240.
125PP 3 items (100) —
126PI 3 items (80) —
Vert. pair with horiz. gutter (10) —
127PP 4 items (80) —
Horiz. pair with vert. gutter (10) —
128PP 4 items (80) —
Horiz. pair with vert. gutter (10) —
125PI Pair (65) —
Horiz. pair with vert. gutter (10) —
126PI Pair (80) —
Vert. pair with horiz. gutter (20) —
127PI Pair (80) —
Horiz. pair with vert. gutter (20) —
128PI Pair (80) —
Horiz. pair with vert. gutter (20) —

Essays similar to No. 125PD have larger numerals and blue text.

New York #129-130
UN Conference on Trade and Development
1964
129PD (6) 250.
130PD (6) 250.
129PI Pair (25) —
130PI Pair (25) —

New York #131-132
Narcotics Control
1964
131PD (2) 250.
132PD (2) 250.
132PDa Card, #131PD-132PD (3) 600.

New York #133
Nuclear Test Ban Treaty
1964
133TC dark red & black, perforated, litho. & engr. (1)
133TC lilac, perforated, engr. (20) 300.
133TCa Card, 2 #133TC dark red & dark brown, litho. & vignette essay, litho. (1) —
133TCb Card, #133TC dark red & black, engr. & 5 vignette essays, engr. (1) —
133TCc Card, 11 #133TC in red, claret, brown rose, brown, dark brown, dull blue, blue, blue violet, gray, dark gray, black, engr. (1) —

New York #134-136
Education for Progress Campaign
1964
135PD (1) —
136PDa Card, #134PD-136PD, with approval stamp (3) —
136PDb Card, #134PD-136PD, without approval stamp (2) 300.
136PDc Card, #134PD, #136PD, without approval stamp (1) 450.
134PP 4 items (80) —
Horiz. pair with vert. gutter (10) —
135PP 4 items (80) —
Horiz. pair with vert. gutter (10) —
136PP 4 items (80) —
Horiz. pair with vert. gutter (10) —
134PI Pair (80) —
Horiz. pair with vert. gutter (20) —
135PI Pair (80) —
Horiz. pair with vert. gutter (20) —
136PI Pair (80) —
Horiz. pair with vert. gutter (20) —

New York #137-138
Special Fund Program
1965
137PD (2) 225.
138PD (2) 225.
138PDa Card, #137PD-138PD, with approval stamp (1) 500.
138PDb Card, #137PD-138PD, without approval stamp (1) —

New York #139-140
UN Peace-Keeping Force in Cyprus
1965
140PDa Card #139PD-140PD, with approval stamp (5) 500.
140PP 3 items (80) —
Vert. pair with horiz. gutter (10) —
139PI Pair (40) —
Vert. pair with horiz. gutter (10) —
140PI Pair (40) —
Vert. pair with horiz. gutter (10) —

Smaller-sized essays (30x38mm) of Nos. 139-140 are in three cards with approval stamps.

New York #141-142
International Telecommunication Union
1965
142PDa Card, #141PD-142PD, with approval stamp (3) 500.
142PDb Card, #141PD-142PD, no approval stamp (3) 450.
142PDc Card, #141PD-142PD, #141TC dated "8.2.65" (3) 925.
141PP 4 items (80) —
Horiz. pair with vert. gutter (10) —
142PP 4 items (80) —
Horiz. pair with vert. gutter (10) —
141PI Pair (80) —
Horiz. pair with vert. gutter (20) —
142PI Pair (80) —
Horiz. pair with vert. gutter (20) —

No. 141TC has orange yellow lines instead of orange lines.

New York #143-145
UN, 20th Anniv. and International Cooperation Year
1965
143PD (3) 275.
143PDa Card, #143PD, 144TC orange red (3) 825.
144PD (3) 275.
144PDa Card, #143PD-144PD, with approval stamp (7) 500.
145PD Imperforate sheet with manuscript printer's instructions (4) —
Issued souvenir sheet, perforated (on printer's card) (1) 110.
145PDa #143PD, #144PD affixed to #145 souvenir sheet margin (5) 600.

New York #146-150
Definitives
1965-66
146PD (7) 200.
148PDa Block of 12 perforated stamps with approval handstamp in margin (2) 140.
148PDb Card, #147-148 perforated, with approval handstamp (3) 500.
149PD Perforated, with approval handstamp (2) 250.
149PDa Card, #149PD (2nd printing), #149PD, first printing, perforated, with approval handstamp (2) 600.
150PD (3) 240.
149TC Prussian blue & dark blue, perforated (1) —
150PP 3 items (80), affixed on cards —
Horiz. pair with vert. gutter (10) —
150PI Pair (161) 375.
Horiz. pair with vert. gutter (19) —

Two cards without approval handstamp have perforated essays of both Nos. 147 and 148. The essay of No. 147 has larger numerals and the essay of No. 148 has bright yellow text at bottom. No. 150PI has had extra glue applied.

New York #151-153
Population Trends and Development
1965
152PDa Card, #151PD-152PD, 153TC, perforated, with approval handstamp (2) 825.

No. 153TC has "Nations Unies" in black instead of gray.

New York #154-155
World Federation of United Nations Associations
1966
155PDa Card, #154-155PD with approval handstamp (3) 500.
154PP 4 items (80) —
Vert. pair with horiz. gutter (10) —
155PP 4 items (80) —
Vert. pair with horiz. gutter (10) —
154PI Pair (80) —
Vert. pair with horiz. gutter (20) —
155PI Pair (80) —
Vert. pair with horiz. gutter (20) —

New York #156-157
World Health Organization
1966
157TCa Card, #156TC-157TC, with approval handstamp (3) 500.
156PP 4 items (50) —
157PP 4 items (80) —
Horiz. pair with vert. gutter (10) —
156PI Pair (65) —
Horiz. pair with vert. gutter (10) —
157PI Pair (80) —
Horiz. pair with vert. gutter (20) —

Nos. 156TC and 157TC have side and front of building the same shade of blue.

New York #158-159
International Coffee Agreement of 1962
1966
159PDa Card, #158PD-159PD (3) 625.

New York #160
UN Observers
1964
160PD (2) on cards dated "3.2.1966" —
160PP 4 items (50) —
160PI Pair (65) —
Vert. pair with horiz. gutter (10) —

Two essays of No. 160 with white text lines larger and cl[ose] together are on cards dated "17.1.1966."

New York #161-163
UNICEF, 20th Anniv.
1966
161PD (3) —
162PD (3) —
163PD (3) —
161PI Pair (72) —
Cross gutter block (1) —
Horiz. pair with vert. gutter (18) —
Vert. pair with horiz. gutter (8) —
162PI Pair (72) —
Cross gutter block (1) —
Horiz. pair with vert. gutter (18) —
Vert. pair with horiz. gutter (8) —
163PI Pair (72) —
Cross gutter block (1) —
Horiz. pair with vert. gutter (18) —
Vert. pair with horiz. gutter (8) —

New York #164-165
UN Development Program
1967
165PDa Card, # 164PD-165PD, dated "6.9.1966" (3) —
165PDb Card, #165PD, 2 #164PD, with approval handstamp, dated "4.10.66" (6) —
164PI Pair (40) —
Horiz. pair with vert. gutter (10) —
165PI Pair (40) —
Horiz. pair with vert. gutter (10) —

New York #166-167
Definitives
1967
166PD (6) —
166PDa Card, 2 #166PD (3) —
167PD (3) —
167TC With brown line separating "UN" in vignette, on card dated "27.4.1966" (3) —
166PP 4 items (80) —
Vert. pair with horiz. gutter (10) —
167PP 3 items (80) —
Horiz. pair with vert. gutter (10) —
166PI Pair (80) —
Vert. pair with horiz. gutter (20) —
167PI Pair (80) —
Horiz. pair with vert. gutter (20) —

New York #168-169
Independence
1967
168PD (2) —
169PD (3) —

New York #170-174
EXPO '67
1967
170PD (1) —
171PD (1) —
172PD (3) —
173PD (1) —
174PD (3) —
170PP 2 items (144) —
Cross gutter block (1) —
Horiz. pair with vert. gutter (8) —
Vert. pair with horiz. gutter (18) —
171PP 2 items (144) —
Cross gutter block (1) —
Horiz. pair with vert. gutter (8) —
Vert. pair with horiz. gutter (18) —
172PP 3 items (144) —
Cross gutter block (1) —
Horiz. pair with vert. gutter (18) —
Vert. pair with horiz. gutter (8) —
173PP 2 items (144) —
Cross gutter block (1) —
Horiz. pair with vert. gutter (8) —
Vert. pair with horiz. gutter (18) —
174PP 2 items (144) —
Cross gutter block (1) —
Horiz. pair with vert. gutter (8) —
Vert. pair with horiz. gutter (18) —
170PI Pair (72) —
Cross gutter block (1) —
Horiz. pair with vert. gutter (8) —
Vert. pair with horiz. gutter (18) —
171PI Pair (72) —
Cross gutter block (1) —
Horiz. pair with vert. gutter (8) —
Vert. pair with horiz. gutter (18) —
172PI Pair (72) —
Cross gutter block (1) —
Horiz. pair with vert. gutter (18) —
Vert. pair with horiz. gutter (8) —
173PI Pair (72) —
Cross gutter block (1) —
Horiz. pair with vert. gutter (8) —
Vert. pair with horiz. gutter (18) —

	Pair (72)	—
	Cross gutter block (1)	—
	Horiz. pair with vert. gutter (8)	—
	Vert. pair with horiz. gutter (18)	—

New York #175-176
International Tourist Year

Da	#175-176, perforated, affixed to printer's card (2)	600.

New York #177-178
Towards Disarmament

D	(3)	—
D	(3)	200.
C	Wall text in copper, gold lines in wall (1)	110.
C	Wall text in copper, blue gray lines in wall (3)	110.
C	Wall text in brown, silver lines in wall (1)	110.
C	Wall text in brown, blue gray lines in wall (3)	110.

New York #179-180
Chagall Stained Glass Windows

P	8 items (29)	—
P	8 items (29)	—
I	Pair on card stock (24)	1,050.
I	Pair on card stock (135)	650.
I	Horiz. pair with vert. gutter, on card stock (15)	—
I	Pair on stamp paper (75)	525.

Essays of Nos. 179-180 in 5c denomination exist.

New York #181-182
UN Secretariat

D	(1)	110.
D	(1)	110.
Da	Card, #181PD-182PD (1)	—
P	5 items (160)	—
	Horiz. pair with vert. gutter (20)	—
P	5 items (160)	—
	Horiz. pair with vert. gutter (20)	—
I	Pair (80)	—
	Horiz. pair with vert. gutter (20)	—
I	Pair (80)	—
	Horiz. pair with vert. gutter (20)	—

New York #183-184
Art at the UN

D	(1)	250.
D	(1)	250.
Da	Card, #183PD-184PD, dated "5.12.67" (2)	—
Ca	Card, #183TC-184TC, dated "10.XI.67" (3)	725.
P	5 items (80)	—
	Vert. pair with horiz. gutter (10)	—
P	5 items (80)	—
	Vert. pair with horiz. gutter (10)	—
I	Pair (65)	—
	Vert. pair with horiz. gutter (10)	—
I	Pair (80)	—
	Vert. pair with horiz. gutter (20)	—

. 183TC has a bright blue frame; No. 184TC a birght red
e.

New York #185-186
UN Industrial Development Orgainzation

D	(4)	325.
D	(3)	500.
C	brown frame, deep blue "ONUDI" (2)	—
P	4 items, affixed to cards (3)	—
P	4 items, affixed to cards (3)	—
I	Pair with security punch (25)	250.
I	Pair with security punch (25)	250.

New York #187
UN Headquarters

C	light gray roof in foreground, numbered 34 or 38, dated July 7, 1967 (2)	140.
C	With wide curved white line under window of General Assembly building, numbered 397 or 404, dated 11.8.1967 (2)	125.
C	With halo around UN emblem, dated Feb. 12, 1968 (2)	240.
P	11 items, on card with staple holes (3)	—
I	Pair with "Specimen" overprint (80)	250.
	Vert. pair with horiz. gutter, with "Specimen" overprint (20)	—
I	Pair without "Specimen" overprint (80)	375.
	Vert. pair with horiz. gutter, without "Specimen" overprint (20)	—

New York #188-189
World Weather Watch

1968

189PDa	Card, #188PD-189PD (1)	500.
188PP	5 items (100)	—
189PP	5 items (100)	—

New York #190-191
International Human Rights Year

1968

190PD	(6)	210.
191PD	(6)	210.
190PP	4 items (100)	—
191PP	4 items (100)	—
190PI	Pair (50)	—
191PI	Pair (50)	—

New York #192-193
UN Institute for Training and Research

1969

193PDa	Card, #192PD-193PD (2)	425.
192PP	6 items (50)	—
193PP	6 items (100)	—
192PI	Pair (15)	425.
193PI	Pair (15)	425.

New York #194-195
Economic Commission for Latin America

1969

195PDa	#194-195, perforated, affixed to printer's card (4)	425.

New York #196
"UN" and Emblem

1969

196PD	With approval handstamp (2)	250.
196TC	Card, #196PD, 196TC dark blue background (2)	—
196PP	3 items (100)	—

New York #197-198
UN International Law Commission

1969

198PDa	Card, #197PD-198PD (9)	650.
197PP	4 items (80)	—
	Horiz. pair with vert. gutter (10)	—
198PP	4 items (80)	—
	Horiz. pair with vert. gutter (10)	—
197PI	(40 pairs)	—
	Horiz. pair with vert. gutter (10)	—
198PI	(40 pairs)	—
	Horiz. pair with vert. gutter (10)	—

New York #199-200
Labor and Development

1969

199PD	With approval handstamp (1)	—
200PD	(1)	—
200PDa	Card, #199PD-200PD, with approval handstamp (1)	425.
199TC	Men in dark blue, perforated (3)	—
200TC	Rose pink background, perforated (3)	—
200PP	4 items (91)	—

Geneva #1-14
Definitives

1969-70

G1PD	(2)	200.
G3PD	(1)	—
G3PDa	Card, 2 #G3PD, with approval handstamp (2)	—
G4PD	(2)	—
G5PD	(3)	325.
G7PD	(1)	250.
G8PD	Perforated, on card with approval handstamp (2)	275.
G8PDa	Perforated layout sheet proof with 4 #G8PD affixed (1)	—
G8PDb	Partial perforated layout sheet proof with 2 #G8PD affixed (1)	—
G9PD	(1)	275.
G10PD	(1)	200.
G11PD	(1)	—
G12PD	(1)	225.
G13PD	(4)	240.
G14PD	(3)	225.
G1TC	Black panel behind "UN" (1)	—
G6TCa	Card, #G6PD, #G6TC pewter emblem, dated "7.10.69" (3)	—
G6TCb	Card, #G6TC silver emblem, 2 #G6PD dated "17.9.69" (3)	—
G6TCc	Card, #G6PD, #G6TC orange denomination, dated "27.8.69" (3)	—
G12TC	gray background, on card marked "Rejected" (2)	325.
G1PP	3 items, perforated (100)	—
G2PP	5 items (160)	—
	Horiz. pair with vert. gutter (20)	—
G3PP	5 items (160)	—
	Horiz. pair with vert. gutter (20)	—
G4PP	5 items (151)	—
	Horiz. pair with vert. gutter (20)	—
G5PP	4 items (160)	—
	Vert. pair with horiz. gutter (20)	—
G6PP	3 items (160)	—
	Horiz. pair with vert. gutter (20)	—
G7PP	4 items (100)	—

G8PP	8 items (150)	—
G9PP	6 items (100)	—
G10PP	8 items (100)	—
G12PP	6 items (100)	—
G13PP	5 items (160)	—
G2PI	Pair (80)	—
	Horiz. pair with vert. gutter (20)	—
G3PI	Pair (80)	—
	Horiz. pair with vert. gutter (20)	—
G4PI	Pair (73)	—
	Horiz. pair with vert. gutter (20)	—
G5PI	Pair (80)	—
	Vert. pair with horiz. gutter (20)	—
G6PI	Pair (80)	—
	Horiz. pair with vert. gutter (20)	—
G7PI	Pair (50)	—
G8PI	Pair (75)	—
G9PI	Pair (50)	—
G10PI	Pair (50)	—
G13PI	Pair (80)	—
	Vert. pair with horiz. gutter (20)	—

Four essays of No. G2 exist, having "0" below "F" jutting out to left. Two essays of No. G10 with small "F.S." are on rejected cards.

New York #201-202
Mosaic Art at the UN

1969

201PD	(3)	210.
202PD	(3)	210.
202PDa	Card, #201PD-202PD (2)	—
201PP	8 items (100)	—
202PP	8 items (100)	—
201PI	Pair (50)	—
202PI	Pair (50)	—

New York #203-204
Peace Bell

1970

204PDa	Card, 2 each #203PD-204PD (2)	1,300.
203PP	5 items (100)	—
204PP	5 items (100)	—

About half of Nos. 203PP and 204PP have faults.

New York #205-206
Lower Mekong Basin Development Project

1970

205PD	(2)	250.
206PD	(2)	250.
205PP	10 items (100)	—
206PP	10 items (100)	—
205PI	Pair (50)	—
206PI	Pair (50)	—

New York #207-208
Fight Cancer

1970

207PD	Perforated, non-glossy paper, on piece of printer's card (1)	—
208PD	Perforated, non-glossy paper, on piece of printer's card (1)	—
208PDa	Card, #207PD-208PD, perforated, non-glossy paper (1)	—
208PDb	Card, 2 #207PD-208PD, perforated, non-glossy paper, with approval handstamp (1)	1,050.
208PDc	#207-208, perforated, glossy paper, on printer's card (2)	—
207PP	2 items (50)	—
208PP	2 items (50)	—
207PI	Pair (50)	—
208PI	Pair (50)	—

New York #209-212
UN, 25th Anniv.

1970

209PD	(2)	—
210PD	(2)	—
211PD	On card (3)	—
211PDa	Card, #209PD-211PD (2)	750.
212PD	(1)	275.
212PDa	Card, #209PD-212PD (1)	—
209PP	4 items (180)	—
	Horiz. pair with vert. gutter (10)	—
210PP	5 items (180)	—
	Horiz. pair with vert. gutter (10)	—
211PP	3 items (180)	—
	Vert. pair with horiz. gutter (10)	—
212PP	5 items (22)	—
209PI	Pair (80)	—
	Horiz. pair with vert. gutter (20)	—
210PI	Pair (80)	—
	Horiz. pair with vert. gutter (20)	—
211PI	Pair (80)	—
	Vert. pair with horiz. gutter (20)	—
212PI	Pair (12)	—

New York #213-214
Peace, Justice and Progress

1970

214PDa	Card, #213PD-214PD (3)	600.
214PDb	Card, 2 each #213PD-214PD (2)	1,300.
213PP	4 items (50)	—
214PP	4 items (50)	—

New York #215, Geneva #15
Peaceful Uses of the Sea Bed

1971

215PD	(2)	200.
G15PD	(1)	—
215PP	6 items (100)	—
G15PP	6 items (100)	—
215PI	Pair (50)	—
G15PI	Pair (50)	—

New York #216-217, Geneva #16
International Support for Refugees

1971

217PDa	Card, #216PD-217PD, #G16PD (2)	775.
216PP	4 items (80)	—
	Horiz. pair with vert. gutter (10)	—
217PP	4 items (80)	—
	Horiz. pair with vert. gutter (10)	—
G16PP	4 items (160)	—
	Horiz. pair with vert. gutter (20)	—
216PI	Pair (80)	—
	Horiz. pair with vert. gutter (10)	—
217PI	Pair (80)	—
	Horiz. pair with vert. gutter (10)	—
G16PI	Pair (80)	—
	Horiz. pair with vert. gutter (20)	—

New York #218, Geneva #17
World Food Program

1971

218PD	(4)	225.
G17PD	(4)	225.
G17TC	(1)	375.
218PP	6 items (100)	—
G17PP	6 items (100)	—
218PI	Pair (50)	—
G17PI	Pair (50)	—

New York #219, Geneva #18
Universal Postal Union

1971

219PDa	Card, #219PD, #G18PD (3)	550.
219PP	5 items (130)	—
	Horiz. pair with vert. gutter (10)	—
G18PP	5 items (150)	—
219PI	Pair (80)	—
	Horiz. pair with vert. gutter (20)	—
G18PI	Pair (80)	—
	Horiz. pair with vert. gutter (20)	—

New York #220-221, Geneva #19-20
International Year Against Racial Discrimination

1971

221PDa	Card, #220PD-221PD, #G19PD-G20PD and 4 similar items with slightly different colors (1)	2,400.
221PDb	Card with affixed plastic sheet with #220PD-221PD, #G19PD-G20PD affixed (1)	600.
221PDc	Cut-up card, #220PD-221PD, G19PD-G20PD (1)	—
220PP	5 items (100)	—
221PP	5 items (75)	—
G19PP	5 items (100)	—
G20PP	5 items (100)	—

New York #222-223
UN Headquarters, New York

1971

222PD	(4)	275.
223PD	(2)	275.
222PP	8 items (91)	—
223PP	5 items (92)	—
222PI	Pair (175)	—

Two sheets of 50 of No. 222PI are "approved."

New York #224-225, Geneva #21
UN International School

1971

225PDa	Card, #224PD-225PD, G21PD, with approval handstamp (2)	750.
225PDb	Card or sheet, #224PD-225PD, 1fr essay of #G21 (3)	925.
224PP	5 items (180)	—
	Vert. pair with horiz. gutter (10)	—
225PP	5 items (100)	—
	Vert. pair with horiz. gutter (10)	—
G21PP	5 items (180)	—
	Vert. pair with horiz. gutter (10)	—
224PI	Pair (80)	—
	Vert. pair with horiz. gutter (20)	—
225PI	Pair (80)	—
	Vert. pair with horiz. gutter (20)	—
G21PI	Pair (80)	—
	Vert. pair with horiz. gutter (20)	—

New York #226, Geneva #22
Definitives

1972

226PD	Perforated on printer's card (3)	225.
G22PD	(5)	225.
226PP	4 items (100)	—
G22PP	4 items (180)	—
	Horiz. pair with vert. gutter (10)	—
226PI	Pair (50)	—
G22PI	Pair (80)	—
	Horiz. pair with vert. gutter (20)	—

New York #227, Geneva #23
Non-proliferation of Nuclear Weapons

1972

227PD	(2)	200.
G23PD	(2)	225.
227PP	6 items (100)	—
G23PP	6 items (100)	—
227PI	Pair (50)	—
G23PI	Pair (50)	—

Two essays each of Nos. 227 and G23 lacking strong gray billowing in center of cloud exist on cards dated "22.Set.1971."

New York #228, Geneva #24, Souvenir Card #1
World Health Day

1972

228PDa	Card, #228PD, #G24PD with approval handstamp (1)	500.
G24PD	(1)	—
SC1PD	Card with stamps with simulated perforations and cancels (2)	600.
228PP	8 items (80)	—
	Vert. pair with horiz. gutter (10)	—
G24PP	8 items (160)	—
	Vert. pair with horiz. gutter (20)	—
G24PI	Pair (180)	—
	Vert. pair with horiz. gutter (20)	—

New York #229-230, Geneva #25-26
UN Conference on Human Environment

1972

229PD	(1)	—
230PDa	Card, #229PD-230PD, #G25PD-G26PD (3)	450.
230PDb	Card, #230PD, #G25PD-G26PD (1)	—
229PP	6 items (288)	—
	Cross gutter block (2)	—
	Horiz. pair with vert. gutter (16)	—
	Vert. pair with horiz. gutter (36)	—
230PP	6 items (288)	—
	Cross gutter block (2)	—
	Horiz. pair with vert. gutter (16)	—
	Vert. pair with horiz. gutter (36)	—
G25PP	6 items (288)	—
	Cross gutter block (2)	—
	Horiz. pair with vert. gutter (16)	—
	Vert. pair with horiz. gutter (36)	—
G26PP	6 items (288)	—
	Cross gutter block (2)	—
	Horiz. pair with vert. gutter (16)	—
	Vert. pair with horiz. gutter (36)	—
229PI	Pair (144)	—
	Cross gutter block (2)	—
	Horiz. pair with vert. gutter (16)	—
	Vert. pair with horiz. gutter (36)	—
230PI	Pair (144)	—
	Cross gutter block (2)	—
	Horiz. pair with vert. gutter (16)	—
	Vert. pair with horiz. gutter (36)	—
G25PI	Pair (144)	—
	Cross gutter block (2)	—
	Horiz. pair with vert. gutter (16)	—
	Vert. pair with horiz. gutter (36)	—
G26PI	Pair (144)	—
	Cross gutter block (2)	—
	Horiz. pair with vert. gutter (16)	—
	Vert. pair with horiz. gutter (36)	—

New York #231, Geneva #27
Economic Commission for Europe

1972

231PDa	Card, #231PD, #G27PD (4)	550.
231PP	8 items (100)	—
G27PP	8 items (50)	—

New York #232-233, Geneva #28-29, Souvenir Card #2
Art at the UN

1972

232PDa	Card, #232PD, #233TC text in dull blue green, #G28PD-G29PD (1)	975.
G28PD	(1)	—
G29PDa	Card, #G28PD-G29PD, #233TC text in dull blue green (1)	—
G29PDb	Card, #G29PD, #233TC text in dull blue green (1)	—
SC2PD	(25)	—
SC2PDa	Defaced card, with corrections marked in blue (8)	—
SC2TC	Untrimmed card, signature in light blue(3)	160.
G28PP	3 items (50)	—
G29PP	3 items (50)	—
232PI	Pair (80)	—
	Vert. pair with horiz. gutter (20)	—
233PI	Pair (80)	—
	Vert. pair with horiz. gutter (20)	—
G28PI	Pair (80)	—
	Vert. pair with horiz. gutter (20)	—
G29PI	Pair (80)	—
	Vert. pair with horiz. gutter (20)	—

New York #234-235, Geneva #30-31, Souvenir Card #3
Disarmament Decade

1973

235PDa	Card, #234PD-235PD, #G30PD-G31PD, with approval handstamp (1)	825.
SC3PD	With printer's stamp or approval handstamp (9)	110.

New York #227... (continued right column)

234PP	8 items (130)	—
	Horiz. pair with vert. gutter (20)	—
235PP	8 items (100)	—
G30PP	8 items (100)	—
	Horiz. pair with vert. gutter (20)	—
G31PP	8 items (100)	—
234PI	Pair (230)	—
	Horiz. pair with vert. gutter (20)	—
235PI	Pair (230)	—
	Horiz. pair with vert. gutter (20)	—
G30PI	Pair (205)	—
	Horiz. pair with vert. gutter (20)	—
G31PI	Pair (230)	—
	Horiz. pair with vert. gutter (20)	—

Two examples of #SC3PD are cut in half.

New York #236-237, Geneva #32
Fight Against Drug Abuse

1973

236PD	(1)	—
237PDa	Card, #236PD-237PD, #G32PD with approval handstamp (4)	—
237PDb	Card, #237PD, #G32PD with approval handstamp (1)	—
237PDc	Card, #237PD, #G32PD, 9c essay of #236 (6)	—
236PP	8 items (75)	—
237PP	8 items (100)	—
G32PP	8 items (50)	—
236PI	Pair (50)	—
237PI	Pair (50)	—
G32PI	Pair (50)	—

New York #238-239, Geneva #33
UN Volunteer Program

1973

239PDa	Card, #238PD-239PD, #G33PD (9)	—
238PP	8 items (80)	—
239PP	8 items (100)	—
G33PP	8 items (50)	—
238PI	Pair (50)	—
239PI	Pair (50)	—
G33PI	Pair (25)	—

New York #240-241, Geneva #34
Namibia

1973

241PDa	Card, #240PD-241PD, #G34PD (1)	—
241PDb	Card, #240PD-241PD, #G34PD, essays of #240-241, #G34 with Africa outlined in gold (3)	—
240PP	8 items (100)	—
241PP	8 items (100)	—
G34PP	8 items (50)	—
240PI	Pair (50)	—
241PI	Pair (50)	—
G34PI	Pair (50)	—

Two cards containing the essays only exist.

New York #242-243, Geneva #35-36, Souvenir Card #4
Universal Declaration of Human Rights, 25th Anniv.

1973

242PD	(9)	—
243PDa	Card, #242PD-243PD, #G35PD-G36PD (6)	—
243PDb	Card, #242PD-243PD (9)	—
243PDc	Card, #243PD, #G35PD-G36PD (1)	—
SC4PD	With approval handstamp (3)	—
242PP	5 items (100)	—
243PP	5 items (100)	—
G35PP	5 items (100)	—
G36PP	5 items (50)	—
SC4PP	2 items (1)	—
SC4PI	untrimmed card (1)	—

No. SC4PP may not be a complete set of progressive pr

New York #244-245, Geneva #37-38
New International Labor Organization Headquarters

1974

245PDa	Card, #245PD, #G37PD-G38PD, 8c essay of #244 (4)	—
244PP	8 items (75)	—
245PP	8 items (75)	—
G37PP	8 items (50)	—
G38PP	8 items (50)	—
244PI	Pair (50)	—
245PI	Pair (50)	—
G37PI	Pair (50)	—
G38PI	Pair (50)	—

New York #246, Geneva #39-40, Souvenir Card
Universal Postal Union, Cent.

1974

246PD	(1)	—
246PDa	Card, #246PD, #G39PD-G40PD (7)	—
G40PDa	Card, #G39PD-G40PD (1)	—
SC5PD	Affixed to card (5)	—
SC5PDa	Card with printer instructions in ink (1)	—
SC5PDb	Progressive proof sheet with printer instructions in ink (1)	—
246PP	6 items (100)	—
G39PP	5 items (50)	—
G40PP	5 items (50)	—

*PI	Pair (25)	—
*PI	Pair (25)	—
*PI	Pair (25)	—

New York #247-248, Geneva #41-42
Art at the UN

*4		
*PDa	Card, #247PD, #G41PD-G42PD, 15c essay of #248 (5)	1,250.
*PDa	Card, #247PD-248PD, #G41PD-G42PD (3)	925.
*PP	8 items (100)	—
*P	8 items (100)	—
*PP	8 items (50)	—
*PP	8 items (50)	—
*I	Pair (50)	—
*I	Pair (50)	—
*PI	Pair (50)	—
*PI	Pair (50)	—

New York #249-251
Definitives

*4		
*PD	Affixed on perforated blank (1)	—
*PD	Affixed on perforated blank (1)	—
*PDa	Taped to card (1)	—
*PDb	Card, #250PD, 251TC with darker brown background, essay of #249 with flat top "S", with "21.DIC.1973" date and approval stamp (2)	—
*PD	Affixed on perforated blank (1)	125.
*PDa	Card, #249PD, #251PD, with "17.ENE.1974" date and approval stamp (2)	500.
TCa	Darker brown background, on cards dated "21.DIC.1973" (3)	—
*PP	10 items (50)	—
*PP	8 items (35)	—
*PI	Pair (200)	—
*PI	Pair (50)	—
*PI	Pair (100)	—

New York #252-253, Geneva #43-44, Souvenir Card #6
World Population Year

*4		
*PDa	Card, #252PD, #G44PD, 21c essay of #253, 40c essay of #G43 in se-tenant strip (5)	725.
PDa	Card, #252PD-253PD, G44PD, 40c essay of #G43 in se-tenant strip (4)	800.
6PD	With approval handstamp (10)	—
*PP	10 items (50)	—
*PP	10 items (50)	—
3PP	10 items (50)	—
4PP	10 items (50)	—
*PI	Pair (50)	—
*PI	Pair (50)	—
3PI	Pair (50)	—
4PI	Pair (50)	—

All examples of No. SC6PD show the 40c essay.

New York #254-255, Geneva #45
Law of the Sea

*4		
5PDa	Card, #254PD-255PD, #G45TC with blue green sky (3)	800.
4PP	10 items (50)	—
5PP	10 items (50)	—
5PP	10 items (50)	—
4PI	Pair (50)	—
5PI	Pair (50)	—
5PI	Pair (50)	—

New York #256-257, Geneva #46-47, Souvenir Card #7
Peaceful Uses of Outer Space

75		
6PDa	Card, #256PD, #G46PD-G47PD (1)	—
7PDa	Cut from #256PDa (1)	—
7PDa	Card, #256PD-257PD, G46PD-G47PD (3)	825.
7PD	with approval handstamp (4)	—
6PP	8 items (150)	—
7PP	8 items (150)	—
6PP	8 items (50)	—
7PP	8 items (50)	—
6PI	Pair (100)	—
7PI	Pair (100)	—
6PI	Pair (50)	—
7PI	Pair (50)	—

New York #258-259, Geneva #48-49
International Women's Year

75		
8PD	On card dated "16 Oct. 1974" (4)	250.
9PD	(4)	250.
8PD	On card dated "16 Oct. 1974" (4)	325.
49PD	(4)	325.
8TC	bright blue background (on cards dated "17 Sep. 1974") (4)	—
48TC	red brown background (on cards dated "17 Sep. 1974") (4)	—
8PP	6 items (50)	—
9PP	6 items (50)	—
48PP	6 items (50)	—
49PP	6 items (50)	—
8PI	Pair (50)	—

259PI	Pair (50)	—
G48PI	Pair (50)	—
G49PI	Pair (50)	—

Six essays of the 18c stamp with "Nations Unies" inscription, and six essays of the 90c stamp with "United Nations" inscription exist.

New York #260-262, Geneva #50-52
UN, 30th Anniv.

1975		
261PDa	Card, #260PD-261PD, #G51PD, #G50TC in olive green, se-tenant (4)	1,200.
262PD	(5)	500.
G52PD	(1)	—
G52TC	With #G52aTC olive green (5)	700.
260PP	6 items (50)	—
261PP	6 items (50)	—
262PP	10 items (6)	—
G50PP	6 items (50)	—
G51PP	6 items (50)	—
G52PP	10 items (6)	—
260PI	Pair (50)	—
261PI	Pair (50)	—
262PI	Pair of souvenir sheets (26)	—
G50PI	Pair (50)	—
G51PI	Pair (50)	—
G52PI	Pair of souvenir sheets (26)	—

New York #263-264, Geneva #53-54
Namibia

1975		
264PDa	Card, #263PD-264PD, #G53PD-G54PD (9)	975.
263PP	8 items (50)	—
264PP	8 items (50)	—
G53PP	8 items (50)	—
G54PP	7 items (50)	—
263PI	Pair (50)	—
264PI	Pair (50)	—
G53PI	Pair (50)	—
G54PI	Pair (50)	—

New York #265-266, Geneva #55-56, Souvenir Card #8
UN Peace-keeping Operations

1975		
266PDa	Card, #265PD-266PD, #G55PD-G56PD (3)	1,300.
266PDb	Card, #266PD, #G55PD-G56PD, 10c essay of #265 (5)	1,200.
SC8PD	With approval handstamp (5)	—
265PI	Pair (25)	—
266PI	Pair (25)	—
G55PI	Pair (25)	—
G56PI	Pair (25)	—

New York #267-271
Definitives

1976		
267PD	(4)	225.
268PD	(3)	350.
269PD	(5)	110.
270PD	(8)	225.
271PD	(4)	200.
271TC	Dark green background (not approved cards dated "30 June 1975" (5)	—
267PP	10 items (25)	—
268PP	8 items (50)	—
269PP	3 items (50)	—
270PP	6 items (50)	—
271PP	10 items (25)	—
267PI	Pair (50)	—
268PI	Pair (50)	—
269PI	Pair (50)	—
270PI	Pair (50)	—
271PI	Pair (50)	—

New York #272-273, Geneva #57, Souvenir Card #9
World Federation of United Nations Associations

1976		
273PDa	Card, #272PD-273PD, #G57PD (4)	825.
SC9PD	With approval handstamp dated "18 Sep 1975" (4)	—
SC9TC	With light blue denominations on 1966 stamp (not approved) (5)	—
272PP	6 items (50)	—
273PP	6 items (50)	—
G57PP	6 items (50)	—
272PI	Pair (50)	—
273PI	Pair (50)	—
G57PI	Pair (50)	—

New York #274-275, Geneva #58
UN Conference on Trade and Development

1976		
G58PDa	Card, #G58PD, non-denominated essays of #274-275 (5)	.725
274PP	5 items (130)	—
275PP	5 items (130)	—
	Vert. pair with horiz. gutter (10)	—
G58PP	5 items (150)	—
274PI	Pair (80)	—
	Vert. pair with horiz. gutter (20)	—
275PI	Pair (80)	—

	Vert. pair with horiz. gutter (20)	—
G58PI	Pair (80)	—
	Vert. pair with horiz. gutter (20)	—

New York #276-277, Geneva #59-60
UN Conference on Human Settlements

1976		
277PDa	Card, #276PD-277PD, #G59PD-G60PD (4)	1,100.
276PP	12 items (50)	—
277PP	12 items (50)	—
G59PP	12 items (50)	—
G60PP	12 items (50)	—
276PI	Pair (50)	—
277PI	Pair (50)	—
G59PI	Pair (50)	—
G60PI	Pair (50)	—

New York #278-279, Geneva #61-62
UN Postal Administration, 25th Anniv.

1976		
279PDa	Card, #278PD-279PD, #G61PD-G62PD (5)	700.
278PP	5 items (64)	—
	Horiz. pair with vert. gutter (4)	—
	Vert. pair with horiz. gutter (4)	—
279PP	5 items (64)	—
	Horiz. pair with vert. gutter (4)	—
	Vert. pair with horiz. gutter (4)	—
G61PP	5 items (72)	—
	Horiz. pair with vert. gutter (4)	—
G62PP	5 items (63)	—
	Horiz. pair with vert. gutter (4)	—
	Vert. pair with horiz. gutter (4)	—

New York #280, Geneva #63, Souvenir Card #10
World Food Council

1976		
280PD	(5)	200.
G63PD	(5)	200.
SC10PD	With approval handstamp (12)	—
280PP	2 items (50)	—
G63PP	2 items (50)	—
280PI	Pair (50)	—
G63PI	Pair (50)	—

New York #281-282, Geneva #64, Souvenir Card #11
World Intellectual Property Organization

1977		
282PDa	Card, #281PD-282PD, #G64PD (4)	650.
SC11PD	With approval handstamp (4)	—
281PP	8 items (50)	—
282PP	8 items (50)	—
G64PP	8 items (50)	—
281PI	Pair (50)	—
282PI	Pair (50)	—
G64PI	Pair (50)	—

New York #283-284, Geneva #65-66
UN Water Conference

1977		
283PD	Cut out from #284PDb (1)	—
284PDa	Card, #283PD-284PD, #G65PD-G66PD (2)	925.
284PDb	Card, #284PD, #G65PD-G66PD (1)	—
284PDc	Card, #284PD, #G66PD (1)	—
283PP	6 items (50)	—
284PP	6 items (50)	—
G65PP	5 items (50)	—
G66PP	5 items (50)	—
283PI	Pair (50)	—
284PI	Pair (50)	—
G65PI	Pair (50)	—
G66PI	Pair (50)	—

New York #285-286, Geneva #67-68
UN Security Council

1977		
286PDa	Card, #285PD-286PD, essays of #G67-G68 with small top Chinese character (4)	975.
G68PDa	Card, #G67PD-G68PD (large Chinese character) (4)	450.
286PP	8 items (50)	—
G67PP	8 items (50)	—
G68PP	8 items (50)	—
285PI	Pair (50)	—
286PI	Pair (50)	—
G67PI	Pair (50)	—
G68PI	Pair (50)	—

A card with the two essays only (a cutout of No. 286PDa) with "not approved" handstamp exists.

New York #287-288, Geneva #69-70, Souvenir Card #12
Combat Racism

1977		
288PDa	Card, #287PD-288PD (4)	425.
G70PDa	Card, #G69PD-G70PD (4)	500.
SC12PD	With approval handstamp and specimen perfin (5)	—
287PP	3 items (50)	—
288PP	3 items (50)	—
G69PP	6 items (150)	—
G70PP	6 items (150)	—
287PI	Pair (175)	—

288PI	Pair (175)	—
G69PI	Pair (225)	—
G70PI	Pair (225)	—

New York #289-290, Geneva #71-72
Peaceful Uses of Atomic Energy

1977

290PDa	Card, #289PD-290PD, #G71PD-G72PD (4)	1,100.
290PDb	Card, #289PD-290PD, #G71PD, essay of #G72 with capital "F" in "Fins" (5)	975.
289PP	8 items (50)	—
290PP	8 items (50)	—
G71PP	6 items (50)	—
G72PP	6 items (50)	—
289PI	Pair (50)	—
290PI	Pair (50)	—
G71PI	Pair (50)	—
G72PI	Pair (50)	—

New York #291-293, Geneva #73
Definitives

1978

291PD	(4)	200.
292PD	(5)	225.
293PD	(4)	200.
G73PD	With approval handstamp (4)	225.
G73TC	Tree in deep brown (with "not approved" handstamp (6)	175.
G73PP	6 items (50)	—
291PI	Pair (50)	—
292PI	Pair (50)	—
293PI	Pair (75)	—
G73PI	Pair (50)	—

Six essays of No. 293 having "C" in Naciones not even with "A" exist on card with "not approved" handstamp.

New York #294-295, Geneva #74-75
Global Eradication of Smallpox

1978

295PDa	Card, #294PD-295PD, #G74PD-G75PD (5)	1,000.
294PP	2 items (50)	—
295PP	2 items (50)	—
G74PP	4 items (50)	—
G75PP	4 items (50)	—
294PI	Pair (50)	—
295PI	Pair (50)	—
G74PI	Pair (50)	—
G75PI	Pair (50)	—

New York #296-297, Geneva #76, Souvenir Card #13
Liberation, Justice and Cooperation for Namibia

1978

296PD	On perforated sheet layout (2)	—
297PD	On perforated sheet layout (1)	—
297PDa	Card, #296-297, #G76, perforated (4)	725.
297PDb	Card, #296-297 perforated, essay of #G76 ("F." and "S." same size, not approved) (5)	725.
G76PD	On perforated sheet layout (9)	—
SC13PD	With approval handstamp (5)	110.
296PP	6 items (50)	—
297PP	6 items (50)	—
G76PP	6 items (50)	—
296PI	Pair (50)	—
297PI	Pair (50)	—
G76PI	Pair (50)	—

The essay of No. G76 exists on a not approved perforated sheet layout.

New York #298-299, Geneva #77-78, Souvenir Card #14
Safety in the Air

1978

298PDa	Card, #298PD, #G77PD-G78PD (1)	—
299PD	Cut out from #298PDa (1)	—
299PDa	Card, #298PD-299PD, #G77PD-G78PD (3)	875.
SC14PD	With approval handstamp (4)	—
298PP	10 items (50)	—
299PP	10 items (50)	—
G77PP	6 items (50)	—
G78PP	6 items (50)	—
298PI	Pair (50)	—
299PI	Pair (50)	—
G77PI	Pair (50)	—
G78PI	Pair (50)	—

New York #300-301, Geneva #79-80
UN General Assembly

1978

301PDa	Card, #300PD-301PD, #G79PD-G80PD (4)	975.
300PP	4 items (50)	—
301PP	5 items (50)	—
G79PP	6 items (50)	—
G80PP	6 items (50)	—
300PI	Pair (25)	—
301PI	Pair (25)	—
G79PI	Pair (25)	—
G80PI	Pair (25)	—

New York #302-303, Geneva #81
Technical Cooperation Conference

1978

303PDa	Card, #302PD-303PD, #G81PD (3)	975.
302PP	10 items (50)	—
303PP	10 items (50)	—
G81PP	8 items (50)	—
302PI	Pair (50)	—
303PI	Pair (50)	—
G81PI	Pair (50)	—

Five not approved cards have essays of the set showing black behind closer cogwheels and text close to bottom frame. Value $725.

New York #304-307
Definitives

1979

304PD	(1)	—
304PDa	Card, #304PD-307PD (9)	—
304PDb	Card, #304PD, essays of #305, 306, 307 with inked-in corrections for printer (2)	875.
307PDa	Card, #305PD-307PD (3)	725.
304PP	8 items (50)	—
305PP	8 items (50)	—
306PP	6 items (50)	—
307PP	4 items (50)	—
304PI	Pair (50)	—
305PI	Pair (50)	—
306PI	Pair (75)	—
307PI	Pair (75)	—

Three cut-up not approved cards exist containing the three essays with inked-in corrections.
Nos. 306PI and 307PI include 25 pairs of reprints.

New York #308-309, Geneva #82-83
UN Disaster Relief Coordinator

1979

309PDa	Card, #308PD-309PD (4)	425.
G82PDa	Card, #G82PD-G83PD (1)	—
G83PDb	Card, #G82PD-G83PD, essays of #308-309 with inked-in corrections for printer (3)	875.
308PP	9 items (50)	—
309PP	9 items (50)	—
G82PP	4 items (50)	—
G83PP	4 items (50)	—
308PI	Pair (50)	—
309PI	Pair (50)	—
G82PI	Pair (50)	—
G83PI	Pair (50)	—

Two not approved cards contain the essays with inked-in corrections for printer.

New York #310-311, Geneva #84-85, Souvenir Card #15
International Year of the Child

1979

310PDa	Card, #310PD, essays of #G84-G85 (with IYC emblem above bottom of children's feet) (1)	—
311PD	Cut out from #310PDa (1)	—
311PDa	Card, #310PD-311PD, essays #G84-G85 (2)	1,350.
G85PDa	Card, #G84PD-G85PD (4)	625.
SC15PD	With manuscript approval (4)	—
310PP	9 items (20)	—
311PP	9 items (20)	—
G84PP	8 items (20)	—
G85PP	10 items (20)	—
310PI	Pair (40)	140.
311PI	Pair (40)	140.
G84PI	Pair (20)	140.
G85PI	Pair (20)	140.

One cut up not approved card contains the two essays. Five essays of No. SC15 marked "not approved" show the stamp essays.

Vienna #1-6
Definitives

1979

V6PDa	Card, #V1PD-V6PD (5)	2,000.
V1PP	5 items (50)	—
V2PP	5 items (150)	—
V3PP	5 items (50)	—
V4PP	5 items (50)	—
V5PP	5 items (50)	—
V6PP	5 items (50)	—
V1PI	Pair (50)	—
V2PI	Pair (150)	—
V3PI	Pair (50)	—
V4PI	Pair (50)	—
V5PI	Pair (50)	—
V6PI	Pair (50)	—

New York #312-313, Geneva #86
Namibia

1979

313PDa	Card, #312PD-313PD, #G86PD (4)	825.
312PP	8 items (50)	—
313PP	8 items (50)	—
G86PP	8 items (50)	—
312PI	Pair (50)	—
313PI	Pair (50)	—
G86PI	Pair (50)	—

One card of No. 313PDa is badly damaged.

New York #314-315, Geneva #87-88, Souvenir Card #16
International Court of Justice

1979

315PDa	Card, #314PD-315PD, #G87PD-G88PD 2 each (4)	
SC16PD	With "not approved" handstamp and "Specimen" perfin (5)	
314PP	4 items (50)	
315PP	4 items (50)	
G87PP	6 items (50)	
G88PP	7 items (50)	
314PI	Pair (50)	
315PI	Pair (50)	
G87PI	Pair (50)	
G88PI	Pair (50)	

New York #316-317, Geneva #89, Vienna #7
New International Economic Order

1980

316PD	(11)	
317PD	(5)	
G89PD	With approval handstamp (5)	
V7PD	(5)	
316PP	4 items (50)	
317PP	4 items (50)	
G89PP	4 items (50)	
V7PP	5 items (50)	
316PI	Pair (50)	
317PI	Pair (50)	
G89PI	Pair (50)	
V7PI	Pair (50)	

Five cards of No. 316PD are marked "not approved" but there are no discernable differences between it and approved proofs. Six "not approved" cards have essays of No. G89 with "Nouvel International Economique Ordre." Six "not approved" cards have essays of No. V7 with the same text.

Vienna #8
Definitive

1980

V8PD	(4)	
V8PP	11 items, perforated (250)	
V8PI	Pair (25)	

New York #318-319, Geneva #90-91, Vienna #9-10, Souvenir Card #17
Decade for Women

1980

318PD	(13)	
319PD	(11)	
G90PD	(13)	
G91PD	(5)	
V9PD	(5)	
V10PD	(5)	
SC17PD	With approval handstamp (5)	
318PP	4 items (50)	
319PP	4 items (50)	
G90PP	4 items (50)	
G91PP	4 items (50)	
V9PP	3 items (50)	
V10PP	2 items (50)	
318PI	Pair (50)	
319PI	Pair (50)	
G90PI	Pair (50)	
G91PI	Pair (50)	
V9PI	Pair (50)	
V10PI	Pair (50)	

New York #320-321, Geneva #92, Vienna #11
UN Peace-keeping Operations

1980

321PDa	Card, #320PD-321PD, #V11PD, essay of #G92 with "de" on top line (3)	
G92PD	(4)	
320PP	2 items (50)	
321PP	8 items (50)	
G92PP	4 items (50)	
V11PP	12 items (50)	
320PI	Pair (50)	
321PI	Pair (50)	
G92PI	Pair (50)	
V11PI	Pair (50)	

New York #322-324, Geneva #93-95, Vienna #12-14
UN, 35th Anniv.

1980

324PDa	Card, #324PD, #G95D, #V14PD (4)	1,0
324PDb	Card, #322PD-324PD, #G93PD-G94PD, #V12PD-V14PD, essay of #G95 with incomplete marginal inscription (3)	1,0
322PP	8 items (50)	
323PP	8 items (50)	
G93PP	6 items (300)	
G94PP	13 items (650)	
V12PP	3 items (50)	
V13PP	8 items (50)	
322PI	Pair (100)	
323PI	Pair (100)	
G93PI	Pair (100)	
G94PI	Pair (100)	
V12PI	Pair (175)	
V13PI	Pair (100)	

New York #325-340
Flags

D	Cut from #340PDa (1)	—
D	Cut from #340PDa (1)	—
Da	Card, #325PD-340PD (4)	3,500.
Db	Card, #326PD-331PD, #333PD-340PD (1)	—
340PP	Set of 20 sheets (1)	—
340PI	Set of 4 sheets (2)	—

Nos. 325-340PP, there are five progressive proof sheets issued sheet.

w York #341-342, Geneva #96-97, Vienna #15-16, Souvenir Card #18
Economic and Social Council

Da	Sheet, #341PD-342PD, #G96PD-G97PD, #V15PD-V16PD (4)	110.
PD	(4)	—
PD	(4)	—
PD	(4)	—
PD	(4)	—
8PD	(4)	—
?P	6 items (50)	—
?P	6 items (50)	—
PP	6 items (50)	—
PP	6 items (50)	—
PP	6 items (50)	—
PI	Pair (50)	—
PI	Pair (50)	—
PI	Pair (50)	—
PI	Pair (50)	—
PI	Pair (50)	—

essay of No. SC18 with curved cancel on 4s stamp has approved" handstamp.

New York #343, Geneva #98, Vienna #17
nalienable Rights of the Palestinian People

TCa	Card, #343TC blue, #G98PD, #V17PD (1)	625.
PD	(5)	—
PD	(5)	—
PP	4 items (50)	—
PP	5 items (50)	—
PP	4 items (50)	—
PI	Pair (50)	—
PI	Pair (50)	—
PI	Pair (50)	—

w York #344-345, Geneva #99-100, Vienna #18-19, Souvenir Card #19
Intl. Year of the Disabled

PD	Cut out from #G100PDa (1)	—
PDa	Card, #344PD, #G99PD-G100PD, #V18PD-V19PD, 31c essay of #345 (4)	1,450.
PDb	Card, #344PD, #G100PD, #V18PD-V19PD (4)	—
00PDa	Card, #G100PD, #V18PD-V19PD (1)	—
19PD	With "not approved" handstamp (9)	110.
PP	6 items (50)	—
PP	2 items (50)	—
9PP	2 items (50)	—
00PP	2 items (50)	—
8PP	6 items (50)	—
9PP	2 items (50)	—
4PI	Pair (50)	—
5PI	Pair (50)	—
9PI	Pair (50)	—
00PI	Pair (50)	—
8PI	Pair (50)	—
9PI	Pair (50)	—

All die proof cards are stamped "not approved." One example No. SC19PD has "35c" covering "31c."

New York #346-347, Geneva #101, Vienna #20
Art at the UN

81

7PDa	Card, #346PD-347PD, #G101PD, #V20PD (1)	1,050.
7PDb	Card, #347PD, #G101PD, #V20PD, 15c essay of #346 (not approved) (6)	—
6PP	5 items (50)	—
7PP	5 items (50)	—
01PP	5 items (50)	—
0PP	5 items (50)	—
6PI	Pair (50)	—
7PI	Pair (50)	—
01PI	Pair (50)	—
0PI	Pair (50)	—

New York #348-349, Geneva #102, Vienna #21, Souvenir Card #20
Conference on New and Renewable Sources of Energy

1981

348PDa	Card, #348PD, #G102PD, #V21PD, 31c essay of #349 (3)	.925
SC20PD	With approval and specimen hand-stamps (4)	—
348PP	6 items (50)	—
349PP	4 items (50)	—
G102PP	6 items (50)	—
V21PP	4 items (50)	—
348PI	Pair (50)	—
349PI	Pair (50)	—
G102PI	Pair (50)	—
V21PI	Pair (50)	—

All examples of No. SC20PD have the 31c essay.

New York #350-365
Flags

1981

357PDa	Card, #350PD-357PD (5)	—
365PDa	Card, #358PD-365PD (5)	2,300.
350-365PP	Set of 19 sheets (1)	—
350-365PI	Set of 4 sheets (2)	4,600.

On Nos. 350-365PP, there are four progressive sheets for the issued sheet containing Nos. 354-357, and five progressive proof sheets per issued sheet for the issued sheets containing Nos. 350-353, 358-361 and 362-365. Two sets of imperforate sheets of Nos. 350-353 and two sets of imperforate sheets of Nos. 354-357 exist with 15c denominations are essays.

New York #366-367, Geneva #103-104, Vienna #22-23
Volunteers Program, 10th Anniv.

1981

367PDa	Card, #367PD, #G103PD-G104PD, #V22PD-V23PD, 20c essay of #366 (3)	1,450.
G103TC	white background (1)	—
V22TC	white background (1)	—
V23TC	white background (1)	—
366PI	Pair (50)	—
367PI	Pair (50)	—
G103PI	Pair (50)	—
G104PI	Pair (50)	—
V22PI	Pair (50)	—
V23PI	Pair (50)	—

New York #368-370, Geneva #105-106, Vienna #24
Definitives

1982

370PDa	Card, #368PD-370PD, #G106PD, #V24PD, essay of #G105 with no "l" before "apartheid" (5)	1,450.
368PP	5 items (50)	—
369PP	5 items (50)	—
370PP	5 items (50)	—
G105PP	4 items (50)	—
G106PP	5 items (50)	—
V24PP	5 items (50)	—
368PI	Pair (50)	—
369PI	Pair (50)	—
370PI	Pair (50)	—
G105PI	Pair (50)	—
C106PI	Pair (50)	—
V24PI	Pair (50)	—

One example of No. 370PDa has all stamps canceled and #G105 altered.

New York #371-372, Geneva #107-108, Vienna #25-26, Souvenir Card #21
Environment Program, 10th Anniv.

1982

372PDa	Card, #371PD-372PD, #G107PD, #V25PD-V26PD, 1.30fr essay of #G108 (5)	1,600.
372PDb	Card, #372PD, #G107PD-G108PD, #V25PD-V26PD, 18c essay of #371 (4)	1,450.
SC21PD	(5)	—
371PP	8 items (50)	—
372PP	7 items (50)	—
G107PP	12 items (50)	—
G108PP	8 items (50)	—
V25PP	7 items (50)	—
V26PP	11 items (50)	—
371PI	Pair (50)	—
372PI	Pair (50)	—
G107PI	Pair (50)	—
G108PI	Pair (50)	—
V25PI	Pair (50)	—
V26PI	Pair (50)	—

One copy of No. 372PDb has had some stamps defaced. Five essays of No. SC21PD show the 18c essay, with one altered to change 18c to 20c.

New York #373, Geneva #109-110, Vienna #27, Souvenir Card #22
Exploration and Peaceful Uses of Outer Space

1982

373PDa	Card, #373PD, #G109PD-G110PD, #V27PD (4)	925.
G109PD	(4)	—
G110PD	(4)	—
V27PD	(4)	—
SC22PD	(4)	—
373PP	6 items (50)	—
G109PP	6 items (50)	—
G110PP	14 items (50)	—
V27PP	14 items (50)	—
373PI	Pair (50)	—
G109PI	Pair (50)	—
G110PI	Pair (50)	—
V27PI	Pair (50)	—

New York #374-389
Flags

1982

381PDa	Card, #374PD-381PD (5)	2,000.
389PDa	Card, #382PD-389PD (4)	2,000.
374-389PP	Set of 20 sheets (1)	—
374-389PI	Set of 4 sheets (2)	5,250.

On Nos. 374-389PP, there are five progressive proof sheets per issued sheet.

New York #390-391, Geneva #111-112, Vienna #28-29
Conservation and Protection of Nature

1982

390PDa	Card, #390PD, #G111PD, #V29PD, essays of #G112 and #V28 (1)	—
391PD	(1)	—
391PDa	Card, #390PD-391PD, #G111PD, #V29PD, essays of #G112 and #V28 (3)	1,400.
G112PD	(3)	250.
V29PD	(3)	200.
390PP	10 items (50)	—
391PP	10 items (50)	—
G111PP	10 items (50)	—
G112PP	10 items (50)	—
V28PP	10 items (50)	—
V29PP	10 items (50)	—
390PI	Pair (50)	—
391PI	Pair (50)	—
G111PI	Pair (50)	—
G112PI	Pair (50)	—
V28PI	Pair (50)	—
V29PI	Pair (50)	—

Essays of No. G112 have snake with lighter stripes. Essays of No. V28 have umlaut missing one dot.

New York #392-393, Geneva #113, Vienna #30
World Communications Year

1983

392PD	(5)	225.
393PD	(4)	200.
G113PD	(4)	200.
V30PD	(5)	200.
392TC	Dark blue and green colors switched (4)	300.
V30TC	Dark blue and green colors switched (3)	325.
392PP	10 items (50)	—
393PP	15 items (50)	—
G113PP	15 items (50)	—
V30PP	10 items (50)	—
392PI	Pair (50)	—
393PI	Pair (50)	—
G113PI	Pair (50)	—
V30PI	Pair (50)	—

New York #394-395, Geneva #114-115, Vienna #31-32, Souvenir Card #23
Safety at Sea

1983

395PDa	Card, #394PD-395PD & G114PD-G115PD, #V31PD-V32PD, #394TC-395TC, #G114TC (1)	—
395PDb	Card, #394PD-395PD, #G114PD (4)	750.
G115PDa	Card, #G115PD, #V31PD-V32PD, #394TC-395TC, #G114TC (10)	—
SC23PD	(5)	—
SC23TC	(6)	—
394PP	10 items (50)	—
395PP	8 items (50)	—
G114PP	11 items (50)	—
G115PP	5 items (50)	—
V31PP	5 items (50)	—
V32PP	8 items (50)	—
394PI	Pair (50)	—
395PI	Pair (50)	—
G114PI	Pair (50)	—
G115PI	Pair (50)	—
V31PI	Pair (50)	—
V32PI	Pair (50)	—

Nos. 394TC and G114TC have orange buoy lights instead of red, and No. 395TC has red violet line in ship instead of orange. These appear on No. SC23TC.

New York #396, Geneva #116, Vienna #33-34
World Food Program

1983

396PD	(3)	225.
G116PD	(3)	225.
V33PD	(3)	200.
V34PD	(3)	225.
396PI	Pair (25)	—
G116PI	Pair (25)	—
V33PI	Pair (25)	—
V34PI	Pair (25)	—

New York #397-398, Geneva #117-118, Vienna #35-36, Souvenir Card #24
UN Conference on Trade and Development
1983

398PDa	Card, #397PD-398PD, #G117PD-G118PD, #V35PD-V36PD, approval handstamp (4)	—
398PDb	Card, #397PD-398PD, #G117PD, #V36PD, essays of #G118 and #V35, (not approved, undated) (5)	1,300.
398PDc	As #398PDb, with red dot essays (not approved, dated) (5)	—
SC24PD	With approval handstamp (4)	—
SC24TC	With "not approved" handstamp (5)	—
397PP	5 items (50)	—
398PP	7 items (50)	—
G117PP	5 items (50)	—
G118PP	6 items (50)	—
V35PP	6 items (50)	—
V36PP	7 items (50)	—
397PI	Pair (50)	—
398PI	Pair (50)	—
G117PI	Pair (50)	—
G118PI	Pair (50)	—
V35PI	Pair (50)	—
V36PI	Pair (50)	—

Essays of Nos. G118 and V35 have blue rectangle instead of blue and yellow triangles on bottom row of flags, along with other differences. No. 398PDb has essays showing flag with green dot in 3rd row; No. 398PDc has red dot on this flag. No. SC24TC has Nos. G118 and V35 with lighter box bottom.

New York #399-414
Flags
1983

403PD	With approval handstamp (1)	240.
406PDa	Card, #399PD-402PD, 404PD-406PD, #403 essay (5)	1,600.
414PDa	Card, #407PD, 409PD-414PD, #408 essay (5)	2,100.
399-414PP	Set of 20 sheets (1)	—
399-414PI	Set of 4 sheets (2)	5,000.

The essay of No. 403 has fewer sun rays than on the issued stamp. The essay of No. 408 has incomplete ring above crest and thinner garlands at left and right. Nos. 413PD-414PD are marked "not approved" on No. 414PDa, but there is no appreciable difference between these and the issued stamps. On Nos. 399-414PP, there are five progressive proof sheets per issued sheet.

New York #415-416, Geneva #119-120, Vienna #37-38
Universal Declaration of Human Rights, 35th Anniv.
1983

415PD	mounted on presentation folder, perforated	450.
416PD	mounted on presentation folder, perforated	450.
G120PDa	Card, #G119PD-G120PD (10)	500.
V37PD	mounted on presentation folder, perforated	325.
V38PD	mounted on presentation folder, perforated	400.
415PP	7 items, with "Muster" overprint (32)	—
415PPa	6 items, without "Muster" overprint (24)	—
	Horiz. pair with vert. gutter, without "Muster" overprint (4)	—
416PP	7 items, with "Muster" overprint (24)	—
	Horiz. pair with vert. gutter, with "Muster" overprint (16)	—
416PPa	6 items, without "Muster" overprint (24)	—
	Horiz. pair with vert. gutter, without "Muster" overprint (4)	—
G119PP	7 items, with "Muster" overprint (24)	—
G119PPa	6 items, without "Muster" overprint (24)	—
	Horiz. pair with vert. gutter, without "Muster" overprint (4)	—
G120PP	7 items, with "Muster" overprint (24)	—
	Horiz. pair with vert. gutter, with "Muster" overprint (16)	—
G120PPa	6 items, without "Muster" overprint (24)	—
	Horiz. pair with vert. gutter, without "Muster" overprint (4)	—
V37PP	7 items, with "Muster" overprint (24)	—
	Horiz. pair with vert. gutter, with "Muster" overprint (16)	—
V37PPa	6 items, without "Muster" overprint (24)	—
	Horiz. pair with vert. gutter, without "Muster" overprint (4)	—
V38PP	7 items, with "Muster" overprint (24)	—
	Horiz. pair with vert. gutter, with "Muster" overprint (16)	—
V38PPa	6 items, without "Muster" overprint (24)	—
	Horiz. pair with vert. gutter, without "Muster" overprint (4)	—
415PI	Pair (64)	—
	Horiz. pair with vert. gutter (16)	—

416PI	Pair (64)	—
	Horiz. pair with vert. gutter (16)	—
G119PI	Pair (64)	—
	Horiz. pair with vert. gutter (16)	—
G120PI	Pair (64)	—
	Horiz. pair with vert. gutter (16)	—
V37PI	Pair (64)	—
	Horiz. pair with vert. gutter (16)	—
V38PI	Pair (64)	—
	Horiz. pair with vert. gutter (16)	—

On Nos. 415PP-416PP, G119PP-G120PP, V37PP-V38PP, one of the items with "Muster" overprint is a finished imperforate.

New York #417-418, Geneva #121, Vienna #39, Souvenir Card #25
Intl. Conference on Population
1984

417PD	(4)	240.
418PD	(4)	250.
G121PD	(4)	250.
V39PD	(4)	250.
SC25PD	With "not approved" handstamp (9)	—
417PP	8 items (50)	—
418PP	7 items (50)	—
G121PP	8 items (50)	—
V39PP	8 items (50)	—
417PI	Pair (50)	—
418PI	Pair (50)	—
G121PI	Pair (50)	—
V39PI	Pair (50)	—

No. 418PP does not include the blue progressive proof found in No. 417PP.

New York #419-420, Geneva #122-123, Vienna #40-41
World Food Day
1984

419PD	(5)	—
420PDa	Card, #419PD-420PD, #G122PD-G123PD, #V40PD-V41PD with "not approved" handstamp (8)	1,500.
419PP	6 items (50)	—
420PP	6 items (50)	—
G122PP	6 items (50)	—
G123PP	6 items (50)	—
V40PP	6 items (50)	—
V41PP	6 items (50)	—
419PI	Pair (50)	—
420PI	Pair (50)	—
G122PI	Pair (50)	—
G123PI	Pair (50)	—
V40PI	Pair (50)	—
V41PI	Pair (50)	—

There is no appreciable difference between approved and not approved examples of No. 419PD.

New York #421-422, Geneva #124-125, Vienna #42-43
World Heritage Sites
1984

422PDa	Card, #421PD-422PD, with approval handstamp (4)	875.
G125PDa	Card, #G124PD-G125PD, with approval handstamp (4)	625.
V43PDa	Card, #V42PD-V43PD, with approval handstamp (4)	625.
V43TCa	Card, #V42PD (darker sky), V43PD prussian blue sky, "not approved" handstamp (8)	875.
421PP	6 items (80)	—
	Horiz. pair with vert. gutter (10)	—
422PP	6 items (80)	—
	Horiz. pair with vert. gutter (10)	—
G124PP	6 items (80)	—
	Horiz. pair with vert. gutter (10)	—
G125PP	6 items (80)	—
	Horiz. pair with vert. gutter (10)	—
V42PP	6 items (80)	—
	Horiz. pair with vert. gutter (10)	—
V43PP	6 items (80)	—
	Horiz. pair with vert. gutter (10)	—
421PI	Pair (80)	—
	Horiz. pair with vert. gutter (20)	—
422PI	Pair (80)	—
	Horiz. pair with vert. gutter (20)	—
G124PI	Pair (80)	—
	Horiz. pair with vert. gutter (20)	—
G125PI	Pair (80)	—
	Horiz. pair with vert. gutter (20)	—
V42PI	Pair (80)	—
	Horiz. pair with vert. gutter (20)	—
V43PI	Pair (80)	—
	Horiz. pair with vert. gutter (20)	—

Four cards like No. 422PDa with "not approved" handstamp contain essays with slightly different vignettes having taller sky area that is brighter blue and with less distinct designs. Four cards like No. G125PDa contain essays lacking "F.S." before denominations.

New York #423-424, Geneva #126-127, Vienna #44-45
Future for Refugees
1984

424PDa	Card, #423PD-424PD, #G126PD-G127PD, #V44PD-V45PD (2)	—
424PDb	Card, #423PD, #G127PD, 2 each #424PD, #G126PD, #V44PD-V45PD (3)	—

424PDc	Card, #423PD-424PD, #G126PD-G127PD, #V44PD-V45PD, #423TC-424TC, #G126TC-G127TC, V44TC-V45TC (5)	—
424TCa	Card, #423TC-424TC, #G126TC-G127TC, #V44TC-V45TC (1)	
423PP	2 items (50)	—
G126PP	2 items (50)	—
G127PP	2 items (50)	—
V44PP	2 items (50)	—
V45PP	2 items (50)	—
423PI	Pair (50)	—
424PI	Pair (25)	—
G126PI	Pair (50)	—
G127PI	Pair (50)	—
V44PI	Pair (50)	—
V45PI	Pair (50)	—

Trial color items have backgrounds in buff.

New York #425-440
Flags
1984

432PDa	Card, #429PD-432PD (1)	
432PDb	Card, 2 each #429PD-432PD (2)	
436PDa	Card, #425PD, 427PD, 433PD-436PD, essays of #426, 428 (5)	
440PDa	Card, #437PD-440PD (1)	
440PDb	Card, 2 each #437PD-440PD (2)	
425-440PP	Set of 21 sheets (1)	
425-440PI	Set of 4 sheets (2)	

Essays of Nos. 426 and 428 have country name in sm type. On Nos. 425-440PP, there are six progressive p sheets for the issued sheet containing Nos. 429-432, and progressive proof sheets for the issued sheets containing 425-428, 433-436 and 437-440.

New York #441-442, Geneva #128, Vienna #46-Souvenir Card #26
Intl. Youth Year
1984

441PD	With approval handstamp (4)	
442PD	With approval handstamp (3)	
G128PD	With approval handstamp (4)	
V46PD	(4)	
V47PD	(4)	
SC26PD	With approval handstamp (4)	
G128TC	Greenish black strand in center (not approved) (5)	
SC26TC	With #G128TC "not approved" handstamp (5)	
441PP	7 items (50)	
442PP	9 items (50)	
G128PP	9 items (50)	
V46PP	7 items (50)	
V47PP	7 items (50)	
441PI	Pair (50)	
442PI	Pair (50)	
G128PI	Pair (50)	
V46PI	Pair (50)	
V47PI	Pair (50)	

Five "not approved" essays of No. 441 and four of No. have "N" in "Nations" not touching white frame at bottom. A with a cutout version of the approved No. 442, but with a approved handstamp, and a card with a cutout essay of 442 with an "approved" handstamp exist, probably in error.

New York #443, Geneva #129-130, Vienna #48
Souvenir Card #27
Intl. Labor Organization
1985

443PD	Card, imperforate sheet of 50 stamps (1)	
443PDa	Card, #443PD (single), #G129PD (single) (4)	
G130PDa	Card, #G130PD (single), #V48PD (single) (4)	5
V48PD	Card, imperforate sheet of 50 stamps (4)	
SC27PD	With approval handstamp (4)	
443PI	Pair (50)	
G129PI	Pair (50)	
G130PI	Pair (50)	
V48PI	Pair (50)	

Essays of No. SC27 exist which have the 1954 stamp wit buff background.

New York #444, Geneva #131-132, Vienna #49
UN University
1985

444PDa	Card, #444PD, #G131PD-G132PD, #V49PD, with approval handstamp (5)	1,
G132TC	Bright colors in background ("not approved" handstamp) (6)	4
444PP	6 items (50)	
G131PP	6 items (50)	
G132PP	6 items (50)	
V49PP	6 items (50)	
444PI	Pair (50)	
G131PI	Pair (50)	
G132PI	Pair (50)	
V49PI	Pair (50)	

New York #445-446, Geneva #133-134, Vienna #50-51

Definitives

5		
Da	Card, #445PD, #G133PD-G134PD, #V50PD-V51PD, #446TC ("not approved handstamp") (4)	1,600.
Da	Card, #445PD-446PD, #G134PD (4)	775.
P	4 items (50)	—
P	5 items (50)	—
PP	7 items (50)	—
PP	3 items (50)	—
P	5 items (50)	—
P	5 items (50)	—
I	Pair (50)	—
I	Pair (50)	—

. 446TC has a lighter blue emblem. Other items in No. Da were declared "not approved," but do not have any eciable difference from approved items.

New York #447-449, Geneva #135-137, Vienna #52-54

UN, 40th Anniv.

5		
Da	Card, 4 each #447PD, #G135PD, #V52PD (1)	—
Da	Card, 4 each #448PD, #G136PD, #V53PD (1)	—
PDa	Card, #447PD-449PD, #G135PD-G137PD, #V52PD-V54PD (1)	1,850.
PDb	Card, #449PD, #G137PD, #V54PD (4)	—
P	5 items (50)	—
P	5 items (50)	—
P	6 items (36)	—
PP	5 items (50)	—
PP	5 items (50)	—
PP	6 items (36)	—
PP	5 items (50)	—
PP	5 items (50)	—
PP	6 items (36)	—
I	Pair (50)	—
I	Pair (50)	—
I	Pair of souvenir sheets (27)	—
5PI	Pair (50)	—
6PI	Pair (50)	—
7PI	Pair of souvenir sheets (27)	—
I	Pair (50)	—
I	Pair (50)	—
I	Pair of souvenir sheets (27)	—

New York #450-465

Flags

5		
PDa	Card, #450PD-455PD, 457PD-465PD, essay of #456 (5)	2,900.
-465PP	Set of 24 sheets (1)	—
-465PI	Set of 4 sheets (2)	4,000.

ssay of Nos. 456 has thin-lined star. On Nos. 425-440PP, e are six progressive proof sheets per issued sheet.

New York #466-467, Geneva #138-139, Vienna #55-56, Souvenir Card #28

UNICEF Child Survival Campaign

35		
PD	(4)	300.
PD	Card, with cut-up pane of 50 (1)	—
PD	(4)	300.
PDa	Card, with cut-up pane of 50 (1)	—
38PD	(4)	300.
38PDa	Card, with cut-up pane of 50 (1)	—
39PD	(4)	225.
39PDa	Card, with cut-up pane of 50 (1)	—
5PD	(4)	300.
5PDa	Card, with cut-up pane of 50 (1)	—
6PD	(4)	250.
6PDa	Card, with cut-up pane of 50 (1)	—
28PD	(4)	—
5PP	5 items (50)	—
7PP	5 items (50)	—
38PP	5 items (50)	—
39PP	5 items (50)	—
5PP	5 items (50)	—
6PP	5 items (50)	—
5PI	Pair (50)	—
7PI	Pair (50)	—
38PI	Pair (50)	—
39PI	Pair (50)	—
5PI	Pair (50)	—
6PI	Pair (50)	—

New York #468, Geneva #140, Vienna #57

Africa in Crisis

86		
8PDa	Card, #468PD, #G140PD, essay of #V57 (4)	—
8PP	5 items (50)	—
40PP	4 items (50)	—
7PP	4 items (50)	—
8PI	Pair (50)	—
40PI	Pair (50)	—
7PI	Pair (50)	—

One example of No. 468PDa has essay of No. V57 corrected show small loop of "8" at top as in the issued stamp.

New York #472a, Geneva #144a, Vienna #61a

UN Development Program

1986		
472aPD	(4)	825.
472aPDa	Card, pane of 10 blocks (2)	—
G144aPD	(4)	825.
G144aPDa	Card, pane of 10 blocks (2)	—
V61aPD	(4)	825.
V61aPDa	Card, pane of 10 blocks (2)	—
472aPP	6 items (10 blocks)	—
G144aPP	6 items (10 blocks)	—
V61aPP	6 items (10 blocks)	—
472aPI	Pair (20)	—
G144aPI	Pair (20)	—
V61aPI	Pair (20)	—

Geneva #145

Definitive

1986		
G145PD	(5)	—
G145PP	5 items (50)	—
G145PI	Pair (50)	—

New York #473-474, Geneva #146-147, Vienna #62-63, Souvenir Card #29

Philately

1986		
473PDa	Partial pane of 39 with approval handstamp on reverse (1)	—
473PDb	Full pane of 50 with approval handstamp on reverse (3)	—
474PDa	Imperforate pane of 50 with approval handstamp on reverse (4)	—
G146PDa	Imperforate pane of 50 with approval handstamp on reverse (4)	—
G147PDa	Partial pane of 41 with approval handstamp on reverse (1)	—
G147PDb	Full pane of 50 with approval handstamp on reverse (3)	—
V62PDa	Imperforate pane of 50 with approval handstamp on reverse (4)	—
V63PDa	Partial pane of 41 with approval handstamp on reverse (1)	—
V63PDb	Full pane of 50 with approval handstamp on reverse (4)	—
SC29PD	(3)	—
473TC	greenish black (5)	725.
474TC	purple (1)	725.
474TC	blue (1)	725.
474TC	red brown (1)	725.
474TC	olive brown (1)	725.
474TC	dark green (1)	725.
G146TC	purple (1)	725.
G146TC	blue (1)	725.
G146TC	reddish purple (1)	725.
G146TC	greenish black (1)	725.
G146TC	dark olive brown (1)	725.
G147TC	dark blue (5)	775.
V62TC	purple (1)	725.
V62TC	blue (1)	725.
V62TC	red brown (1)	725.
V62TC	greenish black (1)	725.
V62TC	dark olive brown (1)	725.
V63TC	greenish black (5)	775.

New York #475-476, Geneva #148-149, Vienna #64-65, Souvenir Card #30

International Peace Year

1986		
475PD	(4)	300.
475PDa	Card, imperforate pane of 50 (1)	—
476PD	(4)	250.
476PDa	Card, imperforate pane of 50 (1)	—
G148PD	(4)	450.
G148PDa	Card, imperforate pane of 50 (1)	—
G149PD	(4)	250.
V64PD	(1)	300.
V65PD	(4)	—
V65PDa	Card, imperforate pane of 50 (1)	—
SC30PD	(4)	—
475PP	4 items (50)	—
476PP	4 items (50)	—
G148PP	4 items (50)	—
G149PP	4 items (50)	—
V64PP	4 items (50)	—
V65PP	3 items (50)	—
475PI	Pair (50)	—
476PI	Pair (50)	—
G148PI	Pair (50)	—
G149PI	Pair (50)	—
V64PI	Pair (50)	—
V65PI	Pair (50)	—

Essays of No. V64 with 7s denominations exist in three cards with singles and one card with an imperforate pane of 50.

New York #477-492

Flags

1986		
492PDa	Card, #477PD-492PD (5)	3,250.
477-492PP	Set of 24 sheets (1)	—
477-492PI	Set of 4 sheets (2)	4,000.

On Nos. 477-492PP, there are six progressive proof sheets per issued sheet.

New York #493, Geneva #150, Vienna #66

World Federation of UN Associations, 40th Anniv.

1986		
493PD	(3)	525.
493PDa	Imperforate souvenir sheet with cancel lines added (1)	—
G150PD	(3)	300.
G150PDa	Imperforate souvenir sheet with cancel lines added (1)	—
V66PD	(3)	400.
V66PDa	Imperforate souvenir sheet with cancel lines added (1)	—
493PP	8 items (16)	—
G150PP	11 items (16)	—
V66PP	6 items (16)	—
493PI	souvenir sheets (32)	—
G150PI	souvenir sheets (32)	—
V66PI	souvenir sheets (32)	—

New York #494, Geneva #151, Vienna #67

Trygve Lie

1987		
494PD	On imperforate sheet layout (1)	—
494PDa	Card, #494PD, #G151PD, V67PD (4)	725.
G151PD	On imperforate sheet layout (1)	—
V67PD	On imperforate sheet layout (1)	—
494PP	10 items (50)	—
G151PP	10 items (50)	—
V67PP	10 items (50)	—
494PI	Pair (50)	—
G151PI	Pair (100)	—
V67PI	Pair (50)	—

Geneva #152-153

Definitives

1987		
G152PD	(1)	375.
G153PD	(4)	—
G153TCa	Card, 2 #G153TC dark blue panel (5)	—
G153TCb	Card, imperforate pane of 50 #G153TC dark blue panel (2)	.525
G152PP	6 items (50)	—
G153PP	5 items (50)	—
G152PI	Pair (50)	—
G153PI	Pair (50)	—

Six essays of No. G152 with design 33mm high exist on cards marked "approved text only."

New York #495-496, Geneva #154-155, Vienna #68-69, Souvenir Card #31

International Year of Shelter for the Homeless

1987		
496PDa	Card, #495PD-496PD, #G154PD-G155PD, #V68PD-V69PD (4)	1,350.
SC31PD	(3)	—
495PP	6 items (80)	—
	Horiz. pair with vert. gutter (10)	—
496PP	6 items (80)	—
	Horiz. pair with vert. gutter (10)	—
G154PP	6 items (80)	—
	Horiz. pair with vert. gutter (10)	—
G155PP	6 items (80)	—
	Horiz. pair with vert. gutter (10)	—
V68PP	6 items (80)	—
	Horiz. pair with vert. gutter (10)	—
V69PP	6 items (80)	—
	Horiz. pair with vert. gutter (10)	—
495PI	Pair (80)	—
	Horiz. pair with vert. gutter (20)	—
496PI	Pair (80)	—
	Horiz. pair with vert. gutter (20)	—
G154PI	Pair (80)	—
	Horiz. pair with vert. gutter (20)	—
G155PI	Pair (80)	—
	Horiz. pair with vert. gutter (20)	—
V68PI	Pair (80)	—
	Horiz. pair with vert. gutter (20)	—
V69PI	Pair (80)	—
	Horiz. pair with vert. gutter (20)	—

New York #497-498, Geneva #156-157, Vienna #70-71

Fight Drug Abuse

1987		
498PDa	Card, #497PD-498PD, #G156PD-G157PD, #V70PD-V71PD with approval handstamp (5)	1,450.
497PP	8 items (50)	—
498PP	8 items (50)	—
G156PP	8 items (50)	—
G157PP	8 items (50)	—
V70PP	8 items (50)	—
V71PP	8 items (50)	—
497PI	Pair (100)	—
498PI	Pair (100)	—
G156PI	Pair (100)	—
G157PI	Pair (100)	—
V70PI	Pair (100)	—
V71PI	Pair (100)	—

Six "not approved" cards contain essays of the six stamps, each lacking the white line separating the halves of the vignette.

Vienna #72-73
Definitives

1987

V73PDa	Card, #V72PD-V73PD (5)	575.
V72PP	8 items (50)	—
V73PP	7 items (50)	—
V72PI	Pair (100)	—
V73PI	Pair (100)	—

New York #499-514
Flags

1987

511PDa	Card, #500PD, 501PD, 503PD, 507PD, 509PD, 511PD (1)	—
514PDa	Card, #499PD-514PD (5)	3,750.
514PDb	Card, #499PD, 500PD, 502PD, 504PD 506PD, 508PD, 510PD, 512PD-514PD (1)	—
499-514PP	Set of 24 sheets (1)	—
499-502PI	Sheet (2)	—
503-506PI	Sheet (2)	—

On Nos. 499-514PP, there are six progressive proof sheets per issued sheet.

New York #515-516, Geneva #158-159, Vienna #74-75
United Nations Day

1987

515PDa	Card, #515PD, #V74PP, essay of #G158 (1)	—
516PDa	Card, #516PD, #G159PP, #V75PD (1)	—
516PDb	Card, #515PD-516PD, #G159PD, #V74PD-V75PD, essay of #G158 (4)	1,250.
515PP	8 items (36)	—
	Cross gutter block (3)	—
	Horiz. pair with vert. gutter (6)	—
	Vert. pair with horiz. gutter (18)	—
516PP	8 items (36)	—
	Cross gutter block (3)	—
	Horiz. pair with vert. gutter (6)	—
	Vert. pair with horiz. gutter (18)	—
G158PP	8 items (36)	—
	Cross gutter block (3)	—
	Horiz. pair with vert. gutter (6)	—
	Vert. pair with horiz. gutter (18)	—
G159PP	8 items (36)	—
	Cross gutter block (3)	—
	Horiz. pair with vert. gutter (6)	—
	Vert. pair with horiz. gutter (18)	—
V74PP	8 items (36)	—
	Cross gutter block (3)	—
	Horiz. pair with vert. gutter (6)	—
	Vert. pair with horiz. gutter (18)	—
V75PP	8 items (36)	—
	Cross gutter block (3)	—
	Horiz. pair with vert. gutter (6)	—
	Vert. pair with horiz. gutter (18)	—
515PI	Pair (12)	—
516PI	Pair (12)	—
G158PI	Pair (28)	—
	Cross gutter block (3)	—
	Horiz. pair with vert. gutter (6)	—
	Vert. pair with horiz. gutter (18)	—
G159PI	Pair (28)	—
	Cross gutter block (3)	—
	Horiz. pair with vert. gutter (6)	—
	Vert. pair with horiz. gutter (18)	—
V74PI	Pair (28)	—
	Cross gutter block (3)	—
	Horiz. pair with vert. gutter (6)	—
	Vert. pair with horiz. gutter (18)	—
V75PI	Pair (28)	—
	Cross gutter block (3)	—
	Horiz. pair with vert. gutter (6)	—
	Vert. pair with horiz. gutter (18)	—

Essay of No. G158 lacks accent in "Journée."

New York #517-518, Geneva #160-161, Vienna #76-77, Souvenir Card #32
Immunize Every Child

1987

518PDa	Card, #517PD-518PD, #G161PD, #V76PD-V77PD, 35c essay of #G160 (11)	1,500.
SC32PD	(11)	—
517PP	11 items (50)	—
518PP	11 items (50)	—
G160PP	11 items (50)	—
G161PP	12 items (50)	—
V76PP	12 items (50)	—
V77PP	9 items (50)	—
517BPI	Pair (50)	—
518PI	Pair (50)	—
G160PI	Pair (75)	—
G161PI	Pair (75)	—
V76PI	Pair (75)	—
V77PI	Pair (75)	—

All examples of No. SC32PD have the essay of No. G160. No appreciable difference could be found between approved and not approved examples of Nos. 518PDa or SC32PD.

New York #519-520, Geneva #162-163, Vienna #78-79
International Fund for Agricultural Development

1988

520PDa	Card, #519PD-520PD, #G162PD-G163PD, #V78PD-V79PD (4)	1,550.
519PP	8 items (50)	—
520PP	8 items (50)	—
G162PP	9 items (50)	—
G163PP	9 items (50)	—
V78PP	9 items (50)	—
V79PP	9 items (50)	—
519PI	Pair (50)	—
520PI	Pair (50)	—
G162PI	Pair (50)	—
G163PI	Pair (50)	—
V78PI	Pair (50)	—
V79PI	Pair (50)	—

New York #521, Geneva #164
Definitives

1988

521PD	(4)	575.
G164PD	(6)	300.
521PP	6 items (50)	—
G164PP	11 items (50)	—
521PI	Pair (50)	—
G164PI	Pair (50)	—

New York #523a, Geneva #166a, Vienna #81a
Survival of the Forests

1988

523aPDa	Card, imperforate pane of 6 pairs with approval handstamp (6)	2,750.
523aPDb	Card, perforated pane of 6 pairs with approval handstamp (1)	—
G166aPDa	Card, imperforate pane of 6 pairs with approval handstamp (7)	2,400.
V81aPDa	Card, imperforate pane of 6 pairs with approval handstamp (7)	2,400.
523aPP	8 items (6 pairs)	—
G166aPP	8 items (6 pairs)	—
V81aPP	8 items (6 pairs)	—
523aPI	Pair (12)	—
G166aPI	Pair (24)	—
V81aPI	Pair (24)	—

Panes on Nos. 523aPDa, 523aPDb, G166aPDa, V81aPDa are not affixed to cards but are between stamp mounts.

New York #524-525, Geneva #167-168, Vienna #82-83, Souvenir Card #33
Intl. Volunteer Day

1988

524PDa	Card, #524PD, #G167PD-G168PD, #V82PD-V83PD with approval handstamp (4)	1,400.
525PDa	Card, #525PD, #G168PD, #V83PD, essays of #524, #G167, #V82 with "not approved" hand-stamp (4)	875.
SC33PD	(4)	—
SC33TC	light blue signature (4)	—
524PP	6 items (40)	—
525PP	6 items (40)	—
525PPa	Horiz. se-tenant pair with vert. gutter, #524PP-525PP (10)	—
G167PP	6 items (40)	—
G168PP	6 items (40)	—
G168PPa	Horiz. se-tenant pair with vert. gutter, #G167PP-G168PP (10)	—
V82PP	6 items (40)	—
V83PP	6 items (40)	—
V83PPa	Horiz. se-tenant pair with vert. gutter, #V82PP-V83PP (10)	—
524PI	Pair (70)	—
525PI	Pair (70)	—
G167PI	Pair (70)	—
G168PI	Pair (70)	—
V82PI	Pair (70)	—
V83PI	Pair (70)	—

Essays have incomplete dates at bottom.

New York #526-527, Geneva #169-170, Vienna #84-85, Souvenir Card #34
Health in Sports

1988

526PD	With approval handstamp (2)	250.
526PDa	Card, #526PD, #527TC	—
526PDb	Card, imperforate pane of 50 #526PD (1)	—
527PD	(6)	150.
527PDa	Card, 2 #527PD (1)	—
527PDb	Card, imperforate pane of 50 #527PD (2)	—
G169PD	(6)	350.
G169PDa	Card, 2 #G169PD (1)	—
G169PDb	Card, imperforate pane of 50 #G169PD (2)	—
G170PD	With approval handstamp (2)	350.
G170PDa	Card, #G170PD, #G170TC (1)	—
G170PDb	Card, imperforate pane of 50 #G170PD (1)	—
V84PD	With approval handstamp (2)	450.
V84PDa	Card, #V84PD, #V84TC (1)	—
V84PDb	Card, imperforate pane of 50 #V84PD (1)	—
V85PD	(6)	450.
V85PDa	Card, 2 #V85PD (1)	—
V85PDb	Card, imperforate pane of 50 #V85PD (2)	—

SC34PD	With approval handstamp (5)	—
526TC	Card, darker brown in LL part of vignette (not approved) (4)	—
526TCa	Card, imperforate pane of 50 #526TC (1)	—
G170TC	Card, black "F.S." (not approved) (4)	—
G170TCa	Card, imperforate pane of 50 #G170TC (1)	—
V84TC	Card, red splotches in UL of vignette (not approved) (4)	—
V84TCa	Card, imperforate pane of 50 #V84TC (109)	—
SC34TC	With #526TC (not approved) (4)	—
526PP	4 items (50)	—
527PP	4 items (50)	—
G169PP	4 items (50)	—
C170PP	4 items (50)	—
V84PP	5 items (50)	—
V85PP	4 items (50)	—
526PI	Pair (50)	—
527PI	Pair (50)	—
G169PI	Pair (50)	—
G170PI	Pair (45)	—
V84PI	Pair (50)	—
V85PI	Pair (50)	—

No appreciable difference could be seen between appr and not approved examples of Nos. 527PD, G169PD V85PD.

New York #528-543
Flags

1988

543PDa	Card, #540PD, 543PD (2)	—
543PDb	Card, #540PD, 543PD, 22c es-says of #528-539, 541-542 (2)	—
528-543PP	Set of 24 sheets (1)	—
528-543PI	Set of 4 sheets (1)	3

Nine cards each containing 22c essays of Nos. 528-543 Value $2,900 each. On Nos. 528-543PP, there are six prog sive proof sheets per issued sheet.

New York #544-545, Geneva #171-172, Vienn #86-87
Universal Declaration of Human Rights, 40th Anniv.

1988

545PDa	Card, #544PD-545PD, #G171PD-G172PD, #V86PD-V87PD (5)	2
G172PDa	Card, #172PD, 90c essay of #G172 (6)	
544PP	6 items (50)	—
545PP	6 items (1)	—
G171PP	6 items (50)	—
G172PP	6 items (1)	—
V86PP	6 items (50)	—
V87PP	6 items (1)	—
544PI	Pair (50)	—
545PI	souvenir sheets (2)	—
G171PI	Pair (50)	—
G172PI	souvenir sheets (2)	—
V86PI	Pair (50)	—
V87PI	souvenir sheets (2)	—

New York #546-547, Geneva #173-174, Vienn #88-89, Souvenir Card #35
World Bank

1989

547PDa	Card, #546PD-547PD, #G173PD-G174PD, #V88PD-V89PD with ap-proval handstamp (4)	1,
547PDb	Card, #547PD in slightly lighter col-ors, #V88PD, #G173TC, essays of #546, #G174, #V89 (5)	1,
SC35PD	With "29 Aug. 1988" handstamp on back (4)	—
546PP	6 items (40)	—
547PP	6 items (40)	—
547PPa	Vert. se-tenant pair with horiz. gut-ter, #546PP-547PP (10)	—
G173PP	6 items (40)	—
G174PP	6 items (40)	—
G174PPa	Vert. se-tenant pair with horiz. gut-ter, #G173PP-G174PP (10)	—
V88PP	6 items (40)	—
V89PP	6 items (40)	—
V89PPa	Vert. se-tenant pair with horiz. gut-ter, #V88PP-V89PP (10)	—
546PI	Pair (40)	—
547PI	Pair (40)	—
G173PI	Pair (70)	—
G174PI	Pair (70)	—
G174PIa	Vert. se-tenant pair with horiz. gut-ter, #G173PI-G174PI (10)	—
V88PI	Pair (50)	—
V89PI	Pair (50)	—

No. G173TC has lighter orange background. Essays of N 546, G174, and V89 have incomplete years at bottom.

New York #548, Geneva #175, Vienna #90
UN Peace-keeping Force

1989

548PD	Imperforate pane of 50 with "not ap-proved" handstamp (1)	
548PDa	Card, #548PD, #G175PD, #V90PD (5)	
G175PD	Imperforate pane of 50 with "not ap-proved" handstamp (1)	
V90PD	Imperforate pane of 50 with "not ap-proved" handstamp (1)	

PP	6 items (90)	—
	Horiz. pair with vert. gutter (5)	—
5PP	6 items (90)	—
	Horiz. pair with vert. gutter (5)	—
PP	6 items (90)	—
	Horiz. pair with vert. gutter (5)	—
PI	Pair (70)	—
5PI	Pair (138)	—
	Horiz. pair with vert. gutter (10)	—
PI	Pair (138)	—
	Horiz. pair with vert. gutter (10)	—

o appreciable difference could be seen between approved
not approved examples of No. 548PDa.

New York #549
Definitive

9		
PD	(9)	—
PP	6 items (64)	—
	Cross gutter block (1)	—
	Horiz. pair with vert. gutter (8)	—
	Vert. pair with horiz. gutter (8)	—
PI	Pair (24)	—

o appreciable difference could be seen between approved
not approved examples of No. 549PD.

New York #550-551, Geneva #176-177, Vienna #91-92, Souvenir Card #36
World Weather Watch

89		
PDa	Card, #550PD-551PD, #G176PD-G177PD, #V91PD-V92PD (9)	—
36PD	(4)	—
PP	6 items (40)	—
PP	6 items (40)	—
PPa	Vert. se-tenant pair with horiz. gutter, #550PP-551PP (10)	—
76PP	6 items (40)	—
77PP	6 items (40)	—
77PPa	Vert. se-tenant pair with horiz. gutter, #G176PP-G177PP (10)	—
1PP	6 items (40)	—
2PP	6 items (40)	—
2PPa	Vert. se-tenant pair with horiz. gutter, #V91PP-V92PP (10)	—
PI	(50 pairs)	—
1PI	(50 pairs)	—
76PI	(70 pairs)	—
77PI	(70 pairs)	—
77PIa	Vert. se-tenant pair with horiz. gutter, #G176PI-G177PI (10)	—
1PI	(50 pairs)	—
2PI	(50 pairs)	—

No appreciable difference could be seen between approved
d not approved examples of No. 551PDa.

New York #552-553, Geneva #178-179, Vienna #93-94
Offices in Vienna, 10th Anniv.

89		
2PD	With approval handstamp (4)	—
3PD	(4)	—
78PD	(4)	—
79PDa	Card, #G179PD, #G179TC orange background, #G179TC dull green background (4)	—
3PD	(4)	—
4PD	(9)	—
2PP	10 items (25)	—
3PP	12 items (25)	—
178PP	10 items (25)	—
179PP	10 items (25)	—
3PP	10 items (25)	—
4PP	10 items (25)	—
2PI	(24 pairs)	—
3PI	(24 pairs)	—
178PI	(24 pairs)	—
179PI	(24 pairs)	—
3PI	(24 pairs)	—
4PI	(24 pairs)	—

Five not approved essays of #552 have clearly defined cross-
atching in background. There is no appreciable difference
etween approved and not approved examples of No. V94PD.
he item from No. G179PP and V93PP is blank as it is from
ogressive proof sheet showing only black sheet margins.

New York #554-569
Flags

989		
58PDa	Card, #558PD-561PD, 563PD, 564PD, 566PD-568PD (6)	—
69PDa	Card, #554PD-569PD (5)	—
54-569PP	Set of 24 sheets (1)	—
54-569PI	Set of 4 sheets (2)	—

On Nos. 554-569PP, there are six progressive proof sheets
er issued sheet.

New York #570-571, Geneva #180-181, Vienna #95-96
Human Rights

989		
70PD	Strip of 3 + 3 labels (4)	—
71PD	Strip of 3 + 3 labels (4)	—
71PDa	Card, #570PD-571PD, #G180PD-G181PD, #V95PD-V96PD (5)	—
180PD	3 singles or strip of 3 + 3 labels (4)	—

G181PD	Strip of 3 + 3 labels (4)	—
V95PD	Strip of 3 + 3 labels (4)	—
V96PD	3 singles or strip of 3 + 3 labels (4)	—
570PP	6 items (20)	—
	Cross gutter block (1)	—
	Horiz. pair with vert. gutter (2)	—
	Vert. pair with horiz. gutter (10)	—
571PP	6 items (20)	—
	Cross gutter block (1)	—
	Horiz. pair with vert. gutter (2)	—
	Vert. pair with horiz. gutter (10)	—
G180PP	6 items (20)	—
	Cross gutter block (1)	—
	Horiz. pair with vert. gutter (2)	—
	Vert. pair with horiz. gutter (10)	—
G181PP	6 items (20)	—
	Cross gutter block (1)	—
	Horiz. pair with vert. gutter (2)	—
	Vert. pair with horiz. gutter (10)	—
V95PP	6 items (48)	—
	Cross gutter block (1)	—
	Horiz. pair with vert. gutter (2)	—
	Vert. pair with horiz. gutter (10)	—
V96PP	6 items (48)	—
	Cross gutter block (1)	—
	Horiz. pair with vert. gutter (2)	—
	Vert. pair with horiz. gutter (10)	—
570PI	(12 pairs)	—
	Cross gutter block (1)	—
	Horiz. pair with vert. gutter (2)	—
	Vert. pair with horiz. gutter (10)	—
571PI	(12 pairs)	—
	Cross gutter block (1)	—
	Horiz. pair with vert. gutter (2)	—
	Vert. pair with horiz. gutter (10)	—
G180PI	(20 pairs)	—
	Cross gutter block (1)	—
	Horiz. pair with vert. gutter (2)	—
	Vert. pair with horiz. gutter (10)	—
G181PI	(20 pairs)	—
	Cross gutter block (1)	—
	Horiz. pair with vert. gutter (2)	—
	Vert. pair with horiz. gutter (10)	—
V95PI	(20 pairs)	—
	Cross gutter block (1)	—
	Horiz. pair with vert. gutter (2)	—
	Vert. pair with horiz. gutter (10)	—
V96PI	(20 pairs)	—
	Cross gutter block (1)	—
	Horiz. pair with vert. gutter (2)	—
	Vert. pair with horiz. gutter (10)	—

New York #572, Geneva #182, Vienna #97
International Trade Center

1990		
572PDa	Card, #572PD, #G182PD, #V97PD with approval handstamp (5)	—
572TCa	Card, #572TC blue green ship, #G182TC red orange ship, #V97TC light pink building, with "not approved" handstamp (6)	—
572PP	9 items (50)	—
G182PP	7 items (50)	—
V97PP	8 items (50)	—
572PI	(50 pairs)	—
G182PI	(75 pairs)	—
V97PI	(50 pairs)	—

Geneva #183, Vienna #98
Definitives

1990		
G183PD	(6)	—
V98PD	Proof on large sheet with approval or "not approved" handstamp, and set of 7 progressive proofs on large sheets (9)	—
G183PP	9 items (1)	—
V98PP	7 items (50)	—
G183PI	(50 pairs)	—
V98PI	(50 pairs)	—

The not approved proofs of No. V98PD are slightly lighter
than the approved proofs.

New York #573-574, Geneva #184-185, Vienna #99-100, Souvenir Card #37
Fight AIDS Worldwide

1990		
573PDa	Card, #573PD, #G184PD, #V99PD (4)	—
574PDa	Card, #574PD, #G185PD, #573TC white background, #G184TC white background, #V99TC white background, 10s essay of #V100 (4)	—
SC37PD	(4)	—
573PP	7 items (50)	—
574PP	6 items (50)	—
G184PP	7 items (50)	—
G185PP	7 items (50)	—
V99PP	7 items (50)	—
V100PP	6 items (50)	—
573PI	(50 pairs)	—
574PI	(50 pairs)	—
G184PI	(75 pairs)	—
G185PI	(75 pairs)	—
V99PI	(75 pairs)	—
V100PI	(75 pairs)	—

New York #575-576, Geneva #186-187, Vienna #101-102
Medicinal Plants

1990		
576PDa	Card, #575PD-576PD, #G186PD-G187PD, #V101PD-V102PD (4)	—
G187PD	(4)	—
G186PP	6 items (50)	—
G187PP	6 items (50)	—
V101PP	6 items (50)	—
V102PP	6 items (50)	—
575PI	(50 pairs)	—
576PI	(50 pairs)	—
G186PI	(50 pairs)	—
G187PI	(50 pairs)	—
V101PI	(50 pairs)	—
V102PI	(50 pairs)	—

New York #577-579, Geneva #188-190, Vienna #103-105
United Nations, 45th Anniv.

1990		
578PDa	Card, #577PD-578PD, #G188PD-G189PD, 6s essay of #V103, 8s essay of #V104 (4)	—
579PDa	Card, #579PD, #G190PD, #V105PD (4)	—
577PP	8 items (320)	—
	Horiz. pair with vert. gutter (40)	
578PP	8 items (320)	—
	Horiz. pair with vert. gutter (40)	
579PP	8 items (100)	—
G188PP	10 items (160)	—
	Horiz. pair with vert. gutter (20)	
G189PP	8 items (320)	—
	Horiz. pair with vert. gutter (40)	
G190PP	9 items (100)	—
V103PP	8 items (320)	—
	Horiz. pair with vert. gutter (40)	
V104PP	8 items (320)	—
	Horiz. pair with vert. gutter (40)	
V105PP	8 items (100)	—
577PI	(80 pairs)	—
	Horiz. pair with vert. gutter (10)	
578PI	(80 pairs)	—
	Horiz. pair with vert. gutter (10)	
579PI	(100 souvenir sheets)	—
G188PI	(260 pairs)	—
	Horiz. pair with vert. gutter (40)	
G189PI	(260 pairs)	—
	Horiz. pair with vert. gutter (40)	
G190PI	(100 souvenir sheets)	—
V103PI	(260 pairs)	—
	Horiz. pair with vert. gutter (40)	
V104PI	(260 pairs)	—
	Horiz. pair with vert. gutter (40)	
V105PI	(100 souvenir sheets)	—

New York #580-581, Geneva #191-192, Vienna #106-107, Souvenir Card #38
Crime Prevention

1990		
581PDa	Card, #580PD-581PD, #G191PD-G192PD, #V106PD-V107PD, #SC38PD (5)	—
580PP	8 items (50)	—
581PP	8 items (50)	—
G191PP	8 items (50)	—
G192PP	8 items (50)	—
V106PP	8 items (100)	—
V107PP	8 items (100)	—
580PI	(50 pairs)	—
581PI	(50 pairs)	—
G191PI	(75 pairs)	—
G192PI	(75 pairs)	—
V106PI	(75 pairs)	—
V107PI	(75 pairs)	—

New York #582-583, Geneva #193-194, Vienna #108-109,
Human Rights

1990		
582PDa	Strip of 3 + 3 labels (9)	—
583PDa	Strip of 3 + 3 labels with approval handstamp (4)	—
G193PDa	Strip of 3 + 3 labels (9)	—
G194PDa	Strip of 3 + 3 labels (9)	—
V108PDa	Strip of 3 + 3 labels (9)	—
V109PDa	Strip of 3 + 3 labels (9)	—
583TCa	Strip of 3 + 3 labels (chocolate panels) with "not approved" handstamp (5)	—
582PP	6 items (20)	—
	Cross gutter block (1)	
	Horiz. pair with vert. gutter (2)	
	Vert. pair with horiz. gutter (10)	
583PP	6 items (20)	—
	Cross gutter block (1)	
	Horiz. pair with vert. gutter (2)	
	Vert. pair with horiz. gutter (10)	
G193PP	6 items (20)	—
	Cross gutter block (1)	
	Horiz. pair with vert. gutter (2)	
	Vert. pair with horiz. gutter (10)	
G194PP	8 items (20)	—
	Cross gutter block (1)	
	Horiz. pair with vert. gutter (2)	
	Vert. pair with horiz. gutter (10)	
V108PP	6 items (20)	—
	Cross gutter block (1)	
	Horiz. pair with vert. gutter (2)	
	Vert. pair with horiz. gutter (10)	
V109PP	6 items (20)	—

	Cross gutter block (1)	—
	Horiz. pair with vert. gutter (2)	—
	Vert. pair with horiz. gutter (10)	—
582PI	(20 pairs)	—
	Cross gutter block (1)	—
	Horiz. pair with vert. gutter (2)	—
	Vert. pair with horiz. gutter (10)	—
583PI	(20 pairs)	—
	Cross gutter block (1)	—
	Horiz. pair with vert. gutter (2)	—
	Vert. pair with horiz. gutter (10)	—
G193PI	(20 pairs)	—
	Cross gutter block (1)	—
	Horiz. pair with vert. gutter (2)	—
	Vert. pair with horiz. gutter (10)	—
G194PI	(20 pairs)	—
	Cross gutter block (1)	—
	Horiz. pair with vert. gutter (2)	—
	Vert. pair with horiz. gutter (10)	—
V108PI	(20 pairs)	—
	Cross gutter block (1)	—
	Horiz. pair with vert. gutter (2)	—
	Vert. pair with horiz. gutter (10)	—
V109PI	(20 pairs)	—
	Cross gutter block (1)	—
	Horiz. pair with vert. gutter (2)	—
	Vert. pair with horiz. gutter (10)	—

There is no appreciable difference between approved and not approved examples of Nos. 582PD, G193PD, G194PD, V108PD and V109PD.

New York #587a, Geneva #198a, Vienna #113a, Souvenir Card #39
Economic Council for Europe
1991

587aPDa	Card, #587aPD, #G198aPD, #V113aPD with printed perforations (2)	—
587aPDb	Card, #587aPDa, SC39PD (1)	—
SC39PD	(1)	—
587aPP	13 items (20 blocks)	—
G198aPP	13 items (20 blocks)	—
V113aPP	13 items (20 blocks)	—
587aPI	(40 blocks)	—
G198aPI	(40 blocks)	—
V113aPI	(40 blocks)	—

Second sets of blocks of Nos. 587aPP and G198aPP with 10 items, and No. V113aPP with 11 items (some items differing from the 13 item set) exist.

New York #588-589, Geneva #199-200, Vienna #114-115
Namibian Independence
1991

588PDa	Card, #588PD, #G199PD-G200PD, #V114PD-V115PD, 36c essay of #589 (8)	—
589PDa	Card, #588PD-589PD, #G199PD-G200PD, #V114PD-V115PD (1)	—
588PP	7 items (50)	—
589PP	7 items (50)	—
G199PP	8 items (50)	—
G200PP	8 items (50)	—
V114PP	6 items (50)	—
V115PP	6 items (50)	—
588PI	(100 pairs)	—
589PI	(100 pairs)	—
G199PI	(75 pairs)	—
G200PI	(75 pairs)	—
V114PI	(75 pairs)	—
V115PI	(75 pairs)	—

New York #590-592, Geneva #201-202, Vienna #116
Definitives
1991

590PD	With approval handstamp (4)	—
592PD	(4)	—
592PDa	Card, imperforate pane of 50 (1)	—
G201PD	(5)	—
G202PDa	Card, #G201PD-G202PD, #G213PD, #V116PD (4)	—
590TC	deep blue background (not approved) (5)	—
592TC	black (1)	—
590PP	8 items (80)	—
	Horiz. pair with vert. gutter (10)	—
591PP	4 items (150)	—
G201PP	8 items (50)	—
G202PP	7 items (50)	—
V116PP	7 items (50)	—
590PI	(90 pairs)	—
	Horiz. pair with vert. gutter (10)	—
591PI	(175 pairs)	—
592PI	(50 pairs)	—
G201PI	(75 pairs)	—
G202PI	(100 pairs)	—
V116PI	(75 pairs)	—

An essay of No. 592 with emblem in solid color exists.

New York #593-594, Geneva #203-204, Vienna #117-118, Souvenir Card #40
Rights of the Child
1991

593PDa	Card, #593PD, #G203PD-G204PD, #V117PD-V118PD, 90c essay of #594 (6)	—
594PDa	Card, #593PD-594PD, #G203PD-G204PD, #V117PD-V118PD (4)	—
594PDb	Card, #593PD-594PD (4)	—

SC40PD	(4)	—
593PP	9 items (50)	—
594PP	9 items (50)	—
G203PP	8 items (50)	—
G204PP	7 items (50)	—
V117PP	7 items (50)	—
V118PP	7 items (50)	—
SC40PP	15 items (1)	—
593PI	(75 pairs)	—
594PI	(75 pairs)	—
G203PI	(75 pairs)	—
G204PI	(75 pairs)	—
V117PI	(75 pairs)	—
V118PI	(75 pairs)	—

No. SC40PP may not be a complete set of progressive proofs. Five essays of No. SC40PD with the 90c essay of No. 594 exist; one is attached to No. 593PDa.

New York #595-596, Geneva #205-206, Vienna #119-120,
Banning of Chemical Weapons
1991

596PDa	Card, #595PD-596PD, #G205PD-G206PD, #V119PD-V120PD with approval handstamp (5)	—
596PDb	Card, #596PD, #G206PD, #V120PD, essays of #595, #G205, #V119 (each with gray panels taller than numerals) with "not approved" handstamp (4)	—
595PP	9 items (50)	—
596PP	9 items (50)	—
G205PP	9 items (100)	—
G206PP	9 items (100)	—
V119PP	8 items (50)	—
V120PP	8 items (50)	—
595PI	(125 pairs)	—
596PI	(125 pairs)	—
G205PI	(125 pairs)	—
G206PI	(125 pairs)	—
V119PI	(125 pairs)	—
V120PI	(125 pairs)	—

Second sets of six items of Nos. 595PP-596PP, G205PP-G206PP, and V119PP-V120PP exist. Some items differ from those found in the listed sets.

New York #597-598, Geneva #207-208, Vienna #121-122
UN Postal Administration, 40th Anniv.
1991

598PDa	Card, #597PD-598PD, #G207PD-G208PD, #V121PD-V122PD (4)	—
597TCa	Card, #597TC, #G207TC-G208TCD, #V121TC-V122TC (each with white background), 36c essay of #598 (6)	—
597PP	2 items (64)	—
	Cross gutter block (1)	—
	Horiz. pair with vert. gutter (8)	—
	Vert. pair with horiz. gutter (8)	—
598PP	2 items (64)	—
	Cross gutter block (1)	—
	Horiz. pair with vert. gutter (8)	—
	Vert. pair with horiz. gutter (8)	—
G207PP	2 items (64)	—
	Cross gutter block (1)	—
	Horiz. pair with vert. gutter (8)	—
	Vert. pair with horiz. gutter (8)	—
G208PP	2 items (64)	—
	Cross gutter block (1)	—
	Horiz. pair with vert. gutter (8)	—
	Vert. pair with horiz. gutter (8)	—
V121PP	2 items (64)	—
	Cross gutter block (1)	—
	Horiz. pair with vert. gutter (8)	—
	Vert. pair with horiz. gutter (8)	—
V122PP	2 items (64)	—
	Cross gutter block (1)	—
	Horiz. pair with vert. gutter (8)	—
	Vert. pair with horiz. gutter (8)	—
597PI	(120 pairs)	—
	Cross gutter block (3)	—
	Horiz. pair with vert. gutter (24)	—
	Vert. pair with horiz. gutter (24)	—
598PI	(120 pairs)	—
	Cross gutter block (3)	—
	Horiz. pair with vert. gutter (24)	—
	Vert. pair with horiz. gutter (24)	—
G207PI	(120 pairs)	—
	Cross gutter block (3)	—
	Horiz. pair with vert. gutter (24)	—
	Vert. pair with horiz. gutter (24)	—
G208PI	(120 pairs)	—
	Cross gutter block (3)	—
	Horiz. pair with vert. gutter (24)	—
	Vert. pair with horiz. gutter (24)	—
V121PI	(120 pairs)	—
	Cross gutter block (3)	—
	Horiz. pair with vert. gutter (24)	—
	Vert. pair with horiz. gutter (24)	—
V122PI	(120 pairs)	—
	Cross gutter block (3)	—
	Horiz. pair with vert. gutter (24)	—
	Vert. pair with horiz. gutter (24)	—

Four cross gutter blocks, 32 horizontal pairs with vertical gutters and 32 vertical pairs with horizontal gutters can be cut from four perforated sheets of Nos. 597PI-598PI, G207PI-G208PI, V119PI-V120PI. No. 598PI is difficult to distinguish from one item from No. 598PP.

New York #599-600, Geneva #209-210, Vienna #123-124,
Human Rights
1991

599PDa	Strip of 3 + 3 labels with approval handstamp (4)	—
600PDa	Strip of 3 + 3 labels with approval handstamp (4)	—
G209PDa	Strip of 3 + 3 labels with approval handstamp (4)	—
G210PDa	Strip of 3 + 3 labels with approval handstamp (4)	—
V123PDa	Strip of 3 + 3 labels with approval handstamp (4)	—
V124PDa	Strip of 3 + 3 labels with approval handstamp (4)	—
599TC	Strip of 3 (dark gray background) + 3 labels with "not approved" handstamp (5)	—
600TC	Strip of 3 (dark green background) + 3 labels with "not approved" handstamp (5)	—
G209TC	Strip of 3 (light brown in painting) + 3 labels with "not approved" handstamp (5)	—
G210TC	Strip of 3 (dark green background) + 3 labels with "not approved" handstamp (5)	—
V124TC	Strip of 3 (black background) + 3 labels with "not approved" handstamp (5)	—
599PP	6 items (20)	—
	Cross gutter block (1)	—
	Horiz. pair with vert. gutter (2)	—
	Vert. pair with horiz. gutter (10)	—
600PP	6 items (20)	—
	Cross gutter block (1)	—
	Horiz. pair with vert. gutter (2)	—
	Vert. pair with horiz. gutter (10)	—
G209PP	6 items (20)	—
	Cross gutter block (1)	—
	Horiz. pair with vert. gutter (2)	—
	Vert. pair with horiz. gutter (10)	—
G210PP	6 items (20)	—
	Cross gutter block (1)	—
	Horiz. pair with vert. gutter (2)	—
	Vert. pair with horiz. gutter (10)	—
V123PP	6 items (20)	—
	Cross gutter block (1)	—
	Horiz. pair with vert. gutter (2)	—
	Vert. pair with horiz. gutter (10)	—
V124PP	6 items (20)	—
	Cross gutter block (1)	—
	Horiz. pair with vert. gutter (2)	—
	Vert. pair with horiz. gutter (10)	—
599PI	(56 pairs)	—
	Cross gutter block (1)	—
	Horiz. pair with vert. gutter (2)	—
	Vert. pair with horiz. gutter (10)	—
600PI	(56 pairs)	—
	Cross gutter block (1)	—
	Horiz. pair with vert. gutter (2)	—
	Vert. pair with horiz. gutter (10)	—
G209PI	(56 pairs)	—
	Cross gutter block (1)	—
	Horiz. pair with vert. gutter (2)	—
	Vert. pair with horiz. gutter (10)	—
G210PI	(56 pairs)	—
	Cross gutter block (1)	—
	Horiz. pair with vert. gutter (2)	—
	Vert. pair with horiz. gutter (10)	—
V123PI	(56 pairs)	—
	Cross gutter block (1)	—
	Horiz. pair with vert. gutter (2)	—
	Vert. pair with horiz. gutter (10)	—
V124PI	(56 pairs)	—
	Cross gutter block (1)	—
	Horiz. pair with vert. gutter (2)	—
	Vert. pair with horiz. gutter (10)	—

New York #601-602, Geneva #211-212, Vienna #125-126
World Heritage
1992

602PDa	Card, #601PD-602PD (5)	—
G212PDa	Card, #G211PD-G212PD (5)	—
V126PDa	Card, #V125PD-V126PD (5)	—
601PP	6 items (50)	—
602PP	6 items (50)	—
G211PP	6 items (50)	—
G212PP	6 items (50)	—
V125PP	6 items (50)	—
V126PP	6 items (50)	—
601PI	(50 pairs)	—
602PI	(50 pairs)	—
G211PI	(50 pairs)	—
G212PI	(50 pairs)	—
V125PI	(50 pairs)	—
V126PI	(50 pairs)	—

Geneva #213
Definitive
1992

G213PP	6 items (50)	—
G213PI	(75 pairs)	—

See No. G202PDa.

New York #604a, Geneva #215a, Vienna #128a
Clean Oceans

2

aPDa	Card, imperforate pane of 6 #604aPD (2)	—
aPDb	Card, as "a," with one pair removed (1)	—
5aPDa	Card, imperforate pane of 6 #G215aPD (2)	—
5aPDb	(Card, as "a," with one pair removed (1)	—
8aPDa	Card, imperforate pane of 6 #V128aPD (2)	—
8aPDb	Card, as "a," with one pair removed (1)	—
aPP	8 items, vert. pair of pairs with narrow horiz. gutter (20)	—
	Cross gutter block (1)	—
	Horiz. pair of pairs with vert. gutter (4)	—
	Vert. pair of pairs with wide horiz. gutter (10)	—
15aPP	8 items, vert. pair of pairs with narrow horiz. gutter (20)	—
	Cross gutter block (1)	—
	Horiz. pair of pairs with vert. gutter (4)	—
	Vert. pair of pairs with wide horiz. gutter (10)	—
28aPP	8 items, vert. pair of pairs with narrow horiz. gutter (20)	—
	Cross gutter block (1)	—
	Horiz. pair of pairs with vert. gutter (4)	—
	Vert. pair of pairs with wide horiz. gutter (10)	—
4aPI	Vert. pair of pairs with narrow horiz. gutter (20)	—
	Cross gutter block (1)	—
	Horiz. pair of pairs with vert. gutter (4)	—
	Vert. pair of pairs with wide horiz. gutter (10)	—
15aPI	Vert. pair of pairs with narrow horiz. gutter (20)	—
	Cross gutter block (1)	—
	Horiz. pair of pairs with vert. gutter (4)	—
	Vert. pair of pairs with wide horiz. gutter (10)	—
28aPI	Vert. pair of pairs with narrow horiz. gutter (20)	—
	Cross gutter block (1)	—
	Horiz. pair of pairs with vert. gutter (4)	—
	Vert. pair of pairs with wide horiz. gutter (10)	—

New York #608a, Geneva #219a, Vienna #132a
Earth Summit

92

8aPDa	Card, #608aPD, #G219aPD, #V132aPD (5)	—
8aPP	4 items (10)	—
219aPP	4 items (10)	—
132aPP	4 items (10)	—
8aPI	(20 blocks)	—
219aPI	(20 blocks)	—
132aPI	(20 blocks)	—

New York #609-610, Geneva #220-221, Vienna #133-134
Mission to Planet Earth

92

10PDa	Card, #610aPD, G221aPD, #V134aPD (3)	—
C41PD	(3)	—
10aPP	6 items (5)	—
221aPP	6 items (5)	—
134aPP	6 items (5)	—
10aPI	(10 pairs)	—
221aPI	(10 pairs)	—
134aPI	(10 pairs)	—

One item in No. G221aPP is a blank from a sheet showing marginal inscriptions only.

New York #611-612, Geneva #222-223, Vienna #135-136, Souvenir Card #42
Science and Technology for Development

992

11PDa	Card, 2 #611PD, 2 #V136PD (4)	—
12PDa	Card, #611PD-612PD, #G222PD-G223PD, #V135PD-V136PD (4)	—
C42PD	(18)	—
11PP	6 items (50)	—
12PP	6 items (50)	—
222PP	6 items (50)	—
223PP	6 items (50)	—
135PP	6 items (50)	—
136PP	6 items (50)	—
11PI	(100 pairs)	—
12PI	(100 pairs)	—
222PI	(100 pairs)	—
223PI	(100 pairs)	—
135PI	(100 pairs)	—
136PI	(100 pairs)	—

There is no appreciable difference between approved and not approved die proofs.

New York #613-615, Vienna #137-138
Definitives

1992

614PDa	Card, #614PD, #V137PD-V138PD (4)	—
615PDa	Card, #613PD, #615PD (3)	—
613PP	6 items (50)	—
614PP	6 items (50)	—
615PP	6 items (50)	—
V137PP	6 items (50)	—
V138PP	6 items (50)	—
613PI	(50 pairs)	—
614PI	(269 pairs)	—
	Cross gutter block (2)	—
	Horiz. pair with vert. gutter (36)	—
	Vert. pair with horiz. gutter (16)	—
615PI	(50 pairs)	—
V137PI	(269 pairs)	—
	Cross gutter block (2)	—
	Horiz. pair with vert. gutter (16)	—
	Vert. pair with horiz. gutter (36)	—
V138PI	(269 pairs)	—
	Cross gutter block (2)	—
	Horiz. pair with vert. gutter (36)	—
	Vert. pair with vert. gutter (16)	—

Three "not approved" cards containing essays of Nos. 613 and 615 lacking year date and designer inscriptions exist.

New York #616-617, Geneva #224-225, Vienna #139-140
Human Rights

1992

616PDa	Strip of 3 + 3 labels (4)	—
617PDa	Strip of 3 + 3 labels (4)	—
G224PDa	Strip of 3 + 3 labels (4)	—
G225PDa	Strip of 3 + 3 labels (4)	—
V139PDa	Strip of 3 + 3 labels (4)	—
V140PDa	Strip of 3 + 3 labels (4)	—
G225TCa	Strip of 3 (dark brown background under chair) + 3 labels (not approved) (5)	—
616PP	6 items (20)	—
	Cross gutter block (1)	—
	Horiz. pair with vert. gutter (2)	—
	Vert. pair with horiz. gutter (10)	—
617PP	6 items (20)	—
	Cross gutter block (1)	—
	Horiz. pair with vert. gutter (2)	—
	Vert. pair with horiz. gutter (10)	—
G224PP	6 items (20)	—
	Cross gutter block (1)	—
	Horiz. pair with vert. gutter (2)	—
	Vert. pair with horiz. gutter (10)	—
G225PP	6 items (20)	—
	Cross gutter block (1)	—
	Horiz. pair with vert. gutter (2)	—
	Vert. pair with horiz. gutter (10)	—
V139PP	6 items (20)	—
	Cross gutter block (1)	—
	Horiz. pair with vert. gutter (2)	—
	Vert. pair with horiz. gutter (10)	—
V140PP	6 items (20)	—
	Cross gutter block (1)	—
	Horiz. pair with vert. gutter (2)	—
	Vert. pair with horiz. gutter (10)	—
616PI	(32 pairs)	—
	Cross gutter block (4)	—
	Horiz. pair with vert. gutter (8)	—
	Vert. pair with horiz. gutter (40)	—
617PI	(32 pairs)	—
	Cross gutter block (4)	—
	Horiz. pair with vert. gutter (8)	—
	Vert. pair with horiz. gutter (40)	—
G224PI	(32 pairs)	—
	Cross gutter block (4)	—
	Horiz. pair with vert. gutter (8)	—
	Vert. pair with horiz. gutter (40)	—
G225PI	(32 pairs)	—
	Cross gutter block (4)	—
	Horiz. pair with vert. gutter (8)	—
	Vert. pair with horiz. gutter (40)	—
V139PI	(32 pairs)	—
	Cross gutter block (4)	—
	Horiz. pair with vert. gutter (8)	—
	Vert. pair with horiz. gutter (40)	—
V140PI	(32 pairs)	—
	Cross gutter block (4)	—
	Horiz. pair with vert. gutter (8)	—
	Vert. pair with horiz. gutter (40)	—

Five "not approved" cards contain 4.50s essays of No. V139, and five "not approved" cards contain 9.50s essays of No. V140.

New York #618-619, Geneva #226-227, Vienna #141-142
Aging With Dignity

1993

618PDa	Card, #618PD, #G226PD-G227PD, #141PD-V142PD, #619TC yellow flowers (not approved) (5)	—
619PDa	Card, #618PD-619PD, #V141PD-V142PD, #G226TC pink denomination, #G227TC yellow denomination, with approval handstamp (4)	—
619TCb	Card, #618TC-619TC, #G226TC-G227TC, #V141TC-V142TC, each with white denominations (5)	—
618PP	7 items (50)	—
619PP	7 items (50)	—
G226PP	7 items (50)	—
G227PP	7 items (50)	—
V141PP	7 items (50)	—

V142PP	7 items (50)	—
618PI	(50 pairs)	—
619PI	(50 pairs)	—
G226PI	(50 pairs)	—
G227PI	(50 pairs)	—
V141PI	(50 pairs)	—
V142PI	(50 pairs)	—

New York #623a, Geneva #231a, Vienna #146a
Endangered Species

1993

623aPDa	Card, imperforate pane of 4 blocks of #623aPD (3)	—
G231aPDa	Card, imperforate pane of 4 blocks of #G231aPD (4)	—
V146aPDa	Card, imperforate pane of 4 blocks of #V146aPD (3)	—
G231aTCa	Card, imperforate pane of 4 blocks of #G231aTC black (1)	—
G231aPP	6 items (4 blocks)	—
	Cross gutter block (1)	—
	Horiz. pair with vert. gutter (2)	—
	Vert. pair with horiz. gutter (4)	—
V146aPP	6 items (4 blocks)	—
	Cross gutter block (1)	—
	Horiz. pair with vert. gutter (2)	—
	Vert. pair with horiz. gutter (4)	—
623aPI	(20 blocks)	—
	Cross gutter block (8)	—
	Horiz. pair with vert. gutter (8)	—
	Vert. pair with horiz. gutter (16)	—
G231aPI	(44 blocks)	—
	Cross gutter block (10)	—
	Horiz. pair with vert. gutter (10)	—
	Vert. pair with horiz. gutter (20)	—
V146aPI	(20 blocks)	—
	Cross gutter block (8)	—
	Horiz. pair with vert. gutter (8)	—
	Vert. pair with horiz. gutter (16)	—

New York #624-625, Geneva #232-233, Vienna #147-148, Souvenir Card #43
Healthy Environment

1993

625PDa	Card, #624PD-625PD, #V147PD-V148PD, 90c essay of #G232, 1.10fr essay of #G233 (4)	—
SC43PD	(4)	—
624PP	6 items (50)	—
625PP	6 items (50)	—
G232PP	6 items (50)	—
G233PP	6 items (50)	—
V147PP	6 items (50)	—
V148PP	6 items (50)	—
624PI	(50 pairs)	—
625PI	(50 pairs)	—
G232PI	(50 pairs)	—
G233PI	(50 pairs)	—
V147PI	(50 pairs)	—
V148PI	(50 pairs)	—

New York #626, Vienna #149
Definitives

1993

626PD	(5)	—
V149PD	(5)	—
626PP	8 items (144)	—
	Cross gutter block (1)	—
	Horiz. pair with vert. gutter (18)	—
	Vert. pair with horiz. gutter (8)	—
V149PP	5 items (50)	—
626PI	(194 pairs)	—
	Cross gutter block (2)	—
	Horiz. pair with vert. gutter (36)	—
	Vert. pair with horiz. gutter (16)	—
V149PI	(50 pairs)	—

New York #627-628, Geneva #234-235, Vienna #150-151
Human Rights

1993

627PDa	Strip of 3 + 3 labels (4)	—
628PDa	Strip of 3 + 3 labels (4)	—
G234PDa	Strip of 3 + 3 labels (4)	—
G235PDa	Strip of 3 + 3 labels (4)	—
V150PDa	Strip of 3 + 3 labels (3)	—
V151PDa	Strip of 3 + 3 labels (4)	—
627PP	6 items (20)	—
	Cross gutter block (1)	—
	Horiz. pair with vert. gutter (2)	—
	Vert. pair with horiz. gutter (10)	—
628PP	6 items (20)	—
	Cross gutter block (1)	—
	Horiz. pair with vert. gutter (2)	—
	Vert. pair with horiz. gutter (10)	—
G234PP	6 items (20)	—
	Cross gutter block (1)	—
	Horiz. pair with vert. gutter (2)	—
	Vert. pair with horiz. gutter (10)	—
G235PP	6 items (20)	—
	Cross gutter block (1)	—
	Horiz. pair with vert. gutter (2)	—
	Vert. pair with horiz. gutter (10)	—
627PI	(20 pairs)	—
	Cross gutter block (1)	—
	Horiz. pair with vert. gutter (2)	—
	Vert. pair with horiz. gutter (10)	—
628PI	(20 pairs)	—
	Cross gutter block (1)	—
	Horiz. pair with vert. gutter (2)	—
	Vert. pair with horiz. gutter (10)	—
G234PI	(20 pairs)	—
	Cross gutter block (1)	—

G235PI	Horiz. pair with vert. gutter (2)	—
	Vert. pair with horiz. gutter (10)	—
	(20 pairs)	—
	Cross gutter block (1)	—
	Horiz. pair with vert. gutter (2)	—
	Vert. pair with horiz. gutter (10)	—
V150PI	(6 pairs)	—
V151PI	(6 pairs)	—

New York #632a, Geneva #239a, Vienna #155a, Souvenir Card #44
International Peace Day

1993

632aPD	(4)	—
G239aPD	(4)	—
V155aPD	(4)	—
SC44PD	(4)	—
632aPP	7 items (10 blocks)	—
G239aPP	7 items (10 blocks)	—
V155aPP	7 items (10 blocks)	—
632aPI	(40 blocks)	—
G239aPI	(40 blocks)	—
V155aPI	(40 blocks)	—

New York #636a, Geneva #243a, Vienna #159a
Environment & Climate

1993

636aPDa	Card, #636aPD, #V159aPD (4)	—
G243aPD	(4)	—
636aPP	8 items (6 strips)	—
	Horiz. pair of strips with vert. gutter (6)	—
G243aPP	8 items (6 strips)	—
	Horiz. pair of strips with vert. gutter (6)	—
V155aPP	8 items (6 strips)	—
	Horiz. pair of strips with vert. gutter (6)	—
636aPI	(18 strips)	—
	Horiz. pair of strips with vert. gutter (18)	—
G243aPI	(18 strips)	—
	Horiz. pair of strips with vert. gutter (18)	—
V159aPI	(18 strips)	—
	Horiz. pair of strips with vert. gutter (18)	—

New York #637-638, Geneva #244-245, Vienna #160-161, Souvenir Card #45
International Year of the Family

1994

638PDa	Card, #637PD-638PD, #G244PD-G245PD, #V160PD-V161PD (4)	—
SC45PD	(4)	—
637PP	11 items (50)	—
638PP	11 items (50)	—
G244PP	10 items (50)	—
G245PP	10 items (50)	—
V160PP	11 items (50)	—
V161PP	11 items (50)	—
637PI	(100 pairs)	—
638PI	(100 pairs)	—
G244PI	(100 pairs)	—
G245PI	(100 pairs)	—
V160PI	(100 pairs)	—
V161PI	(100 pairs)	—

New York #642a, Geneva #249a, Vienna #165a
Endangered Species

1994

642aPDa	Card, imperforate pane of 4 #642aPD (9)	—
G249aPDa	Card, imperforate pane of 4 #G249aPD (4)	—
V165aPDa	Card, imperforate pane of 4 #V165aPD (4)	—
642aPP	6 items (4 blocks)	—
	Cross gutter block (2)	—
	Horiz. pair with vert. gutter (2)	—
	Vert. pair with horiz. gutter (4)	—
G249aPP	6 items (4 blocks)	—
	Cross gutter block (2)	—
	Horiz. pair with vert. gutter (2)	—
	Vert. pair with horiz. gutter (4)	—
V165aPP	6 items (4 blocks)	—
	Cross gutter block (2)	—
	Horiz. pair with vert. gutter (2)	—
	Vert. pair with horiz. gutter (4)	—
642aPI	(16 blocks)	—
	Cross gutter block (8)	—
	Horiz. pair with vert. gutter (8)	—
	Vert. pair with horiz. gutter (16)	—
G249aPI	(16 blocks)	—
	Cross gutter block (8)	—
	Horiz. pair with vert. gutter (8)	—
	Vert. pair with horiz. gutter (16)	—
V165aPI	(16 blocks)	—
	Cross gutter block (8)	—
	Horiz. pair with vert. gutter (8)	—
	Vert. pair with horiz. gutter (16)	—

There is no appreciable difference between appoved and not approved examples of No. 642aPD. Five cards with imperforate panes of 40c essays of No. G249a and five cards with imperforate panes of 5s essays of No. V165a exist.

New York #643, Geneva #250, Vienna #166
Protection for Refugees

1994

643PDa	Card, #643PD, #G250PD, #V166PD (4)	—
643PP	8 items (50)	—
G250PP	8 items (50)	—
V166PP	6 items (50)	—
643PI	(69 pairs)	—
	Horiz. pair with vert. gutter (8)	—
G250PI	(69 pairs)	—
	Horiz. pair with vert. gutter (8)	—
V166PI	(69 pairs)	—
	Horiz. pair with vert. gutter (8)	—

New York #644-646, Vienna #167-169
Definitives

1994

645PDa	Card, #644PD-645PD, #V167PD-V169PD (5)	—
646PD	(1)	—
644PP	6 items (50)	—
645PP	6 items (50)	—
V167PP	12 items (50)	—
V168PP	11 items (50)	—
V169PP	11 items (50)	—
644PI	(100 pairs)	—
645PI	(100 pairs)	—
646PI	(50 pairs)	—
V167PI	(100 pairs)	—
V168PI	(100 pairs)	—
V169PI	(100 pairs)	—

There is no appreciable difference between approved and not approved examples of No. 645PDa.

New York #650a, Geneva #254a, Vienna #173a
International Decade for Natural Disaster Reduction

1994

650aPDa	Card, #650aPD, #G254aPD, #V173aPD (5)	—
650aPP	6 items (16 blocks)	—
	Cross gutter block (1)	—
	Horiz. pair with vert. gutter (8)	—
	Vert. pair with horiz. gutter (2)	—
G254aPP	6 items (16 blocks)	—
	Cross gutter block (1)	—
	Horiz. pair with vert. gutter (8)	—
	Vert. pair with horiz. gutter (2)	—
V173aPP	6 items (16 blocks)	—
	Cross gutter block (1)	—
	Horiz. pair with vert. gutter (8)	—
	Vert. pair with horiz. gutter (2)	—
650aPI	(48 blocks)	—
	Cross gutter block (3)	—
	Horiz. pair with vert. gutter (24)	—
	Vert. pair with horiz. gutter (6)	—
G254aPI	(48 blocks)	—
	Cross gutter block (3)	—
	Horiz. pair with vert. gutter (24)	—
	Vert. pair with horiz. gutter (6)	—
V173aPI	(48 blocks)	—
	Cross gutter block (3)	—
	Horiz. pair with vert. gutter (24)	—
	Vert. pair with horiz. gutter (6)	—

Geneva #255-257
Definitives

1994

G257PDa	Card, #G255PD-G257PD (5)	—
G255PP	10 items (144)	—
	Cross gutter block (1)	—
	Horiz. pair with vert. gutter (18)	—
	Vert. pair with horiz. gutter (8)	—
G256PP	10 items (144)	—
	Cross gutter block (1)	—
	Horiz. pair with vert. gutter (18)	—
	Vert. pair with horiz. gutter (8)	—
G257PP	11 items (144)	—
	Cross gutter block (1)	—
	Horiz. pair with vert. gutter (18)	—
	Vert. pair with horiz. gutter (8)	—
G255PI	(288 pairs)	—
	Cross gutter block (4)	—
	Horiz. pair with vert. gutter (72)	—
	Vert. pair with horiz. gutter (32)	—
G256PI	(288 pairs)	—
	Cross gutter block (4)	—
	Horiz. pair with vert. gutter (72)	—
	Vert. pair with horiz. gutter (32)	—
G257PI	(288 pairs)	—
	Cross gutter block (4)	—
	Horiz. pair with vert. gutter (72)	—
	Vert. pair with horiz. gutter (32)	—

New York #651-652, Geneva #258-259, Vienna #174-175, Souvenir Card #46
Population and Development

1994

652PDa	Card, #651PD-652PD, #G258PD-G259PD, #V174PD-V175PD (4)	—
SC46PD	(4)	—
G258PP	6 items (40)	—
G259PP	6 items (40)	—
G259PPa	Horiz. se-tenant pair with vert. gutter, #G258PP-G259PP (10)	—
V174PP	6 items (40)	—
V175PP	6 items (40)	—
V175PPa	Horiz. se-tenant pair with vert. gutter, #V174PP-V175PP (10)	—
651PI	(50 pairs)	—
652PI	(50 pairs)	—
G258PI	(70 pairs)	—
G259PI	(70 pairs)	—
G259PIa	Horiz. se-tenant pair with vert. gutter, #G258PI-G259PI (10)	—
V174PI	(70 pairs)	—
V175PI	(70 pairs)	—
V175PIa	Horiz. se-tenant pair with vert. gutter, #V174PI-V175PI (10)	—

New York #653-654, Geneva #260-261, Vienna #176-177
UNCTAD, 30th Anniv.

1994

653PP	15 items (40)	—
654PP	15 items (40)	—
654PPa	Horiz. se-tenant pair with vert. gutter, #653PP-654PP (10)	—
G260PP	16 items (40)	—
G261PP	16 items (40)	—
G261PPa	Horiz. se-tenant pair with vert. gutter, #G260PP-G261PP (10)	—
V176PP	14 items (40)	—
V177PP	14 items (40)	—
V177PPa	Horiz. se-tenant pair with vert. gutter, #V176PP-V177PP (10)	—
653PI	(60 pairs)	—
654PI	(60 pairs)	—
654PIa	Horiz. se-tenant pair with vert. gutter, #653PI-654PI (30)	—
G260PI	(60 pairs)	—
G261PI	(60 pairs)	—
G261PIa	Horiz. se-tenant pair with vert. gutter, #G260PI-G261PI (30)	—
V176PI	(60 pairs)	—
V177PI	(60 pairs)	—
V177PIa	Horiz. se-tenant pair with vert. gutter, #V176PI-V177PI (30)	—

Two items from No. G260PP and one from No. V176PP blank due to color arrangement on progressive proof shee

New York # 655, Geneva #262, Vienna #178
United Nations, 50th Anniv.

1995

655PD	(3)	—
G262PD	(3)	—
V178PD	(3)	—
655PP	8 items (50)	—
G262PP	8 items (50)	—
V178PP	8 items (50)	—
655PI	(100 pairs)	—
G262PI	(200 pairs)	—
V178PI	(200 pairs)	—

New York #656, Geneva #263, Vienna #179, Souvenir Card #47
World Summit for Social Development, Copenhagen

1995

656PDa	Card, #656PD, #G263PD, #V179PD (3)	—
SC47PD	Card, 4 #SC47PD (1)	—
656PP	12 items (25)	—
G263PP	8 items (25)	—
V179PP	8 items (25)	—
656PI	(24 pairs)	—
G263PI	(24 pairs)	—
V179PI	(24 pairs)	—

New York #660a, Geneva #267a, Vienna #183a
Endangered Species

1995

660aPDa	Card, imperforate pane of 4 blocks, #660aPD (5)	—
660aPDb	Card, broken imperforate pane of 4 blocks, #660aPD (1)	—
660aPDc	Card, 2 imperforate panes of 4 blocks, #660aPD (1)	—
G267aPDa	Card, imperforate pane of 4 blocks, #G267aPD (6)	—
G267aPDb	Card, 2 imperforate panes of 4 blocks, #G267aPD (1)	—
V183aPDa	Card, imperforate pane of 4 blocks, #V183aPD with "14. Okt. 1994" handstamp (approved) (3)	—
V183aTCa	Card, imperforate pane of 4 blocks, #V183aTC (violet blue sky on #181TC), not approved (3)	—
V183aTCb	Card, 2 imperforate pane of 4 blocks, #V183aTC, not approved (1)	—
660aPP	6 items (9 blocks)	—
	Cross gutter block (3)	—
	Horiz. pair with vert. gutter (4)	—
	Vert. pair with horiz. gutter (7)	—
G267aPP	6 items (12 blocks)	—
	Cross gutter block (3)	—
	Horiz. pair with vert. gutter (4)	—
	Vert. pair with horiz. gutter (6)	—
V183aPP	6 items (12 blocks)	—
	Cross gutter block (3)	—
	Horiz. pair with vert. gutter (4)	—
	Vert. pair with horiz. gutter (7)	—
660aPI	(11 blocks)	—
	Cross gutter block (3)	—
	Horiz. pair with vert. gutter (4)	—
	Vert. pair with horiz. gutter (7)	—
G267aPI	(16 blocks)	—
	Cross gutter block (3)	—
	Horiz. pair with vert. gutter (4)	—
	Vert. pair with horiz. gutter (6)	—

...aPI — (11 blocks) —
Cross gutter block (3) —
Horiz. pair with vert. gutter (4) —
Vert. pair with horiz. gutter (7) —

...ee cross gutter blocks, four horizontal pairs with vertical ...s, seven vertical pairs with horizontal gutters and nine ...s with untrimmed margins can be cut from perforated ...s of Nos. V180PI-V183PI.

...ew York #661-662, Geneva #268-269, Vienna #184-185, Souvenir Card #48
International Youth Year

...Da — Card, #661PD-662PD, #G268PD-G269PD, #V184PD-V185PD (6) —
...PD — (6) —
...P — 5 items (160) —
Cross gutter block (5) —
Horiz. pair with vert. gutter (25) —
Vert. pair with horiz. gutter (44) —
...P — 8 items (160) —
Cross gutter block (5) —
Horiz. pair with vert. gutter (25) —
Vert. pair with horiz. gutter (44) —
...PP — 6 items (208) —
Cross gutter block (5) —
Horiz. pair with vert. gutter (25) —
Vert. pair with horiz. gutter (44) —
...PP — 5 items (208) —
Cross gutter block (5) —
Horiz. pair with vert. gutter (25) —
Vert. pair with horiz. gutter (44) —
...PP — 7 items (101) —
Cross gutter block (2) —
Horiz. pair with vert. gutter (11) —
Vert. pair with horiz. gutter (12) —
...PP — 6 items (197) —
Cross gutter block (5) —
Horiz. pair with vert. gutter (25) —
Vert. pair with horiz. gutter (44) —
...I — (128 pairs) —
Cross gutter block (5) —
Horiz. pair with vert. gutter (25) —
Vert. pair with horiz. gutter (44) —
...PI — (128 pairs) —
Cross gutter block (5) —
Horiz. pair with vert. gutter (25) —
Vert. pair with horiz. gutter (44) —
...8PI — (128 pairs) —
Cross gutter block (5) —
Horiz. pair with vert. gutter (25) —
Vert. pair with horiz. gutter (44) —
...9PI — (128 pairs) —
Cross gutter block (5) —
Horiz. pair with vert. gutter (25) —
Vert. pair with horiz. gutter (44) —
...4PI — (128 pairs) —
Cross gutter block (5) —
Horiz. pair with vert. gutter (25) —
Vert. pair with horiz. gutter (44) —
...5PI — (128 pairs) —
Cross gutter block (5) —
Horiz. pair with vert. gutter (25) —
Vert. pair with horiz. gutter (44) —

New York #663-665, Geneva #270-272, Vienna #186-188
United Nations, 50th Anniv.

...5
...PDa — Card, # 664PD, #663TC maroon, #663TC dark blue, #663TC green, #664TC dark blue, #664TC green (3) —
...PI — (80 pairs) —
...PI — (80 pairs) —
...PIa — Horiz. se-tenant pair with vert. gutter, #663PI-664PI (40) —
...PI — (8 pairs of souvenir sheets) —
...70PI — (80 pairs) —
...71PI — (80 pairs) —
...71PIa — Horiz. se-tenant pair with vert. gutter, #G270PI-G271PI (40) —
...72PI — (8 pairs of souvenir sheets) —
...86PI — (80 pairs) —
...87PI — (80 pairs) —
...87PIa — Horiz. se-tenant pair with vert. gutter, #V186PI-V187PI (40) —
...88PI — (8 pairs of souvenir sheets) —

Three cards with non-engraved essays of No. 665 in red ...et exist.

New York #666-667, Geneva #273-274, Vienna #189-190
Fourth World Conference on Women

...95
...6PP — 10 items, perforated (275) —
...7PP — 10 items, perforated (250) —
...273PP — 10 items, perforated (100) —
...274PP — 10 items, perforated (250) —
...89PP — 9 items, perforated (275) —
...90PP — 9 items, perforated (275) —
...6PI — (144 pairs) —
...7PI — (144 pairs) —
...273PI — (108 pairs) —
...274PI — (144 pairs) —
...89PI — (132 pairs) —
...90PI — (144 pairs) —

On No. V189PP and V190PP, 125 sets have a red and mul-...olored item while the remaining 150 sets have a blue and ...ulticolored item.

New York #668
UN Headquarters

1995
668PD — (5) —
668PP — 6 items (162) —
Horiz. pair with vert. gutter (9) —
Vert. pair with horiz. gutter (5) —
668PI — (85 pairs) —
Horiz. pair with vert. gutter (9) —
Vert. pair with horiz. gutter (5) —

New York #669-670, Geneva #275-276, Vienna #191-192
United Nations, 50th Anniversary

1995
669PD — (4) —
G275PD — (4) —
V191PD — (4) —
669PP — 6 items (6) —
G275PP — 8 items (6) —
V191PP — 7 items (6) —
669PI — (2 full panes) —
669PIa — (3 pairs of full panes) —
670PI — (3 booklets) —
G275PI — (2 full panes) —
G275PIa — (3 pairs of full panes) —
G276PI — (3 booklets) —
V191PI — (2 full panes) —
V191PIa — (4 pairs of full panes) —
V192PI — (3 booklets) —

New York #671, Geneva #277, Vienna #193, Souvenir Card #49
World Federation of United Nations Associations, 50th Anniv.

1996
671PDa — Card, #671PD, #G277PD, #V193PD (3) —
SC49PD — (4) —
671PP — 6 items (150) —
Horiz. pair with vert. gutter (25) —
G277PP — 6 items (150) —
Horiz. pair with vert. gutter (25) —
V193PP — 6 items (305) —
Cross gutter block (5) —
Horiz. pair with vert. gutter (40) —
Vert. pair with horiz. gutter (30) —
671PI — (155 pairs) —
G277PI — (155 pairs) —
Horiz. pair with vert. gutter (55) —
V193PI — (264 pairs) —
Cross gutter block (11) —
Horiz. pair with vert. gutter (88) —
Vert. pair with horiz. gutter (63) —

New York #672-673, Geneva #278-279, Vienna #194-195
Definitives

1996
673PDa — Card, #672PD-673PD, #G278PD-G279PD, #V194PD-V195PD with approval handstamp (4) —
673PDb — Card, #673PD, #672TC gray in vignette, #G278TC-G279TC tan background in panel, essays of #V194PD-V195PD (larger frames) (not approved) (4) —
673PDc — #673PDa and 673PDb stapled together (1) —
672PP — 8 items (144) —
Cross gutter block (1) —
Horiz. pair with vert. gutter (18) —
Vert. pair with horiz. gutter (8) —
673PP — 8 items (144) —
Cross gutter block (1) —
Horiz. pair with vert. gutter (18) —
Vert. pair with horiz. gutter (8) —
G278PP — 8 items (144) —
Cross gutter block (1) —
Horiz. pair with vert. gutter (18) —
Vert. pair with horiz. gutter (8) —
G279PP — 8 items (144) —
Cross gutter block (1) —
Horiz. pair with vert. gutter (18) —
Vert. pair with horiz. gutter (8) —
V194PP — 8 items (144) —
Cross gutter block (1) —
Horiz. pair with vert. gutter (18) —
Vert. pair with horiz. gutter (8) —
V195PP — 8 items (144) —
Cross gutter block (1) —
Horiz. pair with vert. gutter (18) —
Vert. pair with horiz. gutter (8) —
672PI — (216 pairs) —
Cross gutter block (3) —
Horiz. pair with vert. gutter (54) —
Vert. pair with horiz. gutter (16) —
673PI — (144 pairs) —
Cross gutter block (3) —
Horiz. pair with vert. gutter (54) —
Vert. pair with horiz. gutter (16) —
G278PI — (216 pairs) —
Cross gutter block (3) —
Horiz. pair with vert. gutter (54) —
Vert. pair with horiz. gutter (24) —
G279PI — (216 pairs) —
Cross gutter block (3) —
Horiz. pair with vert. gutter (54) —
Vert. pair with horiz. gutter (24) —
V194PI — (216 pairs) —
Cross gutter block (3) —
Horiz. pair with vert. gutter (24) —

V195PI — Vert. pair with horiz. gutter (36) —
(216 pairs) —
Cross gutter block (3) —
Horiz. pair with vert. gutter (24) —
Vert. pair with horiz. gutter (36) —

New York #677a, Geneva #283a, Vienna #199a
Endangered Species

1996
677aPDa — Card, imperforate pane of 4 blocks, #677aPD (3) —
677aPDb — Card, broken imperforate pane of 4 blocks, #677aPD (1) —
G283aPDa — Card, imperforate pane of 4 blocks, #G283aPD (3) —
G283aPDb — Card, broken imperforate pane of 4 blocks, #G283aPD (1) —
V199aPDa — Card, imperforate pane of 4 blocks, #V199aPD (3) —
V199aPDb — Card, broken imperforate pane of 4 blocks, #V199aPD (1) —
677aPP — 6 items (14 blocks) —
Cross gutter block (5) —
Horiz. pair with vert. gutter (6) —
Vert. pair with horiz. gutter (11) —
G283aPP — 6 items (14 blocks) —
Cross gutter block (5) —
Horiz. pair with vert. gutter (6) —
Vert. pair with horiz. gutter (11) —
V199aPP — 6 items (14 blocks) —
Cross gutter block (5) —
Horiz. pair with vert. gutter (6) —
Vert. pair with horiz. gutter (11) —
677aPI — (25 blocks) —
Cross gutter block (11) —
Horiz. pair with vert. gutter (12) —
Vert. pair with horiz. gutter (23) —
G283aPI — (25 blocks) —
Cross gutter block (11) —
Horiz. pair with vert. gutter (12) —
Vert. pair with horiz. gutter (23) —
V199aPI — (25 blocks) —
Cross gutter block (11) —
Horiz. pair with vert. gutter (12) —
Vert. pair with horiz. gutter (23) —

New York #682a, Geneva #288a, Vienna #204a
City Summit

1996
682aPDa — Card, imperforate pane of 5 strips, #682aPD (4) —
G288aPDa — Card, imperforate pane of 5 strips, #G288aPD (4) —
V204aPDa — Card, imperforate pane of 5 strips, #V204aPD (4) —
682aPP — 10 items (15 horiz. pairs of strips with vert. gutter) —
G288aPP — 10 items (24 horiz. pairs of strips with vert. gutter) —
Cross gutter block of strips (3) —
V204aPP — 10 items (15 horiz. pairs of strips with vert. gutter) —
682aPI — (35 horiz. pairs of strips with vert. gutter) —
G288aPI — (56 horiz. pairs of strips with vert. gutter) —
Cross gutter block of strips (7) —
V204aPI — (35 horiz. pairs of strips with vert. gutter) —

New York #683-685, Geneva #289-291, Vienna #205-207
Sport and the Environment

1996
684PDa — Card, #683PD-684PD (10) —
685PD — (10) —
G290PDa — Card, #G289PD-G290PD (10) —
G291PD — (10) —
V206PD — Card, #V205PD-V206PD (10) —
V207PD — (10) —
683PP — 8 items (88) —
Cross gutter block (2) —
Horiz. pair with vert. gutter (16) —
Vert. pair with horiz. gutter (11) —
684PP — 8 items (88) —
Cross gutter block (2) —
Horiz. pair with vert. gutter (11) —
Vert. pair with horiz. gutter (16) —
685PP — 12 items (25 souvenir sheets) —
G289PP — 8 items (88) —
Cross gutter block (2) —
Horiz. pair with vert. gutter (16) —
Vert. pair with horiz. gutter (11) —
G290PP — 8 items (88) —
Cross gutter block (2) —
Horiz. pair with vert. gutter (11) —
Vert. pair with horiz. gutter (16) —
G291PP — 10 items (25 souvenir sheets) —
V205PP — 8 items (88) —
Cross gutter block (2) —
Horiz. pair with vert. gutter (16) —
Vert. pair with horiz. gutter (11) —
V206PP — 8 items (88) —
Cross gutter block (2) —
Horiz. pair with vert. gutter (11) —
Vert. pair with horiz. gutter (16) —
V207PP — 11 items (25 souvenir sheets) —
683PI — (44 pairs) —
Cross gutter block (2) —
Horiz. pair with vert. gutter (16) —
Vert. pair with horiz. gutter (11) —
684PI — (44 pairs) —
Cross gutter block (2) —
Horiz. pair with vert. gutter (11) —
Vert. pair with horiz. gutter (16) —

685PI   (75 souvenir sheets) —
G289PI   (88 pairs) —
Cross gutter block (4) —
Horiz. pair with vert. gutter (32) —
Vert. pair with horiz. gutter (22) —
G290PI   (88 pairs) —
Cross gutter block (4) —
Horiz. pair with vert. gutter (22) —
Vert. pair with horiz. gutter (32) —
G291PI   (75 souvenir sheets) —
V205PI   (132 pairs) —
Cross gutter block (6) —
Horiz. pair with vert. gutter (48) —
Vert. pair with horiz. gutter (33) —
V206PI   (132 pairs) —
Cross gutter block (6) —
Horiz. pair with vert. gutter (33) —
Vert. pair with horiz. gutter (48) —
V207PI   (75 souvenir sheets) —

New York #686-687, Geneva #292-293, Vienna #208-209
Plea for Peace
1996
687PDa   Card, #686PD-687PD, #G292PD-G293PD, #V208PD-V209PD (4)
686PP   10 items (112) —
Cross gutter block (3) —
Horiz. pair with vert. gutter (14) —
Vert. pair with horiz. gutter (24) —
687PP   10 items (112) —
Cross gutter block (3) —
Horiz. pair with vert. gutter (14) —
Vert. pair with horiz. gutter (24) —
G292PP   10 items (112) —
Cross gutter block (3) —
Horiz. pair with vert. gutter (24) —
Vert. pair with horiz. gutter (14) —
G293PP   10 items (112) —
Cross gutter block (2) —
Horiz. pair with vert. gutter (24) —
Vert. pair with horiz. gutter (14) —
V208PP   10 items (112) —
Cross gutter block (3) —
Horiz. pair with vert. gutter (14) —
Vert. pair with horiz. gutter (24) —
V209PP   10 items (112) —
Cross gutter block (3) —
Horiz. pair with vert. gutter (14) —
Vert. pair with horiz. gutter (24) —
686PI   (104 pairs) —
Cross gutter block (3) —
Horiz. pair with vert. gutter (14) —
Vert. pair with horiz. gutter (24) —
687PI   (104 pairs) —
Cross gutter block (3) —
Horiz. pair with vert. gutter (14) —
Vert. pair with horiz. gutter (24) —
G292PI   (80 pairs) —
Cross gutter block (3) —
Horiz. pair with vert. gutter (24) —
Vert. pair with horiz. gutter (14) —
G293PI   (80 pairs) —
Cross gutter block (3) —
Horiz. pair with vert. gutter (24) —
Vert. pair with horiz. gutter (14) —
V208PI   (80 pairs) —
Cross gutter block (3) —
Horiz. pair with vert. gutter (24) —
Vert. pair with horiz. gutter (14) —
V209PI   (80 pairs) —
Cross gutter block (3) —
Horiz. pair with vert. gutter (14) —
Vert. pair with horiz. gutter (24) —

New York #688-689, Geneva #294-295, Vienna #210-211, Souvenir Card #50
UNICEF, 50th Anniv.
1996
689PDa   Imperforate pane, #689PD (4)
G294PDa   Imperforate pane, #G294PD (4) —
G295PDa   Imperforate pane, #G295PD (6) —
V210PDa   Imperforate pane, #V210PD (on photographic paper) (2) —
V211PDa   Imperforate pane, #V211PD (4) —
SC50PD   (1) —
688PP   10 items (18) —
Cross gutter block (6) —
Horiz. pair with vert. gutter (12) —
Vert. pair with horiz. gutter (15) —
689PP   11 items (18) —
Cross gutter block (6) —
Horiz. pair with vert. gutter (12) —
Vert. pair with horiz. gutter (15) —
G294PP   9 items (18) —
Cross gutter block (6) —
Horiz. pair with vert. gutter (12) —
Vert. pair with horiz. gutter (15) —
G295PP   9 items (18) —
Cross gutter block (6) —
Horiz. pair with vert. gutter (12) —
Vert. pair with horiz. gutter (15) —
V210PP   9 items (18) —
Cross gutter block (6) —
Horiz. pair with vert. gutter (18) —
Vert. pair with horiz. gutter (14) —
V211PP   9 items (18) —
Cross gutter block (6) —
Horiz. pair with vert. gutter (18) —
Vert. pair with horiz. gutter (14) —
688PI   (12 pairs) —
Cross gutter block (18) —
Horiz. pair with vert. gutter (36) —
Vert. pair with horiz. gutter (45) —
689PI   (12 pairs) —
Cross gutter block (18) —

G294PI   Horiz. pair with vert. gutter (36) —
Vert. pair with horiz. gutter (45) —
(12 pairs) —
Cross gutter block (18) —
G295PI   Horiz. pair with vert. gutter (36) —
Vert. pair with horiz. gutter (45) —
(12 pairs) —
Cross gutter block (18) —
V210PI   Horiz. pair with vert. gutter (36) —
Vert. pair with horiz. gutter (45) —
(12 pairs) —
Cross gutter block (18) —
V211PI   Horiz. pair with vert. gutter (36) —
Vert. pair with horiz. gutter (45) —
(12 pairs) —
Cross gutter block (18) —
Horiz. pair with vert. gutter (36) —
Vert. pair with horiz. gutter (45) —

Two of the No. G295PDa items are on photographic paper. Four cards with imperforate panes of 32c Hansel & Gretel essays exist. Four cards with imperforate panes of 5.50s Yeh-Shen essays exist. Four essays of No. SC50 showing these two essay items exist.

New York #690-697
Flags
1997
690-697PP   Set of 20 sheets (1)
690-697PI   Set of 2 sheets (3)

On Nos. 690-697PP, there are ten progressive proof sheets per issued sheet.

New York #698-699, Geneva #296-297, Vienna #212-213
Definitives
1997
698PDa   Card, #698PD, #G296PD-G297PD, #V212PD-V213PD (1)
699PDa   Card, #698PD-699PD, #G296PD-G297PD, #V212PD-V213PD (4)
698PP   8 items (84) —
Cross gutter block (3) —
Horiz. pair with vert. gutter (18) —
Vert. pair with horiz. gutter (14) —
699PP   8 items (84) —
Cross gutter block (3) —
Horiz. pair with vert. gutter (14) —
Vert. pair with horiz. gutter (18) —
G296PP   8 items (84) —
Cross gutter block (3) —
Horiz. pair with vert. gutter (14) —
Vert. pair with horiz. gutter (18) —
G297PP   8 items (84) —
Cross gutter block (3) —
Horiz. pair with vert. gutter (14) —
Vert. pair with horiz. gutter (18) —
V212PP   10 items (84) —
Cross gutter block (3) —
Horiz. pair with vert. gutter (18) —
Vert. pair with horiz. gutter (14) —
V213PP   10 items (84) —
Cross gutter block (3) —
Horiz. pair with vert. gutter (18) —
Vert. pair with horiz. gutter (14) —
698PI   (60 pairs) —
Cross gutter block (3) —
Horiz. pair with vert. gutter (18) —
Vert. pair with horiz. gutter (14) —
699PI   (60 pairs) —
Cross gutter block (3) —
Horiz. pair with vert. gutter (18) —
Vert. pair with horiz. gutter (14) —
G296PI   (60 pairs) —
Cross gutter block (3) —
Horiz. pair with vert. gutter (18) —
Vert. pair with horiz. gutter (14) —
G297PI   (60 pairs) —
Cross gutter block (3) —
Horiz. pair with vert. gutter (18) —
Vert. pair with horiz. gutter (14) —
V212PI   (60 pairs) —
Cross gutter block (3) —
Horiz. pair with vert. gutter (18) —
Vert. pair with horiz. gutter (14) —
V213PI   (60 pairs) —
Cross gutter block (3) —
Horiz. pair with vert. gutter (18) —
Vert. pair with horiz. gutter (14) —

New York #703a, Geneva #301a, Vienna #217a
Endangered Species
1997
703aPDa   Card, imperforate pane of 4 blocks #703aPD, imperforate pane of 4 blocks #G301aPD (4) —
V217aPDa   Card, imperforate pane of 4 blocks #V217aPD (4) —
703aPP   6 items (4 blocks) —
Cross gutter block (2) —
Horiz. pair with vert. gutter (2) —
Vert. pair with horiz. gutter (4) —
G301aPP   6 items (4 blocks) —
Cross gutter block (2) —
Horiz. pair with vert. gutter (2) —
Vert. pair with horiz. gutter (4) —
V217aPP   6 items (4 blocks) —
Cross gutter block (2) —
Horiz. pair with vert. gutter (2) —
Vert. pair with horiz. gutter (4) —
703aPI   (12 blocks) —
Cross gutter block (6) —
Horiz. pair with vert. gutter (6) —
Vert. pair with horiz. gutter (12) —

G301aPI   (12 blocks) —
Cross gutter block (6) —
Horiz. pair with vert. gutter (6) —
Vert. pair with horiz. gutter (12) —
V217aPI   (12 blocks) —
Cross gutter block (6) —
Horiz. pair with vert. gutter (6) —
Vert. pair with horiz. gutter (12) —

New York #707a, 708, Geneva #305a, 306, Vienna #221a, 222
Earth Summit
1997
707aPP   6 items (6 blocks) —
708PP   6 items (1 souvenir sheet) —
708aPP   6 items (1 souvenir sheet) —
C305aPP   6 items (6 blocks) —
V221aPP   6 items (6 blocks) —
707aPI   (15 blocks) —
708PI   (6 souvenir sheets) —
708aPI   (6 souvenir sheets) —
G305aPI   (15 blocks) —
G306PI   (6 souvenir sheets) —
V221aPI   (15 blocks) —
V222PI   (6 souvenir sheets) —

New York #713a, Geneva #311a, Vienna #227a
Transportation
1997
713aPDa   Imperforate pane, #713aPD (9)
G311aPDa   Imperforate pane, #G311aPD (9)
V227aPDa   Imperforate pane, #V227aPD (9)
713aPP   9 items (6 strips) —
Cross gutter block of strips (1) —
Horiz. pair of strips with vert. gutter (6) —
Vert. pair of strips with horiz. gutter (1) —
G311aPP   10 items (6 strips) —
Cross gutter block of strips (1) —
Horiz. pair of strips with vert. gutter (6) —
Vert. pair of strips with horiz. gutter (1) —
V227aPP   9 items (6 strips) —
Cross gutter block of strips (1) —
Horiz. pair of strips with vert. gutter (6) —
Vert. pair of strips with horiz. gutter (1) —
713aPI   (14 strips) —
Cross gutter block of strips (1) —
Horiz. pair of strips with vert. gutter (6) —
Vert. pair of strips with horiz. gutter (1) —
G311aPI   (14 strips) —
Cross gutter block of strips (1) —
Horiz. pair of strips with vert. gutter (6) —
Vert. pair of strips with horiz. gutter (1) —
V227aPI   (14 strips) —
Cross gutter block of strips (1) —
Horiz. pair of strips with vert. gutter (6) —
Vert. pair of strips with horiz. gutter (1) —

New York #714-715, Geneva #312-313, Vienna #228-229, Souvenir Card #51
Philately
1997
715TCa   Card, #714TC-715TC, #G312TC-G313TC, #V228TC-V229TC, all with white denominations (4)
715TCb   Card, #714TC-715TC, #G312TC-G313TC, #V228TC-V229TC, all with light blue green backgrounds (1)
SC51PD   (4)
714PP   11 items (33) —
Horiz. pair with vert. gutter (6) —
715PP   11 items (33) —
Horiz. pair with vert. gutter (6) —
715PPa   Cross gutter block, 2 each #714PP-715PP (2) —
715PPb   Vert. pair with horiz. gutter, #714PP-715PP (11) —
G312PP   11 items (33) —
Horiz. pair with vert. gutter (6) —
G313PP   11 items (33) —
Horiz. pair with vert. gutter (6) —
G313PPa   Cross gutter block, 2 each #G312PP-G313PP (2) —
G313PPb   Vert. pair with horiz. gutter, #G312PP-G313PP (11) —
V228PP   10 items (33) —
Horiz. pair with vert. gutter (6) —
V229PP   10 items (33) —
Horiz. pair with vert. gutter (6) —
V229PPa   Cross gutter block, 2 each #V228PP-V229PP (2) —
V229PPb   Vert. pair with horiz. gutter, #V228PP-V229PP (11) —
714PI   (48 pairs) —
Horiz. pair with vert. gutter (18) —
715PI   (48 pairs) —
Horiz. pair with vert. gutter (18) —
715PIa   Cross gutter block, 2 each #714PI-715PI (6) —
715PIb   Vert. pair with horiz. gutter, #714PI-715PI (33) —
G312PI   (48 pairs) —

	Horiz. pair with vert. gutter (18)	—
PI	(48 pairs)	
	Horiz. pair with vert. gutter (18)	—
PIa	Cross gutter block, 2 each #G312PI-G313PI (6)	—
PIb	Vert. pair with horiz. gutter, #G312PI-G313PI (33)	—
PI	(48 pairs)	
	Horiz. pair with vert. gutter (18)	—
PI	(48 pairs)	
	Horiz. pair with vert. gutter (18)	—
PIa	Cross gutter block, 2 each #V228PI-V229PI (6)	—
PIb	Vert. pair with horiz. gutter, #V228PI-V229PI (33)	—

Nos. 714PP-715PP, G312PP-G313PP and V228PP-V229PP some progressive proof items are blank due to color arrangements on sheets.

New York #716-717, Geneva #314-315, Vienna #230-231
World Heritage

1997

Da	Stapled set of 6 layout sheets with #716PD-717PD, #G314PD-G315PD, #V230PD-V231PD affixed (3)	—
P	10 items (20)	—
P	10 items (20)	—
4PP	10 items (20)	—
5PP	10 items (20)	—
0PP	10 items (20)	—
1PP	10 items (20)	—
PI	(30 pairs)	—
PI	(30 pairs)	—
4PI	(30 pairs)	—
5PI	(30 pairs)	—
0PI	(30 pairs)	—
1PI	(30 pairs)	—

New York #719-726
Flags

8

726PP	Set of 20 sheets (1)	—
726PI	Set of 2 sheets (3)	—

In Nos. 719-726PP, there are ten progressive proof sheets per issued sheet.

New York #727-729, Geneva #317, Vienna #233-234
Definitives

8

PDa	Card, #727PD, #G317TC black (1)	—
PDa	Card, #727PD-729PD, #G317PD, #V233PD-V234PD (4)	—
PP	10 items (84)	—
	Cross gutter block (3)	—
	Horiz. pair with vert. gutter (14)	—
	Vert. pair with horiz. gutter (18)	—
PP	8 items (84)	—
	Cross gutter block (3)	—
	Horiz. pair with vert. gutter (14)	—
	Vert. pair with horiz. gutter (18)	—
PP	9 items (84)	—
	Cross gutter block (3)	—
	Horiz. pair with vert. gutter (18)	—
	Vert. pair with horiz. gutter (14)	—
7PP	10 items (84)	—
	Cross gutter block (3)	—
	Horiz. pair with vert. gutter (14)	—
	Vert. pair with horiz. gutter (18)	—
33PP	8 items (84)	—
	Cross gutter block (3)	—
	Horiz. pair with vert. gutter (18)	—
	Vert. pair with horiz. gutter (14)	—
34PP	10 items (84)	—
	Cross gutter block (3)	—
	Horiz. pair with vert. gutter (18)	—
	Vert. pair with horiz. gutter (14)	—
7PI	(60 pairs)	—
	Cross gutter block (3)	—
	Horiz. pair with vert. gutter (14)	—
	Vert. pair with horiz. gutter (18)	—
8PI	(60 pairs)	—
	Cross gutter block (3)	—
	Horiz. pair with vert. gutter (14)	—
	Vert. pair with horiz. gutter (18)	—
9PI	(60 pairs)	—
	Cross gutter block (3)	—
	Horiz. pair with vert. gutter (18)	—
	Vert. pair with horiz. gutter (14)	—
17PI	(60 pairs)	—
	Cross gutter block (3)	—
	Horiz. pair with vert. gutter (14)	—
	Vert. pair with horiz. gutter (18)	—
33PI	(60 pairs)	—
	Cross gutter block (3)	—
	Horiz. pair with vert. gutter (18)	—
	Vert. pair with horiz. gutter (14)	—
34PI	(60 pairs)	—
	Cross gutter block (3)	—
	Horiz. pair with vert. gutter (18)	—
	Vert. pair with horiz. gutter (14)	—

New York #733a, Geneva #321a, Vienna #238a
Endangered Species

1998

3PDa	Card, imperforate pane of 4 blocks, #733aPD (1)	—
3PDb	Card, broken imperforate pane of 4 blocks, #733aPD (1)	—

G321PDa	Card, imperforate pane of 4 blocks, #G321aPD (1)	—
G321PDb	Card, broken imperforate pane of 4 blocks, #G321aPD (1)	—
V238PDa	Card, imperforate pane of 4 blocks, #V238aPD (1)	—
V238PDb	Card, broken imperforate pane of 4 blocks, #V238aPD (1)	—
733aPP	6 items (4 blocks)	—
	Cross gutter block (2)	—
	Horiz. pair with vert. gutter (2)	—
	Vert. pair with horiz. gutter (4)	—
G321aPP	4 items (4 blocks)	—
	Cross gutter block (2)	—
	Horiz. pair with vert. gutter (2)	—
	Vert. pair with horiz. gutter (4)	—
V238aPP	6 items (4 blocks)	—
	Cross gutter block (2)	—
	Horiz. pair with vert. gutter (2)	—
	Vert. pair with horiz. gutter (4)	—
733aPI	(12 blocks)	—
	Cross gutter block (2)	—
	Horiz. pair with vert. gutter (2)	—
	Vert. pair with horiz. gutter (4)	—
G321aPI	(12 blocks)	—
	Cross gutter block (2)	—
	Horiz. pair with vert. gutter (2)	—
	Vert. pair with horiz. gutter (4)	—
V238aPI	(12 blocks)	—
	Cross gutter block (2)	—
	Horiz. pair with vert. gutter (2)	—
	Vert. pair with horiz. gutter (4)	—

No. G321aPP is not a complete set, as there are no black only and cyan only items.

New York #734, Geneva #322, Vienna #239
International Year of the Ocean

1998

734PD	(not approved) (4)	—
G322PD	(4)	—
V239PD	(4)	—
734PP	6 items (6 panes)	—
G322PP	6 items (6 panes)	—
V239PP	6 items (6 panes)	—
734PI	(18 panes)	—
G322PI	(18 panes)	—
V239PI	(18 panes)	—

New York #735-736, Geneva #323-324, Vienna #240-241
Rain Forests

1998

735PDa	Card, imperforate pane of 20 #735PD (8)	—
736PDa	Card, #736PD, #G324PD, #V241PD (8)	—
G323PDa	Card, imperforate pane of 20 #G323PD (8)	—
V240PDa	Card, imperforate pane of 20 #V240PD (8)	—
735PP	6 items (see note)	—
G323PP	6 items (see note)	—
V240PP	6 items (see note)	—
735PI	(see note)	—
G323PI	(see note)	—
V240PI	(see note)	—

There are two types of Nos. 735PP and V240PP, one with cats lacking spots on the red item, the other with the cat with spots on the magenta item. There are 20 of each type.

There are two types of No. G323PP, one with orangutan with small dots in eyes on the cyan item, the other with large dots in eyes.

Similarly, there are two types of Nos. 735PI, G323PI and V240PI, one with a lighter background, the other with a bolder background. There are 20 pairs of each type.

New York #737-738, Geneva #325-326, Vienna #242-243, Souvenir Card #52
UN Peacekeeping Forces, 50th Anniv.

1998

737TC	Dark blue panel (on Cromalin paper) (5)	—
738TC	Dark blue panel (on Cromalin paper) (5)	—
G325TC	Dark blue panel (on Cromalin paper) (5)	—
G326TC	Dark blue panel (on Cromalin paper) (5)	—
V242TC	Dark blue panel (on Cromalin paper) (5)	—
V243TC	Dark blue panel (on Cromalin paper) (5)	—
SC52PD	(4)	—
737PP	10 items (20)	—
738PP	10 items (20)	—
G325PP	10 items (20)	—
G326PP	10 items (20)	—
V242PP	10 items (20)	—
V243PP	10 items (20)	—
737PI	(20 pairs)	—
738PI	(20 pairs)	—
G325PI	(20 pairs)	—
G326PI	(20 pairs)	—
V242PI	(20 pairs)	—
V243PI	(20 pairs)	—

New York #739-740, Geneva #327-328, Vienna #244-245, Souvenir Card #53
Universal Declaration of Human Rights, 50th Anniv.

1998

740PDa	Card, #739PD-740PD, #G327PD-G328PD, #V244PD-V245PD (4)	—
SC53PD	(4)	—
739PP	8 items (64)	—
	Cross gutter block (2)	—
	Horiz. pair with vert. gutter (8)	—
	Vert. pair with horiz. gutter (16)	—
740PP	8 items (64)	—
	Cross gutter block (2)	—
	Horiz. pair with vert. gutter (8)	—
	Vert. pair with horiz. gutter (16)	—
G327PP	8 items (64)	—
	Cross gutter block (2)	—
	Horiz. pair with vert. gutter (8)	—
	Vert. pair with horiz. gutter (16)	—
G328PP	8 items (64)	—
	Cross gutter block (2)	—
	Horiz. pair with vert. gutter (8)	—
	Vert. pair with horiz. gutter (16)	—
V244PP	8 items (64)	—
	Cross gutter block (2)	—
	Horiz. pair with vert. gutter (8)	—
	Vert. pair with horiz. gutter (16)	—
V245PP	8 items (64)	—
	Cross gutter block (2)	—
	Horiz. pair with vert. gutter (8)	—
	Vert. pair with horiz. gutter (16)	—
739PI	(52 pairs)	—
	Cross gutter block (2)	—
	Horiz. pair with vert. gutter (8)	—
	Vert. pair with horiz. gutter (16)	—
740PI	(52 pairs)	—
	Cross gutter block (2)	—
	Horiz. pair with vert. gutter (8)	—
	Vert. pair with horiz. gutter (16)	—
G327PI	(52 pairs)	—
	Cross gutter block (2)	—
	Horiz. pair with vert. gutter (8)	—
	Vert. pair with horiz. gutter (16)	—
G328PI	(52 pairs)	—
	Cross gutter block (2)	—
	Horiz. pair with vert. gutter (8)	—
	Vert. pair with horiz. gutter (16)	—
V244PI	(52 pairs)	—
	Cross gutter block (2)	—
	Horiz. pair with vert. gutter (8)	—
	Vert. pair with horiz. gutter (16)	—
V245PI	(52 pairs)	—
	Cross gutter block (2)	—
	Horiz. pair with vert. gutter (8)	—
	Vert. pair with horiz. gutter (16)	—

New York #741-743, Geneva #329-331, Vienna #246-248
Schönbrunn Palace

1998

742PDa	Card, blocks of 4, #741PD-742PD (3)	—
742PDb	Card, cut apart blocks of 4, #741PD-742PD (1)	—
G330PDa	Card, blocks of 4, #G329PD-G330PD (3)	—
G330PDb	Card, cut apart blocks of 4, #G329PD-G330PD (1)	—
V247PDa	Card, blocks of 4, #V246PD-V247PD (3)	—
V247PDb	Card, cut apart blocks of 4, #V246PD-V247PD (1)	—
742TCa	Card, block of 4 #742TC dark blue denomination (on photographic paper) (1)	—
743TCa	Card, strips of 3, #743aTC-743cTC bright red violet denomination (on photographic paper) (1)	—
743TCb	Card, blocks of 4, #743dTC-743fTC bright red violet denomination (on photographic paper) (1)	—
743TCc	Entire booklet (black & white, on photographic paper) (1)	—
G330TCa	Card, blocks of 4, #G329TC-G330TC bright red violet denominations (on photographic paper) (1)	—
G331TCa	Card, blocks of 4, #G331aTC-G331cTC bright red violet denomination (on photographic paper) (1)	—
G331TCb	Card, strips of 3, #G331dTC-G331fTC bright red violet denomination (on photographic paper) (1)	—
G331TCc	Entire booklet (black & white, on photographic paper) (1)	—
V247TCa	Card, block of 4 #V247TC bright green denomination (on photographic paper) (1)	—
V248TCa	Card, strips of 3, #V248aTC-V248cTC bright red violet denomination (on photographic paper) (1)	—
V248TCb	Card, blocks of 4, #V248dTC-V248fTC bright red violet denomination (on photographic paper) (1)	—
V248TCc	Entire booklet (black & white, on photographic paper) (1)	—
741PP	10 items (24)	—
	Vert. pair with horiz. gutter (3)	—
742PP	10 items (24)	—

742PPa	Horiz. pair with vert. gutter (3) Cross gutter block, 2 #741PP-742PP (1)	—
742PPb	Vert. pair with horiz. gutter, #741PP-742PP (8)	
G329PP	10 items (24)	
G330PP	Vert. pair with horiz. gutter (3) 10 items (24)	
G330PPa	Horiz. pair with vert. gutter (3) Cross gutter block, 2 #G329PP-G330PP (1)	
G330PPb	Vert. pair with horiz. gutter, #G329PP-G330PP (8)	
V246PP	10 items (24)	
V247PP	Vert. pair with horiz. gutter (3) 10 items (24)	
V247PPa	Horiz. pair with vert. gutter (3) Cross gutter block, 2 #V246PP-V247PP (1)	
V247PPb	Vert. pair with horiz. gutter, #V246PP-V247PP (8)	
741PI	(32 pairs)	
742PI	Vert. pair with horiz. gutter (3) (32 pairs)	
742PIa	Horiz. pair with vert. gutter (3) Cross gutter block, 2 #741PI-742PI (1)	
742PIb	Vert. pair with horiz. gutter, #741PI-742PI (8)	
G329PI	(32 pairs)	
G330PI	Vert. pair with horiz. gutter (3) (32 pairs)	
G330PIa	Horiz. pair with vert. gutter (3) Cross gutter block, 2 #G329PI-G330PI (1)	
G330PIb	Vert. pair with horiz. gutter, #G329PI-G330PI (8)	
V246PI	(32 pairs)	
V247PI	Vert. pair with horiz. gutter (3) (32 pairs)	
V247PIa	Horiz. pair with vert. gutter (3) Cross gutter block, 2 #V246PI-V247PI (1)	
V247PIb	Vert. pair with horiz. gutter, #V246PI-V247PI (8)	

Five cards with blocks of four essays with gold frames over vignette exist for each of the New York, Geneva and Vienna pairings.

New York #744-751
Flags

1999

744-751PP	Set of 20 sheets (1)	—
744-751PI	Set of 2 sheets (4)	—

On Nos. 744-751PP, there are ten progressive proof sheets per issued sheet.

New York #752-753, Geneva #332, Vienna #249
Definitives

1999

752PDa	Card, #752PD, #V249PD (3)	
752PDb	Card, #752PD, #V249PD, #753TC lacking gray in pink frame boxes (1)	—
753PDa	Card, block of 4, #753PD (2)	—
753TC	Lacking gray in pink frame boxes (3)	—
G332TC	red (4)	—
G332TC	brown (4)	—
752PP	9 items (48)	—
	Cross gutter block (1)	—
	Horiz. pair with vert. gutter (6)	—
	Vert. pair with horiz. gutter (8)	—
753PP	10 items (20)	—
V249PP	9 items (48)	—
	Cross gutter block (1)	—
	Horiz. pair with vert. gutter (6)	—
	Vert. pair with horiz. gutter (8)	—
752PI	(24 pairs)	—
	Cross gutter block (3)	—
	Horiz. pair with vert. gutter (18)	—
	Vert. pair with horiz. gutter (24)	—
753PI	(20 pairs)	—
G332PI	(20 pairs)	—
V249PI	(72 pairs)	—
	Cross gutter block (3)	—
	Horiz. pair with vert. gutter (18)	—
	Vert. pair with horiz. gutter (24)	—

New York #754-756, Geneva #333-335, Vienna #250-252
World Heritage

1999

755PDa	Card, pairs of #754PD-755PD, #G333PD-G334PD, #V250PD-V251PD (1)	—
756PDa	Card, pairs of #756aPD-756fPD (1)	—
756PDb	Sheet, pairs of #754PD-755PD, #756aPD-756fPD, #G333PD-G334PD, #G335aPD-G335fPD, #V250PD-V251PD, #V252aPD-V252fPD (2)	—
756PDc	Cut-up section of #756PDb with pairs of stamps issued in sheets (2)	—
756PDd	Cut-up section of #756PDb with pairs of stamps issued in booklets (2)	—
754TC	Black and white image on layout sheet of photographic paper (2)	—
755TC	Black and white image on layout sheet of photographic paper (2)	—

G333TC	Black and white image on layout sheet of photographic paper (2)	—
G334TC	Black and white image on layout sheet of photographic paper (2)	—
V250TCa	Black and white image on layout sheet of photographic paper (2)	—
V250TCb	2 pairs of black and white images on layout sheet of photographic paper, affixed to card (1)	—
V251TCa	Black and white image on layout sheet of photographic paper (2)	—
V251TCb	2 pairs of black and white images on layout sheet of photographic paper, affixed to card (1)	—
754PP	6 items (32)	—
755PP	Horiz. pair with vert. gutter (8) 6 items (32)	—
755PPa	Horiz. pair with vert. gutter (8) Cross gutter block, 2 #754PP-755PP (2)	—
755PPb	Vert. pair with horiz. gutter, #754PP-755PP (8)	—
G333PP	6 items (32)	—
G334PP	Horiz. pair with vert. gutter (8) 6 items (32)	—
G334PPa	Horiz. pair with vert. gutter (8) Cross gutter block, 2 #G333PP-G334PP (2)	—
G334PPb	Vert. pair with horiz. gutter, #G333PP-G334PP (8)	—
V250PP	6 items (32)	—
V251PP	Horiz. pair with vert. gutter (8) 6 items (32)	—
V251PPa	Horiz. pair with vert. gutter (8) Cross gutter block, 2 #V250PP-V251PP (2)	—
V251PPb	Vert. pair with horiz. gutter, #V250PP-V251PP (8)	—
754PI	(52 pairs)	—
755PI	Horiz. pair with vert. gutter (16) (52 pairs)	—
755PIa	Horiz. pair with vert. gutter (16) Cross gutter block, 2 #754PI-755PI (4)	—
755PIb	Vert. pair with horiz. gutter, #754PI-755PI (16)	—
G333PI	(36 pairs)	—
G334PI	Horiz. pair with vert. gutter (8) (36 pairs)	—
G334PIa	Horiz. pair with vert. gutter (8) Cross gutter block, 2 #G333PI-G334PI (2)	—
G334PIb	Vert. pair with horiz. gutter, #G333PI-G334PI (8)	—
V250PI	(36 pairs)	—
V251PI	Horiz. pair with vert. gutter (8) (36 pairs)	—
V251PIa	Horiz. pair with vert. gutter (8) Cross gutter block, 2 #V250PI-V251PI (2)	—
V251PIb	Vert. pair with horiz. gutter, #V250PI-V251PI (8)	—

New York #760a, Geneva #339a, Vienna #256a
Endangered Species

1999

760aPDa	Card, imperf pane of 4 blocks, #760aPD (2)	
760aPDb	Card, 2 each #757PD-760PD (1)	—
G339aPDa	Card, 2 each #G336PD-G339PD (on Cromalin paper), broken pane of 80c essays of #G336-G339 (1)	
V256aPDa	Card, imperf pane of 4 blocks, #V256aPD (3)	
V256aPDb	Card, 2 each #V253PD-V256PD (2)	
760aPP	6 items (4 blocks)	—
	Cross gutter block (2)	—
	Horiz. pair with vert. gutter (2)	—
	Vert. pair with horiz. gutter (4)	—
G339aPP	6 items (4 blocks)	—
	Cross gutter block (2)	—
	Horiz. pair with vert. gutter (2)	—
	Vert. pair with horiz. gutter (4)	—
V256aPP	6 items (4 blocks)	—
	Cross gutter block (2)	—
	Horiz. pair with vert. gutter (2)	—
	Vert. pair with horiz. gutter (4)	—
760aPI	(12 blocks)	—
	Cross gutter block (2)	—
	Horiz. pair with vert. gutter (2)	—
	Vert. pair with horiz. gutter (4)	—
G339aPI	(12 blocks)	—
	Cross gutter block (2)	—
	Horiz. pair with vert. gutter (2)	—
	Vert. pair with horiz. gutter (4)	—
V256aPI	(12 blocks)	—
	Cross gutter block (2)	—
	Horiz. pair with vert. gutter (2)	—
	Vert. pair with horiz. gutter (4)	—

Three cards exist containing imperforate panes of four blocks of the 80c essays.

New York #762a, 763, Geneva #341a, 342, Vienna #258a, 259
UNISPACE III

1999

762aPDa	Card, imperforate pane of 5 pairs, #762aPD (3)	
763PD	With printed perforations on overlay (3)	—
763aPD	With printed perforations on overlay (2)	—

G341aPDa	Card, imperforate pane of 5 pairs, #G341aPD (4)	
G342PD	With printed perforations on overlay (2)	
G342aPD	With printed perforations on overlay (2)	
V258aPDa	Card, imperforate pane of 5 pairs, #V258aPD (4)	
V259PD	With printed perforations on overlay (2)	
762PP	8 items (5 pairs)	
762aPP	8 items (1 souvenir sheet)	
763PP	9 items (1 pair)	
763aPP	10 items (1 souvenir sheet)	
762aPI	(10 pairs)	
763PI	(3 souvenir sheets)	
763aPI	(4 souvenir sheets)	
G341aPI	(10 pairs)	
G342PI	(3 souvenir sheets)	
V258aPI	(10 pairs)	
V259PI	(3 souvenir sheets)	

New York #767a, Geneva #346a, Vienna #263
Souvenir Card #54
Universal Postal Union, 125th Anniv.

1999

767aPDa	Card, #767aPD, #G346aPD, #V263aPD with approval handstamp (4)	
767aTCa	Card, #767aTC, #G346aTCD, #V263aTC (dark blue denominations, not approved (4)	
SC54PD	(4)	
767aPP	8 items (6 blocks)	
G346aPP	8 items (6 blocks)	
V263aPP	8 items (6 blocks)	
767aPI	(12 blocks)	
G346aPI	(12 blocks)	
V263aPI	(12 blocks)	

New York #768-769, Geneva #347-348, Vienna #264-265
In Memoriam

1999

769PDa	Card, #768PD-769PD (4)	
G348PDa	Card, #G347PD-G348PD (4)	
V265PDa	Card, #V264PD-V265PD (4)	
768PP	10 items (66)	
	Cross gutter block (2)	
	Horiz. pair with vert. gutter (12)	
	Vert. pair with horiz. gutter (11)	
769PP	10 items (24 souvenir sheets)	
G347PP	10 items (66)	
	Cross gutter block (2)	
	Horiz. pair with vert. gutter (12)	
	Vert. pair with horiz. gutter (11)	
G348PP	10 items (24 souvenir sheets)	
V264PP	10 items (66)	
	Cross gutter block (2)	
	Horiz. pair with vert. gutter (12)	
	Vert. pair with horiz. gutter (11)	
V265PP	10 items (24 souvenir sheets)	
768PI	(52 pairs)	
	Cross gutter block (2)	
	Horiz. pair with vert. gutter (12)	
	Vert. pair with horiz. gutter (11)	
769PI	(24 souvenir sheets)	
G347PI	(52 pairs)	
	Cross gutter block (2)	
	Horiz. pair with vert. gutter (12)	
	Vert. pair with horiz. gutter (11)	
G348PI	(24 souvenir sheets)	
V264PI	(52 pairs)	
	Cross gutter block (2)	
	Horiz. pair with vert. gutter (12)	
	Vert. pair with horiz. gutter (11)	
V265PI	(24 souvenir sheets)	

New York #770-771, Geneva #349-350, Vienna #266-267
Education

1999

771PDa	Card, #770PD-771PD, #G349PD-G350PD, #V266PD-V267PD with approval handstamp (4)	
771PDb	Card, #770PD, #G350PD, #V266PD-V267PD, #771TC red denomination, #G349TC red violet denomination with "approved with corrections" handstamp (4)	
770PP	9 items (20)	
771PP	8 items (20)	
G349PP	7 items (20)	
G350PP	7 items (20)	
V266PP	7 items (20)	
V267PP	8 items (20)	
770PI	(20 pairs)	
771PI	(20 pairs)	
G349PI	(30 pairs)	
G350PI	(30 pairs)	
V266PI	(30 pairs)	
V267PI	(30 pairs)	

New York #772, Geneva #351, Vienna #268
International Year of Thanksgiving

2000

772PDa	Card, #772PD, #G351PD, #V268PD (4)	
772TCa	Card, #772TC, #G351TC, #V268TC, all with black background (4)	
772PP	12 items (32)	
	Horiz. pair with vert. gutter (4)	

1PP	12 items (32)	—
	Horiz. pair with vert. gutter (4)	—
3PP	12 items (32)	—
	Horiz. pair with vert. gutter (4)	—
PI	(36 pairs)	—
	Horiz. pair with vert. gutter (4)	—
1PI	(36 pairs)	—
	Horiz. pair with vert. gutter (4)	—
8PI	(36 pairs)	—
	Horiz. pair with vert. gutter (4)	—

New York #776a, Geneva #355a, Vienna #272a
Endangered Species

0		
aPDa	Card, imperforate pane of 4 blocks, #776aPD (3)	—
aPDb	Card, 3 each #773PD-776PD (1)	—
55aPDa	Card, imperforate pane of 4 blocks, imperforate pane of 4 blocks, #V272aPD (3)	—
65aPDb	Card, 3 each #G352PD-G355PD, #V269PD-V272PD (1)	—
aPP	6 items (4 blocks)	—
	Cross gutter block (2)	—
	Horiz. pair with vert. gutter (2)	—
	Vert. pair with horiz. gutter (4)	—
55aPP	6 items (4 blocks)	—
	Cross gutter block (2)	—
	Horiz. pair with vert. gutter (2)	—
	Vert. pair with horiz. gutter (4)	—
72aPP	6 items (4 blocks)	—
	Cross gutter block (2)	—
	Horiz. pair with vert. gutter (2)	—
	Vert. pair with horiz. gutter (4)	—
aPI	(12 blocks)	—
	Cross gutter block (2)	—
	Horiz. pair with vert. gutter (2)	—
	Vert. pair with horiz. gutter (4)	—
55aPI	(12 blocks)	—
	Cross gutter block (2)	—
	Horiz. pair with vert. gutter (2)	—
	Vert. pair with horiz. gutter (4)	—
72aPI	(12 blocks)	—
	Cross gutter block (2)	—
	Horiz. pair with vert. gutter (2)	—
	Vert. pair with horiz. gutter (4)	—

New York #777-778, Geneva #356-357, Vienna #273-274
Our World 2000

00		
3PDa	Card, #777PD-778PD, #G356PD-G357PD, #V273PD-V274PD (4)	—
3PDb	Card, #777PD-778PD, #G356PD-G357PD, #V274PD, #V273TC black denomination, with "not approved" handstamp (2)	—
7PP	8 items (64)	—
	Cross gutter block (2)	—
	Horiz. pair with vert. gutter (16)	—
	Vert. pair with horiz. gutter (8)	—
8PP	8 items (64)	—
	Cross gutter block (2)	—
	Horiz. pair with vert. gutter (8)	—
	Vert. pair with horiz. gutter (16)	—
356PP	8 items (64)	—
	Cross gutter block (2)	—
	Horiz. pair with vert. gutter (8)	—
	Vert. pair with horiz. gutter (16)	—
357PP	8 items (64)	—
	Cross gutter block (2)	—
	Horiz. pair with vert. gutter (16)	—
	Vert. pair with horiz. gutter (8)	—
273PP	8 items (64)	—
	Cross gutter block (2)	—
	Horiz. pair with vert. gutter (16)	—
	Vert. pair with horiz. gutter (8)	—
274PP	8 items (64)	—
	Cross gutter block (2)	—
	Horiz. pair with vert. gutter (8)	—
	Vert. pair with horiz. gutter (16)	—
7PI	(52 pairs)	—
	Cross gutter block (2)	—
	Horiz. pair with vert. gutter (16)	—
	Vert. pair with horiz. gutter (8)	—
78PI	(52 pairs)	—
	Cross gutter block (2)	—
	Horiz. pair with vert. gutter (8)	—
	Vert. pair with horiz. gutter (16)	—
356PI	(52 pairs)	—
	Cross gutter block (2)	—
	Horiz. pair with vert. gutter (16)	—
	Vert. pair with horiz. gutter (8)	—
357PI	(52 pairs)	—
	Cross gutter block (2)	—
	Horiz. pair with vert. gutter (16)	—
	Vert. pair with horiz. gutter (8)	—
273PI	(52 pairs)	—
	Cross gutter block (2)	—
	Horiz. pair with vert. gutter (16)	—
	Vert. pair with horiz. gutter (8)	—
274PI	(52 pairs)	—
	Cross gutter block (2)	—
	Horiz. pair with vert. gutter (8)	—
	Vert. pair with horiz. gutter (16)	—

New York #779-781, Geneva #358-360, Vienna #275-277
United Nations, 55th Anniv.

000		
80TCa	Card, #779TC-780TC, #G358TC-G359TC, #V275TC-V276TC (all with white denominations with colored outlines (4)	—

781TCa	Card, #781TC, #G360TC, #V277TC (all with white denominations with colored outlines (4)	—
781TCb	Card, #779TC-781TC ultramarine & silver (2)	—
781TCc	Card, #779TC-781TC blue & silver (2)	—
781TCd	Card, #781TC, #G360TC silver backgrounds, white denominations with colored outlines (5)	—
G359TCa	Card, #G358TC-G359TC brown red & silver (2)	—
G360TCa	Card, #G358TC-G360TC carmine & silver (2)	—
G360TCb	Card, #G358TC-G360TC cerise & silver (2)	—
V277TCa	Card, #V275TC-V277TC green & silver (2)	—
V277TCb	Card, #V275TC-V277TC dark green & silver (2)	—
V277TCc	Silver background, white denominations with green outlines (5)	—
779PP	7 items (128)	—
	Cross gutter block (4)	—
	Horiz. pair with vert. gutter (16)	—
	Vert. pair with horiz. gutter (32)	—
780PP	7 items (128)	—
	Cross gutter block (4)	—
	Horiz. pair with vert. gutter (16)	—
	Vert. pair with horiz. gutter (32)	—
781PP	6 items (60 souvenir sheets)	—
G358PP	9 items (128)	—
	Cross gutter block (4)	—
	Horiz. pair with vert. gutter (16)	—
	Vert. pair with horiz. gutter (32)	—
G359PP	9 items (128)	—
	Cross gutter block (4)	—
	Horiz. pair with vert. gutter (16)	—
	Vert. pair with horiz. gutter (32)	—
G360PP	9 items (60 souvenir sheets)	—
V275PP	10 items (128)	—
	Cross gutter block (4)	—
	Horiz. pair with vert. gutter (16)	—
	Vert. pair with horiz. gutter (32)	—
V276PP	10 items (128)	—
	Cross gutter block (4)	—
	Horiz. pair with vert. gutter (16)	—
	Vert. pair with horiz. gutter (32)	—
V277PP	10 items (60 souvenir sheets)	—
779PI	(84 pairs)	—
	Cross gutter block (4)	—
	Horiz. pair with vert. gutter (16)	—
	Vert. pair with horiz. gutter (32)	—
780PI	(84 pairs)	—
	Cross gutter block (4)	—
	Horiz. pair with vert. gutter (16)	—
	Vert. pair with horiz. gutter (32)	—
781PI	(60 souvenir sheets)	—
G358PI	(84 pairs)	—
	Cross gutter block (4)	—
	Horiz. pair with vert. gutter (16)	—
	Vert. pair with horiz. gutter (32)	—
G359PI	(84 pairs)	—
	Cross gutter block (4)	—
	Horiz. pair with vert. gutter (16)	—
	Vert. pair with horiz. gutter (32)	—
V275PI	(84 pairs)	—
	Cross gutter block (4)	—
	Horiz. pair with vert. gutter (16)	—
	Vert. pair with horiz. gutter (32)	—
V276PI	(84 pairs)	—
	Cross gutter block (4)	—
	Horiz. pair with vert. gutter (16)	—
	Vert. pair with horiz. gutter (32)	—
781PI	(60 souvenir sheets)	—

One item in Nos. G358PP and G359PP is blank, coming from sheet with marginal inscriptions only.

New York #782
International Flag of Peace

2000		
782PD	With approval handstamp (4)	—
782TC	Black and white photocopy of layout of pane of 20, with approval handstamp and signature (1)	—
782PP	9 items (96)	—
	Cross gutter block (2)	—
	Horiz. pair with vert. gutter (16)	—
	Vert. pair with horiz. gutter (8)	—
782PI	(96 pairs)	—
	Cross gutter block (6)	—
	Horiz. pair with vert. gutter (48)	—
	Vert. pair with horiz. gutter (24)	—

An essay with "age 12" after artist's name exists in five cards and a black and white layout of the pane of 20 on photographic paper.

New York #783, Geneva #361, Vienna #278
UN in the 21st Century

2000		
783PDa	Card, #783PD, #G361PD, #V278PD with approval handstamp (4)	—
783TCa	Card, #783TC, #G361TC, #V278TC all with washed-out colors, with "not approved" handstamp (5)	—
783PP	8 items (1)	—
G361PP	8 items (1)	—
V278PP	8 items (1)	—
783PI	(2 sheets)	—
G361PI	(2 sheets)	—
V278PI	(2 sheets)	—

New York #784-786, Geneva #362-364, Vienna #279-281
World Heritage

2000		
785PDa	Card, #784PD-785PD, #G362PD-G364PD, #V279PD-V280PD (4)	—
784TC	Black and white image of pane of 20 on layout sheet on photographic paper (1)	—
785TC	Black and white image of pane of 20 on layout sheet on photographic paper (1)	—
G362TC	Black and white image of pane of 20 on layout sheet on photographic paper (1)	—
G363TC	Black and white image of pane of 20 on layout sheet on photographic paper (1)	—
V279TC	Black and white image of pane of 20 on layout sheet on photographic paper (1)	—
V280TC	Black and white image of pane of 20 on layout sheet on photographic paper (1)	—
784PP	9 items (24)	—
785PP	9 items (24)	—
	Vert. pair with horiz. gutter (3)	—
785PPa	Cross gutter block, 2 #784PP-785PP (1)	—
785PPb	Horiz. pair with vert. gutter, #784PP-785PP (8)	—
786iPPa	9 items, Strip of #786gPP-786iPP, with vert. gutters between (4)	—
G362PP	9 items (24)	—
G363PP	9 items (24)	—
	Vert. pair with horiz. gutter (3)	—
G363PPa	Cross gutter block, 2 #G362PP-G363PP (1)	—
G363PPb	Horiz. pair with vert. gutter, #G362PP-G363PP (8)	—
V279PP	7 items (24)	—
V280PP	7 items (24)	—
	Vert. pair with horiz. gutter (3)	—
V280PPa	Cross gutter block, 2 #V279PP-V280PP (1)	—
V280PPb	Horiz. pair with vert. gutter, #V279PP-V280PP (8)	—
784PI	(32 pairs)	—
	Vert. pair with horiz. gutter (3)	—
785PI	(32 pairs)	—
	Vert. pair with horiz. gutter (3)	—
785PIa	Cross gutter block, 2 #784PI-785PI (1)	—
785PIb	Horiz. pair with vert. gutter, #784PI-785PI (8)	—
786gPI	(5 booklet panes)	—
786hPI	(5 booklet panes)	—
786iPI	(5 booklet panes)	—
786iPIa	Strip of #786gPI-786iPI, with vert. gutters between (4)	—
786jPI	(5 booklet panes)	—
786kPI	(5 booklet panes)	—
786lPI	(5 booklet panes)	—
G362PI	(32 pairs)	—
	Vert. pair with horiz. gutter (3)	—
G363PI	(32 pairs)	—
	Vert. pair with horiz. gutter (3)	—
G363PIa	Cross gutter block, 2 #G362PI-G363PI (1)	—
G363PIb	Horiz. pair with vert. gutter, #G362PI-G363PI (8)	—
G364gPI	(5 booklet panes)	—
G364hPI	(5 booklet panes)	—
G364iPI	(5 booklet panes)	—
G364jPI	(5 booklet panes)	—
G364kPI	(5 booklet panes)	—
G364lPI	(5 booklet panes)	—
V279PI	(82 pairs)	—
	Vert. pair with horiz. gutter (3)	—
V280PI	(32 pairs)	—
	Vert. pair with horiz. gutter (3)	—
V280PIa	Cross gutter block, 2 #V279PI-V280PI (1)	—
V280PIb	Horiz. pair with vert. gutter, #V279PI-V280PI (8)	—
V281gPI	(5 booklet panes)	—
V281hPI	(5 booklet panes)	—
V281iPI	(5 booklet panes)	—
V281jPI	(5 booklet panes)	—
V281kPI	(5 booklet panes)	—
V281lPI	(5 booklet panes)	—

Some pairs of No. V279PI are defaced with blue marker.

New York #787-788, Geneva #365-366, Vienna #282-283, Souvenir Card #55
Respect for Refugees

2000		
787PDa	Card, #787PD, #G365PD, #V282PD (4)	—
788PDa	Card, #788PD, #G366PD, #V283PD (4)	—
SC55PD	(4)	—
787PP	6 items (32)	—
	Horiz. pair with vert. gutter (4)	—
788PP	6 items (20 souvenir sheets)	—
G365PP	6 items (32)	—
	Cross gutter block (1)	—
	Horiz. pair with vert. gutter (6)	—
	Vert. pair with horiz. gutter (8)	—
G366PP	6 items (20 souvenir sheets)	—
V282PP	6 items (32)	—
	Horiz. pair with vert. gutter (4)	—

V283PP	6 items (20 souvenir sheets)	—
787PI	(36 pairs)	
	Horiz. pair with vert. gutter (4)	—
788PI	(20 souvenir sheets)	
G365PI	(44 pairs)	—
	Cross gutter block (1)	—
	Horiz. pair with vert. gutter (6)	—
	Vert. pair with horiz. gutter (8)	—
G366PI	(20 souvenir sheets)	—
V282PI	(36 pairs)	—
	Horiz. pair with vert. gutter (4)	—
V283PI	(20 souvenir sheets)	—

AIR POST STAMPS
New York #C1-C4
Plane and Gull, Swallows and UN Emblem

1951

C1PD	(1)	—
C2PD	(1)	
C3PD	(1)	
C4PD	(1)	—
C1PI	(25 pairs)	—
C2PI	(25 pairs)	—
C3PI	(25 pairs)	—
C4PI	(25 pairs)	—

New York #C5
Airplane Wing and Globe

1957

C5PD	(4)	—
C5TC	brown (not approved) (5)	—
C5TC	indigo (5)	—
C5PI	(40 pairs)	—
	Vert. pair with horiz. gutter (10)	—

New York #C6-C7
Airplane Wing and Globe; UN Flag and Plane

1959

C6PD	(1)	—
C6PDa	Card, #C6PD, 2 #C6TC in slightly different shades (2)	—
C6PDb	Card, 2 #C6PD, 2 #C7TC Prussian blue (1)	—
C7PD	(1)	—
C7PDa	Card, #C7PD, #C7TC Prussian blue, #C7TC dark blue (2)	—
C6TC	black (1)	—
C7TC	black (1)	—
C6PI	(115 pairs)	—
	Vert. pair with horiz. gutter (10)	—
C7PI	(90 pairs)	—
	Horiz. pair with vert. gutter (10)	—

New York #C8-C10
Definitives

1963

C10PDa	Card, #C8PD-C10PD (3)	—
C10PDb	Card, #C8PD, #C10PD, 3 #C9PD (3)	—
C8PP	3 items (80)	—
	Horiz. pair with vert. gutter (10)	—
C9PP	4 items (80)	—
	Vert. pair with horiz. gutter (10)	—
C10PP	4 items (80)	—
	Horiz. pair with vert. gutter (10)	—
C8PI	(80 pairs)	—
	Horiz. pair with vert. gutter (20)	—
C9PI	(80 pairs)	—
	Vert. pair with horiz. gutter (20)	—
C10PI	(80 pairs)	—
	Horiz. pair with vert. gutter (20)	—

New York #C11-C12
Definitives

1964

C11PDa	Card, #C11PD, #C12TC peach and brown background (disapproved) (2)	—
C12PD	(2)	—
C12PDa	Card, #C11PD-C12PD (4)	—
C11PI	(25 pairs)	—
C12PI	(25 pairs)	—

New York #C13
Jet and UN Emblem

1968

C13PD	(3)	—
C13PDa	Card, #C13PD, 2 #C13TC with slightly different shades (2)	—
C13PP	9 items, perforated, mounted on card (1)	—

New York #C14
Wings, Envelopes and UN Emblem

1969

C14PD	(4)	—
C14PP	6 items, perforated (50)	—

New York #C15-C18
Definitives

1972

C15PD	(2)	—
C16PD	With approval handstamp (2)	—
C17PD	(2)	—
C18PD	(2)	—
C16TC	dark blue emblem (dated 16. Oct. 1971) (2)	—
C15PP	4 items (100)	—
C16PP	10 items (100)	—

C17PP	4 items (100)	—
C18PP	10 items (160)	—
	Horiz. pair with vert. gutter (20)	—
C16PI	(50 pairs)	—
C17PI	(50 pairs)	—

New York #C19-C21
Definitives

1974

C19PD	(3)	—
C20PD	(3)	—
C21PD	(3)	—
C19PP	8 items (50)	—
C21PP	5 items (50)	—
C19PI	(50 pairs)	—
C20PI	(50 pairs)	—
C21PI	(50 pairs)	—

Five cards with essays of No. C21 with incorrect Russian inscription exist.

New York #C22-C23
Definitives

1977

C22PD	With approval handstamp (4)	—
C22TC	Gray wings and envelope, with "not approved" handstamp (2)	—
C23PD	(1)	—
C23PDa	Card, #C23PD, #C22TC gray wings and envelope (3)	—
C22PP	6 items (50)	—
C22PI	(50 pairs)	—
C23PI	(50 pairs)	—

ENVELOPES
New York #U1
UN Emblem

1952

U1PD	(1)	—
U1TC	black (1)	—

New York #U2
UN Emblem

1958

U2PD	with manuscript approval (2)	—
U2TC	black, on card, with manuscript approval (1)	—

New York #U3
Stylized Globe and Weather Vane

1963

U3PD	(2)	—
U3PI	Indicia only on small piece of paper (1)	—

See No. UC6PI.

New York #U5
UN Headquarters

1973

U5PD	(41)	—
U5PP	6 items (5)	—
U5PI	Unfolded and uncut (2)	—

New York #U6
UN Headquarters

1975

U6PD	With approval handstamp (5)	—
U6PDa	Die cut and unfolded, without approval handstamp (4)	—

New York #U7
Bouquet of Ribbons

1985

U7PD	Indicia only, in folder (9)	—

Vienna #U1-U2
Donaupark

1995

VU1PD	On Cromalin paper (approved) (6)	—
VU1PDa	On AGFA paper (not approved) (5)	—
VU2PD	On Cromalin paper (approved) (6)	—
VU2PDa	On AGFA paper (not approved) (5)	—

Vienna #U10-U11
Cripticandina

1997

U10PD	On Cromalin paper (4)	—
U11PD	On Cromalin paper (4)	—

Vienna #U3
Landscape

1998

VU3PD	On Cromalin paper (4)	—

AIR POST ENVELOPES & AIR LETTER SHEETS
New York #UC1 Swallows and UN Emblem

1952

UC1PI	(32)	—
UC1PIa	On white paper (22)	—

New York #UC3
UN Flag and Plane Envelope

1959

UC3PD	(1)	

New York #UC4
UN Flag and Plane Letter Sheet

1960

UC4PD	(1)	

Two "not approved" essays exist with diagonal lines ra than bars around envelope.

New York #UC5 Plane and Gull

1961

UC5PD	With approval handstamp (1)	
UC5aPD	With approval handstamp (3)	

New York #UC6
UN Emblem

1963

UC6PDa	Sheet, #UC6PD, #U3PD, with approval handstamp (2)	
UC6PI	(1)	
UC6PIa	Sheet, #UC6PD (2 sizes), #U3PD (2 sizes) (6)	
UC6PIb	As #UC6PIa with one #U3PI removed (1)	

New York #UC7
UN Emblem and Stylized Plane

1968

UC7PD	With specimen perfin and approval handstamp (7)	

New York #UC8
UN Emblem

1969

UC8PD	With specimen perfin at left (4)	

Geneva #UC1
UN Emblem and Stylized Plane

1969

GUC1PD	With specimen perfin and approval handstamp (3)	
GUC1TC	light blue (2)	
GUC1TC	ultramarine (3)	

New York #UC9
UN Emblem, "UN," Globe and Plane

1972

UC9PD	With approval handstamp (2)	

New York #UC10
Birds in Flight

1973

UC10PDa	Small envelope, die cut and folded, with approval handstamp (1)	
UC10PDb	Large envelope, partially folded, with approval handstamp (2)	
UC10PPa	Uncut and unfolded, large and small envelopes (6 items)	

Three sets of essays exist with blue UN inscriptions close.

New York #UC11
Globe and Jet

1975

UC11PD	With approval handstamp (5)	
UC11PDa	Die cut and unfolded, without approval handstamp (1)	

New York #UC12
UN Headquarters

1975

UC12PD	With approval handstamp (1)	

New York #UC13
UN Emblem and Birds

1977

UC13PD	With approval handstamp (2)	

Five "not approved" essays have design flaw at end of orang line.

New York #UC14, Vienna #UC1
Paper Airplane, Dove

1982

UC14PD	With approval handstamp (3)	
UC14PDa	On thin card stock (1)	
VUC1PD	With approval handstamp (3)	
VUC1PDa	On thin card stock (1)	

Vienna #UC3
Birds in Flight and UN Emblem

1987

VUC3PD	On plastic, with approval handstamp (4)	

New York #UC16
UN Headquarters

9
6PD | With approval handstamp (approved) (3) | —
6PDa | With approval handstamp (not approved) (10) | —

Vienna #UC5
Donaupark

2
5PD | On Cromalin paper (3) | —

New York #UC19
Winged Hand With Envelopes Surcharge

5
9PD | On Cromalin paper (1) | —

New York #UC20
Cherry Blossoms

7
20PD | (5) | —

POSTAL CARDS
New York #UX1
UN Headquarters

52
TC | olive brown, on white paper (1) | —
PI | (4 pairs) | —

New York #UX2
UN Headquarters

58
2PD | With approval handstamp (2) | —

New York #UX3
World Map

63
3PD | (2) | —

New York #UX4
UN Emblem and Post Horn

69
4PD | With approval handstamp on reverse (1) | —

Geneva #UX1-UX2
UN Emblem and Post Horn, Stylized Space View

69
X1PD | With approval handstamp (3) | —
X1PI | (53 pairs) | —
X2PI | (52 pairs) | —

New York #UX5
"UN"

73
5PD | (1) | —

Five "not approved" essays similar to #UX5 exist. Ten 7c essays exist, three with approval handstamp, the others lacking any handstamp.

New York #UX6
"UN"

75
6PD | With specimen perfin and approval handstamp (4) | —

ve "not approved" essays have incorrect Russian inscription.

New York #UX7, Geneva #UX3-UX4
UN Emblem, UN Emblem in Rectangles, UN Emblem and Ribbons

77
7PD | With specimen perfin at left (4) | —
JX3PD | With specimen perfin (5) | —
JX4PD | With specimen perfin at left (4) | —

New York #UX8, Vienna #UX1-UX2
"United Nations," Olive Branch, Bird Carrying Olive Branch

82
X8PD | (2) | —
JX1PD | With approval handstamp on reverse (4) | —
JX2PD | With approval handstamp on reverse (16) | —

Geneva #UX5-UX6, Vienna #UX3
Peace Dove, UN Emblem

85
JX5PD | (3) | —
JX6PD | With approval handstamp on reverse (3) | —
JX3PD | (3) | —

One example of No. GUX5PD has inked lines at left of card.
e example of No. GUX6PD has inked lines around address
es.

New York #UX9-UX18
Views of UN Headquarters

1989
UX9PD | Message side (4) | —
UX9PDa | Picture side (4) | —
UX10PD | Message side (4) | —
UX10PDa | Picture side (4) | —
UX11PD | Message side (4) | —
UX11PDa | Picture side (4) | —
UX12PD | Message side (4) | —
UX12PDa | Picture side (4) | —
UX13PD | Message side (4) | —
UX13PDa | Picture side (4) | —
UX14PD | Message side (4) | —
UX14PDa | Picture side (4) | —
UX15PD | Message side (4) | —
UX15PDa | Picture side (4) | —
UX16PD | Message side (4) | —
UX16PDa | Picture side (4) | —
UX17PD | Message side (4) | —
UX17PDa | Picture side (4) | —
UX18PD | Message side (4) | —
UX18PDa | Picture side (4) | —

New York #UX19, Geneva #UX8, Vienna #UX5
UN Headquarters, Palais des Nations, Regschek Painting

1992
UX19PD | On Cromalin paper (4) | —
GUX8PD | On Cromalin paper (4) | —
VUX5PD | On Cromalin paper (4) | —
VUX5PDa | Sheet, #GUX8PD, #VUX5PD on Cromalin paper (1) | —
UX19TC | ultramarine (1) | —

Geneva #UX10, Vienna #UX6-UX7
Palais des Nations, Peoples of the World United, Donaupark

1993
GUX10PD | On Cromalin paper (4) | —
VUX6PD | On Cromalin paper (4) | —
VUX7PD | On Cromalin paper (4) | —

Vienna #UX12
The Gloriette

1999
VUX12TCa | Light blue text (4) | —

AIR POST POSTAL CARDS
New York #UXC1
UN Flag and Plane

1957
UXC1PD | With printer and approval handstamps (6) | —
UXC1PI | (30 pairs) | —

New York #UXC3
Airplane Wing and Globe

1959
UXC3PD | With approval handstamp (3) | —

Six essays of No. UXC3 lacking outlined letters on "Airmail" and "Poste Aerienne" exist.

New York #UXC4
Outer Space

1963
UXC4PD | (2) | —

New York #UXC6
Outer Space

1968
UXC6PD | With "Canceled" perfin (2) | —
UXC6PDa | Strip of 3 cards with 2 "Canceled" perfins (2) | —

New York #UXC7
UN Emblem and Stylized Planes

1969
UXC7PD | (1) | —
UXC7TC | black (2) | —

New York #UXC8
UN Emblem and Stylized Wing

1972
UXC8PDa | Folder with mounted #UXC8PD with approval handstamp, and #UXC8 (2) | —

New York #UXC9
UN Emblem and Stylized Planes

1972
UXC9PD | Folder with mounted #UXC9, with approval handstamp (2) | —

New York #UXC10-UXC11
Clouds; Pathways

1975
UXC10PD | With specimen perfin and approval handstamp (4) | —
UXC11PD | With specimen perfin and approval handstamp (4) | —

UXC10TC | With manuscript "Lighter as on sample," and approval handstamp (not approved) (5) | —

New York #UXC12
Flying Mailman

1982
UXC12PD | With approval handstamp on reverse (5) | —

U.N. TEMPORARY EXECUTIVE AUTHORITY, WEST NEW GUINEA

Located in the western half of New Guinea, southwest Pacific Ocean, the former Netherlands New Guinea became a territory under the administration of the United Nations Temporary Executive Authority on Oct. 1, 1962. The size was 151,789 sq. mi. and the population was estimated at 730,000 in 1958. The capital was Hollandia.

The territory came under Indonesian administration on May 1, 1963. For stamps issued by Indonesia see West Irian in Vol. 6.

100 Cents = 1 Gulden

Catalogue values for all unused stamps in this country are for Never Hinged items.

First Printing (Hollandia)
Netherlands New Guinea Stamps of 1950-60
Overprinted

Overprint size: 17x3½mm. Top of "N" is slightly lower than the "U," and the base of the "T" is straight, or nearly so.

Photo.; Litho. (#4, 6, 8)

1962   Unwmk.   Perf. 12½x12, 12½x13½

1	A4	1c vermilion & yellow, *Oct. 1*	.20	.20
2	A1	2c deep orange, *Oct. 1*	.25	.25
3	A4	5c chocolate & yellow, *Oct. 1*	.25	.25
4	A5	7c org red, bl & brn vio, *Nov. 1*	.25	.35
5	A4	10c aqua & red brown, *Oct. 1*	.25	.35
6	A5	12c green, bl & brn vio, *Nov. 1*	.25	.35
7	A4	15c deep yel & red brn, *Nov. 1*	.50	.50
8	A5	17c brown violet & blue, *Oct. 1*	.60	.75
9	A4	20c lt bl grn & red brn, *Nov. 1*	.60	.75
10	A6	25c red, *Oct. 1*	.35	.55
11	A6	30c deep blue, *Oct. 1*	.80	.80
12	A6	40c deep orange, *Oct. 1*	.80	.80
13	A6	45c dark olive, *Nov. 1*	1.40	1.60
14	A6	55c slate blue, *Nov. 1*	17.50	1.25
15	A6	80c dull gray violet, *Nov. 1*	5.75	5.75
16	A6	85c dark violet brown, *Nov. 1*	3.00	3.00
17	A6	1g plum, *Oct. 1*	9.75	3.00

Engr.

18	A3	2g reddish brown, *Oct. 1*	9.75	22.50
19	A3	5g green, *Oct. 1*	7.75	5.50
		Nos. 1-19 (19)	60.00	48.50

Overprinted locally and sold in West New Guinea. Stamps of the second printing were used to complete sets sold to collectors.

Second Printing (Haarlem, Netherlands)

Overprint size: 17x3½mm. Top of the "N" is slightly higher than the "U," and the base of the "T" is concave.

Photo.; Litho. (#4a, 6a, 8a)

1962   Unwmk.   Perf. 12½x12, 12½x13½

1a	A4	1c vermilion & yellow	.20	.20
2a	A1	2c deep orange	.25	.20
3a	A4	5c chocolate & yellow	.25	.20
4a	A5	7c org red, bl & brn vio	.25	.20
5a	A4	10c aqua & red brown	.25	.20
6a	A5	12c green, bl & brn vio	.25	.20
7a	A4	15c deep yel & red brn	.50	.25
8a	A5	17c brown violet & blue	.60	.35
9a	A4	20c lt blue grn & red brn	.60	.35
10a	A6	25c red	.35	.30
11a	A6	30c deep blue	.80	.35
12a	A6	40c deep orange	.80	.35
13a	A6	45c dark olive	1.40	.75
14a	A6	55c slate blue	1.25	.55
15a	A6	80c dull gray violet	5.75	5.75
16a	A6	85c dark violet brown	3.00	3.00
17a	A6	1g plum	3.50	1.90

Engr.

18a	A3	2g reddish brown	9.75	13.00
19a	A3	5g green	6.00	3.50
		Nos. 1a-19a (19)	35.75	31.60

Overprinted in the Netherlands and sold by the UN in New York.

Third Printing

Overprint 14mm long.

Photo.; Litho. (#4b, 6b, 8b)

1963, Mar.   Photo.   Unwmk.   Perf. 12½x12

1b	A4	1c vermilion & yellow	4.25	2.00
3b	A4	5c chocolate & yellow	4.75	3.00
4b	A5	7c org red, bl & brn vio	20.00	20.00
5b	A4	10c aqua & red brown	4.75	3.00
6b	A5	12c green, bl & brn vio	30.00	30.00
7b	A4	15c deep yel & red brn	97.50	105.00

8b	A5	17c brown violet & blue	11.00	11.00
9b	A4	20c lt blue grn & red brn	6.25	3.75
		Nos. 1b-9b (8)	178.50	177.75

The third printing was applied in West New Guinea and it is doubtful whether it was regularly issued. Used values are for cto.

Fourth Printing

Overprint 19mm long.

Photogravure

1963, Mar.   Unwmk.   Perf. 12½x12

1c	A4	1c vermilion & yellow	45.00	45.00
5c	A4	10c aqua & red brown	130.00	130.00

The fourth printing was applied in West New Guinea and it is doubtful whether it was regularly issued. Used values are for cto.

U.N. INTERIM ADMINISTRATION IN KOSOVO

These stamps were issued by the United Nations Interim Administration Mission in Kosovo and the Post & Telecommunications of Kosovo. Service s local for the first two months, with international use to start in mid-May.

100 pfennigs = 1 mark

Catalogue values for all unused stamps in this country are for Never Hinged items.

Peace in Kosovo — A1

rinted by La Poste, France. Panes of 40. Designed by Shyqri ıani, Kosovo.
esigns: 20pf, Mosaic depicting Orpheus, c. 5th-6th cent., ujeve. 30pf, Dardinian idol, Museum of Kosovo. 50pf, Silver ı of Damastion from 4th cent. B.C. 1m, Statue of Mother esa, Prizren. 2m, Map of Kosovo.

Perf. 13½x13, 13½x13¼ (30pf)

		Litho.		Unwmk.
)0, Mar. 14				
A1	20pf **multicolored**		.40	.40
	First day cover			1.25
A1	30pf **multicolored**		.60	.60
	First day cover			1.25
A1	50pf **multicolored**		1.00	1.00
	First day cover			1.50
A1	1m **multicolored**		2.00	2.00
	First day cover			2.50
A1	2m **multicolored**		4.00	4.00
	First day cover			5.00
	First day cover, #1-5			7.00
	Nos. 1-5 (5)		8.00	8.00

Peace in Kosovo — A2

Designs: 20pf, Bird. 30pf, Street musician. 50pf, Butterfly and ar. 1m, Children and stars. 2m, Globe and handprints.

		Litho.		*Perf. 14*
)1, Nov. 12				
A2	20pf **multicolored**		1.25	1.25
A2	30pf **multicolored**		1.75	1.75
A2	50pf **multicolored**		3.00	3.00
A2	1m **multicolored**		6.50	6.50
A2	2m **multicolored**		12.50	12.50
	Nos. 6-10 (5)		25.00	25.00

Nos. 6-10 were not available to collectors through the United tions Postal Administration.

100 Cents = 1 Euro (€)
Peace in Kosovo Type of 2001 With Denominations in Euros Only

		Litho.		*Perf. 14*
)2, May 2				
A2	10c Like #6		1.40	1.40
A2	15c Like #7		1.90	1.90
A2	26c Like #8		2.75	2.75
A2	51c Like #9		6.25	6.25
A2	€1.02 Like #10		13.00	13.00
	Nos. 11-15 (5)		25.30	25.30

Nos. 11-15 were not available to collectors through the United tions Postal Administration.

Christmas — A3

Designs: 50c, Candles and garland. €1, Stylized men.

			Litho.		*Perf. 14*
2003, Dec. 20					
16	A3	50c **multicolored**		10.00	10.00
17	A3	€1 **multicolored**		18.00	18.00

Nos. 16-17 were not available to collectors through the United Nations Postal Administration.

Return of Refugees — A4

Five Years of Peace — A5

			Litho.		*Perf. 13¼x13*
2004, June 29					
18	A4	€1 **multicolored**		10.50	10.50
19	A5	€2 **multicolored**		13.00	13.00

Aprons — A7

Vests — A8

Designs: 20c, Apron from Prizren. 30c, Apron from Rugova. 50c, Three vests. €1, Two vests.

			Litho.		*Perf. 13x13¼*
2004, Oct. 28					
22	A7	20c **multicolored**		2.75	2.75
23	A7	30c **multicolored**		3.75	3.75
24	A8	50c **multicolored**		7.00	7.00
25	A8	€1 **multicolored**		13.50	13.50
		Nos. 22-25 (4)		27.00	27.00

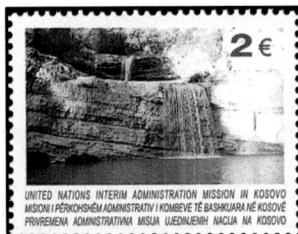

Mirusha Waterfall — A9

			Litho.		*Perf. 13x13¼*
2004, Nov. 26					
26	A9	€2 **multicolored**		10.00	10.00

House — A10

			Litho.		*Perf. 13x13¼*
2004, Dec. 14					
27	A10	50c **multicolored**		3.00	3.00

East Timor

In 2000, the United Nations Transitional Authority in East Timor issued two nondenominated stamps, inscribed "Dom." and "Int.". They are listed in Volume 6 in Timor as Scott Nos. 350-351.

Musical Instruments — A6

			Litho.		*Perf. 13¼x13*
2004, Aug. 31					
20	A6	20c Flute		3.75	3.75
21	A6	30c Ocarina		5.50	5.50

INDEX TO ADVERTISERS – 2007 U.S. SPECIALIZED

DEALERS...TAKE ADVANTAGE OF SCOTT'S ADVERTISING OPPORTUNITIES!

2007
UNITED STATES SPECIALIZED
DEALER DIRECTORY
YELLOW PAGE LISTINGS

This section of your Scott Catalogue contains advertisements to help you conveniently find what you need, when you need it...!

Accessories

BROOKLYN GALLERY COIN & STAMP, INC.
8725 4th Ave.
Brooklyn, NY 11209
PH: 718-745-5701
FAX: 718-745-2775
info@brooklyngallery.com
www.brooklyngallery.com

Albums

THE KEEPING ROOM
PO Box 257
Trumbull, CT 06611
PH: 203-372-8436

Appraisals

DALE ENTERPRISES, INC.
PO Box 539-C
Emmaus, PA 18049
PH: 610-433-3303
FAX: 610-965-6089
daleent@ptd.net
www.dalestamps.com

Auctions

Asia

MICHAEL ROGERS, INC.
Mailing Address:
336 Grove Ave.
Suite B
Winter Park, FL 32789-3602
Walk-in Address:
Ranch Mall
325 S. Orlando Ave.
Suite 14
Winter Park, FL 32789-3608
PH: 407-644-2290
PH: 800-843-3751
FAX: 407-645-4434
Stamps@michaelrogersinc.com
www.michaelrogersinc.com

Auctions

JACQUES C. SCHIFF, JR., INC.
195 Main St.
Ridgefield Park, NJ 07660
PH: 201-641-5566
From NYC: PH: 212-662-2777
FAX: 201-641-5705

R. MARESCH & SON LTD.
5th Floor - 6075 Yonge St.
Toronto, ON M2M 3W2
CANADA
PH: 416-363-7777
FAX: 416-363-6511
www.maresch.com

SAM HOUSTON PHILATELICS
PO Box 820087
Houston, TX 77282
PH: 281-493-6386
PH: 800-231-5926
FAX: 281-496-1445
shduck@aol.com
www.shpauctions.com

SUBURBAN STAMP INC.
176 Worthington St.
Springfield, MA 01103
PH: 413-785-5348
FAX: 413-746-3788
suburbanstamp@earthlink.net

THE STAMP CENTER DUTCH COUNTRY AUCTIONS
4115 Concord Pike
Wilmington, DE 19803
PH: 302-478-8740
FAX: 302-478-8779
scdca@dol.net
www.thestampcenter.com

Auctions-Mail Bid

DALE ENTERPRISES, INC.
PO Box 539-C
Emmaus, PA 18049
PH: 610-433-3303
FAX: 610-965-6089
daleent@ptd.net
www.dalestamps.com

Auctions - Public

ALAN BLAIR STAMPS/ AUCTIONS
5405 Lakeside Ave.
Suite 1
Richmond, VA 23228
PH/FAX: 800-689-5602
alanblair@prodigy.net

China

MICHAEL ROGERS, INC.
Mailing Address:
336 Grove Ave.
Suite B
Winter Park, FL 32789-3602
Walk-in Address:
Ranch Mall
325 S. Orlando Ave.
Suite 14
Winter Park, FL 32789-3608
PH: 407-644-2290
PH: 800-843-3751
FAX: 407-645-4434
Stamps@michaelrogersinc.com
www.michaelrogersinc.com

Classics

GARY POSNER, INC.
1407 Ave. Z, PMB #535
Brooklyn, NY 11235
PH: 800-323-4279
CELL PH: 917-538-8133
FAX: 718-241-2801
garyposnerinc@aol.com
www.garyposnerinc.com
www.gemstamps.com

J. NALBANDIAN, INC.
PO Box 71
East Greenwich, RI 02818
PH: 401-885-5020
FAX: 401-885-3040
nalbandianj@earthlink.net
www.nalbandstamp.com

Auctions - Public

Confed. Stamps & Postal History

ANLEY M. PILLER & SSOCIATES
(OURS BY APPT. ONLY)
0 S. Broadway
ite 201
alnut Creek, CA 94596
: 925-938-8290
X: 925-938-8812
npdlr@aol.com
w.smpiller.com

N COAST STAMP CO.
31 Gulf Gate Dr.
ite 102
rasota, FL 34231
I: 941-921-9761
I: 800-927-3351
X: 941-921-1762
wfam@aol.com

Covers-Zeppelins

NRY GITNER PHILATEL-ISTS, INC.
) Box 3077-S
ddletown, NY 10940
I: 845-343-5151
I: 800-947-8267
X: 845-343-0068
itner@hgitner.com
w.hgitner.com

British Commonwealth

Expertizing

Ducks

MICHAEL JAFFE
PO Box 61484
Vancouver, WA 98666
PH: 360-695-6161
PH: 800-782-6770
FAX: 360-695-1616
mjaffe@brookmanstamps.com
www.brookmanstamps.com

SAM HOUSTON DUCK CO.
PO Box 820087
Houston, TX 77282
PH: 281-493-6386
PH: 800-231-5926
FAX: 281-496-1445
shduck@aol.com
www.shduck.com

TRENTON STAMP & COIN CO./COASTAL BEND DUCK STAMP CO.
Thomas DeLuca
Mail: PO Box 8574
Trenton, NJ 08650
Store: Forest Glen Plaza
1804 Route 33
Hamilton Square, NJ 08690
PH: 800-446-8664
PH: 609-584-8100
FAX: 609-587-8664
TOMD4TSC@aol.com

Errors, Freaks & Oddities

J. NALBANDIAN, INC.
PO Box 71
East Greenwich, RI 02818
PH: 401-885-5020
FAX: 401-885-3040
nalbandianj@earthlink.net
www.nalbandstamp.com

SAM HOUSTON PHILATELICS
PO Box 820087
Houston, TX 77282
PH: 281-493-6386
PH: 800-231-5926
FAX: 281-496-1445
shduck@aol.com
www.shpauctions.com

Expertizing

STANLEY M. PILLER & ASSOCIATES
(HOURS BY APPT. ONLY)
800 S. Broadway
Suite 201
Walnut Creek, CA 94596
PH: 925-938-8290
FAX: 925-938-8812
stmpdlr@aol.com
www.smpiller.com

First Day Covers

HENRY GITNER PHILATEL-ISTS, INC.
PO Box 3077-S
Middletown, NY 10940
PH: 845-343-5151
PH: 800-947-8267
FAX: 845-343-0068
hgitner@hgitner.com
www.hgitner.com

German Colonies

COLONIAL STAMP COMPANY
$1 million photo price list,
$5.00
(refundable against purchase)
5757 Wilshire Blvd. PH #8
Los Angeles, CA 90036
PH: 323-933-9435
FAX: 323-939-9930
Toll Free in North America
PH: 877-272-6693
FAX: 877-272-6694
info@colonialstampcompany.com
www.colonialstampcompany.com

Hawaii Stamps & Postal History

STANLEY M. PILLER & ASSOCIATES
(HOURS BY APPT. ONLY)
800 S. Broadway
Suite 201
Walnut Creek, CA 94596
PH: 925-938-8290
FAX: 925-938-8812
stmpdlr@aol.com
www.smpiller.com

Insurance

COLLECTIBLES INSURANCE AGENCY
PO Box 1200 SSC
Westminster, MD 21158
PH: 888-837-9537
FAX: 410-876-9233
info@insurecollectibles.com
www.collectinsure.com

Japan

MICHAEL ROGERS, INC.
Mailing Address:
336 Grove Ave.
Suite B
Winter Park, FL 32789-3602
Walk-in Address:
Ranch Mall
325 S. Orlando Ave.
Suite 14
Winter Park, FL 32789-3608
PH: 407-644-2290
PH: 800-843-3751
FAX: 407-645-4434
Stamps@michaelrogersinc.com
www.michaelrogersinc.com

Korea

MICHAEL ROGERS, INC.
Mailing Address:
336 Grove Ave.
Suite B
Winter Park, FL 32789-3602
Walk-in Address:
Ranch Mall
325 S. Orlando Ave.
Suite 14
Winter Park, FL 32789-3608
PH: 407-644-2290
PH: 800-843-3751
FAX: 407-645-4434
Stamps@michaelrogersinc.com
www.michaelrogersinc.com

Manchukuo

MICHAEL ROGERS, INC.
Mailing Address:
336 Grove Ave.
Suite B
Winter Park, FL 32789-3602
Walk-in Address:
Ranch Mall
325 S. Orlando Ave.
Suite 14
Winter Park, FL 32789-3608
PH: 407-644-2290
PH: 800-843-3751
FAX: 407-645-4434
Stamps@michaelrogersinc.com
www.michaelrogersinc.com

New Issues

DAVIDSON'S STAMP SERVICE
PO Box 36355
Indianapolis, IN 46236-0355
PH: 317-826-2620
davidson@in.net
www.newstampissues.com

One of A Kind

DALE ENTERPRISES, INC.
PO Box 539-C
Emmaus, PA 18049
PH: 610-433-3303
FAX: 610-965-6089
daleent@ptd.net
www.dalestamps.com

Philatelic Literature

JAMES E. LEE
PO Box 36-YP
Cary, IL 60013
PH: 877-696-8403
PH: 847-462-9130
FAX: 847-462-9140
jim@jameslee.com
www.jameslee.com

LEWIS KAUFMAN
PO Box 255
Kiamesha Lake, NY 12751
PH/FAX: 845-794-8013
PH/FAX: 800-491-5453
mamet1@aol.com

Postal History

JAMES E. LEE
PO Box 36-YP
Cary, IL 60013
PH: 877-696-8403
PH: 847-462-9130
FAX: 847-462-9140
jim@jameslee.com
www.jameslee.com

**STANLEY M. PILLER &
ASSOCIATES**
(HOURS BY APPT. ONLY)
800 S. Broadway
Suite 201
Walnut Creek, CA 94596
PH: 925-938-8290
FAX: 925-938-8812
stmpdlr@aol.com
www.smpiller.com

Proofs & Essays

**HENRY GITNER PHILATEL-
ISTS, INC.**
PO Box 3077-S
Middletown, NY 10940
PH: 845-343-5151
PH: 800-947-8267
FAX: 845-343-0068
hgitner@hgitner.com
www.hgitner.com

**STANLEY M. PILLER &
ASSOCIATES**
(HOURS BY APPT. ONLY)
800 S. Broadway
Suite 201
Walnut Creek, CA 94596
PH: 925-938-8290
FAX: 925-938-8812
stmpdlr@aol.com
www.smpiller.com

Souvenir Cards

AALLSTAMPS
38 N. Main St.
PO Box 249
Milltown, NJ 08850
PH: 732-247-1093
FAX: 732-247-1094
mail@aallstamps.com
www.aallstamps.com

STAMP STORES

California

BROSIUS STAMP & COIN
2105 Main St.
Santa Monica, CA 90405
PH: 310-396-7480
FAX: 310-396-7455

Stamp Shows

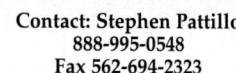
California

**FISCHER-WOLK
PHILATELICS**
24771 "G" Alicia Parkway
Laguna Hills, CA 92653
PH: 949-837-2932
fischerwolk@earthlink.net

NATICK STAMPS & HOBBIES
405 S. Myrtle Ave.
Monrovia, CA 91016
PH: 626-305-7333
natickco@earthlink.net

**STANLEY M. PILLER &
ASSOCIATES**
(HOURS BY APPT. ONLY)
800 S. Broadway
Suite 201
Walnut Creek, CA 94596
PH: 925-938-8290
FAX: 925-938-8812
stmpdlr@aol.com
www.smpiller.com

Colorado

ACKLEY'S ROCKS & STAMPS
3230 N. Stone Ave.
Colorado Springs, CO 80907
PH: 719-633-1153
ackl9@aol.com

SHOWCASE STAMPS
3865 Wadsworth
Wheat Ridge, CO 80033
PH: 303-425-9252
kbeiner@colbi.net
www.showcasestamps.com

Connecticut

SILVER CITY COIN & STAMP
41 Colony Street
Meriden, CT 06451
PH: 203-235-7634
FAX: 203-237-4915

Florida

R.D.C. STAMPS
7381 SW 24th St.
Miami, FL 33155-1402
PH: 305-264-4213
FAX: 305-262-2919
rdcstamps@aol.com

STAMP STORES

Florida

WINTER PARK STAMP SHOP
Ranch Mall (17-92)
325 S. Orlando Ave.
Suite 14
Winter Park, FL 32789-3608
PH: 407-628-1120
PH: 800-845-1819
FAX: 407-628-0091
stamps@winterparkstampshop.com
www.winterparkstampshop.com

Georgia

**STAMPS UNLIMITED OF
GEORGIA, INC.**
133 Carnegie Way
Room 250
Atlanta, GA 30303
PH: 404-688-9161

Illinois

**DR. ROBERT FRIEDMAN &
SONS**
2029 W. 75th St.
Woodridge, IL 60517
PH: 800-588-8100
FAX: 630-985-1588
drbobstamps@yahoo.com
www.drbobfriedmanstamps.com

Indiana

KNIGHT STAMP & COIN CO.
237 Main St.
Hobart, IN 46342
PH: 219-942-4341
PH: 800-634-2646
knight@knightcoin.com
www.knightcoin.com

Massachusetts

KAPPY'S COINS & STAMPS
534 Washington St.
Norwood, MA 02062
PH: 781-762-5552
FAX: 781-762-3292
kappyscoins@aol.com

SUBURBAN STAMP INC.
176 Worthington St.
Springfield, MA 01103
PH: 413-785-5348
FAX: 413-746-3788
suburbanstamp@earthlink.net

Maryland

BULLDOG STAMP COMPANY
4641 Montgomery Ave.
Bethesda, MD 20814
PH: 301-654-1138

Michigan

THE MOUSE AND SUCH
696 N. Mill Street
Plymouth, MI 48170
734-454-1515
weluvstamps@hotmail.com

New Jersey

AALLSTAMPS
38 N. Main St.
PO Box 249
Milltown, NJ 08850
PH: 732-247-1093
FAX: 732-247-1094
mail@aallstamps.com
www.aallstamps.com

New Jersey

**BERGEN STAMPS &
COLLECTIBLES**
717 American Legion Dr.
Teaneck, NJ 07666
PH: 201-836-8987

RON RITZER STAMPS INC.
Millburn Mall
2933 Vauxhall Rd.
Vauxhall, NJ 07088
PH: 908-687-0007
FAX: 908-687-0795
rritzer@comcast.net

**TRENTON STAMP & COIN
CO.**
Thomas DeLuca
Store: Forest Glen Plaza
1804 Route 33
Hamilton Square, NJ 08690
Mail: PO Box 8574
Trenton, NJ 08650
PH: 800-446-8664
PH: 609-584-8100
FAX: 609-587-8664
TOMD4TSC@aol.com

New York

CHAMPION STAMP CO., INC.
432 W. 54th St.
New York, NY 10019
PH: 212-489-8130
FAX: 212-581-8130
championstamp@aol.com
www.championstamp.com

Ohio

HILLTOP STAMP SERVICE
Richard A. Peterson
PO Box 626
Wooster, OH 44691
PH: 330-262-8907
PH: 330-262-5378
hilltop@bright.net

THE LINK STAMP CO.
3461 E. Livingston Ave.
Columbus, OH 43227
PH/FAX: 614-237-4125
PH/FAX: 800-546-5726

Tennessee

HERRON HILL, INC.
5007 Black Road
Suite 140
Memphis, TN 38117
PH: 901-683-9644

Texas

**SAM HOUSTON
PHILATELICS**
14780 Memorial Drive #110
Houston, TX 77079
PH: 281-493-6386
PH: 800-231-5926
FAX: 281-496-1445
shduck@aol.com
www.shpauctions.com

Virginia

**KENNEDY'S STAMPS &
COINS, INC.**
7059 Brookfield Plaza
Springfield, VA 22150
PH: 703-569-7300
FAX: 703-569-7644
j.w.kennedy@verizon.net

LATHEROW & CO., INC.
5054 Lee Hwy.
Arlington, VA 22207
PH: 703-538-2727
PH: 800-647-4624
FAX: 703-538-5210

Topicals-Columbus

COLUMBUS
) Box 1492
nnville, MI 49408
: 269-543-4755
lumbus@accn.org

United States

МSTRONG PHILATELICS
) Box 4089
atsworth, CA 91313-4089
: 818-701-7380
X: 818-701-5915
nstrong@stamp1.com
w.stamp1.com

'S STAMPS
rbara J. Johnson
42 W. Bell Road
endale, AZ 85308
: 623-878-2080
X: 623-412-3456
o@bjstamps.com
w.bjstamps.com

OOKMAN STAMP CO.
) Box 90
ncouver, WA 98666
I: 360-695-1391
I: 800-545-4871
X: 360-695-1616
ve@brookmanstamps.com
w.brookmanstamps.com

LE ENTERPRISES, INC.
) Box 539-C
maus, PA 18049
I: 610-433-3303
X: 610-965-6089
leent@ptd.net
ww.dalestamps.com

United States

U.S.A.

BELOW MARKET PRICES!!

USED   UNUSED

MOST GRADES & PRICE RANGES!

Here is your opportunity to have the older and scarcer stamps of
our country at low, reasonable prices. Issues prior to the year 1950
worth anywhere from 25¢ up to several hundred dollars each.

JUST SEND 39¢ POSTAGE for complete price list. Compare for
PROOF OF LOWEST PRICES before ordering, and find out what you
have missed until you discovered us!!!

LOWELL S. DONALD CO.

P.O. BOX 728,
RUTLAND, VERMONT 05702

United States

MILLER'S STAMP SHOP
41 New London Tpke.
Uncasville, CT 06382
PH: 860-848-0468
millstamps@sbcglobal.net
www.millersstampshop.com

GARY POSNER, INC.
1407 Ave. Z, PMB #535
Brooklyn, NY 11235
PH: 800-323-4279
CELL PH: 917-538-8133
FAX: 718-241-2801
garyposnerinc@aol.com
www. garyposnerinc.com
www.gemstamps.com

U.S.-Back of Book

ARMSTRONG PHILATELICS
PO Box 4089
Chatsworth, CA 91313-4089
PH: 818-701-7380
FAX: 818-701-5915
armstrong@stamp1.com
www.stamp1.com

U.S.-Booklets

DALE ENTERPRISES, INC.
PO Box 539-C
Emmaus, PA 18049
PH: 610-433-3303
FAX: 610-965-6089
daleent@ptd.net
www.dalestamps.com

U.S.-Booklets

WWW.WORLDSTAMPS.COM
242 West Saddle River Road
Suite C
Upper Saddle River, NJ 07458
PH: 201-236-8122
FAX: 201-236-8133
by mail:
Frank Geiger Philatelists
info@WorldStamps.com
www.WorldStamps.com

U.S.-Classics

DALE ENTERPRISES, INC.
PO Box 539-C
Emmaus, PA 18049
PH: 610-433-3303
FAX: 610-965-6089
daleent@ptd.net
www.dalestamps.com

J. NALBANDIAN, INC.
PO Box 71
East Greenwich, RI 02818
PH: 401-885-5020
FAX: 401-885-3040
nalbandianj@earthlink.net
www.nalbandstamp.com

**STANLEY M. PILLER &
ASSOCIATES**
(HOURS BY APPT. ONLY)
800 S. Broadway
Suite 201
Walnut Creek, CA 94596
PH: 925-938-8290
FAX: 925-938-8812
stmpdlr@aol.com
www.smpiller.com

U.S.-Classics/Moderns

WULFF'S STAMPS
PO Box 661746
Sacramento, CA 95866
PH/FAX: 800-884-0656
PH/FAX: 916-489-0656
service@wulffstamps.com
www.wulffstamps.com

U.S.-Collections Wanted

**DR. ROBERT FRIEDMAN &
SONS**
2029 W. 75th St.
Woodridge, IL 60517
PH: 800-588-8100
FAX: 630-985-1588
drbobstamps@yahoo.com
www.drbobfriedmanstamps.com

SUBURBAN STAMP INC.
176 Worthington St.
Springfield, MA 01103
PH: 413-785-5348
FAX: 413-746-3788
suburbanstamp@earthlink.net

U.S.-Errors, Freaks & Oddities

GARY POSNER, INC.
1407 Ave. Z, PMB #535
Brooklyn, NY 11235
PH: 800-323-4279
CELL PH: 917-538-8133
FAX: 718-241-2801
garyposnerinc@aol.com
www. garyposnerinc.com
www.gemstamps.com

SUBURBAN STAMP INC.
176 Worthington St.
Springfield, MA 01103
PH: 413-785-5348
FAX: 413-746-3788
suburbanstamp@earthlink.net

U.S.-Federal Duck Stamps

**HENRY GITNER PHILATEL-
ISTS, INC.**
PO Box 3077-S
Middletown, NY 10940
PH: 845-343-5151
PH: 800-947-8267
FAX: 845-343-0068
hgitner@hgitner.com
www.hgitner.com

SAM HOUSTON DUCK CO.
PO Box 820087
Houston, TX 77282
PH: 281-493-6386
PH: 800-231-5926
FAX: 281-496-1445
shduck@aol.com
www.shduck.com

U.S.-Mint

WWW.WORLDSTAMPS.COM
242 West Saddle River Road
Suite C
Upper Saddle River, NJ 07458
PH: 201-236-8122
FAX: 201-236-8133
by mail:
Frank Geiger Philatelists
info@WorldStamps.com
www.WorldStamps.com

U.S.-Mint Sheets

**HENRY GITNER PHILATEL-
ISTS, INC.**
PO Box 3077-S
Middletown, NY 10940
PH: 845-343-5151
PH: 800-947-8267
FAX: 845-343-0068
hgitner@hgitner.com
www.hgitner.com

U.S.-Plate Blocks

GARY POSNER, INC.
1407 Ave. Z, PMB #535
Brooklyn, NY 11235
PH: 800-323-4279
CELL PH: 917-538-8133
FAX: 718-241-2801
garyposnerinc@aol.com
www. garyposnerinc.com
www.gemstamps.com

U.S.-Postal History

SUN COAST STAMP CO.
3231 Gulf Gate Dr.
Suite 102
Sarasota, FL 34231
PH: 941-921-9761
PH: 800-927-3351
FAX: 941-921-1762
pvwfam@aol.com

U.S.-Postal Stationery

ARMSTRONG PHILATELICS
PO Box 4089
Chatsworth, CA 91313-4089
PH: 818-701-7380
FAX: 818-701-5915
armstrong@stamp1.com
www.stamp1.com

U.S.-Price Lists

DALE ENTERPRISES, INC.
PO Box 539-C
Emmaus, PA 18049
PH: 610-433-3303
FAX: 610-965-6089
daleent@ptd.net
www.dalestamps.com

U.S.-Proofs & Essays

JAMES E. LEE
PO Box 36-YP
Cary, IL 60013
PH: 877-696-8403
PH: 847-462-9130
FAX: 847-462-9140
jim@jameslee.com
www.jameslee.com

J. NALBANDIAN, INC.
PO Box 71
East Greenwich, RI 02818
PH: 401-885-5020
FAX: 401-885-3040
nalbandianj@earthlink.net
www.nalbandstamp.com

SUBURBAN STAMP INC.
176 Worthington St.
Springfield, MA 01103
PH: 413-785-5348
FAX: 413-746-3788
suburbanstamp@earthlink.net

U.S.-Rare Stamps

GARY POSNER, INC.
1407 Ave. Z, PMB #535
Brooklyn, NY 11235
PH: 800-323-4279
CELL PH: 917-538-8133
FAX: 718-241-2801
garyposnerinc@aol.com
www. garyposnerinc.com
www.gemstamps.com

U.S.-Revenues

ARMSTRONG PHILATELICS
PO Box 4089
Chatsworth, CA 91313-4089
PH: 818-701-7380
FAX: 818-701-5915
armstrong@stamp1.com
www.stamp1.com

U.S.-Trust Territories

**HENRY GITNER PHILATEL-
ISTS, INC.**
PO Box 3077-S
Middletown, NY 10940
PH: 845-343-5151
PH: 800-947-8267
FAX: 845-343-0068
hgitner@hgitner.com
www.hgitner.com

Want Lists

BROOKMAN INTERNATIONAL
PO Box 450
Vancouver, WA 98666
PH: 360-695-1391
PH: 800-545-4871
FAX: 360-695-1616
dave@brookmanstamps.com

CHARLES P. SCHWARTZ
PO Box 165
Mora, MN 55051
PH: 320-679-4705
charlesp@ecenet.com

Want Lists-U.S.

GARY POSNER, INC.
1407 Ave. Z, PMB #535
Brooklyn, NY 11235
PH: 800-323-4279
CELL PH: 917-538-8133
FAX: 718-241-2801
garyposnerinc@aol.com
www. garyposnerinc.com
www.gemstamps.com

Wanted-Collections

DALE ENTERPRISES, INC.
PO Box 539-C
Emmaus, PA 18049
PH: 610-433-3303
FAX: 610-965-6089
daleent@ptd.net
www.dalestamps.com

Wanted-Estates

DALE ENTERPRISES, INC.
PO Box 539-C
Emmaus, PA 18049
PH: 610-433-3303
FAX: 610-965-6089
daleent@ptd.net
www.dalestamps.com

Wanted-U.S.

GARY POSNER, INC.
1407 Ave. Z, PMB #535
Brooklyn, NY 11235
PH: 800-323-4279
CELL PH: 917-538-8133
FAX: 718-241-2801
garyposnerinc@aol.com
www. garyposnerinc.com
www.gemstamps.com

SUBURBAN STAMP INC.
176 Worthington St.
Springfield, MA 01103
PH: 413-785-5348
FAX: 413-746-3788
suburbanstamp@earthlink.net

Wanted-U.S. Collections

**THE STAMP CENTER
DUTCH COUNTRY AUCTIONS**
4115 Concord Pike
Wilmington, DE 19803
PH: 302-478-8740
FAX: 302-478-8779
scdca@dol.net
www.thestampcenter.com

Wanted-Worldwide Collections

DR. ROBERT FRIEDMAN & SONS
2029 W. 75th St.
Woodridge, IL 60517
PH: 800-588-8100
FAX: 630-985-1588
drbobstamps@yahoo.com
www.drbobfriedmanstamps.com

SUBURBAN STAMP INC.
176 Worthington St.
Springfield, MA 01103
PH: 413-785-5348
FAX: 413-746-3788
suburbanstamp@earthlink.net

**THE STAMP CENTER
DUTCH COUNTRY AUCTIONS**
4115 Concord Pike
Wilmington, DE 19803
PH: 302-478-8740
FAX: 302-478-8779
scdca@dol.net
www.thestampcenter.com

Websites

ARMSTRONG PHILATELICS
PO Box 4089
Chatsworth, CA 91313-4089
PH: 818-701-7380
FAX: 818-701-5915
armstrong@stamp1.com
www.stamp1.com

J. NALBANDIAN, INC.
PO Box 71
East Greenwich, RI 02818
PH: 401-885-5020
FAX: 401-885-3040
nalbandianj@earthlink.net
www.nalbandstamp.com

Wholesale

**HENRY GITNER PHILATEL-
ISTS, INC.**
PO Box 3077-S
Middletown, NY 10940
PH: 845-343-5151
PH: 800-947-8267
FAX: 845-343-0068
hgitner@hgitner.com
www.hgitner.com

Wholesale-Dealers

GARY POSNER, INC.
1407 Ave. Z, PMB #535
Brooklyn, NY 11235
PH: 800-323-4279
CELL PH: 917-538-8133
FAX: 718-241-2801
garyposnerinc@aol.com
www. garyposnerinc.com
www.gemstamps.com

Wholesale-U.S.

GARY POSNER, INC.
1407 Ave. Z, PMB #535
Brooklyn, NY 11235
PH: 800-323-4279
CELL PH: 917-538-8133
FAX: 718-241-2801
garyposnerinc@aol.com
www. garyposnerinc.com
www.gemstamps.com

Worldwide

WWW.WORLDSTAMPS.COM
242 West Saddle River Road
Suite C
Upper Saddle River, NJ 07458
PH: 201-236-8122
FAX: 201-236-8133
by mail:
Frank Geiger Philatelists
info@WorldStamps.com
www.WorldStamps.com

**METROPOLITAN STAMP CO.,
INC.**
PO Box 657
Park Ridge, IL 60068-0657
PH: 815-439-0142
FAX: 815-439-0143
metrostamp@aol.com
www.metropolitanstamps.com

For a *free sample magazine* and information about membership in America's national philatelic society send the attached card or contact:

American Philatelic Society
100 Match Factory Place
Bellefonte, PA 16823-1367
Phone: 814-933-3803
Fax: 814-933-6128
www.stamps.org

Mail this card to receive information about:

Selling Your Stamps for the Highest Price

s card has been used, see our
age advertisement on the
cover of this catalog!

Mail this card to receive

**YOUR FREE
MYSTIC U.S.
STAMP CATALOG!**

est Edition

r 4,200 Color Photographs

ked with valuable
ecting tips

ums, Supplements
collecting supplies

American Philatelic Society
100 Match Factory Place
Bellefonte, PA 16823-1367

From _____
Address_____
City _____
State/Zip_____

**MYSTIC STAMP COMPANY
ATTENTION: BUYING DEPARTMENT
9700 MILL STREET
CAMDEN NY 13316-9111**

From _____
Address_____
City _____
State/Zip_____

**MYSTIC STAMP COMPANY
DEPT SC06A
9700 MILL STREET
CAMDEN NY 13316-9111**